SLANG

AND ITS ANALOGUES

J. S. Farmer & W. E. Henley

With an Introduction by

Theodore M. Bernstein

Arno Press

A Publishing and Library Service of The New York Times

The original edition of this work was published in seven volumes during the period from 1890 to 1904. In order to reissue the work in a convenient form at a reasonable price, this edition reproduces four original pages on a single page of larger size, without any reduction in the original type size.

Slang and Its Analogues is not only a major work of lexicography; it is also a veritable museum. It reflects the milieu of three centuries of life in England and about a century of life in America. It preserves sparkling specimens of folk language encased in quotations of their time. Many of the specimens are as extinct as the dinosaur in the American Museum of Natural History (one might be able to guess the meaning of *buff-ball*, but who uses the term nowadays?). On the other hand, some specimens are still as alive as they ever were (*stash* shows no signs of senility after two centuries, and *booze*, as is well known, improves with age). Still other specimens have died and been reincarnated in slightly different forms (*bread*, an eighteenth century designation for employment and hence food, reappeared in the 1960's in the not dissimilar sense of money).

Strictly speaking, this monumental compilation is not a dictionary of slang, for it includes material that is not normally classified as slang, such as colloquial and informal language and nicknames. But there is no need to speak strictly; we can accept the compilers' broader scope to embrace everything that might come under the general heading of nonstandard language. Thus it includes *argot* (the speech of thieves and rogues, and, by derived meaning, the "inside" speech of any particular class), *jargon* (the language of a special group — of a science, sect, trade, profession), *dialect* (regional variations of language), and *casualisms* (relaxed, familiar, colloquial language).

As John S. Farmer points out in his Prefatory Note, "The borderland between slang and the 'Queen's English' is an ill-defined territory, the limits of which have never been clearly mapped out." At another point he cites the difficulty of defining slang, but an examination of its characteristics, its purposes, and how and by whom it is formed may obviate the necessity of defining it.

To begin with, slang grows out of the continual efforts to devise new, vigorous, often tough, often humorous ways of communicating, usually within the communicator's own group. Thus, slang usually originates with the experimental young and with such closed groups such as thieves, convicts, narcotics addicts, soldiers, musicians, theater folk, scientists, technicians and even simply men, as opposed (and that's not the word) to women.

The purposes of coining unorthodox words and phrases vary. One is simply to produce humorous effect, as when the students of Cheltenham College spoke of green vegetables as *bunny grub*. A second purpose is to provide an esoteric bond between the users of the particular slang in the usually unexpressed hope that outsiders will feel like outsiders; for instance, *Fanny Adams*, a British naval term for tinned mutton. A third purpose is to provide a kind of shorthand that saves constructing an elaborate phrase or sentence: In England *slap-bang shop* was applied to an eating place where no credit was accepted — only cash. A fourth purpose, somewhat related to the second, is to conceal illicit conduct or intentions from outsiders, as when English thieves spoke of *dead swag*, meaning loot that could not be disposed of.

The world of crime has always been a chief breeding ground for slang. And in criminal slang sexual allusions and references are more common than in the slang of other closed groups, largely because among criminals defiance of convention and decency has matched defiance of law, and because prostitution is a significant element in the crime record. It is the sexual coloration of slang, as G. Legman, "the erotic folklorist," has pointed out, that "in part explains the extreme resistance to and horror of slang in polite circles." This resistance should not be overemphasized, however, because in the 1960's there was a growing acceptance of slang among the better cultivated parts of the population. The process of democratization in America has had a curious leveling-down effect. If there is to be a leveling at all, it must of necessity be downward since education of the masses to the level of the cultivated is not readily achievable, while the intellectuals have no difficulty in lowering themselves. "Democratic manners," says Jacques Barzun in *The House of Intellect*, "prevent a jousting in which somebody might appear stronger, brighter, quicker or richer of mind. . . . Some possessors of intellect try to mask or apologize for it." And at another point he says, "The desire to be inconspicuous, that is, to take on the color of one's surroundings, encourages the use of vogue words and phrases. . . ."

Despite the wide prevalence of sexual terms in criminal cant, Stuart Berg Flexner, in the Preface to the *Dictionary of American Slang*, notes that "sex has contributed comparatively few words to modern slang, but these are among our most frequently used." The reason for the frequent use of such words, as he points out, is undoubtedly that "slang words for sexual attraction and for a variety of sexual acts, positions and relationships are more common than standard words," which are scarce or remote and scientific. There is not, for example, a single transitive verb in respectable or even in scientific language that expresses the idea of the slang verb *fuck*. As to other bodily functions, a somewhat similar situation prevails. There are no words for *shit* and *piss* aside from the correct but stilted verbs *defecate* and *urinate*.

In perusing *Slang and Its Analogues* a reader might

well get the impression that sexual terms are more prevalent there than they really are. On almost every third or fourth page he will find a word that is a synonym for "the female pudendum" or "the penis" or "a prostitute" or "the breast." That is because the words are cross-reference entries to lists of such synonyms. The lists themselves are truly astonishing in the richness of their indecency and because of the humor and inventiveness of our forefathers, to which the lists bear witness. The collections are headed by rather arbitrary titles: "Monosyllable" for the female genitals, "Cream-stick" and "Prick" for the male genitals, "Barrack-hack" and "Tart" for prostitute and "Dairies" for the breast. The oddity of these titles leads Legman to suspect that the authors cunningly chose them in order to spot the lists interestingly throughout the seven volumes of the dictionary.

It seems quite evident that the sexual slang terms are coinages of our forefathers, not our foremothers. Indeed, the overwhelming preponderance of all slang is apparently the invention of males. Its roughness, its occasional savagery, its assertiveness – all suggest masculine origin. In addition, women in general are less inclined to use slang than are men and those women who use it extensively have over the years been considered unfeminine. This masculinity of slang can be explained in part if we go back to the concept of the closed group. By the nature of their work in the world, men tend to constitute a closed group or at least to belong to subgroups. Women lead more isolated lives. If they participate in the working world at all, they are for the most part virtually substitute members of the male group.

There is, to be sure, some female slang, but it tends to be restricted to a few female physical characteristics and to a sparse number of items connected with the home and feminine decor. For instance, menstruation has produced a fair crop of slang terms. This dictionary lists some of them under "flag," but more recent terms include *the curse, the red flag is out, fell off the roof, my cousin from Harvard is visiting* and *have the rag on*. Concerning sexual intercourse, this dictionary contains a goodly list of expressions under "Greens" headed "Of Women Only," and most of these suggest coinage by females: *to do the naughty, to do what mother did before me, to get a wet bottom, to look at the ceiling over a man's shoulder*. As for synonyms for that overworked "female pudendum," female inventions seem few indeed, but there is one gentle one listed specifically in the "Monosyllable" section: *fie-for-shame* (schoolgirls'). In the classification of home-making words and phrases the latter-day crop grows largely out of baby talk: *toidy, didie, a no-no, din-din*. The rest of female slang centers chiefly on various facets of fashion: *updo, bra, panties, flats, undies*.

In general slang strives for quick, out-of-the-ordinary, nonstilted means of expression. It sets great store by vigor, color and often an almost savage kind of toughness. It is no wonder then that slang ranges the whole gamut of rhetorical figures of speech from alliteration to zeugma. Most pronounced is its tendency to go to extremes – the extremes of hyperbole. At the positive extreme a difficult situation has in recent decades been described as *murder*; at the negative extreme an expensive mansion

has been dubbed a *shack*. Since a tough stance entails a depreciatory attitude bordering on cynicism, the negative, underplaying expressions greatly outnumber the positive examples of hyperbole. In addition to hyperbole, slang turns for its coinages to synecdoche, or making the part stand for the whole (*bigtop* = circus); it turns to metonymy, or making an attribute of one thing stand for that thing (*cold shoulder* = aloof treatment); it turns to metaphor, or making a comparison by implying an identity (*coffin nail* = cigarette); it turns to euphemism, or using a mild term to avoid an unpleasant one (one of the drollest entries in this dictionary is *to wrong one's breeches* = to shit), and it turns to figurative locutions (*tickle the ivories, hit the hay*). The list could go on and on.

Some slang derives from fabricated languages, such as pig Latin (*ickiechay the opscay* = chickie the cops) and the type of thing this book lists under "Hypernese." There is also the rhyming slang invented by Cockney laborers, in which *storm and strife* means wife and *glorious sinner* means dinner.

In recent years other linguistic devices have come into play. One is suffixation – the use of terminal affixes to coin new words. Thus we get such words as *aquacade* and *lubritorium*. Blending, to produce what might be called "centaur words," is a source of slang, though not a particularly fruitful one: *brunch* (from breakfast and lunch), *smog* (from smoke and fog), *guesstimate, happenstance*. Then there are instances of what Flexner calls "back clipping": *bus* (from omnibus), *cab* (from taxicab), *burger* (from hamburger). The clipping device and the blending device suggest that people are in a hurry and desire short, explosive forms to replace the normal longer ones. The accelerated tempo of modern living may well account for this and at the same time account for the higher birth rate of such terms today than a century ago.

Finally, there is a source of slang that has attracted little notice among philologists. Some present-day colloquialisms are in effect almost literal translations of standard English words derived from Latin, Greek and other ancient tongues. Here are a few examples: *fed up* (from satiated), *stoned* (from ossified – itself slang), *fire* (from discharge), *setup* (from establishment), *windbag* (from fool – derived from a Latin word meaning bellows), *show (up)* (from appear). Maxwell Nurnberg of New York University, in (of all places) a children's book, *Wonders in Words*, lists a dozen others, including *broke* (from bankrupt), *catch on* (from comprehend or apprehend), *double talk* (from equivocating), *burned up* (from incensed), and *uppity* (from haughty).

One need not search far for the reason for such translations. Quite obviously they developed out of the same desire for quick, nonstilted language that accounts for so many other substandard colloquialisms. No doubt many of them will ultimately be promoted to the category of standard English; of the examples cited, *fire* and *catch on* seem to be fair bets for early advancement. Over the centuries such promotions have always taken place. The number of words classed in the present dictionary as slang or colloquial that are now standard bears witness to that assertion. Such promotions are one way in which the language is enriched and adapted to new things, new ways and new times.

Most slang terms, however, are ephemeral – here today and tomorrow and gone the day after. The present dictionary bears witness to that fact, too. Who today would have the slightest use for the term *barrowbunter*, even after it was explained that it meant a female coster-monger? (And yet the term, together with the 1771 quotation illustrating its use, constitutes a quaint specimen, lending interest to the museum of eighteenth century England.)

On the other hand, the longevity of some slang expressions is astonishing. *Bones*, meaning dice, is in common use today, but Chaucer was rolling the bones as far back as 1386. *Gam* for leg is almost two centuries old. So is *corporation* for a protuberant belly, and *bay window* in the same sense is old enough to find its way into this Farmer and Henley turn-of-the-century compilation. *Clink*, the low-grade term for jail, dates back to 1515, though *jug* is a comparative youngster, having been born somewhere around the 1830's. And then there is *dead as a doornail*, which was in use as far back as 1362. Yet all these sound surprisingly modern.

Mention was made earlier of slang terms that take on new life by reason of new meanings and the example cited was *bread*. There are others worthy of some note. *Old hat* these days means out-of-date or not new. But in the 1700's the now-extinct meaning of the expression was – yes – the female pudendum. The present dictionary quotes the droll entry in Grose's 1785 *Classical Dictionary of the Vulgar Tongue* as follows: "Old hat; a woman's privities: because frequently felt."

Groovy in its twentieth century incarnation means excellent, satisfying, but the same word in the nineteenth century meant settled in habit. There were different frames of reference for the words. The older meaning undoubtedly was related to the idea of being in a rut, whereas the newer one is related to the phrase *in the groove*, an allusion to the phonograph needle.

Boss, from the Dutch *baas*, meaning a master, has retained that sense since 1590 (and, oddly enough, after four centuries is still classed as colloquial). But in recent years it took on, perhaps only briefly, the adjectival meaning of excellent or wonderful.

Still another expression that acquired a second life was *booby trap*. Originally, in schoolboy use in the 1850's, it referred to a practical joke in which bottles were placed atop a door that was slightly ajar. But in the two World Wars it was applied to hidden explosives and then was extended to mean any dangerous or embarrassing situation into which a person might fall.

It is evident that any book that attempts to keep up with contemporary slang should be printed in disappearing ink and bound in loose-leaf form. Such an attempt was not the principal object of John Stephen Farmer and William Ernest Henley in their collaboration on *Slang and Its Analogues*. Most certainly they did try to include all the latest substandard language in their dictionary, but they were at least equally interested in recording slang as it had been used down through the years. They drew upon the earlier compilations that were available, notably Giovanni Florio's *Worlde of Wordes*, published in 1598; *A New Dictionary of the Canting Crew*, by "B.E., Gent.," published toward the end of the seventeenth century; and *A Classical Dictionary of the Vulgar Tongue*, by Captain Francis Grose, published in 1785. Naturally they also ferreted out material from all other manner of publications, both literary and journalistic, in a truly remarkable display of research.

Very little is known about Farmer and even less about the manner of the collaboration between him and Henley. Farmer was born about 1845 and died about 1915. Legman, who has delved into the mystery of the man, says that "he was a scholar and an occultist, and that he wrote or edited some twenty creditable books," including collections of bawdy folk songs, of slang songs and of French erotic dictionaries in translation.

It seems not unlikely that Farmer began work on *Slang and Its Analogues* alone. One piece of evidence supporting this conclusion is that the original first volume dated 1890 of the seven-volume dictionary bears his name alone on the title page. (The revised first volume, issued in sections between 1903 and 1909, does include Henley's name.) A second piece of evidence is that the original first volume carries a Prefatory Note, written in the first-person singular; it is unsigned, but since only the name of Farmer appears on the title page, the presumption must be that he was the author.

On the other hand, it is possible, though not probable, that at first Henley did not wish his name attached to so bawdy a book. It is possible because he was at the time a respected poet; it is not probable because he was a defiant, spirited man. In any event, whatever reluctance he had was overcome because his name does appear on subsequent volumes, though oddly enough his biographers scarcely mention the collaboration.

In the title of this work "Analogues" is a minor element. The analogues themselves – the foreign words and phrases corresponding to English slang – are likewise a minor feature of the compilation. It is, of course, interesting to discover that the English verb *butter*, in the sense of bestowing fulsome flattery, is matched by the French verb *cirer*. But it is even more interesting to learn that *butter* was used in this sense by Congreve well over two centuries ago.

In parentheses after the head word of each entry in the dictionary is a classifying word. Most of these designations are self-explanatory, but a clarifying word may be said about some others. "Colloquial" refers to casual terms used in informal spoken language. "Common" is a step or so below colloquial and terms so described would not normally be used by the well-bred. "Low" is another step down and applies to words that would be used by the great unwashed and would be acceptable to people in that category. At the bottom is "vulgar", which characterizes terms that are boorish, obscene or profane. It should be pointed out that such classifying words do not constitute eternal verities because fashions change in language as in most other human institutions. For instance, *backside* is categorized in this compilation as vulgar, whereas in present-day dictionaries it is standard English, not even slang. Conversely, *arse*, which here is described as "now vulgar," was at one time in good literary use. Farmer and Henley were, of course, presenting slang terms as they were regarded at the turn of the century.

In this, as in other more important respects, the collaborators made a significant philological contribution.

Slang and Its Analogues is without question a basic book in its field. Its treasures have been mined by virtually every twentieth century writer on the subject of common speech and such experts acknowledge it to be a classic. Its new presentation — the seven volumes in one — makes it for the first time comfortably available not only to scholars, but also to the educated public in general. The scholars will find it greatly rewarding, the cultivated reader will find it unusually enlightening, all will find it spicily enjoyable.

Theodore M. Bernstein
Editorial Director
Book and Education Division
The New York Times

SLANG AND ITS ANALOGUES

PAST AND PRESENT.

A DICTIONARY, HISTORICAL AND COMPARATIVE, OF THE
HETERODOX SPEECH OF ALL CLASSES OF SOCIETY
FOR MORE THAN THREE HUNDRED YEARS.

*WITH SYNONYMS IN ENGLISH, FRENCH, GERMAN,
ITALIAN, ETC.*

COMPILED AND EDITED BY

JOHN S. FARMER,

AUTHOR OF

"Americanisms—Old and New": "Ex Oriente Lux": "'Twixt Two Worlds."

VOL. I. — A TO BYZ.

PRINTED FOR SUBSCRIBERS ONLY.

—

MDCCCXC.

PREFATORY NOTE.

 "E that undertakes to compile a dictionary, undertakes that which, if it comprehends the full extent of his design, he knows himself unable to perform. Yet his labours, though deficient, may be useful, and with the hope of this inferior praise, he must incite his activity, and solace his weariness." So wrote the great lexicographer, Dr. Johnson, in the "Advertisement" to the fourth edition of his Dictionary of the English Language, published in 1773. In another place he had already told, in words which have since become classical, of the difficulties he had encountered, and of his own estimate of the shortcomings of his work as compared with the original design. It is in very much the same position that I find myself, now that I have completed the first instalment of my own task, smaller and less important though it be. I am fully conscious of manifold imperfections; yet I hope, and indeed believe, that I have, in my presentation of what is generically known as "slang," advanced the enquiry in some measure. While cordially acknowledging the aid I have derived from the labours of my predecessors in the field, I cannot but recognise that, again and again, having adopted a new mode of treatment, I have found myself forced to "blaze" the way into what was practically a *terra incognita*.

The difficulties were manifold, and crowded upon one at every turn from the very outset. First and foremost came the question of deciding whether any given word, phrase, or turn of expression could with justice be relegated to the limbo of unorthodox speech — in short to decide, What is Slang? As a matter of fact, I have not yet discovered, nor have I been able to formulate any definition which covers the whole of the ground to be traversed. As Dr. Murray truly observes, "there is absolutely no defining line in any direction: the circle of the English language has a well-defined centre, but no discernible circumference." Authorities differ between themselves, and often with themselves when asked to set down in plain scientific terms the marks which distinguish the vagrant words of slang from correct and orthodox English. Nor is the difficulty removed or lessened by an analysis of the genesis, or the application of this vast and motley crowd of heterodox words: of a verity the borderland between slang and the "Queen's English" is an ill-defined territory, the limits of which have never been clearly mapped out. It is, therefore, not without hesitation, that I have ventured to explore this "Dark Continent" of the World of Words. If I cast a ray of light where before was darkness, or reduce to some sort of order where much was confusion — well and good: if, on the other hand, my steps at times chance to falter, others will, in such a case, be able to profit by my experience as I have by that of my predecessors.

Hence — bearing in mind the ill-defined character of much of the enquiry — my title, "Slang and its Analogues," which I think fairly and accurately describes

the scope and intent of the present work, though it may not satisfy those critics who, without examination, seek to decry or put aside that which it has cost years of labour and research to produce. For the rest, however, a conscientious worker may well be content to abide the result of careful and honest criticism, whether for praise or demerit.

Great as was the initial difficulty in regard to a dividing line between the three great divisions of colloquial English —dialectical, technical, and slang— it was clearly and obviously necessary to draw the line somewhere. After careful consideration, I adopted, as a standard between literary and non-literary English, Annandale's edition of Ogilvie's *Imperial English Dictionary*. With but few exceptions, it will be found that no word is here included which is there set down as forming part of the orthodox inheritance of "the noble English tongue." The next great difficulty with which I found myself confronted was the determination of the exact meanings of slang words and expressions. Frequently I discovered I had to deal with a veritable Proteus—slang used to-day in one sense shades off to-morrow into many modifications. This fact I have had to keep steadily in mind. It will account, in some instances, for what may, at first sight, appear to be an unnecessarily extended list of illustrative quotations; in such cases it will generally be found, on examination, that different shades of meaning are exemplified.

As regards treatment, I have adopted, though not in its entirety, what is commonly known as the "historical method," supplementing this by an attempt at the comparative study of slang, *i.e.*, the presentation of unorthodox English in juxtaposition with the argots of other European nations, notably those of the French, German, Italian, and Spanish peoples. The historical usage of slang is amply illustrated by the quotations appended to each example. These comprise in their range the whole period of English literature from the earliest down to the present time, my plan having been to give the first ascertainable use of any given word or phrase, tracing it down century by century, winding up with an example "down to date." These illustrative quotations, roughly speaking, number upwards of 100,000 for the whole work. I was fortunate enough shortly after commencing my final task of revision to have about 12,000 quotations placed at my disposal by Mr. G. L. Apperson, of Wimbledon, who for many years has had special knowledge of the requirements of such work, having sub-edited certain sections of the *New English Dictionary*. I am glad to be able to make special mention of my indebtedness in this respect; as also to Mr. G. A. King, of Croydon, an old Wykehamist, for invaluable aid in connection with public school words and phrases.

Copious materials for a comparative study of English and foreign slang will be found in the often-times lengthy lists of analogous and synonymous terms appended to the more important and more commonly used examples in the body of the work. This branch of my study I shall deal with more fully in an article to follow the completion of the vocabulary proper, and I purpose to enhance the usefulness of that portion of the dictionary by a complete alphabetical list of all the foreign slang words and phrases herein used, with full references to page and column.

For the rest, my method will, I think, need little elucidation. I have endeavoured to make each example, with its explanation, derivation, synonyms, and illustrative quotations, as far as possible, complete in itself. Over and above this, however, the cross-references will be found of considerable value for the purpose of comparison, and will, I hope, be acceptable. I may also add that, wherever possible, I have given a reference indicating where synonymous or analogous words may be found. The arrangement of these synonyms has been a matter of considerable thought; first, as to the most fitting place for inclusion; and second, so to distribute them throughout the dictionary as to present a piece of work evenly balanced, and ready of reference.

There are certain sources of information of which I must make special acknowledgment. Among books, first and foremost, comes that invaluable store-house, *Notes and Queries*. I have freely drawn for information upon this inestimable periodical from its very first issue, invariably making a note of my indebtedness, and to whom, in the text. The *New English Dictionary* has also been of service in supplying, at times, earlier examples of the use of a slang word or phrase than those of which I was already possessed. It is not, however, without a certain amount of perhaps pardonable satisfaction that I, working single-handed, am often able to give much earlier illustrations of the slang side and usage of our mother tongue, than occurs elsewhere.

As regards French *Argot*, Francisque Michel, Lorédan Larchey, and A. Barrère, respectively, are the chief authorities to whom I wish to render due acknowledg-

ment; Avé-Lallemant and Kahle have also been specially useful in connection with the German *Gaunersprache*. The dates of quotations have, wherever possible, been finally verified by comparison with the comprehensive and useful appendix to Dr. Brewer's *Reader's Handbook*.

It may not be out of place to give some indication of the complete scheme (subject to slight modification) of SLANG AND ITS ANALOGUES. The work will comprise:—

I. A dictionary of ancient and modern English slang, treated historically, including copious lists of English, French, German, and Italian synonyms, etc.

II. A chapter on the comparative study of the subject; this embraces English cant and slang, French *Argot*, German *Gaunersprache*, Italian *Fourbesque*, Spanish *Germania*, and Portuguese *Calaõ*.

III. A new and exhaustive Bibliography, with copious entries of foreign books treating of the subject.

IV. A list of authorities and references to periodical literature, with full titles and dates as mentioned throughout the dictionary.

V. A complete vocabulary of all foreign slang words and expressions occurring throughout the body of the work, with detailed references to example, page, and column. This will form in itself a comprehensive dictionary of foreign slang.

List of Abbreviations, Signs, etc.

Adj. = Adjective.	M.H.G. = Middle High German.
Adj. phr. = Adjectival phrase.	[N.] = Nares (quoted from).
Adv. = Adverb.	O.E. = Old English.
Adv. phr. = Adverbial phrase.	O.H.G. = Old High German.
C. c. = *Circa*, about.	*ppl.* = participial or participle.
Cf. cf. = *Confer*, compare.	*phr.* = phrase.
f. = feminine.	*pl.* = plural.
F. or Fr. = French.	pop. = popular.
Heb. = Hebrew.	*ppl. adj.* = participial adjective.
imp. = imperative.	(*q.v.*) = *quod vide*, which see.
int. = interjection.	*subs.* = substantive.
intr. = intransitive.	*trans.* = transitive.
It. = Italian.	U.S. or U.S.A. = United States of America.
lit. = literally.	
[M.] = Murray (quoted from *New English Dictionary*).	When a word is printed in small capitals it should be referred to for further information.
m. = masculine.	
M.E. = Middle English.	

A · Dictionary · of
❋ Slang · and · its · Analogues. ❋

 (vulgar) — ["ă" as in *bat*]. — A common vulgarism in speaking for (1) "have," (2) "I," (3) "he," (4) "at," (5) "on," etc. It occurs in these connections for more than 300 years; all were used by Shakspeare, as well as by Beaumont and Fletcher and other writers of the Elizabethan period.

A1 or **A1 Copper-Bottomed,** *adj. phr.* (popular). — Applied to men or things, A1 is synonymous with a high degree of praise. 'He must be a first-rater,' said Sam. 'A1,' replied Mr. Roker. [1837, *Pickwick Papers*.]

The derivation of this colloquialism from the symbols used in registering ships at Lloyd's is pretty well known. Letters—A.A. (in black and red), Æ (in black), E, etc.—are employed to denote various degrees of excellence in the hulls of vessels, figures being

added to show the quality of the equipments, such as masts and rigging in sailing vessels, or boilers and engines in steamers. When hull and fittings alike are of the best, a vessel is classed A1. Hence, in mercantile circles, the expression has become popularly current, in a figurative sense, to signify the highest commercial credit; and, by a process of expansion, excellence of quality in general, *i.e.*, first-class; first-rate. The form varies, being rendered by FIRST-CLASS LETTER A; A1 COPPER-BOTTOMED; and, in the U.S.A., A1 AND NO MISTAKE. The earliest reference given in the *New English Dictionary* for the colloquially figurative usage bears date 1836, but it was employed at least two years previously in a quarter which seems definitely to fix, not only the period of its adoption, but the process of transition as well. A1 was a perfectly natural colloquialism in the hands of Captain Marryat, at once an experienced seaman and a practised writer.

ABADDON, *subs.* (old). — A thief who, to general nefarious practices, adds perfidy to his companions. Rarely, and perhaps only locally used. It is obviously derived from ABADDON, the destroyer or angel of the bottomless pit (Revelation ix., 11).

ABANDANNAD, ABANDANNAAD, *subs.* (thieves'). — 1. A nearly obsolete term to designate primarily a pickpocket, whose chief quarry is pocket handkerchiefs or bandannas; and, hence

2. A petty thief, *i.e.*, one whose depredations are regarded by the fraternity as not worth the risk incurred. Brewer writes down the word as a contraction of 'a bandanna lad.' With this derivation is connected the story of an incident said to have been a prime factor in the movement resulting in the passing of Sir Samuel Romilly's Act for the abolition of capital punishment for highway robberies under 40s. value. Briefly told, it is that a footpad robbed a woman of a bandanna shawl, valued at 9d., an offence for which a notorious highwayman was hanged. Subsequently, however, he was proved to have been innocent, whereupon the fact of her mistaken accusation having done an innocent man to death so preyed upon the woman's mind that she became raving mad. The incidents touched the public conscience, an agitation ensued, and the law was amended as stated.

ABANDONED HABITS, *subs. phr.* (popular). — The riding costumes of the ladies of the demi-monde in Hyde Park—(*Slangiana*). The punning and sufficiently obvious

innuendo involved in the appellation hardly calls for further comment.—*See* ANONYMA.

ABBESS or **LADY ABBESS,** *subs.* (old). — The keeper of a house of ill-fame; also a procuress. It has been suggested that the origin of this term for the mistress of a brothel, as also that of ABBOT (*q.v.*), the name given to the male associate of the mistress, may be traced to the alleged illicit amours of Abelard and Héloïse. In this connection it is significant that, according to Francisque Michel's *Etudes Comparées sur l'Argot*, a common woman was, in the old French cant, said to come from *l'abbaye des s'offre à tous*. The keeper of such an establishment was called *l'abbesse*, and her associate *le sacristain*. The analogy was carried still further, by the inmates being termed 'nuns' and 'sisters of charity.' This depravation in the meaning of words, usually applied only to the holders of sacred offices, may possibly, without undue license, be regarded as resulting from the mockery born of the degradation, in the popular mind, of the priestly office; or, it may naturally flow from the loose way in which the title of 'abbot' was often applied to the holders of non-monastic offices. Thus, the first step toward degeneration may have occurred in applying the term to the principal of a body of clergy, as an episcopal rector; or, as amongst the Genoese, to a chief magistrate. The second stage was reached when, in the middle ages, 'abbot' was applied ironi-

1883. MARRYAT, *Peter Simple*, ch. xliii. 'Broached molasses, cask No. 1, LETTER A.'

1876. C. HINDLEY, *Life and Adventures of a Cheap Jack*, p. 229. 'Here's spoons for six, and tea and sugar for one. Sold again! and this time to my old sweetheart of all. She's a prime girl, she is; she is a NUMBER ONE, COPPER-BOTTOMED, and can sail as well in her stays as out of her stays; she is full rigged, and carries a lot of canvas. But I must not tell tales out of school.'

1882. *Punch*, lxxxii. 181, 1. IN VINO (ET CETERA) VERITAS. 'What's up, old man? You seem to be out of sorts!' 'Snappe's been here. I begged him to give me his candid opinion about my pictures. He did! 'Ah! I see! It differs from *yours*! Now when I want a fellow's candid opinion about my pictures, I ask him to dinner, give him a first-rate bottle of claret, a cup of A1 coffee, a glass of old cognac, and the best cigar money can buy, and *then* I show him my pictures, and I always find that his candid opinion coincides with my own.'

ENG. SYNONYMS. All brandy; the pure quill; about East (American); about right; at par; the cheese; all there; bang up; a corker; up to Dick; downy; fizzing; that's Bible; splash up; up to the nines; up to the knocker; down to the ground; slap up, etc.

FRENCH SYNONYMS. *Abracadabrant, adj.* (from Abracadabra); *aux petits oignons* (literally 'like small onions.' *Cf.*, English, 'like a thousand of bricks,' and 'like winkey'); *bath* (adj.: also *bate*. In *Argot and Slang* the origin of the term is thus stated:—Towards 1848 some Bath notepaper was hawked about in the streets of Paris, and sold at a low price. Thus 'papier bath' became synonymous of (*sic*) excellent paper. In a short time the qualifying term alone remained and received a general application);

arriver bon premier (literally 'to arrive a good first').

(Fenian). — Sometimes erroneously No. 1. In the copy of Hotten's *Slang Dictionary*, annotated by H. J. Byron, the playwright, now in the British Museum, this is given as 'a title for the commander of 900 men.''

AARON, *subs.* (thieves'). — 'The AARON,' says H. O. Manton in *Slangiana*, 'is the chief or captain of a gang or school of thieves. The title is invariably preceded by the prefix *The*—par excellence the first—similar to the eldest representatives of certain Irish and Scotch clans or families, such as *The* O'Connor Don, *The* Chisholm, etc. As AARON was the first high priest . . . . it is probably of Jewish origin in its slang application. An AARON was an old cant term for one of a class of cadgers, who combined begging with acting as guide to the summits of mountains, chiefly to evade the laws against vagabondage, no doubt a play, in its slang sense, on its Hebrew equivalent, lofty.' In this last connection a closer relationship probably exists than that just stated, inasmuch as Gesenius thinks that the Hebrew AARON is a derivative of *Hāron*, a mountaineer. It is to be remarked that leaders of the church were also called AARONS.

A. B., or **A. B. S.** (commercial). — An able-bodied seaman.—*See* BOTTLE SUCKER.

1875. *Chambers' Journal*, No. 627. Of all the European sailors by far the most reliable were five stalwart A.B's.

cally to the heads of various guilds and associations, and to the leaders in popular assemblages and disorderly festivities, *e.g.*, the Abbot of Bell-ringers, the Abbot of Misrule, the Abbot of Unreason. Henceforward deterioration was both easy and rapid to the point when 'abbot' and its co-relative ABBESS, signified a steward and stewardess of the STEWS (*q.v.*). The terms are now obsolete on both sides of the Channel. In England the modern equivalent for ABBESS is MOTHER (*q.v.*); and in France *la maca, mère maca, la maquecée,* or *l'institutrice*, do similar duty.

1782. WOLCOT [P. Pindar], *Odes to the Pope*, Ode ii. in *Works* (Dublin, 1795), vol. II., p. 492.
So an old ABBESS, for the rattling rakes, A tempting dish of human nature makes, And dresses up a luscious maid.

1840. W. KIDD, *London and all Its Dangers*. The infernal wretches who traffic in the souls and bodies of their helpless victims are called LADY ABBESSES.

ABBEY LUBBER, *subs. phr.* (old).— [From ABBEY + LUBBER.]

1. An old term of contempt for an able-bodied idler who grew sleek and fat upon the charity of religious houses; also sometimes, especially subsequent to the Reformation, applied to monks. In this sense it has long fallen into disuse.

1680. DRYDEN, *Spanish Friar*, III. 3. This is no huge, overgrown ABBEY LUBBER.

2. The term survives, however, and is still occasionally used by seafaring men, although 'lubber' is now more common amongst our Jack tars for a lazy, thriftless individual. If a sailor wishes to express

the utmost scorn for laziness and meanness, he finds a very much more forcible expression in a 'dirty dog and no sailor.'—*See* LUBBERS' HOLE.

ABBOT, *subs.* (old). — The husband or 'fancy man' of an ABBESS (*q.v.*); now called a PONCE (*q.v.*) In the old French argot these gentry were dignified by the title of *sacristain*. They were occasionally spoken of as CROZIERED ABBOTS, or ABBOTS ON THE CROSS, in which case the establishments over which they mounted guard were not so much brothels as PANEL CRIBS (*q.v.*), where prostitution served mainly as a cloak for robbery.

ABBOTT'S PRIORY, *subs. phr.* (popular). — The King's Bench Prison was formerly so-called; perhaps from Chief Justice Abbott.

ABBREVIATIONS. — These occasionally partake most clearly of the nature of slang. As illustrative examples may be mentioned : — K.D.Gs., the King's, now the First Dragoon Guards.—O.K., all right; 'orl krect.'—B.T.I., a big thing on ice.—Q.T., generally 'on the strict Q.T.', *i.e.*, quiet.—T.T., too thin.—Cri., the Criterion (restaurant or theatre).—The Ox., the Oxford Music Hall.—Tec., detective.—B.P., British Public.—B. and S., brandy and soda.—P.D.Q., pretty d——d quick.

A.B.C.'s (London).—1. The Aërated Bread Co.'s establishments are, familiarly speaking, *A.B.C.'s*.
2. (Christ's Hospital.)—*A*le, *B*read and *C*heese on 'going home night.'

As EASY AS A. B. C., *adv. phr.* (popular). — Extremely facile; the acme of ease, *i.e.*, from an adult's point of view; children, however, probably view the matter in a different light. In this, as in much else, distance lends enchantment to the scene. This colloquialism is by no means of modern growth; Shakspeare speaks of answer 'coming like A. B. C. book.'

A-BEAR, *v.* (provincial and vulgar).—To suffer, or to tolerate. [From old English *abearan*, to bear or carry].—This term, though hoary with age, and long of honorable usage (from A.D. 885 downward), must now be classed with degenerate words, or at all events with non-literary English. Though still largely dialectical, its use amongst people of education is reckoned vulgar. It is now invariably employed in conjunction with 'cannot' — 'I can't ABEAR furriners.'

ABELWHACKETS. — *See* ABLEWHACKETS.

ABERDEEN CUTLET, *subs. phr.* (familiar).—A dried haddock.—*Cf.*, BILLINGSGATE PHEASANT.

ABIDE, *v.* (vulgar).—To tolerate; to put up with. This, like ABEAR (q.v.), has ancient sanction for its use. In the senses of to endure, suffer, bear, or sustain—meanings which are now obsolete—the word can be traced back as far as A.D. 1205; the modern vulgar usage, rarely employed affirmatively, dates from about A.D. 1526, when Tindale translated John viii. 43, by 'He cannot ABYDE the hearyng of my words.' ABIDE, therefore, may be classed amongst those words which, once respectable, have now fallen into disrepute. Shakspeare puts into the mouth of one of his characters a phrase which, to those acquainted with the speech of the uneducated classes, has a very modern appearance, 'I cannot ABIDE the smell of hot meat.'

ABIGAIL, *subs.* (popular).—A lady's maid. There can be little doubt that the familiar use of this name for the genus 'waiting woman,' was primarily an allusion to the title of handmaid assumed by ABIGAIL, the wife of Nabal, in speaking to the servants of King David. 'Behold, let thine handmaid be a servant to wash the feet of the servants of my Lord' (1 Sam. xxv. 41). Other names recorded in the Bible, and for the matter of that elsewhere, have been used much in the same way as marking distinctive character. ABIGAIL has thus become associated with the idea of a female servant; so, too, a giant is spoken of as a Goliath; a patient man as a Job; a shrew as a Jezebel; a coward as a Bob Acres, *cum multis aliis*. In Beaumont and Fletcher's comedy of *The Scornful Lady* (1616), one of the characters, Mrs. Youngton, a 'waiting gentlewoman,' is named ABIGAIL. This play, having a long run of public favour,—Pepys in his *Diary* [1666], iv. 195, specially mentions it,—possibly led to the popularization of the nickname. At all events it subsequently appeared on more than one occasion in the same connection

in the plays of the period. There is no reason to suppose that the term was derived from the notorious ABIGAIL Hill, better known as Mrs. Masham, a poor relative of the Duchess of Marlborough, by whom she was introduced to a subordinate place about the person of Queen Anne; nor will the contention that it was first established in public usage by Dean Swift, who employed it in a letter to Stella, hold good; although likely enough he caused it to take deeper root than before. The terms on which he was with the Mashams rendered him the last person in the world likely to have used such a term, unless it had been so long in familiar use as to be deprived of all appearance of personal allusion to them.

1663. T. KILLIGREW, *Parson's Wedding*, II., vi. in Dodsley, *O.P.* (1780), xi., 425. [In this play, a waiting woman is termed an ABIGAIL.]

1750. FIELDING, *Tom Jones*, book XI., ch. ii. The mistress was no sooner in bed than the maid prepared to follow her example. She began to make many apologies to her sister ABIGAIL for leaving her alone in so horrid a place as an inn.

1858. G. ELIOT, *Mr. Gilfil's Love-Story*, ch. iii. The next morning, Mrs. Sharp, then a blooming ABIGAIL of three-and-thirty, entered her lady's private room.

It has been stated that Old English writers used the word ABIGAIL to signify a termagant woman, and also a female bigamist, but there is no evidence to support these views. It may be mentioned that the French use the word in the popular English sense. A waiting woman was also formerly called a COMB-BRUSH (*q.v.*).

ABLEWHACKETS, also **ABELWHACKETS, ABELWACKETS**, *subs.* (nautical). —[From ABLE (uncertain, perhaps alluding to able seaman) + WHACK]. A game of cards played by sailors, in which the loser receives a whack or blow with a knotted handkerchief for every game (or point) he loses. Smyth, in his *Sailor's Word Book* [1867], says it is very popular with horny-fisted salts. It is quoted by Grose as far back as 1785, but Clark Russell, in *Sailor's Language* [1883], refers to it as obsolete.

ABOUND, *v.* (American).—To be prominent; *en évidence*.

1873. *Evening Standard*, 28 January. When we are told of a professed wit more than usually ABOUNDING at an evening party, there is no temptation to recruit our dictionaries from the English manufactured in the United States.

ABOUT EAST, *adv. phr.* (American).—To the frontiersman or pioneer, the Eastern or New England States are typical of all that he cherishes most and loves best. The vicissitudes of his rough Western life, the toil and hardships he has undergone while battling with nature and building up a new homestead far from the old homestead, all predispose him to turn with longing eyes and undying, though quaintly exaggerated love to the East—the home of his fathers. A famous Yankee character (Major Jack Downing) makes use of the expression that he would 'Go EAST of sunrise any day to see sich a place.' Everybody and everything connected with the East *i.e.*, his native land, is commendable. To his mind they cannot be surpassed —hence the things he would

hold up to admiration he says are ABOUT EAST, *i.e.*, 'about right.' Indeed, it is surprising what a strong hold this idea has upon the minds of men. Many a familiar phrase recalls the old times and the old folks to memory, which, in this respect, is evergreen. They talk of GOING DOWN EAST, that is, to New England, while the DOWN-EASTER is neither more nor less than the pure and veritable Yankee. — FARMER'S *Americanisms, Old and New.*

ABOUT RIGHT, *adv. phr.* (vulgar).—Correctly; to the purpose; properly—general satisfaction on the part of the speaker concerning a given thing or action. 'Arry sometimes varies the locution by TER RIGHTS (*q.v.*).

1850. F. E. SMEDLEY, *Frank Fairleigh*, ch. iv. 'YOU'RE ABOUT RIGHT, there, Mr. Lawless; you're down to every move, I see, as usual.'

1883. HAWLEY SMART, *Hard Lines*, ch. xxii. 'I am afraid your schemes went a little awry yesterday,' observed Mrs. Daventry . . . 'YOU'RE ABOUT RIGHT; they did.'

ABOUT THE SIZE OF IT, *adv. phr.* (American).—1. An expression covering a wide field—assent, general satisfaction, approval, etc. Synonymous with ABOUT RIGHT; O.K.; TER RIGHTS, etc.

2. Used also for 'how'; 'how much,' etc.—a measure of quantity or quality.

1876 (?). JAMES GREENWOOD, *New 'Roughs' Guide'* in 'Odd People in Odd Places.' Got no home, no wittles, and never a 'a'penny to buy none with. That's ABOUT THE SIZE of how destitoot we are, sir.

1881. *Punch*, May 14, p. 228. SIR G[ORGIUS] M[IDAS] GOES IN FOR CULTURE. "Look 'ere, Clarke. 'Appy thought! I'll make this little room the libery, you know; 'ave a lot o' books. Mind you order me some.' 'Yes, Sir Gorgius. What sort of books shall I order?' 'Oh, the best, of course, with binding and all that to match!' 'Yes, Sir Gorgius, how *many* shall I order?' 'Well,—let me see,—suppose we say a couple o' 'undred yards of 'em, hay? That's ABOUT THE SIZE OF IT, I think.'

ABOVE BOARD, *adv. phr.* (common). —Without disguise or concealment; with an absence of artifice. Jamieson refers this to the language of the gaming table, the players when changing cards putting their hands on, *i.e.*, above the table or board to ensure fair dealing. It appears, however, even in its figurative sense to be a colloquialism of long standing.—*See* MURRAY'S *New English Dictionary.*

ABOVE ONE'S BEND, *adv. phr.* (American).—*See* BEND.

ABOVE PAR, *adv. phr.* (familiar).—Used figuratively in a multitude of senses, *e.g.* (1) in reference to one's health or spirits, in good condition; (2) applied to a man in liquor it signifies a state of moderate drunkenness; or (3) used in regard to pecuniary matters it is synonymous with being 'flush,' having 'the needful'—'best bliss of earth,' as Duncombe puts it. Derived from the technical, commercial meaning. Stocks are said to be *at par* when purchasable at their 'face' value; when at a premium they are ABOVE PAR; and when selling at a decline in value, *i.e.*, at a discount, they are said to be *below par*; hence the colloquial usage. *See* example in quotation. Synonyms, UP TO, or ABOVE THE MARK.

1880. *Punch*, June 5, p. 253. FRED ON PRETTY GIRLS AND PICTURES.

Awful fellow that Ted at his letters!—he
  writes for the *Scanmag*, you know;
And his style never falls below 'PAR.'
  Not my joke, heard him putting it
  so——.
And the pars in the *Scanmag*—he does
  them—are proper, and chock full of
  'go.'
Only paper I care to grind through, never
  preachy, or gushing, or slow!

ABRACADABRA, *subs.* (scientific jargon).——1.—A cabalistic word used in incantations. When written in a manner similar to that shown in accompanying diagram, so as to be read in different directions, and worn as an amulet, it was supposed to cure certain ailments.

A B R A C A D A B R A
A B R A C A D A B R
A B R A C A D A B
A B R A C A D A
A B R A C A D
A B R A C A
A B R A C
A B R A
A B R
A B
A

Hence (2), any word-charm, empty jingle of words, gibberish, nonsense, or extravagant idea. Littré's derivation from the Hebrew—*ab* father, *mach* spirit, and *dabar* word—is regarded by many authorities as fanciful; as also is T. A. G. Balfour's reference of it to a composition of the first letters of the Hebrew words signifying 'Father, Son, and Holy Spirit.' Other authorities, though by no means in accord, generally agree that a Persian origin is the most likely. Mr. R. S. Charnock (*Notes and Queries*, 7 S., iii., 504) thinks it related to the cabalistic word *abraxas* composed of the Greeek letters α, β, ρ, α, ξ, α, ς, making, according to the Greek numeration, the number 365.

Des auteurs beaucoup plus anciens n'ont vu dans le mot *abraxas*, qu'une réunion des lettres numériques, qui étant additionées donnent le nombre 365, ou l'année entière, en sorte qu' *abraxas* serait le symbole du soleil ou de sa révolution annuelle presumée.—*Depping.*

In Persian, according to Grotenford, *abraxas* means the 'Sun God'; if this be so its use as a talisman is easily understood. Yet another derivation is from a corrupt form of the Hebrew—*dabar* is verbū, and *abraca* is benedixit, *i.e.*, verbum benedixit. If, however, the word is Semetic at all, and nothing more than an unintelligible jargon of letters, it could possibly be better explained than by Littré, by *Abra(i) seda bra(i)*, 'Out, bad spirit, out!' as a magic formula for driving out the demon which causes the fever. It is interesting in this connection to compare Mark i. 25, ix. 25, and parallel passages.

1687. AUBREY'S *Remaines of Gentilisme*, p. 124 (1881). [In this work ABRACADABRA is given arranged as a spell.]

1711. *Spectator*, No. 221. They [the signatures] are, perhaps, little amulets or charms to preserve the paper against the fascination and malice of evil eyes; for which reason I would not have my reader surprised, if hereafter he sees any of my papers marked with a Q, a *Z*, a Y, an &c., or with the word ABRACADABRA.

1722. DEFOE, *Journal of the Plague* (ed. Brayley, 1835, p. 56). 'This mysterious word, which, written in the form of a triangle or a pyramid, was regarded as a talisman or charm of wonderful power, is said to have been the name of a Syrian god, whose aid was considered to be invoked by the wearers of the amulet. It originated in the superstitions of a very remote period, and was recommended as an antidote by Serenus Sammonicus, a Roman physician, who lived in the early part of the third century, in the reigns of the emperors Severus and Caracalla. Its efficacy was reputed to be most powerful in agues and other disorders of a febrile kind, and particularly against the fever called by the physicians Hemitritæus.'

1879. *Literary World*, 5 Dec., p.358, col. 2 [M]. The new ABRACADABRA of science, 'organic evolution.'

ABRAHAM, *subs.* (popular). — A clothier's shop of the lowest description, where slop-made garments of shoddy cloth form the staple commodity together with second-hand clothes or HAND-ME-DOWNS (*q.v.*). Chiefly localized in the East End of London, where these establishments are kept by Jews; hence probably the derivation of the term; *adj.* (old cant). — *See* ABRAM.

ABRAHAM-COVE, ABRAHAM-MAN, ABRAM-COVE, ABRAM-MAN, TOM OF BEDLAM'S MAN, or BEDLAM BEGGAR, *subs.* (old cant).— It is difficult now-a-days to trace with certainty the origin of these terms, notwithstanding a wealth of matter on the subject. Nares describes the fraternity as a set of vagabonds who wandered about the country soon after the dissolution of the religious houses; the provision for the poor in those places being cut off and no other substituted. Thus, primarily, an ABRAHAM-MAN was a vagabond, a beggar—tattered, unwashed, unkempt—and a thief withal. 'What an Abram!' an exclamation for a naked fellow. Harman, the earliest authority, refers to them as feigning madness (*see* quot.), and as having been resident in Bethlehem Hospital. Wards in the ancient Bedlam bore distinctive names of some saint or patriarch; that named after Abraham was devoted to a class of mendicant lunatics, who on certain days were permitted to go out begging. It is an open question whether the ward gave the name to the men or *vice versâ*. In either case, however, the use of the term 'Abraham' is in this connection possibly an allusion to the beggar Lazarus in Luke xvii. These mendicants bore a badge, but many assumed the distinction without right, and begged feigning lunacy. Hence, it may be, the more popular signification of the term—

2. An impostor, wandering about the country pretending to be mad, begging in the streets, and laying hands upon all trifles 'considered' or 'unconsidered' in his way. Dekker, in his *English Villanies* [1632], has many curious particulars of the habits of this class of impostors who were said to SHAM ABRAHAM. Shakspeare also, in *King Lear* [1605], Act ii., Scene 3, describes and puts into the mouth of one of these characters the following words:

. . . the basest and most poorest shape,
That ever penury in contempt of man,
Brought near to beast: my face I'll grime with filth;
Blanket my loins; elf all my hair in knots;
And with presented nakedness outface
The winds, and persecutions of the sky.
The country gives me proof and precedent
Of BEDLAM beggars, who, with roaring voices,
Strike in their numb'd and mortified bare arms
Pins, wooden pricks, nails, sprigs of rosemary;
And with this horrible object, from low farms,
Poor pelting villages, sheep-cotes and mills,
Sometime with lunatic bans, sometime with prayers,
Enforce their charity.

The term is now obsolete, though Scott used it as late as 1824, and from the *Quarterly Review* (1813), IX., p. 167, it seems to have then been in pretty general use. The modern prototype is called a tramp or cadger. To SHAM ABRAHAM, *i.e.*, to feign sickness or distress is, however, still in vogue. The French equivalent is *Fagotin* (m). —*See* also ABRAHAM SHAM and ABRAM.

1573. HARMAN, *Caveat* (1814), p. 29. These ABRAHAM MEN be those that fayn themselves to have bene mad, and have bene kept either in Bethlehem, or in some other pryson a good time, and not one amongst twenty that ever came in prison for any such cause.

1625. MASSINGER, *New Way to Pay Old Debts*, II., i. Are they padders or ABRAM-MEN that are your consorts?

1724. E. COLES, *Eng. Dict.* ABRAM cove, naked or poor man.

1825. SCOTT, *St. Ronan's Well*, ch. xxi. 'There is a trick for you to find an ABRAM-MAN, and save sixpence out when he begs of you as a disbanded seaman.'

ABRAHAM GRAINS, *subs.* (thieves').— A publican who brews his own beer.

ABRAHAM NEWLAND, *subs.* (popular). —A bank note. Abraham Newland was chief cashier to the Bank of England, from 1778 to 1807.

1829. SIR W. SCOTT, letter to Croker in *Croker Papers*, vol. II., p. 36. A bank note seems to terrify everybody out of their wits, and they will rather give up their constitution to Hunt and Cobbett than part with an ABRAHAM NEWLAND to preserve it.

ABRAHAM'S BALSAM, *subs.* (old).— Death by hanging.—*See* TO DIE IN ONE'S BOOTS.

ABRAHAM SHAM, *subs.* (old cant).—
1.—Feigned sickness or distress. *See* ABRAHAM-MAN. Usually spoken of as to SHAM ABRAHAM, or ABRAM (*q.v.*). From this primary meaning, joined with an allusion to the name of a once well-known chief cashier of the Bank of England, was derived the secondary meaning of the term SHAMMING ABRAHAM, to forge bank-notes. Abraham Newland was in office in the years 1778-1807, and a popular song of the period ran as follows:

'I have heard people say that SHAM ABRAHAM you may,
But you mustn't SHAM ABRAHAM Newland.'

Further point is added to this stanza by the fact that bank notes were themselves termed ABRAHAM NEWLANDS (*q.v.*), and that forgery was felony by statute.

1759. GOLDSMITH, *Citizen of the World*, cxix. "He swore that I understood my business perfectly well, but that I SHAMMED ABRAHAM merely to be idle."

1849. C. BRONTÉ, *Shirley*, ch. xxxiii. Matthew, sceptic and scoffer, had already failed to subscribe a prompt belief in that pain about the heart; he had muttered some words, amongst which the phrase SHAMMING ABRAHAM had been very distinctly audible.

ABRAHAM SUIT, *subs. phr.* (thieves'). —False pretences; fraudulent representations to excite sympathy. The term is applied to any trick or artifice calculated to extract money from the charitable, whether by means of begging letter, a faked-up appearance, or other contrivance. Those who resort to such practices are said to GO ON THE ABRAHAM SUIT. *Cf.*, ABRAHAM SHAM.

ABRAHAM'S WILLING, *subs. phr.* (rhyming slang).—A shilling.

ABRAHAM WORK, *subs. phr.* (popular). —Shams of all kinds are so designated, from a bubble company down to the most trumpery 'city pen'orth.'

ABRAM, *subs.* (old and also modern sea slang).—1. The same as ABRAHAM-MAN (*q.v.*).—2. A malingerer; one who gets put on the sick list to shirk work.
Adj. (old cant).—1. Mad.
1610. ROWLANDS, *Martin Mark-all*, p. 36 (H. Club's Repr., 1874). ABRAM madde. He maunds ABRAM, he begs as a madde man.

2. Naked, 'she's all ABRAM.'
1671. R. HEAD, *English Rogue*, Part I., ch. v., p. 47(1874). ABRAM, naked.

3. ABRAM or ABRAM COLOURED (old).—Derivation uncertain, but supposed to be a corruption of 'auburn.' In this connection it may be remarked that it is to be found in *Coriolanus*, Act II., scene 3; but where the original reads *Abram* the folio has 'auburn.' TO SHAM ABRAM, *verb.* (old).—Also *see* ABRAHAM SHAM. —The original signification of this word, to feign sickness, led t cits use to describe pretence of any kind; this is specially the case amongst sailors, workmen, etc., who describe malingering as *doing Abram*, the defaulter also being called by the same name.

ABREGOYNS, ABERGOINS, ABROGANS, *subs.* (American).—Vulgarisms for 'aborigines.'

ABRIDGMENTS, *subs.* (nonce word). —Knee breeches. This term for small clothes appears in Bulwer Lytton's comedy, *Money*.
1840. BULWER LYTTON, *Money*, iv. 4. *Frantz* (producing a pair of small clothes, which Toke examines). Your master is von beggar, etc. *Toke.* I accept the ABRIDGEMENTS, but you've forgotten to line the pockets.

ABROAD, *adv.* (old).—1. Confused; staggered; perplexed. More generally retained in this sense in America than in England.

2. (popular).—Generally ALL ABROAD; *i.e.*, wide of the mark; wrong; uncertain in one's estimate; or, 'all at sea.' In this figurative sense the expression is much older than is popularly supposed.—*See* BEDOOZLED.

1821. *The Fancy*, vol. I., p. 255. In the *fourth* round he came in ALL ABROAD, and got a doubler in the bread-basket, which spoiled him for the remainder of the fight.

1840. DICKENS, *Old Curiosity Shop*, ch. lxi. 'My friend!' repeated Kit, 'You're ALL ABROAD, seemingly,' returned the other man. 'There's his letter, take hold.'

1846. THACKERAY, *V. Fair*, ch. v. At the twelfth round the latter champion was ALL ABROAD, as the saying is, and had lost all presence of mind, and power of attack or defence.

3. To be transported. The French have a similar circumlution, *aller en traverse*, and the Italian Fourbesque has *andar a traverso*.

4. (Win. Coll.)—A boy returning to school work after being ill is said to COME ABROAD. When on the sick list he is CONTINENT (*q.v.*) *i.e.*, *continens cameram, vel lectum,* keeping his room or bed. When recovered he is allowed to go *foris*, out of doors, or more colloquially, ABROAD. Adams, in *Wykehamica*, remarks that the use of this term shows the antiquity of the school, dating as it does from the times of the '*patrium sermonem fugito*,

Latinum exerceto, of the *Tabula legum*.' TO BE FURKED ABROAD is a less complimentary term implying that a 'man' has been 'shuffling'; it is specially applied to those who having 'gone continent' in the morning are sent back to school by the doctor at 9 a.m.

ABROADED (society).—*See* quotation, and compare with ABROAD.
1876. H. O. MANTON, *Slangiana*, p. 11 (*See* Bibliography). Fashionable slang for a noble defaulter on the Continent (*sic.*) to avoid creditors. In the police official slang for convicts sent to a colonial or penal settlement, but it is applied by thieves to transportation either at home or in the Colonies.

ABS (Win. Coll.)—1. An abbreviation of 'absent' placed against the name of a boy when absent from the school.

2. *v. tr.*, to take away. Formerly, *circa*, 1840, TO ABS a tolly (candle), meant to put it out; now it would mean to take it away whether lighted or unlighted, the modern 'notion' for putting it out being to 'dump' it.

3. *v. n.* To get away; generally used in the imperative, as, 'ABS!' 'Oh! do ABS!' Sometimes, however, a fellow is said TO ABS quickly, and MESS THINGS (*q.v.*) are ABSED (*trans.*), or put away.

4. TO HAVE ONE'S WIND ABSED is to have it taken away by a violent blow in the stomach.

ABSCOTCHALATER, *subs.* (thieves'). —Quoted by H. O. Manton in *Slangiana* as 'one who is hiding away from the police.' *Cf.*, ABSQUATULATE.

ABSENCE, *subs.* (Eton).—Namescalling, which takes place at 3 p.m. and 6 p.m on half-holidays; and at 11.30 a.m., 3 p.m., and 6 p.m. on whole holidays; at 6 p.m. only in summer half.

ABSENT WITHOUT LEAVE, *adv. phr.* (thieves').—Said of one who has broken prison; or (popular) absconded.

ABSIT, *subs.* (Cambridge). — *See* quotation.
1886. DICKENS's *Dictionary of the University of Cambridge*, p. 3. Every undergraduate wishing to leave Cambridge for a whole day, not including a night, must obtain an 'ABSIT' from his tutor. Permission to go away for a longer period, either at the end of the term or in the middle, is called an 'exeat,' and no undergraduate should go down without obtaining his 'exeat.'

ABSKIZE, ABSCHIZE, *v.* (American). —To depart; go away. Said to be of Western origin, and to have been in use about 1883. Of rare and probably local usage. It has been derived from the Dutch *afscheyden*; Ger. *abscheiden* of similar meaning; a not unlikely origin, bearing in mind the large Dutch and German element in the U.S.A.

ABSQUATULATE, also ABSQUOTILATE, *v.* (American).—To run away; to decamp; with the more or less forcible idea of absconding in disgrace. A factitious word, of American origin and jocular use, simulating a Latin form, perhaps from Latin *ab* and *squat*, *i.e.*, to settle on land, especially public or new lands, without any title or right whether of purchase or permission, though in Australia the term is employed in a more restricted sense for a sub-lessee of the government at a nominal rent. It was first used by Mr. Hackett, as Nimrod Wildfire, a Kentucky character, in a play called 'The Kentuckian,' by Bernard, produced in 1833. It is now less often heard than formerly, having been replaced in some degree by the word SKEDADDLE (*q.v.*). For synonyms, *see* AMPUTATE ONE'S MAHOGANY.

1835-1840. HALIBURTON, *Clockmaker*, 3 S., ch. xiv. 'What's the use of legs but to ABSQUOTILATE with . . . when traps are sot for you.'

1879. *Punch*, Jan. 18, p. 23, col. 1. THE REWARD OF MERIT. *Mrs. Lyon Hunter*, 'How do you do, Mr. Brown?' Let me present you to the Duchess of Stilton! Your Grace, permit me to present to you *Mr. Brown*, the distinguished scholar!' *Her Grace* (affably). 'Charmed to make your acquaintance—er—Mr. Brown!' *Mr. Brown* (with effusion). 'Your Grace is really too kind. This is the *ninth* time I've enjoyed the distinction of being presented to your Grace within the last twelve months; but it's a distinction I value so highly, that without trespassing too much on your Grace's indulgence, I hope I may be occasionally permitted to enjoy it *again*. [*Bows*, and ABSQUATULATES.

1884. *Daily Telegraph*, August 20, p. 6, col. 1. Yet who knows but that some day an accident may happen to the Aberdeenshire works of art . . . the sense of the cartoons be totally subverted —in Rabelaisian phrase, 'absquashed and ABSQUATULATED.'

ACADEMICIAN, *subs.* (old).—The inmate of a brothel.

ACADEMY, *subs.* (old).—1. A disorderly house; a brothel; a bagnio. Grose remarks that these establishments were also called PUSHING SCHOOLS. The old brothels have of late years rapidly disappeared, their places being taken by what are known as BED HOUSES (*q.v.*). These vary in character as regards style, equipment, and cost, but of whatever grade, rooms may be had for longer or shorter periods as required. The French call them *maisons de société*; *maisons de passe*; *foutoirs*, and *gros numéros*, the last from the fact, that these semi-private brothels bear a number of large dimensions over the entrance. The French have also a somewhat analogous term for the mistress of an *académie* in *l'institutrice*, the teacher. In the FINISHING ACADEMY (*q.v.*) the inmates are young prostitutes, the next stage in whose downward career is taken on the streets.

2. According to the N.Y. Slang Dictionary, a penitentiary or prison for minor offences.

3. A thieves' school; also a band of thieves. There are establishments of similar character bearing more distinctive names, *e.g.*:

4. BUZZING ACADEMY (thieves').—A school for thieves, chiefly boys. Fagan, the old Jew in *Oliver Twist*, will occur to mind, as also the devices by which he taught his gang to pick pockets and pilfer adroitly.

5. CANTING ACADEMY (vagrants').—A house of call or common lodging house, frequented by the fraternity; a cadger's dossing ken. The term is also applied to any house where application for food or money is likely to be successful. At the regular 'beggar's house'—establishments which abound more or less in every town—information can be obtained so that the district can be thoroughly and systematically 'worked.'

6. CHARACTER ACADEMY.—At these places false characters are drawn up, to say nothing of the concoction of schemes of robbery.

7. FLOATING ACADEMY (thieves').—The hulks or prison ships were formerly so-called. When the regulations as regards transportation were relaxed, convicts condemned to hard labour were sent on board these vessels.

8. GAMMONING ACADEMY.—A reformatory.

ACAUSE, *conj.* (vulgar).—A corruption of 'because.'

ACCOMMODATION HOUSE, *subs.* (popular).—A brothel. Also frequently applied to what in police court phraseology are known as disorderly houses, *i.e.*, houses where rooms can be hired for shorter or longer periods as desired.—*See* BED HOUSE.

ACCORDING TO COCKER.—*See* COCKER.

ACCORDING TO THE REVISED STATUTES.—*See* REVISED STATUTES.

ACCOUNT. TO GO ON THE ACCOUNT, *verb. phr.* (old nautical).—To join in a fillibustering or buccaneering expedition; to turn pirate. Ogilvie says, probably from the parties sharing, as in a commercial venture.

1812. SCOTT, *Letter to a Friend.* I hope it is no new thing for gentlemen of fortune who are GOING ON THE ACCOUNT to change a captain now and then.

TO ACCOUNT FOR (sporting).—To kill; literally to be answerable for bringing down one's share of the shooting; to make away with.

1846-48. THACKERAY, *Vanity Fair*, ch. xx. The persecuted animals [rats] bolted above ground: the terrier ACCOUNTED FOR one, the keeper for another.

1858. *Letter from Lahore*, 28 September, in *Times*, 19 November. In the course of one week they were hunted up and ACCOUNTED FOR; and you know that in Punjab phraseology ACCOUNTING FOR means the extreme fate due to mutineers. [M.]

ACCOUNTS. TO CAST UP ONE'S ACCOUNTS, *verb. phr.* (old cant).—To vomit. Still common; quoted by Grose [1785]. The expression sometimes runs, amongst seafaring men, TO AUDIT ONE'S ACCOUNTS AT THE COURT OF NEPTUNE.

ENG. SYNONYMS. To shoot the cat; to cat.

FRENCH SYNONYMS. *Semer des miettes* (lit. to sow or scatter crumbs); *piquer le renard* (lit. to goad the fox. *Cf.* 'to shoot the cat.' The old French phrase was *chasser* or *escorcher le renard*, either because, says Cotgrave, 'in spueing one makes a noise like a fox that barks, or because the flaying of so unsavory an animal will make any man spue'; *renverser* (lit. to overturn, to upset); *faire restitution* (lit. to make amends; to restore); *revoir la carte* (lit. to look at the bill of fare again).

(Thieves').—To turn Queen's evidence.

ACCUMULATIVES, *subs.* (American).—These journalistic sparring matches are essentially a 'Yankee notion.' In England they are called CODICILS (*q.v.*), under which see an amusing example which will illustrate their character, as also the length to which American editors sometimes go in heaping Ossa upon Pelion.

ACCUMULATOR, *subs.* (racing).—A bettor, who when successful with one horse, carries forward the stakes to another event.

ACE OF SPADES, *subs. phr.* (old).—A widow. Though obsolete in England, it is quoted by the *New York Slang Dictionary* (1881) as still current in America.

ACK, *intj.* (Christ's Hospital).—No! refusal of a request, *e.g.*, 'Lend me your book.' 'ACK!'

ACKMAN, ACKPIRATE (old), or ACKRUFF (American), *subs.*—A freshwater thief; a ruffian who in conjunction with watermen robs and sometimes murders on the water. [ACK (unknown derivation, unless a corrupted form of ark, a boat; or wherry) + MAN, etc.] Quoted by Grose [1785], and also by Clark Russell, in *Sailor's Language* [1883].

ACKNOWLEDGE THE CORN, *verb. phr.* (American).—To make an admission of failure; to admit being outwitted. The various stories professing to account for derivation are discussed in detail in *Americanisms, Old and New*: the most circumstantial and certainly the best authenticated, runs as follows:—In 1828, the Hon. Andrew Stewart was in Congress discussing the principle of 'Protection,' and said in the course of his remarks, that Ohio, Indiana, and Kentucky sent their haystacks, cornfields, and fodder to New York and Philadelphia for sale. The Hon. Charles A. Wickliffe, from Kentucky, jumped up and said, 'Why that is absurd; Mr. Speaker, I call the gentleman to order. He is stating an absurdity. We never send haystacks or cornfields to New York or Philadelphia.' 'Well, what do you send?' 'Why, horses, mules, cattle, hogs.' 'Well, what makes your horses, mules, cattle, hogs? You feed a hundred dollars' worth of hay to a horse, you just animate and get upon the top of your haystack and ride off to market. How is it with your cattle? You make one of them carry fifty dollars' worth of hay and grass to the Eastern market. Mr. Wickliffe, you send a hog worth ten dollars to an Eastern market; how much corn does it take at thirty-three cents per bushel to fatten it?' 'Why, thirty bushels!' 'Then you put that thirty bushels of corn into the shape of a hog, and make it walk off to the Eastern market.' Mr. Wickliffe jumped up and said: 'Mr. Speaker, I ACKNOWLEDGE THE CORN. [De Vere's *Americanisms* [1872] p. 47.] Latterly the expression has been used in England in the sense of simply to make an admission.

1860. HALIBURTON (SAM SLICK), *The Season Ticket*, No. 9. 'He had a beard that wouldn't ACKNOWLEDGE THE CORN to no man's.'

1865. BACON, *Handbook of America*, p. 361. ACKNOWLEDGE THE CORN, to confess a charge or imputation.

1883. G. A. SALA, *Living London*, p. 97. Mr. Porter ACKNOWLEDGES THE CORN as regards his fourteen days' imprisonment, and is forgiven by his loving consort.

ACORN. A HORSE FOALED OF AN ACORN, *subs. phr.* (old).—The gallows. Euphemisms for hanging, the 'tree' itself, and the victim of the law's majesty were, at the time when the

death penalty was a common punishment, both many and curious. A HORSE FOALED OF AN ACORN, is obviously an allusion to the timber of which the TRIPLE TREE (*q.v.*) was constructed. The widows of those who had suffered the extreme penalty of the law were termed HEMPEN WIDOWS (*q.v.*); the children of such, or those likely to meet with death by hanging, HEMPSEED (*q.v.*); and HEMPEN FEVER (q.v.) represented the dread malady itself.

1760-61. SMOLLETT, *Sir L. Greaves*, ch. viii. I believe as how 'tis no horse, but a devil incarnate; and yet I've been worse mounted, that I have—I'd like to have rid A HORSE THAT WAS FOALED OF AN ACORN (*i.e.*, he had nearly met with the fate of Absalom).

1827. LYTTON, *Pelham*, ch. lxxxii. 'The cove . . . . is as pretty a Tyburn blossom as ever was brought up to ride A HORSE FOALED BY AN ACORN.'

1839. HARRISON AINSWORTH, *Jack Sheppard* [1889], p. 8. Tom Sheppard was always a close file, and would never tell whom he married. Of this I'm certain, however, she was much too good for him. . . . As to this little fellow. . . . he shall never mount A HORSE FOALED BY AN ACORN, if I can help it.

ACQUAINTANCE. TO SCRAPE ACQUAINTANCE, *verb. phr.* (common).—To make acquaintance. Probably from 'bowing and scraping' to a person, in order to curry favor.

1698. FARQUHAR, *Love and a Bottle* [ed. 1711], p. 5, *Lucinda.* Pray good Cæsar, keep off your paws; no SCRAPING ACQUAINTANCE for Heaven's sake.

This phrase has a classical origin, an account of which from the pen of Dr. Doran, F.S.A., appears in the *Gentleman's Magazine* [N.S. xxxix. 230] in an article on 'The Masters of the Roman World during the Happiest Years of the Human Race.'

There is an anecdote connected with Hadrian and the custom of bathing, from which is derived the proverbial saying of SCRAPING AN ACQUAINTANCE. The Emperor, entering a bath, saw an old soldier scraping himself with a tile. He recognised the man as a former comrade—his memory on such points never failed him—and, pitying his condition that he had nothing better than a tile for a flesh-brush, he ordered the veteran to be presented with a considerable sum of money, and a costly set of bathing garments. Thereupon all the old soldiers of the Imperial Army became as anxious to claim fellowship with the Emperor as the Kirkpatricks of Great Britain and Ireland are proudly eager to establish kinship with the Empress of the French. As Hadrian entered the bath the day after that on which he had rewarded his former comrade, he observed dozens of old soldiers scraping themselves with tiles. He understood the intent, but wittily evaded it. 'Scrape one another, gentlemen,' said he, 'you will not SCRAPE ACQUAINTANCE WITH ME!'

ACQUISITIVE, *subs.* (American).—Plunder; booty; pickings. A noun formed from the adjective.

ACREOCRACY, *subs.* (common).—The landed interest. Possibly of American coinage [of simulated Greek formation, from English ACRE + Greek κρατέω, to hold sway or to govern]. Compare with democracy, mobocracy, aristocracy, etc.

1878. *Hallberger's Illustrated Magazine*, p. 622. The introduction of a plutocracy among the aristocracy and the ACREOCRACY though it has tended somewhat to vulgarize our social institutions, etc.

ACRES, *subs.* (theatrical)—A coward. From Bob ACRES, in Sheridan's *Rivals* [1775]; here the character part is of a blusterer, one who talks big, but when put to the push, to use his own words, 'his courage always oozed out of his finger ends.' *Cf.*, Abigail for a waiting maid; Samson for a strong man; Job for a monument of patience, and others.

Across Lots. To GO ACROSS LOTS, *verb. phr.*—To proceed by the shortest route; similarly to do anything in the most expeditious manner. The phrase had its rise in the natural tendency of settlers, in thinly-populated districts, to shorten the distance from point to point by leaving the road and striking *across* vacant *lots*. Brigham Young familiarized its idiomatic use in the now notoriously historic saying attributed to that 'Saint,' — 'We'll send them (the Gentiles) to hell *across lots*.'

1848. LOWELL, *Biglow Papers*.

Past noontime they went trampin' round
An' nary thing to pop at found,
Till, fairly tired o' their spree,
They leaned their guns agin a tree,
An' jest ez they wuz settin' down
To take their noonin', Joe looked roun'
And see (ACROST LOTS in a pond
That warn't mor'n twenty rod beyond),
A goose that on the water sot
Ez ef awaitin' to be shot.

1854. J. C. NEAL, *Charcoal Sketches*, i., p. 35 [to a grumbler]:—'You would cut ACROSS THE LOT, like a streak of lightning, if you had a chance.'

1887. *Scribner's Magazine*. 'I didn't see Crossby go by, did you?' 'He'd have had to foot it by the path CROSS-LOTS, replied Ezra, gravely, from the doorstep.'

Acteon, *subs.* (old).—A cuckold; from the horns planted on the head of Acteon by Diana.

Acting the Deceitful, *verb. phr.* (old theatrical). — Performing; mumming; acting. — *Duncombe.*

Active Citizen, *subs.* (popular).—A louse. For synonyms, *see* CHATES.

Act of Parliament, *subs.* (old).—A military term for small beer, five pints of which, by an Act of Parliament, a landlord was formerly obliged to give gratis to each soldier billetted upon him. For synonyms, *see* COLD BLOOD.

Actual. THE ACTUAL, *subs.* (popular).—Money, when spoken of collectively. The fact of the existence of innumerable synonyms for the 'modern staff of life' goes far to bear out the latter-day contention that it is not the 'evil' itself ['money is the root of all evil'—*Old Saw*] but the lack of it that is to be deplored. The central idea enshrined in many of these terms will well repay comparative study, a vein of subtle, and sometimes grim humor and pathos running through not a few of them This applies equally to English slang, and to the French, Italian, Spanish, and Portuguese argots. Compare for example the English 'feathers' with the Spanish *amigos* (friends), the Italian *agresto* (sour grapes), and the French *du foin* (hay), or *de l'os* (bone), and obviously many a new side-light upon national habits and modes of thought may be obtained therefrom. The English and French, the two nations whose slang vocabularies are by far the most copious extant, have respectively upwards of 130 and 50 synonymous terms for money. The generic names are as follows:—

ENG. SYNONYMS. Ballast; beans; blunt (*i.e.*, specie,—not soft, or rags, *i.e.*, bank-notes); brads; brass; bustle; coal; coppers (copper money, or mixed pence); chink; chinkers; chips; corks; dibs; dimmock; dinarly;

dirt; dooteroomus (or doot); dumps; dust; dye stuffs; feathers; family plate (silver); dollars; gent (silver,—from *argent*); gilt; haddock (a purse of money); hard stuff (or hard); horse nails; huckster; John; John Davis; loaver; lour (the oldest cant term for money); mopusses; muck; needful; nobbings (money collected in a hat by street-performers); ochre (gold); oof; ooftish; pewter; palm oil; pieces; posh; queen's pictures; quids; rags (bank-notes); ready; ready gilt; ready John; redge (gold); rhino; rowdy; shadscales (or scales); shot; shekels; sinews of war; shiners (sovereigns); shin plasters (or plasters); skin (a purse of money); Spanish; spondulics; stamps; stiff (cheques, or bills of acceptance); stuff; stumpy; tin (silver); tow; wad; wedge (silver); wherewith; and yellow-boys (sovereigns). In the 17th century money was often called 'shells'—is this the origin of 'to shell out'?—and 'Oil of Angels' (*q.v.*).

FRENCH ARGOT. *De l'artiche* (thieves': *retirer de l'artiche*, is to pick the pockets of a drunkard); *du morningue; du foin* (lit. hay); *du plâtre* (thieves': lit. plaster); *du poussier* (thieves': lit. coal-dust; *Cf.*, English 'coal' and 'dust'); *des soldats* (thieves': Falstaff, in *Merry Wives of Windsor*, ii., 2, says 'money is a good soldier'); *de la mornifle* (this thieves' term for money, whether good or counterfeit, originally signified false money only; there is a grim suggestiveness between the orthodox meaning of the word, 'a slap on the face,' and its slang signification); *de la sauvette* (also a basket used by rag-pickers and collectors of street refuse); *de l'huile* (lit. oil); *du beurre* (pop.: lit. butter); *de la braise* (pop.: *ma braise* is a term of endearment among the Lyonnais, and is equivalent to *mon trésor*, my treasure); *du bath* (thieves': the tip-top; the excellent. From a superior kind of Bath note paper, which, in 1848, was hawked about the streets of Paris, and sold at a low price. Thus *papier bath* became synonymous with excellent paper. In a short time the qualifying term alone remained, and received a general application.—*Argot and Slang*); *du graissage* (pop.: lit. grease, *Cf.*, 'palm oil,' and 'greasing the palm' in English slang); *de la thune* (thieves': in old French cant the *Roi de la Thune* was the king of the beggars, and the old prison of Bicêtre, where free board and lodging was provided for many of the fraternity, was called *La Thune*. It is easy to see why the name of a place, where beggars congregated in considerable numbers and received relief, should pass into use to signify pecuniary alms); *de la miche de profonde* (pop. and thieves': this exactly corresponds to the English 'loaver'); *de l'oignon pèse* (pop.: lit. heavy onion. *Cf.*, Fourbesque *argume*); *du sable* (pop.: lit. sand); *des pimpions* (thieves': *Qy.*, from *pimpant*, fine, spruce, smart); *de l'os* (familiar: lit. bone); *du nerf* (lit. sinew. *Cf.*, English 'sinews of war'); *des pepettes* (pop.: (*pepette*, a coin of the value of fifty centimes); *des achetoires* (pop.: from *acheter*, to buy); *de la galette* (pop.: lit. sea biscuit); *des picaillons* (pop.: probably a corruption of *picaron*, a Spanish coin); *de ce qui se pousse* (pop.: that which pushes

itself forward. *Cf.*, English proverb, 'It's money makes the mare to go'); *de quoi* (pop.: the wherewithal. *Cf.*, English 'the needful,' the 'ready'); *de l'oignon* (pop.: lit. onion. Fourbesque has also *argume*, lit. in Italian, an onion); *de l'oseille* (pop.: lit. sorrel); *de la douille* (thieves' and pop.: from a kind of large fig much esteemed in Paris); *des jaunets* (lit. buttercups. *Cf.*, English 'yellow-boys'); *des sous* (lit. pence); *de la graisse* (pop. and thieves': lit. 'grease.' *Cf.*, palm oil); *de l'affare* (a thieves' term, probably from the argotic verb *affurer*, to cheat, steal, or deceive); *du metal* (lit. metal); *du zinc* (lit. zinc); *du pèze* (from the Italian *pezzo*, a piece; Spanish *peso*, a silver coin, weighing an ounce); *du pedzale*; *des noyaux* (popular); *des sonnettes plombes* (*plomb* = lead); *des sonnettes* (lit. bells. *Cf.*, English 'chinkers'); *du quantum* (from the Latin); *du gras* (lit. fat); *de l'atout* (lit. trumps in cards); *de l'huile de main* (lit. hand oil, the English 'palm grease'); *des patards* (obsolete copper coins, value ½d.; now applied particularly to a two-sous piece, and to money generally); *de la vaisselle de poche* (lit. pocket plate: *vaisselle* = gold and silver plate); *du carme* (from the game of *Trictrac*); *de la pécune* (lit. cash); *des ronds* (lit. circles; from the shape of coins); *de la bille* (from *billon*); *du "sine quâ non"* (from the Latin; meaning obvious); *du sit nomen* (from the Latin); *quibus* (an abbreviation of *quibus fiunt omnia*).

ITALIAN FOURBESQUE. *Agresto* (lit. sour grapes); *albume* (lit. white of egg); *argume* (lit. onions); *asta, asti* (from Ital. *asta*, a staff); *contramaglia* (silver money); *brunotti* (lit. brownish); *penne* (lit. feathers); *smilzi* (from Ital. *smilzi* = menu); *squame* (lit. chips or scales).

SPANISH GERMANIA. *Amigos* (lit. friends); *florin* (here can be traced the Spanish connection with the Netherlands); *sangre* (lit. blood).

PORTUGUESE CALAÕ.—*Parne*.

GERMAN SYNONYMS (GAUNERSPRACHE).—*See* GILT.

Ad. Adver. *subs.* (printers'). — An abbreviated form of 'advertisement.'

1854. DICKENS, *Household Words*, xiii., 9. The really interesting ADS are in the body of the paper.

1888. *New York Times*, Ap. 6.

[The country editor's wife—] . . . reads the ADS with the editor,
Just to find what each has paid.
'But the column AD of the jeweller, there,'
So he says, 'and the harness, and human hair,
Must be taken out in trade!'
She wears the corsets he gets for ADS,
And rattles his sewing machine;
She uses the butter, and cups, and things,
The country subscriber so faithfully brings,
With a cheerfulness seldom seen.

Adam, *subs.* (old).—A sergeant or bailiff; a master man or foreman. Now used by thieves in the sense of an accomplice. Explained by commentators as a reference to the fact that the buff worn by a bailiff resembled the native buff worn by our first parent, or from his keeping the garden.

1593. SHAKSPEARE, *Comedy of Errors* iv., 3. *Ant S.* . . . . What Adam dost thou mean? *Dro. S.* Not that Adam that kept the Paradise, but that ADAM that keeps the prison: he that goes into the calf-skin that was killed for the prodigal.

1848. *Sinks of London Laid Open*, p. 96. ADAM, a henchman, an accomplice.

Adam's Ale, or sometimes simply **Adam,** and in Scotland **Adam's Wine.**—A colloquialism of long standing for water, humorously suggesting that anything stronger was unknown to our first parents. Duncombe wittily adds a comment that our first father's drink is best with brandy. This also would appear to be the view taken in most of the French and German equivalents.

ENG. SYNONYMS. Fish broth; *aqua pompaginis*.

FRENCH. *Anisette de barbillon* (a popular term); *essence de parapluie* (popular: lit. essence of umbrella); *l'Adam's ale* (a literal translation of the English term); *limonade* (popular: a caustic comment surely upon the virtues of lemonade); *lance* (popular and thieves': this term also does duty for 'rain'; properly written *l'ance*, derived from the Spanish Germania *ansia*, itself an abbreviation of *angustia*, an allusion to the employment of water as a means of torture); *sirop* or *ratafia de grenouilles* (popular: lit. syrup of frogs); *sirop de l'aiguière* (popular: lit. pitcher syrup); *sirop de baromètre* (popular, barometer syrup).

GERMAN GAUNERSPRACHE. *Gänsewein* (lit. goose-wine).

ITALIAN FOURBESQUE. *Lenza* (the remarks on French *lance* quoted above, apply equally here).

1648. PRYNNE, *Sov. Power of Parl.*, II., 32. They have been shut up in prisons and dungeons . . allowed onely a poore pittance of ADAM'S ALE, and scarce a penny bread a day to support their lives. [M.]

1786-9. WOLCOT [P. Pindar], *Lousiad*, c. ii., line 453.

Old ADAM's beverage flows with pride,
From wide-mouth'd pitchers in a plenteous tide.

1884. *Daily Telegraph*, April 1, p. 5, col. 2. The spectral banquet graced now only by ADAM'S ALE, or the sick-room toast and water.

1886. JOHN COLEMAN, *Elfie*, pt. I., ch. ii. For my part, I stuck to ADAM'S ALE, which Elfie brought from the spring.

Adam Tiler, *subs.* (old slang).—A pickpocket's associate; one who receives stolen goods, and then runs off with them. [From ADAM, an accomplice + TILER, a watchman. *Cf.*, Masonic term.] For synonyms, *see* FENCE.

Added to the List (racing).—An abbreviation of 'added to the list of geldings in training.' Among French thieves, *désatiller* is the term employed to signify castration; or, where the operation is performed upon a man, *abélardiser*, *i.e.*, to mutilate a man, as Chanoine Fulbert mutilated Abélard, the lover of his daughter or niece, Héloise.

Addition, *subs.* (old).—A term for various toilet requisites, used by women; such as paint, rouge, powder, etc.

1704. CENTLIVRE, *Platonick Love*, Act iii., Scene 1. *Milliner.* Be pleased to put on the ADDITION madam. *Mrs. Dowdy.* What does she mean now? to pull my skin off, mehap, next. Ha, Peeper, are these your London fashions? *Peeper.* No, no, ADDITION is only paint, madam.

Addition, Division, and Silence! *phr.* (American).—A Philadelphia expression, which, for a time, had a vogue as a catch phrase. It is properly rendered MULTIPLICATION, DIVISION, AND SILENCE! William M. Tweed, or as he is more familiarly known 'Boss' Tweed, is generally credited with this expression. Being asked what in his view was the proper qualification for a member of a ring or trust, in which all play into each other's hands for mutual advantages, he replied MULTIPLICATION, DIVISION, AND SILENCE!

ADDLE COVE, *subs.* (common).—A foolish man; an easy dupe; literally, a RANK SUCKER (*q.v.*), and equivalent to addle-head, addle-pate, addle-plot, all of which are common dictionary words. Why Barrère and Hotten have followed the lead of Grose in classing these words as slang is hardly clear. Dialectical they may have been, but all English was similarly placed prior to the 15th century, and the first reference given by Murray, bears the date of A.D. 1250.

ADEPT, *subs.* (thieves').—An expert amongst the light-fingered gentry. It is quite an open question whether ADEPT, even in a thief's sense, can fairly be classed as slang, the meaning being obviously identical with that commonly attached to the word.

ADJECTIVE JERKER, *subs. phr.* (literary). — A term of derision applied, like INK-SLINGER (*q.v.*), to those who write for the press. The special allusion in the present case is doubtless to the want of discrimination which young writers, and reporters on low-class papers, often exhibit in the use of a plethora of adjectives to qualify a simple statement of fact.

1888. *St. Louis Globe Democrat,* April 29. Genevieve spent four hours last night in constructing a three-line letter, which she sent to an ADJECTIVE JERKER on a society weekly, and in which she said she would spend the summer months in the Rocky Mountains.

ADJUTANT'S GIG, *subs. phr.* (military).—The barrack roller. Men under punishment are generally put to the task of drawing this machine.

ADMIRAL. TO TAP THE ADMIRAL, *verb phr.* (nautical).—A practice otherwise known as 'SUCKING THE MONKEY.' Explained in *Peter Simple* as having originally been used amongst sailors for drinking rum out of cocoa nuts from which the milk had been extracted and replaced by spirits, an evasion of the regulation prohibiting the purchase of ardent liquors when on shore in the tropics. The Germans have an analogous expression *Den affen saugen,* to 'suck the monkey,' with the same signification.

Nowadays it is applied to drinking on the sly from a cask by inserting a straw through a gimlet hole, and to drinking generally.

1897. BARHAM, *Ingoldsby Legends* (the Black Mousquetaire).
What the vulgar call SUCKING THE MONKEY,
Has much less effect on a man when he's funky.

ADMIRAL OF THE BLUE, *subs. phr.* (old).—A publican or tapster; from the colour of his apron; now obsolete. *Cf.,* ADMIRAL OF THE RED.

1731. *Poor Robin* [Pseudonym of Robert Herrick] Almanac.
As soon as customers begin to stir,
THE ADMIRAL OF THE BLUE, cries, 'Coming, sir!'
Or if grown fat, the mate his place supplies;
And says, 'tis not my master's time to rise.

Of all our trades, the tapster is the best,
He has more men at work than all the rest.

ADMIRAL OF THE NARROW SEAS, *subs. phr.* (nautical). — A man who, under drink, vomits into the lap of his neighbour or *vis-à-vis.*

ADMIRAL OF THE RED, *subs. phr.* (popular).—A wine-bibber; one whose face by its redness bears evidence of a fondness for the bottle. Formerly the highest rank of naval officers was divided into three grades or classes denominated from the colours hoisted by them, Admirals of the Red, White, or Blue squadron. Now there are four grades; Admiral of the Fleet, Admiral, Vice-admiral, and Rear-admiral. The French call the bottle or copper-nose possessed by ADMIRALS OF THE RED *betterave* (lit. a beetroot); also *un piton passé à l'encaustique;* and *un piffard. Cf.,* ADMIRAL OF THE BLUE.

ADMIRAL OF THE WHITE, *subs. phr.* (familiar).—Quoted as 'a white-faced person; a coward; a woman in a faint.' Rarely heard, and at best but an extremely weak imitation of kindred phrases, to wit, ADMIRAL OF THE BLUE, and ADMIRAL OF THE RED.

ADMIRALS OF THE RED, WHITE, AND BLUE, *subs. phr.* (familiar).—Beadles; hall-porters; and such-like functionaries when sporting their gorgeous liveries of office.

ADONIZE, *verb.* (rare). [French *adoniser;* from ADONIS+IZE].—To make beautiful or attractive; to adorn oneself with a view of attracting admiration; said only of men.

1818. S. E. FERRIER, *Marriage,* ch. ix. 'Venus and the Graces, by Jove!' exclaimed Sir Sampson, bowing with an air of gallantry; 'and now I must go and ADONIZE a little myself.' The company then separated to perform the important offices of the toilette.

1850. F. E. SMEDLEY, *Frank Fairleigh,* ch. xl. 'He positively refused to face the ladies till he had changed his shooting costume, so I left him up at the hall to ADONIZE.'

ADSUM, *verb.* (Charterhouse). — The response made in answering to names-calling.

1855. THACKERAY, *The Newcomes,* p. 774. 'At the usual evening hour the chapel bell began to toll, and Thomas Newcome's hands outside the bed feebly beat time. And just as the last bell struck, a peculiar sweet smile shone over his face and he lifted up his head a little, and quickly said, 'ADSUM,' and fell back. It was the word we used at school when names were called; and lo, he whose heart was as that of a little child had answered to his name, and stood in the presence of the Master.'

ADULLAMITES, *subs.* (parliamentary).—A nickname, in the first instance, for a party of seceding Liberals, namely, Messrs. Horsman, Lowe, Earl Grosvenor, Lord Elcho, etc., who in 1866 voted with the Tories, when Earl Russell and Mr. Gladstone introduced a measure for the extension of the Franchise, In the debate on the 30th March John Bright said they had agreed to draw back into a political cave of ADULLAM. The reference is to those who, with King David, took refuge in the cave of Adullam (1 Sam. xxii., 1). The political party in question were also known collectively as 'The Cave.'

1878-80. JUSTIN MCCARTHY, *History of Our Own Times,* p. 142. The little third party were at once christened the ADULLAMITES, and the name still survives and is likely long to survive its old political history. *Ibid,* p. 143. The wild cheers of the Conservatives and the ADULLAMITES showed on which 'sword sat laurel victory.' *Ibid,* p. 152. [Lord Derby] had at once invited the leading members of the ADULLAMITE party to accept places in his Administration.

The primary usage has been extended as explained in the following quotations.

1870. *Notes and Queries,* March 5, p. 241. The Scriptural 'CAVE OF ADULLAM' has become an adopted byword for a small clique who unite to obstruct the party with which they usually associate.

1884. *New York Times,* July 19. The Conservative party then presented a tolerably solid front against the extension of the franchise, and received besides a large reinforcement of ADULLAMITES from the Liberal side.

ADVANCE BACKWARD, *verb.* (American).—A rather odd way of expressing retrogression.

1888. *Chicago Inter-Ocean,* Jan. 23. The advice given to his company by a raw Yankee captain TO ADVANCE BACKWARD, seems paralleled in the Chicago *Tribune* of the 18th inst.

ADVANTAGE (Californian). — See POCKET ADVANTAGE.

ÆGER, *subs.* (Univ.). Lat. sick.—Same as ÆGROTAT (*q.v.*).

1870. *Chambers' Journal,* June 18, p. 395. Dick laughed. 'I'll get the receipt from him. I often want a good thing for an ÆGER.'

1888. H. SMART, in *Temple Bar,* February, p. 213. 'Instead of applying for leave to my tutor, I had resorted to the old device of pricking ÆGER.'

ÆGROTAT, *subs.* (Univ.). — [L. he is sick, 3rd pers. sing. pres. ind. of *ægrotare,* to be sick from *ægrotus,* sick, from *æger,* sick]. In English universities a medical certificate given to a student, showing that he has been prevented by sickness from attending to his duties, or his examination; also used for the degree taken by those so excused. Also called ÆGER (*q.v.*).

1794. *Gent. Mag.,* p. 1085. They [at Cambridge] *sported* an ÆGROTAT, and they *sported* a new coat!

1864. BABBAGE, *Passages from the Life of a Philosopher,* 37. I sent my servant to the apothecary for a thing called an ÆGROTAT, which I understood ... meant a certificate that I was indisposed.

READING ÆGROTAT.—In some universities leave taken, commonly in December, in order to get time to read for one's degree.

AFFAIR OF HONOUR *subs.* (old).—Killing an innocent man in a duel. This euphemism was largely in vogue during the Regency days.

AFFIDAVIT MEN, *sub. phr.* (old slang), or, as they also used to be called, KNIGHTS OF THE POST.—False witnesses who attended Westminster Hall and other Courts of Justice, ready to swear anything for hire; they were distinguished by having straws stuck in the heels of their shoes.—*See* STRAW BAIL under BAIL.

AFFINITY, *subs.* (American).—A cant term in frequent use amongst so-called free-lovers. One's AFFINITY is supposed to be a person of the opposite sex, for whom an attachment so strong is felt that even if already married, as more often than not is the case, the husband will abandon his legitimate wife, and *vice versâ,* in favour of the new attraction, or AFFINITY as he or she is called. The argument is generally only

an excuse for unbridled sexual license; indeed, it is inconceivable that it could be otherwise, except in a society of seraphs and archangels.

AFFLICKE, *subs.* (old).—*See* quotation.

1610. ROWLAND'S *Martin Mark-all,* p. 38 (H. Chub's Repr., 1874). AFFLICKE, a theefe.

AFFLICTIONS, *subs.* (drapers').—Mourning goods, half-mourning being designated MITIGATED AFFLICTIONS (*q.v.*).

AFFYGRAPHY, *subs.* (common).—'It fits to an AFFYGRAPHY,' *i.e.,* to a nicety—to a T; also of time—'in an AFFYGRAPHY.'

AFLOAT, *adv.* (common).—On the move; *en évidence.* This term is of nautical origin.

TO HAVE ONE'S BACK-TEETH WELL AFLOAT, is to be well-primed with liquor; in short, to be in one of the many degrees of intoxication.

1888. *Missouri Republican,* Jan. 25. When sober on the bench Judge Noonan is a model of all the virtues. On Friday night, however, in company with Dr. Munford, of Kansas City, ex-Speaker Wood, Mr. Charles Mead, and several other gentlemen, his honor once more drank until, as an onlooker put it, his BACK TEETH WERE WELL AFLOAT.

A-FLY, *adv.* (vulgar).—*See* FLY.

AFTERCLAP, *subs.* (American).—An attempt to unjustly extort more in a bargain or agreement than at first settled upon. Derived from AFTER+CLAP, a blow or shock.] Current in England since the beginning of the fifteenth century, signifying an unexpected subsequent event; something happening after an affair is supposed to be at an end.

AFTER-DINNER MAN; AFTERNOON'S MAN.—Generally read to mean a tippler; one given to long potations after the mid-day meal, formerly the most substantial taken during the twenty-four hours. Smythe Palmer, however, appears to throw a different gloss upon the term, for he says [N. and Q., 5 S., viii., 112], 'AFTERNOONES MEN' — equivalent to AFTER-DINNER MEN. It was the custom, formerly, to dine in the halls of our Inns of Court about noon, and those who returned after dinner to work must have been much devoted to business, or obliged to work at unusual hours by an excess of it.'—*See* quot. from Earle.

1614. OVERBURY, *A wife, etc.* (1638), 196. Make him an AFTERNOONES MAN.

1621. BURTON, *Anat. Mel.* Democr. to Reader (1657), 44. Bervaldus will have drunkards, AFTERNOON MEN, and such as more than ordinarily delight in drink, to be mad.

1628. EARLE, *Microcosmography* (A Player). Your Innes of Court men were undone but for him, hee is their chiefe guest and employment, and the sole businesse that makes them AFTER-NOONES MEN.

1830. *Dublin Sketch Book.* The good Baronet (Sir Francis Burdett) was not only a foxhunter, but a celebrated AFTER-DINNER MAN It must have been a good bout indeed in which he was worsted.

AFTER FOUR, *subs. phr.* (Eton).—From 3 to 6 p.m. on half-holidays; 4 to 5 on whole schoolday.

AFTERNOON FARMER, *subs. phr.* (popular).—This expression for one who procrastinates, or who misses an opportunity is, in reality, a provincialism. It is quoted in more than one of the English Dialect Society's *Glossaries* as a very common phrase for one who is always behind, *i.e.*, late in preparing his land, in sowing or harvesting his crops. It is only slang when used figuratively apart from agricultural pursuits.

After Twelve, *subs. phr.* (Eton).—From noon till 2 p.m.

1861. Whyte Melville, *Good for Nothing*, p. 39. I used to visit him regularly in the dear old college from the AFTER TWELVE.

Against Collar. To work against collar, *verb. phr.* (popular).—To battle or cope with difficulties; 'to kick against the pricks'; 'to pull against the tide.'

1876. C. Hindley, *Life and Adventures of a Cheap Jack*, p. 114. 'It is always thought to be a bad plan to let journeymen Cheap Johns get into debt with their employers. It is bad in two ways, for if they owe their governors a few pounds, they are WORKING AN uphill game, or AGAINST COLLAR, and that don't suit their book, and it destroys the independence which is, and always should be, between the master and the man.'

Against the Grain, *adv. phr.* (popular).—Against the fibres of the wood; hence, in opposition to the wish; unwillingly; unpleasantly; reluctantly. 'It went AGAINST THE GRAIN to do it, but I knew I must,' is a common expression.

1673. Dryden, *Amboyna*, Act i. Seizing their factories I like well enough, it has some savour in't; but for this whoresome cutting of throats, it goes a little AGAINST THE GRAIN.

1693. Dryden, *Juvenal*, i., 202. Though much AGAINST THE GRAIN forc'd to retire.

1709. Steele, *Tatler*, No. 2. Nothing in nature is so ungrateful as story-telling AGAINST THE GRAIN, therefore take it as the author has given it you.

1868. Wilkie Collins, *The Moonstone*, 1st Period., ch. xi. As I had promised for them, the other servants followed my lead, sorely AGAINST THE GRAIN, of course, but all taking the view that I took.

1884. W. C. Russell, *Jack's Courtship*, ch. xxiii. It went AGAINST MY GRAIN to leave the poor chap alone.

Agaze, *adv.* (American thieves').—Astonished; open-eyed.

Aggerawator, *subs.* (common); also **Haggerawator**, both forms being corruptions of 'aggravator.'—A lock of hair brought down from the forehead, well greased, and then twisted in spiral form upon the temple, either toward the ear, or conversely toward the outer corner of the eye. This style of dressing the hair was formerly much affected by costermongers, male and female, and other street folk, but the 'ornament' is now rarely seen. It appears to be known among certain classes in France, especially prostitutes' bullies.

Eng. Synonyms. Kiss-curls; cobbler's knots; cow-licks; Newgate knockers (from a supposed resemblance to the knocker on the prisoner's door at Newgate); number sixes; bell-ropes (being wherewith to *draw* the *belles*); bow-catchers; spit-curls; lovelocks, etc.

French Argot. *Des guiches*; *des rouflaquettes* (from being sported by prostitutes' bullies), *des accroche-cœurs* (lit. heart-hooks).

1836. Dickens, *Sketches by Boz*, p. 132. His hair carefully twisted into the outer corner of each eye, till it formed a variety of that description of semi-curls, usually known as 'AGGERAWATORS.'

From the following they would appear at one time to have formed part of the personal adornment of women in Australia.

1859. Frank Fowler, *Southern Lights and Shadows*, p. 38. The ladies are addicted to . . . straw-coloured gloves, and strained hair, embellished with two or three c's—AGGRAVATORS they call them—running over the temple.

Agility, *subs.* (low).—A woman who, in mounting a stile, or, when being swung, exposes more of her person than is usually counted decent, is said to show her AGILITY. The story told is an absurdly vulgar play upon words.

Agitate the Communicator! *verb. phr.* (common).—Ring the bell!

Agitator, *subs.* (common).—A bell-rope, or knocker.

Agogare, *intj.* (American thieves').—Be quick! a warning signal [from AGOG].—*New York Slang Dictionary.*

Agony. To pile up the agony. *verbal phr.* (popular).—To intensify a statement or relation by exaggerated or blood-curdling details. Newspapers *pile on the agony* when 'writing up' murder, divorce, and other sensations.

1857. C. Brontë, in Mrs. Gaskell's *Life*, ch. xxv. What climax there is does not come on till near the conclusion; and even then, I doubt whether the regular novel-reader will consider the 'AGONY PILED sufficiently high' (as the Americans say), or the colours dashed on to the canvas with the proper amount of daring.

1881. W. Black, *Beautiful Wretch*, ch. vi. 'Sooner or later that organ will shake the Cathedral to bits; the vibrations were fearful. I thought there was a great deal too much noise. You lose effect when you PILE UP THE AGONY like that.'

Agony column, *subs. phr.* (popular).—The second column of the *Times*; originally so-called from the fact of its being devoted to advertisements for missing friends, and private communications, many of which are of a harrowing character. Most London newspapers, for the phrase is chiefly local, have now a similar column. Subjoined are a few examples of these advertisements:—

I AM not sure of identity. Are you Juan of 1873? Longing to see you.—B.

MY darling, how often do I say from my heart come and let us reason together that we may be happy here and live and love for ever. God bless and spare us to meet again.

SATISFIED.—Meet Friday outside Farringdon Street Station, Three p.m. Have slip paper in coat buttonhole.—J. T.

HERBERT WILLIAM BONNETT, who left Bristol on Thursday, Sept. 5, is REQUESTED to COMMUNICATE at once with his uncle at Keynsham. If any shipping agent is aware of his taking passage in any boat leaving England, either London, Liverpool, or elsewhere, please write at once to Mr. J. D. Coates, Keynsham, near Bristol. All expenses will be paid.

The earliest mention in Murray's Dictionary is dated 1880, but from the following quotation it will be seen that the term has been in use for at least twenty years.

1870. L. Oliphant, *Piccadilly*, part II., p. 78. The advertisement of the committee, which appeared in the AGONY COLUMN of the *Times*, who wanted to know how I wished the money applied.

1881. W. Black, *Beautiful Wretch*, ch. xxiii. There were anonymous appeals to the runaways in AGONY COLUMNS.

Agony Piler, *subs.* (theatrical).—An actor who performs blood-curdling parts in sensational plays.

Aground, *adv.* (common).—Stuck fast; stopped; at a loss; ruined; like a boat or vessel AGROUND.

Ain't, sometimes **a'n't**, *verb. phr.* (vulgar).—A corruption for (1) 'am not'; (2) 'are not'; (3) 'is not.' This vulgarism appears to be of much older standing than set down in the *New English Dictionary*, where the earliest example is dated 1778.

1710. Swift, *Journal to Stella*, 24 Nov., Letter ix. I AIN'T vexed at this puppy business of the bishops, although I was a little at first.

1800. Coleridge, *Piccolomini*, II., xiii. *Ter.* Where's the hurry? Come, one other composing draught. . . . *Goetz.* Excuse me—AIN'T able. *Ter.* A thimble-full! *Goetz.* Excuse me.

1835. Dickens, *Sketches by Boz*, p. 275. 'You are a clever fellow, Tottle, AIN'T you?'

Air and Exercise, *subs. phr.* (old).—To have had AIR AND EXERCISE, signified that one had undergone a whipping at the cart's tail. About the beginning of the present century the same operation was termed SHOVING THE TUMBLER (*q.v.*). Among thieves at the present time, AIR AND EXERCISE means penal servitude; in America it is only applied to a short term of imprisonment.

Airing, *subs.* (racing).—When it is not intended that a horse shall win a race for which it is brought to the starting post, it is said to be OUT FOR AN AIRING.

1889. *Evening Standard*, June 25 (Sir Chas. Russell's speech in Durham-Chetwynd case).—What he (Sir C. Russell) meant was that Sir G. Chetwynd never did anything so gross and vulgar as that [tell the jockey to 'pull' horses], and that if horses were pulled, that was not the way in which in any class of turf society instructions were given. A wink was as good as a nod, and trainers and jockeys, from various trivial circumstances, very easily gathered whether a particular horse was only OUT FOR AN AIRING, or whether it was on the job.

Air Line, or **Air Line Road** (American).—To take the air line; to go direct, and by the shortest route; idiomatically, to avoid circumlocution. The origin of this expression is to be found in the straight lines of railway, without expensive detours and grades, which in the New World are rendered possible by the vast expanses of unbroken level. These lines of railway are called AIR LINE ROADS, or STRAIGHT SHOOTS (*q.v.*). De Vere remarks that since the number of such roads has increased in the more thickly settled parts of the Union, the advantages of direct lines between two great centres over others which meander from town to town have become very manifest, and for a few years a tendency to build such AIR LINES has agitated Legislatures, from whom and from financial circles in the States and abroad help is asked. These lines not unfrequently run for long distances by the side of older lines.

1888. *St. Louis Globe Democrat*, Jan. 24. The obese style once admired is now disliked. Many old English authors had too much rhetoric for our age. Of one thing we are profoundly convicted, that we have no time to spare for superfluities. An author must take the AIR LINE or we will not travel.

1888. *Florida Times Union Advertisement*, Feb. 11. Ask for tickets *via* Augusta or Atlanta and the Piedmont AIR LINE.

Air One's Heels, *verb. phr.* (popular).—To loiter; to hang about.

Air One's Vocabulary, *verb. phr.* (old).—To talk for talking's sake; to show off by one's talk; 'to flash the gab.' One of the wits of the time of George IV., when asked what was going on in the House of Commons answered that Lord Castlereagh was AIRING HIS VOCABULARY. The term is now rarely heard, but the practice is with us always.

Airy, *subs.* (vulgar).—A corruption of 'area,' *e.g.*, 'Down the AIRY steps.'

A-Jakes.—*See* Ajax.

Ajax, *subs.* (old). Pronounced with both 'a's' long).—The name of this hero furnished many unsavoury puns to our ancestors, from its similarity in sound to the two English words, A JAKES. In some of the passages the allusion is rather obscure, as in this:

1609. Ben Jonson, *Epicœne, or The Silent Woman*, iv., 5. A stool were better, sir, of Sir AJAX, his invention.

It is plainer in Shakspeare:

1594. *Love's Labour Lost*, v., 2. Your lion, that holds his poll-ax, sitting on a close stool, will be given to AJAX.

The cause of all this vein of low wit was, perhaps, Sir John Harrington, who in 1596 published his celebrated tract called *The Metamorphosis of Ajax*, by which he meant *the improvement of a jakes*, or necessary, by forming it into what we now call a *water-closet*, of which Sir John was clearly the inventor. For this offence to her delicacy, Queen Elizabeth kept him for some time in disgrace. Used directly for a necessary house.

1611. Cotgrave, *Eng. Treasury*, p. 16. Which (like the glorious AJAX of Lincoln's Inne, I saw in London) laps up naught but filth and excrements.

1720. *Hosp. of Incurab. Fooles*, p. 6. Adoring Sterculio for a god, no lesse unworthily then shamfully constituting him a patron and protector of AJAX and his commodities.

To the above work of Sir J. Harrington, Ben Jonson seems to allude, as a masterpiece in its way, when, at the conclusion of a dirty poem, he says,

1574-1637. *On the Famous Voyage*, vol. VI., p. 290:
And I could wish for their eterniz'd sakes,
My muse had plough'd with his that sung A-JAX.

The rhyme here proves that the pronunciation of the time was suited to the English meaning. Even Camden condescends to play upon this word. Speaking of the French word *pet*, he says,

1605. *Remains*, p. 117. Inquire, if you understand it not, of Cloacina's Chaplains, or such as are well read in AJAX.—*See* Jakes.

Akerman's Hotel, *subs.* (obsolete).—Newgate prison was once so called. The governor's name was AKERMAN.—*See* Cage.

Akeybo.—A slang phrase used in the following manner:—He beats AKEYBO, and AKEYBO beat the devil.—*Hotten.*

A-la-Mort.—*See* Amort.

Albany Beef, *subs. phr.* (American).—The popular name of the flesh of the sturgeon. This, in color and taste, has some resemblance to beef, especially when cut in steaks and grilled. Albany is a town on the Hudson River as high as which the fish in question is or was to be caught in large numbers, and as a matter of course, it consequently formed a not inconsiderable factor in the food supply of the inhabitants—hence the term ALBANY BEEF.

ALBERTOPOLIS, *subs.* (popular).— A nickname formerly given by Londoners to the Kensington Gore district, out of compliment to the late Prince Consort. The Albert Hall and the Exhibition buildings of 1862, with which Prince Albert was so closely identified, are situated within the radius; and the Albert Memorial is hard by.

1864. E. YATES, *Broken to Harness*, ch. xxxiii., p. 366 (1877). Mr. Cauthar tripped out of the house, and devoted the remainder of the evening to working out a composition for the nutriment of the hair, which, under the name of Cauthar's Crinibus, has an enormous circulation over the infant heads of ALBERTOPOLIS.

ALBONIZED, *ppl. adj.* (pugilistic).— Whitened. [From L. *albus*, white.]

ALDERMAN, *subs.* (popular).—1. A half-crown. This term is explained by Brewer as containing an allusion to the fact that an alderman is a kind of half-king, whatever that may mean.

1857. SNOWDEN, *Mag. Assistant*, 3 ed., p. 444. Two shillings and sixpence —ALDERMAN.

2. A long pipe; also called a CHURCHWARDEN (*q.v.*); in both instances the name is probably an allusion to the *penchant* these personages had at one time for the long clay.

1859. FAIRHOLT, *Tobacco* (1876), 173. Such long pipes were reverently termed ALDERMAN in the last age, and irreverently yards of clay in the present one.

3. A turkey; a variant is AN ALDERMAN IN CHAINS; *i.e.*, a roast turkey well stuffed and garnished with sausages. The latter are said to be emblematical of the gold chain worn by the civic dignitary—what then about the stuffing?

1782. GEORGE PARKER, *Humorous Sketches*, p. 31. Nick often eat a roast fowl and sausage with me, which in cant is called an ALDERMAN, double slang'd.

4. (thieves').—A JEMMY (*q.v.*); sometimes ALDERMAN JEMMY. A weightier tool is called a Lord Mayor, whereby it is clear that the criminal classes are not without some kind of respect for the city fathers. The tool is used for burglary purposes.

1883. *Daily Telegraph*, May 14, p. 3, col. 7. A complete set of safe-breaking tools had been used and left behind, including wedges, an ALDERMAN JEMMY, a hammer weighing 14 lbs.

1888. *Saturday Review*, 15 Dec., p. 719. One side of slang was illustrated by the burglar Casey in a well-known case of robbery in the City some years ago, who explained in Court that the big jemmy with which iron shutters were prised open was called the 'ALDERMAN,' adding, 'it would never do to be talking about crowbars in the street.'

5. BLOOD AND GUTS ALDERMAN, *subs. phr.* (popular).—A pompous man; one with a 'corporation.' The allusion is to the alleged or real over-eating and drinking of ALDERMEN as a class.

ALDERMAN LUSHINGTON, *subs.* (Australian). — Intoxicating beverages.

ALDERMAN'S PACE.—A slow and stately gait, like that of a burly

man as aldermen are generally represented. The French have an equivalent phrase, *pas d'abbé*.

ALDGATE. A DRAUGHT ON THE PUMP AT ALDGATE, *subst. phr.* (commercial).—A bad bill of exchange. A play on the word 'draught.'

ALECAMPANE.—See ALLACOMPAIN.

ALECIE, ALECY, *subs.* (old nonce words) [from ALE + suffix CIE or CY, as in 'lunacy'].—The state of being under the influence of ale; drunkenness; also balmyness.

1594. J. LYLY, *Mother Bombie*, cc. 9. If he had arrested a mare instead of a horse, it had beene a slight oversight, but to arrest a man, that hath no likenesse of a horse, is flat lunasie, or ALECIE.

ALE-DRAPER, *subs.* (old) [from ALE + DRAPER as in linen-draper].—A humorous title for an alehouse keeper; probably from the ancient custom of measuring ale by the yard. It long survived dialectically, but is now obsolete. Synonyms were RUMCULL, and SQUIRT-QUESTER (*q.v.*).

1593. HENRY CHETTLE, *Kinde-Harts Dreame*. Two milch maydens that had set up a shoppe of ALE-DRAPERY.

1747. In *Parish Register of Scotter, Linc.* [Buried], July 8th, Thomas Broughton, Farmer and ALE DRAPER.

ALE-KNIGHT, *subs. phr.* (old) [from ALE + KNIGHT, used derisively].—A tippler; a boon companion.

1575. *Eccl. Proc., Chester.* [The Vicar of Whalley, Lanc., is charged with being a common dronker and ALE KNIGHT.]

1654. WITT's *Recreations.*
Come all you brave wights,
That are dubbed ALE-KNIGHTS
Now set out youselves in fight:
And let them that crack
In the praises of sack,
Know malt is of mickle might.

1863-64. CHAMBERS' *Bk. of Days*, ii., 597. This man was a regularly dubbed ALE-KNIGHT, loved barley wine to the full.

ALES, *subs.* (Stock Exchange).— The shares in the brewery business of S. Allsopp and Sons, Limited, are thus known.

ALE SPINNER, *subs. phr.* (old) [from ALE + SPINNER, a manufacturer or producer].—A brewer or publican.

ALEXANDRA LIMP, *subs.* (popular).— The name given to an erstwhile fit of semi-imbecility on the part of 'Society.' The Princess of Wales, through a slight infirmity, walks with a suspicion of lameness, and servile imitation of everything pertaining to royalty caused the sudden appearance (*circa* 1860-70) of a crowd of limping petticoated toadies. The craze passed away as suddenly as it came. *Cf.*, GRECIAN BEND.

1876. *Chambers' Journal*, No. 629. Your own advocacy of the Grecian bend and the ALEXANDRA LIMP—both positive and practical imitations of physical affliction. [H.]

ALFRED DAVID, *subs.* (common).— An affidavit—obviously a humorous corruption in pronunciation; also AFFIDAVY; and, by an extended process of curtailment, DAVY. All are common colloquialisms among the uneducated classes. AFTER-DAVY is likewise occasionally heard, generally in connection with a person *in extremis*.

ALGERINE, *subs.* (theat.)—A member of a company who, when 'the ghost' cannot be induced to walk, *i.e.*, when the exchequer is low, and salaries are not paid,

'remonstrates' with the manager. The term is also used to designate the hard-up borrower of petty sums.

ALIVE AND KICKING, *adv. phr.* (popular). — An intensive form of 'ALIVE' in its most colloquial sense of being alert and full of action. In the days of Pierce Egan's *Tom and Jerry*, ALIVE partook far more of the nature of slang than now. Sometimes ALL ALIVE AND KICKING is varied by ALL ALIVO; KNOWING; ALL FLY. The allusion is to a child in the womb after quickening.

1889. *Globe*, Oct. 4, p. 1, col. 3. Next day there appeared a letter from a Mr. Basil Watts Phillips, who proclaimed himself as a son of the playwright, and stated, moreover, that his mother, the playwright's widow, as well as another son, named Gordon, were—to use a popular phrase—'alive and kicking.' Miss Emma, therefore, could hardly be recognised, with fairness, as the 'only living representative of the late Watts Phillips.'

ALLACOMPAIN, *subs.* (rhyming slang). —Forms : ALACOMPAIN, ALICUMPANE, ELECAMPAIN, etc. 1. In the so-called rhyming slang this is the equivalent of rain.

2. (common). — Candy supposed to be made from the root of *inula helenium* or bellwort; it contains, however, little else than colored sugar.

ALL A-FLOAT (rhyming slang).—A coat.

ALL ALIVE, *adv. and adj.* (tailors').— Ill-made garments, and 'misfits,' are said to be ALL ALIVE.

ALL ALONG OF (vulgarism).—On account of; by reason of, etc.

ALL-A-MORT.—See AMORT.

ALL AROUND SPORTS, *sub.* (American).—Obviously a corruption of 'ALL ROUND SPORTSMEN,' *i.e.*, men whose interest in sport is catholic, and all embracing.

ALL AT SEA, *adv. phr.* (popular). —In an uncertain, vague condition. Of nautical origin, and perhaps more colloquial than slang; equivalent to ALL ABROAD (*q.v.*).

ALL BRANDY, *adv. phr.* (common). —When it is desired to commend or speak well of anything it is said to be ALL BRANDY. The use of such a term suggests curious reflections upon the drinking habits of those who employ it.

SYNONYMS. A1; the pure quill; about east; about right; at par; the cheese.

ALL DICKEY.—See DICKEY.

ALLEVIATOR, *subs.* (common). — A drink; refreshment.

1846. MARK LEMON, *Golden Fetters*. If any of you feel thirsty after this exciting interview, I shall be happy to stand an ALLEVIATOR.

SYNONYMS. Gargle; smile; Alderman Lushington; long sleeved 'un (Australian, when taken from a long glass); shout; etc.—See GARGLE.

ALLEY, ALLY, ALAY, *subs.* (schoolboys' term).—A superior kind of marble. Supposed to be a corrupted and abbreviated form of 'alabaster,' of which these superior kind of marbles are sometimes made. ALLEY is the name given to the medium sizes, smaller ones

being called MIVVIES (*q.v.*), and the largest BONCES (*q.v.*). The word sometimes appears as ALLEY TOR, OR ALLEY TAW. De Foe, in 'Duncan Campbell,' as early as 1720, speaks of a large bag of marbles and ALLEYS, and at that time the term was considered vulgar. It is interesting to note that the supposed derivation of ALLEY from alabaster is borne out by the fact, that among school-boys stone marbles are called STONEYS (*q.v.*), and clay ones COMMONEYS (*q.v.*). Additional weight is also given to the accuracy of this derivation, when it is remembered that what are known as 'DUTCH ALLEYS' (*q.v.*), are only STONEYS enamelled or glazed different colours. In old Berlin slang, ALLEY TORS were known as *Kalbacher*.

ALL-FIRED, *adj.* **ALL-FIREDLY**, *adv.* (American).—Thought by most to be a Puritanical corruption of 'hell-fired,' and in that respect a profane euphemistic adjective. In this connection it carries with it the meaning of 'immense,' 'excessive,' or 'inordinate' in general; but, of course, the primary signification of this corruption is perfectly obvious. Some, however, think the word may be taken at its face value [ALL + FIRE + ED.], an intensitive of the merely rhetorical fire. Common now on both sides of the Atlantic.

1755. *The World*, No. 140. How arbitrary is language! and how does the custom of mankind join words, that reason has put asunder! Thus we often hear of HELL-FIRE COLD, of devilish handsome, and the like.

1885. HALIBURTON, *Clockmaker*, 1 S., ch. xxiv. 'Look at that 'ere Dives,' they say, 'what an ALL-FIRED scrape he got into by his avarice with Lazarus'

1861. HUGHES, *Tom Brown at Oxford*, ch. xl. 'I knows I be so ALL-FIRED jealous; I can't abear to hear o' her talkin', let alone writin' to——'

1883. JAMES PAYN, *Thicker than Water*, ch. xvii. 'Well,' he said . . . . 'you've been an ALL-FIRED time you have in selling those jars.'

ALL FLY.—See FLY.

ALL FOURS. TO GO or BE ON ALL FOURS, *verb. phr.* (popular).—From the four legs of a quadruped, or the two legs and two arms of a child or man. Hence to go on ALL FOURS is to go evenly, the figure of speech presented being the reverse of limping like a lame dog. Thence follows the metaphorical use of the phrase in the sense of exact analogy and similarity of relation. It is thus synomyous with 'as like as two peas' (the French say, *comme deux gouttes d'eau*, as like as two drops of water); 'a chip of the old block'; a 'Chinese copy,' etc. At the same time, a show of probability must be conceded to those philologists who refer the phrase to the masonic symbol of the square, emblematic of harmony and completeness. Possibly masons gave its use a fresh impetus.

ALL GAMMON! *phr.* (common).— All nonsense; rubbish! — See ALL MY EYE.

ALL GAY, *adv.* (thieves'). — All serene; all right; the coast is clear. The French *voleur* says, *c'est franco!*

ALL-GET-OUT, *phr.* (American).—That beats ALL-GET-OUT, is an old retort to any extravagant story or assertion. Barrère says, 'oh, get out!' appears to have suggested the phrase, which is, perhaps, not altogether obvious.

ALL HANDS TO THE PUMP, *verb. phr.* (old). — An expression borrowed from seafaring life, signifying concentration of energy in any one direction. Now-a-days we say, 'a long pull, a strong pull, and a pull altogether'; this also is a sailor's phrase.

ALL HOLIDAY AT PECKHAM, *proverbial phr.* (popular).—No work to do; and, as a concomitant, nothing to eat. A play upon words.—*See* PECKISH.

    1811. *Lexicon Balatronicum*. ALL holiday at Peckham . . . . a saying signifying that it is all over with the business or person spoken of or alluded to.

    1848. FORSTER, *Oliver Goldsmith*, bk. I., ch. vi., p. 55 (5ed.) 'Oh, that is ALL A HOLIDAY AT PECKHAM,' said an old friend very innocently one day, is a common proverbial phrase.

It seems that Goldsmith in the early part of his London life passed some miserable months as usher in a school at Peckham, and the memory of this doleful period was ever bitter to him Years afterwards, a friend in conversation happened to speak facetiously of it being 'all holiday at Peckham,' and was surprised to find that this innocent reference to a recognised proverbial phrase was regarded by Goldsmith as an unkind allusion to his past misery, and, therefore, a personal insult.

ALL HOLLOW, *adv.* (popular).—To BEAT, or CARRY ALL HOLLOW, *i.e.*, utterly; completely.

ALL HOT ! *subs.* (common).—A hot potato. A cry used by peripatetic street vendors.

ALL IN, *phr.* (Stock Exchange).—When the market is depressed and a disposition to sell prevails, it is said to be ALL IN. Conversely, ALL OUT signifies that the market is improving.

ALL IN A PUCKER.—*See* PUCKER.

ALL IN FITS, *adv. phr.* (tailors').—Badly made clothes are said to be ALL IN FITS, or to have a paralytic stroke. Such garments are also said to fit where they touch, *i.e.*, nowhere. Now common.

ALL JAW. ALL JAW LIKE A SHEEP'S HEAD, *adv. phr.* (common). — Said of one who is a great talker; or, who has the gift of the gab.

    1876. C. HINDLEY, *Life and Adventures of a Cheap Jack*, p. 41. 'Look at the man! hear him; why, he's ALL JAW LIKE A SHEEP'S HEAD. He was drummed out of the regiment he was in for eating his comrades' knapsacks.'

A synonym is ALL MOUTH.—*See* JAW.

ALL LOMBARD STREET TO A CHINA ORANGE, *phr.* (old); sometimes ALL LOMBARD STREET TO NINE-PENCE.—One of many fanciful forms of betting once current among the sporting fraternity; others were 'Chelsea College to a sentry box,' 'Pompey's Pillar to a stick of sealing wax,' etc.

    1819. THOMAS MOORE, *Tom Cribb's Memorial to Congress*, p. 38 A pause ensued—'till crie of 'Gregson,'

GRANDMOTHER. All nonsense; rubbish. The suggested derivations of this significant retort to a tedious narration containing neither rhyme nor reason are as various as the forms in which the phrase appears. Not so clear, however, is the evidence in support of any of them, although Barrère unwittingly stumbles upon what is probably the true origin. Had he studied the subject of slang historically, he would have been able to adduce adequate proof for what he merely puts forth as a 'more probable' derivation than those of his predecessors. After stating that some have suggested the origin of the phrase in the Welsh, AL MI HIVY, it is very tedious or all nonsense, he says, 'It seems far more probable that it is a contraction of the phrase 'there is as much of it as there is in ALL MY EYE,' the words being made more forcible by closing one of the organs of vision. To express dissent from any statement, or a refusal to comply with a request. French slang has the corresponding term *mon œil!* which is usually accompanied by a knowing wink and a significant gesture as an invitation to inspect the organ.' From a comparative study of the dates and examples which follow, it seems a fair deduction to assume that the original form of the phrase was simply ALL MY EYE, and that the additional tags given above are later importations.

    1653. ARCHBISHOP BRAMHALL, *Answer to the Epistle of M. de la Milletière* [Works, vol. I., pp. 68-9. ed. Ox. 1842.] Fifthly, suppose (all this notwith-

standing) such a conference should hold, what reason have you to promise to yourself such success as to obtain so easy a victory? You have had conferences and conferences again at Poissy and other places, and gained by them just as much as you might PUT IN YOUR EYE and see never the worse.

    1682. *Preface to Julian the Apostate* (London, printed for Langley Curtis). What benefit a Popish successor can reap from lives and fortunes spent in defence of the Protestant religion he may PUT IN HIS EYE; and what the Protestant religion gets by lives and fortunes spent in the service of a Popish successor will be over the left shoulder.

    1768. GOLDSMITH, *Good-natured Man*, Act iii. *Bailiff*. That's ALL MY EYE. The king only can pardon.

    1811. POOLE, *Hamlet Travestied*, i, 1. As for black clothes,—THAT'S ALL MY EYE AND TOMMY.

Hotten's contention, that ALL MY EYE and BETTY MARTIN was a vulgar phrase constructed from the commencement of a Roman Catholic prayer to St. Martin (the patron saint of drunkards), '*Oh, mihi, beate Martine*,' which in common with many another fell into discredit and ridicule after the Reformation, is both fanciful and untrue. In the first place there is no prayer in the Breviary which answers to the description given; and in the second it has been shown that the essential part of the phrase is very much older than the Joe Millerism which first set the copy for every lexicographer of the 'unwritten word,' from Hotten down to Brewer and Barrère, the latter of whom, strangely enough, after pitching on the right track, stultifies himself by an admission that ALL MY EYE AND BETTY MARTIN seems to have been the original phrase. The earliest example of the 'Betty Martin' form, found after

    3

Brought Bob, the poet, on his legs soon,—
My eyes, how prettily Bob writes!
Talk of your camels, hogs and crabs,
And twenty more such *Pidcock* frights—
Bob's worth a hundred of these dabs,
ALL LOMBARD STREET TO NINEPENCE on it.

ALL MOONSHINE, *adverbial phr.* (popular). — Moonshine is in old-fashioned and provincial English 'an illusive shadow,' ' a mere pretence' [Halliwell]. The expression IT IS ALL MOONSHINE is now variously applied, whether as referring to empty professions, to vain boasts, to promises not trustworthy, to questionable statements, or to any kind of extravagant talk. There exist in several languages so many words of *lunar* connection, all implying variableness or inconstancy, that possibly this phrase also, IT IS ALL MOONSHINE, may have been primarily employed to express some degree of fickleness, or caprice; in allusion to the inconstancy or changeableness of the moon, or rather moonlight. When anyone professes or promises great things, which we do not expect to see realized, we say IT IS ALL MOONSHINE, for moonshine is very shifty; one week we have it, another we have it not; nay, it shifts from night to night. 'Lunes' in old English, are not only fits of insanity, but freaks. And the term 'lunatic' itself did not properly signify a person always insane, but one who was mad at intervals, dependent as was supposed on the phases of the moon. This distinction is still very accurately maintained in Spanish philology: 'Lunatics, *El loco, cuya demencia no est continua, sino por intervalos*

que proceden del estado en que se halla la Luna.' Hence also in French, modern and old : ' *Il a des lunes,*' he is whimsical or fantastic. ' *Tenir de la lune,*' to be inconstant, mutable; '*Avoir un quartier de la lune,*' *en la teste,*' or *Il y a de la lune,* he is changeable, giddy, capricious. In the 'language of symbols' the moon is the emblem of hypocrisy, as in the following device :

    'La lune avec ces mots,
    Mentiri didicit.
    (Elle trompe toûjours.)
Pour l'hypocrisie, dont la lune est le symbole.' MENESTRIAR, *Philosophie des Images*, vol. I., p. 266.

Another emblem is the following :

    ' La lune,
Non vultus non color unus,
Pour une personne qui n'est pas sincère.'
    Ibid, I., p. 269.

Moonshine, in conformity with these ideas, was probably employed originally in characterising the talk of persons too mutable to be relied on from one time to another.—*Notes and Queries.*

    1714. *Spectator*, No. 597. Several of my correspondents have been pleased to send me an account how they have been employed in sleep, and what notable adventure they have been engaged in during that MOONSHINE IN THE BRAIN.

    1874. MRS. H. WOOD, *Johnny Ludlow*, 1 S., No. xxii., p. 397.' 'They are all pig-headed together . . . they are blinded by specious arguments that will turn out, I fear, to be ALL MOONSHINE.'

ALL MOUTH, *adv.* (common).—Applied to a loquacious talker. *Cf.*, ALL JAW.

ALL MY EYE, *adv. phr.* (common).—Variations in form are : ALL MY EYE AND BETTY MARTIN—MY ELBOW—TOMMY—and MY

long search, occurs in *Tom Crib's Memorial to Congress*, published in 1819, where it appears simply as ALL MY EYE, BETTY, but that the phrase was known long previously is proved by the extract from Poole quoted above.

Among ENGLISH SYNONYMS of refusal or incredulity, are: Cock and bull story; a wild-goose chase; a mare's nest; fiddle-de-dee; do you see any green in my eye? that's a flam; over the left; go teach your grannie to suck eggs; Walker! you be blowed! I be hanged! Not for Joe! How's your brother, Job? Don't you wish you may get it? Yes, in a horn (American); That's all round my hat.

FR. *Des fadeurs* (lit. insipidity); *C'est des vannes ?* (lit. floodgates or sluices); *des nèfles* (lit. medlars); *des navets !* (lit. turnips); *de l'anis !* (lit. aniseed); *du flan !* (lit. custard); *tu t'en ferais mourir !* (lit. you will die after it); *mon œil !* (my eye); *flûte ! Zut !* (go to the deuce!); *et ta sœur ?* (phrase of the 'who's your hatter' stamp); *des plis !* (don't you wish you may get it); *la peau !* (blow it all!); *de la mousse !* (expression of ironical refusal); *du vent !* (go to pot!); *des emblèmes !* ; *des fouilles !*; *on t'en fricasse !*

ALL NATIONS, *subs.* (old).—1. A mixture of the drainings of all kinds of spirits and malt liquors; it is of an extremely intoxicating character. Sometimes called ALLS, or ALL SORTS.

    2. A parti-colored dress or coat; a Joseph's garment. Also one that is patched.

ALL-NIGHT-MAN, *subs.* (old).—A body snatcher. Now obsolete.

    1861. RAMSAY, *Remin*, ser. ii., 133. The body lifters, or ALL-NIGHT-MEN, as they were wont to be called.

ALL OF A HEAP.—*See* HEAP.

ALL OF A HOUGH, *adv. phr.* (tailors').—Said of an unskilled workman. Equivalent to clumsy; bungling; unworkmanlike. Hotten quotes this as a Suffolk phrase (HOUGH being spelt *hugh*, and pronounced with a grunt). Synonymous with 'all on one side'; falling with a thump.

ALL OF MY LONE, *adv. phr.* (American).—A negro vulgarism for 'ALONE.'

ALL ON THE GO (vulgarism).—*See* GO.

ALL OUT, *adv. phr.* (vulgar).—1. Entirely; completely; by far, as in 'ALL OUT the best.' This vulgarism must now be classed among depraved words; but as far as written English is concerned, it can be traced back to the year 1300. It seems to have fallen out of use about the middle of the seventeenth century.

    1830. CARLETON, *Traits and Stories*, vol. II., p. 102. 'He's now in his grave, and, thank God, it's he that had the dacent funeral ALL OUT.'

    2. Another old English expression, now obsolete, is TO DRINK ALL OUT, to empty a bumper; and hence,—

    3. Used substantively, *e.g.*, an ALL OUT being equivalent to what 'Arry would call now-a-days a BIG DRUNK. The connection between the ancient and modern usage is clear.

4. To BE ALL OUT also signifies to be in error; quite wrong.

5. (turf).—A man is said to be ALL OUT when unsuccessful during the whole of a day's racing.

6. (Stock Exchange).—*See* ALL IN.

7. (athletic). — Exhausted; said of a man or crew who, having exerted him or themselves to the utmost, can do no more.

1886. *Graphic*, April 10, p. 392. Pitman, the Cambridge stroke, after passing the 'Queen's Head,' Mortlake, put on a grand spurt, to which his crew fairly responded, though pretty well ALL OUT.

ALL-OVERISH, *adj.* (colloquial). An indefinite feeling which pervades the body at critical periods, when sickening for an illness, or at a moment of supreme excitement, as when about to 'pop the question' which, says Hotten, 'is sometimes called feeling all over alike, and touching nowhere.' Synonyms are 'to feel all round one's hat,' and 'chippy.'

1851. H. MAYHEW, *London Lab. and Lon. Poor*, vol. III., p. 52. 'When the mob began to gather round, I felt ALL-OVERISH.'

ALL-OVERISHNESS, *subs.* (colloquial).—The state of being all-overish.—*See* foregoing.

1854. AINSWORTH, *Flitch of Bacon*, pt. II., ch. v. 'I feel a sort of shivering and ALL-OVERISHNESS.'

1841. JOHN MILLS, *Old English Gentleman*, ch. xxiv., p. 186 (3 ed.). 'Isn't it natural for a body to feel a sort of a queer ALL-OVERISHNESS on the eve of a wedding, I should like to know?'

ALL OVER PATTERN, *subs. phr.* (common). Used in describing patterns that are intricate, or designs in which the pattern is not of a set character.

1881. F. E. HULME. *Suggestions in Floral Design.* A term [ALL OVER PATTERN] used to denote a design in which the whole of a field is covered with ornament in contradistinction to such as have units only at intervals, leaving spaces of the ground between them. The ornament of the Moors as seen in the decorations of the Alhambra, and that of Eastern nations generally, is most commonly of this nature; the whole surface of the object is covered with decorative forms so as to present to the eye a mass of elaborate detail, the leading lines of which can often only be detected by careful scrutiny. When, as in some Persian surfaces, these lines are often quite lost, the result is unsatisfactory.

ALL OVER THE SHOP, *adv. phr.* (common).—1. A phrase applied to any ubiquitous person, thing or deed.—*See* SHOP.

1883. G. R. SIMS, *Lifeboat, etc.* (*Awful Character*). He kills little babies ALL OVER THE SHOP, each day in a river one thrown is.

2. Disconcerted.

1887. E. E. MONEY, *Little Dutch Maiden*, II., xi., 225. 'Oh, please don't blush; it makes me feel ALL OVER THE SHOP.'

ALLOW, *subs.* (Harrow School).—A boy's weekly allowance.

ALLOWANCES, *subs.* (tailors').—The extra measure in cutting cloth for a garment to permit of turnings in for seams; also the trimmings, such as wadding, buttons, braid, etc. Rather technical than slang.

ALL ROUND, *adj.* (popular).—1. Able in all departments; adaptable in every respect to the purpose in view. Whether applied to sport, business, or indeed any department of life or thought, within a

given circle, it carries with it, *mutatis mutandis*, the same meaning. *Cf.* ALL AROUND SPORTS.

1881. JAMES PAYN, *Grape from a Thorn*, ch. xl. 'He's a bad one ALL ROUND.'

1883. *Graphic*, August 11, p. 138, col. 2. Foremost still as an 'ALL-ROUND' cricketer among the gentlemen stands W. G. Grace.

2. Average; *see* quotation.

1869. *Notes on N. W. Prov. India*, p. 98. We find an ALL ROUND rent of so much per acre charged on the cultivation.

ALL-ROUNDER, *subs.* (popular). [From ALL ROUND+er] he who or that which is ALL ROUND (*q.v.*); as an all round man; particularly applied, however, to a shirt collar the same height all round the neck and meeting in front. Once fashionable, but little worn now.

1857. A. TROLLOPE, *Three Clerks*, ch. xxii. But he had bestowed, perhaps, the greatest amount of personal attention on his collar . . . Some people may think that an ALL-ROUNDER is an ALL-ROUNDER, and that if one is careful to get an ALL-ROUNDER one has done all that is necessary. But so thought not Macassar Jones.

1860. *All the Year Round*, No. 42, 369. That particularly demonstrative type of the [collar] species known as the ALL ROUNDER. [M.]

1865. LORD STRANGFORD, *Selection* (1869), II., 163. Dressed in full uniform, with high stand-up collar; the modern ALL ROUNDER not having got so far into Asia. [M.]

1875. *Chambers' Journal*, No. 586. To present himself in an ALL ROUNDER hat and coat of formal cut on Sunday.

ALL ROUND MY HAT, *adv. phr.* (popular).—1. TO FEEL ALL ROUND ONE'S HAT is to feel queer; out of sorts; all overish.

2. THAT'S ALL ROUND MY HAT is synonymous with gammon! Nonsense! *See* ALL MY EYE. A music hall song [1834] had this phrase as a refrain.

3. SPICY AS ALL ROUND MY HAT, *i.e.*, sensational.

1882. *Punch*, vol. LXXXII, p. 177, col. 1. 'ARRY ON A JEWRY.

Fact is, I have bin on a JURY. New line for yours truly, dear boy, and I 'oped it might be a rare barney, a thing as a chap could enjoy. I am nuts upon Criminal Cases, Perlice News, you know, and all that, And, thinks I, this will be 'tuppence coloured,' and SPICY AS ALL ROUND MY HAT.

ALLS, *subs.*—1. *See* ALL NATIONS.

1868. BREWER, *Phrase and Fable*, s.v. ALLS, tap-droppings. The refuse of all sorts of spirits drained from the glasses, or spilt in drawing. The mixture is sold in gin-houses at a cheap rate.

2. (artisans').—*See* BENS.

ALL'S BLUE.—*See* BLUE.

ALL SERENE! *intj.* (popular).—All right. All's well! This phrase is thought to be of Spanish origin, and to be derived from the word *serena* a countersign used by sentinels in Cuba. The night watchmen in Spain likewise end their proclamation of the hour by '*é sereno!*' It is also equivalent to O.K., and a few years since was the burden of one of the senseless street cries, which, every now and again, have a vogue in large cities. Most of these catches originate in music-hall songs. ALL SERENE, however, was vulgarly colloquial long before the period in question, as will be seen by the following example:

1857. A. TROLLOPE, *Three Clerks*, ch. xlv. 'You're ALL SERENE, then, Mr. Snape,' said Charley; 'you're in the right box.'

ALL SMOKE, GAMMON AND PICKLES. —*See* SMOKE.

ALL SORTS, *subs.* (common).—Explained by quotation.—*See* ALL NATIONS.

1859. SALA, *Gaslight and Daylight*, ch. vi. A counter perforated in elaborately-pricked patterns, like a convivial shroud, apparently for ornament, but really for the purpose of allowing the drainings, overflowings, and out-spillings of the gin-glasses to drop through, which, being collected with sundry washings, and a dash, perhaps, of fresh material, is, by the thrifty landlord, dispensed to his customers under the title of ALL SORTS.

ALL SORTS OF, *adj.* (American).—First rate; excellent. A phrase very common in the South and West, and used in many different ways. It carries with it the idea of smartness and *chic*, as, *e.g.*, when applied to a woman, a horse, or a building.

ALLSPICE, *subs.* (popular.)—A nickname for a grocer; the derivation is obvious.

ALL'S QUIET ON THE POTOMAC, *phr.* (American).—A period of undisturbed rest, quiet enjoyment, or peaceful possession; a phrase dating from the Civil War, when its frequent repetition in the bulletins of the War Secretary made it familiar to the public, who quickly appropriated it in a metaphorical sense. It has since formed the refrain of many a song.

1862. *The Picket Guard.*

ALL QUIET ALONG THE POTOMAC, they say,
Except now and then a stray picket
Is shot on his beat as he walks to and fro,
By a rifleman hid in a thicket.

ALL T. H., *adv. phr.* (tailors cutters').—Said in praise or approval; a tailor's equivalent of A 1; all right; all there—of which last it is possibly an abbreviated form.

ALL THE CABOOSE, *adv. phr.*—*See* CABOOSE.

ALL THE GO, *adv. phr.* (common). — One of the innumerable superlatives of work-a-day English; quite up to the mark; in full demand; 'no deception, gents!'—*See* GO.

ALL THERE, *adv. phr.* (popular).—Up to the mark; first-rate; ready for any emergency; a phrase of general satisfaction and approval; also, in one's element.

1877. *Five Years' Penal Servitude*, ch. iii., p. 220. 'He stayed in a place doing the grand and sucking the flats till the folks began to smoke him as not ALL THERE.'

1880. *Punch*, Aug. 7, p. 59. ALL THERE! *Clerk* (*who has called to see the gas-meter*). 'Is yours a *wet*, or a *dry* meter, madam?' *Young Wife* (*who does not like to show ignorance*). 'Well, it is rather *damp*, I'm afraid!'

1883. JAMES PAYN, *Thicker than Water*, ch. xx. It was his excusable boast, though expressed in somewhat vulgar language, that when anything was wanted he was 'ALL THERE.'

ALL THE SHOOT.—Equivalent to 'THE WHOLE BOILING' (*q.v.*).

ALL THE WAY DOWN, *adv. phr.* (popular). — Synonymous with complete adaptibility to the end in view; sometimes varied by 'UP TO THE KNOCKER,' or 'UP TO THE NINES.'

ALL TO HIS OWN CHEEK. — *See* CHEEK.

ALL TO PIECES, *adverbial phr.* (common).—1. [*Cf.* GO TO PIECES.]

A superlative of all work. To GO ALL TO PIECES is to collapse utterly; to be altogether ruined; to be in a state of utter collapse.

1667. PEPYS, *Diary*, Aug. 29. I find by all hands that the Court is at this day ALL TO PIECES, every man of a faction of one sort or other.

1811. JANE AUSTEN, *Sense and S.*, ch. xxx. 'Fifty thousand pounds! and by all accounts it won't come before its wanted; for they say he is ALL TO PIECES. No wonder! dashing about with his curricle and hunters!'

1882. *Punch*, LXXXII., 185, 2. 'Ah Jerry, we might as well go back to the Shades as be among such a shady crowd.' Young Bob Logic seemed rather nettled at this speech of the Corinthian's, and said, 'Well, don't you know you can't expect a fellow to look very bright till he's had an S. and B., or two and a Kümmel? These pals will be all right after dinner.' 'Let us hope they will,' said the Corinthian, 'for they look ALL TO PIECES now.'

2. When a woman is confined she is said TO GO ALL TO PIECES; variants being TO EXPLODE; TO BUST UP.

3. (rowing).—Collapsed; exhausted; said of a crew when rowing wildly.

1884. *Echo*, April 7, p. 3, col. 1. The Oxford men were now ALL TO PIECES! their boat was full of water.

4. (sporting).—In racing and athletic circles equivalent to want of form.

ALL TO SMASH, *adv. phr.* (common). —Also 'ALL TO PIECES,' *i.e.*, bankrupt; ruined; in a state of utter delapidation; or, complete discomfiture.—*See* SMASH.

1861. CUTHBERT BEDE, *Our New Rector*, ch. x., p. 105. 'There isn't a fellow at school can match *me*, Miss Moore! I beat them ALL TO SMASH!'

ALL UP, *adv. phr.* (common).—'It's ALL UP' with so-and-so, or with such and such a thing, or course of action; *i.e.*, the endeavour is fruitless; utter ruin or collapse is the end of it all; there is nothing left for hope; sometimes also, death. This phrase, indicative of total failure, discomfiture, and destruction, does not appear to be of very ancient standing, and can only be traced back as far as Fielding (*see* quotation). The mock epitaph, which the late Mr. W. J. Conybeare inserted in his novel *Perversion*, fitly illustrates the popular usage of ALL UP. It is supposed to be written in commemoration of a country squire cut off in the midst of festivities.

'Quite well at ten,
Had a few friends to sup with me;
Taken ill at twelve,
And at one it was ALL UP with me.'

Also UP.

Among ENGLISH SYNONYMS may be mentioned:—To have missed stays (nautical); to have gone to pot; to have gone to smash; to have gone to the devil.

1752. FIELDING, *Amelia*, book XII., ch. vi. 'ALL IS UP and undone!' cries Murphy.

1838. DICKENS, *Nicholas Nickleby*, ch. lx. A-double l, all, everything; a cobbler's weapon; u-p, up, adjective, not down; s-q-u-double e-r-s, Squeers, noun substantive, a educator of youth. Total, ALL UP with Squeers.

ALLUS, *adv.* (vulgar).—Always.

ALL WAG BLUE, *subs. phr.* (American). — A frolicing, rollicking time; a spree; a kick-up.

ALLYBEG.—*See* LLYBEGE.

ALMIGHTY, *adj.* (common).—Mighty; great; exceedingly — a superlative of all work. For example, in the 'dialect' of which this word is a component part, an over-officious man is put down as 'ALMIGHTY fast'; or a horse with good points as an 'ALMIGHTY fine beast'; and so on throughout the whole range of superlative merit. It ranks with 'awful,' 'eternal,' 'everlasting,' 'lovely,' and a multitude of other words, orthodox enough when properly handled, but which become the purest slang when used, as is frequently the case, of things finite, and even of trifles. So employed, ALMIGHTY is generally regarded as an Americanism, and is credited to our kinsmen across the sea, a view supported by De Quincey's use of the term. If this be so, there is, in truth, little at which to wonder. The 'wild,' the boundless West is no unlikely nursery for big, high-sounding words; and though one may justly condemn such depravation of our mother-tongue, the fact remains. Thus, amongst the untutored backwoodsmen and rough pioneers of the West a week is an 'eternal' time; a good officer is an ALMIGHTY general; and a spell of rain is spoken of as an 'everlasting' deluge. The foregoing examples by no means exhaust the potentialities of the language; as, *e.g.*, when people talk of a man playing ALMIGHTY 'smash' with his prospects, meaning that he is hopelessly ruining his chances of success: or driving a fellow-citizen into a state of ALMIGHTY 'shivers' through ill-treatment; or of a thing lasting till ALMIGHTY 'crack,' *i.e.*, for an interminable period.

1824. DE QUINCEY, *Works* (1871), XVI., 261. Such rubbish, such ALMIGHTY nonsense (to speak *transatlantice*) no eye has ever beheld.

1833. MARRYAT, *Peter Simple* (1863), 328. An ALMIGHTY pretty French privateer lying in St. Pierre's.

1888. *New York Mercury*, July 21. 'This is a rum world,' said the driver, with a chuckle, as he drove up the street. 'And of all places in it New York is the rummest. And hack-drivin' is the rummest business, leadin' one into the rummest secrets. Another passenger to the "Rookery." I wonder whether the other boys gits as many customers to that place as Luke Hyatt? If they do it must be ALMIGHTY full sometimes.'

In another place De Quincey speaks of a man who cannot live and cannot die as being 'in an ALMIGHTY fix,' and the expression is otherwise frequently used by him. Captain Marryat likewise constantly employs it; in fact, the phrase was well 'acclimatised' on this side of the Atlantic long prior to the publication of *My Novel* [1853], and Prof. Barrère, in attributing its popularisation 'in a certain measure' to Lord Lytton, failed to render due credit, if any, either to De Quincey or Marryat.

ALMIGHTY DOLLAR, *subs.* (American).—The power of money; Mammon regarded as an embodiment of the worship of, and the quest for gold. This phrase is, in reality, an old friend with a new face, for Ben Jonson used the term in its modern sense when speaking of the power of money. Its modern application to dollars is traceable to Washington Irving, who made use of it in a charming little sketch, entitled *A Creole Village*.

1574—1637. BEN JONSON, *Epistle to Elizabeth, Countess of Rutland*.
Whilst that for which all virtue now is sold,
And almost every vice, ALMIGHTIE gold.

1839. WASHINGTON IRVING, *Wolfert's Roost: A Creole Village*, p. 40. The ALMIGHTY DOLLAR, that great object of universal devotion throughout our land, seems to have no genuine devotee in these peculiar villages.

1876. BESANT AND RICE, *Golden Butterfly*, ch. xxii. 'Genius, gentlemen, is apt to be careless of the main chance. It don't care for the ALMIGHTY DOLLAR; it lets fellows like me heap up the stamps.'

1886. G. SUTHERLAND, *Australia*, p. 102. The travelling Yankee, with an overwearing confidence in the ALMIGHTY DOLLAR.

ALOFT. TO GO ALOFT, *verb. phr.* (common).—To die; the figure of speech presented here is nautical in origin.

1790. C. DIBDIN, *Sea Songs: Tom Bowling*.
Here a sheer hulk, lies poor Tom
The darling of our crew; [Bowling,
No more he'll hear the tempest howling,
For death has broached him to.
His form was of the manliest beauty,
His heart was kind and soft;
Faithful below, Tom did his duty,
And now he's GONE ALOFT.

Few expressions synonymous with the act of dying equal this in force or pathos; and it is rarely, moreover, that slang climbs on the wings of hope into a purer atmosphere than that of the vices and follies of men with which it is mainly concerned. By no means few in number, nor wanting in sententiousness and dramatic meaning are the phrases employed in the vulgar tongue to signify the greatest of all human experiences.

ENGLISH SYNONYMS. To kick the bucket; to hop the twig; to go to Davy Jones' locker (nautical); to be put to bed with a shovel; to take an earth bath; to croak; to take a ground sweat; to go under (American: the visible disposal of the body furnishing a simile for the process of death); to go up (compare with foregoing: when the victim of lynch law is enquired after the questioner is told that he has 'gone up,' *i.e.*, been hanged); to lose the number of one's mess (a sailor's phrase); to snuff it (from snuffing a candle); to lay down one's knife and fork; to stick one's spoon in the wall; to give in; to give up; to peg out; to slip one's cable (this, like 'to go to Davy Jones' locker,' is of nautical origin); to pass in one's checks (a euphemism drawn from the game of poker, the simile being that of settling one's earthly accounts and the paying in to the banker of the dues at the end of the game); Kickeraboo (West Indian: a corruption of 'to kick the bucket').

FRENCH. *Passer l'arme à gauche* (popular: 'to lay down one's arms'); *casser sa pipe* (lit. 'to break one's pipe'); *dévisser* or *décoller son billard* (lit. 'to break one's cue'); *graisser ses bottes* (lit. 'to grease one's boots'); *avaler sa langue* (lit. 'to swallow one's tongue'); *avaler sa gaffe* ('to lower one's boat-hook'); *avaler sa cuiller* (lit. 'to lay down one's spoon'); *avaler ses baguettes* (military: lit. 'to lay aside one's drum-sticks'); *n'avoir plus mal aux dents* (lit. 'to have toothache no more.' In Fr. Argot *mal de dents* is also synonymous with love); *poser sa chique* (popular: lit. 'to lay down one's finish, elegance, dash, spirit'—in short all that is distinctive in a man); *claquer* (familiar: lit. 'to chatter

with cold' or 'fear'); *saluer le public* (theat.: lit. 'to make one's bow'—to make one's last appearance on this world's stage, and one's first in that land where 'the dead are many, and the living few'); *recevoir son décompte* (military: lit. 'to receive deferred pay'; *décompte* is also military slang for a 'mortal wound'); *cracher ses embouchures* (an expression of musical origin: the figure is obviously that of losing the power to perform on wind instruments'); *déteindre* (popular: lit. 'to wash off the colour' or 'dye.' Is this a play upon words, or an allusion to death as the great revealer of man as he is?); *donner son dernier bon à tirer* (familiar: equivalent to the American, 'to pass in one's checks.' French printers understand by this phrase 'to send the last proofs to press'); *lâcher la perche* (popular: lit. 'to slip off one's perch'); *éteindre son gaz* (popular: 'to turn off the gas.' *Cf.*, 'to snuff it'); *épointer son foret* (popular: lit. 'to break off the point of the drill,' as in boring); *être exproprié* (popular: lit. 'to be dispossessed'; *exproprier* is a judical term signifying 'to take possession of the landed property of a debtor'); *péter son lof* (sailors'); *fumer ses terres*; *fermer son parapluie* (popular: 'to close one's umbrella'); *perdre son bâton* (popular: 'to lose one's walking stick'); *descendre la garde* (popular: 'to come off guard'); *défiler la parade* (military: 'to file off parade'; equivalent to the English 'to lose the number of one's mess'); *tourner de l'œil* (popular: is there not here an allusion to the phenomenon attendant on genuine sleep; feigned sleep can always be detected by turning up the eyelids of the sleeper, if sleep be genuine only the 'whites' of the eyes will be discoverable); *perdre le goût du pain* (popular: 'to lose one's taste for bread'); *lâcher la rampe* (theatrical: 'to lose sight of the footlights'); *faire ses petits paquets* (popular: 'to pack up one's [small] traps'); *casser son crachoir* (popular: lit. 'to break one's spittoon' or mouth); *remercier son boulanger* (thieves': lit. 'to thank the baker.' It must be explained that *boulanger* baker is a French nickname for the devil); *canner*; *dévider à l'estorgue* (thieves'); *baiser la camarde* (popular: 'to salute,' or 'kiss Death'; *camarde* is a popular euphemism for the 'Messenger of Life'); camarder (popular: *see* previous example); *fuir* (thieves': lit. 'to fly' or 'escape'—from justice or capture); *casser son câble* (popular: 'to slip the cable'—evidently a simile drawn from the sea); *casser son fouet* (popular: 'to break' or 'lay aside one's whip'); *faire sa crevaison* (popular: *crever*, 'to kill' or 'die' is usually only employed in speaking of animals); *déralinguer* (sailors': properly 'to detach from the bolt rope'); *virer de bord* (sailors': lit. 'to tack about'); *déchirer son faux-col* (popular: *verbatim*, 'to burst open one's collar'—the allusion is obvious); *se dégeler* (in good French, 'to thaw'); *couper sa mèche* (coachman's: 'to throw down the whip'); *piquer sa plaque* (sailors'); *mettre la table pour les asticots* (popular: properly 'to lay the table [become food] for worms');

aller manger les pissenlits par la racine (popular: to go and feed off dandelion roots'—observe, by the way, that *pissenlit* is an exact equivalent for one of the English field names of the dandelion, viz., 'piddle-the-bed'); *laisser fuir son tonneau* (familiar: lit. 'to let fly' or 'kick away the cask.' *Cf.*, 'to kick the bucket'); *calancher* (vagrants'); *laisser ses bottes quelque part* (familiar: lit. 'to leave one's boots somewhere'); *déchirer son habit* (popular: properly 'to rend' or 'cast aside one's coat'); *déchirer son tablier* (popular: in literary French this means, 'to throw aside or destroy one's apron'); *souffler sa veilleuse* (popular: meaning lit. 'to blow out one's night-lamp' or 'floating wick.' Compare with 'to snuff it' or 'to put out one's light' in English slang); *pousser le boum de cygne* (popular); *avoir son coke* (familiar); *prendre sa secousse* (popular: *i.e.*, 'to take one's blow' or 'shock'); *rendre sa buche* (tailors': the allusion is an obvious one); *rendre sa canne au ministre* (military: lit. 'to resign one's commission to the Minister [of War]; *rendre sa clef* (gypsy: lit. 'to give up the key'); *rendre son livret* (popular: lit. 'to throw up one's cards').

GERMAN SYNONYMS. *See* HOP THE TWIG.

ITALIAN FOURBESQUE. *Sbasire* (lit. 'to faint away'); *sbasire su le funi* (lit. 'to faint away on the rope').

ALONE, *adv.* (old).—In the flash vocabulary of the time of Pierce Egan's *Tom and Jerry* [*circa* 1800-1825], only an experienced man of the world could be allowed to go ALONE. Such a one was said to be FLY; UP TO SNUFF (*q.v.*), etc.

ALONG OF, *adv.* (vulgar).—A dialectical form for on account of; owing to; pertaining, or belonging to. Formerly ALONG ON, and it so appeared as early as A.D. 880: ALONG OF was used by Chaucer, but it is now mainly confined to the illiterate or vulgar.

1369. CHAUCER, *Troylus* ii., 1001. On me is not ALONG thin evil fare.

1581. W. STAFFORD, *Exam. of Complaints*, p. 16 (New Shaks. Soc.: Ed.). Complaining of general poverty, he says: 'Whereof it is LONGE, I cannot well tell.'

1601. HOLLAND, *Pliny*, p. 25, quoted in Morris' *Elem. Hist. Eng. Gram.*, p. 198. And that is LONG OF contrarie causes.

1858. DICKENS, *Xmas. Stories (going into Society)*, p. 65 (II. ed.). Would he object to say why he left it? Not at all; why should he? He left it ALONG OF a dwarf.

1881. W BLACK, *Beautiful Wretch*, ch. xviii. 'Mayhap the concert didn't come off, ALONG OF the snow.'

ALSATIA, or **ALSATIA THE HIGHER**, *subs.* (old slang).—1. Whitefriars, once a place privileged from arrests for debt, as was also ALSATIA THE LOWER, or the Mint in Southwark. Both were suppressed, in 1697, on account of the notorious abuses committed there. A charter of liberties and privileges had been granted, in 1608, by King James I. to the inhabitants of this district, and it speedily became the haunt of insolvent debtors, cheats, and gamesters, who conferred upon it the jocular cant name of ALSATIA, a Latinised form of Alsace, a province which had long enjoyed the reputation of a 'debateable land.'

1688. SHADWELL, *Sq. of Alsatia I.*, in wks. (1720), IV., 25. Who are these? Some inhabitants of White-fryers; some bullies of ALSATIA.

1822. SCOTT, *Fortunes of Nigel*, ch. xvi. Whitefriars, adjacent to the Temple, then well known by the cant name of ALSATIA.

2. Hence any rendezvous or asylum for loose characters and criminals, where immunity from arrest is tolerably certain; a haunt of thieves, and the criminal classes; a low quarter.

1787. GROSE, *Prov. Glossary, etc.* (1811), p. 82. A 'squire of ALSATIA. A spendthrift or sharper, inhabiting places formerly privileged from arrests.

1861. MISS BRADDON, *Trail of the Serpent*, bk. II., ch. i. So Blind Peter was the ALSATIA of Slopperton, a refuge for crime and destitution.

1876. LORD JUSTICE JAMES, in *ex parte* Saffery *re* Cooke, *Law Times*, 35, p. 718. The Stock Exchange is not an ALSATIA; the Queen's laws are paramount there, and the Queen's writ runs even into the sa·red precincts of Capel-Court.

ALSATIAN, *subs.* (old).—A rogue, or debauchee, such as haunted Alsatia or Whitefriars.

1691. LUTTRELL, *Brief Rel.* (1857), II., 259. The benchers of the Inner Temple having given orders for bricking up their little gate leading into White-fryers. . . . . the ALSATIANS came and pulled it down.

c. 1700. *Gentleman Instructed*, p. 491 [10 ed., 1732]. He spurr'd to London, and left a thousand curses behind him. Here he struck up with sharpers, scourers, and ALSATIANS.

1822. SCOTT, *Fortunes of Nigel*, ch. xvii. 'You shall sink a nobleman in the Temple Gardens, and rise an ALSATIAN at Whitefriars.'

Adj.—Pertaining to Alsatia; roguish; debauched.

1688. SHADWELL, *Sq. of Alsatia I.* in wks. (1720), IV., 27. He came out of White Fryers: he's some ALSATIAN bully.

1822. SCOTT, *Fortunes of Nigel*, ch. xvii. An extravagantly long rapier and poinard marked the true ALSATIAN bully.

1882. BESANT, *All Sorts and Conditions of Men*, ch. vii. The road has come to be regarded with admiration as one of those ALSATIAN retreats, growing every day rarer, which are beyond and above the law.

ALSATIA PHRASE, *subs.* (old).—A slang or cant term, such as was used by Alsatians; or, now-a-days, by thieves and vagrants.

1704. SWIFT, *Tale of a Tub.* Apology for author. The second instance to shew the author's wit is not his own, is Peter's banter (as he calls it in his ALSATIA PHRASE) upon transubstantiation.

Synonymous terms were PEDLER'S FRENCH, ST. GILES' GREEK, etc.

ALTAMEL, ALTEMAL, *subs., adj., adv.*, and *intj.* (American thieves').—

Adv.—All together, as 'Let's anchor ALTEMAL,' *i.e.*, 'Let us come to a stop altogether.'

Subs.— The sum total of a bill or story.

Intj.— An injunction to 'cut it short.'

ALTEMAL is said to be derived from the Dutch *altemal*, but Murray has it as 'altumal' with a different derivation. [From L. *altum*, the deep, *i.e.*, the sea + AL.] Grose leans to the former and quotes DUTCH RECKONING as synonymous; from a verbal account without particulars, such as was given in brothels and sponging houses—accounts which allowed of no sort of verification. *Cf.*, FLEMISH ACCOUNT and remarks under DUTCH.

1711. *Medleys*, 29 Jan. (1712), 186. His ALTUMAL cant, a mark of his poor Traffick and Tar-Education.

1753. CHAMBERS, *Cycl. Supp.* ALTUMAL, a term used to denote the mercantile style, or dialect. In this sense, we

meet with ALTUMAL cant, to denote the language of petty traders and tars.

ALTERING THE JEFF'S CLICK.—*See* JEFF'S CLICK.

ALTHAM, *subs.* (old cant).—A wife; mistress.—*See* quotation.

1560. JOHN AWDELEY, *Fraternitye of Vacabondes* (1869. English Dialect Society's Reprint), p. 4. A curtall is much like to the Vpright man, but hys authority is not fully so great. He vseth commonly to go with a short cloke, like to grey Friers, and his woman with him in like liuery, which he calleth his ALTHAM if she be hys.

ALTITUDES. IN HIS ALTITUDES, *phr.* (old). — In an elevated mood, chiefly from liquor; putting on airs and graces; using lofty phrases; in a state of excitement; and, in a special slang sense, drunk. The phrase has been incorrectly given as '*out* of his ALTITUDES.' The first trace of it is to be found in Beaumont and Fletcher's *Laws of Candy*, II. [1616].

1630. JONSON, *New Inn*, I. I have talked somewhat above my share, at large, and been IN THE ALTITUDES, the extravagants.

1668. DRYDEN, *An Evening's Love*, Act iii. If we men could but learn to value ourselves, we should soon take down our mistresses from all their ALTITUDES, and make them dance after our pipes.

1705. VANBRUGH, *Confederacy*, Act v. *Clar.* 'Who makes thee cry out thus, poor Brass?' *Brass.* 'Why, your husband, madam; he's IN HIS ALTITUDES here.

1785. FRANCIS GROSE, *Dictionary of the Vulgar Tongue.* The man is IN HIS ALTITUDES, *i.e.*, he is drunk.

ALTOCAD, *subs.* (Win. Coll.).—A somewhat venerable paid member of the choir who takes ALTO.

ALYBBEG.—*See* LYBBEGE.

ALYCOMPAINE.—*See* ALLACOMPAIN.

AMBASSADOR, *subs.* (nautical).—A sailor's practical joke upon 'green' hands, similar to the festivities formerly universally observed when 'crossing the line.' These tricks have been common to sailors of every nation. AMBASSADOR was thus managed:—A large tub was filled with water, two stools being placed on either side of it; over the whole was thrown a tarpaulin or old sail, kept tight by two persons, who represented the king and queen of a foreign country, and who were seated on the stools. To the victim was allotted the part of AMBASSADOR, who, after repeating a ridiculous speech dictated to him, was led in great state up to the throne, and seated between the king and queen. They rising suddenly, as soon as the unsuspecting victim was seated, caused him to fall backward into the tub of water.

AMBASSADOR OF COMMERCE, *subs.* (familiar).—A commercial traveller; a BAGMAN (*q.v.*).

AMBIA, *subs.* (American). — A euphemism for the juice of tobacco, as expectorated after chewing. Most frequently heard in the Southern and Western States. Apparently a corruption of 'amber' (indeed it is commonly spelt and pronounced *ambeer*) — presumably from a similarity in colour between expectorated tobacco saliva and the mineralised resinous product.

AMBIDEXTER, also in 17th century, **AMBODEXTER**, *subs.* and *adj.* (old

slang).—[From *ambo*, both + *dexter*, the right hand, *i.e.*, the faculty of using both hands as right hands, or equally well.] Applied first in a slang sense to a lawyer taking fees or bribes from both plaintiff and defendant, AMBIDEXTER gradually became identified with double-dealing of all kinds.

1532. *Use of Dice Play* (1850), 17. Any affinity with our men of law? Never with those that be honest. Marry! with such as be AMBIDEXTERS, and used to play in both the hands. [M.]

1555. RIDLEY, *Works*, 27. They may be called neutrals, AMBIDEXTERS, or rather such as can shift on both sides. [M.]

1691. BLOUNT, *Law Dictionary.* AMBIDEXTER . . . . That Juror o· Embraceor who takes Money on both sides, for giving his Verdict.

1703. DE FOE, *Ref. Manners*, 93. Those AMBODEXTERS in Religion, who Can any thing dispute, yet any thing can do.

1864. SIR F. PALGRAVE, *Norman and Eng. III.*, 278. An AMBIDEXTER, owing fealty to both Counts, and not faithful to either.

AMBUSH, *subs.* (American thieves'). —Fraudulent weights and measures. A punning allusion to the accepted meaning of the word—to lie in wait (lying weight). In juxtaposition to this may be placed the Fourbesque (Italian thieves' argot); *giusta*, a pair of scales, a balance, which in Italian literally means 'correct.' *Cf.*, French thieves' argot, *juste* (an abbreviation of *justice*), for the assizes; also the Spanish Germania *justia*, in a similar sense, the last-named being a shortened form of the Spanish *justicia*.

AMEN CURLER, *subs.* (old slang). —The name formerly given to a parish clerk. In the army the chaplain's clerk is called an AMEN WALLAH (*q.v.*).

AMENER, *subs.* (old).—A nickname given to one who agrees to everything said or done. [From that sense of AMEN = to ratify solemnly + ER.]

AMEN-SNORTER, *subs.* (Australian). —A parson; from which it will be observed that the fifth continent is evolving words and phrases as peculiar to itself as America has already done. For synonyms, *see* DEVIL DODGER.

1888. *Bulletin*, Nov. 24. In Maoriland it is impossible to swing any kind of cat without smiting some variety of AMEN-SNORTER. Still the saints are not happy. They have just held at Wellington a 'United Ker-ristian Conference' to ruminate on the sinfulness of things and the scarcity of the unsanctified threepenny. A Rev. vessel, one Potter, opined that the meagre quantity and inferior quality of family devotion accounted for the depleted condition of the 'treasury of the Loard,' and suggested that steps should be taken 'to find out what families omit this important duty.' Since which all the dead-beats and suspected hen-snatchers plead when before the Binch that they were 'only mouching round to find out whether the family neglected its religious dooties, yer washup.'

AMEN WALLAH, *subs.* (military).—A chaplain's clerk; the allusion is sufficiently obvious. 'Wallah' is Hindustani for 'man' or person. *Cf.*, the old English slang, AMEN CURLER (*q.v.*).

AMERACE, *adv.* (American thieves'). —Jargon signifying near at hand; within call.

AMERICAN SHOULDERS, *subs.* (tailors'). — A particular 'cut,' in which the shoulders of a coat are so shaped as to give the wearer a broad and burly appearance. This is usually done

where a man's shoulders are of the CHAMPAGNE (*q.v.*) order, *i.e.*, like the neck of a wine bottle, with nothing upon which the garment in question can be hung.

AMERICAN TWEEZERS, *subs.* (thieves'). —An ingenious instrument of American invention, by means of which it is possible to turn a key in a door and unlock it from the outside.

AMES ACE, AMBS-ACE, or **AMBES-ACE**, WITHIN AMES ACE, *subs.phr.* (old).—1. Nearly; very near; AMBS-ACE was the double ace, the lowest throw at dice. Hence also

2. Bad luck; misfortune. The expression, according to Murray, dates back to A.D. 1297.

AMINIDAB, *subs.* (old).—A jeering name for a Quaker.—*Grose.*

AMMUNITION, *subs.* (common). — Paper for use at the *cabinet d'aisance*. Also called CURL PAPERS (*q.v.*).

AMMUNITION LEG, *subs.* (military). —A wooden leg. From the attributive use of 'ammunition' as applied to stores supplied to soldiers for equipment or rations. To show the length to which this application of the word has been carried, it may be noted that Robertson, in 1693, speaks of 'an ammunition whore.'—*scortum castrense.*

AMORT, *adv.* and *pred. adj.* (old).— Usually ALL AMORT, an antithetical phrase to ALL ALIVE (*q.v.*), and meaning half dead; in a state of stupor; without spirit; sometimes used as a synonym of BALMY, CRACKED, DOTTY, all of which see. *A-la-mort*, from the French, is regarded as the original form, though it is doubtful which took precedence in literary English. At one time both forms were quite naturalised; they are now of interest as affording an instance of words, gradually lapsing into slang or vulgar usage, and then coming to be regarded as Anglo-French phrases. American thieves still retain them, to signify struck dumb, or confounded; in these senses they are given by Grose in his *Dictionary of the Vulgar Tongue* [1787], which would seem to show they had already commenced their downward career.

AMPERSAND, *subs.* (familiar).—The breech; or posteriors. [From Eng. AND + Latin *per se*, by itself, + Eng. AND; literally, 'and by itself and' used to distinguish the character '&,' which in old nursery books came at the end of the alphabet. Hence, employed to signify the hinder parts.] The word in its slang sense is quite a recent introduction, said to be of American origin. For synonyms, *see* BLIND CHEEKS.

AMPUTATE. TO AMPUTATE ONE'S MAHOGANY OR TIMBER (familiar). —To be off; to begone—the idea being that of quick or violent motion, often, though not always, the result of moral or physical force. [Probably from that sense of AMPUTATE equivalent to 'cut off' or 'away.' *Cf.*, 'cut,' a slang synonym.] A welcher is called a TIMBER-MERCHANT, because he removes himself, or 'cuts his stick' with celerity as occasion requires. Both the English and French have many synonymous words and phrases to express the same idea. Among the more popular may be mentioned:—

ENGLISH SYNONYMS. To skedaddle (an American term); to cut one's lucky; to sling, or take one's hook; to mizzle; to absquatulate; to pad the hoof; to give leg bail; to bolt; to cut and run; to chivey; to walk the trotters; to slip one's cable; to step it; to leg it; to tip the double; to make, or take tracks; to hook it; to make beef (thieves' term); to slope; to cut the cable and run before the wind (obviously a sailor's phrase); to slip it; to abskize; to paddle; to guy (used by thieves); to evaporate; to vamoose (American, from the Spanish imperative *vamos*, let us go); to speele (used by thieves); to skip; to tip one's rags a gallop; to walk one's chalks; to pike; to hop the twig; to turn it up; to cap one's lucky (a phrase mainly confined to American thieves); to crush; to cut dirt; to bunk; to pike it; to stir one's stumps.

FRENCH. *Faire* or *jouer la fille de l'air* (lit. 'to go like the wind,' *fille de l'air*, daughter of air, being a poetical embodiment); *faire le lézard* (a thief's term, and meaning properly 'to imitate a lizard,' an allusion to swiftness of motion); *faire le iat-jat; faire la paire* (lit. 'to go double,' *Cf.*, 'to tip the double'); *faire gille* (a very old French phrase; it means also to become bankrupt. The connection between bankruptcy and decamping is obvious); *se déguiser en cerf* (popular: lit. 'to play the stag'); *s'évanouir* (popular: lit. 'to vanish' or 'fade away'); *se cramper* or *tirer sa crampe* (*cramper* is a popular term for rapid flight, and contains an allusion to the cramp or nervous contraction sometimes caused by violent motion. Old French had the verb *crampir* in the sense of 'to bend' or 'double up.' *Tirer sa crampe* is lit. 'to get cramped'); *se lâcher du ballon* (popular: 'to let loose the balloon,' an allusion to the rapidity with which a balloon shoots up into the air when set free); *se la couler* (exactly equivalent to the English slang 'to slip it'); *se donner de l'air* (popular: *Cf.*, *faire la fille de l'air*); *se pousser du zeph* (popular: properly 'to push forward with the wind.' *Zeph* is a contraction of *zephir*); *se sylphider* (popular: from *sylphide*, a sylph; a reference to what in English racing terminology would be termed the 'light-weight' character of such creatures enabling them to get over the ground quickly); *se faire la débinette; jouer des fourchettes* (popular: 'to put one's forks into play'); *fourchettes* (in French argot = legs or 'pins'); *se la donner* (Michel says *la* here refers to '*la clef des champs*,' an expression synonymous with 'liberty' or 'freedom'); *se la briser* (popular); *ramasser un bidon* (thieves'); *se la casser* (popular); *se la tirer*; *tirer ses granches*; *valser* (lit. to dance); *se tirer les pincettes* (popular: lit. 'to pull along' or to extricate 'one's tongs' or 'nippers.' *Cf.*, English 'nip along'); *se tirer les baladoires*; *se tirer les pattes* (lit. 'to move one's paws'); *se tirer les trimoires* (thieves': *trimoires* is a cant term for legs,

and *trimer* signifies painful progression, or doing most of a journey on foot); *se tirer les flûtes* (popular: *les flûtes* = 'shanks' or 'pegs'); *jouer des guibes* (*guibe* is a popular term for the leg, chiefly employed in burlesque); *jouer des quilles* (this expression is very old. *Quilles* properly signifies 'crutches,' and is popularly employed for the legs); *se carapater* (lit. 'to run on one's paws. *Cf.*, 'to take to one's heels'); *se barrer* (lit. 'to dash over'); *baudrouiller* (thieves': this has the signification of 'to whip up'); *se cavaler* (thieves': *cavaler* was once synonymous with *chevaucher*; therefore, *se cavaler* signifies in reality, 'to go on horseback on oneself,' in which connection it may be compared with 'shanks' mare,' the 'marrow-bone stage' [the Marylebone stage], or the German *Schuhster's Rappen*, the shoemaker's black horses, *i.e.*, the shoes. *Se cavaler* likewise has reference to running away with the tail between the legs when fright has seized hold of an animal, and as employed by thieves conveys the idea of cowardice as well as that of locomotion); *faire une cavale* or *se payer une cavale* (popular: *Cf.*, *se cavaler*); *jouer des* or *se tirer les paturons* (popular and thieves': this may be translated 'to pad the hoof.' *Paturons* is properly the 'pasterns.' The frequent use of *se tirer* in connection with the idea of moving from place to place with a celerity which is oftentimes accentuated by a fear of arrest or unwelcome obstruction is extremely fitting. *Se tirer* means literally to extricate onself; to get through; to pull oneself forward—extra endeavour resulting in rapid progression); *happer le taillis* (thieves': lit. 'to catch, lay hold of' or 'gain the copse'; *i.e.*, a place of concealment); *flasquer du poivre à quelqu'un* or *la rousse* (thieves': *Cf.*, AMUSE; 'to fly from the police'; lit. to shake the pepper box in the eyes of the police; *rousse* is a cant term for a guardian of the peace); *décaniller* (thieves': this word, derived from *canille*, a French provincialism for *chenille*, a caterpillar, is an allusion to the metamorphosis of the grub into a butterfly when it takes unto itself wings); *décarrer* (thieves': to leave prison; *décarrer de belle*, to be released from prison without having been tried); *exhiber son prussien* (popular: *prussien* is a common colloquialism for the posteriors, and the phrase literally means 'to show one's behind,' or 'turn tail.' It may be worth while remarking that the term *prussien* as applied to the breech is no vulgar expression of contempt towards the Prussians. The word is derived, says Michel, from the gypsy *prusiatiñi*, which Borrow translates by pistol. Formerly the French called 'the behind' by the name of a Parisian church, *Saint-Jean le Rond*); *démurger* (thieves': to leave a place; to be set at liberty); *désarrer* (thieves': 'to guy'; to make beef); *gagner les gigoteaux* (also *gagner au trot, au pied, gagner le camp, la colline, le taillis, la guérite*, etc.); *se faire une paire de mains courantes à la mode* (thieves'); *fendre l'ergot* (lit. 'to split the spur,' an allusion to the toes being pressed to the ground, and thus naturally

parted); *filer son nœud*, or *son cable* (sailors' and popular: lit. 'to cut the ropes' or 'cable'); *se défiler* (popular, but derived from the military term, signifying to go off parade: might be translated 'to leg it'); *s'écarbouiller* (popular: properly 'to crush'; compare with the English synonym 'crush'); *esballonner* (popular); *filer son cable par le bout* (sailors'); *faire chibis* (thieves': 'to escape from prison'); *déraper* (common); *fouiner* (popular: this is, in reality, no more slang than the English 'to sneak away'); *se la fracturer* (popular: properly a surgical term, meaning 'to fracture'); *jouer des gambettes* (popular: may be translated 'to leg it'; 'to stir one's stumps'; *gambettes* is from the old French *gambe*, a leg); *s'esbigner* (popular: properly 'to give the slip'); *ramoner ses tuyaux* (popular: lit. 'to sweep one's chimney'; *ramoner*, in its primary cant signification of 'to mutter' or 'to mumble,' is an allusion to the rumbling noise produced by sweeping a chimney. *Se faire ramoner* is 'to go to confession,' or 'to take a purgative'—the one a moral, and the other a physical cleansing. Hence *ramoner ses tuyaux*, 'to run away,' in reference to the speedy locomotion consequent upon the process of purging); *foutre le camp* (popular: equivalent to 'hook it'; a coarse expression); *tirer le chausson* (popular); *se vanner* (thieves: Michel derives this from the Italian *vannare*, 'to flap the wings,' but another authority refers it to the motions of the body and arms of a winnower; the word in literary French signifying 'to sift' or 'to winnow.' Others trace it to the old French *vanoyer*, 'to disappear.' In all cases, however, it would seem to be equivalent to the English 'come shake yourself! be off!'); *ambier* (thieves'); *chier du poivre* (popular: 'to abscond,' or 'to fail to be at hand when needed'); *se débiner*, or *se débiner des fumerons* (popular: 'to stir one's stumps'); *caleter* (popular); *attacher une gamelle* (popular and thieves'); *camper* (low); *affuter ses pincettes* (thieves': lit. 'to sharpen the pins' or 'to leg it'); and many others.

GERMAN SYNONYMS. *Abbaschen* (from *paschen*, 'to smuggle'); *abbauen* (literally 'to remove, or finish' [a building]); *abfocken*; *abhalchen* (from Hebrew *holach*, 'to go'); *schefften*; *abschnurren* (a beggar-musicians' term; also to beg through a lane, town, or district. [M.H.G., *snurren*, *schnurren*, *schnurrant*]); *abtarchenen*; *abtippeln* (to run away secretly); *alchen* (from Hebrew *holach*, 'to go'); *aschween* (Hanoverian: according to Thiele *hascheweine* — probably corrupted from *schuw*; *heschiw*, 'to turn round'); *blättern* (corrupted from *plettern*—Hebrew *pleto*); *caball* (from Latin *caballus*, 'a horse'; hence, to fly quickly as if on horseback); *dippeln* (a Viennese thieves' term) *fucken* or *focken*.

ITALIAN FOURBESQUE. *Sbignare* or *svignare* (these words though given as cant by the author of the *Nuovo Modo* are now received words); *comprare* (lit. 'to buy'); *comprar viole*; *allungare il muro* (lit. 'to lengthen the wall'); *balzare* (lit. 'to caper,' 'to skip,' 'to bounce'); *batter la calcosa* (lit. 'to beat the earth.' *Cf.*, American 'to cut dirt'); *dare a lata*; *scoscare*.

SPANISH GERMANIA. *Piñarse* (an old and now obsolete term); *alar*; *alarse*; *alolargo* (lit. 'at large'); *picar* (lit. 'to use the spurs'); *safarse* (lit. 'to escape' or 'save oneself' [from arrest]).

AMUSE, *verb.* (old cant).—To fling dust or snuff in the eyes of a person intended to be robbed. Also, to invent some plausible tale, to delude shop-keepers and others, thereby to put them off their guard, and so to obtain an opportunity of robbing them.

AMUSERS, *subs.* (old cant and American thieves').—A certain class of thieves' accomplices who throw snuff, pepper, and other noxious substances in the eyes of the person they intend to rob, a confederate then, while apparently coming to the rescue, completing the operation. In this, as in much of the slang of the criminal classes, there runs a vein of brutal cynicism. Though obsolete in England the term survives in America amongst the criminal classes.

ANABAPTIST, *subs.* (old slang).—A pickpocket caught in the act, and punished with the discipline of the pump or horse-pond.—*Grose.*

ANCHOR. TO COME TO AN ANCHOR, *verb. phr.* (nautical and common).—To stop; to sit down; to rest. [From the operation of bringing ships to a standstill by casting anchor.]

ANCHORAGE, *subs.* (common).—An abode; where one dwells. Of nautical origin (*see* ANCHOR). For synonyms, *see* DIGGINGS.

ANCIENT MARINERS, *subs.* (Univ. Oxford).—A term applied to rowing dons.

AND DON'T YOU FORGET IT, *phr.* (American).—A senseless string of words employed indiscriminately in season and out of season. Like 'Who's your hatter?' 'How's your poor feet?' 'Not for Joe!' 'Does your mother know you're out?' 'What! again! so soon?' and many others, which every now and then have caught the 'fancy' of the streets of our large towns, the phrase under consideration has run an almost riotous course through the large centres of population in America. In most cases these strings of words convey no special idea, and can only be described as utterly vulgar, without the slightest scintilation of wit or humour of any kind.

1888. *Boston Weekly Globe*, Feb. 29. There can be no two opposing opinions in that respect. Great capital demands dividends. Dividends can be had only from a prosperous business. A prosperous business must recognise the law of supply and demand, and if the public demand dirt the newspapers will furnish dirt—AND DON'T YOU FORGET IT.

1888. *Detroit Free Press*, Oct. 6. 'Did you see any Quakers in Philadelphia?' was asked of a Detroiter who lately returned from that city.
'Only one that I was sure of.'
'Did he 'thee' and 'thou' you?'
'He did. He got down off his hack and said: 'If thee don't pay me 2 dols. I'll knock thy blamed head off,' and I paid, although I knew the regular fare was twelve shillings. You don't want to fool with those Quakers any, AND DON'T YOU FORGET IT.'

AND HE DIDN'T, *phr.* (tailors').— A phrase of the ALL MY EYE (*q.v.*) stamp, *i.e.*, 'You tell me you have not; but for all that I think you have'—the action referred to being generally of a discreditable character.

AND NO MOGUE? *phr.* (tailors').— Used in a variety of ways to signify doubt and uncertainty. It is equivalent to the street gamin's 'no kid?' when used interrogatively, *i.e.*, 'there's no mistake, is there?' 'Now, joking apart?' Also used as a 'set down' to narrators claiming descent from Baron Munchausen, in which case it is equivalent to the 'You don't say so!' of politer circles; in both cases the spokesman conveys the idea that one's credulity has been somewhat taxed.

AND NO WHISTLE, *phr.* (tailors').— A kind of *tu quoque;* usually applied to a man by a listener desiring to convey to the speaker the idea that no matter what others may think to the contrary, he [the listener] believes that what has been said refers to the person speaking.

ANDREW MILLAR, *subs.* (nautical).— A curious cant name for a ship of war; sometimes simply ANDREW. Its origin is quite unknown; but it has been pointed out that Antonio, in the *Merchant of Venice*, speaks of one of his vessels as his 'wealthy ANDREW'; and it has been conjectured that in this case the ship was named after the celebrated Admiral Andrea Doria, who died in 1560. But to trace any connection between this ANDREW, however general the use of the name may have become, and the ANDREW MILLAR of modern sailors' slang, would be difficult.

1598. SHAKSPEARE, *Merchant of Venice*, i., i., 27.
But I should think of shallows and of flats,
And see my wealthy ANDREW dock'd in sand.

Among Australian smugglers the term still survives for a revenue cutter.

ANGEL or **FLYING ANGEL**, *subs.* (common).—Explained by quotation.

1880. JAMES GREENWOOD, *Seaside Insanity* in *Odd People in Odd Places*, p. 45. It is at this point when the one day excursionist, who, as well as his wife, has an olive-branch or two with him, finds his fortitude suddenly collapse. With the youngest but one (his good lady, of course, carries the baby) bestriding his shoulder, he puts his best foot foremost from the beach to the town so as to be in good time at the station. He is hot and fagged, and his temper is not improved by the knowledge that the cherub to whom he is giving a 'FLYING ANGEL' is smearing his Sunday hat with the seaweed with which its little fists are full.

ANGELICAS.—*See* ANGELICS.

ANGELICS, *subs.* (old).—Unmarried young ladies. Now ANGELICAS.

1821. MONCRIEFF, *Tom and Jerry*, p. 5. (Dicks' ed., 1889.) *Jerry.* You think the cut of my clothes rather too rustic—eh? *Tom.* Exactly; dress is the order of the day. A man must have the *look* of a gentleman, if he has nothing else. We must assume a style if we have it not. This, what do you call it? —this cover-me-decently, was all very well at Hawthorn Hall, I daresay; but here, among the pinks in Rotten Row, the ladybirds in the Saloon, the ANGELICS at Almack's, the top-of-the-tree heroes, the legs and levanters at Tattersall's, nay, even among the millers at the Fives, it would be taken for nothing less than the index of a complete flat.

ANGELIFEROUS, *adj.* (American).— Angelic; also super-excellent; a factitious word. It is interesting to note that 'angelification,' 'angelify,' and 'angelified,' were in use in the seventeenth century, but never to any great extent. [From ANGEL + IFEROUS, a spurious form based on the model of 'auriferous.'] It is said to have been first used by Bird in his novel, entitled *Nick of the Woods.*

ANGELS ALTOGETHER, *subs. phr.* (West Indian).—A sobriquet applied to habitual drunkards. It originated about the year 1876, and was, in the first instance, a *bon-mot* of a well-known sugar planter on the East Coast Demerara. A negro hand, notorious for his hard drinking, applied for a holiday, and the manager having a suspicion that Quashie wanted it simply to go 'on the drink,' bantered him as follows:—'John! you were drunk on Sunday?' 'Yes, massa!' 'Monday too?' 'Yes, massa!' and on the question being repeated as regards Tuesday, Wednesday, Thursday, and Friday, it elicited similar responses, whereupon the 'boss' quietly, but pointedly said, 'But John, you can't be an ANGEL ALTOGETHER, you know!' The story got abroad, caught on, and in a short time the whole colony rang with the expression.

ANGEL'S FOOTSTOOL, *subs. phr.* (nautical). — Yankee skippers, given to high falutin', aver that their craft carry far more canvas than any vessel afloat of 'foreign' origin (the term 'foreign' including British bottoms, as well as those of nations other than Anglo-Saxon. Imaginary sails are crowded on their craft, among these being one which they jokingly call an ANGEL'S FOOTSTOOL. It is pretended to be a square sail, and is supposed to top the SKYSCRAPERS, MOON-SAILS, and CLOUD CLEANERS (*q.v.*).

ANGEL'S GEAR, *subs. phr.* (nautical).—It is thus that 'jolly tars' sometimes speak of female attire. Jack is notoriously most susceptible where a petticoat is concerned.

ANGEL'S-OIL, *subs.* (old).—A seventeenth century colloquialism for money used for bribery; sometimes OIL OF ANGELS. For synonyms, *see* ACTUAL, and BOODLE.

ANGEL'S SUIT, *subs. phr.* (tailors').— A 'combination' garment for males. The coat and waistcoat were made in one, and the 'unmentionables' buttoned on to it. Neither garment nor name was extensively adopted.

ANGEL'S WHISPER, *subs. phr.* (military).—A name given to the call to defaulter's drill. Needless to say it is, as Artemus Ward would express it, 'wrote sarcastic.'

ANGLERS, HOOKERS, or STARRERS, *subs.* (old). — Pilferers or petty thieves, who, with a stick having a hook at the end, steal goods from shop windows, etc. So far Grose; but Duncombe adds that STARRERS are an order of thieves who break show glasses in jewellers' windows and, in the consequent confusion steal the goods. The term is a very ancient one. Dekker in *English Villanies* [1632], thus describes an 'ANGLER for duds':—' He carries a short staff in his hand, which is called a filch, having in the nab or head of it a ferme (that is to say a hole) into which, upon any piece of service, when he goes a filching, he putteth a hooke of iron, with which hook he angles at a window in the dead of night for shirts, smockes, or any other linen or woollen.' It would appear from this that modern thieves are both much more daring and expert. It is not an uncommon thing for a crack thief, in the broad daylight, in the most crowded streets of London, to break a jeweller's window, snatch some valuables, and make off with them. An iron instrument is used for the purpose which is concealed by the coat sleeve. —*See* AREA SNEAK.

ANGLING COVE, *subs.* (thieves').— A receiver of stolen goods. —*See* FENCE.

ANGLING FOR FARTHINGS, *verb. phr.* (old thieves').—Begging out of a prison window with a cap or box, let down at the end of a long string—*Grose.* Such a practice, it is needless to say, would be impossible nowadays.—*See* HOOKER.

ANGLOMANIACS, *subs. phr.* (American).—A club in Boston is thus self-styled. Its members are opposed to anything British in every shape and form. The term is of course a contradiction, and should, to express the policy of its members, be *Anglophobists.*

ANGRY BOYS.—*See* BLOODS.

ANGULAR PARTY, *subs. phr.* (common).—A term given to any gathering of people of which the number is odd; say three, seven, thirteen, etc.

ANIMAL, *subs.* (American).—A new arrival at the United States Military Academy at West Point. *Cf.*, SNOOKER.

TO GO THE WHOLE ANIMAL (American).—A variant of 'to go the whole hog.' In the West Indies it is varied by 'to go the whole dog.'—*See* HOG.

1888. C. DICKENS, *Nicholas Nickleby*, p. . . . . Opposing all half measures, and preferring TO GO THE EXTREME ANIMAL.

1859. G. A. SALA, *Twice Round the Clock*, p. 62 . . . . that they had much better pay first-class, and GO THE ENTIRE ANIMAL.

ANIMULES, *subs.* (American).—This expression is very generally used in the South-western territories, and in California, as a substitute for 'mules.' A witty play upon 'animals' and 'mules.'

1884 (?) *Centre-Pole Bill, in Overland Monthly.* 'Ten miles to town! Waal, stranger, I guess I'll stake out here to-night. Them ANIMULES is too beat to do that. Where's yer water?' 'It's all around you to-night; but you can turn your mules into the corral.'

ANKLE. TO SPRAIN ONE'S ANKLE, *verb. phr.* (old).—When a girl has been seduced she is said to have SPRAINED HER ANKLE. Both French and German slang have analogous expressions; in the former, *elle a mal aux genoux* is said of a woman who is pregnant, *i.e.*, 'she has a bad knee.'

In German, ladies so placed 'lose a shoe'; but of synonyms there are plenty.—*See* LEG.

ANKLE-BEATERS, *subs. phr.* (old).— A class of boys who attended cattle markets for the purpose of driving to the slaughter-house the animals purchased by the butcher. They were called ANKLE-BEATERS from their driving the animals with long wattles, and beating them on the legs to avoid spoiling or bruising the flesh. Also called PENNY-BOYS (*q.v.*), because they received one penny per head as remuneration.

ANNE'S FAN, properly **QUEEN ANNE'S FAN**, *subs. phr.* (common).—Putting the tip of the thumb of either hand to the nose, and then spreading the fingers in the shape of a fan. A gesture of contempt often intensified either by twiddling the digits when in the position named, or by similarly placing the other hand in an extended line. It is also called TAKING A SIGHT (*q.v.*), and BITING THE THUMB (*q.v.*).

ANNEX, *verb.* (American).—To steal; in England the wise it call 'convey.'—*See* BONE.

ANODYNE, *subs.* (American thieves').—A euphemism for death. From the figurative sense of the word—anything that soothes wounded or excited feelings, or that lessens the sense of misfortunes. *Cf.*, Old English slang term for a halter, ANODYNE NECKLACE.

Verb. (American thieves').— To kill. *Cf.*, foregoing; also To COOK ONE'S GOOSE.

ANODYNE NECKLACE, *subs. phr.* (old). —A halter. An *anodyne* is that which allays or extinguishes pain, and the hangman's rope may indeed be regarded, from one point of view, as a cure for all pains. The expression is old, being traced back to 1639. During the period when the death penalty was inflicted for all kinds of comparatively trivial offences—for sheep stealing, and even highway robberies of not more than forty shillings value —synonyms equally grim and sententious were numerous. According to Wilyam Bullein, an ANODYNE NECKLACE was that which 'light fellows merrily will call' . . . neckweede, or SIR TRISTAM'S KNOT, or ST. ANDREW'S LACE (*q.v.*).' Other terms for the hangman's noose were HEMPEN CRAVAT, HORSE'S NIGHT-CAP, TYBURN TIPPET (*q.v.*).

1639. F. BEAUMONT, *Bloody Brother*, Act iii., Sc. 2. [Speaks of the hangman's halter as a 'necklace.']

1766. OLIVER GOLDSMITH, *Vicar of Wakefield* [works, Globe ed., chap. xx., p. 43. [George Primrose's cousin exclaims]. 'May I die by an ANODYNE NECKLACE, but I'd rather be an under-turnkey in Newgate [than an usher in a boarding-school'].

The water poet (John Taylor, a Thames waterman, 1580-1654), explaining the virtue of hemp, says:—

Some call it neck-weed, for it hath a tricke
To cure the necke that's troubled with the crick.

An ANODYNE NECKLACE was also the name of a quack amulet, which, for a long period, was a household word. This famous remedy occupied as prominent a position in the advertising columns of the journals of the middle of the eighteenth as Holloway's pills in the latter part of the nineteenth century. This necklace was of beads artificially prepared, small, like barleycorns, and cost five shillings. For foreign synonyms, *see* HORSE'S NIGHTCAP.

ANOINT, *verb.* (familiar).—To beat soundly; to thrash; humorously derived from the proper meaning of the word, 'to smear' or 'rub over with oil or other unctuous substances.' In the North of England the saying is somewhat more analogous—'to ANOINT with the sap of a hazel rod.'

1175. *Rom. of Partenay* (SKEAT), 5653.
Then thay put hym hout, the kyng away fly,
Which so well was ANOYNTED indede,
That no slene ne pane had he hole of brede.

1708. FULLER'S *Trip to Bridewell*, quoted in Ashton's *The Fleet*, p. 211. The whipper began to NOINT me with his instrument, that had, I believe, about a dozen strings notted at the end.

1748. SMOLLETT, *Rod. Random*, ch. v. 'I'll bring him to the gangway, and ANOINT him with a cat-and-nine-tails.'

1824. W. IRVING, *Tales of a Trav.*, II., 287. Seize a trusty staff and ANOINT the back of the aggressor.

There seems to be some connection, too, between this sense of TO ANOINT, and the depraved use of ANOINTED (*q.v.*) to signify great rascality. *Cf.*, STRAP OIL.

ANOINT OR GREASE THE PALM, *verb. phr.* (common).—To bribe. The Scotch say 'to creesh the luif.' The expression is very old.

1584. KNOX, *Hist. of Reformation, works* [1846] I., 102. Yea, the handis of our Lordis so liberallie were ANOYNTED.

See GREASE THE PALM.

ANOINTED, *ppl. adj.* (old).—1. Used in a depraved sense to signify eminence in rascality. The most probable derivation appears to be that suggested by Prof. Skeat [*N. and Q.*, 3 S., ix., 422]. In a French MS., *Romance of Melusine*, is an account of a man who had received a thorough and severe beating, which is thus referred to:—*Qui anoit este si bien oignt.* The English version [Early English Text Society] translates this, 'which so well was ANOYNTED indeed.' From this it is clear that to ANOINT a man was to give him a sound drubbing, and that the word was so used in the fifteenth century. Thus, an ANOINTED rogue means either one who has been well thrashed or who has deserved to be. *Cf.*, TO ANOINT.

1769. ROBERTSON, *Hist. of Reign of Charles V.* Many assumed the clerical character for no other reason than that it might screen them from the punishment which their actions deserved. The German nobles complained loudly that their ANOINTED malefactors, as they called them, seldom suffered capitally even for the most enormous crimes.

1825. SCOTT, *St. Ronan's Well*, ch. xxxvii. 'But, not being Lord Etherington, and an ANOINTED scoundrel into the bargain, I will content myself with cudgelling him to death.'

2. Knowing; ripe for mischief.—*Duncombe.*

ANONYMA, *subs.* (popular).—A lady of the demi-monde; generally, though not invariably, applied to one of the better class. Women of this status were also called by the *Times* PRETTY HORSEBREAKERS, a notorious ANONYMA (*circa* 1868) having been a good horsewoman. Another and earlier name

was INCOGNITA; this as well as ANONYMA had reference to the unrecognised position these ladies hold in what is called 'Society,' which tries to shut its eyes to a product of its own vice. The French *cocotte* best corresponds to the English term. For synonyms generally, *see* BARRACK HACK.

1864. G. A. SALA, *Quite Alone*, ch. i. Is that ANONYMA driving twin ponies in a low phaeton, a parasol attached to her whip, and a groom with folded arms behind her? Bah! there are so many ANONYMAS nowadays. If it isn't the Nameless One herself, it is Synonyma.

1865. OUIDA, *Strathmore*, ch. vi. 'I'm getting tired of Mondes, one confounds so easily with Demi-monde, and aristocrats that are so near allied to ANONYMA.'

1881. DORAN, *In and about Drury Lane*, vol. II., p. 159. Those ANONYMAS, who dress with such exquisite propriety lest they should be mistaken for modest women.

1889. *Modern Society*, July 13, p. 852. 'Christopher's Honeymoon,' by Mr. Malcolm Watson, produced at the Strand, on Wednesday, is not wholly bad, but it is *too thin.* The honeymooner is surprised at his wedding breakfast by the news that a former wife, whom he thought dead, is still alive. Matters are still further complicated when his mother-in-law mistakes his buxom laundress for a fair ANONYMA.

ANOTHER. YOU'RE ANOTHER, *phr.* (common).—A retort—in usage hardly courteous or suave. Generally spoken in anger or resentment. The quotations which follow specify clearly the manner of use. It is interesting to note how very old is this common rejoinder—nearly 350 years; it is, moreover, an example which fully illustrates the value of the historical method in dealing with slang words and phrases.

c. 1534. N. UDALL, *Roister Doister*, III., v., p. 58 (Arber). R. ROYSTER. If it were another but thou, it were a tenane. M. MERY. YE ARE AN OTHER your selfe, sir. [M.]

1750. FIELDING, *Tom Jones*, bk. IX., ch. vi. 'You mistake me, friend,' cries Partridge, 'I did not mean to abuse the cloth; I only said your conclusion was a *non-sequitur.*' 'YOU ARE ANOTHER,' cries the Serjeant, 'an' you come to that. No more a *sequitur* than yourself.'

1836. DICKENS, *Pickwick*, ch. xv., p. 123. 'Sir,' said Mr. Tupman, 'you're a fellow.' 'Sir,' said Mr. Pickwick, 'YOU'RE ANOTHER.'

1888. SIR W. HARCOURT, *Speech at Eighty Club*, Feb. 21. You know the little urchins in the street have a conclusive argument. They say 'YOU'RE ANOTHER.'

ANOTHER ACROBAT, *phr.* (music-hall).—Another drink—ACROBAT being a play upon the word 'tumbler,' *i.e.*, a glass.

ANOTHER GUESS, *adj.*, or **ANOTHER GUESS SORT OF MAN**, *phr.* (old). A cute man; one who is, in modern lingo, UP TO SNUFF (*q.v.*). 'Guess' suggests an erroneous derivation; the word is really a corruption of 'ANOTHER-GATES' [according to Murray the original genitive case' of another-gate, *i.e.*, of another way, manner, or fashion'].

ANOTHER LIE NAILED TO THE COUNTER, *phr.* (American).—A detected slander. The practice of nailing spurious coins to shop counters is, even yet, not an obsolete custom in country districts; and hence, probably, is derived this colloquialism.

1888. *Texas Siftings*, Oct. 20. 'Who employed you last?' 'A Republican speaker, who had me back up his declaration that Cleveland was in the habit of beating his wife!' 'But that LIE WAS NAILED a good while ago.' 'I know it,' chuckled the C.L., 'but it's easy enough to pull out the nail.'

ANTAGONISE, *verb.* (sporting).—This, 'to act as an opponent,' sounds very like slang; but, as a matter of fact, so long as the antagonising forces are of the same kind the word is legitimate enough. It has been so used from 1634 downwards, by Herbert, Keats, John Stuart Mill, and others. Only when (as for example in America a person in political phraseology is said to ANTAGONISE a measure when it is meant that he opposes it) the word is used in connection with antagonistic forces *not* of a kind can it be regarded as partaking of slang. In the quotation by Barrère from the *Saturday Review* (no date given: refer, however, to *Sat. R.*, Dec. 18, 1886, p. 799) the word is used in a perfectly correct manner.

1886. *Saturday Review* on Sporting Slang, 18 Dec., p. 799, col. 1. Dingley Dell sent Jones and Robinson to the wickets, where they were antagonised with the leather by Alf and the Young Phenomenon.

ANTHONY, or **TO CUFF ANTHONY**, *verb.* (old).—To knock one's knees together from an infirmity. Also called TO CUFF JONAS.

ANTONY, or ANTHONY CUFFIN, *subs.*—A knock-kneed man.

ANTHONY, or **TANTONY PIG**, *subs.* (old).—*See* TANTONY PIG.

1787. GROSE, *Dictionary of the Vulgar Tongue.* The favourite or smallest pig in the litter; to follow like a tantony pig, *i.e.*, St. Anthony's pig, signified to follow close at one's heels. St. Anthony, the hermit, was a swine herd, and is always represented with his bell and pig.

ANTIMONY, *subs.* (printers').—Type; so called from one of its component parts.

ANYHOW. ANYHOW YOU CAN FIX IT, *phr.* (American).—A slang expression of acquiescence as, *e.g.*, 'I don't know if you'll succeed, but ANYHOW YOU CAN FIX IT.'

ANY OTHER MAN! *phr.* (American).—A call to order addressed to prosy, discursive speakers when they give themselves over to the use of synonymous terms.

ANY RACKET, *subs.* (rhyming slang).—A penny faggot.

ANYTHING. LIKE, OR AS ANYTHING, *adv. phr.* (common).—A vulgarism rather than slang. Used in the same manner, as are LIKE ONE O'CLOCK; LIKE OLD BOOTS (*q.v.*), when a person is at a loss for a simile.—*See* WINKEY.

1542. UDALL'S *Erasmus Apoph.*, p. 32. The young maiden, where the lokers on quaked and trembled for feare, daunced without any feare at all emong sweardes and kniues, beyng as sharpe AS ANYTHYNG.

1740. RICHARDSON, *Pamela*, ii., 57. O my dear father and mother, I fear your girl will grow as proud AS ANYTHING.

1840. BARHAM, *I. L.* (*Misadv. at Margate*).
The tear-drop in his little eye again began to spring,
His bosom throbb'd with agony, he cried LIKE ANYTHING.

1873. CARROLL, *Through a Looking Glass*, iv., 73. They wept LIKE ANYTHING to see such quantities of sand.

ANYTHINGARIAN, *subs.* (common).—A contemptuous term for one who is apathetic as regards his political or religious creed, or other matters upon which mankind generally hold decided views. [From ANYTHING + ARIAN, after *trinit*-ARIAN, *unit*-ARIAN.]

1717. *Entertainer*, Nov. 6 [quoted in N. & Q., 7 S., vi., 66]. Nor, which is ten times worse, Free-thinkers, Atheists, ANYTHINGARIANS.

1738. SWIFT, *Polite Conversation* (conv. i.).
Lady Sm. What religion is he of?
Lady Sp. Why, he is an ANYTHINGARIAN.
Lady Ans. I believe he has his religion to chuse, my lord.

1849. C. KINGSLEY, *Alton Locke*, ch. xxii. They made puir Robbie Burns an ANYTHINGARIAN with their blethers.

ANYTHINGARIANISM, *subs.* (popular).—The creed or doctrine of an Anythingarian.—[*See* preceding].

1851. C. KINGSLEY (*Life*, i., 215). Schiller's 'Gods of Greece' expresses, I think, a tone of feeling very common, and which finds its vent in modern Neo-Platonism—ANYTHINGARIANISM.

ANYTHING ELSE.—*See* NOT DOING ANYTHING ELSE.

ANYWHERE DOWN THERE! (tailors').—If, in a workroom or elsewhere where tailors congregate, an article is dropped upon the floor, ANYWHERE DOWN THERE! is used as a kind of catch-phrase.

APARTMENTS. TO HAVE APARTMENTS TO LET, *verb. phr.* (popular).—1. To take rank in the estimation of one's fellows as an idiot; 'a born fool'—one who is empty-headed, not furnished with brains.

ENGLISH SYNONYMS. To be dotty; to have a screw loose; to be balmy; to have a bee in one's bonnet (Scotch); to be off one's chump; to have no milk in the cocoa-nut; to be touched; to be balmy in one's crumpet; to be wrong in the upper storey; to have rats in the upper storey; to have a tile loose; to be half baked.

FRENCH SYNONYMS. *Avoir une écrevisse dans la tourte*, or *dans le vol-au-vent* (popular: that is 'to have a crawfish in the pie,' or 'in the head.' *Cf.*, 'to have rats in the upper storey'); *avoir la boule détraquée* (popular: lit. 'to have one's ball turned'); *avoir le coco fêlé* (popular: lit. 'to have one's cocoa nut cracked.' In English slang the head is also called a 'cocoa-nut'); *avoir le trognon détraquée* (popular: 'to have a bee in one's bonnet.' *Trognon* is also a slang term for the head or 'noddle'); *avoir un asticot dans la noisette* (popular: lit. 'to have a maggot in one's nut.' In English slang the head is likewise 'the nut.' *Cf.*, also the expression 'a worm in the bud'); *avoir un bœuf gras dans le char* (popular); *avoir un cancrelat dans la boule* (popular: lit. 'to have a cockroach in one's ball'—'ball' here referring to the head or 'nut.' *Cancrelat* is properly *kakerlac* or American cockroach); *avoir un hanneton dans le reservoir* (popular: lit. 'to have a May-bug' or 'cockchafer in one's cistern' or 'well.' This seems to be on all fours with 'a bee in one's bonnet.' The phrase sometimes runs *avoir un hanneton dans le plafond*, *i.e.*, to have a cockchafer in one's ceiling, and here the analogy between the two phrases is more clearly marked); *avoir un moustique dans la boite au sel* (popular: lit. 'to have a mosquito in the salt-box or cellar'); *avoir un voyageur dans l'omnibus* (popular); *avoir une araignée dans le plafond* (popular: lit. 'to have a spider in 'the head; *plafond*, 'a ceiling,' be it noted is a slang term for 'the head'); *avoir une grenouille dans l'aquarium* (popular: lit: 'to have a frog in one's aquarium'); *avoir une hirondelle dans le soliveau* (popular: 'to have a swallow in the head'); *avoir une Marseillaise dans le Kiosque* (popular); *avoir une punaise dans le soufflet* (popular: 'to have a bug in one's brain'); *avoir une sardine dans l'armoire à glace* (popular: 'to have a sardine in the head or brain.' *Armoire à glace* = the head); *avoir une trichinne dans le jambonneau* (popular: *jambonneau*, the head); *avoir une sauterelle dans la guitare* (popular: lit. 'to have a grasshopper in the guitar').

For other synonyms, *see* TILE LOOSE.

2. A widow is said TO HAVE APARTMENTS TO LET.

APE-LEADER, *subs.* (old).—An old maid. Leading apes in hell was the employment jocularly assigned to those who neglected to assume marital functions while living.

1581. LYLY, *Euphues* (Arb.), 87. Rather thou shouldest leade a lyfe to thine owne lyking in earthe, than. . . . . LEADE APES IN HELL. [M.]

1605. *Lond. Prodigal*, I.,'2. 'Tes an old proverb, and you know it well, that women dying maids LEAD APES IN HELL.'

1717. Mrs. CENTLIVRE, *Bold Stroke*, II., 1. Poor girl; she must certainly LEAD APES, as the saying is.

1830. GENERAL P. THOMPSON, *Exerc.* (1842), I., 198. Joining with other old women, in LEADING THEIR APES in Tartarus. [M.]

There are several proverbial sayings in which the ape plays an important part. TO SAY AN APE'S PATERNOSTER is to chatter with cold; this corresponds with the French, *dire des pate-* nôtres de singe. TO PUT AN APE INTO ONE'S HOOD or CAP, to make a fool of one, etc.

APES, *subs.* (Stock Exchange).—Atlantic and North-Western Railway first mortgage bonds.

APOSTLES, or THE TWELVE APOSTLES, *subs. phr.* (Cambridge Univ.).—Formerly, when the Poll, or ordinary B.A. degree list was arranged in order of merit, the last twelve were nicknamed THE TWELVE APOSTLES. They were also called THE CHOSEN TWELVE, and the last, St. Poll or St. Paul—a punning allusion to 1 Cor. xv., 9, 'For I am the least of the Apostles, that am not meet to be called an Apostle.' The list is now arranged alphabetically and in classes. Hotten suggests that APOSTLES is a corruption of *post alios, i.e.,* 'after the others.' It may perhaps also be mentioned that in one American University at least, Columbia College, D.C., the last twelve on the B.A. list actually receive the personal names of the Apostles.

1795. *Gentleman's Magazine*, Jan., p. 19. [The last twelve names on the Cambridge list are here called THE TWELVE APOSTLES.]

MANŒUVERING THE APOSTLES, a variant of the familiar expression, 'to rob Peter to pay Paul'; *i.e.,* to borrow from one person to pay another.

APOSTLE'S GROVE, *subs.* (common).—The London district known as St. John's Wood. Also called GROVE OF THE EVANGELIST. Both names are applied sarcastically in allusion to the large numbers of the demi-

monde who live in that quarter of town.

APOTHECARY. TO TALK LIKE AN APOTHECARY, *verb phr.* (old).—To talk nonsense; from the pseudo gravity and affectation of knowledge often assumed by these gentlemen at a time when their status was not legally held under examination and license of the Apothecaries' Company.

APOTHECARIES' BILL, *subs.* (old).—A long bill.

APOTHECARIES', or RAW LATIN, *subs.* (old). — Now called DOG-LATIN (q.v.).

APPLE CART, *subs.* (common). 1. The human body. A slang term similar to 'POTATO TRAP,' 'BREAD-BASKET,' 'BELLOWS,' 'BLUE PLUMB,' 'BACON,' and 'BEER-BARREL' (all of which see). There are numerous variations in usage; *e.g.,* if two men are quarrelling, and a friend of one interferes saying 'I will upset his APPLE CART' it means, 'while you are parleying with the enemy I will knock him down.' Again, if a child falls down, says W. W. Skeat (referring to his early Kentish remembrance of the word), you first enquire if he is much hurt. If he is merely a little frightened you say, 'Well, never mind, then; you've only upset your APPLE CART and spilt the gooseberries.' The child laughs and all is well again.

2. Also employed in a figurative sense. TO UPSET AN APPLE CART sometimes means, not so much to knock a man down, as to prevent him from doing what he wants to do by the upsetting as it were, of an imaginary APPLE CART; *i.e.,* to thwart; to disarrange; to overthrow; to ruin an undertaking. Sometimes the expression is varied by TO UPSET THE OLD WOMAN'S APPLE CART. Barrère's reference of the genesis of the phrase to the costermonger's imaginative powers is 'all conjecture and fancy'; as also is his American derivation of the expression in its more figurative sense. In the first place APPLE CARTS are perfectly familiar objects in all country districts; and, in the second, the phrase is too old a provincialism to need deriving from the peripatetic vendors in question. Further, though TO UPSET HIS APPLE CART AND SPILL THE PEACHES may be an American variation for the second sense, as it appears to have been so used, dialectically, throughout England, the weight of assumption must be given to its English origin, and subsequent transference to America.

ENGLISH SYNONYMS. Beer-barrel; bacon.

FRENCH SYNONYMS. *Acabit* (literally, quality); *cylindre* (popular: lit. 'a cylinder,' or 'barrel.' *Cf.* with English 'beer barrel'); *grosse caisse* (popular: lit. 'a large case,' or 'box'); *paillasse* (popular: lit. 'a straw mattress'); also *place d'armes; casaquin.*

APPLE DUMPLING SHOP, *subs. phr.* (common).—A woman's bosom. For synonyms, *see* DAIRIES.

APPLE-MONGER.—The same as APPLE-SQUIRE (q.v.).

APPLE-PIE BED, *subs. phr.* (common).—A practical joke, which consists in making up a bed with the sheets doubled half way

up, so as to prevent a person from stretching out at full length, and filling the bag thus formed with brushes, soap-dishes, etc. So called, either from the apple-turnover, in which the 'paste' is turned over the apples, or from the French, *à plis,* folded.

1811. C. K. SHARPE, in *Correspondence* (1888), i., 466. After squeezing myself up, and making a sort of APPLE-PYE BED with the beginning of my sheet.

1888. *Saturday Review*, Nov. 3, p. 566, col. 2. Some 'evil-disposed persons' have already visited his room, MADE HIS BED INTO AN APPLE-PIE, plentifully strewn with hair-brushes and razors.

The French have an analogous phrase, '*mettre un lit en portefeuille.*'

APPLE-PIE DAY, *subs. phr.* (Winchester Coll.)—The day on which Six-and-Six (q.v.) is played. It is the Thursday after the first Tuesday in December. So called because hot apple-pies were served on GOMERS (q.v.) in College for dinner.

APPLE PIE ORDER, *subs. phr.* (familiar).—Exact or perfect order. Etymologists have long puzzled themselves concerning this expression, and many derivations have been put forward in explanation. Some have found in it an allusion to the regular order in which the component parts of some varieties of that toothsome delicacy, apple pie, were formerly laid one on the top of, or side by side with each other. Others, on the contrary, scout such a homely origin, and suggest that APPLE PIE ORDER is *cap à pied* order. The authorities who incline to this view point out that *cap à pied* in the sense of 'perfectly appointed' occurs in one of the scenes of *Hamlet.* Though orthographically the transition from one to the other, at first sight, would appear to be somewhat lame and halting, yet phonetically the difference is much less marked. It has further been suggested that APPLE PIE ORDER is a corruption of 'Alpha-beta' *i.e.,* alphabetical order, but this would seem rather far-fetched, as also is the reference of it to the nursery rhyme of 'A was an apple pie; B bit it; C cut it; D divided it,' and so on, the allusion being to the regular order in which the letters of the alphabet occur. Probably the weight of evidence is on the side of the derivation from *cap à pied,* more especially as that phrase was once very familiar.

1813. SCOTT in Lochart, *Life,* IV. (1839), 131. The children's garden is in APPLE PIE ORDER.

1835. MARRYAT, *Jacob Faithful*, viii., 29. Put the craft a little into APPLE PIE ORDER.

1837. BARHAM, I. L. (*Old Woman in Grey*).
I am just in the *order* which some folks
   —though why,
I am sure I can't tell you—would call
apple pie.

APPLES. HOW WE APPLES SWIM! *phr.* (common).—*i.e.,* 'What a good time we are having.' This expression, a very old one, is synonymous with pleasureable experience coupled with brisk action.

1697-1764. HOGARTH (Works by J. Ireland and J. Nichols, London, 1873), III., p. 29. And even this, little as it is, gives him so much importance in his own eyes, that he assumes a consequen-

tial air, sets his arms akimbo, and strutting among the historical artists cries, 'HOW WE APPLES SWIM.'

1860. *Cornhill Mag.* (D. Mallett, *Tyburn*), Dec., p. 737. While tumbling down the turbid stream, Lord, love us, HOW WE APPLES SWIM.

APPLES AND PEARS, *subs. phr.* (rhyming slang).—A pair of stairs.

APPLE-SQUIRE, *subs.* (old).—A harlot's attendant, or FANCY MAN (q.v.); these gentry are now commonly called 'BULLIES' (q.v.). Nares gives 'SQUIRE OF THE BODY' as a synonymous term; also APRON-SQUIRE.

1500. (circa) *Way to Spyttel Hous,* 832 in Hazl. *E. P. P.,* iv., 60. [Here given as APPLESQUYERS.]

[1580-1654] TAYLOR, *Discourse by Sea* (works II., 21).
Are whoremasters decai'd, are bawds all dead,
Are pandars, pimps, and APPLE-SQUIRES all fled? [N.]

1738. *Poor Robin* . . . . Little truth will be found amongst cut-purses, liars, bawds, whores, pimps, pandars, and APPLE-SQUIRES; only the pimp pretends to something more of truth than the other, for if he promise to help you to a whore. he will be sure that she shall not be an honest woman. [N.]

For synonyms, ancient and modern, and also foreign equivalents, *see* FANCY MAN.

APRON. GREEN APRON, *subs.* (old).—A contemptuous term for a lay preacher. — *See* BIBLE-POUNDER.

1654. WARREN, *Unbelievers*, 145. It more befits a GREEN-APRON preacher, than such a Gamaliel. [M.]

1705. HICKERINGILL, *Priestcraft* I. (1721), 21. Unbeneficed Noncons. (that live by Alms and no Paternoster, no Penny, say the GREEN-APRONS). [M.]

1765. TUCKER, *Lt. Nat.,* II., 451. The gifted priestess amongst the Quakers is known by her GREEN APRON. [M.]

APRONEER, *subs.* (old).—A shop-keeper; a tradesman. Murray states that the term was used contemptuously of the Parliamentary party during the Civil Wars.

1659. GAUDEN, *Tears of Church,* 238. Some prating sequestrator, or some surly APRONEER.

1690. D'URFEY, *Collin's Walk,* c. iii., p. 107. But every sturdy APRONEER, arm'd with battoon, did straight appear.

APRON-ROGUE, *subs.* (old). — A labourer; a mechanic.

1663. KILLEGREW, *Parson's Wedding* in Dodsley's Old Plays (1780), XI., 382. APRON-ROGUES with horn hands. [M.]

APRON-SQUIRE. — *See* APPLE-SQUIRE.

APRON-STRING HOLD or TENURE, *subs. phr.* (familiar).—An estate held by a man during his wife's life; or by virtue of her right.

1647. WARD, *Simp. Cobler,* 67. APRON-STRING tenure is very weak. [M.]

1753. RICHARDSON, *Grandison,* iv., 23. He cursed the APRON-STRING tenure, by which he said he held his peace. [D.]

1804. Mrs. BARBAULD, *Richardson* I., 160. All her fortune in her own power—a very APRON-STRING TENURE.

APRON-STRINGS. TO BE TIED TO or ALWAYS AT A WOMAN'S APRON-STRINGS, *verb. phr.* (common).—Under petticoat government; to dangle after a woman. Formerly said only of children; later of all who follow a woman subserviently.

1712. *Spectator,* No. 506. The fair sex are so conscious to themselves, that they have nothing in them which can deserve entirely to ingross the whole man, that they heartily despise one, who, to use their own expression, is always HANGING AT THEIR APRON-STRINGS.

1884. MISS EDGEWORTH, *Helen*, ch. viii. A homebred lordling, who, from the moment he SLIPPED HIS MOTHER'S APRON-STRINGS, had fallen into folly.

1849. MACAULAY, *History of England*, II., 649. He could not submit to be TIED TO THE APRON-STRINGS even of the best of wives.

AQUA, *subs.* (American thieves').—Water. From the Latin.

AQUA POMPAGINIS, *subs. phr.* (old).—Pump water [Dog-Latin; from L., AQUA, water + English, PUMP + simulated Latin termination, *aginis*].

1785. GROSE, *Dictionary of the Vulgar Tongue*. AQUA POMPAGINIS. . . . Apothecaries' Latin.

1839. HARRISON AINSWORTH, *Jack Sheppard* [1889], p. 13. 'Exactly my sentiments,' rejoined Blueskin. 'I wouldn't force him for the world; but if he don't *tip the stivers*, may I be cursed if he don't get a taste of the AQUA POMPAGINIS. Let's have a look at the *kinchen* that ought to have been throttled,' added he, snatching the child from Wood. 'My stars! here's a pretty *lullaby-cheat* to make a fuss about—ho ho!'

1839. HARRISON AINSWORTH, *Jack Sheppard* [1889], p. 15. 'He shall go through the whole course,' replied Blueskin, with a ferocious grin, 'unless he comes down to the last grig. We'll lather him with mud, shave him with a rusty razor, and drench him with AQUA POMPAGINIS.'

For synonyms, *see* ADAM'S ALE.

AQUATICS, *subs.* (Eton college).—The particular game of cricket in which men in the boats play.

AQUA-VITÆ, *subs.* (old).—Formerly an alchemic term; but, after a while, popularly received as a generic name for ardent spirits, such as brandy, whiskey, etc. [From L. = water of life. *Cf.*, French *eau-de-vie*, and Irish *usquebaugh*.]

ARABS, *subs.* (common).—Nicknames for young street vagrants are numerous. They are 'Bedouins,' 'Street Arabs,' and 'Juvenile Roughs' in London; they are 'Gamins' in Paris; 'Bowery Boys' in New York; 'Hoodlums' in San Francisco; and 'Larrikins' in Melbourne. This last phrase is an Irish constable's broad pronunciation of 'larking,' applied to the nightly street performances of these young scamps, there, as elsewhere, a real social pestilence.—*See* STREET ARAB.

1848. GUTHRIE, *Plea for Ragged Schools*. [In this work the homeless wanderers and children of the streets were spoken of as ARABS OF THE CITY, and City Arabs.]

ARBOR VITÆ, *subs.* (old).—The penis. [Latin; = the Tree of Life]. For synonyms, *see* CREAMSTICK.

ARCH.—*See* ARK.

ARCH-COVE or **ARCH-ROGUE**, *subs.* (thieves').—The chief or leader of a gang of thieves. [From Greek, *archo* to be first, to command, to rule + COVE, a slang term for a man.] Formerly also DIMBER DAMBER, UPRIGHT MAN.—*See* COVE and AREA SNEAK.

ARCHDEACON, *subs.* (Oxford Univ.).—Merton strong ale.

ARCH-DELL or **ARCH-DOXY**, *subs.* (old).—The wife or female companion of an ARCH-COVE.—*See* DELL.

ARCHDUKE, *subs.* (old slang).—A buffoon; an eccentric person.

ARCH GONNOF.—*See* DIMBER DAMBER.

ARD, *adj.* (American thieves').—Hot; a corrupted form of 'ardent.' Formerly 'a foot.'—*See* CREEPERS.

AREA-SNEAK, *subs.* (common).—A thief who lurks about areas for the purposes of theft.

1838. DICKENS, *Nicholas Nickleby*, ch. lix., p. 480. 'Why wasn't I a thief, swindler, housebreaker, AREA-SNEAK, robber of pence out of the trays of blind man's dogs?'

1869. *English Mechanic*, 14 May, p. 181, col. 1. [They] would invariably become pickpockets or AREA-SNEAKS.

1883. *Daily Telegraph*, June 13, p. 7, col. 3. The AREA-SNEAK, too, may find his occupation partially gone through the strictness of the rules which encompass the trade of the second-hand dealer.

Among other names for thieves may be mentioned:—

ENGLISH AND AMERICAN. Beak or beaker-hunter (a poultry thief); bug-hunter (speciality—breast pins, studs, etc.); buz-faker (a pickpocket); buttock and file (a shoplifter); bouncer (one who steals while bargaining with a tradesman; a shoplifter); bridle-cull (a highwayman); cracksman (a burglar); crossman (an old term. Literally a man 'on the cross,' or who gets his living surreptitiously); cross-cove (*see* foregoing); conveyancer (a pickpocket); dancer (a thief who gains entrance to houses from the roof); flash-cove (a sharper); flashman (a prostitute's bully who pretends to catch the victim *in flagrante delicto* with his *wife*, and thus makes an excuse for robbery and extortion); finder (a thief who confines his depredations to meat-markets and butchers' shops); gun (a contraction of GONNOF, which *see*); gleaner, hooker, or angler (these are petty thieves, who work with hooks and rods); lob-sneak; lully-prigger (one who steals clothes when they are hanging out to dry); snakesman or sneaksman (a shoplifter; a petty thief); sneeze-lurker (this kind work by first blinding victims with pepper, etc.); moucher (a prowling thief); mill-ben (an old cant term, which *see*); prig; prop-nailer (a 'prop' is a scarf pin); palmer (a thief who 'rings the changes'; but *see* under PALMER); pudding-snammer (an eating-house thief); drummer or drammer (these gentry stupify their victims prior to robbing them); stook-hauler (speciality — pocket-handkerchiefs); tooler (a pickpocket); toy-getter (a watch thief).

FRENCH SYNONYMS. *Un droguiste* (corresponds to the English 'hawk' or 'rook'); *un chêne affranchi* (a 'flash cove'); *un careur*, or *voleur à la care* (thief who robs money-changers while pretending to offer old coins for sale); *un enfant de la matte* ('a child of folly.'—*See* FAMILY MAN); *un tiretaine* (a country thief); *un garçon de cambrouse* (a highwayman); *un garçon de campagne* (same as example last quoted); *un frère de la manicle*; *un philantrope* (a peddlar's term); *un bonjourier* or *voleur au bonjour* (an early morning thief, but *see* under THIEVES); *un philibert* (of the sharper stamp); *un philosophe* (lit. 'a philosopher'); *un enfant de minuit* (formerly, says Cotgrave, *enfants de la messe de minuit*, *i.e.*, companions of the midnight

mass, not for devotion, but for robbery and abuse); *ramastiqueur* (one who swindles by means of pocket-book dropping, etc.—a variety of the confidence trick); *un jardinier*, *un Americain* ('confidence trick' men); *un tirebogue* (a watch thief; in English slang a 'toy-getter'); *un friauche*; *un grinchisseur de bogues* (a watch thief); *un mion de boule* (equivalent to the English 'prig'); *un fil de soie*; *un doubleur* (= English 'prig'; *un doubleur de sorgue*, 'a night thief'); *un voleur à la tire* (a pickpocket); *un tireur* (a pickpocket; literally 'one who draws out'); etc.

GERMAN SYNONYMS. *Broschem-blatter*; *cochem* (a thieves' accomplice; from Hebrew *chochem*, wise, instructed); *ernternackener* (thieves who steal from houses while the owners are away harvesting. From *erndte*, harvest + *machen*, to make); *anstiebler* (one who plans robberies; an instigator to theft. A corrupted form of *anstifter*, an instigator); *achbrosch* (also *achberosch*, *achperosch*, *achprosch*, *approsch*, an infamous thief or robber, a rogue, a sharper. Not so much from the Chaldean *achbero*, a mouse + *rosch*, head, as from the passage *Jer. Baba. Mez.* 8., *achberi reschii*, *i.e.*, 'the mice are vile.' Hence applied primarily to a notorious thief. Thiele says the expressions have not been so much in use since the suppression of the famous Rhenish robber gang; the words, however, particularly *achbrosch*, are not by any means obsolete, being very much in use by cattle and horsedealers, and sharpers generally); *ganof* (Hebrew, 'a thief'; from *gonaw*, 'to steal'); *achelpeter* (an inactive lazy old thief who sponges upon his confederates. From Hebrew *ochal*, to eat + *putzen*, from O.H.G., *bizan*, *pizzan*, 'food'); *golehopser* (a thief who jumps on a loaded cart or other vehicle whilst in motion to steal boxes or small packages. In English slang this kind of thief is called a 'dragsman'); *goleschächter* (the same as preceding, but instead of making off bodily with the booty, the packages are cut open, and the contents thrown down for an accomplice to secure); *bihengst* (a thief who steals bees); *baldower* (a principal, or leader of a gang of thieves; one who advises and plans robberies. *Balhoche* is also a man who has an opportunity for theft; *balspiess* the host of an inn, frequented by thieves and rogues); *brenner* (a thief who preys upon others of his kind, by demanding, under threats of exposure, a share of a successful robbery, without having taken part in it. From *brennen*, 'to claim'; literally 'to burn'; or it may be from *berennen*, 'to run against or blockade'); *chalfan* (also *chalfen*, *chalfener*, *chilfer*, legitimately 'a money changer,' but amongst German thieves the name of the rogue who, in changing money, commits theft. *Cf.*, English, 'ringing the changes'); *chawer* (Hebrew: literally an associate; *chaweress* [*fem.*], a thief's confederate; a comrade. *Chawrusse*, *kabruse*, a gang or confederation of thieves; *chawrusse melochenen*, to form a gang of thieves; *chenneter*, a thief who knows how to conduct himself with tact and address in good society. From

the Hebrew *chono*, gentle, kind, affable); *chessenspiess*, *fem.*, *chessenspiesse* (the landlord or mistress of an inn frequented by thieves—a place where they may find refuge without fear of discovery. From the Hebrew); *chochom* (also *chochem*, *chochemer*,—more frequently spelled with 'K'—from the Hebrew, the wise one. A prudent, cunning thief. *Chochem lehorre*, a dangerous thief, one prepared for the worst; of a similar meaning is *chochem mechutten*, a dangerous companion, a rogue of the worst type); *bahnherr* (also *bohnherr* and *Herr* by itself: literally 'a road-master'; a burglar—one who prepares a robbery); *diffler* (a thoroughly dexterous thief; from *tupfel*, 'a point'); *drängler* (a thief, who, to divert the attention of people from his intention, causes a crowd to assemble); *paddendrücker* (a pickpocket—one whose speciality is purses: *drücker* is a corrupted form of *trecken*, 'to draw' or 'steal' quickly and adroitly. *Drücker*, like *drücken*, 'to steal' is never used by itself, but always with the object of the theft; hence *paddendrücker*, a purse thief; *luppendrücker*, a watch thief; *torfdrücker*, a generic name for a pickpocket); *eintreiber* (a confederate who entices a victim to play so that his comrade may swindle him); *erefschieber* (a thief who goes out at evening time to commit robberies. Also *erefhalchener*, *erefgänger*, *erefhändler*. *Eref* = evening); fichtegänger (a night thief or burglar); *fiesel* (supposed to be derived from *faser*, 'a birch,' 'rod,' or 'fibre.' In Vienna, the scum of society is meant by *fiesel*—the commonest thief, professional vagabond, a protector of brothels and whores of the most repulsive kind. These thieves are of great daring, utterly unscrupulous, and are consequently much dreaded. Some feign to carry on the business of a rag and bone-picker, what in the *fiesellange* or Viennese thieves' lingo is termed, 'going out for profit.' In the sense of 'a rod,' *fiesel* is applied to the *membrum genitale masculi*; hence fiesel as synonymous with strength, *i.e.*, pertaining to the stronger sex. It was formerly used in connection with many other words; *e.g.*, *mädchenfiesel*, 'one who habitually runs after women,' 'a molrower,' a 'loose fish.' *Fiesel*-language means the language of the strong, of those belonging to the fellowship of thieves, burglars, and rowdies); *freikäufer* (a thief whose speciality it is to steal at fairs and markets); *freischupper* (a card sharper; a gambling cheat who carries on his business in crowded places of public resort); *gacheler* (also *gachler*, *gackler*, *kachler*, *kahler*, *kegler*: a pantry thief; one who steals eatables and plate from kitchens whilst servants are attending at table); *gannew* (from Hebrew *gonaw*, 'to steal'); *gaslan* (from Hebrew *gosal*, 'to rob'); *glitscher* (gypsy: *glitschin*, 'the key: a thief who works by means of skeleton keys); *godler chochem* (from Hebrew *godol*, great, strong, celebrated + Hebrew *chochem*, the wise one; hence, a clever rogue, a thief who thoroughly understands his business); *goi gomur* (an utterly unreliable confederate. *Goi*, plural *gojim* is applied to those not Jews, to Christians; in the plural, especially, in the sense of ignorant people, suspicious or two-faced characters; also used as a synonym for Philistine—a man of whom one has to be careful. *Goje* [*fem.*] is almost always used contemptuously for a female); *götte* (also *götti, göde, göttling* [O. H. G., *gataling*] a confederate, a relative—especially used to denote one who has been doing good business); *gutenmorgenwünscher* (literally 'good morning wisher': thieves who break into rooms early in the morning for purposes of robbery. The French have an analogous expression in *bonjourier*, or *voleur au bon jour*). For other synonyms, *see* THIEVES.

ITALIAN SYNONYMS (Fourbesque). *Quadro* (a cut-purse. In the Germania or Spanish argot, *quadro* is used in the sense of 'a poignard,' and *quadrata* in that of 'purse.' Possibly the Fourbesque *quadro* is derived from one of these words. In Italian it is literally 'a square' or 'a rule'); *granchetto* (also 'one who speaks gibberish'); *lavorante di scarpe* (a pickpocket or cut-purse: lit. 'working shoes'); *camuffo*; *fiadetto* (also 'a dolt,' 'a duffer'); *carpione*; *truccante* (also 'a beggar').

SPANISH SYNONYMS (Germania). *Aquila* (a sharper: lit. 'an eagle'); *bolador* (thought to be derived from the French *voleur*); *comendadores de bola* (thieves who work principally at fairs and markets); *gerifalte* (lit. 'a gerfalcon'—one of the 'hawk' species); *lince* (lit. 'a lynx.' This class of thief varies robbery with begging); *piloto* (a thief who directs others to the place of rendezvous, *i.e.*, where a robbery has been planned; lit. 'a pilot'); *trabajar* (lit. 'a traveller').—*See* THIEVES.

PORTUGUESE SYNONYMS (Calaõ). *Pai* (a captain of thieves—an Aaron or arch-cove); *maguino* (a highwayman).

For exhaustive and comparative description of all classes of thieves, both English and foreign, *see* THIEVES—THEIR NAMES AND METHODS.

'ARF, *adj.* (vulgarism).—Half; *e.g.*, ''arf an 'our,' *i.e.*, half an hour.

'ARF AND 'ARF.—*See* FOUR-HALF.

ARGAL.—*See* ARGOL-BARGOL.

ARGOL-BARGOL, *subs.* and *verb.* (old).—ARGOL, sometimes ARGAL, is a corrupt pronunciation of Latin *ergo*, therefore; hence, from that word being frequently used in conversation, a clumsy, unsound piece of reasoning or cavilling; and verbally, to bandy words. Hotten says ARGOL-BARGOL is Scotch, but ARGAL is found in *Hamlet*, v. i., and the fuller form is probably onamatopoetic like 'shilly-shally,' 'hocus-pocus,' etc., unless it comes from the Hebrew through the Yiddish *bar-len* 'to talk or speak' [anyhow].

1596. SHAKSPEAR, *Hamlet* v. i., 21., 1st *Clown.* Here lies the water; good: here stands the man; good: If the man go to this water, it is, will he, nil he, he goes; mark you that: but if the water come to him, he drowns not himself: ARGAL, he that is not guilty of his own death, shortens not his own life.

1823. J. GALT, *The Entail*, i., 53. 'Weel, weel,' said the laird, 'dinna let us ARGOL-BARGOL about it; entail your own property as ye will, mine shall be on the second son.'

1861. *Times*, 23 Aug. Mr. Buckle's argument [is] as absurd an ARGAL as ever was invented by philsopher or gravedigger. [M.]

ARGOL-BARGOLOUS, *adj.* (old).—Quarrelsome.—*See* ARGOL-BARGOL.

1822. J. GALT, *The Provost*, p. 194. No doubt his ARGOL-BARGOLOUS disposition was an inheritance accumulated with his other conquest of wealth from the mannerless Yankees.

ARGUFY, *verb.* (vulgar).—A corrupted form of 'to argue,' usually associated with cavilling or a bandying of words; also, 'to signify'; *e.g.*, 'It doesn't much ARGUFY.'

1758. A. MURPHY, *The Upholsterer*, Act i. Well, it does not signify ARGIFYING.

1837. LYTTON, *Ernest Maltravers*, bk. IV., ch. vii. 'Lord! how I should like to have you on the roadside instead of within these four gimcrack walls. Ha! ha! the ARGUFYING would be all in *my* favour then.'

ARISTIPPUS, *subs.* (old).—1. A diet drink or decoction of sarsaparilla and other drugs, sold at the coffee-houses, and drank as tea.—*Grose.*

2. Also a cant name for canary wine.

1627. (*circa*) MIDDLETON, *Wks.* (Halliwell), II., 422. Rich ARISTIPPUS, sparkling sherry.

ARKANSAS TOOTHPICK, *subs.* (American).—A grimly facetious name for a folding bowie knife of large dimensions.

1854. SIR THEO. MARTIN (with Prof. Aytoun), *Bon Gaultier Ballads*.
'Straightway leaped the valiant Slingby
Into armor of Seville,
With a strong ARKANSAS TOOTHPICK,
Screwed in every joint of steel.'

1881. A. B. GREENLEAF, *Ten Years in Texas*, p. 27. All these (men) irrespective of age, size, or condition in life, could be seen with a Navy six-shooter and an ARKANSAS TOOTHPICK suspended to a raw-hide belt tucked around their waists. Supplement the above equipment with a sore-backed mustang pony, an old army saddle-tree and rope bridle, and you have an exact picture and entire possession of the fifteenth constitutional amendment.

1888. *Detroit Free Press*, Aug. It is not good form to use a TOOTHPICK in ARKANSAS now. A big revolver is the thing in the best society.

For synonyms, *see* CHIVE.

ARK-FLOATER, *subs.* (theatrical).—An actor well advanced in years. [From an allusion to the proverbial saying concerning anything ancient, 'He, or it, must have come out of Noah's ARK,' + FLOATS, the footlights.]

ARKMAN, *subs.* (old).—A Thames waterman. *Cf.*, ACKMAN.

ARK-RUFF, or **ARK-RUFFIAN.**—The same as ACK-MAN (*q.v.*).

ARMOUR. TO BE IN ARMOUR, *verb. phr.* (old).—To be pot-valiant; 'primed'; full of Dutch courage.—*See* SCREWED.

ARMPITS. TO WORK UNDER THE ARMPITS, *verb. phr.* (old).—To sail so far to the windward of the law in petty larceny, that, if caught and tried, the punishment would not amount to more than transportation. On the passing of Sir Samuel Romilly's Act, capital punishment was abolished for highway robberies under 40s. in value. Hence, formerly, TO WORK UNDER THE ARMPITS was to avoid the halter

or NECK-SQUEEZER (*q.v.*), which is applied *above* the armpits.

ARM-PROPS, *subs.* (common).—Crutches; otherwise WOODEN LEGS (*q.v.*).

1825. W. T. MONCRIEFF, *Tom and Jerry*, Act ii., Scene 6. *Beggar*: You did quite right; vell, vile I can get fifteen bob a day by gammoning a maim, the devil may vork for me. If any lady or genman is inclined for a dance, I'll nash my ARM-PROPS in a minute.
(*Throws down his crutches.*)

ARMS AND LEGS, *subs. phr.* (common).—Poor, weak beer, because there is no body in it!—*See* SWIPES.

ARMSTRONG. TO COME CAPTAIN ARMSTRONG.—*See* CAPTAIN ARMSTRONG.

ARROW (vulgarism).—A corruption of 'e'er, a,' or 'ever a.'

1750. FIELDING, *Tom Jones*, bk. V., ch. viii. 'I don't believe there is ARROW a servant in the house ever saw the colour of his money.'

1771. SMOLLETT, *Humphrey Clinker*, i., 126. 'I now carries my head higher than ARROW private gentlewoman of Vales.'

'ARRY, *subs.* (common).—The Christian name Harry without the aspirate. A popular embodiment of the vulgar, rollicking, yet on the whole good-tempered 'rough' of the great metropolis. His 'get-up' is, as he would himself put it, 'immense'; he is seen to most advantage—his own—on Sundays and bank holidays; his 'young woman'—generally 'Arriet'—is *en suite*; taken altogether he is a lively, jovial, but ill-bred 'cuss.' *Mr. Punch* in an inimitable series of sketches has 'hit off' his man 'to a T.'

1880. MILLIKIN, *Punch's Almanac.*
JANUARY! Tailor's bill comes in.
Blow that blooming snip! I'm short of tin.
Werry much enjoyed my autumn Caper,
But three quid fifteen do look queer paper.
Want another new rig out, wuss luck,
Gurl at Boodle's bar seems awful struck.
Like to take her to pantermime;
That and oysters after *would* be prime.
Fan's a screamer; this top coat would blue it,
Yaller at the seams, black ink wont do it.
Wonder if old snip would spring another?
Boots, too, rayther seedy; beastly bother!
Lots o' larks that empty pockets 'queer.'
Can't do much on fifty quid a year.
FEBRYWARY! High old time for sprees!
Now's yer chance the gals to please or tease.
Dowds to guy and pooty ones' to wheedle,
And give all rival chaps the needle.
Crab your enemies,—I've got a many,
You can pot 'em proper for a penny.
My! them walentines do 'it 'em 'ot.
First-rate fun: I always buy a lot.
Prigs complain they're spiteful, lor' wot stuff!
I can't ever get 'em strong enough.
Safe too; no one twigs your little spree,
If you do it on the strict Q.T.
If you're spoons, a flowery one's your plan,
Mem. I sent a proper one to Fan.
MARCH! I'm nuts upon a windy day,
Gurls do get in such a awful way.
Petticoats yer know, and pooty feet;
Hair all flying,—tell you it's a treat.
Pancake day. Don't like 'em—flabby, tough,
Rayther do a pennorth o' plum-duff.
Seediness shows up as Spring advances,
Ah! the gurls do lead us pretty dances.
Days a-lengthening, think I spotted Fan
Casting sheep's eyes at another man.
Quarter-day, too, no more chance of tick,
Fancy I shall 'ave to cut my stick.
Got the doldrums dreadful, that is clear,
Two *d* left!—must go and do a beer!
APRIL! All Fools' Day's a proper time,
Cop old gurls and guy old buffers prime.
Scissors! don't they goggle and look blue,
When you land them with a regular 'do?'
Lor! the world would not be worth a mivvey,
If there warn't no fools to cheek and chivy.
Then comes Easter. Got some coin in 'and,
Trot a bonnet out and do the grand.
Fan all flounce and flower; fellows mad,

Heye us henvious; nuts to me, my lad.
'Ampstead! 'Ampton! Which is it to be?
Fan—no flat—prefers the Crystal P.
Nobby togs, high jinks, and lots o' lotion,
That's the style to go it, I've a notion!
MAY! The month o' flowers. Spooney sell!
'Rum 'ot with,' is wot *I* likes to smell.
Beats yer roses holler. A chice weed,
Licks all flowers that ever run to seed.
Nobby button 'oler very well,
When one wants to do the 'eavy swell;
Otherwise don't care not one brass farden,
For the best ever blowed in Covent Garden.
Fan, though, likes 'em, costs a pretty pile,
Rayther stiff, a tanner for a smile.
Blued ten bob last time I took 'er out,
Left my silver ticker up the spout.
Women are sech sharks! If I don't drop 'er,
Guess that I shall come a hawful cropper!
JUNE! A jolly month; sech stunning weather!
Fan and I have lots of outs together:
Rorty on the river, sech prime 'unts,
Foul the racers, run into the punts.
Prime to 'ear the anglers rave and cuss,
When in quiet 'swims' we raise a muss.
Snack on someone's lawn upon the quiet,
Won't the owner raise a tidy riot
When he twigs our scraps and broken bottles?
Cheaper this than rusty-rongs or hottles.
Whitsuntide 'ud be a lot more gay
If it warn't so near to Quarter-day.
Snip turns sour, pulls 'county-courting' faces,
Must try and land a little on the races.
At JULY! just nicked a handy fiver,
(Twenty-five to one on old 'Screw-driver'!
New rig-out. This mustard colour mixture
Suits me nobly. Fan appears a fixture.
Gurls like style, you know, and colour ketches 'em,
But good show of ochre,—that's what fetches 'em.
Wimbledon! *I'm* not a wolunteer,
Discipline don't suit this child—no fear!
But we 'ave fine capers at the camp,
Proper, but for that confounded scamp:
Punched my 'ead, because I guyed his shooting.
Fan I fancied rather 'igh faluting;
Ogled the big beggar as he propped me,
Would 'a licked 'im if *she* 'adn't stopped me.
AUGUST! Time to think about my outing.
No dibs yet, though, so it's no use shouting.
Make the best of the Bank 'Oliday.
Fan 'engaged'! Don't look too bloomin' gay.
Drop into the bar to do a beer.
Twig her talking to that volunteer.
Sling my 'ook instanter sharp and short,
Took Jemimer down to 'Ampton Court,
Not arf bad that gurl. Got rather screwed,
Little toff complained as I was rude.
'It 'im in the wind, he went like death;
Weak, consumptive cove and short o' breath.
Licked 'im proper, dropped 'im like a shot'—
Only wish that Fan had seen *that* lot.
'Ere's SEPTEMBER! 'Oliday at last!
Off to Margit—mean to go it fast.
Mustard-coloured togs still fresh as paint,
Like to know who's natty, if *I* ain't.
Got three quid; have cried a go with Fan,
Game to spend my money like a man.
But stickin' tight to one gal ain't no fun,—
Here's no end of prime 'uns on the run
Carn't resist me somehow, togs and tile
All A1—make even swell ones smile.
Lor! if I'd the ochre, make no doubt
I could cut no end of big pots out.
Call me cad? When money's in the game,
Cad and swell are pooty much the same.
Now OCTOBER! Back again to collar,
Funds run low, reduced to last 'arf dollar,
Snip on rampage, boots a getting thin,
'Ave to try the turf to raise some tin.
Evenings getting gloomy; high old games;
Music 'alls look up the taking names.
Proper swells them pros! If I'd had my choice,
There's *my* mark. Just wish I'd got a voice;
Cut the old den to-morrow, lots o'cham,
Cabs and diamonds—ain't that real jam?
Got the straight tip for the Siezerwitch,
If I *honly* land it, I'll be rich.
Guess next mornin' wouldn't find me sober—
Allays get the blues about October.
Dull NOVEMBER! Didn't land that lot.
Fear my father's son is going to pot.
Fan jest passed me, turned away 'er eyes,
Guess she ranked me with the *other* guys.
Nobby larks upon the Ninth, my joker
But it queers a chap to want the ochre.

Nothing like a crowd for regular sprees,
Ain't it fine to do a rush, and squeeze?
Twig the women fainting! oh, it's pro-
per!
Bonnet buffers when the blooming cop-
per
Can't get near yer nohow. Then the
fogs!
Rare old time for regular jolly dogs.
If a chap's a genuine 'ot member,
He *can* keep the game up in November!
Dun DECEMBER! Dismal, dingy, dirty.
Still short commons—makes a chap feel
shirty.
Snip rampageous, drops a regular sum-
mons.
Fan gets married; ah! them gurls is rum
'uns!
After all the coin I squandered on 'er!
Want it now. A 'eap too bad, 'pon hon-
our.
Snow! ah, that's yer sort though, and
no error,
Treat to twig the women scud in terror.
Hot 'un in the eye for that old feller;
Cold 'un down 'is neck, burst his um-
breller.
Ha! ha! then Christmas,—'ave a jolly
feast!
The Boss will drop a tip,—'ope so, at
least.
If I don't land some tin, my look-out's
queer.
Well, let's drink, boys—'Better luck next
year!'

ARSE, *subs.* (low).—The posterior;
the breech; the fundament. Once
in polite use, but now considered
very vulgar. As Grose in his
Dictionary of the Vulgar Tongue
[1785] prints the word thus,
'a–e,' it is evident that it had
then fallen into disfavour.
Murray traces the word back to
about A.D. 1000. [A.S., *ears, œurs*;
Icelandic and Swedish, *ars*;
Danish, *arts*, and German, *arsch*].

1060 (*circa*). ÆLFRIC, *Glossary* in
Wright, 44·2 [*Nates*, EARS-lye]. [M.]

1480. CAXTON, *Chronicles of England*,
ccxxxvi., 233. They lete hange fox tailles
. . . . to hele and hyde her ARSES.

1663. BUTLER, *Hudibras* I., iii., 964.
Then mounted both upon their Horses,
But with their Faces to the ARSES. [M.]

1704. SWIFT, *Battle of the Books* (1711),
235. Do you think I have nothing else
to do but to mend and repair after your
ARSE [*i.e.*, behind you, in your rear].

HEAVY-ARSE, a hulking, lazy
fellow; a sluggard.

1580. PALSGRAVE, 436, 2. What up,
HEAVY-ARSE, cannest thou nat aryse?[M.]

TO HANG THE ARSE, to hang
or hold back; to be afraid to
advance.

1633. MASSINGER, *Guardian*, V., v.
Nay, NO HANGING AN ARSE. [M.]

ARSE-UPWARDS in good luck. ·

1600 (*circa*). Timon I., 5 (1842), 20.
This man this daye rose with his ARSE
UPWARDS: To daye a fidler, and at night
a noble.

Also such forms as ARSE-
BOARD, the tail board of a cart—
this is still dialectical; ARSE-
GUT, the rectum; ARSE-LONG;
ARSE-PUSH, a heavy backward
fall; ARSE-ROPES, the intestines.

ARSE-COOLER, *subs.* (low).—A bustle or dress-improver. [From
ARSE, *see* preceding + COOLER;
in reference to the manner in
which this article of feminine
attire extends the dress, and
prevents it clinging to the part
of the body referred to.]
For synonyms, *see* BIRD-CAGE.

ARS-MUSICA, *subs.* (low). — The
podex when used as a noisy vent.
—A play upon words.

ARST (vulgarism).—A mispronunciation of 'asked.'

ARSY-VARSY or ARSY-VERSY, *adv.*
and *adj.* (low).—Topsy-turvy;
topside t'other way; heels over
head; or 'the cart before the
horse.' [From ARSE + Latin
versus 'to turn,' following
model onamatopoetic com-
pounds like 'hirdie-girdie,'
'higgledy-piggledy,' etc.] Once
in polite use, but now confined
to the low and vulgar.

1539. TAVERNER, *Erasm. Prov.*
(1552), 62. Ye set the cart before the
horse . . . cleane contrarily, and ARSY-
VERSY as they say.

1728. BAILEY, *Dictionary.* ARSY-
VERSEY, topsy-turvy, preposterously,
perversely, without order.

Still dialectical. *See* English
Dialect Society's Glossaries,
e.g., *West Somerset Word Book.*

ARTER (vulgarism).—An incorrect
pronunciation of 'after.'

ARTESIAN, *subs.* (Australian).—In
Gippsland, Victoria, a well-
known and popular brew of
beer is manufactured with water
obtained from an artesian well
at Sale—and hence ARTESIAN
as a common nickname for all
Colonial beer.—*See* also CAS-
CADE.

English synonyms for beer
will be found under SWIPES.

ARTFUL DODGER, *subs.* (rhyming and
thieves' slang).—1. A lodger.

1881. *New York Slang Dictionary.*
ARTFUL DODGERS, fellows who dare not
sleep twice in the same place for fear of
arrest.

2. An expert thief. The
ARTFUL DODGER in Dickens'
Oliver Twist' will occur to
mind in this connection.

ARTHUR. KING ARTHUR (old).—A
sailor's game, thus described,
in effect, by Grose. When
near the line, or in a hot latitude, a man who is to represent
King Arthur, is ridiculously
dressed, having a large wig
made out of oakum, or some
old swabs. He is seated on the
side, or over a large vessel of
water, and every person in turn
is ceremoniously introduced to
him, and has to pour a bucket
of water over him, crying out,
'Hail, King Arthur!' If during
the ceremony the person introduced laughs or smiles (to which
his majesty endeavours to excite him by all sorts of ridiculous gesticulations), he changes
places with, and then becomes
King Arthur, till relieved by
some brother tar who has as
little command over his muscles
as himself.—*See* also AMBASSA-
DOR.

ARTICHOKE, *subs.* (American
thieves').—An aged prostitute
of the lowest type. For general
synonyms, *see* BARRACK HACK.

ARTICLE, *subs.* (popular).—1. A
term of contempt for a worthless or insignificant person or
animal—'A pretty ARTICLE he
is.'

1843. DICKENS, *Martin Chuzzlewit*,
ch. xxvi., p. 268. You're a nice ARTICLE,
to turn sulky on first coming home!

2. A woman. In this sense
generally current at the beginning of the century — 'a
prime ARTICLE,' a handsome girl,
or, as the *Lexicon Balatronicum*
[1811] has it, 'a hell of a goer.'

1857. A. TROLLOPE, *Three Clerks*,
ch. xxxi. 'She'd never have done for
you, you know; and she's the very
ARTICLE for such a man as Peppermint.'

See also SAPPY for English
and foreign synonyms.

ARTICLES, *subs.* (thieves').—A suit
of clothes. Formerly current
in England [*circa* 1780-1825];
now surviving principally
amongst American thieves.

ARTICLES OF VIRTUE, *subs. phr.*
(popular). — Virgins. A play
upon the word 'virtue,' in

allusion to the absence of
defloration; and also upon *vertu*
in its special English usage.

ARTIST, *subs.* (American thieves').
—An adroit rogue; a skilful
gamester.—*N.Y.S.D.*

AS . . . . AS THEY MAKE 'EM,
phr. (common).—Generally employed with such adjectives as
'hot,' 'drunk,' 'bad,' etc.; *e.g.*,
AS BAD AS THEY MAKE 'EM.

1889. *Bird o' Freedom*, Aug. 17, p. 3.
On reaching the party it was evident
that one of the Frenchmen was, not to
put too fine a point on it, about AS DRUNK
AS THEY MAKE 'EM. He opened the campaign by asking us to have a drink with
him. Of course, he spoke in French.

ASIA MINOR, *subs.* (popular).—The
Kensington and Bayswater districts in London, on account of
the many Anglo-Indians who,
on their retirement, take refuge
therein. The nickname, however, is a double-barrelled one,
inasmuch as this quarter is also
the headquarters of the Greek
community in the metropolis.
Sobriquets of the kind are not
infrequent. The district between Maida Vale and St. Peter's
Park, Paddington, is called 'the
New Jerusalem,' because of the
large number of Jews who live
there; and the same reason has
given an exactly identical appellation to Brighton, while Cheltenham is nicknamed 'the
Black Hole' from its numerous
Anglo-Indian residents.
A sketch appeared under the
title of 'The Ladies in Parliament' in *Macmillan's Magazine*
[Nov., 1866], wherein Tyburnia
was described as 'the pension'd
Indian's undisturbed retreat.'

1888. *Daily News*, 9 Feb., p. 2, col.
5. The Ladbroke Hall, Notting-hill . .
. . . is in the centre of a district where
Indians in the British metropolis mostly
congregate, a circumstance which has
acquired for this part of London the
nickname of ASIA MINOR, by which it
is sometimes called.

ASK BOGY! *phr.* (old nautical
slang).—An evasive reply.

ASKEW, *subs.* (old cant).—A cuppe.
—Harman [1567].

ASQUIRM.—*See* SQUIRM.

1866. W. D. HOWELLS, *Venetian
Life*, ch. xviii. It is wet and slimy
underfoot, and the innumerable gigantic
eels, writhing everywhere, set the soul
ASQUIRM.

ASS, *subs.* (printers').—A compositor, so nicknamed by pressmen, who, in turn, are called
PIGS (*q.v.*). Ass is sometimes
varied by DONKEY. In French
printing offices compositors are
called *mulets, i.e.*, 'mules.'

ASSAY IT! *intj.* (American thieves').
—Commence! try it! Obvious-
ly from the verb 'to assay,'
and probably introduced by
counterfeit coiners.

ASSIG., *subs.* (old).—An assignation.—*Grose.*

ASTE, *subs.* (old cant).—Nares
quotes this as an old cant term
for money. For modern synonyms, *see* ACTUAL.

1612. *The Passenger of Benvenuto.*
These companions, who in the phisiono-
mie of their forehead, eyes, and nose,
carry the impression and marke of the
pillerie galley, and of the halter, they
call the purse a leafe, and a fleece;
money, cuckoes, and ASTE, and crowns.

ASTRONOMER, *subs.* (old).—A horse
which carries its head high.

ATHANASIAN WENCH, *subs.* (old).
—A forward, abandoned woman,
of obliging disposition—one who
practises prostitution from libid-
inous desire rather than for gain.
Also QUICUNQUE VULT. For
synonyms, *see* BARRACK HACK.

ATLANTIC-RANGER, *subs.* (common).
—A herring. The derivation is
too obvious to need particular-
ization.

1883. *Good Words*, p. 378. Peas-
pudding, and hard-boiled eggs, rubbing
shoulders, as it were, with ATLANTIC
RANGERS (*i.e.*, red herrings).

Among other curious syno-
nyms for this fish may be mentioned BILLINGSGATE PHEA-
SANT; TWO-EYED STEAK; YAR-
MOUTH CAPON; SEA ROVER; and
GLASGOW MAGISTRATE, all of
which *see*. A very common request at Lockhart's coffee-
houses in London is for 'a
door step and a sea rover,' *i.e.*,
a halfpenny slice of bread and
butter and a herring.

ATMOSPHERE, *subs.* (American).—
By the ATMOSPHERE of a thing,
whether book, church, or individual, is meant its tone or
influence. ATMOSPHERE is one
of the most recent introductions into the canting-slang
phraseology of 'Culchaw, don't
you know!' It belongs to the
same category as that which
employs *awfully* and *dreadfully*
for 'very'; or *lovely* for anything pleasing, etc. The number of legitimate words perverted from their legitimate
meanings and used in senses
oftentimes ludicrous is much
larger than most people would
care to admit.

ATOMY, *subs.* (familiar). — 1. A
diminutive, or deformed person.
[From a jocular pronunciation
of 'anatomy.'] As will be seen
from the historical examples
which follow, this expression
has been in the mouths of the
English people for at least 300
years.

1595. SHAKSPEARE, *Romeo and Juliet*,
iv., i., 57.
. . . . I see, Queen Mab hath been with
you.
She is the fairies' midwife; and she
comes
In shape no bigger than an agate-stone
On the forefinger of an alderman,
Drawn with a team of little ATOMIES,
Athwart men's noses as they fall asleep.

1598. SHAKSPEARE, 2 *Henry IV.*,
v., 4, 33. *Host.* Thou ATOMY, thou!
Dot. Come, you thin thing, come,
you rascal.

1822. SCOTT, *The Fortunes of Nigel*,
ch. iii. 'He was an ATOMY when he
came up from the North, and I am sure
he died . . . at twenty stone weight.'

1866. SALA, *Gaslight and Daylight*,
ch. ix. A miserable little ATOMY, more
deformed, more diminutive, more mutilated than any beggar in a bowl.

1884. *Cornhill Magazine*, May, p.
478. 'And ATOMY scarecrow and ATOMY,
what next will you call me? Yet you
want to marry me!

1886. MISS BRADDON, *Mohawks*, ch.
xxii. 'How lovely his young wife looks
to-night; lovely enough to keep that poor
old ATOMY in perpetual torment.'

2. (American thieves').—
Amongst the fraternity ATOMY
has the special meaning of an
empty-headed person, and not
necessarily one deformed or of
small, mean stature.
For synonyms, in first sense,
see SAPPY.

ATTACK, *verb.* (common).—A jocular rendering of the legitimate
word; to commence operations,
not necessarily, however, with
the idea of force, which is always associated with the proper usage. Also as a *subs.*

1812. COMBE (Dr. Syntax), *Pictur.* xvii., 62. The Doctor then . . . pronounced the grace . . . The fierce ATTACK was soon begun.

1849. THACKERAY, *Pendennis*, ch. i. It was a double letter, and the Major commenced perusing the envelope before he ATTACKED the inner epistle.

AT THAT, *adv. phr.* (American and Australian). — An intensive phrase tacked on to the end of an assertion or statement already made. 'He's a slick 'cute rascal, and a pretty demon AT THAT,' *i.e.*, he is a rascal of rascals, an adept at villainy. It is a purely cant phrase, and has achieved a degree of popularity quite out of proportion to its merits—if any. Proctor suggests that the expression is an abbreviation of 'added to that,' but others regard it as the German *dazu*, a theory which is not improbable, in view of the large German element in the States.

1882. PINKERTON'S *Mollie Maguires and Detectives*. A miner from Wadesville, was spoken of as an ancient Mollie—Cooney being actually what the detective assumed to be, and a sharp one AT THAT.

1888. *Forest and Stream*, March 15. Worth a year's subscription, and cheap AT THAT.

1888. *New York Herald*, July 22. Who would have supposed that the self-contained Mr. French, the icily regular T. Henry French, with a disposition as undemonstrative as the Alpine edelweiss, would suffer his temper to go away because of the loss of a hat—aye, and of an old hat AT THAT.

ATTIC or **ATTIC-STOREY**, *subs.* (common).—The head, from its being the highest or crowning member, the body being figuratively regarded as a house. Sometimes UPPER-STOREY. For synonyms, *see* CRUMPET.

1870. ALFORD, in *Life* (1873), 467. Tolerably well all day, but the noise in the ATTIC unremoved

QUEER IN THE ATTIC, etc. Drunk; also weak-minded, or 'cracked.'

ATTIC-SALT, *subs.* (literary).—Well-turned phrases spiced with wit and humour. A reference to the peculiar style and idiom of the Greek language as used by the Athenians, and, says Hotten, 'partly a sly hit at the well-known poverty of many writers.' Whether so, or not, the phrase is one of long standing.

1748. T. DYCHE, *Dictionary* (5 ed.) In *Philology*, we say ATTIC-SALT, for a delicate, poignant kind of wit and humour after the *Athenian* manner, who were particular in this way.

1779. SHERIDAN, *The Critic*, Act i., Sc. 2. I have the plot from the author, and only add — characters strongly drawn—highly coloured—hand of a master—fund of genuine humour—mine of invention — neat dialogue — ATTIC-SALT.

1848. JAS. HANNAY, *King Dobbs*, ch. ix., p. 129 (1856). 'If you joke in that style, we'll lose the day,' said Dobbs. who had some quiet homely superstitions. 'What ? is it unlucky to spill ATTIC-SALT, as well as the ordinary kind ?'

ATTLEBOROUGH, *subs.* (American).—Sham jewelry; used in precisely the same manner as 'Brummagem,' and as widely applied to men and things. It has passed from the classics of thiefdom into general use, and is applied to anything of a sham, pinchbeck, insincere, or doubtful character. Attleborough is a town celebrated for its manufacture of trashy jewelry.

ATTORNEY, *subs.* (popular). — A drumstick of goose, or turkey, grilled and devilled. [From DEVIL = a lawyer who does routine work for another = attorney.]

1828. G. GRIFFIN, *Collegians*, ch. xiii. 'I love a plain beef steak before a grilled ATTORNEY.'

(Thieves').—A shrewd, and often not over honest or scrupulous man who, possessing some knowledge of the law, acts in the capacity of legal adviser to those of the 'crooked craft' unfortunate enough to need assistance. Such men are generally solicitors and others whose names have been struck off the rolls, as also, occasionally, solicitors' clerks who have otherwise failed in life. Their practices are shady, but their fees are low.

ATTORNEY-GENERAL'S DEVIL. — *See* DEVIL.

AUCTIONEER. TO TIP OR GIVE THE AUCTIONEER. — A phrase borrowed from the sale room, and signifying 'to knock a man down.'

1863. G. A. SALA, *Breakfast in Bed*, Essay I., p. 4 (1864). And who, in return for a craven blow, can DELIVER THE AUCTIONEER well over the face and eyes.

AUDIT - ALE, *subs.* (Cambridge Univ.).—A special brew of ale, peculiar to Trinity College, made in the first instance for draught on audit days, whence its name.

1837. BARHAM, *Ingoldsby Legends* (*Lay of S. Dunstan*).
To be sure the best beer
Of all did not appear,
For I've said 'twas in June, and so late in the year
The 'Trinity AUDIT ALE' is not come-at-able,
As I've found to my great grief when dining at that table.

1876. TREVELYAN, *Life of Macaulay* (1884), ch. iv., p. 127. A glass of the AUDIT ALE, which reminded him that he was still a fellow of Trinity.

AUDLEY.—*See* JOHN AUDLEY.

AUFE.—*See* OAF.

AUGER, *subs.* (American thieves').—A person given to prosiness is so called; a bore.

AUGHT, *subs.* (vulgarism).—A common illiteracy for 'naught' when naming the cipher—'o'.

AULD HORNIE, *subs.* (common).—One of the numerous nicknames given to the devil. Others are, old nick; old scratch; old Harry; skipper; old gentleman; deuce; dickens; ruffian, etc.—*See* SKIPPER for synonyms.

AULD REEKIE (popular).—A sobriquet for the old town of Edinburgh. It means 'old smoky.' Of late years it has been applied to the whole city.

1806. MISS PITMAN, in C. K. Sharpe's *Correspondence* (1888), i., 271. We are within two hours-and-a-half of AULD REEKY.

1816. SCOTT, *Antiquary*, ch. vi. 'And what news do you bring us from Edinburgh, Montkbarns?' said Sir Arthur; 'how wags the world in AULD REEKIE?'

1889. *Colonies and India*, July 24, p. 10, col. 1. The Australasian Colony in AULD REEKIE is prospering apace, and it may soon be necessary to plant some gum trees along Princes Street to meet the growing demands of the population.

AULY-AULY, *subs.* (Win. Coll.).—A game formerly played in 'Grass Court' on Saturday afternoons after chapel. It consisted in throwing an india-rubber ball at one another, and everybody was obliged to go down and join in it. 'Haul ye, call ye,' is the supposed derivation; but, as the game, though in vogue in 1830, was not played as late as 1845, there is some difficulty in defining it in detail.

AUNT, *subs.* (old).—Applied, especially during the Elizabethan period, to either a procuress, a prostitute, or a concubine. It survived till the commencement of the present century and then gradually died out. For synonyms, *see* MOTHER.

1608. MIDDLETON, *Trick to Catch the Old One*, II., i. Was it not then better bestowed upon his uncle than upon one of his AUNTS ?—I need not say bawd, for everyone knows what AUNT stands for in the last translation.

1623. SHAKSPEAR, *Winter's Tale*, iv., 3.
Summer songs for me and my aunts,
While we lie tumbling in the hay.

TO GO AND SEE ONE'S AUNT (common).—To go to the W.C. —*See* MRS. JONES.

AUNT SALLY, *subs.* (familiar).—A well-known game, common to race-courses and fairs, which consists in throwing short staves at a wooden head mounted on a stick, placed upright in the ground, and forming a kind of target. In the mouth of the image is placed a clay pipe, and the object of the player, who stands at say twenty or thirty yards distance, is to demolish this. The amusement is not unlike the more popular 'three shies a penny.' The origin of AUNT SALLY is wrapped in mystery; nor is it known whether she is any relation to the black lady whose effigy some few years since was frequently to be met with suspended outside the shops of rag and 'marine store' dealers. A writer in *Notes and Queries* [2 S., x., 117] affirms that AUNT SALLY is the heroine of a popular negro melody, in which the old lady meets with several ludicrous adventures, but evidence in support of this theory is at present wanting.

1866. G. A. SALA, *Gaslight and Daylight*, ch. i., p. 11. They will go to Epsom by the rail, and create disturbances on the course, and among the 'sticks' and AUNT SALLIES.

1883. *Punch*, June 2, p. 264, col. 1. The average number of 'chucks' at cocoa-nuts before achieving success is six, and of 'shies' at AUNT SALLY, four.

AU RESERVOIR! *intj. phr.* (common). —*Au revoir.* A mere play upon sounds. Common in America, where it originated, and now often heard in England.

AUSTRALIAN FLAG, *subs.* (Anglo-Australian). — The tail of a shirt, when, after exertion, it rucks up in folds between the trousers and the waistcoat—an 'up-country' phrase.—*See* CORNSTALK.

AUSTRALIAN GRIP, *subs.* (Australian). —A hearty shake of the hands.

AUTEM, AUTUM, AUTOM, *subs.* (old cant).—A church. The term first appears in Harman's *Caveat* [1573]; again in Rowland's *Martin Mark-all* [1610]; in Head's *English Rogue* [1665]; in Cole's *English Dictionary* [1724]; in Grose's *Dictionary of the Vulgar Tongue* [1785], and in Duncombe's *Sinks of London Laid Open* [1848]. —*See* also AUTEM MORT.

Adj.—Married. So quoted in Cole's *English Dictionary*, whence AUTEM MORT, etc.

AUTEM-BAWLER, *subs.* (old cant).—A parson. [From AUTEM (*q.v.*), a church + BAWLER, a speaker.] For modern English and foreign synonyms, *see* GOSPEL SHARK. Other ancient expressions for a clergyman are AUTEM-JET, AUTEM-CACKLER, and AUTEM-PRICKER; the last two named, however, apply, as a rule, only to Dissenters.

AUTEM-CACKLER, *subs.* (old cant).—A Dissenter; sometimes specially applied to Dissenting ministers.

1876. HINDLEY, *Life and Adventures of a Cheap Jack*, p. 260. 'On one occasion a Jew was selling cocoa-nut, when the AUTEM-CACKLER, *i.e.*, Dissenting minister, came and wanted to impart to the Israelite the sin he committed in carrying on his vocation on such a day [Sunday]. The Jew half listened to what the other said, but kept on calling out "Cocoa-nut a half-penny a slice, a very nice cocoa-nut—cocoa-nut!"'

2. A married woman.—*See* AUTEM. In this sense it is used in a canting song in the *New York Slang Dictionary*, first published in 1881, and which, as a specimen of the verse affected by the light-fingered fraternity, it may not be out of place to give entire. It should be read in connection with the remarks on CANTING SONGS (*q.v.*).

'A HUNDRED STRETCHES (1) HENCE.'

'Oh! where will be the culls of the bing (2)
A hundred stretches hence?
The bene morts (3), who sweetly sing,
A hundred stretches hence?
The AUTUMN-CACKLERS, autumn-coves (4),
The jolly blade who wildly roves;
And where the buffer (5), bruiser (6), blowen (7),
And all the cops (8) and beaks (9) so knowin'
A hundred stretches hence?
'And where the swag (10), so bleakly (11) pinched (12),
A hundred stretches hence?
The thimbles (13), slang (14), and danglers (15) filched,
A hundred stretches hence?
The chips (16), the fawneys (17), chatty-feeders (18),
The bugs (19), the boungs (20), and well-filled readers (21);
And where the fence (22) and snoozing-ken (23),
With all the prigs (24) and lushing men (25),
A hundred stretches hence?
'Played out they lay, it will be said
A hundred stretches hence;
With shovels they were put to bed (26)
A hundred stretches since!
Some rubbed to wit had napped a winder (27),
And some were scragged (28) and took a blinder (29),
Planted the swag and lost to sight,
We'll bid them, one and all, good-night,
A hundred stretches hence?

1, *Stretch*, a year; 2, *culls of the bing* innkeepers, publicans; 3, *bene morts*, pretty girls or women; 4, *autumn cove*, married men; 5, *buffer*, smuggler, rogue, or cheat; 6, *bruiser*, prostitute's bully or prize-fighter; 7, *blowen*, a showy prostitute; 8, *cop*, policeman; 9, *beak*, a magistrate; 10, *swag*, plunder, proceeds of robbery; 11, *bleakly*, cleverly, also handsome; 12, *pinched*, stolen; 13, *thimble*, a watch; 14, *slang*, a watch chain; 15, *danglers*, a bunch of seals; 16, *chips*, money; 17, *fawney*, a ring; 18, *chatty-feeder*, a spoon; 19, *bug*, a breast pin; 20, *boung*, a purse; 21, *reader*, a pocket-book; 22, *fence*, a receiver of stolen goods; 23, *snoozing-ken*, a brothel; 24, *prig*, a thief; 25, *lushing-men*, drinking-men; 26, *put to bed with a shovel*, buried; 27, *to nap a winder—to nap*, to cheat, *winder*, a life sentence; 28, *scragged*, hanged; 29, *to take a blinder*, to drown oneself.

AUTEM CACKLE TUB, *subs.* (old cant). —The meeting house of Dissenters of every description. Also a pulpit.

AUTEM-COVE, *subs.* (old cant).—A married man. [From AUTEM (*q.v.*), a church + COVE, a man.]

AUTEM-DIPPERS or **AUTEM-DIVERS**, *subs.* (old cant).—1. Formerly a nickname for Baptists, from their practice of immersing adult converts, as distinguished from infant sprinkling.

2. Pickpockets who practised in churches were called AUTEM-DIVERS; also churchwardens and overseers of the poor who defrauded, deceived, and imposed upon the parish.

AUTEM-GOGLERS, *subs.* (old cant).—Pretended French prophets—*Grose.* Conjurors, fortune-tellers—*Duncombe.*

AUTEM-JET, *subs.* (old cant).—A parson. [From AUTEM, a church + JET, black, in allusion to the black garments usually worn by 'the cloth.'] For some curious synonyms, see DEVIL-DODGER.

AUTEM, or **AUTEM-MORT**, *subs.* (old cant).—A married woman, *i.e.*, one wedded in a church. [From AUTEM, a church + MORT, or MOT, a woman.] The term belongs to the oldest cant, and is the subject of a long description in Harman's *Caveat.* (See quotation.) The old fraternity of vagabonds (for a full description of which, see CADGERS—ANCIENT AND MODERN) was divided into well marked classes, as also were the women who accompanied them in their peregrinations. The men were not strict monogamists, either as regards lawful companions or those of another grade—

1567. HARMAN, *Caveat* (1814), p. 49. These AUTEM MORTES be maried wemen, as there be but a fewe: For Autem in their language is a church, so

shee is a wyfe maried at the church, and they be as chaste as a cowe I have, that goeth to bull eury moone, with what bull she careth not. These walke most times from their husbands companye a moneth and more to gether, being asociate with another as honest as her selfe. These wyll pylfar clothes of hedges; some of them go with children of ten or xii years of age; yf tyme and place serue for their purpose, they will send them into some house, at the window, to steale and robbe, which they call in their language, Milling of the ken; and wil go with wallets on their shoulders, and slates at their backes. There is one of these AUTEM MORTES, she is now a widow, of fyfty yeres old; her name is Alice Milson: she goeth about with a couple of great boyes, the youngest of them is fast Upon xx yeares of age. . . .

1592. GREENE, *Quip*, in works IX., 283. The pedler as bad or rather worse, walketh the country with his docksey at the least, if he have not two, his *mortes dels*, and AUTEM MORTIS.

1610. ROWLANDS, *Martin Mark-all*, p. 7 (H. Club's Reprint, 1874). Here another [complains] that they could not quietly take their rest in the night, nor keepe his AUTEM, or doxie sole vnto himselfe.

1884. H. AINSWORTH, *Rookwood*, bk. III., ch. v. Morts, AUTEM-MORTS, walking morts, dells, doxies with all the shades and grades of the canting crew, were assembled.

Toward the end of the eighteenth century AUTEM-MORT was used as synonymous with a female beggar alone; then another meaning crept into the word—a prostitute.—*See* CADGER.

AUTEM-PRICKEAR.—The same as AUTEM-CACKLER (*q.v.*).

AUTEM-QUAVER, *subs.* (old cant).—A Quaker. [From AUTEM, a church + QUAVER, referring to the shaking, peculiar to some of the religious exercises of the Society of Friends.]

AUTEM - QUAVER - TUB, *subs.* (old

6

cant). — A Quaker's meeting-house; also a desk therein.

AUTHOR-BAITING, *subs.* (theatrical).—Calling the author of an unsuccessful play before the curtain, and then, wanting all sense of decency and feeling, to overwhelm him with every imaginable source of annoyance—yelling, hooting, bellowing, etc.

AVAST! *intj.* (nautical).—Hold on! Stop! Shut up! Stow it! etc., etc. No word perhaps has more suggested derivations than AVAST! Webster writes it down as from the Italian *basta*, enough; literally, it suffices, from *bastare*, to suffice. He does not, however, seem to have been altogether certain, for he queries whether it is not a worn-down form of the Dutch *houd vast, hou' vast*, hold fast! a derivation which Dr. Murray endorses as 'probable' in his *New Dictionary of the English Language*. Bearing in mind that AVAST, although used colloquially is first and foremost a sailor's term, this derivation does not seem far-fetched; for, the Dutch having been themselves one of the great maritime nations of the past, it is not unlikely that the term should have come from them, especially when it is borne in mind that a large proportion of nautical terms are so derived.

Such are boom; sprit; reef; schooner; skate; sloop; stiver; taffrail; yacht (*jaghten*, ' to chase '), etc.

On the other hand, as regards the Italian *basta*, it is only fair to point out that French work-

men use *basta*, in the sense of enough! no more! The same term occurs also in the Spanish.

Hotten connects it with the old cant BYNGE A WASTE, get out of the way! go hence! but though one cannot speak with certainty, this is not, on the face of it, apparent. There seems no discoverable connection between the two; moreover, the comparative and historical method of dealing with slang shows us that AVAST in its present form and sense can be traced as far back as 1681, within about a hundred years of the publication of Harman's *Caveat* where *bynge a waste* first occurs. The probability therefore is that the two terms are distinct, and that AVAST is derived from a different source to BYNGE A WASTE (*q.v.*) which, as Leland points out, has probably its origin in the Romany.

1681. OTWAY, *Soldiers' Fortune*, iv., i. Hoa up, hoa up; so AVAST there, sir.

1748. SMOLLETT, *Rod. Random*, ch. xli. 'AVAST there, friend: none of your tricks upon travellers.'

1751. SMOLLETT, *Peregrine Pickle*, ch. xcvii. 'And upon this scrap of paper —no, AVAST—that's my discharge from the parish.'

1884. W. C. RUSSELL, *Jack's Courtship*, ch., xiv. But AVAST now! we've had enough of philosophising.

AVOIRDUPOIS-LAY, *subs.* (old thieves' cant).—This is given by Grose as meaning the theft of brass weights off shop counters.

AVUNCULAR-RELATION, *subs.* (common.—A pawnbroker—a facetious variant of UNCLE (*q.v.*), another name for the same individual.

AWAKE, *adv.* (old, and modern American thieves').—On the alert; vigilant. *Cf.*, WIDE-AWAKE, a certain kind of hat, so called, by-the-bye, from its never having a 'nap.' For synonyms, see FLY.

1821. MONCRIEFF, *Tom and Jerry* (Dicks' ed., 1889), p. 6. *Prime.* From the cut of the gentleman's clothes, I presume he's lately come from the Esquimaux Islands.

Tom. Ha! ha! very good, Primefit; I say, Jerry—you see he's down upon you.

Jerry. Yes, he's up, *he's* AWAKE, *he's fly*—Ha! ha!

1838. DICKENS, *Nich. Nickleby*, ch. xxxix., p. 314. 'If you hear the waiter coming, sir, shove it in your pocket and look out of the window, d'ye hear?' 'I'm AWAKE, father,' replied the dutiful Wackford.

AWFUL, *subs.* (common).—A sensational newspaper, tale, or narration; *e.g.*, a penny AWFUL. Sometimes called a DREADFUL; other names for this kind of mental *pabulum* are BLOOD AND THUNDER TALES, and GUTTER LITERATURE.

Adj.—Generally colloquial as an intensitive, conveying no more *awe-full* meaning than 'very,' 'exceedingly,' etc. Strange as it may appear this familiar usage is very old, and was frequently heard north of the Tweed long prior to its use by Southrons. An intermediate stage was its appearance across the Atlantic, whence its re-introduction into the Mother Country may be traced.

1834. LAMB, *Gent. Giantess*, Misc. Wks. (1871), 363. She is indeed, as the Americans would express it, something AWFUL.

b. 1789, *d.* 1880. PLANCHÉ, *Good Woman in the Wood.* 'A poor widow and her orphan chicks Left without fixtures, in an AWFUL fix.'

1888. HAWLEY SMART, *At Fault*, III., v., 82. 'I'm AWFUL glad you two have made acquaintance.'

AWFULLY, the adverbial form, is subjected to the same ill-treatment, as the following examples will show.

1877. *Punch's Pocket Book for 1878*, p. 165. You *should* have come with us. It's too AWFULLY nice, as I told you I thought it would be.

1878. M. E. BRADDON, *Cloven Foot*, ch. vii. 'AWFULLY,' was Miss Clare's chief laudatory adjective [*sic*]; her superlative form of praise was 'quite too AWFULLY,' and when enthusiasm carried her beyond herself she called things 'nice.' 'Quite too AWFULLY nice,' was her maximum of rapture.

1889. *Illustrated Bits*, July 13. AN OLD PROVERB TWISTED. 'The ham of the sandwich was AWFULLY tough',
He said, for, oh, it was dry,
As at first he tried to bite into the stuff,
All in vain, how hard he would try.
But at last, when fairly bit into the thing,
He found that it was all right,
And he said, as happy as any king,
'The bark was worse than the bite.'

French equivalents are, *bigrement; jusqu'à la troisième capucine* ; and *pommé.*

AWKWARD-SQUAD, *subs.* (military and naval). — Recruits when commencing to learn their drill.

AX, AXE, *verb.* (vulgar).—To ask. Though now looked upon as a vulgarism, AX is still largely dialectical, and is really the most correct form of the word. 'Ask' is the northern gloss which has gradually supplanted AX. The latter, down to nearly 1600, says Dr. Murray, was the regular literary form.

c. 1380. CHAUCER, *Tale of Melibeus.* Seint Jame eck saith: If eny fellow have neede of sapiens, AXE it of God.

1474. CAXTON, *Game of the Chesse*, bk. III., ch. viii. He must nedes begge and AXE his breed.

1758. A. MURPHY, *The Upholsterer*, Act i. An old crazy fool—AXING your pardon, ma'am, for calling your father so.

1763. FOOTE, *Mayor of Garratt*, Act ii., Sc. 2. *Mrs. Sneak.* Where is the puppy? *Sneak.* Yes, yes, she is AXING for me.

1861. H. KINGSLEY, *Ravenshoe*, ch. vi. 'I AXED her would she like to live in the great house, and she said no.'

1888. *Echo*, Jan. 25, p. 2, col. 3. To AXE, considered but a vulgarism, for to ask, is good Saxon.

AXE. AN AXE TO GRIND, *phr.* (American). — A much - used phrase of political origin. Men are said to have AXES TO GRIND when suspected of selfish or interested motives. From politics the expression has passed into use among all classes of society. *The Chicago Daily Inter-Ocean* (Feb. 1888) spoke of certain politicians as 'men with AXES TO GRIND.' What

we believe is right is more often so because it GRINDS OUR AXE than otherwise.

1871. (From Hoppe's *Conversations Lexicon*). Miner. 'Who'll turn the grindstones?' When I see a merchant over-polite to his customers, begging them to taste a little brandy, and throwing half his goods on the counter, thinks I, that man has an AXE TO GRIND.

1888. *Detroit Free Press*, Sept. 22, William Black, the novelist, says the only AX a novelist has TO GRIND is the climax.

AXE-MY-EYE! *subs.* (cheap jacks').—One who is up to every trick; a cute fellow.

1876. C. HINDLEY, *Life and Adventures of a Cheap Jack*, p. 232.
Stow your gab and gauffery,
To every fakement I'm a fly;
I never takes no fluffery,
For I'm a regular AXE-MY-EYE.

AYRSHIRES, *subs.* (Stock Exchange).—Glasgow and South-Western Railway Stock.

 NOT TO KNOW B FROM A BATTLEDORE, *phr.* (old). — To be entirely illiterate; very ignorant. This old cant phrase has several variants, all of them alliterative in character. For example, NOT TO KNOW B FROM A BULL'S-FOOT—FROM A BROOMSTICK—CHALK FROM CHEESE, etc. Each and all indicate inability to distinguish between familiar objects that differ. Battledore is an old name for the hornbook from which children used to learn the alphabet.

1401. *Pol. Poems*, II., 57. I know not an A from the wynd-mylne, ne a B FROM A BOLE FOOT. [M.]

1609. DEKKER, *Guls-Hornebooke*, 3. You shall not neede to buy bookes; no, scorne to DISTINGUISH A B FROM A BATTLEDORE; onely looke that your eares be long enough to reach our rudiments, and you are made for ever.

1846. BRACKENRIDGE, *Modern Chivalry*, 43. There were members who SCARCELY KNEW B FROM A BULL'S-FOOT. [M.]

B (fenian).—Mr. H. J. Byron, the playwright, in his annotated copy of the *Slang Dictionary*, mentions this as the title of a captain in the 'army of the Irish Republican Brotherhood.'

B's.—See B FLAT.

BABE, *subs.* (parliamentary).—The last elected member of the House of Commons. The oldest representative of the chamber is called the FATHER OF THE HOUSE (*q.v.*).

(American). — The youngest member of a class at the United States Military College at West Point. A term *sans* wit, *sans* point, *sans* almost everything.

BABE IN THE WOOD, *subs. phr.* (old).—1. A victim of the law's solicitude; in other words, a culprit sentenced to the stocks or the pillory. Obsolete.

2. Dice are also called BABES IN THE WOOD.

BABES, *subs.* (auctioneers').—A set of auction thieves, who attend sales for the express purpose of blackmail. Their *modus operandi* is as follows. In consideration of a small bribe of money or beer, or both, they

the earlier and more legitimate meaning to support, maintain, or strengthen. Possibly in the sense of to wager or support by betting, BACK can hardly nowadays be classed as slang; there seems too, to be long and constant usage to support its claim as a regular dictionary word.

(Uppingham School). — At football, to be ready for a chance.

TO PUT OR SET UP ONE'S BACK, *phr.* (familiar).—To rouse oneself to antipathy; to get angry; to resist. The figure presented is that of a cat, which, when irritated, arches or sets up its back. Also used negatively as an exhortation to keep one's temper. DON'T GET YOUR BACK UP! For synonymous phrases, *see* HOLD YOUR HAIR ON !

1726. VANBRUGH AND CIBBER, *Provoked Husband*, V., iii., 112. O Lud! HOW HER BACK WILL BE UP then when she meets me.

1771. SMOLLETT, *Humphry Clinker*, ch. 66. My uncle's BACK WAS UP in a moment; and he desired him to explain his pretensions.

1855. THACKERAY, *Newcomes*, ch. xvi. 'I know she is flighty, and that; and Brian's BACK IS UP a little. But he ain't a bad fellow; and I wish I could see you and his wife better friends.'

1883. GREENWOOD, *Grandmother Cooper*, in *Odd People in Odd Places*, p 2. 'You don't know what you're sayin'; therefore you don't mean no harm. If so be you think what you just now said, keep it to yourself, don't say it to me. It SETS MY BACK UP, and when my back's set up I'm sometimes orkard.'

TO RIDE ON ONE'S BACK, *phr.* (old).—To deceive successfully.

BACK AND BELLY, *phr.* (vulgar).—1. Back and before; all over.

2. TO KEEP ONE BACK AND

BELLY, *phr.* (old).—To feed and clothe. *Cf.*, BELLY-TIMBER and BACK-TIMBER.

BACK-BREAKER, *subs.* (common).—One who sets, or that which is, an example of more than ordinary human powers of endurance; *e.g.*, in pedestrianism or racing a man or horse whose pace is considerably over the average. In sporting phraseology he or it is called a SCORCHER (*q.v.*) and the pace of such is also eloquently called 'killing.' BACK-BREAKING is therefore synonymous with excessive exertion or effort of all kinds.

BACK-CAP. TO GIVE A BACK-CAP, *phr.* (American).—To expose; to reveal what one knows of another, in a detrimental sense.

1883. MARK TWAIN, *Life on the Mississippi*, p. 462. [A pretended converted thief is made to say]:—i told him all about my being in prison and about you, and how i had almost done giving up looking for work and how the Lord got me the job when i asked him . . . . and then i felt better than ever i had done in my life, for i had given Mr. Brown a fair start with me and now i didn't fear no one GIVING ME A BACK-CAP and running me off the job.

BACK-CHEAT, *subs.* (old cant).—A cloak. Also called a WRAP-RASCAL (*q.v.*).

BACK-DOOR. A GENTLEMAN OF THE BACK-DOOR, *subs. phr.* (common).—A sodomist; formerly a BACKGAMMON PLAYER. The vice itself is called BACK-DOOR WORK. For synonyms, *see* USHER.

BACKDOOR-TROT, *subs.* (provincial).—Diarrhœa. The allusion is obvious. A more common term is JERRY-GO-NIMBLE (*q.v.*).

agree not to oppose the bidding of the larger dealers, who thus dishonestly keep down the price of lots. The practice is generally worked in connection with KNOCK-OUTS (*q.v.*).

(American).—A set of Baltimore rowdies are so-called; at various times they have also received the names of BLOOD TUBS and PLUG-UGLIES (*q.v.*).

BABOO-ENGLISH, *subs.* (Anglo-Indian).—A species of 'ENGLISH AS SHE IS WROTE' (*q.v.*). Its main peculiarity is its grandiloquence, a feature born of an attempt to adapt Western speech to Eastern imagery and hyperbole.

BABY-HERDER, *subs.* (American).—A nurse; a simile drawn from life on the plains, and worked out with true cowboy humour.

BABYLONITISH, *subs.* (Winchester College).—A dressing gown. An abbreviated form of 'Babylonitish garment.'

BABY-PAP, *subs.* (thieves').—A cap; part of the so-called RHYMING SLANG (*q.v.*).

BACCA.—*See* BACCY.

BACCA-PIPES, *subs.* (common).—Whiskers when curled in ringlets, a now obsolete fashion.—*See* MUTTON-CHOPS.

BACCARE! BACKARE! *intj.* (old cant).—Go back! [a humorous form of BACK + a simulated Latin termination]. In use from about 1553-1660.

1592. LYLY, *Midas*, V., 2. The masculine gender is more worthy than the feminine. Therefore, Licio. BACKARE.

1598. SHAKSPEARE, *Taming of the Shrew*, ii.:
Saving your tale, Petruchio, I pray
Let us, that are poor petitioners, speak too;
BACCARE! you are marvellous forward. [N.]

BACCY, also BACCA, *subs.* (common).—A corrupted form of 'tobacco.' Apparently of quite recent introduction. An equivalent term in French is *perlot*, from *perle*.

1833. MARRYAT, *Peter Simple*, ch. ii. 'You must larn to chaw BACCY.'

1861. JAS. CONWAY, *Forays among Salmon and Deer*, p. 228. I lay on an Affghan goat-rug spread over fresh heather, with a pipe filled with good BACCY in my mouth.

BACH or BATCH, *verb.* (American).—To live as a bachelor.

BACHELOR'S BABY, *subs.* (old).—An illegitimate child. For synonyms, *see* BYE-BLOW.

BACHELOR'S-FARE, *subs.* (familiar).—Bread and cheese and kisses—a humorous allusion to the real or alleged 'short commons,' generally assumed to be meted out to a man who is unattached. Like many other proverbial sayings there is more sound than truth in it.

1738. SWIFT, *Polite Conversation*, conv. i. *Lady Ans.* Colonel, some ladies of your acquaintance have promised to breakfast with you, and I am to wait on them; what will you give us? *Col.* Why, faith, madam, BACHELOR'S-FARE, bread and cheese and kisses.

BACK, *verb.* (popular).—To bet or wager; to support by means of money, kind, or influence, on the turf or elsewhere. From

BACK DOWN, *verb.* (common).—To yield; to retreat from a position; to abandon a line of argument; to eat one's words. Originally an American turn of expression.— *See* BACK TRACK and BACK OUT.

Subs. — Usually a SQUARE BACK DOWN; a severe rebuff; sometimes, utter collapse.

BACKED, *ppl. adj.* (old).—Dead—a figurative use of to 'put on one's back,' *i.e.*, to place *hors de combat*.

BACK-END, *subs.* (racing).—The last two months of the racing season. More technical than slang.

1820. *Blackw. Mag.*, Oct., p. 3. When you did me the honour to stop a day or two at last BACK-END.

1888. HAWLEY SMART, *Hard Lines*, ch. xxix. 'Most of what I got over that steeplechase I dropped at the BACK-END over the October handicaps.'

Adj.—The meaning, *mutatis mutandis*, is the same as BACK-END.

1888. *Daily Telegraph*, April 30, p. 3, col. 6. And neither [horse] could beat Palermo on BACK-END form.

BACK-GAMMON PLAYER.—*See* BACK-DOOR.

BACKHAND, *verb.* (common).—To detain the decanter when it is passed round, and thus to drink more than one's share; a more recent phrase is 'not drinking fair.' — *See*, however, BACK-HANDER.

1857. G. A. LAWRENCE, *Guy Livingstone*, ch. viii. 'Livingstone, if you begin BACKHANDING already, you'll never be able to hold that great raking chestnut I saw your groom leading this evening.'

BACK-HANDED TURN (Stock Exchange).—An unprofitable bargain.

BACKHANDER, *subs.* (common).—1. A drink out of turn; also detention of wine at table so as to get an extra share.

1855. THACKERAY, *Newcomes*, ch. xliii. 'Thank you, Mr. Binnie, I *will* take a BACKHANDER, as Clive don't seem to drink.'

1878. *Saturday Review*, p. 798. Long experience has shown us that to get small advantages over us gives the Scotch so much pleasure, that we should not think of grudging them the mild satisfaction, just as a kindly host affects not to notice a valued guest, who, he observes, always helps himself to an innocent BACKHANDER.

2. A blow on the face with the back of the hand.

1836. MARRYAT, *Midshipman Easy*, p. 11. 'Go away, Sarah,' said Johnny, with a BACKHANDER.

1862. FARRAR, *St. Winifred's*, ch. xxxiii. He administered a BACKHANDER to Elgood, as he spoke, and the next minute Charlie, roused beyond all bearing, had knocked him down.

1870. MANSFIELD, *School-Life at Winchester College*. The doctor comes suddenly round a corner, and finds Tibbs [a fag] mopping the rosy fluid from his nose with a rueful countenance, having just received a sharp BACKHANDER from one of his lords and masters.

3. Hence, figuratively, a rebuke; a 'setting down.'

1856. WHYTE MELVILLE, *Kate Coventry*, ch. i. I knew this was what John calls a BACK HANDER at me, but I can be *so* good-natured when I have anything to gain, therefore I only said——

BACKING AND FILLING, *adj.* (colloquial).—A BACKING AND FILLING policy is one that is shifty; irresolute; trifling. A figurative usage derived from BACKING AND FILLING a vessel, *i.e.*, keeping it in the middle of the stream of a narrow river by advancing first to one shore, and then backing to the other, allowing the stream to make the way, the wind blowing in an opposite direction to the stream.

BACKING-ON.—*See* TURNING-ON.

BACKINGS UP, *subs.* (Winchester College). — The unconsumed ends of half-burned fagots. They are collected and sometimes made into surreptitious fires by 'Juniors.'

BACK JUMP, *subs.* (thieves'). — A back window.—*See* JUMP.

BACKMARKED. TO BE BACKMARKED, *verb.* (pedestrian). — In handicapping to receive less start from 'scratch' than previously given—even to being put back to 'scratch.'

BACK OUT, *verb.* (colloquial).—To retreat cautiously and tacitly; from stable phraseology; *e.g.*, the BACKING OUT of a horse. Very much the same as to BACK DOWN (*q.v.*).

1817. SCOTT, *Rob Roy*, ch. viii. Jobson, however, was determined that Morris should not BACK OUT of the scrape so easily.

1855. A. TROLLOPE, *The Warden*, ch. xii. How was he to BACK OUT of a matter in which his name was already so publicly concerned?

1870. L. OLIPHANT, *Piccadilly*, pt. IV., p. 152. I am sure that he had done his best to spread the report of my marriage with his sister for fear of my BACKING OUT.

BACK SCUTTLE, *verb.* (thieves').—The same as BACK-SLANG (*q.v.*).

BACK-SEAM. TO BE DOWN ON ONE'S BACK-SEAM, *phr.* (tailors'). —To be down on one's luck; to be unfortunate.

BACK SEAT. TO TAKE A BACK SEAT, *phr.* (American).—Figuratively, to retire into obscurity; it also sometimes implies a silent confession of failure; an inability to accomplish what one has attempted. The colloquialism has gained a world-wide currency; it received an immense 'send off,' as the Americans say, from Andrew Johnson's famous saying in 1868, that in the work of Reconstruction traitors should TAKE BACK SEATS.

1885. *Society*, Feb. 7, p. 9. This great batting achievement must, however, TAKE A BACK SEAT when compared with the enormous total recently scored by Shaw's Eleven in Australia, against a powerful Colonial team.

1888. *Daily News*, Feb. 24, p. 5, col. 2. Any form of art which is barred by its very nature from perfection must TAKE what the Americans call A BACK SEAT.

1888. *Texas Siftings*, p. 426. Who will say the Britishers are not a forbearing and forgiving race, and the inhabitants of Stratford-on-Avon don't by any means TAKE A BACK SEAT in that line? Ignatius Donnelly actually visited the birthplace of Shakespeare, and wasn't lynched! Far from it, he was hospitably received and entertained.

BACK-SLUM, *subs.* (colloquial).—The lowest and most disreputable quarters of a town or city; generally applied to the dens and rookeries of the criminal and 'outcast' classes.

1821. W. T. MONCRIEFF'S *Tom and Jerry*, Act ii., Scene 5. *Log.* Well, don't grumble—every one must pay for his learning—and you wouldn't bilk the schoolmaster, would you? But, come, I'm getting merry; so if you wish for a bit of good truth, come with me, and let's have a dive among the cadgers in the BACK SLUMS, in the Holy Land. *Jerry.* BACK SLUMS—Holy Land!—I'm at fault again. *Log.* Why, among the beggars in Dyot Street, St. Giles's. *Tom.* Beggars! ah, we shall be very good figures for the part.
(*Turns out his pockets.*)

1876. M. E. BRADDON, *Joshua Haggard's Daughter*, ch. xx. Not in fetid alleys and festering London BACK-SLUMS only is man's fight with difficulty a bitter and crushing battle.

(Australian thieves'.)—A back room or entrance.

BACKSTAIRCASE, *subs.* (common). —A bustle, or 'dress improver.' For synonyms, *see* BIRDCAGE.

BACKSTAIR INFLUENCE, *subs.* (familiar). — Underhand dealing or persuasion; a stab in the dark; intrigue. [From the use of the back or private stairs of a palace, etc., for other than state visitors; hence, a secret mode of approach; and, attributively, applied to indirect, oblique, and unfair intrigue.]

1697. VANBRUGH, *Relapse*, II. He is like a BACKSTAIR minister at Court, who, while the reputed favourites are sauntering in the bed-chamber, is ruling the roast in the closet.

1877. GRENVILLE MURRAY, *Round about France*, p. 77. These men are the most indefatigable retailers of BACK-STAIRS small talk to the little fry of journalism.

BACK-STALL, *subs.* (thieves').—An accomplice who 'covers' the actual thief; especially used in relation to garrote-robberies, in which the BACK-STALL has two functions, first to screen his companion, and then, if necessary, to 'make off' with the booty.

BACK TALK. NO BACK TALK! *phr.* (common).—1. A slang catch-phrase indicating that the matter in question is closed to discussion; 'there's nothing more to be said.'

2. Underhand insinuation.

BACK TEETH. TO HAVE ONE'S BACK TEETH WELL AFLOAT, *phr.* (popular).—A facetiously brutal way of implying that the subject of such a remark is well primed with liquor—even to the verge of drunkenness.—*See* SCREWED.

1888. *Missouri Republican*, Jan. 25. When sober on the bench, Judge Noonan is a model of all the virtues. On Friday night, however, in company with Dr. Munford, of Kansas City, ex-Speaker Wood, Mr. Charles Mead and several other gentlemen, his honour once more drank until, as an onlooker put it, his BACK TEETH WERE WELL AFLOAT.

BACK-TIMBER, *subs.* (old).—Clothes. A humorous term which dates back to the middle of the seventeenth century. Other slang equivalents are TOGS and TOGGERY; also WAR-PAINT in the sense of fine or showy garb. In French argot, *alpague* is used synonymously.

b. 1574, *d.* 1656. BP. HALL, *Works* V., 543. Was there ever more riot and excess in diet and clothes, in belly-cheer and BACK-TIMBER, than we see at this day? [D.]

BACK TOMMY, *subs.* (tailors').—A piece of cloth used to cover the 'stays' at the waist.

BACK-TRACK. TO TAKE THE BACK-TRACK, *phr.* (American). — To retreat from any assumed position; to BACK OUT (*q.v.*).

BACK UP, *verb.* (Winchester College).—To call out. In 'College' various times are called out by Junior in 'Chambers,' such as 'Three quarters!' 'Hour!' 'Bells go single!' 'Bells down!'

BACK-SLANG, *subs.* (street and costermonger). — A species of

slang, in which every word, as far as possible, is pronounced backwards. *See* 'A Comparative and Historical Study of Slang' at the end of this work.

verb. 1. (thieves').—To talk in the BACK-SLANG lingo.

2. (thieves').—To go or come stealthily from a place; to sneak by a roundabout way; also, to go away quickly.

3. (Australian).—Up country in Australia, as in most parts a little out of the beaten tracks of civilization, a traveller is welcome at most of the homesteads in his way. Though unknown to the inmates, and bearing no letter of introduction, it is a common thing for a wayfarer to ride or drive up to a house, maybe call for help, and then take up his quarters for the night. This, in Australia, is called BACK-SLANGING IT, though how the phrase is derived is not quite clear, for there is no suggestion of sneaking or proceeding stealthily in the question.

BACKWARDATION, *subs.* (Stock Exchange). — A penalty paid for an extension of time, by sellers, when unable to deliver stock or shares which they have contracted to deliver by a certain date. BACKWARDATION is the reverse of CONTANGO (*q.v.*). Obviously this sometimes permits the purchase of stock cheaper on credit than for cash.

1850. KEYSER, *Law of the Stock Exchange.* The term BACKWARDATION is employed when stock is more in demand than money, and a premium is given to obtain the loan of stock against its value in money.

1886. *Daily News*, 14 Dec., p. 6, col. 1. The 1873 loan is, on balance, about $\frac{5}{8}$ lower, at 94, after being $93\frac{1}{2}$. The BACKWARDATION on the stock went off at the close.

BACKY, *subs.* (tailors').—A shopmate who works behind another.

BACON, *subs.* (popular). — The human body. A reference probably to the fact that the flesh of the pig forms the staple meat diet of the rural population, and lower classes generally. Formerly, no doubt, the term was applied, at first ironically or contemptuously, to a sleek, gross person; hence such compounds as 'chaw-bacon,' 'bacon-brains,' 'bacon-face,' 'bacon-slicer,' 'bacon-picker,' etc. A transference in sense, and a curtailment in form, in which BACON came to signify the human body was, from this point, easy enough. For synonyms, *see* APPLE-CART.

TO SAVE ONE'S BACON, *phr.* (popular).—To escape narrowly from loss, danger, or damage; to just get off. The term is here an attributive usage of the slang sense, in which BACON signifies the human body. When it is said that a man has just SAVED HIS BACON, it refers to the individual himself. So also in the kindred phrase, 'Oh, SPARE MY BACON,' the suppliant asks to be spared in his own person; and the same idea occurs in 'TO SELL ONE'S BACON,' *i.e.*, one's flesh or body, as in the case of women of the town. Falstaff, in *I. Henry IV.*, Act ii., Sc. 2. 93 [1596] thus applies BACON to human beings—'On! Bacons, on!' So far the general aspect of the question; in regard to particulars, Mr. Thomas

Boys has some curious remarks upon the subject [N. and Q., 2 S., iv., 132] in effect as follows. In connecting the phrase TO SAVE ONE'S BACON with its original meaning, we are carried back to times when imputed heresy was expiated at the stake; and a man was said to have just SAVED HIS BACON (*i.e.*, from *frying*), who had himself narrowly escaped the penalty of being burnt alive. This connection of the two ideas is thus shown. When a pig is killed, it is the custom in some of the southern countries of Europe, as well as in many parts of England, to remove the bristles from the dead pig's hide, not by scalding but by *singeing*. This is an operation of some nicety; for too much singeing would spoil the bacon. But practice makes perfect; and by the aid of ignited stubble, straw, or paper, the object is effected. The bristles are all singed off, and the bacon remains intact. This operation of singeing is in Portugal called *chamuscar*, from *chama* or *chamma*, a flame or blaze. *Chamuscar*, to singe, as pigs, to take off the hair (Moraes). Hence the noun *chamusco*, which is *the smell of anything that has been singed*. Hence also the phrase *cheira a chamusco* (he smells of singeing). This last phrase, however, *cheira a chamusco*, was specially applied to any suspected *heretic*:—*o que merece ser queimado, e faz per onde o seja, o que diziño por afronta aos Judeos encobertos*. That is 'he who deserved to be burnt, and acted in a way that was very likely to lead to it,' was said to *smell* of singeing ('*cheirar a chamusco*'), *i.e.*, to smell of the fire. Consequently, the phrase was contumeliously addressed to anyone who was secretly a Jew (Moraes). Thus the persecuted Israelite, who steadfastly adhered to his forefathers' creed, and lived in daily peril of the stake, was allusively but threateningly and insultingly compared to the abhorred carcass, which, though not yet roasted, boiled or fried, had already the smell of fire. If, after all, he was actually burnt alive, the same allusion was carried out to the end; for he was then said, '*morrer frito*,' to be *fried* to death (literally, '*to die fried*'). But even if not burnt he still had the *chamusco*, or 'smell of fire'; that is, he had only JUST SAVED HIS BACON.

1691. *Weesils*, I., 5. No, they'l conclude I do't to SAVE MY BACON. [M.]

1705. WARD, *Hudibras Redivivus*, vol. I., pt. II., p. 12.
For could their talent be forsaken,
And they unite truth to SAVE THEIR BACON.

1721. MRS. CENTLIVRE, *The Artifice*, v., ii. That pretence shan't SAVE YOUR BACON, you old villain you.

1836. M. SCOTT, *Cringle's Log*, ch. v. 'You know I SAVED YOUR BACON in that awkward affair, when through drunkenness you plumped the *Torch* ashore.'

1856. C. READE, *Never Too Late*, ch. lii. Jem drew a long breath and said brutally, yet with something of satisfaction, 'You have SAVED YOUR BACON this time.'

The French equivalent it may be noticed is somewhat analogous —*sauver son lard*, *i.e.*, 'to save one's bacon.'

Possibly, however, most people will be inclined to take the phrase at its face value, without resort to complicated argumentative derivation. In such a case the figurative use of bacon as signifying the body will suffice to explain its origin.

To PULL BACON, *phr.* (popular). — An operation described by the immortal Ingoldsby in the line—

He put his thumb unto his nose and spread his fingers out.

In other words TO TAKE A SIGHT (*q.v.*), or TO MAKE QUEEN ANNE'S FAN (*q.v.*).

1886. *Household Words,* Oct. 2, p. 453. [This] peculiar action has, I believe, almost invariably been described as 'taking a sight.' A solicitor, however, in a recent police case at Manchester, described it as PULLING BACON.

1887. *Leeds Evening News,* Sept. 15. 'PULLING BACON' AT LEEDS POLICE-MEN.—Before Mr. Goodman and Mr. Farrar Smith, at the Leeds Police Court to-day, George Evans (50), coachman to the Earl of Mexborough, Mexborough Hall, near Methley, was summoned under the Hackney Carriage Bye-laws for having driven on the wrong side of the road. Police-constables Moody and Lockwood were on duty in Boar Lane on the 6th inst., when they saw the defendant driving a pair of horses attached to a carriage on the wrong side of the road for a distance of one hundred yards. The officers spoke to him, when he put his fingers to his nose and PULLED BACON at them. He had been previously cautioned, but had not taken the slightest notice. Defendant said he had been a driver in London for eighteen years, and knew they had policemen in the road there, but he did not understand the law of driving in Yorkshire. He was fined 20s.

BACON-FACED, *adj.* (colloquial).—With sleek, fat face; full faced. Otway in the *Atheist* [1684] speaks of one with a 'BACON FACE like a cherubim.'

BACON-FED, *adj.* (colloquial).—Fat or greasy. The expression occurs in Shakspeare's *King Henry IV.*—*See* BACON.

BACON-SLICER, *subs.* (old). — A rustic.—*See* CHAWBACON.

1653. URQUHART, *Rabelais,* bk. I., ch. xv. (Bohn), I., 149. If he have not a better judgment, a better discourse, and that expressed in better terms than your son, with a complete carriage and civility to all manner of persons, account me for ever hereafter a very clounch, and BACON-SLICER of Brene.

BAD, *adj.* (popular).—Hard; difficult. Used as in quotation.

1884. HAWLEY SMART, *Post to Finish,* ch. xi. 'I have heard you say over and over again that, when they are in the mood, their very temper makes them BAD to beat.'

To GO TO THE BAD, *phr.* (colloquial).—To be ruined; to become depraved. Virgil has a similar phrase *in pejus ruere,* 'to go to the worse.'

1864. M. E. BRADDON, *Aurora Floyd,* ch. xi. 'A reckless man, ready TO GO TO THE BAD by any road that can take me there; worthless alike to myself and to others.'

1880. G. R. SIMS, *Ballads of Babylon* (*Beauty and Beast*). Let him GO TO THE BAD at his own mad pace.

To THE BAD, *i.e.*, on the wrong side of the account; in deficit.

1816. 'Quiz,' *Grand Master,* viii., 25. I've really TO THE BAD some thousand of rupees to add. [M.]

1884. *Pall Mall G.,* 6 Feb., 4. He was between £70 and £80 TO THE BAD. [M.]

WANT 'EM OR HIM BAD, *phr.* (American).—A humorous manner of expressing strong desire.

1888. *Daily Inter-Ocean,* March 9. Myers' absence is seriously annoying to the defense, and does not appear quite as funny as it did when the prosecution called for him on Saturday last. It is not probable that the Court will very long suspend the trial if Myers does not appear. As the case now stands, the defense want Myers, and WANT HIM BAD.

BAD 'APENNY. — *See* BAD HALFPENNY.

BAD-BARGAIN, *subs.* (old). — Formerly a worthless soldier; a malingerer. Nowadays the term is applied to any worthless person or scapegrace.

BAD-BREAK, *subs.* (American).—A corruption of 'bad outbreak,' *i.e.*, riotous conduct, generally attributable to drink.

BAD CROWD GENERALLY, *phr.* (American). — Of Western origin, and equivalent to the English NO GREAT SHAKES (*q.v.*). 'Crowd,' it may be remarked, in America, signifies either *one* or more individuals.

BAD-EGG, *subs.* (familiar). — A scoundrel; a blackguard; a 'loose fish.' In America the meaning attached to the term does not necessarily involve such an idea of depravity as on this side of the Atlantic. In the States the term is also applied to a worthless speculation.

1866. SALA, *Trip to Barbary,* p. 130. The man in black baize with the felt képi, and who had a hatchet face desperately scarred with the small-pox, looked from head to heel a BAD EGG.

1877. *Five Years' Penal Servitude,* ch. ii., p. 123. There is no doubt, but there are many of the officials of the convict prisons who are what the Yankees call BAD EGGS.

ENGLISH SYNONYMS. Bad-lot; bad halfpenny; bad-hat. In Australia 'ne'er-do-wells' are termed sundowners; dry hash; or, a stringy bark.

FRENCH SYNONYMS. *Malfrat* (popular); *mauvais gobet* (popular: *mauvais,* bad; *gobet,* properly a mouthful, morsel, lump, or piece); *ferlampier* or *ferlandier* (thieves': *ferlampié* formerly signified a dunce); *clique* (popular); *mariasse* (popular).

BAD FORM, *subs.* (society). — He who, or that which fails to conform to the shifting fads and fancies of Society, with a big S; and, in a more general sense, anybody or anything vulgar or lacking polish.

1882. *Punch.* ETON BOY. What an awful lot of energy you've got uncle! UNCLE. Pretty well, my boy, for my time of life, I think! E. B. Yes! but energy's such awful BAD FORM, you know!

BADGE, *subs.* (old).—Used in the canting sense, for one branded in the hand. 'He has got his BADGE, and piked'; *i.e.*, 'he was burned in the hand, and is at liberty.—*Grose.*

BADGE-COVE, *subs.* (old).—A parish pensioner; also in the sixteenth, seventeenth, and eighteenth centuries a licensed beggar or almsman. The remarks under ABRAM MAN and ABRAM SHAM are to the point in this connection.

BADGER, *subs.* (old).—1. A river thief. A good account of these gentry appears in Harrison Ainsworth's *Jack Sheppard.*

2. (American thieves'). — In the cant language of the American criminal classes a BADGER or PANEL THIEF (*q.v.*) is one who robs a man after a woman accomplice has enticed the victim into her den.

3. (schoolboy).—A red haired individual.

4. (harlotry). — A common prostitute.—*See* BARRACK-HACK.

5. (nautical). — Sometimes BADGER-BAG. The fictitious individual personating Neptune in the festivities incident to 'crossing the line.'—*See* AMBASSADOR and ARTHUR.

6. (Wellington School).—A fellow who has got his 'badge' for play in the 2nd XV. at football.

verb. (popular).—To tease; to annoy; to confound.

1798. O. KEEFE, *Wild Oats,* I., i. At home, abroad, you will still BADGER me.

1836. DICKENS, *Pickwick,* ch. xxxiv., p. 299. Tracy Tupman, and Augustus Snodgrass, were severally called into the box; both corroborated the testimony of their unhappy friend; and each was driven to the verge of desperation by excessive BADGERING.

1860. DICKENS, *Great Expectations,* ch. xviii., p. 82. 'Which I meantersay,' cried Joe, 'that if you come into my place bull-baiting and BADGERING me, come out!'

The popular French equivalent of TO BADGER is *aguigner.*

To OVERDRAW THE BADGER, *phr.* (popular).—A figurative use of 'drawing the badger'; to overdraw one's banking account.

1843-4. HOOD, *Miss Kilmansegg.*
His cheeks no longer drew the cash,
Because, as his comrades explain'd in flash,
He had *overdrawn his badger.*

BADGER STATE, *subs.* (American).—A popular name for the State of Wisconsin, and so called because of the BADGERS which once abounded there.

BAD GIVE-AWAY.—*See* GIVE AWAY.

BAD-HALFPENNY, *subs.* (popular).—A ne'er-do-weel; an allusion to the frequency with which, like bad coins, they are always 'turning up.' *Cf.*, BAD-EGG.

(Australian).—A failing speculation; a risky venture.

BAD HAT, *subs.* (popular).—The same as BAD EGG (*q.v.*).

1883. BESANT, *They Were Married,* p. II., ch. ix., in *Captain's Room, etc.* There may be one or two BAD HATS among eldest sons; but there is not one, I am sure—there cannot be one—who would dare to take his wife's salary and deprive her of her son.

BAD LOT.—A term derived from auctioneering slang, and now generally used to describe a man or woman of indifferent morals.

1849. THACKERAY, *Pendennis,* ch. lx. 'He's a bad'un, Mr. Lightfoot—a BAD LOT, sir, and that you know.'

1868. MISS BRADDON, *Trail of the Serpent,* bk. I., ch. ii. 'I am good for nothing,' he said, 'I am a BAD LOT. I wonder they don't hang such men as me.'

1872. M. E. BRADDON, *Dead Sea Fruit,* ch. i. 'The impracticable Daniel has a certain kind of influence; and though he rarely cares to use it on his own account—being so BAD A LOT that he dare not give himself a decent character—he will employ it to the uttermost for a spotless nephew.'

BAD MAN, *subs.* (American).—A BAD MAN, in the West, is a somewhat mixed character. The term is generally understood to mean a professional fighter or man-killer, but who, despite this drawback, is said by Roosevelt, in *Ranch Life in the Far West,* to be sometimes, according to his light, perfectly honest. These are the men who do most of the killing in frontier communities; yet it is a noteworthy fact that the men who are killed generally deserve their fate. These men are, of course, used to brawling, and are not only sure shots, but, what is equally important, able to 'draw' their weapon with marvellous quickness. They think nothing whatever of murder, and are the dread and terror of their associates; yet they are very chary of taking the life of a man of good standing, and will often 'weak-

en' and 'backdown' at once if confronted fearlessly. With many of them their courage arises from confidence in their own powers and knowledge of the fear in which they are held; and men of this type often show the white feather when they get into a 'tight place.' Others, however, will face any odds without flinching, and when mortally wounded, have been known to fight with a cool ferocious despair that was terrible. During the last two or three years, stockmen have united to put down these dangerous characters, often by the most summary exercise of lynch law; and, as a consequence, many localities once infested by BAD MEN are now perfectly law-abiding.

BAD MATCH TWIST, *subs. phr.* (hairdressers'). — A man who has red, or carotty hair and black whiskers is said to have a BAD MATCH TWIST.

BADMINTON, *subs.* (common).—1. A cooling drink; a kind of claret-cup, so called because invented at the Duke of Beaufort's seat of the same name. Composed of claret, sugar, spice, soda-water, and ice.

1845. DISRAELI, *Sybil,* bk. I., ch. i. 'Waiter, bring me a tumbler of BADMINTON.'

1853. WHYTE MELVILLE, *Digby Grand,* ch. ix. An enormous measure of BADMINTON, that grateful compound of mingled claret, sugar, and soda-water.

1868. OUIDA, *Under Two Flags,* ch. ix. Looking up out of a great silver flagon of BADMINTON, with which he was ending his breakfast.

2. (pugilistic).—Blood; from the similarity in colour to the summer drink of the same name. CLARET (*q.v.*), for a like reason, is also, in the language of the prize-ring, synonymous with blood.

BAD RECORD.—*See* RECORD.

BAD SHOT, *subs.* (popular).—An abortive attempt; a woman's guess.

1844. KINGLAKE, *Eothen,* viii., 137. I secretly smiled at this last prophecy as A BAD SHOT.

1859. REV. E. BRADLEY ('Cuthbert Bede') in *Notes and Queries,* 2 S., viii., p. 492. A BAD SHOT is one of the worst exposures of his ignorance that a University man when up for examination can make.

See, however, SHOT.

BAD SLANG, *subs.* (circus and showmen's).—Faked up monstrosities; spurious curiosities.

1876. C. HINDLEY, *Life and Adventures of a Cheap Jack,* p. 206. Roderick Palsgrave was considered by all who knew him to be the best showman of a BAD SLANG that ever travelled. He would get hold of any black girl or woman, dress her up, and then show her as one of the greatest novelties ever seen.

BAG, *subs.* (old slang).—1. A woman when *enceinte* was said 'to have a BAG.' *Cf.*, TO BAG. Sense 3.

2. (Westminster School).—Milk.

To EMPTY THE BAG, *phr.* (old).—To tell, or disclose the whole truth; to wind up an argument or discussion.

To GIVE THE BAG, *phr.* (old).—1. Formerly used in varying senses. In the following quotation it conveys, says Nares, the idea of chicanery and cheating. This, however, is doubtful, but compare 'to give the bag to hold.'

1592. GREENE, *Quip,* in *works* IX., 263. You shall be . . . . lighte witted upon every small occasion TO GEUE your maister THE BAGGE.

2. In another respect TO GIVE THE BAG was used in a sense analogous to that conveyed in TO GIVE THE SACK (*q.v.*), *i.e.*, to dismiss a person from one's employment, with this important difference that primarily the 'bag' or 'sack' was not given by the master or mistress to the servant, but *vice versâ*, and, therefore, the expression meant 'to leave without warning.' This was the earliest usage.

1592. *Defence of Conny Catching*, in Greene's *works* XI., 86. If he meane to GIUE HER THE BAGGE, he selleth whatsoever he can, and so leaues hir spoild both of hir wealth and honestie.

1647. *Speedy Hue and Crie*, I. . . . He being sometime an Apprentice on London Bridge . . . . GAVE HIS MASTER THE BAG. [M.]

Gradually the meaning of TO GIVE THE BAG changed to that which, even to-day, is dialectically current, *i.e.*, 'to dismiss a person from one's employment,' though in large centres of population TO GIVE OR RECEIVE THE SACK is, at present, the more popular equivalent. While dealing with variations of this kind, it is noteworthy that 'bag' was, in the seventeenth century, varied by 'canvas,' as Shirley has it ——

1652. SHIRLEY, *The Brothers*, Act ii. I have promis'd him as much as marriage comes to, and I lose my honour, if my don RECEIVE THE CANVAS.

Gifford and Dyce in a note say 'the phrase is taken from the practice of journeymen mechanics who travel in quest of work, with the implements of their profession. When they are discharged by their masters, they are said to RECEIVE THE CANVAS, or THE BAG; because in this their tools and necessaries are packed up, preparatory to their removal.' This suggested derivation would possibly pass muster were it not that, treated historically, the phrase though identical in form is shown to have had an earlier usage, and one, moreover, of an entirely antagonistic character; unless indeed, in the first instance, it was customary for employers to find 'bags' of tools and working implements for their employees, in which case the workman or servant in leaving his work would naturally GIVE the master THE BAG. The transition in sense which the phrase has undergone would then become perfectly clear, as far as the why and wherefore of the change is concerned. *Cf.*, SACK.

TO GIVE ONE THE BAG TO HOLD, *phr.* (old).—To leave in the lurch; to engage a person's attention in order to deceive. *Cf.*, TO GIVE THE BAG, sense 1.

1793. T. JEFFERSON, *Writings* (1859), iv., 7. She will LEAVE Spain THE BAG TO HOLD. [M.]

1823. SCOTT, *Peveril of the Peak*, vii. She GAVE ME THE BAG to hold and was smuggling in a corner with a rich old Puritan.

IN THE BOTTOM OF THE BAG, *phr.* (old).—An expression equivalent to what, in modern slang, is termed 'having a trump card in reserve'; something in hand as a last resource or expedient.

1659. REYNOLDS, in Burton *Diary* (1828), iv., 447. If this be done which is IN THE BOTTOM OF THE BAG, and must be done, we shall . . . be able to buoy up our reputation. [M.]

TO LET THE CAT OUT OF THE BAG, *phr.* (familiar).—To disclose a trick or secret.—*See* CAT.

TO PUT ONE IN A BAG, *phr.* (old).—Usage and derivation explained, as far as known, in quotation.

1662. FULLER, *Worthies, Cardigan* (ii., 579). They (the Welsh) had a kind of play wherein the stronger who prevailed put the weaker into a sack; and hence we have borrowed our English by-word to express such, betwixt whom there is apparent odds of strength, 'He is able to PUT HIM UP IN A BAGGE.' [D.]

1676. EARL OF ROCHESTER, *Hist. of Insipids*, st. 14.
Had haughty *Holms* but call'd in *Spragg*,
Hans had been PUT INTO A BAG.

TO PUT OR GET ONE'S HEAD IN A BAG, *phr.* (printers').—A 'bag' here signifies a pot of beer; hence, to drink. Also in use amongst seafaring men.

1887. *Sat. Review*, 14 May, p. 700. It is slang, and yet purely trade slang, when one printer says of another that he has GOT HIS HEAD IN THE BAG.

TO TURN TO BAG AND WALLET (old).—To become a beggar.

Verb. (popular).—1. To secure for oneself. Most probably a mere extension of the colloquial sporting usage of TO BAG (properly, to put or enclose in a bag), in the sense of to seize, capture, entrap, or otherwise bring within one's reach.

1880. MORTIMER COLLINS, *Thoughts in my Garden*, vol. I., p. 163. The word *beggar* itself is from *bag*—meaning a man who carries a bag; and modern commercial slang reproduces the phrase, saying of a clever man of business that he has BAGGED a good thing.

2. To steal; or to catch (a thief or man). Sometimes rendered by TO COLLAR (*q.v.*).

1881. MOORE, *Fudge Family in Paris*, VI. Who can help TO BAG a few, When Sidmouth wants a death or two?

1862. FARRAR, *St. Winifred's*, ch. xxxv. They would not call it stealing but BAGGING a thing, or, at the worst, 'cribbing it'—concealing the villainy under a new name.

3. (old).—To beget; to conceive; to breed. Also TO BE BAGGED. This usage dates from about A.D. 1400, and was colloquial until about the middle of the seventeenth century. Warner [in *Alb. Eng. VI.*, 148] has the line

Well, Venus shortly BAGGED, and ere long was Cupid bred.

TO GET BAGGY, *phr.* (common).—Said of clothes when loosened by the stretching which arises from wear and tear. Trousers get BAGGY at the knees.

BAG AND BAGGAGE, *phr.* (common).—To clear one out BAG AND BAGGAGE is to get quit of one entirely. A deprecatory expression indicating complete riddance.

BAG AND BOTTLE, *subs. phr.* (old).—Food and drink. The former from being carried in a bag as by beggars and vagrants; the latter also being of similar derivation.

1671. EACHARD, *Observations.* An ill-contriving rascal that in his younger years should choose to lug the BAG AND THE BOTTLE a mile or two to school; and to bring home only a small bit of Greek or Latin most magisterially construed.

BAGGAGE. HEAVY BAGGAGE, *subs. phr.* (old).—1. Women and children.—*Grose.*

2. BAGGAGE is also a fami-

liar colloquialism for a pert, saucy, young woman; like 'wench,' 'rogue,' 'gypsy,' it is often used endearingly.

1698. CONGREVE, *Old Batchelor*, I., iii. I believe the BAGGAGE loves me.

1732. FIELDING, *The Miser*, Act i., Sc. 9. Here's a BAGGAGE of a daughter, who refuses the most advantageous match that ever was offered.

1863. ALEX. SMITH, *Dreamthorpe*, p. 12. And Beauty, who is something of a coquette . . . goes off in a huff. Let the BAGGAGE go!

3. (old).—A whore or strumpet; a woman of loose morals.

4. (old).—Rubbish; 'rot.'

1575. *Touchstone of Complexions*, p. 118. For throughe cruditye and lacke of perfect concoction in the stomacke is engendered great abundance of naughty BAGGAGE and hurtful phlegme.

1576. GASCOIGNE, *The Steele Glas*, p. 79. When brewers put no BAGAGE in their beere.

Adj. (old).—Used contemptuously of individuals and things. *Cf.*, BAGGAGE—a worthless, good-for-nothing woman.

1593. G. HARVEY, *Pierces Superero*, in *works* (Gresart) II., 273. Bibbing Nash, BAGGAGE Nash, swaddish Nash, rogish Nash, the bellweather of the scribling flocke.

1692. HACKET, *Life of Williams*, ii., 128. For four cellars of wine, syder, ale, beer, with wood, hay, corn, and the like, stored up for a year or two, he gave not account of sixpence, but spent it upon BAGGAGE, and loose franions. *Ibid*, p. 123. Booth himself confest, in the hearing of those witnesses, that Pregion had nothing to do with that BAGGAGE woman.

BAGGAGE-SMASHER, *subs.* (American).—1. A railway porter. The why and wherefore of this nickname is abundantly apparent from the following quotations.

1871. DE VERE, *Americanisms*, p. 358. The BAGGAGE-SMASHER, as the porter is commonly called, handles his burdens with appalling recklessness, and responsibility there is none.

1880. *New Viginians*, i., 37. 'Called BAGGAGE-SMASHERS. [M.]

1888. *Texas Siftings*, Nov. 3. Fashionable people who have spent the summer at the watering places or at the seaside, but have now returned to the cities, assert that the BAGGAGE-SMASHER has become more destructive than ever. The BAGGAGE-SMASHER is indeed a terror. In fact there are two of them: the one who flits from station to station and dumps your poor dumb trunk with force enough to drive piles in a government breakwater, and the one who loiters around the depôt watching for his chance to shatter your baggage. The depot baggageman is the most culpable of the two species. In his long and dark career of smashing trunks, he has, evidently, knocked the hoops off his conscience, and there is no remorse brave, foolhardy and reckless enough to tackle his heart-strings and play on them.

2. Also a thief who hangs about 'depôts,' with a view to robbery of luggage.

1861. *New York Tribune*, Nov. 23. Gamblers, ticket-swindlers, emigrant robbers, 'BAGGAGE-SMASHERS, and all the worst classes of the city.

BAGGED, *ppl. adj.* (American).—A term used to signify imprisonment and victimization—probably only an extension of the idea of capture as derived from sport, through the slang 'to bag,' *i.e.*, to steal. *Cf.*, TO BAG.

BAGGING, *subs.* (provincial slang).—In the first instance, food taken between regular meals; now generally applied, especially in Lancashire, to what is known in the South of England as 'high tea.'

1750. J. COLLIER, in *Lancashire Glossary* (E.D.S.). Hoo'l naw cum agen till BAGGIN' TIME. [M.]

1870. *Chambers' Journal*, Oct., p. 661. Lancashire adopts the whole-board or partial-board system very extensively. The local term of BAGGING implies bread and cheese, or pies; and there are all

the varieties of board and lodging, dinner of potatoes and bacon with buttermilk, BAGGING in the forenoon and afternoon, dinner and lunch, and rations allowed for women.

1879. In *Temple Bar Mag.*, 4 Jan. BAGGIN' is not only lunch, but any accidental meal coming between two regular ones.

BAGGING THE OVER.—*See* JOCKEYING THE OVER.

BAGMAN, *subs.* (popular).—1. A commercial traveller. Formerly of respectable usage; now only employed contemptuously.

1765. GOLDSMITH, *Essays*, I. The BAGMAN was telling a better story. [M.]

1840. THACKERAY, *Paris Sketch Book*, p. 20. When all the rest of mankind look hideous, dirty, peevish, wretched, after a forty-hours' coach-journey, a BAGMAN appears as gay and spruce as when he started.

The term BAGMAN took its rise in the saddle-bags in which the commercial traveller of the past century carried his patterns and goods. These saddle-bags being of larger dimensions than those usually carried by travellers on horseback, would designate the commercial traveller *par excellence* as *the* BAGMAN.

2. In sporting slang, a 'bag-fox.'

1875. STONEHENGE, *Brit. Sports*, I., II., iv., § 5. If . . . wild cubs cannot be found, a BAGMAN or two must be obtained. [M.]

BAGNIO, *subs.* (old).—A brothel. [From Italian *bagno*, a bath, properly a hot bath; whence an application as in the case of STEW (*q.v.*), for a house of prostitution.]

1624. MASSINGER, *Parliament of Love*, II., ii. To be sold to a brothel or a common BAGNIO.

1851. THACKERAY, *English Humour*, V. (1858), 243. How the prodigal drinks and sports at the BAGNIO.

1861. WRIGHT, *Domestic Manners in England during the Middle Ages*, 491. They were soon used to such an extent for illicit intrigues, that the name of a hothouse or BAGNIO became equivalent to that of a brothel.

BAG OF BONES, *subs. phr.* (familiar).—A lean, attenuated person; sometimes called a 'walking skeleton.' The French have *un sac à os* (often contracted into *sacdos*)—a literal translation. The term is quite modern, being traced by Murray no further back than 1838, when Dickens used it [in *Oliver Twist*, iv., 64].

BAG O' MOONSHINE, *subs. phr.* (common).—Nonsense.—*See* ALL MOONSHINE.

BAG OF NAILS, *subs. phr.* (American thieves').—A state of confusion or topsy-turveydom. [Qy. from 'bacchanals.']

BAG OF TRICKS, *phr.* (common).—Generally, THE WHOLE BAG OF TRICKS; *i.e.*, every expedient.

BAGPIPE, *subs.* (common).—A windy talker; a senseless chatter-box. The derivation is obviously from the musical instrument of the same name.

Verb. (old).—A lascivious practice; too indecent for explanation.

BAGS, *subs.* (popular).—An ironical nickname for trousers, thought by some to be of University origin, and borrowed from 'the variegated bags' of Euripides —τους θυλάκους τους ποικίλους (Cyclops., 182).

1853. REV. E. BRADLEY ('Cuthbert Bede'), *Adventures of Verdant Green*, p.

51. Just jump into a pair of BAGS and Wellingtons. *Ibid*, p. 5. His black go-to-meeting BAGS.

1870. *Chambers' Journal* (Christmas Number). 'But, holloa!' he cried, as he caught sight of his legs. 'Parsons don't wear light tweed BAGS!' . . . . Jack had to unpack his portmanteau and get out his evening inexpressibles.

1874. M. COLLINS, *Frances*, ch. xv. His well-shapen hip and calf were hidden in loose-fitting BAGS of corduroy.

1880. *Punch*, Jan. 10, p. 6. THE SPREAD OF EDUCATION AND LIBERAL IDEAS.—*His Grace the Duke of Poplar and Bermondsey*. 'Just look at these BAGS you last built me, Snippe! J'ever see such beastly BAGS in your life? I shall always be glad to come and dine with you, old man; but I'll be hanged if you shall ever measure me for another pair of BAGS!' *Mr. Snippe (of Snippe and Son, St. James's Street)*. 'You've *always* grumbled about your BAGS, as you call 'em, ever since you were my fag at Eton; and at Christchurch you were just as bad, even though my poor dear old governor used to come all the way down and measure you himself. It ain't the fault of the BAGS, my dear Popsy—it's the fault of the legs inside 'em! So, shut up, old Stick-in-the-mud, and let's join the ladies—the duchess has promised to give us "Little Billee."'

When made of startling material, or 'cut' in an exaggerated style of fashion they become HOWLING BAGS.

ENGLISH SYNONYMS. Dittoes; kicks; kicksies; bum-bags; sit-upons; unmentionables; continuations; hams; inexpressibles; abridgements; drumstick-cases; and ducks (when made of white material).

FRENCH SYNONYMS. *Dalzar*; *falzar*.

Intj. (schoolboy).—BAGS! or BAGS I! is frequently used to assert a claim to some article or privilege. Analogous schoolboy slang is FAINS OR FAIN IT (*q.v.*) for demanding a truce during the progress of a game, and which is always granted by the opposing party. In other schools PIKE I or PRIOR PIKE serve to lay claim to anything, or for asserting priority of claim. Also BAR! *e.g.*, 'He wanted me to do so and so, but I *barred* not.' *Cf.*, FAIN, PIKE, and BAR.

TO HAVE THE BAGS, *phr.* (popular). — This phrase is erroneously given by Hotten (and Barrère has followed suit), as TO HAVE THE BAGS *off*. The meaning is to be of age, and thus to possess all the rights and privileges of adultship; also to have plenty of money. Obviously an allusion to the transition from child's attire to the garments of manhood.

BAGS OF MYSTERY, *subs. phr.* (common). — Sausages and saveloys are so called—from the often mysterious character of their compounds. Presumably composed of minced 'meat,' but so highly flavoured and seasoned that no man can tell whereof they are made.

TO TAKE THE BAGS (athletic). —To act as 'hare' in 'Hare and Hounds,' a game too well known to need description in this place.

(Stock Exchange).—*B*uenos *A*yres *G*reat *S*outhern Railway Bonds. — Formed from the initial letters, thus *B-A-G-S*.

BAIJAN.—*See* BEJAN.

BAIL. STRAW-BAIL or STRAW-SHOES, *subs.* (common).—A nickname for a person willing for a consideration, to give evidence, or act as bail. Formerly men were much more ostentatious in plying

a vocation of perjury than is now happily possible. It was no uncommon thing for such openly to perambulate the entrances to the law-courts ready for any chance customer. They made known their occupation by wearing a piece of straw just sticking out of their shoes. The *Quarterly Review* (xxxiii., 344) points out that the practice is a very ancient one, Athens having abounded in straw-shoes. The *modus operandi* was much the same then as in later days. When it was 'desirable' to season Attic testimony with bribery and perjury, the scene outside a Greek court of justice might be thus described. An advocate or lawyer who wanted a convenient witness knew by these signs [the straws in the sandals] where to find one, and the colloquy between the parties was brief. 'Don't you remember' said the advocate—(the party looked at the fee and gave no sign: but the fee increased and the powers of memory increased with it). 'To be sure I do!' 'Then come into the court and swear it.' And STRAW-SHOES went into the court and swore it. As B.C., SO A.D. 1754 —before and after.

1754. FIELDING, *Jonathan Wild*, book I., chap. ii. Charity took to husband an eminent gentleman whose name I cannot learn; but who was famous for so friendly a disposition, that he was BAIL for above a hundred persons in one year. He had likewise the remarkable honour of walking in Westminster Hall with a straw in his shoe.

At present lawyers use STRAW-BAIL to designate insufficient bail. Closely allied to this term, and used much in the same manner, is 'a man of straw.' The figure is the effigy of a man, stuffed with straw; hence, 'a man of straw,' the semblance of a man—a person of neither substance nor responsibility; or one put forward to screen a real delinquent. A curious usage, akin to the foregoing, is also sometimes heard among sailors. For example, a strike for wages having taken place amongst the crew of a ship, 'BLACKLEGS' (*q.v.*), or 'straw-yarders' as they were called in nautical phraseology, took the place of the strikers. On the meaning of the expression being asked, it was explained that a 'straw-yarder' was a man about the docks who had never been to sea, and knew little or nothing of the duties of a seaman.

TO GIVE OR TAKE LEG-BAIL, *phr.* (common). — To escape, either from arrest, or from prison; literally, to be indebted to one's legs for flight. For exhaustive list of synonyms, *see* AMPUTATE.

1775. ADAIR, *American Indians*, 277. I had concluded to use no chivalry, but GIVE THEM LEG-BAIL instead of it, by . . . . making for a deep swamp. [M.]

1815. SCOTT, *Guy Mannering*, ch. iii. 'I e'en GAE THEM LEG-BAIL, for there's nae ease in dealing wi' quarrelsome fowk.'

1848. MARRYAT, *Poacher*, xxii. GIVEN THEM LEG-BAIL, I swear.

The phrase is sometimes amplified thus:—TO TAKE LEG-BAIL and GIVE LAND SECURITY.

BAIL UP! also **BALE UP!** *intj.* (Australian).—A bushranger's phrase for 'stand and deliver'! 'Shell out'!

1880. *Blackwood's Mag.*, July, p. 91. [Australian *loq.*] 'BAIL UP! BAIL UP!' shout the two red-veiled attackers, revolvers in hand.

1887. G. L. APPERSON, *All the Year Round*, July 30, p. 68, col. 1. In times gone by, it was by no means an uncommon occurrence [in Australia] for a coach to be 'stuck up' by a band of bushrangers, whose shouts of BAIL UP, an invitation equivalent to our 'shell out,' supported by revolver barrels, terrified the hearts of the passengers. But a coach is now seldom interfered with, and to 'stick up' is applied to less daring attempts to rob.

2. Hence, colloquially, a demand for instant payment. Equivalent to the English FORK OUT! STUMP UP! etc. For synonyms, *see* SHELL OUT.

BAIT, *subs.* (common). — Anger; rage; indignation. Derived from the figurative sense of 'to bait,' *i.e.*, to worry; harass; or tease.

1882. F. ANSTEY, *Vice-Versâ*, ch. v. 'I went calmly on, smoking my cigar as if nothing was the matter. That put the Proctor in a BAIT, I can tell you!'

BAITLAND, *subs.* (nautical).—Admiral Smyth in his *Sailors' Word Book* quotes this as 'an old word, formerly used to signify a port where refreshments could be procured.'

BAKE, *verb.* (Winchester College). —To rest, or lie down.

BAKED, *ppl. adj.* (common). — Collapsed; exhausted; done up; *e.g.*, 'toward the end of the course the crew were regularly BAKED.' A common colloquialism at the beginning of the present century; but the punning idea involved is very ancient. TO BAKE ONE'S BREAD in the sense of 'to do for one' occurs as early as 1380, as will be seen from the following quotation.

1380. SIR FERUMB, 577. For euere MY BRED HAD BE BAKE; myn lyf dawes had be tynt.

HALF-BAKED (common) is said of a dull-witted or imbecile person, *i.e.*, one who is 'soft' or inexperienced, in contrast to one who is BAKED in the sense of 'seasoned,' quick-witted, etc.

1864. *Notes and Queries*, 3 S., vi., 494, 2. He is only HALF-BAKED—put in with the bread, and taken out with the cakes.

BAKER, *subs.* (Winchester College). —A cushion. These were of two kinds; that used in 'College' was of large size, oblong in shape, and green in colour. The other used in 'Commoners' was thin, narrow, much smaller, and of red colour. The term BAKER is also applied to anything placed upon a form to sit upon, *e.g.*, a blotting book or other article; in short, anything comfortable to sit upon.

(American).—A loafer. The word is generally attributed to Baron de Mandat Grancey, who, in his work *Cowboys and Colonels*, innocently translated the word 'loafer' as BAKER.

TO SPELL BAKER (colloquial). —To attempt a difficult task. In the old spelling books 'baker' was frequently the first word of two syllables to which a child came when learning to spell.

BAKER-KNEED, also **BAKER-LEGGED**, *adj.* (common). — 1. Knock-kneed; disfigured by crooked legs. This deformity, incident to bakers, arising from the constrained position in which they knead bread, is said to be the almost certain penalty of habitually bearing any burden of

bulk in the right hand, or of excessive force constantly exerted by the right side of the body. The knees gradually incline inwards until they closely resemble the right side of the letter K.

1607. DEKKER, *Westward Hoe*, Act ii., Sc. 2. Will women's tongues, like BAKERS' LEGS, never go straight?

1692. L'ESTRANGE, *Life of Æsop*. Æsop . . . was . . . flat-nos'd, hunch-back'd. blabber-lipp'd, a long misshapen head; his body crooked all over, big-belly'd, BAKER-LEGG'D, and his complexion so swarthy that he took his very name from 't; for Æsop is the same with Æthiop.

1754. B. MARTIN, *Eng. Dict.*, 2 ed. BAKES-LEGG'D, straddling, with the legs bowing outward.

1812. COLMAN, *Poetical Vagaries*, p. 13. His voice had broken to a gruffish squeak. He had grown blear-eyed, BAKER-KNEED, and gummy.

2. Effeminate. Either an attributive usage of the foregoing, or an allusion to the popular belief that a woman's legs are never straight. Compared physiologically with those of a man this is doubtless true; but otherwise most women would resent the imputation as a libel.

1652. GAULE, *Hagastrom*, 186. BAKER-KNEED signifies effeminate.

BAKER LAYER, *subs.* (Winchester College).—A Junior who used to take a prefect's green BAKER (*q.v.*) in and out of 'Hall' at meal times. The term is now obsolete.

BAKER'S DOZEN, *subs.* (colloquial). —Thirteen reckoned as twelve. Formerly, so careful were 'the powers that be' regarding the supply of bread, that bakers were liable to heavy penalties for any deficiency in the weight of loaves. So hedged in, indeed, was the sale of bread, that the weight of loaves was fixed by law, for every price from eighteenpence down to two-pence, but penny loaves or rolls were not specified in the statute. Bakers, therefore, when selling the latter, in order to be on the safe side, gave, for a dozen of bread, an additional loaf, known as 'inbread.' A similar custom of giving extra quantity was formerly observed with regard to coal, and publishers nowadays reckon thirteen copies of a book as twelve. That the term BAKER'S DOZEN was thoroughly colloquial at the latter end of the sixteenth century is apparent from the first of the following quotations:

1596. NASHE, *Saffron Walden*, in *works* III., ii. Conioyning with his aforesaid Doctor Brother in eightie eight browne BAKER'S DOZEN of Almanackes.

1639. *Will* of Francis Pynner, of Bury, Gent., dated April 26 [Camden Society's 'Bury Wills']. The yerely sume of ffiue pounds p'cell of the said yerely rents to be bestowed in wheaten bread, to be made into *penny* loaves, and upon eu'y Lord's day, called Sonday, throughout eu'y yere of the said terme [40 years or thereabouts], *fowre and twenty* loaves of the said bread, with the *inbread* allowed by the baker for those *twoe dosens* of bread, to be timely brought and sett vpon a forme towards the vpp'end of the chancell of the said p'ish church of St. Marie, and . . . the same *twoe dosens* of bread to be giuen and distributed . . . to and amongst fowre and twentie poore people . . . And they, the said clarke, sexton, and bedell, shall alwaies haue the *inbread* of all the bread aforesaid ovr and besides their shares in the said twoe dosens of bread.

1733. FIELDING, *Don Quixote*, III., vi. I could not number them. I dare swear there were a good round BAKER'S DOZEN, at least.

1825. SCOTT, *St. Ronan's Well*, ch. xxviii. 'As to your lawyer, you get just your guinea's worth from him—not even so much as the BAKER'S BARGAIN, THIRTEEN TO THE DOZEN.'

BAKER'S DOZEN is occasionally used in a somewhat more figurative sense, and is not confined to the technicalities of trade. It is employed to signify thirteen or fourteen. It is so quoted in Grose (1785), but the usage is apparently much older than that, for Hudson, the navigator, when he discovered the bay to which his name is given, designated a cluster of thirteen or fourteen islands on the east shore of it. THE BAKER'S DOZEN, as may be seen on the charts; and even French atlases exhibit these islands as *La Douzaine du boulanger*.

TO GIVE ONE A BAKER'S DOZEN is to pummell a man well; to thrash him soundly—a humorous allusion to the good measure implied by the phrase.

BAKES, *subs.* (American thieves').—A schoolboy.

BAKESTER, *subs.* (Winchester College).—One who bakes (*see* BAKE); a sluggard. The term is now obsolete.

BAKING LEAVE, *subs.* (Winchester College).—Permission to BAKE (*q.v.*) in a study in 'Commoners,' or in a 'scob' place in College. In this sense the term is obsolete; but it is now used of leave to sit in any other person's 'TOYS' (*q.v.*)—a sort of bureau.

BAKING PLACE, *subs.* (Winchester College).—A kind of sofa in 'Studies' of 'Commoners.'

BALAAM, *subs.* (journalistic).—A term applied to all kinds of miscellaneous matter, generally of a trumpery and indifferent character, used as 'padding' in periodical publications. Evidently from Numbers xxii., 30, in which the ass spoke 'with man's voice.' BALAAM hence denotes 'the speech of an ass,' and is well applied to the stupid jokes, and silly paragraphs with which odd corners and short columns are often lengthened out. Brewer claims an American origin, but Webster only calls it 'a cant term.' In any case the term has clearly reference to nonsense to be thrown in to fill space, or nonsense thrown out as refuse. The curious point in the story of Balaam is that the ass talks like a philosopher and the prophet behaves like a donkey. The term was popularised by its frequent use in *Blackwood's Magazine*.

1826. SCOTT, *Mal. Malagr.* iii., 3. How much BALAAM (speaking technically) I have edged out of your valuable paper.

1839. LOCHART, *Scott*, lxx. (1842), 622. BALAAM is the cant name for asinine paragraphs about monstrous productions of nature and the like, kept standing in type to be used whenever the real news of the day leave an awkward space that must be filled up somehow. [M.]

BALAAM-BASKET or **BALAAM-BOX**, *subs.* (journalistic).—1. The receptacle for BALAAM (*q.v.*).

2. When articles or other contributions are rejected they are put in the BALAAM-BASKET, which may either be a pigeon-hole (to await return to the author); the waste paper basket; or, as the readiest mode of extinction, the flames. In any case, the destination is

said to be the BAALAM-BASKET or BOX.

1827. *Blackw. Mag.*, xxi., 340. Several dozen letters on the same subject now in our BALAAM-BOX.

1873. HALL, *Modern English*, p. 17. An essay for the *Edinburgh Review*, in 'the old unpolluted English language,' would have been consigned by the editor to his BALAAM-BASKET.

1877. *Notes and Queries*, 5 S., vii., 270, 2. At the risk of getting into your BALAAM-BOX, I venture to record the whole contents of my bundle as they lie before me.

BALACLAVA-DAY, *subs.* (military).—A soldier's pay day. Balaclava, in the Crimean War [1854-6], was the base of supply for the English troops; and, as pay was drawn, the men went down to make their purchases.

BALANCE, *subs.* (American). — A BALANCE properly is that which balances or produces equilibrium. It is the difference between two sides of an account — the amount of which is necessary to make the one equal to the other. It is not the rest or the remainder, yet we continually hear of the BALANCE of this or that thing. In the sense of 'rest,' 'residue,' or 'remainder,' BALANCE is the purest slang.

1846. *Albany Journal*, Jan. 7. The yawl returned to the wreck, took ten or eleven persons and landed them, and then went and got the BALANCE from the floating cabin. [B.]

1861. *Boston Transcript*, Dec. 27. 'We listened to Wendell Phillips for about half an hour, and having an engagement elsewhere, we were forced to leave, and so lost the BALANCE of his oration.' [DE V.]

The word is thus used very much like the Scottish *lave* (what is left), employed by Burns in the line—

'I'll get a blessing with the *lave*,
And never miss it.'

In some parts of Virginia the word '*shank*' is quaintly used for the same purpose, and one friend will say to another, 'Suppose you come in and spend the *shank* of the evening with me?' The vulgarism is becoming common in England, as witness the following:—

1875. *Blackwood's Magazine*, April, 443. BALANCE, long familiar to American ears, is becoming so to ours. In an account of a ship on fire we read 'Those saved remained the BALANCE of the night watching the burning wreck. [M.]

1883. P. FITZGERALD, *Recreations of a Literary Man*, 170. Everyone is away shooting or riding; a BALANCE of the ladies is left. [M.]

BALBUS, *subs.* (University). — A Latin prose composition. In Arnold's well-known text book, *Latin Prose Composition*, BALBUS turns up at every corner; he is here, there, and everywhere; he appears to be willing and able to do anything, and go anywhere; in fact it is BALBUS this, and BALBUS that, until the wonder is whether BALBUS was not something of a prig or bore, or both. At all events those who used the text book in question, cannot fail to remember that doughty old fossil of a Roman to their dying day.

1870. *Quarterly Review*. BALBUS was in constant use.

BALDERDASH, *subs.* (old).—1. Adulterated wine; a mixture of liquors such as wine and beer, milk and beer, etc.

2. (colloquial).—Frothy talk; nonsense; a jumble of words.

1885. MURRAY, *New English Dictionary*, Art. BALDERDASH, vol. I., p. 633, col. 3. From the evidence at present, the inference is that the current sense was transferred from 1 or 2 [*i.e.*, Froth, frothy liquid, or a jumbled mixture of liquids] either with the notion of 'frothy talk,' or of 'a senseless farrago,' or 'jumble of words.' Most etymologists have, however, assumed 3 [nonsense; frothy talk, etc.] to be the original sense, and sought its explanation in the obvious similarity of *balder* to dialectical *balder*, 'to use coarse language'; Dutch, *balderen*, 'to roar, thunder'; Norwegian, *baldra*; Icelandic, *baldrast*, *ballrast*, 'to make a clatter,' and of *-dash* to the verb *dash* in various senses. The Welsh *baldorddus*, adj., *f. baldordd*, 'idle, noisy talk, chatter,' has also been adduced . . . . Other conjectures may be found in Wedgwood, Skeat, and E. Müller.

BALD-FACE, *subs.* (American).—New whiskey; so villainous is the compound, that only by courtesy can it be recognised as at all approaching the Simon Pure. For synonyms, *see* DRINKS.

BALD-FACED SHIRT, *subs.* (American).—In cowboy lingo, a white shirt; from the fact of being white on the face or front. Ordinarily bald-face is used of animals, *e.g.*, a BALD-FACED STAG. Hereford cattle, too, have white faces, and as cowboys are brought into close contact with all kinds of cattle, the term as applied to a linen shirt is possibly a mere transference in sense. *Cf.*, BOILED SHIRT.

BALD-FACED STAG, *subs.* (common).—A bald-headed man; [from BALD-FACED, having white on face + STAG, a slang term for a man. *Cf.*, STAG PARTY.] For synonyms, *see* BLADDER OF LARD.

BALDHEADED.—TO GO IT BALDHEADED, *phr.* (American). — With eager impetuosity, or great haste; to do a thing with all one's might and main. A suggestion of action without stopping to cover one's head, *i.e.*, on the spur of the moment.

1848-62. J. R. LOWELL, *Biglow Papers*, p. 6.
It ain't by princerples nor men
My preudunt course is steadied,—
I scent which pays the best, an' then
Go into it BALDHEADED.

1869. *Our Young Folks.* Whenever he had made up his mind to do a thing he WENT AT IT BALDHEADED. [DE V.]

1888. *Pall Mall Gazette*, June 22. The Chicago Republicans, to use an Americanism, have gone BALDHEADED for protection. If shouting could win a Presidential contest, Blaine and Protection would be certain.

TO SNATCH BALDHEADED, *phr.* (American). — To defeat a person in a street fight.

1871. R. GRANT WHITE, *Words and Their Uses.*
The crowd than gave a specimen of calumny broke loose,
And said I'd SNATCHED HIM BALDHEADED, and likewise cooked his goose.

BALD-HEADED ROW, *subs. phr.* (American).—The first row of stalls at theatres, especially those which make a feature of ballets. The term is a cynical allusion to the fact that these seats are generally occupied by men of mature age; the innuendo is obvious.—*See* FROG-SALAD.

BALDITUDE, *subs.* (American).—A state of baldness. Probably a nonce word.

1882. S. L. CLEMENS ('Mark Twain'), *The Adventures of Huckleberry Finn*, p. 187. Trouble has done it, Bilgewater, trouble has done it; trouble has brung these gray hairs and this premature BALDITUDE.

BALDOBER or **BALDOWER**, *subs.* (thieves').—A leader; a head man; a spokesman. This term has been imported into the lingo of English thieves from the German Gaunersprache, in which it has very much the same meaning.

BALDUCTUM, *subs.* (old).—Nonsense; rubbish. *Cf.*, BALDERDASH.

BALDY, *subs.* (American).—A colloquial vulgarism for a bald-headed man. *Cf.*, BALDITUDE.

BALFOUR'S MAIDEN, *subs.* (Parliamentary).—A nickname given to a kind of covered battering-ram used by the Royal Irish Constabulary in carrying out evictions in Ireland in the years 1888-9. On many estates the tenants made most desperate resistance to all attempts on the part of the landlords to recover possession, upon which the latter appealed for, and obtained the assistance of the authorities. This but served to intensify the struggle, and the tenants, driven to extremities, in some cases resisted all endeavours, even to throwing boiling water over the soldiers and police employed against them. To protect the evictors, and also to render easier the demolition of the cabins of the wretched people, a kind of covered battering-ram was made, whereupon the Home Rule Party sarcastically gave it, amongst other nick-names, that of BALFOUR'S MAIDEN. The term was first used by Sir Wm. Harcourt in a speech at a monster Home Rule meeting, held at St. James's Hall, on Wednesday, April 10, 1889. An account of the incident runs as follows:—

1889. *Daily News*, April 11. Resolute government has not been absolutely extinguished. Now at Letterkenny, Mr. Balfour has introduced a new invention, the latest development of resolute government. The Government were questioned on the subject, and they accepted the responsibility for the facts. It stated that in view of the Olphert estate evictions, there reached there an iron-headed spiked battering-ram to be used in carrying out the evictions. Why, really, gentlemen, when you read of these things they are like the pictures one sees of the Siege of Jerusalem—(loud laughter)—of the implements, which the Latins called *tormenta*. We are familiar with them in old mediæval castles. You find instruments called 'The Scavenger's Daughter,' and 'The Maiden,' and other implements of that character. I think this last pattern of ram of Mr. Balfour's might be called 'The Unionist's Daughter'—(loud laughter)—or it might be christened 'BALFOUR'S MAIDEN.' (Cheers and laughter.) But not to deprive the Liberal Unionists of their share we might call it 'Chamberlain's Tenants' Protector.' (Renewed merriment.)

BALL, *subs.* (thieves').—1. A prison ration. 2. A drink.

TO OPEN THE BALL, *phr.* (common).—To commence an undertaking; to start off.

1876. *Eton Chronicle*, July 20.
. . . Whatever may seem the mishaps of his team,
Whatever their failings and sinnings,
He who OPENED THE BALL and who saw them all fall,
Scarce deserved that defeat in one innings.

BALLAD-BASKET, *subs.* (old). — A street singer. — *See* STREET PITCHER. A French equivalent is *un braillard*.

BALLAMBANGJANG, *subs.* (nautical).—The Straits of BALLAMBANGJANG, though unnoticed by geographers, are frequently mentioned in sailors' yarns as being so narrow, and the rocks on each side so crowded with trees inhabited by monkeys, that the ship's yards cannot be squared, on account of the monkey's tails getting jammed into, and choking up, the brace blocks.—*Hotten.*

BALLAST, *subs.* (common).—Money. For synonyms, *see* ACTUAL.

WELL-BALLASTED, *adj.* (common).—A rich man is said to be WELL-BALLASTED.

ENGLISH SYNONYMS. 'To be flush'; also 'to have brass; brads,' etc. *See* synonyms for money generally under ACTUAL. Among French equivalents for the solidity arising from the possession of wealth may be mentioned : — *Etre zingué* (popular: literally 'to be covered with zinc') ; *avoir des monacos* (popular: *monaco* is an ironical term for a sou) ; *daim huppé* (popular: *daim*, a slang term for a swell, is properly a 'buck,' and *huppé* also signifies high in station, well-off) ; *homme au sac* (familiar: 'a man with a bag,'—presumably of money) ; *avoir des picaillons* (popular: *picaillons* is thought to be a corruption of *picarons*, a Spanish coin) ; *être de la fête* (popular: *i.e.*, 'to be in luck's way') ; *être sacqué* (popular: meaning obvious) ; *rupin* (thieves' term) ; *avoir de ce qui sonne* (popular: 'to have that which chinks') ; *tailler en plein drap* (popular).

In the Spanish Germania a rich or WELL-BALLASTED man is *florido, i.e.*, 'flowery' or 'agreeable.'

BALL FACE, *subs.* (American).—A contemptuous epithet applied by negroes to white persons. Salem, Mass., 1810-1820.

BALL-KEEPER, *subs.* (Winchester College).—In 'Commoners' an Inferior' appointed to look after cricket and footballs. In return for this service he was exempted from 'kicking in' and 'watching out.' 'Junior in College' has to bring through balls every evening.—*See* BALLS.

BALL OF FIRE, *subs. phr.* (popular).—A glass of fiery and pungent brandy. For all synonyms, *see* DRINKS.

BALLOONING, *subs.* (Stock Exchange).—Inflating the price of stocks by fictitious means, such as newspaper articles, bogus sales, etc.

BALLOON IT, *verb.* (American).—To indulge in rhodomontade; to draw the long bow; to talk big. Obviously from 'to puff or swell out' as a balloon.
1878. T. SINCLAIR, *Mount,* 33. Gas-brained, BALLOONING wandering men. [M.]

BALL O' WAX, *subs.* (common).—A snob, or shoe-maker.—*See* SNOB.

BALLS. TO BRING THROUGH BALLS, *phr.* (Winchester College).— 'Junior in College' collects footballs from the lockers in school, and brings them through at six o'clock to be blown, or repaired, if necessary.

TO MAKE BALLS OF, *verb. phr.* (popular).—To go wrong; to do what 'lands' one in trouble; generally, to make a mistake.

ALL BALLS, *adv.* (popular).—All rubbish; nonsense. For synonyms, *see* ALL MY EYE.

BALLUM RANCUM, *subs.* (old).—A hop or dance, where the women

are all prostitutes; a dance at a brothel. These orgies sometimes take the form of 'buff-balls,' all present dancing in the nude.

BALLY, *adj.* (popular).—A comparatively recent coinage, it is said, of the *Sporting Times*, from 'bally-hooly.' Generally, though not always, used as is 'bloody,' in the lower strata of the body politic. It also signifies intensity, and in cases where the vocabulary at command is limited, BALLY does yeoman's service for such words as 'fearful,' 'dreadful,' 'terrible,' 'outrageous,' 'confounded.'
1889. *Sporting Times,* July 6 (Answers to Correspondents). H. G. Steele:—Thanks. What a BALLY idiot you must be.
1889. *Bird o' Freedom,* Aug. 7, p. 5. Newman Noggs, bringing small boy to carry master's bag, and inculcating manners at the same time, 'Now, what would you say if I was to give you sixpence for taking it?' 'I should say 'twasnt half enough, and you can BALLY well take it yourself,' was the prompt reply. Boys are boys nowadays, and no error, thinks Newman.

BALLY-BOUNDER.—*See* BALLY and BOUNDER.

BALLY-FELLOW.—*See* BOUNDER and BALLY.

BALLY FLAT.—*See* BOUNDER and BALLY.

BALLY FOOL.—*See* BOUNDER and BALLY.

BALLYRAG.—*See* BULLYRAG.

BALM, *subs.* (old).—A lie.—*Duncombe.*

BALMY, *subs.* and *adj.* (common).—Sleep; sleepy. [From the figurative sense of BALMY, *i.e.*, deliciously soft and soothing.]

TO HAVE A DOSE OF THE BALMY; *i.e.*, 'to go to sleep.'
1840. DICKENS, *Old Curiosity Shop,* ch. viii., p. 42. 'As it's rather late, I'll try and get A WINK OR TWO OF THE BALMY.'

ENGLISH SYNONYMS. To doss; to go to BEDFORDSHIRE (*q.v.*)—a play upon words.

FRENCH SYNONYMS. *La pionce* or *pionçage* (popular: *subs., see pioncer*) ; *le somno* (popular: an abbreviated form of *somnolence*) ; *piquage de romance* (a military term) ; *casser une canne*, or *sa canne* (popular: this also means 'to die.' In French as in other languages the analogy between Sleep and Death is fully recognised. Many of the French slang phrases for the former are also used to express the latter. *Mors janua vitæ!*) ; *casser son pif* (popular: *pif* in French argot='the nose.' Amongst the peasants of Normandy and Berry it signifies a 'grog-blossom') ; *pioncer* (popular: from *piausser*, a provincialism for 'to sleep') ; *piquer un chien* (popular: *piquer* a canting verb of action, 'to do'; therefore 'to do as a dog') ; *piquer une romance* (popular) ; *faire son lézard* (popular: *Cf., piquer un chien*) ; *faire son michaud* (thieves': *i.e.*, 'to rest one's head or knowledge box') ; *roupiller* (this term is in general colloquial use) ; *se recueillir* (popular: 'to wrap oneself in meditation') ; *compter des pauses* (musicians': 'to count the beats.' *Cf.*, various suggested remedies

for overcoming insomnia; *e.g.*, counting slowly up to a hundred, etc., etc.) ; *taper de l'œil* (popular: 'to rub the eyes.' *Cf.*, English 'to have sleepy dust in one's eyes') ; *mettre le chien au cran de repos* (popular: 'to curl oneself up like a dog') ; *souffler ses clairs* (popular : 'to blow or put out one's light,' *i.e.*, 'to shut the eyes') ; *fermer maillard* (popular: to close one's shutters, *i.e.*, eyelids. Maillard was the inventor of a particular kind of shutter. Other analogous expressions are *être terrassé par maillard, i.e.*, 'to be extremely sleepy.' Sleep is expressed by *fermeture*) ; *faire schloff* or *schloffer*, from the German *schlafen.*

SPANISH SYNONYM. In the Germania *difunto*, properly 'defunct,' is used for asleep.

A PORTUGUESE SYNONYM for sound sleep is *a bom sornar, i.e.*, 'to sleep on both ears.'

2. Dull-witted; thick-skulled. In this sense BALMY is used up and down the whole gamut of imbecility from mere stolidity to downright insanity. Popularly used, it signifies in most cases little more than shallow-brained or muddle-headed ; or, to use slang equivalents in their most familiar sense, 'to be touched,' 'to be wrong in the upper story,' 'dotty.' Among thieves, however, it is usually applied to insanity, TO PUT ON THE BALMY STICK being, among convicts, to feign madness.
1851. H. MAYHEW, *London Lab. and Lon. Poor,* vol. I., p. 231. List of patterers' words. BALMY—Insane.

A large number of synonyms will be found under APARTMENTS

TO LET, but in addition to those there mentioned may be instanced the following in the French slang: — *Demenager* (popular: 'to remove one's furniture.' It also means 'to die') ; *paumer la sorbonne* (*i.e.*, to punch the head,' *sorbonne* being a slang term for that part of the human body. The Sorbonne is a well-known university and seat of learning. Among thieves, too, *sorbonner* is used in the sense of 'to think') ; *être un peu toc* (*i.e.*, slightly crazy ; *toc* in slang=ridiculous) ; *avoir une pomme de canne felée* (popular : a rather opprobnious expression, meaning 'to have a slate off.' *Cf.*, 'to have a tile loose') ; *avoir une fissure* (literally 'to have a crack') ; *avoir un grain.*

BALMY COVE, *subs.* (common).—A weak-minded individual; one who has 'a tile loose.' [From BALMY (*q.v.*) + COVE, a man.] Among French thieves such an individual is called *un hurlubier* (*hurlublu* is an obsolete term used jestingly for a giddy goose or hair-brained person) ; also *biscayen* from the *Bicêtre* prison which has a lunatic ward for demented convicts. The prison itself is calle *La Biscaye*, but this name has no connection with the province of Biscay as might be supposed.

BALSAM, *subs.* (thieves' and popular). — One of the many generic names for money. A full list of synonyms will be found under ACTUAL. The allusion of course is obvious, *i.e.*, a healing soothing agent or agency; but, in its secondary signification of impertinence,

'brass,' 'cheek,' etc, the reverse of the shield is given. Such reversals in the legitimate meanings of words are not uncommon in slang.

BAM, *subs.* (old slang).—1. A cheat; an imposition; a story intended to hoax the credulous; what nowadays generally goes under the name of chaff or humbug [BAM is thought to be an abbreviated form of BAMBOOZLE (*q.v.*)]. Murray has traced it back to 1762, but it appears nearly twenty years previous in Dyche's dictionary, and also in Martin's, the second edition of which was published in 1754.—*See* verb TO BAM.
1748. T. DYCHE, *Dictionary* (5 ed.). BAM (s.), a sham or pretence, a lying excuse.
1762. FOOTE, *Orators,* Act ii. Why I know that man, he is all upon his fun; he lecture—why 'tis all but a BAM.
1817. SCOTT, *Rob Roy,* ch. ix. 'It's all a BAM, ma'am—all a bamboozle and a bite, that affair of his illness.'

Verb. — To hoax, to bamboozle; to wheedle; to cheat. [Of same formation as substantive, which see above, and *Cf.*, BAMBOOZLE.] The first trace of it appears in Cibber's *Double Gallant* [1707], and is discussed by Swift in his introduction to *Polite Conversation* [1738], where he mentions among 'the exquisite refinements' then in vogue, — BAM for bamboozle, and bamboozle for, God knows what. Whereupon a correspondent of *Notes and Queries* [2 S., Jan. 10, '57, p. 31] alluding to the despair of etymologists in regard to these words remarked that if *from* was put in the place of *for*, it would describe the predicament in which philologists are placed.

1754. H. MARTIN, *Eng. Dict.*, 2 ed. To BAM, or TO BAMBOOZLE, to fun, to fib, to sham.
1760. COLMAN, *Polly Honeycombe,* in *wks.* (1777) IV., 43. 'Lord, how well he behaves! We shall certainly BAM the old gentleman.
1830. MARRYAT, *King's Own,* ch. xlix. 'Now, you're BAMMING me—don't attempt to put such stories off on your old granny.'
1874. E. L. LINTON, *Patricia Kemball,* ch. xxxix. For a moment the thought flashed across him whether 'that tale of Gordon Frere was all a BAM, and had the girl taken a liking for himself?'

BAMBLUSTERCATE, *verb.* (nonce-word).—A factitious creation signifying to embarrass ; confuse ; or hoax in a blustering manner. [From BAM, to hoax, or confuse + BLUSTER, noisy assertion + CATE, a termination in imitation of 'conglomerate'.]—*See* also COMFLOGISTICATE.

BAMBOO, *verb.* (American). — A corruption of bamboozle. To cheat; to victimize; to hoax.—*See*, however, BAM and BAMBOOZLE.

BAMBOOZLE, *verb.* (familiar).—To hoax; deceive; or impose upon. Philologists are all confessedly at sea in regard to the derivation of BAMBOOZLE and its attributive forms, but the general tendency of evidence is to refer it to a gypsy origin. Johnson states it to be a cant word; and Bouchier, in his glossary says, 'it has with great propriety long had a place in the gypsy or canting dictionaries,' it being in his opinion 'the sole invention of gypsies or vagrants.' Leland thinks it 'possibly' the Hindu word *bambhorna*, to humbug, with the gypsy terminative *ăsel.* Wedgwood suggests its origin in the Italian *bamboccio*, a young babe, and metaphorically an old dotard or babyish gull; *imbambolare*, to blear or dim one's sight, also with flatteries and blandishments, to inveigle and make a fool of one. If a verb were made of *bambocciolo* in the same way as *bamboccio-lare*, it would have much the sense of BAMBOOZLE. A. E. Quekett (*N. and Q.*, 5 S., xii., 488) throws a side-light upon this last theory by pointing out that in Shakspeare's *Taming of the Shrew*, Katharina says, 'Belike you mean to make a puppet of me,' and Petruchio replies, 'Why true; he means to make a puppet of thee.' Comparing this passage with the rest of the scene it would seem that Petruchio's answer is not a mere repetition of Katharina's words, but contains a *double entendre* of some kind. He (Quekett) then hazards that perhaps she meant to say, 'Perhaps you mean to treat me as a doll without a will of its own,' while Petruchio appears to mean something very like. 'He wishes to BAMBOOZLE you.'

Be all this as it may, BAMBOOZLE first came into vogue during the early part of the last century; for in the *Tatler* No. 230 [1710], we read, 'The third refinement observable in the letter I send you consists in the choice of certain words invented by some pretty fellows, such as banter, BAMBOOZLE, country-put, and kidney, some of which are now struggling for the vogue, and others are in possession of it'!

So also with the derivatives; *e.g.*, BAMBOOZLE (*subs.*); BAMBOOZLED; BAMBOOZLEMENT; BAMBOOZLER; BAMBOOZLING.

1708. CIBBER, *She Would and She Would Not*, II., i. (1736), 34. Sham proofs, that they propos'd to BAMBOOZLE me with. [M.]

1709. STEELE, *Tatler*, No. 31. But, says I, sir, I perceive this is to you all BAMBOOZLING.

1712. ARBUTHNOT, *History of John Bull*, pt. III., ch. vi. There are a sort of fellows that they call banterers and BAMBOOZLERS, that play such tricks; but it seems these fellows were in earnest!

1731. COFFEY, *Devil to Pay*, Act i., Sc. 3. You juggler, you cheating, BAMBOOZLING villain!

1754. FOOTE, *Knights*, Act ii. You are tricked, imposed on, BAMBOOZLED!

1779. R. CUMBERLAND, *Wheel of Fortune*, Act ii., Sc. 1. You know I love you, Emily, ... and therefore you baffle and BAMBOOZLE and make a bumpkin of me.

1817. SCOTT, *Rob Roy*, ch. ix. 'It's all a bam, ma'am—all a BAMBOOZLE and a bite, that affair of his illness.'

1827. LYTTON, *Pelham*, ch. xxxvi. 'One does not like to be BAMBOOZLED out of one's right of election, by a smooth-tongued fellow, who sends one to the devil the moment the election is over.'

1886. *Sat. Review*, No. 1587, p. 423. The public is a great BAMBOOZABLE body.

(Nautical).—To decoy the enemy by hoisting false colours—merely an extension of the popular sense.

ENGLISH SYNONYMS. 'To throw dust in the eyes'; 'to use the pepper-box'; 'to gild the pill'; 'to throw a tub to a whale'; 'to make believe the moon is made of cream cheese'; 'to jockey'; 'to stick'; 'to bilk'; 'to do'; 'to best'; 'to do brown'; 'to bounce'; 'to take in'; 'to kid'; 'to gammon.'

FRENCH SYNONYMS. *Une monteuse de coups* (a woman who bamboozles her lovers); *monter des couleurs* (popular: 'to de-

ceive by false representations; *couleur* signifies 'pretence,' 'semblance'); *faire la queue à quelqu'un* (popular); *tirer la carotte* (thieves'); *faire voir le tour* (popular); *canarder* (popular: literally 'to shoot at one from a sheltered position'; *i.e.*, to have an advantage, and thus to be able to hoax or humbug); *dindonner* (popular: from *dindon*, a 'goose'); *faire le coup*, or *monter le coup à quelqu'un* (popular: *coup* in French slang is 'a secret process,' 'a knack' or 'dodge'—hence 'to deal one an underhand blow,' or 'to serve one a trick'); *empaler* (popular: 'to deceive by false representations'; literally 'to empale'); *passer des curettes* (popular: 'to make a fool of one'); *monter une gaffe* (popular: *gaffe* in French slang = 'a joke'; a piece of deceit); *monter le job* or *jobarder* (popular: *job* is equivalent to 'simpleton' or 'flat,' and is the same as *jobelin*); *mener en bateau un pante pour le refaire* (thieves': 'to deceive a man in order to rob him'); *monter un batteau* (popular); *donner un pont à faucher* (thieves': 'to lay a trap or snare'); *promener quelqu'un* (popular: 'to make a fool of one.' *Cf.*, 'to rush'); *compter des mistouffles* (familiar: *mistouffle* = 'a scurvy trick'; 'a joke'); *gourrer* (popular: 'to stick'; 'to kid'; 'to deceive'); *affluer* (from *à flouer*, 'to cheat'; 'to diddle out of'); *roustir* (popular and thieves': 'to cheat'); *affûter* (thieves': 'to make unlawful profits'); *bouler* (popular); *juiffer* (popular: literally 'to Jew' as in English); *pigeonner* (familiar: 'to do,' 'to pluck.' In English slang the victims of card and other sharpers are called 'pigeons'); *flancher* (popular: 'to laugh at' or 'ridicule'); *faire la barbe* (popular: *Cf.*, *faire la queue*); *hisser un gandin* (thieves': literally 'to hoist a dandy' or 'swell'); *mettre dedans* (popular: to take a rise out of one; literally to 'take in'); *être l'autre* (popular: *Cf.*, to get left.' The phrase also signifies 'to be the lover,' the mistress); *planter un chou* (familiar).

GERMAN SYNONYMS. —*See* JOCKEY.

ITALIAN SYNONYMS. *Traversare* (literally 'to cross over'); *dar la stolfa*.

SPANISH SYNONYM. *Encantar* (literally 'to enchant,' 'to entertain with soft words').

BAMBOSH, *subs.* (nonce word).—Apparently a variation of BAMBOOZLING, as follows. [BAM + BOSH.] Humbug; deceit; hoaxing.

1865. *Day of Rest*, Oct., 585. I was deaf to all that BAMBOSH. [M.]

BAMBSQUABBLED. — This coined word, which is, however, rarely used except in humorous writings, first saw the light in *The Legend of the American War*. It signifies discomfiture and defeat, or stupefaction; sometimes written BUMSQUABBLED.

1835-40. T. C. HALIBURTON ('Sam Slick'), *The Clockmaker*, 2 S., ch. ii. The judge said, 'He had got too much already, cut him off the other two-thirds, and make him pay all costs.' If he didn't look BUMSQUABBLED it's a pity.

BANAGHAN. HE BEATS BANAGHAN, *phr.* (old).—An Irish saying of one who tells wonderful stories; Banaghan, thought Grose, was a minstrel famous

for dealing in the marvellous—a kind of prototype of Baron Munchausen. Of this, deponent knowing nothing, says the same.

BANAGHER, *verb* (old).—To bang.

BANANALAND, BANANALANDER, *subs.* (Australian).—Queensland, and a native of Queensland respectively. Apparently from a large portion of that section of the fifth continent lying within the tropics, thus allowing of the cultivation of the banana tree (*Musa sapientum*).

1886. *Chamb. Journal*, Feb. 20, p. 124. Booted and spurred 'Cornstalks' and BANANA-MEN (natives of New South Wales and Queensland respectively).

1887. *Melbourne* (Victoria) *Sportsman*, 23 March, p. 7, col. 2. Paddy Slavin came from Queensland with the reputation of having beaten all the BANANALANDERS.

1887. *Sydney* (N.S.W.) *Bulletin*, 26 Feb., p. 6. His friends rallied up to congratulate him, and see him through, after the custom of the simple BANANALANDER.

It may be interesting to note that a native of New South Wales is nicknamed a 'CORNSTALK,' because built somewhat tall and thin. Those whose stature is shorter, with circumference of wider dimensions in proportion to their height are said to be 'NUGGETY.' The gum trees of Tasmania give the elegant nickname 'GUMSUCKER' to its inhabitants. In this practice antipodean colonists follow suit with their cousins across the Atlantic.—*See* NICKNAMES.

BANCO, *subs.* (Charterhouse School).—Evening preparation down at 'house' each day, superintended by a monitor. It answers to the Winchester TOY-TIME.

BANCO-STEERER. — *See* BUNCO-STEERER.

BANDANNA, *subs.* (common).—Formerly a silk handkerchief with white, yellow, or other coloured spots on a dark ground. Now applied to handkerchiefs of all kinds. The name is thought to come from the Spanish *bandano*, a neckerchief.

1752. J. LONG, *Bengal* (1870), 31. Plain taffaties, ordinary BANDANNOES, and chappas.

1855. THACKERAY, *Newcomes*, ch. iv. The Colonel was striding about the room in his loose garments, puffing his cigar fiercely anon, and then waving his yellow BANDANNA.

BANDED, *ppl. adj.* (old).—Hungry. To mitigate the pangs of hunger, starving men tighten the belt round the 'middle.' Bamfylde Moore Carew, the king of the beggars, mentions the practice. *Cf.*, CAFFRE'S TIGHTENER and BANDS.

BANDERO, *subs.* (American).—Widows' weeds; a corruption of the now obsolete 'bandore,' a widow's head-dress. BANDORE was itself a corruption of the French *bandeau*, given by Littré as *anciennement*, *coiffure des veuves*. The term was current about the beginning of the last century, but in 1785 we find it quoted as slang. It appears, however, to have survived in America whilst dropping entirely out of use in the Mother Country. In the English drapery trade mourning goods are sometimes called AFFLICTIONS (*q.v.*).

BAN-DOG, *subs.* (old).—A bailiff, or his assistant. Originally, says

Murray, a dog tied or chained up either to guard a house, or on account of its ferocity; hence generally a mastiff or bloodhound. The transition from this point to the slang sense is clear.

1839. HARRISON AINSWORTH, *Jack Sheppard* [1889], p. 12. 'But where are the lurchers?' 'Who?' asked Wood. 'The traps!' responded a bystander. 'The shoulder-clappers!' added a lady, who, in her anxiety to join the party, had unintentionally substituted her husband's nether habiliments for her own petticoats. 'The BAN-DOGS!' thundered a tall man whose stature and former avocations had procured him the nickname of 'The long drover of the Borough market.' 'Where are they?' 'Ay, where are they?' chorused the mob, flourishing their various weapons, and flashing their torches in the air; 'we'll sarve 'em out.'

BANDS, *subs.* TO WEAR THE BANDS (old cant). — To be hungry.—*See* BANDED.

B. AND S. (popular).—An every-day colloquialism, in the abbreviated form, for brandy and soda.

1868. WHYTE MELVILLE, *White Rose*, ch. xiii. Before the B. AND S.—signifying a beaker of brandy and soda-water—could make its appearance.

1881. W. BLACK, *Beautiful Wretch*, ch. v. 'Come away, and I will get you some tea, though what would be better for you still, would be some B. AND S.'

1882. *Punch*, vol. LXXXII., p. 69, col. 1.

I'll sing you a fine new song, all about a fine young spark,
Who's a fine young London gentleman, quite up to any lark,
Who takes supper very early, and breakfasts in the dark;
Who's a real 'dear old chappie,' as I needn't perhaps remark.
* * * * * * * *
He will say that port and sherry his nice palate always cloy;
He'll nothing drink but 'B. AND S.' and big magnums of 'the boy';
He's the darling of the barmaid and the honest waiter's joy,
As he quaffs his Pommery, 'Extra Sec,' his 'Giesler,' or 'Ivroy.'

BANDY, *subs.* (thieves').—A sixpence; so called, in the first instance, from these coins being often thin, worn, and bent. Also called a CRIPPLE and BENDER, but, for synonyms, see the latter. The term appears in Grose [1785].

1819. T. MOORE, *Tom Crib's Memorial*, p. 25, *n.* A BANDY or *cripple*, a sixpence.

1885. *Household Words*, June 20, p. 155. The sixpence is a coin more liable to bend than most others, so it is not surprising to find that several of its popular names have reference to this weakness. It is called a BANDY, a 'bender,' a 'cripple.'

BANG, *subs.* (colloquial).—1. A blow; Old Norse, *bang*, a hammering. Though a dictionary word, BANG has not yet succeeded in passing from the limbo of vulgarism in many of its uses. For example, a 'BANG of the door' sounds legitimate enough, and is an expression to which even the most pronounced stickler for linguistic purity would scarcely object; yet, a 'BANG on the nose' or 'jaw' would, doubtless, be looked upon as low and vulgar. Only to illustrate such variations, can the word find a fitting entry into these pages. Amongst pugilists and the vulgar, BANG is, without doubt, closely identified with personal castigation; and, in this connection,

ENGLISH SYNONYMS are not rare. To BANG one in the jaw; to spoil one's picture; to give a wipe on the nose; to fetch one a stinger, etc. The blow itself is designated a whopper; wipe; clout; prop; cant; dig; corker; shooting stars (in allusion to the dazed condition of a person so struck, stars being seen dancing before one's eyes).

FRENCH SYNONYMS. *Un gnon* (popular); *un écopage* (familiar); *une dandine* (popular); *un cabochon* (common); *un estaffion* (popular: may be rendered 'a BANG on the nut'); *un coup de gilquin* (popular); *un renfoncement* (colloquial: 'a blow with the fist'; lit. 'an indentation'); *une beugne* (common); *une beigne* (popular); *une dariole* (familiar: properly a kind of pastry); *un coup de tampon* (popular: 'a hard shove'; *tampon*, 'a buffer'); *une balle de coton* (popular); *une baffre* (popular: 'a blow in the face with the fist'); *un pétard* (familiar: either 'a box on the ear' or 'a cant on the gills'); *une paraphe* (popular: *paraphe* is properly the flourish added to one's signature); *dégrader le portrait à quelqu'un* (popular: 'to fetch one a BANG in the mug.' *Cf.*, 'to spoil one's picture'); *détacher un coup de pinceau sur la frimousse* (popular: 'to make pencil marks upon the face'; *i.e.*, 'to spoil one's physiognomy,' — the allusion presumably being to the face as the work of the Divine Artist). For other synonyms, *see* WIPE.

2. A style adopted by women in dressing the hair upon the forehead, generally curled and frizzed, the process being thus described. To make the BANG, one must begin by dividing the front hair at half-inch distances from ear to ear, combing the rest back. This is repeated until the whole front hair has been successfully BANGED. In England these fringes are also called TOFFS (*q.v.*).

1880. W. D. HOWELL, *The Undiscovered Country*, ch. viii. When one lifted his hat to wipe his forehead, he showed his hair cut in front like a young lady's BANG.

1883. *Pall Mall Gazette*, Dec. 19, p. 4, col. 1. It was no doubt unfortunate that when the Empress Eugenie cut her hair across her forehead from sorrow of heart, the women of five continents should imitate her until the BANG became universal.

Verb.—1. To deliver a blow as described under BANG (*subs.* 1); generally, to thump or strike violently; to thrash.

1588. *Marprelate's Epistle*, p. 4 (ed. Arber). His grace will cary to his grave I warrant you the blowes which M. Cartwright gave him in this cause: and, therefore, no marvell though he was loth to have any other so BANGED as he himselfe was to his woe.

1592. JOHN DAY, *Blind Beggar*, Act ii., Sc. 2, p. 37. I am sure my cloak cannot go without hands; and I'll have it again, or I'll BANG it out of the coxcombs of some of them.

b. 1719. H. CAREY, *Sally in our Alley*, st. 3.

My master comes, like any Turk,
And BANGS me most severely.

1731. FIELDING, *The Lottery*, Sc. 2. Ah, think, my lord! how I should grieve to see your lordship BANG'D.

1851-61. H. MAYHEW, *London Lab. and Lon. Poor*, vol. II., p. 47. 'It was good stuff and good make at first, and hasn't been abused, and that's the reason why it always BANGS a slop, because it was good to begin with.'

1884. *Cornhill Mag.*, April, p. 442. 'Davis,' said Toddy, 'you haven't had a BANGING this term, and you're getting cocky.'

2. To dress the hair with a fringe on the forehead, cut squarely across, so that it ends abruptly.

1882. *Century Mag.*, XXV., 192. He was bareheaded, his hair BANGED even with his eyebrows in front.

1888. *Detroit Free Press.*

BANG, Sister, BANG with care;
If your poker's too hot you'll lose your hair.

3. To surpass; to excel. So also BANGING, *adj.*, great or thumping.

4. (Stock Exchange.)—To loudly offer stock with the intention of lowering the price.

To BE BANGED UP TO THE EYES, *phr.* (common).—To be drunk. For synonyms, *see* SCREWED.

BANG-BEGGAR, *subs.* (old).—A constable or beadle. It is not quite clear whether this is not merely a dialecticism. In Lowland Scotch it signifies a strong staff.

BANGER, *subs.* (common).—A lie. Generally, THAT'S A BANGER! This elegant phrase is sometimes varied by 'that's a WHOPPER' (*q.v.*); or the now classical 'THUMPER' (*q.v.*), an invention of the late Lord Iddesleigh.

(Yale College).—A club-like cane or stick; a bludgeon. This word is one of the Yale vocables.—HALL'S *College Words and Customs*.

Yale Lit. Mag., vol. XX., p. 75.

The Freshman reluctantly turned the key,
Expecting a Sophomore gang to see,
Who, with faces masked and BANGERS stout,
Had come resolved to smoke him out.

BANG-OFF, *adv.* (familiar).—Without stopping; right away; *e.g.*, 'I wrote as promised BANG-OFF,' *i.e.*, without delay. [From BANG, a loud, sudden sound + OFF, movement from a place or thing.]

BANG-OUT. To BANG-OUT, *verbal phr.* (common). — To depart hurriedly and with noise.

Adv. phr.—Completely, entirely, combined with suddenness; *e.g.*, 'the candle went BANG-OUT.'

BANG-PITCHER, *subs.* (old). — A drunkard. Possibly only dialectical.

BANGSTER, *subs.* (provincial). — According to Jamieson:—1. A violent and disorderly person, who regards no law but his own will. 2. A victor. 3. A braggart. 4. A loose woman.

1820. SCOTT, *The Abbot*, ch. xix. If the Pope's champions are to be BANGSTERS in our very change houses, we shall soon have the changelings back again. [H.]

1825. SCOTT, *St. Ronan's Well*, ch. xxiii. If you are so certain of being the BANGSTER—so very certain, I mean, of sweeping stakes, what harm will Miss Clara come to by your having the use of her siller.

BANG-STRAW, *subs.* (old).—A nickname for a thresher of corn; a provincialism.

BANG-TAILED, *adj.* (popular).—Short tailed. Usually applied to horses.

1861. HUGHES, *Tom Brown at Oxford*, ch. vi. 'These BANG-TAILED little sinners any good?' said Drysdale, throwing some cock-a-bondies across the table. 'Yes, I never like to be without them and a governor or two.'

BANG-UP, *adj. phr.* (common).—First-rate; quite up to the mark; A 1; slap up; in the height of fashion. Also BANGED-UP.

1812. H. AND J. SMITH, *Rejected Addresses*, p. 188. Dance a BANG-UP theatrical cotillion.

1842. LEVER, *Jack Hinton*, ch. vii. His hat set jauntily on one side, his spotted neckcloth knotted in BANG-UP mode.

1844. *Quarterly Review*, XXIV., 368. We could not resist giving a specimen of John Thorpe . . . . altogether the best portrait of a species which, though almost extinct, cannot yet be quite classed among the Palœotheria, the BANG-UP Oxonian.

1846. THACKERAY, *V. Fair*, vol. I., ch. xxxiv. There appeared on the cliff in a tax cart, drawn by a BANG-UP pony . . . his friends, the Sutbury Pet and the Rottingdean Fibber.

Subs. — Also used substantively as in the following example; that which is quite right; the 'thing'; the 'go.'

1882. *Punch*, LXXXII., 185, 1. *Modern Life in London*, or *Tom and Jerry back again.* The trio turned into the ARCADE, and saw a number of *gay sparks* and *fair ones* promenading. 'Twas a curious sight, a glimpse of LIFE IN LONDON, one of its primest features, and yet, as the CORINTHIAN remarked to his Coz, these people seemed like the '*ghosts* of a former generation.' 'These then are the *dandies*, the *fops*, the *goes* and the BANG-UPS, these the CORINTHIANS of today,' was also Tom's exclamation to young Bob, who said, 'I don't know about being CORINTHIANS, but some of these *fellows* are very 'good form,' and as to being BANG-UP, a good many poor old *chappies* are deuced *hard-up*.'

Verb tr.—To make smart; to produce in first-rate style.

1821. COOMBE, *Dr. Syntax*, *Tour* iii., c. v.

Pat to his neckcloth gave an air
In style, and *á la militaire*;
His pocket too a kerchief bore
With scented water sprinkled o'er;
Thus BANGED-UP, sweeten'd, and clean shav'd,
The sage the dinner-table braved.

BANGY, *subs.* (Winchester College).—'Brown' sugar. From Bangalore, a once coarse-growing sugar country.

Adj.—Colour of brown sugar; *e.g.*, BANGY BAGS, brown trousers. These were also called BANGIES.

So universally was the term BANGY used to designate a brownish hue, that a gate of that colour at Winchester College, formerly leading from Grass Court into Sick House Meads, was called the BANGY Gate. The name is now often used for the gate by Racquet Court, into Kingsgate Street.

BANIAN-DAYS or **BANYAN-DAYS**, *subs.* (nautical).—Those days in which sailors have no flesh meat. Probably derived from the practice of the Banians, a caste of Hindoos, traders or merchants, who entirely abstained from all animal food.

1690. OVINGTON, in Yules' *Anglo-Indian Glossary.* Of kitcheney (butter, rice, and dai) the European sailors feed in these parts, and are forced at such times to a Pagan abstinence from flesh, which creates in them an utter detestation to those BANIAN-DAYS as they call them.

1748. SMOLLETT, *Rod. Random*, ch. xxv. They told me that on Mondays, Wednesdays, and Fridays, the ship's company had no allowance of meat, and that these meagre days were called BANYAN-DAYS, the reason of which they did not know; but I have since learned they take their denomination from a sect of devotees in some parts of the East Indies, who never taste flesh.

1820. LAMB, *Elia* (*Christ's Hospital*). We had three BANYAN to four meat DAYS in the week.

1855. THACKERAY, *Newcomes*, ch. lxiii. If he might be so bold as to carry on the Eastern metaphor, he would say, knowing the excellence of the Colonel's claret and the splendour of his hospitality, that he would prefer a cocoanut day at the Colonel's to a BANYAN-DAY anywhere else.

1876. C. HINDLEY, *Life and Adventures of a Cheap Jack.* [From Strolling Players' bill.] WOOLDRIDGE'S THEATRE. Wanted 700 men, to man that splendid first-class Frigate, 'The Theatre,' commanded by A. J. Wooldridge, now lying at her moorings, in Cheapside. Mr. Wooldridge, with all due respects to his brother Tars, hopes they will lend a hand to man his Vessel. He cannot

offer them a barrel of Ale, but he will make them a promise of his unfeigned thanks and gratitude for this and past favours, with his hearty good wishes for the prosperity of the Town and Trade of Brighton; that his Shipmates, wherever bound, may set sail with fair wind and good passage; that they may never have short allowance—BANYAN DAYS; or a southerly wind in the Bread Basket.

BANJO, *subs.* (common).—A bed-pan; also called a FIDDLE or SLIPPER (*q.v.*)—the latter from an improved shape which allows of its being slipped in without disturbing the patient.

BANK, *subs.* (common).—A lump sum of money; one's fortune.

Verb (thieves').—1. To secure; to obtain (in a pilfering sense).

2. To put in a place of safety.

3. To go shares; to divide fairly with confederates.

4. (prison.)—Millbank prison.

1889. *Answers*, May 25, p. 412. We approached our destination, Millbank—the BANK in a convict's parlance.

BANKERS, *subs.* (old). — Clumsy boots and shoes; now called beetle-crushers. For synonyms generally, *see* TROTTER-CASES.

BANK SHAVING, *subs. phr.* (American.—Before banks were regulated by Act of Congress, a practice prevailed among the least reputable of such institutions of purchasing notes of hand and similar documents at enormously usurious rates of discount. Many were the facilities for sharp practice of every kind. Such banks were called *shaving banks*, and the unfortunate wretch who thus 'raised the wind' was said to GET HIS PAPER SHAVED. The origin of the phrase may be looked for in maritime nomenclature, a shaver from a sailor's point of view being a man who is cute and unscrupulous — possibly from the unpleasant operation of shaving on board ship when crossing the line.

BANKSIDE LADIES, *subs. phr.* (old).—Ladies of more complaisance than virtue. BANKSIDE, Southwark, was once the fashionable theatrical quarter of London. There stood once the Globe, the Swan, the Rose, and the Hope theatres. On the boards of the first-named originally appeared most of Shakspeare's plays. In Old London the neighbourhoods of the principal theatres appear to have been noted for anything but vestal virtue. Covent Garden and Drury Lane, like BANKSIDE, have entered largely into the vicious slang of the past.

1638. RANDOLPH, *Muses' Looking-Glass*, O. Pl., 9., 206. Come, I will send for a whole coach or two of BANKSIDE LADIES, and we will be jovial.

BANK-SNEAK, *subs.* (American).—A variety of the *genus* thief who confines his attention to bank robberies. Smart, clever, well-dressed, they usually work in gangs, two or three confederates being employed as cover whilst the leader does the work. In large towns considerable finesse is exhibited by these men in effecting their purpose; but in the more thinly populated districts polish and *ruse* are abandoned in favour of more drastic methods. The BANK-SNEAK of the West pursues his depredations more as a bandit; his city *confrère* is more adroit, and therefore infinitely more dangerous. For synonyms, *see* AREA-SNEAK.

1888. *Daily Inter-Ocean*, Feb. 16. Buffalo officers to-day picked out from a batch of Erie convicts Watt N. Jones, the notorious BANK-SNEAK and burglar so widely known professionally in every city of the United States and Canada.

BANNER, *subs.* (American news-boys').—The money paid for board and lodging at the homes frequented by these flying mercuries. The origin of the term is unknown.

BANT, *verb* (common.)—To follow the dietary prescribed by Mr. Banting.—*See* BANTING.

BANTING, *subs.* (common).—A course of diet by which fat people seek to reduce their bulk. It consists in strictly discarding as food all articles known to favour the development of adipose tissue. It was introduced about the year 1864 by a Mr. W. Banting—hence the name. The dietary recommended was the use of butcher's meat principally, and abstinence from beer, farinaceous food, and vegetables. Also figuratively, to reduce in any way.

1864. *Times*, 12 Aug., 4. The classics seemed to have undergone a successful course of BANTING.

1868. MISS BRADDON, *Only a Clod*, p. 114. She was a rigid disciplinarian of the school formed by Mr. BANTING. *Ibid*, p. 113. A parlour where all the furniture seemed to have undergone a prolonged course of BANTING.

1883. *Knowledge*, 27 July, p. 49, col. 2. BANTINGISM excludes beer, butter, and sugar.

BANTLING, *subs.* (old).—A young, or small child. This word, once slang, is now a received dictionary word. It is stated in *Bacchus and Venus* [1737], and by Grose, to be a cant term. It was formerly synonymous with bastard. Appended are a few examples of its use when knocking for admittance at the doors of the dictionaries.

1593. DRAYTON, *Eclog.*, vii., 102. Lovely Venus . . . smiling to see her wanton BANTLINGS game.

1635. QUARLES, *Emblems*, II., viii. (1718), 93. See how the dancing bells turn round . . . to please my BANTLING.

1748. SMOLLETT, *Rod. Random*, ch. xlvii. 'That he may at once deliver himself from the importunities of the mother and the suspense of her BANTLING.'

1751. SMOLLETT, *Peregrine Pickle*, ch. lxxx. 'Let the BANTLINGS,' said she, 'be sent to the hospital . . . and a small collection be made for the present support of the mother.'

1758. GOLDSMITH, *Essays*, x. Who follow the camp, and keep up with the line of march, though loaded with BANTLINGS and other baggage.

1822. SCOTT, *Fortunes of Nigel*, ch. xxi. 'Sell me to a gipsy, to carry pots, pans, and beggars BANTLINGS.'

BANTY, *adj.* (American thieves').—Saucy; impudent.

BAPTISED or **CHRISTENED**, *ppl. adj.* (old). — Mixed with water; spirits and wines are said to be BAPTISED when diluted. The French equivalent is *chrétien*; also *baptisé*.

1636. HEALEY, *Theophrastus*, 46. He wil give his best friends his BAPTIZED wine.

BAR, *verb* and *prep.* (colloquial and racing).—1. Used as a verb BAR signifies to exclude; to prohibit; also to object to a person or action. Its lineage is of undoubted respectability, but its usage is now but little removed from the vulgar. As a preposition it is synonymous with 'except' — mainly used in racing; *e.g.*, 'Four to one BAR one.'

c. 1598. SHAKSPEARE, *M. of Venice*, ii., 2, 207. Nay, but I BAR to-night: you shall not gauge me by what we do to-night.

1672. WYCHERLEY, *Love in a Wood*, wks. III. (1712), 382. That were as hard as to BAR a young parson in the pulpit, the fifth of November,—railing at the Church of Rome.

1697. VANBRUGH, *Æsop*, Act ii. What I have in my mind, out it comes: but BAR that; I'se an honest lad as well as another.

1752. FOOTE, *Taste*, Act ii. I don't suppose now, but, BARRING the nose, Roubiliac could cut as good a head every whit.

1818. SCOTT, *Rob Roy*, ch. iii. 'I should like to try that daisy-cutter of yours upon a piece of level road (BARRING canter) for a quart of claret at the next inn.'

1836. DICKENS, *Pickwick*, ch. lv., p. 483. 'I'll bet you ten guineas to five, he cuts his throat,' said Wilkins Flasher, Esquire. 'Done,' replied Mr. Simmery. 'Stop! I BAR,' said Wilkins Flasher, Esquire, thoughtfully. 'Perhaps he may hang himself.'

2. (American thieves'.)—To stop; to cease. Obviously an attributive meaning of the legitimate word.

3. (American colloquial.)—A spurious verb, the signification of which is derived from the drinking-bar. Thus a tippler is said TO BAR too much when given to inordinate drinking.

BARAGAN TAILOR, *subs.* (tailors').—A rough-working tailor.

BARB, *verb* (old cant).—To BARB gold was heretofore a cant term for clipping or shaving it. The modern term is TO SWEAT (*q.v.*). [Apparently from to BARBER, to shave or trim.]

1610. BEN JONSON, *Alchemist*, I., i. Ay, and perhaps thy neck within a noose, for laundring gold, and BARBING it.

BARBER, *verb*. (University). — When impositions are worked off by deputy they are said to be BARBERISED. Tradition relates that a learned barber was at one time frequently employed as a scapegoat in working off this species of punishment inflicted on peccant students—hence the expression. A story *ben trovato esd non e vero!*

THAT'S THE BARBER.—A street catch-phrase, says Grose, about the year 1760. There is nothing new under the sun; not even idiotic and wearisome street cries, which so many good philologists deplore as a sign of the depravity of the times. THAT'S THE BARBER, like 'Who's your hatter?' and 'How's your poor feet?' meant nothing, save a general and indefinite comment on any action, measure, or thing. 'ALL SERENE!' (*q.v.*) is presumably its nearest modern street equivalent.

BARBER'S-CAT, *subs.* (old).—A weak, sickly looking individual. In French such a person is called *un faiblard* and *un astec*, the latter an allusion to the Mexican dwarfs. According to Hotten, the term is also 'used in connexion with an expression too coarse to print.'

BARBER'S-CHAIR, *subs.* (old).—A prostitute; a drab; a strumpet. So called from a BARBER'S-CHAIR being common to all comers. It will be remembered that Shakspeare in *All's Well* [ii., 2.] likens an all-embracing answer to a question to 'a BARBER'S-CHAIR that fits all buttocks; the pin-buttock, the quatch-buttock, the brawn-buttock, or any buttock.'

1621. BURTON, *Anatomy of Melancholy*, III. iv., 1, iii. (1651), 665. A notorious strumpet as common as a BARBER'S-CHAIR. [M.]

1708. MOTTEUX, *Rabelais' Pantagr.*, *Prognost. v. Bonarobaes.* BARBER'S-CHAIRS, hedge whores.

BARBER'S-CLERK, *subs.* (common).—A term of reproach generally applied by mechanics and artisans to overdressed and vaunting clerks and shopmen. In a secondary sense it is used of anyone *over-particular* in his personal appearance. The phrases 'oh, he's just come from the barber's,' and 'one of Truefitt's young men' are common enough.

1835. DICKENS, *Sketches by Boz*, p. 155. 'Tailor!' screamed a third. 'BARBER'S-CLERK!' shouted a fourth. 'Throw him O-VER!' roared a fifth. [D.]

BARBER'S MUSIC, *subs.* (old).—Harsh and roughly discordant music. Barber's shops were formerly places of great resort, and the old plays are full of references to the means by which customers, while waiting their turn, wiled away the time. Amongst other things it was usual to provide a cittern, a musical instrument similar to a guitar, upon which any who chose could try their skill. Many of the old proverbs refer to this circumstance. Ben Jonson in *The Silent Woman* [iii., 5] makes Morose say of his wife whom his barber had recommended, 'I have married his cittern that is common to all men'; and Matheo, in *The Honest Whore*, speaks of a barber's citterne for every serving man to play upon. Therefore, it is little wonder that BARBER'S MUSIC should be synonymous with discord.

1660. PEPYS, June 5. My lord called for the lieutenant's cittern, and with two candlesticks with money in them for symbols (cymbals) we made BARBER'S MUSIC.

BAREFOOTED ON THE TOP OF ONE'S HEAD, *phr.* (American).—Baldheaded. The application of the simile is obvious.

BARGAIN. SELLING A BARGAIN, *phr.* (old).—A species of low wit, much in vogue about the latter end of the reign of Queen Anne, but which is of much more ancient usage. It is frequently alluded to by Swift, who remarks that 'the maids of honor often amused themselves with it.' If so, it seems incredible; and one would say so much the worse for the '*maids of honor.*' It is thus described: A person would come into a room full of company, apparently in a fright, crying out, 'It is white, and follows me!' On any of the company asking what? the bargain was sold by the first speaker naming a certain portion of the body. In another, and happily more decent form, this somewhat senseless 'sell' still has a vogue. This slang expression and practice was apparently well known to Shakspeare, who makes Costard use it in *Love's Labour Lost* [Act iii., Sc. 1], 'The boy hath sold him a bargain.'

BARGE, *subs.* (printers').—1. A 'case' in which there is an undue proportion of some letters, and a corresponding shortness of those which are most valuable.

2. The term is also applied among printers to a card or small box on or in which 'spaces' are put while correcting formes away from 'case.'

Verb.—To abuse; to slang. *Cf.*, BULLYRAG. The allusion is, of course, to the rough mode of speaking peculiar to bargees or bargemen.

1861. ALBERT SMITH, *Medical Student*, p. 102. 'Whereupon they all began to BARGE the master at once; one saying "his coffee was all snuff and chick-weed."'

(Uppingham School.) — To knock against a person; to come into collision with.

BARGE-ARSE, *subs.* (common).—A man or woman of rotund development at the back. [From BARGE, a clumsy vessel, + ARSE, O.E., posterior or buttock.] A low term of ridicule. Also used as an adjective, BARGE-ARSED.

BARGE-POLE, *subs.* (Winchester College).—A large stick or thick bough, of which there was one in each fagot. Also generally used for any large piece of wood.

BARK, *subs.* (common).—1. An Irishman or Irishwoman. *Cf.*, BARKSHIRE.

1869. *Notes and Queries*, 4 S., iii., 406. In Lancashire an Irishman is vulgarly called a BARK.

1876. C. HINDLEY, *Life and Adventures of a Cheap Jack*, p. 191. Mike when asked by some of his countrymen why he called Fairbanks a 'BARK,' *i.e.*, an Irishman, said, 'If I had not put the 'bark' on him he would have put it on me, so I had the first pull.'

2. The skin. This occurs also dialectically. In Alan Ramsay's poems [1758] it is so used.

1843. DICKENS, *Martin Chuzzlewit*, ch. xx., p. 209. To the great detriment of what is called by fancy gentlemen the BARK upon his shins, which were most unmercifully bumped against the hard leather and the iron buckles.

1876. *Family Herald*, 2 Dec., p. 80, col. 1. With the BARK all off his shins from a blow with a hockey stick.

3. (colloquial.) — A cough. *Cf.*, *verb*, To BARK, sense 2.

Verb.—1. To scrape; or rub off the skin; to abraise.

1856. HUGHES, *Tom Brown's School-days*, p. 227. So, after getting up [the tree] three or four feet, down they came slithering to the ground, BARKING their arms and faces.

1859. *Macmillan's Magazine*, Nov., p. 18. The knuckles of his right hand were BARKED.

1872. MARK TWAIN, *Roughing It*, p. 16 (Routledge's ed.). Every time we avalanched from one end of the stage to the other, the 'Unabridged Dictionary' would come too; and, every time it came, it damaged somebody. One trip it BARKED the Secretary's elbow; the next trip it hurt me in the stomach, and the third, it tilted Bemis's nose up till he could look down his nostrils—he said.

2. To cough; generally applied when it is persistent and hacking.

THE WORD WITH THE BARK ON IT, *phr.* (American).—Without mincing the matter; without circumlocution.

1872. MARK TWAIN, *Roughing It*, chap. xv. If ever another man gives a whistle to a child of mine, and I get my hands on him, I will hang him higher than Haman! That is THE WORD WITH THE BARK ON IT.

TO TAKE THE BARK OFF, *phr.* (popular).—To reduce in value, either deliberately, or by accident; a figurative usage of 'to graze,' 'to take the skin off.'

1849. DICKENS, *David Copperfield*, p. 310. I rode my gallant grey so close to the wheel, that I grazed his near foreleg against it and TOOK THE BARK OFF, as his owner told me, to the tune of three pun' sivin.

1853. REV. ED. BRADLEY ('Cuthbert Bede'), *Further Adventures of Verdant Green*, p. 31. That'll TAKE THE BARK FROM your nozzle, and distil the Dutch pink for you, won't it?

TO BARK AT THE MOON (colloquial).—To clamour uselessly; to agitate to no effect; to labour in vain.

1630. TAYLOR'S *Workes*. And thus my booke and comparisons end together; for thus much I know, that I have but all this while BARK'D AT THE MOONE, throwne feathers against the winde, built upon the sands, wash'd a blackmore, and laboured in vaine.

BARKER, *subs.* (popular).—1. A pistol. [From BARKER, a noisy assailant, *i.e.*, one who barks like a dog.] Sometimes called BARKING IRON (*q.v.*). The latter, as far as is known, is the oldest term. An early use of BARKERS bears date of 1815, whilst BARKING IRON occurs in Parker's *Life's Painter*, 1789.

1815. SCOTT, *Guy Mannering*, ch. xxxiii. 'Had he no arms?' asked the Justice. 'Ay, ay, they are never without BARKERS and slashers.'

1837. DICKENS, *Oliver Twist*, ch. xxii. 'BARKERS for me, Barney,' said Toby Crackit. 'Here they are,' replied Barney, producing a pair of pistols.

1857. C. KINGSLEY, *Two Years Ago*, ch. xxiv. I'll give you five for those pistols . . . being rather a knowing one about the pretty little BARKERS.

ENGLISH SYNONYMS. 'Meat in the pot.' (A Texan term, alluding to the means by which meat is literally provided for the pot. Texan figures of speech are often startling enough in originality and sententiousness. Nor is the moral ingenuity revealed by this vernacular less striking; *e.g.*, when revolvers are said 'to make all men equal.') Other synonyms for revolvers of similar character are 'my unconverted friend'; 'a one-eyed scribe' (an argument always persuasive and sometimes unanswerable); 'blue lightning' (sometimes a tragedy in three acts: Act i., a word; Act ii., a flash of blue lightning; and Act iii., certain death); 'whistler' (from the sharp hissing sound of a bullet in its flight); 'peacemaker' (a sarcastic commentary on the proverb that 'short reckonings make long friends'); dag; pop; etc.

FRENCH SYNONYMS. *Un aboyeur* (popular: a literal translation of 'barker'; also 'a tout'); *un pitroux* (thieves': in the old Provencal, *pitrou* bore the sense of a piece of wood or stick, and it is possible that French thieves have here merely transferred the name from one weapon to another); *un pétouze* (a play upon words. In the old cant *pétouze* signified the ancient coin known as a *pistole*); *un bayafe* (thieves': formerly *baillaf*, a term employed by the robbers who infested the highways of Southern France. It is thought to be derived from two words *bailler*, to give, and *affe* or rather *affre*, signifying fear); *un mandolet* (thieves'); *pied de cochon* (military: literally 'a pig's foot'; a variety of weapon of large size and calibre); *un crucifix* or *un crucifix à ressort* (thieves': literally 'a crucifix,' or 'a crucifix with a spring'); *un soufflant* (thieves': *soufflet* = to whisper); *les burettes* (thieves' and popular: literally 'phials').

2. (common.)—A man employed to stand in front of shops and shows to attract the attention of passers-by, and if possible to entice them inside, where he can safely leave them to the tender mercies of the salesmen. The origin of the term is obvious; and, it is interesting to note that BARKER has its exact

equivalent in the French *aboyeur*. Amongst touting photographers, in low neighbourhoods, this individual is called a DOORSMAN, and the term is likewise applied to auction-room touts.

1748. T. DYCHE, *Dictionary* (5 ed.). BARKER (S.), a salesman's servant that walks before his door, to invite customers in to buy cloaths.

1785. GROSE, *Dictionary of the Vulgar Tongue*. BARKER. The shopman of a dealer in second-hand clothes, particularly about Monmouth St., who walks before his shop and deafens every passenger with his cries of clothes, coats, or gowns, 'what d'ye want *gemmen*, what d'ye buy?'

1828. JON. BEE, *Picture of London*, p. 109. *Mock-auctions* and '*selling-off*' shops are not the only pests where BARKERS are kept at the doors to invite unwary passengers to 'walk in, walk in, sale just begun.'

1888. *Texas Siftings*, Oct. 13. I am a BARKER by profession. The pedestrian agility required to pace up and down before the 'Half-dime Museum of Anatomy and Natural History,' soliciting passers-by to enter, is of itself enormous; but where it gets in its base hit is when it increases the appetite. McGinty knows this. McGinty is my friend, but I wouldn't serve a tenth of his unexpired terms for ten dollars. I have peddled clams with McGinty and have seen him eat three bushels of our stock. That is nothing. When the show isn't paying, I have to go out and eat grass. This shows you what nickel-plated, back-action appetites we have.

3. A man with a troublesome cough; his complaint is otherwise known as a 'CHURCH-YARD COUGH,' or a 'NOTICE TO QUIT' (*q.v.*).

4. (nautical.)—Besides being used as a designation for a pistol, BARKER is also employed for lower deck guns on board ship.

1842. COOPER, *Jack O' Lanthorne*, I., 151. Four more carronades with two BARKERS for'ard.

5. *See* quotation, as follows:—

1879. GREENWOOD, *Outcasts of London*. But what was barking? I thought a great deal about the matter, and could arrive at no more feasible conclusion than that a BARKER was a boy that attended a drover, and helped him to drive his sheep by means of imitating the bark of a dog.

6. (University.)—A noisy assertive individual; and, in a complimentary sense, a great swell.

7. (American.)—A noisy coward; a blatant bully.

BARKEY (nautical).—A term of endearment in use amongst seafaring men when speaking of a vessel to which they have got attached. 'She's a BARKEY—she is, my lads!'

BARKING-IRONS, *subs.* (thieves').—Pistols. *Cf.*, BARKER, sense 1. BARKING-IRON is, historically, an older term than BARKER by about a quarter of a century. Formerly applied, in the navy, to large duelling pistols.

1789. GEO. PARKER, *Life's Painter*, p. 173. Pistols, BARKING-IRONS.

1834. H. AINSWORTH, *Rookwood*, bk. II., ch. vi. 'And look you, prick the touch-hole, or your BARKING-IRON will never bite for you.'

BARKING THROUGH THE FENCE, *phr.* (American).—A taking advantage of some obstacle or shield for saying or doing something, which, but for such protection, would not be said or done; or which if done or said might entail unpleasant consequences upon the sayer or doer.

BARKSHIRE, *subs.* (common).—Ireland.—*See* BARK.

BARK UP THE WRONG TREE, *verbal phr.* (American).—Of trapper and pioneer derivation, and idiomatically used to signify that a person is at fault as to his purpose, or the means by which he is endeavouring to attain his object. The expression arose in this way: the Western huntsman found that his prey gradually became more and more wily and cunning in eluding pursuit, and frequently he and his dogs were at fault, supposing they had 'treed' their game when in reality, especially in the case of opossums and squirrels and such-like animals, it had escaped by jumping from the boughs of one tree to another. The dogs consequently were left BARKING UP THE WRONG TREE.

1835. *Richmond Enquirer*, Sep. 8. 'You didn't really go to old Bullion,' said a politician to an office-seeker, 'Why, he has no influence there, I can tell you. You BARKED UP THE WRONG TREE there, my friend, and you deserve to fail.'

1888. *Detroit Free Press*, Oct. Professor Rose who 'hit' this town last spring is around calling us a fugitive from justice, and asking why the police don't do something. Gently, Professor. When we left Xenia, O., the Sheriff patted us on the back and lent us half-a-dollar. We are the only man in this town who doesn't turn pale when the stage comes in, and the only one who doesn't break for the sage brush when it is announced that the United States Marshal is here. We ain't rich or pretty, but we are good, and the Professor is BARKING UP THE WRONG TREE.

BARNABY. TO DANCE BARNABY, *phr.* (popular). — To move expeditiously; irregularly.

BARNACLE, *subs.* (old cant).—1. A pickpocket. For synonyms, *see* AREA SNEAK.

b. 1809, *d.* 1870. MARK LEMON, *Leyton Hall*. The man that stood beside thee is old Crookfinger, the most notorious setter, BARNACLE and foist in the city.

2. (old.)—A good job, or snack easily got. — *Lexicon Balatronicum* (1811).

3. (old.)—A gratuity given to grooms by the buyers and sellers of horses. — *Lexicon Balatronicum* (1811).

4. (old.)—A constant attendant; he who, or that which sticks to one like a barnacle to a ship's bottom.

1607. DEKKER, *Northward Hoe!* III., wks., 1873, III., 39. Ile cashiere all my yong BARNICLES. [M.]

1868. MISS BRADDON, *Trail of the Serpent*, I., i., 7. Slopper found him a species of BARNACLE rather difficult to shake off.

5. (old cant.) — A decoy swindler; from the pertinacity with which such a one fastens on to a victim, and will not be shaken off until the purpose in view is effected. *Cf.*, senses 1 and 4.

1591. GREENE, *Notable Discovery of Coosnage* (1859), 23. Thus doth the Verser and the Setter feign a kind friendship to the Cony . . . As thus they sit tippling, coms the BARNACKLE and thrusts open the doore . . . steps back again: and very mannerly saith I cry you mercy, Gentlemen. I thoght a frend of mine had bin heere.

1608. DEKKER, *Belman of London*, wks. (1885) III., 131. He that . . . before counterfetted the dronken Bernard is now sober and called the BARNACLE.

6. (old.) — An individual speaking with a nasal twang; one who speaks through his nose.

1591. PERCIVALL, *Sp. Dictionary*. *Gango*, a BARNACLE, one that speaketh through the nose, *Chenolopex*. [*Chenalopex* in Pliny, a species of goose.] [M.]

BARNACLES, *subs.* (popular).—1. Spectacles. Formerly applied

only to spectacles with side pieces of coloured glass, and used more as protectors from wind, dust, and glaring light than as aids to the sight. Hence used popularly for all kinds of glasses. The derivation seems uncertain. The principal suggested origins are:—(1) a corruption of *binoculis* [from Latin *bini*, double, + *oculus*, an eye]; (2) an attributive usage of BARNACLES, which, with 'horse-twitchers' or 'brakes,' are tools put on the nostrils of horses when they will not stand still to be shooed; and in support of this it has been pointed out [*N. and Q.*, 1 S., v., 13] the figure of the BARNACLE borne in heraldry sufficiently shows why the term has been transferred to spectacles, which were formerly only kept in position by the manner in which they clipped the nose; (3) that BARNACLES are so called from the similarity in shape to the black streak which proceeds from the upper part of the beak in a line to the corner of, and right round the eye of the bernicle, or BARNACLE goose (*Anser bernicla*). There is a strong resemblance in the mark to a pair of spectacles.

1571. *Damon and Pythias* (Dodsley's Old Plays), Hazlett IV., 81. These spectales put on. *Grim*. They be gay BARNACLES, yet I see never the better.

1653. SIR THOMAS URQUHART, *Translation of Rabelais*, bk. V., ch. xxvii. They had BARNACLES on the handles of their faces, or spectacles at most.

The difference between spectacles and BARNACLES seems to be indicated in this passage. In the original French the phrase reads '*bezicles au nez*.' A later quotation illustrative of the usage is:

1822. SCOTT, *The Fortunes of Nigel*, ch. i. 'Give me the BARNACLES, my good youth, and who can say what nose they may bestride in two years hence?'

ENGLISH SYNONYMS. 'Bossers'; 'gig-lamps'; 'goggles.' A man wearing these aids to sight is sometimes called 'FOUR EYES' (*q.v.*).

FRENCH SYNONYMS. *Les persiennes* (popular: properly 'venetian shutters'); *une vitrine* (popular: literally 'a shop window,' or glass case in a museum).

2. (old cant.)—*See* quotation.

1748. T. DYCHE, *Dictionary* (5 ed.). BARNACLES (S.) . . . . in the *Canting Language*, a pair of spectacles; also the irons or fetters worn by felons are so called; also the gratuity or reward that jockies have for buying horses for gentlemen.

BARNDOOR, *subs.* (sporting).—1. A facetious term for a target too large to be missed; *i.e.*, as large as a BARNDOOR. Hence BARNDOOR PRACTICE as applied to organised battues, in which game is driven within a range from which it is impossible to escape. This can hardly be called sport; rather let it be known as 'slaughter.'

2. (cricket.)—A player who blocks every ball.

BARNET! *intj.* (Christ's Hospital).—Nonsense! humbug! Now obsolete.

BARNET FAIR, *subs.* (thieves').—The hair; part of the RHYMING SLANG (*q.v.*). For synonyms *see* TOP DRESSING.

Barney, *subs.* (popular).—1. A word which varies in sense according to the predelictions of the person using it. Generally speaking it means a jollification; 'lark'; pleasurable outing; picnic. The 'Arries and roughs of London, however, always associate it with a certain amount of rowdyism. Its derivation is unknown, although Barrère gives a long dissertation concerning its origin in the Yiddish. As, however, this is founded mainly upon a misreading of a quotation from *Punch*, it is somewhat beside the mark.

2. Humbug; cheating; a hoax; something pre-arranged—not genuine. In sporting circles it signifies an unfair race of any kind.

1865. B. Brierley, *Irkdale*, II., 19. I won thee i' fair powell one toss an' no barney.

1882. *Evening News*, 2 Sept., p. 1, col. 6. Blackguardly barneys called boxing competitions. [M.]

Murray gives this last in illustration of the secondary sense which he applies to the word, viz., a prize-fight. Barney, it is true, does signify a prize-fight, but it means more than that. A fair contest would not be so named; there must be an element of chicanery in the matter. Besides which, barney is applied to unfair sporting competitions of any kind. A comparison of the different quotations given under this heading will clearly prove that point.

1884. *Referee*, April 13, p. 7, col. 4. Who would believe that Mr. Gladstone shammed being ill, and that Sir Andrew Clark issued false bulletins, and that the whole thing was a barney from beginning to end.

1885. *Bell's Life*, Jan. 3, p. 3, col. 4. Few genuine matches have taken place this season on the Transatlantic waters, though exhibitions and barney contests have been plentiful.

3. (American.)—At Harvard College, about the year 1810, this word was used to designate a bad recitation. To barney was to recite badly.—Hall's *College Words and Customs*.

Barn-Mouse. To be bitten by a barn-mouse, *phr.* (old).—To be tipsy; 'screwed.' The *Lexicon Balatronicum* says 'it is probably an allusion to barley,' presumably as the source of malt liquor. *Cf.*, 'To have on' or 'wear a barley-cap,' to be tipsy; also barley-cap = a tippler.

Barn-Stormer, *subs.* (theatrical).—A deprecatory epithet applied to strolling players.

1884. *Pall Mall Gazette*, 6 June, p. 5, col. 1. If this be barn-storming, Betterton and Garrick were barn-stormers.

1886. *Graphic*, 10 April, p. 399. Travelling players who acted short and highly tragic pieces to audiences of clodpoles in any barn or shed they could get, used to be known as barn-stormers, and a ranting, noisy style of acting and speaking is still called 'barn-storming.'

1887. *Referee*, 21 August, p. 3, col. 1. Mr. Edward Terry has again been elected at the head of the poll as trustee of the charities of Barnes. He is not the first clever actor who has been known as a Barnes-stormer.

The French term for one of such a troupe is *cabotin*.

Barnumese, *subs.* (American).—Barnum, the proprietor of 'the greatest show upon earth,' has at any rate one claim to immortal fame in having, like Boycot, Burke, and Balfour, added a new word to the English tongue. The 'high falutin,' bombastic style of the

great man's announcements are notorious; as much so, in fact, as is the diction of the great London newspaper which claims 'the largest circulation in the world.' From such circumstances we get words like barnumese and telegraphese, to signify exaggeration of style—what in slang parlance is known as the 'putting on of side.'

Verb.—To Barnumize is to talk or assert oneself in the style popularly attributed to Barnum.

Baronet, *subs.* (old).—A humorous variation for sirloin [of beef].

1749. Fielding, *Tom Jones*, bk. IV., ch. x. The sight of the roast beef struck him dumb, permitting him only to say grace, and to declare he must pay his respects to the baronet, for so he called the sirloin.

Barrack-Hack, *subs.* (familiar).—1. In an inoffensive sense applied to young women who attend garrison balls year after year. So used there is no such imputation of lax morals as occurs in sense 2.

2. A soldier's prostitute. There are but few classes of persons to whom a greater number of slang epithets have been applied than to the poor wretched creatures, who from choice, bad-treatment, or as a means of subsistence abandon themselves to a life of prostitution. These names are to be found in plenty for all grades of semi-public or public women. They run the gauntlet from the gilded courtezan to the veriest drab in the last stages of destitution and disease. The list of synonyms is both long and grim; the names in many cases speaking volumes on a subject which it would be painful as well as needless to pursue farther in this place, inasmuch as the epithets both in French and English, and, it must be added, those of other languages as well, speak with a brutal cynicism to which it would be out of place to add a comment.

English Synonyms. Ladies of accommodating morals; ladies of more complaisance than virtue; anonyma; pretty horse-breaker; artichoke; columbine; common Jack; convenient; cow; crack; aunt; ladies of easy virtue; bangster; blowen; garrison-hack; bat; bawdy-basket; bed-fagot; fireship; bit o' muslin; laced mutton; mot; bobtail; bona roba; brevet wife; grass widow; brimstone; black Bess; brown Bessy; bulker; bunter; burick; buttock; cab moll; cat; chauvering donna; chauvering moll; barber's chair; demi-rep; tartlet; trollop; shake; poll; dolly-mop; gay woman; unfortunate; dress-lodger; mauks; quædam (obsolete); woman; bitch; perfect lady; public ledger; necessary; warming-pan; nun.

French Synonyms. *Une persilleuse* (familiar); *une mal peignée* (popular: 'a dirty ill-dressed woman; drab; or draggletail'); *une moellonneuse* (a prostitute who frequents builders' yards); *hirondelle de goguenot* (military: 'a barrack-hack'; in French soldiers' slang *un goguenot* is a tin can used for making coffee or soup); *un chausson* (literally 'a sock' or 'stocking'); *almanach de trente six mille*

adresses (popular: literally 'a directory. *Cf.*, English 'public-ledger'); *une génisse* (popular: literally 'a heifer.' *Cf.*, English 'cow'); *une raccrocheuse* (popular: *raccrocher*, 'to hook'); *une vache à lait* (popular: literally 'a milch cow'); *une fleur de macadam* (popular: 'a roadside flower'; 'a street walker'); *une roulante* (popular: in old French slang *un roulant* = a vehicle. *Cf.*, English 'cab'); *une camelote* (popular: a prostitute of the lowest class; a draggletail); *une morue* (popular: literally 'a cod-fish'); *une marcheuse* (popular: properly 'a walker'; in theatrical parlance, a female super); *une piqueuse de trains* (popular: one who prowls about railway stations). *Piqueuse* = needlewoman); *un pigeon voyageur* (familiar: a girl who travels up and down a railway seeking clients; literally 'a carrier pigeon'); *une pieuvre* (familiar: a kept woman; properly 'an octopus'); *un carcan à crinoline* (popular: *carcan*, applied to either sex is an opprobrious epithet; the phrase also signifies 'a gaunt-woman'); *un omnibus* (popular: *i.e.*, 'one who may be ridden by all'); *un cul crotté* (low: properly 'a dirty bottom'); *une trychine* (popular: an allusion to *trichina spiralis*, the disease-germ in bad pork); *une fenêtrière* (popular: an allusion to the custom of this class to watch at windows and invite passers-by to visit them); *une traîneuse* (familiar: a prostitute who plies her trade at railway stations); *un trumeau* (popular: literally 'a leg of beef'); *une crevette* (popular: 'a prawn' or 'shrimp'); *une boulonnaise* (a girl who 'walks' the Bois de Boulogne); *un matelas ambulant* (popular: properly 'a walking mattress.' *Cf.*, English 'bed-fagot'); *une demoiselle du Pont-Neuf* (popular: this kind haunt the bridge of the name over the Seine); *un demi-castor* (popular: a woman of the demi-monde); *une laqueuse* (familiar: a prostitute frequenting the lake in the Bois de Boulogne); *une pailletée* (common: properly 'spangled'); *un pelican* (familiar: a dressy courtesan); *une ningle* (a literary term); *une maquillée* (popular: 'one with painted face'); *une gueuse* (popular: *gueuse* = beggarly, wretched); *une fille* or *femme du trottoir* (popular: 'a girl' or 'woman of the pavement'); *une vieille garde* (familiar: an old worn-out prostitute); *une biche* (popular: 'a hind' or 'roe'); *une déhanchée* (popular: 'a waddler'); *une demi-mondaine* (general: a woman of the demi-monde; a fashionable prostitute); *une portion* (military: literally 'a share' or 'portion'; one who is shared by many); *une limace* (popular: properly 'a slug'); *une terrinière* (the lowest sort of prostitute; *terrine* = earthen pan); *une terreuse* (a woman who prowls about lonely spots); *une terrière* (popular); *une fille à parties* (popular); *une rivette*; *une voirie* (popular: 'a common sewer'); *une boule rouge* (familiar: a frequenter of the Quartier de la Boule Rouge, Fanbourg Montmartre); *une vessie* (popular: a very low prostitute; *vessie* applied to either sex is an offensive epithet); *une demoiselle de bitume* (familiar); *un pont d'Avignon* (popular); *une pontonnière* (popular: a prostitute who plies

her trade under the arches of bridges; *ponton* = pontoon, 'a bridge of boats'; *pontonnier* = 'a toll gatherer'); *une polisseuse de tuyaux de pipe* (literally 'a polisher of pipe stems'); *une pompe funèbre* (familiar: properly 'funeral pomp'); *une polisseuse de mâts de cocagne en chambre* (popular: an extremely degraded variety of prostitute; literally 'a polisher of greasy poles in a room'); *une punaise* (general: 'a bug'—a public woman of the lowest grade); *une dessalée* (popular: literally 'a knowing woman'); *une mangeuse de viande crue* (popular: 'a devourer of raw meat'); *une cité d'amour* (literally 'a city of love'); *autel de besoin* (popular: 'an altar of necessity'; *Cf.*, English 'necessary'); *une vésuvienne* (familiar: literally 'a vesuvian,' either in allusion to the volcano or the well-known brand of matches; in either case the epithet comes very close to the old English slang 'fireship,' an old and diseased prostitute); *peau*, or *peau de chien* (popular: literally 'dog's skin'); *un grenier à coups de sabre* (a soldiers' term: *grenier*, a granary; *coups de sabre*, thrusts with a broad sword); *une rempardeuse* (a woman who frequents the ramparts); *une femme de terrain* (a draggletailed woman; *femme*, woman, *terrain*, ground); *une saucisse* (popular: *i.e*, 'a small sausage'); *une trainée* (familiar); *une baleine* (popular: 'a whale'); *une lésébombe* (popular); *une fille en brème* (a registered prostitute; *la brème* is the card given to such women by the police); *une fille en carte* (a registered woman: *see* preceding); *une boutonnière à pantalons* (familiar: a kind of semi-prostitute; a sempstress who walks the streets at night; in their own words, they 'work for their living, but do *the naughty* for their clothes'); *une fille de maison* or *une fille à numéro* (familiar: these names are given to girls in brothels; *Cf.*, English 'dress-lodgers'); *une fille de tournure* (familiar: this also is applied to the inmate of a brothel; literally 'a girl of figure'); *une poupée* (popular: 'a doll'); *une mouquette* (popular); *des poules* (popular: the inmates of a brothel are so called; literally 'hens'); *une galvaudeuse* (popular: *galvauder*, 'to scold'); *une planche à boudin* (familiar: literally 'a slice of pudding'; in English harlotry 'to take one's pudding' or 'greens' is to have sexual connection); *une blanchisseuse en chemise* (*blanchisseuse* = laundress; *être dans la chemise de quelqu'un* is to be constantly with one); *un lard* (literally 'bacon' or body); *une gadoue* (properly 'street refuse' or 'mud'); *un sommier de caserne* (military: *sommier* means 'hair-mattress,' and *caserne* = 'barracks'; applied to girls who prowl about barracks); *une grivoise* (this term is now obsolete, but was formerly applied to a garrison town prostitute. It means, literally, 'a jolly canteen woman'); *une paillasse à soldats* (a barrack-hack; literally 'a straw mattress for soldiers'); *un passe-lacet* (properly 'a bodkin'—*i.e.*, 'something to be threaded'); *un chameau* (the term was originally applied to a gaunt, ungainly woman; it now signifies a prostitute also); *un membre de la caravane* (a euphemism for *un chameau, q.v.*); *un lolo* (popular); *une grue* (popular: a kept woman; *faire le pied de grue*, 'to dance attendance'); *une soupeuse* (literally 'one who takes supper'; an allusion to the '*cabinets particuliers*' of French restaurants); *une belle petite* (a young and pretty prostitute of the superior class; literally 'a pretty darling'); *une pêche à quinze sous* (a literary term); *une boulevardière* (a superior class of prostitute frequenting the boulevards); *un camélia* (a kept woman; a reference to the heroine of *La Dame aux camélias* by A. Dumas fils); *une lorette* (a variety of prostitute named after the Quartier Notre Dame de Lorette, the Paris Pimlico); *une petite dame* (literally 'a little lady'); *une impure* (a kept woman; properly 'an unchaste one'); *une agenouillée* (journalistic); *une verticale*; *une horizontale de grande marque* (a fashionable courtezan); *une cocotte* (a generic term); *une pierreuse* (a public woman of the lowest grade who plies her hideous trade in houses in course of building, etc.); *une chamègue*; *un bourdon* (thieves': literally 'a drone'); *une lipète* (popular); *une magneuse* (popular: a woman who depraves herself with members of her own sex. The name is said to be in allusion to a religious community who derived their cognomen from that of their founder, Jeanne Canart, the daughter of Nicholas Colbert, who was the Seigneur de Magneux); *une vielle lanterne* (popular: an old prostitute; *lanterne* = window); *une feuille* (literally 'a leaf'; the term is one used at the Saumur School of Cavalry); *un blanc* (literally 'blank' or 'white'; the derivation is somewhat obscure, but the term is a very ancient one for a public woman. *Mangeur de blanc* is a man who lives upon the earnings of prostitutes and ruins them. Formerly, the expression *mettre à blanc* was used in the sense of 'to ruin'); *une vache* (this term in its popular signification merely means 'a woman of indifferent character'; if a prostitute is intended, the expression is *une vache à lait*, a milch cow); *un veau* (literally 'a calf'; the phrase is applied to a *young* prostitute. *Cf.*, '*vache à lait*'); *une retapeuse* (popular); *un wagon* (popular: a dirty prostitute. *Cf.*, *wagon*, 'a railway carriage' and *un omnibus*); *une taupe* (familiar: literally a mole, an animal that works in the dark; also 'a cunning fox'); *une Jeanneton* (popular: a chambermaid at an inn); *une andre* (an old word; *see* Fourbesque *landra*); *une roulure* (popular: a public woman of the lowest description. *Rouler* signifies 'to roll,' 'to wander,' 'to stroll,' 'to keep going'); *une fille de barrière* (popular: a prostitute plying her trade at the barriers or gates of the city); *une dossière* (thieves': literally 'a back'); *une rouleuse* (familiar: an abandoned woman; literally the name of a species of caterpillar); *une paillasse à troufion* (a soldier's woman); *une paillasse de corps de garde* (military: literally 'a guard-room mattress'); *une marneuse* (popular: a variety of low class prostitute frequenting the river-side; literally 'clayey'); *une Louis* (a bully's mistress; the allusion is to the fancy

which women in brothels often have of powdering and dressing the hair in the fashion of the times of Louis XV.); *une ouvrière* (also a 'bully's' mistress. The term signifies, literally, 'a workwoman.' These wretched creatures support their companions who live and batten on what the woman earns in the sale of her person); *une fesse* (popular: properly 'a breech'); *une marmite* (harlotry: 'a flesh pot'); *un torchon* (a low class of woman; *torchon* = 'a dish clout'); *une sauterelle* (familiar: 'a grass-hopper'); *un prat*; *une femme de carotsi* (thieves': a well dressed prostitute of the boulevards); *une louille*; *une larque* (a registered woman; a corruption of *largue*); *une menesse* (a thieves' term); *une larguèpe*; *une magnuce* (see *une magneuse*); *une casserole* (thieves': literally 'a saucepan'); *une goipeuse* (thieves': a name given to prostitutes who wander about the country); *une ronfle*; *une ronfle à grippart*; *un ronfleur* (thieves': *ronfler* is properly 'to snore'); *un grippeur* (gripper = 'to nab'; crib; clutch); *une panterne*; *une bourre de soie* (a kept woman; *bourre* = *floss* + *soie* = silk); *un asticot* (a bully's or thief's mistress; literally 'a maggot'; it may be stated that *asticot* is also used for both the *membrum virile*, and for vermicelli); *une panuche* (thieves': a term applied to showily dressed women who live in brothels); *une calège* (thieves': a kept woman; *cale*, a kind of head-dress); *une ponante* (thieves': a low-class prostitute); *une môme* or *mômeresse* (thieves'); *une lutainpem* (thieves'); *une laissée* (thieves' and roughs'); *une galupe* (popular: a street walking prostitute); *une ponife*, *poniffe*, or *poniffle* (thieves').

For GERMAN SYNONYMS, *see* TART.

ITALIAN SYNONYMS. *Una sbriso* (this term has another cant signification, *viz.*, 'to be naked'; hence, probably, its attributive usage for a prostitute); *una losena* (this, like other Fourbesque terms for a woman, also means 'a woman of the town'; indeed in most argots there seems to be little, if any distinction drawn between women of easy virtue, and the sex as a whole); *una guagnastra* (*i.e.*, one who acts as a sheath; the allusion is obvious. *Cf.*, English 'broom' and 'broom-handle' for the female *pudenda* and the male *penis* respectively); *una marcona* (said to be an allusion to a certain incident in the history of the Papal States); *una landra* (curiously enough this term signifying, in orthodox Italian, a prostitute is, in the Fourbesque, synonymous also with 'woman.' The French *andre*, a woman of the town, dates back to the sixteenth century); *una brocca* (literally a jug, pitcher, or stupid person); *una brocchiera* (from Italian *brocchiere*, 'a buckler' or 'shield'); *una baia* (*i.e.*, a mistress); *una farfoia* (also a nun, in which connection compare with English ABBESS); *una chierlera* (this term likewise is also used in the sense of a female devotee. Both the English and French slang have 'nun' as an equivalent for a prostitute); *una carniera* or *carnifica* (cant terms for a 'sister,' and 'fox' also); *una cara* (literally 'dear.' *Cf.*, French *belle petite*, 'little darling.')

The Spanish Germania has *gaya* to signify a prostitute. This is an exact equivalent of the French *fille de joie* or 'gay girl'; *gaya* in Spanish signifies 'gay.' Another name is found in *germana*, in explanation of which it may be briefly explained that the Spanish argot or Germania took its name from a band or brotherhood of thieves and robbers; and it would thus appear that *germana*, the name for a female member of the band was also used generically for a prostitute! *Marca*, or *marquida* and *marquisa* are also all used in the sense of a public woman. It may be noted that in the Italian *marchesata* stands for a woman when under menstruation, the physiological fact itself being called *marchese*; *mercenario*, a street walker, also signifies a nun of the religious order of *La Merced*.

BARRACKING, *subs.* (Australian).—Banter; chaff. *Cf.*, BARRIKIN.

BARREL-BOARDER, *subs.* (American).—A loafer in low drinking-saloons.

BARREL-CAMPAIGN, *subs.* (American).—Political contests in which bribery and corruption go hand-in-hand with canvassing and voting. A wealthy candidate for office is said to have originated the phrase by remarking, 'Let the boys know that there's a BAR'L o' money ready for 'em,' or words to that effect. The use of the term in this sense became general about 1876.—*See* BOODLE.

1884. *Boston* (Mass.) *Journal*, 1 Nov., 1. We are accustomed to BARREL-CAMPAIGNS here. Nobody supposes this district to be Democratic, but the Democrats depend upon carrying it with money.

1888. *Florida Times Union*, Feb. 11, p. 4. It will be remembered that Mr. Flower was the nominal candidate of the anti-Cleveland men four years ago, and with the aid of his BARREL they really did achieve some show of success.

BARREL-FEVER, *subs.* (popular).—An indisposition caused by excessive drinking. 'He died of BARREL-FEVER'; *i.e.*, 'he killed himself through drink.' For synonyms, *see* GALLON DISTEMPER.

BARREL-HOUSE, *subs.* (American).—A low groggery.

1888. *Missouri Republican*, Feb. 11. The West-Side police are still arresting BARREL-HOUSE loafers in the hope of catching an expert cracksman among them.

BARRELL'S BLUES, *subs. phr.* (military).—A nickname given to the Fourth Foot. [From its facings and Colonel's name from 1734 to 1739.] They are also called 'the Lions,' from the ancient badge of the regiment.

BARRES, *subs.* (gaming).—Money lost at play, but not paid. The term is an old one, and has long been obsolete. A corrupt form of 'barrace,' an obsolete plural of 'bar.'

BARRIKIN, *subs.* (common).—Gibberish; jargon; a jumble of words. For usage, *see* quotation.

1851-61. H. MAYHEW, *London Lab. and Lon. Poor*, vol. I., p. 15. 'The high words in a tragedy we call jaw-breakers, and say we can't tumble to that BARRIKIN.' *Ibid*, p. 25. Can't tumble to your BARRIKIN [*i.e.*, can't understand you]. *Ibid*, p. 27. The rich has all that BARRIKIN to themselves.

BARRING.—*See* TO BAR.

BARRING OUT, *subs. phr.* (old).—Exclusion from a place by means of locks and bars. More particularly applied to a half serious but oftentimes jocular rebellion of schoolboys against the schoolmaster.

1728. SWIFT, *Journal of a Modern Lady*.

Not schoolboys at a BARRING-OUT,
Raised ever such incessant rout.

1847. TENNYSON, *Princess*, conclusion.

Revolts, republics, revolutions, most,
No graver than a schoolboys' BARRING-OUT.

BARROW-BUNTER, *subs.* (old).—A barrow-woman; a female costermonger.

1771. SMOLLETT, *Humphry Clinker*, i., 140. I saw a dirty BARROW-BUNTER in the street cleaning her dusty fruit with her own spittle.

BARROW-MAN, *subs.* (old).—1. A man who hawks his wares on a barrow; a costermonger. The term dates back to the middle of the seventeenth century. *Un marottier* is the French equivalent for one species of the fraternity, better known in England as a DUDSMAN (*q.v.*).

2. Also formerly a man under sentence of transportation.

BARROW-TRAM, *subs.* (familiar).—An ungainly person; one awkward in gait, and coarse and rawboned in feature.

BARTER, *subs.* (Winchester College).—A half volley. From the Warden of that name famous for disposing of them.

1870. MANSFIELD, *School-Life at Winchester College*, p. 133. What a noble game cricket must be when one loved it so much, notwithstanding the previous training! What genuine excitement when College and Commoners was played; what frantic shouting when Rapid got well hold of a 'BARTER' . . . and sent the ball from 'Spanish Poplar,' right over Mead's wall by 'Log pond.'

1878. ADAMS, *Wykehamica*, p. 327. Barter was the most popular boy of his day with his schoolfellows. Wonderful things are told of his scores at cricket at which he is supposed to have been the hardest hitter of his own times, or of any near him. . . . He was so renowned for the tremendous force with which he was wont to swipe the ball, commonly known to cricketers as a 'half-volley,' that it actually changed its name in the Wykehamical vocabulary, and for fully half a century afterwards—and, for all I know, to the present day—bore the name of a BARTER.

Verb.—To hit a ball hard at cricket.

HITTING BARTERS.—Practice catching; full pitches hit from the middle of 'Turf' towards Ball-Court for catching practice towards the end of 'Long Meads.'

BARTHOLOMEW BABY, *subs.* (old).—A gaudily dressed doll, such as appears to have been commonly sold at Bartholomew Fair.—*See* BARTHOLOMEW-PIG. Also applied to a person gaudily dressed.

1682. *Wit and Drollery*, p. 343.

Her petticoat of sattin,
Her gown of crimson tabby,
Lac'd up before, and spangl'd ore,
Just like a BARTHOLOMEW BABY.

BARTHOLOMEW-PIG, *subs.* (old).—Roasted pigs, says Nares, were formerly among the chief attractions of Bartholomew Fair, West Smithfield, London: they were sold piping hot, in booths and on stalls, and ostentatiously displayed, to excite the appetite of passengers. Hence a BARTHOLOMEW-PIG became a common subject of allusion: the Puritan railed against it.

1614. B. Jons., *Bart. Fair*, i., 6. For the very calling it a Bartholomew-pig, and to eat it so, is a spice of idolatry.

Falstaff, in coaxing ridicule of his enormous figure, is playfully called by his favourite,

1598. Shakspeare, 2 *Hen. IV.*, ii., 4. Thou whoreson little tidy Bartholomew-boar-pig.

Dr. Johnson thought that paste-pigs were there meant: but the true Bartholomew-pigs were substantial, real, hot, roasted pigs; as may be seen throughout the above play of old Ben, where Ursula, the pig-woman, is no inconsiderable personage. Gayton also speaks of the pig-dressers.

Like Bartholomew Fair pig-dressers, who look like the dams, as well as the cooks of what they roasted.
Fest. N., p. 57.

The young wife in Jonson's play pretends a violent longing for pig, that she may be taken to the fair; and it seems that her case was far from uncommon. Davenant speaks of the Bartlemew-pig,

That gaping lies on every stall,
Till female with great belly call.

The fair in its later days got to be a place of too much mobbing and riot for ladies in that condition. There *might* also be paste-pigs, but, if so, they were very inferior objects, and meant only for children. Mrs. Ursula also tells us the price of her pigs; namely, five shillings, five shillings and sixpence, or even six shillings! This was surely as dear in James I.'s time, as a guinea lately. The highest price, of course, was to be asked of a longing woman. The fair was abolished in 1854, having been inaugurated in 1133.—*Nares.*

Barts., *subs.* (medical students').—An abbreviation of 'St. Bartholomew Hospital.'

Bash, *verb* (popular).—To beat; thrash; or crush out of shape. Possibly from the Scandinavian *bask*, a slap; 'box' also seems to have the same derivation. Chiefly appearing in the northern dialects, bash is regarded nowadays in the light of a vulgar colloquialism. Thieves use it synonymously with 'to flog.'—*See* Bashing. In older writers the word appears as pash, the 'p' in this case being simply a harder form than 'b.' An alternative onomatopoetic derivation has, however, been suggested, the 'b' of such words as 'beat' and 'bang' being transferred to the terminal letters of 'dash,' 'gash,' 'smash,' etc.

1592. Nashe, *Strange Newes*, in wks. II., 272. A leane arme put out of the bed shall grind and pash euerie crum of thy booke into pin-dust.

1622. Massinger, *Virgin Martyr*, II., ii. Jove's artillery shot down at once, to pash your gods in pieces.

1882. *Daily Telegraph*, Dec. 9, p. 2, col. 6. A man . . . told witness that he would earn a sovereign if he cared to give a certain woman—the complainant—a couple of black eyes. . . . His instructions were to follow the man he met in the public-house in Bear Street, and to bash the woman he would point out to him in Portland Street.

1882. F. Anstey, *Vice Versâ*, ch. xii. 'If you have got bashed about pretty well since you came back, it's been all your own fault, and you know it.'

1883. *Standard*, March 2, p. 6, col. 7. Mr. Hannay reminded her that when the summons was applied for, the boy's father had said that the boy was bashed on the floor, and received a black eye and a bruised head.

Amongst synonyms may be mentioned the English verb 'bang,' and the French *bûcher*,

which signifies properly to dig or break up ground.—*See* Tan.

Basher, *subs.* (pugilistic).—A prize-fighter. For synonyms, *see* Bruiser.

1882. *Daily Telegraph*, Dec. 16, p. 2, col. 6. According to the statement of the prosecuting solicitor, this was the man who undertook to point out to Leech, the professed basher, the woman whom he was to assault in Portland Street.

Bashi-Bazouk, *subs.* (popular).—A ruffian; and used loosely as a more or less mild term of opprobrium; also applied to anything *bizarre* in character or composition. The expression came into vogue during the period when the Bulgarian atrocities were electrifying the world by their barbarous cruelty. The Bashi-bazouks are properly irregular Turkish soldiery. They are collected hastily in times of emergency; and are, consequently, somewhat impatient of discipline, assuming that such a commodity in its Western sense is known at all to the Tartar-descended Turk—'the unspeakable Turk' as he was fitly called during the period above alluded to. So infamous have these levies become at times, that more than once they have been disbanded in deference to pressure brought to bear upon the Turkish authorities by the Western powers.

Bashing, *subs.* (prison).—A flogging; a taste of the cat-o'-nine-tails. Prisoners condemned to this punishment at the commencement of their term are said by their companions to receive a bashing in; if they also undergo a flogging just previous to their release, it is called a bashing out.

1877. *Five Years' Penal Servitude*, ch. iii., p. 157. There were the evidences of former floggings, or bashings, as the prisoners call them.

Basils, *subs.* (old cant).—Fetters on one leg only.

Basin, *subs.* (American). — A schooner (*q.v.*).

Basing.—*See* That's basing.

Basketed, *ppl. adj.* (old). — From this cockpit expression used of persons unable or unwilling to pay their losses, and who in consequence were relegated for the rest of the day to a basket hung over the cockpit, is derived the figurative usage in the sense of 'to be left out in the cold'; not understood; non-plussed; 'floored.'

b. 1788, *d.* 1841. Hook, *Gerv. Skinner*, ch. iii. Skinner was quite enchanted with the brilliancy of his guests, although now and then a little puzzled at their allusions; there jokes were chiefly local or professional, and very frequently my excellent friend Gervase was, to use a modern phrase of general acceptation, basketed.

1818. P. Egan, *Boxiana*, vol. I., p. 79. The fight was soon over after this circumstance, and the *sweaters* and *trainers* were completely in the basket!

1866. E. Yates, *Land at Last*. . . . And find you in his den, lighting it up like—like—like—I'm regularly basketed, by jove!

To be brought or to go to the basket, *phr.* (familiar).—To be imprisoned; to be reduced to poverty. A basket is here the symbol of daily provision, or alms. Formerly prisoners were dependent on charity for daily sustenance, and it was customary for them to let down

a basket by a string through the gaol windows, soliciting the alms of passers-by.—*See* also Angling for farthings.

1632. Massinger and Field, *Fatal Dowry*, v., 1. *Pontalier* [to Liladam, who is in custody for debt].
Arrested! this is one of those whose base
And abject flattery help'd to dig his grave;
He is not worth your pity, nor my anger;
Go to the basket, and repent.

1700. *Gentleman Instructed* [1732], p. 6. God be praised! I am not brought to the basket, though I had rather live on charity than rapine. [D.]

To be left in the basket, *phr.* (common).—To be rejected; abandoned; unchosen. *Cf.*, second quotation.

1840. Barham, *I. L.* (*House Warning*).
Whatever he wants, he has only to ask it,
And all other suitors are left in the basket.

1874. *Bell's Life*, 26 Dec. The pick of the basket, a compact young greyhound.

Basket-Making, *subs.* (old).—When *enceinte* a woman was formerly said 'to have a kid in the basket.' [*Cf.*, Bay-window.] Hence basket-making to signify the act of copulation.

Bass, *subs.* (popular).—A familiar abbreviation for Bass' ale, brewed at Burton-on-Trent.

1853. Rev. E. Bradley ('Cuthbert Bede'), *Adventures of Verdant Green*, p. 23. The young gentleman exhibited great capacity for the beer of Bass, and the porter of Guiness.

1863. Oudia, *Held in Bondage*, I., p. 65. Those idle lads in the Temple, who smoke cavendish and drink Bass. *Ibid*, p. 126. Discussing Bass and a cold luncheon.

1868. Miss Braddon, *Only a Clod*, I., p. 138. A lot of fellows drinking no end of Bass.

18(?). Annie Thomas, *A Passion in Tatters*, I., p. 110. Bass that was not worthy of its name.

Baste, *verb* (colloquial). — To thrash; to beat soundly. This verb is given a place here for the purpose of comparison, as it is somewhat uncertain whether it can with propriety be classed as slang. Of uncertain origin, but dating from the sixteenth century; to baste, properly 'to sew together loosely,' or 'to apply fat or gravy to a joint,' is, in its figurative usage, of more than passing interest when compared with anoint (*q.v.*), and other words employed in the same figurative sense. It is curious indeed to note the many synonymous analogues for a good beating or thrashing, all of which pertain more or less to slang. R. W. Hackwood [*N. and Q.*, 7 S., vii., 153] mentions several, amongst others colting (*q.v.*), used by Marryat in *Midshipman Easy*. As bearing upon the general idea involved in this class of words, the quotation may be placed side by side with another from the *King's Own* by the same writer.

1830. Marryat, *King's Own*, ch. vii. 'He always carried in his pocket a colt (*i.e.*, a foot and a half of rope, knotted at one end and whipped at the other), for the benefit of the youngsters, to whom he was a most inordinate tyrant.'

1836. Marryat, *Midshipman Easy*, ch. xii. 'Then he colted me for half-an-hour, and that's all.'

Colting like basting is of uncertain derivation. Comparing it, however, with analogous words, may we not take it, continues the writer referred to, as very closely associated

with, if not actually belonging to, the series of synonyms for the operations which derive their origin from the shoemakers, curriers, and allied trades, as we find it in 'a leathering,' 'a strapping,' 'a tanning,' 'a welting,' etc? Indeed, it is worth noting in this connection, from the number of epithets applied to the operation, what a deal of chastising has apparently been required in most trades and occupations, for nearly all—except, perhaps, the carpenter's, where sticks are plentiful—appear to be represented, and even in the domestic circle one can have a choice of 'a towelling,' 'a basting,' 'a clouting,' 'a rubbing down,' 'a dressing,' 'a trimming,' or 'a wiping' when occasion requires.

1533. Bellenden, *Livy*, III. (1822), 223. He departit weil basit and defuleyeit of his clothing.

1599. Greene, *George-a-Greene*, in wks. (Grosart) XIV., 174. Ile baste you both so well, you were neuer better basted in your liues.

1605. *Tryall of Chevalry*, III., i., in Bullen's *Old Plays*, iii., 305. But, had I knowne as much, I would have basted him till his bones had rattled in his skin.

1611. Beaumont, *Knight of Burning Pestle*, II., iv.
Look on my shoulders, they are black and blue;
Whilst to and fro fair Luce and I were winding,
He came and basted me with a hedge-binding.

1660. Pepys, *Diary*, July 22. One man was basted by the keeper, for carrying some people over on his back, through the water.

1754. Martin, *Eng. Dict.*, 2 ed. To baste or bast . . . to beat, or bang soundly.

1874. Mrs. H. Wood, *Johnny Ludlow*, 1 S., xix., p. 328. 'Hold your row, Davvy,' he roared out, wrathfully: 'you'd not like me to come back and give you a basting.'

Among some English Synonyms may also be mentioned:—to give a hiding; to give a walloping; to dust one's jacket; to quilt; to tan; to set about; to walk into; to manhandle; to give one Jesse; to give one gas; to dowse; to pay.

For synonyms generally, *see* Tan.

Baster, *subs.* (American thieves').—A New York cant term for a house thief.

Bastile, *subs.* (vagrants').—A workhouse. For synonyms, *see* Big house. Probably from the Bastile, a famous prison; lock-ups for a long time being generically named Bastiles. Now corrupted into steel.

1883. Cuthbert Bede, in *Graphic*, June 2, p. 558, col. 2. Mister Corbyn had always called the workhouse by the opprobrious epithet of the basteel.

(Thieves'.)—A prison.—*See* Cage. Bastile in this sense is mentioned by Captain Grose [1785].

Bat, *subs.* (old slang).—1. A prostitute who plies her trade by night; an allusion to the nocturnal habits of the flying mammal—indeed, another old term for a woman of the town was literally a fly-by-night. The equivalent French term, *hirondelle de nuit*, *i.e.*, 'a night swallow,' is more poetic. For full lists of synonyms, *see* Barrack-hack.

2. (American.)—A spree; frolic; and sometimes a drunken bout. A contracted form of 'batter.'

1889. *Bird o' Freedom*, Aug. 7, p. 1. *Mr. Pote*: 'I see in the evening paper that a woman has been bitten by a bat, and afterwards died of lockjaw.' *Mrs. P.* (tartily): 'If she had been bitten by the kind of BAT you went on when I was away last Saturday week, she would probably have died of *delirium tremens.*'

3. (athletic.)—Pace; speed (in walking, rowing, etc.). Partly also dialectical, especially Scotch, Craven, and Lincolnshire.

1887. *Daily News*, 18 August, p. 6, col. 3. Here they come, a mixed flock of birds full BAT overhead.

TO BAT ONE'S EYES, *phr.* (American).—1. A South-western term which is explained by quotation.

1846. *Overland Monthly*, p. 79. The ox whip has both parts as long as they can be managed. I have seen a poor fellow from Ohio, totally unused to this enormous affair, swing it round his head in many an awkward twist, while the Texans stood by and laughed to see him knock off his hat and BAT HIS EYES at every twitch, to avoid cutting them out.

Cf., Italian *batter d'occhio*, twinkling of an eye.

2. (American gaming.)—To look on but not to play. *Cf.*, BET.

OFF or ON ONE'S OWN BAT, *phr.* (popular).—On one's own account; by one's own exertions. A figurative usage of a cricketing term; 'OFF ONE'S OWN BAT,' is said of a score made by a player individually.

1845. SYDNEY SMITH, *Fragm. Irish Ch.*, wks. II., 340, 1. He had no revenues but what he got OFF HIS OWN BAT. [M.]

1855. LORD LONSDALE, in *Croker Papers* (1884), vol. III., p. 325. Derby . . . would not make a Ministry FROM his own friends or HIS OWN BAT.

1880. HAWLEY SMART, *Social Sinners*, ch. xxiii. 'You have a weakness for the great world? Good. Score OFF YOUR OWN BAT, and it is the great world comes to you.'

1884. *Sat. Review*, March 8, p. 308, col. 2. He has in the most workmanlike manner, and OFF HIS OWN BAT, lost for the Government an important seat by a crushing majority.

TO CARRY OUT ONE'S BAT, *phr.* (popular).—This also is derived from a cricketing expression. In the game it means to be not out, *i.e.*, the last man in. Figuratively, therefore, TO CARRY OUT ONE'S BAT is to persevere and carry through an undertaking; to outlast all other opponents; and thus to secure the result aimed at.

1874. M. COLLINS, *Frances*, ch. xxviii. The General defended his stumps as he would have defended a fortress, and CARRIED HIS BAT OUT with a score of a hundred and seven.

BATCHELOR'S SON, *subs.* (old).—A bastard.

BATES' FARM or GARDEN, *subs.* (thieves). — Coldbath Fields prison. [From a warder of that name + a certain appropriateness in the initials, C.B.F., the prison initials, and used as a stamp=CHARLEY BATES'FARM.] When, formerly, the convicts were put to the treadmill in this prison, they were said to be 'feeding the chickens on CHARLEY BATES' FARM.' Newgate was also called AKERMAN'S HOTEL, from a former governor, and a similar reason has caused the Melbourne gaol to be nicknamed Castilan's Hotel by Australian thieves.

[*Circa* 1850, but date uncertain.] BATES' FARM.
Good evening pals, how do you do,
  I thought I'd give a call,
And introduce myself to you,
  For I'm glad to see you all.
I'm up to every little *fake*,
  But in me there's no harm,
For it was this *blooming* morning
  That I left OLD BATES' FARM.

CHORUS.
Then, here's success my knowing *kids*,
  I'm filled with ev'ry charm,
I feel so gay this blessed day,
  I've left OLD BATES' FARM.

Now, every morning when you rise,
  You get a starving meal,
And if you don't eat all they send
  You have to work the wheel.
Then so merrily we go,
  To chapel to have prayers,
And for a little pastime work
  The *everlasting stairs.*
    Chorus.

The last time that I went to see
  OLD BATES, he shook my hand,
And said, 'I'm glad to see you,
  You're a chap I understand.'
He said, 'You're here for nothing now?'
  I said 'Yes,' like the rest,
It was only for knocking a *bobby* down,
  And jumping on his chest.
    Chorus.

So now I've got my liberty,
  And once again I'm free,
I mean to '*crack a crib*' to-night.
  But pals don't '*crack on me.*'
So if I should touch lucre,
  For a time I will keep calm,
If I don't see you here some night,
  I shall at BATES' FARM.
    Chorus.

BATH. GO TO BATH! *phr.* (familiar).—This popular saying appears to have two distinct readings, both of which, however, are traceable to the same source.

1. GO TO BATH! *i.e.*, an injunction to desist; to be gone; get out of my sight, or hearing, for you are mad or cracked— a forcible expression of incredulity, sometimes intensified by 'AND GET YOUR HEAD SHAVED.' The saying is applied to those who either relate crack-brained stories, or propose undertakings that raise a doubt as to sanity. The allusion is to the fact that, in former days, persons who showed symptoms of insanity were sent to BATH to drink the medicinal waters; the process of shaving the head being previously resorted to.

1840. BARHAM, I. L. (*Grey Dolphin*). 'GO TO BATH!' said the baron. A defiance so contemptuous roused the ire of the adverse commanders.

1885. *Frank Leslie's Illustrated Newspaper*, Oct. 16, p. 362. You tell a disagreeable neighbour to go to BATH in the sense in which a Roman would have said *abi in malam rem.*

2. Hence, to become a beggar. Bath, especially in the latter part of the last century, and at the beginning of the present one, enjoyed a reputation for its fashion and baths: it was also, naturally enough, for this very reason, the resort of countless numbers of beggars. TO GO TO BATH signified, therefore, amongst vagrants, to proceed to what was in reality one of the first centres of beggardom; presumably to solicit alms. Hence also an additional clue to the process of transition into sense 1. What more natural than to bid an importunate applicant to betake himself to Bath to join his fellows? Fuller in his *Worthies* has a passage which throws some additional light upon the question.

1662. FULLER, *History of the Worthies of England*. *Beggars of Bath.*— Many in that place; some natives there, others repairing thither from all parts of the land; the poor for alms, the pained for ease. Whither should flock fowl in a hard frost, but to the barndoor? Here, all the two seasons, being the general confluence of gentry. Indeed laws are daily made to restrain beggars, and daily broken by the connivance of those who make them; it being impossible when the hungry belly barks, and bowels sound, to keep the tongue silent. And although oil of whip be the proper plaister for the cramp of laziness, yet some pity is due to impotent persons. In a word, seeing there is the Lazar's bath in this city, I doubt not but many a good Lazarus, the true object of charity, may beg therein.

Long previous to 1662, how-

ever, stringent vagrant laws were in force.

1588. WILLIAM LAMBARD, *The Office of the Justices of the Peace*, p. 334. Such two Justices may . . . . License diseased persons (living of almes) to trauell to *Bathe*, or to *Buckstone* [Buxton], for remedie of their griefe.

BATHING MACHINES, *subs.* (nautical). —A name given to the old 10 ton brigs. — RUSSELL'S *Sailor's Language.*

BAT-MUGGER, *subs.* (Winchester College). — A wooden instrument used for rubbing oil into cricket bats.

BATS, *subs.* (thieves').—A pair of bad or old boots. Elworthy in *West Somerset Words* gives this as a heavy laced boot with hobnails.

BATS DOWN? (Winchester and general). — 'How MANY BATS DOWN?' *i.e.*, how many wickets have fallen?

BATTELS, *subs.* (University).—The weekly bills of students at Oxford. The derivation of the term has been the subject of much discussion, and is very uncertain. Murray says much depends on the original sense at Oxford: if this was 'food, provisions,' it is natural to connect it with 'battle,' to feed, or receive nourishment.—*See* quotation.

1886-7. DICKENS, *Dictionary of Oxford and Cambridge*, p. 16. BATTELS is properly a designation of the food obtained from the College Buttery. An account of this, and of the account due to the Kitchen, is sent in to every undergraduate weekly, hence these bills also are known as BATTELS, and the name, further, is extended to the total amount of the term's expenses furnished by the College. In some Colleges it is made essential to the keeping of an undergraduates' term that he should BATTEL, *i.e.*, obtain food in College on a certain number of days each week.

To quote Dr. Murray again, however, it appears that the word has apparently undergone progressive extensions of application, owing partly to changes in the internal economy of the colleges. Some Oxford men of a previous generation state that it was understood by them to apply to the buttery accounts alone, or even to the provisions ordered from the buttery, as distinct from the 'commons' supplied from the kitchen: but this latter use is disavowed by others . . . but whether the BATTELS were originally the provisions themselves, or the sums due on account of them, must at present be left undecided.

1853. CUTHBERT BEDE, *Verdant Green*, pt. II., ch. vii. The Michaelmas term was drawing to its close. Buttery and kitchen books were adding up their sums total; bursars were preparing for BATTELS.

(Eton.)—*See* quotation.

1798. H. TOOKE, *Purley*, 390. BATTEL, a term used at Eton for the small portion of food which, in addition to the College allowance, the collegers receive from their dames.

BATTER, *subs.* (common). — Wear and tear; *e.g.*, 'the BATTER is more than any human being can stand for long. [From one of the ordinary meanings of TO BATTER, to wear or impair by beating or long service, as a BATTERED jade.]

Ppl. adj.—Given up to debauchery; this sense follows upon

TO GO ON THE BATTER, *i.e.*, to walk the streets for purposes of prostitution; but *cf.*, BAT.

BATTLE OF THE NILE, *subs. phr.* (rhyming slang).—A 'tile' = a hat. For synonyms, *see* CADY.

BATTLE ROYAL, *subs.* (colloquial).—A vehement quarrel.

1698. HOWARD, *All Mistaken*, Act i. *1st Nurse.* Your husband is the noted'st cuckold in all our street. *2nd Nurse.* You lie, you jade; yours is a greater. *Phil.* Hist—now for a BATTLE-ROYAL.

18(?). THACKERAY, *Shabby Genteel Story*, ch. vi. A BATTLE-ROYAL speedily took place between the two worthy mothers-in-law.

1865. *Sketches from Cambridge*, p. 137. Our brethren there [in Oxford] seem to be always indulging in BATTLES-ROYAL.

BATTLINGS, *subs.* (public schools').—A weekly allowance of money. At Winchester it is 1s., while at Repton it is only 6d.

1864. *Household Words*, p. 188. The business of the latter was to call us of a morning to distribute amongst us our BATTLINGS, or pocket-money.

1870. MANSFIELD, *School-Life at Winchester College*, p. 184. The expense was defrayed by the boys subscribing the last three BATTLINGS (*i.e.*, the weekly shilling allowed each boy). This was rather an illusory coin, for we seldom actually fingered it, as some one of the College servants generally had a kind of prescriptive right to a benefit; and whenever Saturday arrived, Præfect of Hall's valet was sure to come round to ask the boys if they would give their BATTLING to Rat Williams, or Dungy, or Purver, or Long John, or some other equally deserving individual.

1883. TROLLOPE, *Autobiogr.* (1883), I., 13. Every boy had a shilling a week pocket-money, which we called BATTELS. [This is probably a misprint — the Winchester term, as that used at other schools, is BATTLING. It was advanced out of the pocket of the second master.]

BATTNER, *subs.* (old). — An ox; beef being apt to batten or fatten those that eat it. 'The cove has hushed the BATTNER,' *i.e.*, has killed the ox.—*Grose* [1785].

BATTY, *subs.* (general).—Wages; perquisites. Derived from BATTA, an extra pay given to soldiers while serving in India.—*Hotten.* Col. Yule says in Indian banking, agio or difference in exchange; discount on coins not current; or of short weight.

1824. T. HOOK, *Sayings and Doings*, 1 S., *Merton*, ch. viii. Whether he could draw full BATTA in peace-time.

1868. BREWER, *Phrase and Fable*, 5 S. 'Batta.' BATTA or BATTY (Hindustanee). Perquisites; wages. Properly, an allowance to East Indian troops in the field.

BAULK, *subs.* (Winchester College). —A false report (especially that a master is at hand), which is SPORTED (*q.v.*), not spread.

(Popular.)—A false shot; a mistake.

BAUM, *verb* (American Univ.).—To fawn; to flatter; to curry favour.—HALL'S *College Words and Phrases.*

BAWBELS or BAWBLES, *subs.* (old). —A man's testicles. Originally, a provincialism. For synonyms, *see* CODS.

BAWCOCK, *subs.* (old).—A burlesque term of endearment. [From either French *beau*, fine, + French *coq*, cock = a fine or good 'feller'; or from English BOY + COCK = a young dandy or strut.]

1599. SHAKSPEARE, *Henry V.*, iii., 2, 25. *Pist.* Be merciful, great duke, to men of mould! . . . Good BAWCOCK 'bate thy rage!

1861. H. AINSWORTH, *Constable of the Tower*, p. 131. One of the gamesome little BAWCOCK's jests.

Bawd, *subs.* (old).—A female procuress. A CARTED BAWD meant one who had been placed in a cart and led through the town to make her person known to the inhabitants. *Cf.*, ABBESS. *See* also CART and BARRACK-HACK for synonyms

Bawde Phisicke.—*See* quotation.

1560-1. AWDELEY, *The XXV. orders of Knaues*, (ed. 1869), p. 14. BAWDE PHISICKE, is he that is a Cocke, when his Maysters meate is euyll dressed, and he challenging him therefore, he wyl say he wyll eate the rawest morsel thereof him selfe. This is a sausye knaue, that wyl contrary his Mayster alway.

Bawdy Banquet, *subs.* (old). — Whoremongering. [From BAWDY, lewd, + BANQUET.]

1567. HARMAN, *Caveat* (1869), p. 63. 'Where haue I bene?' quoth he, and began to smyle. 'Now, by the mas, thou hast bene at some BAUDY BANQUET.'

Bawdy Banquet, *subs.* (old).—A running after loose women; molrowing.

Bawdy Basket, *subs.* (old cant).—1. The twenty-third rank of canters (*see* Harman), who carried pins, tape, ballads, and obscene books to sell, but lived mostly by stealing,

1567. HARMAN, *Caveat* (ed. 1869), p. 65. These BAWDY BASKETS be also wemen, and go with baskets and Capeases on their armes, where in they haue laces, pynnes, nedles, white ynkell, and round sylke gyrdles of al coulours. These wyl bye conneyskins and steale linen clothes of on hedges. And for their trifles they will procure of mayden seruaunts, when [leaf 20, back] their mystres or dame is oute of the waye, either some good peece of béefe, baken, or chéese, that shalbe worth xij pens, for ii pens of their toyes. And as they walke by the waye, they often gaine some money wyth their instrument, by such as they sodaynely mete withall. The vpright men haue good acquayntance with these, and will helpe and relieue them when they want. Thus they trade their lyues in lewed lothsome lechery. Amongest them all is but one honest woman, and she is of good yeares; her name is Ione Messenger. I haue had good proofe of her, as I haue learned by the true report of diuers.

1671. R. HEAD, *English Rogue*, pt. I., ch. v., p. 39 (1874). [In list of orders of thieves], BAWDY-BASKETS.

2. A prostitute; an alternative and earlier form of BAWD (*q.v.*).

1589. PUTTENHAM, *Art of Eng. Poesie*, bk. III., ch. xix.
Many a faire lasse in London towne,
Many a BAWDIE BASKET borne vp and downe:
Many a broker in a thridbare gowne,
Many a bankrowte scarce worth a crowne. In London.

1608. DEKKER, *Belman of London*, in wks. (Grosart) III., 86. The victualers to the campe are women, and to those some are *Glymerers*, some BAWDY-BASKETS, some *Autem-Morts*.

Bawdy House Bottle, *subs. phr.* (old).—A very small one, short measure, being among the many means used by the keepers of those houses, to gain what they call an honest livelihood; indeed, this is one of the least reprehensible, the less they give a man of their infernal beverages for his money, the kinder they behave to him.—*Grose*.

Bayard of Ten Toes. TO RIDE BAYARD OF TEN TOES, *phr.* (old).—To go on foot. Bayard was a horse famous in old romances.—*See* MARROW BONE STAGE.

1606. BRETON, *Good and Badde*, p. 14. Breton says of the 'honest poore man,'—his trauell is the walke of the woful, and his horse BAYARD OF TEN TOES.

1662. FULLER, *Worthies, Somerset* (ii., 291). At last he [Coryat] undertook to travail into the East Indies by land, mounted on AN HORSE WITH TEN TOES.

Bay Window, *subs.* (common).—A slang phrase applied to women when pregnant, or men who have 'corporations.' The allusion is obvious.

B. C., *subs.* (common).—A name jokingly applied to a person who brings a trumpery action for libel against another. Dr. Brewer in *Phrase and Fable* thus, in effect, explains the allusion:—A young woman complained to Mr. Ingham [the magistrate at Bow Street Police Court and now (1889) Sir James Ingham] of having been abused by a woman who called her a B. C. On being asked the meaning, the young woman said C meant 'cat' but the B——, well, it was too shocking to utter, and the magistrate allowed her to whisper the word in his ear. It was a well-known word of sanguinary sound; but, though B.C. was hardly a pretty epithet, yet his worship could hardly grant a summons for libel against the person of whom complaint was made for using it.

Beach-Cadger, *subs.* (old). — A beggar whose 'pitch' is at watering-places, and sea-ports. [From BEACH, the sea-shore + CADGER, a beggar.]

Beach-Comber, *subs.* (nautical).—1. One who hangs about the sea-shore on the look-out for jobs. It was chiefly applied to runaway seamen, deserters from whalers, who lived along the beach in South America, the South Sea Islands, etc. It is a term of contempt.—CLARK RUSSELL'S *Sailors' Language*.

1847. *Blackwood's Magazine*, LXI., 757. A daring Yankee BEECH-COMBER. [M.]

1880. *Athenæum*, 18 Dec., p. 809, col. 2. The white scamps who, as BEECH-COMBERS, have polluted these Edens and debauched their inhabitants.

1885. A. LANG, in *Longm. Mag.*, VI., 417, *note*. BEACH-COMBER is the local term for the European adventurers and long-shore loafers who infest the Pacific Archipelagoes. There is a well-known tale of an English castaway on one of the isles, who was worshipped as a deity by the ignorant people. At length he made his escape, by swimming, and was taken aboard a British vessel, whose captain accosted him roughly. The mariner turned aside and dashed away a tear: 'I've been a god for months and you call me a (something alliterative) BEACH-COMBER!' he exclaimed, and refused to be comforted.

2. A river boatman.

3 A thief who prowls about the sea-shore; a plunderer of wrecks; a picker-up of waifs and strays. This is derived from sense 4.

4. (American.)—A long wave rolling in from the ocean. Hence applied to those whose occupation it is to pick up, as pirates or wreckers, whatever these waves wash in to them.

Beach-Tramper, *subs.* (nautical).—A coastguardsman. [From BEACH, the shore of the sea + TRAMP, to walk along + ER.]

Bead. TO DRAW A BEAD [ON ONE], *phr.* (American).—To attack an opponent by speech or otherwise. The phrase has passed into colloquial use from backwoods parlance, where it signifies the process of taking aim and firing. The front sight of a gun is in appearance like a BEAD.

1841. CATLIN, *North American Indians* (1844), I., x., 77. I made several attempts to get near enough TO DRAW A BEAD upon one of them.

1870. BRET HARTE, *Society on the Stanislaus* (in *Poems and Prose*). It is not a proper plan, to lay for that same member for TO PUT A BEAD ON HIM.

188(?) S. CLEMENS ('Mark Twain'), *Adventures of Huckleberry Finn*, p. 48. Iwas pretty close to the Shanty, and I thought I heard the old man coming all the time; but I got her hid; and then I out and looked around a bunch of willows, and there was the old man down the path apiece just DRAWING A BEAD on a bird with his gun.

1889. *Albany Journal*, Aug. 6. If Jake's not careful I'll DRAW A BEAD ON HIM. Very little more will make me go for him tooth and nail.

TO RAISE A BEAD.—To bring to the point; to ensure success. The figure is taken from brandy, rum, or other liquors, which will not 'raise a bead,' unless of the proper strength.

1846. *N. Y. Tribune*, *Letter from Ohio*. The result was, if the convention had been then held, the party wouldn't have been able TO RAISE A BEAD. [B.]

Beagle, *subs.* (old).—A spy; informer; man-hunter; policeman; also a general term of contempt. [From BEAGLE, a small hound, which tracks by scent, formerly used for hunting.]

1599. *Myrr. Mag.*, *Jack Cade*, xix., 2. That restless BEGLE sought and found me out. [M.]

1607. DEKKER, *Westward Hoe*, Act iii., Sc. 4. *Mon.* I beseech you, Mistress Tenterhook,—before God, I'll be sick, if you will not be merry. *Mist. Ten.* You are a sweet BEAGLE.

1748. T. DYCHE, *Dictionary* (5 ed.). BEAGLE (s.) . . . . also a contemptuous name given to a boy or man, as to say, *you are a special* BEAGLE, is the same as, you are good for nothing.

1837. CARLYLE, *French Revolution*, III., VII., v., 377. Attorneys and Law-BEAGLES, which hunt ravenous on this Earth.

Beak, *subs.* (old cant).—1. A policeman or guardian of the peace. As far as is known, this (as 'beck') is the oldest cant term for a member of a class of men, who, perhaps, above all o hers, have been the recipients of nicknames and epithets, and these, be it noted, not always of a complimentary character. In Harman's *Caveat* (1573), *harman* BECK is explained as 'the counstable,' *harmans* being 'the stockes.' The derivation of BECK or BEAK is doubtful. Especially vague seems that which finds its source in the Saxon *beag*, a gold collar worn by civic magistrates, and an emblem of authority. This genesis appears to be based on the later and secondary sense of BEAK, a magistrate, a meaning which it still retains. But, against this must be placed the fact that, as the name for a watchman or guardian of the peace, BEAK boasts a much older usage. Sir John Fielding, half brother of the author of *Tom Jones*, and an active Middlesex Justice in the last century, was popularly known as the 'Blind Beak' [*c.* 1750]; but beyond this date no instance of this sense has been found. If, therefore, BEAK originally signified a policeman, it is difficult to discover any connection with the Saxon *beag*, inasmuch as watchmen are not known to have been decorated with gold collars. The following quotations will give other illustrations, and also show that, meaning a policeman, the term has not long been obsolete.

1609. DEKKER, a Gypsy song, in *Lanthorne and Candlelight, etc.*
The Ruffin cly the nab of the HARMAN BECK,
If we mawnd Pannam, lap or Ruff-peck,

Or poplars of yarum; he cuts, bing to the Ruffmans.
Or else he sweares by the lightmans,
To put our stamps in the Harmans.
The Ruffian cly the ghost of the HARMAN BECK.
If we heaue a booth we cly the Jerke.
If we niggle or mill a bousing ken.
Or nip a bung that has but a win,
Or dup the giger of a gentry cofes ken:
To the quier cuffing we bing,
And then to the quier-Ken to scowre the Cramp-ring,
And then to the Trin'de on the chates, in the lightmans,
The Bube and Ruffian cly the HARMAN BECK and Harmans.

[This is thus 'Englished' by DEKKER].

The Deuill take the Constable's head,
If we beg Bacon, Butter-milke or bread.
Or Pottage, to the hedge he bids us hie,
Or sweares (by this light) i'th' stocks we shall lie.
The Deuill haunt the Constable's ghoast,
If we rob but a booth, we are whip'd at a poast.
If an ale-house we rob or be tane with a whore,
Or cut a purse that has iust a penny, and no more,
Or come but stealing in at a gentleman's dore:
To the Justice straight we goe,
And then to the Jayle to be shakled: And so
To be hang'd on the gallows i'th' day time: the pox
And the Deuill take the Constable and his stocks.

1821. W. T. MONCRIEFF, *Tom and Jerry*, Act ii., Sc. 6.
Land. Gentlemen vagabonds; the *traps* are abroad, and half a thousand beadles and *beaksmen* are now about the door.
Billy. De BEAK! oh curse a de BEAK!
Jemmy. Gemmen!—gemmen! (*Knocking on table to command attention.*)
Jack. Silence for the chair!
Jemmy. Put out the lights, put out the lights, every one shift for himself. Here, Bob, carry me up the ladder, good luck to you do, Bob.

1840. THACKERAY, *Catherine*, ch. x. But Mrs. Polly, with a wonderful presence of mind, restored peace by exclaiming, 'Hush, hush! the BEAKS, the BEAKS!' Upon which, with one common instinct, the whole party made a rush for the garden gates, and disappeared into the fields. Mrs. Briggs knew her company: there was something in the very name of a constable which sent them all a-flying.

ENGLISH SYNONYMS. 'Blue' (traceable to Queen Elizabeth's days when the colour of the uniform was the same as now); 'men in blue'; 'Royal Regiment of Footguards Blue'; 'bluebottle' (used by Shakspeare); 'blew coate' (also a Shakspearian term, and still in use); 'Dogberry' (an allusion to *Much Ado about Nothing*); 'charley' (one of the old watchmen); 'bobby'; 'peeler'; 'copper' (a thieves' term, from 'to cop' to lay hold of); 'crusher' (thieves'); 'slop' (a back slang corruption of 'police' = esclop, with *c* not sounded and shortened to 'slop'); 'scufter' (a northern term, as also is the example next following); 'bulky' (used by Bulwer Lytton); 'philip' (from a thieves' signal); 'cossack'; 'philistine'; 'frog' (from pouncing upon criminals); 'Johnnie Darby' (a corruption of *gendarme*); 'Johnnie'; 'pig' (a plain clothes man); 'worm'; 'nose'; 'nark'; 'dee' (a detective); 'tec'; the C.T.A. (a circus man's term); 'demon' (Australian thieves'); 'reeler'; 'raw lobster' (this like 'blue,' etc., would appear to be a reference to the colour of the uniform).

FRENCH SYNONYMS. *Un rousse* (popular and thieves': *roux* signifies 'red,' and red hair has always been held in contempt as indicative of treachery and craft; hence its application by the criminal classes to their natural enemies); *un roussin* (thieves': of same derivation as foregoing); *un bâton de réglisse* (popular: 'a stick of liquorice'); *un baladin* (properly 'a mountebank, juggler, or buffoon'); *une cagne* (popular: 'a dog,' *i.e.*, 'a worthless fellow,' 'a slut'; *cagne* or *caigne* in Old French signified 'dog,' and was derived from the Latin *canis*, whence *caignot*, 'a little dog.' It may also be noted that, prior to the establishment of the modern *gendarmerie*, the archers of the watch were known as *chiens-courants*); *un cogne* (thieves': another form of *cagne*); *un balai* (hawkers': properly 'a broom, brush, or besom'); *un serin* (popular: properly 'a canary'; *serin* is also slang for 'a foolish fellow,' 'a greenhorn'); *un pousse* (thieves': the guardians of public order formerly known in Paris as *serjents* or *archers de l'écuelle* were called *pousse-culs*); *une vache* (literally 'a cow'); *un arnif* (thieves'); *une peste* (thieves': literally 'a plague' or 'torment'); *une tronche à la manque*; *un flaquadard*; *un cabestan* (thieves': properly 'a hand-winch'; Michel thinks this is derived either from *cabe*, 'a dog'; or from *capitan*, 'a captain.' The latter, be it noted, has also the signification of 'hector' or 'braggadocio'); *un raille* or *railleux* (thieves': a detective. Michel derives it from *raillon*, a weapon with which the police were formerly armed. Victor Hugo thought it came from the English word 'rascal,' but there seems little, if any, authority for this); *un sacre* (Nicot gives this as 'a bird of prey,' but Henri Estienne adds that it was used to denote 'one who lays hands on everything that comes in his way'; also 'a gourmand'); *un grive* (thieves': 'a warder' or 'military patrol'); *un laune* (thieves'); *un flique* (popular: also a petty police magistrate. Thought to be a corruption of *friquet*, another opprobrious term for a police man); *un bec du gaz*; *un estaffier* (familiar: also, among thieves, 'a cat'); *une bourrique* (thieves': also 'an informer'); *un pousse trottoir* (*pousse* from *pousser*, 'to push'; *trottoir*, a footpath); *un lampion rouge* (thieves'); *un escargot de trottoir* (popular: literally 'a snail of the footpath'); *un cierge* (thieves': properly 'a wax taper'); *un sergo* (popular); *un grippe-Jesus* (a term used by thieves in the north of France, and by seafaring men which, says Michel, might lead one to suppose that gendarmes only arrested innocent persons); *un pince sans rire* (thieves': a sly, malicious person); *un pot à tabac* (popular: 'a tobacco jar'); *un singe de la rousse* (*singe* = monkey, *de la rousse*, 'of the police force').

For GERMAN SYNONYMS, *see* COPPER.

ITALIAN SYNONYMS. *Un' zaffo* (literally 'a bung' or 'tipstaff'); *un' foco* or *un' fuoco* (literally 'fire').

SPANISH SYNONYMS. *Uno mastin* (literally 'a mastiff' or 'bulldog'; 'a clumsy fellow'; 'a clown'); *una harpia* (*un harpeo* = 'grapnel' or 'grappling-iron'); *una fiera* (properly 'a wild beast').

2. (popular.)—A magistrate. *Cf.* foregoing, much of which has reference to this secondary meaning of BEAK. Sometimes called A BEAK OF THE LAW.

1837. DICKENS, *Oliver Twist*, ch. viii. 'My eyes, how green!' exclaimed the young gentleman. 'Why a BEAK'S a madgst'rate.'

18(?) HOOD, *Tale of a Trumpet*.
The pies and jays that utter words,
And other Dicky gossips of birds,
Who talk with as much good sense and decorum,
As many BEAKS who belong to the quorum.

1881. *Punch*, Dec. 3, 258. A PAIR OF ANTI-VIVISECTIONISTS. *Sir Slangsby Jaunter.* 'See that old fellow, Miss Diana? That's Doctor Katchett, who swears he's going to find a cure for *lunatics*! Just got into trouble. Been trying the effects of extreme terror and bodily fatigue on a rabbit, and *without chloroform*, too, the old ruffian! And then he killed it, and dissected its brain. Going to be had up before the BEAK for it! Bow St., you know!' *Miss Diana.* 'Serve him right, horrid man! Don't want to know about such people. But talking of rabbits, what a splendid run that second *Hare* gave us to-day! Thirty minutes gallop without a check!—Wasn't it lovely!—And I was in at the death!'

1889. *Pall Mall Gaz.*, Oct. 12, p. 5, col. 2. Taken before some French BEAK whom he did not know, and an interpreter brought, the 'cotched' culprit was made to pay 20 f., his friend escaping because he was not caught red-handed.

An ENGLISH SYNONYM is 'queer cuffin' (old cant).

FRENCH SYNONYMS. *Un sapeur* (thieves': properly 'a sapper,' *i.e.*, 'one who undermines' [one's chances of wrong doing]); *un pante en robe* (*pante* in French slang is equivalent to 'a man' or 'cove'; *en robe* = 'in a robe'); *un endormi* (popular: properly 'a sleepy-head'); *un grignon* (thieves': probably from *grigner les dents*, 'to show one's teeth threateningly'; or from *grognon*, 'grumbler,' 'growler'); *un gerbier*; *un curieux* (thieves': *i.e.*, 'the curious one'; from the *adj. curieux*. Michel, however, adds that *curieux* formerly signified 'a courtier'); *un singe à rabat* (thieves': possibly *rabat* is an abbreviated form of *rabat-joie*, 'a wet blanket.' The phrase would then mean 'a baboon with a wet blanket,' 'a damper'; or it may be derived from *singe*, a monkey + *rabat*, slang for 'a cloak.' *Cf.*, *singe de la rousse*); *un lustre* (thieves': properly 'renown'; 'distinction'); *un pant' de la magistrat' muche* (thieves').

ITALIAN SYNONYM. *Un antigo* (literally 'an old one'; also 'a master,' 'a boss').

SPANISH SYNONYM. *Sombrador* (thieves' and popular: from *sombra*, 'shade'; *i.e.*, one who puts in the shade. *Poner à la sombra* is 'to imprison').

3. (popular.) — The nose. For synonyms, *see* CONK.

1598. FLORIO. *Naso adunco*, a BEAKE-nose. [M.]

1854. THACKERAY, *Newcomes*, I., 296. The well-known hooked BEAK of the old countess. [M.]

1865. E. C. CLAYTON, *Cruel Fort*, I., 143. A large, fat, greasy woman, with a prominent BEAK.

1876. E. C. GRENVILLE MURRAY, *The Member for Paris*, I., p. 80. It was not the most agreeable thing in the world to be suddenly interrupted in a mantel-shelf conversation by a gentleman with a firm BEAK-NOSE and a red rosette in his button-hole.

4. (Eton and Marlborough Schools.)—A master.

BEAKER, *subs.* (thieves').—A fowl. Sometimes shortened into BEAK. The derivation is obviously an illusion to the beak or horny mandibles of poultry. Formerly called CACKLING-CHEAT (*q.v.*), and by French thieves *une estable*, or *une estaphle*.

BEAKER-HUNTER, *subs.* (thieves').—A poultry yard thief. Also BEAK-HUNTER.

1857. SNOWDEN, *Mag. Assistant*, 3 ed., p. 445. A poultry stealer. A BEAKER-HUNTER.

BEAK-GANDER, *subs.* (common).—A judge of the Superior Courts. [From BEAK (*q.v.*), a magistrate + GANDER, a humorous term for an old man.]

BEAKSMAN, *subs.* (old).—*See* BEAK (sense 1), of which it is an alternative form.

BEAM ENDS. TO BE THROWN ON ONE'S BEAM ENDS, *phr.* (nautical).—1. To be in bad circumstances; to be at one's last shift; hard-up; a metaphor drawn from sea-faring life. A ship is said to be on her BEAM ENDS when she is so prostrated on her side by stress of weather, or shifting of cargo, as to submerge her lee rail.

1843. DICKENS, *Martin Chuzzlewit*, xl. In short, he laughed the idea down completely; and Tom, abandoning it, was THROWN UPON HIS BEAM ENDS again for some other solution. [H.]

1851. HENRY MAYHEW, *London Labour and London Poor*, III., 121. When a fellow is ON HIS BEAM ENDS, as I was then, he must keep his eyes about him, and have impudence enough for anything, or else he may stop and starve. [H.]

2. Also, less figuratively, to be thrown to the ground; to be reduced to a sitting or lying posture.

1830. MARRYAT, *King's Own*, xxvi. Our first lieutenant was . . . ON HIS BEAM ENDS, with the rheumatiz.

1853. REV. E. BRADLEY ('Cuthbert Bede'), *Adventures of Verdant Green.* You get on stunningly, gig-lamps, and haven't been ON YOUR BEAM ENDS more than once a minute.

BEAN or **BIEN**, *subs.* (popular).—A sovereign. Formerly a guinea. In America five-dollar gold pieces are now called BEANS. *See* also HALF-BEAN and HADDOCK OF BEANS. In the old French cant, *biens* meant money or property. For synonyms, *see* CANARY.

1811. *Lexicon Balatronicum.* BEAN, a guinea. HALF-BEAN.

1834. H. AINSWORTH, *Rookwood*, bk. III., ch. ix. Zoroaster took long odds that the match was off; offering a BEAN to *half a quid* (in other words, a guinea to a half guinea).

1885. D. C. MURRAY, *Rainbow Gold*, bk. V., ch. vi. 'Here's some of the BEANS,' he continued figuratively, as he drew five sovereigns from the same pocket, and surveyed them in his great brown palm.

FULL OF BEANS, *phr.* (society).—In good form or condition; as full of health, spirits, or capacity as a horse after a good feed of beans. Among the ancients the word signified venery; possibly, therefore, a more esoteric meaning may be attached to it than commonly supposed.—*See* BEANY.

1889. *Sporting Times*, June 29. The tennis-ground [was] a pretty place, overlooking the harbour, and surrounded by trees and female beauty. The game began. 'Ich dien,' shouted Jack, as FULL OF BEANS as the Prince of Wales' plume, and immediately sent a ball which went bang through the window of an adjoining house.

TO GIVE BEANS, *phr.* (common).—To chastise; to give a good drubbing. For synonyms, *see* TAN.

LIKE BEANS, *adv. phr.* (common).—In good form, style, time, etc.; with force; a general expression of approval and praise. *Cf.*, LIKE BLAZES, BRICKS, OR ONE O'CLOCK.

NOT TO CARE, or BE WORTH A BEAN.—To hold in little esteem; to think lightly of; to be of little value. The allusion is to

the small worth, or value of a bean, or 'the black of a bean.' A variant is NOT WORTH A STRAW (*q.v.*). Both phrases are old, NOT WORTH A BEAN being traced back to 1297.

TO BE BEANY, *phr.* (common).—To be in good humour—a metaphor also drawn from the stable.

TO KNOW BEANS, *phr.* (American).—To be well informed. The phrase is incorporated into many expressions in a very strange way; and is an allusion to the fondness of New Englanders in general, and Bostonians in particular, for baked beans and pork, combined with a sly hit at the assumption of superior culture on which they are supposed to insist. TO KNOW BEANS, therefore, is to be sharp and shrewd; to be within the charmed circle of the 'cultured elect'—in short to be fully equipped in the 'upper storey.'

1888. *Portland Transcript*, March 7. The pudding was pronounced a success by each member of the assembled family, including a dainty Boston girl who, of course, KNOWS BEANS.

1888. *Chicago Herald.* One has to KNOW BEANS to be successful in the latest Washington novelty for entertainment at luncheons.

An alternative derivation may, however, be found in the English form.

TO KNOW HOW MANY BLUE BEANS MAKE FIVE WHITE ONES, *phr.* (common).—This is generally put in the form of a question, the answer to which is 'Five, if peeled,' and those who fail to get tripped by the 'catch' are said 'TO KNOW HOW MANY,' etc.; in other words to be cute; knowing; wide awake.

1830. GALT, *Laurie, T.* (1849), II., i. 42. Few men who better knew HOW MANY BLUE BEANS IT TAKES TO MAKE FIVE. [M.]

1886. *Zoological Comparisons*, in *Broadside Ballad.*
Nature and art improves us, the girls with smiles are moving us,
Which very often ruin us there's no gammon about that;
Then just as we begin to know 'HOW MANY BEANS MAKE FIVE,'
The ladies call us puppies when we at that age arrive;
You may perchance become a deer, if in favour with some lass,
If not you're called a donkey, and often-times an ass.

1889. *Daily News*, 4 Nov., p. 6, col. 5. Mr. Gladstone and *The Saturday Review*. Sir,—My master, who is a good Conservative, lends me *The Saturday Review* to improve my mind. . . . It says that there were eighty-six Parnellites, and that if Mr. Gladstone, by his wickedness, could make them leave off voting for the Tories, and vote for him, instead of being in a minority of four, he would have had a majority of 80. Why, Sir, the dunce of the school knows that if you take 80 from one side and add it on to the other, the difference is not 80, but 160. It is as simple as HOW MANY BLUE BEANS MAKE FIVE. I think some people are losing their wits faster than Mr. Gladstone.—I am, Sir, yours respectfully, A SCHOOLBOY.

THREE BLUE BEANS IN A BLUE BLADDER.—Nares confesses his inability to discover the origin of this whimsical combination of words, but points out that it is at least of long standing. The subjoined quotations would seem to indicate the meaning as noisy, frothy talk; clap-trap.

1600. DEKKER, *Old Fortunatus*, iii., p. 128.
F. Hark, does't rattle?
S. Yes, like THREE BLUE BEANS IN A BLUE BLADDER, rattle, bladder, rattle.

1717. MATHEW PRIOR, *Alma* (cant), I., v., 25.
They say———
That putting all his words together,
'Tis THREE BLUE BEANS IN ONE BLUE BLADDER.

Bean Belly, *subs.* (old).—A nickname for a Leicestershire man; from a real or supposed fondness of the inhabitants of this county for beans.

Bean-Feast, *subs.* (common).—An annual feast given by employers to their work-people. The derivation is uncertain, and, at present, their is little evidence to go upon. Some have suggested its origin in the prominence of the bean goose, or even beans at these spreads; others refer it to the French *bien*, good, *i.e.*, a good feast (by-the-bye, tailors call all good feeds BEAN-FEASTS); whilst others favour its derivation from the modern English *bene*, a request or solicitation, from the custom of collecting subscriptions to defray the cost. All three suggestions are, at the best, unsatisfactory, and numerous objections crop up at every turn to each of them. An annual outing of this kind is also called a WAYZGOOSE (*q.v.*).

1882. *Printing Times*, 15 Feb., 26, 2. A BEAN-FEAST dinner served up at a country inn. [M.]

1884. *Bath. Jour.*, 26 July, 6, 1. The annual grant of £20 for their BEAN-FEAST. [M.]

Bean-Feaster, *subs.* (common).—One who takes part in a BEAN-FEAST (*q.v.*).

1884. *Cornh. Mag.*, Jan., 621. For the delectation of the bold BEAN-FEASTERS. [M.]

Beano, *subs.* (printers').—The same as BEAN-FEAST (*q.v.*).

Bean Traps, *subs.* (American thieves').—A swell mobsman, or stylish sharper. BEANS (*q.v.*) are five-dollar gold pieces, and the insinuation is obvious. In old English cant a BEAN meant a guinea, probably from the French *biens*, property.

Beany, *adj.* (common).—Full of vigour; fresh, like a bean-fed horse. Or, it may be an allusion to the meaning of venery, which Aristotle says was attached to the word BEANS.

1852. KINGSLEY, in *Life* (1876), I., 278. The very incongruity keeps one BEANY and jolly.

1870. *Daily News*, 27 July, 5. The horses . . . looked fresh and BEANY. [M.]

Bear, *subs.* (Stock Exchange).—1. Applied, in the first instance, to stock sold by jobbers for delivery by a certain date on the chance of prices falling in the meantime, thus allowing the seller to re-purchase at a profit. The phrase was probably at first 'to sell the BEAR-SKIN,' the buyers of such bargains being called BEAR-SKIN JOBBERS (*see* quot.), in allusion to the proverb, 'To sell the bear's skin before one has caught the bear.' So far, the origin of the phrase seems pretty clear; of the date of its introduction, however, nothing is known. It was a common term in Stock Exchange circles, at the time of the bursting of the South Sea Bubble in 1720, but it does not seem to have become colloquial until much later. In these transactions no stock was passed, the 'difference' being settled according to the quotation of the day, as is the practice now in securities dealt with for 'the account.' At present the term for such an arrangement is TIME-BARGAIN.

1709. STEELE, *Tatler*, No. 38, p. 3. Being at that General Mart of stock-jobbers called Jonathans . . . he bought the BEAR of another officer. [M.]

1719. *Anatomy of Change Alley* (*N. and Q.*, 5 S., vi., 118). Those who buy Exchange Alley bargains are styled 'buyers of BEAR-SKINS.' [M.]

1778. BAILEY, *Dictionary* (24 ed.). To sell A BEAR, to sell what one hath not.

2. Hence a dealer who speculates for a fall. The earliest instance noted of this transferred usage is in

1744. *London Magazine*, 86. These noisy devotees were false ones, and in fact were only bulls and BEARS. [M.]

1768. FOOTE, *Devil upon Two Sticks*, Act i. A mere bull and BEAR booby; the patron of lame ducks, brokers, and fraudulent bankrupts.

1774. COLMAN, *Man of Business*, iv., i., in wks. (1777) II., 179. My young master is the bull, and Sir Charles is the BEAR. He agreed for stock expecting it to be up at three hundred by this time; but, lack-a-day, sir, it has been falling ever since.

1817. SCOTT, *Rob Roy*, ch. iv. The hum and bustle which his approach was wont to produce among the bulls, BEARS, and brokers of Stock-alley.

1860. PEACOCK, *Gryll Grange*, ch. xviii. In Stock Exchange slang, bulls are speculators for a rise, BEARS for a fall.

1889. *Ally Sloper's H. H.*, Aug. 3, p. 242, col. 3. Mrs. Spingles says she doesn't wonder that the Stock Exchange at times resembles a menagerie let loose, seeing what a lot of bulls, BEARS and stags they have at Capel Court.

The French Bourse equivalent is *un baissier*. *See* the analogous terms BULL; STAG; and LAME DUCK.

3. (old.)—The pupil of a private tutor, the latter being called a BEAR-LEADER (*q.v.*). From the general roughness and uncouthness of boys; a reference to the heavy build and ungainliness of the plantigrade in question. Even now the youth of the rising generation are sometimes called 'unlicked cubs.' Also called formerly BRIDLED-BEAR.

1832. *Legends of London*, II., 247. When I was the youthful BEAR—as the disciple of a private tutor is called at Oxford. [M.]

Verb.—To act as a BEAR (*q.v.*).

1861. *New York Tribune*, Nov. 29. There is no truth in the startling developments, implicating British officials, in the *Herald's* despatch . . . His Lordship is wholly guiltless of the charge which the *Herald*, in its anxiety to BEAR THE MARKET, has brought against him.

ARE YOU THERE WITH YOUR BEARS? *phr.* (colloquial).—A greeting of surprise at the re-appearance of anybody or anything; are you there again; or, in the words of its most recent slang equivalent, 'What, again! so soon?' The phrase is explained by Joe Miller, as the exclamation of a man who, not liking a sermon he had heard on Elisha and the BEARS, went next Sunday to another church, only to find the same preacher and the same discourse.

1642. JAMES HOWELL, *Instructions for Forreine Travell*, sec. 3. Another when at the racket court he had a ball struck into his hazard, he would ever and anon cry out, *estes vous là avec vos ours?* ARE YOU THERE WITH YOUR BEARS? which is ridiculous in any other language but English.

1740. RICHARDSON, *Pamela*, III., 335. O no, nephew! ARE YOU THERE-ABOUTS WITH YOUR BEARS?

1820. SCOTT, *Abbot*, xv. Marry, come up. 'ARE YOU THERE WITH YOUR BEARS'? muttered the dragon.

TO PLAY THE BEAR, *phr.* (common).—To behave in a rough and rude manner.

1579. TOMSON, *Calvin's Serm. Tim.*, p. 473, col. 1. When we haue so turned all order vpsidowne . . . there is nothing but . . . PLAYING THE BEARE amongst vs.

BEAR A BOB, *verbal phr.* (nautical).—1. To lend a hand; look sharp! look alive!

2. (popular.)—To aid, to assist, to take part in anything.

Bearded Cad, *subs.* (Winchester College).—A porter, employed by the College to convey luggage from the railway station to the school. The term originated in an extremely hirsute individual, who, at one time, acted in the capacity.

Beard-Splitter, *subs.* (old).—A man much given to the company of prostitutes; nowadays called A HOT MEMBER, or MOLROWER, which *see* for synonyms. [From BEARD, a tuft of hair + SPLITTER, one who divides. The allusion is obvious.]

Bearer-Up.—*See* BEAR UP and BONNET.

Bear-Garden Jaw, *subs.* (old).—Rough, unmannerly speech; talk akin to that used in bear gardens and other places of low resort. Quoted by Grose, 1785. [From BEAR-GARDEN, a place set apart for bear baiting and other rough sports + JAW, talk or speech.]

1848. JOHN FORSTER, *Life of Oliver Goldsmith*, bk. IV., chap. xi. He called Burke a BEAR-GARDEN RAILER.

1871. ARCHIBALD FORBES, *My Experience of the War between France and Germany*, p. 301. THE BEAR-GARDEN-LIKE BABEL was rather more noisy than usual.

Be-Argered, *adj.* (familiar).—Drunk.

Bearing, *ppl. adj.* (Stock Exchange).—Acting as a BEAR (*q.v.*); or using artifices to lower the price of stock to suit a 'bear' account.

Bearings. TO BRING ONE TO ONE'S BEARINGS, *verbal phr.* (colloquial).—To bring one to reason; to act as a check. A nautical term.

Bear-Leader, *subs.* (old).—A travelling tutor. In the days when it was customary to send 'young hopefuls' on the Grand Tour, the expression was much more common and significant than is nowadays the case. The simile is taken from a person who leads about a tame bear for exhibition.

1749. WALPOLE, *Lett. to Mann*, 4 June (1883), vol. II., p. 392. I shall not wonder if she takes me for his BEAR-LEADER, his travelling governor!

1756. FOOTE, *Englishman Returned from Paris*, Act i.
Serv. My young master's travelling tutor, sir, just arrived.
Crab......Shew him in. This BEAR-LEADER, I reckon now, is either the clumsy curate of the knight's own parish church, or some needy highlander.

1812. COMBE, *Dr. Syntax*, *Tour I* ch. xxiii.

And as I almost wanted bread,
I undertook a BEAR TO LEAD,
To see the brute perform his dance
Through Holland, Italy, and France;
But it was such a very Bruin,
. . . .
I took my leave, and left the *cub*
Some humbler Swiss to pay and drub.

1848. THACKERAY, *Book of Snobs*, ch. vii. They pounced upon the stray nobility, and seized young lords travelling with their BEAR-LEADERS.

Bearskin-Jobber, *subs.* (Stock Exchange).—*See* BEAR, *subs.*, sense 1.

Bear Up, *verb* (common).—To cheat; to swindle in any way; more particularly applied to the action of 'decoys' and confederates.—*See* BONNET. The derivation is obviously from that sense of TO BEAR UP, signifying support or backing up.

1828. G. SMEETON, *Doings in London*, p. 40. The billiard-marker refused to make any division of the spoil, or even to return the £10 which had been lost to him in BEARING UP the cull.

1883. *Referee*, Dec. 2, p. 2, col. 4. This looks as if the BEARING UP and 'bonneting' which has been done by friendly writers in response to my remarks is all thrown away.

Beast, *subs.* (common).—1. Applied to anything unpleasant; or, to that which displeases; *e.g.*, 'It's a perfect BEAST of a day,' for 'it's an unpleasant day.'—*See* BEASTLY.

2. (American cadet.)—A name given to new cadets at the U.S. Military Academy at West Point.—*See* SNOOKER.

3. (Cambridge University.)—Anyone who has left school and come up to Cambridge for study, before entering the University, is called a BEAST, because 'he is neither man nor boy.'

Beastly, *adv.* (popular).—In modern colloquial usage applied to whatever may offend the taste. Akin also to 'awful,' 'everlasting,' etc.—when used as mere intensitives, *i.e.*, 'very,' 'exceedingly.' [Originally from BEASTLY, of, or pertaining to the nature of a beast; hence, figuratively, brutish, irrational, unmanly; whence, through a series of transitions, its slang significations.]

1611. DEKKER, *Roaring Girle*, wks., 1873, III., 159. I thought 'twould bee a BEASTLY iourney.

1778. JOHNSON, in D'Arblay *Diary, etc.* (1876), vol. I., p. 37. 'It moves my indignation to see a gentleman take pains to appear a tradesman. Mr. Braughton would have written his name with just such BEASTLY flourishes!'

1865. *Daily Telegraph*, 24 Oct., p. 5, col. 3. He was in good health . . . looked almost 'BEASTLY well,' as I once heard it described. [M.]

1882. F. ANSTEY, *Vice Versâ*, ch. i. He had a troublesome dryness in his throat, and a general sensation of dull heaviness, which he himself would have described—expressively enough, if not with academical elegance—as 'feeling BEASTLY.'

Beast with Two Backs, *subs. phr.* (old).—Explained in second quotation.

1602. SHAKSPEARE, *Othello*, Act i., Sc. 1. *Brabantio*: What profane wretch art thou? *Iago*: I am one, Sir, that comes to tell you, your daughter and the Moor are now making the BEAST WITH THE TWO BACKS.

1785. GROSE, *Classical Dictionary of Vulgar Tongue*. BEAST WITH TWO BACKS, a man and woman in the act of copulation.

Beat, *subs.* (American).—1. This word is used in many ways, its precise meaning often depending on its qualifying adjective. It is said of both men and things; for example, a *live* BEAT is anybody or anything that surpasses another, and the sense is not derogatory in the least. A *dead* BEAT, on the other hand, is the name given to a man who sponges on his fellows. [Probably from that sense of BEAT signifying to overcome; to show oneself superior to, either in a good or bad sense.]

1888. *New York Tribune*, May 16. As we pay big money for our special news, we can't afford to throw it away on account of a little mistake in the name. So we shove her in with the single remark that it is better to have a Carrot for a President than a DEAD BEAT for a son-in-law. In this way, we again score a LIVE BEAT on the galoot 'The Rip-snorter.' Whoopee! Now is the time to subscribe.

1888. *New York Mercury*, Aug. 7. But not only steamboats and locomotives were used by reporters for BEATS, but one newspaper man named Monroe F. Gale made a trip across the Atlantic in a pilot-boat, to get some peculiar news in his own fashion. All things taken into consideration, there never was a bolder voyage over the Atlantic than this made by the 'Romer,' all for the sake of a few 'points' in news.

2. (popular.)—The round of a policeman or watchman when on duty; one's daily round of duty, work, etc.; and, figuratively, one's sphere of influence.

1788. G. A. STEVENS, *Adv. of a Speculist*, i., 211. The first evening I took my stand in Fleet Street, to look out for a fare, I was drove from street to street by women of my own profession, who swore I should not come in their BEATS until I had paid my 'footing.'

1835. DICKENS, *Sketches by Boz*, p. 31. The costermongers repaired to their ordinary BEATS in the suburbs.

1862. *Saturday Review*, 15 March, 295. Ask him why anything is so-and-so, and you have got out of his BEAT. [M.]

Faire sa nouveauté is said of a French prostitute when seeking fresh fields and pastures new.

Ppl. adj. (popular.)—1. Overcome; exhausted; 'done up.' Generally DEAD-BEAT (*q.v.*). [A shortened form of BEATEN.] —See BEATEN OUT.

1832. MOORE, *Jerome*, etc., wks. II. (1862), 558. Till fairly BEAT, the saint gave o'er. [M.]

1859. H. KINGSLEY, *Geoffery Hamlyn*, ch. xxxvii. 'The lad was getting BEAT, and couldn't a'gone much further.'

2. Hence also, figuratively, to be baffled; defeated.

Verb (American).—To swindle; to deceive; to cheat.

1888. *Daily Inter-Ocean*, Ap. 12. Later he heard of her marriage to some lawyer or artist named Diss Debar. Previous to this she had been in Montreal and telegraphed that she was dying. She BEAT the hotel out of a hundred dollars.

DAISY BEAT (American thieves').—A swindle of the first water; a robbery of magnitude.

TO BEAT HOLLOW—TO STICKS —TO RIBANDS—TO FITS—ALL CREATION—TO SHIVERS, etc. (popular.)—To excel; to surpass.

1759. TOWNLEY, *High Life Below Stairs*, I., ii. Crab was BEAT HOLLOW, Careless threw his rider, and Miss Slammerkin had the distemper.

1847. BARHAM, *Ingoldsby Legends* (1877), p. 55. Many ladies . . . were BEAT ALL TO STICKS by the lovely Odille. [M.]

1854. WHYTE MELVILLE, *General Bounce*, ch. i. Talk of climate! a real fine day in England, like a really handsome Englishwoman, BEATS CREATION.

1856. WHYTE MELVILLE, *Kate Coventry*, ch. i. I rode a race against Bob Dashwood the other morning, . . . and BEAT HIM ALL TO RIBANDS.

1879. LOWELL, *Poetical Works*, 418. And there's where I shall BEAT THEM HOLLOW.

1889. *Modern Society*, 19 Oct., p. 1302. (How the Nobility live in Germany.) Germans BEAT THE ENGLISH HOLLOW at drinking beer; the ladies drink it, and the children also, like milk; and it seems to agree with them, for they are very robust. They are not ceremonious at any meal, and eat as if in a hurry for a train, cutting up all on their plate first, then forking it in with the aid of bread or their fingers.

The French say *arriver bon premier*, 'to arrive' or 'be a good first.' *Cf.*, synonyms in A1.

TO GET A BEAT ON is to get the advantage of. The same idea is expressed in the phrase TO BEAT ONE'S WAY THROUGH THE WORLD; in other words, to push one's interests with vigour and pertinacity. As used by thieves and their associates, TO

GET A BEAT ON ONE, besides conveying the idea of obtaining an advantage, also implies that the point has been scored by underhand, secret, or unlawful means.

TO BEAT THE BOOBY or GOOSE, *phr.* (nautical).—To strike the hands across the chest and under the armpits to warm them. Formerly TO BEAT JONAS.

1888. *Times*, 15 March, p. 9, col. 6. The common labourers at outdoor work were BEATING GOOSE to drive the blood from their fingers. [M.]

TO BEAT THE ROAD, *phr.* (American).—To travel by rail without paying.—See DEADHEADS and TO BEAT, sense 1.

THAT BEAT'S THE DUTCH!—See DUTCH.

BEAT DADDY MAMMY (old military). —To tattoo; to practice the elements of drum beating.

BEATEN DOWN TO BED-ROCK, *adv. phr.* (American).—See BEDROCK.

BEATEN OUT, *ppl. adj.* with *adv.* (common).—Impoverished; in one's last straits; hard up.

1851. MAYHEW, *London Labour and London Poor*, I., p. 351. The BEATEN OUT mechanics and artisans, who, from want of employment in their own trade, take to making small things. *Ibid*, p. 400. The last class of street sellers is the BEATEN OUT mechanic or workman.

BEATER-CASES, *subs.* (old).—Boots or shoes. Nearly obsolete. TROTTER-CASES (*q.v.*) is the usual term nowadays.—See BEATERS.

BEATERS, *subs.* (American).—The feet. [A transferred sense of BEATER, originally signifying one who 'beat' or walked the streets. Barclay, in *Shyp of Folys* (1509), speaks of 'night watchers and BETERS of the stretes.'] For synonyms, see CREEPERS.

BEAT THE HOOF, *verbal phr.* (popular.)—To walk; to plod; to prowl. [From BEAT, in the sense of to strike the ground in walking, etc., + HOOF, a humorous term for the foot.] TO BEAT THE HOOF is an older form of the modern PAD THE HOOF (*q.v.*).

1596. SHAKSPEARE, *Merry Wives of Windsor*, Act i., Sc. 3. Falstaff: Hold, sirrah, [to *Robin*] bear you these letters tightly;
Sail like my pinnace to these golden shores.—
Rogues, hence, avaunt! vanish like hailstones, go;
Trudge, PLOD AWAY, O' THE HOOF; seek shelter, pack!

1691. WOOD, *Ath. Oxon.*, II., 412. They all BEATED IT ON THE HOOF to London. [M.]

BEAT THE RIB.—See RIB.

BEAU TRAP, *subs.* (old).—1. A loose stone in a pavement, under which water lodges, and which, on being trodden upon, squirts it up, to the great damage of clean clothes.

2. (old.)—Also a well-dressed sharper, on the look out for raw country visitors and such like.

3. (old.) — A fop, well-dressed outwardly indeed, but whose linen, person, and habits generally, are unclean.

BEAUTY, *subs.* (American cadet). —A term applied, on the rule of contrary, to the plainest or ugliest cadet in the class at the United States Military Academy

at West Point. *Cf.*, SNOOKER and BABE.

BEAUTY-SLEEP, *subs.* (familiar).—Sleep before midnight, the idea being that early hours conduce to health and beauty.

1850. SMEDLEY, *Frank Fairleigh*, II., p. 120. The fair pupils have talked themselves to sleep, which, if report does not belie them, is not until they have forfeited all chance of adding to their attractions by getting a little BEAUTY-SLEEP before twelve o'clock.

1857. KINGSLEY, *Two Years Ago*, ch. xv. 'Are you going? it is not late; not ten o'clock yet.' 'A medical man, who may be called up at any moment, must make sure of his BEAUTY-SLEEP.'

1869. BLACKMORE, *Lorna Doone*, ch. lxiv. Would I please to remember that I had roused him up at night, and the quality always made a point of paying four times over for a man's loss of his BEAUTY-SLEEP. I replied that his loss of BEAUTY-SLEEP was rather improving to a man of so high a complexion.

1880. JAS. PAYN, *Confid. Agent*, ch. iii. 'You must get your BEAUTY-SLEEP,' cried he to his wife when Barlow had departed, 'or you will have no colour in your cheeks to-morrow.'

BEAVER, *subs.* (common).—1. An old term for a hat; GOSS or CADY, however, is more frequently heard nowadays. At one time hats were made of beaver's fur—hence the name; the term is still occasionally applied to tall 'chimney-pot hats,' in spite of the fact that for many years silk has replaced the skin of the rodent in their manufacture.

1528. Roy, *Sat.* To exalte the thre folde crowne Of anti-christ hys BEVER. [M.]

1661. PEPYS, *Diary*, 27 June. Mr. Holden sent me a BEVER, which cost me £4 5s.

1712. GAY, *Trivia*, bk. II., l., 277. The broker here his spacious BEAVER wears,
Upon his brow sit jealousies and cares.

1855. THACKERAY, *Newcomes*, ch. ix. 'Had you not better take off your hat?' asks the Duchess, pointing . . . to the foring cove's' BEAVER, which he had neglected to remove.

1857. O. W. HOLMES, *Autocrat of the Breakfast Table*, ch. x. We know this of our hats, and are always reminded of it when we happen to put them on wrong side foremost. We soon find that the BEAVER is a hollow cast of the skull, with all its irregular bumps and depressions.

IN BEAVER, *phr.* (University). —In a tall hat and non-academical garb, as distinguished from cap and gown.

1840. *New Monthly Magazine*, lix., 271. He . . . went out of College in what the members of the United Service called mufti, but members of the University BEAVER, which means not in his academics—his cap and gown. [M.]

See also BEVER.

BECK, *subs.* (old cant).—1. A constable.—See BEAK and COPPER.

2. A parish beadle. Apparently the term was applied to all kinds of watchmen.—See HARMAN-BECK.

Verb (thieves'). — To imprison. Amongst Dutch thieves *bekaan* has the same signification, imprisoned.

1861. READE, *Cloister and Hearth* ch. lv. The circle with the two dots was writ by another of our brotherhood, and it signifies as how the writer . . . was BECKED, was asking here, and lay two months in Starabin.

BED. TO PUT TO BED WITH A PICKAXE AND SHOVEL (common). —To bury. For analogous expressions, *see* LADDER.

c. 1881. *Broadside Ballad*, 'Hands off'—
Kitty Crea, some fine day, when I'm laid in the clay,
PUT TO BED WITH A SPADE in the usual way,

And yourself on the shelf a neglected old maid,
Troth, your conscience will sting you, I'm greatly afraid.

BEDDER, *subs.* (Cambridge University).—A charwoman; one who makes the beds and performs other necessary domestic duties for residents in college.

BED-FAGOT, *subs.* (familiar). — 1. Applied contemptuously to a woman; *Cf.*, 'hussy,' 'witch,' etc.

2. Synonymous with prostitute. For full list of analogous terms, see BARRACK-HACK.

BEDFORDSHIRE, *subs.* (familiar).—A humorous term for bed. There are several other phrases of a kindred character; as, for example, SHEET ALLEY (*q.v.*); BLANKET FAIR (*q.v.*); THE LAND OF NOD (*q.v.*), etc.

1665. COTTON, *Poet. Wks.* (1765), 76. Each one departs to BEDFORDSHIRE. And pillows all securely snort on. [M.]

1738. SWIFT, *Polite Conversation* (conv. iii.)
Lady Ans. I'm sure 'tis time for all honest folks to go to bed.
Miss. Indeed my eyes draw straws (she's almost asleep)—
Col. I'm going to the Land of Nod.
Ner. Faith, I'm for BEDFORDSHIRE.

1845. HOOD, *Miss Kilmansegg*.
The time for sleep had come at last,
And there was the bed, so soft, so vast,
Quite a field of BEDFORDSHIRE clover.

BED-HOUSE, *subs.* (common).—A place of assignation where beds can be hired for a longer or shorter period as required — hence the name. For synonyms generally, *see* NANNY SHOP.

BEDOOZLE, *verb* (American).—To confuse; to bewilder. Probably a corrupt 'form of the old English verb 'bedazzle,' used by Shakspeare in *Taming of the Shrew*, iv., 5, 46. [1593.]

BEDPOST. IN THE TWINKLING OF A BEDPOST, *phr.* (familiar).—Instantaneously; with great rapidity. Originally IN THE TWINKLING OF A BEDSTAFF. This phrase has given rise to not a little speculation; first, as to what use the BEDSTAFF was put; and, secondly, as to its possible connection with rapidity of motion. The generally received explanation is that the staff referred to was, as Johnson puts it, 'a wooden pin stuck anciently on sides of the bedstead to hold the cloaths from slipping on either side.' Dr. Murray, however, points out that the great lexicographer gave no authority, and also that 'no corroborative evidence has been found.' Still it seems certain that bedstaffs were used and kept near beds for *some* purpose by our ancestors. Bobadil, in *Every Man in his Humour* [1596], uses one to display his skill with the rapier, and the following explanation has been suggested by Mr. Thomas Boys [*Notes and Queries*, 2 S., vi., 437]. The bedstaff was an *upright* peg, fixed into the side of the bedstead after the manner of a pin, and projecting upwards to keep the bed clothes in their place. Consequently, as offering the means of exhibiting the use of the rapier, the wooden bedstaff may have afforded a very available as well as harmless implement. Suppose then the bedstaff to have been an upright peg or pin fitting into a hole or socket in the side of the bedstead, and, in length, about equal to the rapier. The socket is a few inches deep; and the bedstaff has (to steady it) a projecting rim which overlays the socket like a lid. The part of the bedstaff which enters the socket will then be the *hilt* of the rapier; the projecting rim will be the *guard*; and the rest of the staff will do duty as the *blade*. In the bedstaff we have then the form of a rapier; and, with this implement of wood, Captain Bobadil would have no difficulty in exhibiting his *passado* and *stoccado*. The rapier of the sixteenth and seventeenth centuries, moreover, was by no means the light and foil-like weapon now known as the small sword. It was of great length and heavy, and a bedstaff such as that suggested above, with a species of guard, and most likely about the weight of a heavy single-stick, would have been no bad instrument wherewith to indoctrinate a tyro in the noble art of self defence.

Hence, probably, if this be so, the derivation of the expression, IN THE TWINKLING OF A BEDSTAFF; more especially if, as would occasionally be the case, it were used as a weapon of defence against intruders, when possibly even life itself might hang upon a dexterous use of the implement.

1660. *Charac. Italy*, 78. IN THE TWINKLING OF A BEDSTAFF he disrobed himself . . . and was just skipping into bed. [M.]

1676. T. SHADWELL, *Virtuoso*, I., i. 'Gad, I'll do it instantly, IN THE TWINKLING OF A BEDSTAFF.

1698. WARD, *London Spy*, pt. XI., 259. Shake 'em off and leap into bed, IN THE TWINKLING OF A BEDSTAFF.

1854. F. E. SMEDLEY, *Harry Coverdale*, ch. i. 'I'll adown and be with you IN . . . THE TWINKLING OF A BEDPOST.'

Among ENGLISH SYNONYMS may be included:—In a jiffy; in two two's; in a brace of shakes; before you can say Jack Robinson; in a crack; in the squeezing of a lemon.

BETWEEN YOU AND ME AND THE BEDPOST, *phr.* (familiar).—A humorous tag to an assertion; *i.e.*, 'between ourselves';—'I know what you say, but, BETWEEN YOU AND ME, etc. . . . the thing is absurd.' Sometimes the last word is varied by 'post,' 'door post,' or 'gate post'—any prop seems to serve.

1831. BULWER LYTTON, *Eugene Aram*, p. 234. Ah, sir, all very well to say so; but, BETWEEN YOU AND ME AND THE BEDPOST, young master's quarrelled with old master.

1838. DICKENS, *Nicholas Nickleby*, p. 127. And BETWEEN YOU AND ME AND THE POST, sir, it will be a very nice portrait too.

1879. *Punch*, March 8, p. 108. Discussing an absent friend. 'Yes, Robinson's a clever feller, and he's a modest feller, and he's a honest feller; but BETWIXT YOU AND I AND THE POST, Mr. Jones,' said Brown, confidentially, picking his wisdom tooth with his little finger nail, 'Robinson ain't got neither the Looks, nor yet the Language, nor yet the Manners of a Gentleman.'

'Right you are, sir!' said Jones, shovelling the melted remains of his Ice Pudding into his Mouth with a Steel Knife (which he afterwards wiped on the Table Cloth). 'You've 'it 'im orf t' a T!'

BEDROCK. TO GET DOWN TO BEDROCK [in anything; whether in an enquiry, or in one's circumstances, etc.].—To the bottom; to the lowest level. A miner's term, alluding to the solid rock underlying superficial and other formations. Therefore, metaphorically, 'to reach BEDROCK'

is to attain a solid basis or foundation; BEDROCK FACTS are the 'chiels that winna ding'—the incontestible and uncontrovertible truth.

1870. BRET HARTE, *Poems and Prose*, p. 113. 'No! no!' continued T. hastily. 'I play this yer hand alone. To COME DOWN TO THE BEDROCK it's just this,' etc.

1875. *Scribner's Magazine*, p. 277. Getting to the real character of a man is COMING TO THE BEDROCK.

1888. *Louisiana Press*, March 31. Thomas J. Whiteman, of Carrol county, is a Republican candidate for Governor of Missouri. You can bet your BEDROCK dollar that the next governor of Missouri will be a white man, although his first name isn't apt to be Thomas.

BEE. TO HAVE A BEE IN THE HEAD OR BONNET, *phr.* (familiar).—To be possessed of queer ideas; 'half-cracked'; flighty. This phrase is of considerable antiquity, being traced back to a Scotch writer, Gawin Douglas by name [1474-1521], Bishop of Dunkeld, who used it in a translation of Virgil's *Æneid*.

1512-3 (translated: published in 1553). GAWIN DOUGLAS, *Æneis*, VIII., Prol. 120. Quhat bern be thou in bed with HEID FULL OF BEIS.

1657. SAMUEL COLVIL, *Whigg's Supplication, or Scotch Hudibras* [1710]. Which comes from BRAINS WHICH HAVE A BEE.

1825. SCOTT, *St. Ronan's*, ch. xvii. 'Maybe ye think the puir lassie has A BEE IN HER BONNET; but ye ken yoursell if naebody but wise folk were to marry, the warld wad be ill peopled.'

1853. BULWER LYTTON, *My Novel*, III., 307. It is not an uncommon crochet amongst benevolent men to maintain that wickedness in necessarily a sort of insanity, and that nobody would make a violent start out of a straight path unless stung to such disorder by a BEE IN HIS BONNET.

For synonyms, *see* APARTMENTS TO LET.

1868. DR. BREWER, *Dictionary of Phrase and Fable*, p. 77, col. 2. YOU HAVE A BEE IN YOUR BONNET OR YOUR HEAD IS FULL OF BEES; [*i.e.*] full of devices, crotchets, fancies, inventions, and dreamy theories. The connection between bees and the soul was once generally maintained . . . . the moon was called a *bee* by the priestesses of Cerēs, and the word lunatic or moonstruck still means one with 'BEES IN HIS HEAD.'

BEEF, *subs.* (common).—1. Human flesh (a transferred sense); *i.e.*, obese; stolid; or fleshy like an ox.

1862. *Cork Examiner*, March 28. Chelmsford stood higher in the leg, and showed less BEEF about him. [M.]

2. (nautical.)—By a further transition BEEF has also come to signify men; strength; or 'hands'; 'More BEEF!' a bo'sun's exhortation to extra exertion.

1863. *Cornhill Magazine*. Feb., 'Life on Board a Man of War.' Useful at the heavy hauling of braces, etc., where plenty of BEEF is required. [M.]

3. (common.) — The penis. For synonyms, *see* CREAMSTICK.

TO BE IN BEEF, *phr.* (old).—Said only of women. It means to have carnal knowledge.

TO BE IN A MAN'S BEEF, *phr.* (old).—To wound with a sword. —*Grose.*

TO CRY OR GIVE BEEF, OR HOT BEEF, *phr.* (thieves').—To give an alarm; to pursue; to set up a hue and cry. It has been suggested that BEEF in this case is a rhyming synonym to 'thief.' For synonyms, *see* TO GUY.

TO BE DRESSED LIKE CHRISTMAS BEEF, *phr.* (common).—To be decked out in one's best raiment; in allusion to the

'dressing' of Christmas beef by butchers.

TO MAKE BEEF, *phr.* (thieves').—To run away; to decamp. For synonyms, *see* AMPUTATE.

BEEF! *intj.* (Australian).—'Stop thief.' *Cf.*, TO CRY OR GIVE BEEF.

BEEF UP! *phr.* (common).—'Put on your strength!' 'Give a long pull and a strong pull!'

BEEF-BRAINED, *adj.* (common).—Doltish; obtuse; thickheaded; a reference to the heavy, dullness of appearance of oxen.

BEEF-HEAD, *subs.* (common).—A dolt; a stupid, thickheaded person. *Cf.*, BEEF-BRAINED.

BEEF IT, *verb* (common).—Considered originally a provincialism, but now common. The lower classes in the East End of London frequently speak of BEEFING IT, either in reality or anticipation (mostly latter), when referring to a meat meal, more particularly when it happens to be beef.

BEEFMENT. ON THE BEEFMENT, *adv. phr.* (thieves').—On the alert; on the look out.

BEEF-STICK, *subs.* (military).—The bone in a joint of beef. At mess it is 'first come, best served'; and those who come last sometimes get little more than the BEEF-STICK.

BEEF STRAIGHT.—*See* STRAIGHT.

BEEF TO THE HEELS, LIKE A MULLINGAR HEIFER, *phr.* (Irish).—A stalwart man, or a fine woman; *i.e.*, one whose superiority is manifest from the crown of the head to the sole of the foot; literally, ALL BEEF DOWN TO THE HEELS.

c. 1880. RHODA BROUGHTON, *Cometh up as a Flower*, p. 193. Dolly was not a fine woman as they say, at all; not BEEF TO THE HEELS, by any means; in a grazier's eye she would have had no charm whatsoever.

BEEF-WITTED, *adj.* (common).—*See* BEEF-BRAINED.

1594. NASHE, *Terrors of the Night*, in wks. (Grosart) III., 257. Lies there anie such slowe yce-braind BEEFE-WITTED gull.

1863. *Reader*, 22 Aug. This British bull-neckedness, this British BEEF-WITTEDNESS. [M.]

BEEFY, *adj.* (common).—Fleshy; unduly thick, or obese. [From BEEF + Y: a transferred sense.] Also BEEFINESS, *subs.*, fleshy development. The ankles of women are sometimes ungallantly spoken of as BEEFY, with which compare BEEF TO THE HEELS. A run of luck and good fortune, generally, is likewise referred to as BEEFY.

1859. SALA, *Gaslight and Daylight*, ch. xi. To see him in his huge shirt-sleeves, with his awkward BEEFY hands hanging inanely by his side, and his great foolish mouth open.

BEE-LINE. TO TAKE OR MAKE A BEE-LINE [for a place or object], *phr.* (originally American; now common).—To go direct; 'as the crow flies'; without circumlocution. Bees, when fully laden with pollen, make for the hive in a straight, or BEE-LINE. One of the American railways is called the BEE-LINE ROAD from the direct route it takes between its termini. *Cf.*, STRAIGHT SHOOT.

1848. J. R. LOWELL, *Biglow Papers*.
The field of Lexin'ton where England tried
The fastest colors thet she ever dyed.
An' Concord Bridge, thet Davis, when he came,
Found was the BEE-LINE TRACK to heaven an' fame,
Ez all roads be by natur', ef your soul
Don't sneak thur shun-pikes so's to save the toll.

1874. M. COLLINS, *Frances*, ch. v. How they could follow an enemy's trail, or STRIKE A BEE-LINE through unpathed woods to the point they sought!

1875. MISS BIRD, *Six Mos. in Sandwich Islands*, Lett. xxix., p. 275 (1886). Horses cross the sand and hummocks as nearly as possible ON A BEE-LINE.

1884. ALDRIDGE, *Ranch Notes*, p. 78. The cattle are in great dread of this pest [the heel-fly], and the instant an animal feels one, it hoists its tail in the air, and TAKES A BEE-LINE for the nearest water.

BEELZEBUB'S PARADISE, *subs.* (popular).—Hell; the infernal regions. Beelzebub is a frequent mis-reading for Beelzebul, the name given by the Jews to the prince of demons. The usage occurs in the New Testament at Matthew x., 25, and xii., 24-27, where Beelzebub should read *Beelzebul*. The former is properly the god of the Philistines, worshipped as the destroyer of flies [from Hebrew *baal*, lord + *zebub*, a fly]; whilst the latter is an opprobrious change on the former [from Hebrew *baal*, lord + *zebul*, dung].

BEEN IN THE SUN, *adv. phr.* (common).—A synonym for 'drunk,' in connection with which *see* SCREWED. An allusion to a flushed, heated appearance.

BEEN MEASURED FOR A NEW UMBRELLA, *phr.* (American).—Said sportively of anyone appearing in new, ill-fitting clothes, or who has struck out a new line of action, the wisdom of which is doubtful. The joke is an old one and refers to a man of whom it was said that nothing fitted him but his umbrella.

BEEN THERE. OH, YES, I'VE BEEN THERE, *phr.* (American), *i.e.*, 'I know what I am about.' A popular exclamation. When it is said of a man that he has BEEN THERE, shrewdness, pertinacity, and experience are implied. A variant may be found in the equally slang expression, 'he got there all the same.'—*See* GOT THERE.

1888. *Atlanta Constitution*, May 4. The Japanese say: 'A man takes a drink; then the drink takes a drink, and next the drink takes the man.' Evidently the Japanese 'have BEEN THERE.'

2. Another and more invidious meaning, however, is attached to the phrase. Women suspected of clandestine meetings with men are said to have BEEN THERE.

BEER, *subs.* (familiar).—To DO A BEER, *i.e.*, to take a drink of beer.

1880. *Punch's Almanac*, p. 3.
Quarter-day, too, no more chance ot tick,
Fancy I shall 'ave to cut my stick.
Got the doldrums dreadful, that is clear,
Two *d.* left!—must GO AND DO A BEER!

1889. *Sporting Times*, July 6. It was the old tale of stony, pebble-beached, block granite Wednesday, and money on the staff there was none. 'Pitcher,' said Shifter, brushing the dust off his tongue, 'got enough for a BEER?' 'Enough for a BEER?' repeated Pitcher. 'Good heavens, I wish I had. If Bass's ale was a ha'penny a barrel I couldn't buy enough to soak a fly-paper!'

Verb.—To drink beer; also, to get drunk.

1780-6. WOLCOT ('P. Pindar') *Odes R. Acad.*, wks., 1794, I., 105. He surely had been brandying it or BEERING, that is, in plainer English, he was drunk. [D.]

TO THINK NO SMALL BEER [of oneself], *phr.* (common).—Small beer is weak beer; hence, figuratively equivalent to a trifle. The expression, TO THINK NO SMALL BEER OF ONESELF, indicates, therefore, a good measure of self-esteem.

1840. DE QUINCEY, *Style*, wks. XI., 174. [I] should express her self-esteem by the popular phrase, that she did not THINK SMALL BEER OF HERSELF.

BEER AND BIBLE, *phr.* (political).—An epithet applied sarcastically to a political party which first came into prominence during the last Beaconsfield Administration. It was called into being by a measure introduced by the moderate Liberals in 1873, with a view to placing certain restrictions upon the sale of intoxicating drinks. The Licensed Victuallers, an extremely powerful association, whose influence extended all over the kingdom, took alarm, and turned to the Conservatives for help in opposing the bill. In the ranks of the latter were numbered the chief brewers; the leaders of the association, moreover, had mostly strong high church tendencies, while one of them was president of the Exeter Hall organization. The Liberals, noting these facts, sarcastically nicknamed this alliance the BEER AND BIBLE ASSOCIATION; the *Morning Advertiser*, the organ of the Licensed Victuallers, was dubbed the BEER AND BIBLE GAZETTE; and lastly, electioneering tactics ascribed to them the war cry of BEER AND BIBLE! This so-called BEER AND BIBLE interest made rapid strides: in 1870 the Conservatives were at their low water mark among the London constituencies; but, in 1880, they had carried seats in the City, Westminster, Marylebone, Tower Hamlets, Greenwich, and Southwark A notable exception to this strange fellowship was Mr. Bass [afterwards Lord Bass], of pale-ale fame, who held aloof from opposition to the measure in question. Anent the nickname BEER AND BIBLE GAZETTE given to the *Morning Advertiser*, it may be mentioned that it had already earned for itself a somewhat similar sobriquet. For a long time this paper devoted one-half of its front page to notices of publicans and tavern-keepers; while the other half was filled up with announcements of religious books, and lists of preachers at the London churches and chapels. This gained for the paper the equally singular sobriquet of the 'Gin and Gospel Gazette.'

BEER AND SKITTLES. Generally, NOT ALL BEER AND SKITTLES, *phr.* (familiar), *i.e.*, not altogether pleasant, or *couleur de rose.* A tap room simile, the allusion being to drinking beer and playing at skittles at one and the same time.

1870. MANSFIELD, *School-Life at Winchester College*, p. 138. But football wasn't all BEER AND SKITTLES to the Fags. There was an institution called 'Kicking in,' which, while it lasted, was much worse than 'watching out' at cricket, although it had the very great merit of not continuing so long; for, even on a whole holiday, we seldom had more than two hours of it.

1889. *Pall Mall Gaz.*, Aug. 13, p. 6. Prince George of Wales is 'learning his

profession,' and finds it is not all BEER AND SKITTLES. That run across the Channel into Queenstown harbour showed our young naval officer the difference between an ironclad and a torpedo boat. The latter is an uncommonly lively craft, and in a choppy sea under a fresh breeze was surprisingly nimble. The commander of No. 79 arrived in the harbour, having shown that at least in one respect he has already something in common with the late admiral, Lord Nelson. The officers of the *Revenge* had the honour to request the pleasure of the company of the Prince and his brother officers to breakfast. The brother officers went, His Royal Highness spent the day in his hammock, and towards evening wrote to his Royal Father a description of the perils of the deep.

BEER-BARREL, *subs.* (common).—The human body. *Cf.*, BACON.

BEERINESS, *subs.*, **BEERY**, *adj.* (common). — Pertaining to a state of, or approaching to drunkenness; intoxicated; fuddled with beer. For synonyms, *see* SCREWED.

1857. DICKENS, *Dorrit*, bk. I., ch. viii., p. 56. The stranger was left to the . . . BEERY atmosphere, sawdust, pipe-lights, spittoons, and repose.

1877. D. C. MURRAY, in *Belgravia*, July, p. 73. There was a BEERY and bloated captain, resident in the inn, who had left the army, as the rumour ran, under disreputable auspices.

1889. *Modern Society*, July 13, p. 838. It is a fact that does not seem to have struck anyone, that Shakspeare's first appearance as a sporting tipster was in the words, 'Lay on Macduff.' We believe, however, that they could at that time have got five to one against him. So sure was the bard of his tip, that he added, in his own classical language, 'Damn'd be he that first cries, Hold, enough,' which is vulgarly translated by the BEERY oracle of the kerbstone, 'Put yer shirt on 'im, cuffs an' all.'

BEER-JERKER, *subs.* (American).—A tippler. — *See* JERKER and SLINGER.

BEEROCRACY, *subs.* (common).—The brewing and beer-selling interest. [A humorous appellation in imitation of aristocracy. From BEER + [O] CRACY, from Greek κρατέω, to rule, to hold.

1881. *World*, 19 Jan., p. 10, col. 2. The startling mixture of peerage and BEEROCRACY . . . was absent this time. [M.]

BEER-SLINGER.—*See* SLINGER; also JERKER.

BEESWAX, *subs.* (old).—1. Poor, soft cheese. Sometimes called SWEATY-TOE CHEESE (*q.v.*).

1821. W. T. MONCRIEFF, *Tom and Jerry*, Act ii., Sc. 3. *Bob:* Now, landlord, 'arter that 'ere drap of max, suppose we haves a *drain o' heavy wet*, just by way of cooling our *chaffers*—mine's as *dry as a chip*—and, I say, do you hear, let's have a twopenny *burster*, half a quartern of BEESVAX, a ha'p'orth o' ingens, and a dollop o' salt along vith it, vill you? *Mace:* Bellay! a burster and BEESVAX—ingens and salt here. (*Calling as he fetches the porter from the side wing*, L.). Now, then, here you are, Master Grimmuzzle.

1849. *Bell's Life.* [From Baumann.] A burster with a slice of BEESWAX.

2. A bore; one who 'buttonholes' another. Generally, OLD BEESWAX.

BEESWAXERS, *subs.* (Winchester College).—Thick boots used for football. Probably from being smeared with beeswax or other substitute for rendering footgear supple. Pronounced *Bēswaxers.*

1870. MANSFIELD, *School-Life at Winchester College*, p. 137. Our costume consisted of a jersey, flannel trousers, BEESWAXERS (lace-up boots), or 'Highlows' (low shoes), with two or three pairs of 'Worsteders' (thick worsted stockings), the feet of all but one pair being cut off.

BEESWING, *subs.* (common).—A gauzy film or 'crust,' in port wines, the result of age. [From BEES + WING; so called from its appearance when broken up in the process of decanting.] Hence also BEESWINGED.

1846. THACKERAY, *Vanity Fair*, III., p. 26. Scott from under bushy eyebrows winked at the apparition of a BEESWING.

1850. D. JERROLD, *The Catspaw*, Act i. Whereupon, the animal spirits are held in suspense, like—like the BEESWING in port.

1873. FITZEDWARD HALL, *Modern English*, p. 32. This port is not presentable unless BEESWINGED.

OLD BEESWING, *subs.* (common).—A nickname for anyone, but especially for one who 'takes to his liquor kindly' as the saying goes.

18(?). MARK LEMON, *Golden Fetters*, II., p. 74. Mr. Clendon did not call Mr. Barnard 'old cock,' 'old fellow,' or OLD BEESWING.

BEETLE - CRUSHER or **BEETLE SQUASHER**, *subs.* (popular).—1. A large foot. The term was popularised by Leech in the pages of *Punch*. For synonyms, *see* HOOF.

2. In a transferred and now more common sense to that originally obtaining, a large boot or shoe. Also BEETLE-CASES. For synonyms, *see* TROTTER-CASES.

1869. W. BRADWOOD, *The O.V.H*, ch. xxi. Writhing yet striving to look pleasant on the infliction which the BEETLE-CRUSHER of a recent arrival had just inflicted on his pet corn.

c. 1880. RHODA BROUGHTON, *Cometh up as a Flower*, II., p. 200. Yes, but what horrible boots! Whoever could have had the atwocity to fwame such BEETLE-CRUSHERS.

3. (military.) — An infantry soldier; the term is applied to them by the cavalry. A variant is MUD-CRUSHER, which *see* for synonyms.

BEETLE-CRUSHING, *adj.* (popular).—With solid tread, such as comes from large heavy feet encased in boots or shoes to match; *e.g.*, the marching of infantry. *Cf.*, BEETLE-CRUSHER, sense 3.

1876. *Anteros*, I., p. 188. The possibility floated before him, now, of sending all his live and dead stock into the market,—of exchange into a sedate BEETLE-CRUSHING corps.

BEETLES, *subs.* (Stock Exchange).—Colorado mine shares.

1887. ATKINS, *House Scraps.*
Oh supposing our creamjugs were broken,
Or BEETLES were sowing the babies.

BEETLE-STICKER, *subs.* (common).—An entomologist.

BEFORE THE WIND, *phr.* (colloquial).—In prosperous circumstances; out of debt or difficulty. From the nautical expression.

BEGAD! *intj.* (common).—A corruption of 'By God!' and, as such a euphemistic oath.—*See* OATHS.

1742. FIELDING, *J. Andrews.* BEGAD! madam . . . 'tis the very same I met.

1848. THACKERAY, *Vanity Fair*, II., iv., 39. Only one, BEGAD! in the world.

BEGGARED. I'LL BE BEGGARED IF, etc., *phr.* (common).—An emphatic form of asseveration; *i.e.*, 'I'll give up everything, even to being reduced to beggary, if,' etc.

BEGGAR-MAKER, *subs.* (old). — A publican.

BEGGARS, *subs.* (cards'). — The small cards from the deuce to the ten are so called.

BEGGAR'S BOLTS.—*See* BEGGAR'S BULLETS.

BEGGAR'S BULLETS or **BOLTS** (old).—Stones.

1584. HUDSON, *Judith*, in Sylvester's *Du Bartas* (1608), 698. A pack of country clowns . . . that them to battail bownes, with BEGGER'S BOLTS and levers. [M.]

1785. GROSE, *Dictionary of the Vulgar Tongue.* 'The BEGGAR'S BULLETS began to fly'; *i.e.*, they began to throw stones.

BEGGAR'S BUSH. TO GO HOME BY BEGGAR'S BUSH, *phr.* (old).—To go to ruin; otherwise explained as follows.

1686. *Twelve Ingenious Characters.* He throws away his wealth as heartily as young heirs, or old philosophers, and is so eager of a goal, or a mumper's wallet, that he will not wait fortune's leisure to undo him, but rides post to BEGGAR'S BUSH, and then takes more pains to spend money than day-labourers to get it. [N.]

1868. BREWER, *Dictionary of Phrase and Fable*, p. 78. BEGGAR'S BUSH. To GO BY BEGGAR'S BUSH (or) GO HOME BY BEGGAR'S BUSH, *i.e.*, to go to ruin. BEGGAR'S BUSH is the name of a tree which once stood on the left hand of the London road from Huntingdon to Caxton, so called because it was a noted rendezvous for beggars. These punning phrases and proverbs are very common.

Russell Hill, near Croydon, where the Warehousemen's and Clerks' Schools are, is locally known as BEGGAR'S BUSH.

BEGGAR'S PLUSH, *subs.* (old)?—Corduroy.—*See* quotation.

1688. *London Gazette*, No. 2379, page 4. A person . . . in a dark grey Cloth Coat . . . Breeches of BEGGAR'S PLUSH. [M.]

BEGGAR'S VELVET, *subs.* (common).—Downy particles which accumulate under furniture from the negligence of housemaids. Otherwise called SLUTS'-WOOL (*q.v.*).

BEGGAR THE THING! *intj.* (common).—Equivalent to 'confound' or 'hang the thing'—used to give additional emphasis to a word or action.

BEGIN UPON [A PERSON], *verb* (common).—To attack; to assault.

BEGOSH! **B'GOSH**! *intj.* (American).—An expletive, probably of negro origin; a half veiled oath; a corruption of 'By God!'—*See* OATHS.

1888. *The Epoch*, May 5. *Art dealer* (descanting on the virtues of the picture). 'You will observe, sir, that the drawing is free, that—' *Agriculturist.* 'Well, if the drawin's free an' you don't tax me too much for the frame B'GOSH I'll take it.'

BEHIND, *subs.* (common).—1. The posterior; the rump.

c. 1830. George IV., in *Saturday Review* (1862), 8 Feb. Go and do my bidding—tell him he lies, and kick his BEHIND in my name. [M.]

2. (Eton and Winchester Colleges.)—A back at football. At Eton called SHORT BEHIND and LONG BEHIND, usually abbreviated to 'short' and 'long.' At Winchester, SECOND BEHIND and LAST BEHIND. These answer to the half-back and back of Association football At Winchester, in the Fifteens, there is also a THIRD BEHIND.

BEHIND ONE'S SIDE, *adv. phr.* (Winchester College).—Said of a man when nearer the opponent's goal than the player of his team who last touched the ball.

Beilby's Ball, *subs.* (old).—An Old Bailey execution.

1785. Grose, *Dictionary of the Vulgar Tongue*. Beilby's Ball,—'he will dance at Beilby's Ball, where the sheriff pays [for] the musick: he will be hanged. Who Mr. Beilby was, or why that ceremony was so called remains with the quadrature of the circle, the discovery of the philosopher's stone, and diverse other desiderata yet undiscovered.

Bejan, Baijan, etc., *subs.* (Scotch University).—A freshman; a student of the first year at the Universities of St Andrew's and Aberdeen: it is now obsolete at Edinburgh. [From the French *bec jaune*, yellow beak, in allusion to the color of the mandibles of young birds.] The term was adopted from the University of Paris; but, signifying 'a novice' it has been in more or less general use for nearly three hundred years. At Aberdeen, the second-class students are 'semi-bejans'; in the third 'tertians'; while those in the highest rank are 'magistrands.' In the University of Vienna the freshman is called *beanus*, and in France 'footing money' is *bejaunia*. For synonymous terms for freshmen and raw recruits, *see* Snooker.

1611. Cotgrave. *Bejaune*, a novice . . or young beginner, in a trade or art.

1865. G. Macdonald, *Alec Forbes*, ch. xxxiv. The benches were occupied by about two hundred students, most of the freshmen or bejans in their red gowns.

1887. *Standard*, Feb. 10, p 5, col. 2. The term baijan, used in one of the Scottish universities to designate a freshman, is from the French *bec jaune*, yellow beak—young birds having usually bills of this hue.

Belch, *subs.* (common).—Beer, especially poor beer. So called because of its liability to cause eructation. The term is probably much older than indicated by quotations. One of Shakspeare's characters in *Twelfth Night* is Sir Toby Belch, a reckless, roystering, jolly knight of the Elizabethan period. For synonyms, *see* Swipes.

1698. Ward, *London Spy*, pt. XV., p. 347. Those *Poor Sots* who are gussling belch at his own *Ale-house*.

1705. Ward, *Hudibras Redivivus*, vol. I., pt. VII., p. 18.
I sneak'd into a little house,
Where porters do their belch carouse.

1748. T. Dyche, *Dictionary* (5 ed.). Belch (s.), common beer or ale sold in publick houses is so called.

1785. Grose, *Dictionary of the Vulgar Tongue*. Belch, all sorts of beer, that liquor being apt to cause eructation.

1858. A. Mayhew, *Paved with Gold*, bk. III., ch. iii., p. 265. 'Let's have a pot of that fourpenny English Burgundy of yours, and, whilst my mates are drinking the belch, I want to talk business with you.'

Belcher, *subs.* (pugilistic).—A neckerchief named after Jim Belcher, a noted pugilist. The ground is blue, with white spots. Also, attributatively, to any handkerchief of a similar pattern. For synonyms, *see* Fogle.

1812. *Examiner*, 21 Sept., 607, 1. The traverser . . . tied a belcher handkerchief round his neck.

18(?). Dickens, *The Ghost of Art*, in *Reprinted Pieces*, p. 215. I saw that the lower part of his face was tied up, in what is commonly called a belcher handkerchief.

1874. *Macmillan's Magazine*, April, p. 506. The spotted blue and white neckerchief, still called a belcher, bears the name of a famous prize fighter.

2. (thieves').—A ring. Described in quotation.

1851. Mayhew, *London Labour and London Poor*, I., p. 399. The best sort of rings for fawney dropping is the belchers. They are a good thick looking ring, and have the crown and V.R. stamped upon them.

3. (circus and showmen.)—A drinker of beer; generally a hard drinker. *Cf.*, Belch.

1876. Hindley, *Life and Adventures of a Cheap Jack*, p. 99. Now it is well known that travelling mummers are all rare belchers . . . I kept them in conversation . . . until the drink took the desired effect, and one by one the princes and kings dropped on the grass floor, and were sound drunk and asleep.

Belial, *subs.* (Oxford University).—A nickname of Balliol College.

Believe. I believe you, *phr.* (common).—This phrase is frequently employed to signify general assent; 'yes.' Sometimes colloquially 'I believe you my boy'; once a favourite catch-phrase of a well-known actor.

1885. Dickens, *Sketches by Boz*, p. 286. 'Now confess: were you not a little surprised?'—'I believe you,' replied that illustrious person.

1849-50. Thackeray, *Pendennis*, I., p. 140. 'Miss Rouney, I gather, was the confidante of the other.' 'Confidant? I believe you.'

1860. George Eliot, *The Mill on the Floss*, p. 199. 'Is she a cross woman?' —'I believe you.'

1879. Dudley Costello, *The Millionaire of Mincing Lane*, p. 204. 'And she hates that fellow?'—'Hates him? I believe you.'

Bell, *subs.* (vagrants').—A song. Tramps' term. Simply diminutive of bellow.—*Hotten*.

Verb (schoolboy).—To bell a marble is to run away with it, but the action scarcely amounts to actual theft.

To ring one's own bell, *phr.* (American).—A variation of 'to blow one's trumpet'; to sound one's praises personally.

Bell-Bastard, *subs.* (provincial slang).—In the West of England the illegitimate child of a woman who is herself illegitimate; why and wherefore is obscure, though possibly a corruption of 'double bastard.'

Bellmare, *subs.* (American).—A political leader, mostly used contemptuously. The term is a slang appropriation from the terminology of Western life, where it seems to be used in regard to mules much in the same way as bell-wether is employed in England in reference to sheep. Why the grey mare, says the author of *A Ride with Kit Carson*, should be the better horse in the estimation of mules I cannot say, but such is certainly the fact. Though very cautious animals when relying solely on their own judgment, they would appear to have a consciousness of their own inferiority, which induces them to entertain a great regard for the sagacity of the horse, and especially for that of a white mare. The wily Californians, taking advantage of this amiable weakness, employ a steady, old, white mare of known gentleness and good character, to act as a kind of mother and guide to each drove of unruly mules.

Bellows, *subs.* (popular).—The lungs. This, etymologically, is the same as 'belly,' both words having passed through a most complicated history. Properly speaking a bellows is an instrument constructed to produce a strong current of air, and the word itself can be traced back to about A.D. 800. Its figurative and slang signification is recorded as follows:—

1615. Latham, *Falconry* (1633), 115. The lungs doe draw a breath . . . When these bellowes doe decay, then health from both doth fade away. [M.]

1730. Jas. Miller, *Humours of Oxford*, Act v., Sc. 2., p. 75 (2 ed.). Heark you, madam, don't abuse my wife—slut quotha! i'gad let me tell you, she has done a cleaner thing than you'll ever do while your bellows blow, old lady.

1821. W. T. Moncrieff, *Tom and Jerry*, Act ii., Sc. 3.
A plague on those malty cove fellows,
Who'd have us in spirits relax;
Drink, they say, and you'll ne'er burn the bellows,
Half water instead of all max;
A glass of good max, had they twigg'd it,
Would have made them, like us, lads of wax;
For Sal swigg'd, and Dick swigg'd,
And Bob swigg'd, and Nick swigg'd,
And I've swigged, and we've all of us swigg'd it,
And, by Jingo, there's nothing like max.
All Max!
By Jingo, there's nothing like max!

1843. Haliburton ('Sam Slick'), *Sam Slick in England*, ch. xxii. He [the servant] is so fat and lazy . . . walkin' put him out o' breath . . . . How I would like to lick him . . . round the park . . . to improve his wind, and teach him how to mend his pace. I'd repair his old bellowses for him, I know.

Though regarded as slang in England, the word is colloquially used in many parts of America, in the duplicated plural form—bellowses.

1848. J. R. Lowell, in *Biglow Papers*, I., p. 23. His bellowses is sound enough.

Bellowsed, *ppl. adj.* (old).—Transported; lagged. *Cf.*, Bellowser, sense 2.

Bellowser, *subs.* (pugilistic).—1. A blow in the pit of the stomach, or wind—one that takes the breath away.

2. (old.)—A sentence of transportation for life.

1856. *Novels and Tales* (from Household Words), Tauch. ed. vi., p. 187. A sigh of the kind which is called by the lower classes a bellowser.

Bellows to Mend, *phr.* (common).—It is said of a broken-winded horse that it has bellows to mend; likewise of a man whose lungs are affected, or one who from any cause is 'out of health.'

1856. Cuthbert Bede, *Verdant Green*, pt. II., ch. iv. To one gentleman he would pleasantly observe, as he tapped him on the chest, 'Bellows to mend for you, my buck!'

Bell-Rope, *subs.* (common).—The same as aggerawators (*q.v.*).

1868. Brewer, *Phrase and Fable*, s.v., 'Love lock.' When men indulge in a curl in front of their ears, the lovelock is called a bell-rope—*i.e.*, a rope to pull the belles after them.

Bells Down! *intj.* (Winchester College).—*See* quotation and Bells go single!

1870. Mansfield, *School-Life at Winchester College*, p. 62. The junior in chamber had a hard time of it; . . . while endeavouring to get through his multifarious duties, he had to keep a sharp ear on the performance of the chapel bell, and to call out accordingly, 'first peal!' 'second peal!' and bells down!

Bells go Single! *intj.* (Winchester College).—A single bell is rung for five minutes before the hour at which chapel commences. For College evening chapel three three's are rung, and then follows a 'bell,' one for every man in College—70.

1878. Adams, *Wykehamica*, p. 256. At a quarter to six the peal again rang out, and the cry of bells go was sounded in shrill tones through every chamber of College and Commoners . . . After ten minutes the peal changed, and only a single bell continued to ring. This was notified by the cry bells go single, and five minutes afterwards, by that of 'bells down.' . . . Presently the head-master . . . would descend from his library: or the second master . . . would appear at the archway near Sixth Chamber, and the warning voice would be heard 'Gabell' or 'Williams through,' 'Williams,' or 'Ridding in.' Straightway there would be a general rush, the college-boys darting across the quadrangle in the rear of the Præfect of Chapel; while the Commoners hurried in, keeping up a continuous stream from their more distant quarters.

Bellswagger.—*See* Belswagger.

Bell-Topped, Bell-Knobbed, *ppl. adj.* (harlotry).—Said of a man whose *penis* is considerably thicker at the top end than at the root or middle.

Bell-Topper, *subs.* (popular).—A silk hat. [From bell, alluding to the shape, + top, from its position when worn, in relation to the rest of the body + er.] For synonyms, *see* Golgotha.

1885. G. A. Sala, in *Daily Telegraph*, Aug. 5, p. 5, col. 4. His very bell-topper hat had been garlanded with flowers.

Belly-Ache, *subs.* (vulgar).—A pain in the bowels; a colic.

1881. *New York Times*, Dec. 18, quoted in *N. and Q.*, 6 S., v., 65. Belly-ache. To grumble without good cause. Employés bellyache at being overworked, or when they fancy themselves underfed, etc.

Belly-Bender, *subs.* (American).—A boy's term for weak and unsafe ice.

Belly-Bound, *adj.* (vulgar).—Constipated; costive.

Belly-Bumper or Belly-Buster. To take a belly-buster, *phr.* (American).—To ride down a hill in a sled lying on one's stomach, an amusement confined, it hardly needs saying, to young America. The idea of tobogganing was derived from this boyish pastime, and the oaken board has been succeeded by the fleet-winged toboggan, made of seasoned maple with handsomely upholstered seats. With the advent of improved ice vehicles the interest in these sports has increased, and instead of being confined to the vulgar boys who used to ride down hill belly-buster fashion, men and even the most fashionable women now partake of this pleasant and invigorating pastime. Also belly-bumbo, belly-guts, or gutter, belly-flounders, belly-flumps, and belly-plumper.

1888. *Chicago Inter-Ocean*. Barney has a sled, on which he hauls the fish in snowy weather. Barney had his sled out yesterday, belly-bumping on a little patch of ice and snow.

Belly-Button, *subs.* (American).—The navel.

Belly-Can (political).—Explained by quotation.

1889. *Pall Mall Gazette*, Mar. 28. Whatever ultimately comes of the Sunday Closing movement, it will at any rate leave behind it a curious addition to the English language. This is the word 'belly-can,' which is (according to the opponents of Sunday Closing) the plebeian counterpart of the more genteel 'small cask'—both things being, of course, contrivances for getting round the legal prohibition of Sunday drinking. Lexicographers may perhaps be glad to have the definitions of the two phrases as given yesterday afternoon by Mr. Cavendish Bentinck:—The 'belly-can' was a tin vessel not unlike a saddle in shape, which men and women, generally the latter—let hon. members note that—got filled with beer and secreted about their clothes, an averaged-sized can holding about four quarts. A more aristocratic method of private Sunday drinking was by means of the 'small cask.' The small cask industry was said to be an exceedingly prosperous one in certain districts. Grocers advertised for casks as a speciality, and one grocer advertised on a Saturday fifty and sixty and sometimes even 100 empty casks.

BELLY-CHEAT or BELLY-CHETE, subs. (old).—An apron; also food. [From BELLY + slang CHEAT, a thing; from Anglo-Saxon *ceat*, a thing.]

1609. DEKKER, *Lanthorne and Candle-light*, wks. (1885) III., 196. A BELLY-CHETE, an apron.

1622. FLETCHER, *Beggar's Bush*, II., i. Each man shall eat his own stol'n eggs and shall possess what he can purchase—back or BELLY-CHEATS.

1811. *Lexicon Balatronicum*. BELLY-CHEAT, an apron.

BELLY-CHEER or BELLY-CHERE, subs. (old).—Food. This term is of considerable antiquity, as also is BELLY-CHEERING for eating and drinking. For synonyms, see GRUB.

1559. *Eliotes Dictionarie*. Abdomini indulgere, to geve hym selfe to BEALY-CHERE.

1612. ROWLANDS, *Knaves of Spades*, etc. Gluttonie mounted on a greedie beare, To BELLY-CHEERE and banquets lends his care.

1699. COLES, *English Dictionary*. BELLY-cheer, Cibaria.

BELLY-CHERE.—See BELLY-CHEER.

BELLY-CHETE.—See BELLY-CHEAT.

BELLY-FULL, subs. (old).—1. A sound drubbing; a thrashing.

1599. NASHE, *Lenten Stuffe*, in wks. V., 265. The churlish frampild waues gaue him his BELLY-FULL of fish broath.

1605. CHAPMAN, *All Fooles*, Act ii., p. 58 (*Plays*, 1874). Walk not too boldly; if the serjeants meet you, you may have swaggering work your BELLY-FULL.

1666. PEPYS, *Diary*, Oct. 28. He says that in the July fight, both the Prince and Holmes had their BELLY-FULLS, and were fain to go aside.

1835. HALIBURTON, *Clockmaker*, 3 S., ch. xvi. Bunker's Hill, where, Mr. Slick observed, 'the British first got a taste of what they afterwards got, a BELLY-FULL.'

2. A woman with child was also formerly said to have her BELLY-FULL.—See BELLY-UP.

BELLY-FURNITURE, subs. (old).—Food; something wherewith to furnish the belly. Cf., BELLY-TIMBER, Back-timber, etc.

1653. URQUHART, *Rabelais*, bk. I., ch. v. (Bohn's), i., 110. Then did they fall upon the victuals, and some BELLY-FURNITURE to be snatched at in the very same place.

BELLY-GO-FIRSTER, subs. (pugilistic).—An initial blow, generally given, say some authorities, in the stomach—whence its classic name!

BELLY-GUT, subs. (old).—A lazy, greedy fellow.

1594. MORYSINE, transl.,*Vives' Introd. Wisd.*, viij. Such as be skoffers, swell feastes ... BELY GUTS. [M.]

1783. BAILEY, *Erasmus*, p. 346. Since then thou would'st not have a BELLY-GUT for thy servant, but rather one brisk and agile, why then dost thou provide for thyself a minister fat and unwieldy?

BELLY-GUTS, subs. (American schoolboys').—1. In Pennsylvania, molasses candy.

2. (American.)—Equivalent to BELLY-BUMPER (q.v.).

BELLY-HEDGES, subs. (Shrewsbury School).—In school steeple-chases, obstructions of such a height that they can easily be cleared—i.e., about 'belly-high.'

BELLY-PIECE, subs. (old).—1. An apron. Cf., BELLY-CHEAT.

1689. SHADWELL, *Bury Fair*. If thou shoulds cry, it would make streaks down thy face; as the tears of the tankard do upon my fat host's BELLY-PIECES.

2. A mistress; a concubine; a whore.

1630. RANDOLPH, *Jealous Lovers*. *Asot:* Come, blush not, bashfull BELLY-PIECE—I will meet thee: I ever keep my word with a fair lady. I will requite that jewell with a richer.

BELLY-PLEA, subs. (old).—A plea of pregnancy, generally adduced by female felons capitally convicted. This they took care to provide for, previous to trial; every gaol had, as the *Beggars' Opera* informs us, one or more child-getters, who qualified the ladies for that expedient. The *plea* still holds good, execution of female convicts in 'an interesting condition' being deferred until after accouchement. In practice, it really means a commutation of the death penalty for life imprisonment. All chances, however, of becoming *enceinte* after arrest are sedulously guarded against by the rules of modern prison life.

BELLY-PLUMPER, subs. (American).—See BELLY-BUMPER.

BELLY-TIMBER, subs. (old).—Food; provisions of all kinds. [From BELLY + TIMBER.] This, like many other words of its class (e.g., BACK-TIMBER, q v.), was once in serious use, but for a long period it has been going down hill, and it is now a thorough-going vulgarism, only surviving dialectically, and as slang. Massinger and the older dramatists employed it seriously; toward the end of the seventeenth century it began to be used in a ludicrous and vulgar sense. Butler employs it thus, and in Charles Cotton's *Scarronides* (1678), the hero we are told—

Lay thinking now his guts grew limber, How they might get more BELLY-TIMBER.

For synonyms generally, see GRUB.

1614. *Terence in English*, Annona cara est. Corne is at a high price; victuals are deare; BELLY-TIMBER IS hard to come by.

1637. MASSINGER, *Guardian*, III., iii. *Ador.* Haste you unto my villa, and take all provisions along with you ... *Car.* Trust me for BELLY-TIMBER.

1663-78. S. BUTLER, *Hudibras*. Through deserts vast, And regions desolate they pass'd, Where BELLY-TIMBER, above ground Or under, was not to be found.

1719. *Poor Robin's Almanack*, Feb. On the 10th day of this month, being Shrove-Tuesday, is like to be a great innundation of BELLY-TIMBER.

1748. T. DYCHE, *Dictionary* (5 ed.). BELLY-TIMBER (s.), all sorts of food.

1820. SCOTT, *Monastery*, ch. xv. 'Yonder comes the monkish retinue ... I hope a'gad, they have not forgotten my trunk-mails of apparel amid the ample provision they have made for their own BELLY-TIMBER'

BELLY-UP, adv. phr. (old).—Applied to women when *enceinte*. From the protrusion of the abdomen which takes place under such circumstances. — See BELLY-FULL.

BELLY-VENGEANCE, subs. (common).—Sour beer, apt to cause gastralgia. The French call this *pissin de cheval*, i.e., 'horse urine.' For synonyms, see SWIPES.

BELONGINGS, subs. (colloquial).—1. Qualities; endowments; faculties.

2. Relations; one's kindred.

3. One's effects; or possessions. In sense 1 BELONGINGS has long been an accepted word; senses 2 and 3 are given by Annandale as 'colloquial and vulgar.'

1852. DICKENS, *Bleak House*. I have been trouble enough to my BELONGINGS in my day.

1866. *Saturday Review*, 24 Feb., p. 244, col. 2. The rich uncle whose mission is to bring prosperity to his BELONGINGS. [M.]

4. (American.) — Used by the prudishly inclined for trousers.—See BAGS.

BELOW THE BELT, adv. phr. (popular).—To strike a man BELOW THE BELT is to hit him unfairly, a term derived from the pugilistic arena. Hence, underhand dealing, and the taking of mean advantage generally. It is akin with 'To stab a man in the back.'

BELSWAGGER, subs. (old).—1. A lewd man; a whoremaster; a pimp. [Thought to be a contracted form of BELLY+SWAGGER, i.e., a man given up to bodily pleasure. Ash has both forms.]

1775. ASH, *Dictionary*. BELSWAGGER, a whoremaster.

2. A bully; a hectoring fellow. This is the older, but least important usage.

1592. GREENE, *Defence of Coney-Catching*. ... the BELSWAGGERS of the country.

1785. GROSE, *Dictionary of the Vulgar Tongue*. BELLSWAGGER, a noisy, bullying fellow.

BELTINKER, subs. and verb (common).—A beating; a drubbing. To thrash; to beat soundly.—For synonyms, see TAN.

BEMUSED, ppl. adj. (common).—Fuddled; as in the stupid stage of drunkenness. [From BE + MUSE + ED, originally to be sunk in reverie, or contemplation.] The expression as generally used now is BEMUSED WITH BEER. This phrase, originally used by Pope, was given a new impetus by G. A. Sala (in *Gaslight and Daylight*). In America, especially, it caught the popular fancy and ran a brief but riotous course throughout the Union to signify one who addicted himself to 'soaking' with beer. The transatlantic usage naturally reacted upon the Mother Country, and from being occasionally employed it became much more popular, and was heard on all sides — a striking instance of 'fashion in words.'

1735. POPE, *Prol. Sat.*, 15. A parson much BE-MUS'D in beer.

1854. WHYTE MELVILLE, *General Bounce*, ch. viii. A fat little man, primed with port, but who, when not thus BE-MUSED, is an influential member of his committee.

1888. R. L. STEVENSON, *The Treasure of Franchard*, ch. iv., in *Longman's Mag.*, April, p. 694. So while the Doctor made himself drunk with words, the adopted stable-boy BEMUSED himself with silence.

For synonyms generally, see SCREWED.

BEN, subs. (theatrical). — 1. A benefit; a performance of which the receipts, after paying expenses, are devoted to one person's special use or benefit.

1872. MISS BRADDON, *Dead Sea Fruit*, I., 190. 'I have played clown

for my BEN,' murmured the great Dr. Mortemas.

1880. G. R. SIMS, *Ballads of Babylon (Forgotten)*. You saw me in Hamlet, Charley, the night that I had my BEN.

2. (old cant.)—A fool.—Grose.—See BENISH.

3. (common.)—A shortened form of BENJAMIN (q.v.), a coat; also of BENJY (q.v.), a waistcoat.

1876. C. HINDLEY, *Life and Adventures of a Cheap Jack*, p. 252. Being at Hailsham, a small market town in Sussex, about the year 1846, I attended the club feast, which was held on the common. At that time we used to buy men's waistcoats of Michael Riley, of Manchester, at £5 per gross, and sell them at 1s. 6d., 1s. 3d., and the lowest price at a shilling each. I had a bale containing twelve dozen arrive that morning, they were red ones; and in offering these BENS, the plan was to put them on to show how well they fitted.

TO STAND BEN (popular).—To stand treat.

BENAR.—See BENE.

BENBOUSE, subs. (old cant).—Good beer. [From the Latin *bene* = good + BOUSE or BOOZE.]

1567. HARMAN, *Caveat* (1869), p. 85. The vpright cofe canteth to the Roge: 'I saye by the Salomon I will lage it of with a gage of BENEBOUSE; then cut to my nose watch.' ['I sweare by the masse, I wull washe it of with a quart of good drynke; then saye to me what thou wylt.']

1622. JOHN FLETCHER, *Beggar's Bush*. I crown thy nab with a gag of BENBOUSE, And stall thee by the salmon into clowes, To maund on the pad and strike all the cheats, To mill from the Ruffmans, and commission and slates. Twang dell's, i' the stiromel, and let the quire cuffin And Herman Beck strine and trine to the Ruffin! *i.e.*, I poure on thy pate a pot of good ale, And by the Rogue's oath, a Rogue the install, To beg on the way and rob all thou meets, To steal from the hedge both the shirt and the sheets, And lie with thy wench in the straw till she twang, Let the Constable, Justice, and Devil go hang!

BENCHER, subs. (old).—A frequenter of taverns; one who hulks about public houses; perhaps with an allusion to the Benchers of the Inns of Court.

BEN CULL or COVE, subs. (thieves').—A friend; a 'pall'; a companion. [From old cant BENE or BEN, good + CULL, a man.] For synonyms, see COVE.

BEND, verb (Scotch).—To tipple; to drink hard. Jamieson, the first lexicographer to draw attention to the word in its slang sense, illustrates his example by quotations from Alan Ramsay. Murray suggests that it is derived from that sense of TO BEND, signifying 'to pull,' 'to strain,' 'to apply oneself.'

1758. A. RAMSAY, *Poems* (1800), I., 215. Brawtippony ... which we with greed BENDED, as fast as she could brew. *Ibid.*, ii., 73. To BEND wi' ye, and spend wi' ye, an evening, and gaffaw. [1860. RAMSAY, *Remin.*, Ser. 1 (ed. 7), 47. BEND weel to the Madeira at dinner, for here ye'll get little o't after.]

ABOVE ONE'S BEND, phr. (common). — Above one's ability, power or capacity; or out of one's reach. Probably a corruption of 'above one's bent.' Shakspeare puts the expression in the mouth of Hamlet, 'to the top of my bent' (iii., 2). In the Southern States [U.S.A.], its place is generally taken by ABOVE MY HUCKLEBERRY (q.v.). An English equivalent is 'above one's hook.'

1848. J. F. COOPER, *The Oak Openings*. It would be ABOVE MY BEND to attempt telling you all we saw among the red skins.

GRECIAN BEND (popular).—A craze amongst women which had a vogue from about 1872 to 1880. It consisted in walking with the body bent forward.

1876. *Chambers' Journal*, No. 629. Your own advocacy for the GRECIAN BEND and the Alexandra limp—both positive and practical imitations of physical affliction.

ON THE BEND, *phr.* (common).—In an underhand, oblique, or crooked way — not 'on the square.'

1863. J. C. JEAFFRESON, *Live It Down*, II., 152. I never have paid anything yet on the square, and I never will. When I die, I'll order my executor to buy my coffin off the square. He shall get it ON THE BEND somehow or other.

BENDER, *subs.* (popular).—1. A sixpence. Thought to be an allusion to the ease with which these coins were liable to be bent in use. At one time the currency was not of such good quality as now.

1789. GEO. PARKER, *Life's Painter*, p. 178. Sixpence. A BENDER.

1836. DICKENS, *Pickwick*, ch. xlii., p. 367. 'Will you take three bob?' 'And a BENDER,' suggested the clerical gentleman. . . . 'What do you say, now? We'll pay you out for three-and-sixpence a week. Come!'

1869. WHYTE MELVILLE, *M. or N.*, p. 66. A ragged boy established, at the crossing, who had indeed rendered himself conspicuous by his endeavours to ferry Puckers over dry-shod, was accosted by a shabby-genteel and remarkably good-looking man, in the following vernacular—'On this minnit, off at six, Buster; two bob an' a BENDER, and a three of eye-water, in?' 'Done for another joey,' replied Buster, with the premature acuteness of youth foraging for itself in the streets of London.

Among synonymous terms for this coin may be mentioned cripple; bandy; crookback; downer; fyebuck; lord of the manor; tanner; sprat; kick; half a borde; tizzy.

2. (Scotch.)—A hard and persistent drinker; a tippler. This should be compared with BEND.

1728. RAMSAY, *Poems* (1848), III., 162. Now lend your lugs, ye BENDERS fine, wha ken the benefit of wine.

1810. TANNAHILL, *Poems* (1846), 53. Or BENDERS, blest your wizzens weetin'.

3. (public schools'.)—In public school phraseology a BENDER is a stroke of the cane administered by the master while the culprit bends down his back.

4. (common.)—The arm. In connection with this *see* the following, and for synonyms, *see* CHALK FARM.

5. (American.)—A drinking bout or spree, in the course of which, to use another slang expression, 'the town is painted red,' and the participants decidedly unbent. This is possibly derived from any one of the three following sources:—(1) from the Scotch usage; (2) from the facetious name given to the arm, which becomes a BENDER from being so frequently bent or 'crooked' to lift the glass to the mouth; (3) from the Dutch *bende*, an assembly, party, or band.

1854. *Putnam's Monthly*, Aug.

I met her at the Chinese room;
  She wore a wreath of roses,
She walked in beauty like the night,
  Her breath was like sweet posies.
I led her through the festal hall,
  Her glance was soft and tender;
She whispered gently in my ear,
  'Say, Mose, ain't this a BENDER?

1864. *Richmond Dispatch*, 3 Jan. 'Most of the owners of these names had

been tempted by the festivities of the day to go on a regular BENDER, and had to pay the penalty for their New Year's frolic by appearing this morning in the police-court.'

1888. *Detroit Free Press*, 4 Aug. He was a character noted for going on frequent BENDERS until he came very near having the jimjams and then sobering up.

6. (American.)—A euphemism employed by the squeamishly inclined for the leg. A similar piece of prudishness is displayed in an analogous use of 'limb.' With a notorious mock-modesty American women decline to call a leg a leg; they call it a *limb* instead. This tendency is the more remarkable when the great freedom extended to American girls and women is borne in mind; unless, indeed, it arises from guilty knowledge. White, who, perhaps, was rather given to excessive incisiveness of speech, remarked that perhaps such persons think that it is indelicate for women to have legs, and that therefore they are concealed by garments, and should be concealed in speech. Professor Geikie, during one of his Canadian tours, also found out that both sexes had *limbs* of some sort; the difficulty was to discover whether they were used to stand on or to hold by. Sensible people everywhere, however, have little part in such prudery.

1849. LONGFELLOW, *Kavanagh*. Young ladies are not allowed to cross their BENDERS in school.

7. (schoolboys'.)—The bow-shaped segment of a paper kite.

1873. DR. BLACKLEY, *Hay Fever*, p. 145. The first kite was six feet in length by three feet in width, and was made of the usual form, namely, with a central shaft or 'standard,' and a semi-circular top or BENDER.

OVER THE BENDER, *phr.* (common).—A variant of 'over the left shoulder'; the connection between BENDER, a slang term for the arm, and the shoulder is sufficiently apparent. There are many analogous expressions, which *see* under OVER THE LEFT.

Intj.—An exclamation of incredulity; also used as a kind of saving clause to a promise which the speaker does not intend to carry into effect. Probably an abbreviated form of OVER THE BENDER.

BENDIGO, *subs.* (common). — A rough fur cap named after a notorious pugilist.

BEND OVER, *intj.* (Winchester College).—A direction to put oneself into position to receive a 'spanking.' This is done by bending over so that the tips of the fingers extend towards the toes, thus presenting a surface as tight as a drum on the part to be castigated.

BENE, BEN, *adj.* (old cant).—Good. This belongs to the most ancient English cant, and is probably a corruption from the Latin. BENAR and BENAT appear to have been used as comparatives of BENE.—(*See* quots.)

1567. HARMAN, *Caveat* (1869), p. 86. What, stowe your BENE, cofe, and cut BENAT whydds, and byng we to rome vyle to nyp a bong. [*i.e.* What, hold your peace good fellow and speak better words, and let us go to London to cut, or steal a purse.]

1610. ROWLANDS, *Martin Mark-all*, p. 37 (H. Club's Repr., 1874). BEN, good.

1611. THOMAS MIDDLETON AND THOMAS DEKKER, *The Roaring Girl or Moll Cut Purse*.

A gage of BEN Rom-bouse,
In a bousing ken of Rom-vile
Is BENAR than a Caster, Peck, pennam, lay
Or popler.

i.e.,

A quart pot of good wine
In a drinking house of London
Is better than a cloak, meat, bread, butter milk (?) or porridge.

1714. *Memoirs of John Hall* (4 ed.), p. 11, list of cant words in. BIEN, good.

1858. A. MAYHEW, *Paved with Gold*, bk. III., ch. iii., p. 265. 'I've brought a couple of BENE coves, with lots of the Queen's pictures in their sacks' [pockets].

Subs. (old cant).—'Stowe your BENE,' *i.e.*, 'hold your tongue.' *See* quotation above from Harman's *Caveat*.

BENE-BOUZE.—*See* BENBOUSE.

BENE-COVE.—*See* BEN-CULL.

BENE DARKMANS! *intj.* (old cant).—Good night! French thieves say *sorgabon*, an inversion of *bonne sorgue*.

BENEDICK, *subs.* (familiar).—1. A sportive name for a newly-married man; especially one who has long been a bachelor. Apparently, however, there is some confusion in the usage (*see* sense 2). The name was derived from Shakspeare's character in *Much Ado About Nothing*.

1599. SHAKSPEARE, *Much Ado About Nothing*, v., 4, 100. *Don Pedro.* How dost thou, BENEDICK, the married man?

1805. REV. J. MARRIOTT, in C. K. Sharpe's *Correspondence* (1888), I., 239. From what I have seen of his lordship, both as a bachelor and as a BENEDICK.

2. A bachelor. *Cf.*, foregoing.

1843. *Life in the West.* He is no longer a BENEDIC, but a quiet married man.

1856. C. BRONTË, *Professor*, ch. xxiv. 'Are you married, Mr. Hunsden?' asked Frances, suddenly.

'No. I should have thought you might have guessed I was a BENEDICK by my look.'

BENE FEAKERS, *subs.* (cant).—Counterfeiters of bills.—*Grose.*

BENE FEAKERS OF GYBES, *subs. phr.* (cant).—Counterfeiters of passes.—*Grose.*

BENE or **BIEN MORT**, *subs.* (old cant).—A fine woman; a pretty girl; a hostess. [From BENE, old cant for 'good,' + MORT, a canting term for a woman.]

1567. HARMAN, *Caveat*, p. 85 (ed. 1869). A BENE MORT hereby at the sign of the prauncer. [*i.e.*, The Horse.]

1671. RICHARD HEAD, *The English Rogue*.

Bing out, BIEN MORTS, and ture and ture,
  Bing out, BIEN MORTS, and toure;
For all your duds are bing'd awast,
  The bien cove hath the loure.

i.e.,

Go forth, brave girls: look out, look out,
  Look out, I say, good maids,
For all your clothes are stole, I doubt,
  And shar'd among the blades.

1822. SCOTT, *Fortunes of Nigel*, ch. xvii. 'Tour out,' said the one ruffian to the other; 'tour the BIEN MORT twiring at the gentry cove.'

1823. SCOTT, *Peveril of the Peak*, ch. xxxvi. Why the BIEN MORTS will think you a chimney-sweeper on May-day.

1881. *New York Slang Dictionary.* [See first stanza of canting song on page 80 ante.]

BENESHIP.—*See* BENSHIP.

1567. HARMAN, *Caveat* (1869), p. 86. The vpright man canteth to the Roge. *Man!* 'That is BENESHYP to our watche.' [That is very good for vs.]

BENESHIPLY, *adv.* (old cant).—Worshipfully.—*Grose.*

BEN-FLAKE, *subs.* (thieves').—A steak.

BENGAL TIGERS, *subs.* (military).—The Seventeenth Foot; so nicknamed from its badge of a royal tiger granted for services in India from 1804-1823. Also called 'The Lily-Whites' from its facings.

1874. *Chambers' Journal*, p. 801. The 17th . . . the BENGAL TIGERS, from their badge—a tiger.

BENGI, *subs.* (military).—An onion.

BENGY.—*See* BENJY.

BENISH, *adj.* (old cant.)—Foolish.—*See* BEN, sense 2.

BENJAMIN, *subs.* (Winchester College).—1. A small ruler.

2. (thieves'.)—A coat. It is said to have been derived from a well-known London advertising tailor of the same name. Formerly this garment was called a JOSEPH, but for synonyms, *see* CAPELLA. An UPPER BENJAMIN = a great coat.

1815. T. PEACOCK, *Nightmare Abbey*, p. 159. His heart is seen to beat through his UPPER BENJAMIN. [M.]

1836. M. SCOTT, *Tom Cringle's Log*, ch. ii. BENJAMINS, and great-coats, and cloaks of all sorts and sizes.

1851. G. BORROW, *Lavengro*, ch. lix., p. 181 (1888). The coachman . . . with narrow-rimmed hat and fashionable BENJAMIN.

1865. *Pall Mall Gazette*, 7 March, p. 3, col. 2. [Quoting East-end slang.]

BEN JOLTRAM, *subs.* (provincial).—Brown bread and skimmed milk; a Norfolk term for a ploughboy's breakfast.—*Hotten.*

BENJY, *subs.* (nautical). — 1. A low crowned straw hat having a very broad brim.

1883. W. CLARK RUSSELL, *Sailors' Language*, p. 14. BENJIE, the name of a straw hat worn by sailors.

2. (common.)—A waistcoat. Also BEN (*q.v.*). For synonyms, *see* FAN.

1821. D. HAGGART, *Life*, Glossary, p. 171. BENJY, a vest.

BENS, *subs.* (American).—A workman's slang term for his tools. In England called ALLS.

BENSHIP or **BEENSHIP**, *subs.* (old cant). — Worship; goodness. This word, evidently from BENESHIP (*q.v.*), is given by Bailey in his Dictionary [1728], and by Coles in 1724.

Adv. (old cant).—Very good.

1567. HARMAN, *Caveat* (1814), p. 65. BENSHIP, very good.

1610. ROWLANDS, *Martin Mark-all*, p. 37 (H. Club's Repr.). BENSHIP, very good.

1665. R. HEAD, *English Rogue*, pt. I., ch. v., p. 47 (1874). BENSHIPLY, very well.

BEONG, *subs.* (thieves' and costermongers').—A shilling. [From Italian *bianco*, white; also the name of a silver coin.] For full list of synonyms, *see* DEANER.

BERAY, *verb* (old cant).—To defile; to befoul; to abuse.

BERKELEYS, *subs.* (common).—A woman's breasts. [It may be noted that in the gypsy, *berk*, or *burk* = breast; plural, *berkia*.] For synonyms, *see* DAIRIES.

BERMUDAS, *subs.* (old).—A district in London, similar to ALSATIA in Whitefriars (*q.v.*), and the Mint in Southwark, privileged against arrests. The BERMUDAS are thought to have been certain narrow and obscure alleys and passages north of the Strand, near Covent Garden, and contiguous to Drury Lane; see, however, the second quotation where the Mint would seem to be indicated.

1616. JONSON, *Devil's an Ass*, II., 1. *Meercraft*. Engine, when did you see my cousin Everhill? keeps he still your quarter in the BERMUDAS? *Eng*. Yes, sir, he was writing this morning very hard.

1839. HARRISON AINSWORTH, *Jack Sheppard*, p. 12. In short, every contrivance that ingenuity could devise was resorted to by this horde of reprobates to secure themselves from danger or molestation. Whitefriars had lost its privileges; Salisbury Court and the Savoy no longer offered places of refuge to the debtor; and it was, therefore, doubly requisite that the ISLAND of the BERMUDA (as the Mint was termed by its occupants) should uphold its rights, as long as it was able to do so.

As regards the derivation of the name, Nares suggests it in the actual practice, which obtained of debtors fleeing to the Bermuda Islands, when first discovered, to elude their creditors. This fact is alluded to in the following. *Cf.*, second quotation already given.

1616. JONSON, *Devil's an Ass*, III., 3. There's an old debt of forty, I ga' my word. For one is run away to the BERMUDAS.

BERTHAS, *subs*. (Stock Exchange).—The nickname in the 'House' and among brokers for the ordinary stock of the London, Brighton and South Coast Railway Company.

1889. *The Rialto*, Mar. 23. The week opened very badly on the Stock Exchange, and two or three days of utter stagnation followed, but yesterday afternoon a revival took place, which was quite dramatic in its suddenness and vigour. Between two o'clock and the closing of the doors at four o'clock, advances were made ranging from 2½ in BERTHAS to an average of 1 in Americans. Tintos climbed to 12¼, and even Kaffirs raised their sickly heads. All the little bulls went home happier than they have been for three weeks.

BERWICKS, *subs*. (Stock Exchange).—The ordinary stock of the North Eastern Railway.

BESPEAK-NIGHT, *subs*. (theatrical).—A benefit.—*See* BEN.

BESS.—*See* BETTY.

BESS-O'-BEDLAM, *subs*. (old).—A lunatic vagrant.

1821. SCOTT, *Kenilworth*, ch. xxvi. 'Why, what BESS OF BEDLAM is this, would ask to see my lord on such a day as the present?'

BEST. TO BEST ONE, *verb* (common).—1. To obtain an advantage; to secure a superior position in a contest or bargain. The meaning of TO BEST, therefore, is really 'to worst.' In this sense, not necessarily to cheat.—*See* sense 2.

1863. TRAFFORD, *World in Ch.*, II., 77. As I am a staunch Churchman I cannot stand quiet and see the Dissenters BEST the Establishment. [M.]

1876. C. HINDLEY, *Life and Adventures of a Cheap Jack*, p. 69. Bob was a good salesman, but of bad temper, who if he could not get rid of any unruly fellow by his chaffing him, would invariably turn to Perdue and say, 'Look at this man; I shan't bother with him, why don't you get him away? He's interrupting me and the business. I can't jolly him down, so you must settle and do away with him, or I must "dry up," for the fellow's BESTED me.'

c. 1879. HAWLEY SMART, *From Post to Finish*, p. 92. His intimates were wont to say there was no trusting Cuddie Elliston, while, as for Sam Pearson, it was a current saying that 'No one had ever BESTED him.' Still, Yorkshire has a certain respect for this faculty; and though Pearson was regarded as a man who carried it rather far, and would have skinned his own brother upon occasion, yet public opinion did not get much further regarding him than that 'Lawyer Pearson knew his away about; and you'd to get up main early in the morning to get a point the BEST of him.'

1883. *Graphic*, Feb. 24, p. 191, col. 1. So there are people who will not scruple TO BEST a railway company, who would be loth to wrong a private person.

2. Sometimes, however, passing the ill-defined border line between sharp practice and down-right roguery, TO BEST is an equivalent of to cheat; to swindle.

1876. C. HINDLEY, *Life and Adventures of a Cheap Jack*, p. 234. His game was BESTING everybody, whether it was for pounds, shillings, or pence. At one time he cheated a poor farming man out of his milch cow in exchange for another. The man was in liquor at the time, and when he came to his senses he went right away to another part of the country, and his poor wife took it so to heart that she died shortly afterwards.

1879. HORSLEY, in *Macmillan's Magazine*, Oct. When I went to the fence he BESTED (cheated) me because I was drunk, and only gave me £8 10s. for the lot. So the next day I went to him and asked him if he was not going to grease my duke (put money into my hand). So he said, 'No.' Then he said, 'I will give you another half-a-quid'; and said, 'Do anybody, but mind they don't do you.' So I thought to myself, 'All right, my lad; you will find me as good as my master,' and left him.

1885. MAY, in *Fortnightly Review*, Oct., p. 578. The quack broker who piles up money by BESTING his clients. [M.]

TO GIVE ONE BEST (thieves').—To leave one; to sever companionship.

1879. HORSLEY, in *Macmillan's Mag.*, Oct. While using one of those places [concerts], I first met a sparring bloke (pugilist), who taught me how to spar, and showed me the way to put my dukes up. But after a time I GAVE HIM BEST (left him) because he used to want to bite my ear (borrow) too often.

BESTER, *subs*. (common).—A cheat; a swindler.—*See* BEST, sense 2. Generally applied to a turf or gaming blackleg.

1851. H. MAYHEW, *Lon. Lab. and Lon. Poor*, IV., 24. Those who cheat the Public . . . 'Bouncers and BESTERS' defrauding, by laying wagers, swaggering, or using threats.

1885. *Evening News*, 21 September, 4, 1. The complainant called her father a liar, 'A BESTER and a crawler.'

BESTING THE PISTOL, *phr*. (pedestrian).—To get away before the signal for starting is actually given. [From BESTING, gaining an advantage, + PISTOL, the firing of which is the signal to 'Go!']

1889. *Polytechnic Magazine*, July 7, p. 330. The third man from scratch was evidently in too great a hurry; twice he tried to BEST THE PISTOL, and as often the whole start had to be made afresh.

BET. YOU BET! *intj*. (American).—You may depend on it; you may be sure; certainly! be assured! Originally a Californian phrase tacked on to an assertion to give it additional emphasis. So popular is the expression that it has been given as a name in the form of UBET to a town in the Canadian Northwest. Oftentimes it is amplified into 'you bet your boots,' 'life,' 'bottom dollar,' and so on. The two former were used in New York and Boston as far back as 1840.

c. 1882. STAVELY HILL, *From Home to Home*. We reached the settlement of *Ubet*. The name had been selected from the slang phrase so laconically expressive of 'You may be sure I will' . . . A night marauder took advantage of a good moon to place a ladder against a window, hoping to secure the property of a gentleman asleep within the chamber. As he lifted the window, and put his head in, the gentleman woke up, and with great promptness presented his six-shooter, shouting out 'You get!' With equal promptness the detected thief exclaimed YOU BET! and slid down the ladder,—*et procul in tenuem ex oculis evanuit auram.*

1870. BRET HARTE, *Poems, etc.*, *The Tale of a Pony*: Ah, here comes Rosey's new turn-out! Smart! YOU BET YOUR LIFE 'twas that!

1872. S. CLEMENS ('Mark Twain'), *Roughing It*, ch. ii. 'The mosquitoes are pretty bad about here, madam!' 'YOU BET!' 'What did I understand you to say, madam?' 'YOU BET!'

1888. *Daily Inter-Ocean*, Mar. 7. Congressional Report. Mr. Boutelle—That is the bravery to which you refer? (Applause on the Republican side.) Mr. O'Ferrall—Well, sir, it is the right kind of bravery: you may BET YOUR BOTTOM DOLLAR on that.

(American.)—TO BET ONE'S EYES is a gambler's term for an onlooker who neither takes part in, nor bets upon the game.

BETHEL, *verb*.—*See* quotation.

1740. NORTH, *Examen*, p. 93. In the year 1680 *Bethel* and Cornish were chosen sheriffs. The former used to walk about more like a corn-cutter than Sheriff of London. He kept no house, but lived upon chops, whence it is proverbial for not feasting to BETHEL the city.

BE THERE, *verbal phr*. (common).—TO BE THERE is to be on the *qui vive*; alive; knowing; in one's element.

BETTER, *adv*. (vulgar).—More; without any idea of superiority. A depraved word; once in good usage, but now regarded as a vulgarism.

1587. FLEMING, *Cont. Holinshed*, III., p. 1382, col. 2. Woorth one hundred and twentie pounds and BETTER. [M.]

1679. PLOT, *Staffordshire* (1686), p. 239. The bodies . . . being BETTER than an inch long. [M.]

1769. GRAY, in *N. Nicholls' Corr.* (1843), p. 87. It is BETTER than three weeks since I wrote to you. [M.]

1851. G. BORROW, *Lavengro*, ch. lxx., p. 217 (1888). Following its windings for somewhat BETTER than a furlong.

1854. AINSWORTH, *Flitch of Bacon*, pt. I., ch. v. 'Pastor of Little Dunmow Church for fifty years and BETTER.'

1857. DICKENS, *Dorrit*, bk. I., ch. x., 75. 'Yes. Rather BETTER than twelve years ago.'

1860. DICKENS, *Xmas Stories* (*Mess. from Sea*), p. 89 (H. ed.). 'He shipped for his last voyage BETTER than three years ago.'

BETTER HALF, *subs*. (colloquial).—A humorous term for a wife. The history of the phrase is thus given by Murray, 'originally my better half, *i.e.*, the more than half of my being; said of a very close and intimate friend'; (*Cf.*, 'the better part of me' Shaks.; '*meæ partem animæ*,' '*animæ dimidium meæ*,' Horace; '*animæ partem* . . . *nostræ majorem*' Statius); especially (after Sidney) used for 'my husband' or 'wife'; now, jocularly appropriated to the latter. Formerly also applied to the soul, as the better part of man.

1580. SIDNEY, *Arcadia*, III., 280. [*Argalus to Parthenia, his wife.*] My deare, my BETTER HALFE (sayd hee), I find I must now leaue thee. [M.]

Circa 1600. SHAKSPEARE, Sonnets, xxxix., 2.

O how thy worth with manners may I sing,
When thou art all the BETTER PART of me?
What can mine own praise to mine own self bring?
And what is't but mine own when I praise thee.

1720. SHEFFIELD (Duke of Buckingham), wks. (1753) I., 274. My dear and BETTER HALF is out of danger. [M.]

1842. THEODORE MARTIN, in *Fraser's Magazine*, Dec., p. 241, col. 2. I . . . shall look out for a BETTER HALF. [M.]

BETTING ROUND, *ppl. adj.* (racing).—Laying fairly and equally against nearly all the horses in a race, so that no great risk can be run. Commonly called GETTING ROUND.—*Hotten*.

BETTOR ROUND, *subs*. (racing).—One who is addicted to BETTING ROUND (*q.v.*).

1882. 'THORMANBY,' *Famous Racing Men*, p. 75. He [John Gully] worked on gradually as a layer of odds—a 'BETTOR ROUND,' or 'leg,' as he was called in those days. [*c.* 1820.]

BETTY or **BESS**, *subs*. (old).—A small instrument used formerly by burglars to force open doors and pick locks. Now called a JENNY; also jemmy; tivvil; twist; or screw. For synonyms, *see* THIEVES, etc.

1671. R. HEAD, *English Rogue*, pt. I., ch. v., p. 47 (1874). BETTY, an instrument to break a door.

1705. WARD, *Hudibras Redivivus*, vol. II., pt. IX., p. 7.

So Ruffains, who, with Crows and BETTIES,
Break Houses, when it dark and late is.

1785. GROSE, *Dictionary of the Vulgar Tongue*. Bring BESS and glym; *i.e.*, bring the instrument to force the door, and the dark lanthorn.

1861. H. MAYHEW, *Lon. Lab. and Lon. Poor*, IV., 339. Expert burglars are generally equipped with good tools. They have a jemmy, a cutter, a dozen of BETTIES, better known as picklocks.

Verb (colloquial).—To potter about; to fuss about. Usually said of a man assuming the domestic functions of a woman.

ALL BETTY! *intj*. (thieves').—A cry of warning; 'it's all up; the game is lost!'

BETTY MARTIN.—*See* ALL MY EYE.

BETWATTLED, *ppl. adj.* (old).—Surprised; confounded; out of one's senses; also bewrayed.—*Grose*.

BETWEEN YOU AND ME AND THE BEDPOST.—*See* BEDPOST.

BEVER, BEVIR, BŒVER, *subs*. (Eton, Winchester, and Westminster Colleges).—An afternoon meal served in hall. An old time term for a repast or snack between meals, especially in the afternoon; it is still dialectical in some parts of England. Murray gives examples of its use dating back to 1500.

1870. MANSFIELD, *School-Life at Winchester College*, p. 83. In summer time we were let out of afternoon school for a short time about four p.m., when there was a slight refection of bread and cheese laid out in Hall. It was called BEEVER-TIME, and the pieces of bread BEEVERS.

1884. M. MORRIS, in *English Illustrated Magazine*, Nov., p. 73. [At Eton, we] came up from cricket in the summer afternoons for BEAVER.

BEVERAGE or **BEVY**, *subs*. (old).—A tip; a vail; equivalent to the French *pourboire*; money for drink, demanded, says Grose [1785], of any one having a new suit of clothes. For synonyms, *see* TIP.

BEWARE, *subs*. (theatrical).—Explained by quotation.

1851-61. H. MAYHEW, *London Labour and London Poor*, vol. III., p. 149. 'We [strolling actors] call breakfast, dinner, tea, supper, all of them "numyare"; and all beer, brandy, water, or soup, are BEWARE.'

B FLATS, *subs*. (common).—Bugs. *Cf.*, F SHARPS, and for synonyms, *see* NORFOLK HOWARDS.

1866. DICKENS, *Household Words*, xx., 326. Mrs. B. beheld one night a stout negro of the flat-back tribe—known among comic writers as B FLATS—stealing up towards the head of the bed.

1868. BREWER, *Phrase and Fable*, s.v. B FLATS.—Bugs. The pun is 'B' (the initial letter), and 'FLAT,' from the flatness of the obnoxious insect.

Bib. To NAP A BIB, or ONE'S BIB, *phr.* (popular).—To weep; to 'blubber'; to 'snivel.'

FRENCH SYNONYMS. *Lâcher les écluses* (popular: 'to let loose the floodgates'; the phrase also means 'to void urine'); *pisser des yeux* (common: 'to urinate with the eyes'); *pleuvoir des châsses* (thieves': *pleuvoir* = 'to rain'; in military slang to void urine; *châsse* = eye); *verver* (thieves': a corrupted form of *verser*, 'to pour out,' to shed); *viauper* (popular: this argotic verb also means 'to go molrowing' or 'to lead a dissolute life'); *chasser des reluits* (popular: *chasser* = 'to expel,' 'to drive out'; *reluits* = 'the eyes,' or 'ogles'); *chier des châsses* (popular: a coarse term); *chigner* (popular); *baver des clignots* (popular: literally 'to drivel, slaver' or 'slobber the eyes'—*cligner* signifying 'to wink' or 'blink'; hence *clignots*, 'the blinkers' or 'winkers'); *beugler* (popular: properly 'to bellow' [like a bull]).

GERMAN SYNONYMS. *Echen eichen* (from the Hebrew *echa*, the first word in the Lamentations of Jeremiah); *flonen*, *phlonen*, *flannen*, *flaussen*, or *flennen* (to pull one's mouth awry, either for laughing or crying, but among German thieves mainly in the former sense); *jalen jaulen*, or *jolen machen* (from the Hebrew *jolal*, whining; 'to howl,' to whine).

ITALIAN SYNONYMS. *Trignare* (this also signifies 'to rain': *Cf.*, the French, *pleuvoir des châsses*); *slenzare* or *slenzire* (also 'to urinate': *Cf.*, French, *lâcher les écluses*); *ventare* (the primary slang sense of *ventare* is 'to moisten,' hence 'to shed tears': properly 'to blow,' 'to be windy'); *lenzare* or *lenzire* (primarily, in a slang sense, 'to soak,' 'to wet'; from this the meaning is transferred to signify 'to make water,' *i.e.*, 'to urinate,' and also 'to shed tears': the word is properly written *l'ance*; the derivation will be found under the French synonyms for ADAM'S ALE, *q.v.*).

In Spanish there is one expression for 'to cry' which is full of poetry—*fabricar las perlas*, *i.e.*, 'to make pearls.' Arabs likewise speak of tears as 'pearls on the face.'

Bibables or **Bibibles**, *subs.* (American).—Drink, as distinguished from food. [A coinage on the model of 'edibles,' 'eatables,' 'drinkables,' etc.; from Latin BIB-*ĕre*, to drink, + ABLE, *i.e.*, able to be drunk.]

1860. WILLIAM HOWARD RUSSELL (Special Correspondent of the *Times*), *My Diary in India in the years* 1858-9, I., p. 8. Could all the pale-ale, soda-water, sherry, porter, and *vin ordinaire*, and the feebler BIBABLES be turned into nectar, etc.

1860. *Pittsburg Despatch*, Aug. The table was loaded and spread with edibles and BIBIBLES of every possible kind. [DE V.]

Bib-All-Night, *subs.* (old). — A toper; a confirmed drunkard. [From BIB-*ĕre*, to drink, + ALL-NIGHT.]

1612. SYLVESTER, *Lacrymæ Lacrymaram*, p. 101. Bats, Harpies, Syrens, Centaurs, BIB-ALL-NIGHTS.

Bible, *subs.* (nautical).—*See* quotations.

1867. ADMIRAL SMYTH, *Sailors' Word Book.* BIBLE, a hand-axe; a small holy-stone [a kind of sand-stone used in cleaning decks], so called from seamen using them kneeling.

1883. W. CLARK RUSSELL, *Sailors' Language*, p. 14. BIBLES. Small holy-stones, no doubt originally so called because they oblige those who use them to kneel. They are also termed 'prayer books' for the same reason.

THAT'S BIBLE, *phr.* (common). —That's the truth; that's A 1.

Bible-Carrier, *subs.* (vagrants').—A person who sell songs without singing them. Often heard in the neighbourhood of Seven Dials.

Bible-Clerk, *subs.* (Winchester College).—A College prefect in full power, appointed for one week. He keeps order in school, reads the lessons in chapel, takes round ROLLS (*q.v.*), and assists at floggings. He is absolved from going up to BOOKS (*q.v.*) during his term of office. The prefect of HALL need not act as BIBLE-CLERK unless he likes, and the prefect of School may choose any week he pleases; the rest take weeks in rotation, in the order of their Chambers in College.—*See* BIBLER AND BIBLING.

1864. *Blackwood's Magazine*, vol. XCV., p. 73. [At dinner] portions of beef were served out to the boys . . . the BIBLE-CLERK meanwhile reading a chapter from the Old Testament. *Ibid*, p. 87. An hour . . . is expected to be employed in working under the superintendence of the BIBLE-CLERK, as the præfect in daily 'course' is termed, who is responsible for a decent amount of order and silence at these hours.

1870. MANSFIELD, *School-Life at Winchester College*, p. 103. Order was kept during school hours by the BIBLE-CLERK and Ostiarus, two of the Præfects, who held these offices in rotation—the former lasting for a week, the latter for one day only. They paraded School armed with sticks, and brought up to the Head and Second Masters (who alone had the power of flogging) the names of the delinquents which had been 'ordered' for punishment; the names of the more heinous offenders being confided to the BIBLE-CLERK, the others to the Ostiarus.

1878. ADAMS, *Wykehamica*, p. 59. There appears to have been no regular BIBLE-CLERK. . . From this it has been inferred that the institution of these offices must have been subsequent, and (some think) long subsequent to the Founder's time.

Bible-Pounder, *subs.* (common).—A clergyman. [From BIBLE + POUNDER, from the practice indulged in by some excitable exponents, of pounding or beating their hands upon the book or desk while preaching.] For synonyms, *see* DEVIL-DODGER.

Bibler, *subs.* (Winchester College). —Now called BIBLING (*q.v.*).

1870. MANSFIELD, *School-Life at Winchester College*, p. 109. The first time a boy's name was ordered, the punishment was remitted on his pleading '*Primum tempus.*' For a more serious breach of duty, a flogging of six cuts (a BIBLER) was administered, in which case the culprit had to 'order his name to the BIBLE-CLERK,' and that individual, with the help of Ostiarius, performed the office of Jack Ketch.

Bibler Under Nail, *subs. phr.* (Winchester College).—*See* BIBLING UNDER NAIL.

1870. MANSFIELD, *School-Life at Winchester College*, p. 109. If a boy was detected in a lie, or any very disgraceful proceeding—a rare occurrence, I am happy to say—he had to stand up in the centre of Junior row during the whole of the School time, immediately preceding the infliction of the flogging; this pillory process was called a BIBLER UNDER THE NAIL.

Bibling, *subs.* (Winchester College).—Formerly called a BIBLER (*q.v.*). A flogging of six cuts on the small of the back, administered by the head or second master. So called because the person to be operated upon

ORDERED (*q.v.*) his name to the BIBLE-CLERK (*q.v.*).

1864. *Blackwood's Magazine*, vol. XCV., p. 79. Underneath is the place of execution, where delinquents are BIBLED. *Ibid*, p. 72. It need hardly be said that it [the rod] is applied in the ordinary fashion: six cuts forming what is technically called a BIBLING—on which occasions the Bible-Clerk introduces the victim; four being the sum of a less terrible operation called a 'scrubbing.'

Bibling-Rod, *subs.* (Winchester College).—The instrument with which a BIBLING (*q.v.*) was administered. It consisted of a handle with four apple twigs in the end, twisted together. It is represented on '*Aut Disce.*' It was invented and first used by Warden Baker in 1454. It is not used now.

Bibling Under Nail, *subs. phr.* (Winchester College).—A BIBLING (*q.v.*) administered for very heinous offences after an offender had stood under NAIL (*q.v.*).—*See* quot. in BIBLER UNDER NAIL.

Biddy, *subs.* (old).—1. A chicken; sometimes CHICK-A-BIDDY. Hence, figuratively.

2. (familiar.) — A young woman, not necessarily Irish. In both these senses the word appears in Grose [1785]. Since that time it would seem to have changed somewhat in meaning as follows.

3. (familiar.) — A woman, whether young or old.

1868. O. W. HOLMES, *Guardian Angel*, ch. xxviii., p. 233 (Rose Lib.). 'Don't trouble yourself about Kitty Fagan, for pity's sake, Mr. Bradshaw. The BIDDIES are all alike, and they're all as stupid as owls, except when you tell 'em just what to do, and how to do it. A pack of priest-ridden fools!'

1887. *Cornhill Mag.*, May, p. 510. How he gave to one old BIDDY 'five guineas to buy a jack,' and to another substantial help towards her boy's schooling.

4. (Winchester College.)—*See* BIDET.

5. (American.)—A servant girl—generally Irish.

Bidet, or **Biddy**, *subs.* (Winchester College).—A bath. Juniors fill these for Præfect. The Winchester term is the French word *bidet*, the name given to the low narrow bedroom bathing stools, used principally by women, but more frequently on the Continent than in England. They are of such a shape that they can be bestridden. In this connection it may be mentioned, that in French *bidet* also signifies 'a small horse' or 'pony.'

1785. GROSE, *Dictionary of the Vulgar Tongue.* BIDET, commonly pronounced *biddy*, a kind of tub, contrived for ladies to wash themselves, for which purpose they bestride it like a little French pony or post horse, called in France BIDETS.

Bien.—*See* BENE.

Biff, *subs.* (American).—A blow. 'To give [one] a BIFF in the jaw'; *Anglicè*, 'to wipe one in the chops.' *Cf.*, BANG, and for synonyms, *see* DIG.

Biffin, *subs.* (familiar).—'My BIFFIN!' *i.e.*, 'my pal!' A biffin is properly a dried apple: Norfolk biffins especially are considered great delicacies.

Big. To TALK or LOOK BIG, *phr.* (familiar).—To assume a pompous style or manner with a view to impressing others with a sense of one's importance; to

talk boastingly. A French equivalent is *se hancher*.

1579. SPENSER, *Shep. Cal.*, Sept., 50.
The shepheards swayne you cannot wel ken,
But it be by his pryde, from other men:
They LOOKEN BIGGE as Bulls.

1604. SHAKSPEARE, *Winter's Tale*, Act iv., Sc. 3. Not a more cowardly rogue, in all Bohemia: if you had but LOOKED BIG, and spit at him, he'd have run.

1771. SMOLLETT, *Humphry Clinker*, l. 26. The squire, in all probability, cursed his punctuality in his heart, but he affected to TALK BIG.

1822. SCOTT, *Fortunes of Nigel*, ch. xv. 'You will gain nought by SPEAKING BIG with me.'

1838. HALIBURTON, *Clockmaker*, 2 S., ch. viii. 'He LOOKED BIG, and TALKED BIG, and altogether was a considerable big man in his own consait.'

1855. ANTHONY TROLLOPE, *The Warden*, p. 207. The Archdeacon waxed wrath, TALKED BIG, and LOOKED BIGGER.

Big as All Outdoors, *phr.* (American).—An expression intended to convey an idea of indefinite size; hugeness; enormous capacity.

1838. HALIBURTON ('Sam Slick'), *The Clockmaker*, 2 S., ch. ii. The infarnal villain! Tell me who he is, and if he was BIG AS ALL OUTDOORS, I'd walk into him. *Ibid*, ch. iv. He is looking as BIG AS ALL OUTDOORS gist now, and is waitin' for us to come to him.

Big-Bellied, *adj.* (colloquial).—Advanced in pregnancy.

1711. ADDISON [Referred to by].

1848. JOHN FORSTER, *Life and Times of Oliver Goldsmith*, bk. II., ch. iv. My desires are as capricious as the BIG-BELLIED woman's.

Big Ben, *subs.* (popular).—A nickname for the clock in the tower of the Houses of Parliament at Westminster. Named after Sir Benjamin Hall, the Commissioner of Works, under whose supervision it was constructed. It was commenced in 1856, and finished in 1857.

1869. *The Register or Mag. of Biography*, p. 213. With Sir Charles Barry's sanction he designed the ornament cast on the Westminster Bell, familiarly known as BIG BEN.

1880. *Punch*, No. 2039, p. 51. BIG BEN struck two, and the house adjourned.

Big Bird. To GET or GIVE THE BIG BIRD, *phr.* (theatrical).—To be hissed on the stage; or, conversely, to hiss. When an actor or actress GETS THE BIG BIRD, it may be from two causes: either it is a compliment for successful pourtrayal of villainy, in which case the GODS (*q.v.*) simply express their abhorence of the *character* and not of the actor; or, the hissing may be directed against the actor, personally, for some reason or other. The BIG BIRD is the goose. For synonyms, *see* GOOSED.

1886. *Graphic*, 10 April, p. 399. To BE GOOSED, or, as it is sometimes phrased, to GET THE BIG BIRD, is occasionally a compliment to the actor's power of representing villainy, but more often is disagreeably suggestive of a failure to please.

Big Bug, *subs.* (popular). —A person of standing or consequence, either self-estimated or in reality. A disrespectful but common mode of allusion to persons of wealth or with other claims to distinction. Variants are BIG-DOG, BIG-TOAD, BIG-WIG, and GREAT GUN (which *see* for general synonyms).

1854. *Widow Bedott Papers*, p. 301. Miss Samson Savage is one of the BIG BUGS,—that is, she's got more money than a'most anybody else in town.

1857. *N. Y. Times*, February. The free-and-easy manner in which the hair-brained Sir Robert Peel described some of the BIG BUGS at Moscow has got him into difficulty.

1872. SCHELE DE VERE, *Americanisms*, p. 392. Persons of great wealth and distinction are irreverently called BIG BUGS, and I-street, in Washington, is thus said to be inhabited by the foreign ambassadors and other BIG BUGS. J. C. Neal makes a nice distinction when he says of a rich man without social importance: 'He is one of your BIG BUGS, with more money than sense.'

1888. *Texas Siftings*, Sep. 15. Don't appear unduly surprised or flustrated if, on answering the front door bell, you find Mr. Gladstone wiping his feet on the door mat. Invite him to walk in in a cool, collected tone of voice . . . Show him you have entertained BIG BUGS before.

BIG COUNTRY, *subs.* (hunting).—The open country.

BIG DOG OF THE TANYARD, *phr.* (American).—A consequential, pompous individual; one who will neither allow others a voice in any matter, or permit dissent from his own views. The obvious derivation is from the customary guarding of tan-yards by ferocious watch-dogs. For synonyms, *see* GREAT GUN.

BIG DOG WITH THE BRASS COLLAR, *phr.* (American).—The chief in any undertaking or enterprise; a leader. A simile evidently derived from the stable or kennel. The phrase is sometimes shortened to BIG DOG. For synonyms, *see* GREAT GUN.

1848. J. R. BARTLETT, *Americanisms*, p. 42. In some parts of the country, the principal man of a place or in an undertaking is called the BIG DOG WITH A BRASS COLLAR, as opposed to the little curs not thought worthy of a collar.

1882. ALAN PINKERTON, *The Molly Maguires*, p. 24. 'Yes,' said Dormer, 'Lawler is the BIG DOG in these parts now; besides he kapes a good tavern, and will see no old-timer, or young one either, for that matther, sufferin' from want while he can relieve him!'

BIG DRINK, *subs.* (familiar).—1. The ocean; more particularly applied to the Atlantic. Also called the BIG POND, HERRING POND, the PUDDLE (*q.v.*).

1882. MISS BRADDON, *Mount Royal*, ch. xiii. 'I was coming across the BIG DRINK as fast as a Cunard could bring me.'

2. (Western American.)—When a Western plainsman talks of the BIG DRINK, he is always understood to mean the Mississippi river.

TO TAKE A BIG or LONG DRINK is to partake of liquor from a large glass. It is very customary when calling for refreshment to state whether a LONG or SHORT DRINK is required.

BIG FIGURE. TO GO THE BIG FIGURE, *phr.* (common).—A variant of 'to go the whole hog,' or 'to go the whole animal.' It signifies embarking upon an enterprise of magnitude. The phrase is mainly current in the Southern States, and is derived from a term used in poker.

1868. *Pickings from the Picayune*, p. 226. When I saw that, I thought I might as well GO THE BIG FIGURE, you see, and so I grabbed the bag; but mischief would have it, that just then the policeman grabbed me and took me to the caboose.

BIGGEST, *adj.* (American).—A superlative often used in the sense of 'the best' or 'the finest.'

1848. RUXTON, *Life in Far West*, p. 129. The thermal springs are regarded by the trappers as the breathing-places of his Satanic majesty; and considered, moreover, to be the BIGGEST kind of medicine to be found in the mountains.

1888. *Washington (Pa.) Review*. *The Pittsburg Times* is as breezy a journal as comes to this office. It is the BIGGEST little paper we are acquainted with.

BIGGEST TOAD IN THE PUDDLE, *phr* (American).—One of the many bold, if equivocal metaphors to which the West has given rise. The BIGGEST TOAD IN THE PUDDLE is the recognised leader or chief whether in politics, or in connection with the rougher avocations of pioneer life. Equivalent to THE BIG DOG WITH THE BRASS COLLAR (*q.v.*).—*See* also BIG BUG, and for synonyms generally, GREAT GUN.

1848. J. R. BARTLETT, *Americanisms*, p. 42. BIGGEST TOAD IN THE PUDDLE. A Western expression for a head-man; a leader of a political party, or of a crowd. Not an elegant expression, though sometimes well applied. Thus a Western newspaper, in speaking of the most prominent man engaged in the political contest for one of the Presidential candidates before Congress, says: 'Mr. D. D. F.—is the BIGGEST TOAD IN THE PUDDLE.'

BIGGIN, *subs.* (Winchester College).—A coffee machine in two parts—a strainer, and a coffee-pot for the infusion. It took its name from the inventor, a Mr. Biggin, who received letters patent 'some years' previous to 1803. (*Gent. Mag.*, lxxiii., p. 1094.)

BIGGITY, *adv.* (American).—Consequential; giving oneself airs. A negro term.

c. 1884. S. L. CLEMENS, *Life on the Mississippi*, p. 511. These railroads have made havoc with the steamboat commerce. The clerk of our boat was a steamboat clerk before these roads were built. In that day the influx of population was so great, and the freight business so heavy, that the boats were not able to keep up with the demands made upon their carrying capacity; consequently the Captain was very independent and airy — pretty BIGGITY as Uncle Remus would say.

BIG GUN, *subs.* (familiar).—A person of consequence. Possibly of sporting origin. For synonyms, *see* GREAT GUN.

1888. *Texas Siftings*, Oct. 13. 'Who's a BIG GUN? You don't consider that insignificant ink-slinger across the way a BIG GUN, do you?' 'My wife can hardly wait to get it out of the mail,' shouted Jones, desperately.

BIG-HEAD. TO HAVE A BIG-HEAD, *phr.* (American).—1. To be conceited; bumptious. Also applied to men or youths who are 'cocksure' of everything, or affected in manner.—*See* also SWELL-HEAD.

1848. J. R. BARTLETT, *Americanisms*, p. 43. Boys who smoke cigars, chew tobacco, drink strong liquors, gamble, and treat their parents and superiors as their inferiors—of such a boy it is said, 'He has GOT THE BIG-HEAD.'

1888. *Texas Siftings*, Oct. 20. If we were to base our calculation upon the corpulency of his iron hat and helmet, we should say it was a case of BIG-HEAD, while his legs were long as a pair of duplex pinchers, his arms like the fans of a windmill, his feet like the foot of Mont Blanc, while his digital annex is like an inverted ham.

2. The phrase also signifies the after effect of a debauch.

TO GET THE BIG-HEAD. To get drunk. For synonyms, *see* SCREWED.

BIG HOUSE, *subs.* (common).—The workhouse,—a phrase used by the very poor; sometimes called the LARGE HOUSE.

1851-61. H. MAYHEW, *London Lab. and Lon. Poor*, vol. I., p. 52. 'As long as they kept out of the BIG HOUSE (the workhouse), she would not complain.' *Ibid*, *II.*, p. 251. The men hate the thought of going to the BIG HOUSE.

BIG MOUTH, *subs.* (American).—Excessive talkativeness; loquacity. *Cf.*, ALL MOUTH. For synonyms, *see* GAS.

BIG NUTS TO CRACK, *subs. phr.* (American).—An undertaking of magnitude; one not easy to perform. [From a presumed difficulty in cracking large nuts.]

BIG ONE or **BIG 'UN**, *subs.* (old).—A man of note or importance. The current colloquialism is BIG-WIG, but at one time BIG-ONE was the more frequently-used expression. For synonyms, *see* GREAT GUN.

1819. MOORE, *Tom Crib's Memorial to Congress*, p. 42. Then up rose Ward, the veteran Joe, And, 'twixt his whiffs, suggested briefly That but a few at first should go, And those, the light-weight Gemmen chiefly; As if too many BIG ONES went, They might alarm the Continent!

BIG PEOPLE, *subs.* (familiar).—Persons of standing or consequence. *Cf.*, GREAT GUN.

1858. ANTHONY TROLLOPE, *Dr. Thorne*, I., p. 43. He would n no way assume a familiarity with bigger men than himself; allowing to the bigger men the privilege of making the first advances. *Ibid*, p. 81. When one is absolutely in the dirt at their feet, perhaps these BIG PEOPLE won't wish one to stoop any further.

BIG POND, *subs.* (popular).—The Atlantic. Also called THE BIG DRINK (*q.v.*).

1838. HALIBURTON ('Sam Slick'), *The Clockmaker*, 3 S., ch. xviii. He [old Clay] is all sorts of a hoss, and the best live one that ever cut dirt this side of the BIG POND, or t'other side either.

1883. SALA, *Living London*, p. 204. Next time Miss Ward crosses the BIG POND, I earnestly hope that she will cross the 'Rockies,' and triumphantly descend the Pacific slope.

BIG POT, *subs.* (familiar).—A person of consequence. For synonyms, *see* GREAT GUN.

1880. *Punch's Almanac*, *The Cad's Calendar*. Lor! if I'd the ochre, make no doubt, I could cut no end of BIG POTS out. Call me cad? When money's in the game, Cad and swell are pooty much the same.

BIG-SIDE, *subs.* (Rugby School).—The combination of all the bigger fellows in the school in one and the same game or run; also the ground specially used for the game so denominated. Used also at other public schools.

BIG-SIDE RUN, *subs.* (Rugby School).—A paper chase, in which picked representatives of all houses take part, as opposed to a house run.

BIG TAKE, *subs.* (American).—That which takes the public fancy; a great success, etc.,—in short, anything that 'catches on.'—*See* TAKE.

BIG TALK, *subs.* (popular).—Pompous speech; a pedantic use of long words.

1874. *Saturday Review*, Feb., p. 280. [With regard to words like 'psithurism,' 'cheirognomy,' 'scintillating eyes,' 'the phaesimbrotous sun'] perhaps they have been grown so accustomed to BIG TALK that, etc.

BIG-WIG, *subs.* (popular).—A person of consequence; one high in authority or rank. [From BIG + WIG, an allusion to the large and ornate headgear of men of importance in former times.] The term is used both contemptuously and humorously. For synonyms, *see* GREAT GUN.

1703. *English Spy*, p. 255. Most noble cracks, and worthy cousin trumps,—permit me to introduce a brother of the togati, fresh as a new-blown rose, and innocent as the lilies of St. Clements. Be unto him ever ready to promote his wishes, whether for spree or sport, in term and out of term,—against the Inquisition and their bull-dogs—the town-raff and the bargees—well-blunted or stiver-cramped—against dun or don—nob or BIG WIG—so may you never want a bumper of bishop.

1846. THACKERAY, *Vanity Fair*, ch. xx. We live among bankers and city BIG-WIGS, and be hanged to them, and every man, as he talks to you, is jingling his guineas in his pocket.

1859. H. KINGSLEY, *Geoffrey Hamlyn*, ch. xlv. So you are going to sit among the BIG-WIGS in the House of Lords.

1876 *circa*. *Broadside Ballad*, 'Justice and Law.'
The Penge Case you know took a curious twist,
But how it occurred, we can't guess,
Unless, unexpected, some turn of the wrist,
Has got some 'BIG-WIG' in a mess.
To some folks it seems rather queer, now, you see,
When 'Sentence of Death' had been passed,
That one of the four is allowed to go free,
And her prison doors wide open cast.
Chorus.

1880. A. TROLLOPE, *The Duke's Children*, ch. xxvi. 'The Right Honorable gentleman no doubt means,' said Phineas, 'that we must carry ourselves with some increased external dignity. The world is BIGWIGGING itself, and we must buy a bigger wig than any we have got, in order to confront the world with proper self-respect.'

BIG-WIGGED, *ppl. adj.* (popular).—Pompous; consequential. [From BIG-WIG (*q.v.*) + [G] ED.]

1851. CARLYLE, *John Sterling*, pt. I., ch. vii. And along with obsolete spiritualisms, he sees all manner of obsolete thrones and BIG-WIGGED temporalities.

BIG-WIGGERY, *subs.* (popular).—A display of consequence, or pomposity. [From BIG-WIG (*q.v.*) + [G] ERY, a condition.]

1848. THACKERAY, *Book of Snobs*, ch. ii. Whilst Louis XIV., his old squaretoes of a contemporary—the great worshipper of BIGWIGGERY—has always struck me as a most undoubted and Royal Snob.

1855. *Household Words*, xii., 250. All this solemn BIGWIGGERY—these triumphs, ovations, sacrifices, orations.

BIG-WIGGISM, *subs.* (popular).—Pomposity. [From BIG-WIG (*q.v.*) + [G] ISM, a state or condition.]

1871-72. G. ELIOT, *Middlemarch*, ch. xvii. I determined not to try anything in London for a good many years at least. I didn't like what I saw when I was studying there—so much empty BIG-WIGGISM and obstructive trickery.

BIG WORDS, *subs.* (familiar).—Pompous speech; 'crack-jaw' words. *Cf.*, TO TALK BIG, and BIG TALK.

1879. GRENVILLE MURRAY, *Member for Paris*, I., p. 103. 'I don't like such cynicism!' 'Oh, cynicism is a BIG WORD.'

BILBO or **BILBOA**, *subs.* (old).—A sword. Bilboa in Spain was once renowned for well-tempered blades. Grose [1785] quotes the term as slang; this, however, is somewhat doubtful.

1592. GREENE, *Disputation, etc.*, in wks. X., 236. Let them doe what they dare with their BILBOWE blades, I feare them not.

1693. CONGREVE, *Old Batchelor*, Act iii., Sc. 7. Tell them, I say, he must refund—or BILBO's the word, and slaughter will ensue.

1713. *Guardian*, No. 145. 'He that shall rashly attempt to regulate our hilts, or reduce our blades, had need to have a heart of oak . . . BILBO is the word, remember that and tremble.'

1816. SCOTT, *Old Mortality*, ch. iv. 'It was all fair play; your comrade sought a fall, and he has got it.'
'That is true enough,' said Bothwell, as he slowly rose; 'put up your BILBO, Tom.'

2. A kind of stock—a long iron bar with sliding shackles for the ankles of prisoners, and a lock by which to fasten the bar at one end to the ground. The derivation is very uncertain.

1557. HAKLUYT, *Voy.*, I., 295. I was also conveyed to their lodgings . . . where I saw a pair of BILBOWES.

1594. NASHE, *Terrors of the Night*, in wks. (Grosart) III., 255. He that is spyced with the gowte or the dropsie, frequently dreameth of fetters and manacles, and being put on the BILBOWES.

1596. SHAKSPEARE, *Hamlet*, Act v., Sc. 2. *Ham.* . . . Methought I lay worse than the mutines in the BILBOES.

1695. CONGREVE, *Love for Love*, Act iii., Sc. 6. Now a Man that is marry'd, has as it were, d'ye see, his Feet in the BILBOES, and may-hap mayn't get 'em out again when he wou'd.

1714. *Memoirs of John Hall* (4 ed.), p. 19. And are those shear'd, or put into BILBOES, and handcufft.

1748. T. DYCHE, *Dictionary* (5 ed.). BILBOES, the punishing a person at sea, by laying or putting the offender in irons, or a sort of stocks, but more severe than the common stocks.

1815. SCOTT, *Guy Mannering*, ch. xxxiv. 'And now let us talk about our business.' '*Your* business, if you please,' said Hatterick; 'hagel and donner!—mine was done when I got out of the BILBOES.'

BILE, *subs.* (old).—1. The female *pudenda*. For synonyms, *see* MONOSYLLABLE.

2. (common.)—A vulgarism for 'boil.'

BILGEWATER, *subs.* (common). — Bad beer. Properly the name given to the drainings to the lowest part of a ship; being difficult to get at, these become, at times, exceedingly foul and offensive. For synonyms, *see* SWIPES.

BILK, *subs.* (common).—A word, formerly in general use, to which a certain stigma of vulgarity is now attached. Uncertain in derivation—possibly a corrupted form of 'balk'—it was first employed technically at cribbage to signify the spoiling of an adversary's score in the crib. Among obsolete or depraved usages may be mentioned.

Subs. 1. (obsolete.)—A statement or string of words without sense, truth, or meaning, jointly or severally.

1663. JONSON, *Tale of a Tub*, I., i. *Tub.* He will have the last word, though he talk BILK for't. *Hugh.* BILK! what's that. *Tub.* Why nothing; a word signifying Nothing. [Note refers to Cole's *English Dict.* (n.d. given) and to Halliwell, *Arch. and Prov. Words*, s.v.]

1740. NORTH, *Examen*, p. 213. Bedloe was sworn, and being asked what he knew against the prisoner, answered, Nothing . . . . Bedloe was questioned over and over, who still swore the same BILK.

2. (common.)—A hoax; an imposition; a humbug. For synonyms, *see* SELL. *Cf.*, BITE.

1664. BUTLER, *Hudibras*, II., iii., 376. Spells, Which over ev'ry month's blank-page In th' Almanack strange BILK'S presage. [M.]

1694. CONGREVE, *Double Deal*, III., x. There he's secure from danger of a BILK. [M.]

1733 *circa*. NORTH, *Lives*, i., 260. After this BILK of a discovery was known. [M.]

3. (common.)—A swindler; a cheat. This is the most familiar current use of the word in its substantive form, and is applied mainly to persons who cheat cabmen of their fares, or to men who swindle prostitutes out of their wretched earnings. Also BILKER. For synonyms, *see* SELL. *Cf.*, BITE.

1790. SHERIDAN, in *Sheridaniana*, 109. Johnny W[i]lks, Johnny W[i]lks, Thou greatest of BILKS.

1836. MARRYAT, *Japhet*, ch. ix. After a little delay, the wagoner drove off, cursing him for a BILK, and vowing that he'd never have any more to do with a 'larned man.'

4. (American.)—A strongly offensive term used in the West to signify a person who habitually sponges upon another, and who never by any chance makes

a return or even offers to do so. In English slang it means a downright cheat or swindler (*see* sense 3). It will therefore be seen that the Western American usage has considerably softened its meaning.

1840. MCCLURE, *Rocky Mountain*, p. 211. The term was entirely novel to me, and I first asked its meaning of a landlord, who explained to me by saying that a BILK is a man who never misses a meal and never pays a cent.

Adj. (obsolete).—Fallacious; without truth or meaning.

1740. NORTH, *Examen*, p. 129. To that [Oates's plot] and the author's BILK account of it I am approaching.

Verb (common).— To cheat; defraud; evade one's obligations; escape from, etc. (*see subs.*, sense 2, and compare with quotations). For synonyms, *see* STICK. *Cf.*, BITE.

1677. WYCHERLEY, *Plain Dealer*, Act v., Sc. 3. 1 *Knight:* Ay, a great lawyer that shall be nameless BILKED me too.

1729. GAY, *Polly*, Act ii., Sc. 9. Honour plays a bubbles part, ever BILK'D and cheated.

1748. T. DYCHE, *Dictionary* (5 ed.). BILK (v.), to cheat, balk, disappoint, deceive, gull, or bubble; also to go out of a publick-house or tavern, without paying the reckoning.

1750. FIELDING, *Tom Jones*, bk. XIV., ch. iv. 'I promise you,' answered Nightingale, 'I don't intend to BILK my lodgings; but I have a private reason for not taking a formal leave.'

1785. GROSE, *Dictionary of the Vulgar Tongue*. BILKE. 'Let us BILK the rattling cove'; let us cheat the hackney coachman of his fare: bilking a coachman, a box keeper, or a poor whore, was formerly among men of the town thought a gallant action.

1847. LYTTON, *Lucretia*, pt. II., ch. xix. 'Are you playing me false? Have you set another man on the track with a view to BILK me of my promised fee?'

TO BILK THE BLUES, *phr.* (thieves').—To evade the police. —*See* BLUES.

TO BILK THE SCHOOLMASTER, *phr.* (common). — To obtain knowledge or experience without paying for it.

1821. W. T. MONCRIEFF, *Tom and Jerry*, Act ii., Sc. 5. *Log.* Well, don't grumble — every one must pay for his learning—and you wouldn't BILK THE SCHOOLMASTER, would you? But, come, I'm getting merry; so if you wish for a bit of good truth, come with me, and let's have a dive among the cadgers in the back slums, in the Holy Land.

BILKER, *subs.* (common). — A cheat; a swindler. Sometimes abbreviated to BILK (sense 3).

BILKING, *subs.* (common). — The action of cheating or swindling.

BILL, *subs.* (Eton College).—1. A list of the boys who have to go to the head master at 12 o'clock; also of those who get off ABSENCE (*q.v.*), or names-calling, *e.g.*, an eleven playing in a match are thus exempt.

1876. BRINSLEY RICHARDS, *Seven Years at Eton*. Some of the small boys whom this delightful youth tempted to ape his habits, had often occasion to rue it when they staggered back to college giddy and sick, carrying with them a perfume which told its tale to their tutors, and caused them to be put in the BILL.

2. (Harrow School.)—Names-calling.

TO HANG UP A BILL, *phr.* (American political).—Explained by quotation.

1887. *Cornhill Magazine*, June, p. 628. To HANG UP A BILL is to pass it through one or more of its stages, and then to lay it aside and defer its further consideration for a more or less indefinite period.

TO RUSH A BILL, *phr.* (American political).—To expedite the passing of a bill through the Senate and Congress. *Cf.*, RUSH.

1887. *Cornhill Magazine*, June, p. 628. TO RUSH A BILL is an expression well known in the American Senate, and occasionally also used here.

LONG OR SHORT BILL, *subs. phr.* (thieves').—A long or short term of imprisonment.

TO PAY A BILL AT SIGHT, *phr.* (old).—Said of a man or woman who is always ready for sexual commerce.

BILLBRIGHTER, *subs.* (Winchester College).—A small fagot used for lighting coal fires in Kitchen. So called from a servant, Bill Bright, who was living in 1830.

1870. MANSFIELD, *School-Life at Winchester College*, p. 89. The Kitchen is a spacious apartment with a vaulted roof, occupying the entire height of the building on the west side of the quadrangle, and at least half its length; here we might see a few Fags endeavouring to coax Jem Sims, John Coward, or Mother Mariner (the cooks), for an extra supply of mashed potatoes, till Kitchen is cleared by the exasperated Manciple, who has just detected a delinquent in the act of secreting under his gown an armful of the small faggots used for lighting the Kitchen fires (called BILL BRIGHTERS), an opportunity for purloining which was never allowed to slip by a Junior of a properly regulated mind.

BILLED UP, *ppl. adj.* (military).—In the Guards' regiments to be BILLED UP signifies to be confined to barracks.

BILLET, *subs.* (popular).—A situation; a 'berth.' [From BILLET, an official military order requiring food and shelter to be provided for the soldier bearing it.]

TO GET A BILLET, *phr.* (thieves')—When in prison to obtain promotion to duties which carry with them certain privileges.

BILLIARD BLOCK, *subs.* (society).—An epithet applied to one who puts up with disagreeables for the sake of pecuniary or other advantages; also, occasionally, to one who acts as 'jackal' for another and to TAME CATS (*q.v.*).

1831. MRS. GORE, *Mothers and Daughters*, p. 75. The Duke of L. was fortunate in somewhat more than the usual apportionments of *souffre-douleurs*, doubles, BILLIARD-BLOCKS, living hunters, younger brothers, to talk to the young lady nieces, etc.

BILLIARD-SLUM, *subs.* (Australian thieves').—False pretences.

TO GIVE ON THE BILLIARD-SLUM.—*See* MACE.

BILLINGSGATE, *subs.* (popular).—Foul, coarse language; scurrilous vituperation. From the evil reputation which the market of the same name has enjoyed for centuries. In the seventeenth century references to the violent and abusive speech of those frequenting the place were very numerous. In French an analogous reference is made to the Place Maubert, long noted for its noisy market.

1677. WYCHERLEY, *Plain Dealer*, Act iii. *Quaint.* . . . Whose reputation, though never so clear and evident in the eye of the world, yet with sharp invectives— *Wid.* Alias, BILLINGSGATE. *Quaint.* With poignant and sour invectives, I say, I will deface.

1711. DEFOE, *The Review*, vol. VII., preface. As long as faction feeds the flame, we shall never want BILLINGSGATE to revile one another with.

1712. *Spectator*, No. 451. Our satire is nothing but ribaldry, and BILLINGS GATE.

1852. THACKERAY, *Esmond*, ch. ix. If she had come with bowl and dagger, would have been routed off the ground by the enemy with a volley of BILLINGSGATE, which the fair person always kept by her.

1876. HINDLEY, *Life and Adventures of a Cheap Jack*. Messrs. Cannon and Co. defied the surgeon or anybody else to say the fish was bad, and kept jabbering away both at the same time and in elegant BILLINGSGATE, until the constable returned; but he came without the doctor, who had gone to attend an urgent case out of the town, and the people at his house could not say when he would return.

TO BILLINGSGATE OR TALK BILLINGSGATE.—To scold; to talk coarsely, or violently; to 'slang.'

1678. A. LITTLETON, *Lat. Dict.* To BILLINGSGATE IT. *Arripere maledictum ex trivio.*

So also, YOU'RE NO BETTER THAN A BILLINGSGATE FISH-FAG, *i.e.*, rude and ill-mannered; BILLINGSGATRY, scurrilous language.

BILLINGSGATE PHEASANT, *subs.* (common).—A red herring or bloater. This is also called a TWO-EYED STEAK, but for synonyms, *see* ATLANTIC - RANGER.

BILL OF SALE, *subs.* (old).—Widow's weeds. Such are also said to have APARTMENTS OR A HOUSE TO LET (*q.v.*).

BILLY, *subs.* (thieves').—1. A pocket or neck-handkerchief, chiefly of silk. The various 'fancies' have been thus described:—BELCHER, darkish blue ground, large round white spots, with a spot in the centre of darker blue than the ground. This was adopted by Jem Belcher, the pugilist, as his 'colours,' and soon became popular amongst 'the fancy.' BIRD'S-EYE WIPE, a handkerchief of any colour, containing white spots. The blue bird's-eye is similar to the Belcher except in the centre. Sometimes a BIRD'S-EYE WIPE has a white ground and blue spots. BLOOD-RED FANCY, red. BLUE BILLY, blue ground, generally with white figures. CREAM FANCY, any pattern on a white ground. KING'S MAN, yellow pattern on a green ground. RANDAL'S MAN, green, with white spots; named after the favourite colours of Jack Randal, pugilist. WATER'S MAN, sky coloured. YELLOW FANCY, yellow with white spots. YELLOW MAN, all yellow. For synonyms generally, *see* WIPE.

1857. SNOWDEN, *Mag. Assistant*, 3 ed., p. 444. A silk handkerchief. A BILLY.

2. (thieves'.)—Stolen metal. —*See* BILLY-HUNTING.

3. (American thieves'.)—A weapon used by desperadoes, and also by the police when apprehending violence or dangerous resistance on the part of the former when pursued. The construction of a BILLY varies, but usually it is composed of a piece of untanned cowhide, as hard as horn itself, some six inches in length, twisted or braided into a sort of handle, and covered from end to end with woollen cloth. One extremity is loaded with three quarters of a pound of lead; to the other is firmly attached a loop, large enough to admit a man's hand, formed of strong linen cord, and intended to allow the BILLY to hang loose from the wrist, and at the same time prevent it being lost or wrenched from the grasp of its owner. At close quarters, it proves a very savage and formidable arm of defence, resembling, but being much more dangerous than

the ordinary slung-shot in use by policemen and others. Twelve ounces of solid lead and raw-hide, dashed against the thickest skull by a strong armed ruffian, would as effectually silence a man as an ounce of the same metal discharged from the bore of a Springfield rifle. It may be remarked that BILLY in English slang is a policeman's staff, a very different weapon.

1888. *Daily Inter-Ocean*, Ap. 4. The condition of the man reported as having been shot twice in the head on Thursday afternoon, is not at all alarming. It transpires that his wounds are not of the gun-shot sort, but were inflicted with a BILLY in the hands of a Pinkerton man.

4. (popular.)—A policeman's staff; a truncheon.

1884. *Daily News*, Ap. 7, p. 5, col. 1. Anderson was first brought down by a pistol shot, and was then corrected with a BILLY, till he declared himself vanquished.

5. (Australian and New Zealand.)—A bushman's tea-pot or saucepan.

1885. G. A. SALA, in *Daily Telegraph*, Sept. 3, 5, 5. They got enough flour from Sydney to make their 'dampers,' and enough tea to boil in their BILLIES.

1886. G. SUTHERLAND, *Australia*, p. 104. A BILLY, or small tin can, for boiling tea or coffee.

1889. *Illustrations*, Oct., p. 22. Refusing a pressing invitation to stay and spend Christmas with the good people with whom I had been boarding, and heeding lightly their remarks as to 'new chum,' 'dangers of the bush,' 'all alone,' 'strange country,' etc., etc., I took a look at the map, and packed my 'swag.' Now a 'swag' proper, usually contains blankets, towels, 'BILLY,' pannikin, and many other articles . . . *Ibid*, p. 28. The 'BILLY' is off, but the roadman (Irish, of course) gives me a grateful cup of beer, and accompanies me to the hotel another mile down the road.

BILLY BARLOW, *subs.* (common).—A street clown; a mountebank —so called from the hero of a slang song. Billy was a real person, semi-idiotic, and though in dirt and rags, fancied himself a swell of the first water. Occasionally he came out with real witticisms. He was a well-known street character about the East-end of London, and died in Whitechapel Workhouse.

1851-61. H. MAYHEW, *London Lab. and Lon. Poor*, vol. III., p. 148. BILLY BARLOW is another supposed comic character, that usually accompanies either the street-dancers or acrobats in their peregrinations. The dress consists of a cocked-hat and red feather, a soldier's coat (generally a sergeant's with sash), white trousers with the legs tucked into Wellington boots, a large tin eye-glass, and an old broken and ragged umbrella.

These merry Andrews are otherwise called JIM CROWS and SALTIMBANCOS; among the French, *un pitre*.

BILLY-BOY, *subs.* (nautical). — A vessel like a galliot, with two masts, the fore-mast square-rigged. They hail mainly from Goole. Also called HUMBER-KEELS.

BILLY-BUTTON, *subs.* (rhyming slang).—1: Mutton.

2. (tailors'.)—A contemptuous term for a journeyman tailor.

1851. MAYHEW, *London Labour and London Poor*, III., p. 117. And there I did Jeremiah Stitchem to his BILLY BUTTON. *Ibid*, p. 142. A laughable sketch entitled BILLY BUTTON'S ride to Brentford, and I used to be Jeremiah Stitchem, a servant of BILLY BUTTON'S, that comes for a 'sitiation.'

BILLY-BUZMAN, *subs.* (thieves').—A thief whose speciality is silk pocket and neckerchiefs. [From BILLY, slang for a pocket-handkerchief, + BUZMAN, slang for a thief.]

BILLY-COCK, *subs.* (popular). — A round, low-crowned hat—generally of soft felt, and with a broad brim. Speculation has been rife as to the derivation of the term. Murray says 'apparently the same as "bully-cocked," used 1721, probably meaning after the fashion of the "bullies" or hectoring "blades" of the period' (*see* quot.). A writer, C. K. C. in *Notes and Queries*, however [6 S., ii., p. 355], points out that 'these hats were first made for "Billy Coke"—or to speak more respectfully, Mr. William Coke—a gentleman well known at Melton Mowbray a quarter of a century ago [*circa* 1853], and used by him at the great shooting parties at Holkham. The old-established hatters in the West-end still call them "Coke hats."' Of the reality of the personality of William Coke of Melton fame there is, and can be no doubt, and although the name of the hat *may* be derived from 'bully-cock,' yet the weight of evidence seems to be against it, unless a slight transference of meaning, very common in slang, has taken place.

1721. AMHERST, *Terræ Filius*, No. 46, p. 246. [A description of an Oxford 'smart' or dandy.] When he walks the street, he is easily distinguish'd by a stiff silk gown, which rustles in the wind, as he struts along; a flaxen tie-wig, or sometimes a long natural one, which reaches down below his waist; a broad BULLY-COCK'D hat, or a square cap of above twice the usual size; white stockings, thin Spanish leather shoes; his cloaths lined with tawdry silk, and his shirt ruffled down the bosom as well as at the wrists. Besides all which marks, he has a delicate jaunt in his gait, and smells very philosophically of essence.

1862. *Life Among Colliers*, 35. I was told to take off my bonnet, and tie a BILLY-COCK [wide-awake] tight down.

1872. FARJEON, *Grif*, p. 14. With the men, mole-skin trousers, pea-jackets, BILLY-COCK hats, and dirty pipes predominated.

1884. *Pall Mall G.*, March 28, p. 11, col. 1. He wore a plaited blouse drawn in at the waist and a dilapidated BILLY-COCK hat.

2. (Australian.)—The BILLY-COCK of the Antipodean colonies differs from the English head-gear known by the name in being made of hard instead of soft felt, and in having a turned up brim.

For synonymous terms of head-gear, *see* DEERSTALKER.

BILLY-FENCER, *subs.* (thieves').—A marine store dealer.—*See* FENCE.

BILLY-GOAT, *subs.* (common). — A tufted beard; similar to that of a goat.

1882. *Standard*, 11 Feb., p. 3, col. 2. Hair turning grey, hazel eyes, BILLY-GOAT beard. [M.]

BILLY-HUNTING, *subs.* (thieves').—1. Collecting and buying old metal.—*See* BILLY-FENCE.

1851-61. H. MAYHEW, *London Lab. and Lon. Poor*, vol. I., p. 465. 'He goes tatling and BILLY-HUNTING in the country (gathering rags and buying old metal).'

2. Going out to steal pocket-handkerchiefs. — *See* BILLY, sense 1.

BILLY NOODLE, *subs.* (American).—This combination stands in American slang for a fellow whose self-conceit leads him to suppose himself specially attractive to the other sex. [From BILLY, a male name, + NOODLE, a fool.]

BILLY-ROLLER, *subs.* (common).—*See* quotations.

1840. MRS. TROLLOPE, *Michael Armstrong*, ch. xiv. 'What is the BILLY-ROLLER?' . . . 'It's a long stout stick, ma'am, that's used often and often to beat the little ones employed in the mills when their strength fails.'

1875. URE, *Dict. Arts*, III., 1166. This is the BILLY-ROLLER, so much talked of in the controversies between the operatives and masters in the cotton-factories, as an instrument of cruel punishment to children, though no such machine has been used in cotton-mills for half a century at least. [M.]

BIM, BIMSHIRE, *subs.* (West Indian). — Nicknames for a Barbadian and the island of Barbadoes. This place is also sometimes jeeringly called LITTLE ENGLAND, and Barbadian is contracted into 'BADIAN.

1887. PATON, *Down the Islands*. Barbadoes is known all the world over as the little island that pays her way; it has never been conquered; its people are enterprising and energetic, go-ahead and driving; in short, the business men of these islands (the Caribbees). Barbadian may therefore be said to mean a man with 'go and grit, energy and *vim*.'

BING.—*See* BYNGE A WASTE.

BINGE, *subs.* (Oxford Univ.)—A drinking bout.

BINGHAM'S DANDIES, *subs.* (military).—The 17th Lancers. From its Colonel (Lord Bingham) causing the men's uniforms to fit so well. It is one of the smartest regiments of the service. They were also at one time christened the HORSE MARINES (*q.v.*). Two troops of this showy corps were employed as marines on board the 'Hermione' frigate during some severe fighting in the West Indies. Hence the sobriquet now almost quite forgotten. But the 17th are still well-known as the DEATH OR GLORY BOYS, from their badge, which consists of a death's head, with the words, 'or glory.'

BINGO, *subs.* (old cant).—Brandy, or other spirituous liquor. Thought by Dr. Murray to be a humorous formation from B. for 'brandy' (*Cf.*, 'B. and S.') and stingo.

1785. GROSE, *Dictionary of Vulgar Tongue*. BINGO, brandy.

1830. BULWER LYTTON, *Paul Clifford*, p. 41.

FIGHTING ATTIE'S SONG.

Air.—'He was famed for deeds of arms
'Rise at six—dine at two—
Rob your man without ado—
Such my maxims—if you doubt
Their wisdom, to the rightabout!'
(*Signing to a sallow gentleman on the same side of the table to send up the brandy bowl.*)
'Pass round the BINGO,—of a gun,
You musty, dusty, *husky son!*'
(*The sallow gentleman in a hoarse voice,*)
'Attie—the BINGO's now with me,
I can't resign it yet, d'ye see!'
(*Attie, seizing the bowl,*)
'Resign, resign it—cease your dust!'
(*Wresting it away, and fiercely regarding the sallow gentleman.*)
'You have resigned it—and you must.'
CHORUS.
'You have resigned it—and you must.'

1861. HUGHES, *Tom Brown at Oxford*, xxxiii. Some soda water with a dash of BINGO clears one's head in the morning.

For all synonyms, *see* DRINKS. Hence BINGO BOY, a tippler; a drunkard. BINGO MORT, a drunken woman.—*See* MORT.

BINGY, *adj.* (trading). — A term largely used in the butter trade to denote bad, ropy butter; nearly equivalent to VINNIED. It may be noted that in the English Dialect Society's Chestere *Glossary*, BINGY is given as a peculiar clouty or frowsty taste in milk—the first stage of turning sour.

1857. MRS. GASKELL, *Life of C. Brontë*, ch. iv. The milk, too, was often BINGY, to use a country expression for a kind of taint that is far worse than sourness, and suggests the idea that it is caused by want of cleanliness about the milk pans, rather than by the heat of the weather.

1860. MRS. GASKELL, *Sylvia's Lovers*, ch. xv. I've heerd my aunt say as she found out as summat was wrong wi' Nancy as soon as the milk turned BINGY, for there ne'er had been such a clean lass about her milk-cans afore that.

BINNACLE WORD, *subs.* (old nautical).—A fine or affected word, which sailors jeeringly offer to chalk up upon the binnacle.—*Grose.*

BIRCH-BROOM, *subs.* (rhyming slang).—A room.

LIKE A BIRCH-BROOM IN A FIT, *phr.* (common).—Said of a rough, towzly head.

1876. HINDLEY, *Life and Adventures of a Cheap Jack*, p. 90. I should like to know what looks worse than to see a young man or woman with their hair in an uproar, LIKE A BIRCH-BROOM IN A FIT, and some of you chaps down there look as if you hadn't had your hair combed since last reaping time, when you did it with a field-rake, which is very harrowing to one's feelings.

BIRCHIN LANE.—TO SEND ONE TO BIRCHIN LANE, *phr.* (old).—To castigate; to flog. A punning allusion to *birch*, a rod. *Cf.*, STRAP OIL, etc.

BIRD, *subs.* (theatrical).—Mr. H. J. Byron says that when a piece is hissed the actors say 'The BIRD's there!';—the bird alluded to being the goose notorious for its hissing capacities.—*See* however, BIG BIRD and GOOSE.

Verb (old).— To thieve; to steal; to look for plunder. So used by Ben Jonson.

BIRD-CAGE, *subs.* (common). — 1. A bustle, an article of feminine attire, used for extending the skirts of the dress. So called because at one time constructed of such a size and in such a manner as to be not altogether unlike an elongated BIRD-CAGE.

1860 *circa*. *Broadside Ballad*, 'The Agricultural Irish Girl,' verse 3.
She has no great education, for
She's not much past her letters;
But for acting like a lady, I
Would like to see her betters:
She does not read Ouida's works,
Nor *Bow Bells'* fashions pages;
And she does not wear those things behind,
The ladies call BIRD-CAGES.

Among ENGLISH SYNONYMS may be mentioned canary cage; backstaircase; false hereafter; bishop.

FRENCH SYNONYMS. *Un volapuk*; *un strapontin*; *un lieutenant* (a pun on *tenant lieu de ce qui manque*); *un nuage* (*parcequ'il cache la lune*; *lune* = the posteriors).

2. (common.)—A four-wheeled cab. For synonyms, *see* GROWLER.

3. (racing.) — The paddock at the Newmarket race-course where saddling takes place. It adjoins the grand stand.

1884. *St. James's Gazette*, May 1, p. 1. All the favourites were brought into the BIRD-CAGE. [M.]

BIRDLIME, *subs.* (rhyming slang). — 1. Time.

2. (old.) — A thief. From the glutinous substance of the same name spread upon twigs for the purpose of catching birds and holding them fast.

1705. VANBRUGH, *Confederacy*, V., 2. That BIRDLIME there stole it.

1705. VANBRUGH, *Confederacy*, III., 2. My rogue of a son has laid his BIRD-LIME fingers on't.

BIRD'S-EYE, BIRD'S-EYE FOGLE, BIRD'S-EYE WIPE, *subs.* (common).—A silk handkerchief spotted with eye-like markings. —*See* also BILLY and WIPE.

1665. PEPYS, *Diary*, May 14. To church, it being Whit-Sunday; my wife very fine in a new yellow BIRD'S-EYE hood, as the fashion is now.

1861. HUGHES, *Tom Brown at Oxford*, ch. xviii. He wore a blue BIRD'S-EYE handkerchief round his neck.

1883. *Daily Telegraph*, August 7, p. 6, col. 2. His neckerchief was of the same hue [silver grey], with a light crimson BIRD'S-EYE.

BIRD-WITTED, *adj.* (old).—Inconsiderate; thoughtless; easily imposed on.—*Grose.*

1605. BACON, *Adv. Learning*, II. (1861), 228. If a child be BIRD-WITTED, that is, hath not the faculty of attention, the mathematics giveth a remedy thereunto.

1650. USSHER, *Ann.*, VI., 360. [He] proved . . . . but a BIRD-WITTED man.

BIRK, *subs.* (back slang).—A 'CRIB' (*q.v.*), *i.e.*, a house. For synonyms, *see* DIGGINGS.

BIRTHDAY SUIT, *subs.* (common).—Naked; in the BUFF (*q.v.*); in the suit in which Adam and Eve first saw each other, and 'were not ashamed.' A French equivalent is *s'habiller en sauvage.*

1771. SMOLLETT, *Humphry Clinker*, I. 61. I went in the morning to a private place, along with the housemaid, and we bathed in our BIRTH-DAY SOOT.

BISHOP, *subs.* (old).—1. A warm decoction of wine, orange or lemon peel, and sugar—but variously compounded. Similar to FLIP and PURL (*q.v.*).

1703. *English Spy*, p. 255. Most noble cracks, and worthy cousin trumps, —permit me to introduce a brother of the togati, fresh as a new-blown rose, and innocent as the lilies of St. Clements. Be unto him ever ready to promote his wishes, whether for spree or sport, in term and out of term,—against the Inquisition and their bull-dogs—the town-raff and the bargees—well-blunted or stiver cramped—against dun or don—nob or big-wig—so may you never want a bumper of BISHOP.

1738. SWIFT, *Women Who Cry Oranges*, wks., 1755, IV., i., 278. Well roasted, with sugar and wine in a cup. They'll make a sweet BISHOP.

1753. *The World*, No. 37. Punch, BISHOP, cool tankard, and negus are equally denied me.

1836. DICKENS, *Pickwick*, ch. xlviii., p. 421. He and the landlord were drinking a bowl of BISHOP together.

2. *subs.* (American).—A bustle—part of feminine attire consisting of a pad worn on the back part of the waist, and designed to give prominence to the skirt. For synonyms, *see* BIRD-CAGE.

1848. BARTLETT, *Dictionary of Americanisms*, p. 42. BISHOP. An appendage to a lady's wardrobe, otherwise called a bustle.
I sing the BISHOP, alias the bustle.

1862-75. SAXE, *Progress.* Imperial Fashion decides the gravest questions which divide the world.
If wrong may not, by circumstance, be right,—
If black cravats be more genteel than white,—
If, by her BISHOP, or her 'grace,' alone
A genuine lady, or a church, is known.

3. (common.)—A chamber utensil; a JERRY; JORDAN; and IT (*q.v.*).

4. (Winchester College.)—The sapling with which a fagot is bound together.

Verb.—1. A term among horse dealers, for burning marks into a horse's teeth, after he has lost them by age; or, by other deceptive arts to give a good appearance to a bad horse. By

BISHOPPING, a horse is made to appear younger than he is. The expression is derived from the name of a person who initiated the practice, and has no connection with 'to bishop,' a provincialism for 'to burn.' For synonyms, *see* FIG.

1727. R. BRADLEY, *Family Dict.*, vol. I., s. v. 'Horse.' This way of making a *horse* look young, is by Horse Coursers called BISHOPING.

1884. *Ill. Lon. News*, 23 August, 171, col. 2. To BISHOP . . . a term . . . signifying the use of deceptive arts to make an old horse appear like a young one.

In French the process is called *masquer en alezan*; also *maquiller un gayet.*

2. To murder by drowning. The term, now obsolete, is like BURKE and BOYCOTT from the name of an individual. A man named Bishop drowned a boy in Bethnal Green, in 1831, to sell the body for dissecting purposes.

1837. BARHAM, *I. L.* (*Account of a New Play*). I burked the papa, now I'll BISHOP the son. [D.]

1864. *Athenæum*, p. 559, col. 1. We have 'to burke,' and 'TO BISHOP.' [M.]

BISMARQUER, *verb* (familiar).—To cheat; to play foul at cards or billiards. A word formed from the name of Prince Bismarck, the German Chancellor, whose policy in 1865-6 roused the indignation of a large section of European thought.

BIT, BITE, BYTE, *subs.* (old).—1. An old cant term for money. For synonyms, *see* ACTUAL.

1532. *Use of Dice Play* (Percy Soc.). Now waxen is he so proud of his gain, because he hath gotten a new chain, fyer new apparel, and some store of BYTE.

1592. *Defence of Conny-Catching*, in Greene's wks. XI., 44. So some that would not stoope a farthing at cardes, would venter all the BYTE *in their boung* at dice.

1607. DEKKER, *Jests to make you Merie*, in wks. (Grosart) II., 328. If they follow you in the street, and once know where the bung and the BIT is, as much as to say your purse and the money.

1608. DEKKER, *Belman of London*, in wks. (Grosart) III., 122. To learne before he play what store of BIT he hath in his *Bay*, that is, what money he hath in his pursse.

1789. GEO. PARKER, *Life's Painter*, p. 149. *Snack the BIT.* To share the money.

1834. H. AINSWORTH, *Rookwood*, bk. III., ch. v. He is caught—he must 'stand and deliver'; then out with the dummy [pocket book], and off with the BIT.

2. (colloquial.)—The name given to coins varying in value according to locality—usually, however, to the silver piece of the lowest denomination. Fourpenny pieces are still called BITS in English slang, but are more popularly known as JOEYS (*q.v.*, for synonyms); and in Demerara the term is in general use for the same coin; in America a 12½ cent piece is called a BIT, and a defaced 20 cent piece is termed a LONG BIT. A BIT is the smallest coin in Jamaica, equal to 6d.

1748. T. DYCHE, *Dictionary* (5 ed.). BIT (s.) . . . In the *West Indies*, it is the least piece of silver coin, which goes current at 7 pence half-penny.

1875. *Scribner's Magazine*, July, p. 277. For a young city, San Francisco is very much wedded to petty traditions. It clings to the BIT with a deathlike tenacity; clings to it against all reason and against its own interests. The BIT is a mythical quantity. It is neither twelve and a half cents, nor half of twenty-five; it is neither fifteen cents nor ten cents. If you buy a BIT'S worth, and throw down twenty-five cents, you get ten cents back; if you offer the same ten cents in lieu of a BIT, you are looked upon as a mild sort of a swindler. And yet, the BIT is the standard of minimum monetary value.

BITCH, *subs.* (low).—1. An opprobrious term for a woman,

generally containing an implication of lewdness and 'fastness.' Not now in literary use, though formerly so. [From its primary sense of a female dog.] It is the most offensive apellation that can be given to an English woman, even more provoking than that of whore.

1400. *Chester Pl.* (1843), 181. Whom calleste thou queine skabde BICHE? [M.]

1575. J. STILL, *Gammer Gurton*, II., ii. Come out, thou hungry needy BITCH. [M.]

1712. ARBUTHNOT, *John Bull* (1755), 9. An extravagant BITCH of a wife.

1750. FIELDING, *Tom Jones*, bk. XVII., ch. iii. There was my lady cousin Bellaston, and my lady Betty, and my lady Catharine, and my lady I don't know who; damn me if ever you catch me among such a kennel of hoop-petticoated BITCHES.

1833. MARRYAT, *P. Simple* (1834), 446. You are a . . . son of a BITCH.

2. (old.)—Applied, opprobriously, as in sense 1, to a man. It has long since passed out of decent usage.

c. 1500. *E. E. Misc.* (1855), 54. He is a schrewed BYCHE, In fayth, I trow, he be a wyche.

1675. HOBBES, *Odyssey*, xviii., 310. Ulysses looking sourly answered, You BITCH. [M.]

1750. FIELDING, *Tom Jones*, bk. XVII., iii. It is an old acquaintance of above twenty years standing. I can tell you landlord is a vast comical BITCH, you will like un hugely.

Verb (low).—1. To go whoring; molrowing; to frequent the company of prostitutes.

2. To yield, or give up an attempt through fear.—*Grose.*

3. (common.)—To spoil; to bungle.

To STAND BITCH.—To make tea, or do the honours of the tea table, or to perform a female part. BITCH is here used generically for a woman.

BITCH BOOBY, *subs.* (old military).—A country girl.—*Grose.*

BITCHERY, *subs.* (low).—Harlotry; lewdness. [From BITCH, sense 1, + ERY.]

1532-3. MORE, *Confut. Tindale*, wks., 648, col. 1. Such marriage is very vnlawfull leckery and plain abhominable BYCHERY.

1598. MARSTON, *Sco. Villanie*, I., iv., 188. He will vnline himselfe from BITCHERY.

1663-1704. THOMAS BROWN, *Works, Serious and Comical*, III., p. 94. Thither run Sots purely to be drunk that they may . . . forget . . . the roguery of their lawyers, the BITCHERY of their paramours, or the ingratitude of the world.

(?). STANYHURST, *Description of Ireland*, p. 14. The quip sat as unseemly in his mouth as for a whore to reprehend BITCHERY, or for an usurer to condemn simony.

BITCH PARTY, *subs.* (popular).—A party composed of women. Originally an Oxford term for a tea-party, tea being considered a beverage only fit for women. [From BITCH, a woman, + PARTY.] Also HEN PARTY (*q.v.*). *Cf.*, STAG PARTY.

1889. C. WHIBLEY, *In Cap and Gown*, Characters of Freshmen, p. 176. 'The studious freshman . . . goeth to a small BITCH-PARTY and findeth his gown taken "by mistake."'

BITE, *subs.* (old).—1. An old slang term for money.—*See* BIT.

2. (old.)—The female *pudenda.* For synonyms, *see* MONOSYLLABLE.

3. An imposition; a piece of humbug; a 'sell' or 'do.' *Cf.*, BILK, BAM, BARGAIN, and SELL, for synonyms. The sense runs

through all stages, from jocular hoaxing to downright swindling. Also in the sense of disappointment, as in the old proverb 'the biter bit.' A man is bitten when he burns his fingers meddling in matters, which, though promising well, turn out failures.—*See* also CROSS BITE.

1711. STEELE, *Spectator*, No. 156, ¶ 2. It was a common BITE with him, to lay Suspicions that he was favoured by a Lady's Enemy.

1721. AMHERST, *Terræ Fil.*, ix., 43. Sharpers would not frequent gaming-tables, if the men of fortune knew the BITE.

1817. SCOTT, *Rob Roy*, ch. ix. 'It's all a bam, ma'am—all a bamboozle and a BITE, that affair of his illness.'

1860. *Sat. Review*, Ap. 14, 475, 2. That form of practical joking, which in the time of 'The Spectator,' was known as a BITE . . . in the popular slang of the day, is designated 'a sell.'

1883. *Daily News*, Ap. 18, p. 5, col. 4. Lord Randolph Churchill, we fear, has been making Mr. Gladstone the victim of what, in the slang of Addison's time, would have been called a BITE, and what in the slang of our own time is called a 'sell.'

4. (old.)—A sharper; cheat; trickster. *Cf.*, BILK. *See* ROOK for synonyms.

1742. FIELDING, *Miss Lucy* (1762), 176. Is this wench an idiot, or a BITE? Marry me, with a pox!

1751. SMOLLETT, *Peregrine Pickle*, ch. xcviii. From which circumstance it was conjectured that Peregrine was a BITE from the beginning, who had found credit on account of his effrontery and appearance, and imposed himself upon the town as a young gentleman of fortune.

1787. S. JENYNS, in *Dodsley*, III., 169. The fool would fain be thought a BITE.

5. (popular.)—Applied in a transferred sense to anybody or anything suspected of being different to what it appears, but not necessarily in a bad sense.

1846. BRACKENRIDGE, *Mod. Chiv.*, 21. The jockeys suspected that the horse was what they call a BITE, that under the appearance of leanness and stiffness, was concealed some hidden quality of swiftness.

6. (common.)—One who drives a hard bargain; a 'close fist.'

7. (familiar.)—A nickname for a Yorkshireman.—*See Daily News*, Sept. 11, 1883, and *Yorkshire Post*, Jan. 9, 1884.

1883. *Daily News*, Sept. 4, p. 5, col. 6. The great and puissant race known indifferently as 'tykes' or BITES.

8. (printers'.)—An irregular white spot on the edge or corner of a printed page, caused by the frisket not being sufficiently cut out.

1677. MOXON, Mech. Exerc. in Savage *Dict. Print*, s.v. BITE. If the frisket is not sufficiently cut away, but covers some part of the form, so that it prints on the frisket, it is called a BITE. [M.]

1884. BLADES, *Caxton*, 130. In 'Speculum Vitæ Christi' we actually find a BITE, half of the bottom line remaining unprinted. [M.]

Verb (old).—1. To deceive; cheat; swindle; to 'do' or 'take in.' In modern colloquial English TO SLICK OR TO SELL (*q.v.*). Formerly used both transitively and passively; now only in latter.

1669. *Nicker Nicked*, in *Hart. Misc.* (ed. Park), ii., 109. Then a rook . . . follows him close, and engages him in advantageous bets, and at length worries him, that is gets all his money, and then they smile and say, 'The lamb is BITTEN.'

1709. STEELE, *Tatler*, No. 12. Nay, he has BIT you fairly enough, that's certain.

1724. *A Journey through England.* Many a poor German hath been BIT by an ordinary or his taylor, after this manner; they have suffered the poor wretch to run in debt, made him an extravagant bill, and then arrested him, and so forced him to pay their demands.

1731. FIELDING, *The Lottery*, Sc. 3. However, Madam, you are BIT as well as I am; for I am no more a lord, than you are a fortune.

1822. [NARES] *Love in a Barn, an old ballad.*
He shall not have my maiden-head,
I solemnly do swear;
But I'll BITE him of a portion,
Then marry with Ralph, my dear.

1838. THACKERAY, *Yellowplush Memoirs*, ch. x. 'You were completely BITTEN, my boy—humbugged, bamboozled—ay, and by your old father, you dog.'

1853. THACKERAY, *Barry Lyndon*, ch. xvii., p. 232. I have no particular pleasure in recalling my Newmarket doings. I was infernally BIT and bubbled in almost every one of my transactions there.

Hence 2. (popular.)—To strike a hard bargain.

3. (old.)—To steal; *e.g.*, 'to BITE the roger,' to steal a portmanteau; 'to BITE the wiper,' *i.e.*, to purloin a handkerchief.

Intj. (old.)—1. Formerly an equivalent to the modern 'Sold!' 'Done!' etc.

1704. CIBBER, *Careless Husband*, Act iii.
Ld. Mo. 'Tis possible I may not have the same regard to her frown that your Lordship has.
Ld. Fop. That's BITE, I'm sure; he'd give a joint of his little finger to be as well with her as I am.

1738. SWIFT, *Polite Conversation* (conv. i.).
Miss. I'm sure the gallows groans for you.
Nev. BITE, Miss; I was but in jest.

1714. ADDISON, *Spectator*, No. 514. It is a superstition with some surgeons who beg the bodies of condemned malefactors, to go to the gaol and bargain for the carcass with the criminal himself. . . . The fellow who killed the officer of Newgate, very forwardly, and like a man who was willing to deal, told him, 'Look you, Mr. Surgeon, that little dry fellow, who has been half starved all his life, is now half dead with fear, cannot answer your purpose . . . Come, for twenty shillings I am your man.' Says the Surgeon, 'Done, there's a guinea.' This witty rogue took the money, and as soon as he had it in his fist, cries, 'BITE, I am to be hanged in chains'

2. (Charterhouse.)—A warning = *Cave!*

TO DO A THING WHEN THE MAGGOT BITES, *phr.* (common), is to do it when the fancy takes one; 'at one's own sweet will.' When a person acts from no apparent motive in external circumstances, he is said to have 'a maggot in his head,' to have 'a bee in his bonnet'; or, in French, *avoir des rats dans la tête*; in Platt-Deutsch, to have a mouse-nest in his head, the eccentric behaviour being attributed to the influence of the internal irritation. *Cf.*, APARTMENTS TO LET.

BITE ONE'S HIPS, *verbal phr.* (tailors').—To regret a word or action.

BITE ONE'S NAME IN, *verbal phr.* (common).—To drink heavily; to tipple; also to drink greedily.

BITE ON THE BRIDLE, *verbal phr.* (old).—To be pinched in circumstances; to be reduced; in difficulties.

BITER, *subs.* (old).—1. A practical joker; a hoaxer; one who deceives; a cheat and trickster. *Cf.*, BITE. The term now only survives in the proverbial expression, 'the biter bit.' For synonyms, *see* ROOK.

1669. *Nicker Nicked*, in *Hart. Misc.* (ed. Park), ii., 108. [BITER is given in a list of names of cheats and thieves'.]

1680. COTTON, *Complete Gamester*, in Singer's *Hist. Playing Cards* (1816), p. 333. *Hectors, setters, gilts, pads*, BITERS, *etc.*, and these may all pass under the general appellation of *rooks*.

1709. STEELE, *Tatler*, No. 12. A BITER, who is a dull fellow, that tells you a lye with a grave face, and laughs at you for knowing him no better than to believe him.

1711. *Spectator*, No. 47. These gentlemen are commonly distinguished by the name of BITERS: a race of men that are perpetually employed in laughing at those mistakes which are of their own production.

1712. *Spectator*, No. 504. A BITER is one who tells you a thing you have no reason to disbelieve in itself, and perhaps has given you, before he bit you, no reason to disbelieve it for his saying it; and if you give him credit, laughs in your face, and triumphs that he has deceived you.

1812. COOMBE, *Syntax, Picturesque*, c. xix.
Pray have you travell'd so far north,
To think we have so little wit,
As by such BITERS to be bit?

2. (old.)—An amorous woman (sexually). *Cf.*, ATHANASIAN WENCH.

BITE THE EAR, *verbal phr.* (thieves').—To borrow. Formerly, a term of endearment; to caress fondly. For synonyms, *see* SHINS.

1879. J. W. HORSLEY, in *Macm. Mag.*, xl., 502. He used to want to BITE MY EAR (borrow) too often.

BITE THE THUMB, *verbal phr.* (old).—To make a gesture of contempt, which was formerly regarded in the light of an insult. Nares says the thumb in the action represented a fig, and the whole was equivalent to 'a fig for you.' There are several gestures of this kind. That best known is probably TAKING A SIGHT (*q.v.*). A similar gesture of contempt is used by the lower orders in France which, there is little doubt, is the 'BITING THE THUMB' spoken of in *Romeo and Juliet*. The person using the gesture placed the nail of his thumb under the front teeth of the upper jaw, and then jerked the thumb forward, using at the same time an expression equivalent to 'I don't care that for you.' Another contemptuous action is placing the thumb between the closed fore and middle fingers; while according to Darwin's *Expression of the Emotions*, it appears that with the Dakota Indians of North America 'contempt is shown . . . conventionally by the hand being closed and held near the breast; then, as the fore arm is suddenly extended, the hand is opened and the fingers separated from each other. If the person at whose expense the sign is made is present, the hand is moved towards him and the head sometimes averted from him.' This sudden extension and opening of the hand perhaps indicates the dropping or throwing away a valueless object.

1595. SHAKSPEARE, *Romeo and Juliet*, i., 1. I will BITE MY THUMB at them; which is a disgrace to them if they bear it.

1596. LODGE, *Wit's Miserie*. Behold next I see Contempt marching forth, giving me the fies, WITH HIS THOMBE IN HIS MOUTH.

1638. RANDOLPH, *Muses' L. Glass*, O. Pl., ix., 220. Dogs and pistols! To BITE HIS THUMB at me! Wear I a sword To see men BITE THEIR THUMBS?

1678. *Rules of Civility*, transl. from French, p. 44. 'Tis no less disrespectful TO BITE THE NAIL OF YOUR THUMB, by way of scorn and disdain, and drawing your nail from between your teeth, to tell them you value not this what they can do.

BITE UP, *subs.* (tailors').—An unpleasant altercation.

BIT-FAKER or **TURNER OUT**, *subs.* (thieves'). — Coiner of bad money. [From BIT, an old canting term for money, + FAKER, one who makes, or does.] Also BIT-MAKER.—*See* TURNER OUT and FAKER.

BIT FAKING, *subs.* (thieves').—Manufacturing base coin; counterfeiting. [From BIT + FAKE + ING. — *See* preceding.] *Cf.*, TURNER OUT.

BITING UP, *subs.* (tailors').—Grieving over a loss or bereavement.

BIT-MAKER, *subs.* (old).—A counterfeiter.—*See* BIT-FAKER.

1857. SNOWDEN, *Mag. Assistant*, 3 ed., p. 447. Coiners—BIT-MAKERS.

BIT-O'-BULL, *subs.* (old). — Beef. The French say *un gobet*; formerly, a dainty morsel.

BIT OF BLOOD, *subs.* (common).—A high-spirited horse; a thoroughbred. The derivation is obvious. For synonyms, *see* PRAD.

1819. MOORE, *Tom Crib's Memorial to Congress*, p. 10.
'Mong the vehicles, too, which were many and various,
From *natty barouche* down to *buggy precarious*,
We twigg'd more than one *queerish* sort of *turn-out*,
C—N N—G came in a *job*, and then canter'd about
On a showy, but hot and unsound, BIT OF BLOOD,
(For a *leader* once meant, but cast off, as no good).

1843. DICKENS, *Martin Chuzzlewit*, II., p. 156. Not that we slacken in our pace the while, not we: we rather put the BITS OF BLOOD upon their mettle.

BIT OF CAVALRY, *subs.* (old).—A horse.

1821. W. T. MONCRIEFF, *Tom and Jerry*, Act i., Sc. 6. *Tom.* You are now at Tattersal's, Jerry, a very worthy fellow, who made his fortune by a horse called Highflyer. *Jerry.* Hum! and if one may judge from the splendour and extent of his premises, he seems to be no small highflyer himself. *Tom.* You are right, Jerry—I shall here buy a BIT OF CAVALRY—that is *a prad*, on your judgment.

BIT OF EBONY, *subs.* (common).—A negro or negress. For synonyms, *see* SNOWBALL.

BIT OF FAT, *subs.* (common).—1. An unexpected pecuniary advantage in a transaction.

2. (printers'.)—*See* FAT.

BIT OF JAM.—*See* JAM.

BIT OF LEAF, *subs.* (thieves').—Tobacco.

BIT OF MUSLIN, *subs.* (common).—A young girl; generally applied only to prostitutes. Also BIT OF STUFF. For synonyms, *see* BARRACK-HACK.

BIT OF MUTTON, *subs.* (familiar).—A woman; generally, a prostitute is meant. *Cf.*, LACED MUTTON, and for synonyms, *see* BARRACK-HACK.

BIT OF STICKS, *subs. phr.* (sporting).—A corpse. For synonyms, *see* DEAD MEAT.

BIT OF STIFF, *subs.* (common).—A bank-note, or other paper money; the equivalent of money when not in specie, *i.e.*, a draft or bill of exchange.

1854. LEVER, *Dodd Family Abroad*, I., 313. I'm sorry that BIT OF STIFF, meaning the bill, wasn't for five thousand francs.

1876. HINDLEY, *Life and Adventures of a Cheap Jack*, p. 234. He liked to have the party's name written across a piece of paper with a stamp attached, commonly called a BIT OF STIFF.

TO DO A BIT OF STIFF, *phr.* (common).—To accept a bill.

BIT OF STUFF, *subs.* (familiar).—An overdressed man; a man with full confidence in his appearance and abilities; a young woman; also called a BIT OF MUSLIN.

1835. MARRYAT, *Jacob Faithful*, ch. xxiii. 'One night he says to me, "Will, come up and I'll show you a devilish fine PIECE OF STUFF." So I walks with him, and he takes me to a shop where they dealed in marine stores, and we goes and finds your mother in the back parlour.'

BIT ON.—*See* ON.

BITTER, *subs.* (popular).—A glass of beer.

TO DO A BITTER.—To drink a glass of bitter. Originally, says Hotten, an Oxford term varied by TO DO A BEER.

1853. REV. E. BRADLEY ('Cuthbert Bede'), *Verdant Green*, 1st., III., ch. x. Mr. Verdant Green and Mr. Bouncer . . . turned into the coffee-room of 'The Mitre' TO DO BITTERS, as Mr. Bouncer phrased the act of drinking bitter beer.

c. 1882. *Comic Song*, 'The West End Boys,' verse 3.
Let fortune frown and friends betray,
There's a class of men that's ever gay,
Where some make troubles, they make joys,
And are known by the title of the West End Boys.
They commence their evening with cigars,
And 'How-d'ye-do, dear,' at the bars,
'Another BITTER, I really can't go,
There's something about you that charms me so.'
Oh, don't they like, etc.

BITTOCK, *subs.* (originally provincial; now common).—A distance of very undecided length. If a North countryman be asked the distance to a place, he will most probably reply, 'a mile and a BITTOCK.' The latter may be considered any distance from one hundred yards to ten miles. Also of time. [From BIT + OCK, a diminutive suffix.]

1802. J. WILSON ('Congleton'), *M.S. Let. to F. Boucher.* BITTOCK, a small Piece or small Bit; *Cheshire.* [M.]

1816. SCOTT, *Old Mortality*, ch. x. 'To Chamwood, madam? It's unco late, and its sax miles an' a BITTOCK down the water.'

1884. *Daily News*, April 15, p. 4, col. 7. Edinburgh University is three hundred years old, or rather, three hundred years and a BITTOCK.

BIT YOU.—A HAIR OF THE DOG THAT BIT YOU.—*See* HAIR.

BIVVY or **GATTER**, *subs.* (provincial).—Beer; 'shant of BIVVY,' a pot or quart of beer; probably from the *Italian*, BEVERE, BERE. *Latin*, BIBERE. *English*, BEVERAGE.

BIZ, *subs.* (originally American, now general).—A vulgar corruption for business, employment, or occupation. 'Good BIZ' is profitable business.

1882. *Democracy*, ch. vii. A number of gentlemen were waiting for interviews with the President, and among them was the whole Pennsylvania delegation, ready for BIZ, as Mr. Tom Lord remarked, with a wink.

1884. *Saturday Review*, Jan. 5, p. 13, col. 2. It is satisfactory to learn from the conductor of the circus that BIZ is very fair.

1889. *Ally Sloper*, Aug. 17, p. 262, col. 1. We understand, though we cannot vouch for the truth of the statement, that a New York lady, moving in the best society, while twisting some worsted, hit upon the idea of applying a little system of her own to a larger field than mere yarn, so she invented a machine for twisting wire rope, and has sold the patent for £10,000 and a royalty upon future sales. Very good BIZ, this, eh!

B. K. S., *subs.* (military). — An abbreviation of 'barracks'; its usage is explained by quotation.

1887. *Standard*, 10 Feb., p. 5, col. 2. B. K. S., used by officers 'in mufti,' who do not wish to give their address.

BLAB, *subs.* (vulgar).—A revealer of that which should be kept secret; a betrayer; a babbler. A depraved word; once in common use, but rarely employed now, except colloquially. Grose [1785] includes it in his *Dictionary of the Vulgar Tongue* as forming part of the slang of his time. These remarks apply with more or less cogency to BLAB when used to signify loose talk or chatter, when employed as a verb, and to the various derivative compounds and allied forms, such as 'blabber,' 'blabbing,' 'blabbing-book,' etc.—a taint of vulgarism now rests upon them all.

BLACK ACT, *subs.* (American).—A corrupted form of BLACK ART (*q.v.*).

BLACKAMOOR'S TEETH, *subs.* (old).—Cowrie shells—the currency of some savage tribes.

1700. W. KING, *Transactioneer*, p. 36. He has shells called BLACKMOORE'S TEETH, I suppose . . . from their Whiteness. [M.]

1719. W. WOOD, *Surv. Trade*, p. 334. Known by the Name of Cowries amongst Merchants, or of BLACKAMORES' TEETH among other Persons. [M.]

BLACK-AND-TAN, *subs.* (vagrants').—Porter or stout and ale, mixed in equal quantities. [From BLACK, in allusion to the dark colour of porter and stout, + AND + TAN, *i.e.*, of the yellowish brown colour of ale.]

BLACK-AND-TAN COUNTRY, *subs. phr.* (American). — The Southern States of North America. [From BLACK, a sobriquet for a negro, + AND + TAN, a pun and an allusion to the slang verb 'to tan,' to thrash or beat + COUNTRY; *i.e.*, the country where the negroes were tanned or beaten.]

BLACK AND WHITE, *subs. phr.* (colloquial).—The black characters of print or writing on white paper. Therefore, to put a thing down in BLACK AND WHITE is to preserve it in writing or in print. BLACK ON WHITE is a variant.

1596. JONSON, *Every Man in His Humour*, IV., ii. I have it here in BLACK AND WHITE. [*Pulls out the warrant.*]

1667. SHIRLEY, *Love Tricks*, Act ii., Sc. 2. *Gov.* [with a letter] . . . Alas, poor gentleman! Little does he think what BLACK AND WHITE is here.

1712. *Spectator*, No. 286. My desire is, Sir, that you will be pleased to give us, in BLACK AND WHITE, your opinion in the matter of dispute between us.

1714. *Spectator*, No. 616. They had like to have dumfounded the justice; but his clerk came in to his assistance, and took them all down in BLACK AND WHITE.

1887. CARLYLE, *French Revolution*, pt. III., bk. II., ch. viii. His accounts lie all ready, correct in BLACK AND WHITE to the uttermost farthing.

1874. MRS. H. WOOD, *Johnny Ludlow*, 1 S., No. xii., p. 202. 'A man can't so much as put on a pair of clean stockings in the morning, but its laid before high quarters in BLACK AND WHITE at mid-day by the secret police!'

BLACK-ARSE, *subs.* (old).—A kettle; a pot. [From BLACK, from its colour, + ARSE, the posterior, hinder, or 'bottom' part.]

BLACK ART, *subs.* (old).—1. Picking of locks; burglary. For synonyms, *see* CRACK.

1591. GREENE, *Conny-Catch.*, wks., 1883, II., x., 72. I can set down the subtiltie of the BLACKE ART, which is picking of lockes.

1608. DEKKER, *Belman of Lond.*, wks., 1884-5, III., 137. This BLACKE ART. . . . is called in English, Picking of Lockes.

1785. GROSE, *Dictionary of the Vulgar Tongue.* BLACK ART, the art of picking a lock.

1811. *Lexicon Balatronicum.* [The definition given is the same as that of Grose, as above-mentioned.]

2. (undertakers'.)—The business of an undertaker. *Cf.*, BLACK WORK.

1861. SALA, *Seven Sons of Mammon*, i., p. 78. Rich men's funerals in the first style of BLACK ART.

BLACK-BALL, *verb* (common).—*See* PILL.

BLACKBALLING, *subs.* (nautical).—Stealing or pilfering. A sailor's word. It originated amongst the employees of the old Black Ball line of steamers between New York and Liverpool. The cruelty and scandalous conduct of officers to men—and sailors to each other—were so proverbial, that the line of vessels in question became known all over the world for the cruelty of its officers, and the thieving propensities of its sailors.

BLACKBEETLES, *subs.* (old).—The lower strata of society. [Apparently a term of contempt derived from the cockroach, generally called a blackbeetle.] Obsolete.

1821. W. T. MONCRIEFF, *Tom and Jerry*, Act ii., Sc. 6. *Jerry*: Tom, here's a group of BLACKBEETLES—do you see those lovely mendicants? *Tom*: Beauty in rags—I do—Cupid imploring charity. I'll relieve him, for I'll be after that match-girl directly. *Jerry*: And I'll chant a few words to that beautiful ballad-singer. *Log*: And I'll take pity on that charming beggar.

BLACKBERRY SWAGGER, *subs.* (common).—A person who hawks tapes, boot-laces, etc.

BLACKBIRD, *subs.* (popular).—Formerly an African captive on board a slaver; now generally understood as referring to a Polynesian indentured labourer, who, if not by name a slave, is often one to all intents and purposes. [Obviously derived from the black or dark-brown colour of these people.]

1881. *Chequered Career*, p. 180. The white men on board knew that if once the BLACKBIRDS burst the hatches . . . they would soon master the ship. [M.]

Verb.—To capture negroes or Polynesians; to kidnap (*see subs.*). Hence the *verbal substantive* and *ppl. adj.* BLACKBIRDING, in the same sense.

1883. *Graphic*, April 21, p. 398, col. 1. The day is not far distant when, to avoid BLACKBIRDING, and the revengeful massacres which these kidnappers provoke, the whole of Oceania will have to be placed under civilised control.

1883. *Academy*, 8 Sep., p. 158. [He] slays Bishop Patteson by way of reprisal for the atrocities of some BLACKBIRDING crew. [M.]

1884. *Pall Mall Gazette*, 19 Aug. p. 2, col. 2. Years ago BLACKBIRDING scoundrels may have hailed from Fiji. [M.]

BLACKBIRD-CATCHING.—*See* BLACKBIRD.

BLACK-BIRDERS, *subs.* (popular).—*See* quotation.

1883. *All the Year Round*, 22 Sep., p. 355. BLACKBIRDERS, the kidnappers for labour purposes on the islands of the Pacific.

BLACK BOX, *subs.* (old).—A lawyer. So given in Grose [1785]; *Lexicon Balatronicum* [1811]; and in Duncombe's *Sinks of London* [1848]. [From the black tin boxes in which clients' papers are kept.]

BLACK-BOY, *subs.* (old).—*See* BLACK-COAT.

BLACK BRACELETS, *subs.* (old).—Handcuffs. For synonyms, *see* DARBIES.

1839. HARRISON AINSWORTH, *Jack Sheppard* [1889], p. 63.
When the turnkey, next morning, stepped into his room,
The sight of the hole in the wall struck him dumb;
The sheriff's BLACK BRACELETS lay strewn on the ground,
But the lad that had worn 'em could nowhere be found.
Tol-de-rol!

BLACK-CATTLE, *subs.* (popular).—1. Clergymen; parsons. [From the prevailing hue of the garments worn by the profession.] Sometimes used in the same way as RED-COATS for soldiers, *e.g.*, BLACK-COATS (*q.v.*); also DEVIL DODGERS, the latter of which, see for synonyms.

2. (old.)—Lice. These are also called ACTIVE CITIZENS and CHATES (*q.v.*).

BLACK-CATTLE SHOW, *subs.* (popular).—A gathering of clergymen. [From BLACK-CATTLE (*q.v.*) + SHOW, in its slang sense of a party or meeting.]

BLACK-COAT, *subs.* (familiar.) — A parson. *Cf.*, BLACK-CATTLE and DEVIL-DODGER.

1627. R. PERROT, *Jacob's Vow*, 52. Let us take heed how these BLACK-COATES get the day of us. [M.]

1671. EACHARD, *Observations*, p. 176. Suppose we should bestow upon a poor low thinking BLACK-COAT, one of our best forms, such as follows; it is five to one he would commit some ecclesiastical blunder or other, in setting his name too near.

1818. SCOTT, *Heart of Midlothian*, i. You are the BLACK-COAT'S son of Knocktarlitie.

1870. EMERSON, *Soc. and Solit.*, ix., p. 197. The BLACK-COATS are good company only for BLACK-COATS. [M.]

BLACK-CUFFS, *subs.* (military).—The Fifty-eight Foot, from the regimental facings which have been black since 1767. They have also been nicknamed THE STEEL BACKS (*q.v.*).

BLACK DIAMONDS, *subs.* (popular).—1. Coals. [A simile in allusion to the colour, and also to the fact that both coal and diamonds are carbon.]

1849. T. MILLER, in *Gabarni in London*, p. 43. Were he even trusted with the favourite horse and gig to fetch a sack of BLACK DIAMONDS from the wharf.

2. Also formerly a rough but clever or good person; this sobriquet, however, has given place to ROUGH DIAMOND (*q.v.*).

BLACK DOG, *subs.* (old). — 1. Applied, *circa* 1702-30, to a counterfeit shilling and other base silver coinage. In this connection it may be pointed out that *black* had long previously been applied to base money. Ruding, in his *Annals of the Coinage* [London, 1817, vol. I., p. 405], having mentioned *black* money, appends this note—'Qy. *Turonenses Nigri?* Copper money struck at Tours.' [*See* Turney's *infra*. Qy. corrupted from Tierney, name of maker.] It is introduced in his account of the Statute of Money, passed at York, 1335, 9 cap., Edward III., which recites that all manner of *black* money which had been commonly current in the king's realm and obeisance should be utterly excluded, so as not to be current in one month after proclamation, on pain of forfeiture of the same. Later on, in 1339, a certain *black* money called 'turneys' was made by

certain persons in Ireland, who circulated it to the injury of the king's sterling money, and to his no little loss and prejudice. Proclamation had, therefore, been ordered to be made to prohibit the circulation of it, on pain of forfeiture of money and goods. But the king having been informed that great inconvenience had arisen from this prohibition on account of the scarcity of sterling money, it was, therefore, commanded that, provided it should be found on due inquiry more advantageous to the public to allow the currency of the said *black* money, proclamation should be made to authorise it until a sufficient quantity of other money was provided.

1706. LUTTRELL, in Ashton's *Reign Queen Anne*, II., p. 225. The Art of making BLACK DOGS, which are shillings, or other pieces of money made only of Pewter, double wash'd. [M.]

1724. SWIFT, *Drapier's Lett.*, wks., 1755, V., ii., 44. Butcher's half-pence, BLACK-DOGS, and others the like. [M.]

2. (common.)—*Delirium tremens*; the horrors; 'jim jams.' BLACK DOG is a frequent figurative expression dialectically for depression of spirits, and melancholy. Among the ancients a black dog and its pups were considered an evil omen. For synonyms, *see* GALLON DISTEMPER.

1861. HUGHES, *Tom Brown at Oxford*, ch. xxxiii. 'Yes, sir,' said the butler, nodding, 'D.T., sir. After one of his rages the BLACK DOG comes, and it's hawful work; so I hope you'll go, sir.'

TO BLUSH LIKE A BLACK DOG, *phr.* (old).—Not to blush at all; to be shameless.—*See* also BLUSH.

1634. WITHAL, *Dictionary*, p. 557 [ed. 1634]. *Faciem perfricuit.* He BLUSHETH LIKE A BLACK DOGGE, hee hath a brazen face.

BLACK DOLL.—*See* DOLLY SHOP.

1835. CHARLES DICKENS, *Sketches by Boz*, p. 174. [Speaking of a marine-store shop]: imagine, in addition to this incongruous mass, a BLACK DOLL in a white frock, with two faces—one looking up the street, the other looking down, swinging over the door.

1838. DOUGLAS JERROLD, *Men of Character*, II., p. 100. Five hundred articles, among which might be found knockers, scrapers, barbers' poles, BLACK DOLLS.

1861. *Cornhill Magazine*, Nov., p. 609. The best price given for old rags—inquire at the sign of the BLACK DOLL.

BLACK-EYE. TO GIVE A BOTTLE A BLACK EYE, *phr.* (old).—To empty it. *Cf.*, DEAD MAN.

BLACK-EYED SUSAN, *subs.* (American).—Texan for a revolver. Among other slang equivalents for this weapon current in the Lone Star State may be mentioned MEAT IN THE POT, BLUE LIGHTNING, THE PEACE-MAKER, MR. SPEAKER, A ONE-EYED SCRIBE, PILL BOX and MY UNCONVERTED FRIEND. For synonyms, *see* MEAT IN THE POT.

BLACK-FLY, *subs.* (old).—A contemptuous name for a clergyman. For synonyms, *see* DEVIL-DODGER.

1811. *Lexicon Balatronicum.* The greatest drawback on the farmer is the BLACK FLY, *i.e.*, the parson who takes tithe of the harvest.

BLACKFRIARS! *intj.* (thieves').—An exclamation of warning; look out! beware!—*See* THIEVES.

BLACKGUARD, *subs.* (common).—A man coarse in speech, and offensive in manner; a scamp; a scoundrel; a disreputable fellow. The term, as now used, is one of the utmost opprobrium, and although a good deal of uncertainty hangs about its history and derivation, it seems pretty clear that a certain amount of odium has always been attached to the word. Between two of its primary significations, however,—(1) a kitchen knave or scullion, and (2) a guard of attendants, black in person, dress, or character, generally in reference to the devil's body-guard—and the modern usage, there is a somewhat marked line to be drawn. The earliest mention is as follows :—

1532. *MS. Churchwarden's Accompts. St. Margaret's, Westminster* (Receipts for burials). Item Receyvid for the lycens of iiij. torchis of the BLAKE GARDE vjd.

What this guard was is not definitely known. Some have suggested that it was a body of soldiers; others that it was a band of torch bearers at funerals; while some incline to the belief that it was comprised of street link-boys.

Better supported by evidence are the senses first mentioned, in which BLACKGUARD signifies (1) a scullion, and (2) a member of the devil's body-guard. But here too, Murray points out that it would be difficult to assign priority. First, however, let the quotations be given in sets :—

SENSE 1 = a scullion.

1535. SIR W. FITZWILLIAMS, 17 Aug., in *Cal. State Papers*. Two of the ring-leaders had been some time of the BLACK GUARD of the king's kitchen. [M.]

1579. FULKE, *Refut. Kastel*, 779. They ought not, nor yet any of the scullerie or BLACKE GARDE. [M.]

SENSE 2 = Devil's body-guard; also other attendants.

1583. FULKE, *Defence*, x., 386. Pelagius, Celestins, and other like heretics of the devil's body-guard. [M.]

1609. DEKKER, *Lanthorne and Candlelight*, wks. [1884-5] III., 214. The Great Lord of Limbo did therefore commaund all his BLACKE GUARD that stood about him, to bestirre them. [M.]

Comparing these one with the other, we are clearly face to face in one set of quotations with a popular superstition—a belief of an age when witchcraft was prevalent, and when hobgoblins and the like were assigned as BLACK GUARDS to his Satanic Majesty. Whether there was any connection in the popular mind between the King's scullions and the Devil's body-guard, cannot now be definitely stated. Still, it is probable; and this view is borne out by later references. It is curious to note the concluding lines of Hudibras' Address to Ralpho, which may perhaps explain the process by which the term of BLACK GUARD may have come to be applied to the lowest class of domestics in the royal kitchens or other great establishments. Still, as stated, priority cannot be given to either; moreover, the use of BLACK GUARD in either sense may have been a mere play on words, whether of 1 on 2, or 2 on 1 is equally uncertain. The quotation from Hudibras is as follows:

1678. BUTLER, *Hudibras*, pt. III., canto 1, line 1403.
I do believe thee, quoth the knight;
Thus far I'm sure thou'rt in the right,
And know what 'tis that troubles thee,
Better than thou hast guess'd of me.
Thou art some paltry, BLACKGUARD *sprite*,
Condemn'd to drudg'ry in the night;
Thou hast no work to do in th' house,
Nor half-penny to drop in shoes;
Without the raising of which sum
You dare not be so troublesome;
To pinch the slatterns black and blue,
For leaving you their work to do.
This is your business, good Pug Robin,
And your diversion, dull dry bobbing.

So also the following :—

1655. FULLER, *Church History* [1845], vol. V., p. 160. For who can otherwise conceive but such a prince-principal of darkness must be proportionately attended with a BLACK GUARD of monstrous opinions.

The BLACK GUARD of Satan, argues a writer in *Notes and Queries* [Sir J. Emmerson Tennent, *N. and Q.*, 1 S., vii., 78], was supposed, in the popular view, to perform the drudgery of the kitchen and servants' hall in the infernal household.

1588-1628. HOBBES, *Microcosmus*, vol. II., p. 134. Since my lady's decay I am degraded from a cook, and I fear the devil himself will entertain me but for one of his BLACKGUARDS, and he shall be sure to have his roast burnt.

Hence came the popular superstition that these goblin scullions, on their visits to the upper world confined themselves to the servants' apartments of the houses which they favoured with their presence, and which at night they swept and garnished; pinching those of the maids in their sleep who, by their laziness, had imposed such toil on their elfin assistants; but slipping money into the shoes of the more tidy and industrious servants whose attention to their own duties before going to rest had spared the goblins the task of performing their share of the drudgery. In allusion to this is Gifford's note on Ben Jonson's plays [vol. II., p. 170],—

In all great houses, but particularly in the Royal Residences, there were a number of mean dirty dependents, whose office it was to attend the woolyard, sculleries, etc. Of these, the most forlorn wretches seem to have been selected to carry coals to the kitchens, halls, etc. To this smutty regiment, who attended the progresses, and rode in the carts with the pots and kettles, which, with every other article of furniture, were then removed from palace to palace, the people, in derision, gave the name of BLACK GUARDS; a term since become sufficiently familiar, and never properly explained.

Many other references also go to prove the connection in the popular mind, so far as usage is concerned, between the two significations. In all this, however, the peculiarly contemptuous odium attached to the word in modern times is absent, and between the old and the modern significations a sharp line may, as already stated, be drawn.

The earliest reference to BLACKGUARD as applied to a vagabond or loafer occurs in 1683. Since that time the word seems gradually to have become more and more depraved, until its present meaning of a low, worthless fellow, one open to, and ready for any villainy has been reached. The following quotations will well repay comparative study.

1683. *MS.*, in Lord Steward's Office, Windsor Castle [*N. and Q.*, 1 S., ix., p. 15]. 7 May, Whereas of late a sort of vicious, idle, and masterless boys and rogues, commonly called the BLACKGUARD, with divers other lewd and loose fellowes, vagabonds, vagrants, and wandering men and women, do usually haunt and follow the Court.

1695. CONGREVE, *Love for Love*, Act iii., Sc. 10. Or if that won't do, I'll bring a Lawyer that shall out-lye the Devil: and so I'll try whether my BLACK-GUARD or his shall get the better of the day.

1744. Nov. 26, WALPOLE, *Lett. to Mann* (1833), II., 57. The whole stage filled with BLACKGUARDS, armed with bludgeons and clubs.

1780. *Parody on the Rosciad, etc.*, p. 13. Like him I'm a BLACKGUARD and sot.

1788. G. A. STEVENS, *Adv. of a Speculist*, i., 59. As BLACK-GUARDS at Newmarket meeting bawl about the lists of horses.

1874. MRS. H. WOOD, *Johnny Ludlow*, 1 S., No. iii., p. 37. 'I must request you to be a little more careful in your language. You have come amidst gentlemen here, not BLACKGUARDS.'

Adj.—Of or pertaining to a blackguard; to the scum or refuse of society; vile; vicious.

1760. SMOLLETT, *Sir L. Greaves*, vol. II., ch. ix. He is become a BLACKGUARD gaol-bird.

1803. C. K. SHARPE, in *Correspondence* (1888), I., 178. His friends were ill-natured, and behaved like BLACKGUARD beasts.

Verb.—To act like a ruffian; to use filthy, scurrilous language; to play the vagabond or scoundrel.

1855. THACKERAY, *Newcomes*, ch. xxix. 'I have been called names, and BLACKGUARDED quite sufficiently for one sitting.'

So also with other derivatives and compounds—BLACKGUARDISM, BLACKGUARDIZE, BLACKGUARDLY, BLACKGUARDRY.

1781. G. PARKER, *View of Society*, I., 124. The talent of common BLACKGUARDISM.

1849. C. KINGSLEY, *Alton Locke*, ch. v. I was awakened by being shoved through the folding-doors of a gin-shop, into a glare of light and hubbub of BLACKGUARDISM.

1861. H. KINGSLEY, *Ravenshoe*, ch. xxvi. 'I beg your pardon, sir, for saying that; I said it in a hurry. It was BLACKGUARDLY.'

1883. WILLIAM MORRIS, reported in *Illust. London News*, March 10, p. 243, col. 3. Almost all ordinary wares now made by man were shabbily and pretentiously ugly . . . Not even the pine-trees and gardens could make the rich men's houses at Bournemouth tolerable. They were simply BLACKGUARDLY; and even as he spoke they were being built by the mile.

BLACK HOLE, *subs.* (Anglo-Indian).—Cheltenham, from the number of retired Anglo-Indians who live there. *Cf.*, ASIA MINOR.

1878. *Notes and Queries*, 5 S., x., p. 234, col. 1. Gained for Cheltenham the . . . title of THE BLACK HOLE.

BLACK HORSE, *subs.* (military).—A nickname of the Seventh Dragoon Guards, so called from the regimental facings, black on scarlet. Occasionally the epithet is shortened into THE BLACKS. During the reign of George II., the corps was known as THE VIRGIN MARY'S GUARD, and is now often called STRAWBOOTS (*q.v.*).

BLACK HOUSE, *subs.* (trade).—A place of business where hours are long, and wages at starvation rates; a sweating house.

1851. MAYHEW, *London Labour and London Poor*, III., p. 234. I have mentioned that the BLACK HOUSES or linen-drapers at the west end of London, were principally supplied from the east end.

BLACK INDIES, *subs.* (old).—Newcastle-on-Tyne, from its wealth in coal. The term is now obsolete, but it was in common use at the latter part of the eighteenth century.

BLACK JACK, *subs.* (Winchester College).—A large leathern jug for beer, holding two gallons. The term was not peculiar to Winchester; in olden times JACKS were common everywhere.

(?) *Simon the Cellarer.* But oh, oh, oh! his nose doth show, How oft the BLACK JACK to his lips doth go.

BLACK JOB, *subs.* (common). — A funeral. Mr. H. J. Byron, in his annotated copy of the *Slang Dictionary* states 'it was the late Lord Portsmouth's hobby to attend all the BLACK JOBS he could hear of.' [From BLACK, in reference to the sombre trappings of funerals + JOB].—*See* BLACK WORK.

1866. YATES, *Land at Last*, I., p. 101. 'What, a funeral mute?' 'Yes, Sir, BLACK-JOB business,' etc.

BLACK JOKE, *subs.* (old). — The female *pudenda*. — *See* MONOSYLLABLE for synonyms. Said to have been the burden of an obscene song, *circa* 1811.

BLACKLEG, *subs.* (common). — 1. A turf swindler; a rook; a welsher; also one who cheats at cards or billiards. Origin unknown; although many speculations have been hazarded, none are satisfactory.—*See* LEG.

1771. B. PARSONS, *Newmarket*, II., 163. The frequenters of the Turf, and numberless words of theirs are exotics everywhere else; then how should we have been told of BLACKLEGS, and of *town-tops . . . taken in . . . beat hollow*, etc. [M.]

1774. COLMAN, *Man of Business*, I., in wks. (1777) II., 133. Countesses and semptresses, lords, aldermen, BLACKLEGS, and Oxonians.

1812. COOMBE, *Dr. Syntax, Picturesque*, ch. x. The crowd with their commission pleas'd, Rudely the trembling BLACK-LEG seiz'd, Who, to their justice forc'd to yield, Soon ran off dripping from the field.

1830. S. WARREN, *Diary of a Late Physician*, ch. xv. 'Mr. T—— is pursuing quite disgraceful courses all night and day, squandering away his money among sharpers and BLACKLEGS.'

2. A workman who, when his fellows are on strike, is willing to go on working. An opprobrious term. *Cf.*, BLACKNOB and SCAB.

1865. *Pall Mall Gazette*, 29 Oct., p. 7. If the timber merchants persist in putting on BLACKLEGS, a serious disturbance will ensue. [M.]

3. Also by another transference of meaning applied to any one failing, or refusing to join his fellows in combination for a given purpose.

1889. *Pall Mall Gazette*, Nov. 21, p. 5, col. 1. It was stated at the meeting that the master bakers were much behind the journeymen in the matter of organisation, and the difficulty of maintaining the price against unscrupulous bakers at 'a living figure' was emphasized. The question of the preparation of a list of master baker 'BLACKLEGS' was also touched upon. These men are selling bread at 4½d. the quartern, and at even a lower rate.

Verb (tailors').—Amongst the fraternity of 'snips,' TO BLACKLEG is used as synonymous with 'to boycott'—*i.e.*, to make things so uncomfortable for a man that he is compelled to leave his work or the town.

TO BLACKLEG IT, *phr.* (trades').—Amongst trades' union men to return to work before the causes of a strike have been removed, or settled to the satisfaction of the leaders.

1888. *Baltimore Herald*, May 6. Early this morning the mountain paths leading to the William Pen colliery were lined with men, dinner in hand, determined to go to work. Some were non-union miners, while the remainder were Knights of Labor who had determined TO BLACKLEG IT, regardless of the jeers and threats of their companions.

BLACK-LEGGISM, BLACK-LEGGERY, *subs.* (common). — Cheating; swindling; the arts and practices of a BLACKLEG (*q.v.*—sense 1).

1832. MAGINN, in *Blackwood's Mag.*, XXXII., 427. From following any profession save the Army, the Navy, Blackapronry and BLACK-LEGGERY. [M.]

BLACK-MAN or **BLACK GENTLEMAN**, *subs.* (old).—The devil. For synonyms, *see* SKIPPER.

1606. DEKKER, in *Newes from Hell*, in wks. (Grosart) II., 113. [Old Nick called the BLACK GENTLEMAN.]

1861. G. MEREDITH, *Evan Harrington*, ch. iii., p. 23 (1885). 'Rich as Crœsus, and as wicked as the BLACK MAN below! as dear papa used to say.'

BLACKMANS.—*See* DARKMANS.

BLACK MARIA, *subs.* (popular).—A prison van or omnibus, used for the conveyance of prisoners. The origin of the phrase is unknown, but BLACK is obviously from the dark and sombre colour of HER MAJESTY'S CARRIAGE as it is sometimes jocularly called. This view is also supported by the fact that a variant is SABLE MARIA (*see* quot.). Julian Marshall, in *Notes and Queries* [6 S., vii., p. 355], suggests that the term MARIA may be allied to 'Marinated,' transported to some foreign plantation, and 'married,' persons chained or handcuffed together, in order to be conveyed to gaol [Grose has this, as also has the *Lexicon Balatronicum*]. In *marinated* evident allusion is made to the compulsory voyage; in *married* to the forced wedlock of convictism. BLACK MARIA may, therefore, possibly be a corruption of one or the other, or both terms. A writer on slang states that the term is said to have originated in Philadelphia in 1838, but gives no evidence in support of the statement.

1877. *Five Years' Penal Servitude*, ch. ii., p. 61. On alighting from the 'SABLE MARIA' we were ushered through a door into a long white-washed passage, with cells on one side.

1880. G. R. SIMS, *Three Brass Balls*, pledge xvii. It is the time when BLACK MARIA, the prison van, stands waiting at the door, and the signal is given that the prisoners are coming out.

1889. *Answers*, Feb. 9. There are two kinds of BLACK MARIAS. One is called the night van and the other the day. The passengers politely term them 'mails.' The day van holds eighteen passengers not including the driver and warder, and the night van a dozen. The vans are divided into two halves, and on each side are small compartments about two feet square with a seat and door, which is carefully locked.

Amongst FRENCH SYNONYMS may be mentioned:—*Le courrier du Palais* (a thieves' term: *courrier*, a post or mail + *Palais*, an abbreviated form of *Palais de Justice*, a police court or sessions house); *un panier à salade* (familiar: 'a salad basket'); *le courrier de la préfecture* (thieves': *Cf.*, *courrier du Palais*. *Préfecture* = the office of a chief magistrate); *l'omnibus pègres* (in slang *un pègre* signifies 'a thief'); *un guimbard* (thieves': *une guimbarde* is properly 'a long cart'); *le service du château* (roughs' and thieves': 'the prison service'; *château* = prison).

For other synonyms, *see* HER MAJESTY'S CARRIAGE.

BLACK-MONDAY, *subs.* (old).—1. A schoolboys' term for the Monday on which, after holidays, school re-opens. Obviously called *black*, from the reluctance with which young hopefuls turn their backs upon the sweets of home and play. BLACK FRIDAY was used of the day on which Overend, Gurney & Co., suspended payment—10 May, 1866. *Cf.*, BLUE MONDAY.

1750. FIELDING, *Tom Jones*, bk. VIII., ch. xi. She now hated my sight, and made home so disagreeable to me, that what is called by school-boys BLACK MONDAY was to me the whitest in the whole year.

1882. F. ANSTEY, *Vice Versâ*, ch. i. There comes a time when the days are grudgingly counted to a BLACKER MONDAY than ever makes a schoolboy's heart quake within him.

2. (popular.)—The Monday on which the death penalty is carried out; these events are generally arranged to fall on the day in question.

BLACK-MUMMER, *subs.* (old).—An epithet applied to one unwashed and unshorn.

BLACK-NOB, *subs.* (trades' union).—A non-unionist; one who, while his fellows are on strike, persists in working at his trade; a BLACKLEG (*q.v.*). [Apparently a humorous variant of BLACKLEG. From BLACK = wicked, atrocious, + NOB, the head, in place of *leg* in BLACKLEG.] They are also called KNOBSTICKS and SCABS (*q.v.*).

BLACK OINTMENT, *subs.* (American thieves').—A term for uncooked meat.

BLACK-POT, *subs.* (old).—A toper; a tippler. [Beer mugs were called BLACK-POTS; also BLACK-JACKS, hence, probably, a transference of the name from the utensil to the drinker.]

1594. GREENE, *Fr. Bacon*, v., 122. I'll be Prince of Wales over all the BLACK-POTS in Oxford.

1636. HEYWOOD, *Love's Mistr.*, II. Iugg, what's shee but sister to a BLACK-POT.

1818. SCOTT, *Heart of Midlothian*, xxxii. A whole whiskin, or BLACK-POT of sufficient double ale.

BLACK PSALM. TO SING THE BLACK PSALM, *phr.* (old).—To cry; a saying used to children.—*Grose.*

BLACKS.—*See* BLACK HORSE.

BLACK SAL or **SUKE**, *subs.* (popular).—A kettle.—*See* SUKEY for synonyms.

BLACK SATURDAY, *subs.* (workmen's).—A Saturday on which an artisan or mechanic has no money to take, having anticipated it by advances. *Cf.*, BLACK MONDAY and BLUE MONDAY.

BLACK-SHEEP, *subs.* (common).—A mildly opprobrious term for a scapegrace; a 'bad lot'; '*un mauvais sujet.*' It is also applied like BLACKLEG and BLACK-NOB to workmen who persist in working when their comrades are on strike. The word is hardly slang now.

1864. LE FANU, *Uncle Silas*, ch. xxvi. 'Your Uncle Silas had injured himself before that in the opinion of the people of his county. He was a BLACK SHEEP, in fact. Very bad stories were told and believed of him.'

1874. M. COLLINS, *Frances*, ch. xxxvii. 'In all cities there are BLACK SHEEP, but in a city like London, sound finance is the rule, I am sure.'

1876. BESANT AND RICE, *Golden Butterfly*, ch. xxviii. 'Many companies, perfectly sound in principle, may be ruined by a sudden decrease in the price of shares; a panic sets in, and in a few hours the shareholders may lose all. And if you bring this about by selling without concert with the other favoured allottees, you'll be called a BLACK SHEEP.

Verb (Winchester College).—When a fellow in 'Junior Part' got above (or 'jockeyed') a fellow in 'Middle Part.'

BLACKSMITH'S DAUGHTER, *subs.* (popular).—A key. Formerly the key with which the doors of sponging houses were unlocked. Also LOCKSMITH'S DAUGHTER, which *see* for synonyms.

1859. C. DICKENS, *Tale of Two Cities.* Place it under the care of the BLACKSMITH'S DAUGHTER.

1864. *Reader* [quoted in *N. and Q.*, 5 S., ix., 263]. BLACKSMITH'S DAUGHTER. A key. I have never met with this word in print, but have heard it frequently in conversation.

BLACK-SPICE RACKET, *subs.* (old).—The practice of robbing chimney sweepers of their tools, bag, and soot.—*Lexicon Balatronicum.*

BLACK SPY, *subs.* (old).—A cant name for the devil. The French equivalent is *le dache*. For synonyms, *see* SKIPPER.

BLACK-STRAP, *subs.* (common).—1. Thick, sweet port. A contemptuous term, in allusion to its dark colour, STRAP being an old name for wine.—(*See* quot.).

1608. DEKKER, *Belman of London*, in wks. (Grosart) III., 131. Sometimes likewise this *Card-cheating*, goes not vnder the name of *Bernard's Lawe*, but is called *Batt fowling*, and then ye *Setter* is the *Beater*, the foole that is caught in the net, the bird, the *Tauerne* to which they repaire to worke the *Feate*, is the *Bush*; the wine the STRAP, and the cardes the *Limetwigs*.

1821. MONCRIEFF, *Tom and Jerry*, p. 3. *Tom* (*taking his seat*): Gentlemen, I beg pardon for being scarce so long; but having to start early, I thought it best to see that the *toggery* was all right and *fly*—I never shirk the BLACK STRAP intentionally, you know. *Jerry*: Don't mention it, my dear Tom.

1853. WH. MELVILLE, *Digby Grand*, ch. x. The orator gets deeper into his subject, till an extremely abrupt conclusion . . . empties every bumper of 'BLACK STRAP' like a shot.

2. (American.) — Properly speaking, gin mixed with molasses, but frequently applied to a compound of any alcoholic liquor with molasses. Beverages of this description were at one time the commonest of drinks among agricultural labourers.

1882. PINKERTON, *Molly Maguires and Detectives*, p. 84. From the great iron kettle a savory incense arose; it came from an admixture of high-wines and common molasses, in about the proportion of one gallon of the latter to four of the spirit. . . . The seething BLACKSTRAP was pronounced ready for use. It rapidly disappeared, and, as it diminished and was imbibed, the fun and hilarity proportionately increased.

3. (old.)—A task of labour imposed on soldiers at Gibraltar as a punishment for small offences.—*Grose.*

BLACK'S YOUR EYE. TO SAY BLACK'S YOUR EYE, *phr.* (old).—To accuse; to find fault with. The phrase was varied by BLACK'S YOUR EYEBROW, NAIL, etc. A more modern rendering is BLACK IS THE WHITE OF YOUR EYE.

1528. ROY, *Sat.* (1845). They eate their belies full . . . . And none sayth BLACKE IS HIS EYE. [M.]

1583. STUBBS, *Anatomie of Abuses*, p. 65. And then no man say BLACKE IS THEIR EYE, but all is well, and they as good Christians, as those that suffer them unpunished.

1647. BEAUMONT AND FLETCHER, *Love's Cure*, iii., 1. I can say BLACK'S YOUR EYE, though it be grey; I have conniv'd at this your friend, and you.

1750. FIELDING, *Tom Jones*, IX., iv. The house is well known to be a house of as good reputation as any on the road, and, though I say it, is frequented by gentry of the best quality, both Irish and English. I defy anybody, to say BLACK IS MY EYE, for that matter.

BLACK-TEAPOT, *subs.* (popular).—A negro footman.

BLACKWORK, *subs.* (common).—Undertaking. The waiters met with at public dinners are often employed during the day as mutes, etc. Omnibus and cab drivers regard BLACKWORK as *un dernier ressort*.—*See* BLACK-JOB.

1859. SALA, *Gaslight and Daylight*, ch. xxvi. A florid man who officiates as a waiter at the London Tavern o'nights, and sometimes takes a spell in the BLACK WORK, or undertaking line of business.

BLADDER OF LARD, *subs.* (popular).—A bald-headed person. [From the supposed similarity of the smooth, hairless cranium to a bag or bladder of lard.]

1886. *Athenæum*, July 31, p. 142. An elderly Jew money-lender, whom she afterwards describes to her admiring friends as a BLADDER OF LARD, a graceful reference to his baldness and tendency to stoutness.

BLADE, *subs.* (common.)—A roysterer; a gallant; a sharp, keen fellow; a free and easy, good fellow. [Probably from BLADE, a sword, a soldier. There seems no warrant for supposing the word connected with the Dutch *bloed*, or with the term 'blood,' a dandy, in use in the time of the Georges in a somewhat similar sense; indeed, the following quotations show a much older usage. In French a 'sly BLADE' is called *un renaré*.

1595. SHAKSPEARE, *Romeo and Juliet*, ii., 4. The pox of such antic, lisping, affecting fantasticoes; these new tuners of accents! *By Jesu, a very good* BLADE !—*a very tall man* !

1632. CHAPMAN AND SHIRLEY, *The Ball*, Act iv.

This came first o' keeping company with the BLADES,
From whom I learnt to roar and run away.

1636. DAVENANT, *The Wits*, Act v.

The old BLADE
Skulks there like a tame filcher, as he had
New stolen 'bove eggs from market-women.

1637. FLETCHER, *Elder Brother*, I., ii.

If he be that old
Rough testy BLADE he always used to be.

1664. PEPYS, *Diary*, Jan. 4. For suffering his man (a spruce BLADE) to be so saucy as to strike a ball while his master was playing in the Mall.

1667. PEPYS, *Diary*, June 3. With his hat cocked like a fool behind, as the present fashion among the BLADES is.

1698. FARQUHAR, *Love and a Bottle*, Act iv., Sc. 2. These London BLADES are all stark mad; I met one about two hours ago, that had forgot his name, and this fellow would persuade me now, that I had forgot mine.

1748. T. DYCHE, *Dictionary* (5 ed.). BLADE (S.) . . . . is sometimes used to signify a beau, spark, or hectoring fellow.

1773. O. GOLDSMITH, *She Stoops to Conquer*, Act i., Sc. 2. 'A troublesome old BLADE, to be sure; but a keeps as good wines and beds as any in the whole country.'

1860. DICKENS, *Great Expectations*, ch. xxiv., p. 115. 'He forged wills, this BLADE did, if he didn't also put the supposed testators to sleep too.'

1883. *Broadside Ballad*, 'Happy Thoughts,' st. 4.

My Uncle Dowle has lots of money;
He's a very knowing looking BLADE.

BLAMED, *ppl. adj.* (popular).—An expletive used to emphasize a statement. It partakes of the nature of an oath, being often used instead of 'doomed' or 'damned.' In America the expression is more of a colloquialism than it is in England.—*See* OATHS.

1835. HALIBURTON ('Sam Slick'), *The Clockmaker*, 3 S., ch. vi. Yes, John Bull is a BLAMED blockhead.

1872. S. CLEMENS, *Roughing It*, ch. ix. The keeper had fired four times at an Indian, but he said with an injured air, that the Indian had 'skipped' around so's to spile everything—and ammunition's BLAMED skurse too.

1873. CARLETON, *Farm Ballads*, p. 18.

And so that pourin' dissentions in our cup;
And so that BLAMED cow-critter was always coming up.

1888. *Detroit Free Press*, Oct. 6. 'Did you see any Quakers in Philadelphia?' was asked of a Detroiter who lately returned from that city. 'Only one that I was sure of.' 'Did he "thee" and "thou" you?' 'He did. He got down off his hack and said: "If thee don't pay me 2 dols. I'll knock thy BLAMED head off," and I paid, although I knew the regular fare was twelve shillings. You don't want to fool with those Quakers any, and don't you forget it.

1888. *Portland Transcript*, May 9. 'Why do you object to your daughter marrying?' 'Wouldn't object ef she wuster marry the right sorter man.' 'Isn't Tom the right sort of man?' 'Not by a BLAMED sight.'

BLAME IT! *intj.* (common).—A round-about oath. Equivalent to 'Damn it!' [A transferred sense of BLAME.]

BLAMENATION! *intj.* (common).—Damnation!—*See* OATHS.

BLANK, BLANKED, BLANKETY, *adj.* (common).—Euphemistic oaths, the derivation of which is clearly an outcome of the practice of representing an oath, for decency's sake in printing, by a dash or blank space; *e.g.*, d——d. The terms are used in America in many combinations (*see* quots.). *Cf.*, OATHS.

1857. C. DICKENS, Farce for the Championship, in *All the Year Round*. Enter a closely shaven, bullet-headed fellow in an ecstasy of excitement at having just seen Cuss, and at the exquisite 'fitness' of that worthy. 'So help me BLANK, BLANK!' he cries delightedly, 'if he ain't a BLANK picter with the weins in his face down 'ere and 'ere, a showin' out just if a BLANK hartist 'ad painted him. Tell yer he's beautiful, fine as a BLANK greyhound, with a BLANK heavy air with him that looks BLANK like winnin'. Take yer two quid to one, guv'nor,' adds the speaker, suddenly picking out a stout purple-faced farmer in the group of eager listeners.

1873. C. READE, *Simpleton*, xxiii. BLANK him! that is just like him; the uneasy fool! [M.]

1878. MRS. EDWARDES, *Jet* iii., 272. '——the colonel of the regiment!' exclaims Mark. . . 'BLANK the colonel of the regiment!' With slow, unmistakable gusto she lingers over the monosyllable 'BLANK.' [M.]

1879. BRET HARTE, *Gabriel Conroy*, in *Hallberger's Illustrated Magazine*, vol. I., p. 378. Because you're religious, BLANK you, do you expect me to starve? Go and order supper first! Stop! Where in BLANK are you going? Here you've been and gone three hours on an errand for me, and blame me if you ain't runnin' off without a word about it.

1888. *Troy Daily Times*, Feb. 3. The captain looked anxious, and an irate fellow-passenger, who had not ceased swearing since we left Tuxpan, declared by all that is sacred and profane that he had known vessels to be hindered thirty days; yes, even three months, by that BLANKETY BLANKETY bar!

1888. *Owosso* (Mich.) *Press*, April. 'Doctor, I'm a dead man!' 'Not right now?' said I, as I kicked his dog out. 'Just as good as dead,' said he, 'or you wouldn't kick that dog in that way with safety. Not by a BLANKETY BLANK BLANK sight.' 'Needn't waste so much profanity, Mr. Starkhill,' said I.

BLANKET. LAWFUL BLANKET, *subs.* (old).—A wife. For synonyms, *see* DUTCH.

BLANKET FAIR, *subs.* (popular).—Bed. *Cf.*, BEDFORDSHIRE, SHEET ALLEY, and LAND OF NOD.

BLANKET HORNPIPE, *subs.* (common).—Sexual commerce. The allusion is obvious. *Cf.*, BASKET MAKING.

BLARMED, *ppl. adj.* (common).—A euphemism for BLESSED (*q.v.*); 'damned'; 'BLOWED' (*q.v.*); or BLAMED (*q.v.*), of the last of which it is probably a corruption.—*See* OATHS.

1867. *No Church*, I., 104. To be in a BLARMED hurry.

1872. JOHN FORSTER, *Life of Dickens*, ch. xxxi. (III., p. 191). He saw a strange sensation among the angry travellers whom he had detained so long; heard a voice exclaim, 'I am BLARMED if it ain't Dickens!' and stood in the centre of a group of *Five Americans!*

BLARM ME! *intj.* (common).—A euphemistic oath.—*See* BLARMED.

BLARNEY, *subs.* (colloquial).—Blandishment; soft speech, or 'sawder'; gross flattery; 'gammon.' [From Castle Blarney in Ireland, in the wall of which, difficult of access, is placed a stone. Whoever is able to kiss this is said thereafter to be able to persuade to anything. BLARNEY is from *bladh-ey*, flowery island, and this may have some connection with the curious tradition. On the other hand, according to Brewer, Cormack Macarthy held the Castle of Blarney in 1602, and concluded an armistice with Carew, the lord president, on condition of surrendering the fort to the English garrison. Day after day his lordship looked for the fulfilment of the terms, but received nothing except protocols and soft speeches, till he became the laughing-stock of Elizabeth's ministers, and the dupe of the lord of Blarney.

1785. GROSE, *Dictionary of the Vulgar Tongue*. He has licked the BLARNEY stone; he deals in the wonderful, or tips us the traveller.

1839. LEVER, *Harry Lorrequer*, ch. xix. They were as cunning as foxes and could tell BLARNEY from good sense.

c. 1876. *Broadside Ballad*, 'A nice young thing.'

Such a nice young thing, such a sweet young thing,
Her name was Kate Carney, she came from Killarney,
So full of her BLARNEY, but fond of her Barney,
Such a fair young thing, a rare young thing,
And just for a lark she had dyed her hair dark,
And they called her the Colleen Dhu.

1884. RUSKIN, in *Pall Mall Gazette*, 17 Nov., p. 11, col. 2. It was bombastic English BLARNEY—not Irish. [M.]

The French have *baliverne* and *pelotage* with the same meaning.

Verb.—1. To wheedle; to coax; to flatter grossly.

2. (American thieves').—Besides the English slang signification of 'to wheedle,' it also bears the secondary meaning, among the low and criminal classes of America, of 'to pick locks.'

BLART OUT, *verb* (American, ? nonce word).—A corruption of 'blurt out'; to utter abruptly.

1835. HALIBURTON ('Sam Slick'), *The Clockmaker*, pref., p. v. It warn't the part of a gentleman for to go and pump me arter that fashion, and then go right off and BLART IT OUT in print. *Ibid*, ch. viii. And there are others again who BLART RIGHT OUT whatever comes uppermost.

BLASÉ, *adj.* (common).—Used up; exhausted with enjoyment; satiated. [From French *blaser*, of unknown derivation.] Its extended colloquial use in England is explained in second quotation.

1823. BYRON, *Don Juan*, ch. xii., st. 81. A little BLASÉ—'tis not to be wondered At, that his heart had got a tougher rind, And though not vainer from his past success, No doubt his sensibilities were less.

1883. G. A. SALA, in *Illustrated London News*, March 10, p. 235, col. 3. There should be a chronology of slang. It is about forty years ago, I think, that the great popularity of a French farce called 'L'Homme BLASÉ' brought the word into colloquial use in England; indeed the first translation of the French piece (at the Princess's, Wright, the low comedian, playing the hero,) was called BLASÉ, with some sub-title that I forget. Subsequently another translation was produced, Charles Mathews playing the principal character. As a title for this version, we borrowed a slang term from the Americans, and 'L'Homme BLASÉ' became 'Used Up'!

BLAST, *verb* (low).—To curse; to damn. An expression of reprobation and hatred. Used in such combinations as BLAST ME! BLAST YOU! BLAST YOUR EYES! etc.—*See* OATHS.

1654. CHAPMAN, *Revenge for Honour*, V., ii. And thus I kiss'd my last breath. BLAST YOU ALL! *Ta.* Damn'd desperate villain!

1752. FIELDING, *Amelia*, bk. X., ch. v. 'I don't know what you mean by ominous,' cries the colonel; 'but, BLAST MY REPUTATION, if I had received such a letter, if I would not have searched the world to have found the writer.'

1759. GOLDSMITH, *Cit. of the World*, lett., 105. 'BLAST ME!' cries Tibbs, 'if that be all, there is no need of paying for that.'

1825. SCOTT, *St. Ronan's Well*, ch. viii. 'Hands, Captain MacTurk!' exclaimed Sir Bingo, in some confusion; 'no, BLAST HIM—not so bad as that neither.'

BLASTED, *ppl. adj.* (low).—Execrable; confounded; often substituted for 'damned,' 'bloody,' it being thought a milder form. Grose has BLASTED FELLOW for an abandoned rogue, and BLASTED BRIMSTONE for a prostitute. [From BLAST, *q.v.*]—*See* OATHS.

1682. DRYDEN, *Medal*, 260. What curses on thy BLASTED Name will fall. [M.]

1750. CHESTERFIELD, *Letters*, 8 Jan. (1870), 169. Colonel Chartres . . . who was, I believe, the most notorious BLASTED rascal in the world. [M.]

1874. PUSEY, *Lent. Sermons*, 79. Balaam after the success of his BLASTED counsel. [M.]

1884. *Good Words*, Nov., p. 767, col. 1. Jim Black states that the BLASTED railway has done away with those journeys.

BLATANTATION, *subs.* (? nonce word).—Noisy effusion; swagger. [From BLATANT, noisy, offensively clamorous, + ATION.] *Cf.*, BLATANCY.

1883. *Graphic*, Feb. 24, p. 199, col. 3. On the ground betting men are conspicuous with their books, BLATANTATIONS, blackguardism, and swell clothes.

BLATER, *subs.* (old).—A calf. [Probably a corruption of 'bleater,' from its cry.]

1714. *Memoirs of John Hall* (4 ed.), p. 11 [list of cant words in]. BLATER, a calf.

1827. LYTTON, *Pelham*, ch. lxxxii. Don't be glim-flashy; why you'd cry beef on a BLATER.

BLATHER, *subs.* (familiar).—Noisy talk; voluble nonsense. *Cf.*, BLETHER.

1864. E. YATES, *Broken to Harness*, ch. xxix., p. 309 (1873). 'There's a letter there from Sir Mordaunt, askin' for more time, and promisin' all sorts of things; but I'm sick of him and his BLATHER.'

Verb.—To talk volubly; noisily; nonsensically.—*See* BLETHER.

1884. W. C. RUSSELL, *Jack's Courtship*, ch. xxiv. Mrs. O'Brien was BLATHERING about the pedigree of the O'Briens and the O'Shandrydans to Mrs. Joyce.

BLATHERSKITE, *subs.* (common).—1. Boastful disputatious swagger. *Cf.*, BLETHERSKITE.

2. A swaggerer; boaster; one who talks volubly and nonsensically. *Cf.*, BLETHERSKITE.

1888. *New York Herald*, July 29. Every BLATHERSKITE republican is filled to the brim and spouting high protection, while the democrats are not prepared to meet them for want of documents.

1888. *Chicago Watchman*. Dr. Brookes, of St. Louis, must be a nice man to live with. He refers to Dr. R. W. Dale and Dr. Parker as 'blatant BLATHERSKITES,' and evidently regards Professor Drummond as beyond reformation.

BLAYNEY'S BLOODHOUNDS, *subs.* (military).—The Eighty-ninth Foot. They obtained this nickname during the Irish Rebellion in 1798. [BLAYNEY, from their Colonel's name + BLOODHOUNDS from their skill in tracking Irish rebels.] They also earned for themselves the sobriquet of THE ROLLICKERS, in allusion to the 'jolly doggish' bearing of the corps.

BLAZE, *subs.* and *verb* (common).—In some of the usages of this word, the precincts of slang are narrowly touched, even if the boundary line is not crossed; as *e.g.*, when a man is said to BLAZE his way through the labyrinths of the metropolis. The original meaning is well known. The early settlers in traversing the vast forests which abounded on the American continent, found it very necessary to mark their route. This they did by the simple expedient of BLAZING the trees at convenient distances. BLAZING consists merely in chopping a piece of the bark off each tree selected in the desired line of march. The mark itself is called a BLAZE. In addition to this, BLAZING was also adopted as an indication that the land within the limits of the trees thus marked had been appropriated by a settler—a rude and informal, but, in early days, a thoroughly well recognised method of securing a title to the land. Some writers affect to derive the word from the old French *blazon*, the armorial bearing of the Normans, and quote the use of 'blazen,' by Shakspeare, in a sense not altogether dissimilar to the meaning conveyed by BLAZING, as proof to this effect.

It is employed generally in America and all English-speaking colonies. The following quotations will exemplify its use both in the original and more figurative senses.—*See* BLAZES.

1737. WESLEY, wks. (1872) I., 68. We then found another BLAZE and pursued it. [M.]

1883. BRET HARTE, *In the Carquinez Woods*, ch. viii. 'I made a blaze hereabouts to show where to leave the trail. There it is,' he added, pointing to a slight notch cut in the trunk of an adjoining tree. . . . They proceeded cautiously at right angles with the BLAZED tree for ten minutes more.

BLAZE-AWAY, *intj.* (common).—Look sharp; 'stir your stumps'—an injunction to renewed and more effective effort.

BLAZER, *subs.* (popular).—Originally applied to the uniform of the Lady Margaret Boat Club of St. John's College, Cambridge, which was of a bright red and was called a BLAZER. Now applied to any light jacket of bright colour worn at cricket or other sports. Prof. Skeat [*N. and Q.*, 7 S., iii., 436] speaking of the JOHNIAN BLAZER, says it was always of the most brilliant scarlet, and thinks it not improbable that the fact suggested the name which subsequently became general.

1880. *Times*, June 19. Men in spotless flannel, and club BLAZERS. [M.]

1885. *Punch*, June 27, p. 304. On the morning of the start for our 'Spin to Brighton,' Harkaway turns up clad in what he calls a BLAZER, which makes him look like a nigger minstrel out for a holiday.

1889. *Daily News*, Aug. 22, p. 6, col. 6. DRESS BY THE SEA. SIR,—In your article of to-day, under the above heading, you speak of 'a striped red and black BLAZER,' 'the BLAZER,' also of 'the pale toned' ones. This is worth noting as a case of the specific becoming the generic. A BLAZER is the red flannel boating jacket, worn by the Lady Margaret, St. John's College, Cambridge, Boat Club. When I was at Cambridge it meant that and nothing else. It seems from your article that a BLAZER now means a coloured flannel jacket, whether for cricket, tennis, boating, or seaside wear.—Yours faithfully, WALTER WREN.

BLAZES, *subs.* (general). — The infernal regions. This, an allusion to the flames of hell, was the original meaning; constant use, however, has lessened the force of the expression, and as in the case of 'bloody,' few who employ such flowers of oratory have any notion of the proper signification. In most cases the word is now a meaningless intensitive, and takes rank with such expressions as LIKE ONE O'CLOCK, LIKE WINKEY, etc. The verb TO BLAZE is likewise employed in a manner closely bordering on slang. Thus one says of an action that it is a blazing shame; that he has a blazing headache; that so-and-so is a blazing thief; that such a job is blazing hard work; that it is a blazing hot day — all figurative uses of the legitimate idea. Appended are illustrations of some of its usages.

(Common.) — The brilliant habiliments of flunkeys. Derived from the episode of Sam Weller and the 'swarry.'

OLD BLAZES, *subs.* (common). —The devil. For synonyms, *see* SKIPPER.

1849. *Southern Literary Messenger*, June. He looked, upon my word, like OLD BLAZES himself, with his clothing all on fire, and rage and despair in his face.

GO TO BLAZES, *phr.* (common). —Go to the devil; go to hell—expressions of contempt used in imprecations.

1851. MAYHEW, *London Labour and London Poor*, III., p. 135. He jumps through a trap in the window with a bottle on it, marked 'Old Tom,' and a scroll falls down, written GONE TO BLAZES.

1861. THACKERAY, *Adventures of Philip*, I., p. 99. Old Parr Street is mined, sir—mined! And some morning we shall be blown into BLAZES,—into BLAZES, sir, mark my words!

1862. MRS. RIDDELL ('F. G. Trafford'), *Too Much Alone*, p. 200. 'Has no one been here this afternoon?' 'Yes, one man, to ask his way to BLAZES, or some place else.'

1880. S. CLEMENS ('Mark Twain'), *Sketch* (*Mr. Skae's Item*). I could have told Johnny Skae that I would not receive his communication at such a late hour, and to GO TO BLAZES with it.

1882. JAS. PAYN, in 'A Failure of Justice', in *Glow Worm Tales*, p. 97. 'Sir,' cried I, authoritatively, 'let me tell you I am a Middlesex magistrate.' 'Oh, yes: a likely story!' was his audacious reply. 'You've got 'Ighbury Barn written on your countenance *you* have, GO TO BLAZES!' and he slammed down the window.

LIKE BLAZES, *adv. phr.* (popular). — Vehemently; with extreme ardour.—*See* ANYTHING and WINKEY.

1845. B. DISRAELI, *Sybil or The Two Nations*, p. 330. Syllabubs LIKE BLAZES, and snapdragon as makes the flunkeys quite pale. *Ibid*, p. 369. 'They pelted the police . . .' 'And cheered the red-coats LIKE BLAZES,' said Mick. *Ibid*. She sets her face against gals working' in mills LIKE BLAZES.

1851. MAYHEW, *London Labour and London Poor*, III., p. 159. She liked this very much, in fact so much, that the other little ones used to cry LIKE BLAZES because I wouldn't let them have a turn at them [the stilts].

1859. CHAS. DICKENS, *Tale of Two Cities*, I., p. 15 (in parts). A BLAZING strange answer.

1864. J. LAWRENCE, *Guy Livingstone or Thorough*. They hate each other LIKE BLAZES.

18(?). DE QUINCEY, *Spanish Nun*, sect. 24. The horse was so maddened by the wound, and the road so steep, that he went LIKE BLAZES.

HOW, WHO, or WHAT THE BLAZES, *phr.* (popular).—A somewhat more intense interrogatory than Who or What or even Who or What the Dickens.

1836. DICKENS, *Pickwick*, ch. lv., p. 479. 'Pell,' he used to say to me many a

time, 'HOW THE BLAZES you can stand the head-work you do, is a mystery to me.'

1884. W. C. RUSSELL, *Jack's Courtship*, ch. xvii. 'WHO THE BLAZES would recognise Jack Seymour in those shore-going duds?'

DRUNK AS BLAZES or BLAIZERS, *phr.* (common). — Very drunk; what is vulgarly called 'beastly' drunk. Whether this expression follows the derivation of the examples given above, or whether we must seek its origin in a totally different direction, is a matter of some doubt. The alternative derivation suggested is that the phrase is really DRUNK AS BLAIZERS, an expression which dates back at least to 1830 [*N. and Q.*, 6 S., i., 434]. Sir Thomas Wyse, in *Impressions of Greece*, speaking (*see Life of Richard Waldo Sibthorp*, by J. Fowler, 1880, p. 227) of the reverence for St. Blaize, in Greece (who is also, as is known, the patron saint of the English woolcombers), and how his feast was observed in the woollen manufactories of the Midland Counties, says, 'Those who took part in the procession were called BLAIZERS, and the phrase AS DRUNK AS BLAIZERS originated in the convivialities common on those occasions! So good 'Bishop and Martyr' Blaize is dishonoured as well as honoured in England, and very probably in Greece. Further data may be found in Chambers' *Book of Days*, vol. I., pp. 219-20.

BLEACH, *verb* (Harvard University.)—To absent oneself from morning prayers.—HALL'S *College Words and Phrases*.

BLEACHED MORT, *subs.* (old).—A fair complexioned wench. — *Grose*. [From BLEACHED, white or fair, + MORT, a girl or woman.]

BLEAK, *adj.* (American thieves').—In the phraseology of American thieves, BLEAK means handsome.

BLEATER, *subs.* (old).—The victim of a sharper or rook. In the following quotation a JACK IN THE BOX (*q.v.*) is an old thieves' term for a swindler or cheat.

1609. DEKKER, *Lanthorne*, wks., 1884-5, III., 290. They that are Cheated by Iacke in a Boxe are called BLEATERS.

1785. GROSE, *Dictionary of the Vulgar Tongue*. BLEATERS, those cheated by Jack in a Box.

1811. *Lexicon Balatronicum*. (Same definition given.)

BLEATING CHEAT, *subs.* (old).—A sheep.—*Grose*. [In the old cant CHEAT or CHETE [from Anglo-Saxon *ceat*] signified a thing; and the names of animals were frequently formed by adding an adjective descriptive of their peculiar noise or cry. Thus a GRUNTING CHEAT was a pig; a CACKLING CHEAT a fowl; a BLEATING CHEAT a sheep.] A sheep is also called a WOOL-BIRD (*q.v.*). Among French thieves this animal is designated *une morne*.

BLEATING CULL, *subs.* (old).—A sheep stealer. [From BLEATING, see preceding, + CULL, a man, honest or otherwise.]

BLEATING PRIG or **RIG**, *subs.* (old).—Sheep stealing. [From BLEATING, *see* BLEATING CHEAT, + PRIG, or RIG, the act of stealing.]

BLEED, *verb tr.* and *intr.* (popular). —1. To be victimised; to lose or part with money so that the loss is felt; to be 'RUSHED' (*q.v.*); to have money drawn or extorted from one. [An allusion to the loss sustained by parting with one's life blood.]

1668. DRYDEN, *An Evening's Love*, Act iv., Sc. 1. In fine, he is vehement, and BLEEDS on to fourscore or an hundred; and I, not willing to tempt fortune, come away a moderate winner of two hundred pistoles.

1748. T. DYCHE, *Dictionary* (5 ed.). BLEED (v.) . . . . also to part with money freely, upon proposing something agreeable to a person's disposition, whether it be in gaming or anything else.

1751. SMOLLETT, *Peregrine Pickle*, ch. lxvi. To whom he was particularly agreeable, on account of his person, address, and BLEEDING freely at play.

1830. S. WARREN, *Diary of a Late Physician*, ch. xxii. The reputed readiness with which she BLED, at last brought her the honour of an old countess, who condescended to win from her, at two sittings, very nearly £5,000.

1849. THACKERAY, *Pendennis*, ch. lxviii. 'You have got a bill of sale for her furniture . . . By Jove, sir, you've BLED that poor woman enough.'

1885. *Manchester Evening News*, 23 June, p. 2, col. 2. Men who give bills have to BLEED for the accommodation.

2. (printers'.) — A book BLEEDS when the margins are 'planed' down so that the edge of the printed portion is cut away.

1876. *Daily Telegraph*, June 9, p. 2, col. 1. So very carelessly has the mechanical part of production been done that, in the phraseology of the craft—half technical, half slang—the pages BLEED in many places—*i.e.*, the binder's knife when cutting the edges has also cut away portions of the printed matter.

BLEEDER, *subs.* (University).—1. A duffer beyond compare; a superlative fool. (common).—A euphemism for 'bloody fool.'

2. (sporting.)—A sovereign. For synonyms, *see* CANARY.

3. (old.)—A spur; an obvious allusion.

BLEEDING, *adj.* — An expletive, which, if meant, would partake of the nature of an oath; as it is there is little enough, sanguinary, either literally or metaphorically about much that is described as BLEEDING. It sounds big and weighty to those who use it, and that suffices.

1877. BESANT AND RICE, *Son of Vulcan*, pt. II., ch. xxiii. 'When he isn't up to one dodge he is up to another. You make no BLEEDING error.'

BLEEDING CULLY, *subs.* (old). — One who parts easily with his money, or bleeds freely.—*Grose*. —[*See* BLEED.]

BLEED THE MONKEY, *verbal phr.* (nautical).—To steal rum from the mess tub called 'the monkey.' The term is exclusively naval, 'monkeys' not being known on merchant ships. The practice is also called SUCKING THE MONKEY, and TAPPING THE ADMIRAL.—*See* ADMIRAL.

1889. *Chambers' Journal*, 3 Aug., p. 495. To SUCK THE MONKEY is a phrase explained in *Peter Simple* as having originally been used among sailors for drinking rum out of cocoa-nuts, the milk having been poured out and the liquor substituted. It is now applied to the act of drinking on the sly from a cask by inserting a straw through a gimlet hole, and to drinking generally. Barham, in the legend of the *Black Mousquetaire* says:

What the vulgar call SUCKING THE MONKEY,
Has much less effect on a man when he's funky.

BLENKER, *verb* (American). — To plunder. A cant phrase much used during the Civil War. Possibly allied to the northern provincialism 'blenk,' a trick or stratagem. 'Blenk' was also used in *Morte d'Arthur* in the sense of 'to bilk,' or 'cheat.'

BLESS, *verb* (popular).—To curse; to damn.—*See* BLESSED.

TO BLESS ONESELF, *verbal phr.* (common).—To be surprised; to be vexed; to be mortified. Generally, 'God bless me!' or 'Bless my eyes!' 'Bless my soul!' 'Lor' bless me!'

1592. SHAKSPEARE, *Midsummer Night's Dream*, iv., 2, 11. *Quin*: Yea, and the best person too: and he is a very paramour, for a sweet voice. *Flu*: You must say, paragon: a paramour is, GOD BLESS US, a thing of nought.

1615. T. ADAMS, *Black Dev.*, 71. He . . . would BLESSE HIMSELFE to think that so little a thing could extend itself to such a capacity. [M.]

1665. PEPYS, *Diary*, 1 Apr. How my Lord Treasurer did BLESS HIMSELF, crying he could do no more, etc.

1759. STERNE, *Tristam Shandy*, ch. xl. Rub your hands thrice across your foreheads—blow your nose—cleanse your emunctories — sneeze, my good people!—GOD BLESS YOU.

1814. MISS AUSTEN, *Mansfield Park*, ch. xviii. Could Sir Thomas look in upon us just now, he would BLESS HIMSELF, for we are rehearsing all over the house.

1843. DICKENS, *Christmas Carol*, p. 77. 'Why, BLESS MY SOUL,' cried Fred, 'who's that?'

1853. BULWER LYTTON, *My Novel*, I., p. 307. After they had lain apart for a little while, very silent and sullen, John sneezed. 'GOD BLESS YOU!' says Joan, over the bolster.

NOT A [PENNY] TO BLESS ONESELF WITH, *phr.* (popular).—Utterly impecunious; 'without a sou.'

1843. DICKENS, *Martin Chuzzlewit*, I., p. 237. He landed there WITHOUT A PENNY TO BLESS HIMSELF WITH.

1849. DICKENS, *David Copperfield*, I., p. 113. I heard that Mr. Mell was not a bad sort of fellow, but HADN'T A SIXPENCE TO BLESS HIMSELF WITH.

1851. MAYHEW, *London Labour and London Poor*, III., p. 55. The most of 'em AIN'T GOT A FARTHING TO BLESS THEMSELVES WITH.

1861. GEORGE ELIOT, *Silas Marner*, p. 38. I HAVE NOT A SHILLING TO BLESS MYSELF WITH.

TO BLESS ONE'S STARS, *verbal phr.* (common).—To thank oneself; to attribute one's good fortune to luck, generally in a ludicrous sense.

1845. HOOD, *Pauper's Christmas Carol*, iii. Ought not I to BLESS MY STARS?

1877. *Five Years' Penal Servitude*, ch. iii., p. 230. Forty-eight marks! a week's remission. The very thought made me savage, but I BLESSED MY STARS I had not lost my class, or my good berth.

BLESSED, BLEST, *ppl. adj.* (popular). —An ironical euphemism; often used like BLAZING for 'cursed,' 'damned,' etc., or as a vow.—*See* quot. from Hindley and OATHS.

1806. WINDHAM, *Let.* in *Speeches* (1812), I., 77. As one of the happy consequences of our BLESSED system of printing debates, I am described to-day . . . as having talked a language directly the reverse of that which I did talk. [M.]

1876. C. HINDLEY, *Life and Adventures of a Cheap Jack*, p. 139. One Maidstone Fair time, I saw one of the gipsy Lees called 'Jemmy,' fighting with a man much bigger than himself. Tom Rosseter, the mumper, was seconding his brother-in-law, Jemmy Lee, when, as Jemmy kept throwing his man very heavily, he said, 'My dear BLESSED brother, don't throw the BLESSED man like that or you will be sure to kill him.' 'Well,' said Jemmy, 'but my dear BLESSED brother, if I don't kill the dear BLESSED man, why the big BLESSED — will be sure to kill me, and so I must keep on throwing the dear BLESSED man, for you see what a BLESSED big dear fellow he is to me.'

1877. *Five Years' Penal Servitude*, ch. iii., p. 245. 'They called in the coppers, and some feller in the shop twigged my old girl as one he'd a-seen before, and BLESSED if they didn't identify her as having lifted some things out of the shop, and she was pinched for seven "stretch."'

1882. *Punch*, Aug. 5, p. 49. *Sir Pompey Bedell*: 'Oh!—er—Mr. Grigsby, I think! How d'ye do?' [extending two fingers]. *Grigsby*: 'I hope I see you well, *Sir Pompey*. And next time you give me two fingers, I'm BLEST if I don't pull 'em off.'

1889. *Sporting Times*, July 6. St. Mannock.—Did you ever hear a still, small voice whispering over its morning shrimps, 'What a pair of BLESSED fools you are!'

BLETHER. BLATHER, *subs.* (Scotch and U.S.A.).—Nonsense; vapid talk; voluble chatter.

b. 1759, *d.* 1796. BURNS, *Tam Samson's Elegy*, st. 12.
Yon auld gray stane, amang the heather,
Marks out his head,
Whare *Burns* has wrote in rhyming BLETHER,
Tam Samson's dead!

1886. *Pall Mall Gazette*, 3 May, 6, 2. Havelock's florid adjurations to his men, the grim veterans of the 78th, bluntly characterized as BLETHER.

Hence BLETHERING (*verb, subs.*) used in the same sense as BLETHER, and as an adjective for 'volubly' or 'foolishly talkative.' *Cf.*, BLETHERSKATE.

b. 1759, *d.* 1796. BURNS, *Holy Fair*, st. 8.
And some are busy BLETHRIN'
Right loud that day.

1816. SCOTT, *Old Mortality*, ch. xiv. 'I hae been clean spoilt, just wi' listening to twa BLETHERING auld wives.'

1883. HAWLEY SMART, *Hard Lines*, ch. vi. He had brought this BLETHERING Irishman down here, and deluyed him with punch for the express purpose of turning him inside out.

BLETHERSKATE, BLATHERSKITE, *subs.* (provincial and American).—1. Boastful swagger, whether in talk or action.

2. A boaster; noisy talker of blatant nonsense. [From BLETHER, to talk nonsensically, + SKATE, allied to Scotch SKYTE, a contemptible fellow.] It occurs in Maggie Lauder, a well-known Scotch song, a fact which Murray says led to its popularisation in the United States. In Ireland it seems to have taken the forms of BLADDER-SKATE and BLADDERUMSKATE.

Circa 1650. F. SEMPILL, *Maggie Lauder*, i. Jog on your gait, ye BLETHERSKATE. [M.]

1825. C. CROKER, *Tradit. S. Ireland*, p. 170. He was, as usual, getting on with his BLETHERUMSKITE about the fairies. [M.]

1870. J. R. O'FLANAGAN, *Lives of the Lord Chancellors of Ireland*. 'Lord Redesdale was speaking of people who learnt to skate with bladders under their arms, to buoy them up if they should fall into a hole and risk being drowned.' 'Ah, my Lord,' said Toler, 'that is what we call BLADDERUMSKATE in Ireland.'

BLEW, *verb* (common).—1. To inform; to 'peach'; to expose; to betray.—*See* BLOW UPON, of which it is a variant.

2. (popular.)—To spend; to waste; generally in connection with money. When a man has spent or lost all his money, he is said to have BLEWED IT. [The derivation is uncertain, that most likely being its reference to a corrupt grammatical use of BLEW, the past tense of 'to blow.' Money spent recklessly and wasted vanishes as if blown away by the wind.]

1884. *Daily Telegraph*, May 28, p. 5, col. 1. 'Which paid him £1,700 compensation, when he took to horses, and BLEWED the blooming lot in eighteen months.'

1889. *Sporting Times*, June 29.
Isabel and Maudie knew the Turf and all its arts—
They had often BLEWED a dollar on a wrong 'un—

And Isabel one evening met a mug from rural parts,
An attenuated Juggins, and a long 'un.

FRENCH SYNONYMS. *Se faire rincer* (popular: 'to be cleared out' [at a game]. *Rincer*, properly 'to drench,' 'to serve out,' also has the slang signification of 'to thrash'); *paumer* (thieves' and vagrants': this verb is very old, and is derived from *palma* = *empoigner*. It also signifies to arrest, lose, etc.); *laumir* (an old cant term); *se faire ratisser* (familiar: literally 'to scrape oneself'); *faire rasoir* (gaming: 'to be penniless'); *se faire enturer* (popular: 'to cut into oneself'; *enture* = incision or cut); *panner quelqu'un* (popular); *mettre dans le sac* (gamesters': *Cf.*, 'be in a hole'); *décavage* (familiar: a term employed to signify the circumstances of a gamester who has 'blewed it'; one who is in 'Queer Street'—from *décavé*, a ruined gamester); *se faire lessiver*: 'to wash oneself.' Michel gives *lessive* = defence, and *lessiveur* = barrister, and remarks that better terms could hardly be given to advocate and speech by those charged with offence, and who wish to return from the same 'white as snow,' or, as police phraseology hath it, without a stain upon one's character. For other synonyms, *see* SHAVE.

BLIMEY, *intj.* (low).—A corruption of 'Blind me!'; an expression little enough understood by those who constantly have it in their mouths.

BLIND, *subs.* (common).—1. The night time—an allusion to the absence of light.—*See* DARKMANS.

2. (familiar.)—A pretence; a shift; an action through which one's real purpose is concealed; that which obstructs; a 'make-believe.'

1663. DRYDEN, *Wild Gallant*, Act iii. He . . . took your court to her, only as a BLIND to your affection for me.

1694. CONGREVE, *Double Dealer*, Act ii., Sc. 5. I know you don't love Cynthia, only as a BLIND for your passion to me.

1703. MRS. CENTLIVRE, *Beau's Dual*, I., i. (1872), i., 70. Am I publish'd to the world as a BLIND for his designs?

1877. E. L. LINTON, *World Well Lost*, ch. xxviii. The excuse was too palpably a BLIND to be accepted as a reason.

1889. *Answers*, July 13, p. 104, col. 3. The Major and the Captain he referred to in his letters were mere 'BLINDS.' The Captain relied upon the fact that not one person in a dozen took the trouble to apply to these gentlemen.

3. (printers'.)—A paragraph [¶] mark is so called; from the eye of the reversed 'P' being filled up.

Adj. (old).—Tipsy; in liquor. Nares says this cant term was used with others in the works of Taylor, the water-poet [1630]. For synonyms, *see* SCREWED.

BLIND AS A BRICKBAT, *adv. phr.* (colloquial).—A facetious simile for very blind—mentally or physically.

1849. DICKENS, *David Copperfield*, III., p. 97. The old scholar . . . is as BLIND AS A BRICKBAT.

WHEN THE DEVIL IS BLIND, *adv. phr.* (common).—Never. The French have three very graphic—though in one case very vulgar—analogues for this expression—*quand les poules pisseront*, which need not be translated; *le trente six du mois, i.e.*, 'on the thirty-sixth day of the month,' and *quand les poules auront des dents, i.e.*, when cocks and hens have teeth.

TO GO IT BLIND.—A luminous figure of speech to convey the idea of entering upon an undertaking without thought as to the result, or inquiry beforehand. This is one of the many slang expressions which owe their origin to the American game of poker, the special form of which known as blind poker, where the cards are betted upon before being looked at, being responsible for the phrase now in question. *Cf.*, also BLIND (*subs.*).

1848. J. RUSSELL LOWELL, *Biglow Papers*, II., p. 118—
'to impress on the popular mind
The comfort and wisdom of GOIN' IT BLIND.'

1871. DE VERE, *Americanisms*, p. 328. *Blind Poker* has given rise to the very common phrase, to GO IT BLIND, used whenever an enterprise is undertaken without previous inquiry.

1882. GENERAL SHERMAN, *Memoirs*, vol. I., p. 342. I know that in Washington I am incomprehensible, because at the outset of the war I would not GO IT BLIND, and rush headlong into a war unprepared and with an utter ignorance of its extent and purpose.

1888. *Chicago Ledger*, May 12. 'And so you've married a jewel, have you, Tom?' 'I have, for a fact, Dick.' 'Lucky dog! You're a man in a million. Mighty few GO IT BLIND and fare as well as you've done.' 'I didn't GO IT BLIND. I employed a detective, and he managed to get board in the family.'

BLIND CHEEKS, *subs.* (common).—The posteriors. [The derivation is from an obvious simile.]

Among ENGLISH SYNONYMS are—Two fat cheeks and ne'er a nose; blind Cupid; ampersand; cheeks; arse; corybungo; dopey; droddum; dummock; feak; bum; nock (*i.e.*, 'a notch'); round mouth; windmill; blind-eye; monocular eyeglass.

FRENCH SYNONYMS. *Un borgne* (low: 'a one-eyed person'); *un cyclope* (the allusion is mythological—from Cyclops, the one-eyed giant, whose optic was placed in the middle of the forehead); *la rose des vents*; *un piffe*; *un pignard*; *boite aux ordures*. GERMAN SYNONYM. *Acherponim* (from Hebrew *achar ponim*; literally 'the face at the back'). For other synonyms, *see* BUM.

BLIND DRUNK, *adj. phr.* (common).—Very intoxicated; so drunk as to be unable to see better than a blind man. Americans say, 'So drunk as not to be able to see through a ladder.' For synonyms, *see* SCREWED.

1845. DISRAELI, *Sybil or the Two Nations*, p. 350. Hang me if I wasn't BLIND DRUNK at the end of it.

BLINDER. TO TAKE A BLINDER, *phr.* (thieves').—To die. For synonyms, *see* ALOFT.

BLIND EYE, *subs.* (common).—The podex.—*See* BLIND CHEEKS.

BLIND HALF HUNDRED, *subs.* (military).—The Fiftieth Regiment of Foot; from so many men suffering from ophthalmia during the Egyptian campaign [1801]; also the DIRTY HALF HUNDRED from the men in action wiping their faces with their black facings during the Peninsula War. HALF HUNDRED is an adaptation of the number of the regiment—the Fiftieth. The corps is also called the 'Gallant Fiftieth,' from its gallantry at the battle of Vimiera, 1808.

1871. *Chambers' Journal*, No. 417, p. 803. The DIRTY HALF HUNDRED was

the curious nickname given to the 50th Foot. Two accounts are given of the origin of this. One asserts that it was from their red uniforms being faced with black and silver lace, and thus giving the regiment a dull and sombre appearance; whilst the other tells us that it was from the men wiping their perspiring faces with the black cuffs of their coats, and thus giving their countenances a somewhat swarthy tint. Whatever may be the origin of this sobriquet, they bear a second about which there can be no doubt. From the glorious charge, led by Colonel Walker, at Vimiera, this regiment is known as the 'Gallant Fiftieth.'

1886. *Tinsley's Magazine*, April, p. 322. Most people have heard of the 'Fighting Fiftieth.' But the 50th are rich in nicknames. They are, or at least they were, the BLIND HALF-HUNDREDTH, having been but too literally blinded by the ravages of ophthalmia when in Egypt with Sir Ralph Abercromby. And when on one occasion the men dried the perspiration from their faces with their cuffs, they for a while became the DIRTY HALF-HUNDREDTH.

BLIND HARPERS, *subs.* (old).—Beggars counterfeiting blindness, playing on fiddles, etc.—*Grose.*

BLIND-MAN'S HOLIDAY, *subs.* (familiar).—Formerly this common colloquialism signified the night or darkness; it is now, however, usually applied to the time 'between lights' when it is too dark to see, but often not dark enough to light up, and a holiday or rest from work is taken. The blind from their infirmity are in general exempted from labour, and in this view keep holiday; when the twilight hour comes, when those that *can* work, or read, etc., can no longer *see* to do so, it is BLIND-MAN'S HOLIDAY to them, and they of necessity rest accordingly. This derivation, one would think, is sufficiently obvious; but, on the other hand, there are those who think the expression a corruption of 'blind-man's *all-day*.' The meaning then would be that the gradual departure of light brings one to the state which the blind man endures all day, or which is all the day the blind man has. Whichever derivation be true, it is, however, interesting to note that this 'household word' of to-day has been in the mouths of the English people for more than three hundred years. It is the English equivalent of the Scotch IN THE GLOAMING, of an equally venerable lineage.

1599. NASHE, *Lenten Stuffe*, in wks. V., 263. And what will not blinde Cupid doe in the night which is his BLINDMAN'S HOLIDAY?

1738. SWIFT, *Polite Conversation* (conv. iii.). Indeed, madam, it is BLINDMAN'S HOLIDAY; we shall soon be all of a colour.

1824. T. FIELDING, *Proverbs, etc.* (*Familiar Phrases*), p. 147. BLINDMAN'S HOLIDAY.

1866. *Aunt Judy's Mag.*, Oct., 358. At meal times, or in BLINDMAN'S HOLIDAY, when no work was to be done. [M.]

BLIND MONKEYS, *subs.* (common).—Hotten thus explains this expression:—An imaginary collection at the Zoological Gardens, which are supposed to receive care and attention from persons fitted by nature for such office and for little else. An idle and useless person is often told that he is only fit to lead the BLIND MONKEYS to evacuate. Another form this elegant conversation takes, is for one man to tell another that he knows of a suitable situation for him. 'How much a week? and what to do?' are natural questions, and then comes the scathing and sarcastic reply, 'Five bob a week at the doctor's—you're to stand behind the door and make the patients sick. They won't want no physic when they sees your mug.'

Blindo, *verb* (military).—To die. For synonyms, *see* Aloft.

Blind One's Trail, *verbal phr.* (American). — Figuratively, to remove the traces of one's actions; to conceal one's intentions. This expression is obviously traceable to the days of Indian warfare, when even the lives of those engaged often depended upon the success with which the trail could be 'blinded,' or obliterated. Also to trash one's trail (*q.v.*).

Blind Side, *subs.* (familiar).—The blind side of a person or thing is that which is weakest; the most assailable side. The expression is much older than the example quoted by Murray [1655].

1606. Chapman, *Gentleman Usher*, Act i., p. 79 (*Plays*, 1874).
For that, we'll follow the blind side of him,
And make it sometimes subject of our mirth.

1663. Dryden, *Wild Gallant*, Act iii. *Con.* My father's credulous, and this rogue has found the blind side of him.

1742. Fielding, *Joseph Andrews*, bk. III., ch. v. Indeed, if this good man had an enthusiasm, or what the vulgar call a blind side, it was this,—he thought a schoolmaster the greatest character in the world, and himself the greatest of all schoolmasters.

1820. Lamb, *Elia* (*Mrs. Battle*). All people have their blind side—their superstitions.

Blink, *verb* (American). — To drink. [Probably of humorous origin, similar to smile (*q.v.*).—and alluding to a wink or blink exchanged between friends and comrades before drinking. A frequent toast is 'I look towards you,' and the transference of sense in such a phrase as 'I wink' or 'blink to you,' and then the use of to blink for 'to drink' is easy enough. *Cf.*, also To go out and see a man.]

Blinker, *subs.* (popular).—1. The eye. [From blink, to move the eyelids, to wink; *Cf.*, Winkers; Peepers; Optics, etc.] For synonyms, *see* Glims.

1816. Quiz, *Grand Master*, I., ii. A patent pair of goggle winkers, Conceal'd from public view his blinkers. [M.]

1888. *American Humorist.* 'Blank your blinkers,' angrily retorted Brudee, 'your business was not to fight, but show us the enemy.'

2. (common.)—*pl.* Spectacles. For synonyms, *see* Barnacles.

1732. M. Green, *Grotto*, 10. Bigots who but one way see through blinkers of authority. [M.]

1803. Bristed, *Pedest. Tour*, I., 38. A little fellow, with blinkers over his eyes. [M.]

1851. Thackeray, *Eng. Hum.*, IV. (1858), 205. Who only dare to look up at life through blinkers. [M.]

3. (provincial.)—In Norfolk, a black eye.

4. (pugilistic.)—A hard blow in the eye.

Blank your blinkers.—A euphemistic oath, equivalent to the more common 'D——n your eyes.'—*See* Oaths.

Blink-Fencer, *subs.* (thieves').—A person who sells spectacles. [From blink, a contracted form of 'blinkers,' spectacles + fence, primarily a receiver of stolen goods, but also applied to a tradesman of any kind, + er.]

Blinko, *subs.* (thieves' and vagrants'). — An amateur entertainment held, generally, at a public house; a free and easy (*q.v.*); a sing song (*q.v.*).

1877. J. Greenwood, *Dick Temple*. 'What is a blinko for instance?' 'Well, it's a kind of entertainment, singing, and that,' replied the old fellow, 'to which strangers are not invited—least of all the police.'

1883. *Daily Telegraph*, August 4, p. 2, col. 1. 'An Harmonic blinko, the proceeds of which will be given towards buying a barrow for Young Duckling, who has got married with no visible means of support.'

Blister, *verb* (common). — Employed euphemistically for 'to damn.' *Cf.*, Blamed.

1840. H. Cockton, *Valentine Vox*, ch. xxvi. 'Where can they be hid?' he exclaimed, with great emphasis. 'Blister 'em! Where can the scoundrels be got to?'

Blizzard, *subs.* (popular). — A poser; a stunning blow; an unanswerable argument, etc., etc. This word, recently brought into prominent notice as the name by which sudden and exceptionally severe snowstorms are known in the Western States of America, is one the etymology of which is dubious. Some authorities derive it from the German *blitz*—lightning, but a correspondent of *N. and Q.* claims it as of English nationality, asserting that the word has been known in the Midland Counties in its present form, or nearly so, for over thirty years; further stating that 'may I be blizzered' is a common oath there. Assuming that the expression is a variation of the more generally familiar 'May God strike me blind' (that is, presumably by lightning), there is nothing antagonistic between the two theories of its genesis, and a further light is perhaps thrown upon the subject, tending to support its German origin, by the fact that, in Pennsylvania, it has been familiar, according to a correspondent of the *New York Sun*, for more than half-a-century, its use and meaning being akin to the instances above mentioned. It appears that in the central counties of the State in question, the word was always used to include the idea of the 'poser,' and even of force, violence, spitefulness, or vindictiveness. If one dealt another a hostile blow he 'gave him a blizzard on the nose,' 'on the jaw,' 'between the eyes,' etc. If a magistrate lectured a litigant severely he 'gave him a blizzard.' If in debate one dealt mercilessly in ridicule he 'gave his opponent a blizzard.' If one man swore at or cursed another he 'gave him a blizzard.' If a man's wife scolded him she 'gave him a blizzard.' When it is remembered that Pennsylvania is the State in which the Dutch or German element most largely predominates, it does not seem far fetched to attribute its origin to a Teutonic source, more especially as there is nothing in the English usage to preclude such a derivation. However this may be, the word invariably seems to imply suddenness combined with violence; and, at any rate, it apparently disposes of the supposition that the word is of Western origin, or a coinage of so recent a date as is frequently supposed. Like most words of its class, which have largely struck the popular taste, it has been generally adopted in an idiomatic sense to signify a stunning blow; an overwhelming argument, or a cool reception.

1834. Crockett, *Tour Down East*, 16. A gentleman at dinner asked me for a toast; and supposing he meant to have some fun at my expense, I concluded to go ahead, and give him and his likes a blizzard.

1871. De Vere, *Americanisms*, p. 443. Blizzard, a term referred back to the German *Blitz*, means in the West a stunning blow or an overwhelming argument.

1884. G. A. S[ala], in *Ill. L. News*, Feb. 23, p. 171, col. 2. Blizzard. The philologers in American Slang refer back to the German *blitz*; and its original meaning in the Western States seems to have been a stunning blow or an overwhelming argument. In the Eastern States a sudden set-in of severe frost is called a 'cold snap.' Query, how many 'cold snaps' does it take to make a 'blizzard'?

1888. *San Francisco News Letter*. I should like to have seen the Colonel's face when he got that very cold, blizzardy letter. I bet that if Minnie had been near him he would have slapped her real hard.

Bloak.—*See* Bloke.

Bloat, *subs.* (American thieves'). —1. A drowned body.

2. A drunkard. The simile which groups the two is, perhaps, not far wrong. [Probably from bloat, an adjective signifying puffed, swollen, inflated. Bloat was also formerly in use in England as a contemptuous name for a human being.]

Bloated Aristocrat, *subs.* (familiar).—An opprobrious epithet for a man swollen with the pride of rank or wealth; also a general sobriquet applied by 'the masses' to 'the classes.' 'Bloated' has long been employed in a similar sense. Swift spoke of a certain statesman as 'a bloated minister' [1731].

1861. Thackeray, *Adventures of Philip*, I., p. 101. What a bloated aristocrat Thingamy has become since he got his place!

1863. G. A. Sala, *Breakfast in Bed*, essay I., p. 17 (1864). Of the two most salient English gentlemen represented, one is a bloated aristocrat of a Baronet hopelessly in debt, the other a rapid brainless nobleman.

1869. M. Twain, *Innocents Abroad*, ch. x. We sat down finally, at a late hour, in the great Casino, and called for unstinted champagne. It is so easy to be bloated aristocrats where it costs nothing of consequence!

Bloater.—*See* My bloater; also Mild bloater.

Blob, *verb* (vagrants').—To talk; to 'patter.' [Probably a corrupted form of blab.] Beggars are of two kinds — those who screeve (introducing themselves with a fakement, or false document) and those who blob, or state their case in their own truly 'unvarnished' language. [*See*, however, second quot.]

1851-61. H. Mayhew, *London Lab. and Lon. Poor*, vol. I., p. 359. 'Of professional beggars there are two kinds—those who "do it on the blob" (by word of mouth), and those who do it by "*screeving*," that is, by petitions and letters.'

1861. Whyte Melville, *Good for Nothing*, ch. xxvi. 'Five minutes more and we shall run into him,' he shouts, sitting well back on his horse, and urging him to his extreme pace, 'when he blobs like that he's getting beat. See how Canvas sticks to him, and the yellow dog hangs back waiting for the turn.'

Block, *subs.* (old).—A stupid person; a hard unsympathetic individual; one of mean, unattractive appearance. [A figurative sense of block, as of wood or stone.]

a. 1534. N. Udall, *Roister Doister*, III., iii., p. 44 (Arber). Ye are such a calfe, such an asse, such a blocke.

1595 Shakspeare, *Two Gentlemen*, Act ii., Sc. 5. *Speed.* What an ass art thou! I understand thee not. *Launce.* What a block art thou, that thou canst not!

1599. Jonson, *Every Man out of his Humour.* Induct. *Cor.* Hang him, dull block!

1624. Massinger, *Bondman*, II., ii. This will bring him on, Or he's a block.

1748. T. Dyche, *Dictionary* (5 ed.). Block (s) . . . sometimes an ignorant, stupid fellow.

1881. Besant and Rice, *Chaplain of the Fleet*, pt. II., ch. iv. She said that her partner was delightful to dance with, partly because he was a lord—and a title, she said, gives an air of grace to any block—partly because he danced well and talked amiably.

2. The head. Possibly an abbreviated form of barber's block (*q.v.*). For synonyms, *see* Crumpet.

1637. Shirley, *Lady of Pleas*, II., i. Buy a beaver For thy own block.

1861. H. Kingsley, *Ravenshoe*, ch. xxxv. 'I cleaned a groom's boots on Toosday, and he punched my block because I blacked the tops.'

Barber's block, *subs.* (common).—1. A transferred sense [from a wooden head for showing off a wig] applied to a showy, over-dressed man; a fop.

1876. E. Lynn Linton, *Hallberger's Illus. Mag.*, p. 72. No, not to men worthy of the name of men—men, not barber's blocks.

2. The head. — *See* Block, sense 2.

1823. Scott, *Peveril of the Peak*, ch. v. (I., p. 67). Were I not to take better care of the wood than you, brother, there would soon be no more wood about the town than the barber's block that's on your own shoulders.

A chip of the same old block, *phr.* (common).—A man or thing exhibiting the same qualities as he or that with which a comparison is made.

1627. Sanderson, *Serm.*, I., 283. Am not I a child of the same Adam, a vessel of the same clay, a chip of the same block, with him. [M.]

1655. L'Estrange, *Charles I.*, 126. Episcopacy, which they thought but a great chip of the old block Popery. [M.]

To cut a block with a razor, *phr.* (old). — Inconsequent argument; futile endeavour; incongruous application of means or ability to the end in view.

1774. Goldsmith, *Retaliation*, 42. 'Twas his fate unemployed or in place, sir, to eat mutton cold and cut blocks with a razor.

To block a hat, *phr.* (popular).—To crush a man's hat over the eyes by a blow; to bonnet (*q.v.*).

Blockers. — *See* Block ornaments.

Block House, *subs.* (old).—A prison; the house of detention. For synonyms, *see* Cage.

1624. Capt. Smith, *Virginia*, III., xi., 85. To stop the disorders of our disorderly Theeues . . . built a Block-house. [M.]

1785. Grose, *Dictionary of the Vulgar Tongue.* Block-houses, Prisons, houses of correction, etc.

1811. *Lexicon Balatronicum.* [Same definition given as in Grose.]

1889. Murray, *New English Dictionary.* [Common since *c.* 1500: of uncertain history. The Ger. equivalent *blockhaus* ('einen steinen Blockhaus') is quoted by Grimm, 1557 and 1602; the Du. *blokhuis* is in Kilian, 1599; Fr. *blocus*, generally considered to be the same word, and orig. in same sense, is quoted by Littré in the 16th c. (*Cf.*, *Bloccuz*). So far as evidence goes, the Eng. is thus the earliest; but we should expect it to be of Du. or Ger. origin. In any case the sense was not originally (as in modern notion) a house composed of blocks of wood, but one which blocks or obstructs a passage. The history and age of the Ger. *blockhaus* and Fr. *blocus* require more investigation.]

BLOCK ISLAND TURKEY, *subs.* (American). — Salted cod-fish. Connecticut and Rhode Island. Slang delights in naming fish as flesh. For some curious examples, *see* TWO-EYED STEAK.

BLOCK ORNAMENTS, or **BLOCKERS**, *subs.* (common). — 1. Small pieces of meat of indifferent quality, trimmings from the joints, etc. Exposed for sale on the blocks or counters of butcher's shops in cheap neighbourhoods.

1848. *Fraser's Mag.*, XXXVII., 396. Forced to substitute a BLOCKER of meat, with its cheap accompaniment of bread and vegetables . . . for poultry and rump steaks. [M.]

1851-61. H. MAYHEW, *London Lab. and Lon. Poor*, vol. I., p. 54. For dinner . . . they buy BLOCK ORNAMENTS, as they call the small, dark-coloured pieces of meat exposed on the cheap butchers' blocks or counters. *Ibid*, p. 516. What they consider a good living is a dinner daily off good BLOCK ORNAMENTS (small pieces of meat, discoloured and dirty, but not tainted, usually set for sale on the butcher's block).

1884. *Punch*, No. 2063, p. 29. And eager-faced women must bargain for tainted BLOCK ORNAMENTS still.

1887. *Standard*, Jan. 20, *The Poor at Market*. Watching a man who stands with his wife and little girl before a butcher's shop, let us see what they have to choose from in buying for the next day's dinner. On the shelves set out in front of the shop meat scraps are offered at 3½d. the lb.; better scraps (or BLOCK ORNAMENTS, as they are termed) at 4d.; somewhat shapeless small joints of beef from inferior parts at 5d., one coarse shoulder of mutton at the same; tolerably good-looking meat at 6d.; mutton chops at 7d. and 8d.; and rump steak at 10d.

2. Applied to individuals, a BLOCK ORNAMENT signifies a queer looking man or woman—one odd in appearance.

BLOKE or **BLOAK**, *subs.* (common). —A man; a fellow. In saying 'not strictly "a man" as Hotten defines it, but a man in a contemptuous sense,' Barrère is himself wide of the mark. The word may *sometimes* be used contemptuously; but, generally speaking, any idea of reproach or praise is absent, and a BLOKE means a man pure and simple. In witness whereof are the following examples of its use.

1851. MAYHEW, *London Labour and London Poor*, III., p. 397. If we met an old BLOKE (man) we propped him.

1857. SNOWDEN, *Mag. Assistant*, 3 ed., p. 446. A gentleman.—A BLOAK.

1860. SALA, *The Baddington Peerage*, II., p. 49. My old BLOKE!

1862. KINGSLEY, in *Macmillan's Mag.*, Dec., 96. Little better than BLOKES and boodles after all. [M.]

1863. OUIDA, *Held in Bondage*, bk. I., p. 245. The girl is stunning, the BLOKES say, so we must forgive you.

1865. MISS BRADDON, in *Temple Bar*, XIII., 483. The society of the aged BLOKE is apt to pull upon the youthful intellect.

1869. J. GREENWOOD, *Seven Curses of London*. It came out in the course of the evidence that the meaning of the word BLOKE was 'a man whom a woman might pick up in the street.'

1873. ROBINSON, *Little Kate Kirby*, I., p. 136. 'Give us a horder then, old BLOKE,' shrieked another gamin.

c. 1875. *Broadside Ballad*, 'Keep it Dark.'

I have heard though may be it isn't a fact,
Keep it dark!
That the present Lord Chancellor's going to be sacked,
Keep it dark!
And Dr. Kenealy, that popular BLOKE,
That extremely warm member, the member for Stoke,
Is about to succeed him, the lawyers to choke—
But, keep it dark!

c. 1869. *Broadside Ballad*, 'Shooting the Moon.' Spoken—Yes, and I used to do very well, until some ragged young urchin said to his pal, don't you varder, don't you know that ere BLOKE, that's the BLOKE we saw the other day with a barrow.

1883. *Daily News*, May 15, p. 7, col. 2. 'When you are coming out into the yard ask the next BLOKE to change numbers with you.'

In each case the 'face value' of the word appears to be simply 'a man,' and in spite of Barrère's assertion that 'in the police newspapers twenty-five years ago a BLOKE was a victim of sharps, a stupid person, a greenhorn,' the evidence is all the other way; in one instance, indeed, the individual in question is reported to be 'a gentleman.' As regards derivation, its origin is uncertain. Hotten and Ogilvie compare it with the Hindustanee *loke*, a man; while Leland traces it to 'the Dutch *blok*, a log, a fool.' For synonyms, *see* COVE.

BLOOD, *subs.* (old). — 1. A fop; dandy; buck; or 'fast' man. Originally in common use, but now obsolete. [From that legitimate sense of the word which attributes the seat of the passions and emotions to the blood. Hence, a man of spirit; one who is worth mention, and, in an inferior sense, he who makes himself notorious, whether by dress or rowdyism.] In the last century, especially during the regency of George IV., the term was largely in vogue to denote a young man of good birth or social standing about town; subsequently, it came to mean a riotous, disorderly fellow.

1562. BULLEYN, *Sicke Men*, etc., 73*a*. A lustie BLOOD, or a pleasaunte brave young roister. [M.]

1606. JOHN DAY, *Ile of Gulls*, Act i., p. 9. *Basil*. Welcome gallants, welcome honord BLOODS. *Ibid*. To which effect we have sent a generall challenge to all the youthfull BLOODS of Africa.

1752. *Adventurer*, No. 15. Our heroes of liberty, whether 'Bucks or BLOODS, or of whatever other denomination, when by some creditor of slavish principles they have been locked up in a prison, never yet petitioned to be hanged.

1839. HARRISON AINSWORTH, *Jack Sheppard* [1889], p. 21. 'Trenchard!' he muttered—'Aliva Trenchard. They were right, then, as to the name. Well, if she survives the accident—as the BLOOD who styles himself Sir Cecil fancies she may do—this ring will make my fortune by leading to the discovery of the chief parties concerned in this strange affair.'

1846. THACKERAY, *V. Fair*, ch. x. A perfect and celebrated BLOOD, or dandy about town, was this young officer.

1853. THACKERAY, *Barry Lyndon*, ch. ii., p. 36. The modern BLOODS have given up the respectful ceremonies which distinguished a gentleman in my time.

2. (old.)—Money. [A comparison of blood, as the vital principle, to money, as that upon which the sustenance of life depends—the 'sinews of war,' the 'needful,' etc.] For all synonyms, *see* ACTUAL.

1748. DODSLEY, *Collection of Poems*, III., 199.

He sticks to gaming, as the surer trade;
Turns downright sharper, lives by sucking BLOOD.

1872. M. E. BRADDON, *Dead Sea Fruit*, ch. iv. 'A man who ought to consider himself uncommonly fortunate never to have known what it was to be hard up, or to have a pack of extravagant sons sucking his BLOOD, like so many modern vampires.'

Verb (familiar).—To deplete of money; to victimise; a figurative usage of 'to bleed'; *i.e.*, surgically, to let or draw blood by opening a vein. *Cf.*, *subs.*, sense 2, and BLEED.

1884. HAWLEY SMART, *From Post to Finish*, p. 187. 'He is very likely to want a thousand pounds at any moment. There's a leaven of the old squire in his composition, and I recollect hearing that he was BLOODED over the Phaeton Leger.' 'You surely can't mean that he has taken to racing? Why, you must be aware that he has no money for anything of that sort.'

BLOOD AND ENTRAILS, *subs.* (American).—The British ensign is so nicknamed by Yankee sailors; English salts return the compliment by jokingly speaking of the American flag as THE GRIDIRON AND DOUGHBOYS (*q.v.*).

BLOOD AND THUNDER, *subs.* (common).—A beverage of port wine and brandy mixed. Port is the BLOOD, from its colour; brandy the THUNDER — the combined effects being, it is held, provocative of 'thundering' headaches.

BLOOD AND THUNDER TALES, *subs. phr.* (originally American, now common).—Low class fiction, the term being generally applied to works dealing with the exploits of desperadoes, cut-throats, and other criminals. Also called AWFULS, PENNY DREADFULS, GUTTER LITERATURE, SHILLING SHOCKERS, etc., all of which *see* for further illustrations.

1876. *Portland Transcript*, May. Here let me say one word to the *Transcript* mothers. Look carefully to your child's reading matter. Beware of the cheap, trashy romances, the BLOOD AND THUNDER TALES by Tom, Dick and Harry, which fill the counters of so many of our bookstores.

1883. *Daily News*, March 26, p. 2, col. 3. The BLOOD AND THUNDER tragedies generally associated with the transpontine drama.

BLOOD-AN'-'OUNS, *phr.* (old).—An abbreviated form of an old and blasphemous oath—'God's blood and wounds!'

1839. HARRISON AINSWORTH, *Jack Sheppard* [1889], p. 58. 'Och! if he's a friend o' yours, my dear joy, there's no more to be said; and right sorry am I I struck him. But, BLOOD-AN'-'OUNS! man, if ould Nick himself were to hit me a blow, I'd be afther givin' him another.'

BLOOD-CURDLER or **BLOOD-FREEZER**, *subs.* (common).—A narration or incident which 'makes the flesh creep'; that which stirs one's feelings strongly, and generally repulsively. Said of a sensational murder, a thrilling ghost-story, etc. *Cf.*, BLOOD AND THUNDER TALES.

BLOOD FOR BLOOD, *phr.* (trade).—When tradesmen exchange wares, setting the cost of one kind off against another instead of making payment in currency, they are said to give BLOOD FOR BLOOD. *Cf.*, BLOOD. (1) the vital fluid; (2) money — hence applied to that upon the sale of which a man is dependent for a livelihood.

1811. *Lexicon Balatronicum*. A hatter furnishing a hosier with a hat, and taking payment in stockings, is said to deal BLOOD FOR BLOOD.

BLOOD-FREEZER.—*See* BLOOD-CURDLER.

BLOOD-RED FANCY, *subs.* (pugilistic).—A particular kind of handkerchief sometimes worn by pugilists and frequenters of prize fights.—*See* BILLY.

1857. SNOWDEN, *Mag. Assistant*, 3 ed., p. 446. Red silk handkerchief. BLOOD-RED FANCY.

BLOOD SUCKERS, *subs.* (military). —The Sixty-third Regiment of Foot.

BLOOD-TUB, *subs.* (American).—A rowdy; a blustering bully; a rough. This nickname was peculiar to Baltimore, which city, perhaps of all cities in the Union, enjoyed, for a time, an unenviable reputation on account of the rowdyism of a section of its inhabitants. More or less, however, these turbulent gangs infest all the more important centres of population, and answer in many respects to the English 'roughs.' They are recruited largely from the labouring and commercial population; they drink, and swear, but commit no crime, save an occasional deed of violence in times when excitement runs unusually high, and are for the most part affiliated with one or other of the two political parties, the Republicans or Democrats. They are known as Dead Rabbits in New York, Moyamensing Hounds in Philadelphia, BLOOD-TUBS in Baltimore, where at other times they have also been designated Babes, Plug-uglies, and Ashlanders. The BLOOD-TUBS are reported to have been mostly butchers, and to have got their epithet from having, on an election day, dipped an obnoxious German's head in a tub of warm blood, and then driven him running through the town,

18 (?). *Song of the Irish Legion.*

BLOOD-TUBS and plug-uglies, and others galore,
Are sick for a thrashing in sweet Baltimore;
Be jabers! that same I'd be proud to inform
Of the terrible force of an Irishman's arm.

BLOODY, *adj.* (low).—An epithet difficult to define, and used in a multitude of vague and varying senses. Most frequently, however, as it falls with wearisome reiteration every two or three seconds from the mouths of London roughs of the lowest type, no special meaning, much less a sanguinary one, can be attached to its use. In such a case it forms a convenient intensitive, sufficiently important as regards sound to satisfy those whose lack of language causes them to fall back upon a frequent use of words of this type. BLOODY occasionally carries with it a suspicion of anger, resentment, or detestation. [For suggested derivations, and some incidental illustrative examples, *see* adverbial usage, which follows.]

1840. R. DANA, *Bef. Mast*, ii., 2. You'll find me a BLOODY rascal. *Ibid*, xx., 61. They've got a man for a mate of that ship, and not a BLOODY sheep about decks. [M.]

1880. RUSKIN, *Fiction, Fair and F.*, § 29. The use of the word BLOODY in modern low English is a deeper corruption, not altering the form of the word, but defiling the thought in it. [M.]

Adv. (low).—Among the vulgar at the present day BLOODY, used adverbially, says G. A. Sala [*Notes and Queries*, 4 S., i., Feb. 8, 1868], simply qualifies the superlative and excessive. Admiral Gambier, who is said to have introduced 'tea and piety' into the navy, very properly discountenanced the practice so long common to naval officers of d——g the sailors' eyes while they were reefing topsails. His tars, scarcely grateful, nicknamed the admiral 'Old Bloody Politeful.' The lower classes use BLOODY indifferently as a term of depreciation or appreciation. Thus, it's a BLOODY shame; and *per contra* in a flash song, the poet (supposed to be languishing in prison) recounts that the chaplain discoursed to the inmates—

'How Jonah lived inside of a whale,
'Twas a BLOODY sight better than county gaol.'

As regards derivation, dual causes seem to have operated in the evolution of BLOODY in its depraved sense. The various stages are summarised by Murray, in so far as evidence will permit, as follows. The origin is not quite certain; but there is good reason to think that it was at first a reference to the habits of the 'bloods' or aristocratic rowdies of the end of the 17th and beginning of the 18th c. The phrase 'BLOODY drunk' was apparently = 'as drunk as a blood' (*Cf.*, 'as drunk as a lord'); thence it was extended to kindred expressions, and at length to others; probably in later times, its associations with bloodshed and murder (*Cf.*, a BLOODY battle, a BLOODY butcher) have recommended it to the rough classes as a word that appeals to their imagination. We may compare the prevalent craving for impressive or graphic intensives, seen in the use of *jolly, awfully, terribly, devilish, deuced, damned, ripping, rattling, thumping, stunning, thundering*, etc. There is no ground for the notion that BLOODY, offensive as from association it now is to ears polite, contains any profane allusion, or has connection with the oath ''sblood!' In this particular it may be noted that Mr. C. G. Leland is in error when he says 'Mr. Hotten thinks this is an expletive without reference to *any* [italics not in original] meaning.' Mr. Hotten neither said nor implied anything of the kind, but just the reverse; and Mr. Leland has hung his remarks upon a misquotation. Hotten's exact words are 'BLOODY, an expletive used, without reference to meaning, as an adjective and an adverb, simply for intensification'—a very different thing; *ergo* as far as Hotten goes he is absolutely correct.

There seems little doubt, however, that the association of BLOODY with bloodshed and murder has had a very large influence in determining its present bad signification in the mouth of a cockney of the lower classes. It is noteworthy, too, that the German *blutig* is sometimes used, says H. Tiedeman [*N. and Q.*, 4 S., i., Feb. 8, 1868], in the same manner as the London BLOODY:—While living in Dresden, I heard many times uttered such phrases as—

'Ich habe keinen *blutigen* Heller mehr,'
[I have no BLOODY penny or 'red cent' more],

for 'I have not a single penny left,' etc. Was, then, the Dresden *blutig* introduced to the London mob in the shape of BLOODY? The Dutch *bloedig* may be used figuratively, just as the French *sanglant*. *Une injure sanglante* might be translated by '*een bloedige beleediging*.' It might, and it is in fact, sometimes used to qualify an adjective. To say '*bloedig schoon*' (literally, 'bloody beautiful'), would be perfectly correct, but then it has not the sense of *exceedingly*; it keeps its original meaning. '*Bloedig schoon*' could not be rendered otherwise than by *sanguinary* and *beautiful*.

1676. SIR G. ETHEREDGE, *Man of Mode* (Act i., Sc. 1), p. 186, ed. 1723.
Dor. Give him half-a-crown.
Med. Not without he will promise to be BLOODY drunk.

1684. DRYDEN, *Prol. Southerne's Disappointment*, line 59. The doughty bullies enter BLOODY drunk. [M.]

1706. FARQUHAR, *Recruiting Officer*, Act iv., Sc. 1. *Plume.* Thou art a BLOODY impudent fellow. [There is no question of fighting in the context.]

1711. SWIFT, *Journal to Stella*, 8 May, letter 22. It was BLOODY hot walking to-day.

1836. M. SCOTT, *Tom Cringle's Log*, ch. ii. 'I've a BLOODY great mind to go down with him,' stuttered another.

From the foregoing examples the word would appear to have been once in literary use; it is not now customary to print it in full, but thus, b——y. In passing it may be mentioned that there is no ground for attributing its derivation to 'By'r Our Lady.'

BLOODY BACK, *subs.* (old).—A soldier; a nickname alluding to the colour of his coat. [From BLOODY = of the colour of blood, *i.e.*, scarlet or blood-red + BACK.]

1811. *Lexicon Balatronicum*. BLOODY BACK. A jeering appellation for a soldier.

BLOODY CHASM. TO BRIDGE THE BLOODY CHASM, *phr.* (American).—A favourite expression with orators who, during the years immediately succeeding the Civil War, sought to obliterate the memory of the struggle. The antithetical phrase is TO WAVE THE BLOODY SHIRT (*q.v.*).

BLOODY ELEVENTH, *subs.* (military). The Eleventh Regiment of Foot. At the battle of Salamanca, fought with the French, the corps was nearly cut to pieces, whence its sanguinary sobriquet. At Fontenoy and Ostend also, it was hard-pressed and nearly annihilated.

BLOODY JEMMY, *subs.* (common).—An uncooked sheep's head.—*See* SANGUINARY JAMES for synonyms.

BLOODY SHIRT. TO WAVE THE BLOODY SHIRT.—A phrase which is only one of many of a similar character, variants such as 'to wave the crimson banner,' 'the ensanguined under garment,' etc., being quite frequently met with in American journalism. Its origin and history is thus explained in *Americanisms, Old and New*:—It is a political phrase used in the States to signify the opening anew or keeping alive of factious strife on party questions. Primarily it was the symbol of those who, during the Reconstruction period at the close of the rebellion of the Southern or Confederate States, would not suffer the Civil War to sink into oblivion out of consideration for the feelings of the vanquished. Perhaps a more odious term never crept into politics than the BLOODY SHIRT; it is alike distasteful to the sense, brutal and vulgar, and capable of misuse. There are still those who, in American politics, in the thousand and one points of difference which continually and inevitably must arise between institutions so diverse in origin, tradition, and practice as those of the North and South, seek for party purposes to estrange the one from the other by keeping alive the exciting memories of the old bitter struggle. When a man is said to have waved the BLOODY SHIRT it is known that he has gone back in spirit and intent to the sorrowful days of the Republic, when the blue and the grey, each confident of battling for the right, were slaying each other in the valleys of the South. He ignores the peace which has settled over the old fields of war, and does not assent to the hand clasp of Federal with Confederate. He tries to open the strife anew, mocks the spirit of forgiveness, and rakes the old ashes over in the hunt for a burning coal. He scoffs at those who fought against the Union, and, because they have come back to it, calls them insincere. He rebukes the veteran who forgave them when together they laid down their arms. This is called WAVING THE BLOODY SHIRT, and to-day, when many of those now in active life cannot remember the time when the Rebellion had closed, and the boys were marching home, there are legislators and journalists who devote their efforts to stirring up a sectional hatred which without these efforts would be but a tradition. Many Southerners keenly resent the spirit which thus traduces the now loyal South, and declares it hypocritical. The BLOODY SHIRTERS, as they are called, rail at the decency which forgives and forgets, and with venomous tongues revile alike those who fell in the lost cause, those who lived to repent, and those who would grant pardon. So long as men lost to honour will do this the action must have a name—it will be called WAVING THE BLOODY SHIRT. From this special meaning it is now passing into general use to indicate similar tactics in regard to any cause. It has recently been introduced into English journalism in connection with the Irish struggle, and the 'Unionist Party' has been accused of WAVING THE BLOODY SHIRT—with how much truth or the reverse there is here no concern. The origin of the expression is to be sought in a Corsican custom now nearly, if not quite, obsolete. In the days of the fierce *vendette*—the feuds which divided the Corsicans, family from family, bloodshed was a common occurrence. Before the burial of a murdered man, the *gridata* was celebrated. This word, which literally means a crying aloud, may be translated 'a wake.' The body of the victim was laid upon a plank; his useless firearms were placed near his hand, and his blood-stained shirt was hung above his head. Around the rude bier sat a circle of women, wrapped in their black mantles, who rocked themselves to and fro with strange wailings. The men, relatives and friends of the murdered man, fully armed stood around the room, mad with thirst for revenge. Then one of the women—the wife or mother or sister of the dead man—with a sharp scream would snatch the BLOODY SHIRT, and waving it aloft begin the *vocero*—the lamentation. This rhythmic discourse was made up of alternate expressions of love for the dead, and hatred of his enemies; and its startling images and tremendous curses were echoed in the faces and amidst the mutterings of the armed mourners. Its application to American politics is credited to Mr. Oliver P. Morton, who, elected United States senator in 1867, and again in 1873, took a prominent part as a leader of the more radical Republicans, favouring a stern policy of coercion in the reconstruction of the Southern States. He was one of the Presidential Candidates at the Cincinnati Convention of 1876, his name standing second on the first ballot. Happily, however, his opinions were too pronounced to unite the factions of his party, and the ultimate choice fell upon Mr. Hayes.

1888. *Coldwater* (Mich.) *Sun*, Jan. The BLOODY SHIRT is gradually fading away. The white-winged dove of peace spreads her wings here and there, patriotism forgets and forgives old differences, sectionalism is gradually giving way to love of country—the whole country. In fact the ill-feeling between the North and South would have died out years ago among the veterans of both sections, had they been left to themselves, and the politicians been as patriotic as they.

1888. *New York Weekly Times*, Mar. 21. It is reprehensible to the last degree for the Bourbons of the South to continue to play on the colour line—the Southern BLOODY SHIRT—and then denounce Republican extremists for doing the same thing at the North.

BLOOMER, *subs.* (Australian prison slang).—A mistake. Said to be an abbreviated form of 'blooming error.'—*See* BLOOMING.

BLOOMING, often **BLOOMIN'**, *ppl. adj.* (common).—This word, similar in type to 'blessed,' 'blamed,' and other words of the kind, is, as used by the lower classes, a euphemism for BLOODY (*q.v.*), but it is also frequently employed as a mere meaningless intensitive. Like the last-named word, little count is taken of its exact primary meaning. Its slang use may be traced to that figurative sense of the orthodox word, which signifies 'in the bloom of health and beauty,' 'in the prime,' 'flourishing,' etc. Some uncertainty exists as to the origin of this not over-ornamental addition to our expletive vocabulary. If the word is used by Granvil (*see* quot.) in its modern sense, then the phrase is very much older than has hitherto been imagined. Barring this, it would seem that we are indebted for it to the Californian coast, although there is little doubt that the chief instrument in its acclimatization in England was Mr. Alfred G. Vance, the comic singer, well-known in connection with 'Jolly dogs,' and other extensively popular music-hall songs. As before stated, it has very largely supplanted 'bloody'; BALLY (*q.v.*) is also used in the same manner. Its applications are manifold. One is requested not to make any BLOOMING mistake or error; another 'showing off,' or 'putting on side,' is told not to be so BLOOMING flash; an excessively stupid man is spoken of as a BLOOMING idiot; and an inquisitive individual is told more forcibly than politely, perhaps, 'you asks me no BLOOMIN' imper'int questions, an' I tells yer no BLOOMIN' lies.'

1726. REV. J. GRANVIL, *Sadducismus triumphatus* [under the head of 'The Demon of Tedworth' (1661). Granvil makes mention that on one occasion the spirit came into a room panting like a dog, and] company coming up, the room was presently filled with a BLOOMING noisome smell.

18(?). COLONEL JOHN HAY, *Ballad*, 'The Mystery of Gilgal.'
He went for his 'leven inch bowie knife:
I tries to foller a Christian life,
But I'll drop a slice of liver or two,
My BLOOMIN' shrub, with you.

1887. G. R. SIMS, *Dagonet Ballads* (*Told to the Missionary*). 'I feels like a BLOOMIN' babby—I gets so infernal weak.'

1877. *Five Years' Penal Servitude*, ch. iii., p. 222. 'Afore that I worked in the galleries, a making the casemates for the guns, and BLOOMING hard work it was.'

1882. *Punch's Almanac*, p. 4. THE STEAM LAUNCH IN VENICE ('Sic Transit Gloria Mundi')—*'Andsome 'Arriet*: 'Ow my! If it 'yn't that BLOOMIN' old Temple Bar, as they did aw'y with out o' Fleet Street!' *Mr. Belleville* (referring to guide book): 'Now it 'yn't. It's the fymous Bridge o' *Sighs*, as Byron went and stood on; 'im as wrote 'Our Boys,' yer know!' *'Andsome 'Arriet*: 'Well, I *never*!'

1880. JAS. GREENWOOD, *Flyfaker's Hotel*, in *Odd People in Odd Places*, p. 59. 'Who's got any music?' presently exclaimed the dirty scoundrel who had been mending the boxing-glove; '—— me, let's have a BLOOMIN' lark! Let's have a tune and a song. Who's got any BLOOMIN' music?'

1884. W. C. RUSSELL, *Jack's Courtship*, ch. xxxviii. 'And if there's fire there ought to be nothen to stop us from cooking a BLOOMIN' old goat.'

1889. *Ally Sloper*, July 6. Injured Innocence: *Indignant Son of Labour.* Well, I'm blowed! If that 'ere BLOOMIN' swell ain't a-himitatin' me!

BLOSS, *subs.* (old, and American thieves').—A generic name for a woman, whether girl, wife, or mistress. Probably from an attributive sense of 'blossom.' For example, Shakspeare, in *Titus Andromicus* [1588, iv., 2, 72], employs it in the sense of one lovely and full of promise. 'Sweet BLOWSE you are a beautious BLOSSOME sure.' Tennyson also [1847] in the *Princess* [v., 79] uses the expression, 'My babe, my BLOSSOM, ah, my child!' *Cf.*, BLOWEN.

1785. GROSE, *Dictionary of the Vulgar Tongue*. BLOSS (cant), the pretended wife of a bully or shop-lifter.

1881. *New York Slang Dictionary*, 'Slang Stories,' p. 42. 'Why, Bell, is it yourself? Tip us your daddle, my bene mort. May I dance at my death, and grin in a class-case, if I didn't think you had been put to bed with a shovel. . . .' 'No, Jim, I only piked into Grassville with a dimber-damber, who couldn't pad the hoof for a single darkman's without his BLOSS to keep him from getting pogy.'

BLOT THE SCRIP, *verbal phr.* (old).—To put an undertaking into writing; the modern phrase is 'to put it in black and white.' Hence

TO BLOT THE SCRIP AND JARK IT (old), *i.e.*, to stand engaged, or bound for anyone.—*Grose*. JARK means a seal, and in Oxford slang, a safe conduct pass; in the former sense it is retained in the patter of modern American thieves, a synonym being JASKER. Jarkman is the name given in America to a begging letter writer, whose accomplishments in this respect are varied by the production of false characters for servants, and other documents of a kindred nature. This is a case, like many others, in which old English cant terms have, across the Atlantic, been invested with a new meaning. Formerly a jarkman was equivalent to an 'Abram-man,' *i.e.*, a licensed beggar.

BLOVIATE, *verb* (American).—To talk aimlessly and boastingly; to indulge in 'high falutin'. [A factitious word probably founded on the verb BLOW, sense 1, on the model of 'deviate.'] Said to have been in use since 1850.

BLOW, *subs.* (common).—1. A shilling.

Amongst SYNONYMS for this coin are beong; borde; button; deaner or deener; bob; bobstick (old slang); breaky-leg; gen (this forms part of the so-called back slang); hog; levy; peg; stag; teviss; twelver; touch-me (this is an abbreviated form of touch-me-on-the-nob, rhyming slang for bob or shilling); Abraham's willing (also rhyming slang for a shilling).

1879. J. W. HORSLEY, in *Macm. Mag.*, XL., 501. But afterwards I got 3s. 9d., and then four BLOW. *Ibid.* I went to the Steel (Bastile—Coldbath Fields Prison), having a new suit of clobber on me and about fifty BLOW in my brigh (pocket).

1885. *Daily Telegraph*, Feb. 5, p. 2, col. 6. They said they could sell some for five BLOWS (shillings), and that he could easily make £158 of the stuff.

2. (Old University.) — A drunken frolic; a spree. *Cf.*, BLOW-OUT, *subs.* For synonyms, *see* JAMBOREE.

Verb.—1. To boast; to brag; to 'gas'—generally to talk boastfully or self-assertingly of oneself or one's affairs. In this sense TO BLOW, long dialectically current, is now regarded as slang. It is also associated with the idea of angry speech, 'storming,' 'fuming.' *Cf.*, BLOW UP, and for synonyms, *see* GAS.

c. 1400. *Apol. Loll.*, 97. BLOUING veynly wip fleschli wit. [M.]

1519. *Four Elements*, in Hazl. *Dodsley*, I., 41. Why, man, what aileth thee so to BLOW? [M.]

1785. BURNS, *Epistle to J. Lapraik*, st. 16. I winna BLAW about mysel; As ill I like my fauts to tell.

1883. *Graphic*, Jan. 27, p. 79, col. 1. The whole team has taught Australia not to BLOW (as they say)—a not unneeded lesson.

1883. MRS. CAMPBELL PRAED, *Sketches of Australian Life*, p. 45. 'He was famous for his coolness and daring, and for BLOWING, in Australian parlance, both of his exploits and of his "bonnes fortunes."'

2. (general.)—To inform; to expose; to betray; to peach. *Cf.*, also BLOW UPON and BLOW THE GAB. [This is a transferred sense of blow = to breathe out; to give forth by breathing; hence, to sound a signal on an instrument; to blaze abroad as by a trumpet.] For synonyms, *see* PEACH.

1575. *Appius and Virg.*, in Hazl. *Dodsley*, IV., 136. Was all well agreed? did nobody BLOW ye? [M.]

1721. DEFOE, *History of Colonel Jack*. 'As for that,' says Will, 'I could tell it well enough, if I had it, but I must not be seen anywhere among my old acquaintances, for I am BLOWN, and they will all betray me.'

1748. T. DYCHE, *Dictionary* (5 ed.). BLOW (v.) . . . also to discover the secrets of another; also when a person undervalues or slights a person or thing, he is said to BLOW upon it.

a. 1859. L. HUNT, *Country Lodgings*, in *Casquet Lit.* (1877), I., p. 42, col. 1. D—n me, if I don't BLOW . . . I'll tell Tom Neville. [M.]

3. (American.)—To lie; and in a slightly less opprobrious sense to 'gas' so much as to be perilously near the border-line which separates boasting exaggeration from absolute untruth.

4. (general.) — Frequently employed euphemistically for 'to damn'—generally in the imperative.—BLOW IT! *i.e.*, 'hang it'! or damn it! *Cf.*, BLOWED, with which it is closely allied in all senses.

1849. C. KINGSLEY, *Alton Locke*, ch. ii. 'Well, if you won't stand a pot,' quoth the tall man, 'I will, that's all, and BLOW temperance.'

1883. MISS BRADDON, *Golden Calf*, ch. xxvi. 'BLOW his station in life! If he was a duke I shouldn't want him.'

5. (general.) — To lose or spend money. *Cf.*, BLUE.

6. (University.)—To indulge in a frolic or spree. *Cf.*, BLOW OUT; also TO GO ON THE BLOW.

7. (Winchester School.)—To blush.

TO BITE THE BLOW, *phr.* (old cant).—To steal goods; to PRIG, which *see* for synonyms.

BLOW A CLOUD, *verbal phr.* (colloquial).—To smoke a cigar or pipe; Hotten says, 'a phrase used two centuries ago' but gives no authority, and Murray's earliest example only dates from 1855, but as will be seen below, it occurs in *Tom Crib* in 1819.

1819. MOORE, *Tom Crib's Memorial to Congress*, p. 39.
. . . His fame I need not tell,
For *that*, my friends, all England's loud with;
But this I'll say, a civiller Swell
I'd never wish to BLOW A CLOUD with.

1870. M. TWAIN, *Innocents Abroad*, ch. vii. And BLOWING suffocating 'CLOUDS' and boisterously performing at dominoes in the smoking-room at night.

FRENCH SYNONYMS. *Tubons en une* (popular: 'let's blow a cloud'; *tuber* = to smoke); *piper*; *la fumerie* (popular: smoking); *faire du brouillard* ('to produce or make a fog or mist'); *en bourrer une*; *bouffarder*. A GERMAN SYNONYM is *Esef schwächen*, or *schweihen*.

BLOW-BOOK, *subs.* (old).—A book containing indelicate or 'smutty' pictures.

1708. *Post Man*, 8 June. Last Sunday a person did pennance in the Chapter-House of St. Paul's, London, for publickly shewing in Bartholomew Fair a book called a BLOW-BOOK, in which were many obscene and filthy pictures: the book was likewise burnt, and the person paid costs.

BLOWED. TO BE BLOWED, *verb* (familiar).—BLOWED is here a euphemism for 'damned'; to all intents and purposes, it is frequently little more than a thinly-veiled oath. Hotten says that Tom Hood used to tell the following story:—'I was once asked to contribute to a new journal, not exactly gratuitously, but at a very small advance upon nothing—and avowedly because the work had been planned according to that estimate. However, I accepted the terms conditionally—that is to say, provided the principle could be properly carried out. Accordingly, I wrote to my butcher, baker, and other tradesmen, informing them that it was necessary, for the sake of cheap literature and the interest of the reading public, that they should furnish me with their several commodities at a very trifling per-centage above cost price. It will be sufficient to quote the answer of the butcher:—"Sir,—Respectin' your note, Cheap literater BE BLOWED! Butchers must live as well as other pepel—and if so be you or the readin' publick wants to have meat at prime cost, you must buy your own beastesses, and kill yourselves.—I remain, etc., John Stokes."'

Cf., BLOW ME!

1835. DICKENS, *Sketches by Boz*, p. 50. Others remonstrating with the said Thomas Sludberry, on the impropriety of his conduct, the said Thomas Sludberry repeated the aforesaid expression, 'YOU BE BLOWED.'

1863. JEAFFRESON, *Live It Down*, III., p. 249. (Cries of 'Chair, Chair,' and 'Order, order.') 'Order BE BLOWED!' exclaimed the infuriated Mr. H.

1864. DICKENS, *Our Mutual Friend*, bk. II., ch. v. 'HOLIDAY BE BLOWED!' said Fledgely, entering, 'What have *you* got to do with holidays?'

1877. *Five Years' Penal Servitude*, ch. iii., p. 244. 'No,' says she, 'we've got some more besides that, and enough, too, to take us to France. BLOWED, old man, if we don't go to Paris, and there we can get £300 for them.'

1879. *Punch's Almanac*, p. 7. Seasonable Slang. For Spring.—YOU BE BLOWED! For Summer.—I'll warm yer! For Autumn.—Not so blooming green! For Winter.—An ice little game all round.

1889. *Ally Sloper's H. H.*, Aug. 3, p. 242, col. 2. 'BLOWED if I'd have made her Mrs. Juggins, if I'd have known she wor going to make a footstool of me!'

BLOWEN or **BLOWING**, *subs.* (old.)—This word appears to have passed through a series of ups and downs in the course of its career. Originally signifying a woman, without special reference to moral character, it subsequently came to mean a showy courtesan, or a prostitute. It still retains the latter meaning, but is frequently used in a more complimentary sense than heretofore to signify a finely built handsome girl. In America among the criminal classes it is only used to designate a mistress. Its derivation is extremely uncertain, the two most important suggestions being that it comes (1) from the reputation having been 'blown upon'; and (2) that in Wilts BLOWEN signifies a blossom—hence BLOWEN a flower; a pet.

1688. SHADWELL, *Sq. of Alsatia*, I., in wks. (1720) IV., 17. What ogling there will be between thee and the BLOWINGS!

1789. GEO. PARKER, *Life's Painter*, p. 143. BLOWEN, a woman.

1812. J. H. VAUX, *Flash Dict.* BLOWEN, a prostitute: a woman who cohabits with a man without marriage.

1847. LYTTON, *Lucretia*, pt. II., ch. ii. 'If she's a good girl, and loves you, she'll not let you spend your money on her.' 'I haint such a ninny as that,' said Beck, with majestic contempt. 'I 'spises the flat that is done brown by the BLOWENS.'

1848. C. KINGSLEY, *Yeast*, ch. xi. Why don't they have a short simple service now and then, that might catch the ears of the roughs and the BLOWENS, without tiring out the poor thoughtless creatures' patience, as they do now?

For synonyms in the sense of prostitute, *see* BARRACK-HACK.

BLOWER, *subs.* (old).—1. A girl; a contemptuous name in opposition to JOMER (*q.v.*); given by Grose [1785].

2. (American and Colonial.)—A good talker; a boaster; a 'gas-bag.' *Cf.*, BLOW, *verb*, sense 1.

1863. MANHATTAN, in *Evening Standard*, 10 Dec. General Grant . . . is not one of the BLOWER generals. [M.]

1864. *Spectator*, 22 Oct., 1202, col. 1. Notorious among our bar and the public as a BLOWER. [M.]

1871. DE VERE, *Americanisms*, p. 584. 'You need not *blow* so, my friend. I don't believe a word of what you say.' Hence also the noun BLOWER, a braggart, with special reference to his success in imitating Baron Munchausen.

3. A pipe. *Cf.*, BLOW A CLOUD.

BLOW GREAT GUNS, *verbal phr.* (popular).—To blow a hurricane; a violent gale. Sometimes varied by to BLOW GREAT GUNS AND SMALL ARMS.

1839. HARRISON AINSWORTH, *Jack Sheppard* [1889], 23. 'Curse me, if I don't think all the world means to cross the Thames this fine night!' observed Ben. 'One'd think it rained fares as well as BLOWED GREAT GUNS.'

Why, there's another party on the stair-head inquiring arter scullers; and, by the mass! they appear in a greater hurry than any of us.'

1854. H. MILLER, *Sch. and Schm.* (1858), 14. It soon began to BLOW GREAT GUNS. [M.]

BLOWHARD, *subs.* (American).—A Western term of revilement, the precise meaning of which it would be difficult to explain, since a newcomer may, in one and the same breath, be called a BLARSTED BRITISHER, a COYOTE, and a BLOWHARD. If all these are synonymous, then indeed the Englishman in America is in a bad way. *Cf.*, BLOWER, sense 2.

BLOW HOT AND COLD, *verbal phr.* (familiar).—To be treacherous; inconsistent; vacillating. There is an allusion in the expression to one of Æsop's fables.

1577. W. BULLINGER, *Decades* (1592), 176. One which out of one mouth, doeth BLOWE BOTH HOAT AND COLDE. [M.]

1756. *The World*, No. 185. This old fellow is of a most capricious, unequal temper, and, like the satyr in the fable, BLOWS HOT AND COLD in the same breath.

1856. MOTLEY, *Dutch Rep.*, V., v., 750. Being constantly ordered 'to BLOW HOT AND COLD with the same breath.'

BLOWING UP, *subs.* (colloquial).—A scolding; a severe reprimand; a jobation.—*See* BLOW UP. The French equivalent is *affres* (*fem. pl.*), *i.e.*, 'agonies.'

1839. HALIBURTON, *Letter-Bag Gt. West*, IV., 42. I would give him a good BLOWING-UP. [M.]

1874. MRS. H. WOOD, *Johnny Ludlow*, I S., No. xxv., p. 448. The waves dashed over the pier, ducking the three or four venturesome spirits who went on there. I was one—and received a good BLOWING UP from Mr. Brandon for my pains.

BLOW IN ONE'S PIPE, *verbal phr.* (American). — A transatlantic equivalent of to BLOW or BLEW [one's money]; *i.e.*, to spend it.

BLOW ME! BLOW ME UP! BLOW ME TIGHT! *intj. phr.* (popular).—Expressions which, like BLOWED (*q.v.*), serve either as half-veiled oaths or as merely big sounding but meaningless exclamations.

1781. G. PARKER, *View of Society*, I., 48. 'BLOW ME UP (says he) if I have had a fellow with such *rum toggys* cross my company these many a day.'

1819. MOORE, *Tom Crib's Memorial to Congress*.
Says Bill 'there's nothing like a Bull
And BLOW ME TIGHT'—Bill Gibbons ne'er
In all his days was known to swear,
Except light oaths, to grace his speeches,
Like '*dash my wig*' or '*burn my breeches*,'
'BLOW ME——'

1876. C. HINDLEY, *Life and Adventures of a Cheap Jack*, p. 25. Here BLOW ME, I'll do such a thing I never did before, I'll say thirty—yes, thirty shillings buys the lot, and I'll have no more nor take no less.

BLOW ONE'S BAZOO, *verbal phr.* (American). — To boast; to swagger; to gasconade. [From the Dutch *bazu*, an abbreviation of *bazuin*, a trumpet; hence an equivalent of the English 'to blow one's own trumpet'.]

BLOW ONESELF OUT, *verb* (common).—To eat heartily; to gorge oneself.—*See* BLOW OUT.

1837. BARHAM, *I. L.* (*Babes in the Wood*).
In the dog-days, don't be so absurd
As to BLOW YOURSELVES OUT with greengages!

BLOW OUT, *subs.* (common). — A gluttonous feast, a heavy 'feed,' or entertainment. Also called a TUCK IN, which *see* for syno-

nyms. *Cf.*, BLOW ONESELF OUT.

1825. SCOTT, *St. Ronan's Well*, II., 264. 'She sent me a card for her BLOW-OUT,' said Mowbray, 'and so I am resolved to go.'

1847. TH. HOOK, *Man of Many Friends*. The giving good feeds is, with many of these worthies, the grand criterion by which the virtues and talents of mankind are measured . . . these persons call a similar favour either a 'spread' or a 'BLOW-OUT.'

1852. H. B. STOWE, *Uncle Tom's Cabin*, ch. viii. 'Get us hot water, and sugar, and cigars, and plenty of the *real stuff*, and we'll have a BLOW-OUT.'

Verb (thieves'). — To steal. For synonyms, *see* PRIG.

BLOWSE, BLOWSY, BLOUZE, BLOWZY, *subs.* (old).—1. A beggar's trull; a wench.

2. A slatternly woman, especially one with dishevelled hair. Thought to be of canting origin. In Grose's time the term was humorously varied by Blowsabella, in reference to the country girl in Gay's pastoral poem, 'The Shepherd's Week,' which depicts rural life in its character of poverty and rudeness, rather than as clothed in the colours of romance.

We, fair, fine ladies, who park out our lives
From common sheep-paths, cannot help the crows,
From flying over; we're as natural still
As Blousalinda.

1557. TUSSER, *Husbandrie*, ch. xvi., st. 37, p. 43 (E.D.S.). Whiles Gillet, his BLOUSE, is a milking thy cow.

1605. CHAPMAN, *All Fooles*, Act iv., p. 68 (*Plays*, 1874).
Wed without my advice, my love, my knowledge,
Ay, and a beggar, too, a trull, a BLOWSE!

1638. FORD, *Lady's Trial*, III., i. Wench is your trull, your BLOUZE, your dowdie.

1705. WARD, *Hudibras Redivivus*, vol. II., pt. VII., p. 20.
So the old Babylonian BLOUZE,
And her demure fanatick Spouse.

1851. THACKERAY, *English Humorists*, p. 167. Are not the Rosalindas of Britain as charming as the BLOUSALINDAS of the Hague?

BLOW THE GAB or **GAFF**, *verbal phr.* (common).—To reveal, or 'let out' a secret; to peach. *Cf.*, GAFF, GAG and GAB. For synonyms, *see* PEACH.

1785. GROSE, *Dictionary of the Vulgar Tongue*. To BLOW THE GAB (cant), to confess, or impeach a confederate.

1833. MARRYAT, *Peter Simple*, ch. xliii. 'One of the French officers, after he was taken prisoner, axed me how we had managed to get the gun up there; but I wasn't going to BLOW THE GAFF.'

1877. *Five Years' Penal Servitude*, ch. ii., p. 122. The prisoner, burning for revenge, quietly bides his time till the chief warder comes round, then asks to speak to him, and 'BLOWS THE GAFF.'

BLOW THE GRAMPUSE, *verbal phr.* (nautical). — To throw cold water on a man who has fallen asleep when on duty.

BLOW THE GROUNDSELS, *verbal phr.* (old).—To have sexual commerce on the ground.

1785. GROSE, *Dictionary of the Vulgar Tongue*. To BLOW THE GROUNDSILS (cant), to lie with a woman on the floor.

BLOW TOGETHER, *verbal phr.* (tailors').—To make garments in a slovenly manner.

BLOW UP, *subs.* (colloquial). — A scolding; a 'wigging'; a railing.

1809. SIR W GELL, in C. K. Sharpe's *Correspondence* (1888), I., 355. There won't be any quarrel, so you need not fear. The only chance is Keppel making a BLOW UP when she abuses me.

1849. THACKERAY, *Pendennis*, ch. lxviii. Morgan had had 'a devil of a BLOW HUP with his own guv'nor, and was going to retire from the business haltogether.'

1855. THACKERAY, *Newcomes*, ch. vii. 'Mind the hice is here in time; or they'll be a BLOW UP with your governor.'

Verb (colloquial).—To scold.

1809. SIR W. GELL, in C. K. Sharpe's *Correspondence* (1888), I., 355. I have heard her daughter BLOW UP Lady Salisbury when she had quarrelled with Lady Sefton.

1883. G. A. S[ALA], in *Illust. L. News*, June 16, p. 599, col. I. That the 'aughty nobleman should BLOW UP the clerk for presuming to take a seat in his presence.

To BLOW UP SKY-HIGH, *phr.* (American). — The American, fond of doing everything with unusual energy, likes to BLOW UP SKY-HIGH, an addition which lends colour to the supposition that probably the phrase is originally a nautical one, and really borrowed from the blowing up of a vessel, much as the meaning of the words must have evaporated before it reached the present stage.

BLOW UPON (old).—To betray; to tell tales of; to discredit; to defame.—*See* BLOW, *verb*, sense 2. Used also with indirect passive.

1402. [? T. OCCLEVE], *Letter of Cupid*, in Arber's *Garner*, vol. IV., p. 61.
Thus they despisèd be, on every side,
Dislanderèd and BLOWN UPON full wide.

1750. FIELDING, *Tom Jones*, bk. X., ch. ii. 'That the reputation of her house, which was never BLOWN UPON before, was utterly destroyed.'

1843. DICKENS, *Martin Chuzzlewit*, II., p. 239. It fortunately occurred to me, that if I gave it him myself, I could be of no farther use. I should have been BLOWN UPON immediately.

1864. DICKENS, *Our Mutual Friend*, bk. III., ch. xii. 'The condition of our affairs is desperate, and may be BLOWN UPON at any moment.'

1877. *Five Years' Penal Servitude*, ch. i., p. 4. Both desisted from their own recriminations as to 'rounding' and 'BLOWING' ON each other.

1882. JAS. PAYN, in *Glow Worm Tales*, p. 301. 'An Improvement on a System.' If Mr. Prince had caught me before his establishment had got 'BLOWN UPON' in the public prints, he might have persuaded me to become an inmate of the Agapemone. I hope I should not have approved of the manner of life in vogue at that institution, but I make no doubt that I should have fallen in with it without much resistance.

BLUB.—*See* BLUBBER, *verb.*

BLUBBER, *subs.* (common). — 1. The mouth. From the figurative use of the word, especially of anything swollen or protruding, as of the lips. For synonyms, *see* POTATO-TRAP.

1785. GROSE, *Dictionary of the Vulgar Tongue*. I have stopped the cull's BLUBBER, I have stopped the fellow's mouth.

2. A woman's breasts.—*See* SPORT BLUBBER, and for synonyms, DAIRIES.

Verb (familiar).—To cry; to weep — used contemptuously. Also shortened into BLUB.

1400. *Test. Love*, II. (1560), 283, I. Han women none other wrech . . . but BLOBER and wepe till hem list stint. [M.]

1748. SMOLLETT, *Roderick Random*, xliv. (1804), 202. He BLUBBERED like a great school-boy who had been whipped.

1826. SCOTT, *Woodstock*, IV. Phœbe Mayflower BLUBBERED heartily for company. [M.]

To SPORT BLUBBER, *phr.* (common).—To show one's breasts, said of women, especially those with large and prominent bosoms.

BLUBBER AND GUTS, *subs.* (common).—Obesity; a low term.

BLUBBER-BELLY, *subs.* (common). —A fat person.

BLUBBER HEAD, *subs.* (common).—A foolish, empty-headed individual.—*See* APARTMENTS TO LET.

BLUCHER (ch. hard), *subs.* (Winchester College).—1. A College præfect in half power. Their jurisdiction does not extend beyond 'Seventh Chamber passage,' though their privileges are the same as those of other præfects. They are eight in number.

1864. *Blackwood*, p. 86. The remaining eight college præfects (called in Winchester tongue, BLUCHERS) have a more limited authority, confined to Chambers and the Quadrangle.

1870. MANSFIELD, *School-Life at Winchester College*, p. 30. The eight senior præfects were said to have 'full power,' and had some slight privileges not enjoyed by the remaining ten, who were generally called BLUCHERS.

2. A non-privileged cab plying at railway stations. The origin of the name and its application, as far as known, is given in the two following quotations.

1864. *Soc. Sc. Review*, I., p. 406. The railway companies recognise two other classes of cabs, called the 'privileged' . . . and the 'BLUCHERS,' named after the Prussian Field-Marshal who arrived on the field of Waterloo only to do the work that chanced to be undone.

1870. *Athenæum*, 5 March, p. 328. Non-privileged cabs, which are admitted to stations after all the privileged have been hired, are known as BLUCHERS.

BLUDGEONER, *subs.* (harlotry).—A bully; pimp; ponce; a man attached to a house of ill-fame for the purpose of terrorising victims, and rendering easier the task of plunder. [From BLUDGEON, a stout stick or club, + ER or EER; *i.e.*, one armed with the weapon in question.]

1852. *Blackwood's Magazine*, p. 224. Those brutal BLUDGEONEERS . . . go out . . . in gangs to poach. [M.]

1855. TROLLOPE, *Warden*, xiv., p. 144. Old St. Dunstan with its smiting BLUDGEONEER has been removed.

BLUDGER, *subs.* (thieves').—A low thief, who does not hesitate to use violence; literally one who will use a bludgeon. *Cf.*, BLUDGET.

1856. H. MAYHEW, *Gt. World of London*, p. 46. Those who plunder with *violence*; as . . . BLUDGERS or 'stick slingers,' who rob in company with low women.

BLUDGET, *subs.* (American).—This is given in the *New York Slang Dictionary* [1881] as 'a low female thief, who decoys her victims into alley-ways, etc., to rob them.' *Cf.*, BLUDGER.

BLUE.—Few words enter more largely into the composition of slang, and colloquialisms bordering on slang, than does the word BLUE. Expressive alike of the utmost contempt, as of all that men hold dearest and love best, its manifold combinations, in ever varying shades of meaning, greet the philologist at every turn. A very Proteus, it defies all attempts to trace the why and wherefore of many of the turns of expression of which it forms a part—why true BLUE should be synonymous with faithful, staunch adherence to one's faith and principles; or why, on the other hand, to look BLUE should signify affected with fear, dismayed, and low-spirited. Curiously enough, the historical method helps but little to decide why in one case an exact reversal of meaning should have taken place in the application of the word; for, as far as the evidence is concerned, both the good and bad shades of meaning appear to run contemporaneously. It is also noteworthy that the word enters largely into the slang of nationalities other than our own; indeed, one of the most curious, as well as one of the most interesting facts connected with the comparative study of slang, is that which reveals the oneness of the human race in its modes of thought and speech, the Tower of Babel notwithstanding. This special feature of slang will, to some extent, be found dealt with at the end of this work; but the subject is too wide, and the field too vast, for one student to have accomplished much single-handed. This, however, may be said; that, comparing the slang of one nation with that of another, one finds the same ideas cropping up, revealing, alas! the same follies and foibles, but also showing, let it be said, in the few cases where slang travels beyond the earthy and the sensual, the same aspirations, the same endeavour, and the same hope.

Subs.—1. A policeman. [From the colour of the uniform.] This epithet can be traced back to Elizabethan days [*see* BLUE-BOTTLE], and the uniform seems to have been blue from time immemorial; indeed, this colour appears from the earliest times to have been the badge of servitude. Pliny tells us blue was the colour in which the Gauls clothed their slaves; and, for many ages, blue coats were the liveries of servants, apprentices, and those in humble stations of life—to wit, the blue-clad beadles, the 'varlets' who wore the blue, the blue-coat boys, and even harlots in a house of correction, who wore blue as a dress of ignominy. The proverb quoted by Ray, 'he's in his better blue clothes,' *i.e.*, 'he thinks himself wondrous fine,' has reference to the livery of a servant. The police more recently have been known collectively as BLUES, the MEN IN BLUE, BLUE-BOYS, BLUE BOTTLES, BLUE-DEVILS, ROYAL REGIMENT OF FOOT-GUARDS BLUE, all nicknames referring to the colour of the uniform. For general synonyms, *see* BEAK.

1877. *Five Years' Penal Servitude*, ch. iv., p. 257. He would chatter gaily and enter with great gusto into the details of some cleverly executed 'bit of business,' or 'bilking the BLUES,'—evading the police.

18(?). HOOD, *Row at the 'Oxford Arms.'*
Well, that's the row, and who can guess
the upshot after all?
Whether Harmony will ever make the
'Arms' her house of call;
Or whether this here mobbing, as some
longish heads fortell it,
Will grow to such a riot that the Oxford
BLUES must quell it.

2. A BLUE is known to licensed victuallers and their customers in certain districts of Wales as a compromise between the half-pint and the pint pot. It is not recognised as a legal measure by the authorities on weights and measures, but it is approaching to something like a status, as it deserves to do in the interests of temperance. Although there is no Board of Trade standard of the BLUE, and inspectors have no power to stamp measures of this denomination for use in trade, the Board of Trade has pointed out to the local authorities that

there is nothing in the Weights and Measures Act to prevent the use of the BLUE or to make its possessor liable to penalties, always provided of course that the vessel is not used as a measure.

3. A scholar of Christ's Hospital; a blue-coat boy. [This nickname is also derived from the colour of the clothes—a blue drugget gown or body with ample skirts to it, a yellow vest underneath in winter time, small clothes of Russia duck, worsted yellow stockings, a leathern girdle, and a little black worsted cap, usually carried in the hand, being the complete costume. This was the ordinary dress of children in humble life during the reigns of the Tudors.]

1834. W. TROLLOPE (*Title*), Christ's Hospital . . . with memoirs of Eminent BLUES.

1877. W. H. BLANCH, *Blue-Coat Boys*, p. 33. To some extent it holds also with regard to Civil Engineers, amongst whom, however, one well-known name is that of a BLUE.

4. Short for BLUE-STOCKING (*q v.*); formerly a contemptuous term for a woman having or affecting literary tastes.

1788. MADAME D'ARBLAY, *Diary* (1876), iv., 219. He was a little the more anxious not to be surprised to-night, but his being too tired for walking should be imputed to his literary preference of reading to a BLUE. At tea Miss Planta again joined us, and instantly behind him went the book; he was very right, for nobody would have thought it more odd or more BLUE.

1823. BYRON, *Don Juan*, ch. xi., st. 50. The BLUES, that tender tribe, who sigh o'er sonnets.

1845. DISRAELI, *Sybil*, p. 76. 'But she was very clever . . .' 'Accomplished?' 'Oh, far beyond that . . .' 'A regular BLUE.'

1853. REV. E. BRADLEY ('Cuthbert Bede'), *Adventures of Verdant Green*, I., p. 7. His Aunt Virginia was as learned a BLUE as her esteemed ancestress in the court of Elizabeth, the very Virgin Queen of BLUES.

5. Female learning or pedantry.

1824. BYRON, *Don Juan*, xvi., 47. She also had a twilight tinge of BLUE. [M.]

6. (University.)—At Oxford and Cambridge a man is said to get his BLUE when selected as a competitor in inter-university sports. The University colours are, for Oxford, dark blue; and for Cambridge, light blue. *Cf.*, TO GET ONE'S SILK, said of a barrister when made Queen's Counsel.

Adj.—1. A contemptuous epithet applied usually to women of literary tastes.—*See* BLUE-STOCKING. The French have *elle est bleue celle-là*; *en voilà une de bleue*; *je la trouve bleue*.

1788. MAD. D'ARBLAY, *Diary* (1842), iv., p. 219. Nobody would have thought it more odd or more BLUE.

1834. SOUTHEY, *The Doctor*, ch. lxxxix. Les Dames des Roches, both mother and daughter were remarkable and exemplary women; and there was a time when Poictiers derived as much glory from those BLUE ladies as from the Black Prince.

1839. LEVER, *Harry Lorrequer*, ch. xi. She was a little, a very little BLUE—rather a babbler in the 'ologies' than a real disciple.

1842. DICKENS, *American Notes*, ch. iii., p. 33. BLUE ladies there are, in Boston; but like philosophers of that colour and sex in most other latitudes, they rather desire to be thought superior than to be so.

1852. F. E. SMEDLEY, *Lewis Arundel*, ch. xxxiii. She had been growing decidedly BLUE. Not only had she, under Bray's auspices, published a series of papers in *Blunt's Magazine*, but she had positively written a child's book.

1864. *Spectator*, No. 1875, p. 660. A clever, sensible woman, rather BLUE.

2. Indecent; 'smutty'; obscene. This may be derived from the blue dress of harlots—*see* preceding, *subs.*, 1—although Hotten suggests it as coming

from the French *Bibliothèque Bleu*, a series of books of very questionable character. Books or conversation of an entirely opposite nature are said to be BROWN or Quakerish, *i.e.*, serious, grave, decent.

3. Gloomy; fearful; depressed; low-spirited. *Cf.*, TO LOOK BLUE, BLUE FUNK, and IN THE BLUES. Possibly an allusion to the blueness of cold.

1857. A. TROLLOPE, *Three Clerks*, ch. xxviii. Charley replied that neither had he any money at home. 'That's BLUE,' said the man. 'It is rather BLUE,' said Charley.

1862. TROLLOPE, *Orley Farm*, I., p. 93. It's BLUE; uncommon BLUE.

1864. YATES, *Broken to Harness*, I., p. 60. 'My dear Charlie,' said the girl . . . 'That certainly is a BLUE look-out,' she continued—for however earnest was her purpose she would not but express herself in her slang metaphor.

1872. S. L. CLEMENS ('Mark Twain'), *Roughing It*, ch. xl. I kept up my BLUE meditations.

1874. S. L. CLEMENS ('Mark Twain'), *Gilded Age*, ch. xxvii. I had forgotten dear, but when a body gets BLUE, a body forgets everything. . . . I am sorry I was BLUE, but it did seem as if everything had been going against me for whole ages.

Verb.—1. To blush. *Cf.*, *subs.*, sense 3.

1709. STEELE AND SWIFT, *Tatler*, No. 71, p. 8. If a Virgin blushes, we no longer cry she BLUES. [M.]

2. To pawn; pledge; spend; actually to get rid of money quickly. *Cf.*, BLEW. There are two suggested derivations of the word when used in this sense; (1) that it is connected with 'blown,' *i.e.*, dissipated or scattered; and (2) that money so squandered has disappeared as effectually as if it had passed into the BLUE, *i.e.*, the sky or the deep sea. The German has *ins blaue hinein*, 'away into the blue,' equivalent to the French *passer au bleu*. *Faire passer au bleu* is to dissipate, spend, or squander. For synonyms, in the sense of to pawn, *see* POP.

1880. *Punch's Almanac*, p. 2. This top coat?—would BLUE IT.

1887. *Punch*, 10 Sept., p. 111. I never minds BLUEING the pieces purvided I gets a good spree.

3. To miscalculate; 'to make a "mess" of anything'; to mull.

4. (thieves'.)—To steal; to plunder. To BE BLUED, to be robbed. For synonyms, *see* PRIG.

BY ALL THAT'S BLUE, *phr.* (popular).—A euphemistic oath; probably meaning 'by Heaven.' It may be compared with the French *parbleu*, synonymous with *par Dieu*.

1840. MARRYAT, *Poor Jack*, xxiii. 'The black cat, by ALL THAT'S BLUE!' cried the Captain.

MEN IN BLUE, *phr.* (popular). —The police.—*See* BLUE, *subs.*, sense 1.

1882. BESANT, *All Sorts and Cond. of Men*, ch. xliii. 'You must now begin to think seriously about handcuffs and prison, and MEN IN BLUE.'

1886. G. A. APPERSON, *Graphic*, 30 Jan., p. 137. The police in recent times have been known as the BLUES and the MEN IN BLUE.

TILL ALL IS BLUE, *phr.* (popular).—1. To the utmost; to the end; for an indefinite period. Smyth, in his *Sailors' Word Book*, says this phrase is borrowed from the idea of a vessel making out of port and getting into deep water.

1835. HALIBURTON, *The Clockmaker*, 2 S., ch. xix. [The land] could be made to carry wheat till ALL'S BLUE again. *Ibid*, 3 S., ch. xx. Your mother kickin' and screamin' till ALL WAS BLUE again.

1850. SMEDLEY, *Frank Fairlegh*, I., p. 184. I'll have at her again, and dance TILL ALL'S BLUE before I give in.

2. When applied to drinking, TILL ALL IS BLUE signifies exceeding tipsy. As will be seen, this usage is somewhat ancient. It is an allusion to the supposed effect of drinking on the eyesight. An analogous French expression is *avoir un coup d'bleu* (to be slightly tipsy).

1616. R. C., *Times' Whis.*, v., 1835. They drink . . . Vntil their adle heads doe make the ground Seeme BLEW vnto them.

1638. FORD, *Lady's Trial*, iv., 2. We can drink TILL ALL LOOK BLUE.

1837. BARHAM, *I. L.* (*Lay of St. Dunstan*).
'I have nothing to do:
And 'fore George, I'll sit here and I'll
drink TILL ALL'S BLUE!'

TO LOOK BLUE, *phr.* (popular). —To be confounded; surprised; astonished; annoyed or disappointed. French equivalents are *en rester tout bleu*; *en être bleu*; *en bailler tout bleu*; and *baba* from *ébahi*, astounded.

c. 1600. *Rob. Hood* ('Ritson'), II., xxxvi., 84. It made the sunne LOOKE BLUE. [M.]

1754. B. MARTIN, *Eng. Dict.* BLUE, adj. . . . 2, blank, or cast down; as, he LOOKED BLUE upon it.

1884. *Cornhill Mag.*, Jan., p. 111. The prudent (and sagacious) officer LOOKED BLUE. But he speedily recovered himself.

TO MAKE THE AIR BLUE, *phr.* (popular).—To curse; to swear; to use profane language. *Cf.*, BLUE, *adj.*, sense 2.

TRUE BLUE, *phr.* (colloquial). —Faithful; genuine; real; an allusion to blue as the colour of constancy. A reference either to the deep blue of the sky or sea suggestive of interminableness; or, it may be derived as was 'Coventry blue,' from a dye that would neither change its colour nor be discharged by washing; hence figuratively, to signify persons or things of sterling character or quality. In neither case is the argument clear or decisive; there is certainly no reason in nature why the colour and cardinal virtue should be thus associated. Blue skies and blue seas are proverbially deceitful, and on the other hand, the expression seems too old a one to owe its origin to the dyer's skill.

1383. CHAUCER, *Squiere's Tale*.
And by hire bedde's hed she made a mew,
And covered it with velouettes BLEW,
In signe of trouthe that is in woman sene.
Ibid, *Court of Love*, line 246.
So you dir folke (quod she) that knele in
BLEW,
They were the colour ay and ever shal,
In signe they were, and ever wil be true,
Withoutin change.

BLUE APRON, *subs.* (common).—A tradesman.

1721. AMHERST, *Terræ Fil.*, xliii., 230. For if any saucy BLUE-APRON dares to affront any venerable person . . . all scholars are immediately forbid to have any dealing or commerce with him.

1868. BREWER, *Dictionary of Phrase and Fable*, p. 98. A BLUE-APRON statesman, a lay politician, a tradesman who interferes with the affairs of the nation. The reference is to the BLUE APRON once worn by nearly all tradesmen, but now restricted to butchers, poulterers, fishmongers, and so on.

BLUEBACKS, *subs.*—1. The paper money of the Confederates. A cant name, originating, as in the case of United States paper currency GREENBACKS, in the colour of the printing on the reverse. A more pronounced slang name, subsequently applied to BLUEBACKS, was 'shucks,' from their worthlessness after the war. 'Shucks' is an old English term for the refuse of peas and similar products when shelled.

1871. De Vere, *Americanisms*, p. 291. The confederate notes bore, for the same reason, the name of BLUEBACKS, which was, however, soon exchanged for the slang term of shucks.

2. The Orange Free State paper money.

1878. Trollope, *South Africa*, II., p. 206. BLUEBACKS, as they were called, were printed. *Ibid*, p. 222. The BLUEBACKS as the Orange Free State bank-notes were called.

Blue Bellies.—A nickname bestowed by Southerners, during the Civil War, upon their opponents of the North, whose uniform was blue. They were also called BOYS IN BLUE, YANKS, etc. The Southerners, on the other hand, received such names as THE SECESH, REBS, and JOHNNY REBS, the latter being sometimes shortened to JOHNNIES. The grey uniform of the Confederates likewise caused them to be styled BOYS IN GREY and GREY-BACKS, the latter epithet cutting two ways, as the Southern soldiers not only wore grey uniforms, but 'greyback' in America as well as England signifies a louse.

1883. *Daily Telegraph*, Feb. 9, p. 5, col. 4. The Confederate armies during the great Civil War in America . . . were known . . . as 'Greybacks,' whereas their Federal opponents, from the light-azure gaberdines which they wore, were dubbed 'BLUE-BELLIES.'

Blue Bills, *subs.* (Winchester College).—The tradesmen's bills sent home to the parents and guardians of students. [So called from the colour of the envelopes generally used.]

Blue Billy, *subs.* (pugilistic).—1. A handkerchief (blue ground with white spots) sometimes worn and used as a colour at prize-fights.—*See* BILLY, sense 1.

2. (mining.)—*See* quotation.

1887. 'Death of BLUE BILLY,' in *Chamb. Jour.*, Dec. 17, p. 812. BLUE BILLY is the technical name given to the lime rendered foul in the purification of the gas.

Blue-Blanket, *subs.* (common).—1. The sky. This simile is an old one; Defoe's use of it may probably have been suggested by Shakspeare's 'blanket of the dark' (Macbeth, I., v.).

c. 1720. Defoe, *Hist. of Devil*, quoted in *N. and Q.*, 7 S., ii., 289; *see* also 7 S., ii., 492. We must be content till we come on the other side the BLUE BLANKET, and then we shall know the whole story.

1877. Greenwood, *Under the Blue Blanket*. The vagrant brotherhood have several slang terms for sleeping out in a field or meadow. It is called 'snoozing in Hedge Square'; dossing with the daisies'; and 'lying under the BLUE BLANKET.'

The French say, '*coucher à l'hotel de l'Etoile*,' *i.e.*, 'to sleep at the Star Hotel'; while in the Fourbesque, or Italian cant, heaven or the sky is termed *copertore*, a covering or blanket.

2. (common.)—A rough over-coat made of coarse pilot cloth.

Blue Blazes.—*See* BLAZES.

Blue Boar, *subs.* (old).—A certain venereal disease.

Blue-Bottle, *subs.* (popular).—1. A policeman. This epithet, at one time applied generally to all wearers of a dark blue uniform, is now invariably understood to mean a guardian of the peace. It is one of the oldest of the nicknames given to members of the force, and occurs as far back as 1598.

Cf., BLUE, sense 1, and *see* BEAK for synonyms.

1598. Shakspeare, 2 *Henry IV.*, v., 4. *Dall* [addressing beadle] . . . you BLUE-BOTTLE rogue, you filthy famished correctioner.

1852. F. E. Smedley, *Lewis Arundel*, ch. lxiv. 'Police, indeed!' muttered Charley, 'the General can't remember that he is out of London . . . These confounded sulky Austrian officials are rather different customers to deal with from our BLUE-BOTTLES.—Messrs. A1 and Co.

1864. Sala, in *Daily Telegraph*, Sept. 13. Caught in his own toils by the BLUE-BOTTLES of Scotland Yard. [M.]

1864. *Blackwood's Mag.*, p. 15. He who could summon to his aid every alphabetical BLUE-BOTTLE that ever handled a truncheon.

1888. Middleton, *Michaelmas Term*. And to be free from the interruption of BLUE BEADLES, and other bawdy officers.

2. A serving-man, blue having been the usual habit of servants. *Cf.*, BLUE-COAT.

1602. *Honest Whore*, O. Pl., iii., 389. You proud varlets, you need not be ashamed to wear BLUE, when your master is one of your fellows.

1608. Dekker, *Belman*, sign E., 3. The others act their parts in *blew coates*, as (if) they were their serving-men.

Hence BLUE-BOTTLE is sometimes a term of reproach for a servant. [*Case Altered*, i., 2. O. Pl., v., 6.] And a *serving-man*, in B. Jonson, says, 'Ever since I was of *the blue order*.'

About 1608, when Middleton's Comedy of *A Trick to catch the Old One* was produced, the *blue-coats* of servants appear to have been changed for cloaks, such as were worn by the upper classes also at that time. Thus, in that comedy [*Act* ii., *Anc. Drama*, v., p. 151]:—There's more true honesty in such a country serving man, than in a hundred of our cloak companions. I may well call 'em companions, for since *blue coats* have been turned into cloaks, one can scarce know the man from the master. B. Jonson [*Mask of Christmas*] introduces New Yeares Gift, In a *blew coat*, serving-man like, with an orange, etc.

1845. G. P. R. James, *Arrah Neil*, p. 325. The personage to whom he addressed himself, was one of the serving-men of that day, known by the general term of BLUE-BOTTLES.

1822. Scott, *Fortunes of Nigel*, ch. x. (I., p. 173). I fancy you would love to move to court like him, followed by a round score of old BLUE-BOTTLES. *Ibid*, ch. xi. My lord, my father . . . has BLUE-BOTTLES enough to wait on him.

Blue Boy, *subs.* (common).—A bubo; a tumour or abscess with inflammation. Specially applied to that kind which is a result of venereal disease.

Blue-Boys, *subs.* (popular).—The police. The expression is generally used in the plural. *Cf.*, BLUE, sense 1, and BEAK, sense 1.

1880. Jas. Greenwood, *Help Myself Society*, in *Odd People in Odd Places*, p. 68. The 'Help Yourselves' are especially strong in instrumental music. They have a friend in Colonel Fraser, the head of the City police, and the excellent band of that branch of the force is at their service, and Sir E. Henderson shows himself to be at heart a 'Help Yourself,' by permitting the instrumental BLUE BOYS belonging to several metropolitan divisions to spend a Saturday night there. Besides these, they have the Polytechnic orchestral band when it is required, and an excellent grand piano with a skilled player and accompanyist.

Blue Butter, *subs.* (common).—Mercurial ointment, used for the destruction of parasites.

Blue-Coat, *subs.*—A constable; a guardian of public order. This, like many of its congeners, has been applied to serving-men, beadles, tailors, and others wearing a uniform of a dark blue colour. Like BLUE BLUE-BOTTLE, etc., its application to a policeman is of some antiquity. *Cf.*, BLUE, sense 1, and BEAK, sense 1.

1610. Rowlands, *Martin Mark-all*, p. 19 (H. Club's Repr., 1874). And being so taken, haue beene carried to places of correction, there wofully tormented by BLEW-COATES, cowardly fellowes, that . . . haue so scourged vs, that flesh and blood could hardly endure it.

1851-61. H. Mayhew, *London Lab. and Lon. Poor*, vol. II., p. 417. 'I thinks them Chartists are a weak-minded set . . . a hundred o' them would run away from one BLUE-COAT.'

Blued or **Blewed**, *ppl. adj.* (common).—Tipsy; drunk. For synonyms, *see* SCREWED.

Blue Dahlia, *subs.* (common).—A colloquialism for something rare or seldom seen; a *rara avis*.

Blue Devils, *subs.* (popular).—1. Dejection; lowness of spirits; hypochondria.

1786. Cowper, *Letters*, No. 219, vol. II., p. 143 (ed. 1834). I have not that which commonly is a symptom of such a case belonging to me,—I mean extraordinary elevation in the absence of Mr. BLUE DEVIL. When I am in the best health, my tide of animal sprightliness flows with great equality.

1790. W. B. Rhodes, *Bombastes Furioso*, Sc. I.
Or, dropping poisons in the cup of joy,
Do the BLUE DEVILS your repose annoy?

1871. Planché, *King Christmas*. There are BLUE DEVILS which defy blue pills.

1880. G. R. Sims, *Three Brass Balls*, pledge iii. He got discontented and had fits of BLUE DEVILS.

Two French equivalents for feeling out of sorts are *s'emboucaner*, and *s'encolifluchete*r.

2. (popular.) — *Delirium tremens*. From the apparitions drunkards often suppose they see. In both this and the foregoing sense BLUE DEVILS is contracted into BLUES.

1818-9. Cobbett, *Resid. U. S.*, 42. It was just the weather to give drunkards the BLUE DEVILS.

1831. Scott, *Demonology*, i., 18. They, by a continued series of intoxication, have become subject to what is popularly called the BLUE DEVILS.

Hence such derivatives as BLUE DEVILAGE; BLUE DEVILRY; BLUE DEVILISM; and an adjectival form BLUE DEVILLY.

1871. Lockhart, *Fair to See*, I., p. 208. On the lower hills the pine-trees loomed through stagnant mists with a dejected and BLUE-DEVILLY aspect.

Blue Fear, *subs.* (popular).—Extreme fright. [From the 'blue' or pallid cast of countenance which fear is supposed to induce. The same as BLUE FUNK (*q.v.*), which is more general.]

1883. R. L. Stevenson, *The Treasure of Franchard*, in *Longman's Mag.*, April, p. 683. Anastasie had saved the remainder of his fortune by keeping him strictly in the country. The very name of Paris put her in a BLUE FEAR.

Blue Flag, *subs.* (common).—A BLUE APRON (*q.v.*). Worn by butchers, publicans, and other tradesmen.

1785. Grose, *Dictionary of the Vulgar Tongue*. He has hoisted the BLUE FLAG, he has commenced publican, or taken a public house, alluding to the blue aprons worn by publicans.

Blue Funk, *subs.* (popular).—Extreme fright, nervousness, or dread. [FUNK is 'to stink through fear'; Wedgwood connects it with the Walloon *funker*, 'to smoke.']

1856. Thomas Hughes, *Tom Brown's School-days*, p. 196. If I was going to be flogged next minute, I should be in a BLUE FUNK.

1861. *Macmillan's Magazine*, p. 211. I was in a real BLUE FUNK.

1861. *Saturday Review*, Nov. 23, 534. We encounter . . . the miserable Dr. Blandling in what is called a BLUE FUNK. [M.]

1871. Maxwell, in *Life* (1882), xvi., 382. Certainly χλωρὸν δέος is the Homeric for a BLUE FUNK.

Blue Hen's Chickens, *subs.* (American).—A slang name for the inhabitants of Delaware. The nickname arose thus: Captain Caldwell, an officer of the first Delaware regiment in the American War of Independence, was noted for his love of cock-fighting. Being personally popular, and his regiment becoming famous for their valour, they were soon known as 'game-cocks'; and as Caldwell maintained that no cock was truly game unless its mother was a blue hen, his regiment, and subsequently Delawareans generally, became known as BLUE HEN'S CHICKENS, and Delaware as the BLUE HEN STATE for the same reason. A boaster is also often brought to book by the sarcasm, 'Your mother was a blue hen no doubt.'

Blue Horse, *subs.* (military).—The Fourth Dragoon Horse, from its facings.

Blue Lightning, *subs.* (American).—One of the grimly facetious names with which Texans have christened revolvers. At times a dispute has literally been a word, a flash of BLUE LIGHTNING and—certain death. For synonyms, *see* BARKER.

Blue Monday, *subs.* (workmen's).—A Monday spent in dissipation and absence from work. One often hears the phrase 'to feel MONDAYISH.' The German has *der blaue Montag*. *Cf.*, BLACK SATURDAY.

1885. *Harper's Magazine*, p. 873, col. 1. The workman getting sober after his usual BLUE MONDAY. [M.]

Blue Moon. ONCE IN A BLUE MOON, *phr.* (popular).—Extremely seldom; an unlimited time; a rarely recurring period. An old phrase, first used in the sense of something absurd. A BLUE MOON, like the Greek Kalends, is something which does not exist. A variant is 'when two Sundays come in a week.' As regards origin nothing is known; barring the extract from Roy and Barlow, authorities give no examples earlier than 1876—a curious fact.

1526. Roy and Barlowe, *Rede me and be not wroth*, p. 114 [ed. Arber, 1871].
Yf they saye the MONE is belewe,
We must beleve that it is true,
Admittynge their interpretacion.

1860. F. W. Robinson, *Grandmother's Money*, I., p. 144. If he talked till a BLUE MOON, etc.

1876. Miss Braddon, *Joshua Haggard's Daughter*, ch. xxiv. Why should she stint as to one or two puddings a week . . . and a fruit pasty ONCE IN A BLUE MOON.

1884. R. E. Francillon, *Ropes of Sand*, ch. xxi. 'I've made bold to take the chance of your being at home for ONCE IN A BLUE MOON, Mr. Carew,' said she.

Blue Murder or **Blue Murders**, *subs.* (common).—A term used to describe cries of terror or alarm; a great noise; an unusual racket. *Cf.*, French *morbleu*.

1887. J. S. Winter, *Eng. Ill. Mag.*, Dec., p. 179. The dingy person dropped his victim and howled what the half-dozen officers . . . graphically described as BLUE MURDER.

BLUENESS, *subs.* (common). — Indecency. Smutty talk is described as BLUE, sense 2 (*q.v.*).

1840. CARLYLE, *Diderot, Ess.*, 240. The occasional BLUENESS of both [writings] shall not altogether affright us.

FRENCH SYNONYMS. *Les horreurs*; *les bêtises*; *les gueulées*. To talk blue is rendered by *décravater ses propos*.

BLUE NOSES, *subs.* (American).—The natives of Nova Scotia. A nickname given them by the Yankees in allusion, it is said, to a potato of that name which Nova Scotians claim to be the best in the world. Proctor, however, thinks differently, and says he would wager that the Nova Scotians were called BLUE NOSES before the potato which they rear was so named, and hazards the suggestion that the nickname refers to the blueness of nose resulting from intense cold.

1837-40. HALIBURTON ('Sam Slick'). Do you know the reason monkeys are no good? Because they chatter all day long,—as do the niggers,—and so do the BLUE NOSES of Nova Scotia.

18(?). SIR GEORGE SIMPSON, *Overland Journey*, vol. I., p. 19. After a run [in the steamer] of fourteen days, we entered the harbour of Halifax, amid the hearty cheers of a large number of BLUE NOSES.

BLUE [or **BLEW**] **ONE'S SCREW**, *verbal phr.* (common).—To waste or squander one's salary. [From BLUE or BLEW (*q.v.*) + SCREW (*q.v.*).]

BLUE PETER, *subs.* (card-players').—The signal or call for trumps at whist. [Properly a blue flag with white square in centre, hoisted as a signal for immediate sailing.]

1875. BEETON, *Handy Book of Games*, p. 358. Since the introduction of BLUE PETER, the necessity of leading through your adversary's hand has become less and less.

BLUE PIGEON, *subs.* (thieves').—Lead used for roofing purposes. *Cf.*, BLUEY and BLUE PIGEON FLYER. Of doubtful origin, but possibly a punning allusion. Lead has long been known as 'bluey,' and pigeons frequently find a resting-place on housetops.

1887. *Judy*, 27 April, p. 200. A burglar whose particular 'lay' was flying the BLUE PIGEON, *i.e.*, stealing lead.

(Nautical.) — The sounding lead.

BLUE PIGEON FLYER, *subs. phr.* (thieves').—A thief who steals lead from the roofs of buildings. Hotten thus explains the *modus operandi*. Sometimes a journeyman plumber, glazier, or other workman, who, when repairing houses, strips off the lead, and makes away with it. This performance is, though, by no means confined to workmen. An empty house is often entered and the whole of the roof in its vicinity stripped, the only notice given to the folks below being received by them on the occasion of a heavy downfall of rain. The term FLYER has, indeed, of late years been more peculiarly applied to the man who steals the lead in pursuance of his vocation as a thief, than to him who takes it because it comes in the way of his work.

1789. GEO. PARKER, *Life's Painter*, p. 165. BLUE PIGEON FLYING. Fellows who steal lead off houses, or cut pipes away.

French equivalents are *un limousineur*; *un gras-doublier*; *un mastarouflcur*.

TO FLY THE BLUE PIGEON, *verbal phr.* (thieves').—To steal lead from the roofs of houses. —*See* BLUE PIGEON. French equivalents are *faire la mastar au gras-double*; *ratisser du gras double*.

1872. J. DORAN, in *Notes and Queries*, 4 S., x., 308. Even at the present day, no rascal would stoop to strip lead from the roof of a house. At least, what honest men would call by that name, he would prettily designate as 'FLYING THE BLUE PIGEON.'

BLUE PILL, *subs.* (popular). — A bullet; also called BLUE PLUM and BLUE WHISTLER. For synonyms, *see* PILL.

1861. *N. Y. Tribune* (*Let. from Missouri*), Nov. 10. Between BLUE PILLS, halters, and the penitentiary, we shall soon work off this element of rascaldom and horse-thieves.

BLUE PLUM, *subs.* (thieves').—A bullet. *Cf.*, BLUE PILL and BLUE WHISTLER.

1785. GROSE, *Dictionary of the Vulgar Tongue*. Surfeited with a BLUE PLUMB, wounded with a bullet; a sortment of George R——'s BLUE PLUMBS, a volley of ball, shot from soldier's firelocks.

1834. HARRISON AINSWORTH, *Rookwood* (1884), p. 95.
Believe me, there is not a game, my brave boys,
To compare with the game of high toby;
No rapture can equal the toby man's joys,
To blue devils, BLUE PLUMBS give the go by.

BLUE RUIN, *subs.* (common).—Gin, generally of inferior quality. For synonyms, *see* DRINKS.

c. 1817. KEATS, *A Portrait*. He sipped no olden Tom or RUIN! BLUE, or Nantz or cherry brandy.

1819. MOORE, *Tom Crib's Memorial to Congress*, p. 39.
A few short words I first must spare,
To him, the Hero, that sits there,
Swigging BLUE RUIN, in that chair.

1821. W. T. MONCRIEFF, *Tom and Jerry*, Act iii., Sc. 3. *Log.* Here, Landlord, more BLUE RUIN, my boy! *Sal.* Massa Bob, you find me no such bad partner; many de good vill and de power me get from de Jack Tar.

1847. LYTTON, *Lucretia*, pt. II., ch. xx. 'The littel un . . . had been a-brought up upon spoon-meat, with a dash o' BLUE-RUIN to make him slim and ginteel.'

1859. SALA, *Gaslight and Daylight*, ch. xxiii. The stuff itself, which in the western gin-shops goes generally by the name of BLUE-RUIN or 'short.'

BLUES, *subs.* (popular).—1. Despondency; hypochondria; depression of spirits. [A shortened form of BLUE DEVILS (*q.v.*).] A French synonym is *se faire des plumes* or *paumer ses plumes*.

1807. WASHINGTON IRVING, *Salmagundi* (1824), p. 96. In a fit of the BLUES. [M.]

1856. WHYTE MELVILLE, *Kate Coventry*, ch. viii. The moat alone is enough to give one the BLUES.

1889. JOHN STRANGE WINTER, *That Imp*, p. 10. 'Miss Aurora,' he said suddenly, one evening after dinner, 'it's awfully dull at Drive now; does it never strike you so?' 'Very often, my dear,' answered Miss Aurora promptly. 'It's as dull as—' 'Ditch-water,' supplied Driver, finding she paused for a word which would express dulness enough. 'I wonder you and Betty don't die of the BLUES.'

2. The police. — *See* BLUE, sense 1.

3. (military.)—The Royal Horse Guards Blue are popularly so known from the blue facings on the scarlet uniform. The corps first obtained the name of 'Oxford Blues' in 1690, to distinguish it from a Dutch regiment of Horse Guards dressed in blue, commanded by the Earl of Portland, the former being commanded by the Earl of Oxford. Subsequently the regiment was, during the campaign in Flanders [1742-45], known as the 'Blue Guards.'

BLUE SKIN, *subs.* (old).—1. Formerly a contemptuous term for

a Presbyterian. Butler, in *Hudibras* [I., p. 26], says:—

'twas Presbyterian *true blue*,
For he was of the stubborn crew
Of errant saints, whom all men grant
To be the true Church Militant.'

Blue is still the Presbyterian colour, and is used as an adjective by them in describing books and people.

2. (West Indian.)—A half-breed—the child of a black woman by a white man.

BLUE SQUADRON, *subs.* (colonial).—One of mixed blood; properly one with a Hindoo strain. Eurasians belong to the BLUE SQUADRON. *Cf.*, TOUCH OF THE TAR BRUSH.

BLUE STOCKING, *subs.* — A literary lady: applied usually with the imputation of pedantry. The generally received explanation is that the term is derived from the name given to certain meetings held by ladies in the days of Dr. Johnson for conversation with distinguished literary men. One of the most eminent of these literati was a Mr. Benjamin Stillingfleet, who always wore BLUE STOCKINGS, and whose conversation at these meetings was so much prized, that his absence at any time was felt to be a great loss, so that the remark became common, 'We can do nothing without the BLUE STOCKINGS,' hence these meetings were sportively called BLUE-STOCKING clubs, and the ladies who attended them BLUE-STOCKINGS. It is stated that the name specially arose in this way. A foreigner of rank refused to accompany a friend to one of these parties on the plea of being in his travelling costume, to which there was the reply, 'Oh! we never mind dress on these occasions; you may come in *bas bleus* or BLUE STOCKINGS,' with allusion to Stillingfleet's stockings, when the foreigner, fancying that *bas bleus* were part of the necessary costume, called the meeting ever after the Bas-bleu Society. In modern slang the term BLUE-STOCKING is abbreviated into BLUE. Derivatives are BLUE-STOCKINGISM, BLUE-STOCKINGER, etc.

b. 1738, *d.* 1819. WOLCOT ('P. Pindar'), *Benevolent Epistle*, in wks. (Dublin, 1795), vol. II., p. 125.
I see the band of BLUE-STOCKINGS arise,
Historic, critic, and poetic dames!

1780. MAD. D'ARBLAY, *Diary*, i., 326. Who would not be a BLUE-STOCKINGER at this rate?

1784. WALPOLE, *Letters*, iv., 381. [Walpole, writing to Hannah More, playfully makes it a verb = to put on BLUE STOCKINGS.] When will you BLUE-STOCKING yourself, and come amongst us?

1877. *Macmillan's Mag.*, May, p. 50. On the airs and graces of the gushing BLUE STOCKINGS who were in vogue in that day . . . . she had no mercy.

1877. MISS MARTINEAU, *Autob.*, vol. I., p. 100. Young ladies (at least in provincial towns) were expected to sit down in the parlour to sew,—during which reading aloud was permitted,—or to practice their music; but so as to fit to receive callers, without any signs of BLUE-STOCKINGISM which could be reported abroad.

BLUE STONE, *subs.* (common). — Gin or whiskey of so bad a quality that it can only be compared to vitriol, of which BLUE-STONE is also a nickname in the north of England and Scotland. For all synonyms, *see* DRINKS.

1880. *Blackwood's Mag.*, June, p. 786. The bar was still thronged, and the effects of the mixture of spirits of wine, BLUESTONE, and tobacco-juice, were to be seen on a miserable wretch who lay stretched in the courtyard.

1882. W. G. BLACK, in *Notes and Queries*, 6 S., v., p. 348. A witness was asked in the Northern Police Court, Glasgow, a few weeks ago, a question relative to the quality of certain whiskey said to have been supplied to him. 'It wasn't whiskey,' he said, 'it was nothing but BLUESTONE.' 'But what?' inquired the magistrate. 'BLUESTONE,' your honour,' was the answer—'poison.' I heard the question and answer, and there can be no doubt that the word was used as a familiar one.

BLUE TAPE, *subs.* (old).—One of the many cant terms for gin. For synonyms, *see* DRINKS.

BLUE WHISTLER, *subs.* (American). — A bullet. For synonyms, *see* PILL.

1888. *New York Herald*, Nov. 4. It was Mr. Barbour's rifle shot which had hit him in the head and caused him to stagger. The pellet of lead passed deep into the brain. The second shot was from the Atlanta drummer, and his thirteen BLUE WHISTLERS tore the brute's liver into shreds and made a great hole in his side. *Ibid.* After a few moments of reflection, being nearest to the quarry, I lifted my double-barrelled shotgun and let drive a volley of BLUE WHISTLERS straight at bruin's yawning jaws.

BLUEY, *subs.* (thieves').—1. Lead. —*See* also BLUE PIGEON. [Supposed to be an allusion to the colour.]

FRENCH SYNONYMS. *Du doussin*; *du noir* (*noir* = black); *du saucisson*. 'To dispose of BLUEY at the fence,' *i.e.*, the receiver of stolen goods—*porter du gras-double au moulin*.

2. (Australian.)—A bushman's bundle, the outside wrapper of which is generally a blue blanket—hence the name. This is also called his SWAG (*q.v.*); likewise a DRUM (*q.v.*).

BLUEY-HUNTER, *subs.* (thieves').—A thief who steals lead, as described under BLUE PIGEON FLYER (*q.v.*), of which BLUEY-HUNTER is a synonym. *Cf.*, BILLY-HUNTER.

1851-61. H. MAYHEW, *Lon. Lab. and Lon. Poor*, IV., 26. BLUEY-HUNTERS, or those who purloin lead from the tops of houses.

1856. H. MAYHEW, *Gt. World of London*, p. 46. BLUEY-HUNTERS, who take lead from the tops of houses.

BLUFF, *subs.* (vagrants' and common).—An excuse; a pretence; that which is intended to hoodwink or 'to blind.' Probably a transferred usage of the American sense.

1851-61. H. MAYHEW, *London Lab. and Lon. Poor*, vol. I., p. 231. [List of patterer's words.] BLUFF, an excuse.

1879. BRET HARTE, *Gabriel Conroy*, ch. xxxix. There is a strong suspicion among men whose heads are level that this Minstrel Variety Performance is a BLUFF of the '*Messenger*' to keep from the public the real motives of the murder.

1884. *Boston* (U.S.) *Journal*, Sept. 25. The offer was only a BLUFF.

Verb (common). — To turn aside; to stop; to hoodwink; to blind as to one's real intention. Properly, to brag; to conceal one's weakness; from the American game of poker.—*See subs.*

1871. DE VERE, *Americanisms*, p. 327. Like its near cousin, suggestively called BLUFF, poker is a mere hazard game, with which, however, is combined great skill in bragging to a purpose. One man offers a bet on his hand; another doubles the bet and 'goes one better'; then the first tries TO BLUFF him off by a still higher bet, and thus the stake rises rapidly to often enormous sums.

1883. *Echo*, April 20, p. 3, col. 5. Subsequently a prominent bookmaker attempted to BLUFF Captain Machell by laying him 2,000 to 1,000 on Goggles against Sweetbread—a merry little bit of financial diplomacy, which was promptly followed by Goggles being struck out.

1885. BRET HARTE, *Ship of '49*, ch. v. 'Far from BLUFFING, Sleight, I am throwing my cards on the table. Consider that I've passed out. Let some other man take my hand.'

It may be remarked that Ray [1674-91] gives BLUFF as to blindfold, and Bailey [1721] as to hoodwink. The German has *blüffen*; the Dutch *bloffen*, 'to bark at,' and *verlüffen*, 'to put out of countenance.'

So also BLUFFING in a similar sense.

1889. *Answers*, July 20, p. 121, col. 2. The youths evidently disagreed as to the nature of my business: one, as far as I could gather, assumed that I was a 'nark,' and that I was BLUFFING (making an excuse), and 'flamming' (lying).

BLUFFER, *subs.* (old).—An innkeeper.—*Grose.* Bailey [1721] also gives the term with the same meaning, and American thieves still retain the word in a similar sense.

2. (nautical.)—A bo'sun.

BLUNDERBUSS, *subs.* (old). — A stupid blundering fellow.—*Grose.*

BLUNT, *subs.* (popular).—Money, especially ready money. For a long list of synonyms, *see* ACTUAL. [There are several suggested derivations; (1) that it is from the French *blond*, sandy or golden colour, and that a parallel may be found in BROWN or BROWNS, the slang for halfpence. Far-fetched as this etymology seems, say Hotten, it may be correct, as it is borne out by the analogy of similar expressions. *Cf.*, BLANQUILLO, a word used in Morocco and Southern Spain for a small Moorish coin. The 'asper' (ἄσπρόν) of Constantinople is called by the Turks *akcheh*, *i.e.*, 'little white'; (2) that it received its name in allusion to the BLUNT rim of coins. A third is that it received the name from Mr. John BLUNT, the chairman of South Sea Bubble.]

1714. *Memoirs of John Hall* (4 ed.), p. 11. [List of cant words.] BLUNT, money.

1821. W. T. MONCRIEFF, *Tom and Jerry*, Act ii., Sc. 3. (*Holding out his right hand for the money, and keeping the porter away with the other.*) *Bob.* That's your sort; give us hold on it. (*Takes Mace's empty hand.*) Vy, vhere? *Mace.* (*Keeping the porter back.*) Vy, here. *Bob.* Oh, you are afeard of the BLUNT, are you? *Mace.* No, it ain't that; only I'm no schollard—so I alvays takes the BLUNT vith von hand, and gives the pot vith t'other. It saves chalk and prevents mistakes, you know.

1837. DICKENS, *Oliver Twist*, ch. xxxix. 'It's all very well,' said Mr. Sikes; 'but I must have some BLUNT from you to-night.' 'I haven't a piece of coin about me,' replied the Jew.

1878. *Notes and Queries*, 5 S., x., p. 315. BLUNT . . . is also a well-known slang term for money.

1882. *Punch*, vol. LXXXII., p. 147, col. 2. 'The New Almacks.' 'It appears, my dear Jerry,' said the Corinthian, 'that anybody can enter here who chooses to "*sport his* BLUNT"'—that is, to pay.

BLUNTED, *ppl. adj.* (old).—Possessed of money.

18(?). *English Spy*, p. 255. Most noble cracks, and worthy cousin trumps,—permit me to introduce a brother of the togati, fresh as a new-blown rose, and innocent as the lilies of St. Clements. Be unto him ever ready to promote his wishes, whether for spree or sport, in term and out of term,—against the Inquisition and their bull-dogs—the town-raff and the bargees—well-BLUNTED or stiver-cramped—against dun or don—nob or big wig—so may you never want a bumper of bishop.

BLUSH LIKE A BLACK OR BLUE DOG, *verbal phr.* (old).—Not to blush at all.

1579. GOSSON, *Apologie of School of Abuse*, p. 75. If it bee my fortune too meete with the learned woorkes of this London Sabinus, that can not playe the

part without a prompter, nor utter a wise worde without a piper, you shall see we will make him to BLUSH LIKE A BLACKE DOGGE, when he is graveled.

ed. 1634. WITHAL, *Dictionary*, p. 557. *Faciem perfricuit.* Hee BLUSHETH LIKE A BLACKE DOGGE, hee hath a brazen face.

1738. SWIFT, *Polite Conversation* (conv. i.).

Lord Sp. (to the Maid). Mrs. Betty, how does your body politick?

Col. Fye, my lord, you'll make Mrs. Betty blush.

Lady Sm. Blush! Ay, BLUSH LIKE A BLUE DOG.

1828. C. K. SHARPE to a lady, in C. K. S.'s *Correspondence* (1888), II., 421. I send you a pair of blue stockings of my own knitting. I BLUSH LIKE A BLUE DOG about the workmanship, for I fear they are too short.

B.N.C., *abbreviation* (University).—For Brasenose; initials of Brasen Nose College. In spite of the nose over the gate, the probability is that the real name was Brasinium. It is still famous for its beer.

1885. *Daily News*, March 13, p. 5, col. 1. As when Corpus bumped B.N.C. years ago, and went head of the river, whereon a spirit of wrath entered into the B.N.C. men, and next night they bumped Corpus back again.

BOARD, *verb* (military).—1. To borrow.

2. (nautical.)—To accost; ask of; make a demand; *i.e.*, to come to close quarters. The allusion is to boarding a ship for a hand-to-hand conflict; originally in a forcible or hostile sense, but now used in a modified form for to 'make up to,' to 'make advances to.' The figure of speech is a very old one, as will be seen from the following examples.

1547. EARL SURREY, *Æneid*, IV., 395. At length her self BORDETH Aeneas thus. [M.]

1596. SHAKSPEARE, *Hamlet*, ii., 2. [*Enter* HAMLET, reading.] *Queen.* But look, where sadly the poor wretch comes reading. *Pol.* . . . I'll BOARD him presently:—O, give me leave.

1672-1726. VANBRUGH, *False Friend*, I., i., 97. What do you expect from BOARDING a woman . . . already heart and soul engaged to another.

1867. SMYTH, *Sailors' Word Book.* BOARD HIM, a colloquialism for I'll ask, demand, or accost him.

TO BOARD IN THE SMOKE, *phr.* (nautical).—To take one unawares, or by surprise. In the midst of a naval fight boarding operations were often successfully carried out under cover of the smoke from a broadside.

ON THE BOARD, *phr.* (tailors').—Enjoying all the privileges and emoluments of a competent workman. When an apprentice becomes a regular journeyman he goes 'ON THE BOARD.' Tailors usually work squatting on a low raised platform—hence possibly the expression.

1877. *Five Years' Penal Servitude*, ch. iii., p. 146. During the term of his imprisonment he became an excellent working tailor, and was ON THE BOARD, as it is termed, among those who are efficient hands.

TO KEEP ONE'S NAME ON THE BOARD, *phr.* (Cambridge Univ.).—To remain a member of a College.

BOARDING HOUSE or **SCHOOL**, *subs.* (old).—A nickname given by thieves in London to Newgate, but it is equally applicable to any gaol. New York thieves apply it to the Tombs. [From that sense of Boarding School = an establishment where persons are boarded and taught, convicts being likened to scholars.] French thieves call such an institution *un collège*. For synonyms, *see* CAGE.

1785. GROSE, *Dictionary of the Vulgar Tongue.* BOARDING SCHOOL. Bridewell, Newgate, or any other prison or house of correction.

BOARDMAN, *subs.* (vagrants').—A standing patterer; explained by quotation. Sometimes called a 'sandwich man.'

1851. H. MAYHEW, *London Labour and London Poor*, I., p. 251. I have no doubt that there are always at least twenty standing patterers—sometimes they are called BOARDMEN—at work in London. *Ibid*, p. 248. They endeavour to attract attention to their papers, or, more commonly, pamphlets . . . by means of a board with coloured pictures upon it, illustrative of the contents of what they sell . . . (This) is what is usually denominated in street technology 'board work.'

BOARD OF GREEN CLOTH, *subs.* (familiar).—A card or billiard table. [From BOARD, a table, + GREEN CLOTH, from the colour of the cloth with which the table is covered.]

1771. P. PARSONS, *New Newmarket*, II., 24. That BOARD OF GREEN CLOTH, the billiard table.

1850. SMEDLEY, *Frank Fairlegh*, p. 23. 'I am going down to F——' 'As usual, the BOARD OF GREEN CLOTH, eh? you will go there once too often, if you don't mind, old fellow.' 'That's my look out,' replied Cumberland.

1853. WHYTE MELVILLE, *Digby Grand*, ch. vi. Often have I seen him rise from the BOARD OF GREEN CLOTH, and turning his chair thrice, from right to left, reseat himself at the play-table, confident that success would follow the mystical manœuvre.

1886. MISS BRADDON, *Mohawks*, ch. viii. The soft seductive sound of the dice sliding gently on to the BOARD OF GREEN CLOTH.

BOAT, *subs.* (old). — Formerly applied to the hulks; latterly to any prison. [The derivation is obvious, old dismasted ships having long served as places of detention for convicts.] For synonyms, *see* CAGE.

1856. H. MAYHEW, *Great World of London*, p. 82, *note.* [List of thieves' names of prisons.] The Hulks, or any Public Works—THE BOAT.

Verb (old).—1. Originally to transport; the term is now applied to penal servitude. To 'get the BOAT,' or to 'be BOATED,' is to be sentenced to a long term of imprisonment, equivalent to transportation under the old system. *Cf.*, BOAT, *subs.*, and for synonyms, *see* COP.

2. (American thieves'.)—To join as partner; evidently a corruption of 'to be in the same boat,' *i.e.*, to be in the same position or circumstances.

TO BAIL ONE'S OWN BOAT, *phr.* (American).—To be self-reliant. A variant is 'to PADDLE ONE'S OWN CANOE.'—*See* CANOE.

BOB, *subs.* (popular).—1. A shilling. [The derivation is obscure, but there are several suggested explanations. Murray points out that there was an old French coin called a *bobe*, but he thinks its survival in English slang is very unlikely. Others think it a corruption of 'baubee' or 'bawbee,' a debased Scotch coin, issued in the reign of James VI. of Scotland, equal in value to a halfpenny. A more likely origin than either of the foregoing is from BOB, a grub used as bait for fish, the allusion being to money as a bribe.] The old cant had BOBSTICK (*q.v.*) as a synonym, and a spurious plural is sometimes formed of BOB, thus BOBBER—TWO BOBBER = a two-shilling piece. *Cf.*, BLOW for synonyms.

1812. J. H. VAUX, *Flash Dictionary.* BOB or BOBSTICK, a shilling.

1821. W. T. MONCRIEFF, *Tom and Jerry*, Act iii., Sc. 3. *Tom.* Now then, what's to pay, landlord? *Mace.* All out, vill be fourteen BOB and a kick, your honour. *Tom.* Well, there's a flimsy for you; serve the change out in max to the covies. (*Gives money.*)

1837. BARHAM, *I. L.* (*Misadventures at Margate*). I changed a shilling—(which in town the people call a BOB).

1882. *Punch*, vol. LXXXII., p. 74, col. 1. ACCOMMODATION. *Swell.* 'Haw—no small change about me.' *Minstrel.* 'Oh, don't mention 't sar. A BOB will do sar, and if you'll call at my club to-morrow, sar, the hall portar will give you sixpence back, sar. My kyard, sar, etc. ! ! '

2. (old.) — A shoplifter's assistant; one who receives and carries off stolen goods. In French he is called *un nonne* or *un noune*.

3. (old.)—Gin.—*See* quotations in BOBSTICK, and DRINKS for synonyms.

1749. 'Honours of the Fleet,' quoted in Ashton's *The Fleet*, p. 286. H' had strain'd his credit for a Dram of BOB.

4. (military.)—An infantry soldier; generally LIGHT-BOB, *i.e.*, a soldier of the light infantry. [This is probably an allusion to their being enlisted with the Queen's shilling or BOB.] For synonyms, *see* MUDCRUSHER.

1844. W. H. MAXWELL, *Sports and Adventures in Scotland*, xxxv., 282. Me, that never . . . listened to a LIGHT-BOB.

1848. THACKERAY, *Vanity Fair*, ch. xxiv. Mr. Stubble, as may be supposed from his size and slenderness, was of the LIGHT-BOBS.

5. (Winchester College.)—A large white jug containing about a gallon in measure, and used for beer.

1870. MANSFIELD, *School-Life at Winchester College*, p. 85. Each end and Præfect's mess had their beer served up in a large white jug, or 'BOB.' The vessel used for the same purpose in Commoners' was called a 'Joram.'

1888. T. A. TROLLOPE, *What I Remember.* Only those 'Juniors' attended whose office it was to bring away the portions of bread and cheese and BOBS of beer for consumption in the afternoon.

Adj. (old).—Lively; nice; in good spirits.

1721. CIBBER, *Refusal*, I., sp. 109. Yesterday at Marybone, they had me all BOB as a Robin. [M.]

1864. MISS YONGE, *Trial*, I., 113. 'That's a nice girl' . . . 'BOBBER than bobtail.' [M.]

Verb (old).—To cheat; to trick; to disappoint. Also to BOB OUT OF.

1605. *Tryall Chev.*, I., in Bullen's *O. Plays*, iii., 273. I had rather dye in a ditch than be BOBD of my fayre Thomasin.

1748. T. DYCHE, *Dictionary* (5 ed.). BOB (v.), to jog, touch, or give notice by some such like sign; also a cant word for to trick or cheat.

Intj. (familiar).—Stop! That's enough!

1889. *Modern Society*, June 6. 'Say when,' said Bonko, taking up a flagon of whiskey and commencing to pour out the spirit into my glass. 'BOB!' replied I.

DRY BOB, *phr.* (old).—Fruitless coition.

DRY BOB, WET BOB, *subs.* (Eton College). — The first-named is one who devotes himself to cricket or football and other land sports; the latter one who goes in for rowing and aquatics generally. The origin of the term is doubtful.—*See* DRY BOB and WET BOB.

1844. DISRAELI, *Coningsby*, p. 42. 'It is settled, the match to-morrow shall be between Aquatics and DRY BOBS,' said a senior boy.

1874. *Saturday Review*, Aug., p. 212. The friendly rivalry between England and America led some while ago to a contest between the WET BOBS, to use an Eton phrase, of either country, and it was only fair that the DRY BOBS should show what they could do.

ALL IS BOB, *phr.* (old).—All's safe; 'serene'; 'gay.' For synonyms, *see* O K.

1785. GROSE, *Dictionary of the Vulgar Tongue.* [ALL'S BOB is defined as foregoing.]

1839. HARRISON AINSWORTH, *Jack Sheppard*, p. 12. A moment afterwards, the street was illumined by a blaze of torchlight, and a tumultuous uproar announced the arrival of the first detachment of Minters. Mr. Wood rushed instantly to meet them. 'Hurrah!' shouted he, waving his hat triumphantly over his head. 'Saved!' 'Ay, ay, it's ALL BOB, my covey! You're safe enough, that's certain!' responded the Minters.

BEAR A BOB! *phr.* (common).—Be brisk! look sharp!

BOB A NOD, *phr.* (common.)—A shilling a head. [From BOB, slang for shilling, + NOD, the head.]

TO GIVE THE BOB, *phr.* (old).—To give the door. An old term used by Massinger—'It can be no other but TO GIVE me THE BOB.'

S'HELP ME BOB, *phr.* (low).—A street oath, equivalent to 'So help me God'; a corrupted form of the legal oath. 'So help' is pronounced *swelp*. There are several variants, such as S'HELP THE CAT—MY GREENS—THE TATURS, etc.

1837. BARHAM, *I. L.* (*Dead Drummer*). For his jaw-work would never, I'm sure, S'ELP ME BOB, Have come for to go for to do sich a job!

1880. JAS. PAYN, *Confid. Agent*, ch. xix. 'Not another word will I say, S'HELP ME BOB.' And John rolled over in his bed like an indignant porpoise.

TO SHIFT ONE'S BOB, *phr.* (common).—To go away. *Cf.*, BOBBING AROUND, 'to go expeditiously from place to place.'

BOBBER, *subs.* (common).—1. A fellow-workman; mate; or 'CHUM' (*q.v.* for synonyms).

1860. W. WHITE, *Round Wrekin*, 34. BOBBER being the equivalent of chum. [M.]

1871. *Daily News*, May 19. As he sells these, the buyers or their BOBBERS carry them off. [M.]

2. A spurious plural of BOB (*q.v.*) = a shilling.

BOBBERY, *subs.* (popular).—A noise; squabble; disturbance; or 'racket.' [An Anglo-Indian representation of *Bāp re!* O father! a common exclamation of surprise or grief.—*Yule.* Murray thinks the evidence for its origination in India is decisive, other plausible derivations to the contrary notwithstanding.] The first of the following quotations shows an earlier use by thirteen years than that given by the *New English Dictionary.*

1803. KENNEY, *Raising the Wind*, II., i. If I don't go back, and kick up such a BOBBERY—

1833. MARRYAT, *Peter Simple*, ch. ii. I'll bet a wager there'll be a BOBBERY in the pigsty before long, for they are ripe for mischief.

1836. MARRYAT, *Midshipman Easy*, ch. xix. 'I can do nothing but there's a BOBBERY at the bottom of it.'

1879. *Punch*, 17 May, 227. I might in quiet hold my own, And not go kicking up a BOBBERY. [M.]

BOBBISH, *adj.* (common).—Frequently PRETTY BOBBISH, *i.e.*, hearty; in good health and spirits; clever; spruce. *Cf.*, BOB, *adj.* So also BOBBISHLY, *adv.*

1819. SCOTT, in *Lockhart*, xliv (1842), 394. I trust you will find me pretty BOBBISH. [M.]

1857. DICKENS, *The Detective Police*, in *Reprinted Pieces*, p. 247. 'Halloa, Butcher! is that you?' 'Yes, it's me, How do you find yourself?' 'BOBBISH,' he says.

1860. DICKENS, *Great Expectations*, ch. iv., p. 13. Every Christmas Day, he retorted, as he now retorted, 'It's no

more than your merits. And now are you all BOBBISH, and how's sixpennorth of halfpence?' meaning me.

1881. W. D. HOWELLS, *Dr. Breen's Practice*, ch. vii. 'I didn't know that I mustn't look downcast. I didn't suppose it would be very polite, under the circumstances, to go round looking as BOBBISH as I feel.'

BOBBLES, *subs.* (common).—The testicles—a corrupted form of BAWBELLS. For synonyms, *see* CODS.

BOBBY, *subs.* (popular).—A policeman. This nickname, though possibly not derived from, was certainly popularised by the fact that the Metropolitan Police Act of 1828 was mainly the work of Mr., afterwards Sir Robert Peel. Long before that statesman remodelled the police, however, the term 'BOBBY the beadle' was in use to signify a guardian of a public square or other open space. There seems, however, a lack of evidence, and examples of its literary use prior to 1851 have not been discovered. For synonyms, *see* BEAK, sense 1.

At the Universities the Proctors are or used to be called BOBBIES.

1851. H. MAYHEW, *London Labour and London Poor*, I., p. 16. It is often said in admiration of such a man that he could muzzle half a dozen BOBBIES before breakfast!

1880. *Punch*, No. 2038. Going round a corner and crying, BOBBY! BOBBY! BOBBY! when he saw a Proctor.

1884. *Punch*, July 26, p. 41, col. 2. But oh, for the grip of the 'BOBBY'S' hand Upon his neck that day.

1889. *The Mirror*, Aug. 26, p. 7, col. 2. On the back seat was perched the perfidious Amelia Ann, the lust of conquest clearly written upon her sinful and perspiring face. She had put her cat in the birdcage, its former occupant being, I presume, inside the cat. . . . In this order the ghastly procession moved off, to the evident amusement of a 'BOBBY,' whose beat seems to include nothing beyond the area-railings of the opposite house.

BOBBY-TWISTER, *subs.* (thieves').—A burglar or thief, who, when resisting pursuit or capture, uses violence. Of obvious derivation.—*See* THIEVES.

BOB-CULL, *subs.* (thieves').—A good fellow; a pleasant companion. [From BOB (*adj.*) = nice, lively + CULL, old cant for a man.]

BOB MY PAL, *subs.* (rhyming slang).—A girl, *i.e.*, 'gal.'

BOBSTICK, *subs.* (old).—A shilling's worth. *Cf.*, BOB, sense 1.

1789. GEO. PARKER, *Life's Painter*, p. 162. BOBSTICK of rum slim. That is, a shilling's worth of punch.

1821. W. T. MONCRIEFF, *Tom and Jerry*, Act ii., Sc. 5. *Tom. Allons donc*—Waiter, bring some wine. *Log.* Hang cards! bring me a BOBSTICK of rum slim, or a glass of Barsac—stay, on second thoughts, I'll have a sniker of green tea punch.

BOB TAIL, *subs.* (old).—1. A lewd woman. For synonyms, *see* BARRACK-HACK.

2. An impotent man or eunuch.

TAG, RAG, AND BOBTAIL; a mob of all sorts of low people; the common herd; the rabble.

1659-60. PEPYS, *Diary*, Mar. 6. The dining-room . . . was full of TAG, RAG, AND BOBTAIL, dancing, singing, and drinking. [M.]

1785. WOLCOT ('P. Pindar'), *Ode to R. A.'s*, ii., wks. (1812) I., 80. TAG-RAGS AND BOBTAILS of the sacred Brush. [M.]

1820. BYRON, *Blues*, ii., 23. The RAG, TAG, AND BOBTAIL of those they call 'Blues.' [M.]

1841. DICKENS, *Barnaby Rudge*, xxxv. 'We don't take in no TAGRAG AND BOBTAIL at our house.' [M.]

BOCO, *subs.* (originally pugilistic, now common).—1. The nose. [Probably from BEAK, sense 3.] The form employed by American thieves is BOKE. For synonyms, *see* CONK.

1880. BESANT AND RICE, *Seamy Side*, ch. i. 'A common keeper, who was in the lot, got a heavy oner on the BOKO for his share.' 'Boys,' said Mr. Hamblin, 'who use slang come to the gallows. BOKO is—' 'Conk or BOKO,' said Nicolas the vulgar. 'It's all the same.'

1889. *Ally Sloper's Half Holiday*, July 6. Dear Old Blistered BOKO,—I trust you will allow me to thank you and your Graphologist for my character I received this morning. My friends say it is correct. I am saving up my pocket-money for a bottle of nose bloomer. I can see your BOKO blushing at the prospect.

1889. *Sporting Times*, July 6. The Gnat, with the Cunning peculiar to the Wicked flew up the Lion's BOKO and Stung hin so Badly, that the Great Beast rent himself to Death with his Own Claws.

2. Nonsense; 'bosh.' [Of unknown derivation, and it seems to have no connection with sense 1.]

1886. *Punch*, 25 Sept., p. 145. Lopsided Free Trade is all BOKO.

BODIER, *subs.* (pugilistic).—A blow on the side of the body.—*See* RIB-ROASTER.

BODKIN, *subs.* (sporting).—Amongst sporting men, a person who takes his turn between the sheets on alternate nights, when an hotel has twice as many visitors as it can comfortably lodge; as, for instance, during a race-week. A transferred sense from

TO RIDE OR SIT BODKIN, *phr.* (common).—To take a place and be wedged in between other persons when the accommodation is intended for two only.

1638. FORD, *Fancies*, IV., i. (1811), 186. Where but two lie in a bed, you must be—BODKIN, bitch-baby—must ye? [M.]

1798. *Loves of the Triangles*, 182. While the pressed BODKIN, punched and squeezed to death, Sweats in the midmost place.

1848. THACKERAY, *Book of Snobs*, ch. xxxiv. The writer supposes Aubrey to come to town in post-chaise and pair, sitting BODKIN probably between his wife and sister.

BODY-COVER, *subs.* (American thieves').—A coat. One is almost tempted to ask whether this is the only garment known to the criminal classes. *Cf.*, WRAP-RASCAL.

BODY OF DIVINITY BOUND IN BLACK CALF, *phr.* (old).—A parson. So quoted in the *Lexicon Balatronicum* [1811]. For synonyms, *see* DEVIL-DODGER.

BODY-SLANGS, *subs.* (thieves').—Fetters. [From SLANG (*q.v.*), a chain.]—*See* quot. and for synonyms, DARBIES.

1819. VAUX, *Memoirs.* BODY-SLANGS are of two kinds. Each consists of a heavy iron ring to go round the waist, to which are attached in one case two bars or heavy chains, connected with the fetters round the ankles, in the other case a link at each side attached to a handcuff. Into these the wrists are locked, and thus held down to the prisoner's sides. The latter are now only to be found in museums.

BODY-SNATCHER, *subs.* (old).—1. A bailiff or runner. [The SNATCH was the trick by which the bailiff captured the delinquent.] These terms are now obsolete, so far as the pursuits mentioned

are concerned. They are mentioned by Parker [1781] in his *View of Society*, II., 70.

2. A policeman. For synonyms, *see* BEAK, sense 1.

1858. A. MAYHEW, *Paved with Gold*, bk. III., ch. i., p. 254. 'Now, if you or I was to do such a dodge as that, we should have the BODY-SNATCHERS (police officers) after us.'

3. (American.)—A generally objectionable individual. This variety is especially known as a MEAN BODY-SNATCHER (*q.v.*).

4. (popular.)—A violator of graves; a 'resurrectionist.'

1833. SIR F. HEAD, *Bubbles from the Brunnen*, 126. Any one of our BODY-SNATCHERS would have rubbed his rough hands. [M.]

1863. *Reader*, Aug. 22. At that time (1827-28) . . . BODY-SNATCHING became a trade.

5. (common.)—An undertaker. For synonyms, *see* COLD COOK.

BOG, *subs.* (prison).—1. The works at Dartmoor, on which convicts labour; during recent years a large quantity of land has been reclaimed in this way.

1877. *Five Years' Penal Servitude*, ch. iii., p. 158. These were the men destined for outdoor work, the BOGS, as the places where the different outside gangs worked were called [at Dartmoor].

2. (low.)—An abbreviated form of BOG-HOUSE (*q.v.*), or BOG-SHOP.

Verb.—To ease oneself; to evacuate.—*See* BURY A QUAKER.

BOGEY.—*See* BOGY.

BOGGLE-DE-BOTCH, BOGGLEDY-BOTCH, *subs.* (colloquial).—A bungle; 'mess'; 'hash.' [From BOGGLE, 'to fumble,' 'to bungle,' + BOTCH, 'to bungle' or 'to construct clumsily.'] BOGGLE by itself is more frequently employed.

1834. MISS EDGEWORTH, *Helen*, ch. xxvi. A fine BOGGLE-DE-BOTCH I have made of it. . . . I am aware it is not a canonical word,—classical, I mean; nor in nor out of any dictionary perhaps—but when people are warm, they cannot stand picking terms.

BOG-HOUSE, BOG-SHOP, *subs.* (low).—A privy; a necessary house. The term, as will be seen, is an old one. [The derivation is probably from BOG, a morass of decaying matter; a soft, spongy place.] For synonyms, *see* BURY A QUAKER and MRS. JONES.

1671. R. HEAD, *English Rogue*, pt. I., ch. xii., p. 123 (1874). Fearing I should catch cold, they out of pity covered me warm in a BOGG-HOUSE.

1703. WARD, *London Spy*, pt. III., p. 47. Its walls being adorn'd with as many unsavoury *Finger-dabs* as an *Inns of Court* BOG-HOUSE.

1754. B. MARTIN, *Eng. Dict.*, 2 ed. BOG-HOUSE, a privy, or necessary-house.

BOGLANDER, *subs.* (old).—An Irishman. [From the boggy and marshy character of a considerable portion of the Emerald Isle.] *Cf.*, BOG-TROTTER.

1698-1700. WARD, *London Spy*, pt. XVI., p. 383. [BOGLANDER is the name applied to an Irishman in this work.]

1785. GROSE, *Dictionary of the Vulgar Tongue.* BOG LANDER, an Irishman. Ireland being famous for its large bogs which furnish the chief fuel in many parts of that kingdom.

1811. *Lexicon Balatronicum.* [The same definition given as in Grose.]

BOG LATIN, *subs.* (Irish).—A spurious mode of speech simulating the Latin in construction.—*See* DOG LATIN.

Bog-Oranges, *subs.* (popular).—Potatoes. The phrase is an allusion to the vegetable in question forming a very substantial food staple of the Irish peasantry, with whom, in the popular mind, potatoes are largely associated. Hence probably the nickname. *Cf.*, MURPHY. [ORANGES, from the shape, + BOG = Irish, Bog-land being a humorous nickname for the Emerald Isle.]

Bog-Trotter, *subs.* (familiar).—A satirical name for an Irishman. Camden, however [*c.* 1605], speaking of the 'debateable land' on the borders of England and Scotland, says, 'both these dales breed notable BOG-TROTTERS.' From this the original sense would appear to have been one accustomed to walk across bogs. As a nickname for an Irishman, it dates at least from 1671.

1671. R. HEAD, *English Rogue*, pt. I., ch. xxvii. (Repr. 1874), p. 232. [Irishmen are spoken of as BOG-TROTTERS in this work.]

1859. SALA, *Gaslight and Daylight*, ch. xxix. Gaunt reapers and BOG-TROTTERS in those traditional blue body-coats, leathern smalls, and bell-crowned hats, that seem to be manufactured nowhere save in Ireland.

BOG-TROTTING, *adj.* (familiar).—A contemptuous epithet applied to one living among bogs; *e.g.*, a BOG-TROTTING Irishman.

1758-65. GOLDSMITH, *On Quack Doctors* (Essays and Poems, 1836), p. 127. Rock advises the world to beware of BOG-TROTTING quacks.

1849. THACKERAY, *Pendennis*, I., p. 169. The impudent, BOG-TROTTING scamp dare not threaten me!

1876. C. HINDLEY, *Adventures of a Cheap Jack*, p. 191. 'What do you mean by calling *me* Irish? it is *you* that are Irish, you——.' 'Ha! ha! ha! ha!' jerked out Fagan. 'There, I tould you so. He can't stand to be called by his true name; the BOG-TROTTING rascal denies his Ould Ireland for a mother.'

Bogus, *adj.* (American, now common).—Spurious: fictitious; a term applied to anything sham, or to that which is not what it professes to be. Various accounts, some of them of a circumstantial character, are given as to the genesis of this word. One thing only seems certain; and that is its American origin. The generally received derivation, hitherto, has been that given by the *Boston Courier* (12 June, 1857) to the effect that the word is a vile corruption of the Italian name Borghese, a notorious swindler, who about the year 1837 literally flooded the Western and South-western States with fictitious cheques, notes, and bills of exchange and similar securities to an enormous amount. It is said that the name was gradually corrupted first to *borges* and then to BOGUS, and the man Borghese being associated in the popular mind with doubtful money transactions, his name so corrupted into BOGUS became applied to fraudulent papers and practices, and latterly to any spurious or counterfeit object, as BOGUS money, hair, diamonds, accusations, etc. Yet another suggestion is one put forward by Mr. Jas. Russell Lowell. He thinks it has descended in a corrupted form from the French *Bagasse*, the refuse of the sugar cane after the juice has been expressed. This worthless product has, it is suggested, given the name to other worthless things having travelled from Louisiana up the Mississippi,

and thence throughout the Union, finally spreading itself over the English speaking world. A few, however, affect to regard it as a corruption of [hocus] pocus, and say that it refers to the German '*Hocus Pocus Imperatus, wer nicht sieht ist blind.*'

The latest light upon the history of the word is thrown, as usual, by the indefatigable Dr. Murray, who, while slily satirising the 'bogus derivations circumstantially given,' makes another attempt to solve the riddle. He says: 'Dr. S. Willard, of Chicago, in a letter to the editor of this Dictionary, quotes from the *Painesville* (Ohio) *Telegraph* of July 6 and Nov. 2, 1827, the word BOGUS as a *subs.*, applied to an apparatus for coining false money. Mr. Eber D. Howe, who was then editor of that paper, describes in his *Autobiography* (1878) the discovery of such a piece of mechanism in the hands of a gang of coiners at Painesville, in May, 1827; it was a mysterious looking object, and some one in the crowd styled it a BOGUS, a designation adopted in the succeeding numbers of the paper. Dr. Willard considers this to have been short for *tantrabogus*, a word familiar to him from his childhood, and which in his father's time was commonly applied in Vermont to any ill-looking object; he points out that *tantarabobs* is given in Halliwell as a Devonshire word for the devil.' [BOGUS seems thus to be related to BOGY, etc.]

1825. HUGHES, in J. Ludlow's *Hist. U. S.*, 338. This precious house of representatives—the BOGUS legislature as it was at once called.

1869. S. L. CLEMENS ('Mark Twain'), *Innocents at Home*, ch. xvii. Nobody had ever received his BOGUS history as gospel before; its genuineness had always been called in question either by words or looks; but here was a man that not only swallowed it all down, but was grateful for the dose.

1874. M. COLLINS, *Frances*, ch. xxxv. 'They've got some good money, as well as BOGUS notes.'

1883. *Saturday Review*, March 31, p. 399, col. 2. M. Soleirol had probably a number of forged autographs of Molière; his whole collection was a BOGUS assortment of frauds.

Bogy, Bogey, *subs.* (common).—A landlord. An attributive usage of the more familiar meanings—(1) the devil; (2) a person much dreaded. The transition from sense 2 to that which signifies a landlord is easy. A French equivalent is Monsieur Vautour; *vautour* = a vulture; and the term is applied to a hard-hearted landlord. In passing, it may perhaps be mentioned (having in view the uncertainty which Murray confesses hangs round the history of this word in its primary meanings) that ASK BOGY, as a reply to a question, occurs in Grose [1785]. It is true it is there associated with a vulgarism which, however, on the face of it, appears to have had little to do with the expression, except perhaps in the not over clean mind of the burly *bon-vivant* who compiled the dictionary in question. It seems to have been used much as the modern 'God knows'! or 'BRAMAH KNOWS' under similar circumstances. This, at any rate, would carry it back, in very much its present form, much earlier than 1825, Murray's earliest trace of it. Grose

says it was 'sea wit,' whatever that may mean.

Adj. (studios').—Sombre, or dark in tint. Said of a painting exhibiting these characteristics.

Bohn, *subs.* (American College).—A translation; a PONY (*q.v.*). The volumes of Bohn's *Classical Library* are in such general use among undergraduates in American Colleges, that BOHN has come to be a common name for a translation.

1855. *Songs, Biennial Jubilee, Yale College.* 'Twas plenty of skin with a good deal of BOHN.

Boil, *verb* (old).—To betray; 'to PEACH,' which *see* for synonyms.

1602. ROWLANDS, *Greene's Coney Catchers*, 16. His cloyer or follower fortwith BOYLES him, that is, bewrayes him. [M.]

1611. MIDDLETON AND DEKKER, *Roaring Girle*, wks., 1873, III., 220. Wee are smoakt . . . wee are BOYL'D, pox on her! [M.]

Boil Down, *verb* (popular).—To reduce in bulk by condensing or epitomizing. When a literary work is reduced to smaller compass by the presentation only of the main or salient features, it is said to be BOILED DOWN. [The expression is a figurative use (quite recent by-the-bye) of BOILING DOWN in the sense of lessening the bulk by boiling.]

1880. *Sat. Review*, No. 1288, 28. It is surprising to see how much research Mr. S. has sometimes contrived TO BOIL DOWN into a single line. [M.]

1885. G. DOLLY, *Dickens as I Knew Him*, p. 125. The newspaper and political elements having been consulted, and their opinions having been BOILED DOWN.

1887. H. FREDERIC, in *Scribn. Mag.*, I., 479. 'To BOIL DOWN' columns of narrative into a few lines of bald, cold statement.

1888. *Polytechnic Mag.*, 25 Oct., p. 258.

Whatever you have to say, my friend,
 Whether witty, or grave, or gay—
Condense as much as ever you can,
 And say in the readiest way;
And whether you write on rural affairs,
 Or particular things in town,
Just a word of friendly advice—BOIL IT
 DOWN.

Boiled Shirt, Biled Shirt or **Boiled Rag**, *subs.* (American).—In the West, BILED SHIRT is the odd name given to a shirt of white linen, and it is not difficult to see the line of reasoning from which the term derives its significance. In the active stirring life of the West little count is taken of the *convenances* of civilization, and only on Sundays and festive occasions would the woollen undergarment be discarded for the white linen article. Indeed, in many cases, the former would be worn until it literally dropped to pieces. Now white shirts are facetiously known as BILED SHIRTS all over the States, and only recently (May, 1888) a question in dispute between the employés of the Chicago Tramway Companies and the managers of the same was whether the former should wear, when on duty, coloured or BILED SHIRTS. *Cf.*, BALD-FACED SHIRT.

1854. MCCLURE, *Rocky Mountains*, p. 412. In order to attend the Governor's reception, I borrowed a BOILED SHIRT, and plunged in with a Byron collar, and polished boots, and also the other necessary apparel.

1869. S. L. CLEMENS ('Mark Twain'), *Innocents at Home*, ch. xii. But they were rough in those times! . . . if a man wanted a fight on his hands without any annoying delay, all he had to do was to appear in public in a white shirt or a stove-pipe hat, and he would be accommodated. For those people hated aris tocrats. They had a particular and malignant animosity toward what they called a BILED SHIRT.

1872. *Dublin Univ. Mag.*, Feb., p. 219. Every man arrays himself in 'store-clothes' and BOILED SHIRTS.

1888. *New York World*, 13 May. Is it possible that the Chicagoans never heard of white shirts before this spring? May be the street-railway presidents never saw a starched shirt (I must deplore the use of the word BILED as applied to shirts) until this year.

Boiler, *subs.* (Winchester College).—1. A plain coffee-pot used for heating water. Called fourpenny and sixpenny boilers, not from their price, but from the quantity of milk they will hold: τὸ πᾶν BOILERS were large tin saucepan-like vessels in which water for hot BIDETS (*q.v.*) was heated.

2. *See* POT BOILER.

Boiler-Plated, *adj.* (American).—Imperturbable; stolid; stoical. [The simile is akin to that contained in expressions like iron-clad, copper-bottomed, etc., drawn mainly from marine phraseology.]

Boilers or **Brompton Boilers**, *subs.* (popular).—1. A name originally given to the new Kensington Museum and School of Art, in allusion to the peculiar form of the buildings, and the fact of their being mainly composed of, and covered with, sheet iron. This has been changed since the extensive alterations in the building, or rather pile of buildings, and the term BOILERS is now applied to the Bethnal Green Museum.—*See* PEPPER-BOXES.

1885. *Daily News*, July 9, p. 5, col. 1. The building is merely a fragment of the old 'BROMPTON BOILERS,' set up originally for the South Kensington Museum.

2. (Royal Military Academy.)—Boiled potatoes. Fried potatoes are called GREASERS.

Boiling or **Biling**. WHOLE BOILING or BILING, *subs. phr.* (common).—The whole lot; entire quantity. [A figurative usage, from a quantity boiled at one time.] Variants are the WHOLE GRIDIRON (*q.v.*) and ALL THE SHOOT.

1835. HALIBURTON ('Sam Slick'), *Clockmaker*, 3 S., ch. xviii. The last mile, he said, tho' the shortest one of the WHOLE BILIN', took the longest [time] to do it by a jug full.

1837. MARRYAT, *Dog Fiend*, xiii. [He] may . . . whip the WHOLE BOILING of us off to the Ingees.

1852. DICKENS, *Bleak House*, ch. lix., p. 496. 'And the WHOLE BILEING of people was mixed up in the same business, and no other.'

1874. E. L. LINTON, *Patricia Kemball*, ch. xxii. 'He have Dora? No, not if he licked my foot for her, and I broke the WHOLE BOILING of them—as I will!'

Boil One's Lobster, *verbal phr.* (old).—To enter the army after having been in the church. [From LOBSTER, a slang term for a soldier, the allusion being to the change in colour which lobsters undergo in the process of boiling, turning from a bluish black to red.] *Cf.*, BLACK COAT and RED COAT.

Boke, *subs.* (American thieves').—The nose. [This may either be derived directly from BEAK, sense 3, or indirectly from BOKO (*q.v.*).] For synonyms, *see* CONK.

Bold as Brass, *adv. phr.* (popular).—Audaciously forward; presumptuous; without shame. The simile, or at least the general idea, seems to be an old one. Shakspeare (*see* quot.) uses the expression 'a face of brass,' and even to this day BRASS, sense I (*q.v.*), is synonymous with impudence or 'cheek.'

1594. SHAKSPEARE, *Love's Labour Lost*, v., 2.
Biron. Thus pour the stars down plagues for perjury.
Can any FACE OF BRASS hold longer out?——

1846. THACKERAY, *Vanity Fair*, II., p. 12. He came in as BOLD AS BRASS.

1854. THACKERAY, *Lovel the Widower*, p. 195. 'A nursery governess at the wages of a housemaid' I continued, BOLD AS CORINTHIAN BRASS.

c. 1882. *Broadside Ballad*, 'Timothy Titus.'
The name belongs to brave men, and I'm as BOLD AS BRASS,
I do not wear the lion's skin and show myself an ass;
I'm full of pluck and can defy, like Ajax, anything,
And if you put me to the test, a proof I soon can bring.

BOLER, also **BOWLER**, *subs.* (popular).—A stiff felt hat. For synonyms, *see* CADY.

1861. *Sat. Review*, Sept. 21, 297. We are informed that he . . . wore, or rather carried in his hand, a white BOWLER hat.

1882. PEBODY, *Eng. Journalism*, xxi., 158. The ministers, in BOWLERS and pea-jackets, are to be found upon the shore of highland locks.

1889. *Answers*, June 8, p. 24. Most of the men were clothed in loud and greasy suits of tweed, and wore what are known as BOWLER hats, many of them much the worse for wear. The ladies affected fine and smart costumes, but as the greater part of their dresses had seen long months of service, the smartness was somewhat of the bedraggled order.

BOLLY, *subs.* (Marlborough College).—Pudding.

BOLT, *subs.* (old).—The throat. [This curious term would seem to be derived from BOLT = to gulp down.]

1821. W. T. MONCRIEFF, *Tom and Jerry*, Act iii., Sc. 3. *Tom.* Here, Dusty, my prince, now then, sluice your BOLT. (*Gives Bob gin.*) *Bob.* Vell, your honours, here's luck. (*Bolts gin.*) That's a regular kwortern, I knows by my mouth.

Verb (at one period slang, now recognised).—I. To escape; to leave suddenly. BOLT is an instance of a word which once orthodox, subsequently fell into disrepute, but which, after having for generations served as a mere slang term, is now nearly as respectable as when Dryden wrote: 'I have reflected on those who, from time to time, have shot into the world, some BOLTING out on the stage with vast applause, and others hissed off.' The following are a few examples of its use. For synonyms, *see* AMPUTATE.

1668. ETHEREGE, *She Would if She Could*, I., i. (1704), p. 94. Is he gone? *Court.* Ay, ay! you may venture to BOLT now.

1712. ARBUTHNOT, *Hist. of John Bull*, pt. IV., ch. vi. Then, of a sudden, BOLTING into the room, he began to tell . . .

1752. FIELDING, *Amelia*, bk. XI., ch. vii. In his way home, Booth was met by a lady in a chair, who immediately upon seeing him . . . BOLTED out of it.

1821. W. T. MONCRIEFF, *Tom and Jerry*, Act i., Sc. 7. *Log.* Come along, then. Now, Jerry, chivey! *Jerry.* Chivey? *Log.* Mizzle? *Jerry.* Mizzle? *Log.* Tip your rags a gallop! *Jerry.* Tip my rags a gallop? *Log.* Walk your trotters! *Jerry.* Walk my trotters? *Log.* BOLT! *Jerry.* BOLT? oh, aye! I'm fly now. You mean go.

1837. BARHAM, *I. L.* (*M. of Venice*). Jessy ransack'd the house, popp'd her breeks on, and when so Disguis'd, BOLTED off with her beau—one Lorenzo.

1843. DICKENS, *Martin Chuzzlewit*, ch. ix., p. 90. He was more strongly tempted . . . to make excursive BOLTS into the neighbouring alleys when he answered the door.

2. (American.)—The usage in the United States indicates the

right of the independently minded to revolt against partisan rule, as 'He BOLTED the party nominations.' Also substantively, as 'He has organized a BOLT.' The word derived this meaning from its sporting application to a horse when it becomes unmanageable on the race-course. *Cf.*, BOLTER. It is rarely used with its dictionary meaning in political connections; and, when so used, is generally misunderstood by the average reader.

1871. *St. Louis Democrat*, 3 April. 'Several of our contemporaries have announced it as a well-established fact, that Carl Schurz has BOLTED from the Republican party. We have the very best authority for denying the report.'

1888. *Daily Inter-Ocean*, 3 Feb. What the Register does object to are the fellows who BOLT the ticket and support the opposition candidate when they can not control nominations.

3. (colloquial.)—To eat hurriedly without chewing; to swallow whole; to gulp down. Wolcot in a note to the first quotation hereunder appended, explains BOLT as a Hampshire word. 'A rapid deglutition of bacon, without the *sober ceremony* of mastication.'

1794. WOLCOT ('P. Pindar'), *Ode to Tyrants*, in wks. (Dublin, 1795), vol. II., p. 527.
Bold push'd the Emp'ror on, with stride so noble,
BOLTING his subjects with majestic gobble.

1843. DICKENS, *Martin Chuzzlewit*, ch. xvi., p. 171. Dyspeptic individuals BOLTED their food in wedges.

1857. DICKENS, *Dorrit*, bk. I., ch. xiii., 101. 'Give me as short a time as you like to BOLT my meals in, and keep me at it.'

1883. *Daily Telegraph*, Jan. 10, p. 5, col. 3. The dangerous habit of BOLTING a light luncheon in two or three minutes.

GETTING THE BOLT, *phr.* (thieves').—Being sentenced to penal servitude. *Cf.*, BOAT.

TO TURN THE CORNER OF BOLT STREET, *phr.* (popular).—A humorous expression for running away. *Cf.*, BOLT, sense I, also QUEER STREET, and for synonyms, *see* AMPUTATE.

BOLTER, *subs.* (old).—I. Explained by quotation. The privileged places referred to were such as Whitefriars, the Mint, Higher and Lower Alsatia, etc.

1748. T. DYCHE, *Dictionary* (5 ed.). BOLTER (s.), a cant name for one who hides himself in his own house, or some privileged place, and dares only peep, but not go out of his retreat.

2. One who 'bolts'; especially applied to horses, but figuratively to persons in the sense of one given to throwing off restraint; in American parlance one who 'KICKS' (*q.v.*).

1840. THACKERAY, *Paris Sk. Bk.* (1872), 244. The engine may explode . . . or be a BOLTER. [M.]

1850. F. E. SMEDLEY, *Frank Fairlegh*, ch. xiii. 'Three of the horses had never been in harness before, and the fourth was a BOLTER.'

1852. DICKENS, *Bleak House*, ch. lviii., p. 483. This sparkling sally is to the effect that, although he always knew she was the best-groomed woman in the stud, he had no idea she was a BOLTER. It is immensely received in turf-circles.

1881. C. J. DUNPHIE, *The Chameleon*, p. 17. It is better to ride a steady old plodder than to trust your neck to a BOLTER.

3. (American.)—One who exercises the right of abstention in regard to his political party. *See* BOLT, *verb*, sense 2.

1883. *Atlantic Monthly*, LII., 327. To whom a 'scratcher' or a BOLTER is more hateful than the Beast. [M.]

1884. *American*, VIII., 100. To denounce the twenty-seven as BOLTERS from their party.

BOLT-IN-TUN, *phr.* (London thieves').—Bolted; run away.

1819. J. H. VAUX, *Memoirs*. A term founded on the cant word 'bolt,' and merely a fanciful variation very common among *flash* persons, there being in London a famous inn so called. It is customary when a man has run away from his lodgings, broken out of jail, or made any other sudden movement, to say 'the BOLT-IN-TUN is concerned,' or 'he's gone to the BOLT-IN-TUN' instead of simply saying, 'he has bolted,' etc.

BOLTSPRIT, BOLTSPREET, BOWSPRIT, *subs.* (common).—An old and humorous term for the nose. [The analogy is between the spar or boom extending beyond the stem of a vessel and the nose as a prominent and projecting feature of the face.] For synonyms, *see* CONK.

1690. SHADWELL, *Amorous Bigot*, Act v. As thou lovest thy ears, or nose, that BOLT-SPRIT of thy face. [M.]

1691. SHADWELL, *Scowerers*, Act v. They do not consider the tenderness of my BOLT-SPRIT. [M.]

1748. T. DYCHE, *Dictionary* (5 ed.). BOLTSPRIT (s.), a cant name for the nose.

BOLT THE MOON, *verbal phr.*—To remove one's goods and chattels under cover of night with a view of evading the payment of rent. A variant of SHOOT THE MOON (*q.v.*); the act itself is called a MOONLIGHT FLITTING (*q.v.*).

BOLUS, *subs.* (common).—An apothecary; a doctor. [From BOLUS, a large pill frequently prescribed by physicians.]

1878. HATTON, *Cruel London*, bk. VI., ch. ii. 'The doctor, up from the Indian bar, came and said I was wanted in London' . . . 'good for old BOLUS,' said Kernan; 'and I believe him.'

BOMAN, *subs.* (old).—A gallant fellow. This is mentioned by Nares, who, however, could find no example illustrating its use.

BOMBAY DUCKS, *subs.* (old).—I. The Bombay regiments of the East India Company's army were so called.

2. A well known delicacy, the exact nature of which is explained by G. A. Sala in the second quotation.

1865. G. A. SALA, in *Daily Telegraph*, 14 August, 5, 4. His *cuisine* was, with the occasional interpolation of a not entirely objectionable curry, accompanied by BOMBAY DUCKS, exclusively old-fashioned English.

1886. G. A. SALA, in *Ill. Lon. News*, 7 August, 138, 2. The BOMBAY DUCK is the Anglo-Indian relation of the Digby chick. Alive, it is a fish called the bummelo; dead and dried, it becomes a DUCK.

BOMBO, BUMBO, *subs.* (common).—A nickname given to various mixtures, but chiefly to cold punch. Smollett, in a note in *Roderick Random*, speaks of it as 'a liquor composed of rum, sugar, water, and nutmeg.'

1748. SMOLLETT, *Roderick Random*, ch. xxxiv. A table well stored with BUMBO and wine.

1867. SMYTH, *Sailors' Word Book*. BOMBO, weak cold punch.

a. 1886. *Northumb. Song*, in *N. and Q.*, 6 March, 195. The pitmen and the keelman . . . drink BUMBO made of gin.

BONA, *subs.* (popular).—A girl; young woman; a belle.

c. 18(?). *Broadside Ballad*, 'Oh, Fred, don't be so frivolous.'
Girls are in vulgar called DONAS,
Some are called Miss and some Mrs.,
The best of them all are called BONAS,
The whole jolly lot's fond of kisses.
I kiss pretty lips, and I squeeze finger tips,
No matter what I have to pay,

If I meet a dear maid who is somewhat afraid,
She'll blush like a virgin and say, 'Oh my.' Chorus.

Adj. (theatrical).—Good. [From the Latin.]—*See* RUMBO.

BONANZA, *subs.* (American).—A happy hit; a stroke of fortune; success. [From the Spanish, a fair wind, fine weather, prosperous voyage.] BONANZA was originally the name of a mine in Nevada, which once, quite unexpectedly, turned out to be a big thing, and of enormous value; now applied to any lucky hit or successful enterprise.

1875. *Scribner's Mag.*, July, p. 272. But a BONANZA with millions in it is not struck every week.

1888. *San Francisco News Letter*, 4 Feb. The mines along the veins running north and south, of which North Belle Isle is the center, are all stayers, and in the east and west ledge Grand Prize has entered a body of ore which may develop into a BONANZA as big as the one which paid millions in dividends in years gone by.

BONA-ROBA, *subs.* (old).—A courtesan; a showy prostitute. [From Italian *buona*, good, + ROBA = a robe or dress.] The term was much in use among the older dramatists. Ben Jonson speaks of a bouncing BONA-ROBA; and Cowley seems to have considered it as implying a fine, tall figure. BONA in modern times is frequently employed to signify a girl or young woman, without reference to morals.

1598. SHAKSPEARE, *2 Henry IV.*, iii., 2. We knew where the BONA-ROBAS were; and had the best of them all at commandment.

b. 1618, *d.* 1667. COWLEY, *Essay on Greatness* (quoted by Nares). I would neither wish that my mistress nor my fortune should be a BONA-ROBA;—but as Lucretius says, *Parvula, pumilio, tota merum sal.*

1822. SCOTT, *Nigel*, xvi. Your lordship is for a frolic into Alsatia? . . . there are BONA-ROBAS to be found there. [M.]

1839. HARRISON AINSWORTH, *Jack Sheppard* [1889], p. 69. The other BONA-ROBA, known amongst her companions as Mistress Poll Maggot, was a beauty on a much larger scale—in fact, a perfect Amazon.

BONCE, *subs.* (popular).—I. The head; [probably a derivative of sense 2, from the analogy between them.] For synonyms, *see* CRUMPET.

2. A large marble [origin unknown, but *see* ALLEY].

BONE, *subs.* (American).—When a traveller, in passing his luggage through the Custom House, tips the officer in the expectation that the latter's examination of his *impedimenta* will be more or less superficial, the fee thus given is termed a BONE. The practice, is, of course, contrary to all regulations; but, human nature being human nature all the world over, it is believed that similar expedients for evading the law are not altogether unknown in England.

Adj. (thieves').—Good; excellent; ◇ is the vagabonds' hieroglyphic for BONE, or good, chalked by them on houses and street corners as a hint to succeeding beggars. [Probably from French *bon*, good. *Cf.*, BOON.]

1851-61. H. MAYHEW, *London Lab. and Lon. Poor*, vol. I., p. 232. He [beggar] mostly chalks a signal on or near the door. I give one or two instances. ◇ 'BONE,' meaning good.

1883. G. A. S [ALA], in *Ill. L. News*, Nov. 10, p. 451, col. 3. It is well known that the lozenge-shaped diagram chalked by beggars and tramps on doors and walls in 'promising' neighbourhoods stands for 'BONE,' a corruption of the French '*bon*,' as a hint to succeeding vagabonds that they will find the happiest of hunting-grounds in the locality.

Verb (popular).—1. To filch; to steal; to make off with; to take into custody. [There are two suggested derivations:—(1) that the figure of speech is drawn from the manner in which a dog makes off with a bone; (2) that BONE is a corruption of 'bonnet' (a gambling cheat who 'sharks' one's money slyly).] For synonyms in sense of to steal, *see* PRIG; in sense of to apprehend, *see* NAB.

1748. T. DYCHE, *Dictionary* (5 ed.). BONE (v.), a cant word to seize or arrest; also to cheat or strip a person of his money or goods.

1819. J. H. VAUX, *Memoirs*, II., 157. Tell us how you was BONED, signifies tell us the story of your apprehension, a common request among fellow-prisoners in a jail, which is readily complied with as a rule; and the various circumstances therein related afford present amusement, and also useful hints for regulating their future operations, so as to avoid the like misfortune.

1838. DICKENS, *Nich. Nickleby*, ch. lvii., p. 467. 'And why you were living so quiet here, and what you had BONED, and who you had BONED it from, wasn't it?'

1861. MISS BRADDON, *Trail of the Serpent*, bk. II., ch. ii. 'I'm blest if he hasn't been and BONED my mug. I hope it'll do him more good than it's done me.'

1871. *Chambers' Journal*, Dec. 9, *A Double Event*, p. 774. It would be a breach of confidence to tell you how it was arranged, but, after some haggling, it *was* arranged that, on the understanding that I gave up the securities, I was to BONE the reward which the detectives had missed.

2. (American.) — To bribe; to 'grease the palm.'—*See* BONE, *subs.*

3. (American cadets').—To study hard. [From BOHN (*q.v.*).]

TO HAVE A BONE IN THE LEG—ARM—THROAT, ETC., *phr.* (common).—A humorous reason for declining to use the member spoken of; a feigned obstacle.

1542. NICHOLAS UDALL, *Erasmus's Apophthegmes* (1877, Reprint of ed. 1562), p. 375. He refused to speake, allegeing that HE HAD A BONE IN HIS THROTE, and he could not speake.

1738. SWIFT, *Polite Conversation* (conv. iii.). *Nev.* Miss, come, be kind for once, and order me a dish of coffee. *Miss.* Pray go yourself; let us wear out the oldest first; besides, I can't go, for I HAVE A BONE IN MY LEG.

BONE-ACHE, *subs.* (old).—The *lues venerea*. [The allusion is obvious.]

1592. NASHE, *Pierce Penilesse*. But *cucullus non facit monachum*—'tis not their newe bonnets will keepe them from the old BOAN-ACK.

1606. SHAKSPEARE, *Tro. and C.*, ii., 3. After this the vengeance on the whole camp! or rather the BONE-ACHE! for that, methinks, is the curse dependent on those that war for a placket.

BONE-BOX, *subs.* (common).—The mouth. [The teeth are here represented as *the* 'bones.' The latter are now more commonly called 'ivories.'] For synonyms, *see* POTATO-TRAP, and compare with BONE-HOUSE.

1785. GROSE, *Dictionary of the Vulgar Tongue*. Shut your BONE-BOX; shut your mouth.

BONE-CRUSHER, *subs.* (sporting).—A heavy bore rifle used for killing big game. [Literally that which crushes or breaks bones by force. *Cf.*, BONE-SHAKER.]

1872. H. M. STANLEY, *How I Found Livingstone* (2 ed.), p. 63. African game require BONE-CRUSHERS; for any ordinary carbine possesses sufficient penetrative qualities, yet has not the disabling qualities which a gun must possess to be useful in the hands of an

African explorer. *Ibid*, p. 342. What is wanted for this country is a heavy bore—No. 10 or 12 is the real BONE-CRUSHER, that will drop every animal shot.

BONED.—*See* BONE, *verb*, sense 1.

BONE-GRUBBER, *subs.* (common).—1. One who lives by collecting bones from heaps of refuse, selling his spoils at the marine stores or to bone grinders. [From BONE + GRUB, to seek by burrowing, + ER.] Also called BONE-PICKER (*q.v.*), and TOT-PICKERS (*q.v.*). *See* first quotation and *cf.* BONE-PICKER form. The French term is *un biffin*, which also signifies a foot-soldier, his knapsack being compared to a rag or bone-picker's basket; also *un chifferton* or *un chiffortin*; *un cupidon* (an ironical allusion to his hook and basket); *un graffin*. For other synonyms, *see* TOT-PICKER.

c. 1750. 'The Hunter's Wedding,' quoted in J. Ashton's *The Fleet*, 1888, p. 366.
Sam the GRUBBER, he having had
warning,
His wallet and broom down did lay.

1851-61. H. MAYHEW, *Lon. Lab. and Lon. Poor*, vol. II., p. 155. The BONE-GRUBBER generally seeks out the narrow back streets, where dust and refuse are cast, or where any dust-bins are accessible. The articles for which he chiefly searches are rags and bones,—rags he prefers,—but waste metal, such as bits of lead, pewter, copper, brass, or old iron, he prizes above all.

1862. MAYHEW, *Crim. Prisons*, 40. A black-chinned and lanthorn-jawed BONE-GRUBBER.

2. A resurrectionist; a violator of graves. Cobbett was therefore called 'a BONE-GRUBBER,' because he brought the remains of Tom Paine from America. *Cf.*, BONE-HOUSE. Latterly, from the quotation which follows, the term seems to have been extended to all having to do with funerals.

1863. G. A. SALA, *Breakfast in Bed*, essay vii., p. 181 (1864). The crowd in Cheapside declared that I was a mute. They called me BONE-GRUBBER.

BONE-HOUSE, *subs.* (familiar). — 1. The human body—an obvious allusion.

1870. EMERSON, *Soc. and Sol.*, vi., 119. This wonderful BONE-HOUSE which is called man. [M.]

2. A coffin. The term is also used to signify a charnel-house, and Americans generally call a cemetery a 'bone-yard.'

1836. DICKENS, *Pickwick Papers*, II., p. 207. Nothing soon—lie in bed—starve—die—Inquest—little BONE-HOUSE—poor prisoner.

1846. WALBRAN, *Guide Ripon*. The celebrated BONE-HOUSE no longer exists.

1848. FORSTER, *Life and Times of Oliver Goldsmith*, II., p. 165 (bk. IV., ch. viii.). The body [of a man who had poisoned himself] was taken to the BONE-HOUSE of St. Andrew's, but no one came to claim it.

BONE MUSCLE, *verbal phr.* (American college). — To practice gymnastics. *Cf.*, BONE, *verb*, sense 3.

BONE-PICKER, *subs.* (common).—1. A footman. [Evidently a contemptuous allusion to sense 2, a footman's duties being to pick up and set in order after his employer.] The French term is *un larbin*.

2. (common.) — A collector of bones, rags, and other refuse from the streets and places where rubbish is placed, for the purpose of sale to marine dealers and bone crushers. The same as BONE-GRUBBER, sense 1 (*q.v.*).

1866. RUSKIN, *Crown of Wild Olives*, p. 25. The deceased was a BONE-PICKER. He was in the lowest stage of poverty, etc.

BONER, *subs.* (Winchester College).—A sharp blow on the spine.

BONES, *subs.* (common).—1. Dice, which are also called ST. HUGH'S BONES (*q.v.*). [So called because made of bone or ivory.] 'To rattle the BONES,' *i.e.*, 'to play at dice.' The term is a very old one, as also seem to be games played with the little cubes in question.

c. 1386. CHAUCER, *Pard. T.*, 328. This fruyt cometh of the bicched BONES two, fforsweryng, Ire, falsnesse, Homycide.

a. 1529. SKELTON, wks. (ed. Dyce) I., 52. On the borde he whyrled a payre of BONES.

1608. DEKKER, *Belman of London*, in wks. (Grosart) III., 123. Who being left by his parents rich in money and possessions, hath to the musicke of square ratling BONES danced so long, that hee hath danced himselfe into the company of beggers.

1698. DRYDEN, *Persius*, III., 96.
But then my study was to cog the dice,
And dexterously to throw the lucky
sice:
To shun ames-ace, that swept my stakes
away;
And watch the box, for fear they should
convey
False BONES, and put upon me in the play.

1772. FOOTE, *Nabob*, Act ii. When your chance is low, as tray, ace, or two deuces, the best method is to dribble out the BONES from the box.

1849. THACKERAY, *Pendennis*, ch. xviii. 'I saw you sit down to *écarté* last week at Trumpington's, and taking your turn with the BONES after Ringwood's supper.'

1861. WHYTE MELVILLE, *Good for Nothing*, ch. xxviii. 'What with speculations failing, and consols dropping all at once, not to mention a continual run of ill-luck with the BONES, I saw no way out of it but to bolt.'

2. (common.) — Pieces of BONES held between the fingers and played Spanish castanet fashion. Generally used as an accompaniment to banjo and other 'negro' minstrel music.

1592. SHAKSPEARE, *Midsummer Night's Dream*, iv., 1, line 27. *Tita.* What, wilt thou hear some music, my sweet love? *Bot.* I have a reasonable good ear in music: let us have the tongs and the BONES.

1851. MAYHEW, *London Labour and London Poor*, III., p. 195. Peter rolling about in his chair like a serenader playing the BONES, and the young Othello laughing as if he was being tickled. *Ibid*, p. 201. The BONES, we've real BONES, rib-of-beef BONES, but some have ebony BONES, which sound better than rib-BONES—they tell best, etc.

1865. *Times*, 17 July. Amateur negro melodists . . . thumped the banjo and rattled the BONES. [M.]

3. (common.) — A member of a 'negro' minstrel troupe; generally applied to one of the 'end' men who plays the BONES (sense 2).

1851. MAYHEW, *London Labour and London Poor*, III. First of all we formed a school of three—two banjos and a tambourine, and after that we added a BONES and a fiddle.

1867. RHODA BROUGHTON, *Cometh up as a Flower*, p. 236. The band clashes out; big fiddle and little fiddle, harp and BONES, off they go.

1884. *Sat. Review*, June 7, 740, col. 1. A single row of negro minstrels seated on chairs . . . while at the end are BONES and Sambo. [M.]

4. (general.)—The bones of the human body, but more generally applied to the teeth. French thieves call these *les piloches* (*f*); and *les osselots* (*m*). *Cf.*, BONE-BOX and BONE-HOUSE, and for synonyms, *see* GRINDERS.

5. (common.)—A surgeon; generally SAWBONES (*q.v.*). A list of curious nicknames for the medical profession will also be found under SQUIRT.

1887. *Chamb. Journal*, Jan. 8, p. 30. 'I have sent for the village BONES, and

if he can but patch me up, it may not yet be too late.

6. (Stock Exchange.)—(1) The shares of Wickens, Pease and Co.; (2) North British 4°/₀ 1st Preference Shares, the 4°/₀ 2nd Preference Stock being nicknamed BONETTAS.

AS DRY OR HARD AS A BONE, *phr.* (common), *i.e.*, as free from moisture as a bone after it has been picked and cleaned, as by a dog.

1833. MARRYAT, *Peter Simple*, i. It's AS DRY AS A BONE.

1837. R. NICOLL, *Poems* (1843), 83. Dubs were HARD AS ONY BANE.

ONE END IS PRETTY SURE TO BE BONE, *phr.* (American).—An old time saying equivalent to an admission that 'all is not gold that glitters'; that the realization of one's hopes never comes up to the ideal formed of them.

1888. *The World*, 13 May. People here (in the west) have to get up and get in order to make both ends meet, and even then ONE END IS PRETTY SURE TO BE BONE.

TO BE UPON THE BONES, *phr.* (vulgar).—To attack.

b. 1616, *d.* 1704. SIR R. L'ESTRANGE (in Annandale). Puss had a month's mind TO BE UPON THE BONES of him, but was not willing to pick a quarrel.

TO FEEL A THING IN ONE'S BONES.—A simile signifying assurance; conviction.

1887. *Scribner's Magazine*. I ain't a-goin' to mention no names but I kin FEEL IT IN MY BONES that things ain't on the square here, there's a nigger in the fence.

1888. *Missouri Republican*, 22 Feb. Nat. M. Shelton, of Lancaster, said: 'I am in the race of attorney-general, and I FEEL IT IN MY BONES that I will get the nomination.

TO MAKE NO BONES, *phr.* (familiar).—To make no scruple; to show no hesitation; to commence and finish a work without difficulty—now restricted to colloquial use; it was formerly current literary coin, and is frequently to be met with in our older literature. Its earlier form was, 'to find bones in,' which clearly shows the phrase to have originated in a reference to bones in soup, or similar food, regarded as obstacles to swallowing. In this sense it is found as early as the middle of the fifteenth century, in the *Paston Letters*. It does not occur in its present shape TO MAKE BONES until a century later; but, from this period on to the end of the seventeenth century it was in constant use.

1459. *Paston Lett.*, 331, I., 444. And FOND that tyme NO BONYS in the matere. [M.]

1542. UDALL, *Apoph. of Erasmus*, p. 133 (1877). Yea, and rather then faill, both whole mainor places, and also whole Lordships, the 'MAKE NO BONES, ne sticke not, quite and cleue to swallow doune the narrow lane, and the same to spue up again.'

1565. SHACKLOCK, *Hatchet of Heresies*. And instede of that whiche he saide, This is my body, they haue MADE NO BONES AT IT, to say, this is my brede.

1590. GREENE, *Francesco's Fortune*, in wks. VIII., 189. Tricke thy selfe vp in thy best reparrell, and MAKE NO BONES at it but on a woing [wooing].

1596. NASHE, *Saffron Walden*, in wks. III., 112. He . . . would MAKE NO BONES to take the wall of *Sir Philip Sidney*.

1677. WYCHERLEY, *Plain Dealer*, Act iii. *Man.* How could I refrain? A lawyer talked peremptorily and saucily to me, and as good as gave me the lie. *Free.* They do it so often to one another at the bar, that they MAKE NO BONES on't elsewhere.

1849. THACKERAY, *Pendennis*, ch. lxiv. Do you think that the Government or the Opposition would MAKE ANY BONES about accepting the seat if it be offered to them?

TO PICK A BONE or BONES WITH ONE, *phr.* (colloquial).—To have an unpleasant matter to settle with one; also, a difficulty to solve; 'a nut to crack.'

1565. COLFHILL, *Answ. Treat. Cron.* (1846), 277. A BONE for you to PICK ON. [M.]

1783. AINSWORTH, *Lat. Dict.* (Morell), I, s.v. *Pick*, To GIVE ONE A BONE TO PICK, *scrupulum alicui injicere.*

1850-68. H. ROGERS, *Ess.*, II., ii. (1874), 103. Many a BONE in these lectures which a keen metaphysician would be disposed TO PICK WITH the author.

BONESETTER, *subs.* (old).—A hard riding horse; a ricketty conveyance; properly one whose occupation is to set broken and dislocated bones. The sarcastic, punning reference is of course to the dire effects which naturally follow the use of an animal of such a description. The odd way in which slang is often derived, strikes one at times as very curious. Not only are words frequently coined which resemble genuine words, such as 'solemncholy' for 'melancholy,' and 'it don't much magnify' for 'it don't much signify,' but the meaning of such factitious words is, in many cases, either subtly reversed or endowed with an extremely cynical tinge of humour and sarcasm. The present instance is a case in point. A more modern term is BONESHAKER (*q.v.*), which is less subtle in its meaning, BONESETTER being certainly far more brutally cynical in its suggestiveness. *See* second quotation for some curious synonyms formerly in use.

1785. GROSE, *Dictionary of the Vulgar Tongue.* BONE SETTER, a hard trotting horse.

1821. W. T. MONCRIEFF, *Tom and Jerry*, Act i., Sc. 7. *Jerry.* I long to be there,—let's hasten to dress at once. *Log.* Aye; call a rattler. *Jerry.* A rattler! I'm at fault again. *Log.* A rattler is a rumbler, otherwise a jarvy! better known perhaps by the name of a hack; handy enough in a wet day, or a hurry. *Jerry.* A hack! If it's the thing we rattled over the stones in to-day, It might more properly be called a BONE-SETTER. *Tom.* Or bone-breaker.—But if you dislike going in a hack, we'll get you a mab. *Jerry.* A mab! I'm at fault again —never shall get properly broken in. *Tom.* A mab is a jingling jarvy!—a cabriolet, Jerry.—But we must mind our flash doesn't peep out at Almack's. 'Tis classic ground there.

BONE-SHAKE, *verb* (popular).—To ride a BONE-SHAKER (*q.v.*), *i.e.*, a heavy bicycle of a very old type.

1889. *Answers*, Feb. 23, p. 195, col. 1. Among those who learnt to BONESHAKE was Charles Dickens, who, had he lived, would have been a devoted cyclist.

BONE-SHAKER, *subs.* (old). — 1. A hard trotting horse.—See BONE-SETTER.

2. (popular.)—An old type of bicycle in use prior to the introduction of india-rubber tires and other manifold improvements. The first bicycle propelled by cranks and pedals was ridden in Paris in 1864. It created enormous excitement. On being introduced into England people went bicycle mad, and the number of persons who suffered in consequence of riding the old BONE-SHAKERS was considerable. Among those who learnt to 'bone-shake' was Charles Dickens, who, had he lived, would have been a devoted cyclist, for he regarded the sport as a grand one, and prophesied a big future for it. In 1868 Mr. Charles Spencer rode to Brighton on a BONE-SHAKER in 14 hours from London. The papers were full

of what was then considered an extraordinary feat, but on Aug. 10, 1889, four riders of the Polytechnic Cycling Club covered the distance to Brighton and back, 108 miles, in 7 hours 50 minutes, which is better time than a most perfectly-appointed modern four-in-hand can be driven over the same course by the aid of unlimited relays of horses kept in readiness to be changed at a moment's notice. Only one machine was used throughout the trial, viz., a safety . roadster, weighing 36 lbs.

1874. A. HOWARD, *Bicycle*, 10. In 1870 and 1871, the low, long BONE-SHAKER began to fall in public esteem. [M.]

1884. G. L. HILLIER, in *Longman's Mag.*, March, p. 487. The BONE-SHAKER, as the ribald cyclist of the present day designates the ancestor of his present bicycle.

1885. *Nineteenth Century*, Jan., p. 92. In the *Field's* report of the performance of the Cambridge Town Bicycle Club we find this entry: 'Half Mile Race on BONE-SHAKERS, not exceeding 36 in.'

BONE STANDING, *verbal phr.* (American college).—To study hard. [Evidently an allusion to the alertness implied by a standing position.]

BONETTAS, *subs.* (Stock Exchange.) —The 4 °/₀ 2nd North British 2nd Preference Stock. — See BONES, *subs.*, sense 6, § 2.

BONG.—See BOUNG.

BONIFACE; *subs.* (popular). — The landlord of a tavern or inn. [Derived from Farquhar's play.]

1707. FARQUHAR, *Beaux Stratagem.* [Boniface is here given as the name of landlord of the inn.]

1803. BRISTED, *Pedest. Tour*, I., 120. To give the characteristic features and to stamp the peculiar traits of honest BONIFACE.

1854. WHYTE MELVILLE, *General Bounce*, ch. xvi. The landlord either could not, or would not, give them any actual information as to his guests. . . So the blue-coated myrmidons of Scotland Yard got but little information from BONIFACE.

BONING ADJUTANT, *verbal phr.* (American cadets').—Aping a military bearing. [From BONE, to study, to imitate.] So also BONING MUSCLE (*q.v.*) is going in largely for gymnastics. To BONE STANDING, to study hard. BONING DEMERIT, giving no cause for complaint as regards one's conduct. All West Point cadet slang.

BONK, *subs.* (travelling showmens').—A short, steep hill. [Possibly only a provincialism, or an obsolete form of 'bank.']

1876. HINDLEY, *Adventures of a Cheap Jack*, p. 302. In Lancashire, Yorkshire, Derbyshire, and Staffordshire, the approaches to some of the large works are either up or down some steep, short hill, usually termed BONK, and the drivers of heavily laden carts with two horses have the breeching on the leading chain-horse, as well as the horse in the shafts, so that when they are going down one of these steep BONKS, the horse is as useful as a help in drawing up.

BONNET, *subs.* (old).—1. A gambling cheat; a decoy at auctions. [So-called because they BONNET or blind the eyes of the victims. —See BONNET, *verb,* sense 1.] Hotten says sometimes called a BEARER-UP. The BONNET plays as though he were a member of the general public, and by his good luck, or by the force of his example, induces others to venture their stakes. BONNETING is often done in much better society than that to be found in the ordinary gaming-rooms. A man who persuades another to buy an article on which he receives commission or percentage, is said to BONNET or bear-up for the seller. Also called a BONNETER. The French has *bonneteur* for one profuse in compliments and bows.

1812. J. H. VAUX, *Flash Dictionary.* BONNET, a concealment.

1841. *Comic Almanack*, October. Or a man at a hell, Playing the part of a BONNETTER well.

1853. WHYTE MELVILLE, *Digby Grand*, ch. xxi. I began to think my military friend was 'a BONNET,' —one of those harpies employed by gambling-house keepers to enhance temptation by the influence of example, and generally selected for their respectable and innocent appearance.

(?) 1868. *Times* (quoted by BREWER, *Phrase and Fable*, p. 104). A man who sits at a gaming-table, and appears to be playing against the table; when a stranger appears, the BONNET generally wins.

1876. HINDLEY, *Life and Adventures of a Cheap Jack*, p. 217. We bid or praised up his goods : in fact, often acted as 'puffers' or BONNETS, to give him a leg up.

1885. *Morning Post*, Sept. 5, p. 7, col. 3. There was no distinct evidence to connect him with a conspiracy to defraud. . . He might have been used as a sort of BONNET to conceal the utter worthlessness of propositions made by the others.

2. (old.)—A pretext; pretence; or 'make believe.'

3. A woman. [This sense is analogous to 'petticoat,' the names of articles of feminine attire being transferred to the wearer.]

1880. *Punch's Almanac*, p. 3. Then comes Easter, Got some coin in hand, Trot a BONNET out and do the grand.

Verb (common).—1. To act as a BONNET (*q.v.*); to cheat; to puff; to 'BEAR UP' (*q.v.*).

1871. 'Hawk's-Eye,' *Budget of Turf Notes*, p. 2. I could point out now what horses he is BONNETING for the 2,000 Guineas and Derby of this year, and the horses whose pretensions he is trying to discredit.

1887. *Referee*, 15 May, p. 1, col. 3. Nobody can suppose that I am anxious to BONNET for the *Times* newspaper.

2. (popular.)—To crush a man's hat down over his eyes.

1835. DICKENS, *Sketches by Boz*, p. 229. Two young men, who, now and then, varied their amusements by BONNETING the proprietor of this itinerant coffee-house.

1836. DICKENS, *Pickwick*, II., p. 216. You are a dutiful and affectionate little boy to come a BONNETIN' your father in his old age.

1843. DICKENS, *Christmas Carol in Prose*, p. 22. Scrooge reverently disclaimed . . . any knowledge of having wilfully BONNETED the Spirit at any period of his life.

1882. *Saturday Review*, LIV., p. 629. The students hustled and 'BONNETTED' a new professor.

TO HAVE A GREEN BONNET, *phr.* (common).—To fail in business. [From the green cloth cap formerly worn by bankrupts.]

BONNET-BUILDER, *subs.*(popular).—A milliner. [The derivation is clear.]—See BUILD.

1839. Song in *The Little Melodist*, quoted in J. Ashton's *The Fleet*, p. 93. Will you go to Bagnigge Wells, BONNET BUILDER, O!

1868. BREWER, *Phrase and Fable*, s.v. 'Build.' A milliner is jestingly called a 'BONNET-BUILDER.'

BONNETER.—1. See BONNET, *subs.*, sense 1.

2. (common.) — A crushing blow on the hat.—See BONNET, *verb,* sense 2.

BONNETS SO BLUE, *subs.* (rhyming slang).—Irish stew.—See RHYMING SLANG.

BONO, *adj.* (circus and thieves').—Good. [From the Latin.]

BOOBY HUTCH, *subs.* (thieves').—A police station; so called no doubt from the light in which the criminal classes regard those who are foolish enough or unfortunate enough to get 'landed' in such places. [Booby = a fool + HUTCH, a box or confined space.]

BOOBY-TRAP, *subs.* (schoolboys').—An arrangement of books, wet sponges, vessels of water, etc., so arranged on the top of a door set ajar that when the intended victim enters the room, the whole falls upon him.

1850. SMEDLEY, *Frank Fairlegh*, ch. iii., p. 28. He had devoted it to the construction of what he called a 'BOOBY-TRAP,' which ingenious piece of mechanism was arranged in the following manner: The victim's room-door was placed ajar, and upon the top thereof a Greek Lexicon, or any other equally ponderous volume, was carefully balanced, and upon this was set in its turn a jug of water. If all these were properly adjusted, the catastrophe above described was certain to ensue when the door was opened.

1882. F. ANSTEY, *Vice Versâ*, ch. xiv. 'I made a first-rate BOOBY-TRAP, though, one day for an old yellow buffer who came in to see you.'

1888. *Sat. Review*, Nov. 3, p. 566, col. 2. On his way down to dinner he is suddenly drenched from head to foot by a BOOBY-TRAP—a sponge soaked in water placed above a half-open door.

BOODLE, *subs.* (American).—1. A crowd; a company; the 'WHOLE BOILING' (*q.v.*). With this meaning the form often appears as CA-BOODLE (*q.v.*). [As regards derivation, which is obscure, Murray, speaking of both senses as here treated, says the U.S. BOODLE, in sense 1, must be the same as Markham's 'buddle' (see quotation given below from *New English Dictionary*); sense 2 (also only in U.S.) may be a different word. BOODLE suggests a Dutch origin from *boedel* pronounced BOODLE, and in its primary sense means ' household stuff,' and refers to property left by a testator. It is curious to note that BODLE was a Scotch coin of the value of one-sixth of a penny.]

1625. F. MARKHAM, *Bk. Honour*, IV., ii. Men curiously and carefully chosen out (from all the BUDDLE and masse of great ones) for their approoued wisedome. [M.]

1857. O. W. HOLMES, *Autocrat*, p. 139. He would like to have the whole BOODLE of them (I remonstrated against this word, but the professor said it was a diabolish good word . . .) with their wives and children shipwrecked on a remote island.

1865. BACON, *Handbook of America*, p. 361. BOODLE, 'the whole BOODLE of them,' *i.e.*, all, the whole. [List of Americanisms.]

1884. E. E. HALE, *Xmas. in Narragansett*, ch. ix., p. 272. At eleven o'clock the 'whole BOODLE of them,' as Uncle Nahum called the caravan . . . had to boot and spur for church. [M.]

2. (American.)—In its second signification this curious word seems to have come into prominent use in politics during the past five years. Its meaning and usage is thus explained in *Americanisms — Old and New.* Some elections cannot be conducted without BOODLE first and last. BOODLE does not mean the capital or stock-in-trade, except the business or trade be something secret, peculiar and illegal. BOODLE always means money; but money has not always been BOODLE (*see* sense 4). Money honestly received and spent, money that circulates in regular and honest channels, that appears in cash-book and

ledger and expense account, is never BOODLE; but when a sum—a thousand dollars, more or less—is given to some one to use in influencing a third party, given perhaps in silence and certainly without requiring any writing of acknowledgment or obligation—that is BOODLE. BOODLE is money used for purposes of bribery and corruption; and the same word is employed to indicate the money that comes as spoils, the result of some secret deal, the profits of which are silently divided. The term is likewise used to cover the ill-gotten gains of the bank robber, or the absconding cashier. 'He carried away so much BOODLE.' In elections the primaries have to be 'fixed,' a great many men have to be 'seen'; in short, the amount of money that it seems necessary in some cases to use to elect a few honest public servants is a thing to wonder at. And when these men are elected, it appears that they often lose the power of distinguishing between 'straight money' and BOODLE. The word seems destined to take its permanent place in the language.—*See* also BOODLERS.

1884. *Boston* (Mass.) *Globe*, Oct. 7. 'Sinews of war,' and 'living issues,' 'soap,' and other synonyms for campaign BOODLE are familiar. [M.]

1888. *Philadelphia Bulletin*, 24 Feb. The best man in the world cannot make an honest living by being a City Councilman. The office is an unsalaried one, and any money that is made out of it is BOODLE. This is the new term for plunder, fraud and every form of stealing that can be practised by office-holders, who, in the practice, add the crime of perjury. It is an easy business for men of easy virtue.

1888. *Puck's Library*, May, p. 3.
In the evening, up the street,
As you see him passing by,
You're convinced his mind's replete
With the legal science high;
That he ponders of divorce,
Or, of BOODLE cases great;
That he spends all day, of course,
Fighting counsel for the State.

3. (American thieves'.)—Amongst the thieving fraternity BOODLE is used to denote money that is actually spurious or counterfeit, and not merely money used for nefarious purposes, but which as currency is genuine enough.

4. (American general.)—Money. This is the latest sense imported into the word. The transition by which it has come to be synonymous with 'dust,' 'pieces,' 'rhino,' 'oof,' etc., is an easy one.—*See* ACTUAL.

1888. *Puck's Library*, Jan., p. 4.
Shakey, take a fader's plessing,
Take it, for you ket it sheap;
Go in hot for making money,
Go in for to make a heap.
Don' you do no dings vot's grooked,
Don' you do no dings vot's mean—
Aber rake right in dot BOODLE,
Qviet, calm, and all serene.

TO CARRY BOODLE is to utter base coinage.—*See* BOODLER.

FAKE-BOODLE, *subs.* (American thieves').—A roll of paper over which, after folding, a dollar bill is pasted, and another bill being loosely wrapped round this it looks as if the whole roll is made up of a large sum of money in bills.

BOODLER, *subs.* (American political).—1. One who bribes or corrupts.—*See* BOODLE, sense 2.

1888. *Omaha World. American.* 'As you are a native of Canada I suppose you think that country is all right, but for my part I should hate most awfully to be a subject of a queen.' *Canadian.* 'The queen is a mere figure-head; there is no difference at all between Canada and the United States.' 'Come to think, I believe you do have elections there.'

'I should say we did. We have elections and campaigns, and political parties, and bosses, and ringsters, and BOODLERS, and——.' 'BOODLERS?' 'Plenty of 'em.' 'Well, well! Why, you are freemen just like us.'

2. (American thieves'.) — BOODLERS and shovers are the men who issue false money (*see* BOODLE, sense 3). Swindlers of this type generally hunt in couples; one carrying the bulk of the counterfeit money, and receiving the good change as obtained by his companion, who utters the BOODLE piece by piece. The game is generally worked so that at the slightest alarm the BOODLE CARRIER vanishes and leaves nothing to criminate his confederate.

BOOGET, *subs.* (old cant).—A travelling tinker's basket. Quoted by Harman [1567].

BOOK, *subs.* (sporting).—1. In betting, more especially in connection with horse racing, an arrangement of bets made against certain horses, and so calculated that the BOOKMAKER (*q.v.*) has a strong chance of winning something whatever the result.

1836. DICKENS, *Pickwick*, I., p. 400. And Wilkins Flasher, Esquire, entered it (the bet) in a little BOOK with a gold pencil-case; and the other gentleman entered it also, in another little BOOK with another gold pencil-case.

1837. DISRAELI, *Henrietta Temple*, p. 260. Am I to be branded because I have made half a million by a good BOOK?

1852. F. E. SMEDLEY, *Lewis Arundel*, ch. liii. 'He has backed the Dodona colt for the Derby, and has got a heavier BOOK on the race than he likes.'

1869. *Gent. Mag.*, July, p. 231. He wins your money with a smile, will accommodate his BOOK to suit what bets you may choose to make.

1879. JAS. PAYN, *High Spirits* (*Change of Views*). He had a knowledge, too, of practical mathematics, which enabled him to make a BOOK upon every great racing event of the year.

1889. *Pall Mall Gazette*, Oct. 21, p. 6, col. 1. Every sporting man is flattered if termed a sportsman, but it would be almost an insult to speak to a sportsman as a sporting man. Wherein does the distinction lie? it may be asked. The one is a lover of sport for the sake of the thing itself. The other is a lover of it for what he can get out of the business. The former may bet, but he does not look at sport through the glasses of a BOOK; the latter always bets, and in fact would not care about it at all if he could not take or give odds.

2. (card-players'.)—The first six tricks at whist.

3. (general.)—The copy of words to which music is set; the words of a play; formerly only applied to the libretto of an opera.

1768. STERNE, *Sentimental Journey*, I., 180. A small pamphlet, it might be the BOOK of the opera.

1889. *Answers*, 8 June, p. 24. The prompter had a little table on the 'prompt' side; that is, the right-hand side looking from the house, and his 'BOOK' was one mass of directions, the margins being covered with little pictures and diagrams of the stage, showing the positions of the leading actors in every scene.

TO KNOW ONE'S BOOK, *phr.* (popular).—To have made up one's mind; to know what is best for one's interest.

c. 1879. *Broadside Ballad*, 'Ain't you glad you didn't.'
Ain't you glad sometimes to know,
A second thought you took,
About a subject upon which
You thought you KNEW YOUR BOOK;
Now first of all you think you will,
And then you think you won't,
While someone says 'Go in and win!'
And someone else says 'Don't.'

TO SUIT ONE'S BOOK, *phr.* (common). — To suit one's arrangements. *Cf.*, BOOK, *subs.*, sense 1, the allusion being to betting books, in which bets are formally entered.

1852. F. E. SMEDLEY, *Lewis Arundel*, ch. vi. 'By which time he expects to be so hard up that he must marry somebody, and as there will be plenty of the needful, she will SUIT HIS BOOK as well as any other.

BOOKED, *ppl. adj.* (common).—Caught; fixed; disposed of; destined, etc. From the book-keeping term—entered in a book, or registered.

1840. HOOD, *Up the Rhine*, p. 6. I am BOOKED for a much longer journey.

1857. SNOWDEN, *Mag. Assistant*, 3 ed., p. 446. BOOKED, caught, taken, or disposed of.

1881. JAS. PAYN, *Grape from a Thorn*, ch. xxiii. 'I don't remember anyone having given *me* an "engaged ring" before; and it's not leap year, neither. However, the lady's BOOKED, which is a great relief.'

French thieves use *être planché* for 'to be booked'; also *être mort* (*i.e.*, 'to be dead'); the adjective is rendered by *faitré*, and the person BOOKED is *un gerbable*.

BOOK-FORM, *subs.* (sporting).—The relative powers of speed or endurance of race-horses as set down in the *Racing Calendar* or 'book.'

BOOKIE or **BOOKY**, *subs.* (sporting).—An abbreviated form of BOOKMAKER (*q.v.*).

1885. *Eng. Ill. Mag.*, April, p. 509. No rowdy ring, but a few quiet and well-known BOOKIES, who were ready enough to lay the odds to a modest fiver.

1889. *Sporting Times*, 29 June.
He now had occasion to speedily hie
To the BOOKIE who laid him the bet,
Who was one of the small and particular fry,
That at times, *when convenient*, forget.

BOOKMAKER, *subs.* (sporting).—The *English Encyclopædia* says:—In betting there are two parties—one called 'layers,' as the BOOKMAKERS are termed, and the other 'backers,' in which class may be included owners of horses as well as the public. The backer takes the odds which the BOOKMAKER lays against a horse, the former speculating upon the success of the animal, the latter upon its defeat; and taking the case of Cremorne for the Derby of 1872, just before the race, the BOOKMAKER would have laid 3 to 1, or perhaps £1000 to £300 against him, by which transaction, if the horse won, as he did, the backer would win £1000 for risking £300, and the BOOKMAKER lose the £1000 which he risked to win the smaller sum. At first sight this may appear an act of very questionable policy on the part of the BOOKMAKER; but really it is not so, because so far from running a greater risk than the backer, he runs less, inasmuch as it is his plan to lay the same amount (£1000) against every horse in the race, and as there can be but one winner, he would in all probability receive more than enough money from the many losers to pay the stated sum of £1000 which the chances are he has laid against the one winner, whichever it is.—*See* also BOOK, *subs.*, sense 1, and BOOKIE.

1862. *London Review*, Aug. 30, p. 188. Betting there seemed to be none . . . we could not perceive a single book or BOOKMAKER.

1880. W. DAY, *Racehorse in Training*, ch. xxiv., p. 245. BOOKMAKERS pursue a legitimate and lucrative trade by laying against all horses as they appear in the market.

1883. HAWLEY SMART, *Hard Lines*, ch. iii. Finding . . . that the BOOKMAKER whom for once they have landed for 'a thousand to thirty' is hopelessly insolvent.

BOOKMAKER'S POCKET, *subs.* (sporting).—A breast-pocket made inside the waistcoat, for notes of large amount.—*Hotten.* — *See* BOOKMAKER.

BOOKS, *subs.* (card-players').—1. A pack of cards. A term used mainly by professional card-players. Also called DEVIL'S BOOKS; BOOK OF BROADS; BOOK OF BRIEFS. The French equivalent is *un juge de paix*; while *une cartouchière à portées* is a prepared pack used by sharpers.

1706. MRS. CENTLIVRE, *Basset Table*, IV., ii., wks. (1872) I., 245.
L. Revel. Clean cards here.
Mrs. Sago. Burn this BOOK, 't has an unlucky air [tears them]. Bring some more BOOKS.

2. (Winchester College.)—(*a.*) The prizes formerly presented by Lord Say and Sele, now given by the governing body, to the 'Senior' in each division at the end of 'Half.' (*b.*) The school is thus divided:—SIXTH BOOK — Senior and Junior Division; the whole of the rest of the School is in FIFTH BOOK — Senior Part, Middle Part, Junior Part, each part being divided into so many divisions, Senior, Middle and Junior, or Senior, 2nd, 3rd and Junior, as the case may require. Formerly there was also 'FOURTH BOOK,' but it ceased to exist about twenty-five years ago.

1876. MANSFIELD, *School-Life at Winchester College*, p. 104. The school was divided into three classes, or BOOKS, as they were called. Of these, the Præfects formed one, SIXTH BOOK; FIFTH BOOK was sub-divided into three parts, called respectively, 'Senior, Middle, and Junior part of the Fifth'; in speaking of them, the words, 'of the Fifth' were generally omitted. The rest of the boys made up 'Fourth Book.'

(*c.*) UP AT BOOKS.—In class; repeating lessons; now called UP TO BOOKS.

1876. MANSFIELD, *School-Life at Winchester College*, p. 101. At each end of school are three tiers of benches rising gradually one above the other,—that on the ground being called 'Senior Row,' and the others 'Middle,' and 'Junior Row' respectively. On these the Classes sit when 'UP AT BOOKS,' *i.e.*, when repeating lessons.

(*d.*) BOOKS CHAMBERS. — Explained by quotation.

1876. MANSFIELD, *School-Life at Winchester College*, p. 103. On Remedies (a kind of whole holiday), we also went into School in the morning and afternoon for an hour or two without masters; this was called BOOKS CHAMBERS; and on Sundays, from four till a quarter to five.

(*e*) TO GET OR MAKE BOOKS.—To make the highest score at anything. *Cf.*, BOOKS, sense 2*a*.

BOOKWORK, *subs.* (University).—Mathematics that can be learned *verbatim* from books—all that are not problems.

BOOM.—This word is a comparatively recent production in its slang sense; and is variously used as a substantive or as a verb. Before particularizing its special usages, it may be interesting to note how, within a few years, it has made its appearance in a variety of combinations; as, 'the whole State is BOOMING for Smith,' or 'the boys have whooped up the State to BOOM for Smith,' or 'the Smith BOOM is ahead in this State,' etc., etc. Stocks and money are said to be BOOMING when active; and any particular spot within a flourishing district is regarded as within the BOOM-BELT. A successful team or party is said to be a BOOMING SQUAD, and we even read of BOOMLETS to express progress of a lesser degree. [Its origin is largely a matter of conjecture, but the most probable derivation is from the nautical phrase 'boom-out,' signifying a vessel running rapidly before the wind; but Murray points out that as various associations are probable, and as the actual use of the word has not been regulated by any distinct etymological feeling, it is not likely that any derivation will account for all its applications.]

Subs.—Commercial activity; rapid advance in prices; a flourishing state of affairs—in all its applications it is synonymous with extreme vigour and effectiveness. The first quotation carries its use back a few years beyond the earliest date given in the *New English Dictionary*.

1875. *Scribner's Mag.*, July, p. 277. Another BOOM in prices is to be looked for.

1883. *Referee*, May 6, p. 3, col. 2. 'The Merry Duchess' is a big BOOM, and I understand that money is being turned away nightly.

1883. M. TWAIN, *Life on the Mississippi*, ch. lvii., p. 499. I lived here in 1857—an extraordinary year there in real-estate matters. The BOOM was something wonderful. Everybody bought, everybody sold . . . anything in the semblance of a town lot, no matter how situated, was saleable.

1888. *Boston Daily Globe*. After the Sheridan reception, of course John Sherman must come to Boston. The Ohio statesman knows where all the real live BOOMS start. If Mr. Blaine is wise he also will come to the 'Hub' without delay.

1888. *Missouri Republican*, 16 Feb. 'Jim, they say thar is a big BUM up at Rome.' 'What's that?' said Jim. 'It's a kind of new tradin' business what swells and shrinks, and the sweller and shrinker stays down in a celler and works the machine. They trade in stock.' 'Horses and mules?' said Jim. 'No, hit's all on paper, and nobody can see what he's buyin'. You put your money in and wait for a swell. If it comes you are all right, but if a shrink comes you are busted, and you feel so ashamed that you don't say anything about it, and it never gets into the papers—nothing but the swells gits into the papers.'

Verb, intr.—To go off with a BOOM.—*See subs.* To make rapid and vigorous progress; to advance by leaps and bounds; *trans.* to push; to puff; to bring into prominence with a rush.

1874. S. L. CLEMENS ('Mark Twain'), *Gilded Age*, ch. xxvii. There's 200,000 dollars coming, and that will set things BOOMING again.

1875. *Scribner's Mag.*, July, p. 272. Stocks may BOOM to-day, but droop to-morrow, and with the crash come remorse and repentance. *Ibid*, p. 277. When stocks are active they are said to be BOOMING.

1884. M. TWAIN, *Huckleberry Finn*, xiii., 3. We BOOMED along down the river, watching for lights and watching for our raft.

1888. *Chicago Daily Inter-Ocean.* The city of Paris is said to be diminishing instead of increasing in population. They don't know how to BOOM a town over there.

As already stated, BOOM enters into many combinations; BOOMER (*q.v.*), BOOM-BELT, BOOMING-SQUAD, etc.

1888. *New Orleans Picayune.* A BOOM in North Carolina is not the kind of phenomenon to which we are accustomed here. Sales of land at from 2 dols. to 10 dols. an acre in a BOOM BELT are not of record hereabout.

1888. *Chicago Herald.* Ben Butterworth, of Ohio, one of the mainstays of John Sherman's BOOMING SQUAD, has just had the title of boss Republican tariff debater conferred upon him by the culture of Boston.

TO TOP ONE'S BOOM OFF, *phr.* (nautical).—To be off, or to start in a certain direction.

1871. G. MEREDITH, *Harry Richmond*, ch. xxxviii., p. 346 (1886). 'And now TOP YOUR BOOM, and to bed here.'

BOOMER, *subs.* (American).—1. One who BOOMS or causes an enterprise to become flourishing, active or notorious. [From BOOM, *subs.*, + ER.]

1883. *Times*, Sept. 26, p. 8. [He] is a North-Western BOOMER of great earnestness. [M.]

1885. *Boston* (Mass.) *Journal*, Aug. 19, p. 2, col. 4. The Oklahoma BOOMERS. [M.]

2. Attributively applied to anybody or anything considerably above the average. Thus, what English people would call a bouncing lie, an American, if given to slang, would call a BOOMER; so also a fine woman, a horse with extra good points, etc., etc.

BOOMERANG, *subs.* (American).—Figuratively used to signify acts or words, the results of which recoil upon the person from whom they originate. The BOOMERANG is properly an Australian missile weapon which, when thrown, can be made to return to the thrower; or which, likewise, can be caused to take an opposite direction to that in which it is first thrown.

1845. HOLMES, *Modest Request*, Poems (1884), 42. Like the strange weapon, which the Australian throws, Your verbal BOOMERANG slaps you on the nose. [M.]

1870. LOWELL, *Among My Books*, 1 S. (1873), 219. The BOOMERANG of argument, which one throws in the opposite direction of what he means to hit. [M.]

BOOMING, *ppl. adj.* (American).—Flourishing; active; in good form; large; astonishing.—*See* BOOM and BOOMER in all senses.

BOOM-PASSENGER, *subs.* (nautical).—A sailor's slang term for a convict on board ship. Derived from the circumstance that prisoners on board convict ships were chained to, or were made to crawl along or stand on the booms for exercise or punishment.—*Hotten*.

BOON-COMPANION, *subs.* (colloquial).—A comrade in a drinking bout; a good fellow. [BOON is evidently a corruption of the French *bon*.]

1566. DRANT, *Med. Morall*, A. v. He is my BONE companion, it's he that cheares up me. [M.]

1592. GREENE, *Quip*, in wks. XI., 220. To seeke good consortes and BOONE COMPANIONS to passe away the day withall.

1594. NASHE, *Terrors of the Night*, in wks. III., 228. Our Poets or BOONE COMPANIONS they are out of question.

1600. W. KEMP, *Nine Days' Wonder*, in Arber's *English Garner*, vol. VII., p. 27. And coming to my inn, where the host was a very BOON COMPANION, I desired to see him.

1712. ARBUTHNOT, *History of John Bull*, pt. I., ch. v. This was occasioned by his being a BOON COMPANION, loving his bottle and his diversion.

1825. SCOTT, *St. Ronan's Well*, ch. xxiii. The morning after a debauch is usually one of reflection, even to the most customary BOON COMPANION.

1827. LYTTON, *Pelham*, ch. lxvii. We went downstairs to our dinner, as charmed with each other as BOON COMPANIONS always should be.

BOON-COMPANIONSHIP, *subs.* (colloquial).—Jollity; conviviality.—*See* BOON-COMPANION.

1592. NASHE, *Strange Newes*, in wks. II., 176. Thinke not, though vnder correction of your BOONE-COMPANIONSHIP, I am disposd to be a little pleasant, I condemne you of anie immoderation, either in eating or drinking.

1849. LYTTON, *Caxtons*, pt. XII., ch. iv. A little society, and BOON-COMPANIONSHIP . . . would take Roland out of those gloomy reveries.

BOONG.—*See* BUNG.

BOORDE.—*See* BORD.

BOOST, *subs.* (American).—A hoisting; a 'shove'; a 'lift'; a 'push up'—a New England vulgarism.

1858. DOW, *Sermons*. Office seekers ask you to give them a BOOST into the tree of office. [M.]

1866. T. A. RICHARDS, *Rice Fields of the South*. [A negro-preacher in South Carolina, *loq.*] 'For, my bredderen, little Zaccheus was bound to see the Lord for once, dough he had to climb up de tree to do it. And how did he get up der tree? Ah, how did he get up der tree, my bredderen? Did he wait for some lazy nigger to bring him a ladder? Ah, no, my bredderen. Did he wait to be BOOSTED? Ah, no, my bredderen. Not a BOOST! He climbed right straight up der tree hisself, like de possum, by his own hands and feet and de grace of God!'

1888. *Puck's Library*, May, p. 11. A genius took hold of the business, and gave it a little BOOST. He was a man of the times, and he applied his reasoning faculties to the problem presented to him. 'What,' he asked, 'is the chief means of success?'

Verb.—To hoist; to lift up; to shove.—*See subs.*

1848-64. J. R. LOWELL, *Biglow Papers*, II., 106. Whereas ole Abram 'd sink afore he'd let a darkie BOOST him.

1872. S. L. CLEMENS ('Mark Twain'), *Roughing It*, ch. vii. You ought to have seen that spider-legged old skeleton go! and you ought to have seen the bull cut out after him, too—head down, tongue out, tail up, bellowing like everything, and actually mowing down the weeds, and tearing up the earth, and BOOSTING up the sand like a whirlwind!

1884. *Harper's Magazine*, Aug., p. 481, col. 1. To BOOST a jurist of so much helpless avoirdupois in through the carriage door.

BOOSY.—*See* BOOZY.

BOOT, *verb* (military).—To beat; to punish with a strap. The punishment is irregular and unconventional, being inflicted by soldiers on a comrade discovered guilty of some serious breach of the unwritten law of comradeship, such as theft, etc. The beating was formerly inflicted with a bootjack—hence the name.

BOOTH, *subs.* (thieves').—A house; 'to heave a BOOTH,' *i.e.*, 'to rob a house.'

BOOTH-BURSTER, *subs.* (theatrical).—A loud and noisy actor. A variant of BARN-STORMER (*q.v.*).

BOOTING, *subs.* (military).—A punishment administered with a strap. *Cf.*, COLTING.

BOOT-JOE, *subs.* (military).—Musketry drill.

BOOT-LEG PLAN.—*See* ON THE BOOT-LEG PLAN.

BOOTLICK, *subs.* (American).—A flunkey; hanger-on; or doer of dirty work. [In England such a one is called a 'bootlicker,' of which BOOTLICK is probably an abbreviated form.]

Verb.—To toady; to hang on; to undertake 'dirty' work.

BOOTS, *subs.* (colloquial).—1. The servant at hotels and places of a kindred character who cleans the boots of visitors. Formerly called boot-catchers, because in the old riding and coaching days part of their duty was to divest travellers of their footgear.

2. (military.)—The youngest officer in a regimental mess.

LIKE OLD BOOTS—BEANS—BRICKS—BLAZES, etc., *phr.* (common).—Thoroughly; vigorously. A simile as general in its application as it is irrelevant. It may mean anything, everything, and nothing. Why old boots and not new boots is beyond comprehension.

1868. MISS BRADDON, *Sir Jasper*, ch. xxvii., p. 282. I'll stick to you LIKE OLD BOOTS.

1874. *Saturday Review*, Jan., p. 55. An Oxford man, nay even a Balliol man . . . introduced in the story a pleasing change by such a phrase as jawing away LIKE OLD BOOTS.

TO BUY OLD BOOTS, *phr.* (old).—To marry or keep the cast-off mistress of another man.

TO DIE IN ONE'S BOOTS (*q.v.*).

BOOTS AND LEATHERS.—*See* COMMONER PEAL.

BOOTY. TO PLAY BOOTY, *phr.* (old).—To play falsely; dishonestly; or unfairly; this with the object of not winning, a previous arrangement having been made with a confederate to share the spoils resulting from the bogus play. Sometimes it takes the form of permitting the victim to win small stakes in order to encourage him to hazard larger sums which, naturally, he is not allowed to win.—*See* quotation from Dyche.

1575. *Frat. of Vacabondes*, p. 13. They wil make as much as they can, and consent as though they wil PLAY BOOTY against him.

1608. DEKKER, *Belman of London*, in wks. (Grosart) III., 133. They . . . haue still an eare how the layes [bets] are made, and according to that leuell doe they throw their bowles, so that be sure the bowlers PLAY BOOTY.

1742. FIELDING, *Joseph Andrews*, bk. I., ch. ii. The best gamesters, before they laid their money, always inquired which horse little Joey was to ride; and the bets were rather proportioned by the rider than by the horse himself; especially after he had scornfully refused a considerable bribe to PLAY BOOTY on such an occasion.

1748. T. DYCHE, *Dictionary* (5 ed.). BOOTY (S.), plunder, spoil, prize; also a cant word signifying a pretence to one thing, and at the same time intends and does the contrary, in order to cheat, impose upon, and draw in a person to lay wagers, play at some game, etc.

1776. COLMAN, *The Spleen*, in wks. (1777) IV., 276. Jubilee started and stumbled but, by-the-bye, I believe his rider PLAYED BOOTY—Duenna won the stakes, and the knowing ones were all taken in.

1817. SCOTT, *Rob Roy*, ch. vii. 'Were he caught PLAYING BOOTY, he would be disarmed, and probably dismounted.'

1831. DISRAELI, *Young Duke*. One thing remained to be lost—what he called his honour, which was already on the scent to PLAY BOOTY.

So also BOOTY = playing BOOTY, and BOOTY-FELLOW, a sharer in the plunder.

BOOZE, *subs.* (popular).—1. Drink; a draught. The older forms are BOUSE or BOUZE (*q.v.*), but BOOZE in its present form appears as early as 1714. For synonyms, *see* DRINKS.

1714. *Memoirs of John Hall* (4 ed.), p. 11. BOOZE, Drink. [List of cant words.]

1821. W. T. MONCRIEFF, *Tom and Jerry*, Act ii., Sc. 6. *Jemmy*. Gemmen, have you ordered the peck and BOOZE for the evening? *Sold. Suke.* Aye, aye, I've taken care of that—shoulder of veal and garnish—Turkey and appendleges—Parmesan—Filberds—Port and Madery.

1889. *Sporting Times*, 6 July. *Kid.* The Music Hall Sports are at Alexandra Park on the 23rd, and there will be rare doings on that occasion. Master and Shifter both give prizes, and there will be BOOZE in our drag.

2. A drinking bout; a tipsy frolic. Murray's first quote for this form and sense is dated 1864; but, from the following,

it will be seen to be at least thirty years older. For synonyms, *see* JAMBOREE.

1834. H. AINSWORTH, *Rookwood*, bk. III., ch. v. 'We'll have a jolly BOOSE when all's over.'

1884. *St. James's Gazette*, 19 Dec., p. 4, col. 1. There was a great BOOZE on board.

Verb (common). — To drink heavily; to tipple; to guzzle. An old term employed in some sense of 'to drink' as early as 1300. Also BOOZE (*q.v.*). For synonyms, *see* SWILL.

1567. HARMAN, *Caveat* (1814), p. 5. The buriall was tourned to BOUSING and belly cheere.

1592. NASHE, *Pierce Penilesse*, in wks. II., 91. They should haue all the companie that resort to them, bye BOWZING and beere-bathing in their BOUSES every after-noone.

1777. COLMAN, *Epilogue to Sheridan's School for Scandal*. While good Sir Peter BOOZES with the squire.

1853. THACKERAY, *Barry Lyndon*, ch. xiii., p. 173. 'I wonder, Sir Charles Lyndon, a gentleman who has been the King's ambassador, can demean himself by gambling and BOOZING with low Irish black-legs!'

So also BOOZED (*ppl. adj.*), drunk, fuddled; BOOZY (*adj.*), drunken, 'screwed'; BOOZING (*verbal subs.*), the act of drinking hard; and BOOZER (*subs.*), a drunkard, a tippler—examples of which respectively will be found hereunder in sections.

b. 1529. SKELTON, *Elynour Rommin*, in *Hart. Misc.* (ed. Park), I., 416.
Droupy and drowsie,
Scurvy and lousie
Her face all BOWSIE.

1592. GREENE, *Quip*, in wks. XI., 253. To marke the BOWSIE drunkard to dye of the dropsy.

1611. COTGRAVE, *Piailleur*: m . . . a tipler, BOWSER.

1616. JONSON, *Devil's an Ass*, V., 4. And in the meantime, to be greasy, and BOUZY.

1671. R. HEAD, *English Rogue*, pt. I., ch. iv., p. 36 (1874). Most part of the night we spent in BOOZING, pecking rumly . . . that is drinking, eating.

1693. DRYDEN, *Juvenal*, x., 288. Which in his cups the BOWSY poet sings.

1705. WARD, *Hudibras Redivivus*, vol. II., pt. IV., p. 14. Amongst a Crowd of Sots, half BOOZY.

c. 1819. WOLCOT, *P. Pindar*, p. 303, ed. 1830.
This landlord was a BOOZER stout,
A snuff-taker and smoker. [D.]

1848. THACKERAY, *Book of Snobs*, ch. xxiii. The BOOZY unshorn wretch is seen hovering round quays as packets arrive, and tippling drams in inn bars where he gets credit.

1848. THACKERAY, *Book of Snobs*, ch. xxxiii. The quantity of brandy-and-water that Jack took showed what a regular BOOZER he was.

1850. P. CROOK, *War of Hats*, 50. BOOZED in their tavern dens, The scurril press drove all their dirty pens.

1866. G. ELIOT, *Felix Holt*, ch. xi. 'Till they can show there's something they love better than swilling themselves with ale, entension of the suffrage can never mean anything for them but entension of BOOZING.'

1889. *Ally Sloper's Half Holiday*, Aug. 24, p. 267, col. 2.
In Canton gardens I have BOOZED;
Beneath the palm-trees I have snoozed;
I've seen the alligator smile,
And peppered at the crocodile.

BOOZING CHEAT, *subs.* (thieves').—A bottle. [From BOOZE (*q.v.*), drink, + CHEAT, from A.S. *ceat*, a thing.]

BOOZING-KEN, *subs.* (old). — A drinking den. [From BOOZE (*q.v.*), drink, + KEN, a place.] A term of long standing. A French equivalent is *une bibine*, but for general synonyms, *see* LUSH CRIB.

1567. HARMAN, *Caveat* (1814), p. 65. A BOWSING-KEN, a ale house.

1610. ROWLANDS, *Martin Mark-all*, p. 37 (H. Club's Repr., 1874). BOWSING-KEN, an Ale-house.

1622. FLETCHER, *Beggar's Bush*, II., i.
When last in conference at the BOOZING-KEN,
This other day we sat about our dead prince.

1714. *Memoirs of John Hall* (4 ed.), p. 11. BOOZING-KEN, an Ale-house. [List of cant words in.]

1834. H. AINSWORTH, *Rookwood*, bk. III., ch. v. The hovel which they termed their BOOZING-KEN.

BOOZINGTON, *subs.* (Australian thieves').—A drunkard. [Apparently a formation from BOOZE (*q.v.*), to drink, on the model of LUSHINGTON (*q.v.*), an English equivalent.] For synonyms, *see* ELBOW CROOKER.

BORACHIO, *subs.* (old).—A nickname for a drunkard; formerly a skin for holding wine. For synonyms, *see* ELBOW CROOKER.

BORAK. TO POKE BORAK, *verbal phr.* (colonial).—To pour fictitious news into credulous ears; to 'stuff'; to 'kid.'

1887. *Notes and Queries*, 7 S., iii., 476. POKE BORAK, applied in Colonial conversation to the operations of a person who pours fictitious information into the ears of a credulous listener.

BORD, BORDE, BOORDE, *subs.* (old cant).—A shilling. The origin is unknown. For synonyms, *see* BLOW.

1567. HARMAN, *Caveat*, p. 85. ROGE, but bouse there a BORD, *i.e.*, but drink there a shilling.

1610. ROWLANDS, *Martin Mark-all*, p. 37 (H. Club's Repr., 1874). BOORD, a shilling; Halfe a BOORD, sixepence.

1611. DEKKER, *Roaring Girle*, wks. (1873) III., 219. My Lord Noland . . . bestowes vpon you two, two BOORDES and a half.

1671. R. HEAD, *English Rogue*, pt. I., ch. v., p. 47 (1874). BORDE, a shilling.

1785. GROSE, *Dictionary of the Vulgar Tongue*. [The same definition.]

BORDEAUX, *subs.* (pugilistic). — Blood [an allusion to the colour of the wine. *Cf.* CLARET and BADMINTON]. For synonyms, *see* CLARET.

BORD YOU! *phr.* (nautical).—An expression used to claim the next turn in drinking.

BORE, *subs.* and *verb* (old slang, but now recognised).—Anybody or anything wearisome or annoying; to weary or to be wearied. [The derivation is unknown, and the word does not appear in English literature prior to 1750. Hotten's reference to Shakspeare, *King Henry VIII.*, i., 1,
At this instant
He BORES me with some trick,
is a misreading, 'bore' in this instance signifying 'to stab,' as the context clearly shows.]

Verb (sporting).—To push or thrust out of the course; and BORING, *subs.*, the practice of 'boring.' Amongst pugilists it signifies to drive an opponent on to the ropes of the ring by sheer weight, whilst amongst rowing men it denotes the action of a coxswain in so steering a boat as to force his opponent into the shore, or into still water, thus obtaining an unfair advantage; also analogously applied to horse-racing. The term, as so used, is a very old one, and is derived from the persistency of motion of a boring tool.

1672. VANBRUGH, *Lover's Quarrels*, 317 in Hazl. *E.P.*, pt. II., 266. He BOR'D him out of the saddle fair.

1819. MOORE, *Tom Crib's Memorial to Congress*. M—rl—y, that very great

Count, stood deploring, He hadn't taught Georgy his new modes of BORING.

1821. *The Fancy*, vol. I., p. 255. Evans BORED in, and upset his man in the first round.

1870. DICKENS, *Edwin Drood*, ch. xvii., p. 129. Their fighting code stood in great need of revision, as empowering them not only to BORE their man to the ropes, but . . . also to hit him when he was down.

BORN DAYS. ALL ONE'S BORN DAYS, *phr.* (colloquial).—One's lifetime.

1740. RICHARDSON, *Pamela*, III., 383. He never was so delighted in his BORN DAYS.

1753. RICHARDSON, *Grandison*, I., 103. There was one Miss Byron, a Northamptonshire lady, whom I never saw before in my BORN DAYS.

1809. MISS EDGEWORTH, *Ennui*, ch. ix. Craiglethorpe will know just as much of the lower Irish as the Cockney who has never been out of London, and who has never in all his BORN DAYS seen an Irishman but on the English stage.

BORN WEAK, *phr.* (nautical).—Said of a vessel feebly built.—CLARK RUSSELL'S *Sailors' Language*.

BOSH, *subs.* (common).—Nonsense; rubbish; 'stuff'; 'rot'—anything beneath contempt. [The derivation is uncertain. Murray says the word became current in England from its frequent occurrence in Morier's Persian novels, *Ayesha* [1834], etc., most of them extremely popular productions. Its source has been suggested in the Turkish *bosh lakerdi*, 'empty talk'; in the German *bosh* or *bossch*, an equivalent of 'swipes'; and in the Gypsy *bosh*, 'a noise,' a fiddle,' from which latter it has been thought that there may be some connection between the exclamation BOSH! and FIDDLE-DE-DEE (*q.v.*).]

1834. MORIER, *Ayesha*, I., 219. This firman is BOSH—nothing. [M.]

1857. C. KINGSLEY, *Two Years Ago*, ch. x. I always like to read old Darwin's *Loves of the Plants*, BOSH as it is in a scientific point of view.

1880. *Punch*, 10 Jan., p. 9, col. 2. 'Prophet,' said I, 'of things evil!' 'Things are going to the devil' Is the formula of fogies, I have heard that BOSH before.

Verb.—To humbug; to spoil; to mar.

1870. *Macmillan's Magazine*, XXI., 71. You BOSH his joke [a man's] by refusing to laugh at it; you BOSH his chance of sleep by playing on the cornet all night in the room next to him. [M.]

1883. MISS BRADDON, *Golden Calf*, ch. xiv. 'And wouldn't he make a jolly schoolmaster?' exclaimed Reginald. 'Boys would get on capitally with Jardine. They'd never try to BOSH *him*.'

Intj.—Nonsense! Rubbish! It's all my eye!—*See* ALL MY EYE.

1852. DICKENS, *Bleak House*, ch. xxi. BOSH! It's all correct.

1889. *Pall Mall Gazette*, October 30, p. 3, col. 1. 'You always learn in front of the looking-glass, do you not, Mr. Brandram?'—'BOSH!' was the laughing reply. 'I generally learn my plays and recitations whilst I am dressing; but you don't think I deliberately stand and make monkey-faces in the looking-glass.

BOSH FAKER, *subs.* (vagrants').—A violin player. [From Gypsy *bosh*, a violin, + FAKER, a performer or player.]

1876. HINDLEY, *Life and Adventures of a Cheap Jack*, p. 231.
Can you rocker Romanie
Can you patter flash,
Can you rocker Romanie
Can you FAKE A BOSH.

BOSHING, *subs.* (American thieves').—A flogging. [Apparently a corrupted form of BASHING.]—*See* BASH.

BOSHY, *adj.* (common). — Trumpery; nonsensical.—*See* BOSH.

1882. F. ANSTEY, *Vice Versâ*, ch. iv. 'There was no dancing, only BOSHY games and a conjuror.'

BOS-KEN, *subs.* (vagrants'). — A farmhouse. An old canting term. [From L. *bos* = ox + KEN, a house.] *Cf.*, KEN.

1851-61. H. MAYHEW, *London Lab. and Lon. Poor*, vol. I., p. 472. 'Up at a BOSKEN (farm-house) they'll get among the servant girls.'

BOSKINESS, *subs.* (popular).—The quality of being fuddled with drink; bemused; a state of drunkenness.

1887. *Judy*, 31 August, p. 101. The Town Councillor had a squabble with his parent . . . and accused him of BOSKINESS.

BOSKY, *adj.* (popular). — Drunk; tipsy; fuddled. [Derivation uncertain; BOSKY = 'wooded,' or bushy,' and there may be an allusion to the obscurity and overshadowing, peculiar to a wooded country. Bailey [1728] has also BOSKY = swelled, but does not give the slang sense of the word, although it appears in the editions 1730-6. It may, therefore, be a figuratively humorous reading of 'swelled,' *i.e.*, 'tight.'] For synonyms, *see* SCREWED.

1748. T. DYCHE, *Dictionary* (5 ed.). BOSKY (A.), fuddled, half or quite drunk.

1824. *Blackw. Mag.*, XVI., 573. He may be tipsy, BOSKY, cut, or anything but drunk.

1886. *Punch*, 17 April, p. 185. I got a bit BOSKY last night. Has the 'eadache got into my rhymes?

BOSMAN, *subs.* (vagrants'). — A farmer. [From the Dutch *bosch-man*, one who lives in the woods; otherwise *Boschjeman*, or bushman.] *Cf.*, BOSKEN.

1851-61. H. MAYHEW, *London Lab. and Lon. Poor*, vol. I., p. 471. 'I've seen the swell BOSMEN (farmers) buy the pills to give the people standing about.'

BOSS, *subs.* (American and English).—1. A master; a head man; one who directs. [From the Dutch *baas*, a master.] Few words have acquired a greater hold on American life than this term, and the primitive meaning of master, overseer, or superior of any kind, though in a large measure retained to this day, has been widened out in every direction. The political BOSS is the leader whose word is law to his henchman. Boss Tweed, of New York, is believed to have been the first to bear the title in a semi-official way. The phrase BOSS RULE is said to have been invented by Mr. Wayne MacVeagh, and employed by him in political speeches in Chicago. It is now in common use in this sense. In the two first quotations the word appears to be used much as in the modern sense. For synonyms, *see* GOVERNOR.

1590. MARLOWE, *Tamburlaine*, pt. I., Act iii., Sc. 3. *Zab.* Base concubine, must thou be placed by me, That am the empress of the mighty Turk? *Zen.* Disdainful Turkess and unreverend BOSS!

1679. M. PHILIPSE, *Early Voyage to New Netherlands* (quoted by De Vere). Here they had their first interview with the female BOSS or supercargo of the vessel.

1848. BARTLETT, *Americanisms*. I have never known a second wife but what was BOSS of the situation.

1850. *New York Herald*, May 24. The Eternal City is in a very curious position. The Pope has returned to his ancestral home; but he has nothing in his pocket, and Rothschild refuses to let him have any more money. A thousand years ago, and the boot would have been on t'other leg. . . . To-day it is very different. The Father of Holiness is the dependent of the Jew, and Rothschild is the real Pope and BOSS of all Europe.

1888. *New York Herald*, Jan. 12. Alderman Campbell—I move an amendment to make Hamline the general superintendent and chief BOSS of this whole gas business.

2. (popular.)—A short-sighted person; also one who squints. *Cf.*, BOSS-EYED and Boss, *verb*, sense 2.

3. (popular.)—A miss; a blunder. *Cf.*, Boss, *verb*, sense 2.

Adj.—Pleasant; first rate; chief.

1884. *Echo*, March 3, p. 1, col. 4. The Americans are acknowledged to be the BOSS artificers in wood.

1888. *Brooklyn Daily Eagle*, March 18. Take it all together, with scarcity of food and little sleep, we had a hard but a BOSS time.

Verb.—1. To manage; direct; control.—*See subs.*, sense 1.

1856. *National Intelligencer*, Nov. 3. The little fellow that BOSSES it over the crowd.

1872. *Athenæum*, March 9. A child wishing to charge his sister with being the aggressor in a quarrel for which he was punished, exclaimed, 'I did not BOSS the job; it was sister.'

1883. *Saturday Review*, April 28, p. 515, col. 1. It is long since the more respectable inhabitants of America have been divided between the convenience of the Irish as hewers of wood and drawers of water, and as voters easily BOSSED or bribed on the one hand, and the manifold nuisance of them on the other.

1885. *Sporting Times*, July 6. The Shah has fairly BOSSED everything this week—he has been chief actor in our social system.

1888. *Texas Siftings*, July.
When lovely woman hires a servant
And BOSSES her around all day,
What makes the girl pray half so fervent
As her desire to run away.

2. (popular.)—To miss one's aim; to make such a shot as a BOSS-EYED (*q.v.*) person would be expected to make. BOSS-SHOT is a common phrase.

1887. *N. and Q.*, 7 S., iii., 236. To BOSS is schoolboy slang for 'to miss.'

So also derivatives—BOSSING, acting as a boss; BOSSISM, a system of management or wire-pulling; BOSSY, pertaining to the qualities of a leader.

BOSSERS, *subs.* (common).—Spectacles.—*See* BARNACLES.

BOSS-EYED, *adj.* (common).—Said of a person with one eye, or rather with one eye injured; a person with an obliquity of vision. In this sense sometimes varied by SQUINNY-EYED and SWIVEL-EYED (*q.v.*). Also used as a *subs.*—BOSS-EYE.

c. 1884. *Broadside Ballad*, 'Put me some Jam Roll by, Jenny.'
Come where the waves roll high, Jenny,
Come where the waves roll high,
Jenny, old girl, I love you,
Come where the waves roll high.
Come where the waves roll high, Jenny,
Come where the sea-sick lie,
Come where we eat salt-junk, love,
Come with your old BOS-EYE.

FRENCH SYNONYMS. *Borgniat*; *cligner des œillets* (a military term, 'to be boss-eyed'); *boiter des calots* ('to be boss-eyed'); *calorgne*.

BOSTRUCHYZER, *subs.* (Oxford University).—A small kind of comb for curling the whiskers.—*Hotten*. Obsolete.

BOT, BOTT, BOTTS, *subs.* (common).—The colic; belly-ache; gripes. Properly a name given to maggots found in the intestines of horses, under the hides of oxen, and in the nostrils of sheep. A French equivalent is *la tourmente*, *i.e.*, 'the torment.'

1787. BURNS, '*Death and Dr. Hornbook*, st. 27.
A countra Laird had ta'en the BATTS,
Or some curmurring in his guts.

1816. SCOTT, *Old Mortality*, ch. viii. 'I ne'er gat ony gude by his doctrine, as ye ca't, but a sour fit o' the BATTS wi' sitting amang the wet moss-hays for four hours at a yoking.

BOTANICAL EXCURSION, *subs.* (old).—A thief's circumlocution for transportation—the allusion being to BOTANY BAY (*q.v.*).

BOTANY BAY, *subs.* (University).—1. At Oxford, Worcester College is so designated on account of its remote situation as regards the bulk of the collegiate buildings. It will be seen that a similar reason has caused a certain portion of Trinity College, Dublin, to receive an identical nickname. The general idea underlying the term is obviously that to get to the places in question one has figuratively to go almost as far as if transported to the real BOTANY BAY, formerly a convict settlement in New South Wales.

1841. LEVER, *Charles O'Malley*, ch. xx., *note*. BOTANY BAY was the slang name given by college men to a new square rather remotely situated from the remainder of the college [*i.e.*, Trinity, Dublin].

1853. REV. E. BRADLEY ('Cuthbert Bede'), *Adventures of Verdant Green*, I., p. 63. A name given to W. College, from its being the most distant college.

2. (thieves' and prison.)—Penal servitude. Formerly convicts [1787-1867] were transported to BOTANY BAY, a convict settlement at the Antipodes. Hence to go to BOTANY BAY was in popular use for a long term of imprisonment.

BOTANY-BAY FEVER, *subs.* (old).—Transportation; penal servitude. Convicts condemned to transportation were said to have died of, or to have BOTANY-BAY FEVER. *Cf.*, HEMPEN FEVER for hanging.

BOTCH, *subs.* (old).—A tailor. [An abbreviated form of 'botcher,' which has been used for a very long period in all the following senses—a cobbler, tailor who does repairs, jobber, and an unskilful workman.] Also called a SNIP, which *see* for synonyms.

BOTTLE. TO TURN OUT NO BOTTLE, *phr.* (sporting).—Not to turn out well; to fail.

BOTTLE-ACHE, *subs.* (common).—Drunkenness; also applied to an attack of *delirium tremens*. [From BOTTLE, in allusion to drink causing indisposition, + ACHE, a pain or sickness.] There are many curious terms for this effect of intemperance, such as Jim-jams, barrel-fever, quartmania; but for full list of synonyms, *see* GALLON DISTEMPER.

BOTTLE-ARSED, *adj. phr.* (printers').—Type thicker at one end than the other—a result of wear and tear.

BOTTLE-HOLDER, *subs.* (common).—1. A second at a prize-fight, hence—

2. One who gives moral support; a backer; an adviser. In the *Times* of 1851, Lord Palmerston was reported to consider himself the BOTTLE-HOLDER of oppressed states: and in *Punch* of the same year, a cartoon appeared representing that statesman as the 'judicious BOTTLE-HOLDER.'

1753. SMOLLETT, *Ct. Fathom* (L.). An old bruiser makes a good BOTTLE-HOLDER.

1816. SCOTT, *Antiquary*, ch. xxxix. Petrie . . . recommends, upon his own experience, as tutor in a family of distinction, this attitude to all led captains, tutors, dependents, and BOTTLE-HOLDERS of every description.

1822. SCOTT, *The Fortunes of Nigel*, ch. ii. Cold water, and a little vinegar, applied according to the scientific method practised by the BOTTLE-HOLDERS in a modern ring.

1860. THACKERAY, *Philip*, ch. xl. 'Do you remember his tremendous fight with Biggs?' 'Remember? who didn't? Marston was Berry's BOTTLE-HOLDER.'

BOTTLE-HOLDING, *verbal subs.* (common).—Backing; supporting.

1878-80. JUSTIN MACCARTHY, *History of Our Own Times*, II., p. 115. The noble lord (Palmerston) told the deputation that the past crisis was one which required on the part of the British Government much generalship and judgment, and that a good deal of judicious BOTTLE-HOLDING was obliged to be brought into play.

BOTTLE OF BRANDY IN A GLASS, *phr.* (common).—A glass of beer; a recent and absurd slang introduction.

BOTTLE OF SPRUCE, *subs.* (rhyming slang).—Twopence. The play of words is upon 'deuce' = two.

BOTTLES, *subs.* (Stock Exchange).—Barrett's Brewery and Bottling Co. Shares.

BOTTLE-SUCKER, *subs.* (nautical).—An able-bodied seaman; the abbreviation is A.B.S., and A BOTTLE-SUCKER is supposed to be a humorous rendering.

BOTTLE-UP, *verb* (old).—To restrain (temper, feelings, etc.); to keep or hold back.

1622. T. Scott, *Belg. Pismire*, 53. Vapours . . . BOTTELED UP in cloudes.

1863. H. KINGSLEY, *Austin Elliot*, ch. xi. Austin played very bad, trumped his partner's . . . knave, led out strong suits of trumps without any suit to follow, BOTTLED them when his partner led them first time round.

1871. *Cincinnati Commercial*, April, p. 637. He will BOTTLE UP his wrath, having had some experience in the line of BOTTLING UP during the war, and pour out his vials upon General Farnsworth's head, whenever the occasion offers.

BOTTOM, *subs.* (colloquial).—1. The posteriors; not now in literary use. For synonyms, *see* BLIND-CHEEKS and BUM.

1794-6. E. DARWIN, *Zoon.* (1801), III., 253. So as to have his head and shoulders much lower than his BOTTOM.

1822-36. J. WILSON, *Noctes. Ambr.*, xxxix. (1864), iv., 79. The Dunghill cock . . . hides his head in a hole . . . unashamed of the exposure of his enormous BOTTOM.

1837. CARLYLE, *Fr. Rev.*, II., iv., i., 185. Patriot women take their hazel wands, and fustigate . . . broad BOTTOM of priests.

2. (popular.)—Capital; resources; stamina; 'grit.'

1662. FULLER, *Worthies* (1840), II., 451. Beginning on a good BOTTOM left him by his father.

1747. CAPTN. GODFREY, *Science of Defence*, p. 54. I have mentioned strength and art as the two ingredients of a boxer. But there is another, which is vastly necessary; that is, what we call a BOTTOM. . . . There are two things required to make this BOTTOM, that is, wind and spirit, or heart, or wherever you can fix the residence of courage.

1819. MOORE, *Tom Crib's Memorial to Congress*, pref., p. xv. The peculiarities of this boxer discussed—his power of standing with his arms extended for two whole days, without any rest, by which means he wore out his adversaries' BOTTOM, and conquered without either giving or taking.

1846. THACKERAY, *V. Fair*, vol. II., ch. xiv. He did not like to dine with Steyne now. They had run races of pleasure together in youth when Bareacres was the winner. But Steyne had more BOTTOM than he, and had lasted him out.

3. (popular.)—Spirit placed in a glass prior to the addition

of water. [From BOTTOM, the lowest surface or part of anything, the foundation, the basis. *See* peculiar American usage in 1883 quot.] Also used as a verb.

1854. SIR THEO. MARTIN, *Bon Gaultier Ballads*. BOTTOMED well with brandy.

1857. A. TROLLOPE, *Three Clerks*, ch. xxxi. Gin and water was the ordinary tipple in the front parlour; and any one of its denizens inclined to cut a dash above his neighbours, generally did so with a BOTTOM of brandy.

1883. *Daily Telegraph*, 2 July, p. 5, col. 3. Soda and DARK BOTTOM is mentioned in a list of American drinks in this article.

TO KNOCK THE BOTTOM OUT OF ONE, *phr.* (American).—To overcome; to defeat, etc.

1888. *Cleveland Leader*. The declination of Mr. Blaine, has knocked the BOTTOM out of Mugwumpery.

BOTTOM DOLLAR, *subs. phr.* (American).—The last dollar. The phrase 'to bet one's BOTTOM DOLLAR' is frequently heard.

BOTTOM FACTS, *subs. phr.* (American).—The exact truth about any matter. To 'get to the BOTTOM FACTS' concerning a subject, is to arrive at an unquestionable conclusion concerning it; or, as is said in England, to get to the root of the question.

1877. S. L. CLEMENS ('Mark Twain'), *Life on the Mississippi*, p. 393. You take a family able to emba'm, and you've got a soft thing. You can mention sixteen different ways to do it—though there aint only one or two ways when you come down to the BOTTOM FACTS of it—and they'll take the highest priced way every time. It's human nature—human nature in grief.

The phrase is also varied by BOTTOM ROCK.

1888. *Omaha World*. BOTTOM ROCK. Conductor (on California train some years hence)—'All out for Pitholeville.' Real Estate Agent (entering car)—'Orange groves and apple orchards, two for a penny.'

BOTTOMLESS PIT, *subs.* (old slang).—A coarse and vulgar name for the female *pudenda*. For synonyms, *see* MONOSYLLABLE.

BOTTY, *subs.* (popular).—An infant's posteriors; the French say *tu tu*.

Adj. (popular).—Conceited; swaggering. TO LOOK BOTTY is in French, *faire sa merde*; *faire son matador*.

BOUGH, *subs.* (old).—The gallows. TREE (*q.v.*) is used in a similar sense.

1590. SWINBURN, *Testaments*, 53. Or in Kent in Gauelkind . . . for there it is said, the father to the BOUGHE, and the son to the ploughe. [M.]

1596. SPENSER, *State Irel.*, wks. (1862), p. 553, col. 2. Some . . . have beene for their goods sake caught up, and carryed straight to the BOUGH.

1870. MORRIS, *Earthly Par.*, III., iv., 77. If she doom thee to the BOUGH.

BOUGHS. UP IN THE BOUGHS, *phr.* (old).—In a passion. Quoted by Grose.

BOUNCE, *subs.* (common).—Brag; swagger; boastful falsehood and exaggeration.

1714. STEELE, *Lover* (1723), 93. This is supposed to be only a BOUNCE.

1748. T. DYCHE, *Dictionary* (5 ed.). BOUNCE (s.) . . . also the huff, brag, or swaggering of a bully or great pretender.

1765. GOLDSMITH, *Haunch of Venison*, l. 14. But hold—let me pause—don't I hear you pronounce this tale of the bacon a damnable BOUNCE?

1856. WHYTE MELVILLE, *Kate Coventry*, ch. i. Only tell a man you think him good-looking, and he falls in love with you directly; or if that is too great a BOUNCE—and indeed very few of them have the slightest pretensions to beauty—you need only hint that he rides gallantly.

1880. *Blackwood's Mag.*, May, p. 670. The whole heroic adventure was the veriest BOUNCE, the merest bunkum!

2. Impudence; cheek; BRASS (*q.v.*).

1872-4. JOHN FORSTER, *Life of Dickens*, ch. ix. It is the face of the Webster type, but without the BOUNCE of Webster's face.

3. A boaster; swaggerer; showy swindler; bully. *Cf.*, BOUNCER.

1812. J. H. VAUX, *Flash Dict.* BOUNCE, a person well or fashionably drest is said to be a RANK BOUNCE.

Verb.—1. To boast; bluster; hector; bully; blow up.

1633. FLETCHER, *Nt. Walkers*, IV., i. I doe so whirle her to the Counsellors' chambers . . . and BOUNCE her for more money.

1698. WARD, *London Spy*, pt. XVIII., p. 428. With lies he tells his Bloody Feats, And BOUNCES like a Bully.

1748. T. DYCHE, *Dictionary* (5 ed.). BOUNCE (v.), to swagger, boast, crack, stump, or pretend to great matters.

1749. WALPOLE, *Lett. to Mann*, 3 May (1833), vol. II., p. 374. The Lords had four tickets a-piece, and each Commoner at first but two, till the Speaker BOUNCED and obtained a third.

1760. COLMAN, *Polly Honeycombe*, in wks. (1777) IV., 55. Nay, nay, old gentleman, no BOUNCING; you're mistaken in your man, sir!

1859. H. KINGSLEY, *Geoffrey Hamlyn*, ch. v. 'He'll be drinking at all the places coming along to get his courage up to BOUNCE me.'

1883. *Daily News*, July 26, p. 4, col. 8. To BOUNCE is simply to prevail on persons whose mirth interferes with the general enjoyment to withdraw from society which they embarrass rather than adorn.

2. To lie; to cheat; to swindle.

1762. FOOTE, *Liar*, II., i. If it had come to an oath, I don't think he would have BOUNCED.

1863. H. KINGSLEY, *Austin Elliot*, ch. x. 'It's them gals, Mr. Austin, got a shilling of mine among un somewhere, and wants to BOUNCE me out of it.'

ON THE BOUNCE, *phr.* (common).—In a state of spasmodic movement; general liveliness.

1889. *Sporting Times*, June 29. Funny to a degree was it to watch some of the select and chosen of Lord Coventry, Major Clements, and those that rule the interior of the Invited Enclosure at Ascot. Several well known defaulters would be observed going to and fro 'ON THE BOUNCE,' including one young gentleman who once signed his surname uninitialled to a cheque which was cashed by a confiding tradesman, who took the said endorsement for that of his baronial parent.

TO GET THE GRAND BOUNCE, *phr.* (American).—This is equivalent, in political parlance, to dismissal, especially in reference to government appointments.

BOUNCEABLE, *adj.* (common).—Prone to bouncing or boasting; 'uppish'; 'bumptious.' [From BOUNCE (*q.v.*) + ABLE.]

1830. S. WARREN, *Diary of a Late Physician*, ch. xvi. As soon as we had exhibited sundry doses of Irish cordial to our friend Tip—under the effects of which he became quite BOUNCIBLE, and *ranted* about the feat he was to take a prominent part in.

1849. DICKENS, *David Copperfield*, ch. iv. I heard that Mr. Sharp's wig didn't fit him; and that he needn't be so BOUNCEABLE—somebody else said 'bumptious'—about it.

BOUNCER, *subs.* (common).—1. A bully; hector; blusterer; one who talks swaggeringly. [From the *verb* BOUNCE, senses 1 and 2, + ER.]

1748. T. DYCHE, *Dictionary* (4 ed.). BOUNCER (s.), a bully or hectoring bravado.

1851-61. H. MAYHEW, *Lon. Lab. and Lon. Poor*, IV., 24. Those who cheat the

20

Public . . . BOUNCERS and Besters defrauding, by laying wagers, swaggering, or using threats.

2. (thieves.')—A thief who steals goods from shop counters while bargaining with the tradesman. The exact French equivalent is *dégringoleur*, and the practice itself is termed *dégringoler à la carre*.

3. (common.)—A lie; a liar. For synonyms, *see* WHOPPER. [This usage in many instances completely overlaps sense 4.]

1762. FOOTE, *Liar*, II., i. He will tell ye more lies in an hour, than all the circulating libraries put together will publish in a year . . . he was always distinguished by the facetious appellation of the BOUNCER.

1833. MARRYAT, *Peter Simple*, ch. xxxi. 'He's . . . such a BOUNCER!! . . . I mean that he's the greatest liar that ever walked a deck.

1872. M. E. BRADDON, *Dead Sea Fruit*, ch. xxii. 'In that case, I should say wait, and put your trust in Time—Time, the father of Truth, as Mary Stuart called him when she wanted to go in for a BOUNCER,—and oh, what an incredible number of royal BOUNCERS were carried to and fro in the despatches of that period!'

4. (common.)—Anything large of its kind; a 'whopper'; a 'thumper'; a 'corker.'

1596. NASHE, *Saffron Walden*, in wks. III., 140. My Book will grow such a BOUNCER, that those which buy it must bee faine to hire a porter to carry it after them in a basket.

5. (American.)—A man who ejects; a 'CHUCKER-OUT' (*q.v.*).

1883. *Daily News*, July 26, p. 4, col. 8. The other fresh American type is less remarkable—the BOUNCER. One might suppose that a BOUNCER was a noisy braggart; but no. A scientific writer in the *Nation* describes a BOUNCER as a 'silent, strong man.' Every one who mixes much in society in Whitechapel will understand the functions of the BOUNCER when we explain that he is merely the English 'chucker-out.'

6. (harlotry.)—A prostitute's companion; ponce; bully. For synonyms, *see* PONCE.

7. (naval.)—A gun that 'kicks' when fired.

BOUNCING, *ppl. adj.* (common).—Vigorous; lusty; exaggerated; excessive; big. This word has manifold meanings, referring, in its various senses, to largeness of size, vigour of action, with the idea of ungainliness rather than elegance. It is, as will be seen, of long continued use.

c. 1563. *Jacke Jugder*, p. 42 (ed. Grosart). And made you a banket [banquet], and BOUNCING cheare.

1588. *Marprelate's Epistle*, p. 14 (ed. Arber). For there must bee orders of ministers in the congregation where you meane this BOUNSING priest should haue superiortie.

1611. MIDDLETON, *Roaring Girle*, Act iii., Sc. 3. The duck that sits is the BOUNCING ramp, that roaring girl my mistress.

1748. SMOLLETT, *Rod. Random*, ch. xix. While I was at work in the shop, a BOUNCING damsel, well dressed, came in.

1846. THACKERAY, *Vanity Fair*, ch. ii. By the side of many tall and BOUNCING young ladies in the establishment, Rebecca Sharp looked like a child.

BOUNCING CHEAT, *subs.* (old).—A bottle. [BOUNCING, probably, says Grose, an allusion to the explosive noise made in drawing a cork, + CHEAT, a thing = Anglo Saxon *ceat* of the same meaning.] The French equivalent is *une rouillarde* or *rouille*, said to be derived from *rouler*. Empty bottles, it may be mentioned, are known as DEAD-MEN; CAMP-CANDLESTICKS; DEAD-MARINES; FELLOW-COMMONERS, etc. For other synonyms, *see* DEAD-MEN.

BOUNDER, *subs.* (popular).—1. A four-wheeled cab or GROWLER (*q.v.*). [Supposed to be an allusion to the jolting motion caused when travelling over a rough road, a fact intensified by the indifferent springs upon which such vehicles are often hung.]

2. (University)—A student whose manners are not acceptable; one whose companionship is not cared for.

3. (University.)—A dog-cart. *Cf.*, sense 1.

4. (common.)—A vulgar though well-dressed man; a superior kind of ''Arry'; one whose dress and personal appearance are correct, but whose manners are of a questionable character. The term is very often used in connection with BALLY (*q.v.*). A BALLY-BOUNDER is one of the most objectionable of the genus. A synonymous term is SNIDE (*q.v.*), and French equivalents are *un mufe* and *un espèce de cafouilleux*. A curious instance of French back-slang is found in another name—*un lof, loff, loffard, loffe*; *lof* here is *fol* reversed, *i.e.*, mad, senseless, foolish.

BOUND TO BE HAD, BOUND TO SHINE, etc., *ppl. adj.* (colloquial).—This expression enters into many slang phrases; for instance, when it seems certain that a man will be out-witted, cheated, or 'bested,' it is said of him that he is BOUND TO BE HAD; similarly, a man fated or resolved to distinguish himself is BOUND TO SHINE. The colloquial use of BOUND dates back as far as 1360, but the peculiar expressions which bring it within the category of slang, are of much later origin. The following quotation will illustrate the usage in question, and further examples will be found under HAD, SHINE, etc.

1864. *Hartford Post*, July 14. When the public have an opportunity of examining this beautiful steamer, they will pronounce her the finest and most comfortable boat they have ever visited, and be satisfied that she is BOUND TO SHINE.

BOUNG.—*See* BUNG.

BOUNG-NIPPER.—*See* BUNG-NIPPER.

BOUNTY-JUMPER, *subs.* (American).—A term applied to men who, receiving a bounty when enlisting, desert, re-enlist, and receive a second bounty. [From BOUNTY, a gratuity given to recruits on joining the army or navy, + JUMPER, a slang term for one who decamps surreptitiously.] The War of the Rebellion is responsible for this, as for many other colloquialisms. As the conflict lengthened out, men became in great request, and large bounties were offered by the North for volunteers. This bounty was found in many cases to be a direct incitement with unprincipled men to bad faith and unfair dealing. Such would enlist, receive their bounty, join their regiment, and then decamp, to reappear in another State, to go through the same performance. Cases were known where this was done many times over, and the practice was called BOUNTY-JUMPING.—*See* JUMPING.

1875. HIGGINSON, *History of United States*, p. 306. Bringing into the service many BOUNTY-JUMPERS, who enlisted merely for money, and soon deserted to enlist again.

ante 1880. *Song of the Bounty-Jumper* (quoted in Bartlett).

My song is of a fast young man whose
name was Billy Wires;
He used to run with the machine, and go
to all the fires:
But as he lov'd a soldier's life, and
wished strange things to see,
So the thought struck him that he would
go and JUMP THE BOUNTI-E.

BOUNTY-JUMPING, *subs.* (American).—Obtaining a bounty by enlisting and then deserting. *Cf.*, BOUNTY-JUMPER.

1887. *Illus. Lon. News*, May 14, 552, 1. In the Civil War in America between the Northern and Southern States, BOUNTY-JUMPING, or enlisting, and obtaining the bounty in several regiments, and then deserting, rose to the dignity of a fine art.

BOURBON, *subs.* (American).—1. A Democrat of the straitest sect; a fire-eater. Applied, for the most part, to the Southern Democrats of the old school. This use of the word probably antedates the Civil War, but no instance of such use has been found in print. Bourbon County, Kentucky, is popularly associated with this kind of Democrat, but we must look to the old Bourbon party in France—uncompromising adherents of political tradition—for its true paternity.

2. A superior kind of whiskey; originally applied to that manufactured in Bourbon, Kentucky. For synonyms, *see* DRINKS.

BOUSE, BOWSE, BOOZE, *subs.* (old).—1. Applied to drink or liquor of any kind. In the sixteenth century BOUSE formed part of the cant of beggars and thieves; latterly the word, whether as substantive or verb, has become colloquial. [Thought to be derived from the Dutch *busen*, to drink to excess.] For synonyms, *see* DRINKS.

1567. HARMAN, *Caveat* (1814), p. 65. BOWSE, drinke.

1610. ROWLANDS, *Martin Mark-all*, p. 37 (H. Club's Repr., 1874). BOWSE, drinke.

1633. MASSINGER, *New Way to Pay Old Debts*, I., i. *Well.* No BOUSE? nor no tobacco?

1785. GROSE, *Dictionary Vulgar Tongue*. BOUZE, etc., drink.

1811. *Lexicon Balatronicum*. As above.

2. (old.)—A drinking bout; a carouse. This sense is more frequently current than sense 1.

Verb.—To drink to excess; to tipple; to 'swill.' Both this and the substantive seem to have been known as early as 1300, but neither came into general use until the sixteenth century, from which period both forms have become more and more colloquial. For synonyms, *see* LUSH.

1567. HARMAN, *Caveat*, p. 32. They bowle and BOWSE one to another, and for the tyme BOUSING belly chere.

1592. NASHE, *Pierce Penilesse*. Who surmise, if there were no playes, they should have all the companie that resort to them bye BOWZING and beere-bathing in their houses everie afternoone.

1615. HARINGTON, *Epigrams*.

Yet such the fashion is of Bacchus crue
To quaffe and BOWZE, until they belch
and spue.
Well, leave it, Marcus, else thy drinking
health,
Will prove an eating to thy wit and
wealth.

So also BOUSER, a toper; BOUSING, hard drinking; and BOUSY, intoxicated or 'screwed.'

BOUSE THE JIB, *verbal phr.* (nautical).—To tipple; to drink heavily.—*See* LUSH.

BOUSING KEN, *subs.* (old).—A tavern; inn; or drinking den;

now applied to a low public house. For synonyms, *see* LUSH CRIB.

1567. HARMAN, *Caveat. Man.* What, stowe your bene, cofe, and cut benat whydds, and byng we to rome vyle. to nyp a bong; so shall we haue lowre for the BOUSING KEN, and when we byng back to the deuseauyel, we wyll fylche some duddes of the Ruffemans, or myll the ken for a bagge of dudes.

1652. BROME, *Jovial Crew*, II., wks. (1873) III., 390 . . . As Tom or Tib When they at BOWSING KEN do swill.

1819. MOORE, *Tom Crib's Memorial to Congress*, p. 27. But notwithstanding the Protean nature of the *Flash* or *Cant* language, the greater part of its vocabulary has remained unchanged for centuries, and many of the words used by the Canting Beggars in Beaumont and Fletcher, and the Gipsies in Ben Jonson's Masque, are still to be heard among the *Gnostics* of Dyot-street and Tothill-fields. To *prig* is still to steal; to *fib*, to beat; *lour*, money; *duds*, clothes; *prancers*, horses; BOUZING-KEN, an alehouse; *cove*, a fellow; a *sou's baby*, a pig, etc., etc.

BOUZY.—*See* BOOZY.

BOW. TWO (or MANY) STRINGS TO ONE'S BOW, *phr.* (colloquial).—To have an alternative; more resources than one. The phrase sometimes formerly ran TO HAVE MANY STRINGS TO THE BOW. Numerous figurative expressions in all languages indicate the dominant pursuits of the respective nations; the English abounds in habitual phrases testifying to the engrossing avocations in all times. It is in this manner that TO HAVE TWO STRINGS TO ONE'S BOW has passed into proverbial usage. In the fourteenth century—a Frenchman, Gaston de Foix, said of our ancestors, 'Of BOWS I know not much, but who would know more, let him go to England, for that is truly their business.' In the olden time, archery, as the dominant pursuit, gave figures of speech to the language—with the very pith of wisdom or Saxon sarcasm. If you made an enemy's machinations recoil upon himself, you 'outshot a man in his own BOW.' If you are a cautious man, 'Always have TWO STRINGS TO YOUR BOW,' and 'Get the shaft-hand of your adversaries,' or 'Draw not thy BOW before thy arrow be fixed.' Of course, if you can 'Kill two birds with one shaft,' so much the better. Never 'shoot wide of the mark'—that is, don't make a foolish guess on a subject you know nothing about. Of useless, silly conversation, our ancestors said — 'The fool's bolt is soon shot'; and if a man evidently exaggerated, he was said to 'draw a long BOW.' If a man's pretensions were not in accordance with the facts of his case—in other words, if he came under the category of 'false pretences'—it was said that he 'had a famous BOW, but it was up at the Castle' Vain military and other boasters were the many who 'talked of Robin Hood, but who never shot his BOW.' 'An archer is known by his aim, and not by his arrows'; that is, if you are not answerable for your materials, at least show your skill in the *modus operandi*; or at all events, don't depend entirely upon your tool.

1562. HEYWOOD, *Prov. and Epigr.* (1867), 30. Ye have MANY STRYNGIS TO THE BOWE. [M.]

1588. *Marprelate's Epistle*, p. 18 (ed. Arber). Doe you not thinke that I haue TWO STRINGS TO MY BOW.

1606. JOHN DAY, *Isle of Gulls*, Act ii., Sc. 2, p. 39. A wise man's BOW goes with a TWO-FOLD STRING.

1748. SMOLLETT, *Rod. Random*, ch. xvii. He was resolved to have TWO STRINGS TO HIS BOW, that in case the one failed, he might use the other.

(?) T. BROWN, wks. IV., 115, ed. 1760. A man in Amsterdam is suffer'd to have but one religion, whereas in London he may have TWO STRINGS TO HIS BOW.

1886. MRS. RIDDELL, *For Dick's Sake*, ch. iv., p. 11 (S.P.C.K.). She had a SECOND STRING TO HER BOW, which suited her far better; and she sent Dick back his letters and his presents, and a note beginning, 'Dear sir,' and ending 'Yours truly.'

TO DRAW THE LONG BOW, *phr.* (colloquial). — To exaggerate; to 'gas'; to 'talk up.'

1819-24. BYRON, *Don Juan*, xvi., 1. They . . . DRAW THE LONG BOW better now than ever.

TO DRAW THE BOW UP TO THE EAR, *phr.* (colloquial).—To do a thing with alacrity; 'to put on full steam'; to exert oneself to the utmost.

1860. *Macmillan's Mag.*, Feb., p. 258. So Miller, the coxswain, took to DRAWING THE BOW UP TO THE EAR at once.

BOW-CATCHER, *subs.* (common).—A kiss-curl. For synonyms, *see* AGGERAWATOR. [A corruption of 'beau-catcher.' *Cf.*, BELL-ROPE.]

BOWDLERIZE, *verb* (colloquial).—To expurgate by removing offensive or questionable words from a book or writing. [From Dr. T. Bowdler's method in editing an edition of Shakspeare, in which, to use his own words, 'Those . . . expressions are omitted which cannot with propriety be read aloud in a family.']

1836. GEN. P. THOMPSON, *Let.* in *Exerc.* (1842), IV., 124. Among the names . . . are many, like Hermes, Nereus, . . . which modern ultra-christians would have thought formidably heathenish; while Epaphroditus and Narcissus they would probably have BOWDLERIZED.

1870. *Notes and Queries*, 4 S., vi., p. 47. No profane hand shall dare, for me, to curtail my Chaucer, to BOWDLERISE my Shakspeare, or to mutilate my Milton.

1874. E. L. LINTON, *Patricia Kemball*, ch. iii. Her uncle had not made her read much beside the Bible and Shakspeare, which last he had BOWDLERISED on his own account with a broad pen and very thick ink.

From this comes BOWDLERIZATION, squeamish emasculation of a work; also BOWDLERIZER, etc.

1882. *Westm. Review*, April, p. 583. The BOWDLERIZATION which the Editor has thought necessary is done in an exceedingly awkward and clumsy fashion.

BOWER, *subs.* (American thieves').—A prison—a transferred usage of the orthodox word. For synonyms, *see* CAGE.

BOWERY BOY, BOWERY GIRL, *subs.* (American).—The 'Arry and 'Arriet of New York of some years ago. The BOWERY is a well known thoroughfare in the American metropolis. [Formerly spelt *bouwerij*, and derived from *bouw*, tillage, or *bouwen*, to till, to cultivate, being equivalent to the modern Dutch word *boerderij*, a farm, or the business of farming. The BOWERY was the farm of Governor Stuyvesant.] *Cf.*, BLOOD TUB.

BOWLAS, *subs.* (common).—Explained by quotation.

1851-61. H. MAYHEW, *London Lab. and Lon. Poor*, vol. I., p. 208. BOWLAS, or round tarts made of sugar, apple, and bread.

BOWLED, *ppl. adj.* (Winchester).—CROPPLED (*q.v.*).

BOWLER.—*See* BOLER.

BOWLES, *subs.* (common).—Shoes. For synonyms, *see* TROTTER-CASES.

BOWL OUT, *verb* (popular).—To overcome; to get the better of; to defeat. [Formerly a cricketing term—to bowl a man out by displacing the bails.] *Cf.*, BOWL OVER. Among thieves it signifies, in a transitive form, to be arrested or 'lagged.'

1812. J. H. VAUX, *Flash Dictionary*. BOWLED OUT, when he [a thief] is ultimately taken, tried, and convicted [he] is said TO BE BOWLED OUT at last.

1817. SCOTT, *Rob Roy*, ch. iii. The polite and accomplished adventurer, who nicked you out of your money at White's, or BOWLED YOU OUT of it at Marybone.

1852. F. E. SMEDLEY, *Lewis Arundel*, ch. xxiv. 'He's handsomer than you are; if you don't mind your play, he'll BOWL YOU OUT.'

1877. *Five Years' Penal Servitude*, ch. ii., p. 121. Now and again a warder does get BOWLED OUT, and comes to grief. At the very least he loses his situation.

BOWL OVER, *verb* (popular).—To defeat; to worst. *Cf.*, BOWL OUT.

1862. *Cornhill Mag.*, p. 729. You have BOWLED me OVER, and I know I can't get up again.

1878. STANLEY, *Through the Dark Continent*, II., p. 291. I sent in a zinc bullet close to the ear, which BOWLED it [the rhinoceros] OVER, dead.

1880. A. TROLLOPE, *The Duke's Children*, ch. xlvii. He confessed to himself that he was completely BOWLED OVER,—'knocked off his pins!'

BOWL THE HOOP, *subs.* (rhyming slang).—Soup.

BOWMAN, *adv.* (old).—*See* quotation.

1839. HARRISON AINSWORTH, *Jack Sheppard* [1889], p. 11. Help! ejaculated Wood, renewing his cries. Arrest! Jigger closed! shouted a hoarse voice in reply. All's BOWMAN, my covey. Fear nothing. We'll be upon the ban-dogs before they can shake their trotters!

BOWSE.—*See* BOOZE.

BOWSING KEN.—*See* BOUSING KEN.

BOWSPRIT, *subs.* (popular).—The nose.—*See* BOLTSPRIT.

TO HAVE ONE'S BOWSPRIT IN PARENTHESIS is to have it pulled. 'To have one's head in Coventry' will occur to mind as another English slang phrase very similar in character.

BOW-WINDOW, *subs.* (common).—A stomach of large proportions. [A bay or BOW-WINDOW is properly a curved window, hence the transference of the term to a big belly.] Also BOW-WINDOWED, *i.e.*, big-bellied.

1840. MARRYAT, *Poor Jack*, ch. i. He was a very large man . . . with what is termed a considerable BOW-WINDOW in front.

1849-50. THACKERAY, *Pendennis*, xxxiv. (1884), 334. Look at that very BOW-WINDOWED MAN. [M.]

1889. *Daily Telegraph*, May 6. She was what is vulgarly called BOW-WINDOWED.

BOW-WOW, *subs.* (common).—1. A childish name for a dog.

1800. COWPER, *Beau's Reply*.
Let my obedience then excuse
My disobedience now,
Nor some reproof yourself refuse
From your aggrieved BOW-WOW.

18(?82). *Broadside Ballad*, 'I haven't for a long time now.'
I used to have a sweetheart, once,
A precious little pearl!
Indeed she was—she really was,
A very charming girl.

I sang outside her door each night
Till her father bought a big BOW-WOW,
But I haven't—haven't—
I haven't for a long time now!

2. (old.)—A Bostonian—a term of contempt.

3. (popular.)—A cavalier; lover; specially applied to a man who dangles after a woman. Also *see* TAME CAT.

1877. *Chamb. Journal*, 12 March, p. 173. Mrs. Brittomart was one of those who never tolerated a BOW-WOW—a species of animal well known in India—and never went to the hills as a 'grass-widow.'

BOW-WOW-MUTTON, *subs.* (old).—Dog's flesh. [From BOW-WOW, a humorous term for a dog, + MUTTON, here used generically for meat.]

BOW-WOW-WORD, *subs.* (common).—A term applied sarcastically by Max Müller to words for which it is claimed that they are in imitation of natural sounds, *i.e.*, onamatopoetic words, of which a full list will be found under CACHUNK.

BOWYER, *subs.* (old).—One who draws a 'long bow'; a dealer in the marvellous; a teller of improbable stories; a liar.—*See* LONG BOW.

BOX, *subs.* (thieves').—A prison cell.

1834. HARRISON AINSWORTH, *Rookwood*, p. 89.
In a BOX of the stone-jug I was born,
Of a hempen widow the kid forlorn
Fake away.

1878. *Notes and Queries*, 5 S., x., p. 214. The BOX in the stone-jug is doubtless a cell.

Verb (Westminster School).—To take possession of; 'to bag.'

TO BE IN A BOX, *phr.* (common).—To be cornered; in a fix; 'stuck' or 'hung up.'

TO BE IN THE WRONG BOX, *verbal phr.* (colloquial).—To be out of one's element; to be in a false position; mistaken. Brewer traces this to Lord Lyttelton, who, being of rather a melancholy disposition, used to tell his friends that when he went to Vauxhall he was always supposing pleasure to be in the next box to his, or at least that he himself was so unhappily situated as always TO BE IN THE WRONG BOX for it. The only objection to be raised to this story is that the phrase is a very old one, of which the derivation is now lost.

1554. RIDLEY ('Foxe,' 1838), vi., 438. Sir, quoth I, if you will hear how St. Augustine expoundeth that place, you shall perceive that you are IN A WRONG BOX.

1588. J. UDALL, *Distrephes*, p. 31. I perceive that you and I are IN A WRONG BOX.

1751. SMOLLETT, *Peregrine Pickle*, ch. xliii. 'That, I grant you, must be confessed: doctor, I'm afraid we have got INTO THE WRONG BOX.'

1836. MARRYAT, *Midshipman Easy*, ch. x. 'Take care your rights of man don't get you IN THE WRONG BOX—there's no arguing on board of a man-of-war.'

ON THE BOX, *phr.* (workmen's).—A man when on strike and in receipt of strike pay is said to be ON THE BOX.

1889. *Daily News*, 19 Nov., p. 6, col. 7. The 'Blackleg' Question Arising. As these have to be allowed strike pay in order to keep them out of temptation, the number of men ON THE BOX, as they say in the North, may be taken to be a thousand.

BOX HARRY, *verbal phr.* (commercial travellers').—Among bag-men to take dinner and tea together;

'dining out,' *i.e.*, doing without a meal at all.

Box Hat, *subs.* (common).—A silk hat. For synonyms, *see* CADY.

Box-Irons, *subs.* (old). — Shoes. For synonyms, *see* TROTTER-CASES.

1789. GEO. PARKER, *Life's Painter*, p. 173. Shoes. *Hockey-dockies*, or BOX-IRONS.

Box of Dominoes, *subs. phr.* (popular).—The mouth. [From BOX + DOMINOES (*q.v.*), a slang term for the teeth.] For synonyms, *see* POTATO-TRAP.

Box the Compass, *verbal phr.* (nautical).—To repeat in succession, or irregularly, the thirty-two points of the compass; beginners on accomplishing this feat are said to be able to BOX THE COMPASS.

1751. SMOLLETT, *Peregrine Pickle*, ch. vi. 'A light, good-humoured, sensible wench, who knows very well how to BOX HER COMPASS.'

1753. CHAMBERS, *Cycl. Supp.* BOXING, among sailors, is used to denote the rehearsing the several points of the compass in their proper order. [M.]

1836. MARRYAT, *Midsh. Easy*, xviii. I can raise a perpendicular . . . and BOX THE COMPASS.

1867. SMYTH, *Sailors' Word Book.* To BOX THE COMPASS. Not only to repeat the names of the thirty-two points in order and backwards, but also to be able to answer any and all questions respecting its division.

Box the Jesuit, *verbal phr.* (old).—*See* COCKROACHES.

Boy, *subs.* (popular).—1. Champagne. [A story, *ben trovato*, is told by the *Sporting Times* of June 30, 1882, as regards the origin of the phrase:—At a shooting party in Norfolk once, a youth was told off to supply the company with champagne. The day being hot and the sportsmen thirsty, cries of 'Boy! Boy! Boy!' were heard all day long. This tickling the fancy of the royal and noble party, the term 'BOY' became applied to champagne.] Also called FIZ and CHAM (*q.v.*). The latter form is nearly reproduced in the French slang, *le champ;* they also brutally speak of this wine as *coco épileptique*, another epithet being *cidre élégant*.

1882. *Punch*, vol. LXXXII., p. 69, col. 2. 'The fine young London Gentleman.'
He will say that port and sherry his nice palate always cloy;
He'll nothing drink but 'B. and S.' and big magnums of THE BOY;
He's the darling of the Barmaid, and the honest waiter's joy,
As he quaffs his Pommery 'Extra Sec,' his 'Giesler' or 'Ivroy,'
Like a fine young London Gentleman, Quite of the present style.

1882. *Punch*, vol. LXXXII., p. 155, col. 1. Dined with Tom and Corky at a new place they had discovered, and raved of. Of course, beastly dinner, but very good BOY. Had two magnums of it.

1883. *Punch*, August 18, p. 84, col. 1. Shall it be B.-and-S., or bumpers of the BOY?

2. (common)—A hump on a man's back. In low circles it is usual to speak of a humpbacked man as two persons—'him and his BOY,' and from this much coarse fun and personality are at times evolved.

3. (Anglo-Indian and colonial.)—A servant of whatever age.

OLD BOY, *subs.* (popular).—1. A familiar term of address. *The* OLD BOY is one's father; the 'guv'nor,' or 'boss.' Sometimes MY BOY.

1602. SHAKS., *Twel. N.*, ii., 4, 122. But di'de thy sister of her loue MY BOY? [M.]

1740. RICHARDSON, *Pamela*, III., 380. Never fear, OLD BOY, said Sir Charles, we'll bear our Parts in Conversation. [M.]

2. The devil. For synonyms, *see* SKIPPER.

1835-40. HALIBURTON, *Clockmaker*, (1862), 140. As we invigorate the form of government (as we must do, or go to the OLD BOY).

YELLOW BOY, *subs.* (common). — A guinea; also, one pound sterling. [From the colour.] As will be seen the term is an old one. For synonyms, *see* CANARY.

1663. DRYDEN, *Wild Gallant*, Act i.
How now, YELLOW BOYS, by this good light!
Sirrah, varlet, how came I by this gold?

1712. ARBUTHNOT, *History of John Bull*, pt. I., ch. vi. There wanted not YELLOW BOYS to fee counsel, hire witnesses, and bribe juries.

1840. DICKENS, *Old Curiosity Shop*, ch. xlii. 'The delight of picking up the money—the bright, shining YELLOW BOYS—and sweeping 'em into one's pocket!'

Boys, *subs.* (popular).—This word is very generally in use in the plural. Thus, bookmakers speak of their fellows, in the aggregate, as the BOYS; and it must be noted as a curious fact that on race-courses the whole army of the swindling and thieving fraternity are so designated.

ANGRY OR ROARING BOYS, *subs.* (old).—A set of young BUCKS, BLOODS or BLADES (*q v.*), of noisy manners and 'fire-eating' tastes. Nares says 'like the MOHAWKS' (*q.v.*) described by the *Spectator*, they delighted to commit outrages and get into quarrels. Early mention is made of such characters. Wilson, in his *Life of James I.* [1653], gives an account of their origin:—The king minding his sports, many riotous demeanours crept into the kingdom; divers sects of vicious persons, going under the title of ROARING BOYS, bravadoes, roysterers, etc., commit many insolencies; the streets swarm, night and day, with bloody quarrels, private duels fomented, etc.

1599. GREENE, *Tu. Quoque*, Old Plays, vii., 25.
This is no ANGRY, nor no ROARING BOY, but a blustering boy.

1609. BEN JONSON, *Epicœne*, i., 4. The doubtfulness of your phrase, believe it, sir, would breed you a quarrel once an hour with the TERRIBLE BOYS, if you should but keep 'em fellowship a day.

1610. BEN JONSON, *Alchemist*, iii., 4.
Sir, not so young, but I have heard some speech
Of the ANGRY BOYS, and seen 'em take tobacco.

1616. BEAUMONT AND FLETCHER, *Scornful Lady*, iv., 1.
Get thee another nose, that will be pull'd
Off, by the ANGRY BOYS, for thy conversion.

Boys of the Holy Ground, *subs. phr.* (old).—Formerly [1800-25] bands of roughs infesting a well-known region in St. Giles.—*See* HOLY LAND.

1819. MOORE, *Tom Crib's Memorial to Congress*, p. 7.
For we are the BOYS OF THE HOLY GROUND,
And we'll dance upon nothing and turn us round.

Brace, *verb* (American thieves').—To get credit by swagger.

BRACE IT THROUGH, *phr.* (American). — To succeed by dint of sheer impudence. *Cf.*, BRACE UP, 'to gird oneself up,' 'to buckle to.'

Bracelets, *subs.* (familiar). — Handcuffs; fetters for the wrist. [Derivation obvious.]

French thieves call them *les alliances*, properly 'wedding rings'; also *la tartouve* and *les lacets*. For synonyms, *see* DARBIES.

1661. *Wit and Drollery*, quoted in Disraeli *Cur. of Wit.* (Tom O'Bedlams.) [Fetters are called BRACELETS in a song in this work.]

1671. R. HEAD, *English Rogue*, pt. I., ch. lv., p. 371 (1874). Fetters confined my legs from stragling, and BRACELETS were clapt upon my arms.

1839. HARRISON AINSWORTH, *Jack Sheppard* (1889), p. 62. 'Thank you—thank you!' faltered Jack, in a voice full of emotion. 'I'll soon free you from these BRACELETS.'

1848. W. H. AINSWORTH, *James the Second*, bk. I., ch. ii. 'It may be, young squire, you'll have to go . . . with a pair of BRACELETS on your wrists, and pay your next reck'nin' to the gov'nor of Newgate.'

1877. *Five Years' Penal Servitude*, ch. v., p. 359. He travels with other people who are also bound to London, and who, seeing him handcuffed, know very well his steel BRACELETS are not the insignia of honour.

Brace of Shakes, *phr.* (popular).—In a moment; 'jiffy'; 'twinkling of an eye,' etc.—*See*, however, SHAKES. The expression is sometimes A COUPLE, instead of A BRACE OF SHAKES. A French equivalent is *far-far*.

1837. BARHAM, *I. L.* (*Babes in the Wood*). I'll be back in a COUPLE OF SHAKES.

1868. OUIDA, *Under Two Flags*, ch. xii. 'But I've a trick with a 'oss that'll set that sort o' thing—if it ain't gone too far, that is to say—right in a BRACE OF SHAKES.'

1884. *Cornhill Mag.*, Jan., p. 101. 'If there were any boys at Oppingbury now like those who were here when I was young, they'd break the window in A COUPLE OF SHAKES.'

Brace Up, *verb* (thieves').—1. To pawn stolen goods—generally to their utmost value.

2. (American.)—To take a drink. [A transferred sense; from BRACE-UP = to string up; to give firmness to.]

1888. *Puck's Library*, Ap., p. 20. Come old boy, let's BRACE UP; a bumper will pull you together again.

Bracket-Faced, *adj.* (old).—Ugly; hard-featured.—*Grose.*

Bracket-Mug, *subs.* (common).—An ugly face. [From BRACKET (*Cf.*, BRACKET-FACED) + MUG, a slang term for the face.] For synonyms, *see* HATCHET-FACE.

Brads, *subs.* (common).—A generic term for money. De Vaux (*see* quot.), though somewhat limiting the meaning, uses the term elsewhere as equivalent to 'pence' or 'coppers.' It possibly originated among shoemakers, BRADS being small rivets or nails largely employed by them. *Cf.*, HORSE-NAILS, and for synonyms, ACTUAL.

1812. J. H. VAUX, *Flash Dict.* BRADS, halfpence; also money in general.

1855. *Punch*, XXIX., 10. [*Cf.*, Punch's suggestion for a 'fast' partner in banks who should enquire of customers] 'Will you take it in flimsies, or will you have it all in tin? Come, look sharp, my downy one, and I'll fork out the BRADS like bricksy wicksy.'

1868. BREWER, *Phrase and Fable*, s.v. 'B Flats.' *Four B's, essential for social success.*—Blood, brains, brass, BRADS [money].—*American.*

1888-9. PAYNE, *Eavesdropper*, pt. II., ch. ii. They used such funny terms: 'BRADS' and 'dibbs' . . . at last it was borne in upon me that they were talking about money.

TIP THE BRADS.—*See* quotation and TIP.

1821. W. T. MONCRIEFF, *Tom and Jerry*, Act i., Sc. 4. [To] TIP THE BRADS—and down with the dust, is to be at

once good, great, handsome, accomplished, and everything that's desirable—money, money, is your universal good,—only get into Tip Street, Jerry.

Brag, *subs.* (thieves').—A usurer; a Jew. *Cf.*, SIXTY-PER-CENT.

Braggadocia, *subs.* (thieves'). — This is explained in Dickens' *Reprinted Pieces* (in a footnote) to mean three months' imprisonment as reputed thieves. It is difficult to trace the connection between this and the ordinary meaning of BRAGGADOCIO.

1857. DICKENS, *Reprinted Pieces* (*Three 'Detective' Anecdotes, The Artful Touch*), p. 253. 'We don't take much by this move, anyway, for nothing's found upon 'em, and it's only the BRAGGADOCIA after all.'

Brain Pan, *subs.* (sporting).—1. The skull, or skull-cap. Also called BRAIN-CANISTER. Hotten quotes the term as of pugilistic origin, but it ante-dates the palmy days of the 'Fancy' by many years. BRAIN PAN in this sense can, perhaps, hardly be classed as slang; not so, however, sense 2. The Scotch equivalent is HARN-PAN.—*See* quotations under sense 2.

2. (common.) — The head itself. For general synonyms, *see* CHUMP.

b. 1529. SKELTON, *Elynoor Rommin*, in *Hart. Misc.* (ed. Park), I., 417.
Upon her BRAIN PAN
Like an Egyptian
Capped about.

1608. DEKKER, *Belman of London*, in wks. (Grosart) III., 91. The spirit of her owne malt walkt in her BRAYNE PAN.

1609. DEKKER, *Gul's Hornbook*, Prœmium. *Tarleton, Kemp,* nor *Singer* . . . never played the clownes more naturally then the arrantest Sot of you all shall if hee will but boyle my Instructions in his BRAINE-PAN.

1622. MASSINGER, *Virgin-Martyr*, ii., 2.
Oh, sir, his BRAIN-PAN is a bed of snakes,
Whose sting shoots through his eyeballs.

1817. SCOTT, *Rob Roy*, ch. xxxiii. 'Weize a brace of balls through his HARN-PAN!'

1822. SCOTT, *Fortunes of Nigel*, ch. xi. 'Were I your master, sirrah, . . . I would make your BRAIN-PAN, as you call it, boil over, were you to speak a word in my presence before you were spoken to.'

Bramble, *subs.* (provincial slang).—In Kent a lawyer is so called; obviously a sarcastic allusion to the 'tangles' of the law.

Bramble-Gelder (provincial slang).—A derisive appellation for an agriculturist; a Suffolk term.

Bran, *subs.* (common).—A loaf. [In all likelihood this is a mere abbreviation of BRAN-LOAF.] For synonyms, *see* TOMMY.

1837. DICKENS, *Oliver Twist*, ch. viii. He purchased a sufficiency of ready-dressed ham and a half-quartern loaf, or, as he himself expressed it, 'a fourpenny BRAN!' *Ibid*, p. 306. Two half-quartern BRANS, pound of best fresh.

Branded Ticket, *subs.* (nautical).—Admiral Smyth [1867] quotes this as 'a discharge given to an infamous man, on which his character is given, and the reason he is turned out of the service.'

Brandy Face, *subs.* (old). — A tippler; a drunkard, especially one whose favourite drink is brandy.

a. 1687. COTTON, *Æneid, II. Burl.* (1692), 85. You goodman BRANDY-FACE, unfist her. [M.]

Brandy-Faced, *ppl. adj.* (general).—Red-faced; bloated. [A reference to the effects upon the physiognomy of excessive indulgence in intoxicating drinks.] The expression is mentioned by Grose as early as 1785, but it is probably still older, for *see* quotation under BRANDY-FACE.

1859. G. A. Sala, *Tw. Round Clock*, 284. Hulking labourers and BRANDY-FACED viragos, squabbling at tavern doors.

Brandy is Latin for Goose or **For Fish**, *phr.* (popular).—This punning vulgarism appears first in Swift's *Polite Conversation*, and Brewer thus states the philological equation.

WHAT IS THE LATIN FOR GOOSE? (Answer) BRANDY. The pun is on the word answer. *Anser* is the Latin for goose, which brandy follows as surely and quickly as an answer follows a question.

1738. Swift, *Polite Conversation* (conv. ii.). *Lord Sm.* Well, but after all, Tom, can you tell me what's Latin for a goose? *Nev.* O my lord, I know that; why, BRANDY IS LATIN FOR A GOOSE, and *Tace* is Latin for a candle.

1835. Marryat, *Jacob Faithful*, ch. xi. 'Art thou forward in thy learning? Canst thou tell me LATIN FOR GOOSE?' 'To be sure,' replied Tom, 'BRANDY.'

As regards the second form, namely, BRANDY IS LATIN FOR FISH, the origin is more obscure, although it is to some extent explained in the following quotation.

1851. Mayhew, *London Labour and London Poor*, I., 125. We are told that the thirst and uneasy feeling at the stomach, frequently experienced after the use of the richer species of fish, have led to the employment of spirit to this kind of food. Hence, says Dr. Pereira, the vulgar proverb, BRANDY IS LATIN FOR FISH.

Brandy Pawnee, *subs.* (Anglo-Indian).—Brandy and water. [From BRANDY + Hindustan *pānī*, water. *Cf.*, PARNEY, also a slang term for water.]

1816. Quiz, *Grand Master*, pref. And died at last with BRANDY PAUNY. [M.]

1855. Thackeray, *Newcomes*, ch. i. 'I'm sorry to see you, gentlemen, drinking BRANDY-PAWNEE,' says he; 'it plays the deuce with our young men in India.'

1860. W. H. Russell, *My Diary in India*, I., p. 120. They had tiffin at two; hot lunch and ale and BRANDY-PAWNEE.

Brandy Smash, *subs.* (popular).—An American drink concocted of brandy and crushed ice. *Cf.*, DRINKS.

1862. E. MacDermott, *Popular Guide to International Exhibition*, 1862, p. 185. In the vestibule of each refreshment room there is an American bar, where visitors may indulge in 'juleps,' 'cocktails,' 'cobblers,' 'rattlesnakes,' 'gum-ticklers,' 'eye-openers,' 'flashes-o'-lightning,' BRANDY-SMASHES, 'stone-fences,' and a variety of similar beverages.

1869. S. Clemens ('Mark Twain'), *Innocents Abroad.* We procured the services of a gentleman experienced in the nomenclature of the American bar . . . a bowing, aproned Frenchman stepped forward and said *Que veulent les messieurs?* Our general said (after naming several other drinks) give us a BRANDY SMASH; the Frenchman began to back away suspicious of the ominous vigour of the last order.

1883. *Daily Telegraph*, 2 July, p. 5, col. 3. [BRANDY-SMASH is mentioned in a list of American drinks.]

1888. *New York Evening Post*, 24 Feb. Philological.—Gallic Tourist—'I do not see how any one ever learns the absurd English. I read on the menu of drinks, 'Sherree Cobblair,' I find in the dictionary—a mender of shoes of sherry wine; 'Santa Cruz Sour,' *La Sainte Croix acide;* BRANDY SMASH, '*Eau de vie écrasé.*' *Bête de langue!*

Bran-Mash, *subs.* (military).—Bread sopped in coffee or tea. *Cf.*, FLOATING BATTERIES.

Brass, *subs.* (popular).—1. Impudence; effrontery; BRASS being a type of unblushing hardness, shamelessness, etc. This colloquialism is by no means of yesterday, having been used by Shakspeare. Sometimes rendered BOLD AS BRASS. *Cf.*, CHEEK, which also *see* for synonyms.

1594. Shakspeare, *Love's Labour Lost*, v., 2, 395. *Biron.* Thus pour the stars down plagues for perjury. Can any face of BRASS hold longer out?

1701. Defoe, *True Born Englishman*, pt. II. By my Old Friend [The Devil], who printed in my face A needful competence of English BRASS.

1703. Farquhar, *Inconstant*, Act i., Sc. 2. Thou hast impudence to set a good face upon anything; I would change half my gold for half thy BRASS, with all my heart.

1740. North, *Examen*, p. 256. She in her defence made him appear such a rogue upon record, that the Chief Justice wondered he had the BRASS to appear in a court of justice.

1773. O. Goldsmith, *She Stoops to Conquer*, Act iii., Sc. 1. 'To me he appears the most impudent piece of BRASS that ever spoke with a tongue.'

1819. Moore, *Tom Crib's Memorial to Congress*, p. 68. Oh, what a face of BRASS was his, Who first at Congress show'd his phyz.

1852. Dickens, *Bleak House*, ch. lv., p. 462. 'I haven't BRASS enough in my composition, to see him in this place and under this charge.'

1876. C. H. Wall, trans. *Molière*, vol. I., p. 18. Gorgibus is a simpleton, a boor, who will readily believe everything you say, provided . . . you have BRASS enough.

1876. C. Hindley, *Life and Adventures of a Cheap Jack*, p. 199. He started with a lot of tin, but had not sufficient BRASS or *physique* to stand the wear-and-tear of the life.

2. (common.)—A generic term for money. At one time money was made of brass, hence probably the slang usage. *Cf.*, TIN.

1526. Tyndale, *Matt.* x., 9. Posses not golde, nor silver, nor BRASSE yn youre gerdels.

1597. Hall, *Satires*, IV., v., 12. Hirelings enow beside can be so base, Tho' we should scorn each bribing varlet's BRASS.

1860. Mrs. Gaskell, *Sylvia's Lovers*, ch. xx. 'There'll be Fosters i' th' background, as one may say, to take t' biggest share on t' profits,' said Bell. 'Ay, ay, that's but as it should be, for I reckon they'll ha' to find the BRASS the first.'

1864. M. E. Braddon, *Aurora Floyd*, ch. xii. 'Steeve's a little too fond of the BRASS to murder any of you for nothing.'

1884. Hawley Smart, *From Post to Finish*, p. 129. 'It's noa use they're telling us afterwards they ain't collared the BRASS.'

1889. *Sporting Times*, June 29. *Billy Wells.* What the dickens is all this about the hats? We have seventy-two telegrams and letters on the subject, and would prefer the BRASS.

Brass-Bound and Copper Fastened, *adj. phr.* (nautical)—Said of a lad dressed in a midshipman's uniform.—*W. Clark Russell.*

Brass-Bounder, *subs.* (nautical).—A midshipman.

Brasser, *subs.* (Christ's Hospital).—A bully.

Brass Farthing or **Farde**.—The lowest limit of value.—*See* quots.

1642. Rogers, *Naaman*, 33. As bare and beggarly as if he had not one BRASSE FARTHING. [M.]

1880. *Punch's Almanac*, p. 5. Nobby button'-oler very well When one wants to do the 'eavy swell; Otherwise don't care not one BRASS FARDEN, For the best ever blowed in Covent Garden.

1880. Besant and Rice, *Seamy Side*, x., 78. I care not one BRASS FARTHING.

Brass Knocker, *subs.* (vagrants').—Broken victuals; the remains of a meal. Specially applied by beggars to the scraps often bestowed upon them in place of money.

Brass-Plate Merchant, *subs.* (common).—Explained by quotation.

1851. H. Mayhew, *London Labour and London Poor*, II., p. 95. The BRASS-PLATE MERCHANT, as he is called in the trade, being a person who merely procures orders for coal, gets some merchant who buys in the coal-market to execute them in his name, and manages to make a living by the profits of these transactions.

Brassy, *adj.* (common).—Impudent; impertinent; shameless. *Cf.*, BRASS, sense 1.

1570-76. Lambarde, *Peramb. Kent* (1826), 156. To make them blush . . . were they never so BRASSIE and impudent.

1661. T. Middleton, *Mayor of Quinborough*, iii., 1. There's no gallant so BRASSY impudent durst undertake the words that shall belong to't.

1738-1819. Wolcot, *P. Pindar*, p. 73, ed. 1830.
No. Mr. Gattle—Betty was too BRASSY,
We never keep a servant that is saucy.

1862. Mrs. H. Wood, *Channings*, ch. xxxii. 'I asked him to leave his name, sir, and he said Mr. Rowland Yorke knew his name quite well enough without having it left for him.' 'As BRASSY as that was he! I wish to goodness it was the fashion to have a cistern in your house roofs'!

Brazen-Faced, *ppl. adj.* (common).—Shameless; impudent; unblushing. With a face as of brass, *see* BRASS. Hotten remarks that such a person is sometimes said to have had his face rubbed with a brass candle-stick.

1571. Golding, *Calvin on Ps.*, xii., 5. With such BRAZENFASTE baldnesse.

1596. Nashe, *Saffron Walden.* in wks. III., 84. Amidst his impudent BRAZEN-FAC'D defamation of Doctor *Ferne.*

1693. Dryden, *Juvenal*, III., 133. Quick-witted, BRAZEN-FAC'D, with fluent tongues.

1714. *Memoirs of John Hall* (4 ed.), p. 10. Thus with an unparallell'd Impudence every BRAZEN-FAC'D Malefactor is harden'd in his Sin.

1874. Mrs. H. Wood, *Johnny Ludlow*, 1 S., viii., p. 137. 'Of all the impudent BRAZEN-FACED rascals that are cheating the gallows, you must be the worst.'

Bread, *subs.* (old).—Employment; a transferred sense, the idea being—no work; no food.

1785. Grose, *Dictionary of the Vulgar Tongue.* Out of BREAD, out of employment.

Bread and Butter Fashion, *phr.* (harlotry).—An expression descriptive of the sexual embrace.

Bread and Butter Warehouse, *phr.* (old).—A nickname given to the old Ranelagh Gardens. An allusion to the scenes of infamy and debauchery which once characterized the place.—*See* BREAD AND BUTTER FASHION.

Bread and Meat, *subs. phr.* (military).—The commissariat.

Bread Bags, *subs.* (military).—A nickname given in the army and navy to any one connected with the victualling department, as a purser or purveyor in the commissariat. At one time called MUCKERS, and amongst French soldiers *riz-pain-sel.*

Bread-Barge, *subs.* (nautical).—The distributing basket or tray containing the rations of biscuits.

Bread-Basket, *subs.* (popular).—The stomach. [An obvious allusion to that part of the body as a receptacle of food.]

English Synonyms. Bread-room; dumpling-depôt; victualling-office; porridge-bowl.

French Synonyms. *La panetière* (common: properly a bag or satchel wherein shepherds put their bread; a pouch. Akin to this is the slang term *la pantière*, the mouth); *panier au pain* (a literal translation of the English term); *le jabot* (popular: formerly heart or breast. *Se remplir le jabot* = to have a 'blow out'); *la halle aux croûtes* (popular: this may be rendered literally as 'Crust' hall; also, a baker's shop); *la place d'armes* (popular: the place of arms, stronghold or arsenal); *la soute au pain* (popular: *soute* = store-room, etc.; thus, the expression would correspond closely to victualling office or BREAD-BASKET. 'Put that in your BREAD-BASKET' is rendered by *colle-toi ça dans le Fusil, i.e.*, 'ram that in your gun').

Italian Synonym. The Fourbesque has *fagiana* (properly a chest or store-house for beans.)

1753. Foote, *Englishman in Paris*, Act 1. Another came up to second time, but I let drive at the mark, made the soup-maigre rumble in his BREAD-BASKET, and laid him sprawling.

1819. Moore, *Tom Crib's Memorial to Congress*, p. 18. Neat *milling* this Round—what with *clouts* on the *nob*, *Home hits* in the BREAD-BASKET, *clicks* in the *gob.*

1821. W. T. Moncrieff, *Tom and Jerry*, Act iii., Sc. 1. *Jerry.* Now, doctor, take care of your BREAD-BASKET—eyes right, look to your napper.

1856. Reade, *Never too Late to Mend*, ch. lxx. When you can't fill the BREAD-BASKET, shut it. Go to sleep till the Southern Cross comes out again.

1876. C. H. Wall, trans. *Molière*, vol. I., p. 194. And get as a reward an ugly piece of cold steel right through my BREAD-BASKET.

Bread-Picker, *subs.* (Winchester College).—The four senior præfects used to appoint 'Juniors' to this office which was nominal, but which carried with it exemption from fagging at meal times. No 'notion' book states in what the office consisted, but it is supposed that it relates to times when Juniors had to secure the bread, etc., served out for their masters.

Bread-Room, *subs.* (old).—The stomach. A variant of BREAD-BASKET, which *see* for synonyms.

1760-61. Smollett, *Sir L. Greaves*, vol. II., ch. v. He ordered the waiter . . . to . . . bring along-side a short allowance of brandy or grog, that he might cant a slug [dram] into his BREAD-ROOM. *Ibid*, ch. xvii. The waiter . . . returned with a quartern of brandy, which Crowe, snatching eagerly, started into his BREAD-ROOM at one cant.

Bread-Room Jack, *subs.* (nautical).—A purser's servant.

Break, *subs.* (thieves').—A collection (of money) usually got up by a prisoner's friends, either to defray the expenses of his defence, or as a 'lift' when leaving prison. Formerly and more generally applied to a pause in street performances to enable the hat to be passed round. *Cf.*, LEAD. French slang has *une bouline* with the same meaning; and, to make a collection is, among mountebanks, *faire la manche.*

1879. J. W. HORSLEY, in *Macm. Mag.*, XL., 502. The mob got me up a BREAK (collection), and I got between five or six foont (sovereigns).

BREAK DOWN, *subs.* (Australian).—1. A measure of liquor.—*See* quotation.

1759. FRANK FOWLER, *Southern Lights and Shadows*, p. 53. To pay for liquor for another is to 'stand,' or to 'shout,' or to 'sacrifice.' The measure is called a 'nobbler,' or a BREAK-DOWN.

2. (common.) — A noisy dance; also, a convivial gathering. The term was, at first, specially applied to a negro dance, but is now in general use in England in a humorous sense. Also used as a verb, *i.e.*, TO BREAK DOWN, to dance riotously; to be boisterous and 'spreeish.' For synonyms, *see* FLARE UP.

1864. YATES, *Broken to Harness*, II., p. 54. And Mr. Pingle retired into the next room, where he indulged in the steps of a comic dance popular with burlesque actors, and known as a nigger BREAK-DOWN.

1873. *Sat. Review*, May, p. 676. We shall not be surprised to learn that they have serious thoughts of engaging a few comic singers and BREAK-DOWN dancers for their next campaign.

1883. *Daily News*, March 26, p. 2, col. 4. A patter song . . . was twice redemanded, chiefly, it appeared, for the sake of a comical 'BREAK-DOWN' danced by the demented king.

BREAK O' DAY DRUM (American thieves'). — A drinking saloon which keeps its doors open all night.

BREAK ONE'S BACK, *verbal phr.* (colloquial).—To become bankrupt; an extension of the figurative usage to overpower; render nugatory; crush.

1601. SHAKSPEARE, *Henry VIII.*, Act i., Sc. 1. *Aber.* I do know Kinsmen of mine, three at the least, that have B y this so sicken'd their estates, that never They shall abound as formerly. *Buck.* O, many Have BROKE THEIR BACKS with laying manors on 'em For this great journey.

1620. MIDDLETON, *Chaste Maid*, iii., 2. [The word is here used in the sense of bankruptcy and ruin.]

1887. BARING GOULD, *The Gamecocks*, ch. xxviii. 'They are very poor, and have made a hard fight to get on. I fear this change would BREAK THEIR BACKS.'

1888. ASHTON, *Mod. Street Ballads*, p. 13. The cesses, rates, and tithes nearly BREAKS THEIR BACKS.

BREAK ONE'S EGG. — *See* CRACK ONE'S EGG.

BREAK OUT ALL OVER or **IN A FRESH SPOT, ETC.**, *verbal phr.* (American).—Expressions in common use—in the one case conveying an idea of completeness; and, in the other, of commencing some new undertaking, or assuming a different position whether in an argument or action. These usages may be traced to the phraseology of medicine.

BREAK SHINS, *verbal phr.* (general).—To borrow money. Hotten thinks the term is a variant of 'to kick,' formerly in use with a similar meaning. This may be so, but it is worthy of note that 'to shin' is colloquial in America in the sense of 'to walk quickly,' 'to gad about'; but having particular reference also, in mercantile phraseology, to the action of a man who, finding himself short of money to meet his engagements, goes round to his friends to borrow what he requires. To BITE THE EAR (*q.v.*) has the same signification; but for synonyms, *see* SHINS.

BREAK THE BALLS, *verbal phr.* (billiards).—To commence playing; a phrase very much akin to 'breaking ground'; indeed few verbs enter more largely into figurative or colloquial combinations than BREAK.

BREAK THE MOLASSES JUG, *verbal phr.* (American).—To come to grief; to make a mistake.

BREAK THE NECK or **BACK OF ANYTHING**, *verbal phr.* (common).—To accomplish the major portion of a task; to be near the end of an undertaking; to be past the middle of same.

BREAKY-LEG, *subs.* (common).—1. Intoxicating drink of any kind. [A humorous allusion to one of the possible effects of confirmed drunkenness, or the weakness produced in one's legs by tippling.] For all synonyms, *see* DRINKS.

2. (thieves'.)—A shilling.

1857. SNOWDEN, *Mag. Assistant*, 3 ed., p. 446. A shilling. BREAKE-LEG.

BREAST FLEET, *subs.* (old).—Roman Catholics; so called from their practice of crossing themselves on the breast as an act of devotion.

1785. GROSE, *Dictionary of the Vulgar Tongue.* He (or she) belongs to the BREAST FLEET; *i.e.*, is a Roman Catholic; an appellation derived from their custom of beating their breasts in the confession of their sins.

BREATH. CHANGE YOUR BREATH, *phr.* (American).—An injunction to adopt a different manner or bearing. An offensive, slang expression which, originating in California, quickly ran its course through the Union.

BREECH, *verb* (schoolboys'). — To flog or be flogged; especially on the posteriors. This verb was formerly in literary use, but has now fallen into disuetude.

1557. TUSSER, *Husbandrie*, ch. lxxiv., st. 6, p. 166 (S.D.S.).
Maides, up I beseech yee
Least Mistres doe BREECH yee.

1637. MASSINGER, *Guardian*, i., 1. How he looks! like a school-boy that had play'd the truant, And went to be BREECH'D.

1821. SCOTT, *Kenilworth*, ch. xxiv. 'Go to,' said Wayland, 'thou art a prating boy, and should be BREECHED for thine assurance.'

BREECHED, *ppl. adj.* (popular).—1. To be well off; to have plenty of money; 'to be well BREECHED,' to be in good circumstances. *Cf.*, BALLASTED. The French have a similar idiom. If a man is bankrupt he is said to be *déculotté*—unbreeched. Given in this sense by Vaux in his *Flash Dictionary* [1812].

BREECHES. TO WEAR THE BREECHES, *phr.* (common). — A phrase said only of women; and signifying to rule; to usurp a husband's prerogative; to be 'master.' An analogous phrase is 'the grey mare is the better horse of the two.' [The derivation is obviously an allusion to BREECHES as the symbol of authority, *i.e.*, of manhood.] Murray traces the expression back to 1553, but it is, in reality, much older. It is found in French as early as 1450.

1450. *Les Quinze Joyes de Mariage: La Dixiesme Joye.* Edition Elzevirienne, Paris (1853), p. 113. Et sachez qu'il est avenu à aucuns que l'en leur faisoit boire de mauvès brouez affin de porter les braies ou pour autres choses pires.

The idea is met with in English at about the same date in a carol, the burden of which is founded on it:—

14(?). *Songs and Carols of the Fifteenth Century*, Percy Soc. Pub., vol. XXIII., p. 65.
Nova, nova, sawe you ever such,
The moste mayster of the hows WERYTH NO BRYCH.

Also a little later, from the same collection:—

The Boke of Maid Emlyn, vol. VI., p. 21.
All women be suche,
Thoughe the man WEAR THE BRECHE.

It is curious to note also that the expression has cropped up in most languages. The Dutch say, '*De vrouw draagd'er de broek*'; the Germans, '*Sie hat die Hosen.*' The Germans have also other 'breeches' sayings; as *e.g.*, '*Das Hertz ist ihm in die Hosen gefallen.*' Other illustrative quotations are:—

1557. TUSSER, *Husbandrie*, ch. lxvii. st. 18, 156 (E.D.S.).
Least some should talke, as is the speech,
The good wiues' husband WEARES NO BREECH.

1591. NASHE, *A Prognostication*, in wks. II., 158. Diverse great stormes are this yere to be feared, especially in houses where the wives WEARE THE BREECHES.

1663. T. KILLIGREW, *Parson's Wedding*, ii., 3, in Dodsley's *O. P.* (1780), xi., 413. Anything that may get rule; I love to WEAR THE BREECHES.

1724. SWIFT, *Misc. Poems*, in wks. (1824) XIV., 199.
Those men, who WORE THE BREECHES least,
Call'd him a cuckold, fool, and beast.

1820. COOMBE, *Syntax, Consolation*, ch. v.
When she doth WEAR THE BREECHES;
And the poor fool dare not resist
The terrors of her threat'ning fist.

1821. W. T. MONCRIEFF, *Tom and Jerry*, Act ii., Sc. 4. *Mrs. T.* No, no—no mischief—harkye, you did me a service just now in the street. *Tom.* I know I did, down by the pump. *Mrs. T.* Well, now, I'll do you one—my husband i asleep: I have the keys; and I WEAR THE BREECHES.

BREECHING, *verbal subs.* (schoolboys').—A flogging. Like BREECH (*q.v.*), formerly in general use.

1520. WHITTINGTON, *Vulg.* (1527), 26. I studye to-day to-daye bycause I fere a BRECHYNG.

1594. NASHE, *Unfortunate Traveller*, in wks. V., 149. Heeres a stirre thought I to my selfe after I was set at libertie, that is worse than an vpbrayding lesson after a BRITCHING.

BREEF.—*See* BRIEF.

BREEZE, *subs.* (general).—A row; quarrel; disturbance; coolness. [From BREEZE, a cool wind.]

1785. GROSE, *Dictionary of the Vulgar Tongue.* To kick up a BREEZE, to breed a disturbance.

1819. MOORE, *Tom Crib's Memorial to Congress*, p. 5. But, though we must hope for such good times as these, Yet, as something may happen to kick up a BREEZE.

1865. *Saturday Review*, 28 Jan., p. 119. 'Don't be angry; we've had our BREEZE. Shake hands!' [M.]

BREKKER, *subs.* (Oxford University).—Breakfast. [Formed by phonetically taking the first syllable of 'breakfast' + ER, a species of slang formation, which originated at Harrow.] —*See* 'Comparative and Historical Study of Slang' at the end of this work.

BREVET HELL, *subs.* (American).—A nickname for a battle, which originated during the Civil War. The meaning is obvious enough. The carnage and bloodshed of a battle-field is only a degree short of the horrors of the theological 'hell.' Compare with BREVET-WIFE, BREVET-RANK.

BREVET-WIFE, *subs.* (general).—A woman who, without being married to a man, lives with him, takes his name, and enjoys all the privileges of a wife. A transferred figurative sense of the legitimate word.

BREW, *verb* (Marlborough School). —To make afternoon tea. Almost always carried on in couples, but sometimes three boys BREW together.

BREWER'S HORSE, *subs.* (old).—A drunkard. For synonyms, *see* ELBOW CROOKER.

BREWING, *verbal subs.* (Marlborough College).—The making of afternoon tea.—*See* BREW.

BRIAN O' LINN, *subs.* (rhyming slang).—Gin. For synonyms, *see* DRINKS.

BRIAR, BRIER, *subs.* (popular).—A colloquialism for 'brier-wood pipe.' The *Erica arborea* or White Heath, a native of the Mediterranean littoral is largely used in the manufacture of pipes. [*Cf.*, Fr. *bruyère* = 'heath.']

1882. *Graphic*, Dec. 16, p. 683, col. 2. Nowadays, every third man you meet has a cigarette or a BRIAR in his mouth.

1886. *Harper's Mag.*, 27 Dec. There is the ever-ready BRIER-root pipe loaded with Caporal.

BRICK, *subs.* (popular).—A good fellow; one whose staunchness and loyalty commend him to his fellows—a highly eulogistic epithet for one man to apply to another. Said to be of University origin, the simile being drawn from the classics. A writer in *Hallberger's Illustrated Magazine* [1878, p. 635], says the expression is logically deduced in the following amusing manner. A brick is 'deep-red,' so a 'deep-read' man is a BRICK. The punning syllogism is carried further. To read like a BRICK is to read till you are deep-'read'; a deep-read man is in University-phrase a 'good man'; a good man is a jolly fellow with non-reading men, *ergo* a jolly fellow is a BRICK.

It has, however, been pointed out that dedicatory columns of various forms have been found bearing Greek inscriptions, records of the great and virtuous. Some of these were *circular* and fluted pillars; but the Athenians are said to have dedicated *square* columns so inscribed, which gave rise to the *style* τετράγ = ωνος ἀνὴρ [*see* Aristotle, *Eth.*, i., 10], one whose worth entitled him to honorary mention on some monumental stone of the *form* described. The *anticipatory* distinction might, therefore, be easily accorded to one worthy of such posthumous honours. From the meritorious notion of the *rectangular* stone or pillar we get the living *type* of genuine or supposititious worth —a regular BRICK. A further analogy may be drawn from the clayey basis of the BRICK, even in a state of combination with *sand* and *ashes*—those types of instability and decay—and we naturally acquire the notion of *solidity*, consistency, and strength. We are thus enabled to apply the above phrase to the *child* of clay, who may chance to resemble it in its constitution, whose moral materials and parts have been originally so carefully formed, so judiciously tempered and skilfully moulded, that, in spite of a frail and infirm nature, he has preserved his shape thus early given. The fiery test but determines his solidity; his sound, staunch, and unshrinking firmness, constitutes him a regular BRICK or hero, the attributes which especially qualify him for that metaphorical appellation. *Cf.*, ON THE SQUARE; STRAIGHT — TRUE — CLEAN AS A DIE.

1837. BARHAM, *Ingoldsby Legends* (*Brothers of Birchington*). In brief I don't stick to declare, Father Dick, So they called him for short, was a regular BRICK; A metaphor taken, I have not the page aright, Out of an ethical work by the Stagyrite.

1850. SMEDLEY, *Frank Fairlegh*, p. 10. 'Mr. Fairlegh, let me introduce this gentleman, Mr. George Lawless; he is, if he will allow me to say so, one of the most rising young men of his generation, one of the firmest props of the glorious edifice of our rights and privileges.' 'A regular BRICK,' interposed Coleman.

1855. THACKERAY, *Newcomes*, ch. x. 'But the others are capital. There is that little chap who has just had the measles—he's a dear little BRICK.'

1856. T. HUGHES, *Tom Brown's School-days*, p. 100. He voted E.'s new crony a BRICK.

1876. GEORGE ELIOT, *Daniel Deronda*, ch. xvi. Their brothers' friend, declared by Hans to be the salvation of him, a fellow like nobody else, and, in fine, a BRICK.

FRENCH SYNONYMS. *Un bon gniasse* (cads' and thieves'); *être d'un bon bouchon* (to be a brick. Michel gives *bouchon* as 'cadet'); *un bon bougre* (popular: Barrère says the word *bougre* is often used with a disparaging sense; *bougre de cochon*, 'you dirty pig'; *bougre de serin*, 'you ass.' Littré derives *bougre* from *Bulgarus*, Bulgarian; the heretic Albigeois, who shared the religious ideas of some of the Bulgarians, received the name of *bougres*); *un zig*, *zigue*, *zigorneau*, *zigard*, or *zingo* (popular: Michel gives *zig* as *camarade*, 'a comrade'; in Italian *zigno* or *petit lézard* which latter (*lézard*) signifies in French argot, a 'bad lot').

Verb (American). — To punish a man by bringing the knees close up to the chin, and lashing the arms tightly to the knees—a species of trussing.

LIKE A BRICK—LIKE BRICKS—(and in an intensive form) LIKE A THOUSAND OF BRICKS, *adv. phr.* (common). — With energy; alacrity; thoroughly; vehemently and with much display. [Derived partly attributively from BRICK (*q.v.*), and partly in allusion to the crash of falling bricks.] There are numerous similes of a kindred character; *e.g.*, LIKE BEANS; LIKE ONE O'CLOCK; LIKE BLAZES, all of which *see*.

1835. DICKENS, *Sketches*, p. 139. Bump they [cab and horse] cums agin the post, and out flies the fare LIKE BRICKS.

1837. BARHAM, *I. L.* (*Ingoldsby Penance*).
For the Friar to his skirts closely sticks,
'Running after him,'—so said the Abbot, —LIKE BRICKS!

1860. *New Orleans Picayune*, April 27 (Police Report). 'When it came to the breakdown, Your Honor, he kicked up a row like a drove of contrary mules, and when we wanted to turn him out, he fell upon us LIKE A THOUSAND OF BRICKS, and threatened to make minced meat of the police and every one of us.

1864. *Western World*, March 5. 'When Mr. Nye had finished, Mr. Stewart rose, and with his irresistible logic and impressive language came down upon him LIKE A THOUSAND OF BRICKS, till he was utterly crushed and demolished.'

BRICK IN THE HAT, *phr.* (American).—A drunken man is said to have a BRICK IN HIS HAT, the allusion being to top-heaviness and inability to preserve a steady gait.

BRICK-DUSTER.—*See* BRICKFIELDER.

BRICKDUSTS, *subs.* (military).—The Fifty-third Regiment of Foot, so nicknamed from its facings, which are scarlet. Another slang appellation is 'THE OLD FIVE-AND-THREEPENNIES,' from its number and the daily pay of an ensign.

BRICKFIELDER or **BRICKDUSTER**, *subs.* (Australian colloquial).—In Sydney the name given to a dust or sand-storm brought by southerly winds from sand hills locally known as the BRICKFIELDS—hence the name. Also called the BUSTER or SOUTHERLY BURSTER.

18(?). MUNDAY, *Our Antipodes*. In October, 1848, as I find by my diary, I witnessed a fine instance of a nocturnal BRICKFIELDER. Awakened by the roaring of the wind I arose and looked out. It was bright moonlight, or it would have been bright but for the clouds of dust, which, impelled by a perfect hurricane, curled up from the earth, and absolulely muffled the fair face of the planet. Pulverised specimens of every kind and colour of soil within two miles of Sydney, flew past the house high over the chimney tops in lurid whirl-winds, now white, now red. It had all the appearance of an American prairie fire, barring the fire.

1853. *Fraser's Mag.*, XLVIII., 515. What the Sydney people call a BRICKFIELDER.

1886. COWAN, *Charcoal Sk.* The buster and BRICKFIELDER: Austral red-dust blizzard and red-hot simoon.

BRICKLAYER, *subs.* (clerical). — A clergyman. [It has been hazarded that the term is a familiar corruption of *Ru*BRICKLAYER, to denote general character for Rubrical exactness—said of men who not only lay down Liturgical law, but obey it. With more propriety, however, may it be held as referring to the important part taken by the mediæval clergy in *ecclesiastical* architecture. Mr. Thomas Boys, in the course of an interesting article on the subject [*N. and Q.*, 2 S., vii., 115], traces its historical derivation somewhat as follows:—It is well known how in former days the building of cathedrals and other sacred edifices was patronised and promoted both by the dignitaries and by the clergy generally; but it is not, perhaps, matter of equal notoriety that many chapters and collegiate bodies had a functionary called a *workman* (*operarius*), on whom devolved the charge of repairing and maintaining the sacred fabric, and who was often *one of their own number*. In fact, he was of the dignitaries of the church. '*Operarius, Dignitas, in Collegiis Canonicorum, et Monasteriis, cui operibus publicis vacare incumbit*' (Carpenter). The office of this *operarius* or workman was called '*operaria*.' '*Operaria. Dignitas Operarii in collegiis canonicorum et monasteriis*' (*ib.*). In Spain, the clerical *operarius* was called by the corresponding Spanish name, *obrero* (a workman). '*Obrero. Se llama tambien el que cuida de las obras, en las Iglesias o Comunidades, que en algunas Cathedrales es dignidad*' (*Dicc. de la Ac. Esp.*); *i.e.*, in some cathedrals the office made the holder of it a dignitary. Salazar de Mendoza, in his 'Cronica del Cardenal Don R. G. de Mendoça,' tells us that, the Cardinal having conceded to the Chapter of the cathedral at Toledo, the administration of the building-fund, the Chapter in 1485, nominated as *workman* (*obrero*) the Canon Juan de Contreras (*Lib.* II., cap. 62, par. 2). May we not conjecture, then, that, if clergymen are now provincially called BRICKLAYERS, it is because their mediæval predecessors were, with a special reference to *building*, called 'workmen'? Possibly, from the appointment of certain ecclesiastics in former days under the name of *operarii* or workmen, for the repair and maintenance of public edifices in the University of Oxford, the title of BRICKLAYERS may have passed, in course of time, to the neighbouring clergy of Oxon and Berks. The use of bricks, which ceased in this country after the decline of the Roman power, is stated by Hallam to have been reintroduced, probably from Flanders, in the early part of the fourteenth century. With perhaps equal propriety the term [BRICKLAYER] is thought to refer to the οἰκοδομὴ τοῦ σώματος τοῦ Χριστοῦ (Eph. iv., 12), trusting that they, like St. Paul, are wise 'master builders'; builders on the only true foundation, 'which is Jesus Christ.' Edify, *edificare* οἰκοδομεῖν have primary reference to houses built with hands, as well as to the spiritual one of building up the Church of Christ.]

BRICKLAYER'S CLERK, *subs.* (nautical). — One of the hundred names given to a lubberly sailor. —*W. Clark Russell.* For synonyms, *see* STRAWYARDER, and *Cf.*, BAIL.

BRICKS, *subs.* (Wellington College). —A sort of pudding.

BRIDGE, *subs.* (cards').—A cheating trick at cards, by which any particular card is cut by previously curving it by the pressure of the hand. Used in France as well as in England, and termed in the Parisian *Argot faire le pont sec*, also *couper dans le pont*. The *modus operandi* of avoiding, or rather of neutralizing the cut, which is the very backbone of the card-sharper's art, is somewhat difficult, and is generally performed by one of two methods, termed respectively the 'BRIDGE' and the 'pass.' In the former method the sharper, at the end of his shuffle—the cards being still held backs uppermost in the left hand—takes some twelve or fifteen of the underneath cards lengthwise between the thumb and first and second fingers of the right hand and throws them on the top of the pack, at the same time giving them a slight squeeze outwards which causes them to assume an imperceptible curve. When placed on the table to be cut, the pack will now, owing to this curve or 'BRIDGE,' present in the middle a very slight gap almost invisible to the eye; and experience shows that the odds are twenty to one that the adversary will cut exactly at that very spot, thus taking off the twelve or fifteen cards thrown on the top and bringing the 'readied' portion of the pack back to its original position.

1851. MAYHEW, *London Labour and London Poor*, I., p. 266. I got my living by card-playing in the low lodging-houses . . . I worked the oracle; they were not up to it. I put the first and seconds on, and the BRIDGE too.

1859. LEVER, *Davenport Dunn*, I., p. 251. I've found out the way that Yankee fellows does the king. It's not the common BRIDGE that every body knows.

1866. YATES, *Black Sheep*, I., p. 70. The genius which had hitherto been confined to BRIDGING a pack of cards, or 'securing' a die, talking over a flat, or winning money of a greenhorn, was to have its vent in launching a great City Company.

Verb (old). — Explained by quotation.

1812. J. H. VAUX, *Flash Dict.* To BRIDGE a person, or to throw him over the bridge, is . . . to deceive him by betraying the confidence he has reposed in you.

BRIDLE-CULL, *subs.* (old).—A highwayman. [From BRIDLE + CULL, a 'man.'] A French equivalent is *un garcon de campagne*; also *un grinche de cambrouse*; *aller au trimar* or *trimard*, 'to become a highwayman.' *Trimar* = road or 'toby.'

1754. FIELDING, *Jonathan Wild*, bk. I., ch. v. A booty of £10 looks as great in the eye of a BRIDLE-CULL, and gives as much real happiness to his fancy, as that of as many thousands to the statesman.

BRIDPORT or **BRYDPORT DAGGER**, *subs.* (old). — The hangman's rope. 'To be stabbed with a BRIDPORT DAGGER' signifies 'to be hanged.' For synonyms, *see* HORSE'S NIGHTCAP, and *Cf.*, ANODYNE NECKLACE.

1662. FULLER, *Worthies, Dorset* (I., 310). 'Stab'd with a BRYDPORT DAGGER.' That is, hang'd or executed at the Gallowes; the best, if not the most, hemp (for the quantity of ground) growing about Brydport.

1787. GROSE, *Prov. Glossary, etc.* (1811), p. 67. Stabbed with a BRYDPORT DAGGER. That is hanged. Great quantity of hemp is grown about this town; and, on account of its superior qualities, Fuller says there was an ancient statute, now disused, that the cables for the royal navy should be made thereabouts.

1807. SOUTHEY, *Espriella's Letters*, i., 35 (3 ed.). The neighbourhood is so proverbially productive of hemp, that when a man is hanged, they have a vulgar saying, that he has been stabbed with a BRIDPORT DAGGER.

BRIEF, *subs.* (thieves').—A ticket of any kind, whether railway pass, pawnbrokers' duplicate, or ticket for a raffle; also a pocket book. Hence BRIEFLESS (*q.v.*).

1879. J. W. HORSLEY, in *Macm. Mag.*, XL., 501. I took a BRIEF (ticket) to London Bridge.

1885. *Daily Telegraph*, Aug. 18, p. 3, col. 2. His usual line of business was 'BRIEF-snatching,' *i.e.*, hovering about the crowd that surrounds a small bookmaker, and snatching from the hands of the unwary the credential they with rash eagerness exhibit, and which they desire to exchange with the man they have bet with for their winnings.

1889. *Sporting Times*, 6 July. They copped the BRIEFS at the next station, and he changed carriages.

BRIEFLESS, *adj.* (common).—Ticketless.—*See* BRIEF.

1889. *Bird o' Freedom*, Aug. 7, p. 3. Following close at the heels of Newman, I soon found myself within the Aquarium, all BRIEFLESS as I was, and without having been asked any questions.

BRIEFS or **BREEFS**, *subs.* (card-sharpers'). — Cards tampered with for the purpose of swindling.—*See* BRIDGE, CONCAVES, and CONVEXES, LONGS, and SHORTS, REFLECTORS, etc. [From the German *briefe*, which Baron Heinecken says was the name given to the cards manufactured at Ulm. *Brief* is also the synonym for a card in the German Rothwalsch dialect, and *briefen* is to play at cards.]

1529. [Edited by] LUTHER, *Liber Vagatorum* (1860), p. 47. 'Item—beware of the Joners (gamblers), who practice Beseflery with the BRIEF (cheating at cards), who deal falsely and cut one for the other, cheat with Boglein and spies, pick one BRIEF from the ground, and another from a cupboard,' etc.

1720. *Old Book of Games*, quoted by Hotten. 'Take a pack of cards and open them, then take out all the honours . . . and cut a little from the edges of the rest all alike, so as to make the honours broader than the rest, so that when your adversary cuts to you, you are certain of an honour. When you cut to your adversary cut at the ends, and then it is a chance if you cut him an honour, because the cards at the ends are all of a length. Thus you may make BREEFS end-ways as well as side-ways.'

BRIEF-SNATCHER, *subs.* (thieves').—Pocket-book thieves. [From BRIEF (*q.v.*, sense 1), slang term for a pocket-book, + SNATCHER.]

BRIGH, *subs.* (thieves').—A pocket.

1879. J. W. HORSLEY, in *Macm. Mag.*, XL., 502. Having a new suit of clobber on me, and about fifty blow in my BRIGH (pocket).

Some ENGLISH SYNONYMS are:—Cly, skyrocket.

FRENCH SYNONYMS are *une grande*; *une profonde*, *parfonde* or *prophête* (thieves': literally deep; also used for 'cave' or 'cellar'); *une fouillouse* (thieves': this term is an old one. *Fouille* = a 'digging' or excavation. There are various forms—*foulle*, *felouse*, *filoche*); *une gueularde* (thieves': *gueulard* = wallet in slang, but properly signifies a stove); *une baguenaude* (thieves' and cads': properly 'a bladder-nut'); *une balade* or *ballade*; *une valade* (thieves': from *avaler*, to swallow up); *une fondrière* (thieves'); *un four banal* (thieves': either used to signify a 'pocket,' a 'false pocket,' or an 'omnibus'); *une sonde* (literally *sonde* = probe).

BRIGHT IN THE EYE, *subs.* (common)—Slightly tipsy. [An allusion to the sparkling appearance of the eyes at an early stage of intoxication; subsequently they become dull and sleepy.] For synonyms, *see* SCREWED.

BRIGHTON TIPPER, *subs.*—A peculiar kind of ale.—*See* quotation.

1843. DICKENS, *Martin Chuzzlewit*, I., p. 347. Requiring . . . a pint of the celebrated staggering ale, or Real Old BRIGHTON TIPPER, at supper. *Ibid*, p. 447. If they draws the BRIGHTON TIPPER here, I takes that ale at night, my love.

BRIM, *subs.* (old).—1. A prostitute. [A contraction of BRIMSTONE (*q.v.*)] For synonyms, *see* BARRACK-HACK.

1730-6. BAILEY. BRIM [*q.* a contraction of Brimstone], a common strumpet. [M.]

1764. T. BRYDGES, *Homer Travest.* (1797), i., 173. Can mortal scoundrels thee [Hera] perplex, And the great BRIM of brimstones vex?

1808. JAMIESON. BRIM, a cant term for a trull.—*Loth.*

2. (common.)—Nowadays the term signifies an angry, violent woman, or a termagant, without reference to moral character. An equivalent French term is *une chipie*. *Cf.*, BRIMSTONE.

1799. *Whim of the Day.* She raved, she abused me, and splenetic was; She's a vixen, she's a BRIM, zounds! She's all that is bad.

BRIMSTONE, *subs.* (old).—1. A violent tempered woman; a virago; a spitfire. [A reference to the inflammable character of the mineral.]

1712. BP. BURNET, in Walpole's *Reminiscences* (1819), p. 75. 'Oh, madam,' said the bishop, 'do not you know what a BRIMSTONE of a wife he had?'

1751. SMOLLETT, *Peregrine Pickle*, ch. vi. 'She is . . . not a BRIMSTONE, like Kate Koddle, of Chatham.'

1760. C. JOHNSTON, *Chrysal*, II., 190. I hate the law damnably ever since I lost a year's pay for hindering our boatswain's mate's brother from beating his wife. The BRIMSTONE swore I beat her husband, and so I paid for meddling.

1859. H. KINGSLEY, *Geoffrey Hamlyn*, ch. xxiii. Who seemed, too, to have a temper of her own, and promised, under circumstances, to turn out a bit of a B—MST—NE.

2. (old.)—A prostitute. For synonyms, *see* BARRACK-HACK.

1785. GROSE. Brim (abbreviation of BRIMSTONE), an abandoned woman; perhaps originally only a passionate or irascible woman, compared to BRIMSTONE for its inflammability.

BRINEY or **BRINY**, *subs.* (popular).—The sea. A 'dip in the BRINEY' once a year is a great attraction to Cockney excursionists. Hotten tells a story of one excursionist saying to another, as they stripped in a double machine, 'Why, 'Arry what dirty feet you've got!' ''Ave I; well yer see I wasn't down last year.' [From the *adj.* signifying, 'of or pertaining to brine or the sea.']

1856. WHYTE MELVILLE, *Kate Coventry*, ch. xiv. The luckless plight in which a stout gentleman had found himself, by the temporary loss of all his apparel, while he was disporting in the BRINY.

1881. *Punch*, Jan. 15, p. 14. *Grigsby.* Hullo, my Jellaby, you here! Come and take a dip in the BRINY, old man. I'm sure you look as if you *wanted* it. *Postlethwaite.* Thanks, no. I never bathe. I always see myself so dreadfully foreshortened in the Water, you know!

1889. *Sporting Times*, June 29. Next day bathing, returning from which we beheld a curious sight, three nymphs carrying down to the strand a bath in which one of them was, apparently with a curious mistrust of the sea, going to try the BRINY.

ENGLISH SYNONYMS. Herring pond; big pond; big drink; the puddle; Davy's locker.

FRENCH SYNONYMS. *La grande tasse* (familiar: properly 'the big cup.' *Boire dans la grande tasse*, 'to be drowned'); *la grande bleue* (popular: the great blue—an allusion to the colour of deep sea water); *le grand salé* (popular: literally 'the great salt.'); *le pré salé* (popular: properly the salted or BRINY meadow.)

BRING DOWN THE HOUSE, *verbal phr.* (general).—To elicit loud applause; and, still more figuratively, to be successful. [The figure of speech is that demonstrative applause will cause the walls to give way. *Cf.*, To RAISE THE ROOF OFF.]

1754. *World*, II., No. 76, 125. His apprehension that your statues will BRING THE HOUSE DOWN.

1853. REV. E. BRADLEY ('Cuthbert Bede'), *Adventures of Verdant Green*, II., p. 23. Why, it would surpass the British sailor's broadsword combat for six, and BRING DOWN THE HOUSE.

1872. FORSTER, *Life of Charles Dickens*, ch. xliv. (IV., p. 252). 'And give us your applause, for that is always just'! which BROUGHT DOWN THE HOUSE with rapture.

1877. MRS. RIDDELL, *Her Mother's Darling*, II., p. 61 (ch. xii). I do not fancy she would ever forgive any of us if Honie were to BRING DOWN THE HOUSE at Elm Vale.

1889. *Bird o' Freedom*, Aug. 7, p. 3. But Samson's crowning feat of all was to break with his fist two steel chains, suspended from a couple of posts. This fairly BROUGHT DOWN THE HOUSE.

BRISKET-BEATER, *subs.* (old). — A Roman Catholic. *Cf.*, BREAST FLEET and CRAW-THUMPER, synonymous terms. Quoted by Grose [1785].

BRISTLES or **BRISTLE DICE**, *subs.* (old).—A method of 'cogging' dice by inserting BRISTLES into them, and thus influencing the position of the cubes when 'thrown.'

1532. *Dice Play* (1050), 28. BRISTLE DICE, be now too gross a practice to be put in use. [M.]

1680. COTTON, in Singer *Hist. Cards*, 335. This they do by false dice, as . . . By BRISTLE-DICE. [M.]

1822. SCOTT, *Fortunes of Nigel*, ch. xxiii. 'Men talk of high and low dice, Fulhams and BRISTLES . . . and a hundred ways of rooking besides.'

BRISTOL MILK, *subs.* (old).—Sherry. [An allusion to sherry being formerly a large import of the city of BRISTOL.] For synonyms, *see* DRINKS.

1644. PRYNNE AND WALKER, *Fiennes' Trial*, 78. Good store of BRISTOL MILK, strong wines and waters. [M.]

1662. FULLER, *Worthies*, *Bristol.* 'BRISTOL MILK'; this metaphorical milk, whereby Xeres or Sherry Sack is intended.

1785. GROSE, *Dictionary of the Vulgar Tongue.* BRISTOL MILK, a Spanish wine called sherry, much drank at that place, particularly in the morning.

1849-61. MACAULAY, *Hist. Eng.*, I., iii. A rich beverage made of the best Spanish wine, and celebrated . . . as BRISTOL MILK.

BROACH CLARET, *verbal phr.* (pugilistic).—To draw blood. — *See*, however, CLARET.

BROAD AND SHALLOW, *phr.* (popular).—An epithet applied to the so-called 'Broad Church,' in contradistinction to the 'High' and 'Low' Churches. —*See* HIGH and DRY.

1886. *Graphic*, 10 April, p. 399. In the Church have we not the three schools of High and Dry, Low and Slow, and BROAD AND SHALLOW?

BROADBOTTOMS, *subs.* (political).—A nickname given to two Coalition Governments, one in the last century [1741], and the other in 1807.—*See* quots.

A pamphlet dated April 18, 1807, has reference to the latter. Its full title is:—'The pigs possessed, or the BROAD-BOTTOM'D litter running headlong into the Sea of Perdition.' The characters are George III., as the British farmer; Lords Sidmouth, Ellenborough, Howick ('Test Act'); Mr. Windham; Lords Holland, Walpole, Carlisle St. Vincent; Earls Temple ('Last Stake'), Grenville ('Catholic Bill'), and of Derby; Lords Erskine, Lauderdale (a Scotch pig), H. Petty, and Moira; the Duke of Bedford, who was Lord Lieutenant of Ireland, marked 'Erin go Bragh'; Earl Spencer, Marquis of Buckingham ('Family'), R. B. Sheridan (Harlequin), Courtney, Tierney, and Whitbread ('Entire'). Courtney is placed in profile between Ellenborough and Sidmouth. He was an intimate friend of Fox. This is said to be the only portrait of him. The print is a supplement to another styled 'More Pigs than Teats.' The pigs represent the Ministers described commonly by the phrase 'All the Talents,' or the 'BROAD-BOTTOMS' who were succeeded, April, 1807, by the Duke of Portland and his supporters. The former are not to be confounded with an earlier 'BROAD-BOTTOM' Administration. The latter was commemorated in the satirical inscription for Fox's tomb, *Hic jacet Pater Broad-Bottomos.*

1742. WALPOLE, *Lett. to Mann* (1833), No. 22, Feb. 18, vol. I., p. 106. The Tories declare against any farther prosecution—if Tories there are, for now one heard of nothing but the BROAD-BOTTOM; it is the reigning cant word, and means, the taking all parties and people, indifferently, into the ministry.

1843. MACAULAY, *Historical Essays*, II., p. 244. The Pelhams had forced the King, much against his will, to part with Lord Carteret . . . They proceeded, after this victory, to form the Government on that basis, called by the cant name of the 'BROAD-BOTTOM.'

1863. JEAFFRESON, *Live It Down*, I., p. 249. The star of Granville is falling, that of Pelham is in the ascendant; and the great coalition on 'The BR. B.' is managing the affairs of the State.

1871. MISS BRADDON, *Robert Ainsleigh*, I., p. 37. A scathing reply from the polished chief of the famous BR. B. Administration.

1887. *Pol. Slang*, in *Cornhill Mag.*, June, p. 628. A Coalition Government in the last century was known by the apt nickname of the 'BROAD BOTTOM.'

BROADBRIM, *subs.* (common).—A Quaker. [The origin of this expression is to be found in the hat once peculiar to the 'Society of Friends.' Hotten says the epithet is now used of any quiet, sedate, old man.]

1712. *Spectator*, No. 276. [BROADBRIM is used as the name of a Quaker correspondent.]

1750. FIELDING, *Tom Jones*, bk. VII., ch. x. This the Quaker had observed, and this, added to the rest of his behaviour, inspired honest BROADBRIM with a conceit that his companion was, in reality, out of his senses.

1864. *Reader* (quoted in *Notes and Queries*, 5 S., ix., p. 263). BROADBRIM, a Quaker. This word clearly owes its origin to the peculiar hat worn by the Society of Friends.

1876. JAS. GRANT, *One of the Six Hundred*, ch. i. The sly BROAD-BRIM, and popularity-hunters of the Peace Society sent a deputation to the Emperor Nicholas.

BROAD-COOPER, *subs.* (brewers').—A person employed by brewers to negotiate with publicans.

BROAD COVES, *subs.* (old).—Card-sharpers. [From BROADS (*q.v.*), cards, + COVE (*q.v.*), a man.] The modern term for swindling at cards is BROAD FAKING (*q.v.*). A French equivalent is *un brêmeur*. For synonyms, *see* ROOK.

1821. W. T. MONCRIEFF, *Tom and Jerry*, Act ii., Sc. 5.
Your swell BROAD COVES, with all their airs
Can't match the kids near Wapping stairs,
They are so down and knowing;
Of lowest life you'll see the best,
At Maces's, All-max, in the East;
So let's at once be going:
Come, toddle along, toddle along, etc.

BROAD-FAKING, *subs.* (card-sharpers'). — Playing at cards. Generally used, however, to denote 'work' of the three card and kindred descriptions.

BROAD-FENCER, *subs.* (thieves').—A 'k'rect card' seller at races. [From BROAD (*q.v.*), a card, + FENCE or FENCER, a 'tradesman.']

BROADS, *subs.* (general).—Playing cards.—*See* STOCK BROADS.

1789. GEO. PARKER, *Life's Painter*, p. 142. Who are continually looking out for flats, in order to do them upon the BROADS, that is *cards.*

1812. J. H. VAUX, *Flash Dict.* BROADS, cards; a person expert at which is said to be a good BROAD-PLAYER.

1834. HARRISON AINSWORTH, *Rookwood*, IV., ii. I nick the BROADS.

1877. *Five Years' Penal Servitude*, ch. iv., p. 262. He . . . became one of a gang who practised with the BROADS card-sharping and the 'confidence trick.'

BROADSMAN, *subs.* (common).—A card-sharper. [From BROADS = cards + MAN.] Formerly called BROAD COVE (*q.v.*). For synonyms, *see* ROOK.

1879. J. W. HORSLEY, 'Autobiography of a Thief,' in *Macm. Mag.*, XL., 502. BROADSMEN (card-sharpers).

1888. G. R. SIMS, in *Cass. Sat. Journal*, 31 March, p. 7. The BROADSMAN is a card-sharper.

BROADY, *subs.* (common).—1. Cloth. [A corruption of BROADCLOTH.]

1851. MAYHEW, *London Labour and London Poor*, I., p. 54. Gentlemen finding their own BROADY can be accommodated.

1883. *Daily Telegraph*, August 7, p. 6, col. 2. The prospectus further intimated that . . . gentlemen 'finding their own BROADY . . . could be accommodated.'

2. (thieves'.)—Anything worth stealing.—*See* BROADY WORKER.

BROADY WORKER, *subs.* (thieves').—A man who goes round selling vile shoddy stuff under the pretence that it is excellent material, which has been 'got on the cross,' *i.e.*, stolen.

BROCK, *verb* (Winchester College).—To bully; to tease; to badger. [BROCK is a north country and Hampshire name for a badger.] In French military schools this is called *faire une brimade* or *faire brimer*.

BROCKSTER, *subs.* (Winchester College).—A bully.—*See* BROCK.

BROGUES, *subs.* (Christ's Hospital).—Breeches. This is, in reality, an obsolete old English term which has survived among the 'Blues.'

BROILED or **BOILED CROW**. TO EAT BOILED CROW.—A newspaper editor, who is obliged by his 'party' or other outside influences, to advocate 'principles' different from those which he supported a short time before, is said to 'EAT BOILED CROW.' Originally the phrase was simply TO EAT CROW, and the following account is that currently accepted as to its derivation.

1888. *Atlanta Constitution.* During the unpleasantness between the States and England, there were located on opposite sides of the Niagara river a British and an American fort, and during an armistice the soldiers of both garrisons were accustomed to go hunting. Among the American troops was one long, lank, stuttering specimen of the genus Yankee, who would persist, in spite of orders to the contrary, in going across the river on his hunting expeditions. One day when on the Canada side he had had poor luck and got nothing, but resolved not to go back entirely empty handed. While passing through the grounds of an English gentleman, he spied a CROW, and, blazing away, brought it down. The Englishman had witnessed the shot and resolved to punish the offender for poaching on his private grounds. As the Yankee was loading his gun he approached, and, complimenting him on his good shot, asked to look at his gun. The unsuspecting Yankee handed it to him, and the Briton, bringing the gun to his shoulder and covering the Yankee, abused him for trespassing on his grounds, and ordered him, on pain of death, to take a bite out of the CROW. The soldier begged and pleaded, but to no avail. The Englishman had the drop on him, so he finally bit a piece from the breast of the CROW. The Englishman, after warning him to keep off his premises in the future, handed him back his gun and bade him clear out. No sooner was his rifle returned than he covered the Briton and ordered him to finish the CROW. Then it was the Englishman's turn to beg off, but the Yankee was firm, and the Englishman, with many a wry face, did succeed in downing several bites of the unsavoury bird. His wounded honour being appeased, the Yankee betook himself back to the fort. The Englishman the next day went to the American commander and told his version of the affair, and demanded that the culprit be punished. From the description given, the American officer knew that the offender must have been the stuttering soldier, and ordered him to be brought

before them. When he came in the captain asked him if he had ever seen the gentleman before. The Yankee shifted uneasily from one foot to the other, and, after several attempts, finally answered that he had. 'When and under what circumstances?' asked the officer. 'I d-dined with him y-y-yesterday, captin,' stuttered the soldier. The story goes that his wit saved the soldier from punishment.

BROKE. DEAD BROKE (*q.v.*)—STONE BROKE (*q.v.*), *adj.* (common).—Ruined; decayed; hard up—said of health or pecuniary circumstances. The French slang has *n'avoir pas un radis*, literally 'not to have a radish'; but for all synonyms, *see* DEAD-BROKE.

1887. G. R. SIMS, *How the Poor Live*, p. 16. 'How do you do when you're STONE BROKE?' I ask him. 'Well, sir, sometimes I comes across a gentleman as gives me a bob and starts me again.'

1889. *Pall Mall Gaz.*, Aug. 14. I see that Sullivan made 21,000 dols. out of his fight, but as he was 'DEAD BROKE' before the battle, there won't be much of it left. Nevertheless, Sullivan has received hundreds of begging letters from folks who want him to pay off mortgages on their homes or buy them houses and lots and things of that sort.

BROKEN FEATHER IN ONE'S WING, *subs. phr.* (popular).—A blot on one's character.

1880. MRS. OLIPHANT, *Phœbe, jun.*, ii., 6. If an angel were to walk about, Mrs. Sam Hurst would never rest till she had found out where he came from. And perhaps whether he had a BROKEN FEATHER IN HIS WING.

BROKEN-KNEED, *ppl. adj.* (common).—Said of a girl or woman who has been seduced. *Cf.*, ANKLE and BROKEN LEGGED; for synonyms, *see* DOCK and LEG. In French theatrical slang, *avoir mal aux genoux*.

BROKEN LEGGED, *ppl. adj.* (common).—Seduced.—*See* DOCK and LEG for synonyms.

BROLLY, *subs.* (general).—An umbrella. Term first used at Winchester, being subsequently adopted at both Oxford and Cambridge Universities.

1885. *Punch*, June 6, p. 273. Pair o' pattens and BROLLY are more in your line.

BRONCHO, *adj.* (American).—Unruly; wild; savage. The epithet is derived from BRONCHO, the name of the native horse of California, a somewhat tricky and uncertain quadruped. The term is familiarly applied to horses that buck and show other signs of vice. The Spanish signification of the word is rough and crabbed little beast, and in truth he deserves this name.

1888. FRANCIS, *Saddle and Mocassin.* Oh! I don't know. He'd been singing the music to 'em' (imitating them). Sam's too BRONCHO.

BRONCHO-BUSTER, *subs.* (American).—A breaker-in of BRONCHOS; also called a FLASH-RIDER. [From BRONCHO (*q.v.*) + BUST, in its slang sense of annihilate, or overcome, + ER.] These men make a profession of their business and perform really marvellous feats, riding with ease the most vicious and unbroken beasts that no ordinary rider would dare tackle. A favourite feat is to sit out the antics of a bucking-horse with silver half-dollars under each knee or in the stirrups under each foot. Their method of breaking-in may be described as the exercise of main force, it being a tussle as to which can hold out the longest, man or BRONCHO. The calling is a dangerous one, and a first-class BRONCHO-BUSTER can always command high wages and constant employment on large ranches.

BRONZE JOHN, *subs.* (American).—A Texas name for yellow fever; Englishmen commonly call it YELLOW JACK (*q.v.*)

BROOM, *subs.* (old).—1. *See* quot.

1815. SCOTT, *Guy Mannering*, ch. xxviii. 'The people got rusty about it, and would not deal, and they had bought so many BROOMS that——' *Ibid*, ch. xxxiii. (II., p. 96). What are you wanting here? Ye'll be come wi' a BROOM in your pocket frae Ellengowan? Got so many warrants out.

2. (harlotry.)—The female *pudenda*. The male *penis* is the BROOMSTICK. For synonyms, *see* MONOSYLLABLE.

Verb (old).—To run away. For synonyms, *see* AMPUTATE.

1821. MONCRIEFF, *Tom and Jerry*, p. 6. *Tom.* That will do—now then Dicky, mizzle!—be scarce!—BROOM! *Prime.* Wouldn't intrude a moment, gentlemen, good morning—order my carriage.

BROOMSTICK, *subs.* (athletic).—A sort of rough cricket bat, very narrow in the blade and all of one piece of wood.

TO JUMP THE BROOMSTICK—HOP THE BROOM—JUMP THE BESOM, *phr.* (common).—To live as man and wife without the legal tie. The allusion is to a *quasi* marriage ceremony performed by both parties jumping over a broomstick.

1811. POOLE, *Hamlet Travestied*, ii., 3. JUMP O'ER A BROOMSTICK, but don't make a farce on The marriage ceremonies of the parson.

1851. MAYHEW, *London Labour and London Poor*, I., p. 336. The old woman (who kept the ken), when any female, old or young, who had no tin, came into the kitchen, made up a match for her with some men. Fellows half-drunk had the old women. There was always a BROOMSTICK wedding. Without that ceremony a couple weren't looked on as man and wife.

1860. DICKENS, *Great Expectations*, ch. xlviii., p. 227. 'They both led tramping lives, and this woman in Gerrard St. here, had been married very young, OVER THE BROOMSTICK (as we say), to a tramping man, and was a perfect fury in point of jealousy.'

c. 18(79). *Broadside Ballad*, 'David Dove that fell in love.' By L. M. THORNTON.

The girl that I had hoped to hear
Pronounce my happy doom, sir,
Had bolted with a carpenter,
In fact HOPPED O'ER THE BROOM, sir.

BROOMSTICKS, *subs.* (old).—Worthless bail. For synonyms, *see* STRAW BAIL and *Cf.*, BAIL.

1812. J. H. VAUX, *Flash Dictionary.* Queer bail are persons of no repute, hired to bail a prisoner in any bailable case. These men are to be had in London for a trifling sum, and are called BROOMSTICKS.

BROSIER or **BROZIER**, *subs.* (Eton College).—A boy when he had spent all his pocket-money. [BROZIER is a Cheshire term for a bankrupt.] A French term for a bankrupt is *un déculotté*, *i.e.*, one unbreeched; also *un bauce* or *bausse fondu*.

BROZIERED, *ppl. adj.*—Cleaned out; done up; ruined; bankrupt.

1796. MERTON, *Way to get Married* (in Inchbald's 'British Theatre,' vol. XXVI). [The term is so used here].

BROZIER-MY-DAME, *verbal phr.* (Eton College).—Eating one out of house and home. At Eton, when a DAME (*q.v.*) keeps an unusually bad table, the boys agree together on a day to eat,

pocket, or waste everything eatable in the house. The censure is well understood, and the hint is generally effective.

1850. *Notes and Queries*, June 15, p. 44. I well remember the phrase BROZIER-MY-DAME, signifying to eat her out of house and home.

1888. REV. W. ROGERS, *Reminiscences*, p. 15. Etonians of my standing will remember John Francis Plumptre, one of the Fellows . . . I once behaved very shabbily to him, for I joined a conspiracy to 'BROZIER' HIM. There were ten or twelve of us [at breakfast], and we devoured everything within reach.

BROTHER-BLADE, *subs.* (old).—A soldier. Formerly BROTHER OF THE BLADE, *i.e.*, of the sword; a fellow-soldier. For synonyms, *see* MUDCRUSHER.

1785. GROSE, *Dictionary of the Vulgar Tongue.* BROTHER OF THE BLADE, a soldier.

1834. H. AINSWORTH, *Rookwood*, bk. IV., ch. ii. 'I heard some devilish good stories of you at D'Osyndar's t'other day; the fellow who told them to me little thought I was a BROTHER BLADE.'

BROTHER CHIP (provincial workmen's).—One of the same calling or trade; formerly a fellow carpenter.

1820. CLARE, *Poems of Rural Life, Familiar Epistle*, st. 3. And, BROTHER CHIP, I love ye dearly, poor as ye be!

BROTHER OF THE BRUSH, *subs. phr.* (old).—An artist; a house-painter.

1687. BP. CARTWRIGHT, in *Hist. Magd. Coll.* (Oxf. Hist. Soc.), 143. Pray make use of my BROTHER OF THE BRUSH. [M.]

1759. STERNE, *Tr. Shandy* (1793), I., 133. The honourable devices which the Pentagraphic BRETHEREN OF THE BRUSH have shewn in taking copies. [M.]

1833. BYRON, wks. (1846), p. 585, col. 1. A young American BROTHER OF THE BRUSH. [M.]

BROTHER OF THE BUNG, *subs. phr.* (old).—A brewer; one of the same trade. [BUNG here is used as an emblem of the trade of a brewer.]

BROTHER OF THE BUSKIN, *subs. phr.* (old).—A player; actor—one of the same profession. [BUSKIN is in allusion to the covering for the foot and leg (*cothurnus*) worn by actors in trag dy among the ancients; in contrast to the sock (*soccus*) worn by comedians. Stage BUSKINS had very thick soles to give an appearance of height. Hence BUSKIN as symbolical of tragedy, but used in the phrase BROTHER OF THE BUSKIN in a transferred and general sense.] Quoted by Grose [1785]. *Cf.*, BARN-STORMER and BOOTH-BURSTER.

BROTHER OF THE COIF, *subs.* (old).—A serjeant-at-law. [The coif was a close-fitting cap worn by the serjeants-at-law—hence the term.] Quoted by Grose [1785].

BROTHER OF THE GUSSET, *subs.* (old).—A pimp or PONCE (*q.v.*). For synonyms, *see* BULLY.

BROTHER OF THE QUILL, *subs. phr.* (old).—An author. [QUILL = pen.] For synonyms, *see* INK-SLINGER.

1754. B. MARTIN, *Eng. Dict.* (2 ed.). BROTHER OF THE QUILL, an author, one of the same profession.

BROTHER OF THE STRING, *subs. phr.* (old).—A fiddler. [A reference to the violin or fiddle as a stringed instrument.]

BROTHER OF THE WHIP, *subs. phr.* (old).—A coachman, the whip being taken, as it were, as an insignia of office.

1756. *The World*, No. 207. He . . . had always greased my heels himself, and upon every one of my birthdays, had treated all his BROTHER WHIPS at his own expence.

1849. T. MILLER, in *Gabarni in London*, p. 39. He is very kind to any poor BROTHER OF THE WHIP whom he sees tugging up-hill in vain, with a weighty load and an ill-fed team.

BROTHER-SMUT, *subs. phr.* (popular).—A term of familiarity. 'DITTO, BROTHER or SISTER SMUT,' *tu quoque*.

BROTHER STARLINGS, *subs.* (old).—Men who cohabit with the same mistress.

1785. GROSE, *Dictionary of the Vulgar Tongue*. BROTHER STARLING . . . one who . . . builds in the same nest.

BROTH OF A BOY, *subs. phr.* (Irish originally, but now common).—A jolly good fellow. *Cf.*, BRICK. [The term is thought to originate from the Irish *Broth*, passion — *Brotha*, passionate, spirited — its meaning being, 'He's a lad of spirit,' though it may come from the ancient Cornish name for the mastiff—*brath*. Hence a BROTH OF A BOY would then mean 'a stout dog of a boy—robust.']

1819-24. BYRON, *Don Juan*, c. viii., st. 24. But Juan was quite A BROTH OF A BOY, a thing of impulse and a child of song.

1877. BESANT AND RICE, *Son of Vulcan*, ch. xx. You ought to have been a preacher and a boy. Faith, and a BROTH OF A BOY, and a BROTH of a preacher you'd have made.

BROUGHTONIAN, *subs.* (old). — A bruiser; boxer; pugilist. [From Broughton, once the best boxer of his day.]

BROWN, *subs.* (common).—1. A halfpenny. [Probably an allusion to the colour of the coin in question.] For synonyms of money generally, *see* ACTUAL.

1812. J. H. VAUX, *Flash Dict.* BROWNS and whistlers, bad halfpence and farthings.

1821. W. T. MONCRIEFF, *Tom and Jerry*, Act ii., Sc. 3. *Bob.* Now then for the stumpy. (*Searching about in his pockets for the money.*) My tanners are like young colts; I'm obliged to hunt 'em into a corner, afore I can get hold on 'em—there!—hand us over three BROWNS out of that 'ere tizzy; and tip us the heavy. (*Landlord receives money, and delivers porter.*)

1837. BARHAM, *I. L.* (*Black Mousquetaire*).
The magic effect of a hand of crowns
Upon people whose pockets boast nothing but BROWNS.

1851. MAYHEW, *London Labour and London Poor*, III., p. 57. If I takes a hat round, they has a plate, and they gets sovereigns where we has only BROWNS. *Ibid.* We keeps it up for half an hour or an hour . . . if the BROWNS tumble in well.

1853. WHYTE MELVILLE, *Digby Grand*, ch. iv. A shower of BROWNS, the coppers mingled with silver, from our private box, rewards their exertions.

c. 1884. *Broadside Ballad*, 'Jimmy Johnson's Holiday.'
But Violet, the Margate pet,
Who always call'd him Teaser,
Said 'She would stick like mortar'd brick,
While Johnson had a BROWN.'

2. (old.)—Porter. [Qy. an abbreviation of 'Brown Stout.']

1820. Glossary at end of Corcoran's *The Fancy*. BROWN, porter; HEAVY BROWN, stout.

Verb.—1. A variant of 'to do brown,' *i.e.*, to do to perfection; to get the better of. [The simile is obviously taken from the browning process which meat undergoes during roasting.]—*See* DO BROWN.

2. To understand; comprehend.

To DO BROWN, *verbal phr.* (common).—To do well; also 'to take in'; deceive; to exceed bounds. *Cf.*, BROWN, *verb*, sense 1. French equivalents for 'to allow oneself to be DONE BROWN' are *godancer* and *être floué*.—*See* second quotation for variation in usage.

a. 1600. JOHN BON, 162 in Hazl. *E. P. P.*, iv., 16. Ha! BROWNE DONE. [M.]

1828. JON. BEE, *Picture of London*, p. 5. 'Those who consider themselves BROWN to every move upon the board' of actual life.

1837. BARHAM, *I. L.* (*The Execution*). 'Why, they'd laugh at and quiz us all over the town, We are all of us DONE so uncommonly BROWN!'

1854. *Harper's Monthly*, January.
'And some of the greenhorns
Resolved upon flight,
And vamosed the ranch
In a desperate plight;
While those who succeeded
In reaching the town,
Confessed they were DONE,
Most exceedingly BROWN.'

1861. *Times* (on American affairs).
John Bull, slyly winkin', then said unto he:
'My dear *Times*, my old covey, go pitch into he;
Let us wallop great Doodle now when he is down;
If we wallops him well, we will DO HIM UP BROWN.'

1876. HINDLEY, *Life and Adventures of a Cheap Jack*, p. 267. I was once done myself with some pigs—I! and DONE BROWN too, and at a time when I ought to have known better.

BROWN BESS, *subs.* (rhyming slang).—1. Yes.

2. (military.)—The old regulation musket. Considerable discussion has taken place over the origin of this term. It first appears in Grose [1785], but the term 'brown musquet' occurs at the beginning of the eighteenth century [1708]. The following suggested derivation appeared in *N. and Q.* [2 S., v., p. 259]. BROWN BESS, in its primary meaning, is equivalent to brown barrel. *Bus*, in Dutch is the barrel of a gun; in Low Germ. *büsse*, in Swed. *byssa*. Hence our English BESS as applied to a gun-barrel. (Conf. in Med. Latin—*bus-bas fragor scloporum et certaminis.*) The Dutch *bus* appears often in composition. *Hand-bus*, a pistol; literally a hand-barrel. *Bus-schieter*, a gunner; literally a barrel-shooter. We have the Dutch *bus* (a barrel) in three English names of fire-arms: namely arque*buse*, *obus*, blunder-*buss*. At the first of these three, *arquebuse*, we must look a little more closely would we trace the term BROWN BESS to its primæval source. The most formidable of cross-bows before fire-arms came into general use, was one which shot a ball or pellet from a *barrel*. Specimens may yet be seen. Now this was the original *arquebuse* (*i.e.*, *arc-bus*, or *arc-et-bus*, bow and barrel). In process of time as gunpowder came into use, the *arc* disappeared, and the *buss* or *barrel* remained. Hence *arquebuse*, though it properly implies a bow fitted with a tube or barrel, came into use as the old appellation of a soldier's firelock. And hence the name of BESS (*bus*, *büsse* or *byssa*), which the musket has borne more recently. BESS or *bus* is the last syllable of the old *arquebuse* or *harquebus* cut off for separate use, just as in the more recent instance of *bus* from *omnibus*. The barrels of firelocks were sometimes BROWNED. Sometimes, however, they were required to be kept bright.

Could we ascertain who first in mercy ordained the browning of the barrel, we might have some prospect of ascertaining the first introduction of the term BROWN BESS. Doubtless it was some hero of the fight, not of the field-day. For a further illustration of the term BROWN BESS, it may be proper to remark that in Northumberland, according to Halliwell, a gun is known by the not very elegant title of *black-bitch*. Now like *bus* in Dutch, *büchse* is in German a gun-barrel. ('*Büchse*, 2, *ein eisernes Rohr zum schiessen*,' *an iron tube for shooting*.) May we not infer, therefore, that *black-bitch* was originally '*black büchse*,' *i.e.*, *black barrel*, in conformity with *brown barrel* or BROWN BESS? 'Formerly,' says Zedler, 'and before the invention of gunpowder, *arquebuse* signified *a bow with a barrel*' (*Bogen Büchse*), which is the literal meaning of the word. Hotten, however, says it is much more likely that the phrase is derived from the fact that 'the soldier is wedded to his weapon,' and some colour is given to this alternative derivation by the fact that the Dutch soldier, mindful of all the care he has to bestow upon his gun, calls it his wife—*mijn geweer is mijn vrouw*. French soldiers call their weapon *la clarinette de cinq pieds*.

1785. GROSE, *Dictionary of the Vulgar Tongue*. BROWN BESS, a soldier's firelock.

1820. COOMBE, *Dr. Syntax*, Tour II., ch. ii.
Religion Jack did never profess,
Till he had shoulder'd old BROWN BESS.

1854. WHYTE MELVILLE, *General Bounce*, ch. xi. The British soldier, with his clothing and accoutrements, . . . — not to mention BROWN BESS, his mainstay and dependence—nothing punishes him so much as wet.

1877. *Chambers' Journal*, No. 720. Such may have been the case in the days of BROWN BESS, but a spinning conical ball from the Martini-Henry will pierce the largest crocodile.

3. (old.)—A prostitute. For synonyms, *see* BARRACK-HACK.

1631. DORE, *Polydorun*. Things proffered and easie to come by diminish themselves in reputation and price, for how full of pangs and dotage is a wayling lover, for it may be some BBOWN BESSIE.

To HUG BROWN BESS, *verbal phr.* (old). — To serve as a private soldier.

BROWN GEORGE, *subs.* (old). — 1. Explained by quotations.

1837. BARHAM, *Ingoldsby L.*, 3 S. 'Jerry Jarvis's Wig.' He looked disdainfully at the wig; it had once been a comely jasey enough, of the colour of over-baked ginger-bread, one of the description commonly known during the latter half of the last century by the name of a BROWN GEORGE.

1882. *Globe*, 24 July, p. 2, col. 1. The King [George III.] wore a brown wig . . . known popularly a century ago as BROWN GEORGE.

2. (common.)—A jug; generally of brown earthenware. *Cf.*, BLACK-JACK.

1861. HUGHES, *Tom Brown at Oxford*, ch. xxiv. He . . . stood behind his oak, holding his BROWN GEORGE, or huge earthenware receptacle, half full of dirty water, in which his bedmaker had been washing up his tea-things.

1881. BESANT AND RICE, *Chap. of the Fleet*, pt. II., ch. iii. His country brother might have been seen at the Crown, over a pipe and a BROWN GEORGE full of strong October.

3. (old.)—A coarse brown loaf; or hard biscuit.

1653. URQUHART, *Rabelais*, bk. IV. Author's Prologue. The devil of one musty crust of a BROWN GEORGE the poor boys had to scour their grinders with.

1693. DRYDEN, *Persius*, V., 215.
Cubb'd in a cabin, on a mattrass laid,
On a BROWN GEORGE, with lousy swabbers fed.

BROWNIE, *subs.* (nautical). — The polar bear.

BROWN JANET, *subs.* (nautical).—A knapsack.

BROWN JOE, *intj.* (rhyming slang).—No. *Cf.*, BROWN BESS for 'yes.'

BROWN-PAPERMEN, *subs.* (thieves').—Low gamblers.—*See* quot.

1851. H. MAYHEW, *London Lab. and Lon. Poor*, vol. I., p. 502. 'But the Little Nick is what we call only 'BROWN PAPERMEN,' low gamblers—playing for pence, and 1s. being a great go.'

BROWN STONE, *subs.* (American thieves').—Beer. For synonyms, *see* SWIPES.

BROWN TALK, *subs.* (common).—Conversation of an exceedingly 'proper' character, Quakerish. Compare BLUE.

BROWSE, *verb* (Marlborough and Royal Military Academy).—To idle; loll; take things easy. [A transferred sense of the legitimate word—to eat lazily.]

Adj.—*See* foregoing. 'A BROWSE morning,' *i.e.*, one in which there is little work.

BRUISE, *verb* (prize-fighters').—1. To fight; box—generally with the idea of mauling.

BRUISE ALONG, *verbal phr.* (hunting).—To pound along.

1865. *Dublin University Magazine*, II., 19. A majority of those who follow them have . . . no notion of hunting, but go BRUISING ALONG.

1872. *Anteros*, xii., p. 110. The baron hunted his five days . . . BRUISING ALONG determinedly.

BRUISER, *subs.* (pugilistic).—1. A prize-fighter; a boxer. [From BRUISE, to maul, + ER.]

1744. Nov. 26, WALPOLE, *Lett. to Mann* (1833), II., 57. He let into the pit great numbers of bear-garden BRUISERS (that is the term), to knock down everybody that hissed.

1753. FOOTE, *Englishman in Paris*, Act i. Dick Daylight and Bob Breadbasket the BRUISERS.

1830. S. WARREN, *Diary of a Late Physician*, ch. xii. The man last named was short in stature, but of a square iron build; and it needed only a glance at his posture to see he was a scientific, perhaps a thorough-bred BRUISER.

1846-48. THACKERAY, *V. Fair*, ch. xi. At college he pulled stroke-oar in the Christchurch boat, and had thrashed all the best BRUISERS of the 'town.'

1860. THACKERAY, *Philip*, ch. xlii. A jolly wag, a fellow of indifferent character, a frequenter of all the alehouses in the neighbourhood, and rather celebrated for his skill as a BRUISER.

1880. JAS. GREENWOOD, *Flyfaker's Hotel*, in *Odd People in Odd Places*, p. 58. Nearly every one seemed to have some little job or other that was necessary to be done at this almost last moment for the business of to-morrow; even one of the two villanous-looking BRUISERS had. They were of the very lowest of the 'rough' type—broken-nosed, besotted, pimple-visaged, and unwholesome-looking fellows, whose foul and blasphemous language seemed to pollute the pestilent air of the place more than anything else that contributed thereto.

2. (thieves'.)—A prostitute's bully or fancy man. For synonyms, *see* BULLY.

3. (common.)—One fond of fighting. *Cf.*, CHUCKER-OUT, and next sense.

4. (American.) — A generic name in large cities for a rowdy or bully. Sometimes, however, the term has been limited in its application to a particular band

of ruffians. This was the case once in Baltimore.

Bruising, *verbal subs.* (prize-fighters'). — Fighting with the fists; boxing.

1751. Smollett, *Peregrine Pickle*, ch. c. The combatants were, in point of strength and agility, pretty equally matched; but the jailer had been regularly trained to the art of bruising.

1855. Thackeray, *Newcomes*, ch. x. At that time the Sunday newspapers contained many and many exciting reports of boxing matches. Bruising was considered a fine manly old English custom.

1860. Thackeray, *Philip*, ch. xxxv. Mugford always persisted that he could have got the better of his great hulking sub-editor, who did not know the use of his fists. In Mugford's youthful time, bruising was a fashionable art.

Ppl. adj. (hunting).—That pounds along.

1872. *Anteros*, by the author of *Guy Livingstone*, I., p. 207. He was a good second-rate shot, and a fair, though by no means bruising rider to hounds. *Ibid*, p. 234. There were not a few admirers of his bruising style, etc.

Brum, *subs.* (old).—1. A counterfeit coin. [Contracted form of Brummagem (*q.v.*).] The term appears to have been given specially to some counterfeit groats [about 1691].

2. (common.) — Something counterfeit; not genuine. [A contraction of Brummagem (*q.v.*).]

1883. *Daily Telegraph*, July 9, p. 3, col. 2. One [earring] might be gold, and the other a Brum, though exactly alike.

3. (common.)—Copper money struck by Boulton and Watt at their works at Soho, Birmingham.

1787. J. West, *Trip to Richmond*, in Ashton's *Eighteenth Century Waifs*, p. 133. My silver I chang'd for a handful of Brums.

4. (common.)—An inhabitant of Birmingham.

1876. Hindley, *Life and Adventures of a Cheap Jack*, p. 321. For Nottingham is a rare place for good eating; here you may buy anything to eat of the commonest person, or in the commonest place with confidence that it is good, clean, and wholesome, very different to dirty Birmingham and the Brums.

Adj. (Winchester College).—Mean; poor; stingy. A superlative form is dead brum. [There are two derivations suggested; viz. (1) from *bruma* = winter; and (2) traditional in 'College' that it is an abbreviated form of *brevissimum*.] A popular French equivalent, used both as a substantive and adjective, is *rapiat*.

Brumby, *subs.* (Australian).—A wild horse. An Antipodean counterpart of the American 'broncho.'

Brummagem, *subs.* (popular).—1. A nickname for Birmingham.

1862. *Cornhill*, Nov., p. 648. We have just touched for a rattling stake of sugar (*i.e.*, a large stake of money) at Brum.

2. (old.)—Base money of various denominations has been so called—especially groats in 17th century—hence its application to anything spurious or unreal—as in adjectival sense. —*See* also Brummagem buttons and Brums.

1691. G. Miege, *New State Eng.*, 235. Bromicham, particularly noted a few years ago for the counterfeit groats made here, and from hence dispersed all over the kingdom. [M.]

1754. B. Martin, *Eng. Dict.*, 2 ed. Bromidgham, money of base metal.

1834. Southey, *The Doctor*, ch. cxl. He picked it up, and it proved to be a Brummejam of the coarsest and clumsiest kind, with a head on each side.

Adj. — Counterfeit; unreal; sham; showy; pretentious.—*See substantive*, senses 1 and 2.

1637. *Calendar Dom. St. Papers*, 105. Those swords which he . . . pretends to be blades of his owne makeing are all Bromedgham blades and forraine blades.

1686. D'Urfey, *Commonwealth of Women*, I., i. A Brummingham, son of a wh—, affront the Noble Admiral!

1866. G. Eliot, *Felix Holt*, ch. v. 'The most of the middle class are as ignorant as the working people about everything that doesn't belong to their own Brummagem life.'

1883. *Echo*, March 28, p. 1, col. 5. There is little of a Brummagem character about the municipal, parochial, and philanthropic work of Birmingham, whatever we may think of some of her industrial productions.

Brummagem Buttons, *subs.* (common).—Counterfeit coin.

1836. Dickens, *Posthumous Papers of the Pickwick Club*, I., p. 11. Bad silver, Brummagem buttons, etc.

1873. *Saturday Review*, Nov., p. 661. They [Brummagem buttons] were marvellously inexpensive, and being such ingenious imitations of the spade guineas and half-guineas then current that many Englishmen might have failed to detect the difference; they must have been of very great 'use to the Indians' indeed.

Brummish, *adj.* (common). — Doubtful; counterfeit. [From Brum (*q.v.*) + ish.]

1805. G. Colman, *John Bull Brit. Theat.*, 55. Two guineas . . . one seems light and t'other looks a little brummish. [M.]

Brums, *subs.* (Stock Exchange).—London and North Western Stock. (Formerly London and Birmingham Ry.).

1887. Atkin, *House Scraps*.
We kneel at the feet of our 'Nancys,'
We load them with 'cottons' and 'tapes.'
If anything tickles our fancy,
We buy them Brums, 'Caleys' or 'Apes.'

Brush.—1. *See* Brother of the brush.

2. *subs.* (old).—A hasty departure. For analogous terms, *see* Amputate.

1750. Fielding, *Tom Jones*, bk. VIII., ch. xii. 'I reminded him, not without blushing, of my having no money. He answered, 'That signifies nothing, score it behind the door, or make a bold brush, and take no notice.'

3. (old.) — A person who decamps hastily, or who evades his creditors.

1748. T. Dyche, *Dictionary* (5 ed.). Brush (v.) . . . also a canting term for one who goes off privately, or runs away from his creditors, or with stolen goods.

Verb (Christ's Hospital).—1. To flog.

2. (old.)—To have sexual intercourse. For synonyms, *see* Ride.

3. (old.)—To run away; to decamp. Also to brush off. For synonyms, *see* Amputate.

1690. B. E., *Dict. Cant. Crew.* Brush, to Fly or Run away. [M.]

1706. E. Coles, *Eng. Dict.* Brush, *c.*, run away.

1764. A. Murphy, *No One's Enemy but his Own*, Act ii. Rascal, says my Master, do as I bid you, and so off he brushed to the tune of an old song.

1776. Foote, *Bankrupt*, I. But I must brush off, for here comes my lady.

1837. Barham, *Ingoldsby Legends* (1877), 204. And one Sergeant Matcham had brush'd with the dibs.

1837. Barham, *I. L.* (*Dead Drummer*). One of their drummers, and one Sergeant Matcham, Had brush'd with the dibs, and they never could catch'em.

Brusher, *subs.* (old). — A full glass.

2. (old.)—*See* quotation.

1748. T. Dyche, *Dictionary* (5 ed.). Brusher (s.) . . . also one that gets or steals away privately.

3. (common and schools'.)—A schoolmaster.

4. (American.)—To humbug by flattery.

Brushing up a flat, *phr.* (general). — Using mealy-mouthed words, or, to employ other slang equivalents, 'laying it on thick,' 'soft soaping one.'

Brute, *subs.* (University). — *See* quot.

1868. Brewer, *Phrase and Fable*, s. v. Brute, in Cambridge University slang, is a man who has not yet matriculated. The play is evident. A 'man,' in college phrase, is a collegian; and as matriculation is the sign and seal of acceptance, a scholar before that ceremony is not a 'man,' and therefore only a 'biped brute.'

Brydport Dagger.—*See* Bridport dagger.

B. T. I., *phr.* (American). — An abbreviation of a big thing on ice. These curtailments of slang phrases are not infrequent in America, and among others may be mentioned p.d.q.; o.k.; n.g. and q.k., etc. (*q.v.*).

Bub, *subs.* (old).—1. Strong drink of any kind, but usually applied to malt liquor. [It is suggested that this term is onamatopoetic, an imitation of the sound of drinking; others, however, incline to regard the word as a derivative of the Latin *bib-ĕre*, to drink. Sometimes spelt bubb.] A common expression for eating and drinking is 'to take bub and grub,' a French equivalent for which is *se caresser l'Angoulême*.

1671. R. Head, *English Rogue*, pt. I., ch. iv., p. 36 (1874). In a short time these four return'd laden with bub and food.

1748. Dodsley, *Collection of Poems*, III., 262.
Tho' beef twice boil'd his meal, with P—n's bub,
And sixpence chang'd defrays the frugal club.

1839. H. Ainsworth, *Jack Sheppard*, ep. II., ch. xi. 'Och! many a mug o' bubb have I drained wi' the landlord.'

2. (common.)—A woman's breast; generally used in the plural—bubbies (*q.v.*).

3. (old.)—A brother.

4. (American.)—Also bubby. A term of affection applied to a little boy. [Said to have originated in Pennsylvania from the German *Bube*.] Likewise used figuratively as a familiar mode of address.

1872. S. Clemens ('Mark Twain'), *Roughing It*. The cayote turns smiles blandly upon him once more, and with a something about it which seems to say: 'Well, I shall have to tear myself away from you, bub—business is business, and it will not do for me to be fooling along this way all day.'

1888. *San Francisco Weekly Examiner*. When she was ready to go home, she did so without carriage or baby. Shortly after bubby kicked up high jinks, and the joker clerk was sent for to take him away.

5. (old.) — An abbreviated form of bubble, *subs.*

1690. B. E., *Dict. Cant. Crew.* Bub or bubble, one that is cheated. [M.]

Verb (old).—1. To drink.—*See substantive.*

1671. R. Head, *English Rogue*, pt. I., ch. vi., p. 54 (1874). We straight betook ourselves to the *Boozing Ken*; and having bubb'd rumly, we concluded an everlasting friendship.

2. (old.)—To bribe; to cheat. *Cf.*, Bubble.

1719. D'Urfey, *Pills*, II., 54. Another makes Racing a Trade . . . And many a Crimp Match has made, By bubbing another Man's Groom.

Bubber, *subs.* (old).—1. A hard drinker; a confirmed tippler. [From bub (*q.v.*) = drink + er.] A synonymous French term is *un bibassier*, but for analogous terms generally, *see* Elbow crooker.

1653. Middleton, *Sp. Gipsy*, ii., 1. Though I am no mark in respect of a huge butt, yet I can tell you great bubbers have shot at me. [There is a play in the word 'butt.']

1674. R. Head, *Canting Acad.*, 191. A bubber . . . goes to the Alehouse, and steals there the Plate.

1785. Grose, *Dictionary of the Vulgar Tongue.* Bubber, . . . a great drinker. A thief that steals plate from publick houses.

2. (old.)—A drinking bowl. *Cf.*, derivation of previous sense.

1690. B. E., *Dict. Cant. Crew.* Bubber, a drinking Bowl; also a great Drinker, and he that used to steal Plate from Publick-houses.

1785. Grose, *Dictionary of the Vulgar Tongue.* Bubber, a drinking bowl, etc.

3. (old.) — A public house thief.—*See* quotation 1690, sense 2; also mentioned by Grose [1785].

4. (American.)—A nickname for an old woman with large pendulous breasts. Rarely heard.

1848. Bartlett, *Americanisms.* Bubber. A stout or stoutly mammalated old woman. Used in Salem, Mass., in 1820, and since. 'Bubber Jones.' (Fr. *poitron*, old woman; Old Fr. *pect. poitron*; Lat. *pectus*, the breast.)

Bubbies, *subs.* (common). — A woman's breasts. An old term of which the derivation is somewhat doubtful, though it may be noted that the ancient cant has bub in the sense of 'to drink,' and also as an abbreviated form of bubby. Arber says that 'bu bu' is the cry of a child needing its mother's milk. —For synonyms, *see* Dairies.

1686. D'Urfey, *New Poems* (1690), 206.
The Ladies here may without Scandal shew,
Face or white bubbies, to each ogling Beau.

1693. Congreve, *Old Batchelor*, Act v., Sc. 7. Did not her eyes twinkle, and her mouth water? Did not she pull up her little bubbies?

1712. Arbuthnot, *Hist. of John Bull*, pt. III., ch. viii. 'To see a handsome, brisk, genteel, young fellow so much governed by a doating old woman! Why don't you go and suck the bubby?'

1715. Vanbrugh, *Country House*, II., v. He talked to me of you, and said you had the charmingest bubbies.

1748. Dodsley, *Collection of Poems*, III., 191. And snowy bubbies pull'd above the stays.

1754. B. Martin, *Eng. Dict.*, 2 ed. Bubbys, a woman's breasts.

Bubbing, *subs.* (old). — Drinking; tippling.

1678. *Poor Robin's Char. of Scold*, 6. She clamours at him so long . . . which makes him seek Bubbing-schools to hide himself in from her fury. [M.]

Bubble, *subs.* (old).—A dupe; gull; also caravan (*q.v.*); and rook (*q.v.*). Grose thinks from the party cheated being like an air-bubble filled with words which are only wind instead of real property. Also apparently used of anything not genuine. Applied to persons, it is older than appears from Murray.

1598. Shakspeare, *All's Well*, iii., vi., 5. *Sec. Lord.* On my life, my lord, a bubble. *Ber.* Do you think I am so far deceived in him?

1688. Shadwell, *Sq. of Alsatia*, III., in wks. (1720) IV., 62. This kinsman a most silly bubble first, and afterwards a betrayer of young heirs.

1697. Vanbrugh, *Provoked Wife*, V., iii. If her conduct has put a trick upon her virtue, her virtue's the bubble, but her husband's the loser.

1711. SWIFT, *Conduct of the Allies.* We are thus become the dupes and BUBBLES of Europe.

1712. ARBUTHNOT, *History of John Bull*, pt. II., ch. iii. He has been my BUBBLE [tool] these twenty years; and to my certain knowledge, understands no more of his own affairs than a child in swaddling clothes.

1750. FIELDING, *Tom Jones*, bk. I., ch. vii. 'This would be to own herself the meer tool and BUBBLE of the man.'

1788. G. A. STEVENS, *Adv. of a Speculist*, I., 69. He persuades his BUBBLE, that he will insure him a certain safe way of getting a sum of money.

1795. R. CUMBERLAND, *The Jew*, Act iii., Sc. 2. If he attempts to raise money upon expectancies, be at their peril who are fools enough to trust him: No prudent man will be his BUBBLE.

1805. G. BARRINGTON, *New London Spy* (4 ed.), p. 24. The shame of being thought a BUBBLE, and exposed to the town, frequently prevents gentlemen from making use of the statute provided in such cases.

Verb (old).—To cheat; humbug; delude as with BUBBLES; to overreach. *Cf.*, *substantive* sense.

1664. ETHERIDGE, *Comical Revenge*, II., iii., in wks. (1704), 24. I believe he's gone down to Receive money; 'twere an excellent design to BUBBLE him.

1685. DRYDEN, *Prol. to Albion and Albanius*, 23.
Freedom and zeal have choused you o'er and o'er;
Pray give us leave to BUBBLE you once more.

1711. *Spectator*, No 89. That she has BUBBLED him out of his youth . . . and that he verily believes she will drop him in his old age, if she can find her account in another.

1752. FIELDING, *Amelia*, bk. XI., ch. iv. He . . . actually BUBBLED several of their money by undertaking to do them services, which, in reality, were not within his power.

1777. SHERIDAN, *Trip to Scarborough*, Act ii. Help the gentleman with a chair, and carry him to my house presently—that's the properest place—[*aside*]—to BUBBLE him out of his money.

1788. G. A. STEVENS, *Adv. of a Speculist*, I., 75. And this was the language which the pretenders to the Philosopher's Stone used to BUBBLE their pigeons with.

1880. MCCARTHY, *Own Times*, III., xli., 235. Some critics declared . . . that the French Emperor had BUBBLED him [Mr. Cobden].

BUBBLEABLE, *adj.* (old).—That can be duped; gullible. [A very rare form from BUBBLE, to cheat, + ABLE.]

1669. *Nicker Nicked*, in *Hart. Misc.* (ed. Park), II., 109. If the winner be BUBBLEABLE, they will insinuate themselves into his acquaintance, and civilly invite him to drink a glass of wine; wheedle him into play, and win all his money.

BUBBLE AND SQUEAK, *subs. phr.* (common).—A compound of cold meat fried up with potatoes and greens. [From the hissing sound produced by the frying; originally nautical.]

1785. GROSE, *Dictionary of the Vulgar Tongue.* BUBBLE AND SQUEAK, beef and cabbage fried together; it is so called from its bubbling up and squeaking whilst over the fire.

1786-89. WOLCOT ('P. Pindar'), *Lousiad*, ch. i., line 366.
Such is the sound (the simile's not weak)
Form'd by what mortals BUBBLE call, and SQUEAK,
When 'midst the frying-pan, in accents savage,
The beef so sorely quarrels with the cabbage.

1853. LYTTON, *My Novel*, bk. VIII., ch. viii. 'Rank and title! BUBBLE AND SQUEAK! No, not half so good as BUBBLE AND SQUEAK. English beef and good cabbage.'

BUBBLE BUFF, *subs.* (old). — A bailiff.

BUBBLE COMPANY, *subs.* (common).—A swindling association, enterprise or project. [From BUBBLE, to cheat, + company.] The South Sea BUBBLE will occur to mind in this connection.

1754. B. MARTIN, *Eng. Dict.* (2 ed.). BUBBLE . . . 5 (in Commerce), a cant name given to certain projects for raising money on imaginary grounds.

1880. HAWLEY SMART, *Social Sinners*, ch. xix. 'My inheritance disappears as if it had been invested in a BUBBLE COMPANY.'

BUBBLED, *ppl. adj.* (old).—Gulled; deceived; befooled. [From BUBBLE, to cheat, + ED.]

a. 1688. OLDHAM, *Wks. and Rem.* (1686), 66. BUBLED Monarchs are at first beguil'd . . . at last depos'd, and kill'd. [M.]

1701. DEFOE, *True Born Englishman*, Introd.
Who shall this BUBBLED nation disabuse,
While they, their own felicities refuse?

1889. *Gentleman's Mag.*, June, p. 598. Towards the end of the century [xvii] a person easily gulled, or BUBBLED was known as a 'caravan,' but earlier the term 'rook,' which is now restricted to a cheat or sharper, appears to have been applied to the person cheated.

BUBBLING SQUEAK, *subs.* (army).—Hot soup.

BUBBLY JOCK, *subs.* (old Scotch).—1. A turkey-cock; a 'gobbler.' [Probably in allusion to the cry of the bird.]

1785. GROSE, *Dictionary of the Vulgar Tongue.* BUBBLY JOCK, a turkey-cock.

1843. THACKERAY, *Irish Sketch Book*, ch. xv. He took but one glass of water to that intolerable deal of BUBBLY JOCK. . . . Three turkey-wings and a glass of water.

1877. BESANT AND RICE, *Son of Vulcan*, pt. II., ch. xviii. Puffing his cheeks like some infuriated BUBBLY JOCK in a stable-yard.

2. (common.) — A stupid boaster.

3. (popular.)—A pert, conceited, pragmatical fellow; a prig; a cad.

1883. G. A. SALA, *Living London*, p. 113. Mr. Benjamin Bunny (Mr. J. L. Toole) is the good-natured husband of a pretty young wife (Miss Winifred Emery). Mr. Bunny is, to use a Scotticism, 'sair owerhanded,' not by a 'BUBBLY JOCK,' but by his wife's aunt.

BUBBY.—*See* BUB and BUBBIES.

BUCCO, *subs.* (American thieves').—A dandy. [A corruption of BUCK (*q.v.*).]

BUCK, *subs.* (common).—1. In the first instance a man of spirit or gaiety of conduct; later a fop, a dandy. [A transferred sense of BUCK, the male of the fallow deer.] In the form 'old BUCK' it is merely a familiar mode of address. The epithet, as applied to a man about town, is somewhat obsolete; MASHER, DUDE, and SWELL having taken its place. *Cf.*, BLOOD.

1725. *New Cant. Dict.* BUCK, as a bold BUCK, is sometimes used to signify a forward daring Person of either Sex.

1752. FIELDING, *Amelia*, bk. X., ch. ii. A large assembly of young fellows, whom they call BUCKS.

1846-48. THACKERAY, *V. Fair*, ch. vi. She had sate by him on the box of his open carriage (a most tremendous BUCK he was, he sat there, serene, in state, driving his greys).

1889. *Answers*, Feb. 9. The ancient BUCK was last seen (at the age of eighty-four) wearing a wig, a pair of stays, 'plumpers,' rouge, and padding, and he daily anointed his face with a compound called 'skin-tightener.' 'Skin-tightener' removes wrinkles, and after the face has been washed with 'bloom of roses,' the wearer can strut forth with the consciousness that all the world takes him for a quarter of a century younger than he is.

2. (common.)—An unlicensed cabdriver. Apparently also applied to a sham fare.—*See* last quotation.

1851-61. H. MAYHEW, *London Lab. and Lon. Poor*, vol. III., p. 362. The long-day men are the parties who mostly employ the BUCKS . . . they are glad to avail themselves of the services of a BUCK for some hours at the end of the day. *Ibid.* The BUCKS are unlicensed cabdrivers, who are employed by those who have a license to take charge of the cab while the regular drivers are at their meals or enjoying themselves.

1865. *Morning Star*, 14 Sept. What is the prisoner? Constable: He is a BUCK, who hangs about an omnibus stand. [M.]

1887. *Daily News*, 5 October, 5, 4. At Bow Street something was further heard of the BUCK. This person . . . is the sham fare whom a cabby drives past the police in order to get up to the theatre doors out of his proper turn, and so increase his chance of securing a legitimate fare.

3. (old.)—A sixpence. [Thought to be a corruption of FYEBUCK (*q.v.*).] The word is rarely used by itself, but generally denotes the sixpence attached to shillings in reference to cost, as, 'three and a BUCK,' three shillings and sixpence. For synonyms, *see* BENDER.

1885. *Household Words*, June 20, p. 155. 'BUCK' is most likely a corruption of 'fyebuck,' a slang name for sixpence, which is now almost, if not altogether, obsolete.

4. (schoolboys'.)—A large marble. *Cf.*, ALLEY, BONCE, MIVEY.

1885. *Household Words*, June 20, p. 155. Readers whose school-days are still green in their memories will also recognise in BUCK the name for the large marble once dear to their boyish hearts.

5. (American.)—A term used in POKER (*q.v.*). *Cf.*, TIGER.

Adj. (American University).—At Princeton College anything which is of an intensive degree, good, excellent, pleasant or agreeable, is called BUCK.

Verb (American). — 1. To oppose; to run counter to. [Possibly a corruption of butt, or from BUCK as applied to a horse.—*See* sense 2.]

2. (Western American.)—As applied to horses this term is used to describe the action of plunging forward and throwing the head to the ground in an effort to unseat the rider—a motion of which probably no domesticated beast is capable, aside from the Texan miserable and treacherous species of horse. A raw hand thus relates his experience:—'When I was told how hard he could BUCK, I only laughed, my impression being that no pony standing on four legs could throw me off. I mounted my new horse, and waving my bran new hat about my head, galloped away in a dignified style. Suddenly the horse stopped. His ears went back, and his hind legs went between his front. The motion was a curious one. But I did not fall. Realizing that the man on his back could ride a little bit, the pony got right down to business. My stomach seemed to fly up into my mouth, and millions of stars floated about my head. I am not prepared to state what kind of hold the pony got on me, but I went sprawling on the ground, my nose making an irrigating ditch. It was all done not more than one hundred yards from where my girl was standing. I stuck on well, however, as the saddle, blanket, gun and bridle came off with me. The wild yell that greeted my exploit nearly drove me mad. While I spit the dirt and curses out of my mouth, I thought that if I had that pony back I'd break him in or break my head. It ran out on the prairie and joined the Government herd. When an old-timer tried to fix things for me in front of my girl by saying, "It's no disgrace, pardnr, that horse can BUCK off a porus plaster," I thanked him from the bottom of my heart.'

3. (commercial.)—A variant of to COOK (*q.v.*), as applied to accounts.

4. (Western American.)—To play against the bank, usually 'to BUCK the tiger.'—*See* following.

1879. BRET HARTE, *Gabriel Conroy*, p. 375. I don't like your looks at all. I'd BUCK against any bank you ran, all night.

1880. BRET HARTE, *Brown of Calaveras.* (Tales of the Arg., p. 81). Why don't you say you want to BUCK agin' faro?

1888. *Hotel Mail.*
A man may hunt the wildest game
Along the Nile or the Niger,
In woods or ranch;
But he will find the sport most tame
Compared with BUCKING the tiger
At dear Long Branch.

5. (Western American.)—To put forth one's whole energy. [An extension of meaning from sense 4.]

1870. *San Antonio Paper.* 'You'll have to BUCK at it like a whole team, gentlemen, or you won't hear the whistle near your diggings for many a year.'

TO RUN A BUCK, *verbal phr.* (old Irish).—To poll a bad vote at an election.—*Grose.*

BUCK OR FIGHT THE TIGER, *verbal phr.* (American). — To gamble. [There are two derivations suggested:—(1) that the phrase is derived from the parti-coloured division or stripes on a gambling table; (2) that it is of Chinese origin. A favourite figure of one of the Chinese gods of gambling is a TIGER standing on his hind-feet, and grasping a large cash in his mouth or his paws. Sometimes the image is made of wood or clay, or drawn on a piece of paper or board. The title of the beast, His Excellency the Grasping Cash TIGER, is frequently written on a piece of paper, and placed in the gambling rooms between two bunches of mock-money suspended under the table or on the wall behind it. This figure is the sign for a gambling house: 'The FIGHTING TIGER.'

1888. *Daily Inter-Ocean*, Feb. 14. Last night and to-day they have succeeded in placing under arrest six of the gaming-house keepers of the city and subpœnaed thirty citizens as witnesses, among whom are said to be prominent city officials and business men. The affair has caused a good deal of talk already, and if reports are anywhere near true, it will create a great sensation when the cases are called, and more than one unsuspecting wife will have her eyes opened to the fact that the wicked TIGER, and not legitimate business has been detaining her husband out so late at night.

BUCK BAIT, *subs.* (thieves').—Bail given by a confederate. *Cf.*, BAIT.

BUCK DOWN, *verbal phr.* (Winchester College). — To be sorry; unhappy. *Cf.*, BUCK UP and BUCKSOME.

BUCKED. TO BE BUCKED, *verb* (Uppingham).—To be tired. *Cf.*, BUCK UP.

BUCKEEN, *subs.* (Irish).—A bully.—*Grose.* Properly a young man of the poorer aristocracy.

BUCKET, *subs.* (American). — An anonymous letter.

Verb (general).—1. To ride hard; not to spare one's beast.

1856. WHYTE MELVILLE, *Kate Coventry*, ch. xi. 'I had rather give Brilliant a good BUCKETING' [Aunt Horsingham shuddered—I knew she would, and used the word on purpose] 'over an even heath or a line of grass, than go bodkin in a chariot.'

1864. YATES, *Broken to Harness*, II., p. 218. There's room in the Row to give him [the horse] a very good BUCKETING.

1868. TOTTENHAM, *C. Villars*, I., 243. BUCKETING his wretched horse home to Cambridge. [M.]

1884. HAWLEY SMART, *From Post to Finish*, p. 342. 'Ten thousand pardons, Dollie, dearest; but I only got your message an hour or so ago, and am so busy I couldn't get here before. As it is I have had to BUCKET my hack unmercifully.

2. (old.)—To cheat; ruin; deceive.

1812. J. H. VAUX, *Flash Dict.*, s. v. To BUCKET a person is synonymous with putting him in the well.

1828. SCOTT, *Diary*, in *Lockhart* (1839), ix., 253. Thurtell . . . must in slang phrase have BUCKETED his palls.

3. (rowing.)—To take the water unfairly—with a scoop at the beginning of the stroke instead of a steady even pull throughout.

1876. BESANT AND RICE, *Golden Butterfly*, ch. xv., p. 130. He was not so straight in the back as an Oxford stroke; and he BUCKETED about a good deal, but he got along.

To GIVE THE BUCKET, *phr.* (old).—To dismiss from one's employment; to 'send a person about his business.'—*Cf.*, BAG and SACK.

1860. MRS. GASKELL, *Sylvia's Lovers*, ch. xxi. He were sore put about because Hester had GI'EN HIM THE BUCKET.

To KICK THE BUCKET, *phr.* (general).—To die. [The bucket here is thought to refer to a Norfolk term for a pulley.] When pigs are killed they are hung by their hind legs on a BUCKET.—For synonyms, *see* ALOFT.

1785. GROSE, *Dictionary of the Vulgar Tongue*. BUCKET; TO KICK THE BUCKET; to die.

1796. WOLCOT ('P. Pindar'), *Tristia*, wks. (1812) V., 242. Pitt has KICKED THE BUCKET.

1840. MARRYAT, *Poor Jack*, xxx. He drained it dry . . . and KICKED THE BUCKET.

1849. KINGSLEY, *Alton Locke*, ch. ii. 'Fine him a pot' roared one, 'for talking about KICKING THE BUCKET. He's a nice young man to keep a cove's spirits up, and talk about a short life and a merry one.'

1876 (?). *Broadside Ballad*, 'Ten Little Niggers.'

Eight little niggers never heard of heav'n,
One KICKED THE BUCKET, and then there were seven.

1889. *Answers*, July 27, p. 141, col. 3. The high-school girl explained to her particular friend yesterday that He KICKED THE BUCKET was slang, and that the polite expression was, 'He propelled his pedal extremities with violence against a familiar utensil used for the transportation of water and other fluids.'

BUCKET AFLOAT, *subs.* (rhyming slang).—A coat.

BUCKET SHOP, *subs.* (American).—1. Primarily a petty stock gambling den carried on in opposition to regular exchange business, and usually of a very doubtful character. The *New York World* recently investigated the whole question, and gave some very interesting details as to the many tortuous ways of these crooked corners of the money world. The conclusion arrived at was that Wall Street and its vicinity did not contain a single 'square and honest' BUCKET-SHOP; all their dealings were nothing but 'a brace gambling game.' By their schemes the customer had 'not the ghost of a chance to win.' Their quotations were obtained surreptitiously, and, in handling them, the BUCKET-SHOP keepers in several ways take unfair advantage of their clients. The term BUCKET SHOP has become common in England, but, fortunately for the community at large, no comparison can be drawn between the establishments known by that name in England, and those which flourish in America under the same title, though in very truth the proceedings of some of the former are scandalous enough. [Possibly from BUCKET (*q.v.*), to cheat, + SHOP. As an alternative derivation, the 'bucket' into which the tape falls may be suggested.

1887. *Daily News*, 14 April, 7, 1. Mr. Charles Fisher said that he carried on business as an agent . . . He did Stock Exchange business, for clients. Mr. Besley: Commonly called a BUCKET SHOP, I think.

1888. *Missouri Republican*, Feb. 12. New York, Feb. 11.—(Special).—Inspector Brynes was seized with another spasm of indignation against the BUCKET-SHOPS this morning, and, accompanied by detectives and a squad of officers, he swooped down upon the lairs of these enemies of the Stock Exchange that abound on Lower Broadway and New Street.

1889. *Pall Mall Gazette*, 12 Nov., p. 3, col. 1. 'The tape is credited with fostering gambling.' 'Well, we know that there are BUCKET-SHOPS, but we have for some time refused to entertain any proposal for a machine if there is the least prospect of its being used for BUCKET-SHOP purposes. There is gambling, of course, but it is unfair to say that the tape is responsible for it. The tape was not originated for that purpose, but in order to inform the public, through the newspapers or otherwise, how securities were going, and it does that. In practice it serves as a check between client and broker, and broker and jobber.'

2. Also applied generally to low groggeries; lottery offices; gambling dens, etc.

BUCK FACE, *subs.* (old).—A cuckold; one who in French slang is said to be *un loger rue du Croissant*.

BUCK FITCH, *subs.* (old).—An old roué; a lecherous old man.

BUCKHARA, *subs.* (American).—A name given in California to a cattle-driver or cowboy.

BUCKHORSE, *subs.* (pugilistic).—A smart blow or box on the ear. [Derived from the name of a celebrated 'bruiser' of that name. BUCKHORSE was a man who either possessed or professed insensibility to pain, and who would for a small sum allow anyone to strike him with the utmost force on the side of the face. His real name was John Smith, and he fought in public 1732-46.]

FRENCH SYNONYMS. (For the blow itself.) *Une boffete* (from the old word *buffet*); *une bouffe*; *une châtaigne*; *une accolade*; *une pamures*. To receive a BUCKHORSE, *encaisser un soufflet*; to give a BUCKHORSE; *donner la savate*.

1864. *Blackwood's Mag.*, II., p. 463 (the Public Schools' Report, 1864—Westminster School). One of the Seniors informs us that the common punishment was BUCKHORSING. 'That was boxing the ears, was it?' 'Yes.' 'BUCKHORSING was rather severe, was it not?' etc. 'I got BUCKHORSED pretty often.'

1876. LORD ALBEMARLE, *Fifty Years of my Life*, quoted in *Temple Bar*, August, 1884, p. 517. He then felled me to the ground by a swinging BUCKHORSE on my right cheek.

BUCKISH, *adj.* (old).—Foppish; dandyish. [From BUCK (*q.v.*) + ISH.] Now colloquial.

1782. D'ARBLAY, *Diary, etc.* (1876), i., 463. A BUCKISH kind of young man of fashion.

1785. WOLCOT ('P. Pindar'), *Apolog. Postscript to Ode upon Ode*, in wks. (Dublin, 1795), vol. I., p. 365. Did not good Nathan tell that BUCKISH youth, David the King, that he stole sheep?

1789. GEO. PARKER, *Life's Painter*, p. 57. Having beat the rounds (as BUCKISH spirits phrase it) of that bustling microcoser, the British metropolis, for eighteen months.

1812. COOMBE, *Dr. Syntax, Picturesque*, ch. xvii.

A BUCKISH blade, who kept a horse,
To try his fortune on the course.

1858. G. ELIOT, *Janet's Repentance*, ch. v. 'I've made him as neat as a new pin this morning, and he says the Bishop will think him too BUCKISH by half.'

1873. W. D. HOWELLS, *A Chance Acquaintance*, ch. xiii. A very BUCKISH young fellow, with a heavy black moustache and black eyes, who wore a jaunty round hat, blue checked trousers, a white vest, and a morning-coat of blue diagonals.

BUCK-JUMP, *subs.* (stable).—A jump made in BUCK (*q.v.*, *verb*, sense 2) fashion.

1864. G. A. LAWRENCE, *Guy Livingstone*, ch. ix. The instant the chestnut was mounted he reared, and indulged in two or three 'BUCK-JUMPS' that would have made a weaker man tremble for his backbone.

BUCKLE, *verb*, *trans.* and *intrans.* (colloquial).—1. To unite or be united in wedlock—a humorous term. For synonyms, *see* SPLICE. French thieves call such a union *l'amadouage*.

1693. DRYDEN, *Juvenal*, vi., 37. Is this an age to BUCKLE with a bride?

1751. SMOLLETT, *Peregrine Pickle*, ch. lxvii. Who . . . declared himself well satisfied with the young man's addresses, and desired that they might be BUCKLED with all expedition.

1822. SCOTT, *The Fortunes of Nigel*, ch. xxxii.

'BUCKLE them, my Lord Bishop, as fast as you can. . . .

The Bishop accordingly opened his book and commenced the marriage ceremony.'

1857. A. TROLLOPE, *Three Clerks*, ch. xlvi. 'We could have half a dozen married couples all separating, getting rid of their ribs and BUCKLING again, helter-skelter, every man to somebody else's wife.'

BUCKLE-BEGGAR, *subs.* (old).—A Fleet prison 'clergyman'; one who celebrated marriage ceremonies therein; thence, one who celebrated irregular marriages; a hedge priest; one who undertook similar offices for gypsies and tramps—a BUCKLE THE BEGGARS.—*See* COUPLE-BEGGAR. [Of Scotch derivation, but *Cf.*, BUCKLE, *verb*, sense 1.]

c. 1700. LD. FOUNTAINHILL, *Diary*, in Larwood, *Bk. Cleric. Anecd.*, 294. He after turn'd a BUCKLE-BEGGAR, *i.e.*, one who married without license. [M.]

1822. SCOTT, *Fortunes of Nigel*, ch. xvii. (II., p. 86). A hedge parson, or BUCKLE-BEGGAR, as that order of priesthood has been irreverently termed. *Ibid*, ch. xxvii. (III., p. 22). Dr. R., who BUCKLES BEGGARS for a tester [sixpence] and a dram of Geneva.

BUCKLED, *ppl. adj.* (thieves').—Arrested; taken into custody; 'scragged.'

BUCKLE DOWN, *verb* (common).—To 'settle down'; to become reconciled to; a variant of to 'KNUCKLE DOWN' (*q.v.*).

1874. JOS. HATTON, *Clytie*, bk. III., ch. iv. 'But you do not BUCKLE DOWN to your position,' said Cuffing . . . 'you wrangle, you higgle.'

BUCKLER, *subs.* (American thieves').—A collar. *Cf.*, ALL-ROUNDER.

BUCKLES, *subs.* (old).—Fetters of any kind. For synonyms, *see* DARBIES.

BUCKLE TO, *verb* (familiar).—To undertake; grapple with; 'slip in'; work vigorously.

1557. TUSSER, *Husbandrie*, ch. xcvi., st. 84, p. 187 (E.D.S.).

Then purchase some pelfe,
by fiftie and three:
or BUCKLE thy selfe,
a drudge for to bee.

1663. BUTLER, *Hudibras*, pt. I., ch. ii., l. 926.

And fitting it for sudden fight,
Straight drew it up, t'attack the Knight,
For getting up on stump and huckle,
He with the foe began to BUCKLE.

1712. ARBUTHNOT, *Hist. of John Bull*, pt. IV., ch. viii. At last Esquire South BUCKLED TO, to assist his friend Nic.

1883. JAMES PAYN, *Thicker than Water*, ch. xxvii. 'Of course it could never have been taken up as a serious occupation; the way you BUCKLED TO at it, as I told Mr. Payton, was something amazing.'

1889. *Modern Society*, 19 Oct., p. 1302. ('How the Nobility live in Germany.') Though, as a rule, courteous to ladies at dinner, when a course is served all BUCKLE TO, and conversation is at an end. Each gentleman forgets his fair neighbour, and minds only number one. Between the courses, when nothing better is on, they converse, and always everything is served *à la Russe*.

BUCKSOME, *adj.* (Winchester College).—Happy; in a state of 'BUCK-UPPISHNESS.'—*See* BUCK-UP.

BUCK UP, *verbal phr.* (Winchester College).—To be glad; pleased. *Cf.*, BUCK DOWN. The usual expression is 'Oh BUCK UP,' a phrase which at Westminster School would have a very different meaning, namely, 'exert yourself.' At Uppingham TO BE BUCKED (*q.v.*) is to be tired.

BUDGE, *subs.* (old).—1. A pickpocket; a general thief.—*See* quots., and for synonyms, AREA-SNEAK and THIEVES.

1671. R. HEAD, *English Rogue*, pt. I., ch. v., p. 48 (1874). BUDGE, one that steals cloaks.

1674. R. HEAD, *Canting Acad.*, 95. The BUDGE . . . his employment is in the dark of the Evening, to go into any door that he seeth open, and . . . take whatever next cometh to hand.

2. (thieves'.)—Also called SNEAKING BUDGE (*q.v.*). In more modern times an accomplice who gains access to a building during the day for the purpose of being locked in. When night comes he is thus easily able to admit his fellow thieves. For synonyms, *see* AREA-SNEAK, and *Cf.*, STANDING BRIDGE.

1752. FIELDING, *Amelia*, bk. I., ch. iii. 'I find you are some sneaking BUDGE rascal' [cant term for pilfering].

3. (old.)—Drink; liquor.—*See* DRINKS. [Thought to be a corruption of BOOZE.] There are several derivatives—BUDGY, 'drunk'; BUDGING-KEN, 'a public house'; COVE OF THE BUDGING-KEN, 'a publican'; BUDGER, 'a drunkard'—all of which *see*.

1821. D. HAGGART, *Life*, Glossary, p. 171. BUDGE, drink.

Verb (old slang, but now colloquial).—To move; 'to make tracks.' For modern synonyms, *see* AMPUTATE, and *Cf.*, BUDGE-A-BEAKE.

BUDGE-A-BEAKE, *verbal phr.* (old).—To run away (presumably from justice). There seems some connection in meaning between this expression and a modern phrase—'TO BILK THE BLUES' (*q.v.*). [From BUDGE (*q.v.*), 'to move away,' 'to decamp,' + A + BEAK (*q.v.*), a policeman.] For synonyms, *see* AMPUTATE.

1610. ROWLANDS, *Martin Mark-all*, p. 37 (H. Club's Repr., 1874). BUDGE-A-BEAKE, runne away.

BUDGER, *subs.* (old).—A drunkard. [From BUDGE, *subs.*, sense 3, 'drink' (*q.v.*) + ER.] For synonyms, *see* ELBOW CROOKER.

BUDGING-KEN, *subs.* (old).—A public house.—*See* BUDGE. [From BUDGE, drink, + KEN (*q.v.*), a place or house.] For synonyms, *see* LUSH CRIB.

1821. D. HAGGART, *Life*, Glossary, p. 171. BUDGE KAIN, a public-house.

BUDGY, *adj.* (old).—Drunk; intoxicated. [From BUDGE (*q.v.*), sense 3, drink.] For synonyms, *see* SCREWED.

BUD OF PROMISE, *subs. phr.* (American).—A facetious term for a young, unmarried woman.—*See* ROSEBUD.

1889. *Charlestown Enterprise.*
The young, unmarried girl, in sport,
Is called a BUD OF PROMISE;
She blooms each year at some resort,
The weather when it is warm is.
And in the Fall a score of men,
Whose hearts till now have harm missed,
Compare sad notes, and find out then
To each the BUD is promised.

BUD SALLOGH (Old Irish).—A term applied to one who practises unmentionable vices.—*See* JESUIT.

BUENOS AYRES (provincial).—The Royal Crescent at Margate at the extreme end of the town used to be so called. The houses remained unfinished for a very considerable time.—*H. J. Byron.*

BUFE, *subs.* (old cant).—A dog. [Murray says, from the sound of its bark.]—*See* BUFFER, and TIKE for synonyms.

1567. HARMAN, *Caveat*, 84. BUFE, a dogge.

1785. GROSE, *Dictionary of the Vulgar Tongue.* BUFE, a dog; BUFE'S NOB, a dog's head.

BUFE-NABBER or **NAPPER**, *subs.* (old).—A dog thief. [From BUFE, old cant for a 'dog,' + NABBER, one who steals or 'nabs.'] For synonyms, *see* AREA-SNEAK.

1785. GROSE, *Dictionary of the Vulgar Tongue.* BUFE-NABBER, a dog-stealer.

BUFF, *subs.* (common).—1. The bare skin. [An allusion to the colour.]

1654. CHAPMAN, *Revenge for Honour*, I., i.
Then for accoutrements you wear the BUFF,
As you believed it heresy to change
For linen: surely most of yours is spent
In lint.

1749. H. FITZCOTTON, *Homer*, I., 38. If you perplex me with your stuff—All that are here shan't save your BUFF. [M.]

1760. JOHNSTON, *Chrysal*, II., 235. 'I have got as many clothes and things of all kinds as would serve to set up a Monmouth-street merchant: if the place had held out but a few days longer, the poor devils must have done duty in their BUFF; ha! ha! ha!' 'And the properest dress for them,' returned the admiral; 'who wants any clothes in such a climate as this?'

1824. HUGHES, *Magic Lay of the One-horse Chay* (Blackwood). When our pair were soused enough, and returned in their BUFF.

1856. H. MAYHEW, *Gt. World of London*, p. 223. 'There's a fine young chap there, stript to the BUFF, and working away hard!

1872. C. KING, *Sierra Nev.*, viii., 176. Stripping ourselves to the BUFF, we hung up our steaming clothes. [M.]

2. (old).—A man; a fellow; also BUFFER (*q.v.*).

1708-15. KERSEY. BUFF . . . a dull Sot, or dronish Fellow. [M.]

1709. *Brit. Apollo*, II, No. 8, p. 3, col. 2. Tell me Grave BUFFS, Partly Gods, partly men. [M.]

1725. *New Cant. Dict.*, s. v. BUFF, a Newgate Cant Word used in familiar Salutation as, How dost do, my BUFF?

1748. SMOLLETT, *Roderick Random*, ch. iv., p. 15. Mayhaps old BUFF has left my kinsman here his heir.

1764. BRYDGES, *Homer Travest.* (1797), II., 420. You seem afraid these BUFFS will flinch.

BUFF IT, *verb* (common).—1. To swear to; to adhere to a statement hard and fast; to stand firm. [Query from 'to bluff.'] To BUFF IT is sometimes enlarged—TO BUFF IT HOME.

1812. J. H. VAUX, *Flash Dict.*, s. v. BUFF, To BUFF to a person or thing, is to swear to the identity of them.

1881. *New York Slang Dictionary.* BUFFING IT HOME is swearing point-blank to anything, about the same as bluffing it, making a bold stand on no backing.

2. (common.)—To strip; to bare oneself to the 'BUFF' or skin.

1851. MAYHEW, *London Labour and London Poor*, II., p. 416. 'You had better BUFF it, Jim,' says I; but Jim wouldn't do it, and kept his trowsers on. *Ibid*, p. 417. So I locks the door, and BUFFS it, and forces myself up, etc.

IN BUFF, *phr.* (common).—Naked; in a state of nudity. Among English equivalents are ABRAM (*q.v.*) and BIRTHDAY SUIT (*q.v.*), but for all synonyms, *see* NATURE'S GARB.

1602. DEKKER, *Satiro-Mastix.* I go in stag, IN BUFF.

1855. *Notes and Queries*, 1 S., xi., p. 467. We say of one in a state of nudity, 'he is IN BUFF.'

TO STAND BUFF, *verbal phr.* (old).—To stand the brunt; to pay the piper; to endure without flinching. [From BUFF, an old pugilistic term for a blow.]

a. 1680. BUTLER, *Hudibras's Epitaph.* And for the good old cause STOOD BUFF 'Gainst many a bitter kick and cuff.

1697. VANBRUGH, *Provoked Wife*, I., i. Would my courage come up to a fourth part of my ill-nature, I'd STAND BUFF to her relations, and thrust her out of doors.

1737. FIELDING, *The Miser*, Act ii., Sc. 2. *Love.* How! rascal, is it you that abandon yourself to those intolerable extravagancies? *Fred.* I must even STAND BUFF, and outface him.

1748. T. DYCHE, *Dictionary* (5 ed.). To STAND BUFF (v.), to stand stoutly to a thing, to be resolute and unmoved, though the danger be great.

1761. COLMAN, *Jealous Wife*, V., i., 139. Stick close to my advice and you may STAND BUFF to a tigress.

1822. SCOTT, *Fortunes of Nigel*, ch. xii. 'STAND BUFF against the reproach of thine over-tender conscience.'

BUFF-BALL, *subs.* (vagrants').—A dancing party in which both sexes dance together naked. [From BUFF (*q.v.*), naked, + BALL.] *Cf.*, BALLUM RANCUM.

1880. GREENWOOD, *In Strange Company.* The most favourite entertainment at this place is known as BUFF-BALL, in which both sexes—innocent of clothing—madly join, stimulated with raw whiskey, and the music of a fiddle and a tin whistle.

BUFFER, *subs.* (old).—1. A dog. [Considerable obscurity surrounds the origin of this term. It occurs in varying forms from 1567 down to the present time. Harman gives it as BUFE (1567) and BUFA (1573); Rowlands as BUFFA (1610); Head as BUGHER (1673); whilst in *The Memorials of John Hall* it first appears as BUFFER.] Synonymous terms will be found under TIKE.

1567. HARMAN, *Caveat* (1814), p. 65. BUFA, a dogge.

1610. ROWLANDS, *Martin Mark-all*, p. 37 (H. Club's Repr., 1874). BUFFA, a Dogge.

1714. *Memoirs of John Hall* (4 ed.), p. 11. BUFFER, a Dog.

1842. LOVER, *Handy Andy*, ch. iv. 'It is not every day we get a badger, you know . . . Reilly the butcher has two or three capital dogs, and there's a wicked mastiff below stairs, and I'll send for my 'BUFFER' and we'd have some spanking sport.'

1876. C. HINDLEY, *Life and Adventures of a Cheap Jack*, p. 162. They had a dog belonging to them that would be sure to begin a quarrel with another BUFFER, whenever his master or mistress found a match.

2. (common.)—A man; a fellow—sometimes used with a slightly contemptuous meaning; generally speaking a familiar mode of address, as in Old Buffer, although even this form may be used disparagingly.

1749. H. FITZCOTTON, *Homer*, I. (1748), 23. You're a BUFFER always rear'd in The brutal pleasures of Bear-garden. [M.]

1837. BARHAM, *I. L.* (*The Bagman's Dog*).
So I'll merely observe, as the water grew rougher,
The more my poor hero continued to suffer,
Till the Sailors themselves cried, in pity,
'Poor BUFFER!'

1882. F. ANSTEY, *Vice Versâ*, ch. xiv. 'I made a first-rate booby-trap, though, one day for an old yellow BUFFER who came in to see you.'

3. (pugilistic.)—A boxer; one of 'the fancy.' [Hotten gives this as of Irish origin, but it would rather seem to come from O.E. BUFF, a blow.]

1819. MOORE, *Tom Crib's Memorial to Congress*, p. 7.
Last Tuesday, at Moulsey, the Balance of Power
Was settled by twelve *Tightish* Rounds in an hour,
The BUFFERS, both 'Boys of the *Holy Ground*.'—*Ibid*, p. 51:—
Yet, sprightly *to the Scratch* both BUFFERS came,
While *ribbers* rung from each resounding frame,
And divers *digs*, and many a ponderous *pelt*,
Were on their broad *bread-baskets* heard and felt.
With roving aim, but aim that rarely miss'd,
Round *lugs* and *ogles* flew the frequent fist;
While showers of *facers* told so deadly well,
That the crush'd jaw-bones crackled as they fell!

4. (old.)—*See* quots.

1690. B. E., *Dict. Cant. Crew.* BUFFER, a Rogue that kills good sound Horses only for their Skins.

1737. *Bacchus and Venus.* BUFFER, a rogue that killed good sound horses for the sake of their skins, by running a long wire into them.

1785. GROSE, *Dictionary of the Vulgar Tongue.* BUFFER, one that steals and kills horses and dogs for their skins.

5. (old.)—One who took a false oath for a 'consideration.' *Cf.*, BAIL.

6. (old.)—A pistol. *Cf.*, BARKER.

1824. SIR W. SCOTT, *Red Gauntlet*, ch. iii. Here be a pair of BUFFERS will bite as well as bark.

7. (old.)—A smuggler; rogue; or cheat.

8. (nautical.)—A navy term for a boatswain's mate, one of whose duties it is—or was—to administer the 'cat.' *Cf.*, O.E. BUFF, a blow.

BUFF HOWARDS, *subs.* (military).—The Third Regiment of Foot; now contracted into BUFFS. It was nicknamed the BUFF HOWARDS, from its facings and Colonel from 1737 to 1749; also the NUT-CRACKERS (*q.v.*); and the RESURRECTIONISTS (*q.v.*), from its re-appearing at the Battle of Albuera after being dispersed by the Polish Lancers; also the 'Old Buffs,' from its facings, and to distinguish it from the 31st, the 'Young

Buffs'; but the most ancient 'Old Buffs' were the 'Duke of York and Albany's Maritime Regiments,' raised in 1664, and incorporated into the 2nd or Coldstream Guards in 1689.

1886. *Tinsley's Mag.*, 'Our Regimental Mottoes and Nicknames,' April, p. 319. The BUFFS—a corps which enjoys the almost unique privilege of marching through the city of London with bayonets fixed. The 3rd Foot owes its immortal cognomen to the fact of its having originally been clad in scarlet, lined and faced with BUFF; its members also had BUFF waistcoats, BUFF breeches, and BUFF stockings. Being the senior regiment thus clothed, they were occasionally styled the 'OLD BUFFS'; and the 31st, raised in 1702, and dressed in a precisely similar fashion, were known as the YOUNG BUFFS. The following tradition, however, offers a more circumstantial account of the latter appellation. Having earned in some hotly-contested action, the good opinion of a general under whom they were serving, and who expressed his approbation by calling out to the 31st, 'Well done, OLD BUFFS!' A few of the men, somewhat excited by close combat, replied, 'We are not the OLD BUFFS, Sir.' Whereupon the general cried, 'Then well done, YOUNG BUFFS!' And so the 'Young BUFFS' they became, and have since remained, although the days of BUFF waistcoats and stockings have long passed away.

BUFFLE, *subs.* (old).—A fool; a stupid person. *Cf.*, BUFFLE-HEAD and BUFF, sense 2. Murray quotes it as occurring in 1655, but the term is, as will be seen, nearly a century older. [After French *buffle*.] For synonymous terms, *see* following:—

ENGLISH SYNONYMS. Buffle-head; Sammy-soft, often contracted into Sammy; sheep's head; crock (the original meaning is rather concerned with a slow worthless horse, but in sporting phraseology it has also come to mean a foolish, good-for-nothing person); duffer; dotty (also used by prostitutes of a low class to designate their protector or fancy man); cuckoo; calf; cabbage-head; cake; block; greenhorn; old curmudgeon; doddering old sheep's head.

FRENCH SYNONYMS. *Un échappé de Charenton* (*échapper* = to escape; *Charenton* is the name of a lunatic asylum in Paris; hence one escaped from Charenton. *Cf.*, English colloquial use of the names of Hanwell, Colney Hatch, and Bedlam in describing idiotic or foolish conversation or behaviour); *échappé d'Herode* (*Cf.*, foregoing); *un vieil embaumé* (this term is applied to a foolish person well advanced in years; an old curmudgeon); *un actionnaire* (literary: properly a shareholder).

GERMAN SYNONYMS. *Amhorez* (literally a countryman; from Hebrew *om*, the people, + *erez*, country); *Blechseppel* (a soldier's term); *Chammer* (a butcher's or knacker's word; it also signifies a donkey, and is derived from the Hebrew *chamor*); *Dilmisch*, *Dilledapp*, *Dilldapp*, *Dilledali*, *Dellemelle*, *Dirledapp*, *Didel*, *Tatidel*, *Dudeldop*, *Dilldan* (all these are popular expressions for a stupid fellow. *Cf.*, *dildalfen* = to exhaust); *Ewil* (from the Hebrew *owal*; the term also stands for a sinner); *Godeschaute* (a great fool, a perfect fool; from the Hebrew *godol*, great, strong, celebrated, + *schoto*, a fool); *Gomol* (used only as a nickname; from the Hebrew *gamal*, a camel); *Hanne* or *Hannes* (a shortened form of *Johannes*, the German for the English John; it is curious that in both languages the nicknames *Hanne* and Jack should, as applied to men, always be used depreciatingly, *see* JACK); *Harbogen, Hornickel, Hornigel* (besides signifying a fool or weak-headed one, these words are used to designate an ox; they are employed indiscriminately); *Heckel, Häckel, Hegel* (also a fop; *heckeln* = to fool anyone, probably from *hacken* or *hecheln*, to hew, to hackle); *Koppel* (a diminutive of Jacob; sometimes written *Jockel*); *Ksil* (from the Hebrew *kossal*; variations in spelling are *Kessil, Kessel*, and in students' slang *Theekessel*); *Nebbich* or *Newich* (among thieves employed to designate the clumsy, stupid fellow who is only entrusted with unimportant tasks connected with a robbery, such for instance as holding the sacks in which the stolen property is placed, or in carrying off the plunder); *Nille* or *Knolle* or *Nolle* (these terms are used to signify a fool, jester, or the male *penis*); *Nowel* or *Newil* or *Nebel* (also a cunning fellow, a rogue or 'sly blade'; *das ist ein Newele*, the equivalent of the Low German *dat is een Aas vun Kêrl* might be rendered by the English 'he is a devil of a fellow'); *Oochbram* or *Ogbrôm* (a fool or rather one whose craziness resembles in extent the traditional stature of Og, King of Bashan — at least authorities agree in thinking this the most likely derivation of the word. Among the Jews Og is taken as an image of gigantic size. When the Israelites advanced on Edrëi, Og sat on the wall of the town, and his feet reached to the ground, so that Moses at first thought he was part of the wall, but when he discovered that it was a man he was seized with terror. *Rum* = on high, therefore *Og b'rum* = the [great] Og on high. *Er hat die Grösse von Og Melech haboschon*, he has the size of Og, King of Bashan. A corresponding expression is found in the Low German, *de lange Rick, i.e.*, a tall, slenderly built fellow); *Schote* or *Schaute* or *Schotte* (from the Hebrew *schoto*; used especially of one who can be cheated or robbed with his eyes open; a tradesman or money changer who can be robbed while transacting business at the counter or while exchanging money); *Sonof* (a Hebrew word signifying properly a tail, and mostly used proverbially of things low and contemptible. It is also employed to designate the male *penis*; the German Gaunersprähe offers frequent examples in which contemptible names are also used synonymously for the male and female organs of generation).

ITALIAN SYNONYMS. *Fiadetto* (besides its meaning of a dolt or duffer, this term is also applied to a thief, rogue, or indeed a villain of any description); *ribeba* or *ribecca* (a goose or simpleton; properly a violin or Jewish harp); *cordovano* (this also means in the Fourbesque, a big man; properly it is the name of Morocco or Spanish leather); *furlana*; *marietta* or *marietto* (a dolt or dunce).

SPANISH SYNONYM. *Dupa* (*Cf.*, English dupe).

1580. *Beehive of the Romish Churche*, fo. 66 *b*. An unlearned BUFFLE did babble.

1655. *Comic Hist. Francion*, iv., 22. He said to the three BUFFLES who stood with their hats in their hands. Tell me you Waggs, etc. [M.]

1710. *Pol. Ballads* (1860), II., 90. To see the chief attorney such a BUFFLE.

BUFFLE-HEAD, *subs.* (old).—An ignoramus; a stupid obtuse fellow. *Cf.*, BUFFLE, and which *see* for synonyms.

1659. *Lady Alimony*, I., ii., in Hazl. *Dodsley*, xiv., 278. What a drolling BUFFLE-HEAD is this!

1663. PEPYS, *Diary*, March 17. But my Lord Mayor a talking, bragging, BUFFLE-HEADED fellow.

1668. PEPYS, *Diary*, Jan. 29. He tells me that Townsend, of the Wardrobe, is the veriest knave and BUFFLE-HEAD that ever he saw.

1677. WYCHERLEY, *Plain Dealer*, Act ii. *Oliv.* You know nothing, you BUFFLE-HEADED stupid creature you.

1686. D'URFEY, *Commonwealth of Women*, I., i. A damn'd huffing fellow yonder, a Rebel, Whiggy BUFFLE-HEAD.

1754. B. MARTIN, *Eng. Dict.*, 2 ed. BUFFLE-HEAD, an ignoramus, or dull sot.

1887. *Dead Man's Rock*, bk. I., ch. v. 'Jonathan's a BUFFLE-HEAD . . . a daft fule like Jonathan.'

BUFFLEHEADED, *adj.* (old).—Stupid; idiotic; foolish. [From BUFFLEHEAD, a foolish fellow (*q.v.*), + ED.]

1883. BARING GOULD, *John Herring*, vol. II., ch. xxv., p. 275. (Tauchnitz ed.) 'A BUFFLEHEADED sort of a chap,' said Joyce.

BUFFS, *subs.* (military).—The Third Regiment of Foot in the British army. From their facings. —*See* BUFF HOWARDS.

1849. MACAULAY, *Hist. England*, I., 295. The third regiment, distinguished by flesh-coloured facings, from which it derived the well-known name of the BUFFS.

1851. MAYHEW, *London Labour and London Poor*, I., p. 232. His father was a captain in the BUFFS, and himself a commissioned officer at seventeen.

1874. *Saturday Review*, p. 95. This regiment [the First or Grenadier Guards] has almost the longest record of any in the service, only yielding, we believe, to the 1st Royals, and to the 3rd BUFFS, which were originally raised for the service of the States-General of Holland.

BUFFY, *adj.* (common). — Intoxicated. For synonyms, *see* SCREWED.

1866. YATES, *Land at Last*, I., p. 85. Flexor was fine and BUFFY when he came home last night, after you was gone, sir.

1872. BESANT AND RICE, *R. M. Mortiboy*, ch. xlii. 'My ideas take me first of all unawares. They generally begin, like a toothache, when I least expect them. Perhaps when I feel a little BUFFY, in the morning; mayhap, after an extra go of grog the night before. Then one comes all of a sudden.'

BUG, *subs.* (thieves').—1. A breast pin.

2. (Old Irish.) — A jeering name for an Englishman — Grose says 'because BUGS were introduced into Ireland by Englishmen!!'

3. (American.) — The term BUG is, in the United States, not confined merely, as in England, to the domestic pest, but is applied to all insects of the Coleoptera order, which includes what in this country are generally called beetles. The English BUG (*Cimex lectularius*) is, in the Southern States, known as the CHINCH. It may be mentioned, however, that at Winchester College a usage akin to that prevailing in America exists. There a BUG merely means an insect, whether belonging to the Coleoptera, Lepidoptera, or any other order. Synonyms for the English domestic pest will be found under NORFOLK HOWARDS.

1642. ROGERS, *Naaman the Syrian*, 74. Do not all as much and more wonder at God's rare workmanship in the Ant, the poorest BUGGE that creeps.

1888. *Grass Valley* (Cal.) *Tidings*. Entomology, or bugology, is now taught to some extent in our public schools. This is well, and is of use. The children ought to learn about the BUGS that are destructive to useful vegetation. It is better to learn much about BUGS than so much about how to solve those arithmetical problems that will never face anybody in the practical affairs of life.

1888. *Daily Inter-Ocean*, March. The Insane Asylum Board some time ago discontinued a bug-killer's employment, and the doctor avers that the old hospital building is swarming with cockroaches, and that these BUGS will soon be large and fat enough to carry out the inmates and take their food and clothes.

4. (American.)—BUG is also used idiomatically in various combinations, as BIG BUGS (*q.v.*), a jocose and vulgar name for persons of wealth or distinction. Thence, similarly, CATTLE-BUGS, that is, wealthy stock-raisers; GOLD-BUGS, or monied men, etc.

1843. HALIBURTON, *Sam Slick in England*, ch. xv. The great guns and BIG BUGS have to take in each other's ladies. *Ibid*, p. 24. Pick out the BIG BUGS and see what sort of stuff they're made of.

1888. *St. Louis Globe Democrat*, March 5. 'Would Senator Allison's well-known views on silver coinage operate materially against him in New York.' 'I think not; I do not think the feeling against silver is anything like as strong as it was. Of course, a few GOLD-BUGS might fight him, but any of the men I have mentioned are reasonably certain to carry New York.'

THAT BEATS THE BUGS, *phr.* (American).—A phrase conveying a high mead of praise; 'that beats cock-fighting.'

Verb (old).—1. A cant word among journeymen hatters, signifying the exchanging some of the dearest materials of which a hat is made for others of less value. Hats are composed of the furs and wools of diverse animals, among which is a small portion of bever's fur. BUGGING is stealing the bever, and substituting in lieu thereof an equal weight of some cheaper ingredient. Bailiffs who take money to postpone or refrain the serving of a writ, are said to BUG the writ.—*Grose.*

2. (thieves'.)—To bribe. In old slang, bailiffs accepting money to delay service were said TO BUG the writ.

3. (thieves'.)—To give; hand over; to deliver. *Cf.*, sense 2.

1812. J. H. VAUX, *Flash Dict.* 'He BUG'D me a quid.' 'BUG OVER the rag.'

BUGAROCH, *adj.* (Old Irish). — Pretty; comely; handsome. —*Grose.*

BUG-BLINDING, *subs.* (military).— Whitewashing operations.

BUGGER, *subs.* (old).—1. A thief whose speciality is stealing breast-pins from drunken men. [From BUG, a cant term for a breast pin, + (G) GER.] Also called a BUG HUNTER. For synonymous terms, *see* AREA-SNEAK and BUG-HUNTER.

2. (low.)—A man; a fellow. A coarse term of abuse without, however, any reference to the legal meaning — a sodomite. The French has an exact equivalent in *Bougre*, which Littré says is *une terme de mépris et d'injure, usité dans le langage populaire le plus trivial et le plus grossier*. The term, as applied to a man, is equivalent to BITCH (*q.v.*), as applied to women. Hence also BUGGERY (*q.v.*).

1719. D'URFEY, *Pills*, I., 59. From every trench the BOUGERS fly. [M.]

1854. M. HOLMES, *Tempest and Sun*, 203. 'If I'd known all you city BUGGERS was comin', I'd a kivered my bar feet.' [M.]

BUGGERY, *adj.* (low). — An indefinite expression signifying disgust; or disapprobation. Of the same type as BLOODY, BLAMED, BLASTED, etc. (*q.v.*), but conveying a somewhat intenser meaning.

1851. MAYHEW, *London Labour and London Poor*, I., p. 23. A BUGGERY fool, why don't he let people go to hell their own way? *Ibid*, p. 180. Here mother, give us one of your BUGGERY trotters.

BUGGY, *subs.* (old). — A leather bottle.

BUGHER.—*See* BUFFER.

BUG-HUNTER, *subs.* (thieves'). —A thief who plunders drunken men. The same as BUGGER, sense 1.

FRENCH SYNONYMS. *Un poivrier* (popular and thieves'); *un allumeur* (this term is also applied to an auction room 'button' or confederate, and to a card-sharper's decoy); *faire un louave*, or *faire les gavés* (to go bug-hunting. *Louave* and *gavé* = drunkard, the latter from *gaver*, to glut).

1856. H. MAYHEW, *Gt. World of London*, p. 46. Those who hocus or plunder persons by *stupefying*; as 'drummers,' who drug liquor, and 'BUG-HUNTERS,' who plunder drunken men.

2. *subs.* (old). — An upholsterer.—*Lexicon Balatronicum.*

BUG-JUICE, *subs.* (common). — 1. Ginger ale.

2. (American.)—The Schlechter whiskey of the Pennsylvania Dutch—a very inferior spirit. Also called BUG-POISON. These terms are now applied to bad whiskey of all kinds. For synonyms, *see* DRINKS.

1888. *Texas Siftings*, 7 July. It is a singular fact, that nearly every character introduced by Charles Dickens into his numerous novels, was addicted to drinking . . . each and every individual took his BUG-POISON with surprising regularity and eminent satisfaction.

BUGLE IT, *verb* (American cadets'). —To abstain from going into class until the last moment— *i.e.*, until the bugle sounds.

BUG WALK, *subs.* (common).—A bed. [Derivation obvious.]

ENGLISH SYNONYMS. Bedfordshire; Sheet Alley; Blanket Fair; Land of Nod; doss; rip; Cloth Market.

FRENCH SYNONYMS. *Un portfeuille* (familiar: properly 'a portfolio'); *la boîte à puces* (popular: this almost exactly corresponds to the English 'BUG WALK,' the French phrase signifying 'the flea box'); *le pucier* (popular: from *puce* = flea); *le tremblant* (popular); *le plumard* (popular); *le fournil* (popular and thieves'); *la halle aux draps* (popular: literally, Sheet Market or Fair. *Cf.*, English 'Blanket Fair'); *le pagne*; *le panier aux ordures*.

BUILD, *subs.* and *verb* (popular).— Properly 'TO BUILD is to construct,' says Murray, 'for a dwelling and by extension of meaning . . . to construct by fitting together of separate parts; chiefly with reference to structures of considerable size . . . (not, *e.g.*, a watch or a piano).' Difficult as it may be at times to draw a dividing line between a literary, or even a colloquial usage and a slang signification, there can be little doubt that when BUILD is applied to the make or style of dress, that it is the purest slang—'It's a tidy BUILD, who made it?' A tailor, it may be noted, is sometimes called a 'trousers' BUILDER.' In the United States, this verb is used with much more latitude than in England. There, as Fennimore Cooper puts it, everything is BUILT. The priest BUILDS up a flock; the speculator a fortune; the lawyer a reputation; the landlord a town; and the tailor, as in England, BUILDS up a suit of clothes. A fire is BUILT instead of made, and the expression is even extended to individuals, to be BUILT being used with the meaning of formed. 'I was not BUILT that way'; and hence in a still more idiomatic sense to express unwillingness to adopt a specified course or carry out any inconvenient plan.—*See* NOT BUILT THAT WAY.

1853. WH. MELVILLE, *Digby Grand*, ch. xx. That creator of manly beauty, who BUILDS your coat on the model of an Apollo.

1853. REV. E. BRADLEY ('Cuthbert Bede'), *Verdant Green*, pt. I., ch. x. If he forswore the primitive garments that his country-tailor had condemned him to wear, and adapted the BUILD of his dress to the peculiar requirements of university fashion.

1871. A. FORBES, *My Experience of the War, etc.*, II., p. 19. I met a gentleman who had got a dress coat BUILT in the place [Versailles].

1880. *Punch*, Jan. 10, p. 6. THE SPREAD OF EDUCATION AND LIBERAL IDEAS.—*His Grace the Duke of Poplar and Bermondsey.* 'Just look at these bags you last BUILT me, Snippe! J'ever see such beastly bags in your life? I shall always be glad to come and dine with you, old man; but I'll be hanged if you shall ever measure me for another pair of bags!' *Mr. Snippe (of Snippe and Son, St. James's Street).* 'You've *always* grumbled about your bags, as you call 'em, ever since you were my fag at Eton; and at Christchurch you were just as bad, even though my poor dear old governor used to come all the way down and measure you himself. It ain't the fault of the bags, my dear Popsy—it's the fault of the legs inside 'em! So, shut up, old Stick-in-the-mud, and let's join the ladies—the duchess has promised to give us "Little Billee."'

BUILD A CHAPEL, *verbal phr.* (nautical).—To steer badly, and so cause a ship to veer round.

NOT BUILT THAT WAY, *phr.* (general).—Not to one's taste, in one's line—a general expression of disapproval or dissent, whether said of persons or things.

1881. *American Humorist*, May 12. We cannot shut our eyes to the fact that mankind is passing through a great era of change; even womankind is not BUILT as she was a few brief years ago.

1888. *Missouri Republican*, Jan. 25. 'Why didn't you roll down?' 'I wasn't BUILT that way.'

BULGARIAN ATROCITIES, *subs.* (Stock Exchange). — Varna and Rutschuk Ry. 3 per cent. obligations.

1887. ATKIN, *House Scraps*.
And we've really quite a crew
Of fancy names to represent a share . . .
But fancy, by the way,
Now, in the present day,
A Varna's a BULGARIAN ATROCITY.

BULGE, *verb* (American).—The legitimate meaning is extended in many odd ways. 'Bags' BULGE, but do not get baggy; and in a similar fashion when a man is 'all attention,' his eyes are said TO BULGE.

1888. *Puck's Library*, May, p. 31. A Phenomenal Fee. 'Yes,' said a pompous young lawyer, on a street-car, to a friend: 'I hadn't been downtown half an hour this morning, before I got a fee of ten dollars!' Then the eyes of a man who was hanging on to a strap began TO BULGE. 'I say, young feller,' he whispered earnestly: 'what saloon d'ye work at? I'm a waiter, myself!'

TO GO OR BE ON A BULGE, *verbal phr.* (American). — To drink to excess.

TO GET THE BULGE ON ONE, *verbal phr.* (American mining slang).—To obtain an advantage over; an equivalent is TO GET THE DROP ON ONE.

1869. S. L. CLEMENS ('Mark Twain'), *Innocents at Home*, p. 18. Well, you've rather GOT THE BULGE ON ME. Or maybe we've both GOT THE BULGE, somehow.

1885. *Household Words*, Oct. 10, p. 466. 'Smart chap, that Jacob, for a nig!' remarked he, as we told him the outlines of our story. 'I guess now he's HAD THE BULGE ON YOU pretty considerable this trip.'

1888. *American Humorist*, May 12. 'Pop! are you up there?' 'Yes, my son.' 'I saw he HAD THE BULGE ON YOU and I got the gun and dropped him!' 'Right, my boy. That's what I was praying for.'

BULGER, *adj.* (common).—Large; synonymous with BUSTER (*q.v.*).

BULK, *subs.* (old).—*See* quots.—*See* also FILE and BULKER, sense 2.

1674. R. HEAD, *Canting Acad.*, 35. BULK and File. The one jostles you, whilst the other picks your pocket.

1725. *New Cant. Dict.* BULK, an assistant to a File or Pickpocket, who jostles a Person up against the Wall, while the other picks his Pocket.

1785. GROSE, *Dictionary of the Vulgar Tongue.* BULK and file, two pickpockets; the BULK jostles the party to be robbed, and the file does the business.

BULKER, *subs.* (old).—1. A prostitute of a low type—generally one who had no settled home; one who slept on a 'bulk,' a kind of sill projecting from a window. For synonyms, *see* BARRACK-HACK.

1691. SHADWELL, *Scowerers*, Act i., Sc. 1. 'Every one in a petticoat is thy mistress, from humble BULKER to haughty countess.'

1728. BAILY. BULKER, a Common Jilt; a Whore.—*Canting term.* [In a later edition (1790) he adds 'one who would lay down on a bulk to anyone.]

2. (old.)—A thief. *Cf.*, BULK.

1669. *Nicker Nicked*, in *Hart. Misc.* (ed. Park), II., 108. BULKER occurs in a list of names of thieves.

1678. *Four for a Penny*, in *Hart. Misc.* (ed. Park), IV., 147. He is the treasurer of the thieves' exchequer, the common fender of all BULKERS and shoplifts in the town.

BULKY, *subs.* (provincial). — A police constable. Said to be a northern term. For synonyms, *see* BEAK.

1821. *Edinburgh Mag.*, August, p. 156. This enterprising ruffian boasts of his success in deceiving the BULKIES on a search, by concealing his stolen notes in the cape of his coat.

1841. LYTTON, *Night and Morning*, bk. V., ch. ii. 'Inquiries about your respectability would soon bring the BULKIES about me.'

Adj. (Winchester College).—Rich or generous, or both. The opposite of BRUM (*q.v.*).

BULL, *subs.* (colloquial.)—1. Formerly a blunder or mistake; now generally understood as an inconsistent statement; a ludicrous contradiction, often partaking largely of the nature of a pun. [BULL in M.E. = to befool; to mock.] The term was current long before the form IRISH BULL is met with.

1642. MILTON, *Apol. for Smect.*, § 6. But that such a poem should be toothless, I still affirm it to be a BULL, taking away the essence of that which it calls itself. For if it bite neither the persons nor the vices, how is it a satire? And if it bite either, how is it toothless?

1673. DRYDEN, *The Assignation*, Act iii., Sc. 1. *Ben.* Faith, lady, I could not sleep one wink, for dreaming of you. *Lan.* Not sleep for dreaming? When the place falls, you shall be BULL master general at court.

1689. SELDEN, *Table Talk*, p. 96 (Arber's ed.). We can make no notion of it, 'tis so full of intricacy, so full of contradiction: 'tis in good earnest, as we state it, half-a-dozen BULLS one upon another.

1705. WARD, *Hudibras Redivivus*, vol. II., pt. I., p. 6. With Stale Quibbles, Puns, and BULLS.

1841. LEVER, *Charles O'Malley*, ch. i. 'I have got into such an infernal habit of making BULLS, that I can't write sense when I want it.'

1859. H. KINGSLEY, *Geoffrey Hamlyn*, ch. xxxix. He was telling the most outrageous of Irish stories, and making, on purpose, the most outrageous of Irish BULLS.

In this connection it may be noted that in French cavalry regiments *portez!* and *remettez!* are mock commands given upon the perpetration of a BULL. *La calinotade* signifies in the popular speech a ludicrous or foolish saying, whilst one given to uttering them is termed *un calino*.

2. (thieves'.)—A crown or five shilling piece. Formerly BULL'S EYE (*q.v.*). [The origin is doubtful. It may be a mere allusion to the circular shape, or it may be of classical derivation, and be a reference to the herds and flocks which at one time constituted a man's wealth. *Cf.*, Latin *pecunia*, from *pecus*, cattle or oxen.]

1812. J. H. VAUX, *Flash Dictionary.* BULL, a crown, or five shillings.

1851-61. H. MAYHEW, *London Lab. and Lon. Poor*, vol. I., p. 232. List of patterers' words. BULL, a crown.

1852. DICKENS, *Bleak House*, ch. xlvi. Four half-BULLS, wot you may call half-crowns.

1857. *Notes and Queries*, 2 S., 4 July. And therefore much as a BULL (or a hog) stand arbitrarily for a five-shilling-piece, half-a-BULL for half-a-crown, a bob for a shilling, a tanner for sixpence, etc., with equal propriety might a plum stand for £100,000.

1889. *Answers*, July 27, p. 136, col. 2. Once found, the 'lurker' is pretty sure to draw a BULL (five shillings), or even a 'counter' (pound).

3. (Stock Exchange.)—Originally a speculative purchase for a rise; *i.e.*, a man would agree to buy stock at a future day at a stated price with no intention of taking it up, but trusting to the market advancing in value to make the transaction profitable. BULL is the reverse of BEAR (*q.v.*). The term is now more frequently applied to the person engaged in the abovementioned tactics, *i.e.*, to one who tries to enhance the value of stocks by speculative purchases or otherwise. Also used as a verb and adjective.

b. 1671, *d.* 1757. CIBBER, *The Refusal, or The Ladies' Philosophy.* *Granger* (to Witling, who has been boasting of his gain): And all this out of 'Change Alley'? *Witling*: Every shilling, Sir, all out of stocks, Pulls, BULLS, Rams, Bears, and Bubbles.

1768. FOOTE, *Devil upon Two Sticks*, Act i. A mere BULL and bear booby; the patron of lame ducks, brokers, and fraudulent foot bankrupts.

1774. COLEMAN, *Man of Business*, IV., i., in wks. (1777) II., 179. My young master is the BULL, and Sir Charles is the bear. He agreed for stock, expecting it to be up at three hundred by this time; but, lack-a-day, sir, it has been falling ever since.

1817. SCOTT, *Rob Roy*, ch. iv. The hum and bustle which his approach was wont to produce among the BULLS, bears, and brokers of Stock Alley.

1860. PEACOCK, *Gryll Grange*, ch. xviii. In Stock Exchange slang, BULLS are speculators for a rise, Bears for a fall.

1881. *Mark Lane Express*, Aug. 8, p. 1085. The speculative movement which has, so far, exerted a BULL influence on the maize market.

On the French Bourse a BULL is called *un haussier*; in Berlin he is known as *liebhaler*; and in Vienna the term used is *contremine*.

4. (nautical.)—*See* BULL THE CASK OR BARREL.

5. (common.)—Explained by quotation.

1887. G. R. SIMS, *How the Poor Live*, p. 148. In these places, too, the lodgers divide their food frequently, and a man, seeing a neighbour without anything, will hand him his teapot, and say, 'Here you are, mate; here's a BULL for you.' A 'BULL' is a teapot with the leaves left in for a second brew.

6. (thieves'.)—Prison rations of meat, an allusion to its toughness; also generally used for meat without any reference to its being either tough or tender. A French equivalent is *la bidoche.* [Its derivation is suggested in the following quot.]

1883. *Echo*, Jan. 25, p. 2, col. 3. Thus from the French '*bouilli*' we probably get the prison slang term BULL for a ration of meat.

7. (American.)—A locomotive; the word is sometimes lengthened into BULLGINE.

8. (Winchester College.)—Cold beef, introduced at breakfast about 1873.

Verb (American University).—At Dartmouth College to recite badly; to make a poor recitation. [From the substantive BULL, a blunder or contradiction, or from the use of the word as a prefix, signifying large, lubberly, blundering.]

STALE BULL, *subs.* (Stock Exchange). — Stock held over for a long period with profit.

BULL AND COW, *subs.* (rhyming slang).—A row.

BULL-BAIT, *verb* (? nonce word).—To bully; hector; badger. [Clearly a figurative usage of the legitimate word.]

1860. DICKENS, *Great Expectations*, ch. xviii., p. 82. 'Which I meantersay,' cried Joe, 'that if you come into my place BULL-BAITING and badgering me, come out!'

BULL-BEEF, *subs.* (old). — A frequently recurring term of contempt. Prisoners apply it to the hard, stringy meat supplied to them, and formerly the expression was in general use. 'As ugly as BULL-BEEF'; 'as big as BULL-BEEF'; 'go and sell yourself for BULL-BEEF'; were common colloquialisms at the end of the last and the beginning of the present century. Sometimes contracted into BULL. *Cf.*, BULLY BEEF.

1579. GOSSON, *Apol. of the Schoole of Abuse*, p. 64 (Arber). I vnderstand they are all in a fustian fume. . . . They haue eaten BUL-BIEF, and threatned highly too put water in my woortes whensoeuer they catche me.

1607. ROWLANDS, *Diogines Lanthorne*, p. 8 (H. Cl. Repr., 1873). How lookes yonder fellow? what's the matter with him trow? has a eaten BUL-BEEFE? there's a lofty slaue indeede, hee's in the altitudes.

1738-1819. WOLCOT ('P. Pindar'), *Rights of Kings, Ode I.*, in wks. (Dublin, 1795), vol. II., p. 219. The Cooks, Bluff on th' occasion, put on BULL'S-BEEF looks.

1782. WOLCOT, *Lyric Odes*, No. 3, in wks. (1809) I., 62.
Yet thou may'st bluster like BULL-BEEF so big.

1860. HALIBURTON ('Sam Slick'), *The Season Ticket*, x. Which look as cheap as BULL-BEEF at one cent a pound.

1868. BREWER, *Phrase and Fable*, p. 524. To look as big as BULL-BEEF. To look stout and hearty, as if fed on BULL-BEEF. BULL-BEEF was formerly recommended for making men strong and muscular.

1888. ASHTON, *Mod. Street Ballads*, p. 61.
For soon he will his trial take,
And hard BULL-BEEF be munching.

BULL CALF, *subs.* (old).—*See* quot.

1785. GROSE, *Dictionary of the Vulgar Tongue*. BULL CALF, a great hulkey or clumsy fellow.

BULL CHIN, *subs.* (old).—Explained by quotation.

1785. GROSE, *Dictionary of the Vulgar Tongue*. BULL CHIN, a fat, chubby child.

BULL-DANCE, *subs.* (nautical).—A dance in which only men take part. *Cf.*, STAG-DANCE, GANDER-PARTY, HEN-PARTY, etc.

1867. SMYTH, *Sailors' Word Book*. BULL-DANCE. At sea it is performed by men only when without women. It is sometimes called a STAG-DANCE.

1887. *Graphic*, March 26, p. 315, col. 3. It is obliged to be a BULL-DANCE. Gentlemen dance with gentlemen, and the pianist is, of course, a gentleman also.

BULL-DOG, *subs.* (old).—1. A sheriff's officer; a bailiff.

1698. FARQUHAR, *Love and a Bottle*, iii., 2. *Mock.* But pray what's the matter, Mrs. Lyric?
Lyric. Nothing, sir, but a shirking bookseller that owed me about forty guineas for a few lines. He would have put me off, so I sent for a couple of BULL-DOGS, and arrested him.

2. (old.)—A pistol; in the naval service a main-deck gun. *Cf.*, BARKER and BULL-DOG BLAZER.

1700. FARQUHAR, *Constant Couple*, iii., 2. He whips out his stiletto, and I whips out my BULL-DOG.

1825. SCOTT, *St. Ronan's Well*, ii., 191. 'I have always a brace of BULL-DOGS about me.' . . . So saying, he exhibited a very handsome, highly-finished, and richly-mounted pair of pistols.

1867. SMYTH, *Sailors' Word Book*. BULL-DOG or MUZZLED BULL-DOG, the great gun which stands housed in the officer's ward-room cabin. General term for main-deck guns.

1881. *Daily News*, Oct. 27, p. 6, col. 2. Revolver cartridges of the ordinary 'BULL-DOG' pattern.

3. (old.)—*See* quot.

1812. J. H. VAUX, *Flash Dict.* BULL-DOG, a sugar-loaf.

4. (University.)—A proctor's assistant or marshall. *Cf.*, quot. from Brewer's *Reader's Handbook*.

1823. LOCKHART, *Reg. Dalton*, I., x. (1842), 59. Long forgotten stories about proctor's bit and BULL-DOGS baffled. [M.]

1841. LYTTON, *Night and Morning*, bk. III., ch. iii. 'The proctor and his BULL-DOGS came up . . . and gave chase to the delinquents . . . the night was dark, and they reached the College in safety.

1847. TENNYSON, *Princess*, Prologue.
We unworthier told
Of college: he had climb'd across the spikes,
And he had squeezed himself betwixt the bars,
And he had breath'd the Proctor's DOGS.

1880. BREWER, *Reader's Handbook*. BULL-DOGS, the two servants of a university proctor, who follow him in his rounds, to assist him in apprehending students who are violating the university statues, such as appearing in the streets after dinner without cap and gown, etc.

5. (University: obsolete.)—A name for a member of Trinity College, Cambridge.

BULL-DOG BLAZER, *subs.* (American).—A revolver. [Probably a mere amplification of the kindred English canting term; BULL-DOG, a pistol, + BLAZER, an allusion to the flash attendant upon firing.] For synonyms, *see* MEAT IN THE POT.

BULL-DOSE, *subs.* (American).—A severe castigation or flogging. *Verb.*—To thrash; to intimidate; to bully. A term of Southern political origin, originally referring to an association of negroes formed to insure, by violent and unlawful means, the success of an election. The phrase has now

passed into general use, political and otherwise, to signify the adoption and use of coercive measures. [The derivation is almost literal—a BULL-DOSE, a flogging with a strip of hide; the action itself being represented by the verb TO BULLDOSE. Though indifferently spelt both with single and double 'l' and with 's' and 'z,' the correct version is BULLDOSE.] Also derivatives BULLDOSER (*q.v.*), and BULL-DOSING, *mutatis mutandis*, of a kindred meaning.

1876. *New York Tribune*, Dec. There was a bad case of 'BULLDOZING' in Cincinnati on Monday night. A handful of bold Democrats had gathered to let out their pent-up desire for Tilden or blood. . . . Mr. C—— was in the chair, and was warming up the faithful with an address, when the Republicans crowded around him in so threatening a manner that he mounted the table, shook his address in their faces, and declared, like a true hero, that he was not to be 'intimidated.'

1880. *Illust. London News*, vol. LXXVII., p. 587, col. 1. The Americans have lately been using a strange word, 'BULL-DOSING,' which signifies, I believe, political intimidation, but not personal molestation.

1881. *Sat. Review*, July 9, p. 40, col. 2. To 'BULL-DOSE' a negro in the Southern States means to flog him to death or nearly to death.

1881. *Sat. Review*, July 9, p. 40, col. 2. A 'BULL-DOSE' means a large efficient dose of any sort of medicine or punishment.

1887. *Cassell's Mag.* (Art. on 'Americanisms'), June, p. 412. To 'BULL-DOZE' is to intimidate, and the word was originally used respecting the alleged interference with negro voters in Louisiana.

1888. *Detroit Evening Journal*, 20 Feb. The Democrats complain of the amounts of money they had to face, but that was not such a source of trouble as the BULLDOZING of voters by the mining bosses. There were driven to the polls, and compelled to vote for Seymour.

A French equivalent is *faire son fendart* (*fendart* signifies 'braggart' or 'swaggerer'; *fendant* in literary French means a hector or bully).

BULL-DOSER, *subs.* (American).—1. A bully; braggart; swaggerer. *Cf.*, BULL-DOSE. French printers call a bully *un mata*, an abbreviation of *matador*. It is curious that this term in the original Spanish not only signifies a killer of bulls (as in a bull-fight), but also a murderer.

1878. *N. American Review*, vol. CXXVII., p. 426. The great 'BULL-DOZER' of Europe.

1882. *New York Tribune*, 3 May. The hotel where he was staying was visited . . . by a mob of BULL-DOZERS. [M.]

2. A pistol.

1881. *Sat. Review*, July 9, p. 40, col. 2. A Californian BULL-DOSER is a pistol which carries a bullet heavy enough to destroy human life with certainty.

BULLET. TO GIVE THE BULLET, *verbal phr.* (common).—To discharge an employé. *Cf.*, TO GIVE THE BAG, sense 2, under BAG, and SACK. [Possibly a punning allusion to the word 'discharge.'] The term is variously used. To SHAKE THE BULLET at anyone, is to threaten with 'the sack,' but not to give actual notice to leave. To GET THE BULLET is to get notice, while TO GET THE INSTANT BULLET is to be discharged upon the spot.

1841. SAVAGE, *Dict. of Art of Printing*. A workman was said to have GOT THE BULLET when he was discharged *instanter*—without the customary notice on either side.

1872. *Chamb. Jour.*, March 9, p. 147. When a fellow GETS THE BULLET from his work, he mostly has a spell at cab-driving.

1887. *Punch*, Sept. 17, p. 126. I have just GOT THE 'BULLET,' Mate—sacked without notice.

BULLFINCH, *subs.* (old).—1. A stupid fellow.

2. (hunting.)—A high thick hedge; one difficult to jump or rush through. [Most authorities agree in suggesting the origin of this term in a corruption of 'bull-fence,' *i.e.*, a fence capable of preventing cattle from straying.]

1832. *Quart. Rev.*, Mar., 226. The BULL-FINCH fence . . . is a quickset hedge of perhaps fifty years' growth, with a ditch on one side or the other, and so high and strong that [one] cannot clear it. [M.]

1864. G. A. LAWRENCE, *Guy Livingstone*, ch. ix. The third is a teaser—an ugly black BULL-FINCH with a ditch on the landing side, and a drop into a ploughed field.

1880. *The Times*, Nov. 2, p. 4, col. 5. They are almost invariably attired in double-stitched shooting coats, that will stand the ordeal of 'BULL-FINCHES' and brambles.

1889. *Man of the World*, June 29. See Harrington, the belted earl, bear down an opponent in the jousts, charging with lance or sword as if he were riding at a South Notts BULL-FINCH.

BULL-JINE, *subs.* (nautical).—A sailor's term for a locomotive. [Thought to be of American origin, New York thieves using the same term, as also an abbreviated form—BULL.]

BULL MONEY, *subs.* (harlotry).—Money extorted from or given by those who in places of public resort have been detected *in flagrante delicto* with a woman, as a bribe to silence.

BULL-NURSE, *subs.* (nautical).—*See* quot.

1885. *Graphic*, April 4, p. 326, col. 3. BULL-NURSES.' Perhaps we ought to apologise for using this word; but years ago (it may be so still) it was the sailors' phrase to indicate a male-attendant on the sick.

BULLOCK, *subs.* (schoolboys').—1. *See* quot.

1855. J. K., in *Notes and Queries*, 1 S., v., 12, 3 Nov., p. 344. BULLOCK, a cheat; but as I think, only when cheating at marbles.

2. (Australian.)—A countryman or bushman. *Cf.*, BULLOCK-PUNCHER.

Verb.—To bully; to bounce over; to intimidate. [Query from BULLY.]

1716. M. DAVIES, *Ath. Brit.*, I., 272. Upon the evidence of that BULLOCKING Fryer Campanella. [M.]

1750. FIELDING, *Tom Jones*, bk. II., ch. vi. 'And then you have charged me with BULLOCKING you into owning the truth.'

1763. FOOTE, *Mayor of Garratt*, Act ii., Sc. 2. She shan't think to BULLOCK and domineer over me.

1785. GROSE, *Dictionary of the Vulgar Tongue*. BULLOCK, to hector, bounce, or bully.

BULLOCK'S HEART.—*See* TOKEN.

BULLOCK'S HORN, *verb* (rhyming slang).—To pawn. For synonyms, *see* POP.

BULL PARTY, *subs.* (old).—A party of men only. *Cf.*, BULL-DANCE, STAG-PARTY, HEN-TEA, etc.

BULL-PUNCHER.—A variant of COW-PUNCHER (*q.v.*).

BULL'S EYE, *subs.* (schoolboys').—1. A sweetmeat of which peppermint is an important ingredient. [It received its name in allusion to its globular shape.]

1825. HONE, *Every-day Bk.*, I., 51. Hardbake, brandy-balls, and BULL'S-EYES. [M.]

1882. *Punch*, vol. LXXXII., p. 83. *Dr. Switcher (who had discovered* BULL'S EYES *about, and traced them to the original donor).* 'Don't you know, Muggins, there's an old proverb that "Fools give feasts and Wise men eat them"? *Muggins.* 'Yes, Sir, and there's another one, sir.' *The Doctor.* 'What's that, sir? Now, Sir?'—*(noticing a reticence)*—'What is it, Sir?'—*(sternly)*—'or else—!' *Muggins (seeing no escape).* 'Please, Sir, "W—— wise men make proverbs and F—— Fools repea——."' [Catches it!]

2. (old.)—A five-shilling piece, otherwise known as a BULL (*q.v.*).

1690. B. E., *Dict. Cant. Crew.* [Mentioned as a cant term for a crown.]

1714. *Memoirs of John Hall* (4 ed.), p. 11. BULL'S-EYE, a Crown.

1785. GROSE, *Dictionary of the Vulgar Tongue*. BULL'S-EYE, a crown piece.

BULL'S-EYE VILLAS, *subs.* (military).—A nickname given to the small open tents used by the Volunteers at their annual gathering. [An allusion to BULL'S-EYE in its meaning of the centre of a target.]

BULL'S FEATHER. TO GIVE [or GET] THE BULL'S FEATHER, *verbal phr.* (old).—To be made, or be a cuckold. *Cf.*, ACTEON. The French say also *planter des plumes de bœuf*.

16(?). *Song of the 17th Century*, quoted by Nares—'The BULL'S FEATHER.'
It chanced not long ago as I was walking,
An echo did bring me where two were a talking,
'Twas a man said to his wife, dye had I rather,
Than to be cornuted and wear a BULL'S FEATHER.
Then presently she reply'd sweet, art thou jealous?
Thou canst not play Vulcan before I play Venus;
Thy fancies are foolish, such follies to gather,
There's many an honest man hath worn the BULL'S FEATHER—
Though it be invisible, let no man it scorn,
Though it be a new feather made of an old horn,
He that disdains it in heart or mind either,
May he be the more subject to wear the BULL'S FEATHER.

1748. RICHARDSON, *Cl. Harlowe*, v., 295. A good whimsical instrument, take it altogether! But what, thinkest thou, are the arms to this matrimonial harbinger? . . . Three crooked horns, smartley top-knotted with ribands; which being the ladies' wear, seem to intimate that they may very probably adorn, as well as bestow, the BULL'S-FEATHER.

BULL THE CASK or **BARREL**, *verbal phr.* (nautical).—To pour water into a rum cask when empty, with a view to keeping the wood moist and preventing leakage. The water, receiving after some time a strong impregnation, is very intoxicating. The authorities, not looking with much favour upon a wholesale brewing of grog in this way, sometimes use salt water as a deterrent, though even this 'SALT WATER BULL' as it is called, when again poured out, has often proved too attractive for seamen to resist. Again it is common to talk in the same way of 'BULLING a teapot,' 'coffee-pot,' etc.; that is; after the first 'brew' has been exhausted, by adding fresh water, and boiling over again, to make a second brew from the old materials. This probably was derived from BULLING THE CASK, but whether the BULLING originally applied to the preserving the water-tight qualities of the cask, or to the making of the second brew is not quite certain. Taking, however, the present acceptation of the term, together with its probable derivation (see below), the latter would appear to be the case. [Thought to have its origin in French *boullir*, whence *bouilloire*, a tea-kettle; *bouillon*, a decoction of meat to which vegetables, salt and pepper have been added.]

1824. COCHRANE, *Narrative of a Pedestrian Journey through Russia and Siberian Tartary*, p. 225. My liquor was at end from the effects of a very common sort of leak—it had been tapped too often. I could do nothing but BULL THE BARREL, that is, put a little water into it, and so preserve at least the appearance of vookey.

1835. MARRYAT, *Jacob Faithful*, ch. xx. 'Why, Jacob, a BULL means putting a quart or two of water into a cask which has had spirits in it.'

1887. G. R. SIMS, *How the Poor Live*, p. 148. In these places, too, the lodgers divide their food frequently, and a man, seeing a neighbour without anything, will hand him his teapot, and say, 'Here you are, mate; here's a BULL for you.' A 'BULL' is a teapot with the leaves left in for a second brew.

BULL-TRAP, *subs.* (American thieves').—A personator of a police constable.

BULLY, *subs.* (old).—1. A 'protector' of a prostitute; a 'fancy man.' The name is often well applied, inasmuch as violence and swagger form the main staple of the stock-in-trade of such men in levying blackmail upon the victims enticed by their women companions.

1706. DEFOE, *Jure Divino*, i., 8. Mars the celestial BULLY they adore, And Venus for an everlasting whore.

FRENCH SYNONYMS. *Poisson* (familiar and popular: one who subsists on the gains of a prostitute, the latter being known as his *marmite*, *i.e.*, 'flesh-pot'; *poisson* signifies literally 'a fish,' and Michel says that such a one was formerly known as *poisson d'avril*, a punning variation of *maquereau* [which *see*], mackerel being fit for food about that month. *Poisson d'avril* properly means a trick or fool's errand; *recevoir un poisson d'avril* is to be made an April-fool); *Alphonse* (a French form of Alphonso, a 'fancy name' for a 'fancy man.' *Cf.*, Adonis for a dandy. *Alphonsisme* is the calling of an *Alphonse*); *baigne-dans-le-beurre* (popular: another allusion to mackerel which is generally served with butter); *barbise* (popular); *barbe* (popular: lit. 'beard'); *barbille* or *barbillon* (a young hand at the business); *barbeau* (popular: properly *barbel*, from L. L. *barbellus*, dim. from *barbus*, a barbel, *i.e.*, the fish, from *barba*, a beard); *marlou* or *marlousier* (general: the second term is the oldest, and Michel derives it from *marlier*, formerly used in the sense of *marguillier*, signifying properly 'churchwarden.' *Cf.*, *Sacristain*); *benoît* (popular); *brochet* (popular: properly this is 'pike' or 'jack'); *dos*, *dos vert*, and *dos d'azur* (general: *dos* = back); *casquette à trois ponts* (popular: so called from a cap often worn by such persons); *chevalier du bidet* (*bidet* = pony; *Cf.*, OMNIBUS); *chevalier de la guiche* (familiar); *chiqueur de blanc* (*chiqueur* = glutton, and *blanc*, a street-walker. *Cf.*, *mangeuse de viande crue*); *bouffeur de blanc* (popular); *costel* (popular); *cravate verte* (popular); *guiche* (popular); *dessous* (thieves': a man for whom 'love' is cherished by a prostitute); *écaillé* (literally 'one with scales,' like those of a fish—allusive of *maquereau*; *fish*, another reference to *maquereau*); *foulard rouge* (popular: lit. 'red silk handkerchief'); *gentilhomme sous marin* (popular); *ambassadeur* (popular); *gonce à écailles* (*gonce* = man; *à écailles* = with scales, an allusion to *maquereau*); *goujon* (general:

? does this come from the Gascon *gouie*, whence comes *gouge*, a prostitute); *lacromuche* (popular); *retrousseur* (popular: *retrousser* properly means 'to turn up,' 'to cock'); *dauphin* (popular: lit. dolphin); *macchoux* (popular); *machabée* (popular: lit. a corpse); *mac* or *macque* (popular; abbreviations of *maquereau*); *macrottin* (familiar); *poisson fraveur* (*frayer* [of fishes] signifies 'to milt'); *releveur de fumeuse* (popular: *Cf.*, *relever le chandelier*, *i.e.*, to lift up the candlestick; from a practice of placing the fees of a prostitute under a candlestick); *maquignon à bidoche* (popular: *maquignon* is properly a 'horsedealer,' and *bidoche* = meat); *mangeur de blanc* (general: a devourer of prostitutes. *Cf.*, *chiqueur de blanc*); *tête de patère* (popular); *marloupatte*, *marloupin* (*see marlou*); *marquant* (thieves'); *mec* (popular and thieves'); *mec de la guiche* (so called from his kiss-curls—*des guiches* = kiss-curls); *monsieur à nageoires* (lit. gentleman with fins); *monsieur à rouflaquettes* (popular: *rouflaquettes* = aggerawators, *q.v.*); *neg en viande chaude* (popular: *neg* is an abbreviation of *négociant*, *i.e.*, merchant, dealer; *viande chaude* = hot meat); *patenté* (popular: *patente* is the name of a cap worn by the fraternity); *porte-nageoires* (*see monsieur à nageoires*); *roi de la mer* (popular: lit. king of the sea. *Cf.*, *maquereau*, *poisson*, etc.); *rouflaquette* (*Cf.*, *monsieur à rouflaquettes*); *roule-en-cul*, *soixante-six* (popular: insulting terms which might be translated by 'pensioner,' with an obscene prefix); *un qui va aux épinards* (popular: one who receives money from a prostitute, *épinards* = spinach. *Cf.*, 'to take one's greens'); *valet de cœur* (popular: the lover of a prostitute); *visqueux* (properly this signifies 'viscous,' 'slimy,' 'clammy'; the term is applied to the lowest type of BULLIES); *bibi* (popular); *bras de fer* (lit. 'arm of iron').

1729. GAY, *Polly*, Act ii., Sc. 7. *Jimmy*: Sure never was such insolence! how could you leave me with this bawdy-house BULLY?

1753. *Adventurer*, No. 100. I learned to pack cards and to cog a die; became a BULLY to whores.

1766. GOLDSMITH, *Vicar of Wakefield*, ch. xx. The lady was only a woman of the town, and the fellow her BULLY and a sharper.

1821. W. T. MONCRIEFF, *Tom and Jerry*, Act. ii., Sc. 4. *M'L.* Plaise your honour, I have brought before your worship a most notorious prostitute and common street walker, who, for her foul doings, has been cooped up in the Poultry Comptor, as often as there are years in a week.—I caught her charging these honest gentlemen (*pointing to Tom and Jerry*) in a most impositious manner, and when I civilly axed her, how she could think of getting drunk, and acting so, she called her BULLIES here. (*Pointing to Kate and Sue.*)

1883. A. DOBSON, *Fielding*, p. 129. Probably a professed *sabreur*, if not a salaried BULLY like Captain Stab in the *Rake's Progress*.

1887. *Daily News*, 15 July, 6, 5. It was not an uncommon thing for a prostitute to solicit a man, and if he refused her importunities, to call upon a 'BULLY,' and complain that she had been assaulted.

2. (Eton College.)—A *melée* at football; the equivalent of the Rugby 'scrimmage' and the Winchester 'hot.' It is where the majority of players play.

3. (nautical)—A term of endearment in use amongst sailors. Equivalent to 'pal,' 'mate,' and similar terms. In this sense it has long been in use, Shakspeare often employing it. Probably hence arose the American and colonial adjectival use of the word in the sense of fine, 'crack.'

4. (American thieves'.)—A weapon formed by tying a stone or a piece of lead in a handkerchief. This is used knuckleduster fashion.

Adj. (American). — Fine; capital; crack; 'spiff.' Applied to persons only, this adjective is traceable as far back as 1681; it seems, however, to have fallen into disuetude and to have been subsequently revived in a much more extended sense in the U.S.A., whence it has made the circuit of the English speaking world. Now applied to anything deserving of commendation, and used very much in the same way and with the same shades of meaning as 'crack.'

ENGLISH SYNONYMS. *See* A1.

FRENCH SYNONYMS. In addition to those given under A1 may be mentioned the following:—*muche*; *pas piqué des hannetons* (popular: literally not bitten or stung by May-bugs or cockchafers).

1681. CHETHAM, *Anglers' Vade Mecum* (1689), pref. From such BULLY fishers this book expects no other reception.

1855. *Cairo City Times.* The BULLY steamboat 'Crystal Palace' passed up to St. Louis on Monday. We have no doubt she left papers.

1870. MEADE, *New Zealand*, p. 331. The roof fell in, there was a 'BULLY' blaze.

1875. *N. Amer. Review*, vol. CXX., p. 128. 'That,' replied Earney, 'is Mercury, the god of merchants and thieves.' 'Good! that's BULLY!' exclaimed Tweed.

1880. BRET HARTE, *A Lonely Ride.* 'I thought you changed horses on the road?' 'So we did. Two hours ago.' 'That's odd. I didn't notice it.' 'Must have been asleep sir. Hope you had a pleasant nap. BULLY place for a nice quiet snooze,—empty stage, sir!'

THAT'S BULLY FOR YOU, *phr.* (American). — Grand or fine; this phrase, during the Civil War, had a remarkably popular run.

1873. JUSTIN MCCARTHY, *Fair Saxon*, ch. xix. 'Darling boy! I had thought of this already.' 'BULLY FOR YOU, mamma! Of course you did.'

BULLY BOY or BULLY BOY WITH THE GLASS EYE, *phr.* (American).—A good fellow.

1815. SCOTT, *Guy Mannering*, ch. xxxiv. 'Well said, my hearty captain!' cried Glossin, endeavouring to catch the tone of revelry. . . . 'That's it, my BULLY BOY! Why, you're alive again now!—'

1817. SCOTT, *Rob Roy*, ch. viii. 'And you, Mr. Frank Osbaldistone, are not the first BULLY-BOY that has said stand to a true man.'

1869. S. L. CLEMENS ('Mark Twain'), *Innocents at Home*, p. 20. You ought to seen him get started once. He was a BULLY BOY WITH A GLASS EYE.

BULLY-BACK or **BULLY-BUCK**, *subs.* (old). — Thus described by Grose: A bully to a bawdy house, one who is kept in pay, to oblige the frequenters of the house to submit to the impositions of the mother abbess or bawd, and who also sometimes pretends to be the husband of one of the ladies, and under that pretence extorts money from greenhorns, or ignorant young men, whom he finds with her. *Cf.*, BULLY-BOSS.

1626. AMHERST, *Terræ Fil.*, xxxiii., 179. They have spirtual bravves on their side, and old lecherous BULLY-BACKS to revenge their cause. [M.]

BULLY BEEF, *subs.* (military). — Tinned meat. Also called IRON RATION (*q.v.*). In the navy by

BULLY-BEEF is meant boiled salt beef. [This may either be a corruption of BULL BEEF or from the French *bouilli*, boiled meat.]

1883. CLARK RUSSELL, *Sailors' Language*, pref., xii. Soup-and-bouilli is another standing sea dish, and, taking it all round, is the most disgusting of the provisions served out to the merchant sailor. I have known many a strong stomach, made food-proof by years of pork eaten with molasses, and biscuit alive with worms, to be utterly capsized by the mere smell of soup-and-bouilli. Jack calls it 'soap and bullion, one onion to a gallon of water,' and thus fairly expresses the character of the nauseous compound.

1887. *Daily News*, July 9, p. 6, col. 4. The rations will be of the kind known to Tommy Atkins as 'BULLY BEEF.' There may be in it a considerable proportion of mutton, but that makes no difference to him.

BULLY-BOSS, *subs.* (American).—The landlord of a brothel or thieves' den. [From BULLY, sense 1 (*q.v.*), + BOSS, a master.]

BULLY-BUCK.—*See* BULLY-BACK.

BULLY COCK, *subs.* (old).—1. *See* quot.

1785. GROSE, *Dictionary of the Vulgar Tongue.* BULLY-COCK, one who foments quarrels in order to rob the persons quarrelling.

2. *subs.* (old).—A low round hat with broad brim.—*See* BILLY-COCK.

3. (old.)—A man who sets other people by the ears, so that, while they quarrel, he may rob them with impunity.

BULLYRAG or **BALLYRAG**, *verb* (colloquial).—To revile; abuse; scold vehemently—usually in vulgar or obscene language; also to swindle by means of intimidation. [The etymology is unknown.]

FRENCH SYNONYMS. *Arranger aux petits oignons*; *monter une gamme* (popular: *gamme* = thrashing or 'walloping'); *habiller quelqu'un de taffetas* (popular: *i.e.*, to clothe anyone with fear; *Cf.*, 'clothed with shame'); *agonir* (popular: 'to haul over the coals'; properly 'to pull to pieces'); *secouer les puces à quelqu'un* (popular: *secouer* = to shake; *puces* = fleas. *Cf.*, 'to send one away with a flea in the ear').

1760. T. WARTON, *Oxford Newsman's Verses.*
On Minden's plains, ye meek Mounseers!
Remember Kingsley's grenadiers.
You vainly thought to BALLARAG us,
Like your fine squadron off Cape Lagos.

1861. CHARLES LEVER, *One of Them*, p. 36. He BULLYRAGGED me.

1876. S. CLEMENS ('Mark Twain'), *Tom Sawyer*, p. 118. I don't want nothing better 'n this; I don't git enough to eat gin'ally,—and here they can't come and pick a feller and BULLYRAG him so.

1880. JAS. GREENWOOD, *Maids in Waiting*, in *Odd People in Odd Places*, p. 143. You should have heard the BULLYRAGGING I got, ma'am, from the mistress and the master as well, and I was turned out in the shameful way I've already explained to you, for doing what was no wrong at all, but only what me good-nature tempted me to.

1884. JAS. PAYN, *Talk of the Town*, ch. v. He had never been 'BALLYRAGGED' in his own house for 'nothing'—except by his wife—before.

BULLYRAGGING, *verb*, *subs.* (colloquial).—Scolding; abuse; and sometimes swindling. [From BULLYRAG (*q.v.*) + ING.] For synonyms, *see* WIGGING.

1863. H. KINGSLEY, *Austin Elliot*, ch. xviii. 'It would be a good thing for *she* . . . if she could bully Miss Eleanor into marrying Captain Hertford, and then that the pair on 'em should have the bullying and BALLY-RAGGING of nine thousand a year.'

1880. MRS. PARR, *Adam and Eve*, xxi., 292. There'll be more set to the score o' my coaxin' than ever 'all be to Adam's BULLY-RAGGING.' [M.]

1882. *Daily Telegraph*, Oct. 19, p. 3, col. 1. 'And you should have heard the BULLY-RAGGING I got, ma'am, from the mistress and the master as well.'

Bully-Rook or **Bully-Rock**, *subs.* (old). — Originally this term seems to have been applied to a pleasant or boon-companion; later, however, to a swaggerer, a bully, a bravo. [Thought by most etymologists to be a combination of BULLY (*q.v.*) + ROOK (*q.v.*), a sharper.]

1596. SHAKSPEARE, *Merry Wives of Windsor*, Act i., Sc. 3. Why says my BULLY-ROOK?

1633. SHIRLEY, *Wittie Faire One*, Act iii., Sc. 4. Such in the spirit of sack, till we be delphic, and prophesy, my BULLY-ROOK.

1697. *Praise of Yorkshire Ale.* My BULLY-ROCKS, I've been experienced long In most of Liquors. [M.]

1754. B. MARTIN, *Eng. Dict.* (2 ed.). Bully, or BULLY-ROCK, 1. a boisterous, hectoring fellow.

Bully Ruffian, *subs.* (old). — A footpad or highwayman, who, to the injury of robbery, added the insult of coarse invective. *Cf.*, BRIDLE-CULL.

Bully Trap, *subs.* (old).—A man who, though of mild outside demeanour, is a match for any ruffian who may attack him. Quoted by Grose [1785].

Bully Up (Uppingham School), *verb.*—To hurry up. Mostly used in the imperative.

Bum, *subs.* (vulgar). — 1. The posteriors; or, as Jamieson puts it, 'the part on which we sit.' [Considerable doubt exists as to the origin of this familiar term. Murray thinks the guess that BUM is an abbreviation of 'bottom' is at variance with the historical fact that the latter, in this sense, is found only from the eighteenth century; besides which there are phonetic difficulties. The origin is probably onamatopoetic.] Besides the synonyms mentioned under BLIND CHEEKS, the following may be cited:

ENGLISH SYNONYMS. Bum-fiddle; bumpkin.

FRENCH SYNONYMS. *Le foiron* (popular: from *foire* = diarrhœa); *le tal* (popular); *le garde-manger* (popular: Michel says this expression is an old one and is to be found in '*Curiositez françoises*' in the sense of 'a necessary house'); *le naze* (equivalent to 'smeller,' or 'smelling cheat'); *le soufflet* (popular: literally 'a pair of bellows'); *le prouas* (the same as *le prose*, of nautical origin); *la contre-basse* (popular: the 'double bass.' *Cf.*, *Ars musica*); *le schaffouse* (popular: a play of words, the town of that name being situated on the Lower Rhine — *chute du Rhein*, and *chute du rein*, the lower part of the back); *le gingin* (popular); *la tabatière* (popular: literally 'the snuff-box'); *la tire-lire* (popular: Rigaud says this term is in allusion to the means of subsistence [daily bread] of prostitutes); *la giberne* (literally 'cartridge-box'); *le proye* (an old canting term); *le cadet* (popular); *la figure* (*i.e.*, 'the face.' *Cf.*, 'cheeks'); *la canonnière* (literally 'a drain pipe' or 'popgun'); *l'oignon* (literally 'the onion'); *la machine à moulures*; *le département du bas Rhin* ('the department of the Lower Rhine; *rein* = back — a play upon words); *le démoc*; *le schelingo-*

phone; *le Prussien* (from the Gypsy *prusiatiñi*, translated by Borrow as 'pistol'); *le panier aux crottes* (*panier* = basket; *crottes* = dung); *le visage de campagne*; *le fignard* (*i.e.*, 'a one-eyed cheek'); *le visage sans nez* (*i.e.*, 'the face without a nose'); *le pétrouskin*; *le face du grand Turc*; *le tortillon*; *le fleurant* (popular: also 'a nose-gay'); *le pedzouille* (familiar: 'a peasant' or 'clod'); *le cadran* or *le cadran lunaise* (*cadran* = dial); *le piffe* (thieves'); *le médaillon* (popular: literally 'a medallion' or 'locket'); *l'arrière-train* (familiar: lit. 'after-carriage'); *le trèfle* (popular: this also signifies 'tobacco'); *messire Luc* (familiar: 'Mr. Luke,' sometimes also '*Nancy*.' *Cf.*, Mrs. Jones); *le moulin à vent* (lit. the 'windmill'); *le ponant* (popular); *la lune* (popular: *lune* in slang means a large full face); *le bienséant* (popular); *le pétard* (popular and thieves': it also stands for *sou*; in the Normandy patois *pétra* is used interchangeably with *pétard*); *le ballon* (popular: *ballon* = balloon; the analogy is obvious); *le moutardier* (*i.e.*, the mustard-pot); *le baril de moutarde* (cads': the mustard barrel); *l'obusier* (lit. the howitzer).

GERMAN SYNONYMS. *Tochas*; *Toges*; *Doges*.

ITALIAN SYNONYM. *Rioppo*.

1387. TREVISA, *Higden Rolls*, 6 S., 357. It semeth that his BOM is oute that hath that euel [*ficus*, *i.e.*, piles]. [M.]

1592. SHAKSPEARE, *Mids. Night's Dream*, ii., 1, l. 51.
The wisest aunt telling the saddest tale,
Sometime for three-foot stool mistaketh me;
Then slip I from her BUM, down topples she,
And *tailor* cries, and falls into a couch;
And then the whole quire hold their hips, and loffe.

1600. DEKKER, *Shoemaker's Holiday*, in wks. (1873) I., 39. Art thou acquainted with neuer a fardingale-maker, nor a French-hood maker, I must enlarge my BUMME.

1609. SHAKSPEARE, *Timon of Athens*, Act i., Sc. 2.
What a coil's here!
Serving of becks, and jutting out of BUMS!

1614. JONSON, *Bartholomew Fair*, iv., 4. Your breeches sit close enough to your BUM.

1729. SWIFT, *Intelligencer*, No. 8, p. 83 (2 ed.).
And first his BUM you see him clap
Upon the Queen of Sheba's lap.

1742. SHENSTONE, *Schoolmistress*, st. 18.
All, but the wight of BUM y-galled, he
Abhors both bench, and stool, and fourm, and chair.

1782. WOLCOT, *Lyric Odes*, No. i., in wks. (1809) I., 12. That lazy BUM-delighting thing, Ridly the Chancellor.

2. (old.)—An abbreviated form of BUM BAILIFF (*q.v.*).

1663. BUTLER, *Hudibras*, I., i. 393.
It had appeared with courage bolder,
Then Sergeant BUM, invading shoulder.

1698-1700. WARD, *London Spy*, pt. VII., p. 153.
The Vermin of the Law, the BUM,
Who gladly kept his distance,
Does safely now in Triumph come.

1845. DISRAELI, *Sybil*, bk. III., ch. i. 'Juggings has got his rent to pay, and is afeard of the BUMS.'

3. (public schools'.)—A birching; 'hiding' or 'tanning.' For synonyms, *see* TANNING. *Cf.*, also BASH and BASTE.

Verb (old).—To arrest. [An obvious allusion to the duty of a BUM or BUM-BAILIFF (*q.v.*).]

CHERRY BUMS, *subs.* (military). —The 11th Hussars. CHERRY-BUM is a corruption of Cherubim; but the obvious reference is to the scarlet trowsers worn by this branch of the service. A simi-

lar nickname is given to the French Chasseurs—*Culs rouges.* —*See* CHERUBIM.

TO TOE ONE'S BUM, *phr.* (low).—An implied threat of physical castigation, rarely, however, carried out literally; to put or 'chuck' out; to show the door to—either will explain the meaning. Sometimes the phrase occurs as 'TO HOOF ONE'S BUM.'

FRENCH SYNONYMS. *Sauter sur la contrebasse* (popular); *filer un coup de trottinet dans l'oignon* (thieves'); *boucher la lumière* (popular: properly 'to stuff up the touch-hole'); *enlever le ballon à quelqu'un* (popular: the allusion is to raising an air balloon with the foot); *donner un coup de pied juste au bon endroit* (popular: 'to give a kick just in the right part'); *botter* (popular: literally 'to make' or 'supply anyone with boots'); *détacher un coup de pinceau dans la giberne* (popular: *coup de pinceau* = 'a kick,' or 'a blow with the foot'; *giberne* = cartridge-box or, in slang, the breech); *crever un œil à quelqu'un* (popular: 'to stave in one's eye.' *Cf.*, CYCLOPS); *graisser le train de derrière* (*i.e.*, 'to grease the hinder carriage.' *Cf.*, Eng. BASTING); *détruire le faubourg à quelqu'un* (popular: properly FAUBOURG = suburb or outskirt); *enlever le schelingophone à quelqu'un* (popular).

Bum Bags, *subs.* (popular). — Trowsers. [From BUM, the posteriors, + BAGS (*q.v.*).]

Bum Bailiff, also **Bum Baily**, *subs.* (old).—An opprobrious name for a bailiff or sheriff's officer. Frequently contracted into BUM or BUMMY. [Thought to be derived from BUM (*q.v.*), an allusion to the proximity of such gentry to debtors' backs, + BAILIFF; there is no reason to suppose, as suggested, that the term is a corruption of BOUND-BAILIFF. The French have *pousse cul*, and it is curious that this term is also, in common use, abbreviated to *cul*, answering to the English contraction, BUM.]

1602. SHAKSPEARE, *Twelfth Night*, Act iii., Sc. 4. *Sir Jo.* Go, Sir Andrew; scout me for him at the corner of the orchard like a BUM-BAILY.

1628. H. SHIRLEY, *Martyr'd Souldier*, Act v. I was first a Varlet, then a BUM-BAILY, now an under Jailor.

1761. DR. HAWKESWORTH, *Edgar and Emmeline*, ii., 1. By the heavens! she has the gripe of a BUM-BAILIFF.

1822. SCOTT, *Fortunes of Nigel*, ch. xvii. 'We are in right opposition to sign and seal, writ and warrant, serjeant and tipstaff, catch-poll and BUM-BAILEY.'

1869. MRS. H. WOOD, *Roland Yorke*, ch. xxxii. 'You know the state we were in all the summer: Gerald next to penniless, and going about in fear of the BUM-BAILIES.'

Bum Bass, *subs.* (old).—Explained by quot.

1809. S. PEGGE, *Anonymiana*, p. 415 (ed. 1809). The humble-bee ought rather, perhaps, to be called the bumble-bee as it is in some parts, from the deepness of the note, just as the violoncello is called by the vulgar a BUM-BASS.

Bumble, *subs.* (common).—A beadle. [This term originated in the name of the beadle in Dickens' *Oliver Twist*, although it may be noted that in the seventeenth century BUMBLE signified a confusion, a jumble. Hence BUMBLER, an idle fellow, or blunderer. A French equivalent is *chasse-coquin* (literally a beggar driver). *Cf.*, BUMBLE-CREW and BUMBLEDOM.]

1883. *Punch*, August 4, p. 51, col. 1.
A helpless 'nuisance' shunned by the Inspector,
Ignored by BUMBLES and by Boards of Works.

Bumble-Crew, *subs.* (popular).—A collective name for corporations, vestries, and other official bodies. [From BUMBLE (*q.v.*) + CREW.]—*See* BUMBLEDOM.

Bumbledom, *subs.* (popular).—A term applied to the spirit of collective petty officialism; red tape fussiness and pomposity. [From BUMBLE (*q.v.*) + DOM.]

1856. *Saturday Review*, II., p. 12, col. 1. The collective BUMBLEDOM of Westminster. [M.]

1884. *Daily News*, Dec. 27, p. 6, col. 1. Our scheme is unfolded to the chief officer—not the slightest trace of BUMBLEDOM about him—a kind-hearted, genial, happy-faced individual.

Bumble Puppy, *subs.* (popular). — Family whist, *i.e.*, 'unscientific' whist. Also applied, says Hotten, to a game played in public houses on a large stone, placed in a slanting direction, on the lower end of which holes are made, and numbered like the holes in a bagatelle-table. The player rolls a stone ball, or marble, from the higher end, and according to the number of the hole it falls into the game is counted. It is undoubtedly the very ancient game of *Trou-le-in-madame*.

1886. *Daily News*, Dec. 25, p. 5, col. 2. Christmas cards, and mince-pies, and another helping of turkey, and family whist, or BUMBLE PUPPY.

Bumbles, *subs.* (general).—Coverings for the eyes of horses that shy in harness. *Cf.*, BLINKERS.

Bumbo, *subs.* (West Indian.)— 1. The female *pudenda*; a term applied by negroes. For synonyms, *see* MONOSYLLABLE.

2. (old.)—Smollett, in a note to the first quotation as follows, says BUMBO was a liquor composed of 'rum, sugar, water, and nutmeg.' Grose gives it as 'brandy, water, and sugar'—the component parts seem to vary according to taste.

1748. SMOLLETT, *Rod. Random*, ch. xxxiv. Who were making merry in the ward-room, round a table well stored with BUMBO and wine.

1756. *Diary of a Sussex Tradesman*, in Sussex *Arch. Coll.*, IX., 188, quoted in *N. and Q.*, 7 S., i., 194. 1756, April 28. I went down to Jones', where we drank one bowl of punch and two muggs of BUMBOO, and I came home again in liquor.

1882. *Northumbrian Minstrelsy, etc.*, p. 113, quoted in *N. and Q.*, 7 S., i., 195.
The pitmen and the keelmen trim,
They drink BUMBO made of gin.

Bum-Brusher, *subs.* (schoolboys'). —A schoolmaster; also applied to an usher. [From BUM, the posteriors, + BRUSHER, in allusion to the office a schoolmaster is sometimes called upon to perform by way of punishment.

ENGLISH SYNONYMS. Flay-bottom; haberdasher of pronouns.

FRENCH SYNONYMS. *Un marchand de soupe* (*marchand* = merchant; *soupe* = soup); *un chien de cour* (*i.e.*, 'a watch-dog'); *un fouette-cul* (a literal translation of BUM-BRUSHER).

1704. T. BROWN, wks. (1760) II., 86. [Dionysius] was forced to turn BUM-BRUSHER.

1788. *New London Magazine*, p. 137. A successor was immediately called from that great nursery of BUM-BRUSHERS, Appleby School.

1832. *Blackwood's Mag.*, Oct., p. 426. To protract existence . . . in the shape of BUM-BRUSHERS, and so forth, after the fashion of the exalted emigrés of 1792?

1838. *Comic Almanac*, Dec. [Schoolmaster's Letter signed] Barnabas BOMBRUSH.

BUM CHARTER, *subs.* (thieves').—Explained by quot.

1819. J. H. VAUX, *Memoirs*. BUM-CHARTER is the name given to bread steeped in hot water by the first unfortunate inhabitants of the English Bastile, where this miserable fare was their daily breakfast, each man receiving with his scanty portion of bread a quart of boiled water from the Cook's Coppers.

BUMCLINK, *subs.* (provincial).—In the Midland counties the inferior beer brewed for haymakers and harvest labourers. [Derivation obvious.] For synonyms, *see* SWIPES.

BUM CURTAIN, *subs.* (Cambridge Univ.).—1. An academical gown when worn scant and short; especially applied to the short black gown worn till 1835 by members of Caius College. *Cf.*, BUM-PERISHER.

1835. (Quoted in Whibley's *Three Centuries of Cambridge Wit* [1889].)
'Tis the College of Caius—'tis the land where the 'BUM
CURTAIN' lately was sported by each jolly chum,
But now black and blue are the gowns that they wear
Like the eye of a drunkard returned from a fair.

BUMF, *subs.* (schooboys').—Paper. [An abbreviation of BUM-FODDER (*q.v.*), an obvious allusion to toilet paper.]

BUMFHUNT, *subs.* (Wellington College).—A paper-chase. [Derived from the popular schoolboy name for paper, *i.e.*, BUMF (*q.v.*).]

BUM FIDDLE, *subs.* (old).—The posteriors. For synonyms, *see* BLIND CHEEKS and BUM.

BUM FIDGET, *subs.* (old).—A restless individual. [Obviously from BUM, the posterior, + FIDGET, *i.e.*, one who cannot sit still.]

BUM FODDER, *subs.* (old).—1. Low class worthless literature; a term once in literary use.—*See* sense 2.

1653. URQUHART, *Rabelais*, I., xiii. Torche-culs, arsewisps, BUM FODDERS.

1753. *Scots' Magazine*, April, p. 208, col. 1 (title). BUM FODDER for the ladies. [M.]

2. (low.) — Toilet paper, otherwise known as CURL PAPER (*q.v.*). *Cf.* BUMF.

1785. GROSE, *Dictionary of the Vulgar Tongue*. BUM FODDER, soft paper for the necessary house, or torche-cul.

BUMMAREE, *subs.* (common).—A Billingsgate middle-man. These men, who are not recognised as regular salesmen by the trade, are speculative buyers of large quantities of fish, which they re-sell in smaller lots. [The origin of the name is unknown, though some have speculated that it may be from the French *bon marée*; others, however, think that it is akin to *bomerie*, a French word for what in England is known as 'bottomry,' *i.e.*, the act of borrowing money and pledging the bottom of the ship, *i.e.*, the ship itself, for the re-payment of the money. It is argued that the leading idea in thus borrowing money on a ship's keel is the hazarding all on a single venture: hence possibly its application to other transactions, especially those connected with

the sea; such as wholesale purchases of fish, in which a large risk is run with an uncertain prospect of return—which is, it must be confessed, a somewhat far-fetched derivation.] This wholesale retailing of fish is also called BUMMAREEING IT.

1786. *Report of Committee of City of London on Price of Provisions*, 31. The BOMAREES will buy up half the fish the Salesmen have, and sell to the Fishmongers. [M.]

1851. MAYHEW, *London Labour and London Poor*, I., 71. In Billingsgate the 'forestallers' or middle men are known as BUMMAREES . . . The BUMMAREE is the jobber or speculator on the fish exchange.

1859. SALA, *Twice Round the Clock*, 4 a.m., p. 17. Any one can be a BUMBAREE . . . The process of BUMBAREEING is very simple. It consists in buying as largely as your means will afford of an auctioneer, hiring a stall for sixpence, and retailing the fish at a swingeing profit.

BUMMED, *ppl. adj.* (old).—Arrested. *Cf. verb*, BUM and BUM-BAILIFF.

BUMMER, *subs.* (old.)—1. A BUM-BAILIFF (*q.v.*).

2. (turf.)—A heavy loss; a severe pecuniary reverse.

3. (American.)—An idler; loafer; sponger; looter (*see* quots.). [From the German *bummler*, with a somewhat similar meaning, save that the term is used good naturedly, and has not altogether the offensive meaning of the American equivalent.] The term came into general use at the time of the Civil War, when it was specially applied to a straggler, hanger-on, or free-lance, particularly in connection with General Sherman's famous march from Atlanta to the sea. Besides its political signification, BUMMER is used as a general term of reproach in the same way as rascal, blackleg, etc., are used in England. Other equivalents are HEELER, STRIKER, STUFFER, and PRACTICAL POLITICIAN.

a. 1865. MAJOR NICHOLS, *Sherman's Great March*. Look hyar, Captain, we BUMMERS ain't so bad after all. We keep ahead of the skirmish line allers; we let's 'em know when an enemy's a comin', and then we ain't allus away from the regiment. We turns over all we don't want ourselves, and we can lick five times as many Rebs as we are any day.

1872. S. L. CLEMENS ('Mark Twain'), *Roughing It*, ch. xxiv. The auctioneer stormed up and down the streets on him for four days, dispersing the populace, interrupting business, and destroying children, and never got a bid—at least never any but the eighteen-dollar one he hired, a notoriously substanceless BUMMER, to make. The people only smiled pleasantly, and restrained their desire to buy, if they had any.

1872. *Sacramento Weekly Union*, Feb. 24, p. 2. All the boys to be trained as scriveners, tape-measurers, counter-hoppers, clerks, pettifoggers, polite loafers, street-hounds, hoodlums, and BUMMERS.

1875. *Scribner's Magazine*, p. 274. San Francisco is the Elysium of BUMMERS. Nowhere can a worthless fellow, too lazy to work, too cowardly to steal, get on so well. The climate befriends him, for he can sleep out of doors four-fifths of the year. He can gorge himself daily for a nominal sum, and get a dinner that a king might envy for fifty cents.

1877. W. BLACK, *Green Past. and Picc.*, ch. xiii. Then the great crowd of BUMMERS and loafers, not finding the soil teeming with nuggets, stampeded off like a herd of buffalo.

1888. *Philadelphia Press*, Jan. 29. Coy is the chairman of the Democratic Central Committee in Marion County, and has wielded great power in politics as the boss of the BUMMERS.

1888. *Detroit Free Press*, May 16. He finds that ten per cent. of the men who patronise these places have a collegiate education; forty per cent. are self-supporting, but prefer this precarious mode of living to anything more

respectable; ten per cent. earn excellent wages, and twenty per cent. are chronic BUMS, who beg or steal the price of their lodgings.

Hence BUMMERISM, to express habits of loafing and petty stealing, and BUMMERISH (*adj.*).

BUMMING, *verb*, *subs.* (Wellington College).—A thrashing, or licking. *Cf.*, BUM, sense 1.

BUMP, *subs.* (University).—When one boat touches another in a race it is said to 'make a BUMP,' and technically beats its opponent. *Cf.*, *verbal* sense, and BUMPING RACE.

Verb.—To overtake and touch an opposing boat, thus winning the heat or race.

1849. THACKERAY, *Pendennis*, ch. iii. He listened, and with respect too, to Mr. Foker's accounts of what the men did at the University of which Mr. F. was an ornament, and encountered a long series of stories about boat-racing, BUMPING, College grass-plats, and milk-punch.

1860. *Macmillan's Magazine*, March, p. 331. The chances of St. Ambrose's making a BUMP the first night were weighed.

1865. *Sketches from Cambridge*, p. 7. I can still condescend to give our boat a stout when it makes a BUMP.

1886-7. DICKENS, *Dictionary of Cambridge*, p. 11. Any boat which overtakes and BUMPS another . . . before the winning post is reached, changes place with it for the next race.

BUMPER, *subs.* (common).—1. Anything of superlative size, whether a 'big lie,' horse, house, or woman. *Cf.*, CORKER, WHOPPER, and THUMPER.

2. (theatrical.)—A full or crowded house.

1838. DICKENS, *Nich. Nickleby*, ch. xxiv., p. 192. 'In the confidence that our fellow-towsmen have not lost that high appreciation of public utility and private worth, for which they have long been so pre-eminently distinguished, we predict that this charming actress will be greeted with a BUMPER.

3. (cards'.)—When, in long whist, one side has scored eight before the other has scored a point, a BUMPER is the result.

BUM-PERISHER, BUM-SHAVER, *subs.* (common).—A short-tailed coat; a jacket. [From BUM, the posteriors, + PERISHER, a slang variant of that which 'perishes,' or fails to protect (from cold, etc.).] *Cf.*, BUM CURTAIN.

BUMPING RACE, *subs.* (University).—Eight-oared inter-Collegiate races, rowed in two divisions of fifteen and sixteen boats respectively, including a SANDWICH BOAT (*q.v.*), *i.e.*, the top boat of the second division, which rows bottom of the first. The boats in each division start at a distance apart of 175 feet from stern to stern in the order at which they left off at the last preceding race, and any boat which overtakes, and BUMPS another (*i.e.*, touches it in any part) before the winning post is reached, changes place with it for the next race.

BUMPKIN, *subs.* (old).—A humorous term for the posteriors.

1658. [In Nares] *Wit Restored*.
And so I take my leave; prithee, sweet Thumkin,
Hold up thy coats, that I may kisse thy BUMKIN.

BUMP-SUPPER, *subs.* (University).—A supper to commemorate the fact of the boat of the college having, in the annual races, 'BUMPED' or touched the boat of another college immediately in front. *Cf.*, BUMPING RACE.

BUMPTIOUS, *adj.* (colloquial).—Arrogant; self-sufficient; on good terms with oneself. [Murray puts this down as a formation from BUMP on the model of 'fractious.' It is of recent introduction.]

1803. MAD. D'ARBLAY, *Diary and Letters*, vi., 324. No, my dearest Padre, BUMPTIOUS! no, I deny the charge *in toto*. [M.]

1849. DICKENS, *D. Copperfield*, ch. vi., p. 53 (C.D.). I heard that Mr. Sharp's wig didn't fit him, and that he needn't be so 'bounceable'—somebody else said 'BUMPTIOUS'—about it, because his own red hair was very plainly to be seen behind.

1883. HAWLEY SMART, *Hard Lines*, ch. xiii. It was all very well while he was fresh, and having things pretty much as he liked. So long he was BUMPTIOUS enough.

BUMPTIOUSNESS, *subs.* (colloquial).—Self-assertiveness; arrogance; self-conceit. [From BUMPTIOUS (*q.v.*) + NESS.]

1865. SALA, *Trip to Barbary*, p. 150. Poor Albert Smith, than whom, with all his occasional BUMPTIOUSNESS, an honester and more clear-sighted hater of snobbery and shams never lived.

BUM ROLL, *subs.* (old).—A pad or cushion worn by women to extend the dress at the back—an equivalent of the modern bustle or dress-improver. [From BUM, the posteriors, + ROLL, in the sense of pad or cushion.] At one time these were called CORK RUMPS, but for synonyms, *see* BIRD-CAGE.

1601. BEN JONSON, *The Poetaster*, II., i. Nor you nor your house was so much as spoken of, before I disbased myself from my hood and my farthingal, to these BUM-ROWLS, and your whale-bone bodice.

1663. KILLIGREW, *Parson's Wedding*, *Old Plays*, XI., 460. Those worthies [of a bawd] rais'd her from the flat petticoat and kercher, to the gorget and BUM-ROLL.

BUMSQUABBLED, *ppl. adj.* (American).—Discomfitted; defeated; stupified. *Cf.*, BUM-FIDDLED, in first quot.

1620. FLETCHER, *The Chances*, I., v. And am I now BUM-FIDDLED with a bastard?

1835-40. HALIBURTON, *The Clockmaker*, p. 251 (ed. 1862). No sooner said than done, Mount Sheer Bullfrog gave the case in our favour in two twos, said Eyetaliano had got too much already, cut him off the other two-thirds, and made him pay all costs. If he didn't look BUMSQUABBLED it's a pity.

BUM SUCKER, *subs.* (general).—A sponger; toady; lick-spittle; hanger-on. [From BUM + SUCKER, allusion obvious.] *Cf.*, BUM. A French equivalent is *une lèche-cul*.

BUM TRAP, *subs.* (old).—A bailiff. *Cf.*, BUM-BAILIFF.

1750. FIELDING, *Tom Jones*, bk. VII., ch. iii. The noble BUM-TRAP, blind and deaf to every circumstance of distress, greatly rises above all the motives to humanity, and into the hands of the jailor resolves to deliver his miserable prey.

BUN, *subs.* (American).—1. A sponger; one who cannot be shaken off.

2. (common).—The female *pudenda*. For synonyms, *see* MONOSYLLABLE.

TO TAKE OR YANK THE BUN, *verbal phr.* (general)—To take first place; to obtain first honours. A variant of TAKE THE CAKE.—*See* CAKE. The French say *décrocher la timballe*.

BUNCE, BUNSE or **BUNT**, *subs.* (old).—Originally money, a signification which it still retains; more generally, however, profit, gain, anything to the good. [Thought to be a corruption of *bonus.*]—*See* quot., 1851. For synonyms in the sense of money, *see* ACTUAL.

1719. D'URFEY, *Pills*, 278. If cards come no better. Oh! oh! I shall lose all my BUNS. [M.]

1851-61. H. MAYHEW, *London Lab. and Lon. Poor*, vol. I., p. 37. There are still other 'agents' among the costermongers, and these are the 'boys' deputed to sell a man's goods for a certain sum, all over that amount being the boys' profit or BUNTS. *Ibid*, p. 526. There are a great number of boys . . . engaged by costermongers or small tradesmen, to sell upon commission, or, as it is termed, for BUNSE (probably a corruption of *bonus*, bone being the slang for good). . . . The mode is this: a certain quantity of saleable commodities is given to a boy whom a costermonger knows and perhaps employs, and it is arranged that the young commission-agent is to get a particular sum for them, which must be paid to the costermonger; I will say 3s. For these articles the lad may ask and obtain any price he can, and whatever he obtains beyond the stipulated 3s., is his own profit or BUNSE. *Ib.*, p. 36. But you see the boys will try it on for their BUNTS.

1881. *A Chequered Career*, p. 270. In the stable, and particularly in livery-stables, there is a box into which all tips are placed. This is called BUNT.

BUNCER, *subs.* (common). — One who sells on commission, as described under BUNCE (*q.v.*).

BUNCH OF FIVES, *subs.* (common).—The hand or fist. [An obvious allusion to the five fingers gathered or bunched together on the hand.]

1847. LYTTON, *Lucretia*, pt. II., ch. vii. 'Is this a h-arm, and this a BUNCH OF FIVES?'

1863. C. READE, *Hard Cash*, ch. xxxiv. 'Now look at that BUNCH OF FIVES,' continued the master; and laid a hand, white and soft as a duchess's, on the table.

1882. *Punch*, vol. LXXXII., p. 133, col. 1. He smote crashingly down . . . with a lead-weighted truncheon he held in his dexter BUNCH OF FIVES.

1883. *Daily Telegraph*, April 30, p. 3, col. 2. The fingers are bent into such an ungraceful BUNCH OF FIVES, as to be suggestive both of chalkstones and of sausages.

ENGLISH SYNONYMS. Mauley; cornstealer; fam or fem (this is said to be of Gypsy origin, and to mean five, *i.e.*, five fingers, but *see Fehm* in German synonyms); famble (*see* preceding); picker; goll (a seventeenth century term — 'make them hold up their spread GOLLS,' says Ben Jonson, in the *Poetaster*); fin; daddle; flipper.

GERMAN SYNONYMS. *Fehm* or *Vehm*, or *Vehn* (more correctly *Fem*. This appears to be the same word as the English seventeenth century colloquialism for the hand [*see* preceding], and is most likely derived from the Swedish and Danish *fem* = five, than from the Gypsy which indeed contains no such word); *Griffling* or *Greifling* (from *greifen*, to seize); *Jad* (Hebrew *jad*, the hand); *Kaf* (from the Hebrew *kaph*; the [hollow] hand).

ITALIAN SYNONYMS. *Tarantola* (an allusion to the many tentacles and close grip of the tarantula spider); *cerra*; *calchi dell' ala* (literally the foot of the arm. *Cf.*, French *doigts du pied*); *grettina* (properly a small sandbank).

SPANISH SYNONYMS. *Labradora* (this, it is curious to note, is an obsolete Spanish term signifying literally a laborious or hard-working woman, and the inference from this fact is obvious); *anclas* (literally anchors).

BUNCO or **BUNCO GAME**, *subs.* (American).—A swindling game

played either with cards or dice, not unlike three card monté. [From the Italian *banco*, a bench or bank].

1883. *Philadelphia Times*, No. 289, 2. 2. Tom's method of BUNCO was the well-known lottery game. [M.]

1888. *Daily Inter-Ocean*, Feb. 2. Robert B. Barnet, a plumber doing business in Grant Street, this city, was arrested in Allegheny to-night, on the charge of being implicated in the recent BUNCO GAME in which William Murdoch, an old and prominent citizen, was robbed of 10,000 dols.

Verb.—1. To rob, cheat, or swindle by means of the BUNCO GAME; or by what in England is known as the confidence trick, etc.

1887. *Cincinnati Enquirer*. Detectives Kirby and Funk last night spotted J. P. Ramby, the person accused of having BUNKOED Ex-County Commissioner Stephens, of Greene Cotnty, out of 2,300 dols. in Xenia recently.

1888. *Chicago Daily Inter-Ocean*, April 14. John Brothers, a farmer living near Canton, Ohio, was BUNKOED out of 2,000 dols. to-day by two sharpers who escaped.

2. From the primary meaning, the verb TO BUNCO has come to be synonymous with any attempt at swindling.

So also with various derivatives, BUNCO-CASE, BUNCO-MAN, BUNCO-STEERER (*q.v*).

BUNCO-STEERER, BUNKO-STEERER, *subs.* (American).—A swindler; confidence-trick man. The means these men adopt to win confidence are always varied and sometimes unique. They are extremely wary, and it is oftentimes with considerable difficulty that the arm of the law, long as it is assumed to be, can lay hold of them. A BUNCO-STEERER may be well known to the police as a ' rofessional swindler, and he may be seen talking to his intended victim, but, unless caught in an overt act, he cannot be interfered with. People whom BUNCO-STEERERS lay their snares for, are generally men who stand high in their communities; consequently it is almost impossible to get victims to become complainants, as they do not care to figure in the police courts, and the thieves get practically a free field for their operations.

1876. BESANT AND RICE, *Golden Butterfly*, p. 235. The BUNCO-STEERER . . . will find you out the morning after you land in Chicago or St. Louis. He will accost you — very friendly, wonderful friendly — when you come out of your hotel, by your name, and he will remind you—which is most surprising, considerin' you never set eyes on his face before—how you have dined together in Cincinnati, or it may be Orleans, or perhaps Francisco, because he finds out where you came from last; and he will shake hands with you; and he will propose a drink; and he will pay for that drink; and presently he will take you somewhere else, among his pals, and he will strip you so clean, that there won't be left the price of a four-cent paper to throw around your face and hide your blushes. In London . . . they do the confidence trick.

1888. *Daily Inter-Ocean*, Feb. 14. Andrew Carnegie fell into the hands of a BUNCO-STEERER in Pittsburg, Saturday night, but was rescued by a detective before he lost anything.

BUNDLE, *verb* (old).—To practise BUNDLING (*q.v.*).

1781. S. PETERS, *Gen. Hist. Connecticut.* It is thought but a piece of civility to ask [a lady] TO BUNDLE.

1797. SEWELL. *Queeston* is an odd way of wooing usual in some sea towns or Isles of Holland, after this manner. When the wench is gone to bed, the fellow enters the room and lays himself down in his clothes upon the blankets, next unto her, with one window of the room open, and thus he talks with her, very innocently—as it is reported.

1809. W. IRVING, *Knickerbocker History of New York.* Van Corlear stopped occasionally in the villages to . . . dance at country frolics, and BUNDLE with the Yankee lasses.

1871. SCHELE DE VERE, *Americanisms*, p. 448. TO BUNDLE, a custom still prevalent in Wales, and not unfrequently practised in the West, of men and women sleeping with all their clothes on, when there is not house-room to provide better accommodation.

BUNDLING or **BUNDLING UP**, *subs.* (old).—A custom now obsolete, but formerly in vogue where bed accommodation was scarce, of men and women sleeping on the same bed together without having removed their clothes. The practice is mentioned by Wright as having been customary in Wales, and it will be remembered that Washington Irving alludes to it in his *Knickerbocker History of New York*. Whatever may have been the case in former times, it does not appear to be a habit either in the Mother Country or the New World at the present day, even in the districts most remote from civilization. No question of immodesty seems to have attached to the custom; indeed, attempts were made to prove that BUNDLING was very right and proper. On this point, however, opinions will vary considerably. Also used in verbal form TO BUNDLE. *Cf.*, CAULK.

1809. W. IRVING, *Knickerbocker History of New York.* Among other hideous customs they [the Yankees] attempted to introduce that of BUNDLING, which the Dutch lasses of the Nederlandts, with their eager passion for novelty and for the fashions, natural to their sex, seemed very well inclined to follow, but that their mothers, being more experienced in the world and better acquainted with men and things, discountenanced all such outlandish innovations.

1814. *Quarterly Review*, X., 517. [The custom spoken of in.]

1842. C. MASSON, *Journal Balochistan, etc.*, III., 287. Many of the Afghan tribes have a custom in wooing, similar to what in Wales is known as BUNDLING-UP.

1868. W. H. DIXON, *Spiritual Wives*, vol. II., p. 31. An old custom, which exists (I believe) in Wales as well as in parts of Pennsylvania and New England, permits under the name of 'BUNDLING,' certain free, but still innocent endearments to pass between lovers who are engaged.

1871. H. R. STYLES, BUNDLING; *its Origin, Progress, and Decline in America*, title. [Contains also its history in England, Wales, Holland, curious songs, etc.]

1878. C. WAKE, *Evol. Moral.*, I., 401. The custom of BUNDLING . . . among Celtic peoples. [M.]

BUNG, BONG, BOUNG, *subs.* (old cant.)—1. A purse. [One of the oldest cant terms in the language, the origin of which is entirely unknown, though, says Murray, 'its resemblance to the O.E. *pung*, "a purse," is worth notice.'] Also called SKIN or POGE (*q.v.*). A French thieves' term is *la plotte*.

1567. HARMAN, *Caveat* (1814), p. 65. BOUNG, a purse. *Ibid*, p. 86.

1591. GREENE, *Second Part Connycatching*, in wks., vol. X., p. 96. The Nip vseth his knife, and if he see a BOUNG lie faire, strikes the stroke.

1610. ROWLANDS, *Martin Mark-all*, p. 37 (H. Club's Repr., 1874). BUNG is now vsed for a pocket, heretofore for a purse.

c. 1658. CLEVELAND, *Cleivelandi Vindiciæ*, p. 99 (ed. 1677). He is in the Inquisition of the Purse an Authentick Gypsie, that nips your BUNG with a canting Ordinance.

1671. R. HEAD, *English Rogue*, pt. I., ch. v., p. 47. BOUNG, a Purse.

1706. E. COLES, *Eng. Dict.* BUNG, a purse.

2. (old.)—A pickpocket. *Cf.*, BUNG, sense 1. BUNG-NIPPER (*q.v.*) was in general usage later.

1598. SHAKSPEARE, *King Henry IV.*, ii., 4. *Doll.* Away, you cut-purse rascal! you filthy BUNG, away! By this wine, I'll thrust my knife in your mouldy chaps, an' you play the saucy cuttle with me.

1658. *An Age for Apes*, p. 232. My BUNG observing this, takes hold of time, Just as this lord was drawing for a prime, And smoothly rims his purse that lay beside him.

3. (common.) — A brewer; landlord of a public house, etc. [An allusion to the BUNGS, or large corks used in the 'mouths' of beer barrels.]

1863. *Cornhill Magazine* (*The Inner Life of a Man-of-War*), Feb. From time immemorial these gentlemen [master's assistants] have had to stand at the grog-butt and see the grog served out—an important duty, the discharge of which has invested them, such is the playfulness of naval humour, with the title of BUNGS.

1884. *Graphic*, Feb. 23, p. 170, col. 1. That Sir Wilfrid Lawson had turned BUNG, and applied for a spirit licence.

Verb (pugilistic).—1. Generally BUNG UP, *i.e.*, to close or shut up the eyes by means of a blow that causes a swelling. Formerly used of the mouth, ears, etc., and in literary use, but now regarded as a vulgarism. *Cf. verb*, sense 2.

1593. G. HARVEY, *Pierces Super.*, in wks. (Grosart) II., 128. That will BUNG-UP their mouthes with a Collyrium of all the stale iestes in a country.

1599. NASHE, *Lenten Stuffe*, in wks. V., 247. The waies beyond sea were so BUNGD VP with your dayly oratours or *Beadsmen* and your crutchet or croutchant friers . . . that a snaile coulde not wriggle in her hornes betwixt them.

1835. HALIBURTON, *Clockmaker*, 1 S., ch. xix. 'I BUNGED UP both eyes for him.'

2. (old.)—To give; pass; hand over; drink; or to perform almost any action. 'BUNG over the rag,' hand over the money. Used by Beaumont and Fletcher, and Shakspeare. Also, to deceive one by a lie, to CRAM, which *see*.

BUNGAY. GO TO BUNGAY! *phr.* (general).—A euphemistic objurgation equivalent to consignment to a region the climate of which is tropical in character. For analogous phrases, *see* GO TO HELL.

BUNG-EYED, *comp. ppl. adj.* (common). — 1. Drunk; fuddled; SCREWED, which *see* for synonyms. [Derivation uncertain: possibly from the Scotch 'bung,' a low word quoted by Jamieson as meaning tipsy or fuddled, with perhaps an indirect allusion to the bunged or crooked distorted eye, the result of a fight or squabble.—*See* sense 2.]

1858. A. MAYHEW, *Paved with Gold*, bk. III., ch. iii., p. 268. One coarse-featured fellow, who was nearly BUNG-EYED over his beer (as they call being drunk).

2. Cross-eyed; unable to see straight; 'boss-eyed' or 'SQUINNY-EYED' (*q.v.*).

BUNGFUNGER, *verb* (American).—To startle; to confuse. Compare with BUMBSQUABBLED. Also used as an adjective for 'confounded.'

1835-40. HALIBURTON, *The Clockmaker*, p. 91 (ed. 1862). 'Well, father, I thought he'd a fainted too, he was so struck up all of a heap; he was completely BUNG-FUNGERED.'

BUNG-JUICE, *subs.* (thieves').—Porter, or beer. [From BUNG, a stopper for casks in which beer is kept, + JUICE. *Cf.*, COW-JUICE for milk, etc.] For synonyms, *see* DRINKS and SWIPES.

Bung Knife or **Boung Knife,** *subs.* (old).—Considerable uncertainty exists as to the nature or use of this implement. It has however been conjectured that as BOUNG was an old cant word for a purse, that BOUNG KNIFE may therefore have been a knife kept in the purse or girdle, but concerning this nothing definite can be stated.

1592. GREENE, *Quip for Upstart Courtier (Hart. Misc.*, V., 407). One of them had on . . . a skeine like a bruer's BOUNG-KNIFE.

Bung Nipper or **Boung Nipper,** *subs.* (old).—A cut-purse; a sharper. [From BUNG (*q.v.*), an old canting term for a purse, + NIPPER, a thief, *i.e.*, one who nips or steals.] In French, to nip a bung is *couper une queue de rat, i.e.*, literally to cut off a rat's tail; but for synonyms, *see* AREA-SNEAK and THIEVES.

Bung Upwards, *adv. phr.* (old).—Said of a person lying on his face.

Bunk, *subs.* (common). — Hasty departure. *Cf.*, BUNK, *verb*. [Of unknown derivation.]

c. 1870. *Broadside Ballad*, 'Peck's Bad Boy.'
Of course you're heard of Peck's bad boy,
that dreadful Yankee lad,
Who's bothered his poor parents so
they've both gone raving mad,
. . . .
He put a pound of old Scotch snuff into
poor Buddha's trunk,
The keeper tried to catch him, but the
bad boy did a BUNK.

Verb (common).—1. To be off; to decamp. For synonyms, *see* AMPUTATE.

c. 1872. *Broadside Ballad*, 'Oh, we are a getting on.'
A stocking used a 'bank' to be,
In the good old days of old,
They didn't run such risks as we
Do now of getting sold.
No sooner does a bank go queer,
You hear the same old strain,
There's another bald-headed Manageer,
Has BUNKED across to Spain.

1885. *Referee*, Feb. 16, p. 7, col. 3.
It was just such a parcel, bless him! he'd
clasped to his noble breast,
And BUNKED with out o' the building.

1887. *Fun*, 9 Nov., p. 201. 'What is a vanishing point?' said the schoolmaster to little Billy. 'The corner you BUNKS round when the "slops" after yer,' warbled the golden-haired child.

2. (Wellington College.)—To expel [from the school].

Bunker, *subs.* (common).—Beer. For synonyms, *see* DRINKS and SWIPES.

Bunkum, Buncombe, Buncome, *subs.* (American). — Talking merely for talking's sake; claptrap of all kinds; gas; tall talk. The employment of the word in its original sense of insincere political speaking or claptrap is ascribed to a member of Congress, Felix Walker, from Buncombe County, North Carolina, who explained that he was merely talking for BUNCOMBE, when his fellow members could not understand why he was making a speech. Judge Haliburton (Sam Slick) in explaining this word says that 'all over America, every place likes to hear of its member of Congress, and see their speeches; and, if they don't, they send a piece to the paper, inquirin' if their members died a natural death, or was skivered with a bowie-knife, for they hante seen his speeches lately, and his friends are anxious to know his fate. Our free and enlightened citizens don't approbate silent members; it don't seem to them

as if Squashville, or Punkinsville, or Lumbertown was right represented, unless Squashville, or Punkinsville, or Lumbertown makes itself heard and known, ay, and feared too. So every feller, in bounden duty, talks, and talks big too, and the smaller the State, the louder, bigger, and fiercer its members talk. Well, when a critter talks for talk's sake, jist to have a speech in the paper to send to home, and not for any other airthly puppus but electioneering, our folks call it BUNKUM.'

The term is now universal on both sides of the water, and, indeed, wherever English is spoken. So much is this the case that the expression may now fairly claim a permanent place in the language. The primary meaning has been somewhat enlarged. 'That's all BUNCOMBE' is equivalent to 'That's all nonsense' or 'an absurdity.'

Also used attributively; for example, a BUNKUM proclamation, BUNKUM logic, BUNKUM politicians, etc.

1841. *Richmond Compiler*, Aug. 17. He was not speaking to the House but to BUNKUM.

1859. SALA, *Tw. Round the Clock*, 2 a.m., par. 9. These tales, full of sound and fury, told by honourable idiots full of unutterable 'BUNKUM' (an Americanism I feel constrained to use, as signifying nothingness, ineffably inept and irremediably fire-perforated windbaggery, and sublimated cucumber sunbeams hopelessly eclipsed into Dis)—

1861. *Blackwood's Mag.*, April. 'This parable, explaining the origin of BUNCOMBE, would form a very useful text to set up, handsomely illustrated, over the Speaker's chair in Parliament.'

1862. *New York Tribune*, Feb. 11. Despatch from Kansas. General Sibley was within thirty miles of Fort Craig, with twenty-five hundred Texans, with artillery, and had issued a BUNKUM proclamation.

1884. *Echo*, May 12, p. 4, col. 2. It will be seen that the wonderful tales about the favourites were like the reports about Richmond's lameness, all BUNKUM.

1888. *Daily Inter-Ocean*, March 3. This thing of trying to rule a husband is all BUNCOMBE; it can't be done. You can coax most men, bribe some, and govern a very few, but that vulgar rubbing of the fur the right way wins every time.

1889. *Pall Mall Gazette*, 18 Oct., p. 6, col. 2. His explanation was contained in the three words, 'Bosh, rubbish, and BUNKUM.' Was it not time, asked the speaker, that the 'great unwashed' should declare that the 'great unpaid' were no longer at liberty to oppress them?

Bunky, *adj.* (Christ's Hospital).—Awkward; ill-finished.

Bunnick, *verb* (common). — To settle; to dispose of.

1886. *Punch*, 17 July, p. 25. 'Owsomever we've BUNNICKED up Gladsting, a barney all patriots enjoy.

Bunny Grub, *subs.* (Cheltenham College). — Green vegetables, such as cabbage, lettuce, and the like. [Obviously from BUNNY, a pet name for a rabbit, + GRUB, a slang term for provender, *i.e.*, food akin to that upon which rabbits are fed.] At the Royal Military Academy and other schools an equivalent is GRASS (*q.v.*).

Bunse.—*See* BUNCE.

Bun-Struggle or **Bun-Worry,** *subs.* (military).—A tea meeting given to soldiers. For synonymous terms, *see* TEA FIGHT.

Bunt.—*See* BUNCE.

Bunter, *subs.* (harlotry). — 1. A prostitute; one who adds theft to her other vocation; also a term of contempt for any low woman. See, however, quot. from Dyche, 1748, and Mayhew, 1851. For analogous terms, *see* BARRACK-HACK.

1705-7. E. WARD, *Hudibras Rediv.*, II., ii. (1715), 25. Punks, Strolers, Market Dames, and BUNTERS. [M.]

1748. SMOLLETT, *Rod. Random*, ch. xlvii. And asked with some heat, if he thought I had spent the evening in a cellar with chairmen and BUNTERS.

1748. T. DYCHE, *Dictionary* (5 ed.). BUNTER (s.), one who goes about the streets to gather rags, bones, etc.

1759. WALPOLE, *Parish Register*.
Here Fielding met his BUNTER Muse,
And, as they quaff'd the fiery juice,
Droll Nature stamp'd each lucky hit,
With unimaginable wit.

1763. *British Magazine*, vol. IV., p. 542. I heard a BUNTER at the Horse-Guards . . . swear she would not venture into the Park.

1765. GOLDSMITH, *Essays*, x. The BUNTERS who swagger in the streets of London.

1851-61. H. MAYHEW, *London Lab. and Lon. Poor*, vol. II., p. 158. They were known by the name of BUNTERS, which signifies properly gatherers of rags.

2. Explained by quotation. [BUNTER here may be a confused variant of BUNKER, one who runs away or 'slopes.']

1851. H. MAYHEW, *London Lab. and Lon. Poor*, IV., 223. There is a class of women technically known as BUNTERS, who take lodgings, and after staying some time run away without paying their rent.

Burdon's Hotel, *subs.* (thieves'). —Whitecross Street Prison, of which the Governor was a Mr. Burdon. Almost every prison has a nickname of this kind, either from the name of the Governor, or from some local circumstance. The Queen's Bench has an immense number of names — SPIKE, PARK, etc.; and every Chief-Justice stands godfather to it. For full list of such names, *see* CAGE.

1861. DUTTON COOK, *Paul Foster's Daughter*, ch. ii. 'David, be respectable, whatever you are, be respectable, and BURDON'S HOTEL is not for you to sojourn at.'

Burick or **Burerk,** *subs.* (old).—Latterly applied to any woman or 'lady,' especially one showily dressed, but formerly a thief's term for a prostitute.

1819. J. H. VAUX, *Memoirs*. BURICK is a prostitute, or common woman.

1851. MAYHEW, *London Labour and London Poor*, I., p. 262. If they can meet with the BURERK (mistress) or the young ladies, etc.

1889. *Answers*, July 20, p. 121, col. 2. Let him ask the loafer what his 'Monekear' (name) is; whether he can drink a 'shant of patter' (pint of beer); whether he finds the 'bone' or 'gammy'—that is good or bad as regards begging; and which sex gives him most—the 'BURERKS' (ladies), or the 'Toffs' (gentlemen).

Amongst French equivalents for a well-dressed woman may be mentioned *une panuche* (this name is also applied to a prostitute living in a brothel); *une dubuge*; *une faraude* (the masculine form, *un faraud*, signifies a vulgar fellow proud of smart clothes—a snob, a swell).

Burke, *verb* (military).—To dye the moustache and whiskers. [BURKE properly is to smother or hush up, and the allusion in the military term is to the practice which once prevailed in smart regiments of dyeing or smothering the natural colour of the hair for the sake of uniformity. The regulations at one time as regards the style of wearing the hair were very stringent and precise.]

Burn, *verb* (thieves').—To cheat; to swindle.

Burnanded, *verb* (? nonce word). —To pilfer plots (of plays, novels, etc.). [Probably only a nonce word; a formation on the same lines as 'Burke,' 'Boycott,' etc., from the name of Mr. F. Burnand, the editor of *Punch*.]

1882. *Echo*, Feb. 11, p. 3. The American papers continue to attack the play [*The Colonel*] vigorously. One of the journals there has invented a new verb to signify the pilfering of plots. 'BURNANDED' is the term.

Burn Crust, *subs.* (old). — A jocular name for a baker. *Cf.*, MASTER OF THE MINT for a gardener; BUNG for a brewer; BALL OF WAX for a shoemaker; QUILL-DRIVER for a clerk; SNIP for a tailor, etc.

Burned. TO BE BURNED, *verb* (old).—To be infected with a venereal disease.—*See* BURNING.

1785. GROSE, *Dictionary of the Vulgar Tongue*. He was sent out a sacrifice, and came home a BURNT offering; saying of seamen who have caught the venereal disease abroad.

Burner, *subs.* (old).—1. A card-sharper.

2. (old.) — The same as BURNING (*q.v.*).

Burning, *verb, subs.* (old). — A venereal disease. Shakspeare alludes to it in *King Lear*, 'No heretics BURN'D, but wenches' suitors.'

Burning Shame. — An obscene practice.—*See* Grose.

Burning the Parade, *phr.* (old). —Thus explained by Grose: 'Warning more men for a guard than were necessary, and excusing the supernumeraries for money. This was a practice formerly winked at in most garrisons, and was a very considerable perquisite to the adjutants and sergeant majors; the pretence for it was to purchase coal and candle for the guard, whence it was called BURNING THE PARADE.'

Burn My Breeches! *phr.* (old).—A mild kind of oath. A few latter day 'fancies' of the same kind will be found under OATHS.

1819. MOORE, *Tom Crib's Memorial*, p. 46.
. . . (Bill Gibbons ne'er
In all his days was known to swear,
Except light oaths, to grace his speeches,
Like '*dash my wig*,' or 'BURN MY
BREECHES.')

Burn the Ken, *verbal phr.* (old).—To live at an inn or tavern without paying for one's quarters. [From BURN (*q.v.*), to cheat, + KEN, an inn, tavern, or place.]

Burr, *subs.* (old).—A hanger on; a dependent; one who sponges. [An allusion to field burrs or prickly seed pods, which when once attached to the clothing are difficult to remove.]

Verb (Marlborough College). —To fight; scrimmage or 'rag.'

Burst, *subs.* (general). — 1. A spree; drunken frolic; big feed; BLOW OUT (*q.v.*). Usually ON THE BURST, an extension of the figurative usage of the word signifying a violent outburst.—*See* BUST.

1880. *Blackwood's Mag.*, June, p. 775. He became a madman when drunk. Once 'ON THE BURST,' as he phrased it, money, horses, cows, furniture, even his wife's wearing apparel, went to feed the insatiable and cruel demon who possessed him.

1881. PRAED, *Policy and Passion*, vol. I., p. 228. When his men go ON THE BURST, what can he do but make his daughters help?

2. (sporting.)—A sudden and vigorous access or display of energy; a lively pace or spurt.

BURSTED, *ppl. adj.* (general).—Hard up. [From BURST, failure or collapse, + ED.]

1873. *Chicago Daily Tribune*, June 30. At the far end [of the room] four lank and BURSTED frontiersmen sang with a doleful want of melody or attention the celebrated ballad by John Hay on the fate of Little Breeches.

BURSTER, *subs.* (racing).—1. A heavy fall; a 'cropper.'

1863. *Evening Standard*, 24 April. Benedict came down a BURSTER, and was out of the race.

2. *See* also BUSTER, sense 1.

BURY. GO BURY YOURSELF! *phr.* (American).—A Californianism which has more of the *fortiter* than the *suaviter* in its composition. Equivalent to 'Go! hide your diminished head.' *Cf.*, CARRY ME OUT AND BURY ME DECENTLY.

TO BURY OR DIG UP THE HATCHET, *verbal phr.* (American).—Amongst Indian tribes certain symbolic ceremonies are connected with the war-hatchet or tomahawk, which are equivalent to a declaration of war, or a compact of peace.——TO BURY THE HATCHET is the emblem of the putting away of strife and enmity; on the other hand, the red skin, before he commences hostilities, digs up afresh the fateful symbol. This picturesque imagery has passed into the colloquial inheritance of the American people, and the expressions of BURYING or DIGGING UP THE HATCHET are frequently applied to the affairs of everyday life. This symbolism though new in form is old in idea. Shakspeare in *The Tempest*, v., 1, 55, says, 'I'le breake my staffe, bury it certaine fadomes in the earth.'

1855-59. WASHINGTON IRVING, *Life of Washington*, I., p. 361. 'They smoked the pipe of peace together, and the colonel claimed the credit of having, by his diplomacy, persuaded the sachem to BURY THE HATCHET.'

1855. LONGFELLOW, *Hiawatha*, 13.
BURIED was the bloody HATCHET;
Buried was the dreadful war-club;
Buried were all warlike weapons,
And the war-cry was forgotten;
Then was peace among the nations.

1873. *Carleton Ballads.*
I don't know what you'll think, sir—I didn't come to inquire—
But I picked up that agreement and stuffed it in the fire;
And I told her we'd BURY THE HATCHET alongside of the cow;
And we struck an agreement never to have another row.

TO BURY A MOLL, *phr.* (general).—To desert or forsake a wife or mistress. [MOLL = woman, wife, or prostitute.]

FRENCH SYNONYMS. *Envoyer une ouistiti* (*ouistiti* signifies properly a striated monkey); *lâcher une femme* (literally to cast off a woman); *balancer une largue.*

TO BURY A QUAKER, *phr.* (Irish slang).—To evacuate; to ease oneself.

ENGLISH SYNONYMS. To go to the crapping castle, casa, or ken (castle, casa, and ken are old canting terms for a place or

house); to the West Central (a punning allusion to the initials W.C. for water closet); to Mrs. Jones; to the chapel-of-ease; to Sir Harry; to the bog-house, rear, dunnock, coffee-shop; to see one's aunt; to crap; to go and sing 'sweet violets'; to go where the queen always goes on foot.

FRENCH SYNONYMS. *Mousser* (popular: literally to foam or effervesce); *enterrer son colonel* (*Cf.*, to bury a Quaker); *aller faire une ballade à la lune* (*i.e.*, 'to go and sing to the moon'; also *ballade* = stroll, walk, or lounge; likewise in French slang *lune* = posteriors); *mouler un sénateur* (popular); *mouler une Venus* (artists'); *gazonner* (literally to 'cover with turf'); *aller au numero cent* (a play upon the word *sent*); *déponer* (Michel thinks that though at first sight this word would seem to be directly derived from the Latin *deponere*, yet it really either comes from the old French *ponant*, signifying posteriors, or from the verb *poner*, used in the thirteenth century in the sense of *pondre*, *i.e.*, to lay eggs); *débourrer sa pipe* (popular); *défalquer* (popular); *tarter* or *tartir* (popular and thieves': in Latin *alvum deponere. Cf.*, Italian Fourbesque *tartire*); *faire une moulure* (*moulure* in architecture = moulding); *aller quelque part* (lit. to go somewhere); *aller à ses affaires* (lit. 'to go to one's business'); *aller où le roi va à pied* (*i.e.*, to go where the king goes on foot. *Cf.*, to go where the queen always goes on foot); *filer* (properly to spin); *aller chez Jules* (to go to Julius. *Cf.*, to go and see one's aunt); *ierchem* (low: *chier*, a disguised obscenity, + *em*); *flasquer* (thieves'); *touser* (this word comes from *tourtouse* and signifies properly *faire de la corde*); *faire corps neuf* (properly to take a new lease of one's life); *déposer une médaille de papier volant*, or *des Pays-Bas* (obsolete); *faire des cordes* (*des cordes* = strings); *mettre une lettre à la poste* (lit. to go and post a letter); *faire le grand* (*grand* = an opprobrious epithet); *faire une commission* (to run an errand); *fogner* (popular); *flaquer* (popular: literally 'to dash' [water or any other liquid]); *écrire à un Juif* (literally to write to a Jew); *déposer une pêche* (popular); *poser une pépin* (popular: *poser* = to place or cast down; *pépin*, in botany a kernel or pip); *poser un factionnaire* (popular: *factionnaire* is properly a sentinel or sentry); *poser une sentinelle* (popular: with same meaning as foregoing); *envoyer une depêche à Bismarck* (popular: this may be a contemptuous usage of the German Chancellor's name, although in French slang *couleur Bismarck* = brown colour); *aller où le roi n'envoie personne* (lit. to go where the king sends no one); *flaquader* (*flaque* = excrement); *fuser* (properly to dissolve); *gâcher du gros* (popular); *galipoter* (another slang meaning of this word is 'to smear'); *pousser son rond* (popular); *faire ronfler la chaire percée — Thomas — le bourrelet — la chaise percée* (*faire ronfler* = to cause to or make snore, *chaire* = Bishop's throne, *chaire percée* = close-stool, and *bourrelet* = padded cushion with hole in centre, *Thomas* = bedroom chamber); *aller voir Bernard* (*Cf.*, *aller chez Jules*); *aller au*

buen-retiro (*buen retiro* properly = a private place of retirement, but in this sense is an ironical allusion to a W.C.); *faire un pruneau* or *poser un pruneau* (Michel thinks this expression is derived from *clos Bruneau*, a facetious name given to the posteriors about the sixteenth century); *filer le cable de proue* (Michel gives this as of nautical origin—seamen's latrines being situated in the fo'cas'le).

ITALIAN FOURBESQUE. *Tartire* (properly to lighten or ease one's conscience by confessing to a Priest).

TO BURY A WIFE, *verbal phr.* (old). — To feast and make merry, an expression used in connection with the jollifications frequently indulged in by apprentices on the completion of their term of indenture, when they became 'full blown' craftsmen.

BUS or **BUSS**, *subs.* (theatrical).—1. A variant of BUSINESS (*q.v.*), of which it is an abbreviation. Pronounced *biz.*

2. (common.)—A contraction of 'omnibus.'

1832. HT. MARTINEAU, *Weal and Woe*, i., 14. If the station offers me a place in a BUSS. [M.]

1852. DICKENS, *Bleak House*, p. 93. He proposed that they should go, per BUSS, a little way into the country.

1861. THACKERAY, *Adventures of Philip*, II., p. 316. We were mortified to see that of the five persons conveyed by the 'BUS, one was a tradesman, etc.

1869. BLACK, *In Silk Attire*, II., p. 205. Annie Brunel got out of the Hampstead 'BUS, and found herself in the muddy highway.

Verb (American).—To punch [one's head].

BUSH or **BE BUSHED**, *verb* (Australian).—Primarily to camp out in the bush; or to get lost in the bush. Hence a slang usage in which the expression is applied to a person in any mental or physical difficulty or muddle.

1887. *All the Year Round*, July 30, p. 68. An Australian says that he IS BUSHED just as an Englishman, equally characteristically, declares that he is fogged.

1889. B. L. FARJEON, *In Australian Wilds.* 'We shall have TO BUSH it, mate,' I said. 'That's so,' said Lilly Trot, unconcernedly; but looking about him sharply, despite his apparent carelessness, for a suitable spot to camp on. *Ibid.* We were on horseback, with blankets before us on our saddles, to provide for our getting BUSHED. We were prepared for rough times. I carried my revolver, and Lilly Trot had a villainous-looking black life-preserver up his sleeve, ready at a moment's notice for any emergency.

BUSHED, *ppl. adj.* (old).—Hard up; without money; destitute.

1812. J. H. VAUX, *Flash Dictionary.* BUSH'D, poor; without money.

BUSHED ON, *verbal phr.* (common).—Pleased; delighted.

BUSHEL BUBBY, *subs.* (old).—A full and large breasted woman. [From BUSHEL, a (large) measure, + BUBBY (*q.v.*), a breast.] *Cf.*, BUBBER.

BUSHWHACKER, *subs.* (American political).—In politics, as in war, simply a 'free-lance.' During the Rebellion deserters from the ranks of both armies infested the country, bands of these marauders making raids upon defenceless houses and even going the length of sacking whole towns. Originally the term was harmless enough in meaning. At a time when

water-communication was the chief means of locomotion, and the rivers, streams, and creeks of densely wooded regions were alive with the advance guards of civilization, BUSHWHACKING was the name given to the means by which lumbermen propelled their craft up and down stream. This was accomplished by pulling the bushes growing by the water side; or, on land, by the cutting away of a thicket in order to obtain a passage. The man who did this, and the instrument—a kind of scythe or cutlass with which, in the latter case, he thus forced his way — were alike called BUSHWHACKERS. The word has gone through yet another transition. Since the war it has also come to mean a 'country bumpkin,' a 'clodpole,' or any other person of a 'verdant' character.

BUSHY PARK, *subs.* (rhyming slang).—A lark.

TO BE IN BUSHY PARK, *phr.* (old).—To be poor.

BUSINESS, *subs.* (old).—1. Sexual intercourse. For synonyms, *see* GREENS.

1630. TAYLOR, *Workes.* And Lais of Corinth, ask'd Demosthenes One hundred crownes for one night's BUSINESSE.

1654. *Wits Recreations.*
What Crispulus is that in a new gown,
All trim'd with loops and buttons up and down,
That learns there on his arm in private chat
With thy young wife, what Crispulus is that?
He's proctor of a court, thou say'st and does
Some BUSINESS of my wives: thou brainless goose,
He does no BUSINESS of thy wives, not he,
He does thy BUSINESS (Coracine) for thee.

2. (theatrical.) — Dramatic action; bye-play.

1753. *The World*, No. 26. We are too much enamoured with what is called intrigue, BUSINESS, and bustle, in our plays.

1820. SCOTT, *The Abbot*, ch. xxvii. (III., p. 6). The . . . went, came, and returned, mingling in every scene of the piece, and interrupting the BUSINESS.

1860. *Cornhill Magazine*, Dec., p. 749. So well do performers understand this principle, that they give the literary composition the utmost contemptuous title of 'words,' while they dignify the movements of the characters with the name of BUSINESS.

1876. C. HINDLEY, *Life and Adventures of a Cheap Jack*, p. 282. Tom observed, I never saw such BUSINESS before; how do you do it with that board thing, for I can't manage it? I have knocked and bruised some of my people about so that they swear they would sooner leave than have such another day.

1880. *Punch*, Sept. 18, 130. 'Quite in his Line.' *Stout Major* (*to Professional Actor, who has been asked down to coach the Garrison Amateurs*): 'Aw—we played *The Bells* at our last Theatricals, of which I've the Management. I—aw—played Irving's part myself. Aw—immense Success!' *Professional* (*drily*): 'Of course you've seen him in it?' *Major*: 'Ya-as—but—aw—I didn't copy him in the least—aw—my own 'BUSINESS.' Aw— Entirely different reading. In fact, every one said it wasn't a bit like him!

1883. H. IRVING, in *Good Words*, Jan., p. 34. Then consider what scope the 'BUSINESS' of the scene gives to the actor's purpose.

TO DO ONE'S BUSINESS FOR ONE, *phr.* (common).— To kill; to cause one's death.

1880. JAS. GREENWOOD, *Grandmother Cooper*, in *Odd People in Odd Places*, p. 4. 'They said it was his hurts as killed him,' said the old lady, 'but it was no use 'em telling me that. It was the bricks and mortar that DID HIS BUSINESS, poor chap.'

BUSINESS END [of a thing], *subs.* (American). — The practical part.

BUSK IT, *verb* (vagrants'). — To sell obscene songs and books at the bars and in the tap-rooms of public houses. Sometimes it implies selling other articles. Also to 'work' public houses and certain spots as an itinerant musician or vocalist. So also BUSKING, *verb subs.* and *ppl. adj.* and BUSKER, a man who thus sings and performs in public houses: an itinerant.

1851. MAYHEW, *London Labour and London Poor*, III., p. 234. From a furniture-carter of this description I received some most shocking details of having to BUSK IT, as this taking about goods for sale is called by those in the trade. *Ibid*, I., p. 229. They obtained a livelihood by BUSKING, as it is termed, or in other words, by offering their goods for sale only at the bars or in the taprooms and parlours of taverns. *Ibid*, III., p. 216. BUSKING is going into public houses and playing and singing and dancing. *Ibid*, p. 222. I now thought I'd try what is termed BUSKING, that is going into public houses and cutting likenesses of the company.

1883. Advt. in *Echo*, May 10, p. 4, col. 6. BUSKING.—A player on the harp and violin wants a mate.

1897. *Referee*, August 21, p. 3, col. 2. Mac himself . . . will appear in the Racecourse scene as a BUSKER.

BUSKER.—*See* under BUSK.

BUSKING.—*See* under BUSK.

BUSNAPPER.—*See* BUZ-NAPPER.

BUSNAPPER'S KINCHIN.—*See* BUZNAPPER'S KINCHIN.

BUSS.—*See* BUS.

BUSS BEGGAR, *subs.* (old).—An old prostitute of the lowest type; a beggar's trull.

BUST, *subs.* (vulgar).—A corrupted form of BURST. So also BUSTING (*adj.*); BUSTED (*ppl. adj.*), etc., etc.

1837. DICKENS, *Oliver Twist*, p. 219. A kind of BUSTING noise.

2. (thieves'.)—A burglary.

18(?79). HORSLEY, *Jottings from Jail*. 'Fatty Bill, from City Road, rem. for a BUST ex. two years,' means that William . . . has been compelled to leave his congenial haunts in the City Road, as he is remanded for a burglary, and anticipates two years' hard labour.

3. (general.) — A frolic; a spree; a drunken debauch. *Cf.*, TO GO ON THE BUST.

1860. BARTLETT (quoted in), *A Californian Song*.
And when we get our pockets full
Of this bright, shinin' dust,
We'll travel straight for home again,
And spend it on a BUST.

4. (American.)—A failure; a fizzle.

Verb (vulgar).—1. To burst; explode.

1838. DICKENS, *Nicholas Nickleby*, II., p. 366. His genius would have BUSTED.

1843. DICKENS, *Martin Chuzzlewit*, I., p. 286. Keep cool, Jefferson . . . don't BUST! *Ibid*, II., p. 124. If the biler of this vessel was Toe BUST Sir . . . and Toe BUST now, it would be a festival day in the calendar of despotism.

2. (thieves'.)—To commit a burglary.

3. (thieves'.) — To inform against an accomplice. A slang variant of 'split' (turn king's evidence, impeach). The person who does this SPLITS or BURSTS the whole concern.

4. (American.)—To fail in business or transactions of any kind.

5. (general.)—To put out of breath; to 'wind.'

c. 1880. *Broadside Ballad*, 'Taking out the Baby.' Spoken—And they had all been taking out the baby, and all had had such a doing—that boy o' mine nearly BUSTED me—and of course they all think they deserve a glass of beer.

6. (American.)—To indulge in a drunken frolic; to go on the spree. *Cf.*, TO GO ON THE BUST.

1869. *New Orleans Picayune*, Feb. 14. 'Because I was a good-natured fellow, I had to go with them, rollicking, teaparting, excursioning, and BUSTING generally.'

7. (American.)—To destroy; to commit suicide; to 'set aside'; to expose.

1880. BRET HARTE, *Chiquita*, p. 22. Did you know Briggs of Tuolumne? BUSTED hisself in White Pine, and blew out is brains.

1888. *North of England Advertiser*, Sept. 1. Then he got the Moabite pottery which Mr. Clement Ganneau BUSTED.

BUST ME! *phr.* (common).—A mild oath—BLOW ME! JIGGER ME! (*q.v.*)—*See* also OATHS.

1859. DICKENS, *Tale of Two Cities*, bk. I., ch. iii. 'BUST ME if I don't think he'd been a drinking!'

TO GO ON THE BUST, *phr.* (common).—To go on a frolic or spree. For synonyms, *see* PAINT THE TOWN RED.

BUSTER, *subs.* (common).—1. A small new loaf; also a coarse cake or bun of large size that fills or blows out the stomach of the eater. [From BUST, a vulgar form of 'burst,' + ER.] *Cf.*, STARVER.

1821. W. T. MONCRIEFF, *Tom and Jerry*, Act ii., Sc. 3. *Bob:* Now, landlord, 'arter that ere drap of max, suppose we haves a *drain o' heavy wet*, just by way of cooling our *chaffers*—mine's as *dry as a chip*—and, I say, do you hear, let's have a twopenny BURSTER, half a quartern of BEESVAX, a ha'p'orth o' ingens, and a dollop o' salt along vith it, vill you? *Mace:* Bellay! a BURSTER and beesvax—ingens and salt here. (*Calling as he fetches the porter from the side wing*, L.) Now, then, here you are, Master Grimmuzzle.

1841. *Comic Almanacks*, 1835-43 (Hotten), p. 295.
Cut us a slap-up slice of Cheshire cheese,
And tip's a twopenny BURSTER if you please.'

1849. *Bell's Life.* [From Baumann.] A BURSTER with a slice of beeswax.

1876. HINDLEY, *Life and Adventures of a Cheap Jack*, p. 192. Mo and his man were having a great breakfast one morning at Newcastle, off a twopenny BUSTER and a small bit of butter, with some wishy-washy coffee . . .

c. 1882. *Broadside Ballad*, 'I can't get at it.
I can't get at it, I can't get at it,
I like the faggots tho' they smell,
But now the penny's down the well,
I can't get at it, I can't get at it,
I thought I'd have a 'BUSTER' but it's all no go!

2. (thieves'.)—A burglar. For synonyms, *see* AREA-SNEAK. *Cf.*, BUST, *subs.*, sense 2, and *verb*, sense 2.

1879. J. W. HORSLEY, 'Autobiography of a Thief,' in *Macm. Mag.*, XL., 582. BUSTERS and screwsmen (burglars).

3. (common.) — Anything of superior size; that has unusual capacity; that causes admiration; a spurt. Hence to 'COME AN AWFUL BUSTER,' 'to fall heavily,' 'to come a cropper'; 'IN FOR A BUSTER,' prepared, ready or determined for a spree.

1852. H. B. STOWE, *Uncle Tom's Cabin*, ch. x. 'Lor, Pete,' said Mose, triumphantly, 'han't we got a BUSTER of a breakfast!' at the same time catching at a fragment of the chicken.

1860. DICKENS, *Great Expectations*, ch. vii., p. 28. 'At such time as when your sister is on the Ram-page, Pip,' Joe sank his voice to a whisper, and glanced at the door, 'candour compels fur to admit that she is a BUSTER.'

1870. *Popular Song on Franco-German War.*
. . . Thank God, my dear Augusta,
We've had another awful BUSTER,
Ten thousand Frenchmen sent below,
Praise God from whom all blessings flow!

c. 1880. *Broadside Ballad*, 'I'll never go courting again.'
A lawyer's niece, next, I admired,
But brief he made my wooing spec;
To a banker's ward then, I aspired,
But got from the banker a check (cheque).
A publican said, other measures
For his girl he'd to carry out,
And a baker he gave me a 'BUSTER,'
With a 'brick,' sent me rolling about.

4. (Australian.) — A heavy storm from the south. Otherwise called in Sydney a BRICK-FIELDER (*q.v.*).

1885. *Household Words*, 10 Oct., p. 463. In anxious expectation we now awaited the result of this curious phenomenon of darkest night in day, which, accustomed to the portents that sometimes herald in the terrific BUSTERS of these southern seas, as most of us were, all declared they had never seen it equalled.

BUSTING, *verb, subs.* (thieves'.)—Informing against accomplices; turning Queen's evidence. *Cf.*, BUST, *verb*, sense 3. For synonyms, *see* PEACHING.

BUSTLE, *subs.* (common).—1. A pad, roll, or wire contrivance worn by women at the back in order to extend the dress, and also with a view to setting off the smallness of the waist. [Origin uncertain.] For synonyms, *see* BIRDCAGE.

1788. T. MONRO, in *Olla Podrida*, No. 40. Such locks the nymphs now wear (in silks who rustle), In rich luxuriance reaching to the BUSTLE. [M.]

1835. *Sketches by Boz*, p. 323. Whether she was pretty, whether she wore much BUSTLE, etc. *Ibid*, p. 488. 'Did you ever,' said a little coquette with a large BUSTLE.

1857. TROLLOPE, *Barchester Towers*, ch. xlv., p. 384. Bertie finished off the countess's BUSTLE.

2. (old.)—Money. A full list of synonyms will be found under ACTUAL.

1812. J. H. VAUX, *Flash Dictionary.* BUSTLE, a cant term for money. *Ibid.* Any object effected very suddenly, or in a hurry, is said to be done on the BUSTLE.

Verb (general).—To confuse; confound; perplex.—*See* previous quot.

1876. HINDLEY, *Life and Adventures of a Cheap Jack*, p. 237. 'Now BUSTLE him,' said Tom Maley; 'you have got him to-rights now. Let go your left straight.'

BUST-MAKER, *subs.* (common).—A molrower; a 'loose fish'; a seducer. For synonyms, *see* MOLROWER. [From BUST, a protuberance, + MAKER.]

BUSY-SACK, *subs.* (common). — A carpet bag. Called in America a GRIP-SACK.

BUTCHER, *subs.* (cards').—1. The king in playing-cards. When card-playing in public houses was common, the kings were called butchers, the queens bitches, and the knaves jacks. The latter term is now in general use. In French slang the king is *un bœuf*.

2. (American.) — A peripatetic 'small-boy' vendor of 'varieties' and 'notions' on railway cars—at once a convenience and a 'terror.'

3. (thieves'.)—The prison doctor. For synonyms, *see* CROCUS.

BUTCHER ABOUT, *verb* (Wellington College). — To make a great noise; to humbug about.

BUTCHER'S MOURNING, *subs.* (common).—A white hat with a black mourning hat-band.

BUTTEKER, *subs.* (old).—A shop.

BUTTER, *subs.* (popular).—Fulsome flattery; unctuous praise; 'soft soap.' A French equivalent is *le cirage*. *Cf.*, *verb*, sense 1. Also BUTTERING-UP.

1819. MOORE, *Tom Crib's Memorial to Congress*, p. 40.
For, knowing how, on Moulsey's plain,
The champion *fibb'd* the Poet's *nob*,
This BUTTERING-UP against the grain,
We thought was curs'd genteel in Bob.

1823 *Blackwood's Magazine*, XIV., p. 309. You have been daubed over by the dirty BUTTER of his applause.

1857. A. TROLLOPE, *Three Clerks*, ch. i. The quantity of BUTTER which he poured over Mr. Hardline's head and shoulders with the view of alleviating the misery which such a communication would be sure to inflict, was very great.

1880. *World*, 13 Oct. A lavish interchange of compliments, the BUTTER being laid on pretty thick.

Verb (common). — 1. To flatter fulsomely; to indulge in rhodomantic praise. French *cirer*.

1700. CONGREVE, *Way of World*, prol. (1866), 259. The squire that's BUTTERED still is sure to be undone. [M.]

1725. *New Canting Dictionary.* To BUTTER signifies also to cheat or defraud in a smooth and plausible manner.

1816. SCOTT, *Antiquary*, ch. xxxviii. 'Keep him employed, man, for half-an-hour or so—BUTTER him with some warlike terms—praise his dress and address.'

1839. LEVER, *Harry Lorrequer*, ch. xii. 'He first BUTTHERS them up and then slithers them down!'

1857. C. KINGSLEY, *Two Years Ago.* I'll BUTTER him, trust me. Nothing comforts a poor beggar like a bit of praise when he is down.

1884. *Saturday Review*, 5 July, p. 27, col. 1. The Lord Chief Justice of England made a tour through America, and generously BUTTERED the natives.

2. (old.)—Jamieson says, 'to increase the stakes every throw or every game.'

1690. B. E., *Dictionary of Canting Crew.* BUTTER, to double or treble the bet or wager to recover all losses.

1785. GROSE, *Dictionary of the Vulgar Tongue.* BUTTER A BET, to double or triple it.

TO LOOK AS IF BUTTER WOULD NOT MELT IN ONE'S MOUTH, *phr.* (old).—A contemptuous saying of a person of somewhat simple demeanour. Murray traces back this familiar phrase to 1530, but a reference to it appears in French literature at a much earlier date.

1475. *Les Evangiles des Quenouilles —Vme Journée.* Edition Elzevirienne. Paris (1855), p. 72. A cette parolle mist dame Mehault ses mains à ses costez et en grant couroux luy respondy que, etc., et que, Dieu merci, aincoires FONDOIT LE BURRE EN SA BOUCHE, combien qu'elle ne peust croquier noisettes, car elle n'avoit que un seul dent.

1530. PALGRAVE, 620, 1. He maketh as thoughe BUTTER WOLDE NOT MELTE IN HIS MOUTH.. [M.]

1562. LATIMER, *Serm. Lord's Prayer*, V., ii., 79. These fellows . . . can speak so finely, that a man would THINK BUTTER SHOULD SCANT MELT IN THEIR MOUTHS.

1687. SEDLEY, *Bellamira. Sil.* He look'd so demurely, I thought BUTTER WOU'D NOT HAVE MELTED IN HIS MOUTH, I hope you will make sure work with him before you send him again.

1738. SWIFT, *Polite Conversation*, i. She LOOKS AS IF BUTTER WOULD NOT MELT IN HER MOUTH, but I warrant cheese won't choak her.

1825. SCOTT, *St. Ronan's Well*, ch. xxviii. (III., p. 26). I am beginning to think ye are but a queer ane, ye LOOK AS IF BUTTER WADNA MELT IN YOUR MOUTH, but I sall warrant cheese no choak ye.

1850. THACKERAY, *Pendennis*, I., p. 149. Telling her landlady how . . . the Mayor was . . . a nice, soft-spoken old gentleman; that BUTTER WOULD'NT MELT IN HIS MOUTH, etc.

WILL CUT BUTTER WHEN IT'S HOT, *phr.* (common).—Said of a knife when blunt. An obvious allusion.

BUTTER AND EGGS, *subs.* (common).—Explained by quotations.

1862. *Macmillan's Mag.*, Jan., p. 238. And I can do BUTTER-AND-EGGS all down the slide. . . . The feat of BUTTER-AND-EGGS consists in going down the slide on one foot and beating with the heel and toe of the other at short intervals.

Compare the foregoing with the following.

1836. DICKENS, *Pickwick Papers*, II., p. 9. Sam Weller, in particular, was displaying that beautiful feat of fancy sliding which is currently denominated 'knocking at the cobblers' door,' and which is achieved by skimming over the ice on one foot, and occasionally giving a two-penny postman's knock upon it, with the other.

BUTTER-BAG or **BUTTER-BOX**, *subs.* (old).—Opprobrious epithets for a Dutchman. [? In allusion to Holland producing large quantities of butter. *Cf.*, quot., 1811.]

1600. DEKKER, *Gentle Craft*, wks. (1873) I., 21. We have not men enow, but wee must entertaine every BUTTER-BOX. [M.]

1650. HOWELL, *Familiar Letters.* And for the latter strength we may thank our countryman Ward, and Dansker the BUTTERBAG Hollander, which may be said to have bin two of the fatallest and most infamoust men that ever Christendom bred.

1811. *Lexicon Balatronicum.* BUTTER-BOX. A Dutchman, from the great quantity of butter eaten by the people of that country.

BUTTER-BOAT. TO EMPTY THE BUTTER-BOAT, *phr.* (common). —To lavish praise; to battle. [From BUTTER-BOAT, a table utensil employed for serving melted butter.]

1865. *Sat. Review*, 7 Jan., p. 16, col. 2. That kind of praise which feels like the BUTTER-BOAT down one's back. [M.]

1866. J. H. SKINNER, *After Storm*, I., 181. He praised some things and gave advice about others, using the BUTTER-BOAT less freely than is customary at volunteer inspections. [M.]

BUTTER-BOX.—*See* BUTTER-BAG.

BUTTERCUPS, *subs.* (common).—A graceful pet name for children.

1877. E. L. LINTON, *World Well Lost*, ch. vii. Hilda was still in the schoolroom, and seldom appeared even at afternoon tea; which in general is licensed to include 'BUTTERCUPS.'

BUTTERED, *ppl. adj.* (old).—1. Whipped. *Cf.*, DUSTED, TANNED, etc. (*q.v.*).

2. (common.)—Flattered.—*See* BUTTER, sense 1.

BUTTERED BUN, *subs.* (old). — A mistress; also a prostitute, especially one who submits to the sexual embrace in quick succession with different men. [In this latter sense, if not in former, from BUTTERED = greased + BUN (*q.v.*), the female *pudenda.*] For synonyms, *see* BARRACK-HACK.

1679. CULLEN, W., *Flock of Court Misses*, in *Roxburgh Ballads* (1884), V., 126. This is the day . . . that sets our Monarch free From BUTTERED BUNS [*i.e.*, Louise de Quérouaille] and Slavery.

1811. *Lexicon Balatronicum.* One lying with a woman that has just lain with another man, is said to have a BUTTERED BUN.

BUTTER-FINGERED, *comp. ppl. adj.* (common).—Apt to let things fall; greasy or slippery-fingered. The nickname of BUTTER-FINGERS is hence given to those who let things slip easily from their grasp.

1615. MARKHAM, *English Housewife*, II., ii. (1668), 51. She must not be BUTTER-FINGERED, sweet-toothed, nor faint-hearted; for the first will let everything fall, etc.

1857. HOOD, *Pen and Pencil Pictures*, p. 141. He was a slovenly player, and went among the cricket lovers by the sobriquet of BUTTER-FINGERS.

1861. G. MEREDITH, *Evan Harrington.* The long-hit-off, he who never was known to miss a catch—BUTTER-FINGERED beast!—he has let the ball slip through his fingers.

1883. MISS BRADDON, *Golden Calf*, ch. xiv. 'I never allow no BUTTER-FINGERED girls in this room, except to sweep or scrub, under my own eye. There's not many ornaments, but what there is is precious, and the apple of master's eye.'

BUTTER-FLAP, *subs.* (rhyming slang). —A trap—*i.e.*, a light cart.

BUTTERFLY, *subs.* (nautical).—1. A river barge.

2. (cabmen's.) — The guard for the reins affixed to the top of a hansom cab.

1883. *Standard*, March 6, p. 6, col. 3. The box covered the whole roof of the cab, preventing him [the cabman] from seeing the BUTTERFLY. [M.]

BUTTERNUTS, *subs.* (American.)— The sympathisers with the South in the North and the Middle States during the American Civil War; the term was derived from the colour of the uniforms worn in the early part of the war by Confederate soldiers in the West, which, being homespun, were dyed brown with the juice of the BUTTERNUT (*Juglans cinerea*).

BUTTER-PRINT, *subs.* (old). — A child; usually one that is illegitimate. *Cf.*, BUTTERCUP.

1620. FLETCHER, *Chances*, I., v. You will be wiser one day, when you have purchased A bevy of these BUTTER-PRINTS. [M.]

1639. BEAUMONT AND FLETCHER, *Wit Without Money*, V., iv. I hope she has brought me no BUTTER-PRINT along with her to lay to my charge. [M.]

1709. *Brit. Apollo*, II., No. 46, p. 3, col. 2. Her Girl and her Boy, For Patterns employ, To make little BUTTER-PRINTS by. [M.]

BUTTOCK, *subs.* (old).—A common prostitute. For synonyms, *see* BARRACK-HACK, and *Cf.*, FILE.

1674. R. HEAD, *Canting Academy*, 105. The Bawds and the BUTTOCKS that lived there round.

1688. SHADWELL, *Squire of Alsatia*, I., wks. (1720) IV., 17. What ogling there will be between thee and the Blowings! . . . Every BUTTOCK shall fall down before thee.

1690. B. E., *Dictionary of the Canting Crew.* BUTTOCK AND FILE, both whore and pickpocket.

BUTTOCK AND FILE, *subs. phr.* (old). —A prostitute and her companion; sometimes BULK AND FILE. Occasionally, too, BUTTOCK AND FILE is used of a single individual — one who unites the *roles* of a thief and prostitute. [From BUTTOCK (*q.v.*), a whore, + FILE (*q.v.*), a pickpocket.]

1671. R. HEAD, *English Rogue*, pt. I., ch. v., p. 48 (1874). BULK AND FILE the Pickpocket and his mate.

1754. FIELDING, *Jonathan Wild*, bk. I., ch. v. The same capacity which qualifies a mill-ben, a bridle-cull, or a BUTTOCK AND FILE to arrive at any degree of eminence in his profession would likewise raise a man in what the world esteem a more honourable calling.

1811. *Lexicon Balatronicum.* BUTTOCK AND FILE, a common whore and a pickpocket.

BUTTOCK AND TONGUE, *subs.* (old). —A scolding woman; a shrew.

BUTTOCK AND TWANG, *subs.* (old).— A common prostitute, but who refrains from theft. *Cf.*, BUTTOCK AND FILE.

BUTTOCK BALL, *subs.* (old).—1. A dance attended by prostitutes. *Cf.*, BALLUM RANCUM and BUFF BALL.

1687. T. BROWN, Lib., *Consc.*, in *Dk. Buckingham's Wks.* (1705), II., 131. Why not into a Bibbing-house, as well as a Dancing School, A BUTTOC-BALL, or the like.

2. (old.)—The sexual embrace; cohabitation. *Cf.*, BAWDY BANQUET and BUTTOCK BANQUETTING.

1811. *Lexicon Balatronicum.* BUTTOCK-BALL, the amorous congress.

BUTTOCK BANQUETTING, *subs.* (old). —Harlotry.

1555. *Fardle Facions*, II., viii., 167. Whiche [wiues] maie neuerthelesse vse BUTTOCKE BANQUETYNG abrode.

BUTTOCK-BROKER, *subs.* (old).—A procuress; a bawd; an ABBESS (*q.v.*).

BUTTOCKING SHOP, *subs.* (old).—A brothel; a house of ill fame used by the lowest class of public women.

BUTTON, *subs.* (old).—1. A shilling. Formerly this applied to good currency; it now only signifies counterfeit coin. For synonyms, *see* BLOW.

2. A decoy of any kind, whether the confederate of confidence trick men, or a sham buyer at an auction. Frequently called a BUTTONER (*q.v.*). *Cf.*, BUNCO-STEERER. Fr. *un allumé.*

1851-61. H. MAYHEW, *London Lab. and Lon. Poor*, vol. I., p. 358. They [cheap Jacks] have a man, or more generally a boy . . . at a fair, to hank, or act as a BUTTON (a decoy), to purchase the first lot of goods put up. *Ibid*, III., p. 121. Then he (the thimble-rigger) turns round to the crowd, and pretends to be pushing them back, and whilst he is saying, 'Come gentlemen, stand more backwarder,' one of the confederates, who is called a 'BUTTON,' lifts up one of the thimbles with a pea under it, and laughs to those around, as much as to say, 'We've found it out.'

1877. BESANT AND RICE, *Son of Vulcan*, ix. The BUTTON, that is the confederate who egged on the flats.

Verb.—To decoy; to act as confederate in swindles. Fr. *aguicher.*

NOT TO CARE A BUTTON—BRASS BUTTON, etc., *phr.* (common).—A very old colloquialism indicative of small value. It has been in continuous use from the beginning of the fourteenth century down to the present time. Americans say 'not worth a cent or a red cent,' while among variants in common use in England may be mentioned 'not to care a fig—a pin—or a sou.'

BUTTON BURSTER or **BUTTON BUSTER**, *subs.* (theatrical).— A low comedian. [The derivation is sufficiently obvious, that is, one who causes his auditors to laugh so that by a figure of speech their buttons are regarded as bursting off their clothes.]

BUTTON-CATCHER, *subs.* (general).— A tailor. There may be mentioned among

ENGLISH SYNONYMS, snip; cabbage contractor; steel-bar driver; goose persuader; sufferer; ninth part of a man, etc.

FRENCH SYNONYMS. *Un gobe-prune* (thieves'); *un emmailloteur* (popular); *un mangeur de prunes* (general); *un pique-poux*; *un pique-prunes*; *un pique-puces*; *un croque-prunes*; *un frus-quineur.*

(Most of these are offensive terms, as will be seen when it is stated that *puces* = fleas; *poux* = lice, and so on.)

BUTTONER, *subs.* (thieves'). — A card-sharper's decoy, an equivalent of BUTTON, *subs.*, sense 2. For synonyms, *see* DECOY-DUCK.

1841. *Blackwood's Mag.*, L., 202. BUTTONERS are those accomplices of thimble-riggers . . . whose duty it is to act as flat-catchers or decoys, by personating flats. [M.]

1857. SNOWDEN, *Mag. Assistant* (3 ed.), p. 446. To entice another to play—BUTTONER.

1860. *Cornhill Mag.*, II., 334. Enticer of another to play — BUTTONER. [M.]

BUTTON-ON. TO HAVE A BUTTON ON, *phr.* (printers').—To have a fit of the blues; to be despondent.—*See* CHOPPER ON.

BUTTON POUND, *subs.* (provincial). — Money. For synonyms generally, *see* ACTUAL.

BUTTONS, *subs.* (common). — A page; sometimes rendered by BOY IN BUTTONS. [In allusion to the numerous BUTTONS which usually adorn the front of a page's jacket.]

1860. THACKERAY, *Lovel the Widower*, p. 289. [Herein quoted as the name of a page.]

1873. *Chambers' Jour.*, p. 605. Even the smallest BOY IN BUTTONS would have been a retainer too costly for us.

1874. H. MAYHEW, *London Characters*, p. 311. Others limit their views to a page, or 'BUTTONS.'

1885. *Ill. Lon. News*, April 11, p. 376, col. 1. Such a man is only fit to be dressed like a BUTTONS, and set to open the door to visitors who come to call on his family.

DASH OR DAMN MY BUTTONS—WIG, etc., *phr.* (general). — A mild oath, the word 'damn' often being represented by a dash. Ordinarily employed to express vexation or surprise.—*See* OATHS.

1860. WM. HOWARD RUSSELL, *My Diary in India*, I., p. 26. DARN MY BUTTONS if I haven't jest a mind to . . .

NOT TO HAVE ALL ONE'S BUTTONS, *phr.* (common).—To be deficient in intellect; slightly cracky; to have a bee in one's bonnet.—*See* APARTMENTS TO LET.

TO HAVE A SOUL ABOVE BUTTONS, *phr.* (common).—To be above one's work or duty; to think one's ability superior to one's position. [The quotation for 1795 to which Murray calls special attention would seem to indicate the possible origin of the phrase.]

1795. G. COLMAN, *Sylv. Daggerwood*, I. (1808), 10. My father was an eminent Button-Maker . . . but I HAD A SOUL ABOVE BUTTONS . . . I panted for a liberal profession. [M].

1833. MARRYAT, *Peter Simple*, ch. i. But my father, who was a clergyman of the Church of England, and the youngest brother of a noble family, had a lucrative living and A SOUL ABOVE BUTTONS, if his son had not.

1855. THACKERAY, *Newcomes*, III., p. 93. If I were to say to Captain Crackthorpe, 'What pretty buttons!' he would be delighted. But you—you HAVE A SOUL ABOVE BUTTONS, I suppose.

TO MAKE BUTTONS, *phr.* (old). —To look sorry; sad; to be in great fear.

1593. G. HARVEY, *Pierces Supererog.*, in wks. II., 238. Thy witt already MAKETH BUTTONS.

1653. MIDDLETON, *Sp. Gipsy*, IV., iii. *Sam.* O Soto, I MAKE BUTTONS!

BUTTON UP, *verb* (American stockbrokers').—When a broker has bought stock on speculation and it falls suddenly on his hands, whereby he is a loser, he keeps the matter to himself, and is reluctant to confess the ownership of a share. This is called BUTTONING UP.

BUTTY, *subs.* (common).—A comrade or partner. Properly and specifically a miner who raises coal or ore by contract at a special price per ton, employing others to do the actual work. Perhaps more provincial than slang, although a writer in *Notes and Queries*, July 30, 1870, suggests its origin in the *Romany:* he says in the gipsy dialect BOOTY is the term for work. BOOTY-pal is a fellow-workman (literally work-brother). As usual when a polysyllable is imported into ordinary use, it loses its tail; so BOOTY - pal, in the mouths of navvies ignorant of its origin, would soon be cut down to BOOTY or BUTTY.

1845. DISRAELI, *Sybil*, wks. III., ch. i. Suppose we were to make a shift for a month or six weeks, . . . and have no tommy out of the shop, what would the BUTTY say to me? [A note to foregoing explains that a BUTTY in the mining districts is a middleman: a Doggy is his manager. The BUTTY generally keeps a Tommy or Truck shop and pays the wages of the labourers in goods.] *Ibid*, p. 385. The BUTTY has given notice to quit in Parker's field this se'nnight. *Ibid*, p. 389. The enemies of the people: all BUTTIES, doggies, dealers in truck and tommy.

1859. H. KINGSLEY, *Geoffrey Hamlyn*, ch. xxxi. 'He and I cottoned together, and found out that we had been prisoners together five-and-twenty years agone. And so I shouted [*stood drinks*] for him, and he for me, and at last I says, 'BUTTY,' says I, 'who are those chaps round here on the lay?'

1876. C. HINDLEY, *Life and Adventures of a Cheap Jack*, p. 101. William Carrol was his partner, or BUTTY, in the 'lollipop' business—a dismal looking man, who had always a burnt short clay pipe in his mouth.

BUVARE, *subs.* (strolling players').—Explained by quotation. *Cf.*, also BEWARE.

1851-61. H. MAYHEW, *London Lab. and Lon. Poor*, vol. III., p. 201. [Ethiopian serenader *loq.*] 'We could then, after our "nunyare" and "BUVARE" (that's what we call eat and drink, and I think it's broken Italian), carry home our 5/- or 6/- each, easy.'

BUY A PROP, *phr.* (Stock Exchange).—A term used to signify that the market has gone flat, and that there is no one to support it.

BUZ or **BUZZ**, *subs.* (common)—A parlour game which is thus described by Hotten, who, however, erroneously limited it to public-houses:—The leader commences saying 'one,' the next on the left hand 'two,' the next 'three,' and so on to *seven*, when 'BUZ' must be said. Every seven and multiple of 7, as 14, 17, 21, 27, 28, etc., must not be mentioned, but 'BUZ' instead. Whoever breaks the rule pays a fine.

1868. MISS ALCOTT, *Little Women*, ch. iii. They . . . were in the midst of a quiet game of 'BUZZ' with two or three other young people who had strayed in, when Hannah appeared.

Verb (general).—1. Some uncertainty exists as to whether TO BUZ signifies to drain a bottle or decanter to the last drop, or whether it means to share equally the last of a bottle of wine, when there is not enough for a full glass to each of the party. [*See*, however, quot. 1795.] Annandale and Hotten incline to the latter; Grose and Murray to the former view, and the following quotations appear to favour the explanation of the

word first noticed as BUZZA by the burly lexicographer of the 'Vulgar Tongue.' [? A corruption of BOOZE or BOUZE, *i.e.*, to drink a bumper or to excess.] The Scotch say BOUSE A', drink all.

1785. GROSE, *Dictionary of the Vulgar Tongue*. To BUZZA ONE, is to challenge him to pour out all the wine in the bottle into his glass, undertaking to drink it, should it prove more than the glass would hold; it is commonly said to one who hesitates to empty a bottle that is nearly out.

1795. *Gent. Mag.*, p. 118. Briskly pushed towards me the decanter containing a tolerable *bumper*, and exclaimed, 'Sir, I'll BUZZ you: come, no *heel taps!*'

1821. W. T. MONCRIEFF, *Tom and Jerry*, Act ii., Sc. 1. *Cribb.* . . . I'll give you, '*May the best man win.*' (*All drink.*) May the best man win. *Green.* May the best man vin. *Log.* With all my heart; but, zounds! we've almost BUZZ'D the bowl. Let's have another, and d'ye hear, Tom, serve it up in your prize cup; Jerry hasn't seen it, and we mustn't omit that.

1846-48. THACKERAY, *Vanity Fair*, II., 138. 'Get some more port, Bowls, old boy, whilst I BUZZ this bottle here—what was I saying?' 'I think you were speaking of dogs killing rats,' Pitt remarked mildly, handing his cousin the decanter to BUZZ.

1871. ARCHIBALD FORBES, *My Experiences of the War between France and Germany*, I., p. 234. The Hotel which I had seen a few days before, where *Von Tümpling's* staff were BUZZING the bottles.

2. To pick pockets. [Probably an allusion to BUZZ in the sense of to talk busily. The victim in BUZZING or BUZ-FAKING (*q.v.*) is generally engaged in conversation with a confederate, while the BUZZER (*q.v.*) is committing the robbery.] For synonyms, *see* PRIG.

1789. GEO. PARKER, *Life's Painter*, p. 158. In order to give them an opportunity of *working* upon the *prig* and BUZ, that is, picking of pockets.

1857. SNOWDEN, *Mag. Assistant*, 3 ed., p. 445. To pick pockets—to BUZZ.

1876. C. HINDLEY, *Life and Adventures of a Cheap Jack*, p. 261. In my young days there used to travel about in gangs, like men of business, a lot of people called 'Nobblers,' who used to work the 'thimble and pea rig' and go BUZZING, that is, picking pockets, assisted by some small boys.

3. (American thieves'.)—To search for; to look about one.

BUZ-BLOKE.—*See* BUZ-NAPPER.

BUZ-COVE.—*See* BUZ-NAPPER.

BUZ-GLOAK.—*See* BUZ-NAPPER.

BUZ-MAN, *subs.* (thieves').—1. A pickpocket. *Cf.*, BUZ-NAPPER.

1856. H. MAYHEW, *Gt. World of London*, p. 111. The London BUZMAN (swell mobsman) can keep his pony by abstracting 'skins' (purses) from gentlemen's pockets.

2. (thieves'.)—An informer. [From BUZZ, to talk or whisper, + MAN.] For synonyms, *see* NARK.

1877. W. BLACK, *Green Past. and Picc.*, ch. xi. What was all this about 'Billy Rowland,' 'Scotland Yard,' 'Spy,' 'BUZMAN,' and the rest?

BUZ-NAPPER, *subs.* (old).—1. A pickpocket. [From BUZ, to pick pockets, + NAPPER or NABBER, one who seizes or snatches. 'Buz-bloke,' 'buz-cove,' 'buz-gloak,' 'buz-man,' and 'buzzer,' are all variants of BUZ-NAPPER; 'bloke,' 'cove,' and 'gloak,' are old canting terms for a man.] For synonyms, *see* AREA-SNEAK.

1781. G. PARKER, *View of Society*, II., 174. A young fry of boys . . . follow the profession of a BUZ-NAPPER.

1819. J. H. VAUX, *Memoirs of Convict Life in Australia.* BUZ-COVE or BUZ-GLOAK, a pickpocket; a person who is clever at this practice is said to be a 'good buz.'

1834. H. AINSWORTH, *Rookwood*, bk. III., ch. v.
Until at last there was none so knowing,
No such sneaksman or BUZ-GLOAK going.

1856. H. MAYHEW, *Gt. World of London*, p. 46. Those who plunder by *stealth*, as . . . 'BUZZERS,' who pick gentlemen's pockets.

1859. SALA, *Twice Round the Clock*, 3 p.m., par. 10. Where these *ruffiani*, these copper captains and cozening BUZ-GLOAKS, are to be found during the day, or even up to midnight . . . must remain a secret.

1862. MAYHEW, *Crim. Prisons*, 46. BUZZERS who pick gentlemen's pockets, and 'wires' who pick ladies' pockets.

1867. *Galaxy*, p. 634. While the [New York] police had no right to arrest pickpockets unless they caught them committing a theft, yet as they had the power to do so, they exercised it, and many were the car-BUZZERS they led captives to police headquarters.

BUZ-NAPPER'S ACADEMY, *subs.* (old).—A school in which young thieves were trained. Figures were dressed up, and experienced tutors stood in various difficult attitudes for the boys to practise upon. When clever enough they were sent on the streets. Dickens gives full particulars of this old style of 'business' in *Oliver Twist*.

1781. G. PARKER, *View of Society*, II., 173. [A BUZ-NAPPER'S ACADEMY is named and described in this work.]

BUZ-NAPPER'S KINCHIN, *subs.* (old).—A watchman. Synonymous terms in the sense of police will be found under BEAK (*q.v.*).

BUZZER.—*See* BUZ-NAPPER.

BUZZING or **BUZ-FAKING**, *subs.* (thieves').—Pocket-picking. *Cf.*, BUZ, *verb*, sense 2.

BY-BLOW, *subs.* (old).—An illegitimate child. [An allusion to the unacknowledged status of the mother, and the 'accident' of the birth of such children.] Also called BY-CHOP and BY-SLIP.

1594. BARNFIELD, *Affectionate Shepherd*. In such a ladies lappe, at such a slipperie BY-BLOW, That in a world so wide could not be found such a wilie Lad; in an age so old, could not be found such an old lad.

1625. MASSINGER, *Parl. of Love*, II., i. Give to each BY-BLOW, I know mine, a farm.

1678. C. COTTON, *Scarronides*, bk. I., p. 21 (ed. 1725).
Now *Venus* was *Æneas* Mother,
In the behalf then of her BY-BLOW,
Which had endured many a dry-Blow,
She weeping came, sighing and throbbing.

1705-7. WARD, *Hudibras Redivivus*, vol. II., pt. II., p. 19.
The poor Man's House abound with Brats,
As country Barn with Mice and Rats;
And Parishes be fill'd with BY-BLOWS
As thick as Butchers' Stalls with Fly-blows.

1748. T. DYCHE, *Dictionary* (5 ed.). BY-BLOW (s.), a bastard or illegitimate child.

1868. BROWNING, *Ring and Bk.*, iv., 612. A drab's brat, A beggar's BYE-BLOW.

1875. OUIDA, *Signa*, vol. I., ch. iii., p. 34. The one who held the child turned his light on the little wet face; . . . 'And whose BY-BLOW is this?' said he. 'The devil knows,' said he who knelt by the mother. 'But it is Pippa.'

BY-CHOP.—*See* BY-BLOW.

1632. JONSON, *Magnetic Lady*, iv., 2.
First I have sent
BY-CHOP away; the cause gone, the fame ceaseth.

BY CRACKY! *intj.*—A meaningless ejaculation conveying no idea beyond that of general surprise.—*See* OATHS.

1888. *Superior Inter-Ocean.* Say, haint Tubbs a Methodist? BY CRACKY! here's where it is, and in we walked.

BYE-DRINK, *subs.* (common).—Liquid refreshment taken at other than meal-times. [From BYE = not in regular course + DRINK.]

1766. KENRICK, *Falstaff's Wedding*, i., 1. I could wish, nevertheless, old white wine stood higher in his lordship's favour; that I may not be stinted at table, or in my BY-DRINKINGS.

1883. *Daily Telegraph*, Jan. 10, p. 5, col. 3. Our business men—and many others who are not men of business—take, as it is, a great many more 'BYE-DRINKS' in the way of 'sherry' and 'whiskey cold' than is good for them.

BY GEORGE! *intj. phr.* (popular).—An ejaculation signifying either surprise, or anger, or used without any special meaning. Phrases of the kind are very numerous, and are mainly employed by those whose poverty of language is otherwise very marked. [BY GEORGE! may either be a reference to St. George, the patron saint of England, or to the predominant Christian name of the early sovereigns of the Brunswick dynasty.]

1731. FIELDING, *Grub Street Opera*, Act iii., Sc. 7. BY GEORGE, I'll make an example of him.

1787. *Bacchus and Venus*, p. 117. 'FORE GEORGE, I'd knock him down.

1852. DICKENS, *Bleak House*, ch. xxxviii. 'I—er—a little subject to this sort of thing—er—BY GEORGE!'

BY GOLDAM! *intj. phr.* (American).—A semi-veiled oath. The Yankee is peculiarly fertile in variations on the name of God, and gives a striking proof of his ingenuity in inventing new forms for the forbidden *I swear*. He has his BY GORRAM! BY GOLDAM! and BY GOSHDANG! by the side of the English oath BY GOLLY! which occurs as early as 1743.—*See* OATHS.

BY GOLLY! *intj. phr.* (popular).—A euphemistic phrase for BY GOD!—*See* OATHS.

1743. W. WARREN, *Five Arguments against Tythes.* 'The first person consulted a gentleman-farmer, and declared that he never read anything so good in his life. 'BY GOLLY,' says he, 'he 'as mauled the parsons.'

1851-61. H. MAYHEW, *London Lab. and Lon. Poor*, vol. III., p. 204. Then I turn round to him and say, 'BY GOLLY, if you don't leave off, I'll broke you over de jaw.'

BY GORRAM!—*See* BY GOLDAM!

BY GOSH! *intj. phr.* (popular).—A compromise for BY GOD!

1804. C. K. SHARPE, in *Correspondence* (1888), I., 210. I promise, BY GOSH (which is the most elegant and classical oath imaginable).

1877. W. BLACK, *Green Past. and Picc.*, ch. xxxv. 'If this goes on,' said he suddenly, 'BY GOSH, I'll heave!'

BY GUM! BY GUMMY! *intj. phr.* (American).—Both these expletives are extracts from the great American *Dictionary of Oaths and Cuss Words*, compiled by descendants of the Puritan Fathers.—*See* OATHS.

1860. HALIBURTON ('Sam Slick'), *The Season Ticket*, No. ix. 'BY GUM, Squire Shegog, we have had the greatest bobbery of a shindy in our carriage you ever knowed in all our born days.'

BY HOOK OR BY CROOK.—*See* HOOK.

By Hooky, *intj. phr.* (popular).—A mild form of swearing.—*See* OATHS.

1882. JAS. PAYN, *For Cash Only*, ch. xxii. 'Pay me what you owe me,' says I, 'or, BY HOOKY, I'll tell your father.'

Byng, Bing, *verb* (old).—To go. BYNGE-AWASTE, to go away.

1567. HARMAN, *Caveat, or Warening for Commen Cursetors*, p. 86. *Man.* What, stowe your bene, cofe, and cut benat whydds, and BYNG we to rome vyle, to nyp a bong; so shall we haue lowre for the bousing ken and when we BYNG back to the deuseauyel, we wyll fylche some duddes of the Ruffemans, or myll the ken for a lagge of dudes. [*i.e.*] What, holde your peace, good fellowe, and speake better wordes, and go we to London, to cut a purse; then shall we haue money for the ale house, and when wee come backe agayne into the country, we wyll steale some lynnen clothes of one hedges, or robbe some house for a bucke of clothes.

1610. ROWLANDS, *Martin Mark-all*, p. 37 (H. Club's Repr., 1874). BING A WAST, get you hence.

1785. GROSE, *Dictionary of the Vulgar Tongue*. BINGED AVAST in a darkmans, stole away in the night. BING we to Rumeville, shall we go to London?

1815. SCOTT, *Guy Mannering*, ch. xxviii. 'BING out and tour [go out and watch] ye auld devil, and see that nobody has scented.'

1822. SCOTT, *Fortunes of Nigel*, ch. xvii. 'I smell a spy,' replied the other, looking at Nigel. . . . 'BING AVAST, BING AVAST!' replied his companion.

By-Scape, *subs.* (old).—A bastard. *Cf.*, BY-BLOW.

1646. EARL MONM., *Biondi's List*, VI., ix., 197. For his being God-son to her Brother, and . . . for that (being very fair) she thought him a BY-SCAPE of his. [M.]

By-Slip, *subs.* (old).—A bastard. *See* BY-BLOW.

1692. HACKET, *Life of Williams*, ii., 37. As Pope Paul the Third carried himself to his ungracious BY-SLIPS (an Incubus could not have begot worse), who made no further inquisition after their horrid facts but to say, They learnt it not of him.

Byte.—*See* BIT.

By the Ever-Living Jumping Moses! *intj. phr.*—An effective ejaculation and moral wastepipe for interior passion or wrath is seen in the exclamation, BY THE EVER-LIVING JUMPING MOSES!—a harmless phrase, that for its length expends a considerable quantity of fiery anger.—*Hotten*.

By the Living Jingo! or **By Jingo!** —*See* JINGO.

By the Wind, *phr.* (nautical).—Hard up; in difficulties. [In reference to the wind being formerly the most important element of success in a sailor's calling.]

END OF VOL. I.

Vol. II.

A · Dictionary · of
Slang · and · its · Analogues.

CAB, *subs.* 1. (University and school boys').—An adventitious aid to study; a 'crib'; a PONY (*q.v.* for synonyms). [From CABBAGE (*q.v.*) = pilferings.]

1853. REV. E. BRADLEY (' Cuthbert Bede'). *Adventures of Verdant Green*. Those who can't afford a coach get a CAB, *alias* a crib, *alias* a translation.

1876. *Academy*, 4 Nov., p. 448, col. 2. The use or translations, 'cribs,' or 'CABS' as boys call them, must at some time or other engage the serious attention of schoolmasters. [M.]

2. (old).—A brothel : in use during the early part of the present century ; now obsolete. [Probably a contracted form of 'cabin,' some of the older senses of which (*e.g.*, a small room, bedroom, or boudoir) are in correspondence. Parallels exist in other languages, and comparison may be made with the Fr. *cabane*, and Sp. *cabaña* ; also with the Latin *taberna* = cabin, hut, and brothel. The It. *bordello* (Eng. bordel) was originally precisely equivalent to *taberna* and *cabaña*, being a diminutive of *borda* = cottage, cabin, shed, house of boards. All these words, and many similar (*e.g.*, Latin *cella*, *cellula*, the *petite maison* of the French) came to be applied in the specifically esoteric sense under discussion, by an obvious euphuism or familiarism, which left the nature of the hut, booth, cell, or cabin to be supplied by those who understood. Further, 'cabin' = an Eng. rendering of the Latin *cella*, *cellula* = brothel. Also CAB-MOLL (*q.v.*), a prostitute, originally the moll or molly of a cabin, *cabane*, or brothel, the present meaning being a popular misuse founded on a mistaken analysis.] For all synonyms, *see* NANNY-SHOP.

1811. *Lexicon Balatronicum*. Mother, how many tails have you in your CAB? *i.e.*, how many girls have you in your bawdy house?

Verb (colloquial).—1. To proceed from one place to another by means of a CAB ; *Cf.*, 'to foot or hoof it,' 'to tram it,' 'to train it,' or 'to 'bus it.'

1836. C. DICKENS, *Pickwick Papers*. He's a CABBING it, I suppose.

I

1882. *Blackwood's Magazine*, Feb., p. 238, col. 1. He . . . CABS off to take advice.

2. (schoolboys').—To pilfer ; to use a crib. *Cf.*, CABBAGE, *verb*, of which it is an abbreviation.

Cabbage, *subs.* (old).—1. Generally applied to pieces purloined by tailors ; attributively to any small profits in the shape of material. Quoted by Johnson as 'a canting term,' but now recognised. There is little chance of CABBAGE nowadays, save amongst those who 'make up gentlemen's own material' ; but the expression is well understood by low-class dressmkers. In America a corresponding term is 'COLD-SLAW (*q.v.*) which consists of finely-cut cabbage, and represents the small remnants known in other quarters as 'carpet-rags' or CABBAGE. *Cf.*, PIGEON SKEWINGS. [The derivation is obscure. Murray traces it back to 1663 (*Hudibras* [spurious]), but points out that Herrick [1648] apparently uses *garbage* and *carbage* for 'shreds and patches used as padding.' He then goes on to say that 'if this was a genuine use at the time, *carbage* may easily have been corrupted to CABBAGE.' This difficulty can, I think, be removed. In the seventeenth century, a style of feminine head-dress, then in vogue, very similar to the modern chignon, was called a CABBAGE. Thus in *Mundus Muliebris* [1690] :

Behind the noddle every baggage, Wears bundle 'choux,' in English CABBAGE.

Now, if this usage (omitted from the *N.E.D.*) be compared with the three quotations first following, it would appear (1)

that the word CABBAGE was in use prior to *carbage* or *garbage* for 'shreds and patches' ; (2) that *carbage* and *garbage* contain a sarcastic reference to the materials with which a woman's CABBAGE, or chignon, was stuffed ; and (3) that in every quotation the play upon words appears to confirm these contentions. Hence, if CABBAGE as a mode of dressing the hair was current during the seventeenth century (I have come across no earlier instance), it is possible that the stages of transition were as follows :—

1 CABBAGE = a well-known vegetable.

2. = A mode of dressing the hair, in such a form as to resemble a cabbage.

3. = The materials with which such a tire was stuffed.

4. = The shreds and pieces appropriated by tailors and others as perquisites.

There is no evidence in support of such guesses as those in, for example, the quotations dated 1853 and 1886.

1638. RANDOLPH, *Hey for Honestey* (Old Play). *Tailor.* Nay, he has made me sharper than my needle ; makes me eat my own CABBAGE.

1648. HERRICK, *Hesperides* (Hazl.), I., 79. *Upon some women*, Pieces, patches, ropes of haire, In-laid GARBAGE ev'rywhere.

1648. HERRICK, *Hesperides* (Hazl.), II.,325. Eupez for the outside of his suite has paide ; But for his heart, he cannot have it made ; The reason is, his credit cannot get The inward CARBAGE for his cloathes as yet.

1663. *Hudibras*, II., 56. For as tailors preserve their CABBAGE, So squires take care of bag and baggage.

SLANG AND ITS ANALOGUES

PAST AND PRESENT.

A DICTIONARY, HISTORICAL AND COMPARATIVE, OF THE HETERODOX SPEECH OF ALL CLASSES OF SOCIETY FOR MORE THAN THREE HUNDRED YEARS.

WITH SYNONYMS IN ENGLISH, FRENCH, GERMAN, ITALIAN, ETC.

COMPILED AND EDITED BY

JOHN S. FARMER and W. E. HENLEY.

VOL. II.—C. TO FIZZLE.

PRINTED FOR SUBSCRIBERS ONLY.

—

MDCCCXCI.

1742. CHARLES JOHNSON *Highwaymen and Pyrates*, p. 343. She takes him into Pissing Alley, in Hollywell Street, otherwise called the backside of St. Clement's in the Strand, so eminently noted for Taylors selling there their CABBAGE.

1748. T. DYCHE, *Dictionary* (5 ed.). CABBAGE (s.) . . . also a cant word to express anything that is pilfered privately, as pieces of cloth or silk retained by taylors, mantua-makers, or others.

1821. COBBETT, *Weekly Register* 28 April, col. 219. Taylor, of Charing Cross, will allow of no thumb-piece and of no CABBAGE.

1853. *Notes and Queries*, 1 S., viii., 315, col. 2. The term CABBAGE, by which tailors designate the cribbed pieces of cloth, is said to be derived from an old word 'cablesh,' *i.e.*, wind-fallen wood. And their 'hell' where they store the CABBAGE, from *helan*, to hide.

1886. G. A. SALA, in *Ill. Lon. News*, 16 Oct., 394, 1. My correspondent's derivation of CABBAGE from *caboged* [*caboged* = 'cabossed' or 'caboched' in heraldry, in Fr. *cabochée*. *See* Littré] is good; but there is another one, namely, *cabas*, a basket in which the pickings and stealings of cloth might be hoarded.

The place where CABBAGE is stored is termed HELL (*q.v.*) or ONE'S EYE (*q.v.*); these terms, as also GOOSE (*q.v.*), a smoothing iron, are responsible for much cheap wit. *Cf.*, MAKINGS and PICKINGS. The Spanish has *sisa* = 'a petty theft.'

2 (old).—A tailor; sometimes CABBAGER, and formerly CABBAGE-CONTRACTOR (*q.v.*). For synonyms, *see* BUTTON-CATCHER and SNIP.

1690. B. E. *Dict. Cant. Crew*. CABBAGE: a Taylor, and what they pinch from the Cloaths they make up.

1725. *New Cant. Dict.* CABBAGE: Taylors are so called, because of their . . . Love of that Vegetable. The cloth they steal and purloin . . . is also called CABBAGE.

3. (old).—A style of dressing the hair similar to the modern chignon. [For suggested derivation, *see* sense 1.] Fr. *un kilo*.

1690. *Mundus Muliebris*. Behind the noddle every baggage, Wears bundle 'choux,' in English CABBAGE.

4. (schoolboys').—A translation or 'crib'; sometimes shortened to CAB (*q.v.*, sense 2).

1868. BREWER, *Dictionary of Phrase and Fable*, p. 129. CABBAGE is also a common schoolboy term for a literary crib, or other petty theft.

5. (common).—A cigar. The French have *une feuille de platane* = a plane-tree leaf; also *un crapulos* or *crapulados*, a Hispanization of *crapule* = filth. For synonyms, *see* WEED.

1843. *Punch's Almanack*, August 12. The cigar dealers, objecting to their lands being cribbed, have made us pay for the CABBAGE ever since.

1848. *Punch*, vol. XIV., p. 298. Q. Are cigars an English invention? A. No! the cigar is a Spanish article, that has been merely CABBAGED by the British manufacturer.

1853. C. S. CALVERLEY, *Verses and Translations*, p. 141 [ed. 1881], *Carmen Sæculare*. O fumose puer nimuim ne crede Baconi Manillas vocat, hoc prætexit nomine caules.

1889. *Ally Sloper's Half-Holiday*, July 6. Last week he offered me a weed—A worse one no man's lips e'er soiled. 'No, thanks,' said, 'I, know the breed; I much prefer my CABBAGE boiled.'

6. (venery).—The female *pudendum*. *Cf.*, GREENS. For synonyms, *see* MONOSYLLABLE.

Verb (old).—1. To purloin or pilfer pieces.

1712. ARBUTHNOT, *History of John Bull*, pt. I., ch. x. Your tailor, instead of shreds, CABBAGES whole yards of cloth.

1870. *New York Evening Sun*, May 24. Report of Speech of Mr Chandler. Let us knock the British crown to flinders; let us arrange for some one or two hundred thousand British graves forthwith, and CABBAGE the whole boundless continent without any further procrastination.

1882. *Notes and Queries*, 6 S., vi., 210. But he said, If I CABBAGE that ring to-night, I shall be all the richer tomorrow.

2. (schoolboys').—To use a translation or other adventitious aid in preparing exercises; to 'crib.'

1837. GEN. P. THOMPSON, *Exerc.* (1842), IV., 234, A speech, which . . . had been what schoolboys call CABBAGED, from some of the forms of oration . . . published by way of caricature [M.]

1862. H. MARRYAT, *Year in Sweden*, II., 387. Steelyards . . . sent by Gustaf Wasa as checks upon country dealers, who CABBAGED, giving short weight. [M.]

So also CABBAGED, *ppl. adj.*, pilfered, or stolen; and CABBAGING, *verbal subs.*, pilfering, purloining.

CABBAGE-CONTRACTOR, *subs.* (old). —A tailor. [From CABBAGE (*q.v.*, *subs.*, sense 1) = CONTRACTOR, a trader.] For synonyms, *see* BUTTON-CATCHER and SNIP.

CABBAGE-GELDER, *subs.* (old).—A greengrocer or market gardener. —*A.B.C. of a New Dictionary of Flash, Cant, and Slang* [1866].

CABBAGE-HEAD, *subs.* (popular).—A fool; a soft-head; a 'go-along.' For synonyms generally, *see* BUFFLE, and more particularly *infra*.

ENGLISH SYNONYMS. Block-head; chuckle-head; chowder-head; cod's-head; chump or chump of wood; dunderhead; flat; go-along; goosecap; greenlander; gulpin; juggins; thick-head; lights; loony; looby; lubber; mooney; mug; muggins; muff; ninny-hammer; nincompoop; nizzie; pigeon; sawney; Simon, or Simple Simon; slow-coach; soft-horn; sop; Tom Tug. To which may be added 'cupboard-headed,' 'half-boiled,' 'not all there,' and 'off one's chump,' used also of one not *compos mentis*; a thick (Winchester College).

FRENCH SYNONYMS. *Une tête de pioche* (popular: *pioche* = pick-axe or mattock); *un poulet d'Inde* (popular: *poule d Inde* = turkey-hen); *un couillé* (popular); *un paroissien de Saint Pierre aux bœufs* (popular); *un noc* (popular = a 'juggins'); *un loffiat* (popular: this is formed from a species of French back slang, *lof* = *fol* reversed. On the same lines we get *la loffitude* = 'stupidity' or 'nonsense'; *bonisseur de loffitudes* = 'a nonsense monger'; also *solliceur de loffitudes* = 'a journalist'); *un Jean-bête* (common: *Cf.*, English 'Johnnie' and 'Jack'); *barré* (= cabbage-headed); *une vieille bouillote* (popular); *une bourriche* (popular: 'a hamper'); *une badouille* (popular: also = 'a hen-pecked husband'); *être déboulonné* (popular: literally = 'unpinned' or 'unbolted'); *un fifilolo* (popular); *un daim* (popular); *être de la tribu des Bénicoco* (military); *être du 14 bénédictins* (popular); *une bestiasse* (this term has passed into the language); *bête comme chou* (= 'extremely stupid'); *bête comme un pôt* (= a perfect ass); *bête comme ses pieds* (= an arrant fool); *un abruti* or *ahuri de Chaillot* (popular: Chaillot, in the suburbs of Paris, is a common butt, much as are Hanwell, Colney Hatch, etc.; *abrutir* = 'to stupify, to besot, to imbrute'); *une tête de boche* (common: = a wooden head; also a German); *un bidon de zinc* (military = 'a can' or 'flask'); *un*

cul or *cul d'âne* (popular: *cul d'âne* = 'the rump of an ass'; *Cf.*, English 'ass'); *un cantaloup* (popular: literally a melon); *un cube* (a 'regular idiot'); *un canarie; être un c* (a euphemistic phrase); *un busard* or *buson* or *une buse* (an allusion to the stupidity of the buzzard); *une couenne* (popular: = 'pig-skin.' '*Est-il couenne!*' 'What an ass!'); *un coquardeau; un couillon* (popular: a cullion, used in friendly jocularity = abashed, crestfallen, and above all idiotic); *un espèce de cafouilleux* (popular = 'a bally bounder'); *un arguche* (thieves'); *battre comtois* (thieves' = to play the fool); *un baveux* (a driveller: one who does not know what he is talking about); *un boniface* (popular); *n'avoir pas cassé la patte à coco* (thieves' = 'as big a bloody mug as they make 'em').

SPANISH SYNONYMS. *Asnazo* (*m*; properly 'a big jackass'); *asno* (*m*); *bambarria* (*m*; also = an accidental but successful stroke at billiards, 'a fluke'); *bobalias* (*m*; a colloquialism for 'a very stupid fellow'); *borro* (*m*; properly a wether not two years old); *echacantos* (*m*); *gentil hombre de placer* (= 'a buffoon' or 'clown'); *guillote* (*m*; literally a husbandman, one who enjoys the produce of a farm. *Cf.*, 'joskin'); *Juan lanas* (vulgar); *mamacallos* or *mamaluco* (*m*); *naranjo* (*m*; properly the *citrus aurantium*); *pandero* (*m*; also 'a timbrel'); *pinchauvas* (*m* = a despicable person); *porra* (*f*); *es un solemne bobo* ('he is a downright booby'); *zamacuco*.

PORTUGUESE SYNONYMS. — *Bamburrio*; *macacada*; *tauso*; *pãosinho*.

1682. MRS. BEHN, *False Count* (1724), III., 146. Thou foul, filthy CABBAGE-HEAD. [M.]

1862. LOWELL, *Biglow Papers*, II., 228. For take my word for 't, when all's come and past, The CABBAGE-HEADS 'll cair the day at last.

c. 1880. *Broadside Ballad*, 'Right before the missis too.' I've had a dreadful row All through a chum named Tommy Sheen, I ought to call him CABBAGE-HEAD, He is so very green.

CABBAGE-LEAF, *subs.* (common).—A bad cigar; usually contracted into CABBAGE (*q.v.*, *subs.*, sense 5). [From a popular theory of material.] In French *un infectados* by a play upon words in two languages, *infect*, Fr. = more than common, vile, and *infectar*, Sp. = 'to infect' or 'be infected'. For synonyms, *see* WEED.

CABBAGE PLANT, *subs.* (old).—An umbrella; GAMP (*q.v.*); or brolly.

CABBAGER, *subs.* (common). — A tailor. [From CABBAGE (*q.v.*, *subs.*, sense 1) + ER.] For synonyms, *see* BUTTON-CATCHER and SNIP.

CABBAGE-STUMPS, *subs.* (common). —The legs. For synonyms, *see* DRUMSTICKS.

CABBAGE-TREE MOB, *subs.* (Australian). Old for what are now called LARRIKINS (*q.v.*). Derived from the low-crowned cabbage-palm hat affected by this section of Australian society.] CABBAGITES was an alternative.

18(?). LIEUT.-COL. MUNDAY *Our Antipodes*. Loafers known as the CABBAGE-TREE MOB, a class whom, in the spirit of the ancient tyrant, one might excusably wish had but one nose in order to make it a bloody one. *Ibid.* Unaware of the propensities of the CABBAGITES, he was by them furiously assailed.

CABBY, *subs.* (colloquial). — A cabman. [From CAB + Y.] Amongst French equivalents are *une hirondelle* (properly = 'a swallow'); *un maraudeur* (*i.e.*, 'a marauder,' one who plies without a license; *Cf.*, PIRATE (*q.v.*), as applied to omnibuses.

1852. F. E. SMEDLEY, *Lewis Arundel*, ch. xxxiii. I was forced to offer him a seat in the cab, but he coolly replied, 'No, thank ye . . . I'll sit beside CABBY.'

1864-5. YATES, *Broken to Harness*, II., p. 41. Easy, CABBY; we don't want to be thrown into the very midst of the aristocracy.

1890. *Standard*, Feb. 11, p. 3, col. 1. There was a Vienna CABBY with his jolly red face and his professional impudence.

CABLE, *verb* (popular).—To send a telegram by ocean (submarine) wire.

TO SLIP or CUT ONE'S CABLE, *subs. phr.* (nautical).—To die. For exhaustive lists of synonymous terms, *see* ALOFT and HOP THE TWIG.

CABLE-HANGER, *subs.* (nautical).—Explained by quotations.

1724-7. DEFOE, *Tour thro' G. Britain* (ed. 1748), I., 150. Persons who dredge or fish for oysters, not being free of the fishery, are called CABLE-HANGERS, and are prosecuted and punished by the Court.

1867. SMYTH, *Sailors' Word Book*. CABLE-HANGER, a person catching oysters. in the River Medway, not free of the fishery.

CAB-MOLL, *subs.* (old).—A prostitute addicted professionally to cabs and trains. [From CAB (*q.v.*, sense 2) + MOLL (*q.v.*), a strumpet.] For synonyms, *see* BARRACK-HACK and TART.

CABOBBLED, *ppl. adj.* (nautical).—Confused; puzzled; perplexed.

CABOODLE, *subs.* (American).—A crowd; generally 'the whole CABOODLE.' [Thought to be an enlarged form of BOODLE which is frequently used in the same sense, and which is supposed by some to be derived from the old English bottel, a bundle (Fr. *botel*, *boteau*, Ger. *beutel*.). *See*, however, BOODLE, *subs.*, sense 1. Another derivation is from the Spanish *cabildo*, a provincialism for the corporation of a town.] CABOODLE is general throughout the States, and has now almost completely supplanted BOODLE (*q.v.*), which is usually applied in a different sense. Sometimes CABOOSE (*q.v.*)

1858. *New Orleans Picayune*, 23 Feb. The whole CABOODLE came out and fell upon me, till I was as soft as a squash, and then they took me up for fighting.

1887. *Scribner's Magazine*. Ye've got ter have faith in Goddle-mighty then, sure, a-swingin' up an' down them mount'n-sides, dark nights or bright, when a rock on the track f'om a landslide 'ud fling the whole CABOODLE down the mount'n an inter kingdom come afo' you'd know it.

CABOOSE, *subs.* (American).—Generally applied to convivial quarters; also to a bachelor's snuggery—a DEN (*q.v.*) or DIGGINGS (*q.v.*). [Properly a ship's cook-house or galley; and in the United States, a car on a freight train for workmen, or for a special purpose.]

THE WHOLE CABOOSE, *phr.* (nonce expression).—Obviously a variation of CABOODLE (*q.v.*).

1870. *London Figaro*, 19 Oct. 'After the Fire.' In this room, sir, said my gallant conductor, lived a bricklayer with his wife and two kids. *He* made that hole in the wall, and got 'em safe through —THE WHOLE CABOOSE on 'em; and a jolly good job he did.

CACAFUEGO, *subs.* (old).—A spitfire; braggart; bully. [From the Latin *cacare* through the Spanish *cagar*, 'to void excrement,' + Spanish *fuego*, fire.] This word, once literary, has long fallen into desuetude. It was regarded as vulgar after the middle of the last century, and thereafter was only included in slang dictionaries.

1625. FLETCHER, *Fair Maid*, III., i. She will be ravisht before our faces, by rascalls and CACAFUGOS, wife, CACAFUGOES. [M.]

1696. PHILLIPS. CACAFUEGO, a Spanish word signifying Shitefire; and it is used for a bragging, vapouring fellow. [M.]

1725. *New Cant. Dict.* [s.v.]

1811. *Lexicon Balatronicum.* CACAFEUGO. A sh-te-fire, a furious braggadocio or bully huff.

CACHUNK! *intj.* (American).—Onomatopœic—the 'bow-wow' word of Max Müller—belonging to a class of exclamations intended to convey an imitation of the sound of a falling body. Uncertain as regards orthography they are largely affected in the Southern and Western States. Mainly of recent origin, though two, KESWOLLOP and KEWHOLLUX rare in the States, are not unfamiliar to English ears. Examples are:—Caswash; Cawhalux; Chewallop; Casouse; Cathump; Kerplunk; Katouse; Katoose; Kelumpus; Kerchunk; Kerplunk; Kerswosh; Kerslosh; Kerswollop; Kerblinkityblunk; and Kerblam.

CACKLE, *subs.* (theatrical).—1. The dialogue of a play; especially used at first, of the patter of clowns, etc., in a circus. [From the figurative usage of CACKLE, to make a noise as a hen after laying an egg, a usage traceable as far back as 1225.]

1887. *Referee*, 21 August, p. 2, col. 3. Those [playgoers] who do not insist upon a very high order of literary quality in the CACKLE.

2. (colloquial).—Idle, inconsequent, noisy chatter.

1676. A. RIVETUS, JUN. *Mr. Smirke*, 18. Bedawb'd with Addle Eggs of the Animadverters own CACKLE.

1887. *Punch*, 10 Sept., p. 111 If a feller would tackle a feminine fair up to Dick, he 'as got to be dabs at the CACKLE.

Verb (old).—To talk idly, especially in the sense of telling secrets. For synonyms, *see* PEACH.

1785. GROSE, *Dictionary of the Vulgar Tongue.* The cull is leaky and CACKLES; the rogue tells all.

1882. *Punch*, LXXXII., 177, 2. The old jokers in scarlet and erming who lounge in their red bedroom-chairs, And the cinder-wig'd toffs in alpaca who CACKLE and give themselves airs.

CACKLE-CHUCKER, *subs.* (theatrical).—A prompter. [From CACKLE, the dialogue of a play, + CHUCKER, one who throws out (from the mouth).]

CACKLE-MERCHANT, *subs.* (theatrical).—A dramatic author. [From CACKLE, the dialogue of a play, + MERCHANT. *Cf.*, CAPER-MERCHANT, a dancing-master.]

CACKLER, *subs.* (old).—1. A fowl. [From CACKLE (*q.v.*) + ER.]—*See* also CACKLING CHEAT.

1673. R. HEAD, *Canting Acad.*, 192. A Prigger of the CACKLERS.

1730–6. BAILEY. CACKLER . . . a humorous word for capons or fowl.

1749. *Life of Bamphylde-Moore Carew.* Oath of the 'Canting Crew.' No dimber damber, angler, dancer, Prig of CACKLER, prig of prancer.

1811. *Lexicon Balatronicum.* CACKLER: a hen.

2. (colloquial).—A noisy talker; a 'blab.'—*See* CACKLE, *verb.*

1400. *Cov. Myst.*, 131. Kytt CAKELERE and Colett Crane. [M.]

1598. FLORIO, *Gracchione* . . . a chatter, a CACKLER. [M.]

1730–6. BAILEY, CACKLER: a Prater, a Tell-tale, a noisy Person.

1878. BROWNING, *Poets of Croisic*, 92. If they dared Count you a CACKLER.

3. (circus and showmen's).—An actor or showman who has a speaking part.

1854. DICKENS, *Hard Times*, bk. I., ch. vi., p. 14 (H. ed.). 'He has his points as a CACKLER still . . . a speaker, if the gentleman likes it better.

CACKLER'S-KEN, *subs.* (old).—A hen-roost; a fowl-house. [From CACKLER (*q.v.*, *subs.*, sense 1), a fowl, + KEN (*q.v.*), a place or house.] A French thieves' equivalent is *une ornière* (from *ornie*, a hen).

CACKLE-TUB, *subs.* (old).—A pulpit. [From CACKLE (*q.v.*) + TUB, in allusion to the shape of old-fashioned pulpits.] For synonyms, *see* HUM-BOX.

1888. MUSGRAVE, *Savage London.* I sorter think if yer'll borrow Lucy's chair to wheel me, I'll go and sit under the CACKLE-TUB in Little Bethel next Sunday.

CACKLING-CHEAT or **CHETE,** *subs.* (old).—A fowl. [From CACKLING, that cackles, + CHEAT, From A.S. *ceat*, a thing.]—*See* CHEAT.

ENGLISH SYNONYMS. Beaker; cackler; margery prater; galeny; partlet; chickabiddy; rooster; chuck-chuck; chuckie.

FRENCH SYNONYMS. *Un becquant* (a thieves' term); *un ornichon* (also a thieves' term for a chicken); *un pique-en-terre* (literally 'a peck-the-ground'); *une estable* or *une estaphle* (thieves'); *bruantez* (Breton slang).

GERMAN SYNONYMS. *Kachni* (from the Gypsy); *mistkratzer.*

ITALIAN SYNONYMS. *Ruspante* or *raspante* (properly 'scratching' or 'scraping').

SPANISH SYNONYMS. *Capiscol* (this, and indeed all the terms here given from the Germania, refer to the cock-bird. *Capiscol* = Fr. *caporal*); *obispo* (properly a bishop); *rey* (literally king).

1567. HARMAN, *Caveat*, p. 86. She has a CACKLING-CHETE, a grunting-chete, ruff pecke, cassan, and poplarr of yarum.

1622. FLETCHER, *Beggar's Bush*, v. 1. Or surprising a boor's ken for grunting-cheats? Or CACKLING-CHEATS?

1785. GROSE, *Dictionary of the Vulgar Tongue.* CACKLING-CHEATS (cant): fowls.

1811. *Lexicon Balatronicum.* CACKLING CHEATS: Fowls (cant).

CACKLING-COVE, *subs.* (theatrical and common).—An actor. [From CACKLING (*see* CACKLE, *subs.*, sense 1) + COVE, an old canting term for a man.]

ENGLISH SYNONYMS. Mummery-cove; mug-faker; mummer; mugger (properly an actor who makes free play with his face); tragedy or comedy merchant; pro; stroller; cackle-faker; barnstormer; surf.

FRENCH SYNONYMS. *Un prêtre* (thieves': literally 'a priest': a curious sidelight on the views concerning religious orders of the criminal classes); *un raze* or *razi pour l'af* (thieves': *raze* or *razi* = priest; and *affe* in old French cant signified 'life' or 'the soul,' but latterly *eau d'affe* = 'brandy.' There seems, however, little connection between either of these readings and the example under consideration); *un Egyptien* (theatrical: a term applied to a bad or inferior actor); *un acteur-guitare* (a term specially applied to one who elicits applause in lacrymose scenes only—an actor with only one string to his bow); *un enleveur* (theatrical: one who plays in such a way as to *enlever la salle*, *i.e.*, 'to bring down the house'); *une doublure* (an understudy); *un cab*, *cabot*, or *cabotin*, (used mainly in contempt, much in the same way as 'mummer.' *Cabotinage* is the life of hardship led by strolling players, and thence, by derivation, the life of the 'profession' generally); *un brûleur de planches* (theatrical: a spirited or restless actor); *un acteur brûlé* (popular: one that has had his day); *un bouch trou* (theatrical: an understudy or stop-gap); *un bouleur* or *une bouleuse* (a substitute, or understudy); *un misloquier* or *une misloquière* (thieves'); *un nom* (theatrical: 'a star').

CACKLING-FART, *subs.* (old).—An egg. [From CACKLING (*see* CACKLE) + FART (*q.v.*) a discharge of wind through the *anus*.] A variant in English is HEN-FRUIT; Fr. *un avergot* (thieves'); the Breton cant has *bruant*, whilst in the German Gaunersprache is found *Dickmann* (also = the *penis* and *testes*); the Fourbesque has *arbifi* and *alberto* (the latter from the Italian *albo*, white).

CAD, *subs.* (popular).—A term of contempt now generally applied to an offensively ill-bred person, irrespective of social position. Formerly used of underlings and others performing menial offices. [Murray favours its origin in *cadet* and the popular forms *cadee* and *caddie*. *See*, however, CADATOR, the quotations under which appear to suggest a collateral, if an independent origin. Some regard the word as a contraction of 'cadger'; whilst others trace it to the Scotch 'cadie' or 'caddie,' an errand boy—now an attendant at golf; or to the slang University sense of the word, a non-member]. The vocable has passed through a variety of meanings.

1. Passengers taken up by coach drivers for their own profit. [M.]

2. (obsolete).—A chum or companion.

3. (old).—An assistant.

4. (old).—An omnibus conductor.

1833. HOOD, *Sk. fr. Road.* Though I am a CAD now, I was once a coachman. [M.]

1836. DICKENS, *Pickwick*, ch. xxxiii., p. 279. He paused, and contemplated, with a face of great calmness and philosophy, the numerous CADS and drivers of short stages who assemble near that famous place of resort [the Mansion-House].

1851-61. H. MAYHEW, *London Lab. and Lon. Poor*, vol. III., p. 355. The conductor, who is vulgarly known as the CAD, stands on a small projection at the end of the omnibus.

5. A messenger or errand boy.

1835. T. HOOK, *Gilbert Gurney*, ch. vii. I will appear to know more of you than one of the CADS of the thimble-rig knows of the pea-holder.

1839 T. HOOD, *Miss Kilmansegg*, p. 230. Not to forget that saucy lad (Ostentation's favourite CAD), The page, who looked so splendidly clad.

1843. J. HEWLETT, *College Life*, I., p. 115. Webb's boy, who went as CAD with the dog.

6. (University and public schools').—A contemptuous term applied to non-school or non-University men. At Cambridge SNOB, the word Thackeray used, has long been a common term for a townsman; now the undergrad says TOWNEE or TOWNER (*q.v.*). The German analogue is *Philister*. Dr. Günther (*Jena and its Environs*) tells that of the old towers and gates which formed the entrance to Jena, the square one to the west alone remains; and is remarkable not only for its prison, called 'The Cheese-Basket,' but for four images of monkeys' heads carved at the several corners of the gate itself. In a quarrel between students and townsfolk in the vicinity of the Johannis-Thor, the former dubbed the watchmen there 'the monkey watchmen.' The guard vowed vengeance, and one evening killed a student who had taken no part in the disturbance. The ecclesiastical superintendent, Götz, preached a sermon at the boy's funeral from Judges xvi. 20, 'The Philistines be upon thee, Samson!' and that night his text was heard in the street, *Philister über dir Samson!* Henceforward the citizens were called 'Philister' by the students; and, the name being exported to the other Universities, it came at length to be applied to burgher folk throughout Germany. According to some this fight occurred in 1693. For synonyms, *see* RANK OUTSIDER.

1831. HONE, *Year Book*, 670. Preceded by one or two bands of music in two boats, rowed by CADS.

1856. REV. E. BRADLEY ('Cuthbert Bede'), *Adventures of Verdant Green*, I., p., 117. And I can chaff a CAD.

1860. *Macmillan's Mag.*, March p 327. You don't think a gentleman can lick a CAD, unless he is the biggest and strongest of the two.

1873. *Saturday Review*, September, p. 305. At Oxford the population of the University and city is divided into 'Dons, men and CADS.'

7. (general).—A vulgar, ill-mannered person; a blackguard, *i.e.*, a person incapable of moral decency. For synonyms, *see* SNIDE.

1849. CHARLES KINGSLEY. *Alton Locke.* 'The CADS,' 'the snobs,' 'the blackguards,' looked on with a dislike, contempt, and fear which they were not backward to return.

1860. THACKERAY. *Lovell the Widower*, p. 245. There's a set of CADS in that club that will say anything.

1880. *Punch's Almanack*, 12. Lor' if I'd the ochre, make no doubt I could cut no end of big-pots out. Call me a CAD? When money's in the game, CAD and swell are pooty much the same.

1882. F. ANSTEY, *Vice Versâ*, ch. vii. Perhaps your old governor has been making a CAD of himself then, and you're out of sorts with him.

1889. *Answers*, Feb. 23, p. 205, col. 3. You wouldn't care to know Goodfellow, Miss Smart; he's awfully bad form—a regular CAD, you know.

CADATOR, *subs.* (old).—A beggar in the character of a decayed gentleman.

1703. WARD, *London Spy*, pt. I., p. 7. He is one of those gentile [? genteel] Mumpers, we call CADATORS; he goes a Circuit round England once a year, and under Pretence of a decay'd gentleman, gets both Money and Entertainment at every good House he comes at.

ed. 1760. T. BROWN, *Works*, II., 179. You . . . sot away your time in Mongo's fumitory, among a parcel of old smoak-dry CADATORS.

CADDIE, *subs.* (Scots).—An attendant at golf.

1889. *Scots Observer*, Feb. Oh, my CADDIE, my CADDIE ye're a vera intelligent laddie. But I dinna like yer grinnin When I'm no exactly winnin'.

CADDISH, *adj.* (popular).—Vulgar; offensively ill-bred. [From CAD (*q.v.*, sense 7) + ISH.]

1869. SHIRLEY BROOKS, *Sooner or Later*, II., p. 31. 'Well I don't care about walking on Sundays. Religious scruples, perhaps.' 'I should think not. But it seems so CADDISH—like snobs who can go out on no other day.'

1872. *Civilian*, Aug. 10. There are many sorts of Ministerial insolence at present 'on view' in the House of Commons. Mr. Ayrton's is coarse and CADDISH, the Attorney-General's contemptuously courteous, and Mr. Lowe's cynically and facetiously insulting.

1874. E. L. LINTON, *Patricia Kemball*, ch. xx. 'However, I have brought you here to reason, not to wrangle,' he continued more quietly; 'and wrangling is CADDISH.'

CADE, *subs.* (society).—The Burlington Arcade. [An abbreviated form of 'Arcade.'] *Cf.*, THE ZOO for 'the Zoological gardens,' THE PROMS. for 'the Promenade Concerts,' THE POPS. for 'the Monday Popular Concerts,' and THE CRI. for the 'Criterion Bar.' Somewhat older examples are THE LANE (*q.v.*) and THE HOUSE (*q.v.*).

CADGE, *subs.* (vulgar).—The profession of cadging or begging. —*See* verbal sense.

1812. J. H. VAUX, *Flash Dictionary*. The CADGE is the game or profession of begging.

1832-53. *Whistle-Binkie* (Sc. Songs), Ser. II., 68. He could 'lay on the CADGE' better than ony walleteer that e'er cost a pock o'er his shouther.

Verb tr. and *intr.*—To obtain by begging; to beg. Now applied to vagrants and others who solicit in an artful wheedling manner. [A comparatively modern derivative. CADGER (Scots) a pedlar or carrier, *i.e.*, one who strolls the country with his stock-in-trade in a CADGE, *i.e.*, a panier or basket for the carriage of small wares. *Cf.*, 'to beg,' from 'bag.'] Hence said of anyone who lives by sponging on another, or who gets a livelihood without giving a proper *quid pro quo*. For example, a waiter when hanging about for 'a tip' is said to be CADGING or 'on the CADGE.' Among intimates TO CADGE A DINNER OR SUPPER is now often used without implied reproach.

1811. *Lexicon Balatronicum*. CADGE the swells, beg of the gentlemen.

1846. LYTTON, *Lucretia*, II., xii. 'I be's good for nothin' now, but to CADGE about the streets and steal and filch. [M.]

1848. E. FARMER, *Scrap Book* (ed. 6), 115. Let each CADGE a trifle.

1866. G. A. SALA, *Trip to Barbary*. ch. xiv. Thumping the tom-tom, and CADGING for coppers.

1883. *Daily Telegraph*, Feb. 8, p. 3, col. 1. 'It's as bad a' most as drawing peoples' teeth to CADGE a trifle off them in such winter months as we've had since the Autumn broke.'

ENGLISH SYNONYMS. To mump; to pike; to mouch; to stand the pad; to maund; to tramp; to mike.

FRENCH SYNONYMS. *Bettander* (thieves'); *aller à la chasse avec un fusil de toile* (popular: literally 'to go hunting with a canvas gun,' an allusion to the necessary wallet or bag); *bellander* (tramps'; *Cf.*, *bettander*; possibly some confusion has arisen between these two terms); *balauder* (tramps'); *truquer de la pogne* (tramps'); *trucher* (Old Cant, from *truc*, any kind of open air small trade or artifice. The word appears in various French, Italian and Spanish dialects, whilst MÉRIL in his *Dictionnaire du pâtois Normand* allies it with the English 'trick'); *tendre la demi-aune* (popular:

demi-aune = the arm); *cameloter* (popular: meaning also to sell, cheapen, or tramp); *faire le coup de manche*, or *faire la manche* (to call at people's houses); *mendigoter* (popular).

GERMAN SYNONYMS. *Abgeilen* (to get by begging. From the O.H.G. *gil*); *abschnurren* (to beg through a lane, town, or province; also = to take to one's heels; M.H.G. *snurren*, *schnurren* (*q.v.*, *infra*) and *Schnurrant*, a beggar musician); *bimmeln* (*Bimmler*, *Bummler*, a beggar or vagrant); *benschen* (a corruption of the Latin *benedicere* = to say grace after meat; from praying to begging is but a step); *paternellen* (perhaps, like the foregoing, a formation, from the Latin *pater noster*, signifying to say much *pater*); *noppeln* (vagrants'); *Schnurren*, *schnorren snurren*, (from the O.H.G. *snurren*, to grind, to grind out music on a HURDY-GURDY [*q.v.*], or to grind out prayers. A beggar or vagrant is termed *Schnurrer*, *Schnorrer*, or *Snurrer* = a grinder. *Auf die Pille schnurren* = to beg by feigning epileptic fits; *auf Serffleppe schnurren* = to beg on the pretence of having been 'burnt out'; *Schnurrpilsel*, *Schnurrscheye*, *Scenurrschicksel*, *Schurrkeibelche*, and *Schnurrmädchen*, are epithets for very young girls who are beggars or strumpets as occasion fits; the dual occupation being known as *Kommistarchenen* and *Hemdenschnurren*); *tarchenen*, *targenen*, *dörgen*, *dorchen* ('to beg' or 'to hawk.' The derivation is obscure, but it is possibly to be found in the Hebrew *tirgel*, 'to teach to walk' or 'to guide the foot.' Others trace it to the O.H.G. *Turg*, 'uncertain' or to *storgen* from *Störger*, 'a wandering quack.' The *Fiesellange*, or Viennese thieves' lingo, has *Tarchener* as equivalent to *Kegler*, a kitchen thief); *linkstappeln* (to beg or collect money under false pretences; *see Linkstappler* under CADGER); *prachern* (probably from the Hebrew *berocha*, a blessing: wandering beggars generally introducing themselves with some sort of a benediction); *Schnallendrücken gehen*, or *auf Schnallen*, *drücken gehen* (these terms also signify to walk the streets as a prostitute. *Schnalle* = untruth, cheating, deception, and the female *pudendum*); *stabeln*, *stappeln*, and *stapeln* (the first of these forms is peculiar to Vienna, and all are traceable to *Stiban* or *Stap*, the Anglo-Saxon staff. The meaning is to go with a begging staff, generally with a pretence of having seen better days); *dalfen* and *dalfern* (the corresponding noun *Dalfon* = a poor fellow, is supposed to be derived from *Dalfon*, the only one of the ten sons of Haman, whose name had not the letter *aleph* either at the beginning or end of it [Esther ix. 7-9]. The story goes that because of this he was not only hanged, but mocked into the bargain: the feast in commemoration of Haman's fall being essentially a merrymaking. Thenceforth, a poor man became a *Dalfon*); *deufen gehen* = to go begging with the intention of committing a robbery. *Cf.*, O.H.G. *Diufa*, *Deube* = theft); *jechten*, Viennese thieves' lingo).

ITALIAN SYNONYMS. *Truccare* (identical with the French *truquer q.v.*); *Santocchiare* (also = 'to

say one's prayers'); *calcheggiare* (also = to steal).

CADGE-CLOAK or **GLOAK**, *subs.* (old).—A beggar. For synonyms, *see* CADGER.

1791. CAREW, *Life and Adventures of Bamphylde-Moore Carew*. CADGE-CLOAK, curtal, or curmudgeon; no Whip-Jack, palliard, patrico . . . nor any other will I suffer.

CADGER, *subs.* (common).—Primarily a carrier, pedlar, or itinerant dealer; now mainly applied to a whining beggar; also, occasionally, a 'sponger,' SNIDE (*q.v.*), or 'mean man' (*see* quots.). [From CADGE (*q.v.*) + ER.]

ENGLISH SYNONYMS. Abram man; croaker, Abraham cove; Tom of Bedlam; Bedlam beggar; maunderer, moucher; pikey; traveller; turnpike, or dry land sailor; scoldrum; shyster; Shivering James; silver beggar; skipper-bird; mumper; paper-worker; goose-shearer; master of the black art; durrynacker.

FRENCH SYNONYMS. *Un trucheur*, or *un trucheux* (Old Cant, from *truc*, which *see* under CADGE); *un marcandier* or *une marcandière* (thieves'; a variety of the mendicant tribe which is described in *le Jargon de l'Argot* as 'those who journey with a great purse by their side, with a pretty good coat, and a cloak on their shoulders, pretending they have met with robbers who have stolen all their money); *les millards*. (Old Cant); *un bêcheur*; *une comète* (popular: 'a comet'—one here and there); *les callots*; *un enfant de la loupe* (thieves'); *un loupiat* (popular); *un mendigot* (thieves'); *un lartin* (Old Cant).

GERMAN SYNONYMS. *Daljon* (*see* CADGE); *Techtbrud* (Viennese thieves'); *Gomol* (from the Hebrew, and used only as a nickname); *Hochstappler* (a beggar cheat who has seen better days. *Cf.*, *Stappler* and *Linkstappler*); *Linkstappler* (a beggar by means of false papers; a dealer in sham lottery tickets; or a 'snide' collector for purposes of charity); *Pracher* (possibly from the Hebrew *berocha*, 'a blessing,' in allusion to the mumper's benediction; *Schnallendrücker* (from *Schnalle* = 'an untruth,' 'cheating,' or 'deception,' + *Trecker*, one who pulls); *Schnurrer* (*see* under CADGE); *Stabeler* (*see* under CADGE); *Standjunge* (a beggar frequenting markets, fairs, and public processions).

ITALIAN SYNONYMS. *Campagno di calca* (*campagno* = companion or comrade, *calca* = 'crowd'); *calco* (*see* preceding); *corteggiano* or *cortigiano* (literally 'a courtier'); *cavorante di scarpe* (literally 'working shoes'; specially applied to a beggar who is also a pickpocket); *granchetto* (especially one who PATTERS IN FLASH (*q.v.*); *truccante* (also = a thief); *guido* or *guidone* (literally 'a guide'; also = a 'dog' or a 'companion'); *incatinato* an old and decrepit beggar's boy-leader. Literally one put up or hung up in chains).

SPANISH SYNONYM. *Chita* (a nickname for a deformed vagrant or beggar).

1821.—W. T. MONCRIEFF, *Tom and Jerry*, Act ii., Sc. 6. CADGERS make holiday, Hey, for the maunder's joys, Let pious ones fast and pray, They save us the trouble, my boys.

1851.—MAYHEW, *Lon. Lab. and Lon. Poor*, I., 339. A street seller nowadays is

looked upon as a 'CADGER,' and treated as one.

1882.—*Daily Telegraph*, 5 Oct., p. 3. col. 1. See on a Saturday night, in Whitechapel, the rank hypocritical CADGER, whose coarse disguise of cleanness and respectability would scarcely deceive the most foolish persons at the West-end.

1884.—JAS. GREENWOOD, *The Little Ragamuffins*. I may here remark that amongst people of my born grade no one is so contemptuously regarded as he who is known as a CADGER. The meaning they set on the word is not the dictionary meaning. The CADGER with them is the whining beggar, the cowardly impostor, who being driven or finding it convenient to subsist on charity, goes about his business with an affectation of profoundest humility, and a consciousness of his own unworthiness; a sneaking, abject wretch, aiming to crop a meal out of the despising and disgust he excites in his fellow-creatures.

CADGING, *verbal subs.* (common).—Begging, frequently eked out by petty pilfering. [From CADGE (*q.v.*) + ING.]

1859. H. KINGSLEY, *Geoffrey Hamlyn*, ch. xv. I've got my living by casting fortins, and begging, and CADGING, and such like.

1873. JAS. GREENWOOD, *In Strange Company*. But what one in vain looked for was the 'jolly beggar,' the oft-quoted and steadfastly believed in personage who scorns work because he can 'make' in a day three times the wages of an honest mechanic by the simple process of CADGING.

CADY, *subs.* (common).—A hat. [Derivation unknown.] Sometimes written CADEY and CADDY. For synonyms, *see* GOLGOTHA.

1886. *The A. B. C. of New Dictionary of Flash, Cant, Slang, etc.*, p. 85. CADDY: a man's hat.

1887. *Walford's Antiquarian*, April, p. 251. Sixpence I gave for my CADEY A penny I gave for my stick.

CAFFAN.—*See* CASSAN.

CAFFRE'S LIGHTENER, *subs.* (South African).—A full meal. Fr. *une lichance* (from *licher* = *lécher*, 'to lick').

1864. LADY DUFF GORDON. *Letters from the Cape*. I asked him [a young black shepherd at the Cape] to sing; and he flung himself at my feet, in an attitude that would make Watts crazy with delight, and crooned queer little mournful ditties. I gave him sixpence and told him not to get drunk. He said, 'Oh, no! I will buy bread enough to make my belly stiff; I almost never had my belly stiff.' He likewise informed me that he had just been in the *tronk* [Cape Dutch slang for a prison, answering to the English stone-jug]. and, on my asking why, replied, 'Oh, for fighting and telling lies.'

CAGE, *subs.* (old). — 1. A minor kind of prison for petty malefactors; a country 'lock-up.' [From CAGE, a place of confinement for birds, beasts, and, formerly, human beings.] Once in literary use; now thieves' slang.

1500. *Lancelot*, 2767. As cowart thut schamfully to ly Excludit in to CAGE from chewalry. [M.]

1593. SHAKSPEARE, *II. Henry VI.*, iv., 2. *Dick*. Ay, by my faith, the field is honorable, and there he was born, under a hedge; for his father had never a house but the CAGE.

1748. T. DYCHE, *Dictionary* (5 ed). CAGE (s): a place of confinement for thieves or vagrants that are taken up by the watch in the night-time, to secure them till the proper officer can carry them before a magistrate.

1815. SCOTT, *Guy Mannering*, ch. liii. I was doomed—still I kept my purpose in the CAGE and in the stocks.

1839. HARRISON AINSWORTH, *Jack Sheppard* [1882], p. 78. The CAGE at Willesden was, and is—for it is still standing—a small round building about eight feet high, with a pointed tiled roof, to which a number of boards inscribed with the names of the parish officers, and charged with a multitude of admonitory notices to vagrants and other disorderly persons, are attached.

1841. *Punch*, vol. I., p. 3. 'A synopsis of voting.' He who is incited into an assault, that he may be put into the CAGE.

ENGLISH SYNONYMS. For a prison generally, academy; boat; boarding-house; bower; block-house; bastille; bladhunk; stone-jug; jug; calaboose; cooler; coop; downs; clink; jigger; Irish theatre; quod; shop; stir; clinch; steel; sturrabin; mill; toll shop; floating hell; floating academy; dry room; House that Jack Built; choakee.

Among special names for particular prisons may be mentioned Bates's Farm or Garden (Cold Bath Fields); Akerman's Hotel (Newgate); Castieu's Hotel (Melbourne Gaol); Burdon's Hotel (White Cross Street Prison); Ellenborough Lodge, Spike or Park (the King's Bench Prison, to which, as a matter of fact, every Chief Justice stood god-father); Campbell's Academy (the Hulks); City College and Whittington's College (Newgate); Tench; Pen; and Smith's Hotel (Edinburgh).

FRENCH SYNONYMS. *Le castue* (thieves'); *la caruche* (thieves'); *la boîte aux cailloux* (thieves'); *cailloux* = stones; *Cf.*, 'stone jug'; *le collège* (thieves': Newgate at one time was called the City College); *la cage* (popular); *le château* (thieves': literally a castle, *château de l'ombre* = a convict settlement); *la chambre de sûreté* (the parish prison of the Conciergerie); *le chetard* (thieves'); *le canton* (thieves': according to Ménage in his *Dictionnaire Etymologique*, the original sense of this word is the same as *coin*. From *canton* has been derived the verb, *cantonner*, a military term signifying the billetting of troops in one or more villages); *en ballon* (popular: in prison); *la grosse boîte* (thieves': literally the big box); *la bonde* (thieves': a central prison); *la Biscaye* (thieves'); *l'abbaye de sots bougres* (thieves': obsolete = The Silly Bugger's Arms); *le bloc* (a military prison or cell, *Cf.*, block-house); *la dure* (thieves': a central prison, *dur* is properly hard, merciless, obdurate); *la femme de l'adjudant* (a military lock-up, jigger, or Irish theatre; literally the adjutant's wife); *la bagnole* (popular: a diminutive of *bagne*, of the same meaning); *la motte* (thieves': a central prison or house of correction); *l'hôpital* (thieves': a man in durance is *un malade* = a patient); *la mitre* (thieves': a corruption of *mithridate*, the name of a certain ointment; *mitre* formerly meant 'itch'); *le jetar* (military; the same as *chetar*); *l'ours* (common: a term given to a prison, guard-room, or cell); *la boîte à violon* (a lock-up at a police-station; *violon* itself signifies a prison, the barred windows being compared to the strings of that instrument. *Argot and Slang* says:—The lingo terms *jouer de la harpe*, to be in prison, and *jouer du violon*, to file through the window bars of a cell, seem to bear out this explanation. Some philologists, however, think that the stocks being termed *psaltérion*, *mettre au psaltérion*, to put in the stocks, became synonymous with 'to imprison,' the expression being superseded in time by *mettre au violon* when that instrument itself

superseded the *psaltérion*); *la tuneçon* (Old Cant); *l'austo* (a military prison); *le lycée* (thieves': = 'academy'); *l'école préparatoire* (pop.: a preparatory school for young thieves) *le lazaro* (military: = lazar-house, or 'spike); *le mazaro* (military: = cells); *la matatane* (military: 'a guard room' or the cells); *le loustaud* (thieves'); *la lorcefé* (thieves': the old prison of *La Force*); *le loir* (thieves' = 'dormouse'); *l'hosto* (soldiers' and thieves': also popularly, 'a house or crib'); *la grotte* (thieves': the hulks. Properly a grotto or crypt); *l'hôtel des haricots* (familiar: from the staple of diet, *Cf.*, Ger. *Erbsien* and *Graupenpalais*); *la morte paye sur mer* (obsolete: the hulks) *l'ombre* (popular: = 'shade,' *Cf.*, Ger. *Kühle*); *la maze* (abbreviation of *Mazas*, a central prison in Paris); *là-bas* (prostitutes: St. Lazare; thieves': the convict settlement at New Caledonia, or in Cayenne); *la malle* (military: *Cf.*, English 'box').

GERMAN SYNONYMS. *Antoniklosterl* (Viennese thieves' = a prison in Vienna); *Drillbajis* or *Drillhaus* (a house of drill or correction); *Echetel* (Viennese thieves'); *Erbsien* (Viennese thieves': from the staple of diet —*Erbsen* = peas. *Cf.*, *Graupenpalais*); *Graupenpalais* (a prison in Berlin, from the staple of diet—barley); *Grannigebais* (*Granigire Marochum* = a fortress); *Gymnasium* (*Cf.*, college, academy, *lycée*; *Kaan* or *Kän* (from the Hebrew; *im Kaan scheften*, to be in prison); *Kue* or *Kuh* (*in die Kue sperren*, to imprison); *Kitt* or *Kittchen* (from the Hebrew *Kisse* = a chair, throne, roof, common lodging-house, brothel, workhouse, and prison); *Kille* (literally an assembly); *Kühle* (*im Kühlen sitzen*, literally to sit in the 'cooler' or in the shade; *Cf.*, *être à l'ombre*, and 'to be under a cloud'); *Leck* (Viennese thieves' M.H.G., *luken*, to lock up); *Mifzer* (Hebrew *pozar*, a fortress or prison); *Schofelbajis* (from the Hebrew *schophal*, bad, common, low, or unfortunate. Also a brothel); *Stube* (this, according to Zimmermann, signifies a prison); *Tallesmasky* (Hanoverian: from *tallo*, gallows, + *masky* from *Maskopei*, society, *i.e.*, gallows-birds); *T'fise* (from the Hebrew *tophas*).

ITALIAN SYNONYMS. *Basta*; *casa* (a house. The forms *casaccia* and *cazanza* are also used); *cavagna*; *travagliosa* (literally laborious); *sentina* (properly a sink of vice); *viscola* or *visco losa*.

SPANISH SYNONYMS. *Madrastra*; *angustias* or *ansias* (literally grief or anguish); *banasto* (literally a large round basket); *banco* (properly a bench); *temor* (*i.e.*, fear); *trena* (*f*).

PORTUGUESE SYNONYMS. *Estarim* or *xelro*; *limoeiro* (a cant name for a prison in Lisbon).

2. (common).—An 'improver, or bustle. *See* BIRD-CAGE.

3. (venery). — A bed; also BREEDING-CAGE.

1875. W. E. HENLEY, *Unpublished Ballad*. 'In the BREEDING CAGE I cops her, With her stays off, all a'blowin'!—Three parts sprung.'—

4. (parliamentary). — The Ladies' Gallery in the House of

Commons; sometimes called the CHAMBER OF HORRORS, which appertains more properly to the Peeresses' Gallery in the Upper House.

1870. *London Figaro*, 10 June. 'The Angels in the House.' Mr. Crauford's Motion for the expulsion of strangers (during the debate on The Contagious (Women's) Diseases Act had reference to the CAGE and not to the Reporters' Gallery.

CAGG, *verb* (old military).—Grose says 'a military term used by the private soldiers, signifying a solemn vow or resolution not to get drunk for a certain time; or, as the term is, till their CAGG is out, which vow is commonly observed with the strictest exactness: *e.g.*, "I have CAGG'D myself for six months. Excuse me this time, and I will CAGG myself for a year." Common in Scotland, where the vow is performed with divers ceremonies.'

CAG-MAG, *subs.* (vulgar). — Primarily a provincialism for a tough old goose; now a vulgarism for refuse, or rubbish, or scraps and ends. The transferred sense is older than given in the *N.E.D.* *Cf.*, KEG-MEG. [Brewer derives it, 'from the Gaelic and Welsh,' *cag magu*, whilst others consider it as originally a University slang term for a bad cook, κακὸς μάγειρος. The Latin *magma* (Pliny), = dregs or dross.] Also a plain or dirty woman.

1769. PENNANT, *Tour in Scotland*, 1774, p. 10. Vast numbers [of geese] are driven annually to London; among them, all the superannuated geese and ganders (called here [Lincoln] CAG-MAGS).

1839.—*Comic Almanack*, Sept., p. 188, But here's the greatest grief, and sure it makes one choke to put on A libel to one's neck, just like cheap CAG-MAG-SCRAG of mutton.

1851-61.—H. MAYHEW, *London Lab. and Lon. Poor*, vol. I., p. 133. 'Do I ever eat my own game if it's high? No, sir, never, I couldn't stand such CAG-MAG.'

1864.—*Temple Bar*, vol. X., p. 185. No KAG-MAG wares are sold, no cheap articles are retailed.

CAIN. TO RAISE CAIN, *phr.* (American).—To proceed to extreme measures; to be quarrelsome; to make a disturbance. Of Western origin; primarily applied to men who would have shown no hesitation in shooting or stabbing; generally = merely disputatious or quarrelsome. Variants are TO RAISE HATE, HELL, or HELL AND TOMMY, and TO RAISE NED (*q.v.*). [An allusion to the anger of the first fratricide.]

1849.—RUXTON, *Scenes in the Far West*, p. 117. He had been knocking around all day in every grog-shop and bar-room in town, and when evening came he was seen swaggering down Main Street, his head bare, his eyes bloodshot, and his revolver in hand, shouting: 'Who'll hinder this child? I am going TO RAISE CAIN! Who's got anything to say agin it?'

1869.—MRS. BEECHER STOWE, *Old Town Folks*, p. 116. 'I'll tell you what, Solomon Peters,' said Miss Asphyxia, 'I'd jest as soon have the red dragon in the Revelation a comin' down on my house as a boy! If I don't work hard enough now, I'd like to know, without having a boy around RAISIN' general CAIN.'

CAIN AND ABEL, *subs. phr.* (rhyming slang).—A table.

CAINSHAM - SMOKE, *subs. phr.* (old).—The tears of a wife-beaten husband.—DUNTON. *Ladies' Dictionary* [1694].

CAKE or **CAKEY**, *subs.* (popular).— I. A fool or dullard. Quoted by Grose in his *Dictionary of the Vulgar Tongue* [1785], in various provincial glossaries, and generally colloquial in the lower strata of society. [In punning allusion, some have thought, to the doughy

softness of a cake, a name given at first to any 'flat' kind of sweetened breadstuff. Hence variants, such, for example, as 'flat,' 'soft,' and 'muff.' Others, however, trace it to the Greek κακὸς, bad, and point out that in University slang a clever man is called a good man and the opposite a bad one, or a CAKE.] For synonyms, *see* BUFFLE and CABBAGE-HEAD.

1841. *Comic Almanack*, 'Twelfth Night,' p. 256. And ever since, on fair Twelfth Night, A wand'ring form is seen: A female form, and this its cry:—'Vy vot a CAKE I've been!'

1842. J. R. PLANCHÉ, *The White Cat*, II., iv. Your resignation proves that you must be The greatest CAKE he in his land could see!

1862. MRS. H. WOOD, *Channings*, ch. xxix. If Pye does not get called to order now, he may lapse into the habit of passing over hardworking fellows with trains to exalt some good-for-nothing CAKE with none, because he happens to have a Dutchman for his mother.

2. (American thieves').—A stupid policeman.

3. *subs.* (Christ's Hospital).— A stroke with a cane.

Verb (Christ's Hospital).—To cane.

TO TAKE THE CAKE, *phr.* (common).—To rank the highest; to carry off the honours; to be the best of a kind; 'to fill the bill' (theatrical). [CAKE has long been employed symbolically in this connection; in the seventeenth and eighteenth centuries, 'to get one's share of the cake' was a common colloquialism. The special application has been popularised in the U.S.A. In certain sections of the country 'cake walks' are in vogue among the coloured people. The young bucks get themselves up most elaborately, and walk from one end of the hall to the other, under the gaze of beauty and the critical glance of the judges. The marking is done on a scale of numbers, and the ties are walked off with the utmost finish and a rare attention to style. The prize is a CAKE and the winner TAKES it.] Whimsical variations are TO TAKE or YANK THE BUN; TO SLIDE AWAY WITH THE BANBURY; TO ANNEX THE WHOLE CONFECTIONER'S SHOP. *Cf.*, TO TAKE THE KETTLE = to take the prize for lying.

1885. *San Francisco News Letter*, Between you 'n me, red stockings ain't becomin' to all—ahem—limbs, 'n for cool cheek 'n dash. I back some o'em against any saleslady 't makes a livin' by it, the way 't some o' those girls 'd pin on a *boutonnière* TOOK THE CAKE.

HURRY UP THE CAKES! *phr.* (American) = Look sharp! Buckwheat and other hot cakes form a staple dish at many American tables, but the phrase has now become pure slang.

LIKE HOT CAKES, *phr.* (American).—Quickly; with energy; a variant of LIKE WINKING, or LIKE ONE O'CLOCK (*q.v.*).

1888. *Punch's Library*, p. 15. 'Will go LIKE HOT CAKES.' *Book Seller* (to Clerk). 'Haven't we an overstock of "Jack, the Giant Killer," on hand, James?' *Clerk*. 'Yes, sir.' *Book Seller*. 'Well, take 'm up to the Polo Grounds this afternoon; they'll sell fast enough there.'

CAKEY - PANNUM FENCER.—*See* PANNUM FENCER.

CALABOOSE, *subs.* (American and nautical).—The common gaol. [This word comes into popular use from the Spanish *calabozo* through the French *calabouse*.] So also TO CALABOOSE = to imprison.

1840. R. H. DANA, *Two Years before the Mast*, ch. xxi. A few weeks afterwards I saw the poor wretch sitting on the bare ground, in front of the CALABOZO, with his feet chained to a stake, and handcuffs about his wrists.

1888. *Santa Ana Blade.* Charley Read struck an old tramp in the CALABOOSE the other day, who looked disgusted at his headquarters and remarked 'Well I've been in every jail from Portland to Santa Ana, but this is the d—nest snide of a CALABOOSE I ever struck yet.

CALCULATE, *verb* (U.S. colloquial).—To think; expect; believe; intend; indeed, almost any sense save the legitimate, which is 'to estimate by calculation.' It belongs to the same class of colloquialisms as GUESS and RECKON. CALCULATE is sometimes, especially in New England, corrupted into CAL'LATE.

1830.—GALT, *Lawrie, T.*, II., v. (1849), 56. I CALCULATE, that ain't no thing to make nobody afeard.

1848.—J. R. LOWELL, *Biglow Papers.* The Sarjunt he thout Hosea hedn't gut his i teeth cos he looked a kindo's though he'd jest come down, so he CAL'LATED to hook him in, but Hosy woodn't take none of his sarse.

1851.—MISS WETHERELL, *Queechy*, ch. xix. 'Your aunt sets two tables, I CALCULATE, don't she?'

CALEYS, *subs.* (Stock Exchange).—Caledonian Railway Ordinary Stock.

1881.—ATKIN, *House Scraps.* 'If anything tickles our fancy We buy them, Brums, CALEYS or Apes.'

CALF, *subs.* (colloquial).—An ignoramus; a dolt; a weakling. *Cf.*, CALF LOLLY. For synonyms, *see* BUFFLE and CABBAGE-HEAD.

1553.—UDALL, *Royster D.*, II., iv., in Hazl. *Dodsley*, III., 94. You great CALF, ye should have more wit, so ye should.

1627.—DRAYTON, *Nymphid* (1631), 171. Some silly doting brainless CALFE.

1872. HAMILTON AIDÉ, *Morals and Mysteries*, p. 60. She had a girlish fancy for the good-looking young CALF who had so signally disgraced himself.

TO EAT THE CALF IN THE COW'S BELLY, *phr.* (common).—A variant of 'to count one's chickens before they are hatched.'

1748. RICHARDSON. *Clarissa Harlowe* [ed. 1811], III., 135. I ever made shift to avoid anticipations: I never would EAT THE CALF IN THE COW'S BELLY, as Lord M's phrase is.

CALF-CLINGERS, *subs.* (common).—Pantaloons; *i.e.*, close-fitting trousers. [Derivation obvious.] For synonyms, *see* BAGS and KICKS.

1884.—J. GREENWOOD, *Little Ragamuffins.* Knee-breeches were just going out of fashion when I was a little boy, and CALF-CLINGERS (that is, trousers made to fit the leg as tight as a worsted stocking) were 'coming in.'

CALF, COW, and BULL WEEK, *subs. phr.* (operatives').—Before the passing of the Factory Acts it was customary in manufacturing districts, especially for men, women, and children, to indulge in the practice of working very long hours for a period of three weeks before the Christmas holidays. In the first, which was called 'CALF WEEK,' the ordinary hours of work were but slightly exceeded; in the second, or 'COW WEEK,' they were considerably augmented; and in the third, or 'BULL WEEK,' it was common for operatives to spend the greater portion of the twenty-four of each day in their workshops. The practice resulted in extreme exhaustion and —naturally—indulgence to excess in stimulants.

1871.—*Echo*, 4 Dec. CALF, COW, AND BULL WEEK. We find a good illustration of the beneficial influence of the Factory Acts in the reports of the Government Inspectors just issued. The district inspector expresses the hope that the measures which he took against some offenders in BULL WEEK last year will extinguish for good and all this absurd and illogical custom.

CALF'S HEAD, *subs.* (common).—A stupid, witless individual. For synonyms, *see* BUFFLE and CABBAGE-HEAD.

1600.—SHAKSPEARE, *Much Ado about Nothing*, V., i., CLAUDIO: 'I' faith, I thank him; he hath bid me to a CALF'S HEAD and a capon; the which if I do not carve most curiously, say my knife's naught.

CALF-LICK.—*See* COW-LICK.

CALF-LOLLY, *subs.* (old).—An idle simpleton; a general term of reproach.

1653. URQUHART, *Rabelais*, bk. I., ch. xxv. Jobbinol goosecaps, foolish loggerheads, flutch CALF-LOLLIES.

1708. MOTTEUX, *Rabelais*, iv., xvii. I was a CALF-LOLLY, a doddipole.

CALF-LOVE, *subs.* (common).—A youthful, romantic fancy. [A sarcastic allusion to the blind unreasoning character of boy and girl attachments.]

1823. GALT, *Entail*, I., xxxii., 284. I made a CALF-LOVE marriage. [M.]

1863. MRS. GASKELL, *Sylvia's Lovers*, II., 104. It's a girl's fancy—just a kind o' CALF-LOVE—let it go by.

1884. *Longman's Mag.*, IV., 50. I was still at the early and agonising stage of the passion which is popularly known as CALF-LOVE.

CALFSKIN-FIDDLE, *subs.* (old).—A drum.

1785. GROSE, *Dictionary of the Vulgar Tongue*, s.v.

CALF-STICKING, *subs.* (thieves').—Explained by quotation. [*Cf.*, CALF and STICK].

1883. *Daily Telegraph*, 25 July, p. 2, col. 1. The venerable oarsman grinned, and set me right by explaining that what was called CALF-STICKING by those who practised it was the putting off of worthless rubbish, on the pretence that it was smuggled goods, on any foolish or unscrupulous person who could be inveigled into treating for the same.

CALIBOGUS, *subs.* (American).—A very old name for a mixture of rum and spruce beer, being quoted by Grose in 1785 as 'an American beverage.' The last two syllables of the word are thought to be derived from the French *bagasse*, the refuse of the sugar cane. This view would seem to be supported by the fact that rum is itself a product of the sugar cane.

1861. L. DE BOILEAU. *Recoll. Labrador Life*, p. 162. CALLIBOGUS, a mixture of Rum and Spruce-beer, more of the former and less of the latter.

CALICO, *adj.* (old).—Thin; wasted; attenuated. [Calicut is the name of the Indian city whence the material of the comparison was brought. The earliest reference for original signification given by Murray is 1505; but he omits the cant meaning.]

1733. NATHANIEL BAILEY, *Colloquies of Erasmus* (translated), p. 37. In such a place as that your CALLICO body (*tenui corpusculo*) had need have a good fire to keep it warm.

1861. SALA, *Seven Sons of Mammon.* A shrewd, down-east Yankee once questioned a simple Dutchman out of his well-fed steed, and left him instead a vile CALICO mare in exchange.

CALICO-BALLY, *adj.* (common).—Somewhat 'fast'; applied to

one always on the look out for amusement. [Primarily used of frequenters of CALICO-BALLS.]

18(?). *Broadside Ballad*, 'The Flipperty-Flop Young Man.' I once was a cabby and hack young man, And a little bit CALICO-BALLY; A picture card out of the pack young man, And frequently music hally.

CALIFORNIA.—*See* CALIFORNIAN, sense 2.

CALIFORNIAN, *subs.* (common).—1. A red or hard-dried herring. Further explained by quotations. Also SOLDIER, ATLANTIC RANGER and GLASGOW MAGISTRATE.

1873.—*Cassell's Mag.*, Jan., p. 245, Very large quantities of cured herrings came from North Britain at that time, and, excepting those from the Firth of Forth, they were more cured, dryer and salter than those from Norfolk. Some were sent very dry indeed, as hard as a stick, and of a very deep red colour; such were used, as similar fish now are, for exportation. About the time of the gold discoveries, some one applied the term CALIFORNIAN to these. The word was appropriate, and CALIFORNIANS such highly-coloured herrings are called to this day.

2. [Generally used in the plural—CALIFORNIANS.] Generic for gold pieces.

CALIFORNIA WIDOW, *subs. phr.* (American).—A married woman whose husband is away from her for any extended period; a GRASS WIDOW (*q.v.*) in the least offensive sense. The expression dates from the period of the Californian gold fever, when so many men went West, leaving their wives and families behind them.

CALK, *verb* (Eton College).—To throw.

CALL, *subs.* (Eton College).—The time when the masters do not call ABSENCE (*q.v.*).

TO HAVE OR GET A CALL UPON, *phr.* (American).—To have a preference, or the first chance.

1888.—*Puck's Library*, May, p. 23, *Picture Dealer (to Professional's Husband)*: 'No, sir; I can't sell no more of your wife's pictures unless she gets down some of that flesh, and looks kinder æstheticker. The ethereal and intellectual HAS GOT THE CALL on the old style of beauty now-a-days.

TO CALL A GO, *verbal phr.* (vagrants' and street patterers').—To change one's stand; to alter one's tactics; to give in at any game or business. [From the GO 'call' in cribbage.]

1851-61.—H. MAYHEW, *London Lab. and Lon. Poor*, vol. I., p. 252. TO CALL A GO, signifies to remove to another spot, or adopt some other patter, or, in short, to resort to some change or other in consequence of a failure.

TO CALL A SPADE A SPADE.—*See* SPADE.

TO CALL OVER THE COALS.—*See* WIGGING.

PUT AND CALL.—*See* PUT.

CALLE, *subs.* (old and American thieves').—A cloak or gown. Quoted by Grose [1785], and still in use in the U.S.A. amongst the criminal classes. For synonyms, *see* CASTER.

CALP or KELP, *subs.* (old).—A hat. [Origin unknown.] For synonyms, *see* GOLGOTHA.

CALVERT'S ENTIRE.—The Fourteenth Foot. [Called CALVERT from their colonel, Sir Harry Calvert (1806–1826), and ENTIRE, because three entire battalions were kept up for the good of Sir Harry, when adjutant-general. A play upon words in reference

to Calvert's malt liquors.] This regiment was also called the OLD AND BOLD.

1780. R. TOMLINSON, *Slang Pastoral*, canto viii. Gin! What is become of thy heart-chearing fire, And where is the beauty of CALVERT'S INTIRE?

1871. *Chambers' Journal*, 23 Dec., p. 803, col. 1. The 14th Foot, CALVERT'S ENTIRE.

1886. *Tinsley's Magazine*, April, p. 322. A very curious name, CALVERT'S ENTIRE, used to be attached to the 14th, but this as well as the circumstances which gave rise to it are forgotten.

CALVES. CALVES GONE TO GRASS, *subs. phr.* (old).—Said of spindle shanks; *i.e.*, slender, undeveloped legs, with lack of calves.

THERE ARE MANY WAYS OF DRESSING CALVES' HEADS, *phr.* (old).—Many ways of saying or doing a foolish thing; a simpleton has many ways of showing his folly; or, generally, if one way won't do, we must try another.

CALVES' HEADS ARE BEST HOT, *phr.* (common).—A sarcastic apology for one sitting down to eat with his hat on.—*See* STAND-UP.

CALX, *subs.* (Eton College).—The goal line at football. [From a Latin sense of CALX = a goal, anciently marked with lime or chalk.] At Eton CALX is a space so marked off at each end of WALL; GOOD CALX is the end at which there is a door for a goal; BAD CALX the end where part of an elm tree serves the purpose.

1864. *Daily Telegraph*, Dec. 1. The Collegers were over-weighted . . . and the Oppidans managed to get the ball down into their CALX several times. [M.]

CAMBRIDGE OAK, *subs.* (old).—A willow. [An allusion to the abundance of this tree in the county in question, which is situate in the Fen District.] Formerly many analogous sayings were in vogue; *e.g.*, 'A Cotswold lion' for 'a sheep,' etc. —*See* also CAMBRIDGESHIRE NIGHTINGALE.

CAMBRIDGESHIRE or FEN NIGHTINGALE, *subs. phr.* (common).—A frog. [The county is scored with canals and dykes; the allusion is to the natural preponderance of the croaking of frogs over the singing of nightingales.] *Cf.* CAMBRIDGE OAK and CAPE NIGHTINGALE.

1875. *Chambers' Journal*, No. 581, p. 107, col. 2. The male of the eatable frog is distinguished . . . by . . . a pouch . . . These pouches increase the volume of the croak, and render it so powerful that the possessors have, from the county in which they are particularly plentiful, received the nickname of CAMBRIDGESHIRE NIGHTINGALES.

CAMDEN-TOWN, *subs.* (rhyming slang).—A halfpenny, or 'brown.' For synonyms, *see* MAG.

CAMEL'S COMPLAINT, *subs. phr.* (common).—Low spirits; the HUMP (*q.v.*).

CAMESA, *subs.* (thieves').—A shirt chemise, or 'shimmy.' [From the Spanish *camisa*, or Italian *camicia*.] The word appears in various forms from the beginning of the seventeenth century, *e.g.*, 'camisa,' 'camiscia' 'kemesa,' 'camise,' and in a more genuinely English dress as 'COMMISSION' (*q.v.*), which in turn is shortened into MISH (*q.v.*). For synonyms, *see* FLESH-BAG.

1690.—B.E., *Dict. Cant. Crew.* CAMESA: a shirt or shift.

1785.—GROSE, *Dictionary of the Vulgar Tongue.* CAMESA (*cant, Spanish*): a shirt or shift.

1812.—BYRON, *Childe Harold II., Tambourgi* ii. Oh! who is more brave than a dark Suliote, In his snowy CAMESE and his shaggy capote?

1834.—H. AINSWORTH, *Rookwood*, bk. III., ch. v. With my fawnied famms, and my onions gay, my thimble of ridge, and my driz (laced) KEMESA.

CAMISTER, *subs.* (thieves'). — A preacher or clergyman. From the white gown or surplice. From Latin *camisia*, a linen tunic, alb, or shirt, + (probably) a termination suggested by 'minister.'] For synonyms, *see* DEVIL-DODGER.

1851-61. H. MAYHEW, *London Lab. and Lon. Poor*, vol. I., p. 231. [List of patterer's words.] CAMISTER=Minister.

CAMP. TO GO TO CAMP, *phr.* (Australian).—To go to bed; to take rest. [From the practice in the early settlers' days of forming a camp whenever a halt for the night was called.]

1887. *All the Year Round*, 30 July, p. 66, col. 2. TO GO TO CAMP, by a transference of its original meaning, now signifies, in the mouth of a dweller in houses, simply 'to lie down,' 'to go to bed.'

TO TAKE INTO CAMP, *phr.* (Common).—To kill.

1878. S. L. CLEMENS ('Mark Twain') *Some Rambling Notes of an Idle Excursion*, p. 66. Sure enough one night the trap took Mrs. Jones's principal tomcat into camp, and finished him up.

TO CAMP, *phr.* (Australian).—To surpass; to 'floor.'

18(?) H. KENDALL, *Billy Vickers.* At punching oxen you may guess There's nothing out can CAMP him; He has, in fact, the slouch and dress Which bullock-driver stamp him.

CAMPBELL'S ACADEMY, *subs. phr.* (old).—The hulks, or lighters, on board of which felons were condemned to hard labour. Mr. Campbell was the first director.—*Grose.* — *See* ACADEMY and FLOATING ACADEMY. For synonyms, *see* CAGE.

1781. G. PARKER, *View of Society*, II., 11. He was tried at Guildhall, Westminster, and sentenced to improve as a pupil in Mr. Duncan Campbell's FLOATING ACADEMY for five years.

CAMP-CANDLESTICK, *subs.* (military) —An empty bottle, or a bayonet. Quoted in the *Lexicon Balatronicum* [1811]. For synonyms in the sense of 'an empty bottle,' *see* DEAD-MAN.

CAMP-STOOL BRIGADE, *subs. phr.* (common). — Said in the first place of people who wait outside a place of entertainment to secure the best seats, and bring camp-stools with them to rest themselves.

1889. *Pall Mall Gazette*, 23 Sept., p. 5, col. 2. The first night of the Gaiety Wanderers will not be forgotten in a hurry. Seats for the occasion were booked a year ago last April! Can you wonder that the CAMP-STOOL BRIGADE besieged the pit door as early as 10 a.m.?

CAN, *subs.* (American).—1. A dollar piece.

2. (Scots).—A 'slavey.'

CANACK, CANUCK, KANUCK, K'NUCK, *subs.* (American).—A Canadian, usually a K'NUCK. [Obscure, and limited in its application within the Canadian frontier. There, a CANUCK is understood to be a French Canadian, just as within the limits of the Union only New Englanders are termed Yankees; whereas elsewhere that appellation is given indiscriminately to

natives of all the States. It is by some supposed that CANUCK is a corruption of Connaught, the name applied by French-Canadians to the Irish, from which it would follow that, by a process of inversion, a nickname given by one section of a nation to another has, in course of time, been applied to the whole. Others, however, think the first syllable of 'Canada' has been joined to the Algonkin Indian substantive termination *uc* or *uq*.]

CANARY or **CANARY-BIRD,** *subs.* (thieves').—1. A prisoner; a very old cant term for habitual offenders; or, as Grose says [1785], 'a person used to be kept in a CAGE' (*q.v.*). The same idea occurs in some foreign equivalents, *e.g.*, the French, *oiseau de cage*, and the German, *Kastener*, from *Kasten*, a chest or case. For synonyms, *see* WRONG 'UN.

1673.—HEAD, *Canting Academy*, p. 157. Newgate is a cage of CANARY-BIRDS.

1725.—*New Canting Dictionary.* CANARY-BIRD, a little, arch, or knavish boy; a rogue or whore taken and clapped into the cage or roundhouse.

1839.—HARRISON AINSWORTH, *Jack Sheppard* [1889], p. 55. Now for the cage, my pretty CANARY-BIRD. Before we start I'll accommodate you with a pair of ruffles.

2. (general). — A mistress. [*See* preceding quot. (1725): the term is still in use.] For synonyms, *see* TART.

3. (common). — Formerly a guinea, but now applied to a sovereign [From similarity of colour.]

ENGLISH SYNONYMS. Yellow boy; goldfinch; yellow hammer; shiner; gingleboy; monarch; couter; bean foont; James (from Jacobus); poona; portrait; quid; thick 'un; skin; skiv; dragon; goblin. A guinea was also called a 'ned.'

FRENCH SYNONYMS for the equivalent twenty franc piece are, *un jaunet* (popular: literally 'butter-cup' or 'yellow-boy'); *une sigue, sigle, sigolle* or *cig* (thieves'); *un bonnet jaune* (popular: literally 'yellow-cap' or 'bonnet'); *un bouton* (*i.e.*, 'a master-key'); *une maltaise* (old cant; according to Victor Hugo this gold coin was used on board the convict galleys at Malta); *un moule à boutons* (popular); *une médaille d'or* (popular: = a gold medal).

GERMAN SYNONYMS. *Gelbling* (*gelb* = yellow); *Fuchs* (a gold piece; literally 'a fox').

For synonyms of money generally, *see* ACTUAL and GILT.

1785. GROSE, *Dictionary of the Vulgar Tongue.* CANARY-BIRDS in a canting sense, guineas.

1822. SCOTT, *Fortunes of Nigel*, ch. xvi. Fifty as fair yellow CANARY-BIRDS as e'er chirped in the bottom of a green silk purse.

1842. *Punch*, p. 168. 'Prolusiones etymologicæ,' 13. *Goldfinches*—CANARIES. —Singing birds; the which whose possesseth needeth never to pine for lack of notes.

4. (thieves').—A female watcher or stall; a MOLLISHER (*q.v.*). *Cf.* CROW = a male watcher. Fr. *une marque franche.*

1862. H. MAYHEW, *Lon. Lab. and Lond. Poor*, IV., 337. Sometimes a woman, called a 'CANARY,' carries the tools [of burglars], and watches outside.

5. (Salvation Army).—A written promise of a donation or subscription. At some of the meetings of the 'Army' instead of sending round the plate, the 'officers' distribute slips of paper on which those present are invited to record their benevolent intentions. The original colour of the slips was yellow—hence the nickname.

CANCER. TO CATCH or CAPTURE A CANCER, *phr.* (common).—*See* CRAB.

1857. HOOD, *Pen and Pencil Pictures* p. 141. He had another way of CAPTURING CANCERS, namely, by never putting his oar into the water at all.

CANDLE-KEEPERS, *subs.* (Winchester College). — The eight seniors in college by election who are not præfects. They enjoy most of the privileges of præfects without their powers.

1870. MANSFIELD, *School-Life at Winchester College*, p. 30. The Seven CANDLE-KEEPERS (why so-called, I have no idea, nor have I ever heard any interpretation of the appellation) These were the seven inferiors who had been longest in the school, quite independently of their position in it; they were generally old and tough. Of these, the senior had almost as much power as a præfect; he had a 'valet' in chambers, one or two 'breakfast fags,' and the power of fagging the twenty juniors when in school, or in meads. The junior CANDLE KEEPER was called 'the Deputy,' and had also some slight privileges besides that of having a valet and breakfast fag, which was common to all of them.

1878. ADAMS, *Wykehamica*, p. 278. Presided over by a CANDLE-KEEPER.

CANDLESTICK, *subs.* 1. (Winchester College).—A humorous corruption of the word 'candidate.'

1870. MANSFIELD, *School-Life at Winchester College*, p. 175. Each of these [the Electors] had in turn the privilege of nominating a boy for admission into Winchester till all vacancies were filled, of which there were generally about twelve, but always many more 'Candidates' (or CANDLESTICKS, as they were often called).

1878. H. C. ADAMS, *Wykehamica*, p. 418. CANDLESTICK, merely a facetious version of 'candidate.'

2. *pl.* (London).—The fountains in Trafalgar Square.

1851. MAYHEW, *London Labour and Lon. Poor*, I., p. 529. There was his (Nelson's) pillar at Charing Cross, just by the CANDLESTICKS (fountains).

CANDY, *adj.* (old).—Given by Grose in 1785, and by the *Lexicon Balatronicum*, in 1811, as 'drunk —an Irish term.'

CANDYMAN, *subs.* (northern).—A bailiff or process server. Originally a seller of candy. [In October, 1863, there was a great strike of miners at the collieries of Messrs. Strakers and Love, in the county of Durham. As no adjustment of the difference was possible, the owners determined to eject the miners from their cottages. For this purpose, an army of rascals were engaged, including at least one whose ordinary occupation was that of hawking candy and sweetmeats. The man was recognised and was chaffed; and CANDYMAN, which rapidly became a term of reproach, was soon applied to the whole class; and since that time is come into general use over the two northern counties whenever ejectments take place.]

1863. *Newcastle Chronicle*, Oct. 31. The colliery carts and waggons stood at the doors, and the furniture was handed out, and piled quickly but carefully upon them. It was evident that the CANDYMEN had warmed to their work. The name of CANDYMAN has been given to the loaders because of their avocations of 'candy' hawking, from which they are supposed to have been taken to be put to this work.

1876. *Notes and Queries*, 5 S., v., 405. A term in the North for men employed to carry out evictions against cottage occupiers.

1886. *Notes and Queries*, 7 S., i., p. 445.

CANISTER, *subs.* (general).—1. The head. [A transference of the original meaning, 'a box or case for holding things.'] For synonyms, *see* CRUMPET.

1811. *Lexicon Balatronicum.* To mill his CANNISTER; to break his head.

1821. MONCRIEFF, *Tom and Jerry*, Act ii., Sc. 4. *Tom.* I've nobb'd him on the CANISTER.

1885. *Bell's Life*, Jan. 3, p. 8, col. 4. Once more did the star of Australia rise, but to set from additional raps on the CANISTER. He fell on his knees, and his head droped on his breast.

2. (common).—A hat. [Formerly CANISTER-CAP (*see* sense 1); subsequently shortened to CANISTER.] For synonyms, *see* GOLGOTHA.

1887. ATKIN, *House Scraps.* Turning round, I saw my unfortunate beaver, or CANISTER, as it was called by the gentry who had it in their keeping, bounding backwards and forwards.

CANK, *adj.* (old).—Dumb; silent. [Curiously enough, CANK also signifies 'to chatter,' or 'cackle as a goose'; it only survives in this latter sense.]

1673. R. HEAD, *Canting Acad.*, 36. CANK: dumb.

1785. GROSE, *Dictionary of the Vulgar Tongue.* CANK: dumb.

CANNIBAL, *subs.* (Cambridge University).—In the bumping races at Cambridge, a college may be represented by more than one boat. The best talent is put into the first, but it has sometimes happened that the crew of the second have got so well together that it has disappointed the prophets and bumped the first of its own college. In this case it is termed A CANNIBAL, it having eaten up its own kind, and a fine is enacted from it by the University Boat Club.

CANNIKIN or **CANNIKEN,** *subs.* (old). —The plague. [Grose includes it in his dictionary under the sense of 'a small can,' but this was not a slang usage.]

1688. R. HOLME, *Armoury.* III., iii., § 68. CANNIKIN, the Plague. [M.]

1690. B. E., *Dict. Cant. Crew.* s.v.

CANNIS-COVE, *subs.* (American).—A dog-fancier. [Either from Latin *canis*, a dog, or the Fr. *caniche*, poodle + COVE, a man.]

CANNON.—*See* CANON.

CANNON-BALLS, *subs.* (political).— 1. A nickname, now obsolete, given to the irreconcileable opponents of free trade in England.

1858. *Saturday Review*, 30 Oct., p. 413, col. 2. The amendment . . . which sealed for ever the fate of Protection, was carried [in 1852] with only fifty dissentient voices—the celebrated CANNON-BALLS. [M.]

2. (venery).—The testicles. For synonyms *see* CODS.

CANOE. TO PADDLE ONE'S OWN CANOE, *phr.* (American).—To make one's own way in life; to exhibit skill and energy; to succeed unaided; a slang phrase of Western American origin, but now universal. [Extremely careful and clever manipulation is required in the management of canoes, especially in shooting rapids; otherwise the surging body of water might swamp the boat, or sunken rocks strike and seriously damage it. Hence the adoption of such an expression to signify skill, close attention, and energy.] A variant is TO BAIL ONE'S OWN BOAT; and the French have a proverbial saying, *il conduit* or *il mène bien sa barque.*

1845. *Harper's Magazine*, May. Voyager upon life's sea, to yourself be true; And, where'er your lot may be, PADDLE YOUR OWN CANOE.

1868. *Broadside Ballad*, sung by HARRY CLIFTON. My wants are small, I care not at all, If my debts are paid when due. And to drive away strife on the ocean of life, I PADDLE MY OWN CANOE.

1870. C. H. SPURGEON. At Metropolitan Tabernacle [speaking of Mr. John Magregor said]—He puts his trust in God and PADDLES HIS OWN CANOE.

1871. DE VERE, *English of the New World*, p. 343. The familiarity with boating, which the unsurpassed number of watercourses all over the country naturally produces everywhere, has led to the use, not only of PADDLING ONE'S OWN CANOE, . . . but also of 'bailing one's own boat,' in the sense of 'minding one's own business,' independently and without waiting for help from others.

CANON or **CANNON**, *adj.* (thieves').—Drunk. [The origin of this term is very obscure, although many guesses have been hazarded. Amongst these may be mentioned (1) From the 'can' having been used freely. Rather less absurd is (2) its derivation from the French slang expressions *un canon*, a glass drunk at the bar of a wine-shop; *canonner*, to drink wine at a wine-shop, or to be a habitual tippler; *se canonner*, to get drunk; and *un canonneur*, a tippler, wine-bibber, or drunkard. Yet another suggested origin is (3) from the German *cannon*, a drinking cup, from which is obtained *canonised*, = 'shot' or 'drunk.' A German proverb runs *er ist geschossen*, and Barrère points out that CANON becomes naturally confused with *can*, German *Kaune*, a tankard, and *Canonenstiefel*, or 'canon' (*i.e.*, long boots), a common pattern of tankard.] For synonyms, *see* SCREWED.

1879. J. W. HORSLEY, in *Macm. Mag.*, XL., 502. One night I was with the mob, I got CANON (drunk), this being the first time.

CANOODLE, *verb* (American).—1. To fondle; bill and coo; indulge in endearments.—*See* CANOODLING. [There are two suggested derivations—(1) from CANNIE in the sense of gentle, and (2) that the primary signification may have been 'to act as a noodle,' *i.e.*, to play the fool.] For synonyms, *see* FIRKYTOODLE.

1864. G. A. SALA, *Temple Bar*, Dec., p. 40. He is an adept in that branch of persuasive dialectics known as CONOODLING. He will CONOODLE the ladies (bless their dear hearts! and how sharp they think themselves at making a bargain!) into the acquisition of whole packages of gimcrack merchandise.

1879. *Punch*, March 15, p. 117, col. 2. 'Our Representative Man.' Then he and the matchless one struggle, snuggle, and generally CONOODLE together rapturously. Then the matchless Ecstacy being the wife, not of the Chevalier, but of Charles VI., King of France, she, this impulsive, loving, beautiful, hugging, conoodling young Ecstacy, has the cool impudence to declare that theirs is a 'guiltless love.'

2. (Oxford University).—To paddle or propel a canoe.

1879. E. H. MARSHALL, in *Notes and Queries*, 5 S., xi., 375. When I was an undergraduate at Oxford, to CANOODLE was the slang expression for paddling one's own canoe on the bosom of the Cherwell or the Isis.

3. (American theatrical).—To share profits.

18(?). *Green Room Jokes*. 'Pray, good sir, what is a CANOODLER?' 'Tell you, mum, queer business, mum, but prosperous, money—heaps of it, mum, for you and me'—and he winked significantly, jerked up a chair, and squatted in it, all in a breath. . . . Undeterred, he rattled on:

'I'm an original thinker, mum. Invent business opportunities. Share 'm with actors, and then we CANOODLE—divvy the profits. Me and Sheridan made a big thing on the Japanese advertising screen in "School for Scandal!" Big thing.'

4. (common).—To coax.

CANOODLER.—*See* CANOODLE.

CANOODLING, *verbal subs.* (American).—Endearments.

1859. SALA, *Twice Round the Clock*, 11 a.m., par. 8. A sly kiss, and a squeeze, and a pressure of the foot or so, and a variety of harmless endearing blandishments, known to our American cousins (who are great adepts at sweet-hearting) under the generic name of CONOODLING.

1864 and 1879. [*See* quots. under Canoodle, sense 1.]

CANT, *subs.* and *verb*.—[As regards derivation (whether noun or verb), to signify the speech, phraseology, or whine peculiar to thieves, beggars, and vagrants, authorities differ among and with themselves: the word occurs as early as 1540, and has long since achieved respectability. Grose was probably wrong in thinking it a corruption of *chaunting*, and it was certainly in use long prior to the two Scotch clergymen, Oliver and Andrew Cant, who are said to have preached with such a voice and such a manner as to give their name to all speaking of the same kind. A correspondent of *Notes and Queries* (2 S., vii., 158) suggests as a possible source the ordinary word *mendicant* (fr. Lat. *mendico*), but this is historically improbable, and the weight of evidence is in favour of the Latin *cantus*, singing or song, though it must be observed that neither the ancient nor the modern usage implies a mere sing-song, but rather the whine of one bent on deceit. There is a consciousness of hypocrisy be the canting in connection with religion, politics, begging, or anything else; and this principle is recognized in the attempt on the part of *The Scots Observer* to substitute BLEAT (*subs.* and *verb*) for the cant of æstheticism, the cant which deals with art in the language of sentiment and emotion. It has been further suggested that if the word meant singing, the A.S. *cantere* is a much more probable source of origin than the Latin *canto* or *cantus*; but there is an argument which seems to lend additional weight to the claim of the latter language: the French *chanter*, to sing, is sometimes used in the sense of CANT. In answer to a whining, lying tale (in reply indeed to anything incredible whether whining or brazen), a Frenchman would say, '*Qu'est ce que vous chantez là.*' Whatever the derivation, however, there is little doubt that Andrew Cant has little to do with it; indeed, Pennant in his *Tour in Scotland*, vol. I., p. 122, says that 'Andrew canted no more than the rest of his brethren, for he lived in a whining age.']

Subs.—1. The secret speech or jargon of the vagrant classes—gipsies, thieves, beggars, etc.; hence, contemptuously, the peculiar phraseology of a particular class or subject. Identical with THIEVES' LATIN, ST. GILES' GREEK, PEDDLAR'S FRENCH, etc. (*q.v.*); but for synonyms, *see* FLASH.

1706. In PHILLIPS. [M.]

1748. T. DYCHE, *Dictionary* (5 ed.) CANT (s.): a barbarous broken sort of speech made use of by gypsies.

1856. C. READE, *Never too Late*, ch. xlv. All this not in English, but in thieves' CANT.

Here follow specimens of ancient and modern jargon. Further illustrations will be found in the canting songs in the Appendix.

[ANCIENT CANT.]

1567. HARMAN, *Caveat* (E.E.T. Soc., extra series, IX., 1869), p. 84-86. The vpright Cofe canteth to the Roge. VPRIGHT-MAN.—Bene Lightmans to thy quarromes, in what lipken hast thou lypped in this darkemans, whether in a lybbege, or in the strummell? ROGE.—I couched a hogshead in a Skypper this darkemans. VPRIGHT-MAN.—I towre the strummel trine vpon thy nabchet *and* Togman. ROGE.—I saye by the Salomon I will lage it of with a gage of benebouse; then cut to my nose watch. MAN.—Why, hast thou any lowre in thy bonge to bouse? ROGE.—But a flagge, a wyn, and a make, etc., etc., etc.

[MODERN THIEVES' LINGO.]

1881. *New York Slang Dictionary*. Oh! I'm fly. You mean jumping Jack, who was done last week for heaving a peter from a drag. But you talked of padding the hoof. Why, sure, Jack had a rattler and a prad?' 'Yes, but they were spotted by the harmans, and so we walked Spanish.' 'Was he nabbed on the scent?' 'No; his pal grew leaky and cackled.' 'Well, Bell, here's the bingo—sluice your gob! But who was the cull that peached?' 'A slubber de gullion named Harry Long, who wanted to pass for an out-and-out cracksman, though he was merely a diver.' 'Whew! I know the kiddy like a copper, and saved him once from lumping the lighter by putting in buck. Why, he scarcely knows a jimmy from a round robin, and Jack deserved the tippet for making a law with him, as all coves of his kidney blow the gab. But how did you hare it to Romeville, Bell, for I suppose the jets cleaned you out?' 'I kidded a swell in a snoozing-ken, and shook him of his dummy and thimble.' 'Ah! Bell! you were always the blowen for a rum bing.'

2. (pugilistic)—a blow or toss. [In *Mem. Capt. P. Drake*, II., xiv., 244 (1755), occurs this passage, 'To give me such a CANT as I never had before or since, which was the whole length of the coffee-room; he pitched me on my head and shoulders under a large table at the further end.' Transition from the nautical sense of heeling over to that embodied in 'CANT on the chops,' is easy.] For synonyms, *see* BANG, DIG, and WIPE.

3. (tramps').—Food. Also KANT, but *Cf.*, sense 4.

1851-61. H. MAYHEW, *London Labour and London Poor*, vol. III., p. 415. The house was good for a CANT—that's some food—bread or meat.

1877. BESANT AND RICE, *Son of Vulcan*, pt. I., ch. ix. The slavey's been always good for a KANT, and the cove for a bob.

4. (tramps').—A gift. [Possibly connected with CANT, sense 3, a share or portion.]

1857. SNOWDEN, *Mag. Assistant*, 3, ed., p. 444. Gift of Clothes—CANT of Togs.

Verb.—1. To speak with the beggar's whine.

1567. HARMAN, *Caveat* (1869), 34. 'It shall be lawefull for the to CANT'—that is, to aske or begge—'for thy living in al places.'

1610. ROWLANDS, *Martin Mark-all*, p. 17 (B. Club's Repr., 1874). According to the saying that you [thieves and cadgers] haue among your selues (*If you can* CANT, *you will neuer worke*) shewing that if they haue beene rogues so long, that they can CANT, they will neuer settle themselues to labour againe.

2. To speak the jargon of gipsies, beggars, and other vagrants.—*See* CANTING.

1592. *Defence of Conny-catching*, in Greene's *Works*, XI., 45. At these wordes Conny-catcher and Setter, I was driven into as great a maze, as if one had dropt out of the clowds, to heare a peasant CANT the wordes of art belonging to our trade.

1609. DEKKER, *English Villainies* (1638), And as these people are strange, both in names and in their conditions, so do they speake a language (proper only to themselves) called *Canting*, which is more strange. This word *canting*, seemes to be

derived from the Latine Verbe (*Canto*) which signifies in English to sing, or to make a sounde with words, that is to say, to speake. And very aptly may *Canting* take its derivation, *à cantando*, from singing, because amongst these beggerly consorts that can play on no better instruments, the language of *canting* is a kinde of Musicke, and he that in such assemblies can CANT best, is counted the best musician.

1639. FORD, *Lady's Trial*, V., 1. One can man a gulan, and CANT, and pick a pocket.

1748. T. DYCHE, *Dictionary* (5 ed.) CANT (v.): to talk gibberish like gypsies.

3. To speak; to talk.

1567. HARMAN, *Caveat* (1814), p. 66. To CANTE, to speake.

1881. *New York Slang Dictionary*. 'On the trail.' 'But CANT us the cues. What was the job?' 'A pinch for an emperor's slang. We touched his leather too, but it was very lathy.

CANTAB, *subs.* (colloquial).—A student at Cambridge. [An abbreviation of 'Cantabrigian.']

1750. COVENTRY, *Pompey Litt.* II., x. (1785), p. 18, col. 1. The young CANTAB . . . had come up to London. [M.]

1821. BYRON, *Don Juan*, c. iii., st. 126. And I grown out of many 'wooden spoons' Of verse (the name with which we CANTABS please To dub the last of honours in degrees).

CANTABANK, *subs.* (old).—A common ballad singer. [From Latin *cantare*, to sing, + *banco*, bench; *i.e.*, a singer on a stage or platform.]

1589. PUTTENHAM, *Eng. Poesie* (Arb.), 96. Small and popular Musickes song by these CANTABANQUI vpon benches and barrels heads. [M.]

1834. TAYLOR, *Ph. van Art*, pt. I., iii., 2. He was no tavern CANTABANK that made it, But a Squire minstrel of your Highness' court.

CANTANKEROUS, *adj.* (colloquial).—Cross-grained; ill-humoured; self-willed; productive of strife. *See* also quot. 1773. [Thought to be derived from the M.E. *contak*, *conteke*, contention or quarrelling.] So also CANTANKEROUSLY and CANTANKEROUSNESS. For synonyms, *see* CRUSTY.

1773. GOLDSMITH, *She Stoops to Conquer*, II. There's not a more bitter CANTANKEROUS road in all christendom.

1775. SHERIDAN, *Rivals*, Act v., Sc. 3. But I hope Mr. Faulkland, as there are three of us come on purpose for the game, you wont be so CANTANKEROUS as to spoil the party by sitting out.

1876. M. E. BRADDON, *Joshua Haggard*, ch. xvi. And who was to nurse this peevish, CANTANKEROUS old man.

Hence the American verb, TO CANTANKERATE, and adjective, CANTANKERSOME.

1835. HALIBURTON ('Sam Slick'), *The Clockmaker*, 1 S., ch. xxiv. You may [by contentious writing] happify your inimies [and] CANTANKERATE your opponents. *Ibid.* 3 S., ch. xii. Plato Frisk, a jumpin' Quaker, a terrible cross-grained CANTANKERSOME critter.

CANTE.—*See* CANTER.

CANTEEN MEDAL, *subs. phr.* (military).—A good conduct stripe for the consumption of liquor.

CANTER, *subs.* (old).—A vagrant or beggar; one who CANTS (*q.v.*) or uses the secret language otherwise called Peddlars' French, St. Giles' Greek, etc. The form has varied. Greene using CANTE, whilst many writers speak of the fraternity as the CANTING CREW.—*See* Appendix. [From CANT, *verb*, sense 1, + ER.]

1592. GREENE, *Quip for Upst. Courtiers*, *Harl. Misc*, V., 396. I fell into a great laughter, to see certain Italianate CANTES, humourous cavaliers, youthful gentlemen, etc.

1625. BEN JONSON, *Staple of News*, Act ii. A rogue, a very CANTER I, sir, one that maunds upon the pad.

1630. TAYLOR, ('Water Poet'), wks. II., 239, i. Two leash of oyster-wives hyred a coach on a Thursday after Whitsontide . . . they were so be-madam'd, bemistrist, and ladified by the beggars, that the foolish women began to swell with a proud supposition or imaginary greatness, and gave all their mony to the mendicanting CANTERS.

1878. CHARLES HINDLEY, *Life and Times of James Catnach.* 'Song of the Young Prig.' My mother she dwelt in Dyot's Isle, One of the CANTING CREW, sirs.

CANTICLE, *subs.* (old).—A parish clerk. [From CANTICLE, a song or psalm; one of the duties of a parish clerk being to lead the congregational singing.] So given in Grose [1785], and in the *Lexicon Balatronicum* [1811]. Also called an AMEN CURLER (*q.v.*).

CANTING, *verbal subs.* (old).—The jargon used by beggars, thieves, gipsies, and vagrants. The same as CANT, *subs.*, sense 1, which seems to be an abbreviated and later form of CANTING; *Cf.* 'cab' from 'cabriolet' and 'bus' from 'omnibus.'

1567. HARMAN, *Caveat* (1814), p. 6, Their language which they terms peddelers Frenche or CANTING.

1610. JONSON, *Alchemist*, II. *Supr.* What a brave language here is! next to CANTING.

1688. SHADWELL, *Sq. of Alsatia.* I., in wks. (1720) IV., 27. A particular language which such rogues have made to themselves, called CANTING, as beggars, gipsies, thieves, and jail-birds do.

1742. JOHNSON, *Highwayman and Pyrates*, p. 57. All the CANTING language (which comprehends a parcel of invented words, such as thieves very well know, and by which they can distinguish one another from the other classes of mankind.)

Ppl. adj.—Belonging to the jargon of thieves and beggars.

1592. *Groundwork Coney-Catch*, 99 The manner of their CANTING speech [M.]

1871. *London Figaro*, 13 May, p. 3, col. 2. 'Bill's dead on for a lark with the CANTING bloke,' whispered a lean and hungry-looking 'casual' to a no less half-starved neighbour.

CANTING CREW.—*See* CANTER.

CAN'T SAY NATIONAL INTELLIGENCER, *phr.* (American).—A euphemistic expression equivalent to 'drunk.' [The *National Intelligencer* is an old Washington newspaper.] For synonyms, *see* SCREWED.

CAN'T SEE A HOLE IN A LADDER, *phr.* (American).—Referring to a superlative form of intoxication. For synonyms, *see* SCREWED.

CANUCK.—*See* CANACK.

CANVASS. TO RECEIVE THE CANVASS, *phr.* (old).—A seventeenth century colloquialism for 'to be dismissed'; in modern slang 'to get the sack.'—*See* BAG, sense 2, and SACK.

1652. SHIRLEY, *The Brothers*, Act. ii. As much as marriage comes to, and I lose My honor, if the Don RECEIVES THE CANVAS.

CANVASSEENS, *subs.* (nautical).—Sailors' canvas trousers. For synonyms, *see* BAGS and KICKS.

CANVASS-TOWN, *subs.* (general).—The Volunteer Encampment at Wimbledon or Bisley when the National Rifle Association meets; also any camp or 'baby'-city. *Cf.*, BULL'S-EYE VILLAS.

CAP, *subs.* (thieves').—1. A false cover to a tossing coin, called a COVER-DOWN. The cap showed either head or tail as it was left on or taken off. Obsolete.

2. (old).—The proceeds of an improvised collection. [*Cf.*, 'to send round the cap or hat.']

1851. EUREKA; Sequel Ld. Russell's Post Bag, 21. What amount of CAP is realised out of an average field? [M.]

3. (Westminster School).—The amount of the collection at Play and Election dinners. [From the College cap being passed round on the last night of Play for contributions. *Cf.*, 'to send round the cap.']

Verb (thieves').—1. To stand by a friend; to take part in any undertaking; to lend a hand. Grose has 'to take one's oath.'

1785. GROSE, *Dictionary of the Vulgar Tongue.* I will CAP downright; I will swear home.

2. (public schools' and University).—To take off or touch one's hat in salutation; also TO CAP TO and TO CAP IT.

1593. H. SMITH, *Serm.* (1871) I., 203. How would they CAP me were I in velvets. [M.]

1803. *Gradus ad Cantabrigiam* p. 23. s.v. BORE Other bores are to attend a sermon at St. Mary's on Sunday . . . TO CAP a fellow.

CAP ONE'S LUCKY, *verbal phr.* (American thieves').—To run away. For synonyms, *see* AMPUTATE.

CAP OR CAST ONE'S SKIN, *verbal phr.* (thieves').—To strip naked. For synonyms, *see* PEEL.

TO SET ONE'S CAP AT, *phr.* (colloquial).—To set oneself to gain the affections. Said only of women.

1773. GRAVES, *Spiritual Quixote*, bk. III., ch. xi. I know several young ladies who would be very happy in such an opportunity of SETTING THEIR CAPS AT him.

1773. O. GOLDSMITH, *She Stoops to Conquer*, Act i., Sc. 1. 'Well, if he refuses . . . . I'll only break my glass for its flattery, SET MY CAP to some newer fashion, and look out for some less difficult admirer.

1846. THACKERAY, *V. Fair*, ch. iii. The wily old fellow said to his son, 'Have a care, Joe; that girl is SETTING HER CAP AT you.'

TO CAP A QUOTATION, ANECDOTE, PROVERB, &c., *phr.* (colloquial).—To fit with a second from the same, or another, author; to 'go one better' in the way of anecdote or legend.

1584. PEELE, *Arraignm. Paris*, iv., ii. (1829) 48. Sh'ath CAPT his answer in the cue. [M.]

1856. VAUGHAN, *Mystics* (1860) I., i. v. Now you come to Shakspeare, I must CAP your quotation with another. [M.]

TO PULL CAPS, *phr.* (colloquial).—To wrangle in an unseemly way.—Said only of women.

1763. COLMAN, *Deuce is in Him*, I., in wks. (1777) IV., 120. A man that half the women in town would PULL CAPS for.

1771. SMOLLETT, *Humphry Clinker*, line 19. At length, they fairly proceeded to PULLING CAPS, and everything seemed to presage a general battle.

17(?). WOLCOT, *P. Pindar*, p. 140. Behold our lofty duchesses PULL CAPS, And give each other's reputation raps, As freely as the drabs of Drury's school.

1825. SCOTT, *St. Ronan's Well*, ch. vii. Well, dearest Rachel, we will not PULL CAPS about this man.

CAPE COD TURKEY, *subs. phr.* (American).—A salted cod fish, another name for which is MARBLE-HEAD TURKEY. *Cf.*, BILLINGSGATE PHEASANT, YARMOUTH CAPON, and ALBANY BEEF.

1865. C. NORDHOFF, 1 May (in letter). A salted cod fish is known in American ships as a CAPE COD TURKEY.

1890. *New York Herald*, 3 June. 'Newfoundland Fishery Dispute.' Factories have been established for the production of CAPE COD TURKEYS; *i.e.*, salted cod fish.

CAPELLA, *subs.* (theatrical).—A coat. [From the Italian.]

ENGLISH SYNONYMS. Benjamin; cover-me-decently; upper benjamin (a great coat); joseph; wrap-rascal; bum-cooler or arse-hole-perisher, or shaver (a short jacket); claw-hammer, swallow-tail, steel-pen (all three = a dress coat); M.B. coat; panupetaston; rock-a-low; reliever; pygostole; ulster; monkey-jacket. *See* also CASTER, many synonyms of which = a coat.

FRENCH SYNONYMS. *Un cache-misère* (familiar: specially applied to a coat buttoned close to the throat to conceal the absence of a shirt or the soiled state of one's linen); *un alpague* (also *alpaga* and *alpag*); *un elbeuf; un Berry* (a fatigue jacket); *une menuisière* (pop: a long coat); *un ne-te-gêne-pas-dans-le-parc* (a short jacket; also termed *un saute-en-barque, un pet-en-l'air*, and *un montretout*).

GERMAN SYNONYMS. *Oberhänger* (an overcoat; also a cloak). *Wallnusch* (Hanoverian: corruption from the Hebrew *malbusch* = clothes); *Schwalbenschweif* (a dress-coat, a 'swallow-tail').

ITALIAN SYNONYM. *Tappe* (clothing in general; it also signifies 'feathers').

CAPE-NIGHTINGALE, *subs.* (colonial).—A frog. *Cf.*, CAMBRIDGESHIRE NIGHTINGALE.

1889. H. A. BRYDEN, *Kloof and Karroo: or Sport, Legend, and Natural History in Cape Colony.* The very smell of the water and the din of the huge frogs, CAPE NIGHTINGALES as we call them, revived them.

CAPEOVI, *adj.* (costers').—Sick; SEEDY (*q.v.* for synonyms). *Cf.*, CAPIVI.

CAPER, *subs.* (vagrants').—A device, idea, performance, or occupation. Americans use it in the same sense as RACKET (*q.v.*), *e.g.*, the 'real estate racket' or 'CAPER.' [From the figurative sense of CAPER, signifying a fantastic proceeding, freak, or prank.] Also used in the sense of 'the go,' 'the fad,' *i.e.*, the latest fashionable fancy.

1867. *London Herald*, 23 March, p. 221. 'He'll get five years penal for this little CAPER,' said the policeman.

1870. C. HINDLEY, *Life and Adventures of a Cheap Jack*, p. 220. Charley would reply . . . 'I have just done such and such an amount to-day with these people,' at the same time showing the invoice of the goods he had just purchased at the house where he got change for his fifty sovereigns. The conversation, as a rule, ended in Charley's giving them an order too. Of course, this little CAPER would only 'wash' once.

1884. J. GREENWOOD, *The Little Ragamuffins.* 'Are you goin' a 'tottin'?' 'No,' . . . 'Then what CAPER are you up to?'

TO CUT A CAPER UPON NOTHING, or TO CUT CAPER SAUCE, *phr.* (old).—To be hanged. For synonyms, *see* LADDER.

1708. MOTTEUX, *Rabelais.* IV. xvi. Two of the honestest Gentlemen in Catchpole-land had been made to CUT A CAPER ON NOTHING.

1834. H. AINSWORTH, *Rookwood*, bk. III., ch. v. And my father, as I've heard say, Was a merchant of CAPERS gay, Who CUT HIS LAST FLING with great applause.

CAPER-JUICE, *subs.* (American).—Whiskey. [From CAPER, a freak or antic + JUICE.] For synonyms, *see* DRINKS.

1888. *Portland Transcript*, 29 Feb. Say, fellers, let's take a leetle mo' uv the CAPER JUICE. [*They drink again. Sam and the girl exchange affectionate glances.*]

CAPER-MERCHANT, *subs.* (old).—A dancing master. [From CAPER, a frolicsome leap or step, + MERCHANT.] Also called a HOP-MERCHANT (*q.v.* for synonyms).

1785. GROSE, *Dictionary of the Vulgar Tongue.* [Quoted as above.]

CAPITAL, TO WORK CAPITAL, *verbal phr.* (old).—To commit an offence punishable with death.

1878. CHARLES HINDLEY, *Life and Times of James Catnach.* And though I don't WORK CAPITAL, And do not weigh my weight, sirs, Who knows but that in time I shall.

CAPIVI or **CAPIVVY** (vulgar).—*Balsam copaiba*, a popular remedy for clap.

TO CRY CAPIVVY (sporting).—To be persecuted to the death, or very near it. In *Handley Cross* [1843] Mr. Jorrocks promises to make the foxes CRY CAPIVVY.

CAPON, *subs.* (popular).—Primarily, a red herring; but applied to other kinds of fish, herrings now receiving the distinctive cognomen of YARMOUTH CAPONS. The usage is a very old one, and it is notable that GLASGOW MAGISTRATE, another name for a red herring, was formerly GLASGOW CAPON.

c. 1640. J. SMYTH, *Hundred of Berkeley* (1885), 319. The Sole wee call our Seuverne CAPON. [M.]

1690. B. E., *Dict. Cant. Crew.* YARMOUTH CAPON a Red Herring.

1719. RAMSEY, *Hamilton*, II., iii. A GLASGOW CAPON and a fadge ye thought a feast. [M.]

1812. W. TENNANT, *Anster F.*, iv. Each to his jaws A good Crail's CAPON holds [*note* 'a dried haddock']. [M.]

CAPPADOCHIO, CAPERDOCHY, or **CAPERDEWSIE,** *subs.* (old).—Nares says 'a cant term for a prison.' [The same authority suggests that it is a corruption of Cappadocia: 'The king of Cappadocia, says Horace, was rich in slaves, but had little money.'] For synonyms. *see* CAGE.

1600. HEYWOOD, *I. Edw. IV.* My son's in Dybell here, in CAPERDOCHY, i' the gaol.

1607. W. S., *Puritan*, in *Supp. Shaks.*, II., 510 (N.). How captain Idle? my old aunt's son, my dear kinsman, in CAPPADOCHIO?

1663. BUTLER, *Hudibras*, I., ii., 832. I here engage myself to loose ye, and free your heels from CAPERDEWSIE.

CAPPER, *subs.* (American thieves').—1. A confederate; at cards one who makes false bids in order to encourage a genuine player. [*See* CAP, *verb*, sense 1.]

1871. DE VERE, *Americanisms*, p. 319. In the West a *striker* is not only a shoulder-hitter, as might be suspected, but a runner for gambling establishments, who must be as ready to strike down a complaining victim as to ensnare an unsuspecting stranger . . . CAPPERS they are called, when the game is the famous *Three-Card Monte.*

1881. *New York Slang Dictionary.* Gamblers are called knights of the green cloth, and their lieutenants, who are sent out after greenhorns, are called decoys, CAPPERS, and steerers.

2. (auctioneers').—A dummy bidder whose function is either to start the bidding or to run up the price of articles for sale.

CAPPER-CLAWING.—*See* CLAPPER-CLAWING.

CAPTAIN, *subs.* (general).—1. A familiar and jesting form of address. An equivalent of 'governor,' 'boss,' etc. Very common in U.S.A., where also it signifies the conductor or guard of a train—an analogy being drawn between the phraseology of rail and water traffic. (*see* quot. 1862).

1598. SHAKSPEARE *King Henry IV.* pt. 2, Act ii., Sc. 4. Doll Tearsheet. A CAPTAIN! God's light, these villains will make the word as odious as the word 'occupy.'

1862. RUSSELL, *Diary, North and S.*, I., xiii., 139. All the people who addressed me by name prefixed 'Major' or 'Colonel.' 'CAPTAIN' is very low. . . . The conductor who took our tickets was called 'CAPTAIN.' [M.]

2. (old).—A gaming or bawdy house bully. *Cf.*, Fielding's Captain Bilkum in *Covent Garden Tragedy.* Fr. *un major de table d'hôte.*

1731. *Daily Journal*, Jan. 9. 'List of the officers established in the most notorious gaming-houses.' 12th. A CAPTAIN, who is to fight any gentleman who is peevish for losing his money.

1748. T. DYCHE, *Dictionary* (5 ed.). CAPTAIN (s.) . . . and in the *Cant Phrase*, a CAPTAIN is a bully, who is to quarrel or fight with peevish gamesters, who are testy or quarrelsome at the loss of their money; and sometimes it signifies money itself, as, 'the CAPTAIN is not at home,' that is, there is no money in my pocket.

[CAPTAIN is also a fancy title for a highwayman in a good way of business; Fletcher uses the term COPPER-CAPTAIN, as also does Washington Irving, for one who has no right to the title, and, in modern athletics, we have the CAPTAIN of a club or crew, with the corresponding *verb* TO CAPTAIN.]

3. (old).—Money.—*See* preceding quot. [1748].

4. (knackers').—A glandered (horse).

CAPTAIN ARMSTRONG. TO COME CAPTAIN ARMSTRONG, *phr.* (turf)—To 'pull' a horse and thus prevent him from winning. CAPTAIN ARMSTRONG is often used for a dishonest jockey. [A play upon words, *i.e.*, 'to pull with a strong arm.']

1864. *Sporting Life*, 5 Nov. (Leader). CAPTAIN ARMSTRONG is again abroad, muscular and powerful, riding his favourite hobby in the steeple-chase field, preparing thus early in the season for pulling, stopping, and putting the strings on.

CAPTAIN COPPERTHORN'S CREW. *subs. phr.* (old).—All officers Said of a company where every-one wants to be first.

CAPTAIN CORK, *subs. phr.* (military).—A nickname for a man who is slow in passing the bottle.

CAPTAIN CRANK, *subs. phr.* (old).—The chief of a gang of highway-men.

CAPTAIN GRAND, *subs. phr.* (old).—A haughty, blustering fellow. For synonyms, *see* FURIOSO.

CAPTAIN HACKUM, *subs. phr.* (old).—A hectoring bully.—*Grose.*

CAPTAIN LIEUTENANT, *subs. phr.* (old).—Meat neither young enough for veal, nor old enough for beef. [The simile is drawn from the brevet officer who, while ranking as captain, receives lieutenant's pay.]—*Grose.*

CAPTAIN QUEERNABS, *subs. phr.* (old).—A shabby or ill-dressed man. For synonyms, *see* GUY.

CAPTAIN QUIZ, *subs. phr.* (old).—A mocker.

CAPTAIN SHARP, *subs. phr.* (old).—A cheating bully, or one in a set of gamblers, whose office it is to bully the 'pigeon,' who refuses to pay.—*Grose. Cf.*, CAPTAIN, sense 2.

CAPTAIN TOM, *subs. phr.* (old).—The head or leader of a mob; also the mob itself.—*Grose.*

CARAVAN, *subs.* (old).—1. A dupe; gull; a subject of plunder.—*See* BUBBLE.

1676. ETHEREGE, *Man of Mode*, III., iii., in wks. (1704), 233. What spruce prig is that? A CARAVAN, lately come from Paris.

1688. SHADWELL, *Sq. of Alsatia.* [In list of cant words prefixed to.] CARAVAN: a bubble, the cheated.

1889. G. L. APPERSON, in *Gentleman's Magazine* ('Seventeenth Century Colloquialisms'), p. 598. Towards the end of the century a person easily gulled, or 'bubbled' was known as a CARAVAN, but earlier the term 'rook' which is now restricted to a cheat or sharper, appears to have been applied to the person cheated.

2. (old).—A large sum of money.

1690 B. E., *Dict. Cant. Crew.* CARAVAN: a good round sum of money about a man, and him that is cheated of it.

3. (pugilistic).—A railway train, especially a train expressly chartered to convey people to a prize fight. [Early in the present century CARAVAN, now shortened to 'van,' was applied to a third class covered railway carriage; now a pleasure party is so described; also a gypsy's cart; also the wheeled cages of a travelling menagerie.]

CARAVANSERA, *subs.* (pugilistic).—A railway station. As thus: 'The scratch must be toed at sharp five, so the caravan will start at four from the CARAVANSERA.'—*Hotten. See* CARAVAN, sense 3.

CARD, *subs.* (common).—1. A device; expedient; or undertaking; that which is likely to attain its object, or through which success is sure. Thus we have such expressions as a 'good CARD,' a 'strong CARD,' a 'safe CARD,' a 'likely, or a doubtful CARD.' [Figurative; from card playing.] THAT'S A SURE CARD sounds modern, but as Lowell has pointed out it is to be found in the old interlude of 'Thursytes' (1537).

1690. B. E., *Dic. Cant. Crew.* A SURE CARD, a trusty Tool, or Confiding Man.

1763. FR. BROOKE, *Lady J. Mandeville*, in Barbauld *Brit. Novelists* (1820) xxvii., 23. Poor fellow! I pity him; but marriage is his only CARD. [M.]

1826. SCOTT, *Woodstock*, III., xiv., 358. No CARD seemed to turn up favourable to the royal cause.

2. A character; an odd fish; an eccentric; generally coupled with such adjectives as 'knowing,' 'old,' 'queer,' 'downy,' 'rum,' etc. [Apparently derived from the card-table, such expressions as a 'sure card,' a 'sound card,' being of very ancient use. Osric tells Hamlet that Laertes is the CARD and calendar of gentry.—(*Hamlet*, v., 2.)]

1835. DICKENS, *Sketches by Boz*, 264. Mr. Thomas Potter, whose great aim it was to be considered as a knowing CARD.

1852. DICKENS, *Bleak House*, ch. xx., p. 173. 'Such an old CARD as this; so deep, so sly, and secret.'

1854. WHYTE MELVILLE, *General Bounce*, ch. ii. Frank Hardingstone was, to use their favourite word, 'a great CARD' amongst all the associates of his age and standing.

1854. WHYTE MELVILLE, *General Bounce*, ch. xii. A quaint boy at Eton, *cool hand* at Oxford, a deep CARD in the regiment, man or woman never yet had the best of 'Uppy.'

1864. DICKENS, *Our Mutual Friend.* bk. III., ch. i. 'You're one of the Patriarchs; you're a shaky old CARD; and you can't be in love with this Lizzie.'

3. (common).—The 'ticket'; the 'figure'; the correct thing. [Possibly from the K'RECT CARD (*q.v.*) of racing.]

1851. MAYHEW, *London Labour and London Poor*, II., p. 47. I've got 10s. often for a great coat, and higher and lower, oftener lower in course; but 10s. is about the CARD for a good thing.

Verb.—Also CARDING, *subs.* (Irish Nationalist). A peculiar form of torture, which consists in the application of the card, a spiked or toothed implement used in the preparation of flax and wool, to the naked shoulders, &c., and is commonly reserved for 'unpatriotic' girls and women.

1889. *The Scots Observer.* 'They never told the ramping crowd to CARD a woman's hide.'

TO GIVE ONE CARDS, *phr.* (American).—To give one an advantage. The English equivalent, 'to give points,' is derived from the billiard saloon. An analogous French phrase is *faire un bœuf.*

1888. *Grip* (Toronto), May. You know that Artie found a Chinaman out in 'Frisco who could GIVE HIM CARDS and spades and beat him out.

ON THE CARDS, *phr.* (common).—Within the range of probability. [Dickens popularised the expression, which appears to mean 'possible to turn up,' as anything in the game when the cards are turned up. Still, it is not unlikely that the phrase originated with cartomancy, at a time when cards were frequently consulted as to the issue of enterprises.] *See* N. and Q., 7 s. iv., 507; v. 14, 77, 495.

1749. SMOLLETT, Translation of *il Blas.* I showed them tricks which they did not know to be ON THE CARDS, and yet acknowledged to be better than their own.

1813. SIR R. WILSON, *Diary*, II., 40. It is not OUT OF THE CARDS that we might do more. [M.]

1849. DICKENS, *David Copperfield*, I., p. 219. By way of going in for anything that might be ON THE CARDS, petition to the House of Commons, etc.

1868. W. COLLINS, *Moonstone*, I., p. 149. It's quite ON THE CARDS, sir, that you have put the clue into our hands.

1874. *Saturday Review*, April, p. 488. When they discovered that a Restoration was not at present ON THE CARDS, they became Conservatives.

1890. H. D. TRAILL, *A Bulgarian Appeal.* 'Saturday Songs,' p. 43. I'll be shot if I do, though it's equally true That it's quite ON THE CARDS I'll be shot if I don't.

TO PACK, STOCK, OR PUT UP, THE CARDS, *phr.* (Western American).—To prepare cards for cheating purposes.—*See* CONCAVES, PACK, and STOCK BROADS.

TO SPEAK BY THE CARD, *phr.* (general).—To speak with precision; or with the utmost accuracy. [An allusion to the card of the mariner's compass.]

1596. SHAKSPEARE, *Hamlet*, v., 1, 149. We must SPEAK BY THE CARD, or equivocation will undo us.

1867. YATES, *Forlorn Hope*, i., p. 23. 'Are you SPEAKING BY THE CARD?' said Count Bulow, with the slightest foreign accent.

1879. TROLLOPE, *Thackeray* [in 'English men of Letters' series], p. 186. Henry Esmond . . . however, is not made to SPEAK altogether BY THE CARD, or he would be unnatural.

CARDINAL, *subs.* (old).—1. A red cloak worn by ladies *circa* 1740 and later. [From the colour and shape which suggested a cardinal's vestment.]

1755. *Connoisseur*, No. 62. That fashionable cloak . . . which indeed is with great propriety styled the CARDINAL.

1755. *The World*, No. 127. I have made no objection to their (the ladies) wearing the CARDINAL, though it be a habit of popish etymology, and was, I am afraid, first invented to hide the sluttishness of French dishabille.

1881. BESANT AND RICE, *Chap. of the Fleet*, pt. 1, ch. iv. In the windows of which were hoods, CARDINALS, sashes, pinners, and shawls.

2. (general). — Mulled red wine.

1861. HUGHES, *Tom Brown at Oxford*, ch. xv. He goes up, and finds the remains of the supper, Tankards full of egg-flip and CARDINAL, and a party playing at vingt-un.

3. in *plural* (street).—Shoeblacks. [In allusion to the red tunics of some London brigades. That stationed in the City is now better known as the CITY REDS.]

1889. T. MACKAY [on 'Shoeblacks'], in *Time*, Aug., p. 132. From that hour the Shoeblack Brigade has been firmly established in London . . . costermongers called them CARDINALS.

4. (American).—A lobster; from its colour when cooked. Jules Janin once made a curious blunder and called the lobster *le cardinal de la mer.* CARDINAL HASH = a lobster salad.

5. (common).—A new [1890] variety of red.

CARE. NOT TO CARE OF BE WORTH A [FIG, PIN, RAP, BUTTON, CENT, STRAW, RUSH, OR HANG, etc.], *phr.* (colloquial).—Similes of indifference; to care about a matter not even so much as to the value of a fig, a pin, or a straw. Fr. *s'en battre l'œil.*—*See* NOT WORTH A FIG.

1590. SPENSER, *Fairie Queene*, I., ii., 12. He . . . CARED NOT for God or man A POINT. [M.]

1633. MARMYON, *Fine Compan.*, II., i., 68. I do not CARE A PIN for her. [M.]

1709. STEELE, *Tatler*, No. 50. I do not CARE A FARTHING for you. [M.]

1760. GOLDSMITH, *Citizen of the World*, xlvi. Not that I CARE THREE DAMNS what figure I may cut.

1833. MARRYAT, *Peter Simple*, ed. 1846, vol. I., ch. iii., p. 13. You told him you did not CARE A FIG for him.

1848-62. J. R. LOWELL, *Biglow Papers.* 'Don't fire,' sez Joe, 'it ain't no use, Thet Deacon Peleg's tame wil-'goose'; Seys Isrel, 'I don't CARE A CENT, I've sighted an' I'll let her went.'

1871. *London Figaro*, May 13, p. 4, col. 2. Coster Ballads, 'Found Drowned.' 'Well, sir, to cut it short, she 'ad the chap—'Twos cruel 'ard on me—I don't believe he CARED for 'er A RAP, But so it wos, yer see.'

1889. *Answers*, June 22, p. 49, col. 1. 'Is it for sale?' demanded the visitor, excitedly. 'If it is I want it. I don't CARE A SNAP what it costs.'

I DON'T CARE IF I DO, *phr.* (American).—A street phrase, meaning nothing in particular. Also a form of accepting an invitation to drink: 'Will you peg?' 'I DON'T CARE IF I DO.'

1888. *New York Tribune.* Volapuk will never be popular in Kentucky. It contains no sentence to take the place of that classic phrase, I DON'T CARE IF I DO.

CARE-GRINDER, *subs.* (thieves').—More usually the VERTICAL CARE-GRINDER.—*See* quot. For synonyms, *see* WHEEL OF LIFE.

1883. *Echo*, Jan. 25, p. 2, col 4. The treadmill again, is more politely called . . . the wheel of life, or the VERTICAL CARE-GRINDER.

CARGO, *subs.* (Winchester College).—A hamper from home. The word is still in use.

1870. MANSFIELD, *School Life at Winchester College*, p. 77. The boys, eager for breakfast, tumultuously rushed out from school-court . . . to see if Poole, the porter, had letters, or, what was even more delightful, a CARGO (a hamper of game or eatables from home).

1883. *Every-day Life in our Public Schools.* Scholars may supplement their fare with jam, potted meats . . . or, better still, from the contents of CARGOES, *i.e.*, hampers from home.

CARLER, *subs.* (New York thieves').—A clerk. For synonyms, *see* QUILL-DRIVER.

CARLICUES.—*See* CURLYCUES.

CARNEY or **CARNY,** *subs.* (colloquial).—Soothing and seductive flattery; language covering a design. [The origin is unknown, though some have conjectured the word to be of Irish derivation. As a verb it first appears as a dialecticism, and is now mostly in use as a *ppl. adj.*—CARNEYING (*q.v.*). The word, however, seems to be fast making its way into respectable usage, and is even now largely in literary use.]

Verb, tr. and *intrans.*—To wheedle; coax or insinuate oneself; to act in a cajoleing manner. —*See* CARNEYING.

CARNEYING, *ppl. adj.* (common).—In a wheedling, coaxing, or insinuating manner. *Cf.*, CARNEY.

1851-61. H. MAYHEW, *London Lab. and Lon. Poor*, vol. II., p. 566. When I tried to turn 'em off they'd say, in a CARNYING way, 'Oh, let us stay on,' so I never took no heed of 'em.

1869. H. J. BYRON, *Not such a Fool as He Looks* [French's Acting ed.], p, 12. Sharp old skinflint, downy old robber as he is, he's under Jane Mould's thumb, and well he knows it. (In CARNEYING voice) With many thanks, sir, for your kind attention to my case.

1871. *Daily Telegraph*, 15 May, 'Critique on Mr. H. J. Byron's Play of *An English Gentleman.*' Rachel does not like Brandon's CARNEYING ways.

1884. R. L. STEVENSON in *Eng. Illustr. Mag.*, Feb., p. 305. The female dog, that mass of CARNEYING affectations.

1885. CLEMENT SCOTT, in *Ill. Lon. News*, 3 Oct., p. 339, 2. The change from the CARNEYING, wheedling sneak to the cowardly bully, is extremely clever.

CARNISH, *subs.* (thieves').—Meat. [From the Italian *carne*, flesh, through the Lingua Franca. *Carne*, in French argot, signifies *tough* meat.]

FRENCH SYNONYMS. *La crie, crigne*, or *crignolle* (thieves': Old Cant; Greek, κρίας; Fourbesque, *crea, creata, creatura, criulfa;* Germania, *crioja*); *la criolle* (thieves'); *la niorte* (thieves'); *la barbaque* or *bidoche* (popular); *le choléra* (popular = bad meat); *le mastic* (= bread *or* meat).

GERMAN SYNONYMS. *Kärner* (this is the same as CARNISH and comes from the Italian *carne; Kärnerfetzer* = a butcher).

ITALIAN SYNONYMS. *Bronco* (specially applied to beef); *slavigna; crea* (*see* remarks under *crie* in French synonyms).

CARNISH-KEN, *subs.* (thieves').—A thieves' eating house, or progshop. [From CARNISH, meat, through the Italian *carne*, + KEN, a house or dwelling.] A French equivalent for the proprietor of such a place is *un fripier*, a term which also means a cook, a 'dripping' or old clothes' man.

CARNY.—*See* CARNEY.

CAROON, *subs.* (costermongers').—A five shilling piece. [Hotten and Barrère trace it to the French *couronne*, Spanish and Italian

corona; it is in all probability a mispronunciation of the English word 'crown.']

ENGLISH SYNONYMS. Bull, or bull's-eye; cartwheel, coachwheel, or simply wheel; tusheroon; dollar; thick 'un (obsolete, the term being now applied to a sovereign); case; caser; decus.

The nearest French equivalent, a five franc piece, is called *un roue de derrière* (literally 'a hind wheel,' and corresponding pretty closely to the English WHEEL, CARTWHEEL, and COACHWHEEL); *un bouton de guêtre; un blafard de cinq balles; une drille or dringue; une croix* (the old six franc piece, in allusion to the cross inscribed on it); *une chatte* (a piece of six francs: very old; and formerly prostitutes'); *une médaille* or *médaille de St. Hubert* (popular); *un monarque* (popular); *un œil de bœuf* (= an ox's eye); *un noble étrangère* (literary: = a distinguished stranger).

1859. G. W. MATSELL, *Vocabulum, or the Rogue's Lexicon.* Kersey-mere kicksies, any colour, built very slap with the artful dodge, from three CAROON.

CARPET, *verb* (colloquial).—To reprimand. Equivalents are to 'call over the coals,' to 'give a wigging' or 'earwigging,' etc. The phrase sometimes runs 'TO WALK THE CARPET.' So also CARPETING; for synonyms, *see* WIG.

1823. GALT, *Entail*, III., xxix., 278. Making . . . . her servants WALK THE CARPET. [M.]

1840. H. COCKTON, *Valentine Vox*, xli. They had done nothing! Why were they CARPETED?

1871. *Chester Chronicle*, 11 Feb. 'Report of Affiliation Case at Hawarden Petty Sessions.' [The plaintiff, Louisa Jackson, said] neither did Lunt, the page, say that night if her master knew of her coming home in that state she would be CARPETED for it.

1877. HAWLEY SMART, *Bound to Win*, ch. xxx. There is no hurry; but, before the race, I think Mr. Luxmoore will have to CARPET Sam.

TO BRING ON THE CARPET. To bring up or forward. A slang rendering of *mettre sur le tapis.*

CARPET-BAG, *subs.* used attributively as *adj.* (American).—*See* CARPET-BAGGER for explanation of such phrases as CARPET-BAG rule, CARPET-BAG adventurers, CARPET-BAG government, etc.

1872. *New York Herald*, 22 Aug. Hundreds of millions have been taken from the pockets of the people since the beginning of the war by dishonest contractors, unjust claimants, county robbers, and city plunderers, and CARPET-BAG State Governments. *Ibid.* The Tammany robberies, although trifling in comparison with the old revenue robberies, and the present wholesale plunder of the CARPET-BAG Governments in the South, etc.

1888. *Chicago Record.* The head of the ticket is one of the most vulnerable men who figured in Southern politics in the CARPET-BAG era. No man of that period left a blacker record.

CARPET-BAGGER, *subs.* (American political).—A political adventurer. [After the Civil War, numbers of Northerners went South. Honest or not, they were looked upon with suspicion by the Southerners, and, as they were generally Republican in politics and joined with the freedmen at the polls, the nickname CARPET-BAGGER came to have, and still retains, a political significance. It was unjustly applied to many well-meaning men, but at the same time it fitted the horde of corrupt adventurers who infested the South, and whose only 'property qualification' was contained in the carpet bag with

which they had arrived from the North. Originally, however, a CARPET-BAGGER was a 'wild-cat banker' out West: a banker, that is, who had no local abiding place, his worldly possessions being contained in a carpet bag.] Applied to politics the term has become of general application.—*Cf.*, SCALAWAG.

1868. *Daily News*, Sept. 18. All CARPET-BAGGERS and 'scalawags' are whites. The CARPET-BAGGERS are immigrants from the North who have thrown themselves into local politics, and through their influence with the negroes obtained office.

1871. *New York Post*, April. 'The general drift of public sentiment is, that the CARPET-BAGGERS, scalawags, exslaves, ex-slaveholders, rebels reconstructed, rebels unreconstructed, and Southern loyalists should be left, for a brief period at least, to fight out their own battles, in their own way; and that if the nation is ever again to become a party to their quarrels, it shall be on no slight pretext and for no trivial purpose.'

1877. *Temple Bar*, May, p. 107. At the same moment a swarm of adventurers settled in the conquered states, and became governors, judges, tax-collectors, and so on. These are the CARPET-BAGGERS of history. They came with two shirts, got salaries of (on an average) four thousand dollars per annum, and made fortunes of a million in four years!

CARPET-BAG RECRUIT, *subs. phr.* (military).—A recruit of better than the ordinary standing; one with more than he stands upright in.

CARPET-SWAB, *subs.* (common).—A carpet-bag.

1837. BARHAM, *I.L.* (*Misadv. at Margate*). A little gallows-looking chap —dear me! what could he mean? With a CARPET-SWAB and mucking togs, and a hat turned up with green.

CARRIER, *subs.* (old).—*See* quot., and *Cf.*, CARRIER-PIGEON.

1725. *New Cant. Dict.* CARRIERS: a sett of Rogues . . . employ'd to look out, and watch upon the Roads, at Inns, etc., in order to carry Information to their respective Gangs, of a booty in Prospect.

CARRIER-PIGEON, *subs.* (old).—1. A cheat—especially one who victimised lottery office keepers. *Cf.*, CARRIER.

1781. G. PARKER, *View of Society*, II., 64 [named and described in].

1785. GROSE, *Dictionary of the Vulgar Tongue.* CARRIER PIGEONS; sharpers who attend the drawing of the lottery in Guildhall, and as soon as a number or two are drawn, write them on a card, and run with them to a confederate, who is waiting near at hand, ready mounted; with these numbers he rides full speed to some distant insurance office before fixed on, where there is another of the gang, commonly a decent-looking woman, who takes care to be at the office before the hour of drawing; to her he secretly gives the number, which she insures for a considerable sum, thus biting the biter.

2. (racing).—One that runs from place to place with 'commissions'; a kind of tout.

CARRION, *subs.* (venery).—1. A prostitute. For synonyms, *see* BARRACK-HACK and TART.

2. (common).—The human body; formerly a corpse.

CARRION CASE, *subs.* (common).—A shirt or chemise. [From CARRION, the human body, + CASE, a covering.] For synonyms, *see* FLESH BAG.

CARRION HUNTER, *subs.* (old).—An undertaker. [CARRION was formerly general to signify a corpse]. For synonyms, *see* COLD COOK.

1785. GROSE, *Dictionary of the Vulgar Tongue.* CARRION HUNTER: an undertaker, etc.

CARROTS, *subs.* (popular).—Red hair. Used attributively, and also as a proper name. The

adjectival form is CARROTTY. An analogous colloquialism is GINGER-HACKLED, which *see* for synonyms.

1685. S. WESLEY, *Maggots*, 57. The Ancients . . . Pure CARROTS call'd pure threads of beaten gold. [M.]

1690. B. E., *Dict. Cant. Crew.* CARROTS: Red hair'd People.

1703. T. BAKER, *Tunbridge Walks*, quoted in Ashton's *Social Life in Reign of Q. Anne*, I., 129. Jenny Trapes! What that CARROT-pated Jade.

1748. SMOLLETT, *Rod. Random*, ch. xiv. Not to appear before Mr. Cringer till I had parted with my CARROTY locks.

1848. THACKERAY, *Book of Snobs*, ch. vii. 'Blanche, with her radish of a nose, and her CARROTS of ringle s.'

1855. *Newcomes*, ch. xxii. 'Tom is here with a fine CARROTY beard.

1864. MARK LEMON, *Jest Book*, p. 205. CARROTS CLASSICALLY CONSIDERED. Why scorn red hair? The Greeks, we know (I note it here in charity) Had taste in beauty, and with them The graces were all Χαριται.

1882. *Daily Telegraph*, Oct. 6, p. 2, col. 1. The two elder of the party were a boy and a girl of unmistakably Irish parentage, and with unkempt and CARROTTY heads of hair.

TAKE A CARROT! (common).—A vulgar insult; equivalent to calling one a fool, or telling one to 'go to hell.' The phrase was originally obscene [*Cf.*, *Et ta sœur! aime-t-elle les radis?*] and applied to women only.

CARRY BOODLE, *verbal phr.* (American).—*See* BOODLE.

CARRY COALS, *verbal phr.* (obsolete).—To put up with insults; to endure an affront or injury.

1593. G. HARVEY, *Pierces Supererog.*, in wks. II., 32. Because Silence may seeme suspicious to many: Patience contemptible to some . . . a knowne forbearer of Libellers, a continuall BEARER OF COALES.

1595. SHAKSPEARE, *Romeo and Juliet* i., 1. Gregory o' my word, we'll not CARRY COALS.

1638. H. SHIRLEY, *Martyr'd Souldier*, Act ii., Sc. 1. *Hub.* I can CARRY anything but Blowes, COLES, my Drink, and—the tongue of a Scould.

CARRY CORN, *verbal phr.* (common).—To bear success well and equably. It is said of a man who breaks down under a sudden access of wealth—as successful racing men and unexpected legatees often do—or who becomes affected and intolerant, that 'he doesn't CARRY CORN well.'

CARRYINGS ON, *subs. phr.* (colloquial).—Frolicsome or questionable proceedings; a course of conduct that attracts attention.—*See* CARRY ON.

1663. BUTLER, *Hudibras*, I., ii., 556. Is this the end to which these CARRYINGS ON did tend?

1859. SALA, *Gaslight and Daylight*, ch. xxi. Many have heard her stern demands for rent, and her shrill denunciation of the CARRYINGS ON of her tenants.

1876. M. S. BRADDON, *Joshua Haggard*, ch., iv. 'And what about the rest of the time when he wasn't with you? Fine CARRYINGS ON indeed for a grocer's daughter!'

CARRY-KNAVE, *subs.* (old).—A common prostitute. For synonyms, *see* BARRACK-HACK and TART.

1630. *Taylor's Workes.* And I doe wish with all my heart that the superflous number of all our hyreling hackney CARRY-KNAVES, and hurry-whores, with their makers and maintainers were there.

CARRY ME OUT AND BURY ME DECENTLY, *phr.* (general).—An exclamation or objurgation generally called forth by an incredible story, or by something displeasing to the auditor; varied by 'LET ME DIE!' 'GOOD

NIGHT!' etc., as also by 'CARRY ME HOME!' 'CARRY ME UPSTAIRS!' 'CARRY ME OUT AND LEAVE ME IN THE GUTTER!' A writer in *Notes and Queries* [2 S., iii., 387] states it to have been in use *circa* 1780. [The origin is obscure, but some derive it from the *Nunc dimittis* (Luke ii. 29).]

1857. *Notes and Queries*, 16 May, p. 387, col. 2. CARRY ME OUT AND BURY ME DECENTLY. Do any of your correspondents recollect to have heard this phrase?

1861. HUGHES, *Tom Brown at Oxford*, ch. xlv. And so the president comes out to see the St. Ambrose boat row? Seldom misses two nights running. Then 'CARRY ME OUT, AND BURY ME DECENTLY' Don't be afraid. I am ready for anything you like to tell me.

1864. *The Reader*, Nov. 12. Mr. Hotten has CARRY ME OUT. Well the equivalent 'Federal' is 'D'you tell?'

CARRY ON, *verbal phr.* (colloquial).—To make oneself conspicuous by a certain line of behaviour; to conduct oneself wildly or recklessly; to joke or frolic; also in a special sense applied to open flirtation on the part of both sexes.

French equivalents are *canarder* (based on *canard* = a 'take in,' an extravagant or absurd story); *faire du jardin* (popular).

1856. WHYTE MELVILLE, *Kate Coventry*, ch. iii. With lynx-eyes she notes how Lady Carmine's eldest girl is CARRYING ON with young Thriftless.

1876. BESANT AND RICE, *Golden Butterfly*, ch. xxxv. 'She and I CARRIED ON for a whole season. People talked.

1884. M. TWAIN, *Huckleberry Finn*, ch. xxii., 222. And all the time that clown CARRIED ON so it most killed the people.

CARRY ONE'S REAL ESTATE ABOUT ONE, *verbal phr.* (American).—To neglect the finger nails till they show a black rim; to go so unwashed as to display a considerable amount of what Palmerston called 'matter in the wrong place.'

1877. JOSEPH HATTON, in *Belgravia*, April. p. 221. We looked at the hands of several of the gamblers, and found that they CARRIED THEIR REAL ESTATE with them.

CARRY OUT ONE'S BAT.—*See* BAT.

CARRY THE STICK, *verbal phr.* (Scotch thieves').—To rob in the manner described in quotation.—*See* also TRIPPING UP.

1870. *Times*. 21 Sept [Marlborough Street Police Court Report.] Police Sergeant Cole said the prisoner's plan was for the woman to go up to well-dressed elderly or drunken men, to get them into conversation, and rob them. The male prisoner would then come up, and, pretending to be a detective, make a disturbance, so as to enable the woman to escape. The practice was called in London 'tripping up,' and in Scotland, where it is also practised, CARRYING THE STICK.

CARSEY, *subs.* (thieves').—A house, den, or crib. [From the Lingua Franca *casa* = a house.] For synonyms, *see* KEN.

CART, *verb* (University).—To defeat: in a match, a fight, an examination, a race, &c. We CARTED them home = we gave them an awful licking.

IN THE CART, or CARTED, *phr.* (racing).—1. An employee is said to put an owner IN THE CART when, by some trick or fraud, his horse is prevented from winning. Also IN THE BOX.

1889. *Evening Standard*, 25 June. [Sir Chas. Russell's speech in Durham-Chetwynd case.] It was alleged that in two races run by Fullerton in 1887, Sir George Chetwynd—to use a vulgarism—had been put IN THE cart by his Jockey.

2. (common).—'In the know'; 'in the hunt.'

1883. *Referee*, 1 April, p. 1, col. 1. No one, not even the previously most authoritative—and most IN THE CART—seems at all astonished at the success of Knight of Burghley.

3. (gaming).—The lowest scorer at any point is said to be IN THE CART; sometimes ON THE TAIL-BOARD.

To WALK THE CART, *phr.* (racing). — To walk over the course.

To CART OFF or OUT, or AWAY, *phr.* (colloquial).—To remove.

CART-GREASE, *subs.* (common).—Butter; in the first instance bad butter.

ENGLISH SYNONYMS. Cow-grease; Thames mud; cow-oil; spread; scrape; smear; ointment; sluter.

FRENCH SYNONYM. *Le fondant*

GERMAN SYNONYMS. *Schmierling* (*Schmier* is properly 'grease,' especially 'wheel-grease,' also 'ointment.' The term is, therefore, practically identical with cart-grease); *Schmunk* (used by knackers. *Schmünkig* signifies 'fat' of any kind, but especially that of horses).

CARTS, *subs.* (common).—A pair of shoes. For synonyms, *see* TROTTER-CASES.

CART-WHEEL, *subs.* (popular)—1. A five-shilling piece. A variant is COACH-WHEEL, and both forms are often contracted into WHEEL. For synonyms, *see* CAROON.

1871. *London Figaro*, 15 Feb. 'Mornings at Mutton's.' The coin of the realm in question was the largest that we have known in the present century—so large, that, in the slang language of thieves and costermongers, it is called a CART-WHEEL, 'coach-wheel' and 'thick-'un.' It was, in fact, a crown-piece.

2. (popular).—A broad hint.

3. (popular). — A continuous series of somersaults in which the hands and feet alternately touch the ground, the appearance produced being similar to the spokes of a cart wheel in motion. Otherwise called a CATHARINE WHEEL.

1851. MAYHEW, *London Labour and London Poor*, II., p. 562. We either do the CAT'UNWHEEL (*Sic*) or else we keep before the gentleman and lady, turning head-over-heels. *Ib.*, p. 564: at night I go along with the others tumbling. I does the CAT'ENWHEEL. (*Sic.*)

1864. SALA, in *Daily Telegraph*, Dec. 23. I saw a little . . . blackguard boy turning CARTWHEELS in front of the Clifton House.

CARVER AND GILDER, *subs. phr.* (common). — A match maker. *Cf.*, FINGERSMITH, a midwife.

CASA.—*See* CASE.

CASCADE, *subs.* (Australian).—1. In Tasmania beer is called CASCADE because manufactured from 'cascade' water. *Cf.*, ARTESIAN. For synonyms, *see* SWIPES and DRINKS.

2. (theatrical). — Explained by quotation. Another name for the same effect is HANG OUT.

1851. MAYHEW, *Lon. Lab. and Lon. Poor*, III., p. 156. The principal distinction between pantomimes and ballets is that there are more CASCADES, and trips, and valleys in pantomimes, and none in ballets. A trip is a dance between Harlequin and the Columbine, and CASCADES and valleys are trundling and gymnastic performances, such as tumbling across the stage on wheels, and catching hold of hands and twirling round.

Verb (old).—To vomit. For synonyms, *see* ACCOUNTS.

1771. SMOLLETT, *Humphry Clinker*, III., Oct. 4, iii. She CASCADED in his urn.

1836. M. SCOTT, *Tom Cringle's Log*, ch. ii. I daresay five hundred rank and file, at the fewest, were all CASCADING at one and the same moment.

CASE, *subs.* (colloquial).—1. A certainty in fact, an accentuated or abnormal instance in character. When two persons fall in love, or are engaged to marry, it is said to be a CASE with them. An eccentric person is likewise a CASE. [As a designation for persons, CASE probably had its origin in Journalese and Police-court English; *e.g.*, a CASE of larceny.]

1848. BARTLETT, *Dictionary of Americanisms*. CASE: a character, a queer one; as 'That Sol Haddock is a CASE.' 'What a hard CASE he is,' meaning a reckless scapegrace, *mauvais sujet*.

1859. H. KINGSLEY, *Geoffrey Hamlyn*, ch. xlii. Tossed from workhouse to prison, from prison to hulk—every man's hand against him—an Arab of society. As hopeless a CASE, my lord judge, as you ever had to deal with.

1868. O. W. HOLMES, *Guardian Angel*, ch. iv., p. 35 (Rose Lib.). 'It was a devilish hard CASE,' he said, 'that old Malachi had left his money as he did.'

1872. MISS BRADDON, *To the Bitter End*, ch. xlviii. They have only been engaged three weeks; but from the day we first met Lord Stanmore at a hunting breakfast at Stoneleigh, the business was settled. It was a CASE, as you fast young men say.

1880. HAWLEY SMART, *Social Sinners*, ch. xxiv. He saw people began to make way for him when she was concerned; in short, that they looked upon it as a CASE.

1887. *Cassell's Mag.*, Dec., p. 26. It isn't Mr. and Mrs. Cardewe he comes to see! It's Miss Amy. . . . They have met before; and in my opinion it's a CASE!

2. (thieves')—A bad five-shilling piece; HALF A CASE, a bad half-crown. *Cf.*, CASER. In America a dollar, good or bad. [There are two sources, either of which may have contributed this slang term. (1.) *Caser*, the Hebrew word for a crown; (2.) silver coin is frequently counterfeited by coating or CASING pewter or iron imitations with silver.—*Hotten.*]

1857. SNOWDEN, *Mag. Assistant*, 3 ed., p. 444. Bad five shillings—CASE.

3. (old).—A house, respectable or otherwise. Subsequently restricted to a brothel, and, by derivation, a 'water-closet.' [Presumably from the Italian *casa*, a house, through the Lingua Franca. It is found in various forms, CASA, CASE, CASER, CARSER, CARSEY, the last a phonetic rendering of the usual pronunciation of CASA.] For synonyms, *see* KEN.

1678. MARVELL, wks. (1875) III., 497. A net . . . That Charles himself might chase To Caresbrook's narrow CASE. [M.]

1690. B.E., *Dict. Cant. Crew*. CASE: a House, Shop, or Ware-house.

1785. GROSE, *Dict. of Vul. Tongue*. CASE: a house, perhaps from the Italian *casa*. In the canting *lingo* it meant store or warehouse, as well as dwelling house. Tout that CASE: mark or observe that house. It is all bob, now let's dub the gigg of the CASE: now the coast is clear, let us break open the door of the house.

1883. *Echo*, Jan. 25, p. 2, col. 3. From the Italian we get the thieves' slang term CASA for house.

4. (Westminster School).—The discussion by Seniors and Upper Election preceding a TANNING (*q.v.*), and the tanning itself.

A CASE OF CRABS, *subs. phr.* (colloquial).—A failure.

A CASE OF PICKLES, *subs. phr.* (colloquial).—An incident; a bad break-down; a break up.

A CASE OF STUMP, *subs. phr.* (colloquial).—Said of one absolutely guiltless of the possession of coin.

CASEINE, *subs.* (rare).—The correct thing. A variant of THE CHEESE (*q.v.*) *Cf.*, CASSAN.

1856. C. KINGSLEY, *Letter*, May. Horn minnow looks like a gudgeon, which is the pure CASEINE.

CASER, *subs.* (thieves').—Five shillings.—*See* CASE and CAROON.

1879. J. W. HORSLEY, in *Macm. Mag.*, XL., 501. One morning I found I did not have more than a CASER (5s.).

CASE-VROW, *subs.* (old).—A prostitute in residence in a particular brothel; now called a DRESS-LODGER (*q.v.*). [From CASE (*q.v.*), a house, + Dutch *vrow*, a woman.]

CASEY, *subs.* (thieves').—Cheese.—*See* CASSAN.

CASH.—*See* CASSAN.

EQUAL TO CASH. — Of unquestionable merit. In allusion to the fact that paper currency is largely a medium of exchange.

1835. HALIBURTON, *Clockmaker*, 1 S., chap. xvi. Though I say it, that shouldn't say it, they [the U.S. Americans] fairly take the shine off creation—they are actilly EQUAL TO CASH.

To CASH A PRESCRIPTION, *subs. phr.* (colloquial).—To get a prescription made up.

1890. *The Scots Observer*, p. 399, col. 2. The Socialist, with an ear for Ibsen, and an eye for Wagner, and A PRESCRIPTION in his pocket that only needs TO BE CASHED for the world to forget its past, and belie its present, and bedevil its future.

CASHELS, *subs.* (Stock Exchange).—Great Southern and Western of Ireland Railway Stock. [Said to be derived from the fact that the line originally had no station at Cashel.]

CASH or **PASS IN ONE'S CHECKS**. *verbal phr.* (American). To die. Derived from the game of poker, where counters or CHECKS, purchased at certain fixed rates, are equivalent to coin. The euphemism is drawn from the analogy between settling one's earthly accounts, and paying in dues at the end of the game.

18(?). JOHN HAY, *Jim Bludsoe of the Prairie Belle*. 'How Jimmy Bludsoe PASS'D IN HIS CHECKS The night of the Prairie Belle.'

1870. BRET HARTE, *Outcasts Poker Flat*. Beneath this tree lies the body of J. O. who . . . HANDED IN HIS CHECKS on the 7th December, 1850.

1872. S. L. CLEMENS ('Mark Twain'), *Roughing It*, p. 332. 'You see,' said the miner, 'one of the boys has PASSED IN HIS CHECKS, and we want to give him a good send off.'

1882. DODGE, *Plains of the Great West*. As close a shave as I ever made to PASSING IN MY CHECKS was from a buffalo stampede.

1888. *New York Sun*. Well, I owned the mule for several years after that, and when he finally PASSED IN HIS CHECKS I gave him as decent a burial as any pioneer ever got.

CASH-UP, *verb* (colloquial).—To liquidate a debt by the transfer of money, *i.e.*, cash, or its equivalent. For synonyms, *see* SHELL OUT.

1837. BARHAM, *I. L.* (*M. of Venice*). And Antonio grew In a deuce of a stew, For he could not CASH UP, spite of all he could do.

1843. DICKENS, *Martin Chuzzlewit*, I., p. 213. 'When my father's executors

CASH UP' he used strange expressions now and then, but that was his way.—'CASH UP'S a very good expression' observed Martin, 'when other people don't apply it to you.'

1861. SALA, *Seven Sons of Mammon*, II., p. 197. 'But they may CASH UP.' 'CASH UP! They'll never CASH UP a farthing piece.'

CASK, *subs.* (popular). — A brougham; otherwise a PILL-BOX (*q.v.*). A French equivalent is *une bagniole*.

CASS.—*See* CASSAN.

CASSAN, *subs.* (thieves'). — Old Cant for cheese. Also CASS, CASSON, CASSAM, CASSOM, and CASEY. The oldest form is CASSAN, which is found in Harman's *Caveat or Warening for Common Cursetors*, the first known dictionary of English cant [1567]. CASS, chiefly American thieves, is a latter corruption probably influenced by the Dutch *kaas*, or the M. Dutch *kâse*, Lat. *caseus*. [For suggested derivation, which corresponds to that given in the *N.E.D.*, *see* second quot.]

ENGLISH SYNONYMS. Caz; sweaty-toe; choke-dog.

FRENCH SYNONYMS. *Le renâché* (thieves' term); *une côtelette de menuisier*, *de perruquier*, or *de vâche* (popular terms for a portion of Brie; literally a cabinet-maker's, hair-dresser's, or cow-cutlet); *le dûreme* (thieves); *une boussole de réfroidi* or *de singe* (popular = a Dutch Cheese.)

GERMAN SYNONYMS. *Fendrich* (Old Cant appearing in the *Liber Vagatorum* [1529] as *Wenderich* or *Wendrich*; subsequently modified into *Fähndrich*. The derivation is referable, perhaps, to an old practice, prevalent in North Germany, of using as a board sign [*Fahne*, a flag, standard, banner] with three cheeses pictured); *Gewine* (from the Hebrew *gewino*); *Karnet* or *Kornet*; *Kawine* (a variant of *Gewine*); *Stinkefix* (from the O. H. G. *Stinchan*, to smell, to stink; this is especially applied to *old* cheese).

ITALIAN SYNONYMS. *Tenerosa* (cream cheese); *mascherpo*; *stifello* (literally a kind of flute, in allusion to the holes in some kinds of cheese, notably Gruyère).

SPANISH SYNONYM. *Formage* (evidently a corruption of the French *fromage*).

1567. HARMAN, *Caveat* (1869), p. 86. She hath a Cacking chete, a grunting chete, ruff Pecke, CASSAN, and popplarr of yarum.

1609. DEKKER, *Lanthorne and Candlelight*, in wks. (Grosart) III., 195. CASSAN is cheese, and is a worde barbarously coynd out of the substantive *caseus*, which also signifies a cheese.

1656. BROOME, *Jovial Crew*, Act ii. Here's ruffpeck and CASSAN, and all of the best, And scraps of the dainties of gentry cofe's feast.

1714. *Memoirs of John Hall* (4 ed.), p. 11. CASUM: cheese.

1881. *New York Slang Dictionary*. CASS: cheese.

CASTELL, *verb* (old).—To see or look. [It is uncertain as to whether this word is slang or not. It is not included in the *N.E.D.*] For synonyms, *see* PIPE.

1610. ROWLANDS, *Martin Mark-all*, p. 37 (H. Club's Repr., 1874). To CASTELL: to see or looke.

CASTER, *subs.* (old).—1. A cloak. [*Cf.*, CASTOR, a hat; there seems to be no historical improbability for a similar derivation].

Another Old Cant term for a cloak was CALLE (*q.v.*), and the French have *un bleu*, whilst the Italian Fourbesque has *toppo* and *manto*, the latter probably meaning 'a long black veil'; Calaõ. *tralha*. The Germania renders cloak by *noche* (literally 'night,' and signifying also in a canting sense 'sadness' and 'sentence of death'); *nube* (literally a 'cloud'); *pelosa* (specially applied to a cloak worn in the morning; literally 'shaggy' or 'hairy'); *bellosa* or *vellosa* (a sailor's cloak).

1567. HARMAN, *Caveat* [E. E. Text Soc., 1869], p. 77. He walketh in softly a nights, when they be at their rest, and plucketh of as many garmentes as be ought worth that he may come by, . . . and maketh porte sale at some conuenient place of theirs, that some be soone ready in the morning, for want of their CASTERS *and* Togemans.

1610. ROWLANDS, *Martin Mark-all*, p. 37 (H. Club's Repr., 1874). CASTER: a Clocke.

1785. GROSE, *Dictionary of the Vulgar Tongue* [s.v.].

1811. *Lexicon Balatronicum* [s.v.].

2. (colloquial). — A cast-off or rejected person or thing. [From CAST, thrown, + ER.]

1859. LANG, *Wand. India*, p. 144. The horse which drew the buggy had been a CASTER . . . a horse considered no longer fit for the cavalry or horse artillery, and sold by public auction, after being branded with the letter R on the near shoulder. [M.]

CASTIEU'S HOTEL, *subs. phr.* (Australian thieves').—The Melbourne gaol, so called from Mr. J. B. Castieu. For list of nicknames of this description, *see* CAGE.

18(?). *Australian Printer's Keepsake*. He caught a month, and had to white it out at diamond-cracking in CASTIEU'S HOTEL.

CASTLE-RAG, *subs.* (rhyming slang).—A flag or fourpenny piece. For synonyms, *see* JOEY.

CAST-OFFS, *subs.* (nautical). — 1. Landsmen's clothes. For synonyms, *see* TOGS.

2. In *singular* (general).—A discarded mistress.

CASTOR, *subs.* (old).—A hat. [From Latin *castor*, a beaver, hats having formerly been made of beaver's fur.] For synonyms, *see* GOLGOTHA.

1640. ENTICK, *London*, II., 175. Beaver hats, Demi-CASTERS. [M.]

1754. B. MARTIN, *Eng. Dict.*, 2 ed. CASTOR: lat., 1, a beaver, a beast like an otter. 2, a fine hat made of its fur.

1821. W. T. MONCRIEFF, *Tom and Jerry*, Act ii., Sc. 5. *Jerry*. (Walks about, and, by mistake, takes Logic's hat, which he puts on.) Damn the cards! *Log.* (Following Jerry, and rescuing CASTOR.) Don't nibble the felt, Jerry!

1857. O. W. HOLMES, *Autocrat of the Breakfast Table*, ch. viii. The last effort of decayed fortune is expended in smoothing its dilapidated CASTOR. The hat is the *ultimum morieus* of 'respectability.'

1860. *Morning Post*, Jan. 30. Such as tin for money, CASTOR for hat, brick for good fellow, gemman for gentleman.

CAST SHEEP'S EYES, *verbal phr.* (common).—To ogle; to leer or 'make eyes' at; formerly to look modestly and with diffidence, but always with longing or affection. [Probably in allusion to the quiet, gentle gaze of sheep.] The phrase has been varied by to CAST LAMB'S EYES. Fr. *gingíner*; *lancer son prospectus*, and *un oeil en tirelire* = an eye full of amorous expression.

1590. GREENE, *Francesco's Fortunes*, in wks. VIII., 191. That CASTING A SHEEPE'S EYE at hir, away he goes; and euer since he lies by himselfe and pines away.

1614. JONSON, *Bartholomew Fair*, V., iii. Who chances to come by but fair Nero in a sculler; And seeing Leander's naked leg and goodly calf, CAST at him from the boat A SHEEP'S EYE an' a half.

1748. SMOLLETT, *Rod. Random*, ch. xvi. There was a young lady in the room, and she THREW . . . many SHEEP'S EYES at a certain person whom I shall not name.

1864. G. A. LAWRENCE, *Guy Livingstone*, ch. vii. He would stand for some time CASTING LAMB'S-EYES at the object of his affections—to the amorous audacity of the full-grown sheep he never soared.

1881. HAWLEY SMART, *Gt. Tontine*, ch. xi. It isn't to be expected a well-bred lass like this is going to knock under the minute a young fellow MAKES SHEEP'S-EYES at her.

CAST UP ACCOUNTS.—*See* ACCOUNTS, to which may be added the following.

FRENCH SYNONYMS. *Jeter du cœur*—or *son lest*—*sur carreau* (general: literally to 'throw hearts or diamonds' or 'throw one's heart,' here meaning the stomach, 'on the floor'); *compter ses chemises* (popular); *débecqueter* (popular); *déborder* (popular); *lâcher son goujon* (general); *lâcher une fusée* (popular).

1607. DEKKER, *Westward Ho*, Act v., Sc. 1. *Mist. Wafer.* I would not have 'em CAST UP their ACCOUNTS here, for more than they mean to be drunk this twelvemonth.

1808. R. ANDERSON, *Cumbrld. Ball*, 26. The breyde she KEST UP her ACCOUNTS In Rachel's lap. [M.]

CAT, *subs.* (old).—1. A prostitute. For synonyms, *see* BARRACK-HACK.

[1401. *Pol. Poems*, II., 113. Be ware of Cristis curse, and of CATTIS tailis.] [M.]

1535. LYNDESAY, *Satyre*, 468. *Wantonnes.* Hay! as one brydlit CAT, I brank. [M.]

1690. B. E., *Dict. Cant. Crew.* CAT: a common Whore.

1748. T. DYCHE, *Dictionary* (5 ed.). CAT (s.) . . . also a cant word for a lewd, whorish woman, or street-walker.

2. (popular). — A shortened form of CAT-O'-NINE-TAILS (*q.v.*).

1788. FALCONBRIDGE, *Afr. Slave Tr.*, 40. A CAT (an instrument of correction, which consists of a handle or stem, made of a rope three inches and a half in circumference, and about eighteen inches in length, at one end of which are fastened nine branches, or tails, composed of log line, with three or more knots upon each branch). [M.]

1870. *London Figaro*, 23 Dec. We are delighted to learn that Mr. Baron Bramwell, at the Warwick Assizes, on Saturday, sentenced a batch of street thieves to hard labour for eighteen months, and twenty lashes each, with an instrument called the CAT.

1889. *Globe*, 26 Oct., p. 7, col. 3. The 'CAT.' A companion of the prisoner was convicted last session of being concerned in the assault and robbery, and was sentenced to eighteen months' hard labour and to receive twenty-five lashes.

3. (thieves').—A lady's muff. [Muff = female *pudendum*. *See* sense 4.]

1857. SNOWDEN, *Mag. Assistant*, 3 ed., p. 444. To steal a muff—To free a CAT.

4. (popular). — The female *pudendum*; otherwise a PUSSY; French, *le chat*.

5. (thieves').—A quart pot. Pint pots are called KITTENS. Stealing these pots is termed CAT AND KITTEN SNEAKING.

1851. MAYHEW, *London Labour and London Poor*, II., p. 118. The mistress of a lodging-house, who had conveniences for the melting of pewter-pots (called CATS AND KITTENS by the young thieves according to the size of the vessels). *Ibid.*, I., p. 460. At this lodging-house CATS AND KITTENS are melted down . . . A quart pot is a CAT, and pints and half-pints are KITTENS.

6. (popular).—*See* TAME CAT.

7. (common).—A monster infesting lodging houses, and assimi-

4

lating, with equal readiness, cold meat and coals, spirits and paraffin, etc., etc.

1827. R. B. PEAKE, *Comfortable Lodgings*, Act I., Sc. iii. I wonder whether the CAT ever comes in here, and knocks anything over? · Sir Hippington Miff, here's your health! — Ladies, yours! (*Drinks.*) Bless my soul! the cup's empty! I'll turn it over, and lay the fault at pussy's door.

1871. *Figaro*, 2 July. 'My Landlady.' Who on my viands waxes fat?—Who keeps a most voracious CAT!—Who often listens on my mat? My Landlady.

FLYING CAT, *subs.* (old).—An owl.

1690. B. E., *Dictionary Canting Crew*, s.v. *Flutter.* An owl is a FLYING-CAT.

TO JERK, SHOOT, OR WHIP THE CAT; or simply, TO CAT. To vomit; generally from over indulgence in drink.—*See* ACCOUNTS and CAST UP ACCOUNTS.

1609. ARMIN, *Maids of More-cl.* (1880), 70. Ile baste their bellies and their lippes till we haue IERK'T THE CAT with our three whippes. [M.]

1630. J. TAYLOR ('Water P.'), *Brood Cormor*, wks. III., p. 5, col. 1. You may not say hee's drunke . . For though he be as drunke as any rat He hath but catcht a fox, or WHIPT THE CAT.

1830. MARRYAT, *King's Own*, ch. xxxii. I'm cursedly inclined to SHOOT THE CAT.

TO WHIP THE CAT, otherwise TO DRAW THROUGH THE WATER WITH A CAT, *phr.* (old).—1. To indulge in practical jokes. [For suggested origin, *see* quotation 1785.]

1614. B. JONSON, *Barthol. Fair*, I., iv. [N.]. I'll be DRAWN WITH A GOOD GIB CAT THROUGH THE GREAT POND at home. [M.]

1690. B. E., *Dictionary Canting Crew*. CATTING: DRAWING A Fellow THROUGH A POND WITH A CAT.

1785. GROSE, *Dict. Vulg. Tongue*. CAT-WHIPPING or WHIPPING THE CAT: a trick often practised on ignorant country fellows, vain of their strength; by laying a wager with them, that they may be PULLED THROUGH A POND BY A CAT; the bet being made, a rope is fixed round the waist of the party to be catted, and the end thrown across the pond, to which the cat is also fastened by a pack-thread, and three or four sturdy fellows are appointed to lead and whip the cat; these, on a signal given, seize the end of the cord, and pretending to whip the cat, haul the astonished booby through the water.

2. (tailors', etc.).—To work at private houses. In America the term is also used by carpenters and other itinerants, especially schoolmasters who 'board round.' At one time it was more convenient to pay in kind than in currency; and, in rural New England, a school-teacher would be 'boarded round' amongst his pupils' parents as a part of his remuneration. (*See* Washington Irving's *Legend of Sleepy Hollow.*) This was called WHIPPING THE CAT.

1871. DE VERE, *Americanisms*, 648. WHIPPING THE CAT: an old English phrase, used only by tailors and carpenters, has maintained its existence in New England, Pennsylvania, and a few other States, where it denotes the annual visit of a tailor to repair the clothes of a household. It is said to have originated in a very rough practical joke, which bears the same name in Hampshire, England, and of which, it is surmised, the tailor may have been the victim (J. R. Lowell). The simple tailors of former days liked thus to go from house to house in the rural districts, providing the families with clothing. The chief romance for the happy 'Schneider' was in the abundant and wholesome cheer of the farmer who employed him, and as his annual visits fell in the pudding and sausage season, he was liberally crammed with that kind of 'vegetables,' as he facetiously called them, to his heart's content. The only objection made to CATWHIPPING, was that it afforded no opportunity to 'cabbage,' and in former days this was a serious grievance. The introduction of large manufacturing establishments, low-priced ready-made clothing, and the advent of the sewing-machine, have now nearly made an end to this itinerant occupation. The terms CATWHIPPER and CATWHIPPING were often facetiously, and sometimes very irreverently, applied to other itinerant professions: even 'school-masters'—there was no 'teachers,' much less 'educators,' in those benighted days—were called CATWHIPPERS, when they boarded, as was quite usual, in turns with the parents of their scholars. Itinerating preachers also were, by the initiated, included in this category.

TO SEE HOW THE CAT WILL JUMP, *phr.* (common).—To watch the course of events. An American equivalent is TO SIT ON THE FENCE.—*See* FENCE and JUMPING CAT.

1827. SCOTT, in *Croker Pap.* (1884), I., xi., 319. Had I time, I believe I would come to London merely TO SEE HOW THE CAT JUMPED. [M.]

1853. BULWER LYTTON, *My Novel*, IV., p. 228. 'But I rely equally on your friendly promise.' 'Promise! No—I don't promise. I must first SEE HOW THE CAT JUMPS.'

1859. LEVER, *Davenport Dunn*, III., 229. You'll SEE with half an eye HOW THE CAT JUMPS.

1874. *Sat. Rev.*, p. 139. This dismays the humble Liberal of the faint Southern type, who thinks that there are subjects as to which the heads of his party need not wait TO SEE HOW THE CAT JUMPS.

1887. 'Pol. Slang,' in *Cornhill Mag.*, June, p. 626. Those who sit on the fence—men with impartial minds, who wait to see, as another pretty phrase has it, HOW THE CAT WILL JUMP.

YOU KILL MY CAT AND I'LL KILL YOUR DOG, *phr.* (common). 'Ca' me, 'ca' thee; an exchange in the matter of 'scratching backs'—in Fr. *passez moi la casse, et je t'enverrai la senne.*

TO LET THE CAT OUT OF THE BAG, *phr.* (common).—To reveal a secret; a variant with a slightly modified sense is TO PUT ONE'S FOOT IN IT. [This and the kindred phrase 'to buy a pig in a poke,' are said to have had their origin in the bumpkin's trick of substituting a cat for a young pig and bringing it to market in a bag. If the customer were wary THE CAT WAS LET OUT OF THE BAG, and there was no deal.

1760. *Lond. Mag* XXIX., p. 224. We could have wished that the author . . . had not LET THE CAT OUT OF THE BAG. [M.]

1782. WOLCOT ('P. Pindar'), *Pair of Lyric Epistles* To the Reader But, to use a sublime phrase, as it would be LETTING THE CAT OUT OF THE BAG, I have fortune.

1811. C. K. SHARPE, in *Correspondence* (1888), I., 475. She has LET A wicked CAT OUT OF THE BAG to G. M. respecting his mother.

1855. MRS. GASKELL, *North and South*, ch. xliv. You needn't look so frightened because you have LET THE CAT OUT OF THE BAG to a faithful old hermit like me. I shall never name his having been in England.

1888. MACDERMOTT [on the case of Crawford *v.* Dilke]. This noble representative of everything good in Chelsea, He LET THE CAT, the naughty cat, RIGHT OUT OF THE Gladstone BAG.

WHO ATE OR STOLE THE CAT? *phr.* (common).—A gentleman whose larder was frequently broken by bargees, had a cat cooked and placed as a decoy. It was taken and eaten, and became a standing jest against the pilferers.

TO LEAD A CAT AND DOG LIFE *phr.* (popular).—To quarrel night and day. Said of married (or unmarried) couples.

TO TURN CAT IN THE PAN, *phr.* (old).—To 'rat'; to reverse one's position through self-interest; to play the turncoat. [The derivation is absolutely unknown. The one generally received—that 'cat' is a corruption of 'cate' or 'cake'—is historically untenable.]

c. 1559. *Old Play*, '*Marriage of Witt and Wisdome.*' Sc. 3. Now am I true araid like a phesitien; I am as very a turncote as the wethercoke of Poles; For now I will calle my name Due Disporte. So, so, finely I can TURNE THE CATT IN THE PANE.

1593. 4 *Lett. Conf.*, in wks. (Grosart) II., 286. If it bee a home booke at his first conception, let it be a home booke still, and TURNE NOT CAT IN THE PANNE.

1625. BACON, *Essays* (*of Cunning*), p. 441 (Arber). There is a *Cunning*, which we in *England* call, The TURNING OF THE CAT IN THE PAN, which is, when that which a Man says to another, he laies it, as if Another had said it to him.

c. 1720. *Song*, 'The Vicar of Bray.' 'When George in pudding time came in, And moderate men looked big, sir, He TURNED A CAT-IN-PAN once more, And so became a Whig, sir.'

1816. SCOTT, *Old Mortality*, ch. xxxv. 'O, this precious Basil will TURN CAT IN PAN with any man!' replied Claverhouse.

TO FEEL AS THOUGH A CAT HAD KITTENED IN ONE'S MOUTH, *phr.* (popular).—To 'have a mouth' after drunkenness.

Many other phrases and proverbial sayings might, more or less justifiably, be classed as slang in this connection; *e.g.*, TO FIGHT LIKE KILKENNY CATS; TO GRIN LIKE A CHESHIRE CAT; NOT ROOM ENOUGH TO SWING A CAT; ABLE TO MAKE A CAT SPEAK, AND A MAN DUMB; WHO SHOT THE CAT (the last a reproach addressed to volunteers), etc.

CATAMARAN, *subs.* (colloquial).—A vixenish old woman; also a cross-grained person of either sex. [*Cf.*, CATAMOUNT. Probably associated with the colloquial use of CAT, a quarrelsome, vicious woman]. For synonyms, *see* GEEZER.

1833. MARRYAT, *Peter Simple*, ch. vi. The cursed drunken old CATAMARAN, cried he, I'll go and cut her down by the head.

1855. THACKERAY. *Newcomes*, ch. lxxv. 'What a woman that Mrs. Mackenzie is!' cries F. B. 'What an infernal tartar and CATAMARAN!'

1861. *Macmillan's Magazine*, June, p. 113. She was such an obstinate old CATAMARAN.

CATAMOUNT, CATAMOUNTAIN, or **CAT O'MOUNTAIN**, *subs.* (American).—A shrew. [*Cf.*, CATAMARAN and Beaumont and Fletcher's use of the word for a wild man from the mountains, itself a transferred sense of catamount = a leopard or panther.]

1616. FLETCHER, *Cust. of Country*, I., i. The rude claws of such a CAT O' MOUNTAIN!

1835. HALIBURTON, *Clockmaker*, 1 S., ch., xii. She was a dreadful cross-grained woman, a real CATAMOUNT, as savage as a she-bear that has cubs.

CAT AND MOUSE, *subs.*, *phr.* (rhyming slang).—A house.

CATASTROPHE, *subs.* (old).—The tail or latter end. *Cf.*, the Falstaffism 'I'll tickle your CATASTROPHE.'

CATAWAMPOUS, CATAWAMPTIOUSLY, *adj.* and *adv.* (popular).—With avidity; fiercely; eagerly; or violently destructive. *See* CATAWAMPUS.

1843. DICKENS, *Martin Chuzzlewit*, ch., xxi., 216. There air some CATAWAMPOUS chawers in the small way too, as graze upon a human pretty strong.

1853. LYTTON, *My Novel*, bk. X., ch. xx. If a man like me . . . . is to be CATAWAMPOUSLY champed up by a mercenary selfish cormorant of a capitalist.

18(?). F. BURNAND, *The White Cat.* Don't hurt me; spare a poor unhappy pup, Or I'll be CATAWAMPOUSLY chawed up.

CATAWAMPUS, *subs.*—Vermin, especially those that sting and bite. [Apparently formed from CATAWAMPOUS (*q.v.*).]

1880. MORTIMER COLLINS, *Thoughts in My Garden*, vol. I., p. 244. Look at their [spiders'] value in destroying wasps and blue-bottles, gnats, midges, and all manner of CATAWAMPUSES, as the ladies call them.

CATCH, *subs.* (colloquial).—A man or woman matrimonially desirable; formerly in a canting sense, a prize or booty [*see* quot. 1877]. A woman who is 'no great CATCH' is in French argot termed *une grognotte.*

1593. SHAKSPEARE, *Taming of the Shrew*, Act ii., Sc. 1, 333. *Bap.* The gain I seek is—quiet in the match. *Gre.* No doubt but he hath got a quiet CATCH.

1748. T. DYCHE, *Dictionary* (5 ed.) CATCH (s.) . . . also a cant word for a prize, booty, etc.

1842. *Comic Almanack*, p. 333. Angelina Ampletin was one of the prettiest girls in Pimlico, and if there was any truth in rumour, very far from one of the worst CATCHES.

1877. *Five Years' Penal Servitude*, ch. iii., p. 244. Well, as it was her CATCH, I thought as I'd consult along of her whether we should take the £200.

CATCH or **CUT A CRAB**, *verbal phr.* (common).—There are various ways of CATCHING A CRAB, as for example, (1) to turn the blade of the oar or 'feather' under water at the end of the stroke, and thus be unable to recover; (2) to lose control of the oar at the middle of the stroke by 'digging' too deeply; or (3) to miss the water altogether. An English variant is to 'capture a cancer,' an American form being 'TO CATCH A LOBSTER.'—*See* LOBSTER.

1785. GROSE, *Dict. Vulg. Tongue*, s.v.

1833. MARRYAT, *Peter Simple* [ed. 1846], ch viii., p. 206, s.v.

1844. *Puck*, p. 134. Now, Johnson, thou wilt surely rue! Didst ever pull before? (Brown had been up to fish at Kew. And CAUGHT—of CRABS—a store.

1849. JOHN SMITH (J. D. Lewis) Hark, the gun has gone thrice, and now off in a trice, With the Johnians we're soon on a level. When Hicks, who's no dab, with his oar CUTS A CRAB, And our coxswain he swears like the Devil.

1857. HOOD, *Pen and Pencil Pictures*, p. 144. Awful muff! Can't pull two strokes without CATCHING as many CRABS; he'd upset the veriest tub on the river.

1872. *Daily News*, 10 Sept. 'London Rowing Club Regatta.' The excitement and fun engendered by the numerous scrimmages resulted in 'fouls' and CRABS of most portentous magnitude.

CATCH A TARTAR, *verbal phr.* (popular).—To unexpectedly meet with one's superior; to fall into one's own trap; having a design upon another, to be caught oneself. [Explanation may be found, perhaps, in the horror born of the atrocities of the Tartar hordes who devasted Eastern Europe in the reign of St. Louis of France. *Cf.*, TARTAR, a person of irritable temper.] An American variant is TO CATCH ON A SNAG (*q.v.*).

1682. DRYDEN, *Prol. to King and Queen*, in wks., p. 456 (Globe). When men will needlessly their freedom barter for lawless power, sometimes they CATCH A TARTER.

1748. SMOLLETT, *Rod. Random*, ch. xxx. Who, looking at me with a contemptuous sneer, exclaimed, Ah, ah! have you CAUGHT A TARTER?

1778. FANNY BURNEY, *Diary*, 23 Aug. 'Ah,' he (Johnson) added, 'they will little think what a TARTAR you carry to them.'

1857. O. W. HOLMES, *Autocrat of the Breakfast Table*, ch. v. When the Danish pirates made descents upon the English coast, they CAUGHT A FEW TARTARS occasionally, in the shape of Saxons.

c. 1880. *Broadside Ballad*, 'Unhappy Because it Can't Last.' They say two heads are better than one, so I took a wife and CAUGHT A TARTAR, and found two of a trade could never agree, and proved the proverb that marry in haste repent at leisure.

CATCH-'EM-ALIVE, or **ALIVO**, *subs. phr.* (common).—1. A fly-paper.

[In allusion to the sticky substance smeared over the paper which, attracting the flies, literally 'catches them alive.']

1851-61. H. MAYHEW, *London Lab. and Lon. Poor*, vol. III., p. 38. They used to . . . call 'em Egyptian flypapers, but now they use merely the word 'fly-papers,' or 'fly-destroyers,' or 'fly-catchers,' or 'CATCH 'EM ALIVE, OH'S.'

1857. DICKENS, *Dorrit*, wks. I., ch. xvi., 122 And such coats of varnish that every holy personage served for a fly trap, and became what is now called in the vulgar tongue a CATCH-EM-ALIVE, O.

1890. *Globe*, 16 April, p. 1, col 3. Typhoid microbes take as kindly to sluggish waters as flies do to CATCH-EM-ALIVE-OH'S.

2. (common).—A tooth-comb; a 'louse-trap.'

3. (general).—The female *pudendum.*

CATCH-FART, *subs.* (old).—A footman, or page boy. [A combination of CATCH, in its ordinary sense, + FART (*q.v.*). Fourbesque, *bolognino* and *falcone* ('a falcon').]

CATCH IT, *verb* (colloquial).—To get a scolding or castigation; to get into trouble; to 'come in for it.' For synonyms, *see* TAN and WIG.

1835. MARRYAT, *Jacob Faithful*, ch. xxxviii. We all thought Tom was about to CATCH IT.

1848. MRS. GASKELL, *M. Barton*, xxxi. I shall CATCH IT down stairs, I know.

1872. BLACK, *Adv. Phaeton*, xvi., 218. He CATCHES IT if he does not bring home a fair proportion to his wife.

CATCH ME! or **CATCH ME AT IT!** *phr.* (colloquial).—An intimation that the person speaking will not do such and such a thing. An analogous phrase is DON'T YOU WISH YOU MAY GET IT!

1780. MRS. COWLEY, *The Belle's Stratagem*, Act iii., Sc. 2. *First Gent.* May I be a bottle, and an empty bottle, if you CATCH ME at that! Why, I am going to the masquerade.

1830. GALT, *Lawrie, T.*, V., iv. (1849), 207. CATCH ME again at such costly daffin.

1841. R. B. PEAKE, *Court and City*, I., i. Satisfaction! CATCH ME at that!

1846. DICKENS, *Dombey and Son*, I., p. 112, col. 3. 'You have a committee to-day at three, you know.' 'And one at three, three-quarters,' added Mr. Dombey, 'CATCH YOU at forgetting anything!' exclaimed Carker.

CATCH ON, *verb* (colloquial).—To understand; to grasp in meaning; to apprehend; to attach or fix oneself to; to quickly seize an opportunity and turn it to advantage. [A literal translation, in fact, into the language of slang of the Latin *apprehendere.*] A French equivalent is *piger*, but for synonyms, *see* TWIG.

1884. *Lisbon* (Dakota) *Star*, 27 June. Now is the time to CATCH ON in order to keep up with the procession. [M.]

1889. *The Nation*, 19 Dec., p. 499, col. 1. . . . The farmer knows only the traffic of his market town and his county, and he is slow to CATCH ON to the new and progressive.

1890. *Globe*, Feb. 13, p. 1. col. 5. Well, assuming that the notion were to CATCH ON, and the example of this enterprising mother to be generally imitated in the upper orbits of the social system, would there be a balance of advantage to the nation?

CATCH ON A SNAG, *verbal phr.* (American).—TO CATCH A TARTAR (*q.v.*); to meet with one's superior.

1887. STUART CUMBERLAND, *The Queen's Highway.* In rough Western parlance a man who falls in with such a player (a man, who, bearing a high reputation for all-round godliness, is a crack 'poker' player) CATCHES ON A SNAG, and it is said that everyone who visits the

North-West comes across, sooner or later, the SNAG on which he is TO CATCH.

CATCH ON THE HOP, *verbal phr.* (popular).—Properly to CATCH or HAVE ON THE HIP, as Gratiano catches Shylock.—*See* HOP.

c. 1869. *The Chickaleary Bloke*, sung by Vance. For to GET ME ON THE HOP, or on my 'tibby' drop, You must wake up very early in the morning.

CATCH-POLE, *subs.* (old).—A warrant-officer; a bum-bailiff. A very old term formerly in respectable use, but employed contemptuously from the sixteenth century. [From CATCH, to arrest, or stop, + POLE or POLL, the head.] Fourbesque, *foco* or *fuoco* = fire. *Cf.*, BUMBAILIFF.

1377. LANGL., *P. Pl.*, bk. XVIII., 46. *Crucifige*, quod a CACCHEPOLLE I warante hym a wicche. [M.]

c. 1510. BARCLAY, *Mrr. Good Mann.* (1570), G., iv. Be no towler, CATCHPOLL, nor customer.

1601. B. JOHNSON, *Poetaster*, III. CATCHPOLE, loose the gentlemen, or by my velvet arms, etc.

1751. SMOLLETT, *Peregrine Pickle*, ch. xcvii. The CATCHPOLE, after a diligent search, had an opportunity of executing the writ upon the defendant.

1859. SALA, *Gaslight and Daylight*, ch. xiii. You are brought there by a CATCHPOLE, and kept there under lock and key until your creditors are paid.

CATCH THE WIND OF THE WORD, *verbal phr.* (Irish).—To quickly understand the meaning of what is said. For synonyms, see TWIG.

CATCHY, *adj.* (colloquial).—Vulgarly or cheaply attractive; of a quality to take the eye or ear; easily caught and remembered (as a tune). Wrongly used in quot. 1885.

1831. *Fraser's Mag.*, III., 679. A CATCHY, stage-like effect. [M.]

1885. S. O. ADDY, in *N. and Q.*, 6 S., xii., 143. This seemed to be like one of those CATCHY questions which examiners in law and history are said to 'stump' the candidates.

CATERPILLAR, *subs.* (old).—A soldier. For synonyms, *see* MUDCRUSHER.

CATERWAUL, *verb* (colloquial).—Properly to make a noise like cats at rutting time; to woo, to 'make love.' The quotations show the process of transition from the old figurative usage of the word, to be 'in heat,' 'to be lecherous,' to the current sense. For synonyms, *see* FIRKYTOODLE.

1599. NASHE, *Lenten Stuffe*, in wks. V., 284. The friars and monks CATERWAWLD from the abbots and priors to the novices.

1700. CONGREVE, *Way of the World*, Act i., Sc. 9. An old aunt, who loves CATTERWAULING better than a conventicle.

1771. SMOLLETT, *Humphry Clinker*, l. 64. I hope you have worked a reformation among them [servant-maids], as I exhorted you in my last, and set their hearts upon better things than they can find in junketting and CATERWAULING with the fellows of the country.

1884. HAWLEY SMART, *Post to Finish.* ch. xvii. From what I hear, you came to Riddleton fooling after my daughter. Now, I'll have no CATERWAULING of that sort.

CATEVER, *subs.* (common). — A queer, or singular affair; anything poor or bad. [From the Lingua Franca, and Italian *cattivo*, bad.] Variously spelled by the lower orders.—*Hotten.*

CATFISH DEATH, *subs.* (American).—Suicide by drowning.

c. 1889. *Chicago Press* [quoted by Barrère]. . . . driving his sweetheart to lunacy and a CATFISH DEATH, by his dime-museum freaks.

CATGUT-SCRAPER, *subs.* (common).—A fiddler. [From CATGUT, the material of which fiddle-strings are made, + SCRAPER, one that rubs or scrapes. Sometimes simply SCRAPER or CATGUT; the latter of which is also used to signify the music produced. Also ROSIN-THE-BOW and TEASER OF THE CATGUT.

1633. MASSINGER, *Guardian* IV., ii. Wire-string and CATGUT, men and strong-breathed heautbois. [M.]

1785. BURNS, *Jolly Beggars*. Her charms had struck a sturdy caird, As weel's a poor GUT-SCRAPER.

1796. WOLCOT ('P. Pindar'), *Tristia*, wks. (1812) V., 267. Behold! the CATGUT-SCRAPER with his croud Commands at will the house of hospitality.

1851-61. H. MAYHEW, *London Lab. and Lon. Poor*, vol. I., p. 21. Or they will call to the orchestra, saying, 'Now then you CATGUT-SCRAPERS! Let's have a ha'purth of liveliness.'

CAT HARPING FASHION, *adv. phr.* (nautical).—*See* quot.

1785. GROSE, *Dict. Vulg. Tongue*. Drinking cross ways, and not as usual over the left thumb.

CAT HEADS, *subs.* (old). — The paps. For synonyms, *see* DAIRY.

CATHEDRAL, *subs.* (Winchester College).—A high hat. [So called because only worn when going to the Cathedral.] For synonyms, *see* GOLGOTHA.

Adj. (old). — Old-fashioned; antique.

1690. B. E., *Dictionary Canting Crew*. CATHEDRAL: old-fashioned, out of Date, Ancient.

1755. JOHNSON. CATHEDRAL: in low phrase, antique, venerable, old.

1785. GROSE, *Dictionary of the Vulgar Tongue*. CATHEDRAL: old-fashioned, an old CATHEDRAL bedstead, chair, etc.

CATHARINE PURITANS, *subs. phr.* (University). — Members of St. Catharine's Hall, at Cambridge. [PURITAN from the pun on the words CATHARINE and Καθαίρειν = to purify.] They were also called DOVES (*q.v.*).

CATHERINE HAYES, *subs.* (Australian).—*See* quot. [The derivation may presumedly be traced to the immense popularity of the Irish singer at the antipodes.]

1859. FRANK FOWLER, *Southern Light and Shadows*, p. 53. [A liquor consisting of] claret, sugar, and nutmeg.

CAT'S, *subs.* (University).—A short name for St. Catharine's Hall.

CAT'S MEN, *subs.* (University).—Members of St. Catharine's Hall

CATHERINE WHEEL.—*See* CARTWHEEL.

CAT-LAP, *subs.* (common).—Thin potations of any sort, especially tea. Such a beverage being so feeble as to be only fit for women. For synonyms, *see* SCANDAL BROTH.

1785. GROSE, *Dict. Vulg. Tongue*. CAT-LAP: tea, called also scandal broth.

1824. SCOTT, *Redgauntlet*, ch. xiii. We have tea and coffee aboard . . . You are at the age to like such CATLAP.

1864. M. E. BRADDON, *Aurora Floyd*, ch. xvii. 'I've mashed the tea for 'ee,' said the 'softy'; 'I thought you'd like a coop.' The trainer shrugged his shoulders. 'I can't say I'm particular attached to the CAT-LAP,' he said, laughing.

CAT-MARKET, *subs.* (common).—A number of people all talking at once. 'You make a row like a CAT-MARKET'—a general 'caterwauling.'

CAT-MATCH, *subs.* (old).—*See* quot.

1785. GROSE, *Dict. Vulg. Tongue*. CAT MATCH: when a rook or cully is engaged amongst bad bowlers.

CATOLLER or **CATOLLA,** *subs.* (old).—A noisy, prating fellow.—*See* quot.

1832. PIERCE EGAN, *Book of Sports*, p. 70. [CATOLLA is given as a foolish, betting man.]

CAT-O'-NINE-TAILS or **CAT,** *subs.* (common). — A nine-lashed scourge now used for the punishment of criminals, but until 1881 the authorised means of punishment in the British army and navy. [From CAT, a beast with claws, + O' + NINE TAILS, the nine knotted lashes. History is against the view of some military authorities that the CAT-O'-NINE-TAILS was a Batavian importation of William III., and that the word 'cat' is derived from the Sclavonic *kat*, an executioner, or from *katowae*, to lash or torture. Another theory is that it was introduced at the time of the Armada (1588), when vast numbers of these 'straunge whips' were found in the captured ships of the Spaniards. A ballad of the period declares of the Spaniards that—

> They made such whippes wherewith no man Would seeme to strike a dogge; So strengthened eke with brasen tagges And filde so roughe and thinne, That they would force at every lash The bloud abroad to spinne.

This view is not inconsistent with the quotations, the first of which antedates the earliest given in the *N.E.D.* by thirty years.] In prison parlance the CAT-O'-NINE-TAILS is known as NUMBER ONE or the NINE-TAILED BRUISER (*q.v.*), the birch as NUMBER TWO (*q.v.*).

1665. R. HEAD, *English Rogue*, pt. I., ch. iii., p. 28 (1874). A CAT OF NINE-TAILS (as he called it) being so many small cords.

1702. VANBRUGH, *False Friend*, prologue. You dread reformers of an impious age, You awful CAT-A-NINE TAILS to the stage.

1748. SMOLLETT, *Rod. Random*, ch. v. 'I'll bring him to the gangway, and anoint him with a CAT-AND-NINE-TAILS.'

1837. CARLYLE, *Fr. Rev.*, pt. III., bk. VII., ch. iii. Rash coalised kings, such a fire have ye kindled; yourselves fireless, your fighters animated only by drill-sergeants, mess-room moralities, and the drummer's CAT.

CAT-PARTY; also **BITCH-PARTY,** *subs.* (common).—A party consisting entirely of women. [From CAT, a woman, + PARTY.] *Cf.*, STAG-PARTY, and *see* HEN-PARTY for synonyms.

CATS, *subs.* (commercial).—Atlantic Seconds were formerly so-called for telegraphic purposes.

CATS AND DOGS. To RAIN CATS AND DOGS, sometimes extended to AND PITCHFORKS AND SHOVELS, *phr.* (popular). — To rain heavily. [The French *catadoupe*, a waterfall, has been suggested as the origin. Another etymon has been found in the Greek κατὰ δόξαν in reference to the downpour being out of the common. Possibly Swift, who seems to have been the first to have used the expression, may have evolved it out of his own description of a city shower (1710).

> Now from all parts the swelling kennels flow, And bear their trophies with them as they go. . . . Drown'd puppies, stinking sprats, all drench'd in mud, Dead cats, and turnip-tops, come tumbling down the flood.]

1738. SWIFT, *Pol. Convers.*, dial. 2. I know Sir John will go, though he was sure it would rain CATS AND DOGS.

1819 (Feb. 25). SHELLEY to PEACOCK, in *Letters*, etc. (Camelot), p. 264. After two months of cloudless serenity, it began raining CATS AND DOGS.

1837. BARHAM, *I. L.* (*Blasphemer's Warning*). But it rains CATS AND DOGS and you're fairly wet through Ere you know where to turn, what to say, or to do.

CAT'S FOOT. TO LIVE UNDER THE CAT'S FOOT, *phr.* (old).—To be under petticoat government; hen-pecked. *Cf.*, APRON-STRING.—*See* CAT'S-PAW.

CAT'S HEAD, *subs.* (Winchester College).—The end of a shoulder of mutton; further explained by quotation.

1870. MANSFIELD, *School-Life at Winchester College*, p. 84. His meal [dinner] took place at six o'clock p.m. in College (in Commoners' it was at *one*); it was ample in quantity, and excellent in quality. That of the Præfects was nicely served in joints, that of the Inferiors was divided into portions, (Dispars); there were, if I remember rightly, six of these to a shoulder, and eight to a leg of mutton, the other joints being divided in like proportion. All these 'Dispars' had different names; the thick slice out of the centre was called 'a Middle Cut,' that out of the shoulder a 'Fleshy,' the ribs 'Racks,' the loin 'Long Dispars'; these were the best, the more indifferent were the end of the shoulder, or CAT'S HEAD, the breast, or 'Fat Flab,' etc., etc.

CATSKIN-EARLS, *subs.* (parliamentary).—The three senior earls in the House of Lords, viz., the Earls of Shrewsbury, Derby, and Huntingdon, the only three earldoms before the seventeenth century now existing, save those that (like Arundel, Rutland, etc.), are merged in higher titles, and the anomalous earldom of Devon (1553), resuscitated in 1831. [A correspondent of *Notes and Queries* (7 S. ix., p. 314) suggests that the reason of the application may be that in the seventeenth or late in the sixteenth century an order was issued for the use of ermine instead of the skin of cats—(but were such skins then used?)—for the robes of a peer. If so, however, it is curious that there are not 'catskin dukes' and 'catskin barons' as well. There is yet another theory: an earl's robes consist (now) of but three rows of ermine; but in some early representations they are shown with four, the same as (now) a duke; and it has been suggested that these four rows (*quatre*-skins) may have given the name of catskin.]

1861-75. DEAN HOOK, *Life of Cardinal Pole*, *vide* note, p. 264. The Earl of Huntingdon is one of the three CATSKIN EARLS of the present day.

CAT'S-MEAT, *subs.* (common). — The lungs. [The 'lights' or lungs of animals are usually sold to feed cats.]

CATSO, *subs.* and *intj.* (old).—The *penis*. Murray says: 'Also CATZO. [*a.* It. *cazzo* = *membrum virile*. Also an exclamation, *Cf.*, the English ejaculation, BALLS! Florio says: 'also as *cazzica*, interjection, "What! God's me! God forbid! tush!"'] Frequent in seventeenth century in the Italian senses; also = rogue, scamp, cullion. *Cf.*, Fr. *cul*, *couillé* and *couillon* as terms of contempt; also *see* the later GADSO.

CAT'S-PAW or **CAT'S-FOOT,** *subs.* (common). — A dupe or tool. [A reference to the fable (*Bertrand et Raton*) of a monkey using the paw of a cat, dog, or fox, to pull roasted chestnuts off the fire, current in the sixteenth century, but varying considerably in details. The earliest printed version occurs in John Sambucus' *Emblemata* (Plantin, Antwerp, 1564), where the sufferer is a dog, and not a cat. There is, however, a story of the same kind told (Maiol. Coll. vii., *scil* Simon Maiolus, Astensis, Episcopus Vulturariensis, *Dies Caniculares, h.e. Colloquia XXIII., Physica*, Collog. vii., p. 249, Ursellis, 1600) of Pope Julius II., 1503-13 [*see N. and Q.*, 6 S., viii., 35.]

[1657. M. HAWKE. *Killing is murder.* These he useth as the Monkey did the CAT's PAW to scrape the nuts out of the fire.]

1782. GEO. PARKER, *Humorous Sketches*, p. 140. They lug in Spain, to their assistance, a CAT's-PAW made.

1815. SCOTT, *Guy Mannering*, ch. lvi. Sir Robert, who had rather begun to suspect that his plebeian neighbour had made a CAT's-PAW of him, inclined his head stiffly.

1878. M. E. BRADDON, *Cloven Foot*, ch. xli. He felt angry with himself for having been in some wise a CAT's-PAW to serve the young man's malice.

CAT-STICKS, *subs.* (old). — Thin legs. [In comparison to the stick used by boys in the game of tip-cat.] For synonyms *see* DRUM-STICKS.

1785. GROSE, *Dictionary of the Vulgar Tongue*, s.v.

CAT'S-WATER, *subs.* (common). — Gin. [From CAT, a woman + WATER, a white liquid.] *Cf.*, BITCHES' WINE = champagne. For synonyms, *see* DRINKS.

CATTIE, *adj.* and *adv.* (printers'). — An imperfect or 'smutty' look on a printed sheet, caused by an oily or unclean roller.

CATTING, *verbal subs.* (common). — 1. Vomiting. — *See* CAT, *verb.*

2. (venery). — Running after loose women; MOLROWING (*q.v.*) for synonyms.

1725. *New Canting Dictionary*. CATTING: whoring.

CATTLE, *subs.* (common). — A term of contempt applied to human beings. *Cf.*, QUEER CATTLE, KITTLE CATTLE. The generic names of the lower creation are pretty generally used in such transferred senses; *e.g.*, QUEER FISH, DOWNY BIRD, PIGEON, ROOK, SAD DOG, etc. In England mostly employed disparagingly, but in the U.S.A. BUG — here the name of one of the most offensive of vermin, but there the common term for all varieties of beetles—is used in a good sense; *e.g.*, BIG BUG.

1579. GOSSON, *School of Abuse*, p. 27 (Arber's ed.). We have infinite Poets, and Pipers, and suche peeuishe CATTEL among vs in Englande.

1600. SHAKSPERE, *As You Like It*, Act iii., Sc. 2, 435. Boyes and women are . . . . CATTLE of this colour.

188(?) G. R. SIMS, *Dagonet Ballads* ('Moll Jarvis'). Queer CATTLE is women to deal with? Lord bless ye, yer honour, they are!

[CATTLE is often said of horses. *See* Harrison Ainsworth's *Rookwood*: Have you any horses? Our Cattle are all blown. Also Goldsmith's *She Stoops to Conquer*.]

CATTLE-BUG, *subs.* (American). — *See* BUG, *subs.*, sense 4.

CAUDGE-PAWED, *adj.* (old). — Left-handed. — *Grose.*

CAUGHT ON THE FLY, *phr.* (American). — 'Caught in the act.' An equivalent of 'caught on the hop' or 'hip.' — *See* HOP.

CAULIFLOWER, *subs.* (old). — 1. A clerical wig supposed to resemble

a cauliflower; modish in the time of Queen Anne.

2. (old). — The female *pudendum*. For synonyms, *see* MONOSYLLABLE.

3. (popular). — The foaming head of a tankard of beer. In France, a glass of beer without any head is termed *un bock sans linge* or *sans faux-col*.

1882. *Daily Telegraph*, Oct. 10, p. 5, col. 4. This gave the porter a fine frothy or CAULIFLOWER head. [M.]

4. (military). — In *plural.* — The Forty-seventh Regiment of Foot, so called from its white facings. It is also known as THE LANCASHIRE LADS from its county title.

CAULK, *subs.* and *verb* (nautical). — 1. Sleep; to sleep. In substantive form it sometimes appears as CAULKING. To CAULK formerly meant 'to pick out a soft plank,' *i.e.*, to lie down on deck; to sleep with one's clothes on. [*Cf.*, BUNDLING.]

1836. MARRYAT, *Midshipman Easy*, ch. xix. But it's no go with old Smallsole, if I want a bit of CAULK.

1851. *Chambers' Papers*, No. 52, p. 30. Sleeping upon deck is called, I know not why, CALKING.

2. *Verb.* — To cease; to shut up; *i.e.*, to stop one's talk or leave off talking. [This usage is obviously derived from the legitimate meaning of the word, to stop up crevices and seams.] For synonyms, *see* STOW IT.

3. (common). — To copulate; to do the 'act of kind.' For synonyms, *see* RIDE.

CAULKER, *subs.* (common). — 1. A dram; a stiff glass of grog — generally applied to a finishing bumper. When this happens to be sherry and follows the drinking of red wines it is called a WHITEWASH (*q.v.*). [There are three suggested derivations: (1) that it is a punning reference to caulking, that which serves to keep out the wet; (2) because such a draught takes a deal of swallowing; and (3) that it is a corruption of CORKER (*q.v.*), a regular stopper.] For synonyms, *see* GO.

1808. J. MAYNE, *Siller Gun*, 89 (Jam.). The magistrates wi' loyal din, Tak off their CAU'KERS. [M.]

1836. M. SCOTT, *Cruise of the Midge*, ch vi. We . . . finished off with a CAULKER of good cognac.

1849. C. KINGSLEY, *Alton Locke*, ch. xxi. 'Take a CAULKER? Summat heavy, then?'

1871. A. FORBES, *My Experiences of the War between France and Germany*, II., p. 201. The Mobile officer joins us heartily in a CAULKER, and does not need to be pressed to take a little supper.

1884. W. C. RUSSELL, *Jack's Courtship*, ch. viii. The CAULKER of rum served out under the break of the poop by the light of a bull's-eye lamp.

2. (popular). — A lie; anything surprising or incredible. For synonyms, *see* WHOPPER.

1884. W. C. RUSSELL, *Jack's Courtship*, ch. xxxi. I also took care that she should never afterwards be able to charge me with having told her a real CAULKER.

CAUTION, *subs.* (popular). — A colloquialism used both of men and things. Anything out of the common, or that conveys a warning; something wonderful or staggering; something to be avoided. Anything that causes surprise, wonder, fear, or indeed any uncommon emotion, is a CAUTION to this, that, or the other.

At Oxford in 1865 it was employed to designate a 'guy' or 'cure.'

1835. C. F. HOFFMAN, *Winter in the West*, p. 234. The way the icy blast would come down the bleak shore was a CAUTION.

1853. WH. MELVILLE, *Digby Grand*, ch. ii. 'The way he cleaned out a southerner, a fine young Carolinian, who made a series of matches with him, was, as the Squire himself would have said, a CAUTION.'

1861. WHYTE MELVILLE, *Good for Nothing*, ch. i. Such a clench of the slender hand and stamp of the slender foot as constitute what our American friends term a CAUTION.

CAUTIONARY, *adj.* (American). — Pertaining to that which is a CAUTION (*q.v.*).

1843-4. HALIBURTON, *Sam Slick in England*. Well, the way the cow cut dirt was CAUTIONARY; she cleared stumps, ditches, windfalls, and everything.

CAVAULTING or CAVOLTING, *verbal subs.* (old). — Sexual intercourse. [From the Lingua Franca *cavolta*, the equivalent of HORSING or RIDING, both of which are frequently used in the same sense. Italian *cavaliero* = a rake or debauchee.] *Cf.*, CAVORT. For synonyms, *see* GREENS.

CAVAULTING SCHOOL, *subs.* (old). — A house of ill-fame. — *See* CAVAULTING, and for synonyms, *see* NANNY-SHOP.

CAVE or CAVE IN, *verb* (American). — To give way when opposition can no longer be maintained; to break down; to 'turn up.' [Derived from the practice of navvies in digging earthworks, when the lower part is undermined until it can no longer sustain the overhanging mass. Murray says all the earliest instances of CAVE IN, in print, are from America, and its literary use appears to have arisen there; but, as the word is given as East Anglian by Forby [1830], and is widely used in Eng. dialects, it is generally conjectured to have reached the U.S. from East Anglia.] The French has *barrer*; the Spanish *acomodarse*; and the Fourbesque *battere*.

ENGLISH SYNONYMS. To knuckle under; knock under; give in; sing small; turn it up; chuck it up; jack up; climb down (*q.v.*), throw up the sponge; chuck it; go down; go out; cut it; cut the rope (pugilistic), etc.

1837-40. HALIBURTON, *Sam Slick, Hum. Nat.*, 55 (Bartlett). He was a plucky fellow, and warn't a goin' to CAVE IN that way.

1862. BROWN ('Artemus Ward'), *His Book.* I kin CAVE in enny man's head that, etc.

1869. S. L. CLEMENS ('Mark Twain'), *Innocents at Home.* In the meantime the tropical sun was beating down and threatening to CAVE the top of my head IN.

1883. HAWLEY SMART, *Hard Lines*, ch. xxii. 'The Russians will CAVE when they find we are in earnest.'

CAVE! *intj.* (Eton College). — 'Beware!' A byword among boys out of bounds when a master is in sight. [From the Latin. The modern, 'beware of the dog' was rendered *cave canem* by the Romans.]

CAVIARE, *subs.* (literary). — The obnoxious matter 'blacked out' by the Russian Press Censor. Every foreign periodical entering Russia is examined for objectionable references or 'irreligious' matter, the removal whereof is accomplished in two ways. If the articles or items are bulky,

they are torn or cut out bodily. If they are brief, they are 'blacked out' by means of a rectangular stamp about as wide as an ordinary newspaper column, and 'cross-hatched' in such a way that, when inked and dabbed upon the paper, it makes a close network of white lines and black diamonds. The peculiar mottled or grained look of a page thus treated has suggested the attributive CAVIARE: a memory of the look of the black salted caviare spread upon a slice of bread and butter. A verb has been formed from the noun, and every Russian now understands that 'to caviare' = to 'black out.' Of course as long as the Russian Government permits the entry of letters without censorial examination, any citizen of St. Petersburg or Moscow can write to Berlin, Paris, or London, and ask to have cut out and forwarded in a sealed envelope either a particular article that has been CAVIARED, or all articles relating to Russia that may appear in any specified newspaper or magazine.

1890. *St. James's Gaz.*, 25 April, p. 7, col. 1. Every one of Mr. Kennan's articles in the *Century* has been CAVIARED.

CAVORT, *verb* (American). — To prance; to frisk; to run or ride in a heedless or purposeless manner. [From the Lingua Franca *cavolta* = prancing on horseback. Some, however, derive it from 'curvetting' = capering for show; there are also, as possible sources, the Spanish *cavar*, the pawing of a spirited horse; and the French *courbetter*.] — *See* CAVAULTING.

1848. *Major Jones's Courtship*, 41 (Bartlett). A whole gang . . . came ridin' up, and reinin' in, and prancin', and CAVORTIN'.

1883. BRET HARTE, *In the Carquinez Woods*, ch. i. 'If we hadn't been CAVORTING round this yer spot for the last half-hour I'd swear there was a shanty not a hundred yards away,' said the sheriff.

1889. *Puck's Library*, April, p. 12. Being an educated man, I feel ten thousand woes CAVORTING for the populace In illustrated clothes.

CAWBAWN. — *See* COBBON.

CAW HANDED, or CAW PAWED. — Awkward; not dexterous, ready or nimble. — *Grose* [1785].

CAXTON, *subs.* (theatrical). — A wig. [A corruption of CAXON, a kind of wig.] In Grose's time a CAXON signified an old weather-beaten wig. *Cf.*, CAULIFLOWER.

CAYUSE, *subs.* (American). — A nickname given by Mormon girls to young 'Latter Day Saints': the 'Yahoos' of the Gentiles. [The CAYUSE is properly the common Indian pony. In explanation, it must be noted that there exists among Americans a passionate love of horses. A near and dear friend, an old companion, or men and women whose traits of character command respect and homage, are familiarly 'horses.' A distinguished Kentuckian carried away by enthusiasm for Miss Kemble's acting, started to his feet, and with tremendous energy roared out, 'By heaven she's a "horse."'] *See* OLD HOG.

CAZ, *subs.* (thieves'). — Cheese. — [*See* CASSAN.]

1812. J. H. VAUX, *Flash Dictionary*. CAZ: cheese; 'As good as CAZ,' is a phrase signifying that any projected fraud or robbery may be easily and certainly accomplished.

CAZE, *subs.* (venery).—The female *pudendum.*

CEDAR, *subs.* (Eton College).—1. A pair-oared boat inrigged, without canvas, and very 'crank.' [From the material.]

2. (prison).—A pencil. [This, like the foregoing, is derived from the wood of which both are made.]

CELESTIAL POULTRY, *subs.* (popular).—Angels. [An allusion to the mythological wings of 'men out of the body.']

CELESTIALS, *subs.* (military).—The Ninety-seventh Regiment of Foot. [So nicknamed from its facings of sky blue.]

1856. *Notes and Queries*, 2 S., ii., p. 215. The 97th too is not mentioned by your correspondents as far as I have seen, the CELESTIALS.

1871. *Chambers' Journal*, Dec. 23, p. 801. 'CELESTIALS'—the facings of the . . . corps being sky blue.

2. *sing.* (common).—A 'turn-up' or 'pug' nose. For synonyms, *see* CONK.

3. (colloquial).—The Chinese. The Chinese Empire is spoken of as the Celestial Empire.

CELLIER, *subs.* (old).—An out-and-out, unmitigated lie. [A word of great interest, illustrating the temporary use for certain purposes of the name of a certain person, as in the cases of BURKE, BOYCOTT, BISHOP, and SALISBURY (*q.v.*). The Meal-tub Plot in 1680 was the concoction of Thomas Dangerfield and Elizabeth Cellier, a Roman Catholic midwife. Forged documents which Dangerfield hid in Colonel Mansel's lodgings were upon his deposition found there by Government officers; but the fraud was soon discovered, and Dangerfield was committed to Newgate. On his trial he endeavoured to throw the entire blame on Mrs. Cellier, and asserted that the original papers were all to be found in her house hidden in a meal tub. This turned out to be true, and Mrs. Cellier was committed to prison. On her trial she managed to prove that Dangerfield was wholly unworthy of credit, and her marvellous impudence and vigorous mendacity led to her own acquittal, and made her name for the time the equivalent of 'an out-and-out lie.' After her trial she thanked the jurors for giving her a good deliverance, and offered to 'serve their ladies with the same fidelity in *their* deliveries.'] For synonyms, *see* WHOPPER.

1682. *Pope's Harbinger*, p. 79. That's a CELIER, Sir, a modern and most proper phrase to signifie any Egregious Lye.

CELLAR-FLAP, *subs.* (common).—A step or dance performed within the compass of (say) a CELLAR-FLAP. The object of the Whitechapel artist in the dance is to achieve as many changes of step as possible without shifting his ground: his action being restricted to the feet and legs. An old equivalent is TO CUT CAPERS ON A TRENCHER; also DOUBLE-SHUFFLE (*q.v.*).

1877. *Five Years' Penal Servitude*, ch. iii., p. 219. Others again would indulge in a break-down, or CELLAR-FLAP dance, dreadfully to the discomfort of the men in the cells below.

CENT. NOT WORTH A CENT, *phr.*—*See* CARE and FIG.

CENT PER CENT, *subs.* (common).—A usurer. [Literally one who charges an exorbitant rate of interest, here symbolized as a hundred for every hundred. Quoted by Grose (1785).] For synonyms, *see* SIXTY PER CENT.

CENTRE-OF-BLISS, *subs.* (common).—The female *pudendum.* For synonyms, *see* MONOSYLLABLE.

CENTURION, *subs.* (cricket).—A batsman who scores a hundred runs. [From CENTURION, the commander of a 'century,' in the Roman Army.]

1886. *Graphic*, 31 July, p. 107, col. 2. Some other CENTURIONS have been Chatterton (108) for M.C.C., Shuter (103, not out) for Trent.

CENTURY, *subs.* (turf).—A hundred pounds; or at cricket, etc., a score of a hundred. Originally a division of the Roman Army numbering 100 men. In English it was and is in common use to signify a group of a hundred. Shakspeare, in *Cymbeline*, iv., 2, 391 [1611], writes a 'CENTURY' of prayers. *See* also A. C. Swinburne, *A Century of Rondels* and W. E. Henley, *A Century of Artists* (1889). *Cf.*, MONKEY, PONY, etc.

1864. *Derby Day*, p. 131. 'I'm open to a bet. I'll lay you an even CENTURY about Nimrod.'

1869. *Daily News*, July 29. 'Police Court Report.' After this he said he searched the breeches pockets that were lying by the side of the bed, and took HALF A CENTURY worth of property from them.

1883. *Echo*, Nov. 1, p. 4, col. 2. Golding, . . . purchased Passaic from F. Archer for a CENTURY.

1883. *Graphic*, August 11, p. 138, col. 2. His batting this year has been of the highest order, as witnesses among his many good performances that against the Players, when he marked his CENTURY.

CERT, *subs.* (sporting).—A certainty, of which it is an abbreviation. With special reference in racing circles to events looked upon as absolutely sure. Variants are A DEAD, or MORAL, CERTAINTY; A DEAD 'UN; and A MORAL.

1859. *Letter* from EDWARD S. TAYLOR to John Camden Hotten, 22 Dec. This edition will sell to a DEAD CERTAINTY.

1889. *Man of the World*, June 29. 'Love-in-Idleness is bound to take the Rous Memorial, and I hear Pioneer is a CERT. for the St. James's.'

CERTAINTIES, *subs.* (printers').—Infants of the male sex.—*See* UNCERTAINTIES.

CHAFE, *verb* (old).—To thrash soundly. [Chafe = 'to warm,' 'to rub with the hand.' *Cf.*, ANOINT.] For synonyms, *see* TAN.

1673. R. HEAD, *Canting Acad.*, p. 36

1785. GROSE, *Dictionary of the Vulgar Tongue.* CHAFED: well beaten.

CHAFER, *verb* (common).—To copulate. [Probably a corruption of CHAUVER.] For synonyms, *see* RIDE.

CHAFF, *subs.* (colloquial).—1. Ironical or sarcastic banter; fooling; humbug; ridicule. [A word of uncertain derivation, which, except in two instances, both doubtful, does not appear in English literature, in either its substantive or its verbal form, before the beginning of the present century. Of the two the substantive seems to be the

earlier. If this be correct, Murray thinks it may have arisen from a figurative employment of the orthodox word, in the sense of 'refuse,' 'worthless matter,' etc., connected with which is the proverb 'an old bird is not caught with chaff.' On the other hand there is an Arabic word *Jaf* or *chaf*, 'dry, withered' (like the Greek καρφος), used metaphorically and vulgarly in a sense similar to 'humbug.' To CHAFF a man is *vulgo*, to humbug him; for humbug, like chaff, is what may be scattered before the wind—what is light, trivial, or unfounded—an act of folly or knavery.—*See*, however, *verb*, sense 1.]

[Murray in dealing with this word leads off his illustrative quotations with one (*see* quot. 1648) which he thinks may be uncertainly placed, as it may mean 'scolding.' There is, however, another instance, which, though also uncertain, may be a link in the chain of evidence. In this case CHAFFING may bear its modern slang signification, though as has been said, it is open to another reading.]

For synonyms, *see* GAMMON, sense 1.

164(?). *The Downfall of Charing-Cross.* Percy Ballads, II., p. 327 [ed. 1765]. Undone, undone, the Lawyers are, They wander about the towne, Nor find the way to Westminster, Now Charing-Cross is downe: At the end of the Strand they make a stand, Swearing they are at a loss, And CHAFFING say that's not the way, They must go by Charing-Cross.

1648. JENKYN, *Blind Guide*, iv., 76. You pretend to nothing but CHAFFE and scoffes. [M.]

1821. *The Fancy*, vol. I., 250. He could not of course put up with CHAFF in the streets.

1853. *Diogenes*, II., 79. 'Maxims for Cabmen' If you want oats for your horses you must cease giving CHAFF to your passengers.

1864. *Athenæum*, 29 Oct., No. 1931, p. 557, col. 3. Julius Cæsar passed his boyhood in a vicious locality, where cant phrases abounded, but the latter are not recorded. We have heard of the *Famæ non nimium bonæ puellæ, Quales in mediâ sedent Suburrâ*—but we hear only faint echoes of the CHAFF that was scattered thereupon by the passers-by.

1890. *Globe*, Feb. 13, p. 5, col. 2. The extract you send to me from some letter from Lord Rosebery about the House of Lords looks to me very like CHAFF, and was probably intended as such.

2. (Christ's Hospital).—A small article or plaything, *e.g.*, 'a pocket CHAFF.' Connected with 'chattel,' 'chapman,' etc. —*Blanch.* *Cf.*, *verbal* (sense 2), *adjectival*, and *interjectional* senses.

Verb.—1. To banter; to jest; to 'gammon' or 'quiz.' An analogous term formerly in use was QUEER (*q.v.*). So also CHAFFING and CHAFFINGLY. For synonyms, *see* GAMMON, sense 1.

1851. MAYHEW, *Lon. Lab. and Lon. Poor*, I., p. 35. Though he's only twelve years old he'll CHAFF down a peeler so uncommon severe that the only way to stop him is to take him in charge.

1864. H. AÏDÉ, *Mr. and Mrs. Faulconbridge*, I., 279. 'Pshaw!' said Sir Richard, with a lofty good humour, 'Don't CHAFF your uncle, sir.'

1889. T. MACKAY, on 'Shoeblacks,' in *Times*, Aug., p. 135. I have known courageous men who would rather try to CHAFF a bus driver than a shoeblack.

2. (Christ's Hospital).—To exchange small articles. *Cf.*, *subs.* sense.

1877. W. H. BLANCH, *Blue-coat Boys*, p. 96. CHAFF me your knife.

Adj. (Christ's Hospital).—Pleasant; glad. Sometimes CHAFFY. *Cf.*, *subs.*, sense 2.

Intj. (Christ's Hospital).—An exclamation signifying joy or pleasure.

CHAFF-CUTTER, *subs.* (old).—A back-biter or slanderer.

CHAFFER, *subs.* (colloquial).—1. One given to chaffing. [From CHAFF (*q.v.*) + ER.]

1851-61. H. MAYHEW, *London Labour and London Poor*, vol. I., p. 357. She was considered to be the best CHAFFER on the road; not one of them could stand against her tongue.

1877. *Temple Bar*, p. 536. An actor of very moderate abilities, and so remarkably ill-favoured in person as to be the constant butt of the CHAFFERS in the pit.

2. (popular).—The mouth, [*i.e.*, the organ of chaff, or 'ropery.'] For synonyms, *see* POTATO-TRAP. Also, the tongue.

1821. W. T. MONCRIEFF, *Tom and Jerry*, Act ii., Sc. 3. *Bob.* Suppose we haves a drain o' heavy wet, just by way of cooling our CHAFFERS—mine's as dry as a chip.

1822. DAVID CAREY, *Life in Paris*, p. 194. For there you may damp your CHAFFER In fifty different ways.

TO MOISTEN ONE'S CHAFFER, *phr.* (common).—To drink. [*See* CHAFFER, sense 2.] For synonyms, *see* LUSH.

CHAFFING-CRIB, *subs.* (old).—The place where a man receives his intimates; his 'den,' 'snuggery,' or 'diggings.' [*Cf.*, CHAFF. From CHAFFING, light talk, + CRIB, a place of sojourning.] For synonyms, *see* DIGGINGS.

1821. MONCRIEFF, *Tom and Jerry.* *Jerry.* CHAFFING CRIB! I'm at fault, coz, can't follow. *Tom.* My prattling parlour—my head quarters, coz, where I unbend with my pals.

CHAFFY, *adj.* (colloquial).—Full of banter. [From CHAFF, *subs.*, + Y.]

1889. *Bird o' Freedom*, Aug 7, p. 3. CHAFFY answers were all he got at first.

CHAINED or **CHAIN LIGHTNING**, *subs.*—(American).—Whiskey of the vilest description—a spirit 'warranted to kill at forty rods.' Hence FORTY ROD LIGHTNING, STONE-FENCE, RAILROAD, ROT-GUT, and KILL-THE-CARTER (Scots). For synonyms, *see* DRINKS. In the Western States of America, what is known as forked lightning in England, is called CHAIN-LIGHTNING, from its forming a sequence of zig-zags.

1871. DE VERE, *Americanisms* p. 215. The worst of lickers, as the sign-boards often have it in unconscious irony, is called CHAIN-LIGHTNING, from its terrible strength and stunning effect.

CHAIN-GANG, *subs.* (thieves').—Jewellers; watch-chain makers. The French argot has *un boguiste* (thieves') and *un chaîniste.*

CHAIR. TO PUT IN THE CHAIR, *phr.* (cab-drivers').—*See* quot.

1864. *Social Science Review*, I., 408. A Justice's order is sufficient for the committal to prison of a cab hirer (driver) who will not or cannot pay. . . Some hirers who become inured to prison discipline and prison fare get altogether hardened, and boast of the number of owners whom they have PUT IN THE CHAIR or in polite English neglected to pay.

CHAIRMARKING, *verbal subs.* (cab-owners').—Inserting the date in a cab-driver's licence in words instead of figures: or, endorsing it in an unusually bold, heavy hand: a hint to possible employers that the holder is undesirable. In other trades it is understood that an unexceptionable character, with the adjectives carefully underlined, is to be read as implying just the opposite of what it appears to say.

1890. *Pall Mall Gazette*, Sept. 15. A correspondent writes to protest against the heading 'A Cabman's Odd Complaint,' which was given in these columns on Saturday to a paragraph concerning the CHAIR-MARKING of a licence.

CHALDESE, *verb* (old).—To trick, cheat, or 'take in.' [Thought to be from 'Chaldee,' in allusion to astrology. *Cf.*, to JEW.] For synonyms, *see* STICK.

1664. BUTLER, *Hudibras*, II., iii., 1010. He stole your cloak and pick'd your pocket, Chows'd and CALDES'D you like a blockhead.

1680. *Rem.* (1759), I., 24. Asham'd, that Men so grave and wise, Should be CHALDES'D by Gnats and Flies. [M.]

1697. DENNIS, *Plot and No Plot*, I. I CALDES'D a Judge while he was taking my Depositions. [M.]

CHALK, *subs.* (colloquial).—1. A score, reckoning; and (in a more decidedly slang sense) BY CHALKS, MANY CHALKS, LONG CHALKS, etc., *i.e.*, 'degrees' or 'marks'; also 'credit,' or 'tick.' *Cf.*, CLOCK STOPPED.

1529. SKELTON, *El. Rummyng*, 613. We're fayne with a CHALKE To score on the balke. [M.]

1592. NASHE, *P. Penilesse*, B j b. Hee that hath no money must goe and dine with Sir John best betrust, at the signe of the CHALKE and the Post.

1634. S. R., *Noble Soldier*, v., 3, in Bullen's *O. Pl.*, I., 333. There's lesse CHALKE upon you[r] score of sinnes. [M.]

1704. T. BROWN, *Lat. on Fr. King*, wks. (1730) I., 60. I trespassed most enormously in CHALK. [M.]

1719. D'URFEY, *Pills* (1872), I., 270. This wheedling talk you fancy will rub out my CHALK.

1838-40. HALIBURTON, *The Clockmaker* (ed. 1862), p. 102. They reckon themselves here a CHALK above us Yankees . . .

1864-5. EDMUND YATES, *Broken to Harness*, I., p. 174. 'Can you say that I have deceived or thrown you over in any way? Never!' 'Thank God for that!' says the girl, with some bitterness; 'for that's a CHALK in my favor, at least.'

2. (nautical).—A scratch or scar. *Cf.*, *verb*, sense 2, and CHALKERS, sense 1.

1840. MARRYAT, *Poor Jack*, vi. I got this CHALK.

Adj. (turf).—Unknown or incompetent. [From the practice at race-meetings of keeping blank slides at the telegraph board on which the names of new jockeys can be inscribed in chalk, while the names of well-known men are usually painted or printed in permanent characters. The former were called CHALK-jockeys, and the general public argued that they were incompetent, being unknown.]

Verb (old).—1. To score up, or tick off, in chalk, a material at one time handier than pen-and-ink. Subsequently in pugilistic circles merit marks, etc., were made with the same.

2. (nautical).—To make one 'stand treat' or 'pay his footing.' If an old hand succeeds in CHALKING the shoes of a green hand, the latter has to 'stand drinks all round.'

3. (thieves').—To strike, *Cf.*, CHALKERS, sense 1.

1822. SCOTT, *Fortunes of Nigel*, ch. xvii. (II., p. 84). CHALK him across the peepers with your cheery [which, translated, means slash him over the eyes with your dagger].

TO CHALK UP, OR TO CHALK IT UP, *phr.* (common).—To credit, or take credit; to put to one's account.

1597. *1st Pt. Return Parnass.*, I., i., 451. All my debts stande CHAUKT UPON the poste for liquor. [M.]

1611. CHAPMAN, *May-Day*, Act I., p. 278 (*Plays*, 1874). Faith, sir, she [hostess] has CHALKED UP twenty shillings already, and swears she will CHALK no more.

1843. *Punch's Almanack*, Jan. . . . 'When you wish for beer resort freely to the CHALK, and go on, getting as much as you can upon this principle, until it becomes unproductive, when you may try it in another quarter.'

TO BEAT BY LONG OR MANY CHALKS, *phr.* (common).—To beat thoroughly; to show appreciable superiority.

1837. R. H. BARHAM, *Ingoldsby Legends* (ed. 1862), p. 447. Still Sir Alured's steed was BY LONG CHALKS the best Of the party, and very soon distanced the rest.

1838-40. HALIBURTON, *The Clockmaker*, p. 26 (ed. 1826). 'Yes,' says he, 'your factories down East beat all natur; they go ahead on the English a LONG CHALK.'

1856. C. BRONTË, *Professor*, ch. iii. 'You are not as fine a fellow as your plebeian brother BY A LONG CHALK.'

1883. GRENVILLE MURRAY, *People I Have Met*, p. 133. The finest thing in the world; or, as he himself would have expressed it, 'the best thing out BY MANY CHALKS.'

TO WALK OR STUMP ONE'S CHALKS, *phr.* (popular).—To move or run away; to be off. [Said to be a corruption of 'walk! you're chalked,' the origin of which is found in the ancient practice of lodgings for the royal retinue being taken arbitrarily by the marshal and sergeant-chamberlain, when the inmates were sent to the right about, and their houses designated by a chalk mark. When Mary de Médicis came to England in 1638, Sieur de Labat was employed to mark 'all sorts of houses commodious for her retinue in Colchester.' The same custom is referred to in the *Life and Acts of Sir William Wallace*, To STUMP (*q.v.*) = to go on foot.] For synonyms, *see* AMPUTATE.

1840. HALIBURTON, *Clockmaker*, 3 S., ch. xi. 'The way she WALKS HER CHALKS ain't no matter. She is a regular fore-and-after.'

1843. *Comic Almanack*, p. 366. And since my future walk's chalk'd out—at once I'll WALK MY CHALKS.

1871. DE VERE, *Americanisms*, p. 318. The President, in whom he is disappointed for one reason or another, does not come up to chalk; when he dismisses an official, he is made to WALK THE CHALK.

TO BE ABLE TO WALK A CHALK, *phr.* (popular).—To be sober. [The ordeal on board ship of trying men suspected of drunkenness is to make them walk along a line chalked on the deck, without deviating to right or left. *Cf.*, MAKING CHALKS and TOE THE LINE (*q.v.*).]

MAKING CHALKS, *phr.* (nautical cadets').—A term connected with the punishment of boys on board ship, and in the Royal Naval School. Two chalk lines are drawn wide apart on the deck or floor, and the boy to be punished places a foot on each of these lines, and stoops, thereby presenting a convenient section of his person to the boatswain or master.

TO CHALK THE LAMP-POST, *phr.* (American).—To bribe. For synonyms, *see* GREASE THE PALM.

1857. *Boston Post*, March 5. CHALKING THE LAMP POST. 'The term for bribery in Philadelphia.'

There are other expressions connected with chalk, such as 'to know chalk from cheese,' 'to chalk out,' etc., but these hardly find a place here.

CHALKERS, *subs.* (old).—1. Men of wit in Ireland, who in the night amuse themselves with cutting inoffensive passengers across the face with a knife. They are somewhat like those facetious gentlemen, some time ago known in England by the title of sweaters and mohocks.—*Grose. See Ireland Sixty Years Since* (*p.* 15).

2. *sing.* (common).—A London milkman.—*See* quot. [One who mixes with chalk—an obvious innuendo.] *Cf.*, COW WITH THE IRON TAIL and SIMPSON'S COW.

1865. *Daily Telegraph*, Sept. 7 (?). It is an ominous fact that London milkmen are known in the vocabulary of slang as CHALKERS.

CHALK-FARM, *subs.* (rhyming-slang).—The arm.

ENGLISH SYNONYMS. Bender; hoop-stick; fin; daddle.

FRENCH SYNONYMS. *L'anse* (popular: in old French cant *anse* signified the 'ear'); *les allumettes* (popular: 'the arms'); *l[a]'aile* or *l[e]'aileron* (popular: in the Fourbesque *ala*); *les nageoires* (plural).

ITALIAN SYNONYMS. *Ala* ('a wing'); *barbacana* (literally a kind of advanced fortification); *tarentule* (the Italian has *tarantello*, 'a spider

SPANISH SYNONYMS. *Bracio*; *remo* (properly 'an oar').

CHALK-HEAD, *subs.* (old).—A nickname for a person with a 'good head for figures.' Waiters in London are very commonly so called.—*See* quot. 1861. [From the 'chalks' or score formerly marked up behind a tavern bar, the 'tally' being 'kept in the head' instead of being 'chalked up' on a board or slate.]

1856. *Punch*, vol. XXXI., p. 134. *Billy.* You see, Billy, my heddication war summat neglected, and I haven't got the nateral adwantage of a good CHALK-HEAD.

1861. *Punch*, vol. XLI., p. 129. Among tavern waiters a ready reckoner is called a good CHALK-HEAD.

CHAM or **CHAMMY**, *subs.* (popular).—An abbreviation of 'champagne.' For synonyms, *see* DRINKS. *Cf.*, BOY.

1871. *All the Year Round*, Feb. 18, p. 285. 'Let's have glasses round. Come and have a bottle of CHAM.'

CHAMBER OF HORRORS, *subs. phr.*—1. (parliamentary).—The Peeresses' Gallery in the House of Lords. *Cf.*, CAGE, sense 4.

1876. *Daily News.* There could be no doubt as to the inconvenience, the gallery being generally known as the CHAMBER OF HORRORS.

2. In *plural* (common).—Sausages. [From the possibility of adulteration in this species of food. Also BAGS OF MYSTERY, and SHARP'S ALLEY BLOODWORMS.] In Fourbesque, *carbonata*.

CHAMMING, *verbal subs.* (common).—Indulgence in champagne. [From CHAM, *verb* (on the model of 'to wine,' 'to beer,' etc.), to drink champagne, + ING.]

CHANCE. TO HAVE AN EYE TO THE MAIN CHANCE, *phr.* (colloquial). To keep in view that which will result in advantage, interest or gain. [Thought to have originated in the phraseology of the game of hazard.] Murray, quoting from the *Dict. Cant. Crew*, says that 'to have an eye to the main chance' was a cant phrase in 1699, and that the expression still partakes of the character. All the quotations given in the *N.E.D.* prior to 1699, illustrate a simpler form of the colloquialism, such as to 'stand to the main chance,' but it will be seen that TO HAVE AN EYE TO THE MAIN CHANCE is more than a hundred years older.

1609. JONSON, *Case is Altered*, IV., 4. Juniper, to the door; AN EYE TO THE MAIN CHANCE. [*Removes the dung, and shews him the gold.*]

1693. DRYDEN, *Persius*, VI., 158. Be careful still of the MAIN CHANCE, my son; Put out the principal in trusty hands.

1711. *Spectator*, No. 196. I am very young, and yet no one in the world, dear sir, has the MAIN CHANCE more in HER HEAD than myself.

1844. DICKENS, *Martin Chuzzlewit*, ch. xviii., p. 190. 'Was it politics? Or was it the price of stock?' 'The MAIN CHANCE, Mr. Jonas, the MAIN CHANCE, I suspect.'

CHANCER, *subs.* (tailors').—A liar. Also an incompetent workman: *i.e.*, one who 'chances' what he cannot do.

CHANCERY. IN CHANCERY, *adv. phr.* (common).—'To have or get your man in chancery' is to get his head under your left arm so that you can FIB (*q.v.*) him with your right until he gets it out, or you GO TO GRASS (*q.v.*) together. Primarily pugilistic. Figuratively the expression = in a parlous case; in an awkward fix. The French have adopted the phrases *mettre en chancellerie* and *coup de chancellerie* which are almost literal translations.

1819. THOMAS MOORE, *Tom Crib's Memorial to Congress*, p. 77. Lord St-w-rt's a hero (as many suppose) and the Lady he woos is a rich and a rare one; his *heart* is IN CHANCERY, every one knows, and so would his *head* be, if thou wert his fair one.

1845. *Punch*, vol. IX., p. 9. 'Lord Brougham's Handbook for Political Boxing' Getting the nob INTO CHANCERY is a fine achievement, I once got several nobs INTO CHANCERY: and I certainly gave several of them severe punishment. This CHANCERY manœuvre has been a capital thing for me.

1860. *Chambers' Journal*, vol. XIII., p. 15. Marsden suffered him to approach within distance, dashed his outstretched arms away, and received his transatlantic head INTO CHANCERY.

1883. *Daily News*, 9 Mar., p. 3, col. 7. Thinking the man was a burglar he rode up to assist, and saw the constable holding Burtenshaw, and striking him. The constable had the prisoner IN CHANCERY.

CHANCE THE DUCKS, *phr.* (common).—An expression signifying 'come what may.' [From the colloquial use of CHANCE, to risk, or take one's chance of + DUCKS (*q.v.*), probably a pleonasm. *Cf.*, PLEASE THE PIGS.

1886. T. RATCLIFFE, in *N. and Q.*, 7 S., i., 108. An' CHANCE THE DUCKS—this when a man makes up his mind to a risky venture. He will say, 'I'll do it, an' CHANCE TH' DUCKS.'

CHANCE YOUR ARM, *phr.* (tailors').—'Chance it!' 'Try it on!' etc.—[*See* CHANCE THE DUCKS,—of which it seems a variant.]

CHANEY-EYED, *adj.* (common).—One-eyed. [From CHANEY, a corruption of 'China' or 'Chinese'; hence, eyes as small as those of the Celestials.] *Cf.*, SQUINNY-EYED.

CHANGE.—This word, in the sense of coins of one denomination given in exchange for those of another is responsible for several expressive colloquialisms.

TO GIVE CHANGE, *phr.* (common).—To 'pay out'; to give one his deserts. *Cf.*, TO TAKE ONE'S CHANGE OUT OF.

TO HAVE ALL ONE'S CHANGE ABOUT ONE, *phr.* (common).—To be clever; quick-witted; quite '*compos mentis*'; with 'twelve pence to the shilling about one.'

TO PUT THE CHANGE ON, *phr.* (old).—To deceive, or mislead.

Apparently for a long time a contemporary variant of TO RING THE CHANGES.

1667. DRYDEN, *Sir Martin Marr-all*, Act ii. *Warn.* . . . By this light, she has PUT THE CHANGE UPON HIM! O, sweet womankind! how I love thee for that heavenly gift of lying!

1671. R. HEAD, *English Rogue*, pt. I., ch. xvi., p. 168 (1874). The box-keeper shall walk off, pretending some speedy dispatch of a business concerning the House of Office, etc., whilst your antagonist shall PUT THE CHANGE UPON YOU.

1694. CONGREVE, *Double Dealer*, v., 17. I have so contriv'd that Mellefont will presently, in the chaplain's habit, wait for Cynthia in your dressing-room; but I have PUT THE CHANGE UPON her, that she may be otherwise employed.

1821. SCOTT, *Kenilworth*, ch. iii. You cannot PUT THE CHANGE ON me so easy as you think, for I have lived among the quick-stirring spirits of the age too long to swallow chaff for grain.

TO RING THE CHANGES, *phr.* (common).—To change a better article for a worse. [An allusion to bell-ringing where it signifies to exhaust the combinations of a peal of bells.] In its slang sense TO RING THE CHANGES chiefly refers to the passing of counterfeit money. As thus:—'About five weeks ago, the prisoner went into a tobacconist's shop in Cheapside, and purchased a cheroot, tendering a sovereign in payment. The prosecutor, Mr. Elkin, gave him the change, half-a-sovereign and 9s. 6d. silver. The prisoner said he did not want to distress him by taking away all his silver, and asked for another half sovereign. The prosecutor put down half-a-sovereign, which the prisoner took up, and the latter then said that if he returned the sovereign, he would give him back the change, and the prosecutor, taken off his guard, did so, and received the first half sovereign and the 9s. 6d. in silver, the prisoner walking out of the shop with the second half sovereign.'

1661. *Hist. of Eng. Rebellion* in *Harl. Misc.* (ed. Park), II., 528. Five months ago, our mighty States Were pleas'd to vote *No King*; But two months since, to act new cheats, Their votes the CHANGES RING.

1760. SMOLLETT, *Sir L. Graves*, vol. I., ch. x. Hugging in and RINGING OUT THE CHANGES on the balance of power, the Protestant religion, and your allies on the Continent.

1828. JON. BEE, *Picture of London*, p. 232. He found one piece [of muslin] that was indeed real India, bargained for and bought it, amidst continued attempts to shuffle it between others, for the purpose of RINGING THE CHANGES, as they term the nefarious act.

1877. *Five Years' Penal Servitude*, ch. iii., p. 234. Nothing easier than for some man to have slipped out of bed, night or day, and RUNG THE CHANGES of the bottles.

1880. HAWLEY SMART, *Social Sinners*. ch. xli. The culprit had been guilty of RINGING THE CHANGES or other petty larceny.

TO TAKE THE CHANGE OUT OF [a person or thing], *phr.* (common).—To be revenged upon; to take an equivalent, or *quid pro quo*. Frequently used interjectionally — TAKE YOUR CHANGE OUT OF THAT! with a blow or other rejoinder. An analogous expression is PUT THAT IN YOUR PIPE AND SMOKE IT!

1829. JOHN WILSON, *Noctes Amb.*, wks. II., 174. *Shepherd* (flinging a purse of gold on the table). It'll require a gey strang thaw to melt that, chiels; sae TAK YOUR CHANGE OUT O' THAT, as Joseph [Hume] says, either in champagne, or jile . . . . just whatsumever you like to devour best.

1838. HALIBURTON, *Clockmaker*, 2 S., ch. viii. 'Thinks I to myself, TAKE YOUR CHANGE OUT O' THAT, young man, will you?'

1854. WHYTE MELVILLE, *General Bounce*, ch. xi. If his ammunition be

exhausted he betakes himself to the bayonet, and swears 'the beggars may TAKE THEIR CHANGE OUT OF THAT.

1861. H. KINGSLEY, *Ravenshoe*, ch. xlvi. Turn Lady Ascot once fairly to bay, you would (if you can forgive slang) GET VERY LITTLE CHANGE OUT OF HER.

1863. H. KINGSLEY, *Austin Elliott*, I., 185. Cabman, *log*: 'I never said nothink to you, but without provocation you tell me to go to Putney. Now, I tell you what it is, *I'm blessed if I don't go*, and you may TAKE YOUR CHANGE OUT OF THAT!' And go he did. [*Cf.*, 'GO TO PUTNEY' (*q.v.*).]

QUICK CHANGE ARTISTE, *subs.* (music hall).—A performer, male or female, who sings one song in one costume, retires for a few seconds and returns to sing another in another guise, and so on.

CHANGE-BAGS, *subs.* (Eton).—Grey flannel trousers for cricket, and knickerbockers for football.

CHANGE ONE'S NOTE or **TUNE**, *verbal phr.* (colloquial). — To pass from laughter to tears, or from arrogance to humility; to alter one's mode of speech, behaviour, etc. *Cf.*, CHANGE YOUR BREATH (*q.v.* under BREATH).

1578. *Scot. Poems, 16th c.* (1808), II. 185. Priestes CHANGE YOUR TUNE. [M.]

1708. MOTTEUX, *Rabelais*, V., ix. I'll make him CHANGE HIS NOTE presently.

CHANGE YOUR BREATH.—*See* BREATH.

CHANT or **CHAUNT**, *subs.* (old).—1. *See* quots.

1812. J. H. VAUX, *Flash Dictionary*. CHAUNT: a song . . . To throw off a rum CHAUNT is to sing a good song.

1882. *Daily Telegraph*, 19 Oct., p 5, col. 2. To troll his jovial CHAUNTS . . . in a tavern-parlour. [M.]

2. (old).—*See* quots.

1812. J. H. VAUX, *Flash Dict.* CHAUNT: (a person's) name, address, or designation; . . . a cipher, initials, or mark of any kind, on a piece of plate, linen, or other article; anything so marked is said to be CHANTED . . . an advertisement in a newspaper or handbill, etc.

1824. *Compl. Hist. Murder Mr. Weare*, 258. 'We may as well look and see if there is any CHAUNT about the money'—and they examined the four notes, but there were no marks upon them. [M.]

Verb (old). — 1. To talk; sing; relate the praises of; to 'cry' or 'crack up.' Street patterers and vendors CHANT their songs and wares, oftentimes to an extent not warranted by their quality: hence sense 2. An equivalent amongst French thieves is *pousser la goualante*.

1851. MAYHEW, *London Labour and London Poor*, I., p. 240. A running patterer . . . who also occasionally CHAUNTS.

2. (common).—To sell a horse by fraudulent representations. [Apparently an extended usage of sense 1—'to cry' or 'crack up.'] Fr., *enrosser* = to dissemble a horse's faults.

1816. *Sporting Magazine*, vol. XLIX., p. 305. A number of frauds have been practised lately in the disposal of horses . . . by a gang of . . . swindlers, who technically call it CHAUNTING horses.

1825. *English Spy*, vol. I., pp. 199, 200. Here a church militant is seen Who'd rather fight than preach, I ween, Once major now a parson; With one leg in the grave he'll laugh, CHANT up a prad, or quaintly chaff To keep life's pleasant farce on.

1860. THACKERAY, *Philip*, ch. xx. You may as well say that horses are sold in heaven, which, as you know, are groomed, are doctored, are CHANTED on to the market, and warranted by dexterous horse-vendors as possessing every quality of blood, pace, temper, age.

CHANTER (generally **HORSE-CHANTER**), *subs.* (common). — 1. A horse-dealer who disposes of horses by means of fradulent representations.

1821. W. T. MONCRIEFF, *Tom and Jerry*, Act. i., Sc. 6. Grooms, Jockies, and CHAUNTERS, to Tattersall's bring.

1836. DICKENS, *Pickwick*, xlii., 365. 'He *was* a HORSE-CHAUNTER: he's a leg now.'

1845. W. M. THACKERAY, *Miscellanies*, II. ('Leg. of the Rhine'), p. 88. He is a cogger of dice, a CHANTER of horse-flesh.

1857. DICKENS, *Dorrit*, bk. I., ch. xii., 88. The Plaintiff was a CHAUNTER—meaning, not a singer of anthems, but a seller of horses.

1884. *Daily News*, August 23, p. 5, col. 1. It is for the CHANTER and his attendant bonnet, who officiates as groom, to place the stock.

1890. W. E. HENLEY. *Views and Reviews*, p. 137. An apple woman to mystify, a horse-CHANTER to swindle, a pugilist to study, etc., etc.

2. (vagrants').—A street patterer. More commonly spelt CHAUNTER (*q.v.*).

3. (Scots).—The *penis*.

CHANTEY or **SHANTY**, *subs.* (nautical).—A song sung by sailors at their work.—*See* CHANTEY-MAN. [Obviously a diminutive of CHANT, a song.]

1869. *Chambers' Journal*, 11 Dec., pp. 794-6. [Article on 'Sailors' SHANTIES and Sea-Songs.']

1883. W. CLARK RUSSELL, *Sailors' Language*, preface, xi. But the lack of variety is no obstruction to the sailor's poetical inspiration when he wants the 'old man' to know his private opinions without expressing them to his face, and so the same CHANTEY, as the windlass or halliard chorus is called, furnishes the music to as many various indignant remonstrances as Jack can find injuries to sing about.

1884. W. C. RUSSELL, *Jack's Courtship*, ch. iii. 'Then give us one of the old CHANTEYS,' exclaimed my uncle. 'Haul the Bowline,' or 'Whiskey, Johnny.'

CHANTEY-MAN, *subs.* (nautical).—A singer of CHANTEYS (*q.v.*).

1887. *Saturday Review*, 27 August. A shanty, or, as pedants call it, 'chanty,' is a song sung by sailors at their work. The music is 'to a certain extent traditional,' the words — which are commonly unfit for ears polite—are traditional likewise. The words and music are divided into two parts—the 'shanty' proper, which is delivered by a single voice, with or without a fiddle *obligato*, and the refrain and chorus, which are sung with much straining and tugging, and with peculiar breaks and strange and melancholy stresses, by a number of men engaged in the actual performance of some piece of bodily labour. The manner is this. We will suppose for instance, that what is wanted is an anchor song. The fugleman takes his stand, fiddle in hand, and strikes up the melody of 'Away Down Rio.' Then, everything being ready, he pipes out a single line of the song, and the working party, with a strong pull at the capstan-bars, answers with a long-drawn 'Away Down Rio. He sings a second verse, and this is followed by the full strength of the chorus. . . . And so on, through stave after stave, till the anchor's weighed, and, the work being done, the need for song is gone by.

1890. W. E. HENLEY. *Views and Reviews*, p. 153. He goes down to the docks and loiters among the galiots and brigantines; he hears the melancholy song of the CHANTEY-MAN.

CHANTIE, *subs.* (Scots). — A chamber - pot. For synonyms, *see* IT.

CHANTING (more commonly **HORSE-CHANTING**), *verbal subs.* (common).—1. Tricking into the purchase of unsound or vicious horses.

1825. *English Spy*, vol. I., pp. 199, 200. The servant was a confederate, and the whole affair nothing more than a true orthodox farce of HORSE-CHAUNTING got up for the express purpose of raising a temporary supply.

1870-2. *Gallery of Comicalities.* If I have got an 'orse to sell, You'll never find that Dick is wanting; There's few that try it on so well, Or beat me at a bit of CHAUNTING.

2. (vagrants').—Street ballad-singing.

1851. MAYHEW, *London Labour and London Poor*, I., p. 297. There is a class of ballads, which may with perfect propriety be called street ballads, as they are written by street authors for street singing (or CHAUNTING) and street sale.

1883. *Daily Telegraph*, Feb. 8, p. 3, col. 1. 'The bitterest sort of weather is their [cadgers'] weather, and it doesn't matter if it's house-to-house work or CHANTING, or mud-plunging, it's cold work.'

CHAPEL or **CHAPEL OF EASE**, *subs.* (common).—A water-closet. For synonyms, *see* BURY A QUAKER and MRS. JONES.

CHAPEL OF LITTLE EASE, *subs. phr.* (thieves')—The police station or cells.

1871. *Daily Telegraph*, 27 Jan. [*See* short leader; also 25 Jan.]

1889. *Answers*, 9 Feb. A fourth kind of torture was a cell called LITTLE EASE. It was of so small dimensions, and so constructed, that the prisoner could neither stand, walk, sit, nor lie in it at full length. He was compelled to draw himself up in a squatting posture, and so remain during several days.

CHAPPED or **CHAPT**, *ppl. adj.* (old).—Parched; 'dry'; thirsty. [From CHAP, to crack (as the lips) from want of moisture, + ED.]

1673. R. HEAD, *Canting Acad.*, 37. CHAP'D, Dry, or Thirsty.

1725. *New Canting Dictionary*, s.v.

1785. GROSE, *Dict. Vulg. Tongue.* CHAPT: dry or thirsty.

1811. *Lexicon Balatronicum*, s.v.

CHAPPIE or **CHAPPY**, *subs.* (familiar). — The latest (1890) variety of man about town; a term of intimacy. [From CHAP, a chum, + IE, a diminutive.] For synonyms, *see* DANDY.

1882. *Punch*, vol. LXXXII., p. 69, col. 1. I'll sing you a fine new song, all about a fine young spark, Who's a fine young London gentleman, quite up to any lark, Who takes supper very early, and breakfasts in the dark; Who's a real 'dear old CHAPPIE,' as I needn't perhaps remark.

1883. G. A. S[ALA], in *Illustr. London News*, March 24, p. 290, col. 1. Lord Boodle, a rapid CHAPPIE always ready to bet on everything with anybody.

CHARACTER, *subs.* (colloquial).—A man or woman exhibiting some prominent (and usually contemptible) trait; an eccentric; a CASE (*q.v.*). Generally used with such adjectives as 'low,' 'queer,' 'comic,' etc.—[From CHARACTER = a personage in history or fiction: one who has distinguished him- or herself.] For synonyms, *see* ODD FISH.

1773. GOLDSMITH, *She Stoops to Conquer*, II., 1. A very impudent fellow this! but he's a CHARACTER, and I'll humour him.

1820-33. C. LAMB, *Essays of Elia*, p. 163. You are fond of having a CHARACTER at your table, and truly he is one.

CHARACTERED, *ppl. adj.* (old).—Burnt on the hand; otherwise LETTERED (*q.v.*). [From the legitimate meaning of the word, = 'marked or inscribed with characters.']

1785. GROSE, *Dict. Vulg. T.*, s.v.

1811. *Lexicon Balatronicum.* They have palmed the CHARACTER upon him.

CHARING-CROSS, *subs.* (rhyming slang).—A horse. For synonyms, *see* PRAD.

CHARIOT, *subs.* (thieves').—An omnibus. In the sixteenth century CHARIOT = a vehicle of any kind, and in the eighteenth a light four-wheeled carriage. French thieves call an omnibus *une omnicroche*, or *un four banal*, which last = also a pocket or 'cly.'

CHARIOT-BUZZING, *subs.* (thieves'). — Picking pockets in an omnibus. [From CHARIOT (*q.v.*), an omnibus, + BUZ, *verb* 2 (*q.v.*), to pick pockets, + ING.] French thieves' *faire l'omnicroche.*

CHARLES, HIS FRIEND, *subs.* (theatrical).—*See* FRIEND.

CHARLEY or **CHARLIE,** *subs.* (old). —1. A night watchman, A popular name, prior to the introduction by Sir R. Peel, in 1829, of the present police force; since when it has fallen into desuetude. The CHARLIES were generally old men whose chief duty was crying the hour on their rounds. Boxing a CHARLEY was a favourite amusement with young bucks and bloods, who, when they found a night-watchman asleep in his box, would overturn it, leaving the occupant to escape as best he might. [The origin of the term is uncertain. Some trace it to Charles I., who reorganised the watch system of the metropolis in 1640. If this be tenable it is curious that so long a period elapsed between the event and its recognition in slang. The earliest appears to be that given *infra.* For synonyms, *see* BEAK and COPPER.

1812. J. H. VAUX, *Flash Dictionary.* CHARLEY: a watchman.

1823. CHARLES WESTMACOTT, *Points of Misery,* p. 28. A regular chase between me and the CHARLEYS all the way to Lad Lane.

1845. HOOD, *Tale of a Trumpet,* st. 55. That other old woman, the parish CHARLEY!

1852. *Bentley's Miscellany,* 1 June, p 620. Oh, those dear old CHARLIES of the Dogberry school! How their husky cries of the passing hour mingled with our dreams, letting us know that they were at least wide awake to the thievings of time!

1865. G. F. BERKELEY, *My Life,* etc., I., 106. The night's entertainment ending in the morning before a magistrate, when the roughly used CHARLEYS, as the night-policemen were called, preferred charges of assault supported by black eyes and a few loose teeth carefully preserved for the purpose, and the offenders thought themselves lucky if they got off with only a moderate fine. [*Temp.* George IV.]

1889. *Daily News,* Sep. 28, p. 2, col. 5. THE LAST OF THE CHARLEYS. In the person of Mr. William Mason, who died on Wednesday at the age of 89, we lose the last survivor of the CHARLEYS who used to patrol the streets prior to the establishment in 1849 of the City Police Force.

2. (common).—A small, pointed beard, fashionable in the time of Charles I.; an 'imperial'; in America a GOATEE (*q.v.* for synonyms).

1824. *Gentleman's Magazine,* March 1, p. 295, col. 2. With white pantaloons, watch chains, and Wellingtons, and a CHARLEY at their under lip.

1841. HOOK, *Widow,* x., 145. He ... wore ... a CHARLEY on his under lip.

1861. TAYLOR, *Antiq. Falkland,* 43. That square, short man ... wearing a moustache and CHARLIE is William Laud.

18(?). R. M. JEPHSON, *Girl He Left Behind Him,* ch. i. Dolly himself was occupied in nursing a tuft of hair on his chin termed, grandiloquently, an imperial, familiarly, a CHARLEY.

3. (hunting).—A fox. Fourbesque, *graniera.*

1857. HUGHES, *Tom Brown's School-days,* ch. i., p. 8. A nice little gorse or spinney where abideth poor CHARLEY, having no other cover to which to betake himself for miles and miles, when pushed out some fine November morning by the old Berkshire.

1859. H. KINGSLEY, *Geoffrey Hamlyn,* ch. xxviii. 'And all after a poor little fox!' 'You don't know CHARLEY, I can see,' said Halbert; 'poor little fox indeed!

4. (American thieves').—A watch. [Possibly a pun upon CHARLEY, sense 1, a watch or

watchman.] For synonyms, *see* TICKER.

5. (tailors').—The nap on faced on glossy-surfaced cloth.

6. (tailors'). — A round-shouldered figure.

CHARLEY BATES' FARM, or **GARDEN.**—*See* BATES' FARM.

CHARLEY-LANCASTER, *subs.* (rhyming slang).—A 'handkercher.'

CHARLEY-PITCHER, *subs.* (thieves'). —A prowling sharper who entices greenhorns to take a hand in thimble-rigging, the three-card trick, prick the garter, etc.

1859. G. A. SALA, *Twice Round the Clock* (2 p.m., par. 10), p. 160. Even at remote country race-courses, you may find remnants of the whilom swarming tribe of CHARLEY-PITCHERS, the knavish gentry who pursue the games of 'under seven or over seven,' ... or inveigle the unwary with 'three little thimbles and one small pea.'

1851-61. H. MAYHEW, *Lon. Lab. and Lon. Poor,* IV., 32, *note.* A CHARLEY-PITCHER seems to be one who pitches to the *Ceorla* or countryman, and hence is equivalent to the term *Yokel*-hunter.

1877. BESANT AND RICE, *Son of Vulcan,* pt. I., ch. ix. With them marched the CHARLEY-PITCHERS, who gained an honourable livelihood with the thimble and the pea.

CHARLEY-PRESCOT, *subs.* (rhyming slang).—A waistcoat. For synonyms, *see* FAN.

CHARLEY-WAG. TO PLAY THE CHARLEY-WAG (school-slang).— 1. To absent oneself from school without leave; to play truant. Variants are TO MOUCH; TO WAG; Fr., *tailler* or *caler l'école;* Spanish, *hacer novillos,* and *andar á la tuna.*

1876. C. HINDLEY, *Life and Adventures of a Cheap Jack,* p. 57. Nothing could be done with him at school ... Joe being, in spite of all entreaties, the greatest rapscallion and ringleader of all mischief, and at all times readier TO PLAY THE CHARLEY WAG than to be the first in any prominent position in his class or form.

2. (common). — To disappear [figurative].

1887. W. E. HENLEY, *Villon's Straight Tip to all Cross Coves.* It's up the spout and CHARLEY-WAG With wipes and tickers and what not. Until the squeezer nips your scrag, Booze and the blowens cop the lot.

CHARLIE.—*See* CHARLEY.

CHARLIES, *subs.* (popular). — 1. The paps. For synonyms, *see* DAIRY.

2. (Winchester College). — Thick gloves made of twine. [Introduced by a Mr. Charles Griffith; hence the name.] Obsolete.

CHARM, *subs.* (old).—1. A pick-lock.

1785. GROSE, *Dict. Vulg. Tongue,* s.v.

1811. *Lexicon Balatronicum,* s.v.

1881. *New York Slang Dict.,* s.v.

CHARMS, *subs.* (old).—The paps. Fr., *les appas.* Once in literary use, but now impossible except as slang. FLASHING HER CHARMS =showing her paps.

2. (American). — A generic term for money. For synonyms, *see* ACTUAL and GILT.

1875. *American English,* in *Cham. Journal,* 25 Sept., p. 610. Money has forty or fifty different names; such singular terms as ... shadscales, and CHARMS figuring in the list.

CHARTER THE BAR or **GROCERY,** *verbal phr.* (American).—To buy up the whole of the liquor at a bar and stand drinks all round as

long as it lasts. This freak is not infrequent in the West. In Australia a similar expression is SHOUTING ONESELF HOARSE. (*q.v.*).

18(?). J. G. BALDWIN, *David Bolus, Esq.* Bolus was no niggard. He would as soon treat a regiment, or CHARTER THE GROCERY for the day, as any other way.

CHASING, *verbal subs.* (workmens'). *See* quot.

1884. RAE, *Cont. Socialism,* 361. This is shown ... in their prohibition of CHASING ... *i.e.,* of a workman exceeding a given average standard of production. [M.]

CHASSE, *verb* (society). — To dismiss. [From the French *chasser.*]

1847. THACKERAY, *Lords and Liv.,* III. He was CHASSÉD on the spot. [M.]

1868. YATES, *Rock Ahead,* I., p. 185. If Lord Ticehurst married, more than half Gilbert Lloyd's influence would be gone, if indeed the turf were not abandoned, and the confederate CHASSÉD.

CHAT, *subs.* (thieves').—1. A house. For synonyms, *see* DIGGINGS.

1879. J. W. HORSLEY, in *Macm. Mag.,* XL., 501. I piped a slavey (servant) come out of a CHAT (house).

2. (common). — The female *pudendum.* (From French *chat,* a cat, and by implication the 'pussy.']

3. (common).—The truth; the real state of a case; the proper words to use; the 'correct card.'

1819. THOMAS MOORE, *Tom Crib's Memorial to Congress,* p. 6. And, setting in case there should come such a rumpus, As some mode of settling the CHAT we must compass, With which the tag-rag will have nothing to do, What think you, great swells, of a royal set-to?

1862. TROLLOPE, *Orley Farm,* ch. vi. Has the gentleman any right to be in this room at all, or has he not? Is he commercial, or is he--miscellaneous? That's the CHAT as I take it.

4. (low). — Gabble; chatter; impudence; *e.g.,* None of your CHAT, or I'll give you a shove in the eye.

Verb.—To hang.—*See* CHATES, sense 1. [This reading, however, is problematical.]

1513. G. DOUGLAS, *Æneis,* viii., Prol. 126. Quod. I, churle, ga CHAT the, and chide with ane vthir.

CHATES, *subs.* (old).—1. The gallows. (Also CHATTES and CHATS.) [Doubtful as to derivation, *see* quot. 1610.] For synonyms, *see* NUBBING-CHEAT.

1567. HARMAN, *Caveat* (1814), p. 66. CHATTES: the gallowes.

1610. ROWLANDS, *Martin Mark-all,* p. 37. (H. Club's Repr., 1874). CHATES, the Gallowes: here he [Harman, author of a Caveat for Cursitors-date, *c.* 1570, reprinted as *The Belman of London,* containing list of cant words] mistakes both the simple word, because he so found it printed, not knowing the true originall thereof, and also in the compound; as for CHATES it should be *Cheates,* which word is vsed generally for things, as *Tip me that Cheate,* Give me that thing: so that if you will make a word for the Gallous, you must put thereto this word, *Treyning,* which signifies hanging; and so *Treyning Cheate* is as much to say, hanging things, or the Gallous, and not CHATES.

1671. R. HEAD, *English Rogue,* pt. I., ch. v., p. 48 (1874). CHATS: the gallows.

1690. B. E. *Dict. Cant. Crew,* s.v.

1706. E. COLES, *Eng. Dict.,* s.v.

1725. *New Cant. Dict.,* s.v.

1785. GROSE, *Dict. Vulg. Tongue,* s.v.

1811. *Lexicon Balatronicum,* s.v.

1881. *New York Slang Dict.,* s.v.

2. (old).—Lice. (Also CHATS and CHATTS.) [Grose suggests that CHATTS is an abbreviation of chattels in the sense of cattle —lice being the chief live-stock of beggars, gipsies, and the rest of the canting crew; the his-

tory of the word 'chattel' appears to bear out his contention. The Norman *catel* passed later into *cattell,* and these forms were in the sixteenth century restricted to live-stock, *chattell* passing from legal French into general use for the wider sense—article of property.]

1690. B. E., *Dict. Cant. Crew,* s.v.

1725. *New Cant. Dict.,* s.v.

1812. J. H. VAUX, *Flash Dict.,* s.v.

1864. HOTTEN, *Slang Dict.,* s.v.

ENGLISH SYNONYMS. Active citizens; crabs; crumbs; friends in need; back friends; grey backs; black cattle; Scots Greys; gentleman's companions; creepers; gold-backed 'uns; German ducks; dicky-birds; familiars; saddle-backs; Yorkshire Greys.

FRENCH SYNONYMS. *Les espagnols* (popular: formerly lice were called 'Spanish bugs,' *poux espagnols,* to distinguish them from the *cimex lectuarius,* or common bed bug); *un coquillon* (popular: also 'a pilgrim'); *les goux* (thieves'); *le garnison* (pop. = garrison); *un loupate* (= *poux,* disguised); *un habitant* (= a householder or 'citizen'); *un grenadier* (popular); *un got* (thieves'); *un mousquetaire gris* (pop. = a grey musketeer).

GERMAN SYNONYMS. *Hutterer g' sell'n* (perhaps the nearest German equivalent to the English 'gentleman's companion,' the German word signifying 'skin-society'); *Jokel,* or *Jokelche, Jokelcher, Juckel, Juckeler* (sing.: also = a postillion, 'one who rides,' the latter, however, being more commonly rendered *Post-Juckel.* Ave-Lallement derives it from *Jäckel* or *Jockel,* diminutives of Jacob, but there are the German words, *Jucken,* 'to itch,' and *Juckler,* 'one who itches.' It is quite possible that the two last are later, historically. In connection, *see* next example); *Hans Walter* (in Luther's *Liber Vagatorum* [1529]. *Hanz* literally means Jack, or John [*Cf.,* preceding *Jokel*], the old word *Hansa* refers to a multitude; old German *Hanse,* a society; *Hans,* a companion); *Kinne, pl. Kinnim* (of purely Hebrew origin; *Kinnimachler* = a 'dirty, filthy fellow,' or 'an avaricious man,' literally 'a lice-eater'; *Kinnimer,* a man full of lice. The Fieselsprache has *Kineh* and *Kinehbruder* to signify 'an intimate companion,' or 'chum'; *Marschirer* or *die stillen Marschirer* (Viennese thieves' for lice; literally 'the silent walkers'); *Sand* (used for vermin in general and lice in particular; *sandig sein,* to be lousy).

ITALIAN SYNONYMS. *Grisaldi; grisanti; guallino.*

SPANISH SYNONYM. *Cancano,* (*m;* a low term).

CHAT-HOLE, *subs.* (prison).—A hole made by convicts in a wall, to carry on a conversation. [From CHAT, an abbreviation of chatter, + HOLE.]

CHATS, *subs.* (old).—1. *See* CHATES.

2. (thieves').—*See* quot.

1821. D. HAGGART, *Life,* Glossary, p. 171. CHATS, seals.

3. (Stock Exchange). — London, Chatham and Dover Railway Stock.

CHATTER-BASKET, *subs.* (common). —A prattling child. Originally dialectical, CHATTER-BASKET being the Lancashire form; while in West Somerset they say CHATTER-BAG. *Cf.*, CHATTERBOX.

CHATTER-BONES, CHATTER-CART, and **CHATTER-BLADDER,** *subs.* (common).—Variants of CHATTERBOX (*q.v*). For synonyms, *see* CLACK-BOX.

1842. DICKENS, *American Notes*, ch. xi., p. 94. That little girl of fifteen with the loquacious chin: who, to do her justice, acts up to it . . . for of all the small CHATTERBONES that ever invaded the repose of drowsy ladies' cabin, she is the first and foremost.

CHATTERBOX, *subs.* (colloquial).—An incessant talker; used contemptuously of adults and playfully of children. [From CHATTER, gabble + BOX, a receptacle; metaphorically, a box full of chatter *Cf.*, BAG OF BONES.] A variant is CHATTERBONES (*q.v.*). For synonyms, *see* CLACK-BOX.

1785. GROSE, *Dictionary of the Vulgar Tongue.* CHATTER BOX, one whose tongue runs twelve score to the dozen; a chattering man or woman.

1840. C. DICKENS, *Old Curiosity Shop* [C. D. ed.], p. 93. A set of idle CHATTERBOXES.

1878. E. JENKINS, *Haverholme*, p. 52. A mere political CHATTERBOX.

CHATTER-BROTH, *subs.* (old).—Tea; the beverage and the party. A Yorkshire equivalent is CHATTER-WATER. Quoted by Grose [1785]. Variants are CAT-LAP and SCANDAL-BROTH (*q.v.*).

CHATTERER, *subs.* (pugilistic).—A heavy blow upon the mouth; or, says Peter Corcoran, 'a blow that tells.' For synonyms *see* DIG.

1827. REYNOLDS ('Peter Corcoran'), Sonnet on *The Fancy.* I've left the Fives-Court rush,—the flash—the rally The noise of 'Go it, Jack'—the stop—the blow—The shout—the CHATTERING hit—the check—the sally.

CHATTERERS, *subs.* (common).—The teeth. For synonyms, *see* GRINDERS.

CHATTERY, *subs.* (thieves').—*See* quot.

1821. D. HAGGART, *Life*, Glossary, p. 171. CHATTERY, cotton, or linen goods.

CHATTY, *subs.* (old).—A filthy man. [From CHAT (*q.v.*), a louse, + Y.] English variants are CHATTY-DOSSER, CRUMMY-DOSSER. Amongst French equivalents may be mentioned *un bifteck à maquart* (Maquart is the name of a well-known knacker); *un sale pâtissier* (literally a dirty pastry-cook); *un kroumir; un gorgniat; un pégocier.*

Adj. (common).—Filthy; lousy. [For derivation, *see subs.*] A French equivalent is *graphiqué*—itself a very 'telling,' 'speaking,' or 'chatty' expression; also *malastiqué.*

1812. J. H. VAUX, *Flash Dictionary.* CHATTY: lousy.

CHATTY-FEEDER, *subs.* (old).—A spoon. [A vague reference to the mouth as the place of 'chat' or 'chatter.'] For synonyms *see* WEDGE-FEEDER.

1881. *New York Slang Dictionary.* 'And where the swag so bleakly pinched, A hundred stretches hence? . . . The chips, the fawneys, CHATTY-FEEDERS

CHAUNT, *subs.* (old).—A song.—*See* CHANT, *subs.*, sense I.

Verb (vagrants').—To sing ballads, etc., in the streets.—*See* CHANT, *verb*, sense I.

TO CHAUNT THE PLAY, *verbal phr.* (thieves').—To explain the tricks and manœuvres of thieves.

CHAUNTED, *ppl. adj.* (streets').—Sung of, and celebrated, in street ballads. [From CHAUNT, to sing street ballads, + ED.]—*See* CHANTING, *subs.*, sense 2.

1827. REYNOLDS ('Peter Corcoran'). Lines to Philip Samson in *The Fancy.* 'Be content that you've beat Dolly Smith, and been CHAUNTED, And trained—stripped—and petted, and hit off your legs!'

CHAUNTER, *subs.* (vagrants').—I. A street singer of ballads, dying speeches, etc. Rarely heard now except in the poorest neighbourhoods. His practice is peculiar. One man gets as far as he can, and when his voice cracks his companion takes things up. For this reason the business is conducted by a brace of men, by a man and woman, or by a woman and child.—*See* quot. 1851. [From CHAUNT, to sing, + ER.] Also called a PAPER-WORKER (*q.v.*); and DEATH-HUNTER (*q.v.*). FRENCH SYNONYMS are *un chanteur à la balade* or *au baladage; un goualeur* or *une goualeuse* (*see* EUGENE SUE *Mystères de Paris*); *une cigale* (popular: a female street-singer); and *un braillard.* Fourbesque, *granchetto* (a term also applied to one who speaks gibberish or thieves' lingo).

1851-61. H. MAYHEW, *London Lab. and Lon. Poor*, vol. I., p. 229. The CHAUNTERS, or those who do not cry, but (if one may so far stretch the English language) *sing* the contents of the 'papers' they vend. *Ibid*, p. 240. The running patterer . . . is accompanied generally by a CHAUNTER . . . The CHAUNTER not only sings, but fiddles.

2. (common).—*See* CHANTER, sense I.

CHAUNTER-COVE, *subs.* (thieves').—A reporter. [From CHAUNT, to 'crack' or 'cry up,' + ER + COVE, a man.]

CHAUNTER-CULL, *subs.* (old).—A writer of ballads and street literature for the use of CHAUNTERS or 'street patterers.' They haunted certain well-known public-houses in London and Birmingham, and were open to write ballads 'to order' on any subject, the rate of remuneration varying from half-a-crown to seven-and-sixpence. The chaunter having practically disappeared, his poet has gone with him.

1781. G. PARKER, *View of Society*, II., 58. [Named and described in.]

1785. GROSE, *Dict. Vulg. Tongue.* CHAUNTER-CULLS: Grub Street writers, who compose songs, carrols, etc., for ballad singers.

1834. H. AINSWORTH, *Rookwood*, bk. IV., ch. vi. I trust, whenever the CHAUNTER-CULLS and last-speech scribblers get hold of me, they'll at least put no cursed nonsense into my mouth.

CHAUNTER UPON THE LEER, *phr.* (old).—An advertiser.

CHAUNTING.—*See* CHANTING.

CHAUVERING DONNA or **MOLL,** *subs.* (old). — A prostitute. [From CHAUVERING, sexual intercourse. + DONNA (*q.v.*), a woman, or MOLL (*q.v.*), a loose female.] For synonyms, *see* BARRACK-HACK.

CHAW, *subs.* (common).—I. A countryman; a yokel; a bumpkin. [A contraction of CHAW-BACON (*q.v.*). In common use at Harrow School.]

1856. T. HUGHES, *Tom Brown's School-days*, pt. I., ch. i. There's nothing like the old country-side for me, and no music like the twang of the real old Saxon tongue, as one gets it fresh from the veritable CHAW in the White Horse Vale.

2. (vulgar).—A mouthful; a 'gobbet'; in the mouth at once;

e.g., a quid of tobacco; a dram of spirits, etc. [From CHAW, *verb*, *q.v.*]

1749. 'Humours of the Fleet,' quoted in Ashton's *The Fleet*, p. 286. And in his nether jaw Was stuff'd an elemosynary CHAW.

1772. *Gentleman's Magazine*, XLII., 191. The tars . . . Took their CHAWS, hitched their trousers, and grinn'd in our faces. [M.]

1833. MARRYAT, *Peter Simple*, xiv. The boy was made to open his mouth, while the CHAW of tobacco was extracted.

1838. GLASCOCK, *Land Sharks and Sea Gulls*, II., 123. 'I'm blest if I'm fit for work, 'thout a raw CHAW.'

1864. *Daily Telegraph*, 26 July. The gentleman have often 'that within that passeth show,' to wit, a CHAW of tobacco: this is not very conducive to volubility in conversation.

3. (University).—A trick; device; or 'sell.'

Verb (vulgar).—I. To eat or chew noisily and roughly. To bite (*see* quot., 1890). Once literary; now degenerate, and vulgarly applied; specifically 'to chew tobacco.'

1890. *The Oont*, RUDYARD KIPLING in *Scots Observer*, . . . We socks him with a stretcher-pole, and 'eads him off in front, And when we saves his bloomin' life, he CHAWS our bloomin' arm.

2. (University).—To deceive, trick, 'sell,' or impose upon one.

TO CHAW OVER, *verbal phr.* (common).—To create ridicule by repeating one's words.

TO CHAW UP, *phr.* (American).—To get the better of; to demolish; 'do for'; smash or finish. CHAWED UP: utterly done for.

1843. DICKENS, *Martin Chuzzlewit*, ch. xvi., p. 162, 'Here's full particulars of the patriotic loco-foco movement yesterday, in which the Whigs was so CHAWED UP.

1862. C. F. BROWNE, *Artemus Ward: His Book*, p. 66. We CHAWED 'em UP, that's what we did.

TO CHAW UP ONE'S WORDS, *phr.* (American).—To retract an assertion; 'to eat one's words.'

CHAW-BACON, *subs.* (colloquial).—A country bumpkin. [From CHAW, a vulgar form of chew, to masticate or chew, + BACON, the staple food of agricultural labourers.] Other nicknames for a countryman are bacon-slicer; clodhopper; barn-door savage; clodpole; cart-horse; Johnny; cabbage-gelder; turnip-sucker; joskin; jolterhead; yokel; clodcrusher, etc.

1811. *Lexicon Balatronicum.* CHAW BACON. A countryman. A stupid fellow.

1822. *Blackwood's Magazine*, XII., 379. You live cheap with CHAW-BACONS and see a fine, flat country. [M.]

1854. WHYTE MELVILLE, *General Bounce*, ch. v. 'Give *me* the pail, you lop-eared buffoon—do you call that the way to feed a pig?' and the General, seizing the bucket from an astonished CHAW-BACON, who stood aghast, as if he thought his master was mad, managed to spill the greater part of the contents over his own person and gaiters.

CHAWS, *subs.* (venery).—Copulation. For synonyms, *see* GREENS.

CHEAP. ON THE CHEAP, *adv. phr.* (colloquial).—At a low rate [of money]; economically; keeping up a showy appearance on small means.

1884. *Cornhill Mag.*, June, p. 614. His being's end and aim, both by day and night, is to obtain as much drink as possible ON THE CHEAP.

CHEAP AND NASTY, *adv. phr.* (colloquial).—Said of articles which, though pleasing to the eye, are 'shoddy' in fact. For special application, *see* quot.

1864. *Athenæum*, Oct. 29. CHEAP AND NASTY, or, in a local form, 'CHEAP AND NASTY, LIKE SHORT'S IN THE STRAND,' a proverb applied to the deceased founder of cheap dinners.

TO FEEL CHEAP, *verb phr.* (common).—To 'have a mouth on;' to be suffering from a night's debauch.

DIRT CHEAP or DOG CHEAP, *adv. phr.* (colloquial).—Inexpensive; as cheap as may be. DOG CHEAP is the earliest form in which this colloquialism appears in English literature, DIRT CHEAP not being found earlier than 1837.

1577. HOLINSHED, *Chron. Descr. Irel.*, iii. They afourded their wares so DOGGE CHEAPE, that etc. [M.]

1837. C. DICKENS, *Oliver Twist*, xxxvii. 'I sold myself,' said Mr. Bumble . . . 'I went very reasonable. Cheap, DIRT CHEAP!'

CHEAPSIDE. HE CAME HOME BY WAY OF CHEAPSIDE, *phr.* (old).—That is 'he gave little or nothing for it'; 'he got it cheap.'

CHEAT, *subs.* (old).—A general name for any object. [From Anglo-Saxon *ceat*, a thing. *Cf.*, quot., 1608.] A term which, with a descriptive adjective, appears in a variety of forms in Old Cant. The CHEAT *par excellence* was the gallows, also known as the NUBBING, TOPPING, or TREYNING-CHEAT. The word is variously spelt—CHET, CHETE, CHEATE, CHEIT, CHATE. CHEAT. The following combinations will serve to illustrate its use.

BELLY-CHETE	=	An Apron.
BLETING-CHETE	=	A sheep or calf.
CACKLING-CHETE	=	A fowl.
CRASHING-CHEATS	=	The teeth.
GRUNTING-CHETE	=	A pig.
HEARING-CHETES	=	The ears.
LOW'ING-CHETE	=	A cow.
LULLABY-CHEAT	=	An infant.
MOFLING-CHETE	=	A napkin.
NUBBING-CHEAT	=	The gallows.
PRATTLING-CHETE	=	The tongue.
QUACKING-CHETE	=	A duck.
SMELLING-CHETE	=	The nose.
TOPPING-CHEAT	=	The gallows.
TREYNING-CHEAT	=	The gallows.
TRUNDLING-CHEAT	=	A cart or coach.

All of which *see.*

1567. HARMAN, *Caveat* [ed. 1869], p. 86. Now we have well bous'd, let vs strike some CHETE [that is], now we have well dronke, let us steale some thinge.

1608. DEKKER, *Belman of London*, in wks. (Grosart) III., 117. The *Cheating* Law or the Art of winning money by false dyce. Those that practise this studie call themselues *Cheators*, the dyce *Cheaters*, and the money which they purchase *Cheates*: borrowing the tearme from our common Lawyers, with whome all casuals as fall to the Lord at the holding of his Leetes, as Waifes, Strayes, and such like, are said to be *Escheated to the Lord's vse*, and are called *Cheates.*

1611. SHAKSPEARE, *Winter's Tale*, iv., 2, 28. With dye and drab, I purchas'd this Caparison, and my Reuennew is the silly CHEATE. Gallowes, and Knocke, are too powerfull on the Highway.

1754. FIELDING, *Jonathan Wild*, bk. IV., ch. ii. See what your laziness is come to; to the CHEAT, for thither will you go now, that's infallible.

CHEATS, *subs.* (old).—Sham cuffs or wristbands. *Cf.*, DICKY and SHAMS.—*See* also quot., 1688.

1688. R. HOLME, *Armoury*, III., p. 96, col. I. A . . . kind of Waistcoats are called CHATES, because they are to be seen rich and gaudy before, when all the back part is no such thing. *Ibid*, III., p. 258, col. I. Such Gallants weare not CHEATS or half Sleeves, but . . . their Waistcoats are the same clear throughout. [M.]

1690. B. E., *Dictionary Canting Crew.* CHEATS . . . also Wristbands or sham Sleeves worn for true, or whole ones.

1785. GROSE, *Dict. Vulg. Tongue.*
1811. *Lexicon Balatronicum.* }
Sham sleeves to put over a dirty shift or shirt.

CHECKS, *subs.* (American).—Money in general; cash. [A term derived from poker, in which game counters or CHECKS, bought at certain fixed rates, are equivalent to current coin.] For synonyms, *see* ACTUAL and *Cf.*, CHIPS.

TO PASS OR HAND IN ONE'S CHECKS, *phr.* (American).—*See ante*, TO CASH (or PASS IN) ONE'S CHECKS. To die. For synonyms, *see* ALOFT and *Cf.*, CHIPS.

CHEEK, *subs.* (colloquial).—1. Insolence; jaw; *e.g.*, 'none of your cheek' or 'chat' and 'none of your jaw.' Equivalents are LIP, CHAT, IMPERANCE, MOUTH, CHIN, CHIRRUP, and NINE SHILLINGS; the last a corruption of 'nonchalance!' Among foreign equivalents may be mentioned the French *avoir un toupet de bœuf*; and the Spanish adjectives *cariraido* ('impudent') and *desollado* (from *desollar*, 'to skin, flay'); *desuellacaras* (*m*; an impudent, shameless person); *paparrucha* (*f.* impertinence).

1840. MARRYAT, *Poor Jack*, xxii. The man, who was a sulky, saucy sort of chap . . . gives CHEEK.

1848. J. MITCHELL, *Jail Jrnl.*, July 20. I once asked . . . what fault a man had committed who was flogged. . . . 'For giving CHEEK, sir.' [M.]

1884. G. MOORE, *Mummer's Wife* (1887), p. 133. If he gives me any of his CHEEK I'll knock him down.

2. Audacity; confidence; impudence; 'brass'; 'face.' Formerly 'brow' was used in the same sense.—(*See* quot., 1642.)

1642. FULLER, *Holy State*, bk. IV., ch. xi. They were men of more BROW than brain, being so ambitious to be known, that they had rather be hissed down than not come upon the stage.

1851. MAYHEW, *London Labour and London Poor*, I., p. 471. They [the Crocusses] 'd actually have the CHEEK to put a blister on a cork leg. *Ibid*, p. 404 (provided with) a noggin o' rum to 'give him CHEEK,' and make him speak up to his victims.

1882. *Daily News*, Oct. 10, p. 5, col. 6. Of this fact, I know no more signal instance than the seizing of the Citadel of Cairo. As I stood on the spot the other day I realised for the first time the—if you will pardon me the use of a vulgar but expressive colloquialism—astounding CHEEK of the feat.

1889. *Answers*, p. 59, col. 2. The whole suggestion savoured so much of what our Transatlantic brothers call MONUMENTAL CHEEK, that the Duke hardly knew what to say, or what emotions to express.

1890. *Athenæum*, Feb. 22, p. 253, col. 2. In various disguises Miss Palmer sings, dances, and exhibits her powers of coquetry and CHEEK.

Verb.—To address a person saucily.

1851. MAYHEW, *London Labour and London Poor*, I., p. 452. (They) persuaded me to go and beg with them, but I couldn't CHEEK it.

1857. DICKENS, *Our Vestry*, in *Reprinted Pieces*, p. 292. Dogginson . . . informed another gentleman . . . that if he CHEEK'D him he would resort to the extreme measure of knocking his blessed head off.

1890. *Saturday Review*, Feb. 1, p. 151, col. 1. Not only was Dick always ready to CHEEK his employer, and by his own account usually capable of getting the better of him, but he was on the same sort of terms with his pupils.

TO ONE'S OWN CHEEK, *phr.* (colloquial).—To one's own share; all to oneself. Sometimes used in the sense of allowance, *i.e.*, 'Where's my CHEEK?'

1841. LEVER, *Charles O'Malley*, ch. lxxxviii. And though he consumed something like a prize on to HIS OWN CHEEK, he at length had to call for cheese.

1855. *Punch*, vol. XXVIII., p. 10. [From day to day, for near a week,] 'I had a boiled salt round of beef On Monday ALL TO MY OWN CHEEK Whereon my hunger sought relief.'

TO CHEEK UP, *verbal phr.* (colloquial).— = CHEEK, to answer saucily.—*See* CHEEK, *verb.*

1867. *North Briton*, June 5. 'Royal Dramatic College.' We shall not soon forget seeing, during our visit to the Fair last July, a number of ladies dressed up as jockeys, confined, like so many chattering monkeys, in a cage, CHEEKING UP to gentlemen, selling them 'k'rect cards,' etc.

CHEEK-ACHE. TO HAVE THE CHEEK-ACHE, *phr.* (common).—To be made to blush; to be abashed. [From CHEEK, the face, + ACHE, a metaphorical exaggeration of the pain of blushing.]

CHEEKINESS, *subs.* (colloquial).—Impudence; effrontery; cool audacity.

1847. *Illustrated London News*, 28 Aug. p. 142, col. 1. They were beat . . . by their slow, loggy stroke, and by their CHEEKINESS. [M.]

1854. MARTIN AND AYTOUN, *Bon Gualtier Ballads*, 'Francesca da Rimini.' There's wont to be at conscious times like these. An affectation of a bright-eyed ease, — A crispy-CHEEKINESS, if so I dare, Describe the swaling of a jaunty air.

1857. A. TROLLOPE, *Three Clerks*, ch. xliv. He lived but on the CHEEKINESS of his gait and habits; he had become member of Parliament, Government official, railway director, and club aristocrat, merely by dint of cheek.

CHEEKISH, *adj.* (colloquial).—Audacious; impudent; saucy. [From CHEEK + ISH.]

1851. MAYHEW, *London Labour and London Poor*, I., p. 248. Being CHEEKISH (saucy) to the beadle.

CHEEKS, *subs.* (old).—1. The posteriors. For synonyms, *see* BLIND-CHEEKS: to which may be added toby; stern; catastrophe; latter-end; jacksy-pardo; and juff.

1785. GROSE, *Dict. Vulgar Tongue.*

2. (old).—An accomplice.

1857. SNOWDEN, *Mag. Assistant*, 3 ed., p. 448. I have seen CHEEKS (a flash name for an accomplice).

CHEEKS AND EARS.—A fantastic name for a kind of head-dress, of temporary fashion.

(?) *Lond. Prod.*, iv., 3, Suppl. to Sh., II., 511, *Fr.* O then thou canst tell how to help me to CHEEKS AND EARS. *L.* Yes, mistress, very well. *Fl. S.* CHEEKS AND EARS! why, mistress Frances, want you CHEEKS AND EARS? methinks you have very fair ones. *Fr.* Thou art a fool indeed, Tom, thou knowest what I mean. *Civ.* Ay, ay, Kester; 'tis such as they wear a' their heads.

CHEEKS THE MARINE, *subs. phr.* (nautical).—Mr. Nobody. An imaginary personage on board ship created and popularised by Captain Marryat. The epithet has, likewise, passed into a byword as a sarcastic rejoinder to a foolish or incredible story—'tell that to CHEEKS THE MARINE.'

1833. MARRYAT, *Peter Simple* (ed. 1846), vol. I., ch. vii., p. 36. I enquired who, and he said CHEEKS THE MARINE.

1878-80. JUSTIN MCCARTHY, *History of Our Own Times*, II., ch. xiii., p. 15 (1848). CHEEKS THE MARINE was a personage very familiar at that time to the readers of Captain Marryat's sea stories, and the name of that mythical hero appeared with bewildering iteration in the petition.

1883. CLARK RUSSELL, *Sailors' Language.* CHEEKS THE MARINE: an imaginary being in a man-of-war.

CHEEKY, *adj.* (colloquial).—Coolly presumptuous; impudent or saucy. Fr., *insolpé.*

1859. H. KINGSLEY, *Geoffrey Hamlyn*, ch. xxvi. 'You will find, Sir,' said Lee, 'that these men in this here hut are a rougher lot than you think for; very like they'll be CHEEKY.'

1860. *Punch*, vol. XXXIX., p. 30. 'The Volunteer on July fourteenth.' But that Ass SNIVENS—a coming it as CHEEKY as could be.

1889. *Pall Mall Gaz.*, 8 Nov., p. 2, col. 3. The CHEEKY boy, with the natural ingratitude of youth, often makes a long nose at his master, even when showing off all that the master has taught him.

CHEESE. THE CHEESE, *phr.* (common).—1. Anything first-rate or highly becoming; the expression runs up and down the whole gamut of 'cheese nomenclature' from THE STILTON, DOUBLE GLOSTER, to THE PURE LIMBURGER. [It has been variously traced to the Anglo-Saxon *ceosan*, to choose; German, *kiesen*; French, *chose*; Persian, *chiz*; Hindu, *cheez*, thing. Summing up the evidence, the expression—(barring a solitary reference in the *London Guide* of 1818, where it is referred to a bald translation of *c'est une autre chose*, *i.e.*, that is another CHEESE, subsequently coming to signify that is the real thing)—appears to have come into general vogue about 1840. This contention is borne out in some measure by a correspondent to *Notes and Queries* (1853, I S., viii., p. 89), who speaks of it as about 'ten or twelve years old,' a calculation which carries it back to the date when it appears to have started in literature. Yule, writing much later, says the expression was common among young Anglo-Indians, *e.g.*, 'my new Arab is the real *chiz*,' *i.e.*, 'the real thing,' a fact which points to a Persian origin.] For synonyms, *see* A1.

1835. HALIBURTON ('Sam Slick'), *The Clockmaker*, 3 S., ch. xiv. Whatever is the go in Europe will soon be THE CHEESE here.

1837. R. H. BARHAM, *Ingoldsby Legends*, p. 418. Cries Rigmaree, rubbing her hands, 'that will please—My "*Conjuring cap*"—it's the thing;—it's THE CHEESE.'

1842. *Punch*, vol. III., p. 33. 'I hopes my love will excuse me if I'm not quite—quite— '*Comme il faut*, George.' 'I don't mean that, love—not quite THE CHEESE.'

1860. *Punch*, vol. XXXIX., p. 97. Were the custom [of putting mottoes on garments, *temp.* Rich. II.] now revived we can conceive what stupid mottoes would be sported by the Œntish who always mock and maul the fashion of their betters:—'*I wish my gal to please: O, aint I just* THE CHEESE' would doubtless be a popular device for a new shirt front.

1863. CHAS. READE, *Hard Cash*, II., 186. 'Who ever heard [said Mrs. Dodd] of a young lady being married without something to be married *in?*' 'Well [said Edward], I've heard Nudity is not THE CHEESE on public occasions.

2. *subs.* (schools and University).—An adept; one who 'takes the shine out of another' at anything; at Cambridge an overdressed dandy is called a HOWLING CHEESE. [An extended usage based on sense 1.]

1864. *Eton School-days.* 'Do you know Homer, Purefoy?' asked Chudleigh. 'No, I have not looked at the lesson yet.' 'I am sure I don't know why you ever do; you are such a CHEESE. I want you to give me a construe.'

HARD CHEESE, *phr.* (common).—What is barely endurable; hard lines; bad luck.

TIP-CHEESE.—Probably the same as TIP-CAT (*q.v.*).

1836. C. DICKENS, *Pickwick Papers*, p. 282 (ed. 1857). All is gloom and silence in the house; even the voice of the child is hushed; his infant sports are disregarded when his mother weeps; his '*alley tors*' and his '*commoneys*' are alike neglected; he forgets the long familiar cry of '*knuckle down*,' and at TIP-CHEESE, or odd and even, his hand is out.

CHEESE IT! *phr.* (thieves').—Leave off! Have done! Be off! [Thought to be a corruption of 'cease it!'] For synonyms, *see* STOW IT!

1811. *Lexicon Balatronicum*, CHEESE IT, the coves are fly; be silent, the people understand our discourse.

1859. SALA, *Gaslight and Daylight*, ch. xxviii. Two or three 'hallos!' and 'now thens!' accompanied by a strong recommendation to CHEESE IT (*i.e.*, act of cessation), causes these trifling annoyances to cease.

1864. *Times*, 7 December. He shouted 'Murder!' as well as he could, and the cries he made bringing assistance, he heard one of the men just before they let go of him call out 'CHEESE IT, CHEESE IT,' which a policeman said meant make off.

1871. *London Figaro*, May 13, p. 3, col. 3. 'CHEESE THAT,' cried Bill. 'The genelman's agoin' to read, and I am agoin' to listen.'

CHEESE-BOXES, *subs.* (American).—A Confederate nickname for vessels of the 'Monitor' type; first applied during the Civil War [1860-65]. *Cf.*, TINCLADS (*q.v.*).

1871. DE VERE, *Americanisms*, p. 335. The great inventor has not made it known what induced him to choose the name ['Monitor']: hence etymologists have evolved it out of their inner consciousness that he must have borrowed it from Gray's *Monitor Dracæna*, a large lizard covered with impenetrable armour. Irreverent Confederates called the hideous-looking vessels CHEESE-BOXES, and apparently one designation is, etymologically, though not æsthetically, as good as the other.

CHEESECUTTER, *subs.* (common).—1. A prominent, aquiline nose. For synonyms, *see* CONK.

2. (common).—A large, square peak to a cap; the *abat-jour* of the Zouaves.

3. (in plural).—Bandy-legs. For synonyms, *see* DRUMSTICKS.

CHEESE-KNIFE, *subs.* (military).—A sword. For synonyms, *see* CHEESE-TOASTER.

CHEESEMONGERS. — A popular name for the First Lifeguards until the Peninsular War. The term then fell into desuetude; but at Waterloo the commanding officer of the regiment had not forgotten it, and when leading to the charge, he called out, 'Come on, you damned CHEESEMONGERS!' an invitation accepted so heartily that the title was restored, with the difference that it was no longer a word of reproach. [Some say that the nickname came from their exclusive home service until the time of the Peninsular War; others that it was bestowed on account of the old gentlemen in the corps declining to serve when it was remodelled in 1788, on the ground that the ranks were no longer composed of gentlemen, but of CHEESEMONGERS.] Also called THE CHEESES.

CHEESER, *subs.* (old).—An eructation. The Spanish has *una pluma* (*f*; literally 'a feather'); *zullenco* (a common colloquialism); *soltar el preso* (*soltar* = 'to unloose,' or 'to untie'; *preso* = 'a prisoner').

CHEESES.—*See* CHEESEMONGERS.

CHEESE-TOASTER, *subs.* (military).—A sword.

ENGLISH SYNONYMS. Toasting-fork; toasting iron; sharp; knitting-needle; iron; cheese-knife; toll; poker.

FRENCH SYNONYMS. *Un astic* (thieves': from the German *Stich*); *l'aiguille à tricoter les côtes* (military: *l'aiguille à tricoter* = knitting-needle, *côtes* = ribs); *l'entrecôte* (popular); *un charlemagne* (military; a bayonet-sabre); *un Bon-Dieu* (military); *une curette* (military: a cavalry sword, as also is *un bancal*); *une côte de bœuf* (thieves'); *un grand couteau* (military: a cavalry sword. Literally 'a large knife'); *un fauchon* (popular); *un fauchon de satou* (a wooden sword); *une gaudille* or *gandille*; *Joyeuse* (the name of the sword of Charlemagne); *une flambe* or *flamberge* (the sword of Roland); *une paille de fer* (=cold steel); *une latte* (a cavalry sword); *une lardoire* (popular).

GERMAN SYNONYM. *Michel* (from the Hebrew *michael*, an executioner's sword; also *Langmichel*).

ITALIAN SYNONYM. *Martina.*

SPANISH SYNONYMS. *Fisberta*; *centella* (literally 'spark,' 'thunder,' 'lightning'); *respeto* (properly 'respect'); *garrancha*; *durindana.*

1785. GROSE, *Dict. Vulg. Tongue*, CHEESE-TOASTER: a sword.

1857-59. THACKERAY, *Virginians*, x. I'll drive my CHEESE-TOASTER through his body.

CHEESY, *adj.* (common).—Fine or showy. The opposite of 'dusty.' [From CHEESE (*q.v.*) + Y.] For synonyms, *see* UP TO DICK.

1858. R. S. SURTEES, *Ask Mamma*, xlviii., 211. To see him at Tattersall's sucking his cane, his CHEESY hat well down on his nose. [M.]

CHEMILOON, *subs.*—Chemise and drawers in one; a COMBINATION (*q.v.*).

CHEPEMENS, *subs.* (old). — *See* quot.

1610. ROWLANDS, *Martin Mark-all*, p. 37 (H. Club'sRepr., 1874). CHEPEMANS: Cheape-side Market.

CHEQUE. TO HAVE SEEN THE CHEQUE, *phr.* (common).—To know positively; to be possessed of exact knowledge concerning a matter. For synonyms, *see* KNOWING.

CHERRILETS, *subs.* (old). — The nipples.

1599. SYLVESTER, *Miracle of the Peace.* Then those twins, thy strawberry teates, Curled, purled CHERRILETS?

1654. *Witt's Recreations.* Then nature for a sweet allurement sets Two smelling, swelling, bashful CHERRYLETS.

CHERRY, *subs.* (thieves').—A young girl. *Cf.*, CHERRY-RIPE and ROSEBUD.

CHERRY-BREECHES.—*See* CHERUBIMS.

CHERRY-COLOURED, *adj.* (common).—Either red or black; a term used in a cheating trick at cards. When the cards are being dealt, a 'knowing' one offers to bet that he will tell the colour of the turn-up card. 'Done,' says Mr. Green. The sum being named, Mr. Sharp affirms that it will be CHERRY-COLOUR; and as cherries are either black or red, he wins. Grose [1785] has CHERRY-COLOURED CAT for one either black or white in colour.

1834. HARRISON AINSWORTH, *Rookwood.* And forth to the heath is the scamps-man gone, His matchless CHERRY BLACK prancer riding.

1886. *Ill. London News*, Jan. 23, p. 78, col. 2. A favourite hoax is the great exhibition, wherein a CHERRY-COLOURED cat and a rose-coloured pigeon (the meeting between Wellington and Blucher), etc., are to be shown. The former consists of a black cat and a white pigeon.

CHERRY-MERRY, *adj.* (old). — 1. Convivial; slightly inebriated.

1602. MIDDLETON, *Blurt*, I., i. [Tricks, tricks, KERRY MERRY buff!]

1775. *Cont. Sterne's Sent. Jour.*, 219. That every convivial assistant should go home CHERRY-MERRY.

2. *subs.* (Anglo-Indian).—A present of money. CHERRY-MERRY-BAMBOO, a beating.

CHERRY-PICKERS, *subs.* (military).—*See* CHERUBIMS.

CHERRY-PIE, *subs.* (common).—A girl. [Possibly only an amplification of CHERRY (*q.v.*).] For synonyms, *see* TITTER.

CHERRY-PIPE, *subs.* (rhyming slang).—A woman, the 'rhyme' being with 'ripe,' from CHERRY-RIPE (*q.v.*). For synonyms, *see* PETTICOAT.

CHERRY-RIPE, *subs.* (thieves').—1. A woman. *Cf.*, CHERRY = a young girl. For synonyms, *see* PETTICOAT.

2. (old).—A 'redbreast' or Bow Street Runner. [So called from the scarlet waistcoat which formed part of the uniform.]

3. (common).—A footman in red plush.

4. (rhyming slang).—A pipe.

CHERUBIMS, *vulgo*, **CHERRY-BUMS**, *subs.* (military). — 1. The Eleventh Hussars. [From their crimson overalls.] Also CHERRY-BREECHES and CHERRY-PICKERS.

1865. *Notes and Queries*, 3 S., vii., p. 49. 11th Hussars — CHERUBIMS and CHERRY PICKERS, having had some men taken while on out-post duty in a fruit garden in Spain.

1871. FORBES, *Exper. War between France and Germany*, II., 149. When [Lord Cardigan] commanded the CHERRY-BREECHES there were generally more sore backs among them than in any other regiment in the service.

1871. *Chambers' Journal*, Dec. 23, p. 802. The 11th Hussars, the 'CHERUBIMS and CHERRY PICKERS.'

2. (common).—Peevish children. [A facetious allusion to a passage in the *Te Deum*—'To Thee cherubin and seraphin continually do cry.'] Quoted by Grose [1785].

3. (common).—Chorister boys. [Either founded on the allusion quoted in sense 2, or in reference to the fact that little more than the heads of choristers is visible to the general congregation.]

TO BE IN THE CHERUBIMS, *phr.* (old).—To be in good humour; in the clouds; unsubstantial; fanciful.

1542. UDAL, *Erasmus's Apophth.*, p. 139. Diogenes mocking such quidificall trifles, that were al IN THE CHERUBINS, said, Sir Plato, your table and your cuppe I see very well, but as for your tabletee and your cupitee I see none soche.

CHESHIRE CAT. TO GRIN LIKE A CHESHIRE CAT [CHEWING GRAVEL, EATING CHEESE, or EVACUATING BONES, is sometimes added], *phr.* (common). — To laugh broadly—to 'laugh all over one's face.' Used disparagingly. [Origin unknown.]

1782. WOLCOT ('P. Pindar'), *Pair of Lyric Epistles*, in wks. (Dublin, 1795), vol. II., p. 424. Lo, like a CHESHIRE CAT our Court will GRIN!

1811. *Lexicon Balatronicum*, s.v.

1855. THACKERAY, *Newcomes*, ch. xxiv. In fact, Mr. Newcome says to Mr. Pendennis, in his droll, humourous way, 'that woman grins like a CHESHIRE CAT!' Who was the naturalist who first discovered that peculiarity of the cats in Cheshire?

1859. *Letter* from EDWARD S. TAYLOR to John Camden Hotten, 22 Dec. CHESHIRE CAT EATING CHEESE—I have always heard 'evacuating bones,' which if less decent is more expressive.

1866. DODGSON ('Lewis Carroll'), *Alice in Wonderland*, ch. viii.

CHEST. TO CHUCK OUT ONE'S CHEST, *phr.* (common).—To pull oneself together; stand firm; 'keep a stiff upper lip.'

CHESTNUT, *subs.* (American).—A stale joke or story; an old 'Joe'; something frequently said or done before. As to the variants of this phrase—their name is legion. The old songs are CHESTNUT songs; he who would foist a stale jest is implored to spare the CHESTNUT tree, not to rustle the CHESTNUT leaves, not to set the CHESTNUT bell a-ringing. [The *Philadelphia Press* (1888) attributes the introduction of the phrase to Mr. William Warren, a veteran Boston comedian. In a forgotten melodrama, by William Dillon, called *The Broken Sword*, there were two characters, one a Capt. Xavier, and the other the comedy part of Pablo. Says the captain, a sort of Munchausen, 'I entered the woods of Colloway, and suddenly from the thick boughs of a cork tree'—when Pablo interrupts him with the words: 'A CHESTNUT, captain, a CHESTNUT. 'Bah!' replies the captain. 'Booby, I say a cork tree.' 'A CHESTNUT,' reiterates Pablo, 'I should know as well as you, having heard you tell the tale these twenty-seven times.' Warren, who had often played Pablo, was at a stage-dinner, where one of the men told a story of doubtful age and originality. 'A CHESTNUT,' quoth Warren, 'I have heard you tell the tale these twenty-seven times.' The application pleased, and when the party broke up each member helped to spread the story and the commentary. This is the most plausible of many explanations.]

1882. HALKETT LORD, in *N. and Q.*, 7 S., vii., 53. I first heard the word [CHESTNUT] in 1882, in a theatrical chop-house (Brown's) in New York. The explanation given to me by Mr. Brown—once a well-known member of Wallack's company—was 'CHESTNUT, because it is old enough to have grown a beard,' alluding to the prickly bristly husk of the nuts.

1886 *Dram. Rev.*, March 27, p. 86 col. 2. Minnie Palmer will give £1000 to any one who will submit to her an idea for legitimate advertising . . . CHESTNUT ideas not wanted. [M.]

1888. *New York Sun*, Jan. 24. 'May I venture to tell the old, old story, Miss Maud,' he said, tremulously; 'the old, old, yet ever new, story of—' 'Pardon me, Mr. Sampson, if I cause you pain,' interrupted the girl, gently, 'but to me the story you wish to tell is a CHESTNUT.' 'A CHESTNUT?' 'Yes, Mr. Sampson, I'm already engaged; but I will be a sister—' 'It isn't as wormy as that one,' murmured Mr. Sampson, feeling for his hat.

CHETE.—*See* CHEAT.

CHEW, *subs.* (common).—A small portion of tobacco; a quid. *Cf.*, CHEW THE CUD.

1880. JAS. GREENWOOD, *Gaol Birds at Large.* A piece as large as a horse-bean, called a CHEW, is regarded as an equivalent for a twelve-ounce loaf and a meat ration.

TO CHEW ONESELF, *verbal phr.* (American).—To get angry. For synonyms, *see* NAB THE RUST.

TO CHEW THE CUD, *verbal phr.* (common).—To chew tobacco.

TO CHEW THE RAG or FAT, *verbal phr.* (military). — To grumble.

c. 1887. BRUNLEES PATTERSON, *Life in the Ranks.* Some of the 'knowing blokes,' prominent among whom will be the 'grousers,' will, in all probability, be CHEWING THE RAG or FAT.

CHEWALLOP! *intj.* (American).—An onomatopœia, representing, it is thought, the sound of an object falling heavily to the ground or into water—*See* CACHUNK.

1835. HALIBURTON ('Sam Slick'), *The Clockmaker*, 3 S., ch. ii. I felt . . . only one stop more [and I] was over head and ears CHEWALLOP in the water.

1888. HOPPE, *Englisch-Deutsches Supplement-Lexikon*, p. 215. It means 'flat down,' and is a strong expression. If a woman, for ex., falls head over heels and flat to the ground, they say, 'she fell CHEWALLOP.'

CHEWRE, *verb* (Old Cant).—To steal.

CHIC, *subs.* (popular).—Finish; elegance; spirit; dash; style—any quality which marks a person or thing as superior. [Originally a French slang term of uncertain origin, Littré being inclined to trace it to *chicane*, tact or skill. The French *chic* originally signified subtlety, cunning, skill; and, among English painters, TO CHIC UP A PICTURE, or TO DO A THING FROM CHIC = to work without models and out of one's own head.]

1856. LEVER, *Martins of Cro' M.*, 321. The French have invented a slang word . . . and by the expression CHIC have designated a certain property, by which objects assert their undoubted superiority over all their counterfeits.

1866. YATES, *Land at Last*, I., p. 110. A certain piquancy and CHIC in her appearance.

1871. *London Figaro*, 28 Feb. Those rollicking break-downs, those screeching girls who are so much admired for their CHIC, invariably give me a headache.

Adj. (common). — Stylish; elegant; 'up to Dick.' So also CHICDOM. [From CHIC + DOM.]

1873. *Daily News*, 9 June. She must be ready to stick on a bow here and there, to give herself an air of CHICDOM. The youthful student, however, must not go too far in the direction of CHIC, . . . the chief thing which distinguishes the dress of a lady is the absence of those prominent and inharmonious decorations, etc.

CHICKABIDDY, *subs.* (costers').—A young girl. — *See* BIDDY. [A nursery name for a chicken, commonly used as an endearment.] For synonyms, *see* TITTER.

CHICK-WOMAN.—*See* 'Much Ado about Nothing.' Act I, Sc. iii.

CHICKALEARY COVE or **BLOKE**, *subs. phr.* (costers').—An 'artful member,' otherwise a DOWNY COVE (*q.v.*, for synonyms).

c. 1869. VANCE, *Broadside Ballad.* I'm a CHICKALEARY COVE, with my one, two, three; Whitechapel was the village I was born in.

CHICKEN, *subs.* (thieves').—A pint pot. *Cf.*, HENS AND CHICKENS and CAT AND KITTENS.

1851. MAYHEW, *London Labour and London Poor*, I., p. 276. The HENS AND CHICKENS, of the low lodging-houses are the publican's pewter measures; the bigger vessels are hens, the smaller CHICKENS.

NO CHICKEN, *adv. phr.* (common). — Elderly. [The term CHICKEN is often applied to children.]

1720. SWIFT, *Stella's Birthday.* Pursue your trade of scandel-picking, Your hints that Stella is NO CHICKEN.

1738. SWIFT, *Polite Conversation* (conv. i). I swear she's NO CHICKEN; she's on the wrong side of thirty if she be a day.

1742. FIELDING, *Joseph Andrews*, bk. II., ch. ix. Adams, who was NO CHICKEN, and could bear a drubbing as well as any boxing champion in the universe.

1771. SMOLLETT, *Humphry Clinker*, I., 68. The knight swore he was NO SUCH CHICKEN, but a tough old rogue, that would live long enough to plague all his neighbours.

1717-1797. HORACE WALPOLE, *Letters*, III., 308. I made a visit yesterday to the Abbess of Panthemont, General Oglethorpe's niece, and NO CHICKEN.

1859. SALA, *Gaslight and Daylight*, ch. v. I am NO CHICKEN (though not the gray-headed old fogy that insulting Squirrel presumes to call me).

TO COUNT ONE'S CHICKENS BEFORE THEY ARE HATCHED, *verbal phr.* (colloquial). — To reckon beforehand upon a successful issue. The Latins said, 'Don't sing your song of triumph before you have won the victory' (*ante victoriam canere triumphum*). 'Don't hallo till you are out of the wood' has a similar meaning, and in French, to lose a game as good as won = *la perdre belle.* The expression was doubtless popularised by Butler in his *Hudibras* [*see* quot., 1664], but it was known long prior.

1579. GOSSON, *Ephem.*, 19a. I woulde not have him TO COUNTE HIS CHICKENS SO SOONE BEFORE THEY BE HATCHT. [M.]

1664. BUTLER, *Hudibras*, II., iii., 923. To swallow gudgeons ere they're catch'd. And COUNT THEIR CHICKENS ERE THEY'RE HATCHED.

CHICKEN-BUTCHER, *subs.* (old).—A poulterer; also a sportsman's term for anyone shooting immature game.

1811. *Lexicon Balatronicum*, s.v.

CHICKEN-FIXINGS, *subs.* (American).—Properly a hash, stew, or fricassee of chicken, but the term is now applied to any fare out of the common, and also to show of any kind. French, *la gueulardise. Cf.*, COMMON DOINGS.

1864. *A Trip to the South.* An extraordinary sight were the countless waiters, held up to the car-windows at Gordonsville by turbaned negro-women, filled with coffee-cups, eggs, and the inevitable CHICKEN-FIXINGS, which it was henceforth our fate to meet at every railway depot, till we reached New Orleans.

18(?). CARLTON, *New Purchase*, vol. II., p. 240. These preachers dress like big bugs, and go ridin' about on hundred-dollar horses, a-spungin' poor priest-ridden folks, and a-eaten CHICKEN-FIXINS so powerful fast that chickens has got scarce in these diggins.

CHI-IKE or **CHY-ACK**, *subs.* (costers').—A street salute; a word of praise.—*See* COO-EY.

c. 1869. VANCE. *The Chick-a-leary Cove.* Now my pals I'm going to slope, see you soon again, I hope, My young woman is avaiting, so be quick, Now join in a CHYIKE, the 'jolly' we all like.

1885. *Daily Telegraph*, April 6, p. 6, col. 1. A prosperous butcher . . . gives him what Mr. Poleaxer calls a CHI-HIKE at his gate as he passes that way in his cart, between five and six a.m.

1864. HOTTEN, *Slang Dictionary*, s.v.

Verb.—1. To salute or hail.

1886. *Sporting Times*, 17 July, 7, 2. There was no charge for admission. Enough. They came, they saw, and they CHI-IKED.

2. (tailors'). — To chaff unmercifully. For synonyms, *see* GAMMON, sense 1.

TO GIVE CHI-IKE WITH THE CHILL OFF, *phr.* — To scold; abuse. For synonyms, *see* WIG.

CHILD.—*See* THIS CHILD.

CHILDREN'S SHOES. — *See* MAKE CHILDREN'S SHOES.

CHILL or **TAKE THE CHILL OFF** [of liquids]. *verb* (popular). — To warm. CHILL is a contraction of the fuller phrase.

1835. DICKENS, *Sketches by Boz*, p. 264. A pint pot, the contents of which were CHILLING on the hob.

WITH THE CHILL OFF, *phr.* (popular).—An expression of (1) dissent, (2) depreciation, or (3) disbelief. A variant of OVER THE LEFT (*q.v.*).

CHIME, *verb* (thieves').—To praise; extol; puff; canoodle: especially with a view to personal advantage.

CHIMNEY, *subs.* (common). — A great smoker; Fr., *un locomotive.*

CHIMNEY CHOPS, *subs.* (old).—A negro. [An allusion to colour.] For synonyms, *see* SNOWBALL.

CHIMNEY-POT, *subs.* (common). — The silk hat worn by men, as also by women on horseback. Also called a STOVE-PIPE, BEAVER, BELL-TOPPER, etc., but for synonyms, *see* GOLGOTHA. [An allusion to shape and colour.] The French has *une cheminée,*

1861. *Punch*, vol. XLI., p. 258, 'The Riding-Hat Question.' *Lucy.* 'Now tell me, Mary, which *is* the best?' *Mary (who is rather horsey).* 'Well, dear, for tea in the arbour and that sort of thing, perhaps the little round one; but if you want to look like going across country, the CHIMNEY-POT all to nothing.'

1864. *Spectator*, p. 356. The CHIMNEY-POT hat, for the power of its transcendant ugliness beat all the artists, penmen, and men of taste in England, ten years ago.

1871. *Echo*, 2 March. 'London Trades—Hatters.' The shape of the CHIMNEY-POT is constantly changing, as we all know.

1880. *Punch's Almanack*, p. 10. Now, why should not gentlemen content themselves with mere underclothing, and discard the hideous CHIMNEY-POT, Frock Coat, and Trousers of the Period, so fatal to Pictorial Design?

1890. *Daily Graphic*, Jan. 7, p. 9, col. 4. Then the crowd go mad. Up fly head-gear, CHIMNEY-POT, and wide-a-wake alike, their owners careless of their fate.

CHIMNEY-SWEEP, *subs.* (common). —1. A black draught. *Cf.*, CUSTOM-HOUSE OFFICER.

2. A clergyman. [In allusion to the black wear of 'the cloth.'] For synonyms, *see* DEVIL-DODGER. Sweeps are nicknamed CLERGYMEN.

CHIN, *subs.* (American thieves').—A child. [? A corruption of *kinchin.*]

Verb (American). — 1. To talk; to chatter.

1883. *Bread-winners* (1884), 161. You haven't done a thing but . . . eat pea nuts and hear Bott CHIN. [M.]

1887. *New York World.* They CHIN about the best methods of relieving poverty. [M.]

18(?). FRANCIS, *Saddle and Moccasin.* He was a worker, and liked nothing better than to get into a circle of young cow-punchers, and CHIN and josh with them.

2. To talk or act with brazen effrontery.

CHINAS, *subs.* (Stock Exchange). Eastern Extension Australasian and China Telegraph Shares.

CHIN-CHOPPER, *subs.* (pugilists'). —A drive under the chin. For synonyms, *see* DIG.

CHINK, *subs.* (old). — 1. Money; ready cash; also CHINKERS, or JINK. For synonyms, *see* ACTUAL and GILT.

1557. TUSSER, *Husbandrie*, ch. lvii., st. 43, p. 134 (E.D.S.). To buie it the cheaper, haue CHINKES in thy purse.

1595. SHAKSPEARE *Romeo and Juliet*, Act i., Sc. 5. I nursed her daughter, that you talk'd withal; I tell you he that can lay hold of her Shall have the CHINKS.

1603. JOHN DAY, *Law Tricks*, Act i. They know me rich, Horatio,—CHINKE, CHINKE! Whilst this holds out, my cause shall never sincke

1630. JONSON, *New Inn*, I. Where every jovial tinker, for his CHINK, May cry, Mine host, to crambe! 'Give us drink.'

1754. B. MARTIN, *Eng. Dict.*, 2 ed., s.v.

18(?). MISS WETHERELL, *Glenham-Family*, ch. xxviii. 'I guess it's something else,—*she* had CHINK enough to buy shoes with, *I* know.'

2. (general). — The female *pudendum.* For synonyms, *see* MONOSYLLABLE.

CHINKERS, *subs.* (old).—1. Money —*See* CHINK.

1834. TAYLOR, *Ph. van Artevelde*, pt. II., iii., 1. We're vile crossbow-men, and a knight are you, But steel is steel, and flesh is still but flesh, So let us see your CHINKERS.

1887. BAUMANN, *A Slang Ditty.* Rum coves that relieve us of CHINKERS and pieces, Is gin'rally lagged, Or, wuss luck, they gits scragged.

2. (thieves').—Handcuffs united by a chain. [Derivation obvious.] For synonyms, *see* DARBIES.

CHIN-MUSIC, *subs.* (American). — Talk; chatter; oratory. *Cf.*, CHIN-WAG. The French say *casser un mot.*

1872. S. L. CLEMENS ('Mark Twain'), *Roughing It*, p. 332. The thing I'm now on is to roust out somebody to jerk a little CHIN-MUSIC for us.

1874. S. L. CLEMENS ('Mark Twain'), *Gilded Age.* Whereupon a young sprig . . . began to sass [sauce] the conductor with his CHIN-MUSIC.

1876. BESANT AND RICE, *Golden Butterfly*, ch. xxvi. 'I am not,' said he, 'going to orate. You did not come here, I guess, to hear me pay out CHIN-MUSIC.

1883. *Bread-Winners*, 77. If we have joined this order to listen to CHIN-MUSIC the rest of our lives.

CHINNING, *verbal subs.* (American). —Chatting; talking.

CHINNY, *adj.* (American). — Talkative. [From CHIN, *verb*, sense 1, + NY.]

CHINQUA SOLDI, *subs. phr.* (theatrical).—Fivepence. [From the Italian.]

CHINSE, *subs.* (Winchester College). —a chance. [Apparently a corrupted form of the word.]

CHIN-WAG, *subs.* (common).—Talk; chatter; officious impertinence.

1879. *Punch*, No. 2061, p. 4. I'd just like to have a bit of CHIN-WAG with you on the quiet.

CHIP, *subs.* (American).—1. [In plural.] Items of news, more especially LOCALS (*q.v.*).

2. A reporter who collects CHIPS, sense 1.

3. (common).—A sovereign. —*See* CHIPS, sense 5.

1883. MISS BRADDON, *Phantom Fortune*, ch. xli. Where sheafs of bank notes were being exchanged for those various coloured counters which represented divers values, from the respectable 'pony to the modest CHIP.

4. (gaming). — *See* CHIPS, *subs.* sense 2.

Verb (American).—To understand. For synonyms, *see* TWIG

18(?). FRANCIS, *Saddle and Moccasin.* I knew at once that they had got scared, and had trenched up like a bevy of quails; so I said to Jim, 'Now you let me do the talking, when they begin to sing "Indians" —don't you CHIP?'

TO CHIP IN, *verb* (common).—To contribute one's share in money or kind; to join in an undertaking; to interpose smartly.

1884. BRET HARTE, *In the Tunnel.* When you'll hear the next fool Asking of Flynn—Just you CHIP IN, Say you knew Flynn.

1869. S. L. CLEMENS ('Mark Twain'), *Innocents at Home*, p. 22. Pard, he was a great loss to this town. It would please the boys if you could CHIP IN something like that, and do him justice.

1888. *American Magazine*, Sept. A man who won't CHIP IN to charity is always an object of suspicion.

1888. *Star*, 12 Dec., p. 3, col. 3. Justice Smith here CHIPPED IN with the remark that counsel . . . had not curtailed their cross-examination.

NOT TO CARE A CHIP. — *See* CARE and FIG.

BROTHER CHIP, *subs. phr.* (common).—'Brother smut'; one of the same trade or profession, *Cf.*, CHIP OF THE OLD BLOCK.

1862. *Penny Newsman*, 'Mr. Bernal Osborne on Pigs and Politics.' I must say I never saw a set of gentlemen, who were in such excellent condition without verging upon obesity (considerable laughter). I could have wished, gentlemen, that there had been a larger show to-day. At the same time as a BROTHER CHIP (a laugh)—Oh, gentlemen, I am a farmer (hear). I am one of those farmers that don't understand my business as well as I ought.

CHIP OF THE SAME, or THE SAME OLD, BLOCK, sometimes abbreviated to CHIP, *phr.* (common), A person reproducing certain familiar or striking characteristics, CHIP = also a man or thing, and in this sense is equivalent to BLOKE, COVE, CHEAT, etc., all of which *see.*

c. 1626. *Dick of Devonshire*, in Bullen's *Old Plays*, ii., 60. Your father used to come home to my mother, and why may not I be A CHIPP OF THE SAME BLOCKE, out of which you two were cutt?

1762. COLMAN, *Musical Lady*, II., iii. You'll find him his father's own son, I believe; A CHIP OF THE OLD BLOCK, I promise you!

1843. DICKENS, *Martin Chuzzlewit*, ch. xviii., p. 189. 'Yes, yes, Chuffey, Jonas is a CHIP OF THE OLD BLOCK. It's a very old block now, Chuffey,' said the old man.

1860. *Funny Fellow*, May 7, p. 1. Hollo, my kiddy, stir your stumps, And chuck yourself about; Make haste, young CHIP, my boots to shine, Or your shine I'll quick take out.

1865. M. E. BRADDON, *Henry Dunbar*, ch. xxxviii. I was in love myself once, though I do seem such a dry old CHIP.

CHIP IN PORRIDGE, BROTH, etc., *phr.* (common).—An old phrase signifying a thing of no moment; a nonentity.

1686. GOAD, *Celest. Bodies*, I., xvii., 108. The Sextile is no CHIP IN BROTH . . . but a very considerable Engine. [M.]

1688. *Vox Cleri Pro Rege*, 56. A sort of CHIP IN POTTAGE, which (he hopes) will not do Popery much good, nor the Church of England much harm. [M.]

1849. SIR CHAS. NAPIER, as quoted in *N. and Q.*, 1 S., i., p. 383. 'The reviews which the Commander-in-Chief makes of the troops are not to be taken as so many CHIPS IN PORRIDGE.'

1880, *Church Times*, 25 June. The Burials Bill . . . is thought . . . to resemble the proverbial CHIP IN PORRIDGE, which does neither good nor harm. [M.]

CHIPPER, *adj.* (American).—'Fit'; active; ready to 'chip in.'

CHIPPY, *adj.* (common).—Unwell; seedy. Generally used to describe the results of over-indulgence in eating, drinking, etc. *Cf.*, CHEAP.

1877. *Belgravia*, April, p. 235. After two copious libations of the above [B. and S.], a man is apt to feel CHIPPY next morning.

1884. HAWLEY SMART, *From Post to Finish* [Ry. ed.], p. 157. A dozen cigars a day make one feel dreadfully CHIPPY in the morning.

CHIPS, *subs.* (old).—1. A carpenter. Fourbesque equivalents are *gangherino* and *zangarino*, whilst the Gaunersprache has *Mepaie.*

1785. GROSE, *Dict. Vulg. Tongue.* A nick-name for a carpenter.

1851. *Chambers' Paper*, No. 52, p. 20. The carpenter, a rough hardy Swede, rejoicing in the name of Burstrome, was not offended in the slightest degree at being called CHIPS even by the black cuddy servant.

1883. CLARK RUSSELL, *Sailors' Language*, pref., xii. The carpenter is more politely termed CHIPS.

2. (gaming).—Counters used in games of chance. *Cf.*, CHECKS.

1869. S. L. CLEMENS ('Mark Twain'), *Innocents at Home*, ch. ii. Don't put up another CHIP till I look at my hand.

3. (American).—Cards. [Mr. C. Nordhoff writing to Mr. John Camden Hotten, on 1 May, 1865, states that 'CHIPS = slang for cards.']

4. (common).—Money. [This usage is derived through sense 2, and passes naturally to sense 5 (*q.v.*).]

1877. W. BLACK, *Green Past. and Picc.*, ch. xlix. You kent fool away your hand and keep the CHIPS.

1885. *Sporting Times*, 23 May. 'The Chorister' Promise.' The landlady came and knocked at the door—(Sing Fulham Road), Saying she'd have to clear out, and swore She'd distrain on her wardrobe what was more (Because of the CHIPS she owed).

5. (general). — A sovereign. Used both in *sing.* and *pl.*—*See* quot. under CHIP, sense 3, and *Cf.*, preceding sense.

6. (Wellington College). — A kind of grill, so called from its hardness.

TO HAND IN ONE'S CHIPS, *phr.* (gamblers').—To die. [For probable derivation, *see* CHECKS.]

CHIRP, *verb* (thieves').—1. To talk. For synonyms, *see* PATTER. Grose has CHIRPING MERRY= exhilarated with liquor.

1884. J. GREENWOOD, *The Little Ragamuffins*. I firmly resolved to CHIRP, when I was taken before the magistrate to give evidence, as little as possible.

2. To inform. For synonyms, *see* PEACH.

CHIRPER, *subs.* (common).—1. A singer.

2. (common), — A glass or tankard.

1862. GEORGE MEREDITH, *Juggling Jerry Poems*. Hand up the CHIRPER! ripe ale winks in it; Let's have comfort and be at peace. Once a stout draught made me light as a linnet. Cheer up! the Lord must have his lease.

3. (common). — The mouth. For synonyms, *see* POTATO TRAP.

4. (music-hall).—One of a gang frequenting the stage doors of music-halls to blackmail the singers. If money be refused them, they go into the auditorium and hoot, hiss, and groan at the performer. [*Cf.*, CHIRRUP, quot., 1888.]

1889. *Daily News*, 2 July, p. 2. Singularly enough the Canterbury Music hall . . . was mentioned in one of the night charges, two men known as CHIRPERS or CHIRRIPERS being brought before Mr. Biron.

CHIRPY, *adj.* (colloquial).—Cheerful; lively. [From CHIRP = babble of birds, + Y.]

1837. J. BATES, in Ht. Martineau, *Soc. Amer.*, III., 332. It makes me CHIRPY to think of Roseland.

1879. JUSTIN McCARTHY. *Donna Quixote*, ch. xxxv. To Charlton this appeared gravely ominous . . . Paulina, on the other hand, was what she would herself have called CHIRPY.

1882. BESANT, *All Sorts and Conditions of Men*, ch. xx., p. 146. Her ladyship pu quite a CHIRPY face upon it.

CHIRRUP, *verb* (music-hall).—To cheer or applaud under a system of blackmail. [The term appears to have come into vogue in the early part of 1888.—*See* quots. under CHIRRUPER; also *Cf.*, CHIRPER, sense 4, and CHIRRUPING.]

CHIRRUPER.—*See* CHIRPER, senses 1 and 4. Fr., *un intime*.

1888. *Pall Mall Gazette*, 6 Mar., p. 4, col. 2. A CHIRRUPER . . . excused himself at the Lambeth Police Court yesterday by alleging that 'he thought there was no harm in it.'

1888. J. PAYN, in *Illustrated London News*, 17 Mar., p. 268. The . . . singers in music-halls cannot . . . do without him (the CHIRRUPER). [M.]

CHIRRUPING, *verbal subs.* (music-hall) — Hanging about stage doors to intercept the 'artistes,' and extort money with a statement that the performer who 'parts' will be applauded. [For suggested, but very dubious, derivation, *see* quot., and *Cf.*, CHIRPER, sense 4.]

1888. *Pall Mall Gazette*, 9 March, p. 14. CHIRRUPING. Mr. Rintoul Mitchell writing from the Savage Club [asks] to add a hint as to the etymology of the word. It is not remote. The French argot for blackmail is *chantage*. Such paltry operations as those reported from the Lambeth music-hall do not merit the description of singing—they are simply twittering or CHIRRUPING.

CHISEL, CHIZZLE, or **CHUZZLE**, *verb* (common). — To cheat. [Possibly an extension of the orthodox meaning of the verb in the sense of 'to cut, shave, or pare with a chisel to an excessive degree.' Jamieson (1808) gives CHISEL as to cheat, or act deceitfully. Current during the first half of the present century, it seems first to have appeared in literature about 1840. *Cf.*, GOUGE, SHAVE, SKIN, and other words of a kindred type.] For synonyms, *see* STICK.

1844. *Illustrated London News*, 25 May. 'The Derby.' They have CHISELED the peaman and no mistake about that.

1851-61. H. MAYHEW, *London Lab. and Lon. Poor*, vol. III., p. 78. When we got home at night we shared 2s. a piece. There was five of us altogether; but I think they CHISSELLED me.

1858. *Savannah Republican*, 17 May. When the books were overhauled by the Committee, it was found that . . the stockholders would be CHISELLED out of a pretty considerable sum.

1865. *Saturday Review*, April. Mr. Hotten has given the supposed classical originals of 'Dickey' and of 'Skedaddle.' He might have traced the slang verb TO CHISEL to the Latin *deascio* and *deruncino*.

1865. G. A. SALA, *Trip to Barbary*, ch. xx. To '*carrotter*' any one, say an uncle or a creditor, is to CHIZZLE or 'chouse' or 'do' him out of his property amidst assurances of high-flown benevolence and exalted integrity.

TO GO FULL CHISEL, *phr.* (American).—To go at full speed or 'full drive'; to show intense earnestness; to use great force; to go off brilliantly.

1835. HALIBURTON, *Clockmaker* (1862), 95. The long shanks of a bittern . . . a drivin' away like mad, FULL CHISEL arter a frog.

1878. MRS. STOWE, *Poganuc P.*, ix., 76. Then he'd turn and run up the narrow way, FULL CHISEL. [M.]

CHISELLING, *verbal subs.* Cheating. [*Cf.*, CHISEL, *verb.*] Variants are BAMMING; BITING; BESTING; GOUGING, etc.

1871. DE VERE, *Americanisms*, p. 298. Other efforts at cheating are designated as CHISSELLING—not as some have believed from the practice of CHISELLING, that is, opening by means of cold chisels the safes of banks and merchants, since the term is much older than the introduction of safes.

CHIT, *subs.* (Anglo-Indian).—1. A letter; corruption of a Hindoo word.

1785. In *Seton-Karr*, I., 114. [They] may know his terms by sending a CHIT. [M.]

1887. *Chamb. Jour.*, 25 June, p. 411. He had brought a note or CHITTI, as they call it in those parts [Bengal].

2. (society). — An order for drinks in clubs, etc. [Obviously an extended use of sense 1. In India the practice of writing CHITS or notes on the smallest provocation has always been carried to excess.]

3. (common).—A girl, under age and undersized. For general synonyms, *see* TITTER.

4. *subs.* (Scots). Food eaten in the hand: as a THUMBER (*q.v.*), a workman's lunch, and a child's PIECE (*q.v.*).

CHITTERLINGS, *subs.* (old).—The shirt frills once fashionable. [Properly the entrails of a pig, to which they are supposed to bear some resemblance.]

CHITTY, *subs.* (tailors').—An assistant cutter or trimmer.

CHITTY-FACED, *adj.* (old).—Thin; weazened; baby-faced. *Cf.*, CHIT, sense 3.

1601. MUNDAY, *Downf. R. Earl of Huntingdon*, I., iii. You halfe-fac't groat, you thick [? thin] cheekt CHITTI-FACE. [M.]

1621. BURTON, *Anat. of Melan*, [2nd ed.], p. 519. A thin, lean, CHITTY-FACE.

1690. B. E., *Dict. Cant. Crew.*

1725. *New Cant. Dict.*

1785. GROSE, *Dict. Vulg. Tongue.*

1811. *Lexicon Balatronicum.*

1859. HOTTEN, *Slang Dict.*

CHIV.—*See* **CHIVE.**

CHIVALRY, *subs.* (old).—Coition. [From the Lingua Franca or O. F. *chevaulcher.*] For synonyms, *see* GREENS and *Cf.*, RIDE.

CHIVE or **CHIV**, *subs.* (thieves').—1. A knife. [The Gypsy has CHIVE, to stab.]

ENGLISH SYNONYMS. Arkansas toothpick (a bowie knife); cabbage-bleeder; whittle; gully; jocteleg (a clasp knife: a corruption of Jacques de Liége); snickersnee (nautical); cuttle; cuttlebung; pig-sticker.

FRENCH SYNONYMS. *Un bince* (thieves'); *un coupe-lard* (popular: literary 'a bacon slicer,' *lard* being used as the English 'bacon' for the human body); *un coupe-sifflet* (thieves': *couper le sifflet à quelqu'un* = 'to cut any one's throat'); *un lingre* or *lingue* (thieves': from Langres, a manufacturing town); *un trente-deux* or *un vingt-deux* (thieves': originally terms used by Dutch and Flemish thieves'); *un chourin* or *surin* (thieves': possibly from the Gypsy *churi*, 'a knife'); *un pliant* (thieves'); *une petite flambe* (thieves': also a sword, said by Michel to be derived from *Flamberge*, the name of the sword of Renaud de Montauban. *Mettre flamberge au vent* = 'to draw').

GERMAN SYNONYMS. *Hechtling*; *Kaut* (possibly connected with the English 'cut'); *Mandel* or *Mandle*: (Viennese thieves': in the Gaunersprache = 'a man,' especially a little one); *Sackin*, *Sackem*, *Sackum*, *Zackin*, *Zacken* (from the Hebrew *sochan*); *Schorin* or *Schorie* (from the Gypsy *churi*, which in Hanover appears as *Czuri*).

ITALIAN SYNONYM. *Bacchetto.*

PORTUGUESE SYNONYM. *Sarda.*

1674. R. HEAD, *Canting Academy*, 12. He takes his CHIVE and cuts us down.

1714. *Memoirs of John Hall* (4 ed.), p. 11. CHIEVE, knife.

1785. GROSE, *Dict. of the Vulgar Tongue*, s.v.

1828. JON. BEE, *Picture of London*, p. 26. Some of these accomplices also carry a CHIV, or knife.

1837. DISRAELI, *Venetia*, ch. xiv. 'Berwnu,' he shouted, 'gibela CHIV for the gentry cove.'

1879. J. W. HORSLEY, in *Macm. Mag.*, XL., 503. So we had a fight, and he put the CHIVE (knife) into me.

2. *See* CHIVEY.

Verb.—To stab; to 'knife.'

1725. *New Cant. Dict.* To CHIVE his Darbies: to saw asunder his Irons.

1812. J. H. VAUX, *Flash Dict.*, s.v. To CHIV a person is to stab or cut him with a knife.

1868. *Cassell's Magazine*, May, p. 80. He [a bushranger] was as good a man as Jacky at any weapon that could be named, and if Jacky were game for a CHIVING (stabbing) match, he (Kavanagh) was ready for him.

1879. J. W. HORSLEY, in *Macm. Mag.*, XL., 503. After the place got well where I was CHIVED.

CHIVE-FENCER, *subs.* (costers').—A street hawker of cutlery. [From CHIVE, a knife, + FENCE or FENCER, a receiver of stolen property.]

CHIVEY or **CHIVVY**, *subs.* (common).—A shout; greeting or cheer. *Cf.*, CHI-IKE.

Verb (common).—To 'guy'; to chase round or hunt about; to throw or pitch about. Also CHEVY. [Mr. C. G. Leland says in *Annandale* (vol. I., 460) CHIVVY is a common English word, meaning to goad, drive, vex, hunt, or throw as it were here and there. It is purely Gypsy. *Chiv* in Rommany means anything sharp-pointed, as a dagger, goad, or knife. The old Gypsy word *chiv* among its numerous meanings has exactly that of casting, throwing, pitching, and driving. Murray, however, inclines to derive it from Chevy Chase, the scene of a famous Border skirmish; in any case the usage is modern, but see quot., 1821.] So also CHIVIED, CHIVEYING, etc.

1821. MONCRIEFF, *Tom and Jerry*, I., vii. *Log.* Come along, then. Now, Jerry, CHIVEY! *Jerry.* CHIVEY? *Log.* Mizzle! *Jerry.* Mizzle? *Log.* Tip your rags a gallop! *Jerry.* Tip my rags a gallop? . . . *Log.* Bolt! *Jerry.* Bolt? Oh, aye! I'm fly now. You mean go.

1840. GEN. P. THOMPSON, *Exerc.* (1842), V. 50. The other side are to blame, if they do not, as we should say in the dragoons 'CHEVY' them back again.

1851-61. H. MAYHEW, *London Lab. and Lon. Poor*, vol. III., p. 44. I never had patience enough to try and kill fleas by my process; it would be too much of a CHIVEY to please me.

1863. H. KINGSLEY, *Austin Elliot*, ch. xxxix. The dog . . . used to CHIVY the cats into the window among the bon bons, and play the deuce and all.

1864. *Eton School-days*, ch. xiv., p. 168. Burke, however, ran the faster of the two, and after a short CHIVEY, succeeded in capturing him.

1868. MISS BRADDON, *Trail of the Serpent*, bk. VI., ch. iv. The Board of Health came a-CHIVVING of us to take up our floorings, and limewash ourselves inside.

1871. *Daily News* Report, 'A Republican Demonstration in Hyde Park, on Sunday, April 17.' A comparatively decent man selling 'A History of Ireland' was mobbed and CHIVIED from side to side.

CHIVING LAY, *subs. phr.* (old).—Cutting the braces of coaches behind, whereupon, the coachman quitting the box, an accomplice broke and robbed the boot. Also cutting through the back of the coach to snatch the large and costly wigs then fashionable. —*Grose.* [From CHIVE, a knife.]

CHIVY or **CHEVY**, *subs.* (thieves').—The face. For synonyms, *see* DIAL.

c. 1886. Music Hall Song. ''Aint he got an artful CHEVY.'

Verb.—To scold; to bullyrag. For synonyms, *see* WIG.

CHOAKEE.—*See* CHOKEY.

CHOCK, *verb* (streets').—To strike a person under the chin. [Probably a corruption of TO CHUCK, *i.e.*, 'chuck under the chin.']—*See* CHOCKER.

CHOCKER, *subs.* (streets').—A man. Generally OLD CHOCKER, and thus comparable with OLD CODGER (*q.v.*). The term is not however, used in contempt; presumably, therefore, it signifies a manly man, *i.e.*, one who is capable of 'chocking.'—*See* CHOCK.

CHOCOLATE. TO GIVE CHOCOLATE WITHOUT SUGAR, *phr.* (old).—To reprove.—*Grose* [1785], and *Lexicon Balatronicum* [1811].

CHOKE-DOG, *subs.* (common).—Cheese; especially that made in Devonshire.

1870. *Good Words*, March. As I have said before, the Dorsetshire hind is undoubtedly under-fed. Bread and CHOKE-DOG, as he calls his county's cheese, etc. —these, as I have said before, are the chief items in his bill of fare.

CHOKE OFF, *verb* (common).—To get rid off; to put a stop to; and in a milder sense, 'to run contrary to.' [In the first instance the idea was associated with the throttling of bull-dogs to make them loose their hold; but the editor of a recent edition of the *Slang Dictionary* (Mr. Henry M. Sampson of *The Referee*) adds *en parenthèse*, 'Of course by those who don't know the scientific way used in canine exhibitions and dog-fights—of biting their tails till they round to bite the biter.']

ENGLISH SYNONYMS. To shut off; to shunt; to fub off; to rump; to cold shoulder. For synonyms in a more emphatic sense, *see* FLOOR.

FRENCH SYNONYMS. *Envoyer quelqu'un s'asseoir* (popular: *Cf.*, 'to set one down'); *arrêter les frais* ('to put a stop to proceedings.')

1818. COBBETT, *Pol. Reg.*, XXXIII., 72. The Duke's seven mouths . . . made the Whig party CHOAK OFF Sheridan. [M.]

1848. *New York Exp.*, 21 Feb. (Bartlett). In the House . . . of . . . Representatives. The operation of CHOKING OFF a speaker was very funny, and reminded me of the lawless conduct of fighting school-boys.

1864. *Derby Day*, p. 155. 'That will do, mother,' he said; 'I think I have had my five shillings' worth'; but the gipsy would not be CHOKED OFF until she had finished the patter she had learnt by heart.

1870. *London Figaro*, 26 November. The hair-oil vendor was proceeding in this strain of eulogium on the virtues of his particular invigorating application when he was gently but firmly CHOKED OFF.

1883. *Graphic*, July 7, p. 11, col. 2. English dealers attend these fairs with the object of purchasing these noble-looking animals, but prices have now risen to £20 per head, and the English demand is being CHOKED OFF.

CHOKER, *subs.* (common).—1. A cravat; primarily the large neckerchief once worn high round the neck. Sometimes WHITE CHOKER (*q.v.*), the white neckerchief peculiar to evening dress.

ENGLISH SYNONYMS. Neckinger; tie (this is now technical, but was formerly a slang term); crumpler.

FRENCH SYNONYMS. *Un collier* or *coulant*; *un blave* or *blavin*; *un épiploon* (students').

1848. THACKERAY, *Book of Snobs*, ch. i., p. 146. The usual attire of a gentleman, viz., pumps, a gold waistcoat, a crush hat, a sham frill, and a WHITE CHOKER.

1853. WH. MELVILLE, *Digby Grand*, ch. xix. Cram on a wrap-rascal and a shawl CHOAKER. Never mind the gold-laced overalls and spurs.

1853. REV. E. BRADLEY ('Cuthbert Bede'), *Verdant Green*, pt. I., p. 72. I'll take off his CHOKER and make him easy about the neck, and then we'll shut him up and leave him. Why, the beggar's asleep already.

1855. THACKERAY, *Newcomes*, ch. vii. There's Mr. Brown, who oils his hair, and wears rings, and WHITE CHOKERS—my eyes! such WHITE CHOKERS!—and yet we call him the handsome snob!

1869. *Orchestra*, 20 August. I found myself elbowing a fellow-countryman in a button-up waistcoat, and WHITE CHOKER!

1871. *London Figaro*, 13 May, p. 3, col. 3. 'Bill ain't hungry this morning,' she repeated; 'or the cove with the WHITE CHOKER 'ud be safe to collar. But look!'

2. (popular).—An all-round collar. *Cf.*, ALL-ROUNDER.

1869. *New York Herald*, 6 Sept. 'Prince Arthur in Canada.' A neat and elegant black dress coat, closely buttoned, pants of a light drab hue, a CHOKER collar of enormous size, and a black silk tile, were the garments most conspicuous

3. (common).—A garotter.—*See* WIND-STOPPER.

4. (thieves').—A cell; prison; lock up.—*See* CHOKEY.

1884. *St. James's Gazette*, Jan. 4, p. 12, col. He preferred to go to CHOKER.

5. (thieves').—The hangman's rope or 'squeezer'; a halter. For synonyms, *see* HORSE'S NIGHTCAP.

WHITE-CHOKER, *subs.* (common).—A clergyman. [In allusion to the white ties worn by 'the cloth.'] For synonyms, *see* DEVIL-DODGER.

1849. *Punch's Almanack.* The Swell Mobsman's Almanack. Plant about Exeter 'All, in May take old ladies on way to 'All, as they generally hempties into the plate. The VITE CHOKERS may be fingured on their way 'ome as they mostly brings hoff a pocketful.

1852. *Comic Almanack.* 'Modes of addressing persons of various ranks.' The *Clergy* as a body, you will speak of as the WHITE-CHOKERS, The lay aristocracy are simply styled *The Nobs.*

CHOKERED, *ppl. adj.* (common).—Wearing a CHOKER (*q.v.*).

1866. *London Review*, 7 April, p. 388, col. 1. A whitebait waiter is admirably CHOKERED.

CHOKEY, CHOKY, CHOKEE or **CHOKER**, *subs.* (common).—1. A prison. [Indian: from Hindī *chaukī*, a shed, station, or lock-up. In use from 1698 onwards and transferred to English slang early in the present century.] The Queen's Bench prison has been called the QUEEN'S CHOKEY. For synonyms, *see* CAGE.

1836. MICHAEL SCOTT, *Cruise of the Midge* (ed. 18), p. 107. Lord, but it's CHOKEY!

1866. *London Miscellany*, March 3, p. 58, col. 1. I've jist crept out o' CHOKEY. This is the twenty-ninth time I've been took that way, and I'm jist gone twenty.

1877. *Five Years' Penal Servitude*, ch. ii., p. 131. Both were marched off to CHOKEE, and I have no doubt got punished.

1877. BESANT AND RICE, *This Son of Vulcan*, II., ch. vi., p. 223. Find out this stranger, and, by God, I'm a justice of the peace, and I'll cool his heels in CHOKEE for a month.

1884. *Daily News*, Sept. 24, p. 3, col. 1. Wright . . . would get two or three days' CHOKY (*i.e.*, bread and water).

2. (prison).—A cell, specially a punishment cell. For synonyms, *see* CLINCH.

1889. *Answers*, 30 March, p. 280, col. 2. But I am reminded that I have not yet described that horrible institution known as the dark cell—CHOKEY, we convicts called it.

CHONKEYS, *subs.* (common).—*See* quot.

1851-61. H. MAYHEW, *London Lab. and Lon. Poor*, vol. I., p. 208. CHONKEYS, or a kind of mincemeat baked in crust.

CHOP, *subs.* (old).—1. A blow. Once (in the sixteenth and seventeenth centuries) literary; and still respectable in a 'chopping'—*i.e.*, a beating 'sea.'

2. An exchange; a barter. *Cf.*, CHOP AND CHANGE.

1876. C. HINDLEY, *Life and Adventures of a Cheap Jack*, p. 140. I purchased, or more properly speaking, had a CHOP with a wooden bowl maker from Chesham.

Verb (colloquial).—1. To exchange; to barter: as, TO CHOP LOGIC = to give argument for argument; and TO CHOP STORIES = to 'cap' one anecdote with another. Also to change quarters: as 'the wind CHOPPED round to the north.' *Cf.*, SWAP.

1554. LATIMER, wks. (1845), II., 433. Shall we go about to CHOP away this good occasion, which God offereth us. [M.]

1693. SHADWELL, *Volunteers*, IV. (1720), iv., 467. Horses that are jades . . . may be CHOPT away or sold in Smithfield. [M.]

1871. *City Press*, Jan. 21. 'Curiosities of Street Literature.' He hangs out in Monmouth-court, And wears a pair of blue-black breeches, Where all the 'Polly Cox's crew' do resort, To CHOP their swag for badly-printed dying speeches.

2. To eat a chop.

1841. MRS. GORE, *Cecil*, xx. I would rather have CHOPPED at the 'Blue Posts' as I once did, fifteen years before. [M.]

1887. SALA, *Illustrated London News*, Feb. 5, 144. I went one day . . . to CHOP at the 'Cock.' [M.]

3. (colonial).—*See* quot.

1871. *Sheffield Telegraph*, April. West African (New Calabar) slang for cannibalistic practice. He's CHOPPED, *i.e.*, he is eaten.

CHOP AND CHANGE, *subs. phr.* (colloquial).—Ups and downs; vicissitudes; changes of fortune.

1759-67. STERNE, *Tristam Shandy* [ed. 1772], I., ch. xi. [Surnames] which, in a course of years, have generally undergone as many CHOPS AND CHANGES as their owners.

1835. MARRYAT, *Jacob Faithful*, xvi. At last we were all arranged . . . although there were several CHOPS AND CHANGES about until the order of precedence could be correctly observed.

1845. HOOD, *To Kitchener*, iii. Like Fortune, full of CHOPS AND CHANGES.

1849-50. THACKERAY, *Pendennis*, III., p. 423. I have heard of all that has happened, and all the CHOPS AND CHANGES that have taken place during my absence.

1851. MAYHEW, *London Labour and London Poor*, II., 238. The accounts of such transactions for a series of years, with all their CHOPS AND CHANGES.

Verbal phr., *trs.* and *intrs.*—To barter; buy and sell; exchange; change tactics; veer frequently from one side to the other; vacillate, etc.

1485. *Digby Myst.* (1882), v., 641. I . . . CHOPPE AND CHAUNGE with Symonye, and take large yiftes. [M.]

1593. G. HARVEY, *Pierces Super.*, in wks. II., 115. To mangle my sentences, hack my arguments, CHOPP AND CHANGE my phrases.

1672. WYCHERLEY, *Love in a Wood*, wks. V. (1713), 431. We have CHOP'D AND CHANG'D, and hid our Christina's so long, and often, that at last, we have drawn each of us our own?

1706. E. COLES, *Eng. Dict.* CHOP Church, CHANGING of one Church for another.

1883. PRINCIPAL SHAIRP, in *Good Words*, Jan., p. 27. The politicians seemed bent on making the Church a tool which they might CHOP AND CHANGE as the political wind blew.

FIRST CHOP, SECOND CHOP, etc. (*q.v.*).

CHOP-CHOP, *adv.* (pidgin).—Immediately; quickly.

1878. JAS. PAYN, *By Proxy*, ch. ii. 'Chow-chow is not fish, but food,' explained Conway, laughing, 'and CHOP-CHOP only means directly.'

CHOPPER or **CHOPPING BLOW**, *subs.* (pugilistic).—1. *See* quotation. For synonyms, *see* DIG, BANG, and WIPE.

1819. THOS. MOORE, *Tom Crib's Memorial to Congress*, pref., p. 30. A CHOPPER is a blow, struck on the face with the back of the hand. Mendoza claims the honour of its invention, but unjustly; he certainly revived, and considerably improved it. It was practised long before our time—Broughton occasionally used it; and Slack, it also appears, struck the CHOPPER in giving the return in many of his battles.

2. (trade).—A sausage maker.

1865. *Pall Mall Gazette*, 4 Sept., p. 9, col. 2. I was glad to get it off to a CHOPPER at last. . . . Dr. Letheby explained that a CHOPPER is the trade term for a sausage maker.

TO HAVE A CHOPPER, or BUTTON, ON, *phr.* (printers').—To be miserable; 'down in the dumps' or in a fit of the 'blues.'

CHOPPING, *adj.* (old).—Sexually forward; said of girls unduly 'vain and amatorious.' [An extension in sense of CHOPPING = strapping, thumping, bouncing, etc.] The French express it by *avoir la cuisse gaie.*

CHOPPING-BLOCK, *subs.* (pugilistic).—A man like a butcher's block, *i.e.*, who takes an immense amount of 'punishment' in a fight without the science or the strength to return it.

CHOPS. TO LICK THE CHOPS, *phr.* (common).—*See* quots. [CHOPS = the mouth, lips, jaws.] Fr., *les jaffes.*

1655. FELLOWES, tr., *Milton's 2nd Defence*, 227. The sight of this egg . . . caused our monarchy-men . . . to LICK THEIR CHOPS. [M.]

1841. *Punch*, vol. I., p. 6. *Manager.* Of course then the Tories will take office? *Punch.* I raythur suspect they will. Have they not been LICKING THEIR CHOPS for ten years outside the Treasury door while the sneaking Whigs were helping themselves to all the fat tit-bits within?

DOWN IN THE CHOPS or MOUTH, *phr.* (colloquial).—Sad, melancholy. *Cf.*, TO HAVE A CHOPPER ON.

1830. SIR E. B. LYTTON, *Paul Clifford*, p. 28, ed. 1854. 'Vy, Paul, my kid, you looks DOWN IN THE CHOPS; cheer up, care killed a cat.'

1868. BREWER, *Phrase and Fable.* DOWN IN THE CHOPS—*i.e.*, down in the mouth; in a melancholy state; with the mouth drawn down. Chop or chap is Saxon for mouth; we still say a pig's chap.

CHOP THE WHINERS, *verbal phr.* (thieves').—To say prayers. [From an extended use of CHOP in the sense of to bandy words—hence to speak + WHINERS (*q.v.*), prayers.] Fr., *manger sa paillasse.*

1830. BULWER LYTTON, *Paul Clifford*, p. 2, ed. 1854. I tells you, I vent first to Mother Bussblour's, who, I knows, CHOPS THE WHINERS morning and evening to the young ladies, and I axes there for a Bible, and she says, says she, 'I 'as only a Companion to the *Halter*! but you'll get a Bible, I think at Master Talkins the cobbler as preaches.'

1857. *Punch*, 31 Jan. For them coves in Guildhall and that blessed Lord Mayor, Prigs on their four bones should CHOP WHINERS I swear.

CHORTLE, *verb* (popular). — To chuckle; to laugh in one's sleeve; to 'snort.' [Introduced by Lewis Carrol in *Through the Looking Glass.—See* quot.]

1872. LEWIS CARROL, *Through Looking Glass*, i. 'O frabjous day! Callooh! Callay!' He CHORTLED in his joy.

1876. BESANT AND RICE, *Golden Butterfly*, xxxii., 242. It makes the cynic and the worldly-minded man to chuckle and CHORTLE with an open joy.

1887. *Athenæum*, 3 Dec., p. 751, col. 1. A means of exciting cynical CHORTLING.

1888. *Daily News*, 10 Jan., p. 5, col. 2. So may CHORTLE the Anthropophagi. [M.]

CHOSEN TWELVE.—*See* APOSTLES.

CHOUSE, *subs.* (colloquial).—1. A trick; swindle; sham; or 'SELL' (*q.v.*). [From CHOUSE, a cheat, trickster, or swindler, through the verb. The derivation is thus discussed and weighed by Dr. Murray: 'As to the origin of the Eng. use, Gifford (1814), in a note on the quot. from Ben Jonson, says, 'In 1609, Sir Robt. Shirley sent a messenger or CHIAUS to this country, as his agent from the Grand Signior and the Sophy to transact some preparatory business.' The latter CHIAUSED the Turkish and Persian merchants of £4,000,' and decamped. But no trace of this incident has yet been found outside of Gifford's note; it was unknown to Peter Whalley, a previous editor of Ben Jonson, 1756; also to Skinner, Henshaw, Dr. Johnson, Todd, and others who discussed the history of the word. Yet most of these recognised the likeness of CHOUSE to the Turkish word, which Henshaw even proposed as the etymon on the ground that the Turkish CHIAUS 'is little better than a fool.' Gifford's note must therefore be taken with reserve.'] The word is also used at Eton in this sense, but *see* sense 2, which is the commoner. Variously spelt CHIAUS, CHEWS, SHOWSE, GHOWSE, and CHOUSE.

1610. BEN JONSON, *Alchymist*, I., ii., 25. '*D.* What do you think of me? That I am a CHIAUSE? *Face.* What's that? *D.* The Turk [who] was here. As one would say, doe you think I am a Turke?'

1639. FORD, *Lady's Trial*, II., i. Gulls, or Moguls, Tag, rag, or other, hogen-mogen, vanden, Skip-jacks, or CHOUSES.

1672. WYCHERLEY, *Love in a Wood*, I., i., wks. (1713), 343. You are no better than a CHOUSE, a cheat.

1673. WYCHERLEY, *Gent. Danc. Master*, III., in wks. (1713), 295. He a dancing-master, he's a CHOUSE, a cheat, a meer cheat.

1754. B. MARTIN, *Eng. Dict.* (2 ed.).

2. (Eton College).—A shame; an imposition.

1864. *Athenæum.* When an Eton boy says that anything is 'a beastly CHOUSE,' he means that it is a great shame; and when an Eton peripatetic tradesman is playful enough to call his customer 'a little CHOUSER,' he means that a leaf has been taken out of his own book by one on whom he has practised.

1883. BRINSLEY RICHARDS, *Seven Years at Eton.* The boy . . . was told that what he had done was an awful CHOUSE.

Verb (colloquial).—To cheat. [For suggested derivation, *see subs.*, sense 1.] Synonyms will be found under STICK.

1659. SHIRLEY, *Honoria and Mam.*, II., iii. We are in a fair way to be ridiculous . . . CHIAUS'D by a scholar! [M.]

1663. PEPYS, *Diary*, May 15. The Portugalls have CHOUSED us, it seems, in the Island of Bombay, in the East Indys.

1708. CENTLIVRE, *Busie Body*, Act iii. You and my most conscionable *Guardian* here . . . plotted and agreed, to CHOUSE a very civil, honest, honourable gentleman, out of a Hundred Pound.

1742-4. ROGER NORTH, *Lives of the Norths*, I., 90. The judge held them to it, and they were CHOUSED of the treble value.

1823. *Hints for Oxford*, p. 26. Everything in common use at Oxford, with the exception, perhaps, of books, is charged at an exorbitant rate; and, what is worse . . . you are often having yourself CHOUSED with abominable trash.

1890. *Academy*, Feb. 22, p. 125, col. 1. Susan Burney's letters, with charming naïveté, confess that, in the expectation of an early visit from the delightful mimic, she for four mornings was up at seven o'clock, only to find herself, borrowing the slang phrases of the day, 'CHOUSED, for he nick'd us entirely, and never came at all.'

So also CHOUSED, *ppl. adj.*, CHOUSING, *verbal subs.*, and CHOUSER, *subs.*

CHOUT, *subs.* (East London).—An entertainment.—*Hotten.*

CHOVEY, *subs.* (costermongers').—A shop. A shopman is known amongst the fraternity as a MAN-CHOVEY, and a shop-woman as ANN-CHOVEY.

1857. SNOWDEN, *Mag. Assistant* (3 ed.), 444. A shop—CHOVEY.

FRENCH SYNONYMS. *Une boutogue* (thieves'); *une boutanche* (thieves'); *un boucard* (thieves'); *un rade* or *radeau* (thieves'); also primarily, a till.

GERMAN SYNONYM. *Chenwene* (a market stall, the stock itself, or a box full of goods; *Chenwener*, the owner of such a place—a merchant or shop-keeper).

CHOW, *subs.* (theatrical).—Talk; 'lip'; jaw; *e.g.*, to have 'plenty of CHOW' = to have a good deal to say.

Verb (theatrical). — To talk incessantly; to grumble. A variant is to CHIP. [CHOW is apparently a form of 'chew,' now fallen into desuetude.]

CHOWDER-HEADED, *adj.* (American). — Stupid. [The term though only dialectical in England is pretty general in U.S.A. It is given by Murray as a variant of CHOLTER-HEADED, which in turn is another form for jolt or JOLTER-HEADED. Chowder is properly a kind of hotch-potch, and applied to the intellectuals would imply 'confusedness,' and hence idiocy.]

1819. SCOTT, *Lett.*, 15 April, in Lockhart. I hesitate a little about Raeburn . . . [he] has twice already made a very CHOWDER-HEADED person of me.

1851. H. MELVILLE, *Whale*, xv., 73. What's that stultifying saying about CHOWDER-HEADED people? [M].

18(?). S. L. CLEMENS ('Mark Twain'), *Launch of the Steamer 'Capital.'* The Showman . . . grabbed the orchestra and shook him up, and says, 'That lets you out, you CHOWDER-HEADED old clam.'

CHRISTEN, *verb* (thieves')—1. To erase the markings from a watch, and substitute a fictitious inscription, with a view to preventing identification. An Old Cant variant was TO CHURCH (*q.v.*), the derivation being analogous. French thieves, in speaking of a CHRISTENED watch or other 'faked' silver, use *convert.*

1781. G. PARKER, *View of Society*, II., 74. This alteration is called CHRISTENING, and the watch thus transformed faces the world without fear of detection.

1811. *Lexicon Balatronicum*, s.v.

1857. SNOWDEN, *Mag. Assistant*, 3 ed., p. 444. To alter the maker's name in a watch—to CHRISTEN a yack.

1868. DORAN, *Saint and Sinn.*, II., 290. The pietist thieves . . . CHRISTEN daily as soon as they have stolen a watch. This thieves' CHRISTENING consists in erasing the maker's name and supplying another. [M.]

1872. *Standard*, 'Middlesex Sessions Report.' William Miller, the detective officer in the case, being called upon by the judge to state what he knew of the prisoner, said he knew him by his trade as a baker, but he mixed up with watch thieves and housebreakers, and the tools found in his possession he used for CHRISTENING stolen watches and putting new bows to them.

2. (colloquial).—To mix water with wine; to mix liquors generally. Fr., *Maquiller le vitriol* = to adulterate brandy; *monter sur le tonneau* (vinters' = to add water to a cask of wine). A Spanish equivalent is exactly translated *bautizar el vino.* TO DROWN THE MILLER (*q.v.*), = to add too much water.

1824. SCOTT, *Redgauntlet*, let. xiii. We'll CHRISTEN him with the brewer (here he added a little small beer to his beverage).

3. (low).—To souse from a chamber utensil.

4. (common).—To take a dram; or 'do a drain,' in celebration of something, as the purchase of a new pair of boots, a removal, etc.

CHRISTIAN, *subs.* (common).—A good fellow; a decent or presentable person. [A human being as distinguished from the brute creation, in which sense it is used by Shakspeare; the modern slang usage was apparently introduced by Dickens.] — *See* quots. in various senses.

1595. SHAKSPEARE, *Two Gentlemen of Verona*, Act iii., Sc. 1, 272. Thee hath more qualities than a Water-Spaniell, which is much in a bare CHRISTIAN.

1811. *Lexicon Balatronicum*, CHRISTIAN: a tradesman who has faith, *i.e.*, will give credit.

1843. DICKENS, *Martin Chuzzlewit*, xxxiv. You must take your passage like a CHRISTIAN; at least, as like a CHRISTIAN as a fore-cabin passenger can.

1859. *Times*, 20 April. Grey parrot for sale, the property of a lady. She talks like a CHRISTIAN, and is in first-rate condition. Price, including cage, £15. Apply, etc., etc.

Adj. (common).—Decent; respectable, etc.—[*See subs.*]

CHRISTIAN PONY, *subs. phr.* (old Irish slang).—The chairman or president of a meeting.

CHRISTIANS, *subs. pl.* (Cambridge Univ.). — Members of Christ's College. — [Of obvious derivation.]

CHRISTMAS, CHRISTMASSING, *subs.* and *verbal subs.* (colloquial).—Holly and mistletoe.

1836. C. DICKENS, *Pickwick Papers*, p. 228 (ed. 1857). The fat boy pointed to the destination of the pies. 'Wery good,' said Sam, 'stick a bit o' CHRISTMAS in 'em.'

1851. H. MAYHEW, *Lon. Lab. and Lon. Poor*, vol. I., p. 141. In London a large trade is carried on in CHRISTMASING, or in the sale of holly and mistletoe for Christmas sports and decorations. . . . 'Look,' said a gardener to me, 'what's spent on a CHRISTMASING the churches!'

CHUCK, *subs.* (prison).—1. Bread; meat; in fact, refreshment of any kind.

1850. *Lloyd's Newspaper*, Oct. 6. 'Inquest on murder of Rev. Mr. Hollest, Frimley Grove, Surrey.' Macey, the village constable, stated that the prisoner,

upon coming to his cottage door had tried hard to get some CHUCK out of him, but had failed.

1877. *Five Years' Penal Servitude*, ch. i., p. 4. Two large slices of bread, . . . the allowance given out to some prisoner who . . . had forgotten to eat what in prison slang is called his 'toke' or CHUCK.

1877. S. L. CLEMENS ('Mark Twain') *Life on the Mississippi*, ch. lii., p. 463. i wish i was nere you so i could send you CHUCK (*refreshments*) on holidays.

2. (common). — Scraps of meat; BLOCK ORNAMENTS (*q.v.*). For synonyms, *see* DUCK.

1871. *Echo*, 11 Dec. 'Sunday amongst the Silk Weavers.' Few regular butchers ply their trade on Sunday morning—money is only to be made by the vendors of nauseous substitutes for wholesome meat—the refuse portion of beef and mutton, tough, coarse, and meagre pork, flaccid tripe, lean little sheeps' CHUKS, as the natives call them, the savourless saveloy of Old England.

1887. *Standard*, 20 Jan. 'The Poor at Market.' From a sort of ludicrous spirit of snobbery a labourer will term a fellow he dislikes a 'beggar who eats CHUCK,' CHUCK being a low-priced part of the carcase.

3. (Billingsgate).—*See* quot.

1851-61. MAYHEW, *London Lab. and Lon. Poor*, vol. I., p. 73 Sprats . . . are sold at Billingsgate by the 'toss,' or CHUCK, which is about half a bushel, and weighs about 40 lbs. to 50 lbs.

4. (colloquial).—A toss or throw.

1883. *Punch*, June 2, p. 264, col. 1. The average number of CHUCKS at cocoa-nuts before achieving success is six.

5. (nautical). — Sea biscuit. *Cf.*, senses 1 and 6. A sailor's variant is 'chow-dow.'

1864. *Standard*, 13 Dec. Of naval slang Mr. Hotten has missed the words CHUCK, used by sailors for biscuit, and BARGE, the box or cask in which the CHUCK is kept by the messes on the lower deck.

6. (military).—Mealy bread. *Cf.*, nautical usage, sense 5.

7. Westminster School).—A schoolboy's treat.

1864. HOTTEN, *Slang Dict.*, p. 101, s.v.

Verb (colloquial).—1. To throw; especially to throw away; to pitch.

1593. *Prodigal Son*, iv., 112. Yes, this old one will I give you (CHUCKS him old hose and doublet). [M.]

1627. DRAYTON, *Agincourt*, 63. In the Tauerne, in his cups doth rore, CHOCKING his crownes. [M.]

1753. *Adventurer*, No. 43. I . . . was kicked about, hustled, tossed up, and CHUCKED into holes.

1771. SMOLLETT, *Humphry Clinker*, I. 36. Dirt and trash CHUCKED into it by roguish boys for the joke's sake.

1820. COOMBE, *Dr. Syntax*, tour II., ch. i. Yes, faith, as I've a soul to save, I will for nothing dig her grave; Yes, I would do it too as willing As if her hand had CHUCK'D a shilling.

1836. DICKENS, *Pickwick*, ch. xxxix., p. 342. I'm not only ready but villin' to do anythin' as'll make matters agreeable; and if CHUCKIN' either o' them sawbonesses out of winder u'll do it, I'm the man.

1851. H. MAYHEW, *Lon. Lab. and Lon. Poor*, vol. I., p. 150. Many a time I walked through the streets and picked a piece of bread that the servants CHUCKED out of the door.

1864. DICKENS, *Our Mutual Friend*, bk. IV., ch. i. 'When you're ready for your snooze,' said the honest creature, 'CHUCK yourself on my bed in the corner.'

2. (vagrants').—To eat.—*See subs.*, sense 1. For synonyms, *see* GRUB.

1876. HINDLEY, *Life and Adventures of a Cheap Jack*, p. 192. Mo and his man were having a great breakfast one morning . . . Mo exclaimed to his man, 'CHUCK rumbo (eat plenty), my lad.'

3. (pigeon fanciers').—To despatch a pigeon. *Cf.*, sense 1, and TO CHUCK IT; also HARD CHUCK.

4. (general).—To spend extravagantly. For synonyms, *see* DUCKS AND DRAKES.

1876. BESANT AND RICE, *Golden Butterfly*, ch. xviii. Next to unlimited CHUCKING of his own money, the youthful Englishman would like—what he never gets—the unlimited CHUCKING of other people's.

5. (old).—To desire (sexually); to be 'warm,' or a HOT MEMBER (*q.v.*).

TO CHUCK, CHUCK IT, or CHUCK UP, *verbal phr.* To abandon; 'turn up'; dismiss; turn out of doors; to give up. Also CHUCK IT UP='drop it.' [From the custom of throwing up the sponge at a prize fight in sign of defeat. Often corrupted into JACK UP.—*See* SPONGE. A French equivalent is *laisser tout en plan.*

1869. *Daily Telegraph*, 6 Sept. 'Season at Baden.' Why is it that Englishwomen can never combine their colours, or put on their clothes? Are their maids used to haymaking when at home, and do they 'pitch' on the petticoats, and give three cheers and have beer when they finish the work by CHUCKING UP the dress?

1883. HAWLEY SMART, *Hard Lines*, ch. xxvi. 'But here, Cis, if you mean business, take my advice and CHUCK that corps.'

1883. MISS BRADDON, *Phantom Fortune*, ch. xxv. She knows on which side her bread is buttered. Look how easily she CHUCKED you UP because she did not think you good enough.

TO GET or GIVE THE CHUCK, *phr.*—To dismiss, or be dismissed. *Cf.*, BAG and SACK.

1889. *Sporting Times* [quoted in *Slang, Jargon, and Cant*]. And I shall GET THE blooming CHUCK as well as fourteen days.

CHUCK UP THE SPONGE.—*See* SPONGE.

TO CHUCK [ONESELF] ABOUT or INTO, *phr.*—To move expeditiously. For synonyms, *see* AMPUTATE and SKEDADDLE. Also, to fall into.

1860. *Funny Fellow*, 7 May, p. 1. Hollo, my kiddy, stir your stumps, And CHUCK YOURSELF ABOUT.

CHUCK HER UP, *phr.* (cricket).—An expression of delight. [From the practice of throwing the ball into the air after a successful catch.]

[The verb, TO CHUCK, is attached in an active sense to any number of objectives, and may be taken as equivalent to 'to perform' or 'do.' Thus 'to chuck a fag'=to 'give a beating'; to 'chuck a turd'=to 'rear,' to evacuate; to 'chuck a tread'=to have intercourse; to 'chuck a jolly'=to undertake a bout of chaff; to 'chuck a fit'=to have an epileptic, or apoplectic, seizure; to 'chuck a cram' or 'a kid'=to lie, etc.]

HARD-CHUCK (pigeon fanciers').—A long distance; also a trying flight. From Gravesend to London is considered a HARD-CHUCK, as the low, flat country is bare of landmarks.

CHUCK A CURLY, *verbal phr.* (military).—To feign sickness; to malinger. [For possible derivation, *see* general remarks on CHUCK, in a preceding paragraph, + CURLY, 'doubling up,' or writhing, as in pain.]

CHUCK A JOLLY, *verbal phr.* (costermongers').—To bear up or 'bonnet': as when a costermonger praises the inferior article his mate or partner is trying to sell. This process is usually commenced with a CHI-IKE (*q.v.*). Also to undertake a bout of chaff.

CHUCK A STALL, *verb phr.* (thieves').—To attract a person's attention while a confederate picks his pockets, or otherwise robs him. [STALL=an accomplice; and as a verb, to keep watch or spy upon.]

1884. GREENWOOD, *Seven Years' Penal Servitude.* I said to my pal 'CHUCK ME A STALL and I'll have that.' What

did I mean? Why, keep close to me, and cover what I'm doing.

CHUCKED. TO BE CHUCKED or CHUCKED UP, *verbal phr.* (thieves').—1. To escape committal; to be acquitted or released.

1887. HORSLEY, *Jottings from Jail*, Rit from 7 dials; remanded innocent on two charges of pokes, only out 2 weeks for a drag, expects to be fullied or else CHUCKED.

1889. *Evening News* [quoted in *Slang, Jargon, and Cant*, p. 251, col. 1]. When I was CHUCKED UP they took me to an old Jew's in Dudley Street for my clothes.

1889. *Answers*, 9 Feb. He was fortunate enough to get CHUCKED, to escape, that is to say, as the evidence against him was not strong enough.

2. (common). — [Generally CHUCKED OUT.] To be forcibly ejected. [From CHUCK, *verb*, sense 1, + ED + OUT.] *Cf.*, CHUCKER-OUT.

3. (common). — Slightly intoxicated. For synonyms *see* SCREWED.

1889. *Ally Sloper's Half-Holiday*, Aug. 17, p. 258, col. 2. His back being nearly broken from your constantly falling over him when you've been CHUCKED.

4. (prostitutes'). — Amorous; and hence 'fast.' French, *galoper une femme*=to make hot love to a woman. *Cf.*, MOLROWER.

FRENCH SYNONYMS. *S'allumer* or *allumer son pétrole* or *son gaz* (the first of these terms is in general use, the others being employed chiefly by prostitutes); *battre du beurre* (popular: used more in the sense of 'to be fast,' but also=to speculate on 'Change and to dissemble).

GERMAN SYNONYM. *Spannen* (to ogle prostitutes; to waylay women in order to make overtures; generally to lear with concupiscence).

SPANISH SYNONYMS. *Apacentar* (properly to tend cattle); *desbeber* (also = to make water); *despepitarse* (literally to give a loose to one's tongue or to act imprudently); *rabanillo* (*m*= an ardent longing).

5. (common).—To be disappointed; put out in one's calculations; put to shame; 'sold.'

c. 1879. *Broadside Ballad.* 'CHUCKED again.' CHUCKED again, CHUCKED again! Whatever may happen I get all the blame, Wherever I go, it is always the same—Jolly well CHUCKED again!

CHUCKED-IN, *adv. phr.* (popular).—Into the bargain. *Cf.*, LAGNIAPPE. [From CHUCK, sense 1, + ED + IN.]

1880. *Punch*, No. 2055, p. 245. Happy thought! CHUCKED IN an extra chapter on Literature.

1884. *Punch*, Oct. 11. ''Arry at a Political Picnic.' Went to one on 'em yesterday, Charlie; a regular old up and down lark. The Pallis free gratis, mixed up with a old country fair in a park, And Rosherville Gardens CHUCKED IN.

CHUCKER, *subs.* (cricketers').—1. A volunteer who does not keep a promise to play.

2. A bowler who throws the ball.

CHUCKER-OUT, *subs.* (colloquial).—A man retained to eject or 'chuck out' from public meetings, taverns, brothels, and hells.—*See* quot., 1880.

1880. *Punch*, No. 2040, p. 63. Lord Grey was about to resume his rôle of CHUCKER-OUT to the proposed measures of his own party.

1883. *Saturday Review*, March 31, p. 398, col. 1. We hired a smiling but stalwart assistant to act in the capacity of CHUCKER-OUT.

1884. *Good Words*, June, p. 400, col. 1. He had done twelve months [in prison] for crippling for life the CHUCKER-OUT of one of these pubs. [M.]

1885. *All the Year Round*, Nov., 226. Dens to which Brickey is attached in the capacity of CHUCKER-OUT. [M.]

1887. *Guardian*, 2 March, p. 343, col. 1. Bogus meetings, where the chairman, committee, reporters, audience, and CHUCKERS-OUT were all subsidised. [M.]

1890. *The Scots Observer*, p. 394, col. 2. The result of which was the resolution to appoint a body of CHUCKERS-OUT to keep delegates in order, and to show the Commons what to do with its Healys and its Tanners.

CHUCK-FARTHING, CHUCK, CHUCK-AND-TOSS, or **PITCH-AND-TOSS**, *subs. phr.* (common).—Games played with money, which is PITCHED at a line, gathered, shaken in the hands, and TOSSED up into the air so as to fall 'heads and tails' until the stakes are guessed away. A parish clerk was formerly nicknamed a CHUCK-FARTHING.

1690. B.E., *Dict. Cant. Crew.* CHUCK FARTHING: a Parish Clerk (in the Satyr against Hypocrites) also a Play among Boies.

1703. WARD, *London Spy*, pt. XIII., p. 317. Where Mumpers, Soldiers and Ballad-Singers, were as busie at CHUCK-FARTHING and *Hussle-Cap*, as so many Rooks at a gaming Ordinary.

1712. *Spectator*, No. 509. The unlucky boys with toys and balls were whipped away by a beadle, I have seen this done indeed of late, but then it has been only to chase the lads from CHUCK, that the beadle might seize their copper.

1759. STERNE, *Tristram Shandy*, vol. I., ch. x. The spinning-wheel forgot its round,—even CHUCK-FARTHING and shuffle-cap themselves stood gaping till he had got out of sight.

1821. CLARE, *Vill. Minstr.*, I., 174. With CHUCK and marbles wearing Sunday through.

1851. MAYHEW, *Lon. Lab. and Lon. Poor*, II., p. 398. They frequently had halfpence given to them. They played also at CHUCK AND TOSS with the journeymen, and of course were stripped of every farthing.

c. 1868. BROUGH, *Field of the Cloth of Gold.* From PITCH-AND-TOSS to manslaughter's my game.

1878. M. E. BRADDON, *Cloven Foot*, ch. xlii. 'I remember when I was a little chap, at Dr Prossford's grammar school, playing CHUCK-FARTHING.'

1888. *Illus. London News*, Summer Number, p. 26, col. 1. Having replaced the musty documents upon the shelf, that ingenious youth adjourned to indulge in the passionately exhilarating game of CHUCK-FARTHING.

CHUCK IN, *verb* (pugilistic).—To challenge.—[From the custom of throwing a hat into the ring; a modern version of throwing down the gauntlet. Also, 'to compete'; *e.g.*, I shall have a CHUCK IN='I shall try my luck'—with a woman, a raffle, a personal encounter, and so on.

CHUCKING-OUT, *subs.* (popular).—Ejection. [From CHUCK, *verb*, sense 1, through CHUCK UP (*q.v.*), + ING + OUT.] Also as an *adj.*

1881. *Sportsman*, Jan. 31, p. 3 col. 5. We were the first to take the part of the pit against a CHUCKING-OUT policy. [M.]

1887. *Pall Mall Gaz.*, Feb. 23, p. 11, col. 1. Evictions in Glenbeigh . . . and CHUCKINGS-OUT in London. [M.]

1887. G. R. SIMS, *How the Poor Live*, p. 83. It is fair to say that the youths seemed quite ready for the emergency, and took their CHUCKING-OUT most skilfully.

CHUCKS! *intj.* (school).—A boy's signal on a master's approach. A French schoolboy's equivalent is *Vesse!*

CHUCK THE DUMMY, *verbal phr.* (thieves'). — To feign sickness, especially epilepsy; a common dodge in prisons to get an order for the infirmary.

CHUFF IT! *intj.* (common).—Be off! Take it away! For synonyms, *see* HOOKEY WALKER!

CHUL or **CHULL**, *verb* (Anglo-Indian).—*See* quot.

1886. G. A. SALA, in *Ill. L. News*, June 19, p. 644. In Calcutta CHUL is a word that you hear fifty times a day. A lady tells you that her new Ayah will not CHUL at all; the proprietor of that popular weekly journal, the *Hooghly Dacoit* . . . tells you that he is going home for six months; but that he has an able editor, and that the paper will CHUL very well during his absence. The CHUL, I apprehend, means to go on, to proceed, to do.

CHUM, *subs.* (colloquial).—A close companion; a bosom friend; an intimate. Formerly a chamber-fellow or mate. [Johnson calls it a term used in the Universities, and the earliest quot. seems to bear him out. The derivation is uncertain, and Dr. Murray says 'no historical proof connecting it with "chamber-fellow" or "chamber-mate" has been found.']

1684. CREECH, *Theocritus, Idyll* XII. Ded. to my CHUM, Mr. Hody of Wadham College. [M.]

1690. B. E., *Dict. Cant. Crew.* CHUM: a Chamber-fellow, or constant Companion.

1714. *Spectator*, No. 617. Letter written by University man to a friend begins 'Dear CHUM.'

c. 1750. *Humours of the Fleet*, quot. in Ashton's *Eighteenth Century Waifs*, p. 249. When you have a CHUM, you pay but fifteen pence per week each.

1828–45. T. HOOD, *Poems*, vol. II., p. 201 (ed. 1846). The very CHUM that shared my cake Holds out so cold a hand to shake It makes me shrink and sigh.

1855. THACKERAY, *Newcomes*, ch. v., The Colonel, as has been stated, had an Indian CHUM or companion, with whom he shared his lodgings.

1889. *Pall Mall Gazette*, Nov. 21, p. 6, col. 2. His [Allingham's] own chosen friend was Dante Gabriel Rossetti, his CHUMS the Pre-Raphaelite brotherhood.

ENGLISH SYNONYMS. Gossip; pal; pard (American); marrow (north-country); cully (theatrical); cummer; ben cull; butty; bo' (nautical); mate or matey; ribstone; bloater.

FRENCH SYNONYMS. *Une branche* (literally a branch or bough); *un amar* or *amarre* (thieves', *Cf.*, *amarre*, a cable, rope, hawser); *un aminche*, *aminchemar*, or *aminchemince* (thieves': *aminche d'af*= an accomplice or stallsman); *amis comme cochons* (popular, *m. pl.*: literally 'as thick as pigs.' *Cf.*, AS THICK AS THIEVES); *un matelot*; *une coterie* (popular); *un bon attelage* (cavalry=a couple of good friends; literally 'a good team'); *un artiste* (popular); *un camerluche* or *camarluche* (popular); *vieux frère la côte* (sailors'); *un camaro*; *une faridole* (prostitutes' = a female pal); *un fanande*, or *fanandel* (thieves').

GERMAN SYNONYMS. *Gleicher* (also 'a brother'); *Kineh* or *Kinehbruaer* (Viennese thieves': German thieves use *Kinne*; from the Hebrew *Kinnim*, 'a louse'; *Kinnemachler*, literally 'lice eater'=a dirty, filthy fellow; also=a miser. *Kinimer* = a man full of lice).

ITALIAN SYNONYMS. *Furbo* ='an imposter, rogue, or sharper'); *foneo*; *calcagno*; *guido*, or *guidone* (literally a 'guide.' Also a 'dog' or 'beggar').

SPANISH SYNONYMS. *Cirinco* (*m*); *compinche* (*m*).

PORTUGUESE SYNONYM. *Filhos do Golpe* (literally 'children of the crowd').

2. (military).—A brother-in-arms.

1890. RUDYARD KIPLING. *Plain Tales* (3rd ed.), p. 264. Oh! where would I be when my froat was dry? Oh! where would I be when the bullets fly? Oh! where would I be when I came to die? Why, Somewheres anigh my CHUM.

Verb, trs. and *intrs.* (colloquial).—To occupy a joint lodging, or share expenses; to be on the closest terms of intimacy with another; to be 'thick as thieves'; or 'thick as hops.' French slang has *être dans la chemise de quelqu'un*; also *être du dernier bien avec quelqu'un.*

1730. WESLEY, wks. (1872) XII., 20. There are . . . some honest fellows in College, who would be willing to CHUM in one of them. [M.]

1762. CHURCHILL, *The Ghost*, bk. II. Old Maids and Rakes are join'd together. Coquettes and Prudes, like April weather, Wits forc'd to CHUM with Common Sense.

1836. C. DICKENS, *Pickwick Papers*, p. 339 (ed. 1857). 'Why I don't rightly know about to night,' replied the stout turnkey. 'You'll be CHUMMED on somebody to-morrow, and then you'll be all snug and comfortable.'

1864. *Temple Bar*, Nov., p. 587. We choose our own carriages, and either leave our fellow trippers altogether, or, making a selection, CHUM in parties of three or four.

1871. MORTIMER COLLINS, *Mrq. and Merch.*, II., v., 143. She . . . found herself CHUMMED upon a young person who turned out to be . . . a . . . slattern. [M.]

1877. BESANT AND RICE, *With Harp and Crown*, ch. xii. Here are City clerks, who, by CHUMMING together, are able to afford one festive evening in the week at the Oxford.

NEW CHUM, *subs.* (Australian).—A new arrival in the colony; a 'greenhorn'; or 'tenderfoot.' For general synonyms, *see* SNOOKER.

1861. EARLES, *Ups and Downs of Australian Life*, p. 199. 'I suppose you're a stranger, or as we calls 'em, a NEW CHUM, ain't you?'

1886. E. WAKEFIELD, *Nineteenth Century*, Aug., p. 173. In these colonies [Australia], where pretty nearly every one has made several sea voyages, that subject is strictly tabooed in all rational society. To dilate upon it is to betray a NEW CHUM.

1889. *Town and Country*, 16 Feb. 'Answers to Correspondents.' NEW CHUM (Forbes):—The first instalment will be due, etc.

CHUMMAGE, *subs.* (old).—Money procured by the practice of chumming together; but various extensions of meaning appear to have been in vogue at different periods.—*See* quots. [The practice alluded to in quot. 1777, was the rough music made with pokers, tongs, sticks, and saucepans, for which ovation the initiated prisoner had to pay or 'fork out' a certain sum of money, or submit to being deprived of its equivalent from among his personal effects; otherwise called CHUMMING UP.]

1777. HOWARD, *State of Prisons in England and Wales*, quoted in J. Ashton's *The Fleet*, p. 295. A cruel custom obtains in most of our Gaols, which is that of the prisoners demanding of a new comer GARNISH, FOOTING, or (as it is called in some London Gaols) CHUMMAGE.

1785. GROSE, *Dict. Vulg. Tongue.* CHUMMAGE: money paid by the richer sort of prisoners in the Fleet and King's Bench to the poorer for their share of a room . . . A prisoner who can pay for being alone, chooses two poor chums, who for a stipulated price, called CHUMMAGE, give up their share of the room.

1836. DICKENS, *Pickwick*, xlii. The regular CHUMMAGE is two-and-sixpence.

1859. G. A. SALA, *Twice Round the Clock* (1861), 103. The time-honoured system of CHUMMAGE, or quartering two or more collegians in one room, and allowing the richest to pay his companions a stipulated sum to go out and find quarters elsewhere.

Also used as an adjective.

1836. DICKENS, *Pickwick*, ch. xlii., p. 364. You'll have a CHUMMAGE ticket upon twenty-seven in the third, and them as is in the room will be your chums.

CHUMMERY, *subs.* (common).—Chumhood; also the quarters occupied by 'chums.' [From CHUM + ERY; *cf.*, ROOKERY, SNUGGERY, &c.].

1877. BESANT AND RICE. *Son of Vulcan*, p. 196. Jack and her father lived in bachelor CHUMMERY.

CHUMMY, *subs.* (colloquial).—1. A chimney-sweep's climbing boy. [A corruption of 'chimney' through 'chumley.']

1835. DICKENS, *Sketches by Boz*, p. 169. Vereas he 'ad been a CHUMMY—he begged the cheerman's parding for using such a vulgar hexpression, etc.

1844. THACKERAY, *Greenwich*, wks. (1886) XXIII., 380. The hall . . was decorated with banners and escutcheons of deceased CHUMMIES. [M.]

1851-61. H. MAYHEW, *London Lab. and Lond. Poor*, vol. II., p. 417. A CHUMMY (once a common name for the climbing-boy, being a corruption of chimney).

1859. W. GREGORY, *Egypt*, I., 154. His shrill voice, high up aloft, like a CHUMMY'S on a London summer morn. [M.]

2. A diminutive form of CHUM (*q.v.*).

1864. GILBERT, *Bab Ballads, Etiquette.* Old CHUMMIES at the Charter-house were Robinson and he. [M.]

3. (common).—A low-crowned felt hat. For synonyms, *see* GOLGOTHA.

Adj. (colloquial).—Very intimate; friendly; sociable. The analogous French terms are *chouette*; *chouettard*; *chouettaud*.

1884. *Harper's Magazine*, Sept., p. 536 col. 2. I . . . saw them form into small CHUMMY groups. [M.]

1888. W. BESANT, *Herr Paulus*, bk. III., ch. xi., vol. III., p. 204. I liked the fellow, I confess, and we got CHUMMY in the evenings.

1889. *Answers*, May 11, p. 380. When I was at Pentonville, a man in the same ward, who had got rather CHUMMY with his warder, asked him to post a letter to his friends in Manchester.

CHUMP, *subs.* (common).—1. A blockhead.

1883. HAWLEY SMART, *At Fault* II., i., 29. Such a long-winded old CHUMP at telling a story one don't often see, thank goodness.

1887. *Pall Mall Gazette*, 2 Feb., p. 10, col. 1. Frank audibly remarked: 'This man is a CHUMP. I could go . . . this minute and do better than that.' [M.]

2. (popular).—A variant of CHUM, *subs.* (*q.v.*). French *ma vieille branche* = my old chump.

1884. *Punch*, 11 Oct. ''Arry at a Political Picnic.' All my Saturday arfs are devoted to Politics. Fancy, old CHUMP, Me doing the sawdusty reglar, and follering swells on the stump.

3. (popular). — The head; especially in the phrase OFF ONE'S CHUMP (*q.v.*). For synonyms, *see* CRUMPET.

CHUMP-OF-WOOD, *subs. phr.* (rhyming slang).—No good. Also a blockhead.

OFF ONE'S CHUMP, *phr.* (vulgar).—Insane. *Cf.*, OFF ONE'S HEAD, NUT, etc. For synonyms, *see* APARTMENTS.

c. 1860. *Broadside Ballad*, 'We are a merry family.' The fire is out, the fender's broke, And father's out on strike, Sister Ann's gone OFF HER CHUMP, In fact, we're all alike.

1866. *Broadside Ballad*, 'Oh, She Was Such a Beautiful Girl.' She diddled me, she fiddled me, She sent me OFF MY CHUMP.

1877. BESANT AND RICE, *Son of Vulcan*, II., xxiv., p. 377. 'Master,' he said, 'have gone OFF HIS CHUMP—that's all.'

1883. BESANT, *Captain's Room*, ch. vii., p. 85 (1885). He . . . was engaged to be married to the king's sister . . . unfortunately, only the week before I arrived, he was killed and devoured by a lion, and the princess was gone OFF HER royal CHUMP.

TO GET ONE'S OWN CHUMP, *phr.* (thieves').—*See* quot.

1877. *Five Years' Penal Servitude*, ch. iii., p. 242. 'Cut her own grass! Good gracious, what is that?' I asked. 'Why, PURVIDE HER OWN CHUMP—earn her own living,' the old man replied.

CHUMPY, *adj.* (common). — The same as OFF ONE'S CHUMP.

CHUNK, *subs.* (colloquial).—1. A thick piece or lump of wood, bread, coal, etc.

1691. RAY, *S. and E. Country Wds.* (E. D. S.) *Chuck*, a great chip . . . In other countries [= districts] they call it a CHUNK. [M.]

1787. GROSE, *Prov. Glossary*, 'Chuck.' *Chuck*, a great chip, Suss. In other counties called a CHUNK or junk.

1876. BESANT AND RICE, *Golden Butterfly*, ch. xxix. Why not keep a clerk to read for you, and pay out the information in small CHUNKS? I should like to tackle Mr. Carlyle that way.

c. 1880. *Broadside Ballad*, 'The Hungry Man from Clapham.' He'd eat everything there was in the place, He bit a CHUNK from his mother-in-law's face.

2. (streets').—A school-board officer.

18(?). THOR FREDUR, *Sketches from Shady Places.* Here they gambol about like rabbits, until somebody raises the cry, 'Nix! the CHUNK' (the slang term for School Board officer).

CHURCH, *verb* (thieves').—To take out the works of a watch and substitute another set, so that identification is impossible.—*See* CHRISTEN, *verb*, sense 1.

1857. SNOWDEN, *Mag. Assistant*, 3 ed., p. 445. To have the works of a watch put into another case—TO CHURCH A YACK.

1868. DORAN, *Saints and Sinn.*, II., 290. The (thieves') CHURCH THEIR YACKS when they transpose the works of stolen watches to prevent identification. [M.]

TO TALK CHURCH, *verbal phr.* (colloquial).—To TALK 'SHOP' (*q.v.*).

1851. NEWLAND, *Erne*, 217. Looking at those wretched people and TALKING CHURCH. [M.]

CHURCHWARDEN, *subs.* (general).—A clay pipe with a long stem.—*See* quot., 1864, under CLAY. The following are general variants.

ENGLISH SYNONYMS. Alderman; steamer; yard of clay; clay.

FRENCH SYNONYMS. *Une bouffarde; une Belge; une chiffarde* (thieves'); *une marseillaise*; *une gambier* (pop. from a manufacturer's name).

GERMAN SYNONYMS. *Lülke* (M. H. G. *lullen* or *löllen* = to suck; *lülken*, to smoke); *Massel* (Swabian: also = a street-walker; *masseln* = to smoke); *Nagel*; *Pilmerstab* (only in Zimmermann); *Sarcherstock* (from the Hebrew *sorach*, through *särchen*, to stink or to smoke. *Sarcher*, tobacco; *Sarcherkippe* or *Sarchertiefe*, tobacco-box; *Sarcherhanjo*, tobacco-pouch); *Selcher* (Viennese thieves': from *selchen*, to smoke); *Schmalfink*.

1857. HOOD, *Pen and Pencil Pictures*, p. 269. Give me my willow-tube for a lance, the lid of a cigar-box for a shield. Thrust me a pair of cutties into my girdle for pistols; hang a CHURCHWARDEN by my side for a sabre.

1863. ALEX. SMITH, *Dreamthorpe*, p. 262. He . . . lifted a pipe of the kind called CHURCHWARDEN from the box on the ground, filled and lighted it.

1864. DR. RICHARDSON, on 'Tobacco,' before Brit. Assoc. Meeting at Bath. Cigars are more injurious than any form of pipe; and the best pipe is unquestionably what is commonly called a CHURCHWARDEN or long clay.

CHURL. TO PUT A CHURL UPON A GENTLEMAN.—*See* GENTLEMAN.

CIDER. ALL TALK AND NO CIDER, *phr.* (American).—Purposeless loquacity; 'Much cry and little wool.' Literally, much ado about nothing. [For suggested derivation, *see* quot., 1871.]

1835-40. HALIBURTON ('Sam Slick'), *Clockmaker*, 1 S., ch. xxi. It is an expensive kind of honour that, bein' Governor . . . Great cry and little wool! ALL TALK AND NO CIDER.

1858. *Notes and Queries*, 2 S., v., 233. ALL TALK AND NO CIDER. This expression is applied to persons whose performances fall far short of their promises.

1862. C. F. BROWNE, *Artemus Ward: His Book*, p. 135. What we want is more CIDER and less TALK.

1871. DE VERE, *Americanisms*, p. 591. This phrase originated at a party in Bucks County, Pennsylvania, which had assembled to drink a barrel of superior cider; but politics being introduced, speeches were made, and discussion ensued, till some malcontents withdrew on the plea that it was a trap into which they had been lured, politics and not pleasure being the purpose of the meeting, or, as they called it, ALL TALK AND NO CIDER.

CIDER AND, *subs. phr.* (colloquial).—Cider mixed with some other ingredient. *Cf.*, COLD WITHOUT, HOT WITH, etc.

1742. FIELDING, *Joseph Andrews*, bk. I., ch. xvi. She then asked the doctor and Mr. Barnabas what morning's draught they chose, who answered, they had a pot of CIDER-AND at the fire.

CIG, *subs.* (common).—A cigar. [An abbreviation of the legitimate word.] For synonyms, *see* WEED.

CINCH, *verb* (American).—To get a grip on; to 'corner'; to put the screw on; also, in the passive sense, to come out on the wrong side in speculations. [From the Spanish *cincha*, a belt or girdle; *cinchar*, to girdle. Properly used of the saddling of horses with the huge Mexican saddle. To CINCH a horse, however, is by no means the same as girthing him. The two ends of the tough cordage which constitute the CINCH terminate in long narrow strips of leather called *latigos*—thongs—which connect the CINCHES with the saddle, and are run through an iron ring and then tied by a series of complicated turns and knots known only to the craft.]

1875. *Scribner's Mag.*, July, p. 277. A man is CINCHED = he is hurt in a mining transaction (San Francisco localism).

1881. *New York Times*, Dec. 18, quoted in *Notes and Queries*, 6 S., v. 65. CINCH. To subdue, to forcibly bind down and overcome. Thus it is unfairly said that the Northern Pacific Company intends to CINCH the settlers by exacting large prices for its lands. Query, from Latin *cingere*.

1888. *Daily Inter-Ocean*, 2 Feb. Black and Blue thinks the Dwyers have a CINCH on both the great events.

1888. *New York World*, 22 July. The bettor, of whom the pool-room bookmaker stands in dread, however, is the racehorse owner, who has a CINCH bottled up for a particular race, and drops into the room an hour or two before the races begin.

CINCINNATI OLIVE, *subs.* (American).—A pig. [A spurious 'olive oil' is manufactured from lard, and Cincinnati is one of the largest centres of the 'pork packing industry' in America.] *Cf.*, CINCINNATI OYSTERS.

CINCINNATI OYSTERS, *subs.* (American).—Pigs' trotters. A curious interchange of names occurs between fish, flesh, and fowl. In CINCINNATI OYSTERS we have flesh presented in the guise of fish; and the reverse is the case when the sturgeon is spoken of as ALBANY BEEF. Amongst other examples may be quoted MARBLE-HEAD TURKEY, for a codfish; also, in Nova Scotia a DIGBY CHICKEN = a herring smoked and dried in a peculiar fashion.

In England a BILLINGSGATE PHEASANT is a fresh herring; whilst a Yarmouth bloater is sometimes a TWO-EYED STEAK.

CINDER, subs. (common).—1. Any strong liquor as brandy, whiskey, sherry, etc., mixed with a weaker, as soda-water, lemonade, water, etc., to fortify it.

1864. HOTTEN, Slang Dictionary, s.v.

1883. Referee, March 18, p. 2, col. 4. Having rushed out to get a glass of cold water with a CINDER in it to take the chill off.

2. (sporting).—A running path or track; merely an abbreviation of 'cinder-path,' it being laid with 'cinders.'

CINDER-GARBLER, subs. (old).—A female servant. Grose [1785] says the term was 'Custom House wit,' but gives no particulars.

ENGLISH SYNONYMS. Marchioness; slavey; cinder-grabber; cinderella; can (Scots); pisskitchen; Julia.

FRENCH SYNONYMS. Un extrait de garni (popular); un chambrillon; une bobonne (for bonne); une larbine; une cambrouse; une jeanneton; une groule or groulasse.

GERMAN SYNONYMS. Schifche or Schifches; Schammesch or Schammes (from the Hebrew).

SPANISH SYNONYM. Famula (f).

CIRCLING-BOY, subs. (old).—A 'rook'; swindler. Nares says a species of roarer; one who in some way drew a man into a snare, to cheat or rob him. See Gifford.—Ben Jonson, Barth. Fair, iv., 3, p. 481.

CIRCS, subs. (common).—Circumstances.

CIRCUMBENDIBUS, subs. (old).—A roundabout; a long-winded story. [From Lat. circum, around, + Eng. BEND, with a Latin termination.]

1681. DRYDEN, Sp. Friar, V., ii. I shall fetch him back with a CIRCUMBENDIBUS, I warrant him. [M.]

1768. LORD CARLISLE, in Jesse's Selwyn, II., 317 (1882). I can assure you it grieved me that anything of yours should make such a CIRCUMBENDIBUS before it came to my hands.

1773. O. GOLDSMITH, She Stoops to Conquer, Act v., Sc. 2. 'And from that, with a CIRCUMBENDIBUS, I fairly lodged them in the horse-pond at the bottom of the garden.'

1849. LYTTON, Caxtons, pt. VIII. ch. i. The cabman, to swell his fare, had thought proper to take a CIRCUMBENDIBUS.

1890. Notes and Queries, 7 S., ix., 29 March. . . . No choice but to deliver himself of a malediction with a CIRCUMBENDIBUS.

CIRCUMLOCUTION OFFICE, subs. (common). — A centre of redtape; a roundabout way. [A term invented by Charles Dickens (see quot., 1857), and applied at first in ridicule to public offices, where everybody tries to shuffle off his responsibilities upon some one else.

1857. C. DICKENS, Little Dorrit, I., x. The CIRCUMLOCUTION OFFICE was the most important Department under Government. Ibid. Whatever was required to be done, the CIRCUMLOCUTION OFFICE was beforehand with all the public departments in the art of perceiving—How not to do it.

1870. Graphic, Feb. 19, in 'By the Bye.' To complete the contretemps a portion of the telegraphs struck work on the very first day of the Government taking them in hand. Of course the great tribe

of evil-wishers ran about chuckling, and rubbing their hands gleefully. 'I told you so,' cried Rubasore. CIRCUMLOCUTION OFFICE again, sneered Crossgrain.

CIRCUMSLOGDOLOGIZE. — See STOCKDOLLAGIZE.

CIRCUMSTANCE. NOT A CIRCUMSTANCE, etc., phr. (American).—Not to be compared with; a trifle; of no account—unfavourable comparison.

18(?). J. H. BEADLE, Western Wilds, p. 28. I took a broadhorn to Noo Orleens, and when I was paid off on the levee, I was the worst lost man you ever did see. In the middle of the thickest woods in the world WASN'T A CIRCUMSTANCE TO IT.

1848. J. R. LOWELL, Biglow Papers. For Jacob WARN'T A SUCKESTANCE to Jeff at financierin'; He never'd thought of borryin' from Esau like all nater An' then cornfiscatin' all debts to sech a small pertater.

TO WHIP [something] INTO A CIRCUMSTANCE = to surpass. Thus a newspaper correspondent writes that 'the streets of Georgetown, Demerara, are broad, smooth, and well laid out. Georgetown could give points to New York in its roads, and WHIP IT INTO A CIRCUMSTANCE.'

CIRCUS-CUSS, subs. (thieves').—A circus-rider.

CITIZEN, subs. (thieves').—A wedge for 'prizing open' safes, before the ALDERMAN (q.v.), and JEMMY (q.v.). — See also CITIZENS' FRIEND.

CITIZENS' FRIEND, subs. (thieves'). —A smaller wedge than the CITIZEN (q.v.), for 'prizing open' safes. The order in which the tools are used is (1) CITIZENS' FRIEND; (2) CITIZEN; (3) the ALDERMAN (i.e., a JEMMY); and sometimes (4) a LORD MAYOR. For synonyms, see JEMMY and BETTY.

CITY COLLEGE, subs. (thieves').—Newgate. In New York = 'The Tombs.' For synonyms, see CAGE.

CITY STAGE, subs. (old).—The gallows, formerly in front of Newgate. For synonyms, see NUBBING CHEAT.

CIVET, subs. (general).—The female pudendum. For synonyms, see MONOSYLLABLE.

CIVIL RECEPTION.—See HOUSE OF CIVIL RECEPTION.

CIVIL-RIG, subs. (vagrants'). — A trick to obtain alms by a profuse show of civility and obsequiousness.

CIVVIES, subs. (military).—Civilians' clothes, as opposed to regimentals. [A corruption of the legitimate word.]

CLACK, subs. (colloquial).—1. Idle, loquacious talk; gossip; prattle —an exceedingly old usage. For synonyms, see PATTER.

c. 1440. YORK, Myst. XXXIV., 211. Ther quenes vs comeres with her CLAKKE. [M.]

1599. NASHE, Lenten Stuffe, in wks. V. 251. Their CLACKE or gabbling to this purport.

1678. BUTLER, Hudibras, pt. III., ch. ii. And, with his everlasting CLACK, Set all men's ears upon the rack.

1748. SMOLLETT, Rod. Random, ch. liv. I dreaded her unruly tongue, and felt by anticipation the horrors of an eternal CLACK!

1812. H. AND J. SMITH, Rejected Addresses ('Punch's Apotheosis'). See she twists her mutton fists like Molyneux

or Beelzebub, And t'other's CLACK, who pats her back, is louder far than Bell's hubbub.

1888. J. PAYN, Myst Mirbridge (Tauchn.) II., xviii., 197. The old fellow would have had a CLACK with her. [M.]

2. (common).—The tongue [i.e., that which CLACKS (q.v.), verb.] A more ancient form was CLAP dating back to 1225.

ENGLISH SYNONYMS. Glib; red-rag; clapper; dubber; velvet; jibb; quail-pipe.

FRENCH SYNONYMS. La diligence de Rome (popular); un battant (thieves': also 'heart,' 'stomach,' and 'throat'); un bon battant ('a nimble tongue.' Cf., 'clapper'); une chiffe or un chiffon rouge (popular); une gaffe; le grelot.

GERMAN SYNONYM. Lecker (literally 'the licker').

ITALIAN SYNONYMS. Serpentina; dannoso (literally 'damagable'); zavarina (properly 'a trifling old woman').

SPANISH SYNONYM. La desosada (i.e., Old Boneless).

1598. GREENE, Jas. IV., wks. (Gros.) XIII., 210. Haud your CLACKS, lads. [M.]

1748. T. DYCHE, Dictionary (5 ed.). CLACK (s.) . . . also a nickname for a woman's tongue; a prattler or busybody.

1828. D'ISRAELI, Chas. I., II., i., 23. Who, as washerwomen . . . at their work, could not hold their CLACK. [M.]

1864. E. SARGENT, Peculiar, III., 76. To hermetically seal up this Mrs. Gentry's CLACK. [M.]

Verb. To gabble. For synonyms, see PATTER.

CLACK-BOX, subs. (common).—1. The mouth. For synonyms, see POTATO-TRAP.

2. (common).—A chatterbox.

ENGLISH SYNONYMS. A mouth almighty; poll parrot; babble-merchant; slammer.

FRENCH SYNONYMS. Un parlotteur (familiar); un dévideur or une dévideuse (popular: literally 'a winder'); un bagoulard (popular: c'est un fameux bagoulard = he is the bloke to slam); un chambert: abuser du crachoir (said of a chatterbox who does too much with the 'spitter').

SPANISH SYNONYMS. Hablatista (m; jocular); hablantin or hablanchin (m; colloquial); ladrador (m; properly 'a barker'); prosador (m; properly 'a sarcastic and malicious babbler'); gazetilla (f; a farthing newspaper'); garlador; fuelle (m; properly 'a pair of bellows'); ya escampa (it is importunate babbling; escampar signifies literally 'to clean or clear out a place'); cotorrera (= a gossip; cotorreria = loquacity; a term specially applied to women); comadre (f; jueves de comadres = Cummers' Thursday, the last before Shrove Tuesday); una chicharra (a prattler; chicharra = 'a froth worm' or 'harvest fly'); charlantin.

CLACK-LOFT, subs. (popular). — A pulpit. [From CLACK, verb, + LOFT, an elevated room or place.] For synonyms, see HUM-BOX.

CLAIM, verb (thieves').—To steal. (A locution similar in character to 'annex,' 'convey,' etc., and derived from a sense of the legitimate word signifying 'to demand on the ground of right.') For synonyms, see PRIG.

1879. J. W. HORSLEY, in Macmillan's Mag., XL., 501. So I CLAIMED (stole) them.

TO JUMP A CLAIM, phr. (American and colonial). — To take forcible possession; to defraud; specifically to seize land which has been taken up and occupied by another settler, or squatter. The first occupant is, by squatter law and custom, entitled to the first claim on the land.—See JUMP.

1846. E. H. SMITH, Hist. of Black Hawk. When I hunted claims, I went far and near, Resolved from all others to keep myself clear; And if, through mistake, I JUMPED a man's CLAIM, As soon as I knew it I jumped off again.

18(?). F. MARRYAT, Mountains and Molehills, p. 217. If a man JUMPED my CLAIM, and encroached on my boundaries, and I didn't knock him on the head with a pickaxe, I appealed to the crowd, and, my claim being carefully measured and found correct, the jumper would be ordered to confine himself to his own territory.

1883. R. L. STEVENSON, The Silverado Squatters, p. 221. The CLAIM was JUMPED; a track of mountain-side, fifteen hundred feet long by six hundred wide . . . had passed from Ronalds to Hanson, and in the passage changed its name from the 'Mammoth' to the 'Calistoga.'

CLAM, subs. (American).—1. A blockhead. Anglicé, 'as stupid as an oyster.' Shakspeare (Much Ado About Nothing, ii. 3) has 'Love may transform me to an oyster; but I'll take my oath on it, till he hath made an oyster of me, he shall never make me such a fool.'—See CHOWDER-HEADED; chowder is a favourite form of serving clams.

1871. S. L. CLEMENS ('Mark Twain'), Sketches, I., 46. A fine stroke of sarcasm, that, but it will be lost on such an intellectual CLAM as you.

2. The mouth or lips. Also CLAM-SHELL. 'Shut your CLAM-SHELL' = 'Shut your mouth.' The padlock now used on the United States mail-bags is called the 'Clam-shell padlock.' For synonyms, see POTATO-TRAP.

1825. J. NEAL, Bro. Jonathan, I., 143. Shet your CLAM, our David.

1848. J. R. LOWELL, Biglow Papers, II., p. 19. You don't feel much like speakin', When if you let your CLAM-SHELLS gape, a quart of tar will leak in.

1848. BARTLETT, Dict. Americanisms. SHUT UP YOUR CLAM-SHELLS. Close your lips together; be silent. Common along the shores of Connecticut and Rhode Island, where clams abound. Same as 'shut your head.'

CLAM-BUTCHER, subs. (American). —A man who opens clams; the attendant at an oyster bar is an 'oyster-butcher.'

CLANK, subs. (thieves').—A pewter tankard; formerly a silver one.

1785. GROSE, Dict. Vulg. Tongue. CLANK: a silver tankard.

1837. DISRAELI, Venetia, ch. xiv. Tip me the CLANK like a dimber mort as you are.

CLANKER, subs. (old).—1. A great lie.—Grose. Cf., CLINKER. For synonyms, see WHOPPER.

2. (old).—Silver plate. Cf., CLANK.

CLANK NAPPER, subs. (old).—A thief whose speciality is silver-plate. [From CLANK, subs. + NAPPER (q.v.), a thief.] For synonyms, see THIEVES.

CLAP (or CLAPPER), subs. (common).—1. The tongue. [From CLAP = chatter; a babbler's tongue is said to be hung in the middle, and to sound with both ends.] For synonyms, see CLACK.

a. 1225. Ancr. R., 72. þeone Ru ðen heo neuere astunten hare CLEPPE.

1609. DEKKER, *Guls' Horne-Booke*, ch. vi. And to let that CLAPPER (your tongue) be tost so high, that all the house may ring of it.

1633. MASSINGER, *New Way to Pay Old Debts*, III., 2. *Greedy.* Sir Giles, Sir Giles! *Over.* The great fiend, stop that CLAPPER!

1750. FIELDING, *Tom Jones*, bk. VII., ch. xv. My landlady was in such high mirth with her company that no CLAPPER could be heard there but her own.

1835. HALIBURTON, *Clockmaker*, I S., ch. xix. I thought I should have snorted right out two or three times . . . to hear the critter let her CLAPPER run that fashion.

1861. HUGHES, *Tom Brown at Oxford*, ch. vi. But old Murdoch was too pleased at hearing his own CLAPPER going, and too full of whiskey, to find him out.

1878. JOHN PAYNE, tr. *Poems of Villon*, p. 139. Enough was left me (as warrant I will) To keep me from holding my CLAPPER still, When jargon that meant 'You shall be hung' They read to me from the notary's bill: Was it a time to hold my tongue?

2. (vulgar). — Gonorrhœa; once in polite use. [Origin uncertain; *cf.*, *Old Fr. clapoir*, bosse, bubo, *panus inguinis*; *clapoire*, *clapier*, '*lieu de débauche*,' '*maladie q'on y attrape*']. For synonyms, *see* LADIES' FEVER.

1587. *Myrr. Mag.*, *Malin* iii. Before they get the CLAP.

1706. FARQUHAR. *The Recruiting Officer.* Five hundred a year besides guineas for CLAPS.

1709. SWIFT. *Adv. Relig.* Works [1755] II., i. 99, *s.v.*

1738. JOHNSON, *London*, 114. They sing, they dance, clean shoes, or cure a CLAP.

1881. In *Syd. Soc. Lex.*

Verb (vulgar).—To infect with CLAP; *see subs.* Also figuratively.

1658. OSBORN. *Jas. I.* [1673], 514. Atropos CLAPT him, a Pox on the Drab!

1680. BUTLER, *Rem.* [1759], I. 249. [They] had ne'er been CLAP'D with a poetic itch.

1738. *Laws of Chance.* Pref. 9. It is hardly 1 to 10 . . . that a Town-Spark of that Age has not been CLAP'D.

CLAPPER-DUDGEON, *subs.* (old).—A whining beggar.

1567. HARMAN, *Caveat* (1814), p. 26. These Palliards be called also CLAPPER DOGENS, these go with patched clokes, and haue their morts with them which they cal wiues.

1625. JONSON, *Staple of News*, II. Here he is, and with him—what? a CLAPPER-DUDGEON! That's a good sign, to have the beggar follow him so near.

1705-7. WARD, *Hudibras Redivivus*, vol. I., pt. V., p. 10. Says he, there is an old curmudgeon, A hum-drum, preaching, CLAPPERDUDGEON.

1863. SALA, *Capt. Dang.*, II., vii., 225. Rogues, Thieves . . . and CLAPPER-DUDGEONS . . . infested the outskirts of the Old Palace. [M.]

CLAP OF THUNDER, *subs. phr.* (old).—A glass of gin: a variant of FLASH OF LIGHTNING (*q.v.*).

1821. P. EGAN, *Tom and Jerry* [Ed. 1890], p. 79. I have not exactly recovered from the severe effects of the repeated 'flashes of lightning' and strong CLAPS OF THUNDER, with which I had to encounter last night.

CLAP-SHOULDER, *subs.* (old).—A term applied to the officers of justice who laid their hands upon people's shoulders when they arrested them. *Cf.*, CATCH-POLE.

1630. TAYLOR, *Workes.* CLAP-SHOULDER serjeants get the devill and all, By begging and by bringing men in thrall.

CLAPSTER, *subs.* (vulgar). — An habitual sufferer from gonorrhœa; by implication, one much and often in the way of getting clapped.

CLARAS, *subs.* (Stock Exchange). —Caledonian Railway Deferred and Ordinary Stock.

1887. ATKIN, *House Scraps.* For we have our Sarahs and CLARAS. Our Noras and Doras for fays.

CLARET, *subs.* (pugilistic).—Blood. Variants are BADMINTON, BORDEAUX, and COCHINEAL-DYE. French *le vermeil* or *le vermois*.

1604. DEKKER, *Honest Whore*, II., 45, wks. [1873]. This should be a Coronation day: for my head runs CLARET lustily.

1819. THOMAS MOORE, *Tom Crib's Memorial to Congress*, p. 25. . . . This being the first Royal CLARET let flow, Since Tom *took* the Holy Alliance *in Tow*, The *uncorking* produced much sensation about, As *bets* had been *flush* on the first *painted snout*.

1878. BESANT AND RICE, *By Celia's Arbour*, ch. xxxix. The lieutenant picked him up, and placed him—because he declined to stand; and, indeed, the CLARET was flowing freely—in the President's arm chair.

TO TAP ONE'S CLARET, *phr.*—To draw blood.

CLARET JUG, *subs.* (pugilistic).—The nose. [From CLARET, blood, + JUG, a receptacle.] For synonyms, *see* CONK.

1859. *Punch*, vol. XXXVII., p. 22. 'A Chapter on Slang.' A man's broken nose, is his CLARET-JUG smashed.

CLARIAN, *subs.* (Cambridge University).—A member of Clare Hall, Cambridge; also a GREYHOUND (*q.v.*).

1889. C. WHIBLEY. *Cap and Gown.* E'en stuke-struck Clarians strove to stoop.

CLASS, *subs.* (athletic).—The highest quality or combination of highest qualities among athletes. He's not CLASS enough, *i.e.*, not good enough. There's a deal of CLASS about him, *i.e.*, a deal of quality. The term obtains to a certain extent among turfites.

1884. *Referee*, March 23, p. 1, col. 3. The elasticity necessary for anything like CLASS at sprinting departs comparatively early.

CLAW, *subs.* (prison).—A lash of the cat-o'-nine-tails. *Cf.*, CLAWED-OFF, sense 1.

1876. GREENWOOD, *A Night in a Work-house.* Oh! cuss that old Kerr, who condemned me to twenty-five CLAWS with the cat.

CLAWS FOR BREAKFAST, *subs. phr.* (prison).—*See* quot.

1873. GREENWOOD, *In Strange Company.* A ruffian being uncertain as to the morning when he is to have, as he himself would say, CLAWS for breakfast, is in the habit of lying night after night in a sweat of terror.

CLAWED-OFF, *adv. phr.* (old).—1. Severely beaten or whipped. *Cf.*, CLAW.

2. (old).—Venereally infected.

CLAW-HAMMER, *subs.* (Irish). — A dress coat. [From a supposed similarity in the cut of the tails to a CLAW HAMMER, one end of which is divided into two claws, for extracting nails from wood.] Also called STEEL-PEN COAT and SWALLOW-TAIL. For synonyms of evening dress generally, *see* WAR-PAINT.

1863. NATHANIEL HAWTHORNE, *Passages from English Note-books*, I., 538. Sea-captains call a dress-coat a CLAW-HAMMER.

1883. *Punch*, July 21, p. 29, col. 2. An 'Impressionist' is not impressive In a CLAW-HAMMER on a public platform.

1889. *Pall Mall Gazette*, Nov. 11, p. 7. col. 1. After the CLAW-HAMMER crowd had been exhausted, he sent up an invitation to the great army of unvarnished.

CLAY, *subs.* (colloquial). — A clay pipe. *Cf.*, YARD OF CLAY, but for synonyms, *see* CHURCHWARDEN.

1859. FAIRHOLT, *Tobacco* (1876), 173. Such long pipes were reverently termed ALDERMEN in the last age, and irreverently YARDS OF CLAY in the present one.

1861. HUGHES, *Tom Brown at Oxford*, ch. xxi., p. 223. 'He is churchwarden at home, and can't smoke anything but a long CLAY.'

1866. *London Miscellany*, 19 May, p. 235, col. 2. Surely these men, who win and lose fortunes with the stolidity of a mynheer smoking his CLAY YARD, must be of entirely different stuff from the rest of us.

1871. CALVERLEY, *Verses and Tr. Ode Tobacco.* Jones . . . daily absorbs a CLAY after his labours.

TO MOISTEN, SOAK, or WET ONE'S CLAY, *verbal, phr.*—To drink. [Clay = the human body.]

1708. *Brit. Apollo*, No. 80, 3, 1. We were MOISTENING OUR CLAY.

1711. ADDISON, *Spectator*, No. 72, par. 9. TO MOISTEN THEIR CLAY, and grow immortal by drinking.

1731. FIELDING, *Letter Writers*, Act ii., Sc. 2. A soph, he is immortal, And never can decay; For how should he return to dust Who daily WETS HIS CLAY?

1790. RHODES, *Bombastes Furioso.* MOISTENING OUR CLAY and puffing off our cares.

1800. *Morning Chronicle* (in Whibley, p. 92). Cram not your attics With dry mathematics, But MOISTEN YOUR CLAY with a bumper of wine.

1836. DICKENS, *Pickwick*, ch. xxxix., p. 345. Ever and anon MOISTENING HIS CLAY and his labours with a glass of claret.

1837. BARHAM, *I. L.* (*The Monstre Baloon*). And they're feasting the party, and SOAKING THEIR CLAY, With Johannisberg, Rudesheimer, Moselle, and Tokay.

1864. LOWELL, *Fireside Trav.*, 119. When his poor old CLAY WAS WET with gin. [M.]

CLEAN, *adj.* and *adv.* (colloquial and expletive).—1. Entirely; altogether; *e.g.*, CLEAN GONE, CLEAN BROKE, etc. Employed by the best writers until a recent date, and scarce colloquial even now.

1888. W. E. HENLEY. *A Book of Verses*, 'Ballade of a Toyokuni Colour Print.' Child, although I have forgotten CLEAN, I know That in the shade of Fuji-san, What time the cherry orchards blow, I loved you, once, in old Japan.

1890. MARK RUTHERFORD ('Reuben Shapcott'), *Miriam's Schooling*, p. 11. The memory of the battle by the hill Moreh is CLEAN forgotten.

2. Expert; smart.

1878. CHARLES HINDLEY, *Life and Times of James Catnach.* The CLEANEST *angler* on the *pad*, In daylight or the *darky*.

CLEAN-OUT, *verbal phr.* (colloquial) —To exhaust; strip; 'rack'; or ruin. Fr., *se faire lessiver*.

1812. J. H. VAUX, *Flash Dict.* CLEANED OUT: said of a gambler who has lost his last stake at play; also, of a flat who has been stript of all his money.

1819. THOS. MOORE, *Tom Crib's Memorial to Congress*, p. 38. *All Lombard-street to ninepence* on it, Bobby's the boy would CLEAN them OUT!

1840. DICKENS, *Old Curiosity Shop*, ch. xxix., p. He never took a dice-box in his hand, or held a card, but he was plucked, pigeoned, and CLEANED OUT completely.

c. 1880. *Broadside Ballad*, 'When I was Prince of Paradise.' I introduced 'loo'—in an hour or two, I'd CLEANED all their pockets right OUT.

CLEAN POTATO, *phr.* (general).—The right thing. Of an action indiscreet or dishonest, it is said that 'It's not the CLEAN POTATO.'

CLEAN STRAW, *subs.* (Winchester College).—Clean sheets. [Before 1540 the beds were bundles of straw on a stone floor. At that date Dean Fleshmonger put in oaken floors, and provided proper beds, such as existed in 1871 in Third, and later in the case of the Præfect of Hall's unused beds in Sixth. The term has never been used, as stated by Barrère, in reference to mattresses of any kind, straw or other.]

CLEAN WHEAT. IT'S THE CLEAN WHEAT, *phr.* (general). The

best of its kind. For synonyms, *see* A1 and FIZZING.

CLEAR, *adj.* and *adv.* (old).—Thick with liquor. [Apparently on the principle *lucus a non lucendo*.]

1688. SHADWELL, *Sqr.*, *Alsatia*, I., iv. Yes, really I was CLEAR; for I do not remember what I did.

1690. B. E., *Dict. Cant. Crew.* CLEAR; very Drunk.

1699. VANBRUGH, *Relapse*, IV., iii. I suppose you are CLEAR—you'd never play such a trick as this else.

1725. *New Cant. Dict.*, s.v.

1785. GROSE, *Dict. Vulg. Tongue.* The cull is CLEAR let's bite him.

1811. *Lexicon Balatronicum*, s.v.

Verb.—*See* CLEAR OUT.

CLEAR AS MUD, *adv. phr.* (common) = Not particularly lucid.

CLEAR CRYSTAL, *subs.* (popular).—White spirits, as gin and whisky, but extended to brandy and rum.

CLEAR GRIT, *subs.*—1. (Canadian). —A member of the colonial Liberal party.

1884. *Fortnightly Review*, May, 592. There arose up [in Canada] a political party of a Radical persuasion, who were called CLEAR GRITS, and the CLEAR GRITS declared for the secularisation of the Clergy Reserves.

2. (American). — The right sort; having no lack of spirit; unalloyed; decided.

1835-40. HALIBURTON ('Sam Slick'), *Clockmaker*, 3 S., ch. xxxii. I used to think champagne no better nor mean cider . . . but if you get the CLEAR GRIT there is no mistaking it.

1861. *New York Tribune*, 10 Oct. Nor do we think the matter much mended by a CLEAR GRIT Republican convention, putting one or two Democrats at the foot of their tickets.

CLEAR OUT (or **CLEAR OFF**), *verbal phr.* (colloquial).—1. To depart.

1825. J. NEAL, *Bro. Jonathan*, II., 151. Like many a hero before him, he CLEARED OUT.

1861. *Harper's Monthly*, August. You'll have to CLEAR OUT, and that pretty quick or I'll be after you with a sharp stick.

1885. *Truth*, 28 May, 1847. I would have the Canal under the control of an International Commission . . . and then I would CLEAR OUT of the country.

1888. J. RICKABY, *Moral Philos.*, 205. To warn the visitor to CLEAR OFF.

2. (popular).—To rid of cash; to ruin; to 'clean out.'

1849-50. THACKERAY, *Pendennis.* The luck turned from that minute . . . came away CLEARED OUT, leaving that infernal check behind me.

1884. *Illustrated London News*, Christmas Number, p. 6, col. 2. He CLEARED you OUT that night, old man.

CLEAVE, *verb* (old).—To be wanton; used of women. [Quoted by Grose, 1785.]

CLEFT, *subs.* (common). — The female *pudendum*. For synonyms, *see* MONOSYLLABLE.

CLEGG, *subs.* (Scots).—A horse-fly.

CLENCHER.—*See* CLINCHER.

CLERGYMAN, *subs.* (common).—A chimney-sweep. [In allusion to the colour of 'the cloth.'] Clergymen in their turn = 'chimney sweeps.'

ENGLISH SYNONYMS. Black draught; knuller; flue-faker; querier; chummy.

FRENCH SYNONYMS. *Un artiste*; *Jean de la suie.*

ST. NICHOLAS' CLERK or CLERGYMAN (old).—A highwayman.

1589. R. HARVEY, *Pl. Perc.*, I, A quarrel, by the highway side, between a brace of SAINT NICHOLAS CLARGIE MEN. [M.]

1597. SHAKSPEARE, *King Henry IV.*, i. 1. Sirrah, if they meet not with ST. NICHOLAS' CLERKS, I'll give thee this neck.

CLERKED, *ppl. adj.* (old). Imposed upon; 'SOLD' (*q.v.*).

1785. GROSE, *Dick. Vulg. Tongue.* The cull will not be CLERKED.

CLERKS. — *See* ST. NICHOLAS' CLERK.

CLERK'S BLOOD, *subs.* (old).—Red ink. A common expression of Charles Lamb's.

CLEVER SHINS, *phr.* (school). — Sly to no purpose.

CLEYMES, *subs.* (old).—Artificial sores, made by beggars to excite charity.

CLICK, *subs.* (pugilistic).—A blow. For synonyms, *see* DIG, BANG and WIPE. Also a hold in wrestling.

1819. T. MOORE, *Tom Crib's Memorial*, p. 18. *Home-hits* in the *bread-basket* CLICKS in the *gob*. *Ibid*, p. 30.

1871. *Daily Telegraph*, 8 April. C. and W. Wrestling Society. The various competitors struggled hard and put on all they knew in 'hipes,' 'hanks,' 'CLICKS,' 'strokes,' and 'buttockings.'

Verb (old). — *See* quots., and *Cf.*, CLICKER.

1748. T. DYCHE, *Dictionary* (5 ed.). CLICK (v.) . . . or to stand at a shop-door and invite customers in, as salesmen and shoemakers do.

1785. GROSE, *Dict. Vulg. Tongue.* To CLICK a nab; to snatch a hat.

CLICKER, or **KLICKER**, *subs.* old). —1. A shop-keeper's tout. [Formerly a shoemaker's doorsman or BARKER (*q.v.*), but in this particular trade the term is nowadays appropriated to a foreman who cuts out leather and dispenses materials to workpeople; a sense not altogether wanting from the very first.]

c. 1690. B. E. *Dict. Cant. Crew.* CLICKER: the shoemaker's journeyman or servant, that cutts out all the work, and stands at or walks before the door, and saies, 'What d'ye lack, sir? what d'ye buy, madam?'

1698. WARD, *London Spy*, pt. V., p. 117. Women were here almost as Troublesome as the Long-Lane CLICKERS.

1748. T. DYCHE, *Dictionary* (5 ed.). CLICKER (s.): the person that stands at a shoe-maker's door to invite customers to buy the wares sold there.

1864. HOTTEN, *Slang Dictionary.* CLICKER: a female touter at the bonnet shops in Cranbourne Alley. In Northamptonshire, the cutter out in a shoemaking establishment.

2. (popular). — A knockdown blow.—*See* CLICK, *subs.*, sense.

3. (thieves'). — One who apportions the booty or 'regulars.'

1785. GROSE, *Dict. Vulg. Tongue*, s.v.

CLIFT, *verb* (thieves').—To steal. For synonyms, *see* PRIG.

CLIMB DOWN, *subs.* and *verb* (colloquial).—The abandonment of a position; downward or retrograde motion; the act of surrender. At first American.

1871. REV. H. W. BEECHER, *Star Papers*, p. 41, quoted in De Vere's *Americanisms*. To CLIMB DOWN the wall was easy enough, too easy for a man who did not love wetting. *Ibid.* I partly CLIMBED DOWN, and wholly clambered back again, satisfied that it was easier to get myself in than to get the flowers out.

1889 *St. James's Gazette*, 22 Nov, p. 12, col. 2. I am particularly pleased (adds our correspondent) with the noble

conduct of the Bread Union, the first to CLIMB DOWN, and the promptest to send in its little bill.

1890. *Globe*, 7 April, p. 2, col. 2. It is satisfactory to learn on no less an authority than that of the *New York Herald* that the general election may at the moment be regarded remote. This is indeed a CLIMB DOWN on the part of the chief disseminator of the Dissolution rumour.

1890. *Globe*, 19 Feb., p. 2, col. 2. Mr. MacNeill's 'personal statement' in the House yesterday was distinctly in the nature of a CLIMB DOWN.

CLINCH, *subs.* (thieves').—A prison cell. [? From CLINCH, to clutch, grip, and hold fast. *Cf.*, CLINK.] Variants in English are BOX, COB, SALT-BOX, CHOKEY and SHOE. Fr., *une cachemitte*, *une cachemar* or *cachemince* (all thieves', from *cachot*, 'a black hole'); also *un clou* (military); *maison de campagne* (military); *un mazaro*, or *lazaro*; *une matatane* (military); *un ours* (popular); *un abattoir* (thieves'; properly 'a slaughter house.' This last, the name of the condemned cell in the prison of La Roquette, corresponds to the Newgate Salt Box). In German: *Näck* (only in Zimmermann; single cell in a prison; probably from the U.G. *Noche* and the M.H.G. *Nacke* = boat, from its shape; derivation from the Hebrew *Nekef* = hole, is also possible).

TO GET or KISS THE CLINCH or CLINK, *verbal phr.* (thieves'). —To be imprisoned. For synonyms, *see* COP.

1864. HOTTEN, *Slang Dict.*, p. 102. *s.v.*

CLINCHER or **CLENCHER**, *subs.* (colloquial).—1. That which decides a matter, especially a retort which closes an argument; a 'finisher,' 'settler,' 'corker.' [From CLINCH, 'to secure or make fast,' through its obsolete meaning of 'to pun or quibble,' + ER.]

1754. B. MARTIN, *Eng. Dict.* CLINCHER . . . an unanswerable reason or argument.

1839. PIERCE EGAN, *Finish to Life in London*, p. 13. Death comes but once, the Philosophers say And 'tis true my brave boys, but that once is a CLENCHER It takes us from drinking and loving away And spoils at a blow the best tippler and wencher.

1836. DICKENS, *Pickwick*, ch. xvi., p. 136. 'Why cannot I communicate with the young lady's friends?' 'Because they live one hundred miles from here, sir,' responded Job Trotter. 'That's a CLINCHER,' said Mr. Weller, aside.

2. (common). — An unsurpassed lie; a 'stopper-up,' [This sense flows naturally from sense 1 and the accepted usages of CLINCH, verb and noun. *Cf.*, CLINKER, WHOPPER, THUMPER, WHACKER, etc.] For synonyms, *see* WHOPPER.

CLING-RIG.—*See* CLINK-RIG.

CLINK, *subs.* (old).—1. A prison or lock-up; specifically applied, it is thought, to a noted gaol in the borough of Southwark; subsequently to places—like Alsatia, the Mint, etc.—privileged from arrests; and latterly, to a small dismal prison or a military guard room. For synonyms, *see* CAGE.

1515. BARCLAY, *Egloges*, I. (1570) A. 5, 4. Then art thou clapped in the Flete or CLINKE. [M.]

1642. MILTON, *Apol. for Smect*, § ii., in wks. (1806) I., 237. And the divine right of episcopacy was then valiantly asserted, when he who would have been respondent, must have bethought himself withal how he could refute the CLINK or the Gatehouse.

1835. MARRYAT, *Jacob Faithful*, ch. xix. Come along with me; we've a nice CLINK at Wandsworth to lock you up in.

1839. H. AINSWORTH, *Jack Sheppard*, ep. I., ch. vi. The old and ruinous prison belonging to the liberty of the Bishop of Winchester (whose palace formerly adjoined the river); called the CLINK.

2. (thieves'). — Silver plate; also CLINCH.—*See* CLANK.

1781. G. PARKER, *View of Society*, II. He wouldn't have been hobbled but the melting-pot receiver proved his selling the CLINK to him.

3. (Scotch colloquial).—Money. *Cf.*, CHINK.

1724-40. RAMSAY, *Tea-t. Misc.*, 14. The Warld is rul'd by Asses, And the WISE are sway'd by CLINK.

1789. BURNS, *Let. J. Tennant*, May ye get . . . Monie a laugh, and monie a drink, An' aye enough o' needfu' CLINK.

1817. HOGG, *Tales and Sk.*, II., 2, 3. Such young ladies as were particularly beautiful . . . and had the CLINK. [M.]

4. (colloquial). Also BUM-CLINK.—A very indifferent beer made from the gyle of malt and the sweepings of hop bins, and brewed especially for the benefit of agricultural labourers in harvest time.

1863. SALA, *Capt. Dang.*, I., ix., 266. A miserable hovel of an inn . . . where they ate their rye-bread and drank their sour CLINK. [M.]

TO KISS THE CLINK, *verbal phr.* (old).—To be imprisoned. [From CLINK, *subs.*, sense 1.] For synonyms, *see* COP.

1588. JOHN UDALL, *State of the Ch. of England, etc.*, p. 22 (Arber's ed.) DIOTR. Awaye, thou rayling hypocrite, I will talke with thee no longer, if I catche thee in London, I will make thee KISS THE CLINKE for this geare. PAUL. In deede the CLYNKE, Gate-house, White-lyon, and the Fleet, haue bin your onely argumentes whereby you haue proued your cause these many yeeres.

1889. *Gentleman's Magazine*, p. 598. *s.v.*

CLINKER, *subs.*—1. (*in plural*, old). —Fetters. For synonyms, *see* DARBIES.

1690. B. E., *Dict. Cant. Crew*, CLINKERS: the Irons Felons wear in Gaols.

1785. GROSE, *Dict. Vulg. Tongue*, CLINKERS: irons worn by prisoners.

1811. *Lexicon Balatronicum*, s.v.

2. (old).—A crafty, designing man.

1690. B. E., *Dict. Cant. Crew*, CLINKER: a crafty fellow.

1785. GROSE, *Dict. Vulg. Tongue*, s.v.

1811. *Lexicon Balatronicum*, s.v.

3. (thieves').—A chain of any kind, whether fetter or watch chain. *Cf.*, sense 1.

4. (pugilistic). — A well-delivered blow; a 'hot-'un.'

c. 1863. THACKERAY, *Men's Wives*, *Frank Berry*, ch. i. Berry goes gallantly in, and delivers a CLINKER on the gown-boy's jaw.

5. (colloquial, chiefly sporting).—Any thing or person of first-rate and triumphant quality; also a CLINCHER (*q.v.*); a 'settler.' *Cf.*, sense 4.

1733. SWIFT, *Life and Character Dean S——t.* A protestant's a special CLINKER. It serves for sceptic and free-thinker. [M.]

1869. *Daily Telegraph*, 5 April. Despite the indifferent manner in which Vagabond cut up at the finish of the Metropolitan, quite sufficient was seen of him to prove that at a mile and a half he is a CLINKER.

1871. *Daily News*, 17 April, p. 2., col. 1. Ripponden and Cheesewring performed so indifferently as to strengthen the doubts whether they are really CLINKERS.

6. (common). — Deposits of fæcal or seminal matter in the hair about the *anus* or the female *pudendum*.

7. (common).—A lie. For synonyms, *see* WHOPPER.

TO HAVE CLINKERS IN ONE'S BUM, *phr.* (vulgar).—To be uneasy; unable to sit still.

CLINKERUM. The same as CLINK, sense 1.

CLINKING, *ppl. adj.* (common).— First-rate; extra good; about the best possible. *Cf.*, CLIPPING, THUMPING, WHOPPING, BATTLING, etc.

1868. *Daily Telegraph*, 6 June. Vermouth was a CLINKING good horse.

1887. *Sporting Times*, 12 March, p. 2, col. 2. Prince Henry must be a CLINKING good horse when in the humour to go.

1889. *Polytechnic Mag.*, 24 Oct., p. 263. Soon afterwards the Poly. obtained a free kick, and Young notched a point for them. Heard again steered the ball to the Clapham goal, and Toghill put in a CLINKING shot which just shaved the upright.

CLINK-RIG or **CLING-RIG**, *subs.* (old).—Stealing silver tankards from public-houses, etc. [From CLINK, plate, + RIG, a theft, or dodge.]

1781. G. PARKER, *View of Society*, II., 174, *s.v.*

1864. HOTTEN, *Slang Dict.*, s.v.

CLIP, *subs.* (colloquial).— A smart blow, *e.g.*, a CLIP in the eye. For synonyms, *see* DIG, BANG, and WIPE.

1830. MARRYAT, *King's Own*, xxvi. The master fires and hits the cat a CLIP on the neck.

1835. HALIBURTON ('Sam Slick'), *The Clockmaker* (1862), 89. He made a pull at the old-fashioned sword . . . and drawing it out he made a CLIP at him.

1860. *Police Gazette*, 17 November. He ran up to him, hit him a severe CLIP, and dashed through the window.

Verb (colloquial). — To move quickly. For analogous terms, *see* AMPUTATE. [Probably originally a falconry term = to fly swiftly.]

1833. M. SCOTT, *Tom Cringle*, xii. (1859), 281. He CLIPPED into the water with the speed of light.

1835-40. HALIBURTON ('Sam Slick'), *The Clockmaker* (1862), 46. He sees a steam-boat a CLIPPIN it by him like mad.

1843-4. *Sam Slick in England*, viii. (Bartlett). I ran all the way, right down as hard as I could CLIP.

CLIPE, *verb* (school). — To tell tales; to 'split'; to PEACH; *q.v.* (for synonyms).

CLIPPER, *subs.* (colloquial). — A triumph in horses, men, or women; a splendid man; a brilliant or very stylish woman; an admirable horse. [From CLIPPER, = a vessel built with a view to fast sailing; previous to which the term was applied to a hack for the road.]

1835. HALIBURTON, *Clockmaker*, 1 S., ch. xv. A perfect pictur' of a horse, and a genuine CLIPPER; could gallop like the wind.

1846. THACKERAY, *V. Fair*, ch. xvi. You have head enough for both of us, Beck, said he. You're sure to get us out of the scrape. I never saw your equal, and I've met with some CLIPPERS in my time, too.

1851. MAYHEW, *Lon. Lab. and Lon. Poor*, I., p. 133. They [wild ducks] come over here when the weather's a CLIPPER; for you see cold weather suits some birds and kills others.

CLIPPING or **CLIPPINGLY**, *ppl. adj.* and *adv.* (common).—Excellent; very showy; first-rate. [From that sense of clipping = that flies or moves fast.—*See* quot., 1643.] For synonyms, *see* A1 and FIZZING.

1643. P. QUARLES, *Emblemes*, B. IV., ii., p. 194 (ed. 1648). O that the pinions of a CLIPPING Dove Would cut my passage through the Empty Air, Mine eyes being sealed, how would I mount above The reach of danger and forgotten care!

1860. THACKERAY, *Philip*, ch. i., p. 46. What CLIPPING girls there were in that barouche.

1864. E. YATES, *Broken to Harness*, ch. xxiii. [Mr. Commissioner Beresford loq.:] CLIPPING riders, those girls! good as Kate Mellon anyday!

Cloak, *subs.* (thieves').—A watch case. [From CLOAK, an outer garment.]

1839. HARRISON AINSWORTH, *Jack Sheppard* [1889], p. 70. Near to these hopeful youths sat a fence, or receiver, bargaining with a clouter, or pickpocket, for a 'suit,' or, to speak in more intelligible language, a watch and seals, two 'CLOAKS;' commonly called watch-cases and a 'wedge-lobb,' otherwise known as a silver snuff-box.

Cloak-Twitchers, *subs.* (old).—Thieves who made a special business of robbing the lieges of their CLOAKS. [From CLOAK + TWITCH, to snatch, + ER.] In the old French cant these rogues were termed *tirelaines, i.e.*, wool-pullers (*tirer* = pull). For synonyms, *see* THIEVES.

1785. GROSE, *Dict. Vulg. Tongue*, s.v.

1811. *Lexicon Balatronicum*, s.v.

Clobber, *subs.* (common). — Primarily old, but now also applied to new clothes. For synonyms, *see* TOGS.

1879. J. W. HORSLEY, *Macm. Mag.*, XL., 502. Having a new suit of CLOBBER on me.

1889. *Answers*, 11 May, p. 374, col. 3. The CLOBBER (old clothes) which have been presented by charitable persons are exchanged and sold.

1889. *Sporting Times*, quoted in *Slang, Jargon, and Cant*, p. 255. If you are hard up always tell the dear things that you are a gentleman's valet. This will account for your good CLOBBER.

Verb.—Also CLOBBER UP. 1 To patch; revive; or 'translate' clothes. [Properly applied to cobbling of the lowest class. *Cf.*, CLOBBERER.]

1865. *Cassell's Paper*, Article, 'Old Clo'.' They are now past 'CLOBBERING,' 'reviving,' or 'translating,' they are, in fact, at the lowest point of Fortune's wheel: but the next turn puts them in its highest point again.

2. To dress smartly; to rig oneself out presentably. For synonyms, *see* RIG OUT.

1879. J. W. HORSLEY, *Macm. Mag.*, XL., 501. I used to get a good many pieces about this time, so I used to CLOBBER myself up and go to the concert-rooms.

1886. W. E. HENLEY, *Villon's Good-Night.* You judes that CLOBBER for the stramm.

1889. *Fun* [quoted in *S., J., and C.* p. 256]. 'D'you know, if you were CLOBBERED up I shouldn't mind taking you out?' She promised to be presentable. In her own words she said, 'I'll come CLOBBERED UP like a dukess.'

TO DO CLOBBER AT A FENCE, *phr.* (thieves').—To sell stolen clothes. Fr., *laver les harnais.*

Clobberer, *subs.* (common).—*See* quot. and *Cf.*, CLOBBER, *subs.* and *verb.*

1864. *The Times*, Nov. 2. Old clothes that are intended to remain in this country have to be tutored and transformed. The CLOBBERER, the 'reviver,' and the 'translator' lay hands upon them. The duty of the CLOBBERER is to patch, to sew up, and to restore as far as possible the garments to their pristine appearance.

Clock, *subs.* (thieves').—A watch. A RED CLOCK = a gold watch; a WHITE CLOCK = a silver watch. Generally modified into 'red'un' and 'white'un,' but for synonyms, *see* TICKER.

1886. *Tit-Bits*, 5 June, p. 121. Thus Fillied for a CLOCK and Slang, reveals the fact that the writer stole a watch and chain, was apprehended, and has been fully committed for trial.

TO KNOW WHAT'S O'CLOCK, *phr.* (common).—To be on the alert; in full possession of one's senses; a DOWNEY COVE: generally KNOWING (*q.v.* for synonyms). A variant is to KNOW THE TIME O'DAY.

1835. DICKENS, *Sketches by Boz*, p. 451. Our governor's wide awake, he is,

I'll never say nothin' agin him, nor no man; but he knows WHAT'S O'CLOCK, he does, uncommon.

1849-50. THACKERAY, *Pendennis*, I., p. 138. I'm not clever, p'raps, but I *am* rather downy, and partial friends say that I know WHAT'S O'CLOCK tolerably well.

CLOCK STOPPED.—*See* TICK.

Clod-Crushers, *subs.* (popular). —1. Clumsy boots. [In agriculture an implement for pulverising clods. *Cf.*, BEETLE-CRUSHERS, and for synonyms, *see* TROTTER-CASES.]

2. (common). — Large feet. [A transferred usage.—*See* sense 1.]

Clods and Stickings, *subs. phr.* (paupers').—*See* quot.

1871. *Daily Telegraph*, 24 Oct., Henry Melville's (the pauper) passionate, 'beutiful,' for Stepney Workhouse is a grotesque reflex of Marie Stuart's pathetic farewell to France. Is the skilly we wonder most 'beutiful' at Stepney, or are the CLODS AND STICKINGS unusually free from bone.

Cloister-Roush, *subs.* (Winchester College: obsolete).—*See* quot.

1870. MANSFIELD, *School Life at Winchester College*, p. 117. We had some singular customs at the commencement of Cloister time. Senior part and Cloisters, just before the entrance of the Masters into School, used to engage in a kind of general tournament; this was called CLOISTER ROUSH.

Clootie (Scots).—The Devil.—*See* CLOOTS.

1786 BURNS, *Address to the Deil.* Auld Hornie, Satan, Nick, or CLOOTIE.

Cloots (Scots), *subs.* —Hooves.

1786. BURNS, *The Death and Dying Words of Puir Mailie.* An' no to rin and wear his CLOOTS, Are ither menseless, graceless brutes.

Close as Wax, *adv. phr.* (general). —Miserly; niggardly; secretive. [A simile derived mainly from CLOSE, *adj.* = hidden or reticent.]

1863. C. READE. *Hard Cash*, I., 231. Then commenced a long and steady struggle, conducted with a Spartan dignity and self command, and a countenance as CLOSE AS WAX.

Close-File, *subs.* (old).—A person secretive or 'close'; not 'open' or communicative. [From CLOSE, *adj.* = secretive + FILE = a man.]

1839. HARRISON AINSWORTH, *Jack Sheppard* [1889], p. 8. Tom Sheppard was always a CLOSE FILE, and would never tell whom he married.

Cloth. [Generally THE CLOTH], *subs.* (colloquial). — Primarily clergymen; the members of a particular profession. For synonyms, *see* DEVIL-DODGER.

1836. C. DICKENS, *Pickwick Papers* (about 1827), p. 363 (ed. 1857). 'I maintain that that 'ere song's personal to THE CLOTH,' said the mottle-faced gentleman.

1864. *Daily Review*, Nov. 3. It might have seemed more decorous to draw our illustration of the Doctor's [Revd.] ingenuity from an incident related of two persons who have some right to be considered as in a sense belonging to THE CLOTH—The Abbess and Novice of Andouillets.

Clothes-Line. ABLE TO SLEEP UPON A CLOTHES-LINE, *phr.* (common).—Capable of sleeping anywhere or in any position; said of those able and willing to rest as well upon the roughest 'shake-down' as upon the most comfortable bed. [*Cf.*, TWO-PENNY ROPE and PLANK-BED.] Also applied in a transferred sense—a synonym for general capacity and ability.

Clothes-Pin. THAT'S THE SORT OF CLOTHES-PIN I AM, *phr.* (popular).—That's the sort of man I am. In the case of women THAT'S THE SORT OF HAIR-PIN (*q.v.*).

Cloth-Market, *subs.* (old).—A bed. [Of obvious derivation. *Cf.*, Fr., *la halle aux draps.*] For synonyms, *see* BUG-WALK and KIP.

1738. SWIFT, *Pol. Convers.*, dial i. I hope your early rising will do you no harm. I find you are but just come out of the CLOTH MARKET.

1824. T. FIELDING, *Proverbs, etc.* (*Familiar Phrases*), p. 148. He's in the CLOTH MARKET. In bed.

Cloud. — *See* BLOW A CLOUD. CLOUD originally signified tobacco smoke. — [*Grose*, 1785.] Fr., *en griller une* = to smoke a pipe or cigarette; also *en griller une sèche* and *en griller une bouffarde.*

Cloud-Cleaner, *subs.* (nautical).—*See* quot. ANGEL'S FOOTSTOOL, and *Cf.*

1883. W. CLARK RUSSELL, *Sailors' Word Book*, p. 31. CLOUD-CLEANER, an imaginary sail jokingly assumed to be carried by Yankee ships.

Clout, *subs.* (vulgar).—1. A blow; a kick. For synonyms, *see* BANG, DIG, and WIPE.

1785. GROSE, *Dict. Vulg. Tongue.* CLOUT: a blow (cant), I'll give you a CLOUT on your jolly nob; I'll give you a blow on the head.

1811. *Lexicon Balatronicum*, s.v.

1864. M. E. BRADDON, *Aurora Floyd*, ch. xx. 'If *you* had a father that'd fetch you a CLOUT of the head as soon as look at you, *you'd* run away perhaps.

2. (thieves').—A pocket-handkerchief. [A.S. *clút*, a clout or patch; Dan. *klud*, Swed. *klut*, or perhaps from the Keltic; hence, any worthless piece of cloth.] For synonyms, *see* WIPE, sense 2.

1574-1637. BEN JONSON, *Metam. Gipsies.* And Tidslefoot has lost his CLOUT, he says, with a three-pence and four tokens in't.

1714. *Memoirs of John Hall*, 4 ed., p. 11. [List of Cant Words in.] CLOUT: a handkerchief.

1754. FIELDING, *Jon. Wild*, bk. I., ch. ix. A neat double CLOUT, which seemed to have been worn a few weeks only, was pinned under her chin.

1785. GROSE, *Dict. Vulg. Tongue.* A handkerchief.

1811. *Lexicon Balatronicum.* A handkerchief (cant). Any pocket handkerchief except a silk one.

1864. HOTTEN, *Slang Dict.* CLOUT, or Rag, a cotton pocket handkerchief (old cant).

3. *plural* (low).—A woman's under-clothes, from the waist downwards. Also her complete wardrobe, on or off the person.

4. (common). — A woman's 'bandage'; 'diaper'; or 'sanitary.'

Verb (low). — 1. To strike. Fr., *jeter une mandole.* For synonyms, *see* TAN.

1576-1625. BEAUMONT AND FLETCHER [quoted in Annandale's ed. of Ogilvie's Imperial Dict.]. Pay him over the pate, CLOUT him for all his courtesies.

2. (old).—To patch; to tinker.

17(?). *Scots Ballad.* I'll CLOUT my Johnnie's grey breeks For a' the ill he's done me yet.

1785. BURNS, *The Jolly Beggars.* In vain they searched when off I marched To go and CLOUT the caudron.

Clouter, *subs.* (old).—A pickpocket — especially one who steals handkerchiefs. [From CLOUT, sense 2 (*q.v.*), a pocket-handkerchief, + ER.] *Cf.*, CLOUTING, sense 2. For synonyms, *see* STOOK-HAULER.

1839. W. H. AINSWORTH, *J. Sheppard*, p. 158, ed. 1840. Near to these hopeful youths sat a fence, or receiver, bargaining with a CLOUTER, or pickpocket.

Clouting, *verbal subs.* (common). 1. A beating, basting, or TANNING (*q.v.* for synonyms).—*See* also BASTE.

2. (thieves').—Stealing handkerchiefs. *Cf.*, CLOUTER.

Cloven, Cleaved, Cleft, *adj.* (old).—Terms applied to a sham virgin. (CLEFT, *subs.* = the female *pudendum.*)

IN CLOVER, *adv. phr.* (colloquial).—Well-off; comfortable; *e.g.*, like a horse at grass in a clover field.

Clow, *subs.* (Winchester College). Pronounced *clō.*—A box on the ear. [Possibly from CLOUT (*q.v.*) on the model of 'bow' from 'bout,' and 'low' from 'lout.' Halliwell gives 'clow' as a Cumberland word, meaning 'to scratch.'] *Cf.*, BASTE, and for general synonyms, *see* BANG, DIG, and WIPE.

1870. MANSFIELD, *School-Life at Winchester College*, p. 140. The juniors did not get much fun out of the regular games, as their part consisted solely in kicking in the ball, and receiving divers kicks and CLOWS in return for their vigilance. *Ibid*, p. 39. Nor, when ordered to 'hold down,' (*i.e.*, put your head in a convenient position) for a CLOW, would the victim dare to ward off the blow.

Verb.—To box one on the ear. It was customary to preface the action by an injunction to 'hold down.'—*See* quot., 1870, under *subs.*, sense.

Clowes, *subs.* (old).—Rogues.—*Grose* [1785].

Cloy, Cligh, or **Cly**, *verb* (old). —To steal. For synonyms, *see* PRIG. An old Gloucestershire vulgarism for the hands is CLEES.

1610. ROWLANDS, *Martin Mark-all*, p. 8 (H. Club's Repr., 1874). They are sure to be CLYD in the night by the angler, or hooker, or such like pilferers that liue upon the spovle of other poore people.

1622. HEAD AND KIRKMAN, Canting Song, in *English Rogue.* I met a Dell, I viewed her well, She was benship to my watch; So she and I did stall and CLOY, Whatever we could catch.

1671. R. HEAD, *English Rogue*, pt. I., ch. v., p. 48 (1874). CLOY: to steal.

1706. E. COLES, *Eng. Dict.* CLOY: to steal.

1785. GROSE, *Dict. Vulg. Tongue*, s.v. To CLOY the clout, to steal the handkerchief. To CLOY the lour, to steal money.

1811. *Lexicon Balatronicum*, s.v.

Cloyer, *subs.* (old).—A thief who intruded on the profits of young sharpers, by claiming a share.

1611. MIDDLETON, *Roaring Girl*, *O. Pl.*, vi., 113. Then there's a CLOYER, or snap, that dogs any new brother in that trade, and snaps,—will have half in any booty.

1659. *The Catterpillars of this Nation Anatomised.* [CLOYER = a pick-pocket.]

Cloyes, *subs.* (old). — Thieves; robbers, etc. [In Grose, 1785, and *Lexicon Balatronicum*, 1811.] —*See* CLOY and CLOYER.

Cloying, *verbal subs.* (old) Stealing.

1739. *Poor Robin.* Money is now a hard commodity to get, insomuch that some will venture their necks for it, by padding, CLOYING, milling, filching, nabbing, etc., all of which in plain English is only stealing.

Club, *verb* (military).—In manœuvring troops, so to blunder the word of command that the soldiers get into a position from which they cannot extricate themselves by ordinary tactics.

18(?). THACKERAY, *Novels by Eminent Hands.* 'Phil Fogarty.' 'CLUBBED, be jabers!' roared Lanty Clancy. 'I wish we could show 'em the Fighting Onety-Oneth, Captain, darlin'!'

1854. WHYTE MELVILLE, *General Bounce*, ch. xi. If you're in difficulties, ask Sergeant File what is best to be done, only don't CLUB 'em, my boy, as you did at Limerick.

Subs. (venery).—The *penis.*

CLUMP, *subs.* (common).—A blow, generally a heavy one, with the hand.—*See* quots. under verbal sense. For synonyms, *see* BANG, DIG, and WIPE.

Verb (common).—To strike; to give a heavy blow. Fr., *faire du bifteck.* For synonyms, *see* TAN.

1864. *Derby Day,* p. 52. 'We can't give 'em in charge now.'... 'Because why? I'll tell you ... we shouldn't know when to *spot* 'em. No I want to CLUMP them. It will spoil sport to call in the *bobbies.*'

1874. W. E. HENLEY, *MS. Ballad.* Which they calls me the Professor, But I'm only Hogan's Novice, Bloody artful with the mufflers, And a mark on fancy CLUMPING.

1888. *Daily News,* 2 Jan., p. 7, col. 1. The prisoner CLUMPED (struck) both of them, and then ran away.

CLUMPER, *subs.* (common).—1. A thick, heavy boot for walking. [Clumps in shoemakers' technology = extra fore or half soles.] *Cf.,* quot. under CLUMPING. For synonyms, *see* TROTTER-CASES.

2. (common).—One that clumps; a 'basher.'

CLUMPERTON, *subs.* (old).—A countryman. For synonyms, *see* JOSKIN.

1870. *All the Year Round,* Mar. 5. 'Byegone Cant (Geo. II.).' CLUMPER-TONS agape at the giant proportions of the still somewhat new St. Paul's would turn from their wondering walks to shudder and shrink at the ghastly gallows exhibition at Newgate.

CLUMPING, *verbal subs.* (common).—Walking heavily and noisily: as in hob nails or in clogs.

1864. [From Hotten's *MS.* Collection, n.d.] 'Why, woman! dost 'oo think I'se had naught better to do than go CLUMPING up and down the sky a-searching for thy Tummas?'

CLY, *subs.* (thieves').—1. A pocket; purse; sack; or basket. For synonyms, *see* BRIGH and SKY-ROCKET.

1714. *Memoirs of John Hall* (4 ed.). p. 12. CLY: a pocket.

1742. CHARLES JOHNSON, *Highwaymen and Pirates,* p. 252. Filing a CLY which is picking pockets of watches, money, books or handkerchiefs.

1748. T. DYCHE, *Dict.* (5 ed.). CLY (s.): the cant term for ... purse or pocket.

1818. MAGINN, from VIDOCQ. *The Pickpocket's Chaunt.* A regular swell cove lushy lay. To his CLIES my hooks I throw in, Tol, lol, etc.

1834. AINSWORTH, *Rookwood.* No knuckler so deftly could fake a CLY.

1858. A. MAYHEW, *Paved with Gold,* bk. II., ch. i., p. 69. They're just made for hooking a fogle [handkerchief] out of a CLYE.

1878. CHARLES HINDLEY, *Life and Times of James Catnach.* Frisk the CLY and fork the rag, Draw the fogles plummy.

2. (thieves').—Money.

1748. T. DYCHE, *Dictionary* (5 ed.), CLY (s.): the cant name for money, a purse, or a pocket.

1785. GROSE, *Dict. Vulg. Tongue,* CLY: money.

1811. *Lexicon Balatronicum,* s.v.

Verb (old).—1. To take; have; receive; pocket: in fact, 'to COP.'

1567. HARMAN, *Caveat* (1814), p. 66. The ruffian CLY thee, the deuil take thee.

1609. DEKKER, a Gypsy song, in *Lanthorne and Candlelight, etc.* The Ruffin CLY the nab of the Harman beck. If we mawnd Pannam, lap or Ruff-peck.

CLY-FAKER, *subs.* (thieves').—A pickpocket. [From CLY, a pocket, + FAKE, to steal. + ER.] For synonyms, *see* STOOKHAULER.

1827. LYTTON, *Pelham,* ch. lxxxii. They were gentlemen-sharpers, and not vulgar cracksmen and CLYFAKERS.

1839. HARRISON AINSWORTH, *Jack Sheppard* [1889], p. 14. 'Oh, I see!' replied Blueskin, winking significantly.... 'Now! slip the purse into my hand. Bravo! the best CLY-FAKER of 'em all; couldn't have done it better.'

1852. *Punch,* vol. XXIII., p. 161.

1864. HOTTEN, *Slang Dict.,* p. 103. CLY-FAKER: a pickpocket.

CLY-FAKING, *subs.* (thieves').—Pocket-picking. For synonyms, *see* PUSH.

1851. BORROW, *Lavengro,* ch. xxxi., p. 112 (1888). 'What do you mean by CLY-FAKING?' 'Lor, dear! no harm; only taking a handkerchief now and then.'

1861. H. KINGSLEY, *Ravenshoe,* ch. lx. Well, sir, I won't deny that the young woman is Bess, and perhaps she may be on the cross, and I don't go to say that what with flimping, and with CLY-FAKING, and such-like, she mayn't be wanted.

CLY-OFF, *verb* (old).—To carry off. *Cf.,* CLY, *verb,* sense 1.

1656. BROME, *Jovial Crew.* Act ii. Here safe in our skipper Let's CLY OFF our peck, And bowse in defiance O' th' Harman-beck.

CLYSTER-PIPE, *subs.* (old).—An apothecary. [From CLYSTER = an injection for costiveness.] Fr., *un flûtencul,* a play upon words. For synonyms, *see* GALLIPOT.

1785. GROSE, *Dic. Vulg. Tongue,* s.v.

1811. *Lexicon Balatronicum,* s.v.

CLY THE GERKE or JERK, *verbal phr.* (old).—*See* quots.

1567. HARMAN, *Caveat* (1814), p. 66. To CLY THE GERKE, to get a whipping! *Cf.,* to COP A HIDING.

1610. ROWLANDS, *Martin Mark-all,* p. 38 (H. Club's Repr., 1874), s.v.

1706. E. COLES, *Eng. Dic.,* s.v.

1827. LYTTON, *Pelham,* ch. lxxxii. You deserve to CLY THE JERK for your patter.

COACH, *subs.* (formerly University and public schools'; now common).—A private tutor; and in a transferred sense one who trains another in mental or physical acquirements, *e.g.,* in Sanskrit, Shakspeare, cricket, or rowing. Analogous terms are CRAMMER, FEEDER, and GRINDER.

1850. F. E. SMEDLEY, *Frank Fairleigh,* ch. xxix., p. 240. Besides the regular college tutor, I secured the assistance of what, in the slang of the day, we irreverently termed a COACH.

1853. C. BEDE, *Verdant Green,* pt. I., pp. 63-4. 'That man is Cram, the patent safety. He's the first COACH in Oxford.' 'A COACH,' said our freshman in some wonder. 'Oh, I forgot you didn't know college slang. I suppose a royal mail is the only gentleman COACH you know of. Why, in Oxford a COACH means a private tutor you must know'; and those who can't afford a COACH, get a cab *alias* a crib *alias* translation.

1864. *Eton School-days,* ch. ix., p. 103. Lord Fitzwinton, one of the smallest and best COACHES—in aquatics—in the school.

1871. *Times.* 'Report of the Debate in House of Lords on University Test Bill.' The test proposed would be wholly ineffective ... while it would apply to the college tutors, who had little influence over the young men, it would not affect the COACHES, who had the chief direction of their studies.

1889. *Pall Mall Gazette,* 29 Nov., p. 1, col. 3. The schoolmaster is concerned with the education of boys up to eighteen; all beyond that falls either to the COACH or the professor.

Verb (common).—To prepare for an examination by private instruction; to train: in general use both by coacher and coachee.

1846. THACKERAY, *Vanity Fair,* ch. v. The superb Cuff himself ... helped him on with his Latin verses, COACHED him in play-hours.

1870. *London Figaro,* June 10. 'Quadrille Conversation.' It is, we fear, Quixotic to hope that ladies and gentlemen invited to the same ball would COACH with the same master.

COACHEE, *subs.* (colloquial).—A coachman. *Cf.,* CABBY.

1819. THOS. MOORE, *Tom Crib's Mem. Cong,* p. 79. This song ... in which the language and sentiments of COACHEE are transferred so ingeniously.

1825. *English Spy,* I., pp. 134-5.

COACHING, *verbal subs.* (common).—1. Instruction; training, etc.—*See* COACH, *subs.* French students call it *la barbe.*

1836. *Pluck Examination Papers for Candidates at Oxford and Cambridge,* by SCRIBLERUS REDIVIVUS [Oxford]. The system of COACHING pupils considerably improved by the examiners becoming pupils.

2. (Rugby School).—A flogging. Now obsolete.

COACHMAN, *subs.* (anglers').—A fly-fisher's rod. [In allusion to whipping the stream.]

COACH-WHEEL, *subs.* (popular).—A crown-piece, or five shillings. For synonyms, *see* CART-WHEEL.

1785. GROSE, *Dict. Vulg. Tongue.* COACH WHEEL: a half crown piece is a *fore* COACH WHEEL, and a crown piece a *hind* COACH WHEEL, the fore wheels of a coach being less than the hind ones.

COAL.—*See* COLE.

TO TAKE IN ONE'S COALS, or WINTER COALS, *phr.* (nautical).—To contract a venereal disease. For synonyms, *see* LADIES' FEVER.

COAL-BOX, *subs.* (musical).—A chorus. [Obviously 'music-hally' or 'circussy' in derivation: a cross between rhyming slang and a clown's WHEEZE (q.v.).]

1809-70. MARK LEMON, *Up and Down London Streets.* The slang word for chorus, COAL BOX, if we might mention anything so ungenteel.

COALEY, *subs.* (common).—A coal-heaver, or porter.

1880. JAS. GREENWOOD, 'Diddler Domesticus,' in *Odd People in Odd Places,* p. 93. With such arguments the bargain is driven to a conclusion, and the grateful COALEY takes his departure.

1889. *Star,* 3 Dec., p. 3, col. 4. The COALIES demonstrated last night in right novel fashion at St. Pancras Arches.

COALING or COALLY, *adj.* (theatrical).—Among 'pros' a COALLY or COALING part is one that is grateful to the player. [Hotten says it means ' profitable,' and derives it from COLE = money, but this is doubtful.—*See* quot.]

1872. M. E. BRADDON, *Dead Sea Fruit,* ch. xiv. The gorger's awful COALLY on his own slumming, eh? ... I mean to say that our friend the manager is rather sweet upon his own acting.

COAL-SCUTTLE, *subs.* (common).—A poke bonnet; modish once, but now reserved for old-fashioned Quakeresses and 'Hallelujah Lasses.' [From the shape.]

1838. DICKENS, *Nicholas Nickleby.* There was Miss Snevellici ... glancing from the depths of her COAL-SCUTTLE bonnet at Nicholas.

COAT. TO GET THE SUN INTO A HORSE'S COAT, *phr.* (racing).—Explained by quot.

1889. *Standard.* 'Sir Chas. Russell's Speech in Durham-Chetwynd Case,' June 25. An owner says to his trainer, 'I suppose, Mr. Jones, we'll have very good luck to-morrow?' (laughter). 'Well no, sir,' says the trainer; 'I don't think the horse has any chance to-morrow. The fact is, he isn't fit.' A fortnight elapses, and on comes another meeting at Newmarket, and the owner goes down again, and he sees the horse. To his uninitiated eye the horse seems as well as when he saw it on the previous occasion. In the interval the trainer had 'slipped in a lot of work into him,' I think that is the term, and the owner, who thinks he knows something about horses (laughter) says to his trainer 'You're going to run this horse

to-morrow?' 'Oh, I think so, sir,' says the trainer. 'But look here,' says the owner, 'This is a much better class. He is meeting this horse upon no better terms than before.' 'But, sir,' says the trainer, 'he has greatly improved. The SUN HAS GOT INTO HIS COAT.'

COAX, *verb* (old).—To dissemble in the shoes the soiled or ragged parts of a pair of stockings.—[Grose, 1785.]

COB, *subs.* (prison).—1. A punishment cell. For synonyms, *see* CLINCH.

2. (nautical).—Money. Especially given to a Spanish coin formerly current in Ireland, worth about 4s. 8d. Also the name still given at Gibraltar to a Spanish dollar.

1805. *Plymouth Newspaper* of Feb. 24, quoted in 'Autobiography of a Seaman,' by Earl of Dundonald, vol. I., ch. x., p. 174. His Lordship sent word to Plymouth that, if ever it was in his power he would fulfil his public advertisement (stuck up here) for entering seamen, of filling their pockets with Spanish 'pewter' and 'cobs,' nicknames given by seamen to ingots and dollars.

3. (Winchester College).—A hard hit at cricket. Of modern introduction. *Cf.,* BARTER.

Verb (schoolboys').—1. To detect, catch, etc.

2. (popular).—To humbug; deceive; TO GAMMON (q.v.).

3. To hit hard.—*See* subs., sense 3.

COBB, *verb* (general).—To spank; to smack the posteriors with (say) a tailor's sleeve-board.

1830. MARRYAT, *King's Own.* Gentlemen, gentlemen, if you must COBB Mrs. Skrimmage, for God's sake *let it be over all.*

COBBER, *subs.* (common).—A prodigious falsehood; *i.e.,* 'a THUMPER'; WHOPPER (q.v.).

COBBLE-COLTER, *subs.* (old).—A turkey. Fr., *une ornie de balle* and *un Jésuite. Cf.,* ALDERMAN IN CHAINS.

1785. GROSE, *Dict. Vulg. Tongue,* s.v.

1837. DISRAELI, *Venetia,* p. 69. 'Come, old mort,' said the leader, in a very different tone to the one in which he addressed his young guest, 'tout the COBBLE-COLTER; are we to have darkmans upon us?

COBBLED, *ppl. adj.* (schoolboys').—Caught; detected; spotted. [From COB, *verb,* sense 1.]

COBBLERS' KNOCK. TO GIVE THE COBBLER'S KNOCK or TO KNOCK AT THE COBBLER'S DOOR, *verbal phr.* (provincial).—A sort of fancy sliding in which the artist raps the ice in triplets with one foot while progressing swiftly on the other.

1836. DICKENS, *Pickwick,* vol. ii., ch. 2. SamWeller, in particular was displaying that beautiful feat of fancy sliding which is currently called KNOCKING AT THE COBBLER'S DOOR, and which is achieved by skimming over the ice on one foot and occasionally giving a postman's knock upon it with the other.

COBBLERS' MARBLES, *subs. phr.* (vulgar).—A corrupt pronunciation of *cholera morbus,* once a name for Asiatic cholera.

COBBLER'S THUMB, *subs.* (Irish localism).—A small fish; the bull-head, called in English the MILLER'S THUMB.

1839. LEVER, *Harry Lorrequer,* ch. xxvii. His hands and feet, forming some compensation by their ample proportions, give to his entire air and appearance somewhat the look of a small fish, with short, thick fins, vulgarly called a COBBLER'S THUMB.

COCHINEAL DYE, *subs.* (pugilistic).—Blood. [From the colour.] For synonyms, *see* CLARET.

1853. REV. E. BRADLEY ('Cuthbert Bede'), *Verdant Green*, pt. II., p. 31. He would kindly inquire of one gentleman, 'What d'ye ask for a pint of your COCHINEAL DYE?'

1883. *Referee*. It certainly seemed that their stock-in-trade was largely composed of COCHINEAL DYE; there was in truth no lack of the gory accessory of the fight

COCK, *subs.* (common).—1. The *penis*. *Cf.*, Ger., *Hahn*, *Hänchen*. [Possibly related to 'cock' = turn-valve.] For synonyms, *see* CREAM-STICK.

1600. SHAKSPEARE, *King Henry V.*, ii. 1.—*Cf.*

1647. BEAUMONT AND FLETCHER. The *Custom of the County*, v., 4. The mainspring's weakened that holds up his COCK.

1730 BAILEY *Dict.*, s.v.

1737. RABELAIS. Trans. I., 185., s.v.

1807. RABELAIS. Trans. [LONGMAN'S ed.]. s.v., I., 169.

1849. RABELAIS. Trans. [BOHN'S ed.], s.v., I., 135.

2. (colloquial).—A chief or leader; particularly in such phrases as COCK OF THE WALK, SCHOOL, etc. [A simile drawn from the barndoor.] *Cf.*, sense 3, and *adj.*

1711. *Spectator*, No. 131. Service to the knight. Sir Andrew is grown the COCK OF THE CLUB since he left us, and if he does not return quickly will make every mother's son of us commonwealth's men.

1729. SWIFT, *Grand Question Debated*. But at cuffs I was always the COCK OF THE SCHOOL.

1764. O'HARA, *Midas*, I., 1. COCK OF THE SCHOOL. He bears despotic rule.

1811-63. W. M. THACKERAY, *Miscellanies*, II., 275. There is no more dangerous or stupifying position for a man in life than to be a COCK OF SMALL SOCIETY.

1862. MRS. H. WOOD, *Channings*, ch. xxix. 'Were I going in for the seniorship, and one below me were suddenly hoisted above my head, and made a COCK OF THE WALK, I'd know the reason why.

3. (common).—A familiar address; *e.g.*, OLD COCK, or JOLLY OLD COCK. [Probably derived from sense 1.] Amongst similiar expressions may be mentioned OLD MAN, MY PIPPIN, and in French, *mon vieux zig*, or *lapin*.

1639. MASSINGER, *Unnatural Combat*, II., i. He has drawn blood of him yet: well done, OLD COCK.

1749. FIELDING, *Tom Jones*, bk. XVIII., ch. x. Then give me thy fist, a't as hearty an honest COCK as any in the kingdom.

1825. *The English Spy*, vol. I., p. 215. The low-bred, vulgar, Sunday throng, Who dine at two, are ranged along On both sides of the way; With various views these honest folk Descant on fashions, quiz and joke, Or mark the SHY COCK down.*

1836. C. DICKENS, *Pickwick Papers* (about 1827), p. 367 (ed. 1857). 'Do you always smoke arter you goes to bed, OLD COCK?' inquired Mr. Weller of his landlord, when they had both retired for the night. 'Yes, I does, young Bantam,' replied the cobbler.

1841. *Punch*, vol. I., p. 278. The people down here are a queer lot, but I have hunted up two or three JOLLY COCKS, and we contrive to keep the place alive between us.

1855. THACKERAY, *Newcomes*, ch. xvi. Shrewd OLD COCK, Mr. Binnie. Has brought home a good bit of money from India.

1870. *London Figaro*, 19 Oct. What on earth is the meaning of Mr. Santley's voice being over-*crowed* by a mammoth orchestra? I never heard before that fiddles crowed, or that Mr. Santley was a COCK. He is what is known as a JOLLY COCK, but there his similarity to the noisy fowl ends.

4. (racing).—A horse not intended to win the race for which it is put down, but kept in the lists to deceive the public.

1887. *Field*, May 29. In the phraseology of slangy turfites, the horse was a COCK; *i.e.*, it had been liberally backed, but was never intended to run.

* The Sunday men, as they are facetiously called in the fashionable world, are not now so numerous as formerly; the facility of a trip across the channel enables many a SHY COCK to evade the eye . . . of the law.

5. (common).—Primarily the fictitious narratives in verse or prose of murders, fires, etc. (*see* quot., 1851), produced for sale in the streets. Famous manufactories of COCKS were kept by 'Jemmy' Catnach and Johnny Pitts, called the Colburn and Bentley of the 'paper' trade. They fought bitterly, and Catnach informed the world that Pitts had once been a 'bumboat woman,' while Pitts declared—

That all the boys and girls around, Who go out prigging rags and phials, Know Jemmy Catnach ! ! ! well, Who lives in a back slum in the Dials.

Catnach got at last to be 'Cock of the Walk,' and remained so till his retirement in 1839. [Hotten thought the word might be a corruption of *cook*, a 'cooked' or garbled statement, or a coinage from 'cock and bull story.'] Fr., *une goualante*.

1851-61. H. MAYHEW, *Lon. Lab. and Lon. Poor*, vol. I., p. 228. What are technically termed COCKS, which, in polite language, means accounts of fabulous duels between ladies of fashion, of apocryphal elopements . . . or awful tragedies, etc.

Hence applied to any incredible story.

1870. *London Figaro*, 1 Feb. We are disposed to think that COCKS must have penetrated to Eastern Missouri.

6. (thieves').—An abbreviation of 'cockney.'

7. (printers').—In gambling or playing with 'quads,' a COCK is when one (or more) of the nine pieces does not fall flat but lodges crosswise on another. The player is then given another chance.

8. (tailors').—GOOD COCK—POOR COCK. A good and bad workman respectively.

Adj. (colloquial).—Chief; first and foremost. *Cf.*, COCK, *subs.*, sense 2.

1676. ETHEREGE, *Man of Mode*, II., ii., in wks. (1704), 211. Why the very COCK-fool of all those fools, Sir Fopling Flutter.

1856. T. HUGHES, *Tom Brown's School-days*, pt. II., ch. vi. They'll make the old Madman COCK medicine-man and tattoo him all over.

Verb (venery).—1. To copulate. Usually employed by women and in the passive sense: *e.g.*, 'to want cocking,' or 'to get cocked.' For synonyms, *see* RIDE.

2. (common).—To smoke.

COCK THE EYE, *verbal phr.* (colloquial).—To shut or wink one eye; to leer; to look incredulous. Fr., *cligner des œillets*. *Cf.*, COCK-EYED. [In venery a woman with A COCK IN HER EYE = a woman in a condition of sexual excitement, a woman that 'means business.' *Cf.*, PINTLE-KEEK (*q.v.*) and LOOK PRICKS.] Of the kindred phrase, to COCK THE CHIN, an illustration appears in *Elegant Extracts*.

As Dick and Tom in fierce dispute engage, And face to face the noisy contest wage; 'Don't COCK YOUR CHIN at me,' Dick smartly cries. 'Fear not, his head's not charg'd,' a friend replies.

The French equivalent is *s'aborgner* (literally 'to make oneself blind of one eye by closing it').

1751. SMOLLETT, *Peregrine Pickle*, ch. ii. He . . . made wry faces, and, to use the vulgar phrase, COCKED HIS EYE at him, to the no small entertainment of the spectators.

1836. MARRYAT, *Japhet*, ch. iv. Timothy put on his hat, COCKED HIS EYE at me, and left us alone.

1859. J. EASTWOOD, in *Notes and Queries*, 2 S., viii., 461. The phrase COCK YOUR EYE is not at all an uncommon one in Yorkshire—meaning 'direct your eye, give a glance.'

TO COCK SNOOKS, *verbal phr.* (common).—*See* COFFEE-MILLING and SNOOKS.

THAT COCK WON'T FIGHT. *phr.* (common).—Originally cock-pit slang. Said of things problematical or doubtful.

1844. *Puck*, p. 124. 'Song of the First Tragedian . . . having pawned his properties.' Suppose I told my uncle what I fear he'd not believe, That I'll certainly repay him the money ere I leave; That my benefit when it comes off is sure to prove a hit, I don't think, with a screw like him, THAT COCK WOULD FIGHT A BIT.

BY COCK OR BY COCK AND PYE. *phr.* (old).—'Cock' is here a corruption, or disguise of 'God.' We find also 'cocks-passion,' 'cocks-body,' and other allusions to the Saviour, or His body, as supposed to exist in the Host: the expression surviving the belief. In BY COCK AND PYE, the PIE, or Sacred Book of Offices is added. BY COCK AND PIE AND MOUSEFOOT, is quoted from the old play of *Soliman and Perseda*, *Orig. of Drama*, ii., p. 211.

1571. EDWARDS, *Damon and Pythias*, Old Pl., i., 216. *W.* By the masse I will boxe you. *J.* BY COCKE I will foxe you.

1596. SHAKSPEARE, *Hamlet*, iv., 5. BY COCKE they are to blame.

1598. SHAKSPEARE, *Henry IV.*, pt. II., Act v., Sc. 1. BY COCK AND PIE, sir, you shall not away to-night.

1606. WILY, *Beguilede*. NOW BY COCK AND PIE, you never spoke a truer word in your life.

KNOCKED A-COCK, *adv. phr.* (pugilistic).—Knocked 'all of a heap,' or 'out of time.' Obviously adapted from the lingo of the cock-pit, and suggested by the sight of the beaten bird laid on his back.

COCK-A-DOODLE BROTH, *subs. phr.* (? nonce phrase).—*See* quot.

1856. READE, *Never Too Late to Mend*, ch. lxxxv. He complains that 'he can't peck,' yet continues the cause of his infirmity, living almost entirely upon COCK-A-DOODLE BROTH,—eggs beat up in brandy and a little water.

COCK-A-HOOP or **COCK-ON** (or **IN A**)-**HOOP,** *adj.* (colloquial).—Strutting; triumphant; high-spirited; 'uppish.' [Ray suggested that it refers to the practice of taking out the spigot (an old synonym for the *penis*, by the way) and laying it on the top of a barrel with a view to drinking the latter dry; a proceeding that would naturally induce a certain swagger in the actors. There seems, however, no doubt that the true derivative is the French *coq à houppé*. *Houppé*, in French, is a tuft, *touffe* (and *toupet*, is kindred). Littré says, *terme de blason*, tuft of silk or tassel hanging from a hat: '*Elle sert de timbre au chapeau des cardinaux*, etc. *Houppée* is the foam on the top of a wave. *Houppe* is the tuft on a trencher cap: '*Qui distingue*,' says Tarver, '*le bonnet des nobles de celui des autres*' at the universities—hence tuft-hunter, *coureur de houppes*. Also, '*Il trouve à se fourrer parmi les plus huppés*' = he contrives to vie with those at the very top of fashion. The *Hoopoe*, (Lat. *Upupa*), is a crested bird. Hence *coq à houppé* is a crested cock, and by analogy one swaggering, triumphant, exulting; so 'cock-a-hoop' is 'cock-a-top,' 'cock-a-crest,' elated beyond reason—'cocky,' as schoolboys say—'cock of the walk,' 'cock at the top.' In cock-fighting, the 'cock-a-top' is he that gets the vantage stroke. '*Abattre l'orgueil des plus huppés*'; to bring down the

crest of the highest. COCK-A-HOOP is plainly the original expression, and COCK-ON-THE-HOOP a later form adopted when the original meaning had vanished.] English equivalents are 'IN FULL FEATHER,' and 'A-COCK-HORSE' (*q.v.*), while colloquial French has *s'en pourlécher la face* and *s'émérillonner* (to become cheerful through repeated potations).

1595. SHAKSPEARE, *Romeo and Juliet*, Act i., Sc. 5. Am I the master here or you? Go to . . . You will set COCK-A-HOOP! you'll be the man.

1623. JONSON, *Tale of a Tub*, V., ii. John Clay agen! nay then—set COCK-A-HOOP: I have lost no daughter, nor no money, justice.

1707. WARD, *Hudibras Redivivus*, ol. II., pt. XII., p. 20. Those cruel, sanctify'd Pretenders, Now rais'd by Fortune, COCK-A-HOOP.

1853. *Diogenes*, II., 195. 'Our Foreign News Summary.' All the COCK-A-HOOP BEYS in the Sultan's dominions Have taken to expressing their individual opinions.

1885. D. C. MURRAY, *Rainbow Gold*, bk. IV., ch. vi. He's a fine lad, a fine lad, but COCK-A-WHOOP, and over certain for his years

COCK-ALE, *subs.* (old).—A homely aphrodisiac.—[*Grose*, 1785.] [An allusion to the *penis* and the stirring tendency of strong beer.] Nares says it was 'a sort of ale which was very celebrated in the seventeenth century for its superior quality.'

1675. *Woman Turn'd Bully* [quoted in Nares]. *Spr.* How, Mr. Trupenny, not a drop worth drinking? Did you ever taste our COCK-ALE?

1698. WARD, *London Spy*. My friend by this time (knowing the entertainment of the house) had called for a bottle of COCK-ALE, of which I tasted a glass, but could not conceive it to be anything but a mixture of small beer and treacle. If this be COCK-ALE, said I, e'en let cockscombs drink it. [N.]

1738. *Poor Robin*. Notwithstanding the large commendations you give the juice of barley, yet if compar'd with canary, it's no more than a mole-hill to a mountain; whether it be COCK-ALE, China ale, etc. [N.]

Also COCK-BROTH, etc.

COCK ALLEY, *subs.* (old).—The female *pudendum*. Other derivations of the same make are COCK-CHAFER, COCK HALL, COCK INN, COCK LANE, COCK-LOFT, COCK-PIT, COCKSHIRE, and COCK-SHY. For synonyms, *see* MONOSYLLABLE.

COCKALORUM or **COCKYLORUM,** *subs.* (common).—1. A half contemptuous address.—*See* quot.

1815-23. T. C. CARTER, in *Daily News*, 7 Dec., 1889, p. 3, col. 5. In 1823 was displayed in a shop window in Pilgrim Street, Ludgate Hill, a picture entitled 'Seizure for Rent.' It represented the interior of a room; the only article of furniture a bottomless chair, on the edge of which was seated a half-clad man smoking a pipe. The doorway was filled up by a very fat beadle in full uniform; behind him in the shade could be seen two men, each with a porter's knot. To the beadle the tenant was saying: 'Now then, old COCKALORUM jig, seize away.' In my school days, from 1815 to 1820, we often heard in the playground: 'Now little COCKALORUM, out of that,'

2. (schoolboys').—A rough and tumble game described as follows by a correspondent of the *Pall Mall Gazette* (1890, Jan. 4, p. 2, col. 1):—

When I went to Harrow, thirty years ago, I found a winter evening game in force there, called 'high COCKALORUM,' of which I send you a sketch. The players used to divide into two opposing bands of from twelve to fourteen each—in fact, the more the merrier. One side 'went down,' so as to constitute a long 'hogsback'—the last boy having a couple of pillows between himself and the wall, and each boy clasping his front rank man, and carefully tucking his own 'cocoa-nut' under his right arm, so as to prevent fracture of the vertebræ. When the hogsback was thus formed, the other side came on, leap-frogging on to the backs of those who were down, the best and steadiest jumpers being sent first. Sometimes the passive line was broken quite easily by the ruse of a short high jump, coming with irresistible impulse on a back which was not expecting weight just yet. Sometimes a too ambitious leap-frogger ruined his party by overbalancing and falling off. It was, however, as the last two or three leap-froggers came on that the real excitement more generally began. There was absolutely no back-space belonging to the other party left to them; and they were obliged to pile themselves one upon another—'Pelion on Ossa' as it was called. When the last man was up it was his duty to say, 'High COCKALORUM jig jig jig—high COCKALORUM jig jig jig—high COCKALORUM jig jig jig—off, off, off,' and then alone was it permissible for tortured and perspiring human nature to fall in one indistinguishable heap to the ground. The repeater of the shibboleth often fell off himself as he was uttering the above incantation—thus losing the victory for his side. It was a splendid game. I understood from family inquiries that it was played at Harrow in my great grandfather's time.

COCK AND-BREECHES, *subs.* (common).—A sturdy, little man, or boy.

COCK-AND-BULL-STORY, *subs.* (colloquial).—An idle or silly story. [Presumably from some old legend of a cock and a bull, *apropos* to which it should be noted that the French equivalent is *coq-à-l'âne*, a cock-and-ass.']

1603. JOHN DAY, *Law Trickes*, Act iv., p. 66. Didst marke what a tale of a COCK AND A BULL he tolde my father whilst I made thee and the rest away.

1759. STERNE, *Tristram Shandy*, vol. IX., ch. xxxiii. L—d! said my mother, what is all this about? A COCK AND A BULL, said Yorick—and one of the best of its kind I ever heard.

1857. O. W. HOLMES, *Autocrat of the Breakfast Table*, ch. v. That sounds like a COCK-AND-BULL STORY, said the young fellow whom they call John. I abstained from making Hamlet's remarks to Horatio and continued.

1874. MRS. H. WOOD, *Johnny Ludlow*, I S., xxiv., p. 432. 'Giving ear to a COCK-AND-BULL STORY that can't be true!'

COCK-AND-HEN-CLUB, *subs.* (common).—1. A free and easy gathering, or 'sing-song,' where females are admitted as well as males. [From COCK-AND-HEN, the male and female bird, and used figuratively for men and women, + CLUB.]

1819. THOS. MOORE, *Tom Crib's Mem. to Congr.*, p. 78. A Masquerade, or *Fancy* Ball, given lately at one of the most fashionable COCK-AND-HEN CLUBS in St. Giles's.

1828. G. SMEETON, *Days in London*, p. 40. Introduced him to one of the COCK-AND-HEN HOUSES near Drury Lane Theatre well primed with wine.

2. A club for both sexes; *e.g.*, The Lyric.

COCK-AND-PINCH, *subs.* (old).—The old-fashioned beaver of forty years since. [From its being COCKED back and front, and PINCHED at the sides.] For synonyms, *see* GOLGOTHA.

COCKATOO-FARMER, *subs.* (Australian).—In Victoria and New South Wales a small farmer or selector. A term of contempt used by large holders in describing agricultural squatters with small capital. [Probably an allusion to their numbers: a comparing to the rush for land, the swooping of cockatoos in myriads in new sown corn.]

1865. H. KINGSLEY, *Hillyars and Burtons*, ch. lx. The small farmers [in Australian wool districts] contemptuously called COCKATOOS are the fathers of fire, the inventors of scab, the seducers of bush-hands for haymaking and harvesting [and many other heinous crimes].

1886. G. SUTHERLAND, *Australia*, p. 64. The shepherd king tries to steal a march upon the poor COCKATOO, as he contemptuously calls the small farmer.

1887. G. A. SALA, in *Ill. L. News*, 12 March, 282, col. 2. I venture to differ from my correspondent when, in telling

me that 'cocky' is Australian argot for a small farmer, adds, 'by-the-by, you never hear the word "farmer" over there . . . many scores of times at the Antipodes I have heard agriculturists, whose holdings were small, spoken of, not as "cockies" but as "COCKATOO FARMERS."'

COCKATRICE, *subs.* (old).—1. A common prostitute; also a mistress or 'keep.' [Nares says 'probably from the fascination of the eye,' alluding to the fabulous monster hatched from a cock's egg by a serpent. Shakspeare speaks of 'the death-dealing' eye of a COCKATRICE.] For synonyms, *see* BARRACK-HACK and TART.

1600. BEN JONSON, *Cynth Rev.*, IV., 4. And withall, calls me at his pleasure I know not how many COCKATRICES and things.

1604. MARSTON AND WEBSTER, *Malcontent*, O. P., iv., 93. No courtier but has his mistress, no captain but has his COCKATRICE.

1630. TAYLOR, *Workes* [quoted by Nares]. And amongst souldiers this sweet piece of vice Is counted for a captaines COCKATRICE.

1664. KILLEGREW, *Pandora*. Some wine there, That I may court my COCKATRICE. *Care*. Good Captaine, Bid our noble friend welcome.

1740. *Poor Robin*. Some gallants will this month be so penurious that they will not part with a crack'd groat to a poor body, but on their COCKATRICE or punquetto will bestow half a dozen taffety gowns, who in requital bestows on him the French pox.

2. (common).—A baby.

COCK-A-WAX, *subs.* (common).—1 A cobbler. [From COCK a man (*q.v.*), + A + WAX, an adjunct of the cobbler's trade.] For synonyms, *see* SNOB.

2. A familiar address.

COCK-BAWD, *subs.* (old).—A male brothel keeper. [Quoted in Grose (1785).]

COCKCHAFER, *subs.* (thieves').—1. The treadmill. For synonyms, *see* WHEEL OF LIFE.

1851-61. H. MAYHEW, *London Lab. and Lon. Poor*, vol. II., p. 59. 'He enpiated,' as it is called, this offence by three months' exercise on the COCKCHAFER (treadmill).

1864. *Glasgow Citizen*, Nov. 19. The Jeremy Diddler who forges his honest name to a fakement, incurring thereby a drag at the COCKCHAFER.

2. (venery). — The female *pudendum*.

3. (venery). — *See* COCK-TEASER.

COCKED-HAT. TO BE KNOCKED INTO A COCKED HAT, *verbal phr.* (common).—To be limp enough to be doubled up and carried flat under the arm [like the COCKED HAT of an officer.]

ENGLISH SYNONYMS. To be doubled up; knocked into the middle of next week; spifflicated; beaten to a jelly; knocked a-cock; wiped out; sent all of a heap; bottled up; settled; to get beans, or snuff; sent, done, or smashed to smithereens, etc.—*See* also TAN, TANNING, and WIPE.

FRENCH SYNONYMS. *Effondrer quelqu'un* (popular: literally 'to dig into one'; *effondrer une volaille* = to draw a fowl); *tatouiller quelqu'un* (popular: *tatouiller* is a slang term for a thrashing); *soigner quelqu'un* (popular: properly 'to take care of,' or 'to attend,' 'to nurse'); *se faire écharpiller* (popular); *déboulonner la colonne à quelqu'un* (popular); *décarcasser quelqu'un* (popular); *manger le nez à quelqu'un* (popular: literally 'to eat one's nose').

1870. *Daily Telegraph*, 20 Aug., 'Speech of Mr. Ralph Harrison at the Crystal Palace.' The publication of the

Morning Star on March 17, 1856, it was prophesied, would knock the *Daily Telegraph* into A COCKED HAT.

1877. C. READE, *The Jilt*, I., in *Belgravia*, March, p. 59. I never knew a Welsh girl yet who couldn't dance an Englishman into A COCKED HAT.

1881. HAWLEY SMART, *Gt. Tontine*, ch. xxx. I think now we may consider Bob Pegram's marriage as knocked pretty well into A COCKED HAT.

1889. *Pall Mall Gaz.*, 18 Sept. p. 2, col. 3. You give in the *Pall Mall* of tonight three translations of Plato's well-known epigram. Permit me to give you another which in my opinion KNOCKS ALL THE REST INTO A COCKED HAT.

Also in the moral sense to be amazed to stupefaction and speechlessness.

COCKER, ACCORDING TO COCKER, *adv. phr.* (colloquial).—According to rule; properly, arithmetically, or correctly done. [From old Cocker, a famous writing master in Charles II. time, author of a treatise on arithmetic. Professor de Morgan notes 'that it became a proverbial representative of arithmetic from Murphy's farce of *The Apprentice* (1756), in which the strong point of the old merchant Wingate is his extreme reverence for COCKER and his arithmetic.'] In America a similar locution is according to GUNTER (*q.v.*). Gunter was a famous arithmetician a century before Cocker, and the American is no doubt the older phrase. The old laws of Rhode Island say, 'All casks shall be gauged by the rule commonly known as "gauging by Gunter."' Among sailors, the standard of appeal is ACCORDING TO JOHN NORIE—the compiler of a popular *Navigator's Manual.*

1851. MAYHEW, *Lon. Lab. and Lon. Poor.* 'Answers to Correspondents.' Surely, to increase the quantity of labour, while the amount expended in the direct purchase of that labour remains the same, is ACCORDING TO COCKER—to decrease the wages in precisely the same proportion.

1861. T. HUGHES, *Tom Brown at Oxford*, ch. xxxii., p. 337. Well, so you ought to be, ACCORDING TO COCKER, spending all your time in sick rooms.

1883. G. A. S[ALA], in *Ill. L. News*, Nov. 24, p. 499, col. 2. The average American may not know what we mean by ACCORDING TO COCKER; while the average Englishman may be unaware of the meaning of 'according to Gunter.' They both mean the same thing; implying irreproachable accuracy in computation.

1888. GRANT ALLEN, *This Mortal Coil*, ch. ii. ACCORDING TO COCKER nought and nought make nothing.

COCK-EYED, *adj.* (common). — Squinting. [*Cf.*, COCK THE EYE.] For synonyms, *see* SQUINNY-EYE.

1884. *Daily News*, Nov. 27, p. 2, col. 2. I am told the proper description of him would be a little man with a COCK-EYE.

COCK-FIGHTING. THAT BEATS COCK FIGHTING, *phr.* (common).—A general expression of approval—up to the mark; A 1. [From the esteem in which the sport was held.]

1659. GAUDEN, *Tears of the Church*, p. 228. Ministers' scufflings and contests with one another is BEYOND ANY COCK FIGHTING or Bear-baiting to the vulgar envy, malice, profaneness, and petulancy.

1884. W. C. RUSSELL, *Jack's Courtship*, ch. vi. 'Well, roast me!' cried he, viewing me with a kind of admiration; 'if this don't BEAT COCK FIGHTING.'

COCK-HORSE, *adv. phr.* (old).—Triumphant; in full swing; cock-a-hoop. Halliwell says, 'a somewhat slang expression not quite obsolete.'

COCKING.—*See* COCK, *verb*, sense 1.

COCKISH, *adj.* (old).—Wanton; 'on heat.' [From COCK, the *penis*, + ISH.] Latham quotes COCKISH in the sense of 'pert,' from the strutting of the barn-door cock.

1785. GROSE, *Dict. Vulg. Tongue.* A COCKISH wench: a forward, coming girl.

COCK IT, *verb* (tailors').—To examine; see; or speak of (a thing).

COCKLES, *subs.* (venery).—The *labia minora.*

COCKLES OF THE HEART, *subs. phr.* (common).—A jocose vulgarism encountered in a variety of combinations; *e.g.*, 'that will rejoice' or 'tickle' or 'warm the COCKLES OF YOUR HEART,' etc. [It is suggested (*N. and Q.*, 7 S., iv., 26) that a hint as to its origin may be found in Lower, an eminent anatomist of the seventeenth century, who thus speaks in his *Tractatus de Corde* (1669), p. 25, of the muscular fibres of the ventricles.

'Fibræ quidem rectis hisce exteri oribus in dextro ventriculo proximè subjectæ obliquè dextrorsum ascendentes in basin cordis terminantur, et spirali suo ambitu helicem sive *cochleam* satis aptè referunt.'

The ventricles of the heart might, therefore, be called *cochlea cordis*, and this would easily be turned into COCKLES OF THE HEART.] The French say, *Tu t'en pourlècheras la face* (that'll rejoice the cockles of your heart).

1671. EACHARD, *Observations* [Wright]. This contrivance of his did inwardly rejoice the COCKLES OF HIS HEART.

1822. SCOTT, *Fortunes of Nigel*, ch. xxvi. Which would have cheered the COCKLES of the reigning monarch.

1834. MARRYAT, *Jacob Faithful*, ch. xii. 'There now, master, there's a glass of grog for you that would float a marling-spike. See if that don't warm the COCKLES OF YOUR OLD HEART.'

1839. W. H. AINSWORTH, *Jack Sheppard*, p. 49 (ed. 1840). 'There, Mr. Wood,' cried David, pouring out a glass of the spirit, and offering it to the carpenter, 'that'll warm the COCKLES OF YOUR HEART.'

TO CRY COCKLES, *verbal phr.* (common). — To be hanged. [From the gurgling noise made in strangulation.] For synonyms, *see* LADDER.

COCK-LOFT, *subs.* (old).—The head. [A COCK-LOFT is properly a small loft, garret, or apartment at the top of a house. *Cf.*, GARRET, UPPER STOREY, etc.] An old proverb runs, 'All his gear is in his COCK-LOFT'; *i.e.*, 'all his wealth, work, or worth is in his head.' For synonyms, *see* CRUMPET.

1642. THOMAS FULLER, *Holy and Profane State*, And. Ad. fen. 1. Often the COCKLOFT is empty, in those whom nature hath built many stories high.

COCKNEY, *subs.* (colloquial).—One born within the sound of bow-bells. [The origin of COCKNEY has been much debated; but, says Dr. Murray, in the course of an exhaustive statement (*Academy*, May 10, 1890, p. 320), the history of the word, so far as it means a person, is very clear and simple. We have the senses (1) 'cockered or pet child,' 'nestle-cock,' 'mother's darling,' 'milksop,' the name being applicable primarily to the child, but continued to the squeamish and effeminate man into which he grows up. (2) A nickname applied by country people to the inhabitants of great towns, whom they considered 'milksops,' from their daintier habits and incapacity for rough work. York, London, Perugia, were, according to Harman, all nests of cockneys. (3) By about 1600 the name began to be attached especially to Londoners, as the representatives *par excellence* of the city milksop. One understands the disgust with which a cavalier in 1641 wrote that he was 'obliged to quit Oxford at the approach of Essex and Waller, with their prodigious number of cockneys.']

1607. DEKKER, *Westward Ho*, Act ii., Sc. 2. As Frenchmen love to be bold . . . and Irishmen to be costermongers, so COCKNEYS, especially SHE-COCKNEYS, love not aqua-vitæ when 'tis good for them.

1760. FOOTE, *Minor*, Act i. But you COCKNEYS now beat us suburbians at our own weapons.

1840. THACKERAY, *Paris Sketch Book*, p. 28. 'You 'ad such an 'eadach', sir,' said British, sternly, who piques himself on his grammar and pronunciation, and scorns a COCKNEY.

1889. *Pall Mall Gaz.*, 6 Nov., p. 3, col. 2. London mist, when turned into London black fog by the poisonous carbonic anhydride and sulphurous anhydride with which it is loaded, encompasses all COCKNEYS, good or bad with a real danger to health and life

COCKNEY-SHIRE, *subs.* (common).—London. [From COCKNEY, a native of London, + SHIRE.]

COCK PIMP, *subs.* (old).—The husband, real or supposed, of a bawd or procuress. [From COCK, male, + PIMP, a procurer.]—*Grose* [1785].

COCKQUEAN, *subs.* (obsolete).—A man who interests himself in women's affairs. The common form is 'cotquean.' *Cf.*, MOLLY.

COCKROACHES. TO GET OR EAT COCKROACHES, *verbal phr.* (old).—To practise masturbation. For synonyms, *see* FRIG.

COCK-ROBIN, *subs.* (old).—A soft, easy fellow.—*Grose* [1785].

COCK-ROBIN SHOP, *subs. phr.* (printers').—A small printing office, for cheap work done at vile wages. In other trades a SLOP SHOP.

1888. R. R., in *Notes and Queries*, 7 S., v., 333. Let me advise collectors of such things [cheap books] to avoid the regular booksellers, and try the COCK-ROBIN SHOPS, and the general dealers in small wares, down back streets.

COCKS, *subs.* (popular).—1. *See* COCK, *subs.*, sense 2.

2. (trade). — Explained by quotation. The word appears to be slang for anything fictitious. *Cf.*, COCKS, *subs.*, sense 2.

1880. *Daily News*, Nov. 4. [Quoted in *N. and Q.*, 6 S., ii., p. 387.]

3. (Charterhouse).—A lavatory where changing for games, washing before meals, etc., goes on. [From the taps over the basins.] It is equivalent to the Winchester MOAB (*q.v.*).

COCK'S EGG. TO GIVE ONE A COCK'S EGG, *phr.* (common).—To send one on a fool's errand; to GAMMON (*q.v.* for synonyms). The expression is of the same type as 'to send one to buy pigeon's milk,' 'oil of strappum,' 'strap oil,' etc

COCK-SHY, *subs.* (popular). —A mark, butt, or target; any person or thing that is the centre of jaculation.

c. 1834. MARRYAT, *Rattlin the Reefer*, p. 92. What a fine COCKSHY he would make, said Master Blubberlips.

18(?) LORD STRANGFORD, *Letters and Papers*, p. 215. This was as if the great geologists . . . had invited two rival theorists to settle the question of a

geological formation by picking up the stones and appealing to the test of a COCKSHY.

1849. THACKERAY, *Pendennis*, ch. iii. He had seen Tom Ricketts, of the fourth form, who used to wear a jacket and trousers so ludicrously tight, that the elder boys could not forbear using him in the quality of a butt or COCKSHY.

1876. HINDLEY, *Life and Adventures of a Cheap Jack*, p. 262. A desperate fight ensued, the 'nobblers' arming themselves with COCK-SHY sticks.

COCK-STAND, *subs.* (venery).—An erection of the *penis*. For synonyms, *see* HORN and *Cf.*, STAND.

COCK-SUCKER, *subs.* (venery).—A *feliatrix*.

COCKSURE, *adj.* (colloquial).—Confidently certain; pertly sure. [Probably a corruption of 'cocky sure.' We call a self-confident, overbearing prig a cocky fellow, from the barnyard despot. Shakspeare (*I Henry IV.*, ii., 1) employs the phrase in the sense of 'sure as the cock of a firelock.'

We steal as in a castle, COCKSURE:

and still earlier usages imply its derivation from the fact that the cock was much surer than the older fashioned match.]

1549. LATIMER, *Sermon on the Ploughers*, p. 32 (Arber's ed.) For the Deuyll was dysapoynted of his purpose for he thoughte all to be hys owne. And when he had once broughte Christe to the crosse, he thought all COCK-SURE.

1603. JOHN DAY, *Law Trickes*, Act iii., p. 39. Then did I learn to . . . . Make false conueyances, yet with a trick, Close and COCK-SURE, I cony-catch'd the world.

1667. DRYDEN, *Sir Martin Marr-all*, Act. iv. Nothing vexes me, but that I had made my game COCK-SURE, and then to be backgammoned.

b. 1738, *d.* 1819. WOLCOT ('Paul Pindar'), *Odes to the Pope*, II., in wks. (Dublin, 1795) V. ii., p. 492. Yet deem themselves, poor dupes, COCKSURE of Heav'n.

1837. R. H. BARHAM, *The Ingoldsby Legends* (ed. 1862), 320. Last of all, gentle Reader, don't be too secure!—Let seeming success never make you COCK-SURE.

1849. T. CARLYLE, IV., 108. [Yes, Manning was shot there; he had told us Hyde was COCKSURE.]

1884. W. C. RUSSELL, *Jack's Courtship*, ch. iii. 'Hawke will not get his daughter to have him, he may be COCKSURE of that.'

1889. *The Star*, Aug. 24, p. 3, col. 4. In his most insolent and COCKSURE manner he declared, etc.

COCKTAIL, *subs.* (common).—1. A prostitute; a wanton.

2. (common).—A coward.

3. (American).—A drink composed of spirits (gin, brandy, whisky, etc.), bitters, crushed ice, sugar, etc., the whole whisked briskly until foaming, and then drunk 'hot.'

COCKTAIL or **COCKTAILED**, *adj.* (military).—Unsoldierlike; uneven; showing bad form; and in its specifically military sense, anything unworthy of the regular army. For example, at one time the Volunteer auxiliaries were described as 'such a COCKTAILED CREW.'

1877. *Five Years' Penal Servitude*, ch. ii., p. 67. He confessed he not only urged his brother into it, but compelled him to be as bad as himself, and had thrashed him many times for turning COCKTAIL.

COCK-TEASER, or **COCKCHAFER**, *subs.* (venery).—A girl in the habit of permitting all familiarities but the last.

COCK-UP, *subs.* (printers').—What is technically known as a 'superior'; *e.g.*, the smaller letters in the following examples:

Y^e^ Limt^d^ Comp^y^; J^no.^ Smith, Senr.; N^o.^; London [1]

COCKED-UP, *adj.*—*See* COCKY.

COCK UP ONE'S TOES, *verbal phr.* (thieves').—To die. For synonyms, *see* ALOFT and HOP THE TWIG.

1820. REYNOLDS. ('Peter Corcoran'), *The Fancy*. 'King Tims the First.' Now I see a neighbour COCK HIS TOE—Walk by his side in black—in well paid woe.

1864. E. D. FORGUES, in *Revue des deux Mondes*, Sep. 15, p. 472, note. COCK ONE'S TOES. Cette . . . locution, si bizarre au premier coup d'œil, doit s'expliquer par un des phénomènes de la retraction cadavérique; les pieds du mort, ramenés en arrière, ont pu rappeler la position que prend le *chien* de la batterie quand le fusil est armé.

COCKY or **COCKING**, *adj.* (popular).—1. Pert or saucy; forward; coolly audacious; over confident, 'botty.' [Formerly COCKING. An allusion to the strut of the barndoor bird.] Fr., *se gourer*, to be cocky; also *se gonfler*, *faire sa merde*, and *faire son matador*.

1711. *Spectator*, No. 153. But the COCKING young fellow who treads upon the toes of his elders, and the old fool who envies the saucy pride he sees in him, are the objects of our present contempt and derision.

1820. CLARE, *Poems of Rural Life, Familiar Epistle*, st. 5. I've long been aggravated shocking, To see our gentry folks go COCKING

1856. T. HUGHES, *Tom Brown's School-days*, pt. II., ch. vi. 'It seems so COCKY in me to be advising you.'

1864. *Glasgow Citizen*, Nov. 19. Cotgrave (1672) gives us '*Herr*, master or sir; a rogue.' Aleman ['The Spanish Rogue'] *Vous faite du Herr*. 'You are very COCKIT, or lusty; you take too much upon you.' Is it not gratifying to know that COCKINESS is older than this century, in which it has been developed to so alarming an extent?

1872. *The Scotsman*, 29 Oct. 'Sir J. Pakington at Stourbridge.' He should be inclined to offer him a little homely advice, and to tell him in somewhat plain language 'Not to be too COCKY.'

1884. *Cornhill Mag.*, April, p. 442. 'Davis,' said Toddy, 'you haven't had a banging this term, and you're getting COCKY.'

2. (Stock Exchange).—Brisk; active—applied to the money market.

1871. *Figaro*, 3 June. 'Notes on Change.' Everything again brisk, and the market, what is expressly termed COCKY.

COCOA-NUT, *subs.* (general).—The head. Fr. *le coco*. For synonyms, *see* CRUMPET.

1834. W. H. AINSWORTH, *Rookwood*, p. 176 (ed. 1864). 'A thousand pities that so fine a fellow should have a sconce like a COCOA-NUT!'

1840. HALIBURTON, *Clockmaker*, 3 S., ch. iii. 'The Major a-pokin' along with his COCOA-NUT down, a-studyin' over somethin' or another quite deep.'

c. 1880. *Broadside Ballad*, 'Waltzing Round the Water-butt.' Gaily the troubadour will waltz round the water-butt, Blissful the happy thoughts that float round my COCOA-NUT, Moonlight and spooning 'neath the old hazel tree!

THAT ACCOUNTS FOR THE MILK IN THE COCOA-NUT, *phr.* (common). — A rejoinder upon having a thing explained for the first time.

TO HAVE NO MILK IN THE COCOA-NUT, *phr.*—To be insane; silly; 'cracked.'—*See* APARTMENTS.

COCUM, KOCUM, *subs.* (common).—1. Shrewdness; ability; luck; cleverness. [From the Hebrew

chochum, *chochem*, or *cochem*, crafty; learned, wise, or a wise man. The term is found *passim* in early Hebrew literature, especially in the BOOK OF PROVERBS: 'A COCHEM will hear and increase learning' (Prov. i. 5). The slang sense has been introduced by the Whitechapel Jews. In Yiddish *cochemer* or *cochem*, the pronunciation of which is not dissimilar to COCUM, means wisdom; *cochumwirth* = a thieves' landlord. (*Cf.*, paragraph on German analogues.) *Cocma* is another Hebraism used by London Jews in a similar sense, but it has not made its way into slang.

ENGLISH ANALOGUES. Real jam (this in the sense of anything exceptionally good or lucky); all beer and skittles (extremely pleasant); rattling (extremely jolly, pleasant, or well appointed); to be in clover (happiness and luck); to stand on velvet (a variant of the last mentioned); to be cracking a tidy crust (to be doing very well); to be having a good swim (thieves' for a good run of luck, *i.e.*, being a long time out of the policeman's clutches); well ballasted; on the spot; up to Dick; on it; right; and so forth.

FRENCH ANALOGUES. *Etre de la bonne* (popular: to be lucky); *décrocher la timballe* (popular); *être de la fête* (popular and thieves'); *avoir des as dans son jeu* (popular: to have an advantage, 'to be in luck's way'); *avoir l'assiette au beurre* (popular: to be fortunate in life); *bidard* (*m.* lucky); *être de la bate* (popular).

GERMAN ANALOGUES. *Chochom*, *Chochem*, *Chochemer* (which Hebraism is the root of the English COCUM. Among German thieves who more frequently spell the word *Kochem*, *Kochemer*, the meaning is almost identical with that given it by their English brethren, except that the wisdom, profit, or luck, applies almost solely to the results of crooked ways and dealings. *Chochom* and its variants signify, therefore, the cunning, prudent, and successful vagabond; *Chochem lehorre* = a dangerous vagabond, one who is prepared for the worst; *Chochem mechutten* = a bad patron, a dangerous companion, a rogue of the worst type; *Chochme* = wisdom, cunning, circumspection, or the practice of swindling).

ITALIAN ANALOGUES. *Cavazzonare* (literally 'to place well or be well placed'); *aver primavera* (this applies to COCUM as represented by pleasure; literally 'to have spring').

SPANISH ANALOGUES. *Cucarachera* (*f*; a vulgarism for luck or good fortune); *harlarse buena cucarachera* (to be lucky or fortunate); *potroso* (a colloquialism signifying lucky; literally 'afflicted with a rupture'); *charanguero* (*m*; a lucky fellow, one with COCUM); *hijo de la gallina blanca* (a lucky bird).

1851-61. H. MAYHEW, *London Lab. and Lon. Poor*, vol. I., p. 279. 'It's decent and comfortable too, and it's abou 6d. a night to me for singing and patter in the tap-room. That's my COKUM (advantage).'

1861. EARL, *Ups and Downs of Australian Life*, p. 224. 'No one was to get drunk, the governor said as how it wasn't COKUM, and he wouldn't have it,—and so we were all fit for work the next day.'

1864. HOTTEN, *Slang Dict.*, s.v. 'Jack's got COCUM, he's safe to get on, he is,' viz., he starts under favourable circumstances.

c. 1886. *Broadside Ballad*, 'The Flippity Flop Young Man.' I once was a Member-for-Slocum young man, And for Parliament had a strong fancy, A know-pretty-well-what-is-KOCUM young man When addressing a constituency.

2. (publishers'). —A sliding scale of profit. [Publishers sometimes issue books without fixing the published price. These they sell to the retail trade at a fixed sum, leaving the bookseller to make what he can.

TO FIGHT or PLAY COCUM, *verbal phr.* (common). To play double; to be wary, cunning, or 'artful.'

1857. SNOWDEN, *Mag. Assistant* (3 ed.), p. 445, s.v. To be cunning, wary, or sly.

1885. *Referee*, April 26, p. 1, col. 2. The best show in the Crawfurd Plate—that is, unless a lot of the pulling-up division were PLAYING COKUM—was that of Ptolemy.

COD, *subs.* (common).—**1.** A fool. [*Cf.*, COD'S HEAD, of which it is possibly an abbreviation.] For synonyms, *see* BUFFLE and CABBAGE-HEAD.

2. (tailors').—A drunkard.—[*See verb*, sense 2.]

3. (thieves'). —A purse; a COD of money = a large sum of money. [A.S. *cod* or *codd*, a small bag.] For synonyms, *see* POGE.

4. (street). —A, 'pal' or friend; generally prefixed to a surname. [Here COD is the diminutive of 'codlin,' an old endearment.] *Cf.*, CODD.

Verb (common).—**1.** To play the fool; to MONKEY (*q.v.*).

2. (tailors'). —To go on the drink; generally, to act loosely.

3. (common). — To chaff; hoax; 'take a rise out of.'

1865. *Evening Citizen*, 28 Nov. CODDING a Town Council.—The *Fife Circular*, Kirkcaldy, says:—According to usual practice, several members of the new Town Council attended divine service at the Parish Church on Sunday forenoon last. The Rev. M. J. Bryden officiated, and preached an eloquent and appropriate sermon *to the Council* from these words in the 10th chapter of St. Matthew:—'Ye are of more value than many sparrows.'

1884. W. C. RUSSELL, *Jack's Courtship*, ch. xxxi. 'What do you think of that, cook?' 'Think?' answered the cook, who had a rather sour eye; 'why, that that rough sailor man was a-CODDIN' of you, sir.'

CODD or **COD**, *subs.* (Charterhouse). —A pensioner of the Charterhouse.—*See* quot., and *Cf.*, COD, sense 4.

1855. THACKERAY, *Newcomes*, II., p. 333. Yonder sit some three score of gentlemen, pensioners of the hospital, listening to the prayers and psalms. You hear them coughing feebly in the twilight—the old reverend blackgowns. Is CODD Ajax alive, you wonder?—the Cistercian lads called these old gentlemen CODDS, I know not wherefore—I know not wherefore—but is old CODD Ajax alive, I wonder? or CODD Soldier? or kind old CODD Gentleman? or has the grave closed over them?

CODDAM or **CODDOM**, *subs.* (common). —A public-house game played three, four, or more a side. The only 'property' required is a coin, a button, or anything which can be hidden in the clenched hand. The principle of the game, which is simplicity itself, is that of 'Guess whose hand it's in.' If the guesser 'brings it home,' his side takes the 'piece,' and the centre man 'works' it. If the guess be wrong, a chalk is taken to the holders, who go on again.

1884. J. GREENWOOD, *Seven Years Penal Servitude*. The convicts take advantage of that to the extent sometimes of playing a gambling game called CODDOM

1885. *Good Words*, August, p. 530. Some prefer CODDAM, and risk their pint of beer on the discovery of the coin.

1890. *Pall Mall Gaz.*, March 1, p. 5, col. 2. The boys were playing a game called CODDOM, a guessing game.

CODDING, *verbal subs.* (common).—Nonsense; humbug; chaff. [From COD (*q.v.*, *verb*, sense 3).]

CODGER, *subs.* (common). — A familiar term of address, especially in OLD CODGER; a curious old fellow; an odd fish; a 'rum' character; a precise, and sometimes a mean or miserly man.

ENGLISH SYNONYMS. Most of the general slang terms for a man or fellow correspond in usage to 'old codger,' *e.g.*, old chap; ben cull; old man; my pippin; old cock, etc.

FRENCH SYNONYMS. *Un béquillard* (popular: French thieves give the same name to the executioner); *vieux canasson* (popular: 'old man,' 'old cock'); *un birbe; ma vieille branche.*

ITALIAN SYNONYM. *Fuino* (literally a pole-cat).

1760. COLMAN, *Polly Honeycombe*, in wks. (1777) IV., 39. A clear coast. I find. The OLD CODGER'S gone, and has locked me up with his daughter.

1760. SMOLLETT, *Sir L. Greaves*, vol. I., ch. iii. She twisted her hand in Grove's neckcloth without ceremony, crying—'Sha't then, I tell thee, OLD COGER.'

1796. MAD. D'ARBLAY, *Camilla*, bk. IX., ch. iv. He gave himself the airs of an old justice of the peace, and said if he did not find the affair given up, nothing should induce him ever to help me again. What a mere CODGER that lad has turned out!

1837. BARHAM, *I. L.* (*Lay of St. Nicholas*). How a thirsty OLD CODGER, the neighbours call'd Roger, With them drank cold water in lieu of old wine.

1859. DICKENS, *Tale of Two Cities*, bk. II., ch. xxiv. Why, I am a boy, sir, to half-a-dozen OLD CODGERS here.

1876. HINDLEY, *Life and Adventures of a Cheap Jack*, p. 61. His father, a rum OLD CODGER, had been a captain in the army.

1883. F. R. STOCKTON, *Rudder Grange*, ch. xi. I knew that any sensible man would rather have me in charge of his tent than a young CODGER like that.

1887. BAUMANN, *Londinismen, Slang u. Cant.* pref., vi. So from hartful young dodgers, From vaxy OLD CODGERS, From the blowens we got Soon to know vot is vot.

CODICILS, *subs.* (American journalists').—A kind of literary sparring match; also called ACCUMULATIVES (*q.v.*). Some editor will make a remark or a joke—with a capital J; another will cite it with comments; and, in his turn, he will be handled by a third. There are cases in which the original paragraph has gone the round of twenty or thirty prints. [A codicil is properly a writing by way of supplement to a will.]

1889. *Polytechnic Mag.*, 24 Oct., p. 253. 'How many apples did Adam and Eve eat?' Some say Eve 8 and Adam 2—a total of 10. Now, we figure the thing out far different. Eve 8, and Adam 8 also—total 16.—*Boston Journal.* We think the above figures are entirely wrong. If Eve 8, and Adam 8-2, certainly the total will be 90. Scientific men, however, on the strength of the theory that the antidiluvians were a race of giants, and consequently great eaters, reason something like this:—Eve, 8-1st, and Adam 8-2—total, 163.—*Gloucester Advertiser.* Wrong again; what could be clearer than if Eve 8-1-1st, and Adam 8-1-2, would not the whole be 1,623?—*Boston Journal.* Now we think these figures are not according to Cocker. The following is probably the true solution:—Eve 8-1-4 Adam, Adam 8-1-2-4 Eve—total, 8,698.—*Veritas.* Stop friend; still another calculation is as follows:—If Eve 8-1-4 Adam, Adam 8-1-2-4-2 oblige Eve—total, 82,056. We think, however, this is not a sufficient quantity; for, if we admit that Eve 8-1-4 Adam, Adam, if he 8-0-8-1-2-4-2 keep Eve company—total,

1,082,056.—*New York Mail.* You do the fair thing by Adam, brother, but you slight Eve. This poor smit 10-1-8-1-4-2 please the serpent, and Adam, of course, if he as good husbands do of-10-8-0-8-1-2-4-2 keep Eve company—total, 109,099,384.—*Syracuse Journal.* The American newspaper calculators, with the savagery of all other historians, meanly stigmatise the woman. Adam, a mere dupe, lacked the nobility to try a dangerous experiment first. Eve eat an apple for dinner: Adam, forgetting the injuries to many an unborn 1,000,000-8-1-4 millions more—the coward! True total, 1,000,000,814,-000,000. Whoopee! Now is the time to subscribe.—*Polytechnic Magazine.*

CODLAND, *subs.* (American).—Newfoundland. *Cf.*, COD-PRESERVES.

CODLINGS.—*See* CODS.

COD-PRESERVES, *subs.* (nautical). —The Atlantic Ocean. [An obvious allusion. *Cf.*, CODLAND = Newfoundland; also BRINEY.]

CODS, *subs.* (venery).—**1.** The testicles. [From A.S. *cod* or *codd* = a small bag.] Also CODLINGS.

ENGLISH SYNONYMS. Bawbels, baubels, or bobbles; bollocks; balls; beef (the *penis* and *testes*); bird's-eggs; bobbies; bullets; bum-balls; cannon-balls; clock-weights; culls (old); dowsetts (old); gingambobs; jelly-bags (more properly in sing = the *scrotum*); knackers; love-apples; marbles; nick-nacks; pebbles; seals (*Cf.*, WATCH-AND-SEALS = the male *pudenda*); spunk-holders; stones; thingambobs.

FRENCH SYNONYMS. *Les antilles* (thieves': *f. pl.*); *les virolets* (obsolete: in allusion to a man's virility); *les sonnettes* (common: literally bells); *les frères siamois* (popular: an allusion to the Siamese twins); *les prunes* (common); *les grains* (*leger de deux grains* = an eunuch).

GERMAN SYNONYM. *Dickmann* (also 'an egg,' and 'the *penis*.' *Dick* = *enciente*; *dick machen*, to deflower and quicken. *Dick* means literally 'thick').

SPANISH SYNONYM. *Cojones.*

2. (old).—*See* quot.

1871. *Bookseller*, 4 Nov. The CODS and Hooks were the Whigs and Tories of Dutch William's land.

COD'S-HEAD, *subs.* (old).—A stupid fellow; a fool.—*See* BUFFLE and CABBAGE-HEAD.

1675. *The Woman turn'd Bully. Dash.* Sweet sir, I think it is neer *octa hora.* Your servant, gentlemen. *Good.* Farewell, CODS-HEAD.

1694. DUNTON, *Ladies' Dictionary.* You confounded toad, you, where were your eyes, in your heels? that you should be such a bungling CODS-HEAD to see no better.

COFE.—*See* COVE.

COFFEE, *subs.* (American thieves'). —Beans.

1859. G. W. MATSELL, *Vocabulum, or Rogue's Lexicon*, p. 19, s.v.

GREASED COFFEE, *subs. phr.* (American).—Pork and beans.

COFFEE-HOUSE or **COFFEE-SHOP**, *subs.* (common).—**1.** A water-closet. For synonyms, *see* MRS. JONES, and *Cf.*, BURY A QUAKER.

2. (venery). — The female *pudendum.* For synonyms, *see* MONOSYLLABLE.

COFFEE-HOUSING, *subs.*—*See* quot.

1877 HAWLEY SMART *Play or Pay* ch. iv. 'Not going to hunt? Why Miss Bazing told me you had a regular string of horses coming down!' 'Ah, Bessie's wrong. I always was a changeable beggar, you know. The string consists of a hack, just good enough to do a little bit of COFFEE-HOUSING occasionally.

COFFEE-MILL, *subs.* (old). — The mouth: a 'grinder' itself, and furnished with 'grinders'—American 'cogs,'—as well. For synonyms, *see* POTATO-TRAP.

1821. W. T. MONCRIEFF, *Tom and Jerry*, Act ii., Sc. 2. *Gas.* Come, come, silence your COFFEE-MILL.

COFFEE-MILLING, *subs. phr.* (common).—**1.** Grinding; working hard. *Cf.*, TO COCK SNOOKS (*see* SNOOKS) or 'take a sight' by putting the thumb of one hand to the nose and grinding the little finger with the other, as if you worked an imaginary coffee mill.

1837. DICKENS, *Pickwick*, p. 249.

1854. AYTOUN AND MARTIN, *The Bon Gaultier Ballads.* 'The Lay of the Lovelorn.' When I went the pace so wildly, caring little what might come, COFFEE-MILLING care and sorrow, with a nose-adapted thumb.

COFFINS, *subs.* (Stock Exchange). —The Funeral Furnishing Company's Shares.

ANOTHER NAIL IN ONE'S COFFIN.—*See* NAIL.

COG, *subs.* (American thieves'). —A tooth.—*Matsell* [1859]. *Cf.*, COFFEE-MILL.

COKE. GO AND EAT COKE, *verb. phr.* (vulgar).—A phrase indicative of contempt. A corollary is 'and evacuate, or s—t cinders.'

COKER, *subs.* (old).—A lie.—*Grose* [1785]. For synonyms, *see* WHOPPER.

COLCHESTER CLOCKS, *subs.* (streets').—A breed of large oysters.

1865. *Daily Telegraph*, 13 Sep. For the big, uncompromising COLCHESTER CLOCK, which we see on stalls and shudder at, with unlimited vinegar and pepper, the East-ender willingly gives his penny.

COLD. TO HAVE A BAD COLD, *verbal phr.* (common).—Said of one who keeps his door closed against all comers for fear of duns; also of one who has 'shot the moon.' Also of one that has taken clap.

1863. *Chambers' Journal*, vol. XX., p. 5. 'It's no good your ringing,' remarked the book-boy, when I had discovered that fact for myself;' 'Mr. Cranium ain't at home, he ain't. He's GOT A WERRY BAD COLD.' After a few minutes, however, and many genial impertinences, I discovered that HAVING A BAD COLD means, in Camden Town, being in debt, while A VERY BAD COLD implies that the sufferer has taken clandestine departure from his lodgings.

TO LEAVE OUT IN THE COLD, *verbal phr.*—To neglect; shut out, or abandon.

1861. *New York Tribune*, July, The 'Assents' continue to come in freely at the Erie Railroad office; and the appearances are that at the closing of the books . . . there will be few shares or bonds LEFT OUT IN THE COLD.

COLD BLOOD, *subs.* (licensed victuallers').—A house licensed for the sale of beer 'not to be drunk on the premises.'

COLD COFFEE, *subs. phr.* (Oxford University).—**1.** A sell; a hoax; a trumpery affair.

2. (common). — Misfortune; ill-luck. A variant is COLD GRUEL; also TO HAVE ONE'S COMB CUT; in French, to experience a run of ill-luck is expressed by *être abonné au guignon*; literally 'to become a subscriber to ill-luck'; in Spanish, *dar al traste con los negocios*, signifies, colloquially, 'to fail' or 'to be unfortunate in business.'

3. (familiar).—An unpleasant return or snub for a proffered kindness.

COLD COMFORT, *subs. phr.* (trade).—An expression used of articles sent out on approval and returned. [Merely an extension of the literal meaning *i.e.*, what is barren of consolation : a usage dating from the sixteenth century.]

COLD COOK, *subs.* (popular).—An undertaker. [Literally one who has to deal with cold meat, *i.e.*, the lifeless human body.] *Cf.*, COLD MEAT and its derivatives.

ENGLISH SYNONYMS. Carrion hunter ; body snatcher ; death hunter ; black worker (*see* BLACK WORK).

FRENCH SYNONYMS. *Un emballeur de refroidis* (thieves' : an undertaker's man ; literally 'a packer of cold meat').

1785. GROSE, *Dict. Vulg. Tongue*, s.v.

1864. HOTTEN, *Slang Dict.*, s.v.

COLD COOKSHOP, *subs. phr.* (popular). — An undertaker's premises.— *See* COLD COOK.

COLD CREAM.—*See* CREAM OF THE VALLEY.

COLD DECK, *subs.* (American hieves').—A prepared pack of cards. *Cf.*, CONCAVES AND CONVEXES and STOCK BROADS. More politely a good hand obtained on first dealing and without drawing fresh cards.

1880. S. L. CLEMENS ('Mark Twain'). *Screamers.* I never have gambled from that day to this — never once—without a COLD DECK in my pocket. I cannot even tell who is going to lose in games that are being played unless I deal myself.

COLD GRUEL.—*See* COLD COFFEE, sense 2.

COLD MEAT, *subs.* (common).—A corpse. [The human carcass is compared to butchers' wares.] For synonyms, *see* DEAD MEAT. Among medical students the term COLD MEAT OR PICKLES (*q.v.*) = specimens direct from the subject.

1819. THOS. MOORE, *Tom Crib's Mem. to Con.*, p. 25. In the Twelfth and Last Round Sandy fetched him a *downer*, That left him all's one as COLD MEAT for the Crowner.

TO MAKE COLD MEAT OF ONE, *verbal phr.* (common).—To kill. For synonyms, *see* COOK ONE'S GOOSE.

1836. C. DICKENS, *Pickwick Papers*, p. 148 (ed. 1857). 'You mustn't handle your piece in that 'ere way, when you come to have the charge in it, sir,' said the tall gamekeeper, gruffly, 'or I'm damned if you won't MAKE COLD MEAT OF some of us!'

COLD-MEAT BOX, *subs. phr.* (common).—A coffin. [From COLD-MEAT, a corpse, + BOX, a receptacle.] For synonyms, *see* ETERNITY BOX.

1889. *Sporting Times*, 3 Aug., p. 1, col. 3. 'Well, s'pose I perched first?' 'Well, replied Pitcher, I should just come in where you were lying in the COLD-MEAT BOX, and I should whisper in your ear,' etc.

COLD-MEAT CART, *subs. phr.* (common).—A hearse. [From COLD-MEAT, a corpse, + CART.] Fr., *mannequin à refroidis*. *Cf.*, COLD-MEAT TRAIN.

1820. REYNOLDS ('Peter Corcoran'). *The Fancy*, p. 46. He's gone—how very muddy some folks die!—He's for the COLD-MEAT CART, and so am I.

COLD-MEAT TRAIN, *subs. phr.* (popular).—Generally, the funeral trains to Brookwood, Kensal Green, and other cemeteries.

Specifically, the last train at night per S.W.R., by which officers can reach Aldershot in time for their morning duties. It starts about 2 a.m. from Nine Elms, and is properly a goods train, but a carriage is attached which is known as the 'Larky Subaltern.' [It is an error to suppose that this particular train received its nickname for taking corpses to Woking Cemetery. It carries nothing more dreadful than a portion of the beef and mutton for the morning ration to the troops in camp; and, as before stated, a few belated officers.]

1876. R. M. JEPHSON, *Girl He Left Behind Him*, ch. xi. The train by which Dorrien journeyed to Aldershot was that one known as the COLD-MEAT.

COLD PIG. TO GIVE COLD PIG, *verbal phr.* (common). — To waken a sleeper either by sluicing him with cold water, or by suddenly stripping him of his bed-clothes.

1818. J. R. PLANCHÉ, *Amoroso, King of Little Britain.* For if the Queen should come this way, As sure as fate and quarter day, COLD PIG will be your fare.

1837. *Comic Almanack*, June. I've given him strap,—a thick rope's end,—COLD PIG! In vain!—There lies the stupid clown, As if the Night Mare held him down.

1846. THACKERAY, *Jeames's Diary* (in *Punch*, vol. 11., p. 72). 'What was it I red there? What was it that made me spring outabed as if sumbady had given me COLD PIG?—I red Rewin in that share list—the Pannick was in full hoporation.'

1869. W. BRADWOOD, *The O. V. H.*, ch. xxxv. Then he came back rosy and hungry, and revenged himself by an administration of COLD PIG to the still slumbering Ralph.

Subs. (thieves').—1. A person robbed of his clothing. *Cf.*, sense 2.

2. (thieves').—A corpse. For synonyms, *see* DEAD MEAT.

3. (commercial travellers').—The 'empty returns' sent back by rail to wholesale houses.

COLD SHIVERS, *subs. phr.* (common).—A figure of speech describing the effect of illness, intense fear or any violent emotion. An American equivalent is a 'cold shake,' which may refer alike to a period of cold weather, and an attack of fever and ague.

1864. *Derby Day*, p. 50. 'There's our friend the Littl'un,' he resumed; 'he's all shivery shaky as if he got the staggers or the COLD SHIVERS, and was going wurra, wurra, wurra, between his teeth, as if he couldn't help himself.'

COLD SHOULDER. TO GIVE, SHOW, OR TURN THE COLD SHOULDER, *verbal phr.* (colloquial). — To treat a person with studied coldness, neglect, or contempt; to 'cut,' in a modified form. The phrase appears to have been first used by Scott in the *Antiquary*, in the glossary to which it is explained as 'to appear cold and reserved.' Jamieson localizes it in the South of Scotland.

1816. SCOTT, *Antiquary*, ch. xxxiii. The countess's dislike didna gang farther at first than just SHOWING O' THE CAULD SHOUTHER.

1840. DICKENS, *Old Curiosity Shop*, ch. lxvi. He GIVES me THE COLD SHOULDER on this very matter, as if he had had nothing to do with it, instead of being the first to propose it.

1880. G. R. SIMS, *Three Brass Balls*, pledge iii. They were not received everywhere with open arms. He was, of course, but the wife was occasionally COLD SHOULDERED.

c. 1882. *Broadside Ballad*, 'Where's the Cat?' She GAVE HIM THE COLD SHOULDER, and quickly told him to depart.

COLD SLAW.—*See* CABBAGE, sense 1.

COLD TEA, *subs.* (common). — Brandy — a seventeenth and eighteenth century colloquialism. For synonyms, *see* DRINKS.

1690. *Dict. Cant. Crew.* COLD TEA : brandy.

1693. *Remonstrance of the Batchelors*, in *Harl. Misc.* (ed. Park), IV., 505. Since their sex has been so familiar with brandy (blasphemed by the name of COLD TEA).

1857. *Notes and Queries*, 2 S., iii., p. 59, s.v.

1888. C. J. DUNPHIE, *The Chameleon*, p. 235. It is worthy of remark that COLD TEA was a slang name for Brandy in the 18th century.

COLD WATER ARMY, *subs. phr.* (colloquial).—The general body of total abstainers.

COLD WITHOUT, *subs. phr.* (common).—Spirits and cold water without sugar. *Cf.*, CIDER AND; also HOT WITH.

1837. R. H. BARHAM, *Ingoldsby Legends*, p. 156 (ed. 1862). On the fire, too, she pops some nice mutton-chops, And she mixes a stiff glass of COLD WITHOUT.

1853. BULWER LYTTON, *My Novel.* I laugh at fame. Fame, sir! not worth a glass of COLD WITHOUT.

COLE or **COAL**, *subs.* (popular).—Money. For synonyms, *see* ACTUAL and GILT.

1671. R. HEAD, *English Rogue*, pt. I., ch. v., p. 52 (1874). *Tip the* COLE *to Adam Tyler*, give what money you pocket-pickt to the next party, presently.

1676. *A Warning for Housekeepers* (canting song). But when that we come not agen, As we walk along the street, We bite the Culley of his COLE.

1688. SHADWELL, *Sq. of Alsatia*, I., in wks. (1720) IV., 16. *Cheat.* My lusty rustick, learn, and be instructed. COLE is, in the language of the witty, money; the *ready*, the *rhino*.

16(?). *Song of Seventeenth Century*, (quoted in Halliwell and Wright's ed. of *Nares' Glossary*). The twelfth a trapan, if a cull he doth meet, He naps all his COLE, and turns him i' th' street.

1741. WALPOLE, ballad in *Letters to Mann*, i., 22. This our captain no sooner had finger'd the COLE, But he hies him aboard with his good Madam Vole.

1837. R. H. BARHAM, *The Ingoldsby Legends* (ed. 1862), p. 398. Moreover—the whole Of the said cash or COLE, Shall be spent for the good of the said Old Woman's soul!

1844. *Puck*, p. 146. Thank you for the offer of your bill; but I can wait until you can finger the COLE, when I shan't stand on ceremony about taking a cool hundred or two. . .

TO POST OR TIP THE COLE, *phr.* (common).—To hand over money; to 'shell' or 'fork out.'—*See* 1671 quot., *subs.* sense.

1839. HARRISON AINSWORTH, *Jack Sheppard* [1889], p. 13. 'Will he POST THE COLE? Will he come down with the dues? Ask him that,' cried Blueskin. *Ibid.* If he don't TIP THE COLE without more ado, give him a taste of the pump, that's all.

1883. G. A. S[ALA], in *Ill. L. News*, Nov. 10, p. 451, col. 3. The lamented J. B. Buckstone, at a Theatrical Fund Dinner, once entreated the guests present to POST THE COLE, *i.e.*, to be prompt with their subscriptions and donations.

COLFABIAS or **COLFABIS**. — *See* quot.

1864. HOTTEN, *Slang Dict.* COLFABIAS, a Latinized Irish phrase signifying the closet of decency, applied as a slang term to a place of resort in Trinity College, Dublin.

COLIANDER or **COLIANDER-SEEDS**, *subs.* (old). — Money. — *Grose* [1785]. For synonyms, *see* ACTUAL and GILT.

COLLAR, *verb* (common).—To seize: appropriate; steal; *e.g.*, 'COLLAR his dragons,' *i.e.*, steal his sovereigns. [Properly 'to seize by the collar'; hence, by transition, 'to lay hold of anything forcibly.'] For synonyms, *see* NAB and PRIG.

1841. LEMAN REDE, Song, 'Kit Clayton,' in *Sixteen-String Jack*, Act i., Sc. 3. Ve COLLAR'D the blunt, started off

for town, With the dashy, splashy, leary, little stringer, Horses knock'd up, men knocked down—Phililoo!

1852. DICKENS, *Bleak House*, ch. lvii., p. 476. Look well after your own money, for they are dead certain to COLLAR it, if they can.

1866. *London Miscellany*, March 3, p. 58. I slept in Holborn Workhouse. While I was asleep the other coves tore every rag up and COLLAR'D my toke.

1866. HINDLEY, *Life and Adventures of a Cheap Jack*, p. 242. Old Sir John Collywobbles had six black horses, six white horses, and six pied horses. So I recommended my father-which-is-in-law to COLLAR the lot.

1884. W. BESANT, *Julia*, ch. iv. Your grandmother tells me you've plucked up spirit at last and won't let her COLLAR more than half the wages.

TO COLLAR THE BUN, CAKE, BANBURY, OR CONFECTIONER'S SHOP, *verb. phr.* (common).—To be easily first; to surpass. —*See* CAKE.

OUT OF COLLAR, *adv. phr.* (colloquial).—Out of work; out of cash; not in training. Conversely, IN COLLAR = in work; in comfortable circumstances; and, as regards training, 'fit' or 'in form.' [Simile taken from the stable, in allusion to a horse, *i.e.*, with his collar on or off.]

FRENCH SYNONYMS. *Balloter* (tailors' = 'to be out of work'); *caler* (popular and nautical = 'to sink'); *envoyer à la comédie* (popular: to dismiss a workman for want of work to give him. *Cf.*, *remporter une veste*); *être à la comédie* ('to be out of work'); *un panas* (popular: 'one out of work'); *un inspecteur des pavés* (literally 'an inspector of the pavement'); *avoir de la laine* (to be in work).

1857. DUCANGE ANGLICUS, *The Vulgar Tongue.* A decent allowance made to seedy swells, head robbers, and flunkeys OUT OF COLLAR.

1867. *Scottish Journal*, p. 39, col. 1. There is nothing that so materially and frequently effects the well-being and social position of a working man as the circumstances arising from being, in his own phrase, 'OUT OF COLLAR'—that is, his being unable to obtain work when he is able to do it and anxious to get it to do. *Ibid.* A workman on tramp will, if he is tolerably well known in the trade, and if he have, when IN COLLAR, shown a disposition to assist those who were out, often be kept among his former shopmates.

1880. MILLIKIN, *Punch's Almanack.* Now October! Back again to COLLAR, Funds run low, reduced to last 'alf dollar.

c. 1880. *Broadside Ballad*, 'Why Did She Leave her Jeremiah?' When I was IN COLLAR I loved a fair maid, With eyes of a sweet dark blue.

AGAINST COLLAR, *adv. phr.* (common). — Uphill; working against difficulties, or against the grain.

TO BE PUT TO THE PIN OF THE COLLAR, *verbal phr.* (common). — To be driven to extremities; to come to the end of one's resources.

TO WEAR THE COLLAR, *verbal phr.* (colloquial).—To be subject to control not altogether to one's liking. The antithesis of 'to have the whip hand' and 'to wear the breeches'; etc.

COLLAR AND ELBOW, *subs. phr.* (wrestling).—A term for a peculiar style of wrestling—the Cornwall and Devon style.

COLLAR-DAY, *subs.* (old).—Hanging day. [In allusion to the hangman's noose.] Also WRY-NECK-DAY (*q.v.*); Fr., *jour de la St. Jean Baptiste*.

COLLARED. TO BE COLLARED, *verbal phr.* (gaming). — To be unable to play one's usual game owing to temper, 'funk,' or other causes.

COLLARED UP, *ppl. adj.* (colloquial).—Kept close to business. *Cf.*, OUT OF COLLAR.

COLLAR or GET THE BIG BIRD.—*See* BIG BIRD, and for synonyms, GOOSED.

COLLAR WORK, *subs. phr.* (colloquial). Laborious work.—*See* AGAINST COLLAR.

1883. *Daily Telegraph*, July 3, p. 2, col. 1. The bald patches on their shoulders testified to their intimate acquaintance with COLLAR WORK and tugging on stoney roads with heavy loads behind them.

1888. ANT. TROLLOPE, *What I Remember*. And when Lucca was reached there were still fourteen miles, nearly all COLLAR WORK, between that and the baths.

COLLECTOR, *subs.* (old).—A highwayman or footpad.

COLLEGE, *subs.* (thieves'). — A prison; the inmates are called COLLEGIANS or COLLEGIATES (*q.v.*); Newgate was formerly called 'the CITY COLLEGE.' The Spanish *Germania* has *colegio* and *collège* is found in the argot of French thieves.

1703. *Title*, 'The History of Whittington's COLLEDGE otherwise (vulgarly) called Newgate. London, Printed in the Year 1703.'

1785. GROSE, *Dict. Vulg. Tongue*. COLLEGE, Newgate, or any other prison.

1836. DICKENS, *Pickwick Papers* (about 1827), p. 370 (ed. 1857). 'Mornin', gen'l'mem', said Sam, entering at the moment with the shoes and gaiters; 'avay vith melancholly, as the little boy said ven his schoolmissus died. Welcome to the COLLEGE, gen'l'mem.'

1859. MATSELL, *Vacabulum, or Rogue's Lexicon*, p. 20. COLLEGE: a State prison.

1889. *Answers*, 8 June, p. 25. I have since met several men whom I knew in prison at one time or other, and most of them have recognised me; but only one other has stopped me to remind me that we were at 'COLLEGE' together.

COLLEGE CHUM.—*See* COLLEGIATE.

COLLEGER, *subs.* (University and public schools').—A square cap, otherwise known as a MORTAR-BOARD. For general synonyms, *see* GOLGOTHA.

COLLEGIAN.—*See* COLLEGIATE.

COLLEGIATE, COLLEGIAN or COLLEGE CHUM, *subs.* (thieves').—The inmate of a prison.—[*See* COLLEGE.]

1743. NORTH, *Life of Lord Guildford*, I., 123. His beginnings were debauched, and his study and first practice in the gaol. For having been one of the fiercest town-rakes and spent more than he had of his own, his case forced him upon that expedient for a lodging, and there he . . . busied himself with the cases of his fellow-COLLEGIATES.

1785. GROSE, *Dict. Vulg. Tongue*, s.v.

1836. DICKENS, *Pickwick Papers* (about 1827), p. 369 (ed. 1857). 'I say—do you expect anybody this morning? Three men—devilish gentlemanly fellows—have been asking after you downstairs, and knocking at every door on the hall flight: for which they've been most infernally blown up by the COLLEGIANS that had the trouble of opening 'em.'

1859. G. W. MATSELL, *Vocabulum, or the Rogue's Lexicon*, COLLEGE CHUM: a fellow-prisoner.

1884. DICKENS. [Quoted in Supplement to Annandale's ed. of Ogilvie's *Imperial Dict.*] It became a not unusual circumstance for letters to be put under his door at night enclosing half-a-crown . . . for the father of the Marshalsea, 'with the compliments of a COLLEGIAN taking leave.'

LADIES' COLLEGE, *subs.* (general).—A brothel. For synonyms, *see* NANNY-SHOP.

COLLOGUE, *verb* (colloquial).—To confer confidentially and secretly; to conspire; to wheedle; or flatter. The term is also used in a humorous sense. [From Lat. *col*, toge-

ther + Lat. *loquor*, to speak, influenced probably by 'colleague' and 'colloquy.']

1596. NASHE, *Saffron Walden*, in wks. III., 136. For once before I had bin so cousend by his COLLOGING, though personally we neuer met face to face.

1676. EARL OF ROCHESTER, *Hist. of Insipids*, st. 9. When to give Money he can't COLOGUE 'um, He doth with Scorn prorogue, prorogue 'um.

1748. T. DYCHE, *Dictionary* (5 ed.). COLLOGUE (v.): to treat with a person underhandedly, to cheat, flatter, coax, or sooth a person in order to get a secret out of him.

1818. SCOTT, *Rob Roy*, ch. xxxvii. It was hardly possible two such d—d rascals should COLLOGUE together without mischief to honest people.

1857. BARHAM, *I. L.* (*House-warming*). Miss Alice, in short, was supposed to COLLOGUE—I Don't much like the word—with the subtle old rogue, I'Ve heard call'd by so many names,—one of them's Bogy.

1858. G. ELIOT, *Mr. Gilfil's Love-Story*, ch. iv. 'We shall be poisoned wi' lime an' plaster, and hev the house full o' workmen COLLOGEING wi' the maids, an' makin' no end o' mischief.'

1861. G. ELIOT, *Silas Marner*, ch. ix. 'And how long have you been so thick with Dunsey that you must COLLOGUE with him to embezzle my money?'

COLLY-MOLLY, *adj.* and *adv.* (old).—Melancholy. [A jocular corruption of the word. *Cf.*, SOLEMNCHOLY and (in *Dr. Marigold's Prescriptions*) LEMON-JOLLY.]

17(?). *Decl. of Pop. Imp.* sign. Q. 3. (quoted in Nares). The devil was a little COLLI-MOLLIE and would not come off.

COLLY WOBBLES, *subs.* (common).—The stomach-ache; also the rumblings of flatulency; figuratively, the stomach.

ENGLISH SYNONYMS. Wiffle-waffles; gripes; mulligrubs.

FRENCH SYNONYMS. *Mal au brèchet*; also *gargouillade*.

1853. CUTHBERT BEDE, *Verdant Green*, pt. I., ch. viii. 'Peakyish you feel, don't you, now, with a touch of the mulligrubs in your COLLYWOBBLES?'

c. 1880. *Broadside Ballad*, 'Complaints' or 'The Ills of Life.' Then I've had the colic, spasms, dizziness, and swimmings, Mullygrubs and COLLYWOBBLES, with delicious trimmings.

COLOUR, *subs.* (sporting).—1. The handkerchief worn as a badge by prize-fighters and other professional athletes. Each man chooses his own, and it was once a practice to sell them to backers to be worn at the ring-side. The present rules of the Ring provide as follows:—'That every man shall be provided with a handkerchief of a colour suitable to his own fancy, and that the seconds proceed to entwine these handkerchiefs at the upper end of one of the centre stakes of the ring; that these handkerchiefs shall be called the COLOURS, and that the winner of the battle at its conclusion shall be entitled to their possession as the trophy of victory.' For a description of various 'fancies,' *see* BILLY. In racing circles the COLOURS are the owner's and are shown in the jockeys' caps and jackets.

1818. P. EGAN, *Boxiana*, vol. I., p. 170. The Chicken now sported the blue-spotted silk handkerchief, as the champion's COLOUR.

1858. A. MAYHEW, *Paved with Gold*, bk. II., ch. xii., p. 189. Each of the men had, previous to the fight, done a little profitable business by selling pocket-handkerchiefs, which they called their COLOURS.

2. (popular).—Used of money; *e.g.*, 'I have not seen the COLOUR of his money' = I have not received payment.—*See* quots.

1736. FIELDING, *Don Quixote*, I., iii. If I have seen the COLOUR of gold this fortnight, may I never see Teresa Pancha again.

1836. MARRYAT, *Midshipman Easy*, ch. xix. The padrone informed them that he should like to see the COLOUR of their money before they went on board.

COLOURED ON THE CARD, *phr.* (racing). — Having the colours in which a jockey is to ride inserted on the card of the race.

OFF COLOUR, *adv. phr.* (common).—Exhausted; run down; 'seedy.'

c. 1876. *Broadside Ballad*, 'That's Where The Money Goes.' London's Police will be made up of men, Cold Rabbit Pie will be OFF COLOUR then.

COLOUR ONE'S MEERSCHAUM, *verbal phr.* (common).—To get brandy-faced; to drink one's nose into a state of pimples and scarlet.

COLQUARRON, *subs.* (old) —The neck. For synonyms, *see* SCRAG.

1785. GROSE, *Dict. Vulg. Tongue*. COLQUARRON: a man's neck (*cant*), his COLQUARRON is just about to be twisted, he is just going to be hanged.

1830. SIR E. B. LYTTON, *Paul Clifford*, p. 5 (ed. 1854). ''Tis a rum business, and puzzles I! but mum's the word, for my own little COLQUARREN.'

COLT, *subs.* (popular).—1. A person new to office, or, to the exercise of any art; *e.g.*, a professional cricketer during his first season; a first-time juryman; a thief in his novitiate. [Properly a COLT is a young male horse.]

1785. GROSE, *Dict. Vulg. Tongue*, s.v.

1885. *Daily News*, 28 August, p. 3, col. 7. A match arranged for the benefit of the young players of the county was commenced yesterday at Manchester, when the Lancashire Eleven were opposed to Twenty-six COLTS.

2. (nautical).—*See* quots.

1830. MARRYAT, *King's Own*, ch. viii. He always carried in his pocket a COLT (*i.e.*, a foot and a half of rope, knotted at one end, and whipped at the other), for the benefit of the youngsters, to whom he was a most inordinate tyrant.

1836. MARRYAT, *Midshipman Easy*, ch. xii. 'He knocked me down—and when I got up again he told me that I could stand a little more—and then he took out his COLT, and said he was determined to ride the high horse.'

3. (thieves').—A thief's weapon; otherwise known as a BILLY (*q.v.*). For synonyms, *see* NEDDY.

4. (thieves'). — A man who hires horses to burglars. In America he is called a COLT-MAN. [Quoted by Grose, 1785.]

5. (legal).—*See* quot.

1887. SIR F. POLLOCK, *Pers. Remembr.*, vol. I., p. 212. In April I accompanied the newly-made Chief Baron [of Exchequer] as his COLT (the so-called attendant on a serjeant at his making) to the Lord Chancellor's private room at Westminster.

Verb (nautical).—1. To thrash; [From COLT, sense 2.] *Cf.*, BASTE, and for synonyms, *see* TAN.

1836. MARRYAT, *Midshipman Easy*, ch. xii. 'Then he COLTED me for half-an-hour, and that's all.'

2. (common). — To cause a person to stand treat by way of being 'made free' of a new place; to make one 'pay one's footing.' *Cf.*, *subs.*, sense 1.

COLTAGE, *subs.* (old).—The footing paid by COLTS (*q.v.*, *subs.*, sense 1) on their first appearance.

COLTING, *verbal subs.* (common).—A thrashing. For general synonyms, *see* TANNING and BASTE.

COLT-MAN. — *See* COLT, *subs.*, sense 4.

COLT'S TOOTH. TO HAVE A COLT or COLT'S TOOTH, *verbal phr.* (old).—To be fond of youthful pleasures; in the case of elderly persons, to have juvenile tastes; to be of wanton disposition and capacity. [In allusion to a supposed desire to shed the teeth and see life over again.]

1500. MARLOWE, 2 *Tamburlaine*, iv., 4. Nay, we will break the hedges of their mouths, And pull their kicking COLTS out of their pastures.

1606. SIR GYLES GOOSECAPPE, v., 2, in Bullen's *Old Plays*, iii., 87. I shood doe my country, and Court-ship good service to beate thy COALTS TEETH out of thy head, for suffering such a reverend word to passe their guarde.

1637. FLETCHER, *Elder Brother*, II., iii. He should love her now, As he hath a COLT'S TOOTH yet.

1753. WALPOLE, *Lett. to Mann*, 27 April (1833), vol. III., p. 89. I hear that my Lord Granville has cut another COLT'S TOOTH—in short, they say he is going to be married again . . . there are not above two or three-and-forty years difference in their ages.

1770. COLMAN, *The Portrait*, in wks. (1777) IV., 215. Tho' not in the bloom of my youth, Yet still I have left a COLT'S TOOTH.

1812. C. K. SHARPE, in *Correspondence* (1888), II., 5. Tyndall and I always fought about noblemen, tho' I suspected his COLT'S TOOTH with regard to Lord Apsley, who is a mighty good sort of man, but only captivating.

COLUMBINE, *subs.* (theatrical).—A prostitute. For synonyms, *see* BARRACK-HACK and TART.

COLUMBUS, *subs.* (theatrical). — Failure. A REGULAR COLUMBUS = an utter failure; 'dead frost.' Fr., *Il pleut!* = the play is a failure.

COMB-BRUSH, *subs.* (old).—A lady's maid. [A word compounded from the names of two familiar toilet requisites. *Cf.*, WHIP = a coachman.]—*See* ABIGAIL.

1750. FIELDING, *Tom Jones*. The maid who at present attended on Sophia was recommended by Lady Bellaston, with whom she had lived for some time in the capacity of a COMB-BRUSH.

COMB CUT. TO HAVE ONE'S COMB CUT, *verbal phr.* (popular).—To be mortified; disgraced; down on one's luck. [A simile drawn from cock-fighting.]

COMB DOWN.—*See* COMB ONE'S HAIR.

COMBIE, *subs.* (university). – A familiar abbreviation for 'Combination room,' the parlour in which college dons drink wine after Hall. Also a garment; *see* COMBINATION.

COMBINATION, *subs.* (general).—A woman's undergarment, shift and drawers in one. Also COMBIE, and (American) CHEMILOON (*q.v.*), itself a combination of 'chemise' and 'pantaloon.'

COMB ONE'S HAIR, *verbal phr.*, *trs.* and *intr.* (common).—To take to task; to scold; to keep in order. Sometimes to thrash, and generally ill-treat. Variants are TO COMB DOWN; TO COMB ONE'S NODDLE WITH A THREE-LEGGED or JOINT STOOL. [A.S. *cemban*; O.E. *kemben*; German, *kämmen* = to comb. Halliwell gives *kemb* (a Border form) = to comb; also COMB = to cut a person's comb, to disable him. The word seems to have always involved the idea of personal castigation, either physical or figurative. In this connection, *cf.*, quot., 1593.] Fr., *donner une peignée* and *laver la tête*; but for synonyms in the sense of 'to scold,' *see* WIG; and in the sense of 'to thrash,' *see* TAN.

1593. SHAKSPEARE, *Taming of the Shrew*, i., 1. Kath . . . doubt not her cares should be to COMB YOUR NODDLE WITH A THREE-LEGG'D STOOL, And paint your face, and use you like a fool.

1769. JOHN WALLIS, *Antiquities of Northumberland*. [Speaking of Wark Castle.] On the west side are the outworks, now called the Kemb, *i.e.*, the camp of the militia designed to KEMB or fight an enemy; KEMB being a word often used by the borderers when they threaten in a passionate tone to beat an assailant, —they will KEMB him, *i.e.*, drub him heartily.

1836. W. KIDD, *London and all its Dangers*. 'Magistrates,' p. 12. The Magistrate of Hatton Garden has lately HAD HIS 'HAIR COMBED' by the Home Secretary for his brutal conduct.

1852. DICKENS, *Bleak House*, ch. xxvii., p. 236. 'If you had only settled down, and married Joe Pouch's widow when he died in North America, *she'd* have COMBED YOUR HAIR for you.'

1866. G. ELIOT, *Felix Holt*, ch. xliii. But you see, these riots—it's been a nasty business. I shall HAVE MY HAIR COMBED at the sessions for a year to come.'

1869. . . . . *Ino* (played at Strand Theatre). 'Since Ino's COMBED MY WOOL it's ceased to grow.'

COMB THE CAT, *verbal phr.* (nautical). —*See* quot.

1867. SMYTH, *Sailors' Word Book*. COMBING THE CAT: the boatswain, or other operator, running his fingers through the cat-o'-nine tails to separate them.

COME, *verb* (venery).—1. To experience the sexual spasm; to achieve emission; TO SPEND (*q.v.*). The expression (which applies to the agents only: never to the proof, or effect, of their activity) is common to both the sexes. *Cf.*, CREAM (*q.v.*); SPENDINGS; *q.v.*; and LETCHWATER (*q.v.*).

2. (general). — To practice; to understand; to act the part of. *Cf.*, COME OVER and COME TRICKS.

1883. GREENWOOD, *Tag, Rag, and Co.* We ain't two by ourselves as COMES that dodge.

3. (old).—To lend.

1785. GROSE, *Dict. Vulg. Tongue*. Has he COME IT? *i.e.*, has he lent it?

TO MAKE DRUNK COME, *phr.* (American).—To become intoxicated. For synonyms, *see* SCREWED.

COME ABOUT [ONE], *verbal phr.* (old).—1. To circumvent. *Cf.*, COME OVER and COME ROUND.

1755. JOHNSON, *Dict. Eng. Lang.* (11 ed., 1816), s.v. 'About' in common language they say to COME ABOUT a man, 'to circumvent him.'

2. (venery). — To copulate. (Said only of men by women).

COME A BUSTER. — *See* BUSTER (*subs.*, sense 3).

COME A CROPPER.—*See* CROPPER.

COME AND SEE YOUR PA, *phr.* (common). — An invitation to drink. For synonyms, *see* DRINKS.

COME CAPTAIN ARMSTRONG.—*See* CAPTAIN ARMSTRONG.

COME-DOWN, *subs.* (popular).—A fall, whether of pride or worldly prospects; an abandonment of something for something else of less value or moment.

Verb.—[Used either independently or in combination: *e.g.*, TO COME DOWN; TO COME DOWN HANDSOME, or TO COME DOWN WITH THE DUST, DUES, DIBS, READY, OOF, SHINERS, BLUNT, NEEDFUL, etc.] (common).—1. To pay, *i.e.*, to 'part'; or

to lay down (as in payment); to 'fork out.' For synonyms, *see* SHELL OUT.

1701. STEELE, *The Funeral*, Act ii., Sc. 1. I must do according to my orders . . . except you'd COME DOWN a little deeper than you talk of:—You don't consider the charges I've been at already.

1727. GAY, *Beggar's Opera*, Act iii., Sc. 1. Did he tip handsomely?—How much did he COME DOWN with?

1842. *Punch*, vol. III., p. 136. 'Bolt!' she falter'd, 'from the gov'nor? Oh, my Colin, that won't pay; He will ne'er COME DOWN, my love, nor Help us, if we run away.'

1849. THACKERAY, *Pendennis*, ch. lxix. My uncle augurs everything from the Begum's generosity, and says that she will COME DOWN very handsomely.

1889. BARRÈRE, *Sl., Jar., and Cant*, (quoted in). Do you keep the gentleman in discourse while I speak to the prisoner, and see how he can COME DOWN.

2. (trade).—To abate prices.

COME DOWN FROM THE WALLS, *verbal phr.* (American). — To abandon a position. *Cf.*, BACK SEAT.

COMEDY-MERCHANT, *subs.* (common).—An actor. For synonyms, *see* CACKLING-COVE.

COME IT, *verb* (colloquial).—1. To proceed at a great rate; to make a splash and dash (in extravagance); to 'cut a figure.' *Cf.*, COME IT STRONG and GO IT.

1840. THACKERAY, *Paris Sketch Book*, p. 22. 'I think the chaps down the road will stare,' said Sam, 'when they hear how I've been COMING IT.'

2. (thieves'). — To inform. For synonyms, *see* PEACH.

1857. SNOWDEN, *Mag. Assistant*, 3 ed., p. 444. To inform=TO COME IT.

1864. HOTTEN, *Slang Dict.*, p. 126. The expression COME IT (to inform, tell, or disclose) is best known to the lower and most dangerous classes.

1889. *Daily Telegraph*. He heard one of the others say in reply, 'COME IT, meaning to tell—to be quiet.

3. (pugilistic).—To show fear.

4. (American).—To succeed. Especially in YOU CAN'T COME IT, *i.e.*, you cannot succeed: an expression of disbelief in the ability of another. Probably a survival of old English usage. *Cf.*, COME OVER.

COME IT STRONG, *verbal phr.* (popular). — To exaggerate; to 'lay it on thick'; to carry to extremes. For synonyms, *see* LONGBOW. *Cf.*, COME IT.

1836. C. DICKENS, *Pickwick Papers*, p. 356 (ed. 1857). 'Vell, sir,' rejoined Sam, after a short pause, 'I think I see your drift; and if I do see your drift, it's my 'pinion that you're a COMIN' IT A GREAT DEAL TOO STRONG, as the mail-coachman said to the snow-storm, ven it overtook him.'

1837. BARHAM, *I. L.* (*Lay of St. Gengulphus*), ed. 1862, p. 157. He here shook his head,—Right little he said, But he thought she was COMING IT RATHER TOO STRONG.

1846. W. M. THACKERAY, *Yellowplush*. 'Mr. Deuceace at Paris.' Now, though master was a scoundrill and no mistake, he was a gentleman and a man of good breeding; and miss CAME A LITTLE TOO STRONG (pardon the vulgarity of the expression), with her hardor and attachment for one of his taste.

1869. BRET HARTE, *The Heathen Chinee*. In his sleeves, which were long, He had twenty-four packs. Which was COMING IT STRONG.

COME JOHN, or LORD, AUDLEY.—*See* JOHN AUDLEY.

COME OFF, *verbal phr.* (colloquial). —To happen; to occur; to result from. — *See* also COME, sense 1.

1609. JONSON, *Case is Altered*, IV., iii. His muse sometimes cannot curvet, nor prognosticate, and COME OFF as it should; no matter, I'll hammer out a paraphrase for thee myself.

1857. DICKENS, *The Detective Police*, in *Reprinted Pieces*, p. 239. In consequence of which appointment the party CAME OFF, which we are about to describe.

1870. WILKIE COLLINS, *Man and Wife*, in *Cassell's Mag.*, p. 292, col. 1. 'The betting's at five to four, my dear. And the race COMES OFF in a month from this.'

1872. *Civilian*, 10 Aug. Unfortunately, the event, to use the language of the turf, did not COME OFF, and considerable disappointment was manifested.

1883. *Graphic*, August 11, p. 138, col. 2. Batting is his forte, though he does not always COME OFF.

COME OFF THE GRASS, or THE TALL GRASS! *phr.* (American). — 'None of your airs!' 'Don't put it on so!' 'Don't tell any more lies!' The French say, *As-tu fini tes manières* or *magnes? ne fais donc pas ta Sophie*; and *ne fais donc pas ton fendart*.

COME OUT, *verbal phr.* (common).—1. To make an appearance; to display oneself; to express oneself vigorously; to make an impression (especially in sense 2). Sometimes in an intensified form TO COME OUT STRONG. *Cf.*, COME IT STRONG.

[The first quot. is doubtful, but it looks like an anticipation.]

1637. SL. RUTHERFORD, *Letters*, No. 167, vol. I., p. 390 (ed. 1862, 2 vols.). Christ . . . who hath given you eyes to discern the devil COMING OUT in his whites.

1855. THACKERAY, *Newcomes*, II., 14. The more he [Clive] worked, the more he was discontented with his performance, somehow; but J. J. was COMING OUT VERY STRONG; J. J. was going to be a stunner.

1865. G. F. BERKELEY, *Life, etc.* II., 135. Our inclination to quiz him [Lord Wm. Lennox] on the subject increased when in later years he CAME OUT STRONG in magazines and reviews, as a sporting writer.

1865. *Cornhill Magazine*, IV., 218. 'A county ball.' The native COMES OUT STRONG in waistcoats—his array in that respect being gorgeous.

1870. *Good Words*, April. 'The Hand Nailer.' In the nailing communities, as elsewhere, woman manages somehow to COME OUT EXTENSIVELY on Sundays.

18(?). AYTOUN, *The Dreepdaily Burghs*, p. 2. Let me confess it. I had of late COME OUT RATHER TOO STRONG. When a man has made money easily, he is somewhat prone to launch into expense.

2. (common).—To turn out; to result; *e.g.*, How did it COME OUT? *Cf.*, COME OFF.

3. (colloquial).—To make a first appearance in society.

TO COME OUT OF THE LITTLE END OF THE HORN, *phr.* (American).—To fare badly; in allusion to the thin end of the CORNUCOPIA.

COME OVER, *verbal phr.* (colloquial). —To influence; to overreach; to cheat. (If the quots. are compared chronologically it will be seen that there has been a gradual deterioration in the meaning of this colloquialism.) *Cf.*, COME ROUND; GET OVER.

1609. DEKKER, *Gul's Horne-Booke*, ch. ii. Care not for those coorse painted cloath rimes, made by ye University of *Salerne*, that COME OUER you, with . . . sweete candied councell.

1667. SHIRLEY, *Love Tricks*, Act ii., Sc. 1. I do not see what fault she can find with me; and if I had some good word to COME OVER her—but I must help it out, an need be, with swearing.

1785. GROSE, *Dict. Vulg. Tongue*. To COME OVER any one: to cheat or overreach him.

1794. *Gent. Mag.*, p. 1085. I lately CAME OVER him for a good round sum.

c. 1860. *Broadside Ballad*, I'm a young man from the country, But you don't GET OVER me.

c. 1879. *Music Hall Song* (sung by Jenny Hill, the 'Vital Spark'). You may GET OVER water-butts, You may GET OVER fountains, But I'll take particular notice that you don't GET OVER Sal.

1884. *Daily Telegraph*, March 11, p. 2, col. 1. 'But don't you try and COME IT OVER me, or you'll find yourself in the wrong box.'

COME [THE OLD SOLDIER, or any person or thing] OVER ONE, *verbal phr.* (colloquial).—To imitate; to overbear; to wheedle; to rule by an assumption of authority. Fr., *essayer de monter un bateau à quelqu'un*; or *monter le coup* or *un battage*.

1713. C. SHADWELL, *Humours of the Army*, Act iii. The Devil a Farthing he owes me—but however, I'll PUT THE OLD SOLDIER UPON him.

1825. SCOTT, *St. Ronan's Well*, ch. xviii. Were it not that I think he has scarce the impudence to propose such a thing to succeed, curse me but I should think he was COMING THE OLD SOLDIER OVER ME, and keeping up his game.

1836. DICKENS, *Pickwick Papers* (about 1827), p. 369 (ed. 1857). 'Ah, by jove, he has!' replied Smangle. 'Hear him COME THE FOUR CATS IN THE WHEELBARROW—four distinct cats, sir, I pledge you my honour Now you know that's infernal clever '

1839. *The Druid*. 'Post and Paddock.' The only way his crime to cover, To hide his shame from children's eye, Is not to try and COME THE LOVER But stable-wards at once to fly.

1855. W. M. THACKERAY, *The Newcomes*, II., 253. 'I had a letter this morning from my liberal and punctual employer, Thomas Potts, Esquire, of the *Newcome Independent*, who states, in language scarcely respectful, that Sir Barnes Newcome Newcome is trying TO COME THE RELIGIOUS DODGE, as Mr. Potts calls it.'

1877. W. BLACK, *Green Past. and Picc.*, ch. i. 'She's rather serious, you know, and would like to COME THE MATERNAL OVER YOU.'

1877. *Five Years' Penal Servitude*, ch. iii., p. 167. To hear him speak, one might imagine him as innocent as a lamb, and as green as a schoolboy, but just try TO COME THE HANKY-PANKY and PLAY THE OLD SOLDIER WITH him.

1877. J. GREENWOOD, *Dick Temple*. Permit me, if you and your two friends think of COMING what is vulgarly called THE OLD SOLDIER over me, to make you understand that you had better abandon the intention.

COME ROUND, *verbal phr.* (colloquial).—To influence; to circumvent; to persuade. *Cf.*, COME OVER, and COME ABOUT, sense 1.

1846. THACKERAY, *V. Fair*, ch. xi. Finally, the reports were that the governess had COME ROUND everybody, wrote Sir Pitt's letters, did his business, managed his accounts — had the upper hand of the whole house.

COME SOUSE, *verbal phr.* (pugilistic).—To fall heavily. Also COSOUSE.

1819. T. MOORE, *Tom Crib's Mem. to Cong.* As it was, Master Georgy CAME SOUSE with the whack, And there sprawled, like a turtle turned queer on its back.

COME THE GUM GAME, *verbal phr.* (Western American).—To overreach by concealment. [From the preference shown by hunted opossums and racoons for *gum* trees as places of refuge.]

1869. *Kansas City Advertiser*, 7 May. You can't COME THAT GUM GAME over me any more; I've been to the land-office and know all about the place.

COME THROUGH A SIDE DOOR, *verbal phr.* (common).—To be born illegitimately.

c. 1880. *Broadside Ballad*, 'The Blessed Orphan.' I don't think I was born at all, No parents own I came here; I was left at a house of call, Close by a Pickford's van here, Some wicked wretches say, but I My indignation smother, That I CAME THROUGH A SIDE DOOR In this world from the other.

COME TO STAY, *verbal phr.* (American).—To be endowed with permanent qualities. Thus the *New York Morning Journal* announces that earth fuel, a new material for cooking and firing purposes, has COME TO STAY, *i.e.*, its commercial success is assured.

1888. *Pittsburg Bulletin.* In the realm of advertising, the illustration has evidently COME TO STAY. It attracts and retains the eye, and so serves a double purpose.

COME TO, or UP TO, TIME, *verbal phr.* (pugilistic).—To answer the call of 'Time!' after the thirty seconds' rest between round and round; hence, by analogy, to be on the alert; to be ready.

1869. WHYTE MELVILLE, *M. or N.*, p. 11. The surprise staggered him like a blow. From such blows, however, we soon COME TO TIME, willing to take any amount of similar punishment.

COME TRICKS.—*See* COME, sense 2.

COME UP SMILING, *verbal phr.* (pugilistic).—To laugh (or grin) at 'punishment'; hence (generally) to be superior to rebuff or disaster; to face defeat without flinching.

1887. JOHN STRANGE WINTER, *That Imp*, p. 67. And yet COME UP SMILING at the end of it.

COME UP TO THE CHALK.—*See* SCRATCH.

[Some other slang uses of the verb To COME are To COME THE ARTFUL = to essay to deceive; To COME THE HEAVY = to affect a vastly superior position; To COME THE UGLY = to threaten; To COME THE NOB, or THE DON = to put on airs; To COME THE LARDY-DARDY = to dress for the public and 'look up to your clobber'; To COME THE SERJEANT = to issue peremptory orders; To COME THE SPOON = to make love; To COME THE GYPSY = to try to defraud; To COME THE ROTHSCHILD = to pretend to be rich; and To COME THE TRAVIATA (prostitutes', now obsolete) = to feign consumption, to put on 'the Traviata cough' (*q.v.*) with a view to beguiling charitable males.]

COMFLOGISTICATE, *verb* (American).—To embarrass; put out of countenance; confuse; or hoax.—*See* BAMBLUSTERCATE.

COMFOOZLED, *adj.* (rare).—Overcome; exhausted.

1836. DICKENS, *Pickwick*, ch. xxxix., p. 340. 'Well,' said Sam, 'he's in a horrid state o' love; reg'larly COMFOOZLED, and done over with it.'

COMFORTABLE IMPORTANCE or **COMFORTABLE IMPUDENCE,** *subs.* (old).—A wife; also a mistress in a wife's position. Fr., *Mon gouvernement.* For synonyms, *see* DUTCH.

COMICAL, *subs.* (common).—A napkin.

TO BE STRUCK COMICAL, *verb. phr.* (popular).—To be astonished.

COMING, *ppl. adj.* (old).—1. Wanton; forward; sexual.—*See* COME, sense 1.

1750. FIELDING, *Tom Jones*, ch. xii. I dares to swear the wench was as willing as he, for she was always a forward kind of body. And when wenches are so COMING, young men are not so much to be blamed neither, for to be sure they do no more than what is natural.

1785. GROSE, *Dict. Vulg. Tongue*, s.v.

2. (old).—Sexually capable.—*See* COME, sense 1.

COMMERCIAL, *subs.* (thieves')—*See* quot.

1886. *Tit-Bits*, 31 July, p. 252. He is one of the cleverest COMMERCIALS (this is the polite name for rogues and vagabonds generally) on the road.

2. (common).—An abbreviation of 'commercial traveller.'

COMMISSION or **MISH,** *subs.* (old).—A shirt. [From the Italian.—

See CAMESA.] For synonyms, *see* FLESH BAG.

1567. HARMAN, *Caveat* (1814), p. 65, s.v.

1610. ROWLANDS, *Martin Mark-all*, p. 37 (H. Club's Repr., 1874), s.v.

1622. JOHN FLETCHER, *The Beggar's Bush.* I crown thy nab with a gag of benbouse, And stall thee by the salmon into clowes To maund on the pad and strike all the cheats To mill from the Ruffmans, and COMMISSION, and slates.

1630. TAYLOR ('The Water Poet') wks. quoted in Nares. As from our beds we doe oft cast our eyes, Cleane linnen yeelds a shirt before we rise, Which is a garment *shifting* in condition, And in the canting tongue is a COMMISSION; In weale or woe, in joy or dangerous drifts, A *shirt* will put a man unto his *shifts.*

1671. R. HEAD, *English Rogue*, pt. I., ch. v., p. 48 (1874), s.v.

COMMISTER, *subs.* (old).—A clergyman. The same as CAMISTER (*q.v.*). For synonyms, *see* DEVIL-DODGER.

COMMODITY, *subs.* (old).—The female *pudendum.* For synonyms, *see* MONOSYLLABLE.

1596. SHAKSPEARE, *King John*, ii., 2. Tickling COMMODITY; COMMODITY—the bias of the world.

1785. GROSE, *Dict. Vulg. Tongue*, s.v.

1811. *Lexicon Balatronicum*, s.v.

COMMON-BOUNCE, *subs.* (low).—One using a lad as a decoy to prefer a charge of unnatural intercourse.

1886. M. DAVITT, *Leaves from a Prison Diary*, p. 109. THE COMMON BOUNCE Of all the scoundrels that stalk abroad in the world unhung for ur detected enormities, this is the most infamous.

COMMON-DOINGS, *subs.* (American).—Every-day fare. [A phrase of Western origin, at first restricted in its meaning, but now including ordinary transactions as compared to those either large or peculiarly profitable; applied to men, actions, and things. 'What shall we do?' says a poor frontiersman's wife, when she hears of a Federal Officer who is to take up his quarters at her cabin for a day; 'I can't give him COMMON-DOINGS.']

1835. HALIBURTON ('Sam Slick'), *The Clockmaker*, 3 S. I guess I'll order supper. What shall it be? Cornbread and COMMON DOINS, or wheatbread and chicken fixins?

COMMONER-GRUB, *subs.* (Winchester College).—A dinner formerly given by Commoners to College after cricket matches. [Commoners are boys not on the foundation.]

COMMONEY, *subs.* (schoolboys').—A clay marble. *Cf.*, ALLEY.

1836. C. DICKENS, *Pickwick Papers* (about 1827), p. 28 (ed. 1857). On one occasion he patted the boy on the head, and after inquiring whether he had won any alley tors or COMMONEYS lately (both of which I understand to be a particular species of marbles much prized by the youth of this town), made use of this remarkable expression—'How should you like to have another father?'

COMMON-JACK, *subs.* (military).—A prostitute. For synonyms, *see* BARRACK-HACK and TART.

COMMON-PLUGS, *subs.* (American).—Ordinary members of society.

COMMONSENSICAL, *adj.* (colloquial).—Marked with common sense.

1880. *Frazer's Magazine*, Sep., p. 308. The manner in which he (Alexander Russell) begins must have delighted the COMMONSENSICAL mind of old Charles Maclaren.

COMMON SEWER, *subs. phr.* (common).—1. A drink; dram; or 'go.' [From common sewer = 'a drain.'] For synonyms, *see* GO.

2. (venery).—A prostitute.

COMMUNICATOR. AGITATE THE COMMUNICATOR, *verbal phr.* (common).—To ring the bell.

COMP, *subs.* (printers').—A compositor. [An abbreviated form of 'companion' now peculiar to compositors, but originally applied to pressmen who work in couples, as well as to compositors who work in a 'companionship,' or SHIP (*q.v.*).] GALLEY-SLAVE (*q.v.*) is a variant; so are ASS (*q.v.*) and DONKEY (*q.v.*). *Cf.*, PIG.

1870. *Sportsman*, 17 Dec. 'A Chapel Meeting.' I stood before the world a journeyman COMP.

1886. *Tit-Bits*, 31 July, p. 252. At provincial newspaper offices and other establishments applications for work from travelling COMPS are frequent.

1888. W. BLADES, in *Notes and Queries*, 7 S., vi., 365. The printers who work together in one room are to this day called COMPS.

COMPANY. TO SEE COMPANY, *verbal phr.* (prostitutes').—To live by prostitution; TO TAKE IN FANCY WORK (*q.v.*).

1811. *Lexicon Balatronicum*, s.v.

COMPETITION WALLAH, *subs. phr.* (Anglo-Indian).—One who enters the Indian Civil Service by examination. [From COMPETITION + Hindustani *wallah*, 'a man' or 'person.']

1863. G. O. TREVELYAN, Title, THE COMPETITION WALLAH.

1886. *Ill. Lon. News*, 9 Jan., p. 31, col. 3. It is quite certain that, if justice is ever to be done to India, our COMPETITION WALLAHS must not be encouraged to look upon it as a mere Tom Tidler's ground, where they are to remain just so long as they require for picking up gold and silver (in the form of pension and savings).

COMPO, *subs.* (nautical).—A sailor's term for his monthly advance of wages.

COMPY-SHOP, *subs.* (workmen's).—A truck-shop. [Probably a corruption of 'company-shop': workmen before the passing of certain Truck Acts, having been frequently compelled to make their weekly purchases at shops either kept by, or worked to the profit of, their employer.]

1870. *Globe*, 24 Sept. The Acts of Parliament which have been passed from time to time in reference to truck are easily evaded, for as a rule no workman is told that he must buy at the COMPY-SHOP, but the workmen well know that if they did not resort thither they would soon be dismissed their employment.

CON, *subs.* (Winchester College).—A rap on the head with the knuckles, or with anything hard, such as a cricket ball. [For suggested derivations, *see verbal* sense.]

Verb.—To rap with the knuckles. [The derivation formerly accepted at Winchester was from κονδυλον = a knuckle, but the editors of the *Wykehamist* suggest its origin in the North Country *con*, 'to fillip,' with which the French *se cogner* exactly corresponds.]

CONCAVES AND CONVEXES, *subs. phr.* (cardsharpers'). Cards prepared for cheating. All from the eight to the king are cut CONVEX, and all from the deuce to the seven CONCAVE; so that by cutting the pack broadwise you cut CONVEX, and by cutting them

lengthwise you cut CONCAVE. Sometimes they are shaped the reverse way, so that, if suspicion arise, a pack so treated may be substituted for the other to the same effect. In this trick the sharper has less in his favour than in others, because the intended victim may cut in the usual way, and so cut a low card to the dealer. But the certainty of being able to cut or deal a high or low card at pleasure, gives him an advantage against which skill is of none avail. Other modes of sharping are by means of REFLECTORS (*q.v.*); LONGS AND SHORTS (*q.v.*); PRICKED CARDS (*q.v.*); THE BRIDGE (*q.v.*); SKINNING (*q.v.*); WEAVING (*q.v.*); THE GRADUS OR STEP (*q.v.*); PALMING (*q.v.*); and THE TELEGRAPH (*q.v.*). A French term for prepared cards is *les aiguilles à tricoter les côtes* (*Anglicé* = OLD GENTLEMEN, *q.v.*); also *une cartouchière à portées* (a pack of prepared cards); and *les harnais* = STOCKED BROADS (*q.v.*).—*See* also STOCK BROADS.

CONCERN, *subs.* (general).—The *pudenda*, male or female.—*See* CREAMSTICK and MONOSYLLABLE respectively for synonyms.

CONCERNED, *ppl. adj.* (old).—Drunk. For synonyms, *see* SCREWED.

1686. *Magdalen College and King James II.* (Oxford Hist. Soc.), quoted in *Athenæum*, 8 Jan., 1887, p. 56. When Mr. Anthony Farmer came to the Lobster about eleven at night, he came much CONCERNED in drink.

17(?). SWIFT. [Quoted in DAVIES' *Supp. Lex.*] (Mary, the cook-maid to Dr. Sheridan.) Which, and I am sure I have been his servant four years since October, And never call'd me worse than sweetheart, drunk or sober; Not that I know his Reverence was ever CONCERN'D to my knowledge; Tho' you and your come-rogues keep him out so late in your wicked college.

1834. TAYLOR, *Ph. van Art.*, pt. II., iii., 3. Oh, she's a light skirts! yea, and at this present A little, as you see, CONCERN'D with liquor.

CONCHERS, *subs.* (Australian).—Tame or quiet cattle.

CONDIDDLE, *verb* (old).—To purloin or steal. [From Latin *con*, a pleonastic prefix, + DIDDLE, 'to cheat.' CONDIDDLED is quoted by Grose in the *Provincial Glossary*, 1787, as signifying 'dispersed.']

1825. SCOTT, *St. Ronan's Well*, ch. iv. 'Twig the old connoisseur,' said the Squire to the Knight, 'he is CONDIDDLING the drawing.'

CONDOG, *verb* (common).—To agree with. [A facetious variation of 'concur'; 'cur' = dog.]

CONFAB, *subs.* (colloquial).—Familiar talk. [A contraction of confabulation; Latin *confabulatio.*]

1778. D'ARBLAY, *Diary, etc.* (1876), vol. I., p. 37. We had a very nice CONFAB about various books.

1789. WOLCOT ('P. Pindar'), *Subjects for Painters*, in wks. (Dublin, 1795), vol. II., p. 26. For lo, with *many* a King and *many* a Queen, in close CONFAB the gentleman is seen.

1841. *Punch*, vol. I., 75. Sibthorp, meeting Peel in the House of Commons after congratulating him on his present enviable position, finished the CONFAB with the following unrivalled conundrum.

1850. F. E. SMEDLEY, *Frank Fairleigh*, ch. xxv. 'Mr. Harry . . . called Mr. Archer into his own room, and they had a CONFAB.'

1884. W. C. RUSSELL, *Jack's Courtship*, ch. viii. This ended our CONFAB and half an hour afterwards I stood in the hall shaking hands all round.

Verb.—To talk in a familiar manner; to chat.—*See subs.*, sense.

1778. D'ARBLAY, *Diary, etc.* (1876), vol. I. p. 85. Mrs. Thrale and I were dressing, and, as usual, CONFABBING.

CONFECTIONERY, *subs.* (American).—A drinking bar. An analogous term is GROCERY, but for synonyms, *see* LUSH-CRIB.

CONFIDENCE TRICK, DODGE, or **BUCK,** *subs. phr.* (common).—A process of swindling, the basis of which consists in obtaining trust with the deliberate intention of betraying it to your own advantage. A greenhorn meets (or rather is picked up by) a stranger who invites him to drink. The stranger admires him openly, protests his CONFIDENCE in him, and to prove his sincerity hands him over a large amount of money [snide] or valuables [bogus], with which to walk off and return. The greenhorn does both, whereupon the stranger suggests that it is his turn next, and being favoured with certain proofs of 'confidence,' which in this case are real, decamps and is no more seen. This is the simplest form of the trick, but the CONFIDENCE MAN is inexhaustible in devices. In many cases the subject's idiosyncrasy takes the form of an idiotic desire to overreach his fellows; *i.e.*, he is only a knave, wrong side out, and it is upon this idiosyncrasy that the operator works. He offers a sham gold watch at the price of a nickel one; he calls with presents from nowhere where none are expected; he writes letters announcing huge legacies to persons absolutely kinless; and as his appeal is addressed to the sister passions of greed and dishonesty he seldom fails of his reward. Fr., *mener en bateau un pante pour le refaire* = 'to stick a jay and flap him.'

CONFLABBERATED, *ppl. adj.* (common).—Bothered; upset; 'flummoxed.'

CONFLABBERATION, *subs.* (common).—A confused wrangle; a 'hullabaloo.'

CONFOUNDED, *adj.* (colloquial).—Excessive; odious; detestable; *e.g.*, a CONFOUNDED nuisance, lie, humbug, etc. [CONFOUND is properly 'to mistake one for another,' or 'to throw into consternation.' In its colloquial sense CONFOUNDED is misused much as are 'awful,' 'beastly,' and other 'strumpets of speech.']

1766. O. GOLDSMITH, *Vicar of Wakefield*, ch. vii. (ed. 1827), p. 42. Mr Thornhill, *loq.*: 'For what are tythes and tricks but an imposition, all CONFOUNDED imposture.'

CONFUBUSCATE, *verb* (popular).—*See* quot., and *Cf.*, CONFUSTICATE.

1880. *Broadside Ballad*, 'You mustn't tickle me.' I hope I don't CONFUBUSCATE, I'se Topsy from the Georgia State.

CONFUSTICATE, *verb* (American).—To confuse.

CONIACKER, *subs.* (thieves'). — A counterfeiter; smasher; or 'queer-bit' faker. [Obviously a play upon COIN, money, and HACK, to mutilate.] Fr., *un mornifleur tarte.*

1871. DE VERE, *Americanisms*, p. 296. False coins, the makers of which are curiously called CONIACKERS.

CONISH, *adj.* (old).—*See* quot.

1830. SIR E. B. LYTTON, *Paul Clifford*, p. 29 (ed. 1854). 'Paul, my ben cull,' said he with a knowing wink, and nudging the young gentleman in the left side, 'vot do you say to a drop o' blue ruin? or, as you likes to be CONISH (genteel), I doesn't care if I sports you a glass of port.'

CONK, *subs.* (popular).—The nose. [Hotten says: possibly from the Latin *concha*, a shell. Greek, κόγχη—hence anything hollow. A parallel is *testa* = an earthenware pot, a shell, in Latin; and in later Latin = a skull; whence the French *teste* or *tête* = head. *Cf.*, quot., 1838.]

ENGLISH SYNONYMS. Boko or boco; proboscis; smeller; bowsprit; claret-jug; gig; muzzle; cheese-cutter; beak; snuff-box; snorter; post-horn; paste-horn; handle; snout; nozzle; smelling-cheat; snotter; candlestick; celestial; snottle-box; snuffler; trumpet; snorer; peak.

FRENCH SYNONYMS. *Une bouteille* (popular: literally 'a bottle'); *un Bourbon* (popular: an abbreviated form of *nez à la Bourbon*. In allusion to the thick, prominent, and almost aquiline Bourbon nose); *un blair* or *blaire* (popular); *un caillou* (popular: properly 'a flint.' In allusion to a Bardolphian, a light-giving, quality); *un tubercule* (familiar: applied to a big nose. In medicine 'a tumour,' 'swelling,' or 'protuberance'); *un pivase* (popular: a nose of large dimensions. Michel derives the word from *pive* = 'a grog-blossom' or 'pin-point,' properly a fir-apple); *un piton* (popular: literally a geographical term meaning 'a peak.' *Un piton passé à l'encaustique*, a red or 'copper-nose'); *un pif* or *pifre* (general); *une trompe* (literally 'a horn' or 'trumpet'); *une truffe* (popular: literally 'a truffle,' for which pigs are trained to search. Hence a Frenchman when he wants to call a man a pig, says *il a un nez à chercher des truffes*); *une trompette* (popular: literally 'a trumpet'); *un naze* (popular and thieves': a Provençalism); *un nazaret* (popular); *un chandelier* (popular); *une tasse* (popular); *un sabot* (popular); *un os à moelle* (thieves': literally 'a marrow-bone.' *Faire juter l'os à moelle* = to use the fingers as a handkerchief); *un éteignoir* (popular: a large nose; literally, 'an extinguisher'); *un nazonnant* (popular); *un minois* (thieves': obsolete); *un mirliton* (popular); *un morviau* (popular).

GERMAN SYNONYMS. *Muffer* or *Muffert* (from *muffen*, *muffeln*, or *murfeln* = 'to smell'); *Schneitzling* or *Schnäuzling*; *Schnut* (a North German form of *Schnauze*. *Schnut* is a favourite nickname among thieves, especially for those who possess long noses; also a pet name for a sweet-heart or doxy. *Schnutenmelech* or *Schnutenkönig*: the nosey king, or nosey one); *Schniffling.*

ITALIAN SYNONYMS. *Soffiante* (this exactly corresponds to the English 'snorter'; it signifies literally 'blowing' or 'breathing'); *fiauto* or *flauto* (properly 'a flute'); *maremagno* (literally 'the great sea').

1838. *Comic Almanack*, p. 158. I have inserted a small item from my surgeon's bill, for repairs of his companions' noses, damaged by his passion for CONCHOLOGY.

1840. H. COCKTON, *Valentine Vox*, ch. xxviii. He fancied it proper to put on his nose before he alighted from the cab. 'Oh! oh! there's a CONK! there's a smeller! Oh! oh!' exclaimed about fifty voices in chorus.

1859. *Punch*, vol. XXXVII., p. 54. 'Essence of Parliament.' *July 25, Monday.* Lord Lyndhurst let fly and caught him what (if pugilistic terms be not out of place when one is alluding to so pacific a personage) may be designated an extremely neat one on the CONK.

1860. *Chambers' Journal*, vol. XIII., p. 348. His nose is his CONK.

1887. ATKIN, *House Scraps.* His 'dexter ogle' has a 'mouse'; His CONK'S devoid of bark.

1889. *Answers*, 9 Feb. That portion of his countenance which is euphemistically described in the language of lower London as a CONK.

CONOODLE.—*See* CANOODLE.

CONSCIENCE, *subs.* (theatrical).—Thus explained in *Slang, Jargon, and Cant*: A kind of association in a small company for the allotment of shares in the profits, etc. The man who is lucky enough to have a concern of his own, generally a very small affair, however badly he may act, must be the leading man or first low comedian, perhaps both. He becomes the manager, of course, and thus has one share for 'fit-up,' one for scenery, one and a half for management, one for wardrobe, one and a half as leading man; and the same is given to the wife, who, of course, will not play anything but the juvenile lead, but who at any other time would be glad to play first old woman.

CONSIDERABLE BEND. TO GO ON THE CONSIDERABLE BEND *verb. phr.* (common).—To go in for a bout of dissipation.

CONSONANT - CHOKER, *subs.* (common). — One that clips his G's and muffles his R's.

CONSTABLE. TO OUT OF OVER-RUN THE CONSTABLE, *verbal phr.* (common).—To live beyond one's means and get into debt; also, in a figurative sense, to escape from a bad argument; 'to change the subject'; to talk about what is not understood.

1663. BUTLER, *Hudibras*, pt. I., canto iii., l. 1367. Quoth Hudibras, Friend Ralph, thou hast OUT-RUN THE CONSTABLE at last; For thou art fallen as a new Dispute, as senseless as untrue, But to the former opposite, And contrary as black to white.

1748. SMOLLETT, *Rod. Random*, ch. xxiii. He inquired, 'how far have you OVERRUN THE CONSTABLE?' I told him that the debt amounted to eleven pounds.

1766. ANSTEY, *New Bath Guide*, letter vii. And some people think with such haste he began, That soon he THE CONSTABLE greatly OUTRAN.

1782. WOLCOT ('P. Pindar'), *Rights of Kings*, ode xi. Got deep in debt, THE CONSTABLE OUT-RAN.

1836. DICKENS, *Pickwick*, ch. xli., p. 357. 'He RUN a match agin THE CONSTABLE, and vun it.' 'In other words, I suppose,' said Mr. Pickwick, 'he got into debt.' 'Just that, sir,' replied Sam.

CONSTICIAN, *subs.* (theatrical).—A member of the orchestra.

CONSTITUTIONAL, *subs.* (colloquial).—A walk undertaken for the sake of health and exercise [*i.e.*, for the benefit of the constitution]. *Tronchiner*, from Doctor Tronchin, is French for the verb, *tronchinade* for the act.

1850. F. E. SMEDLEY, *Frank Fairleigh*, ch. xxix. One evening, about a week before the examinations were to begin, I was taking my usual CONSTITUTIONAL after Hall.

1853. REV. E. BRADLEY ('Cuthbert Bede'), *Verdant Green*, pt. II., p. 41. At one time he was a great friend of Cocky Palmer's, and used to go with him to the Cock fights at Wheatley—that Village just on the other side Shotover Hill—where we did a CONSTITUTIONAL the other day.

1871. *City of London Directory.* 'Facts and Anomalies.' The valetudinarian has not much choice in the city for a CONSTITUTIONAL, seeing that it possesses but three walks, and 'Long Walk' is the shortest.

CONTANGO, *subs.* (Stock Exchange).—A fine paid by the buyer to the seller of stock for carrying over the engagement to another settling day, and representing a kind of interest for a fourteen days' extension. [Thought to be a corruption of 'continuation.']

1853. *Notes and Queries*, 17 Dec., p. 586, col. 2. CONTANGO: a technical term in use among the sharebrokers of Liverpool, and I presume elsewhere, signifying a sum of money paid for accommodating either a buyer or seller by carrying the engagement to pay money or deliver shares over to the next account day.

1871. *Daily News*, 27 Feb. A large amount of money was offered in the Stock Exchange, in connection with the fortnightly settlement, which began this morning, and the CONTANGOES on British railway securities were light, while the supply of stock was small.

1872. *Evening Standard*, 11 Dec. 'City Intelligence.' Erie Shares are steady; the CONTANGO is 3d. to 9d.

1884. *Daily News*, Nov. 13, p. 5, col. 1. City shop is not less baffling, and it is perhaps impossible for laymen to understand what CONTANGO means. CONTANGO, by the way, would be a proud motto for an ennobled stockbroker, and would look well under a crest.

1887. ATKIN, *House Scraps.* B stands for broker, for bull and for bear, C's the CONTANGO that's paid by the bull.

CONTENT, *adv.* (old).—Dead. For synonyms, *see* ALOFT and HOP THE TWIG.

1785. GROSE, *Dict. Vulg. Tongue.* The cull's CONTENT: the man is past complaining (cant), saying of a person murdered for resisting the robbers.

CONTINENT, *adv.* (Winchester College).—Ill; on the sick list. [From *continens cameram vel lectum*, keeping one's room or bed.] —*See* ABROAD.

1870. MANSFIELD, *School Life at Winchester College*, p. 146. When a boy felt ill, or inclined to quit school for a period, he had to get leave CONTINENT which was done by sending a boy in the morning first to get leave from his tutor, and then from the Head Master.

1878. ADAMS, *Wykehamica*, p. 224 We suggested the 'CONTINENT room'; and on being required to say what was to become of the sick boys? replied, that it was notorious that there was never anything the matter with them!

CONTINENTAL. NOT TO CARE OF BE WORTH A CONTINENTAL or CONTINENTAL DAMN, *phr.* (American).—To be worthless; not to care in the least degree. [CONTINENTAL was the common qualification at the time of the Revolution of whatever concerned the American Colonies before they were united into a confederacy; hence CONTINENTAL congress, CONTINENTAL money, CONTINENTAL troops; while the people themselves were generally spoken of as CONTINENTALLERS or CONTINENTALS. CONTINENTAL DAMN, a term almost universally applied to the worthless CONTINENTAL paper money of those days is, nevertheless held by James Grant White (*Words and their Uses*) to be a counterpart, if not a mere modification, of other phrases of the same kidney—a tinker's or trooper's damn, etc.—and as the colonial troops were called CONTINENTALLERS or CONTINENTALS during the war, and for many years afterwards, it is probable that it began as a CONTINENTAL'S DAMN. Passing to the general phrase 'not worth a damn' Mr. White thinks that the 'damn' = A.S. *cerse.* = watercress. Piers Ploughman (1362) says 'wisdom and witt nowe is not worth a kerse' and transition, by reason of identity of sound and a love of variety, from 'not worth a curse' to 'not worth a damn' is easy.]—*See* CARE and CURSE.

1869. S. L. CLEMENS ('Mark Twain'), *The Innocents at Home*, p. 20. He didn't give a CONTINENTAL for anybody. Beg your pardon, friend, for coming so near saying a cuss-word.

1888. *Missouri Republican*, 16 Feb. I am not worrying about the nomination, though. I DON'T CARE A CONTINENTAL if I don't receive it.

CONTINUATIONS, *subs.* (general).—Trousers. [Of analogous derivation to INEXPRESSIBLES; UNMENTIONABLES; MUSN'T-MENTION'EMS; UNTALKABOUTABLES, etc.] For synonyms, *see* BAGS and KICKS.

1841. *Punch*, vol. I., p. 4, col. 1. Like the London dustmen, the Newmarket jockeys, the peripatetic vendors, or buyers of 'old clo',' or the Albert CONTINUATIONS at *one pound one*, they appear to be *made to measure for the same*.

1853. WHYTE MELVILLE, *Digby Grand*, ch. xx. To whose wonderfully-fitting CONTINUATIONS, 'pants' he calls them, the 'Ananyridians' themselves are but as a Dutchman's drawers.

CONTRAPTIONS, *subs.* (American).—Small articles; tools; and so forth.

1838. J. C. NEAL, *Charcoal Sketches*. For my part, I can't say as how I see what's to be the end of all of them new-fangled CONTRAPTIONS. [DE V.]

CONTROL FORTUNE, *verbal phr.* (card-sharpers'). — To cheat at cards.—*See* ROOK.

CONVENIENCE, *subs.* (common).—A water-closet or chamber-pot.

CONVENIENT, *subs.* (old).—A mistress. For synonyms, *see* BARRACK-HACK and TART.

1676. ETHEREGE, *Man of Mode*, III., iii., in wks. (1704), 233. Dorimant's CONVENIENT, Madam Loveit.

1688. SHADWELL, *Sq. of Alsatia*, II., in wks. (1720), iv., 47. But where's your lady, captain, and the *blowing*, that is to be my *natural*, my CONVENIENT, my *pure? Ibid*, I., iv., p. 22. *Shamwell*. Thou art i' th' right; but, captain, where's the CONVENIENT, the Natural? *Hackum*. Why, at my house; my wife has brought her into a good humour; she is very pretty.

1785. GROSE, *Dict. Vulg. Tongue*, s.v.

1811. *Lexicon Balatronicum*, s.v.

CONVEXES. —*See* CONCAVES.

CONVEY, *verb* (old).—To steal. [In law, to transfer from one person to another; by which it will be seen that there is a certain humour in the expression.] For synonyms, *see* PRIG, *Cf.*, ANNEX.

1596. SHAKSPEARE, *Merry Wives of Windsor*, Act i., Sc. 3. *Nym*. The good humour is, to steal at a minute's rest. *Pist*. CONVEY, the wise it call.

1607. MARSTON, *What You Will*, II., 260. But, as I am Crack, I will CONVEY, crossbite, and cheat upon Simplicius.

1883. A. DOBSON, *Old World Idylls*, p. 237. If they hint, O Musician, the piece that you played Is nought but a copy of Chopin or Spohr; That the ballad you sing is but merely CONVEYED From the stock of the Arnes and the Purcells of yore.

1889. *Pall Mall Gaz.*, 31 Oct., p. 3, col. 1. Three great works of research and collaboration have been projected and partially or wholly executed in England within the lifetime of the present generation. They are the *Encyclopædia Britannica*, the *Dictionary of National Biography*, and the *New English Dictionary*. Each of these, but especially the last (from which the Century crew have CONVEYED freely) is as perfect in its way as any human undertaking can be.

1890. *Scots Observer*, 14 June, p. 98, col. 1. Lest this may seem an ungenerous suspicion, I hasten to say that it would never have crossed my mind had not so many of the other characters in this remarkable production (?) been obviously CONVEYED (delicious word!) from well-known novels.

CONVEYANCE, *subs.* (old).—A theft. —[*See* CONVEY and CONVEYANCER.]

1592. SHAKSPEARE, *I. Hen. VI.*, i., 3. Since Henry's death, I fear there is CONVEYANCE.

1712. *Spectator*, No. 305. Provided the CONVEYANCE was clean and unsuspected, a youth might afterwards boast of it.

CONVEYANCER, *subs.* (old). — A thief. [From CONVEY, to steal. In law, one whose occupation is to draw conveyances or transfers of property, deeds, etc.]—*See* CONVEYER.

1857. SNOWDEN, *Mag. Assistant* (3 ed.), p. 445. To pick pockets: to buzz, buzzmen, clyfakers, CONVEYANCERS.

CONVEYANCING, *verbal subs.* (common).—Thieving. [In law, the act or practice of drawing up deeds, leases, etc., for transferring the title to property from one person to another. *Cf.*, CONVEY, to steal.]

1865. MR. SMOLLETT, in House of Commons, 14 March. 'Speech on the Nawab of the Carnatic.' Pickpockets in London, when they appropriated purses or watches, called the transaction CONVEYANCING.

1889. *Modern Society* (quoted in *S., J. and C.*), p. 269. The green youth who attempted to decamp with ——'s watch . . . was properly punished for his verdancy in the art of CONVEYANCING.

CONVEYER, *subs.* (old).—A thief. [One who conveys or steals.] Fr., *emposteur*.

1597. SHAKSPEARE, *Richard II.*, iv., *sub. fin.* O good *convey!* CONVEYERS are you all, That rise thus nimbly by a true king's fall.

CONY or **TOM CONY**, *subs.* (old).—A simpleton. [From the proverbial simplicity of the rabbit or CONY.]—*See* CONY-CATCH, *verb*, and for synonyms, BUFFLE-HEAD and CABBAGE-HEAD.

1785. GROSE, *Dict. Vul. Tongue*, s.v.

CONY-CATCH, *verb* (old).—To cheat; deceive; trick; or 'BITE' (*q.v.*). [Literally 'to catch conies.'] Dekker, in his *English Villainies*, describes the system which is obviously the equivalent of the modern CONFIDENCE TRICK (*q.v.*). A society of sharpers of this type was called 'a warren,' and their dupes 'rabbit-suckers' (that is, baby rabbits), or conies. At other times the gang were 'bird-catchers,' and their quarry was 'a gull,' etc. For synonyms, *see* STICK.

1593. SHAKSPEARE, *Taming of the Shrew*, v., 1. Take heed, signor Baptista, lest you be CONNY-CATCHED in this business.

1596. NASHE, *Saffron Walden*, in wks. III., 158. Hereby hee thought to CONNY-CATCH the simple world.

1604. DEKKER, *Honest Wh.*, in wks. (1873) II., 12. Why, sister, do you thinke He CONNY-CATCH you, when you are my cozen?

CONY CATCHER, *subs.* (old).—A cheat; sharper; or trickster. [From CONY-CATCH, *verb* (*q.v.*), + ER.] For synonyms, *see* ROOK.

1592. JOHN DAY, *Blind Beggar*, Act iii., Sc. 3, p. 57. We'll go seek out those CONY-CATCHERS; and ere I catch them, I'll make them pay soundly all for their roguery.

1599. MINSHEW, *Dict.*, s.v. A CONIE-CATCHER: a name given to deceivers, by a metaphor, taken from those that rob warrens, and conie-grounds, using all means, sleights, and cunning to deceive them, as pitching of haies before their holes, fetching them in by tumblers, etc.

1602. ROWLANDS, *Greene's Ghost*, p. 3. (Hunterian Club's Repr.) And the name of CONICATCHERS is so odious, that now a dayes it is had vp, and vsed for an opprobrious name for euerie one that sheweth the least occasion for deceit.

1822. SCOTT, *Fortunes of Nigel*, ch. xxiii. Marry, thou hast me on the hip there, thou old miserly CONY-CATCHER!

CONY-CATCHING, *verbal subs.* (old).—Cheating; trickery; swindling after the manner of CONY-CATCHERS (*q.v.*). Shakspeare, says Nares, has once used it to express harmless roguery, playing jocular tricks, and no more [*see* quot., 1593]. For synonyms, *see* SELL.

1592. GREENE, *Groundwork of Conny-Catching*, p. 2. . . . this booke, wherein thou shalt find the ground-worke of CONNY-CATCHING.

1593. SHAKSPEARE, *Taming of the Shrew*, iv., 1. Come, you are so full of CONYCATCHING.

1608. MIDDLETON, *Trick to Catch the Old One*, III., iv. Thou hast more CONY-CATCHING devices than all London.

1703. WARD, *London Spy*, pt. XI., p. 260. And being almost Drunk, their Brains ran on CONEY-CATCHING.

1884. *Daily News*, Jan. 5, p. 5, col. 2. CONEY-CATCHING, or its modern equivalent, the confidence trick.

Ppl. adj. (old).—*Mutatis mutandis*, the same as the substantive (*q.v.*).

1596. SHAKSPEARE, *Merry Wives of Windsor*, i., 1. Marry, sir, I have matter in my head against you; and against your CONEY-CATCHING rascals, Bardolph Nym, and Pistol.

1596. BEN JONSON, *Every Man in His Humour*, iii., 1. Whoreson CONEY-CATCHING rascal! I could eat the very hilts for anger.

COO-E-E-E, or **COO-EY**, *subs.* (Australian). — A signal cry of the Australian blackfellow, adopted by the invading whites. The final 'e' is a very high note, a sort of prolonged screech, that resounds for miles through the bush, and thus enables parties that have lost each other to ascertain their relative positions.

1883. *Graphic*, July 7, p. 6, col. 3. COO-E-E is the Australian cry for help. When the two hands are used, and the coo properly pitched, it can be heard a wonderful distance. Whenever a COO-E-E is heard in the bush it is a matter of conscience to answer it and see what is amiss.

1887. G. L. APPERSON, in *All the Year Round*, 30 July, p. 67, col. 1. A common mode of expression is to be 'within COOEY' of a place. Originally, no doubt, this meant to be within the distance at which the well-known COOEY or bush cry, could be heard; now it simply means within easy reach of a place. To be 'within COOEY' of Sydney is to be at the distance of an easy journey therefrom.

1889. E. S. RAWSON, *In Australian Wilds*. 'A Queensland Mystery.' It is solely on this, or the mad theory, that one could account for the startling effects of Jim's COOEE or otherwise to the belated wanderer it would have been a revelation of joy and rescue.

COOK, *verb* (colloquial). — **1**. To tamper with, garble, or falsify. Accounts are COOKED when so altered as to look better than they are. Pictures are COOKED when dodged-up for sale. Painters say that a picture will not COOK when it is so excellent as to be beyond imitation.

1751. SMOLLETT, *Peregrine Pickle*, ch. xcviii. Some falsified printed accounts, artfully COOKED up, on purpose to mislead and deceive.

1856. *Punch*, vol. XXXI., p. 189. 'Advertisement of Bubble Bank Book-keeping,' by Prof. McDooall. It is remarkable especially for the facilities it offers for COOKING the accounts, as it entirely prevents any possibility of checking them.

1863. C. READE, *Hard Cash*, II., p. 19. When A has been looking up to B for thirty years, he cannot look down on him all of a sudden, just because he catches him falsifying accounts. Why, man is a COOKING animal; commercial man especially.

1871. *The Athenæum*, 4 Feb. The great work of art of Ivan Turgeneff, the *Notes by a Sportsman* had been what is vulgarly called COOKED for the French markets.

1872. SPENCER, *Study of Sociology*, ch. vi., p. 119 (9 ed.). The dishonesty implied in the adulterations of tradesmen and manufacturers . . . in COOKING of railway accounts and financial prospectuses.

1888. GRANT ALLEN, *This Mortal Coil*, ch. v. Where Warren Relf was seated COOKING a sky in one of his hasty seaside sketches.

1890. *Saturday Review*, 1 Feb., p. 134, col. 1. We referred, in our last article upon this [gambling] subject, to the *Paris Mutuels*, and explained their working. Now money has to be found somehow for the poorer classes to get to the *Mutuel* and back their fancies, and the clerk COOKS his books, and the shop-boy 'fingers the till.'

2. *See* COOK ONE'S GOOSE, of which it is an abbreviation.

3. (colloquial). — To swelter with heat and sweat. In this sense the Fourbesque has *ansare*; literally 'to be out of breath.'

TO COOK ONE'S GOOSE, *verbal phr.* (common). — To 'settle'; 'worst'; kill; or ruin.

ENGLISH SYNONYMS. To anodyne; to put to bed; to snuff out; to give, or cook one's gruel; to corpse; to cooper up; to wipe out; to spiflicate; to settle, or settle one's hash; to squash; to shut up; to send to pot; to smash; to finish; to do for; to bugger up; to put one's light out; to stop one's little game; to stop one's galloping; to put on an extinguisher; to clap a stopper on; to bottle up; to squelch; to play hell (or buggery) with; to rot; to squash up; to stash; to give a croaker. For synonyms in the sense of circumvention, *see* FLOORED.

FRENCH SYNONYMS. *Avoir son affaire* (familiar: this also means to have got 'a settler,' and 'to be absolutely drunk'); *buter* (thieves' = 'to kill' or 'execute'); *escarper* (thieves'); *envoyer essayer une chemise de sapin* (military: literally 'to send one to try on a deal shirt.' *Cf.*, 'wooden surtout' = coffin); *faire suer un chêne* (popular: *suer* = to sweat; *chêne* = cove); *faire passer le goût du pain* (familiar = 'to give one his gruel'); *coffier* (thieves': an abbreviation of *escoffier*, to kill); *conir* (thieves'); *ébasir* (thieves': formerly *esbasir*; Fourbesque *sbasire* and Germania *esbasir*); *mettre à l'ombre* (general = to put in the shade); *endormir* (thieves'); *entailler* (thieves'); *abasourdir* (thieves': properly 'to astound'); *chouriner* or *suriner* (thieves': '*chourin*' or *surin* = a knife); *estourbir* (thieves'); *scionner* (thieves': from *scion* = a knife); *faire un machabée* (thieves': in cant *machabée* = a drowned corpse. Michel thinks the expression originated either in the reading of *II. Macabees*, ch. xii., which is still retained in the Mass for the Dead, or through *la danse macabre*, the Dance of Death shown in the engravings of the fourteenth and fifteenth centuries); *faire flotter un pante* (popular = to cook one's goose by drowning. *Flotter* = to float. *i.e.*, like a corpse); *crever la paillasse* (popular: literally 'to rip open the mattress'); *laver le linge dans la saignante* (thieves': to wash linen in blood): *dévisser le trognon à quelqu'un* (popular); *entonner* (popular: *see* Michel); *estrangouiller* (popular = 'to strangle'; from a veterinary term *étranguillon* = 'the strangles'); *tortiller la vis*, or *le gaviau* (thieves'); *terrer* (thieves': to 'guillotine'); *faire la grande soulasse* (thieves': *soulas*, Old French = 'solace' or 'comfort'); *rebâtir un pante* (thieves'); *sonner* (popular); *lingrer* (popular); *envoyer ad patres* (popular = 'to send to one's fathers'); *envoyer en paradis* (general = 'to send to kingdom-come'); *envoyer en parade* (thieves' = 'to send on parade'); *capahuter* (thieves' = to get rid of an accomplice to secure his share of the booty; sometimes rendered by *refroidir à la capahut*); *décrocher* (military: literally 'to unhook' 'to take down'); *descendre quelqu'un* (popular = to bring down); *couper le sifflet* (popular = to cut one's whistle); *watriniser* (popular: in reference to M. Watrin, who was murdered by the Decazeville miners in 1886. *Cf.*, the English 'to burke'); *moucher le quinquet* (popular: 'to snuff the lamp'); *faire saigner du nez* (thieves' = 'to give a bloody nose'); *sabler* (thieves'); *faire banque* (common); *suager* (thieves': from *suer*, 'to sweat').

GERMAN SYNONYMS. *Abfetzen* (to kill by cutting or stabbing); *abmeken*, *abmacken* (Hebrew *mocho* = to put aside, to destroy, or to give 'tit for tat.' North German *afmurksen*); *bekern machen* (from the Hebrew *peger*. Used of animals it is the equivalent of *krepieren*); *hargenen* or *horeg sein* ('to kill' or 'murder.' *Horeg*, the murderer; *Horug*, the murdered; *nehrog*, murdered; *nehrog werden*, to be murdered; *Hereg* or *Harigo*, the murder); *heimthun*, or *heimerlich spielen* (*heim*, a corruption of the Hebrew *chajim* = life); *Kappore machen* or *fetzen* (literally 'to make purified.' From the Hebrew *kophar*); *memissen* or *mĕmissren*; *die Neschome nehmen* (Hebrew *neschomo*, the soul or life); *pegern* or *peigern*; *rozechenen* or *rozchenen* (Hebrew, *rozach* = to kill); *schächten* (Hebrew, *schochat*).

ITALIAN SYNONYM. *Sbasire* (literally 'to cause to faint' or 'swoon.' *Sbasire su le funi* = to swoon on the rope, *i.e.*, to be hanged).

SPANISH SYNONYMS. *Apretar á uno la nuez* (properly to clutch the Adam's apple, *i.e.*, the throat); *apiolar* (properly 'to gyve a hawk' or 'to tie game together by the legs'; and metaphorically, 'to seize' or apprehend); *despabilar* (literally 'to snuff a candle.' *Cf.*, Fr. *moucher le quinquet* and the Eng. 'to put on an extinguisher'); *apercollar* (also, 'to seize one by the collar').

1851-61. H. MAYHEW, *London Lab. and Lon. Poor*, vol. III., p. 360. When the clarences, the cabs that carry four, came in, they COOKED the hackney-coachmen in no time.

1853. REV. E. BRADLEY ('Cuthbert Bede'), *Adventures of Verdant Green*, p. 270. Billy's too big in the Westphalia's gig-lamps, you're the boy to COOK Fosbrooke's GOOSE.

1861. A. TROLLOPE, *Framley Parsonage*, ch. xlii. Chaldicotes, Gagebee, is a COOKED GOOSE, as far as Sowerby is concerned. And what difference could it make to him whether the Duke is to own it or Miss Dunstable.

1865. G. A. SALA, *Trip to Barbary*, ch. v. The first Napoleon . . . once nearly killed himself by his addictedness to Provençal cookery. Yes; a mess of mutton and garlic—'tis said it was poisoned—very nearly COOKED THE GOOSE of Achilles.

1877. *Five Years' Penal Servitude*, ch. ii., p. 128. Seeing how the fellow was acting he sent him two 'shise' notes, which gave him a dose that COOKED him. I saw the man myself, serving his time at Dartmoor.

1888. *Puck's Library*, May, p. 10. When the chromo first emerged from chaos, the producers of that kind of picture insisted that the GOOSE of the artist was COOKED.

COOKEY or **COOKIE**. To BET A COOKIE, *verbal phr.* (American).—The custom of preparing the cakes still known in Scotland as COOKIES was part and parcel of American life. [The COOKEY, like the English pancake on Shrove Tuesday, and the hot cross bun on Good Friday, forms a special old-fashioned dainty at Christmas-tide and New Year. From the Dutch *kœkje*, dim. of *kœk*, a cake.]

1870. BRET HARTE, *Luck of Roaring Camp*, p. 227. Don't know what he is! He lost every hoof and hide, I'll BET A COOKEY!

1872. *Lloyd's Weekly*, 28 April. 'Probate Court Report.' Might have said she would BET A COOKEY that the will was in America. (Laughter.)

1888. *Detroit Free Press*, 31 March. A book has just been published to instruct reporters in the use of proper phrases. We BET A COOKEY no reporter will ever read it.

COOKEYSHINE, *subs.* (old Scots).—An afternoon meal at which COOKIES (*q.v.*) form a staple dish. *Cf.*, TEA-FIGHT, MUFFIN-WORRY, etc. (*q.v.*). [From COOKEY, a small cake, + SHINE (*q.v.*), an entertainment.]

1863. C. READE, *Hard Cash*, I., 103. Dr. Sampson, *loq.*: We shall see whether we are on the right system: and if so, we'll dose her with useful society in a more irrashinal forrm; conversazionys, COOKEYSHINES, et cetera. And if we find ourselves on the wrong tack, why then we'll hark back.

COOK-RUFFIAN, *subs.* (old).—A bad or indifferent cook, 'who would cook the devil in his feathers.'

COOL, *adj.* (colloquial).—1. Impertinent; audacious; calmly impudent.

1870. *Figaro*, 22 May. It is considered to be COOL to take a man's hat with his name written in it, simply because you want to get his autograph.

COOL AS A CUCUMBER, *phr.* (common).—Without heat; also, metaphorically, calm and composed.

2. (In reference to money; *e.g.*, a COOL hundred, thousand, etc.) Commonly expletive; but sometimes used to cover a sum a little above the figure stated.

1750. FIELDING, *Tom Jones*, bk. VIII., ch. xii. Mr. Watson, too, after much variety of luck, rose from the table in some heat, and declared he had lost a COOL hundred, and would play no longer.

1771. SMOLLETT, *Humphry Clinker*, I. 41. I'll bet a COOL hundred he swings before Christmas.

1825. MISS EDGEWORTH, *Love and Law*, i., 2. Suppose you don't get sixpence costs, and lose your COOL hundred by it, still it's a great advantage.

1841. LYTTON, *Night and Morning*, bk. II., ch. x. Borrowed his money under pretence of investing it in the New Grand Anti-Dry-Rot Company; COOL hundred—it's only just gone, sir.

1890. *Illustrated Bits*, 29 March, p. 8, col. 2. I made three thousand last year, but if I have good luck this year I shall make a COOL fifty thousand.

3. (Eton College).—*See* COOL KICK and the following.

Verb (Eton College).—To kick hard.

COOL-CRAPE, *subs.* (old).—A shroud, or winding sheet.—*Grose.*

COOLER, *subs.* (old).—1. A woman.—*Grose* [1785]. For synonyms, *see* PETTICOAT.

1742. CHARLES JOHNSON, *Highwaymen and Pyrates* p. 293. 'Not I,' replied Jones, very readily, 'I neither know nor

care who you are, tho' before you spoke I took you for a brewer because you travel with your COOLER by your side.'

2. (American thieves').—A prison. For synonyms, *see* CAGE.

3. (common).—Ale or stout after spirits and water. Sometimes called 'putting the beggar on the gentleman'; also DAMPER (*q.v.*).

1821. P. EGAN, *Tom and Jerry* (ed. 1890), p. 76. Many persons . . . in order to allay the heat or thirst arising from the pernicious use of such quantities of ardent spirits, frequently take a glass of porter, which is termed a COOLER, 'a damper,' etc.

COOL-KICK, *subs.* (Eton College).—When a BEHIND (*q.v.*) or 'back' gets a kick with no one up to him.

COOL-LADY, *subs.* (old).—A female follower of the camp who sells brandy.—*Grose* [1785].

COOL-NANTZ, *subs.* (old).—Brandy. For synonyms, *see* DRINKS.

COOL ONE'S COPPERS, *verbal phr.* (popular).—To allay the morning's thirst after a night of drink. *Cf.*, HOT-COPPERS and DRY AS A LIME BASKET.

1861. T. HUGHES, *Tom Brown at Oxford*, ch. iii. We were playing Van John in Blake's rooms till three last night, and he gave us devilled bones and mulled port. A fellow can't enjoy his breakfast after that without something TO COOL HIS COPPERS.

1870. *Sportsman*, 17 Dec. 'A Chapel Meeting.' Bring me a mouthful, George, shouted a grasping Typo one day to his chum, who, at the trough in the furthest corner of the room, was COOLING HIS COPPERS with cold water.

COON, *subs.* (American).—1. A man. [COON, a curtailment of 'racoon' (*Procyon lotor*), is thought to be of Indian origin (Algonquin, *aroughcun*, the scratcher), though some trace it to the French *raton*. The contraction dates from about 1840, when the racoon was used as a kind of political totem.]

1860. *Punch*, vol. XXXIX., p. 227. 'The Baby in the House.' I sign him, said the Curate Howe, O'er Samuel Burbott George Bethune, Then baby kicked up such a row As terrified that reverend COON.

2. (American). — A nigger, *e.g.*, a coons' bawdy house = a house where none are kept but girls of colour.

GONE COON, *subs. phr.* (American).—One in a serious or hopeless difficulty. A Scots equivalent is GONE CORBIE, *i.e.*, a dead crow. *Cf.*, GONE GOOSE. [The explanation generally given is that during the American War a spy dressed in racoon skins ensconced himself in a tree. An English rifleman (the nationalities are reversible) levelled his piece at him, whereupon the American exclaimed: 'Don't shoot, I'll come down. I know I am a GONE COON.']

1845. MR. GIDDINGS, in Congress (quoted in De Vere). Besides the acquisition of Canada, which is put down on all sides as a GONE COON.

1857. DICKENS, *Lying Awake*, in *Reprinted Pieces*, p. 192. I must think of something else as I lie awake; or, like that sagacious animal in the United States who recognised the colonel who was such a dead shot, I am a GONE COON.

1864. *Derby Day*, p. 51. We shan't get to your advice till the crack's *hocussed and done for*, and we're all RUINED AS SAFE AS COONS.

1867. *London Herald*, 23 March, p. 221, col. 3. 'We're safe to nab him; safe as houses. He's a GONE COON, sir.'

1883. CALVERLEY, *Fly Leaves*, p. 83. 'On the Brink.' She stood so calm, so like a ghost, Betwixt me and that magic moon, That I already was almost A FINISHED COON.

TO GO THE WHOLE COON, *verbal phr.* (American). = 'To go the whole hog.'

COON'S AGE, *subs. phr.* (American).—A long time; 'a blue moon.' The racoon is held to be a long-lived animal.

b. 1780, *d.* 1851. AUDUBON, *Life*, I., p. 178. 'Wall, Pete, whar have you been? I hav'n't seen you this COON'S AGE.'

COOP, *subs.* (thieves').—A prison. For synonyms, *see* CAGE.

1866. *London Miscellany*, 3 Mar., p. 58, col. 3. I don't think that's no little letdown for a cove as has been tip-topper in his time, and smelt the insides of all the COOPS in the three kingdoms.

1877. J. GREENWOOD, *Dick Temple.* You say that you have been in the COOP as many times as I have.

COOPED-UP, *ppl., adj., phr.* (old).—Imprisoned. [From COOP (*q.v.*), a place of detention.] For synonyms, *see* LIMBO.

COOPER or **COOPER UP**, *verb* (thieves' and vagrants').—1. To destroy; spoil; settle; or finish.

2. (thieves').—To forge.

3. (American).—To understand. For synonyms, *see* TWIG.

COOPERED, *ppl. adj.* (racing, thieves', and vagrants').—Hocussed; spoiled; ruined; *e.g.*, a house is said to be COOPERED when the importunity of many tramps has caused its inmates to cold-shoulder the whole fraternity; a COOPERED horse is a horse that has been 'got at' with a view to prevent its running.

1851-61. H. MAYHEW, *London Lab. and Lon. Poor*, vol. I., p. 232. 'COOPER'D,' spoiled by the imprudence of some other patterer.

COORED, *adj.* (old).—Whipped.—D. HAGGART, *Life*, Glossary, p. 171 [1821].

COOT, *subs.* (American).—A stupid fellow; generally 'a silly' or 'mad old COOT.' Stupid as a COOT is a common English provincialism. [The *fulica altra*, the bald or common COOT, like the ostrich, is said to bury its head when pursued, thinking none can see it, as it cannot see itself.] For synonyms, *see* BUFFLE-HEAD and CABBAGE-HEAD.

COOTER.—*See* COUTER.

COP, *subs.* (common).—A policeman. [From COP, *verb*, sense 1.] For synonyms, *see* BEAK, sense 1, and COPPER.

1859. MATSELL, *Vocabulum, or Rogue's Lexicon*, p. 124. Oh! where will be the culls of the bing . . . And all the COPS and beaks so knowin', A hundred stretches hence?

1879. *Punch*, 3 May, p. 201, col. 1. I suppose if the Toffs took a fancy for chewing a stror or a twig, Like a tout or a hostler, or tumbled to carryin' a bludgeon as big As a crib cracker's nobby persuader, Pall Mall would be jolly soon gay With blue-blooded blokes a green COP might mistake for foot-pads on the lay.

Verb (common).—1. To seize; steal; catch; take an unfair advantage in a bet or bargain. [COP has been associated with the root of the Latin *cap-io*, to seize, to snatch; also with the Gypsy *kap* or *cop* = to take; Scotch *kep*; and Gallic *ceapan*. Probably, however, its true radix is to be found in the Hebrew *cop* = a hand or palm. Low-class Jews employ the term, and understand it to refer to the act of snatching.]

[COP like CHUCK (*q.v.*), is a sort of general utility verb. Thus to COP THE

Needle = to get angry; to Cop the Bullet or the door = to get the sack; to Cop it Hot = to be severely clapped; to Cop it (said of women) = to be got with child; and to Cop the Brewer = to be drunk.]

For synonyms in the sense of to steal, *see* Prig; and in the sense of to seize, *see* Nab.

1864. *Manchester Courier*, 13 June. 'Copper' . . . a slang name for a policeman derived from cop, which is a well known and generally used vulgarism for 'catch.'

1879. J. W. Horsley, in *Macm. Mag.*, XL., p. 500. I was taken by two pals (companions) to an orchard to cop (steal) some fruit.

1883. *Punch*, Sept. 29, p. 146, col. 2. 'Bill's not such a fool as you think; He'll cop my truncheon, pat, Jam the whistle into my mouth, And stretch the Peeler flat.'

1887. W. E. Henley, *Villon's Straight Tip to all Cross Coves.* Booze and the blowens cop the lot.

2. *trs.* and *intrs.* (thieves').—To arrest; imprison; betray; ensnare.

English Synonyms. To give the clinch; to make one kiss the clink; to accommodate; to nobble; to bag; to box; to fist (old); to scoop; to take up; to victimize; to run in; to give or get one the boat; to buckle; to smug; to nab; to collar; to pinch; to nail; to rope in; to snake; to pull up.

French Synonyms. *Empioler* (thieves'); *tomber au plan* (thieves' = to be apprehended); *être mis au plan* (thieves' = to be imprisoned); *enfourailler* (thieves'); *bâcler* or *boucler* (thieves': literally to buckle, put a ring to); *bloquer* (military: properly to blockade); *être le bon* (popular = to be arrested; also to be the right man); *boulotter de* or *coucher à la boîte* (military = to get frequently locked up. *La grosse boîte* = a prison; *boîte aux réflexions* = a prison cell); *mettre quelqu'un dans la blouse* (familiar = to 'pocket,' as at billiards); *se faire cuire* (popular = to be arrested); *clouer* (popular: *clou* = guard-room or cell); *coller au bloc* (popular: *coller* is properly to stick, as with glue, but in a slang sense it carries the meaning of to place or put; *bloc* = prison); *piper* (familiar); *poisser* (popular and thieves'); *grimer* (popular); *coquer* (thieves': also, to peach or inform); *enflacquer* (thieves'); *mettre* or *fourrer dedans* (familiar: literally to put inside); *mettre à l'ombre* (common: literally to put in the shade); *mettre au violon* (popular: see *violon* under Cage); *grappiner* (popular); *poser un gluau* (thieves' = to lime, as in snaring birds); *empoigner* (popular = to fist; possibly a dictionary word); *piger* (popular); *emballer* (popular and thieves'; properly to pack up); *gripper* (this has passed into the language); *encoffrer* (popular = to 'box up'); *encager* (familiar = to cage); *accrocher* (properly to hook); *ramasser de la boîte* (military: also *ramasser quelqu'un* and *se faire remasser*); *souffler* (thieves'); *faire tomber malade* (popular = to make one ill); *agrafer* (literally to hook or clasp; *avoir son linge lavé* (thieves' = to have one's linen washed).

German Synonyms.—*Bekaan scheften* (from the Hebrew *kaan*); *im Kühlen sitzen* (literally to sit in the cold. *Cf.*, Fr., *mettre à l'ombre*); *krank werden* (literally

to fall ill; equivalent to the Fr. *faire tomber malade*); *ins Leck baun* (Viennese thieves.' M.H.G. *luken* = to lock up); *millek sein* (to be imprisoned); *trefe fallen* (to be apprehended under grave circumstances; *e.g.*, with burglar's instruments or stolen goods); *versargen* (to imprison for a long time); *abfassen* (students' slang); *ankappen* (popular colloquialism); *klemmen* (M.H.G. *klembern* = to press heavily); *taffen*, *tofes nehmen*, *tofes lokechnen*, or *tofes lekichnen* (from the Hebrew *tophas*); *vercheweln*, *vercheifeln* or *verheifeln* (from the Hebrew *chobal*; also to bind or gag).

Copbusy, *verb* (thieves'). — *See* quot.

1857. Snowden, *Mag. Assistant*, 3 ed., p. 445. To hand over the booty to a confederate or girl—to copbusy.

Copper, *subs.* (popular).—A policeman. [From cop, *verb*, senses 1 and 2, (*q.v.*), to catch, + er; literally a catcher.] Equivalents are robin or robin-redbreast; M.P. (*i.e.*, *member of police*); copperman (an Australian prison term); but for synonyms, *see* Beak, to which may be added the following.

French Synonyms. *Un chasse-coquin* (popular: also = a 'beadle' and 'bad wine.' Literally 'a beggar-driver': *Cf.*, *chasse-chien* = a beadle employed to drive away dogs); *un chasse-noble* (thieves'); *le cadratin* (police; a term applied to the detective force; properly what printers call an 'em quad'); *l'enplaque* (thieves'); *une fauvette à tête noire* (thieves': literally 'a black-cap'); *un bricul* or *briculé* (thieves': an inspector of police); *une casserole* (thieves' = a detective; also a prostitute. Properly 'a saucepan' or warming-pan); *un emballeur* (thieves': properly 'a packer'); *un ficard* (thieves'); *un arnacq* or *arnache* (thieves'); *un vesto de la cuisine* (thieves' = a detective. *Vesto* = haricot bean; *cuisine* = detective force); *rabatteur de pantes* (thieves' = a beater of game, man being the quarry); *un bigorneau* (properly a periwinkle); *un cognac* (thieves'); *un quart* (pop: *faire son quart* = to be on the watch); *un radis noir* (common: also = a priest or devil-dodger); *un renifleur* (thieves': *renifler* = to sniff); *mari Robin* (thieves'); *un marchand* or *solliceur de lacets* (thieves': *lacets* = hand-cuffs); *lapin ferré* (a mounted policeman); *un liège* (thieves').

German Synonyms. *Blaukragen* (Viennese thieves': for an armed policeman; literally 'a blue collar,' in allusion to the uniform); *Blitzableiter* (literally 'the lightning conductor'); *Bosser-Isch* (a play upon words is involved in this term. It is derived from the Hebrew *bosar* = meat. *Bosser-Isch* signifies literally 'meat-man,' *i.e.*, a butcher, or translated into literary German, *Fleischmann*. In the first half of the last century a certain Lieutenant Fleischmann was especially zealous in 'persecuting' the robber gangs infesting the district between Frankfurt and Darmstadt. Every hunter of rogues and vagabonds has since then been called a *Bosser-Isch* or *Fleischmann*. Hence its application to the police); *Greiferci* (specially applied to the 'criminal' police);

Hadatsch or *Hatschier* (Viennese thieves'); *aie Herren* (the police force generally; literally 'the gentlemen'); *Husche*, *Huscher*, *Husskiefel* or *Husskopf* (a mounted policeman); *Iltis* or *Iltisch* (thieves'); *Kapdon* (from the Hebrew *kophad*: literally 'to draw together,' or intransitively 'to cut off'; applied to a clever policeman); *Karten* (the police. *Cf.*, *Garden* = guards); *Koberer* (the officer in charge of the regulations over registered prostitutes; *Koberer* = 'fancy-man,' or 'protector'); *Klisto* (a mounted policeman; from the Hanoverian gypsy *glisto*); *Kreuzritter* (Viennese thieves' = a policeman who is also a soldier; more correctly, a police-soldier); *Laileschmir* (a night policeman; from the Hebrew *lailo*, 'the night'); *Laterne* (Viennese thieves'); *Lederzeug* (a mounted policeman); *Mischpoche* (a Hebrew word signifying 'the family,' 'the relations'; gang of robbers; the inmates of a prison; the police force taken as a whole); *Polenk* or *Polente* (Hanoverian slang for the police; possibly from the Gypsy *polontschero* = 'the night-watchman' or 'herdsman'); *Poliquetsch* (a term applied either to the force or to a single member); *Quetsch* (*Cf.*, foregoing); *Schin* (an abbreviation, being the Hebrew letter ש, for the turnkey of a prison, a policeman, etc.; *ein platter Schin*, a policeman who makes common cause with a burglar; *miser Schin*, a policeman who is hated); *Spinatwächter* (soldiers' for a police-soldier; in allusion to the green uniform); *Spitz* or *Spitzl* (a vigilant policeman, from *Spitz* = pointed, from which is derived *Spitz-bube*, a thief); *Teckel* (Hanoverian for foot-police); *Zaddik* (from the Hebrew signifying 'the just' or 'pious one'; used sarcastically as a nickname for the guardians of the right); *Zenserei* (Viennese thieves'; *Zenserer* = a police superintendent. Apparently the modern form of the old *Sens*, *Sins*, *Söns*, *Sims*, or *Simser*, of which the derivation is clearly to be found in *Zent* or *Cent*, from the *Centenæ* of the Frankish kings, who divided the counties into *Centenæ* and *Decaniæ* for the purposes of administration).

Italian Synonyms. *Falcon de draghetti* (literally 'a hawk preying on schoolboys'); *sbirre*.

Spanish Synonym. *Abrazador* (*m*; literally 'one who embraces'; *abrazar* = to hug, or clasp).

1859. Matsell, *Vocabulum, or Rogue's Lexicon*, p. 21. 'The knuck was copped to rights, a skin full of honey was found in his kick's poke by the copper when he frisked him'; [*i.e.*] the pick-pocket was arrested, and when searched by the officer a purse was found in his pantaloons pocket full of money.

1864. *Manchester Courier*, 13 June. The professors of slang, however, having coined the word, associate that with the metal, and as they pass a policeman they will, to annoy him, exhibit a copper coin, which is equivalent to calling the officer copper.

1877. *Five Years' Penal Servitude*, ch. iii., p. 237. I daresay the coppers quite expected us the next night, and looked out for us. . . . Coppers, I may inform the reader, is slang for police.

1889. *Punch*, 3 Aug., p. 49, col. 2. Young 'Opkins took the reins, but soon in slumber he was sunk—(*Indignantly*) When a interfering copper ran us in for being drunk!

Copperheads, *subs.* (American).—A nickname applied to different sections of the American nation: first to the Indian; then to the Dutch colonist (*see* Irving, *Knickerbocker*); lastly, during the Civil War, to certain Northern Democrats who sympathised with the South. [Properly the *Trigonocephalus contortrix.*]

1864. Walt. Whitman, *Diary*, 10 April [in *Century Mag.*, Oct., 1888]. Exciting times in Congress. The copperheads are getting furious, and want to recognise the Southern Confederacy.

1872. *Daily Telegraph*, 29 Aug. Should he [Mr. Greeley] be elected, he will owe his victory to . . . the copperhead ring of the Democratic party.

1881. W. D. Howells, *Dr. Breen's Practice*, ch. ix. He lived to cast a dying vote for General Jackson, and his son, the first Dr. Mulbridge, survived to illustrate the magnanimity of his fellow-townsmen during the first year of the civil war, as a tolerated copperhead.

1888. *Daily Inter-Ocean*, 2 March. Gay was executed, I think, in November, 1862, at Indianapolis. He was . . . a virulent copperhead.

Copperman, *subs.* (Australian prison).—A policeman. *Cf.*, Copper.

Copper-Nose, *subs.* (old).—The swollen, pimply nose of habitual drunkards. A 'jolly' or 'bottle' nose; in Fr., *une bette-rave*, *i.e.*, a beetroot; also *un piton passé à l'encaustique*. *Cf.*, Grog-blossom. For synonyms for the nose generally, *see* Conk.

1822. Scott, *Fortunes of Nigel*, ch. x. 'The stoutest raven dared not come within a yard of that copper nose.

Copper's Nark, *subs.* (thieves').—A police spy; one in the pay of the police. [From copper (*q.v.*), a policeman, + nark, a spy; used as a verb nark signifies to watch or look after.]

1879. Thos. Satchell, in *Notes and Queries*, 5 S., xi., 406. Copper's Nark: A police spy.

1887. W. E. Henley, *Villon's Good Night.* Likewise you coppers' narks and dubs What pinched me when upon the snam.

1889. *Answers*, 20 July, p. 121, col. 1. He instructed me . . . on no account to appear to be anxious to pry into their secrets, lest I should be mistaken for a copper's nark, *i.e.*, a person in the pay of the police.

Copperstick, *subs.* (venery).—The *penis*. For synonyms, *see* Creamstick.

Copus, *subs.* (Univ.).—A wine or beer cup, which was commonly imposed as a fine upon those who talked Latin in hall or committed other breaches of etiquette. Dr. Johnson derives it from *episcopus*, and if this be correct it is doubtless the same as Bishop.

Copy of Countenance, *subs. phr.* (old).—A sham; humbug; pretence.

1579. Gosson, *Apol. of the Schoole of Abuse*, p. 64 (Arber). They have eaten bulbief, and threatned highly, too put water in my woortes, whensoeuer they catche me; I hope it is but a coppy of their countenance.

1607. Dekker, *Westward Ho*, Act ii., Sc. 1. I shall love a puritan's face the worse, whilst I live, for that copy of thy countenance.

1637. Fletcher, *Elder Brother*, V., i. Nor can I change my copy, if I purpose to be of your society.

1754. Fielding, *Jonathan Wild*, bk. III., ch. xiv. This, as he afterwards confessed on his death-bed, *i.e.*, in the court at Tyburn, was only a copy of his countenance; for that he was at that time as sincere and hearty in his opposition to Wild as any of his companions.

1756. Foote, *Englishman from Paris*, Act i. And if the application for my advice is not a copy of your countenance, a mask; if you are obedient, I may set you right.

CORAL BRANCH, *subs. phr.* (venery).—The *penis*.

CORE, COREING, *verb* and *verbal subs.* (old).—*See* quot.

1821. D. HAGGART, *Life*, Glossary, p. 171. COREING: picking up small articles in shops.

CORINTH, *subs.* (old).—A brothel. For synonyms, *see* NANNY-SHOP. *Cf.*, CORINTHIAN and CORINTHIANISM.

1609. SHAKSPEARE, *Timon of Athens*, Act ii., Sc. 2. Would we could see you at Corinth!

1785. GROSE, *Dict. Vulg. Tongue*, s.v.

1859. MATSELL, *Vocabulum, or Rogue's Lexicon*, s.v.

CORINTHIAN, *subs.* (old).—1. A rake; a loose liver; sometimes specifically, a fashionable whore. Shakspeare has it, 'a lad of mettle,' but in another place he uses CORINTH as above. In the slang sense an allusion to the notoriety of Corinth as a centre of prostitution, *i.e.*, the temple-city of Aphrodite. **Κορινθιάζεσθαι**, = to CORINTHIANISE was Greek slang. Hence the proverb—**Οὐ παντὸς ἀνδρὸς εἰς Κόρινθον ισθ' ὁ πλοῦς**: and *Horace*, Epist. lib. 1, xvii., 36—

'Non cuivis homini contingit adire Corinthum.'

Also used as an adjective, a verbal form being TO CORINTHIANIZE. *Cf.*, Shakspeare's use of EPHESIANS in II. King Henry IV., ii. 2. For synonyms, *see* MOLROWER.

1598. SHAKSPEARE, *I Henry IV.*, Act ii., Sc. 4. And tell me flatly I am no proud Jack, like Falstaff; but a CORINTHIAN, a lad of mettle, a good boy.

b. 1608. *d.* 1674. MILTON, *Apology for Smect.* And raps up, without pity, the sage and rheumatic old prelatess, with all her young CORINTHIAN laity.

1890. *Daily Telegraph*, 25 Feb., p. 4, col. 7. Is it not curious that hotel proprietors [at Monte Carlo] should countenance, if not encourage, a Tom and Jerry tone and a wild CORINTHIAN element, even in well-conducted restaurants?

1890. HENLEY AND STEVENSON, *Beau Austin*, iii., 1. I assure you, Aunt Evelina, we are CORINTHIAN to the last degree.

2. A dandy; specifically applied in the early part of the present century to a man of fashion; *e.g.*, CORINTHIAN Tom, in Pierce Egan's *Life in London*. For synonyms, *see* DANDY.

1785. GROSE, *Dict. Vulg. Tongue*, s.v.

1819. T. MOORE, *Tom Crib's Memorial*, p. 9. 'Twas diverting to see, as one *ogled* around, How CORINTHIANS and *Commoners* mixed on the ground.

1832. PIERCE EGAN, *Book of Sports*, p. 210. 'I would be a CORINTHIAN to the end of the chapter if I could—but the truth is, I was not lucky enough to be born a swell.'

1853. WH. MELVILLE, *Digby Grand*, ch. iv. Where the hospitable 'Jem' received his more aristocratic visitors, and to which, as CORINTHIANS, or 'swells,' we were immediately admitted.

1854. THACKERAY, *Leech's Pictures* in *Quarterly Review*, No. 191, Dec. CORINTHIAN, it appears, was the phrase applied to men of fashion and ton . . . they were the brilliant predecessors of the 'swell' of the present period.

CORINTHIANISM, *subs.* (old and modern).—*See* CORINTHIAN, in both senses of which, *mutatis mutandis*, CORINTHIANISM is employed.

CORK, *subs.* (common).—1. A bankrupt. For analogous terms, *see* QUIZBY.

2. (Scotch).—The general name in Glasgow and neighbourhood for the head of an establishment, *e.g.*, of a factory, or the like.

TO DRAW A CORK, *verbal phr.* (pugilistic).—To draw blood. A variant is TO TAP ONE'S CLARET.

1818. P. EGAN, *Boxiana*, vol. I., p. 136. Severa blows exchanged, but no CORKS were DRAWN.

1819. THOS. MOORE, *Tom Crib's Mem. to Cong.*, p. 25. . . . This being the first Royal *claret* let flow, Since Tom *took* the Holy Alliance *in tow*, The UNCORKING produced much sensation about, As bets had been *flush* on the first *painted snout*.

1837. S. WARREN, *Diary of a Late Physician*, ch. xii. Tap his claret cask—DRAW HIS CORK!

CORK-BRAINED, *adj. phr.* (old).—Light headed; foolish.

CORKER, *subs.* (common).—1. That which closes an argument, or puts an end to a course of action; a SETTLER; a FINISHER (*q.v.*); specifically a lie. *Cf.*, WHOPPER.

2. Anything unusually large, or of first-rate quality; remarkable in some respect or another; *e.g.*, a heavy blow; a monstrous lie.—*See* WHOPPER.

1835. HALIBURTON, *Clockmaker*, 1 S., ch. xix. 'Then I lets him have it, right, left, right, jist three CORKERS, beginning with the right hand, shifting to the left, and then with the right hand ag'in.'

TO PLAY THE CORKER.—To indulge in the uncommon; to exhibit exaggerated peculiarities of demeanour; specifically in school and university slang to make oneself objectionable to one's fellows.

1882. F. ANSTEY, *Vice Versâ*, ch. vii. 'Why, you're sticking up for him now!' said Tom . . . astonished at this apparent change of front. 'If you choose to come back and PLAY THE CORKER like this, it's your look-out.'

CORKS, *subs.* (general).—1. A butler. [An allusion to one of the duties of the office.] *Cf.*, BURN-CRUST, a baker; MASTER OF THE MINT, a gardener; CINDER-GARBLER, a maid-of-all-work, etc.

2. (nautical).—Money. [A facetious allusion to money as the means of 'keeping afloat.'] For synonyms, *see* ACTUAL and GILT.

CORKSCREWING, *verbal subs.* (common).—The straggling, spiral walk of tipsiness.

CORKSCREWS, *subs. pl.* (general)—Very stiff and formal curls, once called BOTTLE-SCREWS.

1890. *Notes and Queries*, 5 April. BOTTLE-SCREWS.—Dr. Murray has this word in the *N.E.D.* as obsolete, meaning CORK-SCREWS, as we now call them.

CORKY, *adj.* (colloquial).—Sprightly; lively. [An allusion to the buoyancy of a cork.] Shakspeare uses it in *King Lear*, iii., 7. *Com.*, 'Bind fast his CORKY arms'; but with him (1605) it = 'withered.'

CORN, *subs.* (American).—1. Food; sustenance; GRUB. [A figurative usage of the legitimate word.]

1870. *Green Bay* (Wis.) *Gaz.*, Oct. I therefore take thus to forewarn You not to trust her with a straw, For I will never pay her CORN Unless compelled to by the law.

2. (American).—An abbreviated form of CORN-JUICE (*q.v.*), *i.e.*, whiskey.

1843. JOHN S. ROBB. 'The Standing Candidate.' 'Ef you war a babby, just new born, 'Twould do you good this juicy CORN!

TO ACKNOWLEDGE THE CORN, *phr.* (American).—*See* ACKNOWLEDGE, and the following quote:

1846. *New York Herald*, 27 June. The Evening Mirror very naively comes out and ACKNOWLEDGES THE CORN, admits that a demand was made, etc.

CORNED, *ppl. adj.* (common).—1. Drunk. [HOTTEN: 'possibly from soaking or pickling oneself like salt-beef.' BARRÈRE: 'almost beyond doubt . . . an Americanism from CORN, a very common name for whisky.' Both are wrong; the verb 'to corn' is a common provincialism and Scotticism signifying 'to be drunk.'] For synonyms, *see* SCREWED.

1785. GROSE, *Dict. Vulg. Tongue*, s.v.

1808. JAMIESON, *Etymolog. Dict. Scottish Lang.* The lads are weel CORNED.

1835. HALIBURTON, *The Clockmaker*, p. 257 (ed. 1862). 'I was pretty well CORNED thet arternoon, but still I knew what I was about.'

2. (sailors').—Pleased.

CORNER, *subs.* (colloquial).—1. —*See verbal* sense.

1884. HAWLEY SMART, *From Post to Finish*, p. 309. Mr. Bill Greyson thought it much more likely that a syndicate of bookmakers had plotted to make a good thing out of the horse by working him in the betting-market like any other CORNER on the Stock Exchange.

2. (sporting).—Tattersall's Subscription Rooms once situate at the top of Grosvenor Place, near Hyde Park Corner; now removed to Albert Gate, but still known by the old nickname.

1848. W. M. THACKERAY, *Book of Snobs*, ch. x. He is a regular attendant at the CORNER, where he compiles a limited but comfortable libretto.

1874. G. A. LAWRENCE, *Hagarene*, ch. v. She heard how—without anticipating the stable commission, or making any demonstration at the CORNER—the cream of the long odds against the Pirate had been skimmed.

3. (sporting).—Short for Tattenham Corner, a crucial point on the Derby course on Epsom Downs.

4. (thieves').—A share; an opportunity of 'standing in' for the proceeds of a robbery.

Verb (colloquial).—To get control of a stock or commodity and so monopolize the market; applied to persons, to drive or force into a position of difficulty or surrender, *e.g.*, in an argument. [Probably American, being a simple extension of the legitimate meaning of the word to drive or force into a corner or place from which there is no means of escape.] French equivalents are *être en fine pègrène*, and *se mettre sur les fonts de baptême*. Tailors speak of a man as CORNERED who has pawned work entrusted to him, and cannot redeem it. Also used as a *ppl. adj.*

1848. LOWELL, *Fable for Critics*, p. 24. Such [books] as Crusoe might dip in, altho' there are few so Outrageously CORNERED by fate as poor Crusoe.

1851. HAWTHORNE, *House of Seven Gables*, ch. v. A recluse, like Hepzibah, usually displays remarkable frankness, and at least temporary affability, on being absolutely CORNERED, and brought to the point of personal intercourse.

1883. *Graphic*, April 21, p. 406, col. 2. Chief member of a ring which has CORNERED colza oil this winter to such an extent that the price has been very considerably enhanced during the last few months.

TO BE ROUND THE CORNER, *verbal phr.* (common).—To get round or ahead of one's fellows

by dishonest cuts, doublings, twists, and turns. For synonyms, *see* KNOWING.

TO TURN THE CORNER, *phr.* (common).—To get over the worst; to begin to mend in health or fortune.

TO BE CORNERED, *verbal phr.* (common).—To be in a 'fix.' Fr., *être dans le lac.*

CORNER-MAN OR COVE, *subs.* (common).—1. A loafer; literally a lounger at corners.

1851. H. MAYHEW, *Lon. Lab. and Lon. Poor*, IV., 445. I mean by CORNER-COVES them sort of men who is always a standing at the corners of the streets and chaffing respectable folks a-passing by!

1885. *Chamb. Journal*, Feb. 28, p. 136. Curley Bond was well known in the district as a loafer and CORNER-MAN.

2. (music hall).—The 'Bones' and 'Tambourine' in a band of negro minstrels.

CORN IN EGYPT, *subs. phr.* (colloquial).—Plenty of all kinds. [Biblical.]

CORNISH DUCK, *subs.* (trade).—A pilchard. *Cf.*, YARMOUTH CAPON.

CORN-JUICE, *subs.* (American).—Whiskey. For synonyms, *see* DRINKS.

1888. *Detroit Free Press*, May. . . . Don't be for ever loafing whar the CORN-JUICE flows.

CORNSTALK, *subs.* (Australian).—Generic for persons of European descent, but especially applied to girls. The children of Anglo-Australians are generally taller and slighter in build than their parents. Originally a native of New South Wales; now general. *Cf.*, BANANALANDER.

1885. *Chambers' Journal*, March 21, p. 191. The stockman—a young six-foot CORNSTALK (or native of New South Wales).

1887. G. L. APPERSON, in *All the Year Round*, 30 July, p. 67, col. 2. A native of New South Wales is known as a CORNSTALK.

1888. *Colonies and India*, 14 Nov. Auld Jamie Inglis has written 'anither buik, ye ken' . . . . for the delectation of the youthful CORNSTALK'S mind.

CORNSTEALERS, *subs.* (American).—The hands. For synonyms, *see* BUNCH OF FIVES and DADDLE.

1835. HALIBURTON ('Sam Slick'), *The Clockmaker*. 'How is you been, my old bullock?' and he squeezed his CORNSTEALERS till the old gineral began to dance like a bear on red-hot iron.

CORNY-FACED, *adj.* (old).—Red and pimply with drink. [From CORN, to render intoxicated, + FACED.]

CORONER, *subs.* (common).—A severe fall. [Literally a fall likely to produce a coroner's inquest.]

CORPORAL, TO MOUNT A CORPORAL AND FOUR, *verbal phr.* (old).—To practice masturbation.—*See* FRIG.

CORPORATION, *subs.* (colloquial).—A protuberant stomach. For synonyms, *see* BREAD-BASKET and VICTUALLING OFFICE.

1785. GROSE, *Dict. Vulg. Tongue.*

1849. C. BRONTË, *Shirley*, ch. xvi. The former, looming large in full canonicals, walking as became a beneficed priest, under the canopy of a shovel hat, with the dignity of an ample CORPORATION.

1887. W. P. FRITH, *Autobiog.*, i., 49. Very stout men . . . . each possessing larger CORPORATIONS than are commonly seen.

CORPSE, *subs.* (sporting).—A horse in the betting for market purposes alone; otherwise A STIFF'UN.—*See* COCK, *subs.*, sense 4.

Verb (theatrical).—1. To confuse; 'to queer'; to blunder and so 'put out' one's fellows: to spoil a scene.—*See* REGULAR CORPSER.

1864. HOTTEN, *Slang Dict.*, s.v.

1886. *Graphic*, April 10, p. 399. An actor who forgets his words is said to 'stick,' or be 'CORPSED.'

1886. *Cornhill Mag.*, Oct., p. 436. He expressed a hope that Miss Tudor 'wouldn't CORPSE his business' over the forge-door again that evening.

2. (common).—To kill (literally to make a corpse of one). A Fr. equivalent is *parler sur quelqu'un*. For synonyms, *see* COOK ONE'S GOOSE.

1884. EDITOR of *Notes and Queries* [in 'Answers to Correspondents' (6 S., ix., 120), says that]. 'To CORPSE . . . is one of many customary and coarse ways of menacing the infliction of death. It is horribly familiar in London.'

1887. W. E. HENLEY AND R. L. STEVENSON, *Deacon Brodie*, Act 4. MOORE. And is he thundering well CORPSED? . . . Then damme, I don't mind swinging.

CORPSE-PROVIDER, *subs.* (common). —A doctor or physician. For synonyms, *see* CROCUS.

CORPSE REVIVER, *subs. phr.* (American). — A mixed drink.—*See* DRINKS.

1871. *Birmingham Daily Post*, 22 Dec. And our American refreshment bars, In drinks of all descriptions cut a dash, From CORPSE REVIVERS down to 'brandy smash.'

1883. *Daily Telegraph*, March 8, p. 7, col. 1. In winter the dash into the open air or the standing for a few minutes in a line of comrades will certainly enhance the joys of the English equivalents for the Yankee CORPSE REVIVER.

CORRECT or **K'RECT CARD**.—*See* CARD.

CORROBOREE, *subs.* (Australian).—A disturbance. [Properly a tremendous native dance.]

Verb. — To boil. — *See* preceding.

CORSICAN, *subs.* (sporting).—Something out of the common; a 'buster.' [A 'Burnandism.']

1889. *Polytechnic Mag.*, 18 April, p. 232, col. 2. This heat was a CORSICAN.

CORYBUNGUS, *subs.* (pugilistic).—The posteriors.—*See* BLIND CHEEKS, BUM, and MONOCULAR EYE GLASS.

COSH, *subs.* (popular and thieves'). —A 'neddy'; a life-preserver; a short, loaded bludgeon. Also a policeman's truncheon.

COSOUSE.—*See* COME SOUSE.

COSSACK, *subs.* (common).—A policeman. For synonyms, *see* BEAK and COPPER.

1886. *Graphic*, Jan. 30, p. 130, col. 1. A policeman is also called a 'COSSACK,' a 'Philistine,' and a 'frog.'

COSTARD, *subs.* (old).—The head. [Properly an apple.] For synonyms, *see* CRUMPET.

1534. N. UDALL, *Roister Doister*, III., v., p. 58 (Arber). I knocke youre COSTARDE if ye offer to strike me.

1605. SHAKSPEARE, *King Lear*, Act iv. Sc. 6. *Edg.* . . . Nay, come not near th' old man; keep out, che vor ye, or ise try whether your COSTARD or my bat be the harder.

1787. GROSE, *Prov. Glossary*, COSTARD, the head; a kind of opprobrious word, used by way of contempt, probably alluding to a costard apple.

1817. SCOTT, *Rob Roy*, ch. xii. 'It's hard I should get raps over the COSTARD.'

COTCH, *verb* (vulgar).—To catch. [A corruption.] Also *ppl. adj.*, COTCHED.

1889. *Pall Mall Gaz.*, Oct. 12, p. 5, col. 2. Taken before some French beak whom he did not know, and an interpreter brought, the COTCHED culprit was made to pay 20 f.

COTS, *subs.* (Christ's Hospital).—*See* quot. [A corruption of 'cotton.']

1810. CHARLES LAMB, *Recollections of Christ's Hospital* [1835], p. 24. The COTS, or superior Shoe Strings of the Monitors.

COTSOLD or **COTSWOLD LION**, *subs. phr.* (old).—A sheep. Mentioned by Ray in his proverbs. For synonyms, *see* WOOL-BIRD.

1615. HARINGTON, *Epigrams*, bk. III., ep. 18. Lo then the mystery from whence the name Of COTSOLD LYONS first to England came.

COTTON-LORD or **KING**, *subs.* (common).—A wealthy cotton manufacturer.

1883. HAWLEY SMART, *Hard Lines*, ch. xix. 'But, Mr. Fulsby [a Manchester man], the country will never . . . do away with the army because you COTTON LORDS consider it unnecessary.'

COTTONOPOLIS, *subs.* (general).—Manchester. [In allusion to the staple.] *Cf.*, ALBERTOPOLIS, CUBITOPOLIS, HYGEIAPOLIS.

1884. *Echo*, May 12, p. 4, col. 2. For the big race [Manchester Cup] at COTTONOPOLIS a fine lot are let in.

COTTONS, *subs.* (Stock Exchange). —Confederate Bonds. [From the staple of the Southern States.]

COTTON TO, *verb* (common).—To take a fancy to; to unite with; to agree with. In the last sense it is found occasionally in the Elizabethan writers, and is American by survival. [As regards derivation, it comes from the Welsh *cytuno*, to agree, to consent.]

Some French analogues are:—*Avoir un béguin pour quelqu'un* and *avoir un pépin pour une femme*; one who COTTONS TO another is by students called *un colleur*; while concubinage by sheer force of habit is damned as *le collage*.

1582. STANYHURST, *Virgil*, p. 19 (Arber). If this geare COTTEN, what wight wyl yeelde to myn aulters Bright honor and Sacrifice.

1605. *Play of Stucley*, I., 290. John a Nokes and John a Style and I cannot COTTON.

1837. BARHAM, *I. L.* (*The Bagman's Story*). For when once Madam Fortune deals out her hard raps, It's amazing to think, How one COTTONS to drink!

1846. *Punch*, vol. II., p. 12. I agree in the words of Mrs. Judy, who says, 'My dear, I hope one day to see Peel and Cobden COTTON together.

1864. *Derby Day*, p. 152. 'You stop here and COTTON UP TO the gipsies,' exclaimed Charley Brickwood.

1880. OUIDA, *Moths*, ch. vii. 'Ride? Ah! That's a thing I don't COTTON TO anyhow,' said Miss Fuschia Leach, who had found that her talent did not lie that way.

TO DIE WITH COTTON IN ONE'S EARS, *phr.* (obsolete).—*See* quots.

1821. P. EGAN, *Tom and Jerry* [ed 1890), p .92. Many of the most hardened and desperate offenders, from the kindness, attention, and soothing conduct of the Rev. Mr. Cotton [the chaplain at Newgate, 1821], who is indefatigable in administering consolation to their troubled minds, have become the most sincere penitents.

1864. *Athenæum*, 29 Oct., No. 1931. Rev. of *Sl. Dict.* When a late chaplain

of Newgate [Rev. Mr. Cotton] used to attend poor wretches to the scaffold, standing by their side to the last moment, they were said to 'DIE WITH COTTON IN THEIR EARS!' Let us add here, that Rowe invented the phrase 'launched into eternity,' to signify the simple but solemn matter of hanging.

This was by no means the only instance of a popular punning allusion to the name of Cotton. The Jesuit Father Coton, having obtained a great ascendency over Henri IV., it was remarked by that monarch's subjects that, unfortunately, 'HIS EARS WERE STUFFED WITH COTTON.'

COTTON-TOP, *subs.* (obsolete).—A woman loose in fact, but keeping up some sort of appearance. [In allusion to cotton stockings with silk feet.]

COUCH A HOGSHEAD, *verbal phr.* (old).—To lie down and sleep. [COUCH, to lie down, was in common use in Shakspeare's time (*Merry Wives of Windsor*, v., 2). HOGSHEAD = the head.]—*See*, however, quot., 1610, and for synonyms, *see* BALMY.

1567. HARMAN, *Caveat* (1814), p. 66. To COUCH A HOGSHEAD: to ly downe and slepe. *Ibid*, I COUCHED A HOGSHEAD in a skypper this darkemans.

1610. ROWLANDS, *Martin Mark-all*, p. 38 (H. Club's Repr., 1874). COWCH A HOGSHEAD: to lie doune and sleepe; this phrase is like an Alminacke that is out of date: now the duch word to *slope* is with them vsed, to sleepe, and *liggen*, to lie downe.

1671. R. HEAD, *English Rogue*, pt. I., ch. iv., p. 37 (1874). The fumes of drink had now ascended into their brain, wherefore they COUCHT A HOGS-HEAD, and went to sleep.

1706. E. COLES, *Eng. Dict.*, s.v.

1818. SCOTT, *Heart of Midlothian*, ch. xxx. 'We'll COUCH A HOGSHEAD, and so better had you. They retired to repose, accordingly.

COUNCILLOR OF THE PIPOWDER COURT, *subs.* (old).—A pettifogging lawyer. [The Pipowder Court was one held at fairs, where justice was done to any injured person before the dust of the fair was off his feet; the name being derived from the French *pié poudré*. Some, however, think that it had its origin in *pied-pouldreux*, a pedlar, and signifies a pedlars' court.

COUNCIL-OF-TEN, *subs. phr.* (common).—The toes of a man who walks DUCK-FOOTED (*q.v.*). *Cf.*, TEN COMMANDMENTS. Fr., *arpions*.

COUNSELLOR, *subs.* (Irish).—A barrister. Fr., *un gerbier*.

1889. *Answers*, 9 Feb. I referred him to my solicitors, who very kindly lent their services for nothing, giving the £3 he had to the COUNSELLOR (thieves always call barristers COUNSELLORS) employed.

COUNT, *subs.* (common).—A man of fashion; a swell.—*See* quot., 1883, and DANDY for synonyms.

1859. SALA, *Twice Round the Clock*, 6 p.m., par. 20. Tremendous COUNTS are the clerks in the secretary's office, jaunty bureaucrats, who ride upon park hacks, and are 'come for' by ringlets in broughams at closing time.

1883. G. A. S[ALA], in *Ill. London News*, April 21, p. 379, col. 2. Fops flourished before my time, but I can remember the 'dandy,' who was superseded by the COUNT, the 'toff,' and other varieties of the 'swell.

COUNTER, *verb* (pugilistic). — To strike while parrying. Also used as a *verbal subs.*, COUNTERING. Figuratively, to oppose; to circumvent.

1853. C. BEDE, *Verdant Green*, pt. I., p. 106. His kissing traps COUNTERED, his ribs roasted.

1857. O. W. HOLMES, *Autocrat of the Breakfast Table*, ch. vii. He will certainly knock the little man's head off, if he strikes him. Feinting, dodging, stopping, hitting, COUNTERING—little man's head not off yet.

1871. *Daily News*, 17 April, p. 2, col. 2. The Jockey Club met on Wednesday last, when they COUNTERED the Hunt Committee . . . by refusing to father the said 'wrangling stakes' by a majority of eleven to three.

1873. *Conservative*, 15 Feb. If 'The Druid' is the prettier sparrer, 'The Ædile' must be admitted to have shown unexpected powers of COUNTERING, and has stood up gamely to his bigger opponent.

ANOTHER LIE NAILED TO THE COUNTER.—*See* ANOTHER.

COUNTERFEIT-CRANKE, *subs.* (old). — Explained in quots. — *See* CRANKE.

1567. HARMAN, *Caveat*. These that do COUNTERFET THE CRANKE be yong knaves and yonge harlots, that deeply dissemble the falling sickness.

1621. BURTON, *Anatomy of Melancholy*, p. 159. A lawyer of Bruges hath some notable examples of such COUNTERFEIT CRANKS. *Ibid*, 436. Thou art a COUNTERFEIT CRANK, a cheater.

1622. FLETCHER, *Beggar's Bush*, ii., 1. And these, what name or title e'er they bear, Jarkman, or Patrico, CRANKE, or Clapper-dudgeon, Frater, or *Abram-man*, I speak to all That stand in fair election for the title Of king of beggars.

1671. R. HEAD, *English Rogue*, pt. I., ch. v., p. 39 (1874), s.v.

COUNTER-JUMPER (or **SKIPPER**), *subs.* (common).—A draper's assistant; a shopman. Fr., *chevalier du mètre*. For synonyms, *see* KNIGHT OF THE YARD. Also COUNTER-JUMP = to act as a shop-assistant, and COUNTER-JUMPING, *verbal subs.*

1855. C. KINGSLEY, *Westward Ho.* 'Why,' said he, stifling his anger, 'it seems free enough to every COUNTER-JUMPER in the town.'

1860. *Guide to Eton*, p. 236. They are like the young COUNTER-JUMPER, mentioned by Dickens, on the outside of a coach, who lighted a great many cigars, and threw them away when he thought no one was looking.

1863. C. READE, *Hard Cash*, II., 189. Mamma, dear, you open that gigantic wardrobe of yours, and I'll oil my hair, whitewash my mug (a little moan from Mrs. D.), and do the COUNTER-JUMPING business to the life.

1864. G. A. SALA, in *Temple Bar*, Dec., p. 40. He is as dextrous as a Regent Street COUNTER-JUMPER in the questionable art of 'shaving the ladies.'

1876. M. E. BRADDON, *Joshua Haggard*, ch. viii. I don't want my son and heir to keep company with COUNTER JUMPERS.

COUNT-NOSES, *verbal phr.* (parliamentary).—To count the 'Ayes' and 'Noes.' [A punning allusion to the latter.] Generally, to take the sense of any assembly.

COUNTRY, *subs.* (cricket). — That part of the ground at a great distance from the wicket; thus, a fielder at 'deep-long-off,' or 'long-on' is said 'to be in the COUNTRY,' and a ball hit to the far boundary is 'hit into the COUNTRY.'

COUNTRY-PUT, *subs.* (old).—An ignorant, country fellow. For synonyms, *see* JOSKIN.

1717. MRS. CENTLIVRE, *Bold Stroke for a Wife*, Act iv., Sc. 2. *Col. F.* Enough. Now for the COUNTRY-PUT.

COUNTY-CROP, *subs.* (general).—The hair cut close to the skull; a mode once common to all prisoners, but now to convicts only. Also PRISON-CROP. [An abbreviation of COUNTY-PRISON CROP.] Used likewise adjectively.

1867. JAS. GREENWOOD, *Unsent. Journeys*, xxv., 199. A slangy, low-browed, bull-necked, COUNTY-CROPPED . . . crew.

COUPLE- (also BUCKLE-) BEGGAR, *subs.* (old).—A celebrant of irregular marriages—as the Chaplain of the Fleet; a hedge priest. A Spanish colloquialism for such a marriage is *bodijo.*

1737. SWIFT, *Proposal for Badges to the Beggars.* Nay, their happiness is often deferred until they find credit to borrow, or cunning to steal, a shilling to pay their popish priest, or infamous COUPLE-BEGGAR.

1842. LEVER, *Handy Andy,* ch. xxix. This was a degraded clergyman, known in Ireland under the title of COUPLE-BEGGAR, who was ready to perform irregular marriages on such urgent occasions as the present.

COUPLE OF SHAKES.—*See* BRACE OF SHAKES.

COUPLING-HOUSE, *subs.* (old).—A brothel. [From COUPLING, the act of copulating, + HOUSE.] For synonyms, *see* NANNY-SHOP.

COURANNE.—*See* CAROON.

COURT-CARD, *subs.* (old).—A beau, or 'swell.' For synonyms, *see* DANDY.

COURT HOLY WATER or COURT PROMISES, *subs. phr.* (old).—Fair speeches without performance.

COUSIN BETTY, *subs.* (colloquial).—A half-witted person. For synonyms, *see* BUFFLE and CABBAGE-HEAD.

1860. MRS. GASKELL, *Sylvia's Lovers,* ch. xiv. I dunnot think there's a man living—or dead for that matter—as can say Foster's wrong him of a penny, or gave short measure to a child or a COUSIN BETTY.

COUSIN-TRUMPS, *subs.* (old).—One of a kind: brother smut; brother chip.

1825. *English Spy,* p. 255. Most noble cracks, and worthy COUSIN-TRUMPS, etc.

COUTER or COOTER, *subs.* (common).—A sovereign. For synonyms, *see* CANARY, sense 3. HALF A COUTER = half-a-sovereign.

1857. SNOWDEN, *Mag. Assistant* (3 ed.), p. 444, S.V.

1877. *Five Years' Penal Servitude,* ch. iii., p. 243. 'A foulcher, with flimsies and COUTERS for a score of quid in it.'

1880. JAMES PAYN, *A Confidential Agent,* I., 207. 'Well, he gave us half a COUTER at all events,' pleaded John in mitigation.

COVE, COVEY, COFE, CUFFING, and, in the feminine, COVESS, *subs.* (general).—1. A person; a companion. [Some derive COVE from the Gypsy *cova, covo* = that man, *covi* = that woman; *Cova,* says Pott (quoted in Annandale), has a far wider application than the Latin *res;* there is no expression more frequent in a gypsy's mouth. Others connect it with the north country *coof,* a lout or dolt.] COVE enters into many combinations: *e.g.,*

CROSS-COVE = a robber.
FLASH-COVE = a thief or swindler.
KINCHIN-COVE = a little man.
FLOGGING-COVE = a beadle.
SMACKING-COVE = a coachman.
NARRY-COVE = a drunkard.
TOPPING-COVE = a highwayman.
ABRAM-COVE = a beggar.
QUEER-COVE = a rogue.
NUBBING-COVE = the hangman.
GENTRY-COVE = a gentleman.
DOWNY-COVE = a shrewd man.
RUM-COVE = a doubtful character.
NIB-COVE = a gentleman.

etc., etc., etc., all which *see.*

ENGLISH SYNONYMS. Boy; chap; cull; cully; customer; kiddy; homo or omee; fish; put; bloke; gloak; party; cuss; codger; buffer; gaffer; damber; duck; chip.

FRENCH SYNONYMS. *Bête à pain* (popular: literally a bread-eater; also a man who 'keeps' a woman); *un bonhomme* (familiar); *un type* (prostitutes' = a dupe); *un gonce, gonse* or *gonze,* and *une gonzesse* (thieves'); *un goncier* (thieves'); *un gonsalé* (thieves'); *un gadouille; un nière* or *niert; un pante* (thieves': from *pantin,* a puppet); *un mastic* (thieves': properly cement or putty); *une mazette* (military); *une mecque* (thieves'); *un marquant* (thieves': especially applied to bullies or Sunday-men); *un marpaut* or *marpeau* (old cant); *un lancier* (thieves'); *un lascar* (thieves'); *un messier* or *messière* (thieves': from *mézière,* a fool); *un orgue* (thieves'); *un gas* (thieves'); *un gosselin* (popular = Eng. covey; *une fignolé gosseline* = a 'natty piece'); *un gniasse* (thieves'); *un loncegue* (thieves').

GERMAN SYNONYMS. *Raal* (perhaps one of the most comprehensive terms in the *Gaunersprache,* and signifying not only a 'cove' [*i.e.,* an individual], but also a master, husband, possessor, artist, expert, artisan—in fact, one owning or capable of anything. Combinations are *Balbajis, Balbos* [fem. *Balboste, Balboèste*] = master of the house; *Baldower* = a principal or leader of a gang, an adviser, the creator of opportunities, the spy; *Baleze, Baleïze* = an adviser, also a chief of police; *Balhoche* [from *Baal* and

hocho (there)], prostitutes' = 'one in possession' but removeable; *Balhoche* (thieves') = one with an opportunity of theft; *Balhei* is merely the abbreviation of *Baalhe* or *hei; Balmassematten* [*massoumattan*], the business man, the leader of a gang; *Balmelocho,* the artisan; *Balmelochestift,* the artisan's apprentice; *Balplete, Balpleite,* the runaway; *Balschochad,* any official who takes bribes; *Balspiess* = a common lodging-house; *Balm, Balmach, Balmachan, Palm, Palmer, Palmach, Pallmack, Pallmagen* = a soldier; the Hanov. has *Palemachome* [*Palemachen, Pallemacher*]; *Balverschmai* = an inquisitor or judge; *Brooker* (Hanoverian = one in trousers, from the North German *Broek* or *Bracca,* trousers); *Gatscho* (from the Gypsy *gaxo*); *Isch* (from the Hebrew *isch*).

1567. HARMAN, *Caveat.* COFE: a person.

1609. DEKKER, *Lanthorne and Candlelight,* in wks. (Grosart) III., 196. The word COVE, or COFE, or CUFFIN, signifies a Man, a Fellow, etc.

1654. WITTS, *Recreations.* As priest of the game, And prelate of the same, There's a gentry COVE here.

1714. *Memoirs of John Hall* (4 ed.), p. 12, S.V.

1837. DICKENS, *Oliver Twist,* ch. x. 'Do you see that old COVE at the book-stall?'

1849. C. KINGSLEY, *Alton Locke,* ch. ii.: [a misquotation of a far older song.] 'The ministers talk a great deal about port, And they makes Cape wine very dear, But blow their hi's if ever they tries, To deprive a poor COVE of his beer.'

1871. *Figaro,* 15 April. We need hardly say that the COVE in question is not a man.

[For examples of the use of COVEY and COVESS, *see* same.]

2. (Up-country Australian).—The master, 'boss,' or 'gaffer' of a sheep station.

COVE OF DOSSING-KEN, *subs. phr.* (thieves').—The landlord of a common lodging-house. Fr., *marchand de sommeil.*

COVENT-GARDEN, *subs.* (rhyming slang).—A 'farden' or farthing.

COVENT-GARDEN ABBESS, *subs.* (old).—A procuress. [Covent Garden at one time teemed with brothels: as Fielding's *Covent Garden Tragedy* (1751-2) suggests. *Cf.,* BANKSIDE LADIES, and BARNWELL AGUE.]—*See* COVENT-GARDEN AGUE and ABBESS. For synonyms, *see* MOTHER.

COVENT-GARDEN AGUE, *subs. phr.* (old).—A venereal disease. [An allusion to brothels in the neighbourhood in question.] *Cf.,* BANKSIDE LADIES. For synonyms, *see* LADIES' FEVER.

COVENT-GARDEN NUN, *subs. phr.* (old).—A prostitute.—[*See* COVENT-GARDEN AGUE and NUN.]

COVENTRY. TO SEND ONE TO, or TO BE IN COVENTRY, *verbal phr.* (colloquial).—To exclude from social intercourse, or notice; to be in disgrace. [Variously but indecisively explained:—(1) From Coventry Gaol, as a place of imprisonment for Royalists during the Parliamentary war. (2) From the fact that in Coventry, as elsewhere, the privilege of trading was anciently confined to certain privileged persons. (3) As a corruption of PUT or SENT INTO QUARANTINE, the transition from 'Coventry' formerly pronounced and written *Cointrie*

—('his breech of Cointrie blewe.' DRAYTON'S *Dowsabell:* 1593) —being easy and natural, in which connection, *see* quot., 1821. The expression appears first in Grose, but 'Quarantine' used analogically is found in Swift.]

1785. GROSE, *Dict. Vulg. Tongue,* S.V.

1821. CROKER, in *Croker Papers,* vol. I., p. 203. I found MacMahon in A KIND OF COVENTRY, and was warned not to continue my acquaintance with him.

1838. LYTTON, *Alice,* bk. IV., ch. iii. 'If any one dares to buy it, we'll SEND HIM TO COVENTRY.'

1869. SPENCER, *Study of Sociology,* ch. x., p. 244 (9 ed.). The skilful artizan, who in a given period can do more than his fellows, but who dares not do it because he would be SENT TO COVENTRY by them.

1872. *Post,* 21 June. Another representation on behalf of Lieutenant Tribe, of the 9th Lancers, now for some months past in COVENTRY, will be made in the course of a few days to the Minister for War and to his Royal Highness Commanding-in-Chief.

COVER, *subs.* (thieves').—A pickpocket's confederate: one who 'fronts,' *i.e.,* distracts the attention of, the victim; a STALL (*q.v.*).

Verb (thieves').—1. To act as a pickpocket's confederate.

1858. *Glasgow Gazette,* 13 Nov. 'A Sensitive Thief.' I saw Merritt lift up the tail of a gentleman's coat and thrust his hand into the pocket. . . . Jordan and O'Brien were COVERING Merritt while so acting. I knew them all to be regular thieves.

2. (American).—To drink. For synonyms, *see* LUSH.

3. (venery).—To 'have' or 'possess' a woman. [Properly used of a stallion and a mare.]

1653. URQUHART, Translation of *Rabelais.* Madam, it would be a very great benefit to the commonwealth, delightful to you, honourable to your progeny, and necessary for me, that I COVER you for the propagating of my race.

13

COVER-ARSE GOWN, *subs. phr.* (Univ., obsolete).—A gown without sleeves.

1803. *Gradus ad Cantabrigiam,* S.V.

COVER-DOWN, *subs.* (thieves').—An obsolete term for a false tossing coin.—*See* CAP.

COVER-ME-DECENTLY, *verbal phr.* (old).—A coat. For synonyms, *see* CAPELLA.

1821. MONCRIEFF, *Tom and Jerry,* p. 5. (Dicks' ed., 1889.) *Tom.* This, what do you call it?—this COVER-ME-DECENTLY, was all very well at Hawthorn Hall, I daresay.

COVESS, *subs.* (old).—A woman.—See COVE.

1789. GEO. PARKER, *Life's Painter,* p. 144. He was well acquainted with the COVE and COVESS.

1827. SIR E. B. LYTTON, *Pelham,* p. 310 (ed. 1864). Ah, Bess my COVESS, strike me blind if my sees don't tout your bingo muns in spite of the darkmans.

COVEY, *subs.* (common).—A man; a diminutive of COVE (*q.v.*).

1821. W. T. MONCRIEFF, *Tom and Jerry,* Act iii., Sc. 3. *Tom.* Well there's a flim-sy for you; serve the change out in max to the COVIES.

1837. DICKENS, *Oliver Twist,* ch. viii. Upon this, the boy crossed over; and, walking close up to Oliver, said, 'Hullo, my COVEY! what's the row?'

1854. AYTOUN AND MARTIN, *The Bon Gaultier Ballads.* 'The Laureate's Tourney.' 'Undo the helmet! cut the lace! pour water on his head!' 'It ain't no use at all, my lord; 'cos vy? the COVEY's dead.'

1876. C. HINDLEY, *Life and Adventures of a Cheap Jack,* p. 19. Ah! Ah! you half-starved, hungry, ugly-looking COVEY, why, if they had you in the country where I came from they'd boil you down for the pigs.

COW, *subs.* (old).—1. A woman. The term is now opprobious; but in its primary and natural

sense the usage is ancient. Howell [1659] says: 'There are some proverbs that carry a kind of authority with them, as that which began in Henrie the Fourth's time. "He that bulls the cow must keep the calf." For synonyms, *see* PETTICOAT.

2. (general). — A prostitute. [By analogy from sense 1.] Fr., *une vache.* For synonyms, *see* BARRACK-HACK and TART.

3. (sporting).—A thousand pounds. Other slang terms for sums of money are:—

PONY = £25.
CENTURY = £100.
MONKEY = £500.
PLUM = £100,000.
MARIGOLD = £1,000,000.

but for complete list, *see* MONKEY.

1870. *Athenæum,* 10 Sept. 'Liverpool.' All over Lancashire a horse is called a COW, which everywhere else where slang prevails is a cant term for a thousand pounds.

TO TALK THE HIND LEG OFF A COW or DOG.—*See* TALK.

TUNE THE COW DIED OF.—*See* TUNE.

COWAN, *subs.* (common).—A sneak or prying individual. Among masons the uninitiate in general.

COW-AND-CALF, *verb* (rhyming slang).— To laugh.

COWARD'S-CASTLE or CORNER, *subs. phr.* (popular).—A pulpit. [Because a clergyman may deliver himself therefrom without fear of contradiction or argument.] For synonyms, *see* HUM-BOX.

1883. *Notes and Queries,* 6 S., viii., p. 147. COWARD'S CASTLE . . . . An epithet . . . . in use not inaptly for a pulpit. *Ibid*, p. 238. I have often heard the pulpit called the COWARD'S CASTLE, it being said to be 'six feet above argument.'

COWCUMBER, *subs.* (vulgar).—A corruption of 'cucumber.'

1821. W. T. MONCRIEFF, *Tom and Jerry*, Act iii., Sc. 3. *Bob.* Very vell, two pound, vith a pickled COWCUMBER, and a pen'orth o' ketchup.

1843. DICKENS, *Martin Chuzzlewit*, ch. xxv. In case there should be such a thing as a COWCUMBER in the house will you be so kind as bring it, for I'm rayther partial to 'em myself, and they does a world of good in a sick room.

COW- (also **BUSHEL-** and **SLUICE-**). **CUNTED**, *adj. phr.* (venery). — A term of opprobium applied to women deformed by parturition or debauchery.

COW-GREASE or **COW-OIL**, *subs.* (common).—Butter. For synonyms, *see* CART-GREASE.

COW-JUICE, *subs.* (popular).—Milk. *Cf.*, BUNG-JUICE and COW-GREASE. For synonyms, *see* SKY-BLUE.

COW-LICK, *subs.* (common).—A peculiar lock of hair, greased, curled, brought forward from the ear, and plastered on the cheek. Once common amongst costermongers and tramps. For synonyms, *see* AGGERAWATORS.

COW-OIL.—*See* COW-GREASE.

COW-PUNCHER, *subs.* (American).—A cowboy or herdsman.

1888. *Detroit Free Press*, 21 July. He was a cowboy, or, in Western parlance, a COW-PUNCHER.

COW-QUAKE, *subs.* (Irish).—The roar of a bull.

COWS-AND-KISSES, *subs.* (rhyming slang).—The 'missus,' or mistress; also women generally.

1887. HORSLEY, *Jottings from Jail.* Come, COWS-AND-KISSES, put the battle of the Nile on your Barnet fair, and a rogue and villain in your sky-rocket.

COW'S-BABY or **BABE**, *subs.* (common).—A calf. In Old Cant BLEATING-CHEAT (*q.v.*). For synonyms, *see* MOOER; *Cf.*, COW-JUICE and COW'S-SPOUSE. Also a poltroon; Fr., *un fouinard*, *un fouetteux de chats*, *un fouailleur*, *un foie*, *un flemard* or *flaquadin*, or *un frileux*.

1785. GROSE, *Dict. Vulg. Tongue*, s.v.

COW-SHOOTER, *subs.* (Winchester College).—A 'deerstalker' hat: only worn by præfects and 'candle-keepers.'

COW'S-SPOUSE, *subs.* (old).—A bull.—*Grose* [1785].

COW WITH THE IRON TAIL, *subs. phr.* (general).—A pump; the source of the 'cooling medium' for 'regulating' milk. Thus, Dr. Wendell Holmes, in *The Professor at the Breakfast Table* (1860): —It is a common saying of a jockey that he is all horse, and I have often fancied that milkmen get a stiff upright carriage, and an angular movement that reminds one of a pump and the working of a handle. Also BLACK-COW; ONE-ARMED MAN; and SIMPSON'S COW (*q.v.*).

1867. *Punch.* The Rinderpest does not affect the COW WITH THE IRON TAIL.

1872. *Standard*, 25 Dec. Simpson . . . is, however, universally accepted as the title for that combined product of the Cow natural, and the COW WITH THE IRON TAIL.

1876. *Once a Week*, 23 August. Every drop of milk brought into Paris is tested at the harriers by the lactometer, to see if the IRON TAILED COW has been guilty of diluting it; if so, the whole of it is remorselessly thrown into the gutter—the Paris milk is very pure in consequence.

COXY, *adj.* (public schools'). — Stuck up; conceited; impudent.

1856. HUGHES, *Tom Brown's School-days*, p. 202. He's the COXIEST young blackguard in the house—I always told you so. *Ibid*, p. 214. 'Confoundly COXY those young rascals will get if we don't mind,' was the general feeling.

1882. F. ANSTEY, *Vice Versâ*, ch. iv. 'Now then young Bultitude, you used to be a decent fellow enough last term, though you were COXY. So, before we go any further—what do you mean by this sort of thing?'

COYDUCK, *verb* (old).—To decoy. [An ingenious blend of *conduct* and *decoy*.]

1829. *A Laconic Narrative of the Life and Death of James Wilson.* That awful monster, William Burke. Like Reynard sneaking on the lurk, COYDUCKED his prey into his den And then the woeful work began.

COYOTE, *subs.* (old).—The female *pudendum.* For synonyms, *see* MONOSYLLABLE.

COZZA, *subs.* (cheap Jacks').—*See* quot.

1876. HINDLEY, *Life and Adventures of a Cheap Jack*, p. 28. Mo . . . declared he would never eat another bit of COZZA, *i.e.*, pork, as long as he lived.

CRAB, *subs.* (auction).—The same as BONNET (*q.v.*), *subs.*, sense I.

Verb (thieves').—To expose; to inform; to offend or insult; and especially to interrupt, to get in the way of, to spoil. [Properly to render harsh, sour, or peevish; to make crabbed.] Also used adjectively. For synonyms, *see* PEACH and RILE, respectively.

1825. *The English Spy*, vol. I., p. 179. LIVERYMAN, EGLANTINE. What coming CRABB over us, old fellow? Very well, I shall bolt and try Randall, and that's all about it.

1851-61. H. MAYHEW, *London Lab. and Lon. Poor*, vol. I., p. 232. If a patterer has been CRABBED, that is offended at any of the 'cribs' (houses), he mostly chalks a signal on or near the door. *Ibid*, vol. II., p. 568. 'We don't CRAB one another when we are sweeping; if we was to CRAB one another, we'd get to fighting and giving slaps of the jaw to one another.'

1876. HINDLEY, *Life and Adventures of a Cheap Jack*, pp. 5-6. Others, however, would be what we termed CRABBED.

1880. MILLIKIN, *Punch's Almanack.* CRAB your enemies,—I've got a many, You can pot 'em proper for a penny.

TO CATCH A CRAB; also TO CUT A CRAB; TO CATCH or CUT A CANCER or LOBSTER, *verbal phr.* (common). — There are various ways of CATCHING A CRAB, as, for example, (1) to turn the blade of the oar or 'feather' under water at the end of the stroke, and thus be unable to recover; (2) to lose control of the oar at the middle of the stroke by 'digging' too deeply; or (3) to miss the water altogether.

CRAB LOUSE, *subs.* (old).—The *pulex pubis*, the male whereof is called a cock, the female a hen.—*Grose* [1785].

CRABS, *subs.* (thieves').—1. The feet. [A punning comparison of the feet and ten toes to the ten-footed, short-tailed crustaceans popularly known as 'crabs.'] For synonyms, *see* CREEPERS. In Haggart (*see* Glossary, 1821) CRABS = shoes.

2. (old).—Lice. For synonyms, *see* CHATES, sense 2.

3. (gaming).—A pair of aces, or deuce-ace—the lowest throw at hazard.

1768. LORD CARLISLE, in Jesse's *Selwyn*, II., 238 (1882). I hope you have left off hazard. If you are still so foolish, and will play, the best thing I can wish you is, that you may win and never throw CRABS.

1837. BARHAM, *Ingoldsby Legends* (*Hard Times*), p. 4, ed. 1851. Well, we know in these cases Your CRABS and '*Deuce Aces*' Are wont to promote frequent changes of places.

1874. G. A. LAWRENCE, *Hagarene*, ch. iii. 'My annuity drops with me; and if this throw comes off CRABS, there won't be enough to bury me, unless I die a defaulter.'

TO TURN OUT CRABS or A CASE OF CRABS, *verbal phr.* (common). —A matter TURNS OUT CRABS when it is brought to a disagreeable conclusion. [*Cf.*, CRAB, *verb*, in the sense of to interrupt; to get in the way of; to spoil.]

CRABSHELLS, *subs.* (popular). — Shoes. [From CRABS, *subs.*, sense 1 (*q.v.*), + SHELLS, an outer covering.] For synonyms, *see* TROTTER-CASES.

1785. GROSE, *Dict. Vulg. Tongue*, s.v.

1851-61. H. MAYHEW, *London Lab. and Lon. Poor*, vol. III., p. 210, 'Now these 'ere shoes,' he said . . . 'even now, with a little mending, they'll make a tidy pair of CRAB-SHELLS again.'

1889. *Answers*, July 20, p. 121, col. 2. The state of my CRABSHELLS, or boots, pointed to the fact that I had come down in the world.

CRACK, *subs.* (old).—A crazy person, or soft-head. [From CRACK = to impair, or to be impaired.] For synonyms, *see* BUFFLE and CABBAGE-HEAD.

1609. DEKKER, *Lanthorne and Candlelight*, in wks. (Grosart) III., 212. A Foyst nor a Nip shall not walke into a Fayre or a Play-house, but euerie CRACKE will cry looke to your purses.

b. 1672, *d.* 1719. ADDISON (quoted in Annandale). I cannot get the Parliament to listen to me, who look upon me as a CRACK.

2. (old). — A prostitute, *see* sense 4. For synonyms, *see* BARRACK-HACK and TART.

1698. FARQUHAR, *Love and a Bottle*, Act v., Sc. 3. You imagine I have got your whore, cousin, your CRACK.

1705-7. WARD, *Hudibras Redivivus*, vol. II., pt. II., p. 27. Old Leachers, Harridans, and CRACKS.

1715. VANBRUGH, *Country House*, II., v. For you must know my sister was with me, and it seems he took her for a CRACK, and I being a forward boy he fancied I was going to make love to her under a hedge, ha, ha.

1748. T. DYCE, *Dictionary* (5 ed.), s.v.

1785. GROSE, *Dict. Vul. Tongue*, s.v.

1811. *Lexicon Balatronicum*, s.v.

3. (old).—A lie. *Cf.*, CRACKER (the modern form), and for synonyms, *see* WHOPPER.

1773. GOLDSMITH, *She Stoops to Conquer*, Act ii. *Miss N.* There's something generous in my cousin's manner. He falls out before faces to be forgiven in private. *Tony.* That's a damned confounded CRACK.

4. (venery). — The female *pudendum.* For synonyms, *see* MONOSYLLABLE.

5. (thieves').—A burglary. *Cf.*, CRACK A CRIB, and for synonyms, *see* PANNY. [The term originated about the beginning of the present century. Fr., *une fraction.*]

1834. W. H. AINSWORTH, *Rookwood* p. 120 (ed. 1864). We'll overhaul the swag here, when the speak is spoken over. This CRACK may make us all for life.

1837. DICKENS, *Oliver Twist*, p. 124. The CRACK failed, said Toby, faintly.

1841. G. W. REYNOLDS, *Pickwick Abroad*, ch. xxvi. But should the traps be on the sly, For a change we'll have a CRACK.

1841. LEMAN REDE, *Sixteen-String Jack*, Act i., Sc. 5. Come on, then! A sweet ride of a dozen miles, just to cool one's head, then for the CRACK; and then back to London.

1889. *Answers*, 13 April, p. 313. Such inscriptions as 'Poor Joe from the Dials in for a CRACK,' meaning 'Poor Joe from Seven Dials in for a burglary,' are numerous.

6. (thieves'). — A burglar. [*See* sense 5, and *cf.*, CRACKSMAN.]

1749. *Life of Bampfylde-Moore Carew.* Sufler none, from far or near, With their rights to interfere; No strange Abram, ruffler CRACK.

1857. *Punch*, 31 Jan. (from slang song). That long over Newgit their Worships may rule, As the High-toby, mob, CRACK, and screeve model school.

7. (colloquial).—An approach to perfection. *Cf.*, sense 8.

1825. *English Spy*, p. 255. Most noble CRACKS and worthy cousin trumps, permit me to introduce a brother of the togati.

1864. *Glasgow Herald*, 5 April. 'Report of R. N. Y. Club.' This vessel (one of Fyfe's CRACKS) being almost new, and coppered, will be free from the objectionable fouling which is so great a drawback to the use of iron yachts.

1871. *London Figaro*, 17 Oct. Does it mean that the CRACK is a thing of the past, and that the learned author is no longer to be considered as a CRACK?

1889. *Answers*, March 23, p. 265, col. 3. Warders are not, thank goodness, first-rate shots, but even a CRACK would find it difficult to hit a man's head appearing for only a moment or two in probably a heavy fog.

8. (turf).—A racehorse eminent for speed. Hunting: a famous 'mount.' [An extension of the usage in sense 7.]

1853. *Diogenes* II., 271. 'The Betting Boy's Lament.' Cesarewitch, Cambridgeshire now No longer for me have a charm; the CRACKS may be ranged in a row, But for me they've no fear nor alarm.

1864. *Derby Day*, p. 38. Sir Bridges Sinclair would not scratch a horse—no, not if it was ever so, let alone a Derby CRACK.

1871. *Standard*, 6 Nov. Unlimited gossip as to the welfare and chances of forthcoming CRACKS.

1883. *The Echo*, Feb. 7, p. 3, col. 6. I give below a few of the probable starters for the Waterloo Cup, including all the CRACKS.

1884. HAWLEY SMART, *From Post to Finish*, p. 155. Of course he was *au courant* with all the rumours concerning the Panton Lodge CRACK.

9. (vagrants').—Dry firewood.

1851-61. H. MAYHEW, *London Lab. and Lon. Poor*, vol. I., p. 358. The next process is to look for some CRACK (some dry wood to light a fire).

Adj. (colloquial).—Approaching perfection; used in a multitude of combinations. A CRACK hand is an adept or 'dabster'; a CRACK corps, a brilliant regiment; a CRACK whip, a good coachman; etc. As a connecting link between the adjective and the earlier use of CRACK, *cf.*, THE CRACK.

1836. W. H. SMITH, *The Individual*, 13 Nov. 'The Thieves' Chaunt.' Her duds are bob—she's a kinchin CRACK, and I hopes as how she'll never back.

1839. THACKERAY, *Fatal Boots* (July). And such a CRACK-shot myself, that fellows were shy of insulting me.

1859. WHITTY, *Political Portraits*, p. 106. But he [the Earl of Shaftesbury] has insisted on a recognition of the facts of our appalling civilisation, and *that* was a good deal to do, which none other than a Peer and CRACK Christian could hope to do. *Ibid*, p. 288. The whippers-in will never receive instructions to find the addresses of the brilliancies of Union debating clubs, bar messes, and CRACK newspapers.

1865. M. E. BRADDON, *Henry Dunbar*, ch. xx. Who was moreover a CRACK shot, a reckless cross-country-going rider, and a very tolerable amateur artist.

Verb (old).—1. To talk to; to boast. [The verb was once good English, and in the sense of to talk or gossip is still good Scots. The modern form TO CRACK-UP, is well within the borderland between literary and colloquial English. The following quots., together with those under CRACK-UP, form an unbroken series].

1597. G. HARVEY, *Trimming of Nashe*, in wks. (Grosart) III., 31. So you may CRACKE your selfe abroad, and get to be reported the man you are not.

1621. BURTON, *Anat of Mel.*, I., II., III., xiv., 199, (1876). Your very tradesmen, if they be excellent, will CRACK and brag, and show their folly in excess.

1654. WITTS, *Recreations*. And let them that CRACK In the praises of sack, Know malt is of mickle might.

1785. GROSE, *Dict. Vulg. Tongue*, s.v.

2. (thieves').—To force open; to commit a burglary. [A shorter form of CRACK A CRIB (*q.v.*).]

1837. DICKENS, *Oliver Twist*, ch. xix. The crib's barred up at night like a jail; but there's one part we can CRACK, safe and softly.

3. (American thieves').—To forge or utter worthless paper. [An extension by analogy of 'to crack,' *i.e.*, 'to force,' and 'cracksman,' a burglar.]

4. (colloquial).—To fall to ruin; to be impaired. *Cf.*, *subs.*, sense 1.

b. 1631. *d.* 1701. DRYDEN [quoted in *Annandale*]. The credit of the exchequer CRACKS when little comes in and much goes out.

5. (thieves'). — To inform; to PEACH (*q.v.* for synonyms).

c. 1850, but date uncertain. *Broadside Ballad*, 'Bates' Farm.' I mean to CRACK a crib to-night, but pals don't CRACK on me.

TO CRACK A BOTTLE or A QUART, *verbal phr.* (colloquial).—To drink. Analogous and equally old is 'to crush a cup.' Fr., *étouffer une négresse* or *un enfant de chœur*. For synonyms, *see* LUSH.

1598. SHAKSPEARE, *II. Henry IV.*, v., 3, 66. *Shal.* By the mass, you'll CRACK A QUART together.

1711. *Spectator*, No. 234. He hems after him in the public street, and they must CRACK A BOTTLE at the next tavern.

1750. FIELDING, *Tom Jones*, bk. VIII., ch. vii. 'What,' says the wife, 'you have been tippling with the gentleman! I see.' 'Yes,' answered the husband, 'we have CRACKED A BOTTLE together.'

1817. SCOTT, *Rob Roy*, ch. viii. 'You have CRACKED MY SILVER-MOUNTED COCOA-NUT OF SACK, and tell me that you cannot sing!'

1853. THACKERAY, *Barry Lyndon*, ch. xvii., p. 221. I chose to invite the landlords of the 'Bell' and the 'Lion' to CRACK A BOTTLE with me.'

TO CRACK A CRIB, SWAG, or KEN, *verbal phr.* (thieves').—To commit a burglary; to break into a house. [From CRACK, to force open, + CRIB, a house.]

ENGLISH SYNONYMS. To stamp a ken or crib; to work a panny; to jump a house (also applied to simple robbery without burglary); to do a crack; to practice the black art; to screw; to bust a crib; to flimp; to buz; to tool; to wire; to do a ken-crack-lay.

FRENCH SYNONYMS. *Faire un cassement de porte* (thieves'); *faire une condition* (thieves'); *faire copeaux* (thieves': in allusion to the splinters from a forced door); *écorner une boutanche* or *un boucard* (thieves') = to enter shops burglariously); *faire un vol à l'esquinte* (thieves');

maquiller une cambriole (thieves': *maquiller* = to do, to 'fake'—an almost universal verb of action); *faire fric-frac*; *nettoyer un bocart* (thieves').

GERMAN SYNONYMS. *Aufnollen* (to 'burgle' with skeleton keys); *aufplatzen* (literally 'to wrench' or 'break open'); *aufschränken* (*schränken* [from *Schranke*, O. H. G. *screnchan*, M. H. G. *schranne*, *schrange*, *schrand*] = a burglary with violence. *Schränker* = burglar. Up to the middle of the present century burglars used to be called *Schränker a zierlicher*; *Schränkmassematten* = a burglary with violence; *Schränkzeug*, *Schränkschaure*, *Schränkschurrich* = burglars' tools); *blaupfeifen* (Viennese thieves'); *Cassne handeln* or *melochenen* (to commit burglary with open violence); *einen Massematten handeln* (*Massematten* is a word whose Hebraic components very nearly correspond to the English 'debit and credit'; it signifies commerce and activity—of the kind that pertains to cracksmanship; *e.g.*, *einen Massematten baldowern*, to make an opportunity for theft; *einen Massematten stehen haben*, to have 'dead-lurked' a crib, or prepared a burglary; *Massematten bekoach* a burglary with violence.)

1830. BULWER LYTTON, *Paul Clifford*, p. 297, ed. 1854. And you 'members as how I met Harry and you—there, and I vas all afeard at you—cause vy? I had never seen you afore and ve vas a going to CRACK a swell's CRIB.

1841. LEMAN REDE, *Sixteen-String Jack*, Act i., Sc. 5. *Jer.* Now comes the grand spec; we go to CRACK A KEN; Kit's in, so's the captain. Steady's the word; I go first, you all follow.

1871. *Standard*, 26 Dec. If their pals outside, the gentry who hocus Jack ashore in the east, pick the pockets of Lord Dundreary in the west, and CRACK CRIBS in the lonely outskirts could only realise how miserable the Christmas-day was for them, we might look out for a needful retrenchment in the estimates of penal expenditure.

1871. *Morning Advertiser*, 11 May. 'Leader.' He took to burglary, employing professional burglars to assist him, whenever it became necessary to CRACK A CRIB.

1887. W. E. HENLEY, *Villon's Straight Tip*. Dead-lurk a crib, or do a CRACK.

TO CRACK A JUDY (or HER TEA CUP), *verb. phr.* (common).—To deflower a maid.

TO CRACK A CRUST, *phr.* (common).—To rub along in the world. A superlative for doing very well is, TO CRACK A TIDY CRUST.

1851-61. H. MAYHEW, *Lon. Lab. and Lon. Poor*, vol. III., p. 445. I am now just managing to CRACK AN HONEST CRUST; and while I can do that I will never thieve more.

TO CRACK A KEN, *verb. phr.* (thieves').—To commit a burglary; to CRACK A CRIB (*q.v.*).—[*See* CRACK, *verb*, sense 2 and KEN.]

TO CRACK A WHID, *verb. phr.* (thieves').—To talk. [WHID (*q.v.*) = a word: Old Cant.] *Cf.*, CUT, *verb*, sense 1. For synonyms, *see* PATTER.

1876. HINDLEY, *Life and Adventures of a Cheap Jack*, p. 22. The WHIDS as the words or set phrases used by Cheap Johns in disposing of their articles are called are very much alike . . . many little circumstances occur when they (the WHIDS) are being CRACKED which are lost to a reader.

TO CRACK ON, *verb. phr.* (common).—To 'put on speed'; increase one's pace.

1835. HALIBURTON, *Clockmaker*, 1 S., ch. xi. 'I shot a wild goose at River Philip last year, with the rice of Varginny fresh in his crop; he must have CRACKED ON near about as fast as them other geese, the British travellers.'

1876. *Broadside Ballad* [quoted in C. G. Leland's *Captain Jonas*]. We carried away the royal yards, and the stunsle boom was gone. Says the skipper, 'they may go or stand, I'm darned if I don't CRACK ON.

TO CRACK UP, *verbal phr.* (colloquial).—To praise; eulogize. A superlative is TO CRACK UP TO THE NINES. Fr., *faire l'article*, (commercial travellers') and *faire son boniment* or *son petit boniment* (cheap jacks' and showmen's).

1843. DICKENS, *Martin Chuzzlewit*. Ch. . . . We must be CRACKED UP, said Mr. Chollop, darkly.

1856. HUGHES, *Tom Brown's School-days*, p. 139. Then don't object to my CRACKING UP the old school house, Rugby.

1878. JAS. PAYN, *By Proxy*, ch. i. 'We find them CRACKING UP the country they belong to, no matter how absurd may be the boast.'

THE CRACK, or ALL THE CRACK, *phr.* (general).—The GO (*q.v.*); 'the thing'; the 'kick'; the general craze of the moment.

IN A CRACK, *phr.* (colloquial).—Instantaneously; in the twinkling of an eye. For synonyms, *see* BEDPOST.

1725. RAMSAY, *Gentle Shepherd*, Act i. I trow, when that she saw, WITHIN A CRACK, She came with a right thieveless errand back.

1763. FOOTE, *Mayor of Garrett*, Act i. Nic Goose, the taylor, from Putney, they say, will be here IN A CRACK.

1819. BYRON, *Don Juan*, ch. i., st. 135. 'They're on the stair just now, and IN A CRACK will all be here.'

1842. *Punch*, vol. III., p. 136. IN A CRACK the youth and maiden To a flowery bank did come.

CRACKED or **CRACKED-UP**, *ppl. adj. phr.* (colloquial).—1. Ruined; 'bust up'; 'gone to smash' or to 'pot.' For synonyms, *see* DEAD BROKE.

1851. H. MAYHEW, *Lon. Lab. and Lon. Poor*, vol. I., p. 2 [also pp. 24, 47]. If a Catholic coster,—there's only a very few of them—is CRACKED UP (penniless) he's often started again, and the others have a notion that it's through some chapel fund. *Ibid*, p. 22. 'If we're CRACKED UP, that is, if we're forced to go into the Union.'

1870. *Britannia*, June. 'Speculation in 1870.' Of these there only remain now 122 companies, with a capital of a hundred and eighty millions, the rest having one and all CRACKED UP, as the Americans would say.

2. (common). — Crazy. For synonyms, *see* APARTMENTS and TILE LOOSE.

1872. *Daily Telegraph*, 3 Sept. 'Police Court Report.' Mr. Bushby: Is her head affected? The Prisoner: Am I CRACKED? Of course—in the nut. You'll be to-morrow.

3. (common). — Deflowered. Also CRACKED IN THE RING.

CRACKER, *subs.* (common).—Anything approaching perfection. Used in both a good and bad sense; *e.g.*, a rattling pace, a large sum of money, a bad fall, an enormous lie, a dandy (male or female) of the first magnitude, and so forth. [*Cf.*, CRACK, *subs.*; senses 3 and 7, *adj.*, and *verb*, sense 1.]

1861. WHYTE MELVILLE, *Good for Nothing*, ch. vi. 'I remember . . . Belphegor's year. What a CRACKER I stood to win on him and the Rejected!'

1863. C. READE, *Hard Cash*, I., 28. You know the University was in a manner beaten, and he took the blame. He never cried; that was a CRACKER of those fellows.

1869. *Daily News*, Nov. 8. 'Leader.' Now he's gone a CRACKER over head and ears.

1871. *Daily News*, Nov. 1. 'Prince of Wales' Visit to Scarborough.' The shooting party, mounting their forest ponies, came up the straight a CRACKER, Lord Carrington finishing a good first.

1883. *Graphic*, March 24, p. 303, col. 1. He [the Oxford stroke] could also depend on his own men for not falling to pieces through being taken off at a CRACKER.

CRACKEY.—*See* CRIKEY.

CRACK-HALTER, or **CRACK-ROPE**, *subs.* (old).—A vagabond; an old equivalent of JAIL-BIRD. *Cf.*, HEMP-SEED.

1566. GASCOIGNE, *Supposes*, i., 4. You CRACKHALTER, if I catch you by the ears, I'll make you answer directly.

1607. DEKKER, *Northward Hoe*, IV., i. Featherstone's boy, like an honest CRACK-HALTER, laid open all to one of my prentices.

1639. MASSINGER, *Unnatural Combat*, II., ii. Peace, you CRACK-ROPE!

1818. SCOTT, *Heart of Midlothian*, ch. xxx. 'Hark ye, ye CRACK-ROPE padder, born-beggar, and hedge-thief,' replied the hag.

CRACK-HUNTER, or **HAUNTER**, *subs.* (venery).—The *penis*. *Cf.*, CRACK, *subs.*, sense 4. For synonyms, *see* CREAMSTICK.

CRACKING, *verbal subs.* (thieves').—House-breaking. [From CRACK, *verb*, sense 2.]

1862. *Cornhill Mag.*, vol. VI., 651. We are going a-flimping, buzzing, CRACKING, tooling, etc.

CRACKISH, *adj.* (old).—Wanton, said only of women. [From CRACK, *subs.*, sense 4.] *Cf.*, COMING.

CRACK-JAW WORDS, NAMES, etc., *subs.* (colloquial).—Long words difficult to pronounce. [From CRACK, to break, + JAW, speech.] Variants are HALF-CROWN WORDS, JAW-BREAKERS, and CRAMP WORDS.

1876. M. E. BRADDON, *Joshua Haggard's Daughter*, ch. vii. 'He brings her plants with CRACKJAW NAMES.',

1883. *Daily Telegraph*, June 25, p. 3, col. 1. 'Some of the ways with the CRACK-JAW NAMES of cooking it would give it a foreign flavour to me.'

CRACKLE or **CRACKLING**, *subs.* (University).—The velvet bars on the gowns of the Johnian 'HOGS' (*q.v.*). [From their resemblance to the scored rind on roast pork.] The covered bridge between one of the courts and the grounds of John's is called the Isthmus of Suez (Latin *sus*, a swine).

1885. CUTHBERT BEDE, in *Notes and Queries*. 6 S., xi., 414. The word CRACKLE refers to the velvet bars on the students' gowns.

CRACKMANS or **CRAGMANS**, *subs.* (old).—A hedge.

1610. ROWLANDS, *Martin Mark-all*, p. 57 (H. Club's Repr., 1874), s.v.

1671. R. HEAD, *English Rogue*, pt. I., ch. v., p. 48 (1874), s.v.

1785. GROSE, *Dict. Vulg. Tongue*. The cull thought to have loped, by breaking through the CRACKMANS, but we fetched him back by a nope.

CRACK or **BREAK ONE'S EGG**, or **DUCK**, *verbal phr.* (cricket).—To begin to score. [To make no run is to 'lay, or make, a duck's egg'; to make none in either innings is 'to get a double-duck,' or to come off with a pair of spectacles.]

1890. *Polytechnic Magazine*, 5 June, p. 367, col. 2. Watson bowled splendidly, taking 8 wickets at a very small cost, two of his foemen being unable to CRACK THEIR EGG.

CRACK-POT, *subs.* (popular).—A pretentious, worthless person. For synonyms, *see* SWASH-BUCKLER.

1883. *Broadside Ballad*, 'I'm Living with Mother now.' My aunty knew lots, and called them CRACK-POTS.

CRACK-ROPE.—*See* CRACK-HALTER.

CRACKSMAN, *subs.* (popular).—1. A housebreaker. [From CRACK, *verb*, sense 2, + MAN; literally one who CRACKS or forces his way into a house.] For synonyms, *see* THIEVES.

1811. *Lexicon Balatronicum.* The kiddy is a clever CRACKSMAN.

1830. LYTTON, *Paul Clifford*, p. 298, ed. 1854. I have no idea of a gentleman turning CRACKSMAN.

1837. DICKENS, *Oliver Twist*, p. 123. You'll be a fine young CRACKSMAN afore the old file now.

1837. BARHAM, *I. L.* (*Lay of St. Aloys*). Your CRACKSMAN, for instance, thinks night-time the best To break open a door or the lid of a chest.

1839. AINSWORTH, *Jack Sheppard* (1889), p. 70. I'll turn CRACKSMAN, like my father.

1889. *Pall Mall Gaz.*, 21 Nov., p. 6, col 1. The latest dodge among CRACKSMEN is to personate an electric-light man.

2. (common). — The *penis*. —*See* CRACK, *subs.*, sense 4.

CRADLE, ALTAR, AND TOMB COLUMN, *subs. phr.* (American). — The births, marriages, and deaths column in newspaper. An English equivalent is HATCH, MATCH, AND DISPATCH COLUMN.

CRAG.—*See* SCRAG.

CRAM, *subs.* (popular).—1. A lie; oftentimes CRAMMER. [The idea is that of stuffing with nonsense.] For synonyms, *see* WHOPPER.

1842. *Punch*, vol. II., p. 21, col. 2. It soundeth somewhat like a CRAM: but our honour is at stake, and we repeat the 'mile.'

1864. LE FANU, *Uncle Silas*, ch. xxxviii. 'It is awful, an old un like that elling such CRAMS as she do!'

1864. *Quiver*, 4 June. By some delicate distinction the falsehood presented itself under the guise of a CRAM, and not of a naked lie.

1887. W. E. HENLEY, *Villon's Good Night.* You magsmen bold that work the CRAM.

2. (colloquial).—Hard, forced study. Resulting rather in a test of memory than of capacity.

1872. *Morning Post*, Oct. 15. Poor Toots, the head boy of Dr. Blimber's academy . . . bloomed early and had by CRAM been enabled to answer any given set of questions, and to work any papers at an 'exam.'

1872. *Daily Telegraph*, July 25. 'Speech Day at King's College School.' Dr. Maclear also said a few words on the advantage of boys going up straight from school to college without any interval of CRAM.

1878. JAS. PAYN, *By Proxy*, ch. xii. They have gained their position by CRAM of the philosophic kind.

3. (colloquial).—One who prepares another for an examination; a coach; a 'grindstone.'

1861. DUTTON COOK, *Paul Foster's Daughter*, ch. ix. 'I shall go to a coach, a CRAM, a grindstone.'

4. (University).—An adventitious aid to study; a translation; a 'crib.' For synonyms, *see* PONY.

1853. REV. E. BRADLEY ['C. Bede'), *Verdant Green*, pt. II., p. 68. The infatuated Mr. Bouncer madly persisted . . . . in going into the school clad in his examination coat, and padded over with a host of CRAMS.

Verb (colloquial).—1. To study at high pressure for an examination. Also to prepare one for examination. *Cf.*, DIG and COACH.

1803. *Gradus ad Cantabrigiam*, s.v.

1825-27. HONE, *Every-day Book*, Feb. 22. Shutting my room door, as if I was 'sported in' and CRAMMING Euc

1836. DICKENS, *Pickwick*, chap. li., p. 446. 'He CRAMMED for it, to use a technical but expressive term; he read up for the subject, at my desire, in the *Encyclopædia Britannica*.'

1844. *Puck*, p. 13. Though for Great Go and for Small, I teach Paley, CRAM and all.

1872. BESANT AND RICE, *My Little Girl.* The writer of one crushing article CRAMMED for it, like Mr. Pott's young man.

2. (general).—To lie; to deceive. [Literally to stuff with nonsense.] For synonyms, *see* STICK.

1794. *Gent. Mag.*, p. 1085. Luckily, I CRAMMED him so well, that at last honest Jollux tipped me the cole [money].

1822. SCOTT, *Fortunes of Nigel*, ch. xviii. A thousand ridiculous tales. . , with some specimens of which our friend Richie Moniplies had been CRAMMED . . . by the malicious apprentice.

CRAMMER, *subs.* (general). 1. A liar; one who tells CRAMS (*q.v.*). [From CRAM (M a lie, + ER.]

2. (common).—A lie; the same as CRAM, sense 1.

1861. H. C. PENNELL, *Puck on Pegasus*, p. 17. I sucked in the obvious CRAMMER kindly as my mother's milk.

1880. A. TROLLOPE, *The Duke's Children*, ch. xxxviii. 'What on earth made you tell him CRAMMERS like that?' asked Silverbridge.

c. 1884. *Broadside Ballad*, 'On Monday I Met Mary Ann.' I thought t'would last for ever and I never should be sold, Because I was so clever in the CRAMMERS that I told.

3. (general).—One who prepares men for examination; a coach, or GRINDER (*q.v.*, for synonyms).

1812. MISS EDGEWORTH, *Patronage*, ch. iii. Put him into the hands of a clever *grinder* or CRAMMER, and they would soon cram the necessary portion of Latin and Greek into him.

1872. *Evening Standard*, 16 Aug. 'The Competition Wallah.' The CRAMMER follows in the wake of competitive examinations as surely as does the shadow the body.

CRAMMING, *verbal subs.* (common). —The act of studying hard for an examination. [From CRAM (*q.v.*, sense 2) + ING.] American, BONING.

1841. *Punch*, vol. I., p. 201, col. 1. Aspirants to honours in law, physic, or divinity, each know the value of private CRAMMING.

1863. CHARLES READE, *Hard Cash*, I., p. 16. 'All this term I have been ('training' scratched out and another word put in: c—r oh, I know) CRAMMING.' 'CRAMMING, love?' 'Yes, that is Oxfordish for studying.'

1869. SPENCER, *Study of Sociology*, ch. xv., p. 574 (9 ed.). And here, by higher culture, I do not mean mere language-learning, and an extension of the detestable CRAMMING system at present in use.

1872. *Daily News*, Dec. 20. Competitive examinations for the public service defeated in a great measure, the object of their promoters, which was to place rich and poor on an equality, because success was made to depend very largely on successful CRAMMING, which meant a high-priced crammer.

CRAMPED or **CRAPPED**, *ppl. adj.* (old).—Hanged; also killed. For synonyms, *see* LADDER.

CRAMPING-CULL, *subs.* (old).—The hangman. [From the CRAMPING of the rope, + CULL, a man.] *Cf.*, CRAMP RINGS (*q.v.*).

CRAMP IN THE HAND, *subs. phr.* (common). — Meanness; stinginess.

CRAMP-RINGS, *subs.* (old).—Bolts; shackles; fetters. [Properly a ring of gold or silver, which after being blessed by the sovereign, was held a specific for cramp and falling-sickness.] For synonyms, *see* DARBIES.

1609. DEKKER, *Lanthorne and Candlelight* [ed. Grosart, III., 203]. Straight we're to the Cuffin Queer forced to bing; And 'cause we are poor made to scour the CRAMP-RING.

1671. HEAD AND KIRKMAN, *The English Rogue*, 'Canting Song.' Till CRAMPRINGS quire, tip Cove his Hire, And Quire-ken do them catch.

1706. E. COLES, *Eng. Dict.*, s.v.

1785. GROSE, *Dict. Vulg. Tongue*, s.v.

CRAMP-WORDS, *subs.* (old).—1. Hard, unpronounceable vocables; CRACKJAW WORDS (*q.v.*).

1748. T. DYCHE, *Dictionary* (5 ed.). CRAMP WORDS (s.): hard, difficult, unusual or uncommon words.

1779. MRS. COWLEY, *Who's the Dupe?* II., ii. I've been in the Dictionary this half-hour, and have picked up CRAMP WORDS enough to puzzle and delight the old gentleman the remainder of his life.

1812. COOMBE, *Tour in S. of Picturesque*, C. xxv. Who get CRAMP WORDS, and cant the Muse In Magazines and in Reviews.

2 (thieves'). — Sentence of death. [A figurative usage of sense 1.]

1748. DYCHE, *Dict.*, 5 ed. CRAMP-WORDS (s) . . . also in the canting dialect the sentence of death pass'd by the judge upon a criminal.

1785. GROSE, *Dict. Vulg. Tongue.* He has just undergone the CRAMP-WORD.

CRANBERRY-EYE, *subs.* (American). A blood-shot eye resulting from alcoholism.

CRANK, *subs.* (old).—1. Sometimes CRANKE.—*See* quots. and COUNTERFEIT CRANK.

1567. HARMAN, *Caveat* (1814), p. 33. These that do counterfet the CRANKE be yong knaues and yonge harlots, that deeply dissemble the falling sicknes. For the CRANK in their language is the fallinge evill.

1610. ROWLANDS, *Martin Mark-all*, p. 38 (H. Club's Repr., 1874). CRANCKE, the falling sickenesse: and thereupon your Rogues that counterfeit the falling sickenes, are called counterfeit CRANCKS.

2. (old). — Gin and water. — *Grose* [1785].

3. (American).—An eccentric, a crotcheteer. [From the colloquial CRANKY (*q.v.*) = full of crotchets; crazy.] *Cf.*, COUNTERFEIT CRANK.

1886. *Florida Times Union*, 22 May. I know perfectly well that I shall probably be called an old fogy, if not a CRANK, for presuming to think that anything in the past can be better than in the present.

1887. *New York Tribune*, 4 Nov. A good deal of ridicule, mostly good-natured, is showered upon the base-ball CRANK, as everybody persists in calling the man or woman who manifests any deep interest in the great American game.

1888. *Daily Inter-Ocean*, 2 Feb. The man was evidently a CRANK, and said that 4,000 dollars were due him by the Government.

Adj. (nautical).—Easily upset: *e.g.*, 'the skiff is very CRANK.'

CRANK-CUFFIN, *subs.* (old).—One of the canting-crew whose specialty was to feign sickness. [From CRANK (*q.v.*, sense 1), the 'falling - sickness,' + CUFFIN (*see* COVE), a man.]

1749. BAMPFYLDE MOORE-CAREW, *Oath of the Canting Crew.* I, CRANK-CUFFIN, swear to be True to this fraternity.

CRANKY, *adj.* (colloquial).—Crotchetty; whimsical; ricketty; not to be depended upon; crazy. [*Cf.*, quot., 1787.]

ENGLISH SYNONYMS. Dicky; maggotty; dead-alive; yappy; touched; chumpish; comical; dotty; rocketty; queer; faddy; fadmongering; twisted; funny.

FRENCH SYNONYMS. *Chevrotin* (popular: applied to a bad or irritable temper); *être comme un crin* (popular); *avoir sa chique* (familiar: said of the temper).

1787. GROSE, *Prov. Glossary.* CRANKY, ailing, sickly; from the Dutch *crank*, sick.

1840. DICKENS, *Old Curiosity Shop*, ch. vii., p. 33. Adding to this retort an observation to the effect that his friend appeared to be rather CRANKY in point of temper.

1863. C. READE, *Hard Cash*, II., 113. He had repeatedly been called into cases of mania described as sudden, and almost invariably found the patient had been CRANKY for years.

1873. MRS. EDWARDS, *A Vagabond Heroine*, in *Temple Bar*, June. 'On goes the CRANKY carriage, on goes the swearing driver and the high souled Burke.'

1874. MRS. H. WOOD, *Johnny Ludlow*, 1 S., No. III., p. 42. 'What's the matter now?' asked Mrs. Hall, in her CRANKY way.

CRANNY, *subs.* (venery). — The female *pudendum*. For synonyms, *see* MONOSYLLABLE.

CRANNY-HUNTER, *subs.* (venery).— The *penis*. For synonyms, *see* CREAMSTICK.

CRAP, *subs.* (old).—1. Money; sometimes CROP. For synonyms, *see* ACTUAL and GILT.

1748. T. DYCHE, *Dictionary* (5 ed.), s.v.

1787. GROSE, *Prov. Glossary* and *Dict. Vulg. Tongue* [1785]. CRAP . . . In the north it is sometimes used for money.

2. (old).—The gallows. For synonyms, *see* NUBBING CHEAT.

1830. BULWER LYTTON, *Paul Clifford*, p. 255 (ed. 1854). 'Ah!' said Long Ned, with a sigh, 'that is all very well, Mr. Nabbem; but I'll go to the CRAP like a gentleman.'

1834. HARRISON AINSWORTH, *Rookwood.* And what if, at length, boys, he comes to the CRAP Even rack punch has *some* bitter in it.

3. (printers').—Type that has got mixed; technically known as 'pi.' [Here compared to excrement.]

Verb, trs. and *intrs.* (old).—1. To hang; to be CRAPPED = to be hanged.

2. (common).—To ease oneself by evacuation. For synonyms, *see* BURY A QUAKER and MRS. JONES.

CRAPPED, *ppl. adj.* (old).—Hanged. [From CRAP (*q.v.*, *subs.*, sense 2), + ED.]—*See* CROPPED.

1785. GROSE, *Dict. Vulg. Tongue.* s.v.

CRAPPING CASA, CASE, CASTLE or **KEN**, *subs.* (common).—A water-closet. [From CRAP, *verb*, sense 2 (*q.v.*), to ease oneself, + ING + CASA or KEN, a house.] For synonyms, *see* BURY A QUAKER and MRS. JONES.

CRAPPING-CASTLE, *subs.* (hospital). —A night-stool.

CRASH, *subs.* (old).—1. Entertainment. Probably a cant word.— *Nares.*

2. (theatrical).—The machine used to suggest the roar of thunder; a noise of desperate (and unseen) conflict; an effect of 'alarums, excursions' generally.

Verb (old).—To kill. For synonyms, *see* COOK ONE'S GOOSE.

CRASHING - CHEATS or **CHETES**, *subs.* (old).—1. The teeth. [From CRASH, to break to pieces. + ING + CHEAT, a thing, from A.S. *ceat.*] For synonyms, *see* GRINDERS.

1567. HARMAN, *Caveat* (1814), p. 64, s.v.

1671. R. HEAD, *English Rogue*, pt. I., ch. v., p. 48 (1874), s.v.

1706. E. COLES, *Eng. Dict.*, s.v.

1785. GROSE, *Dict. Vulg. Tongue*, s.v.

1811. *Lexicon Balatronicum*, s.v.

2. (old).—*See* quots.

1567. HARMAN, *Caveat* (1814), p. 66. CRASHING CHETES: appels, peares, or any other fruit.

1610. ROWLANDS, *Martin Mark-all*, p. 37 (H. Club's Repr., 1874), CRASHING CHEATES: apples.

CRATER, CRATUR, or CREATURE, *subs.* (old).—Formerly, any kind of liquor, but now, Irish whiskey. [Fuller speaks of water as 'a CREATURE so common and needful,' and Bacon describes light as 'God's first CREATURE.' Transition is easy.] THE SKIN OF THE CREATURE = the bottle. For synonyms, *see* DRINKS.

1598. SHAKSPEARE, *II. King Henry IV.*, ii. 2. My appetite was not princely got; for, by my troth, I do now remember the poor CREATURE, small beer.

1663. HOWARD, *The Committee*, Act iv. *Mrs. Day.* Oh fie upon't! who would have believ'd that we should have liv'd to have seen Obadiah overcome with the CREATURE.

1683. S.B. *Anacreon done into English out of the original Greek.* Oxford. There goes a very pleasant Story of him, that once having took a Cup too much of CREATURE, he came staggering homewards through the Market Place, etc.

1772. GRAVES, *Spiritual Quixote*, bk. VII., ch. ii. You will never be able to hold out as Mr. Whitfield does. He seems to like a bit of the good CRETUR as well as other folks.

1816. SCOTT, *Old Mortality*, I., p. . . . I do most humbly request. . . that . . . thou wilt take off this measure, called by the profane a gill, of the comfortable CREATURE, which the carnal do denominate brandy.

1836. M. SCOTT, *Tom Cringle's Log*, ch. xiv. He produced two bottles of brandy . . . so we passed the CREATURE round, and tried all we could to while away the tedious night.

1842. *Punch*, vol. II., p. 23. And reaching home refresh myself with a 'kervartern of the CRATUR!'

1864. *Good Words*, p. 952. Well as an Irishman—who had already paid for one pot of porter and a drop of the CRATER besides—I was not going to hear anything against ould Ireland.

CRAWL, *subs.* (tailors').—A workman who curries favour with a foreman or employer; a 'lickspittle' or 'bum-sucker.'

CRAWLER, *subs.* (common).—1. A cab that leaves the rank and 'crawls' the street in search of fares.

1860. *Daily News.* It is said the question of making increased provisions for cab-stands, with a view to the restriction of the wandering cabs called CRAWLERS, is now under the consideration of the Chief Commissioner of Police.

1885. *Daily News*, August 7, p. 5, col. 1. How often does the driver of the CRAWLER increase his pace just as he sees some one venturing to attempt a crossing.

2. (common). — A contemptible person, especially a 'bum-sucker' or 'lickspittle.' For synonyms, *see* SNIDE.

1885. *Evening News*, 21 Sept., p. 4, col. 1. The complainant called her father a liar, a bester, and a CRAWLER.

CRAWTHUMPERS, *subs.* (old). — 1. Roman Catholics, 'the Pope's cockrels' (1629). Also called BRISKET-BEATERS and, collectively, the BREAST-FLEET. In America a CRAWTHUMPER = an Irishman or DICK, *i.e.*, an Irish Catholic.

1782. WOLCOT, *Lyric Odes*, No. 7, in wks. (1809) I., 69. We are no CRAWTHUMPERS, no *devotees*.

1811. *Lexicon Balatronicum.* CRAW THUMPERS: Roman Catholics, so called from their beating their breasts in the confession of their sins.

1889. *Philadelphia Public Ledger* [quoted in *S. J. & C.*, p. 279]. Wanted a servant-maid. No pulings or CRAWTHUMPERS need apply.

CREAM, *subs.* (venery).—The seminal fluid; Marlowe's 'thrice-decocted blood'; the 'white-blow' and the 'father-stuff' of Whitman. A single drop is called A SNOWBALL (*q.v.*).

ENGLISH SYNONYMS. Butter; buttermilk; fuck; white honey; jelly; baby-juice; homebrewed; jam; 'delicious jam' (Whitman); lather; 'lewd infusion'; love-liquor; milk; milt; ointment; the oyster; roe; seed; soap; spendings; sperm; spermatic juice (Rochester); spume; spunk; starch; stuff; the tread.—*See* COME.

PORTUGUESE SYNONYMS. *Leite* (=milk); *esporra*; *langouha* (= a kind of thick gum).

CREAM CHEESE. TO MAKE ONE BELIEVE THE MOON IS MADE OF CREAM (or GREEN) CHEESE, *verbal phr.* (popular).—To humbug; to deceive; to impose upon. For synonyms, *see* BAMBOOZLE and JOCKEY.

CREAM FANCY.—*See* BILLY, *subs.*, sense 1.

CREAM JUGS, *subs.* (Stock Exchange).—1. Charkof-Krementschug Railway Bonds.

1887. ATKIN, *House Scraps.* Oh! supposing our CREAM-JUGS were broken, Or 'Beetles' were souring the 'Babies.'

2. (common).—The paps.

CREAM OF THE VALLEY, also **COLD CREAM,** *subs. phr.* (common).—Gin. *Cf.*, MOUNTAIN DEW = whiskey. For synonyms, *see* DRINKS.

1858. A. MAYHEW, *Paved with Gold*, ch. i., p. 1. 'What's up, Jim? . . . is it CREAM O' THE WALLEY or fits as has overcome the lady?'

1864. *Comic Almanack*, p. 63. COLD CREAM INTERNALLY.—COLD CREAM is an excellent remedy for 'hot coppers.'

CREAM-STICK, *subs.* (common).—The *penis.* [Literally a STICK supplying CREAM (*q.v.*).

ENGLISH SYNONYMS. Aaron's Rod; Adam's Arsenal (the *penis* and *testes*); the Old Adam; *arbor vitæ*; arse-opener; arse-wedge; athenæum; bayonet; bean-tosser; beak; beef (the *penis* and *testes*); bag of tricks (*idem*); belly-ruffian; Billy - my - Nag; bludgeon; Blueskin; bracmard (Urquhart); my body's captain (Whitman); broom-handle; bum-tickler; bush-beater; bush-whacker; butter-knife; catso or gadso; child-getter; chink-stopper; clothes-prop; club; cock; concern; copper-stick; crack-hunter; cracksman; cranny-haunter; cuckoo; cunny-catcher; 'crimson chitterling' (Urquhart); dagger; dearest member (Burns); dicky; dibble (Scots); dirk (Scots); Don Cypriano (Urquhart); doodle; dropping member; drumstick; eye-opener; father-confessor; 'cunny-burrow ferret' (Urquhart); fiddle-bow; o-for-shame; flute; fornicator; garden-engine and gardener (garden = the female *pudendum*); gaying instrument; generation tool (C. Johnson and Urquhart); goose's neck; cutty gun (Scots); gut-stick; hair-(or beard-)splitter; hair-divider; Hanging Johnny; bald-headed hermit; Irish root; Jack-in-the-box; Jack Robinson; jargonelle; Jezebel; jiggling-bone (Irish); jock (*q.v.*); Dr. Johnson; 'Master John Goodfellow' (Urquhart); John-Thomas; Master John Thursday' (Urquhart); man Thomas; jolly-member (Urquhart); Julius Cæsar; 'knock-Andrew' (Urquhart); lance of love; Langolee (Irish); leather-stretcher; life-preserver; live sausage (Urquhart); Little Davy (Scots); lollipop; lullaby; machine; 'man-root' (Whitman); marrow-bone; marrow-bone-and-cleaver;

Member for Cockshire; merry-maker; middle-leg; mouse; mole; mowdiwort (Scots); Nebuchadnezzar (*cf.*, GREENS); nilnisistando (Urquhart); Nimrod; nudinnudo (Urquhart); 'nine-inch knocker' (Urquhart); old man; peace-maker; pecker; pecnoster; pego; pestle; pike (Shakspeare); pike-staff; pile-driver; pintle; pizzle; ploughshare; plug-tail; pointer; 'poperine pear' (Shakspeare); Polyphemus; 'pond-snipe' (Whitman); prick (Shakspeare and Fletcher); 'prickle'; privates, and private property (the *penis* and *testes*); 'privy member' (Biblical); quim-stake; ramrod; 'Rector of the females' (Rochester); Roger; rolling-pin; root; rudder; rump-splitter; Saint Peter (who 'keeps the keys of Paradise'); 'sausage' (Sterne); sceptre; shove-straight; sky-scraper; solicitor-general; spigot; 'split-rump' (Urquhart); spindle; sponge (*cf.*, RAMROD); staff of life; stern-post; sugar-stick; tarse; tent-peg; thing; 'thumb of love' (Whitman); 'tickle-gizzard' (Urquhart); tickle-toby; tool; toy; trifle (tailors'); trouble-giblets; tug-mutton; unruly-member; vestry-man; watch-and-seals (the *penis* and *testes*); wedge; whore-pipe (Rochester); wimble; yard; Zadkiel (almanack) = the female *pudendum*.

FRENCH SYNONYMS. *Le sansonnet* (popular: literally a starling); *le gluant* (thieves' = Old Slimy. In *Argot* also 'a baby'); *l'asticot* (properly = a flesh-worm); *le jambot* (Villon).

GERMAN SYNONYMS. *Bletzer* (from *Bletz*=a wedge; *bletzen* = to beget); *Breslauer* (Viennese thieves' = *magnum membrum virile*; also, a head-piece, and a large glass, or indeed any quantity of brandy); *Bruder* (also an expression belonging to the *Fiesellange*; literally a brother. *Cf.*, *Schwesterlein*, little sister = the female *pudendum*); *Butzelmann* (in Luther's *Liber Vagatorum* [1529]; *Buze*=little man); *Fiesel* (supposed to be from *Faser* a birch-rod or fibre; the Eng. *feaze* is also connected with it. Thus, *Mädchenfiesel*, a 'hot member'; *Pechfiesel*, a shoemaker, etc. *Fiesellange* signifies the language of the strong, *i.e.*, those of the 'fellowship' of thieves, burglars, and rowdies [Fr., *coupeur*], etc. In Vienna *Fiesel* = the lowest and most dangerous type of bawdy-house bully). *Dickmann* (also, an egg, or testicle); *Pinke* or *Finke* (Low German); *Schmeichaz* or *Schmeigaz* (O.H.G. *smeichen* = to flatter, to laugh); *Schwanz* (also, a fool or boaster).

PORTUGUESE SYNONYMS. *Pae de todos* (=father of all); *porra* (=a strong stick); *virgolleiro* (= that which deprives of virginity); *pica* (=lance; also, a measure equal in length to the handle of a long spear; *cf.*, Eng. YARD); *bacamarte* (=a milk-giving gun); *a montholia de Pastor* (= an oil-flask).

CREAMY, *adj.* (general).—Excellent; first-rate. For synonyms, *see* A1 and FIZZING.

CREATION. TO BEAT OR LICK CREATION, *verbal phr.* (American).—To overpower; excel; surpass; to be incomparable. English variants are 'to beat hollow, to sticks, or to fits,' etc. *Cf.*, BIG AS ALL OUTDOORS.

1848. BARTLETT, *Dict. of Amer.* '*Proverbs.*' When a man runs his head against a post, he curses the post first, ALL CREATION next, and something else last, and never thinks of cursing himself.

1862. *Among the Mermaids.* 'An Old Sailor's Yarn,' p. 86. The notion of finding the capting's cask pleased me mightily cos I knowed it would TICKLE the old man LIKE ALL CREATION.

1888. *Detroit Free Press*, 14 Aug. I'm willin' to take advice. BEATS ALL CREATION how I mistook, but I shan't go agin yer words.

CREEME, *verb* (old).—To slip or slide anything into the hands of another.—*Grose* [1785].

CREEPER, *subs.* (general).—One who cringes and 'curries favour'; a 'skunk,' or SNIDE (*q.v.*, for synonyms).

CREEPERS, *subs.* (common). — 1. The feet.

ENGLISH SYNONYMS. Dew-beaters; beetle-crushers; under-standings; trotters; tootsies; stumps (also the legs); ever-lasting shoes; hocks; boot-trees; pasterns; ards (Old Cant: now used as an adjective. = 'hot'); double-breasters; daisy-beaters; kickers; crabs; trampers; hockles; hoofs; pudseys.

FRENCH SYNONYMS. *Les trottins* (popular: *trottiner*, to go a jog-trot; *aller chercher les pardons de Saint-Trottin*, to take a walk instead of going to church); *les reposoirs* (common: properly [in *sing.*] a resting place or pause; also an altar set up in the streets for a procession); *les ripatons* (popular); *les palerons* (thieves': properly, in *sing.*, a shoulder-blade); *les paturons* (thieves': properly pasterns); *les harpions* (thieves': also hands. Cotgrave has *harpe d'un chien* = a dog's claw or paw; also, *Il mania très bien ses harpes*, He stirred his fingers very nimbly. [*Cf.*, 'pickers and stealers' = fingers]; *les mains courantes* (popular: literally running hands).

GERMAN SYNONYMS. *Tretter* (*Cf.*, English 'trotter'); *Trittling*, or *Trittchen* (Hanoverian = shoe, boot, foot, or staircase); *Trittlingspflanzer* or *Trittlingsmelochner* (the shoemaker).

ITALIAN SYNONYMS *Calcioso*; *pisante*; *bottiero*; *mazzo*.

2. (general). — Lice. For synonyms, *see* CHATES.

CREEPS, *subs.* (common).—The peculiar thrill resulting from an undefinable sense of dread. [Literally a 'crawling' of the flesh as with fear.] Also known as GOOSE-FLESH, COLD SHIVERS, and COLD WATER DOWN THE BACK.

1836. DICKENS, *Pickwick Papers.* I wants to make yer flesh CREEP.

1864. E. YATES, *Broken to Harness*, ch. xiii. [Late Autumn.] Dreary down in the old country mansions . . . where the servants, town-bred, commence to be colded, sniffy, to have shivers and CREEPS.

1870. *London Figaro*, 27 June. 'A River Romance.' Talking about bodies, I could give you the CREEPS with what I've seen.

1883. *The Lute*, 15 Jan., p. 18, col. 2. We see the great tragedian holding on to a chair, and giving his audience CREEPS with the 'Dream of Eugene Aram.'

1890. *Globe*, 22 May, p. 1, col. 4. Miss Gertrude is the sister of Mrs. Chanler-Rives (better known as Amélie, or still better as the writer of *The Quick or the Dead*, by which many ladylike persons have been given 'the CREEPS').

CREVECŒUR.—*See* HEARTBREAKER.

CREVICE, *subs.* (venery). — The female *pudendum.* For synonyms, *see* MONOSYLLABLE.

CRI, *subs.* (popular). — The Criterion, theatre and restaurant, at Piccadilly Circus.

c. 1886. *Broadside Ballad*, 'Another Fellah's.' Round into the CRI ev'ry evening I slip, And deep in the pale sparkling bitter I dip.

CRIB, *subs.* (old).—1. The stomach. *Cf.*, CRIBBING, sense 1. [A transferred sense of CRIB = a manger, rack, or feeding place. *Cf.*, Isaiah i., 3, 'The ox knoweth his owner, and the ass his master's CRIB.'] For synonyms, *see* BREAD-BASKET and VICTUALLING OFFICE.

1656. BROME, *Jovial Crew*, Act. ii. Here's pannum and lap, and good poplars of Yarrum, To fill up the CRIB, and to comfort the quarron.

2. (colloquial). — A house; place of abode; apartments; lodgings; shop; warehouse; 'den,' 'diggings,' or 'snuggery.' For synonyms, *see* DIGGINGS. [From A.S., *crib*, or *cribb* a small habitation.]

1598. SHAKSPEARE, *King Henry IV.* Why, rather, sleep, liest thou in smoky CRIBS, Than in the perfumed chambers of the great?

1830. BULWER LYTTON, *Paul Clifford*, p. 80 (ed. 1854). Now, now in the CRIB, where a ruffler may lie, Without fear that the traps should distress him.

1837. DICKENS, *Oliver Twist*, ch. xix. The CRIB'S barred up at night like a jail.

1847. *Illus. London News*, 22 May. The burglar has his CRIB in Clerkenwell.

1860. *Chambers' Journal*, vol. XIII., p. 212. He said he was awful flattered like by the honour of seeing two such gents at his CRIB.

1882. *Daily News*, 5 Oct., p. 5, col. 2. To manage escapes from prison successfully is only an application of the principles which enable the burglar to crack the rural CRIB and appropriate the swag of her Majesty's peaceful subjects.

3. (popular). — A situation, 'place,' or 'berth.' [The transition from *subs.*, sense 2, is easy and natural.]

4. (school and University).— A literal translation surreptitiously used by students; also a theft of any kind; specifically, anything copied without acknowledgment.—[*See verb.*, sense 2.] For synonyms, *see* PONY.

1841. *Punch*, vol. I., p. 185. He has with a prudent forethought stuffed his CRIBS inside his double-breasted waistcoat.

1853. C. BEDE, *Verdant Green*, pt. I., p. 64.

1855. THACKERAY, *Newcomes*, ch. xxii. I wish I had read Greek a little more at school . . . when we return I think I shall try and read it with CRIBS.

1856. T. HUGHES, *Tom Brown's School-days*, pt. II., ch. vi. Tom, I want you to give up using vulgus books and CRIBS.

1889. *Globe*, 12 Oct., p. 1, col. 4. Always, it seems likely, there will be men 'going up' for examinations; and every now and again, no doubt, there will be among them a wily 'Heathen Pass-ee' like him of whom Mr. Hilton speaks—who had CRIBS up his sleeve, and notes on his cuff.

5. (thieves').—A bed.—[*See subs.*, senses 2 and 3.]

1827. MAGINN, from Vidocq. Lend me a lift in the family way. You may have a CRIB to stow in.

Verb (colloquial).—1 To steal or pilfer; used specifically of petty thefts. For synonyms, *see* PRIG.

1748. T. DYCHE, *Dictionary* (5 ed.). CRIB (v.): to with-hold, keep back, pinch,

or thieve a part out of money given to lay out for necessaries.

1772. FOOTE *Nabob*, Act i. There are a brace of birds and a hare, that I CRIBBED this morning out of a basket of game.

1846. T. HOOD, *Ode to Rae Wilson, Esqr.*, wks., vol. IV., p. 224. Yet sure of Heaven themselves, as if they'd CRIBB'D Th' impression of St. Peter's keys in wax.

1855. ROBERT BROWNING, *Men and Women. Fra Lippo Lippi*, ed. 1863, p. 351. Black and white I drew From good old gossips waiting to confess Their CRIBS of barrel-droppings, candle-ends.

1889. *Answers*, 27 July, page 141, col. 1. He knew that if the manuscript got about the Yankees would think it a smart thing to CRIB it.

2. (school and University).— To use a translation; to cheat at an examination; to plagiarise.

1841. *Punch*, vol. I., p. 177. CRIBBING his answers from a tiny manual of knowledge, two inches by one-and-a-half in size, which he hides under his blotting-paper.

1856. T. HUGHES, *Tom Brown's School-days*, pt. II., ch. iii. Finishing up with two highly moral lines extra, making ten in all, which he CRIBBED entire from one of his books.

TO CRACK A CRIB.—*See* under CRACK.

CRIBBAGE-FACE and **CRIBBAGE-FACED**, *subs.* and *adj. phr.* (common).—Pock-marked and like a cribbage - board. Otherwise COLANDER - FACED, CRUMPET-FACED, PIKELET - FACED, and MOCKERED (*q.v.*).

FRENCH SYNONYMS. *Avoir un grenier à lentilles* (popular: a cock-loft, granary, or garret, for the storage of lentils); *ne pas s'être assuré contre la grêle* (popular: *grêle*=hail); *un morceau de gruyère* (popular: that cheese being honeycombed with holes); *avoir un moule à gaufres* (popular: *moule* = mould; *gaufre* = a cake); *une écumoire* (familiar: properly a skimmer); *poêle à châtaignes* (*poêle* = frying pan and *châtaignes* = chestnuts; the colander-like shovel for roasting chestnuts).

1785. GROSE, *Dict. Vulg. Tongue.* CRIBBAGE-FACED: marked with the small-pox, the pits bearing a kind of resemblance to the holes in a cribbage-board.

CRIBBER, *subs.* (military). — A grumbler. [A horse that gnaws his crib or manger.] *Cf.*, CRIB-BITER, and for synonyms, *see* RUSTY-GUTS.

CRIBBEYS or **CRIBBY-ISLANDS**, *subs.* (old).—Blind alleys, courts, and bye-ways; Fr., *culs-de-sac.*

CRIBBING, *verbal subs.* (old).—1. Food and Drink. *Cf.*, CRIB, sense 1.

1656. R. BROME, *A Jovial Crew.* For all this ben CRIBBING and Peck let us then, Bowse a health to the gentry cofe of the ken.

2. (schools' and University and general).—Stealing; purloining; using a translation. *Cf.*, CRIB, *subs.*, sense 4.

1862. FARRAR, *St. Winifred's*, ch. xxxv. They would not call it stealing but bagging a thing, or, at the worst, CRIBBING it—concealing the villainy under a new name.

CRIB-BITER, *subs.* (common).—An inveterate grumbler. [Properly a horse that worries his crib, rack, manger, or groom, and at the same time draws in his breath so as to make the peculiar noise called wind-sucking.] French equivalents are *un gourgousseur*; *un rême*; *un renâcleur*; and *un renaudeur.*—*See* CRIBBER.

CRIB-CRACKER, *subs.* (general).—A housebreaker.

1880. G. R. SIMS, *How the Poor Live*, p. 11. The little boys look up half with awe and half with admiration at the burly Sikes with his flash style, and delight in gossip concerning his talents as a CRIB-CRACKER, and his adventures as a pickpocket.

CRIB-CRACKING, *verbal subs.* (thieves').—Housebreaking.

1852. *Punch*, vol. XXIII., p. 161. With higher ambition Bill Sykes he burned, And becoming experter as he grew older, From cly-faking to CRIB-CRACKING turned.

CRIES.—*See* STREET CRIES.

CRIKEY! CRACKY! CRY! *intj.* (common).—Formerly, 'a profane oath'; now a mere expression of astonishment. [A corruption of 'Christ.']

1837. R. H. BARHAM, *The Ingoldsby Legends* (ed. 1862), p. 276. It would make you exclaim, 'twould so forcibly strike ye, If a Frenchman *Superbe!*—if an Englishman CRIKEY!

1841. *Comic Almanack*, p. 275. Oh! CRIKEY, Bill; vot a conch that lady's got!

1853. *Diogenes*, II., 54. O, CRIKEY! the switching I got, At the hand of the cruel old miser.

1888. W. E. HENLEY. 'Culture in the Slums.' 'O CRIKEY, Bill!' she says to me, she ses. 'Look sharp,' ses she, 'with them there sossiges.'

CRIMINI, CRIMINEY, or **CRIMES!**— *See* CRIKEY. [Possibly the latter usage has been influenced by *crimen meum*, my fault.]

1700. FARQUHAR, *Constant Couple*, Act iv., Sc. 1. Murder'd my brother! O CRIMINI!

1816. SCOTT, *Antiquary*, ch. xvi. 'A monument of a knight-templar on each side of a Grecian porch, and a Madonna on the top of it!—O CRIMINI!

1841. *The Comic Almanack*, p. 280. 'A Lament for Bartlemy Fair.' Oh! lawk; oh! dear; oh! CRIMENY me; what a downright sin and a shame.

CRIMSON. TO MAKE THINGS LOOK CRIMSON, *verbal phr.* (American). —To indulge in a drunken frolic; to PAINT THE TOWN RED (*q.v.*).

CRIMSON CHITTERLING, *subs. phr.* (old). — The *penis.* Used by Urquhart. For synonyms, *see* CREAMSTICK.

CRINCLE-POUCH, *subs.* (old).—A sixpence. For synonyms, *see* BENDER.

1593. '*Bacchus' Bountie*,' *Harl. Misc.*, II., p. 270 [ed. 1808-11]. See then the goodnes of this so gracious a god, al yee, which in the driest drought of summer, had rather shroude your throates with a handfull of hemp, than with the expence of an odde CRINCLEPOUCH, wash yourselues within and without, and make yourselues as mery as dawes.

CRINKUM-CRANKUM, *subs.* (old). —The female *pudendum.* [Properly a winding way.] For synonyms, *see* MONOSYLLABLE.

CRINKUMS, *subs.* (old).—A venereal disease. *Cf.*, CRINKUM-CRANKUM. For synonyms, *see* LADIES' FEVER.

CRINOLINE, *subs.* (common).—A woman. For synonyms, *see* PETTICOAT.

CRIPPLE, *subs.* (old).—1. A 'snid' (Scots) or sixpence.—[*See* quots., 1785 and 1885.] For synonyms, *see* BENDER.

1785. GROSE, *Dict. Vulg. Tongue.* CRIPPLE: six pence, that piece being commonly much bent and distorted.

1789. GEO. PARKER, *Life's Painter*, p. 178, s.v.

1819. T. MOORE, *Tom Crib's Memorial*, p. 25, *n.* A bandy or CRIPPLE, a sixpence.

1885. *Household Words*, 20 June, p. 155. The sixpence is a coin more liable to bend than most others, so it is not surpris-

ing to find that several of its popular names have reference to this weakness. It is called a bandy, a 'bender,' a CRIPPLE.

2. (common). — An awkward oaf; also a dullard. Fr., *malapatte* (popular: properly *mal à la patte*). [Figurative for one that creeps, limps, or halts— whether physically or mentally.] *Cf.*, sense 3, and GO IT, YOU CRIPPLES.

3. (Wellington College).—A dolt; literally one without a leg to stand on. *Cf.*, sense 2, and GO IT, YOU CRIPPLES.

GO IT, YOU CRIPPLES! *phr.* (general).—A sarcastic comment on strenuous effort; frequently used without much sense of fitness; *e.g.*, when the person addressed is a capable athlete. WOODEN LEGS ARE CHEAP is sometimes added as an intensitive.

1840. THACKERAY, *Cox's Diary.* 'Striking a balance,' p. 229. 'O! come along.' said Lord Lollypop, 'come along this way, ma'am! Go IT, YE CRIPPLES.

CRISP, *subs.* (popular).—A banknote. For synonyms, *see* SOFT.

CRISPIN, *subs.* (common).—A shoemaker. [From Saints Crispin and Crispianus, the patrons of the 'gentle craft,' *i.e.*, shoemaking.]

1785. GROSE, *Dict. Vulg. Tongue*, s.v.

1861. *Punch*, vol. XLI., p. 246. CRISPIN, everybody knows to be a name for a shoemaker.

ST. CRISPIN'S LANCE, *subs. phr.* (old). — An awl. [From CRISPIN (*q.v.*) + LANCE, a weapon.] Fr., *une lance.*

CRISPIN'S HOLIDAY, *subs. phr.* (old). —Every Monday throughout the year, but most particularly the 25th of October, being the anniversary of Crispinus and Crispianus.

CROAK, *subs.* (thieves').—A dying speech, especially the confession of a murderer. Also the same as printed for sale in the streets by a 'FLYING STATIONER. [From the *verbal* sense (*q.v.*).]

1887. A. BARRÈRE, *Argot and Slang*, p. 272. The criminal . . . would perhaps, utter for the edification of the crowd his 'tops, or CROAKS,' that is, his last dying speech.

1887. W. E. HENLEY, *Villon's Straight Tip.* Go crying CROAKS, or flash the drag.

Verb.—To die. For synonyms, *see* ALOFT.

CROAKER, *subs.* (old).—1. A sixpence. For synonyms, *see* BENDER.

2. (old).—A beggar.

1857. SNOWDEN, *Mag. Assistant*, 3 ed., p. 444, s.v.

3. (common).—A dying person.—*See* CROAK, *verbal* sense.

4. (common). — A corpse. [From CROAK, *verb.* sense, through CROAKER, senses 2 and 3.] For synonyms, *see* DEAD-MEAT.

5. (provincial).—*See* quot.

1886. *Ulster Echo*, 31 July, p. 4. The inspector of nuisances said the meat was known as CROAKER, or the flesh of an animal which had died a natural death.

6. (prison).—A doctor [connected with CROCUS, but influenced by CROAKER, *subs.*, senses 2, 3, and 4.]

1889. *Evening News* [quoted in *Slang, Jargon, and Cant*]. One man who had put his name for the 'butcher' or CROAKER, would suddenly find that he had three ounces of bread less to receive, and then a scene would ensue.

7. (common).—A person, male or female, who sees everything *en noir*, and whose conversation is likened to that of the raven, which is a bird of ill-omen.—*See* Goldsmith's *Good Natured Man*. Fr., *un glas*=also a passing bell.

CROAKUMSHIRE, *subs.* (old).—Northumberland. [Grose: 'from the particular croaking in the pronunciation of the people of that county, especially about Newcastle and Morpeth, where they are said to be born with a burr in their throats, which prevents their pronouncing the letter 'r.']

CROCK, *subs.* (common).—A worthless animal; a fool; said of a horse it signifies a good-for-nothing brute; of a man or woman, a duffer, a 'rotter.' [Most likely from the Scots CROCK = an old sheep.]

1887. *Sporting Times*, 12 March, p. 2, col. 5. The wretched CROCKS that now go to the post will be relegated to more appropriate work.

1889. *Bird o' Freedom*, 7 Aug., p. 3. For five minutes that CROCK went about twice as fast as it had ever done.

1889. *Illustrated Bits*, 13 July, 'I say,' said the Lumberer to the Old Hermit, as they stood at the mouth of the Cave listening to the song birds, 'you are getting a bit of a CROCK—failing fast, I should say.'

CROCKETTS, *subs.* (Winchester College).—A kind of bastard cricket, sometimes called 'small CROCHETTS.' Five stumps are used and a fives ball, with a bat of plain deal about two inches broad, or a broomstick.

1870. MANSFIELD, *School-Life at Winchester College*, p. 122. The more noisily disposed would indulge in . . . playing Hicockolorum, or CROCKETTS.

TO GET CROCKETTS, *verbal phr.*—To fail to score at cricket; to make a duck's egg.

CROCODILE, *subs.* (University).—A girl's school walking two and two.

CROCUS, CROCUS-METALLORUM or **CROAKUS,** *subs.* (common).—A doctor; specifically, a quack. [Conjecturally, a derivative of CROAK=to die. *Cf.*, quot. 1781, under CROCUSSING RIG.]

ENGLISH SYNONYMS. Pill; squirt; butcher; croaker; corpse-provider; bolus; clyster; gallipot. [Several of these terms also =an apothecary.]

FRENCH SYNONYMS. *Un dragueur* (popular: literally a dredging machine); *un cliabeau* (a doctor at St. Lazare); *un bénévole* (popular: a young doctor, especially one walking the hospitals); *un marchand de morts subites* (common: literally 'a dealer in sudden death.' *Cf.*, CORPSE PROVIDER).

GERMAN SYNONYM. *Rofe* or *Raufe* (from the Hebrew).

ITALIAN SYNONYMS. *Maggio* (signifying God, king, lord, and pope); *posteggiatore* (literally 'he that places'; used of any charlatan, but particularly of a quack doctor); *dragon di farda*.

1785. GROSE, *Dict. Vulg. Tongue*. CROCUS OR CROCUS METALLORUM: a nickname for the surgeons of the army and navy.

1851-61. H. MAYHEW, *London Lab. and Lond. Poor*, vol. I., p. 231 (quoted in list of patterer's words).

1857. SNOWDEN, *Mag. Assistant*, 3 ed. p., 444, s.v.

CROCUS-CHOVEY (vagrants' and thieves').—A doctor's shop. From [CROCUS = doctor + CHOVEY, a shop.]

CROCUS-PITCHER, *subs.* (vagrants' and thieves').—A quack ambulant. [From CROCUS (*q.v.*), a doctor, + PITCHER, one that stands in the street to hold forth concerning his business.]

CROCUSSING-RIG, *subs.* (old).—Travelling from place to place as a quack doctor. [From CROCUS (*q.v.*), a doctor, + ING + RIG, a performance or trick.]

1781. G. PARKER, *View of Society*, II., 171. CROCUSSING RIG is performed by men and women, who travel as Doctors or Doctoresses.

CRONE, *subs.* (showmen's).—A clown or buffoon.

CROOK, *subs.* (old).—1. A sixpence. [An abbreviation of CROOKBACK (*q.v.*).]

1789. GEO. PARKER, *Life's Painter*, p. 178, s.v.

2. (general).—A thief; swindler; one who gets things ON THE CROOK (*q.v.*).

1887. *Orange Journal*, 16 April. Strange as the statement may seem, the public know nothing of the work of a really clever CROOK, and the police themselves know very little more. The explanation of this ignorance is a very simple one. A CROOK whose methods are exposed is a second-rate CROOK.

ON THE CROOK, *adv. phr.* (thieves').—The antithesis of ON THE STRAIGHT (*q.v.*). *Cf.*, ON THE CROSS.

1879. J. W. HORSLEY, in *Macm. Mag.*, XL., 503. Which he had bought ON THE CROOK (dishonestly).

TO CROOK (or COCK) THE ELBOW, or the LITTLE FINGER, *verbal phr.* (popular).—To drink. [A French colloquialism, identical in meaning, is *lever le coude*; a hard drinker is *un adroit du coude*.] For synonyms, *see* LUSH.

1871. DE VERE, *Americanisms*. To CROOK THE ELBOW, is one of the many slang terms for drinking.

1877. BESANT AND RICE, *With Harp and Crown*, ch. xix. The secretary . . . might have done great things in literature but for his unfortunate CROOK OF THE ELBOW. As he only CROOKS it at night, it does not matter to the hospital.

1888. *Detroit Free Press*, 3 May, p. 4, col. 1. I'll . . . . ask him to take a drink, chat with him while he CROOKS HIS ELBOW.

CROOK-BACK, *subs.* (old).—A sixpenny piece, many of the slang names of which suggest a bashed and battered appearance; *e.g.*, 'bender,' 'cripple,' 'crook,' CROOKBACK, etc. Quoted by Grose [1785]. For synonyms, *see* BENDER.

CROOKED, *ppl. adj.* (colloquial).—Disappointing; the reverse of STRAIGHT (*q.v.*); pertaining to the habits, ways, and customs of thieves.—*See* ON THE CROOK. So also, *mutatis mutandis*, CROOKEDNESS=rascality of every kind.

1837. *Comic Almanack*, p. 94. Things have gone very CROOKED.

1877. *Five Years' Penal Servitude*, ch. ii., p. 126. The prisoner's friend was also a 'fly' man, and he immediately saw how he could thoroughly pay off the CROOKED officer.

1884. *Daily Telegraph*, 22 Jan., p. 3, col. 1. My time was up the same day as that of two lads of the CROOKED school; it was through them that I took to thieving.

1884. *Echo*, 28 Jan., p. 4, col. 1. Last season will be long remembered in the racing world for the CROOKEDNESS of some owners.

1888. *Detroit Free Press*, 3 Nov. 'What are you trying to get out of me?' 'I am going to see that to-night you are better lodged to begin with. I may decide to do more, but that will depend pretty much on yourself.' 'Nothing CROOKED, is it?' asked the other, suspiciously!

CROOKED AS A VIRGINIA (or SNAKE) FENCE, *phr.* (American).—Uneven; zig-zag; said of matters or persons difficult to keep 'straight.' TO MAKE A VIRGINIA FENCE is to walk unsteadily, as a drunkard. The Virginia fences zigzag with the soil.

CROOKY, *verb* (common).—To hang on to; to lead; to walk arm-in-arm; to court or pay addresses to a girl. For synonyms, *see* TROT OUT.

CROP.—*See* CRAP, sense 1.

CROPPED, *ppl. adj.* (old).—Hanged. For synonyms, *see* LADDER and TOPPED.

1781. G. PARKER, *View of Society*, II., 30. Sentencing some more to be CRAPPED (*sic*) [hanged].

CROPPER, *subs.* (common).—A heavy fall or failure of any kind; generally 'to come a CROPPER.' [Originally hunting.] Analagous French phrases are *avoir une discussion avec le pavé* (literally 'to argue with the pavement'); *prendre un billet de parterre* (a punning play upon words: the pit of a theatre is *parterre*; *par terre* = on the ground: hence to take a ticket for the pit); *se lithographier* (popular). For synonyms in a metaphorical sense, *see* GO TO POT.

1868. *Echoes from the Clubs*, 23 Dec. 'Pleasures of the Hunting Field.' In short, it is fox-hunting which . . . induces the belief that life is a mistake without occasional CROPPERS.

1869. H. J. BYRON, *Not such a Fool as He Looks* [French's Acting ed.], p. 8. Mr. Topham Sawyer missed his own tip as well as his victim's, and CAME DOWN A CROPPER on a convenient doorstep.

1880. A. TROLLOPE, *The Duke's Children*, ch. lxvii. Talking to his father he could not quite venture to ask what might happen if he were TO COME A CROPPER.

1883. *Daily News*, 24 Jan., p. 5, col. 3. Ouida treads 'alone, aloft, sublime' where Astræa might fear to pass, and though she COMES what men call CROPPERS over a thousand details, she is sublimely unconscious of her blunders.

CROPPIE or **CROPPY,** *subs.* (old).—Originally applied to criminals CROPPED as to their ears and their noses by the public executioner; subsequently, to convicts, in allusion to their close CROPPED hair; hence to any person whose hair was cut close to the head; *e.g.*, the Puritans and the Irish Rebels of 1789.

1870. SIR G. C. LEWIS, *Letters*, p. 410. Wearing the hair short and without powder was, at this time, considered a mark of French principles. Hair so worn was called a 'crop.' Hence Lord Melbourne's phrase, 'crop-imitating wig' [*Poetry of Anti-Jacobin*, p. 41]. This is the origin of CROPPIES, as applied to the Irish rebels of 1789.

1877-79. GREEN, *Short Hist. Eng. People*, ch. x., The CROPPIES, as the Irish insurgents were called in derision from their short-cut hair.

CROPPLED. TO BE CROPPLED, *verbal phr.* (Winchester College).—To fail in an examination; to be sent down at a lesson.

CROPPY.—*See* CROPPIE.

CROPS, *verbal phr.*—TO GO AND LOOK AT THE CROPS=to leave the room for the purpose of consulting MRS. JONES (*q.v.*).

CROSS, *subs.* (thieves').—1. A pre-arranged swindle. In its special sporting signification a CROSS is an arrangement to lose on the part of one of the principals in a fight, or any kind of match. When both principals conspire that one shall win, it is called a DOUBLE CROSS (*q.v.*). [Obviously a shortened form of CROSS-BITE (*q.v.*, *verbal* sense).]

1834. W. H. AINSWORTH, *Rookwood*. Two milling coves, each vide avake, Vere backed to fight for heavy stake; But in the mean time, so it vos, Both kids agreed to play a CROSS.

1864. *Derby Day*, p. 39. 'As sure as the sun shines, Askpart 'll lick 'em; if so be,' he added significantly, 'as there ain't no CROSS.'

1867. A. TROLLOPE, *Claverings*, ch. xxx. I always suppose every horse will run to win; and though there may be a CROSS now and again, that's the surest line to go upon.

2. (thieves').—A thief; also CROSS-MAN, CROSS-COVE, CROSS-CHAP, SQUIRE, KNIGHT, or LAD, OF THE CROSS, etc. [Literally a man ON THE CROSS (*q.v.*).] For synonyms, *see* THIEVES.

1830. BULWER LYTTON, *Paul Clifford*, p. 72, ed. 1854. There is an excellent fellow near here, who keeps a public-house, and is a firm ally and generous patron of the LADS OF THE CROSS. *Ibid*, p. 140. Gentlemen of the Road, the Street, the Theatre and the Shop! Prigs, Toby-men, and SQUIRES OF THE CROSS!

1834. H. AINSWORTH, *Rookwood*, bk. IV., ch. ii. Never a CROSS COVE of us all can throw off so prime a chant as yourself.

1864. *Cornhill Magazine*, II., 336. In the following verse, taken from a pet flash song, you have a comic specimen of this sort of guilty chivalry:—'A CROSS COVE is in the street for me, And I a poor girl of low degree; If I was as rich as I am poor, Ye never should go on the cross no more.'

Verb.—1. To play false in a match of any kind.

1887. W. E. HENLEY AND R. L. STEVENSON, *Deacon Brodie*, Act iv., Sc. 3. What made you CROSS the fight and play booty with your own man?

2. (venery).—To possess or 'cover' a woman.

CROSS IN THE AIR, *subs. phr.* (volunteers').—A rifle carried butt-end upwards.

3. (colloquial).—To thwart; to baffle; to spoil.

1709. MATTHEW PRIOR, *The Thief*, *etc.* There the squires of the pad and the knights of the post, Find their fears no more balked and their hopes no more CROSSED.

TO PLAY A CROSS, *verbal phr.*—*See* CROSS, *subs.*, sense 1; and *verb*, sense 1.

1834. W. H. AINSWORTH, *Rookwood*, p. 257 (ed. 1864), Zoroaster was just the man to lose a fight; or, in the language of the Fancy, to PLAY A CROSS.

TO SHAKE THE CROSS, *verbal phr.* (American thieves').—To quit the CROSS and go ON THE SQUARE (*q.v.*).

1877. S. L. CLEMENS ('Mark Twain'), *Life on the Mississippi*. ch. lii., p. 459. The day my time was up, you told me if I would SHAKE THE CROSS and live on the square for three months, it would be the best job i ever done in my life.

TO BE CROSSED, *verbal phr.* (University).—Thus explained in a University Guide:—For not paying term bills to the bursar (treasurer), or for cutting chapels, or lectures, or other offences, an undergrad can be CROSSED at the buttery, or kitchen, or both, *i.e.*, a CROSS is put against his name by the Don, who wishes to see him, or to punish him.

1853. REV. E. BRADLEY, ('Cuthbert Bede'), *Verdant Green*, pt. II., ch. x. Sir!—You will translate all your lectures; have your name CROSSED on the buttery and kitchen books; and be confined to chapel, hall, and college.

See also CROSS, *verb*, sense 1.

ON THE CROSS, *phr.*—The opposite of ON THE SQUARE (*q.v.*). *Cf.*, ON THE CROOK.

1861. H. KINGSLEY, *Ravenshoe*, ch. xxxv. [*Chas. Ravenshoe to Shoeblack*] 'Have you any brothers?' 'Five altogether. Jim was gone for a sojer, it appeared; and Nipper was sent over the water, Harry was gone ON THE CROSS.' 'ON THE CROSS?' said Charles. 'Ah,' the boy said, 'he goes out *cly-faking* and such. He's a *prig*, and a smart one, too. He's *fly*, is Harry.'

1868. OUIDA, *Under Two Flags*, ch. v. Rake had seen a good deal of men and manners, and, in his own opinion at least, was 'up to every dodge ON THE CROSS' that this iniquitous world could unfold.

1877. *Five Years' Penal Servitude*, ch. iii., p. 244. We went down to a bloke I knew up in one of the streets leading off the Euston road who did a little ON THE CROSS now and again, to see what he'd stand for the £300.

1884. *Echo*, 1 March, p. 3, col. 6. Prisoner knew they were stolen, and said he could get rid of any quantity of similar articles that were got ON THE CROSS, a slang expression for stolen goods.

1889. *Answers*, 8 June, p. 25. One of them then came a little nearer, and produced a good gold scarf pin, worth, perhaps, £2 or £3, and asked if I would buy it, adding it was ON THE CROSS (stolen), and I could have it for 2s., as they wanted a shilling to get a bed.

CROSS-BELTS, *subs.* (military).—The Eighth Hussars. [The regiment wears the sword belt over the right shoulder in memory of the Battle of Saragossa, where it took the belts of the Spanish cavalry. This privilege was confirmed by the King's Regulations of 1768.

CROSS-BITE, *subs.* (old).—*See* CROSS-BITING.

Verb (old).—To cheat; to scold; to hoax. [Nares thinks it a compound of CROSS and BITE. It has suffered a double abbreviation, both its components being used substantively and verbally in the same sense.] For synonyms, *see* STIFF.

1581. RICHE, *Farewell to Militarie Profession*. She was such a devill of her tongue, and would so CROSSEBITE hym with suche tauntes and spightful quippes.

1593. G. HARVEY, *New Letter*, in wks. I., 274 (Grosart). If he playeth at fast and loose . . . whom shall he conny catch, or CROSBITE, but his cast-away selfe.

1717. PRIOR, *Alma*, canto iii. As Nature slily had thought fit For some by ends to CROSS-BIT wit.

1822. SCOTT, *Fortunes of Nigel*, ch. xxiii. I know—I know—ugh—but I'll CROSS-BITE him.

CROSS-BITER, *subs.* (old).—A cheat; swindler; or hoaxer. [From CROSS-BITE, *verb* (*q.v.*), + ER.] Fr., *un goureur*.

1592. ROBERT GREENE, *Blacke Bookes Messenger* [part of title]. Laying open the Life and Death of Ned Browne, one of the most notable Cutpurses, CROS-BITERS, and Coneycatchers.

1669. *Nicker Nicked*, in *Harl. Misc.* (ed. Park), II., 108, s.v.

1681. *A Dialogue, etc.*, in *Harl. Misc.* (ed. Park), II., 126. I think nobody knows what he is; but I take him to be a CROSS-BITER.

CROSS-BITING, *verbal subs.* (old).—A deception; cheat; or hoax. *Cf.*, CROSS-BITE, *verb*.

1576. WHETSTONE, *Rocke of Regard*, p. 50. CROSBITING, a kind of cousoning, under the couler of friendship; and in his epistle to the readers, The cheter will fume to see his CROSBITING and cunning shiftes decyphered.

1586. MARLOWE, *Jew of Malta*, IV., v. Like one that is employed in catzerie [knavery] and CROSSBITING.

1610. ROWLANDS, *Martin Mark-all*, p. 53 (H. Club's Repr., 1874). He [Lawrence Crosbiter] first vsed that art which now is named CROSBITING, and from whose name this damned art (CROSBITING) tooke her first call, as if *Laurence Crosbiter* first inuented the same.

1839. W. H. AINSWORTH, *J. Sheppard*, p. 126, ed. 1840. 'The devil,' ejaculated Jonathan. 'Here's a CROSS-BITE.'

CROSS-BUTTOCK, *subs.* (athletics').—A peculiar throw in wrestling. Also used as a *verb* and *verbal subs.*

1690. D'URFEY, *Collin's Walk*, c. ii., p. 74. When th' hardy Major, skilled in Wars, To make quick end of fight prepares, By Strength or'e BUTTOCK CROSS to hawl him, And with a trip i' th' Inturn maul him.

1742. 'Handbill,' in P. Egan's *Boxiana*, vol. I., p. 45. I doubt not but I shall prove the truth of what I have asserted, by pegs, darts, hard blows, falls, and CROSS-BUTTOCKS.

1760. SMOLLETT, *L. Greaves*, vol. II., ch. viii. He was on his legs again . . . but, instead of accomplishing his purpose, he received a CROSS-BUTTOCK.

1836. M. SCOTT, *Cringle's Log*, ch. xii. While the old woman keelhauled me with a poker on one side, he jerked at me on the other, until at length he gave me a regular CROSS-BUTTOCK.

1860. *Chambers' Journal*, vol. XIII., p. 347. He is initiated into all the mysteries of 'hitting' and 'counterhitting,' 'stopping,' and 'infighting,' 'the suit in chancery,' and the CROSS-BUTTOCK.'

CROSS-CHAP.—*See* CROSS, *subs.*, sense 2.

CROSS-COVE.—*See* CROSS, *subs.*, sense 2.

CROSS-CRIB, *subs.* (thieves' and vagrants').—A thieves' hotel. [From CROSS (*q.v.*, *subs.*, sense 2), a thief, + CRIB (*q.v.*, *subs.*, sense 2), a place of abode.]

CROSS-DRUM, *subs.* (thieves').—A thieves' tavern. [From CROSS (*q.v.*, *subs.*, sense 2), a thief, + DRUM, a house or lodging.]

CROSSER, *subs.* (sporting).—One who arranges or takes part in a CROSS (*q.v.*, *subs.*, sense 1).

1834. AINSWORTH, *Rookwood*. The mill is o'er, the CROSSER crost, The loser's won, the vinner's lost!

CROSS-FAN or **CROSS-FAM**, *subs.* (thieves').—Robbery from the person done CROSS-FAMMED, that is, with one hand (FAM) across, and dissembling the action of, the other.

c. 1869. *Broadside Ballad*, 'The Chickaleary Cove.' Off to Paris I shall go, to show a thing or two, To the 'dipping blokes' what hangs about the caffies, How to do a CROSS-FAN for a 'super' or a 'slang.'

Verb (thieves').—To rob from the person.—*See subs.*

CROSS-KID or **CROSS-QUID**, *verb* (thieves').—To question; cross-examine. [KID = to quiz; hoax, or jest.] Fr., *faire la jactance*; also *faire saigner du nez*.

1879. J. W. HORSLEY, in *Macmillan's Mag.*, XL., 502. A reeler [policeman] came to the cell and CROSS-KIDDED (examined) me.

CROSS-MAN.—*See* CROSS, *subs.*, sense 2.

CROSS-PATCH, *subs.* (colloquial).—An ill-natured, ill-tempered person. As in the old nursery rhyme:

CROSS-PATCH, Draw the latch, Sit by the fire and spin.—*Lit.*

Not mentioned in Ash.

1785. GROSE, *Dict. Vulg. Tongue*. CROSS-PATCH: a peevish boy or girl.

1841. *Comic Almanack*, p. 258. Miss Pigeon's trying to look shy, *He's* calling her CROSSPATCH!

CROSS THE DAMP-POT, *verbal phr.* (tailors').—To cross the Atlantic.—*Cf.*, BIG DRINK, DAMP-POT, PUDDLE, and HERRING-POND.

CROW, *subs.* (thieves').—1. A confederate on watch whilst another steals. Generally a man, but occasionally a woman acts as a CROW; the latter is also called a CANARY (*q.v.*, *subs.*, sense 4).

1851–61. H. MAYHEW, *Lon. Lab. and Lon. Poor*, IV., 286. One keeps a look-out to see there is no person near to detect them. This person is termed a 'CROW.' If anyone should be near, the 'CROW' gives a signal, and then decamps.

1862. *Cornhill Mag.*, VI., 648. Occasionally they [women] assist at a burglary . . . remaining outside and keeping watch; they are then called CROWS.

1889. *Answers*, 18 May, p. 390, col. 2. A CROW (confederate) is next planted outside, or in an upper window, if there be one, to give notice, by means of signals or a cord reaching to the workers, of the approach of a peeler or chance passer-by.

2. (common).—A piece of unexpected luck; a 'fluke'; generally 'a REGULAR CROW.' [Originally billiards' in which it = a hazard not played for, *i.e.*, a 'fluke': no doubt a corruption of the Fr. *raccroc*.] A French equivalent is *mettre dans le mille*.

TO EAT CROW.—*See* BROILED CROW.

A CROW TO PLUCK, TO PULL, or TO PICK WITH ONE, *phr.* (colloquial). Something demanding explanation: a misunderstanding to clear; a disagreeable matter to settle. Sometimes, A BONE TO PICK, etc.

1593. SHAKSPEARE, *Comedy of Errors*, iii., 1. If a crow help us in, sirrah, we'll PLUCK A CROW TOGETHER.

1599. NASHE, *Lenten Stuffe*, in wks. V., 302. So I coulde PLUCKE A CROWE WYTH Poet *Martiall* for calling it *putre halec*.

1659. HOWELL, *Proverbs*. I have a GOOSE TO PLUCK WITH YOU.

1664. BUTLER, *Hudibras*, pt. II., 2. If not, resolve before we go, That YOU AND I MUST PULL A CROW.

1785. GROSE, *Dict. Vulg. Tongue*. TO PLUCK A CROW: To reprove anyone for a fault committed; to settle a dispute.

1819. SCOTT, *Bride of Lammermoor*, ch. xv. If these Ravenswood cases be called over the coals in the House of Peers, you will find that the Marquis will have A CROW TO PLUCK WITH YOU.

CROWD, *subs.* (old).—A fiddle.

CROWDER, *subs.* (theatrical).—1. A large audience.

1883. *Referee*, 18 March, p. 3, col. 2. If the proprietors want, in the way of audiences, to be able to boast of CROWDERS, they should take care to avoid giving pain.

2. (old).—A fiddler.

CROW-EATER, *subs.* (colonial).—A lazybones who prefers subsisting upon what he can pick up, as the crows do, to putting himself to the trouble of working for it. For synonyms, *see* LOAFER.

CROW-FAIR, *subs.* (old).—A gathering of clergymen.

CROWN, *verb* (thieves').—To inspect a window with a view to operations.

CROWN AND FEATHERS, *subs. phr.* (venery).—The female *pudendum*. For synonyms, *see* MONOSYLLABLE.

CROWNER, *subs.* (old colloquial).—A coroner. [A corruption of 'coroner.']

1596. SHAKSPEARE, *Hamlet*, Act v., Sc. 1. *Sec. Cl.* The CROWNER hath sat on her, and finds it Christian burial.

1599. NASHE, *Lenten Stuffe*, in wks. V., 220. And if any drowne themselues in them, their CROWNERS sit vpon them.

1835. HALIBURTON, *Clockmaker*, 3 S., ch. ii. You'll be to Connecticut afore they can wake up the CROWNER and summon a jury.

CROWN-OFFICE, *subs.* (old).—The head. For synonyms, *see* CRUMPET. Quoted by Grose [1785].

CROW'S-FOOT, *subs.* (thieves').—The Government broad arrow: also (in *pl.*) wrinkles at the outside corners of the eyes.

CRUEL or **CRUELLY**, *adj.* and *adv.* (colloquial).—Extremely; very; great. A fashionable intensitive; an Americanism by survival. *Cf.*, AWFUL and BEASTLY.

1662. PEPYS, *Diary*, 31 July. Met Captain Brown, of the 'Rosebush,' at which he was CRUEL angry. *Ibid*, 1666-7, 21 Feb. W. Batten denies all, but is CRUEL mad.

1848. BARTLETT, *Dict. of Americanisms*, p. 170. Oh, doctor, I am powerful weak, but CRUEL easy.

CRUELTY-VAN or **BOOBY-HUTCH**, *subs.* (common).—A four-wheeled chaise.

CRUG, *subs.* (Christ's Hospital).—1. At Hertford, a crust; in the London school, crust and crumb alike.

1820. LAMB, *Elia* (*Christ's Hospital*), p. 322, wks. [ed. 1852]. He had his tea and hot rolls in a morning, while we were battening upon our quarter of a penny loaf—our CRUG.

2. (Christ's Hospital).—A BLUE; especially an 'old boy.'

1877. BLANCH, *Blue Coat Boys*, p. 80. All CRUGS will well remember, etc.

CRUGANALER, *subs.* (Christ's Hospital). A biscuit given on St. Matthew's Day. [Orthography dubious. Blanch inclines to the following derivation: 'The biscuit had once something to do with those nights when bread and beer, with cheese, were substituted for bread-and-butter and milk. Thence the term "crug and aler." The only argument against this is the fact that the liquid was never dignified with the name of ale, but was invariably called "the swipes." By another derivation = "hard as nails." It is then spelt CRUGGY-NAILER.']

CRUGGY, *adj.* (Christ's Hospital).—Hungry. [From CRUG (*q.v.*).]

CRUISERS, *subs.* (old).—1. Beggars, or highway spies: 'those who traversed the road,' says Grose, 'to give intelligence of a booty'; also, rogues 'ready to snap up any booty that may offer.'

2. in *sing.* (common).—A street-walker.

CRUMB, *subs.* (military).—A pretty woman. *Cf.*, CRUMMY, *adj.*, senses 1 and 2.

CRUMB AND CRUST MAN, *subs. phr.* (common).—A baker. *Cf.*, BURN-CRUST and MASTER OF THE ROLLS. Fr., *un marchand de larton*.

CRUMBS.—*See* PICK UP ONE'S CRUMBS and CHATES.

CRUMMY, *adj.* (popular).—1. Fat; plump; well-developed. Especially said of high-bosomed and full-figured women: *e.g.*, a CRUMMY piece of goods. [From a provincialism, crum or crom = to stuff, whence CRUMMY = fat or well stuffed.] Fr., *fort en mie* (an almost literal translation); *elle a de ça*; Sp., *carrilludo* = plump-faced.

1748. T. DYCHE, *Dictionary* (5 ed.). CRUMMY (A.): . . . also fat, rich, plump, or fleshy.

1819. T. MOORE, *Tom Crib's Memorial to Congress*, p. 14. For they saw, notwithstanding Crib's honest endeavour, To train down the CRUMMY, 'twas monstrous as ever!

1828. JON. BEE, *Pict. of London*, p. 60. A nice, CRUMMY, young woman, who seemed surprised and interested at his situation.

1843. DICKENS, *Martin Chuzzlewit*, ch. xxix., p. 289. 'There's the remains of a fine woman about Sairah. Poll, . . . Too much CRUMB, you know,' said Mr. Bailey; 'too fat, Poll.'

1865. HENRY KINGSLEY, *The Hillyars and the Burtons*. You're CRUMMY and I ain't a going to deny it. But you ain't what I'd call fat.

2. (American). — Comely. *Cf.*, sense 1.

3. (thieves' and soldiers').—Lousy.

4. (thieves').—Plump in the pockets. [Probably an extended use of sense 1.]

CRUMMY-DOSS, *subs.* (thieves').—A lousy bed. [From CRUMMY (*q.v.*, sense 3), lousy, + DOSS (*q.v.*), a bed.]

CRUMP, *subs.* (Winchester College).—A hard hit; a fall. Used also as a verb in very much the same sense as to COB (*q.v.*). *Cf.*, BARTER.

CRUMPET, *subs.* (common).—The head.

ENGLISH SYNONYMS. Brain-pan; nut; chump; jazey; steeple; tib or tibby; weather-cock; turnip; upper extremity; top end; twopenny; upper storey; canister; attic; garret; costard; sconce; bonce; nob; lolly; lobb; knowledge-box; block; cocoa-nut; Crown-Office; calabash; top-knot; crust; chimney-pot; onion; chevy; cockloft; top-flat; gable; pumpkin; hat-peg; billiard ball; upper-crust; mazzard; cabaza; dome.

FRENCH SYNONYMS. *Le michaud* (thieves'); *un caillou* (popular; properly a pebble or flint); *une baigneuse* (thieves'); *un baptême* (popular); *une cafetière* (thieves' and vagrants'); *une façade* (popular); *une armoire à glace* (popular); *une bille* (popular: properly a billiard ball); *un béguin* (popular); *une citrouille* or *un citrouillard* (thieves': literally a pumpkin or gourd); *un citron* (thieves'); *une ardoise* (popular); *un coco* (popular: literally a cocoa-nut); *une calebasse* (popular = a calabash); *une cocarde* (popular: properly a cocade); *un caisson* (common: literally a chest or locker); *une coloquinte* (thieves'); *un chapiteau* (popular: literally a capital); *une balle* (popular); *un moule de bonnet* (popular: literally a cap-mould); *le grenier à sel* (popular: properly the [Attic] salt-loft); *le baldaquin* (a canopy); *la boule* (popular: the bowl, ball, or sconce); *une ciboule* (popular: properly a scallion, green onion, or eschalot); *la boussole* (familiar: in nautical phraseology, the compass); *la pomme* (popular and thieves'); *le tesson* (roughs'); *la bobine* (popular: literally a bobbin or spool); *la poire* (popular); *la boîte au sel* (familiar: the [Attic] salt-box); *la boîte à sardines* (popular = sardine box); *la boîte à surprises* (general: box of surprises); *la tirelire* (popular: literally money-box); *la hure* (properly the head of a wild boar); *la gouache* (popular); *la noisette* (popular: literally nut); *le char* (popular); *le réservoir* (popular: reservoir or cistern); *le bourrichon* (popular); *la goupine*

(thieves'); *la tourte* (popular: properly tart or fruit pie); *la tronche* (thieves' = chunk (or 'chump' of wood); *le trognon* (popular); *la guitare* (common); *la guimbarde* (popular: properly a Jew's harp); *le soliveau* (popular; properly a small joist); *le bobéchon* (popular); *la bobinasse* (popular); *le kiosque* (familiar); *le vol-au-vent* (general); *l'omnibus* (common); *la sorbonne* (*see* remarks under BALMY, sense 2); *la caboche* (possibly a language word); *le soufflet* (popular: literally bellows; also the head of a carriage); *le jambonneau* (popular: properly a small ham); *le schako* (popular).

GERMAN SYNONYM. *Kiefel.*

ITALIAN SYNONYMS. *Chiurla* or *ciurla* (a popular term); *elmo* (literally a helmet); *borella* (properly a ball); *grinta* (in orthodox Italian, ringworm of the scalp).

SPANISH SYNONYMS. *Chimenea* (*fem.*; literally a chimney. *Se le subió el humo á la chimenea*, = the smoke has got into his head; said of one who is affected with drink); *cholla* (*fem.*); *cabezorro* (*mas.*; a big head, an augmentative of *cabeza*); *caletre* (*mas.*; an abusive term, properly understanding, judgment, discernment); *campanario* (*mas.*; properly a belfry).

BALMY IN ONE'S CRUMPET. — *See* BALMY, sense 2, and the foregoing.

CRUMPET-FACE, *subs.* (common).—A pock-pitted face.—*See* CRIBBAGE-FACE.

CRUMPET-SCRAMBLE, *subs.* (popular).—A tea party; TEA-FIGHT, MUFFIN-WORRY, MUFFIN-FIGHT, BITCH-PARTY or COOKY-SHINE (*q.v.*).

1864. *Derby Day*, p. 16. There *are* men who do not disdain muffin-worries and CRUMPET-SCRAMBLES.

CRUMPLER, *subs.* (common).—1. A cravat.

2. (acrobats').—*See* quot.

1874. G. A. LAWRENCE, *Hagarene*, ch. xxxviii. Pete knew how to fall as well as any acrobat, and thought no more of a common 'CRUMPLER,' than ordinary hunting folks do of a 'peck' or stumble.

CRUSH, *subs.* (colloquial). — A fashionable name for any large social gathering.

1854. WHYTE MELVILLE, *General Bounce*, ch. xiii. We fear he had rather go to a CRUSH at Lady Dinadam's than sup with Boz.

1872. *Pall Mall Gaz.*, 23 June. It would possibly be found that one week of political reunions, concerts, balls, and CRUSHES would be as disastrous in its effects as two months of absinthe drinking.

1890. H. D. TRAILL, *Tea Without Toast*. 'Saturday Songs,' p. 100. It appeared to us a feast wouldn't help the cause the least, And we settled that to give a CRUSH at nine Would be greatly more effectual, and far more intellectual, Than at six o'clock to, greatly daring, dine.

Verb (general).—To run away; to decamp. For synonyms, *see* AMPUTATE and SKEDADDLE.

TO CRUSH DOWN SIDES, *verbal phr.* (Northern).—To keep tryst; also to run to a place of safety.

TO CRUSH OR BURST A POT, CUP, OR BOTTLE, *phr.* (old).—To drink (generally in company). *See* CRACK A BOTTLE. [From the Italian *crosciare* = to decant.] Shakspeare, in *The Taming of the Shrew*, induction, Sc. 1, uses BURST in a similar sense to CRACK and CRUSH.

1592. *Defence of Conny-catching*, in Greene's wks., xi., 43. If euer I brought my Conny but to CRUSH A POTTE OF ALE with mee.

1595. SHAKSPEARE, *Romeo and Juliet*, Act I., Sc. 2. And if you be not of the house of Montagues, I pray, come and CRUSH A CUP of wine.

1822. SCOTT, *Fortunes of Nigel*, ch. vii. I CRUSHED A QUART with that jolly boy Jenkin.

CRUSHER, *subs.* (popular).—1. A policeman. [Possibly from the slang verb to CRUSH = to run. CRUSH! was once a favourite signal of the 'pea and thimble' and other race-course sharpers, the meaning being: 'Run! the police!' The word came into general use, and was ultimately converted into CRUSHER = a policeman.] For synonyms, *see* BEAK, sense 1, and COPPER.

c. 1840. THACKERAY, *The Organ-Boy's Appeal*. Though you set in Vestminster surrounded by your CRUSHERS, Harrogant and habsolute like the Hortocrat of hall the Rushers.

1842. *Punch*, vol. II., p. 137. 'Proverbial Philosophy.' There is not one CRUSHER who is proof against the waistcoat pocket.

1853. *Diogenes*, II., 46. Here in came [to the Court] a CRUSHER (Beg pardon—mean usher), Dragging in a Pot-boy, With great show of joy.

1859. SALA, *Tw. Round the Clock*, 5 p.m., par. 19. A CRUSHER, or policeman, there is indeed.

1877. *Five Years' Penal Servitude*, ch. iii., p. 223. Oh, that's one of the cleverest gentlemen cracksmen out. . . . The blooming CRUSHERS were precious glad when they 'pinched' 'im.

2. (popular). — Anything large, fine, or extraordinary. [From CRUSH, to overwhelm or subdue.] Akin to WHOPPER, STINGER, CORKER, BOUNCER, etc. (*q.v.*).

1849. THACKERAY, *Pendennis*, ch. iv. She *is* a CRUSHER, ain't she now?

1870. *New York Herald*, Jan. The Fenians in England received rather a CRUSHER, if I may use so slang a word, two days ago.

CRUSHING, *ppl. adj.* (colloquial).—Excellent; first-rate. For synonyms, *see* A1 and FIZZING.

CRUST or **UPPER CRUST**, *subs.* (common).—1. The head. For synonyms, *see* CRUMPET.

UPPER-CRUST (*q.v.*), also = Society with a capital S.

CRUSTY-BEAU, *subs.* (old).—One that uses paint and cosmetics to obtain a fine complexion.—*Grose.*

CRUTCH, *subs.* (colloquial).—The 'fork,' or inner angle of the thigh.

CRUTCHES ARE CHEAP. — *See* WOODEN-LEGS.

CRY, *subs.* (common). — A large number; a quantity. [From CRY, a pack of dogs.] As in Shakspeare's *Coriolanus*, Act iii., Scene 3. 'You common CRY of curs.'

GREAT CRY AND LITTLE WOOL, *phr.* (general).—Much ado about nothing. The original text of the proverb was, 'GREAT CRY AND LITTLE WOOL, as the devil said when he sheared the hogs.' Hudibras alters it into 'All cry and no wool.'

TO CRY CARROTS AND TURNIPS, *verbal phr.* (old).—*See* quot.

1747. CHARLES JOHNSON, *Highwaymen and Pyrates*, p. 254. He came off with CRYING CARROTS AND TURNIPS, a term which rogues use for whipping at the cart's arse.

TO CRY [or CALL] A GO, *verbal phr.* (common).—To give in, as one unable to proceed. An expression borrowed from cribbage signifying that the player who makes use of it has nothing playable in his hand, and is compelled to 'CRY A GO.'] *Cf.*, PASS

1880. *Punch's Almanack.* Got three quid; have CRIED A GO with Fan, Game to spend my money like a man.

TO CRY CUPBOARD, *verbal phr.* (common).—To be fasting, hungry, BANDED (*q.v.*). Fr., *n'avoir rien dans le cornet*; *avoir le buffet vide*; and *danser devant le buffet.*

1738. SWIFT, *Polite Conversation* (conv. iii.), *Footman.* Madam, dinner's upon the table. *Col.* Faith, I'm glad of it; my belly began to CRY CUPBOARD.

CRY MATCHES! *intj. phr.* (American).—An exclamation of surprise. [Variously derived: (1) a corruption of 'Crime hatches'; (2) CRY = *XPI* or Christ, no suggestion being offered to account for 'MATCHES'; and (3) a conversion of the Fr. *cré matin*, presumably Canadian. *Cf.*, CRIMINI.] Quoted in *N. and Q.*, 5 S., viii., 491, and ix., 55, 318.

CRY OFF, *verb* (general).—To retreat; to back out from an engagement.

1866. *London Miscellany*, 5 May, p. 201. 'London Revelations.' 'Why this gent told me to bid,' said the dealer, patting his tingling fingers sharply, 'and now he wants to CRY OFF.'

TO CRY STINKING FISH.—*See* STINKING FISH.

C.T.A., *phr.* (circus and showmen's)—The police.

CUB or **UNLICKED-CUB**, *subs.* (colloquial). — An awkward, sulky girl; a mannerless, uncouth lout of a boy. [In allusion to the clumsiness of bear cubs till their dam has 'licked them into shape.'] *Cf.*, BEAR-LEADER.

1602. SHAKSPEARE *Twelfth Night*, Act v., I., 167. *Duke.* O thou dissembling CUB! what wilt thou be When time hath sow'd a grizzle on thy case?

1693. CONGREVE, *Old Batchelor*, Act iv., Sc. 8. A country squire, with the equipage of a wife and two daughters, came to Mrs. Snipwell's shop while I was there—but, oh Gad! two such UNLICKED CUBS!

1762. FOOTE, *Liar*, II., ii. I don't reckon much upon him: for you know, my dear, what can I do with an awkward, raw, college CUB?

1773. O. GOLDSMITH, *She Stoops to Conquer*, Act iv., Sc 1. 'A poor contemptible booby that would but disgrace correction.' . . . 'An insensible CUB.'

1880. A. TROLLOPE, *The Duke's Children*, ch. ix. And Tommy, you are an uncivil young,—young,—young,—I should say CUB if I dared, to tell me that you don't like dining with me any day of the week.

1855. THACKERAY, *Newcomes*, ch. xxix. I don't see why that infernal young CUB of a Clive is always meddling in our affairs.

CUBITOPOLIS, *subs.* (obsolete).—The Warwick and Eccleston Square districts. [From the name of the builders, *see* quot., 1864.] *Cf.*, ALBERTOPOLIS, MESOPOTAMIA, ASIA MINOR, THE NEW JERUSALEM, SLOPERS' ISLAND, etc. (*q.v.*).

1864. *The Press*, 12 Nov. CUBITOPOLIS received its felicitous cognomen from Lady Morley.

1866. E. YATES, *Land at Last*, ch. iii. There are men yet living among us whose mothers had been robbed on their way from Ranelagh in crossing the spot, then a dreary swampy marsh, on which now stands the city of palaces known as CUBITTOPOLIS.

CUCKOO, *subs.* (popular).—1. A fool. For synonyms, *see* BUFFLE and CABBAGE-HEAD.

1598. SHAKSPEARE, *Henry IV.,* Part I, Act i, Scene 4. O'horseback, ye CUCKOO; but afoot he will not budge a foot.

2. (old).—A cuckold.

1594. SHAKSPEARE, *Love's Labour Lost,* Act v, Scene 2. CUCKOO, CUCKOO, O word of fear Unpleasing to a married ear

3. (schoolboys').—The *penis.* For synonyms, see CREAMSTICK.

CUCKOOS, *subs.* (old).—Money, For synonyms, see ACTUAL and GILT.

1612. *The Passenger of Benvenuto.* These companions, who . . . carry the impression and marke of the pillerie galley, and of the halter, they call the purse a leafe, and a fleece; money, CUCKOES, and aste, and crowns.

CUCKOO'S NEST, *subs.* (venery).— The female *pudendum.* For synonyms, see MONOSYLLABLE.

CUCUMBER-TIME, *subs.* (tailors').— The dull season. [A correspondent of *Notes and Queries* (1 S., viii., 439) says it is of German origin, and remarks that many hundreds of London tailors are of German nationality. The German phrase is *die saure Gurken Zeit* (pickled gherkin-time). Hence, it is said, the expression 'Tailors are vegetarians,' because they live now on 'cucumber' and now on 'cabbage.' Quoted by Grose (1785).] *Cf.,* quot., 1821.

1821. P. EGAN, *Tom and Jerry* [ed. 1890], p. 60. The chap in the corner . . . has been chaffing Spendall . . . about his being so CUCUMBERISH as to be compelled to 'gammon the draper' [which means when a man is without a shirt, and is buttoned up close to his neck, with merely a handkerchief round it to make an appearance of cleanliness, it is termed, 'gammoning the draper.']

CUD, *subs.* (popular).—A chew of tobacco; a quid. [An allusion to 'chewing the cud.']

Adj. (Winchester College).— 1. Pretty; handsome. [Thought to be derived from *kudos.*]

2. (Christ's Hospital).—Severe.

CUDDIE, *subs.* (Scots).—A donkey.

CUDDLING, *verbal subs.* (athletic and pugilistic).—Wrestling.

CUDDY, *adj.* (Christ's Hospital).— Hard; difficult; said of a lesson. Also *Hertfordicé* for PASSY (*q.v.*). [There is a common hard biscuit called a 'cuddy-biscuit' which doubtless has this derivation.]

CUE, *verb* (thieves').—To swindle on credit.

CUFF, *subs.* (old).—1. A foolish old man. [Probably a contraction of CUFFIN (*q.v.*).]

1678. C. COTTON, *Scarronides,* bk. I., p. 3 (ed. 1725). The lustiest Carles thereabouts. Rich CUFFS and very sturdy Louts.

1708. CENTLIVRE, *Busie Body,* Act i. A very extraordinary Bargain I have made truly, if she should be really in Love with this old CUFF now.

1760. COLMAN, *Polly Honeycombe,* in wks. (1777) IV., 38. They are just here! ten to one the old CUFF may not stay with her: I'll pop into this closet.

2. (tailors').—A religious man, either real or sham.

TO CUFF ANTHONY, *phr.*— See ANTHONY.

TO BEAT or CUFF JONAS, *phr.* =TO BEAT THE BOOBY or GOOSE (*q.v.* under BEAT).

CUFFEN.—See CUFFIN.

CUFFER, *subs.* (military).—1. A lie; an exaggerated and improbable story.—*See* quot., under TO SPIN CUFFERS, and for synonyms, see WHOPPER.

2. (American thieves').—A man; also CUFFIR. [*Cf.,* COFE, COVE, and CUFFIN, from one of which the American form is doubtless derived.]

1859. MATSELL, *Vocabulum, or Rogue's Lexicon,* s.v.

TO SPIN CUFFERS, *phr.*— To tell extremely improbable stories; to yarn; TO DRAW THE LONG BOW (*q.v.*).

1888. *Colonies and India,* 14 Nov. The Australian youth can develop the art of SPINNING CUFFERS very successfully on his own account, without any adventitious assistance from a passing Minister of Public Instruction.

CUFFIN, CUFFEN, or CUFFING, *subs.* (Old Cant).—A man.

1567. HARMAN, *Caveat,* s.v.

1857. *Punch,* 31 Jan., p. 49. 'Dear Bill, this Stone-jug.' In the day-rooms the CUFFINS [warders] we queer at our ease, And at Darkmans we run the rig just as we please.

QUEER-CUFFIN, *subs.* (old).— A magistrate. [From QUEER, an old canting term for bad, + CUFFIN, a man; literally a bad man—from a rogue's point of view. Some of the old canting terms are curious enough: *e.g.,* 'quyer cramprings' = bolts or fetters; 'quyer kyn'=a prison house.] For synonyms, see BEAK, sense 2.

1609. DEKKER, *Lanthorne and Candle-light* [ed. Grosart, III., p. 203]. To the QUIER CUFFING we bing.

1837. DISRAELI, *Venetia,* p. 71. The gentry cove will be romboyld by his dam said a third gypsy. 'QUEER CUFFIN' [magistrate or queer man] will be the word if we don't tout.

CUFF-SHOOTER, *subs.* (theatrical).— A beginner; one who gives himself 'airs'; literally one who shoots his cuffs: having a greater regard for the display of his linen than for his work as an actor.

CULE, CULL, CULING, CULLING, *verb* and *verbal subs.* (thieves').— To purloin from the seats of carriages; the act of snatching handbags and other *impedimenta* therefrom. [Either an abbreviation and corruption of RETICULE, or from CULL, to gather.]

1857. SNOWDEN, *Mag. Assistant,* 3 ed., p. 444. Snatching reticules from a carriage—CULING.

CULL or CULLY, *subs.* (old).—A man; companion; partner. Specifically, a fool; one tricked or imposed upon. Grose seems to make a distinction, for he quotes CULL = 'a man honest or otherwise,' and CULLY='a fop, fool, or dupe to women,' in which sense it was current in the seventeenth century. Thus Rochester (in *Satire on the Times*), 'But pimpfed Ratcliffe's not a greater CULLY. —*See* also quot., 1771. [Probably a contraction of CULLION (Fr., *couillon*; It., *coglione*); but derived by Annandale from the Sp. Gypsy *chulai,* a man; Turkish Gypsy, *khulai,* a gentleman.]

1671. R. HEAD, *English Rogue,* pt. I., ch. v., p. 48 (1874). CULLE: a sapheaded fellow.

1676. *A Warning for Housekeepers.* As we walk along the street, We bite the CULLEY of his cole.

1693. CONGREVE, *Old Batchelor,* Act iii., Sc. I. Man was by nature woman's CULLY made: We never are but by ourselves betrayed.

1712. ARBUTHNOT, *Hist. of John Bull,* pt. IV., ch. i. I won't let him make me over, by deed and indenture, as his lawful CULLY.

1748. T. DYCHE, *Dictionary* (5 ed.) CULL (s.): a cant word for a man, either good or bad, but generally means one that a wench has picked up for some naughty purpose.

1760. JOHNSTON, *Chrysal,* ii., 17. Your secret, grave, old, rich CULLS, just fit to do business with.

1771. HENRY MACKENZIE, *The Man of Feeling,* vol. I., ch. xxvi. Harley . . . sallied forth with a blush of triumph on his face, without taking notice of the sneer of the waiter who, twirling the watch in his hand, made him a profound bow at the door, and whispered to a girl who stood in the passage something in which the word CULLY was honoured with a particular emphasis.

1825. SCOTT, *St. Ronan's Well,* ch. xxx. 'Na, Na,' answered the boy: 'he is a queer auld CULL, he disna frequent wi' other folk.'

1830. BULWER LYTTON, *Paul Clifford,* p. 75 (ed. 1854). A famous CULL is my friend Attie—an old soldier—has seen the world, and knows what is what.

1839. W. H. AINSWORTH, *Jack Sheppard* (1889), p. 14. Capital trick of the CULL in the cloak to make another person's brain stand the BRUNT for his own—capital!

1889. *Puck's Library,* April, p. 18. *Showman:* Look-a-here, CULLY, yer don't 'xpect ter git a lecture on nat'l history 'n'a free ticket ter the antipoads fer a quarter, do yer?

RUM CULL, *subs.* (theatrical).— The manager of a theatre; also called a CULLY-GORGER.

CULLS, *subs.* (old).—The *testes.*

b. 1574, d. 1637. BEN JONSON. Claw a churl by the CULLS, and he'll shite in your fist.

CULLY-GORGER, *subs.* (theatrical). —The manager of a theatre; a companion or brother actor. [CULLY (*q.v.*)=a man+GORGER (*q.v.*), a swell, employer, or boss; literally a well - dressed man.]

CULLY-SHANGY, *subs.* (common).— Copulation. For synonyms, see GREENS.

18(?). CAREY, *Life in Paris,* p. 276, s.v.

CULMINATE, *verb* (University: obsolete).—To mount a coach-box.

1803. *Gradus ad Cantabrigiam,* s.v.

CULTY-GUN, *subs.* (venery).—The *penis.* For synonyms, see CREAMSTICK.

CUM-ANNEXIS, *subs.* (West Indian). —One's belongings; specially applied to one's wife and children. [In allusion to a legal locution connected with land transfer in Demerara. The outlying farms of estates come under this general description; *e.g.,* Belair, (a well-known property) CUM ANNEXIS includes, amongst others, estates formerly known as La Penitence, Turkeyen, Cuming's Lodge, Industry, etc., and in official documents this congeries of estates is spoken of as Belair CUM ANNEXIS.]

CUMMER, *subs.* (common).—An intimate. For synonyms, *see* CHUM.

CUNDUM, *subs.* (old).—An obsolete appliance worn in the act of coition, to prevent infection: so-called from the name of its inventor, a colonel in the Guards, *temp.,* Charles II.: the modern equivalent is known as a FRENCH LETTER (*q.v.*).

1767. ROCHESTER, ROSCOMMON, AND DORSET, *A Panegyric upon Cundum,* p. 208. Happy the man who in his pocket keeps, Whether with green or scarlet riband bound, A well-made CUNDUM.

CUNNILINGE, *verb* (venery).—To tongue a woman. [Latin *cunnilingus,* a form which occurs in Martial, from *cunnus*=the female *pudendum* + *lingo. Cf.,* TIP THE VELVET.

CUNNILINGIST, *subs.* (venery).—A man (or woman) addicted to the practice of tonguing the female *pudendum.*

CUNNY-HAUNTED, *adj. phr.* (popular).—Lecherous.

CUNNY-THUMBED, *adj.* (old).—1. Said of a person who doubles the fist with the thumb turned inwards.

2. (schoolboys').—Said of one who shoots his marble—as at ring-taw or shoot hole—with the first phalange of the thumb from the second of the forefinger, instead of with the knuckle of the thumb from the first of the forefinger.

CUNT, *subs.* (common).—The female *pudendum;* Latin *cunnus.* A language word, but vulgar in usage. Diminutives of varying degrees are CUNNICLE, CUNNIKIN, CUNTKIN, CUNTLET, CUNNY. Derivatives, the result of an obvious play upon words (old), are CUNNY-CATCHER and CUNNY-BURROW FERRET (Urquhart), for which *see* CREAM-STICK; CUNNY-HUNTER=a whoremonger; and CUNNY-SKIN (Durfey), for which *see* FLEECE. For synonyms, see MONOSYLLABLE.

1383. CHAUCER, *The Miller's Tale.* Full prively he caught her by the QUEINT, And sayde Ywis but if I have my will, For derne love of thee, lemman, I spill.

1622. FLETCHER, *Spanish Curate.* They write *sunt* with a C, which is abominable.

1647-80. ROCHESTER, *The Royal Angler.* However weak and slender in the string, Bait it with CUNT, and it will hold a king.

1768. STERNE, *The Sentimental Journey,* So that, when I stretched out my hand, I caught hold of the fille-de-chambre's ——.

CUNT-PENSIONER, *subs.* (vulgar).— A male keep; one who lives by the prostitution of a wife, a mistress, a daughter, or any other female connection.

CUNT-STRUCK, *adj.* (vulgar).— Enamoured of women: who may, in turn, be either COCK-SMITTEN or PRICK-STRUCK (*q.v.*).

CUP-AND-SAUCER PLAYER, *subs. phr.* (theatrical).—A term of derision applied to the players associated with the late T. W. Robertson's comedies.

CUPBOARD LOVE, *subs. phr.* (popular).—Interested affection: a variant of the saw that 'the way to a man's heart is through his stomach.' *Cf.,* RICE-CHRISTIAN.

c. 1661. *Poor Robin* [HERRICK]. A CUPBOARD LOVE is seldom true, A love sincere is found in few.

1787. MISS SEWARD, *Letters* [ed. 1811], vol. II., p. 103. This last and long-enduring passion [of Dr. Johnson] for Mrs. Thrale was, however, composed perhaps of CUPBOARD LOVE, Platonic love, and vanity tickled and gratified.

1885. *Girl's Own Paper,* VI., 830. When tea-time comes and milk, she's not above Increasing her caresses, till we hear A whisper now and then of CUPBOARD LOVE.

CUPID.—See FANCY JOSEPH.

CUPS. IN ONE'S CUPS, *adv. phr.* (colloquial).—Drunk. *Cf.,* CUP-SHOT, and for synonyms, see SCREWED.

1593. NASHE, *Christ's Teares,* in wks. IV., 228 (Grosart). Those whom the Sunne sees not in a month together, I nowe see IN THEIR CUPPES and their jolitie.

1688. SHADWELL, *Sq. of Alsatia* III., in wks. (1720), iv., 64. I shall take my leave: you are in YOUR CUPS: you will wish you had heard me.

1693. DRYDEN, *Juvenal*, x 288. Which IN HIS CUPS the bowsy poet sings.

1712. ARBUTHNOT, *History of John Bull*, pt. II., ch. iv. She used to come home IN HER CUPS, and break the china and the looking-glasses.

1837. BARHAM, *I. L.* (*Brothers of Birchington*). Gets tipsy whenever he dines or he sups, And is wont to come quarrelsome home IN HIS CUPS.

1864. MARK LEMON, *Jest Book*, p. 185 [of one remarkable at once for Bacchanalian devotion and large and startling eyes]. 'I always know when he has been IN HIS CUPS by the state of his saucers.'

CUP-SHOT, *adj.* (old).—Drunk.

1639. FULLER, *Holy War*, bk. III., ch. xvi. The spring-tide of their mirth so drowned their souls that the Turks coming in upon them cut every one of their throats, to the number of twenty thousand, and quickly they were stabbed with the sword that were CUP-SHOT before.

1785. GROSE, *Dict. Vulg. Tongue*, s.v.

CUP-TOSSER, *subs.* (common).—*See* quot.

1868. BREWER, *Phrase and Fable*, s.v. CUP TOSSER: a juggler (French *joueur de gobelet*). The old symbol for a juggler was a goblet. The phrase and symbol are derived from the practice of jugglers who toss in the air, twist on a stick, and play all sorts of tricks with goblets or cups.

CURATE, *subs.* (common).—A small poker, or TICKLER (*q.v.*), used to save a better one; also a pocket-handkerchief in actual use as against one worn for show. The better article is called a RECTOR. Similarly, when a tea-cake is split and buttered, the bottom half, which gets the more butter, is called the RECTOR, and the other, the CURATE.

CURB, *verb* (old).—To steal. For synonyms, *see* PRIG.

1615. GREENE, *Thieves Falling Out* (*Harl. Misc.*, VIII., 389). Though you can foyst, nip, prig, lift, CURBE, and use the black art, yet you cannot crossbite without the helpe of a woman.

CURBSTONE-BROKER, *subs.* — *See* GUTTER-SNIPE.

CURBSTONE-SAILOR, *subs.* (popular).—A prostitute. For synonyms, *see* BARRACK-HACK and TART, and *cf.*, CRUISER, sense 2.

CURE, *subs.* (common).—An eccentric; a fool; also a funny fellow. Originally applied in many connections, *see* quot.

1856. *Punch*, vol. XXXI., p. 201.

WHAT'S A CURE.

Punch has no mission to repeat
The Slang he hears along the street,
But when a curious phrase he seizes,
Punch does—as always—what he pleases.
He finds then in the following word
No merit save that it's absurd,
But as it's likely to endure
He asks a question, 'What's a CURE'?
He heard upon a river boat
The steersman told to move his coat,
The fellow grunted like a boor,
The captain said, 'Well you're a CURE,'
The mud was thick, the crossing clean—
A well-dressed man, genteel of mien—
Walked through the first (he might be poor)—
The sweeper muttered 'He's a CURE.'
Two youths talked 'chaff' (in phrase polite),
Each asked where 'tother slept last night,'
'Me? Up a spout.' 'Me? Down a sewer.'
The first: 'Ain't you a precious CURE.'
A child more apt to eat than spell
Espied his little sweetheart Nell:
Embraced her with affection pure,
And cried, 'You darling little CURE.'
Before a shop stood maidens two
Where fine mock diamonds mocked their view:
'Oh, Julia! That's the Koh-i-noor.'
'That!' Julia said, 'You silly CURE.'
Lastly, he heard the word applied
To Lord Mayor Finnis in his pride;
A female shouted, 'Well I'm sure!
Call him a mayor—he looks a CURE.'
Thus having heard the word he mentions
Spoken with seven distinctions,
Punch doth the slangy world adjure
To state whence derivation 'CURE'

CURIOUS. TO DO CURIOUS, *verbal phr.* (common).—To act strangely.

CURL. OUT OF CURL, *adv. phr.* (common).—Out of sorts; out of condition.

TO CURL UP, *verbal phr.* (familiar). — To be silent; to 'shut up.'

TO CURL ONE'S HAIR, *verb. phr.* (common).—To administer chastisement; to 'go for' one.

TO CURL ONE'S LIVER OR TO HAVE ONE'S LIVER CURLED, *verbal phr.* (common).—To make one feel intensely. *Cf.*, TURN THE LIVER (*q.v.*).

1877. S. L. CLEMENS ('Mark Twain'), *Life on the Mississippi*, pp. 414-415. This is sport that makes the body's VERY LIVER CURL with enjoyment.

CURLE, *subs.* (old).—Clippings of money.—*Grose.*

CURL PAPER, *subs.* (common).—Paper for the W.C.; toilet paper; 'wipe - bummatory' (Urquhart), or 'sanitary' paper; bum-fodder; bumf; ammunition.

CURLYCUES or **CARLICUES**, *subs.* (common).—Fantastic ornaments worn on the person or used in architecture; also, by implication, a strange line of conduct. Used by Burns in *The Merry Muses.*

1858. *Home Journal*, 24 July. Architects have a wonderful predilection for all manner of CURLYCUES and breaks in your roof.

CURRANTS AND PLUMS, *subs. phr.* (rhyming slang).—A threepenny bit; or THRUMS (*q.v.*).

CURRENCY, *subs.* (Australian).—A colonist born in Australia, those of English birth being STERLING (*q.v.*). [In allusion to the colonial and home mintages, which, identical in value, present one or two strongly marked points of difference.]

1856. C. READE, *Never Too Late*, ch. lxxxv. When gold was found in Victoria he crossed over to that port and robbed. One day he robbed the tent of an old man, a native of the colony, who was digging there with his son, a lad of fifteen. Now these CURRENCY lads are very sharp and determined.

CURSE. NOT TO CARE OR BE WORTH A CURSE, *phr.* (common). —To care or be worth little—or nothing at all. [CURSE may either = (1) the wild cherry; or (2) a corruption of A.S. *cerse*, watercress. *Cf.*, CONTINENTAL (*q.v.*).

1362. WILLIAM LANGLAND, *Vision of Piers Ploughman*. Wisdom and witt nowe is NOT WORTH A KERSE, But if it be carded with cootis as clothers Kemble their woole.

1838. DICKENS, *Nicholas Nickleby*, ch. xvi., p. 124. With regard to such questions . . . which one can't be expected to CARE A CURSE ABOUT.

187(?). G. R. SIMS, *Dagonet Ballads* (*In the Workhouse*). I CARE NOT A CURSE for the guardians.

CURSE OF GOD, *subs. phr.* (old).—A cockade. — *Lexicon Balatronicum* [1811].

CURSE OF SCOTLAND, *subs. phr.* (popular). — The nine of diamonds. [The suggested derivations are inconclusive. The locution has nothing to do with Culloden and the Duke of Cumberland, for the card was nicknamed the JUSTICE-CLERK, in allusion to the Lord Justice-Clerk Ormistone, who, for his severity in suppressing the

Rebellion of 1715, was called the CURSE OF SCOTLAND. Other suggestions are: (1) That it is derived from the game of Pope Joan, the nine of diamonds there being called the 'pope,' of whom the Scotch have always stood in horror. (2) The word 'curse' is a corruption of *cross*, and the nine of diamonds is so arranged as to form a St. Andrew's Cross. (3) That it refers to the arms of Dalrymple, Earl of Stair (viz., or, on a saltire azure, nine lozenges of the field), who was held in abhorrence for the Massacre of Glencoe; or to Colonel Packer, who attended Charles I. on the scaffold, and had for his arms nine lozenges conjoined, or in the heraldic language, GULES, a cross of lozenges. These conflicting views were discussed at length in *Notes and Queries*, 1 S., i., 61, 90; iii., 22, 253, 423, 483; v., 619; 3 S., xii., 24, 96; 4 S., vi., 194, 289; also, *see Chambers' Encyclopædia.*]

1791. *Gent. Mag.*, vol. LXI., p. 141. The Queen of Clubs is . . . called *Queen Bess* . . . The Nine of Diamonds, the CURSE OF SCOTLAND.

CURSITOR or **CURSETOR**, *subs.* (old). —A low tramp or vagabond. [Properly, a CURSITOR (*unde* Cursitor Street, in Chancery Lane) was a clerk in the Court of Chancery, whose business was to make out original writs; also a courier or runner. From the Latin.]

CURTAIN-RAISER, *subs.* (theatrical). —A short 'piece' to bring up the curtain and play in the house. Fr., *lever de rideau.*

1889. *Daily News*, 2 Sept., p. 3, col. 4. Miss Grace Hawthorne is about to try an original experiment in what are known as CURTAIN-RAISERS.

CURTALL or **CURTAIL**, *subs.* (old).—A vagabond and thief. — *See* quots.

1560. JOHN AWDELEY, *Fraternitye of Vacabondes* (1869. English Dialect Society's Reprint), p. 4. A CURTALL is much like to the Vpright man, but hys authority is not fully so great. He vseth commonly to go with a short cloke, like to grey Friers, and his woman with him in like liuery, which he calleth his altham if she be hys.

1785. GROSE, *Dict. Vulg. Tongue.* CURTAILS: thieves who cut off pieces of stuff hanging out of shop windows; the tails of women's gowns, etc.; also thieves wearing short jackets.

Verb (old).—To cut off. Originally a cant word—*vide Hudibras*, and *Bacchus and Venus*, 1737.

CUSE, *subs.* (Winchester College).—A book in which a record is kept of the 'marks' in each division: its name to dons is 'classicus paper'; also used for the weekly order.

CUSHION, *verb* (thieves').—To hide or conceal. Variants are, STALL OFF; STOW; SLUM. Sp., *Hacer la agachadiza* = to hide oneself.

TO DESERVE THE CUSHION, *verbal phr.* (old).—On the birth of a child a man was said TO DESERVE THE CUSHION; *i.e.*, the symbol of rest from labour.

CUSHION-SMITER or **-THUMPER**, *subs.* (common).—A clergyman. [Derivation obvious.] For synonyms, *see* DEVIL-DODGER

1843. THACKERAY, *Irish Sketch Book*, ch. xx. For what a number of such loud nothings, windy, emphatic tropes and metaphors, spoken, not for God's glory, but the preacher's, will many a CUSHION-THUMPER have to answer!

1849. THACKERAY, in *Scribn. Mag.*, June, 1887, p. 686. CUSHION-THUMPERS and High and Low Church extatics.

1889. *Modern Society*, 19 Oct., p. 1294, col. 1. On a recent occasion a

CUSHION-THUMPER received a challenge from the miserable sinner whom he so volubly denounced.

CUSS, *subs.* (American).—A man, COVE, or CULL. Generally, but not necessarily, disparaging. [Of uncertain derivation: may be either from 'curse' or from 'customer.'] For synonyms, *see* COVE. Also *see* specific use in quot., 1883.

1883. *Daily Telegraph*, 25 July, p. 2, col. 1. I'll give Tom his due, and say of him that for flumoxing a CUSS (Custom House Officer) or working the weed, I don't know any one he couldn't give a chalk to and beat 'em.

1888. F. R. STOCKTON, *Rudder Grange*, ch. xii. The man that lives up this lane is a mean, stingy CUSS, with a wicked dog, and it's no good to go there.

CUSSEDNESS, *subs.* (American).—Generally in such phrases as 'pure CUSSEDNESS,' the 'CUSSEDNESS of things,' etc. Mischievousness, or resolution, or courage may be implied; but in the Coventry plays CURSYDNESSE signified sheer wickedness and malignity.

18(?). COL. JOHN HAY, *Song of the Prairie Belle.* Through the hot, black breath of the burnin' boat Jim Bludsoe's voice was heard, And they all had trust in his CUSSEDNESS, And knowed he would keep his word.

1886. *Detroit Free Press*, Aug. A more mischievous boy never came under my observation. Pure CUSSEDNESS was spread out all over him.

1888. . . . *Mr. Potter of Texas* (Ry. ed.), p. 122. The extraordinary belief he had of transatlantic blood - thirstiness, scalping, and general CUSSEDNESS engendered by these books.

1890. *Notes and Queries*, 7 S., ix., 29 Mar., p. 244. To swear at something when 'the CUSSEDNESS of things' manifests itself in any specially exasperating shape seems to be recognised as a necessity by a large majority of the adult male population of the globe.

1890. *Pall Mall Gaz.*, 22 May, p. 4, col. 2. The cause of the difficulty is the pestilent CUSSEDNESS of the working man.

CUSS OUT, *verb* (common).—To talk down, to FLUMMOX BY THE LIP (*q.v.*).

1881. *New York Times*, 18 Dec. [quoted in *N. and Q.*, 6 S., v., 65]. He CUSSED that fellow OUT, *i.e.*, he annihilated him verbally.

CUSTOMER, *subs.* (common).—A man; fellow; cove; cuss; or chap; with a certain qualification, *e.g.* An 'ugly CUSTOMER = a dangerous opponent; a queer CUSTOMER = a suspicious person, one to be suspected; a 'rum CUSTOMER' = an odd fish. For synonyms, *see* COVE.

1818. P. EGAN, *Boxiana*, I., 19. Here . . . many an ugly CUSTOMER has met with his match, and been frightened in his turn.

1854. WHYTE MELVILLE, *General Bounce*, ch. vi. Some of these good-looking young gentlemen are 'ugly CUSTOMERS' enough when their blood is up.

1870. *London Figaro*, 8 Oct. Customers would then know the kind of 'CUSTOMERS' of tradesmen with whom they had to deal.

CUSTOMHOUSE-OFFICER, *subs.* (common).—An aperient pill. [Because it effects a clearance.] *Cf.*, CHIMNEY-SWEEP.

CUT, *subs.* (common).—1. A stage or degree.

1835. DICKENS, *Sketches by Boz*, p. 183. It looked so knowing, with the front garden, and the green railings, and the brass knocker, and all that—I really thought it was a CUT above me.

1843. DICKENS, *Martin Chuzzlewit*, ch. iv., p. 29. Any other man in the wide world, I am equal to; but Sylme is, I frankly confess, a great many CUTS above me.

1851. MAYHEW, *London Labour and London Poor*, vol. II., p. 123. He's a CUT above me a precious sight.

2. (popular). — A refusal to acknowledge acquaintance, or to associate, with another person.—*See verbal* sense. A CUT DIRECT

or DEAD CUT is a conspicuous non-acknowledgment of an acquaintance.

1821. P. EGAN, *Tom and Jerry* [ed. 1890], p. 55. His acquaintances were numerous, but they seldom lasted longer than a few days, when he made no hesitation in giving them the CUT-DIRECT.

1836. MARRYAT, *Japhet*, ch. lii. He was a noted duellist, had killed his three or four men, and a CUT DIRECT from any person was, with him, sufficient ground for sending a friend.

3. (theatrical). — Mutilation of the 'book' of a play, opera, etc.

1779. SHERIDAN, *The Critic*, Act ii., Sc. 2. *Puff* (speaking of the mutilation of his play): Hey, what the plague!—what a CUT is here!

1883. *Saturday Review*, 21 April, p. 501, col. 2. Mr. Mackenzie had not only modified the energy of the orchestra, but had shortened the opera by some judicious CUTS.

4. (general).—A snub or set-down. *Cf.*, sense 2.

1876. HINDLEY, *Life and Adventures of a Cheap Jack*, p. 143. One of the greatest CUTS I ever knew was once when a man was speaking of Chris. Newman and saying what a good sort he was, upon which the other said, 'What do you mean by saying that? Why, d— me, sir, he never called for a bottle of champagne in his life!'

Adj. (old).—Tipsy; ON THE CUT = on the spree. For synonyms, *see* SCREWED.

1748. T. DYCHE, *Dictionary* (5 ed.). CUT (A.) . . . also an epithet applied to one who is drunk, as, He is deeply CUT, that is, he is so drunk, that he can neither stand nor go.

1830. PIERCE EGAN, *Finish to Life in London*, p. 214. Terry was terribly CUT.

1848. THACKERAY, *Book of Snobs*, ch. xli. I was so CUT last night, old boy! Hopkins says to Tomkins (with amiable confidence).

1859. *Punch*, vol. XXXVII., p. 22. Our friend prone to vices you never may see, Though he goes on the Loose, or the CUT, or the Spree.

Verb (old).—1. To talk.

1567. HARMAN, *Caveat* 1814), p. 66
To CUTTE, to say.
To CUT BENLE, to speake gentle.
To CUT BENE WHYDDS, to speake or give good words.
To CUTTE QUYER WHYDDES, to geue euil words or evil language.

1622. HEAD AND KIRKMAN, *The English Rogue*. This Doxie Dell can CUT BIEN WHIDS, and drill well for a win.

1815. SCOTT, *Guy Mannering*, ch. xxviii. Meg's true-bred; she's the last in the gang that will start—but she has some queer ways, and often CUTS queer words.

1834. W. H. AINSWORTH, *Rookwood* p. 230 (ed. 1864). Here I am, pal Peter; and here are my two chums, Rust and Wilder. CUT the whid.

1849. THACKERAY, *Pendennis*, ch. ix. The infatuated young man went on CUTTING his jokes at the Admiral's expense, fancying that all the world was laughing with him.

2. (colloquial).—To disown, ignore, or avoid associating with, a person. Sometimes to CUT DEAD.—*See* CUT, *subs.*, sense 2. An article in the *Monthly Magazine* for 1798 cites CUT as a current peculiarity of expression, and says that some had tried to change it into 'spear,' but had failed.

1634. S. ROWLEY, *Noble Souldier*, Act ii., Sc. 1. Why shud a Souldier, being the world's right arme, Be CUT thus by the left, a Courtier?

1794. *Gent. Mag.*, p. 1085. I no sooner learned he was at the 'Black Bull' than I determined to CUT the old codger completely.

1811. MISS AUSTEN, *Sense and Sensibility*, ch. xliv. That he had CUT me ever since my marriage, I had seen without surprise or resentment.

1855. THACKERAY, *Newcomes*, ch. xli. 'You are angry with her because she CUT you,' growls Clive. 'You know you said she CUT you, or forgot you; and your vanity's wounded.'

1864. G. A. LAWRENCE, *Guy Livingstone*, ch. viii. It was only a slight satisfaction to hear that she has utterly lost

sight of my rival, and promises to CUT him DEAD the first time they meet.

1870. *Daily News*, 26 May, 'Leader.' The old Greeks dedicated an altar to the Unknown God, for fear of CUTTING some jealous but obscure deity through ignorance of his existence and attributes.

Also as *verbal substantive*, CUTTING.

1840. MRS. GORE, *The Dowager*, ch. xiii. [On the Continent.] Every person's place in Society is so definite . . . that except in cases of some enormous breach of propriety, no person once established can ever be expelled. Unless for cogent reasons, he could not have been there at all . . . There is no talk of 'CUTTING.' Such an outrage would reflect on the perpetrator rather than on the person '*cut*.' All the vulgar caprices consequent on a shifting state of society are unknown.

3. (general).—Also TO CUT AND RUN, CUT IT, CUT ONE'S LUCKY, CUT ONE'S STICK, CUT OFF, CUT AWAY, etc. To depart more or less hurriedly and perforce. [Originally nautical—to CUT the cable AND RUN before the wind.] CUT OVER and CUT AWAY formerly bore precisely the same meanings. For synonyms, *see* AMPUTATE and SKEDADDLE.

1570. LAMBARDE, *Perambulation of Kent*. Let me CUT OVER to Watling Streete.

1593. NASHE, *Countercuffe to Martin Junior*, in wks., vol. I., p. 79. He came latelie ouer-sea into *Kent*, fro thence he CUT OUER into *Essex* at *Grauesende*.

1678. C. COTTON, *Scarronides*, bk. IV., p. 86 (ed. 1725). Put on the Wings that used to bear ye, And CUT AWAY to Carthage quickly.

1841. *Punch*, vol. I., p. 51. Explain the philosophical meaning of the sentence. 'He CUT AWAY from the crushers as quick as a flash of lightning thro' a gooseberry bush.'

1857. DICKENS, *Little Dorrit*, bk. I., ch. xxxi., p. 238. 'I see precious well,' said Mr. Tip, rising, 'that I shall get no sensible or fair argument here to-night, and so the best thing I can do is to CUT.'

1888. RIDER HAGGARD, *Mr. Meeson's Will* [in *Illus. Lond. News*, Summer Number], p. 2, col. 3. Off you go! and mind you don't set foot in Pompadour Hall, Mr. Meeson's seat, unless it is to get your clothes. Come, CUT.

4. (trade).—To compete in business; to under-sell. A CUTTING trade is one where profits are reduced to a minimum. Also CUT UNDER.

1874. H. MAYHEW, *London Characters*, p. 469. All agreed in referring their misery to the spirit of competition on the part of the masters—the same universal desire to CUT UNDER.

1883. L. OLIPHANT, *Altiora Peto*, II., xxiii., 78. So we dissolved partnership, and I went in with another chap, to work on some kind of principle, but Ned was all the time CUTTING UNDER us by bringing out some new contrivance—he's great on electricity, Ned is.

5. (common). — To excel.— *See* quot., 1853. Also CUT OUT (*q.v.*).

1853. WH. MELVILLE, *Digby Grand*, ch. viii. There have been instances of the weaker sex . . . CUTTING DOWN, from sheer nerve and determination, the bearded sons of Nimrod themselves.

1884. *Referee*, 13 April, p. 1, col. 4. George's performance in the ten miles handicap at Stamford Bridge on Monday —51 min. 20 sec.—is hardly likely to be disturbed for a long time to come, unless he CUTS himself.

6. (theatrical). — To strike out portions of a dramatic production, so as to shorten for representation. *Cf.*, *subs.*, sense 3.

7. (University).—To avoid; to absent oneself from. Thus, TO CUT LECTURE, TO CUT CHAPEL, TO CUT HALL, TO CUT GATES are common phrases.

1794. *Gentleman's Mag.*, Dec., s.v.

1889. WHIBLEY, *In Cap and Gown*, s.v.

CUT A CAPER or **CAPERS**, *verbal phr.* (colloquial). — To play a trick or prank; to behave bois-

terously or fantastically. [From CUT, a verb of action, + CAPER (*q.v.*) a freakish proceeding or prank.] *Cf.*, CUT DIDOES. Fr., *battre un huit*.

1602. SHAKSPEARE, *Twelfth Night*, Act i., Sc. 3. *Sir And.* Faith, I can CUT A CAPER.

c. 1626. *Dick of Devonshire*, in Bullen's *Old Plays*, ii., 68. *Pike*, Could I shake those chaines off I would CUTT CAPERS: poore *Dick Pike* would dance though Death pip'd to him.

1712. *Spectator*, No. 324. Others are called the dancing-masters, and teach their scholars to CUT CAPERS by running swords through their legs.

1751. SMOLLETT, *Peregrine Pickle*, ch. lxxxvii. He . . . . hied him home to his bride, to communicate his happiness, CUTTING CAPERS, and talking to himself all the way.

1780. MRS. COWLEY, *The Belle's Stratagem*, Act iv., Sc. 1. *Har.* Why, isn't it a shame to see so many stout, well-built young fellows, masquerading, and cutting courants here at home, instead of making the French CUT CAPERS to the tune of your cannon; or sweating the Spaniards with an English fandango?

1843. DICKENS, *Martin Chuzzlewit*, ch. xx., p. 208. Jonas only laughed at this, and getting down from the coach-top with great alacrity, CUT a cumbersome kind of CAPER in the road.

CUT A DASH, SPLASH, or **SHINE,** *verbal phr.* (general).—To make a show; to attract attention through some idiosyncrasy of manner, appearance, or conduct. In the United States to CUT A SPLURGE or CUT A SWATHE Fr., *flamber*; *faire du flafla*; and *faire flouer*.

1771. FOOTE, *Maid of Bath*, I. But the squire does not intend to CUT A DASH till the spring.

1835. HALIBURTON, *Clockmaker*, 1 S., ch. xxii. Well, they CUT as many SHINES as Uncle Peleg. One frigate they guessed would captivate, sink, or burn our whole navy.

1857. A. TROLLOPE, *Three Clerks*, ch. xxxi. Gin and water was the ordinary tipple in the front parlour; and any one of its denizens inclined to CUT A DASH above his neighbours generally did so with a bottom of brandy,

1884. S. L. CLEMENS ('M. Twain'), *Hucklebury Finn*, xxiii., 227. It would a made a cow laugh to see the SHINES that old idiot CUT.

1885. G. A. SALA, in *Daily Telegraph*, 1 Sept., p. 5, col. 4. It is while they are in the land of the living that I should like to see the Australian Crœsuses spending their money. Why don't they—to use a very vulgar but very expressive locution—CUT A SPLASH with their magnificent revenues?

CUT A FIGURE, *verbal phr.* (common).—To make an appearance, good or bad.

1759. STERNE, *Tristram Shandy*, vol. II., ch. ii. You will CUT NO contemptible FIGURE in a metaphysic circle.

1766. GOLDSMITH, *Vicar of Wakefield*, ch. x. When Moses has trimmed them [the horses] a little, they will CUT A VERY TOLERABLE FIGURE.

1839. LEVER, *Harry Lorrequer*, ch. i. He certainly CUT A DROLL FIGURE.

CUT AND COME AGAIN, *phr.* (colloquial).—Plenty: *i.e.*, if one cut does not suffice plenty remains to come at again.

1738. SWIFT, *Polite Conv.*, dial. ii. I vow, 'tis a noble sir-loyn. *Neverout*. Ay; here's CUT AND COME AGAIN.

1821. COOMBE, *Dr. Syntax*, tour III., ch. iv. Something of bold and new design Dug from the never-failing mine, That's work'd within your fertile brain, Where all is CUT AND COME AGAIN.

Subs. (venery). — The female *pudendum*.

CUT-AWAY, *subs.* (common).—A morning coat. [From comparison to a frock-coat, the lappets in front being 'CUT AWAY.'] For synonyms, *see* CAPELLA.

1866. *London Miscellany*, 5 Jan., p. 201. 'London Revelations.' He wore a Newmarket CUTAWAY, with huge flaps and pockets monopolising the whole of the skirts, suggestive of being receptacles for plunder.

1870. *London Figaro*, 8 June. It may be taken as an axiom that if a CUT-AWAY has been made for a fashionable man six feet high and broad in proportion, it will never sit nicely on the form of a wee little weaver of five feet two.

1889. *Pall Mall Gaz.*, 29 Oct., p. 3, col. 1. Off flies the frock coat and the flowing necktie; on goes the little red bow and the seedy brown 'CUTAWAY.'

CUT or **CUT UP DIDOES, SHINDIES, SHINES,** etc., *verbal phr.* (colloquial).—To play pranks or tricks; the same as CUT CAPERS.

18(?). *Pickings from the Picayune*, p. 147. This 'ere Frenchman has been CUTTING UP DIDOES in my house now for several days; he aint sober onst a week, and breaks all my cheers and tables Mr. Recorder.

1851. *New York Tribune*, 10 April. Had the Free States been manly enough, true enough, to enact the Wilmot Proviso as to all present or future territories of the Union, we should have had just the same DIDOES CUT UP by the chivalry that we have witnessed, and with no more damage to the Union.

CUT DIRT (American), or **CUT ONE'S STICK, LUCKY,** etc., *verbal phr.* (common).—To make off; to escape. TO CUT DIRT is clearly an allusion to the throwing up of mud and dust by a horse's hoofs in fast trotting. Originally, TO CUT ONE'S STICK refers to the cutting of a staff from a hedge or tree on the occasion of a journey CUT OVER and CUT AWAY, though vulgarly colloquial in the nineteenth, were in literary use in the sixteenth and seventeenth centuries. A curious and noteworthy parallel is found in Zechariah xi. 10, where the 'cutting of a stick' is described as the symbol of breaking a friendly covenant. CUT ONE'S STICK is sometimes elaborated into AMPUTATE ONE'S MAHOGANY (*q.v.*). CUT ONE'S LUCKY is a simple reference to a 'lucky' escape. A Latin equivalent of CUT ONE'S STICK is to be found in Juvenal's *Collige sarcinulas* ('collect the bags'). For synonyms, *see* AMPUTATE. To CUT ONE'S LUCKY also signifies to die.

1829. *Negro Song* [quoted in *S. J. and C.*, p. 287]. He jump up fo' sartin—he CUT DIRT and run, While Sambo follow arter wid his 'tum, tum, tum.'

1836. C. DICKENS, *Pickwick Papers* (about 1827), p. 79 (ed. 1857). Hold still, sir; wot's the use o' runnin' arter a man as has MADE HIS LUCKY, and got to t'other end of the Borough by this time.

1840. DICKENS, *Old Curiosity Shop*, ch. xl. 'And now that the nag has got his wind again,' said Mr. Chuckster, rising in a graceful manner, 'I'm afraid I must CUT MY STICK.'

1841. *Punch*, vol. I., p. 136. He [James II.] is the only English sovereign who may be said to have amputated his bludgeon, which, if we were speaking of an ordinary man and not a monarch, we should have rendered by the familiar phrase of CUT HIS STICK.

1841. *Comic Almanack*, p. 278. As sune as ve arived at the sumat had a Werry hextensif vew off Prinse lewy a CUTTIN HIS UNLUKKY, folowd by his folowers at Hi pressure spede.

1843. W. M. THACKERAY, *Lyra Hibernica*. 'The Battle of Limerick.' . . . the best use Tommy made Of his famous battle blade, Was to CUT HIS OWN STICK from the Shannon shore.

1851-61. H. MAYHEW, *London Lab. and Lon. Poor*, vol. I., p. 150. A man got me to go for some in a orchard, and told me how to manage; but I CUT MY LUCKY in a minute

1853. *Western Scenes*. Now you CUT DIRT, and don't let me see you here again for a coon's age, you hear?

1855. J. RICHARDSON, *Recollections of Last Half Century*, vol. II., p. 172. In less than half an hour he swallowed the whole undiluted contents of the bottle, and having done so CUT HIS LUCKY, and retired.

ante 1871. *Border Adventures*, p. 231. Now, I say, old hoss, if you don't hurry up and CUT DIRT like streak-lightnin', this child goes arter you, and you look out for a windin' sheet, you hear?

1880. *Punch's Almanack*, p. 3.

CUTE, CUTERER, and **CUTELY**, *adj.* and *adv.* (colloquial).—Sharp; clever; 'fly to wot's wot.' [A corruption of ACUTE.] Fr., *avoir le nez creux.* For synonyms, *see* KNOWING. So also CUTENESS, the quality or character of being CUTE.

1748. T. DYCHE, *Dictionary* (5 ed.). CUTE (A): sharp, witty, ingenious, ready, etc.

1754. B. MARTIN, *Eng. Dict.* (2 ed.). CUTE (a low word used instead of (*Acute*): witty.

1762. FOOTE, *Orators*, Act i. I did *speechify* once at a vestry concerning new lettering the church buckets, and came off CUTELY enough.

1765. FOOTE, *Commissary*, III. I did not know but they might be after, more CUTERER now in catching their larniug.

1768. GOLDSMITH, *Good Natured Man*, Act ii. Well, who could have thought so innocent a face could cover so much 'CUTENESS!

1768. GOLDSMITH, *Good Natured Man*, Act iv. Truly, madam, I write and indite but poorly. I never was 'CUTE at my learning.

1874. M. COLLINS, *Frances*, ch. xxxv. We can leave them to their own devices; they're both pretty 'CUTE.

1884. C. GIBBON, *By Mead and Stream*, ch. xx. Dressed in the latest City fashion—for there is a City fashion, designed apparently to combine the elegance of the West end with a suggestion of superhuman 'CUTENESS.'

CUT FINE, *verbal phr.* (common).—To narrow down to a minimum.

CUT IN, *verbal phr.* (common).—To join in suddenly and without ceremony; to intrude, or CHIP IN (*q.v.*). Also substantively.

1819. SCOTT, *Bride of Lammermoor*, ch. xxi. He was afraid you would CUT IN and carry off the girl.

1843. DICKENS, *Martin Chuzzlewit*, ch. xxiv., p. 246. I advise you to keep your own counsel, and to avoid tittle-tattle, and not to CUT IN where you're not wanted.

1849. THACKERAY, *Pendennis*, ch. vii. 'Most injudicious,' CUT IN the Major.

1864. G. A. LAWRENCE, *Guy Livingstone*, ch. vi. Keeping all her after-supper waltzes for him religiously, though half the men in town were trying to CUT IN.

1883. *Referee*, 17 June, p. 7, col. 4. I am anxious to have a CUT IN and get a big advertisement for nothing.

1884. W. C. RUSSELL, *Jack's Courtship*, ch. v. 'In short,' CUT IN my uncle unceremoniously, 'you have seen enough of Jack's life to know something about it?'

CUT INTO, *verbal phr.* (Winchester College).—Originally to hit one with a 'ground ash.' The office was exercised by Bible-clerks upon a 'man' kicking up a row when 'up to books.' Now generally used in the sense of to correct in a less formal manner than TUNDING (*q.v.*).

CUT IT, *verbal phr.* (common).—To move off quickly; to run away, or CUT DIRT (*q.v.*). For synonyms, *see* AMPUTATE and SKEDADDLE.

1885. *Indoor Paupers*, p. 36. Once a week we CUT IT From the workhouse gate.

Intj. phr. (common).—'Cease!' 'Stow it!' 'Stash it!'—A forcible injunction to desist and be off. Also CUT THAT! or simply CUT!

1863. C. READE, *Hard Cash*, II., 240. Then first he seemed to awake to his danger, and uttered a stentorian cry of terror, that rang through the night, and made two [unprofessional] of his three captors tremble. 'CUT THAT,' said Green [professional] sternly, 'or you'll get into trouble.' Mr. Hardie lowered his voice directly.

CUT IT FAT, *verbal phr.* (general).—To show off; to make a display; to 'come it strong'; 'put on side,' or CUT A DASH (*q.v.*).

1835. DICKENS, *Sketches by Boz*, p. 54. Gentlemen, in alarming waistcoats,

and steel watch-guards, promenading about, three abreast, with surprising dignity (or as the gentleman in the next box facetiously observes, 'CUTTING IT UNCOMMON FAT!')

1841. *Comic Almanack*, 'Christmas Fair.' A goose, even tailors have, who CUT IT FAT, And use the *goose* itself to get a *flat*.

1887. BAUMANN, *Londonismen.* 'A slang ditty,' p. v. But, there, it don't matter, Since to CUT IT STILL FATTER, By 'ook and by crook Ve've got up this book.

CUT MUTTON, *verbal phr.* (old).—To partake of one's hospitality. *Cf.*, 'to break bread' with one.

1849. THACKERAY, *Pendennis*, ch. xxxii. Bungay . . . hoped to have the pleasure of seeing both gents to CUT MUTTON with him before long.

CUT OFF ONE'S HEAD, *verbal phr.* (American political).—Used when an official's term of office has come to an end through change of Government, or supercession in other ways. Also TO DECAPITATE and TO BEHEAD.

1869. *New York Herald*, 5 Aug. 'The axe,' wrote a correspondent from Washington, 'is still doing its bloody work, and HEADS ARE FLYING OFF in all directions. The clerks in the Treasury Department begin to feel anxious, as the work of *decapitation* will soon make an end of them also.'

1872. *Daily Telegraph*, 5 Jan. 'Leader.' At the commencement of any fresh Presidency, hundreds of Democratic *employés* have their HEADS CUT OFF to make room for Republicans who, in their turn, will be decapitated when the Democrats get the upper hand again.

CUT OF ONE'S JIB, *subs. phr.* (nautical).—The general appearance. [From the foremost sail of a ship, which is frequently indicative of a vessel's character. A strange sail is judged by the CUT OF ITS JIB.]

1833. MARRYAT, *Peter Simple* [ed. 1846], vol. I., ch. ii., p. 9. I axes you because I see you're a sailor by the CUT OF YOUR JIB.

1835. HALIBURTON, *Clockmaker*, 3 S., ch. iv. For I seed by the CUT OF THE FELLER'S JIB that he was a preacher.

1836. MICHAEL SCOTT, *Cruise of the Midge* (ed. 18), p. 363. Oh, I see—*there* is a smart hand, in the gay jacket there, who does not seem to belong to your crew—a good seamen, evidently, by the CUT OF HIS JIB.

1881. BUCHANAN, *God and the Man*, ch. xvi. By the voice of you, by the rigs of you, and by the CUT OF YOUR PRECIOUS JIB.

1884. W. C. RUSSELL, *Jack's Courtship*, ch. iii. My democratic wide-awake and the republican CUT OF MY JIB, said he looking down at his clothes.

CUT ONE'S CART, *verbal phr.* (vagrants')—*See* quot.

1851-61. H. MAYHEW, *London Lab. and Lon. Poor*, vol. I., p. 339. I've seen them doze and sleep against the door. They like to be there before anyone CUTS THEIR CART (exposes their tricks).

CUT ONE'S COMB, *verbal phr.* (common).—To snub; to lower conceit.

1593. G. HARVEY, *Pierces Supererog.*, in wks. II., 283. Can . . . loue quench, or Zeale luke warme, or valour manicle, or, excellencie mew-vpp, or perfection geld, or supererogation COMBE-CUTT itselfe?

1608. MIDDLETON, *Trick to Catch the Old One*, IV., iv. To see ten men ride after me in watchet liveries, with orange-tawny caps,—'twill CUT HIS COMB, i' faith.

ed. 1717. NED WARD, wks. II., 302. If you prate one word more, I shall SLICE A SLIVER OFF YOUR COXCOMB, and teach you a little more manners before I've done with you.

1822. SCOTT, *The Fortunes of Nigel*, ch. ii. I will take my own time; and all the Counts in Cumberland shall not CUT MY COMB.

CUT ONE'S EYES, *verbal phr.* (thieves').—To get suspicious.

CUT ONE'S EYE (or **WISDOM**) **TEETH**, *verbal phr.* (common).—To learn 'what's what.' [A play

upon the word 'eye,' with an allusion to the canine teeth.]

CUT ONE'S OWN GRASS, *verbal phr.* (prison).—To get one's own living. *Cf.*, PADDLE ONE'S OWN CANOE.

CUT OUT, *verbal phr.* (colloquial).—To debar; deprive of advantage; supersede. *Cf.*, CUT, *verb*, sense 5. [Originally a nautical term; from CUTTING OUT a ship in an enemy's port.]

1779. R. CUMBERLAND, *Wheel of Fortune*, Act iv., Sc. 3. I suspect your heart inclines to Captain Woodville; and now he is come to England, I suppose I am likely to be CUT OUT.

1856. C. BRONTË, *Professor*, ch. iii. There's Waddy—Sam Waddy—making up to her; won't I CUT HIM OUT?

1863. HON. MRS. NORTON, *Lost and Saved*, p. 182. One woman has often CUT ANOTHER OUT, whose superiority, if dissected and analysed, would be found to be composed of the carriage that whirled her up to the door, the nimble footman who rapped at it, the soft carpet on the handsome staircase, the drawing-room to which it led, and the gilt stand full of geraniums, heliotropes, and roses in the curtained window.

1864. G. A. LAWRENCE, *Guy Livingstone*, ch. xxv. Here, as elsewhere, she pursued her favourite amusement, remorselessly. Fallowfield called it 'her CUTTING OUT expeditions.' She used to watch till a mother and daughter had, between them, secured a good matrimonial prize, and then employ her fascinations on the captured one.

CUT OUT OF, *verbal phr.* (common).—To 'do,' or be done, out of.

CUTS, *subs.* (tailors'). — Scissors. 'SMALL CUTS' = button-hole scissors.

CUT SAUCY.—*See* SAUCY.

CUT SHORT. (Generally CUT IT SHORT!) *phr.* (common). — A common injunction not to be prolix. For synonyms, *see* STOW IT.

1852. DICKENS, *Bleak House*, ch. lvii., p. 478. 'Come, then!' he gruffly cried to her, 'You hear what she says. CUT IT SHORT, and tell her.'

1878. JAS. PAYN, *By Proxy*, ch. xvi. Let us CUT THIS SHORT, Pennicuick. There is nothing more of importance to be said, and such talk is painful to both of us.

CUTTER, *subs.* (old).—A robber; a bully. [From committing acts of violence like those ascribed to the Mohocks; or, from cutting purses. Cotgrave translates CUTTER (or swash-buckler) by *balaffreux, taillebras, fendeur de naseaux.* Coles has, 'A CUTTER (or robber), gladiator, *latro.*'] This ancient cant word now survives in the phrase, 'to swear like a CUTTER.'

c. 1589. NASHE, *Month's Mind*, in wks., vol. I., p. 152. These like lustie CUTTERS . . . . aduentured to lay holde fast on our purses, and like strong theeues in deed proffered to robbe vs of all our monnie.

1633. ROWLEY, *Match at Midn.*, O. Pl., vii., 353. He's out of cash, and thou know'st, by CUTTER'S law we are bound to relieve one another.

1663. ABRAHAM COWLEY, *The Cutter of Coleman St.* [Title of play.]

1822. SCOTT, *Fortunes of Nigel*, ch. xxiii. Fifty thousand decuses, the spoils of five thousand bullies, CUTTERS, and spendthrifts.

CUT THE LINE, ROPE, or **STRING**, *verbal phr.* (thieves').—To cut a story short; to stop yarning.—*See* CAVE.

CUT THE PAINTER, *verbal phr.* (nautical). 1. To decamp; make off—secretly and suddenly. For synonyms, *see* AMPUTATE and SKEDADDLE.

2. To die.—*See* ALOFT and HOP THE TWIG.

CUTTING, *verbal subs.* and *ppl. adj.* (trade).—1. The process of underselling; synonymous with competition of the keenest kind.—*See* CUT, *verb*, sense 4.

1851-61. H. MAYHEW, *London Lab. and Lon. Poor*, vol. I., p. 372. There is great competition in the trade, and much of what is called CUTTING, or one tradesman underselling another. *Ibid.*, vol. II., p. 232. Those employers who seek to reduce the prices of a trade are known technologically as CUTTING employers, in contradistinction to the standard employers, or those who pay their workpeople, and sell their goods at the ordinary rates.

1863. *Once a Week*, vol. VIII., p. 552. At first sight it would seem that the poor men got a better article for less money than the rich and well-to-do classes; but a little inquiry into the method by which these CUTTING bakers 'make things pleasant' soon dissipate this seeming anomaly.

1863. *Once a Week*, vol. VIII., p. 179. If she is accustomed to frequent CUTTING SHOPS, where the stock is periodically thrown into a state of convulsions in its efforts to sell itself off, of course she expects to be done.

2. (colloquial).—Disowning or ignoring a person.—*See* CUT, *verb*, sense 2.

1854. AYTOUN AND MARTIN. *Bon Gaultier Ballads.* 'The Doleful Lay of the Honble. I. O. Uwins.' Uselessly down Bond Street strutting, Did he greet his friends of yore: Such a universal CUTTING, Never man received before.

CUTTLE or **CUTTLE BUNG**, *subs.* (old).—A knife used by cutpurses. [From Latin *cultellus*, a knife; *unde*, a cutlass.] For synonyms, *see* CHIVE.

1592. GREENE, *Second Part Connycatching*, in wks., vol. X., p. 3. And feeling if his CUTTLE BOUNG were glibbe and of a good edge, went to this mealeman to enter combate hand to hand with his purse.

1599. NASHE, *Lenten Stuffe* (*Harl. Misc.*, VI., 172). [He] unsheathed his CUTTLE-BONG, and from the nape of the necke to the taile dismembered him.

1608. DEKKER, *Belman of London*, in wks. (Grosart) III., 154. He that cuts the purse is called the *Nip* . . . The knife is called a CUTTLE-BUNG.

1610. ROWLANDS, *Martin Mark-all*, p. 37 (H. Club's Repr., 1874). A Roome CUTTLE: a sword. A CUTTLE BUNG: a knife to cut a purse.

CUTTY-EYED, *adj.* (thieves').—Suspicious looking; leering.

CUT UP, *verbal phr.* (colloquial).—1. To run down; to mortify.

1759. GOLDSMITH *The Bee*, No. 5, p. 390 (Globe ed.). The pack of critics, who probably have no other occupation but that of CUTTING UP everything new.

1819. SHELLEY, Letter to Ollier, in *Letters* (Camelot), p. 309. I read the article . . . I am glad, however, to see the *Quarterly* CUT UP, and that by one of their own people.

1874. MORTIMER COLLINS, *Frances*, ch. xvii. The slashing writers who delight to CUT UP a book, especially if the author is a friend or a rival.

2. (common).—To come up; turn up; become; show up.

3. (thieves'). — To divide plunder; to share; to 'nap the regulars.' *Cf.*, CUT UP FAT.

1779. R. CUMBERLAND, *Wheel of Fortune*, Act iv., Sc. 3. *Sir D. D.* A gentleman, who trusts to servants in his absence, is sure to be CUT UP. *Emily*, CUT UP! what's that. *Sir D. D.* Why, 'tis a common phrase.

1870. J. K., *Good Words*, April. 'The Nailmakers' Lamentation.' Now, what's twelve shillings to CUT UP, To pay so many things.

1879. J. W. HORSLEY, in *Macm. Mag.*, XL., 505. We had between sixty and seventy quid to CUT UP (share).

1880. G. R. SIMS, *How the Poor Live.* These . . . were mostly '*ramps*,' or swindles, got up to obtain the gate-money, and generally interrupted by circumstances arranged beforehand by those who were going to CUT UP the plunder.

4. (common).—To behave.

1856. T. HUGHES, *Tom Brown's School-days*, pt. I., ch. v. You see, a great deal depends on how a fellow CUTS UP, at first. If he's got nothing odd about him, and answers straightforward, and holds his head up, he gets on.

1883. *Illust. London News*, 12 May, p. 463, col. 2. Export again CUT UP wretchedly in the Burwell Stakes, which fell to Blue Glass, and one of the best of the American three-year-olds.

CUT UP FAT, *verbal phr.* (common). — To leave a large fortune. *Cf.*, CUT UP, sense 3.

1824. T. HOOK, *Sayings and Doings*, 1 S., *Danvers*, p. 13 ('Colburn's Stand. Novels'). His property was immense . . . and few people ventured to guess . . . what he would CUT UP for.

1831. DISRAELI, *The Young Duke*, bk. IV., ch. vii., p. 228 (ed. 1866). 'You think him rich?' 'Oh, he will CUT UP VERY LARGE,' said the Baron.

1848. THACKERAY, *Book of Snobs*, ch. vii. The old banker died in course of time, and to use the affectionate phrase common on such occasions, CUT UP prodigiously well.

1860. O. W. HOLMES, *The Professor at the Breakfast Table*, xi., p. 351. In the midst of these kind expressions, the gentleman with the diamond, the Koh-i-noor, as we called him, asked in a very unpleasant sort of way, how the old boy was likely to CUT UP, — meaning what money our friend was going to leave behind.

1872. *Civilian*, 2 March. Time wears on, and old Stubbs pays the debt of nature, and CUTS UP SPLENDIDLY. His colossal fortune is the making of his needy sons-in-law.

CUT UP [ROUGH, RUSTY, SAVAGE, STIFF, UGLY, etc.], *verbal phr.*—To become quarrelsome or dangerous.

1836. DICKENS, *Pickwick*, ch. xliii., p. 377. 'I'll trouble you for the loan of five-and-twenty pound.' 'Wot good 'ull that do?' inquired Mr. Weller. 'Never mind,' replied Sam. 'P'raps you may ask for it five minits arterwards; p'raps I may say I von't pay, and CUT UP ROUGH.'

1849. THACKERAY, *Pendennis*, ch. l. I didn't mean any offence—beg pardon —hang it! you CUT UP QUITE SAVAGE.

1855–7. W. M. THACKERAY, *Miscellanies*, II., 272. It is true that Natty [Edward's Julia's younger brother] called many times in Pocklington Square, and complained to Edward that he, Nat, could neither see his Mar nor the Gurls, and that the old gent CUT UP UNCOMMON STIFF.

1864. A. TROLLOPE, *The Small House at Allington*, ch. iv. She's always talking of Lupex being jealous! if he was TO CUT UP ROUGH, you wouldn't find it pleasant.

CUT UP WELL, *verb. phr.* (venery).—To strip well; to be an engaging bed-fellow.

TO BE CUT UP (common).—To be vexed; hurt; dejected; sometimes simply CUT. Formerly, to be in embarrassed circumstances.

1821. P. EGAN, *Tom and Jerry* [ed. 1890], p. 60. But, owing to a combination of unfortunate circumstances, such as gambling, dissipation, etc., Jem is so CUT UP, that all his old pals have turned their backs upon him.

1846. THACKERAY, *V. Fair*, vol. I., ch. xxv. 'I should have liked to see the old girl before we went,' Rawdon said. 'She looks so CUT UP and altered that I'm sure she can't last long.'

1855. W. M. THACKERAY, *Newcomes*, II., p. 201. It's not when a fellow's down and CUT UP, and riled,—naturally riled—as you are,—I know you are, Marquis; it's not then that I'm going to be angry with you . . .

1864. *Glasgow Herald*, 28 Dec. Not a word was said. I felt confoundly CUT, and every mouthful of that dinner felt as if it would choke me.

CUTTY, *subs.* — A short pipe; a NOSE-WARMER, (*q.v.*).

CUZ, *subs.* (printers').—A workman free of the 'chapel.'

CYMBAL, *subs.* (thieves').—A watch. For synonyms, *see* TICKER.

D *subs.* (common). --1. A penny, or (in *pl.*) pence; *e.g.*, two D; three D, etc., = two-pence, three-pence, etc. [The initial letter of the Latin *denarius*.]

1880. *Punch's Almanack*, p. 3. Got the doldrums dreadful, that is clear. Two D left! must go and do a beer!

2. (common).—A detective; among thieves, a policeman. For synonyms, *see* BEAK and NARK.

1879. THOR FREDUR, *Sketches from Shady Places*. Still I play Shoeblack odd times. I have a few friends among the D's (detectives), who give me the job to watch a house occasionally.

TO USE A BIG D, *verbal phr.* (common). — 'To swear'; the 'D' stands for 'damned.'

1878. GILBERT AND SULLIVAN, *Her Majesty's Ship 'Pinafore.'* What, never USE A BIG, BIG D?'

1890. H. D. TRAILL, *Saturday Songs*, p. 3. Do we fight the senseless duel, do we SLING THE BIG, BIG D, No; our strongest word is 'Bother,' and revolvers all we see.

THE TWO D's, *phr.* (military). —Army regulations enact that a soldier's pay must not be so docked in fines as to leave him less than two-pence a day. Hence, if a man, from any cause, is put on short pay, he is said to be 'on THE TWO D's.'

DAB, *subs.* (colloquial).—1. An expert; a DABSTER. [Thought to be a corruption of 'adept' (Latin *adeptus*) a dep; a dap; a dab.] *Cf.*, 'dabbler,' one who meddles without mastery; a superficial meddler. Fr., *dab*, *dabe*, or *dade*.

1733. Letter of LORD CHESTERFIELD to Lady Suffolk, 17 Aug. [Suffolk Correspondence, 1824, ii., 64.] . . . known DABS at finding out mysteries.

1748. T. DYCHE, *Dictionary* (5 ed.). DAB (s.) . . . also an expert gamester is so called [also 1754, MARTIN, *Eng. Dict.* (2 ed.), s.v.].

1759. GOLDSMITH, *The Bee*, No. 1. One writer, for instance, excels at a plan or a title-page, another works away the body of the book, and a third is a DAB at an index.

1838. *Comic Almanack*, p. 148. Such a DAB to get up a commission.

1849. J. D. LEWIS, in WHIBLEY, p. 231. When Hicks, who's no DAB, with his oar cuts a crab, And our coxswain he swears like the devil.

1860. DICKENS, *Great Expectations*, ch. xlii., p. 200. He was a smooth one to talk, and was a DAB at the ways of gentlefolks.

2. (common).—A bed. For synonyms, *see* BUG-WALK and KIP.

1823. W. T. MONCRIEFF, *Tom and Jerry*, Act iii., Sc. 3. *Mace*: . . . Vhen ve've had the liqvor, ve'll kick up a reel, and all go to our DABS.

3. (river-side thieves').—The drowned corpse of an outcast woman.

4. (old).—A trifle.

1745. WALPOLE *to Mann*, ii., 53. The Count may have procured for her some dirty DAB of a negotiation about some acre of territory more for Hanover.

Adj. (colloquial).—1. Clever; skilled; expert.—*See subs.*, sense 1. Fr., *avoir le pouce long*, or *rond*, *i.e.*, 'to have a long or round thumb.'

2. (back slang).—Bad. A DABHENO, a bad market, day, or sale. DOOGHENO = a good day, etc.; DAB TROS = a bad sort.

1877. DIPROSE, *London Life*. I've been doing awful DAB with my tol (lot) or stock, have'nt made a yennep (penny).

RUM-DABE, *subs.* (old).—The same as DAB, *subs.*, sense 1. [RUM (*q.v.*) is Old Cant for 'good.']

DAB DOWN, *verbal phr.* (common).—To pay; hand over; to 'post' or 'SHELL OUT' (*q.v.* for synonyms).

TO DAB IT UP [with a woman], *verbal phr.* (old).—To pair off; to agree to cohabitation.

DABSTER, *subs.* (colloquial).—An expert or DAB (*q.v.*).

1877. J. GREENWOOD, *Dick Temple*, ch. iii. 'Not in the least like the performance of an amateur DABSTER,' remarked Jack Mallet, admiringly. 'Much more like the work of an old master for style and finish.'

DACE, *subs.* (old).—Two-pence; in America, two cents. [From 'deuce.']

DACHA-SALTEE, *subs.* (thieves' and vagrants').—A franc; or tenpence English. [From the Italian *dieci soldi.*]—*See* SALTEE.

1861. READE, *Cloister and Hearth*, ch. lv. What with my crippledom and thy piety, a wheeling of thy poor old dad, we'll bleed the bumpkins of a DACHA-SALTEE.

DAD-BINGED (also **-BLAMED, -FETCHED**), **-GASTED, -GONED, -ROTTED**, or **-SNATCHED**, *ppl. adj.* (American). — Half veiled oaths; 'whips to beat the devil round the stump.' [DAD is a corrupted form of 'God,' which, with other forms, (DOD-, Dog-, etc.), is found in various combinations, as above.] For synonyms, *see* OATHS.

1887. *Scribner's Magazine*, 'DADGUM ye!' cried Jeff, irritably, 'whut — by grabs, hit's a human critter!'

1888. S. L. CLEMENS ('Mark Twain'), *Adventures of Huckleberry Finn*, p. 122. A chile er two, mo 'er less, warn't no consekens to Sollermun, DAD-FETCH him. *Ibid.* 'Why, Mars Tom, I doan want no rats. Dey's de DAD-BLAMEDEST creturs to 'sturb a body . . . I ever see.'

DAD-DAD, MUM-MUM or **DADDY-MAMMY**, *subs. phr.* (military).—A beginner's practice on the drum.

DADDLE, *subs.* (common). — The hand; or fist. TO TIP THE DADDLE, to shake hands. For synonyms, *see* BUNCH OF FIVES, to which may be added the following lists:—

ENGLISH SYNONYMS. Chalk-farm; claw; clutch; cornstealer; duke; fam; famble; feeler; fin; flapper; flipper; forceps; fore-foot; fork; grappling-iron or

hook; goll (old); oar; paddle; palette; paw; plier; shaker; wing; Yarmouth mitten.

FRENCH SYNONYMS. *Les abatis* or *abattis* (popular: a term applied to both hands and feet; properly giblets); *l'agrafe* (common; hook or clasp); *la croche* (thieves': properly a quaver; possibly influenced by *croc* = hook, grapnel, or drag; an allusion to the hooked appearance of the musical note); *la cuiller* (popular: literally a spoon); *les brancards* (popular: this expression, like *abatis*, is also used of the feet; properly = shafts, as of a cart); *l'arguemine* (thieves'); *le battoir* (popular: properly a washerwoman's 'bat'); *un gigot* (popular: a large, thick hand, a 'mutton fist'); *le grappin*; *les harpions* (also = feet).

ITALIAN SYNONYM. *Gramoso* (properly 'a wretch'); *cerra*.

1785. GROSE, *Dict. Vulg. Tongue*, s.v.

1789. GEO. PARKER, *Life's Painter*, p. 143, s.v.

1819. T. MOORE, *Tom Crib's Mem. to Cong.*, p. 23. From this to the finish, 'twas all *fiddle-faddle*, Poor Georgy, at last, could scarce hold up his DADDLE. *Ibid.* With DADDLES high uprais'd, and *nob* held back, In awful prescience of th' impending thwack.

1827. SCOTT, *Two Drovers*, ch. ii. Ah, this comes of living so long with kilts and bonnets—men forget the use of their DADDLES.

1842. *Punch*, vol. III., p. 136. And her DADDLE link'd in his'n gone to roam as lovers use.

1849. C. KINGSLEY, *Alton Locke*, ch. v. 'Tip us your DADDLE, my boy,' said the second speaker.

DADDY, *subs.* (general).—1. The superintendent of a casual ward; generally an old pauper.

2. (theatrical). — A stage manager.—*See* quot.

1886. *Graphic*, 10 April, p. 399. The manager himself is sometimes known as the 'gorger,' and DADDY is the stage-manager.

3. (common).—A confederate of 'workers' of mock raffles, lotteries, etc.; generally the person selected to receive the prize.

DADDYISM, *subs.* (American).—Pride of birth.

1871. KATE FIELD, in *Harper's Bazaar*, Aug. An Eastern man commending the services of a young Philadelphian to a Chicago tradesman, said: 'He comes of a very good family; his grandfather was a distinguished man.' 'Was he?' replied the man of Chicago. 'That's of no account with us. There's less DADDYISM here than any part of the United States. What's he himself.'

DAFFY or **DAFFY'S ELIXIR**, *subs.* (common).—Gin. [From a popular medicine sold as early as the beginning of the eighteenth century: *see* advertisements (1709), in Ashton's *Social Life in the Reign of Queen Anne*, i., pp. 7, 8: now known as 'Tincture of Senna.'] For synonyms, *see* DRINKS.

1821. *The Fancy*, vol. I., p. 304. While carrying on his new vocation of publican, Jack did not deny himself the use of drops of DAFFY.

1841. LEMAN REDE, *Sixteen-String Jack*, Act i., Sc. 2. Take some DAFFY to the back parlour.

1851. H. MAYHEW, *Lon. Lab. and Lon. Poor*, IV., 430. When I goes in where they are a havin' their DAFFIES—that's drops o' gin, sir.

1871. *London Figaro*, 15 April. [If the baby] should bawl persistently . . . he would . . . thoroughly dose it with DAFFY.

1882. *Punch*, vol. LXXXII., 193. They had low foreheads, and wore big buttonholes, for so they termed the flowers, it was 'the thing' to wear. A good many of them, too, had been partaking freely of DAFFY.

DAFFY-DOWN-DILLY, *subs.* (old).—A dandy; one 'got up regardless.' For synonyms, *see* DANDY.

1841. LEMAN REDE, *Sixteen-String Jack*, Act i., Sc. 2. *Bob*: I'm here, my DAFFY-DOWN-DILLY!

DAGEN, *subs.* (old).—An 'artful member.' [From DAGEN, a sword or dagger.] For synonyms, *see* DOWNY COVE. DAGGER = the *penis*.

DAGGER-CHEAP, *adj. phr.* (old).—'Dirt' cheap. [From an ordinary of low repute in Holborn, notorious for the coarseness of its entertainment.—*See* Jonson's *Alchemist*, v., 2, and *Devil is an Ass*, i., 1.]

1631. BISHOP ANDREWES, *Sermons* (posthumous). We set our wares at a very easy price; he (the devil) may buy us even DAGGER-CHEAP, as we say.

DAGS, *subs.* (common).—A feat; a performance or work, *e.g.*, I'll do your DAGS = an incitement to emulation. [From DAG, the old Saxon form of 'day.' *Darg* for a day's work is common in Scotland. A *love-darg* is a day's free help given to a farmer by his neighbours.]

1879. *Notes and Queries*, 5 S., xii., 15 Aug., p. 128. 'I'll do you (or your) DAGS.' An expression used by children of young, and sometimes of older, growth, meaning, 'I'll do something that you cannot do.'

1886. *Fun.* He was very fond of what, in schoolboy days, we used to call doing DAGS.

DAILY LEVY, *subs.* (journalistic).—The *Daily Telegraph*. [This London daily was established by Mr. Edward Levy Lawson.]

DAIRY, *subs.* (common).—The paps. TO AIR THE DAIRY = to expose the breast.

ENGLISH SYNONYMS. Bubs or bubbies; charlies; blubber; butter-boxes; butter-bags; berkeleys; cat-heads; diddies; globes; dugs; milk-walk; milk-shop; milky way; dumplings; udder (Browning); 'Nature's founts'; feeding bottles; 'charms'; hemispheres; apple-dumpling shop; meat market; poonts; titties; cabman's rests (rhyming); baby's bottom.

FRENCH SYNONYMS. *Les avantages* (familiar); *l'avant-cœur* (popular = the fore-heart; as *l'avant-bras* = the fore-arm); *l'avant-main*; *les avant-scènes* (properly that goes before; the front of a stage); *les avant-postes* (literally, the outposts); *l'oranger* (popular = the orange-tree. *Cf.*, *des oranges sur l'étagère*); *les nénais* or *nénets* (popular); *deux œufs sur le plat* (common); *le monzu* or *mouzu* (Old Cant); *des blagues à tabac* (popular = tobacco-pouches); *des bessons* (common = twins); *une étagère* or *un étal* (properly a butcher's stall; *étalage* = goods exposed for sale; *Cf.*, *étaler sa marchandise* = to wear a low-necked dress); *la doublure de la pièce* (popular); *devant de gilet* (popular: *un gilet à la mode* = well-developed paps); *une livraison de bois devant sa porte* (popular); *le ragoût de la poitrine* (*ragoût* = pleasure, *poitrine* = breast); *la mappe-monde* (popular: literally a map of the two hemispheres); *les nichons* (familiar); *il y a du monde au balcon* (said of one with large paps); *les bossoirs* (sailors'; *gabarit sans bossoirs* = thin or withered paps); *les calebasses* (= gourds); *les éclaireurs* (popular: scouts); *des gibasses* (popular: skinny paps); *des œufs sur la place d'armes* (popular).

GERMAN SYNONYM. *Gleishaus* (*i.e.*, milk-house; *Gleis* = milk).

ITALIAN SYNONYM. *Tetta*.

SPANISH SYNONYMS. *Balsopeto* (*m*; properly = a large pouch carried near the breast); *chiche* or *chichi* (*f*; a Mexican vulgarism); *pechera* (*f*; also = a stomacher or frill on the bosom of a shirt).

1811. *Lexicon Balatronicum*, s.v.

DAISIES, *subs.* (general). — Boots. *Cf.*, DAISY-ROOTS, and for synonyms, *see* TROTTER-CASES.

1879. J. W. HORSLEY, in *Macm. Mag.*, XL., 503. While waiting for my pal I had my DAISIES cleaned.

TO TURN UP ONE'S TOES TO THE DAISIES. — To die. For synonyms, *see* ALOFT and HOP THE TWIG.

1837. BARHAM, *Ingoldsby Legends* (*Babes in the Wood*). Be kind to those dear little folks When our TOES ARE TURNED UP TO THE DAISIES.

DAISY, *subs.* (American).—A man or thing first-rate of a kind. Also equivalent to DANDY, *subs.*, sense 4.

c. 1876. *Broadside Ballad*, 'Mrs. Brady's Daughter.' She's such a DAISY, she sets me crazy.

1888. *Denver Republican*, May. Jack Dempsey is beyond compare a pugilistic DAISY.

1890. RUDYARD KIPLING, *Fuzzy Wuzzy*, in *Scots Observer*, iv., p. 439, col. I. 'E's a daisy, 'e's a ducky, 'e's a lamb.

Adj. (American).—First-rate; AI.

1889. *Puck's Library*, April, p. 7. Big scene of boats ascending Nile cataracts—new sensation, never done before—and chance for DAISY effects in the desert.

DAISY BEAT.—*See* under BEAT.

DAISY-BEATERS.—*See* CREEPERS.

DAISY-CUTTER, *subs.* (common).—1. A horse whether good or bad. Also DAISY-KICKER. Fr., *un rase-tapis*.

1785. GROSE, *Dict. Vulg. Tongue*, s.v.

1817. SCOTT, *Rob Roy*, ch. iii. I should like to try that DAISY-CUTTER of yours upon a piece of level road (barring canter) for a quart of claret at the next inn.

1834. W. H. AINSWORTH, *Rookwood*. Song, 'The Game of High Toby.' But what DAISY-CUTTER can match that black tit.

1866. C. READE, *Griffith Gaunt*, ch. i. Others galloped uselessly about pounding the earth, for DAISY-CUTTERS were few in those days.

2. (cricket).—A ball which travels more than half the 'pitch' along the ground without rising; a 'sneak.' Wykehamicè, 'a ramrod.'—*See* GRUB.

DAISY-KICKER, *subs.* (old).—1. A horse. *Cf.*, DAISY-CUTTER and GROGHAM. For synonyms, *see* PRAD.

1781. G. PARKER, *View of Society*, II., 48. The hostler then says, 'He has a choice nag or DAISY-KICKER to sell or SWAP.'

2. (old).—An ostler. [By implication from sense 1.]

1781. G. PARKER, *View of Society*, II., 39. DAISY-KICKERS are Hostlers belonging to large inns; and are known to each other by this name.

DAISY-ROOTS (rhyming slang).—Boots. Also DAISIES. For synonyms, *see* TROTTER-CASES. Fr., *des salaires*.

1879. J. W. HORSLEY, in *Macm. Mag.*, XL., 501. I piped [saw] three or four pair of DAISY-ROOTS (boots).

TO PICK A DAISY, *verbal phr.* (common).—To evacuate in the open air; also, to retire to make water.

DAISYVILLE, *subs.* (thieves').—The country. Also DEUSEAVILLE.

ENGLISH SYNONYM. Monkery.

FRENCH SYNONYMS. *La camplouse*; *la cambrouse*; *le pasclin* or *pasquelin*.

ITALIAN SYNONYMS. *Longa* (literally = an expanse); *polverosa* (literally = dusty); *graziosa* (literally = graceful).

1622. HEAD AND KIRKMAN, 'Canting Song.' This Doxie Dell can cut bien whids, And drill well for a win; And prig and cloy so benshiply, All the DEUSEA-VILE within.

DAKMA, *verb* (thieves').—To silence.

1859. MATSELL, *Vocabulum, or Rogue's Lexicon*, s.v.

1881. *New York Slang Dict.* I had to DAKMA the bloke to cly the swag.

DAM. NOT TO CARE or **BE WORTH A DAM**, *phr.* (common).—To care or be worth nothing. [The DAM or DAWM is an Indian coin worth barely the fortieth part of a rupee.] *Cf.*, CARE and FIG.

DAMAGE, *subs.* (colloquial).—The cost of anything; the sum total in the sense of recompense. 'What's the DAMAGE?' 'what's to pay?' also What's the SWINDLE? (*q.v.*). [An allusion to damages at law.]

b. 1788, *d.* 1824. BYRON [quoted in Annandale]. Many thanks, but I must pay the DAMAGE and will thank you to tell me the amount of the engraving.

1852. H. B. STOWE, *Uncle Tom's Cabin*, ch. xiv. Well, now, my good fellow, what s the DAMAGE, as they say in Kentucky; in short, what's to be paid out for this business.

1871. DE VERE, *Americanisms*, p. 576. When he wishes to know what he has to pay, he asks, What's the DAMAGE? or not so charitably, What's the *swindle*?

DAMAGED, *ppl. adj.* (common).—Drunk; SCREWED (*q.v.* for synonyms).—*See* DRINKS.

DAMBER, *subs.* (old). — A man, COVE, or CULL belonging to the fraternity of vagabonds. For synonyms, *see* COVE.

DAMME, **DAMMY** or **DAMMY-BOY**, *subs.* (old). — A sixteenth and seventeenth century royster; a blustering fellow. [So called from the excess to which swearing was carried by the rakes of the day.]

1654. WITTS, *Recreations*. To valiant DAMMEE. DAM-ME, thy brain is valiant, 'tis confest; Thou more, that with it every day dar'st jest Thy self into fresh braules; but call'd upon, With swearing DAM-ME, answer'st every one. Keep thy self there, and think thy valour right, He that dares DAMNE himself, dares more than fight.

1687. CLEVELAND, *Works*. Depriver of those solid joys, Which sack creates; author of noise Among the roaring punks and DAMMY-BOYS.

DAM NASTY OATH, *subs. phr.* (American). — A corruption of AMNESTY OATH. [Southerners, at the close of the Civil War, were required, as an outward sign of submission to the Union, to subscribe to certain conditions, upon which a free pardon was granted. The terms were deemed unpalatable—hence DAM NASTY OATH.]

DAMNED-SOUL, *subs.* (old).—A Customs House clearing clerk. [Because to avoid perjury he was alleged to have taken a general oath never to swear truly in making 'declarations.'] [*Lexicon Balatronicum*, 1811.]

DAMP (Generally, SOMETHING DAMP), *subs. phr.* (common).—

A drink; or 'GO' (*q.v.* for synonyms).

1836. DICKENS, *Pickwick*, ch. xxvii., p. 228. 'So we'll just give ourselves a DAMP, Sammy.' Saying this, Mr. Weller mixed two glasses of spirits and water, and produced a couple of pipes.

DAMPER, *subs.* (thieves').—1. A till or 'lob.' DRAWING A DAMPER = robbing a till, *i.e.*, 'lob-sneaking.'

1857. SNOWDEN, *Mag. Assistant*, 3 ed., p. 445, s.v.

2. (tailors').—A sweater; one who takes as much as possible out of workmen for a minimum of pay.

3. (colloquial).—He or that which damps, chills, or discourages.

4. (old). — Ale or stout after spirits and water.—*See* COOLER.

5. (old). —A snack between meals.—*See* senses 6 and 7.

6. (schoolboys'). — A suet pudding served before meat. *Cf.*, senses 4 and 5.

7. (Australian). — Unleavened bread made of flour and water and baked in thin cakes, in a frying pan or on a flat stone in wood ashes.

1885. G. A. SALA, in *Daily Telegraph*, 3 Sept., p. 5, col. 5. They got enough flour from Sydney to make their DAMPERS.

1886. G. SUTHERLAND, *Australia*, p. 77. They must at least receive a 'pannikin' of flour and be allowed to bake it up into a piece of DAMPER at the cooking fire.

DAMP ONE'S MUG, *verbal phr.* (common). — To drink. For synonyms, *see* LUSH.

DAMP-POT, *subs.* (tailors')—The sea; specifically the Atlantic. For synonyms, *see* BRINY and PUDDLE.

DAMP THE SAWDUST, *verbal phr.* (licensed victuallers')—To 'crack a bottle' with friends 'for luck' on starting a new 'house.'

DAMSON-PIE, *subs.* (Black Country).—A Birmingham and 'black country' term for 'Billingsgatry.'

1888. W. BLACK, *Strange Adv. of House Boat*, ch. viii. Even if you were to hear some of the Birmingham lads giving each other a dose of DAMSON-PIE . . . you wouldn't understand a single sentence.

DANCE, *subs.* (thieves'). — A staircase or flight of steps. A contraction of the older form—DANCERS. [*Ducange Anglicus*, 1857.]

Verb (old).—1. To be hanged. Also TO DANCE UPON NOTHING and TO DANCE THE PADDINGTON FRISK. Fr., *danser une danse où il n y a pas d'plancher* and *faire la bénédiction du pied en l'air*. For synonyms, *see* LADDER.

1839. H. AINSWORTH, *Jack Sheppard*, ch. xxxi. 'My limbs feel so light, now that my irons are removed,' he observed with a smile, 'that I am half inclined to dance.' 'You'll DANCE UPON NOTHING, presently,' rejoined Jonathan, brutally.

1840. HOOD, *Miss Kilmansegg*. Just as the felon condemned to die, With a very natural loathing, Leaving the sheriff to dream of ropes, From his gloomy cell in a vision elopes To a caper on sunny greens and slopes Instead of the DANCE UPON NOTHING.

1864. *Daily News*, 2 Dec. Another synonym for being hanged is DANCING ON NOTHING IN A HEMPEN CRAVAT.

2. (printers').—Type DANCES if letters drop out when the forme is lifted.

TO DANCE BARNABY. — *See* BARNABY.

DANCE OF DEATH, *subs. phr.* (old).—Hanging. *Cf.*, DANCE, *verb*, sense 1.

DANCERS, *subs.* (thieves') — 1. Stairs ; a flight of steps. Fr., *les grimpants*.

1671. R. HEAD, *English Rogue*, pt. I., ch. v., p. 52 (1874). Track up the DANCERS, go up the stayres.

1785. GROSE, *Dict. Vulg. Tongue*, s.v.

1847. LYTTON, *Lucretia*, pt. II., ch. vii. 'Bob, track the DANCERS. Up like a lark — and down like a dump.' Bob grinned . . . and scampered up the stairs.

1858. LYTTON, *What will he do with it?* bk. III., ch. xvi. Come, my Hebe, track the DANCERS, that is, go up the stairs.

2. *sing.* (thieves').—Also DANCING MASTER. A thief whose speciality is prowling about the roofs of houses and effecting an entrance through attic and upper storey windows ; a GARRETEER (*q.v.*). [In allusion to dexterity of walk.] For synonyms, *see* AREA-SNEAK.

DANCING-MASTER, *subs.* (old).—1. A species of Mohock or dandy, *temp.* Queen Anne. [Who made his victims caper by running his sword through the legs ; for detailed description, *see Spectator* (1712), No. 324.] For list of synonyms, *see* DANDY.

2. (thieves').—*See* DANCERS, sense 2.

3. (old). — The hangman ; Jack Ketch.—*See* DANCE, *verb*, sense 1.

D AND D, *phr.* (police).—'Drunk and disorderly' (in connection with charge sheet cases). A synonym is LUSHY AND STROPOLUS.

1889. *Answers*, 2 March, p. 218, col. 1. Last New Year's Day he took over 14s. to my certain knowledge, for the old man was up for D AND D, trying to break a window with his broom.

DANDER, *subs.* (colloquial).—Anger. TO RAISE ONE'S DANDER or GET ONE'S DANDER UP or RIZ = to make or get angry. [Derivation uncertain ; provincial in several English counties.]

1843. DICKENS, *Martin Chuzzlewit*, ch. xxi., p. 223. I do my duty ; and I RAISE THE DANDER of my feller critters, as I wish to serve ; . . . they rile up rough, along of my objecting to their selling Eden off too cheap.

1848-62. J. RUSSELL LOWELL, *Biglow Papers*. Wut'll make ye act like freemen? Wut'll GIT YOUR DANDER RIZ?

1849. THACKERAY, *Pendennis*, ch. xliii. Don't talk to me about daring to do this thing or t'other, or when my DANDER IS UP, it's the very thing to urge me on.

1863. *Punch*, 7 Feb. If John Bull had RIZ OUR DANDER, Settin' foot on yonder shore, Then we should have holler'd grander Than the broad Atlantic's roar.

1872. *Chamb. Journal*, 14 Dec., p. 791. They knew he'd never find out who did it, for he was in such an awful DANDER.

DANDERED, *ppl. adj.* (colloquial).—Angry ; 'mad.'

1890. H. D. TRAILL, *Saturday Songs*, 'The Precipitate Grandmother,' p. 30. Whose way of tackling DANDERED snakes Is to perpitiate the critters With hominy an' buckwheat cakes And pumpkin-squash an' apple fritters.

DANDO, *subs.* (common).—A great eater ; a glutton ; specifically a sharper who subsists at the expense of hotels, restaurants, or oyster bars. [From one DANDO, a 'bouncing, seedy swell,' hero of a hundred ballads, notorious for being 'charged' at least twice a month with bilking.]

18(?). THACKERAY, *The Professor*. 'What a flat you are,' shouted he in a voice of thunder, 'to think I'm agoing to pay! Pay! I never pay—I'm DANDO.'

1850. MACAULAY, *Journal in Life*, by Trevelyan, ch. xii., p. 539 (1884), April 27.—To Westbourne Terrace, and passed an hour in playing with Alice . . . I was DANDO at a pastry cook's and then at an oyster shop.

1885. *Ill. London News*, 15 Aug., p. 154, col. 3. One day we are told that the couplet should be :—Oysters, you'll find, are best by far In every month which ends with an *r*. Next day this is pooh-poohed, and we are to read, instead :—Oysters, you'll find, are best by far In every month which contains an *r*. Spiritualists might be kind enough to consult DANDO, who would, no doubt, have the true version at his finger's ends, so as to rap it out on the instant.

DANDY, *subs.* (formerly slang, now recognized).—1. A fop ; a coxcomb ; a man who pays excessive attention to dress. The feminine forms, 'dandilly' and 'dandizette,' did not 'catch on.' DANDY was first applied half in admiration, half in derision to a fop about the year 1816. John Bee (*Slang Dict.*, 1823) says that Lord Petersham was the chief of these successors to the departed Macaronis, and gives, as their peculiarities, 'French gait, lispings, wrinkled foreheads, killing king's English, wearing immense plaited pantaloons, coat cut away, small waistcoat, cravat and chitterlings immense, hat small, hair frizzled and protruding.' In common English DANDY has come to be applied to such as are neat and careful in dressing according to fashion. [From DANDY-PRATT (*q.v.*).]

ENGLISH SYNONYMS. Beau ; blade ; blood ; buck ; chappie ; corinthian ; count ; court-card ; cheese ; daffy-down-dilly ; dancing-master ; dude ; dundreary ; exquisite ; flasher ; fop ; gallant ; gommy ; gorger ; Jemmy Jessamy ; Johnny ; lounger ; macaroni ; masher ; mohawk ; nerve ; nicker ; nizzie ; nob ; oatmeal ; scourer ; smart ; spark ; sweater ; swell ; toff ; tip-topper ; tumbler ; yum-yun.

FRENCH SYNONYMS. *Un gandin* (popular = a frequenter of the old Boulevard de Gand) ; *un gommeux ; un mouchard ; un mouget ; un petit maître ; un talon-rouge* (from the red heels worn in the seventeenth century); *un incroyable* (a 'swell' of the Directoire period, as also *un merveilleux*) ; *un mirliflore* (an allusion to *millefleurs*, a favourite perfume) ; *un muscadin ; un élégant ; un dandy ; un lion ; un fashionable ; un cocodès ; un crevé ; un petit crevé ; un col-cassé ; un luisant ; un poisseux ; un boudiné ; un pschutteux ; un exhumé ; un gratiné ; un faucheur ; un bécarre ; un daim ; un excellent bon ; un fade ; un fadard ; un gilet en cœur ; un muguet* (properly lily of the valley. *Cf.*, DAFFY-DOWN-DILLY).

SPANISH SYNONYMS. *Don guindo ; hopeo ; pisaverde.*

1818. CARLYLE, in *Early Letters* (Norton), vol. I., p. 158 When I walk along the streets, I see fair women . . . . and fops (DANDIES as they are called in current slang), shaped like an hour-glass—creatures whose life and death, as Crispin pithily observes, 'I esteem of like importance, and decline to speak of either.'

1821. COOMBE, *Syntax, Wife*, c. iv. I met just now, upon the stairs, A DANDY in his highest airs.

1835. HALIBURTON, *Clockmaker*, 2 S., ch. viii. Great DANDY was Mr. Bobbin ; he looked just as if he had come out of the tailors' hands.

1847. LYTTON, *Lucretia*, pt. I., ch. i., What is now the DANDY was then [1880] the Buck.

1866. W. D. HOWELLS, *Venetian Life*, ch. xx. He is a DANDY, of course,—all Italians are DANDIES,—but his vanity is perfectly harmless, and his heart is not bad.

1890. LORD LAMINGTON, *The Days of the Dandies* [Title].

2. (thieves'). — A bad gold coin. [In allusion to its careful make and composition, this coin containing a certain proportion of pure gold.]

1883. JAS. GREENWOOD, *Tag, Rag, and Co.*, p. 24. It is not in paltry pewter 'sours' with which the young woman has dealings, but in DANDYS, which, rendered into intelligible English, means imitation gold coin—half-sovereigns and whole ones.

3. (Irish).—A 'small whiskey.'

1838. *Blackwood's Mag.*, May, 'Father Tom and the Pope.' 'Dimidium cyathi vero apud Metropolitanos Hibernicos dicitur DANDY.'

1883. HAWLEY SMART, *Hawkins*, ch. vi. It's beautiful punch—ah, well, as you're so pressing, I'll just take another DANDY.

4. (American). — Anything first-rate ; a DAISY (*q.v.*). Also used adjectively.

1888. *Superior Inter-Ocean*. Dr. H. Conner has invested in a fine piece of horse-flesh. The animal was purchased in Oshkosh, and has a record of 3'37. It is said to be a DANDY.

1888. *St. Louis Globe Democrat*, 21 Jan. My box ain't no good mister, but I know a feller over dere dat's got de DANDY one.

1888. *Missouri Republican*, 2 Feb. I'm a terror from Philadelphia, and I can lick any man in the world. I'm a DANDY from away back ; the farther back they come the DANDIER they are, and I come from the furthest back.

THE DANDY, *adv. phr.* (common).—All right ; 'your sort' ; 'the ticket.' *Cf.*, DANDY, sense 4. A north-country song has the line, 'The South Shields lasses are THE DANDY O!'

1835. HALIBURTON, *Clockmaker*, 1 S., ch., xxvi. I guess our great nation may be stumped to produce more eleganter liquor than this here. It's THE DANDY, that's a fact.

1884. *Notes and Queries*, 6 S., ix., p. 35. I not long since heard a carpenter whose saw did not cut, wanting, as he expressed it, 'to be sharpn'd,' and who took up another in better condition, say, 'Ah! that's THE DANDY.'

DANDY-MASTER, *subs.* (thieves').—The head of a gang of counterfeiters ; who makes the coin, but does not himself attempt to pass it. [From DANDY, *subs.*, sense 2, + MASTER.]

1883. GREENWOOD, *Tag, Rag, and Co.* The spirits obtained being mostly bottled and labelled, and unopened, find a ready sale at public-houses known to the DANDY-MASTER, so that no serious loss is experienced in that direction.

DANDYPRATT or **DANDIPRATT,** *subs.* (old).—Primarily a dwarf ; a page ; by implication a jackanapes. In all likelihood, the etymon of the modern 'dandy,' erroneously derived from the French *dandin* = a fool, as in Molière, *Georges Dandin*. [From DANDIPRATT, a half farthing of the time of Henry VII.]

1580. *Lingua, or the Five Senses*, O. Pl., v., 172. This Heuresis, this invention, is the proudest Jackanapes, the pertest, self-conceited boy that ever breathed ; because, forsooth, some odd poet, or some such fantastic fellows, make much on him, there's no ho with him ; the vile DANDIPRAT will overlook the proudest of his acquaintance.

1622. MASSINGER, *Virgin-Martyr* II., i. The smug DANDIPRAT smells us out, whatsoever we are doing.

1657. MIDDLETON, *More Dissembler besides Women*, Anc. Dr., IV., 372. There's no good fellowship in this DANDIPRAT, this divedapper [didapper], as in other pages.

1706. R. ESTCOURT, *Fair Example*, Act iii., Sc. 3, p. 40. *Boy.* A candle, sir! 'tis broad daylight yet. *Whims.* What then, you little DANDYPRAT? If we have a mind to a candle we will have a candle.

1821. SCOTT, *Kenilworth*, ch. xxvi. It is even so, my little DANDYPRAT, but who the devil could teach it thee.

DANG IT! *phr.* (provincial).—A euphemism for 'damn it!' Also DANG MY BUTTONS! and DANG ME!

DANGLERS, *subs.* (thieves'). — A bunch of seals.

1859. MATSELL, *Rogue's Lexicon*, p. 124. And where the swag, so bleakly pinched, A hundred stretches hence? The thimbles, slang, and DANGLERS filched, A hundred stretches hence?

DAN TUCKER, *subs. phr.* (rhyming slang).—Butter. For synonyms, *see* CART-GREASE.

DARBIES, *subs.* (common). — 1. Handcuffs. [Origin uncertain. Father Derby's name (he is supposed to have been a noted usurer) was already proverbial in 1576, but that is all now known of him.]

ENGLISH SYNONYMS. Black-bracelets ; buckles ; Father derbie's bands ; ruffles ; wife ; snitchers ; clinkers ; government securities ; twisters ; darbies and joans (= fetters coupling two persons).

FRENCH SYNONYMS. *Les alliances* (popular = wedding rings) ; *une bride* (thieves' = a convicts' chain) ; *le bouclage* (thieves' : also = imprisonment) ; *une cadenne* (thieves' : applied to a neck-chain) ; *un cabriolet* (thieves' = a small rope or strap) ; *une guirlande* (a chain for two).

ITALIAN SYNONYM. *Trionfo* (literally = triumph).

SPANISH SYNONYM. *Calceta* (properly = understocking).

1576. GASCOIGNE, *Steel Glas*, I., 787. To binde such babes in father DERBIE'S BANDS.

1592. GREENE, *Quip for an Upstart Courtier* (*Harl. Misc.*, V., 405). Then hath my broker an usurer at hand, as ill as himself, and he brings the money ; but they tie the poor soul in such DARBIES' BANDS [*i.e.*, bonds], what with receiving ill commodities [*i.e.*, goods in lieu of cash], and forfeitures upon the bond, that they dub him 'Sir John had Land,' before they leave him ; and share, like wolves, the poor novice's wealth betwixt them as a prey.

1602. CAREW, *Survey of Cornwall*, p. 15 (ed. 1769). [Speaking of the hard dealings and usurious tricks of the marchant Londoners in their dealings with the Cornish tinners of his day, this writer tells the wiles by which the poor wretches became bound 'in DARBYE'S BONDS.']

1676. *Canting Song*, 'A Warning for Housekeepers.' But when that we come to the Whitt, Our DARBIES to behold.

1714. *Memoirs of John Hall* (4 ed.), p. 12, s.v.

1819. T. MOORE, *Tom Crib's Memorial to Congress*, p. 77. Thus a new set of DARBIES, when first they are worn, Makes the jail-bird uneasy, though splendid their ray.

1836. MARRYAT, *Japhet*, ch. lvii. We may as well put on the DARBIES, continued he, producing a pair of handcuffs.

1890. *Standard*, 7 April, p. 6, col. 3. (Addressing the officer): Didn't you take me by the scruff of the neck, and hold me whilst others put the DARBIES on me?—I did not.

2. (common). — Sausages. Also BAGS OF MYSTERY and CHAMBERS OF HORRORS (*q.v.*).

DARBLE, *subs.* (old).—The devil. [A corruption of French *diable*.]

DARBY, *subs.* (old).—Ready money. [One Derby is supposed to have been a noted sixteenth century usurer.—*See* quots. under DARBIES, sense 1.] For synonyms, *see* ACTUAL and GILT.

1688. SHADWELL, *Squire of Alsatia* (list of cant words), s.v.

c. 1712. R. Estcourt, *Prunella*, Act i., p. 4. Come nimbly lay down DARBY; Come, pray sir, don't be tardy.

1785. Grose, *Dict. Vulg. Tongue*, s.v.

1811. *Lexicon Balatronicum*, s.v.

DARBY ALLEN, *subs. phr.* (Lancashire). — Cajolery; 'chaff'; 'gammon.'

DARBY-ROLL, *subs.* (old).—A gait peculiar to felons of long standing: the result of long shackles-wearing. *Cf.*, BAKER-KNEED.

DARBY'S-DYKE, *subs.* (old).—The grave; also death.

DARBY'S-FAIR, *subs.* (old).—The day of removal from one prison to another for trial.

DARD, *subs.* (old).—The *penis*. For synonyms, see CREAMSTICK.

DARK. TO GET THE DARK, *verbal phr.* (prison).—To be confined in the punishment cell.

DARK-CULL or CULLY, *subs.* (old). —A married man with a secret mistress.—[*Grose*, 1785.]

DARK-HORSE or DARK'UN, *subs.* (turf).—A horse whose pace is unknown to the backers; figuratively, a candidate about whom little is known.

1831. Disraeli, *Young Duke*, ch. v., p. 66 (ed. 1866). All the ten-to-oners were in the rear, and a DARK HORSE, which had never been thought of, and which the careless St. James had never even observed in the list, rushed past the grand stand in sweeping triumph.

1853. *Diogenes*, vol. II., p. 271. Farewell! oh, farewell to the lists On whose varying prices I've hung; I care nought for the DARK-HORSE that lives Unknown, who shall put me all right.

1884. Hawley Smart, *Post to Finish*, ch. i. He had beaten everything that was

going to oppose him, with the exception of some two or three DARK COLTS, of which little was expected.

DARK-HOUSE, *subs.* (old).—A madhouse. Shakspeare (*All's Well*, etc., ii., 3) used it to denote the seat of gloom and discontent.

DARKMANS, DARKS, DARKY, *subs.* (old).—The night; also twilight.

1567. Harman, *Caveat* (1814), p. 84. Bene Lightmans to thy quarromes, in what lipken hast thou lypped in this DARKEMANS, whether in a lybbege or in the strummell?

1667. Dekker, *Lanthorne and Candlelight*. 'Canting Rithmes.' Enough —with bowsy Cove Maund Nace, Tour the Parting Coue in the DARKEMAN'S Case.

1706. E. Coles, *Eng. Dict.*, s.v.

1815. Scott, *Guy Mannering*, ch. xxviii. I think we should be down upon the fellow, one of these DARKMANS, and let him get it well.

1857. *Punch*, 31 Jan. 'Dear Bill, this Stone Jug.' And at DARKMANS we run the rig just as we please.

ENGLISH SYNONYMS. Blackmans; blind; blindman's holiday (twilight).

FRENCH SYNONYM. *La sorgue*, or *sorne*.

GERMAN SYNONYMS. *Mittelaile* (midnight); *Choschech, Chauschech*, or *Koschech* (from the Hebrew *choschach* = a moonless night); *Eref* (specifically the eve of a Sabbath or festival); *Fichte* (literally a fir-tree); *Ratt* (Gypsy); *Schwärze* = (the black 'un); *Zofon* or *Zofen* (from Hebrew *zophan* = to hide).

ITALIAN SYNONYMS. *Bruna* or *brunora* (Fr. *brune*); *materna* (properly = the maternal.

SPANISH SYNONYM. *Sorna*.

PORTUGUESE SYNONYM. *Zona.*

DARKMAN'S BUDGE, *subs. phr.* (old). —A housebreaker's confederate, who slips into a house during the day, hides there, and opens the door at night.—[*Grose*, 1785.]

DARKY, or DARKEY, *subs.* (old).— 1. A dark lantern; a bull's eye.

1811. *Lexicon Balatronicum*. Stow the DARKEE and bolt, the cove of the cub is fly.

2. (old). — The night; the twilight. Also (nautical) DARKS.

1789. Geo. Parker, *Life's Painter*, p. 124. Bless your eyes and limbs, lay out a *mag* with poor Chirruping Joe. I don't come here every DARKEY.

1851-61. H. Mayhew, *London Lab. and Lon. Poor*, vol. III., p. 216. We could average our 'duey bionk peroon a DARKEY,' or two shillings each, in the night.

1878. C. Hindley, *Life and Times of Jas. Catnach*. The cleanest angler on the pad in daylight or the DARKEY.

3. (common).—A negro. [From his complexion.] For synonyms, see SNOWBALL.

1840. Dana, *Two Years before the Mast*, ch. xvii. Tom Cringle says that no one can fathom a negro's affection for a pig; and I believe he is right, for it almost broke our poor DARKY's heart when he heard that Bess was to be taken ashore.

1870. *Negro Hymn*. Walk in, DARKIES, troo de gate; Hark, de kullered angels holler; Go 'way, white fokes, ye're too late, We's de winnin' kuller! Wait, Till de trumwet blow to foller!

1871. De Vere, *Americanisms*, p. 594. I wish de legislatur' would set dis DARKIE free, Oh! what a happy place den de DARKIE land would be; We'd have a DARKIE Parliament An' DARKIE codes of law, An' DARKIE judges on the bench, DARKIE barristers and aw'.

DARN, DARNED, *verb* and *ppl. adj.* (colloquial).—Euphemistic forms

of 'damn' and 'damned'; used to avoid 'cussing bar'-foot.' Also DARNATION, DANGNATION, DARN BURN IT, and DARN or DASH MY BUTTONS or WIG.—*See* DADBINGED and OATHS for synonyms.

c. 1840. *West of England Ballad* [quoted in *Literary World*, 11 Apr., 1890, p. 347, col. 1]. But if he'd know'd he'd got so much money He DARNED HIS BUTTONS if he'd gi'ed 'un the shillin'.

1880. G. R. Sims, *Zeph and other Stories*, p. 87. I shall bring you to your senses, Bess, now, my girl, and you won't be so DARNED fast refusin' a good offer.

1888. *Harper's Magazine*. My experience has taught me that in Colorado the man who tells the first story has a DARNED poor show.

DART, *subs.* (pugilistic). — A straight-armed blow.

D.A.'s, *subs.* (general).—The menstrual flux. [An abbreviation of DOMESTIC AFFLICTIONS (*q.v.*) and for synonyms see FLAG-UP.]

DASH, *subs.* (old).—1. A tavern waiter.

2. (common).—A small quantity; a 'drink'; a 'GO' (*q.v.* for synonyms). Also a small quantity of one fluid to give a flavour to another, *e.g.*, a lemon and a dash = a bottle of lemonade with just a suggestion of bitter beer in it.

Verb (brewers').—1. To adulterate.

1871. *Times*, 4 April. 'Leader on Licensing Bill.' The brewers are careless of the characters of their tenants; they compel them to take all their beer from themselves, and too often at such prices that they are driven to adulterate or DASH the liquor.

2. Also DASH IT! or DASH MY BUTTONS, WIG, TIMBERS, etc., *intj. phr.* (common). - Colloquial

---

expletives; also employed euphemistically = 'to damn.'—*See* BUTTONS and OATHS.

1819. Moore, *Tom Crib's Memorial to Congress*, p. 46. Except light oaths, to grace his speeches, Like 'DASH MY WIG!' or 'burn my breeches!'

1839. Harrison Ainsworth, *Jack Sheppard* [1889], p. 22. You may try, but DASH MY TIMBERS if you'll ever cross the Thames to-night!

1842. *Punch*, vol. II., p. 20, col. 2. Yet henceforth—DASH MY WIG! I'll live with thee, with thee I'll hop the twig!

1849. C. Kingsley, *Alton Locke*, ch. iv. Gunpowder is your true leveller— DASH physical strength! A boy's a man with a musket in his hand, my chap!

1864. Dickens, *Our Mutual Friend*, bk. IV., ch. iii. And if you hadn't come round to me to-night, DASH MY WIG if I wouldn't have come round to you to-morrow.

1880. G. R. Sims, *Three Brass Balls*, pledge ii. 'DASH IT ALL!' said the police-surgeon, 'that's two fatal cases I've had to-day.'

CUT A DASH.—*See* CUT.

TO HAVE A DASH ON, *verbal phr.* (turf).—To speculate largely or wildly; 'to go it strong.'

DASHER, *subs.* (old).—1. A showy prostitute. (*Cf.*, sense 2).

1790. C. Dibdin, *Sea Songs*, 'Old Cunwell the Pilot.' My Poll, once a DASHER, now turned to a nurse.

2. (colloquial).—An ostentatious or extravagant man or woman; an impetuous person; a 'clipper'; also latterly, — the word has shown progress towards literary English throughout—a man or woman of fashion; a person of brilliant qualities, mental or physical. Fr., *genreux-se*; *une femme catapulteuse* (a fine woman, as also *une cocodète*). Spanish equivalents are *damaza* and *sibila*, while *tiene garabato* is

said of women who 'hook' men by their manner and grace (*garabato* = a meat-hook).

1843. Dickens *Martin Chuzzlewit*, ch. xxix., p. 289. 'Why, you look smarter by day,' said Poll, 'than you do by candlelight. I never see such a tight young DASHER.'

1856. Miss Edgeworth, *Almeria*, p. 292. She was astonished to find in high life a degree of vulgarity of which her country companions would have been ashamed: but all such things in high life go under the general term dashing. These young ladies were DASHERS.

DAUB, *subs.* (common).—1. An artist. *Verb*.—*See* DAWB.

2. A bad picture.

DAVID, *subs.* (common).—1.—*See* DAVY, sense 1.

2. (American).—A torpedo.

1872. *Morning Advertiser*, 3 April.

DAVID JONES or DAVID JONES'S LOCKER.—*See* under DAVY.

DAVID'S SOW. DRUNK AS DAVID'S, or DAVY'S, SOW, *adv. phr.* (old). —Beastly drunk. [For a somewhat far-fetched derivation, *see* GROSE'S *Dict. Vulg. Tongue*.]

c. 1720. Gay, *New Song of New Similes*. Though as DRUNK AS DAVID'S SOW.

1733. Bailey, *Erasmus*, p. 127. When he comes home, after I have been waiting for him till I do not know what time at night, as DRUNK AS DAVID'S SOW, he does nothing but lie snoring all night long by my side.

1836. Marryat, *Midshipman Easy*, ch. xiv. Fellows who have no respect for the articles of war, and who get as DRUNK AS DAVID'S SOW.

DAVY, *subs.* (colloquial).—1. An affidavit. Synonymous, by implication, with 'God,' in SO HELP, or S'WELP ME DAVY, or

17

ALFRED DAVY (*q.v.*). Fr., *Je t'en fous mon billet* or *mon petit turlututu* = I'll take my DAVY on it.

1764. O'Hara, *Midas*, II., iv. And I with my DAVY will back it, I'll swear.

1835. Haliburton, *Clockmaker*, 1 S., ch. xxii. 'I'll take my DAVY,' says the captain, 'it's some Yankee trick.'

1842. *Punch*, vol. III., p. 136. Tell me on thy DAVY; whether thou dost dear thy Colin hold.

1884. *Daily Telegraph*, 4 Sept., p. 2, col. 2. You may take your DAVY I didn't care anything about that.

2. (nautical).—Also OLD DAVY and DAVY JONES (*q.v.*).

DAVY JONES, DAVY, or OLD DAVY, *subs. phr.* (nautical).—The spirit of the sea; specifically the sailors' devil. [For suggested derivation, *see* DAVY JONES'S LOCKER, and for synonyms, SKIPPER.]

1751. Smollett, *Peregrine Pickle*, ch. xiii. This same DAVY JONES, according to the mythology of sailors, is the fiend that presides over all the evil spirits of the deep.

1790. C. Dibdin, *Sea Songs*. And if to OLD DAVY I should go, friend Poll, Why you will ne'er hear of me more.

c. 1800. C. Dibdin, *The Birthday*, Act I., Sc. 2. June. When your back's turn'd she's for . . . sending you in a gale to OLD DAVY.

DAVY JONES' (or DAVY'S) LOCKER, *subs. phr.* (nautical).— The ocean; specifically, the grave of them that perish at sea. The popular derivation (= a corruption of 'Jonah's locker,' *i.e.*, the place where Jonah was kept and confined, and by implication the grave of all gone to the bottom, drowned or dead) is conjectural. The following, however, may be an additional link in the chain of evidence.

1628. Bishop Andrewes, *Ninety-six Sermons*, p. 515 (fol.). Of any, that hath beene in extreme perill, we use to say: he hath beene where Ionas was; by Iona's going downe the Whales throat, by Him againe comming forth of the Whales mouth, we expresse, we even point out, the greatest extremity, and the greatest deliverence that can be.

[*Cf.*, quots. under DAVY JONES.]

1785. Grose, *Dict. Vulg. Tongue*, s.v.

1836. Marryat, *Midshipman Easy*, ch. xxvii. By de holy poker, Massa Easy, but that terrible sort of gale the other day, anyhow. I tink one time we all go to DAVY JONES'S LOCKER.

1842. *Comic Almanack*, p. 324. There is no reason right why Jones's kid Should be consign'd to DAVY JONES'S LOCKER.

1851. *Notes and Queries*, 1 S., iii., p. 478. If a sailor is killed in a sea-skirmish, or falls overboard and is drowned, or any other fatality occurs which necessitates the consignment of his remains to the 'great deep,' his surviving messinates speak of him as one who has been sent to DAVY JONES'S LOCKER.

DAVY PUTTING ON THE COPPERS FOR THE PARSONS, *phr.* (nautical).—The indications of a coming storm.

DAVY JONES' NATURAL CHILDREN, *subs. phr.* (nautical). — Smugglers; sea-rovers; pirates.

DAVY'S DUST, *subs. phr.* (common). —Gunpowder. [DAVY (*q.v.*) = the devil.]

1864. G. W. Reynolds, *Pickwick Abroad*, ch. xxvi. Let DAVY'S DUST and a well-faked claw, For fancy coves be the only law.

DAWB or DAUB, *verb* (old).—To bribe.

1785. Grose, *Dict. Vulg. Tongue*, s.v. The cull was scragged because he could not DAWB.

DAYLIGHT, *subs.* (University).— A glass that is not a bumper; also SKYLIGHT (*q.v.*). Obsolete.

To BURN DAYLIGHT, *verbal phr.* (colloquial).—To use artificial light before it is really dark; to waste time.

1595. SHAKSPEARE, *Romeo and Juliet*, Act i., 4. Mercutio. Come, we BURN DAYLIGHT.

To LET or KNOCK DAYLIGHT INTO ONE, INTO THE VICTUALLING DEPARTMENT, or INTO THE LUNCHEON RESERVOIR, *phr.* (common).—To stab in the stomach (or breadbasket); in the breadroom, potato-store, or giblet-pie, etc., and by implication to kill. Fr., *bayafer*. For synonyms, *see* COOK ONE'S GOOSE.

1841. *Punch*, vol. I., p. 101, col. 2. A gentleman in a blue uniform has thrown himself into an attitude *à la Crib*, with the facetious intention of LETTING DAYLIGHT INTO THE WITTLING DEPARTMENT.

DAYLIGHTS, *subs.* (common).—1. The eyes. *Cf.*, quots. under DARKEN THE DAYLIGHTS. For synonyms, *see* GLIMS.

1785. GROSE, *Dict. Vul. Tongue*, s.v.

1823. BEE, *Sl. Dict.* [quoted in]. The hero (Achilles) in his tent they found, His DAY-LIGHTS fixed upon the cold, cold ground.

2. (general).—The space in a glass between liquor and brim: inadmissible in bumpers at toasts: the toast-master cries 'no DAYLIGHTS nor heeltaps!'

To DARKEN ONE'S DAYLIGHTS, *verbal phr.* (pugilistic).—1. To give a black-eye; 'to sew up one's sees.'

1752. FIELDING, *Amelia*, bk I., ch. x. If the lady says such another word to me, d—n me, I will DARKEN HER DAYLIGHTS.

1786. *The Microcosm*, No. 2 The nobility and gentry were taught theoretically as well as practically, to bruise the bodies, and (to use a technical term) DARKEN THE DAYLIGHTS of each other, with the vigour of a Hercules, tempered with the grace of an Apollo.

1819. T. MOORE, *Tom Crib's Memorial*, p. 3. If the Fine Arts Of *fibbing* and *boring* be dear to your hearts; If to *level*, to *punish*, to *ruffian* mankind, And to DARKEN THEIR DAYLIGHTS, be pleasures refin'd.

1822. DAVID CAREY, *Life in Paris*, p. 200. So here's at DARKENING HIS DAYLIGHTS for the advantage of his mummer.

DEACON, *verb* (American).—To pack fruit, vegetables, etc., the finest on the top. [Either derived by inversion, or in allusion to the Yankee proverb—'All deacons are good, but there is odds in deacons.']

1868. MISS ALCOTT, *Little Women*, ch. xi. The blanc-mange was lumpy, and the strawberries not as ripe as they looked, having been skilfully DEACONED.

To DEACON A CALF, *verbal phr.* (American).—To kill.

To DEACON LAND, *verbal phr.* (American).—To filch land by removing one's fences into the highway or other common property.

To DEACON OFF, *verbal phr.* (American).—To give the cue; to lead in debate. [From a custom, once universal but now almost extinct, in the New England Congregational churches. An important function of the deacon's office was to read aloud the hymns given out by the minister one line at a time, the congregation singing each line as soon as read. This was called DEACONING OFF.]

1848. J. R. LOWELL, *Biglow Papers*. To funk right out o' p'lit'cal strife ain't thought to be the thing, Without you DEACON OFF the tune you want your folks should sing.

1890. H. D. TRAILL, *Saturday Songs*, p. 7. We grieve, too, that of all men you

Your own great Union's stout defender Should DEACON OFF the craven crew, Who here are clamouring for surrender.

DEACON-SEAT, *subs.* (American lumberers').—In log cabins the sleeping apartment is partitioned off by poles. The bed is mother earth, the pillow is a log, the foot-board a long pole six feet from the fire and in the centre of the cabin. The DEACON SEAT is a plank fixed over and running parallel with the footboard so as to form a kind of settee in front of the fire. [Probably in allusion to the seats round a pulpit, facing the congregation, reserved for deacons.]

DEACON'S HIDING PLACE, *subs. phr.* (American).—A private compartment in oyster saloons and *cafés*; the Fr. *cabinet particulier*.

DEAD, *subs.* (turf).—An abbreviation of 'dead certainty.'—*See* CERT.

1889. *Bailey's Magazine* [quoted in *S. J. & C.*]. 'Dealers in the DEAD' did well then.

Adj. (various). — Stagnant; 'quiet' (of trade); 'flat' (as of beer or aërated waters after exposure); cold (Am., *see* quot., 1888); good; thorough; complete (*Cf.*, *subs.*, sense). Also as an *adv.* as in DEAD BEAT, DEAD BEST, DEAD DRUNK, DEAD ROLLED (or FLUMMOXED), DEAD NUTS, DEAD BITCHED, etc.

1602. SHAKSPEARE, *Othello*, ii., 2. Why, he drinks you, with facility, your Dane DEAD-DRUNK.

1819. MOORE, *Tom Crib's Memorial to Congress*, p. 36. As DEAD hands at a mill as they, and quite as ready after it.

1843. DICKENS, *Martin Chuzzlewit*, ch. xvii., p. 187. 'I wish you would pull off my boots for me,' said Martin, dropping into one of the chairs, 'I am quite knocked up. DEAD BEAT, Mark.'

1845. *Punch*, vol. IX., p. 163. The general opinion is that the Premier is DEAD BEAT.

1860. *Punch*, vol. XXXIX., p. 37. A DEAD take-in is swipes too thin.

1864. *Punch*. Veal is as DEAD as mutton.

1872. *Derby Mercury*, 1 May. 'Freemasonry in New Zealand.' He was not dead, but only DEAD DRUNK.

1884. W. C. RUSSELL, *Jack's Courtship*, ch. vii. So surely do I intend to try my DEAD BEST—all that I know—to win Florence's love and possess her as a wife.

1888. *Puck's Library*, May, p. 27. Hungry Guest. Please bring me some clam fritters. Count (in disguise). Live 'r DEAD? Hungry Guest. Why, DEAD, of course! (And he got them stone-cold.)

DEAD AS A DOOR-NAIL, MUTTON, A HERRING, A TENT-PEG, JULIUS CÆSAR, etc., *adv. phr.* (common).—Utterly, completely dead. DEAD AS A DOOR-NAIL is found in Langland's *Piers Plowman* [1362]; all other forms are modern. [The door-nail is the striking-plate of the knocker. Herrings die sooner after capture than most fish.]

1593. G. HARVEY, *Pierces Super.*, in wks. II., 71. If you will needes strike it as DEAD AS A DORE NAILE.

1596. NASHE, *Saffron Walden*, in wks. III., 182. Wee'l strike it as DEAD AS A DOORE-NAILE.

1598. SHAKSPEARE, *II. King Henry IV.*, iii. *Falstaff*. What! is the old king DEAD? *Pistol*. AS NAIL IN DOOR.

1608. ARMIN, *Nest of Ninnies*. But now the thought of the new come foole so much moved him, that he was as DEAD AS A DOORE-NAYLE, standing on tip-toe, looking toward the door to behold arivall.

1700. FARQUHAR, *Constant Couple*, Act iv., Sc. 1. He's as DEAD AS A DOOR-NAIL; for I gave him seven knocks on the head with a hammer.

1790. RHODES, *Bombastes Furioso*, Ay, DEAD AS HERRINGS—herrings that are red.

1843. C. DICKENS, *Christmas Carol*, s.v.

1864. D. W. THOMPSON, *Daydreams of a Schoolmaster*, p. 230. The boat of Charon will push a difficult furrow through innumerable bodies, brick-bat laden, of purrless, soul-less DEAD-AS-DOOR-NAIL cats. Poor pussies.

1878. BESANT AND RICE, *By Celia's Arbour*, ch. xlviii. Quite dead he was, DEAD AS A DOOR-NAIL.

IN DEAD EARNEST, *adv. phr.* (colloquial).—Without doubt; in very truth.

1880. E. BELLAMY, *Dr. Heidenhoff's Process*, p. 11. I am sure that you never had a more sincere, more DEAD-IN-EARNEST convert than I was.

DEAD AGAINST, *adv. phr.* (colloquial).—Decidedly opposed to.

1835. HALIBURTON, *Clockmaker*, 1 S., ch. vii. You know I was always DEAD AGIN your tariff bill.

DEAD-ALIVE or **DEAD-AND-ALIVE**, *adj.* (colloquial).—Dull; stupid; mopish; formerly deadly-lively.

1884. H. D. TRAILL, in *Eng. Ill. Mag.*, I., 541. The city has greatly revived of late . . . it has ceased to belong to the category of the DEAD-ALIVE, and has entered that of the lively.

DEAD-AMISS, *adv. phr.* (turf).—Incapacitated through illness from competing in a race; said of horses.

DEAD-BEAT, *subs.* (American).—1. A sponger; loafer; sharper. *Cf.*, DEAD-HEAD and BEAT, *subs.*, sense 1.

1865. *Glasgow Herald*, 25 Dec. 'Trial Swanborough *v.* Sotheran.' I returned the whole of the receipts, and about £4 16s. for DEAD BEATS—free admissions who took advantage of the occasion and got paid—which caused great discontent.

1884. S. L. CLEMENS ('Mark Twain'), *The Adventures of Huckleberry Finn*, p. 284. These uncles of your'n ain't no uncles at all; they're a couple of frauds—regular DEAD-BEATS.

1888. *Bulletin*, 24 Nov. All the DEAD-BEATS and suspected hen-snatchers plead when before the Bench that they were 'only mouching round to find out whether the family neglected its religious dooties, yer washup.

2. (American).—A pick-me-up compounded of ginger, soda, and whiskey.

Verb (American).—To sponge; loaf; cheat. *Cf.*, BEAT, *verb*, and DEAD-HEAD.

1880. *Boston Journal*. No party can DEAD-BEAT his way on me these hard times.

Adj.—Exhausted; *e.g.*, Billy romped in as 'fresh as paint, but the rest were DEAD-BEAT.

1821. P. EGAN, *Tom and Jerry* [ed. 1890], p. 34. Logic was at length not only so DEAD-BEAT, as to be compelled to cry for quarter, but to seek a temporary retirement, in order to renovate his constitution.

DEAD BROKE, *adv. phr.* (general).—Utterly penniless; ruined. Also FLAT or STONE BROKE; used verbally, to DEAD-BREAK.

1866. *Cincinnatti Enquirer*, 1 June. When he left the gambling-house, he was observed to turn toward a friend with the words, DEAD-BROKE! and then to disappear round the corner.

ENGLISH SYNONYMS. Wound up; settled; coopered; smashed up; under a cloud; cleaned out; cracked up; done up; on one's back; floored; on one's beam ends; gone to pot; broken-backed; all U. P.; in the wrong box; stumped; feathered; squeezed; dry; gutted; burnt one's fingers; dished; in a bad way; gone up; gone by the board; made mince meat of; broziered; willowed; not to have a feather to fly with; burst; fleeced; stony; pebble-beached; in Queer Street; stripped; rooked; hard up; broke; hooped-up; strapped; gruelled.

FRENCH SYNONYMS. *Enfoncé* familiar: also—done brown); *centré* (popular); *désossé* (popular: properly = boned); *eréné* (popular); *atigé* (thieves'); *panné* (= in Queer Street); *see* also BEAT.

ITALIAN SYNONYM.—*Ferrare* (to be ruined; also = to spoil or corrupt).

DEAD-CARGO, *subs.* (thieves').—Booty of a disappointing character.

DEAD CERTAINTY, *subs. phr.* (colloquial).—That which is sure to occur; usually contracted to DEAD or CERT, both of which *see*.

18(?). AYTOUN. *The Dreepdaily Burghs*, p. 4. Everybody is realising; the banks won't discount; and when your bills become due, they will be, to a DEAD CERTAINTY, protested.

DEAD CUT.—*See* CUT.

DEAD DUCK, *subs. phr.* (American).—That which has depreciated to the verge of worthlessness.

1888. *New York Clipper*. Long Branch is said to be a DEAD DUCK. But for the investments made at Elberon the Branch proper would probably have been abandoned long ago.

DEADER, *subs.* (military).—1. A funeral; a BLACK-JOB (*q.v.*).

2. (common).—A corpse.

DEAD FROST, *subs.* (theatrical).—A fiasco; a COLUMBUS (*q.v.*). Fr., *un four noir*.

DEAD-GIVE-AWAY.—*See* GIVE DEAD-AWAY.

DEAD GONE, *adv. phr.* (colloquial). Utterly collapsed.

DEAD-HEAD, DEAD-BEAT or **DEAD-HAND**, *subs.* (American).—One who obtains something of commercial value without special payment or charge; a person who travels by rail, visits theatres, etc., by means of free passes (*cf.*, PAPER); a SPONGE (*q.v.*). Also a loafing sharper.—*See* BEAT and DEAD-BEAT.

1861. *Morning Post*, 'New York Correspondence.' The editor had evidently been travelling as a DEAD-HAND, as it is called, and paid his bill by a laudatory notice.

1871. DE VERE, *Americanisms*. The DEAD-HEAD receives his newspapers without subscribing, travels free of charge on steamboat, railroad, and stage, walks into theatres and shows of every kind unmolested, and even drinks at the bar and lives at the hotel without charge.

1883. *Daily Telegraph*. 21 May, p. 3, col. 1. 'Lucia di Lammermoor' is stale enough to warrant the most confirmed DEADHEAD in declining to help make a house.

Also TO DEAD-HEAD, DEAD-HEADISM, etc.

1871. *New York Tribune*, March. Elder Knapp, the noted revivalist, advertised that he would furnish a free pass to glory, but very few of the unrighteous population seemed anxious to be DEAD-HEADED on this train.

1888. *Portland Transcript*, 14 March. Unless we count those which had to do with the stage business and went DEAD-HEAD.

DEAD-HEAT, *subs.* (colloquial).—A race with an equal finish. Formerly DEAD.

1635. QUARLES, *Emblems*, Epig. 10. Mammon well follow'd, Cupid bravely led; Both touchers; equal fortune makes a DEAD; No reed can measure where the conquest lies; Take my advice; compound, and share the prize.

1828-45. T. HOOD, *Poems*, vol. I., p. 170 (ed. 1846). Away! Away! she could ride a DEAD HEAT With the Dead who rides so fast and fleet.

1884. *Ill. London News*, 18 Oct., p. 362, col. 3. St. Gatien, the horse that ran a DEAD-HEAT for the Derby.

DEAD-HORSE, *subs.* (common).—1. Work, the wages for which have been paid in advance; by implication, distasteful, or thankless labor. Fr., *la bijouterie*. To PULL THE DEAD HORSE = to work for wages already paid. [Seamen, on signing articles, sometimes get pay in advance, and they celebrate the term of the period thus paid for by dragging a canvas horse, stuffed with straw, round the deck and dropping him into the sea amidst cheers.] Fr., *manger du salé* (to eat salt pork.)

1651. CARTWRIGHT, *Siedge. Ply.* Now you'l wish I know, you ne'r might wear Foul linnen more, never be lowzy agen, Nor ly perdue with the fat sutler's wife In the provoking vertue of DEAD HORSE, Your dear delights, and rare camp pleasures.

1669. *Nicker Nicked*, in *Harl. Misc.* (ed. Park), ii., 110. Sir Humphry Foster had lost the greatest part of his estate, and then (playing, as it is said, for a DEAD HORSE) did, by happy fortune, recover it again.

1824. T. FIELDING, *Proverbs*, etc. (*Familiar Phrases*), p. 148, s.v.

1857. *Notes and Queries*, 2 S., iv., p. 192. A workman 'horses' it when he charges for more in his week's work than he has really done. Of course he has so much unprofitable work to get through in the ensuing week, which is called DEAD HORSE.

2. (West Indian).—A shooting star. Among Jamaican negroes the spirits of horses that have fallen over precipices are thought to re-appear in this form.

TO FLOG THE DEAD HORSE, *verb. phr.* (common).—To work to no purpose; to dissipate one's energy in vain; to make 'much ado about nothing.'

1872. *Globe*, 1 Aug. 'In the House,' For full twenty minutes by the clock the Premier... might be said to have rehearsed that particularly lively operation known as FLOGGING A DEAD HORSE.

DEAD-LETTER, *subs.* (colloquial).—Anything that has lost its force or authority by lapse of time or other causes.

1755. FIELDING, *Voyage to Lisbon*, p. 145. And to enact laws without doing this, is to fill our statute-books, much too full already, still fuller with DEAD LETTER, of no use but to the printer of the Acts of Parliament.

1859. SALA, *Gaslight and Daylight*, ch. xxi. The Metropolitan Buildings' Act is a DEAD LETTER in Tattyboys Rents, for nobody ever thinks of building.

1861. *Chambers' Encyclopædia*, s.v. *Bunkum*. Many laws, agitated for by popular factions, remain a DEAD LETTER, unless they happen to be enforced by clubs organized for the purpose.

DEADLIGHTS, *subs.* (nautical). — The eyes. For synonyms, *see* GLIMS.

DEAD LURK, *subs.* (thieves').—*See* quot.

1851-61. H. MAYHEW, *London Lab. and Lon. Poor*, vol. i., p. 403. The DEAD LURK, for instance, is the expressive slang phrase for the art of entering dwelling-houses during divine service.

DEADLY, *adv.* (colloquial).—Very; extremely; excessively. In ARBUTHNOT: 'So DEADLY cunning a man.'

DEADLY LIVELY, *adv. phr.* (common).—Jovial against the grain and to no purpose.

DEADLY NEVERGREEN, *subs. phr.* (old).—The gallows. Also known as THE LEAFLESS TREE and THE TREE THAT BEARS FRUIT ALL THE YEAR ROUND. For synonyms, *see* NUBBING CHEAT.

1785. GROSE, *Dict. Vulg. Tongue* s.v.

DEAD MAN, *subs. phr.* (common).—1. An empty bottle: said also to bear Moll Thompson's mark (*i.e.* M.T. = empty).

ENGLISH SYNONYMS.—Camp-candlestick; fellow-commoner; corpse; dummy; dead marine; dead recruit; dead 'un.

FRENCH SYNONYMS. — *Une fillette* (= a half-bottle); *un corps mort* (popular: literally, a corpse; *une négresse morte* (popular: a reference to color as well as condition).

1738. SWIFT, *Polite Convers.*, Dial. 2. *Ld. S.* Come, John, bring us a fresh bottle. *Col.* Ay, my lord; and pray, let him carry off the DEAD MEN, as we say in the army [*meaning the empty bottles*].

1825. *The English Spy*, vol I., p. 152. On the right was the sleeping room and at the foot of a neat French bed, I could perceive the wine bin, surrounded by a regiment of DEAD MEN (empty bottles).

1853. REV. E. BRADLEY ('Cuthbert Bede'), *Verdant Green*, pt. I., p. 59. Talk of the pleasures of the dead languages, indeed! why, how many jolly nights have you, and J. Larkyns passed 'down among the DEAD MEN.'

1871. *London Figaro*, 15 April. We knew that, in practical use, imperials were inconvenient and wasteful; and that, moreover, it was far from easy to dispose of their corpses when they became DEAD MEN.

1879. BRADDON, *Vixen*, ch. viii. And added more DEAD MEN to the formidable corps of tall hock bottles, which the astonished butler ranged rank and file in a obby outside the dining room.

1888. E. ZOLA. 'Translation of *L'Assommoir*, ch. vii., p. 208. In a corner of the shop, the heap of DEAD MEN increased, a cemetery of bottles.

2. (bakers').—A loaf, overcharged, or marked down though not delivered. In London, DEAD 'UN is a popular term for a half-quartern loaf. Also, by implication, a baker.

1819. T. MOORE, *Tom Crib's Memorial*, p. 16. DEAD MEN are bakers, so called from the loaves falsely charged to their master's customers.

3 (tailors').—In *pl.* Misfits; hence, a scarecrow.

DEAD MAN'S LURK, *subs. phr.* (thieves').—Extortion of money from the relatives of deceased persons. [LURK = a sham, swindle, or imposition of any kind.]

DEAD MARINE.—*See* DEAD MAN.

DEAD-MEAT, *subs.* (common).—A corpse. [By comparison to butchers' wares.] *Cf.*, COLD MEAT.

ENGLISH SYNONYMS. — Cold meat; pickles (medical students': for specimens direct from the subject); croaker; stiff; stiff 'un; dustman; cold pig.

FRENCH SYNONYMS. — *Un engourdi* (thieves': properly, torpid, heavy, dull); *une falourde engourdie* (popular: *falourde* = a heavy piece of firewood); *un dégelé* (pop: *dégel* = death); *un rebouis* (thieves': one who has been 'polished off'); *un refroidi* (thieves': *refroidir* = to cool, to chill; in cant, to kill); *les conserves* (popular: literally, preserves; *cf.*, 'pickles': specifically used of murdered bodies recovered from the water).

DEAD - MEAT TRAIN. — *See* COLD-MEAT TRAIN.

DEAD MEN'S SHOES, *subs. phr.* (common).—A situation, property, or possession formerly occupied or enjoyed by a person who is dead and buried. WAITING FOR DEAD MEN'S SHOES = looking forward to inheritances.

b. 1584, *d.* 1660. PHINEAS FLETCHER, *Poems*, p. 256. And 'tis a general shrift, that most men use, But yet 'tis tedious waiting DEAD MEN'S SHOES.

1758. A. MURPHY, *The Upholsterer*, Act i. I grant ye, ma'am, you have very good pretensions; but then it's waiting for DEAD MEN'S SHOES.

1764. WILKES [in P. FITZGERALD's *Life of*] (1888), vol. I., p. 244. As they have no other relation but Miss Wilkes, I therefore suppose they will leave everything to her, independent of me. Yet this is, after all, waiting for DEAD MEN'S SHOES.

1878. C. H. WALL, tr. *Molière* II., 218. Death is not always ready to indulge the heir's wishes and prayers, and we may starve while waiting for DEAD MEN'S SHOES.

DEAD-NAP, *subs.* (provincial).—A thorough-going rogue.

DEAD-NIP, *subs.* (provincial).—A plan or scheme of little importance which has turned out a failure.

DEAD-OH, *adv.* (naval).—In the last stage of intoxication. For synonyms, *see* DRINKS and *cf.*, SCREWED.

DEAD ON, or **DEAD NUTS ON,** *adv. phr.* (common).—Originally, having some cause of complaint or quarrel; also, very fond of; having complete mastery over; sure hand at. *Cf.*, DEATH ON, DERRY ON and DOWN ON, all of which are variants. — *See* also NUTS ON, an older form.

1877. *Five Years' Penal Servitude*, ch. iv., p. 288. Davies was DEAD NUTS upon cutting men's hair. The whole evening long was he calling men out to be operated upon.

DEAD-SET, *subs.* (colloquial).—A pointed and persistent effort or attempt.

1781. G. PARKER, *View of Society*, I., 196. He then gave me what I term the DEAD SET with his eye.

1877. *Five Years' Penal Servitude*, ch. iii., p. 145. He was made a DEAD SET at by some other prisoners, who schooled him for a career of vice and crime.

1889. *Globe*, 2 Nov., p. 6, col. 2. Certain persons of the 'thoughtful' kind, says *Rod and Gun*, are making a DEAD SET against the field sports of Britain.

DEAD SOW'S EYE, *subs. phr.* (tailors'). — A badly worked button-hole.

DEAD STUCK, *adv. phr.* (theatrical).—Said of actors who break down in the midst of a performance through sudden lapse of memory.

DEAD SWAG, *subs.* (thieves').—'Dead stock' or DEAD CARGO (*q.v.*); plunder that cannot be disposed of. [SWAG = booty.]

DEAD TO RIGHTS, *adv. phr.* (common).—Certain; without doubt. An amplification of TO RIGHTS (*q.v.*).

1888. *Cincinnatti Weekly Gazette*, 22 Feb. Hill claims he has the thing down DEAD TO RIGHTS, and that he will make the farmers sweat who have been asserting that his claim was 'N.G.'

DEAD-'UN, *subs.* (thieves').—1. An uninhabited house. The cracksman who confines his attentions to 'busting' of this kind is, in Fr., *un nourrisseur*.

1879. J. W. HORSLEY, in *Macm. Mag.*, xl., 505. Me and the screwsman went to Gravesend, and I found a DEAD 'UN (uninhabited house).

2. (common).—A half-quartern loaf. *Cf.*, DEAD MAN, sense 2.

3. (turf).—A horse destined to be scratched or not intended to win, and against which odds may be safely laid; a SAFE 'UN (*q.v.*).

1864. *Bailey's Magazine*, June. These *al fresco* speculators have their DEAD 'UNS, and carry 'milking pails,' like their more civilised brethren, privileged with the *entrée* to the clubs and the Corner.

1868. *London Review*, 11 July, p. 38, col. 2. The stable and owners might safely lay against what was technically a DEAD 'UN from the first.

1880. HAWLEY SMART, *Social Sinners*, ch. v. Lord, what DEAD 'UNS he did back, to be sure!

4. (common).—An empty bottle. For synonyms, *see* DEAD MAN.

1889. *Bird o' Freedom*, 7 Aug., p. 3. We submitted, and with her help were soon surrounded with a formidable array of DEAD 'UNS.

5. (theatrical).—An unpaid super.

DEAD UNIT FOR [or **AGAINST**], *adv. phr.* (colloquial).—Collective advocacy of (or opposition to) a subject, principle, or line of action. *Cf.*, TO GO THE WHOLE HOG.

1888. *The Solid Muldoon* (Ouray, Colorado), The Eastern Press is a DEAD UNIT against the passage of the Postal Telegraph Bill.

DEAD-WOOD EARNEST, *adv. phr.* (American).—Quite earnest; 'dead on.' *Cf.*, IN DEAD EARNEST.

1876. S. L. CLEMENS ('Mark Twain'), *Tom Sawyer*. No! oh, good licks, are you in real DEAD-WOOD EARNEST?

DEAD WRONG 'UN.—*See* WRONG 'UN.

DEADY (modern American, **DEAD-EYE**), *subs.* (old).—Gin; a special brand of full proof spirit, also known as STARK-NAKED (*q.v.*). [From Deady, a well-known gin-spinner.] For synonyms, *see* DRINKS.

1819. T. MOORE, *Tom Crib's Memorial to Congress*, p. 35. As we'd been summon'd thus, to quaff our DEADY o'er some state affairs.

1834. SOUTHEY, *The Doctor*, interchapter xvi. Some of the whole-hoggery in the House of Commons he would designate by DEADY, or Wet and Heavy; some by Weak Tea, others by Blue-Ruin.

DEAL. THERE'S A DEAL OF GLASS ABOUT, *phr.* (common).—Said of men and things; used as a compliment = showy, 'its the thing.'

TO WET THE DEAL, *verb. phr.* (common).—To ratify a bargain by drinking; to 'shake.'

1876. C. HINDLEY, *Life and Adventures of a Cheap Jack*, p. 268. I shall be back again shortly, when we will WET THE DEAL.

TO DO A DEAL, *verb. phr.* (common).—To conclude a bargain.

DEAL-SUIT, *subs.* (common).—A coffin; especially one supplied by the parish. [In allusion to the wood of which cheap coffins are made.] For synonyms, *see* ETERNITY BOX.

DEAN, *subs.* (Winchester College).—A small piece of wood bound round a BILL-BRIGHTER (*q.v.*); that securing a fagot is called a BISHOP.

DEANER, *subs.* (thieves').—A shilling. [Origin uncertain; possibly related to Latin *denarius*. In the 16th and 17th centuries, *denier* = a coin—*vide* Nashe, Shakspeare, Johnson, etc. Others trace it to (*a*) the Cornish *dinair*; (*b*) Yiddish *dinoh*, a coin; (*c*) Gypsy *deanee*, a pound; (*d*) Lingua Franca *dinarly*.] For synonyms, *see* BLOW.

1857. SNOWDEN, *Mag. Assistant*, 3rd ed., p. 444. Shilling, DEANER, also twelver.

1864. *Times*, 12 October, p. 11, col. 6. One woman said where's the DEANER?

1879. J. W. HORSLEY, in *Macm. Mag.*, xl., 501. I had been down three or four days running, and could not buy anything to earn a DEANER (shilling) out of.

DEAREST MEMBER.—The *penis*.

DEATH. TO BE DEATH ON, *verb. phr.* (common).—Very fond of, or thoroughly master of—a metaphor of completeness; the same as DEAD ON, A MARK ON, or SOME PUMPKINS ON. *Cf.*, NUTS ON. [Literally to prosecute or pursue any course of action to the death.]

TO DRESS TO DEATH (colloquial).—To attire oneself in the very extreme of fashion. In America TO DRESS WITHIN AN INCH OF ONE'S LIFE; TO DRESS UP DRUNK and TO DRESS TO KILL. An old Cornish proverb has DRESSED TO DEATH LIKE SALLY HATCH (*N. and Q.*, 3 ser., vi., 6). [Apparently a pun on KILLING (*q.v.*).]

1869. *Newfoundland Fisheries* [quoted in De Vere]. The next day I met Davis and Nye, my two chums, on board the Little Rhody, DRESSED TO DEATH and trunk empty, as they said of themselves.

DEATH-HUNTER, *subs.* (common).—1. A vendor of the last dying speeches, or confessions of criminals; a running patterer or stationer.

1738. [From J. W. Jarvis and Son: Cat. No. 40, p. 38]. *Ramble through London, containing observations on Beggars, Pedlars, Petticoat Pensioners*, DEATH HUNTERS, *Humours of the Exchange*, etc., by a True-born Englishman [Title].

1851-61. H. MAYHEW, *London Lab. and Lon. Poor*, vol. I., 228. The latter include the 'running patterers,' or DEATH-HUNTERS; being men (no women) engaged in vending last dying speeches and confessions.

2. (popular).—An undertaker. For synonyms, *see* COLD COOK.

? *Old Song*, 'Life's a Chase.' And e'en the DEATH-HUNTER, in coffins who deals Is at last hunted into a coffin.

1785. GROSE, *Dict. Vulg. Tongue*, s.v.

DEATH OR GLORY BOYS.—*See* BINGHAM'S DANDIES.

DEBBLISH, *subs.* (South African).—A penny. For synonyms, *see* WINN.

DECAPITATE.—*See* CUT OFF ONE'S HEAD.

DECENT, DECENTLY, DECENTISH, *adj.* and *adv.* (colloquial).—Moderate; tolerable; passably; fairly good.

DECOY-BIRD or **DUCK**, *subs.* (colloquial).—One employed to decoy persons into a snare; a BUTTONER or BUG-HUNTER (*q.v.*). Fr., *un allumeur, un chatouilleur*, or *un arrangeur*.

DECUS, *subs.* (old).—A crown piece. [From the Latin, the motto *decus et tutamen* on the rims of these coins.] For synonyms, *see* CAROON.

1688. T. SHADWELL, *Squire of Alsatia*, ed. 1720, 2, vol. IV., p. 48. Madam Hackum, to testify my gratitude, I make bold to equip you with some Meggs, DECUS's, and Georges.

1822. SCOTT, *Fort. of Nigel*, ch. xxiii. 'You see,' he said, pointing to the casket, 'that noble Master Grahame, whom you call Green, has got the DECUSES and the *smelts*.'

DEE, *subs.* (vagrants').—1. A pocket-book or reader. For synonyms, *see* LEATHER.

2. (common).—A detective; also 'TEC, (*q.v.*). *Cf.*, DEEKER, and for synonyms, *see* NARK.

1886. *Graphic*, 30 Jan., p. 130, col. 1. A detective is known as a DEE and a teck; the former is principally used by tramps and gipsies, and is properly D, the initial letter of the word.

3. (common).—*See* D, sense 2.

DEEKER, *subs.* (old).—*See* quot.

1821. D. HAGGART, *Life*, Glossary, p. 171. DEEKER, a thief kept in pay by a constable.

DEEP, *adj.* (colloquial).—Artful; *e.g.*, 'a DEEP one.' [An extension

of the figurative sense = remote from comprehension, hard to penetrate — usages frequent in Biblical language.

1672-1726. VANBRUGH, *The Mistake*, Act I. When you take us for fools, we never take you for wise men. For my part, in this present case, I take myself to be mighty DEEP.

1688. SHADWELL, *Sq. of Alsatia*, III., in wks. (1720) iv., 63. Fools! nay, there I am sure you are out: they are all DEEP, they are very DEEP, and sharp.

1841. *Punch*, vol. I., p. 268. I can scarcely believe my eyes. Oh! he's a DEEP one.

1880. A. TROLLOPE, *The Duke's Children*, ch. vi. He was, too, very DEEP, and some men, who could put up with his other failings, could not endure that.

1890. *Pall Mall Gaz.*, 17 Oct., p. 2, col. 2. His Majesty the Sultan is 'a DEEP one,' it is clear.

DEERSTALKER, *subs.* (popular).—A felt hat. For synonyms, *see* GOLGOTHA.

1870. *London Figaro* [letter dated Dec. 9]. Either the wind must be bottled up or the P. of W. must start the fashion of wearing DEERSTALKERS ... in the windy weather.

DEFERRED STOCK, *subs.* (city).—Inferior soup. [A play upon words.] For synonyms, *see* GLUE.

1871. *Pall Mall Gaz.*, 22 May. A few years ago, at an economical Chancellor of Exchequer's dinner on the Queen's Birthday, the Chairman of one of the Revenue Boards, after tasting the soup, asked the Governor of the Bank of England, who happened to be sitting next to him at the table, 'What is this?' 'DEFERRED STOCK, I suspect,' replied the Governor.

DEGEN, DEGAN, or **DAGEN**, *subs.* (old).—A sword. [From the German.]

1785. GROSE, *Dict. Vulg. Tongue*, Nun the DEGEN, steal the sword.

1827. BULWER LYTTON, *Pelham*, p. 325. ed. 1864. Tip him the DEGEN.

DELICATE, *subs.* (vagrants').—A LURKER'S (*q.v.*) false subscription book.

DELL, *subs.* (old).—1. A young girl; a virgin; a young wanton. Later, a mistress: *cf.*, DOXY. For synonyms, *see* TITTER.

1567. HARMAN, *Caveat*, p. 75. A DELL is a yonge wenche, able for generation, and not yet knowen or broken by the vpright man.

1574-1637. BEN JONSON, *Metam. Gipsies*. Sweet doxies and DELLS My Roses and Nells.

1609. THOMAS DEKKER, *Lanthorne and Candlelight*. Docked the DELL, for a Coper meke His wach shall feng a Prounces Nab-chete.

1622. HEAD AND KIRKMAN, *English Rogue*. I met a DELL, I viewed her well.

1694. DUNTON, *Ladies' Dictionary*. DELLS are young bucksom wenches, ripe, and prone to venery, but have not yet been debauch'd.

1706. E. COLES, *Eng. Dict.* DELL, Doxy, a wench.

1834. H. AINSWORTH, *Rookwood*, bk. I., ch. ix. He was seized ... by the bailiff of Westminster when dead drunk, his liquor having been drugged by his DELLS — and was shortly afterwards hanged at Tyburn.

DELOG, *subs.* (back slang).—Gold. For synonyms, *see* REDGE.

DELO-NAMMOW, *subs.* (back slang).—An old woman. For synonyms, *see* OLD GEEZER.

DELVE IT, *verb. phr.* (tailors').—To hurry with one's work, head down and sewing fast. *Cf.*, DIG, *verb*.

DEMAND THE BOX, *verb. phr.* (nautical).—To call for a bottle.

DEMAUNDER FOR GLYMMAR, *subs. phr.* (old).—*See* quot.

1567. HARMAN, *Caveat*, p. 61. These DEMAUNDERS FOR GLYMMAR be for the moste parte wemen; for glymmar

in their language, is fyre. These goe with fayned lycences and counterfayted wrytings, hauing the hands and seales of suche gentlemen as dwelleth nere to the place where they fayne them selues to haue bene burnt, and their goods consumed with fyre. They wyll most lamentable demaunde your charitie, and wyll quicklye shed salte teares, they be so tender harted. They wyll neuer begge in that Shiere where their losses (as they say) was.

DEMI-DOSS, *subs.* (vagrants').—*See* quot.

1886. *Daily News*, 3 Nov., p. 5, col. 5. Others, unable to find the coin wherewith to obtain even a DEMI-DOSS, *i.e.*, penny sleep.

DEMI-REP, *subs.* (old slang, now recognised).—A woman of doubtful repute. [A contraction of demi-reputation.] For synonyms, *see* BARRACK HACK and TART.

1750. FIELDING, *Tom Jones*, bk. XV., ch. ix. That character which is vulgarly called a DEMI-REP; that is to say, a woman who intrigues with every man she likes, under the name and appearance of virtue ... in short, whom everybody knows to be what nobody calls her.

1754. *Connoisseur*, No. 4. An order of females lately sprung up ... usually distinguished by the denomination of DEMI-REPS; a word not to be found in any of our dictionaries.

1846-48. THACKERAY, *Vanity Fair*, vol. II., ch. xx. So they went on talking about dancers, fights, drinking, DEMI-REPS, until Macmurdo came down.

DEMNITION BOW-WOWS, *subs. phr.* (common). — The 'dogs' which spell 'ruin.' Originally a Dickensism (*see* quot., 1838). For analogues, *see* DEAD BROKE.

1838. DICKENS, *Nicholas Nickleby*, II., 32. 'I beg its little pardon,' said Mr. Mantalini, dropping the handle of the mangle, and folding his arms together, 'It's all up with its handsome friend. He has gone to the DEMNITION BOW-WOWS.

1888. *New York Herald*, 25 March. There are some men who, if they don't make twice as much as they expect to make, will cry hard times, and say that general business is going to the DEMNITION BOW-WOWS, but these men would say the same thing in any event.

1889. *The Nation*, 19 Dec., p. 499, col. 1. Our great farming industry—the very soil of National growth—is not going to the DEMNITION BOW-WOWS.

DEMNITION HOT, *adv. phr.* (American).—Exceedingly warm; a heat supposed to be akin to that of the place where they don't rake out the fires at night.

1888. *San Francisco Weekly Examiner*, 22 March. It was DEMNITION HOT, and I commenced to hunt for soft spots in my saddle.

DEMON, *subs.* (Australian prison).—1. A policeman. For synonyms, *see* BEAK and COPPER.

2. (colloquial). — A super-excellent adept; *e.g.*, THE DEMON BOWLER = Mr. Spofforth; THE DEMON JOCKEY = Fordham or Fred Archer, and so forth.

DEN, *subs.* (common). — A place where intimates are received; one's 'diggings' or 'snuggery.' [In Anglo-Saxon = a bed, cave, or lurking place.] For synonyms, *see* DIGGINGS.

1865. *Punch*, vol. XLVIII., p. 111 col. 2, s.v.

DENNIS, *subs.* (old). — A small walking stick.

DEP, *subs.* (common).—1. A deputy; specifically the night porter or chamberlain at padding or doss-ing kens.

1870. C. DICKENS, *Mystery of Edwin Drood*, ch. v. I'm man-servant up at the Travellers' Twopenny in Gas Works Garding, this thing explains, all man-servants at Travellers' Lodgings is named DEPUTY

2. (Christ's Hospital).—A deputy GRECIAN, *i.e.*, a boy in the form below the GRECIANS.

DERBY.—*See* DARBY.

DERREY, *subs.* (thieves').—An eye-glass. TO TAKE THE DERREY, (tailors') = to quiz, ridicule.

DERRICK, *subs.* (old).—The gallows. [A corruption of Theodoric, the name of the public hangman at the end of the sixteenth and the beginning of the seventeenth centuries.] Now the name of an apparatus, resembling a crane. Also, used as a verb = to hang; apparently the earliest recorded sense. For synonyms, *see* NUBBING CHEAT.

1600. W. KEMP, *Nine Days' Wonder*, in Arber's *English Garner*, vol. VIII., p. 37. One that ... would pol his father, DERRICK his dad! do anything, how ill soever, to please his apish humour.

1607. DEKKER, *Jests to Make you Merie*, in wks. (Grosart), ii., 318. For might I have beene her Judge, shee should haue had her due, and danst DERRIKS dance in a hempen halter.

1609. DEKKER, *Gul's Horne-Booke*, chap. ii. The *Neapolitan* will (like DERICK, the hangman) embrace you with one arme, and rip your guts with the other.

DERWENTER, *subs.* (Australian).—A convict. [From the penal settlement on the banks of the Derwent, Tasmania.]

DESPATCHERS, *subs.* (gamesters').—False dice with two sides, double four, five, and six.

1856. *Times*, 27 Nov., s.v.

DESPERATE, and **DESPERATELY**, *adj.* and *adv.* (colloquial).—A metaphor of excessiveness; *e.g.*, DESPERATELY MASHED = over head and ears in love.

DETRIMENTAL, *subs.* (society).—An ineligible suitor; also a male flirt.

1841. *Punch*, vol. I., p. 133, col. 1. Defining that zero of fortune to stand below which constitutes a DETRIMENTAL.

1859. WHITTY, *Political Portraits*, p. 113. The fact is, that the DETRIMENTALS won't work; born into shifty affluence, it is easier to struggle on in a false position than to struggle out of it.

1886. *Household Words*, 13 March, p. 400. A DETRIMENTAL, in genteel slang, is a lover, who, owing to his poverty is ineligible as a husband; or one who professes to pay attentions to a lady without serious intention of marriage, and thereby discourages the intentions of others.

DETRIMENTAL-CLUB, *subs.* (society).—The Reform Club.

DEUCE, DEWCE, or **DEUSE**, *subs.* (common).—1. The devil; perdition. Also used as an ejaculative, *e.g.*, THE DEUCE! WHAT THE DEUCE! WHO THE DEUCE! DEUCE TAKE YOU! etc. [WEDGWOOD: 'The evolution of DEUCE from *Thurs.*, the name of a Scandinavian demon is fully vouched.' SKEAT: Latin *deus*, God, *deus*, borrowed from French usage, being found as an interjection in early English works. Low German *duus*, Ger. *daus* are used similarly and may have the same origin; others connect it with Armor. *dus*, *teuz*, a goblin.] For synonyms, *see* SKIPPER.

b. 1670, *d.* 1729. CONGREVE. It was the prettiest prologue as he wrote it; well, the DEUCE take me if I ha'n't forgot it.

1754. B. MARTIN, *Eng. Dict.* (2nd ed.), s.v. DEWCE.

1780. MRS. COWLEY, *The Belle's Stratagem*, Act v., Sc. i. *Miss C.* DEUCE take her! She's six years younger than I am.

1827. R. B. PEAKE, *Comfortable Lodgings*, Act I., Sc. iii., *De C.* I am the Intendant of Police, sir. *Sir H.* The DEUCE you are!

1837. BARHAM, *I. L.* (*Jackdaw of Rheims*). There's a cry and a shout, And a DEUCE of a rout, And nobody seems to know what they're about.

1854. AYTOUN AND MARTIN, *Bon Gaultier Ballads.* 'To a forget-me-not.' I can't tell WHO THE DEUCE it was That gave me this Forget-me-not.

2. (vagrants').—Twopence.

1714. *Memoirs of John Hall* (4th ed.), p. 12, s.v.

1851-61. H. MAYHEW, *London Lab. and Lon. Poor*, vol. I., p. 276. 'Give him a DEUCE' (2d.).

3. (gamesters').—The two at dice or cards.

TO PLAY THE DEUCE or DEVIL WITH, *verb. phr.* (common).—To send, or be sent, to rack and ruin.

1881. JAS. PAYN, *Grape from a Thorn*, ch. i. I have a presentiment that the cooking will PLAY THE DEUCE with my digestion.

1885. *Indoor Paupers*, p. 89. Her drinking PLAYED THE DEUCE with the shop.

THE DEUCE TO PAY, *phr.* (common).—Unpleasant or awkward consequences to be faced; *see* DEVIL TO PAY.

1854. THACKERAY, *The Rose and the Ring*, p. 69. There has been such a row, and disturbance, and quarrelling, and fighting, and chopping of heads off, and THE DEUCE TO PAY, that I'm inclined to go back to Cumtartary.

1869. MRS. H. WOOD, *Roland Yorke*, ch. xxxiii. One or both of 'em . . report me for negligence! I get a curt telegram to come to town, and here's THE DEUCE TO PAY!

DEUCED, *adj.* (common).—Devilish; excessive; confounded. Also adverbially. [From DEUCE (*q.v.*), + ED.]

1836. MICHAEL SCOTT, *The Cruise of the Midge*, vol. I. [ed. 1860], p. 160. Quacco all this while was twisting and turning himself, and, although evidently in a DEUCED quandary, trying to laugh the affair off as a joke.

DEUSEA-VILLE, *subs.* (old).—The Country.—*See* DAISYVILLE.

DEUSEA-VILLE STAMPERS, *subs. phr.* (old).—Country carriers.

DEVIL, *subs.* (common).—1. Formerly a barrister who DEVILS, or 'gets up,' a case for a leader; as in *A Tale of Two Cities*, Sydney Carton for Mr. Stryver. Now common for anyone hacking for another.—(*See* quots., 1889.)

1872. *Echo*, 14 Nov. Mr. Archibald, the Attorney-General's DEVIL is to be made a judge. Well, other DEVILS have been made judges of. Sir James Hannen, we are told, was a DEVIL once.

1873. *Daily Telegraph*, 12 Feb. It will not be possible even to send a telegram to a French journal during a sitting. Not a word must be printed until the President's DEVIL has distributed the *Officiel* to the different office boys who will henceforth, etc.

1889. *Telegram.* M— 84, B— Street, London, E.C. Strange letter received. Will you please see DEVIL at my chambers? R—. [In original telegram the word 'devil' was queried by the P.O. authorities!]

1889. GEORGE R. SIMS, *The Author's Ghost.* 'Who are you?' I asked in dismay. 'I'm a DEVIL . . .' 'A what!' I exclaimed with a start. 'A DEVIL . . . I give plots and incidents to popular authors, sir, write poetry for them, drop in situations, jokes, work up their rough material: in short, sir, I DEVIL for them.'

1890. *Speaker*, 22 Feb., p. 211, col. 2. No one who is not in the swim can have any conception of the amount of work and worry that devolves upon a counsel in leading practice at the criminal bar. . . . He has to do the best he can, with the assistance of juniors and DEVILS.

2. (printers').—An errand boy or young apprentice; in the early days of the craft, the boy who took the printed sheets as they came from the press. Fr., *un attrape-science.*

1754. *Connoisseur*, No. 9. Our publisher, printer, corrector, DEVIL, or any other employed in our service.

1757. FOOTE, *Author*, Act I. A printer's prime minister, called a DEVIL.

1859. *Punch*, vol. XXXVI, p. 82. 'An author's paradise.' A place where there are no printers' DEVILS.

1863. ALEX. SMITH, *Dreamthorp*, p. 211. He wrote in a leisurely world, when there was plenty of time for writing and reading; long before the advent of the printer's DEVIL or of Mr. Mudie.

3. (nautical).—*See* quot.

1883. *Illustrated London News*, 16 June, p. 603, col. 2. It is proposed to prevent the use of the DEVIL, a kind of sharpened anchor, at the bows of a trawler for cutting the nets of drifters in the North Sea.

4. (old). —A firework.

1742. FIELDING, *Joseph Andrews*, bk. III., ch. vii. The captain, perceiving an opportunity, pinned a cracker or DEVIL to the cassock, and then lighted it.

5. (licensed victuallers'). —Gin seasoned with capsicums. *Cf.*, following sense.

1823. G. SMEATON, *Doings in London.* The extract of Capsicums or extract of Grains of Paradise is known in the gin-selling trade by the appellation of the DEVIL. They are manufactured by putting a quantity of small East India chillies into a bottle of spirits of wine and keeping it closely stopped for about a month.

6. (common).—A grilled bone seasoned with mustard and cayenne. *Cf.*, ATTORNEY.

7. (military).—A sand-storm.

1889. *Daily News*, 8 July. 'The Camp at Wimbledon.' They raised also clouds of dust that went whirling across the common in spiral cones like desert DEVILS.

8. (common).—A species of firewood soaked in resin.

THE or A DEVIL OF [A THING], *adj.* and *adv.* (colloquial).—An indefinite intensive: *e.g.*, DEVIL of a mess, of a woman, of a row, etc.

1602. SHAKSPEARE, *Twelfth Night*, ii., 3. The DEVIL, a puritan that he is, or anything constantly.

1836. MICHAEL SCOTT, *Cruise of the Midge* [ed. 1860], p. 102. A DEVIL OF A good fight he made of it.

1836. MICHAEL SCOTT, *Cruise of the Midge* [ed. 1860], p. 298. The DEVIL A THING was there in sight, not even a small white speck of a sail.

AMERICAN DEVIL, *subs. phr.* (workmen's).—A steam whistle or 'hooter'; used in place of a bell for summoning to work.

1872. *Manchester Guardian*, 24 Sept. Mr. Powell's Bill contains abundant powers for suppressing the vile nuisance known as the AMERICAN DEVIL, and should any man suffer from it in future he will have nobody to thank but himself.

BLUE DEVILS.—*See ante.*

LITTLE (or YOUNG) DEVIL, *subs. phr.* (common). — A half playful, half sarcastic, address; a term of endearment; *e.g.*, YOU LITTLE DEVIL. *Cf.*, YOU YOUNG TINKER.

1841. R. B. PEAKE, *Court and City*, Act i., Sc. 1. My wife was such an unreasonable LITTLE DEVIL, as to ask me forty questions about my staying out so late.

Verb (common).—1. To act as a DEVIL (*q.v.*, *subs.*); to perform routine or detail work for another.

1872. *Daily Telegraph*, 30 Nov. Letter 'Called to the Bar.' Then I took legislative rambles in the Courts, so that I might see practice, and that practitioners might see me; and then I DEVILLED and reported a little.

1883. *Graphic*, 12 May, p. 478, col. 2. The practice prevailing among eminent counsel of undertaking more cases than they can possibly manage, and handing over some to the juniors who DEVIL for them.

2. (American cadet). — To victimize.

WHAT, WHO, WHEN, WHERE, or HOW THE DEVIL, *phr.* (common). — An expletive of wonder, vexation, etc.

b. 1688, *d.* 1744. POPE [quoted in Annandale]. The things we know are neither rich nor rare; But wonder HOW THE DEVIL they got there.

1776. DAVID GARRICK, *Bon Ton, or High Life Above Stairs*, Act ii., Sc. 1. *Sir. T.* Why, WHAT THE DEVIL do you make one at these masqueradings.

1780. MRS. COWLEY, *The Belle's Stratagem*, Act i., Sc. 3. *Har.* WHO THE DEVIL could have foreseen that?

1827. R. B. PEAKE, *Comfortable Lodgings*, Act i, Sc. 3. WHAT THE DEVIL is all this about?

1836. MICHAEL SCOTT, *Cruise of the Midge* [Ry. ed. 1860], p. 134. HOW THE DEVIL can you get anything out of an empty vessel?

TO PLAY THE DEVIL WITH, *verb. phr.* (colloquial).—To ruin or molest.

1821. EGAN, *Tom and Jerry*, p. 46. The passions, as I've said, are far from evil, But if not well confined they PLAY THE DEVIL.

TO PULL THE DEVIL BY THE TAIL, *phr.* (colloquial).—To go to ruin headlong; also to be reduced to one's last shift. *Cf.*, TO PLAY THE DEVIL WITH.

1890. *European Mail*, 2 Aug., p. 30, col. 2. The immense disproportion between the solid assets and the liabilities of the enterprise made experienced Parisian financiers say from the first that the company was PULLING THE DEVIL BY THE TAIL, and a perusal of M. Monchicourt's report must confirm this view.

TO WHIP THE DEVIL ROUND THE STUMP, *verb. phr.* (American).—To enjoy the sweets of wickedness and yet escape the penalty.

1857. *New York Evening Post*, While Mr. Jones is describing his wants in the money line, and telling the president how near through he is, that officer is carrying on a mental addition it may be after this manner: Jones, you're a clever fellow, but Smith tells me you are engaged in a coal-stock operation. I have heard also that you have been dabbling in Erie. There is a want of candor now, I perceive, in the statement of your affairs. There, you are now WHIPPING THE DEVIL AROUND THE STUMP: I see his foot.

1871. DE VERE, *Americanisms*, p. 187. Nor is the slang phrase: TO WHIP THE DEVIL AROUND THE STUMP to be traced very clearly to the backwoods.

1872. HALDEMAN, *Pennsylvania Dutch.* I WHIPPED THE DEVIL ROUND THE STUMP, And gave a cut at every jump.

HAUL DEVIL, PULL BAKER, *phr.* (colloquial). — To contend with varying fortunes. In the sense of endeavouring to overreach, a variant is DIAMOND CUT DIAMOND.

1889. *Cornhill Mag.*, July, p. 99. I can't get proper accounts from her; and it's a regular case of PULL DEVIL, PULL BAKER, whenever I want to look at the trades-people's books.

AND THE DEVIL KNOWS WHAT or WHO, *phr.* (colloquial).—A term used vaguely and indefinitely to include details not specifically mentioned or known.

1717. MRS. CENTLIVRE, *A Bold Stroke for a Wife*, Act iii., Sc. 1. *Per.* Why, what a pack of trumpery has this rogue picked up! His pagod, poluflosboio, his zonos moros musphonons, AND THE DEVIL KNOWS WHAT.

TO GO TO THE DEVIL, *phr.* (colloquial).—To go to rack and ruin. GO TO THE DEVIL! = begone! A summary form of dismissal with no heed as to what may become of the person who is sent about his business.

1801. T. DIBDIN, *The Birthday*, Act i., Sc. 2. *Capt.* Hold your tongue, Junk; you are a libellous rascal. You, and your box, too, may GO TO THE DEVIL.

TO HOLD A LIGHT or CANDLE TO, or BURN A CANDLE BEFORE, THE DEVIL, *phr.* (colloquial).—To propitiate through fear; to assist or wink at wrong doing. Shakspeare (*Merchant of Venice*, Act ii., Sc. 6), employs 'What! must

I hold a candle to my shame,' in much the same sense. [From the practice of burning candles before the images of saints, etc.]. NOT FIT TO HOLD A CANDLE TO THE DEVIL = a simile of inferiority. TO HOLD A CANDLE TO ANOTHER = to assist in, occupy a subordinate position, or (*see* quot., 1859) to compare to another.

c. 1461. In *Paston Letters*, II., 73 (ed. Gairdner). For it is a common proverbe, 'A man must sumtyme SET A CANDEL BEFOR THE DEVYLE;' and therefor thow it be not alder most mede and profytabyl, yet if ij harmys the leste is to be take.

1557. TUSSER, *Husbandrie*, p. 148. Though not for hope of good, Yet for the feare of euill, Thou maist find ease so proffering up A CANDELL TO THE DEUILL.

1672. WYCHERLEY, *Love in a Wood*, I., i., wks. (1713), 346. You cannot HOLD A CANDLE TO THE DEVIL.

1705. WARD, *Hudibras Redivivus*, vol. I., pt. III., p. 17. TO HOLD A CANDLE TO THE DEVIL, Is not the means to stop this evil.

1828. SCOTT, *Fair Maid of Perth*, ii., 213. Here have I been HOLDING A CANDLE TO THE DEVIL, to show him the way to mischief.

1859. H. KINGSLEY, *Geoffrey Hamlyn*, ch. xxxii. A Frenchman is conceited enough, but, by George, he can't HOLD A CANDLE to a Scotchman.

THE DEVIL, or THE DEVIL AND ALL TO PAY, *phr.* (colloquial). — A simile of fruitless effort; awkward consequences to be faced. [Nautical: originally, 'There's the devil to pay and no pitch hot'; the 'devil' being any seam in a vessel, awkward to caulk, or in sailors' language 'to pay.' Hence by confusion THE DEUCE TO PAY (*q.v.*).]

1711. SWIFT, *Journal to Stella*, 28 Sept. Letter 31. And then there will be THE DEVIL AND ALL TO PAY.

1761. COLMAN, *Jealous Wife*, III., in wks. (1777), i., 69. There's the DEVIL TO PAY in meddling with them.

1762. FOOTE, *Liar*, iii., 3. Sir, here has been the DEVIL TO PAY within.

1836. MICHAEL SCOTT, *Cruise of the Midge.* [Ry. ed. 1860], p. 127. Here was the DEVIL TO PAY with a vengeance.

1837. R. H. BARHAM, *The Ingoldsby Legends.* The Execution (ed. 1862). p. 198. Hollo! Hollo! Here's a rum go. Why, Captain!—My Lord!—Here's THE DEVIL TO PAY!—The fellow's been cut down and taken away!

1866. G. ELIOT, *Felix Holt*, ch. xxi. He made a fool of himself with marrying at Vesoul; and there was THE DEVIL TO PAY with the girl's relations.

TALK OF THE DEVIL AND YOU'LL SEE HIS HORNS or TAIL, *phr.* (colloquial). — Said of a person who, being the subject of conversation, unexpectedly makes an appearance. Fr., *parlez des anges et vous en voyez les ailes.*

b. 1664, *d.* 1721. M. PRIOR. *Hans Carvel.* Since therefore 'tis to combat evil, 'Tis lawful to employ the Devil, Forthwith the Devil did appear, For NAME HIM and HE'S ALWAYS NEAR.

DEVIL-MAY-CARE, *adj.* (colloquial).—Rollicking; reckless; rash.

1822-36. JNO. WILSON, *Noctes Amb.* I., 274. [The shepherd has thrown back to the fire a live coal.] Belyve the blisters 'll be rising like foam-bells; but DEIL MAY CARE.

1836. DICKENS, *Pickwick*, ch. xlix., p. 428. He was a mighty free and easy, roving, DEVIL-MAY-CARE sort of person, was my Uncle, gentlemen.

1839. LEVER, *Harry Lorrequer*, ch. xii. There was also a certain DEVIL-MAY-CARE recklessness about the self-satisfied swagger of his gait.

1849. ALBERT SMITH, in *Gabarni in London (Acrobats).* Unsettled, wandering, and DEVIL-MAY-CARE as his disposition may be, he cannot be called idle.

1863. HON. MRS. NORTON, *Lost and Saved*, p. 33. Treherne had a hot twinge of doubt, in spite of his DEVIL-MAY-CARE style of writing, whether Lewellyn would answer him at all.

1865. *Punch*, vol. XLVIII., p. 106. Fechter's acting [as Robert Macaire] in *The Roadside Inn* may be described as the DEVIL-MAY-CARE style.

DEVIL TAKE, or FETCH, or SEND, or SNATCH, or FLY AWAY WITH, YOU, ME, HIM! etc., *phr.* (colloquial). — An imprecation of impatience. Fr., *le boulanger t'entrolle en son pasclin.*

1837. R. H. BARHAM, *Ingoldsby Legends* (ed. 1862), p. 330. Don't use naughty words, in the next place, and ne'er in your language adopt a bad habit of swearin'. Never say, 'DEVIL TAKE ME,' or 'SHAKE ME,' or 'BAKE ME,' or such-like expressions. Remember Old Nick, To take folks at their word, is remarkably quick.

THERE'S THE DEVIL AMONG THE TAILORS, *phr.* (common). — A row is going on. [Edwards: — Originating in a riot at the Haymarket when Dowton announced the performance for his benefit, of a burlesque entitled 'The Tailors: a Tragedy for Warm Weather.' Many thousands of journeymen tailors congregated, and interrupted the performances. Thirty-three were brought up at Bow Street next day.—*See Biographica Dramatica* under 'Tailors.']

WHEN THE DEVIL IS BLIND, *adv. phr.* (colloquial). — Never, *i.e.*, in a month of Sundays; said of anything unlikely to happen. For synonyms, *see* GREEK KALENDS.

DEVIL DODGER, *subs.* (common).—A clergyman. Also, by implication, anyone of a religious turn of mind.

ENGLISH SYNONYMS. — Devil catcher, driver, pitcher, or scolder; snub devil; bible pounder; duck that grinds the gospel mill; commister; camister; sky-pilot; chimney-sweep; rat; rum (Johnson); pantiler; cushion smiter, duster, or thumper; couple, or buckle, beggar; rook; gospel grinder; earwig; one-in-ten (tramps' = a tithe-monger); finger-post; parish prig; parish bull; holy Joe; green apron; black cattle (collectively); crow; the cloth (collectively); white choker; patrico; black coat; black fly; glue pot; gospel postillion; prunella; pudding - sleeves; puzzle - text; schism - monger; cod; Black Brunswicker; spiritual flesh - broker; head-clerk of the Doxology Works; Lady Green; fire-escape; gospel sharp; padre (Anglo-Indian); pound-text.

FRENCH SYNONYMS. — *Un radicon* (thieves'); *un otage* (popular: = hostage, in allusion to events under the Commune of 1871); *un radis noir* (familiar: also a police officer. In allusion to 'the cloth'); *un ratichon* (pop. from *ratissé, rasé* = shaved); *un sanglier* (thieves': a wild boar, but also a play upon words *sans* without, + *glier*, the infernal regions); *un raze* or *razi* (thieves'); *un rochet* (thieves': a surplice); *un pante en robe* (thieves': 'a cove in a gown,' also a judge); *un chasublard* (popular); *une calotte* (fam.: *le régiment de la calotte* = the skull-cap brigade, *i.e.*, the company of the Society of Jesus); *un corbeau* (pop.: = crow); *un couac* (popular); *un babillard* (thieves': especially a confessor, a 'blab-monger'); *un bichot* (a bishop); *une enseigne de cimetière* ('a cemetery signpost.' *Cf.*, SKY-PILOT and FINGER-POST); *un bâton de réglisse* (thieves': = a stick of liquorice. Also a police-officer); *un barbichon* (popular: a preaching friar. From *barbe* = beard, in allusion to the long beard characteristic of the order).

GERMAN SYNONYMS.—*Herrle* (especially applied to Catholic priests). *Lefranz* or *Lefrenz* (a transposition of Franzle or Fränzle = the Franciscan. *Liber Vagatorum Lefrenzin*, = a priest's harlot, still popular in N. Germany); *Schocherer* (from Hebrew *schochar* = black. *Cf.*, analogous English terms); *Schwarzfärber* (*Schwarz* = black; *Färber* = a dyer).

ITALIAN SYNONYMS.—*Chiodrino*; *capellano rosso* (a cardinal; 'a red chaplain'); *farfoio* (= a monk; *farfoia*, a nun); *rossignolo* (= 'a nightingale'); *pisto* or *pistolfo* (Michel: '*parce qu'il suit le condamné à la piste*').

SPANISH SYNONYM.—*Cleriguillo* (= a little cleric: both insult and endearment).

1791. LACKINGTON, *Memoirs*, Letter vi. [ed. 1803]. These DEVIL-DODGERS happened to be so very powerful (that is, noisy) that they soon sent John home, crying out he should be damn'd.

1889. *Cornhill Mag.*, Jan., p. 50. He's just a kind of a fine-haired cuss—a gambler, or a DEVIL-DODGER. I reckon . . . I'm open ter bet he's a preacher.

DEVIL-DRAWER, *subs.* (old).—An indifferent artist.

DEVILISH, *adv.* (colloquial).—Used intensitively. *Cf.*, AWFULLY, and BEASTLY.

1755. *The World*, No 140. How arbitrary is language! and how does the custom of mankind join words, that reason has put asunder. Thus we often hear of hell-fire cold, of DEVILISH handsome, and the like.

1780. MRS. COWLEY, *The Belle's Stratagem*, iii., 1. I tell you, sir, that, for all that, she's DEV'LISH sensible.

1871. SIR M. LOPEZ, Speech on Army Bill, H. of C., 3 July. It was DEVILISH hard—he meant very hard—to lay it.

DEVIL'S BED-POSTS, or **DEVIL'S FOUR-POSTER**, *subs. phr.* (cards').—The four of clubs; held as an unlucky 'turn-up.'

1879. J. C. J., in *N. and Q.*, 5 S., xii., 473. In London I have always heard the four of clubs called the DEVIL'S BEDPOST, and also that it is the worst turn-up one could have.

DEVIL'S-BONES, *subs.* (old).—Dice; also DEVIL'S TEETH. *Cf.*, DEVIL'S BOOKS.

1664. ETHEREGE, *Comical Revenge*, II., iii., in wks. (1704), 27. I do not understand dice: I understand good pasture and drink—hang the DEVIL'S BONES.

1822. SCOTT, *Fortunes of Nigel*, ch. xxiii. A gamester, one who deals with the DEVIL'S BONES and the doctors.

DEVIL'S-BOOKS, *subs.* (common).—Cards. [Of Presbyterian origin; in reproof of a synonymous term —KING'S BOOKS, or more fully, THE HISTORY OF THE FOUR KINGS (Fr., *livre des quatre rois*).] Also BOOKS OF BRIEFS (Fr., *la cartouchière à portées*).

1729. SWIFT, *Intelligencer*, No. 4, p. 43 (2nd ed.). Cards are the devil's own invention, for which reason, time out of mind, they are and have been called the DEVIL'S BOOKS.

18(?). THACKERAY, *Character Sketches* (*Capt. Rook and Mr. Pigeon*). I often think that the DEVIL'S BOOKS, as cards are called, are let out to us from Old Nick's circulating library.

DEVIL'S-CLAWS, *subs.* (thieves').—The broad arrow on convicts' uniforms.

DEVIL'S-COLOURS or **LIVERY**, *subs.* (common).—Black and yellow.

DEVIL'S - DAUGHTER, *subs.* (common).—A shrew.

DEVIL'S-DELIGHT. TO KICK UP THE DEVIL'S DELIGHT, *verbal phr.* (common). — To make a disturbance.

1854. WHYTE MELVILLE, *General Bounce*, ch. xv. His wives, five or six on 'em, was yowlin', and cryin', and KICKIN' UP THE DEVIL'S DELIGHT.

1863. CHAS. READE, *Hard Cash*, I., 278. Well then, speak quick, both of you, said Sharpe, or I'll lay ye both by the heels. Ye black scoundrels, what business have you in the Captain's cabin, KICKING UP THE DEVIL'S DELIGHT?

DEVIL'S - DOZEN, *subs.* (old). — Thirteen; the original BAKER'S-DOZEN (*q.v.*). [From the number of witches supposed to sit down together at a 'Sabbath.' In Fr. *le boulanger* (the baker) = the devil.]

DEVIL'S - DUNG, *subs.* (old).—Asafœtida: the old pharmaceutical name. [From the smell.] Now recognised.

1604. DEKKER, *Honest Wh.*, in wks. (1873), ii. 40. *Fust.* The DIVEL'S DUNG in thy teeth: I'll be welcome whether thou wilt or no.

1759. STERNE, *Tristram Shandy*, vol. VIII., ch. xi. 'Tis all pepper, garlic, staragen, salt, and DEVIL'S DUNG.

1804. C. K. SHARPE, in *Correspondence* (1888), i. 203. I devoured loads of DEVIL'S DUNG rounded into pills.

DEVIL'S-DUST, *subs.* (trade). — 1. Old cloth shredded for re-manufacture. [In allusion both to the swindle and to the 'DUST' or 'flock' produced by the disintegrating machine which is called a 'devil.' The practice and the name are old. Latimer, in one of his sermons before Edward the Sixth, treating of trade rascality, remarked that manufacturers could stretch cloth seventeen yards long, into a length of seven-and-twenty yards: 'When they have brought him to that perfection,' he continues, 'they have a pretty feat to thick him again. He makes me a powder for it, and plays the pothicary. They call it flock-powder, they do so incorporate it to the cloth, that it is wonderful to consider; truly a good invention. Oh that so goodly wits should be so applied; they may well deceive the people, but they cannot deceive God. They were wont to make beds of flocks, and it was a good bed too. Now they have turned their flocks into powder, to play the false thieves with it.' Popularised by Mr. Ferrand in a speech before the House of Commons, March 4, 1842 (*Hansard*, 3 S, lxi., p. 140) when he tore a piece of cloth made from DEVIL'S DUST, into shreds to prove its worthlessness.] *Also* SHODDY (*q.v.*).

1840. CARLYLE, *Misc.*, iv., 239. Does it beseem thee to weave cloth of DEVIL'S DUST instead of true wool, and cut and sew it as if those were not a tailor but the fraction of a very tailor?

1851. MAYHEW, *London Lab. and Lon. Poor*, II., p. 30.

1864. *Times*, 2 Nov. It is not many years since Mr. Ferrand denounced the DEVIL'S DUST of the Yorkshire woollen manufacturers; this DEVIL'S DUST arises from the grand translation of old cloth into new.

2. (military)—Gunpowder.

1883. HAWLEY SMART, *Hard Lines*, ch. i. One looks up at the snow-white walls . . and then remembers grimly what a mess the DEVIL'S DUST, as used by modern artillery, would make of them in these days.

DEVIL'S GUTS, *subs.* (old).—A surveyor's chain.

1785. GROSE, *Dict. Vulg. Tongue*, s.v.

DEVIL'S OWN, *subs.* (military).—1. The Eighty-Eight Foot. [A contraction of THE DEVIL'S OWN CONNAUGHT BOYS, a name given by General Picton for their gallantry in action and their irregularity in quarters during the Peninsular War, 1809-14.]

2. (volunteer)—The Inns of Court Volunteers [in allusion to the legal *personnel*].

1864. MARK LEMON, *Jest Book*, p. 211. At a review of the volunteers, when the half-drowned heroes were defiling by all the best ways, the DEVIL'S OWN walked straight through. This being reported to Lord B——, he remarked, 'that the lawyers always went through *thick* and *thin.*'

1872. *Daily Telegraph*, 28 Nov. In Richmond Park the Inns of Court Rifle Volunteers, more familiarly known as the DEVIL'S OWN, were inspected by Colonel Daubeney.

DEVIL'S-PATERNOSTER. TO SAY THE DEVIL'S PATERNOSTER, *verb. phr.* (old).—To grumble.

1614. TERENCE, in English. *D.* What DEVILS PATER NOSTER is this he is saying? what would he? what saist thou honest man?

DEVIL'S PLAYTHINGS, *subs. phr.* (common).—Cards.—*See* DEVIL'S BOOKS.

DEVIL'S-SHARPSHOOTERS, *subs.* (American).—Clerics who took part in the Mexican War.

DEVIL'S-SMILES, *subs.* (common).—April weather with alternations of sunshine and rain.

DEVIL'S-TATTOO, *subs.* (common). Drumming the fingers on any resonant surface, or tapping the floor with one's feet, acts of vacancy or impatience.

1817. SCOTT, *Search after Happiness*, st. xv. His sugar-loaves and bales about he threw, And on his counter beat the DEVIL'S TATTOO.

1837. R. H. BARHAM, *Ingoldsby Legends* (ed. 1862), p. 181. Her tears had ceased; but her eyes were cast down, and mournfully fixed upon her delicate little foot, which was beating the DEVIL'S TATTOO.

1841. LYTTON, *Night and Morning*, bk. III., ch. vi. Mr. Gawtrey remained by the fire beating the DEVIL'S TATTOO upon the chimney-piece.

1855. THACKERAY, *The Newcomes*, II., 130. Lady Kew (*loq.*): 'Have you been quarrelling as much as usual?' 'Pretty much as usual,' says Barnes, drumming on his hat. 'Don't beat that DEVIL'S TATTOO.'

DEVIL'S TEETH. — *See* DEVIL'S BONES.

[Also to note in this connexion are DEVIL'S OWN BOY = a young blackguard; IMP OF THE DEVIL = *idem*; DEVIL'S OWN SHIP = a pirate; DEVIL'S OWN LUCK = uncommon, or inexplicable, good fortune; TO LEAD ONE THE DEVIL'S OWN DANCE = to baffle one in the pursuit of any object; THE DEVIL A BIT SAYS PUNCH = a jocular yet decided negative; and NEAT BUT NOT GAUDY, AS THE DEVIL SAID WHEN HE PAINTED HIS BOTTOM PINK AND TIED UP HIS TAIL WITH PEA GREEN, a locution employed of aged ladies dressed in flaming colours.]

DEVILTRY, *subs.* (low).—A vulgar form of 'devilry.'

DEVOR, *subs.* (Charterhouse).—Plum Cake. [From the Latin.]

DEVOTIONAL-HABITS, *subs.* (stable).—Said of a horse that is apt to 'say his prayers,' *i.e.*, to stumble and go on his knees.

DEW - BEATERS, **- DUSTERS**, or **- TREADERS**, *subs.* (old). - 1. Pedestrians out early in the morning, *i.e.*, before the dew is off the ground.

1692. HACKET, *Life of Williams*, i., 57. It is not equity at lust and pleasure that is moved for, but equity according to decrees and precedents foregoing, as the DEW-BEATERS have trod their way for those that come after them.

2. (common).—The feet. [An extension of sense 1.] For synonyms, *see* CREEPERS.

1811. *Lexicon Balatronicum*, s.v.

1823. SCOTT, *Peveril*, ch. xxxvi. First hold out your DEW-BEATERS till I take off the darbies. Is that usual? said Peveril, stretching out his feet.

3. (tramps').—Shoes. [*Cf.*, senses 1 and 2.] In Norfolk, heavy shoes for wet weather.—*Forby*.

DEW-BIT, *subs.* (common).—A snack before breakfast. *Cf.*, DEW-DRINK and DEW-BEATERS.

DEW-DRINK, *subs.* (common).—A drink before breakfast. *Cf.*, DEW-BIT and DEW-BEATERS. Fr., *une goutte pour tuer le ver*, *i.e.*, 'to drown the maggot,' or 'to crinkle the worm.' Not, of course, the 'early worm of the proverb, but his spiritual cousin, the worm that never dies.

DEWITT, *verb* (old).—To lynch. [The two De Witts, opponents of William of Orange, were massacred by the mob in 1672, without subsequent enquiry.] *Cf.*, BOYCOTT, BURKE, CELLIER.

1690. *Modest Enquiry into the Present Disasters* (*Life of Ken*, p. 561). It is a wonder the English Nation . . . have not in their fury DE-WITTED some of these men who have brought all this upon us. And I must tell them that the crimes of the two unhappy brothers in Holland (which gave rise to that word) were not fully so great as some of theirs.

b. 1664, *d.* 1721. PRIOR, *The Viceroy*. To her I leave thee, gloomy peer, Think on thy crimes committed; Repent, and be for once sincere, Thou ne'er wilt be DE-WITTED.

1849-1861. MACAULAY, *Hist. of England*. One writer . . . expressed his wonder that the people had not . . . DE-WITTED the nonjuring prelates.

DEWSE-A-VYLE.—The country.—*See* DAISYVILLE. *Cf.*, ROM-VILE = London.

1567. HARMAN, *Caveat*, etc., s.v.

1609. DEKKER. *Lanthorne and Candle-light*, in wks. (Grosart), iii., 200, s.v.

1610. ROWLANDS, *Martin Mark-all*, p. 38. (H. Club's Repr., 1874), s.v. 1714. *Memoirs of John Hall* (4th ed.), p. 12, s.v.

DEWSKITCH, *subs.* (tramps').—A thrashing. For synonyms, *see* TANNING.

1851-61. H. MAYHEW, *London Lab. and Lon. Poor*, vol. i., p. 244. It means a DEWSKITCH (a good thrashing).

DIAL or **DIAL-PLATE**, *subs.* (common).—The face. TO TURN THE HANDS ON THE DIAL = to disfigure the face.

ENGLISH SYNONYMS.—Frontispiece; gills (the jaws); chump (also the head); phiz; physog; mug; jib; chivy, or chevy; roach and dace (rhyming); signboard; door-plate; front-window.

FRENCH SYNONYMS.—*La binette* (familiar: *quelle sale binette* = what an ugly mug); *un abcès* (pop. = 'a red or bloated face'); *la fertille* (thieves': also straw); *la fiole* (fam. = phial); *la bobine* (pop: from O. F. *bobe* = grimace); *une balle d'amour* (prostitutes': a handsome face); *une balle* (pop.: also = a franc piece and head); *une glutouse* (thieves'); *une gargouille*, *gargouine*, or *gargue* (popular); *une gargarousse* (thieves'); *une gargagoitche* (thieves'); *une frime* (thieves': *une frime à la manque* = ugly face).

GERMAN SYNONYMS.—*Bonum* or *Bunem* (Hanoverian: from Heb. *ponim* = face); *Ponim* (*see* preceding); *Rauner* (also = the eye; *im Rauner halten* = to keep an eye upon one).

ITALIAN SYNONYMS.—*Berlo*; *baleffo* (literally, a gash or scar: primarily = the mouth).

SPANISH SYNONYMS. — *El mundo* (also = the world); *el geme* (a woman's face. Properly, the space between the extended ends of thumb, and forefinger).

1811. *Lexicon Balatronicum*, s.v.

1889. *Bird o' Freedom*, 7 Aug., p. 3. An absinthe tumbler which caught him a nasty crack across the DIAL finally convinced him that discretion was the better part of valour.

1890. *Polytechnic Magazine*, 21 March. 'Boxing Brutalities.' Now if there is a rule that no competitor may strike another with a force greater than a fixed number of pounds, it will be easy to disqualify a man whose opponent's DIAL shows a greater amount of punishment.

DIALS, *subs.* (prison).—Convicts and thieves hailing from Seven Dials.

DIAMOND-CRACKING, *subs.* (Australian thieves').—1. Stonebreaking.

1885. *Australian Printer's Keepsake*. He caught a month, and had to white it out at DIAMOND-CRACKING in Castieu's Hotel [Melbourne Gaol].

2. (English miners').—Working in a coal mine. *Cf.*, BLACK DIAMONDS.

DIBBLE, *subs.* (common). — The *penis*. For synonyms, *see* CREAMSTICK.

DIBS or **DIBBS**, *subs.* (common).—Generic for money. [Said to be a corruption of *diobs*, *i.e.*, *diobolus*, a classic coin = 2½d. Another derivation is from the hucklebones of sheep, popularly DIBBS, used for gambling; Scots 'chuckies.'] For synonyms, *see* ACTUAL and GILT. TO BRUSH WITH THE DIBS = to abscond with the cash; TO TIP OVER THE DIBS = to pay down or 'shell out'; TO FLASH THE DIBS = to show money, etc.

1837. BARHAM, *I. L.* (*Dead Drummer*). One of their drummers, and one Sergeant Matcham, Had BRUSH'D WITH THE DIBS, and they never could catch 'em.

1842. *Comic Almanack*, p. 313. Governor,—Science can't be purchased without DIBBS. When we want subjects we must shell out.

1862. *Penny Newspaper*. The other informed him that if he did not TIP OVER THE DIBS he would blow his —— brains out.

1880. *Punch's Almanack*, p. 7. Time to think about my outing. No DIBS yet, though, so it's no use shouting.

1887. W. E. HENLEY, *Villon's Straight Tip*. The merry little DIBBS you'll bag.

DICE. TO BOX THE DICE, *verb. phr.* (legal).—To carry a point by tricking or swindling.

DICK, *subs.* (common). — 1. A dictionary; a RICHARD (*q.v.*); also, by implication, fine language or long words.—*See* SWALLOW THE DICK.

1860. HALIBURTON ('Sam. Slick'), *The Season Ticket*, No. xii. Ah, now you are talking 'DIC.,' exclaimed Peabody, and I can't follow you. When I talk——You use the *vulgar tongue*, retorted the Senator.

2. (coachman's). — A riding whip.

3. (military). — The *penis*. For synonyms, *see* CREAMSTICK.

4. (common).—An affidavit.

1861. DUTTON COOK, *Paul Foster's Daughter*, ch. xxvi. No. I'd take my dying DICK he hasn't got a writ in his pocket, or he couldn't move along so easy as that.

5. (American). — An Irish Catholic.—*See* CRAWTHUMPER.

Verb (thieves').—To look; to PIPE (*q.v.*); *e.g.*, the bulky's DICKING = the policeman is watching you. [From the gypsy *dikk*.] Fr., *gaffer*. For synonyms, *see* PIPE.

DICK IN THE GREEN, *phr.* (thieves').—Weak; inferior. *Cf.*, DICKY.

1812. VAUX, *Memoirs*, s.v.

IN THE REIGN OF QUEEN DICK, *adv. phr.* (common).—Never; 'when two Sundays come in a week.' For synonyms, *see* GREEK KALENDS.

1811. *Lexicon Balatronicum*, s.v.

1864. *Standard*, 13 Dec., *Rev. of St. Dicy*. Moreover . . a few days since, a 'bus driver in altercation with his conductor, who threatened him with paying off soon, replied, 'Oh yes, IN THE REIGN OF QUEEN DICK,' which, on inquiry we found to be synonymous with 'Never,' or 'Tib's eve.'

TO SWALLOW THE DICK, *verb. phr.* (common). — To use long words without knowledge of their meaning; TO HIGH FALUTE (American).

UP TO DICK, *adv. phr.* (common).—Not to be 'taken in'; 'artful'; 'fly'; wide-awake. For synonyms, *see* DOWNY. Also = up to the mark, *i.e.*, perfectly satisfactory.

1877. J. GREENWOOD, *Under the Blue Blanket*. 'Ain't that UP TO DICK, my biffin?' 'I never said it warn't.'

1887. *Walford's Antiquarian*, April, p. 251. Betwixt you and me I think you'll agree That of course I look 'UP TO DICK.'

DICKENS, *subs.* (old).—The DEVIL (*q.v.*) or DEUCE (*q.v.*); used interchangeably. [A corruption of NICK (*q.v.*).] For synonyms, *see* SKIPPER.

1596. SHAKSPEARE, *Merry Wives of Windsor*, Act III., Sc. ii. I cannot tell what the DICKENS his name is.

1653. URQUHART, *Rabelais*, bk. I., prol. (Bohn), vol. I., p. 99. But hearken, joltheads, you vie-dayes, or DICKENS take ye.

1727. JOHN GAY, *Beggar's Opera*, Act I. Sc. 1. *Peach*. What a DICKENS is the woman always whimpering about murder for! No gentleman is ever looked upon the worse for killing a man in his own defence.

1754. FOOTE, *Knights*, Act II. Mally Pengrouse! Who the DICKENS is she?

1824. R. B. PEAKE, *Americans Abroad*, i., 1. Oh! the DICKENS—I'm stunded.

1880. G. R. SIMS, *Zeph*. ch. xv. 'Inez is fretting after Pedro,' he said to himself, 'but what the DICKENS is Totty blubbering about?'

1889. C. HADDON CHAMBERS, *Ne'er-do-Well*, 'In Australian Wilds.' What the DICKENS could I do? I believe I swore a little at first, and then I flourished my whip.

DICKER, *subs.* and *verb*: also DICKERING, *subs.* (American).—Barter; SWAP (*q.v.*): generally applied to trade in small articles.

1830. COBBETT, in *Rural Rides*, I., 199 (1886). It is barter, truck, change, DICKER, as the Yankees call it, but, as our horse-jockeys call it, swap, or chop.

1831-90. WHITTIER, *Poems*. For peddling DICKER, not for honest sales.

1888. *New York Weekly Times*, 28 March. He had perhaps been considering the advisability of making a DICKER with his old political opponents in the hope of bettering his condition.

1888. *Denver Republican*, 7 April. After some DICKERING a style of coffin was selected and a price decided upon.

DICKEY, *subs.* (old).—1. A woman's under petticoat.

1811. *Lexicon Balatronicum*, s.v.

2. (common).—A donkey.

b. 1766, *d.* 1823. BLOOMFIELD, *Richard and Kate*. But now, as at some nobler places Amongst the leaders 'twas decreed Time to begin the DICKY races, More famed for laughter than for speed.

1841. JOHN MILLS, *Old Eng. Gentleman*, ch. vii., p. 60 (3rd ed.). A young DICKEY, in the full kick of youth, mistook some sweet briar for a thistle.

3. (common).—A sham shirt front, formerly a worn-out shirt.

Cf., sense 4. [Hotten: originally TOMMY (from the Greek, τομή, a section), a word once used in Trinity College, Dublin.] Also, by implication, any sham contrivance; *see* quots.

1781. G. PARKER, *View of Society*, I., 82, note. DICKEY: cant for a worn-out shirt.

1811. *Lexicon Balatronicum*, s.v. A sham shirt.

1835-40. HALIBURTON, *Clockmaker*, 2 S., ch. ix. She made frill, shirt-collar, and DICKY fly like snow.

1836. WILLIS GAYFORD CLARKE, *The Olla Podriana Papers*. For a handkerchief I had flourished a common DICKEY, the strings whereof fell to my feet.

1848. THACKERAY, *Book of Snobs*, ch. xx. Those wretched Beaux Tibbs's of society, who sport a lace DICKEY, and nothing besides.

1857. HOOD, *Pen and Pencil Pictures*, p. 206. Do not take off that article of apparel which Fanny Fern distinguishes by a name which, on this side the Atlantic, is the familiar for a YOUTHFUL RICHARD. Spare it, we say . . . although it may be (and we guess, from the absence of cuffs and sleeves, it is) an imitation, a sham, a make-shift!

1872. *Public Opinion*, 24 Feb., p. 241. 'Inside Newgate.' What is she here for? I asked, pointing to a florid-looking girl who was taking a deep professional interest in ironing a DICKEY.

1876. JAS. GREENWOOD, *Low Life Deeps*. 'I saw a laden waggon bearing the name of one of the cheap advertising firms you speak of.' . . . 'Ah, bearing the name . . . you saw a waggon wearing a DICKY, you mean—a false front-plate with a name on it which slips on and off like them on the wans that the pianoforte-makers borrow.'

1883. JAS. GREENWOOD, 'Veteran of Vauxhall,' in *Odd People in Odd Places*, p. 38. Besides these articles there was a pair of what had once been white linen cuffs, a DICKEY of the same dubious complexion, and a white tie.

4. (American: New England).—A shirt collar. *De Vere*. *Cf.*, sense 3.

5. (nautical).—A ship's officer or mate; generally, SECOND DICKEY, *i.e.*, second mate.

6. (London).—A swell. For synonyms, *see* DANDY.

7. (schoolboys').—The *penis*.

Adj. (common). — 1. Sorry; inferior; paltry and poor in quality. DICKEY DOMUS (theatrical) = a poor 'house.'

2. (London). — Smart. A corruption of UP TO DICK (*q.v.*). *Cf.*, *subs.*, sense 6.

ALL DICKEY WITH [ONE], *adv. phr.* (common).—Queer; gone wrong; 'all up with.'

1811. POOLE, *Hamlet Travestied*, III., vi. O, Hamlet! 'tis ALL DICKEY WITH us both You've done my business by a blow, 'tis true; But I—Oh! I—have done the same for you.

1819. MOORE, *Tom Crib's Memorial*, p. 21. 'Twas ALL DICKY WITH Georgy, his *mug* hung so dead.

1837. THACKERAY, in *Fraser's Magazine*, 10 Oct. Sam, the stable boy [who from living chiefly among the hosses and things has got a sad low way of talking], said it was ALL DICKY, and bid us drive on to the nex' page.

1837. BARHAM, *I. L.* (*Brothers of Birchington*). Here a monk, whose teeth funk and concern made to chatter, Sobs out as he points to the corpse on the floor, 'Tis ALL DICKEY WITH poor Father Dick—he's no more'

1882. *Daily Telegraph*, 3 Oct., p. 2, col. 2. I was coolly told that 'anyhow, all the actual meat there was in, say half a pound of cheap German sausage, couldn't do any one much harm if it was ever so DICKY.'

DICKEY-BIRD, *subs.* (common).—1. A louse. For synonyms, *see* CHATES.

2. *pl.* (theatrical)—Professional singers of all grades.

3. (venery). — A prostitute; generally NAUGHTY DICKY-BIRD. For synonyms, *see* BARRACK-HACK and TART.

c. 1830. *Broadside Ballad*, GEORGE BARNWELL. When he had put the shutters up He went to see his DICKEY-BIRD, And when he came back next morning, Blowed if he could speak a word.

DICKEY-DIAPER, *subs.* (old). — A linendraper.

DICKEY-DIDO, *subs.* (popular).—An idiot. For synonyms, *see* BUFFLE and CABBAGE-HEAD.

DICKEY-LAGGER, *subs.* (common).— A bird catcher. [From DICKEY, a pet name for a bird + LAGGER, one who lays hold of.]

1881. W. BLACK, *Beautiful Wretch*, ch. xviii. 'They're starved out in this weather, Miss; and then the boys come out wi' their guns; and the DICKY-LAGGERS are after them too.' 'The what?' 'The bird-catchers, Miss.'

DICKEY-SAM, *subs. phr.* (common). —A native of Liverpool.

1870. *Athenæum*, 10 Sept. We cannot even guess why a Liverpool man is called a DICKEY SAM.

1884. *Book Lore*, Dec., p. 27. The natives of Liverpool call themselves, or are called by others, DICKY SAMS.

DICKY, *subs.* (Scots').—1. The *penis*. For synonyms, *see* CREAMSTICK.

2. *See* DICK in all senses.

DIDDIES, *subs.* (common). — The paps. For synonyms, *see* DAIRY.

DIDDLE, *subs.* (old).—1. Gin. For synonyms, *see* DRINKS. In America, liquor generally.

1858. H. MAYHEW, *Paved with Gold*, bk. iii., ch. i, p. 252. And there's a first-rate 'DIDDLE cove' (publican) keeps a gin-shop there.

2. (schoolboys').—The *penis*. For synonyms, *see* CREAMSTICK.

3. (common).—A swindle or 'do.'—*See verb*, sense 1.

1885. *Punch*, 5 Sept., p. 110. And something whispered me—in diction chaste —It's all a DIDDLE!

Verb (common).—1. To cheat. For synonyms, *see* STICK.

1811. POOLE, *Hamlet Travestied.*

1819. MOORE, *Tom Crib's Memorial*, 1. DIDDLING your subjects, and *gutting* their *fobs.*

1825. SCOTT, *St. Ronan's Well*, ch. v. And Jack is DIDDLED, said the Baronet.

1841. *Comic Almanack*, p. 266. Thus, while pig and tail the villagers DIDDLE, My tale's in the middle, my tale's in the middle!

1880. HAWLEY SMART, *Social Sinners*, ch. xv. He had me, and no mistake. Done, yes, DIDDLED; and I thought I had rather an easy-going lawyer to deal with.

1887. *Lic. Vict. Gazette*, 2 Dec, 362, 1. You have been done, regularly DIDDLED, by that fellow.

2. (venery).—To copulate. *Cf.*, DIDDLE, *subs.*, sense 2. For synonyms, *see* RIDE.

3. (Scots' colloquial). — To shake.

DIDDLE-COVE, *subs.* (American).— A landlord. *Cf.*, DIDDLER.

1859. MATSELL, *Rogue's Lexicon*, s.v.

DIDDLER, *subs.* (common). — A cheat; a dodger. [From DIDDLE (*q.v.*) + ER.] For synonyms, *see* ROOK.—*See* JEREMY DIDDLER (KENNY's *Raising the Wind*). Also a chronic borrower. DIDDLING = cheating; also borrowing.

DIDDLY-POUT, *subs.* (venery).—The female *pudendum*. For synonyms, *see* MONOSYLLABLE.

DIDOES, *subs.* (American).—Pranks; tricks; fantastic proceedings.— *See* CUT DIDOES, and CUT CAPERS.

1835. HALIBURTON, *Clockmaker*, 1 S., ch. xvii. I met a man this mornin' . . . frum Halifax, a real conceited lookin' critter as you e'enamost ever seed, all shines and DIDOES.

1851. *New York Tribune*, 10 April, Had the Free States been manly enough, true enough, to enact the Wilmot Proviso as to all present or future territories of the Union, we should have had just the same DIDOES CUT UP by the chivalry that we have witnessed, and with no more damage to the Union.

DIE or **DEE**, *subs.* (American thieves').—A pocket-book. MATSELL'S *Vocabulum* [1859]. For synonyms, *see* LEATHER.

DIE-BY-THE-HEDGE, *subs. phr.* (provincial).—The flesh of animals deceased by accident or of disease; by implication, inferior meat.

DIE-HARDS, *subs.* (military).—The Fifty-Seventh Foot. [From the rallying call at Albuera (1811) its Colonel (Inglis) calling to the men, 'Die hard, my men, die hard,' when it had thirty bullets through the King's Colour, and only had one officer out of twenty-four, and one hundred and sixty-eight men out of five hundred and eighty-four, when left standing.]

DIE IN ONE'S BOOTS or **SHOES**, *verb. phr.* (old).—1. To be hanged. For synonyms, *see* LADDER.

1653. URQUHART, *Rabelais.*

1837. R. H. BARHAM, *Ingoldsby Legends.* 'The Execution' (ed. 1862), p. 196. And there is McFuze And Lieutenant Tregooze, And there is Sir Carnaby Jenks of the Blues All come to see a man DIE IN HIS SHOES.

1888. *Denver Republican*, 9 April. When in liquor he was quarrelsome and the prediction was commonly made that he would DIE WITH HIS BOOTS ON.

2. (American).—To 'die standing': at work, 'in harness,' in full possession of one's faculties.

1887. *Scribner's Magazine.* These stiff prairie plants bever wilt— they DIE IN THEIR BOOTS.

1888. *Cincinnatti Enquirer*, Title: DIED WITH HIS BOOTS ON. The killing of the notorious Desperado Leo Renfro.

DIE WITH ONE'S EARS STUFFED WITH COTTON.—*See* COTTON.

DIG, *subs.* (colloquial).—1. A blow, thrust, punch, or poke; in pugilism = a 'straight left-hander' delivered under the guard on the 'mark.'

1819. MOORE, *Tom Crib's Memorial*, p. 51. While *ribbers* rung from each resounding frame, and divers DIGS, and many a ponderous *pelt.*

1876. C. W. WALL, trans. *Molière*, vol. i., p. 80. The DIGS in the ribs I gave you with such hearty good will.

ENGLISH SYNONYMS. — Auctioneer; biff; bang; buck-horse; buster; chatterer; chin-chopper; chopper; clip; click; clinker; clout; cock; cork; comber; cuff; cant; corker; dab; downer; douser; ding; domino; floorer; ferricadouzer; fibbing; facer; flush-hit; finisher; gooser; hot 'un; jaw-breaker; lick; mendoza; muzzler; noser; nobbler; nose-ender; nope; oner; punch; stock-dollager; stotor; spank; topper; twister; whack; wipe.

FRENCH SYNONYMS. — *Un coup d'encensoir* (popular: a tap on the nose; 'one on the smeller'); *un coup de tampon* (pop.: *tampon* = buffer); *un coup de Garibaldi* (thieves': a butt in the stomach); *un moule de gant* (popular: 'a mould for a glove'); *une mornifle* (colloquial: 'a wipe in the jaw');

une mandole (popular: from *torgnole*); *une gnole* (popular); *un coup de gilquin* (popular); *un cataplasme de Venise* (popular); *un gnon* (popular); *une dariole* (pop.: also, a cream-cake); *une beugne* (popular); *une dandine* (popular: 'a twister'); *une baffre* (popular); *des castagnettes* (military: punches); *une châtaigne* (popular); *une couleur* (popular); *une bouffe* (popular: *bouffée* = gust or blast); *un cabochon* (popular); *un estaffion* (popular); *une estaphe* (popular); *une accolade*; *une balle de coton* (thieves').—*See* also TAN, *verb.*

GERMAN SYNONYM. *Azkes malaikes* (Viennese thieves': = a blow with the fist on the throat. The derivation may be: *azke* from Heb. *osak*, to quarrel + *malaikes* from Heb. *melocho*, work).

SPANISH SYNONYMS. — *Duros* (whip-strokes; also = harsh, merciless); *tapaboca* (a 'corker': also any action or observation which cuts one short); *pasagonzalo* (a quick hit); *capon* (generally colloquial); *chamorrada* (a butt with the head); *mojada* (a stab); *zumbido* or *zumbo* (literally, a humming or buzzing); *tantarantin* (a thwack; also = beat of a drum); *tarja* (also = a target).

ITALIAN SYNONYM. *Ramenghi d'alta foia* (blows with a stick).

2. (American). — A diligent student. [By implication from the *verb* (*q.v.*); also study; *e.g.*, To have a DIG at Cæsar or Livy.

Verb (American) —To work hard; especially to study.

1876. MISS ALCOTT, *Little Wives*, ch. ix. He . . . turned studious, and gave out that he was going to DIG, intending to graduate in a blaze of glory.

DIG A DAY UNDER THE SKIN, *verb. phr.* (common).—To make a shave serve for two days.

TO DIG UP THE HATCHET.— *See* BURY.

DIGESTER. — *See* PATENT DIGESTER.

DIGGED.—*See* JIGGED.

DIGGERS, *subs.* (common). — 1. Spurs; 'persuaders.'

1789. GEO. PARKER, *Life's Painter*, p. 173, s.v.

1811. *Lexicon Balatronicum*, s.v.

2. (cards).—The spades suit; also DIGGUMS. BIG DIGGER = ace of spades.

3. (vulgar).—The finger nails.

1859. MATSELL, *Vocabulum*, s.v.

1881. *New York Slang Dict.* 'On the Trail.' 'If you do,' returned Bill, 'I will fix my DIGGERS in your dial-plate and turn it up with red.

DIGGERS'-DELIGHT, *subs.* (New Zealand).—A wide-brimmed felt hat. For synonyms, *see* GOLGOTHA.

DIGGINGS, *subs.* (common).—A place of residence or employment. [First used at the Western lead mines in the U.S.A. to denote whence ore was dug.]

ENGLISH SYNONYMS.—Birk; box; case; crib; chat; den; dry-lodgings; drum; place; pig-sty; pew; cabin; castle; chaffing-crib; caboose; sky-parlour; shop; ken; dossing-ken; hole; rookery; hutch; hang-out.

FRENCH SYNONYMS. — *Une bagnole* (pop.: from *bagne* = hulks); *un bazar* (military: also, a brothel); *un bocal* (pop.: also = stomach); *une baraque* (common: in disparagement); *une baite* (thieves'); *une case* (thieves'); *une carrée* (thieves'); *une cambriole* (thieves'); *une cambuse* (popular); *une condition* (thieves'); *un creux* (thieves'); *une piole* or *piolle* (thieves').

GERMAN SYNONYM. — *Bes, Beth*, or *Bajis.*

ITALIAN SYNONYMS. — *Bacchia*; *clocchia* or *cloccia* (also = a bell); *coschetto delle Fantasime.*

SPANISH SYNONYMS. — *Caverna* ('a cavern'; *cf.*, English DEN); *aduana* (also = a brothel, and thieves' resort); *nido* ('a nest'; *nido de ladrones*, a 'cross-drum'; a thieves' resort); *percha* ('a perch').

1838. J. C. NEAL, *Charcoal Sketches*, II., 119. Look here, Ned, I reckon it's about time we should go to our DIGGINGS; I am dead beat.

1871. DE VERE, *Americanisms*, p. 171. The miner in California and Nevada has been known, in times of a *rush*, to speak of a place where he could stand leaning against a stout post, as his DIGGINGS for the night.

1883. *Referee*, 1 July, p. 3, col. 2. Mr. and Mrs. Bancroft are changing their DIGGINGS, and clearing out of Cavendish-square.

1884. W. C. RUSSELL, *Jack's Courtship*, ch. viii. Oh, he lives round the corner. You may see his DIGGINGS from your daughter's bedroom window, sir.

1888. C. J. DUNPHIE, *The Chameleon*, p. 86. 'DIGGINGS' I call my dwelling, according to the prevalent slang.

DIGGUMS, *subs.* (provincial).—1. A gardener.

2. (gamesters'). — The suit of spades; also DIGGERS (*q.v.*).

DILBERRIES, *subs.* (common). — Fæcal and seminal deposits in the hair of the *anus* and the female *pudendum*; CLINKERS.

DILBERRY-BUSH, *subs.* (common).—The hair about the female *pudendum* or the *anus*.—*See* DILBERRIES.

DILDO, *subs.* (old).—An instrument (of wax, horn, leather, india-rubber, gutta-percha, etc., and other soft material), shaped like, and used by women as a substitute for, the *penis*. Now called a BROOM-HANDLE or BROOMSTICK, the *pudendum* in this connection = BROOM (*q.v.*). [BAILEY: from It., *diletto*, a woman's delight or from DALLY = to toy.] In Lombardy, *passo tempo.*

c.1672. BUTLER, *Dildoides* (Occasioned by Burning a hogshead of DILDOES at Stocks Market).

1886. BURTON, *The Thousand Nights and a Night*, vol. x, p. 239. Of the *penis succedaneus*, that imitation of the *Arborvitæ*, or *Sotor-Kosmou*, which the Latins called *phallus* and *fascinum*, the French *godemiché*, and the Italians *passatempo* and *diletto* (whence our DILDO), every kind abounds, varying from a stuffed 'French Letter' to a cone of ribbed horn, which looks like an instrument of torture.

Verb (old).—To wanton with a woman. *Cf.*, *subs.*, sense. For synonyms, *see* FIRKYTOODLE.

DILLY, *subs.* (common).—A night cart; formerly a coach. [From Fr., *diligence.*]

17(?). *The Anti-Jacobin.* So down thy hill, romantic Ashbourne glides, The Derby DILLY having four inside.

1833. MARRYAT, *Peter Simple*, ch. ix. One which they called a DILLY.

DILLY-BAG, *subs.* (Australian).—A wallet; or scran-bag.

1880. A. C. GRANT. Their own DILLY-BAGS have nothing of value or interest in them.

DILLY-DALLY, *verb* (colloquial). — To loiter; hesitate; trifle. [A duplication of DALLY.]

1740. RICHARDSON, *Pamela*, i., 275. What you do, sir, do; don't stand DILLY-DALLYING.

1750. FIELDING, *Tom Jones*, bk. XVIII., ch. xii. But if I had suffered her to stand shill I shall I, DILLY DALLY, you might not have had that honour yet awhile.

1869. W. S. GILBERT, *The Bohemian Girl*. When at a pinch you should never DILLY-DALLY.

DIMBER, *adj.* (old).—Pretty, neat, lively. Variants are SCRUMPTIOUS; NATTY. Fr., *batif* (thieves'); *fignole* (thieves'); *girofle* (thieves').

1671. R. HEAD, *English Rogue*, pt. I., ch. v., p. 48 (1874), s.v.

1706. E. COLES, *Eng. Dict.*, s.v.

DIMBER COVE = a sprightly man, a gentleman: DIMBER MORT = a pretty girl. Fr., *une largue girofle*. *Cf.*, DIMBER-DAMBER.

1837. DISRAELI, *Venetia*, book I., ch. xiv. 'Tis a DIMBER COVE, whispered one of the younger men to a companion: *Ibid*, Tip me the clank like a DIMBER MORT.

DIMBER-DAMBER, *subs.* (old).—A captain of thieves or vagrants. [From DIMBER (*q.v.*), skilful, etc., + DAMBER (*q.v.*), a chief or head man.]

1671. R. HEAD, *English Rogue*, pt. 1, ch. v., p. 48 (1874).

1724. E. COLES, *Eng. Dict.*

1749. *Life of Bampfylde-Moore Carew*, 'Oath of the Canting Crew.' . . No DIMBER DAMBER, angler, dancer, prig of cackler, prig of prancer.

1834. H. AINSWORTH, *Rookwood*, bk. III., ch. v. No; no refusal, exclaimed a chorus of voices. Dick Turpin must be one of us. He shall be our DIMBER DAMBER.

DIMMOCK, *subs.* (common).—Money. For synonyms, *see* ACTUAL and GILT.

1834. H. AINSWORTH, *Rookwood*, bk. IV., ch. i. 'I have . . . pocketed the DIMMOCK (here 'tis,' continued he, parenthetically slapping his pockets).

DINAHS, *subs.* (Stock-Exchange).—Edinburgh and Glasgow Railway Ordinary Stock.

DINARLY or **DINALI**, *subs.* (theatrical).—Money. For synonyms, *see* ACTUAL and GILT. NANTEE or NANTI DINARLY = no money. Sp., *dinero*; Lingua Franca, *niente dinaro* = not a penny.

1851-61. H. MAYHEW, *London Lab. and Lon. Poor*, vol. III., p. 149. 'I have got no money' is, 'My nabs has nanti DINALI' [among strolling actors].

1870. *South London Press*, 8 Oct., *Advt.* So don't forget when you've the tin To here spend your 'DINARLEY.'

DINE-OUT, *verb. phr.* (common).—To go dinnerless, TO DINE WITH DUKE HUMPHREY (*q.v.*). Variants: TO TAKE A SPITALFIELDS' BREAKFAST (*q.v.*), or AN IRISHMAN'S DINNER (*q.v.*), also TO GO OUT AND COUNT THE RAILINGS (*q.v.*). Fr., *Se coucher bredouille* = to go to bed supperless; *aller voir défiler les dragons* = to go and watch the dragoons march past; *diner en ville* = to dine in town, *i.e.*, to munch a roll in the street or to eat nothing; *lire le journal*.

1888. *All the Year Round*, 9 June, p. 542. To 'dine with Duke Humphrey, or, as it is now sometimes more shortly phrased, to 'DINE OUT,' in both cases meaning not to dine at all.

DINE WITH DUKE HUMPHREY, *verb. phr.* (old).—To go dinnerless; to DINE OUT (*q.v.*).—[Origin uncertain; supposed, however, to refer to Humphrey, Duke of Gloucester, the youngest son of Henry the Fourth, who, though really buried at St. Alban's, was reputed to have a monument in

Old St. Paul's, from which one part of the church was termed Duke Humphrey's Walk. Old Paul's was a regular promenade, especially for lackeys out of livery, and ruffians and sea-captains out of luck. Thus Falstaff explains of Bardolph that he 'got him in Paul's,' while Jonson actually lays the scene of *Every Man Out of His Humour* (1599), in 'The Middle Aisle of St. Paul's,' to introduce his cavaliero Shift. Shift and Bardolph, in fact, were what is now called 'inspectors of public buildings'; they walked in Paul's on the chance of a pick-up, and they dined by looking at the monuments. The Bodleian Library was founded by the same Duke Humphrey, and the *Gentleman's Mag.* (1794, p. 529) records that when a student stayed on during the dinner hour, at which time it used to be closed, he was said to DINE WITH DUKE HUMPHREY. An alternative traces the saying to the report that Duke Humphrey was starved to death. Chambers, in his *Historical Sketch of St. Giles's Cathedral*, Edinburgh, records a similar pleasantry concerning the tomb of the Earl of Murray, and quotes a Scots poet, one Sempill (16th cent.), who makes a hungry idler say: I dined with saints and gentlemen, E'en sweet St. Giles and the Earl of Murray. *See* WHARTON, *Hist. of Eng. Poetry* (ed. 1824), vol. IV., p. 361.

1592. NASHE, *Pierce Penilesse*, in wks., ii., 18. I . . . . retired me to Paules, to seeke my dinner WITH DUKE HUMFREY.

1592. GAB. HARVEY, *Four Letters*. To seek his dinner in Poules WITH DUKE HUMPHREY.

1608. *The Penniless Parliament of Threadbare Poets*. And if I prove not that a mince-pie is the better weapon, let me DINE twice a week AT DUKE HUMPHRY'S TABLE.

1664. H. PEACHAM, *Worth of a Penny*, in Arber's *Garner*, vol. VI., p. 273. Who, having been troubled with over much money, afterward, in no long time, have been fain, after 'A LONG DINNER WITH DUKE HUMPHREY,' to take a nap on 'penniless bench,' only to verify the old proverb, 'A fool and his money is soon parted.'

1748. SMOLLETT, *Rod. Random*, ch. lv. My mistress and her mother must have DINED WITH DUKE HUMPHREY, had I not exerted myself in their behalf.

1884. *Daily Telegraph*, 22 Jan., p. 5, col. 3. In future, not even the most impecunious of diners-out must accept an invitation from DUKE HUMPHREY.

DING, *verb* (Old Cant, in some senses).—Used as a colloquialism (as in Scott) it signifies to knock, to strike down, to pound or (as in quot., 1786) to give way: while in slang it means to get rid of; to pass to a confederate; 'to steal by a single effort.' TO DING A CASTOR = to snatch a hat and run with it: the booty being DINGED if it has to be thrown away. GOING UPON THE DING = to go on the prowl. DING THE TOT! = Run away with the lot!

c. 1340. HAMPOLE, *Pricke of Conscience*, 7015 (ed. Morris). Right swa þe devels salle ay DYNG, on þe synfulle, withouten styntyng.

1600. *Sir John Oldcastle*, Act III., Sc. ii. For the credit of Dunstable, DING down the money to-morrow.

1610. JONSON, *Alchemist*, V., iii. *Sur.* [*without*]. Down with the door. *Kas.* [*without*]. 'Slight, DING it open.

1773. O. GOLDSMITH, *She Stoops to Conquer*, Act II. If I'm to have any good, let it come of itself; not to keep DINGING it, DINGING it into one so.

1786. BURNS, *A Dream*. But facts are chiels that winna DING.

1821. PIERCE EGAN, *Tom and Jerry* [ed. 1890], p. 78. Oh I took him such a lick of his mummer, and DINGED his rattle clean out of his hand.

b. 1793, *d.* 1872. DEAN RAMSEY. Our meenister's DINGED the guts out of twa Bibles.

1846. DICKENS, *Dombey*, ch. ix., p. 74. These were succeeded by anchor and chain-cable forges, where sledge hammers were DINGING upon iron all day long.

DING-BAT, *subs.* (American). — Money. For synonyms, *see* ACTUAL and GILT.

DING-BOY, *subs.* (old).—A rogue; a bully.

1785. GROSE, *Dict. Vulg. Tongue*, s.v.

DING-DONG. TO GO AT IT, or TO IT, DING-DONG, *verb. phr.* (colloquial).—To tackle with vigor, or in right good earnest. Formerly, helter-skelter, (GROSE, 1785).

1887. H. SMART, *Saddle and Sabre*, ch. xx. For the next hundred yards it was a DING-DONG struggle between them.

DINGE, *subs.* (Royal Military Academy).—A picture or painting.

DINGED, *adj.* (American).—A euphemism for 'darned' = dammed. Sometimes DING-GONED. — *See* OATHS.

DINGER, *subs.* (old).—1. A thief who throws away his booty to escape detection. [From DING (*q.v.*), to throw away + ER.]

2. in *pl.* (conjurers').—Cups and balls; Fr., *gobelets et muscades*.

DING-FURY, *subs.* (provincial).—Huff; anger.

DING-GONED.—*See* DINGED.

DINGLE, *adj.* (old).—Hackneyed; used up.

1786. *The Microcosm*, No. 3. Your Mic is *dead-lounge*—dissipates insufferable *ennui* of tea-table,—fills boring intervals of *conversazione*, . . . By the by, in your next propose some new *lounge*.—They are all so DINGLE at present, they are quite a bore.

DINING-ROOM, *subs.* (common).—The mouth. For synonyms, *see* POTATO-TRAP.

DINING-ROOM CHAIRS, *subs. phr.* (common). — The teeth; also DINNER-SET (*q.v.*). For synonyms, *see* GRINDERS.

DINING-ROOM POST, *subs. phr.* (old).—Petty pilfering done from houses by sham postmen.

DINK, *adj.* (Scots' colloquial). — Dainty; trim.

1794. BURNS, *My Lady's Gown*. My lady's DINK, my lady's drest.

DINNER-SET, *subs.* (common). — The teeth. 'Your DINNER-SET wants looking to' = you need to go to the dentist. For synonyms, *see* GRINDERS.

DIP, *subs.* (thieves').—1. A pickpocket; also DIPPER and DIPPING-BLOKE. For synonyms, *see* STOOK-HAULER.

1859. MATSELL, *Vocabulum*, p. 26, s.v.

1866. VANCE, *The Chickaleary Cove*. Off to Paris I shall go to show a thing or two To the DIPPING-BLOKES wot hangs about the *cafés*.

1888. *St. Louis Globe Democrat*. A DIP touched the Canadian sheriff for his watch and massive chain while he was reading the Riot Act.

2. (American).—A stolen kiss, especially one in the dark.

3. (Westminster School). — A pocket inkstand.

4. (colloquial).—A candle made by dipping the wick in tallow.

19

1837. BARHAM, *I. L.* (*Ingoldsby Penance*.) None of your rascally DIPS, but sound, Best superfine wax-wicks, four to the pound.

Verb (thieves').—1. To pick pockets. TO DIP A LOB = to rob a till. Also TO GO ON THE DIPE = to go pocket-picking. For synonyms, *see* FRISK.

1817. *Sporting Mag.* Defence of Groves at Bristol Assizes. I have DIPPED into 150 . . . pockets and not found a shilling.

2. (old).—To pawn; mortgage.

1693. DRYDEN, *Persius*, vi., 160. Put out the principal in trusty hands: Live of the use; and never DIP thy lands.

1711. *Spectator*, No. 114. What gives the unhappy man this peevishness of spirit is, that his estate is DIPPED, and is eating out with usury; and yet he has not the heart to sell any part of it.

1860. THACKERAY, *Philip*, ch. xiv. You have but one son, and he has a fortune of his own, as I happen to know. You haven't DIPPED it, Master Philip?

3. (thieves').—To be convicted; to get into trouble.

TO DIP ONE'S BEAK, *verb. phr.* (common).—To drink. For synonyms, *see* LUSH.

DIPE.—*See* DIP, *verb*, sense 1.

1877. S. L. CLEMENS ('Mark Twain') *Life on the Mississippi*, p. 460. I felt very rough and was thinking I would have TO GO ON THE DIPE again.

DIPPED IN WING, *adv. phr.* (popular).—Worsted.

DIPPER, *subs.* (old).—1. A baptist.—[GROSE, 1785.]

2. *See* DIP, *subs.*, sense 1.

DIPPING-BLOKE.—*See* DIP, *subs.*, sense 1.

DIPS, *subs.* (nautical).—1. The purser's boy.

2. (colloquial).—A grocer.

DIPSTICK, *subs.* (old).—A gauger.

DIRK, *subs.* (Scots'). — The *penis*. For synonyms, *see* CREAMSTICK.

DIRT, *subs.* (American).—Money. For synonyms, *see* ACTUAL and GILT.

TO EAT DIRT, *verb. phr.* (colloquial).—To submit to insult; TO EAT BROILED CROW, or HUMBLE PIE (*q.v.*); to retract.

1854. WHYTE MELVILLE, *General Bounce*, ch. x. Though they bow before a calf, is it not a golden one? though they 'EAT DIRT,' is it not dressed by a French cook?

1861. *New York Evening Post*, 4 Jan. After EATING so much DIRT, are we asked to swallow free soil?

TO FLING DIRT OR MUD, *verb. phr.* (colloquial).—To abuse; to vituperate.

1689. SELDEN, *Table Talk*, p. 104 (Arber's ed.). One that writes against his Adversary, and THROWS all the DIRT he can in his Face.

1705. WARD, *Hudibras Redivivus*, vol. I., pt. ii., p. 11. Scurrility's a useful trick, Approv'd by the most politick; FLING DIRT enough, and some will stick.

1875. OUIDA, *Signa*, vol. I., ch. xv., p. 358. A wicked old tongue that could THROW DIRT with any man's or woman's either.

1885. J. S. WINTER, *Bootles' Baby*, p. 66. I suppose he wants to daub Bootles with some of his own MUD. Thinks if he only THROWS enough some of it's sure to stick.

TO CUT DIRT.—*See* CUT.

DIRT-BAILLIE, *subs.* (Scots').—An inspector of nuisances.

DIRT-SCRAPER *subs.* (American).—An advocate who rakes up unpleasant facts in a witness's past.

DIRTY-DISHES, *subs.* (common).—Poor relations.

DIRTY HALF-HUNDRED, *subs. phr.* (military).—The Fiftieth Foot. [From the fact that, in action, during the Peninsular War, the men wiped their faces with their black facings.] Also nicknamed the BLIND HALF-HUNDRED.

1841. LEVER, *Charles O'Malley*, ch. xciv. A kind of neutral tint between green and yellow, like nothing I know of except the facings of the 'DIRTY HALF-HUNDRED.'

DIRTY-PUZZLE, *subs.* (old). — A slut.—*Grose* [1785].

DIRTY SHIRT MARCH, *subs. phr.* (vulgar).—On Sunday mornings the male population of Drury Lane, Whitechapel, and other crowded districts loaf about the streets, before attiring themselves in their Sunday clothes. This promenade is called a 'DIRTY SHIRT MARCH.'

DIRTY-SHIRTS, *subs.* (military).—The Hundred and First Foot. [They fought in their shirt-sleeves at Delhi in 1857.]

1887. *Daily News*, 11 July. As the old Bengal European Regiment . . . . . they [the 2nd Munster Fusiliers] had won their honourable sobriquet of the DIRTY SHIRTS, half-a-century earlier.

DISGRUNTLED, *adj.* (old).—Offended: still colloquial in U.S.A. UNDISGRUNTLED = unoffended.

1785. GROSE, *Dict. Vulg. Tongue*, s.v.

1869. *Springfield Republican*, 20 Nov. Rev. Dr. Newman Hall, of London, tells how when he was journeying to Chicago, an apple-peddling boy, on the cars, without any preliminaries took hold of and immediately examined his breast-pin. Nevertheless the reverend gentleman, quite UNDISGRUNTLED, remarked, 'Was it not there to be seen? Was he not a man and a brother?'

1877. *Providence Journal*, 1 March. We have had enough exercise of extraordinary power, and this continual grasping after authority for the purpose of meeting the individual case of some DISGRUNTLED persons should receive the stamp of this committee's disapprobation.

DISGUISED, *adj.* (old). — Drunk. For synonyms, *see* DRINKS and SCREWED.

1622. MASSINGER, *Virgin Martyr*, III., iii. *Harp.* I am a prince disguised. *Hir.* DISGUISED! How? Drunk!

1625. JONSON, *Staple of News*, IV. Come, I will shew you the way home, if drink Or too full diet have DISGUISED you.

1663. DRYDEN, *Wild Gallant*, Act I. *Fail.* Will not ale serve the turn, Will? *Bib.* I had too much of that last night; I was a little DISGUISED, as they say.

1704. STEELE, *Lying Lover*, Act IV., Sc. i. *Sim.* You are a little DISGUIS'D in Drink tho' Mr. *John*.

1773. GOLDSMITH, *She Stoops to Conquer*, Act IV. A damned up and down hand, as if it was DISGUISED in liquor.

1884. W. C. RUSSELL, *Jack's Courtship*, ch. xvi. I met a third mate I knew, slightly DISGUISED in liquor.

DISH, *verb* (common).—To cheat; to circumvent; to disappoint; to ruin.

1798. *Monthly Mag.* [quoted in *N. and Q.*, 1 S., iv., p. 313. In the *Monthly Mag.*, in 1798, is a paper on peculiarities of expression among which are . . . 'done up,' DISH'D, etc.

1811. E. NARES, *Thinks I to Myself*, i., 208. He was completely DISHED—he could never have appeared again.

1819. MOORE, *Tom Crib's Memorial*, p. 26. . . . Could old Nap himself, in his glory, have wish'd To *show up* a fat Gemman more handsomely DISH'D?

1821. MONCRIEFF, *Tom and Jerry*, i. 7. No, I'm out of spirits because I have been DISHED and doodled out of forty pounds to-day.

1884. W. C. RUSSELL, *Jack's Courtship*, ch. xvi. I oughtn't to show a youngster like you any sympathy in this job of DISHING a parent's hopes.

DISH-CLOUT, *subs.* (common).—A dirty, slatternly woman.

TO MAKE A NAPKIN OF ONE'S DISH-CLOUT, *verb. phr.* (old).—To marry one's cook; to contract a *mésalliance*.

1785. GROSE, *Dict. Vulg. Tongue*, s.v.

DISHED, *ppl. adj.* (printers').—Said of electrotypes when the centre of a letter is lower than its edges.

DISMAL-DITTY, *subs.* (old). — *See* quot.

1748. T. DYCHE, *Dictionary* (5th ed.). DISMAL DITTY . . . also a cant expression for a psalm sung by a criminal at the gallows (s.v. *Ditty*).

DISPAR, *subs.* (Winchester College). —*See* CAT'S-HEAD.

DISPATCHES, *subs.* (old). — False dice; so contrived as always to throw a nick.—*See* DOCTOR.

1811. VAUX, *Memoirs*, s.v.

1866. *Times*, 27 Nov.

DISSECTING-JOB, *subs.* (tailors').—Garments requiring extensive alteration.

DISTILLER, *subs.* (Australian thieves').—A man easily vexed, and unable to dissemble his condition.

DITTO-BLUES, *subs.* (Winchester College).—A suit of clothes all of blue cloth. *Cf.*, DITTOES.

DITTO BROTHER, or **SISTER, SMUT**. —*See* BROTHER SMUT.

DITTOES, *subs.* (colloquial). — A complete suit of clothes of the same material. Fr., *un complet*, Occasionally applied to trousers only.

1880. HAWLEY SMART, *Social Sinners*, ch. x. A slight, dark man, of middle height, clad in an ordinary suit of DITTOES, entered the room.

1882. JAMES PAYN, *Thicker than Water*, ch. ix. His attire, though quite as faultless and more equable—he was never seen in DITTOS even in September—was not so splendid as of some members of the Aglaia.

DITTY-BAG, *subs.* (common).—A handy bag, used by sailors as a 'huswife.' [From DEFT, DIGHT = neat, active, handy.]

DIVE, *subs.* (American). — A drinking-saloon; also a brothel.

1888. *Troy Daily Times*, 7 Feb. A plot to entrap young women for the DIVES of Northern Wisconsin has been discovered at Eau Claire, Wis.

1888. *St. Louis Globe Democrat*, 27 Feb. Even fallen women, when the rose is gone from their cheeks, are pushed aside, and from a gilded house to the lowest DIVE is the last and quickest step of all.

Verb (old).—To pick pockets. *Cf.*, DIP, and for synonyms, *see* FRISK. Also DIVING = picking pockets.

1631. BEN JONSON, *Metam. Gipsies*. Or using your nimbles [fingers], in DIVING the pockets.

1712 GAY, *Trivia*, bk. III., l., 80. Guard well thy pocket; for these sirens stand To aid the labours of the DIVING hand.

1748. T. DYCHE, *Dictionary* (5th ed.). DIVE (v.) . . . and in the *Canting Language*, to pick pockets in a crowd, church, etc.

1785. GROSE, *Dict. Vulg. Tongue*, s.v.

1859. MATSELL, *Vocabulum, or The Rogue's Lexicon*, s.v.

A DIVE IN THE DARK, *subs. phr.* (venery).—The 'act of kind.'

TO DIVE INTO ONE'S SKY, *verb. phr.* (common).—To put one's hands into one's pockets.

TO DIVE INTO THE WOODS, *verb. phr.* (American).—To conceal oneself.

DIVER, or **DIVE** [*see* quot., 1608], *subs.* (old). — A pickpocket (as Jenny Diver in 'The Beggar's Opera'); A DIP (*q.v.*). For synonyms, *see* STOOK-HAULER.

1608. DEKKER, *Belman of London*, in wks. (Grosart), III., 140. [One who steals from houses by putting a boy in through a window to hand out to him the plunder—is called a DIVER.]

c. 1626. *Dick of Devonshire*, in Bullen's *Old Plays*, ii., 40. Your horse and weapons I will take, but no pilferage. I am no pocketeer, no DIVER into slopps.

1705. WARD, *Hudibras Redivivus*, vol. I., pt. i., p. 24 [2nd ed.). So expert DIVERS call aloud, Pray mind your pockets, to the crowd.

1748. T. DYCHE, *Dictionary* (5th ed.). DIVER (s.) . . . also a cant name for a pick-pocket.

1828. JON. BEE, *Picture of London*, p. 56. Thieves frequently go well-dressed, especially pickpockets; good *toggery* being considered a necessary qualification for his calling, without which the DIVER could not possibly mix in genteel company nor approach such in the streets.

1887. BAUMANN, *Londismen*, V. Smashers and DIVERS and noble contrivers.

DIVERS, *subs.* (common). — The fingers. For synonyms, *see* FORKS.

DIVIDE THE HOUSE WITH ONE'S WIFE, *verb. phr.* (old).—To turn her out of doors.

DIVING-BELL, *subs.* (common).—A cellar-tavern. *Cf.*, DIVE. For synonyms, *see* LUSH-CRIB.

DO, *subs.* (colloquial).—1. A fraud.

1812. VAUX, *Memoirs*, s.v.

1835. DICKENS, *Sketches by Boz*, p. 17. I thought it was a DO, to get me out of the house.

1837. R. H. BARHAM. *Ingoldsby Legends.* (ed. 1862.) p. 418. I should like to see you Try to *sauter le coup* With this chap at short whist or unlimited loo, By the Pope you'd soon find it a regular DO.

1846. *Punch*, vol. XI., p. 114. What is the meaning of the rise? I'm sure I cannot tell—can you? Yes, fame with hundred tongues replies, 'Tis in one word A DO! A DO!

2. (colloquial). — One's duty; a success; performance what one has to do; once literary.

1663-78. BUTLER, *Hudibras*. No sooner does he peep into the world but he has done his DOE.

1851. H. MAYHEW, *Lon. Lab. and Lon. Poor*, vol. I., p. 162. Well, I heard how a man . . . was making a fortune at the hot-eel and pea-soup line. . . . So I thought I'd have a touch at the same thing. But you see I never could rise money enough to make a DO of it.

Verb (colloquial). — 1. To cheat. For synonyms, *see* GAMMON.

1789. GEO. PARKER, *Life's Painter*, p. 142. Who are continually looking out for flats, in order to DO them upon the *broads*, that is, *cards*.

1803. KENNEY, *Raising the Wind*, I., i. I wasn't born two hundred miles north of Lunnun, to be DONE by Mr. Diddler, I know.

1831. DISRAELI, *The Young Duke*, bk. iv., ch. vi., p. 220 (ed. 1866). There was the juvenile Lord Dice, who boasted of having DONE his brothers out of their miserable £5,000.

1835. DICKENS, *Sketches by Boz*, p. 265. I should have a much better opinion of an individual if he'd say at once, in an honourable and gentlemanly manner, as he'd DONE everybody he possibly could.

1843. *Comic Almanack*, p. 373. England expects every man to do his duty, a strong recommendation to every man 'to DO' the authorities who collect the duty at the Custom-house.

1871. *Public Opinion*, 4 Feb. Do you suppose that you can do the landlord in the 'Lady of Lyons?' asked a theatrical manager of a seedy actor in quest of an engagement. If I can't DO him, was the reply, he will be the first landlord I ever had anything to do with that wasn't DONE by me.

1889. *Answers*, 9 Feb. The regular hotel thieves are constantly inventing new dodges to DO us.

2. (pugilistic).—To 'punish.'

3. (common). — To visit a place; *e.g.*, 'to DO Italy,' 'to DO the Row,' 'to DO the High' (at Oxford), etc. Early quots. are given; latterly the phrase is common enough. The Fr., *faire* is used in the same sense; *faire ses Acacias*, *i.e.*, to walk or drive in the *Allée des Acacias*.

1857. G. A. LAWRENCE, *Guy Livingstone*, ch. xxxii. We DID Venice very severely, with the exception of Forrester, who . . . declined seeing anything more than what he could view from his gondola.

1858. SHIRLEY BROOKS, *The Gordian Knot*, p. 53. You have been in Egypt? asked Margaret, with much interest. I DID Egypt, as they say, about two years back, [said Philip].

4. (colloquial).—To perform; to 'come'; *e.g.*, TO DO THE POLITE = to be polite; TO DO A BOOK = to write one; TO DO THE HEAVY, THE GRAND, or THE GENTEEL = to put on airs.

1767. COLMAN, *Eng. Merchant*, I., in wks. (1777), ii. 17. I compose pamphlets on all subjects, compile magazines, and DO newspapers.

1835. DICKENS, *Sketches by Boz*, p. 224. He used to talk politics to papas, flatter the vanity of mammas, DO the amiable to their daughters.

1836. DICKENS, *Pickwick*, ch. xv., p. 125. There was the young lady who DID the poetry in the Eatanswill Gazette, in the garb of a sultana.

1855. THACKERAY, *Newcomes*, ch. xxiv. A great number of the descriptions in Cook's Voyages, for instance, were notoriously invented by Dr. Hawkesworth, who DID the book.

1856. WHYTE MELVILLE, *Kate Coventry*, ch. iii. A vision of John DOING the polite, and laughing as he ceremoniously introduced Captain Lovell and Miss Coventry.

1864. *Glasgow Citizen*, 29 Nov. Is not the exhilarating short-length of being known beyond our own Queen Street that it is not registered here? And we miss the rag trade whose worthy members DO the above-named *goes*.

1880. MILLIKEN, *Punch's Almanack*. Nobby button 'oler very well, When one wants to DO the 'eavy swell.

5. (counterfeiters'). — To utter base coin or QUEER (*q.v.*).

DO AS I DO, *phr.* (common).—An invitation to drink. — *See* DRINKS.

TO DO A BEER, or A BITTER, or A DRINK, or A DROP, *verb. phr.* (common). — To take a drink.

1853. BRADLEY ('Cuthbert Bede'), *Verdant Green*, ch. x. TO DO BITTERS, as Mr. Bouncer phrased the act of drinking bitter beer.

1880. MILLIKEN, *Punch's Almanack*. Got the doldrums dreadful, that is clear, Two *d* left!—must go and DO A BEER.

TO DO A BILK.—*See* BILK.

TO DO A BILL, *verb. phr.* (commercial).—To utter an acceptance or bill of exchange. *Cf.*, TO FLY PAPER or KITES.

1837. R. H. BARHAM, *Ingoldsby Legends* [ed. 1862], p. 257. Now, then, old sinner, let's hear what you'll say As to DOING A BILL at three months from to-day.

1849. THACKERAY, *Pendennis*, ch. lxii. Sir Francis Clavering . . . had managed to sign his respectable name to a piece of stamped paper, which . . . Mr. Moss ABRAMS had carried off, promising to have the BILL DONE by a party with whose intimacy Mr. Abrams was favoured.

TO DO A BISHOP, *verb. phr.* (military).—To parade at short notice.

TO DO A BIT, *verb. phr.* (common). — To eat something. *Cf.*, TO DO A BEER. Also (venery), to have a woman.

TO DO A BUNK or SHIFT, *verb. phr.* (vulgar). — To ease nature.—*See* BURY A QUAKER and

Do. 295 Do.

MRS. JONES. Also (colloquial), to go away.

TO DO A CRIB, *verb. phr.* (thieves').—To break into a house, to burgle. Fr., *maquiller une cambriole.* For synonyms, *see* CRACK A CRIB.

TO DO A GUY, *verb. phr.* (thieves').—I. To run away; to make an escape. [From DO, verb of action + GUY, an escape.] For synonyms, *see* AMPUTATE and SKEDADDLE.

1889. *Answers*, 6 April, p. 297. They all dispersed at once—to put it in their own language, they DID A GUY.

2. (workman's). — To absent oneself when supposed to be at work.

TO DO A NOB, *verb. phr.* (circus and showmen's). — To make a collection.

TO DO A PITCH.—*See* PITCH.

TO DO A RUSH.—*See* RUSH.

TO DO A SNATCH. — *See* SNATCH.

TO DO A STAR PITCH, *verb. phr.* (theatrical).—To sleep in the open air. Fr., *loger à la belle étoile.* For synonyms, *see* HEDGE SQUARE.

TO DO A BROWN.—*See* under BROWN; also BAMBOOZLE. Also TO DO BROWN and TO DO IT UP BROWN.

TO DO FOR, *verb. phr.* (common).—I. To ruin. Also, to kill, in which sense, *cf.*, quots., 1650 and 1877. For synonyms, *see* DEAD BROKE and COOK ONE'S GOOSE respectively.

1650. HOWELL, *Familiar Letters.* The Emperor, who, rather than becom

captif to the base Tartar, burnt his castle, and DID AWAY himself, his thirty wives, and children.

1752. FIELDING, *Amelia*, bk. vi., ch. iv. He said something, too, about my master . . . he said he would DO FOR him, I am sure he said that; and other wicked, bad words, too, if I could but think of them.

1811. JANE AUSTEN, *Sense and S.*, ch. xli. He has DONE FOR himself completely! shut himself out for ever from all decent society!

1877. *Five Years' Penal Servitude*, ch. iii., p 233. He called out, He's DONE FOR me; he's DONE FOR me; send at once for Doctor Howell.

2. (common).—To attend on (as landladies' on lodgers).

3. (thieves').—To convict; to sentence. DONE FOR=convicted.

TO DO A GRIND, A MOUNT, A TREAD, etc., *verb. phr.* (venery). —To copulate.

TO DO or PLAY GOOSEBERRY. —*See* GOOSEBERRY.

TO DO GOSPEL, *verb. phr.* (common).—To go to church.

TO DO THE HANDSOME or THE HANDSOME THING, *verb. phr.* (colloquial).—To behave extremely well to one.

TO DO IT AWAY, *verb. phr.* (thieves').—To dispose of stolen goods. Also TO DO THE SWAG (*q.v.*); TO FENCE (*q.v.*).

TO DO IT ON THE B. H., *verb. phr.* (common).—To perform with ease. [B=bloody; H=head].

1877. *Five Years' Penal Servitude*, ch. iii., p. 221. 'What's yer dose?' Looking on to my badge, 'Five, oh, you can do that little lot on yer 'ED EASY.'

TO DO IT UP, *verb. phr.* (old). —To accomplish an object in view; to obtain one's quest. TO DO IT UP IN GOOD TWIG=to live an easy life by one's wits.

TO DO ONE PROUD, *phr.* (colloquial). — To flatter: *e.g.*, Will you drink?' 'You DO ME PROUD.'

1836. W. G. CLARK, *Ollapodriana Papers.* To this damsel I addressed myself, and solicited her hand in the dance. She assented; and with my brain reeling with fancies of wine and women, I really thought, for the moment, that 'she DID ME PROUD.'

1887. SIDNEY LUSKA, *Land of Love*, in 'Lippincott's Mag.,' p. 241. Ah? So? The frank confession DOES YOU PROUD.

TO DO OUT, *verb. phr.* (American thieves').—To plead guilty and exonerate an accomplice.

TO DO OVER, *verb. phr.* (common).—I. To knock down; to persuade; to cheat; to ruin.

1789. GEO. PARKER, *Life's Painter*, p. 50. Who could, at any time, DO him OVER, as they phrased it, for half-a-crown or half-a-guinea.

1836. C. DICKENS, *Pickwick Papers*, p. 326 (ed. 1857). Well, said Sam, he's in a horrid state o' love; reg'larly comfoozled, and DONE OVER with it.

2. (thieves').—To search a victim's pockets without his knowing it. *Cf.*, RUN THE RULE OVER.

3. (venery). — To seduce; also to copulate. For synonyms, *see* DOCK and RIDE respectively.

TO DO POLLY, *verb. phr.* (American prison). — To pick oakum in gaol.

1859. MATSELL, *Vocabulum, or the Rogue's Lexicon*, s.v.

TO DO ONE'S BUSINESS, *verb. phr.* (common).—To kill. For synonyms, *see* COOK ONE'S GOOSE. *Cf.*, BUSINESS. Also (vulgar), to evacuate; and (venery), to serve a woman.

1750. FIELDING, *Tom Jones*, bk. VIII., ch. x. He concluded he had pretty well DONE THEIR BUSINESS, for both of them, as they ran off, cried out with bitter oaths, that they were dead men.

1849. THACKERAY, *Pendennis*, ch. xii. Then he took down his venerable and murderous duelling-pistols, with flint locks, that had DONE THE BUSINESS of many a pretty fellow in Dublin.

1856. C. READE, *Never Too Late*, ch. xvi. She was stronger than he was for a moment or two, and that moment would have DONE HIS BUSINESS. She meant killing.

TO DO THE DOWNY, *verb. phr.* (common). — To lie in bed. DOWNY FLEA PASTURE=a bed. *Cf.*, BALMY.

1841. LEMAN REDE, *Sixteen-String Jack*, Act i., Sc. vi. *Jer.* The family's GONE TO DOWNY NAP this half-hour. Why don't the captain give the signal.

1853. C. BEDE, *Verdant Green*, pt. ii., p. 59. This'll never do, Giglamps! Cutting chapel TO DO THE DOWNY.

TO DO THE SWAG, *verb. phr.* (thieves').—To sell stolen property, Fr., *laver la camelote* or *les fourgueroles. Cf.*, TO DO CLOBBER.

TO DO THE TRICK, *verb. phr.* (colloquial). —To accomplish one's object; specifically (venery), to do the 'act of kind' effectually, and (for woman), to get rid of one's maidenhead.

1864. *Derby Day*, p. 38. If the little 'un don't DO THE TRICK me an' him'll fall out.

1870-2. *Gallery of Comicalities.* Star of the stable ! Ostler Dick, Still in your calling wide awake; I warrant you can DO THE TRICK—A cunning cove, and no mistake.

18(?). W. C. RUSSELL, *Representative Actors*, p. 476. Edmund Kean then whispered in his son's ear 'Charlie, we are DOING THE TRICK.'

TO DO TIME, *verb. phr.* (thieves').—To serve a term of imprisonment.

1871. *Times*, Dec. Both . . . fled to New York to save DOING TIME on the treadmill.

1884. *Cornhill Mag.*, June, p. 614. He has repeatedly DONE TIME for drunks and disorderlies, and for assaults upon the police.

1888. *Referee*, 15 April, 3, 1. The robbers-in-chief, who had DONE TIME before, were sentenced to five years' penal servitude.

TO DO TO DEATH, *verb. phr.* (colloquial).—To repeat *ad nauseam.*

TO DO TO TIE TO, *verb. phr.* (American).—To be fit to associate with; to be trustworthy.

TO DO UP, *verb. phr.* (common).—To use up; finish; or quiet. DONE UP = tired out; ruined; 'sold up.' For synonyms, *see* FLOORED.

1594. NASHE, *Unf. Traveller*, in wks. v., 170. I was cleane spent and DONE, there was no hope of me.

1667. DRYDEN, *Ann. Mir.*, st. 70. Not so the Holland fleet, who, tired and DONE, Stretch'd on their decks like weary oxen lie.

1815. SCOTT, *Guy Mannering*, ch. xxxiv. 'How did he get back from India?' 'Why, how should I know? The house there was DONE UP, and that gave us a shake at Middleburgh.'

1831. DISRAELI, *The Young Duke*, bk. iv., ch. xii., p. 245 (ed. 1866), 'The Universe' and 'The New World' announced that the young duke was DONE UP.

1851-61. H. MAYHEW, *London Lab. and Lon. Poor*, vol. iii., p. 264. A man's DONE UP at fifty, and seldom lives long after, if he has to keep on at coal-portering.

1870. L. OLIPHANT, *Piccadilly*, pt. iii., p. 130. I am awfully DONE, said Spiffy. I never went to bed at all last night.

[For the rest, DO, like CHUCK and COP, is a verb-of-all-work, and is used in every possible and impossible connection. Thus, TO DO REASON and TO DO RIGHT= to honour a toast; TO DO A BIT OF STIFF = to draw a bill; TO DO A CHUCK = to eject, or to go away; TO DO A RUB-UP

=to masturbate; TO DO A SIP (back slang) = to make water; TO DO A CAT = to vomit; TO DO A HALL or A THEATRE= to visit a music hall or a playhouse; TO DO A FLUFF (theatrical)=to forget one's part; TO DO A PITCH (showman's or street artists') =to go through a performance; TO DO A MOUCH or A MIKE= to go on the prowl; TO DO A GROUSE = to go questing for women; TO DO A DOSS = to go to sleep; TO DO A CADGE=to go begging; TO DO A TUMBLE or A SPREAD=to lie down to a man; TO DO A PERPENDICULAR or KNEE-TREMBLER=to copulate standing; TO DO A SCRAP=to engage in combat; TO DO A RURAL =to 'rear' by the wayside; TO DO A DIVE in THE DARK=to copulate; etc.

DOASH, *subs.* (Old Cant).—A cloak. For synonyms, *see* CAPELLA.

DOBBIN, *subs.* (old). — Ribbon. DOBBIN RIG=stealing ribbon.

DOCK, *subs.* (printers'). — I. The weekly work bill or POLE (*q.v.*).

2. (popular).—The hospital.

Verb (old).—I. To deflower; hence, by implication, to possess; [Gypsy *dükker*, to ravish]. Feminine analogues are TO HAVE DONE THE TRICK; TO HAVE HAD IT; TO HAVE DONE IT AT LAST; TO BE CRACKED IN THE RING; TO HAVE BROKEN HER TEA-CUP; TO HAVE HAD IT THERE; TO HAVE GONE STAR-GAZING ON HER BACK; TO HAVE GIVEN HER PUSSY A TASTE OF CREAM; TO HAVE LET THE PONY OVER THE DYKE (Scots'); TO HAVE BROKEN HER KNEES or HER LEG; TO HAVE SPRAINED HER ANKLE. Fr., *avoir vu le loup; laisser aller le chat au fromage;* and *avoir vu la lune;* whilst *l'avoir encore* and *avoir encore l'avoine* is said of maids. Sp., *desvirgar* = to deflower: DOCKED=possessed.

1567. HARMAN, *Caveat* [ed. 1869, E. E. T. Soc.], p. 87. He DOKTE the dell.

1609. DEKKER, *Lanthorne and Candlelight.* 'Canting Rithmes.' DOCKED the dell for a Coper meke.

1611. MIDDLETON and DEKKER, *Roaring Girl*, v., 1. And couch till a pallyard DOCKED my dell.

2. (Winchester College).—To scratch out; to tear out (as from a book); also to strike down.

TO GO INTO DOCK, *verb. phr.* (nautical).—To undergo salivation.

TO BE DOCKED SMACK SMOOTH, *verb. phr.* (old).—To have suffered amputation of the *penis.*

DOCKER, *subs.* (legal).—I. A brief handed to counsel by a prisoner in the dock. Legal etiquette compels acceptance if 'marked' with a minimum fee of £1 3s. 6d.

2. (colloquial). — A dock labourer.

DOCK-WALLOPER, *subs.* (American).—A loafer; one who loiters about docks and wharves; also an unemployed emigrant.

1871. DE VERE, *Americanisms*, p. 344. . . A DOCK-WALLOPER is an object of great contempt to Jack.

DOCKYARDER, *subs.* (nautical).— A skulker. *Cf.*, STRAWYARDER (*q.v.*).

DOCKYARD-HORSE, *subs.* (naval).— An officer better at correspondence than at active service.

DOCTOR, *subs.* (old). — I. A false die; sometimes a manipulated card.—*See* TO PUT THE DOCTOR ON ONE.

1688. SHADWELL, *Sq. of Alsatia*, I., in wks. (1720), iv., 18. *Belf. Sen. Tatts*, and DOCTOR! what's that? *Sham.* The tools of sharpers, false dice.

1709. CENTLIVRE, *Gamester*, Act i. Now, sir, here is your true dice, a man seldom gets anything by them; here is your false, sir; hey, how they run! Now, sir, those we generally call DOCTORS.

1750. FIELDING, *Tom Jones.* Here, said he, taking some dice out of his pockets, here are the little DOCTORS which cure the distempers of the purse.

1822. SCOTT, *Fortunes of Nigel*, ch. xxxiii. A gamester, one who deals with the devil's bones and the DOCTORS.

1823. SCOTT, *Peveril*, ch. xxviii. The dicers with their DOCTORS in their pockets, I presume.

2. (common).—An adulterant. *Cf.*, TO KEEP THE DOCTOR.

1785. GROSE, *Dict. Vulg. Tongue*, s.v. A composition used by distillers to make spirits appear stronger than they really are.

1828. G. SMEATON, *Doings in London.* Maton, in his 'Tricks of Bakers Unmasked,' says alum, which is called the DOCTOR, ground and unground, is sold to the bakers at fourpence per pound.

3. (licensed victuallers'). — Brown sherry. [Because a 'doctored' (*q.v.*) wine. *Cf.*, sense 2.]

4. (nautical and up-country Australian).—A ship's cook.

5. (Winchester College).—The head master.

1870. MANSFIELD, *School Life at Winchester College*, p. 27. The head master, or the DOCTOR as he is always called, lives in 'Commoners' buildings.

6. (Old gamesters').—The last throw of dice or ninepins.

Verb (common).—I. To patch; adulterate; falsify; 'cook.'

1837. R. H. BARHAM, *Ingoldsby Legends* [ed. 1862], p. 464. She DOCTOR'D the punch and she DOCTOR'D the negus, Taking care not to put in sufficient to flavour it.

1862. H. GREELEY, in *N. Y. Independent.* The news [of success to the United States armies, said the English leading journals] all came through Northern channels, and was DOCTORED by the government which controlled the telegraph.

2. (sporting).—To poison a horse.

TO KEEP THE DOCTOR, *verb. phr.* (licensed victuallers').—To make a practice of adulterating the liquor sold. *Cf.*, DOCTOR, *subs.*, sense 2.

TO PUT THE DOCTOR ON ONE, *verb. phr.* (common).—To cheat.

DOCTOR DRAW-FART, *subs. phr.* (common).—A wandering quack.

DOCTORED, *ppl. adj.* (common).—Patched; adulterated; falsified; 'cooked.'

1866. G. ELIOT, *Felix Holt*, ch. xxviii. The Cross-keys . . . had DOCTORED ale, an odour of bad tobacco, and remarkably strong cheese.

DOD BURN IT! *intj.phr.* (American). A euphemistic oath; on the model of DADBINGED (*q.v.*).

DODDER, *subs.* (Irish).—Burnt tobacco taken from the bottom of a pipe and placed on the top of a fresh plug to give a stronger flavor.

DODDERER, *subs.* (street). — A meddler; always used in contempt. Sometimes DODDERING OLD SHEEP'S HEAD, which also = a fool.

DODDY, *subs.* (provincial). — In Norfolk a person of low stature. Sometimes HODMANDOD and HODDY-DODDY, all head and no body. DODMAN in the same dialect = a snail.

DODFETCHED, *adj.* (American).—A euphemistic oath. [Dod = God.] Most of its kind have originated in New England, where the descendants of the Puritans form the largest portion of the population.

1888. *Texas Siftings*, 7 July. Then the poet was sore grieved, and he said unto himself, 'I'm a DODFETCHED fool.'

DODGASTED, *adj.* (American).—*See* DODFETCHED.

1888. *Detroit Free Press.* It's a DODGASTED funny thing, Uncle Zeke, but it's a fact, never knew it to fail; straight as a string, too.

DODGE, *subs.* and *verb*, [and derivative. DODGING, *verb. subs.*] (colloquial). — To trick; to swindle; to elude. Once slang, now recognised. Used in various combinations: THE PIOUS DODGE = a pretence of piety; THE TIDY-DODGE = begging in the streets with tidily but poorly dressed children, etc. Also, to 'nart.' For synonyms, *see* LAY.

1708. SWIFT, *Abolishing of Christianity* in prose wks. (Camelot Cl.), p. 235. The chaffering with Dissenters, and DODGING about this or the other ceremony.

1754. B. MARTIN, *Eng. Dict.* (2nd ed.). To DODGE . . . 2. To be off and on. 3. To prevaricate, or play shifting tricks.

1836. C. DICKENS, *Pickwick Papers*, p. 135 (ed. 1857). 'It was all false, of course?' 'All, sir,' replied Mr. Weller, 'reg'lar do, sir; artful DODGE.'

1851-61. H. MAYHEW, *London Lab. and Lon. Poor*, vol. i., p. 227. Conscious how much their own livelihood depends upon assumption and trickery, they naturally consider that others have some DODGE, as they call it, or some latent object in view when any good is sought to be done them.

1856. *Punch*, vol. XXXI., p. 217. Long though your sentence and your task severe, The pious DODGE a ticket soon will send.

1865. *Spectator*, 2 Dec., *Women's Tact.* [Mrs. Caudle.] Nagged, and

nagging is universally useful only with maids. She lost her temper occasionally, and the suffering angel DODGE is a very much more effective as well as Christian resource.

1865. *Spectator* (On the Academy Dinner), p. 492. Earl Russell . . . broke loose from one conventionality of public dinners to fall into another. He DODGED the toast of Her Majesty's Ministers, and did not promise the Academy.

1883. *Daily Telegraph*, 23 March, p. 6, col. 1. He is naturally anxious to ascertain if any new DODGE has been brought to light, and what was the amount of the penalty imposed for its perpetration.

DODGER, *subs.* (common).—1. A trickster. *Cf.*, The 'Artful Dodger' (DICKENS, *Oliver Twist*, ch. viii.). Fr., *être ficelle* = 'to be a dodger.'

1611. COTGRAVE, *Dict.*, *Caqueraffe*, a base micher, scurvie hagler, lowsie DODGER, etc.

1825. SCOTT, *St. Ronan's Well*, ch. xxviii. A sly cock, this Frank Tyrrel, thought the traveller; a very complete DODGER—but no matter—I shall wind him, were he to double like a fan.

1887. BAUMANN, *Londonismen*, vi. So from hartful young DODGERS, From vaxy old codgers, From the blowens ve got Soon to know vot is vot.

2. (popular).—A dram; provincially, a NIGHTCAP. For synonyms, *see* GO.

3. (American).—A hard-baked cake or biscuit, more usually termed CORN-DODGER. When mixed with beef, BEEF-DODGERS.

4. (American).—A handbill.

1888. *Texas Siftings*, 15 Sept. Then I would have a great quantity of little DODGERS printed to throw around everywhere.

DODO, *subs.* (old). — A stupid, old man.

DODROTTED, *ppl. adj.* (American). —A euphemistic oath. *See* OATHS.

1887. *Century Magazine.* You ketch us with yer DODROTTED foolin', says he; we hain't the kind to be fooled.

DOES IT? *phr.* (common).—A sarcastic retort.—*See* DOES YOUR MOTHER KNOW YOU'RE OUT?

DOES YOUR MOTHER KNOW YOU'RE OUT? *phr.* (streets').—A popular locution, vague as to meaning and inexact in application—an expression expressive of contempt, incredulity, sarcasm, anything you please.—*See* ALL MY EYE, STREET CRIES, and *infra*.

ENGLISH VARIANTS. — Has your mother sold her mangle? Not to-day, or it won't do, Mr. Ferguson! Sawdust and treacle! Draw it mild! And the rest! Who are you? All round my hat! Go it, ye cripples! Shoo, fly! How does the old thing work? Well, you know how it is yourself! How's your poor feet? Why, certainly! I'll have your whelk! Not to-day, baker, call to-morrow, and we'll take a crusty one! Do you see any green in my eye? Put that in your pipe and smoke it! Where are you going on Sunday? Go to Putney! Who stole the donkey: the man in the white hat! Cough, Julia! Over the bender! There you go with your eye out! etc., etc.

FRENCH VARIANTS.—*Et les mois de nourrice* = (and the rest!); *du combustible* (popular: = go it you cripples); *tu t'en ferais péter le cylindre* (popular: = don't you wish you may get it); *chiche!* (popular: a defiant refusal); *chaleur!* (popular: expressive of contempt, disbelief, and ironical admiration); *croyez ça et buvez de l'eau* (popular: = believe that and

drink water); *à Chaillot* = 'go to Bath and get your head shaved'); *tu t'en ferais crèver* (pop.: = don't you wish you may get it); *colle-toi ça dans l'cornet* (pop.: = put that in your pipe and smoke it!) *je la connais* (pop.: = do you see any green?'); *j'entrave pas dans tes vannes* (thieves': = you don't take me in); *de la bourrache!* (popular: = no go); *un sale truc pour la fanfare* (popular: an expression of disgust); *de quoi* (popular: what next? also = wealth, money, etc.); *allez donc raconter cela à dache* (thieves': = tell that to the marines!); *des dattes!* (pop.: = take a carrot!); *et ta sœur* (popular: indicative of refusal, contempt, and insult); *faut pas m'la faire* (popular: = Walker!); *et le pouce* (pop.: = and the rest!)

1841. *Punch*, vol. I., p. 6, col. 2. Where are they that *should* protect thee In this darkling hour of doubt? Love *could* never thus neglect thee! DOES YOUR MOTHER KNOW YOU'RE OUT?

1864. *Sun*, 28 Dec. 'Review of Hotten's Slang Dictionary.' Ridiculous street cries, such as DOES YOUR MOTHER KNOW YOU'RE OUT? or, Has your Aunt sold her mangle? or, You don't lodge here, Mr. Fergusson — whatever those sapient remarks may mean.

DOG, *subs.* (colloquial).—1. A man; sometimes used contemptuously (*Cf.*, Cat = a woman), but more frequently in half-serious chiding; *e.g.*, a sad DOG, gay DOG, old DOG, etc. For synonyms, *see* COVE. Sometimes adjectively = male; *see* quot., 1856. AN OLD DOG AT IT = expert, or accustomed to.

1596. NASHE, *Have with you*, Epis. Ded. par. 5. O, he hath been olde DOGGE at that drunken, staggering kinde of verse.

1697. VANBRUGH, *Æsop*, part II., Sc. iii. Why, I'm a strong young DOG, you old gent, you.

1703. MRS. CENTLIVRE, *Stolen Heiress*, I., wks. (1872), i., 336. She is in love, forsooth, with a young beggarly DOG not worth a groat.

1736. FIELDING, *Don Quixote*, II. iv. A comical DOG, I fancy; go, give my service to him.

b. 1764, *d.* 1817. J. G. HOLMAN, *Abroad and at Home*, I., 3. And my praise to withhold none so currish, With a girl so divine! Such dinners! such wine! What a d—d clever DOG was Jack Flourish!

1810. CRABBE, *The Borough*, Letter 6, *Law.* For he'd a way that many judg'd polite, A cunning DOG—he'd fawn before he'd bite.

1836. C. DICKENS, *Pickwick Papers*, p. 369. (ed. 1857). Curse me, they're friends of mine from this minute and friends of Mivins, too. Infernal pleasant, gentlemenly, DOG Mivins, isn't he? said Smangle, with great feeling.

1856. WHYTE MELVILLE, *Kate Coventry*, ch. vii. Then comes Ascot, for which meeting they leave the metropolis, and enjoy some quiet retreat in the neighbourhood of Windsor, taking with them many potables, and what *they* call a DOG cook.

2. (thieves').—A burglar's iron. For synonyms, *see* JEMMY.

1888. *American Humorist*, 31 Mar. The safe was rifled, and every appearance of robbery was manifest. In this case the murderer was discovered by means of a DOG, which was described in the newspapers as having certain peculiar scratches on it.

Verb (venery). — To copulate on all fours.

TO GO, OR THROW TO THE DOGS.—*See* GO and DEMNITION BOW-WOWS.

HAIR OF THE DOG THAT BIT YOU.—*See* HAIR.

TO BLUSH LIKE A BLUE DOG. —*See* BLUSH.

DOGBERRY, *subs.* (common).—A stupid constable, or magistrate. [From *Much Ado about Nothing.*] For synonyms, *see* BEAK and COPPER.

1864. M. E. BRADDON, *Aurora Floyd*, ch. xxxviii. The detective had reason to know that the DOGBERRIES of Doncaster, . . were on the wrong scent.

1869. *Gent. Mag.*, July, p. 195. I trust I shall not be accounted a DOGBERRY, lavish in my tediousness, if I bestow one more anecdote upon my readers.

DOG BITING DOG, *adv. phr.* (theatrical). — Said of actors who spitefully criticise each others performance.

DOG-CHEAP, *adj.* (colloquial). — Very cheap; of little worth; foolish. [SKEAT: from Swed., *dog*, = very; LATHAM: the first syllable is god = good, transposed + CHEAP, from chapman, a merchant—hence, a good bargain (Fr., *bon marché*).]

1598. SHAKSPEARE, 1 *Henry IV.*, iii. 3. The sack . . . would have bought me lights as GOOD-CHEAP at the dearest chandler's in Europe.

1606. DEKKER, *Newes from Hell*, in wks. (Grosart), ii., 116. Three things there are DOG-CHEAP, learning, poore men's sweat, and others.

1663. DRYDEN, *Wild Gallant*, Act II. No fat over-grown virgin of forty ever offered herself so DOG CHEAP, or was more despised.

1772. FOOTE, *Nabob*, Act II. DOG-CHEAP; neck-beef; a penny-loaf for a halfpenny.

1830. MARRYAT, *King's Own*, ch. xxx. I'll sell mine, DOG-CHEAP, if any one will buy it.

1851. CARLYLE, *John Sterling*, pt. I., ch. x. There lay in a certain neighbouring creek ot the Irish coast, a worn-out royal gun-brig condemned to sale, to be had DOG-CHEAP.

DOG-COLLAR, *subs.* (common).—A 'stand-up' shirt collar; an ALL-ROUNDER (*q.v.*).

1883. GRENVILLE-MURRAY, *People I have Met*, p. 42. The DOG-COLLAR which rose above the black cloth was of spotless purity.

DOG-DRAWN (old), *adj. phr.*—Said of a bitch from which a dog has been removed by force during coition. Sometimes applied to women.

DOGGER, *verb* (Charterhouse).—To cheat; to sell rubbish.

DOGGERY, *subs.* (popular). — 1. Transparent cheating. *Cf.*, DOGGER.

[Carlyle in *Frederick* uses DOGGERY = the doings of a scurvy set of soldiers.]

2. (American).—A low drinking saloon.

1871. DE VERE, *Americanisms*, p. 315. DOGGERIES are only found near the shanties of Irish laborers or in remote western and southern settlements.

DOGGONED, *adj.* (American).—A euphemistic oath.—*See* OATHS.

1852. GLADSTONE, *Englishman in Kansas*, p. 46. If there's a DOG-GONED abolitionist aboard this boat, I should like to see him. I'm the man to put a chunk o' lead into his woolly head right off.

1873. CARLTON, *Farm Ballads*, p. 80. But when that choir got up to sing, I couldn't catch a word; They sung the most DOG-GONDEST thing A body ever heard!

1879. EGGLESTON, *The Hoosier Schoolmaster.* I never knowed but one gal in my life as had cyphered into fractions, and she was so DOG ON stuck up, that she turned up her nose one night at an *applepeelin'* bekase I tuck a sheet off the bed to splice out the table-cloth, which was rather short.

DOGGY, *subs.* (mining).—*See* quot.

1845. DISRAELI, *Sybil*, bk. III. ch. i., note. A Batty in the mining districts is a middleman; a DOGGY is his manager.

Adj. (colloquial). — 1. Connected with, or relating to dogs.

1883. *Graphic*, 24 Feb., p. 199. col. 3. Liverpool and the Adelphi Hotel in particular, are now [time of Altcar coursing meeting] the headquarters of all the DOGGY men of the three kingdoms.

2. (colloquial).—Stylish.

DOG IN A BLANKET, *subs. phr.* (colloquial).—A pudding of preserved fruit spread on thin dough, rolled up, and boiled; also called ROLY-POLY and STOCKING.

1887. G. A. SALA, in *Ill. Lon. News*, 12 Feb., p. 174, col. 3. Bubble and squeak . . . is a colloquialism, and no more slangy than 'toad in the hole' or DOG IN A BLANKET.

LIKE A DOG IN SHOES, *adv. phr.* (Irish).—A pattering sound; as the noise of a brisk walk.

DOG IN THE MANGER, *subs. phr.* (colloquial). — A selfish churl; who does not want himself, yet will not let others enjoy. [From the fable.]

1621. BURTON, *Anat. of Mel.*, I., II., III., xii., 189 (1836). Like a hog, or DOG IN THE MANGER, he doth only keep it, because it shall do nobody else good.

1673. DRYDEN, *Amboyna*, Act ii. You're like DOGS IN THE MANGER, you will neither manage it yourselves nor permit your neighbours.

1757. GARRICK, *Irish Widow*, II. That's the DOG IN THE MANGER; you can't eat the oats, and won't let those who can.

1836. MARRYAT, *Japhet*, ch. lxxii. Why, what a DOG IN THE MANGER you must be—you can't marry them both.

DOG-LATIN, *subs.* (colloquial). — Barbarous or sham Latin; also KITCHEN, BOG, GARDEN, or APOTHECARIES' LATIN.

1856. H. MAYHEW, *Great World of London*, p. 149. A Spaniard . . . who called himself a physician, and who, being unable to speak English, communicated with the doctor in a kind of Spanish DOG-LATIN.

DOGS, *subs.* (university).—1. Sausages; otherwise BAGS OF MYSTERY (*q.v.*), or CHAMBERS OF HORRORS (*q.v.*).

2. (Stock Exchange).—Newfoundland Land Company's shares; now amalgamated with the Anglo-American United, and called ANGLOS.

TO GO TO THE DOGS.—*See* under GO.

TO LET SLEEPING DOGS LIE.—*See* SLEEPING DOGS.

DOG'S-BODY, *subs.* (nautical).—Pease pudding.

1851. *Chambers' Papers*, No. 52, p. 16. Peas-pudding (*alias* DOG'S BODY) is often allowed upon pork days.

1883. W. CLARK RUSSELL, *Sailors' Language*, p. 42. DOGS-BODY.—A mess made of pea-soup, powdered biscuit, and slush.

1889. *Chambers' Journal*, 3 Aug., p. 495, col. 1.

DOG'S-EARED, *adj.* (colloquial).—Crumpled, as the leaves of a page with much reading.

DOG'S MATCH. TO MAKE A DOG'S MATCH OF IT, *verb. phr.* (vulgar).—To copulate by the wayside.

DOG'S MEAT, *subs.* (colloquial).—Anything worthless; as a bad book, a common tale, a villainous picture, etc.

DOG-SHOOTER, *subs.* (old).—1. A volunteer.

2. (Royal Military Academy).—*See* quot.

1889. BARRÈRE, *Slang, Jargon and Cant*, p. 317. Cadets thus term a student who accelerates, that is, who, being pretty certain of not being able to obtain a commission in the engineers, or not caring for it, elects to join a superior class before the end of the term.

DOG'S-NOSE, *subs.* (common). — A mixture of gin and beer.—*See* DRINKS.

1812. VAUX, *Flash Dict.*, s.v.

1836. DICKENS, *Pickwick*, ch. xxxiii., p. 285. DOG'S NOSE . . . your committee find upon enquiry, to be compounded of warm porter, moist sugar, gin, and nutmeg.

1861. HUGHES, *Tom Brown at Oxford*, ch. xl. Ah! that's not bad tipple after such a ducking as we've had. DOG'S NOSE, isn't it?

DOG'S-PASTE, *subs.* (common).—Sausage or mince-meat. *Cf.*, BAGS OF MYSTERY and CHAMBERS OF HORROR (*q.v.*).

DOG'S-PORTION, *subs.* (common).—'A lick and a smell,' *i.e.*, next to nothing.

DOG'S SLEEP, *subs. phr.* (colloquial). — The lightest possible form of slumber.

DOG'S-SOUP, *subs.* (common). — Water. For synonyms, *see* ADAM'S ALE and FISH BROTH.

1836. W. H. SMITH. 'The Thieves' Chaunt.' For she never lushes DOG'S-SOUP or lap.

DOG'S-TAIL, *subs.* (nautical).—The constellation of *Ursa minor* or Little Bear.

DOG-STEALER, *subs.* (common).—A dog-dealer; applied sarcastically.

1854. WHYTE MELVILLE, *General Bounce*, ch. xiii. Now nodding to a trainer, now indulging in quaint *badinage*, which the vulgar call 'chaff,' with a DOG-STEALER.

DOLDRUMS, *subs.* (colloquial).—Low spirits; the DUMPS or HUMP (*q.v.*). [Properly parts of the ocean near the Equator abounding in calms and light, baffling winds.]

1865. M. BROWNE, in the 'Argosy,' I., 36. *An Apology for the Nerves.* All I say is, do not let us have any abuse of he nerves. Do not confound nervousness with the megrims, or the DOLDRUMS, or any other complaint. Do not confound it with cowardice or ill-temper.

1883. JAMES PAYN, *The Canon's Ward*, ch. xi. She treated all subjects in the same light way; . . . from aversion to serious thoughts of any kind, which she stigmatised generally as the DOLDRUMS.

DOLE, *subs.* (Winchester College).—A stratagem or trick. [From Latin *dolus*.]

DOLIFIER, *subs.* (Winchester College).—One who contrives a trick.—*See* DOLE.

DOLLAR, *subs.* (common).—A five-shilling piece. HALF-DOLLAR = half-a-crown, or two shillings. For synonyms, *see* CAROON.

DOLLOP, *subs.* and *verb* (common). A lot; ALL THE DOLLOP = the whole thing. *Cf.*, quot., 1812. In Norfolk TO DOLLOP = to dole out; also to 'plank.' DOLLOPING = throwing down.

1812. VAUX, *Flash Dict.*, s.v. = the whole sum of money.

1853. *Notes and Queries*, 16 July, p. 65, col., 2. Applied to lumps of any substances, whether food or otherwise. Such a phrase as this might be heard: What a DOLLOP of fat you have given me.

1871. *Bell's Life*, 23 Dec. All we wish to convey is, that a *large* bait is absolutely necessary to a heavy bag of chub. Exceptions may arise, as giants may dally with crumbs, but as a rule these fish desire a DOLLOP.

1876. HINDLEY, *Life and Adventures of a Cheap Jack*, p. 28. I have known men literally give their goods away, or to throw them at each other, which is termed DOLLOPING.

1883. *Daily Telegraph*, 8 March, p. 4, col. 1. A DOLLOP of something having a mortar-like appearance, imaginatively styled pudding.

DOLLY, *subs.* (venery). — 1. A mistress. For synonyms, *see* BARRACK-HACK and TART.

1647-48. HERRICK, *Hesperides*, p. 38. Drink, and dance, and pipe, and play, Kisse our DOLLIES night and day.

1843. *Punch*, vol. V., p. 8. Dol is a pure Anglo-Saxon word signifying *dull*, erring—whence the English DOLLY, any one who has made a *faux pas*.

2. (tailors').—A piece of cloth used as a sponge.

3. (venery).—The *penis*. For synonyms, *see* CREAMSTICK.

Adj. (popular).—Silly.

1864. DICKENS, *Our Mutual Friend*, bk. I., chap. 4. You are a chit and a little idiot, returned Bella, or you wouldn't make such a DOLLY speech.

DOLLY-MOP, *subs.* (common).—Specifically, a professional strumpet, but *see* quot., 1851. For synonyms, *see* BARRACK-HACK and TART.

1833. MARRYAT, *Peter Simple*, ch. iv. The captain says we are to take the young gentleman on board directly. His liberty's stopped for getting drunk and running after the DOLLY-MOPS!

1851. H. MAYHEW, *Lon. Lab. and Lon. Poor*, IV., 234. Those women who, for the sake of distinguishing them from the professionals, I must call amateurs, are generally spoken of as DOLLY-MOPS.

DOLLY-SHOP, *subs.* (common).—A marine store: really an illegal pawn-shop and FENCE (*q.v.*); also LEAVING-SHOP. No questions are asked; all goods are received on the understanding that they may be repurchased within a given time; so much per day is charged; no duplicate is given; and no books are kept. [From the BLACK DOLL (*q.v.*) suspended outside as a sign.]

1851-61. H. MAYHEW, *London Lab. and Lon. Poor*, vol. I., p. 142. If she hasn't, or if the neighbours hasn't it, she borrows it at a DOLLY-SHOP (the illegal pawnshop).

1860-68. *Chambers' Encyclopædia*, s.v.

1871. *Echo*, 16 March. Chimney sweeps having lent their machines to DOLLY-SHOP keepers for the price of a spree, could not redeem them to commence business.

DOME, *subs.* (common).—The head. For synonyms, *see* CRUMPET.

DOMESTIC-AFFLICTIONS, *subs.* (common).—The menstrual flux; a woman's flower-time. For synonyms, *see* FLAG-UP.

DOME-STICK, *subs.* (common).—A 'domestic' servant.

DOMINIE, *subs.* (old).—A clergyman; modern Scots = a pedagogue or schoolmaster. [From Latin *dominus*, a lord or master.]

1616. BEAUMONT AND FLETCHER, *Scornful Lady*, II., i. *Wel.* [addressing parson], Adieu, dear DOMINE!

1754. FOOTE, *Knights*, Act ii. She alls in love with young Sleek, her father's chaplain; . . what does me I, but slips on DOMINE'S robes, you; passed myself upon her for him, and we were tacked together.

1819. MOORE, *Tom Crib's Memorial*, p. 21. And, take him at *ruffianing* work (though, in common, he *Hums* about Peace and *all that*, like a DOMINE.

1883. BRINSLEY-RICHARDS, *Seven Years at Eton*, xii., 122. The Scotch DOMINIE, from whom he had learnt Latin . . . knew nothing of elegiacs.

DOMINIE DO-LITTLE, *subs. phr.* (old).—An impotent old man.

DOMINO! *intj.* (common). — An ejaculation of completion: *e.g.*, for sailors and soldiers at the last lash of a flogging; and for 'bus conductors when an omnibus is full inside and out [*N. and Q.*, 6 S., v., 229]; also, by implication, a knock-down blow, or the last of a series. [From the call at the end of a game of dominoes.]

DOMINO-BOX, *subs.* (old). — The mouth. For synonyms, *see* POTATO-TRAP.

1812. VAUX, *Flash Dictionary*, s.v.

DOMINOES, *subs.* (popular). — 1. The teeth. For synonyms, *see* GRINDERS.

1823. MONCRIEFF, *Tom and Jerry*, ii., 6. *Mr. J.* Sluice your DOMINOS—vill you? *Green.* Vot! I never plays at dominos—It's too wulgar. *Mr. J.* Vy, then vash your ivories? *Green.* I've got no hiveries to vash. *Mr. J.* Drink, vill you? don't you understand Hinglish?

1856. H. MAYHEW, *Gt. World of London*, p. 6, *note*. Fanciful metaphors contribute largely to the formation of slang. It is upon this principle that the mouth has come to be styled the 'tater-trap'; the teeth, DOMINOES.

1864. E. D. FORGUES, in *Revue des deux Mondes*, 15 Sept., p. 470. Le mot 'dents' est remplacé par celui de DOMINOS aussi bien sur les bordes de la Tamise que sur ceux de la Seine.

2. (colloquial).—The keys of a piano.

TO SLUICE ONE'S DOMINOES, *verb. phr.* (common).—To drink.—*See* quot., 1823 *ante*.

DOMINO-THUMPER, *subs.* (common).—A pianist.

DOMMERAR, DOMMERER, or **DUMMERER**, *subs.* (old).—A beggar feigning to be deaf and dumb; also, a madman.

1567. HARMAN, *Caveat*, p. 57. These DOMMERARS are leud and most subtyll people: the moste part of these are Walch men, and wyll neuer speake, vnlesse they haue extreame punishment, but wyll gape, and with a maruelous force wyll hold downe their toungs doubled, groning for your charyty, and holding vp their handes full pitiously, so that with their deepe dissimulation they get very much.

1621. BURTON, *Anat. of Mel.*, I., II., IV., vi., 233 (1836). It compels some miserable wretches to counterfeit several diseases, to dismember, make themselves blind, lame, to have a more plausible cause to beg . . . we have DUMMERERS, Abraham men, etc.

1671. R. HEAD, *English Rogue*, pt. I., ch. v. (Repr. 1874), p. 49. DOMMERAR, a Madman.

1706. E. COLES, *Eng. Dict.* DOMMEROR, a Madman.

1785. GROSE, *Dict. Vulg. Tongue*, s.v.

1859. MATSELL, *Vocabulum.* DOMMERER, a fellow that pretends to be deaf and dumb.

DON, *subs.* (colloquial).—An adept; a swell; also a man that 'puts on side.' At the Universities a fellow or officer of a college; whence the vulgar usage. [From Latin, *dominus*, a lord, through the Spanish title.]

1665. DRYDEN, *Indian Emperor*, Epilogue, 21. For the great DONS of wit—Phœbus gives them full privilege alone, To damn all others, and cry up their own.

1698-1700. WARD, *London Spy*, pt. xiii., p. 299. Like the Great Old DONS of the Law, when they dance the Measures in an *Inns-of-Court Hall* upon the first day of *Christmas*.

1730. JAS. MILLER, *Humours of ford*, Act I., p. 7 (2 ed.) The old DONS . . . will come cringing, cap in hand, to offer to show the ladies the curiosities of the college.

1826. REYNOLDS ('Peter Corcoran') *Song on the Fancy*. Dull innocence! Twaddle on, Thy weary worshipper—and fain Would give thee up, to be a DON, And beat the watch in Drury Lane.

1855. THACKERAY, *Newcomes*, ch. xi. Does not go much into society, except . . . . once or twice to the houses of great country DONS who dwell near him in the country.

c. 1880. *Broadside Ballad*, sung by JENNY HILL. ''Arry, 'Arry, There you are now, 'Arry, I say, 'Arry, by Jove, you are a DON.'

Adj. (common).—Clever, expert; first rate. [From the *subs.* sense.]

DONA, DONNA, DONNY, or **DONER,** *subs.* (vulgar).—A woman. [From the Italian.] For synonyms, *see* PETTICOAT.

1875. *Athenæum,* 24 April, p. 545, col. 2. A circus man almost always speaks of a circus woman, not as a woman, but a DONA.

DONAKER, *subs.* (old).—A cattle-lifter.

1669. *Nicker Nicked,* in *Harl. Misc.* (ed. Park), ii., 10⁹.

DONE! *intj.* (common).—An interjection of acceptance or agreement.

1602. DEKKER, *Honest Whore,* in wks. (1873), ii., 17. *Cast.* . . . I'le wage a hundred duckats upon the head on't, that it moves him, frets him, and galles him. *Pio.* DONE, 'tis a lay, joyne gols [hands] on't.

1761. COLMAN, *Jealous Wife,* IV., in wks. (1777), i., 106. Why, it's a match, miss! it's DONE and DONE on both sides.

1762. GOLDSMITH, *Life of Nash,* in wks., p. 546 (Globe). Why, if you think me a dab I will get this strange gentleman, or this, pointing to the flat. DONE! cries the sailor, but you shall not tell him.

1840. THACKERAY, *Paris Sketch-book,* p. 196. 'I will bet thee thy water for a year that none of the three will pray for thee.' 'DONE!' said Rollo. 'DONE!' said the daemon.'

Ppl. adj. (common).—Exhausted; ruined; cheated; convicted.

[*See* DO in most of its senses.]

DONE-OVER, *adj.* (common).—1. Intoxicated. For synonyms, *see* SCREWED.

2. (venery). Possessed in kind; said only of women.

DONKEY, *subs.* (printers').—1. A compositor; pressmen are in turn called PIGS (*q.v.*).

ENGLISH SYNONYMS. — Ass; moke; galley-slave.

FRENCH SYNONYMS. — *Un mulet* (printers'); *un compositeur mie de pain* (an unskilled or clumsy workman; *mie de pain* also = a louse); *un marron* (a compositor working on his own account with another printer's plant); *un homme de lettres* (= a man of letters); *un singe* (=a monkey); *un amphibie* (a compositor who is DONKEY and PIG [*q.v.*] together).

1857. In *Notes and Queries,* 2 S., iv., 192. Compositors are jocosely called mokes or DONKEYS.

2. (nautical).—A sailor's chest.

3. (colloquial).—A blockhead. For synonyms, *see* CABBAGE-HEAD and BUFFLE.

A PENNY, TWOPENCE or THREEPENCE MORE AND UP GOES THE DONKEY, *phr.* (common).—An exclamation of derision. [Street acrobats': the custom was to finish off the pitch by balancing a donkey at the top of a ladder on receipt of 'tuppence more'; which sum, however often subscribed, was always re-demanded, so that the donkey never 'went up' at all.]

1841. *Punch,* vol. I., p. 41, col. 2. Mr. Joseph Muggins begs to inform his old crony, Punch, that the report of Sir John Pullon, 'as to the possibility of elevating an ass to the head of the poll by bribery and corruption' is perfectly correct, provided there is no abatement in the price. Let him canvass again, and Mr. J. M. pledges himself, whatever his weight, if he will only stand ONE PENNY MORE, UP GOES THE DONKEY!

1850. F. E. SMEDLEY, *Frank Fairleigh,* ch. xv. He . . . has left the key in the lock; so I shall take the liberty of exploring a little; I've a strong though undeveloped taste for architectural antiquities. TWOPENCE MORE, AND UP GOES THE DONKEY! Come along! So saying, he flung open the door.

WHO STOLE THE DONKEY? *phr.* (common).—A street cry once in vogue on the appearance of a man in a white hat. With a similar expression 'Who stole the leg of mutton'? applied to the police, it had its rise in a case of larceny. J. H. Dixon, writing to Hotten, Nov. 6th, 1864, remembered both. The first occurred at Hatton Garden Police Court, where a man, wearing a white hat, was charged with stealing a costermonger's donkey.

1889. *Sporting Times,* 3 Aug., p. 3, col. 5. WHO STOLE THE DONKEY? The man with the white hat! This was a very popular street colloquy some years ago.

TO RIDE THE DONKEY, *verb. phr.* (common).—To cheat with weights and measures. Also DONKEY - RIDING = cheating as aforesaid. *Cf.,* AMBUSH.

1859. MATSELL, *Vocabulum, or Rogue's Lexicon.* DONKEY - RIDING. Cheating in weight or measure; miscounting.

TO TALK THE HIND LEG OFF A DONKEY.—See TALK.

DONKEY-DROPS, *subs. phr.* (cricket).—See quot.

1890. THE HON. AND REV. E. LYTTELTON, *Cricket,* p. 69. Slow round-hand bowling, such as is seldom seen in good matches, but is effective against boys, and is known by the contumelious designation of DONKEY-DROPS.

DONKEY'S-EARS, *subs.* (old).—An old-fashioned shirt - collar with long points.

DONNA.—*See* DONA.

DONNISH, *adj.* **DONNISM, DONNISHNESS,** *subs.* (University).—Arrogant; arrogance. [From DON (*q.v.*).]

1823. *Hints for Oxford,* p. 66. The Bachelors, we imagine, are the most pleasant set of beings in Oxford . . . They have luckily not been so long emancipated as to have become stiff, and DONNISH, and disagreeable.

c. 1830. *Ballad,* quoted in *N. and Q.,* 2nd S., xii., 154. Our Yankee, who'd commenced the fight and rather to be DONNISH meant, *Sam squabbled* felt (*as well he might*) with genu-*ine* astonishment.

1853. THACKERAY, in *Scribner's Mag.,* Oct., 1887, p. 415. At Boston is very good literate company indeed; it is like Edinburgh for that,—a vast amount of toryism and DONNISHNESS everywhere.

1888. MRS. WARD, *Robt. Elsmere,* vol. I., bk. I., ch. ii., p. 48. He was a curious man, a refined-looking, melancholy creature, with a face that reminded you of Wordsworth, and cold DONNISH ways, except to his children and the poor.

DONNY.—See DONA.

DONOVANS, *subs.* (old).—Potatoes. *Cf.,* MURPHY. [Donovan, like Murphy, is a common Irish patronym.]

DON'S WEEK, *subs. phr.* (tailors').—The week before a general holiday.

DON'T GET YOUR BACK UP.—See BACK, and HOLD YOUR HAIR ON.

DON'T-NAME-'EMS, *subs. phr.* (common). — Trousers. For synonyms, *see* KICKSIES.

DON'T YOU WISH YOU MAY GET IT, *phr.* (street).—A retort forcible.

1837. BARHAM, *Ingoldsby Legends* (ed. 1862), p. 179. A thousand marks, continued the confessor. . . Sir Guy shrank from the monk's gaze; he turned to the window, and muttered to himself something that sounded like, 'DON'T YOU WISH YOU MAY GET IT?'

1841. *Punch,* vol. I., p. 22, col. 2. Who would own her heart thine, Though a monarch beset it, And love on unchanged, DON'T YOU WISH YOU MAY GET IT?'

1844. *Puck,* p. 14. The Proctor caught him in a spree, Asked his name and college with courtesie; 'DON'T YOU WISH YOU MAY GET IT?' and off he ran, Did my spicy swell small college man.

DOODLE, *subs.* (old). -- 1. A dolt. For synonyms, *see* BUFFLE and CABBAGE-HEAD. [Thought to be a corruption of DAWDLE, to trifle.]

1775. ASH, *Eng. Dict.,* s.v.

1830. S. WARREN, *Diary of a Late Physician,* ch. v. I know it was every word composed by that abominable old addlehead, Dr. ——, a DOODLE that he is!

2. (old). — The *penis.* For synonyms, *see* CREAMSTICK.

1785. GROSE, *Dic. Vulg. Tongue,* s.v.

DOODLED, *ppl. adj.* (old).—Cheated, 'done.'

1823. MONCRIEFF, *Tom and Jerry,* i., 7. No, I'm out of spirits because I have been dished and DOODLED out of forty pounds to-day.

DOODLE-DASHER, *subs.* (venery).— A masturbator. [From DOODLE, the *penis* + DASHER.]

DOODLE-DOO-MAN, *subs.* (old cock-pit).—A cockfighter or breeder. [From the childish name for poultry.]

DOODLESACK, *subs.* (old). — The female *pudendum.* Also DOODLE-CASE and DOODLE-TRAP. For synonyms, *see* MONOSYLLABLE.

DOOG, *adj.* (back-slang).—Good.

DOOKIE, *subs.* (theatrical).—A penny show or unlicensed theatre. *Cf.,* GAFF.

DOOKIN and **DOOKERING,** *subs.* (thieves' and gypsies').—Fortune-telling.

1857. SNOWDEN, *Mag. Assistant,* 3rd ed., p. 444.

DOOKIN-COVE, *subs.* (common).—A fortune-teller. [From DOOKIN =fortune-telling=COVE, a man.]

DOOR-NAIL. DEAD AS A DOOR-NAIL.—See DEAD.

DOORSMAN, *subs.* (common).—See BARKER and CLICKER.

DOORSTEP, *subs.* (common). — A thick slice of bread and butter. Fr., *une fondante.*

1885. MISS TENNANT, in *Eng. Ill. Mag.,* June, p. 604. DOORSTEPS, I found, were thick slices of bread spread with jam.

1890. *Spectator,* 3 May, Rev. of vol. I., 'Slang and its Analogues.' . . . The extraordinary 'bouncer' that a very common request at Lockhart's coffee-houses in London is for 'a DOORSTEP and a sea-rover,' *i.e.,* for a halfpenny slice of bread and butter and a herring, &c.

DOOTEROOMUS or **DOOT,** *subs.* (American).—Money. For synonyms, *see* ACTUAL and GILT.

1871. DE VERE, *Americanisms,* s.v.

DOPE, *verb* (American). — To drug with tobacco. Also DOPING = the practice.

DOPEY, *subs.* (old).—1. A beggar's trull.

1785. GROSE, *Dict. Vulg. Tongue,* s.v.

2. (old).—The *podex.*

DOR, *subs.* (Old Westminster School).—1.—*See* quot.

1715. J. KERSEY, *English Dictionary. Sub voce,* a term used at Westminster School for leave to sleep awhile.

2. (old).—An affront.

1600. JONSON, *Cynthia's Revels.*

DORAS, *subs.* (Stock Exchange).—South-Eastern Railway Deferred Ordinary Stock, sometimes applied to the 'A' Stock.

DORBIE, *subs.* (Scots Masonic).—An initiate.

THE DORBIES' KNOCK, *subs. phr.*—A peculiar rap given by masons as a signal amongst themselves. It may be represented by the time of the following notes :

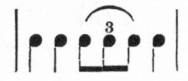

DORCAS, *subs.* (colloquial), — A sempstress; especially one employing herself for charitable purposes.

DORSE.—See DOSS.

DOSE, *subs.* (thieves').—1. A sentence of imprisonment; specifically three months' hard labour.

ENGLISH SYNONYMS.—Spell, time, drag, three moon, length, stretch, seven-pennorth, sixer, twelver, lagging.

FRENCH SYNONYM. — *Une marque.*

1877. *Five Years' Penal Servitude,* ch. iii., p. 22. 'What's yer DOSE?' looking on to my badge; 'five, oh, you can do that little lot on yer 'ed easy.'

2. (thieves').—A burglary.

1859. MATSELL, *Vocabulum, or Rogue's Lexicon,* s.v.

3. (pugilistic).—A beating.

1819. MOORE, *Tom Crib's Memorial to Congress,* p. 17. Sandy tipp'd him a DOSE of that kind, that, when taken, It isn't the *stuff,* but the *patient* that's shaken.

4. (colloquial). — As much liquor as one can hold.

TO HAVE A DOSE OF THE BALMY, *verbal phr.* (common).—To 'do a sleep.'—See BALMY and DOSS.

TO TAKE A GROWN MAN'S DOSE, *verb. phr.* (common).—To take a very large quantity of liquor.

DOSS or **DORSE,** *subs.* (vagrants').—A bed, or lodging; also a sleep, or LIB (*q.v.*). [Origin uncertain.] For synonyms, *see* KIP and BALMY.

1789. GEO. PARKER, *Life's Painter,* p. 165. *Dorsed.* The place where a person sleeps, or a bed. 'I DORSED there last darkey.'

1858. MAYHEW, *Paved with Gold,* p. 118. Into this branch curtained retreat, the lads crept on all fours, one after another, to enjoy their DOSS, as, in their slang, they called sleep.

1883. *Daily News,* 3 April, p. 3, col. 5. He replied that he had only come there to have a DOSS (sleep).

1889. *Pall Mall Gazette,* 9 Sep., p. 3, col. 2. If you want a DOSS, a DOSS is provided. A wooden framework, about as wide as the widest part of a coffin, and a wooden pillow and a blanket of leather.

Verb (vagrants')—To sleep. For synonyms, *see* BALMY and *infra.* Also DORSE.

ENGLISH SYNONYMS.—To go to the arms of Murphy (*q.v.*); to have forty winks; to go to Bedfordshire; to take a little (or do a dose) of the balmy; to chuck (or do) a doss; to snooze; to go to by-by; to read the paper; to shut one's eyes to think; to retire to the land of Nod.

FRENCH SYNONYMS.—*Battre la couverte* (military); *se foutre un coup de traversin* (=to have a little turn up with the bolster) ; *se bâcher, pagnotter* or *percher* (to roost) ; *se mettre dans la bâche* ; *se bourser* (popular) ; *éteindre son gaz* (popular : to put out one's light ;=also to die) ; *entrer aux quinze-vingts* (*Les Quinze-vingts* =a government hospital for the blind) ; *dormir en chien de fusil* (*i.e.*, to sleep sitting, the head between the knees) ; *dormir en gendarme* (popular : 'to sleep with one eye round the corner') ; *fermer les châssis* (to put up shutters or 'peepers') ; *se coller dans le pieu* (popular).

SPANISH SYNONYMS.—*Acostarse con las gallinas* (= to go to bed by cock-light) ; *encamarse* ; *tomarle á uno el sueño* ; *tumbar* (literally, to tumble down).

1785. GROSE, *Dict. Vulg. Tongue*, s.v. To DORSE with a woman signifies to sleep with her.

1846. *Punch*, vol. XI., p. 165. Then silent flowed the tears of those maidens as perforce, Each saw her favourite champion sent, as *Bell's Life* says, DORSE.

1850. *Lloyd's Weekly*, 3 Feb., 'Low Lodging House of London.' One said, Mate, how long have you been knocking about ; where did you DOSS? I didn't know what they meant, and when they'd told me, they meant, where did I sleep?

DOSSER, *subs.* (vagrants').—One who frequents a DOSS HOUSE (*q.v.*).

'APPY-DOSSERS, *subs.* (vagrants').—Houseless vagrants who creep in, sleep on stairs, in passages, and in empty cellars.

1880. G. R. SIMS, *How the Poor Live*, p. 43. A 'APPY DOSSER can make himself comfortable anywhere. I heard of one who used to crawl into the dust-bin, and pull the lid down.

1883. *Referee*, 15 July, p. 7, col. 2. The Lazaruses of to-day don't lie exactly at Dives's front door—the police are too active to allow such HAPPY DOSSING as that.

THE DOSSER, *subs.*—The father of a family.

DOSS-HOUSE or **DOSSING-CRIB** or **KEN**, *subs.* (vagrants').—A common lodging-house. [From DOSS, to sleep + CRIB, or KEN, a place of abode.] Fr., *un bastengue* and *un garno*. English variants : LIBKEN, TWO-PENNY-ROPE, PADDING-KEN, and KIDDEN (all of which *see*). DOSS - MONEY = the price of a night's lodging.

1838. *Comic Almanack*, April. The hulks is now my bowsing-crib, the hold my DOSSING-KEN.

1851-61. H. MAYHEW, *London Lab. and Lon. Poor*, vol. I., p. 150. When their funds are insufficient to defray the charge of a bed, or a part of one, at a country DOSSING - CRIB (his lodging-house).

1885. *Daily Telegraph*, 22 August, p. 2. col. 1. Her's is no common DOSSING-CRIB, with a squalid kitchen, common to all comers.

1889. *Globe*, 29 Aug., p. 2, col. 2. Various other smart people who are at present residing in the DOSS-HOUSES of London.

1890. *Speaker*, 22 Feb., p. 211, col. 1. Equally bad DOSS-HOUSES exist in Notting Hill and near Drury Lane.

DOSSY, *adj.* (common).—Elegant, 'SPIFF' (*q.v.*).

DOT, *subs.* (old).—A ribbon. DOT-DRAG = a watch ribbon.

1821. D. HAGGART, *Life*, Glossary, p. 171, s.v.

DOT-AND-CARRY-, or **GO-ONE**, *subs. phr.* (common).—1. Properly, a man with a wooden leg ; by implication, a HOPPING - GILES or LIMPING JESUS (*q.v.*). Fr., *un* (or *une*) *banban*. *Cf.*, verbal sense.

1785. GROSE, *Dict. Vulg. Tongue*, s.v.

1822. SCOTT, *The Fortunes of Nigel*, ch. v. That was his father . . . You old dotard. DOT-AND-CARRY-ONE that you are.

1837. BARHAM, *Ingoldsby Legends* (*Lay of S. Nicholas*). How he rose with the sun, limping DOT AND GO ONE.

1841. LEMAN REDE, *Sixteen String Jack*, Act i., Sc. 4. *Kit.* Of all the rummy chaps I ever did see, that DOT-AND-CARRY-ONE-OF-old poetry is the queerest ; he's as green as a babby, and as deep as a wooden spoon.

2. (old).—A writing-master or teacher of arithmetic. [GROSE, 1785.]

Verb (old). — To 'hirple' ; especially applied to a person with one leg shorter than the other, or, 'with an uneven keel.'

DO TELL! *intj.* (American). — A useful interjection, for listeners who feel that some remark is expected; equivalent to the English Really? and Indeed? A similar phrase in the South is the old English, You don't say so? which a Yankee will vary by, I want to know! DO TELL is also used with inexperienced Munchausens who by its means may often be lured to repeat themselves.

1824. R. B. PEAKE, *Americans Abroad*, Act I., Sc. ii. *Mrs. L.* But when they order nothing at all— *Dou*: What then, DU PRAY TELL?

1854. *N. and Q.*, 1 S., x., p. 84, *R.* Does Jeremiur behave well now? *S.* No, he's very ugly. He tried to burn the barn. *R.* DO TELL!

1871. DE VERE, *Americanisms*, p. 598 s.v.

DOTS, *subs.* (American journalist).—1. Items of news.

2. (popular). — Money. For synonyms, *see* ACTUAL and GILT.

DOTTER, *subs.* (common). —A reporter ; penny-a-liner. *Cf.*, DOTS, sense 1.

DOTTLE, *subs.* (common). — The same as DODDER (*q.v.*).

1885. JOHN COLEMAN, in *Longm. Mag.*, VII., 69. During the performance of 'It's Never Too Late to Mend,' some gentleman of the proletariat, in knocking out the burning DOTTLE of his pipe, succeeded in setting the gallery on fire.

DOTTY, *adj.* and *adv.* (common).—1. Feeble ; dizzy ; idiotic ; *e.g.*, DOTTY IN THE CRUMPET = weak in the head ; DOTTY IN THE PINS = unsteady on the legs. [TOTTY is given in Cole's *Eng. Dict.* (1724) = dizzy, but *cf.*, DOTISH and DOTAGE.] For synonyms, *see* APARTMENTS, BALMY, and *Cf.*, CABBAGE-HEAD.

1870. *Sportsman*, 9 April. Although he begins to go a little stiff in his limbs and DOTTY on his feet he enjoys good health.

1884. *Daily Telegraph*, 9 April, p. 2, col. 6. His bad leg grows worse . . and, as usual, he [a race-horse] pulled up in a DOTTY condition.

1889. *Ally Sloper's Half Holiday*, 3 Aug., p. 242, col. 3. As poor Doody on his knees had dropt In front of lovely Tottie, And the fatal question just had pop't. He really look'd quite DOTTY.

Subs. (common).—The fancy man of prostitutes of the lowest type.

DOUBITE, *subs.* (old).—A street.

1859. MATSELL, *Vocabulum, or Rogue's Lexicon*, s.v.

DOUBLE, *subs.* (colloquial).—1. A trick.

2. (theatrical).—An actor playing two parts in the same piece ; used also as a verb.

1825. EGAN, *Life of an Actor*, 'The Country Manager.' I make no *reserve* for myself, like all other managers ; indeed, I am to DOUBLE any character, and only anxious to make the most of every little bit.

3. (thieves').—*See* quot.

1879. J. W. HORSLEY, in *Macm. Mag.*, xl., 501. I piped a slavey (servant) come out of a chat (house), so when she had got a little way up the DOUBLE (turning) I pratted (went) in the house.

4. (printers').—Repetition of a word or sentence.

[DOUBLE, *adj.* and *adv.*, is also used as an intensive in many obscene or offensive connotations : *e.g.*, DOUBLE-ARSED = large in the posteriors ; DOUBLE-DUGGS (and DOUBLE - DUGGED or DIDDIED) = heavy breasted ; DOUBLE-GUTS (and DOUBLE - GUTTED) = excessively corpulent ; DOUBLE-CUNTED = stretched beyond service ; DOUBLE - HOCKED = abnormally thick ankled ; DOUBLE-SHUNG = extravagantly large in the genitals ; DOUBLE-MOUTHED = mouth-almighty (*q.v.*) ; and so forth.]

TO PUT THE DOUBLE ON, *verb. phr.* (colloquial). — To circumvent.

TO TIP or GIVE THE DOUBLE, *verb. phr.* (common).—To run or slip away openly or unperceived ; to double as a hare ; formerly to escape one's creditors. Also to TIP ONE THE DUBLIN PACKET. For synonyms, *see* AMPUTATE and SKEDADDLE.

1781. G. PARKER, *View of Society*, I., 174, s.v.

1860. *The Druid*, 'Post and Paddock.' Alas! my innocent rural police, Your fondest hopes were a bubble ; Your attempts to prevent a breach of the peace, Your race o'er the Derbyshire stubble ; You must freely own that you felt like geese, When Sam Rogers GAVE YOU THE DOUBLE.

1870. *Daily News*, 26 May. 'The Metropolitan Police.' The policeman must do his best to 'keep square' with the sergeant who looks after him and his beats, who can be down upon him at any moment and DOUBLE UPON HIM three or four times a-night.

1884. HAWLEY SMART, *Post to Finish*, ch. i. Old Gregson would never PUT THE DOUBLE UPON US. No, it's right enough, you may depend upon it.

DOUBLE-BACK, *verb. phr.*—(colloquial).—To go back upon oneself ; an action ; an opinion.

DOUBLE-BARREL, *subs.* (popular).—A field or opera glass.

1890. H. D. TRAILL, *Saturday Songs*, p. 61. Intently as the masher plies O'er all the stage his DOUBLE-BARREL That Eightyer mute had fixed his eyes Upon his honoured guest's apparel.

DOUBLE-BARRELLED, *adj.* (venery). —Said of a harlot working both before and behind.

DOUBLE - BOTTOMED, *adj.* (colloquial). — Insincere ; saying one thing and meaning another.

DOUBLE-BREASTED FEET, *subs. phr.* (common). — Club feet. Also DOUBLE BREASTERS.

DOUBLE-CROSS or **DOUBLE-DOUBLE**, *subs.* (sporting). -- Winning or doing one's best to win after engaging to lose or 'MIKE' ; (*q.v.*).

1887. *Referee*, 21 Aug., 1, 3. When the pair raced before, Teemer declared, and Hanlan did not deny, that a DOUBLE CROSS was brought off. Teemer promised to sell the match, and finished by selling those who calculated on his losing.

DOUBLE - DISTILLED, *adj.* (colloquial). — Superlative : *e.g.*, 'a double - distilled whopper' = a tremendous lie.

DOUBLE-DUTCH, *adj.* (colloquial). —Unintelligible speech ; jargon ; gibberish. 'It was all DOUBLE-DUTCH to me' = I didn't understand a word of it.

DOUBLE-EVENT, *subs.* (sporting). —1. Backing a horse for two races.

1883. GRENVILLE MURRAY, *People I Have Met*, p. 155. His lordship, who had won largely on a DOUBLE EVENT.

2. (venery).—Gonorrhœa and syphilis at once. Said also of simultaneous defloration and impregnation.

DOUBLE-FINN, *subs.* (common).—A £10 note.—[*See* FINN.]

1879. J. W. HORSLEY, in *Macm. Mag.*, xl., 505. Yes, there it was, fifty quid in DOUBLE FINNS (£10 notes).

DOUBLE-HEADER, *subs.* (common). —A false coin with a head on the obverse and reverse, made by soldering two split coins. *Cf.*, COVER and HEADING 'EM.

1887. *Walford's Antiquarian*, p. 252. A DOUBLE-HEADER is the usual property of the gutter sharper.

DOUBLE-JUGGS, *subs.* (old).—The posteriors (Burton). For synonyms, *see* BLIND CHEEKS, BUM, and MONOCULAR EYEGLASS.

DOUBLE-LINES, *subs.* (nautical).—Ship casualties. So called from the manner of entering at Lloyd's.

DOUBLER, *subs.* (pugilistic). — A blow in the side or stomach, causing a man to bend from pain or lack of wind. *Cf.*, DOUBLE UP, sense 1. For synonyms, *see* DIG.

1821. *The Fancy*, vol. I., p. 255. In the *fourth* round he came in all abroad, and got a DOUBLER in the bread-basket, which spoiled him for the remainder of the fight.

DOUBLE-RIBBED, *adj. phr.* (common). — Pregnant. For synonyms, *see* LUMPY.

DOUBLE-SHOTTED, *adj.* (colloquial. —Said of a whiskey (or brandy) and soda, containing twice the normal quantity of alcohol.

DOUBLE-SHUFFLE, *subs.* (common). 1. A hornpipe step in which each foot is shuffled twice in succession, the more rapidly and neatly the better.

1835. DICKENS, *Sketches by Boz*, p. 47. The waterman . . . is dancing the DOUBLE SHUFFLE, in front of the pump, to keep his feet warm.

1851-61. H. MAYHEW, *London Lab. and Lon. Poor*, vol. i., p. 542. I used to talk to him and whistle. I *can* just whistle . . . and to dance him the DOUBLE-SHUFFLE.

1871. *Echo*, 11 Dec., 'Sunday among the Silk Weavers.' The clumsy high low with which they execute scientific 'elephant dances' and DOUBLE-SHUFFLES.

2. *subs.* (common).—A trick or fakement.

DOUBLE-SLANG.—*See* SLANGS.

DOUBLE-SUCKER, *subs.* (venery). —A term descriptive of an abnormal development of the tissues of the *labia majora*.

DOUBLET, *subs.* (thieves'). — A doctored diamond or other precious stone. *Cf.*, TRIPLET. [The quots. show derivation.]

1706. E. COLES, *Eng. Dict.* DOUBLET, a precious stone of two pieces joyned.

1822. SCOTT, *Fortunes of Nigel*, ch. xxxi. Your een are sharp enough to look after gowd and silver, gems, rubies, and the like of that . . . Look at them—they are a'right and tight, sound and round, not a DOUBLET crept in amongst them.

1877. *Five Years' Penal Servitude*, ch. iv., p. 273. Most jewellers and pawnbrokers are well acquainted with what are called DOUBLETS. These are rubies or emeralds made of two pieces. The face is a real ruby, emerald, or sapphire, as the case may be, and this is backed up by a piece of coloured glass.

DOUBLE-THUMPER, *subs.* (common).—A prodigious lie.

DOUBLE-TONGUED, *adj.* (colloquial). — Mendacious ; given to change opinions in changing company.

DOUBLE-TONGUED SQUIB, *subs. phr.* (common). — A double-barrelled gun. For synonyms, *see* SQUIB.

1864. G. W. REYNOLDS, *Pickwick Abroad.* A DOUBLE-TONGUED SQUIB to keep in awe The chaps that flout at me.

DOUBLE-UP, *verb* (pugilistic).—1. To punish. Also to be collapsed. *Cf.*, DOUBLER.

1819. MOORE, *Tom Crib's Memorial*, p. 20. DOUBLED him UP, like a bag of old *duds*.

1827. REYNOLDS, ('Peter Corcoran') *The Fancy*, note on p. 89. Randall DOUBLES UP an opponent, as a friend lately declared, as easily as though he were picking a flower or pinching a girl's cheek.

1830. S. WARREN, *Diary of a Late Physician*, ch. xii. Accompanied by a tremendous DOUBLING UP body-blow, as in an instant brought him senseless to the ground.

1845. *Punch*, vol. IX., p. 163. Ben's reference to the Premier's friend, Canning, completely DOUBLED him UP.

1849. THACKERAY, *Dr. Birch*, p. 6. I reflect as I go up and set him a sum, that he [Champion] could whop me in two minutes, DOUBLE UP Prince and the other assistant and pitch the Doctor out of the window.

1866. *London Miscellany*, 5 May, p. 202. DOUBLED you UP, I mean, sir. Smashed you.

2. (common).—To pair off, to chum with.

1885. W. WESTALL, *Larry Lohengrin*, ch. iii. He . . . promised the steward a handsome tip if nobody were DOUBLED UP with him,—*i.e.*, if no other person were put into the same cabin.

DOUGH, *subs.* (public schools')—Pudding.

DOUGH-BAKED, *adj. phr.* (colloquial). — Deficient in intellect. U. S. A. = Easily moulded: said of politicians. For synonyms, *see* APARTMENTS.

1675. WYCHERLEY, *Country Wife*, IV., iv. in wks. (1713), 212. These DOW-BAKED, senseless, indocile animals, women.

DOUGHY, *subs.* (common). — A baker.—*See* BURNCRUST, and for synonyms, MASTER OF THE ROLLS.

DOUSE.—*See* DOWSE.

DOVER, *subs.* (hotel). —A made dish; hash; *rechauffé*.

DOVERS, *subs.* (Stock Exchange). — South Eastern Railway Ordinary Stock. [From one of the termini on the line.]

DOVES, *subs.* (University).—Members of St. Catharine's College, Cambridge. — *See* quot. Obsolete.

1888. C. WHIBLEY, *Three Centuries of Cambridge Wit*, p. xxix. It is said that the members of St. Catharine's Hall were first of all called 'Puritans,' from the derivation of the name of their patroness from καθαίρειν. The 'dove' being the emblem of purity, to change a name from 'Puritans' to DOVES was but one short step.

SOILED - DOVES, *subs.* (common). — High-class prostitutes. For synonyms, *see* BARRACK-HACK and TART.

DOVE-TART, *subs.* (colloquial).—A pigeon pie. (DOO-TAIRT is excellent Scots for the same thing.) *Cf.*, SNAKE TART=eel pie.

1857. REV. E. BRADLEY ('Cuthbert Bede'), *Verdant Green*, pt. II., ch. vii. Why, a DOVE TART is what mortals call a pigeon-pie.

DOWLAS, *subs.* (common). — A draper. [From DOWLAS, now a kind of towelling, but mentioned by Shakspeare (1 *Henry IV.*, III., iii., 1597) as a material for shirts.

Popularised as a sobriquet by Colman's Daniel Dowlas in *The Heir at Law*.—*See* DICKEY DIAPER, and *cf.*, DRIPPING=cook; GRINDO = miller; GALLIPOT = chemist; LINT-SCRAPER=surgeon, (*q.v.*).

DOWLING, *subs.* (public school).—*See* quot.

1871. Newspaper Report, 18 Feb., of of a charge of assault against the head boy of Shrewsbury School. Mr. Chandler addressed the Bench for the defence. He said the game of DOWLING was practised at Eton, Harrow, Rugby, Westminster and other large schools, etc.

1877. *Everyday Life in our Public Schools.* There are four or five compulsory games a week (football) known as DOWLINGS δοῦλος.

DOWN, *subs.* (thieves'). — 1. Suspicion; alarm; a diversion. THERE IS NO DOWN=All is quiet, it is safe to go on.

1821. D. HAGGART, *Life*, Glossary, p. 171. DOWN, alarm; rose the DOWN, gave the alarm.

2. (American). — Small beer. UP=bottled ale.

Adv. (colloquial).—1. Dispirited; hard-up; in disgrace. Found in various combinations: *e.g.*, DOWN IN THE MOUTH, or DUMPS = dejected; DOWN ON ONE'S LUCK = reduced in circumstances; DOWN AT HEEL=shabby; DOWN ON ONE'S BACK-SEAM = out of luck; DOWN TO BED-ROCK (American)=penniless, etc., etc.

1608-11. BISHOP HALL, *Epistles*, i., 6. The Roman orator was DOWN IN THE MOUTH; finding himself thus cheated by the money-changer.

1693. CONGREVE, *Old Batchelor*, Act iv., Sc. 9. *Sir J. Witt.* Now am I slap-dash DOWN IN THE MOUTH, and have not one word to say!

1751. SMOLLETT, *Peregrine Pickle*, ch. xlix. He . . . . told the physician that he was like the root of the tongue, as being cursedly DOWN IN THE MOUTH.

1836. C. DICKENS, *Pickwick Papers*, p. 6, (ed. 1857). I see—never ruined—accidents will happen — best regulated families—never say die—DOWN UPON YOUR LUCK—pull him up.

1840. *Comic Almanack*, p. 208. Let's not be DOWN UPON OUR LUCK Nor out of heart at our condition.

1846. THACKERAY, *Vanity Fair*, vol. II., ch. xxix. They say, that when Mrs. Crawley was particularly DOWN ON HER LUCK, she gave concerts and lessons in music here and there.

1851. H. MAYHEW, *Lon. Lab. and Lon. Poor*, vol. I., p. 58. If the hucksters know that the person calling the raffle is DOWN, and that it is necessity that has made him call it, they will not allow the property put up to be thrown for.

1861. MARIAN EVANS (G. Eliot), *Silas Marner*, ch. viii. Well, here's my turning, said Bryce, not surprised to perceive that Godfrey was rather DOWN; so I'll bid you good-day.

1864. EDMUND YATES, *Broken to Harness*, ch. x. What won't do? asked Prescott, with flaming face, Why, this Kate Mellon business, Jim. It's on hot and strong, I know. You've been DOWN IN THE MOUTH all the time she was away.

1880. A. TROLLOPE, *The Duke's Children*, ch. xlvii. I'm sorry you're so DOWN IN THE MOUTH. Why don't you try again?

1880. JAS. GREENWOOD, *Veteran of Vauxhall* in 'Odd People in Odd Places,' p. 40. Then I got DOWN AT HEEL, as the saying is; and when a man is reduced to one bare suit of black, and that one so shaky with long wear that it wants as tender handling as an invalid, he hasn't got much of a chance to get on well as a waiter.

2. (old). — Acquainted with; 'FLY' (*q.v.*); UP TO (*q.v.*). Also in combination: DOWN TO, DOWN ON, and DOWN AS A HAMMER.

1610. JONSON, *Alchemist*, IV., iv. Thou art so DOWN UPON the least disaster! How would'st thou ha' done, if I had not help't thee out?

1825. *The English Spy*, vi., p. 162. Dick's a *trump*, and no *telegraph*—up to every *frisk*, AND DOWN TO every *move* of the domini, thoroughbred and no *want of courage*.

1839. W. H. AINSWORTH, *Jack Sheppard*, p. 138, [ed. 1840.] Awake! to be sure I am, my flash cove, replied Sheppard, I'm DOWN AS A HAMMER.

1850. F. E. SMEDLEY, *Frank Fairleigh*, ch. iv. You're about right there, Mr. Lawless, you're DOWN TO every move, I see, as usual.

1865. G. F. BERKELEY, *Life, etc.*, II., 103. *Crib.* I said . . . . I'm DOWN ON it all; the monkey never bit your dog.

3. (old). — Hang-dog. *Cf.*, *adv.*, sense 1.

1703. WARD, *London Spy*, pt. xv., p. 353. He describes a swarthy, black, ill-looking Fellow, with a DOWN look, or the like.

1879. JAS. PAYN, *High Spirits* (*Number Forty-seven*). 'Well, he was rather a DOWN-looking cove. 'Hang-dog?' said I. 'Well, yes, to be frank, hang-dog.'

4. *Verb* (common).—To put on one's back: whether by force or by persuasion: *e.g.*, TO DOWN A WOMAN = to lay her out for copulation.—*See* also quot.

1874. HENLEY, *Unpublished Ballad.* Then I DOWNS my bleedin' Judy, And I puts a new head on her.

TO BE DOWN A PIT, *verb. phr.* (theatrical).—To be very much 'taken' with a part.

TO BE, or COME DOWN UPON ONE, *verb. phr.* (colloquial).—To be-rate; to attack; to oppose. Sometimes with a tag: *e.g.*, LIKE A THOUSAND, or A LOAD, OF BRICKS; LIKE ONE O'CLOCK; LIKE A TOM-TIT ON A HORSE-TURD, etc.

1815. SCOTT, *Guy Mannering*, ch. xxviii. I think we should BE DOWN UPON the fellow one of these darkmans, and let him get it well.

1823. MONCRIEFF, *Tom and Jerry* (Dicks' ed., 1889), p. 6. *Prime.* From the cut of the gentleman's clothes, I presume he's lately come from the Esquimaux Islands. *Tom.* Ha! ha! very good, Primefit; I say, Jerry—you see he's DOWN UPON you.

1864. *London Review*, 28 May. There are no loungers in this mortal sphere who so nicely judge a horse's points, or who are so inexorably DOWN UPON any blemish as this careless fringe of observers upon those two fashionable promenades.

1877. *Five Years' Penal Servitude*, ch. iii., p. 167. Let him only find out a man in some artful little game, and he would BE DOWN ON him and hunt his life out almost.

TO BE DOWN PIN, *verb. phr.* (skittle alley).—To be out of sorts, or despondent. *Cf.*, DOWN, *adv.*, sense 1.

TO DROP DOWN TO ONE, *verb. phr.* (old). — To discover one's character or designs.

TO PUT A DOWN UPON ONE, *verb. phr.* (old).—To peach so as to cause detection or failure.

TO PUT ONE DOWN TO [A THING], *verb. phr.* (old).—To apprize, elucidate, or explain; to coach or prime; to 'let one into the know.

TO TAKE DOWN A PEG.—*See* PEG.

DOWNED, *ppl. adj.* (common).—Tricked; beaten; 'sat upon.' [*Cf.*, DOWN, *adv.*, sense 1.]

DOWNER, *subs.* (old).—1. A sixpence. In U.S.A., a five-cent. piece. [*Cf.*, DEANER (*q.v.*); now corrupted into TANNER (*q.v.*).] For synonyms, *see* BENDER.

1857. SNOWDEN, *Mag. Assistant*, 3rd ed., p. 444. Sixpence, DOWNER, also sprat.

1861. WHYTE MELVILLE, *Good for Nothing*, ch. vi. It's not the first DOWNER I've had by a good many; and if it was not for leaving *you* I shouldn't care so much about it!

1885. *Household Words*, 20 June, p. 155. Two more names for a sixpence are a DOWNER and a 'tanner.'

2. (pugilistic).—A knock-down blow. *Cf.*, BENDER, DOUBLER, and DIG, for synonyms.

1819. MOORE, *Tom Crib's Mem. Cong.*, p. 25. In the twelfth and last round Sandy fetch'd him a DOWNER.

DOWN-HILLS, *subs.* (old).—Dice cogged to run on the low numbers. [1785, GROSE.]

DOWNS, *subs.* (thieves').—Tothill Fields Prison. For analagous terms, *see* CAGE.

1856. H. MAYHEW, *Great World of London*, p. 82, note, s.v.

DOWNSTAIRS, *subs.* (old).—Hell.

1837. BARHAM, *I. L.* (*Brothers of Birchington.*) Now if *here* such affairs Get wind unawares, They are bruited about, doubtless much more DOWNSTAIRS, Where Old Nick has a register-office they say, With commissioners quite of such matters *au fait*.

DOWN THE ROAD, *adj.* and *adv. phr.* (common). — Vulgarly showy; 'flash.'

1859. SALA, *Tw. Round the Clock*, 4 p.m., par. 9. A knot of medical students, who should properly, I take it, in this sporting locality, have a racing and DOWN-THE-ROAD look, but who, on the contrary, have the garb and demeanour of ordinary gentlemen.

DOWN TO DANDY.—*See* UP TO DICK.

DOWN TO THE GROUND, *adv. phr.* (old). — Entirely; thoroughly; to the last degree. Formerly, UP AND DOWN. *Cf.*, UP TO THE KNOCKER or THE NINES, UP TO THE HANDLE, UP TO DICK, etc. [Literally, from top to bottom.]

1542. UDAL'S, *Erasmus's Apophth.*, p. 324 [ed. 1877]. He [Phocion] was euen Socrates VP AND DOWNE in this pointe and behalfe, that no man euer sawe hym either laughe or weepe.

1606. JOHN DAY, *Ile of Guls*, Act v., p. 98. For, saies my mother, a thinge once wel done is twice done: and I am in her mind for that, VP AND DOWNE.

1878. M. E. BRADDON, *Cloven Foot*, ch. xlv. Some sea coast city in South America would suit me DOWN TO THE GROUND.

1883. *Echo*, 6 Aug., p. 4, col. 1. A post which would suit the noble lord . . . DOWN TO THE GROUND.

1889. JOHN STRANGE WINTER, *That Imp*, p. 3. A name that suited him well—DOWN TO THE GROUND, the officers of the Royal Horse said.

DOWN UPON THE NAIL.—*See* NAIL.

DOWNY, *subs.* (common). A bed. *Cf.*, DOWNY FLEA PASTURE.

1857. A. TROLLOPE, *Three Clerks*, ch. ix. I've a deal to do before I get to my downy. . . . Good night, Mr. Scott.

Adj. (common). — Artful; KNOWING (*q.v.*, for synonyms). [*Cf.*, DOWN, *adv.*, sense 2, of which DOWNY is a derivative.]

1823. W. T. MONCRIEFF, *Tom and Jerry*, Act ii., Sc. 3. *Bob.* You're a DOWNEY von — you'll not give a chance avay if you knows it.

1842. *Punch*, vol. II., p. 217, c. 2.

1849. DICKENS, *David Copperfield*, ch. xxii., p. 198. Up to mischief, I'll be bound. Oh, you're a DOWNY fellow.

1849. THACKERAY, *Pendennis*, ch. x. I'm not clever, p'r'aps, but I *am* rather DOWNY; and partial friends say I know what's o'clock tolerably well.

1860. *Punch*, vol. XXXVIII., p. 230. You never come across A cove more DOWNIER, I'll be bound, But you knows that 'ere 'oss.

1869. H. J. BYRON, *Not Such a Fool as He Looks* [French's acting ed.], p. 12. . . . . Sharp old skinflint, DOWNY old robber as he is, he's under Jane Mould's thumb.

TO DO THE DOWNY.—*See* DO.

Downy Bit, *subs. phr.* (venery).—A half-fledged girl.

Downy Cove, (or **Bird**, or in *pl.*, The Downies), *subs. phr.* (common).—A clever rogue.

English Synonyms.—Mizzler; leary bloke or cove; sly dog; old dog; nipper; file; Greek; one that knows what's o'clock; one who knows the ropes, or his way about; don; dodger; dab; doll's-eye-weaver; dammacker; shaver; dagen; chickaleary-cove; ikey bloke; artful member; one that is up to the time of day; fly cove; one that's in the know; one that has his eyeteeth skinned, or that has cut his wisdoms.

French Synonyms.—*Un gaspard* (popular); *un fouinard* (pop.: *fouiner*=to slink off); *un ficellier* (popular); *être d'affût* (thieves') =to be on the track or scent); *un arcasien* (thieves': from *arcane*= a secret); *un pante désargoté* (thieves': one 'fly to the time of day'); *un mariolle* (thieves' =English file [*q.v.*]); *un lapin* (popular); *un écopeur* (pop.: a safe hand); *un emberlificoteur* (O.F., popular).

German Synonyms. *Barje* or *Borje* (from the Hebrew *birjah*: also = a fop); *Bochur*, *Bacher*, or *Bocher* (from Hebrew *bochur*: also an official who understands thieves' lingo); *Chochom*, *Chochem*, or *Chochemer* (more frequently spelled with 'k': from Hebrew *chochom*); *Lowon* (also= silver, shining).

Spanish Synonyms. — *Candonguero* (applied to one who is mischievous as well as cunning); *zarapeto*; *zorrastron*; *perro viejo*; *estuche* (also = a pair of scissors); *guitarron* (also=a large guitar); *perillan*; *pua* (also = a sharp point: *es buena pua* = he is a keen blade); *carlancon*; *es un buen sastre* (=he is a sly dog or cunning blade. *Sastre*=tailor); *soga*; *alpargatilla*; *sobon* or *sobonazo* (also=a lazy fellow).

Portuguese Synonym. — *Tinente*.

1821. Egan, *Tom and Jerry* (ed. 1890), p. 95. Mr. Mace had long been christened by the downies, the 'dashing covey.'

1841. Leman Rede, *Sixteen-String Jack*, ii., 4. Tom Bullock, the downiest cove, the leary one that never goes to sleep.

1877. Greenwood, *Dick Temple*, Downy-looking Cove, the fair 'un; a mug like that ought to be worth a fortune to him.

Downy Flea-pasture, *subs. phr.* (common).—A bed. For synonyms, *see* Bug Walk and Kip.

Dowry, *subs.* (common).—A lot; a great deal; dowry of parny= lot of rain or water.

Dowse or **Douse**, *verb* (old).—1. A verb of action.—*See* quots.

1785. Grose, *Dict. Vulgar Tongue*. Dowse your dog vane = take the cockade out of your hat. Dowse the glim = put out the candle. Dowse on the chops =a blow in the face.

1815. Scott, *Guy Mannering*. Dowse the glim!

1860. *Punch*, vol. XXXVIII., p. 252. 'The Death and Burial of poor little Bill.' And who'll put on mourning 'Not we,' said the House 'The Reform flag we'll douse, But we won't put on mourning.'

1863. C. Reade, *Hard Cash*, I., 212. At nine p.m., all the lights were ordered out. Mrs. Beresford had brought a novel on board and refused to comply; . . . The master-at-arms, finding he had no chance in argument, doused the glim—pitiable resource of a weak disputant—then basely fled the rhetorical consequences.

Dout, *verb* (provincial).—Literally =to do out; as Dup (*q.v.*)=to do up, and Don=to do on. *Cf.*, *Hamlet*, iv. Then up he rose and donned his clothes, And dupped the chamber door.

1874. Mrs. H. Wood, *Johnny Ludlow*, 1 S., No. VIII., p. 131. The guard seemed not to hear it, so lost was he in astonishment at there being no light. Why, what can have douted it? he cried aloud.

Doxology-Works, *subs.* (common). — A church or chapel. For synonyms, *see* Gospel Mill.

Doxy, *subs.* (old).—A mistress; a prostitute; occasionally, a jade, a girl, even a wife. In West of England, doxy=a baby. For synonyms, *see* Barrack-hack and Tart.

1567. Harman, *Caveat* (1814), p. 14. And thither repayre at accustomed tymes, their harlotes which they terme mortes and doxes.

1592. Greene, *Quip*, in wks., xi., 283. The Pedler as bad or rather worse, walketh the country with his docksey at the least.

1610. Rowlands, *Martin Mark all*, p. 14 (H. Club's Repr., 1874). You decypher and point out a poore Rogue, or a doxie that steale and rob hedges of a few ragged clothes.

1611. Chapman, *May-Day*, Act IV., p. 299 (*Plays*, 1874). He called me . . . pandar, and doxy, and the vilest nicknames.

1617. C. Shadwell, *Fair Quaker of Deal*, Act v. Thou couldst not have picked out a wife so fit for thee, out of a whole regiment of doxies.

1694. Dunton, *Ladies' Dict. Prostitute* doxies are neither wives, maids, nor widows; they will for good victuals, or for a very small piece of money, prostitute their bodies, and then protest they never did any such thing before, that it was pure necessity that now compell'd them to do what they have done, and the like; whereas the jades will prove common hacknies upon every slight occasion.

1727. John Gay, *Beggar's Opera*, Act III., Sc. 3. Finale. Thus I stand like the Turk, with his doxies around, From all sides their glances his passion confound.

1748. T. Dyche, *Dictionary* (5th ed.). Doxy (s.) a she-beggar . . . the female companion of a foot-soldier travelling tinker, etc.

1851-61. H. Mayhew, *London Lab. and Lon. Poor*, vol. I., p. 231. List of patterers' words. Doxy—a wife.

Dozing-crib, *subs.* (old).—A bed. For synonyms, *see* Bug Walk and Kip.

D.Q., On the D.Q., *phr.* (American).—On the dead quiet. *Cf.*, Strict Q.T., etc.

Drab, *subs.* (common).—1. Poison; also medicine. [From the gypsey.] Also used as a verb.

1851. G. Borrow, *Lavengro*, ch. lxxi., p. 226 (1888). At him, juggal [a dog], at him; he wished to poison, to drab you.

2. (colloquial). — A strumpet. Also drabbing=strumming.

Drabbut, *verb* (provincial). — A vague and gentle form of imprecation. Drabbut your back =Confound you.

Draft on Aldgate Pump, *subs.* (old).—A fictitious banknote or fraudulent bill. *See N. and Q.*, 7 S., i., 387-493.

17(?). Fielding, *Essay on Character of Men*, in wks., p. 647, ed. 1840 (*b.* 1754). This is such another instance of generosity as his who relieves his friend in distress by a draught on Aldgate pump. [A footnote says] A mercantile phrase for a bad note.

1828. Jon Bee, *Picture of London*, p. 187. Why, he might as well have accosted Aldgate-pump with a bill for payment.

Drag, *subs.* (old: now recognised). —1. A cart of any kind; now usually applied to a four-horse coach.

1819. Moore, *Tom Crib's Memorial*, p. 11. While Eld—n, long doubting between a *grey* nag And a *white* one to mount, took his stand in a drag.

1820. Reynolds ('Peter Corcoran'). Glossary at end of *The Fancy*, s.v.

1839. Lever, *Harry Lorrequer*, ch. x. He turned out what he calls a four-in-hand drag which dragged nine hundred pounds out of my pocket.

1855. Thackeray, *Newcomes*, ch. xxviii. Lord Kew's drag took the young men to London; his lordship driving, and the servants sitting inside.

2. (old).—A chain.

1821. D. Haggart, *Life*, Glossary, p. 171, s.v.

3. (old).—A street or road; Back-drag = a back street.

1851-61. H. Mayhew, *London Lab. and Lon. Poor*, vol. I., p. 232. He 'patters' very little in a main drag (public street).

4. (thieves').—Three months' imprisonment; also three moon. For synonyms, *see* Dose.

1851-61. H. Mayhew, *London Lab. and Lon. Poor*, vol. 1., p. 233. Sometimes they are detected, and get a drag (three months in prison).

1883. Horsley, *Jottings from Jail*. But neither Snuffy (Reeves, the identifier), nor Mac (Macintyre) knew me, so I got a drag and was sent to the Steel.

1884. Greenwood, *Seven Years' Penal Servitude*. Well, sir, as I was saying, I only got a drag for that last job. Oh, I beg pardon, a drag means three months. Three weeks is called a drag, too—a cadger's drag.

5. (general).—Feminine attire worn by men. To go on, or flash the drag = to wear women's attire for immoral purposes.

1870. *Reynold's*, 29 May, 'Police Proceedings.' He afterwards said, that instead of having a musical party he thought he would make it a little fancy dress affair, and said, We shall come in drag, which means men wearing women's costumes.

1870. *London Figaro*, 23 June. There is a good deal about Tom and Jerry which our superior refinement might term low—not quite so low though, as going about in drag or consorting with creatures who do.

6. (common).—A lure; trick; stratagem.

7. (hunting).—A fox prepared with herring or aniseed and brought to covert in a bag.

1869. W. Bradwood, *The O.V.H.*, ch. v. He subscribed to the drag at Oxford, though his first season had taught him to seek a less emulous scene of horsemanship.

1887. *Cassell's Mag.*, Dec., p. 27. He was thrown from his horse, near London, they say, huntin' with a drag.

8. (old).—*See* Dragging.

Done for a drag, *phr.* (old). —Convicted of dragging (*q.v.*). *Cf.*, drag = term of imprisonment.

To put on the drag, *verb. phr.* (colloquial).—To ease off or go slow; also to put on pressure.

Drag-cove, *subs.* (old).—A carter or driver of a drag (*q.v.*, sense 1).

Dragging, *verb. subs.* (old).—Robbing vehicles.

Drag-lay, *subs.* (old) — The practice of robbing vehicles. [Grose, 1785.]

Dragon, *subs.* (common).—1. A sovereign. [From the device.] For synonyms, *see* Canary.

1827. Maginn, *Translation of Vidocq*. And collar his dragons clear away.

1859. Matsell, *Vocabulum, or Rogue's Lexicon*, s.v.

2. (venery).—A wanton. *Cf.*, St. George (*q.v.*).

d. 1625. Fletcher, How our St. George's will be stride the dragons! The red and ramping dragons!

To water the dragon, *verb. phr.* (common). — To urinate; 'pump ship;' 'rack off.'

Dragsman.—A coachman; also a Drag-sneak (*q.v.*).

1832. Egan, *Book of Sports*, p. 2. The Swell dragsman or in plain English a well-dressed stage coachman.

1851. H. Mayhew, *Lon. Lab. and Lon. Poor*, IV., 332. This locality is much infested with pickpockets and also with dragsmen, *i.e.*, those persons who steal goods or luggage from carts and coaches.

Drag-Sneak, *subs.* (old).—A thief who makes a speciality of robbing vehicles.—[*See* Drag, sense 1.] Also Dragsman and Dragger, *see* quot., 1781.

1781. G. Parker, *View of Society*, II., 151. Draggers [named and described in].

1856. H. Mayhew, *Gt. World of London*, p. 46. Belonging to the first variety, or those who sneak off with goods, are drag-sneaks, who make off with goods from carts or coaches.

Drag the Pudding, *verb. phr.* (tailors'). — To 'get the sack' just before Christmas-time.

Drain, *subs.* (common).—A drink. For synonyms, *see* Go. To do a drain, wet (*q.v.*), or Common Sewer (*q.v.*)=to take a friendly drink.

1835. Dickens, *Sketches by Boz*, p. 106. Those two old men who came in just to have a drain, finished their third quartern a few seconds ago.

1883. *Daily Telegraph*, 2 July, p. 5, col. 3. The drinking portion of the Americans are excessively partial to perpendicular drains of cocktails and other drams with more or less preposterous names.

2. (old).—Gin. [From its diuretic qualities.] For synonyms, *see* Drinks.

3. (venery). — The female *pudendum*. For synonyms, *see* Monosyllable.

Drains, *subs.* (nautical).—A ship's cook; otherwise the doctor (*q.v.*).

Drammer.—*See* Drummer.

Draper. — *See* Gammon the Draper.

Drat, *verb*, and Dratted, *adj.* (colloquial).—A mild and indefinite imprecation of contempt, or impatience. [A corruption of 'God rot it.'] For synonyms, *see* Oaths.

1846. *Punch*, vol. XI., p. 40, col. 2.

1852. Dickens, *Bleak House*, ch. xxi., p. 178. Drat you, be quiet! says the good old man.

1864. *Churchman's Family Magazine*, Nov., p. 420.

1869. Mrs. H. Wood, *Roland Yorke*, ch. v. If that dratted girl had been at her post indoors . . . it might never have happened.

1883. James Payn, *Thicker than Water*, ch. xxix. An observation which, I am sorry to say, . . . she supplemented with 'Drat the girl!'

Draught, *subs.* (colloquial). — A privy. For synonyms, *see* Mrs. Jones.

1602. Shakspeare, *Troilus and Cressida*, v. 1. Sweet draught! [Sweet quoth 'a! sweet sink, sweet sewer!

1633. Harrington, *Epigrams*. A godly father sitting on a draught, To do as need and nature hath us taught, Mumbled (as was his manner) certaine prayers.

Draw, *subs.* (popular).—1. An undecided contest. [An abbreviation of 'drawn game.']

2. (common). -- An attraction; *e.g.*, an article; a popular preacher; a successful play; and so forth.

1883. *Saturday Review*, 21 April, p. 497, col. 2. The insinuation that umbrellas are the creation of the devil to tempt otherwise honest men . . . is an unfailing DRAW, whether in a comic paper or an after-dinner speech.

3. (cricket).—A stroke with the surface of the bat inclined to the ground.

Verb (common).—1. To attract public attention.—*See subs.*, sense 2.

1883. HAWLEY SMART, *At Fault*, III., xx., 238. Like a judicious theatrical manager, he usually kept 'his show' running as long as it would DRAW.

2. (thieves').—To steal; to pick pockets. TO DRAW A WIPE or TICKER = to prig a handkerchief or watch; TO DRAW A DAMPER = to empty a till.

1785. GROSE, *Dict. Vulg. Tongue*, s.v. To DRAW a swell of a clout, To pick a gentleman's pocket of a handkerchief.

1878. CHARLES HINDLEY, *Life and Times of James Catnach. Chorus.* Frisk the Cly and fork the rag, DRAW the fogles plummy, Speak to the tattler, bag the swag, And finely hunt the dummy.

3. (common). — To tease into vexation; take in; make game of.

4. (colloquial). — To bring out; to cause to act, write, or speak, by flattery, mis-statement, or deceit. Also TO DRAW OUT; Fr., *tirer les vers du nez.*

1860. THACKERAY, *Philip*, ch. vi. The wags who call upon Mrs. Brandon can always, as the phrase is, 'DRAW' her father, by speaking of Prussia, France, Waterloo, or battles in general.

1883. GREENWOOD, *Tag, Rag, and Co.* The older tramp was in conversation with him, and evidently DRAWING HIM OUT.

1889. *Colonies and India*, 24 July, p. 11, col. 1. Any libel or unjust criticism on Western Australia is sure to DRAW that sturdy friend of the Colony in London, Mr. Charles Bethell.

1890. *Pall Mall Gazette*, 16 July, p. 4, col. 2. They had the satisfaction last night of seeing him regularly DRAWN by Mr. Morley.

5. (colloquial). — To ease of money: *e.g.*, 'I DREW him for a hundred'; 'She DREW me for a dollar'!

6. (venery). — Cf., DOG-DRAWN (q.v.).

TO DRAW ON [A MAN], verb. phr. (common and American).—To use a knife.—See BEAD.

1885. *Saturday Review*, 7 Feb., p. 167. I'll never DRAW a revolver ON a man again as long as I live.

TO DRAW A BEAD ON, verb. phr. (common and American).—To attack with rifle or revolver.

1886. *World*, 11 August, p. 12. It is said that twice A BEAD WAS DRAWN UPON him, but fortunately the shots missed.

TO DRAW A STRAIGHT FURROW, verbal phr. (American).—To live uprightly.

TO DRAW ONE'S FIREWORKS (or TO DRAW ONE OFF), verb. phr. (venery). — To cool one's ardour by coition (said of men by women).

TO DRAW PLASTER, verb. phr. (tailors').—To 'fish' for a man's intentions.

TO DRAW STRAWS, verb. phr. (old).—See quot.

1728. SWIFT, *Polite Conversation* (conv. iii.) *Lady Ans.* I'm sure 'tis time for all honest folks to go to bed. *Miss.* Indeed my eyes DRAW STRAWS (she's almost asleep) . . . *Col.* I'm going to the Land of Nod. *Ner.* Faith, I'm for Bedfordshire.

TO DRAW TEETH, verb. phr. (old).—To wrench knockers and handles from street doors.

TO DRAW THE BADGER.—See BADGER, verb.

TO DRAW BLANKS, verb. phr. (colloquial).—To fail; to be disappointed. [From drawing a blank in a lottery.]

TO DRAW THE BOW UP TO THE EAR.—See Bow.

TO DRAW or PULL THE LONG BOW, verb. phr. (colloquial).—See Bow and quots., *infra.*

1849. THACKERAY, *Pendennis*, ch. xxx. What is it makes him PULL THE LONG BOW in that wonderful manner?

1883. A DOBSON, *Old World Idylls*, p. 134. The great Gargilius, then, behold! His LONG BOW hunting tales of old Are now but duller.

TO DRAW THE CORK, verb. phr. (pugilistic).—To make blood to flow; TO TAP THE CLARET (q.v.).

1860. *Chambers' Journal*, vol. XIII., p. 348.

TO DRAW THE KING'S or QUEEN'S PICTURE, verb. phr. (common). — To manufacture counterfeit coins.

1785. GROSE, *Dict. Vulg. Tongue*, s.v.

TO DRAW WOOL or WORSTED, verb. phr. (tailors').—To irritate; to foment a quarrel. Cf., COMB ONE'S HAIR.

DRAW IT MILD! phr. (common). — An interjection of (1) derision; (2) incredulity; (3) supplication. Cf., COME IT STRONG.

1837. R. H. BARHAM, *Ingoldsby Legends* (ed. 1862.), p. 322. It was not so much for that vulgar child, And I said, 'A pint of double X, and please to DRAW IT MILD.'

1841. *Punch*, vol. I., p. 60, col. 2. DRAW IT MILD! as the boy with the decayed tooth said to the dentist.

1841. *Comic Almanack*, p. 271. Vehement cries of 'bravo!' and 'DRAW IT MILD!' here interrupt the speaker; but he declares he cannot DRAW IT ANY MILDER.

1850. SMEDLEY, *Frank Fairleigh*, p. 10. DRAW IT MILD, old fellow! interrupted the young gentleman in question.

1851-61. H. MAYHEW, *London Lab. and Lon. Poor*, vol. I., p. 154. This caused angry words, and Nancy was solemnly requested to DRAW IT MILD, like a good soul.

1854. MARTIN and AYTOUN, *Bon Gaultier Ballads.* 'The Biter Bit.' And if you'd please, my mother dear, your poor desponding child, Draw me a pot of beer, mother, and mother! DRAW IT MILD.

DRAW-BOY, subs. (trade).—A superior article ticketed and offered at a figure lower than its value. Cf., DRAW, sense 2.

DRAWER - ON, subs. (colloquial).—An appetiser: used only of food as PULLER-ON (q.v.) of drink. Both are in Massinger.

DRAWERS, subs. (old). — Embroidered stockings. Fr., *bas-de-tire*; *tirants brodanchés.* Spanish, *denias*; *tirantes.* German, *Zehnling.* It., *tiranti.*

1567. HARMAN, *Caveat* (1814), p. 65, s.v.

1610. ROWLANDS, *Martin Mark-all*, p. 38 (H. Club's Repr., 1874), s.v.

1671. R. HEAD, *English Rogue*, pt. I., ch. v., p. 48 (1874), s.v.

1706. E. COLES, *Eng. Dict.*, s.v.

DRAW-FART (or DOCTOR DRAW-FART), subs. (common).—A wandering quack.

DRAW-LATCH, subs. (old).—A thief; also a loiterer.

1631. CHETTLE, *Hoffman.* Well, phisitian, attend in my chamber, heere, till Stilt and I returne; and if I pepper him not, say I am not worthy to be cald a duke, but a DRAWLATCH.

1706. E. COLES, *Eng. Dict.* DRAW LATCHES, Roberdsmen, Night thieves.

1811. *Lexicon Balatronicum*, s.v.

[Date uncertain]. *Nursery Rhyme.* Cross-patch, DRAW THE LATCH, sit by the fire and spin.

DRAW-OFF, verb (pugilistic).—To throw back the body to strike; 'he DREW OFF, and delivered on the left peeper.' A sailor would say, 'he hauled off and slipped in.'

DREADFUL, subs. (common).—A 'sensational' story, newspaper, or print. For variants, see AWFUL, and SHILLING SHOCKER.

1890. *Academy*, 1 Feb., p. 78, col. 1. Mr. George Manville Fenn is old hand at a story with an alarming title, and he seldoms fails to live up to it. The only thing we can say against his last 'DREADFUL' is that it is a little deficient in 'BODY.'

DREDGERMAN, subs. (common).—Explained in quot.

1857. DICKENS, *Down with the Tide*, in *Reprinted Pieces*, p. 269. Besides these, there were the DREDGERMEN, who, under pretence of dredging up coals and such like from the bottom of the river, hung about barges and other undecked craft, and when they saw an opportunity, threw any property they could lay their hands on overboard: in order, slyly, to dredge it up when the vessel was gone. Sometimes, they dexterously used their dredges to whip away anything that might lie within reach. Some of them were mighty neat at this, and the accomplishment was called dry dredging.

DRESS, subs. (Winchester College).—The players who come next in order after SIX or FIFTEEN. [So called because they come down to the matches ready dressed to act as substitutes if required.]

DRESS A HAT, verb. phr. (common).—To exchange pilferings: *e.g.*, to swap pickings from a hosier's stock with a shoemaker's assistant for boots or shoes.

DRESS DOWN, verb. phr. (colloquial).—To beat; also to scold.—See TAN and WIG respectively for synonyms. Cf., DRESSING.

1715. MRS. CENTLIVRE, *Gotham Election*, Sc. v. I'll DRESS her DOWN, I warrant her. and she be for fighting.

DRESSED LIKE XMAS BEEF. — See BEEF.

DRESS-HOUSE, subs. (common).—A brothel. Cf., DRESS-LODGER.

DRESSING, or DRESSING-DOWN, subs. (colloquial). — Correction, whether manual or verbal; also defeat. Cf., BASTE. For synonyms, see TANNING.

1811. JANE AUSTEN, *Sense and S.*, ch. xxx. If ever I meet him again I will give him such a DRESSING as he has not had this many a day.

1855. THACKERAY, *Newcomes*, ch. xxviii. The *Scourge* flogged him heartily . . . . and the *Penny Voice of Freedom* gave him an awful DRESSING.

DRESS-LODGER, subs. (common).—A woman boarded, fed, and clothed by another, and paying by prostitution.

1836. KIDD, *London and all its Dangers*, p. 32. DRESS LADIES are a class of Cyprians who deserve no pity. They are voluntarily the property of an old hag who clothes them elegantly for the wages of their prostitution, and their only aim is to enjoy themselves, and cheat her of half her perquisites.

1869. GREENWOOD, *Seven Curses of London.* You would never dream of the deplorable depth of her destitution if you met her in her gay attire. . . . She is absolutely poorer than the meanest beggar that ever whined for a crust. These women are known as DRESS LODGERS.

DRESS TO DEATH, DRESS WITHIN AN INCH OF ONE'S LIFE, or DRESS TO KILL, verb. phr. (colloquial). To DRESS in the extreme of fashion.

1859. *Notes and Queries*, S. 2, viii., 490. 'He was got up very extensively, said of a man who is DRESSED WITHIN AN INCH OF HIS LIFE or DRESSED TO DEATH.

DRESSY, adj. (colloquial). — Fond of dress.

DRILLED, ppl. adj. (old). — Shot through the body.

1833. MARRYAT, *Peter Simple* [ed. 1846], I., iv., 17. And what is winged and DRILLED? enquired I.

DRINKS.—The subjoined lists will be of interest.

INVITATIONS TO DRINK.—What'll you have? Nominate your pizen! Will you irrigate? Will you tod? Wet your whistle? How'll you have it? Let us stimulate! Let's drive another nail! What's your medicine? Willst du trinken? Try a little anti-abstinence? Twy (zwei) lager! Your whiskey's waiting. Will you try a smile? Will you take a nip? Let's get there. Try a little Indian? Come and see your pa? Suck some corn juice? Let's liquor up. Let's go and see the baby.

RESPONSES TO INVITATIONS TO DRINK.—Here's into your face! Here's how! Here's at you! Don't care if I do. Well, I will. I'm thar! Accepted, unconditionally. Well, I don't mind. Sir, your most. Sir, your utmost. You do me proud! Yes, sir-ree! With *you*—yes! Anything to oblige. On time. I'm with you. Count me in. I subscribe.

SYNONYMS FOR A DRINK [*i.e.*, a portion], generally, or when taken at specified times.—Anti-lunch; appetiser; ball; bullock's eye (a glass of port); bead; bosom friend; bucket; bumper; big-reposer; chit-chat; cheerer; cinder; corker; cobbler; damper, or something damp; dannie; drain; dram; deoch-an-doras; digester; eye-opener; entr'acte; fancy smile; flash; flip; facer; forenoon; go; gill; heeltap; invigorator; Johnny; joram; morning rouser; modicum; nip, or nipperkin; night cap; nut; pistol shot; pony; pill; quantum; refresher; rouser; reposer; shout; smile; swig; sleeve-button; something; slight sensation; shant; sparkler; settler; stimulant; soother; thimble-full; tift; taste; toothful; Timothy. For other synonyms, see Go.

GENERAL SYNONYMS FOR DRINK. — Breaky - leg; bub; crater (also = whiskey); fuddle; gargle; grog; guzzle; lap; lush; neck-oil; nectar; poison; slumgullion; swizzle; stingo; tipple; tittey; toddy. For other synonyms, see TIPPLE.

SYNONYMS FOR BEER (including stout).—Act of Parliament; artesian; barley; belch; belly - vengeance; bevy or bevvy; brownstone; bum-clink; bung - juice; bunker; cold-blood; down (see UP); English burgundy (porter); gatter; half-and-half; heavy-wet; John Barleycorn; knock down or knock-me-down; oil of barley; perkin; ponge, pongelow, or ponjello; rosin; rot-gut; sherbert; stingo; swankey; swipes; swizzle; up (bottled ale or stout). For other synonyms, see SWIPES.

SYNONYMS FOR BRANDY.—Ball of fire; bingo; cold-tea; cold-nantz; French elixir or cream. For other synonyms, see FRENCH ELIXIR.

SYNONYMS FOR WHISKEY.—*Aqua vitæ*; bald-face; barley-bree; breaky-leg; bottled-earthquake; bum-clink; caper-juice; cappie; curse of Scotland; family-disturbance; farintosh; forty-rod lightning; grapple-the-rails; hard stuff; hell-broth; infernal compound; kill-the-beggar; lightning; liquid fire; moonlight; moonshine; mountain-dew; old man's milk; pine-top; railroad; red-eye; rotgut; screech; Simon pure; sit-on-a-rock (rye whiskey) soul-destroyer; square-face; stone-fence; tangle-foot; the real thing; the sma' still; white-eye. For other synonyms, *see* OLD MAN'S MILK.

SYNONYMS FOR GIN.—Blue ruin; blue-tape; Brian O'Lynn (rhyming); cat-water; cream of the valley; daffy; diddle; drain; duke; eye-water; frog's wine; juniper; jackey; lap; max; misery; old Tom; ribbon; satin; soothing-syrup; stark-naked; strip-me-naked; tape; white satin, tape, or wine. For other synonyms, *see* SATIN.

SYNONYMS FOR CHAMPAGNE.—Cham or chammy; boy; fiz; dry; bitches' wine.

SYNONYMS FOR PORT.—Red fustian (*q.v.*).

SYNONYMS FOR SHERRY.—Bristol milk; white wash.

TERMS IMPLYING VARIOUS DEGREES OF INTOXICATION.—All mops and brooms; at rest; *Bacchi plenus*; battered; be-argured; beery; been at a ploughing match, crooking the elbow, drowning the shamrock, having a cooler or warmer, having the eyes opened, in the sun, looking through a glass, lifting the little finger, making fun, on sentry, talking to Jamie Moore or trying Taylor's best; bemused; been bit by a barn mouse; blued; boosed or boosy; bosky; bright in the eye; buffy; canon; can't see a hole in a ladder; can't say National Intelligencer; chirping-merry; clear; corned; croaked; crooked; cup-shot; cut; damaged; dipped rather deep; disguised; doing the lord or emperor; done over; down with barrel fever; dry; electrified; elevated; elephant's-trunk (rhyming); far-gone; feeling right royal; flushed; flustered; flawed; been flying rather high; foggy; fou', or fou' as a piper; fuddled; full; foxed; glorious; got a drop in the eye; got the back teeth well afloat; greetin' fu'; groggy; got the gravel rash; half-cut; half-seas-over; hard-up; hazy; hearty; helpless; in a difficulty; in liquor; in the altitudes; in one's cups; inspired; in the blues, shakes, or horrors; jolly; kisky; been lapping the gutter; loose; looking lively; lumpy; lushy; mellow; miraculous; mortal; moony; muggy; muddled; muzzy; nappy; obfuscated; on; on his fourth; on the batter, beer, bend, fuddle, loose, muddle, ramble, ran-tan, ree-raw, rampage, skyte, or spree; off his nut; out of funds; overcome; overtaken; paralysed; peckish; ploughed; podgy; pruned; pushed; raddled; rather touched; reeling; roaring; salubrious; screwed; scammered; sewed-up; shaky; slewed; smee kit; smelling of the cork; soaked; spiffed; spreeish; sprung; stolling; starchery; swipey; tavered; taking it easy; thirsty; three-sheets-in-the-wind; tight; tipsy; top-heavy; unco' happy; under the influence; up a tree; waving a flag of defiance; with the mainbrace well spliced; got the sun in the eyes;

whittled; wet; winey; yaupish, yappy, or yaupy. For other synonyms, *see* SCREWED, and *cf.*, DRUNK AS DAVY'S SOW.

See also lists under ELBOW-CROOKER; DRUNK; LUSH; GALLON DISTEMPER; GLADSTONE; PISTOL; FLESH AND BLOOD; and RAZORS.

DRIPPER, *subs.* (old).—A gleet.

DRIPPING, *subs.* (common).—A cook; especially an indifferent one. Fr., *un fripier* and *une daube*. *Cf.*, DOCTOR and SLUSHY (*q v.*) = a ship's cook.

DRIVE, *subs.* (common).—A blow. *Cf.*, 'LET DRIVE' = to aim a blow; to strike. 'Four rogues in buckram LET DRIVE at me.'—*Shakspeare.* For synonyms, *see* DIG.

1863. H. KINGSLEY, *Austin Elliot*, ch. xix. Lord Charles, after three or four attempts, had managed to give him a violent 'DRIVE' on the shins under the table.

Verb (cricket).—To send a ball off the bat with full force horizontally.

TO DRIVE AT, *verb. phr.* (colloquial).—To aim at: *e.g.*, What are you DRIVING AT? = What do you mean?

1697. VANBRUGH, *Relapse*, Act iii., Sc. 2. I can't imagine what you DRIVE AT, Pray tell me what you mean.

1730. JAS. MILLER, *Humours of Oxford*, Act iii., p. 41 (2 ed.). *Tru.* What does the coxcomb DRIVE AT?

1752. FIELDING, *Amelia*, bk. IX., ch. iii. 'O, your servant, sir,' said the Colonel, 'I see what you are DRIVING AT.'

1861. H. KINGSLEY, *Ravenshoe*, ch. xii. Howld yer impudence, ye young heretic doggrel-writer; can't I see what ye are DRIVING AT?

TO DRIVE A BARGAIN, *verb. phr.* (colloquial).—To conduct a negotiation; to make the best terms you can; to dispute a condition or a price; to succeed in a 'deal.' *Cf.*, TO DRIVE A HUMMING TRADE.

1580. SIDNEY, *Arcadia*. My true love hath my heart, and I have his, There never was a better BARGAIN DRIVEN.

1638. FORD, *Lady's Trial*, V., ii. Love DROVE THE BARGAIN, and the truth of love confirmed it.

1668. ETHEREGE, *She Would if She Could*, V., in wks. (1704), p. 172. How . . . goes the business between you and these ladies? Are you like to DRIVE A BARGAIN?

1688. SHADWELL, *Sq. of Alsatia*, ii., in wks. (1720), iv., 43. He never . . . . drinks hard, but upon design, as DRIVING A BARGAIN, or so.

1697. VANBRUGH, *Provoked Wife*, II., i. Why, madam, TO DRIVE A Quaker's BARGAIN, and make but one word with you, if I do part with it, you must lay down your affectation.

1712. *Spectator*, No. 450. I do not remember I was ever overtaken in drink, save . . . . five times at DRIVING OF BARGAINS.

1837. LYTTON, *Ernest Maltravers*, wks. IV., ch. vii. You'll DRIVE A much better BARGAIN with me than with her.

1855. MRS. GASKELL, *North and South*, ch. xxvii. As it affected his branch of the trade he took advantage of it, and DROVE hard BARGAINS.

TO DRIVE A HUMMING OR ROARING TRADE, *verb. phr.* (colloquial).—To do well in business.

1625. JONSON, *Staple of News*, II. And as you say, DRIVE A QUICK PRETTY TRADE still.

1736. FIELDING, *Don Quixote*, III., iv. You are to DRIVE A HUMMING TRADE here.

1883. HAWLEY SMART, *Hard Lines*, ch. vii. The vendors of apples, oranges, and gingerbread . . . . were DRIVING A ROARING TRADE.

1883. A. DOBSON, *Hogarth*, p. 71. The gentleman at the sign of the 'Three Balls' is DRIVING A ROARING TRADE.

TO DRIVE ONESELF TO THE WASH, *verb. phr.* (common).—To drive in a basket-chaise.

TO DRIVE PIGS TO MARKET, *verb. phr.* (common).—To snore.—*See* quot. Fr., *jouer à la ronfle* or *de l'orgue*; also *fumer*.

1787. GROSE, *Prov. Glossary, &c.*, p. 64 (1811). He is DRIVING HIS HOGS OVER SWARSTON-BRIDGE. This is a saying used in Derbyshire, when a man snores in his sleep. Swarston-bridge (or bridges, for there are several of them, one after another) is very long, and not very wide, which causes the hogs to be crowded together, in which situation they always make a loud grunting noise.

TO DRIVE TURKEYS TO MARKET, *verb. phr.* (common).—To reel and wobble in drink.

TO DRIVE FRENCH HORSES, *verb. phr.* (common).—To vomit. [From the '*Hue donc*' of French carters to their teams.] For synonyms, *see* ACCOUNTS.

DRIVER'S PINT, *subs. phr.* (military).—A gallon.

DRIZ, *subs.* (thieves').—Lace. Fr., *la miche* (pop., in allusion to the holes in a loaf of bread); *la gratouse* (thieves': *gratousé* = adorned with lace); *la paille* (thieves': also, straw, or chaff); *la galuche* (thieves'); *le rayon de miel* (thieves').

1812. DE VAUX, *Flash Dict.*, s.v.

1834. H. AINSWORTH, *Rookwood*, bk. III., ch. v. [*see* CAMESA].

1851-61. H. MAYHEW, *London Lab. and Lon. Poor*, vol. 1., p. 233. Scotch Mary, with 'DRIZ' (lace), bound to Dover and back.

DRIZ-FENCER, *subs.* (thieves').—A seller of lace; also a receiver of stolen material. [From DRIZ + FENCE.]

1851-61. H. MAYHEW, *London Lab. and Lon. Poor*, vol. I., p. 429. Among street-people the lace is called driz, and the sellers of it DRIZ-FENCERS.

DR. JOHNSON, *subs. phr.* (old).—The *penis*. For synonyms, *see* CREAMSTICK.

DRODDUM, *subs.* (Scots').—The posteriors. For synonyms, *see* BLIND CHEEKS, BUM, and MONOCULAR EYEGLASS.

1786. BURNS, *To a Louse*.—O for some rank mercurial rozet, Some fell, red smeddum, I'd gie ye sic a hearty doze o't, Wad dress your DRODDUM!

DROMAKY, *subs.* (provincial).—A prostitute: north of England, particularly N. and S. Shields. [From a strolling actress who personated Andromache.]

DROMEDARY, *subs.* (old).—A bungler; specifically, a bungling thief. Also PURPLE DROMEDARY (*q.v.*).

DROP, *subs.* (old).—*See* DROP-GAME.

Verb (common).—1. To lose, give, or part with.

1812. VAUX, *Flash Dict.* He DROPPED me a quid, He gave me a guinea.

1849. THACKERAY, *Pendennis*, ch. xliii. That rascal Blackland got the bones out, and we played hazard on the dining-table. And I DROPPED all the money I had from you in the morning.

1870. *London Figaro*, 7 June. The money DROPPED by the turf prophets in the investment of advertisments, postage-stamps, and 'an office for the transaction of the increasing business of their numerous clients,' is quickly returned to them.

1876. BESANT and RICE, *Golden Butterfly*, ch. xxxi. Ladds is hard at work at ecarté with a villainous-looking stranger. And I should think, from the way Tommy is sticking at it, that Tommy is DROPPING pretty heavily.

1880. A. TROLLOPE, *The Duke's Children*, ch. lxiii. Nobody could have been more sorry than me that your Lordship DROPPED your money.

2. (colloquial).—To relinquish; abandon; leave: *e.g.*, TO DROP AN

ACQUAINTANCE = to gradually withdraw from intercourse. *Cf.*, CUT, *verb*, sense 2. TO DROP THE MAIN TOBY = to turn out of the main road.

1711. *Spectator*, No. 89. He verily believes she will DROP him in his old age, if she can find her account in another.

1751. SMOLLETT, *Peregrine Pickle*, ch. lxxxi. They attempted to make a proselyte of me; but finding the task impracticable on both sides, we very wisely DROPPED each other.

1855. THACKERAY, *Newcomes*, ch. xxiv. What do these people mean by asking a fellow to dinner in August, and taking me up after DROPPING me for two years?

1872. DR. DORAN, *A Lady of the Last Century*. 'Mrs. Montague, sir,' said Dr. Johnson, 'has DROPT me.'

3. (pugilistic).—To knock down. *Cf.*, TO DROP INTO = to thrash.

4. (sporting and duelling).—To bring down with a shot.

1852. F. E. SMEDLEY, *Lewis Arundel* ch. v. But when you *do* make a hit, DROP your man if possible; it settles him and frightens the rest.

TO DROP ANCHOR, *verb. phr.* (racing).—To pull up a horse.

TO DROP ONE'S ANCHOR, *verb. phr.* (colloquial).—To sit (or settle) down.

TO DROP A COG.—*See* DROP-GAME.

TO DROP ONE'S FLAG (colloquial).—To salute; also to submit; to lower one's colours.

TO DROP, HANG, SLIP, OR WALK INTO, *verb. phr.* (colloquial).—To attack. *Cf.*, DROP ON TO.

1852. DICKENS, *Bleak House*, ch. xxiv., p. 217. He's welcome TO DROP INTO me, right and left, if he likes.

1884. *Punch*, 10 May, p. 217, col. 2. If I ever drop into tune, I deserve to be DROPPED INTO by the critics afterwards.

TO DROP OFF THE HOOKS, *verb. phr.* (common).—To die. For synonyms, *see* ALOFT and HOP THE TWIG.

1857. DUCANGE ANGLICUS, *The Vulgar Tongue*, s.v.

TO DROP ONE'S LEAF, *verb. phr.* (common).—To die. [From the 'fall of the leaf' in nature] For synonyms *see* ALOFT and HOP THE TWIG.

TO DROP ON ONE, *verb. phr.* (colloquial).—To accuse or call to account without warning. Also = to thrash. *Cf.*, TO DROP INTO.

1877. *Five Years' Penal Servitude*, ch. iv., p. 258. During the weeks or months that the siege is going on, and the plans are working, do the police ever DROP UPON the parties and frustrate their plans?

TO DROP THE SCABS IN, *verb. phr.* (tailors').—To work button-holes.

TO DROP ONE'S WAX, OR TO DROP A TURD (vulgar).—To evacuate or 'rear.'

TO GET OR HAVE THE DROP ON, *verb. phr.* (American).—To hold at disadvantage; to forestall.

1888. *Troy Daily Times*, 8 Feb. I also kept my revolver handy and did not propose that he should GET THE DROP ON me. When he found that I was prepared for him, he did not try to shoot me.

1888. *Texas Siftings*, Aug. At any rate, we will not let Arcturus GET THE DROP ON the reading public.

TO HAVE A DROP IN THE EYE, *verb. phr.* (common).—To be slightly drunk. For synonyms, *see* SCREWED.

1738. SWIFT, *Polite Conversation*. O faith, Colonel, you must own you HAD A DROP IN YOUR EYE, for when I left you you were half-seas over.

1785. GROSE, *Dict. Vulg. Tongue*, s.v.

DROP IT! *phr.* (colloquial). — Cease! CUT IT! CHEESE IT (*q.v.* sense 2).

1854. WHYTE MELVILLE, *General Bounce*, ch. xxvi. A jackdaw on the roof brings their hearts into their mouths; were it not for the case-bottle they would DROP IT even now.

1859. DICKENS, *Tale of Two Cities*, bk. II., ch. xix. You might as well flop as meditate. You may as well go again me one way as another. DROP IT altogether.

1872. *Public Opinion*, 24 Feb., p. 241. 'Inside Newgate.' Do you know Newgate? I said to a cabman whom I hailed in Piccadilly on Saturday afternoon. He looked at me angrily, and briefly answered, DROP IT.

DROP-GAME, *subs.* (old).—A variety of the confidence trick:—The thief picks out his victim, gets in front of him, and pretends to pick up (say) a pocket-book, (snide) which he induces the greenhorn to buy for cash. The object is a COG, and the operator a DROPPER or DROP-COVE.

1785. GROSE, *Dict. Vulg. Tongue*, s.v.

1859. MATSELL, *Vocabulum, or Rogue's Lexicon*, s.v.

DROPPED ON, *adv. phr.* (tailors'). – Disappointed.

DROPPER, *subs.* (old).—A specialist in the DROP-GAME (*q.v.*). Also DROP-COVE.

1669. *Nicker Nicked*, in *Harl. Misc.* (ed. Park), ii. 108. [In list of names of thieves.]

DROPPING, *verb. subs.* (old Royal Military Academy).—A beating; 'I'll give you a good DROPPING *i.e.*, I'll thrash you severely. For synonyms, *see* TANNING.

DROPPING-MEMBER, *subs.* (old).—The *penis*; specifically one affected with gonorrhœa.

DROPPINGS, *subs.* (vulgar).—The excrement of horses and sheep.

DROWN THE MILLER.—*See* MILLER.

DRUDGE, *subs.* (American). — Whiskey in its raw state, as used in the manufacture of alcohol. For synonyms, *see* DRINKS.

1869. S. S. HALDEMAN, *Pennsylvania Dutch*. DRUDGE, another name for raw whiskey, originating in the Eastern States. I doubt whether the word DRUDGE is thirty years old.

DRUG, *verb* (colloquial).—To administer a narcotic.

A DRUG IN THE MARKET, *subs. phr.* (colloquial).—Anything so common as to be not vendible.

DRUM, *subs.* (old).—1. An entertainment; now a tea before dinner; a KETTLE-DRUM (*q.v.*).

1750. FIELDING, *Tom Jones*, bk. XVII., ch. vi. A DRUM, then, is an assembly of well-dressed persons of both sexes, most of whom play at cards and the rest do nothing at all, while the mistress of the house performs the part of the landlady at an inn.

1854. WHYTE MELVILLE, *General Bounce*, ch. i. We recollect it well, not so many years ago, lit up for one of those great solemnities which novelists call 'a rout,' but which people in real life, equally martially as well as metaphorically designate 'A DRUM.'

2. (thieves').—A road, street, or highway. [From the Gr. δρομός through the Gypsy *drom*.]

ENGLISH SYNONYMS. Drag; toby; high or main toby; pad; donbite; finger and thumb (rhyming).

FRENCH SYNONYMS. *La trime* (thieves'); *le Général Macadam* (popular, also = the public).

SPANISH SYNONYM. *Calca.*

1851-61. H. MAYHEW, *London Lab. and Lon. Poor*, vol. i., p. 231. We . . . slink into the crib (house) in the back DRUM (street).

3. (pugilistic).—The ear. For synonyms, *see* HEARING-CHEAT.

4. (old).—A building; HAZARD-DRUM = a gambling hell; FLASH-DRUM = a brothel; CROSS-DRUM = a thieves' tavern. For synonyms, *see* KEN. In U.S.A., a drinking place.

1867. JAS. GREENWOOD, *Unsent. Journeys*, xxvi., 204. 'Come along; I shall be a pot to your pot.' 'Where shall we go?' 'Oh, to the old DRUM, I suppose.'

1890. *Illustrated Bits*, 29 March, p. 11, col. 1. The two chums were footing it to the 'ancient DRUM,' as they called the Norwich theatre.

5. (Australian). — A bundle carried on tramp; generally worn as a roll over the right shoulder and under the left arm. Also BLUEY and SWAG (*q.v.*). *Cf.*, SWAGSMAN.

1887. G. A. SALA, in *Ill. London News*, 12 March, 282/2. Here are a few more items of Australian slang kindly forwarded to me by a correspondent:—'To hump one's swag,' or 'DRUM,' *i.e.*, to pack up a bundle to be carried on the shoulders.

1890. *Family Herald*, 8 Feb., p. 227. I was just debating whether I had better 'hump my DRUM.'

6. (tailors').—A small workshop. *Cf.*, sense 4.

DRUMMER, *subs.* (old).—1. A horse, the action of whose forelegs is irregular. [*Grose*—1785.]

2. (old).—A thief who before robbing narcotises or otherwise stupifies his victim.

1856. H. MAYHEW, *Great World of London*, p. 46. Those who hocus or plunder persons by *stupifying*; as 'DRUMMERS' who drug liquor.

3. (general). — A commercial traveller; also AMBASSADOR OF COMMERCE or BAGMAN (*q.v.*); Fr., *un gaudissart* (from one of Balzac's novels); *une hirondelle* (= a swallow). [*Cf.*, DRUM = a road; and old-time pedlars announced themselves by beating a drum at the town's end.]

1827. SCOTT, to C. K. Sharpe, in C. K. S.'s *Correspondence* (1888), ii. 398. Dear Charles,—I find the Nos. of Lodge's book did not belong to the set which I consider yours, but were left by some DRUMMER of the trade upon speculation, so I must give you the trouble to return it. [In another letter on next page S. again refers to the 'scoundrelly DRUMMER.']

ante 1871. [in DE VERE], *A Country Merchant out West*, p. 217. Look at that man, he's DRUMMER for A. T. Stewart.

1877. M. TWAIN, *Life on the Mississippi*, ch. xxxix., p. 365. It soon transpired that they were DRUMMERS—one belonging in Cincinnati, the other in New Orleans.

1885. G. A. SALA, *Daily Telegraph*, 14 August, 5, 3. Among whom were conspicuous sundry DRUMMERS, or representatives of American commercial firms, bound for Australasia, there to push their wares.

4. (tailors').—A trousers'maker, or KICKSEYS'-BUILDER (*q.v.*).

DRUMSTICK-CASES, *subs.* (common).—Trousers. [From DRUMSTICK = a leg + CASE, a cover.] For synonyms, *see* BAGS and KICKS.

DRUMSTICKS, *subs.* (common).—1. The legs—especially of birds.

ENGLISH SYNONYMS. Cheese-cutters (bandy legs); stumps; cabbage-stumps; pins; gams; notches; shanks; stems; stumps; clubs; marrow-bones; cat-sticks; trap-sticks; dripping sticks; trams; trespassers; pegs; knights of the garter.

FRENCH SYNONYMS. *Les brancards* (popular, *les brancards de laine* = weak or lame legs); *des baguettes de tambour* (popular = thin legs; properly DRUMSTICKS); *un bâton de tremplin* (mountebanks' = a leg; *tremplin* is properly a spring-board); *des cotrets* (popular: 'a fagot'; *jus de cotret* = stirrup-oil, a 'lathering'); *des flûtes* or *flûtes à café* (popular); *des flageolets* (popular); *des gambettes* (popular: from O. F. *gambe* = leg; *des gambilles* is of similar derivation); *des fumerons* (popular); *des fuseaux* (popular: also = a spindle or distaff); *des jambes en manche de reste* (popular = bandy-legs; *des jambes de coq* = spindle-shanks; *des jambes de coton* = weak legs); *numéro onze* (popular = Shank's mare); *des guibes, guiboles, guibolles*, or *guibonnes* (popular and thieves'); *des merlins* (popular); *des fourchettes* (popular, literally, forks; *fourchettes d'Adam* = fingers); *les chevaux à double semelles* (popular. *Cf.*, English Shank's mare).

ITALIAN SYNONYMS. *Ramo* (literally, 'a branch'); *calcha*; *colonna* (literally, 'a column').

SPANISH SYNONYM. *Gamba* (*Cf.*, O. F. *Gambe*).

1770. FOOTE, *Lame Lover*, I. What, d'ye think I would change with Bill Spindle for one of his DRUMSTICKS.

1837. BARHAM, *Ingoldsby*, 'Lay of St. Nicholas.' He helped his guest to a bit of the breast, And he sent the DRUMSTICKS down to be grilled.

2. In *sing.* (venery). — The *penis*. For synonyms, *see* CREAM-STICK.

DRUNK, *subs.* (vulgar).—A debauch; by implication, a drunkard. ON THE DRUNK = 'on the drink, *i.e.*, drinking for days on end.

1871. *Philadelphia Inquirer*, 6 July. It seems that Gamble went on a DRUNK last Monday evening.

1879. G. R. SIMS, *Dagonet Ballads* (told to the Missionary). I was out on the DRUNK and caught it—lor, what a cuss is drink!

[Among other meridians are drunk as a brewer's fart; drunk as Bacchus; drunk as Chloe; drunk as the devil; drunk as hell; drunk as buggery; drunk as a Gosport fiddler; drunk as a fly; drunk as he (or she) can stick (or hang together); drunk as a lord; drunk as an owl (American, a biled owl); drunk as a tapster; drunk as a piper; blind drunk; crying drunk; pissing drunk; dead drunk; so drunk that you can't see a hole through a ladder; drunk as blazes; and so drunk that he opens his shirt collar to piss; tumbling drunk].

DRUNK AS DAVY'S SOW.—Excessively drunk. — *See* DAVY'S SOW.

DRUNKARD. TO COME THE DRUNKARD, *verb. phr.* (colloquial).—To feign drunkenness; also to be drunk.

TO BE QUITE THE GAY DRUNKARD (colloquial), *verb. phr.*—To be more or less in liquor.

DRUNKEN-CHALKS, *subs.* (military). —Good conduct badges.—*See* CHALK.

DRUNKS, *subs.* (colloquial). — An abbreviation of 'drunk and disorderly.'

1883. *Daily Telegraph*, 26 March, p. 2, col. 8. Of the twenty-nine night charges, by far the greater number were of DRUNKS.

1884. W. D. HOWELLS, *Lady of the Aroostook*, ch. xvii. If you could see how my mother looks when I come out of one of my DRUNKS.

1890. *Globe*, 26 Feb., p. 1, col. 4. 'A Short Way with DRUNKS.' At Buenos Ayres it is customary to punish drunkards, . . . by setting them to sweep the public streets for eight days or so.

DRURY-LANE AGUE, *subs. phr.* (old).—A venereal disease.—*See* LADIES' FEVER.

DRURY-LANE VESTAL, *subs.* (old). —A prostitute. *Cf.*, COVENT GARDEN NUN, and BANK-SIDE LADIES.

DRY AS A LIME-BASKET. — *See* LIME-BASKET.

DRY-BOB, *subs.* and *verb* (venery). —Coition without emission (said of men only).

DRY-BOOTS, *subs.* (old).—A dry humorist. [*Grose*—1785.]

DRY-HASH, *subs.* (Australian).—A miser; or BAD EGG; also, by implication, a loafer.

1887. *All the Year Round*, 30 July, p. 66. In Australian parlance . . . a DRY HASH, or a stringy bark, that is, a ne'er-do-weel.

DRY-LAND! *intj.* (rhyming). — 'You understand!

DRYLAND SAILOR.—*See* TURNPIKE SAILOR.

DRY-LODGING, *subs.* (common).—Accommodation without board.

DRY-NURSE, *subs.* (old).—A guardian; a bear-leader, or tutor; a junior who instructs an ignorant chief in his duties.

1614. JONSON, *Bartholomew Fayre*, I. *Quar.* Well, this DRY NURSE, I say still, is a delicate man.

c. 1640. [SHIRLEY], *Captain Underwit*, in Bullen's *Old Plays*, ii. 322. *Tho.* But, sir, you must have a DRY NURSE, as many Captaines have. Let me see: I can hire you an old limping decayed sergeant at *Brainford* that taught the boyes.

1747. WALPOLE, *Lett. to Mann*, 10 May (1833), vol. II., p. 292. This curious Minister . . . used to . . . walk in the Park with their daughters, and once went DRY-NURSE to Holland with them.

1852. F. E. SMEDLEY, *Lewis Arundel*, ch. xxv. Oh, some poor devil old Grant has picked up cheap as DRY-NURSE to his pet idiot . . . half valet, half tutor.

1868. BREWER, *Phrase and Fable*, s.v. When a superior officer does not know his duty, and is instructed in it by an inferior officer, he is said to be dry-nursed. The inferior nurses the superior as a DRY-NURSE rears an infant.

DRY-ROOM, *subs.* (thieves'). — A prison. For synonyms, *see* CAGE.

DRY-SHAVE, *subs.* (common).—Rubbing the chin with the fingers; also used as a verb. The action implies a certain effrontery.

DRY-UP, *subs.* (theatrical). — A failure or COLUMBUS (*q.v.*); contrast with DRAW, sense 2.

Verb (colloquial).—To cease talking; to abandon a purpose or position; to stop work. As an interjection = Hold your jaw!

1865. *The Index*, 2 Feb. With which modest contribution we DRY UP with reference to the subject.

1872. *Daily Telegraph*, 4 July. An audience which should cause defeated Boston to hang her diminished head, DRY UP, and feel small.

1876. C. HINDLEY, *Life and Adventures of a Cheap Jack*, p. 69. I must DRY UP for the fellow's bested me.

1884. *Cornhill Mag.*, June, p. 617. DRY UP! is the slangy and impatient exclamation with which he cuts short the occasional attempts of his mother to lecture him.

1887. O. W. HOLMES, *Our Hundred Days*, p. 131. There were frequent . . interruptions, something like these: 'That will do, sir!' or, 'You had better stop, sir!' . . . With us it would have been DRY UP! or Hold on!

1888. R. HAGGARD, *Mr. Meeson's Will* [in *Illus. Lond. News*, Summer No. p. 3, col. 1]. He . . . suddenly DRIED UP as he noticed the ominous expression on the great man's brow.

DRY-WALKING, *subs.* (military).—A hard-up soldier's outing.

D. T'S., *subs. phr.* (common).—*Delirium tremens.* For synonyms, *see* JIM-JAMS. Also THE D. T. = *Daily Telegraph.*

1864. *Soiled Dove*, p. 266. I wish to God I could get D. T., and then I should go mad and cut my throat, or pitch myself out of the window.

1868. *Public Opinion*, 1 Aug. Frightful diseases, one of the commonest of which is jocularly spoken of by tipplers as D. T.

1880. G. R. SIMS, *Ballads of Babylon (Beauty and Beast).*—And had sold her child to a titled churl, Who had just got round from a bad D.T.

1883. *Globe*, 7 July, p. 1, col. 5. One of the daily papers, which boasts the largest circulation in the world, is familiar to all as the D.T.

1887. JAS. PAYN, *Glow-worm Tales*, vol. i., p. 209. As certain as D.T. is the end of drinking.

DUB, *subs.* (old). — 1. A key; specifically a master key. [From DUP or DUB, to open; to do up; *see verb*, sense.] For synonyms, *see* LOCKSMITH'S DAUGHTER.

1789. GEO. PARKER, *Life's Painter*, p. 153. A bunch of young DUBS by her side, which are a bunch of small keys.

1821. D. HAGGART, *Life*, Glossary, p. 171. DUB, a key.

1839. HARRISON AINSWORTH, *Jack Sheppard* [1889], p. 39. That's the kinchin as was to try the DUB for us, ain't it? muttered Smith.

Verb (old).—To open, 'DUB your mummer' = Open your mouth. *Cf.*, DUBBER; 'DUB the jigger' = open the door.—*See* quot., 1848. Also by confusion, to shut or fasten.

1567. HARMAN *Caveat* [E. E. T. Soc., 1869], p. 85. DUP the gygger, and maund that is bene shyp.

1596. SHAKSPEARE, *Hamlet*, Act iv. Sc. 5. Then up he rose and donned his clothes, and DUPPED the chamber door.

1848. DUNCOMBE, *Sinks of London Laid Open*, p. 106. DUB the jigger, fasten the door.

DUB AT A KNAPPING JIGGER, *subs. phr.* (old).—A turnpike keeper.

1812. VAUX, *Flash Dict.*, s.v.

DUBBER, *subs.* (old).—1. The mouth or tongue; mum your DUBBER = hold your tongue. (*Cf.*, DUB YOUR MUMMER, under DUB).

1789. GEO. PARKER, *Life's Painter*, p. 150. DUBBER mum'd. To keep your mouth shut, or be obliged to hold your tongue.

2. (old).—A picklock. [From DUB, a key + ER.]—*Grose*, 1785.

DUB-COVE.—*See* DUBSMAN.

DUB-LAY, *subs.* (old).—Using picklocks. [From DUB (*q.v.*), a key + LAY (*q.v.*).]—*Grose*, 1785.

DUBLIN-DISSECTOR, *subs.* (medical students').—A cudgel.

1841. *Punch*, vol. I., p. 154. At first he perpetually carries a DUBLIN DISSECTOR under his arm.

DUBS, *adj.* (Winchester College).—Double.

DUBSMAN, or **DUBS**, *subs.* (old).—A turnkey or gaoler. [From DUB (*q.v.*) = key + MAN.]

1812. VAUX, *Flash Dict.*, s.v.

1887. HENLEY, *Villon's Good Night.* For you, you coppers' narks, and DUBS, What pinched me when upon the snam.

ENGLISH SYNONYMS. Jigger-dubber; screw.

FRENCH SYNONYMS. — *Un gaffier* (thieves'); *un gaffe* (thieves' = boat hook); *un oncle* (thieves' = uncle); *un boye* (thieves': also an executioner at Cayenne or New Caledonia); *le Duc de Guiche* (thieves': from *guichettier* = jailer); *un artoupan* (thieves'); *un barbeaudier* (thieves'); *le Comte de Castue* (thieves': *Castue* = prison); *un chat* (thieves' = a cat); *le Comte de Canton* (thieves': *Canton* = prison or 'stir'); *le Comte de la Caruche* (thieves').

SPANISH SYNONYMS.—*Banastero* (= basket-maker); *banquero* (= banker).

1839. HARRISON AINSWORTH, *Jack Sheppard* [1889], 30. Quoth a DUBSMAN, who gazed on the shattered wall, 'You have carved your epitaph, Claude du Val, With your chisel so fine, tra la!'

DUB UP, *verb. phr.* (colloquial).—To hand over; pay; fork out. [*Cf.*, provincial DUBS = money.] Fr., *foncer*; *abouler*. Formerly, to lock up or secure; to button one's pocket.

1840. *Comic Almanack*, p. 237. Come, DUB UP! roars a third: and I don't mind telling you, in confidence, that I was so frightened that I took out the sovereign and gave it.

DUCATS, *subs.* (theatrical). — 1. Money. [Probably from Shylock and *The Merchant of Venice.*] For synonyms, *see* ACTUAL and GILT.

1853. WH. MELVILLE, *Digby Grand*, ch. vi. The Jews have always appeared to me a calumniated race. From spendthrift King John downwards, the Christian has ever pocketed the DUCATS, and abused the donor.

2. (thieves').—Specifically a railway ticket; also pawnbroker's duplicate; raffle-card, or BRIEF (*q.v.*). Also DUCKET.

1879. J. W. HORSLEY, in *Macm. Mag.*, xl., 501. So I took a DUCAT (ticket) for Sutton in Surrey.

DUCE, *subs.* (old). — Twopence. [From the Latin.]

1812. VAUX, *Flash Dict.*, s.v.

1823. MONCRIEFF, *Tom and Jerry*, ii., 6. If any body offers you less nor a mag, or a DUCE, vy, you may say with the poet, Who vou'd his farthings bear? ven he himself might his quivetus make vith a bare bodkin,

DUCK, *subs.* (common).—1. Scraps of meat; otherwise BLOCK-ORNAMENTS, STICKINGS, FAGGOTS, MANABLINS, or CHUCK (*q.v.*).

2. (Winchester College).—The face. TO MAKE A DUCK = to make a grimace. For synonyms, *see* DIAL.

3. (common).—A 'draw' or decoy. [An abbreviation of DECOY-duck.]

4. (colloquial). — A term of endearment; also used in admiration; *e.g.*, a DUCK of a bonnet. Also DUCKY: DUCK OF DIAMONDS being a superlative. For synonyms, *see* MY TULIP.

1837. *Comic Almanack*, p. 78. You won't grudge your poor rib a few ribbons, will you, DUCK?

1841. LEMAN REDE, *Sixteen String Jack*, i., 2. *Nel.* Oh, isn't he a DUCK of a fellow? *Bob.* He's the very flower of the flock.

1846. *Punch*, vol. XI., p. 164. Though somewhat out at elbows, he's what the ladies call a 'DUCK.'

5. (cheap jacks'). — A metal-cased watch; *i.e.*, old watch movements in German silver cases.

1876. C. HINDLEY, *Life and Advent. of Cheap Jack*, p. 38. What appeared to the roughs a fine old English and valuable watch, but what in reality was an almost worthless DUCK.

TO MAKE A DUCK, or DUCK'S EGG, *verb. phr.* (cricketers').—To make no score; *Cf.*, TO CRACK ONE'S EGG, and PAIR OF SPECTACLES. [From the shape of the 'O.']

1868. *St. Paul's Magazine*, Aug. You see by the twitch of the hand, the glove rapidly raised to the face, and replaced on the bat-handle, the jerk of the elbow, and perhaps the uneasy lifting of the foot, that his fear of a DUCK—as, by a pardonable contraction from 'DUCK'S-EGG,' —a nought is called in cricket play—etc.

1870. *London Figaro*, 21 June. J. C. Shaw is a host in himself; he took six wickets, and all of them for DUCKS.

1872. *Weekly Dispatch*, 9 June. The next ball from Brice sends Caffyn's bails flying: and out comes the last man—Southerton—and he is used to DUCK'S EGGS.

1883. *Echo*, 15 May, p. 4, col. 2. Out of the eleven Surrey batsmen who played against Notts yesterday, no less than five were credited with DUCKS.

DUCK THAT RUNS, or GRINDS THE GOSPEL MILL, *subs. phr.* (American).—A clergyman. For synonyms, *see* DEVIL-DODGER.

1869. S. L. CLEMENS ('Mark Twain') *Innocents at Home*, p. 17, 18. Are you the DUCK THAT RUNS THE GOSPEL MILL NEXT DOOR?

LAME DUCK (*q.v. post*).

GERMAN DUCK (*q.v. post*).

TO DO A DUCK, *verb. phr.* (thieves').—To hide under the seat of a public conveyance with a view to avoid paying the fare. [From DUCK = to bow or stoop.]

1889. *Sporting Times.* DOIN' A DUCK, macin' the rattler, ridin' on the cheap, on the odno, under the bloomin' seat.

DUCKET.—*See* DUCAT.

DUCK-FOOTED, *adj. phr.* (common).—Said of people who walk like a duck; *i.e.*, with the toes turned inwards.

DUCKING. TO GO DUCKING, *verb. phr.* (common).—To go courting. [From DUCK (*q.v.*) = a term of endearment + ing.] *See* GOOSE-AND-DUCK.

DUCKS, *subs.* (colloquial).—1. Linen trousers; generally WHITE DUCKS. [From the material and colour.] At Eton worn only by men in the boats. For synonyms, *see* BAGS and KICKS.

1835. DICKENS, *Sketches by Boz*, p. 248. There's our man, Tom; he can have a pair of DUCKS of mine, and a check shirt of Bob's.

1846. *Punch*, vol. X., p. 263. I wore my Russian DUCKS, In their beautiful WHITENESS.

1888. MRS. MUSGRAVE, *Savage London.* Billy should do the thing proper, and be married in a pair of white DUCKS.

2. (Stock Exchange].—Aylesbury Dairy Co. shares.

3. (Anglo-Indian). — Officials of the Bombay service.

CHANCE THE DUCKS (*q.v.*, *ante.*)

TO MAKE DUCKS AND DRAKES OF ONE'S MONEY, *verb. phr.* (common).—To squander money as lavishly as stones are squandered at 'ducks and drakes.' [In allusion to the childish game. Lempriére (*Art.* Scipio Africanus the Younger) refers to Scipio and Lælius taking to 'ducks and drakes' as a supplementary recreation to shell-gathering, and an early notice of the game occurs in Minucius Felix (*Octavius* cap. iii.):—From the beach they choose a shell, thin and polished by the waves; they hold it in a horizontal position, and then whirl it along as near the surface of the sea as possible, so as to make it skim the surge in its even motion, or spring up and

bound from time to time out of the water. That boy is conqueror whose shell both runs out farthest and bounds oftenest.] Variants are TO BLUE ONE'S PILE; TO SWEAT (*q.v.*). *Fr.*, *galvauder*; *manger sa légitime.*

1605. CHAPMAN, etc., *Eastward Hoe!* Act i. Do nothing, be like a gentleman, be idle . . . MAKE DUCKS AND DRAKES with shillings.

1664. H. PEACHAM, *Worth of a Penny*, in Arber's *Garner*, vol. VI., p. 259. I remember, in Queen Elizabeth's time, a wealthy citizen of London left his son a mighty estate in money; who, imagining he should never be able to spend it, would usually MAKE 'DUCKS AND DRAKES' in the Thames, with Twelve pences [= 5/- now], as boys are wont to do with tile sherds and oyster shells.

d. 1680. S. BUTLER, *Character of a Miser*, in *Remains*, vol. II., p. 343 (ed. 1759). And he that MADE DUCKS AND DRAKES with his Money enjoyed it every way as much.

1698. WARD, *London Spy*, pt. xvi., p. 372. They hook in the old fool again TO MAKE DUCKS AND DRAKES with his money.

1700. *Gentleman Instructed*, p. 18. I would neither fawn on money for money's sake, nor DUCK AND DRAKE it away for a frolick.

1849. THACKERAY, *Pendennis*, ch. lviii. We've tied up the property, so that he can't MAKE DUCKS AND DRAKES with it.

1858. MARIAN EVANS (G. Eliot), *Janet's Repentance*, ch. xxv. They say Mrs. Dempster will have as good as six hundred a year at least. . . . It's well if she doesn't MAKE DUCKS AND DRAKES of it somehow.

DUCK'S-BILL, *subs.* (printers').—A tongue cut in a piece of stout paper and pasted on at the bottom of the tympan sheet. [From the shape.]

DUCKY or **DUCK OF DIAMONDS.**—*See* DUCK, sense 4.

DUDDER, DUDSMAN, or **DUFFER**, *subs.* (old). — A pedlar of so-called smuggled wares — gown-pieces, silk waistcoats, etc. The term and practice are both obsolete, though in a few seaports, London especially, they survived till recently in a modified form. [From DUDS (*q.v.*) = clothes.] Fr., *un marottier* (thieves'). *See* also WHISPERING DUDDER and BARROW-MAN.

1781. G. PARKER, *View of Society*, II., 160. A DUDDER happened some time ago to meet a countryman in a dark lane, and sold him a waistcoat-piece for two guineas and a half, which stood himself in only four-and-sixpence.

DUDE, *subs.* (American).—A swell; fop; 'masher.' For synonyms, *see* DANDY. [From Scots DUDS = clothes; *Cf.*, quot., 1870.] Derivatives are DUDETTE and DUDINETTE = a young girl affecting the airs of a belle; DUDINE = a female masher.

1870. *Putnam's Magazine*, Feb. Think of her? I think she is dressed like a DUD; can't say how she would look in the costume of the present century.

1883. *Graphic*, 31 March, p. 319, col. 1. The one object for which the DUDE exists is to tone down the eccentricities of fashion. . . . The silent, subfuse, subdued 'DUDE' hands down the traditions of good form.

1889. *Puck's Library*, April, p. 3. For the front rows two styles are recommended—DUDE, No. 16, and Bald-headed Man, No. 41—both original in design and exquisite in finish.

DUDE HAMFATTER, *subs. phr.* (American). — A wealthy pig-jobber. [From DUDE, a swell + HAMFATTER, in allusion to occupation.]

1888. *New York National Police Gazette.* It seems that the DUDE HAMFATTERS, after trying various games to skip unseen, conceived the idea of making up as a couple of well-dressed women.

DUDS, *subs.* (colloquial).—Clothes; sometimes old clothes or rags. [Scots *dud*, Dutch *todde*, a rag;

O. E. *dudde*=cloth. DUDDERY =a clothiers' booth (DE FOE'S *Tour of Gt. Brit.*, p. 125).] In America applied to any kind of portable property (*Cf.*, quots., 1622, 1780, and 1884). To ANGLE FOR DUDS, *see* ANGLERS; TO SWEAT DUDS=to pawn (*see* SWEAT).

1440. *Prompt. Parv.*, ed. Way, i, 134. DUDDE, cloth.

1567. HARMAN, *Caveat* (1869), p. 86. When we byng back to the deuseauyel, we wyll fylche some DUDDES of the Ruffemans.

1610. ROWLANDS, *Martin Mark-all*, p. 38 (H. Club's Repr., 1874). DUDES, clothes.

1622. HEAD AND KIRKMAN, *English Rogue*. 'Canting Song.' For all your DUDS [goods] are binged avast.

1780. R. TOMLINSON, *Slang Pastoral*, IX. No DUDS in my pocket, no sea-coal to burn.

1787. GROSE, *Prov. Glossary*. DUDDS, rags. Also clothes.

1819. MOORE, *Tom Crib's Memorial*, p. 20. *Doubled* him *up*, like a bag of old DUDS!

1822. SCOTT, *Fortunes of Nigel*, ch. v. A ragged rascal, every DUD upon whose back was bidding good-day to the other.

1841. LEMAN REDE, *Sixteen String Jack*, ii. 3. Crissy, odsbuds! I'll on with my DUDS.

1871. *New York Tribune*, 23 Jan. The three [railway] Commissioners, in whose appointment you had no choice, decide that you must get out, leave your house, bundle out your DUDS, and be off.

1881. A TROLLOPE, *Marian Fay*, ch. iii. To see her children washed and put in and out of their DUDS was perhaps the greatest pleasure of her life.

1884. *Athenæum*, 19 July, p. 74, col. 2. A writer in 1784 [in *Gent. Mag.*, Gomme, vol. II.] says, for instance, that DUDS signifies rags, tatters, and that it comes from the Celtic. We do not believe in the derivation, but will not at present endeavour to refute it; we are sure the meaning is given wrongly, though it has the authority of Halliwell and Wedgwood in recent times. DUDS, in the northern dialects means small things, or things of little account, whether articles of clothing, trade, or merchandise. We have frequently heard the word applied to workmen's tools; and in an unprinted churchwarden's account of an eastern shire we find in the year 1501 mention of 'CLOCKE-DUDES.' From the context it is evident that the small wheels belonging to the town clock are meant.

DUDSMAN.—*See* DUDDER.

DUES, *subs.* (old). — Money. TO TIP THE DUES=to pay; to hand over a share. For synonyms, *see* ACTUAL and GILT. [A colloquial extension of DUE= toll, tribute, fee, etc.]

1812. VAUX, *Flash Dict.* So a thief, requiring his share of booty from his *palls*, will desire them to *bring the* DUES *to light*.

1839. HARRISON AINSWORTH, *Jack Sheppard* [1889], p. 13. Will he come down with the DUES.

DUFF, *verb* (thieves').—1. Specifically, to sell flashy goods as pretended contraband or stolen; hence to cheat. DUFFERS, or MEN AT THE DUFF=pedlars of flash. (*Cf.*, DUDDER). DUFFING =the practice; used as an adjective =spurious.

1781. G. PARKER, *View of Society*, II., 158. 'The DUFF' [smuggled goods, so named and described in.]

1811. *Lexicon Balatronicum*. DUFFERS: cheats who pretend to deal in smuggled goods, stopping all country people, or such as they think they can impose on; which they frequently do, by selling them Spital-fields goods at double their current price.

1851-61. H. MAYHEW, *London Lab. and Lon. Poor*, vol. II., p. 23. They have been regularly 'DUFFED' out of the streets, so much cheap rubbish is made to sell.

1888. G. R. SIMS, in *Cass. Sat. Journal*, 31 March, p. 7. The MAN AT THE DUFF palms off false jewellery as real.

2. (common).—To rub up the nap of old clothes so as to make them look almost as good as new.

DUFFER= one who performs this operation, whilst the article operated upon is also a DUFFER by virtue of the fact itself. *Cf.*, DUFFER.

DUFFER, *subs.* (old: now recognised).—1. A pedlar; specifically a hawker of BRUMMAGEM (*q.v.*), and so-called smuggled goods (hence senses 2 and 3). In the population returns of 1831 DUFFER = one who gets a living by cheating pawnbrokers.—*See* DUDDER and DUFF.

1796. COLQUHOUN, *Police of the Metropolis*, p. 176. A class of sharpers who are known by the name of DUFFERS, who go about from house to house, and attend public-houses, inns, and fairs, pretending to sell smuggled goods.

1843. DICKENS, *Martin Chuzzlewit*, ch. xxxvii., p. 361. Nor did it mark him out as the prey of ring-droppers, pea and thimble-riggers, DUFFERS, touters, or any of those bloodless sharpers, who are, perhaps, a little better known to the police.

1849. THACKERAY, *Pendennis*, ch. lx. Now it is a fact that Colonel Altamont had made a purchase of cigars and French silks from some DUFFERS in Fleet Street about this period.

1851-61. H. MAYHEW, *London Lab. and Lon. Poor*, vol. i., p. 413. An intelligent street-seller, versed in all the arts and mysteries of this trade, told me that he understood by a DUFFER, a man who sold goods under false pretences, making out that they were smuggled, or even stolen, so as to enhance the idea of their cheapness.

2. (colloquial).—Anything (or person) worthless; anything sham. [From sense 1.]

d. 1845. HOOD [quoted in Annandale]. DUFFERS (if I may use a slang term which has now become classical, and which has no exact equivalent in English proper) are generally methodical and old. Fosset certainly was a DUFFER.

1869. MRS. H. WOOD, *Roland Yorke*, ch. xi. Don't you think, Hamish, he must have been a great DUFFER to go and marry before he knew how he could keep a wife?

1872. *Standard*, 12 Sept. 'Who is to blame?' we ask, in the interests of our government, and natural curiosity. 'That DUFFER in feathers' is the curt reply, pointing with the finger of scorn at one hero whom we had mistaken for something little short of a field marshal.

1877. *Five Years' Penal Servitude*, ch. iv., p. 264. I'd several sovs.—good ones —with me, and also a whole lot of DUFFERS.

1884. HAWLEY SMART, *From Post to Finish*, p. 10. He made no bones about calling her stupid, and was more apt to call her a little DUFFER than to sympathise with her when she got into trouble.

1889. *Answers*, 29 June, p. 66, col. 1. If the note is a genuine one the water-mark will then stand out plainly. If a DUFFER it will almost disappear.

3. (nautical). — A female smuggler.

DUFFER-OUT, *verb. phr.* (Australian miners').—To get exhausted.

1887. FINCH-HATTON, *Advance Australia*. He then reported to the shareholders that the lode had DUFFERED OUT, and that it was useless to continue working.

DUFFING, *ppl. adj.* (colloquial).— False; counterfeit; worthless; *Cf.*, DUFF and DUFFER.

1862. *London Herald*, 27 Dec. 'Answers to Correspondents.' Houses burdened with ninety years' repairing leases and heavy ground rents are run up by the 'DUFFING' builder, merely for sale.

1873. *Times*, Jan. We know now that so-called 'DUFFING' jewellery is scattered far and wide over the land.

1877. *Five Years' Penal Servitude*, ch. iii., p. 239. A 'shise' half-bull and a 'DUFFING' tanner: half-a-crown and a sixpence quietly palmed off on this man out of his half-sovereign.

DUGS, *subs.* (old).—The paps; once used without reproach of women; now only in contempt, except of animals. [From same stem as 'daughter.'] For synonyms, *see* DAIRY.

DUKE, *subs.* (old).—1. Gin. For synonyms, *see* DRINKS.

1859. SALA, *Gaslight and Daylight*, ch. xxiii. The stuff itself, which in the Western gin-shops goes generally by the name of 'blue ruin,' or 'short,' is here called . . . DUKE.

2. (cabmen's).—A horse. For synonyms, *see* PRAD.

3. (thieves').—Any transaction in the shape of a burglary; *e.g.*, 'I was Jemminy to their DUKE'= 'I was privy to the robbery.'

DUKE HUMPHREY. TO DINE WITH DUKE HUMPHREY.—*See* DINE.

DUKE OF LIMBS, *subs. phr.* (common). — An awkward, uncouth man; specifically one with ungainly limbs. [*Grose*, 1785.]

DUKE OF YORK, *verb. phr.* (rhyming slang).—To walk; also, to talk.

DUKES, *subs.* (common). — The hands. For synonyms, *see* BUNCH OF FIVES and DADDLE.

1879. J. W. HORSLEY, in *Macm. Mag.*, xl., 501. So I said I would not go at all if he put his DUKES (hands) on me.

1888. *Lic. Vict. Gazette*, 27 Jan., p. 55, 3. The men . . . put up their DUKES to fight for supremacy.

TO GREASE THE DUKES, *verb. phr.* (common).—To bribe; also to pay.

1883. J. W. HORSLEY, *Jottings from Jail*. I went to him and asked him if he was not going TO GREASE MY DUKE.

TO PUT UP THE DUKES, *verb. phr.* (common).—To put up one's hands for combat.

1885. *Home Tidings*, p. 369. 'Boxing Club Report.' The two contestants PUT UP THEIR DUKES, and soon warmed up to their work.

DUKEY.—*See* DOOKIE and GAFF.

DULCAMARA, *subs.* (colloquial).—A quack-doctor. [From the name of a character in Donizetti's *l'Elixir d'Amour* (1845).]

DULL IN THE EYE, *adv. phr.* (common). — Intoxicated. For synonyms, *see* DRINKS and SCREWED.

DULL-SWIFT, *subs.* (old).—A sluggish messenger.

DUMB-FOGGED, *ppl. adj.* (common). —Confused.

DUMB-FOOZLED, *ppl. adj.* (common). —Confounded; puzzled.

1883. HAWLEY SMART, *At Fault*, I., x., 240. Considering you built the theatre, it struck me you weren't very good at finding your way about, you seemed regularly DUMBFOOZLED.

DUMBFOUND, DUMFOUND, *verb* (Also **DUMBFOUNDING**, *subs.*, **DUMBFOUNDED** or **DUMFOUNDERED** [Scots], *adj.* [Old Slang, now colloquial]).—To perplex; to confound.

1690. DRYDEN, Prologue to *Prophetess*. Then think on that bare bench my servant sat. I see him ogle still, and hear him chat. Selling facetious bargains, and propounding That witty recreation called DUMBFOUNDING.

1703. WARD, *London Spy*, pt. xvi., p. 379. This unexpected retort of the parsons, quite DUMB-FOUNDED the Quaker.

1706. R. ESTCOURT, *Fair Example*, Act. III., Sc. i., p. 30. And if I can but DUMB-FOUND my husband with a dream, I shall be able to make my word good.

1714. *Spectator*, No. 616. They grew a little mutinous for more liquor. They had like to have DUMFOUNDED the justice; but his clerk came in to his assistance.

1766. MORTIMER, *Falstaff's Wedding*, I., ii. They let fly their jests so thick at me, and peppered me so plaguily with small wit, that I was DUMFOUNDED.

1855. A. TROLLOPE, *The Warden*, ch. xi. At any other time how exquisitely valuable would have been that touch! but now he was distraught, DUMB-FOUNDED, and unmanned.

1861. H. KINGSLEY, *Ravenshoe*, ch. v. He utterly DUMFOUNDERED Charley, by asking abruptly 'How's Jim?'

1880. G. R. SIMS, *Three Brass Balls*, Pledge xx: White as a ghost, DUMBFOUNDERED, and trembling, Dan attempted to explain that he was innocent.

1882. *Democracy*, ch. vii. She lost her command of thought, and sat DUMBFOUNDED.

1883. W. E. NORRIS, *Thirlby Hall*, ch. ix. I was too DUMBFOUNDERED to speak.

DUMB-GLUTTON, *subs.* (venery).— The female *pudendum*. For synonyms, *see* MONOSYLLABLE.

DUMB-SQUINT, *subs.* (venery).— The female *pudendum*. For synonyms, *see* MONOSYLLABLE.

DUMMACKER, *subs.* (old). — A knowing person. For synonyms, *see* DOWNY COVE.

DUMMERER.—*See* DOMMERAR.

DUMMOCK, *subs.* (common).—The posteriors. For synonyms, *see* MONOCULAR EYE-GLASS.

DUMMY, *subs.* (colloquial).—A deaf mute; also an idiot; sometimes a DUFFER, sense 2.

c. 1884. G. R. SIMS, *Dagonet Ballads* (*Mott Jarvis*). And she left us like open-mouthed DUMMIES a-waggin' our heads at the moon.

2. (colloquial). — Generic for sham substitutes for real objects: *e.g.*, empty bottles and drawers in an apothecary's shop; wooden half-tubs of butter, bladders of lard, hams, cheeses, and so forth; DUMMIES in libraries generally take the form of works not likely to tempt the general reader. Hence, by implication, anything sham.

1846. *Punch*, vol. XI., p. 185. A DUMMY list of Causes has long since been preferred, to enable Thompson to ascertain whether 'we are retained on the other side when a brief is brought on behalf of either party.

1856. H. MAYHEW, *Gt. World of London*, p. 112. The doorway is set round with sprucely-dressed 'DUMMIES' of young gentlemen that have their gloved fingers spread out like bunches of radishes.

1869. MRS. H. WOOD, *Roland Yorke*, ch. ix. The large imposing stock turned out to be three parts DUMMIES.

1871. *Daily News*. 'Leader,' 28 April. The Bill is not yet in the hands of members or public, the document placed on the table of the Lords being what is, in parliamentary slang, called a 'DUMMY.'

3. (cards').—The open hand at an imperfect game of whist

1853. LYTTON, *My Novel*, bk. XI., ch. iv. We might cheer the evening with a game at whist—double DUMMY.

4. (thieves').—A pocket book.

1785. GROSE, *Dict. Vulg. Tongue*. Frisk the DUMMEE of the screens=take all the bank notes out of the pocket book: Ding the DUMMEE, and bolt, they sing out beef=Throw away the pocket book, and run off, as they call out 'stop thief.'

1834. H. AINSWORTH, *Rookwood*, bk. III., ch. v. He is caught—he must 'stand and deliver'; Then out with the DUMMY, and off with the bit [money].

1878. CHARLES HINDLEY, *Life and Times of James Catnach*. (Chorus)— Speak to the tattler, bag the swag, And finely hunt the DUMMY.

[Other colloquial usages are: (1) = dumb-waiter; (2) = a locomotive furnished with condensing engines, and hence without the noise of escaping steam; (3) = a fireman's term for a jet from the main or chief water pipe; (4) = a hatter's pressing iron; *Cf.*, tailor's GOOSE; (5) = a piece of cloth rolled tight and saturated with oil, for rubbing hard places to be cut; (6) = an actor or actress who has nothing to say, etc.]

DUMMY-DADDLE DODGE, *subs. phr.* (thieves').—Picking pockets under cover of a sham hand or DADDLE (*q.v.*).

1883. GREENWOOD, in *Daily Telegraph*. Asked by the friendly warder what he thought of the DUMMY-DADDLE DODGE,

Mr. Mobbs said he rather thought that game was played out. A woman, he proceeded to explain, can work with a DUMMY-DADDLE in an omnibus or a railway carriage much better than a man, because, without appearing conspicuous, she can wear any kind of loose shawl or cloak as concealment for her real hand.

DUMMY-HUNTER, *subs.* (old).—A pickpocket who confined his operations to pocket-books. [From DUMMY (*q.v.*) = a pocket book + HUNTER.]

1785. GROSE, *Dict. Vulg. Tongue*, s.v.

1834. H. AINSWORTH, *Rookwood* [ed. 1884] p. 89. No DUMMY HUNTER had forks so fly, No knuckler so deftly could fake a cly.

1843. *Punch*, vol. IV., p. 129. While ears are cramm'd with humbug, boys! The DUMMY-HUNTERS ply An easy trade.

DUMP, *subs.* (old).—A metal counter.

Verb (colloquial). — 1. To throw down so as to produce a heavy noise: *e.g.*, to DUMP down coals.

2. (Winchester College).—To put out. 'DUMP THE TOLLY!' = Extinguish the candle!

DUMP FENCER, *subs.* (old). — A button-merchant.

DUMPIES, *subs.* (military). — The Nineteenth Hussars. [From the diminutive size of the men when the regiment was first raised.] Obsolete. DUMPY = squat or undersized.

DUMPLING-DEPÔT, *subs.* (common). —The stomach. For synonyms, *see* BREAD-BASKET.

DUMPLING-SHOP, *subs.* (common). —The paps. For synonyms, *see* DAIRY.

DUMPS, *subs.* (common).—Money. For synonyms, *see* ACTUAL and GILT.

1837. BARHAM, *Ingoldsby Legends* (Sir Rupert). May I venture to say when a gentleman jumps In the river at midnight for want of the DUMPS He rarely puts on his knee-breeches and pumps.

IN THE DUMPS, *adv. phr.* (colloquial). — Cast down; ill at ease; unpleasantly situate.

1592. GREENE, *Groatsworth of Wit*, in wks. xii., 115. Whence spring these DUMPS?

1596. JONSON, *Every Man in His Humour*, III., iii. How now, Master Knowell, IN DUMPS, IN DUMPS! Come, this becomes not.

1600. SHAKSPEARE, *Much Ado about Nothing*, ii., 3. Sing no more ditties, sing no mo Of DUMPS so dull and heavy.

1711. *Spectator*, No. 176. When I come home she is IN THE DUMPS, because she says she is sure I came so soon only because I think her handsome.

1717. MRS. CENTLIVRE, *Bold Stroke for a Wife*, v., 1. What art thou IN THE DUMPS for?

1771. FOOTE, *Maid of Bath*, II. She seems got quite I' THE DUMPS.

1847. W. B. RHODES, *Bombastes Furioso*, p. 19. My happiness is chang'd to doleful DUMPS, Whilst, merry Michael, all thy cards were trumps.

1855. TRENCH, English, *Past and Present* (2nd ed.), p. 131. In the great ballad of Chevy-Chase a noble warrior, whose legs are hewn off, is described as being IN DOLEFUL DUMPS. Holland's translation of Livy represents the Romans as being IN THE DUMPS after the battle of Cannæ. It was in elegant use then.

1885. *Daily Telegraph*, 19 Jan., p. 5, col. 2. Everybody who suffers now and then from a fit of THE DUMPS is counselled to read amusing books.

DUN, *subs.* and *verb* (originally slang: now recognised).—An importunate creditor; to persist in demanding payment. [A. S. *dynian* = to clamour, to din; possibly influenced by the memory of a certain Joe Dunn, a famous

English bailiff, *temp.* Henry VII.] Fr., *un loup* (= wolf); *un Anglais* = an Englishman). Also DUNNER and DUNNING.

1663. T. KILLEGREW, *Parson's Wedding*, III., v., in Dodsley, *O.P.* (1780), xi., 452. We shall have the sport, and be revenged upon the rogue for DUNNING a gentleman in a tavern.

1675. WYCHERLEY, *Country Wife*, I., in wks. (1713), 136. The most insatiable sorts of DUNS, that invade our lodgings in a morning.

1677. WYCHERLEY, *Plain Dealer*, Act V., Sc. ii. *Man.* No, no. Those you have obliged most, most certainly avoid you, when you can oblige 'em no longer; and they take your visits like so many DUNS.

1678. C. COTTON, *Scarronides*, bk. i., p. 43 (ed. 1725). Have what you want, nor will I DUN ye, But pay me when you can get mony.

1707. FARQUHAR, *Beaux Stratagem*, Act III., Sc. iii. I remember the good days when we could DUN our masters for our wages, and if they refused to pay us, we could have a warrant to carry 'em before a Justice.

1712. *Spectator*, No. 454. Though they never buy, they are ever talking of new silks, laces, and ribbons, and serve the owners, in getting them customers as their common DUNNERS do in making them pay.

1731. *Daily Journal*, 9 Jan. ['List of the officers established in the most notorious gaming-houses.'] 9th.: A DUNNER, who goes about to recover money lost at play.

1742. FIELDING, *Joseph Andrews*, bk. III., ch. iii. Poverty and distress, with their horrid train of DUNS, attorneys, bailiffs, haunted me day and night.

1777. SHERIDAN, *Trip to Scarborough*, Act I., Sc. ii. What, hast spent all, eh? And art thou come to DUN his lordship for assistance?

1821. SCOTT, *Kenilworth*, ch. xv. I refused him admittance as flatly, Blount, as you would refuse a penny to a blind beggar; as obstinately, Tracy, as thou didst ever deny access to a DUN.

1838. DICKENS, *Nicholas Nickleby*, ch. ix., p. 66. To fetch three new boys, and DUN the relations of two old ones for the balance of a small account.

1888. C. J. DUNPHIE, *The Chameleon* p. 6. DUNNING for payment which may not be convenient to *them*, and which would in no sense conduce to the honour of the DUNNERS.

DUNAKER, *subs.* (old).—A cattle-lifter.

16(?). Poem of 17th Century (quoted by Nares). The seventeenth a DUN-AKER, that maketh his vows To go i' the country and steal all their cows.

1693. HERRICK ('*Poor Robin*'). Mercury is in a conjunction with Venus, and when such conjunctions happen, it signifies a most plentiful crop that year, of hectors . . . . DONNAKERS, cross-biters, etc.

1811. *Lexicon Balatronicum*, s.v.

DUNDERHEAD, *subs.* (old).—A fool. For synonyms, *see* BUFFLE and CABBAGE-HEAD.

DUNDREARY, *subs.* and *adj.* (colloquial).—Specifically, a stammering, foolish, and long-whiskered fop—the Lord Dundreary of *Our American Cousin* (1858)—generally, a foppish fool. *Cf.*, JUBILEE JUGGINS.

1876. JAS. GRANT, *One of the Six Hundred*, ch. iii. His whole air had the 'used up' bearing of those miserable DUNDREARYS who affect to act as if youth, wealth, and luxury were the greatest calamities that flesh is heir to, and that life itself was a bore.

DUNDREARIES, *subs.* (colloquial). —A pair of whiskers cut sideways from the chin, and grown as long as possible. A fashion (now obsolete) suggested by Sothern's make-up in *Our American Cousin*.

1882. F. ANSTEY, *Vice-Versâ*, ch. xvii. Bushy black whiskers, more like the antiquated DUNDREARY type than modern fashion permits.

DUNG, *subs.* (workmen's). — An operative working for less than 'society' wages. Formerly, according to Grose, 'a journeyman taylor who submits to the law for regulating journey-men's taylors'

wages, therefore deemed by the FLINTS (*q.v.*) a coward.'

DUNG-FORK (also **DUNG-CART**), *subs.* (colloquial). — A country bumpkin. For synonyms, *see* JOSKIN.

DUN-IN-THE-MIRE, *subs. phr.* (obsolete).—An antiquated game.

1595. SHAKSPEARE, *Romeo and Juliet*, i., 4. *Mercutio.* If thou art DUN we'll draw thee from the MIRE Of this (save reverence) love, wherein thou stick'st Up to the ears.

DUNNAGE, *subs.* (nautical).—Baggage; clothes. *Cf.*, DUDS. [Properly wood or loose fagots laid across the hold of a vessel, or stuffed between packages to keep cargo from damage by water or shifting.]

1849. J. F. COOPER, *The Sea Lions*, ch. v. Not only was the chest more than half empty, but the articles it did contain were of the coarsest materials . . . 'There is little here to pay a man for crossing from the Vineyard,' observed Roswell Gardiner . . . 'What is to be done with all this DUNNAGE, deacon?'

1851-61. H. MAYHEW, *London Lab. and Lon. Poor*, vol. i., p. 262. If they can meet with . . . the young ladies, they 'put it on them for DUNNAGE' (beg a stock of general clothing.)

DUNNAKIN or **DUNNYKEN**, *subs.* (old). — A privy; in U.S.A., a chamber-pot. For synonyms, *see* BURY and MRS. JONES.—[GROSE —1785.]

DUNOP, *subs.* (back-slang). — A pound.

DUP, *verb* (old).—To open.

1567. HARMAN, *Caveat* (1814), p. 66. To DUP ye gyger, to open the dore.

1596. SHAKSPEARE, *Hamlet*, iv. And DUPPED the chamber door.

1609. DEKKER, *Lanthorne and Candlelight*. If we . . . DUP but the gigger of a country-cove's ken, from thence at the chats we trine in the Lightmans.

1665. R. HEAD, *English Rogue*, pt. I., ch. v., p. 49 (1874), s.v.

1691. *Academia*, quoted in *Notes and Queries*, 6 S., xii., 416. Beside, it cost me twopence more, To one that sits to DUP a dore.

1724. E. COLES, *Eng. Dict.* DUP = enter (the house).

DURHAM-MAN, *subs.* (old). — A knock-kneed man.

DURIA, *subs.* (old).—Fire.

1857. DUCANGE ANGLICUS. *The Vulgar Tongue*, s.v.

DURRYNACKER, *subs.* (thieves').—A female hawker of lace; generally practised as an introduction to fortune-telling. Also DURRYNACKING. [Described in H. Mayhew's *London Labor and London Poor*, vol. i., p. 472, 1851.]

DUST, *subs.* (common). — Money. [Said to be from 'gold-dust,' but this is a mere guess.]

1655. FULLER, *Ch. Hist.*, vi., 299. My lord, quoth the king, presently deposit your hundred pounds in gold, or else no going hence all the daies of your life . . . The abbot down with his DUST, and glad he escaped so, returned to Reading.

1671. EACHARD, *Observations.* If they did intend to trade with Christ they must down with the DUST instantly, for to his knowledge the Papists did offer a vast sum of money for England's Christ.

1748. T. DYCHE, *Dictionary* (5 ed.). DUST . . . also a cant name for money, as down with your *dust*, put, pay, or lay down your money, etc.

1834. H. AINSWORTH, *Rookwood*, bk. III., ch. xiii. You have thrown away a second chance. Play or pay, all the world over . . . Down with the DUST.

1840. *Comic Almanack.* 'The Dust about the Gold Dust,' p. 217. She cried, 'Come, down, now, with your DUST!'

1890. *Welfare*, March, p. 5, col. 1. 'Strange Sermons.' It is related of Dean Swift that, preaching of charity, he comprised his sermon within a single short sentence. His text was from Proverbs xix., 17: 'He that hath pity upon the poor

lendeth unto the Lord.' His treatment of the subject consisted of the words: 'If you approve the security, down with your DUST!'

TO DUST ONE'S JACKET, CASSOCK, or COAT, *verb. phr.* (colloquial).—To thrash; metaphorically, to criticise severely.—*See* quot., 1557, and *cf.*, BASTE.

1557. TUSSER, *Husbandrie*, ch. 49, st. *b.*, p. 107 (E.D.S.). What fault deserves A BRUSHED COTE.

1612. *Passenger of Benvenuto.* Observe, my English gentleman, that blowes have a wonderfull prerogative in the feminine sex; for if shee be a bad woman, there is no more proper plaister to mend her, then this: but if (which is a rare chance) she be good, to DUST her often hath in it a singular, unknowne, and as it were an inscrutable vertue to make her much better, and to reduce her, if possible, to perfection.

1698. FARQUHAR, *Love and a Bottle*, Act v., Sc. ii. Tell me presently where your master is, sirrah, or I'll DUST the secret out of YOUR JACKET.

1771. SMOLLETT, *Humphry Clinker*, l. 26. Prankley, shaking his cane, bid him hold his tongue, otherwise he would DUST HIS CASSOCK for him.

1837. BARHAM, *I. L.* (*M. of Venice*). Old Shylock was making a racket, and threatening how well he'd DUST EVERY MAN'S JACKET, Who'd help'd her in getting aboard of the packet.

1865. *Saturday Review*, Ap. If he will turn to Theocritus, v., 119, he will learn that there is a good and respectable Greek ancestry for the cant phrase, to DUST ONE'S JACKET:—ὅκα μάν τοκα τεῖδέ τυ δάσας Εὐμάριδας ἐκάθηρε, where ἐκάθηρε means, 'purgavit te,' 'dressed you,' 'gave you a dressing,' DUSTED YOUR JACKET. So great is the similarity of ideas in all nations and languages, of which, indeed, there is abundant illustration in other passages of Theocritus.

1872. *Fun*, Sept. The difference is I DUSTS his [coat] off his back, and he DUSTS mine on my back.

TO GET UP AND DUST, or TO DUST OUT OF, *verb. phr.* (American).—To move quickly; to leave hurriedly. For synonyms, *see* ABSQUATULATE.

TO HAVE DUST IN THE EYES, *verb. phr.* (colloquial). — To be sleepy; to DRAW STRAWS (*q.v.*). Said mainly of children: *e.g.*, 'The DUSTMAN is coming.'

TO KICK UP, OR RAISE A DUST, *verb. phr.* (colloquial).—To make a disturbance, or much ado.

1759. SMOLLETT, *Letter to Wilkes*, quoted in D. Hannay's *Smollett* (1887), p. 132. If the affair cannot be compromised, we intend to KICK UP A DUST, and die hard.

1766. H. BROOKE, *Fool of Quality*, ii., 41. Our lay and ecclesiastical champions for arbitrary power . . . have RAISED such A DUST, and kept such a coil about the divine, hereditary, and indefeasible right of kings.

1815. SCOTT, *Guy Mannering*, ch. xxxiii. 'Is there not a strong room up yonder in the old castle?' 'Ay, is there, sir; my uncle the constable once kept a man there for three days in Auld Ellangowan's time. But there was an unco-DUST about it—it was tried in the Inner-house afore the feifteen.'

TO THROW DUST IN THE EYES, *verb. phr.* (colloquial).—To mislead; to dupe.—*See* BAMBOOZLE.

TO BITE THE DUST, *verb. phr.* (colloquial).—To knock under; to be mortified, or shamed.

DUST-BIN, *subs.* (common). — A grave.

DUSTED, *ppl. adj.* (colloquial).—Drubbed; severely criticised.—*See* DUST ONE'S JACKET and TANNING.

DUSTER, *subs.* (tailors'). —A sweetheart. For synonyms, *see* JOMER.

DUST-HOLE, *subs.* (theatrical). —1. The late Prince of Wales' Theatre in Tottenham Court Road. [From the fact that, fifty years ago, under the management of Mr. Glossop, the sweepings of the house were deposited and suffered to accumulate under the pit.]

1886. JOHN COLEMAN, in *Temple Bar*, Feb., p. 225. During his management of THE DUSTHOLE (since known as 'The Prince of Wales's'), in Tottenham Court Road.

2. (University).—Sidney Sussex College, Cambridge. Obsolete.

DUSTMAN, *subs.* (common).—1. A personification of sleep: 'the DUSTMAN'S coming' = you are getting sleepy. *Cf.*, DUST IN THE EYES.

1821. PIERCE EGAN, *Tom and Jerry*, p. 111. A social glass of wine beguiled an hour or two, till the DUSTMAN made his appearance and gave the hint to Tom and Jerry that it was time to visit their beds.

2. (old).—A dead man.

1811. *Lexicon Balatronicum*, s.v.

DUSTY. NOT SO DUSTY, *adv. phr.* (common).—A term of approval; 'not so bad'; 'so-so.'

1854. F. E. SMEDLEY, *Harry Coverdale*, ch. xlii. 'Why is the fact of the contents of a backgammon-board having been thrown out of the window like Milton's *chef d'œuvre*?' Do you give it up? 'Because it's a *pair o'dice lost*.' NONE SO DUSTY that—eh? for a commoner like me?

1884. HAWLEY SMART, *From Post to Finish*, p. 28. 'Well, my dear,' said Butters in the most patronising way, 'I know I'm NOT SO DUSTY, and if it wasn't for my disgusting weight I'd pretty soon let 'em see at Newmarket what I can do.'

DUSTY-BOB, *subs.* (common).—A scavenger.

DUSTYPOLL or DUSTY-NOB, *subs.* (old).—A miller. [DUSTY = floury, + POLL, or NOB = the head.]

DUTCH. An epithet of inferiority. A witness, no doubt, to the longstanding hatred engendered by the bitter fight for the supremacy of the seas between England and Holland in the seventeenth century.

Subs. (common).—A wife. [Probably an abbreviation of DUTCH CLOCK.]

ENGLISH SYNONYMS.—Mollisher; rib; grey-mare; warming-pan; splice; lawful blanket; autem-mort; comfortable impudence; comfortable importance; old woman; evil; missus; lawful jam; yoke-fellow; night-cap; legitimate, or legiti; weight-carrier; mutton-bone; ordinary; pillow-mate; supper-table; Dutch clock; chattel; sleeping-partner; doxy; cooler; mount; bed-fagot.

FRENCH SYNONYMS.—*Une marque de cé* (thieves'); *une légitime* (fam. =legitimate); *mon gouvernement* (pop. = my old woman); *mon associée* (printers' = my partner); *mon bien* (popular, *bien* = chattel); *une gerce* (thieves': also a mattress).

GERMAN SYNONYMS.—*Keibe, Keibel, Keife* (also=woman or concubine: from O. H. G. *Chebisa*, M. H. G. *Kebese, Kebse* = illegitimate); *Krönerin* (literally a 'horneress'; *Kröne*=to be provided with horns); *Rammenin* (Hanoverian: from the gypsy *romnin*).

TO DO A DUTCH, *verb. phr.* (military).—To desert; to run away. For synonyms, see AMPUTATE.

THAT BEATS THE DUTCH, *phr.* (common).—A sarcastic superlative.

1775. *Revolutionary Song* [New Eng. Hist., Reg. Ap. 1857], p. 191. And besides all the mortars, bombs, cannons, and shells, And bullets and guns, as the

newspaper tells, Our cargoes of meat, drink, and cloaths BEAT THE DUTCH; Now who would not tarry and take t'other touch?

TO TALK DUTCH, DOUBLE-DUTCH, or HIGH-DUTCH, *verb. phr.* (common).—To talk gibberish; by implication, nonsense.

1604. MARLOWE, *Faustus*, Sc. ii. *Wag.* Villain—call me Master Wagner, and let thy left eye be diametarily fixed upon my right heel, with *quasi vestigiis uostris insistere*. *Clown.* God forgive me, he SPEAKS DUTCH FUSTIAN.

1790. DIBDIN, *The Sweet Little Cherub*. And, my timbers! what lingo he'd coil and belay, Why 'twas just all as one as HIGH DUTCH.

1876. C. H. WALL, trans. *Molière*, vol. I., p. 116. He never taught me anything but my prayers, and though I have said them daily now these fifty years, they are still DOUBLE DUTCH to me.

THE DUTCH HAVE TAKEN HOLLAND, *phr.* (common).—A quiz for stale news. *Cf.*, QUEEN BESS (or QUEEN ANNE) IS DEAD; THE ARK RESTED ON MOUNT ARARAT, etc.

DUTCH-AUCTION or SALE, *subs.* (cheap-jacks').—A sale at minimum prices; a mock-auction.

1872. *Daily Telegraph*, 30 Nov. So thoroughly corrupt and vicious has the existing system become that it would be well-nigh a relief to fall back on the old DUTCH AUCTION, by which an article was put up at a high price, and, if nobody accepted the offer, then reduced to a lower, the sum first required being gradually decreased until a fair value was attained.

1885. *Punch*, 21 Feb., p. 93. Gives up India to Russia, Africa to Germany, puts up garrisoned fortresses and coaling stations at DUTCH AUCTION, and lets colonies run loose.

DUTCH-BARGAIN, *subs.* (old).—A bargain all on one side.

'In matters of commerce the fault of the Dutch, Is giving too little and asking too much!'

DUTCH-CLOCK, *subs.* (music-hall).—1. A wife. *Cf.*, DUTCH and sense 2.

2. (common).—A bed-pan.

DUTCH-CONCERT or MEDLEY, *subs.* (common).—A sing-song whereat everybody sings and plays at the same time as everybody else; a hubbub.

1814. SCOTT, *Waverley*, ch. xi. And now the Demon of Politics envied even the harmony arising from this DUTCH CONCERT, merely because there was not a wrathful note in the strange compound of sounds which it produced.

1871. *Daily Telegraph*, 23 Mar. 'Lord Derby on Pauperism.' It happens that instead of the harmony which should exist where good men and good women are, working together for a common object, you have something like what is popularly known as a DUTCH CONCERT, or in other words, every man playing his own tune on his own instrument.

DUTCH CONSOLATION, *subs.* (common).—Job's comfort; unconsoling consolation.

1888. *All the Year Round*, 9 June, p. 542. The expression often heard, 'Thank Heaven, it is no worse,' is sometimes called DUTCH CONSOLATION.

DUTCH-COURAGE, *subs.* (common).—Pot-valiancy. *Cf.*, Fielding's DUTCH-DEFENCE=sham-defence.

1872. SPENCER, *Study of Sociology*, ch. viii., p. 185 (9th ed.) A dose of brandy, by stimulating the circulation, produces DUTCH COURAGE, as it is called.

1887. Mrs. LOVETT CAMERON, *Neck or Nothing*, ch. iv., p. 50. Bob waited half a second for an answer, glancing uneasily at his friend's face, and then he dashed on again with a sort of DUTCH COURAGE, for, to tell the truth he wasn't quite sure how Jack would take it.

DUTCH-FEAST, *subs.* (old).—See quot.

1888. *All the Year Round*, 9 June, p. 542. DUTCH FEAST is a phrase now obsolete; it was formerly applied to an entertainment where the host got drunk before his guests.

DUTCH-GLEEK, *subs.* (old). Drinks.

1654. GAYTON, *Fest. Notes*, p. 96. Nor could be partaker of any of the good cheer, except it were the liquid part of it, which they call DUTCH GLEEK, where he plaied his cards so well, and vied and revled so often, that he had scarce an eye to see withall.

DUTCHMAN. I'M A DUTCHMAN IF I DO, *phr.* (common).—A strong refusal. [During the wars between England and Holland, Dutch was synonymous with all that was false and hateful; therefore, 'I would rather be a Dutchman' = the strongest term of refusal that words could express.]

1855. EARL RUSSELL, *Memoirs of Thomas Moore*. Cope mentioned a good specimen of English-French, and the astonishment of the French people who heard it, not conceiving what it could mean—'Si je fais, je fais; mais si je fais, je suis un Hollandais.' 'If I do, I do; but IF I DO, I'M A DUTCHMAN.'

DUTCHMAN'S-BREECHES, *subs.* (nautical).—Two streaks of blue in a cloudy sky.

DUTCHMAN'S-DRINK, *subs.* (common).—A draught that empties the pot.

DUTCH-TREAT, *subs.* (common).—An entertainment where everyone pays his shot.

1887. *Lippincott's Mag.*, Aug., p. 191. 'You'll come along too, won't you?' Lancelot demanded of Ormizon! DUTCH TREAT, *vous savez!*

DUTCH UNCLE. I WILL TALK TO YOU LIKE A DUTCH UNCLE, *phr.* (common).—I will reprove you smartly. [The Dutch were renowned for the brutality of their discipline. Uncle is the Latin notion of *pat'ruus*, 'an uncle,' 'severe guardian,' or 'stern castigator.' Hence Horace, 3 Od. xii. 3, *Metuentes patrua verbera linguæ* (dreading the castigations of an uncle's tongue); and 2 Sat. iii. 88, *Ne sis patruus mihi* (Don't come the uncle over me). A DUTCH UNCLE = therefore, an uncle of peculiar fierceness.]

1853. *Notes and Queries*, 1 S., vii., 65. In some parts of America, when a person has determined to give another a regular lecture, he will often be heard to say, I WILL TALK TO HIM LIKE A DUTCH UNCLE; that is, he shall not escape this time.

1869. *East Anglian*, vol. III., p. 350. [In list of Suffolk sea words]: 'There were the squires on the bench, but I took heart, and TALKED TO 'EM LIKE A DUTCH UNCLE.'

DUTCH-WIDOW, *subs.* (old).—A prostitute. For synonyms, see BARRACK-HACK and *cf.*, GRASS-WIDOW.

1608. MIDDLETON, *Trick to Catch the Old One*, III., iii. *Dra.* Yes, a DUTCH WIDOW. *Hoa.* How? *Dra.* That's an English drab, sir.

DUTCH-WIFE, *subs.* (common).—A bolster.

DYING IN A HORSE'S NIGHTCAP. Dying by the rope; *cf.*, HORSE'S NIGHTCAP.

EAGLE-TAKERS, *subs.* (military).—The Eighty-Seventh Foot. [The title was gained at Barossa (1811), when it captured the eagle of the 8th French Light Infantry. Its colours also bear 'the plume of the Prince of Wales' and 'the harp and crown,' an eagle with a wreath of laurel.] It was also nicknamed 'The Old Fogs'; also 'The Faugh-a-Ballagh Boys,' from *Fag an bealac!* = 'Clear the Way,' the regimental march, and the war-cry at Barossa.

EAR. TO SEND AWAY WITH A FLEA IN THE EAR, *verb. phr.* (common).—To dismiss peremptorily and with a scolding. Fr., *mettre la puce à l'oreille*=to get angry.

1764-1817. J. G. HOLMAN, *Abroad and at Home*, ii., i. I could not think of Miss Hartley being troubled with such a brute of a fellow . . . . so, an't please you, my lady, I SENT HIM AWAY WITH A FLEA IN HIS EAR.

1841. *Comic Almanack*, p. 280. One thing is very clear, If they ain't off of their own accord, the Lord Mayor will SOON HELP 'EM OFF WITH A FLEA IN THEIR EAR.

1884. HAWLEY SMART, *From Post to Finish*, p. 202. Her husband had with difficulty restrained her from SENDING FORREST AWAY WITH what in homely language is denominated A FLEA IN HIS EAR.

TO BITE THE EAR.—See BITE and BREAK SHINS.

TO GET UP ON ONE'S EAR, *verb. phr.* (American).—To bestir oneself; to rouse oneself for an effort.

1870. RICHARD GRANT WHITE. *Words and their Uses*. They called me bully boy, altho' I've seen nigh three-score years, And said that I was lightning when I GOT UP ON MY EAR.

1888. *Puck's Library*, May, p. 15. A man who walked on HIS EAR out of a store said 'he came out on the Erie route.'

EARL OF CORK, *subs. phr.* (Irish).—The ace of diamonds.—[See quots.]

1830. W. CARLETON, *Traits and Stories of the Irish Peasantry*. 'What do you mean by the Earl of Cork?' asked Mr. Squander. 'The ace of diamonds, your honour. It's the worst ace, and the poorest card in the pack, and is called the EARL OF CORK, because he's the poorest nobleman in Ireland.'

1864. *Athenæum*, 29 Oct. The ace of diamonds acquired the name of 'the EARL OF CORK' because his lordship happened to be the poorest nobleman in Ireland.

EARL OF MAR'S GREY BREEKS, *subs. phr.* (military).—TheTwenty-First Foot. [In allusion to the colour of the men's breeches and to the original title of the regiment, The Earl of Mar's Fuzileers.] Obsolete.

EARLY. TO GET UP EARLY, *verb. phr.* (common).—To be astute; ready; wide-awake. *Cf.*, 'It's the early bird that catches the worm.'

1738. SWIFT, *Polite Convers.*, Dial. 3. They must RISE EARLY that would cheat her of her money.

c. 1869. VANCE, *Broadside Ballad.* For to get me on the hop, or on my 'tibby' drop, You must WAKE UP VERY EARLY in the morning.

1880. A. TROLLOPE, *The Duke's Children*, ch. xlvi. It was said of him that . . . . if you wished to take him in you must GET UP EARLY.

EARLY-RISER, *subs.* (common).—An aperient. *Cf.*, CUSTOM-HOUSE OFFICER and TWO GUNNERS AND A DRIVER.

EARLY-WORM, *subs.* (common).—A man who searches the streets at daybreak for cigar stumps.

EARTH-BATH, *subs.* (old).—A grave. TO TAKE AN EARTH-BATH = to be buried; *cf.*, GROUND SWEAT.

1785. GROSE, *Dict. Vulg. Tongue*, s.v.

1859. MATSELL, *Vocabulum, or Rogue's Lexicon*, s.v.

EARTHQUAKE. BOTTLED EARTH-QUAKE, *subs. phr.* (American).—Intoxicating drinks.

EARTH-STOPPERS, *subs.* (old).—Horse's feet.

1823. MONCRIEFF, *Tom and Jerry*, i., 6. There's action for you—there's one to tip 'em the go-bye at a mill,—there's EARTH-STOPPERS—quiet to drive, quiet in harness, trots fifteen miles in less than an hour.

EARTHY, *adj.* (colloquial).—Gross; common; devoid of 'soul.'

EAR-WIG, *subs.* (old).—A private prompter or flatterer; also (thieves') a clergyman. [From the popular delusion that the ear-wig lodges itself in the ear with a view to working its way into the brain when it causes death.]

1639. BEAUMONT AND FLETCHER, *Bloody Brother.* Dram. Personæ, Latorch Rollo's *Earwig.*

1789. GEO. PARKER, *Life's Painter* p. 77. And the court, mercy on us! there are no words equal to the just painting of its EAR-WIGS, its sycophants, pensioners, placemen, scouters, masters of the ceremonies, etc.

1822. SCOTT, *Fortunes of Nigel.* A pack of mouthers, and flatterers, and EAR-WIGS.

Verb (common).—To prompt; to influence by covert statements; to whisper insinuations.

1842. MARRYAT, *Percival Keene*, xiii. And by way of a hint, make him your friend if you can, for he EARWIGS the captain in fine style.

1879. JAS. PAYN, *High Spirits (Confiscated Weeds).* He is a sound divine and politician, but a little apt to be led away by specious arguments on the subject of education; and Carker was in the habit . . . of EARWIGGING him.

EASE, *verb* (common).—1. To rob; Fr., *soulager. Cf.*, ANNEX and CONVEY. TO EASE A BLOKE = to rob a man.

1630. JONSON, *New Inn*, I. EASE his pockets of a superfluous watch.

1817. SCOTT, *Rob Roy*, ch. viii. 'The law's hard—very severe—hanged poor Jack Winterfield at York, despite family connexions and great interest, all for

1874. MRS. H. WOOD, *Johnny Ludlow*, 1 S., No. xxv., p. 446. And I fit to EAT MY HEAD off with having nothing to do.

EAT ONE'S HEAD, HAT, BOOTS, etc., *verb. phr.* (common).—A locution of emphatic asseveration. [Probably Dickensonian, influenced by the proverbial saying, 'To eat one's heart out'—to undergo intense struggle, and also TO EAT ONE'S HEAD OFF (*q.v.*).]—*See Notes and Queries*, 7 S., iii., 7, 94, 197, 352, 433.

1836. DICKENS, *Pickwick*, xlii., 367. 'Well, if I knew as little of life as that, I'd EAT MY HAT and swallow the buckle whole,' said the clerical gentleman.

1837. DICKENS, *Oliver Twist*, ch. xiv. This was the handsome offer with which Mr. Grimwig backed and confirmed nearly every assertion he made; and it was the more singular in his case because, even admitting, for the sake of argument, the possibility of scientific improvements being ever brought to that pass which will enable a man to EAT HIS OWN HEAD in the event of his being so disposed, Mr. Grimwig's head was such a particularly large one that the most sanguine man alive could hardly entertain a hope of being able to get through it at a sitting, to put entirely out of the question a very thick coating of powder.

1887. E. E. MONEY, *Little Dutch Maiden*, II., viii., 148. And if you don't run up against him next day in Bond Street, you may EAT YOUR HAT!

TO EAT ONE'S TERMS, *verb. phr.* (legal).—To go through the prescribed course of study for admission to the bar. [In allusion to the dinners a student has to attend in the public hall of his inn.]

TO EAT ONE'S WORDS, *verb. phr.* (colloquial).—To retract a statement; to own a lie.

TO EAT UP, *verb. phr.* (colloquial). — To vanquish; to ruin. [Originally Zulu.]

1890. *National Observer*, 13 Dec., p. 88, col. 2. But buttons tarnish, hot gospelling palls, the EATING-UP of white men is in strictest consonance with regal tradition and the regal habit.

EAVES, *subs.* (American).—A hen-roost.

1859. MATSELL, *Vocabulum, or Rogue's Lexicon*, s.v.

EAVESDROPPER, *subs.* (American). —A chicken thief; also generally, any petty pilferer.

1859. MATSELL, *Vocabulum, or Rogue's Lexicon*, s.v.

EBENEZER, *subs.* (Winchester College). — A stroke at fives: when the ball hits 'line' at such an angle as to rise perpendicularly into the air.

EBONY, *subs.* (common). — 1. A negro; otherwise BLACKBIRD (*q.v.*)and BLACK IVORY. Thomas Fuller (1608–1661) spoke of the negro race as 'God's images cut in ebony.' For synonyms, see SNOWBALL.

2. The publisher of *Magn.*: *i.e.*, BLACKWOOD.—(*See Noctes Ambrosianæ passim.*)

EBONY-OPTICS, *subs.* (old).—Black eyes. EBONY-OPTICS ALBONIZED = black eyes painted white.

EDGABAC, *subs.* (back slang). — Cabbage.

EDGE. STITCHED OFF THE EDGE, *phr.* (tailors').—Said of a glass not filled to the top.

SIDE-EDGE, *subs.* (tailors').—Whiskers.

SHORT TOP EDGE, *subs. phr.* (tailors'). — A turn-up nose or CELESTIAL (*q.v.*).

23

EASING a fat West-country grazier of the price of a few beasts.

1840. THACKERAY, *Paris Sketch Book*, p. 109. His was the place at the écarté table, where the Countess would EASE him nightly of a few pieces.

1849. *Punch*, November, 'The Swell Mobsman's Almanack.' Remember, wen you've EASED a cove in a fogg, never cut away in an 'urry, or crushers stop you.

2. (venery). — To content a woman.

1861. A. C. SWINBURNE, *Poems and Ballads.* 'Hermaphroditus.' Hath made him man to EASE a woman's sighs.

TO EASE ONESELF, *verb. phr.* (colloquial).—1. To 'rear.' For synonyms, see BURY A QUAKER.

2. (venery).—To ejaculate.

EASON, *verb* (American thieves'). —To tell.

1859. MATSELL, *Vocabulum, or Rogue's Lexicon*, s.v.

EAST-AND-SOUTH, *subs.* (rhyming slang). — The mouth. Also SUNNY SOUTH. For synonyms, see POTATO-TRAP.

1857. DUCANGE ANGLICUS, *The Vulgar Tongue*, s.v.

EASTERY, *subs.* (cheap-jacks').—Private business.

1876. C. HINDLEY, *Life and Adventures of a Cheap Jack*, p. 107. At one EASTERY Aaron Jessell was going to cry the place.

EASY. TO MAKE EASY, *verb. phr.* (old).—To gag or kill. [GROSE, 1785.]

EASY AS DAMN IT, (or AS MY EYE), *adj. phr.* (popular).—Excessively easy: 'easy as lying' [Shakspeare].

EASY DOES IT! *verb. phr.* (popular). — An exclamation of

encouragement and counsel = 'Take your time and keep your coat on.'

EASY OVER THE PIMPLES, (or OVER THE STONES), *verb. phr.* (popular).—An injunction = 'go slow,' or 'mind what you're about.'

EASY VIRTUE.—*See* LADY OF EASY VIRTUE.

EAT, *verb* (American). — To provision: *e.g.*, a steamer is said to be able to EAT 400 passengers and sleep about half that number.

ante 1871. *Pickings from the Picayune*, p. 47. Hoosier—' Squire, what pay do you give?' Contractor — 'Ten bits a day.' Hoosier—'Why, Squire, I was told you'd give us two dollars a-day and EAT us.'

1887. R. A. PROCTER, on 'Americanisms' in *Knowledge*, s.v. Sometimes a host may EAT his guests in another sense. I once, when staying at an hotel, found a finely coloured motto rather unfortunately spelt; it ran, 'Watch and Prey.' Its owner carried out the idea.

EAT COKE.—*See* COKE.

EAT CROW.—*See* CROW.

EAT A FIG, *verb. phr.* (rhyming slang).—To 'crack a crib'; to break a house.

TO EAT ONE'S HEAD OFF, *verb. phr.* (colloquial). — To be retained for service and stand idle; also (quot., 1850) to cost more in 'keep' than it is worth.

1850. F. E. SMEDLEY, *Frank Fairleigh*, ch. xiv. I'd rather keep her for a week than a fortnight, I can tell you; she'd EAT HER HEAD OFF in a month, and no mistake.

1872. *Times*, 27 Aug. 'The Autumn Manœuvres.' The country never would stand the maintenance all the year round of some 1,500 horses which would have nothing to do for nine months out of the twelve but EAT THEIR HEADS OFF.

EDGE IN, *verb. phr.* (colloquial).—To slip in; insinuate: *e.g.*, To EDGE IN a word (or a remark).

EDGE OFF (or OUT OF), *verb. phr.* (colloquial).—To slink away; to gradually desist. TO TAKE THE EDGE OFF [a thing, or person, or idea] = to become acquainted with; to enjoy to satiety. *Cf.*, *Hamlet*, iii., 2. 'It would cost you a groaning TO TAKE OFF MY EDGE.'

EDGENARO, *subs.* (back slang).—An orange.

EDGE-WAYS. NOT ABLE TO GET A WORD IN EDGE-WAYS, *phr.* (colloquial). — Having but the barest opportunity of taking part in a discussion.

EEL-SKINS, *subs.* (old). — Tight trousers. For synonyms, *see* BAGS and KICKS.

1827. BULWER LYTTON, *Pelham*, ch. xlix., p. 190. He only filched a two-penny halfpenny gilt chain out of his master, Levy, the pawnbroker's window, and stuck it in his EEL-SKIN to make a show.

E-FINK, *subs.* (back slang). — A knife.

EFTER, *subs.* (thieves').—A theatre thief.

EGG.—*See* BAD EGG.

EGG ON, *verb. phr.* (colloquial). —To encourage.

EGGS. SURE AS EGGS IS EGGS, *phr.* (popular).—Of a certainty; without doubt. [From the formula, '*x is x.*']

TO TEACH ONE'S GRANDMOTHER TO ROAST or SUCK EGGS, *verb. phr.* (colloquial).—Tolecture elders and superiors; Fr., *les oisons veulent mener les oies paître* = the goslings want to drive the geese to pasture.

EGHAM, STAINES, AND WINDSOR, *subs. phr.* (common).—*See* quot.

1886. G. A. SALA, in *Ill. Lon. News*, 23 Oct., 418, 2. Is not the three-cornered hat of an English gentleman's coachman in gala livery known as an 'EGHAM, STAINES, AND WINDSOR'?

EGYPTIAN-HALL, *subs.* (rhyming slang).—A ball.

EIGHTER, *subs.* (prison).—An eight-ounce loaf.

EKAME, *subs.* (back slang). — A MAKE (*q.v.*), or swindle.

EKOM, *subs.* (back slang).—A MOKE (*q.v.*), or donkey.

ELBOW, *verb* (American thieves'). — To turn a corner; to get out of sight.

1859. MATSELL, *Vocabulum, or Rogue's Lexicon*, s.v.

TO SHAKE THE ELBOW, *verb. phr.* To play dice. [From the motion of the arm in 'casting.']

1680. COTTON, *Compleat Gamester* [gaming is compared to] a paralytical distemper which, seizing the arm the man cannot chuse but SHAKE HIS ELBOW.

1705. VANBRUGH, *Confederacy*, Act i. He's always SHAKING his heels with the ladies and HIS ELBOWS with the lords.

1709. MRS. CENTLIVRE, *Gamester*, I. (1872), i., 134. He is at SHAKING his ELBOWS over a table . . . courting the dice like a mistress, and cursing them when he is disappointed.

1713. *Guardian*, No. 120. But what would you say, should you see the Sparkler SHAKING HER ELBOW for a whole night together, and thumping the table with a dice-box?

1822. SCOTT, *Fortunes of Nigel*, ch. xvii. To eke out your living By the WAG OF YOUR ELBOWS.

TO CROOK THE ELBOW, *verb. phr.* (common). — To drink. — See ELBOW - CROOKER. [From the action of the arm.] For synonyms, see LUSH.

ELBOW-CROOKER, *subs.* (common). —A hard drinker. See *infra* and DRINKS.

ENGLISH SYNONYMS. — Borachio ; boozington ; brewer's horse ; bubber ; budger ; mop ; lushington ; worker of the cannon ; wet-quaker ; soaker ; lapper ; pegger ; angel altogether ; bloat ; ensign-bearer ; fiddle-cup ; sponge ; tun ; tosspot ; swill-pot ; wet subject ; shifter ; potster ; swallower ; potwalloper ; wetster ; dramster ; drinkster ; beer-barrel ; ginnums ; lowerer ; moist 'un ; drainist ; boozer ; mopper-up ; piss-maker ; thirstington.

FRENCH SYNONYMS. — *Un louave* (thieves') ; *un litronneur* (popular : *litre* = 1·760 pint) ; *une grosse culotte* (popular = bigbreeches or fat-arse) ; *un gavé* (thieves' : *gaver* = to stuff) ; *une lampe à mort* (pop. : a confirmed drunkard ; = a death-lamp) ; *un zingueur* (popular) ; *un boyau rouge* (pop. = red-guts) ; *un marquant* (thieves' : = conspicuous, striking, etc.); *un canonneur* (pop. : *canon* = a glass of wine ; *cf.*, English CANNON); *un camphrier* (pop.: a dram-drinker ; also = a camphortree) ; *un fioleur* (pop. : *fiole* = phial : *cf.*, TOSS-POT and SWILLPOT) ; *une éponge* (pop. : = a sponge ; also a p ramour, a fool, an attorney) ; *un bibard* (thieves':

bibcron = sucking-bottle) ; *un buvard* (popular: = blotting book) ; *un pochard* (colloquial) ; *adroit du coude* (pop. = artful elbowed) ; *un artilleur* (pop. : = a cannoneer ; *cf*, CANNON) ; *un boissonneur* (pop. : *boisson* = drink) ; *un buvailleur* or *buvaillon* (pop.: a man easily drunk) ; *un chocaillon* (pop. : a female drunkard) ; *un poivrot* (familiar) ; *un sac à vin* (pop. = a wine butt).

GERMAN SYNONYM. — *Mattobolo* (*matto balo* = a drunken pig : from the gypsy *matto* = drunk).

ITALIAN SYNONYMS. — *Fransoso* (= a Frenchman) ; *chiaritore* ; *chiaristante*.

SPANISH SYNONYMS. — *Cuero* (= a goat-skin bag for wine or oil) ; *coladra* (= a wooden pail in which wine is measured and retailed) ; *cuba* (= a measure for wine) ; *difunto de taberna* (lit., a public-house corpse) ; *odre* (= a wineskin) ; *pellejo* (= a liquor skin dressed and pitched) ; *peneque* ; *potista* ; *odrina* (= an ox-hide bottle).

ELBOWER, *subs.* (American thieves'). —A runaway. [*Cf.*, ELBOW.]

ELBOW-GREASE, *subs.* (colloquial). — Energetic and continuous manual labour : *e.g.*, 'ELBOW-GREASE is the best furniture oil.' Fr., *huile de bras* or *de poignet* ; *du foulage*.

1779-1839. GALT [quoted in *Imperial Eng. Dict.*]. He has scartit and dintit my guid mahogany past a' the power o bees-wax and ELBOW-GREASE to smooth.

1785. GROSE, *Dict. Vulg. Tongue*, s.v.

1859. G. ELIOT, *Adam Bede*, bk. I., ch. vi. Nowhere else could an oak clock-case and an oak table have got to such a

polish by the hand : genuine ELBOW-POLISH, as Mrs. Poyser called it, for she thanked God she never had any of your varnished rubbish in her house.

1870. *London Figaro*, 31 Oct. Often have I been . . . frequently admonished to put some ELBOW-GREASE into my work.

1876. M. E. BRADDON, *Joshua Haggard's Daughter*, ch. xi. There's no such polish in Devonshire, I should think, as poor Phœbe's ELBOW-GREASE.

ELBOW-SCRAPER, or JIGGER, *subs.* (common).—A fiddler.

ELBOW-SHAKER, *subs.* (old).—A gambler.—See ELBOW.

1748. T. DYCHE, *Dictionary* (5th ed.). ELBOW-SHAKER (s.) a gamester, one that practises dice-playing.

ELBOW-SHAKING, *subs.* (common). —Gambling.—See ELBOW.

1849. THACKERAY, *Pendennis*, ch. lx. 'It's been doosedly dipped and cut into, sir, by the confounded extravygance of your master, with his HELBOW SHAKIN', and his bill discountin'.

ELECTRIFIED, *ppl. adj.* 1. (American). — Moderately drunk. For synonyms, see DRINKS and SCREWED.

2. (colloquial). — Violently startled.

1837. BARHAM, *Ingoldsby Legends*. 'The Lay of St. Gengulphus.' Pig, pudding, and soup. The ELECTRIFIED groups, Pop under the sofa.

ELEGANT, *adj.* (colloquial).—Excellent.

ELEGANT-EXTRACTS, *subs.* (military).—1. The Eighty-Fifth Foot. [This regiment was remodelled in 1812, after a long sequence of court-martials : when the officers were removed, and others set in their room.]

1871. *Chambers' Journal*, 23 Dec., p. 803. 'ELEGANT EXTRACTS' was the

name given to the 85th on its being reformed with officers picked out from those of other regiments.

2. (Cambridge University).—Students who, though 'plucked,' were still given their degrees. A line was drawn below the poll-list, and those allowed to pass were nicknamed the ELEGANT EXTRACTS. There was a similar limbo in the honour-list, called the Gulf : for 'Between them (*in the poll*) and us (*in the honour lists*) there is a great gulf fixed.']

ELEPHANT, *subs.* (American thieves').—A wealthy victim. *Cf.*, TO SEE THE ELEPHANT.

1859. MATSELL, *Vocabulum, or Rogue's Lexicon*, s.v.

TO SEE THE ELEPHANT, *verb. phr.* (American).—1. To see the world ; to 'go out for wool and come home shorn' ; by implication, to 'go on the loose.' Sometimes, TO SEE THE KING.

b. 1533, d. 1592. MONTAIGNE, *Arrien. Hist. Ind.*, ch. 17. Aux Indes Orientales la chasteté y estant en singulière recommandation, l'usage pourtant souffroit qu'une femme mariée se peust abandonner à qui luy presentoit un ÉLÉPHANT, et cela avec quelque gloire d'avoir esté estimée à si hault prix.

1841. KENDALL, *Narrative of the Texan Santa Fé Expedition*, i., p. 109. When a man is disappointed in any thing he undertakes, when he has seen enough, when he gets tired and sick of any job he may have set himself about, he has SEEN THE ELEPHANT.

1870. L. OLIPHANT, *Piccadilly*, pt. ii., p. 39. So had Mr. Wog, who went up to town to SEE what he called THE ELEPHANT, — an American expression, signifying 'to gain experience of the world.'

1872. BESANT and RICE, *R. M. Mortiboy*, ch. xxxiv. Just like the Americans, when they go to see a great sight, say they are going to SEE THE ELEPHANT.

1888. *Boston Globe*, 4 March. It was in Hanover Street dispensary, where the tillers of the soil love to congregate, when

they are down to Bosting, INSPECTING THE Athenian white ELEPHANT.

1889. *Puck's Library* Ap., p. 25. Forepaugh says that elephants have a natural liking for whiskey. We have often wondered, when a man went out to SEE THE ELEPHANT, why he always brought back such a strange odour with him. This seems to explain it.

2. (common).—To be seduced ; Fr., *avoir vu le loup*. For synonyms, see LEG.

ELEPHANT-DANCE. — See CELLAR-FLAP and DOUBLE-SHUFFLE.

ELEPHANT'S-TRUNK, *subs.* (rhyming slang).—Drunk. For synonyms, see DRINKS and SCREWED.

ELEVATE, *verb* (colloquial).— To make or become slightly drunk.— See ELEVATED.

ELEVATED, *ppl. adj.* (colloquial). —Slightly drunk. For synonyms, see DRINKS and SCREWED.

1664. ETHEREGE, *Comical Revenge*, IV., iii. in wks. (1704), 51. The wine makes the rogue witty. . . . I will keep him thus ELEVATED 'till he has married Grace.

1748. SMOLLETT, *Rod. Random*, ch. xvii. The liquor mounted up to our heads, and made us all extremely frolicsome. In particular, was much ELEVATED.

1748. T. DYCHE, *Dictionary* (5th ed.). ELEVATED (A.). . . . sometime spoke of a person that has drank a little too freely.

1836. DICKENS, *Pickwick*, ch. l., p. 434. Except when he's ELEVATED, Bob's the quietest creature breathing.

1837. DISRAELI, *Venetia*, p. 274.

ELEVATION, *subs.* (colloquial).—1. A phase of drunkenness. — See ELEVATED.

1823. SCOTT, *Peveril*, ch. iii. The unwonted agitation of her voice attracted the attention of the refractory steward, notwithstanding his present state of ELEVATION.

2. (common).—Opium.

1849. C. KINGSLEY, *Alton Locke*, 'What's ELEVATION?' 'Opium, bor alive.'

ELFEN, *verb* (American thieves'). — To walk lightly ; to go on tiptoe.

1859. MATSELL, *Vocabulum, or Rogue's Lexicon*, s.v.

ELLENBOROUGH LODGE, or SPIKE, or PARK, *subs. phr.* (old).—The King's Bench. [From Lord Chief-Justice Ellenborough.] For synonyms, see CAGE. ELLENBOROUGH'S TEETH = the *chevaux de frize* round the prison wall.

ELRIG, *subs.* (back slang).—A girl.

ELYCAMPANE or ELECAMPANE. — See ALLACOMPAIN and quot.

1823. W. T. MONCRIEFF, *Tom and Jerry*, ii., 4. Go and get a pennyworth of ELYCAMPANE. *Jerry.* There's a pair of men-milliners.

EMAG, *subs.* (back slang).—Game : *e.g.*, 'I know your little EMAG.'

EMBROIDER, *verb* (common).—To exaggerate ; to add to the truth.

1877. S. L. CLEMENS ('Mark Twain'), *The Mississippi Pilot*. Tom tried to make himself appear to be a hero too, and succeeded to some extent, but then he always had a way of EMBROIDERING.

EMBROIDERY, *subs.* (common).— Exaggeration ; the American SASS AND TRIMMIN'S (*q.v.*).—[See EMBROIDER.]

1890. *Standard*, 5 April, p. 2, col. 1. Fanny Burney had many good qualities, no doubt, but we fancy that when she tells us with such evident unction how great folks loved and admired her she puts a good deal of EMBROIDERY into her narrations.

EMMA.—See WHOA EMMA and STREET-CRIES.

EMPEROR, *subs.* (American thieves'). — A drunken man. [An intensification of 'drunk as a lord' ; whence 'drunk as an emperor.']

1881. *New York Slang Dict.* 'On the Trail.' A pinch for an EMPEROR's slang.

DRUNK AS AN EMPEROR, *phr.* (common). — An intensive of 'drunk as a lord.' Fr., *saoul comme trente mille hommes*, or *un âne*.

1785. GROSE, *Dict. Vulg. Tongue*, s.v.

EMPTY THE BAG.—See BAG.

ENCUMBRANCES, *subs.* (common).— Children.—See CERTAINTIES and UNCERTAINTIES.

END. TO BE ALL ON END, *verb. phr.* (American). — To be very angry ; irritated. Also expectant.

AT LOOSE ENDS, *adv. phr.* (common). — Neglected ; precarious.

END ON, *adv. phr.* (colloquial). —Straight ; full-tilt.

TO BE END ON, *verb. phr.* (venery).—To have an erection.

TO KEEP ONE'S END UP, *verb. phr.* (American).—To rub along.

END OF THE SENTIMENTAL JOURNEY, *subs. phr.* (venery). —The female *pudendum*. For synonyms, see MONOSYLLABLE.

ENEMY, *subs.* (common).—Time : *e.g.*, 'How goes the ENEMY'= what's o'clock? 'To kill the ENEMY'=to kill time.

1839. DICKENS, *Nich. Nickleby*, ch. xix., p. 149. 'How goes the ENEMY, Snobb?' asked Sir Mulberry Hawke. 'Four minutes gone.

1864. *Glasgow Citizen*, 19 Nov. The swell who is bored by his efforts to 'kill the ENEMY.'

ENGLISH BURGUNDY, *subs. phr.* (old). - Porter.—See DRINKS.

1785. GROSE, *Dict. Vulg. Tongue*, s.v.

1859. MATSELL, *Vocabulum, or Rogue's Lexicon*, s.v.

ENIF, *adj.* (back slang).—Fine.

ENIN GEN, *subs. phr.* (back slang). —Nine shillings. ENIN YANNEPS = Ninepence.

ENJOY, *verb* (old).—To 'possess' a woman.

1594. Shakspeare. *The Rape of Lucrece*, st. 74. 'Lucrece,' quoth he, 'this night I must ENJOY thee ; if thou deny, then force must work my way.'

ENO, *adj.* (back slang).—One.

1850. *Lloyd's Weekly*, 3 Feb. 'Low Lodging Houses of London.' There's people there will rob their own brother. There's people there talk backward—for one they say ENO, for two *owt*, for three *eerht*, for four *ruof*, for five *evif*, for six *exis*. I don't know any higher.

ENSIGN-BEARER, *subs.* (old). — A drunkard ; especially one with a red nose and blotchy face.—See ELBOW-CROOKER.

1785. GROSE, *Dict. Vulg. Tongue*, s.v.

EPHESIAN, *subs.* (old).—A boon companion ; a 'spreester.' *Cf.*, CORINTHIAN.

1596. SHAKSPEARE, *Merry Wives of Windsor*, iv., 5. Art thou there? it is thine host, thine EPHESIAN, calls.

1598. SHAKSPEARE, *2 Henry IV.*, ii. 2. P. H. What company? Page. EPHESIANS, my lord, of the old church.

EPIP, *subs.* (back slang).—A pipe.

EPSOM-RACES, *subs.* (rhyming slang).—A pair of braces.

EQUAL TO THE GENUINE LIM-BURGER.—*See* LIMBURGER.

EQUIPPED, *ppl. adj.* (American thieves').—Rich ; well-dressed ; in good circumstances. *Cf.,* WELL-BALLASTED.

ERIF, *subs.* (back slang).—Fire.

ERIFF, *subs.* (American thieves').—A young thief.

1881. *New York Slang Dict.* 'On the Trail.' It's the gait all them ERIFFS dances, observed the one-eyed man.

ERRAND. TO SEND A BABY ON AN ERRAND, *verb. phr.* (common).—To undertake what is pretty sure to turn out badly.

ERROR.—*See* NO ERROR.

ERTH (back slang).—THREE. ERTH GEN = Three shillings. ERTH - PU = Three-up, a street game, played with three halfpence. ERTH SITH - NOMS = Three months' imprisonment ; a 'drag.' ERTH YANNEPS = Threepence.

ESCLOP (back slang).—A police-constable ; ESCLOP is pronounced 'slop' the *c* is never sounded. For synonyms, *see* BEAK and COPPER.

ES-ROCH (back slang).—A horse. For synonyms, *see* PRAD.

ESSEX-LION, *subs.* (old).—A calf : *e.g.,* 'as valiant as an ESSEX-LION. *Cf.,* COTSWOLD LION, CAMBRIDGESHIRE NIGHTINGALE, etc.

1787. GROSE, *Prov. Glossary,* s.v. ESSEX LIONS. Calves, great numbers of which are brought alive in carts to the London markets.

ESSEX-STILE, *subs.* (old).—A ditch.

1787. GROSE, *Prov. Glossary.* Explained to be either real stiles which, because of the very small enclosures in Essex, are very frequent or the 'narrow bridges, such as are laid between marsh and marsh in the hundreds of this county, only jocularly called stiles, as the loose stone walls in Derbyshire are ludicrously called hedges.'

ESUCH (back slang).—A house. For synonyms, *see* KEN.

ETERNITY-BOX, *subs.* (common).—A coffin.

ENGLISH SYNONYMS. — Cold meat box ; wooden surtout ; coffee-shop ; deal suit.

FRENCH SYNONYMS. — *Boîte à dominos* (popular) ; *étui à lorgnette* (popular) ; *boîte à doche* (thieves') ; *redingote de sapin* (popular).

GERMAN SYNONYMS. — *Pron* (from the Hebrew) ; *Teba* (Hebrew leba).

EVAPORATE, *verb* (common).—To run away ; to disappear. For synonyms, *see* AMPUTATE and SKEDADDLE.

1852. DICKENS, *Bleak House,* ch. xxii., p. 191. Upon which the young man, looking round, instantly EVAPORATES.

1854. AINSWORTH, *Flitch of Bacon,* pt. I., ch. x. You may EVAPORATE if you think proper, Sir G. ; but split me if I stir a step.

1857. CUTHBERT BEDE, *Verdant Green,* pt. II., ch. ix. Mr. Bouncer EVAPORATES with a low bow, leaving the ladies to play with their parasols, and converse.

EVATCH, *verb* (back slang).—To have : *e.g.,* 'EVATCH a kool at the elrig ' = Have a look at the girl.

EVERLASTING-SHOES, (also EVER-LASTINGS) *subs.* (common). — The naked feet. For synonyms, *see* CREEPERS.

EVERLASTING-STAIRCASE, *subs.* (thieves').—The treadmill. For synonyms, *see* WHEEL OF LIFE.

1851-61. H. MAYHEW, *London Lab. and Lon. Poor,* vol. i., p. 300. Why we should be very soon taking reg'lar exercise on Colonel Chesterton's EVERLASTING STAIRCASE. We has a great respect for the law—O, certainly !

1874. H. MAYHEW, *London Characters,* p. 349. I had 'done' my quarter of an hour on the EVERLASTING STAIRCASE (treadmill).

EVERTON-TOFFEE, *subs.* (rhyming slang).—Coffee.

EVERYTHING IS LOVELY AND THE GOOSE HANGS HIGH, *phr.* (American). — Everything is going swimmingly. [An allusion to the 'sport' of gander pulling. A gander was plucked, thoroughly greased, especially about the head and neck, and tied tight by the feet to the branch of a tree. The game was then to ride furiously at the mark, catch it by the head or neck, and attempt to bear it away. With every failure the fun would get more uproarious].

1867. *Round Table,* 30 July. I am not aware that any one has asked you the meaning of the slang phrase, EVERYTHING GOES LOVELY AND THE GOOSE HANGS HIGH ; but doubtless . . . it is derived from the Southern sport (!) of 'Gander-pulling.'

EVE'S CUSTOM-HOUSE, *subs. phr.* (venery).—The female *pudendum.*

EVIF, *adj.* (back slang). — Five EVIF-GEN = A crown, or five shillings. EVIF-YANNEPS = five pence.

EVIL, *subs.* (old). — A wife. For synonyms, *see* DUTCH.

1859. MATSELL, *Vocabulum, or Rogue's Lexicon.* EVIL. A wife ; a halter ; matrimony.

EVLENET-GEN, (back slang). — Twelve shillings. EVLENET SITH-NOMS = twelve months : generally known as a 'stretch.'

EWE.—*See* WHITE EWE and OLD EWE.

EWE-MUTTON, *subs.* (common).—An elderly strumpet or 'piece.'

EXALTED, *ppl. adj.* (old).—Hanged. For synonyms, *see* LADDER. *Cf.,* elevated = drunk.

1836. MICHAEL SCOTT, *Cruise of the Midge,* p. 226. Your great-grandfather was EXALTED, was he?—that is hanged, I suppose?

EXAM, *subs.* (school).—An abbreviation of 'Examination.'

1883. JAMES PAYN, *Thicker than Water,* ch. xxi. It's a mere question of political economy ; I read all about it for my EXAM.—the supply will exceed the demand.

EXASPERATE, *verb* (common).—To over-aspirate the letter H.

1857. CUTHBERT BEDE, *Verdant Green,* pt. II., ch. ix. Mr. Bouncer replies, with a footman's bow, and a footman's hEXASPERATION of his h's.

EXCELLERS, *subs.* (military).—The Fortieth Foot. [A pun upon its number, XL + ERS.]

EXCRUCIATORS, *subs.* (common).—Tight boots ; especially with pointed toes.

EXECUTION-DAY, *subs.* (common).—Washing day.

EXES, *subs.* (common).—1. An abbreviation of ' expenses.'

1871. *Fun,* 4 Nov. ' The Policeman's Complaint.' Nay oft I'm told I've been deceived, And of my x's I'm bereaved ; So on the whole I muchly grieved By information I received.

1883. *Referee,* 18 March, p. 3, col. 3. The piece was ready, but the ' pieces' were not, and without the EXES Morton would not allow the gas to be lighted or the curtain to go up. It was a case of no pay no play.

1890. MONTAGU WILLIAMS, *Leaves of a Life,* I., p. 153. He was out for a spree at the races, and I suppose he thought he'd like to pay his EXES.

2. (colloquial). — An abbreviation of 'ex-officials,' 'ex-ministers,' and so forth. As in TOM MOORE'S ' We x's have proved ourselves not to be wise.'

EXIS-EVIF-GEN, (back slang).—Six times five shillings, *i.e.,* 30s. All monies may be reckoned in this manner, either with YANNEPS or GENS. EXIS - EVIF - YANNEPS, literally, 'sixpence and fivepence = elevenpence.' EXIS GEN = six shillings. EXIS SITH-NOMS = six months. EXIS YANNEPS = Sixpence.

EXPECTING, *ppl.* (colloquial).—With child.

EXPERIENCE DOES IT, *phr.* (common).—A dog-English rendering of *Experienta docet.*

EXPLATERATE, *verb* (American).—To hold forth ; explain in detail. [From O. E. Explate = to unfold.]

EXPLOSION, *subs.* (common). — A delivery.

EXQUISITE, *subs.* (common). — A fop. For synonyms, *see* DANDY.

EXTENSIVE, *adv.* (common).—Formerly applied to a person's appearance or talk ; 'rather EX-TENSIVE that !' intimating that the person alluded to is showing off, or ' cutting it fat.'

EXTINGUISHER, *subs.* (common).—A dog's muzzle.

1890. *Standard,* 12 May, p. 5, col. 4. I had to appear before Mr. Curtis-Bennett, at West Kensington, to answer the charge of the dog being at large without his EX-TINGUISHER *en évidence.*

EX TRUMPS, *adv. phr.* (Winchester College). — Extempore. TO GO UP TO BOOKS EX TRUMPS = to go to class without preparing one's lesson.

EYE.—*See* ALL MY EYE.

TO PULL WOOL OVER THE EYES.—*See* PULL WOOL.

TO KEEP THE EYES CLEAN, SKINNED, or PEELED, *verb. phr.* (American). — To be watchful ; alert ; with all one's wits about one.

1837. C. GILMAN, *Negro Domestic's Recollections.* Mans Ben ax 'em for sing one hymn for 'em, cause he EYE CLEAN.

1865. *New York Herald.* My son, afore you leave yer home, I want ter say ter you, Thar's lots of pitfalls in the world ter let young roosters through ; So keep a padlock on yer mouth and SKIN YER WEATHER EYE, But never advertise yerself as being monstrous fly.

TO HAVE A DROP IN THE EYE, *verb. phr.* (common). — To be drunk. For synonyms, *see* DRINKS and SCREWED.

1738. SWIFT, *Pol. Convers.,* Dial. I. You must own you had a DROP IN YOUR EYE ; when I left you, you were half seas over.

1837. BARHAM, *I. L. (Black Mousquetaire).* In vain did he try With strong waters to ply His friend, on the ground

that he never could spy Such a thing as a ghost with a DROP IN HIS EYE.

IN THE TWINKLING OF AN EYE.—*See* BEDPOST.

TO BET ONE'S EYES.—*See* BET.

MY EYES ! *intj. phr.* (common).—An expression of surprise.

1837. DICKENS, *Oliver Twist,* ch. viii. ' MY EYES, how green !' exclaimed the young gentleman. ' Why a beak's a madgst'rate.'

EYELASHES. TO HANG ON BY THE EYELASHES or EYEBROWS, *verb. phr.* (common). — To be very tenacious ; also, by implication, to be in a difficulty. *Cf.,* HANG ON BY THE SPLASH-BOARD.

EYE-LIMPET, *subs.* (common).—An artificial eye.

EYE-OPENER, *subs.* (American).—1. Drink generally ; specifically, a mixed drink.

2. (general). — Anything surprising or out of the way.

1879. *Notes and Queries,* 5th S., xi., 140. His lecture must have been a lively and profitable EYE-OPENER for the somnolence of a cathedral town.

1888. *Cornhill Mag.,* March, p. 228. If Joanna was ever so blessed as to hear her sing ' Houp la !' it would be a regular EYE-OPENER to her.

1889. *Answers,* 23 Feb., p. 194, col. 1. No doubt the enclosed will be an EYE-OPENER for you.

3. (venery).—The *penis.* For synonyms, *see* CREAMSTICK.

EYETEETH. TO HAVE CUT ONE'S EYETEETH, *verb. phr.* (colloquial).—To have learned wisdom.

1748. T. DYCHE, *Dictionary* (5th ed). EYE-TEETH (s.), those immediately under the eye ; also quickness or sharpness of understanding and parts, are sometimes so called.

1835. HALIBURTON, *Clockmaker* I S., ch. xvi. Them 'ere fellers CUT THEIR EYE-TEETH afore they ever sot foot in this country, I expect.

EYE-WATER, *subs.* (common).—Gin. For synonyms, *see* DRINKS.

1869. WHYTE MELVILLE, *M. or N.,* p. 66. On this minnit, off at six, Buster ; two bob an' a bender, and a three of EYE-WATER, in ?

1886. *Judy,* 4 August, p. 58. He imbibed stupendous quantities of jiggered gin, dog's nose, and Paddy's EYE-WATER.

FACE, subs. (colloquial).—1. Confidence; boldness; also (more frequently) impudence: e.g., 'I like your FACE' =I like your cheek. Once literary; Cf., CHEEK, JAW, GAB, BROW, MOUTH, LIP, etc.

1610. BEN JONSON, The Alchemist. 'Dramatis Personæ.'—FACE.

1617. MIDDLETON, A Faire Quarrell, II., ii. I that had FACE enough to do the deed, Cannot want tongue to speak it.

1668. ETHEREGE, She Would if She Could, I., i. (1704), p. 95. I admire thy impudence, I could never have had the FACE to have wheadled the poor knight so.

1676. ETHEREGE, Man of Mode, V., i., in wks. (1704), 265. I am amazed to find him here! How has he the FACE to come near you?

1702. DEFOE, Shortest Way, in Arber's Garner, vol. VII., p. 590. You have butchered one king! deposed another king! and made a mock king of a third! and yet, you could have the FACE to expect to be employed and trusted by the fourth.

1714. Spectator, No. 566. A man has scarce the FACE to make his court to a lady, without some credentials from the service to recommend him.

1854. F. E. SMEDLEY, Harry Coverdale, ch. liii. I can hardly suppose even Phil Tirrett would have the FACE to throw me over and ride for O'Brien.

1870. London Figaro, 3 June. 'Look at that girl in pink, Sancho,' he said; 'that's Lord Rubric's daughter. Ran away with the family organist—that's he with her. I like their FACE, though, to come here; it's awfully good.'

2. (common). — Credit. To PUSH ONE'S FACE = to get credit by bluster. — [See sense I and cf., FACE-ENTRY.]

1765. GOLDSMITH, Essays, VIII. There are three ways of getting into debt: first, by PUSHING A FACE; as thus: 'You, Mr. Lutestring, send me home six yards of that paduasoy, damme; but, harkee, don't think I ever intend to pay you for it, damme.' At this the mercer laughs heartily; cuts off the paduasoy, and sends it home; nor is he, till too late, surprised to find the gentleman had said nothing but the truth, and kept his word.

1865. BACON, Handbook of America, p. 365. To RUN ONE'S FACE, to make use of one's credit, TO RUN ONE'S FACE for a thing is to get it 'on tick.'

1875. American English in Chamb. Journal, 25 Sept., p. 610. To RUN YOUR FACE, which means, to go upon credit.

3. (common).—A qualification of contempt: e.g., 'Now FACE! where are you a-shoving of?'

Verb (old).—To bully.—See all senses, especially TO FACE WITH A CARD OF TEN.

1593. SHAKSPEARE, Taming of the Shrew, iv., 3. FACE not me; thou hast brav'd many men; brave not me; I will neither FAC'D nor brav'd.

To FACE or OUT-FACE WITH A CARD OF TEN, verb. phr. (old).—To browbeat; to 'bluff.' [NARES: derived from some game (possibly primero) wherein the standing boldly upon a ten was often successful. The phrase originally expressed the confidence of one player who with a ten, as at brag, FACED or OUTFACED one who had really a faced card against him.]

1460-1529. SKELTON [quoted by Nares]. First pycke a quarrel and fall out with him then, And so OUT FACE HIM WITH A CARD OF TEN.

1593. SHAKSPEARE, Taming of the Shrew, ii. A vengeance on your crafty wither'd hide, Yet I have FAC'D IT WITH A CARD OF TEN.

1630. B. JONSON, New Inn, i., 3. Some may be coats, as in the cards; but then Some must be knaves, some varlets, bawds, and ostlers, As aces, duces, CARDS o' TEN TO FACE IT OUT, i' the game which all the world is.

To FACE THE KNOCKER, verb. phr. (tailors'). — To go begging. For synonyms, see CADGE.

To HAVE NO FACE BUT ONE'S OWN, verb. phr. (old).—To be penniless; or (gamesters') to hold no court cards. Fr., n'avoir pas une face = 'not to have a sou.'

1785. GROSE, Dict. Vulg. Tongue, s.v.

To MAKE FACES, verb. phr. (prison).—1. To go back, or 'round' upon a friend. [In allusion to the convicts' habit of distorting their features under the lens.]

2. (old).—To beget children. Cf., FACE-MAKING.

To FACE THE MUSIC, verb. phr. (American).—To meet an emergency; also to show one's hand. [J. Fenimore Cooper derived it from the green-room, whence actors go on the boards and literally FACE THE MUSIC. Another traces it to militia musters, where every man is expected to appear equipped and armed, when in rank and file, FACING THE MUSIC. A third derives it from drumming out of the army.]

1857. Worcester Spy, 22 Sept. Although such reverses would seem to fall with crushing weight upon some of our most substantial citizens, a strong determination to FACE THE MUSIC is everywhere manifested.

1888. Daily Inter-Ocean, 20 Feb. I am sure Fred can explain everything satisfactorily. I hope he hasn't read the newspaper stories about him, for it might scare him, and he'd very foolishly skip out. That would be the worst thing he could do. He must FACE THE MUSIC.

FACE-ENTRY, subs. (theatrical).—Freedom of access, the personal appearance being familiar to attendants.

FACE-MAKING, verb. subs. (old).—Begetting children. Cf., MAKING FEET FOR CHILDREN'S STOCKINGS.

FACER, subs. (pugilistic). — 1. A blow in the face.

1785. GROSE, Dict. Vulg. Tongue, s.v.

1819. MOORE, Tom Crib's Memorial, p. 24. In short, not to dwell on each FACER and fall, Poor Georgy was done up in no time at all.

1834. HARRISON AINSWORTH, Rookwood. 'The Double Cross.' No claret flows, No FACERS sound — no smashing blows.

1837. BARHAM, I.L. (The Ghost). Whom sometimes there would come on A sort of fear his spouse might knock his head off, Demolish half his teeth, or drive a rib in, She shone so much in FACERS and in 'fibbing.'

1862. Athenæum, 1 Nov., p. 557, col. I. Before his unknown adversary well

knew what was coming, the skilled fist of the Professor had planted such a FACER as did not require repetition.

1868. C. READE, Foul Play, ch. ii. This was followed by a quick succession of staggering FACERS, administered right and left, on the eyes and noses of the subordinates.

2. (common). — A sudden check; 'a spoke in one's wheel.' [By implication from sense I.]

1860. THACKERAY, Philip, ch. xl. In the battle of life every man must meet with a blow or two, and every brave one would take his FACER with good humour.

1869. WHYTE MELVILLE, M. or N., p. 189. Dick Stanmore took his punishment with true British pluck and pertinacity. It was a FACER.

3. (Irish).—A dram.

4. (old).—A bumper. [Grose, 1785.]

5. (common).—A tumbler of whiskey punch.

6. (American thieves').—An accomplice; a STALL (q.v.) or FENCE (q.v.).

1859. MATSELL, Vocabulum, or Rogue's Lexicon, s.v.

1881. New York Slang Dict., s.v.

FACEY, subs. (tailors').—A fellow workman vis-à-vis. FACEY ON THE BIAS = one in front either to right or left; FACEY ON THE TWO THICK = one working immediately behind one's opposite.

FACINGS.—TO BE PUT, or GO, THROUGH ONE'S FACINGS, verb. phr. (popular).—To be called to account or scolded; to exemplify capacity; to 'show off.' [Military.]

SILK-FACINGS, subs. (tailors').—Stains upon work caused by droppings of beer. [In allusion to the 'watered' silk trimmings in front of a regimental jacket or coat.]

FAD-CATTLE, subs. (old). — Easy women. For synonyms, see BARRACK-HACK and TART. [Cf., FADDLE = to toy + CATTLE (q.v.).]

FADDIST (also FADMONGER), subs. (colloquial).—A person (male or female) devoted to the pursuit of public fads: as 'social purity,' moral art, free-trade in syphilis, and so-forth.

FADDLE, verb (obsolete).—To toy or trifle: as a subs. = a busybody; a 'nancified' affected male. Also FADDY = full of fads.

FADGE, subs. (common).—A farthing.

ENGLISH SYNONYMS. — Fiddler; farden; gig, or grig; quartereen.

1789. GEO. PARKER, Life's Painter, p. 178, s.v.

1811. Lexicon Balatronicum, s.v.

1848. DUNCOMBE, Sinks of London, s.v.

Verb (old).—To suit; to fit; to agree with; to come off. [A.S., fégan, fégean, to join, to fit. Nares says, 'probably never better than a low word: it is now confined to the streets.']

1593. NASHE, 4 Lett. Conf., in wks. (Grosart) II., 215. They haue brought in a new kind of a quicke sight, which your decrepite slow-mouing capacitie cannot FADGE with.

1594. SHAKSPEARE, Love's Labour Lost, V., i., 154. We will haue, if this FADGE not, an Antique.

1599. MASSINGER, Old Law, IV., ii. Clean. My Lord! Sim. Now it begins to FADGE.

1636. T. HEYWOOD, Love's Mistress, Act IV. Vulcan . . . . I keep a dozen journeymen at least, besides my Ciclops and my Prentises, yet 'twill not FADGE.

1639. BEAUMONT AND FLETCHER, Wit without Money, III., iv. Clcthes I must get; this fashion will not FADGE with me.

1678. Quack's Academy, in Harl. Misc. (ed. Park), ii., 32. That could never make their untoward handicrafts FADGE to purpose.

1750. WALPOLE, Lett. to Mann, 18 Oct. (1833), vol. II., p. 485. Alack! when I came to range them, they did not FADGE at all.

1819. SCOTT, in C. K. Sharpe's Correspondence (1888), ii., 197. Pray let me know . . . how matters FADGE in the great city of Edinburgh.

1830. SCOTT, Doom of Devorgoil, Act II., Sc. I. If this same gear FADGE right, I'll cote and mouth her, And then! whoop! dead! dead! dead!

1851. G. BORROW, Lavengro, ch. lv., p. 173 (1888). Any new adventure which I can invent will not FADGE well with the old tale.

FADGER, subs. (glaziers').—A glazier's frame; otherwise a 'frail.'

FADMONGER, subs. (colloquial).—A FADDIST (q.v.). FADMONGERING, verb. phr. (colloquial) = dealing as a FADDIST (q.v.) with fads.

FAG, subs. (public schools').—1. A boy who does menial work for a schoolfellow in a higher form. [From FAG, to grow weary.]

1855. THACKERAY, Newcomes, ch. xviii. Bob Trotter, the diminutive FAG of the studio, who ran on all the young men's errands, and fetched them in apples, oranges, and walnuts.

1857. G. A. LAWRENCE, Guy Livingstone, ch. i. Is still enumerated among the feats of the brave days of old, by the FAGS over their evening small beer.

2. (Christ's Hospital). — See quot.

1850. L. HUNT, Autobiography, ch. iii. FAG, with us [at Christ's Hospital], meant eatables. The learned derived the word from the Greek phago, to eat.

3. (American thieves'). — A lawyer's clerk.

1859. MATSELL, Vocabulum, or Rogue's Lexicon, s.v.

Verb (public schools').—1. To do menial work for a schoolfellow in a higher form. Cf., FAG, subs., sense I.

1884. Temple Bar, August, p. 514. He must have completely marred his chance of happiness at the school when he refused to FAG and took countless thrashings, snivelling.

2. (old).—To beat.

1754. B. MARTIN, Eng. Dict. (2nd ed.).

1811. Lexicon Balatronicum, s.v. FAG the bloss, beat the wench.

FAGGER, FIGGER, or FIGURE, subs. (old).—A boy thief whose duty is to enter houses by windows and either open the doors to his confederates (as Oliver Twist with Bill Sykes), or hand out the 'swag' to them; also LITTLE SNAKESMAN (q.v.); cf., DIVER.

1785. GROSE, Dict. Vulg. Tongue, s.v.

1848. DUNCOMBE, Sinks of London, s.v.

FAGGING, or FAGGERY, subs. (public schools').—Waiting upon and doing menial work for a school-fellow in a higher form. Also used adjectively.

1853. DE QUINCEY, Autob. Sketches, i., 210. FAGGERY was an abuse too venerable and sacred to be touched by profane hands.

1873. Pall Mall Gazette, 17 May. The Winchester 'tunding' system, with all its faults, is hardly less objectionable than the FAGGING system pursued in the Scotch endowed hospitals.

FAGGOT, subs. (common).—1. A term of opprobrium to women; a 'baggage.' [At one time a faggot was a popular symbol of recantation of opinions thought worthy only of burning (Bailey, 1728), and heretics who had thus escaped the stake were required either to bear a faggot and burn it in public, or to wear an imitation on the sleeve as a badge.] Also used in combination: *e.g.*, BED- (or STRAW-) FAGGOT = a wife, or mistress; TUMBLE-FAGGOT = a whoremaster; CARRY-FAGGOT = a mattress; and SPIKE- (or TICKLE)- FAGGOT (obsolete) = the *penis*.

1820. REYNOLDS ('P. Corcoran'), *The Fancy*, p. 16. I have got a FAGGOT here, Aye, and quite a bad one; Were I married, p'rhaps my dear Might think that *he* too had one.

2. (common).—*See* quot., 1851.

1851-61. H. MAYHEW, *London Lab. and Lon. Poor*, vol. ii., p. 255. He then made his supper, or second meal, for tea he seldom touched, on FAGOTS. This preparation . . . is a sort of cake, roll, or ball, a number being baked at a time, and is made of chopped liver and lights, mixed with gravy, and wrapped in pieces of pig's caul. It weighs six ounces, so that it is unquestionably a cheap [it costs 1d. hot] and, to the scavager, a savoury meal, but to other nostrils it's odour is not seductive.

1870. *London Figaro*, 2 July. Have you more than a penny? A glorious perspective opens out before you of all the delicacies of the season, commencing with trotters—the harmless mutton, or the succulent swine; 'FAGGOTS,' etc.

1884. *Cornhill Mag.*, June, p. 615. They can obtain hot FAGGOTS, hot baked potatoes, hot fried fish, or a cut of pork with hot pease-pudding.

3. (old).—A 'dummy' soldier; one hired to appear at a muster to hide deficiencies. Many names of dummies would appear on the muster-roll: for these the colonel drew pay, but they were never in the ranks.

1672-1719. ADDISON [quoted in *Imperial Dict.*]. There were several counterfeit books which were carved in wood, and served only to fill up the number like FAGOTS in the muster of a regiment.

1728. BAILEY, *Dict.*, s.v.

1785. GROSE, *Dict. Vulg. Tongue*, s.v.

Verb (old).—1. To bind hand and foot; to tie [as sticks into a faggot]. Fr., *un fagot* = a convict, because bound to a common chain on their way to the hulks.

1728. BAILEY, *Dict.*, s.v.

1785. GROSE, *Dict. Vulg. Tongue* s.v. FAGGOT the culls, bind the men.

1859. MATSELL, *Vocabulum, or Rogue's Lexicon*, s.v.

2. (venery).—To copulate; also to frequent the company of loose women.

FAGGOT-BRIEFS, *subs.* (political).—Bundles of dummy papers sometimes carried by briefless barristers. [*Cf.*, FAGGOT, sense 3.]

1859. SALA, *Twice Round the Clock*, 10 a.m. Par. 10. The counsel chat and poke each other in the ribs; the briefless ones, in the h gh back rows, scribble caricatures on their blotting-pads, or pretend to pore over FAGGOT BRIEFS.

1887. *Cornhill Mag.*, June, p. 627. FAGGOT BRIEFS . . . those bundles of dummy papers sometimes carried by the briefless ones.

FAGGOTEER, (also FAGGOT-MASTER), *subs.* (venery).—A whoremonger. For synonyms, *see* MOLROWER.

FAGGOT-VOTE, *subs.* (political).—A vote secured by the purchase of property under mortgage, or otherwise, so as to constitute a nominal qualification without a substantial basis. [Derived by some from FAGGOT, sense 3; by others from the mode of manufacture, *i.e.*, by the purchase of property which is divided into as many lots as will constitute separate votes, and given to different persons.]

1854. *Notes and Queries*, vol. X., p. 403. FAGGOT-VOTE.—Can you inform me of the origin of the term used to denote a spurious or fictitious vote, formed usually by the nominal transfer of a sufficient qualification to an otherwise unqualified man; this is called a FAGGOT VOTE.

1879. GLADSTONE, *1st Midl. Speech*, 25 Nov. Why, gentlemen, quite apart from every question of principle, nothing, I venture to say, can be so grossly imprudent as that which is familiarly known in homely but most accurate phrase as the manufacture of FAGGOT VOTES.

1887. *Cornhill Mag.*, June, p. 627. FAGGOT VOTES . . . . the name is probably taken from an old military term.

FAINS! FAINITS! FAIN IT! *intj.* (schoolboys').—A call for truce during the progress of a game without which priority or place would be lost; generally understood to be peferred 'in bounds,' or when out of danger. [Thought to be a corruption of 'fend.']—*See* BAGS!

FAIR-GANG, *subs.* (old).—Gypsies. [From their habit of visiting fairs.]

FAIR-RATIONS, *subs.* (sporting).—Fair dealings.

FAIR-SHAKE, *subs.* (American).—A good bargain. [From a measure well shaken down. *Cf.*, SHAKE.

FAIR-TRADE, *subs.* (nautical).—Smuggling.

FAITHFUL. ONE OF THE FAITHFUL, *subs. phr.* (old).—1. A drunkard. For synonyms, *see* ELBOW-CROOKER.

1609. *The Man in the Moone.* This fellow is ONE OF THE FAITHFULL, as they prophanelie terme him, said Opinion; no Heliogabalus at meat, but he will drinke many degrees beyond a Dutchman.

2. (common).—A tailor giving long credit.

1785. GROSE, *Dict. Vulg. Tongue*, s.v.

1859. MATSELL, *Vocabulum, or Rogue's Lexicon.* FAITHFUL. A tailor that gives long credit. 'I say, Sam, what kind of crib was that you cracked?' 'Oh! it belonged to ONE OF THE FAITHFUL.

FAITHFUL DURHAMS, *subs. phr.* (military).—The Sixty-Eight Foot.

FAKE, *subs.* (common).—An action; a proceeding; a manœuvre; a mechanical contrivance—an affair of any kind irrespective of morals or legality: generally used in a sense specifically detrimental. In America, a swindler. [Origin dubious: Barrère says, 'a very ancient cant word,' but gives no evidence. FAKEMENT (*q.v.*) appears to be the older *subs.* form (1785), while the verbal usage is traced to Ainsworth's 'FAKE away'! in *Rookwood* (1834). Conjecturally derived from the Latin *facere*, to make, to do: compare to which the French slang use of *faire.*]

1827. MAGINN, in *Blackwood's Mag.* . . . the fogle-hunters doing Their morning FAKE in the prigging lay.

[*Circa*, 1850, but date uncertain.] 'Bates' Farm.' I'm up to every little FAKE, But in me there's no harm.

1851-61. H. MAYHEW, *London Lab. and Lon. Poor*, vol. I., p. 237. After that we had a fine FAKE—that was the fire of the Tower of London—it sold rattling.

1871. *London Figaro*, 21 Oct. Yet they've been known for many a FAKE To coolly set a trap.

1883. GREENWOOD, *Tag, Rag, and Co.* Naming the house in the ridiculous way it was named was merely a FAKE to draw attention to it.

1888. *New York Mercury.* Both ladies then came to the conclusion that the fortune-teller was a FAKE, and they decided to notify the police.

1889. *Globe*, 23 July, p. 2, col. 2. Good Gladstonites, flock up and take One bottle of the Parnell FAKE.

Verb (common).—1. To do anything; to fabricate; to cheat; to deceive, or devise falsely; to steal; to forge. A general verb-of-all-work. In America FIX (*q.v.*) is employed much in the same way, whilst the French slang has *faire*; *maquiller*; *aquiger* or *quiger*; and *goupiner*.

[In combination TO FAKE A SCREEVE = to write a begging letter; TO FAKE ONE'S SLANGS = to file through one's fetters; TO FAKE A CLY (*q.v.*) = to pick a pocket; TO FAKE THE SWEETENER = to kiss; TO FAKE THE DUCK = to adulterate, to dodge; TO FAKE THE RUBBER = to stand treat; TO FAKE THE BROADS = to pack the cards, or to work the three-card trick; TO FAKE A LINE (theatrical) = to improvise a speech; TO FAKE A DANCE, OR A STEP, OR A TRIP (theatrical) = to perform what looks like, but is not, dancing.]

1851-61. H. MAYHEW, *London Lab. and Lon. Poor*, vol. I., p. 390. The ring is made out of brass gilt buttons, and stunning well: it's FAKED up to rights, and takes a good judge even at this day to detect it without a test.

1861. READE, *Cloister and Hearth*, ch. lv. There the folk are music-bitten, and they molest not beggars, unless they FAKE to boot, and then they drown us out of hand.

2. (sporting).—To hocus; to nobble; to tamper.

1872. *Morning Post*, 7 Nov. Since the FAKING of the scales in Catch-'em-alive's year the oldest *habitué* of Newmarket cannot recall so sensational a Cambridgeshire week as the last one.

3. (theatrical).—Also TO FAKE UP. To paint one's face; to make up a character.

1885. *Sporting Times*, 23 May. 'The Chorister's Promise.' The landlady left, and the chorister fair FAKED herself UP, and frizzed her hair.

4. (American thieves').—To cut out the wards of a key.

1859. MATSELL, *Vocabulum, or Rogue's Lexicon*, s.v.

FAKE AWAY! *intj. phr.* (common).—An ejaculation of encouragement.

1834. HARRISON AINSWORTH, *Rookwood.* The knucks in quod did my schoolmen play, FAKE AWAY!

1846. *Punch's Almanack*, 'Song of September.' The partridge on its tender wing Is up at break of day, But down the bird my gun shall bring: Bang! fizz, boys! FAKE AWAY!

FAKE-BOODLE.—*See* BOODLE.

FAKED, *ppl. adj.* (common).—Counterfeit; sometimes FAKED-UP. Fr., *lophe*.

1889. *Answers*, 15 June, p. 41, col. 1. In order to prevent any chance of a dishonest person winning by means of a FAKED puzzle we shall provide a number of puzzles ourselves, and these will be used by all competitors.

FAKEMENT, *subs.* (old).—1. A counterfeit signature; a forgery; specifically a begging letter or petition. Fr., *brasser des faffes* = to forge documents, *i.e.*, 'TO SCREEVE FAKEMENTS'; *un fafiot* (also a bank note, or shoe); and *une luque* or *un luquet*.

1785. GROSE, *Dict. Vulg. Tongue.* Tell the macers to mind their FAKEMENTS, desire the swindlers to be careful not to forge another person's signature.

1856. H. MAYHEW, *Gt. World of London*, p. 46. Dependents of beggars; as screevers or the writers of 'slums' (letters) and FAKEMENTS (petitions).

1857. DUCANGE ANGLICUS, *The Vulgar Tongue*, p. 39. Lawyer Bob draws FAKEMENTS up; he's tipped a peg for each.

1889. *Answers*, 27 July, p. 137, col. 1. I have drawn up FAKEMENTS for sham members of almost every trade, always using a leading name at the head of the list of donors.

2. (common).—Generic for dishonest practices; but applied to any kind of action, contrivance, or trade.—*See* FAKE, *subs.*, of which it is an older usage. *Cf.*, KIDMENT.

1838. GLASCOCK, *Land Sharks and Sea Gulls*, II., 4. That's right; I see you're fly to every FAKEMENT.

1857. DUCANGE ANGLICUS. *The Vulg. Tongue*, p. 44. For every day, mind what I say, Fresh FAKEMENTS you will find.

1859. H. KINGSLEY, *Geoffry Hamlyn*, ch. v. I cultivated his acquaintance, examined his affairs, and put him up to the neatest little FAKEMENT in the world.

1876. C. HINDLEY, *Life and Adventures of a Cheap Jack*, p. 232. Stow your gab and gauffery, To every FAKEMENT I'm a-fly. *Ibid.*, p. 233. I have got a pair of highly polished steel spring snuffers with extra FAKEMENT; they will either snuff a candle out or snuff a candle in.

1877. *Five Years' Penal Servitude*, ch. iv., p. 254. You worked that little FAKEMENT in a blooming quiet way, . . . said my late neighbour.

1883. *Daily Telegraph*, 7 Aug., p. 6, col. 2. Pair of moleskins [trousers], any colour . . . with a double FAKEMENT down the sides, and artful buttons at the bottom.

3. (theatrical).—Small properties; accessories.

FAKEMENT-CHARLEY, *subs. phr.* (thieves').—An owner's private mark.

1864. HOTTEN, *Slang Dict.*, s.v.

FAKER, *subs.* (common).—1. One who makes, does, or 'fakes' anything; specifically a thief. Found in many combinations: *e.g.*, BIT-FAKER; FLUE-FAKER; GRUB-FAKER; SHAM-FAKER, TWAT-FAKER, etc.

1851. G. BORROW, *Lavengro*, ch. xxxi., p. 112 (1888). We never calls them thieves here, but prigs and FAKERS.

1857. DUCANGE ANGLICUS, *Vulg. Tongue.* FAKER, a jeweller (theatrical).

1869. GEORGE MACDONALD, *Robert Falconer*, pt. III., ch. x. Them pusses is mannyfactered express for the convenience o' the FAKERS.

1885. *Daily Telegraph*, 1 August, p. 2, col. 1. 'I've turned FAKER of dolls and dolls' furniture; like what you see us working on now.' 'And when you say FAKER you mean—'Renowater,' struck in Miss Menders.

1887. BAUMANN, *Londonismen*, p. 5. Piratical FAKERS Of bosh by the acres.

2. (circus).—A circus rider or performer.

3. (venery).—A prostitute's FANCY-MAN (*q.v.*).

FAKES AND SLUMBOES, *subs. phr.* (theatrical).—Properties; accessories of any kind.

FAKING, *verb. subs.* (common).—The act of doing anything. [From FAKE (*q.v.*) + ING.] Fr., *le maquillage* or *le goupinage*.

FALL, *verb* (thieves').—1. To be arrested.

1883. HORSLEY, *Jottings from Jail* [in *Echo*]. A little time after this I FELL again at St. Mary Cray for being found at the back of a house.

2. (venery).—To conceive. For synonyms, *see* LUMPY.

FALL OF THE LEAF, *subs. phr.* (old).—Hanging. [In allusion to the fall of the drop.] For synonyms, *see* LADDER.

1789. G. PARKER, *Variegated Characters.* He was knocked down for the crap the last sessions. He went off at the FALL OF THE LEAF at Tuck'em Fair.

FALSE-HEREAFTER, *subs.* (American).—A bustle. For synonyms, *see* BIRD-CAGE.

FAM.—*See* FAMBLING-CHEAT and FAMBLE.

FAMBLE, FAM, or **FEM**, *subs.* (old).—The hand. *Cf.*, FAMBLING-CHEAT. For synonyms, *see* BUNCH OF FIVES and DADDLE. [German slang has *Fehm*, *Vehm*, or *Vehn*, and is apparently the same word as he English FAM. A likely etymon is the Swed. and Dan. *fem*, five.]

1567. HARMAN, *Caveat* (1814), p. 64, s.v. 1610. ROWLANDS, *Martin Mark-all*, p. 38 (H. Club's Repr., 1874). FAMBLES. handes.

1662 FLETCHER, *Beggar's Bush*, ii., I. We clapt our FAMBLES.

1724. E. COLES, *Eng. Dict.*, s.v.

1815. SCOTT, *Guy Mannering*, ch. xxviii. If I had not helped you with these very FAMBLES (holding up her hands).

1819. MOORE, *Tom Crib's Memorial*, p. 28. Allowing for delicate FAMS, which have merely Been handling the sceptre, and that, too but queerly.

1878. C. HINDLEY, *Life and Times of James Catnach*. So kiddy is my FAMBLE.

Verb (old).—To touch; to handle; especially with a view to ascertaining the whereabouts of valuables. Also termed TO FAM FOR THE PLANT, and TO RUN A RULE OVER. TO FAM A DONNA=to take liberties with a woman; to FIRKY-TOODLE (*q.v.*); to CROSS-FAM (*q.v.*).

FAMBLERS, FAMBLING - CHEATS (*q.v.*) or **FAM-SNATCHERS** (*q.v.*), *subs.* (old).—Gloves.

1610. ROWLANDS, *Martin Mark-all*, p. 38 (H. Club's Repr., 1874), s.v.

FAMBLING-CHEAT, FAMBLE, or **FAM,** *subs.* (old).—A ring; also (about 1694) gloves, which later still were also called FAM-SNATCHERS (*q.v.*). [From FAM-BLE, a hand + A.S. CHETE (*q.v.*), a thing.]

1567. HARMAN, *Caveat* (1814), p. 64. A FAMBLING CHETE, a ring on thy hand.

1610. ROWLANDS, *Martin Mark-all*, p. 38 (H. Club's Repr., 1874). FAMBLING CHEATES, Rings.

1688. SHADWELL, *Sq. of Alsatia*, II., in wks. (1720), iv., 47. Look on my finger, sirrah, look here; here's a FAMBLE.

1694. DUNTON, *Ladies' Dict.*, s.v. Famble-cheats, rings or gloves.

1724. E. COLES, *Eng. Dict.* FAMBLE CHEATS, rings or gloves.

1789. GEO. PARKER, *Life's Painter*, p. 180. FAM, A gold ring.

FAM - GRASP, *verb* (old). — To shake hands. Also substantively, hand-shaking.

1785. GROSE, *Dict. Vulg. Tongue*, s.v.

FAMILIARS, *subs.* (common).—Lice. For synonyms, see CHATES.

FAMILIAR-WAY, *subs.* (common).— With child.

FAMILY DISTURBANCE, *subs.* (American). — Whiskey. For synonyms, see DRINKS.

FAMILY - HOTEL, *subs.* (old).—A prison. For synonyms, see CAGE. [*Cf.*, FAMILY-MAN.]

1857. *Punch*, 31 Jan. In a ward with one's pals, Not locked up in a cell, To an old hand like me its a FAM-LY HOTEL.

FAMILY-MAN, *subs.* (old).—A thief; specifically, a FENCE (*q.v.*). [In allusion to the fraternities into which thieves were at one time invariably banded.]—See THIEVES.

1749. BAMFYLDE MOORE - CAREW. 'Oath of the Canting Crew.' No dummerar, or romany; No member of THE FAMILY.

1788. G. A. STEVENS, *Adv. of a Specialist*, i., 221. Let the people say what they will against gamesters, gamblers, or FAMILY-MEN.

1838. GLASCOCK, *Land Sharks and Sea Gulls*, II., 100. This house . . . was a favourite resort of THE FAMILY, or, to speak with less reserve, it was a thieves' house.

1857. SNOWDEN, *Mag. Assistant*, [3rd ed.], p. 444. Thieves: FAMILY-MEN.

FAMILY OF LOVE, *subs. phr.* (venery).—A company of prostitutes.

FAMILY-PLATE, *subs.* (common).— Silver money. For synonyms, see ACTUAL and GILT.

FAMILY-POUND, *subs.* (common).— A family grave.

FAM-LAY, *subs.* (thieves'). — Shoplifting. [From FAM, a hand + LAY, a performance.]

1785. GROSE, *Dict. Vulg. Tongue*, s.v.

1859. MATSELL, *Vocabulum, or Rogue's Lexicon*, s.v.

FAM-SNATCHERS, *subs.* (old).— Gloves. *Cf.*, FAMBLING-CHEAT.

c. 1824. PIERCE EGAN, *Finish to Life in London*. To Jerry Hawthorn, Esq., I resign my FAM-SNATCHERS, *i.e.*, my gloves.

FAM - SQUEEZE, *subs.* (old).— Strangulation.

FAM - STRUCK, *adj.* and *adv.* (thieves'). — Baffled in ascertaining the whereabouts of valuables on the person of an intended victim; also handcuffed.

FAN, *subs.* (thieves').—A waistcoat; said by Hotten (1864) to be a Houndsditch term, but quoted in Matsell (1859) as American.

ENGLISH SYNONYMS. — Ben; benjie; M.B. waistcoat; Charley Prescot.

FRENCH SYNONYMS.—*Un gilmont* (thieves'); *un georget* (popular : = a breast-plate); *un casimir* (popular); *une camisole* (popular : properly, a kind of petticoat-bodice worn by women); *un croisant* (popular).

GERMAN SYNONYMS.—*Brustmalbisch* ; *Kreuzspanne* (Hanoverian) ; *Nefesch* (Ave-Lallement

suggests identity with the *Fischness* of Zimmermann, a word said to be derived from the English 'fashion.' Probably, however, the true etymon is the Hebrew *nephesch*, in allusion to a waistcoat covering the chest and heart, the seat of life. German ladies call a scarf or shawl [which protects the same region] *Seelenwärmer, i.e.*, a soul-warmer) ; *Zwängerling* (=fitting closely to the body ; *cf., Weitling,* Hanoverian *Weitchen*, the trousers=wide).

1857. SNOWDEN, *Mag. Assistant*, 3rd ed., p. 444, s.v.

Verb (old).—1. To beat; to be-rate. For synonyms, see BASTE and TAN.

1785. GROSE, *Dict. Vulg. Tongue*. I FANND him sweetly, I beat him heartily.

1887. W. O. TRISTRAM, in *Eng. Ill. Mag.,* v., 228. The coachman now has recourse to all the dark arts of persuasion and the whip, FANNING them, which, in the tongue of coachmen, is whipping them.

2. (thieves'). — To feel ; to handle (with a view to ascertain if a victim has anything valuable about his person). [*Cf.*, FAM, of which it is possibly a corruption.] Also to steal from the person.

1851-1861. H. MAYHEW, *Lon. Lab. and Lon. Poor*, IV., 319. Before Joe said anything to me, he had FANNED the gentleman's pocket, *i.e.*, 'had felt the pocket and knew there was a handkerchief.

QUEEN ANNE'S FAN. — *See* ANNE'S FAN.

FANCY, *subs.* (old).—The fraternity of pugilists : prize-fighting being once regarded as THE FANCY *par excellence.* Hence, by implication, people who cultivate a special hobby or taste. *Cf.*, FANCY-BLOKE.

1818. P. EGAN, *Boxiana*, vol. I., p. 355. The various gradations of THE FANCY hither

---

resort, to discuss matters incidental to pugilism.

1848. THACKERAY, *Book of Snobs*, ch. xiv. Mr. William Ramm, known to THE FANCY as the Tutbury Pet.

1860. *Chambers' Journal*, vol. XIII., p. 153.

FANCY-BLOKE, *subs.* (common).— 1. A sporting man. [From FANCY (*q.v.*) + BLOKE, a man.]

2. (venery).—*See* FANCY-MAN.

FANCY-HOUSE, *subs.* (venery). — A brothel ; also a HOUSE OF ACCOMMODATION (*q.v.*). For synonyms, see NANNY-SHOP.

FANCY-JOSEPH, *subs.* (venery).—A prostitute's boy, or apple-squire, or CUPID (*q.v.*). For synonyms, *see* BULLY and FANCY-MAN.

FANCY-LAY, *subs.* (old).—Pugilism. [From FANCY (*q.v.*) + LAY (*q.v.*) = an undertaking or pursuit.]

1819. MOORE, *Tom Crib's Memorial*, p. 36. We, who're of the FANCY-LAY, As dead hands at a mill as they, And quite as ready, after it, To share the spoil and grab the bit.

FANCY-MAN or **BLOKE,** *subs* (venery).—A prostitute's lover, husband, or pensioner. [There are two suggested derivations ; (1) that FANCY here bears its face value ; (2) that it is a corruption of the Fr. *fiancé.*] FANCY-WOMAN=a mistress or KEEP (*q.v.*). For synonyms, see BULLY and *infra*.

1821. P. EGAN, *Tom and Jerry*, p. 20. Although 'one of the fancy,' he was not a FANCY MAN.

1839. HARRISON AINSWORTH, *Jack Sheppard* [1889], p. 70. 'And me,' insinuated Mrs. Maggot. 'My little FANCY MAN'S quite as fond of me as of you, Bess. Ain't you, Jacky darling ?'

1851-61. H. MAYHEW, *Lon. Lab. and Lon. Poor*, vol. I., p. 186. The women of

the town buy of me, when it gets late, for themselves and their FANCY MEN.

1857. SNOWDEN, *Mag. Assistant*. (3rd ed.), p. 446, s.v.

1885. *Indoor Paupers*, p. 38. The most degraded are the men who subsist by fastening upon street harlots and sharing their wretched earnings. When their mistresses come to grief, and are placed under lock and key, which happens frequently, the FANCY MAN generally manages to skulk out of the mischief and escape scot-free.

ENGLISH SYNONYMS. Apple-squire ; faker ; bully ; ponce ; pensioner ; Sunday-man ; fancy-Joseph ; squire of the body ; fucker ; apron - squire ; cunt-pensioner ; petticoat pensioner ; prosser ; twat - faker ; twat-master ; stallion ; mack ; bouncer ; bruiser ; buck.

FRENCH SYNONYMS. *Un Des Grieux* (popular : the hero of *Manon Lescaut*) ; *un aquarium* (pop. : an assembly of fancy-men ; *cf., maquereau*=a mackerel) ; *un cousin de Möise* (pop. : a 'fast' man who has married a *demi-mondaine* ; Delvau says, ' *dans l'argot du peuple, qui fait allusion aux deux lignes de feu dont sont ornées les tempes du législateur des Hébreux*') ; *un caprice* (pop. : *un caprice sérieux* =a man who keeps a mistress) ; *un paillasson* (pop. :=a mattress) ; *un dos* ; *un marlou*.

GERMAN SYNONYMS. *Balhoche* (from Hebrew *baal*, a man + *hocho*, here, there. Literally, one in possession but removable) ; *Strichler* or *Strichhube* (*Strich* = a fast locality) ; *Strawes* ; *Straweszunder* (Viennese : from *strizeln* = to run quickly).

ITALIAN SYNONYM. *Bramoso*.

SPANISH SYNONYMS. *Comblezado* (obsolete : applied to a

---

married man whose wife lives in adultery with another) ; *mandilejo* (vulgar).

FANCY-PIECE, *subs.* (venery).—A prostitute. For synonyms, *see* BARRACK-HACK and TART.

FANCY-WORK. TO TAKE IN FANCY WORK, *verb. phr.* (popular).—To play the prostitute on the sly ; in the language of venery, ' to work for one's living and do the naughty for one's clothes.' Said of women (as milliners, dressmakers, shop girls, and so forth) in receipt of low wages yet dressing well and having plenty of money. ' How does she do it ? ' ' Oh ! she TAKES IN FANCY-WORK ! ' *Cf.*, FANCY-HOUSE and RIDE.

FANG-FAKER, *subs.* (common).— A dentist. [From FANG, a long pointed tooth + FAKER (*q.v.*).] FANG-CHOVEY=a dental establishment.—*See* CHOVEY.

FANNING, *verb. subs.* (thieves').— 1. Stealing ; CROSS-FANNING = robbery from the person, the arms of the manipulator being folded.

2. (old).—A beating. [From FAN (*q.v.*), to beat + ING.]

FANNY (also FANNY-ARTFUL and FANNY-FAIR), *subs.* (venery).— The female *pudendum.* For synonyms, see MONOSYLLABLE.

FANNY ADAMS, *subs. phr.* (naval).— Tinned mutton.

FANNY BLAIR, *subs. phr.* (rhyming slang).—The hair. For synonyms, *see* TOP-DRESSING.

1859. MATSELL, *Vocabulum, or Rogue's Lexicon*, s.v.

FANTAIL, *subs.* (common).—A sort of round hat with a long leathern fan-shaped flap at the back ; worn by coal-heavers and dustmen ; a SOU'-WESTER (*q.v.*).

1851-61. H. MAYHEW, *London Lab. and Lon. Poor*, vol. II., p. 199. He had good strong lace boots, gray worsted stockings, a stout pair of corduroy breeches, a short smockfrock and FANTAIL.

1877. J. GREENWOOD, *Dick Temple*, ch. xiii. I fancy I see you, for example, with knee breeches and calves and a FANTAIL, shouldering an inky sack and shooting its contents into a hole in the pavement.

FANTEAGUE. ON THE FANTEAGUE, *adv. phr.* (colloquial).—On the 'burst,' or on the 'loose.'

FAR-BACK, *subs.* (tailors'). — An indifferent workman ; an ignoramus.

FARDEN, *subs.* (common). — A farthing. For synonyms, see FADGE.

1880. MILLIKEN, *Punch's Almanack*, May. Otherwise don't care one brass FARDEN, For the best ever blowed in Covent Garden.

FARM, *subs.* (common). — 1. An establishment where pauper children were lodged and fed at so much a head ; also for illegitimate children. Also verbally =to contract to feed and lodge pauper or illegitimate children.

1838. DICKENS, *Oliver Twist*, ch. ii. The parish authorities magnanimously and humanely resolved, that Oliver should be FARMED, or, in other words, that he should be despatched to a branch workhouse some three miles off, where twenty or thirty other juvenile offenders against the poor-laws, rolled about the floor all day, without the inconvenience of too much food or too much clothing, under the parental superintendence of an elderly female, who received the culprits at and for the consideration of sevenpence-halfpenny per small head per week.

1869. GREENWOOD, *Seven Curses of London*. There can be no question that he has a better chance . . . though his treacherous 'adopter' deserts him on a doorstep, than if he were so kindly cruel as to tolerate his existence at the FARM.

2. (prison).—The prison infirmary. TO FETCH THE FARM = to be ordered infirmary diet and treatment.—See FETCH.

FARMER, subs. (old).—1. An alderman.

1848. DUNCOMBE, Sinks of London, s.v. 1859. MATSELL, Vocabulum, or Rogue's Lexicon, s.v.

2. (common).—One who contracts to lodge and feed pauper or illegitimate children.

1869. GREENWOOD, Seven Curses of London. These are not the FARMERS who append to their advertisements the notification that children of ill-health are not objected to.

FART, subs. (vulgar).—An eruption of wind through the anus. [A.S. feort.] By implication a contemptible person. Also verbally = to discharge wind through the anus. Fr., lâcher une pastille.

1383. CHAUCER, The Miller's Tale. This Nicholas anon let fleen a FART As gret as it had been a thonder dint.

1610. BEN JONSON, The Alchemist, i., 1. Thy worst! I FART at thee.

1750. FIELDING, Tom Jones. 'I don't give a FART for 'n,' says the squire, suiting the action to the word.

1785. BURNS, Death and Dr. Hornbook. But Dr. Hornbook with his art And cursed skill, Has made them baith no worth a F——T.

FART-CATCHER, subs. (vulgar).—A footman. [That is, one who follows another closely; cf., FART.] Other names are flunkey; John Thomas; James; catchfart; and CALVES (q.v.).

FART-DANIEL, subs. (venery).—The female pudendum. For synonyms, see MONOSYLLABLE.

FARTHING. NOT TO CARE A BRASS FARTHING, phr. (common).—To care nothing. Chaucer uses the expression 'no farthing of grease' as equivalent to a small quantity. [James II. debased the coinage and issued brass pence, halfpence, and farthings.]

FARTICK (also FARTKIN), subs. (vulgar).—A diminutive of FART (q.v.).

FARTING-CRACKERS, subs. (old).—Breeches. For synonyms, see BAGS and KICKS.

FARTING-TRAP, subs. (Irish).—A jaunting car. [An allusion to the effects of the rough-driving character of these vehicles.]

FARTLEBERRIES, subs. (vulgar).—Excrement on the hair about the anus; also DILBERRIES (q.v.) or CLINKERS (q.v.).

FART-SUCKER, subs. phr. (common).—A vile parasite; an 'arse-hole creeper.'

FAST, adj. and adv. (colloquial).—1. Embarrassed; 'hard-up'; 'in a tight place.'

2. (colloquial). — Dissipated; addicted to GOING THE PACE (q.v.): e.g., a FAST man = a rakehell, or spendthrift; a FAST woman = a strumpet; a FAST life = a life of debauchery; a FAST house = a brothel, or a sporting tavern; to dress FAST = to dress for the town; to live FAST = to 'go the pace,' and so forth.

1751. SMOLLETT, Peregrine Pickle ch. lxxxviii. He returned to his former course of FAST living among the bucks of the town.

1846. THACKERAY, V.F., vol. i., ch. xxvi. 'He's going it pretty FAST,' said the clerk. 'He's only married a week, and I saw him and some other military chaps handing Mrs. Highflyer to her carriage after the play.'

1860. The Atlas, 7 July. Lord William belongs to the genus FAST and we presume to the species soft — contradictions more apparent than real.

1870. Daily Telegraph, 11 July. Having a delightful air of being mildly FAST and decorously on the loose.

1880. G. R. SIMS, Three Brass Balls, Pledge xi. She knew he could not afford to gamble and keep FAST company night after night.

3. (common). — Impudent; 'cheeky': e.g., 'Don't you be so FAST' = Mind your own business.

TO PLAY FAST AND LOOSE, verbal phr. (colloquial).—To be variable; inconstant; to say one thing and do another. [From the ancient game now known as PRICK THE GARTER (q.v.).]

1557. Tottel's Miscellany, p. 157 (Arber's ed.), 'Of a new maried student that PLAIED FAST OR LOSE' [Title of Epigram].

1593. G. HARVEY, New Letter, in wks., i., 274 (Grosart). If he PLAYETH AT FAST AND LOOSE (as is vehemently suspected by strong presumptions) whom shall he cunny catch, or cros-bite, but his cast-away selfe?

1599. JONSON, Ev. Man out of his Hum., I. Nor how they PLAY FAST AND LOOSE with a poor gentleman's fortunes, to get their own.

1632. CHAPMAN AND SHIRLEY, The Ball, Act ii. Fr. Is't come to this? if lords PLAY FAST AND LOOSE, What shall poor knights and gentlemen?

1710. WARD, Vulgus Britannicus, ch. iv., p. 50. On second Thoughts, we should excuse, The People's PLAYING FAST AND LOOSE.

1852. DICKENS, Bleak House, ch. lvii., p. 477. I'm a practical one, and that's my experience. So's this rule. FAST AND LOOSE in one thing, FAST AND LOOSE in everything.

FASTENER, or FASTNER, subs. (old).—A warrant.

1811. Lexicon Balatronicum, s.v.; 1859. MATSELL, Vocabulum, or Rogue's Lexicon, s.v.

FAST-FUCK, subs. (prostitutes').—An act of trade done standing, or at least in quick time: as opposed to trade with an all-night lodger.

FAT, subs. (thieves').—1. Money; Fr., de la graisse (= grease or tallow). For synonyms, see ACTUAL and GILT.

1859. MATSELL, Vocabulum, or Rogue's Lexicon, s.v.

2. (printers'). — Composition full of blank spaces or in many lines. Verse is FAT, while this dictionary, with its constant change of type, is LEAN (q.v.). Hence, work that pays well. Fr., une affaire juteuse = a 'fat job.'

1811. Lexicon Balatronicum. FAT amongst printers means void spaces.

1856. Notes and Queries, 2 S., I., 283, s.v.

1868. O. W. HOLMES, Guardian Angel, ch. xxiv., p. 203 (Rose Lib.). If collected and printed in large type, with plenty of what the unpleasant printers call FAT ensuring thereby blank spaces upon . . . thick paper.

1885. Athenæum, 27 June, p. 817, col. 1. With the aid of wide margins and a liberal amount of FAT, as the printers call it, the text is doled out in pages of but nineteen lines each, and thus the three articles are successfully expanded into a booklet of over two hundred pages.

3. (theatrical).—A good part; telling lines and conspicuous or commanding situations. [Cf., sense 2.] Fr., avoir des côtelettes = to have a BIT OF FAT (Dictionnaire Historique et Pittoresque du Théâtre. Paris, 1884).

1883. Referee, 18 March, p. 2, col. 4. They look miserable because they have nothing to do, all the FAT having been seized by Terry.

1888. Referee, 15 April, 3, 1. I don't want to rob Miss Claremont of her FAT, but her part must be cut down.

Adj. (general). — 1. Rich; abundant; profitable.

1785. GROSE, Dict. Vulg. Tongue, s.v. FAT cull, a rich fellow.

1888. Puck's Library, May, p. 25. This would make the labour so much lighter, that every time a girl went to set a pound of candy she would consider that she had a good FAT take.

2. (Australian).—Good. [An old English usage.]

d. 1626. MIDDLETON [works, II., 422]. O, for a bowl of FAT canary, Rich Aristippus, sparkling sherry! Some nectar else from Juno's dairy, O, these draughts would make us merry.

1890. Speaker, 22 Feb., p. 212, col. 2. As 'good' in English is FAT in Australian, the story is probably true about the missionary—not a story of Dr. Lumholtz's. After many years of work in the field, this good missionary was taken apart by some anxious but meagre inquirers in his flock. Sir, said they, must a man be very FAT to enter the Kingdom of Heaven? He was able to reassure them.

CUT IT FAT.—See CUT.

CUT UP FAT.—See CUT UP.

BIT OF FAT, subs. phr. popular).—See subs., senses 2 and 3; also adj. in both senses: and (venery) connection with a stout woman.

ALL THE FAT'S IN THE FIRE, phr. (common).—Said of failures and of the results of sudden and unexpected revelation; disappointments: i.e., it is all 'over' or 'up' with a person or thing. A late equivalent is, 'And then the band played.'

FAT AS A HEN'S FOREHEAD, adv. phr. (old). — Meagre; SKINNY (q.v.).

FAT- (also BARGE-, BROAD- and HEAVY-) ARSED, adj. phr.

(common).—Broad in the breech; and, by implication, in Richard Baxter's Shove to Heavy Arsed Christians, thick-witted and slow to move.

FAT- (also THICK-) CHOPS, subs. (common). — A contumelious epithet.

FAT-COCK, subs. (common).—An epithet rather jocular than derisive for a stout and elderly man; also (venery) a DOUBLE-SUCKER (q.v.).

FATER, FAYTOR, or FATOR, subs. (old).—A fortune-teller. Lexicon Balatronicum [1811]. In Spencer = a doer; in Bailey = an idle fellow; a vagabond. [From Fr. faiteur.]

FAT-FANCIER, (or -MONGER,) subs. (venery).—An amateur of stout women.

FAT-FLAB. subs. (Winchester School).—A cut off the fat part of a breast of mutton.—See CAT'S HEAD.

FAT- (or FULL-) GUTS, subs. (common).—An opprobrious epithet for a fat man or woman.

FAT-HEAD, subs. (common). — A dolt.

FAT-HEADED, -SKULLED, -THOUGHTED, -PATED, -BRAINED, and -WITTED (colloquial) = dull; stupid; slow.

1885. Mrs. J. H. RIDDELL, Mitre Court, ch. xix. He is a FATHEAD—a great blundering John Bull.

FATHER, subs. (thieves').—1. A receiver of stolen property; a FENCE (q.v.).

2. (general). — A chief in authority; an elder: e.g., THE FATHER OF THE HOUSE = the oldest member of the House of Commons (cf., BABE); among printers, the chairman of the CHAPEL, the intermediary between master and men; in naval circles, the builder of a man-of-war or Government 'bottom.'

FATHER DERBIES' BANDS.—See DARBIES.

FATHER'S BROTHER, subs. phr. (common).—A pawnbroker; MY UNCLE (q.v.).

FAT JACK OF THE BONE-HOUSE, subs. phr. (common).—A contumelious epithet for a very stout man.

FAT-MUTTON, subs. (venery).—A FAT BIT (see BIT OF FAT), i.e., a stout bed-fellow.

FATNESS, subs. (common).—Wealth. Cf., FAT = rich.

FATTEN-UP, verb (theatrical).—To write FAT (subs., sense 3) into a part.

FAT-UN, subs. (common).—An emission of wind from the anus of peculiar rankness; a 'roarer' (Swift).

FATTY (or FATYMUS, or FATTYMA), subs. (colloquial). — A jocular epithet for a fat man; a comic endearment for a fat woman.

FAUGH-A-BALLAGH BOYS, subs. phr. (military). — The Eighty-Seventh Foot; also known as THE EAGLE-TAKERS (q.v.), and THE OLD FOGS (q.v.). [From Fag an bealac = 'Clear the Way,' the name of the regimental march.]

FAULKNER, subs. (old).—A tumbler; juggler. Lex. Balat. [1811] and Duncombe's Sinks of London [1848].

FAWNEY, or FAUNEY, subs. (common).—1. A ring; Fr., une brobuante; une broquille; un chason; Fourbesque, cerchiosa.

2. A swindle (also called FAWNEY-DROPPING, or RIG), worked as follows:—A ring (snide) is let drop in front of a passer-by, who picks it up, and is confronted by the dropper, who claims to share. In consideration of immediate settlement he offers to accept something less than the apparent value in cash. Also done with pocket-books, meerschaum pipes, etc. FAWNEY-DROPPER = one that practices the ring-dropping trick; FAWNEY-BOUNCING = selling rings for a pretended wager; FAWNIED = ringed.

1789. GEO. PARKER, Life's Painter, p. 174. Fawny. An old, stale trick, called ring-dropping.

1851-61. H. MAYHEW, London Lab. and Lon. Poor, vol. I., p. 471. He wears a stunning FAWNY (ring) on his finger.

1851-61. H. MAYHEW, London Lab. and Lon. Poor, vol. I., p. 389. I do a little in the FAWNEY DROPPING line; (FAWNEYS are rings).

1857. DUCANGE ANGLICUS, The Vulgar Tongue, p. 39. FAWNEY-DROPPERS gammon the flats and take the yokels in.

1859. MATSELL, Vocabulum, or Rogue's Lexicon, p. 124. And where . . . The Chips, the FAWNEYS, Chatty-feeders, The bugs, the boungs, and well-filled readers.

FEAGER, subs. (old).—See quot. and cf., FEAKER.

1610. ROWLANDS, Martin Mark-all, p. 38 (H. Club's Repr., 1874). A FEAGER of Loges, one that beggeth with counterfeit writings.

FEAGUE, verb (old). — To send packing; to whiff away.

1826. SCOTT, *Journal* [pub. 1890], I., 205. Though this be Monday, I am not able to FEAGUE it away, as Bayes says— [The reference, as furnished by Dr. Murray to Mr. David Douglas, editor of the *Journal* (1890), is to certain editions of Buckingham's farce, *The Rehearsal*: 'I lay my head close to it with a snuff-box in my hand, and FEAGUE it away.]

FEAK, subs. (old).—The fundament. *Lex. Balat.* [1811].

FEATHER, subs. (colloquial). — 1. Kind; species; company; cf., BIRDS OF A FEATHER. For synonyms, see KIDNEY.

1608. DEKKER, *Belman of London*, in wks. (Grosart), III., 140. And he delivers it either to a Broker or some Bawd (for they all are of one FEATHER).

1609. SHAKSPEARE, *Timon of Athens*, Act i., Sc. 1. I am not of that FEATHER, to shake off My friend when he must need me.

2. *in pl.* (common).—Money; wealth.—[*See* FEATHER ONE'S NEST.] For synonyms, see ACTUAL AND GILT.

3. (venery). — The female pubic hair (PRIOR and T. MOORE). For synonyms, see FLEECE.

IN FULL FEATHER, adv. phr. (colloquial). — 1. Rich. — [*See* sense 2.]

1871. MRS. H. WOOD, *Dene Hollow*. ch. xxx. And now things went on swimmingly. Captain Clanwaring, IN FEATHER as to cash, at least temporarily, was the gayest of the gay.

1886. *Graphic*, 30 Jan., p. 130, col. 2. On these generally convivial occasions, Watty, by reason of his office [butler], was of course always IN FULL FEATHER.

2. (colloquial).—In full costume; 'with all one's war paint on.'

IN HIGH or FULL FEATHER, adv. phr. (colloquial).—Elated; brilliant; conspicuous.

1852. H. B. STOWE *Uncle Tom's Cabin*, ch. viii. Sam was in the HIGHEST POSSIBLE FEATHER, and expressed his exultation by all sorts of supernatural howls and ejaculations.

1856. T. HUGHES, *Tom Brown's School-Days*, pt. II., ch. iv. Martin leads the way IN HIGH FEATHER; it is quite a new sensation to him, getting companions, and he finds it very pleasant, and means to show them all manner of proofs of his science and skill.

TO FEATHER ONE'S NEST, verb. phr. (colloquial). — To amass money; specifically to enrich oneself by indirect pickings and emoluments. [From birds collecting feathers (*see* also sense 2) to line their nests.]

1590. GREENE, *Francesco's Fortunes*, in wks., viii., 138. She sees thou hast FETHRED THY NEST, and hast crowns in hy purse.

1662. PEPYS, *Diary*, 7 June. Mr. Coventry had already FEATHERED HIS NEST in selling of places.

1700. CONGREVE, *Way of the World*, Act v., Sc. 1. You have forgot this, have you, now you have FEATHER'D YOUR NEST.

1705. VANBRUGH, *Confederacy*, I., ii., 25 (1734). If I don't FEATHER MY NEST, and get a good husband, I deserve to die.

1858. G. ELIOT, *Janet's Repentance*, ch. xiii. Dempster must have FEATHERED HIS NEST pretty well; he can afford to lose a little business.

TO FEATHER AN OAR, verb. phr. (aquatics).—In rowing, to turn the blade horizontally, with the upper edge pointing aft, as it leaves the water, for the purpose of lessening the resistance of the air upon it.

d. 1814. DIBDIN, *The Waterman*. He FEATHERED HIS OARS with such skill and dexterity, Winning each heart and delighting each eye.

Whence HIGH or LOW IN THE FEATHER.

1819. T. MOORE, *Tom Crib's Memorial to Congress*, p. 5. The swells in HIGH FEATHER.

1878. LANG, *Ballad of the Boat-race*. They catch the stroke and they slog it through, With Cambridge heavy and LOW IN THE FEATHER, The standing sin of the fair Light Blue.

TO SHOW THE WHITE FEATHER, verb. phr. (colloquial).—To turn cur; to prove oneself a coward. [Among game cocks a cross-bred bird is known by a white feather in the tail. Of old the breed was strictly preserved in England, for though birds of all descriptions were reared in the farm-yard, special care was taken that game fowls did not mix with them; but this would occasionally happen, and while the game birds were only red and black, white feathers would naturally appear when there was any cross. The slightest impurity of strain was said to destroy the bird's courage, and the half-breeds were never trained for the pit. It became an adage that any cock would fight on his own dunghill, but it must be one without a white feather to fight in the pit.]

1842. *Comic Almanack*, p. 306. Precluding the possibility of anyone, at any time, SHOWING A WHITE FEATHER.

FEATHER-BED AND PILLOWS, subs. phr. (venery).—A fat woman.

FEATHER-BED LANE, subs. phr. (old).—A rough or stony lane.

FEATHER-BED SOLDIER, subs. phr. (old colloquial).—A practised and determined whoremonger.

FECK, verb (old).—To discover the safe way of stealing or swindling.

1848. DUNCOMBE, *Sinks of London*, p. 106, s.v.

FEED, subs. (colloquial).—A meal; SPREAD (q.v.), or BLOW-OUT (q.v.). Fr., *une lampie* (from *lamper* = to gulp down). [From the stable usage = an allowance of provender. An analogue, however, is found in Milton: 'For such pleasures till that hour AT FEED or fountain never had I found.']

1830. BULWER LYTTON, *Paul Clifford*, p. 22, ed. 1854. Like most single men, being very much the gentlemen so far as money was concerned, he gave them plenty of FEEDS, and from time to time a very agreeable hop.

1853. REV. E. BRADLEY ('C. Bede'), *Verdant Green*, pt. III., p. 90 (q.v.).

1861. A. TROLLOPE, *Framley Parsonage*, chap. iii. . . . It's deuced shabby of him, not hunting here in his own county. He escapes all the bore of going to lectures, and giving FEEDS to the neighbours; that's why he treats us so.

1864. E. YATES, *Broken to Harness*, ch. xxxiii. He had been accustomed to describe Mr. Schröder as 'a good old cock, sir; a worthy old party; kind-hearted, and all that, and giving no end of good FEEDS.

18(?). BRET HARTE, *The Man of no Account*. When the 'Skyscraper' arrived at San Francisco we had a grand FEED.

1883. G. A. S[ALA], in *Illustr. L. News*, 7 July, p. 3, col. 1. To be able to escape from a large public FEED is, indeed, a sweet boon; but there are some big dinners at which attendance is a case of 'must.'

Verb (football).—1. To support; back up.

2. (theatrical).—To prompt.

3. (university).—To teach or CRAM (q.v.) for an examination.

AT FEED, subs. phr. (colloquial).—At meat.

1890. *National Observer*, V., p. 138 col. 1. Statesmen AT FEED.

d. 1674. MILTON. For such pleasures till that hour AT FEED or fountain never had I found.

TO BE OFF ONE'S FEED, verb. phr. (common).—To have a distaste for food. [From the stable.]

1836. M. SCOTT, *Cringle's Log*, ch. ix. Shall I fill you a cup of coffee, Obed? . . . Why, man, you are OFF YOUR FEED.

1863. C. READE, *Hard Cash*, ii., 218. No, doctor; I'm OFF MY FEED for once.

1881. JAS. PAYN, *Grape from a Thorn*, ch. liii. I won't take a rasher this morning, thank you; nor yet any pigeon pie. I'm rather OFF MY FEED.

TO FEED THE DUMMY or THE DUMB-GLUTTON (q.v.), verb. phr. (venery).—To have connection. For synonyms, see RIDE.

TO FEED THE FISHES, verb. phr. (common).—To be sea-sick; also to be drowned.

1884. *Home Tidings*, 22 Nov., p. 398. Although I fed myself shortly before arriving abreast of Eddystone, I FED THE FISH shortly afterwards.

TO FEED THE PRESS, verb. phr. (journalistic).—To send up copy slip by slip.

FEEDER, subs. (common).—1. A spoon; among thieves a silver spoon. TO NAB A FEEDER = to steal a spoon.

1785. GROSE, *Dict. Vulg. Tongue*, s.v.

1821. D. HAGGART, *Life*, Glossary, s.v.

2. (university). — A tutor; CRAMMER (q.v.); COACH (q.v.). —(*See* Dr. Blimber's Mr. Feeder in *Dombey and Son*.)

1766. O. GOLDSMITH, *Vicar of Wakefield*, chap. vii. (ed. 1827), p. 41. Mr. Thornhill came with a couple of friends, his chaplain and FEEDER.

1864. *Glasgow Herald*, 9 Nov. [Review of Hotten's Slang Dictionary.] FEEDER is given here as 'old cant' for a spoon.

FEEDING-BOTTLE, subs. (colloquial). —The paps. For synonyms, see DAIRY.

FEEL, verb (venery).—To take liberties with a woman. For synonyms, see FIRKYTOODLE.

FEEL A THING IN ONE'S BONES. —See BONES.

FEELE, subs. (common).—A girl or daughter. For synonyms in the former sense, see TITTER. [Fr., *fille*; It., *figlia*.] FEELES = mother and daughter.

FEELER, subs. (colloquial) —1. A device or remark designed to bring out the opinions of others.

1841. *Tait's Mag.*, Sept. 'Political Register.' The *Times* is putting out FEELERS on the corn-law question.

1889. *Pall Mall Gazette*, 29 Nov., p. 6, col. 3. The efforts made to purchase the Halliwell-Phillips collection by private subscription in Birmingham, have (says the local *Times*) utterly failed. A FEELER was sent out by the Free Libraries Committee.

2. (common).—The hand. For synonyms, see BUNCH OF FIVES and DADDLE.

1877. *Five Years' Penal Servitude*, ch. iv., p. 259. I one day asked a man . . . if the hard work of prison did not spoil his hands for delicate manipulations. 'Oh, bless you, no!' he replied; . . . In a week or two a man can bring his hooks and FEELERS into full working trim again and no mistake.

FEET. MAKING FEET FOR CHILDREN'S STOCKINGS, verb. phr. (old). — Begetting or breeding children.

OFFICER OF FEET, subs. phr. (old military). — An officer of infantry.—GROSE [1785].

HOW'S YOUR POOR FEET? phr. (common). — A street catch

phrase in the early part of the sixties. [For suggested derivation cf., quot., 1890.] — See STREET CRIES.

1863. *All the Year Round*, p. 180, col. 1. 'How's YOUR POOR FEET?' a year ago cheated half the natives of Cockaigne into the belief that they were gifted with a special genius for repartee.

1890. *Town and Country* (Sydney), 11 Jan., p. 19, col. 4. Henry Irving's revival of 'The Dead Heart' has revived a bit of slang. . . . When the play was brought out originally, where one of the characters says, 'My heart is dead, dead, dead!' a voice from the gallery nearly broke up the drama with 'How ARE YOUR POOR FEET?' The phrase lived.

TO LIE FEET UPPERMOST, verb. phr. (venery).—To 'take' a man.

FEET-CASEMENTS, subs. (common). —Boots or shoes. For synonyms, see TROTTER-CASES.

FEEZE [also FEAZE, FEIZE, and PHEEZE], verb (old).—1. To copulate. For synonyms, see RIDE.

1612. BEAUMONT AND FLETCHER, *The Coxcomb* (q.v.).

2. (old).—To beat.

FEINT, subs. (old).—A pawnbroker. For synonyms, see MY UNCLE.

1848. DUNCOMBE, *Sinks of London*, s.v.; 1859. MATSELL, *Vocabulum, or Rogue's Lexicon*, s.v.

FEKER, subs. (American thieves'). —Trade; profession; cf., FECK.

1859. MATSELL, *Vocabulum, or Rogue's Lexicon*, s.v.

FELL A BIT ON, verb. phr. (tailors'). —To act craftily; in an underhand manner.

FELL-AND-DIDN'T, phr. (tailors').— Said of a man walking lame.

FELLOW.—See OLD FELLOW.

FELLOW-COMMONER, subs. (university).—An empty bottle. For synonyms, see DEAD MAN.

1794. *Gent. Mag.*, p 1084. One [student at Cambridge] was a *Harry Soph*; another a fellow-commoner and senior *Soph*, and occasionally jocularly called an empty bottle, whilst *è contrà*, a bottle decanted was, from time to time, denominated a FELLOW-COMMONER.

FELT, subs. (old).—A hat of felted wool. For synonyms, see GOLGOTHA.

1609. DEKKER, *Gul's Horne-Booke*, chap. iv. For, in my opinion, ye braine that cannot choose his FELT well (being the head ornament) must needes poure folly into all the rest of the members.

1614. J. COOKE, *Green's Tu Quoque*, in *Anc. Brit. Drama* (1810), ii., 567. *Sir Lion.* Aye, but son Bubble, where did you two buy your FELTS? *Scat.* FELTS! by this light mine is a good beaver.

1823. W. T. MONCRIEFF, *Tom and Jerry*, Act ii., Sc. 5. Don't nibble the FELT, Jerry.

1841. THYNNE, *Deb. between Pride and Lowliness*. A faire cloke on his backe, and on his head a FELT.

FEM.—See FAMBLE.

FEN, subs. (thieves').—A prostitute or procuress.—GROSE [1785].

Verb (schoolboys').—(also FEND, FAIN, FAINITS, etc.). A term of warning, or of prohibition: as to prevent any change in the existing conditions of a game; *e.g.*, at marbles, FEN-PLACINGS = no alteration in position of marbles is permissible; FEN-CLEARANCES = removal of obstacles is forbidden. [FEND = M.E. defend in sense of 'to forbid.'] FAIN, FAIN I, (with which cf., BAGS I) are corruptions. At Winchester, FINGY YOU or FINGY THAT are anala gous; but at Christ's Hospital FIN='I won't have,' the reverse of BAGS I.

ante. 1815. E. C. HARRINGTON, in *N. and Q.*, 5 S., vii., 98. Respecting the word FEN . . . I can testify to the use of the term by schoolboys prior to the battle of Waterloo . . . meaning that we protested against an exceptional action.

1852. DICKENS, *Bleak House*. 'I'm fly,' says Jo. 'But FEN larks, you know.'

1877. *Notes and Queries*, 5 S., vii., 178. A comical application, was, I remember well, 'FEN live lumber'! which, if pronounced in time, would disable your opponent from moving a bystander out of the way of his shot.

FENCE, *subs.* (common).—1. A purchaser or receiver of stolen goods. —*See* verbal sense, and THIEVES.

ENGLISH SYNONYMS. Fencing master, or cully; billy-fencer; angling cove; stallsman; Ikey; family-man; father.

FRENCH SYNONYMS. *Une crosse* (thieves'); *un carreur* (thieves'); *un attriqueur* or *une attriqueuse* (thieves'); *un franc de maison* (also = landlord of a thieves' lodging-house or 'flash ken'); *un fourgue, fourgat*, or *fourgasse* (thieves'); *une nourrice* (a female fence ; =nurse); *un meunier* (=a miller; *porter au moulin* = to fence the swag); *un ogre* (thieves').

GERMAN SYNONYMS. *Pascher* or *Verpascher* (from *paschlnisenen* =to peddle illegally); *Sarser*, or *Sasser* (= a go - between); *Tschorrgoi* (gypsy).

PORTUGUESE SYNONYM. *Entrujão*.

1714. *Memoirs of John Hall* (4th ed.), p. 3. The FENCE and he [a thief], are like the Devil and the Doctor, they live by one another.

1748. T. DYCHE, *Dictionary* (5th ed.). FENCE (s.) . . . and in the *Canting Language*, signifies one who receives and disposes of stolen goods for the robbers.

1834. W. H. AINSWORTH, *Rookwood*, p. 171 (ed. 1864). The FENCE and he are like the devil and the doctor, they live by one another; and, like traitors, 'tis best to keep each other's counsel.

1837. DICKENS, *Oliver Twist*, p. 60 What are you up to? Ill-treating the boys, you . . . insatiable old FENCE.

1851. MAYHEW, *London Labour and the London Poor*, vol. II., p. 106. In one of my inquiries among the young thieves and pickpockets in the low lodging-houses, I heard frequent accounts of their selling the metal goods they stole to FENCES, and in one particular instance to the mistress of a lodging house, who had conveniences for the melting of pewter pots (called '*cats and kittens*' by the young thieves according to the size of the vessels).

1883. *Daily Telegraph*, 13 June, p. 7, col. 2. The criminal who, without the aid of the professional FENCE, would experience much difficulty in disposing of his booty.

1885. *Indoor Paupers*, p. 73. The articles bore the workhouse stamp, were much worn, and would not have brought the thief more than a couple of pence, even supposing that he could find a FENCE, who would venture to purchase.

2. A place where stolen goods are purchased or received. [From sense 1.] Also a DOLLY-, LEAVING-, or SWAG - SHOP—(*q.v.*); FENCING-CRIB. Fr., *un moulin*.

1847. *Illus. Lon. News*, 2 May. The keeper of the FENCE loves to set up in business there [Clerkenwell]—low public-houses abound, where thieves drink and smoke—Jew receivers work the corners.

1848. *Punch*, vol. xiv., p. 149. If Citizen Blanc hold to his opinions of 1839, we may expect no law of international copyright from the Republic. Let M. Galignani rejoice; and let his Bibliotheque in the Rue Vivienne still remain the greatest literary FENCE in Europe.

Verb (old).—1. To purchase or receive stolen goods.

1610. ROWLANDS, *Martin Mark-all* p. 38 (H. Club's Repr., 1874). To FENCE property, to sell any thing that is stolen.

1789. GEO. PARKER, *Life's Painter*, p. 153. FENCED. Is disposing of anything stolen for a quarter of the value.

1828. JON BEE, *Picture of London*, p. 212. Even though he be a thief himself, or more harmfully engaged in FENCING others' thefts.

1830. BULWER LYTTON, *Paul Clifford*, p. 298, ed. 1854. Vell, ven ve came out, you minds as on the voman had a bundle in her arms, and you spake to her, and she answered you roughly, and left us all and vent straight home; and ve vent and FENCED the swag that wery night, and afterwards napped the regulars.

1885. *Chamb. Journal*, 21 Feb., p. 126. Moreover, he was strongly suspected of FENCING—that is, purchasing stolen property.

2. (common). — To spend money.

1728. BAILEY, *Dict.*, s.v.

TO BE, SIT, or RIDE ON THE FENCE, *verb. phr.* (American).— To be neutral; to be ready to join the winning side; to wait 'to see how the cat will jump.' Also, TO SIT ON BOTH SIDES OF THE HEDGE. [*Cf.*, Latin *prævaricato* =straddling with distorted legs.] —*See* JUMPING CAT.

1862. J. RUSSELL LOWELL, *Biglow Papers*, II., p. 97. A kind o' hangin' round an' SETTIN' ON THE FENCE, Till Providence pinted how to jump an' save the most expense.

1887. 'Political Slang,' in *Cornhill Mag.*, June, p. 626. Those who SIT ON THE FENCE—men with impartial minds, who wait to see, as another pretty phrase has it, 'how the cat will jump.'

1888. *Texas Siftings*, 7 July. While Democratic papers will claim that Judge Thurman is as hearty and well at seventy-five as he was at fifty-five, journals ON THE other side of the FENCE will represent him to be a weak, feeble old man, much better fitted for the invalid than the vice-presidential chair.

Those who thus seek to run with the hare and hunt with the hounds are called FENCE-MEN. The operation is FENCE-RIDING, which sometimes qualifies for RAIL-RIDING (*q.v.*).

1848. *New York Herald*, 14 Oct. All the FENCE-MEN, all the doubters, all the seekers after majorities, will now bustle up, come out, and declare that General Taylor is the most popular man in the country, and that he was always their first choice.

1868. *Congressional Globe*, 17 July, This question is one of clear right and wrong, and there can be no FENCE-RIDING, when the rights of four millions of men are at stake.

FENCER, *subs.* (tramps'). — A hawker of small wares; a tramp: generally used in connection with another word; thus, DRIZ-FENCER (*q.v.*) = a pedlar of lace.

FENCING - CRIB or **KEN**, *subs.* (thieves').—A place where stolen goods are purchased or secreted. —*See* FENCE, *subs.*, sense 2.

1785. GROSE, *Dict. Vulg. Tongue*, s.v.

1839. W. H. AINSWORTH, *Jack Sheppard*, p. 277, ed. 1840. 'It only leads to the FENCING CRIB,' replied Wild. 'There's no outlet that way.'

FENCING-CULLY, *subs.* (thieves').— A receiver of stolen goods.—*See* FENCE.

1720. BAILEY, *Dict.*, s.v.

FEN-NIGHTINGALE, *subs.* (common). — A frog. Also CAMBRIDGESHIRE, and CAPE NIGHTINGALE.

FERGUSON. YOU CAN'T LODGE HERE, MR. FERGUSON, *phr.* (street).—A street cry, popular about 1845-50; used in derision or denial. [Mr. J. H. Dixon, writing to Mr. John Camden Hotten, under date Nov. 6, 1864, says the phrase originated thus:—A young Scotsman, named Ferguson, visited Epsom races, where he got very drunk. His friends applied to several hotel keepers to give him

a bed, but in vain. There was no place for Mr. Ferguson. He was accordingly driven to London by his companions, who kept calling out, FERGUSON, YOU CAN'T LODGE HERE. This was caught up by the crowd, repeated, and in a week was all over London, and in a month all over the kingdom. Mr. Dixon states he was introduced to Mr. Ferguson, and that two of his companions were intimate friends.]—*See* STREET-CRIES.

FERM, *subs.* (Old Cant).—A hole; with Spencer=a prison.

1632. DEKKER, *English Villanies* He [an angler for duds] carries a short staff in his hand which is called a filch, having in the nab or head of it a FERME (that is to say a hole).

FERRET, *subs.* (thieves'). — 1. A barge-thief.

2, (old).—A dunning tradesman.

1811. *Lexicon Balatronicum*, s.v.

3. (common).—A pawnbroker. For synonyms, *see* MY UNCLE.

1848. DUNCOMBE, *Sinks of London*, s.v.

FERRETING, *subs.* (venery). — The act of connection.

FERRET OUT, *verb. phr.* (colloquial).—To be at pains to penetrate a mystery of any kind by working underground.

FERRICADOUZER, *subs.* (pugilist). —A knock - down blow; a thrashing. [From the Italian *fare cadere*, to cause to fall + *dosso*, back.] For synonyms, *see* DIG.

1851-61. H. MAYHEW, *London Lab. and Lon. Poor*, vol. I., p. 244. Then there wasn't no risk with Haynan . . . no fear of a FERRICADOUZER for the butcher . . . What does it mean? It means a denskitch (a good thrashing).

FESS, *verb* (colloquial).—To confess; to own up. Fr., *norguer*.

Adj. (school).—Proud.

FESTIVE, *adj.* (colloquial).—Loud; fast; a kind of general utility word. GAY AND FESTIVE CUSS (Artemus Ward) = a rollicking companion.

FETCH, *subs.* (old).—1. A stratagem; indirectly bringing something to pass.

1576. J. SKELTON, *Merie Tales*, xiii. Yea sayde Skelton, if thou have such pretie FETCHIS, you can dooe more then thys; and therefore if thou dooeste not one thynge that I shel tell thee, I wil folowe the lawe on thee. What is that sayde the Myller. If that thou dooeste not stele my cuppe of the table when I am sette atte meate thou shalt not eskape my handes.

1727. JOHN GAY, *Beggar's Opera*, Act II., Scene 2. *Mac.* Be pacified, my dear Lucy; this is all a FETCH of Polly's, to make me desperate with you, in case I get off. If I am hanged, she would fain have the credit of being thought my widow. Really, Polly, this is no time for a dispute of this sort; for whenever you are talking of marriage, I am thinking of hanging.

1780. MRS. COWLEY, *Belle's Stratagem*, v. 1. Why, my illness was only a FETCH, man, to make you marry Letty.

1848. LOWELL, *Fable for Critics*, p. 19. But as Cicero says he won't say this or that (a FETCH, I must say, most transparent and flat), After saying whate'er he could possibly think of.

2. (colloquial).—A success.

3. (old).—A likeness: *e.g.*, the very FETCH of him=his very image or SPIT (*q.v.*). Also an apparition.

Verb (colloquial). — 1. To please; to excite admiration; to arouse attention or interest.

1607. DEKKER, *Westward Ho!* Act ii., Sc. 2. *Earl.* Ha! *Bird.* O, I thought I should FETCH you: you can 'ha' at that; I'll make you hem anon.

1610. JONSON, *Alchemist*, II. This will FETCH 'em, And make them haste towards their gulling more. A man must deal like a rough nurse, and fright Those that are froward, to an appetite.

1727. GAY, *Beggar's Opera*, Act I., Sc. 8. *Polly.* Give her another glass, Sir; my Mama drinks double the quantity whenever she is out of order. This, you see, FETCHES her.

1864. E. YATES, *Broken to Harness*, ch. v., p. 48 (1873). But now he was certainly FETCHED, as his friends would call it, and began to feel an interest in Miss Townshend, which he had never felt for any other person.

1867-70. C. G. LELAND, *Hans. Breitmann's Ballads*. Dot FETCHED him. He shtood all shpell-bound.

1879. JUSTIN MCCARTHY, *Donna Quixote*, ch. xvii. She was quite clever enough to take on any part that might best commend her to the people she sought to please; and she thought she had hit upon the best way to FETCH Gabrielle, as she would herself have put it.

1882. BESANT, *All Sorts and Cond. of Men*, ch. xxx. You shall be my assistant: you shall play the piano and come on dressed in a pink costume, which generally FETCHES at an entertainment.

1883. *Referee*, 1 April, p. 2, col. 4. There were scenes, though, wherein she fairly FETCHED her audience.

1884. S. L. CLEMENS ('M. Twain'), *Huckleberry Finn*, xxi., 205. Hamlet's soliloquy, you know; the most celebrated thing in Shakespeare. Ah, it's sublime, sublime! Always FETCHES the house.

1884. G. A. SALA, in *Ill. Lon. News*, 17 May, p. 470, col. 3. The maritime conflagration FETCHED the audience, especially the pit and gallery.

2. (colloquial). — To get; to do.

[Some combinations are TO FETCH THE FARM = to get infirmary treatment and diet; TO FETCH A STINGER (colloquial) = to get in a heavy blow; TO FETCH A LAGGING (thieves') = to serve one's term; TO FETCH A HOWL=to cry; TO FETCH A CRACK =to strike; TO FETCH A CIRCUMBENDIBUS = to make a detour; TO FETCH THE BREWER=to get drunk.]

TO FETCH AWAY, *verb. phr.* (colloquial). — To part; *e.g.*, 'a fool and his money are soon FETCHED AWAY.'

TO FETCH UP, *verb. phr.* (common).—1. To stop; to run against.

2. (popular).—to startle.

3. (American).—To come to light.

4. (common). — To recruit one's strength after illness.

FETCHING, *ppl. adj.* (colloquial).— Attractive (as of women); pleasing (as of a dress or bonnet).

c. 1882. *Broadside Ballad.* 'You May Lay Odds on That.' Some most FETCHING dresses the ladies now wear, You may lay odds on that.

1889. *Ally Sloper's Half Holiday*, 17 August, p. 262, col. 2. How can they show off a pretty figure and a FETCHING bathing costume if they go in further than knee deep?

1889. *Bird o' Freedom*, 7 Aug., p. 3. Quite delighted at being at last understood and appreciated by one of the FETCHING sex, Stewart made the running so fast that I couldn't see the way he went.

FETTLE. IN GOOD or IN PROPER FETTLE, *adv. phr.* (colloquial). — Drunk. [From provincial English FETTLE = a state of fitness.]

FEW. A FEW, or JUST A FEW, *adv. phr.* (colloquial).—Originally (*cf.*, quot., 1778) a little. Hence, by implication, on the *lucus a non lucendo* principle, considerably; *e.g.*, 'Were you alarmed?' 'No, but I was astonished A FEW!' *i.e.*, 'I was greatly surprised. *Cf.*, RATHER = a good deal.

1778. D'ARBLAY, *Diary, etc.*, 6 July, vol. I., ch. i., p. 15 (1876). So I trembled A FEW, for I thought, ten to one but he'd say: 'He?—not he—I promise you!'

1852. DICKENS, *Bleak House*, ch. xx., p. 173. I appeal to our mutual friend, Smallweed, whether he has or has not heard me remark, that I can't make him out. Mr. Smallweed bears the concise testimony, A FEW.

FIB, *verb* (Old Cant).—1. To beat; specifically (pugilism) to get in a quick succession of blows, as when you get your man round the neck (*i.e.*, into chancery) and pommel his ribs or face.

1665. R. HEAD, *English Rogue*, pt. I., ch. v., p. 49 (1874). FIB, to beat.

1724. E. COLES, *Eng. Dict.* FIB, to beat.

1811. SOUTHEY, *Letters* (ii., 236). I have been taking part in the controversy about 'Bell and the Dragon,' as you will see in the *Quarterly*, where I have FIBBED the Edinburgh (as the fancy say) most completely.

1853. THACKERAY, *Men's Wives Frank Berry*, ch. 1. For heaven's sake my boy, FIB with your right, and *mind his left hand!*

1853. REV. E. BRADLEY ('C. Bede'). *Verdant Green*, pt. I., p. 106. His whole person put in chancery, stung, bruised, FIBBED, propped . . . . and otherwise ill-treated.

1865. G. F. BERKELEY, *My Life etc.*, I., 311. As there was no room to hit out, in the phraseology of the ring, I FIBBED at half a dozen waistcoats and faces with all my might and main.

2. (colloquial and recognised).—To lie.

1694. CONGREVE, *Double Dealer*, Act iv., Sc. iij. You FIB, you baggage, you do understand, and you shall understand.

1712. ARBUTHNOT, *Hist. of John Bull*, pt. IV., ch. iv. Whereby one may know when you FIB, and when you speak truth.

1755. JOHNSON, *Dict. of Eng. Lang.*, s.v. FIB, a cant word amongst children.

1863. ALEX. SMITH, *Dreamthorp*, p. 11. Could I have FIBBED in these days; Could I have betrayed a comrade?

Also, used substantively = (1) a lie; (2) a liar; *see* quot., 1862.

1738. SWIFT, *Polite Convers.*, Dial. 2. If I had said so I should have told a FIB.

1750. FIELDING, *Tom Jones*, bk. III., ch. iv. Those who will tell one FIB will hardly stick at another.

1773. GOLDSMITH, *She Stoops to Conquer*, Act iii. Ask me no questions, and I'll tell you no FIBS.

1861. H. KINGSLEY, *Ravenshoe*, chap. 58. 'Oh! you dreadful FIB,' said Flora.

1883. HAWLEY SMART, *Hard Lines*, ch. xix. Mrs. Charrington saw no harm . . . . in the utterance of a pretty FIB; but she refused to place a deliberate lie upon paper.

FIBBER, *subs.* (colloquial).—A liar. [From FIB.]

1748. T. DYCHE, *Dictionary* (5th ed.). FIBBER (s.) a liar, one who speaks falsely, etc.

1785. WOLCOT, *Lyric Odes*, No. 6, in wks. (1809), i., 67. Your royal grandsire (trust me, I'm no FIBBER) Was vastly fond of Colley Cibber.

1882. JAS. PAYN, *For Cash Only*, ch. xxvi. For one's lover to be a FIBBER is bad enough, but to be a forger

FIBBERY, *subs.* (colloquial).—Lying.

1857. DUCANGE ANGLICUS, *Vulg. Tongue*. 'The Leary Man.' And if you come to FIBBERY You must mug one or two.

FIBBING, *subs.* (pugilist).—1. Pummelling an opponent's head while 'in chancery'; a drubbing. Fr., *bordée de coups de poings*. [From FIB (*q.v.*).]

1819. MOORE, *Tom Crib's Mem. to Cong.*, p. 2. And if the Fine Arts Of FIBBING and loving be dear to your hearts.

1834. W. H. AINSWORTH, *Rookwood*, p. 268 (ed. 1864). Resolved his FIBBING not to mind.

1837. BARHAM, *I. L. (The Ghost)*. Whom sometimes there would come oh a sort of fear his Spouse might knock his head off, Demolish half his teeth, or drive a rib in, She shone so much in 'facers' and in FIBBING.

2. (colloquial).—Lying.

FIBBING-GLOAK, *subs.* (Old Cant). —A pugilist. For synonyms, *see* HITTITE. [From FIB, sense 1 + GLOAK, a man.]

FIBBING-MATCH, *subs.* (thieves').—A prize-fight.—*See* FIB, sense 1.

FIBSTER, *subs.* (colloquial). — A liar. [From FIB, *verb*, sense 2.]

1861. H. KINGSLEY, *Ravenshoe*, ch. xx. You wicked old FIBSTER! Didn't you hesitate, stammer, and blush, when you said that?

FIDDLE, *subs.* (common). — 1. A sharper; sometimes OLD FIDDLE. For synonyms, *see* ROOK.

2. (American).—A swindle. For synonyms, *see* SELL.

3. (thieves').—A whip.

4. (thieves').—*See* quot.

1877. *Five Years' Penal Servitude*, ch. i., p. 44. The taskmaster warder came in, bringing with him the FIDDLE on which I was to play a tune called 'Four pounds of oakum a day.' It consisted of nothing but a piece of rope and a long crooked nail.

5. (Stock Exchange).—One-sixteenth part of a pound.

1887. ATKIN, *House Scraps*. Done at a FIDDLE.

6. (old). — A watchman's or policeman's rattle.

1832. W. T. MONCRIEFF, *Tom and Jerry*, Act II., Sc. 2. There's one! go it, Jerry!—Come, Green. *Log.* Aye, come, Jerry, there's the Charlies' FIDDLES going. *Jerry.* Charlies' FIDDLES?—I'm not fly, Doctor. *Log.* Rattles, Jerry, rattles! you're fly now, I see. Come along, Tom! Go it, Jerry!

1848. DUNCOMBE, *Sinks of London*, s.v.

7. (colloquial).—A sixpence; also a fiddler; *Cf.*, FIDDLER'S MONEY.

8. (venery).—The female *pudendum*. For synonyms, *see* MONOSYLLABLE.

Verb (colloquial).—1. To trifle, especially with the hands.

1663. PEPYS, *Diary*, 13 July. Where all the ladies walked, talking and FIDDLING with their hats and feathers, and changing and trying one another's by one another's heads, and laughing.

1738. SWIFT, *Polite Convers.*, Dial. 2. He took a pipe in his hand, and FIDDLED with it till he broke it.

1748. T. DYCHE, *Dictionary* (5th ed.). FIDDLE (v.) . . . also to spend a person's time about matters of small or no importance.

1883. HAWLEY SMART, *Hard Lines*, ch. iii. That second charger of Mr. Harperley's is smart, but they've had him FIDDLING about so long in the school, he's most likely forgot how to gallop.

2. (thieves').—To cheat; specifically, to gamble.

1851-61. H. MAYHEW, *London Lab. and Lon. Poor*, vol. III., p. 140. She is supposed to bring in all the money she has taken, but that we don't know, and we are generally FIDDLED most tremendous.

3. (common).—To earn a livelihood by doing small jobs on the street.—*See* FIDDLING.

4. (American).—To intrigue.

5. (common).—To take liberties with a woman; for synonyms, *see* FIRKYTOODLE.

6. (pugilistic).—To strike.

SCOTCH-FIDDLE, *subs.* (common).—The itch.

TO HANG UP THE FIDDLE.—To abandon an undertaking.

TO PLAY FIRST OR SECOND FIDDLE, *verb. phr.* (colloquial) —To take a leading or a subordinate part. Among tailors SECOND FIDDLE = an unpleasant task

1843. DICKENS, *Martin Chuzzlewit*, ch. xii., p. 122. To say that Tom had no idea of PLAYING FIRST FIDDLE in any social orchestra but was always quite satisfied to be set down for the hundred and fiftieth violin in the band, or thereabouts, is to express his modesty in very inadequate terms.

1847. THACKERAY, *Letter*, 2 Jan., to W. E. Ayton in *Memoirs*. If my friend will shout, Titmarsh for ever, hurrah for etc., etc., I may go up with a run to a pretty fair place in my trade, and be allowed to appear before the public as among the FIRST FIDDLES.

1886. JAS. PAYN, *Grape from a Thorn*, ch. xi. She had inherited from her mother an extreme objection to PLAYING, in any orchestra whatsoever, the SECOND FIDDLE.

FIT AS A FIDDLE, *phr.* (colloquial).—In good form or condition.

1886. JAS. PAYN, *Heir of the Ages* (Ry. ed. 1888), p. 63.

Intj.—*See* FIDDLE-DE-DEE.

FIDDLE-BOW, *subs.* (venery).—The *penis*. For synonyms, *see* CREAMSTICK.

FIDDLE-FACED, *adj.* (colloquial).—Wizened, also substantively.

1885. W. WESTALL, *Larry Lohengrin*, ch. v. Tell me how far, in your opinion, I answer to this flattering description of yours—white-chokered, strait-laced, and FIDDLE-FACED?

FIDDLE-FADDLE, *subs.* (colloquial). —Twaddling; trifling; 'little nothings'; ROT (*q.v.*). Fr., *oui, les lanciers!*

1593. G. HARVEY, *Pierces Super.* in wks. II., 98. Or who of judgment, will not cry? away with these paultringe FIDLE-FADLES.

1657. *Political Ballads* (ed. Wilkins, 1860), vol. I., p. 139. After much FIDDLE-FADDLE The egg proved addle.

1712. *Spectator*, No. 299. Their mother tells them . . . . that her mother danced in a ball at Court with the Duke of Monmouth; with abundance of FIDDLE-FADDLE of the same nature.

1876. C. H. WALL, trans. *Molière*, vol, i., p. 157. I see nothing about here but white of eggs, milk of roses, and a thousand FIDDLE-FADDLES that I know nothing about.

Adj. Trifling; fussing; fluffing.'

1712. ARBUTHNOT, *Hist. of John Bull*, pt. III., ch. viii. She was a troublesome, FIDDLE-FADDLE old woman, and so ceremonious that there was no bearing of her.

b. 1811, *d.* 1863. THACKERAY, *Character Sketches (Fashionable Authoress)*. She interlards her works with fearful quotations from the French, FIDDLE-FADDLE extracts from Italian operas, German phrases, fiercely mutilated, and a scrap or two of bad Spanish.

Verb. To toy; to trifle; to talk nonsense; to gossip; to make 'much cry and little wool.'

1761. DR. HAWKSWORTH, *Edgar and Emmeline*, I., ii. Here have I had a young, tempting girl FIDDLE-FADDLING about me these two hours to dress me.

1873. MISS BROUGHTON, *Nancy*, ch. xxxvii. I am idly FIDDLE-FADDLING with a piece of work.

Also FIDDLE-FADDLER, one inclined to FIDDLE-FADDLES.

FIDDLE-HEAD, *subs.* (nautical).—A plain prow as distinguished from a figure-head. Hence FIDDLE-HEADED = plain; ugly.

1833. MARRYAT, *Peter Simple*, III., i., 316 (ed. 1846). She has a d——d pretty run; but I hope Captain O'Brien will take off her FIDDLE-HEAD and get one carved: I never knew a vessel do much with a FIDDLE-HEAD.

1854. WHYTE MELVILLE, *General Bounce*, ch. v. 'Zounds! you've broke it, you FIDDLE-HEADED brute!' exclaimed a choleric voice . . . , startling the ladies most unceremoniously, and preparing them for the spectacle of a sturdy black cob trotting rebelliously down the farm-road.

FIDDLER, *subs.* (old).—1. A trifler; a careless, negligent, or dilatory person. [From FIDDLE, to trifle.]

1748. T. DYCHE, *Dictionary* (5th ed.) s.v.

2. (common).—A sharper; a cheat; also FIDDLE (*q.v.*).

3. (pugilistic).—A prize-fighter; one who depends more on activity than upon strength or 'stay.'

4. (common). — A sixpence. [From the old custom of each couple at a dance paying the fiddler a sixpence. *Cf.*, FIDDLER'S MONEY.]

1885. *Household Words*, 20 June, p. 155. Why a sixpence should be a 'magpie' it would be hard to say. A more easily explained name . . . is a FIDDLER. This probably from the old custom of each couple at a dance paying the fiddler sixpence, and, moreover 'fiddler's money' is generally small money.

5. (common). — A farthing. For synonyms, *see* FADGE.

1885. *Household Words*, 20 June, p. 155. FIDDLER. This same word also does duty as an equivalent for a farthing.

FIDDLERS' - FARE, *subs.* (old).—Meat, drink, and money—*Grose*, 1785.

FIDDLERS'-GREEN, *subs.* (nautical). —A sailor's elysium (situate on the hither and cooler side of hell) of wine, women, and song.

1837. MARRYAT, *Snarley-Yow*, ch. ix. At FIDDLER'S GREEN, where seamen true, When here they've done their duty, The bowl of grog shall still renew, And pledge to love and beauty.

1842. LOVER, *Handy Andy*, ch. xii 'He would as soon go into Squire Egan's house as go to FIDDLER'S GREEN.' 'Faith, then, there's worse places than FIDDLER'S GREEN,' said Andy, 'as some people may find out one o' these days.'

1884. HENLEY and STEVENSON, *Admiral Guinea*, iv., 4. Jack Gaunt, . . . it's thanks to you I've got my papers, and this time I'm shipped for FIDDLER'S GREEN.

FIDDLERS'-MONEY, *subs.* (old).—Sixpences. [From the custom at country merry-makings of each couple paying the fiddler sixpence.] Also generically, small silver.

FIDDLESTICK! *intj.* (colloquial).—Nonsense; sometimes FIDDLE-STICK'S END and FIDDLE-DE-DEE.

1600. NASHE, *Summer's Last Will*, in wks. (Grosart) VI., 130. A FIDDLE-STICKE! ne're tell me I am full of words.

1701. FARQUHAR, *Sir Harry Wildair*, Act IV., Sc. ii. Golden pleasures! Golden FIDDLESTICKS—What d'ye tell me of your canting stuff?

1834. SOUTHEY, *The Doctor*, ch. clxxxix. At such an assertion he would have exclaimed, a FIDDLESTICK! Why and how that word has become an interjection of contempt I must leave those to explain who can.

Subs.—1. *See* quot.

1821. D. HAGGART, *Life*, Glossary, p. 172. FIDDLESTICK, a spring saw.

2. (venery).—The *penis*. For synonyms, *see* CREAMSTICK.

3. (old).—A sword.

1596. SHAKSPEARE, *Romeo and Juliet*, iii., 1. Here's my FIDDLESTICK: here's that shall make you dance.

FIDDLING, *subs.* (streets').—1. A livelihood got on the streets, holding horses, carrying parcels, etc.

1851-61. H. MAYHEW, *London Lab. and Lon. Poor*, vol. I., p. 211. A lad that had been lucky FIDDLING (holding horses, or picking up money anyhow).

2. *See* quot. and *cf.*, quot., *subs.*, sense 1.

1850. *Lloyd's Weekly*, 3 Feb. 'Low Lodging Houses of London.' I live on 2s. a week from thieving, because I understand FIDDLING—that means, buying a thing for a mere trifle, and selling it for double, or for more, if you're not taken in yourself.

3. (colloquial).—Idling; trifling.

4. (gamesters').—Gambling.

Adj. (colloquial). — Trifling ; trivial ; fussing with nothing.

b. 1667, *d.* 1745. SWIFT [quoted in 'Annandale']. Good cooks cannot abide what they call FIDDLING work.

1802. C. K. SHARPE, in *Correspondence* (1888), i., 152. He is a mighty neat, pretty little, FIDDLING fellow, and exceedingly finely bred.

1880. HAWLEY SMART, *Social Sinners*, ch. xiii. I will look in at that time, and trust to find you have settled all these FIDDLING preliminaries.

FID-FAD, *subs.* (old).—A contracted form of FIDDLE-FADDLE (*q.v.*) ; also applied to persons.

1754. *The World*, No. 95. The youngest, who thinks in her heart that her sister is no better than a slattern, runs into the contrary extreme, and is, in everything she does, an absolute FIDFAD.

1874. E. L. LINTON, *Patricia Kemball*, ch. xvi. The FIDFADS, called improvements, which were not wanted and seldom properly managed.

FIDLAM-BENS or **COVES**, *subs.* (thieves'). — Thieves who steal anything they can lay hands on. Also ST. PETER'S SONS.

1785. GROSE, *Dict. Vulg. Tongue*, s.v.

FIE-FOR-SHAME, *subs. phr.* (school-girls').—The female *pudendum.* For synonyms, *see* MONOSYLLABLE.

FIELD. TO CHOP THE FIELD, *verb. phr.* (racing). — To win easily [FIELD=the horses taking part in a race.]

FIELDER, *subs.* (betting).—A backer of the field [*i.e.*, the RUCK (*q.v.*), as against the favorite]. At cricket, a player in the field as against the team at the wickets.

1853. WH. MELVILLE, *Digby Grand*, ch. vi. I accommodate a vociferous FIELDER with 6 to 4 in hundreds as my concluding stake.

1883. *Graphic*, 11 August, p. 138, col. 2. As a batter, bowler, and FIELDER combined . . . he has yet no equal.

FIELD-LANE DUCK, *subs. phr.* (common).—A baked sheep's head.

1811. *Lexicon Balatronicum*, s.v.

1848. DUNCOMBE, *Sinks of London*, s.v.

FIENT, *intj. phr.* (Scots colloquial). —An expression of negation : *e.g.*, FIENT a hair care I=Devil a hair I care.

FIERI FACIAS. TO HAVE BEEN SERVED WITH A WRIT OF FIERI FACIAS, *verb. phr.* (legal).—Said of a red-nosed man. [A play upon words.]

1594. NASHE, *Unf. Traveller*, in wks. v., 44. Should I tell you how many pursenants with red noses, and sargeants with precious faces, shrunke away in this sweat, you would not belieue me . . . . a pursenant or a sargeant at this present, with the verie reflexe of his FIRIE FACIAS, was able to spoile a man a farre of.

1608. *Penniles Parl*, in *Harl. Misc.* (ed. Park), I., 182. They that drink too much Spanish sack, shall, about July, be served with a FIERY FACES.

1663. DRYDEN, *Wild Gallant*, Act ii. *Vour.* You are very smart upon one another, gentlemen. *Fail.* This is nothing between us ; I was to tell him of his title, FIERY FACIAS ; and his setting dog, that runs into ale-houses before him.

FIERY LOT, *subs. phr.* (common).— FAST (*q.v.*) ; rollicking ; applied to a HOT MEMBER (*q.v.*).

FIERY SNORTER, *subs. phr.* (common).—A red nose.

FIFER, *subs.* (tailors').—1. A waist-coat 'hand.'

---

2. (Scots' colloquial). — A native of the KINGDOM (*q.v.*), *i.e.*, the county of Fife.

FI-FI or **FIE-FIE**, *adj.* (common).— Indecent ; 'blue' or 'smutty.' [From FIE=an exclamation signifying contempt, impatience, or disapproval.] A Thackerayean term.

1861. A. TROLLOPE, *Framley Parsonage*, ch. vi. And then Mrs. Proudie began her story about Mr. Slope, or rather recommenced it. She was very fond of talking about this gentleman who had once been her pet chaplain, but was now her bitterest foe ; and, in telling the story, she had sometimes to whisper to Miss Dunstable, for there were one or two FIE-FIE little anecdotes about a married lady, not altogether fit for young Mr. Robart's ears.

1874. M. COLLINS, *Frances*, ch. xviii. Flood was a gay bachelor, with a few FIE-FIE stories floating through club atmosphere about him.

FIFTEENER, *subs.* (bibliographical). —A book printed in the 15th century.

1890. 'Grangerising' in *Cornhill Mag.*, Feb., p. 139. Some of them torn from FIFTEENERS, or 'incurables,' books of the fathers of printing.

FIFTH RIB. TO HIT, DIG, or POKE ONE UNDER THE FIFTH RIB, *verb. phr.* (common).—To deliver a heavy blow ; to dumbfound.

1890. *Globe*, 26 Feb., p. 1, col. 5. It strikes the man who has been dallying with strange tailors . . . UNDER THE FIFTH RIB.

FIG, *subs.* (colloquial). — 1. A gesture of contempt made by thrusting forth the thumb between the fore and middle fingers : whence the expression 'I do not care, or would not give, a fig for you.' Fr., *je ne voudrais pas en donner un ferret d'aiguillette*. *Cf.*, CARE, and for

other similes of worthlessness, *see* CURSE, STRAW, RUSH, CHIP, CENT, DAM, etc. [Italian : When the Milanese revolted against the Emperor Frederick Barbarossa, they set his Empress hind before upon a mule, and thus expelled her. Frederick afterwards besieged and took the city, and compelled all his prisoners, on pain of death, to extract with his (or her) teeth a fig from the fundament of a mule and, the thing being done, to say in announcement, 'ecco la fica.' Thus *far la fica* became an universal mode of derision. Fr., *faire la figue* ; Ger., *die Feigen weisen* ; It., *far le fiche* ; Dutch, *De vyghe setten.*

1599. SHAKSPEARE, *Henry V.*, iii., 6. *Pistol.* Die and be damned and FICO for thy friendship. *Fluellen.* It is well. *Pistol.* The FIG of Spain.

1610. BEN JONSON, *The Alchemist*, i 1. *Subtle.* What to do? Lick FIGS out of mine arse.

1821. PIERCE EGAN, *Tom and Jerry* [ed. 1890], p. 106. A FIG for each bum.

1861. T. HUGHES, *Tom Brown at Oxford*, ch. vi. A FIG for Poll Ady and fat Sukey Wimble ; I now could jump over the steeple so nimble ; With joy I be ready to cry.

1882. *Punch*, vol. LXXXII., p. 185, col. 2 (*q.v.*).

2. (common).—Dress. [From FIG, *verb.* sense = that which shows off a man or woman, as a fig of ginger shows off a horse. *Cf.*, quot., 1819, in FIG UP.] IN FULL FIG=in full dress.

1861. T. HUGHES, *Tom Brown at Oxford*, ch. i. He waits on me in hall, where we go IN FULL FIG of cap and gown at five, and get very good dinners, and cheap enough.

1873. *Cassell's Magazine*, Jan., p. 246, col. 2. 'London Cured.' They are rather prone to dress flashily, and wear when IN FULL FIG no end of jewellery.

---

3. (venery). — The female *pudendum.* For synonyms, *see* MONOSYLLABLE.

Verb (stable). —. To ginger a horse. [For origin, *see* subs. sense.]

TO FIG OUT, *verb. phr.* (colloquial).—To show off ; to dress ; to don one's WAR PAINT (*q.v.*). [From the verb.]

1825. *The English Spy*, vol. 1, p. 177. *Eglantine* (to the ostler). Well, Dick, what sort of a stud, hey? Come, FIG OUT two lively ones.

1884. W. C. RUSSELL, *Jack's Courtship*, ch. vi. He began to inveigh against the waiter's costume, as he styled the dress I had FIGGED myself OUT in.

TO FIG UP, *verb. phr.* (colloquial.—To restore ; to reanimate (as a gingered horse).

1819. T. MOORE, *Tom Crib's Memorial*, p. 24. In vain did they try to FIG UP the old lad, 'Twas like using persuaders upon a dead prad.

FIGARO, *subs.* (common).—A barber. [From *Le Nozze di Figaro.*]

1886. *Globe*, 18 March, p. 3, col. 2. [Referring to recent order of French War Minister permitting soldiers to wear their beards.] There is wailing and weeping among a certain section of that army, the FIGAROS, which has been despoiled at one fell swoop.

FIGDEAN, *verb* (old). — To kill. For synonyms, *see* COOK ONE'S GOOSE.

1785. GROSE, *Dict. Vulg. Tongue*, s.v.

1859. MATSELL. *Vocabulum, or Rogue's Lexicon*, s.v.

FIGGED.—See JIGGED.

FIGGER or **FIGURE.**—See FAGGER.

FIGGING- or **FAGGING-LAY**, *subs. phr.* (old).—Pocket-picking : *cf.*, FAGGER.

FIGHT, *subs.* (common).—A party ; *e.g.*, TEA FIGHT, WEDDING-FIGHT, etc. *Cf.*, SCRAMBLE, and WORRY : also Row (*q.v.*).

TO FIGHT or PLAY COCUM. —See COCUM.

TO FIGHT or BUCK THE TIGER. —See BUCK and quots., *infra.*

1870. *London Figaro*, 20 July. The other day a gentleman of San Francisco, hitherto only noted for deeds of daring in FIGHTING THE TIGER, was seated asleep in the smoking-car of the evening train from Sacramento on the Vallejo route.

1886. *Daily Telegraph*, 18 Oct., p. 5, col. 3. If they subsequently FIGHT THE TIGER at the games of faro or roulette.

ONE THAT CAN FIGHT HIS WEIGHT IN WILD CATS, *subs. phr.* (American). — A brilliant desperado.

1876. BESANT AND RICE, *Golden Butterfly*, John Halkett, as I learned afterwards, could FIGHT HIS WEIGHT IN WILD CATS.

FIGHTING-COVE, *subs. phr.* (tramps').—A professional pugilist : specifically one who 'boxes' for a livelihood at fairs, race-meetings, etc.

1880. GREENWOOD, *Odd People in Odd Places*, p. 56. You see them two there, sitting on t'other end of the table and eating fried fish and bread. That's their mittens they've got tied up in that hankercher. They're FIGHTING COVES.

FIGHTING FIFTH, *subs. phr.* (military)—The Fifth Foot. [So distinguished in the Peninsular.] Other nicknames were THE SHINERS (in 1764 from its clean and smart appearance) ; THE OLD BOLD FIFTH (also Peninsular) ; and LORD WELLINGTON'S BODY GUARD (it was at head-quarters in 1811). *Cf.*, FIGHTING NINTH.

1871. *Chambers' Journal*, 23 Dec., p. 802, col. 2. THE FIGHTING FIFTH was distinguished by its men wearing a white plume in the cap, when the similar ornament of the other regiments was a red and white tuft.

1890. *Standard*, 25 April, p. 3, col. 4, 'St. George's Day.' With the exception of the annual observances by the Northumberland Fusiliers, better known as the FIGHTING FIFTH, and a concert at the Crystal Palace, there does not seem to have been the smallest notice taken of what was, not a hundred years ago, a recognised popular festival throughout the length and breadth of once merrie England.

FIGHTING NINTH, *subs. phr.* (military). — The Ninth Foot. Also HOLY BOYS (Peninsular), from its selling its Bibles for drink.] *Cf.*, FIGHTING FIFTH.

FIGHTING TIGHT, *adv. phr.* (American).—Drunk and quarrelsome. For synonyms, *see* DRINKS and SCREWED.

FIG-LEAF, *subs.* (common).—An apron. In fencing, the padded shield worn over the lower abdomen and right thigh. Fr., *une petite bannette. Cf.*, BELLY-CHEAT and FLAG.

FIGS (also FIGGINS), *subs.* (colloquial).—A grocer.

FIGURE, *subs.* (colloquial). — 1. Appearance ; conduct ; *e.g.*, TO CUT A GOOD or BAD FIGURE, A MEAN FIGURE, SORRY FIGURE, etc.

1712. *Spectator*, No. 479. Men cannot, indeed, make a sillier FIGURE, than in repeating such pleasures and pains to the rest of the world.

1854. WHYTE MELVILLE, *General Bounce*, ch. xvii. Peradventure our youth is fast, and aspires to be a man of FIGURE.

2. (colloquial).—Price ; value ; amount.

d. 1863. THACKERAY [quoted in Annandale]. Accommodating the youngster, who had just entered the regiment, with a glandered charger at an uncommonly stiff FIGURE.

1864. *London Society*, Oct., p. 480. She had saved . . . about four hundred a year out of the wreck . . . and so, on the whole, did not do badly in life. Happiness has been found at even a lower 'FIGURE.'

1883. SALA, *Living London*, p. 184. The 'FIGURE' to be paid to Madame Adelina Patti for her forthcoming season.

1886. *Cornhill Mag.*, March, p. 304. 'About what is their FIGURE?' asked Mr. Corder. 'Slim and graceful,' answered the lady. 'I don't mean that,' said the ex-smoked-mother-of-pearl-button manufacturer ; 'I mean, what is each of them worth in money?'

3. (colloquial).—Paps and posteriors ; said only of women. No FIGURE=wanting in both particulars.

Verb (billiards'). — To single out ; to SPOT (*q.v.*).

[FIGURE, like FETCH, comes in for a good deal of hard work in America. It is colloquially equivalent to 'count upon' ; as, 'you may FIGURE on getting a reply by return mail' ; also = to strive for. TO FIGURE ON [A THING]=to think it over ; TO FIGURE OUT=to estimate ; TO FIGURE UP=to add up ; TO CUT A FIGURE, *see* CUT ; TO GO THE WHOLE FIGURE = to be thorough ; TO GO THE BIG FIGURE = to launch out ; TO MISS A FIGURE=to make a mistake.]

FIGURE-DANCER, *subs.* (thieves').— A manipulator of the face value of banknotes, cheques, and paper security generally.—GROSE [1785]

FIGURE-FANCIER, *subs.* (venery). — An amateur of large-made women.

FIGURE-HEAD, *subs.* (nautical).— The face. For synonyms, *see* DIAL.

FIGURE-MAKER, *subs.* (venery).— A wencher. [In allusion to the enlarged 'figures' of pregnant women.] For synonyms, *see* MOLROWER.

FIGURE (or **NUMBER**) **SIX**, *subs. phr.* (thieves').—A lock of hair brought down from the forehead, greased, twisted spirally, and plastered on the face. For synonyms, *see* AGGERAWATOR.

1851. H. MAYHEW, *Lon. Lab. and Lon. Poor*, v. I., p. 36. As for the hair, they [coster-lads] say it ought to be long in front, and done in FIGURE-SIX curls or twisted back to the ear, 'Newgate-knocker style.'

FILBERT. CRACKED IN THE FILBERT, *adv. phr.* (common).—Crazy; a variant of WRONG IN THE NUT (*q.v.*) or UPPER STOREY. For synonyms, *see* APARTMENTS TO LET and TILE LOOSE.

FILCH, *verb* (Old Cant: now recognised).—1. To steal: specifically to pilfer in small ways [DEKKER: from the 'filches' or hooks used by thieves in stealing out of open windows; SKEAT: for *filk* from O.E. *fele*, Icel. *fela*, to steal, like *talk* and *tell*, *stalk* (*verb*) and *steal* where *k* is a formative element.—*See* Phil. Soc. Trans., 1865, p. 188.] For synonyms, *see* PRIG. FILCH, properly FILCHMAN (*q.v.*), = a hooked staff; ON THE FILCH or FILCHING = stealing.

1567. HARMAN, *Caveat* (1814), p. 66. To FYLCHE, to robbe.

1580. TUSSER, *Husbandrie*, ch. 63, st. 13, p. 143 (E. D. S.). The champion robbeth by night, And prowleth and FILCHETH by day.

1611. MIDDLETON, *Roaring Girl*, Act iv., Sc. 1. What she leaves Thou shalt come closely in and FILCH away.

1729. SWIFT, *Intelligencer*, No. 4, p. 35 (2nd ed.). The servants having all that time to themselves to intrigue, to junket, to FILCH and steal.

1830. MARRYAT, *King's Own*, ch. x. I could FILCH a handkerchief as soon as I was high enough to reach a pocket, and was declared to be a most promising child.

1877. *Five Years' Penal Servitude*, ch. iii., p. 246. She were an out-and-outer in going into shops on the FILCH.

2. (old). — To beat. For synonyms, *see* BASTE and TAN.

1610. ROWLANDS, *Martin Mark-all*, p. 38 (H. Club's Repr., 1874), s.v.

Subs. (old).—A thief. [From the verb.] Also FILCHER (*q.v.*). For synonyms, *see* AREA-SNEAK.

1810. POOLE, *Hamlet Travestie*, II., iii. A very FILCH, that more deserves to hang, Than any one of the light-finger'd gang.

FILCHER or **FILCH** (*q.v.*). *subs.* (Old Cant: now recognised). A thief. [From FILCH (*q.v.*) = to steal + ER.] For synonyms, *see* AREA-SNEAK and THIEVES.

1580. TUSSER, *Husbandrie*, ch. 10, st. 54, p. 25 (E.D.S.). Purloiners and FILCHERS, that loveth to lurke.

1596. JONSON, *Every man in his Humour*, IV., ix. How now, Signior Gull! are you turned FILCHER of late? Come, deliver my cloak.

1636. DAVENANT, *The Wits*, Act. V., The old blade Skulks there like a tame FILCHER, as he had New stolen 'bove eggs from market-women, Robb'd an orchard, or a cheese-loft.

1887. J. W. EBSWORTH, *Cavalier Lyrics* (*In Alsatia, etc.*). FILCHERS, who grabble at other folks' chink.

FILCHMAN or **FILCH**, *subs.* (old).—A thief's hooked staff used as described in quot., 1632.

1567. *Frat. of Vacabondes*, p. 3. The trunchion of a staffe, which staffe they cal a FILTCHMAN.

1589. NASHE, *Countercuffe to Martin Junior*, in wks., vol. I., p. 80. Pasquill met him . . . with a Hatte like a sawcer vppon hys crowne, a FILCH-MAN in his hande.

1610. ROWLANDS, *Martin Mark-all*, p. 38 (H. Club's Repr., 1874), s.v.

1632-48. DEKKER, *English Villanies* He carries a short staff in his hand, which is called a FILCH, having in the nab or head

of it a ferme (that is to say a hole) into which, upon any piece of service, when he goes a FILCHING, he putteth a hooke of iron, with which hooke he angles at a window in the dead of night for shirts, smockes, or any other linen or woollen.

1665. R. HEAD, *English Rogue*, pt. I., ch. v., p. 49 (1874), s.v.; 1724. E. COLES, *Eng. Dict.*, s.v.

FILE, *subs.* (old). 1. A pickpocket. Also FILE CLOY or BUNG-NIPPER; *cf.*, BUTTOCK. Fr., *une poisse à la détourne*.

1754. FIELDING, *Jon. Wild*, bk. IV., ch. xii. The greatest character among them was that of a pickpocket, or, in truer language, a FILE.

1837. C. DICKENS, *Oliver Twist*, p. 123. You'll be a fine young cracksman afore the old FILE now.

1859. MATSELL, *Vocabulum, or Rogue's Lexicon*. The FILE is one who is generally accompanied by two others, one of whom is called the 'Adam tyler,' and the other the 'bulker,' or 'staller.' It is their business to jostle or 'ramp' the victim, while the FILE picks his pocket, and then hands the plunder to the 'Adam tyler,' who makes off with it.

2. (common).—A man: *i.e.*, a COVE (*q.v.*). Thus SILENT FILE (Fr., *un lime sourde*) = a dumb man; CLOSE-FILE = a miser, or a person not given to blabbing; HARD-FILE = a GRASPER (*q.v.*); OLD FILE = an elder; and so forth.

1821. P. EGAN, *Tom and Jerry* (ed. 1890), p. 54. He was one of the deepest FILES in London; indeed, he was 'awake' on every suit.

1836. C. DICKENS, *Pickwick Papers* p. 360 (ed. 1857). 'Wot a perverse old FILE it is!' exclaimed Sam, 'always agoin' on about werdicks and alleybis, and that. Who said anysthings about the werdick?'

1837. C. DICKENS, *Oliver Twist*, p. 233. The Dodger . . . desired the jailer to communicate the names of them two FILES as were on the bench.

1849. THACKERAY, *Hoggarty Diamond*, ch. xi. 'You beat Brough; you do, by Jove! for he looks like a rogue—anybody would swear to him: but you! by Jove, you look the very picture of honesty!' 'A deep FILE,' said Aminadab, winking and pointing me out to his friend, Mr. Jehoshaphat.

1876. BESANT and RICE, *Golden Butterfly*, ch. xiii. If you were not such a steady old FILE I should think you were in love with her.

Verb (old).—To pick pockets.

FILING-LAY, *subs.* (thieves').—Pocket-picking. [From FILE = to steal from the person + LAY = business, occupation.

1754. *Jon. Wild*, bk. IV., ch. ii. I am committed for the FILING-LAY, man, and we shall be both nubbed together.

FILLING AT THE PRICE, *adv. phr.* (common).—Satisfying.

1870. *London Figaro*, 28 May. 'Penny Pleasures.' We believe that baked taturs are accepted as Penny Pleasures, and as being FILLING AT THE PRICE.

FILL ONE'S PIPE, *verb. phr.* (obsolete).—To attain to easy circumstances.

1821. P. EGAN, *Tom and Jerry* (ed. 1890), p. 32. It has often been the subject of sincere regret that such persons, with very few exceptions, have lived just long enough, according to a vulgar phrase, TO FILL THEIR PIPE, and leave others to enjoy it.

FILL THE BILL, *verb. phr.* (theatrical).—To excel in conspicuousness: as a star actor whose name is 'billed' to the exclusion of the rest of the company. Hence, by implication, out of the common run of things; *e.g.* THAT FILLS THE BILL = 'that takes the cake,' for a lie, an effect, an appearance—anything.

FILL THE BIN, *verb. phr.* (American).—To be beyond question; to come up to the mark; *e.g.*, 'Is the news reliable?' Yes, it FILLS THE BIN. *Cf.*, TO FILL THE BILL.

1862. *Speech of W. G. Brownlow of Tenn.* in *N. Y. Herald*, 16 May. 'Sir,' said he,—and he [W. L. Yancey] is a beautiful speaker and personally a very fine-looking man,—'are you the celebrated Parson Brownlow?' 'I'm the only man on earth,' I replied, 'that FILLS THE BIN.'

FILLUPEY, *adj.* and *adv.* (obsolete).—Satisfying. [From FILL + UP + Y.]

1853. *Diogenes*, II., 195. Champagne is FILLUPEY, so is Auber's music.

FILLY, *subs.* (common).—A girl; specifically a wanton. Among thieves, a daughter.

1668. ETHEREGE, *She Would if She Could*, II., ii. (1704), p. 112. I told you they were a couple of skittish FILLIES, but I never knew 'em boggle at a man before.

1846. THACKERAY, *V. Fair*, ch. xi. Well, I heard him say, 'By jove, she's a neat little FILLY!' meaning your humble servant, and he did me the honour to dance two country dances with me.

FILLY-HUNTING, *subs.* (venery).—Questing adventures; GROUSING (*q.v.*).

FILTH, *subs.* (old venery).—A prostitute.

1602. SHAKSPEARE, *Othello*, v., 2. *Iago*, FILTH, thou liest!

1609. SHAKSPEARE, *Timon of Athens*, iv., 1. To general FILTHS Convert, o' the instant, green virginity.

FIMBLE-FAMBLE, *subs.* (common).—A lame excuse; a prevaricating answer.

FIN, *subs.* (common). — 1. The arm; also the hand. [Fr., *nageoire*, but for synonyms, *see* DADDLE. TO TIP THE FIN = to shake hands.

1785. GROSE, *Dict. Vulg. Tongue*, FIN, an arm.

1836. MICHAEL SCOTT, *Cruise of the Midge*, p. 116. I wagged my head at this one, and nodded to another, and salaam'd with my FINS with all the grace of a wounded turtle, to a third.

1836. DICKENS, *Pickwick*, ch. xxxvii., p. 323. 'Smauker, my lad, your FIN,' said the gentleman with the cocked hat. Mr. Smauker dovetailed the top joint of his right hand little finger into that of the gentleman with the cocked hat, and said he was charmed to see him looking so well.

1844. *Puck*, p. 134. The sun shines fair in Carey Street, And eke in Lincoln's Inn, When Brown and Johnson gaily meet And shake the friendly FIN.

1849. THACKERAY, *Pendennis*, ch. lv. The young surgeon . . . succeeded in getting the General's dirty old hand under what he called his own FIN.

1850. F. SMEDLEY, *Frank Fairleigh*, p. 152. I'll drive you there instead; it will be better for your scorched FIN (pointing to my injured arm), than jolting about outside a horse.

2. Also FINN or FINNIE.—*See* FINNUP.

Intj.—*See* FAIN.

FIND, *subs.* (Harrow).—A mess of three or four upper boys which teas and breakfasts in the rooms of one or other of the set. FIND-FAG = a fag who provides for or 'finds' upper boys.

FINDER, *subs.* (thieves').—1. A thief; specifically a meat-market thief.

2. (Oxford University).—A waiter; especially at Caius'.

FINE, *subs.* (thieves').—Punishment; a term of imprisonment. For synonyms, *see* DOSE. TO FINE = to sentence. [From the payment of money imposed as a punishment for an offence.]

1785. GROSE, *Dict. Vulg. Tongue* s.v.

1859. MATSELL, *Vocabulum, or Rogue's Lexicon*. The cove had a FINE of two stretches and a half imposed upon him for relieving a joskin of a load of cole.

TO CUT IT FINE.—*See* CUT FINE.

TO GET ONE DOWN FINE AND CLOSE, *verb. phr.* (American).—To find out all about a man; to deliver a stinging blow.

ALL VERY FINE AND LARGE, *adj. phr.* (common).—An interjection of (1) approval; (2) derision; and (3) incredulity. [The refrain of a music-hall song excessively popular about 1886-88.]

FINE AS FIVEPENCE. — *See* FIVEPENCE.

FINE DAY FOR THE YOUNG DUCKS, *subs. phr.* (colloquial).—A very wet day.

FINE WORDS BUTTER NO PARSNIPS, *phr.* (colloquial).—A sarcastic retort upon large promises.

FINE-DRAWING, *subs.* (tailors').—Accomplishing an end without discovery.

FINEER, *verb*, **FINEERING**, *subs.* (old).—*See* quot.

1765. GOLDSMITH, *Essays*, VIII. The second method of running into debt is called FINEERING; which is getting goods made in such a fashion as to be unfit for every other purchaser, and if the tradesman refuses to give them on credit, then threatens to leave them upon his hands.

FINE-MADAM, *subs. phr.* (common).—An epithet of envy or derision for a person (feminine) above her station.

FINGER, *subs.* (American). — A 'nip'; usually applied to spirituous liquors. Thus, Three FINGERS of clear juice = Three 'goes' of whiskey.

1888. *Newport Journal*, 25 Feb. Which is correct, spoonfuls or spoons-ful, uncle?' Denver uncle—'Um—er—the fact is I don't know, my boy. In Denver, we don't use either, we say FINGERS.'

Verb (venery). — To take liberties with a woman. For synonyms, *see* FIRKYTOODLE.

TO PUT THE FINGER IN THE EYE, *verb. phr.* (colloquial).—To weep. For synonyms, *see* NAP A BIT.—[GROSE, 1785.]

A BIT FOR THE FINGER, *phr.* (venery). — A lascivious endearment.

FINGER AND THUMB, *subs. phr.* (rhyming slang). — A road or highway, *i.e.*, 'drum.' For synonyms, *see* DRUM.

FINGER-BETTER, *subs.* (American).—A man who bets on credit; also one who points out cards.

FINGER - FUCKING, *subs. phr.* (venery).—Masturbation (said of women only). For synonyms, *see* FRIG.

FINGER-POST, *subs.* (common).—A clergyman. For synonyms, *see* DEVIL-DODGER.

1785. GROSE, *Dict. Vulg. Tongue*. A parson: so called, because . . . Like the FINGER-POST he points out . . . the way to heaven.

FINGER-SMITH, *subs.* (thieves').—1. A pickpocket.

1883. HORSLEY, *Jottings from Jail* [in *Echo*], 25 Jan., p. 2, col. 4. The delicate expression FINGERSMITH, as descriptive of the trade which a blunt world might call that of a pickpocket.

2. (common). — A midwife. Fr., *Madame tire-monde* or *tire-pouce* (Rabelaisian); *Madame tire-mômes* (*môme* = 'kid'); *une mômière* (thieves'); *Madame tâte-*

minette, *Madame guichet* or *Madame portière du petit guichet* (17th century phrases). *Cf.*, CARVER AND GILDER.

FINISH, *verb* (common).—To kill. For synonyms, see COOK ONE'S GOOSE.

FINISHER, *subs.* (colloquial).— Something that gives the last, the settling touch to anything. *Cf.*, CORKER, CLINCHER, etc.

1788-1841. TH. HOOK [quoted in Annandale]. 'This was a FINISHER,' said Lackington.

FINJY! *intj.* (Winchester College). —An exclamation excusing one from participation in an unpleasant or unacceptable task, which he who says the word last has to undertake.

FINNUF.—See FINNUP.

FINNUP, (also FINNIP, FINNUF, FINNIF, FINNIE, FINN, or FIN), *subs.* (thieves').—A five-pound note or FLIMSY (*q.v.*). [A Yiddish pronunciation of German *fünf* = five.] Also FINNUP-READY (ready = money). In America FINNUP = a five dollar bill. DOUBLE FINNUP = a ten pound note.

1851-61. H. MAYHEW, *London Lab. and Lon. Poor,* vol. III., p. 396. The notes were all FINNIES (£5 notes), and a good imitation.

1857. SNOWDEN, *Mag. Assistant,* 3rd ed., p. 444. Five-pound notes, FINNIPS, ten-pound notes, DOUBLE FINNIPS.

1883. HORSLEY, *Jottings from Jail.* When we got into the rattler they showed me the pass. Yes, there it was, fifty quids in DOUBLE FINNS.

FIPPENNY, *subs.* (Australian thieves'). — A clasp knife. For synonyms, see CHIVE.

FIRE, *subs.* (thieves').—Danger.

1859. MATSELL, *Vocabulum, or Rogue's Lexicon.* This place is all on FIRE; I must pad like a bull or the cops will nail me.

LIKE A HOUSE ON FIRE, *adv. phr.* (common). — Easily and rapidly. *Cf.,* HOUSE, WINKING, ONE O'CLOCK, CAKE, BRICK, etc.

TO FIRE A SHOT, *verb. phr.* (venery).—To emit. Fr., *tirer un coup.*

TO FIRE A SLUG, *verb. phr.* (old).—To drink a dram. [GROSE, 1785.]

TO FIRE IN THE AIR, *verb. phr.* (venery).—TO SHOOT IN THE BUSH (*q.v.*).

TO FIRE A GUN, *verb. phr.* (old).—To introduce a story by head and shoulders; to lead up to a subject.—[GROSE, 1785.]

TO PASS THROUGH THE FIRE, *verb. phr.* (venery).—To be CLAPPED (*q.v.*), or POXED (*q.v.*).

TO SET THE THAMES ON FIRE, *verb. phr.* (colloquial)—To be clever, or the reverse; used in sarcasm.

FIRE AND LIGHT, *subs. phr.* (nautical).—A master-at-arms.

FIRED, *adj.* (American).—Arrested; turned out; and (among artists) rejected.

FIRE-EATER, *subs.* (common).—In Old Cant a quick-worker; and in modern English, a duellist or bully. Also FIRE-EATING.

1841. SAVAGE, *Dict. Art. of Printing,* s.v. A quick compositor.

1854. WHYTE MELVILLE, *General Bounce,* ch. xii. Sir Ascot was none of your sighing, despairing, FIRE-EATING adorers.

1868. OUIDA, *Under Two Flags,* ch. xv. A soldier, who . . . was one of the most brilliant FIRE-EATERS of his regiment.

FIRE-ESCAPE, *subs.* (common).—A clergyman. For synonyms, see DEVIL-DODGER.

FIRE-PRIGGER, *subs.* (old). — A thief whose venue is a conflagration.—GROSE [1785].

FIRESHIP, *subs.* (old).—A tainted whore. For general synonyms, see BARRACK-HACK and TART.

FIRE-SPANIEL, *subs.* (military).— A soldier who 'nurses' the barrack-room fire. Some English synonyms are, fire-dog; fire-worshipper; chimney-ornament; fender-guard; and cuddle-chimney.

FIREWATER, *subs.* (American).— Ardent spirits.

1861. T. HUGHES, *Tom Brown at Oxford,* ch. xiv. Yes. And awful FIRE-WATER we used to get. The governor supplied me, like a wise man.

FIREWORKS, *subs.* (common).— A state of disturbance; mental excitement: *e.g.,* FIREWORKS ON THE BRAIN = to be in a fluster.

FIRK, *verb* (old).—To beat.

1599. SHAKSPEARE, *Henry V.,* iv., 6. *Pistol.* I'll fer him, and FIRK him, and ferret him.

FIRKYTOODLE, *verb* (common).— To indulge in sexual endearments. Also FIRKYTOODLING = preliminary caresses.

ENGLISH SYNONYMS. — To canoodle; to fiddle; to mess (or pull) about; to slewther (Irish); to spoon; to crooky; to fam; to dildo; to caterwaul;

to feel; to finger; to fumble; to grope; to clitorize; to touch up; to tip the long (or middle) finger; to guddle (Scots.)

FRENCH SYNONYMS. *Mignoter* (popular); *jouer de la harpe* (familiar: Leroux, in *Dict. Comique,* says: 'Jouer de la harpe signifie jouer des mains auprès d'une femme, la patiner, lui toucher la nature, la farfouiller, la clitoriser, la chatouiller avec les doigts); *la petite oie* (= preliminary favours); *faire des horreurs* (popular: *des horreurs* = broad or 'blue' talk; *dire des horreurs* = to talk bawd); *bécoter* (popular: = to make hot love); *chouchouter* (familiar: *chouchou* = darling).

SPANISH SYNONYMS. *Garatusa* (= an act of endearment); *caroca* (generally used in plural, *carocas* = endearments); *amoricones* (vulgar.)

FIRMED.—See WELL-FIRMED.

FIRST-CHOP, *adj.* (common).—First rate. [From Hind., *chaap,* a stamp, an official mark on weights and measures; hence used to signify quality.] Also SECOND-CHOP (*q.v.*).

1855. THACKERAY, *Newcomes,* ch. iv. 'As for poetry, I hate poetry.' 'Pen's not FIRST-CHOP,' says Warrington.

1880. A. TROLLOPE, *The Duke's Children,* ch. lxviii. Old Beeswax thinks that if he can get me up to swear that he and his crew are real FIRST-CHOP hands, that will hit the governor hard.

FIRST FLIGHT. IN THE FIRST FLIGHT, *subs. phr.* (sporting).— Those first in at the finish; in fox-hunting those in at the death.

1852. F. E. SMEDLEY, *Lewis Arundel,* ch. xxxix. Then you promise you will dine with me at Lovegrove's, on Thursday,

---

and I'll pick up half-a-dozen fellows that I know you'll like to meet, regular top-sawyers, that you're safe to find in the FIRST FLIGHT, be it where it may.

FIRST-NIGHTER, *subs. phr.* (journalistic).—An *habitué* of first performances.

1886. G. SUTHERLAND, *Australia,* p. 125. The FIRST-NIGHTER is almost unknown in the colonies.

FIRST-NIGHT WRECKER.—See WRECKER.

FISH, *subs.* (common).—1. A man; generally in contempt or disparagement as ODD FISH, LOOSE FISH, QUEER FISH, SCALY FISH, SHY FISH (all of which see). *Cf.,* COVE.

2. (tailors'). — Pieces cut out of garments to make them fit close.

3. (venery).—Generic for the female *pudendum*: *e.g.,* A BIT OF FISH = A GRIND (*q.v.*); FISH-MARKET = a brothel; and TO GO FISHING = to go GROUSING (*q.v.*).

Verb (colloquial).—To attempt to obtain by artifice; to seek indirectly; to curry favour.

PRETTY KETTLE OF FISH, *subs. phr.* (colloquial).—A perplexing state of affairs; a quandary.

TO HAVE OTHER FISH TO FRY, *verb. phr.* (colloquial).—To have other business on hand.

1785. GROSE, *Dict. Vulg. Tongue,* s.v.

1836. MICHAEL SCOTT, *Cruise of the Midge,* p. 90. He shouted to us, and pointed to his cargo; but we HAD OTHER FISH TO FRY, and accordingly never relaxed in our pulling.

TO BE NEITHER FISH NOR FLESH, *verb. phr.* (colloquial).—

To be neither one thing nor another; said of waverers and nondescripts; sometimes extended to NEITHER FISH, FLESH, FOWL, NOR GOOD RED HERRING.

1598. SHAKSPEARE, II. *Henry IV.,* iv., 3. *Falstaff.* Why, she's NEITHER FISH NOR FLESH; a man knows not where to have her.

1631-1700. DRYDEN [quoted in Annandale]. Damned neuters in their middle way of steering, Are NEITHER FISH, NOR FLESH, NOR GOOD RED HERRING.

FISH-BROTH, *subs.* (common). — Water. For synonyms, see ADAM'S ALE, to which may be added: Fr., *le bouillon de canard* (thieves'); *l'agout* (thieves'): Four. *vetta.*

1599. NASHE, *Lenten Stuffe.* The churlish frampold waves gave him his belly-full of FISH-BROATH.

FISHER, *subs.* (common).—A lick-spittle; only used contemptuously.

FISHHOOKS, *subs.* (common).—The fingers. For synonyms, see FORKS.

1848. DUNCOMBE, *Sinks of London,* s.v.

FISHMARKET, *subs.* (gaming).— The lowest hole at bagatelle; SIMON (*q.v.*). — See also FISH, *subs.,* sense 3.

FISHY, *adj.* (common). — Effete, dubious, or seedy (of persons); unsound, or equivocal (of things). Also FISHINESS = UNSOUNDNESS.

1858. SHIRLEY BROOKS, *The Gordian Knot,* p. 14. Highly FISHY they were. Something about breach of trust, and the embezzling his brother's money—a man in India.

1859. *Punch,* vol. XXXVI., p. 82. The affair is decidedly FISHY. However somebody must have the place, and so our friend Sam Warren . . . takes the mastership, resigning his seat.

26

1868. *Orchestra,* 29 Feb., p. 365. When he commented on the words in the libel of Greek derivation, he professed to have forgotten all he ever learnt at school, said that ichthyophagous meant FISHY, a word that thoroughly described the plaintiff's case.

1870. *London Figaro,* 31 Oct. Captain Spratt is the right man in the right place, though his appointment to such a post is certainly, on the face of it, FISHY.

1884. F. ANSTEY, *Giant's Robe,* ch. xxii. There's something FISHY about it all, and I mean to get at it.

1890. *St. James' Gazette,* 9 April, p. 3, col. 1. Unfortunately the Bill is FISHY; and there are 'very awkward and stiff considerations about it.'

FIST, *subs.* (common).—1. Handwriting. Fr., *la cape.*

1864. *Derby Day,* p. 8. Must say though that your friend writes a tolerable FIST.

2. (tailors'). — A workman. GOOD FIST = a good workman.

3. (printers').—An index hand.

Verb. 1.—To apprehend.

1598. SHAKSPEARE, II. *Henry IV.,* ii., 1. *Fang.* An I but FIST him once! An a' come but within my vice.

2. (colloquial).—To take hold, *e.g.,* Just you FIST that scrubbing-brush, and set to work.

3. (venery).—To FIST IT = to take a man by the *penis,* for intromission or masturbation.

TO PUT UP ONE'S FIST, *verb. phr.* (tailors').—To acknowledge a fact; *cf.,* FILL THE BIN and ACKNOWLEDGE THE CORN.

FIST-FUCKING, *subs. phr.* (venery).—Masturbation. For synonyms, see FRIG.

FIT, *adj.* and *adv.* (colloquial).— Suitable; in good form.

1882. *Punch,* vol. LXXXII., p. 155, col. 1, (*q.v.*).

1884. A. LANG, in *Longman's Mag.,* IV., 140. The really best moment in life is that which finds us young and FIT, bowling on a lively wicket, and conscious that we have considerable command of the ball.

1889. *Evening Standard,* 25 June. 'Sir C. Russell's Speech in Durham-Chetwynd Case.' Now, Mr. Lowther, I am not suggesting—and I wish to be perfectly understood—that to run a horse that is not perfectly FIT does not stand alone as an offence against the honourable conduct of any man on the turf.

FIT AS A FIDDLE, *adj. phr.* (colloquial).—AWFULLY FIT, *i.e.,* in perfect condition.

TO FIT LIKE A BALL OF WAX, *verb. phr.* (common). — To fit close to the skin.

TO FIT LIKE A SENTRY BOX, *verb. phr.* (common). — To fit badly.

TO FIT LIKE A GLOVE, *verb. phr.* (colloquial). — To fit perfectly.

TO FIT TO A T, *verb. phr.* (colloquial).—To fit to a nicety. [In reference to the T square used in drawing.]

1791. BOSWELL, *Johnson.* You see they'd have FITTED HIM TO A T.

TO FIT UP A SHOW, *verb. phr.* (artists').—To arrange an exhibition.

TO FIT ENDS (or END TO END), *verb. phr.* (venery). — To copulate. For synonyms, see RIDE.

FITCH'S GRENADIERS, *subs. phr.* (military). — The Eighty-Third Foot. [From the small stature of the men and the name of the first colonel.]

FITS. TO BEAT INTO FITS, *verb. phr.*—See BEAT and CREATION.

FITTER, *subs.* (thieves').—A burglar's locksmith.

FIT UP, *subs. phr.* (theatrical).—A small company. Also used adjectively; *see* CONSCIENCE.

1889. *Answers*, p. 40. One young fellow, who had come down with me, shook his head when he found that the company was one known as a FIT UP, that is to say, one where the stage is really carried about with the company.

FIVE-FINGERS, *subs. phr.* (cards).—The five of trumps in the game of 'Don' or 'Five Cards.'

1611. CHAPMAN, *May-Day*, V., ii., in wks. (1873), ii., 401. For my game stood, me thought, vpon my last two tricks, when I made sure of the set, and yet lost it, hauing the varlet and the FIUE FINGER to make two tricks.

1674. COTTON, *Compleat Gamester* [at the game of five-cards]. The FIVE FINGERS (*alias*, five of trumps) is the best card in the pack . . . the Ace of Hearts wins the Ace of Trumps, and the FIVE FINGERS not only wins the Ace of Trumps, but also all other cards whatever.

FIVER, *subs.* (colloquial).—Anything that counts as five; specifically a five-pound note. *Cf.*, FINN.

1853. WH. MELVILLE, *Digby Grand*, ch. i. Spooner . . . . loses a five-pound note, or, as he calls it, a FIVER, to my antagonist.

1864. E. YATES, *Broken to Harness*, ch. xxv. Wouldn't lend me a FIVER to save me from gaol.

1871. *Daily News*, 26 Dec. 'Workhouse Xmas Depravity.' Why, there's Jemima Ann . . . has . . . been bleeding me of a FIVER to send to some Christmas Dinner Fund for juvenile mudlarks.

1872. *Fun*, Sept. I lent a FIVER unto a friend—He managed somehow that to spend.

1890. *Tit-Bits*, 8 Feb., p. 273, col. 2. Lend me a FIVER, will you, Gus?

FIVE OVER FIVE, *adv. phr.* (common).—Said of people who turn in their toes.

FIVEPENCE. AS FINE, (or AS GRAND), AS FIVEPENCE (or AS FIPPENCE), *phr.* (colloquial).—As fine as possible. *Cf.*, AS NEAT AS NINEPENCE.

1672. WYCHERLY, *Love in a Wood*, V., wks. (1713), 421. Whilst his mistress is as FINE AS FIPPENCE, in embroidered sattens.

1720. GAY, *New Song of New Similes*. As FINE AS FIVE-PENCE is her mien.

1738. SWIFT, *Polite Convers.*, Dial. 3. Pray how was she drest? *Lady Sm.* Why, as FINE AS FI'PENCE.

1857. A. TROLLOPE, *Barchester Towers*, ch. xxxix. There's . . . the lot of 'em all sitting AS GRAND AS FIVEPENCE in madam's drawing-room.

1866. G. A. SALA, *Trip to Barbary*, ch. xiii. They [the Jews] continue to sit 'all of a row' with their daughters dressed 'all in green,' or all in pink or salmon-colour, and AS FINE AS FIVEPENCE on their ceremonial days, waiting, waiting, always waiting, for the restoration of the Temple and the end of the dolour.

FIVES, *subs.* (common).—1. The fingers. BUNCH OF FIVES = the fist. Formerly also = the feet. For synonyms, *see* FORKS.

c. 1629. Ballad in Arber's *English Garner*, vol. VII., p. 13. Her cheeks were like the cherry . . . Her waist exceeding small. The FIVES did fit her shoe.

1836. DICKENS, *Pickwick*, ii., 7. Smart chap that cabman—handled his FIVES well.

1887. *Judy*, 18 May, p. 236. Both the men of sin handled their FIVES with almost professional dexterity.

2. (streets').—A fight. [From sense 1.]

FIX, *subs.* (common).—A dilemma; frequently in conjunction with AWFUL (*q.v*). and REGULAR (*q.v.*), *e.g.*, AN AWFUL FIX = a terrible position. Variants are CORNERED; UP A TREE; UP A CLOSE; UNDER A CLOUD; IN A

SCRAPE. Fr., *avoir des mots avec les sergots* = to run amuck of the police.

1837. R. H. BARHAM, *The Ingoldsby Legends*, (ed. 1862), p. 405. But, alas! and alack!—He had stuffed her sack So full that he found himself quite IN A FIX.

1840. DICKENS, *Old Curiosity Shop*, ch. lxi. It can't be helped you know. He ain't the only one in the same FIX.

1858. SHIRLEY BROOKES, *The Gordian Knot*, p. 88. John Claxton, what a FIX I am in. That Mrs. Spencer will never go out of town.

1864. *Tangle Talk*, p. 271. Just as you are in a capital FIX, exquisitely placed for being made a laughing stock, your friend will turn round upon you.

1869. MRS. H. WOOD, *Roland Yorke*, ch. xxi. Oh, but I could tell you of worse FIXES than that.

Verb (old).—1. To arrest. For synonyms, *see* NAB and COP.

1789. G. PARKER, *Variegated Characters*. If any of us was to come in by ourselves and should happen to take a snooze you'd snitch upon us and soon have the traps FIX us.

2. (American colloquial).—A general verb of action. Everything is FIXED except the meaning of the word itself. The farmer FIXES his fences, the mechanic his work-bench, the seamstress her sewing-machine, the fine lady her hair, and the schoolboy his books. The minister has to FIX his sermon, the doctor to FIX his medicines, the lawyer to FIX his brief. Dickens was requested to 'UN-FIX his straps'; eatables are FIXED for a meal; a girl UNFIXES herself to go to bed, and FIXES HERSELF UP to go for a walk. At public meetings it is FIXED who are to be the candidates for office; rules are FIXED to govern an institution, and when the arrangements are made the people contentedly say, 'Now everything is FIXED nicely.' [This use is thought by Proctor to have arisen from some confusion between 'fingency' and 'fixation': as if the word had the meaning of the Latin *fingo, fingere*, instead of that of the Latin *figo, figere*. At least there is no use of FIX in American which would not fairly represent the meaning of both.—*See Philol. Soc. Trans.* for 1865, p. 188.] The universality of the verb is only equalled by its antiquity, for, as J. R. Lowell points out, as early as 1675, the Commissioners of the United Colonies ordered 'their arms well FIXED and fit for service.'

TO FIX THE BALLOT BOX = to tamper with returns.

1842. DICKENS, *American Notes*, ch. x., p. 86. You call upon a gentleman in a country town, and his help informs you that he is FIXING himself just now, but will be down directly: by which you are to understand that he is dressing. You inquire, on board a steamboat, of a fellow-passenger, whether breakfast will be ready soon, and he tells you he should think so, for when he was last below, they were FIXING the tables; in other words, laying the cloth. You beg a porter to collect your luggage, and he entreats you not to be uneasy, for he'll FIX IT presently, and if you complain of indisposition, you are advised to have recourse to Doctor so and so, who will FIX you in no time.

1888. *Scribner's Mag.* I do hope you'll like everything; it's the first time we ever took boarders, but we try to FIX things nice.

ANYHOW, OR NOHOW, YOU CAN OR CAN'T FIX IT.—*See* ANYHOW.

TO FIX ONE'S FLINT, *verb. phr.* (American).—'To settle one's hash.' For synonyms, *see* COOK ONE'S GOOSE.

1835-40. HALIBURTON, *Clockmaker*, S., ch. xii. Their manners are rude, overbearin', and tyrannical. They want their FLINTS FIXED for 'em as we did last war.

FIXINGS, *subs.* (American). — A noun of all work. Applied to any and everything.

1842. DICKENS, *American Notes*, ch. x., p. 86. 'Will you try,' said my opposite neighbour, handing me a dish of potatoes, broken up in milk and butter, 'will you try some of these FIXINGS.'

1872. *Daily Telegraph*, 30 Sept. Still stoutly asserted by some sceptical Down-Easter to have been an itinerant dealer in hardware and kitchen FIXINGS from Salem, Mass.

FIX UP, *verb. phr.* (American).—To settle; to arrange. *Cf.*, FIX.

FIZ, or FIZZ, *subs.* (common).—Champagne; sometimes lemonade and ginger-beer. For synonyms, *see* BOY.

1864. *Punch*, vol. XLVII., p. 100. So away we went to supper For hungry we had grown, And ordered some FIZZ, which the right thing is, With a devilled turkey bone.

1869. *St. James' Mag.*, July. Her great object is to get one of these fellows to order the champagne. On each bottle of this stuff disposed of she has a percentage. She terms it FIZZ, and will pretend to fall into ecstacies at the prospect of a glass of the chemical essence of gooseberry sweetened up with tartaric acid and sugar of lead.

1871. *Morning Advertiser*, 11 Sept. Shall the Admirals of England now their former prowess drop, All courage ooze from tarry hands, like FIZ from uncorked 'pop?'

1879. JUSTIN MCCARTHY, *Donna Quixote*, ch. xvii. I can open a bottle of soda or FIZZ . . . and never as much as wink.

1883. *Referee*, 22 April, p. 3, col. 3. I have seen you wince when it has come to your turn to stand treat, and you have been called upon to pay twelve shillings for a bottle of FIZZ.

FIZ-GIG, *subs.* (schoolboys'). — A firework.

FIZZER, *subs.* (common). — Anything first-rate. *Cf.*, FIZZING.

1866. *London Miscellany*, 19 May, p. 235. If the mare was such a FIZZER why did you sell her?

FIZZING, *adj.* (common).—First-rate.

ENGLISH SYNONYMS. — A1; cheery; clean wheat; clipping; crack; creamy; crushing; first chop; first class; first-rate, or (in America) first-rate and a half; hunky; jammy; jonnick; lummy; nap; out-and-out; pink; plummy; proper; real jam; right as ninepence; ripping; rooter; rum; screaming; scrumptious; shipshape; slap-up; slick; splendacious; splendiferous; to rights; tip-top; true marmalade; tsing-tsing.

FRENCH SYNONYMS. — *Aux oiseaux* (pop.: very fine, very good); *bath* or *bate* (pop.: tip-top; for origin *see* under A1); *c'est du flan* (thieves': it is excellent); *c'est hurf* (general: = true marmalade); *c'est un peu ça* (popular); *c'est bath aux pommes* (*cf.*, BATH *ante*); *chenâtre* (thieves'); *chic* or *chique* (*chique* is literally a quid of tobacco); *chicard, chicancardo* or *chicandard* (superlatives of *chic*); *chocnoso, chocnosof, chocnosogue* or *kosenoff* (= crushing; nobby); *chouette, chouettard*, or *chouettaud* (*chouette* = literally a screech-owl); *épatarouflant* or *épatant* (general = stunning); *farineux* (lit. farinaceous); *flambant* (lit. blazing, flaming); *frais* (used ironically); *grand 'largue* (*largue* = offing); *mirobolant* (fam. and pop. = slap-up); *muche* (= bully or ripping); *numéro un* (*i.e.*, A1); *obéliscal* or *obélisqual* (common); *ruisselant d'inouisme*

(familiar); *rup* (popular); *schpile* (popular); *sgoff* (popular); *snoboye* (fam. and pop.); *superlificoquentieux* (= splendiferous).

1885. *Daily Telegraph*, 1 August, p. 2, col. 2. 'She'll do FIZZING,' remarked Mr. Menders, regarding the transformed effigy admiringly, 'to stick up at the head of the barrer.'

FIZZLE, *subs.* (American). — A ridiculous failure; a flash in the pan. [The figure is adapted from wet powder which burns with a hiss, and then goes out.] In many of the United States colleges, the term = a blundering recitation. To hit just one third of the meaning constitutes 'a perfect FIZZLE.'—*Hall's College Words.* The 'Brunonian,' Feb. 24, 1877, defines the word to mean 'where the student thinks he knows, but can't quite express it,' or 'he tries to express it, and the professor thinks he doesn't quite know.'

1849. *Tomahawk*, November. Here he could FIZZLES mark, without a sigh, And see orations unregarded die.

1851. *National Intelligencer*, 8 Dec. The speech was as complete a FIZZLE as has ever disgraced Congress, and we hope sincerely the honourable member from Massachusetts will take the lesson to heart.

1865. Letter in the *D. Telegraph*, 30 March. The famous 'Jack o' Clubs,' from which so much was expected, is a dead FIZZLE. The half of the men had to leave the mines and go to the low country for want of work; and wages, which always were $10 a-day, were reduced to $80 per month, with board.

1883. *Echo*, 16 March, p. 4, col. 1. What promised at first to be a magnificent Parliamentary 'row' ended in a mere unsensational FIZZLE.

1890. *St. James' Gaz.*, 1 May, p. 4, col. 2. Altogether it begins to look as though the terrible demonstrations of down-trodden labour which were to shake society to its foundations would end in something like FIZZLE.

Verb (American).—To fail in reciting; to recite badly. Also (said of an instructor) to cause one to fail at reciting. At some American colleges FLUNK (*q.v.*) is the common word for an utter failure. To FIZZLE = to stumble through at last. In the 'Yale Literary Messenger,' 'FIZZLE = To rise with modest reluctance, to hesitate often, to decline finally; generally, to misunderstand the question.' Also to FLAT OUT (*q.v.*). Four. *Far une yappa.*

1847. *The Yale Banger*, 22 Oct. My dignity is outraged at beholding those who FIZZLE and flunk in my presence tower above me.

1850. *Yale Lit. Mag.*, p. 321. FIZZLE him tenderly, Bore him with care; Fitted so slenderly, Tutor, beware.

END OF VOL. II.

SLANG AND ITS ANALOGUES

PAST AND PRESENT.

A DICTIONARY, HISTORICAL AND COMPARATIVE, OF THE HETERODOX SPEECH OF ALL CLASSES OF SOCIETY FOR MORE THAN THREE HUNDRED YEARS.

WITH SYNONYMS IN ENGLISH, FRENCH, GERMAN, ITALIAN, ETC.

COMPILED AND EDITED BY

JOHN S. FARMER and W. E. HENLEY.

VOL. III.—Fla. to Hyps.

PRINTED FOR SUBSCRIBERS ONLY.

MDCCCXCIII.

A · Dictionary · of Slang · and · its · Analogues.

LABBERGAST, *verb*. (colloquial). To astound; to stagger, either physically or mentally. [O. E., FLAB = to frighten + GAST = to scare.] Fr., *abalober*; *baba* (from *ébahi* = astounded); *épater* (= flatten out). Sp., *quedarse de*, or *hecho*, *una pieza* (= 'knocked all of a heap'). See FLOORED.

1772. *Annual Register*, 'On New Words.' Now we are FLABBERGASTED and bored from morning to night.

1823. BEE, *Dict. of the Turf*, etc., p. 79. His colleagues were FLABBERGASTED when they heard of Castlereagh's sudden death.

1837. BARHAM, *Ingoldsby Legends* ('Brothers of Birchington'). He was quite FLABBERGASTED to see the amount.

1841. *Punch*, vol. I., p. 261. We rather just imagine they will be not a little puzzled and FLABBERGASTED to discover the meaning or wit of some of those elegant phrases.

1864. *Derby Day*, p. 67. You're sort of FLABBERGASTED. It's taken all the wind out of you like, and you feel like an old screw a blowing up Highgate Hill.

1889. *Licensed Victuallers' Gazette*, 18 Jan. Poor Clarke was completely FLABBERGASTED.

1891. *National Observer*, 1 Aug. In no other sport is the *laudator temporis acti* so completely FLABBERGASTED as here.

FLABBERDEGAZ, *subs.* (theatrical). Words interpolated to dissemble a lapse of memory; GAG (*q.v.*). Also, imperfect utterance or bad acting.

FLAG, *subs.* (old).—1. A groat, or fourpenny piece. Also FLAGG, and FLAGGE. For synonyms, see JOEY.

1567. HARMAN, *Caveat* (1814), p. 65. *Roge*. But a FLAGGE, a wyn and a make. (But a groat, a penny, and a half-penny.)

1610. ROWLANDS, *Martin Mark-all*, p. 38 (H. Club's Rept. 1874) s.v.

1714. *Memoirs of John Hall* (4th ed.), p. 12, s.v.

1725. JONATHAN WILD, *Canting Dict.*, s.v.

1851-61. H. MAYHEW, *Lond. Lab. and Lond. Poor*, vol. I., p. 269. A tremendous black doll bought for a FLAG (fourpence) of a retired rag-merchant.

2. (common). — An apron; hence a badge of office or trade; *cf.*, FLAG-FLASHER. Equivalents are BELLY-CHEAT and FIG-LEAF.

1851-61. H. MAYHEW, *Lond. Lab. and Lond. Poor*, vol. I., p. 232 (List of patterer's words), s.v.

1872. *Dundee Advertiser*, 20 April. 'Report of Meeting of Domestic Servants. It was contended that they were compelled to wear what was generally known as a FLAG.

1887. W. E. HENLEY, *Villon's Straight Tip*. Suppose you try a different tack, And on the square you flash your FLAG.

3. (obsolete).—A jade.

1539. DAVID LYNDSAY, *Thrie Estaitis*. Works [Ed. Laing, 1879], ii. 109. Ane fistand FLAG.

4. (common).—The menstrual cloth. Variants are bandage; clout; danger-signal; diaper; double clout (Durfey); gentleman's pleasure garden padlock; periodicity rag; the red rag; sanitary towel; window-curtain.

THE FLAG (or DANGER-SIGNAL) IS UP = " The Captain's at home " (GROSE), *i.e.*, the menstrual flux is on.

ENGLISH SYNONYMS. — To have domestic afflictions, or the D.A.'s; to have the FLOWERS (*q.v.*); to have one's grandmother, or little friend, or auntie, with one; to have them (or it) on; to be in a state of 'no thoroughfare'; to have the red rag on; to be roadmaking; to have the street up for repairs; to be at Number One, London; to have 'the gate locked and the key lost.'

FRENCH SYNONYMS. — *Avoir ses cardinales* (literally, — to have one's reds); *avoir les histoires*; *avoir les affaires* (common); *avoir ses anglais* (in allusion to the scarlet of English soldiers); *broyer des tomates* (= tomato - crushing); *avoir son marquis* (COTGRAVE); *avoir les fleurs rouges*; *avoir sa chemise tachée* (COTGRAVE); *voir Sophie*; *avoir les ordinaires*.

ITALIAN SYNONYMS. — *Marchese* (FLORIO), *marchesano* (= menses. Michel says, Art. *marque* = a month, a woman. " Il ne saurait être douteux que ce nom ne soit venu à cette division de l'année, de l'infirmité périodique qu'ont les *marques*, ou femmes, lors que la Lune, pour tenir sa diette et vaquer à ses purifications menstruelles, fait *marquer* les logis feminins par son fourrier, lequel pour escusson n'a que son impression rouge ").

TO FLY THE FLAG, *verb. phr.* (tailors').—To post a notice that 'hands' are wanted. See also FLY THE FLAG, *post*.

FLAG OF DEFIANCE, *subs. phr.* (old nautical).—A drunken roysterer. For synonyms, *see* ELBOW-CROOKER.

TO HANG OUT THE FLAG OF DEFIANCE (or BLOODY FLAG), *verb. phr.*—To be continuously drunk. [An allusion to the 'crimson face' (COTGRAVE) and the pugnacity of certain terms of inebriety.] For synonyms, *see* RINKS.

1690. B. E., *New Dict. of the Canting Crew*, s.v. THE FLAG OF DEFIANCE IS OUT (among the Tarrs) the Fellow's Face is very Red, and he is Drunk.

1785. GROSE, *Dict. Vulg. Tongue*, s.v.

FLAG-FLASHER, *subs.* (common).— One sporting a badge or other ensign of office (cap, apron, uniform, etc.) when off duty.—*Cf.*, FLAG, sense 2.

FLAG-ABOUT, *subs.* (old).—A strumpet. [From FLAG, a paving-stone]. For synonyms, *see* BARRACK-HACK and TART.

FLAG-FLYING.—See FLAG.

FLAG OF DISTRESS, *subs. phr.* (common).—1. A card announcing 'lodgings,' or 'board and lodgings.' Hence, any overt sign of poverty.

2. (common).—A flying shirt-tail; in America, a LETTER IN THE POST-OFFICE (*q.v.*).

FLAGGER, *subs.* (common). — A street - walker. For synonyms, *see* BARRACK-HACK and TART.

1865. *Daily Paper*, 'Police Report.' She wasn't a low sort at all—she wasn't a FLAGGER, as we call it. So I replies, 'I am well, thankee; and am happy to say I feel as such.'

FLAGS, *subs.* (common). — Linen drying and flying in the wind. For synonyms, *see* SNOW.

FLAG UNFURLED, *subs. phr.* (rhyming).—A man of the world.

FLAG-WAGGING, *subs.* (military).— Flag-signal drill.

FLAM, *subs.* (colloquial). — Nonsense (for synonyms, *see* GAMMON); humbug; flattery; or, a lie : as A REGULAR FLAM (for synonyms, *see* WHOPPER). *Cf.* FLIM-FLAM.

1598. FLORIO, *A Worlde of Wordes*, [*Cf.*, FLIM-FLAM.]

1647. BEAUMONT and FLETCHER, *Humourous Lieutenant*, iv., 1. With some new FLAM or other, nothing to the matter.

1664. BUTLER, *Hudibras*, pt. II., ch. iii., p. 29. A FLAM more senseless than the roguery of old aruspicey and aug'ry.

1742-4. ROGER NORTH, *Lives of the Norths*, ch. i., p. 368. They must have known his Lordship better and not have ventured such FLAMS at him.

1760. FOOTE, *Minor*, Act II. Had the FLAM been fact, your behaviour was natural enough.

1762. FOOTE, *Liar*, bk. II., ch. ii. Can't you discern that this FLAM of Sir James Elliot's is a mere fetch to favour his retreat?

1830. SIR E. B. LYTTON, *Paul Clifford*, p. 298 (ed. 1854). Harry . . . told you as ow it was all a FLAM about the child in the bundle!

1837. BARHAM, *Ingoldsby Legends* (ed. 1862), p. 325. No trick nor FLAM, but your real Schiedam.

1849. C. KINGSLEY, *Alton Locke*, ch. ii. And their pockets full they crams by their patriotic FLAMS, And then swear 'tis for the good of the nation.

1850. D. JERROLD, *The Catspaw*, Act II. Though the story of that scoundrel Coolcard, Augustus Coolcard—and I was never before deceived—never—is a FLAM—all a FLAM.

1870. *London Figaro*, 22 Sept. Is not your boasted power a FLAM?

1887. W. E. HENLEY, *Villon's Good Night*. You flymy titters fond of FLAM.

2. (old).—A single stroke on the drum.--[GROSE, 1785.]

Adj. (old).—False.

1692. SPRAT, *Relation of Young's Contrivance* (Harl. Misc. vi. 224). To amuse him the more in his search, she addeth a FLAM story that she had got his hand by corrupting one of the letter-carriers in London.

Verb (colloquial).—1. To take in; to flatter; to lie; to foist or fob off. FLAMMING = lying.

1658. Rowley and Ford, &c., *Witch of Edm.*, ii., 2. Was this your cunning? and then flam me off with an old witch, two wives, and Winnifride.

1688. Shadwell, *Sq. of Alsatia*, II. in wks. (1720) iv. 41. Does he think to flam me with a lye?

1830. S. Warren, *Diary of a Late Physician*, ch. v. But I'll show him whether or not I, for one of them, am to be jeered and flammed with impunity.

1835. Marryat, *Jacob Faithful*, ch. xxviii. How she did flam that poor old Domine.

(American University). — To affect, or prefer, female society; to Grouse (*q.v.*). [A corruption of flame (*q.v.*)] *See* Molrowing.

Flambustious, *adj.* (American).—Showy; gaudy; pleasant.

1868. *Putnam's Magazine*. We will have a flambustious time. [*Cf.*, Shakspeare (1608), *Antony and Cleopatra*, iii., 11. Let's have one other gaudy night.]

Flamdoodle, *subs.* (American).—Nonsense; vain boasting. Probably a variant of flap-doodle (*q.v.*).

1888. *New York Sun*. We wasn't goin' to have any high falutin' flam-doodle business over him.

Flame, *subs.* (colloquial). — 1. A sweetheart; a mistress in keeping. Old flame = an old lover; a cast-off mistress. Also (2) a venereal disease.

b. 1664. *d.* 1721. Mathew Prior [in Palgrave's "Golden Treasury of Songs and Lyrics," ed. 1885]. Euphelia serves to grace my measure, but Chloe is my real flame.

1757. Foote, *Author*, Act I. Let's see, Mr. and Mrs. Cadwallader, and your flame, the sister, as I live.

1846-8. Thackeray, *Vanity Fair*, ch. xiv. On this Rebecca instantly stated that Amelia was engaged to be married to a Lieutenant Osborne, a very old flame.

1859. Matsell, *Vocabulum, or Rogue's Lexicon*, s.v.

Flamer, *subs.* (colloquial).—A man, woman, thing, or incident above the common. [Literally conspicuous to flaming point, *i.e.*, as a light in the dark]. For synonyms, *see* Stunner.

1840. H. Cockton, *Valentine Vox*, ch. ii. Concocting a criticism on the evening's performance, which certainly was, according to the signor's own acknowledgment, a regular flamer.

Flames, *subs.* (old).—A red-haired person. *Cf.*, Carrots and Ginger.

1823. Jon Bee, *Dict. of the Turf*, etc., p. 79. Who should I fling my precious ogles upon but flames—she as lived at the 'Blue Posts.'

Flaming, *ppl. adj.* (colloquial).—Conspicuous; ardent; stunning (*q.v.*). For synonyms, *see* A 1 and Fizzing.

1738. Swift, *Polite Conv.*, Dialogue II. *Lord Sparkish*. My Lady Smart, your ladyship has a very fine scarf. *Lady Smart*. Yes, my lord, it will make a flaming figure in a country church.

1776. Rubrick, *The Spleen*, ii. I'l send a flaming paragraph of thei wedding to all the newspapers.

1872. Besant and Rice. *Ready Money Mortiboy*, ch. xxx. He called one of the children, and sent her for a bill. She presently returned with a flaming poster.

Flanderkin, *subs.* (old).—*See* quot.

1690. B. E., *New Dict. of the Canting Crew*, s.v. A very large fat man or horse; also natives of that country.

Flanders Fortunes, *subs. phr.* (old). — Of small substance. — B.E., *New Dict. of the Canting Crew* (1690).

Flanders Pieces, *subs. phr.* (old). —*See* quot.

1690. B. E., *New Dict. of the Canting Crew*. Flanders pieces, pictures that look fair at a distance, but coarser near at hand.

Flank, *verb* (common).—1. To crack a whip; also, to hit a mark with the lash of one.

1830. Sir E. B. Lytton, *Paul Clifford* (ed. 1854), p. 18. He then, taking up a driving whip, flanked a fly from the opposite wall.

1833. 'An Anglo-sapphic Ode (Whibley, *Cap and Gown*, p. 136). Kicks up a row, gets drunk, or flanks a tandem whip out of window.

2. (colloquial).—To deliver—a blow or a retort; to push; to hustle; to quoit (Shakspeare). Fr., *flanquer*: as in *flanquer à la porte*, and *Je lui ai flanqué un fameux coup de pied au cul!*

A Plate of Thin Flank, *subs. phr.* (common).—A 'sixpenny cut' off the joint. *See* N. Twill in *Fancy Too Late for Dinner*.

To Flank the whole bottle, *verb. phr.* (American soldiers').—To dodge, *i.e.*, to outflank, to achieve by strategy. For synonyms, *see* Stick.

1871. De Vere, *Americanisms*, p. 286. When the men wished to escape the attention of pickets and guards by slipping past them, they said they flanked them; drill, and detail, and every irksome duty was flanked, when it could be avoided by some cunning trick. Soon, however, honesty itself was thus treated, and the poor farmer was flanked out of his pig and his poultry, and not infrequently even the comrade out of his pipe and tobacco, if not his rations. The height of strategy was employed in these various *flank manœuvres*, when the Commissary could be made to surrender some of his whiskey, and thus it came about, in the South at least, that to flank the whole bottle was a phrase expressive of superlative cunning and brilliant success.

Flanker, *subs.* (common). — A blow; a retort; a kick. *Cf.*, Flank, sense 1.

Flankey, *subs.* (common).—The posteriors. For synonyms, *see* Blind Cheeks and Monocular Eyeglass.

1848. Duncombe, *Sinks of London*, s.v.

Flannel. *See* Hot Flannel.

Flannels. To get one's flannels, *verb. phr.* (schools').—To get a place in the school football or cricket teams, or in the boats. *Cf.*, 'to get one's colours,' or 'one's blue.'

Flap, *subs.* (thieves').—1. Sheet-lead used for roofing. Fr., *doussin*; *noir*. *Cf.*, Bluey.

2. (old).—A blow.

1539. David Lyndsay, *Thrie Estaitis*. Works [Laing, 1879], ii. 73. And to begin the play, tak thair ane flap.

Verb (thieves').—1. To rob; to swindle. For synonyms, *see* Prig and Stick.

2. (common).—To pay; 'to fork out.' *Cf.*, Flap the Dimmock.

3. (venery). — To possess a woman. For synonyms, *see* Greens and Ride.

To Flap a Jay, *verb. phr.* (thieves').—To swindle a greenhorn; to sell a pup (*q.v.*).

1885. *Daily Telegraph*, Aug. 18th, p. 3., col. 1. He and three others of the 'division' had 'cut up' £70 between them, obtained by flapping a jay, which, rendered into intelligible English, means plundering a simple-minded person.

To Flap the Dimmock, *verb phr.* (common).—To pay. [From Flap, a verb of motion + Dimmock = money]. *Cf.*, Flap.

Flapdoodle, *subs.* (colloquial).—1. Transparent nonsense; "kid."

Also Flamdoodle and Flam-sauce, or Flap-sauce. For synonyms, *see* Gammon.

1833. Marryat, *Peter Simple*, ch. xxviii. 'It's my opinion, Peter, that the gentleman has eaten no small quantity of flapdoodle in his lifetime.' 'What's that, O'Brien,' replied I. 'Why, Peter, it's the stuff they feed fools on.'

1861. Hughes, *Tom Brown at Oxford*. I shall talk to our regimental doctors about it, and get put through a course of fools' diet—flapdoodle they call it, what fools are fed on.

1884. S. L. Clemens ('Mark Twain'), *Huck. Finn*, xxv., 247. A speech, all full of tears and flapdoodle about its being a sore trial for him and his poor brother to lose the diseased [deceased].

2. (venery). — The *penis*. (Urquhart). For synonyms, *see* Creamstick and Prick.

To talk Flapdoodle. *verb. phr.* (American).—To brag; to talk nonsense.

1888. *Daily Inter-Ocean*, Mar. 2. Possibly rich men will turn from sharp dealing, from debauchery, from flapdoodle fashion to a common-sense recognition of a situation, which clearly shows that wealth is no longer what it used to be—autocratic, absolute, the ruler of all else.

Flapdoodler, *subs.* (American).—A braggart agitator; one that makes the eagle squeal (*q.v.*).

Flap-dragon, *subs.* (old). — The pox or clap (*q.v.*). For synonyms, *see* Ladies' Fever.

1690. B. E., *New Dict. of the Canting Crew*, s.v. Flapdragon, a clap or pox.

Verb. (old).—To gulp down hastily, as in the game of flap-dragon.

1604. Shakspeare, *Winter's Tale*, Act III., Sc. 3. But, to make an end of the ship: to see how the sea flap-dragoned it!

Flapman, *subs.* (prison). — A convict promoted for good behaviour to first or second class.

Flapper, *subs.* (common). — 1. The hand; also flapper-shaker. For synonyms, *see* Daddle and Mauley.

1833. Marryat, *Peter Simple*, ch. vii. My Dear Mr. Simple, extend your flapper to me for I'm delighted to see you.

1859. Matsell, *Vocabulum or Rogues' Lexicon*, s.v.

1866. *London Miscellany*, May 19, p. 235. 'There's my flapper on the strength of it.' Guy shook hands with the eccentric stranger heartily.

2. (common). — A little girl. [Also a fledgeling wild duck.]

3. (venery).—A very young prostitute; *cf.*, sense 2.

4. (common). — A dustman's or coal-heaver's hat; a fantail (*q.v.*).

5. (in. pl.). — Very long-pointed shoes worn by 'nigger' minstrels.

6. (venery).—The *penis*. (For synonyms, *see* Creamstick and Prick).

7. (colloquial). — A parasite; a remembrancer. (*Cf.* Swift, *Gulliver*, 'Laputa.')

Flapper-shaking, *subs.* (common).—Hand-shaking.

1853. Bradley ('Cuthbert Bede'), *Verdant Green*, pt. II., ch. iv. Wondering whether . . . if the joining palms in a circus was the customary flapper-shaking before 'toeing the scratch' for business.

Flap-sauce. *See* Flapdoodle.

Flare, *subs.* (nautical).—1. Primarily a stylish craft; hence, by implication, anything out of the common. For synonyms, *see* Stunner.

2. (colloquial). — A row; a dispute; a 'drunk'; or spree. *Cf.*, flare-up.

Verb. (thieves'). — 1. Specifically to whisk out; hence, to steal actively, lightly, or delicately.

1850. *Lloyd's Weekly*, 3 Feb. Low Lodging Houses of London. B. tried his pocket saying, 'I'll show you how to do a hankerchief'; but the baker looked round and B. stopped; and just after that I flared it (whisked the handerchief out); and that's the first I did.'

1851-61. Mayhew, *Lond. Lab. and Lond. Poor*, I., 457. Just after that I flared it (a handerchief).

2. (common).—To swagger; to go with a bounce.

1841. Leman Rede, *Sixteen-String Jack*, ii., 3. Crissy Odsbuds, I'll on with my duds, And over the water we'll flare.)

All of a flare, *adv. phr.* (thieves').—Bunglingly.

1839. Brandon, *Poverty, Mendicity, and Crime*, p. 113. Some of the girls at Milberry's pick pockets at night: while one talks to the man, the other robs him; but they are not dextrous, they pull it out all of a flare.

Flaring, *adj.* and *adv.* (colloquial). — Excessive: *e.g.*, a flaring lie; flaring drunk; a flaring whore; *see* Flaming.

Flare-up (or -**Out**), *subs.* (popular). An orgie; a fight; an outburst of temper. Also a spree.

1838. Haliburton, *Clockmaker*, 2 Ser. ch. x. Some of our young citizens . . . got into a flare-up with a party of boatmen that lives in the Mississippi; a desperate row it was too.

1847. *Punch*, vol. XIII., p. 148, Address at the Opening of a Casino. In for flare-up and frolic let us go, And polk it on the fast fantastic toe.

1851. Mayhew, *Lond. Lab. and Lond. Poor*, I., p. 160. These (hot eel) dealers generally trade on their own capital; but when some have been having a flare-up, and have 'broke down for stock' to use the words of my informant, they borrow £1 and pay it back in a week or a fortnight.

1879. Justin M'Carthy, *Donna Quixote*, ch. xvii. Paulina had a hard struggle many a time to keep down her temper, and not to have what she would have called a flare-out.

English Synonyms.—Barney; batter; bean-feast; beano; breakdown; burst; booze (specifically a drinking-bout); caper; devil's delight; dust; fanteague; fight; flare; flats-yad (back slang); fly; gig; hay-bag; hell's delight; high jinks; hooping up; hop; jagg; jamboree; jump; junketting; lark; drive; randan; on the tiles; on the fly; painting the town (American); rampage; razzle-dazzle; reeraw; ructions; shake; shine; spree; sky-wannocking; tear; tear up; toot.

French Synonyms. — *La nocerie* (popular: *une noce à tout casser*; or, *une noce de bâtons de chaise* = a grand jollification); *faire des crêpes* (= to have a rare spree); *badouiller* (popular: especially applied to drinking bouts).

Italian Synonym. — *Far festa alle campane.*

Spanish Synonyms.—*Trapisonda* (a drunken revel); *holgueta.*

Verb (common).—To fly into a passion.

1849. Mahoney, *Rel. Father Prout*, I., 319. 'Vert-Vert, the Parrot.' Forth like a Congreave rocket burst, And storm'd and swore, flared up, and curs'd.

1855. THACKERAY, *Newcomes*, ch. xii. He was in the 'Cave of Harmony,' he says, that night you FLARED UP about Captain Costigan.

1871. *Daily Telegraph*, 8 June, 'Paris in Convalescence.' On this he FLARED UP like a Commune conflagration, and cried out, 'Shame, in the name of religion, art, and history!'

FLASH, *subs.* (old).—1. The vulgar tongue; the lingo of thieves and their associates. TO PATTER FLASH = to talk in thieves' lingo. [The derivation of FLASH, like that of French *argot*, is entirely speculative. It has, however, been generally referred to a district called FLASH (the primary signification as a place name is not clear), between Buxton Leek and Macclesfield: there lived many chapmen who, says Dr. Aiken ("*Description of Country round Manchester*"), 'were known as FLASH-MEN . . . using a sort of slang or cant dialect.']

1718. HITCHIN. *The Regulator of Thieves, etc., with Account of* FLASH *words, etc.* (Title).

1781. G. PARKER, *View of Society*, II., 69. Jigger, being cant or FLASH for door.

1819. MOORE, *Tom Crib's Memorial*, p. 25. With respect to that peculiar language called FLASH, or St. Jiles' Greek, etc.

1830. SIR E. B. LYTTON, *Paul Clifford*, ch. viii. Here a tall gentleman marched up to him, and addressed him in a certain language, which might be called the freemasonry of FLASH.

1839. HARRISON AINSWORTH, *Jack Sheppard* (1889), p. 12. 'What does he say?' roared the long drover. 'He says he don't understand FLASH,' replied the lady in gentleman's attire.

1843-4. HOOD, *Miss Kilmansegg*. His cheeks no longer drew the cash. Because, as his comrades explain'd in FLASH, He had overdrawn his badger.

1827. MAGINN, *Vidocq's Song*. Pattered in FLASH like a covey knowing.

1864. *Athenæum*, 29 Oct. The northern village of ill-repute, and bearing that name (FLASH) gave to felonious high-flying the term FLASH.

1884. HAWLEY SMART, *From Post to Finish*, p. 278. Why, when the late Lord Lytton wrote *Pelham* it was brought against him that 'his knowledge of FLASH was evidently purely superficial.' FLASH, my sister, is merely recondite slang or thieves' argot.

ENGLISH ANALOGUES.—Back Slang or Kacab-Genals (the main principle consists in roughly pronouncing the word backwards, as *erif* for *fire*, *dab* for *bad*, etc.: the practice exists in most languages); CANT (*q.v.*); Centre Slang (the central vowel is made the initial letter, vowels and consonants being added at pleasure); Gammy (North country: mainly composed of Gypsy words); Gibberish (formed by inserting a consonant between each syllable of a word, the result being the F, G, H, M or S gibberish, according to the letter used: thus, "goming mout tomdaym," or "gosings outs tosdays?" = going out to-day?); jargon; the Green Lingo (French thieves'); Marrowskying or Hospital Greek (manufactured by transferring the initial letters of words; *plenty of rain* thus becomes *renty of plain*: the 'Gower St. dialect' of Albert Smith, *Mr. Ledbury*); Pedlar's French (old cant: FLORIO, 1598; COTGRAVE, 1612); RHYMING SLANG (*q.v.*) SLANG (*q.v.*); St. Giles' Greek (last century for Slang as distinguished from Cant); Thieves' Latin; the Vulgar Tongue; YOB-GAB (*q.v.*); NOTIONS (*q.v.*); ZIPH (*q.v.*).

FRENCH AND OTHER ANALOGUES.—*Argot* or *arguche*; *la langue verte* (properly gamesters'); *le langage soudardant* (soldiers'

lingo); *le jars*; *le jargon jobelin*; (COTGRAVE, *Dictionarie*, 1611. *Jargon* = 'Gibridge, fustian language, Pedlar's French, a barbarous jangling'); *le langage de l'artis*; *langage en lem* (formed by prefixing "l" and adding the syllable "em," preceded by the first letter of the word); thus "*main*" becomes "*lainmem*." A similar mode of dealing with words of more than one syllable is to replace the first consonant by the letter "l," the word being followed by its first syllable preceded by "du"; thus, "*jaquette*" becomes "*laquette du jaq*," or if "m" be used as a key-letter, "*maquette du jaq*," etc.; *le javanais* — here the syllable "av" is interpolated; *e.g.*, "*jave l'avai vavu javeudavi*" = (*je l'ai vu jeudi*). GERMAN.—*Rothwalsch* (from *Roter* = beggar or vagabond + *walsch* = foreign); *Gaunersprache* (= thieves' lingo). ITALIAN.—*Lingua gerga* (abbreviated into *gerga*; (FLORIO, 1598 '*gergo* = Pedlar's French, fustian, or roguish language, gibbrish'); *lingua franca* (Levantine: the source of some English slang); *lingua furbesca*. DUTCH.—*Bargoens*. SPANISH.—*Germania* (the Gypsies were supposed to have come from Germany); *jeriganza*. PORTUGUESE.—*Calaõ* (*Zincali* or *Calo* = Gypsy).

2. Hence, at one period, especially during the Regency days, the idiom of the man about town, of Tom and Jerrydom.

1819. MOORE, *Tom Crib's Memorial*, p. xxix. To the cultivation in our times, of the Science of Pugilism, the FLASH language is indebted for a considerable addition to its treasures.

1823. JON BEE, *Dict. of the Turf*, etc. They were invariably thieves and gamblers who used FLASH formerly; but other kinds of persons, now-a-day, who may be rippishly inclined, adopt similar terms and phrases, to evince their uppishness in the affairs of life. These gentlemen also consider all terms of art and of science as FLASH; . . . . of course those words and sayings which are appropriate to the turf, the ring, and field sports, are equally considered as FLASH by them, and the word has been applied (too generally we allow), to all this species of *quid pro quo* lingo.

3. (old).—See quot. and *cf.*, with a Shaksperian gloss of FLASH = a burst of wit or merriment.

1748. T. DYCHE, *Dict.* (5th ed.), FLASH (s.), also a boast, brag, or great pretence made by a spendthrift, quack, or pretender to more art or knowledge than he really has.

4. (old).—A showy swindler. (*e.g.*, the Sir Petronel Flash of quot.); a blustering vulgarian.

1605. MARSTON, JONSON, and CHAPMAN, *Eastward Hoe!* iv. 1. 'Sir Petronel Flash, I am sorry to see such FLASHES come from a gentleman of your quality.

1632. SHIRLEY. *Love in a Maze*, i., 2. The town is full of these vainglorious FLASHES.

5. (old).—A peruke or perriwig.

1690. B. E., *New Dict. of the Canting Crew*, s.v.

1785. GROSE, *Dict. of the Vulgar Tongue*. Rum FLASH, a fine long wig. Queer FLASH, a miserable weather-beaten caxon.

6. (common).—A portion; a drink; or GO (*q.v.*). *Cf.*, FLASH OF LIGHTNING, sense 1.

Adj. (common).—1. Relating to thieves, their habits, customs, devices, lingo, etc.

1782. GEO. PARKER, *Humorous Sketches*, p. 34 No more like a kiddy he'll roll the FLASH song.

1830. LYTTON, *Paul Clifford*, 'Long Ned's Song.' And rarely have the gentry FLASH, In sprucer clothes been seen.

1837. DICKENS, *Oliver Twist*, ch. viii. I suppose you don't know what a beak is, my FLASH com-pan-i-on.

1852. SNOWDON, *Mag. Assistant*' 3rd ed., p. 448. I have seen Cheeks (a FLASH name for an accomplice).

1863. C. READE, *Hard Cash*, II., 244. He used some FLASH words, and they were shown into a public room.

1864. *Cornhill Magazine*, ii., 336. In the following verse, taken from a pet FLASH song, you have a comic specimen of this sort of guilty chivalry.

2. (thieves').—Knowing; expert; showy. *Cf.*, DOWN, FLY, WIDE-AWAKE, etc. Hence (popularly), by a simple transition, vulgarly counterfeit, showily shoddy: possibly the best understood meanings of the word in latter-day English. TO PUT ONE FLASH TO ANYTHING = to put him on his guard; to inform.

1819. MOORE. *Tom Crib's Memorial*, p. 19. Another philosopher, Seneca, has shown himself equally FLASH on the subject.

1835. DICKENS, *Sketches by Boz*, p. 17. Laying aside the knowing look, and FLASH air, with which he had repeated the previous anecdote.

1836. MARRYAT, *Japhet*, etc., ch. lvii. He considered me as . . . a FLASH pickpocket rusticating until some hue and cry was over.

1839. W. H. AINSWORTH, *Jack Sheppard*, p. 138 (ed. 1840). 'Awake! to be sure I am, my FLASH cove,' replied Sheppard.

1865. M. E. BRADDON, *Henry Dunbar*, ch. v. He . . . took out the little packet of bank-notes. 'I suppose you can understand these,' he said. The languid youth . . . looked dubiously at his customer. 'I can understand as they might be FLASH uns,' he remarked, significantly.

1888. C. D. WARNER, *Their Pilgrimage*, p. 157. The FLASH riders or horse-breakers, always called 'broncho busters,' can perform really marvellous feats.

3. (originally thieves', now general). — Vulgar, or blackguardly; showy; applied to one aping his betters. Hence (in Australia), vain glorious or swaggering. The idea conveyed is always one of vulgarity or showy blackguardism.

1830. Sir E. B. LYTTON, *Paul Clifford* (ed. 1854), p. 21. A person of great notoriety among that portion of the *élite* which emphatically entitles itself FLASH.

1861. A. TROLLOPE, *Framley Parsonage*, ch. ix. If the dear friendship of this FLASH Member of Parliament did not represent that value, what else did do so?

1880. G. R. SIMS, *Three Brass Balls*, Pledge xi. The speaker was one of the FLASH young gentlemen who haunt suburban billiard-rooms, who carry chalk in their pockets, and call the marker 'Jack.'

4. (common).—In a set style. Also used substantively.

1819. VAUX, *Flash Dict.*, p. 173. s.v. A person who affects any peculiar habit, as swearing, dressing in a particular manner, taking snuff, etc., merely to be taken notice of is said to do it out of FLASH.

1828. *The English Spy*, vol. I., p. 189. The man upon that half-starved nag Is an Ex S——ff, a strange wag, Half-FLASH and half a clown.

1851. MAYHEW, *Lon. Lab. and Lon. Poor*, i., p. 36. They all of them (coster lads) delight in dressing FLASH as they call it. . . . They try to dress like the men, with large pockets in their cord jackets, and plenty of them. Their trousers, too, must fit tight at the knee, and their boots they like as good as possible. A good 'kingsman,' a plush skull-cap, and a seam down the trousers are the great points of ambition with the coster boys.

[Hence, in combination, FLASH-CASE, CRIB, DRUM, HOUSE, KEN, OR PANNY (*see* FLASH-KEN); FLASH COVE (*q.v.*); FLASH-DISPENSARY (American = a boarding house), especially a swell brothel; FLASH-GENTRY (= the swell mob or higher class of thieves); FLASH-GIRL, MOLL, -MOLLISHER, -PIECE OR -WOMAN (= a showy prostitute); FLASH-JIG (costers' = a favourite dance); FLASH-KIDDY (= a dandy); FLASH-LINGO, OR SONG (=

'patter,' or a song interlarded with cant words and phrases); FLASH-MAN (*q.v.*); FLASH-NOTE (= a spurious bank-note); FLASH-RIDER (American, *see* BRONCHO-BUSTER); FLASH TOGGERY (= smart clothes; FLASH VESSEL (= a gaudy looking, but undisciplined ship)].

1821. EGAN, *Tom and Jerry*, [1890,] p. 58. The rusticity of Jerry was fast wearing off . . . and he bid fair, etc. . . to chaff with the FLASH MOLLISHERS.

1834. AINSWORTH, *Rookwood*, p. Soon then I mounted in Swell St. High, And sported my FLASHIEST TOGGERY.

1851-61. MAYHEW, *Lond. Lab. and Lond. Poor*, I., p. 14. The other dances are jigs—FLASH JIGS—hornpipes in fetters—a dance rendered popular by the success of the noted Jack Sheppard.

Verb (common).—1. To show; to expose.

[Among combinations may be mentioned, TO FLASH ONE'S IVORIES = to show one's teeth, to grin (*Grose*); TO FLASH THE HASH = to vomit (*Grose*); TO FLASH THE DICKEY = to show the shirt front; TO FLASH THE DIBS = to show or spend one's money; TO FLASH A FAWNEY = to wear a ring; TO FLASH ONE'S GAB = to talk, to swagger, to brag; TO FLASH THE BUBS = to expose the paps; TO FLASH THE MUZZLE (*q.v.*); TO FLASH ONE'S TICKER = to air one's watch; TO FLASH THE DRAG = to wear women's clothes for immoral purposes; TO FLASH THE WHITE GRIN = *see* GRIN; TO FLASH IT (*q.v.*), OR TO FLASH ONE'S MEAT (*cf.*, MEAT-FLASHER); TO FLASH A BIT (*q.v.*); TO FLASH THE FLAG = to sport an apron; TO FLASH THE WEDGE = to 'fence' the swag, etc.]

1812. VAUX, *Flash Dict.* Don't FLASH YOUR STICKS, don't expose your pistols.

1819. MOORE, *Tom Crib's Memorial*, p. 2. His lordship, as usual, that very great dab At the flowers of rhet'ric, is FLASHING HIS GAB.

1823. JON BEE, *Dict. of the Turf*, etc. He FLASHED THE BLUNT, made a show of money to dazzle the spectators.

1825. E. KENT, *Modern Flash Dict.* FLASHING HIS IVORY, shew his teeth.

1834. W. H. AINSWORTH, *Rookwood*, (ed. 1864), p. 176.

1837. BARHAM, *Ingoldsby Legends*. 'The Dead Drummer.' When trav'lling, don't FLASH YOUR NOTES OR YOUR CASH Before other people—its foolish and rash.

1887. W. E. HENLEY, *Villon's Good-Night*. Likewise you molls that FLASH YOUR BUBS, For swells to spot and stand you sam.

1887. W. E. HENLEY, *Straight Tip*. Go crying croaks, or FLASH THE DRAG.

TO FLASH A BIT, *verbal phr.* (venery).—To show up; to permit examination; 'TO SPREAD' (*q.v.*); to behave indecently. Said of women only.

TO FLASH IT, OR TO FLASH ONE'S MEAT. — To expose the person. [Hence MEAT-FLASHER] (*q.v.*). Said usually of men.

TO FLASH THE MUZZLE (old). —To produce a pistol.

c. 1823. *Ballad* (quoted in *Don Juan* xi.). On the high toby spice FLASH THE MUZZLE In spite of each gallows old scout.

TO FLASH IT ABOUT, OR TO CUT A FLASH OR DASH, *verbal phr.* (common). — To make a display; to live conspicuously and extravagantly.

1877. *Five Years' Penal Servitude*, ch. iii., p. 220. He FLASHED IT ABOUT a good deal for a long time, going from one place to another. Sometimes he was a lord, at others an earl.

TO GO FLASHING IT, *verb. phr.* (venery).—To have sexual intercourse. For synonyms, *see* GREENS and RIDE.

FLASH-CASE (or -CRIB, -HOUSE, -DRUM, -KEN, -PANNY, etc).—1. A house frequented by thieves, as a tavern, lodging-house, fence (*q.v.*).

1690. B. E., *New Dict. of the Canting Crew* FLASH-KEN, *c.*, a house where thieves use, and are connived at.

1785. GROSE, *Dict. of the Vulgar Tongue*, s.v.

1821. D. HAGGART, *Life*, 'Glossary, p. 172, FLASH-KAIN, a house for receiving stolen goods. [Haggart's spelling, being that of the respectable Edinburgh lawyer who took down his 'confessions' is generally misleading and inaccurate.]

1828. SMEETON, *Doings in London*, p. 39. It is a game in very great vogue among the macers, who congregate nightly at the FLASH-HOUSES.

1830. LYTTON, *Paul Clifford*, p. 50 (ed. 1854). There is one Peggy Lobkins who keeps a public house, a sort of FLASH-KEN called 'The Mug' in Thames Court.

1839. AINSWORTH, *Jack Sheppard* (ed. 1840), p. 271. I've been to all the FLASH-CASES in town, and can hear nothing of him or his wives. . . . *Ibid*, p. 135. 'The Black Lion!' echoed Terence, 'I know the house well; by the same token that it's a FLASH-CRIB.'

2. (common).—A brothel; a haunt of loose women.

1811. *Lexicon Balatronicum* (Flash song quoted under FLASH-PANNEYS). Next for his favourite mot the kiddey looks about, And if she's in a FLASH-PANNY he swears he'll have her out; So he fences all his togs to buy her duds, and then He frisks his master's lob to take her from the bawdy ken.

1830. LYTTON, *Paul Clifford*, ch. xvi. (ed. 1840). You know how little I frequent FLASH-HOUSES.

1837. BARHAM, *Ingoldsby Legends* (ed. 1862), p. 380. Those troublesome swells, Who come from the play-houses, FLASH-KENS, and hells.

1840. MACAULAY, *Essays*: 'Lord Clive.' The lowest wretches that the company's crimps could pick up in the FLASH-HOUSES of London.

1852. BRISTED, *Upper Ten Thousand*, p. 34. That is Mary Black who keeps the greatest FLASH HOUSE in Leonard Street.

FLASH-COVE (also FLASH-COMPANION), *subs.* (common). — A thief; a sharper; a FENCE (*q.v.*).

1825. E. KENT, *Modern Flash Dict.* FLASH-COVE, the keeper of a place for the reception of stolen goods.

1839. H. AINSWORTH, *Jack Sheppard* (1889), p. 60.—'Awake! To be sure I am, my FLASH-COVE!' replied Sheppard.

FLASH-MAN, *subs.* (old). — Primarily a man talking FLASH (*see* quots., 1823 and 1862); hence, a rogue, a thief, the landlord of a FLASH-CASE (*q.v.*). Also a FANCY-JOSEPH (for synonyms, *see* FANCY-MAN). In America, a person with no visible means of support, but living in style and 'showing up' well.

1789. GEO. PARKER, *Life's Painter*, p. 141. A FLASHMAN is one who lives on the hackneyed prostitution of an unfortunate woman of the town.

1823. MONCRIEFF, *Tom and Jerry*, II., 1. Soon one is floored upon the ground. While loud her FLASHMAN cries, 'Arise, my ladybird, arise!'

1823. JON BEE, *Dict. of the Turf*, etc., p. 80. Derived from his language, and this again has its appellation ('tis suggested) from the first FLASH-MEN being highwaymen, that then generally abounded (circa 1770). He is the favorite, or protector of a prostitute, whose FLASH-MAN he is; and she is called inversely, his FLASH-WOMAN.

c. 1833. *Broadside Ballad.* My FLASH-MAN has gone to sea.

1849. *New South Wales, Past, Present, and Future*, ch. i., p. 14. This man was known to Mr. Day to be what is termed a FLASH-MAN; and, seeing his own imminent danger, he instantly spoke to him and called him a cowardly rascal, and offered to give him shot for shot, while he was re-loading.

1859. H. KINGSLEY, *Geoffrey Hamlyn*, ch. v. You're playing a dangerous game, my FLASHMAN.

1862. SMILES, *Lives of the Engineers*, vol. I., pt. 5, ch. i., p. 307. Those articles were sold throughout the country by pedestrian hawkers, most of whom lived in the wild country called THE FLASH, from a hamlet of that name situated between Buxton, Leek, and Macclesfield . . . . Travelling about from fair to fair, and using a cant or slang dialect, they became generally known as FLASH-MEN, and the name still survives (to which may be added: They paid, at first, ready money, but when they had established a credit, paid in promissory notes which were rarely honored.

a. 1873. *Lyra Flagitiosa.* [Quoted in HOTTEN.] My FLASH MAN's in quod, And I'm the gal that's willin', So I'll turn out to-night, And earn an honest shillin'.

FLASH OF LIGHTNING, *subs. phr.* (old).—1. A glass of gin; a dram of neat spirit. *See* GO and DRINKS. Latterly, an 'American drink.' *See* quot. 1862.

1789. GEO. PARKER, *Life's Painter*, p. 164, s.v.

1821. P. EGAN, *Tom and Jerry* (ed. 1890), p. 79. I have not exactly recovered from the severe effects of the repeated FLASHES OF LIGHTNING and strong claps of thunder, with which I had to encounter last night.

1823. JON BEE, *Dict. of the Turf* (quoted in). But ere they homeward pik'd it, A FLASH OF LIGHTNING was sarv'd round to every one as lik'd it.

1830. LYTTON, *Paul Clifford*, (ed. 1854), p. 141. The thunders of eloquence being hushed, FLASHES OF LIGHTNING, or, as the vulgar say, 'glasses of gin' gleamed about.

1851-61. MAYHEW, *Lond. Lab. and Lond. Poor*, i., p. 168. The stimulant of a FLASH OF LIGHTNING . . . for so a dram of neat spirit was then called.

1862. E. MACDERMOTT, *Popular Guide to International Exhibition*, 1862, p. 185. In the vestibule of each refreshment room there is an American bar, where visitors may indulge in . . . gum-ticklers, eye-openers, FLASHES OF LIGHTNING . . . and a variety of similar beverages.

2. (nautical). The gold braid on an officer's cap.

FLASH IN THE PAN, *subs. phr.* (venery). — Connection without emission. *Cf.* DRY-BOB (*q.v.*). Also verbally.

1719. DURFEY, *Pills*, v., 340. Still hawking, still baulking, You FLASH IN THE PAN.

FLASHY, *adj.*, and **FLASHILY**, or **FLASHLY**, *adv.* (old: now colloquial). Empty; showy; tawdry; insipid.

1637. MILTON, *Lycidas*, 123. Their lean and FLASHY songs Grate on their scrannel pipes of wretched straw.

1693. CONGREVE, *Old Batchelor*, Act I., sc. iv. It is oftentimes too late with some of you young, termagant, FLASHY sinners.

1719. DURFEY, *Pills*, etc., ii., 12. A FLASHY town beau.

1748. T. DYCHE, *Dictionary*, (5th ed.) FLASHY (*a*), vain, bragging, boasting, foolish, empty; also anything waterish and unsavoury.

1755. *The World*, No. 149. Whose melodious voices give every syllable (not of a lean and FLASHY, but of a fat and plump song) its just emphasis.

1830. LYTTON, *Paul Clifford*, p. 13, (ed. 1854). Vy it be . . . the gemman vot payed you so FLASHLY.

1857. Song in DUCANGE ANGLICUS, *The Vulgar Tongue*, p. 42. Your fogle you must FLASHLY tie.

1863. SPEKE, *Journal of the Discovery of the Nile*, p. 154. FLASHILY dressed in coloured cloths and a turban, he sat down in one of our chairs.

1864. BRADDON, *Henry Dunbar*, ch. v. But he evinced no bad taste in the selection of a costume. He chose no gaudy colours, or FLASHILY cut vestments.

1873. *Cassell's Magazine*, Jan., p. 246, col. 2. They are rather prone to dress FLASHILY, and wear, when in full fig, no end of jewellery.

1874. MORTIMER COLLINS, *Frances*, ch. xvii. That wild set of people Captain Heath picked up with—members of Parliament and FLASHY young women—all driving four horses, I don't know where.

1882. *Century Magazine*, xxvi., 295. As stones, they were cheap and FLASHY.

FLASH-TAIL, *subs.* (common).—A prostitute.—*See* TAIL.

1868. *Temple Bar*, xxiv., p. 538-9. Picking-up Moll. . . . a FLASHTAIL? a prostitute who goes about the streets at nights trying to pick up toffs.

FLASHER, *subs.* (old). — A highflyer; a fop; a pretender to wit. For synonyms, *see* DANDY. Also (quot. 2), a BONNET (*q.v.*).

1779. D'ARBLAY, *Diary*, etc. (1876). vol. I., p. 185. They are reckoned the FLASHERS of the place, yet everybody laughs at them for their airs, affectations, and tonish graces and impertinences.

1880. *Derbyshire Gatherer*, p. 128. Long before this date (*circa* 1800) the cant name of FLASHER was applied to the man who sat by the table in the gambling-house to swear how many times he had seen lucky gamesters break the bank.

FLASHERY, *subs.* (old).—Inferior, or vulgar, elegance, dash, distinction, display.

FLASH-YAD, *subs.* (back-slang).—A day's enjoyment. For synonyms, *see* FLARE-UP.

FLASHY BLADE or **SPARK**, *subs. phr.* (old).—A DANDY (*q.v.*); now a cheap and noisy swell, whether male or female; *Cf.*, FLASHER.

1719. DURFEY, *Pills, etc.*, vi., 104. In youth a nauseous FLASHY FOP, in elder days a bore.

1819. MOORE, *Tom Crib's Memorial*, p. 40. For though all know that FLASHY SPARK, etc.

FLAT, *subs.* (colloquial).—1. A greenhorn; noddy; gull. For synonyms, *see* BUFFLE and CABBAGE-HEAD; also SAMMY-SOFT.

1762. GOLDSMITH, *Life of Nash*, in wks. p. 546 (*Globe*). Why, if you think me a dab I will get this strange gentleman, or thi-, pointing to the FLAT. Done! cries the sailor, but you shall not tell him.

1789. G. PARKER, *Life's Painter*, p. 142. Who are continually looking out for FLATS, in order to do them upon the broads, that is, cards.

1819. MOORE, *Tom Crib's Memorial*, p. 59. Poor Johnny Raw, what madness could impel, So rum a FLAT to face so prime a swell.

1837. BARHAM, *Ingoldsby Legends*. 'Misadventures at Margate.' He's been upon the mill, And cos he gammons all the FLATS we calls him Veepin Bill.

1841. LYTTON, *Night and Morning*, bk. II., ch. ix. 'Did he pay you for her?' 'Why, to be sure, he gave me a cheque on Coutt's.' 'And you took it? My eyes? what a FLAT.'

1847. THACKERAY, *Vanity Fair*, ch. xiv. I won two hundred of him at the Cocoa-tree. He play, the young FLAT!

1847. *Punch*, vol. XIII., p. 148. It mayn't precisely please the moral FLAT. You won't find fault with it, kind friends, for that.

1848. THACKERAY, *The Book of Snobs*, ch. x. When he does play he always contrives to get hold of a good FLAT.

1857. DUCANGE ANGLICUS, *The Vulgar Tongue*, p. 39. Fawney-droppers gammon the FLATS and take the yokels in.

1866. YATES, *Black Sheep*, I., p. 70. The genius which had hitherto been confined to bridging a pack of cards, or 'securing' a die, talking over a FLAT, or winning money of a greenhorn.

1880. MORTIMER COLLINS, *Thoughts in My Garden*, vol. II., p. 180. Their quack medicines that will cure everything, and their sales of invaluable articles at a loss, and a thousand other devices to catch FLATS.

1887. W. E. HENLEY, *Villon's Good-night.* You FLATS and joskins great and small.

1889. *Pall Mall Gazette*, Sept. 21, p. 3, col. 1 (In a London Gambling Hell). The FLATS who play faro (Cross-heading).

2. (American thieves').—An honest man.

3. (American). A lover's dismissal; a jilting.

Adj. (colloquial and literary). —Downright; plain; straightforward; as in THAT'S FLAT? a FLAT LIE, "FLAT BURGLARY," etc.

1598. SHAKSPEARE, 1 *King Henry IV*, Act I., Sc. 3. *Wor.*: You start away, And lend no ear to my purposes. Those prisoners you shall keep. *Hot.*: Nay, I will; THAT'S FLAT.

1835-40. HALIBURTON, *The Clockmaker*, p. 6, preface (ed. 1862).

1848. LOWELL, *Fable for Critics*, p 19. (A fetch, I must say, most transparent and FLAT).

[There are other usages, more or less colloquial: *e.g.*, Insipid; tame; dull: as in Macaulay's "FLAT as champagne in decanters." On the Stock Exchange, FLAT = without interest: Stock is borrowed FLAT when no interest is allowed by the lender as security for the due return of the scrip.]

Verb (American). To jilt. *Cf.*, *subs.*, sense 3. For synonyms, *see* MITTEN.

1871. DE VERE, *Americanisms*, p. 602. To FLAT, in the West, means to jilt, and is probably derived from another slang phrase, 'to feel flat,' denoting the depression which is apt to follow such a disappointment.

TO FEEL FLAT, *verb. phr.* (American). — 1. To be low-spirited; out of sorts; OFF COLOUR (*q.v.*).

1838. J. C. NEAL, *Charcoal Sketches*. Not to hurt a gentleman's feelings and to make him FEEL FLAT afore the country.

2. (American).—To fail; to give way. Also used substantively.

FLAT AS A FLOUNDER (or PANCAKE), *phr.* (colloquial). — Very flat indeed. Also FLAT AS BE BLOWED.

1882. *Punch*, vol. LXXXII, p. 177, col. 1.

TO BRUSH UP A FLAT. *See* BRUSHER.

TO PICK UP A FLAT, *verb. phr.* (prostitutes'). To find a client. Fr., *lever* or *faire un miché* (*miche* = bread, from *michon* = money. Compare BREADWINNER: under MONOSYLLABLE (*q.v.*)).

1869. GREENWOOD, *Seven Curses of London*. On the chance that she will, in the course of the evening, PICK UP A FLAT.

TO HAVE (OR DO) A BIT OF FLAT, *verb. phr.* (venery).—To indulge in sexual intercourse. For synonyms, *see* GREENS and RIDE.

FLAT-BACK, *subs.* (common).—A bed-bug. For synonyms, *see* NORFOLK HOWARD.

FLAT-BROKE, *adj.* (colloquial).—Utterly ruined; DEAD-BROKE (*q.v.*).

FLAT-CATCHER, *subs.* (common).—An impostor.

1823. MONCRIEFF, *Tom and Jerry*, i., 6. *Cope* (speaking of a horse). Well, Master Gull'em, do you think we shall get the FLAT-CATCHER off to-day?

1841. *Blackwood's Mag.*, I., 202. Buttoners are those accomplices of thimble-riggers . . . whose duty it is to act as FLAT-CATCHERS or decoys, by personating flats.

1856. MAYHEW, *Great World of London*, p. 46. And FLAT-CATCHERS, or 'ring-droppers,' who cheat by pretending to find valuables in the street.

1864. *London Review*, June 18, p. 643. 'The Bobby' or chinked-back horse, is another favourite FLAT-CATCHER.

1869. WHYTE-MELVILLE, *M. or N.*, p. 110. Rather a FLAT-CATCHER, Tom? said that nobleman, between the whiffs of a cigar.

FLAT-CATCHING, *subs.* (common). —Swindling.

1821. EGAN, *Tom and Jerry*, p. 118, The no-pinned hero, on being elevated. gave, as a toast, 'Success to FLAT-CATCHING,' which produced roars of laughter and shouts of approbation.

1869. GREENWOOD, *Seven Curses of London*. To mark the many kinds of bait that are used in FLAT-CATCHING, as the turf slang has it.

FLATCH, *adj.* (back-slang).—A half. FLATCH-KENNURD = half drunk; FLATCH-YENORK = half-a-crown; FLATCH-YENNEP = a half-penny (*see subs.*, sense 1).

Subs. 1.—A half-penny. [An abbreviation of FLATCH-YENNEP.] For synonyms, *see* MAG.

c. 1866. VANCE, *The Chickaleary Cove*. I doesn't care a FLATCH as long as I've a tach.

2 (coiners'). — A counterfeit half-crown. For synonyms, *see* MADZA.

FLAT-CAP, *subs.* (old).—A nickname for a citizen of London. [In Henry the Eight's time flat round caps were the pink of fashion; but when their date was out, they became ridiculous. The citizens continued to wear them long after they were generally disused, and were often satirized for their fidelity].

1596. BEN JONSON, *Every Man in H.*, ch. ii., v. 1. Mock me all over From my FLAT-CAP unto my shining shoes.

1602. DEKKER, *Honest Whore*. Old Plays, iii., 304. Come, Sirrah, you FLAT-CAP, where be those whites?

1605. MARSTON, *Dutch Court*, ii., 1. Wealthy FLAT-CAPS that pay for their pleasure the best of any men in Europe.

1613. BEAUMONT and FLETCHER, *Hon. Man's Fort.*, v. 3. Trade? to the city, child: a FLAT-CAP will become thee.

FLAT-COCK, *subs.* (old).—A female. [GROSE, 1785.] For synonyms, see PETTICOAT.

FLAT-FEET, *subs.* (common).—Specifically the Foot Guards, but also applied to other regiments of the line. Also (generally with some powerful adjective), applied to militia men to differentiate them from linesmen. For synonyms, see MUD-CRUSHER.

FLAT-FISH, (generally, A REGULAR FLAT-FISH) *subs.* (common).—A dullard. [A play upon FLAT =stupid, and FISH = something to HOOK or catch.] For synonyms, see BUFFLE, CABBAGE-HEAD, and SAMMY-SOFT. *Cf.*, Fr., *platpied* = a contemptible fellow.

FLAT-FOOTED, *adj.* (American).—Downright; resolute; honest. [Western: the simile, common to most languages, is of a man standing, his back to the wall, resolute to accomplish his purpose.]

1858. *Harper's Magazine*, Sept. His herculean frame, and bold, FLAT-FOOTED way of saying things, had impressed his neighbours, and he held the rod in terrorism over them.

1871. *Philadelphia Bulletin*, Mar. 23. 'The row at St. Clement's Church.' Now the Committee of the vestry put their FOOT FLATLY down on auricular confession and priestly absolution.

1887. R. A. PROCTOR, *Knowledge*, June 1. When, in America, General Grant said he had PUT HIS FOOT DOWN and meant to advance in that line if it took him all the summer, he conveyed . . . the American meaning of the expression FLAT-FOOTED.

FLAT-HEAD, *subs.* (American).—A greenhorn; a SAMMY-SOFT (*q.v.*).

FLAT-IRON, *subs.* (common).—A corner public house. [From the triangular shape.]

FLATTIE or **FLATTY**, *subs.* (common).—A gull. [A diminutive of FLAT, sense I.] Formerly cheap-jacks' = one in a new 'pitch.'

1851-61. MAYHEW, *Lond. Lab. and Lond. Poor*, vol. I., p. 232. They betray to the FLATTIES (natives) all their profits and proceedings.

FLAT-MOVE, *subs.* (old). — An attempt or project that miscarries; folly and mismanagement generally.—GROSE.

FLATS, *subs.* (old). 1. Playing cards. For synonyms, see KING'S Books.

1821. HAGGART, *Life*, p. 56. We played at FLATS in a budging-crib.

2. (old). — False dice. For synonyms, see FULHAMS.

3. (old).—Base money.

MAHOGANY FLATS, *subs. phr.* (common).—Bed-bugs. For synonyms, see NORFOLK HOWARDS.

FLATS AND SHARPS, *subs. phr.* (old).—Weapons.

1818. SCOTT, *Heart of Midlothian*, ch. xxx. 'I have known many a pretty lad cut short in his first summer upon the road, because he was something hasty with his FLATS AND SHARPS.'

FLATTEN OUT, *verb. phr.* (American). —To get the better of (in argument or fight). For synonyms, see FLOOR. FLATTENED-OUT = ruined; beaten.

FLATTER-TRAP, *subs.* (common).—The mouth. Fr., *la menteuse*, but for synonyms, see POTATO-TRAP.

1859. MATSELL, *Vocabulum, or Rogue's Lexicon*, s.v.

FLATTY-KEN, *subs.* (thieves')—See quot.

1851-61. MAYHEW, *Lond. Lab. and Lond. Poor*, vol. I., p. 261. Some take up their abode in what they call FLATTY-KENS, that is, houses the landlord of which is not 'awake' or 'fly' to the 'moves' and dodges of the trade.

FLAWED, *ppl. adj.* (common).—1. Half drunk; 'a little crooked'; quick-tempered.—GROSE. For synonyms, see DRINKS and SCREWED.

2. (venery).—'Cracked in the ring'; *i.e.*, deflowered.

FLAY (or FLAY THE FOX), *verb. phr.* (old).—To vomit: 'from the subject to the effect,' says COTGRAVE; 'for the flaying of so stinking a beast is like enough to make them spue that feel it.'

Now, TO SHOOT THE CAT. For synonyms, see ACCOUNTS and CAST UP ACCOUNTS. *Cf.*, FOX, *verb*, sense I.

1653. URQUHART, *Rabelais*, bk. I., ch. xi. He would FLAY THE FOX.

2. (American).—To clean out by unfair means.

TO FLAY or SKIN A FLINT, *verb. phr.* (old).—To be mean or miserly. See SKINFLINT.

1690. B. E., *New Dict. of the Canting Crew*, s.v. He'll FLAY or SKINN A FLINT of a Meer Scrat or Miser.

1833. MARRYAT, *Peter Simple*, vol. II., p. 194 (ed. 1846). Report says she would SKIN A FLINT if she could.

FLAYBOTTOM or **FLAYBOTTOMIST**, *subs.* (common). — A schoolmaster, with a play on the word phlebotomist = a blood-letter.—GROSE. Fr., *fouette-cul*; and (COTGRAVE) "*Fesse-cul*, a pedantical whip-arse."

FLAVOUR, TO CATCH (or GET) THE FLAVOUR. *verb. phr.* (common). — 1. To be intoxicated. For synonyms, see DRINKS and SCREWED.

2. (venery). To be 'half-on' for coition; to wax PROUD (*q.v.*): said of men and women both.

FLAX, *verb.* (American).—To beat severely; TO GIVE IT HOT (*q.v.*). For synonyms, see TAN.

FLAX-WENCH, *subs.* (old). — A prostitute. For synonyms, see BARRACK-HACK and TART.

1604. SHAKSPEARE, *Winter's Tale*, i., 2. My wife's a hobby-horse; deserves a name As rank as any FLAX-WENCH.

2

FLEA. TO SEND AWAY WITH A FLEA IN THE EAR. *verb. phr.* (common).—To dismiss with vigour and acerbity.

1854. *Notes and Queries*, 8 Apl., p. 322, col. 2. The luckless applicant is peremptorily dismissed with an imperative flee!' . . . or, facetiously, WITH A FLEE IN HIS EAR.

TO HAVE A FLEA IN THE EAR = (1) to fail in an enterprise; and (2) to receive a scolding, or annoying suggestion.

TO SIT ON A BAG OF FLEAS. *verb. phr.* (common). — To sit uncomfortably; ON A BAG OF HEN FLEAS = very uncomfortably indeed.

TO CATCH FLEAS FOR, *verb. phr.* (venery).—To be on terms of extreme intimacy: *e.g.*, 'I catch her fleas for her' = She has nothing to refuse me. *Cf.*, Shakspeare (*Tempest*, III. 2.), 'Yet a tailor might scratch her wheree'er she did itch.'

IN A FLEA'S LEAP, *adv. phr.* (old).—In next to no time; INSTANTER (*q.v.*).

FLEA-AND-LOUSE, *subs.* (rhyming slang). A house. For synonyms, see KEN.

FLEA-BAG, *subs.* (common). — A bed; Fr. *un pucier*. For synonyms, see KIP.

1839. LEVER, *Harry Lorrequer*, ch. xl. 'Troth, and I think the gentleman would be better if he went off to his FLEA-BAG himself.'

LEA-BITE, *subs.* (old).—A trifle.

1630. TAYLOR, *Works*. If they doe lose by pirates, tempests, rocks, 'Tis but a FLEABITE to their wealthy stockes; Whilst the poore cutpurse day and night doth toile, Watches and wardes, and doth himselfe turmoile.

1785. GROSE, *Dict. Vulg. Tongue*, s.v.

FLEA-BITING, *subs.* (old).—A trifle.

1621. BURTON, *Anatomy of Melancholy*. Their miseries are but FLEA BITINGS to thine.

FLEA- (or FLAY-) **FLINT**, *subs.* (old.)—A miser: *Cf.*, SKIN FLINT (*q.v.*).

1719. DURFEY, *Pills*, etc., i., 141 The FLEA-FLINTS . . . strip me bare.

FLEAR, *verb.* (old).—To grin. A FLEARING FOOL = a grinning idiot.

1690. B. E., *New Dict. of the Canting Crew.*

FLEECE, *subs.* (old). — An act of theft. *Cf.*, old proverb, 'to go out to shear and come home shorn.' For synonyms, see SKIN.

1690. B. E., *New Dict. of the Canting Crew*. FLEECE, to Rob, Plunder, or strip.

1703. MRS. CENTLIVRE, *Beau's Duel*, ii., 2. Had a FLEECE at his purse.

2. (venery). — The female pubic hair. Fr. *toison* (BAUDELAIRE); It., *barbiglioni* (FLORIO). For foreign synonyms, see MOTT.

ENGLISH SYNONYMS. — Banner (Durfey); bandoliers (old); beard; bearskin; belly-bristles; belly-thicket; belly-whiskers; Boskage of Venus; broom; brush; bush; cat-skin; cloverfield; cunny-skin (Durfey); Cupid's Arbour; cunt-curtain; damber-, dilberry-, gooseberry-, furze-, quim-, or whin-bush; down; Downshire; front-doormat; feather (Prior and Moore); fluff; forest (Donne); fud (Burns); fur; fur-below (old catch); 'grove of eglantine' (Carew); hedge on

the dyke; lower-wig (Burton); moss; mott-carpet; mustard-and-cress; nether eye-brow (or -lashes); nether-whiskers; parsley (Durfey); plush; quim-whiskers; quim-wig; scut (Shakspeare); shaving-brush (*cf.*, LATHER); scrubbing-brush; shrubbery; sporran; stubble (*see* POINTER); sweet-briar; thatch; tail-feathers; 'toupee;' 'tufted honours'; twat-rug.

Verb (now recognised). — To cheat; to shear or be shorn (as a sheep).

1593. NASHE, *Christ's Teares*, in wks. (Grosart) IV. 140. Tell me (almost) what gentleman hath been cast away at sea, or disasterly souldiourizd it by lande, but they (usurers) have enforst him thereunto by their FLEECING.

1598. SHAKSPEARE, *I King Henry IV.*, ii., 2. Down with them: FLEECE them!

1620. DEKKER, *His Dreame*, in wks. (Grosart) III. 52. Catchpolles and varlets, who did poore men FLEECE (To their undoing) for a twelve-peny peece.

1712. ARBUTHNOT, *Hist. of John Bull*, pt. IV., ch. ii. When a poor man has almost undone himself for thy sake, thou art for FLEECING him.

1822. SCOTT, *Fort. of Nigel*, ch. xxiii. He is now squeezed and FLEECED by them on every pretence.

1836. M. SCOTT, *Cruise of the Midge*, p. 106. He was stabbed by the Ragamuffin he had FLEECED.

1849. THACKERAY, *Pendennis*, ch' xxxi. Bloundell is a professional blackleg, and travels the Continent, where he picks up young gentlemen of fashion and FLEECES them.

1859. *Times*, 25 Oct. 'Review of Dean Ramsay's *Reminiscences*.' I don't know whether they are black or white sheep, but I know that if they are long there they are pretty certain to be FLEECED.

1891. *Licensed Victuallers' Gazette*, 16 Jan. How you would be FLEECED! You've got a lot to learn yet.

Hence FLEECED = ruined; DEAD-BROKE (*q.v.* for synonyms).

FLEECER, *subs.* (old).—A thief.

1600-69. PRYNNE, *Breviate*. Not FLEECERS, but feeders.

FLEECE-HUNTER, or **-MONGER**, *subs. phr.* (venery).—A whoremaster. For synonyms, see MOLROWER.

FLEETER-FACE, *subs.* (old.)—A pale-face; a coward. *Cf.*, Shakspeare's 'cream-faced loon.'

1647. BEAUMONT and FLETCHER, *Queen of Corinth*. You kncw where you are, you FLEETER-FACE.

FLEET-NOTE, *subs.* (old).—A forged note.

1821. *Real Life in London.*

FLEET OF THE DESERT, *subs. phr.* (common). — A caravan; *cf.*, SHIP OF THE DESERT = camel.

FLEET-STREET, *subs. phr.* (colloquial).—The estate of journalism, especially journalism of the baser sort.

FLEET-STREETER, *subs.* (colloquial).—A journalist of the baser sort; a spunging PROPHET (*q.v.*); a sharking dramatic critic; a SPICY (*q.v.*) paragraphist; and so on.

FLEET-STREETESE, *subs. phr.* (colloquial). — The so-called English, written to sell by the FLEET-STREETER (*q.v.*), or baser sort of journalist: a mixture of sesquipedalians and slang, of phrases worn threadbare and phrases sprung from the kennel; of bad grammar and worse manners; the like of which is impossible outside FLEET-STREET (*q.v.*), but which in FLEET-STREET commands a price, and enables not a few to live.

FLEG, *verb.* (old). — To whip. BAILEY.

FLEMISH ACCOUNT, *subs. phr.* (old).—A remittance less than was expected; hence, an unsatisfactory account. [Among the Flemings (the merchants of Western Europe when commerce was young) accounts were kept in livres, sols, and pence; but the livre or pound only = 12s., so that what the Antwerp merchant called one livre thirteen and fourpence would in English currency be only 20s.]

1668. T. BROWN, *The Accurate Accomptant*, etc. Quoted in *N. and Q.* I. S. I., 286. London, August 10th, 1668. To Roger Pace, Factor, etc., for 10 pieces cont. 746 Ells Fl. at 10s. Flem. per Ell is £373 Flem. Exchange at 35s. makes Sterling Money £213 2s. 10d.

1774–1826. *Typ. Antiq.*, p. 1773. A person resident in London is said to have had most of Caxton's publications. He sent them to Amsterdam for inspection, and on writing for them was informed that they had been destroyed by accident. 'I am very much afraid,' says Herbert, 'my kind friend received but a FLEMISH ACCOUNT of his Caxton's.

1785. GROSE. *Dict. Vulg. Tong.* FLEMISH ACCOUNT, a losing or bad account.

FLESH, *subs.* (old).—Generic for the organs of generation, male or female. Also (of women) FLESHLY-PART.

1604. SHAKSPEARE, *Winter's Tale*, iv., 3. She would not exchange FLESH with one that loved her.

1605. *Cymbeline*, i., 5. If you buy ladies' FLESH at a million a dram you cannot preserve it from tainting.

1620. PERCY. *Folio MSS.* [Hales & Furnivall, 1867]. 'As I was ridinge by the way.' Sweet hart, shall I put my FLESH in thine?

FLESH, *verb.*, or, **FLESH IT**; or, **TO BE FLESHED IN** (venery).—To have carnal knowledge of—to be 'one flesh with'—a woman. [For synonyms, *see* GREENS and RIDE.] An equivalent in the passive sense is TO FEEL HIS FLESH IN ONE'S BODY (said by women only).

1598. FLORIO, *A Worlde of Wordes*, *Andar in Carnafau*. To go a FLESHING or a wenching: (*Carnafau*=the brat-gettingplace; the hole of content).

FLESH AND BLOOD, *subs. phr.* (common).—Brandy and port in equal proportions. *See* DRINKS.

FLESH-BAG, *subs.* (common). — A shirt or chemise.

ENGLISH SYNONYMS.—Biled rag (American); camesa; carrion-case; commission; dickey (formerly a worn-out shirt); gad (gips); lully; mill tog; mish; narp (Scots'); shaker; shimmy (=a chemise, Marryat); smish.

FRENCH SYNONYMS. — *Une liquette* or *limace* (thieves': from the Gypsy. The form also occurs also in the Italian *lima*); *un panais* (popular).

GERMAN SYNONYMS.—*Kamis*, *Kamsel*, *Kemsel*, or *Gemsel* (from med. Lat., *Camisiale*; Fr. *camisole*); *Kesones*, *Kusones*, or *Ksones* (also = cotton and underclothing); *Staude* or *Stauden*; *Hanfstandt* (*Liber Vagatorum*: literally *hempshrub*).

ITALIAN SYNONYM. — *Lima* (*see* Fr., *limace*).

1820. *London Magazine*, I., 29. They are often without a FLESH-BAG to their backs.

FLESH-BROKER, *subs.* (old).—1. A match-maker.

1690. B.E., *New Dict. of the Canting Crew.* FLESH-BROKER, a match-maker; also a bawd; between whom but little difference, for they both (usually) take money.

2. A procuress [GROSE]. *Cf.*, FLESH-FLY, FLESH-MONGER, and FLESH-MARKET. For synonyms, *see* MOTHER.

FLESH-FLY (also, FLESH-MAGGOT), *subs.* (old). — A whoremaster. For synonyms, *see* MOLROWER.

1781. COWPER, *Progress of Error*, 323-324. Oh! that a verse had power, and could command far, Far away, these FLESH-FLIES of the land.

FLESH-MARKET, or **FLESH-SHAMBLES**, *subs.* (common).—A brothel or FLASH-HOUSE (*q.v.*); also the pavement, in Piccadilly or Regent-street, for instance, where whores do congregate. *Cf.*, MEATMARKET.

1668. JOHN DAY, *Humour out of Breath*, II. *I Asp.* . . . . She may bee well discended; if shee be, Shee's fit for love, and why not then for me. *Boy.* And you be not fitted in Venice 'tis straunge, for 'tis counted the best FLESH-SHAMBLES in Italie.

FLESH-MONGER, *subs.* (old).—A procurer; a whore-master. [From Eng. FLESH + MONGER]. For synonyms, *see* MOTHER and MOLROWER. *Cf.*, FLESH-FLY, FLESH-MARKET, and FLESH-BROKER.

1603. SHAKSPEARE, *Measure for Measure*, V., 1. And was the duke a FLESH-MONGER, a fool, and a coward, as you then reported him to be?

FLESHMONGERING. TO GO FLESH-MONGERING, *verb. phr.* (venery).—To quest for women; to GO ON THE PROWL (*q.v.*)., or AFTER MEAT. *See* GREENS and RIDE.

FLESH-POT. SIGHING FOR THE FLESH-POTS OF EGYPT. *phr.* (common).—Hankering for good things no longer at command. [Biblical].

1884. HAWLEY SMART, *From Post to Finish*, p. 131. Do you think it is a HANKERING AFTER THE FLESH-POTS, and that the canon's cook reconciles me to the canon's opinions?

FLESH-TAILOR, *subs.* (old). — A surgeon. For synonyms, *see* SAWBONES.

1633. FORD, *'Tis Pity She's a Whore*, iii. Oh, help! help! help! Oh, for a FLESH-TAILOR quickly.

FLESHY, *subs.* (Winchester College).—*See* CAT'S HEAD.

FLETCH, *subs.* (prison). A spurious coin. *Cf.*, FLATCH.

FLICK, or **FLIG**, *subs.* (colloquial). —1. A cut with a whip-lash; hence, a blow of any sort. A FLICKING is often administered by schoolboys with a damp towel or pocket-handkerchief. For synonyms, *see* TANNING.

1750. FIELDING, *Tom Jones*, bk. VI., ch. ii. 'I do know you are a woman,' cries the squire, 'and it's well for thee, that art one; if had'st been a man, I promise thee I had lent thee a FLICK long ago.

1787. GROSE, *Provincial Glossary*, s.v. VLICK.

2. (common).—A jocular salutation; usually OLD FLICK. *Cf.*, CODGER and MY TULIP.

1883. *Punch*, 28 July, p. 38, col. 1. Well, last night, They'd a feet in these gardens, OLD FLICK, as was something too awfully quite.

Verb. (thieves').—1. To cut.

1690. B.E., *New Dict. of the Canting Crew.* FLICKING, *c.*, to cut, cutting.

1728. BAILEY, *Eng. Dict.* (FLICK is given as a 'country word').

1785. GROSE, *Dict. Vulg. Tongue.* FLICK me some pannam and cassan, cut me some bread and cheese; FLICK the peter, cut off the cloak bag or portmanteau.

1791. CAREW, *Life and Adventures*, q.v.

1837. DISRAELI, *Venetia*, ch. xiv. FLICK the bread, cut the bread.

1859. MATSELL, *Vocabulum or Rogue's Lexicon*, s.v. FLICK the Peter and rake the swag for I want to pad my beaters.

2. (colloquial). — To strike with, or as with, a whip.

1836. DICKENS, *Pickwick*, ch. xliii. Near him, leaning listlessly against the wall, stood a strong-built countryman, FLICKING with a worn-out hunting whip the top-boot that adorned his right foot.

1852. DICKENS, *Bleak House*, ch. xxvii. Who . . . receives this compliment by FLICKING Mr. George in the face with a head of greens.

1854. *Our Cruise in the Undine*, p. 103. It appeared to us that one of the most frequent, and therefore we supposed the principal stroke aimed at (in a Heidelberg duel), was to strike your sword low down, perhaps four inches from the handle, upon your adversary's bandaged arm, so that the end of the weapon (the only part that is sharpened) should FLICK itself against your opponent's face.

1863. HON. MRS. NORTON, *Lost and Saved*, p. 29. Drivers shouting, swearing, and FLICKING at the horses.

FLICKER, *subs.* (Old Cant). — A drinking glass.

1690. B.E., *New Dict. of the Canting Crew.* FLICKER, *c.*, a drinking-glass. FLICKER SNAPT, *c.*, the glass is broken; NIM THE FLICKER, *c.*, steal the glass; RUM FLICKER, *c.*, a large glass or rummer; QUEER FLICKER, *c.*, a green or ordinary glass.

FRENCH SYNONYMS. — *Une lampe* (masons'); *un guindal* (popular); *un godet* (very old); *une gobette* (thieves'); *un gobeson* (thieves').

Verb. 1. To drink.—MATSELL.

2. (old).—To laugh wantonly; also to kiss, or lewdly fondle a woman.—PALSGRAVE. For synonyms, *see* FIRKYTOODLE.

1690. B. E., *New Dict. of the Canting Crew*, s.v. FLICKER, to grin or flout.

Also FLICKING = (1) drinking, and (2) wanton laughter.

LET HER FLICKER, *phr.* (American).—Said of any doubtful issue: 'let the matter take its chance.'

FLICKET-A-FLACKET, *adv.* (old). —Onomatopoetic for a noise of flapping and flicking.

1719. DURFEY, *Pills*, etc., ii., 20. Their bellies went FLICKET-A-FLACKET.

FLIER or **FLYER**, *subs.* (racing and yachting).—1. A horse or boat of great speed; also (American railway) a fast train; hence, by implication, anything of excellence. *Cf.*, DASHER, DAISY, etc. Also *adj.*, = keen for.

1865. BRADDON, *Henry Dunbar*, ch. xxii. The mare's in splendid condition; well, you saw her take her trial gallop the other morning, and you must know she's a FLIER, so I won't talk about her.

1884. HAWLEY SMART, *From Post to Finish*, p. 156. Atalanta might be a FLYER, but an artist like Pycroft, with a clever colt like Newsmonger under him, was quite likely to outride whatever boy Mr. Pipes might now be able to pick up.

1888. *St. Louis Globe-Democrat*, 2 Mar. In spite of the strike passenger trains, what are known as the FLYERS, are running with reasonable regularity.

1890. *Bird o' Freedom*, 19 Mar., p. 1, col. 1. Clearly the G.O.M. is no FLIER over this course.

1891. *Licensed Victuallers' Gazette*, 20 Mar. Although he may doubtless be made a good deal better he may turn out to be no FLIER.

1891. BURY AND HILLIER. *Cycling*, p. 6. A moderate rider, not being an athlete or a FLIER . . . can . . . get over in an hour seven or eight miles of ground on a tricycle.

1891. *Anti-Jacobin*, 23 May, p. 400. When Dangerous, Plenipotentiary, Bay Middleton, and other FLYERS ran.

1891. *Morning Advertiser*, 28 Mar. In any event, he was never a FLYER at breakfast. But late at night, and when, perhaps, he tumbled across something equivalent to woodcock, tripe and onions, or a hot lobster, say, why then, take my word for it, he made up for previous abstinence.

1891. *National Observer*, 1 Aug. It remains to be seen whether large yachts constructed on the same principle will be equally invincible: that is, if the FLYERS we have are one and all to disappear.

2. (football).—A shot in the air. *See* MADE-FLYER.

3. (American).—A small handbill; a DODGER (*q.v.*).

TO TAKE A FLIER (American trade).—1. To make a venture; to invest against odds.

2. (venery). — To copulate in haste (GROSE); to do a FAST-FUCK (*q.v.*).

FLIES, *subs.* (rhyming). — Lies. Hence, nonsense; trickery; deceit.

THERE ARE NO FLIES ON ME, ON HIM, etc., *phr.* (common).—'I am dealing honestly with you;' 'he is genuine, and is not humbugging.' In America, the expression is used of (1) a man of quick parts, a man who 'knows a thing without its being kicked into him by a mule'; and (2) a person of superior breeding or descent. Sometimes the phrase is corrupted into 'no fleas.' *See* GAMMON.

1868. DIPROSE, ST. CLEMENT DANES, *Past and Present.* To Deaf Burke, the celebrated pugilist, is attributed the old story of the 'flies and the gin and water;' and hence the term 'no flies' became prevalent. Burke had ordered . . . . some 'hot and strong and a dash of lemon,' The goblet was brought . . . . Burke raised . . . the nectar to his lips, and beheld some dissipated flies lying at the bottom of the tumbler; he placed the glass on the table, and deliberately removed the flies with the spoon, five or six in number, and laid them side by side before him, and then giving a hearty pull at the gin and water, he as deliberately replaced the flies . . . . and passed it to his friend. His companion stared angrily. 'Do you dare to insult me, and in the presence of company?' said the irate *vis-à-vis*. 'Pardon me,' replied Burke, quietly handing the glass a second time, 'though I don't drink FLIES myself, I didn't know but what others might.'

1888. *Detroit Free Press*, 25 Aug. THERE AIN'T NO FLIES ON HIM, signifies, that he is not quiet long enough for moss to grow on his heels, that he is wide awake.

1888. *Missouri Republican*, 24 Feb. People who are capable of descending to New York and Boston English are fully justified in saying that THERE ARE NO FLIES ON ST. LOUIS or the St. Louis delegation either.

FLIGGER (also FLICKER), *verb.* (old). —To grin.

1720. DURFEY *Pills*, etc., vi., 267. He FLIGGERED, and told me for all my brave alls He would have a stroke.

FLIM.—*See* FLIMSY.

FLIM-FLAM, *subs.* (old).—An idle story; a sham; a ROBINHOOD TALE (*q.v.*). A duplication of FLAM (*q.v.*).

1589. *Pappe with an Hatchet* (ed. 1844) p. 39. Trusse up thy packet of FLIM-FLAMS, and roage to some countrey faire, or read it among boyes in the belfrie.

1630. TAYLOR, *Workes.* They with a courtly tricke, or a FLIM-FLAM, do nod at me, whilst I the noddy am.

1750. FIELDING, *Tom Jones*, bk. XVIII., ch. xii. I thought thou had'st been a lad of higher mettle than to give way to a parcel of maidenish tricks. I tell thee 'tis all FLIM-FLAM.

1780. MRS. COWLEY, *The Belle's Stratagem*, iii., 1. Mr. Curate, don't think to come over me with your FLIM-FLAMS, for a better man than ever trod in your shoes is coming over-sea to marry me.

1805. ISAAC DISRAELI, FLIM-FLAMS; *or the Life and Errors of my Uncle, and the Amours of my Aunt* [title].

1825. C. LAMB, *Munden* (in *London Magazine*) Feb. I wonder you can put such FLIM-FLAMS upon us, sir.

Adj. (old).—Idle; worthless.

1589. NASHE, *Month's Minde*, in wks. Vol. I., p. 174. But to leaue thy FLIM-FLAM tales and loytering lies.

1598. FLORIO, *A Worlde of Wordes*. *Filastroccola*, FLIM-FLAM tales, old wiues tales as they tell when they spinne, a tale without rime or reason, or head or foote.

1633. T. NEWTON, *Lennie's Touchstone of Complexions*, p. 120. Reporting a FLIM-FLAM tale of Robin Hood.

1750. OZELL'S *Rabelais*, vol. V., p. 247. Glibly swallow down every FLIM-FLAM story that's told them.

1853. LYTTON, *My Novel*, bk. X., ch. xix. I wish you'd mind the child—it is crumpling up and playing almighty smash with that FLIM-FLAM book, which cost me one pound one.

FLIMP, *verb.* (thieves')—1. To hustle or rob. TO PUT ON THE FLIMP = to rob on the highway. For synonyms, *see* CRACK and PRIG.

1839. BRANDON, *Poverty, Mendicity, and Crime*, p. 111. To take a man's watch is to FLIMP him, it can only be done in a crowd, one gets behind and pushes him in the back, while the other in front is robbing him.

1857. SNOWDEN, *Mag. Assistant*, 3rd ed., p. 445, s.v.

2. (venery). — To copulate. For synonyms, *see* RIDE.

FLIMPING, *subs.* (thieves').—Stealing from the person.

1857. DUCANGE ANGLICUS, *The Vulgar Tongue*, p. 38. He told me as Bill had FLIMPED a yack.

1862. *Cornhill Mag.*, vol. vi., p. 651. We are going a-FLIMPING, buzzing, cracking, etc.

1861. H. KINGSLEY, *Ravenshoe*, ch. lx. FLIMPING is a style of theft which I have never practised, and, consequently of which I know nothing.

FLIMSY, or **FLIM**, *subs.* (common).—1. A bank-note. [From the thinness of the paper.] SOFT-FLIMSY = a note drawn on 'The Bank of Elegance,' or 'The Bank of Engraving.' For synonyms, *see* SOFT.

1811. *Lexicon Balatronicum*, s.v.

1818. P. EGAN, *Boxiana*, iv., 443. Martin produced some FLIMSIES and said he would fight on Tuesday next.

1837. BARHAM, *Ingoldsby Legends* ('Merchant of Venice'). Not 'kites, manufactured to cheat and inveigle, But the right sort of FLIMSY, all sign'd, by Monteagle.

1855. *Punch*, XXIX., 10. 'Will you take it in FLIMSIES, or will you have it all in tin?'

1870. *Chambers' Journal*, 9 July, p. 448. 'What would it be worth?' 'A FLIM, Sam.'

1884. *Daily Telegraph*, 8 Apl., col. 3. One of the slang terms for a spurious bank-note is a SOFT-FLIMSY.

1891. HUME NISBET, *Bail Up!* p. 149. Next morning when I went to the bank to collect the swag, they stopped the FLIMSY, and had me arrested before I could look round.

2. (journalists').—News of all kinds; POINTS (*q.v.*). [From the thin prepared paper used by pressmen for making several copies at once]. First used at Lloyd's.

1861. *Cornhill Magazine*, iv., 199 'At Westminster,' my lord is neither a mumbling nor a short-tempered judge; he will . . . read them a great deal of his notes, which are a thousand-fold clearer, fuller, and more accurate than the reporter's FLIMSY.

1865. *Morning Star* ('The Flaneur'). A London correspondent, who, by the aid of FLIMSY misleads a vast number of provincial papers.

1870. *London Figaro*, 23 Sept. 'Special Lining.' We do not think it is

altogether worthy of the high repute of the *Pall Mall Gazette* to publish FLIMSY as a special correspondence.

1876. BESANT and RICE, *Golden Butterfly*, ch. xviii. The sharpest of the reporters had his FLIMSY up in a minute, and took notes of the proceedings.

FLINDERS, *subs.* (common). — Pieces infinitesimally small.

1870. *New York Evening Sun*, 24 May. Report of Speech of Mr. Chandler. Let us knock the British crown to FLINDERS; let us arrange for some one or two hundred thousand British graves forthwith, and cabbage the whole boundless continent without any further procrastination.

FLING, *subs.* (colloquial).—1. A fit of temper.

2. (common). — A jeer; a jibe; a personal allusion or attack.

1592. SHAKSPEARE, *I Henry VI.*, iii., 1. Then would I have a FLING at Winchester.

1888. *Star*, 10 Oct. Those writers who had a FLING at Iddesleigh after his poor running at Stockton will have to take their words back some day.

1890. *Pall Mall Gazette*, 24 July, p. 4. col. 2. As the disputants warmed up, little personal FLINGS were of course introduced

Verb (old).—1. To cheat; to get the best of; to DO (*q.v.*) or diddle.—GROSE.

1830. LYTTON, *Paul Clifford*, ch. xxi. FLUNG the governor out of a guinea.

2. (Scots).—To dance.

1790. BURNS, *Tam O' Shanter*. To tell how Maggie lapt and FLANG (A souple jaud she was, and strang).

3. (venery).—To move in the act; to BACK-UP (*q.v.*). Fr., '*frizer la queue* = to wriggle the tayle (in leachering).' — COTGRAVE.

1539. DAVID LYNDSAY, *Three Estaitis*, Works (Ed. Laing, Edinburgh, 1879), I traist sche sal find you FLINGING your fill.

TO FLING OUT, *verb. phr.* (colloquial). — To depart in a hurry, and, especially, in a temper.

TO FLING (or FLAP) IT IN ONE'S FACE, *verb. phr.* (prostitutes')—To expose the person.

IN A FLING, *adv. phr.* (colloquial).—In a spasm of temper.

TO HAVE ONE'S FLING, *verb. phr.* (colloquial).—To enjoy full liberty of action or conduct. *Cf.*, HIGH OLD TIME.

1624. BEAUMONT AND FLETCHER, *Rule a Wife, &c.*, iii., 5. I'll have a FLING.

1846-8. THACKERAY. *Vanity Fair*, ch. xiii. Hang it; the regiment's just back from the West Indies, I must HAVE A LITTLE FLING, and then when I'm married I'll reform.

1855. THACKERAY, *Newcomes*, II., 118. I don't want to marry until I HAVE HAD MY FLING, you know.

1880. GILBERT, *Pirates of Penzance*. Peers will be peers, And youth will HAVE HIS FLING.

1891. HUME NISBET, *Bail Up!* p. 253. If policy (police) show up, then you let me HAVE MY FLING, eh?

TO FLING DIRT.—*See* DIRT.

FLINGER, *subs.* (Scots).—A dancer.

1821. SCOTT, *Pirate*, ch. ix. That's as muckle as to say, that I suld hae minded you was a FLINGER and a fiddler yoursel', Maister Mordaunt.

FLING-DUST, *subs.* (old).—A street-walker. For synonyms, *see* BARRACK-HACK and TART.

FLINT, *subs.* (workmen's). A man working for a 'Union' or 'fair' house; non-Unionists are DUNG (*q.v.*). Both terms occur in Foote's burlesque, *The Tailors: a Tragedy for Warm Weather*, and they received a fresh lease of popularity during the tailors'

strike of 1832. *See* quots. *Cf.*, SCAB SOC, SNOB, SNOB-STICK, and KNOBSTICK.

1785. GROSE, *Dict. Vulg. Tongue*, FLINTS, journeyman taylors who, on a late occasion, refused to work for the wages settled by law. Those who submitted were by the mutineers stiled dungs, *i.e.*, dunghills.

1832. P. EGAN, *Book of Sports*, p. 34. Jack Reeve is without a rival; the throne of the FLINTS is decidedly freehold property to him.

1834. *Noctes Amb.*, xxxiv., vol. IV., p. 83. (The company is discussing the tailors' strike). TICKLER. The FLINTS flash fire, and the day of the dungs is gone.

OLD FLINT, *subs. phr.* (common). A miser: one who would 'skin a flint,' *i.e.*, stoop to any meanness for a trifle.

1840. DICKENS, *Old Curiosity Shop*, ch. vii., p. 34. It's equally plain that the money which the OLD FLINT—rot him—first taught me to expect that I should share with her at his death, will all be hers.

TO FIX ONE'S FLINT. *See* FIX.

TO FLINT IN, *verb. phr.* (American). To act with energy; not to stand on ceremony; to pitch into; to tackle. A verb of action well-nigh as common as FIX (*q.v.*).

FLIP, *subs.* (common). — 1. Hot beer, brandy, and sugar; also, says Grose, called SIR CLOUDESLEY after Sir Cloudesley Shovel. *See* DRINKS.

1690. B. E., *New Dict. of the Canting Crew*. FLIP, Sea Drink, of small beer (chiefly) and brandy, sweetened and spiced upon occasion.

1690. WARD, *London Spy*, part II., p. 41. After the drinking a Kan of Phlip or a Bowl of Punch.

1705. WARD, *Hudibras Redivivus*, vol. I., pt. 4, p. 8. So have I seen on board of ship, Some knawing beeff, some spewing FLIP.

1748. SMOLLETT, *Rod. Random*, ch xxiv. He . . . sent for a can of beer, of which he made excellent FLIP to crown the banquet.

1810. CRABBE, *The Borough*, Letter 16. Nay, with the seamen working in the ship, At their request, he'd share the grog and FLIP.

1875. C. D. WARNER, *Backlog Studies*, p. 18. It was thought best to heat the poker red-hot before plunging it into the mugs of FLIP.

2. (popular). — A bribe or douceur.

3. (common).—A light blow, or snatch.

1821. HAGGART, *Life*, p. 23. Barney made a very unceremonious FLIP at the bit.

Verb (thieves').—To shoot.

1819. VAUX, Flash Dict., s.v.

1834. AINSWORTH, *Rookwood* (ed 1864), p. 273. FLIP him, Dick; fire, or I'm taken.

TO FLIP UP *verb. phr.* (American).—To spin a coin.

1879. *New York Tribune*, 4 Oct. The two great men could FLIP UP to see which should have the second place.

FLIP-FLAP, *subs.* 1 (old).—1. A flighty creature.

1702. VANBRUGH, *False Friend*. 1. The light airy FLIP-FLAP, she kills him with her motions.

2. (popular). A step-dance; a CELLAR-FLAP (*q.v.*). Also (acrobats'); a kind of somersault, in which the performer throws himself over on his hands and feet alternately.

1727. GAY, *Fables*, 'Two Monkies. The tumbler whirls the FLIP-FLAP round. With sommersets he shakes the ground.

1872. BRADDON, *Dead Sea Fruit*, ch. xiv. There ain't nothing you can't do, Morty, from Shylock to a FLIP-FLAP.

1889. *Pall Mall Gazette*, 12 Nov., p. 6, col. 2. There were the clowns who danced, turned somersaults, FLIP-FLAPS, and contorted themselves.

3. (American). A kind of tea-cake.

1876. BESANT and RICE, *Golden Butterfly*, ch. xviii. The first evening I took tea with Mrs. Scrimmager. 'It must be more than a mite lonely for you,' she said, as we sat over her dough-nuts and FLIP-FLAPS.

4. (nautical). The arm. For synonyms, *see* BENDER.

5. (venery). The *penis*.

1653. URQUHART, *Rabelais*, I., 20. I might have cleft her water-gap And joined it close with my FLIP-FLAP.

FLIPPER, *subs.* (nautical and common). 1. The hand. TIP US YOUR FLIPPER = give me your hand. [From the flipper or paddle of a turtle.] For synonyms, *see* DADDLE and MAULEY.

1837. BARHAM, *Ingoldsby Legends*. 'Lay of St. Gengulphus.' With those great sugar-nippers they nipp'd off his FLIPPERS, As the clerk, very flippantly, termed his fists.

1884. *Punch*, 11 Oct. 'Arry at a Political Picnic.' Old Bluebottle TIPPED ME HIS FLIPPER, and 'oped I'd 'refreshed,' and all that.

2. (common). *See* FLAPPER.

3. (theatrical). Part of a scene, hinged and painted on both sides, used in trick changes.

FLIRTATIOUS, *adj.* (American). — Flighty.

1881. W. D. HOWELLS, *D. Breen's Practice*, ch. i., "Oh, you needn't look after *her*. Mr. Libby! There's nothing FLIRTATIOUS about Grace," said Mrs. Maynard.

FLIRT-GILL, **FLIRTGILLIAN**, or **GILL-FLIRT**, *subs.* (old). A wanton; a CHOPPING GIRL (*q.v.*); specifically a strumpet. For synonyms, *see* BARRACK-HACK and TART.

1595. SHAKSPEARE, *Romeo and Juliet*, ii., 4. Scurvy knave! I am none of his FLIRT-GILLS.

1713. *Guardian*, No. 26. We are invested with a parcel of FLIRT-GILLS, who are not capable of being mothers of brave men.

1729. GAY, *Polly*, ii. 4. While a man is grappling with these GILL-FLIRTS, pardon the expression, Captain, he runs his reason aground.

1822. SCOTT, *Fort. of Nigel*, ch. v. She is a dutiful girl to her god-father, though I sometimes call her a JILL-FLIRT.

FLIRTINA COP-ALL, *subs. phr.* (common). A wanton, young or old; a MEN'S WOMAN (*q.v.*).

FLOAT, *subs.* (theatrical).—The footlights: before the invention of gas they were oil-pans with floating wicks. *Cf.*, ARK-FLOATER.

1886. *Saturday Review*, 24 July, p. 108. To an actor the FLOAT is not what it is to a fisherman.

1889. *Answers*, 8 June, p. 24. He slapped me on the back, put me in a hansom, and cried, 'We'll have you behind the FLOAT (footlights) in a week.'

IF THAT'S THE WAY THE STICK FLOATS. *See* STICK.

FLOATER, *subs.* (Stock Exchange).—An Exchequer bill; applied also to other unfunded stock.

1871. *Temple Bar*, XXXI., 320. On the Stock Exchange, where slang abounds, FLOATERS is a term which would puzzle outsiders. FLOATERS are Exchequer bills and their unfunded stock.

2. (common).—A suet dumpling in soup.

3. (political).—A vendible voter.

1883. *Graphic*, 17 Mar., p. 279, col. 3. 'How many voters are there?' asked a candidate in one of these pure-blooded

Yankee townships. 'Four hundred.' 'And how many FLOATERS, i.e., purchasable?' 'Four hundred.'

1888. *New York Herald*, 4 Nov. The Building Materials Exchange people were in line to the number of about 200, with a band, and were followed by a sixteen-horse stage of the 'Long Tom' shape containing a lot of FLOATERS and some fifers and drummers.

4. (Western American). — A candidate representing several counties, and therefore not considered directly responsible to any one of them.

1853. *Texas State Gazette*, 16 July. J. W. Lawrence, Esq., requests us to withdraw his name as a candidate for FLOATER in the district composed of the counties of Fayette, Bastrop, and Travis.

5. (venery).—The *penis*. For synonyms, *see* CREAMSTICK and PRICK.

FLOATING ACADEMY, *subs. phr.* (old).—The hulks; also CAMPBELL'S ACADEMY (*q.v.*), and FLOATING HELL (*q.v.*). For synonyms, *see* CAGE.

FLOATING BATTERIES, *subs. phr.* (military). — 1. Broken bread in tea; also SLINGERS (*q.v.*).

2. (American). — The Confederate bread rations during the Secession.

FLOATING COFFIN, *subs. phr.* (nautical).—A rotten ship.

FLOATING HELL, or HELL AFLOAT, *subs. phr.* (nautical).—A ship commanded by (1) a brutal savage, or (2) a ruthless disciplinarian. *See* also FLOATING ACADEMY.

FLOCK, *subs.* (colloquial).—A clergyman's congregation. Also any body of people with a common

haunt or interest: *e.g.*, a family of children, a company of soldiers, a school of girls or boys, 'a cabful of molls,' and such like.

TO FIRE INTO THE WRONG FLOCK, *verb. phr.* (American pioneers'). — To blunder. A variant is TO BARK UP THE WRONG TREE.

1858. *New York Herald*, 9 Nov. When Mr. Saulsbury rose and called the Speaker's attention to the alleged blunder in the Secretary's report, his own friends jumped up in great excitement and pulled him down; he soon found out that he had FIRED INTO THE WRONG FLOCK.

FLOCK OF SHEEP, *subs. phr.*—1. (gaming). A hand at dominoes set out on the table.

2. (colloquial).—White waves on the sea: WHITE HORSES (*q.v.*).

FLOG, *subs.* (American thieves').— 1. A whip. A contraction of FLOGGER (*q.v.*). TO FLOG (now recognised), is cited by B. E. (1690), GROSE, and the author of *Bacchus and Venus* as Cant.

TO BE FLOGGED AT THE TUMBLER, *verb. phr.* (old).—To be whipped at the cart's tail. *See* TUMBLER.

1690. B. E., *New Dict. of the Canting Crew.*

TO FLOG THE DEAD HORSE, *verb. phr.* (common). — 1. To work up an interest in a bygone subject; to try against heart; to do with no will nor liking for the job. [Bright said that Earl Russell's Reform Bill was a DEAD HORSE (*q.v.*), and every attempt to create enthusiasm in its favour was FLOGGING THE DEAD HORSE.]

2. (nautical).—To work off an advance of wages.

TO FLOG A WILLING HORSE, *verb. phr.* (common).—To urge on one who is already putting forth his best energies.

FLOGGER, *subs.* (old).—1. A whip; *cf.*, FLOG. GROSE gives the word as Cant. Fr., *un bouis.*

1789. GEO. PARKER, *Life's Painter*, p. 173, s.v.

2. (theatrical).—A mop (*i.e.*, a bunch of slips of cloth on a handle) used in the painting room to whisk the charcoal dust from a sketch.

FLOGGING, *ppl. adj.* (old).—Careful; penurious.

FLOGGING-COVE, *subs. phr.* (prison)—1. An official who administers the CAT (*q.v.*).

1690. B. E., *New Dict. of the Canting Crew.* FLOGGING COVE, c. the Beadle, or Whipper in Bridewell, or any such place.

1785. GROSE, *Dict. Vulg. Tongue*, s.v. FLOGGING-COVE, the beadle, or whipper, in Bridewell.

2. *See* FLOGGING CULLY.

FLOGGING CULLY, *subs. phr.* (venery). — A man addicted, whether from necessity or choice, to flagellation; a WHIPSTER (*q.v.*).

1690. B. E., *New Dict. of the Canting Crew.* FLOGGING, c. a Naked Woman's whipping (with rods) an Old (usually) and (sometimes) a young Lecher.

FLOGGING STAKE, *subs. phr.* (old).—A whipping post.

1690. B. E., *New Dict. of the Canting Crew*, s.v.

1785. GROSE, *Dict. of the Vulgar Tongue*, s.v.

FLOGSTER, *subs.* (old). — One addicted to flogging. Specifically (naval), a nickname applied to

the Duke of Clarence (afterwards William IV).

FLOOR, *verb.* (colloquial).—1. To knock down. Hence to vanquish in argument; to make an end of; to defeat; to confound. *See* FLOORED and DEAD-BEAT.

1785. GROSE, *Dict. Vulg. Tongue.* FLOOR the pig, knock down the officer.

1821. HAGGART, *Life*, p. 15. That moment the farmer let fly at the drover, which FLOORED him.

1857. G. A. LAWRENCE, *Guy Livingstone*, ch. xxi. 'When I saw him so FLOORED as not to be able to come to time, I knew there had been some hard hitting going on thereabouts, so I kept clear.'

1821. EGAN, *Tom and Jerry*, p. 10. Then (apostrophising 'Maga') FLOOR me not. *Ibid.*, p. 60, The Corinthian, being no novice in these matters, FLOORED two or three in a twinkling.

1835. COLERIDGE, *Table Talk* (published posthumously). The other day I was what you may called FLOORED by a Jew.

1836. C. DICKENS, *Pickwick Papers* p. 425 (Ed. 1857). Even Mr. Bob Sawyer . . . . was FLOORED.

1862. MRS. H. WOOD, *The Channings*, ch. v. 'So if the master is directing his suspicions to the seniors, he'll get FLOORED.'

1870. L. OLIPHANT, *Piccadilly*, Pt. V., p. 196. 'Whenever the mammas object to asking her on account of that horrid Lady Wylde,' I FLOOR all opposition by saying, 'Oh, Lady Jane Helter will bring her.'

1888. *Sportsman*, 28 Nov. Pope, who was the fresher, started at a terrific pace and drove his man all over the ring, ending by FLOORING him.

TO FLOOR THE ODDS. (betting men's).—Said of a low-priced horse that pulls off the event in face of the betting.

1882. *Daily Telegraph*, 16 Nov. The odds were, nevertheless, FLOORED from an unexpected quarter.

1889. *Echo*, 24 Jan. As the odds betted on Miss Jessie II. were easily FLOORED by Marsden.

2. (drunkards'). — To finish; to get outside of. *E.g.*, 'I FLOORED three half-pints and a nip before breakfast.'

1837. *Punch*, 31 Jan. Dear Bill, this stone jug. . . . Is still the same snug, Free-and-easy old hole, Where Macheath met his blowens, and Wylde FLOORED his bowl.

18(?). *Macmillan's Magazine* (quoted in *Century Dict.*). I have a few bottles of old wine left: we may as well FLOOR them.

3. (university). — To pluck; to PLOUGH (*q.v.*).

TO FLOOR A PAPER, LESSON, EXAMINATION, EXAMINER, etc., *verb. phr.* (university). — To answer every question; to master; to prove oneself superior to the occasion.

1852. BRISTED, *Five Years in an English University*, p. 12. Somehow I nearly FLOORED the paper.

1861. HUGHES, *Tom Brown at Oxford.* I've FLOORED my Little Go.

TO FLOOR ONE'S LICKS, *verb. phr.* (common).—To surpass one's self; to CUT-AROUND (*q.v.*).

1844. PUCK, p. 14. Now slowly rising, raised his pewter and FLOORED HIS LICKS.

TO HAVE, HOLD, or TAKE THE FLOOR. *verb. phr.* (colloquial). — To rise to address a public meeting; in Ireland, to stand up to dance; and, in America, 'to be in possession of the House.'

1882. McCABE, *New York*, xxi., p. 342. A member making a bid below or an offer above the one which HAS THE FLOOR.

1888. *St. Louis Globe-Democrat.* After a half hour's recess Mr. Glover TOOK THE FLOOR.

1889. *Pall Mall Gazette*, 11 Nov., p. 6, col. 1 The Duke of Rutland, however, who 'TOOK THE FLOOR' non-politically at the end of the evening, was really 'felicitous' in his few remarks.

FLOORED, *ppl. adj.* (colloquial).— 1. Vanquished; brought under; ruined. For synonyms, *see* DEAD-BEAT and *infra.*

ENGLISH SYNONYMS.—Basketed; bitched; bitched-up; bowled out; broken up; buggered up; busted; caved in; choked-off; cornered; cooked; coopered up; dead-beat; done brown; done for; done on toast; doubled up; flattened-out; fluffed; flummoxed; frummagemmed; gapped; gone through St. Peter's needle; gone under; gravelled; gruelled; hoofed out; in the last of pea-time, or last run of shad; jacked-up; knocked out of time; knocked silly; looed; mucked-out; petered out; pocketed; potted; put in his little bed; queered in his pitch; rantanned; sat upon; sewn up; shut-up; smashed to smithereens; snashed; snuffed out; spread-eagled; struck of a heap; stumped; tied up; timbered; treed; trumped; up a tree.

FRENCH SYNONYMS. — *Mon linge est lavé* (pop. : = I have thrown up the sponge); *coller sous bande* (= to put in a hole: at billiards, *bande* = cushion); *avoir son affaire* (pop. : = to have got a 'settler'); *aplatir* (*fam.* : = to flatten out); *aplomber* (thieves' : = to brazen down; to bluff); *être pris dans la balancine* (pop. : = to be in a fix); *se faire coller* (familiar); *envoyer quelqu'un s'asseoir*, or *s'asseoir sur quelqu'un* (popular).

ITALIAN SYNONYM.— *Traboccare* (= to overturn).

SPANISH SYNONYMS.—*Pesado* (doubled-up: from *peso* = weight); *aculado* (from *acular* = to corner); *arrollar* (= to sweep away, as a torrent); *aturrullar* (= to shut up); *cogite!* (= 'I've got you,' or, 'there I have you !')

2. (common). — Drunk; in Shakspearean 'put down': as Sir Andrew Aguecheek, 'Never in your life, I think, unless you see Canary PUT ME DOWN.' (*Twelfth Night*, i., 3). For synonyms, *see* SCREWED.

3. (painters').—Hung low at an exhibition; in contradistinction to SKYED (*q.v.*), and ON THE LINE (*q.v.*).

FLOORER, *subs.* (common). — 1. An AUCTIONEER (*q.v.*); or knock-down blow; *cf.*, DIG, BANG, and WIPE. Hence, sudden or unpleasant news; a decisive argument; an unanswerable retort; a decisive check. Sp., *peso.*

1819. T. MOORE, *Tom Crib's Memorial*, p. 20 For in these FANCY times, 'tis your hits in the MUNS, And your CHOPPERS and FLOORERS that govern the funds.

1839. SWINTON, *Trial of Wm. Humphreys*, p. 297. It is a downright FLOORER to the Crown.

1856. BRADLEY ('Cuthbert Bede'), *Adventures of Mr. Verdant Green.* The Putney Pet stared . . . The inquiry for his college was, in the language of his profession, a 'regular FLOORER.'

1861. H. C. PENNELL, *Puck on Pegasus*, p. 20. What a FLOORER to my hopes is this performance on the ropes! Miss Marianne *suspensa scalis*—(Would twere sus. per coll instead)

1868. *Cassell's Magazine*, 4 Jan., p. 213. 'Ah, she hasn't told you of the strokes I have had, one arter the other—clean FLOORERS, and left like a log of wood in my bed.'

2. (schools').—A question, or a paper, too hard to master.

3. (bowling alley).—A ball that brings down all the pins.

4. (thieves').—A thief who trips his man, and robs in picking him up; a RAMPER (*q.v.*).

1809. G. ANDREWS, *Dict. of the Slang and Cant Languages*, s.v.

FLOORING, *subs.* (pugilists').— Knocking down. Hence, to vanquish in all senses.

1819. MOORE, *Tom Crib's Memorial*, p. xii. Cross-buttocking . . . being as indispensable an ingredient, as nobbing, FLOORING, etc.

FLOOR-WALKER, *subs.* (American). —A shop-walker.

FLOP, *subs. and verb.* (American university).—1. A BITE (*q.v.*); a successful dodge.

1856. HALL, *College Words and Customs.* Any 'cute' performance by which a man is sold is a good FLOP, and by a phrase borrowed from the base-ball ground is 'rightly played.' If the discomfited individual declares that they 'are all on a side,' and gives up, or 'rolls over,' by giving his opponent 'gowdy.' A man writes cards during examinations to 'feeze the profs'; said cards are 'gumming cards,' and he FLOPS the examination if he gets a good mark by the means. One usually FLOPS his marks by feigning sickness.

2. (common).—A sudden fall or 'flop' down.

3. (common).—A collapse or breakdown.

4. (For FLAP or FLIP, old).— A light blow.

1662. *Rump Songs*, ii., 3. The good the Rump will do, when they prevail, Is to give us a FLOP with a fox's tail, Which nobody can deny.

Verb. (colloquial).—1. To fall, or flap down suddenly. A variant of 'flap.' Fr., *prendre un billet de parterre.*

1742. FIELDING, *Joseph Andrews,* bk. iv. ch. v. She had FLOPPED her hat over her eyes.

1859. DICKENS, *Tale of Two Cities* bk. ii. ch. i. If you must go FLOPPING yourself down.

1870. *Public Opinion,* 12 Feb. But even if they were more numerous and greater than they are, we should hold aloof from the crowd that FLOPS in his presence with love and awe, as the dismal wife of Jerry Cruncher FLOPPED in pious misery.

1883. *The Theatre,* Feb., p. 93. She is able to call in tumbling to the aid of tragedy, and bring the plastic arts to the portrayal of the passions; to FLOP through four such acts as these night after night, and finish with a death-scene warranted correct, to the very last kick and quiver.

1891. HUME NISBET, *Bail Up!* p. 118. He cursed under his breath each time he rose to follow, and smothered a yell of pain and horror each time he FLOPPED DOWN.

2. (pugilists').—To knock down; to FLOOR (q.v.).

1888. *Sporting Life,* 15 Dec. 'E carnt FLOP a bloke.

Adv. (colloquial).—An onomatopœia expressive of the noise of a sudden and sounding fall. Often used expletively, as SLAP (q.v.) is, and the American RIGHT (q.v.).

1726. VANBRUGH, *Journey to London,* Act I., Sc. 2. That down came I FLOP o' my feace all along in the channel.

1860. *Punch,* v. 38, p. 255, 'Twixt two stools, FLOP, he let me drop, The fall it was my murther.

1881. JAS. PAYN, *Grape from a Thorn,* ch. vi. 'She'll roll down, papa, and come FLOP.'

TO FLOP OVER, *verb. phr.* (colloquial).—To turn heavily; hence (in America), to make a sudden change of sides, association, or allegiance.

FLOP-UP, *subs.* (American). — A day's tramp, as opposed to a SOT-DOWN=half a day's travel.

1888. *Detroit Free Press,* 15 Sept. 'Stranger, did ye lope it?' (come on foot.) 'Yes.' 'A mile or a sot down?' 'More'n that. About a dozen FLOP-UPS.'

FLOP-UP-TIME=Bedtime.

[FLOP, too, is something of a vocable of all-work. Thus TO FLOP IN=(venery) to effect intromission; TO FLOP ROUND =to loaf; to dangle; TO FLOP A JUDY=to lay out, or 'SPREAD' (q.v.), a girl; TO DO A FLOP=(colloquial) to sit, or to fall, down, and (venery) to lie down to a man; TO FLOP OUT = to leave the water noisily and awkwardly; belly-FLOPPING=belly-bumping, coition; a FLOP in the gills=a smack in the mouth.]

FLORENCE, *subs.* (old)—'A wench that has been touzed and ruffled.'

1690. B. E., *New Dict. of the Canting Crew,* and (1785) GROSE, s.v.

FLOSTER, *subs.* (common). — A mixed drink: sherry, noyau, peach-leaves, lemon, sugar, ice, and soda-water. Cf., FLESH-AND-BLOOD.

FLOUCH. TO FALL (or GO), FLOUCH (or FLOUSH), *verb. phr.* (colloquial).—To come to pieces; to sag suddenly on the removal of a restraining influence: as a pair of stays.

1819. MOORE, *Tom Crib,* p. 13. Old Georgy went FLOUSH, and his backers look'd shy.

FLOUNCE, *verb.* (colloquial).—To move with violence, and (generally) in anger. Said of women, for whom such motion is, or rather was, inseparable from a great flourishing of flounces.

FLOUNDER, *subs.* (riverside thieves'). —1. A drowned corpse. Cf., DAB, and for synonyms, see STIFF.

of the viands) to generate FLUE. . . . *Ibid.* 'Refreshment for Travellers.' Take the old established Bull's Head . . . . with its old-established FLUE under its old established four-post bedsteads.

3. (common).—A contraction of 'influenza.'

Verb (common).—To put in pawn.

IN (or UP) THE FLUE, *phr.* (common). — Pawned. For synonyms, *see* POP.

1821. *Real Life, etc.,* I., p. 566.

1851. MAYHEW, *Lond. Lab. and Lond. Poor,* II., p. 250. I've had sometimes to leave half my stock IN FLUE with a deputy for a night's rest.

UP THE FLUE (or SPOUT), *adj. phr.* (colloquial). — Dead; collapsed, mentally or physically.

TO BE UP ONE'S FLUE, *verb. phr.* (colloquial).—To be awkward for one. THAT'S UP YOUR FLUE=That's a 'facer,' or that's up against you.

FLUE-FAKER (or SCRAPER), *subs.* (common).—A chimney-sweep. [From FLUE + FAKER (q.v.).] MINOR CLERGY=young chimney sweeps. For synonyms, *see* CLERGYMAN.

1821. EGAN, *Tom and Jerry,* p. 60. The 'office' has been given to 'shove' the poor FLUE-FAKER against Tom's light drab coat.

1859. MATSELL. *Vocabulum, or Rogue's Lexicon,* s.v.

1882. *Punch.* LXXXII., p. 185, col. 2.

FLUFF (or FLUFFINGS), *subs.* (railway clerks').—1. Short change given by booking-clerks. The practice is known as FLUFFING. Cf., MENAVELINGS. Fr., *des fruges* (= more or less unlawful profits of any sort).

1890. *Star,* 27 Jan. Many porters on this line are but getting 15s. per week, and with regard to 'tips,' or, as we say, 'FLUFF'—well, would you not think it mean to tell your servant when you engaged him that such were strictly forbidden by punishment with dismissal, and then proclaim to the world that with good wages and tips your servant was well paid.

2, (theatrical).—'Lines' half learned and imperfectly delivered. Hence, TO DO A FLUFF =to forget one's part.

1891. W. ARCHER, *The World,* p. 28. col. 1, line 34. But even as seen through a cloud of FLUFF the burlesque is irresistibly amusing.

3. (venery).—The female pubic hair. For synonyms, *see* FLEECE.

Verb. (railway clerks').—1. To give short change.

2. (common).—To disconcert, to FLOOR (q.v.). Cf., FLUFF IN THE PAN=a failure.

3. (theatrical). — To forget one's part. Also TO DO A FLUFF.

FLUFF IT! *Intj.* (common).—An interjection of disapproval: 'Be off!' 'Take it away!'

FLUFFER, *subs.* (common).—1. A drunkard. Cf., FLUFFINESS.

2. (theatrical). — A player 'rocky on his lines'; *i.e.,* given to forgetting his part.

3. (old).—A term of contempt.

FLUFFINESS, *subs.* (common).—1. Drunkenness. Cf., FLUFFY and FLUFFER.

1886. *Fun,* 4 August, p. 44. A sullen-faced, clerical-looking young man, charged with FLUFFINESS in a public conveyance, said he was sober as a judge when taken into custody.

---

2. (Stock Exchange).—To sell, and afterwards re-purchase a stock, or *vice versâ.*

1889. *Echo,* 1 Feb. A third expedient offers itself—namely, to turn round and buy; but this operation goes by the name of 'FLOUNDERING' especially when the speculator loses both ways.

FLOUNDER-AND-DAB, *subs. phr.* (rhyming).—A cab. For synonyms, *see* GROWLER.

FLOUR, *subs.* (American).—Money. For synonyms, *see* ACTUAL and GILT.

FLOURISH, *subs.* (venery).—Coition in a hurry; FLYER (q.v.); a FAST-FUCK (q.v.). Also verbally. For synonyms see GREENS and RIDE.

1796. GROSE, *Dict. of the Vulgar Tongue* (3rd ed.), s.v. To enjoy a woman with her clothes on or without going to bed.

Verb (colloquial.)—To be in luck: *e.g.,* 'I flourish'='I am well off'; 'Do you flourish,' or 'Are you flourishing?'='Have you got any money?'

FLOURISHING, *adj.* (colloquial). —A retort to the enquiry, 'How are you?' The equivalent of 'Pretty well, thank you?'

TO FLOURISH IT, *verb. phr.* (venery).—To expose the person.

FLOWER, *subs.* (venery).—1. The female *pudendum.* Also FLOWER-POT. For synonyms, *see* MONO-SYLLABLE.

2. *In pl.* (conventional).—The menstrual flux. Cf., FLAG, sense 3.

1598. FLORIO, *A Worlde of Wordes.* Biancuria, the monthly FLOWERS that women have.

1611. COTGRAVE, *Dictionaire. Le fourrier de la lune a marqué le logis,* applicable to a woman that hath her FLOWERS.

FLOWER-FANCIER, *subs. phr.* (venery).—A whore-master.

FLOWERY, *subs.* (thieves').—Lodging; entertainment; 'square the omee for the FLOWERY' = pay the landlord for the lodging. [*Lingua Franca.*]

FLOWERY LANGUAGE, *subs. phr.* (colloquial).—A euphemism for blasphemous and obscene speech.

FLOWER OF CHIVALRY, *subs. phr.* (venery). — The female *pudendum.* For synonyms, *see* MONO-SYLLABLE.

FLOWING-HOPE, *subs.* (military).—A forlorn hope.

FLUB-DUB-AND-GUFF, *subs. phr.* (American). — Rhetorical embellishment; HIGH-FALUTIN' (q.v.).

1888. *Detroit Free Press,* August. Rev. Mr. Selah (to desk editor of the *Daily Roarer*)—'Mr. Seezars, are you going to publish my prayer in full?' Desk Editor—'In full? Well, I guess not.' (Changing his tone)—'However, we'll do what we can for you. By swiping out the FLUB-DUB-AND-GUFF, I guess we'll have room to put in the points.'

FLUE, *subs.* (old). 1. The recorder of London or any large town. BAMFYLDE MOORE-CAREW.

2. (colloquial). — The filth, part fluff, part hair, part dust, which collects under ill-kept beds, and at the junctures of sofas and chairs; BEGGAR'S VELVET (q.v.).

1860. DICKENS, *Uncommercial Traveller.* 'Arcadian London.' A power they possess of converting everything into FLUE. Such broken victuals as they take by stealth appear (whatever the nature

2. (theatrical).—The trick, or habit, of forgetting words.

FLUFFY, *adj.* (common and theatrical).—Unsteady; of uncertain memory. Cf., FLUFFER (sense 2), and FLUFFINESS (sense 2).

1885. *Referee,* July 26, p. 3, col. 2. In the last act Groves and one or two others were either what actors call FLUFFY in their lines, or else Mr. Cross was guilty of irritating tautology.

FLUKE, *subs.* (common). — In billiards, an accidental winning hazard; in all games a result not played for; a CROW (q.v.). In yachting an effect of chance; a result in which seamanship has had no part. Hence, a stroke of luck. Sp., *bambarria.*

1857. *Notes and Queries,* 2 S. IV., p. 208, col. 1. In playing at billiards, if a player makes a hazard, etc., which he did not play for, it is often said that he made a crow. . . . Another term is, 'He made a FLOOK (or FLUKE).'

1869. WHYTE MELVILLE, *M or N,* p. 100. 'Only lost a pony on the whole meeting,' answered Dick triumphantly. 'And even that was a FLUKE, because Bearwarden's Bacchante filly was left at the post.

1873. BLACK. *Princess of Thule,* ch. xix. 'These conditions are not often fulfilled—it is a happy FLUKE when they are.

1880. HAWLEY SMART, *Social Sinners,* ch. xxxii. 'I suppose, by your asking the question, you have become acquainted with Mr. Solamo's past.' 'That's just it, Mr. Prossiter; by an odd FLUKE I have.'

1891. HUME NISBET, *Bail Up!* p. 144. He was now being cured only to be hanged, most kely, unless by some happy FLUKE he got off with imprisonment for life.

Verb (common and billiards).— 1. To effect by accident.

1888. *Sportsman,* 20 Dec. Fortune once more assisted Mitchell, who, in trying to make a red loser, FLUKED a cannon, from which he got on the spot, and made forty-three winners in a break of 161.

2.—(schoolboys').—To shirk.

1864. *Eton School Days,* ch. xvi., p. 203. 'By Jove! I think I shall FLUKE doing Verses; I should like to see Paddy drive tandem through College,' said Butler Burke.

TO CUT FLUKES OUT, *verb. phr.* (nautical).—To mutiny; to turn sulky and disobedient.

TO TURN FLUKES, *verb. phr.* (nautical).—To go to bed; *i.e.,* TO BUNK (q.v.), or turn in.

FLUKY, or FLUKEY, *adj.* (common). —Of the nature of a FLUKE (q.v.); *i.e.,* achieved more by good luck than good guidance.

1882. *Standard,* 3 Sept. Bonnor got a FLUKEY three to square leg.

1891. *Licensed Vict. Gazette,* 20 March. Now, Grady was a smart young Irishman who had thrashed Stevens twice in days gone by, and had won a somewhat FLUKEY victory over Young Norley.

Hence FLUKINESS=abounding in FLUKES.

1886. *Ill. Sport. and Dram. News,* 20 Feb., p. 579. There is no FLUKINESS about him: he makes his runs because he is an excellent batsman, and takes his wickets because he is an excellent bowler.

FLUMMADIDDLE, *subs.* (American). —1. Nonsense; FLUMMERY (q.v.).

2. (nautical).—A sea-dainty.

1884. G. A. SALA, in *Ill. London News,* July 19, p. 51, col 2. I suppose that when the friendly skippers GAM (q.v.), they feast on FLUMMADIDDLE, a dish composed, I am given to understand, of stale bread, pork fat, molasses, cinnamon, allspice, and cloves.

FLUMMERGASTED, *ppl. adj.* (colloquial).—Astonished; confounded. A variant of FLABBERGASTED (q.v.).

1849. *New South Wales: Past and Present*, ch. i., p. 14. This coolness so completely FLUMMERGASTED the fellow, that he kept talking until Mr. Day shot him through the shoulder.

FLUMMERY, *subs.* (colloquial). 1. Nonsense; GAMMON (*q.v.*); flattery.

1785. GROSE, *Dict. of the Vulgar Tongue*, s.v. Oatmeal and water boiled to a jelly; also compliments: neither . . . over-nourishing.

1836. M. SCOTT, *Tom Cringle's Log*, ch. i. I shall . . . blow off as much of the froth as I can, in order to present the residuum free of FLUMMERY.

1846. THACKERAY, *Yellow Plush Papers.* She swallowed Lord Crabs' FLUMERY just as she would so many musheruims.

1854. WHYTE MELVILLE, *General Bounce*, ch. xii. None of the dubious, half-expressed, sentimental FLUMMERY.

2. (American nautical).—A kind of bread pudding.—NORDHOFF.

3. (old).—Oatmeal and water boiled to a jelly.—GROSE (1785).

FLUMMOX, FLUMMOCKS, or FLUMMUX, *verb.* (colloquial).—1. To perplex, dodge, abash, or silence; to victimize; to BEST (*q.v.*); to disappoint. Also CONFLUMMOX. TO FLUMMOX (or CONFLUMMOX) BY THE LIP = TO OUTSLANG (*q.v.*), or talk down; TO FLUMMOX THE COPPERS = to dodge the police; TO FLUMMOX THE OLD DUTCH = to cheat one's wife, etc. For synonyms, *see* FLABBERGAST.

2. (theatrical).—To confuse, to QUEER (*q.v.*). *Cf.*, CORPSE.

3. (American).—Used in the passive sense = to abandon a purpose; to give in; to die.

Subs. (American University).—A bad recitation; a failure.

FLUMMOXED, *ppl. adj.* (thieves' and general).—1. Spoilt; ruined; drunk; SENT DOWN (*q.v.*); BOSHED (*q.v.*); defeated; disappointed; silenced; FLOORED (*q.v.*).

1836. DICKENS, *Pickwick*, ch. xxxiii., p. 283. 'And my 'pinion is, Sammy, that if your governor don't prove an alleybi, he'll be what the Italians call reg'larly FLUMMOXED, and that's all about it.'

1840. WHIBLEY, *Cap and Gown*, p. 170. So many of the men I know Were FLUMMOXED at the last great go.

1861. H. C. PENNELL, *Puck on Pegasus*, p. 17. I felt FLUMMOX'D in a brown (*study* understood) old fellow.

1864. *Cornhill Magazine*, Dec., p. 742. 'I say, Tom.' 'Yes, mate.' 'If I should have a fit heave a bucket of water over me.' Tom was too astonished, or, as he expressed it, CONFLUMMOXED to make any reply.

1883. *Daily Telegraph*, 25 July, p. 2, col. 1. I'll give Tom his due, and say of him that for FLUMMOXING a cuss (Custom House Officer) or working the weed, I don't know any one he couldn't give a chalk to and beat 'em.

1890. *Punch*, 30 Aug., p. 97. I'm fair FLUMMOXED, and singing, 'Oh, what a surprise!'

FLUMMOCKY, *adj.* (colloquial).—Out of place; in bad taste.

1891. F. H. GROOME. *Blackwood's Mag*, March, p. 319. 'It is a nice solemn dress,' she said, as she lifted a piece to examine it more closely; 'there's nothing FLUMMOCKY about it.'

FLUMMUT, *subs.* (vagrants').—A month in prison. *See* FLUMMOXED. For synonyms, *see* DOSE.

1889. *Answers*, 20th July, p. 121 col. 2. If you want to get rid of an importunate tramp tell him to 'stow his patter,' or you will get him a FLUMMUT.

1851-61. H. MAYHEW, *Lond. Lab. and Lond. Poor*, vol. I., p. 232. He [patterer] mostly chalks a signal on or near the door. I give one or two instances. . . . 'FLUMMUT,' sure of a month in quod.

FLUMP, *verb*, (colloquial).—To fall, put, or be set, down with violence or a thumping noise. Onomatopœic. Also to COME DOWN WITH A FLUMP *Cf.*, PLUMP and CACHUNK.

1840. THACKERAY, *Paris Sketch Book*, ch. v. Chairs were FLUMPED down on the floor.

1865. H. KINGSLEY, *The Hillyars and the Burtons*, ch. lxii. Before my mother had been a week in the partly-erected slab-house, the women began to come in, to FLUMP down into a seat and tell her all about it.

FLUNK, *subs.* (American colloquial).—1. An idler, a LOAFER (*q.v.*) or LAWRENCE (*q.v.*).

2. (Also FLUNK-OUT).—A failure, especially (at college) in recitations; a backing out of undertakings.

1853. *Songs of Yale.* In moody meditation sunk, Reflecting on my future FLUNK.

1877. *Brunonian*, 24th Feb. A FLUNK is a complete fizzle; and a DEAD FLUNK is where one refuses to get out of his seat.

1888. *Missouri Republican*, 11th Feb. Riddleberger forced the presidential possibilities of the senate to a complete FLUNK.

Verb (American).—To retire through fear; to fail (as in a lesson); to cause to fail. *Cf.*, FUNK.

1838. NEAL, *Charcoal Sketches*, IV. Why, little 'un, you must be cracked, if you FLUNK OUT before we begin.

1847. *The Yale Banger*, 22 Oct. My dignity is outraged at beholding those who fizzle and FLUNK in my presence tower above me.

1853. *Amherst Indicator*, p. 253, They know that a man who has FLUNKED. because too much of a genius to get his lesson, is not in a state to appreciate joking.

1871. JOHN HAY, 'Jim Bludso of the Prairie Bell.' in *New York Tribune*, Jan. But he never FLUNKED, and he never lied, I reckon he never know'd how.

FLUNKEY, *subs.* (nautical).—1. A ship's steward.

2. (American.)—An ignorant dabbler in stock; an inexperienced jobber.

1862. *A Week in Wall St.*, p. 90. A broker, who had met with heavy losses, exclaimed: 'I'm in a bear-trap,—this won't do. The dogs will come over me. I shall be mulct in a loss. But I've got time; I'll turn the scale; I'll help the bulls operate for a rise, and draw in the FLUNKIES.

3. (American University.)—One that makes a complete failure in a recitation; one who FLUNKS (*q.v.*).

1859. *Yale Lit. Magazine.* I bore him safe through Horace, Saved him from the FLUNKEY'S doom.

4. (colloquial).—A man-servant, especially one in livery. Hence, by implication, a parasite or TOADY (*q.v.*). Fr., *un larbin.*

1848. THACKERAY, *Book of Snobs*, ch. v. You who have no toadies; you whom no cringing FLUNKEYS or shopmen bow out of doors.

Whence, FLUNKEYISM = Blind worship of rank, birth, or riches. Fr., *la larbinerie.*

1857. J. E. RITCHIE. *Night Side of London*, p. 23. Our trading classes, becoming richer and more sunk in FLUNKEYISM every day.

FLURRYMENT, *subs.* (common.)—Agitation; bustle; confusion; nervous excitement. [Pleonastic, from FLURRY.]

1848. JONES, *Sketches of Travel*, p. II. Mary and all on em was in a monstrous FLURRYMENT.

FLURRY ONE'S MILK, *verb. phr.* (common).—To be worried, angry, or upset; TO FRET ONE'S KIDNEYS (*q.v.*); TO TEAR ONE'S SHIRT, or ONE'S HAIR (*q.v.*).

FLUSH, *subs.* (gamesters').—A hand of one suit.

Adj. (colloquial).—1. With plenty of money; the reverse of HARD UP (*q.v.*); WARM (*q.v.*)., Also abounding in anything: *e.g.* FLUSH OF HIS PATTER = full of his talk; FLUSH OF THE LOTION = liberal with the drink; FLUSH OF HIS NOTIONS = prodigal of ideas; FLUSH OF HER CHARMS = lavish of her person; and so forth.

1603. DEKKER, *Batchelors' Banquet*, ch. viii. Some dames of the company, which are more FLUSH in crownes than her good man.

1605. *The Play of Stucley*, l. 538. They know he hath received His marriage money: they perceive he's FLUSH And mean to share with him ere all be gone.

1663. DRYDEN, *Wild Gallant*, Act II. *Con.* Since you are so FLUSH, sir, you shall give me a locket of diamonds of three hundred pounds.

1690. B. E., *New Dict. of the Canting Crew.* FLUSH in the pocket *c.* full of money. The cull is FLUSH in the fob, the Spark's pocket is well lined with money.

1767. O'HARA, *Two Misers*, Act I. What stops many an hopeful project? lack of cash—[*looking archly at him*]. Are you FLUSH, Sir?

1785. GROSE, *Dict. of the Vulgar Tongue*, s.v.

1846. THACKERAY, *V. F.*, vol. I. ch. xxviii. The expenses were borne by Jos and Osborne, who was FLUSH of money and full of kind attentions to his wife.

1861. A. TROLLOPE, *Framley Parsonage*, ch. viii. Allow me to draw on you for that amount at three months. Long before that time I shall be FLUSH enough.

1864. *Economist*, 29 Oct. The world was then, if such a *very* colloquial expression could be pardoned, 'FLUSH of cash,' and it sent in that cash rapidly and at once.

2. (common).—Intoxicated (*i.e.*, full to the brim); also FLUSHED. For synonyms, *see* DRINKS and SCREWED.

3. (colloquial).—Level: *e.g.*, FLUSH with the top, with the water, with the road, with the boat's edge, etc.

Verb. (common).—1. To whip.

ENGLISH SYNONYMS.—To bludgeon; to bumbaste; to breech (Cotgrave); to brush; to club; to curry; to dress with an oaken towel; to drub; to drybeat; to dry-bob; to drum; to fib; to flap; to flick; to flop; to jerk; to give one ballast; to hide; to lamm; to larrup; to paste; to punch; to rub down; to swinge; to swish; to switch; to trounce; to thump; to tund (Winchester); to wallop. *See* also TAN.

FRENCH SYNONYMS.—*Donner l'avoine* (pop. = to give a feed of hay); *allumer* (popular); *bouiser* (thieves': *un bouis* = a whip).

ITALIAN SYNONYMS.—*Smanegrare; cotillare; corillare; cerire.*

2. (colloquial).—To clean by filling full, and emptying, of water: *e.g.*, to FLUSH a sewer; to wash, swill, or sluice away. Also to fill with water: *e.g.*, to FLUSH a lock.

1884. HENLEY and STEVENSON, *Admiral Guinea*, i., 8. Pray for a new heart; FLUSH OUT your sins with tears.

3. (shooting).—To start or raise a bird from covert: *e.g.*, TO FLUSH a snipe, or a covey of partridges. Hence (venery) TO FLUSH A WILD DUCK = to single out a woman for GROUSING (*q.v.*).

TO COME FLUSH ON ONE, *verb. phr.* (colloquial).—To come suddenly and unexpectedly (Marvell); to overwhelm (as by a sudden rush of water).

FLUSHED ON THE HORSE, *phr.* (prison).—Privately whipped in gaol.

FLUSH-HIT, *subs. phr.* (pugilistic).—A clean blow; a hit full on the mark and straight from the shoulder. For synonyms, *see* DIG.

1891. *Lic. Vict. Mirror*, 30 Jan., p. 7, col. 2. Landed a very heavy FLUSH HIT on the mouth.

Adv. (colloquial).—Full; straight; RIGHT ON (*q.v.*).

1888. *Sporting Life*, 15 Dec. Both cautious, Wilson with marked frequency leading off, and getting the left FLUSH on the face.

FLUSTER, *verb.* (old).—To excite; to confuse, abash, or FLUMMOX (*q.v.*); to upset, or be upset, with drink.

1602. SHAKSPEARE, *Othello*, I., 3. The very elements of this warlike isle,—Have I to-night FLUSTER'D with flowing cups.

1711. *Spectator*, No 87. It is very common for such as are too low in constitution to ogle the idol upon the strength of tea, to FLUSTER themselves with warmer liquors.

1719. DURFEY, *Pills*, etc., ii., 261. When I vext proud Celia just come from my glass, She tells me I'm FLUSTERED, and look like an ass.

1731. FIELDING, *Letter Writers.* Act II., Sc. 5. Who hath taken me to the tavern, and, I protest, almost FLUSTER'D me.

FLUSTERED (or **FLUSTRATED**), *ppl. adj.* (old).—Excited by drink, circumstances, another person's impudence, etc; also mildly drunk. *Cf.*, FLUSTICATED. For synonyms, *see* SCREWED.

1686. *Common. of Women*, Prol. Another to compleat his daily task, FLUSTER'D with claret, seizes on a mask.

1690. B. E., *New Dict. of the Canting Crew.* FLUSTERED, drunk.

1709. STEELE, *Tatler*, No. 3. I . . . therefore take this public occasion to admonish a young Nobleman, whocame FLUSTERED into the box last night.

1748. T. DYCHE, *Dict.* (5th ed.) FLUSTERED (*a*) . . . somewhat intoxicated with liquor.

1750. FIELDING, *Tom Jones*, bk. XIV. ch. ix. This latter, though not drunk, began to be somewhat FLUSTERED.

1779. *The Mirror*, No. 57. All of them FLUSTERED, some of them perfectly intoxicated.

1785. GROSE, *Dict. of the Vulgar Tongue*, s.v.

FLUSTICATED, or **FLUSTRATED**, *ppl. adj.* (old and colloquial).—Confused; in a state of heat or excitement. *Cf.*, FLUSTERED.

1712. *Spectator*, No. 493. We were coming down Essex Street one night a little FLUSTRATED.

1766. COLMAN, *Cland. Marriage V.*, in works (1777) i. 271. Your mind is too much FLUSTRATED, and you can neither eat nor drink.

1843. *Maj. Jones' Courtship*, I. Somehow I was so FLUSTRATED that I tuk the rong way.

1847. PORTER, *Big Bear, &c.*, p. 98. I sot down, being sorter FLUSTICATED like, thinkin' of that skrape, last time I was there.

FLUSTRATION, *subs.* (old and colloquial).—Heat; excitement; bustle; confusion; FLURRY (*q.v.*).

1771. SMOLLET, *Humphrey Clinker*, I., 126. Being I was in such a FLUSTRATION.

1843. *Major Jones' Courtship*, viii. The old woman's been in a monstrous FLUSTRATION 'bout the comet.

1847. PORTER, *Quarter Race, etc.*, p. 177. My wife is in a delicut way, and the frite might cause a FLUSTRATION.

1848. JONES, *Studies of Travel*, p. 21. The old woman was in such a FLUSTRATION she didn't know her lips from anything else.

1872. MORTIMER COLLINS, *Two Plunges for a Pearl*, vol. II., ch. vii. Then was this pretty little actress whom he admired in a great state of FLUSTRATION.

FLUTE, *subs.* (old).—1. The recorder of a corporation.

1598. FLORIO, *A Worlde of Wordes. Tibia*, a FLUTE, a *recorder*, a pipe.

1690. B. E., *New Dict. of the Canting Crew.* FLUTE, c. The recorder of London or of any other town.

1785. GROSE, *Dict. of the Vulgar Tongue*, s.v.

1825 KENT, *Modern Flash Dict.* FLUTE—the recorder of any town.

2. (venery).—The *penis*. Also the ONE-HOLED, THE LIVING, or THE SILENT FLUTE. TO PLAY A TUNE ON THE ONE-HOLED FLUTE=to have connection. *Cf.*, Dryden (*Sixth Juvenal*, line 107). 'And stretch his QUAIL-PIPE till they crack his voice.' For synonyms, *see* CREAMSTICK and PRICK.

1720. DURFEY, *Pills*, etc, vi., 31. He took her by the middle, And taught her by the FLUTE.

1736. *Cupid*, p. 163. The Flute is good that's made of Wood And is, I own, the neatest; Yet ne'ertheless I must confess, The SILENT FLUTE'S the sweetest.

FLUTTER, *subs.* (common).—1. An attempt, or SHY (*q.v.*), at anything; a venture in earnest; a spree; a state of expectancy (as in betting). Hence gambling.

1883. *Echo*, 26 Feb. p. 4, col. 2. I have no stable tip, but I fancy the animal named will at any rate afford backers a FLUTTER for their money.

1889. *Licensed Vict. Gazette*, 8 Feb. Of course he told her he only went in for a little FLUTTER occasionally.

1890. *Saturday Review*, 1 Feb., p. 134, col. 1. They find out the addresses of people whom they see at the races—people whom they suspect to be fond of a FLUTTER, and then an invitation is sent to a little *soirée intime*.

1887. HENLEY, *Culture in the Slums*, iii. I likes a merry little FLUTTER, I keeps a Dado on the sly, In fact my form's the blooming Utter.

2. (common).—The act of spinning a coin.

3. (venery).—Connection defloration. TO HAVE HAD A FLUTTER = (1) TO HAVE BEEN THERE (*cf.*, GREENS); and (2) to have lost one's maidenhead.

Verb. (common).—1. To spin a coin (for drinks); also to gamble.

2. (common).—To go in for a bout of pleasure.

TO FLUTTER THE RIBBONS, *verb. phr.* (common)—To drive.

1864. *Eton School Days*, chap. 1, p. 11. As I was going to be saying, I used to FLUTTER THE RIBANDS of the London, Croydon and South Coast coach.

[FLUTTER, if not a word of all-work, is a word with plenty to do. Thus, TO HAVE (or DO) A FLUTTER=to have a LOOK IN (*q.v.*), to go on the spree, and (of both sexes) to have carnal connection; TO BE ON THE FLUTTER=to be on the spree, and also (venery) to be ALL THERE (*q.v.*) or ON THE SPOT (*q.v.*); TO FLUTTER A JUDY=both to pursue and to possess a girl; TO FLUTTER A BROWN=to spin a coin; TO FLUTTER (or FRET) ONE'S KIDNEYS=to agitate, to exasperate; TO FLUTTER A SKIRT=to walk the streets; and so forth.]

FLUX, *verb* (old).—1. To cheat; to cozen; to overreach. For synonyms, *see* STICK.

1785. GROSE, *Dict. of the Vulgar Tongue*, s.v.

2. (old.)—To salivate. Grose, (1785).

FLY, *subs.* (old).—A familiar; hence, by implication, a parasite or SUCKER (*q.v.*). [In the sixteenth and seventeenth century it was held that familiar spirits, in the guise of flies, lice, fleas, etc., attended witches, who for a price professed to dispose of the power for evil thus imparted.]

1596. LODGE, *Incarnate Devils.* This divel prefers an Ephimerides before a Bible; and his Ptolemey and Hali before Ambrose, golden Chrisostome, or S. Augustine: promise him a familiar, and he will take a FLIE in a box for good paiment.

1610. BEN JONSON, *Alchemist* i. You are mistaken, doctor, Why he does ask one but for cups and horses, A rifling FLY, none of your great familiars.

1622. MASSINGER, *Virgin Martyr*, ii., 2. Courtiers have FLIES That buzz all news unto them.

2. (old).—A printer's devil; specifically a boy who lifted the printed sheets from the press. [Now the vibrating frame used for the same purpose.]

1688. R. HOLME, *Academy of Armory.* These boys do in a printing-house commonly black and bedaub themselves, when the workmen do jocosely call them devils, and sometimes spirits, and sometimes FLIES.

3. (trade).—A customer.

4. (common).—The act of spinning a coin. *Cf.*, FLUTTER.

5. (old).—A public wagon: afterwards (colloquial) a four-wheel hackney coach. Fr., *mouche* (fly)=a public boat on the Seine.

1714. *Memoirs of John Hall*, s.v.

6. (common).—A policeman. For synonyms, *see* BEAK and COPPER.

1857. SNOWDEN, *Magistrates' Assistant*, 3rd ed., p. 446. A policeman; a FLY.

Adj. (common).—1. Knowing; ARTFUL (*q.v.*); up to every move; cute. Also FLY TO, A-FLY, FLY TO THE GAME, and FLY TO WHAT'S WHAT. *Cf.*, AWAKE, and, for synonyms, *see* KNOWING; FLY DOG (*q.v.*).

1811. *Lexicon Balatronicum*, Cheese it, the coves are FLY=be silent, the people understand our discourse.

1823 W. T. MONCRIEFF, *Tom and Jerry*, Act II., Sc. 2. *Jerry.* Charlies' fiddles?—I'm not FLY, Doctor. *Log.* Rattles, Jerry, rattles Jerry rattles! you're FLY now, I see.

1838. GLASCOCK, *Land Sharks and Sea Gulls*, II., 4. That's right; I see you're FLY to every fakement.

1850. *Lloyd's Weekly*, 3 Feb. 'Low Lodging Houses of London.' They say the FLIEST is easy to take in sometimes—that's the artfullest; but I could do no good there.

1851-61. H. MAYHEW, *Lond. Lab. and Lond. Poor*, vol. I., p. 260. 'We were too FLY to send anybody to market but ourselves.'

1861. H. KINGSLEY, *Ravenshoe*, ch. xxxv. [*Chas. Ravenshoe to Shoeblack*]. 'On the cross?' said Charles. 'Ah,' the boy said, 'he goes out *cly-faking* and such. He's a *prig*, and a smart one, too, He's FLY, is Harry.

1876. MISS BRADDON, *Dead Men's Shoes*, ch. lii. 'Go and fetch the cleverest police officer in Liverpool, and let him wait outside this door till I want him.' 'I'm FLY,' answers the youth, brightening at the prospect of excitement and remuneration. 'Case of 'bezzlement, I suppose, Sir?'

1877. *Five Years' Penal Servitude*, ch. ii., p. 125. A certain prisoner, who was what is termed a very FLY man, *i.e.*, a clever, scheming fellow . . . sounded him as to getting tobacco and other matters.

188(?). JENNY HILL *Broadside Ballad.* I've cut my wisdom teeth, some at top, some underneath. . . . So you needn't try it on; I'm FLY.

1890. *Punch*, 30 Aug., p. 9. Briggs, Junior, a lobsculler called me; I wasn't quite FLY to his lay.

1891. *Licensed Victuallers' Gazette*, 9 Jan. If you get among a FLY lot, why they'd skin you in less than no time.

2. (common).—Dextrous.

1834. AINSWORTH, *Rookwood*, bk. III., ch. v. No dummy hunter had forks so FLY.

1839. REYNOLDS, *Pickwick Abroad*, p. 223. We'll knap a fogle with fingers FLY.

3. (venery).—Wanton. FLY-GIRL, -WOMAN, or -DAME = a prostitute.

1888. *San Francisco News Letter*, 4 Feb. 'I'm just gettin' sick'n tired o' the way 't them FLY dames go on, 'n the way t the fellahs hang round 'em 'n dance with 'em 'n so forth.'

Verb. (thieves').—1. To toss; to raise; TO FLY THE MAGS =to toss up half-pence (*cf.*, *subs.*, sense 4).

1857. SNOWDEN, *Magistrates' Assistant*, 3rd ed., p. 447. To lift a window. to FLY a window.

2. (pugilistic).—To give way: as, china FLIES in the baking.

1865. G. F. BERKELEY, *My Life*, II. 296. Heenan . . . told me his right hand was worth nothing to him, and we have since seen that his left FLIES, or, in other words, becomes puffed, softened, or severely damaged by the force of his own blows.

TO FLY AROUND, *verb. phr.* (American).—To bestir oneself; to make haste. Also TO FLY AROUND AND TEAR ONE'S SHIRT.

1851. HOOPER, *Widow Rugby's Husband*, p. 44. Old 'ooman, FLY AROUND, git somethin' for the Squire and Dick to eat.

TO FLY THE FLAG, *verb. phr.* (colloquial).—1. To walk the streets.

2. (vulgar).—To experience the menstrual flux.

See also FLAG.

TO FLY HIGH (or RATHER HIGH).—1. *verb. phr.* (common). —To get, or be drunk. For synonyms, *see* DRINKS and SCREWED.

2. (colloquial).—To keep the best company, maintain the best appearances, and affect the best aims: *i.e.*, to be a HIGH-FLIER (*q.v*). Also, to venture for the biggest stakes in the biggest way.

TO FLY LOW, *verb. phr.* (colloquial).—To make as little of oneself as possible; to SING SMALL (*q.v.*); and (among thieves) to keep out of the way when WANTED (*q.v.*).

TO FLY OFF THE HANDLE, *verb. phr.* (American pioneer).—To lose temper; to fail of a promise; to jilt; to die; also TO SLIP OFF THE HANDLE (*q.v.*); to disappoint in any way. [In pioneer life for an axe to part company with its handle is a serious trial to temper and patience.]

1843-4. HALIBURTON, *The Attaché.* You never see such a crotchical old critter as he is. He FLIES RIGHT OFF THE HANDLE for nothing

1867. *Home Journal* (New York), 21 July (speaking of a man who had succeeded to a large fortune it says) he WENT OFF THE HANDLE in England rather unexpectedly.

1871. DE VERE, *Americanisms*, p. 195 If a fair lady loses her temper, or worst of all, if she breaks the tender promise, she is said to FLY OFF THE HANDLE, and the disappointment is as serious to the unlucky lover as a lost axe to many a settler.

1888. *Pittsburg Chronicle.* 'I can't say that I'am stuck on Sue Fitzpercy,' remarked Amy. 'She is liable TO FLY OFF THE HANDLE.

TO FLY OUT, *verb. phr.* (colloquial).—To get angry; to scold.

1612. CHAPMAN, *Widow's Tears*, Act II., p. 317 (*Plays*, 1874). For wherefore rage wives at their husbands so when they FLY OUT? for zeal against the sin?

1665-6. PEPYS, *Diary*, 17 Jan. It is to be feared that the Parliament will FLY OUT against him and particular men, the next Session.

1712. *Spectator*, No. 479. He (Socrates) has said, My dear friend, you are beholden to Xantippe, that I bear so well your FLYING OUT in a dispute.

1855. THACKERAY, *Newcomes*, ch. xx. 'And then the Colonel FLIES OUT about his boy, and says that my wife insulted him!'

TO MAKE THE FUR (or FEATHERS) FLY, *verb. phr.* (common).—To attack effectively; to make a disturbance; to quarrel noisily, like two tom cats on the tiles, who are said (in American) to pull fur, or to pull wool.

1847. PORTER, *Big Bear*, etc., p. 132. Thar, they've got him agin, and now the FUR FLIES.

1888. *Denver Republican*, 29 Feb. 'Wait until the National Committee assembles on February 22,' said the organizer, 'and you will see the FUR FLY from the Cleveland hide.'

TO TAKE ON THE FLY, *verb. phr.* (vagrants').—To beg in the streets; a specific usage of adverbial sense.

1851-61. MAYHEW, *Lond. Lab. and Lond. Poor*, II., p. 59. The 'first move' in his mendicant career was TAKING THEM ON THE FLY, which means meeting the gentry on their walks, and beseeching or at times menacing them till something is given.

TO FLY A KITE, *verb phr.* (common).—To raise money by means of accommodation bills; TO RAISE THE WIND (*q.v.*).

1812. From an old Dublin *Jester.* [The story, however, with slight variations, is told of other judges. See *N. and Q.*, 6 S. ix., 326-394.] In a case before the Lord Chancellor of Ireland Mr. Curran, on behalf of the suitor, prayed to be relieved from the payment of some bills for which he had not received consideration, but only lent his name as an accommodation. Mr. Curran, in the course of his pleadings, mentioned the terms KITE and RAISING THE WIND several times, when his lordship requested to know the meaning of the words. 'My lord,' Mr. Curran replied, 'in your country (meaning England) the wind generally raises the kite, but with *us*, significantly looking at the gentlemen of the bar, THE KITE RAISES THE WIND.'

1848. *Punch*, XIV., p. 226. 'The Model Gentleman.' He never does 'a little discounting' nor lends his hand to 'FLYING A KITE.'

1849. *Perils of Pearl Street*, p. 87. FLYING THE KITE is rather a perilous adventure.

1880. G. R. SIMS, *Ballads of Babylon* (Little Worries). You have a KITE you cannot FLY, and creditors are pressing.

1891. *Licensed Victuallers' Gazette*, 23 Jan. Prince Alexis Soltykoff, who has been FLYING KITES, and getting into trouble thereby, is the only son of Prince Soltykoff, the steward of the Jockey Club.

2. (thieves')—To go out by the window.

3. (lodging-house).—To evacuate from a window.

4. (colloquial).—To attempt; to set one's cap at.

1863. H. KINGSLEY, *Austin Elliot*, ch. xii. 'They say that you FLEW YOUR KITE at that girl of George Cecil's who has married that prig, Lord Mewstone.'

TO FLY THE BLUE PIGEON, *verb. phr.* (thieves').—To steal lead from roofs. *See* BLUE-PIGEON. Fr., *faire la mastar au gras-double*, or *la faire au mastar*.

1785. GROSE, *Dict. of the Vulgar Tongue*, s.v.

1789. G. PARKER, *Life's Painter*, Thieves who FLY THE BLUE PIGEON, that is, who steal lead off houses, or cut pipes away . . . cut a hundredweight of lead, which they wrap round their bodies next to the skin. This they call a BIBLE (*q.v.*), and what they steal and put in their pockets, they call a TESTAMENT (*q.v.*).

1887. *Judy*, 27 April, p. 200. A burglar whose particular LAY was FLYING the BLUE PIGEON, *i.e.*, stealing lead.

TO LET FLY, *verb. phr.* (colloquial).—To hit out. [From cock-fighting.]

1859. *Punch*, vol. XXXVII., p. 54. 'Essence of Parliament.' Monday, 25 July. Lord Lyndhurst LET FLY and caught him what (if pugilistic terms be not out of place when one is alluding to so pacific a personage) may be designated an extremely neat one on the conk.

NOT A FEATHER TO FLY WITH, *adv. phr.* (common).—Penniless and ruined; DEAD-BROKE (*q.v.* for synonyms).

TO BREAK A FLY ON A WHEEL, *verb. phr.* (colloquial). To make a mountain of a molehill. *Cf.*, TO CRACK A NUT WITH A NASMYTH HAMMER = to lavish force or energy.

THE FLY ON THE WHEEL, *subs. phr.* (colloquial).—One who fancies himself of mighty importance. [From the fable.]

I DON'T RISE TO THAT FLY, *phr.* (common) = I don't believe you ; you won't catch me with such bait as that. [From fly-fishing.]

OFF THE FLY, *adv. phr.* (colloquial).—On the quiet ; laid up in dock ; doing nothing : said of a strumpet retired from business, or a man (or woman) who has given over the pursuit of pleasure.

ON THE FLY, *adv. phr.* (popular). — 1. Walking the streets ; out for a LARK (*q.v.*) ; OFF WORK (*q.v.*) ; out on the SPREE (*q.v.*).

2. (thieves')—In motion : *e.g.*, 'I got in one ON THE FLY' = I landed a blow while I was running.

1868. *Temple Bar*, xxiv., p. 538. I prigged an old woman's poke ON THE FLY.

FLY-BLOW, *subs.* (common).—A bastard ; *cf.*, BYE-BLOW. A nonce word.

1875. OUIDA, *Signa*, vol. I., ch. viii., p. 140. No doubt that little FLY-BLOW is his own.

FLY-BLOWN, *adj.* (common).—1. Intoxicated. For synonyms, see DRINKS and SCREWED.

1877. *Judy*, 18 May, p. 236. The officer assisted the pastor out, and hinted that he was slightly 'FLY-BLOWN.'

2. (Australian). — Cleaned-out ; without a rap ; HARD-UP (*q.v.* for synonyms).

1889. *Star*, 3 Jan. Our diggers go into Castlemaine to get their hair cut, and once there, they get on the spree, and come back FLY-BLOWN.

3, (common).—Used, or done-up ; WASHED-OUT (*q.v.*).

4. (venery).—Deflowered. Also STALE (*q.v.*) ; 'known for a wanton.' Also suspected of disease.

FLY-BY-NIGHT, *subs.* (old). — 1. A sedan chair on wheels ; a usage of the Regency days.

2. (common).—A defaulting debtor ; one who SHOOTS THE MOON (*q.v.*). Also applied to the act.

3. (venery). — A prostitute. See BAT, and for synonyms, BARRACK-HACK and TART.

4. (common).—A noctambulist for business or for pleasure : *i.e.*, a burglar or a common SPREESTER (*q.v.*).

5. (obsolete). — A term of opprobrium.

1796. GROSE, *Dict. of the Vulgar Tongue* (3rd ed.), s.v. An ancient term of reproach to an old woman, signifying that she was a witch, and alluding to the nocturnal excursions attributed to witches who were supposed to fly abroad to their meetings mounted on brooms.

6. (venery). — The female *pudendum*. For synonyms, see MONOSYLLABLE.

FLY-CAGE, *subs.* (venery). — The female *pudendum*. For synonyms, see MONOSYLLABLE.

FLY-CATCHER, *subs.* (venery).—1. The female *pudendum*. For synonyms, see MONOSYLLABLE.

2. (common). — An open-mouthed ignoramus ; a GAPE-SEED (*q.v.*) — SYDNEY SMITH. Fr., *gobe-mouche.*

FLYCOP, *subs.* (American). — A sharp officer ; one well broken in to the tricks of trade. [From FLY = knowing + COP, a policeman.]

1859. MATSELL, *Vocabulum or Rogue's Lexicon*, s.v.

FLY-DISPERSER SOUP, *subs. phr.* (common).—Oxtail.

FLYER. — 1. See FLIER in all senses.

2. (old). — A shoe. For synonyms, see TROTTER-CASE.

1690. B. E., *New Dict. of Terms*, etc., s.v.

1785. GROSE, *Dict. of the Vulgar Tongue*, s.v.

1791. *Life and Adventures of Bamfylde Moore Carew*, s.v.

1851. MAYHEW, *Lond. Lab. and Lond. Poor*, vol. II., p. 34. There is another article called a FLYER, that is, a shoe sold without being welted.

3. (Winchester).—A half-volley at football. A MADE-FLYER is when the bound of the ball is gained from a previous kick, by the same side, against canvas or any other obstacle, or is dropped, as in a 'drop-kick.' This is now confused with a 'kick-up.'

FLY-FLAPPED, *adj.* (obsolete).—Whipped in the stocks, or at the cart's tail.—GROSE.

FLY-FLAPPER, *subs.* (old). — A heavy bludgeon.

FLY-FLAT, *subs.* (turf).—A would-be connoisseur and authority. [From FLY = knowing + FLAT = a fool.]

FLYING. — TO LOOK AS IF THE DEVIL HAD SHIT HIM (or HER) FLYING (common and proverbial). —Said in derision of one odd-looking, filthy, or deformed.

FLYING-ANGEL.—See ANGEL.

FLYING BRICKLAYERS, *subs. phr.* (military).—The mounted Royal Engineers.

FLYING CAMPS, *subs. phr.* (old).— Couples or gangs of beggars.

1699. B. E., *Dict. of the Canting Crew.* Beggars plying in FLYING CAMPS. Beggars plying in bodies at funerals.

1785. GROSE, *Dict. of the Vulgar Tongue*, s.v.

FLYING-CAPER, *subs.* (thieves')—An escape from prison ; LEG-BAIL (*q.v.*).

1864. *Daily Paper*, 'Police Report.' The blues are always ready to spot a fellow who has tried on the FLYING-CAPER with them, and given them leg-bail.

FLYING-CAT.—See CAT.

FLYING COUNTRY, *subs. phr.* (hunting).—A country where the GOING (*q.v.*) is fast and good.

1856. WHYTE MELVILLE, *Kate Coventry*, ch. xii. The heavy-top hounds are an establishment such as, I am given to understand, is not usually kept in Leicestershire, Northamptonshire, and other so-called 'FLYING COUNTIES.'

FLYING COVE, *subs. phr.* (American thieves').—An impostor who gets, or tries to get, money from persons who have been robbed by pretending to give such information as will lead to recovery. Formerly, FLYING-PORTER (GROSE).

1859. MATSELL, *Vocabulum or Rogues' Lexicon*, s.v.

FLYING-DUSTMAN.—See STIFF-UN.

FLYING-DUTCHMAN, *subs.* (common).—The London and Exeter express (G.W.R.). See also FLYING SCOTCHMAN and WILD IRISHMAN. *Cf.*, DEAD-MEAT TRAIN and LARKY SUBALTERN'S COACH.

FLYING-HORSE (or MARE), *subs.* (wrestling).—The throw by which an opponent is sent over the head. Introduced, says Bee, by Parkins.

1754. FOOTE, *Knights*, Act I. But we don't wrestle after your fashion ; we ha' no tripping ; fath and soul ! we all go upon close hugs or the FLYING-MARE.

1884. *Referee*, 23 March, p. 1., col. 1. In the third and last bout, Klein brought his man clean over his head—holding him by his own—with a sort of FLYING - MARE, and elicited thunders of applause.

1886. *Pall Mall Gazette*, 5 July, p. 4. On a Mississippi steamer he astonished a rowdy who was shocked at his unnatural objection to whisky, by performing upon him the feat known to British wrestlers as 'the FLYING MARE.'

FLYING-JIGGER OR GYGGER, *subs.* (thieves'). — A turnpike gate. JIGGER = a door or gate.]

1785. GROSE, *Dict. of the Vulgar Tongue*, s.v.

1859. MATSELL, *Vocabulum or Rogue's Lexicon*, s.v.

FLYING-MAN, *subs.* (football).—A skirmisher good at taking, and running with, the ball.

1864. *Eton School Days*, ch. 23, p. 255. He possessed good wind, and was a very good 'kick-off,' and he could 'bully' a ball as well as any one. He was a little too heavy for 'FLYING-MAN,' but he made a decent 'sidepost,' and now and then he officiated as 'corner.'

FLYING-MARE. See FLYING-HORSE.

FLYING PASTY, *subs. phr.* (obsolete). —Excrement wrapped in paper and thrown over a neighbour's wall. [GROSE.]

FLYING-PORTER. See FLYING COVE.

FLYING-STATIONER, *subs.* (street)—A hawker of street ballads ; a PAPERWORKER (*q.v.*), or RUNNING PATTERER (*q.v.*). *Cf.*, CROAK. 'Printed for the FLYING-STATIONER' is the *imprimatur* on hundreds of broadsheets from the last century onwards.

1785. GROSE, *Dict. of the Vulgar Tongue*, s.v. Ballad singers and hawkers of penny histories.

1851-61. H. MAYHEW, *Lond. Lab. and Lond. Poor*, Vol. I., p. 228. That order or species of the pattering genus known as FLYING STATIONERS, from the fact of their being continually on the move while describing the attractions of the 'papers' they have to sell.

1886. *Athenæum*, 31 July, p. 139. Scores of tracts were issued in the Newgate region, from Giltspur Street to Blowbladder Street, whence numbers of FLYING STATIONERS drew their supplies long before either of the Catnachs were born.

FLYMY. *Adj.* (streets).—Knowing, FAST (*q.v.*) ; roguish ; sprightly. From FLY (*q.v.*).

1887. W. E. HENLEY, *Villon's Good Night.* You FLYMY titters fond of flam.

FLY-MY-KITE, *subs. phr.* (rhyming). —A light.

FLYMY-MESS, TO BE IN A FLYMY-MESS, *verb. phr.* (military).—To be hungry and have nothing to eat. For synonyms, see PECKISH.

FLY-SLICER, *subs.* (common).—A cavalry-man ; *cf.*, MUDCRUSHER. French lancers are *allumeurs de gaz*, their weapons being likened to a lamplighter's rod.

1785. GROSE, *Dict. of the Vulgar Tongue*, s.v. FLY-SLICERS: Life-guardmen, from their sitting on horseback, under an arch, where they are frequently observed to drive away flies with their swords.

FLY THE GARTER, *subs. phr.* (school-boys').—Leap-frog.

1863. G. A. SALA, *Breakfast in Bed*, Essay VIII., p. 187 (1864). He was very probably been playing FLY-THE-GARTER in the gutter instead of waiting his turn at the office.

FLY-TRAP, *subs.* (common). — 1. The mouth. For synonyms, see POTATO-TRAP.

2. (venery).—The female *pudendum*. For synonyms, see MONOSYLLABLE.

FOALED, *adj.* (hunting).—Thrown from a horse. Fr., *faire parache.*

FOB, or FUB, *subs.* (old).—1. A cheat ; a trick ; a swindle. To COME THE FOB = to impose upon ; to swindle ; *cf.*, COME OVER.

1690. B. E., *Dict. of the Canting Crew.* FOB c., a cheat trick.

1785. GROSE, *Dict. of the Vulgar Tongue*, FOB, s.v.

1852. JUDSON, *Mysteries of New York*, ch. vii. He come ze FOB on some of ze nobilitie, and zey invite him to go to Amerique.

2. (old : now recognised)—A breeches pocket ; a watch pocket.

1678. BUTLER, *Hudibras*, III., i., 107. Had rifled all his pokes and FOBS Of gimcrack whims and gimgumbobs.

1690. B. E., *Dict. of the Canting Crew.* FOB, c., also a little pocket.

1703. MARVELL, *Poems on Affairs of State.* 'Royal Revolutions.' When plate was in pawn and FOB at an ebb. *Ibid.* 'Last Instructions,' etc. More gold in's FOB, more lace upon his coat.

1785. GROSE, *Dict. of the Vulgar Tongue*, s.v.

3. (common).—A watch chain or ribbon, with buckle and seals, worn hanging from the fob.

Verb. (old).—1. To rob ; to cheat ; to pocket ; also TO FOB OFF.

1700. CONGREVE, *Way of the World*, i., 9. There were items of such a treaty in embrio ; and if it shou'd come to life poor *Mirabell* wou'd be in some sort unfortunately FOBB'D, i'faith.

1703. MRS. CENTLIVRE, *Stolen Heiress*, III., iv., wks. (1872), i., 358. I shall be FOBBED of my mistress by and by. Why, Frank, why, thou wilt not FOB me, wilt thou?

1731. FIELDING, *Grub Street Opera*, i., 5. While ev'ry one else he is FOBBING, He still may be honest to me.

1789. WOLCOT [P. Pindar], *Rowland for an Oliver*, in wks. (Dublin. 1795), Vol. II., p. 159. To use a cant phrase, we've been finely FOBB'D, Indeed, have very dext'rously been robb'd.

1840. HOWITT, *Visits to Remarkable Places*, p. 170. Very pretty sums he has FOBBED now and then.

1842. *Punch*, III., p. 239, col. 2. The world turns its back on you, and neither by cards nor dice can you FOB your brother mortal out of a single guinea.

2. (old).—To deceive ; trifle with ; disappoint ; to put off dishonestly or unfairly.

1598. SHAKSPEARE, *2 Henry IV.*, ii., 1. A hundred mark is a long loan for a poor lone woman to bear, and I have borne, and borne, and borne, and have been FUBBED off and FUBBED off.

1602. SHAKSPEARE, *Othello*, IV., 2. I think it is scurvy, and begin to find myself FOBBED in it.

1610. SHAKSPEARE, *Coriolanus*, I., 1. You must not think to FOB off our disgrace with a tale.

1884. *Fortnightly Review*, XXXVI., p. 75. In nothing are amateur backers of horses FOBBED OFF by professionals with less than the legitimate odds than in backing double and triple events.

1864. *The Tramp Exposed*, p. 7. A miserable, a job lot of humanity as had ever been FOBBED OFF on a defrauded universe.

TO GUT A FOB, *verb. phr.* (old). — To pick pockets. *Cf.*, FOB, verbal sense 1. For synonyms, *see* PRIG.

1819. MOORE, *Tom Crib's Memorial*, 1. Diddling your subjects, and GUTTING their FOBS.

FOBUS, *subs.* (old). — An opprobrious epithet.

1677. WYCHERLEY, *Plain Dealer*, II., 1. Ay, you old FOBUS.

2. (venery). — The female *pudendum*. For synonyms, *see* MONOSYLLABLE.

FODDER, *subs.* (common). — Paper for the closet, BUM-FODDER (*q.v.*).

FŒTUS. TO TAP THE FŒTUS, *verb. phr* (medical). — To procure abortion.

FOG, *subs.* (old) — Smoke.—GROSE [1785]; *Modern Flash Dict.* [1823]; MATSELL [1859]. [*Cf.*, FOGUS.]

IN A FOG, *subs. phr.* (colloquial).—In a condition of perplexity, doubt, difficulty, or mystification: as, 'I'm quite in a FOG as to wha you mean.'

Verb (old).—1. To smoke.

2. (colloquial).—To mystify; to perplex; to obscure.

1836. W. H. SMITH, '*The Thieves' Chaunt.*' There's a nook in the boozingken, Where many a mug I FOG.

1883. *Punch*, May, p. 210, col. 1. So large a picture, treated so ideally—Not that *that* means stricture—FOGS us to find room for it.

1883. *Daily Telegraph*, 29 Sept. We turns what we say into tangle talk so as to FOG them.

FOGEY, or **FOGY**, **FOGAY**, or **FOGGI**, *subs.* (old).—An invalid or garrison soldier or sailor. Whence the present colloquial usages: (1) a person advanced in life, and (2) an old-fashioned or eccentric person; generally OLD FOGEY. [Derivation doubtful; suggestions are (1) from Su. G. *fogde* and (2) from Eng. *folk*. *See Notes and Queries*, 1 S. vii., 354, 559, 632; viii., 64, 154, 256, 455, 652; 6 S. ix., 10, 195.]

1785. GROSE, *Dict. of the Vulgar Tongue*, s.v.

1812. Letter quoted in *Notes and Queries*, 6 S., ix., 10:. My company is now forming into an invalid company. Tell your grandmother we will be like the Castle FOGGIES.

1855. THACKERAY, *The Ballad of Bouillabaisse*. When first I saw ye, *cari luoghi*, I'd scarce a beard upon my face, And now, a grizzled, grim OLD FOGY, I sit and wait for Bouillabaisse.

1864. *Tangled Talk*, p. 104. An OLD FOGEY, who particularly hated being '*done*.'

1867. NESMITH, 'Reminiscences of Dr. Anthon,' in *The Galaxy*, Sept., p. 611. The adherents of 'progress' mostly regard classics as OLD FOGEY, and 'see no use' in the laborious years which youth spend upon them.

1883. JAMES PAYN, *The Canon's Ward*, ch. xv. 'He would have preferred some bookish sneak like Adair, or some OLD FOGEY like Mavors.'

1888. *Sporting Life*, 10 Dec. So it is with the sister art of music, for I (myself something of an OLD FOGEY in such matters).

So also FOGEYISH = old-fashioned; eccentric. FOGEYDOM = the state of FOGEYISHNESS; and FOGEYISM = a characteristic of FOGEYDOM.

1877. BESANT and RICE, *Golden Butterfly*, ch. i. They repaired arm-in-arm to their club—the Renaissance, now past its prime, and a little FOGYISH.

1883. *Saturday Review*, 31 March, p. 403, col. 1. Not the least among the pleasures of FOGEYDOM, so ably depicted by Thackeray, is the confidence that it inspires in the hearts of the fairer sex.

FOGGAGE, *subs.* (colloquial).—Fodder, especially green-meat.

1785. BURNS, *To a Mouse.* And naething now to bigg a new ane O'FOGGAGE green.

FOGGED, *ppl. adj.* (common).—1. Drunk. *Cf.*, FOGGY. For synonyms, *see* DRINKS and SCREWED.

2. (common). — Perplexed; bewildered; at a loss. [From FOG (*q.v.*), to perplex]. For synonyms, *see* FLABBERGASTED.

1883. *Illust. London News*, 6 Jan., p. 6, col. 3. They were all treading on one another's heels, trying to do their best, but hopelessly FOGGED.

1887. *All the Year Round*, 30 July, 30, p. 68. An Australian says that he is bushed just as an Englishman, equally characteristically, declares that he is FOGGED.

FOGGER, *subs.* (old).—1. A huckster; a cringing, whining beggar; a pettifogger.

1614. *Terence in English.* I shall be exclaimed upon to be a beggarly FOGGER, greedily hunting after heritage.

2. (old).—A farm servant whose duty is to feed the cattle; *i.e.*, to supply them with FOGGAGE (*q.v.*).

FOGGY, *adj.* (common).—1. Drunk; *i.e.*, CLINCHED or HAZY (*q.v.*) For synonyms, *see* DRINKS and SCREWED.

2. (colloquial).—Dull; fatwitted; THICK (*q.v.*).

FOGLE, *subs.* (thieves'). — A silk handkerchief; also generic. [*Cf.*, Ital., *foglia* = a pocket, a purse: Fr., *fouille* = a pocket]. A cotton handkerchief is called a CLOUT.

ENGLISH SYNONYMS. — Bandanna; belcher; billy; clout; conch-clout; fam-cloth; flag; kent-rag; madam; muckender; mucketer (FLORIO); nose-wipe; pen-wiper; rag; sneezer; snottinger or snot-rag; stook; wipe. *See* BILLY.

FRENCH SYNONYMS. — *Un cachemire* (popular); *un blave* or *blavin* (thieves'; from O.F., *blave* = blue); *une fassolette* (thieves': It., *fazzoletto*); *un chiffon* or *chiffornion* (popular = a rag); *un moufion* (popular); *les mouchettes* (popular = wipes).

GERMAN SYNONYMS.—*Schneitzlingsschneiche* (*cf.*, SNOT-RAG); *Flammert* or *Flamme* (also a neckerchief and an apron); *Wisch* (= also clothing of any kind).

1785, GROSE, *Dict. of the Vulg. Tongue*, s.v.

1821. EGAN, *Tom and Jerry* (1890), p. 74. Jerry's sneezer was touched with some convulsive efforts so that his FOGLE was continually at work.

1834. AINSWORTH, *Rookwood* bk. iii., ch. 5. FOGLES and fawnies soon went their way.

1837. DICKENS, *Oliver Twist*, ch. xviii. 'If you don't take FOGLES and tickers——' 'What's the good of talking in that way?' interposed Master Bates: 'he don't know what you mean.' 'If you don't take pocket-handkerchiefs and watches,' said the Dodger

1841. *Tait's Edinburgh Mag.*, viii., p. 220. Fawnies or FOGLES, onions gay, all were the same to me.

1849. *Punch's Almanack*, 'The Swell Mobsman's Almanack.' Their FOGLES fetch next to nothing.

1858. A. MAYHEW, *Paved with Gold*, bk. II., ch. i., p. 60. They're just made for hooking a FOGLE [handkerchief] out of a clye.

FOGLE-HUNTER, *subs.* (thieves').—A thief whose speciality is FOGLES (*q.v.*) Fr. *un blaviniste* or *un chiffonier*, but for synonyms, *see* STOOKHAULER.

1827. MAGINN, in *Blackwood's Mag.* . . . . the FOGLE HUNTERS doing Their morning fake in the prigging lay.

1830. LYTTON, *Paul Clifford*, ch. xvi. Who's here so base as would be a FOGLE-HUNTER?

1837. DICKENS, *Oliver Twist*, p. 44. 'What's the matter now?' said the man, carelessly. 'A young FOGLE-HUNTER,' replied the man who had Oliver in charge.

1843. *Punch*, IV., p. 129. Rich charities the chapel throng. The swell mob they are there, The Bishop's sermon is not long, The FOGLE-HUNTER ware!

FOGLE-HUNTING (or **DRAWING**), *subs. phr.* (thieves').—Stealing pocket-handkerchiefs; *i.e.*, 'prigging of wipes.'

1823. BEE, *Dict. of the Turf*, etc., p. 82. *Q.* 'Where's Teddy?' *A.* 'He's out a FOGLE-HUNTING.' Sometimes 'tis said 'drawing FOGLES,' and 'FOGLE-DRAWING.'

FOGRAM, or **FOGRUM**, *subs.* (old).—A fussy old man. [*Cf.*, colloquial sense of FOGEY.]

1785. GROSE, *Dict. of the Vulgar Tongue*, s.v.

1793. BUTT, *Poems.* We teach old maxims, neither less nor more, Than Locke, or humble Hooker taught before, Those FOGRUMS, quizzes, treats, and bores, and gigs, Were held in some account with ancient prigs.

1798. O'KEEFE, *Fontainbleau*, II., 3. Never mind, old FOGRUM, run away with me.

1859. MATSELL, *Vocabulum, or Rogue's Lexicon*, s.v.

Adj. (old).—Fogeyish; stupid.

1777. FOOTE, *Trip to Calais*, i, Father and mother are but a couple of FOGRUM old fools.

Hence FOGRAMITY = (1) FOGEYISM (*q.v.*), and (2) the state of FOGEYISHNESS.

1796. D'ARBLAY, *Camilla*, ii., 5. Nobody's civil now, you know, it is a FOGRAMITY quite out of date.

FOGUE, *adj.* (American thieves')—Fierce; fiery.

1859. MATSELL, *Vocabulum, or Rogue's Lexicon*, s.v.

FOGUS, *subs.* (old).—Tobacco. [*Cf.*, FOGUS.] For synonyms, *see* WEED.

1671. HEAD, *English Rogue*, I., v., p. 49 (1874), s.v. 1724. COLES, *English Dict.*, s.v. 1785. GROSE, *Dict. of the Vulg. Tongue.* Tip me a gage of FOGUS.

1821. HAGGART, *Life*, p. 133. A hole in the roof of my cell, through which I handed her plenty of FOGUS.

1834. H. AINSWORTH, *Rookwood*, bk. III., ch. v. Troll us a stave, my antediluvian file, and in the meantime tip me a gage [pipe] of FOGUS, Jerry.

1859. MATSELL, *Vocabulum, or Rogue's Lexicon*, s.v.

FOILER, *subs.* (old).—A thief.

1669. *Nicker Nicked*, in *Harl. Misc.* [ed. Park], ii., 108. Given in list of names of thieves.

FOIN, *verb.* (obsolete).—To copulate, *i.e.*, to thrust, TO POKE (*q.v.*). Also *subs.*

1598. FLORIO, *A Worlde of Wordes. Scazzata*: A thrust, a push, a FOYNE, or the serving to a woman of a man's pricke.

1598. SHAKSPEARE, 2 *Henry IV.*, ii., 4. Thou whoreson little tidy Bartholomew boar pig, when wilt thou leave fighting o'days, and FOINING o'nights, and begin to patch up thine old body for heaven?

FOIST, **FOYST**, or **FYST**, *subs.* (old).—1. A cheat; a swindler; a sharper.

1592. JOHN DAY, *Blind Beggar* (Bullen), p. 21. Your nipper, your FOYST, your rogue, your cheat.

1596. BEN JONSON *Every Man in His Humour* iv., 7. Prate again, as you like this, you whoreson FOIST you.

1607. DEKKER, *Jests to Make you Merie* in wks. (Grosart) II., 326. Now to our FOYSTS, *alias* pickpocket, *alias* cutpurse.

1609. DEKKER, *Lanthorne and Candelight*, in wks. (Grosart) III., 212. A FOYST nor a Nip shall not walke into a Fayre or a Play-house.

1611. MIDDLETON, *Roaring Girl*, O. Pl., vi., 113. This brave fellow is no better than a FOIST. FOIST! what is that? A diver with two fingers; a pickpocket; all his train study the figging law, that's to say cutting of purses and FOISTING.

2. (old).—A trick; a swindle; an imposture. Also FOYSTER and FOISTER.

1605. BEN JONSON, *Volpone or the Fox*, iii., 9. Put not your FOISTS upon me. I shall scent 'em.

3. (old).—A silent emission of wind through the anus (see quot., sense 2); a CHEESER. *See* FART and FOUSTY. [Coles has to *fyst*, vissio; which in his Latin part he renders to *fizzle*. Also FYSTING CUR; and in Sherwood's English Dictionary, subjoined to Cotgrave, FYSTING CURS, and other offenders of the same class, are fully illustrated.]

1598. FLORIO, *A Worlde of Wordes. Loffa*, a fizle, a FISTE, a close fart.

1605. JONSON, *Eastward Hoe*, pl. iv., 270. Marry, FYST o' your Ruidess. I thought as much.

1662. *Rump Songs*, II., 3. That a reason be enacted (if there be not one), Why a fart hath a voice, and a FYST hath none, Which nobody can deny.

1690. B. E., *Dict. of the Canting Crew.* FOYST . . . also a close strong stink, without noise or report.

1785. GROSE, *Dict. of the Vulgar Tongue*, s.v. FICE or FOYSE.

Verb. (old).—1. To trick; to swindle; to pick pockets.

1607. DEKKER, *Jests to Make You Merie*, in wks. (Grosart) II., 332. But now to the manner of the FOYSTING of a pocket, the sharing of the money, and how honest men may avoide them.

1610. ROWLANDS, *Martin Mark-all*, p. 38 (H. Club's Rept., 1874). To FOYST, to picke a pocket.

1653. MIDDLETON, *Spanish Gipsy*, ii., 1. I mean fitching, FOISTING, nimming.

2. (old).—To fart. Also to copulate (URQUHART).

1539. DAVID LYNDSAY, *Thrie Estaitis* (Works, Laing, 1879), ii., 109. Ane FISTAND flag.

1598. FLORIO, *A Worlde of Wordes. Loffare*, s.v.

1611. COTGRAVE, *Dictionnarie*, *Vessir*, s.v.

FOISTER, or **FOYSTER**, *subs.* (old).—A pick-pocket; a cheat.

1598. FLORIO, *A Worlde of Wordes. Barattiere*, a barterer, a trucker, a marter, an exchanger, a briber, a cheater, a false gamester, a cousener, a broker, a fripper, a chaffrer, a cogger, a FOYSTER, a deceiuer, a coni-catcher, a bareter, a prowler.

(?). *Mirrour for Magistrates*, p. 483, When facing FOISTERS, fit for Tiburn. fraies, Are food-sick faint.

FOLLOWER, *subs.* (colloquial).—A maid-servant's sweetheart; a beau. For synonyms, *see* JOMER.

1838. DICKENS, *Nicholas Nickleby*, ch. xv. Five servants kept. No man. No FOLLOWERS.

1860. *Chambers' Journal*, XIII., p. 32. No FOLLOWERS allowed.

1870. *Spectator*, 15 Jan. It is safer, unkind as it may seem, to forbid the presence of a 'FOLLOWER' in the house. A girl is less likely to get into mischief when she is walking with her friend in the street or talking with him over the area gate, than when she receives him alone in the kitchen.

1872 *The Ladies*, 29 June, p. 335. If you take into consideration that 'FOLLOWERS' are in most houses strictly forbidden, what wonder is it that girls are now and then caught flirting with the butcher and the baker at the area railings?

FOLLOW-ME-LADS, *subs. phr.* (common). — Curls or ribands hanging over the shoulder; *cf.*, Fr., *suivez-moi-jeune-homme* = ribbons flying behind a lady's dress. Also FOLLOWERS.

1872. *Spectator.* 'FOLLOW-ME-LADS' are not in themselves very pretty, though, like any other fashion, they become the Princess, and they are exceedingly costly.

FOLLOW ON, *subs. phr.* and *verb* (cricket). — A team eighty runs behind the other in the first innings is obliged to FOLLOW ON; *i.e.*, to take to the wickets a second time. A run more, and it SAVES THE FOLLOW ON.

1891. *Pall Mall Gazette*, 5 Aug. 'Notts. *v.* Surrey. The game, with a possible prospect of the FOLLOW-ON, being saved.

FOLLOW YOUR NOSE! *intj. phr.* (streets'). — A retort on asking the way. The full phrase is, 'Follow your nose, and you are sure to go straight.'

1620. PERCY, *Folio MSS.*, p. 462. He went to the sea syde, and FFOLLOWED HIS NOSE.

1854. *Notes and Queries*, x., p. 66. In what collection of tales published in 1834 shall I find the tale entitled FOLLOW YOUR NOSE?

FOO-FOO, *subs.* (American). — A person of no account; an insignificant idiot; a POOP (*q.v.*).

1837. *A Glance at New York* (in Bartlett). Don't know what a FOO-FOO is? Well, as you're a greenhorn, I'll enlighten you. A FOO-FOO, or an outsider, is a chap that can't come the big figure.

FOOL, *subs.* (colloquial.)—A dish of gooseberries, boiled with sugar and milk. [Fr., *groseilles en foule.*] Also, a GULL (*q.v.*).

1719. DURFEY, *Pills*, etc., III., 9. 'Praise of the Dairy Maid.' A lady, I heard tell, Not far off did dwell, Made her husband a FOOL, and it pleased him quite well.

1774. GOLDSMITH, *Retaliation.* And by the same rule, Magnanimous Goldsmith's a gooseberry FOOL.

NO FOOL, *subs. phr.* (American colloquial).—A phrase laudatory, applied to neuter nouns. *Cf.*, NO SLOUCH.

1848. JONES, *Sketches of Travel*, p. 33. I tell you what, Charlston ain't no FOOL of a city.

TO MAKE A FOOL OF, *verb. phr.* (colloquial).—To delude. Specifically (venery), to cuckold, or to seduce under promise of marriage.

TO FOOL ABOUT (or AROUND), *verb. phr.* (American). — To dawdle; to trifle with; to be infatuated with; to hang about; to defraud.

1837. *A Glance at New York.* Mose —Now look a-here, Liz,—I go in for Bill Sykes, 'cause he runs wid our machine; but he mustn't come FOOLIN' ROUND my gal, or I'll give him fits.

1884. HAWLEY SMART, *Post to Finish*, ch. xvii. From what I hear, you came to Riddleton, FOOLING after my daughter. Now, I'll have no caterwauling of that sort.

1891. GUNTER, *Miss Nobody of Nowhere*, p. 124. I should think you had too much ed-u-cash to FOOL ABOUT such a going on.

FOOL-FINDER, *subs.* (obsolete).—A bum-bailiff.—GROSE.

FOOLISH, *adj.* (prostitutes')—Said of a man that pays. 'Is he FLASH (*q.v.*) or FOOLISH = Is he the cully or the other.'—GROSE.

FOOL-MONGER, *subs.* (colloquial).— A person, male or female, living by their wits, *e.g.*, a PROMOTER (*q.v.*); a betting-man; a swindler. Also FOOL-CATCHER and FOOL-TRAP (*q.v.*).

FOOLOMETER, *subs.* (colloquial).— A standard, positive or neuter, whereby to gauge the public taste.

FOOL'S FATHER, *subs. phr.* (theatrical).—The pantaloon or OLD 'UN. (*q.v.*)

FOOL-STICKER, *subs. phr.* (venery). —The *penis.* For synonyms, *see* CREAMSTICK and PRICK. Also FOOL-MAKER.

FOOL'S WEDDING, *subs. phr.* (common).—A party of women. For synonyms, *see* HEN PARTY.

FOOL-TRAP, *subs.* (colloquial).—1. A FOOL-MONGER (*q.v.*).

2. (venery).—The female *pudendum.* For synonyms, *see* MONOSYLLABLE.

3. (colloquial).—A high-class harlot.

FOONT, *subs.* (thieves')—A sovereign [Probably a corruption of Ger. *Pfund.*] For synonyms, *see* CANARY.

1879. J. W. HORSLEY, in *Macm. Mag.*, XL., 502. The mob got me up a break (collection), and I got between five or six FOONT (sovereigns).

FOOT, *verb.* (common). — 1. To acknowledge payment; *e.g.*, TO FOOT A BILL; *cf.*, FOOT-UP.

1848. DURIVAGE, *Stray Subjects*, p. 183. If our plan succeeded the landlord was to FOOT the bill, and stand treat.

2. (football and colloquial).— To kick; to HOOF (*q.v.*). *Cf.*, *Merchant of Venice*, I., 3, You, that did void your rheum upon my beard, And FOOT me, as you spurn a stranger cur.

1852. BRISTED, *Upper Ten Thousand*, p. 223. Both teams were FOOTING their very best.

TO FOOT IT, *verb. phr.* (colloquial).—To walk. For synonyms, *see* PAD THE HOOF.

1892. PRICE, *From Arctic Ocean to Yellow Sea.* The discomfort of having to FOOT IT.

TO FOOT-UP, *verb. phr.* (American colloquial).—To sum up the total (of a bill); to TOT UP (*q.v.*). Hence, to pay; to discharge one's obligations; to RECKON UP (*q.v.*); to summarize both merits and defects, and strike a balance. FOOTING-UP = the reckoning, the sum total. Fr., *gomberger.*

1865. SALA, *A Trip to Barbary.* The Arab abhors statistics. He won't be tabulated if he could help it, and were you to go to Algeria, Doctor Colenso, you would find a deeply rooted objection among the people to the reckoning, or FOOTING-UP, as the Americans call it, of anything animate or inanimate.

1871. DE VERE *Americanisms*, p. 310. To FOOT A BILL, by paying the amount at the bottom of the account, is a phrase equally well known abroad and with us.

1882. McCABE, *New York*, XXI., 333. The transactions of 'the Street' FOOT UP an almost fabulous sum daily.

1884 G. A. S[ALA], in *Ill. Lon. News*, 29 March, p. 294, col. 3. They FOOT UP (American English) to an almost alarming amount in thousands of dollars.

TO PUT ONE'S BEST FOOT (or LEG) FOREMOST, *verb. phr.* (colloquial).—To use all possible despatch; to exert oneself to the utmost.

1596. SHAKSPEARE, *King John*, iv., 2. Nay, but make haste; the BETTER FOOT BEFORE.

TO PUT ONE'S FOOT INTO ANYTHING, *verb. phr.* (colloquial).— To make a mess of it; to get into a scrape. THE BISHOP (*i.e.*, the Devil) HAS PUT HIS FOOT IN IT (Old English proverb) is said of burned porridge or over-roasted meat.—GROSE. Fr., *faire une gaffe.*

1823. BEE, *Dict. of the Turf*, s.v.

1888. *Daily Telegraph*, 7 May. *Faire une gaffe*, in modern Parisian slang, may be best rendered as to PUT YOUR FOOT IN IT.

TO HAVE ONE FOOT (or LEG) IN THE GRAVE. *verb. phr.* (common). — On one's last legs; MEASURED FOR A FUNERAL SERMON. Also as *adj.*

1825. *English Spy*, i., pp. 199-200. With ONE LEG IN THE GRAVE he'll laugh.

1890. *Globe*, 15 May, p. 5, col. 2. ONE-FOOT-IN-THE-GRAVE paralytic sort of people.

TO PULL FOOT, *verb. phr.* (American). — To make haste. Variants are TO TAKE ONE'S FOOT IN ONE'S HAND, and TO MAKE TRACKS; but for synonyms, *see* ABSQUATULATE and SKEDADDLE.

1825. NEAL, *Brother Jonathan*, Bk. I., ch. iv., How they PULLED FOOT when they seed us commin.

1836. MICHAEL SCOTT. *Tom Cringle's Log*, ch. viii. 'Why, PULL FOOT, captain,' promptly replied Paul.

1843-4. HALIBURTON, *Sam Slick in England.* I look'd up; it was another shower, by gosh. I PULLS FOOT for dear life.

TO TAKE MR. FOOT'S HORSE, *verb. phr.* (old).—To walk; to GO BY SHANK'S MARE (*q.v.*) For synonyms, *see* PAD THE HOOF.

TO KNOW THE LENGTH OF ONE'S FOOT, *verb. phr.* (old).— To be well acquainted with one's character.

1581. LILLY, *Euphues*, etc. But you shall not know the LENGTH OF MY FOOT, untill by your cunning you get commendation.

1614. *Terence in English.* He measures an other MAN'S FOOTE BY HIS OWNE LAST. Hee considers an other mans meaning by his owne intent.

FOOTER, *subs.* (Harrow: once common).—1. Short for 'football.'

2. (University).—A player of football according to Rugby rules.

FOOT-HOT, *adv.* (Old English).—In hot haste; HOT-FOOT (*q.v.*)

1848. *Burton Waggeries*, etc., p. 65. I'm darned if I don't streak it to the Squire's FOOT-HOT.

FOOTING, *subs.* (common).—Money paid on entering upon new duties, or on being received into a workshop or society: as at sea when a comrade first goes aloft. Formerly FOOT-ALE: *cf.*, GARNISH. Fr., *arroser ses galons* = to christen one's uniform.

1777. HOWARD, *State of Prisons in England and Wales*, quoted in J. ASHTON'S *The Fleet*, p. 295. A cruel custom obtains in most of our Gaols, which is that of the prisoners demanding of a new comer garnish, FOOTING, or (as it is called in some London Gaols) chummage.

1781. G. PARKER, *View of Society*, I., 48. I must instantly pay down two shillings for my FOOTING.

1788. G. A. STEVENS, *Adv. of a Speculist*, i., 211. I was drove from street to street by women of my own profession, who swore I should not come in their beats until I had paid my FOOTING.

1830. CARLETON, *Collegian's Colleen Bawn*, 94. 'Pay your FOOTING now, Master Kyrle Daly, before you go farther,' said one.

1840. HALIBURTON, *Clockmaker*, 3 S., ch. iii. 'Waiter, half-a-dozen of iced champagne here, to pay for Mr. Slick's FOOTIN'.'

1891. CLARK RUSSELL, *An Ocean Tragedy*, p. 86. I was going aloft and wished to PAY MY FOOTING.

FOOTLE, *verb.*, and **FOOTLING,** *adj.* (colloquial). — To dawdle, trifle, potter; dawdling, trifling, pottering; MESSING ABOUT (*q.v.*).

FOOTLICKER, *subs.* (old).—A servant: a lickspittle.

1609. SHAKSPEARE, *The Tempest*, IV., 1. Do that good mischief which may make this island Thine for ever, and I, thy Caliban, For aye thy FOOT-LICKER.

FOOTLIGHTS. TO SMELL THE FOOTLIGHTS, *verb. phr.* (theatrical). — To acquire a taste for theatricals. [Footlights = the FLOAT (*q.v.*); the row of burners in front of the stage.]

TO SMELL OF THE FOOTLIGHTS. To carry theatrical concerns and phraseology into private life; to TALK SHOP (*q.v.*).

FOOTMAN'S INN, *subs. phr.* (old).— A poor lodging; a jail. Fr., *Hôtel de la modestie* = the Poor Man's Arms.

1608. *Penniles Parliament of Threedbare Poets.* Those that depend on destiny, and not on God, may chance look through a narrow lattice at FOOTMAN'S INN.

1612. ROWLAND, *Knave of Hearts.* Which at the heeles so hants his frighted ghost, That he at last in FOOTMAN'S-INNE must host, Some castle dolorous compos'd of stone, Like (let me see) Newgate is such a one.

FOOTMAN'S MAUND, *subs. phr.* (old).—An artificial sore, as from a horse's bite or kick. The FOX'S BITE of schoolboys. Also the SCALDRUM DODGE, or MAUND (*q.v.*). MAUND = a cadger's sale-basket. *Cf.*, MASONS' MAUND.

1690. B. E., *Dict. of the Canting Crew*, s.v. An artificial sore made with unslacked lime, soap, and the rust of old iron, on the back of a beggar's hand, as if hurt by the bite or kick of a horse.

1785. GROSE, *Dict. of the Vulg. Tongue*, s.v.

FOOT-RIDING, *subs.* (cyclists').— Walking and wheeling one's machine instead of riding it.

1887. T. STEVENS, *Round the World on a Bicycle.* Already I realise that there is going to be as much FOOT-RIDING as anything for the first part of my journey.

FOOT-SCAMP, *subs.* (old).—A footpad.—G. PARKER.

FOOTSTOOL. *See* ANGELS' FOOTSTOOL.

FOOT-WOBBLER, *subs.* (old, soldier's').—An infantryman. For synonyms, *see* MUDCRUSHER.

1785. GROSE, *Dict. of the Vulg. Tongue*, s.v.

FOOTY, *adj.* (old).—Contemptible; worthless. *Fr.*, *foutu.*—GROSE.

1836. MICHAEL SCOTT, *Tom Cringle's Log*, ch. v. My eye, Captain, no use to dodge from her; it is only dat FOOTY little King's cutter on de Jamaica station.

FOOZLE, *subs.* (common and sporting).—1. A boggle; a miss.

2. (common). — A bore; a fogey; and (in America) a fool; a GREEN 'UN. For synonyms, *see* BUFFLE, CABBAGE-HEAD, and SAMMY SOFT.

1867. RHODA BROUGHTON, *Cometh up as a Flower*, ch. xxvi. Frumps and FOOZLES in Eaton Square.

Verb. (common).—To miss; to boggle; to MUFF (*q.v.*).

1888. *Field*, 25 Feb. Park FOOZLED his second stroke.

FOOZLED (or FOOZLEY), *adj.* (colloquial). — Blurred in appearance and effect; fuzzy; MUFFED (*q.v.*). Often said of badly painted pictures, or parts of pictures.

FOP-DOODLE, *subs.* (old). — An insignificant man; a fool.

1689. SHADWELL, *Bury Fair.* Come come, you brace of FOP-DOODLE

FOP'S ALLEY, *subs. phr.* (old).—*See* quot. 1883.

1782. D'ARBLAY, *Cecilia*, bk. II., ch iv. Sir Robert Floyer, sauntering down FOP'S ALLEY.

1883. SALA, *Echoes of the Year*, p. 369. FOP'S ALLEY was the gangway running parallel to the footlights, between the last row of the stalls and the first row of the pit in Her Majesty's Theatre, and in its palmiest days it was always graced by the presence of a subaltern of the Guards in full uniform, daintily swinging his bear-skin.

FORAKERS, *subs.* (Winchester College). — The water-closet. [Formerly spelt *foricus* and probably a corruption of *foricas*, an English plural of the Latin *forica.*] For synonyms, *see* MRS. JONES.

FORAMINATE, *verb* (venery).—To copulate. For synonyms, *see* GREENS and RIDE.

FORCE, *subs.* (colloquial). — The police; properly a body of men trained for action. For synonyms, *see* BEAK and COPPER.

1868. BRADDON, *Trail of the Serpent*, bk. IV., ch. vi. 'I should like to . . . bring a child up from the very cradle to the police detective line, to see whether I couldn't make that 'ere child a ornament to the FORCE.'

1883. *Daily Telegraph*, 5 April, p. 2, col. 1. But in all my experience of THE FORCE, I think I never saw a policeman's eyes so expressive of gratitude.

TO FORCE THE VOUCHER, *verb. phr.* (turf).—It is customary for sporting tricksters to advertise selections and enclose vouchers (similar to those sent out by respectable commission agents) for double or treble the current odds. The correspondent is informed that, in consequence of early investments, the extra odds can be laid; a remittance is requested; the VOUCHER IS FORCED; and then the firm 'dries up,' and changes its name and address.

FORCEMEAT BALL, *subs. phr.* (old). —Something endured from compulsion: as (1) a rape: (2) going to prison; (3) transportation; (4) an affiliation order; (5) abstention (from drink, pleasure, etc.) through impecuniosity.

FORCEPS, *subs.* (old).—The hands. [Properly a pair of surgeon's pincers.] — For synonyms, *see* DADDLE.

FORE-AND-AFT, *verb.* (venery).— To copulate. *See* GREENS and RIDE.

FORE-AND-AFTER, *subs. phr.* (American).—1. *See* quot.

1840. HALIBURTON, *Clockmaker*, 3 S., ch. xi. 'The way she walks her chalks ain't no matter. She is a regular FORE-AND-AFTER.'

2. (venery).—A DOUBLE-BARRELLED (*q.v.*) harlot. [As in the song attributed to an eminent living man of letters: "Sing whore, sing whore, Behind and before, Her price is a shilling— She never gets more."]

FORE-BUTTOCKS, *subs.* (old).—The paps.—For synonyms, *see* DAIRY.

a. 1745. SWIFT, POPE, and ARBUTHNOT, *Misc.* iv., 222. Now her FORE-BUTTOCKS to the navel bare.

FORECASTER, *subs.* (venery). The female *pudendum*. For synonyms, *see* MONOSYLLABLE.

FORE-COACH-WHEEL, *subs.* (common). — A half-crown. For synonyms, *see* CAROON.

FORE-COURT, *subs. phr.* (venery). —The female *pudendum*. Also FORE-HATCH, FORE-CASTLE, and FORE-ROOM. For synonyms, *see* MONOSYLLABLE.

FOREFOOT, *subs.* (old).—The hand.

1599. SHAKSPEARE, *Henry V.*, II., 1. Give me thy fist; thy FOREFOOT to me give.

1785. GROSE, *Dict. of the Vulgar Tongue.*

FOREGATHER, *verb.* (old). — To share the sexual embrace. For synonyms, *see* RIDE.

FOREHATCH, *subs.* (venery).—The female *pudendum*. For synonyms, *see* MONOSYLLABLE. Also FORECASTLE.

FOREMAN, *subs.* (old).—1. The *penis*. For synonyms, *see* CREAMSTICK and PRICK. [*Cf.*, FOREWOMAN.]

1647. *Ladies' Parliament* (*q.v.*).

FOREMAN OF THE JURY, *subs. phr.* (old).—A babbler; one with the GIFT OF THE GAB (*q.v.*).

1690. B. E., *Dict. of the Canting Crew.* FOREMAN OF THE JURY, he that engrosses all the talk to himself.

1785. GROSE, *Dict. of the Vulgar Tongue*, s.v.

FORESKIN HUNTER, *subs. phr.* (venery).—A harlot. For synonyms, *see* BARRACK-HACK and TART.

FOREST, *subs.* (venery). — The female pubic hair. For synonyms, *see* FLEECE.

1573-1631. DONNE, *Elegies*, xviii. Yet ere thou be where thou would'st be embayed, Thou must upon another FOREST set, Where many shipwreck and no further get

1720. DURFEY, *Pills*, etc., vi., 146. Give me the Country lass, That trips it o'er the field, And opes her FOREST to the first.

FORE-STALL, *subs.* (thieves').—In garotting, a look-out in front of the operator, or UGLY-MAN (*q.v.*); the watch behind is the BACK-STALL (*q.v.*). [From FORE + STALL (*q.v.*).]

FOREWOMAN, *subs.* (old). — The female *pudendum*. For synonyms, *see* MONOSYLLABLE.

FORK, *subs.* (old). 1. A pickpocket. Fr., '*Avoir les mains crochues* = to be a light-fingered or lime-fingered filcher; every finger of his hand as good as a lime-twig.'—COTGRAVE.

1690. B. E., *Dict. of the Canting Crew*, s.v.

1785. GROSE, *Dict. of the Vulgar Tongue.*

2. (thieves').—A finger. The FORKS = the fore and middle fingers; also *cf.*, (proverbial) 'Fingers were made before FORKS.'

ENGLISH SYNONYMS.—Claws; cunt-hooks (Grose); daddles (also the hands); divers; feelers; fives; flappers; grapplers; grappling irons; gropers; hooks; nail-bearers; pickers and stealers (Shakspeare); corn-stealers; Ten Commandments; ticklers; pinkies; muck-forks.

FRENCH SYNONYMS. — *Les apôtres* (thieves': = the ten Apostles); *les fourchettes*, or *les fourchettes d'Adam* (popular: = Adam's forks); *le peigne d'allemand* (thieves': RABELAIS).

GERMAN SYNONYMS. — *Ezba* (= the finger, especially the first or fore-finger. The names of the others are: *Godel* = the thumb; *Ammo* = the middle-finger; *Kemizo* = the ring-finger; *Seres*, *i.e.*, 'span' = the little finger); *Griffling* (= also the hand. From *greifen* = to seize).

SPANISH SYNONYMS. — *Mandamiento* (= a commandment: *cf.*, TEN COMMANDMENTS); *tijeras* (= the fore- and middle fingers; MINSHEU (1599) *Dictionarie*, *tijeras* = 'small sheares, seizers, snuffers.').

PORTUGUESE SYNONYM. — *Medunhos.*

1821. HAGGART, *Life*, p. 121. My FORKS were equally long, and they never failed me.

1834. AINSWORTH, *Rookwood.* 'Nix my Dolly.' No dummy hunter had FORKS so fly. *Ibid. Jack Sheppard* (1889), p. 20. I'll give him the edication of a prig—teach him the use of his FORKS betimes.

1841. *Tait's Edinburgh Mag.*, VIII., p. 220. My FORKS were light and fly, and lightly faked away.

1891. *Licensed Victuallers' Gazette*, 9 Feb. Up they came briskly with smiling mugs, shook hands, then stepped back a pace or two, put up their FORKS, and the spectators were hushed into silence, for they saw that the battle was about to begin.

3. In plural (common). — The hands.

4. (old).—A gibbet; in the plural = the gallows. [FORK is often applied to anything resembling a divarication (as of a tree, river, or road), etc.: *Cf.*, sense 2. *Cf.*, Cicero (*de Div.*, i., 26). *Ferens furcam ductus est*: a slave so punished was called *furcifer.*]

5. (old).—A spendthrift.

1725. *New Canting Dict.*, s.v.

6. (tailors' and venery).—The CRUTCH (*q.v.*), NOCKANDRO (*q.v.*), or TWIST (*q.v.*). [Thus, A BIT ON A FORK = the female *pudendum*; a GRIND (*q.v.*).] Fr., '*Fourcheure*, that part of the bodie from whence the thighs depart.'—COTGRAVE.

Verb (old).—1. To steal; specifically to pick a pocket by inserting the middle and forefinger. Also TO PUT ONE'S FORKS DOWN: Fr., *vol à la fourchette.*

1690. B. E., *Dict. of the Canting Crew.* LET'S FORK HIM, c. Let us pick that man's pocket, the newest and most dextrous way; it is to thrust the fingers straight, stiff, open, and very quick into the pocket, and so closing them hook what can be held between them.

1785. GROSE, *Dict. of the Vulgar Tongue.* Let us FORK him.

1830. LYTTON, *Paul Clifford*, ch. xvi. Yet so keen was his appetite for the sport, that the veteran appropriator absolutely burst into tears at not having 'FORKED more.'

1878. C. HINDLEY, *Life and Times of James Catnach.* Frisk the Cly and FORK the Rag, Draw the fogles plummy.

2. (venery).—To open up, or SPREAD (*q.v.*).

TO FORK OUT, or OVER (sometimes abbreviated to FORK). *Verb. phr.* (common).—To hand over; to pay; TO SHELL OUT (*q.v.*).

1830. LYTTON, *Paul Clifford*, ch. xxxi. The person FORKS him OUT ten shiners.

1836. DICKENS, *Sketches by Boz*, p. 84. His active mind at once perceived how much might be done in the way of . . . shoving the old and helpless into the wrong buss, and carrying them off . . . till they was rig'larly done over, and FORKED OUT the stumpy.

1837. BARHAM, I. L., *The Execution.* He Pulls up at the door of a gin-shop, and gaily Cries, 'What must I FORK OUT to night, my trump, For the whole first-floor of the Magpie and Stump?'

1840. *Comic Almanack.* 'Tom the Devil,' p. 214. 'That's a nate way of doin' business, sure enough,' was the commentary; 'ounly I can't larn the sinse of going to a private lodging, where, if you ordher a kidney for breakfast, you're expected to FORK OUT to the butcher.

1852. H. B. STOWE, *Uncle Tom's Cabin*, ch. viii. You've got to FORK OVER fifty dollars, flat down, or this child don't start a peg.

1864. DICKENS, *Our Mutual Friend*, Bk. III., ch. i. 'Now,' said Fledgeby, 'FORK OUT your balance in hand, and prove by figures how you make it out that it ain't more.'

1867. *Albany Argus*, 5 Sept. Now, sir, you will please FORK OVER that money to me, and pay your bill, or I'll have the law out of you, as sure as you are born.

1887. *Lippincott's Magazine*, Aug., p. 199. Just calculate my percentage of our liabilities, and allow me to FORK OVER.

1888. *Detroit Free Press*, 9 Sept. The dozen screw-drivers came up C. O. D. and he had to FORK OVER for them.

TO FORK ON, *verb. phr.* (American).—To appropriate. *Cf.*, TO FREEZE ON TO.

TO PITCH THE FORK, *verb. phr.* (popular).—To tell a pitiful tale.

TO EAT VINEGAR WITH A FORK, *verb. phr.* (common).—A person either over-shrewd or over-snappish is said to have EATEN VINEGAR WITH A FORK. Fr., *Avoir mangé de l'oseille.* *See* NETTLE.

FORKER, *subs.* (nautical).—A dockyard thief or FENCE (*q.v.*). [From FORK = to steal + ER.]

FORKING, *subs.* (thieves'). — 1. Thieving. *See* FORK.

2. (tailors'). — Hurrying and SCAMPING (*q.v.*).

FORKLESS, *adj.* (thieves').—Clumsy; unworkmanlike; as without FORKS (*q.v.*).

1821. HAGGART, *Life*, p. 40. I met George Bagrie, and William Paterson, alias old Hag, two very willing, but poor snibs, accompanying a lushy cove, and going to work in a very FORKLESS manner

FORLOPER, *subs.* (South African).— A teamster guide.

FORLORN HOPE, *subs. phr.* (colloquial).—A gamester's last stake. —GROSE.

FORM, *subs.* (turf).—1. Condition; training; fitness for a contest. IN or OUT OF FORM = in or out of condition, *i.e.*, fit or unfit for work. BETTER or TOP FORM, etc. (in comparison). *Cf.*, COLOUR.

1861. WALSH, *The Horse*, ch. vi. If it be supposed that two three-year-olds, carrying the same weight, could run a mile and a-half, and come in abreast, it is said that the FORM of one is equal to that of the other.

1884. HAWLEY SMART, *Post to Finish*, ch. xxxv. When fillies, in racing parlance, lose their FORM at three years old, they are apt to never recover it.

1868. WHYTE MELVILLE, *White Rose*, ch. xxxiv. That mysterious property racing men call 'FORM.'

2. (colloquial). — Behaviour (with a moral significance: as GOOD FORM, BAD FORM = agreeable to good manners, breeding, principles, taste, etc., or the opposite). This usage, popularised in racing circles, is good literary English, though the word is commonly printed in inverted commas (" "): SHAKSPEARE (*Two Gentlemen of Verona*, 4), says, 'Can no way change you to a milder FORM,' *i.e.*, manner of behaviour.

1871. *Orchestra*, 13 Jan. This squabble at the Globe may most fitly, perhaps, be characterised by the words 'BAD FORM.'

1871. *The Drawing Room Gazette*, Dec. 9, p. 5. It is an open question, whether snubbing be not, like cutting, in the worst possible 'FORM.'

1873. *Belgravia*, Feb. The demeanour and conduct which the 'golden youth' of the period call 'GOOD FORM' was known to their fathers as bad manners.

1881. JAS. PAYN, *Grape from a Thorn*, ch. xvii. It would be considered what they call 'BAD FORM' in my daughter Ella if she were known to be a contributor —for pay—to the columns of a magazine.

1890. *Speaker*, 22 Feb., p. 211, col. 2 Still, after all, we doubt very much whether it be fair, or right, or even prudent —it certainly is not 'GOOD FORM'—to publish to a world of Gallios a lot of irreverent bar-mess and circuit 'good stories,' worked up about living Lord Chancellors, Lord Justices, and other present occupants of the judicial bench.

3. (common).—Habit; GAME (*q.v.*): *e.g.*, 'That's my FORM = That's what I'm in the way of doing'; or 'That's the sort of man I am.'

1884. *Punch*, 11 Oct. 'Arry at a Political Picnic.' Athletics ain't hardly my FORM.

FORNEY, *subs* (thieves').—A ring; a variant of FAWNEY (*q.v.*).

1871. EGAN, *Finish of Tom and Jerry*, p. 243. He sports a diamond FORNEY on his little finger.

FORNICATING-ENGINE (-MEMBER; -TOOL), *subs. phr.* (venery).—The *penis*. For synonyms, *see* CREAM-STICK and PRICK.

FORNICATOR, *subs.* (venery).—1. The *penis*. For synonyms, *see* CREAM-STICK and PRICK.

2. In *pl.* (obsolete),—The old-fashioned flap trousers.

FORNICATOR'S HALL, *subs. phr.* (venery).—The female *pudendum*. For synonyms, *see* MONOSYLLABLE.

FORT, *subs.* (venery).—The female *pudendum*. For synonyms, *see* MONOSYLLABLE.

1620. PERCY, *Folio MSS.* [Hales & Furnivall, 1867]. 'Come, Wanton Wenches.' When they your FFORT beleauger; grant but a touch or a kisse ffor a tast.

FORTUNE-BITER, *subs.* (obsolete).—A sharper.

1719. DURFEY, *Pills*, etc., ii. 'Hey! for Richmond Ball'! FORTUNE-BITERS, Hags, bum-fighters, Nymphs of the Woods, And stale City goods.

FORTUNE-TELLER, *subs.* (old).—A magistrate.

1690. B. E., *Dict. of the Canting Crew*. FORTUNE-TELLERS, c. the Judges of Life and Death, so-called by the Canting Crew.

1785. GROSE, *Dict. of the Vulg. Tongue*. FORTUNE-TELLER, or cunning man; a judge who tells every prisoner his fortune, lot, or doom; to go before the FORTUNE-TELLER, lambskin man or conjuror, to be tried at an assize.

1871. EGAN, *Finish of Tom and Jerry*, p. 242. He had been werry cruelly used by the FORTUNE-TELLERS.

FORTY. TO TALK FORTY (more commonly NINETEEN) TO THE DOZEN, *verb. phr.* (colloquial).—To chatter incessantly; to gabble. TO WALK OFF FORTY TO THE DOZEN = to decamp in quick time.

1891. FARJEON, *Mystery of M. Felix*, p. 107. He run agin me, he did, and I ased, 'Who are yer pushing of?' He didn't say nothink, but walked off FORTY TO THE DOZEN.

ROARING FORTIES, *subs. phr.* (nautical).—The Atlantic between the fortieth and fiftieth degrees of latitude; also applied to the same region in southern latitudes.

FORTY-FACED, *adj.* (colloquial).—An arrant deceiver: *e.g.*, a FORTY-FACED liar, a FORTY-FACED flirt, and so forth.

FORTY-FIVE, *subs.* (American).—A revolver. For synonyms, *see* MEAT IN THE POT.

FORTY-FOOT or **FORTY-GUTS**, *subs.* (common).—A fat, dumpy man, or woman. In contempt.

ENGLISH SYNONYMS.—'All arse, and no body'; arse-and-corporation; all-belly (Cotgrave); all guts (idem); bacon-belly; barrel-belly; belly-god; bladder-figured; bosse-belly; Bosse of Billingsgate (Florio = a fat woman); chuff (Shakspeare); Christmas beef; double-guts; double-tripe; fat-cock; fat-guts (Shakspeare and Cotgrave); fatico; fattymus or

fattyma; fubsy; fat Jack of the bonehouse; fat-lips; flanderkin; fustiluggs (Burton); fussock; gorbelly; grampus; gotch-guts; grand-guts (Florio); gulche (Florio); gullyguts; gundiguts; guts; guts-and-stomach; guts-and-garbage; guts-to-sell; hoddy-doddy; humpty-dumpty; hogshead; hopper-arse; Jack Weight; loppers; lummox; paunch; pod; porpoise; pot-guts; princod; pudding-belly; puff-guts; ribs; 'short-and-thick-like-a-Welshman's-cock'; slush-bucket; sow (a fat woman); spud; squab; studgy-guts; tallow-guts; tallow-merchant; thick-in-the-middle; tripes; tripes and trullibubs; tubs; waist; water-butt; walking ninepin; whopper.

FRENCH SYNONYMS. *Un gros bajaf* (popular); *un bout de cul* (popular); *un bas de plafond, or de cul* (popular); *un brasset* (= a tall, stout man); *un berdouillard*.

SPANISH SYNONYM. *Angelon de retablo* (generally applied to a pot-bellied child).

FORTY-JAWED, *adj.* (colloquial).—Excessively talkative.

FORTY-LUNGED, *adj.* (colloquial).—Stentorian; given to shouting; LEATHER-LUNGED (*q.v.*).

FORTY-ROD or **FORTY-ROD LIGHTNING**, *subs. phr.* (American).—Whiskey; specifically, spirit of so fiery a nature that it is calculated to kill at Forty Rods' distance, *i.e.*, on sight. *Cf.*, ROT-GUT. For synonyms, *see* DRINKS and OLD MAN'S MILK. *Cf.*, FLORIO (1598), *Catoblepa*, 'a serpent in India so venomous that with his looke he kils a man a mile off.'

1884. M. TWAIN, *Huck. Finn*, ch. v., p. 36. He got powerful thirsty and clumb out on to the porch-roof and slid down a stanchion, and traded his new coat for a jug of FORTY-ROD.

FORTY-TWA, *subs.* (Scots).—A common jakes, or BOGSHOP (*q.v.*).—in Edinburgh: 'so called from its accommodating that number of persons at once' (*Hotten*). [Long a thing of the past.]

FORTY WINKS, *subs. phr.* (colloquial).—A short sleep or nap. *See* DOG'S SLEEP.

1866. G. ELIOT, *Felix Holt*, ch. xliii. She was prevented by the appearance of old Mr. Transome, who since his walk had been having 'FORTY-WINKS' on the sofa in the library.

1871. EGAN. *Finish to Tom and Jerry*, p. 87. On uncommanly big gentlemen, told out, taking FORTY-WINKS.

[Forty is often used to signify an indefinite number; *cf.*, Shakspeare's usage, 'I could beat forty of them' (*Cor.* iii., 1); 'O that the slave had forty thousand lives' (*Othello* iii., 1); 'forty thousand brothers' (*Hamlet*, v., 1); 'The Humour of Forty Fancies' (*Taming of the Shrew*); and Jonson 'Some forty boxes' (*Silent Woman*).]

FOSSED, *ppl. adj.* (American thieves').—Thrown; *cf.*, [foss = a ditch].

FOSSICK, *verb* (Australian miners').—To work an abandoned claim, or to wash old dirt; hence to search persistently. [Halliwell: = to take trouble, but *cf.*, fosse, a ditch or excavation.] Also FOSSICKING = a living got as aforesaid; FOSSICKER = a man that works abandoned claims; FOSSICKING ABOUT = (American) SHINNING AROUND, or in England FERRETING (*q.v.*).

1870. *Notes and Queries*, 4 S., vi., p. 3.

1878. *Fraser's Mag.*, Oct., p. 449, They are more suited . . . to plodding, FOSSICKING, persevering industry, than for hard work.

1887. SALA, in *Ill. Lond. News*, 12 Mar., p. 282, col. 2. 'To FOSSICK' in the old digging days was to get a living by extracting gold from the refuse wash-dirt which previous diggers had abandoned as worthless.

1890. *Illustrations*, Jan., p. 158. After some 'FOSSIKING' we discover three or four huts within 'cooee,' all diggers, all 'hatters,' and mostly good fellows.

FOU, or **FOW**, *adj.* (old English and Scots' colloquial).—Drunk; variants are BITCH-FOU; GREETIN'-FOU; PIPER-FOU; ROARING-FOU; FOU AS BARTY (Burns); PISSING-FOU; and so forth. For synonyms, *see* DRINKS and SCREWED. Also (Scots') = full of food or drink, as in quot. under date 1815.

1697. VANBRUGH, *Provoked Wife*, III., ii. (quoted in). Then sit ye awhile, and tipple a bit, For we's not very FOU, but we're gayly yet.

1787. BURNS, *Death and Dr. Hornbook*, st. 3. I was na FOU, but just had plenty.

1815. SCOTT, *Guy Mannering*, ch. xlvi. 'Are ye FOU or fasting?' 'Fasting from all but sin.'

1857. J. E. RITCHIE, *Night Side of London*, p. 166. The time admits of a man getting FOU between the commencement and the close of the entertainment.

FOUL, *subs.* (nautical and aquatic).—A running into; a running down.

Verb. (idem).—To run against; to run down. Also TO COME (or FALL) FOUL OF.

[FOUL, *adj.* and *verb.* is used in two senses: (1) = dirty, as a FOUL word, a FOUL shrew (Dickens), to FOUL the bed, &c.; and (2) = unfair, as a FOUL (*i.e.*, a felon) stroke, a FOUL blow, and so forth.]

1626. CAPTAIN JOHN SMITH, *Accidence for Seamen*, in wks. (Arber), p. 796. Boord and boord, or thwart the hawse, we are FOULE on each other.

1724. E. COLES, *Eng. Dict.* FOUL, hindred or intangled with another ship's ropes, etc.

1754. *Connoisseur*, No. 3. Which sailed very heavy, were often a-ground, and continually ran FOUL on each other.

1861. HUGHES, *Tom Brown at Oxford*, ch. xiii. Their coxswain . . . had to pull his left hand hard or they would have FOULED the Oxfordshire corner.

1885. *Illus. London News*, March 28, p. 316, col. 1. In 1849 there were two races in the course of the year; Cambridge won the first, Oxford the second, on a FOUL (the only time the race has been so won).

1889. *Licensed Victuallers' Gaz.*, 18 Jan. Dick was done out of the stakes on an appeal of FOUL.

TO FOUL A PLATE WITH, *verbal phr.* (old, colloquial).—To dine or sup with.—GROSE.

FOULCHER, *subs.* (thieves').—A purse.

1877. *Five Years' Penal Servitude*, ch. iii., p. 243. 'A FOULCHER, with flimsies and couters for a score of quid in it.'

FOUL-MOUTHED, *adj.* (colloquial).—Obscene or blasphemous in speech.

FOUND IN A PARSLEY-BED. *See* PARSLEY-BED and GOOSEBERRY-BUSH.

FOUNTAIN OF LOVE, *subs. phr.* (venery).—The female *pudendum*. For synonyms, *see* MONOSYLLABLE.

FOUR-AND-NINE (or **FOUR-AND-NINEPENNY**), *subs. phr.* (old).—A hat. [So-called from the price at which an enterprising Bread Street hatter sold his hats, *circa* 1844, at which date London was hideous with posters displaying a large black hat and '4s. and 9d.' in white letters.]

1844. *Advertisement Couplet*. When-e'er to slumber you incline, Take a short nap at FOUR-AND-NINE.

1846. THACKERAY, *Yellow Plush Papers*, p. 152 (ed. 1887). You may, for instance, call a coronet a coronal (an 'ancestral coronal,' p. 74) if you like, as you might call a hat a 'swart sombrero,' a 'glossy FOUR-AND-NINE,' 'a silken helm to storm impermeable, and lightsome as the breezy gossamer;' but in the long run it is safer to call it a hat.

1847. THACKERAY, *Mrs. Perkins's Ball* (*The Mulligan*). The Mulligan has withdrawn his custom from the 'infernal FOUR-AND-NINEPENNY scoundthrel,' as he calls him. The hatter has not shut up shop in consequence.

1849. VIATOR, *Oxford Guide*. He then did raise his FOUR-AND-NINE, And scratched his shaggy pate.

1867. JAS. GREENWOOD, *Unsent. Journeys*, xxx., 229. Because he wore a FOUR-AND-NINE, and had a pencil stuck behind his ear.

FOUR-BONES, *subs.* (thieves').—The knees.

1857. *Punch*, 31 Jan. 'Dear Bill, This Stone-jug.' For them coves in Guildhall and that blessed Lord Mayor, Prigs on their four bones should chop whiners I swear.

FOUR-EYES, *subs.* (common).—A person in spectacles: 'a chap that can't believe his own eyes.'

FOUR-HOLED MIDDLINGS, *subs. phr.* (Winchester College).—Ordinary walking shoes; *cf.* BEESWAXERS. Obsolete.

FOUR KINGS. THE HISTORY (or BOOK) OF THE FOUR KINGS. *subs. phr.* (old).—A pack of cards; otherwise, a CHILD'S BEST GUIDE TO THE GALLOWS, or THE DEVIL'S PICTURE BOOKS. Fr., *Livre des quatre rois*.

FOUR-LEGGED BURGLAR-ALARM, *subs. phr.* (common).—A watch dog.

FOUR-LEGGED FROLIC, *subs. phr.* (venery).—The act of kind: a reminiscence of the proverb, 'There goes more to a marriage than four bare legs in a bed.' For synonyms, *see* GREENS and RIDE.

FOUR-POSTER, *subs. phr.* (colloquial).—A four-post bedstead.

1836. DICKENS, *Pickwick*, ch. xliv. 'Vill you allow me to en-quire vy you make up your bed under that ere deal table?' said Sam. ''Cause I was always used to a FOUR-POSTER afore I came here, and I find the legs of the table answer just as well,' replied the cobbler.

FOUR SEAMS AND A BIT OF SOAP, *subs. phr.* (tailors').—A pair of trousers. *See* KICKS.

FOUR—(more commonly **THREE**)—**SHEETS IN THE WIND**, *adv. phr.* (nautical).—Drunk; *cf.*, HALF SEAS OVER. For synonyms, *see* DRINKS and SCREWED.

FOURTEEN HUNDRED, . . . *phr.* (Stock Exchange).—A warning cry that a stranger is in the 'House.'

1887. ATKIN, *House Scraps*. So, help me Got, Mo, who is he? Instead of replying in a straightforward way, Mo raised his voice as loud as he could, and shouted with might and main, 'FOURTEEN HUNDRED new fives!' A hundred voices repeated the mysterious exclamation.

1890. *Cassell's Saturday Journal*, 26 April. The cry of 'FOURTEEN HUNDRED' is said to have had its origin in the fact that for a long while the number of members never exceeded 1,399; and it was customary to hail every new comer as the fourteen hundredth. It has, in its primary sense, long since lost significance, for there are now nearly three thousand members of the close corporation which has its home in Capel Court.

FOURTEENTH AMENDMENT PERSUASION, *subs. phr.* (American).—Negroes. [From the number of the clause amending the Constitution at the abolition of slavery.]

1888. *Times Democrat*, 5 Feb. To take the law is one of the greatest privileges in the estimation of the colored folk that the FOURTEENTH AMENDMENT conferred, and, whether offender or defendant, they take a pride in summonses beyond describing.

FOURTH, *subs.* (Cambridge University).—A REAR (*q.v.*) or jakes. [Origin uncertain; said to have been first used at St. John's or Trinity, where the closets were situated in the Fourth Court. Whatever its derivation, the term is now the only one in use at Cambridge, and is frequently heard outside the university.] The verbal phrase is TO KEEP A FOURTH (*see* KEEP).

ON HIS FOURTH, *phr.* (common).—Hopelessly drunk. For synonyms, *see* DRINKS and SCREWED.

FOURTH ESTATE, *subs. phr.* (literary).—The body of journalists; the 'Press.' [Literally the Fourth Estate of the realm, the other three being Queen, Lords, and Commons.]

1855. *Notes and Queries*. I S. xi., p. 452.

1857. J. E. RITCHIE, *Night Side of London*, p. 202. Let me say a word about these exceedinglyseedy-looking individuals connected with the FOURTH ESTATE.

FOUR-WHEELER, *subs.* (common).—A steak.

2. (colloquial).—A four-wheeled cab; a GROWLER (*q.v.*).

1873. BLACK, *Princess of Thule*, ch. 10. Having sent on all their luggage by a respectable old FOUR-WHEELER.

FOUSTY, *adj.* (colloquial).—Stinking [probably derived from FOIST, sense 3].

FOUTER, *verb*, and **FOUTERING**, *subs.* (common).—To meddle, importune, waste time and tongue; the act of meddling, importunity, wasting time and tongue. *E.g.*, 'Don't come FOUTERING here!' [From the French, *foutre*: the sense of which is intensified in a vulgarism of still fuller flavour].

FOX, *subs.* (old).—A sword; specifically, the old English broadsword. [Derivation dubious. Suggestions are: (1) from a maker's name; (2) from the fox sometimes engraved on the blade; (3) from the Latin *falx*.] For synonyms, *see* CHEESE-TOASTER and POKER.

1598. SHAKSPEARE, *Henry V.*, 4. O signieur Dew, thou dy'st on point of FOX.

1614. JONSON, *Bartholomew Fair*, ii. A fellow that knows nothing but a basket-hilt, and an old FOX in't.

c. 1640. [SHIRLEY], *Captain Underwit*, in Bullen's *Old Plays*, ii., 321. *Un.* An old FOX blade made at *Hounsloe* heath.

1667. SHIRLEY, *Love Tricks*, Act II., Sc. I. They say your swords most commonly are FOXES, and have notable metal in them.

1700. CONGREVE, *Way of the World*, Act V., Sc. 10. Sir, I have an old FOX by my thigh shall hack your instrument of *ram vellum* to shreds, Sir.

1821. SCOTT, *Kenilworth*, ch. iv. 'Come, come, comrade,' said Lambourne, 'here is enough done, and more than enough, put up your FOX, and let us be jogging.'

Verb (old).—1. To intoxicate. FOXED = drunk; TO CATCH A FOX = to be very drunk; while TO FLAY THE FOX (Urquhart) = to vomit, to shed your liquor, *i.e.*, to get rid of the beast.

1611. BARRY, *Ram Alley*, Act IV. They will bib hard; they will be fine sunburnt, Sufficient FOX'D or columber'd now and then.

1633. HEYWOOD. *Eng. Travellers*, IV., v., p. 266 (Mermaid Series). *Rioter.* Worthy Reginald. *Reig.* Will, if he now come off well, FOX you all, Go, call for wine.

c. 1640. [SHIRLEY], *Captain Underwit*, in Bullen's *Old Plays*, ii., 375. Then to bee FOX'D it is no crime, Since thickest and dull braines It makes sublime.

1661. T. MIDDLETON, *Mayor of Quinborough*, V., i. Ah, blind as one that had been FOX'D a sevennight.

1673. SHADWELL, *Epsom Wells*, IV., in wks. (1720), ii., 248. But here's my cup. Come on. Udsooks, I begin to be FOX'D!

1719. DURFEY, *Pills*, etc., i., 194. Come, let's trudge it to Kirkham Fair: There's stout liquor enough to FOX me.

1738. SWIFT, *Polite Convers.*, Dial. 2. *Lady Sm.* But, Sir John, your ale is terrible strong and heady. . . . *Sir John.* Why, indeed, it is apt to FOX one.

1748. T. DYCHE, *Dictionary* (5th ed.). Fox (v.) . . . also to make a person drunk or fuddled.

1891. *Sporting Times*, 11 April. And so to bed well nigh seven in the morning, and myself as near FOXED as of old.

2. (old).—To cheat; to trick; to rob (colloquial at Eton). For synonyms, *see* GAMMON.

1631. MAYNE, *City Match*, iii., 1. Fore Jove, the captain FOXED him rarely.

1866. *Notes and Queries*, 3, S. x., 123. Where the tramps . . . out of their gout are FOXED.

3. (common).—To watch closely. Also TO FOX ABOUT. *Cf.*, FOX'S SLEEP. For synonyms, *see* NOSE.

1880. GREENWOOD, *Odd People in Odd Places*, p. 61. 'You keep it going pretty loud here, with a couple of policemen FOXING about just outside.

4. (colloquial).—To sham.

1880. *One and All*, 6 Nov., p. 296, 'Let us look at these vagabons; maybe they're only FOXIN'.' The two men who had received such tangible mementos of the whip-handle and the blackthorn lay perfectly still.

5. (American).—To play truant.

6. (booksellers').—To stain; to discolour with damp; said of books and engravings. FOXED = stained or discoloured.

1881. C. M. I[NGLEBY] in *Notes and Queries* (6th S., iv., 96). Tissue paper harbours damp, and in a damp room will assuredly help to FOX the plates which they face.

1885. AUSTIN DOBSON, *At the Sign of the Lyre*, 83. And the Rabelais FOXED and flea'd.

7. (theatrical).—To criticise a 'brother pro's' performance.

8. (common).—To mend a boot by 'capping' it.

TO SET A FOX TO KEEP ONE'S GEESE, *phr.* (common).—To entrust one's money, or one's circumstances, to the care of sharpers. Latin, *Ovem lupo commisisti.*

TO MAKE A FOX PAW, *verb. phr.* (common).—To make a mistake or a wrong move; specifically (of women) to be seduced. [A corruption of the Fr. *faux pas.*]

1785. GROSE, *Vulg. Tongue.*

FOX'S SLEEP, *subs. phr.* (common).—A state of feigned yet very vigilant indifference to one's surroundings. [Foxes were supposed to sleep with one eye open.]

1830. SIR J. BARRINGTON, *Personal Sketches*, Vol. III., p. 171 (ed. 1832). Mr. Fitzgerald, he supposed, was in a FOX'S SLEEP, and his bravo in another, who, instead of receding at all, on the contrary squeezed the attorney closer and closer.

FOXY, *adj.* (colloquial).—1. Red-haired; *cf.*, CARROTTY.

1828. G. GRIFFIN, *Collegians*, ch. ii. Dunat O'Leary, the hair-cutter, or FOXY Dunat, as he was named in allusion to his red head.

2. (colloquial).—Cunning; vulpine in character and look. Once literary. Jonson (1605) calls his arch-foist VOLPONE, the second title of his play being '*The Fox*;' and Florio (1598) defines *Volpone* as 'an old fox, an old reinard, an old, crafty, sly, subtle companion, sneaking, lurking, wilie deceiver.'

d. 1536. TYNDALE, *Workes*, p. 148. Oh, FOXY Pharisay, that is thy leuen, of which Christ so diligently bad vs beware.

1849. DICKENS, *David Copperfield*, ch. xlix., p. 429 Whatever his state of health may be his appearance is FOXY, not to say diabolical.

3. (American cobblers').—Repaired with new toe-caps. *See* FOX, verb, sense 8.

1877. M. TWAIN, *Life on the Mississippi*, ch. lvii., p. 503. It was the scarecrow Dean—in FOXY shoes, down at the heels; socks of odd colours, also 'down.'

4. (booksellers').—A term applied to prints and books discoloured by damp; *see* FOX, verb, sense 6.

5. (painters': obsolete).—Inclined to reddishness.

d. 1792. SIR J. REYNOLDS, *Notes on Dufresnoy*. That (style) of Titian, which may be called the Golden manner, when unskilfully managed, becomes what the painters call FOXY.

6. (common).—Strong-smelling. Said of a red-haired man or woman.

FOY, *subs.* (old).—A cheat; a swindle.

1615. GREENE, *Thieves Falling Out*. You be crossbites, FOYS, and nips.

FOYL-CLOY, *subs.* (old).—A pickpocket; a rogue—B.E. [1690].

FOYST, *subs.* and *verb.* *See* FOIST.

FOYSTER. *See* FOISTER.

FRAGGLE, *verb.* (Texas).—To rob.

FRAGMENT, *subs.* (Winchester College).—A dinner for six (served in College Hall, after the ordinary dinner), ordered by a Fellow in favour of a particular boy, who was at liberty to invite five others to join him. Obs. A fragment was supposed to consist of three dishes.—*Winchester Word-book* [1891].

FRAMER, *subs.* (American thieves').—A shawl.

1859. MATSELL, *Vocabulum, or Rogue's Lexicon*, s.v.

FRATER, *subs.* (old).—A beggar working with a false petition.

1567. HARMAN, *Caveat*, s.v. FRATER, a beggar wyth a false paper.

1622. FLETCHER, *Beggar's Bush*, ii., 1. And these what name or title e'er they bear, Jarkman, or Patrico, Cranke, or Clapper-dudgeon, FRATER, or *Abram-man*, I speak to all That stand in fair election for the title Of king of beggars.

1791. *Life of Bamfylde Moore-Carew.* 'Oath of Canting Crew.' Rogue or rascal, FRATER, maunderer, Irish toyle, or other wanderer.

FRAUD. *subs.* (colloquial).—A failure; anything or body disappointing expectation; *e.g.*, an acquaintance, a picture, a book, a play, a picture, a bottle of wine. Actual dishonesty is not necessarily implied.

1882. *Punch*, LXXXII., p. 177, col. 1. A FRAUD, Charlie!

FRAZE. *See* VESSEL.

FREAK, *subs.* (American showmen's). A living curiosity: as the Siamese Twins, the Two-headed Nightingale. [Short for 'freak of nature.']

FREE, *adj.* (Oxford University).—Impudent; self-possessed.

1864. TENNYSON, *Northern Farmer*, (Old Style), line 25.—But parson a coomes an' a goos, an' a says it eäsy an' FREEÄ.

Verb. (old).—To steal; *cf.*, ANNEX and CONVEY. For synonyms, *see* PRIG.

1857. SNOWDEN, *Magistrates' Assistant*, 3rd ed., p 444. To steal a muff. To FREE a cat.

1859. MATSELL, *Vocabulum, or Rogue's Lexicon*, s.v.

1882. McCABE, *New York*, ch. xxxiv., p. 509. (Given in list of slang terms.)

FREE-FUCKING, *subs.* (venery).—General lewdness. Also the favour gratis. Also fidelity to the other sex at large.

FREE OF FUMBLER'S HALL, *adv. phr.* (venery).—Impotent; unable to do 'the trick.' [FUMBLER'S HALL = female *pudendum.*]

1785. GROSE, *Vulg. Tongue* s.v., A saying of one who cannot get his wife with child.

FREE, GRATIS,—FOR NOTHING, *phr.* (common).—A pleonastic vulgarism. *Cf.*, ON THE DEAD.

TO MAKE FREE WITH BOTH ENDS OF THE BUSK, *verb. phr.* (venery).—To take liberties with a woman. *Cf.*, BOTH ENDS OF THE BUSK.

FREE OF THE HOUSE, *adj. phr.* (colloquial).—Intimate; privileged to come and go at will.

FREE OF THE BUSH, *adj. phr.* (venery).—On terms of extreme intimacy. *See* BUSH.

[For the rest, the commonest sense of FREE is one of liberality: *e.g.*, FREE OF HIS FOOLISHNESS = full of chaff; FREE-HANDED = lavish in giving; FREE-HEARTED = generously disposed; FREE OF HER FAVOURS = liberal of her person: FREE OF HIS PATTER = full of talk.]

FREE-AND-EASY, *subs.* (common).—A social gathering where you smoke, drink, and sing; generally held at a public house.

1796. (In BEE's *Dict. of the Turf*, published 1823, s.v.). Twenty seven years ago the cards of invitation to that (FREE-AND-EASY) at the 'Pied Horse,' in Moorfields, had the notable 'N.B.—Fighting allowed.'

1810. CRABBE, *The Borough*, Letter 10. Clubs. Next is the club, where to their friends in town, Our country neighbours once a-month come down; We term it FREE-AND-EASY, and yet we Find it no easy matter to be free.

1811. *Lexicon Balatronicum*. FREE-AND-EASY JOHNS. A society which meets at the Hole in the Wall, Fleet Street, to tipple porter, and sing bawdry.

1821. EGAN, *Tom and Jerry* (ed. 1890), p 91. Blew a cloud at a FREE-AND-EASY.

1843. MACAULAY. *Essays: Gladstone on Church and State.* Clubs of all ranks, from those which have lined Pall-Mall and St. James's Street with their palaces, down to the FREE-AND-EASY which meets in the shabby parlour of the village inn.

1869. MRS. H. WOOD, *Roland Yorke*, ch. xii. He tilted himself on to a high stool in the middle of the room, his legs dangling, just as though he had been at a FREE AND-EASY meeting.

1880. JAS. GREENWOOD, *Odd People in Odd Places*, p. 64. A roaring trade is done, for instance, on a Saturday evening at the 'Medley' in Hoxton, a combination of theatre and music-hall, and serves as a FREE-AND-EASY chiefly for boys and girls.

1891. *Cassell's Saturday Journal*, Sept., p. 1068, col. 3. The FREE AND EASY of to-day among us is a species of public-house party, at which much indifferent liquor and tobacco are consumed, songs are sung, and speeches are got rid of.

FREEBOOKER, *subs.* (journalists').—A 'pirate' bookseller or publisher; a play on the word freebooter.

FREE FIGHT, *subs.* (colloquial).—A general mellay.

1877. W. MARK, *Green Past. and Picc.*, ch. xxx. That vehement German has been insisting on the Irish porters bringing up all our luggage at once; and as there has been a sort of FREE FIGHT below he comes fuming upstairs.

FREE-FISHERY, *subs. phr.* (venery).—The female *pudendum*. For synonyms, *see* MONOSYLLABLE.

FREEHOLDER, *subs.* (venery).—1. A prostitute's lover or FANCY-MAN. *Cf.*, FREE-FISHERY, and for synonyms, *see* JOSEPH.

2. (old).—A man whose wife insists on accompanying him to a public house.

1690. B. E., *Dict. of the Canting Crew*, s.v. 1785. GROSE, *Dict. of the Vulg. Tongue*, s.v.

FREE-LANCE, *subs.* (common). — An habitual adulteress.

c 1889. (Quoted from *Spectator* in 'Slang, Jargon, and Cant'). Sooner than be out of the fashion they will tolerate what should be most galling and shaming to them—the thought that by these they are put down among the FREE-LANCES.

Also said of a journalist attached to no particular paper.

FREEMAN, *subs.*, (venery). — A married woman's lover.

FREEMAN OF BUCKS, *subs. phr.* (old).—A cuckold. [In allusion to the horn.] GROSE.

TO FREEMAN, OR TO MAKE A FREEMAN OF, *verb. phr.* (schoolboys').—To spit on the *penis* of a new comer. Also TO FREEMASON.

FREEMAN'S QUAY. TO DRINK, or LUSH, AT FREEMAN'S QUAY, *verb. phr.* (old).—To drink at another's expense. [Freeman's Quay was a celebrated wharf near London Bridge, and the saying arose from the beer that was given to porters, carmen, and others going there on business.]

1811. *Lexicon Balatronicum*, s.v.

FREEZE, *subs.* (colloquial).—1. The act or state of freezing; a frost.

2. (old). — Hard cider. — GROSE.

Verb. (American).—To long for intensely; *e.g.*, 'to FREEZE to go back,' said of the home-sick; 'to FREEZE for meat.'

1848. RUXTON, *Life in the Far West* (1887), p. 129. Threats of vengeance on every Redskin they met were loud and deep; and the wild war songs round their nightly camp-fires, and grotesque scalp-dances, borrowed from the Indians, proved to the initiated that they were, one and all, HALF-FROZE for hair.'

2. (thieves').—Hence, to appropriate; to steal; 'to stick to.'

3. (old). — To adulterate or BALDERDASH (*q.v.*) wine with FREEZE (*q.v.* sense 2).—GROSE.

TO FREEZE TO (or ON TO), *verb phr.* (American). — To take a strong fancy to; to cling to; to keep fast hold of; and (of persons) to button-hole or shadow.

1883. *Graphic*, 17 March, p. 287, col. 1. If there was one institution which the Anglo-Indian FROZE to more than another, it was his sit-down supper and—its consequences.

1888. *Daily Inter-Ocean*, 2 March. The competence of a juror was judged by his ability to shake ready-formed opinions and FREEZE ON TO new ones.

TO FREEZE OUT, *verb. phr.* (American).—To compel to withdraw from society by cold and contemptuous treatment; from business by competition or opposition; from the market by depressing prices or rates of exchange.

FREEZER, *subs.* (common).—1. A tailless Eton jacket; *cf.*, BUM-PERISHER. For synonyms, *see* MONKEY-JACKET.

2. (colloquial).—A very cold day. By analogy, a chilling look, address, or retort.

FRENCH-ELIXIR (CREAM, LACE, or ARTICLE), *subs. phr.* (common).—Brandy. [The custom of taking of brandy with tea and coffee was originally French.—Whence French Cream. LACED TEA = tea dashed with spirits].

1815. SCOTT, *Guy Mannering*, ch. ix. 'Get out the gallon punch-bowl, and plenty of lemons. I'll stand for the FRENCH ARTICLE by the time I come back, and we'll drink the young Laird's health.'

1821. *Real Life*, i., p. 606. Not forgetting blue ruin and FRENCH LACE.

ENGLISH SYNONYMS. — Ball-of-fire; bingo; cold tea; cold nantz; red ribbon.

FRENCH SYNONYMS.—*Le parfait amour du chiffonnier* (*i.e.*, ragman's happiness = coarse brandy); *le trois-six* (popular: = ROT-GUT); *fil-en-quatre*, *fil-en-trois*, *fil-en-six* (specifically, old brandy, but applied to spirits generally); *le dur* (= a drop of hard: common); *le raide* (popular = a drop of stiff): *le chenique or chnic* (popular:); *le rude* (popular: = a drop of rough, *i.e.*, coarse brandy); *l'eau d'affe* (thieves'); *le pissat d'âne* (popular: = donkey's piss; sometimes applied to bad beer, which is likewise called *pissat de vache*); *l'avoine* (military = hay, as who should say 'a nose bag'); *le blanc* (popular = brandy or white wine); *le possédé* (thieves': BINGO); *le raspail* (popular:); *le cric* (popular: also *crik*, *crique*, or *cricque* = rough brandy:); *le schnaps* (popular); *le schnick* (common: = bad brandy); *le camphre* (popular: = camphor; applied to the coarsest spirit); *le sacré-chien* or *sacré-chien tout pur* (common: = the vilest sold); *casse-poitrine* (common: = brandy heightened with pepper; *cf.*, ROT-GUT); *le jaune* (rag-pickers': = a drop of yellow); *tord-boyaux* (popular = twist-gut); *la consolation* (popular = a drop of comfort); *requiqui* (workmen's); *eau de mort* (common: = death - water); *le Tripoli* (rank brandy); *casse-gueule* (= 'kill the-carter'; applied to all kinds of spirits).

FRENCH FAKE. *subs. phr.* (nautical).—The fashion of coiling a rope by taking it backwards and forwards in parallel bands, so that it may run easily.

FRENCH GOUT (or DISEASE, FEVER, etc.), *subs. phr.* (common).—Sometimes CLAP (*q.v.*), but more generally and correctly syphilis, *Morbus Gallicus*, especially with older writers. For synonyms, *see* LADIES FEVER. Also THE FRENCHMAN. FRENCH POX = a very bad variety of syphilis. The French themselves always refer to the ailment as the *mal de Naples*, for which *see* MARSTON (1598) and his 'Naples canker,' and FLORIO (1598) *mal di Napoli* = French pocks. *Cf.*, SHAKSPEARE, *Henry V.*, v., 1. News have I that my Nell is dead i' the spital Of malady of France.

1598. FLORIO, *A Worlde of Wordes*. *Lue*, a plague . . . . It is also used for the FRENCH POXE.

1611. COTGRAVE, *Dictionarie*, *Mal de Naples*, the FRENCH POCKS.

1690. B. E. *Dict. of the Canting Crew.* (s.v.).

1740. *Poor Robin*. Some gallants will this month be so penurious that they will not part with a crack'd groat to a poor body, but on their cockatrice or punquetto will bestow half a dozen taffety gowns, who in requittal bestows on him the FRENCH POX.

1785. GROSE, *Dict. of the Vulgar Tongue*, s.v. He suffered by a blow over the snout with a French faggot-stick; *i.e.*, he lost his nose by the POX.

FRENCHIFIED, *adj.* (old).—Clapped; more generally and accurately poxed.

1690. B. E., *New Dict. of the Canting Crew*, s.v.

1785. GROSE, *Dict. of the Vulgar Tongue*, s.v. FRENCHIFIED, infected with the venereal disease; the mort is FRENCHIFIED = THE WENCH IS INFECTED.

FRENCH LEAVE, TO TAKE FRENCH LEAVE. *verb. phr.* (colloquial).—(1) To decamp without notice; (2) to do anything without permission; (3) to purloin or steal; (4) to run away (as from an enemy). [Derivation obscure; FRENCH, probably traceable to the contempt engendered during the wars with France; the compliment is returned in similar expressions (*see* Synonyms) + LEAVE = departure or permission to depart. Sense 1 is probably the origin of senses 2, 3, and 4. *See* Notes and Queries, 1 S. i, 246; 3 S. vi, 17; 5 S. xii, 87; 6 S. v, 347, 496; viii, 514; ix, 133, 213, 279; 7 S. iii, 5, 109, 518.]

ENGLISH SYNONYMS.—To retire up (one's fundament); to slope; to smouge; to do a sneak; to take the Frenchman; to vamoose.

FRENCH SYNONYMS.—*S'escarpiner* (popular: = to flash one's pumps; *escarpin* = a dancing shoe; *jouer de l'escarpin* = to ply one's pumps, (16th century); *s'échapper*, *s'esquiver*, *filer*, *disparaître*, *s'éclipser*, *se dérober*, *se retirer*, and *s'en aller à l'anglaise* (= to take English leave); *pisser à l'anglaise* (= to do an English piss, *i.e.*, affect a visit to the urinal); *prendre sa permission sous son coude* (popular: literally to take one's leave under one's arm); *ficher* or *foutre le camp*.

GERMAN SYNONYMS. — *Französischen Abschied nehmen* (= to take French leave: from GUTZKOW, R. 4, 88, etc, born 1811); *französischer Abschied* (IFFLAND, 1759-1814, 5, 3, 117); *auf gut französisch sich empfehlen* (BLUMAUER, 2, 72, 1758-1798: also GUTZKOW, R., 4, 88); *hinter der Thur urlaub* (= to take leave behind [or outside] the door, *i.e.*, after one has got outside it: quoted by SANDERS, from FISCHART, 1550-1589); *hinter der Thüre Abschied nehmen* (= to say good-bye outside, to take French leave); also, *er beurlaubte sich in aller Stille*, explained as *er stahl sich*, *schlich sich davon*, and translated 'he took French leave'; also, *sich aus einer Gesellschaft stehlen*.—HILPERT'S Dict., 1845.

SPANISH SYNONYM. — *Despedirse á la francesa* (= to take French leave).

1771. SMOLLETT, *Humphrey Clinker*, p. 54. He stole away an Irishman's bride, and took a FRENCH LEAVE of me and hi master.

1805. *Newspaper* (quoted in *Notes and Queries*, 5, S. xii., 2 Aug., 79, p. 87, col. 2). On Thursday last Monsieur J. F. Desgranche, one of the French prisoners of war on parole at Chesterfield, took FRENCH LEAVE of that place, in defiance of his parole engagement.

1854. F. E. SMEDLEY, *Harry Coverdale*, ch. lviii. 'I thought I would avoid

all the difficulties . . . by taking FRENCH LEAVE, and setting off in disguise and under a feigned name.'

1885 STEVENSON, *Treasure Island*, ch. xxii., p. 178 (1886). My only plan was to take FRENCH LEAVE, and slip out when nobody was watching.

1892. *Globe*, 25 Mar., p. 5, col. 1. They finally resolved to go on FRENCH LEAVE to the place.

FRENCH- (also AMERICAN, SPANISH, and ITALIAN) LETTER, *subs. phr.* (colloquial). — A sheath —of india-rubber, gold beater's skin, gutta-percha—worn by a man during coition to prevent infection or fruition. Usually described in print as SPECIALITIES (*q.v.*). or CIRCULAR PROTECTORS and (in U.S.A.) as SAFES (*q.v.*). *See* CUNDUM. Fr., *capote anglaise*.

FRENCH PIGEON, *subs. phr.* (sportsman's). — A pheasant killed by mistake in the partridge season. Also MOKO and ORIENTAL (*q.v.*).

FRENCH PIG, *subs. phr.* (common). —A venereal bubo; a BLUE BOAR (*q.v.*), or WINCHESTER GOOSE (*q.v.*).

FRENCH PRINTS, *subs.* (colloquial). —Generic for indecent pictures.

1849-50. THACKERAY, *Pendennis II.*, ch. xxxi. Young de Boots of the Blues recognised you as the man who came to barracks, and did business, one-third in money, one-third in eau-de-Cologne, and one third in FRENCH PRINTS, you confounded, demure, old sinner.

FRENCH VICE, *verb. phr.* (venery). — A euphemism for all sexual malpractices; LARKS (*q.v.*). First used (in print) in the case of Crawford *v.* Crawford and Dilke.

FRENCHY, *subs.* (colloquial). — A Frenchman.

FRESH, *adj.* (University).—1. Said of an undergraduate in his first term.

1803. *Gradus ad Cantabrigiam*, s.v.

1866. TREVELYAN, *Horace at Athens*. When you and I were FRESH.

2. (common). — Slightly intoxicated; elevated. For synonyms *see* DRINKS and SCREWED. (Scots' = sober).

1829. MARRYAT, *Frank Mildmay*, ch. xiii. Drinking was not among my vices. I could get FRESH, as we call it, when in good company and excited by wit and mirth; but I never went to the length of being drunk.

3. (Old English and modern American).—Inexperienced, but conceited and presumptuous; hence, forward, impudent.

1596. SHAKSPEARE, *King John*, iii., 4. How green you are and FRESH in this old world.

1886. FRANCIS, *Saddle and Mocassin*. 'Has Peggy been too FRESH?' Her sunburnt cheeks flushed.

4. (common). — Fasting; opposed to eating or drinking.

FRESH AS PAINT, AS A ROSE, AS A DAISY, AS A NEW-BORN TURD, etc., *phr.* (common).—Full of health, strength, and activity; FIT (*q.v.*).

1864. E. YATES, *Broken to Harness*, ch. xix. This is his third day's rest, and the cob will be about as FRESH AS PAINT when I get across him again.

1880. *Punch's Almanack*, p. 12.

FRESH ON THE GRAFT, *adj. phr.* (common). — New to the work. *Cf.*, FRESH BIT.

FRESH BIT, *subs. phr.* (venery).— A beginner; also a new mistress. *Cf.*, BIT OF FRESH = the sexual favour: MEAT, or MUTTON, or FISH (*q.v.*), being understood.

FRESHEN ONE'S WAY, *verb. phr.* (nautical).—To hurry; to quicken one's movements. [The wind FRESHENS when it rises.]

FRESHEN UP, *verb. phr.* (colloquial). To clean; to vamp; to revive; to smarten.

FRESHER, *subs.* (University).—An undergraduate in his first term.

FRESHERS. THE FRESHERS, *subs.* (University).—That part of the Cam which lies between the Mill and Byron's Pool. So called because it is frequented by FRESHMEN (*q.v.*).

FRESHMAN (or FRESHER), *subs.* (University).—A University man during his first year. In Dublin University he is a JUNIOR FRESHMAN during his first year, and a SENIOR FRESHMAN the second year. At Oxford the title lasts for the first term. Ger., *Fuchs*.

1596. NASHE, *Saffron Walden*, in wks. iii., 8. When he was but yet a FRESHMAN in Cambridge.

1611. MIDDLETON, *Roaring Girl*, Act iii., Sc. 3. *S. Alex.* Then he's a graduate. *S. Davy.* Say they trust him not. *S. Alex.* Then is he held a FRESHMAN and a sot.

1767. COLMAN, *Oxonian in Town*, ii., 3. And now I find you as dull and melancholy as a FRESHMAN at college after a jobation.

1841. LEVER, *Charles O'Malley*, ch. xiv. 'This is his third year,' said the Doctor, 'and he is only a FRESHMAN, having lost every examination.'

1891. *Sporting Life*, 20 Mar. The mile, bar accidents, will be a gift to B. C. Allen, of Corpus, who has more than maintained the reputation he gained as a FRESHER.

Adj. (University). — Of, or pertaining to, a FRESHMAN, or a first year student.

FRESHMANSHIP, *subs.* (old).—Of the quality or state of being a freshman.

1605. JONSON, *Volpone, or the Fox*, iv., 3. Well, wise Sir Pol., since you have practised thus, Upon my FRESHMANSHIP, I'll try your salt-head With what proof it is against a counter-plot.

FRESHMAN'S BIBLE, *subs. phr.* (University). — The University Calendar.

FRESHMAN'S CHURCH, *subs. phr.* (University).—The Pitt Press at Cambridge. [From its ecclesiastical architecture.]

FRESHMAN'S LANDMARK, *subs. phr.* (University). — King's College Chapel, Cambridge. [From the situation.]

FRESHWATER MARINER (or SEAMAN), *subs. phr.* (old).—A beggar shamming sailor; a TURNPIKE SAILOR (*q.v.*).

1567. HARMAN, *Caveat* (1869), p. 48, These FRESHWATER MARINERS, their shipes were drowned in the playne of Salisbury. These kynde ... counterfet great losses on the sea.

1690. B. E., *New Dict. of the Canting Crew*. FRESHWATER SEAMEN, that have never been on the Salt, or made any Voyage, meer Land-Men.

FRESHWATER SOLDIER, *subs. phr.* (old).—A raw recruit.

1598. FLORIO, *A Worlde of Wordes*, Biancone. A goodly, great milke-soppe, a FRESH WATER SOLDIER.

1603. KNOLLES, *Hist. of the Turkes*. The nobility, as FRESHWATER SOLDIERS, which had never seen but some slight skirmishes, made light account of the Turks.

1696. *Nomenclator*. Bachelier aux armes, nouveau ou jeune soudard. A FRESHWATER SOULDIER: a young souldier: a novice: one that is trayned up to serve in the field.

FRET, TO FRET ONE'S GIZZARD, GUTS, GIBLETS, KIDNEYS, CREAM, etc., *verb. phr.* (common).—To get harassed and worried about trifles; TO TEAR ONE'S SHIRT (*q.v.*).

FRIAR, *subs.* (printers').—A pale spot in a printed sheet. Fr., *un moine* (= monk).

FRIB, *subs.* (old).—A stick. For synonyms, see TOKO.

1754. *Discoveries of John Poulter*, p. 43. A Jacob and FRIB; a ladder and stick.

FRIBBLE, *subs.* (old).—A trifler; a contemptible fop. [From the character in Garrick's *Miss in her Teens* (1747).]

1785. GROSE, *Dict. of the Vulgar Tongue*, s.v.

1860. THACKERAY, *Four Georges. George IV.* That FRIBBLE, the leader of such men as Fox and Burke!

FRIDAY-FACE, *subs.* (old). — A gloomy, dejected-looking man or woman. [Probably from Friday being. ecclesiastically, the banyan day of the week.] Fr., *figure de carême*.

1592. GREENE, *Groatsworth of Wit*, in wks. xii., 120. The Foxe made a FRIDAY-FACE, counterfeiting sorrow.

1785. GROSE, *Dict. of the Vulg. Tongue*, s.v.

1889. *Gentleman's Mag.*, June, p. 593. FRIDAY-FACE is a term still occasionally applied to a sour-visaged person; it was formerly in very common use.

FRIDAY-FACED, *adj.* (old).—Mortified; melancholy; 'sour-featured' (Scott).

1592. JOHN DAY, *Blind Beggar*, Act ii., Sc. 2, p. 57. Can. No, you FRIDAY-FAC'D frying-pan, it was to save us all from whipping or a worse shame.

1606. *Wily Beguiled* (Hawkins *Eng. Dr.*, iii., 356). Marry, out upon him! What a FRIDAY-FAC'D slave it is! I think in my conscience his face never keeps holiday.

FRIEND (or LITTLE FRIEND), *subs.*— The menstrual flux or DOMESTIC AFFLICTIONS (*q.v.*), whose appearance is sometimes announced by the formula 'My little friend has come.' Conventionalisms are queer; poorly; changes (Irish); 'the Captain's at home' (GROSE). See FLAG.

TO GO AND SEE A SICK FRIEND, *verb. phr.* (venery).—To go on the loose. See GREENS.

FRIEND CHARLES. See CHARLES HIS FRIEND.

FRIENDLY LEAD, *subs. phr.* (thieves').—An entertainment (as a sing-song) got up to assist a companion in TROUBLE (*q.v.*), or to raise money for the wife and children of a 'quodded pal.'

1871. *Daily Telegraph*, 4 Dec. This was the secret business, the tremendous conspiracy, to compass which it was deemed necessary to act with infinitely more caution than the friends of Bill Sikes feel called on to exercise when they distribute tickets for a FRIENDLY LEAD for the benefit of Bill, who is 'just out of his trouble.'

1889. *Cassell's Saturday Journal*, 5 Jan. The men frequently club together in a FRIENDLY LEAD to help a brother in distress.

1892. *Ally Sloper*, 2 Apr., p. 106, col. 3. My father takes the chair at FRIENDLY LEADS.

FRIENDS IN NEED, *subs. phr.* (common).—Lice. For synonyms, see CHATES.

FRIG, *verb trans. and refl.* (venery). — To masturbate. Also *subs.* = an act of masturbation. Known sometimes as KEEPING DOWN THE CENSUS. [Latin, *fricare* = to rub.]

ENGLISH SYNONYMS. — To bob; to box the Jesuit ['St. Omer's lewdness,' Marston,

'*Scourge*' (1598)]; to chuff; to chuffer; to claw (Florio); to digitate (of women); to eat (or get) cock-roaches; to bring up (or off) by hand; to fight one's turkey (Texan); to finger or finger-fuck (of women); to friggle (Florio); to fuck one's fist (of men); to fetch mettle (Grose); to handle; to indorse; to jerk, play, pump, toss, or work off; to lark; to milk; to mount a corporal and four; to mess, or pull about; to play with (school-boys); to rub up; to shag; to tickle one's crack (of women); to dash one's doodle; to touch up; to play paw-paw tricks (Grose); to wriggle (old). For foreign synonyms, see WRIGGLE.

1598. FLORIO, *A Worlde of Wordes*. Fricciare ... to FRIG, to wriggle, to tickle.

1611. COTGRAVE, *Dictionaire*. Branler la pique, To FRIG.

1728. BAILEY, *Dict.*, s.v. FRIG, to rub.

c. 1716-1746. ROBERTSON of Struan. *Poems*, 83. So to a House of office ... a School-Boy does repair, To ... fr—bis P— there.

1785. GROSE, *Dict. of the Vulgar Tongue.*, s.v.

FRIGATE, *subs.* (common). — A woman.

1690. B. E., *New Dict. of the Canting Crew*. FRIGGAT well rigg'd, a woman well drest and gentile.

1785. GROSE, *Vulg. Tongue*. A well-rigg'd FRIGATE, a well-dressed wench.

FRIGGING, *subs.* (venery).—1. The act of masturbation; the 'cynick friction' (Marston, *Scourge*); otherwise SIMPLE INFANTICIDE.

2. (old). — Trifling [GROSE, 1785.]

Adj. and adv. (vulgar).—An expletive of intensification. Thus, FRIGGING BAD = 'bloody' bad; a FRIGGING IDIOT = an absolute fool. See also FOUTERING and FUCKING.

FRIGHTFULLY, *adv.* (colloquial). —Very. An expletive used as are AWFULLY, BEASTLY, BLOODY, etc. (*q.v.*).

FRIG-PIG, *subs.* (old).—A finnicking trifler.

1785. GROSE, *Dict. Vulg. Tongue*, s.v.

1811. *Lexicon Balatronicum*, s.v.

FRIGSTER (in fem. FRIGSTRESS) *subs.* (venery).—A masturbator; an INDORSER (*q.v.*, also = a Sodomite).

FRILLERY, *subs.* (common). — Feminine underclothing. For synonyms, see SNOWY. TO EXPLORE ONE'S FRILLERY (venery) = to grope one's person.

FRILLS, *subs.* (American). — Swagger; conceit; also accomplishments (as music, languages, etc.); and culture; *cf.*, MAN WITH NO FRILLS.

1870. *Sacramento Paper* (quoted in *De Vere*). 'I can't bear his talk, it's all FRILLS.'

1884. CLEMENS ('Mark Twain'), *Adventures of Huck, Finn.* 33. I never see such a son. I bet I'll take some of these FRILLS out of you before I'm done with you.

TO PUT ON ONE'S FRILLS, *verb. phr.* (American).—To exaggerate; TO CHANT THE POKER; to swagger; to put on SIDE (*q.v.*); to SING IT (*q.v.*). Fr., *se gonfler le jabot*, and *faire son lard*.

1890. RUDYARD KIPLING *National Observer*, March, 1890, p. 69. 'The Oont.' It's the commissariat camel PUTTING ON HIS BLOOMING FRILLS.

2. (venery).—To get wanton or PRICK-PROUD (*q.v.*); in a state of MUST (*a.v.*).

TO HAVE BEEN AMONG ONE'S FRILLS, *verb. phr.* (venery).—To have enjoyed the sexual favour. For synonyms, see GREENS.

FRINT, *subs.* (old).—A pawnbroker. For synonyms, see UNCLE.

1821. *Real Life in London*, i., p. 566.

FRISCO, *subs.* (American).—Short for San Francisco.

1870. BRET HARTE, *Poems*, 'Chiquita.' Busted hisself at White Pine, and blew out his brains down in FRISCO.

1890. *Sporting Life*, 8 Nov. The battle . . . took place in the theatre, Market St., FRISCO.

FRISK, *subs.* (old). — 1. A frolic; an outing; a LARK (*q.v.*); mischief generally.

1697. VANBRUGH, *Provoked Wife*, iii., 1. If you have a mind to take a FRISK with us, I have an interest with my lord; I can easily introduce you.

1785. GROSE, *Vulg. Tongue*, s.v.

1825. *The English Spy*, vi., p. 162. Dick's a *trump*, and no *telegraph*—up to every FRISK, and down to every *move* of the domini, thoroughbred and no *want of courage*.

1852. DICKENS, *Bleak House*, ch. xx., p. 171. 'When you and I had the FRISK down in Lincolnshire, Guppy, and drove over to see that house at Castle Wold.'

2. (old).—A dance.

1719. DURFEY, *Pills*, etc., i., 274. Let's have a neat FRISK or so, And then rub on the law.

1782. COWPER, *Table Talk*, 237. Give him his lass, his fiddle, and his FRISK, Is always happy, reign whoever may

1880. OUIDA, *Moths*, ch. xiv. And her fancy-dress FRISKS, and her musical breakfasts, were great successes.

3. (venery).—The act of copulation. See GREENS and RIDE.

Verb (thieves').—1. To search; TO RUN THE RULE OVER (*q.v.*); Especially applied to the search made, after arrest, for evidence of character, antecedents, or identity. Hence, careful examination of any kind.

1781. G. PARKER, *Life's Painter*, p. 179. They FRISK him? That is search him. *Ibid.*, p. 122. Putting a lap-feeder in our sack, that you or your blowen had prig'd yourselves though we should stand the FRISK for it.

1828. JON. BEE, *Pict. of London.* p. 69. The arms are seized from behind by one, whilst the other FRISKS the pockets of their contents.

1852. JUDSON, *Mysteries, etc. of New York*, ch. vii. Vel sare, the offisare 'ave FRISK me: he 'ave not found ze skin or ze dummy, eh?

1859. MATSELL, *Vocabulum, or Rogue's Lexicon*, p. 21. The knuck was copped to rights, a skin full of honey was found in his kick's poke by the copper when he FRISKED him'; [i.e.] the pickpocket was arrested, and when searched by the officer a purse was found in his pantaloons pocket full of money.

2. (thieves'). — To pick pockets; to rob. TO FRISK A CLY = to empty a pocket.

1852. JUDSON, *Mysteries, etc. of New York*, ch. iv. You're as good a knuck as ever FRISKED a swell.

1883. *Daily Telegraph*, 13 June, p. 7, col. 3. The ragged little wretches who prowl in gangs about the suburbs, who crawl on their hands and knees into shops in order to 'FRISK the till.'

3. (venery).—To 'HAVE (*q.v.*) a woman.' For synonyms, see RIDE.

TO DANCE THE PADDINGTON FRISK, *verb. phr.* (old). — To dance on nothing; *i.e.*, to be hanged. [Tyburn Tree was in Paddington.] For synonyms, see LADDER.

FRISKER, *subs.* (old).—A dancer.

1719. DURFEY, *Pills*, etc., ii., 20. At no Whitsun Ale there e'er yet had been Such Fraysters and FRISKERS as these lads and lasses.

FRIVOL or **FRIVVLE**, *verb.* (colloquial). — To act frivolously; to trifle. [A resuscitation of an old word used in another sense, viz., to annul, to set aside].

1883. W. BLACK, *Yolande*, ch. xx. 'Mind, I am assuming that you mean business—if you want to FRIVOLE, and pick pretty posies, I shut my door on you but, I say, if you mean business, I have told Mrs. Bell you are to have access to my herbarium, whether I am there or not.'

FROG, *subs.* (common). — 1. A policeman. For synonyms, *see* BEAK and COPPER.

1881. *New York Slang Dict.*, 'On the Trail.' I must amputate like a goaway, or the FROGS will nail me.

1886. *Graphic*, 30 Jan., p. 130, col. 1. A policeman is also called . . . a 'frog, the last-named because he is supposed to jump, as it were, suddenly upon guilty parties.

2. (common).—A Frenchman. Also FROGGY and FROG-EATER. [Formerly a Parisian; the shield of whose city bore three toads, while the quaggy state of the streets gave point to a jest common at Versailles before 1791: Qu'en disent les grenouilles? *i.e.*, What do the FROGS (the people of Paris) say?]

1883. *Referee*, 15 July, p. 7, col. 3. While Ned from Boulogne says '*Oui mon brave*,' The Froggies must answer for Tamatave.'

3. (popular). — A foot. For synonyms, *see* CREEPERS.

TO FROG ON, *verb. phr.* (American).—To get on; to prosper FROGGING-ON = success.

FROG-AND-TOAD, *subs.* (rhyming) —The main road.

FROG-AND-TOE, *subs.* (American thieves'). — The city of New York.

1859. MATSELL *Vocabulum, or Rogue's Lexicon*, p. 35. Coves, let us FROG-AND-TOE, coves, let us go to New York.

FROGLANDER, *subs.* (old). — A Dutchman. *Cf.*, FROG, sense 2.

1690. B. E., *New Dict. of the Canting Crew*, s.v.

1852. JUDSON, *Mysteries, etc. of New York*, ch. xiv. The funny swag which they raised out of the FROGLANDER coves.

FROG-SALAD, *subs.* (American).—A ballet; *i.e.*, a LEG-PIECE (*q.v.*).

FROG'S MARCH. TO GIVE THE FROG'S MARCH, *verb. phr.* (common). — To carry a man face downwards to the station; a device adopted with drunken or turbulent prisoners.

1871. *Evening Standard*, 'Clerkenwell Police Report,' 18 April. In cross-examination the police stated that they did not give the defendant the FROG'S MARCH. The FROG'S MARCH was described to be carrying the face downwards.

1884. *Daily News*, Oct. 4, p. 5, col. 2. They had to resort to a mode of carrying him, familiarly known in the force, we believe, as the FROG TROT, or sometimes as the FROG'S MARCH. . . . The prisoner is carried with his face downwards and his arms drawn behind him.

1888. *Daily Telegraph*, 22 Dec. Whether the 'bobbies' ran the tipsy man in, treating him meanwhile to a taste of the FROG'S MARCH, and whether he was fined or imprisoned for assaulting the police, is not upon the record.

1890. *Bird o' Freedom*, 19 Mar., p. 1 col. 1. And then he gets the FROG'S MARCH to the nearest Tealeafs.

FROG'S WINE, *subs. phr.* (old).—Gin. For synonyms, *see* DRINKS and SATIN.

1811. *Lexicon Balatronicum*, s.v.

FROLIC, *subs.* (common).—A merry-making.

1847. ROBB. *Squatter Life*, p. 133. At all the FROLICKS round the country, Jess was hangin' onter that gal.

FROSTY-FACE, *subs.* (old).—A pox-pitted man. Grose (1785).

FRONT, *verb* (thieves').—To conceal the operations of a pickpocket; to COVER (*q.v.*).

1879. J. W. HORSLEY in *Macmillan's Mag.*, XL., 506. So my pal said, 'FRONT me (cover me), and I will do him for it.'

FRONT-ATTIC (or **-DOOR**, **-GARDEN**, **-PARLOUR**, **-ROOM**, or **-WINDOW**). *subs. phr.* (venery).—The female *pudendum*. For synonyms, *see* MONOSYLLABLE. TO HAVE (or DO) a BIT OF FRONT-DOOR WORK = to copulate.

1823. BEE, *Dict. of the Turf*, s.v. Mrs. Fubb's FRONT-PARLOUR (*vide* Tom Rees) is not to be mistaken for any part of any building.

FRONT-DOOR MAT, *subs. phr.* (venery).—The female pubic hair. For synonyms, *see* FLEECE.

FRONT-GUT, *subs.* (venery).—The female *pudendum*. For synonyms, *see* MONOSYLLABLE.

FRONTISPIECE, *subs.* (pugilists').—The face. For synonyms, *see* DIAL.

1818. P. EGAN, *Boxiana*, I., p. 221. Tyne put in right and left upon the Jew's FRONTISPIECE two such severe blows, that Crabbe's countenance underwent a trifling change.

1845. BUCKSTONE, *Green Bushes*, i., 1. It's a marcy my switch didn't come in contract with your iligant FRONTISPIECE.

1860. *Chambers' Journal XIII.*, p. 368. His forehead is his FRONTISPIECE.

1864. A. TROLLOPE, *Sm. Ho. at Allington* (1884), vol. ii., ch. V., p. 47. He said that he had had an accident—or rather, a row—and that he had come out of it with considerable damage to his FRONTISPIECE.

1891. *Sporting Life*, 28 Mar. It must be confessed that the ludicrous was attained when Griffiths subsequently appeared with a short black pipe in his distorted and battered FRONTISPIECE.

FRONT-WINDOWS, *subs.* (common). —1. The eyes; also the face.

2. In *sing.* (venery). — The female *pudendum*. *Cf.*, FRONT-ATTIC; and for synonyms, *see* MONOSYLLABLE.

FROST, *subs.* (common).—A complete failure. *Cf.*, Fr., *un four noir*. Also *un temps noir* = a blank interval; a prolonged silence (as when an actor's memory fails him).

1885. *Saturday Review*, 15 Aug., p. 218. He is an absolute and perfect FROST.

1885. *Bell's Life*, 3 Jan., p. 3, col. 6. We regret we cannot write favorably concerning this matter, the affair being almost as big a FROST athletically as it was financially.

1889. *Star*, 17 Jan. The pantomime was a dead FROST.

2. (common). — A dearth of work; TO HAVE A FROST = to be idle.

FROUDACIOUS, **FROUDACITY**, *adj.* and *subs.* *See* quots.

1888. *Colonies and India*, 14 Nov. The word 'FROUDACITY,' invented by Mr. Darnell Davis in his able review of *The Bow of Ulysses*, recently published, has reached the height of popularity in the Ausralasian Colonies, where it has come into everyday use. In the Melbourne Assembly the other day an hon. member observed—speaking of some remarks made by a previous speaker—that he never heard

such FROUDACIOUS statements in his life. The colonial papers are beginning, also, to spell the word with a small 'f,' which is significant.

1889. *Graphic*, 16 Feb. By exposing some of Mr. Froude's manifold errors (the most dangerous is that which assumes the sour Waikato clays to be rich because they grow fern) he justifies the Australian adjective FROUDACIOUS.

FROUST, *subs.* (Harrow School).—1. Extra sleep allowed on Sunday mornings and whole holidays. Fr., *faire du lard*.

2. (common).—A stink; stuffiness (in a room).

FROUSTY, *adj.* (common).—Stinking.

FROUT, *adj.* (Winchester College).—Angry; vexed.

FROW (or **FROE**, or **VROE**), *subs.* (old).—A woman; a wife; a mistress. [From the Dutch.]

1607. DEKKER, *Westward Ho*, Act V., Sc. 1. Eat with 'em as hungerly as soldiers; drink as if we were FROES.

1690. B. E., *New Dict. of the Canting Crew*, V. Brush to your FROE and wheedle for crap, c. whip to your mistress and speak her fair to give or lend you some Money.

1754. B. MARTIN, *Eng. Dict.* (2 ed.), s.v.

1789. PARKER, *Life's Painter*, p. 119 A flash of lightning next Bess tipt each cull and FROW.

FRUITFUL VINE, *subs. phr.* (venery). —The female *pudendum*. For synonyms, *see* MONOSYLLABLE.

1811. *Lexicon Balatronicum*, s.v. FRUITFUL VINE. A woman's private parts, *i.e.*, that has flowers every month, and bears fruit in nine.

FRUMMAGEMED, *adj.* (old). — Choked; strangled; spoilt.

1671. R. HEAD, *English Rogue*, Pt. I., ch. v., 49 (1874). FRUMMAGEM, Choakt.

1724. E. COLES, *Eng. Dict.* FRUMMIGAM, *c.* choaked.

1785. GROSE, *Vulg. Tongue*, s.v. Choaked, strangled, or hanged. Cant.

1815. SCOTT, *Guy Mannering*, ch. xxviii. 'If I had not helped you with these very fambles (holding up her hands), Jean Baillie would have FRUMMAGEM'D you, ye feckless do-little!'

1819. MOORE, *Tom Crib's Memorial*, p. 21. There he lay, almost FRUMMAGEM'D.

FRUMP, *subs.* (old). — 1. A contemptuous speech or piece of conduct; a sneer; a jest.

1553. WILSON, *Art of Rhetorique*, p. 137. (He) shall be able to abashe a right worthie man, and make him at his witte's ende, through the sodaine quicke and vnlooked FRUMPE giuen.

1589. GREENE, *Menaphon*, p. 45. For women's paines are more pinching if they be girded with a FRUMPE than if they be galled with a mischiefe.

1598. FLORIO, *A Worlde of Wordes*. *Bichiacchia*, jestes, toyes, FRUMPS, flimflam tales, etc.

1606. T. DEKKER, *Seven Deadly Sinnes*, p. 44 (ed. Arber). The courtiers gives you an open scoffe, ye clown a secret mock, the citizen yat dwels at your threshald, a ieery FRUMP.

1630. TAYLOR, *Works*. But yet, me thinkes, he gives thee but a FRUMPE, In telling how thee kist a wenches rumpe.

1662. *Rump Songs*, 'Arsy-Varsy, etc., ii., 47. As a preface of honor and not as a FRUMP, First with a Sir reverence ushers the Rump.

1668. DRYDEN, *An Evening's Love* Act IV. Sc. 3. Not to be behindhand with you in your FRUMPS, I give you back your purse of gold.

2. (common). — A slattern; more commonly a prim old lady; the correlative of FOGEY (*q.v.*). Fr., *un graillon*.

1831. J. R. PLANCHÉ, *Olympic Revels*, Sc. i. Cheat, you stingy FRUMP! Who wants to cheat?

1837. BARHAM, *Ingoldsby Legends*, I., p. 157. Get into the hands of the other old FRUMPS.

1857. THACKERAY, *Virginians*, ch. xxxi. She is changed now, isn't she? What an old Gorgon it is! She is a great patroness of your book-men, and when that old FRUMP was young they actually made verses about her.

3. (old).—A cheat; a trick.

1602. ROWLAND, *Greene's Ghost*, 37. They come off with their . . . FRUMPS

Verb (old).—To mock; to insult.

1589. NASHE, *Month's Mind*, in Works, Vol. I., p. 158. One of them . . . maketh a iest of *Princes*, and '*the troubling of the State, and offending of her Maiestie*,' hee turneth of with a FRUMPING *forsooth*, as though it were a toie to think of it.

1593. G. HARVEY, *Pierces Super*, in Works II., 107. That despiseth the graces of God, floweth the constellations of heaven, FRUMPETH the operations of nature.

1609. *Man in the Moone*. Hee . . . FRUMPETH those his mistresse frownes on.

1757. GARRICK, *Irish Widow*, I., i. Yes, he was FRUMPED, and called me old blockhead.

FRUMPER, *subs.* (old).—A sturdy man; a good blade.

1825. KENT, *Modern Flash Dict.*, s.v.

FRUMPISH, *adj.* (colloquial). — Cross-grained; old-fashioned and severe in dress, manners, morals, and notions; ill-natured; given to frumps. Also FRUMPY.

1589. GREENE, *Tullies Love*, in wks. vii., 131. Who were you but as fauourable, as you are FRUMPISH, would soone censure by my talke, how deepe I am reade in loues principles.

1701. FARQUHAR, *Sir Harry Wildair*, Act. V., Sc. 5. She got, I don't know how, a crotchet of jealousy in her head. This made her FRUMPISH, but we had ne'er an angry word.

1757. FOOTE, *Author*, Act II. And methought she looked very FRUMPISH and jealous.

1764. O'HARA, *Midas*, I., 3. La! mother, why so FRUMPISH?

1864. DICKENS, *Our Mutual Friend*, Bk. I., ch. xi. 'Don't fancy me a FRUMPY old married woman, my dear; I was married but the other day, you know.'

1889. *Modern Society*, 12 Oct., p 1271, col. 2. Quite an elderly and superannuated look is given to the toilette which is finished off by a woollen cloud or silken shawl, and only invalids and sixty-year-old women should be allowed such FRUMPISH privileges.

FRUSHEE, *subs.* (Scots').—An open jam tart.

FRY, *verb* (common).—To translate into plain English. *Cf.*, BOIL DOWN.

1881. JAS. PAYN, *Grape from a Thorn*, ch. xxx. 'I shall repose the greatest confidence in you, my dear girl, which one human being can entrust to another.' was one of its sentences, which, when it came 'to be FRIED,' meant that she should delegate to her the duties of combing Fido and cutting her canary's claws.

GO AND FRY YOUR FACE, *phr.* (common).—A retort expressive of incredulity, derision, or contempt.

FRYING-PAN. TO JUMP FROM THE FRYING-PAN INTO THE FIRE, *verb. phr.* (common). — To go from bad to worse. *Cf.*, 'from the smoke into the smother' (As You Like it, i., 2.). Fr., *tomber de la poêle dans la braise*.

1684. BUNYAN, *Pilgrim's Progress*, Part II. Some, though they shun the FRYING-PAN, do leap into the fire.

TO FRY THE PEWTER, *verb phr.* (thieves').—To melt down pewter measures.

F SHARP, *subs. phr.* (common). —A flea; *cf.*, B flat.

FUANT, *subs.* (old).—Excrement.—B.E., *Dict. of the Canting Crew*.

FUB, *verb.* (old).—To cheat; to steal; to put off with false excuses. Also FUBBERY = cheating, stealing, deception.

1598. SHAKSPEARE, 2 *Henry IV.*, II., 1. I have borne, and borne, and borne, and have been FUBBED OFF, and FUBBED OFF from this day to that day.

1604. MARSTON, *Malcontent*, i., 3. O no; but dream the most fantastical. O heaven! O FUBBERY! FUBBERY!

1619. FLETCHER, *Mons. Thomas*, ii., 2. My letter FUBB'D too.

1647. CARTWRIGHT, *Ordinary* iv., 4. I won't be FUBBED.

FUBSEY or **FUBSY**, *adj.* (old).—Plump; fat; well-filled. FUBSY DUMMY = a well-filled pocket book; FUBSY wench = a plump girl.

1785. GROSE, *Vulg. Tongue*, s.v.

1825. *English Spy*, I., p. 188. Old dowagers, their FUBSY faces, Painted to eclipse the Graces.

1837. MARRYAT, *Snarley-yow*, I., ch. viii. Seated on the widow's little FUBSY sofa.

FUBSINESS, *subs.* (common).—Any sort of fatness.

FUCK, *subs.* (venery).—1. An act of coition. For synonyms, *see* GREENS.

2. (venery). — The seminal fluid. For synonyms, *see* CREAM.

Verb. (common).—To copulate. For synonyms, *see* GREENS and RIDE.

c. 1540. DAVID LYNDSAY, *'Flyting with King James.'* Aye FUKKAND like ane furious fornicator.

1568. CLERK, *Bannatyne MSS.*, Hunterian Soc. Publication, p. 298. He clappit fast, he kist, he chukkit, As with the glaikkis he wer ourgane; Yit be his feiris he wald haif FUKKIT.

1568. Anonymous, *Bannatyne MSS.*, Hunterian Soc. Publication, p. 399. 'In Somer when Flouris will Smell.' Allace! said sch, my awin sweit thing, Your courtly FUKKING garis me fling, Ye wirk sae weill.

1598. FLORIO, *A Worlde of Wordes*, *Fottere.* To jape; to sarde, to FUCKE; to swive; to occupy.

1620. PERCY, *Folio MSS.*, p. 459. [Hales and Furnivall, 1867.] A mighty mind to clipp, kisse, and to FFUCK her.

1647-80. ROCHESTER, *'Written under Nelly's Picture.'* Her father FUCKED them right together.

1683. EARL OF DORSET, *'A Faithful Catalogue.'* From St. James's to the Land of Thule, There's not a whore who F——S so like a mule.

c. 1716-1746. ROBERTSON of Struan, *Poems*, 256. But she gave proof that she could f——k, Or she is damnably bely'd.

1728. BAILEY, *English Dict.*, s.v. FUCK . . . *Feminam subigitare.*

1785. GROSE, *Vulg. Tongue.* F——K, to copulate.

c. 1790(?). BURNS, *Merry Muses.* And yet misca's a poor thing That FUCKS for its bread.

FUCKABLE, *adj.* (venery). — Desirable. Also FUCKSOME.

FUCKER, *subs.* (common).—1. A lover; a FANCY JOSEPH (*q.v.*).

2. (common). — A term of endearment, admiration, derision, etc.

FUCK-FINGER, *subs. phr.* (venery). —A fricatrix.

FUCK-FIST, *subs. phr.* (venery).—A FRIGSTER (*q.v.*); a masturbator. For synonyms, *see* MILKMAN.

FUCK-HOLE, *subs. phr.* (venery).—The female *pudendum*. For synonyms, *see* MONOSYLLABLE.

FUCKING, *subs.* (venery).—Generic for the 'act of kind.'

1568. SCOTT, *Bannatyne MSS.*, Hunterian Soc. Publication, p. 363. 'To the Derisioun of Wantoun Wemen.' Thir foure, the suth to sane, Enforsis thame to FUCKING . . . Quod Scott.

1575. *Satirical Poems, etc.*, Scottish Text Soc. Pub. (1889-90) i., 208. 'A Lewd Ballat.' To se forett the holy frere his fukking so deplore.

Adj. (common). — A qualification of extreme contumely.

Adv. (common).—1. Intensitive and expletive; a more violent form of BLOODY (*q.v.*). *See* FOUTERING.

FUCKISH, *adj.* (venery).—Wanton; PROUD (*q.v.*); inclined for coition.

FUCKSTER, *subs.* (venery). — A good PERFORMER (*q.v.*); one specially addicted to the act. A WOMAN-FUCKER (FLORIO), but in feminine FUCKSTRESS.

FUD, *subs.* (venery).—The pubic hair. For synonyms, *see* FLEECE. Also the tail of a hare or rabbit.

1785. BURNS, *The Jolly Beggars.* They scarcely left to co'er their FUDS.

FUDDLE, *subs.* (common). — 1. Drink. [Wedgwood: A corruption of FUZZ.]

1621. BURTON, *Anatomy of Melancholy.* The university troop dined with the Earl of Abingdon and came back well FUZZED.

1690. B. E., *New Dict. of the Canting Crew*, s.v. FUDDLE, Drink. 'This is rum FUDDLE, *c.* this is excellent Tipple.'

1705. WARD, *Hudibras Redivivus*, *I.*, Pt. iv., p. 18. And so, said I, we sipp'd our FUDDLE, As women in the straw do caudle, 'Till every man had drown'd his noddle.

1733. BAILEY, *Erasmus*, p. 125 (ed. 1877). Don't go away; they have had their dose of FUDDLE.

2. (common). — A drunken bout; a DRUNK.

1864. *Glasgow Citizen*, 9 Dec. Turner is given to a FUDDLE at times.

Verb. (colloquial). — To be drunk.

1720. DURFEY, *Pills*, etc., vi., 265. All day he will FUDDLE.

1754. B. MARTIN, *Eng. Dict.* (2nd ed.). To FUDDLE. 1. To make a person drunk. 2. To grow drunk.

1770. FOOTE. *Lame Lover*, iii. Come, Hob or Nob, Master Circuit—let us try if we can't FUDDLE the serjeant.

1855. THACKERAY, *Newcomes*, ch. x. He boxed the watch; he FUDDLED himself at taverns; he was no better than a Mohock.

1889. *Echo*, 15 Feb. If rich, you may FUDDLE with Bacchus all night, And be borne to your chamber remarkably tight.

FUDDLECAP (or **FUDDLER**), *subs.* (common).—A drunkard; a boon companion. For synonyms, *see* LUSHINGTON.

1607. DEKKER, *Jests to make you Merie*, in wks. (GROSART) ii., 299. And your perfect FUDDLECAP [is known] by his red nose.

d. 1682. T. BROWNE, *Works*, iii., 93. True Protestant FUDDLECAPS.

1690. B. E., *New Dict. of the Canting Crew.* FUDDLECAP, a drunkard.

1748. T. DYCHE, *Dictionary* (5th ed.) FUDDLECAP (S.) one that loves tippling, an excessive drinker, or drunkard.

1785. GROSE, *Vulg. Tongue*, s.v.

FUDDLED, *adj.* (colloquial). — Stupid with drink. For synonyms, *see* DRINKS and SCREWED.

1661. PEPYS, *Diary*, 8 March After dinner, to drink all the afternoon . . . at last come in Sir William Wale, almost FUDDLED.

1713. *Guardian*, No. 145. It was my misfortune to call in at Tom's last night, a little FUDDLED.

1730. THOMSON, *Autumn*, 537. The table floating round, And pavement faithless to the FUDDLED foot.

1838. DICKENS, *Nich. Nickleby*, ch. lx., p. 485. You're a little FUDDLED to-

night, and may not be able to see this as clearly as you would at another time.

1841. *Punch*, I., p. 74. The Sultan got very FUDDLED last night with forbidden juice in the harem, and tumbled down the ivory steps.

1864. *Glasgow Citizen*, 19 Nov. No other word has so many equivalents as 'drunk.' . . . One very common and old one has escaped Mr. Hotten — FUDDLED.

1888. *Daily News*, 28 Nov. Music halls would soon decrease in numbers if drink were not sold in them, for sober people would not go to see spectacles only attractive to those who were half FUDDLED.

FUDGE, *subs.* (colloquial). — Nonsense; humbug; an exaggeration; a falsehood. [Provincial French, *fuche*, *feuche*; an exclamation of contempt from Low Ger. *futsch* = begone; *see*, however, quots. 1700 and 1712.] Also as an exclamation of contempt.

1700. ISAAC DISRAELI, *Notes on the Navy.* There was, in our time, one Captain Fudge, a commander of a merchant-man; who, upon his return from a voyage, always brought home a good cargo of lies; insomuch that now, aboard ship, the sailors, when they hear a great lie, cry out FUDGE.

1712. W. CROUCH, *A Collection of Papers.* In the year 1664 we were sentenced for banishment to Jamaica by Judges Hyde and Twisden, and our number was 55. We were put on board the ship Black Eagle; the master's name was FUDGE, by some called LYING FUDGE.

1766 GOLDSMITH, *Vicar of Wakefield*, ch. xi. Who . . . would cry out FUDGE! an expression which displeased us all, and, in some measure, damped the rising spirit of the conversation.

1841. LYTTON, *Night and Morning*, Bk. II., ch. vii. Very genteel young man—prepossessing appearance—(that's a FUDGE!)—highly educated; usher in a school—eh?

1850. THACKERAY, *Rebecca and Rowena*, ch. i. Her ladyship's proposition was what is called bosh . . . or FUDGE in plain Saxon.

1861. *Cornhill Magazine*, iv., 102. 'A Cumberland Mare's Nest.' . . . Up jumped the worthy magistrate, And seizing 'Burn,' Of justices the oracle and badge, he straight Descended to! his 'lion's den' (a *sobriquet* in FUDGE meant) Where he, 'a second Daniel,' had often 'come to judgment.'

1864. *Tangled Talk*, p. 108. It is FUDGE to tell a child to 'love' every living creature—a tapeworm, for instance, such as is bottled up in chemists windows.

1865. *Morning Star*, 1 June. Old as I am and half *woor* out, I would *lay* (too bad, Mr. Henley, this) upon my back and hallo FUDGE!

1882. *Daily Telegraph*, 5 Oct., p. 2, col. 2. Much that we hear concerning the ways and means of the working classes is sheer FUDGE.

Verb. (colloquial). — 1. To fabricate; to interpolate; to contrive without proper materials.

1776. FOOTE, *The Bankrupt*, iii., 2. That last 'suppose' is FUDGED in.

1836. MARRYAT, *Midshipman Easy*, ch. xviii. By the time that he did know something about navigation, he discovered that his antagonist knew nothing. Before they arrived at Malta, Jack could FUDGE a day's work.

1858. SHIRLEY BROOKS, *Gordian Knot.* Robert Spencer was hiding from his creditors, or FUDGING medical certificates.

1859. G. A. SALA, in *John Bull*, 21 May. I had provided myself with a good library of books of Russian travel, and so FUDGED my *Journey Due North.*

2. (schoolboys') — To copy; to crib; to dodge or escape.

1877. BLANCH, *The Blue Coat Boys* p. 97. FUDGE, *verb.*, *trans.* and *intrans.* To prompt a fellow in class, or prompt oneself in class artificially. Thence to tell; *e.g.*, 'FUDGE me what the time is.'

3. (common).—To botch; to bungle; to MUFF (*q.v.*)

4. (schoolboys').—To advance the hand unfairly at marbles.

FUG, *verb* (Shrewsbury School).—To stay in a stuffy room.

FUGEL, *verb.* (venery).—To possess; TO HAVE (*q.v.*).

1719. DURFEY, *Pills*, etc., i., 126. Who FUGELLED the Parson's fine Maid.

FUGGY, *subs.* (schoolboys').—A hot roll.

Adj. (Shrewsbury School).—Stuffy.

FUGO, *subs.* (obsolete). — The rectum, or (COTGRAVE) 'bunghole.'

1720. DURFEY, *Pills*, etc., vi., 247. This maid, she like a beast turned her FUGO to the East.

FULHAMS or **FULLAMS**, *subs.* (old). —Loaded dice; called 'high' or 'low' FULHAMS as they were intended to turn up high or low. *Cf.*, GOURDS. [Conjecturally, because manufactured at Fulham, or because that village was a notorious resort of blacklegs.] For synonyms, *see* UPHILLS.

1594. NASHE, *Unf. Traveller*, in wks. v., 27. The dice of late are growen as melancholy as a dog, high men and low men both prosper alike, langrets, FULLAMS, and all the whole fellowshippe of them will not affoord a man his dinner.

1596. SHAKSPEARE. *Merry Wives of Windsor*, i., 3. Let vultures gripe thy guts! for gourd, and FULLAM holds, And *high* and *low* beguile the rich and poor.

1599. JONSON, *Every Man out of His Hum.*, iii., 1. *Car.:* Who! he serve? 'sblood, he keeps high men, and low men, he! he has—fair living at Fullam. [Whalley's note in Gifford's *Jonson*, 'The dice were loaded to run high or low; hence they were called *high men* or *low men*, and sometimes high and low FULLAMS. Called FULLAMS either because F. was the resort of sharpers, or because they were chiefly made there.]

1664. BUTLER, *Hudibras*, Part II., C. i., l. 642. But I do wonder you should chuse This way t' attack me with your muse, As one cut out to pass your tricks on, With FULHAMS of poetic fiction.

[Note in Dr. Nash's Ed., vol. I., p. 272 (Ed. 1835). 'That is, with cheats or impositions. FULHAM was a cant word for a false die, many of them being made at that place.']

1822. SCOTT, *Fortunes of Nigel*, ch. xxiii. Men talk of high and low dice, FULHAMS and bristles . . . and a hundred ways of rooking besides.

2. (colloquial). — A sham; a MAKE-BELIEVE (*q.v.*). [From sense 1.]

1664. BUTLER, *Hudibras*, ii., 1, FULHAMS of poetic fiction.

FULHAM VIRGIN, *subs. phr.* (colloquial).—A fast woman. *Cf.*, BANKSIDE LADY; COVENT GARDEN NUN; ST. JOHN'S WOOD VESTAL, etc.

FULK, *verb* (old schoolboys').—To use an unfair motion of the hand in plumping at taw.—GROSE.

FULKE, *verb* (venery).—To copulate. [A euphemism suggested by Byron in *Don Juan*, the first and last words of which, so adepts tell you, are 'I' and 'FULKE.']

FULKER, *subs.* (old).—A pawnbroker. For synonyms, *see* UNCLE.

1566. GASCOIGNE, *Supposes*, ii., 3. The FULKER will not lend you a farthing upon it.

FULL, *adj.* (colloquial).—1. Drunk. For synonyms, *see* DRINKS and SCREWED.

1888. *Detroit Free Press*, 15 Dec. When he was FULL the police came and jugged.

2. (turf). Used by bookmakers to signify that they have laid all the money they wish against a particular horse.

FULL-GUTS, *subs. phr.* (common).—A swag-bellied man or woman.

A FULL HAND, *subs. phr.* (American waiters'). Five large beers. For analogous expressions, *see* GO.

FULL IN THE BELLY, *subs. phr.* (colloquial).—With child.

FULL IN THE PASTERNS (or THE HOCKS), *subs. phr.* (colloquial). Thick-ankled.

FULL TEAM, *subs. phr.* (American). An eulogium. A man is a FULL TEAM when of consequence in the community. Variants are WHOLE TEAM, or WHOLE TEAM AND A HORSE TO SPARE. *Cf.*, ONE-HORSE = mean, insignificant, or strikingly small.

FULL IN THE WAISTCOAT, *adj. phr.* (colloquial).—Swag-bellied.

FULL OF 'EM, *adj. phr.* (common).—Lousy; nitty; full of fleas.

FULL TO THE BUNG, *adj. phr.* (colloquial).—Very drunk. For synonyms, *see* DRINKS and SCREWED.

TO HAVE (or WEAR) A FULL SUIT OF MOURNING, *verb. phr.* (pugilists').—To have two black eyes. HALF-MOURNING = one black eye. For synonyms, *see* MOUSE.

TO COME FULL BOB, *verb. phr.* (old colloquial).—To come suddenly; to come full tilt.

1672. MARVELL, *Rehearsal Transposed* (in Grosart, iii., 414). The page and you meet FULL BOB.

FULL AGAINST, *adv. phr.* I. Dead, or decidedly opposed to, a person, thing, or place.

FULL-BOTTOMED (or -BREECHED, or -POOPED), *adv. phr.* (colloquial).—Broad in the behind; BARGE-ARSED (*q.v.*)

FULL-FLAVOURED, *adv. phr.* (colloquial). — Peculiarly rank: as a story, an exhibition of profane swearing, an emission of wind, etc.

FULL-FLEDGED, *adv. phr.* (venery).—Ripe for defloration.

FULL-GUTTED, *adv. phr.* (colloquial).—Stout; swag-bellied.

FULL OF EMPTINESS, *adv. phr.* (common).—Utterly void.

FULL ON, *adv. phr.* (colloquial). —Set strongly in a given direction, especially in an obscene sense: *e.g.*, FULL ON FOR IT or FULL ON FOR ONE = ready and willing *au possible.*

AT FULL CHISEL, *adv. phr.* (American).—At full speed; with the greatest violence or impetuousity. Also FULL DRIVE; FULL SPLIT. *Cf.*, HICKETY SPLIT; RIPPING; STAVING ALONG; TWO-THIRTY, etc.

IN FULL BLAST, SWING, etc., *adv. phr.* (colloquial).—In the height of success; in hot pursuit.

1859. SALA, *Twice Round the Clock*, 5 a.m., Part I. At five a.m. the publication of the *Times* newspaper is, to use a north-country mining expression, in 'FULL BLAST.'

1884. *Daily News*, Feb. 9, p. 5, col. 2. If he visit New York in that most pleasant season, the autumn, he will find that the 'fall' trade is 'in FULL BLAST.'

1888. *Daily Telegraph*, 17 Nov. By half-past ten o'clock the smoking-room was IN FULL SWING.

IN FULL DIG, *adv. phr.* (common).—On full pay.

IN FULL FEATHER, *see* FEATHER.

IN FULL FIG.—I. *See* FIG (to which may be added the following illustrative quotations).

1836. M. SCOTT, *Cruise of the Midge*, p. 178. In front of this shed—FULL FIG, in regular Highland costume, philabeg, short hose, green coatee, bonnet and feather, marched the bagpiper.

1836. M. SCOTT, *Cringle's Log*, ch. xi. Captain Transom, the other lieutenant, and myself in full puff, leading the van, followed by about fourteen seamen.

1838. HALIBURTON, *Clockmaker*, (2nd ed.), ch. viii. 'Lookin' as pleased as a peacock when it's IN FULL FIG with its head and tail up.'

1841. *Punch*, i., p. 26, col. 1. Dressed IN FULL FIG—sword very troublesome—getting continually between my legs.

1874. MRS. H. WOOD, *Johnny Ludlow* (1st ed.), No. IV., p. 62. When our church bells were going for service, Major Parrifer's carriage turned out with the ladies all IN FULL FIG.

2. *adv. phr.* (venery).—Said of an erection of the *penis*; PRICK-PROUD (*q.v.*). For synonyms, *see* HORN.

LIKE A STRAW-YARD BULL: FULL OF FUCK AND HALF STARVED, *phr.* (venery). A friendly retort to the question, 'How goes it?' *i.e.*, How are you?

FULL OF IT, *phr.* (common).—With child.

FULL OF GUTS, *phr.* (colloquial).—Full of vigour; excellently inspired and done: as a picture, a novel, and so forth. *See* GUTS.

FULL OF BEANS, *see* BEANS.

FULL OF BREAD, *see* BREAD.

FULLER'S EARTH, *subs. phr.* (old).—Gin. For synonyms, *see* SATIN.

1821. *Real Life in London*, i., 394. The swell covies and out-and-outers find nothing so refreshing, after a night's spree, when the victualling office is out of order, as a little FULLER'S EARTH, or dose of Daffy's.

1823. MONCRIEFF, *Tom and Jerry*, iii., 3. Bring me de kwarten of de FULLER'S EARTH.

FULLIED. TO BE FULLIED, *verb. phr.* (thieves').—To be committed for trial. [From the newspaper expression, 'Fully committed.'] Fr., *être mis sur la planche au pain.*

1851-61. H. MAYHEW, *London Lab. and Lon. Poor*, Vol. iii., p. 397. He got acquitted for that there note after he had me 'pinched' (arrested). I got FULLIED (fully committed).

1879. HORSLEY, 'Autobiography of a Thief,' in *Macmillan's Magazine*, xl., 506. I . . . was then FULLIED and got this stretch and a half.

1889. *Answers*, 13 April, p. 313. At the House of Detention I often noticed such announcements as 'Jack from Bradford FULLIED for smashing, and expects seven stretch,' *i.e.*, fully committed for trial for passing bad money, and expects seven years' penal servitude.

FULNESS. THERE'S NOT FULNESS ENOUGH IN THE SLEEVE TOP. *phr.* (tailors').—A derisive answer to a threat.

FUMBLER, *subs.* (old).—An impotent man.

1690. B. E., *New Dict. of the Canting Crew.* FUMBLER, c., an unperforming husband; one that is insufficient; a weak Brother.

1719. DURFEY, *Pills*, etc., vi., 312. The old FUMBLER (title).

1785. GROSE, *Vulg. Tongue*, s.v.

c 1790. BURNS, 'David and Bathsheba,' p. 40. 'By Jove,' says she, 'what's this I see, my Lord the King's a FUMBLER.'

FUMBLER'S HALL, *subs. phr.* (venery).—The female *pudendum. See*, however, quot. 1690. For synonyms, *see* MONOSYLLABLE.

1690. B. E., *New Dict. of the Canting Crew.* FUMBLER'S HALL, the place where such (FUMBLERS, *q.v.*) are to be put for their non-performance.

FREE OF FUMBLER'S HALL, *phr.*—Said of an impotent man.

FUMBLES, *subs.* (thieves').—Gloves

1825. KENT, *Modern Flash Dict* s.v.

1859. MATSELL, *Vocabulum, or Rogue's Lexicon* s.v.

1881. *New York Slang Dict.*, s.v.

FUN, *subs.* (old).—I. A cheat; a trick.

1690. B.E., *New Dict. of the Canting Crew* s.v.

2. (old).—The posteriors, or WESTERN END (MARVELL). Probably an abbreviation of fundament. For synonyms, *see* BLIND CHEEKS and MONOCULAR EYE-GLASS.

1690. B. E., *New Dict. of the Canting Crew.* I'll kick your FUN, c., I'll kick your arse.

1785. GROSE, *Vulg. Tongue*, s.v.

Verb. (old).—I. To cheat; to trick. Also TO PUT THE FUN ON.

1690. B. E., *New Dict. of the Canting Crew.* What do you FUN me? Do you think to Sharp or Trick me? *Ibid.* He put the FUN upon the cull, c., he sharp'd the Fellow. *Ibid.* I FUNN'D him, c., I was too hard for him; I outwitted or rook'd him.

1785. GROSE, *Vulg. Tongue*, s.v.

1859 MATSELL, *Vocabulum, or Rogue's Lexicon*, s.v.

TO POKE FUN AT, *verb. phr.* (colloquial).—To joke; to ridicule; to make a butt.

1837. BARHAM, *Ingoldsby Legends*, i., p. 280. O fie! Mister Noakes,—for shame, Mr. Noakes! To be POKING YOUR FUN at us plain-dealing folks.

1855. HALIBURTON ('Sam Slick') *Human Nature*, p. 124. I though' you was POKIN' FUN at me; for I am a poor ignorant farmer, and these people are always making game of me.

1865. NEAL, *Charcoal Sketches* (in Bartlett). Jeames, if you don't be quit POKING FUN at me, I'll break your mouth, as sure as you sit there.

TO HAVE BEEN MAKING FUN, *verb. phr.* (common).—Intoxicated. For synonyms, *see* DRINKS and SCREWED.

TO HAVE (or DO) A BIT OF FUN, *verb. phr.* (venery).—To procure or enjoy the sexual favour. For synonyms, *see* GREENS..

FUNCTIOR or FUNCTURE, *subs.* (Winchester College).—An iron bracket candlestick, used for the nightlight in college chambers. [The word, says *Winchester Notions*, looks like *fulctura*, an earlier form of *fulture*, meaning a prop or stay with phonetic change of *l* into *n.*]

1870. MANSFIELD, *School Life at Winchester*, p. 68. Beside the window yawned the great fireplace, with its dogs, on which rested the faggots and bars for the reception of the array of boilers. Above it was a rushlight, fixed in a circular iron pan fastened to a staple in the wall; it was called the FUNCTIOR.

FUNDAMENTAL FEATURES, *subs. phr.* (common).—The posteriors. For synonyms, *see* BLIND CHEEKS and MONOCULAR EYE-GLASS.

1818. MOORE, *Fudge Family*, ix., Aug. 21. O can we wonder, best of speechers, When Louis *seated* thus we see, That France's 'FUNDAMENTAL FEATURES' Are much the same they used to be?

FUNDS, *subs.* (colloquial).—Finances; *e.g.* 'my FUNDS are very low.'

FUNERAL. IT'S NOT MY (or YOUR) FUNERAL, *verb. phr.* (American). —*i.e.*, It is no business of mine, or yours. Fr., *nib dans mes blots* (= that is not my affair). Also used affirmatively.

1867. MRS. WHITNEY, *A Summer in Leslie Goldthwaite's Life*, p. 183. 'It's NONE OF MY FUNERAL, I know, Sin Saxon,' said Miss Craydocke. 'I'm only an eleventh-hour helper; but I'll come in for the holiday business . . . that's more in my line.'

1871. DE VERE, *Americanisms*, p. This is NONE OF YOUR FUNERAL is heard quite frequently as an indirect rebuke for intermeddling, with the ludicrous undercurrent of thought, that the troublesome meddler has no right to be crying at a strange man's funeral.

1877. *Hartford Times*, 17 Oct. Senators Blaine and Barnum passed down to New York, *en route* to Washington, on Wednesday last, when Barnum asked Blaine how he liked the news from Ohio. 'Oh, that ISN'T MY FUNERAL, I want you to understand,' replied the plucky Maine Senator.

1888. *Missouri Republican*, 8 Apr. After a lot of slides had been exhibited the audience howled for Miss Debar. It got so noisy that Mr. Marsh reluctantly exclaimed—'Well, is this YOUR FUNERAL or mine?'

FUNGUS, *subs.* (old).—An old man.

FUNK, *subs.* (old).—I. Tobacco smoke; also a powerful stink. *Cf.*, Ger., *funke*; Walloon *funki.*

1690. B. E., *New Dict. of the Canting Crew.* What a FUNK here is! What a thick smoke. Smoak of Tobacco is here! *Ibid.* Here's a damn'd FUNK, here's a great stink.

2. (vulgar).—A state of fear; trepidation, nervousness, or cowardice; a STEW (*q.v.*). Generally, with an intensitive, *e.g.*, a 'mortal,' 'awful,' 'bloody,' 'blue,' or 'pissing' FUNK. Fr., *la guenette; le flubart* (thieves'); *la frousse* (also = diarrhœa). It., *filo* = thread.

1796. WOLCOTT, *Pindarina*, p. 59. If they find no brandy to get drunk, Their souls are in a miserable FUNK.

1819. MOORE, *Tom Crib's Memorial*, p. 21. Up he rose in a FUNK.

1821. P. EGAN, *Tom and Jerry* (1890), p. 91. I was in a complete FUNK.

1837. BARHAM, I. L., *Look at the Clock*, ed. 1862, p. 39. Pryce, usually brimful of valour when drunk, Now experienced what schoolboys denominate FUNK.

1848. RUXTON, *Life in the Far West*, p. 9. The mules, which was a-snorting with FUNK and running before the Injuns . . . followed her right into the corral, and thar they was safe.

1850. *Literary World* (New York), 30 Nov. So my friend's fault is timidity . . . I grant, then, that the FUNK is sublime, which is a true and friendly admission.

1856. THOMAS HUGHES, *Tom Brown's School-days*, p. 196. If I was going to be flogged next minute, I should be in a blue FUNK.

1859. WHITTY, *Political Portraits*, p. 30. Lord Clarendon did not get through the business without these failures, which result from the intellectual process termed freely FUNK.

1861. *Macmillan's Magazine*, p. 211. I was in a real blue FUNK.

1861. HUGHES, *Tom Brown at Oxford*, ch. xxxvi. I was in a real blue FUNK and no mistake.

1870. *London Figaro*, 19 Oct. After the Fire. He was in a mortal FUNK, no doubt.

1871. MAXWELL, in *Life* (1882), xvi., 382. Certainly χλωρὸν δέος is the Homeric for a blue FUNK.

1888. *Cassell's Saturday Journal*, 29 Dec., p. 305. You're always in a FUNK about nothing at all.

3. (schoolboys').—A coward.

1882. F. ANSTEY, *Vice Versâ*, ch. v. Bosher said, 'Let's cut it,' and he and Peebles bolted. (They were neither of them FUNKS, of course, but they lost their heads.)

Verb. (common).—I. To smoke out. *See* FUNK THE COBBLER.

1720. DURFEY, *Wit and Mirth*, vi., 303. With a sober dose Of coffee FUNKS his nose.

1578. GROSE, *Vulg. Tongue*. FUNK, to smoke, figuratively to smoke or stink through fear.

1823. MONCRIEFF, *Tom and Jerry*, ii., 2. *Tom.* But, I say, only see how confoundedly the dustman's getting hold of Logic—we'll FUNK him. (*Tom and Jerry smoke Logic*), *Log.* Oh, hang your cigars, I don't like it; let's have no FUNKING.

1841. *Punch*, I,, p. 172. Look here . . . isn't it considerable clear they're a all FUNKING like burnt cayenne in a clay pipe, or couldn't they have made a raise somehow to get a ship of their own, or borrow one to send after that caged-up coon of a Macleod.

2. (common).—To terrify; to shrink or quail through nervousness or cowardice.

1858. A. MAYHEW, *Paved with Gold*, Bk. III., ch. vi., p. 294. Perhaps we're only FUNKING ourselves useless, and it mayn't be the farm chaps at all.

3. (colloquial).—To fear; to hesitate; to shirk; and (among pugilists) TO COME IT (*q.v.*).

1836. SMITH, *The Individual*, 'The Thieves' Chaunt.' But dearer to me Sue's kisses far Than grunting peck or other grub are, And I never FUNK the lambskin men When I sits with her in the boozing ken.

1846. *Punch*, X., p. 163. But as yet no nose is bleeding, As yet no man is down; For the gownsmen FUNK the townsmen, And the townsmen FUNK the gown.

1848. J. R. LOWELL, *Biglow Papers*. To FUNK right out o' p'lit'cal strife ain't thought to be the thing

1873. M. COLLINS, *Squire Silchester's Whim*, ch. xvii. Come along! don't FUNK it, old fellow.

ENGLISH SYNONYMS.—To come it; to lose one's guts; to shit one's breeches; to get the needle (athletic).

FRENCH SYNONYMS. — *Paniquer* (thieves': *Panique*=sudden fright); *blaguer* (familiar: = to swagger: *Il avait l'air de blaguer mais il n'était pas à la noce*=he put on a lot of side, but he didn't like it); *avec la cœur en gargousse* (sailors' = with sinking heart); *avoir une fluxion* (popular: *fluxion* = inflammation); *avoir la flemme* (popular: also = to be idle); *avoir le trac* or *trak* (general); *foirer* (popular: *foire* =excrement); *léziner* (popular: also = to cheat).

SPANISH SYNONYM. — *Pajarear*.

ITALIAN SYNONYM. — *Filare* (= to run: Fr., *filer*).

4. (colloquial).—To be nervous; to lose heart.

1827. 'Advice to Tommy,' *Every Night Book* (by the author of 'The Cigar'). Do not go out of your depth, unless you have available assistance at hand, in case you should FUNK.

1856. HUGHES, *Tom Brown's School Days*, ii., p. 5. He's FUNKING; go in Williams!

1857. MONCRIEFF, *The Bashful Man*, ii., 4. Ah! Gyp, hope I sha'n't get *plucked*; FUNK confoundedly: no matter, I must put a bold face on it.

1857. HOOD, *Pen and Pencil Pictures*, p. 144. I have seen him out with the governor's hounds: he FUNKED at the first hedge, and I never saw him again!

1863. READE, *Hard Cash*, ii., p. 135. I told him I hadn't a notion of what he meant! 'O yes I did,' he said, 'Captain Dodd's fourteen thousand pounds! It had passed through my hands.' Then I began TO FUNK again at his knowing that. . . . I was flustered, ye see.

1865. H. KINGSLEY, *The Hillyars and the Burtons*, ch. xxxiii. The sound of the table falling was the signal for a

---

rush of four men from the inner room, who had to use a vulgar expression, FUNKED following the valiant scoundrel Sykes, but who now tried to make their escape, and found themselves hand to hand with the policemen.

1871. *Morning Advertiser*, 11 Sept. 'Holy Abr'ham!' mused he vauntingly, 'shall British sailors FUNK, While tracts refresh their spirits, tea washes down their junk?'

1890. *Pall Mall Gazette*, 17 Oct. p. 2, col. 1. They wanted badly to get one steamer loaded and sent to New Zealand. The non-union men FUNKED loading her on account of the union men.

1891. *Licensed Vict. Gazette*, 13 Feb. Smith's friends thought he was FUNKING, and shouted to Tom to go in and punch him.

5. (schoolboys').—To move the hand forward unfairly in playing marbles; to FUDGE (*q.v.*).

1811. *Lexicon Balatronicum*. FUNK, to use an unfair motion of the hand in plumping at taw.

1851-61. MAYHEW, *Lond. Lab. and Lond. Poor*, i., p. 144. I've noticed them, too, playing at ring-taw, and one of their exclamations is 'Knuckle down fair, and no FUNKING.'

TO FUNK THE COBBLER, *verb. phr.* (schoolboys').—To smoke out a schoolmate: a trick performed with asafœtida and cotton stuffed into a hollow tube or cow's horn; the cotton being lighted, the smoke is blown through the keyhole.

1698-1700. WARD, *London Spy*, Pt. IX., p. 197. We smoak'd the *Beans* almost as bad as unlucky schoolboys us'd to do the COBLERS, till they sneak'd off one by one, and left behind 'em more agreeable Company.

1785. GROSE, *Dict. of the Vulg. Tongue*, s.v.

See also PETER FUNK.

FUNKER, *subs.* (old).—I. A pipe; a cigar; a fire. [From FUNK = to smoke + ER.]

2. (thieves').—A low thief.

1848. DUNCOMBE, *Sinks of London*, etc., s.v.

1859. MATSELL, *Vocabulum, or Rogue's Lexicon*. FUNKERS, the very lowest order of thieves.

3. (colloquial).—A coward.

4. (prostitutes').—A girl that shirks her trade in bad weather.

FUNKING-ROOM, *subs.* (medical).—The room at the Royal College of Surgeons where the students collect on the last evening of their final during the addition of their marks, and whence each is summoned by an official announcing failure or success.

1841. *Punch*, I., p. 225, col. 2. On the top of a staircase he enters a room, wherein the partners of his misery are collected. It is a long, narrow apartment, commonly known as the FUNKING-ROOM.

FUNKSTER, *subs.* (Winchester College).—A coward; one that FUNKS (*q.v.*).

FUNKY, *adj.* (colloquial).—Nervous; frightened; timid.

1845. NAYLOR, *Reynard the Fox*, 46. I do seem somewhat FUNKY.

1863. C. READE, *Hard Cash*, I., 143. On his retiring with twenty-five, scored in eight minutes, the remaining Barkingtonians were less FUNKY, and made some fair scores.

1876. HINDLEY, *Life and Adventures of a Cheapjack*, p. 237. The second round commences with a little cautious sparring on both sides, the bouncing Elias looking very FUNKY.

1891. HUME NISBET, *Bail Up!* p. 51. 'I'll noy FUNKY,' returned the Chinaman impressively.

FUNNEL, *subs.* (common). — The throat. For synonyms, *see* GUTTER ALLEY.

1712. BLACKMORE, *Creation*, Bk. VI Some the long FUNNEL's curious mouth extend, Through which the ingested meats with ease descend.

FUNNIMENT, *subs.* (colloquial).—I. A joke, either practical or verbal.

2. (venery). — The female *pudendum*. For synonyms, *see* MONOSYLLABLE.

FUNNY, *subs.* (nautical).—A clinker-built, narrow boat for sculls.

1837. BARHAM, I. L., *Sir Rupert the Fearless*. Sprang up through the waves, popped him into his FUNNY, Which some others already had half-filled with money.

1882. *Field*, 28 Jan. The only obtainable craft, besides FUNNIES, pair-oars, and randans, were a couple of six-oars.

TO FEEL FUNNY, *verb. phr.* (common). — To be overtaken with (1) emotion, or (2) drink: *e.g.*, to wax amorous, or GET THE FLAVOUR (*q.v.*); to begin to be the worse for liquor.

FUNNY BIT, *subs. phr.* (venery).— The female *pudendum*.

FUNNY BONE, *subs.* (popular).—The elbow, with the passage of the ulnar nerve connecting the two bones: the extremity of the *humerus*.

1837. BARHAM, I. L. (*Blondie Jacke*). They have pull'd you down flat on your back! And they smack, and they thwack, Till your FUNNY BONES crack, As if you were stretch'd on the rack.

1853. THACKERAY, '*Shabby Genteel Story*,' ch. ix. He had merely received a blow on that part which anatomists call the FUNNY BONE.

1870. *Lowell Courier*. Thanks for your kind condolence; I would write A merry rhyme in answer if I might; But then—confound the fall!—the very stone That broke my *humerus* hurt my FUNNY BONE!

FUNNY-MAN, *subs.* (common).—A circus clown. Also a joker in private life.

1851-61. MAYHEW, *Lond. Lab. and Lond. Poor.*, III., p. 129. What I've earned as clown, or the FUNNY MAN.

FUR, *subs.* (venery).—The pubic hair. For synonyms, *see* FLEECE.

TO MAKE THE FUR FLY.—See FLY.

TO HAVE ONE'S FUR OUT, *verb. phr.* (Winchester College).—To be angry. For synonyms, *see* NAB THE RUST.

FUR AND FEATHERS, *subs. phr.* (sporting).—Generic for game.

FUR-BELOW, *subs.* (venery).—The female pubic hair. For synonyms, *see* FLEECE.

16(?). *Old Catch*. Adam caught Eve by the FUR-BELOW, And that's the oldest catch I know.

FURIOSO, *subs.* (old).—A blusterer; Ital., *furioso*=raving.

1692. HACKET. *Life of Archbishop Williams*, ii., p. 218. A violent man and a FURIOSO was deaf to all this.

ENGLISH SYNONYMS.—Barker; blower; bobadil; bouncer; bulldozer (American); cacafogo; Captain Bounce; Captain Bluff; Captain Grand; Captain Hackam; cutter; fire-eater; hector; huff-cap; humguffin; gasser; gasman; mouth; mouth-almighty; pissfire; pump-thunder; ramper; roarer; ruffler; shitefire; slangwhanger; spitfire; swashbuckler; swasher; teazer; Timothy Tearcat.

FRENCH SYNONYMS.—*Un avale-tout-cru* (popular := an eat-all-he-kills); *un fendart* or *fendart*

(popular := a cutter); *un avaleur de charrettes ferées* (popular); *un mata* (printers' : from *matador*=a bull-fighter); *un bousineur* (popular : *bousin*=uproar, shindy); *un bourreau de crânes* (military) := a scull-destroyer; *un bœufier* (popular : =an ugly customer); *un mauvais gas* (familiar : from *garçon*); *un homme qui a l'air de vouloir tout avaler* (familiar : a man who looks as though he'd swallow the world); *un croquet* (popular).

SPANISH SYNONYMS. — *Perdonavidas*; *fierabras*(*fiera*=a wild beast); *botarate*; *macareno cacafuoco*(= a shitfire).

FURK, FERK, FIRK, *verb.* (Winchester College).—To expel; to send (as on a message); to drive away. Also TO FURK UP and FURK DOWN. [Old English *fercian*, High German *ferken*, Middle English to lead or send away.]

FURMEN, *subs.* (old).—Aldermen. From their fur-trimmed robes.

1690. B. E., *New Dict. of the Canting Crew*, s.v.

1785. GROSE, *Vulg. Tongue*, s.v.

FURMITY-FACED, *adj. phr.* (old).—White - faced (FURMITY is described by GROSE as 'wheat boiled to a jelly'). To simper like a FURMITY kitten (GROSE), *see* SIMPER.

FURNISH, *verb.* (common).—To fill out; to improve in strength and appearance.

FURNITURE PICTURE, *subs. phr.* (artists').—A 'picture' sold not as a piece of art but as a piece of upholstery, such things being turned out by the score, as pianos are, or three-legged stools; the worst and cheapest kind of POT-BOILER (*q.v.*).

FURROW, *subs.* (venery). Also CUPID'S (or the ONE-ENDED) FURROW, etc.—The female *pudendum*. For synonyms, *see* MONOSYLLABLE. TO DRAW A STRAIGHT FURROW. *See* DRAW.

TO FALL IN THE FURROW, *verb. phr.* (venery).—To achieve emission.

TO FAIL (or DIE) IN THE FURROW, *verb. phr.* (venery).—To do a DRY-BOB (*q.v.*).

FURRY TAIL, *subs. phr.* (printers').—A non-unionist; a RAT (*q.v.*). Specifically, a workman accepting employment at less than 'Society' wages. *Cf.*, DUNG, FLINT, etc.

FURTHER. I'LL SEE YOU FURTHER FIRST, *phr.* (colloquial). — A denial. I'LL SOONER DIE FIRST (*q.v.*).

1851-61. MAYHEW, *Lond. Lab. and Lond. Poor*, i. p. 29. I gave a country lad 2d. to mind him (the donkey) in a green lane there. I wanted my own boy to do so, but he said, I'LL SEE YOU FURTHER FIRST. A London boy hates being by himself in a lone country part. He's afraid of being burked.

FUR TRADE, *subs. phr.* (old).—Barristers.

1839. REYNOLDS, *Pickwick Abroad*, ch. xxvi. Let nobs in the FUR TRADE hold their jaw, And let the jug be free.

FURZE-BUSH, *subs. phr.* (venery). The female pubic hair. For synonyms, *see* FLEECE.

FUSSOCK, and **FUSSOCKS**, *subs.* (old).—Opprobrious for a fat woman.

1690. B. E., *New Dict. of the Canting Crew.* FUSSOCKS, a meer FUSSOCKS, a Lazy Fat-Arsed Wench, a fat FUSSOCKS, a Fulsom, Fat, Strapping Woman.

1785. GROSE, *Dict. of the Vulg Tongue*, s.v.

FUST (or **FUST OUT**), *verb.* (American).—To end in smoke; to go to waste; to end in nothing. *Cf.*, FIZZLE.

FUSTIAN, *subs.* and *adj.* (old).—1. Bombast; bad rhetoric; sound without sense: bombastic; ranting. Now accepted.

1598. SHAKSPEARE, *2 Henry IV*, II., 4. Thrust him downstairs; I cannot endure such a FUSTIAN rascal.

1602. SHAKSPEARE, *Twelfth Night* II., 5. A FUSTIAN riddle.

1602. SHAKSPEARE, *Othello*, II., 3. And discourse FUSTIAN with one's own shadow.

1690. B. E., *New Dict. of the Canting Crew.* FUSTIAN-verse, verse in words of lofty sound and humble sense.

1828-45. HOOD, *Poems*, i., p. 105 (ed. 1846). The saints!—the bigots that in public spout, Spread phosphorous of zeal on scraps of FUSTIAN, And go like walking 'Lucifers' about These living bundles of combustion.

2. (common).—Wine; WHITE FUSTIAN = champagne; RED FUSTIAN = port.

1834. W. H. AINSWORTH, *Rookwood*, p. 51 (ed. 1864). I'm as dry as a sandbed. Famous wine this—beautiful tipple—better than all your red FUSTIAN. Ah, how poor Sir Piers used to like it!

FUSTILARIAN, *subs.* (old).—A low fellow; a common scoundrel.

1598. SHAKSPEARE, *2 Henry IV.*, II., I. Away, you scullion! you rampallian! you FUSTILARIAN! I'll tickle your catastrophe.

FUSTILUG (or **FUSTILUGS**), *subs.* (old).—A piece of grossness, male or female; a coarse and dirty Blowzalinda; a foul slut; a fat stinkard.

1690. B. E., *New Dict. of the Canting Crew.* FUSTILUGGS, a Fulsom, Beastly, Nasty Woman.

1739. JUNIUS (quoted in *Encly. Dict.*). You may daily see such FUSTILUGS walking in the streets, like so many tuns.

1785. GROSE, *Dict. of the Vulgar Tongue.*

FUTTER, *verb.* (venery). — To copulate. Fr., *foutre.* [A coinage of Sir. R. Burton's, who makes continual use of it in the *Thousand Nights and a Night.*] For synonyms, *see* GREENS and RIDE. Also TO DO A FUTTER.

1885. BURTON, *Thousand Nights*, II., 332. Eating and drinking and FUTTERING for a year of full twelve months.

1890. BURTON, *Priapeia*, Ep. xii. Thee, my girl, I shalt FUTTER.

FUTURE, TO DEAL IN FUTURES, *verb phr.* (Stock Exchange).—To speculate for a rise or fall.

1869. *Globe*, 1 Dec. He DEALS IN FUTURES, *i.e.*, speculates in cotton with Stock Exchange folks, or speculates in securities.

FUZZ, *verb.* (old).—1. 'To shuffle cards minutely; also to change the pack.' [GROSE.]

2. (old).—To be, or to make, drunk.

1685. *Life of Amb. Wood*, 14 July. Came home well FUZD.

FUZZINESS, *subs.* (old).—The condition of being in drink. Hence blurredness; incoherence; bewilderment.

FUZZY, *adj.* (common).—1. Drunk. For synonyms, *see* DRINKS and SCREWED. Hence blurred (as a picture); tangled; incoherent or inconsequent.

1876. HINDLEY, *Life and Adventures of a Cheap Jack*, p. 324. Her husband or any other man might have drunk six glasses, with no more hurt than just making him a little FUZZY.

2. (popular).—Rough; as in a FUZZY head; a FUZZY cloth; a FUZZY bit (= a full-grown wench); a FUZZY carpet; etc.

FUZZY-WUZZY, *subs.* (military). A Soudanese tribesman.

1890. RUDYARD KIPLING, *National Observer*, 8 Mar., p. 438, col. 1. So 'ere's to you FUZZY-WUZZY And your 'ome in the Soudan, You're a pore benighted 'eathen but a first-class fighting man; And 'ere's to you FUZZY-WUZZY with your 'ay-rick 'ead of 'air, You big, black bouncing beggar, for you bruk a British square.

FYE-BUCK, *subs.* (old).—A sixpence. For synonyms, *see* BENDER.

1781. G. PARKER, *View of Society*, II., 56. You give a shilling to buy a comb, for which he gives sixpence, so *works* you for another FYE-BUCK.

1885. *Household Words*, 20 June, p. 155. 'Buck' is most likely a corruption of FYE-BUCK, a slang name for sixpence, which is now almost, if not altogether, obsolete.

FYLCHE.—*See* FILCH.

FYST.—*See* FOIST.

AB, *subs.* (vulgar).—1. The mouth; also GOB. For synonyms, *see* POTATO-TRAP.

1785. GROSE, *Dict. of the Vulgar Tongue*, s.v.

1785. BURNS, *Jolly Beggars.* And aye he gies the touzie drab The tither skelpin kiss, While she held up her greedy GAB, Just like an aumos dish.

1820. SCOTT, *The Abbot*, ch. xiv. 'And now, my mates,' said the Abbot of Unreason, 'once again digut your GABS and be hushed—let us see if the Cock of Kennaguhair will fight or flee the pit.'

1890. *Rare Bits*, 12 Apr., p. 347. 'Clap a stopper on your GAB and whack up, or I'll let 'er speak !'

2. (vulgar).—Talk; idle babble. Also GABB, GABBER, and GABBLE.

1712. *Spectator*, No. 389. Having no language among them but a confused GABBLE, which is neither well understood by themselves or others.

1811. POOLE, *Hamlet Travestied*, I., 3. Then hold your GAB, and hear what I've to tell.

1863. C. READE, *Hard Cash*, ch. xxxiv. 'Hush your GAB,' said Mr. Green, roughly.

1887. *Punch*, 10 Sept., p. 111. Gladstone's GAB about 'masses and classes' is all tommy rot.

Verb (vulgar: O. E., and now preserved in GABBLE).—To talk fluently; to talk brilliantly; to lie.

1383. CHAUCER, *Canterbury Tales* 1652. I GABBE nought, so have I joye or blis.

1402. [? T. OCCLEVE], *Letter of Cupid*, in Arber's *Garner*, vol. IV., p. 59. A foul vice it is, of tongue to be light, For *whoso mochil clappeth, gabbeth* oft.

1601. SHAKSPEARE, *Twelfth Night*, Act II., Sc. iii. *Mal.* . . . Have you no wit, manners, nor honesty, but to GABBLE like tinkers at this time of night.

1663. BUTLER, *Hudibras*, pt. I., ch. i., p. 5. Which made some think when he did GABBLE Th' had heard three Labourers of Babel.

1786. BURNS, *Earnest Cry and Prayer*, st. 10. But could I like Montgomeries fight, Or GAB like Boswell.

1880. G. R. SIMS, *Zeph*, ch. vii. An elderly clergyman . . . GABBLED the funeral service as though he were calling back an invoice at a draper's entering desk.

1887. *Punch*, 10 Sept., p. 111. Gals do like a chap as can GAB.

GIFT OF THE GAB (or GOB), *subs. phr.* (colloquial).—The gift of conversation; the talent for speech. Fr., *n'avoir pas sa langue dans sa poche.*

d. 1653. Z. BOYD, *Book of Job*, quoted in Brewer's *Phrase and Fable*, s.v., 'GAB. There was a good man named Job, Who lived in the land of Uz, He had a good gift of the GOB.

1690. B. E., *New Dict. of the Canting Crew.* GIFT OF THE GOB, a wide, open Mouth; also a good Songster, or Singing-master.

1785. GROSE, *Dict. of the Vulgar Tongue*, s.v.

1820. SHELLEY, *Œdipus Tyrannus*, Act I. You, Purganax, who have the GIFT O' THE GAB, Make them a solemn speech.

1837. DICKENS, *Oliver Twist*, ch. xliii. And we'll have a big-wig, Charley : one that's got the greatest GIFT OF THE GAB : to carry on his defence.

1851-61. MAYHEW, *Lond. Lab. and Lond. Poor*, I., 250. People reckon me one of the best patterers in the trade. I'm reckoned to have the gift — that is, THE GIFT OF THE GAB.

1869. WHYTE-MELVILLE, *M. or N.*, p. 29. I've GOT THE GIFT OF THE GAB, I know, and I stick at nothing.

1870. *Lond. Figaro*, 18 Sept. 'Of all gifts possessed by man,' said George Stephenson, the engineer, to Sir William Follett, 'there is none like the GIFT OF THE GAB.'

1876. HINDLEY, *Life and Adventures of a Cheap Jack*, p. 193. Others, although they have the GIFT OF THE GAB when they are on the ground, as soon as they mount the cart are dumbfounded.

TO BLOW THE GAB, *verb. phr.* (vulgar).—To inform ; TO PEACH (*q.v.*). Also TO BLOW THE GAFF (*q.v*).

1785. GROSE, *Vulg. Tongue*, s.v.

1834. AINSWORTH, *Rookwood*, bk. III., ch. 5. Never BLOW THE GAB or squeak.

TO FLASH THE GAB, *verb. phr.* (common).—To SHOW OFF (*q.v.*) in talk ; *cf.*, AIR ONE'S VOCABULARY.

1819. MOORE, *Tom Crib's Memorial*, p. 2. While his Lordship . . . that very great dab At the flowers of rhet'ric is FLASHING HIS GAB.

GABBLE, *subs.* (colloquial).—1. A gossip. Also GABBLER, GABBLE-GRINDER, GABBLE-MERCHANT, and GABBLE-MONGER.

2. (colloquial). — A voluble talker.

GABBLE-MILL, *subs.* (American).—1. The United States Congress. Also GABBLE-MANUFACTORY.

2. (common).—A pulpit. For synonyms, *see* HUMBOX.

3. (common).—The mouth. For synonyms, *see* POTATO-TRAP.

GABLE, *subs.* (common).—The head. Also GABLE-END. For synonyms, *see* CRUMPET.

GABSTER, *subs.* (common). — A voluble talker, whether eloquent or vain ; one having the GIFT OF THE GAB (*q.v.*).

GAB-STRING.—*See* GOB-STRING.

GABY (also GABBEY and GABBY), *subs.* (common).—A fool ; a babbler ; a boor. Icl. *gapi* = a foolish person, from *gapa* = to gape.

1811. *Lexicon Balatronicum*, s.v.

1856. T. HUGHES, *Tom Brown's School Days*, pt. 1, ch. iii. Two boys, who stopped close by him, and one of whom, a fat GABY of a fellow, pointed at him and called him young 'mammy-sick.'

1859. H. KINGSLEY, *Geoffrey Hamlyn*, ch. ix. Don't stand laughing there like a great GABY.

1875. OUIDA, *Signa*, vol. I., ch. iv., p. 47. 'You have never dried your clothes, Bruno,' said his sister-in-law, 'What a GABY a man is without a wife !'

GAD, *subs.* (common).—An idle slattern. An abbreviation of GAD-ABOUT (*q.v.*).

Intj. (common).—An abbreviation of BY GAD ! *Cf.* AGAD, EGAD—themselves corruptions of BY GOD, *Lit.*

ON THE GAD, *adv. phr.* (old).—1. On the spur of the moment.

1605. SHAKSPEARE, *Lear*, i., 2. All this is done UPON THE GAD.

2. (colloquial).—On the move, on the gossip.

1818. AUSTEN, *Persuasion.* I have no very good opinion of Mrs. Charles' nursery maid. . . . She is always UPON THE GAD.

3. (colloquial).—On the spree (especially of women); and, by implication, on the town.

TO GAD THE HOOF, *verb. phr.* (common).—To walk or go without shoes; TO PAD THE HOOF (*q.v.*). Also, more loosely, to walk or roam about.

1852. SNOWDEN, *Mag. Assistant*, 3rd ed., p. 447. Going without shoes, GADDING THE HOOF.

GADABOUT, *subs.* (colloquial).—A trapesing gossip; as a housewife seldom seen at home, but very often at her neighbours' doors [From GAD=to wander, to stray (*Cf.*, *Lycidas:* 'the gadding vine') + ABOUT.] Used also as an adjective; *e.g.*, 'a GAD-ABOUT hussey.'

GADSO, *subs.* (old) — The *penis.* Italian *cazzo.* For synonyms, *see* CREAMSTICK and PRICK.

Intj. (old: still literary and colloquial).—An interjection. [A relic of phallicism with which many popular oaths and exclamations have a direct connection, especially in Neo-Latin dialects. A Spaniard cries out, CARAJO! (=the member), or COJONES! (=the testicles); an Italian says CAZZO (the *penis*); while a Frenchman exclaims by the act itself, FOUTRE! The female equivalent, (COÑO with the Spaniard, CONNO with the Italian, CON with the Frenchman, and CUNT with ourselves), was, and is, more generally used as an expression of contempt, which is also the case with the testicles. (*Cf.*, *ante*, ALL BALLS!) Germanic oaths are profane rather than obscene; except, perhaps, in POTZ! and POTZTAUSEND! and the English equivalent POX! which last is obsolete. *See* CATSO. [In Florio (*A Worlde of Wordes*, 1598), *Cazzo*='a man's privie member,' and *cazzo di mare*=a pintle fish; while *cazzica* = 'an interjection of admiration and affirming. What? Gad's me, Gad forfend, tush.']

1697. VANBRUGH, *Provoked Wife*, iii., 1. *Sir?* GADSO! we are to consult about playing the devil to night.

1770. FOOTE, *Lame Lover*, i. Gadso! a little unlucky.

1838. DICKENS, *Oliver Twist*, ch. iv. 'GADSO!' said the undertaker . . . 'that's just the very thing I wanted to speak to you about.'

GADZOOKS! *intj.* (old and colloquial).—A corruption of GADZO (*q.v.*).

GAFF, *subs.* (old).—1. A fair.

1754. *Discoveries of John Poulter*, p. 32. The first thing they do at a GAFF is to look for a room clear of company.

1811. *Lexicon Balatronicum*, s.v. The drop coves maced the joskins at the GAFF; the ring-droppers cheated the countryman at the fair.

1821. HAGGART, *Life*, p. 22. We stopped at this place two days, waiting to attend the GAFF.

1823. JON. BEE, *Dict. of the Turf*, etc., s.v. A fair is a GAFF as well as all the transactions enacted there.

2. (common).—A cheap, low music-hall or theatre; frequently PENNY-GAFF, *Cf.*, quot. 1823, sense 1. Also DOOKIE. Fr., *un beuglant* (=a low music-hall; *beugler*=to bellow); *un bouisbouis* (*boui* = brothel); *une guinche* (popular). *See* also quot. 1889.

1851-61. MAYHEW, *Lond. Lab. and Lond. Poor*, I., p. 46. They court for a time, going to raffles and GAFFS together, and then the affair is arranged.

1869. GREENWOOD, *Seven Curses of London*, p. 68. A GAFF is a place where stage plays, according to the strict interpre-

tation of the term, may not be represented. The actors of a drama may not correspond in colloquy, only in pantomime; but the pieces brought out at the GAFF are seldom of an intricate character, and the not over-fastidious auditory are well content with an exhibition of dumb-show and gesture.

1870. *Orchestra*, 18 Feb. The absolute harm done by these GAFFS does not consist in the subjects represented.

1889. *Notes and Queries*, 7 S. vii., p. 395. I have often heard the British soldier make use of the word when speaking of the entertainment got up for his benefit in barracks.

3. (prison).—A hoax; an imposture. *Cf.*, Fr., *gaffe*=joke, deceit.

1877. *Five Years' Penal Servitude*, ch. iv., p. 312. I also saw that Jemmy's blowing up of me wos all GAFF. He knew as well as I did the things left the shop all right.

1892. HUME NISBET, *Bushranger's Sweetheart*, p. 227. Can you put me up to this other GAFF.

4. (old sharpers'). — A ring worn by the dealer. [From *gaffe* =a hook.]

5. (American cock-pit). — A steel spur.

6. (anglers') — A landing spear, barbed in the iron.

Verb. (old). — 1. To toss for liquor. *See* GAFFING.

1823. JON BEE, *Dict. of the Turf*, s.v.

2. (theatrical).—To play in a GAFF (*q.v.* sense 2).

TO BLOW THE GAFF, or GAB (*q.v.*), *verb. phr.* (common). To give information; to let out a secret. For synonyms, *see* PEACH.

1785. GROSE, *Vulg. Tongue.* To BLOW THE GAB (cant), to confess, or impeach a confederate.

1833. MARRYAT, *Peter Simple*, ch. xliii. One of the French officers, after he was taken prisoner, axed me how we had managed to get the gun up there; but I wasn't going to BLOW THE GAFF.

1877. *Five Years' Penal Servitude*, ch. ii., p. 122. The prisoner, burning for revenge, quietly bides his time till the chief warder comes round, then asks to speak to him, and BLOWS THE GAFF.

1891. *Referee*, 8 Mar. Under sacred promise not to BLOW THE GAFF I was put up to the method.

GAFFER, *subs.* (old). — 1. An old man; the masculine of GAMMER (*q.v.*). Also a title of address: *e.g.*, 'Good day, GAFFER!' *Cf.*, UNCLE and DADDY. Also (*see* quot. 1710), a husband.

1710. *Dame Hurdle's Letter* (quoted by NARES). My GAFFER only said he would inform himself as well as he could against next election, and keep a good conscience.

1714. GAY, *Shepherd's Week.* For GAFFER Treadwell told us, by-the-bye, Excessive sorrow is exceeding dry.

1842. TENNYSON, *The Goose.* Ran GAFFER, stumbled Gammer.

2. (common).—A master; an employer; a BOSS (*q.v.*); (athletic) a pedestrian trainer and 'farmer'; and (navvies') a gang-master or GANGER (*q.v.*).

1719. DURFEY, *Pills*, etc., iv., 123. In comes our GAFFER Underwood, And sits him on the bench.

1748. T. DYCHE, *Dict.* (5th ed.) GAFFER (S.) a familiar word mostly used in the country for master.

1885. *Daily News*, 24 Jan., p. 3, c. 1. They go and work at fivepence, and some on 'em as low as threepence halfpenny, an hour; that's just half what we get, and the GAFFERS keep 'em on and sack us.

1888. *Sportsman*, 20 Dec. Comic enough were some of the stories 'Jemmy' told of his relations with 'the GAFFER.'

1889. *Broadside Ballad*, 'The Gaffers of the Gang.' We are the boys that can do the excavations, We are the lads for the 'atin' and the dhrinkin', With the ladies we are so fascinatin', Because we are the GAFFERS of the gang.

3. (old).—A toss-penny; a gambler with coins. From GAFFING (*q.v.*).

1828. JON BEE, *Living Picture of London*, p. 241. If the person calling for 'man' or 'woman' is not right or wrong at five guesses, neither of the GAFFERS win or lose, but go again.

Verb. (venery).—To copulate. For synonyms, *see* GREENS and RIDE.

GAFFING, *subs.* (old).—*See* quot.

1821. PIERCE EGAN, *Life in London*, p. 279. GAFFING was unfortunately for him introduced. *Ibid.* NOTE.—A mode of tossing for drinks, etc., in which three coins are placed in a hat, shaken up, and then thrown on the table. If the party to 'call' calls 'heads' (or 'tails') and all three coins are as he calls them, he wins; if not, he pays a settled amount towards drinks.

1839. BRANDON, *Poverty, Mendicity, and Crime*, s.v.

GAG, *subs.* (common).—1. A joke; an invention; a hoax.

1823. JON BEE, *Dict. of the Turf*, s.v. GAG—a grand imposition upon the public; as a mountebank's professions, his cures, and his lottery-bags, are so many *broad* GAGS.

1871. *All the Year Round*, 18 Feb., p. 288. You won't bear malice now, will you? All GAG of mine, you know, about old Miss Ponsonby.

1885. *Daily News*, 16 May, p. 5, c. 2. 'The Mahdi sends you lies from Khartoum, and laughs when you believe them,' said a native, lately. We need not gratify the Mahdi by believing any bazaar-GAG he may circulate.

2. (theatrical). — Expressions interpolated by an actor in his part: especially such as can be repeated again and again in the course of performance. Certain plays, as *The Critic*, are recognised 'gag-pieces,' and in these the practice is accounted legitimate. *Cf.*, *Hamlet*, iii., 2: 'And let those, that play your clowns, say no more than is set down for them.' *Cf.*, WHEEZE. Fr., *la cocotte* (specifically additions to vocal scores). A typical example is the 'I believe you, my boy!' of the late Paul Bedford. In the quot. under 1851-61, it is probable that GAG=PATTER (*q.v.*)

1841. *Punch*, i., p. 105. I shall do the liberal in the way of terms, and get up the GAG properly.

1851-61. MAYHEW, *Lond. Lab. and Lond. Poor*, iii., p. 148. When I go out I always do my own GAG, and I try to knock out something new.

1866. W. D. HOWELLS, *Venetian Life*, ch. v. . . . I have heard some very passable GAGS at the Marionette, but the real *commedia a braccio* no longer exists.

1889. *Globe*, 12 Oct., p. 4, c. 4. In a high-class music hall it is a rule that no song must be sung till it is read and signed by the manager, and this applies even to the GAG.

1890. *Pall Mall Gazette*, 5 Mar., p. 4, c. 3. Mr. Augustus Harris pointed out that if the clause were carried the penalty would, in many cases, be incurred twenty times in one scene, for actors and singers were continually introducing GAG into their business.

3. (American).—A commonwealth of players in which the profits are shared round. *Cf.*, CONSCIENCE.

1847. DARLEY, *Drama in Pokerville*, p. 124. The artist . . . . merely remarking that he had thought of a GAG which would bring them through, mounted a ladder, and disappeared.

4. (American).—A fool; *i.e.*, a thing to laugh at. For synonyms, *see* CABBAGE- and BUFFLE-HEAD and SAMMY SOFT.

1838-40. HALIBURTON, *The Clockmaker*, p. 46. 'Sam,' says he, 'they tell me you broke down the other day in the House of Representatives and made a proper GAG of yourself.'

5. (Christ's Hospital).—Boiled fat beef. GAG-EATER=a term of reproach.

1813. LAMB, *Christ's Hospital*, in wks., p. 324 (ed. 1852). L. has recorded the repugnance of the school to GAGS, or the fat of fresh beef boiled; and sets it down to some superstition. . . . A GAG-EATER in our time was equivalent to a ghoul . . . and held in equal estimation.

6. (Winchester College).—An exercise (said to have been invented by Dr. Gabell) which consists in writing Latin criticisms on some celebrated piece, in a book sent in about once a month. In the Parts below Sixth Book and Senior Part, the GAGS consisted in historical analysis. [An abbreviation of 'gathering.']

1870. MANSFIELD, *School-life at Winchester College*, p. 108. From time to time, also, they had to write . . . an analysis of some historical work; these productions were called GATHERINGS (or GAGS).

Verb, trs. and *intrs.* (theatrical). — 1. To speak GAGS (*q.v.*), sense 2. Fr., *cascader.*

1851-61. MAYHEW, *Lond. Lab. and Lond. Poor*, III., 149. He has to GAG, that is, to make up words.

1852. DICKENS, *Bleak House*, ch. xxxix. The same vocalist GAGS in the regular business like a man inspired.

1883. *Referee*, 15 April, p. 3, c. 1. Toole . . . cannot repress a tendency to GAG and to introduce more than is set down for him by the author.

2. (old).—To hoax; to puff.

1781. G. PARKER, *View of Society*, II., 154. Having discovered the weak side of him he means to GAG.

1823. JON BEE, *Dict. of the Turf*, etc., s.v. A showman cries 'Walk in, ladies and gentlemen, they're all alive,' but the spectators soon perceive *'tis all stuff*, reproach Mr. Merryman, and he, in excuse, swears he said 'they *were*' and not 'are alive.' He thus GAGS the public.

1876. HINDLEY, *Life and Adventures of a Cheap Jack*, p. 325. Then they GAG the thing up, and send their bills out about the immense cost of scenery and dresses, and other expenses they are at, etc.

3. (thieves').—To inform; to ROUND ON (*q.v.*); also TO BLOW THE GAG. *Cf.*, GAFF, GAB, etc. For synonyms, *see* PEACH.

1891. *Morning Advertiser*, 28 Mar. She . . . besought them with (crocodile) tears not to GAG on them, in other words not to give information to the police.

ON THE HIGH GAG., *adv. phr.* (old).—On the whisper; telling secrets; *cf.*, *verb*, sense 3.

1823. KENT, *The Modern Flash Dict.*, s.v.

1848. DUNCOMBE, *Sinks of London*, etc., s.v.

ON THE LOW GAG, *adv. phr.* (old).—On the last rungs of beggary, ill-luck, or despair.

1823. KENT, *The Modern Flash Dict.*, s.v.

1848. DUNCOMBE, *The Sinks of London*, etc., s.v.

TO STRIKE THE GAG, *verb. phr.* (old).—To cease from chaffing.

1839. AINSWORTH, *Jack Sheppard* (ed. 1889), p. 43. 'A clever device,' replied Jonathan; 'but it won't serve your turn. Let us pass, sir. STRIKE THE GAG, Blueskin.'

GAGE (GAUGE or GAG), *subs.* (old). —1. A quart pot (*i.e.*, a measure). Also a drink or GO (*q.v.*).

1567. HARMAN, *Caveat* (1814), p. 65. A GAGE, a quart pot.

1610. ROWLANDS, *Martin Mark-all*, p. 38 (H. Club's Rept., 1874). GAGE, a quart pot.

1622. J. FLETCHER, *Beggar's Bush.* I crown thy nab with a GAGE of benbouse.

1656. BROOME, *Jovial Crew*, Act ii., I bowse no lage, but a whole GAGE Of this I bowse to you.

1690. B. E. *New Dict. of the Cant. Crew*. GAGE, *c.* A pot or pipe. Tip me a GAGE, *c.* give me a pot, or pipe.

1714. *Memoirs of John Hall* (4th ed.), p. 12. GAGE, a pot.

1785. GROSE, *Vulg. Tongue*. GAGE, a quart pot, also a pint (cant).

1821. HAGGART, *Life*, p. 40. We drank our GAUGE and parted good friends.

2. (18th century).—A chamber-pot.

3. (old).—A pipe.

1690. B. E., *New Dict. of the Cant. Crew* (See quot. 1690 under sense 1).

1796. GROSE, *Vulg. Tongue* (3rd Ed.), s.v.

1834. H. AINSWORTH, *Rookwood*, Bk. III., ch. v. In the mean time, tip me a GAGE of fogus, Jerry.

4. (American).—A man. For synonyms, *see* COVE.

1859. MATSELL, *Vocabulum or Rogue's Lexicon*. Deck the GAGE, see the man.

GAGERS, *subs.* (American).—The eyes. For synonyms, *see* GLIMS.

1859. MATSELL, *Vocabulum*, s.v.

GAGGA, *subs.* (old).—See quot.

1796. GROSE, *Vulg. Tongue* (3rd Ed.) Cheats who by sham pretences and wonderful stories of their sufferings impose on the credulity of good people.

GAGGER, *subs.* (theatrical). — A player who deals in GAGS (*q.v.*), sense 2. Also GAGGIST, GAG-MASTER, and GAGSTER.

1841. *Punch*, Vol. I., p. 169. Men with 'swallows' like Thames tunnels, in fact accomplished GAGGERS and unrivalled 'wiry watchers.'

1887. BURNAND and A'BECKETT in *Fortn. Review*, April, p. 548. Robson . . . was an inveterate GAGGER.

1890. *Globe*, 3 March, p. 1, c. 4. The low comedy was much toned down . . . In other words, the GAGGERS were gagged.

GAGGERY, *subs.* (theatrical).—The practice of GAGGING (*q.v.*), sense 3.

GAGGING, *subs.* (old).—1. BLUFF (*q.v.*); specifically, BUNCO-STEER-ING (*q.v.*), the art of talking over and persuading a stranger that he is an old acquaintance. *Cf.*, GAG, *verb*, sense 2.

1828. G. SMEATON, *Doings in London*, p. 28. One of the modes of raising money, well known in town by the flash name of GAGGING, has been practised of late to a considerable extent on simple country-men, who are strangers to the 'ways of town.'

2. (cabmen's).—Loitering about for 'fares'; 'crawling.'

1851-61. H. MAYHEW, *Lond. Lab. and Lond. Poor*, Vol. III., p. 366. The means used are GAGGING, that is to say, driving about and loitering in the thorough-fares for jobs.

3. (theatrical). — Dealing in GAGS (*q.v.*), sense 1. Also as *ppl. adj.*

1883. *The Echo*, 5 Jan., p. 2, c. 3. A protest, by no means unneeded, against the insolence or ignorance of some play-wrights, and GAGGING actors.

1889. *Answers*, 27 July, p. 143, c. 2. GAGGING is a thing about which the public know little.

GAGGLER'S COACH, *subs. phr.* (old). —A hurdle.

1823. KENT, *Modern Flash Dict.*, s.v.

1848. DUNCOMBE, *Sinks of London* s.v.

GAIL, *subs.* (old).—A horse. For synonyms, *see* PRAD.

1781. G. PARKER, *View of Society*, i., 207. A compound of Player, Soldier, Stroller, Sailor, and Tinker! An odd GALLIMAUFRY!

1860. HALIBURTON (Sam Slick), *The Season Ticket*, No. 7. This portion of my journal, which includes a variety of topics and anecdotes, some substantial like solid meat, some savoury as spicy vegetable ingredients, and some fragments to swell the bulk, which, though not valuable as materials, help to compound the GALLIMAUFRY.

2. (old).—A hodge-podge of scraps and leavings.

1724. COLES, *Eng. Dict.*; 1728. BAILEY, *Eng. Dict.*; 1785. GROSE, *Vulg. Tongue*; 1811. *Lexicon Bala-tronicum*.

3. A mistress.

1596. SHAKSPEARE, *Merry Wives*, ii., 1. He loves thy GALLYMAWFRY; Ford, perpend.

4. (venery).—The female *pu-dendum*. For synonyms, *see* MONOSYLLABLE.

GALL, *subs.* (common).—Effrontery; CHEEK (*q.v.*); BRASS (*q.v.*); *e.g.*, 'Ain't he got a GALL on him?'

1789. GROSE, *Vulg. Tongue* (3rd Ed.), s.v. His GALL is not yet broken, a saying used in prisons of a man just brought in who appears melancholy and dejected. [*i.e.*, 'He is not yet embittered enough to care for nothing, and meet every-thing with a front of brass.']

1811. *Lexicon Balatronicum*, s.v.

a 1891. *New York Sun* (quoted in *Slang, Jargon, and Cant*, s.v.). 'What do you think he had the GALL to do to-day?' Brown: 'He has the GALL to do anything.' Dumley: 'He asked me to drink with him; but he'll never repeat the impudence.'

GALLANT, *subs.* (old).—A DANDY (*q.v.*); a ladies' man; a lover; a cuckold-maker, whether *in posse* or *in esse* [Shakspeare].

1596. SHAKSPEARE, *Merry Wives*, ii. One that is well-nigh worn to pieces with age to show himself a young GALLANT!

1598. SHAKSPEARE, 1 *Henry IV.*, ii., 4. GALLANTS, lads, boys, hearts of gold, all the titles of good fellowship come to you.

1663. DRYDEN, *The Wild Gallant* [Title.]

1690. B.E., *A New Dict.* GALLANT a very fine man; also a Man of Metal, or a brave Fellow; also one that Courts, or keeps, or is Kept by, a Mistress.

1719. DURFEY, *Pills*, etc., iv., 110 There's never a GALLANT but sat at her hand.

1751-4. JORTIN, *Eccles. Hist.* (quoted in *Encyclopædic Dict.*). As to Theodora, they who had been her GALLANTS when she was an actress, related that dæmons, or nocturnal spirits, had often driven them away to lie with her themselves.

Adj. (old). — (1). Valiant (2) showy; (3) amorous.

1719. DURFEY, *Pills*, etc., i., 40. O London is a fine town, and a GALLANT city.

Verb. (old).—To sweetheart; to squire; to escort; to pursue or to enjoy.

To GALLANT A FAN. *verb. phr.* (old). — To break with design, to afford an opportunity of presenting a better. — B.E. (1690).

GALLANT FIFTIETH, *subs. phr.* (military).—The Fiftieth Foot. [For its share in Vimiera, 1808.] Also, BLIND HALF HUNDRED (*q.v.*); and DIRTY HALF HUNDRED (*q.v.*).

GALLANTRY, *subs.* (1). SPARKISH-NESS (*q.v.*); dandyism; (2) the habit, or pursuit, of the sexual favour. A LIFE OF GALLANTRY =a life devoted to the other sex.

GAILY-LIKE, *adj.* (American). — Showy; expensive: BANG-UP (*q.v.*).

1872. CLEMENS (Mark Twain), *Undertaker's Chat*. Now, you know how difficult it is to roust out such a GAILY-LIKE thing as that in a little one-horse town like this.

GAIN-PAIN, *subs.* (old).—A sword; specifically, in the Middle Ages, that of a hired soldier. [From Fr., *gagner* = to gain + *pain* = bread. *Cf.*, BREADWINNER (prostitutes') and POTBOILER (artists').] For synonyms, *see* CHEESE-TOASTER and POKER.

GAIT, *subs.* (colloquial).—Walk in life; profession; mode of making a living; GAME (*q.v.*).

1859. MATSELL, *Vocabulum*. 'I say, Tim, what's your GAIT now?' 'Why, you see, I'm on the crack' (burglary).

GAITERS, *subs.* (American collo-quial). — Half boots; shoes.

GAL, *subs.* (common).—1. A girl; a servant-maid; a sweetheart. BEST GIRL=favourite flame.

2. (common). — A prostitute. For synonyms, *see* BARRACK-HACK and TART.

1851-61. MAYHEW, *Lond. Lab. and Lond. Poor*, I., p. 535. Upon the most trivial offence in this respect, or on the suspicion of an offence, the GALS are sure to be beaten cruelly and savagely by their 'chaps.'

3. (American). — A female rough.

GALANEY. *See* GALENY.

GALANTY (GALLANTY or GALANTEE) SHOW, *subs. phr.* (common). — A shadow panto-mime: silhouettes shown on a transparency or thrown on a white sheet by a magic lantern. Specifi-cally, the former. *See* PUNCH AND JUDY.

1851-61. H. MAYHEW, *Lond. Lab. and Lond. Poor*, Vol. III., p. 81. The GALANTEE show don't answer, because magic lanterns are so cheap in the shops.

1884. *Cassell's Technical Educator*, pt. 10, p. 244. That reminiscence of the nursery, the GALANTY SHOW.

1888. *Notes and Queries*, 7 S. v., p. 265. A flourish on the panpipes and a rumble on the drum was followed by the cry, GALANTY-SHOW!

GAL-BOY, *subs.*, (American). — A romp; a TOM-BOY (*q.v.*).

GALEN, *subs.* (common). — An apothecary. For synonyms, *see* GALLIPOT.

GALENA, *subs.* (American).—Salt pork. [From Galen, Ill., a chief hog-raising and pork-packing centre].

GALENY (or GALANY), *subs.* (old).—The domestic hen; now (West of England) a Guinea fowl. [Latin, *gallina*]. For synonyms, *see* CACKLING-CHEAT.

1887. *Temple Bar*, Mar., p. 333 It's a sin to think of the money you'd be spending on girls and things as don't know a hen's egg from a GALEENY'S.

GALIMAUFREY, *subs.* (old).—1. A medley; a jumble; a chaos of differences. [Fr., *gallimaufrée*= a hash].

1592. NASHE, *Pierce Penilesse*, in wks., ii., 93. Coblers, Tinkers, Fencers, none escapt them, but they mingled them all on one GALLIMAUFREY of glory.

1592. JOHN DAY, *Blind Beggar*, Act iv., Sc. 1, p. 75. Can. Let me be torn into mammocks with wilde Bears if I make not a GALLIMAUFRY of thy heart and keep thy Skull for my quaffing bowl.

1604. SHAKSPEARE, *Winter's Tale*, Act iv., Sc. 4. And they have a dance which the wenches say is a GALLIMAUFRY of gambols, because they are not in't.

1690. DURFEY, *Collin's Walk*, ch. ii., p. 58. But, like thy Tribe of canting Widgeons, A GALLIMAUFRY of Religions.

GALLERY, *subs.* (Winchester College).—A commoner bedroom. [From a tradition of GALLERIES in Commoners.] *See* GALLERY-NYMPHS.

TO PLAY TO THE GALLERY, *verb. phr.* (colloquial).—To act so as to win the applause of the vulgar: *i.e.*, to abandon dis-tinction and art for coarseness of means and cheapness of effect. Said indifferently of anyone in any profession who exerts himself to win the suffrages of the mob; as a political demagogue, a 'popular' preacher, a 'fashion-able' painter, and so on.

1872. *Standard*, 23 Oct. 'New York Correspondence.' His dispatches were, indeed, too long and too swelling in phrase; for herein he was always PLAYING TO THE GALLERIES.

Hence, GALLERY-HIT, SHOT, STROKE, etc.=a touch designed for, and exclusively addressed to, the non-critical.

TO PLAY THE GALLERY, *verb. phr.* (colloquial).—To make an audience; to applaud.

1870. *Echo*, 23 July, p. 5, c. 4. He seemed altogether a jovial, amusing sort of fellow, and as we were close by him, and constantly called in to PLAY THE GALLERY to his witty remarks, we asked him, when his friends left him, to join our party.

GALLERY NYMPH, *subs. phr.* (Winchester College).—A house-maid. *See* GALLERY.

GALLEY—PUT A BRASS GALLEY DOWN YOUR BACK, *verb. phr.* (printers').—An admonition to appear before a principal; imply-ing that the galley will serve as a screen.

GALLEY-FOIST, *subs.* (old).—The state barge, used by the Lord Mayor when he was sworn in at Westminster.

1609. BEN JONSON, *Silent Woman*, iv., 2. Out of my doores, you sons of noise and tumult, begot on an ill May day, or when the GALLEYFOIST is afloate to West-minster.

1785. GROSE, *Vulg. Tongue*, s.v.
1811. *Lexicon Balatronicum*, s.v.

GALLEY-GROWLER or -STOKER, *subs.* (nautical).—A loafer; a MALINGERER (*q.v.*); a GRUMBLE-GUTS (*q.v.*).

GALLEY-HALFPENNY, *subs.* (old). —A base coin, *tempus* Henry IV. [So called because it was com-monly imported in the Genoese galleys. See Leake, *English Money*, p. 129; Ruding, *Annals of Coinage*, i., 250; and Stow, *Survey* (ed. 1842) p. 50.]

GALLEY-SLAVE, *subs.* (printers').— A compositor. [From the oblong tray whereon the matter from the composing stick is arranged in column or page.] For synonyms, *see* DONKEY.

1683. MOXON, s.v.

GALLEYWEST, *adj.* or *adv.* (American).—An indefinite super-lative. *Cf.*, ABOUT-EAST.

1884. CLEMENS, (M. Twain) *Huck. Finn*, xxxvii., 382. Then she grabbed up the basket and slammed it across the house, and knocked the cat GALLEYWEST.

1887. FRANCIS, *Saddle and Mocassin* (quoted in *Slang, Jargon, and Cant*). I'll be darned if this establishment of yours, Hunse, don't knock any one of them GALLEY-WEST!—GALLEYWEST, sir, that's what it does.

GALLEY-YARN (or NEWS), *subs. phr.* (nautical).—A lying story; a swindle or TAKE-IN (*q.v.*). Frequently abbreviated to 'G.Y.'

1884. HENLEY and STEVENSON, *Admiral Guinea*, iii., 4. What? lantern and cutlass yours; you the one that knew the house; you the one that saw; you the one overtaken and denounced; and you spin me a GALLEY-YARN like that.

GALLIED, *ptl. adj.* (old). — 'Harried; vexed; over-fatigued; perhaps like a galley-slave' (GROSE, *Vulg. Tongue*, s.v.). In Australia, frightened.

GALLINIPPER, *subs.* (West Indian). —A large mosquito.

1847. PORTER, *Big Bear*, etc., p. 119. In the summer time the lakes and snakes . . . musketoes and GALLINIPPERS, buffalo gnats and sandflies . . . prevented he Injins from gwine through the country.

1888. *Lippincott's Magazine*. I thought the GALLINIPPERS would fly away with me before the seed ticks had sucked all my blood.

GALLIPOT, *subs.* (common).—An apothecary.

1785. GROSE, *Vulg. Tongue*, s.v

1836. M. SCOTT, *Cringle's Log*, ch. xiv. In truth, sir, I thought our surgeon would be of more use than any outlandish GALLIPOT that you could carry back.

1848. THACKERAY, *Book of Snobs*, ch. xxvii. 'Half-a-dozen little GALLIPOTS,' interposed Miss Wirt.

ENGLISH SYNONYMS.—Bolus; bum-tender; clyster-giver; clyster-pipe; croaker; crocus; drugs; Ollapod (from a creation of the Younger Coleman's); gage-monger; Galen (from the great physician); jakes-provider; pill-box; pill-merchant; pills; squirt; salts-and-senna; squire of the pot.

FRENCH SYNONYMS. — *Un miranςu* (obsolete: a play on *mire en cul*, respecting which *cf.*, Béralde, in Molière, *Malade Imaginaire*: *'On voit bien que vous n'avez pas accoutumé de parler à des visages'*); *un limonadier de postérieurs* (popular: *cf.*, 'bum-tender'; *un flûtencul* (common); *un insinuant* (popular: one who 'insinuates' the clyster-pipe).

GERMAN SYNONYMS.—*Rokeach, Raukeach*, or *Raukack* (from the Hebrew).

GALLIVANT, *verb*. (colloquial).—1. To gad about with, or after, one of the other sex; to play the gallant; to 'do the agreeable.'

1838. DICKENS, *Nicholas Nickleby*, ch. lxiv. You were out all day yesterday, and GALLIVANTING somewhere, I know.

1862. H. BEECHER STOWE, in *The Independent*, 27 Feb. What business had he to flirt and GALLIVANT all summer with Sally Kittridge?

1886. HAWLEY SMART, *Struck Down*, xi. The ramparts is a great place for GALLIVANTING.

1863. H. KINGSLEY, *Austin Elliot*, i., 112. It's them gals, Mr. Austin. Come in afore she sees you, else she'll not be at home. She is GALLIVANTING in the paddock with Captain Hertford.

2. (colloquial).—To TRAPES (*q.v.*); to fuss; to bustle about.

1859. *Boston Post*, 10 Dec. Senator Seward is GALLIVANTING gaily about Europe. Now at Compiègne, saying soft things to the Empress and studying despotism, now treading the battle-field of Waterloo, then back at Paris, and so on.

1871. C. D. WARNER, *My Summer in a Garden*. More than half the Lima beans, though on the most attractive sort of poles, which budded like Aaron's rod, went GALIVANTING off to the neighboring grape trellis.

1848. RUXTON, *Far West*, p. 145. The three remaining brothers were absent from the Mission . . . Fray Jose, GALLIVANTING at Pueblo de los Angeles.

1863. NORTON, *Lost and Saved*, p. 255. A pretty story, if, when her services were most wanted by the person who paid for them, she was to be gadding and GALLIVANTING after friends of her own.

1865. M. E. BRADDON, *Henry Dunbar*, ch. x. A pretty thing it would have been if your pa had come all the way from India to find his only daughter GALLIVANTING at a theaytre.

1870. *London Figaro*, 6 Dec. You're never content but when you're GALAVANTING about somewhere or other.

GALLIVATE, *verb* (American).—To frisk; to 'figure about'; *cf.*, GALLIVANT.

GALLON. WHAT'S A GALLON OF RUM AMONG ONE? *phr.* (American). —The retort sarcastic; applied, *e g.*, to those with 'eyes too big for their stomach'; to disproportionate ideas of the fitness of things, and so forth.

GALLON DISTEMPER, *subs. phr.* (common).—1. Delirium tremens; (2.) the lighter after-effects of drinking.

ENGLISH SYNONYMS.—(1) For the former, barrel-fever; black-dog; blue-devils; blue Johnnies (Australian); B. J's. (*idem.*); blues; bottle-ache; D. T.; horrors; jim-jams; jumps; pink-spiders; quart-mania; rams; rats; shakes; snakes in the boots; trembles; triangles; uglies.

2. For the latter: a head; hot-coppers; a mouth; a touch of the brewer; a sore head (Scots).

FRENCH SYNONYMS. — *Avoir mal aux cheveux* (familiar = the hair-ache); *les papillons noirs* (*Cf.*, pink spiders; also = hypochondria); *avoir fumé dans une pipe neuve* (= sick of a new clay).

GALLOPER, *subs.* (old).—1. A blood horse; a hunter.

1811. *Lexicon Balatronicum*, s.v. The toby gill clapped his bleeders to his GALLOPER and tipped the straps the double.

2. (military). — An aide-de-camp.

GALLOW-GRASS, *subs. phr.* (old).—Hemp. [*i.e.*, halters in the rough.]

1578. LYTE, *Trans. of Dodoens History of Plantes*, fol. 72. Hempe is called in . . . . English, Neckweede, and GALLOWGRASS.

GALLOWS, *subs.* (old). — 1. A rascal; a wretch deserving the rope.

1594. SHAKSPEARE, *Love's Labour Lost*, v., 2. A shrewd unhappy GALLOWS too.

1754. B. MARTIN, *Eng. Dict.* (2nd ed.). s.v. = a wicked rascal.

1837. DICKENS, *Oliver Twist*. (*To Oliver*). Now, young GALLOWS.

1838. JAS. GRANT, *Sketches in London*, ch. ii., p. 58. Blow me tight, young GALLOWS, if I don't pound your ribs to powder!

2. (common: generally *in. pl.* – GALLOWSES). — A pair of braces

1835. HALIBURTON, *Clockmaker*, 1 S., ch. xv. Chock-full of spring, like the wire end of a bran new pair of trouser GALLUSES.

1848. DURIVAGE, *Stray Subjects*, p 168. If I wouldn't spile his picter bust my boots and GALLOWSES.

1851-61. H. MAYHEW, *Lond. Lab. and Lond. Poor*, vol. I., p. 431. The braces, which in some parts of the country are called 'GALLOWSES.'

c. 1852. *Traits of American Humor*, p. 58. Hole on, dod drot you, wait till I unbutton my GALLOWSES.

1864. JAMES, etc, *Italian-English Dict.* GALLOWSES, *batilla*.

1883. G. A. S[ALA], in *Ill. Lond. News*, Sept. 22, p. 275, c. i. Braces (which, when I was young, used, in the north of England, to be known by the expressive name of GALLOWSES.)

Adv. (old).—Excessively; same as BLOODY, BLEEDING, (*q.v.*), etc. (As *adj.*) great; uncommon; real.

c. 1551. L. SHEPHERD. *John Bon* in Arber's *Garner*, Vol. IV., p. 109. Ye, are much bound to God for such a spittle holiness. A GALLOWS gift!

1789. PARKER, *Life's Painter*, p. 120. Some they pattered flash with GALLOWS fun and joking.

1827. EGAN, *Anecdotes of the Turf*, etc., p. 44. Then your blowen will wax GALLOWS haughty! [Also quoted in notes to *Don Juan*.]

1830. LYTTON, *Paul Clifford*, p. 293 (ed. 1854). Ah, Dame Lobkin, if so be as our little Paul vas a vith you, it would be a GALLOWS comfort to you in your latter hend!

1851-61. MAYHEW, *Lond. Lab. and Lond. Poor*, III., 90. I'll be smothered if I'm going to look down that GALLOWS long chimney.

1861. H. KINGSLEY, *Ravenshoe*, ch. xli. And the pleece come in, and got GALLUS well kicked about the head.

1869. GREENWOOD, *Seven Curses of London*, p. 244. Put it on your face so GALLUS thick that the devil himself won't see through it.

GALLOWS-BIRD (also NEWGATE-BIRD), *subs.* (common).—1. A son of the rope; an habitual criminal; a vagabond or scoundrel, old or young; a crack-rope or wag-halter (COTGRAVE); a gallows-clapper (FLORIO). Fr., *gibier de Cayenne*, or *de potence*.

1785. GROSE, *Vulg. Tongue*, s.v. One that deserves hanging.

1822. SCOTT, *Fortunes of Nigel*, ch. xi. That very GALLOWS-BIRD were enough to corrupt a whole ante-chamber of pages.

2. (common).—A corpse on, or from, the gallows.

1861. READE, *Cloister and Hearth*, ch. xxviii. I ne'er minced (dissected) ape nor GALLOWS-BIRD.

GALLOWS-FACED, *adj.* (old)—Evil-looking; hang-dog. Also GALLOWS-LOOKING.

1766. H. BROOKE, *Fool of Quality*, ii. 16. Art thou there, thou rogue, thou hang-dog, thou GALLOWS-FACED vagabond?

1768. GOLDSMITH, *Good-natured Man*, Act v. Hold him fast, he has the GALLOWS in his FACE.

1837. BARHAM, I. L. (*Misadv. at Margate*). A little GALLOWS-LOOKING chap—dear me! what could he mean?

GALLOWS-MINDED, *adj.* (colloquial).—Criminal in habit and idea; also, evil-hearted.

GALLOWSNESS, *subs.* (old).—Rascality; recklessness; mischievousness.

1859. G. ELIOT, *Adam Bede*, ch. vi. I never knew your equal for GALLOWSNESS.

GALLOWS-RIPE, *adj.* (old).—Ripe for the rope.

1837. CARLYLE, *French Revolution*, Pt. II., bk. v., ch. iii. Loose again, as one not yet GALLOWS-RIPE.

GALLUS.—*See* GALLOWS.

GALLY-FOIST—*See* GALLEY-FOIST.

GALLYSLOPES, *subs.* (Old Cant).—Breeches. For synonyms, *see* KICKS.

GALOOT (also GALLOOT and GEELOOT), *subs.* (general).—A man (sometimes in contempt); also (in America) a worthless fellow (or thing, *see* quot. 1888); a rowdy; a CAD (*q.v.*).

1835. MARRYAT, *Jacob Faithful*, ch. xxxiv. Four greater GALLOOTS were never picked up, but never mind that.

1869. S. L. CLEMENS (Mark Twain) *Innocents at Home*, p. 22. He could lam any GALOOT of his inches in America.

1871. JOHN HAY, *Jim Bludso*. I'll hold her nozzle agin the bank Till the last GALOOT'S ashore.

1885. *Saturday Review*, Feb. 7, p. 167. I'll never draw a revolver on a man again as long as I live.' . . . 'Guess I'll go for the GALOOT with a two-scatter shoot-gun.

1888. *New York Tribune*, May 16. It is better to have a Carrot for a President than a dead beat for a son-in-law. In this way we again score a live beat on the GALOOT.

1892. R. L. STEVENSON and L. OSBOURNE, *The Wrecker*, p. 137. 'My dear boy, I may be a GALOOT about literature, but you'll always be an outsider in business.

ON THE GAY GALOOT, *adv. phr.* (common).—On the spree,

1892. MILLIKEN, *'Arry Ballads*, p. 3. I'm off ON THE GAY GALOOT somewheres.

GALOPTIOUS or **GALUPTIOUS**, *adj.* (popular).—Delightful; a general superlative.

1887. *Judy*, 21 Sept., p. 140. Four young ladies represented the GALOPSHUS sum of 20,000,000 dollars.

GALORE (also GALLORE and GOLORE), *adv.* (old; now recognised).—In abundance; plenty. [Irish and Gaelic *go leor* = in plenty.]

1785. GROSE, *Vulg. Tongue*, s.v.

1848. RUXTON, *Life in the Far West*, p 14. GALORE of alcohol to ratify the trade.

1856. C. READE, *Never Too Late*, ch. lx. He found rogues GALORE, and envious spirits that wished the friends ill.

1891. *Licensed Vic. Mirror*, 30 Jan., p. 1, c. 1. Of chit-chat this week we have GALORE, and the difficulty is how to sift the wheat from the chaff.

GALUMPH, *verb.* (American).—To bump along (Onomatopœia).

1888. *New York World*, 13 May. The young man tackled the driver of a green bobtail car that GALUMPHED through Lewis Street at a high rate of speed.

GALVANISED YANKEE, *subs. phr.* (American Civil War).—A GREY-BACK (*q.v.*) who took the oath to the North and served in its armies.

GAM, *subs.* (thieves').—1. Pluck; gameness.

1888. *Cassell's Saturday Journal*, 8 Dec., p. 260. I'm not so sure about his lack of cunnin', speed, or GAM.

2. (American thieves')—Stealing (MATSELL, 1859).

Verb. (American thieves').—1. To steal.

2. (American). — To engage in social intercourse; to make a call; to have a chat. *See* GAMMING.

GAMALIEL, *subs.* (colloquial).—A pedant; a person curious of the letter and the form: *e.g.*, 'these GAMALIELS of the theory' = these ultra-puritans, to whom the spirit is nothing.

GAMARUCHE, *subs.* (venery).—*See* CUNNILINGIST and COCK-TEASER. *Verb* (venery). — To irrumate; to BAG-PIPE (*q.v.*). Also to CUNNILINGE (*q.v.*). Fr., *gamahucher*.

GAMB (or **GAM**), *subs.* (old).—A leg. In use also in this sense as an heraldic term. [It., *gambe*; Fr., *jambe*; probably through Lingua Franca.] For synonyms, *see* DRUMSTICKS and PINS.

1789. GEO. PARKER, *Life's Painter*, p. 143. If a man has bow legs, he has queer GAMS, GAMS being cant for legs.

1796. GROSE, *Vulg. Tongue* (3rd ed.), s.v.

1819. MOORE, *Memorial*, p. 61. Back to his home, with tottering GAMS.

1887. HENLEY, *Villon's Good Night*. At you I merely lift my GAM.

[To FLUTTER A GAM = to dance; TO LIFT A GAM = to break wind; TO GAM IT = to walk; to run away; TO LEG IT (*q.v.*)].

GAMBLE, *subs.* (colloquial). — A venture: a FLUTTER (*q.v.*).

1892. R. L. STEVENSON and L. OSBOURNE, *The Wrecker*, p. 250. And you know the Flying Scud was the biggest GAMBLE of the crowd.

GAMBLER, *subs.* (old, now recognised). *See* quots.

1778. BAILEY, *Eng. Dict.* GAMBLER, a guinea-dropper; one class of sharpers.

1785. GROSE, *Vulg. Tongue*. GAMBLER, a sharper; a tricking gamester.

1816. JOHNSON, *Eng. Dict.* (11th ed.). GAMBLER, a cant word, I suppose. A knave whose practice it is to invite the unwary to game and cheat them.

1890. *Cassell's Enc. Dict.* GAMBLER, one given to playing for a stake.

GAMBOL, *subs.* (booking clerks'). A railway ticket.

1882. *Daily News*, 6 Sept., p. 2, c. 5. . . . Mr. Chance [the magistrate] asked what GAMBOLS meant. The inspector said doubtless the railway tickets.

GAM-CASES, *subs.* (old). Stockings (PARKER, *Life's Painter*). [From GAM = leg + CASE.]

GAME, *subs.* (old).—1. The proceeds of a robbery; SWAG (*q.v.*).

1676. *Warning for Housekeepers*. Song. When that we have bit the bloe, we carry away the GAME.

2. (old).—A company of whores. A GAME-PULLET = a young prostitute, or a girl inclined to lechery; *cf.*, *adj.*, sense 8.

1690. B.E., *New Dictionary*, s.v. . . also a Bawdy house, lewd women.

1785. GROSE, *Vulg. Tongue*, s.v. GAME . . . Mother, have you any GAME, Mother, have you any girls?

3. (old).—A gull; a simpleton. For synonyms, *see* BUFFLE and CABBAGE-HEAD.

1690. B. E., *New Dictionary*. GAME, *c.* Bubbles drawn in to be cheated.

1785. GROSE, *Vulg. Tongue*, s.v.

4. (thieves').—Specifically, THE GAME = thieving; also (nautical), slave trading; and (venery), the practice of copulation (*e.g.*, good at THE GAME = an expert and vigorous bedfellow. *Cf.*, SHAKSPEARE, *Troilus*, iv., 5, 'Spoils of opportunity, daughters of the GAME'). In quot. (1639) it would seem that HEN OF THE GAME = a shrew, a fighting woman.

1639-61. *Rump*, ii., 185. 'Free Parliament Litany.' From a dunghill Cock and a HEN OF THE GAME.

1640. *Ladies' Parliament*. Stamford she is for THE GAME, She saies her husband is to blame, For her part she loves a foole, If he hath a good toole.

1668. ETHEREDGE, *She Would if She Could*, i., 1. A gentleman should not have gone out of his chambers but some civil officer of the GAME or other would have . . . given him notice where he might have had a course or two in the afternoon.

17(?). BURNS, *Merry Muses*, 'Jenny Macraw' (old song). Jenny Macraw was a bird of THE GAME.

1839. BRANDON, *Poverty, Mendicity, and Crime, Glossary*. On THE GAME—thieving.

1851-61. MAYHEW, *Lond. Lab. and Lond. Poor*, i., 263. Whether the GAME got stale, or Peter became honest, is beyond the purport of my communication to settle.

1852. SNOWDEN, *Mag. Assist.* (3rd ed.), p. 444, s.v.

1859. MATSELL, *Vocabulum or Rogue's Lexicon*, s. v. The particular line of rascality the rogue is engaged in; thieving; cheating.

1860. *Chambers' Journal*, Vol. 13, p. 281. I asked him if he meant by a trading voyage, the GAME.

5. (colloquial).—A source of amusement; a LARK (*q.v.*): a BARNEY (*q.v.*); as, *e.g.*, It was such a GAME!

6. (colloquial).—A design; trick; object; line of conduct: *e.g.*, What's your little GAME = What are you after? Also, None of your little GAMES! = None of your tricks! *See* HIGH OLD GAME.

1854. WHYTE MELVILLE, *General Bounce*, ch. ix. *Honesty*, indeed! if honesty's the GAME, you've a right to your share, what Mrs. Kettering intended you should have.

1857. DUCANGE ANGLICUS, *The Vulg. Tongue*, p. 9. GAME n. Intention. 'What's your GAME?' or, 'What are you up to?' (very generally used).

1870. *Standard*, 27 Sept. If we accept the meaner GAME which the *Times* indicates for us, it can only be by deliberate choice.

1879. JUSTIN MCCARTHY, *Donna Quixote*, ch. xiii. Come, what's your little GAME?

1883. EDW. E. MORRIS, in *Longman's Mag.*, June, p. 176. A youth, who left England, and then carried on the same GAME in Australia.

1889. *Standard*, 1 May, p. 5, c. 1. The 'GAME of law and order' is not up, in Paris.

1890. *Punch*, 30 Aug., p. 97. Mug's GAME! They'll soon find as the Marsters ain't going to be worried and welched.

1891. J. NEWMAN, *Scamping Tricks*, p. 46. She knew how to work THE GAME of fascination right.

1892. R. L. STEVENSON and L. OSBOURNE, *The Wrecker*, p. 349, 'It was the thing in your times, that's right enough; but you're old now, and THE GAME'S up.

Adj. (old).—1. Plucky; enduring; full of spirit and BOTTOM (*q.v.*). [Cock-pit and pugilists'. The word may be said to have passed into the language with the rise to renown of Harry Pearce, surnamed the GAME CHICKEN.]

1747. CAPT. GODFREY, *Science of Defence*, p. 64. Smallwood (a boxer) is thorough GAME, with judgment equal to any, and superior to most.

1819. MOORE, *Tom Crib's Memorial*, p. 57. Pitying raised from earth the GAME old man.

1821. P. EGAN, *Tom and Jerry* (ed. 1891), p. 38. Tom, however, was too GAME to acknowledge any sort of alarm at this slight visitation.

1823. E. KENT, *Mod. Flash Dict.* GAME, s.v. Sturdy, hardy, hardened.

1827. REYNOLDS, *Peter Corcoran, The Fancy*. 'The Field of Tothill.' The highest in the fancy—all the GAME ones, Who are not very much beneath her weight.

1855. A. TROLLOPE, *The Warden*, ch. viii. He was a most courageous lad, GAME to the backbone.

1891. *Licensed Vict. Gaz.*, 19 June, p. 395. The round had lasted sixteen minutes, and no one present had ever seen GAMER or more determined fighting.

2. (common).—Ready; willing; prepared. [Also from cock-fighting. *See* sense 1].

1836. DICKENS, *Pickwick*, p. 99, (ed. 1857). 'All alive to-day, I suppose?' 'Regular GAME, sir.'

1856. READE, *Never Too Late* ch. xxi. I'm GAME to try.

1865. *Bentley*, p. 182, 'The Excursion Train.' Again to London back we came The day the excursion ticket said, And really both of us felt GAME To travel round the world instead.

1880. *Punch's Almanack*. Got three quid; have cried a go with Fan, GAME to spend my money like a man.

1891. FARJEON, *The Mystery of M. Felix*, p. 103. 'I'm GAME,' said Sophy, to whom any task of this kind was especially inviting.

1891. HUME NISBET, *Bail Up!* p. 51. 'Yes, I am GAMEY, you bet!' exclaimed the Chinaman, softly.

1891. J. NEWMAN *Scamping Tricks*, p. 121. It is nearly midnight. I am GAME for another hour, are you?

3. (old).—Lame; crooked; disabled: as in GAME LEG.

1787. GROSE, *Prov. Glossary*. GAME-LEG, a lame leg.

1825. SCOTT, *St. Ronan's Well*, ch. i. Catching hold of the devil's GAME leg with his episcopal crook.

1851. G. BORROW, *Lavengro*, ch. lxvii., p. 204 (1888). Mr. Platitude, having what is vulgarly called a GAME leg, came shambling into the room.

1875. JAS. PAYN, *Walter's Word*, ch. i, Well, you see, old fellow, with a GAME-arm (his left arm is in a sling), and a GAME-leg (he has limped across the platform with the aid of his friend, and also of a crutch), one feels a little helpless.

4. (thieves').—Knowing; wide-awake; and (of women) FLASH (*q.v.*), or inclined to venery. *E.g.*, GAME-COVE = an associate of thieves; GAME-woman = a prostitute: *i.e.*, a woman who is GAME (sense 2); GAME-PULLET (GROSE) = a girl that will show sport, a female GAME-COCK; GAME-SHIP (old) = a ship whose commander and officers could be corrupted by bribes to allow the cargo to be stolen (CLARK RUSSELL).

1676. ETHEREDGE, *Man of Mode*, ii. Go on, be the GAME mistress of the town and entice all our young fops as fast as they come from travel.

COCK OF THE GAME, *subs. phr.* (old).—A champion; an undoubted blood; a star of magnitude (cock-pit).

1719. DURFEY, *Pills*, iii., 329. Now all you tame gallants, you that have the name, And would accounted be COCKS OF THE GAME.

1822. SCOTT, *Nigel*, xiv. I have seen a dung-hill chicken that you meant to have picked clean enough; it will be long ere his lordship ruffles a feather with a COCK OF THE GAME.

TO MAKE GAME OF, *verb. phr.* (colloquial).—To turn into ridicule; to delude; to humbug.

1671. MILTON, *Samson*, 1331. Do they not seek occasion of new quarrels, On my refusal, to distress me more; Or MAKE A GAME OF my calamities?

1690. B. E., *New Dictionary*. What you GAME me? c. do you jeer me, or pretend to expose me to MAKE A May-GAME OF me?

1745. *Hist. of Coldstream Guards*, 25 Oct. If the militia are reviewed to-morrow by his Majesty, the soldiers of the third regiment of Guards are to behave civilly and not to laugh or to MAKE ANY GAME OF them.

TO DIE GAME, *verb. phr.* (colloquial).—To maintain a resolute attitude to the last; to show no contrition.

1785. GROSE, *Vulg. Tongue*. To DIE GAME, to suffer at the gallows without showing any signs of fear or repentance.

1815. SCOTT, *Guy Mannering*, ch. liv. The ruffian lay perfectly still and silent. 'He's gaun to die GAME ony how,' said Dinmont.

1836. DICKENS, *Pickwick* (ed. 1857), p. 363. I say that the coachman did not run away; but that he DIED GAME—GAME as pheasants; and I won't hear nothin' said to the contrary.

1869. SPENCER, *Study of Sociology*, ch. viii., p. 183 (9th ed.). Nor should we forget the GAME-cock, supplying, as it does, a word of eulogy to the mob of roughs who witness the hanging of a murderer, and who half condone his crime if he DIES GAME.

1871. *Times*, 30 Jan. *Critique on London*, etc. The principal was acquitted, and though his accomplices were hung in Pall Mall at the scene of their act, they DIED GAME.

TO GET AGAINST THE GAME, *verb. phr.* (American).—To take a risk; to chance it. [From the game of poker].

TO PLAY THE GAME, *verb. phr.* (colloquial).—To do a thing properly; to do what is right and proper.

1889. GEOFFREY DRAGE, *Cyril*, ch. vii. I really think he is . . . not PLAYING THE GAME.

THE FIRST GAME EVER PLAYED, *subs. phr.* (venery).—Copulation. For synonyms, *see* GREENS and RIDE.

GAMECOCK, *adj.* (old).—Hectoring; angry; valiant out of place.

1838. LEVER, *Handy Andy*. Smoke and fire is my desire, So blaze away my GAMECOCK squire.

GAMENESS, *subs.* (colloquial).—Pluck; endurance; the mixture of spirit and bottom.

1861. HUGHES, *Tom Brown at Oxford*, ch. xxiv. There was no doubt about his GAMENESS.

1884. *Referee*, 23 March, p. 1, c. 4. Carter fought with great GAMENESS, but he never had a look in.

GAMESTER, *subs.* (old).—1. A prostitute. For synonyms, *see* BARRACK-HACK and TART.

1598. SHAKSPEARE, *All's Well*, v. 3. She's impudent, my lord, and was a common GAMESTER to the camp.

1614. JONSON, *Bartholomew Fair* ii. 1. Ay, ay, GAMESTERS, mocke a plain soft wench of the suburbs. do.

1620. PERCY, *Folio MSS.*, p. 404. Be not att ffirst to nice nor coye when GAMSTERS you are courting.

2. (old).—A ruffler; a gallant; a wencher; a man fit and ready for anything; also a player.

1639-61. *Rump*, i., 253, 'A Medley. Room for a GAMESTER that flies at all he sees.

1676. ETHEREDGE, *Man of Mode*, v., 1. Live it also like a frank GAMESTER, on the square.

GAMEY, *adj.* (colloquial).—1. High-smelling; offensive to the nose; half-rotten.

2. (colloquial).—Frisky; plucky.

1843. DICKENS, *Martin Chuzzlewit*, ch. xi. There's something GAMEY in it, young ladies, ain't there.

1869. S. BOWLES, *Our New West*, p. 275. Horses are fresh and fat and GAMEY.

GAMINESS, *subs.* (colloquial).—The malodorousness proceeding from decay and—by implication—filthiness.

GAMING-HOUSE, *subs.* (old).—A house of ill-repute—hell, tavern, or stews.

1611. COTGRAVE, *Dictionarie, Berlan*, a common tippling house, a HOUSE OF GAMING, or of any other disorder.

GAMMER, *subs.* (old).—An old wife; a familiar address; the correlative of GAFFER (*q.v.*).

1551. *Gammer Gurton's Needle* Title).

1706. *Hudibras Redivivus*, Part VI. And monkey faces, yawns, and stammers, Delude the pious dames and GAMMERS To think their mumbling guides precation So full of heavenly inspiration.

1842. TENNYSON, *The Goose*. Ran Gaffer, stumbled GAMMER.

GAMMING, *subs.* (nautical).—A whaleman's term for the visits paid by crews to each other at sea.

1884. G. A. SALA, in *Illus. Lon. News*, July 19, p. 51, c. 2. When two or more American whalers meet in mid-ocean, and there are no whales in sight, it is customary to tack topsails and exchange visits. This social intercourse the whalemen call GAMMING . . . I cannot help fancying that 'gam' is in greater probability an abbreviation of the Danish 'gammen,' sport, or that it has something to do with the nautical 'gammoning,' the lasting by which the bowsprit is bound firmly down to the cutwater.

1890. *Century*, Aug. To GAM means to gossip. The word occurs again and again in the log-books of the old whalers.

GAMMON, *subs.* (colloquial).—1. Nonsense; humbug; deceit. Sometimes GAMMON AND SPINACH. No GAMMON = no error, no lies.

[SKEAT says from Mid. Eng. *Gamen* = a game; but R. SHERWOOD (*Eng. Dict.*, 1660), gives 'a beggar or seller of gammons of Bacon; and in COTGRAVE (1611), *jambonnier* = a beggar, also a seller of bacon, or gammons of bacon.']

c. 1363. *Chester Plays*. i. 102. This GAMMON shall begin.

1781. G. PARKER, *View of Society*, I. 208. I thought myself pretty much a master of GAMMON, but the Billingsgate eloquence of Mrs. P. . . . . exceeded me.

1811. *Lexicon Balatronicum*, s.v. GAMON. What rum GAMON the old file pitched to the flat.

1823. *Mod. Flash Dict.* GAMMON—Falsehood and bombast.

1828-45. HOOD, *Poems* (ed. 1846), vi., p. 96, Behold yon servitor of God and Mammon, Who, binding up his Bible with his ledger, Blends Gospel texts with trading GAMMON.

1836. DICKENS, *Pickwick*, ch. xxvii. Lord bless their little hearts, they thinks its all right, and don't know no better, but they're the wictims o' GAMMON, Samivel, they're the wictims o' GAMMON.

1837. BARHAM, I. L. *Blasphemer's Warning*. When each tries to humbug his dear Royal Brother, in Hopes by such GAMMON to take one another in.

1839. *Comic Almanack*, Jan. But if you wish to save your bacon, Give us less GAMMON.

1849. DICKENS, *David Copperfield*, ch. xxii., p. 199. 'Oh, my goodness, how polite we are!' exclaimed Miss Mowcher. . . . . 'What a world of GAMMON AND SPINNAGE it is!'

1890. HUME NISBET, *Bail up!* p. 92. I'm real grit and no GAMMON.

2. (thieves').—A confederate whose duty is to engage the attention of a victim during robbery; a BONNET (*q.v.*) or COVER (*q.v.*).

Verb (colloquial). — 1. To humbug: to deceive; to take in with fibs; to KID (*q.v.*).

1700. *Step to the Bath*, quoted in Ashton's *Soc. Life in Reign of Queen Anne*, v. ii., p. 111. We went to the *Groom Porter's* . . . . there was Palming, Hodging, Loaded Dice, Levant, and GAMMONING, with all the Speed imaginable.

1823. MONCRIEFF, *Tom and Jerry*, ii., 6. Vile I can get fifteen bob a day by GAMMONING a maim, the devil may vork for me.

1825. BUCKSTONE, *The Bear Hunters*, ii. There! that's just the way she GAMMONS me at home.

1836. M. SCOTT, *Tom Cringle's Log*, ch. ii. Why, my lad, we shall see to-morrow morning; but you GAMMONS so bad about the rhino that we must prove you a bit; so Kate, my dear,—to the pretty girl who had let me in.

1836. DICKENS, *Pickwick*, ch. xiii. So then they pours him out a glass o' wine, and GAMMONS him about his driving, and gets him into a reg'lar good humour.

1837. BARHAM, *Ingoldsby Legends*, 'Misadventures at Margate.' And 'cause he GAMMONS so the flats, ve calls him Veeping Bill!

1840. HOOD, *Tale of a Trumpet*. Lord Bacon couldn't have GAMMONED her better.

1890. HUME NISBET, *Bail Up!* p. 70. Oh, don't try to GAMMON me, you cunning young school-miss.

ENGLISH SYNONYMS.—To bam; to bamblustercate; to bamboozle; to bambosh; to barney; to be on the job; to best; to bilk; to blarney; to blow; to bosh; to bounce; to cob; to cod; to cog; to chaff; to come over (or the artful, or Paddy, or the old soldier over) one; to cram; to do; to do brown; to doctor; to do Taffy; to fake the kidment; to flare up; to flam; to flummox; to get at (round, or to windward of) one; to gild the pill; to give a cock's egg; to gravel; to gull; to haze: to jimmify; to jaw; to jockey; to jolly; to kid; to make believe the moon is made of green cheese (Cotgrave); to mogue; to palm off on; to pickle; to plant; to plum; to poke bogey (or fun) at; to pro-moss; to put the kibosh on; to put in the chair, cart, or basket; to pull the leg; to queer; to quiz; to roast; to roorback; to run a bluff, or the shenanigan; to sell; to send for pigeon's milk; to sit upon; to send for oil of strappum, etc.; to shave; to slum, or slumguzzle; to smoke; to snack; to soap, soft soap, sawder, or soft sawder; to spoof; to stick; to stall; to string, or get on a string; to stuff; to saw-dust, or get on sawdust and treacle; to suck; to suck up; to sugar; to swap off; to take a rise out of; to rot; to tommy-rot; to take in, or down; to take to town; to take to the fair; to tip the traveller; to try it on; to throw dust in the eyes; to throw a tub to a whale; to pepper; to throw pepper in the eyes; to use the pepper box; to whiffle; to work the poppycock racket (Irish American). [NOTE.—Many of the foregoing are used substantively, *e.g.*, a bam, a barney, a sell, bambosh = nonsense; deceit; a hoax, etc.]

FRENCH SYNONYMS.—*Donner un pont à faucher* (also, thieves' = to lay a trap); *dindonner* (popular: from *dindon* = a gull, a gobbler); *battre à la Parisienne* (thieves': = to cheat; to come the cockney); *se ficher de la fiole*, or *de la bobine, de quelqu'un* (popular: to get on with it, *i.e.*, to try to fool); *envoyer chercher le parapluie de l'escouade* (military: *parapluie de l'escouade* = the squad's umbrella: to send on a fool's errand; *cf.*, to send for pigeon's milk, etc.); *la faire à quelqu'un* (popular); *faucher* (thieves' = to best); *enfoncer* (familiar: to let in: also to surpass); *cabasser* (popular); *monter des couleurs, le Job*, or *un schtosse* (= to do up brown); *faire le coup*, or *monter le coup, à quelqu'un* (popular: = to take a rise); *bouffer la botte* (military: = to SELL (*q.v.*) or BILK, as a woman refusing congress after receiving the SOCKET-MONEY (*q.v.*) in advance); *bouler* (popular: also to WHOP (*q.v.*)); *être l'autre* (popular: = to GET LEFT (*q.v.*)); *mettre dans le sac* (thieves': = to bag, *i.e.*, to trap); *coller* or *poser un lapin* (popular: = to MAKE A HARE OF (*q.v.*); also more generally, to BILK (*q.v.*)); *emblémer* (thieves': = to stick); *faire voir le tour* (popular: = to show how it's done; *connaitre le tour* = to know the game); *faire la queue à quelqu'un* (popular: = to pull one's leg); *tirer la carotte* (thieves'); *canarder* (popular: = to bring down); *empaler* (popular: = to stick); *passer des curettes* (popular: = to befool); *monter une gaffe* (popular: *gaffe* = a joke, a hoax); *jobarder* (popular: *job* = simpleton, and is the same as *jobelin*); *mener en bateau un pante pour le refaire* (thieves': = to take a man on); *monter un bateau* (popular); *promener quelqu'un* (popular: *cf.*, to take to town); *compter des mistoufles* (fam.: *mistoufle* = a scurvy trick); *gourrer* (popular: = to bosh); *affluer* (from *flouer* = to cheat, to diddle); *rouster* (popular and thieves'); *affûter* (thieves' = to run down, also to make unlawful profits); *bouler* (popular); *juiffer* (popular = to Jew); *pigeonner* (popular to PLUCK A PIGEON (*q.v.*)); *flancher* (popular = to KID (*q.v.*)); *faire la barbe* (popular = to SHAVE (*q.v.*)); *monter* or *hisser un gandin* (thieves' = literally to hoist a swell); *fourrer* or *mettre dedans* (popular = to take in and do for); *planter un chou* (fam.); *être marron* (popular); *interver dans les vannes* (= to let oneself be sucked-up); *monter un godan à quelqu'un* (popular); *griller quelqu'un* (popular = to cuckold); *passer en lunette* (popular); *goujonner* (*i.e.*), to hook like a gudgeon); *fourguer* (thieves' = also to FENCE (*q.v.*)); *pousser une blague* (popular = to cram); *paqueliner* (thieves'); *se baucher* (thieves'); *balancer* popular).

GERMAN SYNONYMS.—*Zinkennen an Almoni peloni* (= to send one after Cheeks the Marine [*q.v.*]. *Almoni* and *peloni* are used mockingly in combination and also singly for a non-existent person); *anbeulen* (= to fool); *jemanden arbeiten* (= to haze, to cram); *bekaspern*, or *bekaschpern*, or *beschwatzen* (= to fool: from *Heb. kosaw* = to cheat).

SPANISH SYNONYMS.—*Disparar* (= also to talk nonsense; to

blunder); *hacer á uno su dominguillo*, or *hacer su dominguillo de uno* (colloquial: *dominguillo* = a figure made of straw and used at bull fights to enrage the bulls); *freirsela á alguno* (*freir* = to fry: to deceive: *Cf.*, to ROAST, or have one ON TOAST); *pegar una tostada á alguno* (= to put one on toast: more generally to play a practical joke); *echar de baranda* (= to EMBROIDER (*q.v.*)); *bola* (*subs.* = humbug; a hoax); *borrufalla* (*subs.* = bombast); *chicolear* (= to jest in gallantry); *engatusar* (= to rob, or hurt; also to trick without intention); *candonguear* (also = to jeer); *abrir á chasco* (also to jeer); *encantar* (= to enchant).

ITALIAN SYNONYMS. *Ganezzarre; dar la stolfa; traversare* (*cf.*, TO COME OVER); *scamuffare* = to disguise oneself).

2. (thieves').—To act as BONNET (*q.v.*) or COVER (*q.v.*) to a thief.

Intj. (colloquial).—Nonsense; SKITTLES! (*q.v.*).

1827. R. B. PEAKE, *Comfortable Lodgings*, i., 3. *Sir H.* (*aside*). GAMMON!

1836. M. SCOTT, *Tom Cringle's Log*, ch. vii. GAMMON, tell that to the marines: you're a spy, messmate.

1854. THACKERAY, *The Rose and the Ring*, p. 100. Ha! said the king, you dare to say GAMMON to your sovereign.

1861. A. TROLLOPE, *Framley Parsonage*, ch. iv. GAMMON, said Mr. Gowerby; and as he said it he looked with a kind of derisive smile into the clergyman's face.

GAMMON AND PATTER. *subs. phr.* (thieves'). — 1. (old).—The language used by thieves; 2. (modern). — A meeting; a PALAVER. (*q.v.*). 3. Commonplace talk of any kind.

1789. GEO. PARKER, *Life's Painter*, p. 150. GAMMON AND PATTER is the language of cant, spoke among themselves: when one of them speaks well, another says he GAMMONS well.

1811. *Lex. Bal.* s.v. GAMMON AND PATTER. Commonplace talk of any kind.

TO GIVE (or KEEP) IN GAMMON. *verb. phr.* (thieves').—To engage a person's attention while a confederate is robbing him.

1719. CAPT. ALEX. SMITH, *Thieves' Grammar*, s.v.

1821. HAGGART, *Life*, p. 51. Bagrie called the woman of the house, KEPT HER IN GAMMON in the back room, while I returned and brought off the till. *Ibid.*, p. 68. I whidded to the Doctor and he GAVE ME GAMMON.

TO GAMMON LUSHY (or QUEER, etc.). *verb. phr.* (thieves'). — To feign drunkenness, sickness, etc.

TO GAMMON THE TWELVE. *verb. phr.* (thieves').—To deceive the jury.

1819. VAUX, *Life*. A man who has been tried by a criminal court and by a plausible defence has induced the jury to acquit him, or to banish the capital part of the charge and so to save his life, is said by his associates to have GAMMONED THE TWELVE in prime twig, alluding to the number of jurymen.

GAMMONER, *subs.* (old).—1. One who GAMMONS (*q.v.*); a nonsense-monger. Fr., *bonisseur de loffitudes; blagueur; mangeur de frimes*.

1823. MONCRIEFF, *Tom and Jerry* i. Fly to the GAMMONERS, and awake to everything that's going on.

2. (thieves').—A confederate who covers the action of his chief; a BONNET, a COVER, a STALL, all which *see*.

1821. HAGGART, *Life*, p. 66. The Doctor played the part of the GAMMONER so well that I made my escape without being observed.

GAMMY, *subs.* (tramps').—1. Cant.

1785. GROSE, *Vulg. Tongue*, s.v. Do you stoll the GAMMY? Do you understand cant?

2. (common).—A nickname for a lameter; a HOPPING JESUS; (*q.v.*).

3. (Australian).—A fool.

1892. HUME NISBET, *Bushranger's Sweetheart*, p. 191. Well, of all the GAMMIES you are the gammiest, Slowboy, to go and string yourself to a woman, when you might have had the pick of Melbourne.

Adj. (tramps'). — 1. Bad; impossible. Applied to householders of whom it is known that nothing can be got. *See* BEGGARS' MARKS. GAMMY-VIAL = a town in which the police will not allow unlicensed hawking. (VIAL = Fr., *Ville*).

1839. BRANDON, *Poverty, Mendicity, and Crime, Glossary*, s.v.

1851-61. MAYHEW, *Lond. Lab.*, i., 466. No villages that are in any way GAMMY are ever mentioned in these papers. *Ibid.*, i., 404. These are left by one of the school at the houses of the gentry, a mark being placed on the door post of such as are bone or GAMMY, in order to inform the rest of 'the school' where to call, and what houses to avoid.

2. Forged; false; spurious: as a GAMMY-MONEKER = a forged signature; GAMMY-LOUR = counterfeit money, etc.

1839. BRANDON, *Poverty, Mendicity, and Crime*, s.v.

1852. SNOWDEN, *Mag. Assistant* (3rd. ed.), p. 445. Spurious medicine, GAMMY stuff, bad coin, GAMMY LOWER, p. 446.

1889. C. T. CLARKSON and J. HALL RICHARDSON, *Police*, p. 321. Bad money (coin). . . . GAMMY LOWER.

3. (theatrical).—Old; ugly.

4. (common). — Same as GAME, sense 3: *e.g.*, a GAMMY arm = an arm in dock. GAMMY-eyed = blind; sore-eyed; or afflicted with ecchymosis in the region of the eyes. GAMMY-leg = a lame leg. Also (*subs.*) a term of derision for the halt and the maimed.

GAMP, *subs.* (common). — 1. A monthly nurse; a FINGERSMITH (*q.v.*). [After Mrs. Sarah Gamp, a character in *Martin Chuzzlewit* (1843).] Also applied to a fussy and gossiping busybody.

1864. *Sun*, 28 Dec. A regular GAMP . . . a fat old dowdy of a monthly nurse.

1868. BREWER, *Phr. and Fab.* (quoted from *Daily Telegraph*). Mr. Gathorne Hardy is to look after the GAMPS and Harrises of the Strand.

2. (common).—An umbrella; specifically, one large and loosely-tied; a LETTUCE (*q.v.*). [The original Sarah always carried one of this said pattern.] Sometimes a SARAH GAMP. For synonyms, *see* RAIN-NAPPER.

1870. *Lond. Figaro*, 15 June. Though —shattered, baggy, shivered GAMP!

1883. G. R. SIMS, *Life Boat*. He donned his goloshes and shouldered his GAMP.

1890. *Daily Chron.*, 5 Mar. Sainte-Beuve insisted that though he was prepared to stand fire he was under no obligation to catch cold, and with his GAMP over his head he exchanged four shots with his adversary.

1892 *Ally Sloper*, 2 Apr., p. 106, c. 3. I never had a brand new tile, a glossy silk or swagger brown, But I left home without a GAMP, And rain or hail or snow came down

3. (journalists').—*The Standard*.

Adj. (common). — Bulging. Also GAMPISH.

1864. *Derby Day*, p. 18. I wasn't joking, there is an air of long-suffering about you, as if you had been mortifying the flesh by carrying a GAMPISH UMBRELLA up Piccadilly, and back again.

1881. *Mac. Mag.*, Nov., p. 62. Grasping his GAMP umbrella at the middle.

GAMUT, *subs.* (artists'). — Tone; general scheme; SWIM (*q.v.*). Thus IN THE GAMUT = a picture, a detail, or a shade of colour, in tone with its environment.

GAN (also GANE), *subs.* (old).—The mouth. [A.S., *ganian* = to yawn.] Occasionally = throat, lip. For synonyms, *see* POTATO-TRAP.

1512-13. DOUGLAS, *Virgil*, 250, 29. To behald his ouglie ene twane, His teribill vissage, and his grislie GANE.

1567. HARMAN, *Caveat* (1814), p. 64. GAN, a mouth.

1610. ROWLAND, *Martin Mark-all*, p. 38. (H. Club's Rept., 1874). GAN, a mouth. *Ibid.* A gere peck in thy GAN.

1656. BROOME, *A Jovial Crew*, Act ii. This bowse is better than rombowse, it sets the GAN a giggling.

1671. R. HEAD, *English Rogue*, Pt. I., ch. v., p. 49. (1874.) GAN, a lip.

1690. B. E., *Cant. Crew.* GANNS, the lips.

1785. GROSE, *Vulg. Tongue*, s.v.

1881. *New York Slang Dict.*, s.v.

GANDER, *subs.* (colloquial). — A married man; in America one not living with his wife; a GRASS-WIDOWER (*q.v.*).

Verb. (old).—To ramble; to waddle (as a goose). Also, to go in quest of women; TO GROUSE (*q.v.*).

1859. H. KINGSLEY, *Geoff. Hamblyn*, ch. x. Nell might come GANDERING back in one of her tantrums.

1861. H. KINGSLEY, *Ravenshoe*, ch. xlvii. She GANDERED upstairs to the dressing-room again.

GONE GANDER. — *See* GONE COON.

TO SEE HOW THE GANDER HOPS, *verb. phr.* (American.)— To watch events. A variant of To see how the cat jumps.

1847. PORTER, *Big Bear*, p. 96. SEEIN' HOW THE GANDER HOPPED I jumped up and hollered, Git out, Tromp, you old raskel!

WHAT'S SAUCE FOR THE GOOSE IS SAUCE FOR THE GANDER, *phr.* (common).—A plea for consistency.

GANDER-MONTH, *subs.* (common). —The month after confinement; when a certain license (or so it was held) is excusable in the male. Also GANDER-MOON, the husband at such a period being called a GANDER-MOONER. *Cf.*, BUCK - HUTCH and GOOSE-MONTH.

1617. MIDDLETON, *A Faire Quarrell*, iv., 4. Wondering GANDER-MOONERS.

1653. BROME, *English Moor* in *Five New Playes.* I'le keep her at the least this GANDER-MONTH, while my fair wife lies-in.

1785. GROSE, *Vulg. Tongue*, s.v.

1811. *Lexicon Balatronicum*, s.v.

GANDER-PARTY, *subs.* (common).— A gathering of men; a STAG-PARTY (*q.v.*); also BULL-DANCE, GANDER-GANG, etc. *Cf.*, HEN-PARTY = an assembly of women.

GANDER-PULLING. *See* GOOSE-RIDING.

GANDER'S WOOL, *subs. phr.* (common.)—Feathers.

GANG, *subs.* (old: now recognised). —A troop; a company.

1639-61. *Rump*, i., 228. 'The Scotch War.' With his gay GANG of Blue-caps all. *Ibid* ii., 104, 'The GANG; or, the Nine Worthies, etc.'

1690. B. E., *Cant. Crew*, s.v. GANG, an ill knot or crew of thieves, pickpockets or miscreants; also a society of porters under a regulation.

1704. CIBBER, *Careless Husband*, i., 1. *Sir C.* Who was that other? *More.* One of Lord Foppington's gang.

1754. FIELDING, *Jonathan Wild*, bk. i., c. 14. What then have I to do in the pursuit of greatness, but to employ a GANG, and to make the use of this GANG centre in myself? *Idem.* bk. iii., c. 14. But in an illegal society or GANG, as this of ours, it is otherwise.

1785. GROSE, *Vulg. Tongue*, s.v.

1859. MATSELL, *Vocabulum.* GANG, company, squad, mob.

GANGER, *subs.* (old: now recognised). —An overseer or foreman of a gang of workmen; one who superintends. For synonyms, *see* GOVERNOR.

1851-61. MAYHEW, *Lond. Lab.*, ii., 487. The GANGER, or head of the working gang, who receives his orders from the inspector, and directs the men accordingly.

1884. *Cornhill Mag.*, June, p. 614, The mother and boy do the work, while the father constitutes himself contractor for and GANGER over their labour.

GANYMEDE, *subs.* (old). — 1. A sodomist. For synonyms, *see* USHER.

1598. FLORIO, *Worlde of Wordes*, *Catamito*, a GANIMED, an ingle, a boie hired to sinne against nature. [And in COTGRAVE (1611) under GANYMEDES; Any boy that's loved for carnal abuse, an Ingle.]

1598. MARSTON, *Satyres*, ii. But Ho! What GANIMEDE is it doth grace The gallant's heels.

2. (popular).—A pot-boy (*i.e.*, a cup-bearer). The masculine of HEBE (*q.v.*).

1659. FLORIO-TORRIANO, *Vocabolario. Mescitore*, a skinker or filler of wine; also a mingler, a GANIMEDE.

1841. *Punch* I., p. 101, c. 1. Lo! GANYMEDE appears with a foaming tankard of ale.

GAOL-BIRD, *subs.* (old: now recognised).—A person who has been often in gaol; an incorrigible rogue. Fr., *un chevronné.* For synonyms, *see* WRONG 'UN.

1680. *Hist. of Edward II.*, p. 146. It is the piety and the true valour of an army, which gives them heart and victory; which how it can be expected out of ruffians and GAOL-BIRDS, I leave to your consideration.

1701. DEFOE, *True Born Englishman*, part II. In print my panegyrics fill the street, And hired GAOL-BIRDS, their huzzas repeat.

1762. SMOLLETT, *L. Greaves*, vol. II., ch. ix. He is become a blackguard GAOL-BIRD.

1857. C. READE, *Never Too Late* ch. xi. The GAOL-BIRDS who piped this tune were without a single exception the desperate cases of this moral hospital; they were old offenders.

1882. *Pall Mall Gaz.*, 5 Oct. Liberating the GAOL-BIRDS in Alexandria.

GAOLER'S COACH, *subs. phr.* (old). —A hurdle to the place of execution.

1785. GROSE. *Vulg. Tongue*, s.v.

1811. *Lexicon Balatronicum*, s.v.

GAP, *subs.* (venery).—The female *pudendum*: also SPORTSMAN'S GAP and WATER-GAP (*q.v.*). For synonyms, *see* MONOSYLLABLE.

d. 1746. ROBERTSON of Struan, *Poems*, p. 84. O gracious Hymen! Cure this dire Mishap, Sew up this mighty rent, or fill the GAP.

TO BLOW THE GAP, *verb. phr.* (old).—The same as TO BLOW THE GAFF (*q.v.*).

1821. EGAN, *Real Life*, etc., i., 557 He should like to smack the bit without BLOWING THE GAP.

GAPER, *subs.* (venery). — The female *pudendum.* Also, GAPER (and GAPE) OVER THE GARTER. For synonyms, *see* MONOSYLLABLE.

GAPES, *subs.* (colloquial).—A fit of yawning; also the open mouth of astonishment.

1818. AUSTEN, *Persuasion.* Another hour of music was to give delight or the GAPES.

1838. HALIBURTON, *Clockmaker* (ed. 1862), p. 373. But what gave me the GAPES was the scenes (at the theatre).

GAPESEED, *subs.* (common). — 1. A cause of astonishment; anything provoking the ignorant to stare with open mouth. Also TO SEEK A GAPE'S NEST.

1598. FLORIO, *Worlde of Wordes. Ansanare* . . . to go idly loytring vp and downe as we say, to go seeking for a halfepenie worth of GAPING SEEDE.

1600. NASHE, *Summer's Last Will*, in wks. (Grosart), vi., 144. That if a fellow licensed to beg, Should all his life time go from faire to faire, And buy GAPESEEDE, having no businesse there.

1690. B. E., *Cant. Crew.* GAPESEED, whatever the gazing crowd idly stares and gapes after; as Puppet-shows, Rope-dancers, Monsters and Mountebanks, anything to feed the eye.

1694. *Poor Robin.* 'Tis plainly clear, They for their GAPES-SEED do pay dear.

1856. *N. and Q.*, 2 S 1., 362. Plenty of persons were sowing GAPESEED.

1870. B. F. CLARK, *Mirthfulness* p. 24. Do you wish to buy some GAPESEED?

1884. *Daily News*, 8 Oct. Title (at head of sporting column).

2. (common). — An open-mouthed loiterer.

1885. *Sportsman*, June 23, p. 2, c. 4. The yearlings bred by Messrs. Graham were offered to a rather select audience of buyers, though the ring was surrounded by a fairly strong crowd of GAPESEEDS.

GAPPED, *ppl. adj.* (old).—Worsted; FLOORED (*q.v.* for synonyms).

1753. RICHARDSON, *Sir Chas. Grandison.* I will never meet at hard-edge with her; if I did . . . I should be confoundedly GAPPED.

GAP-STOPPER, *subs.* (old).—1. A whoremaster. For synonyms, *see* MOLROWER.

2. (venery). — The *penis.* [GAP = female *pudendum*]. For synonyms, *see* CREAMSTICK and PRICK.

GAR. *See* BY GAR!

GARBLE, TO GARBLE THE COINAGE, *verb. phr.* (old).—*See* quot. [GARBLE = to pick and choose.]

1875. JEVONS, *Money*, etc., p. 81. A practice amongst money-lenders of picking out the newest coins of full weight for export or re-melting, and passing the light ones into circulation.

GARDEN, *subs.* (various). — 1. (greengrocers', fruiterers', etc.) = Covent Garden Market; 2. (theatrical) = Covent Garden Theatre; 3. (diamond merchants') = Hatton Garden. *Cf.*, HOUSE, LANE, etc.

[THE GARDEN (= Covent Garden) was frequently used for the whole neighbourhood, which was notorious as a place of strumpets and stews. Thus, GARDEN-HOUSE = a brothel; GARDEN-GODDESS = a woman of pleasure; GARDEN-GOUT = the pox or clap; GARDEN-WHORE = a low prostitute, etc.]

1733. BAILEY, *Erasmus.* When young men by whoring, as it commonly falls out, get the pox, which, by the way of extenuation, they call the Common GARDEN-GOUT.

1782. GEO. PARKER, *Humorous Sketches*, p. 90 No more the GARDEN female orgies view.

1851-61. W. MAYHEW, *Lond. Lab. and Lond. Poor*, Vol. I., p. 85. Not only is the GARDEN itself all bustle and activity, but the buyers and sellers stream to and from it in all directions, filling every street in the vicinity.

1884. JAS. PAYN, in *Cornhill Mag.*, Mar., p. 257. She [Miss O'Neill] talked of the GARDEN and 'the Lane,' and was very fond of recitation.

1890. *Tit-Bits*, 29 Mar., p. 389, c. 1. Let me describe the GARDEN. A long, straight street, stretching almost due north and south, from Holborn Circus to Clerkenwell Road. *Ibid.* c. 2. The cut stones are chiefly sold to the large dealers in the GARDEN.

2. (venery).—The female *pudendum.* [The simile is common to all nations, ancient and modern. Shakspeare, in Sonnet 16, seems to play upon this double meaning; *e.g.*, Now stand you on the top of happy hours; And many maiden-GARDENS, yet unset, With virtuous wish would bear you living flowers.] Also GARDEN OF EDEN. For synonyms, *see* MONOSYLLABLE.

TO PUT ONE IN THE GARDEN, *verb. phr.* (thieves').—To defraud a confederate; to keep back part of the REGULARS (*q.v.*), or SWAG (*q.v.*).

GARDENER, *subs.* (common).—1. An awkward coachman. [In allusion to the gardener who on occasion drives the carriage.] *Cf.*, TEA-KETTLE COACHMAN.

1859. SALA, *Twice Round the Clock.* Noon: Par. I. He can drive neither to the right nor to the left, nor backwards nor forwards. . . . A sarcastic saloon omnibus driver behind jeeringly bids him keep moving, accompanying the behest by the aggressive taunt of GARD'NER.

2. (venery). — The *penis.* GARDEN (*q.v.*) = female *pudendum.* Also GARDEN-ENGINE. For synonyms, *see* CREAMSTICK and PRICK.

GARDEN-GATE, *subs. phr.* (rhyming).—1. A magistrate. For synonyms, *see* BEAK.

2. (venery).—The *labia minora.* [GARDEN-HEDGE = the pubic hair.]

GARDEN-LATIN, *subs.* (colloquial).— Barbarous or sham Latin. Also APOTHECARIES', BOG, DOG, and KITCHEN-LATIN.

GARDEN-RAKE, *subs. phr.* (common). — A tooth-comb. Also SCRATCHING-RAKE or RAKE.

GARDY-LOO, *subs.* (old Scots).— A warning cry; 'take care!' [Fr. *gardez'* (*vous de*) *l'eau!* Used before emptying slops out of window into the street. Hence the act of emptying slops itself, as in quotation dated 1818.]

1771. SMOLLET, *Humphry Clinker*, (British Novelists), xxxi., p. 57. At ten o'clock the whole cargo is flung out of a back windore that looks into some street or lane, and the maid calls GARDY-LOO to the passengers, which signifies 'Lord have mercy on you!'

1818. SCOTT, *Heart of Midlothian*, ch. xxvii. She had made the GARDY-LOO out of the wrong window.

GARGLE, *subs.* (formerly medical students', now common). — A drink; also generic. *Cf.*, LOTION, and for synonyms, *see* GO.

1889. *Sporting Times*, 3 Aug., p. 3, c. 1. We're just going to have a GARGLE —will you join us?

Verb. (common).—To drink; to 'liquor up.' For synonyms, *see* DRINKS and LUSH.

1889. *Sporting Times*, 3 Aug., p. 5. c. 5. We GARGLED . . .

1891. *Morning Advertiser*, 2 Mar. It's my birthday; let's GARGLE.

GARGLE-FACTORY, *subs.* (common). —A public house. For synonyms, *see* LUSH CRIB.

GARN, *intj.* (vulgar).—A corruption of Go on! Get away with you!

1888. RUNCIMAN, *The Chequers*, p. 80. GARN, you farthin' face! She your neck.

1892. *Ally Sloper*, 19 Mar., p. 90, c. 3. GAR'N, you men ain't got no sense.

1892. *National Observer*, 6 Feb. p. 307, c. 2. And so simple is the dictum, so redolent of the unlettered Arry that we long to add GARN, oo're you gettin' at?

GARNISH, subs. (old).—1. A fee or FOOTING (q.v.); specifically one exacted by gaolers and old prisoners from a newcomer. The practice was forbidden by 4 Geo. IV., c. 43, sec. 12. Also GARNISH-MONEY.

1592. GREENE, Quip, in works, xi., 256. Let a poore man be arrested into one of the counters [prisons] . . . he shall be almost at an angel's charge, what with GARNISH [etc.].

1606. T. DEKKER, Seven Deadly Sinnes, p. 28 (Arber's ed.). So that the Counters are cheated of Prisoners, to the great dammage of those that shoulde have their morning's draught out of the GARNISH.

1632. JONSON, Magnetic Lady, v. 6. You are content with the ten thousand pounds Defalking the four hundred GARNISH-MONEY?

1704. STEELE, Lying Lover, Act iv., Sc. iv. But there is always some little trifle given to prisoners, they call GARNISH.

1752. FIELDING, Amelia, Bk. I., ch. iii. Mr. Booth . . . was no sooner arrived in the prison, than a number of persons gathered round him, all demanding GARNISH.

1759. GOLDSMITH, The Bee, No. 5, p. 385 (Globe ed.). There are numberless faulty expenses among the workmen—clubs, GARNISHES, freedoms, and such like impositions.

1815. SCOTT, Guy Mannering, ch. xliv. [Jailor log.] Thirty shillings a week for lodgings, and a guinea for GARNISH.

2. (thieves').—Fetters; handcuffs. For synonyms, see DARBIES.

Verb. (thieves').—To fit with fetters; to handcuff.

GARRET, subs. (common).—1. The head; COCKLOFT (q.v.); or UPPER STOREY (q.v.). For synonyms, see CRUMPET.

1625. BACON, Apothgm, No. 17. My Lord St. Albans said that wise Nature did never put her precious jewels into a GARRET four stories high, and therefore that exceeding tall men had ever very empty heads.

1811. Lexicon Balatronicum., s.v.

1837. BARHAM, Ingold. Leg. What's called the claret Flew over the GARRET.

2. (old).—The fob-pocket.

TO HAVE ONE'S GARRET UNFURNISHED, verb. phr. (common). To be crazy, stupid, lumpish. For synonyms, see APARTMENTS and BALMY.

GARRETEER, subs. (thieves'). A thief whose speciality is to rob houses by entering skylights or garret-windows. Also DANCER and DANCING-MASTER. For synonyms, see THIEVES.

2. (journalists').—An impecunious author; a literary hack.

1849-61. MACAULAY, Hist. of Eng., ch. xxv. GARRETEERS, who were never weary of calling the cousin of the Earls of Manchester and Sandwich an upstart.

1886. SHELLEY (quoted in Dowden's Life), i., 47. Show them that we are no Grub-street GARRETEERS.

1892. National Observer, 18 Mar., p. 453. Has proclaimed urbi et orbi that governments have no business to manufacture specious sentiment by greasing the palms of ignorant and greedy GARRETEERS.

GARRET-MASTER, subs. (trade).—A cabinet-maker who works on his own account, selling his manufacture to the dealers direct.

1851-61. MAYHEW, Lond. Lab., ii., p. 376. These trading operatives are known by different names in different trades. In the shoe trade, for instance, they are called 'chamber-masters,' in the cabinet trade GARRET-MASTERS, and in the cooper's trade the name for them is 'small trading-masters.'

GARRISON-HACK, subs. (common).—1. A woman given to indiscriminate flirtation with officers at a garrison.

1889. Daily Telegraph, 14 Feb. Lord Normantower, Philip's dearest friend, to whom she, when a GARRISON-HACK, had been engaged, and whom she had thrown over simply because he was poor and prospectless.

1890. Athenæum, 8 Feb., p. 176, c. 1. The heroine is a GARRISON-HACK, but the hero is an Australian.

2. (common).—A prostitute; a soldier's trull. For synonyms, see BARRACK HACK and TART.

GARROTTE, subs. (common).—A form of strangulation (see verb). [From the Spanish la garrota = a method of capital punishment, which consists in strangulation by means of an iron collar.]

Verb. (common). 1. A method of robbery with violence, much practised some years ago. The victims were generally old or feeble men and women. Three hands were engaged: the FRONT-STALL who looked out in that quarter, the BACK-STALL at the rear, and the UGLY or NASTY-MAN who did the work by passing his arm round his subject's neck from behind, and so throttling him to insensibility.

1869. GREENWOOD, Seven Curses of Lond. Committed for trial for GARROTTING and nearly murdering a gentleman.

1873. TROLLOPE, Phineas Redux, ch. xlvi. In those days there had been much GARROTTING in the streets.

2. (cards).—To cheat by concealing certain cards at the back of the neck.

GARROTTER, subs. (common).—A practitioner of GARROTTING (under verb, sense 1.)

1869. GREENWOOD, Seven Curses of London, p. 201. The delectable epistle was written by GARROTTER Bill to his brother.

GARROTTING. 1. See GARROTTE (verb, sense 1).

2. (gamblers').—Hiding a part of one's hand at the back of the neck for purposes of cheating.

GARTER, subs. (nautical).—1. in pl. the irons, or bilboes. For synonyms, see DARBIES.

TO GET OVER THE GARTER, verb. phr. (venery).—To take liberties with a woman.

TO FLY or PRICK THE GARTER. See PRICK THE GARTER.

GARVIES, subs. (Scots').—1. Sprats. Sometimes GARVIE-HERRING.

1845. P. ALLOA, Statis. Acc., viii., 597. They are often very successful in taking the smaller fish, such as herrings, GARVIES or sprats, sparlings or smelts.

2. (military).—The Ninety-fourth Foot. [From the small stature of the earlier recruits.]

1869. Notes and Queries, 4 S. iii., p. 349. GARVIE. The soubriquet points to the low average height of the recruits in the Fifeshire regiments, which, however, may not now be the case, since recruiting has become less local.

GAS, subs. (common). — Empty talk; bounce; bombast.

1847. PORTER, Quarter Race, etc., p. 120. The boys said that was all GAS to scare them off.

1867. Chambers' Jour., 29 June. I've piped off Sabbath GAS in my time I don't deny, but under the woods we mostly tell the truth.

1868. Chambers' Jour., 15 Feb., p. 110. I don't, an' never could splice ends with them as blow off GAS about gold-digging—saying it's plunder easy come an' easy gone, seeking the root of evil, an' other granny talk which hasn't no meaning.

a. 1871. EMERSON (quoted in De Vere's Amer.). 'Tis odd that our people should have not water on the brain, but a little GAS there.

1889. Globe, 31 Oct., p. 4, c. 4. It went on to state that the petitioner's talk about a divorce was all GAS, and made a further appointment.

Verb. (common). — 1. To talk idly; to brag; to bounce; to talk for talking's sake. Fr., faire son cheval de corbillard (in American 'to be on the tall grass.') See LONG BOW.

1872. Lond. Figaro, 14 Dec. There is no good to be got out of GASSING about rallying around standards, uniting as one man to resist, etc.

1875. 'American English' in Chambers' Jour., 25 Sept., p. 610. To GAS is to talk only for the purpose of prolonging a debate.

1885. Society, 7 Feb., p. 7. Agitators and place-seekers may GAS as much as they please, but they cannot make black appear white.

2. (common).—To impose on by 'GAS'; TO PILL (q.v.); TO SPLASH (q.v.). For synonyms, see GAMMON.

TO TAKE THE GAS OUT OF ONE, verb. phr. (common).—To take the conceit out of; to take down a peg.

TO TURN ON THE GAS, verb. phr. (common).—To begin bouncing; also to GAS (q.v.).

TO TURN OFF THE GAS, verb. phr. (common).—To cease, or cause to cease, from bouncing, vapouring, or GAS (q.v.).

TO GAS ROUND, verb. phr. (common).—To seek information on the sly; also to GAS (q.v.).

GAS-BAG, subs. (common). — A man of words or GAS (q.v.); a gasconader. Also GASOMETER. For synonyms, see MOUTH ALMIGHTY.

1889. Referee, 6 Jan. That great GAS-BAG of modern days.

GASH, subs. (American).—1. The mouth. For synonyms, see POTATO-TRAP.

1878. H. B. STOWE, Poganuc People, ch. xiv., p. 122. Ef Zeph Higgins would jest shet up his GASH in town-meetin', that air school-house could be moved fast enough.

2. (venery). — The female pudendum. For synonyms, see MONOSYLLABLE.

GASHLY, adj. (common).—A vulgarism for GHASTLY.

GASKINS, subs. (old).—Wide hose; wide breeches. [From GALLI-GASKINS. Johnson says, 'an old ludicrous word.']

GASP, subs. (common). — A dram of spirits. For synonyms, see GO.

Verb. (common).—To drink a dram, e.g., 'Will you GASP?' = Will you take something neat.

GASPIPE, subs. (nautical).—1. An iron steamer, whose length is nine or ten times her beam. [At one time a ship's length but rarely exceeded four and a half to five times the beam.]

2. (printers').—Bad rollers.

3. (common).—A rifle; specifically the Snider.

1883. Daily Telegraph, 9 July, p. 5, col. 7. The old Snider — the despair-breeding GAS-PIPE of our Volunteers — continues to be used in many of the competitions.

GASPIPE-CRAWLER, subs. phr. (common).—A thin man. Cf., LAMP-POST.

GASSER, subs. (common). — A braggart. For synonyms, see MOUTH ALMIGHTY.

GASSY (or GASEOUS), adj (common).—1. Likely to take umbrage or to flare-up.

1863. North American Review, cxiii., p. 220. GASSY politicians in Congress.

2. (colloquial).—Full of empty talk or GAS (q.v.).

1872. WHITNEY, Life and Growth of Lang., p. 17. As when we call an empty and sophistical but ready talker GASSY.

GASTER, subs. (nonce-word).—A fine and curious eater (Thackeray). In Rabelais = the belly and the needs thereof: a coinage adopted by Urquhart.

GAT, subs. (schoolboys').—A quantity; e.g., a GAT of grub = plenty to eat. Also GATS.

1803. Every-day Life in our Public Schools. They are called up in GATS of three at a time.

GATE, subs. (colloquial).—1. The attendance at a race or athletic meeting, held in enclosed grounds; the number of persons who pass the gate.

1888. Sportsman, 20 Dec. The Birmingham man, on account of the large GATE that would be secured, wanted the affair to be brought off in that town, whereas Regan favoured Wolverhampton.

2. Money paid for admission to athletic sports, race course, etc.; the same as GATE-MONEY (q.v.).

1891. Telegraph, 21 Mar. The leading clubs are now commercial corporations, dependent for revenue on the GATES at the matches.

3. in. pl. (University).—The being forbidden to pass outside the gate of a college. See verb, sense 1.

18(?). BRADLEY, Tales of College Life, p. 19. That's the ticket; that will just land me in time for GATES.

1881. LANG, xxxii. Ballades, 'Of Midsummer Term.' When freshmen are careless of GATES.

Verb. (University). — To confine wholly or during certain hours within the college gate for some infraction of discipline.

1835. The Snobiad (WHIBLEY, Cap and Gown, p. 141). Two proctors kindly holding either arm Staunch the dark blood and GATE him for the term.

1853. BRADLEY, Verd. Green, I., ch. xii. He won't hurt you much, Gig-lamps! GATE and chapel you!

1861. HUGHES, Tom Brown at Oxford, ch. xii. Now you'll both be GATED probably, and the whole crew will be thrown out of gear.

1865. Cornhill Mag., p. 227. He is requested to confine himself to college after a specified hour, which is familiarly termed being GATED.

1870. Morning Advertiser, 23 May. The two least culpable of the party have been GATED.

THE GATE, subs. phr. (various).—Among fishmongers, Billingsgate; among thieves, Newgate. Cf., LANE, ROW, GARDEN, etc.

1877. Five Years' Penal Servitude, ch. i., p. 5. The 'steel,' a slang name of the large metropolitan prisons, as the GATE is for Newgate.

TO BREAK GATES, verb. phr. (University).—To stay out of college after hours.

TO BE AT GATES, verb. phr. (Winchester College).—To assemble in Seventh Chamber passage, preparatory to going Hills or Cathedral.

1870. MANSFIELD, School Life, p. 149. Soon after morning chapel on a holiday or a remedy all the boys assembled at GATES.

ON THE GATE, adv. phr. (thieves').—On remand.

GATE-BILL, *subs.* (University).—The record of an undergraduate's failure to be within the precincts of his college at, or before, a specified time at night.

1803. *Gradus ad Cant.*, p. 128. To avoid GATE-BILLS he will be out at night as late as he pleases . . . climb over the college wall, and fee his gyp well.

GATE-MONEY, *subs.* (colloquial).—The charge for admission to a race-meeting. *See* GATE, *subs.*, sense I.

1885. *Daily News*, 25 May, p. 3, c. 2. The truth of the matter is, that so far as sport goes, open meetings like those at Bath and Salisbury cannot stand up against GATE-MONEY meetings such as Manchester.

1888. *Sporting Life*, 10 Dec. The comfort that is brought home at our great GATE-MONEY meetings gatherings to every visitor.

GATE-OF-HORN, *subs. phr.* (venery). The female *pudendum*. *Cf.*, HORN, and for synonyms, *see* MONOSYLLABLE.

GATE-OF-LIFE, *subs.* (venery).—The female *pudendum*. Also GATE-OF-HORN. For synonyms, *see* MONOSYLLABLE.

GATER, *subs.* (Winchester College), —A plunge head foremost into a POT (*q.v.*).

GATE-RACE (or **-MEETING**), *subs.* (sporting). Formerly, a contest not got up for sport but entrance money; now a race or athletic meeting to which admission is by payment.

1881. *Daily News*, 14 July. Few of these athletics care to compete at GATE-MEETINGS.

GATH, *subs.* (colloquial).—A city or district in PHILISTIA (*q.v.*); often used, like ASKELON (*q.v.*) for PHILISTIA itself. Hence, TO BE MIGHTY IN GATH = to be a PHILISTINE (*q.v.*) of the first magnitude; TO PREVAIL AGAINST GATH = to smite the Philistines hip and thigh, as becomes a valiant companion of the *Davidsbund;* and so forth.

TELL IT NOT IN GATH, *verb. phr.* (colloquial).—An interjection of derision, signifying that the person exclaimed against has done something the knowledge of which would bring on him the wrath, or the amazement, of his friends.

GATHER. TO GATHER UP, *verb. phr.* (American).—To lead away.

1847. *Chronicles of Pineville*, p. 182. 'GATHER him UP, boys,' said the judge, 'the sentence of the law must be executed.'

TO GATHER THE TAXES, *verb. phr.* (tailor's).—To go from workshop to workshop seeking employment. Hence, TAX-GATHERER = a man out of work and looking for a job. *Cf.*, INSPECTOR OF PUBLIC BUILDINGS.

OUT OF GATHERS, *adv. phr.* (colloquial).—In distress. *Cf.*, OUT AT ELBOWS.

GATHERINGS. *See* GAGS.

GATTER, *subs.* (common).—Beer; also liquor generally. SHANT OF GATTER = a pot of beer. Fr., *la moussante*. For synonyms, *see* DRINKS.

1818. MAGINN, *Vidocq Versified*. Lots of GATTER, says she, is flowing. Lend me a lift in the family way.

1841. *Punch*, I., p. 243, GATTER is but threepence a pot, and that's the price of a reasonable 'pike ticket.

1851-61. H. MAYHEW, *Lond. Lab. and Lond. Poor*, Vol. i., p. 232. They have a 'shant of GATTER' (pot of beer) at the nearest 'boozing-ken' (alehouse).

GAUDEAMUS, *subs.* (colloquial).—A feast; a drinking bout; any sort of merry-making. [German students', but now general and popular.] From the first word of the mediæval (students') ditty. For synonyms, *see* JAMBOREE.

GAUDY (or **GAUDY-DAY**), *subs.* (common).—A feast or entertainment: specifically the annual dinner of the fellows of a college in memory of founders or benefactors; or a festival of the Inns of Court. (Lat. *gaudere* = to rejoice.)

1724. E. COLES, *Eng. Dict.* GAUDY DAYS, college or Inns of Court festivals.

1754. B. MARTIN, *Eng Dict.*, 2nd ed. GAUDIES, double commons, such as they have on GAUDY or grand DAYS in colleges.

1760. FOOTE, *Minor*, Act i. Dine at twelve, and regale, upon a GAUDY DAY, with buns and beer at Islington.

1803. *Gradus ad Cantab.*, p. 122. Cut lectures . . . give GAUDIES and spreads.

1820. LAMB, *Elia* (*Oxford in the Vacation*). Methought I a little grudged at the coalition of the *better Jude* with Simon—clubbing (as it were) their sanctities together, to make up one poor GAUDY-DAY between them.

1822. SCOTT, *Fortunes of Nigel*, ch. xxiii. We had a carouse to your honour . . . we fought, too, to finish off the GAUDY.

1878. BESANT AND RICE, *By Celia's Arbour*, ch. xxxiii. Champagne . . . goes equally well with a simple luncheon of cold chicken, and with the most elaborate GAUDY.

Adj. (colloquial). — Good; frolicsome; festive. *Cf.*, Shakspeare's 'Let's have one other GAUDY night.'—*Ant. and Cleo.*, iii, 13.

1884. HAWLEY SMART. *From Post to Finish*, p. 176. 'Yes,' answered the trainer, slowly, 'he's right enough; but a Leger's a Leger, and I don't think they are likely to give him a very GAUDY chance.'

NEAT BUT NOT GAUDY, AS THE DEVIL SAID WHEN HE PAINTED HIS BOTTOM PINK, AND TIED UP HIS TAIL WITH PEA-GREEN, *phr.* (common).—A locution used to ancient ladies dressed in flaming colours.

GAUGE. *See* GAGE.

TO GET THE GAUGE OF. *verb. phr.* (colloquial). — To divine an intention; to read a character; to SIZE, (or RECKON) UP (*q.v.*). Hence, That's about the GAUGE of it = That's a fair description.

GAULEY. *See* BY GOLLY.

GAWF, *subs.* (costers'). — A red-skinned apple.

1851-61. MAYHEW, *Lond. Lab.*, i., 63. A cheap red-skinned fruit, known to costers as GAWFS, is rubbed hard, to look bright and feel soft, and is mixed with apples of a superior description. GAWFS are sweet and sour at once, I was told, and fit for nothing but mixing.

GAWK, *subs.* (colloquial).—A simpleton, especially an awkward one, whether male or female. For synonyms, *see* BUFFLE and CABBAGE-HEAD. [Scots GOWK = a cuckoo; a fool; whence, TO GOWK = to play the fool. As in the 'Derision of Wanton Women' (*Bannatyne, MS.*, 1567), 'To gar them ga in GUCKING' = to make them play the fool.]

1837. H. MARTINEAU, *Soc. in America*, i., 299. They proved such GAWKS that they were unable to learn.

1882. MCCABE, *New York*, p. 217. I wasn't half as awkward as some of the GAWKS about me.

1887. H. FREDERIC, *Seth's Brother's Wife*, ch. iv. Girls brought up to be awkward GAWKS, without a chance in life.

Verb. (colloquial).—To loiter round; to PLAY THE GOAT. [The same verb is used by JONSON (*Magnetic Lady*, iii., 4, 1632) in the sense of amazed, or bamboozled, *i.e.*, absolutely befooled: Nay, look how the man stands, as he were GOWKED!]

1888. F. R. STOCKTON, *Rudder Grange*, ch. xvi. That afternoon we GAWKED around, a-lookin' at all the outside shows, for Jone said he'd have to be pretty careful of his money now.

GAWKINESS, *subs.* (colloquial).—Awkwardness; silliness; GREENNESS (*q.v.*).

1873. MISS BROUGHTON, *Nancy*, ch. xxxvii. The crude GAWKINESS of the raw girl he has drifted into marrying.

GAWKING, *subs.* (colloquial).—Loitering and staring; GATHERING HAYSEED (*q.v.*).

GAWKY, *subs.* (colloquial). — An awkward booby; a fool. 'Now SQUIRE GAWKY' = a challenge to a clumsy lout. For synonyms, *see* BUFFLE and CABBAGE-HEAD.

1686-1758. RAMSAY, *Poems*, ii., 299. Or, gentle born ye be; but youths in love you're but a GAWKY.

1777. SHERIDAN, *School for Scandal*, Act ii., Sc. 2. *Crab.* Yes, and she is a curious being to pretend to be censorious—an awkward GAWKY, without any one good point under heaven.

1825. NEAL, *Bro. Jonathan*, ii., ch. 18. Great, long, slab-sided GAWKEYS from the country.

1878. C. H. WALL, tr. *Molière*, ii., 197. Our big GAWKY of a viscount.

Adj. (colloquial). — Lanky; awkward; stupid.

1759. TOWNLEY, *High Life Below Stairs* i., 1. Under the form of a GAWKY country boy I will be an eye-witness of my servants' behaviour.

1855. THACKERAY, *Newcomes*, ch. xlviii. Even for his cousin Samuel Newcome, a GAWKY youth with an eruptive countenance, Barnes had appropriate words of conversation.

GAWNEY (or **GONEY**), *subs.* (common).—A fool. For synonyms, *see* BUFFLE and CABBAGE-HEAD.

GAY, *adj.* (colloquial).—1. Dissipated; specifically, given to venery: As in the French, *avoir la cuisse gaie* = to be addicted to the use of men. Hence GAY WOMAN, or GIRL, or BIT = a strumpet; GAY HOUSE = a brothel; TO BE GAY = to be incontinent; GAY IN THE LEGS, IN THE GROIN, IN THE ARSE = SHORT-HEELED (*q.v.*); GAYING INSTRUMENT = the *penis* [*Lexicon Balatronicum*, 1811, s.v.]; GAY MAN = a wencher; GAY LADIE (old) = a mistress; GAYING IT = copulating.

1383. CHAUCER, *Canterbury Tales*, 3767. What eyeleth you? Some GAY girl, God it wot, Hath brough you thus upon the very trot.

1754. *Adventurer*, No. 124. The old gentleman, whose character I cannot better express than in the fashionable phrase which has been contrived to palliate false principles and dissolute manners, had been a GAY man, and was well acquainted with the town.

1854. LEECH, *Pictures of Life and Character*. How long have you been GAY?

1857. J. E. RITCHIE, *Night Side of London*, p. 40. Here in Catherine-street vice is a monster of a hideous mien. The GAY women, as they are termed, are worse off than American slaves.

1868. *Sunday Times*, 19 July. As soon as ever a woman has ostensibly lost her reputation, we, with a grim inappositeness, call her GAY.

2. (common).—In drink. For synonyms, *see* SCREWED.

ALL GAY (or ALL SO GAY). *adv. phr.* (common).—All right; first-rate; ALL SERENE (*q.v.*).

TO FEEL GAY. *verb. phr.* (colloquial).—Inclined for sport, venereal or other; TO FEEL NAUGHTY (*q.v.*).

GAY TYKE BOY, *subs. phr.* (old).—A dog fancier.

1848. DUNCOMBE, *Sinks of London*, s.v.

GAZEBO, *subs.* (old).—A summer-house commanding an extensive view. [Dog-Latin, GAZEBO = I will gaze.]

1785. GROSE, *Vulg. Tongue*, s.v.

1811. *Lexicon Balatronicum*, s.v.

GEACH, *subs.* (thieves').—A thief. For synonyms, *see* THIEVES.

1821. HAGGART, *Life*, p. 56. He was a tolerable GEACH.

Verb. (thieves').—To steal. For synonyms, *see* PRIG.

1821. HAGGART, *Life*, p. 73. A small dross scout . . . which I knew had been GEACHED.

GEAR, *subs.* (venery). — 1. The private parts, both male and female. ['Geere, *besognes; aussi les parties honteuses*' (ROBERT SHERWOOD'S *Dictionarie, English and French*, appended to COTGRAVE, 1660). '*Besongner* . . . also to do or leacher with' (COTGRAVE). Anglo-Saxon: *gearwe* (strong feminine plural) ornaments. SKEAT says original sense of gear was 'preparation.']

1598. FLORIO, *Worlde of Wordes*, *Mozza*, a wench, a lasse, a girle. Also a woman's GEERE or cunnie.

1620. PERCY, *Folio MSS.* 'Ffryar and Boye.' I sweare, by night nor day thy GEARE is not to borrow.

1659. TORRIANO, *Vocabulario*, s.v.

2. (obsolete). — Work, BUSINESS (*q.v.*). Thus: Here's goodly GEAR = Here's fine doings; Here's a pretty kettle of fish. As in *Romeo and Juliet* (ii., 2, 106).

GEE, *subs.* (colloquial).—*See* GEE-GEE.

Verb. (colloquial).—1. To go or turn to the off-side; used as a direction to horses. *Cf.*: It.: *gio* = Get on!

1480. *Dialogus Creaturum.* Et cum sic gloriaretur, et cogitaret cum quanta gloria duceretur ad illum virum super equum, dicendo, '*Gio! Gio!*' cepit pede percutere terram quasi pungeret equum calcaribus.

2. (colloquial). — To move faster: as a teemster to his horses, 'Gee up!'

1824. *Blackwood's Mag.*, Oct. Mr. Babb GE-HUPPED in vain, and strove to jerk the rein, Nobbs felt he had his option to work or play.

3. (colloquial).—To stop: as 'Gee whoa!'

TO GEE WITH, *verb. phr.* (colloquial).—To agree with; to fit; to be congenial; to go on all fours with; to do.

1690. B. E., *Dict. of the Cant. Crew*, GEARS, s.v. . . . It won't GEE, it won't hit or go.

1785. GROSE, *Vulg. Tongue*. GEE, it won't GEE, it won't hit or do, it does not suit or fit.

1850. SEAWORTHY, *Nag's Head*, ch. v., p. 35. It don't seem to GEE! said Isaac, as he was trying to adjust the stove.

1888. *Missouri Repub.*, 8 April. He and Mrs. Barnay did not GEE.

GEE-GEE (or **GEE**).—*subs.* (common).—1. A horse. *See* GEE, *verb.* in all senses. For synonyms, *see* PRAD.

1888. *Referee*, 15 April, 1/2. In nearly all other races they see most of the GEES do a canter on their way up the course.

1889. *Pall Mall Gaz.*, 14 April. He knows as much about GEE-GEE'S as a professional trainer.

1890. *Licensed Vict. Gaz.* 8 Feb. The GEES were all broken to the stable.

2. (colloquial). — The nickname among journalists (of the interviewer, type) of Mr. G(eorge) G(rossmith), better known, perhaps, as the Society Clown.

GEE-GEE DODGE, *subs. phr.* (trade).—Selling horseflesh for beef.

1884. GREENWOOD, *Veiled Mysteries*. The GEE-GEE DODGE . . . was seldom or ever practised . . . it was impossible . . . to bargain for a regular supply.

GEEKIE, *subs.* (Scots thieves').—A police-station.

GEELOOT. See GALOOT.

GEESE, ALL HIS GEESE ARE SWANS, *phr.* (colloquial).—He habitually exaggerates, or EMBROIDERS (*q.v.*); or, He is always wrong in his estimates of persons and things.

THE OLD WOMAN'S PICKING HER GEESE (proverbial).—Said of a snowstorm. [The other leg of the couplet (schoolboys') runs : 'And selling the feathers a penny a piece.']

LIKE GEESE ON A COMMON (colloquial).—Wandering in a body, aggressive and at large : *e.g.*, as FADDISTS (*q.v.*) in pursuit of a FAD; or members of Parliament in recess, when both sides go about to say the thing which is in them.

GEEWHILIKENS! *intj.* (Western American).—An exclamation of surprise; also JEEWHILIKENS.

1888. *Detroit Free Press*. It is on time? No? Three hours late? GEEWHILIKENS!

GEEZER, *subs.* (popular). — An appellation, sometimes, but not necessarily, of derision and contempt; applied to both sexes, but generally to women. Usually, OLD GEEZER. For synonyms, *see* WITCH.

1885. *Truth about the Stage*, p. 16. If we wake up the old GEEZERS we shall get notice to quit without compensation

1886. *Broadside Ballad*. 'Her Mother's Got the Hump.' This frizzle-headed old GEEZER had a chin on her as rough—well, as rough as her family, and they're rough 'uns.

1890. A. CHEVALIER, 'Knocked 'Em in the Old Kent Road.' Nice old GEEZER with a nasty cough.

1892. ANSTEY, *Voces Populi*, p. 82. Our old GEESER's perdoocin' the custimary amount o' sensation.

GELDING, *subs.* (old).—A eunuch.

1380. WYCLIFFE, *Trans. of the Bible*, Acts viii. 39. . . . the spirit of the Lord ravysched Filip, and the GELDYNGE say him no more.

1659. TORRIANO, *Vocabolario*, s.v.

1785. GROSE, *Vulg. Tongue*, s.v.

1811. *Lexicon Balatronicum*, s.v.

TO ENTER FOR THE GELDINGS' STAKES, *verb. phr.* (old).—To castrate a man; also used to describe a eunuch.

GELT, *subs.* (old).—Money; GILT (*q.v.*). Also GELTER.—(DUNCOMBE, 1848).

1690. B. E., *Dict. of the Cant. Crew*, s.v. There is no GELT to be got, Trading is very dull.

1785. GROSE, *Vulg. Tongue*, s.v.

1811. *Lexicon Balatronicum*, s.v.

GEMINI! (or **GEMINY!** or **JIMINY!**) *intj.* (common).—An exclamation of surprise; a mild oath. [Generally referred to the Lat. : Gemini = the Twins (*i.e.*, Castor and Pollux, the objects of an old Roman oath); but Palmer (*Folk Etymology*), traces the interjection to the German, *O Gemine!*; Dutch, *Jemy Jemini!*; both abbreviated from the Latin, *O Jesu Domine!*; or merely from *Jesu meus!*; Italian, *Giesu mio!* It seems to have come in at the Restoration.] Also O JIMMINY!;

O JIMMINY FIGS! O JIMMINY GIG! etc.: for the phrase has pleased the cockney mind, and been vulgarised accordingly.

1672. DRYDEN, *The Assignation*, Act ii., Sc. 3. *Ben.* O GEMINI! is it you, sir?

1704. STEELE, *Lying Lover*, Act iv., Sc. 3. *Sim.* I stay with you? Oh GEMINI! Indeed, I can't.

1731. FIELDING, *The Lottery*, Sc. 2. Lord Lace! Oh GEMINI! who's that?

1780. MRS. COWLEY, *The Belle's Stratagem*, iv., 2. Oh GEMINI! beg the petticoat's pardon.

1797. M. G. LEWIS, *Castle Spectre*, iii., 3. Oh GEMINI! what would he use with me, lady?

1798. MORTON, *Secrets Worth Knowing*, i., 1. A parcel of lazy chaps, I dare say—but I'll make them stir their stumps. Well, here we are at last.—Oh GEMINI GIG how my poor bones do ache!

1836. M. SCOTT, *Tom Cringle's Log*, ch. i. 'GEMINI! what is that now?' quoth Tip again.

1863. READE, *Hard Cash*, I., 125. O, JIMINY! This polite ejaculation was drawn out by the speaker's sudden recognition of Alfred.

GEMMAN, *subs.* (vulgar).—A contraction of gentleman.

1550. *Docteur Double-All* (the word occurs in this play).

c. 1551. L. SHEPHERD, *John Bon* in Arber's *Garner*, iv., 107. Ye be the jolliest GEMMAN that I ever saw in my life.

1767. COLMAN, *Oxonian in Town*, i., i. I am glad to see your honour's well. I hope you left all the GEMMIN well at Oxford.

1818. BYRON, *Beppo*, st. 86. At home our Bow-street GEMMEN keep the laws.

1834. AINSWORTH, *Rookwood*, bk. iii., ch. v. . . . but knock down a GEMMAN.

1851. BORROW, *Lavengro*, ch. 26. Here the gipsy GEMMAN see.

GEN, *subs.* (costers').—A shilling. Back slang, but *cf.* Fr., *argent*. For synonyms, *see* BLOW.

1851-61. H. MAYHEW, *Lond. Lab. and Lond. Poor*, vol. i., p. 19. I'll try you a GEN (shilling) said a coster.

1887. *Saturday Review*, 14 May, p. 700. The difficulty of inverting the word shilling accounts for 'generalize,' from which the abbreviation to GEN is natural as well as affectionate.

GENDER, *verb.* (old). — To copulate. [An abbreviation of ENGENDER.] For synonyms, *see* GREENS and RIDE.

1602. SHAKSPEARE, *Othello*, iv., 2. A cistern for foul toads To knot and GENDER in.

1659. TORRIANO, *Vocabolario*, s.v.

1778. BAILEY, *Eng. Dict.*, s.v.

1816. JOHNSON, *Eng. Dict.*, s.v.

1892. *Bible*, Lev. xix., 19. Thou shalt not let thy cattle GENDER with a diverse kind.

FEMININE GENDER, *subs. phr.* (schoolboys').—The female *pudendum*. [As in the old (schoolboys') rhyme : *Amo, amas*, I loved a lass, And she was tall and slender, *Amas, amat*, I laid her flat, And tickled her FEMININE GENDER. Quoted (with modifications) by Marryat in *Jacob Faithful*, 1835.]

GENERALIZE, *subs.* (costers').—A shilling. *See* GEN.

GENERATING PLACE, *subs. phr.* (venery).—The female *pudendum*.

GENERATION TOOL, *subs. phr.* (venery).—The *penis*. For synonyms, *see* CREAMSTICK and PRICK.

GENEVA PRINT, *subs. phr.* (old).—Gin. For synonyms, *see* DRINKS and SATIN.

1584-1640. MASSINGER (quoted in *Slang, Jargon, and Cant*). And if you meet an Officer preaching of sobriety, Unless he read it in GENEVA PRINT, Lay him by the heels.

GEN-NET, *subs. phr.* (back slang).—Ten shillings.

GENNITRAF, *subs.* (back slang).—A farthing.

GENOL, *adj.* (back slang).—Long.

GENT, *subs.* (once literary : now vulgar). — 1. A showily-dressed vulgarian. [A contraction of 'gentleman.']

1635. [GLAPTHORNE], *Lady Mother*, in Bullen's *Old Plays*, ii., 114. Hees not a GENT that cannot parlee. I must invent some new and polite phrases.

1785. BURNS, *Epistle to J. Lapraite*, st. 11. Do ye envy the city GENT, Behint a kist to lie and sklent?

1843. THACKERAY, *Irish Sketch Book*, ch. viii. The crowd of swaggering GENTS (I don't know the corresponding phrase in the Anglo-Irish vocabulary to express a shabby dandy), awaiting the Cork mail.

1844. DISRAELI, *Coningsby*, bk. IV., ch. ii. 'Ah, not in business! Hem! professional?' 'No,' said Coningsby, 'I am nothing.'—'Ah! an independent GENT; hem! and a very pleasant thing too.'

1846. *Sunday Paper*, 24 May. Mr. Rawlinson (Magistrate at Marylebone Police Court). What do you mean by GENT? There is no such word in our language. I hold a man who is called a GENT to be the greatest blackguard there is.

1848. *Punch*, vol. XIV., p. 226. His aversion for a GENT is softened by pity.

1869. *Blue Budget*. The GENT indicates a being who apes the gentility without the faintest shadow of a claim to it.

2. (Old Cant.) — Money. [From Fr., *argent*.] For synonyms, *see* ACTUAL and GILT.

1864. *Revue des Deux Mondes*, 15 Sept., p. 470. Les voleurs anglais disent GENT pour 'argent.'

3. (colloquial).—A sweetheart, a mistress : *e.g.*, My GENT = my particular friend.

Adj. (old literary).—Elegant comely; genteel.

1383. CHAUCER, *Canterbury Tales*. 'Miller's Tale.' [Skeat, 1878, i., 194]. As any wesil her body GENT and small.

1553-99. SPENSER. He loved as was his lot, a lady GENT. *Idem.* A knight had wrought against a lady GENT.

1704. *Mad. Knight's Jour.*, p. 44. Law you, sais she, it's right GENT, do you take it—'tis dreadfull pretty.

GENTILE, *subs.* (colloquial). Any sort of stranger, native or foreign; among the Mormons, any person not professing the Gospel according to Joe Smith. Hence, IN THE LAND OF THE GENTILES = (1) in foreign parts; and (2) in strange neighbourhoods or alien society.

GENTLE, *subs.* (anglers'). — A maggot; vulgarly, GENTILE.

1811. *Songs of the Chase*. 'The Jolly Anglers.' We have GENTLES in our horns.

GENTLE CRAFT, *subs.* (old).—1. The trade of shoemaking. [From the romance of Prince Crispin, who is said to have made shoes.]

1662. *Rump Songs*. 'A Hymn to the Gentle Craft,' etc., ii. 152. Crispin and he were nere akin: The GENTLE CRAFT hath a noble kin.

2. (anglers').—Angling.

1892. MILLIKEN, *'Arry Ballads*, p. 65. Sez I, GENTLE CRAFT, said I.

GENTLEMAN, *subs.* (thieves'). — A crowbar. For synonyms, *see* JEMMY.

TO PUT A CHURL (or BEGGAR) **UPON A GENTLEMAN**, *verb. phr.* (old). — To drink malt liquor immediately after wine.—GROSE.

GENTLEMAN OF THE (THREE, or FOUR, or FIVE) **OUTS** (or INS), *subs. phr.* (old). — A

varying and ancient wheeze, of which the following are representative:—

Out of money, and out of clothes; Out at the heels, and out at the toes; Out of credit, and in debt.

A man in debt, in danger, and in poverty; or in gaol, indicted, and in danger of being hanged.

1785. GROSE, *Vulg. Tongue*, s.v.

1830. LYTTON, *Paul Clifford*, ch. iv. Paul became A GENTLEMAN OF THREE OUTS—out of pocket, out of elbows, and out of credit.

1834. H. AINSWORTH, *Rookwood*, Bk. III., ch. v. Jerry Juniper was what the classical Captain Grose would designate A GENTLEMAN WITH THREE OUTS and, although he was not entirely without wit, nor his associates avouched, without money, nor certainly, in his own opinion, had that been asked, without manners.

GENTLEMAN OF THE BACK (or BACKDOOR), *subs.* (old).—A sodomist. For synonyms, *see* USHER.

GENTLEMAN OF FORTUNE, *subs. phr.* (common). — An adventurer.

1890. R. L. STEVENSON, *Treasure Island*, p. 149. 'Why, in a place like this, where nobody puts in but GENTLEMEN OF FORTUNE, Silver would fly the jolly roger, you don't make no doubt of that.

GENTLEMAN OF OBSERVATION, *subs. phr.* (turf).—A tout.

GENTLEMAN OF THE ROUND, *subs. phr.* (old).—An invalided or disabled soldier, making his living by begging.

1596. JONSON, *Every Man in*, etc., 2. Your decaied, ruinous, worme-eaten GENTLEMEN OF THE ROUND.

GENTLEMAN OF THE SHORT STAFF, *subs. phr.* (old). — A constable.

1839. AINSWORTH, *Jack Sheppard* (1889), p. 12. In the language of the GENTLEMAN OF THE SHORT STAFF an important caption could be effected.

GENTLEMAN OF THE FIST, *subs. phr.* (pugilists').—A prize-fighter.

1819. MOORE, *Tom Crib*, p. 44. Furnish such GENTLEMEN OF THE FIST.

GENTLEMAN IN BROWN, *subs. phr.* (common). — A bed bug. For synonyms, *see* NORFOLK HOWARD.

1885. G. A. SALA in *Daily Telegraph*, 14 Aug., 5/3. Bed bugs, the convertible term for which is 'chintzes,' are the disagreeable insects known in modern polite English as 'Norfolk Howards,' or GENTLEMEN IN BROWN.

THE LITTLE GENTLEMAN IN BROWN VELVET, *subs. phr.* (obsolete).—A mole. [The Tory toast after the death of William III., whose horse was said to have stumbled over a mole-hill.]

GENTLEMAN OF THE GREEN BAIZE ROAD, *subs. phr.* (gamesters').—A card sharper.

GENTLEMAN COMMONER, *subs. phr.* (University). — 1. A privileged class of commoners at Oxford, wearing a special cut of gown and a velvet cap.

2. (common). — An empty bottle. Also FELLOW-COMMONER (*q.v.*). [A sarcastic allusion to the mental capacity of this class of student.] For synonyms, *see* DEAD-MAN.

1785. GROSE, *Vulg. Tongue*, s.v.

GENTLEMAN-RANKER, *subs.* (military).—A broken gentleman serving in the ranks.

1892. KIPLING, *Barrack Room Ballads*. 'Gentlemen Rankers.' GENTLEMAN-RANKERS out on the spree, Damned from here to eternity, God ha' mercy on such as we, Baa! Yah! Bah!

Gentleman's Companion, *subs. phr.* (common).—A louse. For synonyms, *see* Chates.

1785. Grose, *Vulg. Tongue*, s.v.

Gentleman's Master, *subs. phr.* (old).—A highwayman.—Grose.

Gentleman's (or **Ladies'**) **Piece**, *subs. phr.* (colloquial).—A small or delicate portion; a tit-bit.

Gentleman's Pleasure-garden, *subs. phr.* (venery).—The female *pudendum*. For synonyms, *see* Monosyllable. [Hence, Gentleman's Pleasure Garden Padlock = menstrual cloth.]

Gentlemen's Sons, *subs. phr.* (common).—The three regiments of Guards.

Gently! *intj.* (stables' and colloquial).—An interjection = stand still (*q.v.*); hence, colloquially, = don't get into a passion, go slow (*q.v.*).

Gentry Cove (or **Cofe**), *subs.* (old cant).—A gentleman; a nib-cove (*q.v.*). Fr., *un messire de la haute*.

1567. Harman, *Caveat*, s.v.

1656. Brome, *Joviall Crew*, Act ii. For all this bene Cribbing and Peck let us then, Bowse a health to the gentry cofe of the Ken.

1654. *Witts' Recreations*. As priest of the game, And prelate of the same. There's a gentry cove here.

1785. Grose, *Vulg. Tongue*, s.v.

1822. Scott, *Fortunes of Nigel*, ch. Tour the bien mort twiring the gentry cove.

1837. Disraeli, *Venetia*, p. 71. The gentry cove will be ramboyled by his dam.

Gentry Cove's Ken (or **Gentry-Ken**), *subs. phr.* (Old Cant).—A gentleman's house.

1567. Harman, *Caveat* (1814), p. 65. A gentry cofe's ken, a noble or gentleman's house. A gentry cofe, a noble or gentle man.

1610. Rowlands, *Martin Mark-all*, p. 38 (H. Club's Rept., 1874). Gentry cove's ken, a gentleman's house.

1690. B. E., *Dict. of the Cant. Crew*, s.v.

1785. Grose, *Vulg. Tongue*, s.v.

Gentry Mort, *subs. phr.* (old cant).—A lady.

1567. Harman, *Caveat* (1814), p. 65. A gentry mort, a noble or gentle woman.

1610. Rowlands, *Martin Mark-all*, p. 38 (H. Club's Rept., 1874). Gentry mort, a gentlewoman.

1728. Bailey, *Eng. Dict.*, s.v.

1785. Grose, *Vulg. Tongue*, s.v.

Genuine, *subs.* (Winchester College).—Praise.

Adj. (colloquial).—Trustworthy; not false nor double-faced.

Verb. (Winchester College).—To praise. 'He was awfully quilled and genuined my task.' [Probably from calling a thing genuine. *Cf.*, to blackguard, to lord, etc. But fifty years ago it was a *subs.* only.—*Notions.*]

Geordie, *subs.* (North Country).—1. A pitman; also, a Northumbrian in general.

2. (nautical).—A North Country collier.

3. *See* George.

George (or Scots' diminutive **Geordie**), *subs.* (old). 1.—A half crown. Also (obsolete), the noble = 6*s*. 8*d*., *temp.*, Henry VIII

1688. Shadwell, *Sq. of Alsatia*, *List of cant words*. George, half-a-crown.

1690. B. E., *Dict. of the Cant. Crew*. He tipt me Forty Georges for my earnest, He paid me Five Pounds for my Share or Snack.

1785. Grose, *Vulg. Tongue*, s.v.

2. (old).—A guinea; also more frequently Yellow George.

1785 Grose, *Vulg. Tongue*, s.v.

1787. Burns, *The Twa Dogs*. The yellow-lettered Geordie keeks.

3. (old).—A penny.

1820. Reynolds, *The Fancy*, Glossary. A Penny-piece—a georgy.

Brown George.—*See Ante.*

By Fore, or By George.—*See* By George.

George Horne, *intj.* (printers').—A derisive retort on a piece of stale news. Also G. H.! [From a romancing compositor of the name.]

Georgy-Porgy, *verb* (colloquial).—To pet; to fondle; to beslobber.

1883. R. L. Stevenson, *The Treasure of Franchard*, ch. iii., in *Longman's Magazine*, April, p. 685. He must be spoken to with more respect, I tell you; he must not be kissed and georgy-porgy'd like an ordinary child.

German. The German, *subs. phr.* (New York).—A round dance.

German Duck, *subs. phr.* (obsolete).—1. Half a sheep's head, stewed with onions.—Grose.

2. (common).—A bed bug. For synonyms, *see* Norfolk Howard.

German Flutes, *subs. phr.* (rhyming).—A pair of boots.

Germantowner, *subs.* (American billiards').—A pushing shot—when the balls played with, and at, are jarred together. *Cf.*, Whitechapeller.

Gerry, *subs.* (Old Cant).—Excrement.

1567. Harman, *Caveat*, s.v.

Gerry Gan, *intj.* (Old Cant).—A retort forcible. Stow it! (*q.v.*). [From Gerry = excrement + Gan = mouth, *i.e.*, literally, Shit in your mouth.] The common form is: Shit (or a turd) in your teeth; as in Ben Jonson, *Bartholomew Fair*, 1614. Fr., *Tais ta gueule ou j'te chie dedans.*

1567. Harman, *Caveat*. Gerry gan, the ruffian cly thee.

Gerrymander (pronounced with the 'g' hard, as in 'get'), *verb*, (political American).—To arrange the electoral subdivisions of a State to the profit and advantage of a particular party.

[The term, says Norton, is derived from the name of Governor Gerry, of Massachusetts, who, in 1811, signed a Bill readjusting the representative districts so as to favour the Democrats and weaken the Federalists, although the last-named party polled nearly two-thirds of the votes cast. A fancied resemblance of a map of the districts thus treated led Stuart, the painter, to add a few lines with his pencil, and say to Mr. Russell, editor of the *Boston Sentinel*, 'That will do for a Salamander.' Russell glanced at it: 'Salamander,' said he, 'call it a Gerrymander!' The epithet took at once, and became a Federalist war-cry, the caricature being published as a campaign document.]

1871. *Boston Daily Advertiser*, 6 Dec. Gerrimander was the name printed under a picture of a pretended monster, whose shape was modified from the distorted geography which Mr. Gerry's friends inflicted on part of the State for the sake of economizing majorities.

Gerrymandering, *subs.* (political American). *See* Gerrymander.

1872. *New York Sunday Mercury*, 31 March. The Legislature of Ohio intends to prove itself a veritable master in the gerrymandering business.

1890. *Athenæum*, 22 Feb. p. 23 8, c. 1. Whatever faults can be found with Sir John's administration, it has been good and successful enough to afford excuse for all the gerrymandering with which he is charged by his critics.

1891. *Belfort's Mag.*, Aug., p. 439. The Democrats of Michigan have carried the art of gerrymandering to such an extent that they have thoroughly disgusted their opponents.

Gerund-Grinder, *subs.* (common).—A schoolmaster, especially a pedant. Also Gerund-Grinding.

1759-67. Sterne *Tristam Shandy*, iv., 112. Tutors, governors, gerund-grinders, and bear-leaders.

1788. Knox, *Winter Evenings*, 59. A pedant, a mere plodder, a petty tyrant, a gerund-grinder.

1825-7. Hone, *Every Day Book*, II., p. 33. Gerund-Grinding and parsing are usually prepared for at the last moment.

Get, *subs.* (old).—1. A cheating contrivance; a Have (*q.v.*).

2. (old).—A child; the result, that is, of an act of procreation or begetting. Thus, one of his gets = one of his making; whose get is that? = Who's the father? It's his get, anyhow = At all events he got it.

1570. Scottish Text Society, *Satirical Poems*, I., 171, 'Treason of Dumbarton' (1891). Ganelon's gets, relicts of Sinon's seed.

d 1796. Burns, *Merry Muses*. 'For a' that.' O' bastard getts some had a score, An' some had mair than a' that.

1891. N. Gould, *Double Event*, p. 41. This, again, is unusual for a Chester, as his get are generally quiet and docile, but a bit lazy.

Get! (or You Get!) *intj.* (American).—Short for Get out! Usually, Git! (*q.v.*).

1892. Hume Nisbet, *Bushranger's Sweetheart*, p. 176. None of your damned impertinence. Get!

To get at, *verb. phr.* (colloquial).—1. To quiz; to banter; to aggravate; to take a rise out of. Also To get back at.

1891. *Sloper's Half Holiday*, 3 Jan. 'Your family don't seem to get on, missie.' '*On!*' replied the child, with dignity flashing from her great blue eyes; '*on!* I've got a father *on* the booze, a sister *on* the music 'all, an' a brother *on* the treadmill. *On!* who're ye gettin' at?'

2. (racing and colloquial).—To influence; to bribe; to nobble (of horses), and to corrupt (of persons); applied to horse, owner, trainer, jockey, and vet. alike.

1870. *Spectator*, 23 April. That, of course, makes it profitable for owners to withdraw horses they have secretly betted against, and for scoundrels to get at horses.

1871. *Saturday Review*, 9 Sept. It is quite clear that some of the foreign working men have been got at.

1883. *Graphic*, 17 March, p. 262, c. 2. The House of Commons . . . can also be trusted to decide in local questions without any suspicion of being got at, as is sometimes the case elsewhere.

1883. Badminton Library, *Steeple-chasing*, p. 404. Suspicions that the mare had been got at, that is to say, drugged, were afterwards noised abroad.

1888. *Daily Telegraph*, 17 Nov. It was strongly suspected that he had been got at.

1890. *Globe*, 11 Aug., p. 1, c. 1. Fancy the professional agitator trying to get at such men as these—men who gloried in being soldiers and nothing else!

1892. *Pall Mall Gazette*, May 10, p. 3, c. 3. The scoundrels (verily of the lowest form) who have tried to get at Orme.

1892 *National Observer*, vii. 630. If the horse were got at, then a bookie who stood heavily to lose is probably assumed.

To get about. *verb. phr.* (venery).—To do the act of intromission. For synonyms, *see* Greens and Ride.

To get back at, *verb. phr.* (colloquial).—To satirise; to call to account.

1888. *Daily Inter-Ocean.* The newspapers are getting back at Sam.

Get back into your box! *phr.* (American).—An injunction to silence; stow it! (*q.v.* for synonyms).

To get encored, *verb. phr.* (tailors').—To have a job returned for alterations.

To get even with, *verb. phr.* (common).—To take one's revenge; to give tit for tat.

To get it, *verb. phr.* (colloquial).—To be punished (morally or physically); to be called over the coals. Also (venery) to catch a clap.

To get off, *verb. phr.* (colloquial).—To (1) escape punishment, to be let off; (2) to utter, to deliver oneself of, to perpetrate—as to get off a joke; and (3) to get married.

To get on, *verb. phr.* (colloquial).—1. To back a horse; to put a bit on (*q.v.*).

2. (colloquial).—To succeed; or, simply, to fare. Thus, How are you getting on? may signify (1) To what extent are you prospering? or (2) How are you doing?

1871. *Pall Mall Gaz.*, 29 Dec. That great Anglo-Saxon passion of rising in the world, or getting on—that is, rising into the class above him.

1892. A. W. Pinero, *The Times: a Comedy*, v. 1. We used to go very early to such places and stay right through, now that papa has got on, we arrive late everywhere and murmur an apology!

To get one in the cold, *verb. phr.* (American).—To have at an advantage; to be on the windward side (*q.v.*); to have on toast (*q.v.*).

To get one on, *verb. phr.* (pugilists').—To land a blow.

To get down fine (or close), *verb. phr.* (American).—To know all about one's antecedents; and (police) to know where to find one's man.

To get into, *verb. phr.* (venery).—To occupy (*q.v.*). Also To get in and To get up. For synonyms, *see* Greens and Ride.

1620. Percy, *Folio MSS.*, p. 197. Gett vp againe, Billy, if that thou louest me.

To get over, *verb. phr.* (colloquial).—To seduce, to fascinate, to dupe. Also To come over and To get round.

To get outside of, *verb. phr.* (colloquial).—1. To eat or drink; also to accomplish one's purpose.

1892. S. Watson, *Wops the Waif*, p. 9. Tickle urged Wops again and again to drink, but Wops's only reply was, 'Yer go on, Tickle; git outside the lot, if yer can; it'll do yer good, Cully.'

2. (venery).—To receive the sexual embrace: of women only.

To get out of bed on the wrong side, *verb. phr.* (colloquial).—To be testy or cross-grained. [A corruption of an old saying, 'To rise on the right side is accounted lucky'; hence the reverse meant trials to temper, patience, and luck.]

1607. Marston, *What You Will.* You rise on your right side to-day, marry.

1608. Machin, *Dumb Knight*, iv., 1. Sure I said my prayers, ris'd on my right side, Wash'd hands and eyes, put on my girdle last; Sure I met no splea-footed baker, No hare did cross me, nor no bearded witch, Nor other ominous sign

1614. *Terence in English. C.* What doth shee keepe house alreadie? *D.* Alreadie. *C.* O good God! ; WE ROSE ON THE RIGHT SIDE to-day.

1647. BEAUMONT and FLETCHER, i. *Women Pleased.* You ROSE O' YOUR RIGHT SIDE.

1890. *Globe*, 15 May, p. 2, col. 2. Some of them had—if we may employ such a vulgar expression—GOT OUT OF BED ON THE WRONG SIDE.

TO GET OUT (or ROUND), *verb. phr.* (racing).—To back a horse against which one has previously laid; to HEDGE (*q.v.*).

1884. HAWLEY SMART, *From Post to Finish*, p. 318. He had an idea Johnson was this time cleverly working a very well authorised commission, and that he personally had taken more than one opportunity of what is termed GETTING OUT.

TO GET SET, *verb. phr.* (cricketing). — 1. To warm to one's work at the wicket, and collar the bowling; to get one's eye well in.

TO GET THERE, *verb. phr.* (colloquial). — To attain one's object; to be successful; TO MAKE ONE'S JACK (*q.v.*); TO GET THERE WITH BOTH FEET = to be very successful.

1887. FRANCIS, *Saddle and Mocassin.* He said as he'd been gambling, and was two hundred dollars ahead of the town. He GOT THERE WITH BOTH FEET at starting.

1888. *New York Herald*, 29 July. Although not a delegate he GOT THERE all the same.

2. (common).—To get drunk. For synonyms, *see* DRINKS and SCREWED.

3. (venery). — To enjoy the sexual favour.

TO GET THROUGH, *verb. phr.* (colloquial).—To pass an examination; to accomplish.

1853. BRADLEY, *Verd. Green*, II. ch. xii. So you see, Giglamps, I'm safe to GET THROUGH.

TO GET UP AND DUST, *verb. phr.* (American). — To depart hastily. For synonyms, *see* SKEDADDLE and AMPUTATE.

TO GET UP BEHIND (or GET BEHIND) A MAN, *verb. phr.* (common).—To endorse or back a bill.

1880. *Life in a Debtor's Prison*, p. 87. In other cases he figured as the drawer, or simply as endorser. This, Mr. Whipper described as GETTING UP BEHIND.

TO GET UP THE MAIL, *verb. phr.* (thieves').—To find money (as counsels' fees, etc.) for defence.

1889. CLARKSON and RICHARDSON, *Police*, 322, s.v.

[GET enters into many other combinations. *See* BACK TEETH; BAG OF SACK; BEAD; BEANS; BEAT; BIG BIRD and GOOSE; BIG HEAD; BILLET; BIT; BOAT; BOLT; BOOKS; BULGE; BULLET; BULL'S FEATHER; CROCKETTS; DANDER and MONKEY; DARK; DROP; EYE; FLANNELS; FLINT; GAME; GRAND BOUNCE; GRAVEL - RASH; GRIND; GRINDSTONE; HAND; HANG; HAT; HEAD; HIP OF HOP; HOME; HORN; HOT; JACK; KEEN; LENGTH OF ONE'S FOOT; MEASURE; MITTEN; NEEDLE; RELIGION; RISE; RUN; SCOT, SWOT, or SCRAPE; SET; SHUT OF; SILK; SNUFF; STRAIGHT; SUN; TICKET OF LEAVE; WOOL; WRONG BOX.]

GETAWAY, *subs.* (American thieves').—A locomotive or train; a PUFFER (*q.v.*).

GETTER. A SURE GETTER, *subs. phr.* (Scots).—A procreant male with a great capacity for fertilization.

GET-UP, *subs.* (colloquial). — 1. Dress; constitution and appearance; disguise. *See* GET-UP, *verb*, sense 1.

1856. WHYTE MELVILLE, *Kate Coventry*, ch. xiv. Is that killing GET UP entirely for your benefit, John? I asked.

1865. G. A. SALA, *Trip to Barbary*, ch. x. Altogether the GET UP of a Mauresque *en promenade* is livelier and smarter than that of a Turkish woman.

1866. G. ELIOT, *Felix Holt*, ch. xii. The graceful, well-appointed Mr. Christian, who sneered at Scales about his GET UP, having to walk back to the house with only one tail to his coat.

1882. *Graphic*, 9 Dec., p. 643, c. 2. Comic GETS UP, which will make the house roar presently, are elaborated with the business air of a judge in *banc*, or a water-rate collector.

1889. *Mirror*, 26 Aug., p. 2, c. 1. I cannot, however, congratulate F. C. G. on his sketch of Blowitz; it isn't much like the great man, and the GET UP is quite too absurd.

1890. *Daily Telegraph*, 25 Feb., p. 7. col. 7. Dressed as a *copurchic*, and, giving himself out as an Italian count—thinking to entrap some Transatlantic heiress by his title, fascinating appearance, and gorgeous GET UP.

Verb. phr. (colloquial).—(1). To prepare (a part, a paper, a case); (2) to arrange (a concert); (3) to dress (as GOT UP REGARDLESS, TO THE NINES, TO THE KNOCKER, TO KILL, WITHIN AN INCH OF ONE'S LIFE); (4) to disguise (as a sailor, a soldier, Henry VIII., a butcher, a nun). *See* also GET INTO.

1828. L. HUNT, *Essays* (Camelot ed.), p. 13. The pocket-books that now contain any literature are GOT UP, as the phrase is, in the most unambitious style.

1856. WHYTE MELVILLE, *Kate Coventry*, ch. xviii. Three very gentleman-like, good-looking men, GOT UP to the utmost extent of hunting splendour.

1864. *Eton School Days*, ch. xviii., p. 207. He felt confident in his power of GETTING UP so that no one would recognise him.

1866. *New York Home Journal*, Jan. While that admirable old dame, Nature, has been strangely neglectful of much which might be conducive to our comfort, she has GOTTEN UP, REGARDLESS OF EXPENSE, a few articles which are good for some purposes, as the witty Hood has told us.

1871. *London Figaro*, 11 Mar. It is GOT UP very much in the style of the Paris journals, and is very inferior compared with any respectable journal in England.

1889. *Polytechnic Magazine*, 24 Oct., p. 261. He came specially GOT UP in piebald trousers.

1892. CHEVALIER. 'The Little Nipper.' I've knowed 'im take a girl on six feet tall; 'E'd GIT 'IMSELF UP dossy, Say 'I'm goin' out wi' Flossie.'

G.H. *See* GEORGE HORNE.

GHASTLY, *adj.* and *adv.* (colloquial).—Very: a popular intensitive; *Cf.*, AWFUL, BLOODY, FUCKING.

GHOST, *subs.* (common). — One who secretly does artistic or literary work for another person taking the credit and receiving the price. [The term was frequently used during the trial of Lawes *v.* Belt in 188(?).] *Cf.*, DEVIL.

1890. *Daily Telegraph*, 8 Feb. The sculptor's GHOST is conjured up from the vasty deep of bygone lawsuits.

1892. *National Observer*, vii., 327 Would not the unkind describe your 'practical man' as a GHOST?

Verb. (common).—To prowl; to spy upon; TO SHADOW (*q.v.*).

THE GHOST WALKS (or DOES NOT WALK) *phr.* (theatrical). — There is (or is not) money in the treasury.

1853. *Household Words*, No. 183. When no salaries are forthcoming the GHOST DOESN'T WALK.

1883. *Referee*, 24 June, p. 3, c. 2. An Actor's Benevolent Fund box placed on the treasurer's desk every day when THE GHOST WALKS would get many an odd shilling or sixpence put into it.

1885. *The Stage*, p. 112. The rogues seldom appear at a loss for a plausible story when it is time for the GHOST TO WALK. *Ibid.* The next day THE GHOST DECLINES TO WALK.

1889. J. C. COLMAN (in *Slang, Jargon, and Cant*), p. 405. GHOST-WALKING, a term originally applied by an impecunious stroller in a sharing company to the operation of 'holding the treasury,' or paying the salaries, which has become a stock facetiæ among all kinds and descriptions of actors. Instead of enquiring whether the treasury is open, they generally say—'Has the GHOST WALKED?' or 'What, has this thing appeared again?' (Shakspeare).

1890. *Illustrated Bits*, 29 Mar., p. 11, c. 1. And a few nights with empty benches LAID THE GHOST completely. It could not even WALK to the tune of quarter salaries.

THE GHOST OF A CHANCE, *subs. phr.* (colloquial). — The faintest likelihood, or the slightest trace: *e.g.*, He hasn't THE GHOST OF A CHANCE.

1891. *Sportsman*, 26 Mar. He did not give THE GHOST OF A CHANCE.

GHOUL, *subs.* (American.)—1. A spy; specifically a man who preys on such married women as addict themselves to assignation houses.

2. (journalistic). — A newspaper chronicler of the smallest private tittle-tattle.

GIB, *subs.* (colloquial).—1. Gibraltar. Once a penal station: whence—2. A gaol.

1877. *Five Years' Penal Servitude*, ch. iii., p. 221. I did a lagging of seven, and was at the GIB three out of it.

1892. *Pall Mall Gazette*, 23 Mar., p. 6, c. 1. 'Stormy Weather at GIB.' The weather here has been fearful; 51 inches of rain have been registered, and the land for miles round Gibraltar is submerged.

TO HANG ONE'S GIB, *verb. phr.* (colloquial).—To pout. *See* JIB.

GIBBERISH (or GEBBERISH, GIBBERIDGE, GIBRIGE, etc.), *subs.* (old: now recognised).—Originally the lingo of gipsies, beggars, etc. Now, any kind of inarticulate nonsense. [From GIBBER, a variant of JABBER.] *See* CANT, SLANG, PEDLAR'S FRENCH, etc.

1594. NASHE, *Unf. Traveller*, in wks., v., 68. That all cried out upon him mightily in their GIBRIGE, lyke a companie of beggers.

1598. FLORIO, *Worlde of Wordes. Gergare*, to speak fustian, pedlers french, or rogues language, or GIBBRISH.

1611. COTGRAVE, *Dictionarie. Jargon*, GIBRIDGE fustian language, pedler's French, a barbarus jangling.

1638. H. SHIRLEY, *Martyr'd Souldier*, Act iii., Sc. 4. Feele my pulse once again and tell me, Doctor, Tell me in tearmes that I may understand —I doe not love your GIBBERISH,—tell me honestly Where the Cause lies, and give a Remedy.

1659. TORRIANO, *Vocabolario*, s.v.

1748. T. DYCHE, *Dictionary* (5th ed.). GIBBERISH (s.) an unintelligible jargon, or confused way of speaking, used by the gipsies, beggars, etc., to disguise their wicked designs; also any discourse where words abound more than sense.

1748. SMOLLETT, *Rod. Random*, ch. xxx. He repeated some GIBBERISH which by the sound seemed to be Irish.

1817. SCOTT, *Rob Roy*, ch. viii. Since that d——d clerk of mine has taken his GIBBERISH elsewhere.

1850. D. JERROLD *The Catspaw* Act i. Odds and ends . . . writ down in such a kind of GIBBERISH that I can't make out one of 'em.

1858. G. ELIOT, *Mr. Gilfil's Love Story*, ch. iv. It'll learn to speak summat better nor GIBBERISH, an' be brought up i' the true religion.

1892. R. L. STEVENSON and L. OSBOURNE, *The Wrecker*, p. 129. It was Fo'c's'le Jack that piped and drawled his ungrammatical GIBBERISH.

GIBBLE-GABBLE, *subs.* (colloquial). —Nonsense; GIBBERISH (*q.v.*). [A reduplication of GABBLE (*q.v.*).]

1600. DEKKER, *Shoemaker's Holiday*, in wks. (1873) i., 21. Hee's some uplandish workeman, hire him good master, That I may learne some GIBBLE GABBLE, 'twill make us worke the faster.

1659. TORRIANO, *Vocabolario*, s.v.

1748. T. DYCHE, *Dictionary* (5th ed.). GIBBLE-GABBLE (s), silly, foolish, idle talk.

GIB-CAT, *subs.* (old),—A tom-cat. [An abbreviation of Gilbert = O. Fr.: *Tibert*, the cat in the fable of Reynard the Fox.]

1360. CHAUCER, *Romaunt of the Rose*, 6204 (*Thibert le Cas* is rendered by GIBBE, our cat).

1598. SHAKSPEARE, 1 *Henry IV.*, Act i., Sc. 2. I am as melancholy as a GIB-CAT.

1614. JONSON, *Bartholomew Fair*, i., 1. Before I endure such another day with him, I'll be drawn with a good GIB-CAT through the great pond at home.

1663. *Rump Songs.* 'Rump Carbonadoed,' ii., 71. As if they had less wit and grace than GIB-CATS.

1785. GROSE, *Vulg. Tongue*, s.v.

GIBE, *verb.* (American).—To go well with; to be acceptable. *See* GEE.

GIBEL, *verb.* (thieves').—To bring.

1837. DISRAELI, *Venetia*, bk. i., ch. xiv. GIBEL the chive, bring the knife.

GIB-FACE, *subs.* (colloquial). — A heavy jowl; an UGLY-MUG (*q.v.*). *Cf.*, TO HANG ONE'S GIB.

GIBLETS, *subs.* (common).—1. The intestines generally; the MANIFOLD (*q.v.*). *Cf.*, TROUBLE-GIBLETS.

1864. BROWNING, *Dramatis Personæ* 'Flight of the Duchess.' Is pumped up briskly through the main ventricle, And floats me genially round the GIBLETS.

2. (colloquial).—A fat man; FORTY-GUTS (*q.v.*). Also DUKE OF GIBLETS.

TO JOIN GIBLETS, *verb. phr.* (venery) — To copulate. Also TO HAVE OR DO A BIT OF GIBLET-PIE. For synonyms, *see* RIDE. Hence to cohabit as husband and wife; TO LIVE TALLY. *Cf.*, PLASTER OF WARM GUTS.

1785. GROSE, *Vulg. Tongue*, s.v.

1887. *Notes and Queries*, 7 S., iv., 511. 'TO JOIN GIBLETS.'—This expression may occasionally be heard in this district, among the lowest and vulgarest, and has a very offensive meaning.

TO FRET ONE'S GIBLETS, *verb. phr.*—*See* FRET.

GIBRALTAR, *subs.* (American).—A party stronghold: *e.g.*, the GIBRALTAR of Democracy. — NORTON.

GIBSON (or SIR JOHN GIBSON), *subs.* (old coachbuilders').—A rest to support the body of a building coach.

GIBUS, *subs.* (colloquial).—1. An opera, or crush hat. Fr., *un accordéon*. [From the name of the inventor.]

1867. JAS. GREENWOOD, *Unsent. Journeys*, iii., 21. West-End aristocrats, with spotless jean coats and GIBUS hats.

1871. *Figaro*, 2 Sept. Much fun may be made by wearing a GIBUS, and collapsing it at the moment of contact with the funnel.

1885. *Punch*, 4 Apr., p. 160. Giving his comic, shiny, curly-brimmed hat to the swell who couldn't by any possible chance have mistaken it for his own GIBUS.

1887. ATKIN, *House Scraps*, p. 144. Their GIBUS hats are cock'd awry.

GIDDY, *adj.* (colloquial).—Flighty; wanton : *e.g.*, TO PLAY THE GIDDY GOAT = to live a fast life ; to be happy-go-lucky.

1892. *Ally Sloper*, 19 Mar., p. 91, c. 2. Fanny Robinson was flighty ; she PLAYED THE GIDDY OX—I mean heifer.

GIFFLE-GAFFLE, *subs.* (old).—Nonsense ; a variant of GIBBLE-GABBLE (*q.v.*).

1787. GROSE, *Prov. Glossary.* GIFF-GAFF, unpremeditated discourse.

GIF-GAF (or **GIFF-GAFF**), *subs.* (Scots').—A bargain on equal terms. Whence the proverb : GIF-GAF maks guid friens. Fr. : *Passe-moi la casse et je t'enverrai la senne.*

GIFT, *subs.* (colloquial).—1. Anything lightly gained or easily won.

2. (common).—A white speck on the finger nails, supposed to portend a gift.

1811. *Lexicon Balatronicum*, s.v.

3. (printers').—See GIFT-HOUSE.

AS FULL OF GIFTS AS A BRAZEN HORSE OF FARTS, *phr.* (old).— Mean ; miserly ; disinclined to PART (*q.v.*).

1811 *Lexicon Balatronicum*, s.v

GIFT OF THE GAB.—See GAB.

GIFT-HOUSE (or **GIFT**), *subs.* (printers').—A club ; a house of call ; specifically for the purpose of finding employment, or providing allowances for members.

GIG (**GIGG**, **GIGGE**), *subs.* (old).—1. a wanton ; a mistress ; a flighty girl. *Cf.*, GIGLET.

1373. CHAUCER, *House of Fame*, iii. 851. This house was also ful of GYGGES.

1690. B. E., *Dict. of the Cant. Crew.* A young GIG, a wanton lass.

1780. D'ARBLEY, *Diary*, etc., (1876), i., 286. Charlotte L—— called, and the little GIG told . . . of the domestic life she led in her family, and made them all ridiculous, without meaning to make herself so.

1825. PLANCHÉ, *Success in Extravaganzas* (1879) I., 26. He! he! What a GIG you look in that hat and feather !

1832. MACAULAY in *Life*, by TREVELYAN (1884), ch. v., p. 188. Be you Foxes, be you Pitts, You must write to silly chits, Be you Tories, be you Whigs, You must write to sad young GIGS.

2. (old).—A jest ; a piece of nonsense ; anything fanciful or frivolous. Hence, generally, in contempt.

1590. NASHE, *Pasquil's Apologie*, in wks. Vol. I., p. 234. A right cutte of the worde, withoute GIGGES or fancies of haeretical and newe opinions.

1793. BUTT, *Poems*. . . . Fograms, quizzes, treats, and bores, and GIGS, Were held in some account with ancient prigs.

1856. WHYTE MELVILLE, *Kate Coventry*, ch. xiv. Such a set of GIGS, my dear, I never saw in my life ; large underbred horses, and not a good-looking man amongst them.

3. (old).—The nose. For synonyms, *see* CONK. TO SNITCHELL THE GIG = to pull the nose. GRUNTER'S GIG = a hog's snout.

1690. B. E., *Dict. of the Cant. Crew*, s.v.

1785. GROSE, *Vulg. Tongue*, s.v.

4. (venery). — The female *pudendum*. For synonyms, *see* MONOSYLLABLE. [Possibly from GIG = a top, *i.e.*, a toy ; possibly, too, from It. *giga* = a FIDDLE (*q.v.*) ; but see *post* sense 8.]

1690. B. E., *Dict. of the Cant. Crew*, s.v.

1785. GROSE, *Vulg. Tongue*, s.v.

5. (old : now recognised).—A light two-wheeled vehicle drawn by one horse.

1785. GROSE, *Vulg. Tongue*, s.v.

1809. WINDHAM, *Speech*, 25 May. Let the former riders in GIGS and whiskeys, and one horsed carriages continue to ride in them.

6. (old). — A door. *See* GIGGER.

1785. GROSE, *Vulg. Tongue*. It is all bob, now let's dub the GIGG of the case : now the coast is clear, let us break open the door of the house.

7. (Eton).—A fool ; an overdressed person. For synonyms, *see* SAMMY-SOFT.

1797. COLMAN, *Heir at Law*, iv., 3. *Dick.*—What a damn'd GIG you look like, *Pangloss.*—A GIG ! umph ! that's an Eton phrase — the Westminsters call it Quiz.

1870. *Athenæum*, 16 Apr. He would now be what Eton used to call a GIG, and Westminster a Quiz.

8. (old).—Fun ; a frolic ; a spree. [Possibly from Fr. : *gigue* = a lively dance movement. *Cf.*, *gigue et jon* = a Bacchanalian exclamation of sailors. In Florio, too, *frottolare* = ' to sing GIGGES, rounds, or . . . . wanton verses.'] FULL OF GIG = full of laughter, ripe for mischief.

1811. MOORE, *Twopenny Post-bag*, Letter 3. We were all in high GIG—Roman punch and tokay travelled round, till our heads travelled just the same way.

1820. RANDALL, *Diary*. In search of lark, or some delicious GIG, The mind delights on, when 'tis in prime twig.

1823. MONCRIEFF, *Tom and Jerry*, i., 3. I hope we shall have many a bit of GIG together.

1888. BESANT, *Fifty Years Ago*, p. 134. A laughter-loving lass of eighteen who dearly loved a bit of GIG.

9. (old).—The mouth. For synonyms, *see* POTATO-TRAP.

1871. *Finish to Tom and Jerry*, p. 175 [ed. 1872]. The bit of myrtle in his GIG.

10. (old).—A farthing. Formerly GRIG (*q.v.*).

11. American).—*See* POLICY DEALING.

Verb. (old).—To hamstring.

1785. GROSE, *Vulg. Tongue*, s.v. To GIG a Smithfield hank, to hamstring an overdrove ox.

BY GIGS ! *intj.* (old). — A mild and silly oath. *See* OATHS.

1551. *Gammer Gurton's Needle*, ii., 51. Chad a foule turne now of late, chill tell it you, BY GIGS !

GIGAMAREE, *subs.* (American).—A thing of little worth ; a pretty but useless toy ; a GIMCRACK (*q.v.*).

1848. JONES, *Sketches of Travel*, p. 9. Byin' fineries and northern GIGAMAREES of one kind or another.

Ibid. I ax'd the captain what sort of a GIGAMAREE he had got up there for a flag.

GIGANTOMACHIZE, *verb.* (old). — To rise in revolt against one's betters. Gr., *Gigantomachia* = the War of the Giants against the Gods. [Probably a coinage of Ben Jonson's.]

1599. JONSON, *Every Man Out*, Act v., 4. Slight, fed with it the whoreson, strummel-patched, goggle-eyed grumbledores would have GIGANTOMACHIZED their Maker.

GIGGER, *subs.* (tailors')—1. A sewing machine. (In allusion to noise and movement).

2. *See* JIGGER.

GIGGLES-NEST. HAVE YOU FOUND A GIGGLES-NEST? *phr.* (old). — Asked of a person tittering, or one who laughs immoderately and senselessly.

GIG-LAMPS, *subs.* (common).—1. Spectacles. For synonyms, *see* BARNACLES.

1848. BRADLEY, in *Letter to J. C. H.* GIG-LAMPS (certainly a university term. I first heard it in 1848 or 1849, long before Mr. Verdant Green was born or thought of).

1877. *Five Years' Penal Servitude*, ch. ii., p. 140. You with the GIG-LAMPS, throw us your cigar.

1887. *Punch*, 30 July, p. 45. Jack's a straw-thatched young joker in GIG-LAMPS.

1892. F. ANSTEY, *Voces Populi.* ' At the Tudor Exhibition.' Stop, though, suppose she *has* spotted me ? Never can tell with GIGLAMPS.

2. (common).—One who wears spectacles ; a FOUR EYES (*q.v.*). [Popularised by Verdant Green.]

GIGLER (or **GIGLET**, **GOGLET**, **GIGLE**, **GIG**), *subs.* (old).—A wanton ; a mistress. GIGLET (West of England) = a giddy, romping girl ; and in Salop a flighty person is called a GIGGLE. *Cf.*, GIG, sense 1.

1533. UDAL, *Floures for Latine Spekynge*, fo. 101. What is the matter, foolish GIGLOTTE ? What meanest thou ? Whereat laughest thou ?

1567. HARMAN, *Caveat*, leaf 22, *back.* Therefore let us assemble secretly into the place where he hath appoynted to meet this GYLEOT that is at your house.

1603. SHAKSPEARE, *Measure for Measure*, v., 1. Let him speak no more : away with those GIGLOTS too, and with the other confederate companion.

1611. COTGRAVE, *Dictionarie. Gadrouillette*, minx, GIGLE, flirt.

1620. MASSIENGER, *Fatal Dowry*, Act. iii. If this be The recompence of striving to preserve A wanton GIGLET honest, very shortly 'Twill make all mankind pandars.

1690. B. E., *Cant. Crew*, s.v.

1785. GROSE, *Vulg. Tongue.* GIGGIERS, wanton women.

Adj. (old). — Loose in word and deed. Also GIGLET-LIKE, and GIGLET-WISE = like a wanton.

1598. SHAKSPEARE, 1 *Henry IV.*, Act v., Sc. 1. Young Talbot was not born To be the pillage of a GIGLOT wench.

1600. FAIRFAX, *Jerusalem Delivered*, vi., 72. That thou wilt gad by night in GIGLET-WISE, Amid thine armed foes to seek thy shame.

GILD, *verb.* (old). — To make drunk ; to flush with drink.

1609. SHAKSPEARE, *Tempest*, Act v., Sc. 1. This grand liquor that hath GILDED them.

1620. FLETCHER, *Chances*, iv., 3. Is she not drunk, too? A little GILDED o'er, sir.

TO GILD THE PILL, *phr.* (colloquial).—To say, or do, unpleasant things as gently as may be ; to impose upon ; to BAMBOOZLE (*q.v.*).

GILDED ROOSTER, *subs. phr.* (American).—A man of importance ; a HOWLING SWELL (*q.v.*); sometimes THE GILDED ROOSTER ON THE TOP OF THE STEEPLE. *Cf.*, BIG-BUG ; BIG DOG OF THE TANYARD, etc.

1888. *New York Herald.* We admit that as a metropolis Chicago is the GILDED ROOSTER ON TOP OF THE STEEPLE, but even GILDED ROOSTERS have no right to the whole corn bin.

GILDEROY'S KITE. TO BE HUNG HIGHER THAN GILDEROY'S KITE, *verb. phr.* (old).—To be punished more severely than the very worst criminals. ' The greater the crime the higher the gallows ' was at one time a practical legal axiom. Hence, out of sight ; completely gone.

GILES' GREEK. *See* ST. GILES' GREEK.

GILGUY, *subs.* (nautical). — Anything which happens to have slipped the memory ; equivalent to WHAT'S-HIS-NAME or THINGA-MYTIGHT.

GILKES, *subs.* (old). — Skeleton keys.

1610. ROWLANDS, *Martin Mark-all*, p. 38 (H. Club's Rept., 1874). GILKES for the Gigger, false keyes for the doore or picklockes.

GILL (or **JILL**), *subs.* (old).—1. A girl ; (2) a sweetheart : *e.g.*, ' every Jack must have his GILL ' ; (3) a wanton, a strumpet (an abbreviation of GILLIAN). For synonyms, *see* JOMER and TITTER.

1586-1606. WARNER, *Albion's England*, bk. vii., ch. 37. The simplest GILL or knave.

1598. FLORIO, *A Worlde of Wordes. Palandrina*, a common queane, a harlot, a strumpet, a GILL.

1620. PERCY, *Folio MSS.*, p. 104. There is neuer a Jacke for GILL.

1659. TORRIANO, *Vocabolario*, s.v.

2. (common).—a drink ; a GO (*q.v.*).

1785. BURNS, *Scots Drink.* Haill breeks, a scone, and WHISKY GILL.

3. *in. pl.* ' g ' hard (colloquial).—The mouth or jaws ; the face. *See* POTATO-TRAP and DIAL.

1622. BACON, *Historia Naturalis.* Redness about the cheeks and GILLS.

1632. JONSON, *Magnetic Lady*, i. He . . . draws all the parish wills, Designs the legacies, and strokes the GILLS of the chief mourners.

b. 1738. WOLCOT, *Pindar's Works* (1809), i., 8. Whether you look all rosy round the GILLS, Or hatchet-fac'd like starving cats so lean.

1820. LAMB, *Elia (Two Races of Men).* What a careless, even deportment hath your borrower ! what rosy GILLS !

1855. THACKERAY, *Newcomes*, ch. viii. Binnie, as brisk and rosy about the GILLS as chanticleer, broke out in a morning salutation.

1884. *Punch.* He went a bit red in the GILLS.

4. *in. pl.* (common).—A very large shirt collar ; also STICK-UPS and SIDEBOARDS. Fr. : *cache-bonbon-à-liqueur* = a stick-up.

1859. SALA, *Twice Round the Clock*, 6 p., in Part 7. With a red face, shaven to the superlative degree of shininess, with GILLS white and tremendous, with a noble white waistcoat.

1884. *Daily Telegraph*, July 8, p. 5, c. 4. Lord Macaulay wore, to the close of his life, ' stick-ups,' or GILLS.

TO GREASE THE GILLS. — *verb phr.* (common).—To have a good meal ; TO WOLF (*q.v.*).

TO LOOK BLUE (or QUEER, or GREEN) ABOUT THE GILLS, *phr.* (common).—To be downcast or dejected ; also to suffer from the effects of a debauch. Hence, conversely, TO BE ROSY ABOUT THE GILLS = to be cheerful.

1836. M. SCOTT, *Tom Cringle's Log*, ch. ii. Most of them were very white and BLUE IN THE GILLS when we sat down, and others of a dingy sort of whitey-brown, while they ogled the viands in a most suspicious manner.

1892. G. MANVILLE FENN, *Witness to the Deed*, ch. ii. You look precious seedy. WHITE ABOUT THE GILLS.

A CANT (or DIG) IN THE GILLS, *phr.* (pugilists'). — A punch in the face. *See* BANG.

GILL-FLIRT, *subs.* (old).—A wanton ; a flirt. For synonyms, *see* BARRACK HACK and TART.

1598. FLORIO, *A Worlde of Wordes*

1611. COTGRAVE, *Dictionarie. Gaultiere*, a whore, punke, drab, queane, GILL FLIRT.

1690. B. E., *Dict. of the Cant. Crew*, s.v. A proud minx.

1785. GROSE, *Vulg. Tongue*, s.v.

1811. *Lexicon Balatronicum*, s.v.

GILLY, *subs.* (American).—A fool. For synonyms, *see* BUFFLE and CABBAGE-HEAD.

GILLY-GAUPUS, *subs. phr.* (Scots). —A tall loutish fellow.

1785. GROSE, *Vulg. Tongue*, s.v.

GILT, *subs.* (popular).—1. Money. [Ger. : *Geld.* ; Du. : *Gelt.*]

ENGLISH SYNONYMS.—Add to those under ACTUAL :—Charms ; checks ; cole or coal ; coliander seeds ; corn in Egypt ; crap ; darby ; dots ; ducats ; gingerbread; kelter; lowie; lurries; moss; oil of palms ; palm-oil ; peck ; plums ; rhino ; rivets ; salt ; sawdust ; scad ; screen ; scuds ; shigs ; soap ; spoon ; steven ; sugar ; tea-spoons ; tinie.

FRENCH SYNONYMS. — *Le galtos* (popular) ; *l'odeur de gousset* (obsolete); *l'onguent* (= palm grease, Sp., *unguento* ; the simile is common to most languages) ; *le morlingue* (thieves') ; *la menouille* (popular) ; *le michon* (thieves' : from *miche*, a loaf, *cf.*, LOAVER) ; *les monacos* (popular) ; *le monarque* (prostitutes' : primarily a five franc piece) ; *le blé* = corn or loaver) ; *les étoffes* (thieves').

SPANISH SYNONYMS.—*La lana* (= wool) ; *la morusa* (colloquial) ; *la mosca* (= the flies) ; *lo numerario* ; *la pelusa* (= down) ; *lozurraco* (colloquial) ; *lo unguento de Mejico* (= Mexican Grease) ; *a' toca teja* (colloquial : ready money) ; *caire.*

ITALIAN SYNONYMS.—*Cucchi* ; *cuchieri* ; *cucchielli* ; *lugani.*

GERMAN SYNONYMS.—*Fuchs* (= fox : an allusion to the ruddy hue of gold pieces ; *fuxig* or *fuxern* = golden, red ; *fuchsmelochener* = goldsmith) ; *gips* or *gyps* (Viennese thieves', from the Latin, *gypsum*) ; *hora* (= ready-money : from the Hebrew *heren*) ; *kall* (Han : especially small change : from Heb. *kal* = lowly light) ; *kis, kies, kiss* (applied both to money in general and the receptacle or purse in which it is carried) ; *lowe, love* (Han.) ; *mepaie* (from the Fr., *payer*) *mesumme, linke mesumme* = counterfeit money) ; *moos* (from Heb., *mĕo* = a little stone) ; *pich, picht,* or *pech* ; *staub* (= dust).

1599. SHAKSPEARE, *Henry V.*, Act ii. *Chorus.* These corrupted men . . . have for the GILT of France (O guilt, indeed) Confirmed conspiracy.

1714. *Memoirs of John Hall* (4th ed.), p. 9. And from thence conducted (provided he has GILT) over the way to Hell.

1885. *Daily News*, 25 May, p. 3, c. 1. Disputatious like mobs grouped together to discuss whether Charrington or Crowder had the most GILT.

2. *subs.* (old). — A thief; a pick-lock ; also GILT- or RUM-DUBBER, GILTER, etc.

1669. *Nicker Nicked* in *Harl. Misc.* (ed. Park), ii., 108 (given in list of names of thieves).

1673. *Character of a Quack Astrologer.* For that purpose he maintains as strict a correspondence with GILTS and lifters.

1676. *Warning for Housekeepers*, p. 3. The GILTER is one that hath all sorts of picklocks and false keys.

1680. COTTON, *Complete Gamester*, p. 333. Shoals of muffs, hectors, setters, GILTS, pads. biters, etc. . . . may all pass under the general appellation of snobs.

1785. GROSE, *Vulg. Tongue*, s.v.

1882. MCCABE, *New York*, ch. xxxiv., 509. GILT-DUBBER, a hotel thief.

3. (thieves'). — Formerly a pick-lock or skeleton key ; now a crow-bar. For synonyms, *see* JEMMY.

1671. R. HEAD, *English Rogue*, Pt. 1, ch. v., p. 50 (1874). GILT, a pick-lock.

1724. E. COLES, *Eng. Dict.* GILT, c. a pick-lock.

1839. W. H. AINSWORTH, *Jack Sheppard*, p. 183 (ed. 1840). We shall have the whole village upon us while you're striking the jigger. Use the GILT, man!

TO TAKE THE GILT OFF THE GINGERBREAD, *verb. phr.* (colloquial).—To destroy an illusion ; to discount heavily.

1884. HAWLEY SMART, *From Post to Finish*, p. 171. You see we had a rattling good year all round last, bar the Dancing Master. He TOOK THE GILT OFF THE GINGERBREAD considerably.

GILT-DUBBER, *see* GILT, sense 2.

GILT-EDGED, *adj.* (American). — First-class ; the best of its kind ; a latter - day superlative. For synonyms, *see* A1 and FIZZING.

c. 1889. *Chicago Tribune* (quoted in *Slang, Jargon, and Cant*). He's a GILT-EDGED idiot to play the game.

1891. *Standard*, 18 June, p. 2, c. 1. 'GILT-EDGED mutton' is the latest of glorified and 'boomed' American products.

1891. *Tit Bits*, 8 Aug., p. 286, c. 2. Another accomplishment, peculiar to the GILT-EDGED academy, is learning to eat asparagus, oranges, grapes, etc.

GILTER, *see* GILT, sense 2.

GILT-TICK, *subs.* (costermongers'). Gold.

GIMBAL- (or **GIMBER-**) **JAWED**, *adj.* (common). — Loquacious ; talking NINETEEN TO THE DOZEN (*q.v.*). [Gimbals are a combination of rings for free suspension ; hence applied to persons the joints of whose jaws are loose in speech.]

GIMCRACK (**GINCRACK**, or **JIMCRACK**), *subs.* (old). — 1. A showy simpleton, male or female ; a DANDY (*q.v.*).

1618. BEAUMONT and FLETCHER, *Loyal Subject*, iv., 3. These are fine GIMCRACKS ; hey, here comes another, a flagon full of wine in his hand.

1637. FLETCHER, *Elder Brother*, iii.,3. You are a handsome and a sweet young lady, And ought to have a handsome man yoked to ye. An understanding too ; this is a GIMCRACK That can get nothing but new fashions on you.

1690. B. E., *Dict. of the Canting Crew.* GIMCRACK, a spruce wench.

1706. MRS. CENTLIVRE, *Basset Table*, II., *Works* (1872), i., 122. The philosophical GIMCRACK.

1785. GROSE, *Vulg. Tongue*, s.v.

2. (colloquial). — A showy trifle ; anything pretty to look at but of very little worth.

1632. CHAPMAN and SHIRLEY. *The Ball*, Act iv. *Lu.* There remains, To take away one sample. *Wi.* Another GIMCRACK?

1678. BUTLER, *Hudibras*, pt. 3, ch. i. Rifled all his pokes and fobs. *Cf.*, GIMCRACKS, whims, and jiggumbobs.

1698-1700. WARD, *London Spy*, pt. 7, p. 148. I suppose there being little else to lose except scenes, machines, or some such JIM-CRACKS.

1843. THACKERAY, *Irish Sketch Book*, ch. i. There was the harp of Brian Boru, and the sword of some one else, and other cheap old GIMCRACKS with their corollary of lies.

1892. MILLIKEN, *'Arry Ballads*, p. 63. Such rum-looking GIMCRACKS, my pippin.

3. (provincial).—A handy man ; a JACK-OF-ALL-TRADES (*q.v.*).

1785. GROSE, *Vulg. Tongue*, s.v. A GIMCRACK also means a person who has a turn for mechanical contrivances.

4. (venery). — The female *pudendum.* [A play on sense 2, and CRACK, (*q.v.*).] For synonym, *see* MONOSYLLABLE.

Adj. (colloquial). — Trivial ; showy ; worthless.

1855. THACKERAY, *Newcomes*, ch. ix. No shops so beautiful to look at as the Brighton GIMCRACK shops, and the fruit shops, and the market.

1891. W. C. RUSSELL, *An Ocean Tragedy*, p. 30. Soberly clothed with nothing more GIMCRACK in the way of finery upon him than a row of waistcoat-buttons.

1892. *Tit Bits*, 19 Mar., p. 425 c. 2. A large cabinet or wardrobe, beautifully carved, and very substantial, no GIMCRACK work.

GIMCRACKERY, *subs.* (colloquial). — The world of GIMCRACK (*q.v.*).

1884. A. FORBES, in *Eng. Illustr. Mag.*, Jan., p. 230. The inner life of the Empire was a strange mixture of rottenness and GIMCRACKERY.

GIMLET-EYE, *subs.* (common).—A squint-eye ; a PIERCER (*q.v.*). Fr. : *des yeux en trou de pine.*

GIMLET - EYED, *adj.* (common).— Squinting, or squinny-eyed ; cock-eyed. As in the old rhyme : 'Gimlet eye, sausage nose, Hip awry, bandy toes.'

1785. GROSE, *Vulg. Tongue*, s.v.

GIMMER, *subs.* (Scots').—An old woman. A variant of 'cummer.'

GIN, *subs.* (Australian). — An Australian native woman.

1857. KINGSLEY, *Two Years Ago*, ch. xiii. An Australian settler's wife bestows on some poor slaving GIN a cast-off French bonnet.

1890. HUME NISBET, *Bail Up*, p. 30.

2. (Australian). — An old woman. For synonyms, *see* GEEZER.

GIN-AND-GOSPEL GAZETTE, *subs. phr.* (journalists').—The *Morning Advertiser* : as the organ of the Licensed Victualling and Church of England party. Also the TAP-TUB and BEER - AND - BIBLE GAZETTE.

GIN-AND-TIDY, *adv. phr.* (American). — Decked out in 'best bib and tucker.' A pun on 'neat spirits.'

GIN-CRAWL, *subs.* (common).—A TIPPLE (*q.v.*) on gin.

1892. A. CHEVALIER, 'The Little Nipper.' I used to do a GIN CRAWL ev'ry night, An' very, very often come 'ome tight.

GINGAMBOBS (or **JIGGUMBOBS**), *subs.* (common).—1. Toys ; baubles.

1690. B. E. *Dict. of the Cant. Crew*, s.v.

1785. GROSE, *Vulg. Tongue*, s.v.

2. (venery). — The testicles ; also THINGAMBOBS. For synonyms, *see* CODS.

GINGER, *subs.* (common).—1. A fast, showy horse ; a beast that looks FIGGED (*q.v.*).

1859. *Notes and Queries*, 17 Dec. p. 493. A GINGER is a showy fast horse.

2. (common).—A red-haired person ; CARROTS (*q.v.*). [Whence the phrase (venery) 'Black for beauty, GINGER for pluck.']

1885. MISS TENNANT in *Eng. Illustrated Magazine*, June, p. 605. The policemen are well known to the boys, and appropriately named by them. There is 'Jumbo,' too stout to run ; GINGER, the red-haired.

3. (common).—Spirit ; dash ; GO (*q.v.*). TO WANT GINGER = to lack energy and PLUCK (*q.v.*).

1888. *The World*, 13 May. You will remark that your spinal column is requiring a hinge, and that considerable GINGER is departing from your resolution to bear up and enjoy yourself.

1891. GUNTER, *Miss Nobody of Nowhere*, p. 124. If father objects send him to me, I'll take the GINGER out of him in short order.

1892. R. L. STEVENSON and L. OSBOURNE, *The Wrecker*, p. 207. Give her GINGER, boys.

Adj. (common).—Red-haired ; FOXY (*q.v.*) ; JUDAS-HAIRED (*q.v.*). Also GINGER-PATED, GINGER-HACKLED, and GINGERY.

1785. GROSE, *Vulg. Tongue*, s.v. Red-haired ; a term borrowed from the cock-pit, where red cocks are called GINGERS.

1839. H. AINSWORTH, *Jack Sheppard*, ch. xii. Somebody may be on the watch —perhaps that old GINGER-HACKLED Jew.

1852. DICKENS, *Bleak House*, ch. xix., p. 160. The very learned gentleman who has cooled the natural heat of his GINGERY complexion in pools and fountains of law, until he has become great in knotty arguments for term-time.

1878. M. E. BRADDON, *Cloven Foot*, ch. iv. The landlady was a lean-looking widow, with a false front of GINGERY curls.

GINGERBREAD, *subs.* (old).—1. Money : *e.g.*, 'He has the GINGERBREAD' = he is rich.

1690. B. E. *Dict. of the Cant. Crew*, s.v.

1785. GROSE, *Vulg. Tongue*, s.v.

1834. AINSWORTH, *Rookwood.* Your old dad had the GINGERBREAD.

1864. *Standard*, 13 Dec. We do not find . . . the word GINGERBREAD used for money, as we have heard it both before and within the last six months. The origin of the use of the word may probably be the old fairy legends wherein the coin obtained over night from the elves was usually found in the morning to have turned into little gingerbread cakes.

2. (colloquial).—BRUMMAGEM (*q.v.*) ; showy, but worthless ware.

Adj. (colloquial).—Showy but worthless ; tinsel. Fr., *en pain d'épice.* GINGERBREAD WORK (nautical) = carved and gilded decorations ; GINGERBREAD QUARTERS (nautical) = luxurious living.

1757. SMOLLETT, *Compendium of Voyages and Travels.* The rooms are too small and too much decorated with carving and gilding, which is a kind of GINGERBREAD work.

TO TAKE THE GILT OFF THE GINGERBREAD. *See* GILT.

GINGERLY, *adj.* and *adv.* (old : now recognised).—As *adj.*, delicate ; fastidious ; dainty ; as *adv.*, with great care ; softly.

1533. UDAL, *Floures for Latine Spekynge.* We stayghe and prolonge our goyng, with a nyce or tendre and softe, delicate, or GINGERLY pace.

c. 1563. *Jacke Jugeler*, p. 40 (ed. Grosart). We used to call her at home Dame Coye, a pretie GINGERLIE pice [piece].

1592. NASHE, *Pierce Penilesse*, in *Wks.*, ii., 32. That lookes as simperingly as if she were besmeared, and sits it as GINGERLY as if she were dancing the Canaries.

1611. CHAPMAN, *May-Day*, Act iii., p. 294 (*Plays*, 1874). Come, come, GINGERLY ; for God's sake, GINGERLY.

1659. TORRIANO, *Vocabolario*, q.v.

1690. B. E., *Dict. of the Cant. Crew*, s.v. Gently, softly, easily.

1759-67. STERNE, *Tristram Shandy*, vol. V., ch. v. My mother was going very GINGERLY in the dark.

1785. GROSE, *Vulg. Tongue*, s.v. To go GINGERLY to work, *i.e.*, to attempt a thing gently, or cautiously.

1874. MRS. H. WOOD, *Johnny Ludlow*, 1 S. 12, p. 207 The Squire went in GINGERLY, as if he had been treading on a spiked ploughshare.

GINGER-POP, *subs.* (colloquial).— 1. Ginger-beer.

2. (rhyming).—A policeman ; a SLOP (*q.v.*).

1887. DAGONET, *Referee*, 7 Nov., p. 7, c. 3. Ere her bull-dog I could stop, She had called a GINGER-POP.

GINGER-SNAP, *subs.* (American).— A hot-tempered person, especially one with carrotty hair.

GINGHAM, subs. (common).—An umbrella; specifically one of this material. For synonyms, see MUSHROOM.

1868. MISS BRADDON, Trail of the Serpent, Bk. I., ch. vii. Mr. Peters therefore took immediate possession by planting his honest GINGHAM in a corner of the room.

1889. Sportsman, 2 Feb. It would really put a premium on the many little mistakes of ownership concerning GINGHAMS at present so common.

GINGLE-BOY, subs. (old).—A coin; latterly a gold piece. Also GINGLER. See ACTUAL and CANARY.

1622. MASSINGER and DEKKER, Virgin Martyr, ii., 2. The bag of GINGLEBOYS hangs at the door of our pockets.

GINGUMBOBS. See GINGAMBOBS.

GINICOMTWIG, verb. (venery).—To copulate. For synonyms, see RIDE.

1598. FLORIO, Worlde of Wordes, Scuotere il pellicione. To GINICOMTWIG or occupie a woman.

GIN-LANE (or TRAP), subs (common).—1. The throat. For synonyms, see GUTTER-ALLEY. GIN-TRAP, also = the mouth. For synonyms, see POTATO-TRAP.

1827. EGAN, Anecdotes of the Turf, p. 67. Never again could . . . he feel his ivories loose within his GIN-TRAP.

2. (common). — Generic for the habit of drunkenness.

1839. AINSWORTH, Jack Sheppard [1889], p. 8. Let me advise you on no account to fly to strong waters for consolation, Joan. One nail drives out another, it's true; but the worst nail you can employ is a coffin nail. GIN LANE's the nearest road to the churchyard.

GIN-MILL, subs. (American).—A drinking saloon. For synonyms, see LUSH-CRIB.

1872. Belgravia, Dec. 'A Presidential Election.' Then goes off to rejoin his comrades, to adjourn to the nearest GIN-MILL.

GINNIFIED, subs. (common). — Dazed, or stupid, with liquor.

GINNUMS, subs. (common).—An old woman: especially one fond of drink.

GINNY, subs. (old).—A housebreaker's tool; see quot., 1754.

1690. B. E., Dict. of the Cant. Crew, s.v.

1754. Scoundrels' Dict. An instrument to lift up a grate or grating, to steal what is in the window. 'The ninth is a GINNY, to lift up the grate, If he sees but the Lurry, with his Hooks he will bait.'

1785. GROSE, Vulg. Tongue, s.v.

GIN-PENNY, subs. (costermongers').—Extra profit, generally spent in drink.

GIN-SLINGER, subs. (common).—A gin-drinker. For synonyms, see LUSHINGTON.

GIN-SPINNER, subs. (old).—A distiller; a dealer in spirituous liquors. Cf., ALE-SPINNER.

1785. GROSE, Vulg. Tongue, s.v.

1827. EGAN, Anecdotes of the Turf, p. 179. Just as she was about to toddle to the GIN-SPINNER's for the ould folk and lisp out for a quartern of Max.

1888. F. GREEN, in Notes and Queries, 7 S., vi., 153. I have always understood that a GIN SPINNER is a distiller who makes gin, but could never find out why so called.

GIN-TWIST, subs. (common).—A drink composed of gin and sugar, with lemon and water.

1841. Comic Almanac, p. 271 What, for instance, but GIN-TWIST could have brought Oliver Twist to light?

Fr., aller en donner. For synonyms, see WIG and TAN respectively.

1612. CHAPMAN, Widow's Tears, Act i., p. 312 (Plays, 1874). This braving wooer hath the success expected; the favour I obtained made me witness to the sport, and let his confidence be sure, I'll GIVE IT HIM home.

1835. DICKENS, Sketches by Boz, p. 134. 'Take that,' exclaimed Mr. Samuel Wilkins. . . . 'GIVE IT HIM,' said the waistcoat. . . . Miss J'mima Ivins's beau and the friend's young man lay gasping on the gravel, and the waistcoat and whiskers were seen no more.

1889. J. M. BARRIE in Time, Aug. p. 148. When he said he would tell everybody in the street about there being a baby, I GAVE HIM ONE IN THE EYE. Ibid. If it's true what Symons Tertius says, that Cocky has gone and stolen my reminiscences about Albert's curls, putting it into his reminiscences like as if it was his own, I'll GIVE HIM IT HOT.

TO GIVE IN (or OUT), verb. phr. (colloquial). — To admit defeat; to yield; to be exhausted; TO THROW UP THE SPONGE. See FLOORED and CAVE IN.

1748. SMOLLETT Rod. Random, ch. xviii. Strap, after having received three falls on the hard stones, GAVE OUT, and allowed the blacksmith to be the better man.

1760-1. SMOLLETT, L. Greaves, vol. II., ch. viii. By this time the doctor had GIVEN OUT, and allowed the brewer to be the better man.

1819. MOORE, Tom Crib, p. 25. Poor Georgy GAVE IN.

1837. LYTTON, Ernest Maltravers, bk. IV., ch. ix. Your time is up . . . you have had your swing, and a long one it seems to have been—you must now GIVE IN.

1847. ROBB, Squatter Life, p. 99. Jest about then both on our pusses GIN OUT.

1850. BUFFUM, Six Months in the Gold Mines, p. 73. After working three days with the machine, the earth we had been washing began to GIVE OUT.

1852. DICKENS, Bleak House, ch. xxiv., p. 217. I am surprised to hear a man of your energy talk of GIVING IN.

TO GIVE AWAY, verb. phr. (American).—To betray or expose inadvertently; TO BLOW UPON (q.v.): TO PEACH (q.v. for synonyms). Also TO GIVE DEAD AWAY. Largely used in combination: e.g., GIVE-AWAY = an exposure; GIVE-AWAY CUE = an underhand revelation of secrets.

1883. F. M. CRAWFORD, Doctor Claudius, ch. vi., p. 100. It always amused him to see sanguine people angry. They looked so uncomfortable, and GAVE THEMSELVES AWAY so recklessly.

1886. A. LANG, Longman's Mag., VII., 321. I know not whether the American phrase, to GIVE A PERSON AWAY, to GIVE YOURSELF AWAY, meaning to reveal your own or another's secret, is of provincial English origin. Did it cross over with the Pilgrim Fathers in the May Flower, or is it a recent bit of slang? 'Who GIVETH THIS WOMAN AWAY?' asked the rural American parson in the wedding service. 'I could,' came the voice of a young man from the gallery, 'but I'd never be so mean.'

1888. Detroit Free Press, Aug. Careful what we say, For it will GIVE US DEAD AWAY.

1889. Answers, 20 Apr., p. 326. My closely cropped hair, however, GAVE ME AWAY.

1892. R. L. STEVENSON and L. OSBOURNE, The Wrecker, p. 195. For the sake of the joke I'll GIVE MYSELF AWAY.

TO GIVE ONE BEST, verb. phr. (schoolboys').— 1. To acknowledge one's inferiority, a defeat. Also (thieves') to leave, TO CUT (q.v.).

1887. HORSLEY, Jottings from Jail. But after a time I GAVE HIM BEST (left him), because he used to want to bite my ear (borrow) too often.

TO GIVE THE COLLAR, verb. phr. (American).—To seize; to arrest; TO COLLAR (q.v.). For synonyms, see NAB.

TO GIVE THE BULLET (SACK, BAG, KICK-OUT, PIKE, ROAD, etc.), verb. phr. (common).—To discharge from an employ.

GIN UP, verb. (American).—To work hard; to make things lively or HUM (q.v.). For synonyms, see WIRE IN.

1887. FRANCIS, Saddle and Moccassin. They were GINNING her UP, that's a fact.

GIP, subs. (American thieves').—1. A thief. 2. Also (Cambridge University) a college servant. See GYP. For synonyms, see THIEVES.

GIRL, subs. (common). — 1. A prostitute; in. pl. = the stock in trade of a brothel. See BARRACK HACK, TART, and GAY. Fr., fille.

2. (colloquial).—A mistress; a MASH (q.v).

3. In. pl. (venery). — The sex—or that part of it which is given to unchastity—in general; hence THE GIRLS = lechery.

AFTER THE GIRLS. HE's BEEN AFTER THE GIRLS, verb. phr. (common).—Said of one with clap or pox.

GIRL AND BOY, subs. phr. (rhyming). A saveloy.

GIRLERY, subs. (colloquial).—A brothel. Also a theatre for burlesque and comic opera.

GIRL-GETTER, subs. (colloquial).—A mincing, womanish male.

GIRLING. To GO GIRLING, verb. phr. (venery). — To quest for women; to go on the LOOSE (q.v.).

GIRLOMETER, subs. (venery).—The penis. Also, GIRL-CATCHER. For synonyms, see CREAMSTICK and PRICK.

GIRL-SHOP, subs. phr. (common).—A brothel.

GIRL-SHOW, subs. phr. (common).—A ballet, a burlesque, a LEG-PIECE (q.v.).

GIRL STREET. In HAIR COURT, GIRL STREET, subs. phr. (common).—Generic for fornication. Also the female pudendum.

GIRL-TRAP, subs. phr. (common).—A seducer; a MUTTON-MONGER (q.v.).

GIT! (or YOU GIT!), intj. (American).—Be off with you! An injunction to immediate departure; WALKER! (q.v.). Sometimes a contraction of GET OUT! Also GET OUT AND DUST!

1851. SEAWORTHY, Bertie, p. 78. Thrue as the tin commandhers! GIT AOUT!

TO HAVE NO GIT UP AND GIT, phr. (American). — To be weak, vain, mean, or slow—generally deprecatory.

GIVE, verb. (vulgar).—1. To lead to; to conduct; to open upon: e.g., 'The door GAVE upon the street.' Cf. the idiomatic use, in French, of donner.

2. (American).—An all-round auxiliary to active verbs; TO GIVE ON PRAYING = to excel at prayer; TO GIVE ON THE MAKE = to be clever at making money, etc.

TO GIVE IT TO, verb. phr. (old).—1. To rob; to defraud.—GROSE.

2. (common).—To scold; to thrash. Also TO GIVE WHAT FOR; TO GIVE IT HOT; TO GIVE SOMETHING FOR ONESELF; TO GIVE ONE IN THE EYE, etc.

GIVE US A REST! phr. (American). — Cease talking! An injunction upon a bore.

TO GIVE NATURE A FILLIP, verb. phr. (old).—To indulge in wine or women.—B.E. (1690).

TO GIVE WAY, verb. phr. (colloquial).—To permit the sexual embrace: by women only.

1870. Weekly Times, 1 May. She was sorry to say, she GAVE WAY to him. (Laughter.) Mr. Maude remarked she was a foolish woman, and, being a widow, ought to have known what GIVING WAY would come to.—Complainant said of course she did, but she thought he meant to marry her.

[Other combinations will be found under the following; AUCTIONEER; BACK CAP; BAG; BAIL; BASTE; BEANS; BEEF; BIFF; BLACK EYE; BONE; BUCKET; BULLET; BULL'S FEATHER; CLINCH; DOUBLE; FIG; GAS; GO BY; GRAVY; HOIST; HOT BEEF; JESSE; KENNEDY; KEY OF THE STREET; LAND; LEG UP; LIP; MILLER; MITTEN; MOUTH; NEEDLE; OFFICE; POINTS; PUSSY; RUB OF THE THUMB; SACK; SKY-HIGH; SLIP; TAIL; TASTE OF CREAM; TURNIPS; WEIGHT; WHITE ALLEY; WORD.]

GIVER, subs. (pugilistic).—A good boxer; an artist in PUNISHMENT (q.v.).

1824. REYNOLDS, ('Peter Corcoran'), The Fancy, p. 73. She knew a smart blow from a handsome GIVER Would darken lights.

GIXIE, subs. (obsolete).—A wanton wench; a strumpet; an affected mincing woman.

1598. FLORIO, Worlde of Wordes. Faina, a mincing, coie, nice, puling, squeamish woman, an idle huswife, a flurt, a GIXGI. Also as Foina [i.e., 'a polecat'; while Foirare= 'to lust for beastly leacherie, to be salt as a bitch.']

1611. COTGRAVE, Dictionarie, s.v. Gadrouillette, a minx, gigle, flirt, callet GIXIE: (a fained word applyable to any such cattell). [See further, gadriller (a wench)= 'to rump or play the rig'].

GIZZARD, TO FRET ONE'S GIZZARD, verb. phr. (common).—To worry oneself. See FRET.

TO STICK IN ONE'S GIZZARD, verb phr. (common).—To remain as something unpleasant, distasteful or offensive; to be hard of digestion; to be disagreeable or unpalatable.

c. 1830. Finish of Tom and Jerry, p. 241. It had always STUCK IN HIS GIZZARD to think as how she had been werry cruelly used.

TO GRUMBLE IN THE GIZZARD, verb. phr. (common).—To be secretly displeased. Hence, GRUMBLE-GIZZARD (q.v.).

GLADSTONE, subs. (common)—1. Cheap claret. [Mr. Gladstone, when in office in 1869, reduced the duty on French wines.] See DRINKS.

1876. BESANT and RICE, Golden Butterfly, ch. ix. Claret certainly good, too—none of your GLADSTONE tap; sherry probably rather coarse.

1885. A. BIRRELL, Obiter Dicta, p. 86. To make him unbosom himself over a bottle of GLADSTONE claret in a tavern in Leicester Square.

2. colloquial).—A travelling bag. [So named in honour of Mr. Gladstone.]

GLADSTONIZE, verb (colloquial).—To talk about and round; to evade or prevaricate; to speak much and mean nothing.

GLANTHORNE, subs. (old). — Money. For synonyms, see ACTUAL and GILT.

1789. PARKER Life's Painter, p. 42. Drop the GLANTHORNE = part with money.

GLASGOW GREYS, *subs. phr.* (military).—The 70th Foot. [Which in the beginning was largely recruited in Glasgow.]

1886. TINSLEY'S *Mag.*, Apr., p. 321. The 70th were long known as the GLASGOW GREYS.

GLASGOW MAGISTRATE, *subs. phr.* (common).—A herring, fresh or salted, of the finest. [From the practice of sending samples to the Baillie of the River for approval.] Also GLASGOW BAILLIE.

1855. STRANG, *Glasgow and its City Clubs*. This club . . . . better known by the title of the Tinkler's club, particularly when the brotherhood changed the hour of meeting . . . . and when the steak was exchanged for a 'Welsh rabbit' or GLASGOW MAGISTRATE.

ENGLISH SYNONYMS (for herrings generally). — Atlantic ranger ; Californian ; Cornish duck ; Digby chicken ; Dunbar wether ; gendarme ; Gourock ham ; magistrate ; pheasant (or Billingsgate pheasant) ; reds ; sea-rover ; soldier ; Taunton turkey ; two-eye'd steak ; Yarmouth capon. Fr. : *gendarme*.

GLASS, *subs.* (American thieves').—An hour. [An abbreviation of 'hour-glass.']

1859. MATSELL, *Vocabulum*, s.v. The badger piped his Moll about a GLASS and a half before she cribbed the flat.

THERE'S A DEAL OF GLASS ABOUT, *phr.* (common). — 1. Applied to vulgar display='IT'S THE THING' (*q.v.*).

2. (common).—Said in answer to an achievement or assertion. A memory of the proverb, 'People who live in glass houses should not throw stones.'

WHO'S TO PAY FOR THE BROKEN GLASS? *verb. phr.* (colloquial).—See STAND THE RACKET.

BEEN LOOKING THROUGH A GLASS, *adv. phr.* (common).—Drunk. For synonyms, see DRINKS and SCREWED.

GLASS-EYES, *subs.* (old).—A man wearing spectacles ; FOUR-EYES (*q.v.*) ; GIG-LAMPS (*q.v.*).

1811. *Lexicon Balatronicum*, s.v.

GLASS-HOUSE. TO LIVE IN A GLASS HOUSE, *verb. phr.* (colloquial).—To lay oneself open to attack or adverse criticism.

GLASS-WORK, *subs.* (card-sharpers').—An obsolete method of cheating at cards. A convex mirror the size of a small coin was fastened with shellac to the lower corner of the left palm opposite the thumb, enabling the dealer to ascertain by reflection the value of the cards he dealt.

GLAZE, *subs.* (old).—A window.

1690. B. E., *Dict. of the Cant. Crew*, s.v.

1714. *Memoirs of John Hall* (4th ed.), p. 12. GLAZE, a Window.

1754. *Discoveries of John Poulter*, p. 43. Undub the Jeger and jump the GLAZE.

1852. SNOWDEN, *Mag. Assistant* (3rd ed.), p. 445. A window, GLAZE.

c. 1830. *Finish to Tom and Jerry* [1872], p. 82. A random shot milling the GLAZE.

Verb (old).—To cheat at cards. See quot. and GLASS-WORK.

1821. P. EGAN, *Real Life*, I., 297. If you take the broads in hand in their company, you are sure to be work'd, either by GLAZING, that is, putting you in front of a looking glass, by which means your hand is discovered by your antagonist, or by private signals from the pal.

TO MILL (or STAR A GLAZE), *verb. phr.* (old). — To break a window.

1823. MONCRIEFF, *Tom and Jerry*, iii., 2. *Jerry*. What are you about, Tom? *Tom*. I'm going to MILL THE GLAZE—I ll —(*Is about to break the glass, when Kate and Sue appear as the Miss Trifles*.)

1823. JON BEE, *Dict. of the Turf*. GLAZE, s.v., TO MILL THE GLAZE, the miller may adopt a stick or otherwise, as seems most convenient.

ON THE GLAZE, *adv. phr.* (thieves').— Robbing jewellers' shops by smashing the windows. See GLAZIER.

1724-34. C. JOHNSON, *Highwaymen and Pyrates*, q.v.

1889. *Ally Sloper*, 4 May. Getting a reprieve he went to Dublin ON THE GLAZE.

GLAZIER, *subs., in. pl.* (old).—1. The eyes. For synonyms, *see* GLIMS. Fr. : *les ardents*.

1567. HARMAN, *Caveat* (1814), p. 64. GLASVERS, eyes.

1610. ROWLANDS, *Martin Mark-all*, p. 38 (H. Club's Rept., 1874). GLASIERS, eyes.

1611. MIDDLETON and DEKKER, *Roaring Girl*, v., 1. These GLASIERS of mine, mine eyes.

1656. BROME, *Jovial Crew*, ii. You're out with your GLAZIERS.

1690. B. E., *Dict. of the Cant. Crew*, s.v. The cove has rum GLAZIERS, c. that Rogue has excellent Eyes, or an Eye like a Cat.

1724. E. COLES, *Eng. Dict.* GLAZIERS, c. eyes.

1725. *New Canting Dict.* 'Song.' Her GLAZIERS, too, are quite benighted.

1785. GROSE, *Vulg. Tongue* s.v.

2. (old).—A window thief. *Cf.*, GLAZE.

1725. *New Cant. Dict.* Song. 'The Twenty Craftsmen.' . . . A Glazier who when he creeps in, To pinch all the lurry he thinks it no sin.

1785. GROSE, *Vulg. Tongue*, s.v,

GLEANER, *subs.* (old).—A thief. *Cf.*, HOOKER, ANGLER, etc. For synonyms, *see* THIEVES.

GLIB, *subs.* (common).—1. The tongue. SLACKEN YOUR GLIB= loose your tongue. For synonyms, see CLACK.

2. (old).—A ribbon.

1754. *Discoveries of John Poulter*, p. 42. A lobb full of GLIBBS, a box full of ribbons.

Adj. (old, now recognised).— Smooth ; slippery ; voluble ; GLIB-TONGUED or GLIB-GABBIT (*cf.*, GAB)=talkative ; ready of speech.

1605. SHAKSPEARE, *Lear*, Act i., Sc. 1. I want that GLIB and oily art, To speak and purpose not.

1659. TORRIANO, *Vocabolario*, s.v.

1690. B. E., *Dict. of the Cant. Crew*, s.v. Smooth, without a Rub. GLIB-TONGUED. Voluble or Nimble-tongued.

1890. *Licensed Vict. Gaz.*, 31 Jan. The rest who were so GLIB with their promises.

GLIBE, *subs.* (American thieves').— Writing ; specifically, a written statement.

GLIM (or **GLYM**), *subs.* (old).—1. A candle, or dark lanthorn ; a fire or light of any kind. To DOUSE THE GLIM=to put out the light. Fr. : *estourbir la cabande*. Also short for GLIMMER or GLYMMAR (*q.v.*).

1690. B. E., *Dict. of the Cant. Crew*, s.v. A Dark Lanthorn used in Robbing Houses ; also to burn in the Hand.

1714. *Memoirs of John Hall* (4th ed.), p. 12. GLIM, a Candle.

1728. BAILEY, *Eng. Dict.* GLIM, s.v. A candle or light.

1785. GROSE, *Vulg. Tongue*. Bring bess and GLYM ; *i.e.*, bring the instrument to force the door, and the dark lanthorn.

1823. MONCRIEFF, *Tom and Jerry*, ii., 2. *Tom*. Then catch—here's the gentlemen's tooth-picker, and here's his GLIM— (*Throws stick and lanthorn to Jerry*.)

1834. AINSWORTH, *Rookwood*, bk. III., ch. 5. Every star its GLIM at hiding.

1837. DICKENS, *Oliver Twist*, ch. 16. Let's have a GLIM . . . or we shall be breaking our necks.

1837. LYTTON, *Ernest Maltravers*, Bk. I., ch. 10. 'Hush, Jack!' whispered one ; 'hang out the GLIM and let's look about us.'

1852. JUDSON, *Myst.*, etc., *of New York*, ch. iv. Old Jack bade Harriet trim the GLIM.

1883. R. L. STEVENSON, *Treasure Island*, p. 89. Sure enough, they left their GLIM here.

1884. HENLEY and STEVENSON, *Admiral Guinea*, ii., 6. Now here is my little GLIM ; it aint for me because I'm blind.

2. (old).—A sham account of a fire as sold by FLYING STATIONERS (*q.v.*).

1851-61. MAYHEW, *Lond. Lab. and Lond. Poor*, i., 233. His papers certify any and every 'ill that flesh is heir to' . . . . Loss by fire is a GLIM.

3. *in. pl.* (common). — The eyes.

ENGLISH SYNONYMS.— Blinkers ; daylights ; deadlights ; glaziers ; lights ; lamps ; ogles ; optics : orbs ; peepers ; sees ; squinters ; toplights ; windows ; winkers.

FRENCH SYNONYMS. — *Les quinquets* (popular=bright eyes, Vidocq) ; *les mirettes* (popular and thieves') ; Italian : *mira*= sight) ; *les reluits* (thieves' : also DAY-MANS—or LIGHTMANS [*q.v.*]) ; *les calots* (thieves' = marbles) ; *les châsses* or *les châssis* (popular = hunters') ; *les lampions* (thieves'=LAMPS (*q.v.*)) ; Italian : *lanterna* and *lampante*) ; *les apics* (thieves') ; *les ardents* (thieves' = piercers) ; *les eillets* (popular =eyelets ; *les lanternes de cabriolet* (popular = giglamps) ; *les clig-* nots (popular = winkers) ; *les carreaux* (thieves' = windows) ; *les clairs* (thieves' = shiners) ; *les coquards* (thieves').

ITALIAN SYNONYMS. — *Lanterna* (=a lamp) ; *calchi* ; *balchi* ; *brunotti* (= brownies) ; *lampante*.

SPANISH SYNONYMS.—*Fanal* (= lantern) ; *lanterna* (= *idem*) ; *visantes* (vulgar) ; *vistosos* (vulgar).

GERMAN SYNONYMS. — *Dierling* (from *stieren*=to stare) ; *Linzer* ; *Scheinling* (from *Schein*= DAYLIGHTS (*q.v.*)).

1824. P. EGAN, *Boxiana*, iv., 417. His GLIMS I've made look like a couple of rainbows.

1830. LYTTON, *Paul Clifford*, p. 47 [ed. 1854]. Queer my GLIMS, if that don't little Paul !

1837. BARHAM, *Ingoldsby Legends*, II., 339. Harold escaped with the loss of a GLIM.

1892. MILLIKEN, '*Arry Ballads*, p. 56. A pooty gal, gentle, or simple, as can't use her GLIMS is a flat.

4. *in. pl.* (common).—A pair of spectacles. For synonyms, *see* BARNACLES.

5. (common).—Gonorrhœa or CLAP (*q.v.*). [From sense 1= fire.]

Verb (old).—To brand or burn in the hand.

1690. B. E., *Dict. of the Cant. Crew*, s.v. As the cull was GLIMM'D, he gangs to the Nubb, c., if the Fellow has been Burnt in the Hand, he'll be Hang'd now.

1714. *Memoirs of John Hall*, p. 15. Profligate women are GLIMM'D for that villany, for which, rather than leave it, they could freely die martyrs.

1785. GROSE, *Vulg. Tongue*, s.v.

TO PUFF THE GLIMS, *verb. phr.* (veterinary).—To fill the hollow over the eyes of old

horses by pricking the skin and blowing air into the loose tissues underneath, thus giving the full effect of youth.

GLIM-FENDERS, *subs.* (old).— 1. Andirons, or fire-dogs.

1690. B. E., *Dict. of the Cant. Crew*, s.v. GLIMFENDERS, c. Andirons. RUM GLIMFENDERS, Silver Andirons.

1728. BAILEY, *Eng. Dict.* s.v.

1785. GROSE, *Vulg. Tongue*, s.v.

2. (old). — Handcuffs. [A pun on sense 1.]

1823. JON BEE, *Dict. of the Turf* s.v.

1848. DUNCOMBE, *Sinks of London*, s.v.

GLIMFLASHLY (or **GLIM-FLASHEY**), *adj.* (old). — Angry. See NAB THE RUST and HAIR.

1690. B. E., *Dict. of the Cant. Crew*, s.v. GLIMFLASHLY, c., Angry, or in a Passion. The Cull is GLIMFLASHLY, c. the Fellow is in a Heat.

1785. GROSE, *Vulg. Tongue*, s.v.

1830. LYTTON, *Paul Clifford*, ch. xxxi. No, Captain, don't be GLIM-FLASHEY ! You have not heard all yet.

GLIM-JACK, *subs.* (old).—A link boy ; a MOON-CURSER (*q.v.*) ; but, in any sense, a thief.

1690. B. E., *Dict. of the Cant. Crew*, s.v.

1785. GROSE, *Vulg. Tongue*, s.v.

GLIM-LURK, *subs.* (tramps'). — A beggars' petition, based on a fictitious fire or GLIM (sense 2).

1851-61. H. MAYHEW, *Lond. Lab. and Lond. Poor*, vol. I., p. 233. The patterer becomes a 'lurker,—that is, an imposter ; his papers certify any and every 'ill that flesh is heir to.' Shipwreck is called a SHAKE-LURK ; loss by fire is a GLIM

GLIMMER (or **GLYMMAR**), *subs.* (old).—Fire. See quot.

1567. HARMAN, *Caveat*. These DEMAUNDERS FOR GLYMMAR be for the moste parte wemen.

1610. ROWLANDS, *Martin Mark-all*, p. 38. (H. Club's Rept., 1874). GLYMMER, Fire.

1671. R. HEAD, *English Rogue*, pt. I., ch. v., p. 49 (1874). GLYMMER, Fire.

1724. E. COLES, *Eng. Dict.*, s.v.

1725. *New Canting Dict.*, Song, 'The Maunder's Praise of his Strowling Mort.' Doxy, Oh ! thy Glaziers shine, As GLYMMAR by the Solomon.

1785. GROSE, *Vulg. Tongue*, s.v.

GLIMMERER, *subs.* (old).—A beggar working with a petition giving out that he is ruined by fire. Also GLIMMERING MORT = a female GLIMMERER.

1690. B. E., *Dict. of the Cant Crew*, s.v. GLIMMERER, c., the Twenty-second Rank of the Canting Tribe, begging with Sham Licences, pretending to Losses by Fire, etc.

1785. GROSE, *Vulg. Tongue*, s.v.

GLIMSTICK, *subs.* (old).—A candlestick. [From GLIM = a light + stick.] Fr. : *une occasion*.

1690. B. E., *Dict. of the Cant Crew*, s.v. GLIMSTICK, c., a Candlestick. RUM GLIMSTICKS, c., Silver Candlesticks. QUEER GLIMSTICKS, c., Brass, Pewter, or Iron Candlesticks.

1785. GROSE, *Vulg. Tongue*, s.v.

GLISTER, *subs. phr.* (thieves').—See quot., GLISTER OF FISH-HOOKS.

1889. CLARKSON and RICHARDSON, *Police*, p. 321. A glass of Irish whiskey . . . . a GLISTER OF FISH-HOOKS.

GLISTNER, *subs.* (old).—A sovereign. For synonyms, *see* CANARY.

GLOAK (or **GLOACH**), *subs.* (old).—A man. For synonyms, *see* CHUM and COVE.

1821. D. HAGGART, *Life*, Glossary, pp. 48 and 172. GLOACH, a man; cove.

GLOBE, *subs.* (old).—1. A pewter pot; pewter.

1714. *Memoirs of John Hall*, s.v.

1811. *Lexicon Balatronicum*, s.v.

2. *in. pl.* (common). — The paps. For synonyms, *see* DAIRY.

GLOBE-RANGERS, *subs.* (nautical).—The Royal Marines.

GLOBE-TROTTER, *subs.* (colloquial).—A traveller; primarily one who races from place to place, with the object of covering ground or making a record. Fr.: *un pacquelineur.*

1886. *Graphic*, 7 Aug., 147/1. Your mere idle gaping GLOBETROTTER will spin endless pages of unobservant twaddle, and will record his tedious wanderings with most painful minuteness.

1888. *Academy*, 17 Mar. The inevitable steamboat, the world, and the omnivorous GLOBE-TROTTER.

1889. *Echo*, 9 Feb. The British GLOBE-TROTTER knows Japan as he knows England, and English books about Japan are turned out by the ton.

1890. *Pall Mall Gaz.*, 27 Jan., p. 5, c. 2. This popular definition of a quick-mover has now become effete. Miss Bly is a GLOBE-GALLOPER or she is nothing.

GLOBE-TROTTING, *subs.* (colloquial).—Travelling after the manner of GLOBE-TROTTERS (*q.v.*).

1888. *Academy*, 22 Sept. In fact, GLOBE-TROTTING, as the Americans somewhat irreverently term it, is now frequently undertaken as a mere holiday trip.

GLOPE, *verb.* (Winchester College).—To spit. (Obsolete).

GLORIOUS, *adj.* (common). — Excited with drink; 'in one's altitudes'; BOOZED. For synonyms, *see* DRINKS and SCREWED.

1791. BURNS, *Tam o' Shanter.* Kings may be blessed, but Tam was GLORIOUS, O'er a' the ills of life victorious.

1853. THACKERAY, *Barry Lyndon*, ch. xviii., p. 252. I knew nothing of the vow, or indeed of the tipsy frolic which was the occasion of it; I was taken up GLORIOUS, as the phrase is, by my servants, and put to bed.

1891. *Licensed Vict. Gaz.*, 9 Feb. But as they all began to get GLORIOUS, personalities became more frequent and very much stronger.

GLORIOUS SINNER, *subs. phr.* (rhyming).—A dinner.

GLORY, *subs.* (common). — The after life; KINGDOM COME (*q.v.*). Usually, THE COMING GLORY.

1841. *Punch*, 17 July, p. 2. Clara pines in secret--Hops the twig, and goes to GLORY in white muslin.

IN ONE'S GLORY, *adv. phr.* (colloquial).—In the full flush of vanity, pride, taste, notion, or idiosyncracy.

GLOVES, TO GO FOR THE GLOVES, *verb. phr.* (racing).—To bet recklessly; to bet against a horse without having the wherewithal to pay if one loses—the last resource of the plunging turfite. The term is derived from the well-known habit of ladies to bet in pairs of gloves, expecting to be paid if they win, but not to be called upon to pay if they lose.

1877. HAWLEY SMART, *Play or Pay*, ch. xi. One of the boldest plungers of the day, who had begun badly, was GOING FOR THE GLOVES upon this match.

1886. *Badminton Library*, 'Racing,' p. 255. Hardly worth mentioning are the backers who come in for a hit-or-miss dash at the ring—TO GO FOR THE GLOVES, as it is called in ring parlance.

1891. *Licensed Vict. Gaz.*, 3 Apr. Although we frequently read in stories of the hero backing the right horse at a long price, and so getting out of sundry monetary difficulties, we rarely find the idea realised in practice. Many a bookmaker has GONE FOR THE GLOVES.

GLOW, *adj.* (tailors').—Ashamed.

GLUE, *subs.* (common).—1. Thick soup. (Because it sticks to the ribs.)

ENGLISH SYNONYMS. — Deferred stock; belly-gum; giblets-twist; gut-concrete; rib-tickler; stick-in-the-ribs.

FRENCH SYNONYMS. — *La menêtre* (thieves'); *la lavasse* (= a mess of pot liquor); *la laffe* (thieves'); *la jaffe* (popular); *l'ordinaire* (popular: soup and boiled beef at an ordinary); *le fond d'estomac* (=thick soup); *la mousse*; *la mouillante* (=the moistener).

GERMAN SYNONYMS.—*Jauche*; *Polifke.*

2. (common).—Gonorrhœa.

GLUE-POT, *subs.* (common). — A parson. [Because he joins in wedlock.] For synonyms, *see* DEVIL-DODGER and SKY-PILOT.

1785. GROSE, *Vulg. Tongue*, s.v.

GLUM, *adj.* (old: now recognised).—Sullen; down in the mouth; stern. Fr.: *faire son nez* = to look glum; also, *n'en pas mener large.*

1712. ARBUTHNOT, *Hist. of John Bull*, pt. IV., ch. vii. Nic. looked sour and GLUM, and would not open his mouth.

1785. GROSE, *Vulg. Tongue*, s.v

17(?). *Broadside Ballad.* 'Sam Hall, The parson he will come, And he'll look so bloody GLUM.

1816. JOHNSON, *Dict. of the English Language.* GLUM, s.v., a low cant word formed by corrupting 'gloom.'

1847. THACKERAY, *Vanity Fair*, ii., ch. vi. 'I wonder whether Lady Southdown will go away; she looked very GLUM upon Mrs. Rawdon,' the other said.

1888. *Referee*, 21 Oct. Who found him looking GLUM and gray, And thought his accent gruff and foreign.

1892. A. W. PINERO, *The Times*, v., i. What are you so GLUM about.

GLUMP, *verb.* (provincial). — To sulk. Hence GLUMPY, GLUMPING, and GLUMPISH = sullen or stubborn.

1787. GROSE, *Prov. Glossary.* GLUMPING, sullen, or sour looking. Exm.

1835. TH. HOOK, *Gilbert Gurney.* He was GLUMPY enough when I called.

1860. G. ELIOT, *Mill on the Floss*, Bk. VI., ch. iv. "An it worrets me as Mr. Tom 'ull sit by himself so GLUMPISH, a-knittin' his brow, an' a lookin' at the fire of a night.

GLUTMAN, *subs.* (old).—See quot.

1797. *Police of the Metropolis*, p. 64. An inferior officer of the Customs, and particularly one of that class of supernumerary tide waiters, who are employed temporarily when there is a press or hurry of business. These GLUTMEN are generally composed of persons who are without employment, and, being also without character, recommend themselves principally from the circumstance of being able to write.

GLUTTON, *subs.* (common).—1. A horse which lasts well; a STAYER (*q.v.*).

2. (pugilists'). — A pugilist who can take a lot of PUNISHMENT (*q.v.*).

1819. MOORE, *Tom Crib*, xvi. Thus Theocritus, in his *Milling Match*, calls Amycus a GLUTTON, which is well known to be the classical phrase at Moulsey-Hurst for one who, like Amycus, takes a deal of punishment before he is satisfied.

1891. *Licensed Vict. Mirror*, 30 Jan., p. 6, c. 3. He was known to be an awfully heavy hitter with both hands, a perfect GLUTTON at taking punishment.

GNARLER, *subs.* (thieves'). — A watch dog. For synonyms, *see* TIKE.

GNASP, *verb.* (old).—To vex. For synonyms, *see* RILE.

1728. BAILEY, *English Dict.* s.v.

GNOFF.—*See* GONNOF.

GNOSTIC, *subs.* (colloquial). — A knowing one; a DOWNY COVE (*q.v.*); a WHIPSTER (*q.v.*). [From the Gr., *gnosis*=knowledge.]

1819. MOORE, *Tom Crib*, p. 27. Many of the words used by the Canting Beggars in Beaumont and Fletcher's Masque are still to be heard among the GNOSTICS of Dyot Street and Tothill Fields.

adj. (colloquial). — Knowing, ARTFUL (*q.v.*).

GNOSTICALLY, *adv.* (colloquial).—Knowingly.

1825. SCOTT, *St. Ronan's Well*, ch. iv. He was tog'd GNOSTICALLY enough.

GO, *subs.* (common).—1. A drink; specifically a quartern of gin. (Formerly a GO-DOWN, but *Cf.*, quot. 1811.

[For other combinations *see* ABROAD—ALL FOURS—ALOFT—AUNT—BABY—BACK ON—BAD—BAIL—BALDHEADED—BATH—BATTER—BEDFORDSHIRE—BEGGAR'S BUSH—BETTER—BLAZES—BLIND—BOARD—BODKIN—BULGE—BUNGAY—BURY—BUST—BY-BY—CALL—CAMP—CHUMP—COLLEGE—CRACKED—DEAD BROKE—DEVIL—DING—DING-DONG—DOCK—DOSS—DRAG—FLOUCH—FLUE—GAMBLE—GLAZE—GLORY—GLOVES—GRAIN—GRASS—GROUND—HAIRYFORDSHIRE—HALL—HALVES—HANG—HELL—HIGH FLY—HIGH TOBY—HOOKS—HOOP—JERICHO—JUMP—KITCHEN—MAN—MAJORITY—MILL—MURPHY—PACE—PIECES—PILE—POT—QUEEN—RAKER—RANGE—ROPE-WALK—SALT RIVER—SHALLOW—SHOP—SLOW—SMASH—SNACKS—SNOOKS—SPOUT—STAR-GAZING—SWEET VIOLETS—TOP—WALKER'S BUS—WEST—WHOLE ANIMAL—WOODBINE—WOOLGATHERING—WRONG.

ENGLISH SYNONYMS. — Bender; caulker; coffin nail; common-sewer; cooler; crack; cry; damp; dandy; dash; dewhank; dewdrop; dodger; drain; dram; facer; falsh; gargle; gasp; go-down; hair of the dog, etc.; Johnny; lip; liquor up; livener; lotion; lounce; modest quencher; muzzler; nail from one's coffin; night-cap; nip or nipper; nobbler; old crow; a one, a two, or a three; out; peg; pick-me-up; pony; quencher; reviver; rince; sensation; settler; shift; shove in the mouth; slug; small cheque; smile; snifter; something damp; something short; swig; thimbleful; tiddly; top up; tot; warmer; waxer; wet; whitewash; yard.

FRENCH SYNONYMS. — *Un bourgeron* (popular=a nip of brandy); *un asticot de cercueil* (= a coffin-worm, a play on *verre* and *bière*); *un coup d'arrosoir* (popular: a touch of the watering pot); *un gargarisme* (popular: = a GARGLE [*q.v.*]); *un galopin* (= a PONY [*q.v.*] of beer; *un larme* (= a tear); *un mistiche* (thieves'); *un misérable* (popular: a glass of spirits costing one sou; *une demoiselle* = two sous; *un monsieur*=four sous; *un poisson* =five sous); *un mince de chic* (popular: in contempt); *une coquille de noix* (popular = a thimbleful; a very small GO; a drain); *un jeune homme* (familiar=in capacity four litres); *un Kolback* (popular=a small glass of brandy, or large glass of wine); *une flûte* (familiar); *un extravagant* (popular=a long drink); *un fil* (=a drain); *un*

distingué (popular); *une douleur* (popular=a comforter or PICK-ME-UP); *un ballon* (popular).

ITALIAN SYNONYM.—*Schioppa* (=a long drink: also a large beer glass).

SPANISH SYNONYMS.—*Chisguete* (colloquial); *enjuagadientes* (also = a mouthful of water or wine for rinsing the mouth after eating); *espolada*(=a long drink).

PORTUGUESE SYNONYM.—*Quebrado* (= broken: a small glass).

1690. D'URFEY, *Collin's Walk*, canto 4. And many more whose quality Forbids their toping openly, Will privately, on good occasion, Take six GO-DOWNS on reputation.

1793. GROSE, *Vulg. Tongue*, s.v. GO-SHOP . . . . The Queen's Head in Duke's Court.

1811. *Lexicon Balatronicum.* GO-SHOP, s.v. The Queen's Head, in Duke's Court, Bow Street, Covent Garden, frequented by the under players, where gin and water was sold in three-halfpenny bowls, called GOES; the gin was called Arrack.

1823. JON. BEE, *Dict. of the Turf*, s.v.

1835. DICKENS, *Sketches by Boz*, The Streets: Night. Chops, kidneys, rabbits, oysters, stout, cigars, and GOES innumerable, are served up amidst a noise and confusion of smoking, running, knife-clattering, and waiter-chattering, perfectly indescribable.

1841. *Punch*, Vol. I., p. 11, c. 1. Waiter, a GO of Brett's best alcohol.

1849. THACKERAY, *Hoggarty Diamond*, ch. ii. Two more chairs, Mary, two more tumblers, two more hot waters, and two more GOES of gin!

1850. SMEDLEY, *Frank Fairleigh*, p. 54. Drinking alternate GOES of gin and water with a dustman for the purpose of insinuating myself into the affections of Miss Cinderella Smut, his interesting sister.

1853. *Diogenes*, Vol. II., p. 271. Shall I spend it in theatres? shows? In numerous alcohol GOES?

1870. *Figaro*, 28 May. Their musical performances are evidently inspired by GOES of gin.

1883. *Echo*, 7 Feb., p. 4, c. 3. Witness asked him what he had been drinking. He replied, 'Two half-GOES of rum hot and a half-pint of beer.'

2. (colloquial).—An incident; an occurrence: *e.g.*, a RUM GO= a strange affair, or queer start; a PRETTY GO = a startling business; a CAPITAL GO = a pleasant business.

1803. KENNEY, *Raising the Wind*, i., 3. Ha! ha! ha! Capital GO, isn't it?

1820. *Jack Randall's Diary.* Gemmen (says he), you all well know The joy there is whene'er we meet; It's what I call the primest GO, And rightly named, 'tis—quite a treat.

1835. DICKENS, *Sketches by Boz*, p. 251. A considerable bustle and shuffling of feet was then heard upon the stage, accompanied by whispers of 'Here's a PRETTY GO!—what's to be done?'

1837. BARHAM, *Ingoldsby Legends.* 'Misadventures at Margate.' 'O, Mrs. Jones,' says I, 'look here! Ain't this a PRETTY GO!'

1841. *Punch*, vol. I., p. 162. Stating his conviction that this was raything a RUMMY GO.

1849. THACKERAY, *Pendennis*, ch. lxxiii. Master Frank Clavering . . . had only time to ejaculate the words, 'Here's a JOLLY GO!' and to disappear sniggering.

1869. MRS. H. WOOD, *Roland Yorke*, ch. xli. 'I am about to try what a month or two's absence will do for me.' 'And leave us to old Brown?—that *will* be a NICE GO!'

1876. GEORGE ELIOT, *Daniel Deronda*, ch. vii. A RUM GO as ever I saw.

1880. G. R. SIMS, *Three Brass Balls*, pledge xvi. He . . . exclaimed, 'Well, I'm dashed if this isn't a RUM GO!'

1883. R. L. STEVENSON, *Treasure Island*, p. 55. A pretty RUM GO if squire aint to talk for Doctor Livesey.

1891. N. GOULD, *Double Event*, p. 305. 'It was a NEAR GO,' said Jack.

3. (common).—The fashion; THE CHEESE (*q.v.*); the correct thing. Generally in the phrase ALL THE GO.

1811. *Lexicon Balatronicum*, s.v. He is quite the GO, he is quite varment, he is prime, he is bang up.

1821. EGAN, *Tom and Jerry* [ed. 1891], p. 35. Tom was the GO among the GOES.

1835. HALIBURTON ('Sam Slick'), *The Clockmaker*, 3 S., ch. xiv. Whatever is the GO in Europe will soon be the cheese here.

1837. BARHAM, *Ingoldsby Legends*, I., 251. It was rather the GO With Pilgrims and Saints in the Second Crusade.

1846. *Punch*, vol. X., p. 163. From lowly Queen's quadrangle, Where muffins are the GO.

1880. G. R. SIMS, *Ballads of Babylon* (*Beauty and Beast*). And all day long there's a big crowd stops To look at the lady who's ALL THE GO.

4. (colloquial).—Life; spirit; energy; enterprise; impetus: *e.g.*, PLENTY OF GO = full of spirit and dash. Fr.: *avoir du chien.*

1825. *The English Spy*, i., 178. She's only fit to carry a dean or a bishop. No GO in her.

1865. MACDONALD, *Alec Forbes of Howglen*, II., 269. All night Tibbie Dyster had lain awake in her lonely cottage, listening to the quiet heavy GO of the water.

1882. *Daily Telegraph*, 9 Oct. Mr. Grossmith's music is bright and tripping, full of humour and GO, as, under such circumstances, music should be!

1883. *Illustrated London News*, 10 March, p. 242, c. 3. There was any amount of dash and GO in their rowing.

1887. PATON, *Down the Islands.* Barbadian may therefore be said to mean a man with GO and grit, energy and *vim.*

1889. *Sportsman*, 19 Jan. It all lent a certain zest and GO to the proceedings.

1890. *Pall Mall Gaz.*, 21 Feb., p. 7, c. 1. There was so much heartiness and GO (so to speak) in the work that it reminded me of what I had read about peasant proprietors labouring in Switzerland and elsewhere under a Home Rule Government.

5. (colloquial).—A turn; an attempt; a chance. *Cf.*, NO GO.

TO HAVE A GO AT, *verb. phr.* = to make essay of anything: as a man in a fight, a shot at billiards, and (specifically) a woman.

1836. C. DICKENS, *Pickwick Papers* (about 1827), p. 377 (ed. 1857). Wot do you think o' that for a GO?

1877. *Five Years' Penal Servitude*, ch. iii., p. 221. I've twelve this GO. I did a lagging of seven, and was at the Gib. three out of it.

1878. JAS. PAYN, *By Proxy*, ch. iii. 'I would practise that in the seclusion of my own apartments,' observed Pennicuick; 'and after a few GOES at it, I'll bet a guinea I'd shake the right stick out first.'

1888. HAGGARD, *Mr. Meeson's Will*, ch. x. You have had seven GOES and I have only had six.

6. (American).—A success. TO MAKE A GO OF IT = to bring things to a satisfactory termination.

1888. *Harper's Mag.*, vol. LXXVII., p. 689. Determination to make the venture a GO.

7. (gaming). The last card at cribbage, or the last piece at dominoes. When a player is unable to follow the lead, he calls a GO!

8. (old.)—A DANDY (*q.v.* for synonyms); a very heavy swell indeed, one in the extreme of fashion.

1821. EGAN, *Tom and Jerry* [people's ed.], p. 35. In the parks, Tom was THE GO among the GOES.

Verb (American political).—1. To vote; to be in favour of. *Cf.*, GO FOR.

2. (colloquial).—To succeed; to achieve. *Cf.*, GO DOWN.

1866. *Public Opinion*, 13 Jan., p. 51, c. 1. His London-street railway scheme didn't GO.

1870. H. D. TRAILL, 'On the Watch.' *Sat. Songs*, p. 22. Eh, waddyer say? Don't it GO? Ho, yes! my right honnerble friend. It's GO and GO over the left, it's GO with a hook at the end.

3. (colloquial).—To wager; to risk. Hence to stand treat; to afford.

1768. GOLDSMITH, *Good Natured Man*, Act iii. Men that would GO forty guineas on a game of cribbage.

1876 BESANT AND RICE, *Golden Butterfly*, Prologue ii. The very dice on the counter with which the bar-keeper used to GO the miners for drinks.

1877. S. L. CLEMENS (M. Twain), *Life on the Mississippi*, ch. xliii., p. 390. There's one thing in this world which a person won't take in pine if he can GO walnut; and won't take in walnut if he can GO mahogany. . . . That's a coffin.

c. 1882. *Comic Song*, 'The West End Boys,' verse 3. Another bitter I really can't GO.

1887. *World*, 20 Apr., p. 8. While making up his mind, apparently whether he would GO 'three' or 'Nap.'

4. (racing).—To ride to hounds.

1884. HAWLEY SMART, *From Post to Finish*, p. 219. There would be far too many there who had seen Gerald Rockingham GO with the York and Ainstey not to at once know that he and Jim Forrest were identical.

5. (colloquial).—To be pregnant.

1561-1626. BACON, (quoted by Dr. Johnson). Women GO commonly nine months, the cow and ewe about six months.

1601. SHAKSPEARE, *Henry VIII.*, iv., 1. Great bellied women that had not half a week to GO.

GO DOWN, *verb. phr.* (colloquial).—1. To be accepted, received, or swallowed; to WASH (*q.v.*).

1609. DEKKER, *Lanthorne and Candle-Light*, in wks. (Grosart), III., 272. For the woorst hors-flesh (so it be cheape) does best GOE DOWNE with him.

1659. MASSINGER, *City Madam*, i., 1. But now I fear it will be spent in poultry; Butcher's-meat will not GO DOWN.

1663. PEPYS, *Diary*, 9 Nov. The present clergy will never heartily GO DOWN with the generality of the commons of England.

1742. FIELDING, *Joseph Andrews*, bk. II., ch. xvii. 'O ho! you are a pretty traveller,' cries the host, 'and not know the Levant! . . . . . you must not talk of these things with me, you must not tip us the traveller—it won't GO here.'

1748. SMOLLETT, *Rod. Random*, ch. xxi. He . . . shook his head, and beginning with his usual exclamation said, 'That won't GO DOWN with me.'

1885. W. E. NORRIS, *Adrian Vidal*, ch. vii. In fashion or out of fashion, they always pay and always GO DOWN with the public.

2. (University).—To be under discipline; to be rusticated.

1863. H. KINGSLEY, *Austin Elliot*, i., 179. How dare you say 'deuce in my presence? You can GO DOWN, my Lord.

3. (common).—To become bankrupt. Also, TO GO UNDER.

1892. R. L. STEVENSON and L. OSBOURNE, *The Wrecker*, p. 19. Some one had certainly GONE DOWN.

TO GO DUE NORTH, *verb. phr.* (obsolete).—To go bankrupt. [That is, to go to White-cross Street Prison, once situate in north London]. *See* QUISBY.

TO GO ON THE DUB, *verb. phr.* (old).—To go house-breaking; to pick locks. *See* DUB.

1690. B. E., *Dict. of the Cant. Crew.* Going upon the DUB, *c.* Breaking a House with picklocks.

1785. GROSE, *Vulg. Tongue*, s.v.

1811. *Lexicon Balatronicum*, s.v.

TO GO TO THE DOGS, *verb. phr.* (colloquial).—To go to ruin. [*Cf.*, the Dutch proverb '*Toe goê, toe de dogs*' = money gone, credit gone too.] *See* DEMNITION BOW-WOWS.

1857. A. TROLLOPE, *Three Clerks*, ch. i. The service, he said, would GO TO THE DOGS, and might do for anything he cared and he did not mind h w soon.

1863. H. KINGSLEY, *Austin Elliot*, i, 179. 'Got a second!—bah! The University is going to the '——' Deuce!' suggested Lord Charles, who was afraid of something worse. 'DOGS, Sir, DOGS!

c. 1879. *Broadside Ballad*, 'Old Clo'.' My line of business is played out, it's GOING TO THE DOGS.

TO GO OFF ON THE EAR, *verb. phr.* (American).—To get angry; to fly into a tantrum. *See* NAB THE RUST.

TO GO FOR, *verb. phr.* (colloquial).—1. To attempt; to tackle; to resolve upon; to MAKE FOR (*q.v.*).

1871. JOHN HAY, *Jim Bludso.* He see'd his duty, a dead-sure thing—And he WENT FOR it thar and then.

1890. *Athenæum*, 22 Mar., p. 366, c. 1. The authors have spared neither their creatures nor the reader one iota; whenever an unpleasant effect was obtainable, they straightway seem to have GONE FOR it with unflinching zest.

1891. N. GOULD, *Double Event*, p. 221. Some men had GONE FOR half a dozen, others for two or three, and very few for a single.

1892. HUME NISBET, *Bushranger's Sweetheart*, p. 118. We are strong, my boy, strong now, and are GOING IN FOR the slugging of books also, as well as the immorality of trade.

2. (colloquial).—To attack with violence and directness, whether manually or with the tongue.

1871. *Morning Advertiser*, 2 Feb., 'A curtain lecture.' On . . . arrival home the derelict husband is to be GONE FOR in the most approved style of the late lamented Mrs. Caudle.

1883. JAMES PAYN, *Thicker than Water*, ch. xxxvii. There were occasions . . . when Charley could hardly help GOING FOR the legs of that lofty philosopher, for higher he could not hit him.

1889. *Polytechnic Magazine*, 24 Oct., p. 261. He WENT FOR the jam tarts unmercifully.

1889. *Star*, 24 Aug., p. 4, c. 2. As the enlightened tailor still declined to pay the blackmail one of the anti-machinists WENT FOR him with a chopper.

1892. *Tit Bits*, 19 Mar., p. 424, c. 1. So it comes to much the same thing, with the exception that you cannot indulge in the sad delight of GOING FOR Master Bertie sometimes as you might do were he a member of your own household.

1892. HUME NISBET, *Bushranger's Sweetheart*, p. 123. "Well mate, GO FOR HIM, and we'll keep the cops off till you settle his hash."

3. (colloquial).—To support; to favour; to vote for.

4. (theatrical).—To criticise; specifically, to run down. [An extension of sense 2.] For synonyms, *see* RUN DOWN.

TO GO IN FOR (or AT), *verb. phr.* (colloquial).—To enter for; to apply oneself to (*e.g.*, TO GO IN FOR honours). Also to devote oneself to (*e.g.*, to pay court); to take up (as a pastime, pursuit, hobby, or principle). Closely allied to GO FOR.

1836. C. DICKENS, *Pickwick Papers*, p. 18 (ed. 1857). This advice was very like that which bystanders invariably give to the smallest boy in a street fight; namely, 'GO IN, and win': an admirable thing to recommend, if you only know how to do it.

1849. DICKENS, *David Copperfield*, ch. xviii., p. 162. Sometimes I GO IN AT the butcher madly, and cut my knuckles open against his face.

1864. DICKENS, *Our Mutual Friend*, iii., 3. GO IN FOR money——Money's the article.

1869. WHYTE MELVILLE, *M. or N*, p. 31. Long before he had reached his uncle's house, he had made up his mind to GO IN, as he called it, FOR Miss Bruce, morally confident of winning, yet troubled with certain chilling misgivings, as fearing that *this* time he had really fallen in love.

1870. *Agricultural Jour.*, Feb. Men who GO IN FOR bathing, running, etc.

1872. BESANT AND RICE, *My Little Girl* (in *Once a Week*, 14 Dec., p. 508). He had, after a laborious and meritorious career at Aberdeen, GONE IN FOR Scotch mission work in Constantinople.

1873. MISS BROUGHTON, *Nancy*, ch. xlv. His cheeks are flushed; he is laughing loudly, and GOING IN heavily FOR the champagne.

1883. JAMES PAYN, *Thicker than Water*, ch. xx. This is very nice, but I do wonder, Mrs. Tidman, that you never GO IN FOR curries.

1890. H. D. TRAILL, 'A Noble Watchword,' *Sat. Songs*, p. 58. To GO IN solid for the cause how noble! (though, 'tis true, We must hope at next election that you'll GO IN liquid, too).

TO GO IN UNTO, *verb. phr.* (Biblical).—To have sexual intercourse with. For synonyms, *see* GREENS and RIDE.

1892. *Bible*, Gen. xxx. 3. Behold my maid Bilhah, GO IN UNTO her.

TO GO IT, *verb. phr.* (colloquial).—To act with vigour and daring; to advocate or speak strongly; to live freely. Also to GO IT BLIND, FAST, BALD-HEADED, STRONG, etc. *Cf.*, DASH.

1689 (in ARBER, *Eng. Garner*, vol. VII., p. 365). When these had shared her cargo, they parted company: the French with their shares WENT IT for Petty Guavas in the Grand Gustaphus.

1821. EGAN, *Tom and Jerry* [people's ed.], p. 67. Logic, under the domino, had been GOING IT on a few of his friends with much humour.

Ibid., p. 22. To GO IT, where's a place like London?

1837. R. H. BARHAM, *The Ingoldsby Legends* (Ed. 1862), p. 375. For of this be assured, if you GO IT TOO FAST, you'll be 'dished' like Sir Guy.

1846-48. THACKERAY, *Vanity Fair*, vol. I., ch. 26. 'He's GOING IT PRETTY FAST,' said the clerk.

1849. DICKENS, *David Copperfield*, ch. 6. I say young Copperfield, you're GOING IT.

1841. DOW, *Sermons*, vol. I., p. 176. I would have you understand, my dear hearers, that I have no objection to some of the sons and daughters of the earth GOING IT, while they are young, provided they don't GO IT TOO STRONG.

1864. *Fraser's Mag.*, Aug., p. 54. But what if that O, brave heart? Art thou a labourer? Labour on, Art thou a poet? GO IT STRONG.

1880. MILLIKEN, in *Punch's Almanack* Apr. Nobby togs, high jinks, and lots of lotion, That's the style to GO IT, I've a notion.

Intj. (common).—Keep at it! Keep it up!—a general (sometimes ironical) expression of encouragement. Also GO IT YE CRIPPLES, CRUTCHES ARE CHEAP! (or NEWGATE'S ON FIRE); GO IT, MY TULIP; GO IT MY GAY AND FESTIVE CUSS! (Artemus Ward); or (American) GO IT BOOTS! GO IT RAGS! I'LL HOLD YOUR BONNET! G'LANG! (usually to a man making the pace on foot or horseback.) For similar expressions *see* MOTHER. Fr., *hardi!*

1840. THACKERAY, *Cox's Diary.* Come along this way, ma'am! GO IT, YE CRIPPLES!

1854. THACKERAY, *The Rose and the Ring*, p. 92. 'GO IT, old boy!' cried the impetuous Smith.

1868. MISS BRADDON, *Trail of the Serpent*, bk. I., ch. iii. Three cheers for red! GO IT—GO IT, red!

1890. *Tit Bits*, 1 Mar., p. 325. 'Not for Joe' . . . came from a once popular song. So did GO IT, YOU CRIPPLES.

TO GO OUT, *verb. phr.* (colloquial).—To fall into disuse.

1841. *Punch*, vol. I., p. 113. Pockets, . . . to use the flippant idiom of the day, are GOING OUT.

TO GO OVER, *verb. phr.* (colloquial).—1. To desert from one side to another; specifically (clerical) to join the Church of Rome; to VERT (*q.v.*).

1861. THACKERAY, *Lovel the Widwer*, ch. ii. I remember Pye, of Maudlin, just before he WENT OVER, was perpetually in Miss Prior's back parlour with little books, pictures, medals, etc.

1878. MISS BRADDON, *Open Verdict*, ch. vi. Mr. Dulcimer is a horrid person to tell you such stories; and after this, I shouldn't be at all surprised at his GOING OVER to Rome.

2. (colloquial).—To die; *i.e.*, to GO OVER TO join the majority. Also to GO OFF. TO GO OFF

THE HOOKS, TO GO UNDER, TO GO ALOFT, and TO GO UP.

1848. RUXTON, *Life in the Far West*, p. 4. 'A sight, marm, this coon's GONE OVER.' *Ibid.*, p. 3. Them three's all GONE UNDER.

3. (thieves')—To attack, rifle, and rob.

1889. *Referee*, 2 June. A few who had . . . GONE OVER the landlord, left him skinned.

TO GO OFF, *verb. phr.* (colloquial).—1. To take place; to occur.

1866. MRS. GASKELL, *Wives and Daughters*, ch. xiv. The wedding WENT OFF much as such affairs do.

2. (colloquial).—To be disposed of (as goods on sale, or a woman in marriage).

1835. DICKENS, *Sketches by Boz*, p. 208. Miss Malderton was as well known as the lion on the top of Northumberland House, and had an equal chance of GOING OFF.

3. (colloquial).—To deteriorate (as fish by keeping, or a woman with years).

1883. *Pall Mall Gazette*, 16 Apr., p. 3, c. 2 Shotover rather WENT OFF in the Autumn, and her Leger preparation was not altogether satisfactory.

1892. *Tit-Bits*, 17 Sept., p. 422, c. 3. To those . . . who are apt to GO OFF COLOUR, so to speak, through injudicious indulgence at table.

4. (colloquial).—To die. For synonyms, *see* ALOFT.

1606. SHAKSPEARE, *Macbeth*, v., 7. I would the friends we miss were safe arrived: Some must GO OFF.

1836. C. DICKENS, *Pickwick Papers* (about 1827), p. 368 (Ed. 1857). She's dead, God bless her, and thank him for it!—was seized with a fit and WENT OFF.

GO AS YOU PLEASE, *adj. phr.* (athletics'). — Applied to races where the competitors can run, walk, or rest at will: *e.g.*, in time and distance races. Hence, general freedom of action.

1884. *Punch*, 11 Oct. ''Arry at a Political Picnic.' 'Twas regular GO AS YOU PLEASE.

TO GO TO BATH, PUTNEY, etc.—*See* BATH, BLAZES, HELL, HALIFAX, etc.

TO GO THROUGH, *verb. phr.* (American).—1. To rob: *i.e.*, to turn inside out. Hence, to master violently and completely; to make an end of.

1872. *Evening Standard*, 21 June. The roughs would work their will, and, in their own phrase, GO THROUGH New York pretty effectually.

1888. *Baltimore Sun*. He was garrotted, and the two robbers WENT THROUGH him before he could reach the spot.

Ibid. It was a grand sight to see Farnsworth GO THROUGH him; he did not leave him a single leg to stand upon.

2. (venery).—To possess a woman. For synonyms, *see* RIDE.

TO GO UP (or UNDER), *verb. phr.* (colloquial).—1. To go to wreck and ruin; to become bankrupt; to disappear from society. Also, to die. For synonyms, *see* DEADBROKE.

1864. *The Index*, June. Soon after the blockade, many thought we should GO UP on the salt question.

1879. JAS. PAYN, *High Spirits (Finding His Level)*. Poor John Weybridge, Esq., became as friendless as penniless, and eventually WENT UNDER, and was heard of no more.

1890. *Pall Mall Gaz.*, 29 May, p. 5, c. 1. He asks us further to state that the strike is completely at an end, the society having GONE UNDER.

2. (colloquial).—To die: *Cf.* Ger.: *untergehen*. For synonyms, *see* ALOFT.

18(?). *Hawkeye, The Iowa Chief*, p. 210. Poor Hawkeye felt, says one of his biographers, that his time had come, and

knowing that he must GO UNDER sooner or later, he determined to sell his life dearly.

1849. RUXTON, *Life in the far West*, p. 2. Them three's all GONE UNDER.

1888. *Daily Inter. Ocean*, Mar. All solemnly vowed to see that the mine should be worked solely for the benefit of the girl whether Jim lived or had GONE UNDER.

TO GO UP, *verb. phr.* (American).—To die; specifically to die by the rope.

1867. HEPWORTH DIXON, *New America*, i., 11. Unruly citizens are summarily hung on a cotton tree, and when any question is asked about them, the answer is briefly given, GONE UP—*i.e.*, gone up the cotton tree, or suspended from one of its branches.

TO GO UP FOR, *verb. phr.* (common).—To enter for (as an examination).

1889. *Globe*, 12 Oct., p. 1, c. 4 Always, it seems likely, there will be men GOING UP FOR examinations; and every now and again, no doubt, there will be among them a wily 'Heathen Pass-ee' like him of whom Mr. Hilton speaks—who had cribs up his sleeve, and notes on his cuff.

TO GO WITH, *verb. phr.* (colloquial). — 1. To agree or harmonise with. *See* GEE.

2. (colloquial).—To share the sexual embrace. For synonyms, *see* GREENS and RIDE.

ON THE GO, *adv. phr.* (colloquial).—On the move; restlessly active.

NO GO, *adv. phr.* (colloquial).—Of no use; not to be done; a complete failure. Frequently contracted to N.G.

1835. DICKENS, *Sketches by Boz*, p. 18. I know something about this here family, and my opinion is, it's NO GO.

1853. *Diogenes*, vol. II., p. 271. Dear master, don't think of me ill; If I say—as the lists are NO GO—You've in future no fear for the till!

1884. *Notes and Queries*, 6 S., x., p. 125. There were on the occasion so many rounds and so many NO GOES.

1888. *Puck's Library*, May, p. 12. He thought a moment, and shook his head. It's NO GO was the dictum.

1890. *Punch*, 22 Feb., p. 85. He's a long-winded lot, is Buchanan, slops over tremenjous, he do; . . . But cackle and splutter ain't swimming; so Robert, my nabs, it's NO GO.

1892. J. MCCARTHY and MRS. CAMPBELL-PRAED, *Ladies' Gallery*, p. 84. She sees it is NO GO with the baronet.

A LITTLE BIT ON THE GO, *adv. phr.* (old). — Slightly inebriated; elevated. For synonyms, *see* DRINKS and SCREWED.

1821. EGAN, *Tom and Jerry* [peoples' ed.], p. 58. The Corinthian had made him A LITTLE BIT ON THE GO.

GOAD, *subs.* (old).—1. A decoy at auctions; a horse-chaunter; a PETER FUNK (*q.v.*). [One who goads (*i.e.*, sends up) the prices.]

1609. DEKKER, *Lanthorne and Candle light*, ch. x. They that stand by and conycatche the chapman either with out-bidding, false praises, etc., are called GOADES.

1690. B. E., *Dict. of the Cant. Crew*, s.v. GOADS, those that wheedle in Chapmen for Horse-coursers.

1785. GROSE, *Vulg. Tongue*, s.v.

2. *in. pl.* (old).—False dice.—CHAPMAN. For synonyms, *see* IVORIES.

GOAL, *subs.* (Winchester College).—1. At football the boy who stands at the centre of each end, acting as umpire; and (2) the score of three points made when the ball is kicked between his legs, or over his head without his touching it.

1870. MANSFIELD, *School-Life at Winchester College*, p. 138. Midway between each of the two ends of the line was stationed another boy, as umpire (GOAL, he was called) who stood with his legs wide apart, and a gown rolled up at each foot: if the ball was kicked directly over his head, or between his legs, without his touching it, it was a GOAL, and scored three for the party that kicked it.

GOALER'S COACH. *See* GAOLER'S COACH.

GO-ALONG, *subs.* (thieves'). — A fool; a FLAT (*q.v.*). For synonyms, *see* BUFFLE and CABBAGE HEAD.

1851-61. H. MAYHEW, *Lond. Lab. and Lond. Poor*, vol. I., p. 460. In four days my adviser left me; he had no more use for me. I was a flat: He had me for a GO-ALONG, to cry his things for him.

1853. *Household Words*, No. 183. s.v. 'Slang.'

GOAT, *subs.* (old).—A lecher; a MOLROWER (*q.v.*).

1599. SHAKSPEARE, *Henry V.*, iv., 4. Thou damn'd and luxurious mountain GOAT.

1690. B. E., *Dict. of the Cant. Crew*, s.v. GOAT, a Lecher, a very lascivious person.

1717. CIBBER, *Nonjuror*, i., 1. At the tea-table I have seen the impudent GOAT most lusciously sip off her leavings.

1785. GROSE, *Vulg. Tongue*, s.v.

Verb (common).—1. To thrash. For synonyms, *see* TAN.

1864. *Derby Day*, p. 70. You won't GOAT me? Not this journey.

TO PLAY THE GOAT, *verb. phr.* (common).—1. To play the fool; to MONKEY (*q.v.*). Fr., *faire l'oiseau*.

2. (venery).—To lead a fast life; to be given to MOLROWING (*q.v.*).

TO RIDE THE GOAT, *verb. phr.* (common).—To be initiated into a secret society. [From the vulgar error that a live goat, for candidates to ride, is one of the standing properties of a Masonic lodge.]

GOATEE, *subs.* (colloquial). — A tufted beard on the point of a shaven chin. [In imitation of the tuft of hair on a goat's chin.]

ENGLISH SYNONYMS (for a beard generally).—Charley; imperial; Newgate (or sweep's) frill, or fringe.

FRENCH SYNONYMS. — *Une marmouse* (thieves'); *un impériale* (colloquial: formerly *une royale*); *un bouc* or *une bouquine* (=a goatee); *bacchantes* (thieves': the beard, but more especially the whiskers, from *bâche* = awning).

GERMAN SYNONYM. — *Soken* (from the Hebrew; also = old man).

ITALIAN SYNONYMS. — *Bosco di berlo* (the forest on the face); *settosa* (= full of hair); *spinola* (= thorny).

SPANISH SYNONYM.—*Bosque* (= wood).

1869. *Orchestra*, 18 June. Working carpenters with a straggling GOATEE on the chin, and a mass of unkempt hair on the head.

GOATER, *subs.* (American thieves'). — Dress. For synonyms, *see* TOGS.

GOAT-HOUSE, *subs.* (old). — A brothel. [From GOAT, *subs.*, sense 1.] For synonyms, *see* NANNY-SHOP.

GOATISH, *adj.* (old, now recognised). — Lecherous. [As vieing with a goat in lust.] Hence GOATISHLY, *adv.*, and GOATISHNESS, *subs.*

1622. MASSINGER AND DEKKER, *Virgin Martyr*, iii., 1. Give your chaste body up to the embraces of GOATISH lust.

1605. SHAKSPEARE, *King Lear*, i. 2. An admirable evasion of whoremaster-man, to lay his GOATISH disposition to the charge of a star.

GOAT-MILKER, *subs.* (venery).—1. A prostitute. For synonyms, *see* BARRACK-HACK and TART.

2. (venery).—The female *pudendum*. For synonyms, *see* MONOSYLLABLE.

GOAT'S JIG (or **GIGG**), *subs.* (old).—Copulation. For synonyms, *see* GREENS.—GROSE.

GO-AWAY, *subs.* (American thieves').—A railway-train.

1859. MATSELL, *Vocabulum*, s.v. The knuck was working the GOAWAYS at Jersey City.

GOB (or **GOBBETT**), *subs.* (old: now vulgar). 1. A portion; a mouthful; a morsel. Also a gulp; a BOLT (*q.v.*). [Latin, *gob* = mouth: Old Fr., *gob*=a gulp.] Skeat says the shorter form GOB is rare.

1380. WYCLIFFE, *Trans. of Bible*. Thei token the relifis of broken GOBETIS twelve cofres full.

1542. *Apop. of Erasmus* [1878], p. 14. A bodie thinketh hymself well emende in his substaunce and riches, to whom hath happened some good GUBBE of money, and maketh a great whinyng if he haue had any losse of the same.

1599. NASHE, *Lenten Stuffe*, in wks., v., 261. And thrust him downe his pudding house at a GOBBE.

1605. CHAPMAN, *All Fools*, Act iii., p. 62 (*Plays*, 1874). *Ri.* And do you think He'll swallow down the gudgeon? *Go.* O my life, It were a gross GOB would not down with him.

1611, L. BARRY, *Ram. Alley*, I., i. That little land he gave, Throate the lawyer swallowed at one GOB For less than half the worth.

1689. SELDEN, *Table-Talk*, p. 50 (Arber's ed.). The meaning of the Law was, that so much should be taken from a man, such a GOBBET sliced off, that yet notwithstanding he might live in the same Rank and Condition he lived in before; but now they Fine men ten times more than they are worth.

1690. B. E., *Dict. Canting Crew*, s.v. GOB(c) . . . also a Bit or Morsel; hence GOBBETS, now more in use for little Bits.

1748. T. DYCHE, *Dictionary* (5th ed.). GOB or GOBBET (s.) a piece just big enough, or fit to be put into the mouth at once.

1774. FOOTE, *Cozeners*, ii., 2. The venison was over-roasted, and stunk—but Doctor Dewlap twisted down such GOBS of fat.

1785. GROSE, *Vulg. Tongue*, s.v.

1816. JOHNSON, *Eng. Dict.* (12th ed.) GOB, a small quantity, a low word.

1869. S. L. CLEMENS (M. Twain), *Innocents Abroad*, ch. vii. It is pushed out into the sea on the end of a flat, narrow strip of land, and is suggestive of a GOB of mud on the end of a shingle.

2. (common). — The mouth. SHUT YOUR GOB=an injunction to silence. *See* GAB. A SPANK ON THE GOB = a blow on the mouth. GOB-FULL OF CLARET =a bleeding at the mouth. GIFT OF THE GAB or GOB, *see* GAB. For synonyms *see* POTATO-TRAP.

1690. B. E., *Dict. Cant. Crew*, s.v. GOB, the Mouth.

1819. T. MOORE, *Tom Crib's Memorial*, p. 18. *Home-hits* in the *bread-basket*, clicks in the GOB. *Ibid*, p. 30.

1836. M. SCOTT, *Tom Cringle's Log*, ch. 1. 'All right—all right,' I then exclaimed, as I thrust half a doubled-up muffin into my GOB.

1851-61. H. MAYHEW, *Lond. Lab. and Lond. Poor*, vol. I., p. 469 I managed somehow to turn my GOB(mouth) round and gnawed it away.

3. (common).—A mouthful of spittle. Fr., *un copeau*; It., *smalzo di cavio* (=gutter-butter). For synonyms, *see* SIXPENCES.

Verb. (common). — 1. To swallow in mouthfuls; to gulp down. Also GOBBLE (*q.v.*).

1692. L'ESTRANGE *Fables*. Down comes a kite powdering upon them, and GOBBETS up both together.

2. (common). — To expectorate. Fr., *glavioter* (popular); *molarder*.

GOBBIE, *subs.* (nautical).—A coastguardsman; whence GOBBIE-SHIP, a man of war engaged in the preventive service.

1890. *Scotsman*, 4 Aug. When a meeting takes place the men indulge in a protracted yarn and a draw of the pipe. The session involves a considerable amount of expectoration all round, whereby our friends come to be known as GOBBIES, and in process of time the term came to be applied to the ships engaged in the service. *Ibid.* There are no fewer than three other GOBBIE SHIPS in the channel fleet, each of which carries a considerable number of coastguardsmen putting in their annual period of drill.

GOBBLE (or **GOBBLE UP**), *verb.* (vulgar).—To swallow hastily or greedily; hence (American) to seize, capture, or appropriate. Also GOB: *e.g.*, GOB that!

1602. DEKKER, *Satiro-mastix*, in wks. (1873) i. 233. They will come to GOBBLE downe Plummes.

1728. SWIFT, *Misc. Poems*, in wks. (1824) xiv. 232. The time too precious now to waste, The supper GOBBLED up in haste.

1751. SMOLLETT, *Peregrine Pickle*, ch. cvi. Summoned in such a plaguy hurry from his dinner, which he had been fain to GOBBLE up like a cannibal.

1846-48. THACKERAY, *Vanity Fair*, vol. I, ch. v. Mr. Jos. . . . helped Rebecca to everything on the table, and himself GOBBLED and drank a great deal.

1860. THACKERAY, *Philip*, ch. xiii. There was a wily old monkey who thrust the cat's paw out, and proposed to GOBBLE up the smoking prize.

GOBBLE-PRICK, *subs.* (old). — A lecherous woman.—GROSE.

GOBBLER, *subs.* (old).—1. A duck. —HARMAN.

2. (colloquial). — A turkey cock; a BUBBLY - JOCK (*q.v.*). Also GOBBLE-COCK.

1785. GROSE, *Vulg. Tongue*, s.v.

1851. HOOPER, *Widow Rugby's Husband*, etc., p. 94. Her face was as red as a GOBBLER'S snout.

3. (vulgar).—The mouth. For synonyms, *see* POTATO-TRAP.

4. (colloquial). — A greedy eater. For synonyms, *see* STODGER.

GOBBLING, *subs.* (vulgar).—Gorging.

1846-48. THACKERAY, *Vanity Fair*, ch. iii., vol. I. His mouth was full of it, his face quite red with the delightful exercise of GOBBLING 'Mother, it's as good as my own curries in India.'

GO-BETWEEN, *subs.* (old).—A pimp or bawd. Now an intermediary of any kind.

1596. SHAKSPEARE, *Merry Wives of Windsor*, Act ii., sc. 2. Even as you came into me, her assistant, or GO-BETWEEN, parted from me.

1785. GROSE, *Vulg. Tongue*, s.v.

GOBLIN, *subs.* (old).—A sovereign. For synonyms, *see* CANARY.

1887. W. E. HENLEY, *Villon's Straight Tip*. Your merry GOBLINS soon stravag: Boose and the blowens cop the lot.

GOB-BOX, *subs.* (common). — The mouth. [From GOB, *subs.*] For synonyms, *see* POTATO-TRAP.

1773. FORSTER, *Goldsmith*, Bk. IV., ch. xiv., p. 414 (5th ed.). Shuter protesting in his vehement odd way that 'the boy could patter,' and 'use the GOB-BOX as quick and smart as any of them.'

1819. SCOTT, *Bride of Lammermoor*, ch. i. Your characters . . . . made too much use of the GOB-BOX; they *patter* too much.

GOB-STICK, *subs.* (old).—A silver table-spoon. (In use in America = either spoon or fork); (nautical), a horn or wooden spoon.

1789. PARKER, *Life's Painter*, s.v.

1859. MATSELL, *Vocabulum*, s.v.

GOB-STRING (or **GAB-STRING**), *subs.* (old).—A bridle.

1785. GROSE, *Vulg. Tongue*, s.v.

1811. *Lexicon Balatronicum*, s.v.

GO-BY, *subs.* (colloquial). — The act of passing; an evasion; a deception. To GIVE ONE THE GO-BY = to cut; to leave in the lurch. *Cf.*, CUT (*subs.* sense 2, *verb.* sense 2).

1876. HINDLEY, *Cheap Jack*, p. 214. When we came in contact with a travelling bookseller we could GIVE HIM THE GO-BY with our library.

1892. R. L. STEVENSON, *Kidnapped*, ch. ix. She GAVE US THE GO-BY in the fog — as I wish from the heart that ye had done yoursel'!

1892. *Sala's Journal*, 25 June, p. 194. Now can you understand how it is possible, and, I think, expedient, TO GIVE politics THE GO-BY, so far as one conveniently can?

GO-BY-THE-GROUND, *subs.* (old). —A dumpy man or woman.— GROSE.

GOD, *subs.* (common).—1. *in. pl.*, the occupants of the gallery at a theatre. [Said to have been first used by Garrick because they were seated on high, and close to the sky-painted ceiling.] Fr., *paradis* = gallery; also *poulailler*. In feminine, GODDESS.

1772. CUMBERLAND, *Fashionable Lover* [probably spoken by printer's devil]. 'Tis odds For one poor devil to face so many GODS.

1812. J. and H. SMITH, *Rejected Addresses*, p. 128 [ed. 1869]. Each one shilling GOD within reach of a nod is, And plain are the charms of each gallery GODDESS.

1843. THACKERAY, *Irish Sketch Book*, ch. xxvii. The gallery was quite full . . . one young GOD, between the acts, favoured the public with a song.

1872. M. E. BRADDON, *Dead Sea Fruit*, ch. xiv. There come occasionally actors and actresses of higher repute, eager to gather new laurels in these untrodden regions, and not ill pleased to find themselves received with noisy rapture and outspoken admiration by the ruder GODS and homelier GODDESSES of a threepenny gallery.

1890. *Globe*, 7 Apr., p. 2, c. 2. The GODS, or a portion of them, hooted and hissed while the National Anthem was being performed.

1892. SYDNEY WATSON, *Wops the Waif*, iii., iv. It is only when we have paid our 'tuppence' and ascended to the gallery just under the roof, known as 'among the GODS,' that we begin to understand what is meant by the lowest classes, the 'great unwashed.'

1892. *Pall Mall Gaz.*, 20 Apr., p. 2, c. 3. If theatre managers would only give the public the chance of as good a seat as can be got at the Trocadero or the Pavilion, at the same price, and manage the ventilation of their houses so as not to bake the GODS and freeze the 'pitites,' I venture to think that fewer people would go to the music halls.

2. *in. pl.* (printers'). — The quadrats used in JEFFING (*q.v.*).

3. (tailors').—A block pattern. GODS OF CLOTH = 'classical tailors.'—GROSE. *See* SNIP.

4. (Eton).—A boy in the sixth form.

1881. PASCOE, *Life in our Public Schools*. A GOD at Eton is probably in a more exalted position, and receives more reverence than will ever afterwards fall to his lot.

A SIGHT FOR THE GODS, *phr.* (common).—A matter of wonderment.

1892. HUME NISBET, *Bushranger's Sweetheart*, p. 31. Stringy Bark prepared to greet his native land, was A SIGHT FOR THE GODS to behold with satisfaction, and men to view from afar with awed respect.

GOD PAYS! *phr.* (old).—An expression at one time much in the mouth of disbanded soldiers and sailors (who assumed a right to live on the public charity). The modern form is, 'If I don't pay you, God Almighty will.'

1605. *London Prodical*, ii., 3. But there be some that bear a soldier's form, That swear by him they never think upon; Go swaggering up and down, from house to house, Crying, GOD PAYS.

1630. TAYLOR, in wks. These feather'd fidlers sing, and leape, and play, The begger takes delight, and GOD DOTH PAY.

1640. BEN JONSON, *Epigr. XII.* To every cause he meets, this voice he brays, His only answer is to all, GOD PAYS.

GOD (or BRAMAH) KNOWS: I DON'T, *phr.* (common). — An emphatic rejoinder.

1598. FLORIO, *A Worlde of Wordes. Come Iddio vel dica.*, a phrase, as wee would say: GOD HIMSELFE TELL YOU, I CANNOT.

GODDESS DIANA, *subs. phr.* (rhyming). A sixpence. For synonyms, *see* TANNER.

1864. *The Press*, 12 Nov. GODDESS DIANA is the rhyming equivalent for a tanner which signifies sixpence.

GOD-DOT! *intj.* (old).—An oath. By God! [A contraction of 'God wot!'] For synonyms, *see* OATHS.

GODFATHER, *subs.* (old). — A juryman.

1598. SHAKSPEARE, *Merchant of Venice*, iv. 1. In christ'ning thou shalt have two GODFATHERS, Had I been judge, thou should'st have had ten more, To bring thee to the gallows, not the font.

1616. BEN JONSON, *Devil's An Ass*, v., 5. Not I, If you be such a one, sir, I will leave you To your GOD-FATHERS IN LAW. Let twelve men work.

1638. RANDOLPH, *Muses' Looking Glass*, ix. 251. I had rather zee him remitted to the jail, and have his twelve GODVATHERS, good men and true, condemn him to the gallows.

1785. GROSE, *Vulg. Tongue*, s.v.

TO STAND GODFATHER, *verb. phr.* (common). — To pay the reckoning. [Godfathers being the objects of much solicitude and expectation.]

1811. *Lexicon Balatronicum*, s.v. Will you stand GODFATHER, and we will take care of the brat? = repay you another time.

GO-DOWN, *subs.* (old). — 1. A draught of liquor; a GO (*q.v.*).

2. (American).—*See* quot.

1881. *New York Times*, 18 Dec., quoted in 'N and Q' 6, S. v. 65. *Go Down.* —A cutting in the bank of a stream for enabling animals to cross or to get to water.

GOD-PERMIT, *subs.* (old).—A stage coach. [Which was advertised to start *Deo volente.*]

1785. GROSE, *Vulg. Tongue*, s.v. GOD-PERMIT, a stage coach, from that affectation of piety, frequently to be met with in advertisements of stage coaches or waggons, where most of their undertakings are promised with if GOD PERMIT, or GOD WILLING.

1825. *Modern Flash Dict.*, s.v.

GOD'S-MERCY, *subs.* (old).—Ham (or bacon) and eggs. ['There's nothing in the house but God's mercy': at one time a common answer in country inns to travellers in quest of provant.]

GOD'S-PENNY, *subs.* (old). — An earnest penny.

1690. B. E., *Dict. of the Cant. Crew*, s v. GOD'S PENNY, Earnest Money, to Bind a Bargain.

1765. PERCY, *Reliques*, 'The heir of Linne.' Then John he did him to record draw, And John he cast him a GOD'S PENNIE.

GO-EASTER, *subs.* (American cowboys'). — A portmanteau; a PETER (*q.v.*). [Because seldom used except in going city- or east-wards.]

GOER, *subs.* (old).—1. The foot. For synonyms, *see* CREEPERS.

1557-1634. CHAPMAN, in *Encyclop. Dict.* A double mantle, cast Athwart his shoulders, his faire GOERS grac't With fitted shoes.

2. (colloquial).—An expert or adept; as in drawing, talking, riding; one well up to his (or her) work: generally with an adjective, as *e.g.*, A FAST (or HELL OF A) GOER = a good goer.

1857. G. A. LAWRENCE, *Guy Livingstone*, ch. xx. Nevertheless, she was always deeply engaged, and generally to the best GOERS in the room.

GOFF. *See* MRS. GOFF.

GOGGLES, *subs.* (common).—1. A goggle-eyed person. Also GOGGLER.

1647. BEAUMONT AND FLETCHER, *Knight of Malta*, v., 2. Do you stare, GOGGLES?

1891. CLARK RUSSELL, *Ocean Tragedy*, p. 51. No use sending blind man aloft, GOGGLERS like myself, worse luck.

2. *in. pl.* (common). — The eyes: specifically those with a constrained or rolling stare; also GOGGLE-EYES. GOGGLE-EYED = squint-eyed.

1598. FLORIO, *A Worlde of Wordes. Strabo*, he that looketh a squint or is GOGGLE-EIDE.

c. 1746. ROBERTSON OF STRUAN, *Poems*, 69. An eagle of a dwarfish size, With crooked Beak, and GOGLE EYES.

1691-1763. BYROM, *Dissection of a Beau's Head*. Those muscles, in English, wherewith a man ogles, When on a fair lady he fixes his GOGGLES.

1785. GROSE, *Vulg. Tongue*, s.v.

1821. PIERCE EGAN, *Life in London*, p. 241. Rolling your GOGGLES about after all manner of people.

3. *in. pl.* (common).—Spectacles. For synonyms, *see* BARNACLES.

Verb (colloquial).—GOGGLE = to roll the eyes; to stare.

1577-87. HOLINSHED, *Description of Ireland*, ch. i. They GOGGLE with their eyes hither and thither.

1785. GROSE, *Vulg. Tongue*, s.v. GOGGLE, to stare.

1820-37. WALPOLE, *Letters*, iii., 174. He GOGGLED his eyes.

1880. MILLIKIN, *Punch's Almanack*, April. Scissors! don't they GOGGLE and look blue.

GOGMAGOG, *subs.* (colloquial).—A goblin; a monster; a frightful apparition.—HOOD.

GOING, *subs.* (colloquial). — The condition of a road, a piece of ground, a cinder-path: *i.e.*, the accommodation for travelling. *E.g.*, THE GOING is bad.

1872. *Morning Post*, 19 Aug. The Lamb's starting in the Frankfort steeplechase will depend upon the state of the ground, and, avoiding Wiesbaden, where the GOING is indifferent.

1883. *Daily Telegraph*, 23 Nov. The GOING was wonderfully clean for the time of year.

GOINGS-ON, *subs.* (colloquial). — Behaviour; proceedings; conduct. *Cf.*, CARRYINGS ON.

1845. DOUGLAS JERROLD, *Mrs. Caudle*, Lecture viii. Pretty place it must be where they don't admit women. Nice GOINGS-ON, I daresay, Mr. Caudle.

1870. *Lloyd's Newspaper*, 11 Sept. 'Review.' Elsie is beloved by Gawthwaite, the village schoolmaster, and he takes her to task for her GOINGS-ON.

GOLDARNED (or **GOLDURNED**, **GOLDASTED**, etc.), *adj.* (common).— A mild form of oath: = BLAMED (*q.v.*); BLOODY (*q.v.*). *See* OATHS. As *intj.*, GOLDARN IT! etc.

1888. *American Humorist*. 'Bill, are you hurt?' 'Yes, by gum; I've broke my GOLDARNED neck.'

1888. *Cincinnati Enquirer*. Finally, Deacon Spalding broke out with: 'That GOLDASTED St. Louis mugwump has made suckers of us again with his cracks about coming into the league. I move we adjourn.'

GOLD-BACKED 'UN, *subs.* (common).—A louse. Also GREY-BACKED 'UN. For synonyms, *see* CHATES.

GOLD BUG, *subs. phr.* (American).—A man of wealth and (inferentially) distinction; a millionaire. *See* BUG.

1888. *St. Louis Globe Democrat*, Mar. 5. I do not think the feeling against silver is anything like as strong as it was. Of course, a few GOLD BUGS might fight him.

GOLD-DROPPER, *subs.* (old).—A sharper. An old-time worker of the confidence trick. *See* quots. Also GOLD-FINDER.

1690. B. E., *Cant. Crew*, s.v. GOLD-DROPPERS, Sweetners, Cheats, Sharpers.

1748. T. DYCHE, *Dictionary* (5th ed.). GOLD-FINDER (s.) . . . also a cant name for a cheat, who under the pretence of finding a piece of money, and inviting a by-stander to partake of a treat, etc., out of it, endeavours to get him to play at cards, dice, etc., in order to win or cheat him of his money; they are sometimes also called *guinea-droppers*.

1785. GROSE, *Vulg. Tongue*, s.v. Sharpers who drop a piece of gold, which they pick up in the presence of some unexperienced person, for whom the trap is laid, this they pretend to have found, and, as he saw them pick it up, they invite him to a public house to partake of it: when there, two or three of their comrades drop in, as if by accident, and propose cards, or some other game, when they seldom fail of stripping their prey.

1811. *Lexicon Balatronicum*, s.v.

GOLDEN-CREAM, *subs.* (thieves').—Rum.

1889. CLARKSON and RICHARDSON, *Police*, p. 321, s.v.

GOLD-END MAN, *subs. phr.* (old).—An itinerant jeweller; a buyer of old gold and silver. [GOLD-END = a broken piece of jewellery.] Also GOLDSMITH'S APPRENTICE. *See Eastward Hoe.*

1610. JONSON, *Alchemist*, ii., 1. I know him not, he looks like a GOLD-END MAN.

1622. FLETCHER, *Beggar's Bush*, iii., 1. *Hig.* Have ye any ENDS OF GOLD or silver?

GOLDEN GREASE, *subs. phr.* (old).—A fee; also a bribe. For synonyms, *see* PALM OIL.

GOLDFINCH, *subs.* (old).—1. A well-to-do man; a WARM 'UN (*q.v.*).

1690. B. E., *Dict. Cant. Crew*, s.v. GOLDFINCH, *c.* He that has alwaies a Purse or Cod of Gold in his Fob.

1785. GROSE, *Vulg. Tongue*, s.v.

1852. JUDSON, *Mysteries, etc., of New York*, ch. iv. 'Was the swell a GOLDFINCH?' 'He wasn't nothin' else. Got a clean ten times ten out of him.'

Ibid. 'It'll be a great lay, if the game's fat. Is it a GOLDFINCH?' 'Fifty thousand, hard dust.'

2. (common).—A guinea; a sovereign. For synonyms, *see* CANARY.

1700. FARQUHAR, *Constant Couple*, ii., 2. *Sir H.* Don't you love singing-birds, madam? *Angel (aside).* That's an odd question for a lover; (*aloud*) Yes, sir. *Sir H.* Why, then, madam, here is a nest of the prettiest GOLDFINCHES that ever chirped in a cage.

1822. SCOTT, *The Fortunes of Nigel*, ch. iv. Put your monies aside, my lord; it is not well to be seen with such GOLDFINCHES chirping about one in the lodgings of London.

1826. BUCKSTONE, *Luke the Labourer*, iii., 4. Good-night, noble captain. Pipe all hands at five o'clock, for I've a day's work to do. We'll jig it to-morrow, to the piping of GOLD-FINCHES.

1834. W. H. AINSWORTH, *Rookwood*, p. 101 (ed. 1864). Here's a handful of GOLDFINCHES ready to fly.

GOLDFINCH'S NEST, *subs.* (venery).—The female *pudendum*. For synonyms, *see* MONOSYLLABLE.

1827. *The Merry Muses*, p. 70. And soon laid his hand on the GOLDFINCH'S NEST.

GOLD-FINDER, *subs.* (old).—1. An emptier of privies. Also TOM-TURD-MAN; GONG-MAN; and NIGHT-MAN. Fr., *un fouille-merde; un fifi.* Also *passer la jambe à Jules*=to upset MRS. JONES, *i.e.*, to empty the privy tub.

1611. COTGRAVE, *Dictionarie, Gadouard*, a GOULD-FINDER, Jakes-farmer.

1635. FELTHAM, *Resolves.* As our GOLDFINDERS . . . . in the night and darkness thrive on stench and excrements.

1653. MIDDLETON, *Sp. Gipsy*, ii., 2, p. 398 (Mermaid series). And if his acres, being sold for a maravedii a turf for larks in cages, cannot fill this pocket, give 'em to GOLDFINDERS.

1659. TORRIANO, *Vocabolario*, s.v.

1704. *Gentleman Instructed*, p. 445 (1732). We will commit the further discussion of the poet to a committee of GOLDFINDERS, or a club of rake-kennels.

1785. GROSE, *Vulg. Tongue*, s.v

2. (old).—A thief; a GOLD-DROPPER (*q.v.*).

GOLD HAT-BAND, *subs.* (old University).—A nobleman undergraduate; a TUFT (*q.v.*).

1628. EARLE, *Microcosmography.* His companion is ordinarily some stale fellow that has been notorious for an ingle to GOLD HATBANDS, whom hee admires at first, afterwards scornes.

1889. *Gentleman's Mag.*, June, p. 598. Noblemen at the universities, since known as 'tufts,' because of the gold tuft or tassle to their cap, were then known as GOLD HATBANDS.

GOLDIE-LOCKS, *subs.* (old).—A flaxen-haired woman. GOLDY-LOCKED=golden haired.

1598. FLORIO, *Worlde of Wordes. Biondella* . . . . a golden-lockt wench, as we say a GOLDILOCKS.

1605. BEN JONSON, *The Fox*, i., 1. Thence it fled forth, and made quick transmigration to GOLDY-LOCKED Euphorbus.

GOLD MINE, *subs. phr.* (common).—A profitable investment; a store of wealth, material or intellectual.

1664. H. PEACHAM, *Worth of a Penny*, in Arber's *Garner*, vol. VI., p. 249. Some men . . . when they have met with a GOLD MINE, so brood over and watch it, day and night, that it is impossible for Charity to be regarded, Virtue rewarded, or Necessity relieved.

1830 TENNYSON, *Dream of Fair Women*, p. 274. GOLD-MINES of thought—to lift the hidden ore.

1882. THORMANBY, *Famous Racing Men*, p. 81. Mendicant . . . ran nowhere in the Cup . . . in reality she was destined to prove a GOLD MINE, for ten years afterwards she brought her owner £80,000 through her famous son, Beadsman.

1883. *Sat. Review*, 28 Apr. 533/2. His victory proved a GOLD MINE to the professional bookmakers.

1887. FROUDE, *Eng. in West Indies*, ch. v. Every one was at law with his neighbour, and the island was a GOLD MINE to the Attorney-General.

GOLGOTHA, *subs.* (old).—1. The Dons' gallery at Cambridge; also applied to a certain part of the theatre at Oxford. [That is, 'the place of skulls': *Cf.*, Luke xxiii. 33, and Matthew xxvii. 33, whence the pun: Dons being the heads of houses.]

1730. JAS. MILLER, *Humours of Oxford*, Act ii., p. 23 (2nd ed.). Sirrah, I'll have you put in the black-book, rusticated,—expelled—I'll have you *coram nobis* at GOLGOTHA, where you'll be bedevilled, Muck-worm, you will.

1785. GROSE, *Vulg. Tongue*, s.v.

1791. G. HUDDESFORD, *Salmagundi*, (Note on, p. 150). GOLGOTHA, 'The place of a Scull,' a name ludicrously affixed to the Place in which the Heads of Colleges assemble.

1808. J. T. CONYBEARE in C. K. Sharpe's *Correspondence* (1888), i., 324. The subject then, of the ensuing section is *Oxford News* . . . we will begin by GOLGOTHA . . . Cole has already obtained the Headship of Exeter, and Mr. Griffiths . . . is to have that of University.

2. (common).—Hence, a hat.

ENGLISH SYNONYMS.—Battle of the Nile (rhyming, *i.e.*, a TILE (*q.v.*); bell-topper; billy-cock; beaver; box-hat; cady; canister cap; castor; chummy; cathedral; chimney; chimney-pot; cock; colleger; cock-and-pinch; cowshooter; David; deer-stalker; digger's delight; fantail; felt; Gibus; gomer (Winchester); goss; moab; molocher; mortar-board; muffin-cap; mushroom; nab; nap; napper; pantile; pimple-cover; pill-box; plug-hat; pot; shako; shovel; sleep-less hat; sou'wester; stove-pipe; strawer; thatch; tile; topper; truck; upper-crust; wash-pot; wee-jee; wide-awake.

FRENCH SYNONYMS.—*Un accordéon* (popular: an opera hat); *une ardoise* (= a tile); *une bâche* (thieves': also an awning); *une biscope* or *viscope* (vulgar); *un blockaus* (vulgar: a shako); *un bloumard* or *une bloume* (popular); *une boîte à cornes* (a horn case; *i.e.*, a cover for a cuckold); *un Bolivar* (from the hero of 1820); *un boisseau* (also =a bushel); *un bosselard* (school-boys': from *bosselé* = bruised or dented); *un cabas* (popular: = old hat; also basket or bag); *un cadratin* (printers'=a stove-pipe); *un caloquet* (thieves'); *cambriau*, *cambrieux*, or *cambriot* (popular); *un capet* (from old French, *capel*); *une capsule* (popular=a percussion cap); *un carbeluche galicé* (a silk hat); *une casque* (=helmet); *un chapska* (=a shako); *une cheminée* (popular: = chimney-pot); *une corniche* (popular: = a cornice); *un couvercle* (popular: = pot-lid); *une couvrante*; *un couvre-amour* (military); *un cylindre* (=a stove-pipe); *un Desfoux* (from the maker's name); *un epicéphale* (students': from the Greek); *un gadin* (an old hat); *un galure* or *galurin* (popular); *un Garibaldi; un Gibus* (from the inventor's name); *un lampion* (thieves': = grease-pot); *un loubion* (thieves'); *un marquin* (thieves'); *un monument* (popular); *un nid d'hirondelle*; *un niolle* (thieves': an old hat); *un tromblon* (obsolete = blunder-buss); *un tubard*, *tube*, or *tube à haute pression* (= a cylinder); *une tuile* (= a tile); *une tuyau de poêle* (= a stove-pipe).

GERMAN SYNONYMS.—*Bie* (Viennese); *Kowe* (from the Hebrew, *kowa*).

ITALIAN SYNONYMS.—*Bufala*, *baccha* or *biffacha*; *cresta* or *cristiana* (= a cruet); *fungo* (= mushroom).

SPANISH SYNONYMS.—*Tejado* or *techo* (= tiled roof).

GOLIATH, *subs.* (colloquial).—1. A big man.

2. A man of mark among the PHILISTINES (*q.v.*). [Mr. Swinburne described the late Matthew Arnold as 'David, the son of GOLIATH.']

GOLL, *subs.* (old).—The hand; usually *in. pl.* *See* BUNCH OF FIVES and DADDLE.

1601. B. JONSON, *Poetaster*, v., Bring the whoreson detracting slaves to the bar, do; make them hold vp their spread GOLLS.

1602. DEKKER, *Satiro-Mastrix*, in wks. (1873), i., 203. Holde up thy hand: I ha seene the day thou didst not scorne to holde vp thy GOLLES.

1611. MIDDLETON, *Roaring Girl*, Act i. This is the GOLL shall do't.

1620. MIDDLETON, *Chaste Maid*, ii., 2. What their GOLLS can clutch.

1634. S. ROWLEY, *Noble Souldier*, Act ii., Sc. 2. *Bal.* Saist thou me so? give me thy GOLL, thou art a noble girle.

1659. MASSINGER, *City Madam*, iv., i. All the gamesters are ambitious to shake the golden GOLLS of worshipful master Luke.

1661. T. MIDDLETON, *Mayor of Quinborough*, v., i. Down with his GOLLS, I charge you.

1672. DRYDEN, *The Assignation*, Act iii., Sc. 1. A simperer at lower end of a table, With mighty GOLLS, rough-grained, and red with starching.

1787. GROSE, *Prov. Glossary.* GOLL, a hand or fist; give me thy GOLL.

1803. C. K. SHARPE in *Correspondence* (1888), i., 179. Miss Reid with her silk coat and greasie GOLLS.

GOLLOP, *verb.* (common).—To swallow greedily; to gulp. For synonyms, *see* WOLF.

GOLLUMPUS, *subs.* (old).—A clumsy lout.—GROSE.

GOLLY!—A contraction of BY GOLLY! (*q.v.*).

1890. R. L. STEVENSON, *The Wrong Box*, p. 275. GOLLY! what a paper!

GOLOPTIOUS (or **GOLOPSHUS**), *adj.* (common).—Splendid; fine; delicious; luscious.

1888. *Sporting Life*, 7 Dec. It would better scoop the situation if it were described as GOLOPTIOUS.

GOLOSHES, *subs.* (colloquial).—India rubber overshoes. But *see* GROSE.

1796. GROSE, *Vulg. Tongue*, s.v. GOLOSHES, *i.e.* Goliah's shoes. Large leathern clogs, worn by invalids over their ordinary shoes.

GOMBEEN-MAN, *subs.* (Irish).—A usurer; a money-lender; a sharking middleman. For synonyms, *see* SIXTY-PER-CENT.

GOMER, *subs.* (Winchester College).—1. A large pewter dish used in college.

2. (Winchester College).—A new hat. *See* GOLGOTHA.

GOMMY, *subs.* (old).—1. A dandy. Fr., *gommeux*. [Anglo-Saxon, *guma*=a man; a person: *gomme* =*gommer*=gammer. *Cf.*, GOMUS. Beaumont has GOM=a man.]

2. (colloquial).—*See* quot.

1883. *Weekly Dispatch*, 11 Mar., p. 7, c. 4. There has recently been considerable debate as to the meaning of the term GOMMIE. It is very simple. A GOMMIE is one who calls Mr. Gladstone a G. O. M. [Grand Old Man], and thinks he has made a good joke.

3. (colloquial).—A fool. For synonyms, *see* BUFFLE and CABBAGE-HEAD.

GOMUS, *subs.* (Irish).—A fool. For synonyms, *see* BUFFLE and CABBAGE-HEAD.

GONDOLA, *subs.* (American).—1. A railway platform car, sideless or low-sided. Also a flat-bottomed boat.

GONDOLA OF LONDON, *subs. phr.* (common).—A hansom cab; a SHOFUL (*q.v.*). [The description is Lord Beaconsfield's.]

GONE, *adj.* (colloquial).—1. Ruined; totally undone. Also, *adv.*, an expression of completeness, *e.g.*, GONE BEAVER, CORBIE, COON, GANDER, or GOOSE=a man or an event past praying for: *Cf.*, GO UP and GO DOWN.

1604. SHAKSPEARE, *Winter's Tale*, iv., 3. He must know 'tis none of your daughter nor my sister; we are GONE else.

1843-4. HALIBURTON, *Sam Slick in England*, ch. xviii. If a bear comes after you, Sam, you must be up and doin', or it's a GONE GOOSE with you.

1848. RUXTON, *Life in the Far West*, p. 40. From that moment he was GONE BEAVER; he felt queer, he said, all over.

1857. *Notes and Queries*, 2 S. iii., 519. To call a person a GONE CORBIE, is only to say in other words, it's all up with him.

1862. CLOUGH, *Poems*. He had been into the schools; plucked almost; all but a GONE-COON.

1863. C. READE, *Hard Cash*, I., 178. I shall meet her again next week; will you come? Any friend of mine is welcome. Wish me joy, old fellow; I'm a GONE COON.

GONE ON, *adv. phr.* (colloquial). — Enamoured of; infatuated with; MASHED ON (*q.v.*); SWEET ON (*q.v.*). Generally in contempt. Fr., *aimer comme ses petits boyaux*. For synonyms, *see* SWEET ON.

1887. JOHN STRANGE WINTER, *That Imp*, p. 44. He was a fine fellow, and no mistake. And was GONE ON Lady Lorrimor!

1890. *Illustrated Bits*, 29 Mar. p. 10, c. 3. He must have been terribly GONE ON this woman.

1891. N. GOULD, *Double Event*, p. 113. 'Poor chap, he's very far GONE,' thought Jack.

1892. MILLIKEN, *'Arry Ballads*, p. 31. I'll eat my old boots if she isn't dead GONE ON.

GONER, (or **GONES**, **GONUS**, or **GONEY**), *subs.* (American).—1. A fool; a simpleton. Also GAUNEY (*q.v.*). For synonyms, *see* BUFFLE or CABBAGE-HEAD.

1857. *Punch*, 31 Jan. But the lark's when a GONEY up with us they shut, As ain't up to our lurks, our flash patter, and smut.

1860. HALIBURTON, *Sam Slick*, 'The Season Ticket,' No. X. 'It's only grief, Nabby dear, my heart is broke.' 'Is that all, you GONEY?' says she, 'it's lucky your precious neck ain't broke.'

a. 1871. *The Dartmouth*, vol. iv. One day I heard a Senior call a fellow a GONUS. 'GONUS,' echoed I, 'what does that mean?' Oh,' said he, 'you're a Freshman, and don't understand. A stupid fellow, a dolt, a boot-jack, an ignoramus, is here called a GONUS. All Freshmen,' he continued gravely, 'are GONUSES.'

2. (colloquial).—A person past recovery, utterly ruined, or done for in any way.

1876. S. L. CLEMENS (Mark Twain), *Tom Sawyer*, p. 99. 'Yes, but she ain't dead; and, what's more, she's getting better too.' 'All right, you wait and see. She's a GONER, just as dead sure as Muff Potter's a GONER.'

1888. *Cincinnati Enquirer*. Fortunately, she did not see me, or else I should have been a GONER.

1891. N. GOULD. *Double Event*, p. 261. 'Make a noise or follow me, and you're a GONER,' said Smirk.

1892. HUME NISBET, *Bushranger's Sweetheart*, p. 212. A few more of her meddlings and she's a GONER, that's what she is.

GONG (or **GONG-HOUSE**), *subs.* (old).—A privy. For synonyms, *see* MRS. JONES.

1383. CHAUCER, *Canterbury Tales*. 'The Parsons Tale' [Riverside Ed. (1880)], ii., 241. Thise fool wommen, that mowe be likned to a commune GONG, whereas men purgen hire ordure.

GONG-FARMER (or **GONG-MAN**), *subs.* (old).—An emptier of cess-pools; a GOLD-FINDER (*q.v.*).

1598. FLORIO, *A Worlde of Wordes*. *Curadestri*, a iakes, GOONG, or doong farmer.

GONOF (or **GONNOF** or **GONOPH** or **GNOF**), *subs.* (thieves').—1. A thief; specifically a pick-pocket, and especially an adept. [From the Hebrew. Ancient English; a legacy from the old time Jews. It came into use again with the moderns who employ it commonly. *Cf.*, *gonov* = thief in Ex. xxii, 2 and 6, viz., 'if the *gonov* be found.'] *See* THIEVES.

1857. DICKENS, *On Duty with Inspector Field*, in 'Reprinted Pieces' p. 256. If the smallest GONOPH about town were crouching at the bottom of a classic bath Inspector Field would nose him.

1849. *Morning Chronicle*, 2 Nov. A burglar would not condescend to sit among pickpockets. My informant has known a housebreaker to say with a sneer, when requested to sit down with the GONOFFS, 'No, no, I may be a thief, but at least I'm a respectable one.'

1851-61. H. MAYHEW, *Lond. Lab. and Lond. Poor*, Vol. III., p. 325. The GONAFF (a Hebrew word signifying a young thief, probably learnt from the Jew 'fences' in the neighbourhood).

1852. JUDSON, *Myst., etc., of New York*, ch. vii. He next assumed his present profession, and became a GNOF or pickpocket.

1876. HINDLEY, *Adventures of a Cheap Jack*, p. 146. Oh, you tief! you cheat! you GONNOF!

1889. *Referee*, 12 May. GONOPHS . . . . were frequent in Tattersall's on Friday.

1889. C. T. CLARKSON and J. HALL RICHARDSON, *Police*, p. 321. Boys who creep into houses . . . Young gunneffs or GONOPHS.

2. (old).—A bumpkin; a churl; a clumsy hand; a shameless simpleton.

1383. CHAUCER, *Canterbury Tales*, 3187-8. Whilom there was dwelling in Oxenforde, A rich GNOF, that gertes helde to borde.

c. 1547. SONG (quoted by Hotten). The country GNOFFES, Hob, Dick, and Hick, With clubbes and clouted shoon, Shall fill up Dussin Dale With slaughtered bodies soone.

Verb (old).—To wheedle; to cheat; to steal.

GONOPHING, *subs.* (thieves').—Picking pockets.

1857. DICKENS, *The Detective Police*, in 'Reprinted Pieces,' p. 240. From the swell mob, we diverge to the kindred topics of cracksmen, fences . . . . designing young people who go out GONOPHING, and other 'schools.'

GOOBY, *subs.* (common). — A simpleton; a blockhead. For synonyms, *see* BUFFLE and CABBAGE-HEAD.

1892. *Ally Sloper*, 19 Mar., p. 90, c. 3. Why, you old GOOBY, Mister Sloper will pay us twice as much for the ducks.

GOOD! *subs.* (printers').—An abbreviation of 'Good Night!'

Adj. (colloquial). — Responsible; solvent; principally now with 'for'; *e.g.*, He is GOOD for any amount. Also, expert.

1598. SHAKSPEARE, *Merchant of Venice*, i., 3. Antonio is a GOOD man: my meaning in saying that he is a GOOD man, is to have you understand me that he is sufficient.

1824. REYNOLDS, *Peter Corcoran*, 91 GOOD with both hands and only ten stone four.

GOOD GOODS, *in. pl.*, *subs. phr.* (sporting). — Something worth trying for; a success. In the superlative, 'best' GOODS.

1886. *Sporting Times*, 17 July, 1/4. He was a nice young man for a small tea party, And rather GOOD GOODS at a Sunday-school treat.

1892. MILLIKEN, *'Arry Ballads*, p. 39. Theres Warner in 'Drink'; now, that's business, GOOD GOODS and no error.

BIT (or PIECE) OF GOODS, *subs. phr.* (common).—A woman. For synonyms, *see* PETTICOAT.

GOOD OLD . . . *adj. phr.* (popular).—A familiar address, derisive or affectionate according to circumstances. *See* quots.

1891. *Pall Mall Gaz.*, 16 Sept., p. 6, c. 1. It was Mephisto's greeting to Mary Anne—in Marguerite's garden—'GOOD OLD MARY ANNE!'!!!

Ibid. The famous medico craned his neck out of the window, and, sniffing in the smoke, cried, GOOD OLD LONDON. This is a true story.

Ibid., 17 Sept. Mr. Chirgwin . . . rouses mirth by . . . . exclaiming GOOD OLD SPOT! as he discloses the large white ace of diamonds painted over his right optic.

1892. CHEVALIER 'The Little Nipper.' 'E calls 'is mother 'Sally,' And 'is father 'GOOD OLD pally,' And 'e only stands about so 'igh, that's all!

TO FEEL GOOD, *verb. phr.* (American).—To be jolly; comfortable; 'in form'; to be on perfect terms with oneself.

1887. PROCTOR [in *Knowledge*, 1 Dec., p. 29]. A friend of mine tells me a proposition was once invitingly made to him which, to say the least, involved no virtuous self-abnegation, and he was urged to accept it by the plea that it would make him FEEL GOOD.

1888. *Texas Siftings*, 15 Sept. The saloons are going Saturday afternoon, and the men FEEL pretty GOOD before they come abroad.

TO BE IN ONE'S GOOD BOOKS, *verb. phr.* (colloquial).—To be in favour; in good opinion. Conversely, TO BE IN ONE'S BAD BOOKS = To be in disfavour. *See* BOOK.

GOOD AT IT (or AT THE GAME), *adj. phr.* (venery).—An expert bedfellow, male or female.

TO HAVE A GOOD SWIM.—*See* SWIM.

FOR GOOD (or FOR GOOD AND ALL), *adv. phr.* (colloquial). — Completely; entirely; finally.

1673. WYCHERLEY, *Gent. Danc. Master*, ii., in wks. (1713), 276. If I went, I would go FOR GOOD AND ALL.

1693. CONGREVE, *Old Batchelor*, Act i., Sc. 3. *Sharp.* Faith, e'en give her over FOR GOOD AND ALL: you can have no hopes of getting her for a Mistress.

1875. OUIDA, *Signa*, vol. II., ch. v., p. 66. So the child went up to the hills with Bruno, and stayed there FOR GOOD AND ALL.

GOOD AS WHEAT.—*See* WHEAT.

GOOD AS EVER PISSED, *phr.* (venery).—A qualification of extreme excellence.

1719. DURFEY, *Pills, etc.*, ii., 260. And she is AS GOOD for the game AS E'ER PISSED.

GOOD AS A PLAY.—*See* PLAY.

GOOD AS GOLD, *adv. phr.* (colloquial).—Very good; usually of children.

AS GOOD AS THEY MAKE 'EM.—*See* MAKE 'EM.

GOOD-BYE, JOHN! *phr.* (American).—It's no go; all's U.P.

GOOD CESS, *subs. phr.* (Irish).—Good luck. (Probably an abbreviation of 'success.') BAD CESS = the reverse.

1845. BUCKSTONE, *Green Bushes*, i., 1. *All.* Bravo, Paddy! GOOD CESS to ye, Paddy! Hurrah!

GOODFELLOW (or **GOOD BOY**, or **GOOD MAN**), *subs.* (old).—1. A royster; a boon companion.

1570. ASCHAM, *Scholemaster*. Sir Roger had been a GOOD FELLOW in his youth.

1690. B. E., *Dict. Cant. Crew*, s.v. GOOD FELLOW, a Pot companion or Friend of the Bottle.

1785. GROSE, *Vulg. Tongue*, s.v. A word of various imports, according to the place where it is spoken; in the city it means a rich man; at Hockley in the Hole, or St. Giles's, an expert boxer; at a bagnio in Covent Garden, a vigorous fornicator; at an alehouse or tavern, one who loves his pot or bottle: and sometimes, though but rarely, a virtuous man.

1822. SCOTT, *Fortunes of Nigel*, ch. xvii. Rattling Reginald Lowestoffe of the Temple—I know him; he is a GOOD BOY.

2. (old). — A thief. *See* THIEVES.

1608. MIDDLETON, *Trick to Catch the Old One*, ii., 1. *Luc.* Welcome, GOOD FELLOW. *Host.* He calls me thief at first sight. [Footnote in 'Mermaid Series' Ed. GOOD FELLOW was then the cant term for a thief.]

1870. *Evening Standard*, 11 Feb. 'Police Report.' Police detective said that he believed the two prisoners were GOOD MEN. In reply to the magistrate he explained that he meant they were old thieves.

GOOD GIRL (or **GOOD ONE**), *adj. phr.* (old).—A wanton.

1611. COTGRAVE, *Dictionarie*. *Gaultière*—A whore, punke, drab, queane, gill, flirt, strumpet, cockatrice, mad wench, common hackney, GOOD ONE.

GOODMAN, *subs.* (old).—1. A gaoler; a DUBSMAN (*q.v.*).

1721-2. WOODROW, *History*, ii., 636. The GOODMAN of the Tolbooth came to him in his chamber, and told him he might save his life, if he would sign the petition.

2. (colloquial). — The devil. For synonyms, *see* SKIPPER.

GOODMAN-TURD, *subs.* (old).—A contemptible fellow; a BAD-EGG (*q.v.*).

1598. FLORIO, *Worlde of Wordes*. *Dometa*, an old worde for a shitten fellow, or GOODMAN-TURDE.

GOOD NIGHT! *intj. phr.* (general).—A retort to an incredible statement or a delightful piece of news. *See* CARRY ME OUT!

GOOD-PEOPLE, *subs.* (old colloquial).—The fairies.

1828. G. GRIFFIN, *Collegians*, ch. v. An nothin' shows itself now by night, neither spirits nor GOOD PEOPLE.

1848. FORSTER, *Oliver Goldsmith*, bk. I., ch. 1, p. 8 (5th ed.). A small old parsonage house (supposed afterwards to be haunted by the fairies, or GOOD PEOPLE of the district).

1891. R. L. STEVENSON, *Kidnapped*, p. 168. 'Did ever ye hear tell of the story of the Man and the GOOD PEOPLE?'—by which he meant the fairies.

GOOD (or **GOOD OLD**) **SORT**, *subs. phr.* (popular).—A man of social and other parts.

1892. HUME NISBET, *Bushranger's Sweetheart*, p. 149. Had we not better make a clean breast of it, and trust to his generosity; he seems a GOOD SORT?

GOOD THING, *subs. phr.* (colloquial).—Something worth having or backing; a *bon mot*; GOOD GOODS (*q.v.*). In racing a presumed CERT (*q.v.*).

1844. *Puck*, p. 63. Here's to the GOOD THING whose neatness we prize.

1884. *Saturday Review*, 2 Aug., p. 147, c. 2. The Goodwood Stakes was considered a GOOD THING for Florence, who has proved herself to be an extraordinary mare.

1888. *Sporting Life*, 10 Dec. In a field of four, Livingstone, who was voted a GOOD THING, was served up a warm favourite.

1891. *Daily Telegraph*, 21 Mar. It had been generally anticipated that this was a GOOD THING for Oxford.

1892. *Ally Sloper*, 19 Mar., p. 90, c. 3. That them as trades in rags and bones Makes more than them as writes GOOD THINGS.

GOOD TIME, *subs. phr.* (old).—A carouse; a friendly gathering; an enjoyable bout at anything.

TO HAVE A GOOD TIME, *verb. phr.* (old).—To be fortunate or lucky; to enjoy oneself; to make merry. *See* COCUM.

1596. JONSON, *Every Man in His Humour*, i., 2. As not ten housewives pewter, again a GOOD TIME, shews more bright to the world than he! [=some festival, 'when housewives are careful to set out their furniture to the best advantage.'—Note by Whalley, given in Cunningham's Gifford's *Jonson* (1870)].

1863. A. TROLLOPE, *Rachel Ray*, ii., 6., 109. Eating cake and drinking currant wine, but not having, on the whole, what our American friends call a GOOD TIME of it.

1864. YATES, *Broken to Harness*, ch. xxxviii. And what have you been doing? Had a GOOD TIME?

1883. BRET HARTE, *In the Carquinez Woods*, ch. ix. But we must keep it dark until after I marry Nellie, don't you see. Then we'll have a GOOD TIME all round, and I'll stand the drinks.

1892. R. L. STEVENSON and L. OSBOURNE, *The Wrecker*, p. 14. My idea o'man's chief end was to enrich the world with things of beauty, and have a fairly OOD TIME myself while doing so.

GOOD 'UN, *subs. phr.* (colloquial).—1. A man, woman, or thing of decided and undoubted merit. *Cf.*, GOOD-GIRL.

1828-45. T. HOOD, *Poems*: vi., p. 254 [ed. 1846]. A GOOD 'UN to look at but bad to go.

1854. MARTIN and AYTOUN, *Bon Gaultier Ballads*. 'The Dirge of a Drinker.' Like a GOOD 'UN as he is.

1891. N. GOULD, *Double Event*, p. 160. He's a real GOOD UN, and when his party plank the stuff down it's generally a moral.

2. (colloquial).—An expression of derisive unbelief: *e.g.*, a lie. *See* WHOPPER.

GOOD-WOOLED, *adj. phr.* (American). — Of unflinching courage; of the greatest merit; thoroughly dependable.

1859. MATSELL, *Vocabulum*, s.v.

GOODY, *subs.* (popular). — 1. A matron: the correllative of GOOD-MAN = husband. (Used like AUNTIE, and MOTHER, and GAMMER, in addressing or describing an inferior.) (A corruption of GOOD-WIFE).

1598. FLORIO, *A Worlde of Wordes*. *Mona*, . . . Also a nickname for women as we say gammer, GOODIE, goodwife, such a one.

1689. *Accts. of the Churchwardens of Sprowston*. Paid GOODY Crabbin for washing the surplis and church powrch, 1*s*. 3*d*.

d. 1732. GAY. Swarm'd on a rotten stick the bees I spy'd Which erst I saw when GOODY Dopon dy'd.

d. 1745. SWIFT. Plain GOODY would no longer down: 'Twas Madam in her grogram gown.

1802. BLOOMFIELD, *Rural Tales*, 'Richard and Kate.' Come, GOODY, stop your humdrum wheel.

1816. JOHNSON. *Eng. Dict.* s.v. A low term of civility used to mean persons.

1837. BARHAM, *Ingoldsby Legends*, 'The Witches' Frolic.' Old GOODY Price, Had got something nice.

Hence GOODYSHIP = 'ladyship.'

1663. BUTLER, *Hudibras*, pt. 1, c. 3. The more shame for her GOODYSHIP, To give so near a friend the slip.

2. (colloquial). — A religious hypocrite, male or female; the 'unco guid' of Burns.

1836. KIDD, *London Ambulator*, p. 14. Clapham is celebrated for GOODIES —ladies of a certain age, who not having succeeded in finessing for husbands, betake themselves to a religious life as a *dernier resort*.

Hence GOODY-GOODYISM = sentimental piety.

1892. *Pall Mall Gaz.*, 23 Nov., p. 3., c. 1. The Christmas tale of adventure . . . . has perhaps cast off its element of GOODY-GOODYISM, but the general features and cast are as of old.

3. generally *in. pl.* (colloquial). —Sweetmeats; bon-bons; cakes and buns.

1853. MAYHEW, *Letters Left at a Pastrycook's*. Propped up on each side with bags of oranges, cakes, and GOODIES.

1855. H. A. MURRAY, *Lands of the Slave and the Free*, ch. xii. Adjourning from time to time to some café for the purpose of eating ices or sucking GOODIES.

4. (American).—The kernel of a nut.

Adj. (colloquial). — Well-meaning but petty; officiously pious. *Also* GOODY-GOODY.

1864. D. W. THOMPSON, *Daydreams of a Schoolmaster*, p. 230. I would rather they were not too good; or GOODY. Let us have a little naughtiness, sprinkled in at intervals.

1892. S. WATSON, *Wops the Waif*, p. 7. He knew well enough the whole of this enterprise had sprung from a GOODY-GOODY idea of 'doing something,' born of impulse and whim.

GOODYEAR, *subs.* (old). — The pox. (A corruption of gougeer, from *gouge* = a soldier's trull). For synonyms, *see* LADIES' FEVER.

1605. SHAKSPEARE, *Lear*, v., 3. The GOODYEARS shall devour them.

GOOK, *subs.* (American).—A low prostitute. For synonyms, *see* BARRACK HACK and TART.

GOOSE, *subs.* (common). — 1. A tailor's smoothing iron. (Whose handle is shaped like the neck of the bird.) Hence the old ditton, 'A taylor be he ever so poor is sure to have a goose at his fire. —GROSE. Fr., *un gendarme*.

1606. SHAKSPEARE, *Macbeth*, ii., 3. Come in, taylor; here you may roast your GOOSE.

1606. DEKKER, *Newes from Hell*, in Wks. (Grosart) ii., 114. Every man being armed with his sheeres and pressing Iron, which he calls there his GOOSE.

1638. RANDOLPH, *Hey for Honesty*. . . . *Tailor*. Oh! it is an age that, like the Ostrich, makes me feed on my own GOOSE.

1703. WARD, *London Spy*, pt. xii., p. 276. He grew as hot as a Botcher's GOOSE.

1748. T. DYCHE, *Dictionary* (5th ed.). GOOSE (s.) . . . also the large, heavy iron used by taylors, to press down their seams with when heated very hot.

1766. KENRICK, *Falstaff's Wedding*, iii., 1. Although they had been hissing all the way like a tailor's GOOSE.

1861. SALA, *Twice Round the Clock*, Noon, Par. 12. An Irish tailor who has had a slight dispute with his wife the night before, and has corporeally chastised her with a hot GOOSE — a tailor's GOOSE, be it understood—to the extent of all but fracturing her skull.

1877. *Five Years' Penal Servitude*, ch. ii., p. 89. On the return of the warders from their own breakfast, the tools — scissors, sleeve-boards, irons, or GEESE—are served out.

2. (common). — A simpleton: usually only of women. Also GOOSECAP (*q.v.*).

1591. SHAKSPEARE, *Romeo and Juliet*, ii., 4. *Mercutio*. Was I there with you for the GOOSE? *Rom*. Thou wast never with me that thou wast not for the GOOSE.

1696. B. E., *Dict. Cant. Crew*, s.v.

3. (venery).—*See* WINCHESTER GOOSE.

4. (colloquial).—A reprimand; a WIGGING (*q.v.*); *cf.*, *verb*, sense 1.

1865. G. F. BERKELEY, *My Life* etc., i., 276. On the adventure reaching the ears of the Duke of Wellington, the active experimentalist received considerable GOOSE.

5. (printers'). — *See* WAYZ GOOSE.

6. (colloquial). — A woman: whence, by implication, the sexual favour.

Verb. (common).—1. To hiss; to condemn by hissing. Also TO GET THE GOOSE or THE BIG BIRD (*q.v.*). Among Fr. equivalents are: *appeler* or *siffler Azor* (= to whistle a dog, Azor being a common canine appellation); *boire une goutte* (= to be goosed); *attrapper*; *reconduire*; *se faire travailler*; *empoigner*; *éreinter*; *polisonner*; *égayer*.

1854. DICKENS, *Hard Times*, ch. vi. He was GOOSED last night, he was GOOSED the night before last, he was GOOSED today.

1858. DICKENS *Xmas Stories* (*Going into Soc.*), p. 67 (House. Ed.). Which makes you grind your teeth at him to his face, and which can hardly hold you from GOOSING him audible when he's going through his War-Dance.

1873. *Hornet*, 29 Jan., p. 211, c. 2. *Ferdin*. Fact! My soul is sick on't. GOOSED last night; My salary docked.

1875. T. FROST, *Circus Life*, p. 281. An *artiste* is GOOSED, or GETS THE GOOSE, when the spectators or auditors testify by sibilant sounds disapproval or dissatisfaction.

1886. *Graphic*, 10 Apr., p. 399. To be GOOSED, or, as it is sometimes phrased, 'to get the big bird,' is occasionally a compliment to the actor's power of representing villainy, but more often is disagreeably suggestive of a failure to please.

2. (colloquial).—To ruin; to spoil. *See* COOK ONE'S GOOSE.

1888. *Cassell's Saturday Journal*, 22 Dec., p. 301. We was pretty nigh GOOSED.

3. (cobblers'). — To mend boots by putting on a new front half-way up, and a new bottom; elsewhere called FOOTING boots. *Cf.*, FOX.

4. (venery).—To go wenching; to WOMANIZE (*q.v.*).

5. (venery). — To possess a woman.

GOOSE WITHOUT GRAVY, *subs. phr.* (nautical).—A severe but bloodless blow. *See* WIPE.

TO BE SOUND ON THE GOOSE. *verb. phr.* (American).—Before the civil war, to be sound on the pro-slavery question: now, to be generally staunch on party matters; to be politically orthodox.

1857. *Providence Journal*, 18 June. To seek for political flaws is no use, His opponents will find he is SOUND ON THE GOOSE.

1857. GLADSTONE, *Kansas: or Squatter Life*, p. 43. One of the boys, I reckon? ALL RIGHT ON THE GOOSE, eh? No highfaluten airs here, you know.

1862. LOWELL, *Biglow Papers*, II. Northern religion works wal North, but it's ez suft ez spruce, compar'd to our'n for keepin' SOUND, sez she, UPON THE GOOSE.

1875. *American English* in *Chamb. Journal*, 25 Sept., p. 610. A man who can be depended upon by his party is said to be SOUND ON THE GOOSE.

1892. MILLIKEN, *'Arry Ballads*, p. 22. He didn't acquire quite so SOUND ON THE GOOSE as he ought to ha' done.

TO FIND FAULT WITH A FAT GOOSE, *verb. phr.* (old). — To grumble without rhyme or reason. —B.E. (1690).

TO KILL THE GOOSE FOR THE GOLDEN EGGS, *verb. phr.* (colloquial).—To grasp at more than is due; to over-reach oneself. (From the Greek fable.)

EVERYTHING IS LOVELY AND THE GOOSE HANGS HIGH, *phr.* *See* EVERYTHING.

HE'LL BE A MAN AMONG THE GEESE WHEN THE GANDER IS GONE, *phr.* (old).—Ironical; = 'He'll be a man before his mother.'

GO! SHOE THE GOOSE, *phr.* (old).—A retort, derisive or incredulous = the modern 'To hell and pump thunder.'

UNABLE TO SAY BOH! TO A GOOSE, *phr.* (colloquial).—Said of a bashful person.—GROSE.

1892. MILLIKEN, *'Arry Ballads*, p. 76. And now . . . . he can hardly SAY BOH TO A GOOSE.

See also WILD-GOOSE CHASE.

GOOSE-AND-DUCK, *subs. phr.* (rhyming).—A fuck.

GOOSE AND GRIDIRON, *sub. phr.* (political American). — The American eagle, and the United States flag. *See* GRIDIRON.

1891. *Standard*, 3 Jan., p. 3, c. 1. This is curious, considering the almost fetish-like veneration entertained by the modern American for his Standard, which, coupled with the national bird, tempted the Loyalists in the early days of the war to vent endless rude witticisms on the GOOSE AND GRIDIRON.

GOOSEBERRY, *subs.* (common).—1. A fool. For synonyms, *see* BUFFLE and CABBAGE-HEAD. [Perhaps from GOOSEBERRY FOOL; as in GOLDSMITH'S *Retaliation*: — 'And by the same rule Magnanimous Goldsmith's a GOOSEBERRY FOOL.']

2. (common).—A chaperon; one who takes third place to save appearances or play propriety (*q.v.*); a DAISY- or GOOSEBERRY-PICKER.

3. (common). — A marvellous tale; a MUNCHAUSEN (*q.v.*); a flim-flam. Also GIGANTIC, and GIANT GOOSEBERRY. Hence GOOSEBERRY SEASON = the dull time of journalism, when the appearance of monstrous vegetables, sea serpents, showers of frogs, and other portents is chronicled in default of news. *Cf.*, SILLY SEASON (*q.v.*).

1870. *Figaro*, 22 June. If we have no big GOOSEBERRIES this season, we have at least a big salmon.

1871. *Graphic*, 22 Apr. Mr. Tupper excited a great deal of incredulity a few years ago by announcing in the prodigious GOOSEBERRY SEASON that he had discovered an ancient Roman coin embedded in the heart of an oak tree.

1885. *Ill. London News*, 18 July, p. 50, c. 2. Amongst journalists there is popularly known what they call 'the GIANT GOOSEBERRY season,' the meaning of which is, that when Parliament has risen and the Law Courts are shut and subjects on which to write become scarce, adventurous spirits are apt to discourse in their newspapers of fruit of abnormal size, and other natural prodigies, which, according to current banter, exist only in their own imagination.

4. *in. pl.* (venery).—The testicles. For synonyms, *see* CODS.

TO PLAY (or DO) GOOSEBERRY, *verb. phr.* (common).—To play propriety; also to sit third in a hansom.

1877. HAWLEY SMART, *Play or Pay*. ch. vi. To take care of a pretty girl, . . . with a sister to DO GOOSEBERRY.

1880. G. R. SIMS, *Jeph*, p. 8. Mamma always PLAYED GOOSEBERRY on these occasions.

1883. *Globe*, 6 July, p. 1, c. 5. They will be compelled in self-defence to have a shorthand writer present to PLAY GOOSEBERRY, and to be able to furnish proof that their discourse was innocent.

1892. J. MCCARTHY and MRS. CAMPBELL-PRAED, *Ladies' Gallery*, p. 51. Well, I am not a good hand at PLAYING GOOSEBERRY, and I don't like spoiling sport.

TO PLAY OLD GOOSEBERRY, *verb. phr.* (colloquial).—To play the deuce; to upset or spoil; to throw everything into confusion; but *see* quot. 1811. OLD GOOSEBERRY = The devil (*see* SKIPPER). [*See* Notes and Queries, 2 S x., 307, 376; xii., 336.]

1785. GROSE, *Vulg. Tongue*, s.v.

1811. *Lexicon Balatronicum*, s.v. GOOSEBERRY. He PLAYED UP OLD GOOSEBERRY among them; said of a person who, by force or threats, suddenly puts an end to a riot or disturbance.

1819. MOORE, *Tom Crib*, p. 22. Will PLAY UP OLD GOOSEBERRY soon with them all.

1823. BEE, *Dict. of the Turf*. To PLAY UP GOOSEBERRY; children romping about the house or the parent rating them over.

1837. *Ingoldsby Legends*. 'Bloudie Jacke of Shrewsberrie.' There's a pretty todo! All the people of Shrewsbury PLAYING OLD GOOSEBERRY With your choice bits of taste and *virtù*.

1865. H. KINGSLEY, *Hillyars and the Burtons*, ch. lxii. LAY ON LIKE OLD GOOSEBERRY.

1892. *Globe*, 12 July, p. 2, c. 2. We all know his capacity for playing OLD GOOSBERRY with things in general.

GOOSEBERRY-EYED, *adj.* (old).—Grey-eyed. (*Lex. Bal.*, 1811).

GOOSEBERRY-GRINDER, *subs.* (old). —The breech. For synonyms, *see* MONOCULAR EYEGLASS.

1785. GROSE, *Vulg. Tongue*. GOOSEBERRY-GRINDER, s.v. Ask Bogey the GOOSEBERRY-GRINDER, ask mine a——e.

GOOSEBERRY LAY, *subs. phr.* (thieves').—Stealing linen from a line.

GOOSEBERRY-PICKER, *subs.* (colloquial). — 1. A person whose labour profits, and is credited to, another; a GHOST (*q.v.*).

2. (common). — A chaperon. *See* GOOSEBERRY, *subs.* sense 2.

1884. *Cornhill Mag.*, Dec., p. 578. The good host experienced the sensations of being GOOSEBERRY-PICKER. He sat under a tree, ate, drank, smoked, and finally fell asleep, whilst the Prince and Ottilie explored the Gaulish city and the convent.

GOOSEBERRY - PUDDING, *subs.* (rhyming). — A woman. For synonyms, *see* PETTICOAT.

GOOSEBERRY-WIG, *subs.* (old).—A large frizzled wig. 'Perhaps,' says GROSE (s.v.), 'from a supposed likeness to a gooseberry bush.'

1811. *Lexicon Balatronicum*, s.v.

GOOSECAP, *subs.* (common).—A booby, male or female; a NOODLE. For synonyms, *see* BUFFLE and CABBAGE-HEAD.

1593. G. HARVEY, *Pierce's Super.* in wks. II., 72. A foole, an idiot, a dolt, a GOOSE-CAPP, an asse, and soe fourth.

1604. DEKKER, *Honest Wh.* in wks. (1873), ii., 81. Out, you gulles, you GOOSE-CAPS, you gudgeon-eaters!

1622. BEAUMONT and FLETCHER, *Beggar's Bush*, iv., 4. Why, what a GOOSE-CAP wouldst thou make me!

1763. FOOTE, *Mayor of Garratt*, Act i. My husband is such a GOOSE-CAP that I can't get no good out of him at home or abroad.

1785. GROSE, *Vulg. Tongue*, s.v. A silly fellow or woman.

GOOSE- (or GOOSE'S) EGG, *subs.* (American). — No score. Also GOOSER. *See* DUCK.

1886. *New York Times*, July. With nine unpalatable GOOSE-EGGS in their contest.

1889. *Modern Society*, 12 Oct., p. 1264. An enthusiastic lady cricketer has just bowled over Mr. Jones in a matrimonial match. 'No, Mr. Brown, I cannot marry you. You score a GOOSER this time.'

GOOSE-FLESH (or **GOOSE-SKIN**), *subs.* (colloquial). — A peculiar tingling of the skin produced by cold, fear, etc.; the sensation described as 'cold water down the back'; the CREEPS (*q.v.*).

1824. MISS FERRIER, *Inheritance*, ch. ii. Her skin began to rise into what is vulgarly termed GOOSE-SKIN

GOOSE-GOG (or **GOOSE-GOB**), *subs.* (common).—A gooseberry.

GOOSE-GREASE, *subs. phr.* (venery).—A woman's SPENDINGS (*q.v.*). *See* GOOSE, *subs.*, sense 6.

GOOSE-MONTH, *subs.* (old).—The lying-in month. *Cf.*, GANDER-MONTH.

GOOSE-PERSUADER, *subs.* (common).—A tailor. For synonyms, *see* SNIP.

GOOSER, *subs.* (popular).—1. A settler; a knock-out blow; the act of death. *See* DIG and WIPE.

1851-61. H. MAYHEW, *Lond. Lab. and Lond. Poor*, vol. III., p. 133. It was he who saved my life. If it hadn't been for him it would have been a GOOSER with me.

1857. *Morning Chronicle*, 9 Sept. In the event of my getting a GOOSER.

2. (sporting).—No score; a GOOSE-EGG (*q.v.*).

3. (venery).—The *penis*. For synonyms, *see* CREAMSTICK and PRICK.

GOOSE - RIDING. *See* GANDER-PULLING.

GOOSE'S GAZETTE, *subs.* (old).—A lying story; a flim-flam tale; that is, a piece of reading for a GOOSE, sense 2.

1815. SCOTT, *Guy Mannering*, ch. xxxiv. Lieutenant Brown . . . told him some GOOSE'S GAZETTE about his being taken in a skirmish with the land-sharks.

GOOSE-SHEARER, *subs.* (common). —A beggar. For synonyms, *see* CADGER. [From GOOSE = simpleton + SHEARER = a cheater.]

GOOSE'S-NECK, *subs.* (venery).—The *penis*. For synonyms, *see* CREAMSTICK and PRICK.

GOOSE-STEP, *subs.* (common).—Balancing on one foot and moving the other back and forwards without taking a step. [A preliminary in military drill, the *pons asinorum* of the raw recruit.] Also (more loosely) 'marking time': that is, lifting the feet alternately without advancing.

1840. *Tate's Mag.*, Sept., p. 607 Whether the remarkable evolution [the GOOSE STEP] was called . . . from the nature of the operation requiring the exhibitor to stand on one leg, in imitation of the above-named animal, I am totally at a loss to say.

1890. *Licensed Vict. Gaz.*, 7 Nov. He won his spurs at Punchestown before he had mastered the GOOSE STEP.

GOOSE-TURD GREEN, *adj.* (old). — A light-yellowish green. — COTGRAVE.

GOOSEY-GANDER, *subs.* (common). —A fool. For synonyms, *see* BUFFLE and CABBAGE-HEAD.

GOOSING-SLUM, *subs.* (American). — A brothel. [GOOSING = womanizing; also copulating.] For synonyms, *see* NANNY-SHOP.

GOPHER, *subs.* (American). — 1. A young thief; especially a boy employed by burglars to enter houses through windows, skylights, etc. [In natural history GOPHER = a burrowing squirrel.]

2. (Southern States).—A rude wooden plough.

GOREE, *subs.* (old). — Money; specifically gold or gold - dust. From Fort Goree on the Gold Coast. For synonyms, *see* ACTUAL and GILT.

1696. B. E., *Dict. Cant. Crew*, s.v.

1785. GROSE, *Vulg. Tongue*, s.v.

1859. MATSELL, *Vocabulum*, s.v.

GORGE, *subs.* (vulgar).—1. A heavy meal; a TUCK - IN (*q.v.*); a BLOW-OUT (*q.v.*).

1553. WILSON, *Arte of Rhetorique*, p. 112. The counseler heareth causes with lesse pain being emptie, then he shal be able after a ful GORGE.

1883. *Daily News*, March 24, p. 3, c. 4. The keeper tries these brutes once a week to see whether they are ready for a GORGE, and the python has been known to devour eight ducks at one meal, feathers and all, before signifying enough.

2. (theatrical). — A manager; an abbreviation of GORGER (*q.v.*).

Verb (vulgar).—To eat voraciously; also to gulp as a fish does when it swallows (or gorges) a bait. For synonyms, *see* WOLF.

1572. *Satirical Poems*, Scottish Text Society, 1889-91, 'Lamentacioun,' ii., 232. GORGED waters ever greater grows.

1633. MASSINGER, *New Way to Pay Old Debts*, iii., 2. *Mar.* Come, have patience If you will dispense a little with your worship, And sit with the waiting women, you'll have dumpling, Woodcock, and butter'd toasts too. *Greedy.* This revives me: I will GORGE there sufficiently.

1654. CHAPMAN, *Revenge for Honour*, Act i., Sc. 1. Here men o' th' shop can GORGE their musty maws With the delicious capon, and fat limbs of mutton.

1748. T. DYCHE, *Dictionary* (5th ed.). GORGE (v.), to eat over-much, to cram, glut, or fill unreasonably.

1843. DICKENS, *Martin Chuzzlewit*, ch. xxxiv., p. 336. No man had spoken a word; every one had been intent, as usual, on his own private GORGING; and the greater part of the company were decidedly dirty feeders.

1853. WH. MELVILLE, *Digby Grand*, ch. iii. Who might be such a fine race, if they would only not GORGE their food so rapidly.

GORGER, *subs.* (vulgar). — 1. A voracious eater; a SCRUNCHER (*q.v.*). ROTTEN GORGER = a lad who hangs about Covent Garden eating refuse fruit.

2. (common).—A well-dressed man; a gentleman. [Gypsy, *gorgio* = gentlemen.] Fr., *un gratiné*.

1811. *Lexicon Balatronicum*, s.v. Mung the GORGER; beg child beg, of the gentleman.

3. (common).—An employer; a principal: especially the manager of a theatre. [Perhaps because he takes (or gorges) all the FAT (*q.v.*).] Also CULLY-GORGER. Fr., *amendier*.

1872. M. E. BRADDON, *Dead Sea Fruit*, ch. xiv. The GORGER'S awful coally on his own slumming, eh? . . . I mean to say that our friend the manager is rather sweet upon his own acting.

4. (old). — A neckerchief. [From gorge = throat.]

1320-30. *Gawaine*, 957. That other wyth a GORGER watz gored ouer the swyre.

GORGONZOLA HALL, *subs. phr.* (Stock Exchange). — Formerly the New Hall; now the corporation generally. [From the colour of the marble.]

1887. ATKIN, *House Scraps*, GORGONZOLA HALL got turned into New Billingsgate.

GORM, *verb.* (American University). —To GORGE (*q.v.*). For synonyms, *see* WOLF.

I'M GORMED, *phr.* (popular). —A profane oath. *See* GAUM.

1849. DICKENS, *David Copperfield*, ch. iii. If it [his generosity] were ever referred to, . . . he struck the table a heavy blow with his right hand (had split it on one such occasion), and swore a dreadful oath that HE WOULD BE GORMED if he didn't cut and run for good, if it was ever mentioned again.

1883. *Punch*, May 19, p. 230, c. 2. Why, of course I hardly expects to be believed, but I'M GORMED if there was more than six of one and half-a-dozen of the other.

1884. JULIAN STURGIS, in *Longman's Mag.*, iii., 623. 'GORMED if there ain't that old parson again!' cried Henry, with enthusiasm.

GORMAGON, *subs.* (old). — *See* quots.

1785. GROSE, *Vulg. Tongue*, s.v. A monster with six eyes, three mouths, four arms, eight legs, five on one side and three on the other, three arses, two tarses, and a cunt upon its back; a man on horseback with a woman behind him.

1892. FENNELL, *Stanford Dict.*, s.v., GORMAGON . . . . a member of an English Secret Society which existed in the second quarter of 18 c.

GORMY-RUDDLES, *subs.* (common). —The intestines.

GORRAM (or **GORAM**). — *See* By GOLDAM

GORRY.—*See* BY GORRY!

GOSCHENS, *subs.* (Stock Exchange). —The $2\frac{3}{4}$ per cent. Government Stock created by Mr. Goschen in 1888.

1889. *Man of the World*, 29 June. The nickname GOSCHENS is going out of fashion. The new $2\frac{3}{4}$ stock is now called by the old name.

1891. *Punch*, 4 Apr. Securities yielding a larger return than $2\frac{3}{4}$ GOSCHENS.

GOSH, *see* BY GOSH.

GOSPEL, *subs.* (colloquial). — 1. Anything offered as absolutely true. Also GOSPEL-TRUTH.

1862. H. KINGSLEY, *Ravenshoe*, ch. lx. She is a good young woman, and a honest young woman in her way, and what she says this night about her brother is GOSPEL-TRUTH.

1864. *Derby Day*, p. 35. Apparently unable to resist the powerful influences brought to bear upon him, he replied, in a tone which carried the impress of veracity with it, 'GOSPEL.'

1891. N. GOULD, *Double Event*, p. 175. It was true as GOSPEL.

TO DO GOSPEL, *verb. phr.* (common).—To go to church.

GOSPEL-GAB, *subs.* (common).—Insincere talk concerning religion; cant.

1892. HUME NISBET, *Bushranger's Sweetheart*, p. 146. Yes; when I saw I was in for it, I told them my name and all about my father without any reserve; that, with a little GOSPEL-GAB and howling penitence, got the church people interested in me, and so I was let off easily.

GOSPEL - GRINDER (-POSTILLION, -SHARP, or **-SHARK),** *subs.* (common). — A clergyman or missionary. For synonyms, *see* DEVIL-DODGER and SKY-PILOT;—

FRENCH SYNONYMS. — *La forêt noire* (thieves' = the black forest); *une entonne ramparte* (thieves'); *entonner* = to intone); *une antiffle* (thieves'); *une cavée* (thieves' = a black hole); *une chique* (thieves').

SPANISH SYNONYM.—*Salud.*

ITALIAN SYNONYMS.—*Balza*; *balzana.*

1869. S. L. CLEMENS, *Innocents at Home*, p. 19. 'A what!' 'GOSPEL-SHARP—parson.' 'Oh! why did you not say so before? I am a clergyman—a parson.'

1877. BESANT and RICE, *Golden Butterfly*, ch. viii. Else we should be as stagnant as a Connecticut GOSPEL-GRINDER in his village location.

GOSPELLER, *subs.* (colloquial). — An Evangelist preacher; in contempt. Also HOT-GOSPELLER = a preaching fanatic.)

GOSPEL-MILL (or **-SHOP**), *subs.* (common).—A church or chapel. Also SCHISM-SHOP and DOXOLOGY-WORKS (*q.v.*).

1782. GEO. PARKER, *Humorous Sketches*, p. 88. From Whitfield and Romaine to Pope John range; Each GOSPEL-SHOP ringing a daily change.

1791. *Life of J. Lackington*, Letter xix. As soon as I had procured a lodging and work my next enquiry was for Mr. Wesley's GOSPEL-SHOPS.

1852. JUDSON, *Mysteries of New York*, pt. II., ch. ii., p. 13. On about that ere GOSPEL-SHOP as you was agoin for to crack last week.

1869. S. L. CLEMENS (Mark Twain) *Innocents at Home*, p. 17, 18. Are you the duck that runs the GOSPEL-MILL next door.

1892. MILLIKEN, *'Arry Ballads*, p. 35. It's all GOSPEL-SHOP gruel.

GOSS (or **GOSSAMER**), *subs.* (common).—A hat. (At first a make of peculiar lightness called a FOUR-AND-NINE (*q.v.*).) In quot. 1836 = a white hat. For synonyms, *see* GOLGOTHA.

1836. DICKENS, *Pickwick*, ch. xii. 'That's one thing, and every hole lets in some air, that's another — ventilation GOSSAMER I calls it.' On the delivery of this sentiment, Mr. Weller smiled agreeably upon the assembled Pickwickians.

1838. JAS. GRANT, *Sketches in London*, ch. ix., p. 294. Another passenger inquired whether the hat was 'a vashing beaver von?' while a fourth inquired whether it was 'a GOSSAMER ventilator?'

1851. H. MAYHEW, *Lond. Lab. and Lond. Poor*, Vol. II., p. 49. I have sold hats from 6d. to 3s. 6d., but very seldom 3s. 6d. The 3s. 6d. ones would wear out two new GOSSAMERS, I know.

1884. A. LANG, *Much Darker Days*, p. 25. Yes, the white hat, lying there all battered and crushed on the white snow, must be the hat of Sir Runan! . . . who else would wear the gay GOSSAMER of July in stormy December?

1888. *Harper's Magazine*, LXXVII., 139. Flinging off his GOSSAMER and hanging it up to drip into the pan of the hat rack.

TO GIVE (or GET) GOSS, *verb. phr.* (American).—To requite an injury; to kill; to go strong; to get an opportunity; to PUT IN BIG LICKS (*q.v.*). Sometimes ejaculatory, as 'Give me goss and let me rip!'

1847. ROBB, *Squatter Life*, p. 75. GIN HIM GOSS without sweetin.

1847. DARLEY, *Drama in Porterville*, p. 114. Divers hints passed from one to another among the more excitable citizens, that 'Old Sol' was going to GET GOSS, sure.

1847. PORTER, *Quarter Race*, etc., p. 115. Shouts of 'Fair play,' 'Turn 'em out,' 'GIVE HIM GOSS,' were heard on all sides.

a. 1852. *Traits of American Humour*, II., 261. Ef I don't, the old man will GIVE ME GOSS when I go back.

GOSSOON, *subs.* (colloquial Irish).—A boy. [A corruption of Fr., *garçon* = a boy.]

GOTCH-GUTTED, *adj.* (old).—Pot-bellied; 'a gotch in Norfolk, signifying a pitcher or large round jug.'—GROSE.

GOT 'EM BAD, *phr.* (common).—A superlative of earnestness or excessiveness: *e.g.*, anyone doing his work thoroughly, a horse straining every nerve, a very sick person, especially a patient in the HORRORS (*q.v.*), is said to have GOT 'EM BAD.

GOT 'EM ON (or **ALL ON**), *phr.* (common).—Dressed in the height of fashion. *See* RIGGED OUT.

1880. *Punch*, 28 Aug., p. 90.

188(?). *Broadside Ballad*, ''Arry.' Where are you going on Sunday, 'Arry, now you've GOT 'EM ON?

188(?). *Broadside Ballad*. 'He's GOT 'EM ON.'

GOTH, *subs.* (common). — A frumpish or uncultured person; one behind the times or ignorant of the ways of society.

1712. *Spectator*, No. 367. But I shall never sink this paper so far as to engage with GOTHS and Vandals.

1751. SMOLLETT, *Peregrine Pickle*, ch. lxi. You yourself are a GOTH . . . to treat with such disrespect a production which . . . will, when finished, be a masterpiece of its kind.

1865. OUIDA, *Strathmore*, ch. ii. For God's sake don't suppose me such a GOTH that I should fall in love with a dairymaid, Strath!

GOTHAM, *subs.* (common).—New York City. GOTHAMITE, a New Yorker. [First used by Washington Irving in *Salmagundi* (1807).]

1852. JUTSON, *Mysteries of New York*. ch. xiii. One of the vilest of all hells in GOTHAM.

1852. BRISTED, *Upper Ten Thousand*, p. 37. The first thing, as a general rule, that a young GOTHAMITE does is to get a horse.

GOTHIC, *adj.* (old).—*See* GOTH.

1700. CONGREVE, *The Way of the World*, iv. 4. Ah, rustic, ruder than GOTHIC!

1773. GOLDSMITH, *She Stoops to Conquer*, ii., 8. Why, with his usual GOTHIC vivacity, he said I only wanted him to throw off his wig to convert it into a *tête* for my own wearing.

GO-TO-MEETING BAGS (or **CLOTHES, DRESS**, etc.), *subs. phr.* (common). — Best clothes. [As worn on Sundays, or holiday occasions.]

1837-40. HALIBURTON, *The Clockmaker*, p. 243 (Ed. 1862). If he hadn't his GO-TO-MEETIN' DRESS and looks on this day to the jury, it's a pity.

1854. BRADLEY, *Verdant Green*, Pt. II., p. 5. Besides his black GO-TO-MEETING BAGS please to observe the peculiarity, etc.

1856. HUGHES, *Tom Brown's School-days*, pt II., ch. v. I want to give you a true picture of what every-day school life was in my time, and not a kid-glove and GO-TO-MEETING-COAT picture.

1857. KINGSLEY, *Two Years Ago*. Looks right well in her GO-TO-MEETING CLOTHES.

GOUGE, *subs.* (American). — An imposture; a swindle; a method of cheating.

1845. *New York Tribune*, 10 Dec. R—— and H—— will probably receive from Mr. Polk's administration $100,000 more than respectable printers would have done the work for. There is a clean, plain GOUGE of this sum out of the people's strong box.

Verb. (old).—1. GROSE says, 'To squeeze out a man's eye with the thumb, a cruel practice used by the Bostonians in America.'

1848. RUXTON, *Life in the Far West*, p. 49. His eyes having been GOUGED in a mountain fray.

2. (American).—To defraud.

1845. *New York Tribune*, 26 Nov. Very well, gentlemen! GOUGE Mr. Crosby out of the seat, if you think it wholesome to do it.

1874. W. D. HOWELLS, *Foregone Conclusions*, ch. iii. The man's a perfect Jew—or a perfect Christian, one ought to say in Venice; we true believers do GOUGE so much more infamously here.

1885. BRET HARTE, *A Ship of '49*, ch. i. He's regularly GOUGED me in that 'ere horsehair spekilation.

GOUGER, *subs.* (American). — A cheat; a swindler. For synonyms, *see* ROOK.

GOUGING, *subs.* (American). — Cheating.

GOUJEERS. *See* GOODYEAR.

GOURD, *subs.* (old). — False dice with a cavity within, which in FULLAMS (*q.v.*) was filled with lead to give a bias. *See* also HIGH-MEN and LOW-MEN.

1544. ASCHAM, *Toxophylus*. What false dyse use they? as dyse stopped with quicksilver and heares, dyse of vauntage, flattes, GOURDS, to chop and chaunge when they liste.

1596, SHAKSPEARE, *Merry Wives of Windsor*, i., 3. Let vultures gripe thy guts! for GOURD and fullam holds, And high and low beguiles the rich and poor.

1616. BEAUMONT and FLETCHER, *Scornful Lady*, iv. And thy dry bones can reach at nothing now But GOURDS or nine-pins; pray go fetch a trencher, go.

GOUROCK HAM, *subs.* (common).—A salt herring (Gourock was formerly a great fishing village). For synonyms, *see* GLASGOW MAGISTRATE.

GOVERNMENT-MAN, *subs.* (old Australian).—A convict.

1864. SMYTHE, *Ten Months in Fiji Islands*. q.v.

1883. *Graphic*, 17 Mar., p. 262, c. 3. They never settle down as thousands of our GOVERNMENT MEN cheerfully did in Australia after they had their freedom.

GOVERNMENT-SECURITIES, *subs.* (common). — Handcuffs; fetters generally. For synonyms, *see* DARBIES.

GOVERNMENT-SIGNPOST, *subs.* (old).—The gallows. For synonyms, *see* NUBBING-CHEAT.

1887. A. BARRÈRE, *Argot and Slang*, p. 272. *Montagne du géant*. Fr. (obsolete), *gallows*, scrag, nobbing cheat, or GOVERNMENT SIGNPOST.

GOVERNOR (or **GUV**), *subs.* (common).—1. A father. Also RELIEVING OFFICER; OLD 'UN; PATER; NIBSO; and HIS NIBS. Applied to elderly people in general. Fr., *le géniteur* and *l'ancien* (= the old 'un).

1836. DICKENS, *Pickwick*, ch. xx. p. 169. 'You're quite certain it was them, GOVERNOR?' inquired Mr. Weller, junior. 'Quite, Sammy, quite,' replied his father.

1841. *Punch*, vol. I., p. 28. But—mind! don't tell the GOVERNOR!

1852. *Comic Almanack*, p. 19. Your father: Speaking *to* him, say 'GUVNOR,' or 'Old Strike-a-light;' *of* him, 'The old un.'

1859. *Witty Political Portraits*, p. 111. Unconscious of the constitutional delusions on which his GOVERNOR has thrived.

1889. *Answers*, 20 Apr., p. 323. To call your father 'The GOVERNOR' is, of course, slang, and is as bad as referring to him as 'The Boss,' 'The Old Man,' or 'The Relieving Officer.'

1891. *Licensed Vict. Gaz.*, 9 Jan. It *was* mortifying to be done in that manner by a low fellow like Muggins, that I had always looked upon as a fool, and had made a butt of when the GUV. was out of the way.

1892. HUME NISBET, *Bushranger's Sweetheart*, p. 118. The GOVERNOR is in an awful funk about him.

2. (common). — A mode of address to strangers. Fr., *bourgeois*.

1892. ANSTEY, *Voces Populi* (Second Series). 'At the Guelph Exhibition.' Right, GUVNOR; we'll come.

3. (colloquial).—A master or superior; an employer.

ENGLISH SYNONYMS.—Boss; captain of the waiters; captain; chief; colonel; commander; chief bottle-washer; ganger; head-butler; head-cook and bottle-washer; gorger; omee; rum-cull.

FRENCH SYNONYMS. — *Le pantriot* (popular and thieves': also = a young nincompoop); *le*, or *la*, *pâte* (popular: properly paste or dough); *le naif* (printers': obsolete); *le herz* or *hers* (thieves': obviously from the German); *le loncegué* (thieves': Fr., back-slang; = *gonce*, itself a slang term for a man); *le galeux* (popular) = one with the itch); *le grêle* (popular: specifically a master-tailor); *le singe* (= monkey); *le troploc*; *le nourisseur* = the grubber); *l'ogre* (specifically a FENCE); *le notaire* (= publican); *le patron* (colloquial: = governor).

ITALIAN SYNONYMS. — *Chielmiero* (vulgar).

GOVERNOR'S-STIFF, *subs.* (American).—A pardon.

1859. MATSELL, *Vocabulum*, s.v.

GOWER-STREET DIALECT. *See* MEDICAL GREEK.

GOWK, *subs.* (prison).—A simpleton. (Scots' GOWK = a cuckoo). For synonyms, *see* BUFFLE and CABBAGE-HEAD. Also a countryman. For synonyms, *see* JOSKIN.

1816. SCOTT, *Antiquary*, ch. x. 'Hout awa', ye auld GOWK,' said Jenny Rintherout.

TO HUNT THE GOWK, *verb. phr.* (common). — To go on a fool's errand.

GOWLER, *subs.* (old). — A dog; specifically a howler.

GOWN, *subs.* (Winchester College). — 1. Coarse brown paper. (obsolete).

2. (University).—The schools as distinguished from the TOWN (*q.v.*), *e.g.*, TOWN and GOWN.

1847. THACKERAY, *Punch's Prize Novelists*, 'Codlingsby,' p. 232. From the Addenbrooke's hospital to the Blenheim turnpike, all Cambridge was in an uproar—the College gates closed—the shops barricaded—the shop-boys away in support of their brother townsmen—the battle raged, and the GOWN had the worst of the fight.

1853. BRADLEY, *Verdant Green*, II., ch. iii. When GOWN was absent, Town was miserable.

1891. *Pall Mall Gaz.*, 30 May, p. 4, c. 3. Town and GOWN joined in harmony.

GOWNSMAN (also **GOWN**), *subs.* (university).—A student.

1800. C. K. SHARPE, in *Correspondence* (1888), i., 96. A battle between the GOWNSMEN and townspeople . . . . in spite of the Vice-Chancellor and Proctors.

1850. F. E. SMEDLEY, *Frank Fairleigh*, ch. xxv. The ancient town of Cambridge, no longer animated by the countless throngs of GOWNSMEN, frowned in its unaccustomed solitude.

1861. HUGHES, *Tom Brown at Oxford*. The townsmen . . . . were met by the GOWNSMEN with settled steady pluck.

GRAB, *subs.* (vulgar).—1. A sudden clutch.

1835. HALIBURTON, *Clockmaker*, 1st S., ch. viii. He makes a GRAB at me, and I shuts the door right to on his wrist.

2. (American).—A robbery; a STEAL (*q.v.*). *Cf.*, GRAB-GAINS.

3. (old).—A body-stealer; a resurrectionist.

1830. S. WARREN, *Diary of a Late Physician*, ch. xvi. Sir ——'s dressers and myself, with an experienced GRAB—that is to say, a *professional* resurrectionist—were to set off from the Borough.

4. (gamesters').—A boisterous game at cards.

Verb (vulgar).—1. To PINCH (*q.v.*); to seize; to apprehend; to snatch or steal. GRABBED = arrested.

1811. *Lexicon Balatronicum*. The pigs GRABBED the kiddy for a crack.

1818. MAGINN, *Vidocq's Song*. Tramp it, tramp it, my jolly blowen, Or be GRABBED by the beaks we may.

1837. LYTTON, *Ernest Maltravers*, Wk. I., ch. x. There, man, GRAB the money, it's on the table.

1837. DICKENS, *Oliver Twist*, ch. xiii. Do you want to be GRABBED, stupid?

1839. AINSWORTH, *Jack Sheppard* [1889], p. 39. Don't muddle your brains with any more of that Pharaoh. You'll need all your strength to GRAB him.

1851-61. MAYHEW, *Lond. Lab. and Lond. Poor*, iii., 396. I was GRABBED for an attempt on a gentleman's pocket.

1877. *Five Years' Penal Servitude*, ch. iii., p. 236. I watched a movement, till one of the servant girls had brought another load of grub out, and as she turned her back and went into the house I GRABBED the key, and so they couldn't lock it nohow.

1886. BARING GOULD, *Golden Feather*, p. 23 (S.P.C.K.). There are some folks . . . . so grasping that if they touch a farthing will GRAB a pound.

2. (thieves').—To hold on; to get along; to live.

1851-61. MAYHEW, *Lond. Lab. and Lond. Poor*, iii., 149. I do manage to GRAB on somehow.

GRAB-ALL, *subs.* (colloquial). — 1. An avaricious person; a GREEDY-GUTS (*q.v.*).

1872. *Sunday Times*, 18 Aug. This gentleman, it is well known, has worked with indomitable energy on behalf of the millions, and has succeeded in wresting from the mean and contemptible GRAB-ALLS of that government which professes to study the people's interest those portions of the Embankment which the public money has paid for.

2. (colloquial). — A bag to carry odds and ends, parcels, books, and so forth.

GRABBER, *subs.* (common). — *In. pl.*, the hands. For synonyms, *see* DADDLE and MAULEY.

GRABBLE, *verb.* (old).—1. To seize: a frequent form of GRAB (*q.v.*).

1811. *Lexicon Balatronicum*. To GRABBLE the bit; to seize any one's money.

1859. MATSELL, *Vocabulum*. You GRABBLE the goose-cap and I'll frisk his pokes.

2. (venery). — To grope; to fumble; TO FAM (*q.v.*).

1719. DURFEY, *Pills*, etc., 193. When Nelly, though he teized her, And GRABBLED her and squeezed her.

GRABBY, *subs.* (military). — An infantry-man. [Used in contempt by the mounted arm.] Fr., *marionnette.*

1868. WHYTE MELVILLE, *White Rose*, ch. x. 'Is it a good regiment? How jolly to dine at mess every day!' 'I shouldn't like to be a GRABBY though' (this from the Dandy); 'and after all, I'd rather be a private in the cavalry than an officer in the regiment of *feet!*'

GRAB-GAINS, *subs.* (thieves').—The trick of snatching a purse, etc., and making off.

GRAB-GAME (or-**COUP**, or-**RACKET**), *subs.* (old).—A mode of swindling: the sharpers start by betting among themselves; then the by-standers are induced to join; then stakes are deposited; lastly, there is a row, when one of the gang GRABS the stakes, and decamps. But *see* quot., 1823.

1823. BEE, *Dict. of the Turf*, s.v. GRAB-COUP, modern practice of gambling, adopted by the losers, thus the person cheated, or done, takes his opportunity, makes a dash at the depository of money, or such as may be down for the play, and GRABS as much as possible, pockets the proceeds, and fights his way out of the house.

18(?). *Scenes in the Rocky Mountains*, p. 282. 'I'll bear you company. What d'ye say to that?' 'Just as you like,' responded his two companions, 'that is provided you won't attempt the GRAB GAME on us.'

1892. R. L. STEVENSON and L. OSBOURNE, *The Wrecker*, p. 219. 'Now, boss!' he cried, not unkindly, 'is this to be run shipshape; or is it a Dutch GRAB-RACKET?

GRACE-CARD, *subs.* (Irish).—The Six of Hearts. [For origin *see* N. and Q., 5th Series, iv., 137].

GRACEMANS, *subs.* (old).—Gracechurch Street Market.

1610. ROWLANDS, *Martin Mark-all*, p. 38 (W. Club's Rept., 1874). GRACEMANS, Gratious Streete market.

GRADUATE, *subs.* (turf). — 1. A horse that has been run.

2. (colloquial).—An adept; an ARTFUL MEMBER (*q.v.*).

3. (venery). — An unmarried woman who has taken her degree in carnal lore.

Verb. (colloquial). — To seek and acquire experience: in life, love, society, or trade; and so on.

GRADUS, *subs.* (gamesters'). — A mode of cheating: a particular card is so placed by the shuffler that when he hands the pack to be cut, it projects a little beyond the rest; the chance being that it is the turn-up. Also THE STEP (*q.v.*). [From the Latin.]

GRADUS-AD-PARNASSUM, *subs.* (old literary). — The treadmill. For synonyms, *see* WHEEL-OF-LIFE.

GRAFT, *subs.* (common).—Work; employment; LAY (*q.v.*): *e.g.* What GRAFT are you on now? GREAT - GRAFT = profitable labour; GOOD BIZ (*q.v.*). Also GRAFTING and ELBOW-GREASE.

FRENCH SYNONYMS.—*Le bastimage* (thieves'); *le goupinage* (thieves'); *la laine* (tailors'); *le maquillage* (thieves'); *le massage* (popular); *la masse; le mèche* (printers').

1878. *Graphic*, 6 July, p. 2. According to the well-known maxim in the building trade, 'Scotch masons, Welsh blacksmiths, English bricklayers, Irish labourers' . . . . Perhaps in a generation or two Paddy will fail us. He will have become too refined for hard GRAFTING.

1887. HENLEY, *Villon's Straight Tip.* The merry little dibbs you bag At my GRAFT, no matter what.

1892. *Tit Bits*, 19 Mar., p. 417, c. 1. Millbank for thick shins and GRAFT at the pump.

Verb (common).—1. To work. Fr., *bausser; membrer.*

2. (American).—To steal.

3. (old). — To cuckold; to plant horns.

1690. B. E., *Dict. Cant. Crew*, s.v.
1785. GROSE, *Vulg. Tongue*, s v.

4. (American).—To sole old boots. *Cf.*, GOOSE and TRANSLATE.

GRAMPUS, *subs.* (colloquial).—A fat man. For synonyms, *see* FORTY-GUTS.

TO BLOW THE GRAMPUS. (nautical). — To drench; and (common), to sport in the water.

GRAND, *subs.* (colloquial).—Short for 'grand piano.'

1891. *Morning Advertiser*, 28 Mar. A precocious young relative is now about to take the daïs. There she stands, violin in hand, and there begins the preliminary scramble on the hired GRAND.

Adj. (colloquial).—A general superlative.

1892. MILLIKEN, *'Arry Ballads*, p. 19. Wot we want in a picter is flavour and 'fetch,' and yours give it me GRAND.

TO DO THE GRAND, *verb. phr.* (common).—To put on airs. For synonyms, *see* LARDY-DAH.

GRAND BOUNCE. *See* BOUNCE.

GRANDMOTHER. TO SEE ONE'S GRANDMOTHER, *verb. phr.* (common).—To have a nightmare.

TO SEE (or HAVE) ONE'S GRANDMOTHER (or LITTLE FRIEND, or AUNTIE) WITH ONE. *verb. phr.* (common).—To have the menstrual discharge. *See* FLAG.

TO SHOOT ONE'S GRANDMOTHER, *verb. phr.* (common).—To be mistaken; to have found a mare's nest; to be disappointed. Commonly 'You've shot your grannie.'

TO TEACH ONE'S GRANDMOTHER (or GRANNIE) HOW TO SUCK EGGS, *verb. phr.* (common).—To instruct an expert in his own particular line of business; to talk old to one's seniors.

1811. *Lexicon Balatronicum*, s.v.

1892. *Globe*, 27 Jan., p. 1, c. 5. Evidently he did not consider, as Englishmen seem to do, that GRANDMOTHERS possess no more knowledge than is required to efficiently SUCK EGGS.

1892. HUME NISBET, *Bushranger's Sweetheart*, p. 210. 'Confound you stupid, what do you take me for, that you try to TEACH YOUR GRANDMOTHER TO SUCK EGGS.

1892. MILLIKEN, *'Arry Ballads*, p. 77. She's a TEACHING 'ER GRANDMOTHER, she is, although she's a littery swell.

MY GRANDMOTHER'S REVIEW. *subs. phr.* (obsolete).—The *British Review.* [The nickname was Lord Byron's.]

GRAND-STRUT, *subs.* (old).—The Broad Walk in Hyde Park.

1823. MONCRIEFF, *Tom and Jerry*, i., 4. We'll start first to the show shop of the metropolis, Hyde Park! promenade it down the GRAND STRUT.

GRANGER, *subs.* (American political). —1. A member of the Farmers' Alliance; a secret society, nominally non-political, but really taking a hand in politics when occasion offered to favour agricultural interests. [During the decade of years ending 1870, it attained to great numerical strength, and extended throughout the United States.] *See* AGRICULTURAL WHEEL.

2. (American). — Hence, a farmer; a countryman; anyone from the rural districts. For synonyms, *see* JOSKIN.

GRANGERISE, *verb.* (literary).—To fill out a book with portraits, landscapes, title-pages, and illustrations generally, not done for it.

1883. SALA, *Living Wonders*, p. 497. Mr. Ashton's *Social Life in the Reign of Queen Anne* . . . would be a capital book to GRANGERIZE.

GRANGERISM, *subs.* (literary).—The practice of illustrating a book with engravings, etc., from other sources. [From the practice of illustrating GRANGER'S *Biographical History of England.*]

1883. *Saturday Review*, Jan. 27, p. 123, c. 2. GRANGERISM, as the innocent may need to be told, is the pernicious vice of cutting plates and title-pages out of many books to illustrate one book.

GRANGERITE, *subs.* (literary).—A practitioner in GRANGERISM (*q.v.*).

1890. 'Grangerising,' in *Cornhill Mag.*, Feb., p. 139. Another favourite subject, and suitable also for the GRANGERITE, is 'Boswell's Johnson.' It must be admitted that this delightful book may gain a fresh chance by being thus treated, but 'within the limits of becoming grangerism.'

GRANNAM, *subs.* (old). Corn. [From the Latin.]—Fr., *le grenu*, or *grelu.* It., *re di granata; staffile; corniole:* Sp., *grito.*

1567. HARMAN, *Caveat* (1814), p. 65. GRANNAM, corne.

1610. ROWLANDS, *Martin Mark-all*, p. 38 (H. Club's Rept., 1874). GRANMER, corne.

1671. R. HEAD, *English Rogue*, pt. I., ch. v., p. 49 (1874). GRANNAM, corn.

1706. E. COLES, *Eng. Dict.* GRANNAM, *c.* corn.

1737. *Bacchus and Venus.* 'The Strowling Mort.' GRANNAM ever filled my sack.

GRANNAM'S-GOLD. *subs.* (old).—Wealth inherited. [Grannam = grandmother: *cf.*, BEAUMONT and FLETCHER, *Lover's Progress*, iv., 1. 'Ghosts never walk till after midnight, if I may believe my grannam.']

GRANNY, *subs.* (nautical).—1. A bad knot with the second tie across; as opposed to a reef knot in which the end and outer part are in line. Also GRANNY'S KNOT or GRANNY'S BEND.

2. (common). — Conceit of superior knowledge.

1851-61. MAYHEW, *Lond. Lab. and Lond. Poor*, i., 404. To take the GRANNY off them as has white hands.

Verb (thieves').—To know; to recognise. Also to swindle.

1851-61. MAYHEW, *Lond. Lab. and Lond. Poor*, i., 461. The shallow got so GRANNIED in London.

Ibid., p. 340. If they GRANNY the manley (perceive the signature) of a brother officer or friend.

GRANT. TO GRANT THE FAVOUR, *verb. phr.* (venery).—To confer the sexual embrace; TO SPREAD (*q.v.*).

1720. DURFEY, *Pills*, etc., vi 58. If at last she GRANTS THE FAVOUR, And consents to be undone.

1754. FIELDING, *Jonathan Wild*, iv. 7. I . . . . never would GRANT THE FAVOUR to any man till I had drunk a heavy glass with him.

GRAPE-SHOT, *adj.* (common).—Drunk. For synonyms, *see* DRINKS and SCREWED.

GRAPE-VINE, *subs.* (American).—A hold in wrestling.

GRAPE-VINE TELEGRAPH, *subs. phr.* (American). — News mysteriously conveyed. [During the Civil War bogus reports from the front were said to be BY THE GRAPE-VINE TELEGRAPH.] Also CLOTHES-LINE TELEGRAPH.

GRAPPLE, *subs.* (common).—The hand. Also GRAPPLER. For synonyms, *see* DADDLE and MAULEY.

1852. HAZEL, *Yankee Jack*, p. 9. Give us your GRAPPLER on that, old fellow.

1877. *Five Years' Penal Servitude*, ch. iii., p. 246. Anything she once put her GRAPPLES on she slipped inside.

GRAPPLE-THE-RAILS, *subs.* (Irish). Whiskey. For synonyms, *see* DRINKS and OLD MAN'S MILK.

1785. GROSE, *Vulg. Tongue.* GRAPPLE-THE-RAILS, a cant name used in Ireland for whiskey.

GRAPPLING-IRONS (or **-HOOKS**), *subs.* (old).—1. Handcuffs. For synonyms, *see* DARBIES.

1811. *Lexicon Balatronicum*, s.v.

1830 BUCKSTONE, *Wreck Ashore*, i. 4. I hope the bailiffs have not laid their GRAPPLING IRONS on young Miles.

2. (nautical). — The fingers. For synonyms, *see* FORK. Also GRAPPLERS and GRAPPLING-HOOKS.

GRASS, *subs.* (Royal Military Academy).—1. Vegetables. *Cf.*, BUNNY-GRUB. Fr., *gargousses de la canonnière.*

2. (American).—Fresh mint.

3. (common). — Short for SPARROW-GRASS (*q.v.*) = asparagus.

1851-61. MAYHEW, *Lond. Lab. and Lond. Poor*, I., 539. He sold GRASS, and such things as cost money.

4. (Australian printers'). — A temporary hand on a newspaper; hence the proverb, 'A GRASS on news waits dead men's shoes.' *Cf.*, GRASS-HAND = a raw worker, or green hand.

a. 1889. FITZGERALD, *Printers' Proverbs*, quoted in *Slang, Jargon, and Cant.* Why are the GRASS, or casual news hands not put on a more comfortable footing?

Verb (pugilistic).—To throw (or be thrown); to bring (or be brought) to ground. Hence, to knock down; to defeat; to kill.

1818. EGAN, *Boxiana*, ii., 375. He had much the worst of it, and was ultimately GRASSED.

1819. MOORE, *Tom Crib*, p. 57. The shame that aught but death should see him GRASSED.

1846. DICKENS, *Dombey*, xliv., 385. The Chicken himself attributed this punishment to his having had the misfortune to get into Chancery early in the proceedings, when he was severely fibbed by the Larkey One, and heavily GRASSED.

1881. *Daily Telegraph*, 26 Nov. The Doctor had killed twenty out of twenty-five, while his opponent had GRASSED seventeen out of the same number.

1883. W. BESANT, *All in a Garden Fair.* Intro. It was a sad example of pride before a fall; his foot caught in a tuft of grass, and he was GRASSED.

1888. *Sporting Life*, 11 Dec. Just on the completion of the minute GRASSED his man with a swinging right-hander.

1891. J. NEWMAN, *Scamping Tricks*, p. 119. I saw I was GRASSED, so I took his measurement.

1892. F. ANSTEY, *Voces Populi.* 'The Riding-Class,' p. 108. Didn't get GRASSED, did you?

TO GIVE GRASS, *verb. phr.* (colloquial).—To yield.

TO GO TO GRASS. *verb. phr.* (colloquial). — 1. To abscond; to disappear. Also to HUNT GRASS.

2. (common).—To fall sprawling; to be ruined; to die.

1876. HINDLEY, *Cheap Jack*, p. 237. Elias was SENT TO GRASS to rise no more off it.

3. (common).—To waste away (as of limbs).

TO HUNT GRASS, *verb. phr.* (common).—1. To decamp.

2. (cricket). — To field; to HUNT LEATHER (*q.v.*).

3. (American). To fall; to go to ground; hence, to be puzzled or bewildered.

1869. S. L. CLEMENS, *Innocents at Home*, p. 21. You're most too many for me, you know. When you get in with your left I HUNT GRASS every time.

TO CUT ONE'S OWN GRASS. *verb. phr.* (thieves').—To earn one's own living.

1877. *Five Years' Penal Servitude*, ch iii., p. 242. 'CUT HER OWN GRASS! Good gracious! what is that!' I asked. 'Why, purvide her own chump—earn her own living,' the old man replied.

TO BE SENT TO GRASS. *verb. phr.* (University).—To be rusticated; to RECEIVE A TRAVELLING SCHOLARSHIP (*q.v.*).

1794. *Gent. Mag.*, p. 1085. And was very near *rustication* [at Cambridge] merely for *kicking up a row* after a *beakering party*. 'Soho, Jack!' briskly rejoined another, 'almost presented with a *travelling fellowship*? very nigh being SENT TO GRASS, hey?'

GO TO GRASS! *phr.* (common).—Be off! You be hanged! Go to hell!

1848. DURIVAGE, *Stray Subjects*, p. 95. A gentleman who was swimming about, upon being refused, declared that he might GO TO GRASS with his old canoe, for he didn't think it would be much of a shower, anyhow.

1865. BACON, *Handbook of America*, p. 363. GO TO GRASS! be off! get out!

TO LET THE GRASS GROW UNDER ONE'S FEET, *verb. phr.* (colloquial). — To proceed or work leisurely. Fr., *limer.*

TO TAKE NEBUCHADNEZZAR OUT TO GRASS, *subs. phr.* (venery). — To take a man. [NEBUCHADNEZZAR=*penis.*] For synonyms, *see* GREENS.

GRASS-COMBER, *subs.* (nautical).—A countryman shipped as a sailor.

1886. W. BESANT, *World Went Very Well Then*, ch. xxix. Formerly, Jack would have replied to this sally that, d'ye see, Luke was a GRASS COMBER and a land swab, but that for himself, there was no tea aboard ship, and a glass of punch or a bowl of flip was worth all the tea ever brought from China.

GRASSER, *subs.* (sporting). — A fall.

GRASSHOPPER, *subs.* (common).—1. A waiter at a tea-garden.

2. (rhyming).—A policeman, or COPPER (*q.v.*).

3. (thieves').—A thief. *See* GUNNER.

1893. *Pall Mall Gaz.*, 2 Jan., p. 4, c. 3. Quite a 'school' of youthful GRASSHOPPERS are in possession of one corner of the ice, but on the Westminster side of the park 'pon bridge there is a good sprinkling of old hands.

GRASSING, *subs.* (printers'). — Casual work away from the office. *See* SMOUTING.

GRASSVILLE, *subs.* (old). — The country; *cf.*, DAISYVILLE.

GRASS-WIDOW, *subs.* (old).—1. An unmarried mother; a deserted mistress. *See* BARRACK-HACK and TART.

1690. B. E., *Dict. Cant. Crew*, s.v. Widow's weeds, a GRASS-WIDOW, one that pretends to have been married, but never was, yet has children.

1785. GROSE, *Vulg. Tongue*, s.v. Widow's weeds; a GRASS-WIDOW; a discarded mistress.

2. (colloquial). — A married woman temporarily separated from her husband.

[The usually accepted derivation that grass=Fr., *grâce* is doubtful. Hall (says J. C. Atkinson, in *Glossary of Cleveland Words*) gives as the definition of this word 'an unmarried woman who has had a child'; in Moor's *Suffolk Words and Phrases*, GRACE-WIDOW, 'a woman who has had a child for her cradle ere she has had a husband for her bed'; and corresponding with this is the N. S. or Low Ger., *gras-wedewe*. Again, Sw. D., *gras-anka*, or *-enka*=GRASS-WIDOW, occurs in the same sense as with us: 'a low, dissolute, unmarried woman living by herself.' The original meaning of the word seems to

have been 'a woman whose husband is away,' either travelling or living apart. The people of Belgium call a woman of this description *haeck-wedewe*, from *haecken*, to feel strong desire. . . . . It seems probable, therefore, from the etymology, taken in connection with the Clevel. signification, that our word may rather be from the Scand. source than from the German; only with a translation of the word *enka* into its English equivalent. Dan. D., *graesenka*, is a female whose betrothed lover (fastman) is dead; nearly equivalent to which is German, *strohwittwe*, literally straw-widow. *See* N. and Q. 6 S viii., 268, 414: x. 333, 436, 526; xi. 78, 178.]

ENGLISH SYNONYMS. — Californian widow; widow-bewitched; wife in water colours.

1700. CONGREVE, *Way of the World*, Act iii. If the worst come to the worst,—I'll TURN MY WIFE TO GRASS —I have already a deed of settlement of the best part of her estate, which I wheedl'd out of her.

1877. *Chamb. Journal*, 12 Mar., p. 173. Mrs. Brittomart was one of those who never tolerated a bow-wow—a species of animal well known in India—and never went to the hills as a GRASS-WIDOW.

1878. *London*, A GRASS-WIDOW. And so, you see, it comes to pass That she's a WIDOW OUT AT GRASS And happy in her freedom.

1882. *Saturday Review*, 11 Feb. She is a GRASS-WIDOW, her husband is something in some Indian service.

1885. W. BLACK, *White Heather*, ch. xli. Mrs. Lalor, a GRASS-WIDOW who was kind enough to play chaperon to the young people, but whose effective black eyes had a little trick of roving on their own account.

1889. *Daily Telegraph*, 12 Feb. She had taken up her residence at a house in Sinclair-road, Kensington, where she passed as a GRASS-WIDOW. She represented that her husband was engaged in mercantile pursuits.

GRASS-WIDOWER, *subs.* (common).—A man away from his wife.

1886. *New York Evening Post*, 22 May. All the GRASS-WIDOWERS and unmarried men.

GRAVEL, *verb.* (old).—1. To confound; to puzzle; to FLOOR (*q.v.*).

1593. G. HARVEY, *Pierus Supererog*, in wks. II., 296. The finest intelligencer, or sagest Politician in a state, would undoubtedly have been GRAVELLED in the execution of that rash attempt.

1597. HALL, *Satires*, III., vi., 14. So long he drinks, till the black caravell Stands still fast GRAVELLED on the mud of hell.

1600. SHAKSPEARE, *As You Like It.* When you were GRAVELLED for lack of matter.

1604. MARLOWE, *Faustus*, Act i., Sc. 1. And I, that have with concise syllogisms GRAVELL'D the pastors of the German church.

1659. TORRIANO, *Vocabulario*, s.v.

1667. DRYDEN, *Sir Martin Marr-all*, Act iii. *Warn.* He's GRAVELLED, and I must help him out.

1668. DRYDEN, *An Evening's Love*, Act ii. A difficult question in that art, which almost GRAVELS me.

1857. A. TROLLOPE, *Three Clerks*, ch. xxxiv. He was somewhat GRAVELLED for an answer to Alaric's earnest supplication, and therefore made none till the request was repeated.

1886. R. L. STEVENSON, *Kidnapped*, p. 206. I thought Alan would be GRAVELLED at that, for we lacked the means of writing in that desert.

1893. *National Observer*, 11 Feb., p. 321. In truth to talk of Burns as the apotheosis of Knox is really to GRAVEL and confound your readers; and but for the context one might be suspected that the innuendo hid a touch of sarcasm.

2. (American).—To go against the grain.

1887. CLEMENS, *Life on the Mississippi*, ch. xiv., p. 138. By long habit, pilots came to put all their wishes in the form of commands. It GRAVELS me to this day, to put my will in the weak shape of a request, instead of launching it in the crisp language of an order.

GRAVEL-CRUSHER, *subs.* (military).—A soldier doing defaulter's drill.

GRAVEL-GRINDER, *subs.* (popular).—A drunkard. For synonyms, *see* LUSHINGTON.

GRAVEL-RASH, *subs.* (colloquial).—The lacerations caused by a fall.

TO HAVE THE GRAVEL RASH, *verb. phr.* (colloquial).—To be reeling drunk. For synonyms, *see* DRINKS and SCREWED.

GRAVESEND-BUS, *subs.* (common).—A hearse.

GRAVESEND - SWEETMEATS, *subs.* (popular).—Shrimps.

GRAVESEND-TWINS, *subs.* (common).—Solid particles of sewage.

GRAVE-YARD, *subs.* (common).—1. The mouth. For synonyms, *see* POTATO-TRAP.

TO KEEP A PRIVATE GRAVEYARD, *verb. phr.* (American).—To affect ferocity; to bluster.

GRAVY, *subs.* (venery). — The sexual discharge; the SPENDINGS (*q.v.*) both male and female. [Hence GRAVY-GIVER=the *penis* and the female *pudendum*; and GRAVY - MAKER = the female *pudendum.* Hence, too, TO GIVE ONE'S GRAVY=to SPEND (*q.v.*). *Cf.*, BEEF and MUTTON.]

d. 1796. BURNS, 'Dainty Davie,' in *Merry Muses.* I wot he cam atween my thie, An' creeshed it weel wi' GRAVY.

GRAVY-EYE, *subs.* (common)—A derisive epithet: *e.g.*, Well Old GRAVY-EYE.

GRAWLER, *subs.* (old).—A beggar. For synonyms, *see* CADGER.

1821. D. HAGGART, *Life*, Glossary p. 62. Not so much as would sweeten a GRAWLER in the whole of them.

GRAY, *subs.* (thieves').—1. A coin showing either two heads or two tails; a PONY (*q.v.*).

1828. G. SMEETON, *Doings in London*, p. 40. Breslaw could never have done more upon cards than he could do with a pair of GRAYS (gaffing-coins).

1851-61. H. MAYHEW, *Lond. Lab. and Lond. Poor*, Vol. II, p. 154. Some, if they *can*, will cheat, by means of a half-penny with a head or a tail on both sides, called a GRAY.

1868. *Temple Bar*, Vol. XXIV., p. 539. They have a penny with two heads or two tails on it, which they call a GREY, and of course they can easily dupe flats from the country. How do they call it a GREY, I wonder? I suppose they have named it after Sir George Grey because he was a two-faced bloke.

2. (common).—*See* GRAYBACK, sense 1.

3. *in. pl.* (colloquial).—Yawning; listlessness. *Cf.*, BLUES.

GRAYBACK, *subs.* (common). — 1. A louse. Also SCOTS GREYS. Fr., *un grenadier.* For synonyms, *see* CHATES.

2. (American).—A Confederate soldier. [Partly from the colour of his uniform, and partly because of its inhabitants. *Cf.*, sense 1.] *See* BLUE-BELLIES.

1883. *Daily Telegraph*, 9 Feb., p. 5, c. 4. The Confederate armies, during the great Civil War in America . . . were known . . . as GREYBACKS, whereas their Federal opponents, from the light-azure gaberdines which they wore, were dubbed 'blue-bellies.

1890. *Scribner's Mag.* Mar., p. 283. Mrs. Rutherford stood in such abject fear of the GRAYBACKS that she regarded the possession of so large a sum as simply inviting destruction.

GRAY-BEARD, *subs.* (colloquial).—1. An old man. Mostly in contempt.

1593. SHAKSPEARE, *Taming of the Shrew*, Act ii., Sc. 1. GREY-BEARD, thy love doth freeze.

a. 1845. LONGFELLOW, *Luck of Eden Hall.* The GRAY-BEARD, with trembling hand obeys.

2. (old).—Originally a stoneware drinking jug; now a large earthenware jar for holding wine or spirits. [From the bearded face in relief with which they were ornamented.]

1811. *Lexicon Balatronicum*, GREY-BEARD, s.v. Dutch earthen jugs, used for smuggling gin on the coasts of Essex and Suffolk, are at this time called GREY-BEARDS.

1814. SCOTT, *Waverley*, ch. lxiv. There's plenty of brandy in the GREY-BEARD.

1886. *The State*, 20 May, p. 217. A whisky or brandy which is held in merited respect for very superior potency is entitled [in America] 'reverent,' from the same kind of fancy which led the Scotch to call a whisky jar a GREY-BEARD.

GRAY-CLOAK, *subs.* (common).—An alderman above the chair. [Because his proper robe is a cloak furred with grey amis.]

GRAY-GOOSE, *subs.* (Scots'). — A big field stone on the surface of the ground.

1816. SCOTT, *Black Dwarf*, ch. iv. Biggin a dry-stane dyke, I think, wi' the GREY-GEESE as they ca' thae great loose stones.

GRAYHOUND, *subs.* (general).—1. A fast Atlantic liner; one especially built for speed. Also OCEAN GRAYHOUND.

1887. *Scientific American*, vol. LVI., 2. They [ships] are built in the strongest possible manner, and are so swift of foot, as to have already become formidable rivals to the English GREY HOUND.

2. (Cambridge University).—An obsolete name for a member of Clare College; a CLARIAN.

1889. WHIBLEY, *Cap and Gown*, xxviii. The members of Clare . . . . were called GRAYHOUNDS.

GRAY-MARE, *subs.* (common).—A wife; specifically one who WEARS THE BREECHES (*q.v.*). [From the proverb, 'The gray mare is the better horse' = the wife is master: a tradition, perhaps, from the time when priests were forbidden to carry arms or ride on a male horse: *Non enim licuerat pontificem sacrorum vel arma ferre, vel praeter quam in equuâ equitare.* — *Beda, Hist. Eccl.* ii., 13. Fr., *mariage d'epervier*=a hawk's marriage: the female hawk being the larger and stronger bird. Lord Macaulay's explanation (quot. 1849) is the merest guess-work.]

1546. JOHN HAYWOOD, *Proverbs* [Sharman's reprint, 1874]. She is (quoth he) bent to force you perforce, To know that the GREY MARE is the better horse.

1550. *A Treatyse, Shewing and Declaring the Pryde and Abuse of Women Now a Dayes* (in Hazlitt's *Early Popular Poetry*, iv., 237). What! shall the GRAYE MAYRE be the better horse, And be wanton styll at home?

1605. CAMDEN, *Remains Concerning Britain* [ed. 1870, p. 332]. In list of proverbs. (Is said to be the earliest in English.)

1670. RAY, *Proverbs*, s.v.

1698-1750. WARD, *London Spy*, part II., p. 40. Another as dull as if the GREY MARE was the better Horse; and deny'd him Enterance for keeping late Hours.

1705-1707. WARD, *Hudibras Redivivus*, vol. II., pt. iv., p. 5. There's no resisting Female Force, GREY MARE will prove the better Horse.

1717. PRIOR, *Epilogue to Mrs. Manley's Lucius.* As long as we have eyes, or hands, or breath, We'll look, or write, or talk you all to death. Yield, or she-Pegasus will gain her course, And the GREY MARE will prove the better horse.

1719. DURFEY, *Pills*, etc., p. 240. For the GREY MARE has proved the better horse.

1738. SWIFT, *Polite Convers.*, dial. 3. I wish she were married; but I doubt the GRAY MARE would prove the better horse.

1748. SMOLLETT, *Rod. Random*, ch. xix. By the hints they dropped, I learned the GRAY MARE was the better horse—that she was a matron of a high spirit.

1849. MACAULAY, *Hist. England.* The vulgar proverb, that the GREY MARE is the better horse, originated, I suspect, in the preference generally given to the GREY MARES of Flanders over the finest coach horses of England.

1883. G. A. S[ALA], in *Illustr. London News*, 14 Apr., p. 359, c. 2. She [Mrs. Romford], did not over-accentuate either her strong-mindedness or her jealousy of her flighty husband; but she let him and the audience unmistakably know that she was in all respects the GREY MARE in the Romford stable.

GRAY-PARSON (or **GRAY-COAT PARSON**, *subs.* (old).—A lay impropriator, or lessee of tithes.

1785. GROSE, *Vulg. Tongue.* GREY PARSON, s.v. A farmer who rents the tythes of the rector or vicar.

1830 in COBBETT'S *Rural Rides*, vol. I., p. 123 *note* (ed. 1886). The late editor says, that, having been a large holder of lay tithes, the author applied to Mr. Nicholls, the name of the GREY-COATED PARSON.

GREASE, *subs.* (common).—1. A bribe; PALM-OIL (or -GREASE). (*q.v.* for synonyms). In America BOODLE (*q.v.*). GREASING = bribing.

1823. BEE, *Dict. of Turf*, s.v. A bonus given to promote the cause of anyone.

2. (printers'). — Well-paid work; FAT (*q.v.*).

3. (common. — Fawning; flattery (a figurative use of sense 1).

Verb (old).—1. To bribe; to corrupt by presents; to TIP (*q.v.*). Also more fully TO GREASE IN THE FIST, HAND, or PALM. Fr., *coquer la boucanade.* For synonyms, *see* SQUARE.

1557. TUSSER, *Husbandrie*, ch. 68, pt. 2, p. 159 (E.D.S.). How husbandrie easeth, to huswiferie pleaseth, And manie purse GREASETH With silver and gold.

1578. WHETSTONE, *Promoss and Cassandra*, ii., 3. GREASE them well in their hands,

1592. GREENE, *Quip* in wks., xi., 261 That did you not GREASE THE SEALERS of Leaden Hall throughly in the fist, they should never be sealed, but turned away and made forfiet by the statute.

1619. FLETCHER, *Wild Goose Chase.* Am I GREASED once again?

1649. F. QUARLES, *Virgin Widow*, IV., i., p. 40. GREAZE MY FIST with a Tester or two, and ye shall find it in your penny-worths.

1678. C. COTTON, *Scarronides*, Bk. IV., p. 70 (ed. 1725). Him she conjures, intreats, and prays, With all the Cunning that she has, GREASES HIS FIST; nay more, engages Thenceforth to mend his Quarters-wages.

1693. DRYDEN, *Persius*, iii., 139. And after, envy not the store Of the GREAS'D advocate, that grinds the poor.

1698-1700. WARD, *London Spy*, pt. xv., p. 364. But the Gay Curteyan who trades for gold, That can but GREASE A PALM when she's in hold, No Justice need she dread.

1785. GROSE, *Vulg. Tongue*, s.v.

1878. JAS. PAYN, *By Proxy*, ch. x. His Excellency, your master, has given orders, I presume, that after I have made my compliments—as delicate a phrase as he could think of for GREASING THE HANDS of justice—I shall be at liberty to visit my friend.

1879. HORSLEY, in *Macmillan's Magazine*, Oct. When I went to the fence he bested (cheated) me because I was drunk, and only gave me £8 10s. for the lot. So the next day I went to him and asked him if he was not going to GREASE MY DUKE (put money into my hand).

1891. *Pall Mall Gaz.*, 2 Sept., p. 7, c. 2. Did other people having business with the printing bureau tell you that it would be necessary to GREASE Sénécal?

2. (common).—To fawn; to flatter. Formerly, TO GREASE ONE'S BOOTS.

1598. FLORIO, *A Worlde of Wordes.* *Onger i stivali*, TO GREASE ONES BOOTES, *id est*, to flatter or cog with, to faune vpon one.

3. (old).—To gull; to cheat; to DO.

TO GREASE A FAT SOW IN THE ARSE, *verb. phr.* (old).—To bribe a rich man.—GROSE.

TO GREASE ONE'S GILLS, *verb. phr.* (common). — To make a good or luxurious meal.

GREASED LIGHTNING, *subs. phr.* (American).—An express train.

1871. DE VERE, *Americanisms*, p. 359. The usual Express Train is not half fast enough for the impatient traveller; he must have his *Lightning* Express Train, and in the Far West improves still farther by calling it GREASED LIGHTNING, after a favourite Yankee term.

LIKE GREASED LIGHTNING, *adv. phr.* (American). — Very quick. *See* BED-POST.

1848. DURIVAGE, *Stray Subjects*, p. 72. Quicker than GREASED LIGHTNIN', My covies, I was dead.

1890. *Globe*, 27 Aug., p. 2, c. 5. He is drawn along at a rapid rate, or, as the correspondent puts it, he is whisked all over town like GREASED LIGHTNING.

1891. J. NEWMAN, *Scamping Tricks*, p. 98. He measured again, and then off went his coat LIKE GREASED LIGHTNING, and we all followed suit.

GREASER, *subs.* (American). — 1. A Mexican in general; also a Spanish American: *see* quots. 1848 and 1888. The term originated during the Mexican war.

1848. RUXTON, *Life in the Far West*, p. 3. *Note.* The Mexicans are called Spaniards or GREASERS (from their greasy appearance) by the Western people.

1855. MARRYAT, *Mountains and Mole Hills*, p. 236. The Americans call the Mexicans GREASERS, which is scarcely a complimentary soubriquet; although the term GREASER CAMP as applied to a Mexican encampment is truthfully suggestive of filth and squalor.

1876. BESANT and RICE, *Golden Butterfly*, Prologue i. Behind the leaders followed a little troop of three, consisting of one English servant and two GREASERS.

1883. BRET HARTE, *In the Carquinez Woods*, footnote to ch. vii. GREASERS, Californian slang for a mixed race of Mexicans and Indians.

1888. *Century Mag.*, October. To avenge the murder of one of their number the cowboys gathered from the country round about, and fairly stormed the GREASER—that is, Mexican—village where the murder had been committed, killing four of the inhabitants.

1891. GUNTER, *Miss Nobody*, ch. 2. Don't let the GREASER git his fingers in your ha'r.

2. *in. pl.* (Royal Military Academy). — Fried potatoes, as distinguished from BOILERS = boiled potatoes.

TO GIVE ONE GREASER, *verb. phr.* (Winchester College).—To rub the back of the hand hard with the knuckles.

GREASE-SPOT, *subs.* (common).—The imaginary result of a passage at arms, physical or intellectual.

1844. HALIBURTON, *The Attaché*, ch. xvi. If he hadn't a had the clear grit in him, and showed his teeth and claws, they'd a nullified him so you wouldn't see a GREASE-SPOT of him no more.

GREASY-CHIN, *subs.* (old). — A dinner.

1785. GROSE, *Vulg. Tongue*, s.v.

1837. BARHAM, *Ingoldsby Legends*, 'Lay of St. Gengulphus.' And to every guest his card had express'd 'Half past' as the hour for a GREASY CHIN.

GREAT CRY AND LITTLE WOOL.—*See* CRY.

GREAT GO (or **GREATS**), *subs.* (Cambridge University). — The final examination for the B.A. degree; *cf.*, LITTLE-GO. At Oxford, GREATER.

1841. *Prince of the New-made Baccalere, Oxford.* GREAT-GO is passed.

1861. HUGHES, *Tom Brown at Oxford*, ch. x. Both small and GREAT are sufficiently distant to be altogether ignored, if we are that way inclined.

1856-7. THACKERAY, *King of Brentford's Test.*, st. 7. At college, though not fast, Yet his little-go and GREAT-GO, He creditably pass'd.

1871. *Morning Advertiser*, 28 Apr. Yes, Mr. Lowe has been plucked for his GREAT GO.

1883. *Echo*, 3 May, p. 2, c. 4. But few, indeed, are the men who have been in for GREATS during the last twenty years, and who have not blessed Mr. Kitchin for his edition of the *Novum Organum.*

GREAT GUN, *subs. phr.* (common). —1. A person of distinction; a thing of importance.

ENGLISH SYNONYMS.—Big bug; big dog of the tanyard; big dog with the brass collar; big gun; big head; big one; big (or great) pot; big wig; biggest toad in the puddle; cock of the walk; don; large potato; nob; rumbusticator; stunner; swell; swell-head; topper; top-sawyer.

FRENCH SYNONYMS.—*Un gros bonnet* (familiar = big wig); *un fiérot* (a stuck-up); *un herr* (from the German); *Monsieur Raidillon* or *Monsieur Pointu* (= Mr. STUCK-UP).

1836. M. SCOTT, *Tom Cringle's Log*, ch. ii. A Spanish Ecclesiastic, the Canon of——. Plenty of GREAT GUNS, at any rate—a regular park of artillery.

1843. HALIBURTON, *Sam Slick in England*, ch. xv. The GREAT GUNS and big bugs have to take in each other's ladies.

Ibid., p. 24. Pick out the BIG BUGS and see what sort of stuff they're made of.

1853. WH. MELVILLE, *Digby Grand*, ch. x. The GREAT GUNS of the party, the rector of the parish, the member for the county.

2. (pedlers'). — A peculiar practice; a trick of particular usefulness and importance; a favourite WHEEZE (*q.v.*).

1851. MAYHEW, *Lond. Lab. and Lond. Poor*, i., 256. The street-seller's GREAT GUN, as he called it, was to make up packets, as closely resembling as he could accomplish it those which were displayed in the windows of any of the shops.

TO BLOW GREAT GUNS, *verb. phr.* (nautical).—To blow a gale; also TO BLOW GREAT GUNS AND SMALL ARMS.

1839. HARRISON AINSWORTH, *Jack Sheppard* [1889], 23. 'Curse me, if I don't think all the world means to cross the Thames this fine night!' observed Ben. 'One'd think it rained fares as well as BLOWED GREAT GUNS.

1854. H. MILLER, *Sch. and Schm.* (1858), 14. It soon began to BLOW GREAT GUNS.

1865. H. KINGSLEY, *Hillyars and Burton*, ch. lxxvii. It was BLOWING PRETTY HIGH GUNS, sou' eastern by east, off shore and when we came to the harbour's mouth there was Tom Wyatt with his pilot just aboard.

1869. ARTHUR SKETCHLEY, *Mrs. Brown on Things in General.* I never did see such weather, A-BLOWIN GREAT GUNS as the sayin' is.

1892. R. L. STEVENSON and L. OSBOURNE, *The Wrecker*, p. 340. It BLEW GREAT GUNS from the seaward.

GREAT-HOUSE. *See* BIG-HOUSE.

GREAT-JOSEPH, *subs.* (old).—An overcoat.

GREAT SCOTT! *intj.* (American).—An exclamation of surprise; an apology for an oath. [Possibly a memory of the name of Gen. Winfield Scott, a presidential candidate whose dignity and style were such as to win him the nickname "Fuss-and-Feathers."] Also GREAT CÆSAR.

1888. *New York Mercury.* GREAT SCOTT! you don't say so.

1891. GUNTER, *Miss Nobody of Nowhere*, p. 98. Bob, what's the matter with you? GREAT SCOTT! the mine hain't give out.

1891. *Licensed Vict. Gaz.*, 19 June, p. 396, c 2. GREAT SCOTCH!—no, we mean Scott—well, language worthy of the great Harry prevailed for awhile.

1891. N. GOULD, *Double Event*, p. 305. 'GREAT SCOTT! what the deuce is Wells up to?' said the Squire.

1892. R. L. STEVENSON and L. OSBOURNE, *The Wrecker*, p. 106. GREAT CÆSAR!

1892. *Tit Bits*, 19 Mar., p. 416, c. 1. *He.* GREAT CÆSAR! There you go again! *She.* James will you please remember that it is your wife to whom you are speaking, sir? *He.* No other woman could drive me raving, distracted, crazy, asking silly questions about—*She.* James!

GREAT SHAKES. *See* SHAKES.

GREAT SMOKE, *subs.* (thieves')—London.

GREAT SUN, *intj.* (common).—An exclamation.

1876. BESANT and RICE, *Golden Butterfly.* GREAT SUN! I think I see it now.

GREAT-UNWASHED, *subs.* (colloquial).—The lower classes; the rabble. Also the UNWASHED. [First used by Burke; popularised by Scott.]

1892. SYDNEY WATSON, *Wops the Waif*, ch. iii., p. 4. We begin to understand what is meant by the lowest classes, THE GREAT UNWASHED.

GREAT WHIPPER-IN, *subs. phr.* (common). — Death; OLD FLOORER (*q.v.*).

GRECIAN, *subs.* (old). — 1. A roysterer; a GREEK (*q.v.*).

2. (Christ's Hospital). — A senior boy.

3. (popular).—An Irishman.

GRECIAN ACCENT, *subs.* (popular).—A brogue.

GRECIAN-BEND, *subs.* (common).—A stoop in walking. [Affected by some women *c.* 1869-80.] *Cf.*, ALEXANDRA LIMP, ROMAN FALL, ITALIAN WRIGGLE, KANGAROO DROOP.

1821. *Etonian*, ii., 57. In person he was of the common size, with something of the GRECIAN BEND, contracted doubtless from sedentary habits.

1869. *Daily Telegraph*, 1 Sept. I do not, however, think the 'stoop' our girls now have arises from tight-lacing. Some affect what is called the GRECIAN BEND.

1870. *Orchestra*, 25 Mar. 'Grand Comic Concert.' The ladies have their GRECIAN BEND, our typical gentleman explains a correspondent masculine affectation which he dubs 'The Roman Fall—The Roman Fall.'

1871. *Morning Advertiser*, 4 Dec. A lady of five feet becomes, say, five feet two inches per heels, five feet six inches per hair, five feet again, per GRECIAN BEND.

1876. *Chambers' Journal*, No. 629. Your own advocacy for the GRECIAN BEND and the Alexandra limp—both positive and practical imitations of physical affliction.

1886. *Cornhill Magazine*, Dec., p. 618. You ain't nearly fine enough for a waitress or for 'im, neether. He likes a smart young woman with a GRECIAN BEND.

GREED, *subs.* (thieves). — Money. For synonyms, *see* ACTUAL and GILT.

1857. DUCANGE ANGLICUS, *Vulg. Tongue*, s.v.

1859. MATSELL, *Vocabulum*, s.v.

GREEDY-GUT (or **-GUTS**), *subs.* (old). — A voracious eater; a glutton. [As in the old (schoolboys') rhyme: 'Guy-hi, GREEDY-GUT, Eat all the pudding up.'] For synonyms, *see* STODGER. Fr., *un glafâtre.*

1598. FLORIO, *A Worlde of Wordes*, *Edace*, an eater, a devourer, a GREEDIGUT. *Ibid. Putti occhi*, greedie eies.

1772. COLES, *Eng. Dict.*, s.v.

1811. *Lexicon Balatronicum*, s.v.

GREEK, *subs.* (old).—1. Slang, or FLASH (*q.v.*); usually ST. GILES' GREEK (*q.v.*). *Cf.*, CANT, GIBBERISH, etc.

2. (colloquial).—A card-sharper; a cheat.

1523. ROY and BARLOW, *Rede me and be not wrothe*, p. 117 [ed. Arber, 1871]. In carde playinge he is a goode GREKE And can skyll of post and glycke, Also a prayre of dyce to trolle.

1568. *Satirical Poems*, 'Scottish Text Soc.' [1889-91] i., 77. A cowle, a cowle, for such a GREEK were fitter far to wea're.

1598. FLORIO, *A Worlde of Wordes*. *Grecheggiare* . . . . to play the GREEK.

1602. SHAKSPEARE, *Troilus and Cressida*, v. 6. Come, both you cogging GREEKS; have at you both.

1819. MOORE, *Tom Crib*, xxviii. Most of the cant phrases in HEAD'S *English Rogue*, which was published, I believe, in 1666, would be intelligible to a GREEK of the present day.

1823. MONCRIEFF, *Tom and Jerry*, ii., 5. Come lads, bustle about; play will begin—some of the pigeons are here already, the GREEKS will not be long following.

1834. AINSWORTH, *Rookwood*, bk. IV., ch. i. Jerry was a GREEK by nature, and could land a flat as well as the best of them.

1855. THACKERAY, *Newcomes*, ch. xxxvi. He was an adventurer, a pauper, a blackleg, a regular GREEK.

1861. *Once a Week*, 25 May, p. 97. As the GREEK places the packet [of cards] on the top of the other, he allows it to project the least bit in the world.

1884. *Saturday Review*, 16 Feb., p. 202. Without a confederate the now fashionable game of baccarat does not seem to offer many chances for the GREEK.

3. (old).—An Irishman.

1823. BEE, *Dict. of the Turf*. GREEK, s.v. Irishmen call themselves GREEKS.

1851-61. H. MAYHEW, *Lond. Lab. and Lond. Poor*, Vol. i., p. 240. We had the GREEKS (the lately arrived Irish) down upon us more than once.

1872. *Standard*, 3 Sept. 'Melbourne Correspondence.' The most noticeable point of comparison between the two Administrations is the presence or the absence of the GREEK element from the Cabinet. GREEK, as some of your readers are aware, is colonial slang for 'Irish.'

4. (thieves').—A gambler. Also a highwayman.

MERRY GREEK, *subs. phr.* (old).—A roysterer; a drunkard. COTGRAVE. [In Latin, *Graecare* = to play the Greek—high-living and hard drinking.]

1602. SHAKSPEARE, *Troilus and Cressida*, iv., 4. A woful Cressid 'mongst the MERRY GREEKS.

GREEK FIRE, *subs. phr.* (thieves').—Bad whiskey; ROTGUT (*q.v.*).

1889. CLARKSON and RICHARDSON, *Police*, p. 321, s.v.

GREEK KALENDS, *subs. phr.* (colloquial). — Never. To defer anything to the Greek Kalends is to put it off *sine die*. (The Greeks used no kalends in their reckoning of time.)

c. 1649. DRUMM. of HAWTH. *Consid. Parlt.*, wks. (1711) 185. That gold, plate, and all silver, given to the mint-house in these late troubles, shall be paid at the GREEK KALENDS.

1653. URQUHART, *Rabelais*, bk. I., ch. xx. The judgment or decree shall be given out and pronounced at the next GREEK CALENDS, that is, never.

1823. BYRON, *Don Juan*, c. xiii., st. 45. They and their bills, 'Arcadians both,' are left To the GREEK KALENDS of another session.

1825. SCOTT, *Betrothed*. Intro. Will you speak of your paltry prose doings in my presence, whose great historical poem, in twenty books, with notes in proportion, has been postponed AD GRÆCAS KALENDAS?

1872. O. W. HOLMES, *Poet Breakf. T.* i., 18. His friends looked for it only on the GREEK CALENDS, say on the 31st of April, when that should come round, if you would modernize the phrase.

1882. *Macmillan's Mag.*, 253. So we go on . . . and the works are sent to the GREEK CALENDS.

ENGLISH SYNONYMS.—In the reign of Queen Dick; when the devil is blind; when two Sundays come in a week; at Doomsday; at Tib's Eve; one of these odd-come-shortlys; when my goose pisses; when the ducks have eaten up the dirt; when pigs fly; in a month of Sundays; once in a blue moon.

FRENCH SYNONYMS.—*Mardi s'il fait chaud* (obsolete); *Dimanche après la grande messe* (popular); *quand les poules pisseront; semaine des quatre jeudis* (popular: when four Thursdays come in a week).

GREEN, *subs.* (common). — 1. Rawness; simplicity. Generally, 'Do you see any GREEN in my eye'? = Do you take me for a fool? *See adj.* sense.

1851-61. MAYHEW, *Lond. Lab. and Lond. Poor*, 247. I'm not a tailor, but I understands about clothes, and I believe that no person ever saw anything GREEN in my eye.

1892. *Ally Sloper*, 19 Mar., p. 95, c. 2. Ally Sloper the 'cute, Ally Sloper the sly, Ally Sloper, the cove with no GREEN in his eye.

1892. *Illustrated Bits*, 22 Oct., p. 14, c. 2. Sindin' both shlips is it? How wud Oi have a check on ye? Do ye see inny GREEN IN ME OI?

Adj. (colloquial). — Simple; inexperienced; gullible; UNSALTED (*q.v.*).

1596. SHAKSPEARE, *Hamlet*, Act i., Sc. 3. *Pol.* Affection! pooh! you speak like a GREEN girl.

1605. CHAPMAN, *All Fools*, Act iv., p. 67 (*Plays*, 1874). Shall I then say you want experience? Y'are GREEN, y'are credulous; easy to be blinded.

1748. T. DYCHE, *Dictionary* (5th ed.). GREEN (*a*) . . . so likewise a young or unexperienced person in arts, sciences, etc., is sometimes said to be GREEN, raw, etc.

1823. MONCRIEFF, *Tom and Jerry*. *Tom.* No; you're GREEN! *Jerry.* GREEN! *Log.* Ah! not fly! *Tom.* Yes, not awake!

1837. DICKENS, *Oliver Twist*, ch. viii. 'My eyes, how GREEN!' exclaimed the young gentleman. 'Why a beak's a madgst'rate.'

1841. *Punch*, July 17, p. 6. What a GREEN chap you are, after all. A public man's consistency! It's only a popular delusion.

1850. SMEDLEY, *Frank Fairleigh*, p. 19. Eh! why! what's the matter with you? have I done anything particularly GREEN, as you call it?

1856. T. HUGHES, *Tom Brown's School Days*, pt. I., ch. ii. You try to make us think . . . that you are, even as we, of the working classes. But bless your hearts, we ain't so GREEN.

1869. *Literary World*, 31 Dec., p. 129, c. 2. His fellow-passengers laughed at him for being so GREEN.

1879. *Punch's Almanack*, p. 7. Seasonable Slang. For Spring.—You be blowed! For Summer.—I'll warm yer! For Autumn. —Not so blooming GREEN! For Winter —An ice little game all round.

1887. *Lippincott*, July, p. 104. Within the last day or so a young fellow has arrived who is in danger of being eaten by the cows, so GREEN is he.

1890. *Licensed Vict. Gaz.*, 7 Nov. Being quite GREEN at the time, I rather lost my head over my good fortune.

Verb (colloquial).—To hoax; to swindle. At Eton TO GREEN UP. For synonyms, *see* GAMMON.

1836-41. T. C. BUCKLAND, *Eton*. I was again catechized on many points personal to myself, and some mild attempts were made to GREEN me, as boys call it.

1889. *Answers*, 2 Mar., p. 218, c. 1. Whereupon the old humbug burst into a loud guffaw, as though he were rejoicing at having GREENED the toff.

1892. ANSTEY, *Voces Populi* (Second Series). 'Bank Holiday,' 147. THE DAMSEL (*giggling*). You go on—you don't GREEN *me* that w'y.

GREENS, *subs.* (old).—1. Chlorosis: *i.e.*, the green sickness.

1719. DURFEY, *Pills*, etc., i., 313. The maiden takes five, too, that's vexed with her GREENS.

2. *in. pl.* (printers').—Bad or worn out rollers.

TO HAVE, GET, or GIVE ONE'S GREENS, *verb phr.* (venery).—To enjoy, procure, or confer the sexual favour. Said indifferently of both sexes.

Hence, also, ON FOR ONE'S GREENS = amorous and willing; AFTER ONE'S GREENS = in quest of the favour; GREEN-GROVE = the pubes; GREEN-GROCERY = the female *pudendum*; THE PRICE OF GREENS = the cost of an embrace; FRESH GREENS = a new PIECE (*q.v.*). [Derived by some from the old Scots' *grene* = to pine, to long for, to desire with insistence: whence GREENS = longings, desires; which words may in their turn be referred, perhaps, to Mid. Eng., *zernen*, A.S., *gyrnan*, Icelandic, *girna* = to desire, and Gothic, *gairns* = desirous. Mod. Ger., *begehren* = to desire. *See* DALZIEL, *Darker Superstitions of Scotland*, 1835, p. 106:—'He answered that he wald gif the sum Spanyie fleis callit cantarides, quhilk, gif thou suld move the said Elizabeth to drynk of, it wold mak hir out of all question to GRENE eftir the.' *Trial of Peter Hay, of Kirkland's, and others, for Witchcraft, 25th May, 1601.* But in truth, the expression is a late and vulgar coinage. It would seem, indeed, to be a reminiscence of GARDEN (*q.v.*), and the set of metaphors—as KAIL, CAULIFLOWER, PARSLEY BED, and so forth (all which *see*)—suggested thereby.]

ENGLISH SYNONYMS.—TO BE all there but the most of you; in Abraham's bosom; up one's petticoats (or among one's frills); there; on the spot; into; up; up to one's balls; where uncle's doodle goes; among the cabbages.

TO DANCE the blanket hornpipe; the buttock jig; the cushion dance (*see* MONOSYLLABLE); the goat's jig; the mattress jig; the married man's cotillion; the matrimonial polka; the reels o' Bogie (Scots'); the reels of Stumpie (Scots'); to the tune of THE SHAKING OF THE SHEETS; with your arse to the ceiling, or the kipples (Scots').

TO GO ballocking; beard-splitting; bed-pressing (Marston); belly-bumping (Urquhart); bitching (Marston); bum-fighting; bum-working; bum-tickling; bum-faking; bush-ranging; buttock-stirring (Urquhart); bird's-nesting; buttocking; cock-fighting; cunny-catching; doodling; drabbing; fleshing it; flesh-mongering; goosing: to Hairy-fordshire; jock-hunting; jottling; jumming (Urquhart); leather-stretching; on the loose; motting; molrowing; pile-driving; prick-scouring; quim-sticking; rumping; rump-splitting; strumming; twatting; twat-faking; vaulting (Marston, etc.); wenching; womanizing; working the dumb (or double, or hairy) oracle. twat-raking; tummy-tickling; tromboning; quim-wedging; tail-twitching; button-hole working; under-petticoating.

TO HAVE, or DO, A BIT OF beef (of women); business

(Shakspeare); bum-dancing; cauliflower; cock; cock-fighting; cunt; curly greens; fish; on a fork; fun; off the chump end; flat; front-door work; giblet pie; the gut- (or cream- or sugar-) stick (of women); jam; ladies' tailoring; meat; mutton; pork; quimsy; rough; sharp-and-blunt (rhyming slang); stuff; split-mutton; skirt; summer cabbage.

TO HAVE, or DO, or PERFORM, the act of androgynation (Urquhart); a ballocking; a bit; a lassie's by-job (Burns); a bedward bit (Durfey); a beanfeast in bed; a belly-warmer; a blindfold bit; a bottom-wetter (of women); a bout; a brush with the cue; a dive in the dark; a drop-in; a double fight; an ejectment in Love-lane; a four-legged frolic; a fuck; a futter; a game in the cock-loft; a goose-and-duck (rhyming); the culbatizing exercise (Urquhart); a grind; a hoist-in; a jottle; a jumble-giblets; a jumble-up; an inside worry; a leap; a leap up the ladder; a little of one with t'other (Durfey); a mount; a mow (David Lyndsay, Burns, etc.); a nibble; a plaster of warm guts (Grose); a poke; a put; a put-in; a random push (Burns); a rasp; a ride; a roger; a rootle; a rush up the straight; a shot at the bull's eye; a slide up the board; a squirt-and-a squeeze; a touch-off; a touch-up; a tumble-in; a wet-'un; a wipe at the place; a wollop-in.

SPECIFIC.—TO HAVE, or DO, A BACK-SCUTTLE, (*q.v.*); a BUTTERED BUN (*q.v.*); a DOG'S MARRIAGE (*q.v.*); a KNEE-TREMBLER, PERPENDICULAR, or UPRIGHT (*q.v.*); a MATRIMONIAL (*q.v.*); SPOON-FASHION (*q.v.*); a ST. GEORGE (*q.v.*).

TO PLAY AT, All-fours; Adam-and-Eve; belly-to-belly (Urquhart); brangle-buttock (Urquhart); buttock-and-leave-her; cherry-pit (Herrick); couple-your-navels; cuddle-my-cuddie (Durfey); Hey Gammer Cook (C. Johnson); fathers-and-mothers; the first-game-ever-played; Handie-Dandie; Hooper's Hide (*q.v.*); grapple-my-belly (Urquhart); horses-and-mares (schoolboys'); the close-buttock-game (Urquhart); cock-in-cover; houghmagandie (Burns); in-and-in; in-and-out; Irish-whist (where-the-JACK (*q.v.*)-takes-the ACE [*see* MONOSYLLABLE]); the-loose-coat-game (Urquhart); Molly's-hole (schoolboys'); pickle-me-tickle-me (Urquhart); mumble-peg; prick-the-garter; pully-hauly (Grose); put-in-all; the-same-old-game; squeezem-close; stable-my-naggie; thread-the-needle; tops-and-bottoms; two-handed-put (Grose); up-tails-all.

GENERAL.—To Adam and Eve it; to blow the groundsels; to engage three to one; to chuck a tread; to do (Jonson); to do it; to do 'the act of darkness' (Shakspeare), the act of love, the deed of kind, the work of increase, 'the divine work of fatherhood' (Whitman); to feed the dumb-glutton; to get one's hair cut; to slip in Daintie Davie (Scots'), or Willie Wallace (*idem*); to get Jack in the orchard; to get on top of; to give a lesson in simple arithmetic (*i.e.*, addition, division, multiplication and subtraction); to give a GREEN GOWN (*q.v.*); to go 'groping for trout in a peculiar river' (Shakspeare); to go face-making; to go to Durham (North Country); to go to see a sick friend; to have it; to join faces (Durfey); to join giblets; to make ends meet; to make the beast with two backs (Shakspeare and Urquhart); to make a settlement in tail; to play top-sawyer; to put it in and break it; to post a letter; to go on the stitch; to labor lea (Scots); to tether one's nags on (idem); to nail twa wames thegither (idem); to lift a leg on (Burns); to ride a post (Cotton); to peel one's end in; to put the devil into hell (Boccaccio); to rub bacons (Urquhart); to strop one's beak; to strip one's tarse in; to grind one's tool; to grease the wheel; to take on a split-arsed mechanic; to take a turn in Bushey-park, Cock-alley, Cock-lane, Cupid's-alley, Cupid's-corner, Hair-court, 'the lists of love' (Shakspeare), Love-lane, on Mount Pleasant, among the parsley, on Shooter's-hill, through the stubble; to whack it up; to wollop it in; to labour leather; to wind up the clock (Sterne).

OF WOMEN ONLY.—To get an arselins coup (Burns); to catch an oyster; to do the naughty; to do a spread, a tumble, a back-fall, what mother did before me; a turn on one's back, what Eve did with Adam; to hold, or turn up one's tail (Burns and Durfey); to get one's leg lifted, one's kettle mended, one's chimney swept out, one's leather stretched; to lift one's leg; to open up to; to get shot in the tail; to get a shove in one's bl'nd eye; to get a wet bottom; what Harry gave Doll (Durfey); to suck the sugar-stick; to take in beef; to take Nebuchadnezzar out to grass; to look at the ceiling over a man's shoulder; to get outside it; to play one's ace; to rub one's arse on (Rochester); to spread to; to take in and do for; to give standing room for one; to get hulled between wind and water; to get a pair of balls against one's butt; to take in cream; to show (or give) a bit; to skin the live rabbit; to feed (or trot out) one's PUSSY (q.v.); to lose the match and pocket the stakes; to get a bellyful of marrow pudding; to supple both ends of it (Scots); to draw a cork; to get hilt and hair (Burns); to draw a man's fireworks; to wag one's tail (Pope); to take the starch out of; to go star-gazing (or studying astronomy) on one's back; to get a GREEN GOWN (Herrick and Durfey); to have a hot pudding (or live sausage) for supper; to grant the favour; to give mutton for beef, juice for jelly, soft for hard, a bit of snug for a bit of stiff, a hole to hide it in, a cure for the HORN (q.v.), a hot poultice for the Irish toothache; to pull up one's petticoats to; to get the best and plenty of it; to lie under; to stand the push; to get stabbed in the thigh; to take off one's stays; to get touched up, a bit of the goose's-neck, a go at the creamstick, a handle for the broom.

CONVENTIONALISMS. — To have connection; to have carnal, improper, or sexual intercourse; to know carnally; to have carnal knowledge of; to indulge in sexual commerce; to go to bed with; to lie with; to go in unto (Biblical); to be intimate.

improperly intimate, familiar, on terms of familiarity with; to have one's will of; to lavish one's favours on; to enjoy the pleasures of love, or the conjugal embrace; to embrace; to have one's way with; to perform connubial rites; to scale the heights of connubial bliss; to yield one's favours (of women); to surrender, or give one the enjoyment of one's person (of women); to use benevolence to; to possess. For other synonyms, see RIDE.

TO SEND TO DR. GREEN, verb. phr. (old).—To put out to grass.

1811. *Lexicon Balatronicum*, s.v. My horse is not well, I shall send him to Doctor Green.

S'ELP ME GREENS! (or TATURS!) intj. (common).—A veiled oath of an obscene origin; see GREENS. For synonyms, see OATHS.

1851-61. H. MAYHEW. *Lond. Lab. and Lond. Poor*, vol. iii., p. 144. They'll say, too, s'ELP MY GREENS! and 'Upon my word and say so!'

1891. *Licensed Vict. Gaz.*, 23 Jan. 'Well, s'ELP ME GREENS,' he cried, wiping his eyes and panting for breath, 'if you arn't the greatest treat I ever did meet; you'll be the death o' me, Juggins, you will. Why, you bloomin' idiot, d'ye think if they had'nt been rogues we should have been able to bribe 'em?'

JUST FOR GREENS, adv. phr. (American).—See quot.

1848. JONES, *Sketches of Travel*, p. 7. I've made up my mind to make a tower of travel to the big North this summer, JEST FOR GREENS, as we say in Georgia, when we hain't got no very pertickeler reason for anything, or hain't got time to tell the real one.

GREEN-APRON, subs. (old).—A lay preacher. Also adjectively. For synonyms, see DEVIL-DODGER and SKY-PILOT.

1654. WARREN, *Unbelievers*, 145. It more befits a GREEN-APRON preacher, than such a Gamaliel.

1705. HICKERINGILL, *Priestcraft*, I. (1721) 21. Unbeneficed Noncons. (that live by Alms and no Paternoster, no Penny, say the GREEN-APRONS).

1765. TUCKER, *Lt. Nat.*, II., 451 The gifted priestess amongst the Quaker is known by her GREEN APRON.

GREEN-BACK, subs. (common).—I A frog.

2. (University).—One of Tod-hunter's series of mathematical text-books. (Because bound in green cloth. Cf., BLUE-RUIN.)

3. (American). — The paper issue of the Treasury of the United States; first sent out in 1862 during the civil war. [From the backs being printed in green.] Hence GREEN-BACKER=an advocate for an unlimited issue of paper money.

1873. *Echo*, 8 May. This was accomplished by the issue of legal tender notes, popularly known as GREENBACKS.

1877. CLEMENS, *Life on the Mississippi*, ch. lvii., p. 499. Anything in the semblance of a town lot, no matter how situated, was saleable, and at a figure which would still have been high if the ground had been sodded with GREENBACKS.

1891. GUNTER, *Miss Nobody of Nowhere*, p. 228. Gussie can hear the crinkle of the GREENBACKS as he folds them up.

GREEN BAG, subs. (old).—A lawyer. [From the green bag in which robes and briefs were carried. The colour is now blue, or, in cases of presentation from seniors to juniors, red.]

1690. B. E., *Dict. Cant. Crew*, s.v.

1785. GROSE, *Vulg. Tongue*, s.v.

14

ENGLISH SYNONYMS. — Black box; bramble (provincial); devil's own; gentleman of the long robe; land-shark; limb of the law; mouth-piece; PHILADELPHIA LAWYER (q.v.); quitam; six-and-eightpence; snipe; sublime rascal.

FRENCH SYNONYMS. *Un bavard* (pop. =a talker or mouth-piece); *un blanchisseur* (=white-washer); *un brodancheur à la plaque, aux macarons*, or *à la cymbale* (thieves': a notary-public); *un gerbier* (thieves'); *un grippemini* (obsolete : *grippeminaud* = thief); *un inutile* (thieves': a notary-public); *une éponge d'or* (=a sucker-up of gold: in allusion to the long bills); *un macaron huissier* (popular).

ITALIAN SYNONYMS.—*Dragon del gran soprano*; *dragonetto* (=a dragon, or SUCK-ALL).

SPANISH SYNONYMS.—*Remedio* (=a remedy); *la letraderia* (=a body or society of lawyers); *cataribera* (jocular).

GREEN - BONNET, TO HAVE (or WEAR) A GREEN BONNET, verb. phr. (common). — To fail in business; to go bankrupt. [From the green cloth cap once worn by bankrupts.]

GREEN CHEESE. See CREAM CHEESE and MOON.

GREEN CLOTH. See BOARD OF GREEN CLOTH.

GREEN DRAGOONS, subs. (military).—The fifth Dragoon Guards; also known as the Green Horse. [From their green facings.]

GREENER, subs. (common). — A new, or raw hand; specifically employed of inexperienced workmen introduced to fill the place of strikers; DUNG (q.v.). Cf., FLINT. For synonyms, see SNOOKER.

1889. *Pall Mall Gaz.*, 14 Oct., p. 6, c. 3. A howling mob of Hebrew men and women . . . . in their own Yiddish jargon criticised the new arrivals, or GREENERS, in language that was anything but complimentary.

GREEN-GOODS, subs. (American). —1. Counterfeit greenbacks.

1891. GUNTER, *Miss Nobody of Nowhere*, p. 223. In his opinion Stillman Myth, and Co., were in the GREEN GOODS business.

2. (venery).—A prostitute new to the town; a FRESH BIT (q.v.).

GREEN - GOODS MAN (or OPERATOR), subs. (American).—1. A counterfeiter of spurious greenbacks; a SNIDE-PITCHER (q.v.).

1888. *Troy Daily Times*, 3 Feb. Driscoll was hung, but the GREEN GOODS-MAN escaped, for the only proof against him was that he sold a quantity of paper cut in the shape of bills, and done up in packages of that size.

2. (venery).—A FRESH BIT (q.v.) fancier. Also an amateur of defloration; a MINOTAUR (q.v.).

GREEN-GOOSE, subs. (old). — 1. A cuckold.

2. (old).—A prostitute. For synonyms, see BARRACK-HACK and TART.

1594. SHAKSPEARE, *Love's Labour Lost*, iv., 3. This is the liver vein, which makes flesh a deity; A GREEN GOOSE, a goddess, pure, pure idolatry.

1607. BEAUMONT AND FLETCHER, *Woman Hater*, i., 2. His palace is full of GREEN GEESE.

GREEN-GOWN. TO GIVE A GREEN-GOWN, verb. phr. (old).—To tumble a woman on the grass; to copulate. For synonyms, see GREENS and RIDE.

1647-8. HERRICK, *Hesperides*. 'To Corinna To go a Maying.' Many a GREEN GOWN has been given.

1690. B. E., *Dict. Cant. Crew*. GREEN GOWN, s.v. A throwing of young lasses on the grass and kissing them.

1719. DURFEY, *Pills*, etc., i., 277. Kit GAVE A GREEN GOWN to Betty, and lent her his hand to rise.

1719. SMITH, *Lives of Highwaymen*, i, 214. Our gallant being disposed to give his lady a GREEN GOWN.

1742. C. JOHNSON, *Highwaymen and Pyrates*. Passim.

1785. GROSE, *Vulg. Tongue*, s.v.

GREEN-HEAD, subs. (old). — A greenhorn. For synonyms, see BUFFLE and CABBAGE-HEAD.

1690. B. E., *Dict. Cant. Crew*. GREENHEAD, s.v., A very raw novice or inexperienced fellow.

1785. GROSE, *Vulg. Tongue*, s.v.

GREENHORN (or GREEN-HEAD, or GREENLANDER), subs. (common). —A simpleton; a fool; a GULL (q.v.); also a new hand. For synonyms, see BUFFLE and CAB-BAGE-HEAD. TO COME FROM GREENLAND = to be fresh to things; RAW (q.v.). GREEN-LANDER sometimes=an Irish-man.

1753. *Adventurer*, No. 100. A slouch in my gait, a long lank head of hair and an unfashionable suit of drab-coloured cloth, would have denominated me a GREENHORN, or in other words, a country put very green.

1815. SCOTT, *Guy Mannering*, ch. xliv. 'Why, wha but a crack-brained GREENHORN wad hae let them keep up the siller that ye left at the Gordon-Arms?'

1837. DICKENS, *Oliver Twist*. A new pall . . . Where did he come from? GREENLAND.

1849. THACKERAY, *Pendennis*, ch. ix. All these he resigned to lock himself into a lone little country house, with a simple widow and a GREENHORN of a son.

GREENHOUSE, subs. (London 'bus-drivers'). — An omnibus.

GREEN HOWARDS, subs. phr. (military).—The Nineteenth Foot. [From its facings and its Colonel's name (1738-48), and to distinguish it from the Third Foot, also commanded by a Col. Howard.] Also HOWARD'S GARBAGE.

GREEN KINGSMAN, subs. (pugilistic). — A silk pocket-handkerchief : any pattern on a green ground.

GREEN LINNETS, subs. phr. (military). — The 39th Foot. [From the facings.]

GREENLY, adv. (old).—Like a green-horn; foolishly.

1596. SHAKSPEARE, *Hamlet*, Act iv., Sc. 5. King. . . . We have done but GREENLY, In hugger-mugger to inter him.

GREENMANS, subs. (old). — 1. The fields; the country.

1610. ROWLANDS, *Martin Mark-all*, p. 38 (H. Club's Rept.) 1874. GREENEMANS, the fields.

2. in. sing. (builders').—A contractor who speculates with other people's money.

GREEN-MEADOW, subs. (venery).—The female *pudendum*. For synonyms, see MONOSYLLABLE.

GREENNESS, subs. (colloquial).—Immaturity of judgment; in-experience; gullibility.

1748. T. DYCHE, *Dictionary* (5th ed.). GREENNESS (s) . . . also the rawness, un-skilfulness, or imperfection of any person in a trade, art, science, etc.

1838. JAS. GRANT, *Sketches in London*, ch. vi., p. 205. Instances of such perfect simplicity or GREENNESS, as no one could have previously deemed of possible existence.

GREEN-RAG.—*See* GREENY, sense 1.

GREEN-RIVER. TO SEND A MAN UP GREEN-RIVER, *verb. phr.* (American).—To kill. [From a once famous factory on Green River, where a favourite hunting-knife was made.] For synonyms, *see* COOK ONE'S GOOSE.

1848. RUXTON, *Life in the Far West*, p. 175. A thrust from the keen scalp-knife by the nervous arm of a mountaineer was no baby blow, and seldom failed to strike home UP TO THE GREEN RIVER [*i.e.*, the mark] on the blade.

GREEN-SICKNESS, *subs.* (old).—Chlorosis.

GREEN-TURTLE. TO LIVE UP TO GREEN-TURTLE, *verb. phr.* (American).—To do, and give, one's best. [From the high esteem in which the green fat of turtle is held.]

1888. PATON, *Down the Islands.* People who, as hosts, LIVE UP TO THEIR GREEN TURTLE.

GREENWICH BARBER, *subs.* (old).—A retailer of sand from the Greenwich pits. [A pun upon 'shaving' the banks.]

1785. GROSE, *Vulg. Tongue*, s.v.

GREENWICH-GOOSE, *subs.* (old).—A pensioner of Greenwich Hospital.

1785. GROSE, *Vulg. Tongue*, s.v.

GREENY, *subs.* (old theatrical).—1. The curtain. [From the colour.] Also GREEN-RAG.

1821. EGAN, *Tom and Jerry*, p. 110 [ed. 1890]. It is far more difficult to please the company behind GREENY; I beg pardon, sir, I should have said than the audience before the curtain.

2. (University).—A freshman. For synonyms, *see* SNOOKER.

1834. SOUTHEY, *The Doctor*, ch. i. He was entered among the GREENIES of this famous University.

3. (common).—A simpleton; a GREENHORN (*q.v.*). For synonyms, *see* BUFFLE and CABBAGE-HEAD.

1852. JUDSON, *Myst.*, etc., *of New York*, part III., ch. 9, p. 58. Anybody could know that these was took by a GREENY.

1887. *Congregationalist*, 7 April. Jim said I was a GREENY . . . [and] that he had a lot of houses.

GREETIN' FU', *adv. phr.* (Scots'), Drunk: literally 'crying drunk.' For synonyms, *see* DRINKS and SCREWED.

GREEZE, *subs.* (Westminster School).—A crowd; a PUSH (*q.v.*).

GREGORIAN, *subs.* (old).—A kind of wig worn in the 17th century. [After the inventor, one Gregory, a barber in the Strand.]

1658. *Honest Ghost*, p. 46. Pulling a little down his GREGORIAN.

GREGORIAN-TREE, *subs.* (old).—The gallows. [After a sequence of three hangmen of the name.] For synonyms, *see* NUBBING-CHEAT.

1641. *Mercurius Pragmaticus.* This trembles under the black rod, and he Doth fear his fate from the GREGORIAN TREE.

1785. GROSE, *Vulg. Tongue*, s.v.

GREGORINE, *subs.* (common).—A louse; specifically, head vermin. [From the Italian.] For synonyms, *see* CHATES.

GRESHAMITE, *subs.* (old).—A Fellow of the Royal Society.—B.E. [1690.]

GREY.—*See* GRAY, *passim.*

GRIDDLE, *subs.* (streets').—To sing in the streets. Whence, GRIDDLING = street-singing; GRIDDLER = a street-singer.

1851-61. MAYHEW, *Lond. Lab. and Lond. Poor.* Got a month for GRIDDLING in the main drag.

1877. BESANT AND RICE, *Son of Vulcan*, pt. I., ch. xii. Cardiff Jack's never got so low as to be GRIDDLING on the main drag—singing, I mean, on the high-road.

1888. W. BESANT, *Fifty Years Ago*, ch. iv., p. 53. They [street singers] have not yet invented Moody and Sankey, and therefore they cannot sing 'Hold the Fort' or 'Dare to be a Daniel,' but there are hymns in every collection which suit the GRIDLER.

1890. *Daily Telegraph*, 20 May. Singing or shouting hymns in the streets on Sundays. To this system the name of GRIDLING has been applied. The GRIDLERS, it was stated, were known to boast, as they returned to their haunts in Deptford and Southwark, how much they could make in a few hours.

GRIDIRON, *subs.* (American).—1. The United States' flag; the STARS AND STRIPES. Also STARS AND BARS; BLOOD AND ENTRAILS; GRIDIRON AND DOUGHBOYS; and, in speaking of the Eagle in conjunction with the flag, the GOOSE AND GRIDIRON.

2. (common).—A County Court Summons. [Originally applied to Writs of the Westminster Court, the arms of which resemble a gridiron.]

1859. SALA, *Gaslight and Daylight*, ch. xxi. He collects debts for anybody in the neighbourhood, takes out the abhorred GRIDIRONS, or County Court summonses.

3. (thieves').—The bars on a cell window. Fr., *les gaules de Schtard.*

THE GRIDIRON, *subs. phr.* (common).—The Grafton Club. [Where the grill is a speciality.]

ON THE GRIDIRON, *adv. phr.* (common).—Troubled; harassed; in a bad way; ON TOAST (*q.v.*).

THE WHOLE GRIDIRON, *subs. phr.* (common).—*See* WHOLE ANIMAL.

GRIEF, TO COME TO GRIEF, *verb. phr.* (colloquial).—To come to ruin; to meet with an accident; to fail. In quot., 1891 = trouble.

1855. THACKERAY, *Newcomes*, ch. x. We drove on to the Downs, and we were nearly COMING TO GRIEF. My horses are young, and when they get on the grass they are as if they were mad.

1888. *Cassell's Saturday Jour.*, 8 Dec., p. 249. In the United States he had started a 'Matrimonial Agency,' in which he had COME TO GRIEF, and he had been obliged to return to this country for a similar reason.

1891. *Sportsman*, 28 Feb. The flag had scarcely fallen than the GRIEF commenced, as Midshipmite and Carlo rolled over at the first fence, Clanranald refused at the second, and Dog Fox fell at the third.

GRIFFIN (or **GRIFF**), *subs.* (common).—1. A new-comer; a raw hand; a GREENHORN (*q.v.*) *See* SNOOKER and SAMMY SOFT. [Specific uses are (Anglo-Indian) = a new arrival from Europe; (military) = a young subaltern; (Anglo-Chinese) = an unbroken horse. GRIFFINAGE (or GRIFFINISM) = the state of greenhornism.

1859. H. KINGSLEY, *Geoffry Hamlyn*, ch. xxviii All the GRIFFINS ought to hunt together.

1878. BESANT and RICE, *By Celia's Arbour*, ch. xxx. We were in the Trenches; there had been joking with a lot of GRIFFS, young recruits just out from England.

1882. MISS BRADDON, *Mount Royal*, ch. xxii. There was only one of the lads about the yard when he left, for it was breakfast-time, and the little GRIFFIN didn't notice.

1883. *Graphic*, 17 March, p. 286, c. 3. Many a youngster has got on in his profession . . . . by having the good fortune to make a friend of the old Indian who took him in as a GRIFFIN or a stranger.

2. (colloquial).—A woman of forbidding manners or appearance; a GORGON. Also a caretaker, chaperon, or SHEEP-DOG (*q.v.*) [A reflection of the several griffins of ornithology and of heraldry: the former a feeder on birds, small mammals, and even children; the latter (as in Milton) a perfection of vigilance.]

1824. R. B. PEAKE, *Americans Abroad*, i., 2. It is always locked up by that she-GRIFFIN with a bunch of keys.

3. (thieves').—A signal: *e.g.*, TO TIP THE GRIFFIN = to warn; TO GIVE THE OFFICE (*q.v.*), or TIP (*q.v.*). THE STRAIGHT GRIFFIN = the straight tip.

1888. *Cassell's Sat. Jour.*, 22 Dec., p. 305. Plank yourself at the corner to give the GRIFFIN if you hear or see owt.

1891. N. GOULD, *Double Event*, p. 22. He's got the STRAIGHT GRIFF for something.

1891. J. NEWMAN, *Scamping Tricks*, p. 95. When he wanted to GIVE the chaps in the office THE STRAIGHT GRIFFIN, he used to say, 'Nelson's my guide.'

4. *in. pl.* (trade).—The scraps and leavings from a contract feast, which are removed by the purveyor.

GRIFF-METOLL, *subs.* (old).—Sixpence. For synonyms, *see* TANNER.

1754. *Discoveries of John Poulter*, s.v.

GRIG, *subs.* (old).—1. An active, lively, and jocose person: as in the phrase 'Merry as a GRIG.' [An allusion to the liveliness of the grasshopper, sand-eel, or to GRIG (= Greek: *cf.*, *Troilus and Cressida* i. 2; iv. 4).

1611. COTGRAVE, *Dictionarie. Galebon-temps.* A MERRY GRIG.

1673. WYCHERLEY, *Gent. Danc. Master*, i., 1., wks. (1713) 251. Hah, ah, ah, cousin, dou art a merry GRIGG—ma foy.

1690. B. E., *Dict. Cant. Crew*, GRIG s.v. A merry GRIG; a merry fellow.

1719. DURFEY, *Pills*, etc., i., 43. The statesman that talks on the Woolsack so big, Could hustle to the open as MERRY AS A GRIG.

1765. GOLDSMITH, *Essays VI.* I grew as merry as a GRIG, and laughed at every word that was spoken.

1852. DICKENS, *Bleak House*, ch. xix, p. 159. The learned gentleman . . . is as merry as a GRIG at a French watering-place.

2. (thieves').—A farthing; a GIGG (*q.v.*). For synonyms, *see* FADGE.

1690. B. E., *Dict. Cant. Crew*, s.v Not a GRIG did he tip me, not a farthing would he give me.

1785. GROSE, *Vulg. Tongue*, s.v.

1839. HARRISON AINSWORTH, *Jack Sheppard* [1889], p. 15. 'He shall go through the whole course,' replied Blueskin, with a ferocious grin, 'unless he comes down to the last GRIG.'

Verb. (American).—To vex; to worry.

1855. HALIBURTON [S. Slick], *Human Nature*, p. 83. That word 'superiors' GRIGGED me. Thinks I, 'My boy, I'll just take that expression, roll it up in a ball, and shy it back at you.'

GRIM, *subs.* (American thieves').—A skeleton. Also GRIN.

OLD MR. GRIM, *subs. phr.* (common).—Death. For synonyms, *see* OLD FLOORER.

GRIN, *verb.* (American University, Virginia).—*See* quot.

1887. *Lippincott*, July, p. 99. If here are many 'old men' in the room they immediately begin to GRIN HIM; that is, they strike on their plates with their knives and forks, beat with their feet, and shout at the top of their voices, in the effort to make their victim grin. Woe to him if they succeed; for in that event the same thing will be repeated three times a day, until he ceases to notice it.

TO GRIN IN A GLASS CASE. *verb. phr.* (old).—To be shown as an anatomical preparation. [The bodies and skeletons of criminals were once preserved in glass cases at Surgeon's Hall.—GROSE.]

TO FLASH THE UPRIGHT GRIN, *verb. phr.* (venery).—To expose the person (of women).

GRINAGOG, THE CAT'S UNCLE, *subs. phr.* (old).—A grinning simpleton.—GROSE.

GRINCUMS, *subs.* (old).—Syphilis. For synonyms, *see* LADIES' FEVER.

1608. MIDDLETON, *Family of Love*, B. 1. I had a receipt for the GRINCOMES in his own hand.

1635. JONES, *Adrasta or the Woman's Spleen*, c. 2. You must know, sir, in a nobleman 'tis abusive; no, in him the serpigo, in a knight the GRINCOMES, in a gentleman the Neapolitan scabb, and in a serving man or artificer the plaine pox.

1637. MASSINGER, *Guardian*, iv. The comfort is, I am now secure from the GRINCOMES, I can lose nothing that way.

GRIND, *subs.* (common).—1. A walk; a constitutional: *e.g.*, 'to take a GRIND' or (University) 'to go on the Grandchester (or Gog Magog Hills) GRIND.'

2. (common).—Daily routine; hard or distasteful work.

1853. BRADLEY, *Verdant Green*, pt. III., ch. xi. To a University man, a GRIND did not possess any reading signification, but a riding one. In fact, it was a steeple-chase, slightly varying in its details according to the college that patronised the pastime.

1870. *London Figaro*, 28 July. The world is a wearisome GRIND, love, Nor shirk we our turn at the wheel.

1880. A. TROLLOPE, *The Duke's Children*, ch. xxv. 'Isn't it a great GRIND, sir?' asked Silverbridge. 'A very great GRIND, as you call it. And there may be the GRIND and not the success. But——'

1880. *One and All*, 27 Mar., p. 207. Soul-weary of life's horrid GRIND, I long to come to thee.

3. (schools').—Study; reading up for an examination; also a plodding student, *i.e.*, a GRINDER.

1856. HUGHES, *Tom Brown's School Days*, pt. II., ch. v. 'Come along, boys,' cries East, always ready to leave the GRIND, as he called it.

1887. *Chambers' Jour.*, 14 May, p. 310. Smalls made just such a goal as was required, and the GRIND it entailed was frequently of no slight profit to him.

4. (medical students').—A demonstration: as (1) a 'public GRIND' given to a class and free to all; and (2) a 'private GRIND' for which a student pays an individual teacher. In America, a QUIZ (*q.v.*).

5. (Oxford University).—Athletic sports. Also, a training run.

1872. *Chambers' Jour.*, April. Joe Rullock, the mighty gymnasiarch, the hero of a hundred GRINDS, the unwearied haunter of the palæstra, could never give the lie to his whole past life, and deny his own gymnastics.

6. (venery),—An act of sexual intercourse: *e.g.*, TO DO A GRIND. [MILL and GRINDSTONE (venery) = the female *pudendum.*] For synonyms, *see* GREENS and RIDE.

1598. FLORIO, *A Worlde of Wordes.* *Macinio*, the GRINDING of grist. Also taken for carnal copulation.

1647. *Ladies Parliament.* Digbie's lady takes it ill, that her Lord GRINDS not at her mill.

THE GRIND, *subs. phr.* (Cambridge University). — The ferry-boat at Chesterton.

Verb. (University). — 1. To prepare for examination to study; to read.

1856. T. HUGHES, *Tom Brown's School Days*, pt. II., ch. vii. 'The thing to find out,' said Tom meditatively, 'is how long one ought to GRIND at a sentence without looking at the crib.'

2. (University).—To teach; to instruct; TO COACH (*q.v.*).

3. (common).—To do a round of hard and distasteful work; to apply oneself to daily routine.

1880. *Punch*, 5 June, p. 253. 'Fred on Pretty Girls and Pictures.' And the pars in the *Scanmag*—he does them—are proper, and chock full of 'go.' Only paper I care to GRIND though.

4. (venery).—To copulate.

1811. *Lexicon Balatronicum.* GRIND, s.v.

5. *trans.* (American). — To vex; to 'put out.'

1879. W. D. HOWELLS, *Lady of the Aroostook*, ch. vii. After all, it does GRIND me to have lost that money!

Also GRINDING = (1) the act of reading or studying hard; (2) the act or occupation of preparing students, for an examination; and (3) the act of copulation.

ON THE GRIND, *subs. phr.* (venery).—Said of incontinent persons of both sexes. Also of prostitutes.

TO GRIND AN AXE.—*See* AXE.

TO GET A GRIND ON ONE, *verb. phr.* (American).—To play practical jokes; to tell a story against one; to annoy or vex.

TO GRIND WIND, *verb. phr.* (old prison).—To work the treadmill. *See* EVERLASTING STAIRCASE.

1889. CLARKSON and RICHARDSON. *Police*, p. 322. On the treadmill . . . GRINDING WIND.

GRINDER, *subs.* (college).—1. A private tutor; a COACH (*q.v.*). *Cf.*, CRAMMER.

1812. MISS EDGEWORTH, *Patronage*, ch. iii. Put him into the hands of a clever GRINDER or crammer, and they would soon cram the necessary portion of Latin and Greek into him.

1841. *Punch*, vol. I., p. 201. Then contriving to accumulate five guineas to pay a GRINDER, he routs out his old note books from the bottom of his box and commences to read.

1841. A. SMITH, 'The London Medical Student' in *Punch*, i., p. 229. G was a GRINDER, who sharpen'd the the fools.

1849. THACKERAY, *Pendennis*, ch. v. She sent me down here with a GRINDER. She wants me to cultivate my neglected genius.

2. Usually *in. pl.* (common).—The teeth.

ENGLISH SYNONYMS.—Bones; chatterers; cogs; crashing cheats; dining-room furniture (or chairs); dinner-set; dominoes; front-rails; Hampstead Heath (rhyming); head rails; ivories; park-palings (or railings); snagglers; tushes (or tusks); tomb-stones.

FRENCH SYNONYMS. — *Les soeurs blanches* (thieves' = the 'white sisters' or ivories); *les chocottes* (thieves'); *les cassantes* (thieves' = grinders); *les broches* (popular = head-rails); *les crocs* (popular = tusks); *le clou de girofle* (common = a decayed, black tooth); *les branlantes* (popular = the quakers: specifi-

cally, old men's teeth); *le mobilier* (thieves' = furniture); *les meules de moulin* (popular = millstones); *le jeu de dominos* (thieves' = dominoes); *les osanores* (thieves'); *les osselets* (thieves' = bonelets); *les palettes* (popular and thieves'); *la batterie* (= the teeth, throat, and tongue).

GERMAN SYNONYMS.—*Krächling* (= grinderkin; from *krachen* = to crush).

ITALIAN SYNONYMS.—*Merlo* (= battlement); *sganascio*; *rastrelliera* (= the rack).

1597. HALL, *Satires*, iv., 1. Her GRINDERS like two chalk stones in a mill.

1640. HUMPHREY MILL, *Night's Search*, Sect. 39, p. 194 Her GRINDERS white, her mouth must show her age.

1653. URQUHART, *Rabelais*, bk. IV. Author's Prologue. The devil of one musty crust of a brown George the poor boys had to scour their GRINDERS with.

1690. B. E., *Dict. Cant. Crew.* GRINDER, s.v. The Cove has Rum GRINDERS, the Rogue has excellent Teeth.

1693. DRYDEN, *Juvenal*, x., 365. One, who at sight of supper open'd wide His jaws before, and whetted GRINDERS tried.

1740. WALPOLE, *Correspondence.* A set of gnashing teeth, the GRINDERS very entire.

1751. SMOLLETT, *Peregrine Pickle*, ch. xlv. Like a dried walnut between the GRINDERS of a Templar in the pit.

1817. SCOTT, *Ivanhoe*, c. 16. None who beheld thy GRINDERS contending with these peas.

1819. MOORE, *Tom Crib*, p. 23. With GRINDERS dislodg'd, and with peepers both poach'd.

1834. AINSWORTH, *Rookwood*, bk. iv., ch. i. A GRINDER having been dislodged, his pipe took possession of the aperture.

1836. M. SCOTT, *Cruise of the Midge*, p. 83. Every now and then he would clap his head sideways on the ground, so as to get the back GRINDERS to bear on his prey.

1848. THACKERAY, *Book of Snobs* ch. xiii. Sir Robert Peel, though he wished it ever so much, has no power over Mr. Benjamin Disraeli's GRINDERS, or any means of violently handling that gentleman's jaw.

1871. *Chambers' Jour.*, 9 Dec., p. 772. My GRINDERS is good enough for all the wittels I gets.

1888. *Sporting Life*, 28 Nov. Countered heavily on the GRINDERS.

TO TAKE A GRINDER, *verb. phr.* (common).—To apply the left thumb to the nose, and revolve the right hand round it, as if to work a hand-organ or coffee-mill; TO TAKE A SIGHT (*q.v.*); TO WORK THE COFFEE-MILL (*q.v.*). [A street boy's retort on an attempt to impose on his good faith or credulity.]

1836. DICKENS, *Pickwick*, ch. xxxi. Here Mr. Jackson smiled once more upon the company; and, applying his left thumb to the tip of his nose, worked a visionary coffee-mill with his right hand, thereby performing a very graceful piece of pantomime (then much in vogue, but now, unhappily, almost obsolete) which was familiarly denominated TAKING A GRINDER.

1870. *Athenæum*, 8 July. 'Rev. of *Comic Hist. of United States.*' He finds himself confronted by a plumed and lightly-clad Indian, who salutes him with what street-boys term a GRINDER.

GRINDING-HOUSE, *subs.* (old).—1. The House of Correction. For synonyms, *see* CAGE.

1614. *Terence in English.* The fellow is worthy to be put into the GRINDING-HOUSE.

2. (venery).—A brothel. For synonyms, *see* NANNY-SHOP. [GRINDING-TOOL = the *penis*.]

GRINDING-MILL, *subs.* (common). —The house of a tutor or COACH (*q.v.*) where students are prepared for an examination.

GRIND-OFF (or GRINDO), *subs.* (common).—A miller. [From a character in *The Miller and his Men.*]

GRINDSTONE, *subs.* (common).—1. A tutor; a COACH (*q.v.*).

2. (venery). — The female *pudendum*.

TO BRING (HOLD, PUT, or KEEP) ONE'S NOSE TO THE GRINDSTONE, *verb. phr.* (colloquial).—To oppress, harass, or punish; to treat harshly. To HAVE ONE'S NOSE KEPT TO THE GRINDSTONE = to be held to a bargain, or at work.

1578. NORTH, *Plutarch*, p. 241. They might be ashamed, for lack of courage, to suffer the Lacedæmonians TO HOLD THEIR NOSES TO THE GRINDSTONE.

1690. B. E., *Dict. Cant. Crew*, s.v. HOLD. HOLD HIS NOSE TO THE GRINDSTONE, to keep him Under, or Tie him Neck and Heels in a Bargain.

TO HAVE THE GRINDSTONE ON HIS BACK, *verb. phr.* (common).—Said of a man going to fetch the monthly nurse.—GROSE.

GRINNING-STITCHES, *subs.* (milliners'). — Slovenly sewing; stitches wide apart; LADDERS (*q.v.*).

GRIP (or GRIPSACK), *subs.* (American). — A hand-bag or satchell.

TO LOSE ONE'S GRIP, *verb. phr.* (American). — To fail; to lose one's control.

GRIPE, *subs.* (old).—1. A miser; a usurer. Also GRIPER or GRIPE-FIST (*q.v.*). For synonyms, *see* HUNKS and SIXTY-PER-CENT. GRIPING = extortion.

1690. B. E., *Dict. Cant. Crew.* GRIPE, or GRIPER, s.v. An old covetous wretch. Also a banker, money scrivener, or usurer.

2. *in. pl.* (colloquial).—The colic; the stomach ache; the COLLYWOBBLES. For synonyms, *see* JERRY-GO-NIMBLE.

1684. BUNYAN, *Pilgr. Prog.*, Pt. II. He concluded that he was sick of the GRIPES.

1705. *Char. of a Sneake*, in *Harl. Misc.* (ed. Park), ii., 356. He never looks upon her Majesty's arms but *semper eadem* gives him the GRIPES.

1714. *Spectator*, No 559. Meeting the true father, who came towards him with a fit of the GRIPES, he begged him to take his son again, and give back his cholic.

1812. COOMBE, *Tour in Search of Picturesque*, c. xxvi. That he who daily smokes two pipes, The tooth-ache never has—nor GRIPES.

GRIPE-FIST, *subs.* (common).—A miser; a grasping broker. For synonyms, *see* HUNKS. Also GRIPE-PENNY.

1859. MATSELL, *Vocabulum*, s.v.

GRIST, *subs.* (American).—A large number or quantity. [Swift uses GRIST = a supply; a provision.]

1848. COOPER, *Oak Openings.* There's an unaccountable GRIST of bees, I can tell you.

*a*1852. *Traits of American Humour*, i., 305. I . . . got pretty considerable soaked by a GRIST of rain.

TO BRING GRIST TO THE MILL, *verb. phr.* (colloquial).—To bring profitable business; to be a source of profit.

1719. *Poor Robin's Almanack*, 'May. Lawyers pleading do refrain A while, and then fall to 't again; Strife brings GRIST unto their MILL.

1770. FOOTE, *Lame Lover*, i. Well, let them go on, it brings GRIST TO OUR MILL.

1804. HORSLEY, *Speech*, 23 July. A sly old pope created twenty new saints, TO BRING GRIST TO THE MILL of the London clergy.

1817. SCOTT, *Ivanhoe*, c. 16. Some three or four dried pease—a miserable GRIST for such a mill.

1838. DICKENS, *Nich. Nickleby*, ch. xxxiv., p. 268. Meantime the fools BRING GRIST TO MY MILL.

GRISTLE, *subs.* (venery). — The *penis*. For synonyms, *see* CREAM-STICK and PRICK.

GRIT, *subs.* (originally American: now colloquial).—1. Character; pluck; spirit; SAND (*q.v.*). Also CLEAR GRIT. NO GRIT = lacking in stamina; wanting in courage.

1825. NEAL, *Bro. Jonathan*, bk. II., ch. xiv. A chap who was clear GRIT for a tussle, any time.

1848. BURTON, *Waggeries, etc.*, p. 13. The old folks . . . began to think that she warn't the CLEAR GRIT.

1849. C. KINGSLEY, *Alton Locke*, ch. vi. A real lady—*l'air noble*—the rael genuine GRIT, as Sam Slick says.

1852. H. B. STOWE, *Uncle Tom's Cabin*, ch. vii You're a right brave old girl. I like GRIT, wherever I see it.

1860. THACKERAY, *Philip*, ch. xxxi. If you were a chip of the old block you would be just what he called the GRIT.

1889. *Referee*, 6 Jan. They never did think there was any real GRIT about him.

1890. *Scribner*, Feb., 242. 'Looks like he got GRIT, don't it?' Lige muttered.

1892. R. L. STEVENSON and L. OSBOURNE, *The Wrecker*, p. 249. I am as full of GRIT and work as ever, and just tower above our troubles.

2. (Canadian political). — A member of the Liberal party.

GRITTY, *adj.* (American).—Plucky; courageous; resolute; full of character.

1847. ROBB, *Squatter Life*, p. 106. There never was a GRITTYER crowd congregated on that stream.

GRIZZLE, *verb.* (colloquial).—To fret. Also TO GRIZZLE ONE'S GUTS.

1872. MISS BRADDON, *To the Bitter End*, ch. xvi. 'If the locket's lost, it's lost,' she said philosophically; 'and there's no use in GRIZZLING about it.'

GRIZZLE-GUTS (or GRIZZLE- or GLUM-POT). *subs.* (common).— A melancholy or ill-tempered person; a SULKINGTON (*q.v.*).

GROANER, *subs.* (old).—A thief plying his trade at funerals or religious gatherings.

1848. DUNCOMBE, *Sinks of London*, s.v.

1859. MATSELL, *Vocabulum*, s.v.

GROANING, *subs.* (old).—The act of parturition. Also, *adj.*, parturient; or appertaining to parturition: as in GROANING-MALT (Scots') = drink for a lying-in; GROANING-PAINS = the pangs of delivery; GROANING-WIFE = a woman ready to lie-in.

1591. NASHE, *Unfort. Trav.* (Chiswick Press, 1892), p. 92. As smoothe as a GROANING-WIVE'S bellie.

1596. SHAKSPEARE, *Hamlet*, iii., 2. It would cost you a GROANING to take off my edge.

1786. BURNS, *The Rantin' Dog the Daddie O't*. Wha will bring the GROANING-MALT?

GROATS, *subs.* (nautical).—The chaplain's monthly allowance.

TO SAVE ONE'S GROATS. *verb. phr.* (old University).—To come off handsomely. [At the Universities nine groats are deposited in the hands of an academic officer by every person standing for a degree, which, if the depositor obtains, with honour, are returned to him.—GROSE.]

GROCERY, *subs.* (common). — 1. Small change.

1728. BAILEY, *Eng. Dict.*, s.v.

2. (American). — A drinking bar. Also CONFECTIONERY and GROGGERY.

1847. PORTER, *Quarter Race*, etc. 104. He went into his favourite GROCERY.

3. (common).—Sugar. [A restricted use of a colloquialism.]

1841. LYTTON, *Night and Morning*, Bk. V., ch. ii. A private room and a pint of brandy, my dear. Hot water and lots of the GROCERY.

GROG, *subs.* (old: now recognised).—Spirits and water; strong drink generally. [Till Admiral Vernon's time (1745) rum was served neat, but he ordered it to be diluted, and was therefore nicknamed 'Old Grog,' in allusion to his grogram coat: a phrase that was presently adapted to the mixture he had introduced.] GROGGY = drunk.

Verb. (old).—To dilute or adulterate with water.

1878. *Lincoln, Rutland, and Stamford Mercury*, 8 Mar. The defendants had GROGGED the casks by putting in hot water.

TO HAVE GROG ON BOARD (or TO BE GROGGED), *verb. phr.* (common).—To be drunk. For synonyms, *see* SCREWED.

1842. *Comic Almanack*, October. He stands and listens, sad and dogged, To 'fined five bob' for being GROGGED.

GROG-BLOSSOM, *subs.* (common).—A pimple caused by drinking to excess. Also COPPER-NOSE and JOLLY-NOSE. Fr., *un nez culotté* and *un nez de pompettes*.

1811. *Lexicon Balatronicum*, GROG-BLOSSOM, s.v.

1883. THOS. HARDY, *The Three Strangers*, in *Longman's Mag.*, March, p. 576. A few GROG-BLOSSOMS marked the neighbourhood of his nose.

1888. W. BESANT, *Fifty Years Ago*, ch. xi., p. 169. The outward and visible signs of rum were indeed various. First, there was the red and swollen nose, next, the nose beautifully painted with GROG-BLOSSOMS.

GROG-FIGHT, *subs.* (military).—A drinking party. *Cf.*, TEA-FIGHT.

1876. R. M. JEPHSON, *Girl he Left Behind Him*, ch. i. He had been having a GROG-FIGHT in his room to celebrate the event.

GROGGERY, *subs.* (American).—A public bar; a grog-shop.

GROGGY, *adj.* (colloquial). — 1. Under the influence of drink. For synonyms, *see* DRINKS and SCREWED.

1829. BUCKSTONE, *Billy Taylor*. i., as a gay young woman, will delude Taylor away from Mary, make him GROGGY, then press him off to sea.

1863. *Fun*, 23 May p. 98, c. 2. They fined drunkards and swearers, and there is a record in the parish-books, among others of a similar nature, of a certain Mrs. Thunder who was fined twelve shillings for being, like Mr. Cruikshank's horse at the Brighton Review, decidedly GROGGY.

1872. *Echo*, 30 July. A model of perfection had she not shown more than necessary partiality to her elder friend's brandy bottle during the journey, despite the latter's oft-repeated caution not to become GROGGY.

2. (colloquial).—Staggering or stupified with drink. Also (stable) moving as with tender feet. Also (pugilists') unsteady from punishment and exhaustion. Fr., *locher* = to be GROGGY.

1831. YOUATT, *The Horse*, ch. xvi., p. 380. Long journeys at a fast pace will make almost any horse GROGGY.

1846-8. THACKERAY, *Vanity Fair*, vol. ii., ch. v. Cuff coming up full of pluck, but quite reeling and GROGGY, the Fig-merchant put in his left as usual on his adversary's nose, and sent him down for the last time.

1853. *Diogenes*, vol. ii., p. 177. The anxiety is not confined to the metropolis; as a respectable grazier, who rides a GROGGY horse, on hearing of it at a public-house the other day, affirmed it to be the mysterious cause of the rise in the value of horseflesh.

1888. *Sportsman*, 28 Nov. In the tenth Thompson, who had been growing GROGGY, to the surprise of Evans began to force the fighting.

GROGHAM, *subs.* (old).—A horse; a DAISY-KICKER (*q.v.*). Now mostly in contempt. For synonyms, *see* PRAD.

1785. GROSE, *Vulg. Tongue*, s.v.

GROG-SHOP, *subs.* (common). — The mouth. For synonyms, *see* POTATOE-TRAP.

1843. THACKERAY, *Men's Wives*, Frank Berry, ch. i. Claret drawn in profusion from the gown-boy's GROG-SHOP.

GROG-TUB, *subs.* (nautical).—A brandy bottle.

GROOM, *subs.* (gamesters').—A croupier.

GROOMED. *See* WELL-GROOMED.

GROOVY, *subs.* (American).—A sardine.

Adj. (popular). — Settled in habit; limited in mind.

GROPE, *verb.* (venery).—To feel a woman; to fumble; to FAM (*q.v.*).

1611. COTGRAVE, *Dictionarie. Mariolement.* GROPING of a wench.

1719. DURFEY, *Pills*, etc., i., 194. Smoking, toping, Landlady GROPING.

GROPER, *subs.* (old). — 1. A blind man; HOODMAN (*q.v.*).

1690. B. E., *Dict. Cant. Crew*, s.v.

1728. BAILEY, *Eng. Dict.*, s.v.

1785. GROSE, *Vulg. Tongue*, s.v.

2. (old).—A pocket. For synonyms, *see* BRIGH and SKY-ROCKET.

1789. GEO. PARKER, *Life's Painter*, p. 143. GROPERS. Pockets.

3. (old).—A midwife; a FINGER-SMITH (*q.v.*).

1785. GROSE, *Vulg. Tongue*, s.v.

GROTTO, *subs.* (venery). — The female *pudendum*. For synonyms, *see* MONOSYLLABLE.

GROUND. TO SUIT DOWN TO THE GROUND, *verb. phr.* (common).—To be thoroughly becoming or acceptable.

1878. M. E. BRADDON, *Cloven Foot*, ch. xlv. Some sea coast city in South America would SUIT ME DOWN TO THE GROUND.

1891. *Licensed Vict. Gaz.*, 9 Feb. I knows the very bloke that'll SUIT YOU DOWN TO THE GROUND.

1891. *Sporting Life*, 28 Mar. At Knowle he is SUITED DOWN TO THE GROUND.

1892. MILLIKEN, '*Arry Ballads*, p. ii. They SUIT ME RIGHT DOWN TO THE GROUND.

TO WIPE (or MOP) UP THE GROUND (or FLOOR) WITH ONE, *verb. phr.* (common). — To administer the very soundest thrashing; to prove oneself absolutely superior to one's opposite.

1887. HENLEY and STEVENSON, *Deacon Brodie*, i., 3. Muck! that's my opinion of him; ... I'll mop the FLOOR UP WITH HIM any day, if so be as you or any on 'em 'll make it worth my while.

1888. *Detroit Free Press*, Aug. The Scroggin boy was as tough as a dog-wood knot. He'd WIPE UP THE GROUND WITH HIM; he'd walk all over him.

TO GO (or GET) WELL TO THE GROUND, *verb. phr.* (old colloquial).—To defæcate; TO REAR (*q.v.*). For synonyms, *see* MRS. JONES.

1608. MIDDLETON, *Family of Love*, v. 3. Do you GO WELL TO THE GROUND?

1856. *Notes and Queries*, 2 S., i., p. 324. TO GET TO THE GROUND, in medical phraseology, means to have the bowels opened.

GROUNDER, *subs.* (cricketers').—A ball with a ground delivery; a SNEAK; a GRUB; and (in America) at base-ball, a ball struck low, or flying near the ground.

GROUND-FLOOR. TO BE LET IN ON THE GROUND-FLOOR, *verb. phr.* (American).—To share in a speculation on equal terms with the original promoters.

GROUND-SQUIRREL, *subs.* (old).—A hog; a GRUNTER—*Lex. Bal.* For synonyms, *see* SOW'S BABY.

GROUND-SWEAT. TO HAVE (or TAKE) A GROUND-SWEAT, *verb. phr.* (old).—To be buried.

1690. B. E., *Dict. Cant. Crew.* GROUND SWEAT, s.v., a grave.

1785. GROSE, *Vulg. Tongue*, s.v.

GROUSE. TO DO A GROUSE (or TO GO GROUSING), *verb. phr.* (venery).—To quest, or to run down, a woman; TO MOLROW (*q.v.*). GROUSED = MOLLED (*q.v.*).

GROUSER, *subs.* (popular).—1. A grumbler. For synonyms, *see* RUSTY-GUTS.

2. (venery). — One who goes questing after women; a MOL-ROWER (*q.v.*).

3. (sporting).—A rowing man; a WET-BOB (*q.v.*).

GROUSING, *subs.* (venery).—Going in quest of women; SPARROW-CATCHING (*q.v.*); MOLROWING (*q.v.*).

GROUTE, *verb.* (Marlborough and Cheltenham Colleges).—To work or study hard; to SWOT (*q.v.*). For synonyms, *see* WIRE IN.

GROUTY, *adj.* (common). — Crabbed; sulky.

GROVE OF EGLANTINE, *subs. phr.* (venery).—The female *pudendum*; also the female pubic hair. For synonyms, *see* MONOSYLLABLE and FLEECE.

1772. CAREW, *Poems.* 'A Rapture. Retire into thy GROVE OF EGLANTINE.

GROVE OF THE EVANGELIST. *subs. phr.* (common). — St. John's Wood; also APOSTLE'S GROVE, and the BAPTIST'S WOOD.

GROW, *verb.* (prison).—To be accorded the privilege of letting one's hair and beard grow. Also TO GROW ONE'S FEATHERS.

GROWLER, *subs.* (common).—A four-wheeled cab. *Cf.*, SULKY.

ENGLISH SYNONYMS. — Birdcage; blucher; bounder; fever-trap; flounder-and-dab (rhyming); four-wheeler; groping hutch; mab (an old hackney); rattler; rumbler.

FRENCH SYNONYMS. — *Un bordel ambulant* (common = a walking brothel); *un char numéroté* (popular); *un fiatar* (thieves'); *un foutoir ambulant* (= a fuckery on wheels); *un mylord* (popular).

1870. *Orchestra*, 21 Mar. A recent enigmatical bill-poster on the walls, with the device 'Hie, Cabby, Hie!' turns out to be a Patent Cab Call—an ingenious sort of lamp-signal for remote hansoms and GROWLERS.

1873. *Land and Water*, 25 Jan. The knacker's yard is baulked for a time, while the quadruped shambles along in some poverty-stricken GROWLER.

1883. *Daily Telegraph*, 8 Jan., p. 5, c. 3. But while a great improvement has been made in hansoms of late years, the four-wheeler or GROWLER is still as a rule a disgrace to the metropolis.

1890. *Daily Graphic*, 7 Jan., p. 14, c. 1. What with hansom cabs and GROWLERS and private broughams; what with bonded carmen's towering waggons.

1891. *Globe*, 15 July, p. 1, c. 3. Adapting the words of Waller to the condition of many of our GROWLERS—The cab's dull framework, battered and decayed, Lets in the air through gaps that time has made.

TO RUSH (or WORK) THE GROWLER, *verb. phr.* (American workmen's).—*See* quot. [GROWER = pitcher.]

1888. *New York Herald*, 29 July. One evil of which the inspectors took particular notice was that of the employment by hands in a number of factories of boys and girls, under ten and thirteen years, to fetch beer for them, or in other words TO RUSH THE GROWLER.

GROWN-MAN'S-DOSE, *subs.* (common).—A lot of liquor. Also a LONG DRINK (*q.v.*). For synonyms, *see* GO.

GROWN-UP, *subs.* (colloquial).—An adult: among undertakers, a GROWN.

1864. DICKENS, *Our Mutual Friend*, Bk. ii., ch. I. I always did like GROWN UPS.

GRUB, *subs.* (vulgar).—1. Food.

ENGLISH SYNONYMS.—Belly-cheer (or chere); belly-furniture; belly-timber; Kaffir's tightener (specifically, a full meal); chuck; corn; gorge-grease; manablins (= broken victuals); mouth harness; mungarly; peck; prog; scoff (S. African); scran; stodge; tack; tommy (specifically, bread); tuck; yam. Also, verbally, to bung the cask; to grease the gills; to have the run of one's teeth; to yam. *See also* WOLF.

FRENCH SYNONYMS. — *La becquetance* (popular = peck); *le biffre* (popular); *la frigousse* (popular); *la fripe* (popular, from O. Fr., *fripper* = to eat); *la gringue* (common); *les matériaux* (freemason's = materials); *la briffe* (popular); *la boustifaille* (popular); *le harnois de gueule* (RABELAIS: = mouth-harness); *le coton* (popular, an allusion to a lamp-wick); *les comestaux* (popular = comestibles); *le tortorage* (thieves'); *la broute* (popular = grazing); *la morfe* (O. Fr. Also, in a verbal sense = to feed); *tortiller du bec* (popular = to wag a jaw); *se calfater le bec* (nautical: also = to drink); *becqueter* (popular = to 'peck'); *béquiller* (popular); *chiquer* (popular = to 'chaw'); *bouffer* (popular); *boulotter* (common); *taper sur les vivres* (popular = to assault the eatables); *pitancher* (common: also = to drink); *passer à la tortore* (thieves'); *se l'envoyer*; *casser la croustille* (thieves' = to crack a crust); *tortorer* (thieves); *briffer*; *pass.r à briffe* (popular); *brouter* (VILLON = to browse); *se caler*, or *se caler les amygdales* (popular); *mettre de l'huile dans la lampe* (common = to trim the lamp); *se coller quelque chose dans le fanal, dans le fusil*, or *dans le tube* (popular = to trim one's beacon-light; to load one's gun, etc.); *chamailler des dents* (popular = to 'go it' with the ivories; *jouer des badigoinces* (common: *badigoinces* = chaps); *jouer des dominos* (popular: *dominos* = teeth); *déchirer la cartouche* (military); *gobichonner* (popular); *engouler* (popular = to bolt); *engueuler* (colloquial = to gobble); *friturer* (popular: also = to cook); *gonfler* (popular: to blow out); *morfailler* (Rabelaisian); *mor-*

figner, or ***morfiler*** (From O. Fr., *morfier*; *cf.*, Ital., *morfire* or *morfizzare*); *cacher* (popular=to stow away); *se mettre quelque chose dans le cadavre* (popular=to stoke); *se lester la cale* (nautical: to lay in ballast); *se graisser les balots* (thieves': to grease the gills); *se caresser* (to do oneself a good turn); *effacer* (popular=to put away); *travailler pour M. Domange* (popular: M. Domange was a famous GOLDFINDER or GONG FARMER (*q.v.*); *clapoter* (popular); *debrider la margoulette* (popular=to put one's nose in the manger); *croustiller* (popular); *charger pour la guadaloupe* (popular); *travailler pour Jules* (common: *Jules*=Mrs. Jones); *se faire le jabot* (popular, *jabot*=stomach); *jouer des osanores* (popular: *osanores* = teeth); *casser* (thieves'); *claquer* (familiar=to rattle one's ivories); *klebjer* (popular); *faire trimer les mathurins* (popular=to make the running with one's teeth); *se coller quelque chose dans le bocal* (common: *bocal* = paunch); *estropier* (popular = to maim); *passer à galtos* (nautical); *bourrer la paillasse* (common = to stuff the mattress); *faire trimer le battant* (thieves'); *jouer des mandibules* (popular); *s'emplir le gilet* (popular=to fill one's waistcoat); *se garnir le bocal* (popular: to furnish one's paunch); *se suiver la gargarousse* (nautical: also=to drink); *babouiner* (popular); *charger la canonnière* (popular: *canonnière*=the breech); *gousser* (popular); *gouffier* (obsolete).

GERMAN SYNONYMS.—*Achile*, *Achelinchen*, or *Acheliniken* (from Heb. *Ochal*); *Achelputz* (from Heb. *ochal* + *putzen* from O.H.G. *bizan* or *pizzan* = to eat).

ITALIAN SYNONYMS.—*Artibrio*; and, verbally, *sbattere* (=to beat, to struggle); *intappare il fusto* (=to bung the cask); *smorfire*.

SPANISH SYNONYMS. — *Papar* (colloquial: from *papa* = pap); *hacer el buche* (low: *buche* = craw or crop); *echar* (colloquial); *manducar*; *meter*.

1659. *Dialogue betwixt an Exciseman and Death*, transcribed from a Copy in British Museum, printed in London by J. C[lark]. I'll pass my word this night Shall yield us GRUB before the morning light.

1725. *New Cant. Dict.* GRUB, s.v., victuals.

1781. G. PARKER, *View of Society*, I., 171. How did you procure your GRUB and BUB?

1789. GEO. PARKER, *Life's Painter*, p. 149. BUB AND GRUB. A mighty low expression, signifying victuals and drink.

1836. M. SCOTT, *Tom Cringle's Log*, ch. iii. Poor Purser! de people call him Purser, sir, because him knowing chap; him cabbage all de GRUB, slush, and stuff in him own corner.

d. 1842. MAGINN, *Vidocq's Song*. Any bubby and GRUB, I say?

1857. THACKERAY, *Shabby Genteel Story*, ch. i., p. 9. He used to . . . have his GRUB too on board.

1877. *Five Years' Penal Servitude*, ch. i., p. 45. I at once congratulated myself on not being a large eater, as there was no doubt but my GRUB would run *very* short if it depended on my oakum-picking.

1889. *Star*, 3 Dec., p. 2, c. 6. Of course it was GRUB. It was for food, the food for which they beg, and steal, and go willingly to prison, for a certain good square meal of meat.

1892. HUME NISBET, *Bushranger's Sweetheart*, p. 154. That sad, sad secret about Mary would keep him in GRUB for the next day or two at 'The Rose in Bloom.'

2. (old). — A short thick-set man; a dwarf. In contempt. For synonyms, *see* HOP-O'-MY-THUMB.

3. (colloquial).—A dirty sloven; generally used of elderly people.

4. (American). — A careful student; a hard reader.

1856. HALL, *College Words and Phrases*, quoted from *Williams' Coll. Quarterly*, ii., 246. A hard reader or student: *e.g.*, not GRUBS or reading men, only wordy men.

5. (American). — Roots and stumps; whatever is 'grubbed up.'

6. (cricketers'). — A ball delivered along the ground; a GROUNDER (*q.v.*); a DAISY-CUTTER (*q.v.*). For synonyms, *see* LOB-SNEAK.

1823. BEE, *Dict. of the Turf*. GRUB, s.v.

Verb. (old).—1. To take or supply with food. For synonyms, *see subs.* sense 1.

1725. *New Cant. Dict.* GRUB, s.v., to eat.

1785. GROSE, *Vulg. Tongue*. GRUB, s.v., to dine.

1836. DICKENS, *Pickwick*, ch. xxii., p. 184. I never see such a chap to eat and drink; never. The red-nosed man warn't by no means the sort of person you'd like to GRUB by contract, but he was nothin' to the shepherd.

1883. *Daily Telegraph*, 18 May, p. 3, c. 1. 'They are not bound to GRUB you, don't you know,' said Mr. Sleasey, 'and they try the starving dodge on you sometimes.'

2. (old).—To beg; to ask for alms, especially food.

3. (American).—To study, or read hard; to 'sweat.'

TO RIDE GRUB, *verb. phr.* (old).—To be sulky; CRUSTY (*q.v.*); disagreeable.

1785. GROSE, *Vulg. Tongue*. TO RIDE GRUB, to be sullen or out of temper.

TO GRUB ALONG, *verb. phr.* (common).—To make one's way as best one can; 'to rub along.'

1888. *Daily Telegraph*, 19 Oct. When a youth left school to follow the pursuits of life he found that he had to GRUB ALONG as best he could.

GRUBBING, *subs.* (common).—Eating.

1819. MOORE, *Tom Crib*. What with snoozing, high GRUBBING, and guzzling like Cloe.

GRUBBERY, *subs.* (common).—(1) an eating-house. Also (2) a dining-room, and (3) the mouth.

GRUBBING-CRIB, *subs.* (general).—1. An eating-house. GRUBBING-CRIB FAKER=the landlord of a cheap cookshop. Fr., *le nourrisseur*; Sp., *un ostalero*. *See* GRUB SHOP, sense 2.

ENGLISH SYNONYMS.—Grubbery; grubby-, or grubbing-ken; grub-shop; guttle-shop; hash-house; mungarly casa; prog-shop; slap-bang shop; tuck-shop; waste-butt.

FRENCH SYNONYMS. — *Un bourre-boyaux* (popular = a stuff-your-guts); *un claquedents* (popular, also = a brothel, or punting-house); *une guingette* (general); *une mangeoire* (popular = a grubbery: *manger* = to eat); *un mattais* (popular); *un gargot* (thieves').

GERMAN SYNONYM.—*Achilebajes* (from Heb., *Ochal*=to eat).

SPANISH SYNONYM.—*Ostaleria*, or *Osteria* (also=lush-crib).

1823. BEE, *Dict. of the Turf*, s.v.

2. (tramps').—A workhouse. For synonyms, *see* SPINNIKEN. Sometimes GRUBBIKEN.

1851-61. MAYHEW, *Lond. Lab. and Lond. Poor*, iii., 416. I know all the good houses, and the tidy GRUBBIKENS—that's the unions where there's little or nothing to do for the food we gets.

GRUBBLE, *verb.* (colloquial).—(1) To feel for at random or in the dark; and (2) (venery) TO GROPE (*q.v.*).

1684. DRYDEN, *The Disappointment*. 'Prologue.' The doughty bullies enter bloody drunk, Invade and GRUBBLE one another's punk.

GRUBBY, *subs.* (thieves').—Food. [A diminutive of GRUB (*q.v.*).]

d. 1842. MAGINN, *Vidocq's Song*. I pattered in flash like a covey knowing, Tol lol, etc. Ay, bub or GRUBBY, I say.

Adj. (colloquial). — Dirty; slovenly.

d. 1845. HOOD, *A Black Job*, Like a GRUBBY lot of sooty sweeps or colliers.

GRUB-HUNTING, *subs.* (tramps').—Begging for food.

GRUB-SHITE, *verb.* (old). — To make foul or dirty; to bewray. —GROSE.

GRUB-SHOP, (or -**CRIB**, -**TRAP**, etc.), *subs.* (common).—1. The mouth; and (2) a GRUBBERY (*q.v.*). For synonyms, *see* POTATO-TRAP.

1840. THACKERAY, *Comic Almanack*, p. 229. 'That's the GRUB-SHOP,' said my lord, 'where we young gentlemen wot has money buys our wittles.

3. *See* GRUBBING-CRIB in both senses.

GRUB-STAKE, *subs.* (American).—Food and other necessaries furnished to mining prospectors in return for a share in the 'finds.' Hence, TO GRUB-STAKE = to speculate after this fashion.

1884. BUTTERWORTH, *Zig-zag Journeys*. When miners become so poor that they are not able to furnish the necessary tools and food with which to 'go prospecting, a third party of sufficient means offers to furnish tools and provisions on condition that he is to have a certain interest in anything that may be found.

1891. GUNTER, *Miss Nobody of Nowhere*, p. 100. He GRUB-STAKED us and we used to work on the Tillie mine together.

GRUB-STREET, *subs.* (colloquial).—The world of cheap, mean, needy authors. [Originally a street near Moorfields, changed in 1830 to Milton Street.]

1690. B. E., *Dict. Cant. Crew*, s.v. GRUB-STREET news, false, forg'd.

1728. POPE, *Dunciad*, iii., 135. Shall take through GRUB-STREET his triumphant round.

1785. GROSE, *Vulg. Tongue*, s.v. A GRUB-STREET writer means a hackney author, who manufactures books for the booksellers.

1813. J. and H. SMITH, *Horace in London*, 'The Classic Villa.' GRUB-STREET, 'tis called.

1821. EGAN, *Life in London*, i. Few, if any, writers, out of the great mass of living scribblers, whether of GRUB-STREET fabrication, or of University passport . . . possess souls above buttons.

1892. HUME NISBET, *Bushranger's Sweetheart*, p. 119. We are going it, have got our agents in GRUB STREET.

GRUEL, *subs.* (common).—1. A beating; PUNISHMENT (*q.v.*). For synonyms, *see* TANNING. Hence, TO GET (or GIVE) ONE'S GRUEL =to castigate, or be well beaten; also killed. In the prize ring= to knock a man out for good. GRUELLED = floored; also GRUELLING.

1815. SCOTT, *Guy Mannering*, ch. xxviii. He gathered in general, that they expressed great indignation against some individual. 'He shall have his GRUEL,' said one.

1837. BARHAM, *Ingoldsby Legends*. 'Babes in the Wood.' He that was mildest in mood GAVE THE truculent rascal HIS GRUEL.

1849. C. KINGSLEY, *Alton Locke*, ch. xii. They were as well GRUELLED as so many posters, before they got to the stile.

1888. *Sporting Life*, 15 Dec. Preferred to be easily knocked out to TAKING HIS GRUEL like a man.

1891. *Licensed Vict. Gaz.*, 23 Jan. Both men were badly punished, but George had, of course, the lion's share of the GRUEL.

1891. *Licensed Vict. Mirror*, 30 Jan., p. 7, c. 3. All the advantage rested with the same side for some little time, Paddock getting such a GRUELLING that his head swelled out like a pumpkin.

2. (American thieves'). — Coffee.

1859. MATSELL, *Vocabulum*, s.v.

GRUELLER, *subs.* (common).—A knock-down blow; a settler; a FLOORER (*q.v.*).

GRUMBLE-GUTS, *subs.* (popular).—An inveterate croaker. Also GRUMBLE-GIZZARD.

GRUMBLES. TO BE ALL ON THE GRUMBLES, *verb. phr.* (popular). —To be discontented; cross; ON THE SNARLY-YOW (*q.v.*).

GRUMBLETONIAN, *subs.* (common). —A pattern of discontent: one ever on the grumble. [Grumbleton (during the reigns of the later Stuarts)=an imaginary centre of discontent; hence, GRUMBLETONIAN, a nickname of the County party, distinguished from the Court, as being in opposition.]

1690. B. E., *Dict. Cant. Crew*. GRUMBLETONIANS, malecontents, out of Humour with the Government, for want of a Place, or having lost one.

1705-7. WARD, *Hudibras Redivivus*, vol. I., pt. 1, p. 24 (2nd Ed.). But all the GRUMBLETONIAN throng Did with such violence rush along.

1773. GOLDSMITH, *She Stoops to Conquer*, Act 1. Now, if I pleased, I could be so revenged upon the old GRUMBLETONIAN.

1785. GROSE, *Vulg. Tongue*. GRUMBLETONIAN, s.v., a discontented person.

1849-61. MACAULAY, *Hist. of Eng.*, ch. xix. Who were sometimes nicknamed the GRUMBLETONIANS, and sometimes honoured with the appellation of the County party.

GRUMMET, *subs.* (venery).—The female *pudendum*. For synonyms, *see* MONOSYLLABLE.

GRUMPY (or **GRUMPISH**), *adj.* (colloquial). — Surly; cross; angry.

1840. MRS. TROLLOPE, *Michael Armstrong*, ch. vi. If you blubber or look GRUMPISH.

1859. SALA, *Twice Round the Clock*, 3 a.m., par. 13. Calling you a 'cross, GRUMPY, old thing,' when you mildly suggest that it is very near bed-time.

1868. MISS BRADDON, *Trail of the Serpent*, bk. IV., ch. i. A GRUMPY old deaf keeper, and a boy, his assistant.

1883. *Punch*, 19 May, p. 230, c. 2. They all looked GRUMPY and down in the mouth.

GRUNDY, *subs.* (old).—A short fat man; a FORTY-GUTS (*q.v.*).—*See* MRS. GRUNDY.

1563. FOX, *Acts and Monuments* (London, 1844), iii., 1104. For that he being a short GRUNDY, and of little stature, did ride commonly with a great broad hat.

GRUNTER, *subs.* (old).—1. A pig; a GRUNTING-CHEAT (*q.v.*). In quot. 1652 = pork. For synonyms, *see* SOW'S BABY.

1656. BROME, *Jovial Crew*. Here's GRUNTER and bleater, with tib-of-the-buttry.

1690. B. E., *Dict. Cant. Crew*. GRUNTER, s.v. A sucking pig.

1785. GROSE, *Vulg. Tongue*. GRUNTER, s.v.

1841. *Comic Almanack*, p. 266. And the squeaking GRUNTER is loose on the green.

1847-50. TENNYSON, *Princess*, v. 26. A draggled mawkin, That tends her bristled GRUNTERS in the sludge.

2. (common).—A sixpence. In quot. 1785 = 1s. *Cf.*, Hog and Pig.

1785. Grose, *Vulg. Tongue* Grunter, s.v. A shilling.

1858. A. Mayhew, *Paved with Gold*, bk. III., ch. iii., p. 267. One of the men . . . had only taken three 'twelvers' [shillings] and a grunter.

1885. *Household Words*, 20 June. p. 155. The sixpence . . . is variously known as a 'pig,' a 'sow's baby,' a grunter, and 'half a hog.'

3. (common).—A policeman; a trap (*q.v.*); a pig (*q.v.* sense 2). For synonyms, *see* Beak.

1820. *London Magazine*, i., 26. As a bonnet against . . . grunters.

1859. Matsell, *Vocabulum*. Grunter, s.v., a country constable.

4. (tailors'). — An habitual grumbler; a grumble-guts (*q.v.*).

Grunter's-gig, *subs.* (old).—A smoked pig's chap.—Grose.

Grunting-cheat, *subs.* (old).—A pig. *See* Chete. For synonyms, *see* Sow's Baby.

1567. Harman, *Caveat*, p. 86. She has a cackling-chete, a grunting-chete, ruff pecke, cassan, and poplarr of yarum.

1622. Fletcher, *Beggar's Bush*, v., 1. Or surprising a boor's ken for grunting-cheats? Or cackling-cheats?

Grunting-peck, *subs.* (old). — Pork or bacon.

1690. B. E., *Dict. Cant. Crew* Grunting-peck, s.v., pork.

1728. Bailey, *Eng. Dict.*, s.v.

1785. Grose, *Vulg. Tongue*, s.v.

1836. Smith, *Individual*. 'The Thieves' Chaunt.' But dearer to me Sue's kisses far Than grunting peck or other grub are.

Gruts, *subs.* (common).—Tea; For synonyms, *see* Scandal-broth.

1811. *Lexicon Balatronicum*, s.v.

G. T. T. Gone to Texas, *phr.* (American). — Absconded. [Moonshining gentry used to mark G. T. T. on the doors of their abandoned dwellings as a consolation for inquiring creditors.] Fr., *aller en Belgique*. For synonyms, *see* Swartwort.

1835. Haliburton, *Clockmaker*, 5 S., ch. viii. Before this misfortin' came I used to do a considerable smart chance of business; but now it's time for me to cut dirt, and leave the country. I believe I must hang out the G. T. T. sign.'—'Why, what the plague is that?' says I. 'Gone to Texas,' said he.'

Guage.—*See* Gage.

Gubbins, *subs.* (old). — Fish-offal.

1611. Cotgrave, *Dictionarie*, q.v.

Gudgeon, *subs.* (old).—1. A bait; an allurement. Hence, To gudgeon (or to swallow a gudgeon) = to be extremely credulous or gullible.

1598. Shakspeare, *Merchant of Venice*, i., 1. But fish not with this melancholy bait, For this fool's gudgeon, this opinion.

1598. Florio, *Worlde of Wordes*, *Bersela*, s.v. To swallow a gudgeon . . . to believe any tale.

1785. Grose, *Vulg. Tongue*, Gudgeon, s.v. To swallow the bait, or fall into a trap, from the fish of that name which is easily taken.

1892. *National Observer*, 23 July, vii., 235. It has educated Hodge into an increased readiness to gorge any gudgeon that may be offered him.

2. (colloquial).—An easy dupe; a buffle (*q.v.*).

1785. Grose, *Vulg. Tongue*, s.v.

Guerrilla, *subs.* (American sharpers').—*See* quot.

1859. Matsell, *Vocabulum*, s.v. This name is applied by gamblers to fellows who skin suckers when and where they can, who do not like the professional gamblers, but try to beat them, sometimes inform on them, and tell the suckers that they have been cheated.

Guff, *subs.* (common).—Humbug; bluff; jabber. For synonyms, *see* Gammon.

1889. *Sportsman*, 19 Jan. Hereafter he can have the newspapers to himself, and with that windbag Mitchell fill them with guff and nonsense, but I won't notice them.

Guffy, *subs.* (nautical).—A soldier. For synonyms, *see* Mudcrusher.

Guiders, *subs.* (general).—1. Reins; ribbons (*q.v.*).

2. (common).—Sinews; leaders (*q.v.*).

Guinea. A guinea to a gooseberry, *phr.* (sporting).—Long odds. *See* Lombard Street to a China Orange.

1884. Hawley Smart, *Post to Finish*, ch. vii. What! old Writson against Sam Pearson? Why, it's a guinea to a gooseberry on Sam!

Guinea-dropper, *subs.* (old).—A sharper. Specifically one who let drop counterfeit guineas in collusion with a gold-finder (*q.v.*). For synonyms, *see* Rook.

1712. Gay, *Trivia*, iii., 249. Who now the guinea dropper's bait regards, Tricked by the sharper's dice or juggler's cards.

Guinea-hen, *subs.* (old). — A courtezan. For synonyms, *see* Barrack-hack and Tart.

1602. Shakspeare, *Othello*, i., 3. Ere I would say I would drown myself for the love of a guinea-hen, I would change my humanity with a baboon.

1630. Glapthorne, *Albertus Wallenstein*. Yonder's the cock o' the game About to tread yon guinea-hen, they're billing.

Guinea-pig, *subs.* (old). — 1. A general term of reproach.

1748 Smollett, *Roderick Random*, xxiv. A good seaman he is, as ever stepp'd on forecastle — none of your guinea-pigs,—nor your freshwater, wishy-washy, fair-weather fowls.

2. (old). — Any one whose nominal fee for professional services is a guinea: as vets., special jurymen, etc. Now mainly restricted to clergymen acting as deputies, and (in contempt) to directors of public companies. Hence Guinea-trade = professional services of any kind.

1821. Coombe, *Dr. Syntax*, Tour III., c. iv. 'Oh, oh,' cried Pat, 'how my hand itches, Thou guinea-pig [a 'vet.'], in boots and breeches, to trounce thee well.'

1871. *Temple Bar*, vol. xxxi., p. 320. A much more significant term is that of guinea pigs, the pleasant name for those gentlemen of more rank than means, who hire themselves out as directors of public companies, and who have a guinea and a copious lunch when they attend board meetings.

1880. *Church Review*, 2 Jan. Guinea pigs . . . are, for the most part, unattached or roving parsons, who will take any brother cleric's duty for the moderate remuneration of one guinea.

1883. *Saturday Review*, 25 Aug., p. 246, c. 2. A country parson was suddenly attacked with diphtheria, late in the week. Recourse was had in vain to the neighbours, and it was decided at last to telegraph to London for a guinea pig.

1884. *Echo*, 19 May, p. 1, c. 5. Let us apply the principle further, and imagine . . . limited liability swindlers tried by a jury of guinea-pigs and company promoters.

1884. *Graphic*, 29 Nov., p. 562, c. 3. And the guinea-pig, whose name is on a dozen different Boards, is justly regarded with suspicion.

1886. *Chambers's Jour.*, 24 Apr., p. 258. In order to be considered of any value as Director of a Company, a guinea-pig ought to have a handle to his name.

1887. Payn, *Glow Worm Tales*. 'A Failure of Justice.' He is best known to the public as a guinea-pig, from his habit of sitting at boards and receiving for it that nominal remuneration, though in his case it stands for a much larger sum.

1889. Drage, *Cyril*, vii. The rector has, as usual, got the gout, and we live under a *régime* . . . . . of guinea-pigs.

1890. *Standard*, 26 June, p. 5, c. 4. The least attempt to saddle responsibility for misleading statements upon Boards of Directors would drive prudent, 'respectable' men out of what is vulgarly called the guinea-pig business.

3. (nautical).—*See* quot.

1840. Marryat, *Poor Jack*, ch. xxvi. While Bramble was questioned by the captain and passengers, I was attacked by the midshipmen, or guinea-pigs as they are called.

Guise's Geese, *subs. phr.* (military).—The Sixth Foot or 'Saucy Sixth.' [From its Colonel's name, 1735-63.]

Guiver, *subs.* (theatrical).—(1) Flattery, and (2) artfulness (*q.v.*). For synonyms, *see* Soft Soap.

Adj. (common). — Smart; fashionable; on it (*q.v.*). Guiver lad = a low-class dandy; also an artful member (*q.v.*).

a. 1866. Vance, *Chickaleary Cove*. The stock around my squeeze of a guiver colour see.

Verb (sporting). — To hum-bug; to fool about (*q.v.*); to show off.

1891. *Sporting Life*, 25 Mar. He goes into a ring to *fight* his man, not to spar and look pretty, and run, and dodge, and guiver.

Gulf, *subs.* (old).—1. The throat; also the maw. For synonyms, *see* Gutter-alley.

1579. Spencer, *Shepheardе's Calendar*, Sept. That with many a lamb had glutted his gulf.

2. (Cambridge Univ.).—The bottom of a list of 'passes,' with the names of those who only just succeed in getting their degree.

1852. Bristed, *Five Years in an English University*, p. 205. Some ten or fifteen men just on the line, not bad enough to be plucked, or good enough to be placed, are put into the gulf, as it is popularly called (the examiners' phrase is 'degrees allowed'), and have their degrees given them, but are not printed in the calendar.

3. (Oxford Univ.).—A man who, going in for honours, only gets a pass.

Verb (Cambridge Univ.).—To place in the gulf, *subs.*, sense 2 (*q.v.*); to be gulfed = to be on such a list. [Men so placed were not eligible for the Classical Tripos]. *Cf.*, Pluck and Plough.

1853. Bradley, *Verdant Green*, pt. iii., p. 89. I am not going to let them gulph me a second time.

1863. H. Kingsley, *Austin Elliot*, p. 123. The good Professor scolded, predicted that they would all be either gulfed or ploughed.

1865. *Sporting Gaz.*, 1 Apr. A man who was gulfed for mathematical honours was certainly, in olden time, unable to enter for the classical examination; but though the arrangement is altered, the term is *not* obsolete. A man who is gulfed is considered to know enough mathematics for an ordinary degree, but not enough to be allowed his degree in mathematics only; he is consequently obliged to pass in all the ordinary subjects (except mathematics) for the 'poll,' before taking his degree.

1876. Trevelyan, *Life of Macaulay* (1884), ch. ii., p. 61. When the Tripos of 1822 made its appearance, his name did not grace the list. In short . . . . Macaulay was gulfed.

1852. Bristed, *Five Years in an English University*, p. 297. I discovered that my name was nowhere to be found—that I was gulfed.

Gulf-spin, *subs.* (American cadet). —A rascal; a worthless fellow; a beat (*q.v.*) a shyster (*q.v.*).

Gull, *subs.* (old, now recognised). —1. A ninny. For synonyms, *see* Buffle and Cabbage-head.

1596. Sir J. Davies, *Book of Epigrams*. A gull is he who feares a velvet gowne, And when a wench is brave dares not speak to her; A gull is he which traverseth the towne, And is for marriage known a common wooer; A gull is he, which while he proudly weares A silver-hilted rapier by his side. Indures the lye and knockes about the eares, While in his sheath his sleeping sword doth bide. But to define a gull in termes precise—A gull is he which *seems*, and *is not*, wise.

1598. Florio, *A World of Wordes*, *passim*.

1609. Jonson, *Case is Altered*, iv.,3. *Jun.* Tut, thou art a goose to be Cupid's gull.

1609. Shakspeare, *Timon of Athens*. Lord Timon will be left a naked gull. Which flashes now a phœnix.

1614. Overbury, *Characters*. 'A Roaring Boy.' He cheats young guls that are newly come to town.

1618. Rowlands, *Night Raven*, p. 28 (H. C. Rept., 1872). I know the houses where base cheaters vse, And note what gulls (to worke vpon) they chuse.

1661. Brome, *Poems*, '*The Cure of Care*.' Those gulls that by scraping and toiling.

1818. S. E. Ferrier, *Marriage*, ch. li. The poor gull was caught, and is now, I really believe, as much in love as it is in the nature of a stupid man to be.

1850. D. Jerrold, *The Catspaw*, Act i. Pshaw! some rascal that lives on simpletons and gulls.

1892. R. L. Stevenson and L. Osbourne, *The Wrecker*, p. 231. I was a dweller under roofs; the gull of that which we call civilisation.

2. (old).—A cheat; a fraud; a trick.

1600. Shakspeare, *Much Ado about Nothing*, ii., 3. I should think this a gull, but that the white-bearded fellow speaks it.

1611. Cotgrave, *Dictionarie*, q.v.

3. (Oxford Univ.).—A swindler; a trickster. *Cf.*, Gull-catcher, of which it is probably an abbreviation.

1825. *The English Spy*, v. I., p. 161. 'You'll excuse me, sir, but as you are *fresh*, take care to avoid the gulls.' 'I never understood that gulls were birds of prey,' said I. 'Only in Oxford, sir, and here, I assure you, they bite like hawks.'

Verb (old: now recognised).—To cheat; to dupe; to victimise; to take in (*q.v.*). in any fashion and to any purpose.

1596. Jonson. *Every Man in his Humour*, v. This is a mere trick, a device, you are gulled in this most grossly.

1602. Shakspeare, *Twelfth Night*, ii., 3. *Mar.* For Monsieur Maluolio, let me alone with him; If I do not gull him into a nayword, and make him a common recreation, do not thinke I haue witte enough to lye straight in my bed; I know I can do it.

1607. Rowlands, *Diogenes, his Lanthorne*, p. 11 (H. C. Rept. 1873). He promist me good stuffe *truly*, a great penny-worth *indeed*, and verily did gull me.

1610. Jonson, *Alchemist*, v., 2. Hast thou gulled her of her jewels or her bracelets?

1689. Selden, *Table Talk*, p. 98 (Arber's ed.). Presbyters have the greatest power of any Clergy in the world, and gull the Laity most.

1778. *Sketches for Tabernacle-Frames*, p. 25, *note*. These fanatica Preachers frequently squeeze out Tears to gull their Audience.

1851-61. MAYHEW, *Lond. Lab. and Lond. Poor*, I., 472. It's generally the lower order that he GULLS.

1892. HENLEY and STEVENSON, *Deacon Brodie*, ix. Pay your debts, and GULL the world a little longer.

Hence GULLIBLE, *adj.*, = easily duped.

1841. THACKERAY, *Character Sketches* 'Fashionable Authoress.' And, gulled themselves, gull the most GULLABLE of publics.

GULLAGE, *subs.* (old colloquial).—The act of trickery; the state of being gulled.

1605. B. JONSON, *Volpone*, v., 5. Had you no quirk To avoid GULLAGE, sir, by such a creature?

1611. CHAPMAN, *May Day*, Act II., p. 284 (*Plays*, 1874). For procuring you the dear GULLAGE of my sweetheart, Mistress Franceschina.

GULL-CATCHER (or **GULLER, GULL-SHARPER**, etc.), *subs.* (old).—A trickster; a cheat. *See* GULL, senses 1 and 3.

1602. SHAKSPEARE, *Twelfth Night*, ii., 5. Here comes my noble GULL-CATCHER.

GULLERY, *subs.* (old colloquial).—Dupery; fraud; a cheat's device. *Cf.*, GULLAGE.

1596. JONSON, *Every Man in His Humour*, iii., 2. Your Balsamum and your St. John's wort are all mere GULLERIES and trash to it.

1608. JOHN DAY, *Humour out of Breath*, Act iv., Sc. 3. I am gulld, palpably gulld . . . and mine owne GULLERY grieves me not half so much as the Dukes displeasure.

1630. TAYLOR, *Works*. Neverthelesse, whosoever will but looke into the lying legend of golden GULLERY, there they shall finde that the poore seduced ignorant Romanists doe imitate all the idolatrous fornication of the heathen pagans and infidels.

1633. *Ile of Guls*. Upon you both, so, so, so, how greedily their inventions like beagles follow the sent of their owne GULLERY, yet these are no fooles, God forbid, not they.

1633. MARMION, *Fine Companion. Lit.* What more GULLERIES yet? they have cosend mee of my daughters, I hope they will cheate me of my wife too: have you any more of these tricks to shew, ha?

1689. SELDEN, *Table Talk*, p. 38 (Arber's ed.). And how can it be proved, that ever any man reveal'd Confession, when there is no Witness? And no man can be Witness in his own cause. A meer GULLERY.

1819. H. MORE, *Defence of Moral Cabbala*, ch. iii. The sweet deception and GULLERY of their own corrupted fancy.

1821. SCOTT, *Kenilworth*, ch. xx. Do you think, because I have good-naturedly purchased your trumpery goods at your roguish prices, that you may put any GULLERY you will on me?

GULLET, *subs.* (old: now recognised).—The throat. For synonyms, *see* GUTTER-ALLEY.

1383. CHAUCER, *Canterbury Tales*, 12, 477. [Quoted in *Ency. Dict.*] Out of the harde bones knocken they The mary, for they casten nought away, That may go thurgh the GULLET soft and sote.

1690. B. E., *Dict. Cant. Crew*, GULLET, s.v. A Derisory Term for the Throat, from *Gula*.

1836. DICKENS, *Pickwick*, ch. 15. So he puts a pistol to his mouth, and he fires it down his GULLET.

1893. *National Observer*, x. 168. Through sympathetic GULLETS.

GULL-FINCH, *subs.* (old). — A simpleton; a fool. For synonyms, *see* BUFFLE and CABBAGE-HEAD.

1630. TAYLOR, *Works*. For 'tis concluded 'mongst the wizards all, To make thee master of GUL-FINCHES hall.

GULL-GROPER, *subs.* (old). — A gamesters' money-lender.

1609. DEKKER, *Lanthorne and Candle-light*. The GUL-GROPER is commonly an old mony-monger, who having travaild through all the follyes of the world in his youth, knowes them well, and shunnes them in his age, his whole felicitie being to fill his bags with golde and silver.

1690. B. E. *Dict. Cant. Crew*. GULL-GROPER, s.v. A Bystander that Lends Money to the Gamesters.

1785. GROSE, *Vulg. Tongue*, s.v.

GULLY, *subs.* (common).—1. The throat. For synonyms, *see* GUTTER-ALLEY.

2. (venery). — The female *pudendum*. For synonyms, *see* MONOSYLLABLE.

3. (old and Scots').—A knife. For synonyms, *see* CHIVE.

1653. URQUHART, *Rabelais*, bk. I., ch. xxvii. Fair GULLIES which are little haulch-backed demi-knives.

1785. BURNS, *Death and Dr. Hornbook*. I red ye weel, tak care o' skaith, See, there's a GULLY.

1789. BURNS, *Address to Captain Grose*. The knife that nickit Abel's craig, He'll prove ye fully It was a faulding jocteleg, Or lang-kail GULLY.

Verb (common). — To GULL (*q.v.*); to dupe; to swindle. For synonyms, *see* STICK.

1834. AINSWORTH, *Rookwood*, bk. III., ch. v. I rode about and speechified, and everybody GULLIED.

GULLY-FLUFF, *subs.* (colloquial).—Pocket-filth; BEGGAR'S VELVET (*q.v.*). Also FLUE (*q.v.*).

GULLY-GUT, *subs.* and *adj.* (common).—A glutton. For synonyms, *see* STODGER.

1598. FLORIO, *A Worlde of Wordes*. *Crapulatore*, a surfeiter; a gormand; a glutton; a GULLIE-GUT.

1672. LESTRANGE, *Fables*. A GULLI-GUT friar.

GULLY-HOLE (or **GULLY**), *subs.* (common).—1. The throat, or gullet. For synonyms, *see* GUTTER-ALLEY.

2. (venery). — The female *pudendum*. For synonyms, *see* MONOSYLLABLE.

GULLY-RAKER, *subs. phr.* (venery).—1. The *penis*; and (2) a wencher. For synonyms, *see* CREAMSTICK, PRICK, and MOLROWER.

2. (Australian). A cattle-whip; a cattle-thief.

1881. A. C. GRANT, *Bush Life in Queensland* . . . following up his admonition by a sweeping cut of his GULLY-RAKER, and a report like a musket-shot.

GULPIN, *subs.* (common). — A simpleton; a GAPESEED (*q.v.*). Fr., *un gobemouche*; *une éponge*. For synonyms, *see* BUFFLE and CABBAGE-HEAD.

1886. W. BESANT, *World Went Very Well Then*, ch. xxix. But Jack persisted, and I rose too. 'Go then!' the Admiral roared, with a great oath. 'Go then, for a brace of GULPINS!'

GULPY, *adj.* (common).—Easily duped.

GULSH. TO HOLD ONE'S GULSH, *verb. phr.* (provincial).—To hold one's tongue; to keep quiet.

GUM, *subs.* (old).—1. Chatter; talk; JAW (*q.v.*). Also abuse.

1751. SMOLLETT, *Peregrine Pickle*, ch. xiv. There's no occasion to bowse out so much unnecessary GUM.

1785. GROSE, *Vulg. Tongue*, s.v. Come let us have no more of your GUM.

1824. R. B. PEAKE, *Americans Abroad*, i., 1. *Dou.* Come, none of your GUM—now you are but an underlin', tho' you are so uppish and twistical—where's the chair?

2. (American). — A trick; a piece of dupery; a SELL (*q.v.*). Also GUMMATION.

3. (American). — A golosh; an india-rubber overshoe. [Short for 'gum-shoes.']

1872. *Morning Post*, 9 Jan. Forbidding him again to cross her threshold or to leave his GUM-SHOES in her hall.

Verb (common).—To cheat; to TAKE IN (*q.v.*), to ROAST (*q.v.*) or quiz. For synonyms, *see* GAMMON.

1859. SALA, *Twice Round the Clock*, 6 p.m., par. I. I began to think either that he was quizzing me—GUMMING is the proper Transatlantic colloquialism, I think.

1875. 'American English' in *Chamb. Journal*, 25 Sept., p. 611. To 'gum-tree' is to elude, to cheat [from opossum], and this again is shortened into 'to gum,' as the phrase, 'Now don't you try to GUM me.'

OLD MOTHER GUM, *subs. phr.* (common).—An old woman: in derision.

BY GUM! *intj.* (common).—A mild oath. For synonyms, *see* OATHS.

1860. HALIBURTON ('Sam Slick'), *The Season Ticket*, No. ix. BY GUM, Squire Shegog, we have had the greatest bobbery of a shindy in our carriage you ever knowed in all our born days.

BLESS YOUR (or HIS, HER, ITS, etc.) GUMS, *phr.* (common).—A piece of banter: a facetious way of saying 'Bless your soul!'

GUMMAGY, *adj.* (common).—Snarling; of a scolding habit.

GUMMED, *adj.* (billiards).—Said of a ball close to the cushion.

GUMMY, *subs.* (common). — 1. A toothless person; *i.e.*, with nothing but gums to show. Generally, OLD GUMMY.

2. (thieves').—Medicine. Also GUMMY-STUFF.—MATSELL.

3. (common).—A dullard; a fool. For synonyms, *see* BUFFLE and CABBAGE-HEAD.

Adj. (common). — Puffed; swollen; clumsy.

1785. GROSE, *Vulg. Tongue*, s.v. GUMMEY, clumsy, particularly applied to the ancles of men, or women, and the legs of horses.

TO FEEL GUMMY, *verb. phr.* (University).—To perspire.

GUMP, *subs.* (common).—A dolt. For synonyms, *see* BUFFLE and CABBAGE-HEAD.

1825. NEAL, *Bro. Jonathan*, bk. II., ch. xv. He's . . . sort of a nateral too, I guess; rather a GUMP, hey?

GUMPTION, *subs.* (colloquial).—Cleverness; understanding; NOUS (*q.v.*). Also RUM GUMPTION.

1785. GROSE, *Vulg. Tongue*. GUMPTION, OR RUM GUMPTION, s.v., docility, comprehension, capacity.

1787. GROSE, *Prov. Glossary*, s.v. 'Gawm.' *Gawm*, to understand; I dinna gawm ye, I don't understand you. Hence, possibly, gawmtion, or GUMPTION, understanding.

1834. *Atlantic Club-book*, I., 33. D'ye think I'm a fellow of no more GUMPTION than that?

1843. *Comic Almanack*. Poor beasts, 'tis very clear, To any one possess'd of GUMPTION, That if they'd not come over here, They'd have been carried off by home consumption.

1853. LYTTON, *My Novel*, bk. IV., ch. xii. GUMPTION—it means cleverness.

1883. *Daily Telegraph*, 25 June, p. 3, c. 2. But poor people—leastways, those that have got any GUMPTION—know better than that.

1890. *Notes and Queries*, 7 S., x., 303. As familiar as the Greek word *nous* for what . . . . is known . . . as GUMPTION.

GUMPTIOUS, *adj.* (colloquial).—Shrewd; intelligent; vain.

1853. LYTTON, *My Novel*, bk. IV., ch. xii. *Landlord*. There's gumption and GUMPTIOUS! Gumption is knowing, but when I say that sum un is GUMPTIOUS, I mean—though that's more vulgar like—sum un who does not think small beer of hisself. You take me, sir?

GUM-SMASHER (or **TICKLER**), *subs.* (common). — A dentist. For synonyms, *see* SNAG-CATCHER.

GUM-SUCK, *verb.* (American).—To flatter; to humbug; to dupe For synonyms, *see* GAMMON.

GUM-SUCKER, *subs.* (Australian).—1. *See* quot. *Cf.*, CORN-STALK.

1887. *All the Year Round*, 30 July, p. 67. A GUM-SUCKER is a native of Tasmania, and owes his elegant nickname to the abundance of gum-trees in the Tasmanian forests.

2. (common).—A fool. For synonyms, *see* BUFFLE and CABBAGE-HEAD.

GUM-TICKLER, *subs.* (colloquial).—1. A drink. Specifically, DROP or SHORT, or a dram. For synonyms, *see* GO.

1814. *Quarterly Review*, vol. X., p. 521. A gill, taken fasting, is called a GUM-TICKLER.

1864. DICKENS, *Our Mutual Friend*, bk. IV., ch. iii. I prefer to take it in the form of a GUM-TICKLER.

2. *See* GUM-SMASHER.

GUM-TREE. TO BE UP A GUM-TREE, *verb. phr.* (American).—To be on one's last legs; at the end of one's rope. 'He has seen his last GUM-TREE' = It is all up with him.

GUN, *subs.* (old).—1. A lie. *New Cant. Dict.*, 1725. For synonyms, *see* WHOPPER.

2. (common).—A thief; specifically, a MAGSMAN (*q.v.*) or street-artist. Also GUN-SMITH and GUNNER. GUNNING = thieving. [An abbreviation of GONOF (*q.v.*).] *See* AREA-SNEAK and THIEVES.

1858. A. MAYHEW, *Paved with Gold*, bk. II., ch. i., p. 70. I tell you you ain't a-going to make a GUN (thief) of this here young flat.

1868. *Temple Bar*, xxv., 213. . . . returned to his old trade of GUNSMITH, GUNNING being the slang term for thieving, or going on the cross.

1882. *Cornhill Mag.*, p. 649. Flats graft for GUNS.

1889. CLARKSON and RICHARDSON, *Police*. GUNNERS and grasshoppers sneak about watching their opportunities.

3. (American).—A revolver. For synonyms, *see* MEAT-IN-THE POT.

4. (Irish). — A toddy glass. *See* IN THE GUN.

Verb (American). — 1. To consider with attention.

1859. MATSELL, *Vocabulum*, s.v. GUNNED. The copper GUNNED me as if he was fly to my mug.

2. (American). — To strive hard; to make a violent effort: *e.g.*, to GUN A STOCK = to use every means to produce a 'break'; when supplies are heavy and holders would be unable to resist.

IN THE GUN, *phr.* (old).—Drunk. For synonyms, *see* DRINKS and SCREWED.

1690. B. E., *Dict. Cant. Crew*, s.v.

1785. GROSE, *Vulg. Tongue*. GUN, s.v., he's IN THE GUN, he is drunk, perhaps from an allusion to a vessel called a GUN, used for ale in the universities.

SON OF A GUN. *See* SON.

SURE AS A GUN, *phr.* (common).—Quite certain; inevitable.

1633. JONSON, *Tale of a Tub*, ii., 1. 'Tis right; he has spoke as TRUE AS A GUN, believe it.

1690. B.E., *Dict. Cant. Crew*.

1694. CONGREVE, *Double Dealer*, v., 20. All turned topsy-turvy, as SURE AS A GUN.

1720. GAY, *New Song of New Similes*. SURE AS A GUN she'll drop a tear.

1749. FIELDING, *Tom Jones*, bk. xviii., ch. ix. As SURE AS A GUN I have hit o' the very right o't.

1759. STERNE, *Tristram Shandy*, vol. vi., ch. xxvi. Think ye not that, in striking these *in*,—he might, peradventure, strike something *out*? as SURE AS A GUN.

1825. EGAN, *Life of an Actor*, iv. By gum! he roared out, sir, AS SURE AS A GUN.

d. 1842. FATHER PROUT, *Reliques*, I. 19. 'Vert-Vert, the Parrot.' Scared at the sound,—'SURE AS A GUN, The bird's a demon!' cried the nun.

1849. THACKERAY, *Pendennis*, ch. lviii. In every party of the nobility his name's down as SURE AS A GUN.

1891. N. GOULD, *Double Event*, p. 141. Nobbed, SURE AS A GUN!

1892. MANVILLE FENN, *NewMistress*. xxxv. They were both down there about that school-money Betsey, as SURE AS A GUN.

GUNDIGUTS, *subs.* (common)—A fat man; a FORTY GUTS (*q.v.*).

1690. B.E., *Dict. Cant. Crew*, s.v.

1785. GROSE, *Vulg. Tongue*, s.v.

GUNNER'S DAUGHTER. TO KISS (or MARRY) THE GUNNER'S DAUGHTER, *verb. phr.* (nautical). To be flogged. [GUNNER'S DAUGHTER = the gun to which boys were lashed for punishment.]

1785. GROSE, *Vulg. Tongue*, s.v.

1833. MARRYAT, *Peter Simple*, ch. xxxii. I don't know what officers are made of now-a-days. I'll marry one of you young gentlemen to the GUNNER'S DAUGHTER before long. Quarter-deck's no better than a bear-garden.

GUNPOWDER, *subs.* (old).—An old woman.

1690. B. E., *Dict. Cant. Crew*, s.v.

1785. GROSE, *Vulg. Tongue*, s.v.

GUNTER.—See COCKER.

GUP, *subs.* (Anglo-Indian).—Gossip; scandal.

1868. FLORENCE MARRYATT. *Gup*, xix. With regard to my title . . . GUP is the Hindustani for 'Gossip.' . . . *Voilà tout!*

1883. HAWLEY SMART, *Hard Lines*, ch. xxix. Our Eastern empire is much addicted to what they term GUP, whereby they mean gossip, scandal, or by whatever other equivalent the taking away of one's neighbours' characters may be designated.

TO BE A GUP, *verb. phr.* (American).—To be easy to take or steal.

GURTSEY, *subs.* (American Cadet).—A fat man; a PODGE (*q.v.*). For synonyms, see FORTY-GUTS.

GUSH, *subs.* (colloquial). — The expression of affected or extravagant sentiment.

1883. *Saturday Review*, 3 Feb., p. 148, c. 2. Mr. Picton's style is pleasant and easy, as long as he allows himself to be natural, and does not fall into GUSH.

1886. *Church Times*, 17 Sep. Not mere GUSH or oratorical flip-flap.

Verb (colloquial).—To overflow with extravagant or affected sentiment.

1883. MISS BRADDON, *Golden Calf*, ch. vii. 'Yes, and you saw much of each other, and you became heart-friends,' GUSHED Miss Wolf, beaming benevolently at Brian.

GUSHER, *subs.* (colloquial). — A practitioner of GUSH (*q.v.*). Also GUSHINGTON.

1864. E. YATES, *Broken to Harness*, ch. vi., p. 66 (1873). The enthusiastic GUSHER who flings his or herself upon our necks, and insists upon sharing our sorrow.

1882. MISS BRADDON, *Mount Royal*, ch. viii. 'But, surely there is nothing improper in the play, dear Lady Cumberbridge,' exclaimed the eldest GUSHER, too long in society to shrink from sifting any question of that kind.

GUSHING, *adj.* (colloquial).—Extravagant; affected or irrational in expression; demonstratively affectionate. Also GUSHINGLY.

1864. 'The Campaigner' (No. XVI.), in *Fraser's Mag.*, p. 627. Donald did not belong to what, in the slang of translated Cockneys, is called the GUSHING School.

1864. *Punch's Almanack*, 'Our Growling Bard.' Some, I admit, are Milingtary Dears, As GUSHING ladies say, and some are Muffs.

1872. *Sunday Times*, 18 Aug. This however, was no surprise to the plaintiff, it having been understood from the first that the parties being past the GUSHING age the letters between them should be of a business character.

1880. OUIDA, *Moths*, ch. viii. Your heroics count for nothing. All girls of sixteen are GUSHING and silly.

1883. HARGRAVE JENNINGS, quoted in *Saturday Review*, 28 Apr., p. 536, c. 1. Women are not the laughably credulous creatures that man in his constant condescension and in his appreciation of himself would deem.

1884. F. ANSTEY, *Giant's Robe*, ch. xx. 'It's not precisely GUSHING,' he said to himself, 'but she couldn't very well say more just yet.'

GUSSET, *subs.* (common).—Generic for the female sex. Thus, BROTHER (or KNIGHT, or SQUIRE) OF THE GUSSET = a pimp; GUSSETTING = wenching; GUSSETEER = a wencher; etc.

GUSSET OF THE ARSE, *subs. phr.* (common).—The inside edge of the buttocks.

d. 1796. BURNS, *Merry Muses*, pp. 99-100. An' he grippit her fast by the GUSSET OF HER ARSE.

GUT, *subs.* (vulgar).—The vice or habit of gluttony; the belly [as opposed to the GROIN (*q.v.*).]

2. *in. pl.* (common). — The stomach and intestines.

1609. DEKKER, *Gul's Horne-Booke*, chap. ii. The Neapolitan will (like DERICK, the hangman) embrace you with one arme, and rip your GUTS with the other.

1640. RAWLINS, *The Rebellion*, iii. (DODSLEY, *Old Plays*, 4th ed., 1875, xiv., 48). Thou hast a GUT could swallow a peck loaf.

1661. BROME, *Poems*, 'A Satire on the Rebellion.' The grumbling GUTS, the belly of the State.

1713. BENTLEY, *On Free Thinking*, sect. 53. What then was our writer's soul? Was it brain or GUTS?

1754. FIELDING, *Jonathan Wild*, bk. iv., c. 1. But so it was that the knife, missing these noble parts (the noblest of many) THE GUTS, perforated only the hollow of his belly.

1787. BURNS, *Death and Dr. Hornbook*, st. 27. A ccuntra Laird had ta'en the batts, Or some curmurring in his GUTS.

3. *in. pl.* (old).—A fat man; a FORTY - GUTS (*q.v.*). Also GUTS - AND - GARBAGE. MORE GUTS (also MORE BALLS) THAN BRAINS = a fool.

1598. SHAKSPEARE, *Henry IV.*, pt. 1, ii., 2. Peace, ye fat-GUTS.

1690. B. E., *Dict. Cant. Crew*, s.v. GUTTS, a very fat gross Person.

4. (artists' and colloquial).—Spirit; quality; a touch of force, or energy, or fire: *e.g.*, a picture, a book, an actor. WITH GUTS = a strong thing. Put your GUTS into it (aquatic) = Row the very best you can. He (or it) has NO GUTS in him (or it) = He (or it) is a COMMON ROTTER (*q.v.*). Hence, GUTSY, *adj.* = having GUTS, and GUTSINESS, *subs.* = the condition of being GUTSY.

1738. SWIFT, *Polite Conversation*, I. The fellow's well enough if he had any GUTS in his brain.

1893. *Pall Mall Budget*. No. 1292 (June 29), 1906. The body of the cigar, or what might vulgarly be called the GUTS.

Verb (vulgar).—1. To plunder, or take out all or most of the contents (*i.e.*, intestines) of a place or thing; to drain; to 'clean out': *e.g.*, TO GUT A HOUSE (thieves') = to rifle it; to GUT AN OYSTER = to eat it; TO GUT A BOOK = to empty it of interesting matter; TO GUT A QUART POT = to drain at a draught. Whence, GUTTED = dead-broke.

1690. B. E., *Dict. Cant. Crew*, s.v.

1785. GROSE, *Vulg. Tongue*, s.v.

1819. MOORE, *Tom Crib*, p. 1. Whether diddling your subjects or GUTTING their jobs.

1849-61. MACAULAY, *Hist. of England*. The king's printing-house . . . was, to use a coarse metaphor, which then for the first time came into fashion, completely GUTTED.

1892. R. L. STEVENSON and L. OSBOURNE, *The Wrecker*, p. 373. Well, we've got the GUTS out of you!

2. (schools').—To eat hard, fast, and badly. For synonyms, see WOLF.

TO FRET ONE'S GUTS, *verb. phr.* (common).—To worry.

TO HAVE PLENTY OF GUTS BUT NO BOWELS, *verb. phr.* (common).—To be unfeeling, hard, merciless.

MY GREAT GUTS ARE READY TO EAT MY LITTLE ONES, *phr.* (old).—'I am very hungry.' Also, MY GUTS BEGIN TO THINK MY THROAT'S CUT; MY GUTS CURSE MY TEETH; and MY GUTS CHIME TWELVE.—GROSE.

NOT FIT TO CARRY GUTS TO A BEAR, *phr.* (common).—To be worthless; absolutely unmannerly; UNFIT FOR HUMAN FOOD (*q.v.*).

GUT-ENTRANCE, *subs.* (venery).—The female *pudendum.* Also FRONT-GUT. For synonyms, see MONOSYLLABLE.

GUT-FOUNDERED, *adj.* (old).—Exceedingly hungry.

1690. B. E., *Dict. Cant. Crew*, s.v.

1785. GROSE, *Vulg. Tongue*, s.v.

GUT-PUDDING, *subs.* (old).—A sausage. — *Nomenclator* (1696). For synonyms, see MYSTERIES.

GUT-PULLER, *subs.* (common).—A poulterer; a CHICKEN-BUTCHER (*q.v.*).

GUT-SCRAPER, *subs.* (common).—A fiddler. Also CATGUT SCRAPER, and TORMENTOR OF CATGUT. For synonymns, see KOSIN-THE-BOW.

1719. DURFEY, *Pills*, ii., 218. 'A Song' etc. Strike up, drowsie GUT SCRAPERS.

1785. GROSE, *Vulg. Tongue*, s.v.

1785. BURNS, *Jolly Beggars*. Her charms had struck a sturdy Caird, As weel's a poor GUT-SCRAPER.

1834. W. H. AINSWORTH, *Rookwood*, p. 192 (ed. 1864). Make ready there, you GUT-SCRAPERS, you shawm-shavers; I'll put your lungs in play for you presently. In the mean time—charge, pals, charge—a toast, a toast!

1834. MARRYAT, *Peter Simple*, ch. xxxi. 'You may save yourself the trouble, you dingy GUT-SCRAPER,' replied O'Brien [addressing a fiddler].

GUT-STICK, *subs.* (venery).—The *penis.* For synonyms, see CREAM-STICK and PRICK. TO HAVE A BIT (or A TASTE) OF THE GUT-STICK = to copulate (of women only).

GUT-STICKER, *subs. phr.* (venery). — A sodomite. Also GUT-FUCKER and GUT-MONGER. For synonyms, see USHER.

GUTTER, *subs.* (American thieves').—1. Porter.—MATSELL. [Probably a corruption of GATTER (*q.v.*).]

2. (venery).—The female *pudendum.* For synonyms, see MONOSYLLABLE.

Verb (Winchester College).—To fall in the water flat on the stomach. Fr., *piquer un plat-ventre.*

TO LAP THE GUTTER, *verb. phr.* (common).—To be in the last stage of intoxication. For synonyms, see DRINKS and SCREWED.

CARRY ME OUT AND LEAVE ME IN THE GUTTER, *phr.* (American). — See CARRY ME OUT.

GUTTER-ALLEY (or LANE), *subs.* (common).—The throat. ALL GOES DOWN GUTTER-LANE = 'He spends all on his stomach.'

ENGLISH SYNONYMS. — Beer Street; common sewer; drain; funnel; Gin Lane; gulf; gullet; gully-hole; gutter; Holloway; Peck Alley; Red Lane; the Red Sea; Spew Alley; swallow; thrapple; throttle; whistle.

FRENCH SYNONYMS. — *La carafe* (tramps'); *la creuse* (popular = Holloway); *le corridor*; *le cornet* (popular); *le couloir*; *le lambas*; *la goule* (popular); *le gose* (popular: an abbreviation of *gosier*: also *gésier*); *la gargoine* (thieves'); *la gargarousse* (thieves' = Old Gargles); *le four* (popular = the oven); *le fanal* (popular); *l'entonnoir* (popular = the funnel); *l'avaloir* (thieves' = the swallow).

GERMAN SYNONYM.—*Kollert* (Hanoverian).

SPANISH SYNONYM. — *La gorja.*

1690. B. E., *Dict. Cant. Crew*, s.v.

1785. GROSE, *Vulg. Tongue*, s.v.

1787. GROSE, *Prov. Glossary*, g. (1811), p. 81. All goeth down GUTTER LANE. That is, the throat. This proverb is applicable to those who spend all their substance in eating and drinking.

2. (common).—A urinal. For synonyms, see PISSING-POST.

GUTTER-BLOOD, *subs.* (common).—1. See quot. Also (2) a vulgarian; an upstart from the rabble.

1822. SCOTT, *The Fortunes of Nigel*, ch. v. In rushed a thorough Edinburgh GUTTERBLOOD—a ragged rascal.

GUTTER - CHAUNTER, *subs.* (common).—A street singer.

GUTTER-HOTEL, *subs.* (tramps').—The open air. For synonyms, see HEDGE-SQUARE.

GUTTER-LITERATURE. See BLOOD-AND-THUNDER, and AWFUL.

GUTTER-MASTER, *subs.* (old).—A term of reproach.

1607. MARSTON, *What You Will*, iii, 1. And now my soule is skipt into a perfumer, a GUTTERMASTER.

GUTTER-PROWLER, *subs.* (thieves').—A street thief. For synonyms, see AREA-SNEAK and THIEVES.

GUTTER-SNIPE, *subs.* (common).—1. A street arab. Also GUTTER-SLUSH. For synonyms, see MUD-LARK.

2. (American printers').—A poster for the kerb.

3. (American Commercial).—An 'outside' broker who does business chiefly in the street; a KERBSTONE BROKER (*q.v.*). Fr., *un loup-cervier.*

GUTTIE, *suos.* (golfers')—1. A gutta-percha ball.

2. (colloquial).—A glutton. For synonyms, see STODGER.

3. (colloquial). — A FORTY-GUTS, which see for synonyms.

GUTTLE, *verb.* (vulgar). —To eat greedily; to GORMANDIZE (*q.v.*). Also to drink: *e.g.*, TO GUTTLE A PINT = to take off, or do, a pint; 'He's been GUTTLING swipes'—he's been drinking beer. Hence GUTTLER = a coarse, or greedy eater; a sturdy pot-companion: a GORGER (*q.v.*). Cf., Thackeray's *Book of Snobs* for GUTTLEBURY Fair. See GUZZLE.

1672. LESTRANGE, *Fables*, p. 260. A jolly GUTTLING priest.

GUTTLE-SHOP, *subs.* (Rugby).—A pastry-cook's ; a TUCK-SHOP (*q.v.*).

GUV, *subs.* (common).—An abbreviation of GOVERNOR (*q.v.*).

GUY, *subs.* (colloquial).—1. A Fifth of November effigy ; whence (2) an ill-dressed person. As in the old street cry, 'Hollo, boys, there goes another GUY! (an abbreviation of Guy Fawkes)=a figure of fun).

ENGLISH SYNONYMS.—Caution ; Captain Queer-nabs ; chivey ; comic bird ; ragamuffin ; sight.

FRENCH SYNONYMS. *Un paquet* (popular), *une hallebarde* (popular = a clothes-prop ; *un nippe-mal* (popular) ; *une bécasse* (=a gaby) ; *un carnavale* (popular=a figure of fun).

1806. W. BURRELL, in C. K. Sharpe's *Correspondence* (1888), i., 277. A month ago there was neither shape nor make in use. . . . no GUY ever matched me.

1837. BARHAM, *Ingoldsby Legends.* 'The Nurse's Story.' Did you see her, in short, that mud-hovel within, With her knees to her nose, and her nose to her chin, Leering up with that queer, indescribable grin, You'd lift up your hands in amazement and cry, 'Well!—I never *did* see such a regular GUY!'

1858. G. ELIOT, *Janet's Repentance,* ch. vi. Ned Phipps . . . . whispered that he thought the Bishop was a GUY, and I certainly remember thinking that Mr. Prendergast looked much more dignified with his plain white surplice and black hair.

1871. *Morning Advertiser,* 26 Jan. There is no imperative reason why a constable should be a GUY.

3. (common).—A dark lantern. [Obviously a reminiscence of the Gunpowder Plot].

1811. *Lexicon Balatronicum.* GUY, s.v. Stow the GUY, conceal the lanthorn.

1859. MATSELL, *Vocabulum,* s.v.

4. (streets). — A jaunt ; an expedition.

1889. *Sporting Times,* 3 Aug., p. 5, c. 5. There *was* a gee, there *was* a buggy, but there *wasn't* a punctual Pitcher. So a cheerful GUY to Waterloo was the game.

Verb (common).—1. To quiz ; to chaff ; TO ROAST (*q.v.*) ; TO JOSH (*q.v.*).

1889. *Detroit Free Press,* 26 Jan. His advent here created much merriment, and the operators GUVED him loud enough for him to hear them.

2. (common).—To escape ; TO HEDGE (*q.v.*) ; to run away. Also TO DO A GUY (which also = to give a false name). For synonyms, *see* AMPUTATE and SKEDADDLE.

1879. J.W. HORSLEY, in *Macmillan's Mag.,* xl. 500. I planned with another boy to GUY (run away).

1887. *Fun,* 23 Mar., p. 125. 'Boat-race Day, as per usual,' said the clerk to the court, 'they'll all be DOING GUYS' (giving false names !).

1889. CLARKSON and RICHARDSON *Police,* p. 321. To run away. . . . DO A GUY.

1892. *Punch,* 24 Sept. ''Arry at Arrygate.' I just DID A GUY.

3. (American).—To spoil ; to muddle ; to disfigure or distort.

1591. *New York Herald,* 31 May, p. 12, c. 4. Finally, I would remind them that they are apt to GUY their cause by making 'guys' of themselves, and that the best way of making women a power in the land is by encouraging them to be womanly women.

4. (theatrical).—To damn ; to hiss ; TO SLATE (*q.v.*) OR GIVE THE BIRD (*q.v.*).

GUZZLE (or **GUTTLE**), *subs.* (vulgar). —1. An insatiable eater or drinker. For synonyms, *see* STODGER and LUSHINGTON respectively.

2. (vulgar).—A debauch.

1876. HINDLEY, *Adventures of Cheap Jack,* 58. Doing a GUZZLE with money he earned.

3. (common).—Drink.

1653. URQUHART, *Rabelais,* Bk. II., ch. i., *note.* It signifies rum-booze, as our gipsies call good-GUZZLE.

1690. B. E., *Dict. Cant. Crew,* s.v.

1698-1700. WARD, *London Spy,* part III., p. 47. A Pennyworth of burnt Bread soften'd in a Mug of Porter's GUZZLE.

c. 1795. WOLCOT [P. Pindar] *Peter's Pension,* in wks. (Dublin, 1795), vol. i., p. 484. Lo, for a little meat and GUZZLE, This sneaking cur, too, takes the muzzle.

Verb. (vulgar).—1. To drink greedily, or to excess.

1607. DEKKER, *Westward Ho,* v., 1. My master and Sir Gosling are GUZZLING ; they are dabbling together fathom-deep.

1693. DRYDEN, *Persius,* vi., 51. And, lavish of suspense, Quaffs, crams, and GUTTLES, in his own defence.

1698. FARQUHAR, *Love and a Bottle,* Act i. His education could reach no farther than to GUZZLE fat ale.

1727. GAY, *Beggar's Opera,* i., 3. *Tom Tipple,* a GUZZLING soaking sot, who is always too drunk to stand himself.

1748. T. DYCHE, *Dictionary* (5th ed.). GUZZLE (v.) to tipple, to fuddle, to drink much and greedily.

1782. WOLCOT [P. Pindar], *Lyric Odes,* Ode i. The poet might have GUTTLED till he split.

1849. THACKERAY, *Pendennis,* ch. lxi. Are you . . . to tell me that the aim of life is to GUTTLE three courses and dine off silver?

GUZZLE-GUTS, *subs.* (common).— A glutton ; a hard drinker.—*Lex. Bal.* (1811). See GUZZLE.

a. 1760. T. BROWN, *Works,* iii., 265 [ed. 1760]. Being an eternal GUZZLER of wine, his mouth smelt like a vir.tner's vault.

1841. DICKENS, *Barnaby Rudge,* ch. xiii. To be looked upon as a common pipe-smoker beer-bibber, spirit-GUZZLER, and toss-pot.

GUZZLING, *subs.* (vulgar).—Eating or drinking to excess ; also eating or drinking in a coarse unmannerly fashion.

1690. B. E., *Dict. Cant. Crew,* s.v.

1819. MOORE, *Tom Crib,* p. 28. What with snoozing, high-grubbing and GUZZLING like Chloe.

1882. F. ANSTEY, *Vice Versâ,* ch. xv. There shall be no pocketing at this table, sir. You will eat that pudding under my eye at once, and you will stay in and write out French verbs for two days. That will put an end to any more GUZZLING in the garden for a time, at least.

GUZZUM, *subs.* (American). — Chatter ; noise. For synonyms, *see* PATTER.

1888. *Detroit Free Press,* 22 Dec. 'Now, Jerry, if yer don't stop yer GUZZUM I'll skin yer alive !' she exclaimed as she stood in the door and flourished a skillet at him.

G.Y. ALL A G.Y., *adv. phr.* (North Country).—Crooked ; all on one side ; 'all of a hugh.'

GYBE, *subs.* (old).—A written paper.

1567. HARMAN, *Caveat* (1814), p. 65 A GYB, a writing

1608. DEKKER, *Belman of London,* in wks. (GROSART) III., 104. His office is to make counterfet licences, which are called GYBES.

1724. E. COLES, *Eng. Dict.* GYBE, any Writing or Pass.

1818. SCOTT, *Heart of Midlothian,* ch. xxv. He knows my GYBE [pass] as well as the jark [seal] of e'er a queer cuffin [justice of peace] in England.

Verb (old).—1. To whip ; to castigate. *E.g.,* GYBED at the cart's arse=whipped at the cart's tail.

1690. B. E., *Dict. Cant. Crew* GYBD, jerkt or whipt.

GYBING (also **GIBERY**), *subs.* (old : now recognised).—Jeering.

1690. B. E., *Dict. Cant. Crew,* s.v.

1785. GROSE, *Vulg. Tongue,* s.v.

GYGER. See JIGGER.

GYMNASIUM, *subs.* (venery).—The female *pudendum.* For synonyms, *see* MONOSYLLABLE.

GYP, *subs.* (Cambridge University). — 1. A college servant. At Oxford, a scout, at Dublin, a skip. (Etymology doubtful : according to *Sat. Rev.* an abbreviation of Gipsy Joe ; according to Cambridge undergraduates from the Greek γύψ (GUPS) = a vulture ; from the creature's rapacity.]

1794. *Gent. Mag.,* p. 1085. [A Cambridge college servant is called a JIP.]

1842. *Tait's Mag.,* Oct., 'Reminiscences of Coll. Life.' There is attached to colleges and halls a person more useful than ornamental, and better known than paid, whom Oxonians name GYP, from his supposed moral affinity to a vulture (γύψ). The same is in Dublin denominated a *Skip,* because of the activity which is an indispensable item in his qualifications.

1849. C. KINGSLEY, *Alton Locke,* ch. xii. I'll send you in luncheon as I go through the butteries ; then, perhaps, you'd like to come down and see the race. Ask the GYP to tell you the way.

1850. SMEDLEY, *Frank Fairlegh,* p. 254. Fellow you call the GYP wanted to make me believe you were out—thought I looked too like a governor to be let in, I suppose.

1882. F. ANSTEY, *Vice Versâ,* ch. v. Who should we see coming straight down on us but a Proctor with his bull-dogs (not dogs, you know, but the strongest GYPS in the college).

2. (American).—A thief. For synonyms, *see* THIEVES

GYPSIES OF SCIENCE, *subs. phr.* (literary.)—The British Association.

1846. *Times,* 5 Sept. On Thursday next, *the Gipsies of Science* (the British Association) will have pitched their tents at Southampton.

GYROTWISTIVE, *adj.* (American).— Full of evasions and tricks ; a 'portmanteau word.'

GYTE, *subs.* (common). — 1. A child ; in contempt. [A corruption of goat.]

2. (Scots').—A first year's pupil in the Edinburgh High School.

GYVEL, *subs.* (Scots' venery).—The female *pudendum.* For synonyms, *see* MONOSYLLABLE.

d. 1796. BURNS, *The Merry Muses,* 'Nine Inches for a Lady,' 33-4. Come louse and lug your battering ram, An' thrash him at my GYVEL.

HABERDASHER, *subs.* (old colloquial : now recognised). — 1. A dealer in small wares ; specifically (1) a hatter, and (2, humorously) a publican (*i.e.,* a seller of TAPE (*q.v.*). Now restricted to a retail draper.

1599. MINSHEU, *Dictionarie,* s.v.

1632. JONSON, *The Magnetic Lady,* 'Induction.' Poetaccios, poetasters, poetitos. . . . And all HABERDASHERS of small wit.

d. 1680. BUTLER, *Remains* (1759), ii., 107. He set up HABERDASHER of a small poetry.

1823. MONCRIEFF, *Tom and Jerry,* iii., 5. The HABERDASHER is the whistler, otherwise the spirit-merchant, Jerry—and tape the commodity he deals in.

HABERDASHER OF PRONOUNS, *subs. phr.* (common).—A schoolmaster. For synonyms, *see* BUMBRUSHER.

1690. B. E., *Cant. Crew,* s.v.

1725. *New Cant. Dict.,* s.v.

1785. GROSE, *Vulg. Tongue,* s.v.

HABIT, *subs.* (old University).—See quot.

1803. *Gradus ad Cantabrigiam.* HABIT. College Habit, College dress, called of old, Livery : the dress of the Master, Fellows, and Scholars.

HAB-NAB (or **HOB-NOB** (*q.v.*)), *adv.* (old).—1. At random ; promiscuously ; helter-skelter ; ding-dong.

1602. SHAKSPEARE, *Twelfth Night,* iii., 4. His incensement at this moment is so great that satisfaction can be none but by pangs of death and sepulchre. HOB-NOB is his word ; give't, or take't.

1664. BUTLER, *Hudibras,* ii., 3. Although set down HAB-NAB at random.

1690. B. E., *Cant. Crew,* s.v. HAB-NAB, at a Venture, Unsight, Unseen, Hit or Miss.

1725. *New Cant. Dict.,* s.v.

2. (old).—By hook or by crook ; by fair means or foul.

1581. LILLY, *Euphues,* 109. Philantus determined HABNAB to send his letters.

Verb (old).—To drink with ; giving health for health.

1836. HORACE SMITH, *The Tin Trumpet.* 'Address to a Mummy.' Perchance that very hand now pinioned flat Has HOB-AND-NOBBED with Pharaoh glass for glass.

HACK (or **HACKNEY**), *subs.* (old : now recognised).—1. A person or thing let out for promiscuous use : *e.g.,* a horse, a whore, a literary drudge. Whence (2) a coach that plies for hire ; (3) (stables') a horse for every-day use, as offered to one for a special purpose—hunting, racing, polo. (4) (Cambridge Univ.), *see* quot. 1803. Also HACKSTER.

1383. CHAUCER, *Canterbury Tales,* 16,027. His HAKENEY, which that was a pomele gris.

1540. LYNDSAY, *Satyre of the thri Estaits,* 3237. I may finde the Earle of Rothus best HACKNAY.

1582. HAKLUYT, *Voyages*, i., 400 There they use to put out their women to hire as we do here HAKNEY horses.

1594. SHAKSPEARE, *Love's Labour Lost*, iii., 1. The hobby-horse is but a colt, and your love perhaps a HACKNEY.

1594. NASHE, *Unf. Traveller*, 101 (Chiswick Press, 1890). Out whore, strumpet, sixpenny HACKSTER, away with her to prison!

1672. RAY, *Proverbs*. HACKNEY mistress, HACKNEY maid.

1678. BUTLER, *Hudibras*, pt. iii., c. 1. That is no more than every lover Does from his HACKNEY-LADY suffer.

1690. B. E., *Cant. Crew*, s.v. HACKS, or HACKNEYS, Hirelings. *Ibid*, HACKNEY HORSES. *Ibid*., HACKNEY SCRIBBLERS. *Ibid*., HACKNEY WHORES, Common Prostitutes.

1738. POPE, *Ep. to Sat*. Shall each spurgall'd HACKNEY of the day, Or each new pension'd sycophant, pretend To break my windows?

1754. FIELDING, *Jonathan Wild*, iv., 14. With wonderful alacrity he had ended almost in an instant, and conveyed himself into a place of safety in a HACKNEY-coach.

1785. GROSE, *Vulg. Tongue*, s.v. HACKNEY-WRITER, one who writes for attornies or booksellers.

1803. *Gradus ad Cantabrigiam*. HACKS. HACK Preachers; the common exhibitioners at St. Mary's, employed in the service of defaulters, and absentees.

1819. MOORE, *Tom Crib*. I first was hired to peg a HACK.

1823. MONCRIEFF, *Tom and Jerry*, i., 7. A rattler is a rumbler, otherwise a Jarvy! Better known, perhaps, by the name of a HACK.

1841. LEMAN REDE, *Sixteen String Jack*, ii., 3. I'll get a HACK, be off in a crack.

Verb (colloquial, football).—To kick shins. HACKING=the practice of kicking shins at football.

1857. G. A. LAWRENCE, *Guy Livingstone*, ch. i. I saw, too, more than one player limp out of his path disconsolately, trying vainly to dissemble the pain of a vicious HACK.

1869. SPENCER, *Study of Sociology*, ch. viii. p. 186 (9th ed.). And thus, perhaps, the 'education of a gentleman' may rightly include giving and receiving HACKING of the shins at foot-ball.

1872. *The Echo*, 3 Nov. Some of the modern foot ball players have the tips of their shoes tipped with iron, and others wear a kind of armour or iron plate under their knicker-bockers to avoid . . . what is called HACKING.

HACKLE, *subs*. (common).—Pluck; spirit; BOTTOM (*q.v.*). To SHOW HACKLE = to show fight. [Hackle=a long shining feather on a cock's neck.] Fr., *avoir du foie; n'avoir pas le flubart*, or *avoir du poil au ciel*.

HACKSLAVER, *verb*. (old).—To stammer; to splutter; to hesitate in speech.

HACKUM (or **CAPTAIN HACKUM**, or **HACKSTER**), *subs*. (old).—A bully; a bravo. For synonyms, *see* FURIOSO.

1657. *Lady Alimony*, 1, 3 (DODSLEY, *Old Plays*, 4th ed., 1875, xiv., p. 282). Vowing, like a desperate HAXTER that he has express command to seize upon all our properties.

1690. B. E., *Cant. Crew*, s.v. HACKAM, Fighting Fellow.

1725. *New Cant. Dict.*, s.v.

1785. GROSE, *Vulg. Tongue*, s.v. HACKUM, Captain Hackum, a bravo, a slasher.

1859. MATSELL, *Vocabulum*. HACKUM, a bravado, a slasher, 'Capt. Hackum,' a fellow who slashes with a bowie-knife.

HAD.—*See* HAVE.

HADDOCK, *subs*. (common).—1. A purse. HADDOCK OF BEANS= a purse of money. [Haddock= cod: O. Sw., *Rudde*; Ic., *Koddi* =a small bag. *Cf*., CODPIECE.] For synonyms, *see* POGE.

1598. FLORIO, *Worlde of Wordes*. *Melrusio*, the fish we call a HADOCK, or a cod. *Ibid*. *Metter la faua nel bacello*, to put the beane into the cod.

1834. H. AINSWORTH, *Rookwood*, bk. III., ch. xiii. 'What's here?' cried he, searching the attorney's pockets . . . 'a HADDOCK, stuffed with nothing, I'm thinking.'

2. *in. pl.* (Stock Exchange).—North of Scotland Ordinary Stock.

HADDUMS (or **HAD 'EM**).—*See* quots.

1690. B. E., *Cant. Crew*. The Spark has been at HADDUMS. He is Clapt, or Poxt.

1725. *New Cant. Dict.*, s.v.

1785. GROSE, *Vulg. Tongue*, s.v' He has been at HAD'EM and come home by Clapham, said of one who has caught the venereal disease.

HAG, *subs*. (old: now recognised).—1. A witch. Whence (2) an ugly old woman; a she-monster. Also (3) a nightmare. At Charterhouse, a female of any description; at Winchester, a matron. Hence, HAG-RIDDEN = troubled with nightmare. HAG-BORN = witch-born. HAG-SEED (Shakspeare, *Tempest*) = spawned of a witch. HAG-FACED = foul-featured. In another sense, HAGS =spots of firm ground in a moss or bog.

d. 1529. SKELTON, *Duke of Albany*, Lyke a Scottish HAG.

1606. *Wily Beguiled* (DODSLEY, *Old Plays*, 4th ed., 1875, ix., 277). Like to some hellish HAG or some damned fiend.

1606. SHAKSPEARE, *Macbeth*, iv., 1. How now, you secret, black, and midnight HAGS!

1627. DRAYTON, *The Moon-calf* (CHALMER'S *English Poets*, 1810, iv., 133). The filthy HAG abhoring of the light.

1632. JONSON, *Magnetic Lady*, v. 6. Out HAG!

1637. JONSON, *Sad Shepherd*, ii., 2. As if you knew the sport of witch-hunting, Or starting of a HAG.

1680. COTTON, *Poems*, etc., 'To Poet E.W.' Adulterate HAGS, fit for a common stew.

1690. B. E., *Cant. Crew*, s.v.

1748. THOMSON, *Castle of Indolence*, i., 73. Fierce fiends and HAGS of hell their only nurses were.

1773-83. HOOLE, *Orlando Furioso*, xliii., 998. But such a HAG to paradise conveyed, Had withered by her looks the blissful shade.

1815. SCOTT, *Guy Mannering*, xliii. Hatteraick himself, and the gypsy sailor, and that old HAG.

1892. HUME NISBET, *Bushranger's Sweetheart*, p. 89. Old women were there also, with hideous vice-stamped features, veritable HAGS all of them.

YOUR HAGSHIP! *phr*. (common).—In contempt (of women).

HAG-FINDER, *subs*. (old).—A witch finder.

1637 JONSON, *Sad Shepherd*, ii., 2. That I do promise, or I am no good HAG-FINDER.

HAGGED, *adj*. (old, now [as HAGGARD] recognised).—Ugly; gaunt; hag-like.

1690. B. E., *Cant. Crew*, s.v HAGGED, Lean, Witched, Half-starved.

1716-1771. GRAY, *A Long Story*. The ghostly prudes with HAGGED face.

HAGGISLAND, *subs*. (common).—Scotland.

HAGGLE, *verb*. (old, now recognised).—To bargain keenly; to stick at, or out for, trumpery points; to debate small issues.

1690. B. E., *Cant. Crew*, s.v.

1849-61. MACAULAY, *Hist. Eng.*, ch. xx. HAGGLING with the greedy, making up quarrels.

HAGGLER, *subs*. (old).—Formerly a travelling merchant; a pedlar: now (in London vegetable markets) a middleman. *Cf*., BUMMAREE.

1662. FULLER, *Worthies*; Dorsetshire. Horses, on which HAGLERS used to ride and carry their commodities.

1690. B. E., *Cant. Crew*, s.v. A HAGLER, one that buys of the Country Folks, and sells in the Market, and goes from Door to Door,

1697. VANBRUGH, *Æsop*, , 1. I se no HAGLER, gadswookers and he that says I am—'zbud, he lies!

1851-61. H. MAYHEW *Lond. Lab. and Lond. Poor*, vol. I., p. 83. A HAGGLER being, as I before explained, the middle-man.

HAIL. TO RAISE HAIL (or NED, or CAIN, or HELL), *verb. phr.* (American).—To make a disturbance; to kick up a row.

1888. *Portland Transcript*, 7 Mar. He is determined that they shall have a clear deed to one hundred and sixty acres of land when the question is settled, or he will RAISE HAIL.

TO BE HAIL FELLOW WELL MET, *verb. phr.* (colloquial).—To be on very easy terms: also AT HAIL-FELLOW.

1574-1656. *Hall's Satires*, III., i., p. 40. Now man, that erst HAILE-FELLOW was with beast, Woxe on to weene himselfe a god at least.

1665. *Homer à la Mode*. The cookes too, having done, were set At table HAY FELLOW WELL MET [Quoted by Nares].

1667-1745. SWIFT, *My Lady's Lamentation*. HAIL FELLOW, WELL MET, all dirty and wet; Find out, if you can, who's master, who's man.

1886. R. L. STEVENSON, *Kidnapped*, p. 108. And at first he sings small, and is HAIL-FELLOW-WELL-MET with Sheamus—that's James of the Glens, my chieftain's agent.

TO BE HAILED FOR THE LAST TIME, *verb. phr.* (nautical).—To die. For synonyms, *see* ALOFT.

1891. W. C. RUSSELL, *Ocean Tragedy*, p. 322. He's BEEN HAILED FOR THE LAST TIME.

HAIR, *subs*. (venery).—1. The female pubes. Whence (2) generic for the sex: *e.g*., AFTER HAIR= in quest of a woman; PLENTY OF HAIR=lots of girls; HAIR TO SELL=a woman with a price; HAIR-MONGER=a wencher; BIT OF HAIR = the sexual favour. For synonyms, *see* FLEECE.

TO GO AGAINST THE HAIR, *verb. phr.* (old colloquial).—To go against the grain, or contrary to nature. [From the texture of furs.]

1589. NASHE, *Martin's Months Minde* (Grosart), i., 188. For hee euer WENT AGAINST THE HAIRE.

1596. SHAKSPEARE, *Merry Wives*, ii., 3. If you should fight, you GO AGAINST THE HAIR of your professions.

1661. MIDDLETON, *Mayor of Queenborough*, C. P. xi., 122. Books in women's hands are as much AGAINST THE HAIR, methinks, as to see men wear stomachers, Or night-railes.

BOTH OF A HAIR, *adv. phr.* (colloquial).—Very much alike. Also, two of a trade, and two in a tale.

NOT WORTH A HAIR, *adv. phr.* (colloquial).—Utterly worthless. *Cf*., CENT, RAP, DUMP, etc.

TO A HAIR, *adv. phr.*—(colloquial).—Exactly; to a nicety. *Cf*., TO FIT TO A HAIR = to fit perfectly.

1697. VANBRUGH, *Æsop*, i., 1. Here was a young gentlewoman but just now pencilled me out TO A HAIR.

1738. SWIFT, *Polite Conversation*. *Miss*. Well I love a Lyar with all my Heart; and you FIT ME TO A HAIR.

1891. W. C. RUSSELL, *Ocean Tragedy*, p. 30. The fellow FITS my temper TO A HAIR.

TO SPLIT HAIRS, *verb. phr.* (colloquial).—To cavil about trifles; to quibble; to be over-nice in argument.

1693. CONGREVE, *Old Bachelor*, ii., 2. Now, I must speak; it will SPLIT A HAIR by the Lord Harry.

SUIT OF HAIR, *subs. phr.* (American).—A HEAD OF HAIR (*q.v.*).

TO RAISE (or LIFT) HAIR, *verb. phr.* (Amerian).—To scalp; hence, idiomatically, to defeat; to kill. TO KEEP ONE'S HAIR = to escape a danger.

1848. RUXTON, *Life in the FarWest*, p. 194. Kit Carson . . . had RAISED MORE HAIR from the red-skins than any two men in the Western country.

1891. GUNTER, *Miss Nobody*, p. 101. If you'll take the chances of KEEPING YOUR HAIR.

TO COMB ONE'S HAIR, *verb. phr.* (common).—To castigate; TO MONKEY (*q.v.*). *See* COMB ONE'S HAIR, *ante*.

TO HOLD (or KEEP) ONE'S HAIR (or WOOL) ON, *verb. phr.* (common).—To keep one's temper; to avoid excitement; to take easily. Also TO KEEP ONE'S SHIRT ON, or TO PULL DOWN ONE'S JACKET (or VEST). Fr., *être calme et inodore*.

1885. BRET HARTE, *A Ship of '49*, ch. vi. 'But what the devil——' interrupted the young man impetuously. 'KEEP YER HAIR ON!' remonstrated the old man with dark intelligence.

1892. MILLIKEN, *'Arry Ballads*, p. 78. Do KEEP YOUR 'AIR ON, dear pal.

1892. *Cassell's Sat. Jour.*, 5 Oct., p. 45, c. 1. 'Who make devil's row like that all night?' he asked. 'KEEP YOUR HAIR ON, Moses Trinko,' replied the reception fficer, cheerily.

A HAIR OF THE BLACK BEAR (or B'AR), *subs. phr.* (American).—A spice of the devil.

1848. RUXTON, *Life in the Far West*, . 6. Thar was old grit in him, too, and HAIR OF THE BLACK B'AR at that.

TO GET ONE'S HAIR CUT, *verb. phr.* (venery).—To visit a woman; TO SEE A SICK FRIEND (*q.v.*). For synonyms, *see* GREENS and RIDE.

1892. ANSTEY, *Model Music Hall*, 154. *Tommy*. What, Uncle, going? *The W. U.* (*with assumed jauntiness*). Just TO GET MY HAIR CUT.

TO MAKE ONE'S HAIR STAND ON END, *verb. phr.* (colloquial).—To astonish.

1697. VANBRUGH, *Provoked Wife*, iv., 4. It's well you are come: I'm so frightened, MY HAIR STANDS ON END.

1886. J. S. WINTER, *Army Society* ch. iii. If I were to tell you some incidents of my life since you and I last met, I should make your HAIR STAND ON END.

A HAIR OF THE DOG THAT BIT YOU, *subs. phr.* (common).—A 'pick-me-up' after a debauch. [Apparently a memory of the superstition, which was and still is common, that, being bitten by a dog, one cannot do better than pluck a handful of hair from him, and lay it on the wound. Also figuratively, *see* quot. 1888.]

1531. BOVILLI, *Prov. ii., xvi. siècle*, t. i., p. 192. Du poil de la beste qui te mordis, Ou de son sanc sera guéris.

1546. HEYWOOD, *Proverbs* [1874], 79 What how fellow, thou knave, I pray thee let me and my fellow have A HAIRE OF THE DOG THAT BIT US last night. And bitten were we bothe to the braine aright.

1614. JONSON, *Bartholomew Fayre*, I. 'Twas a hot night with some of us, last night, John: shall we pluck a HAIR OF THE SAME WOLF to-day, proctor John?

1738. SWIFT, *Polite Convers.*, Dial 2 *Lady Gur*. But, Sir John, your ale is terrible strong and heady . . . *Sir John* Why, indeed, it is apt to fox one; but our way is to take a HAIR OF THE SAME DOG next morning.

1841. DICKENS, *B. Rudge*, ch. lii. Put a good face upon it, and drink again Another HAIR OF THE DOG THAT BIT YOU, captain!

1888. *Detroit Free Press*. 'Talk of the Day,' 3 Nov. *Travis*.—'Hello, De Smith! You're looking better thant expected. I understood that you were completely crushed by that love affair. How did you recover?' *De Smith*—'HAIR OF THE DOG THAT BIT ME. Fell in love with another girl.

HAIR-BUTCHER, *subs.* (American).—A barber. For synonyms, *see* NOB-THATCHER.

1888. *Puck's Library*, May, p. 15. 'Oi 'm wullin' thot bloomin' HAIR-BUTCHER shud have a fit, av he wants.

HAIR-COURT, *subs, phr.* (venery).—The female *pudendum*. For synonyms, *see* MONOSYLLABLE. TO TAKE A TURN IN HAIR-COURT = to copulate.

HAIR-DIVIDER (or **-SPLITTER**), *subs.* (venery).—The *penis*. For synonyms, *see* CREAMSTICK and PRICK. Also BEARD-SPLITTER.

1811. *Lexicon Balatronicum*, s.v. HAIR-SPLITTER, a man's yard.

HAIR-PIN, *subs.* (American).—An individual, male or female: *e.g.*, THAT'S THE SORT OF HAIR-PIN I AM = that's my style.

1888. *Detroit Free Press*, 6 Oct. 'That's the kind of HAIRPINS we are,' said the enthusiastic swain.

HAIRY, *adj.* (Oxford University).—1. Difficult.

d. 1861. ARTHUR CLOUGH, *Long Vacation Pastoral.* Three weeks hence we return to the shop and the wash-hand-stand-bason, Three weeks hence unbury Thicksides and HAIRY Aldrich.

1864. *The Press*, 12 Nov. HAIRY for difficult is a characteristic epithet.

2. (colloquial). — Splendid; famous; conspicuous; uncommon.

1892. RUDYARD KIPLING, *Barrack Room Ballads.* 'The Sons of the Widow.' Did you hear of the Widow of Windsor with a HAIRY gold crown on her head?

3. (venery).—Desirable; full of sex; FUCKABLE (*q.v.*). [Said only of women: *e.g.*, HAIRY BIT = an amorous and taking wench.] *See* HAIR.

TO FEEL HAIRY, *verb. phr.* (venery).—To be inclined for coition; to have a MUST (*q.v*).

HAIRYFORDSHIRE, *subs.* (venery).—The female *pudendum*. TO GO TO HAIRYFORDSHIRE = to copulate. For synonyms, *see* MONOSYLLABLE.

HAIRY-ORACLE (or **-RING**), *subs.* (venery).—The female *pudendum* WORKING THE HAIRY-ORACLE = wenching. For synonyms, *see* MONOSYLLABLE.

HALBERT. TO GET THE HALBERT, *verb. phr.* (old military).—To rise to sergeant's rank. [The weapon was carried by sergeants of foot.] TO BE BROUGHT TO THE HALBERTS = to be flogged; TO CARRY THE HALBERT IN ONE'S FACE = to show that one rose from the ranks (of officers in commission).

1785. GROSE, *Vulg. Tongue*, s.v.

HALF. IT'S HALF PAST KISSING TIME AND TIME TO KISS AGAIN. *phr.* (common).—The retort impudent (to females) when asked the time. A snatch from a ballad. [In SWIFT (*Polite Con versation*) = an hour pas hanging time.]

HALF-A-CRACK (or **JIFFY**, or **TICK**).—Half a second.

HALF-AND-HALF, *subs.* (colloquial).—Equal quantities of ale and porter; *Cf.*, FOUR-HALF and DRINKS.

1824. REYNOLDS, *Peter Corcoran*, 41. Over my gentle HALF-AND-HALF.

1835. DICKENS, *Sketches by Boz*, p. 111. We were never tired of wondering how the hackney-coachmen on the opposite stand could . . . drink pots of HALF-AND-HALF so near the last drop.

1841. ALBERT SMITH (in *Punch*). 'The Physiology of the London Medical Student.' HALF-AND-HALF . . . is . . . ale and porter, the proportion of the porter increasing in an inverse ratio to the respectability of the public house you get it from.

1854. MARTIN and AYTOUN, *Bon Gaultier Ballads.* 'My Wife's Cousin.' HALF-AND-HALF goes down before him, Gurgling from the pewter-pot; And he moves a counter motion For a glass of something hot.

1872. *Fun*, July. 'The Right Tap. If the lever, meaning a plumper, were labelled 'stout,' and those recording a split vote HALF AND HALF, the illusion would be complete.

Adj. (common).—Half-drunk; HALF-ON (*q.v.*). For synonyms, *see* DRINKS and SCREWED.

1848. DUNCOMBE, *Sinks of London.* HALF AND HALF, half seas over, tipsy.

HALF-AND-HALF-COVES (or MEN, BOYS, etc.), *subs.* (old).—Cheap or linsey-woolsey dandies; half-BUCKS (*q.v.*) and half-TIGERS (*q.v.*).

1823. MONCRIEFF, *Tom and Jerry*, i., 7. *Jerry.* The HALF-AND-HALF COVES are somewhat different from the swaddies, and gay tyke boys, at the dog pit—Eh, Tom?

HALF-AN-EYE. TO SEE WITH HALF AN EYE, *verb. phr.* (colloquial).—To discern readily; to be quick at conclusions.

HALF-BAKED (or **SOFT-BAKED**), *adj.* (common).—Halfwitted; cracked; SOFT (*q.v.*); DOUGHY (*q.v.*); also HALF-ROCKED (*q.v.*). For synonyms, *see* APARTMENTS and TILE LOOSE. Fr., *n'avoir pas la tête bien cuite.*

1825. SCOTT, *St. Ronan's Well*, ii., 221. He must scheme forsooth, this HALF-BAKED Scotch cake! He must hold off and on, and be cautious, and wait the result, and try conclusions with me, this lump of natural dough!

1857. C. KINGSLEY, *Two Years Ago*, ch. iv. 'A sort of HALF-BAKED body,' said Kate.

1886. W. BESANT, *Children of Gibeon*, Bk. II., ch. xiv. A daughter of seventeen not quite right in her head—HALF-BAKED, to use the popular and feeling expression.

1890. *Answers*, Xmas No., p. 19, c. 3. 'You needn't be so crusty,' said Todkins to his better half. 'Better be a little crusty than not HALF-BAKED,' was the reply of his amiable spouse.

1892. *Pall Mall Gaz.*, 1 Nov., p. 2, c. 3. Mr. Vane Tempest as serenest of HALF-BAKED cynics, and Mr. H. Vincent as most credulous of bibulous optimists.

HALF-BREED, *subs.* (American political).—A nick-name applied to certain New York Republicans, who wavered in their allegiance during an election to the Senate in 1881.—NORTON.

HALF-COCKED, *adv.* (common).—Half-drunk. For synonyms, *see* DRINKS and SCREWED.

1887. H. SMART, *Saddle and Sabre*, ch. xvii. 'Black Bill,' as he was called by his brother jockeys, was very often HALF-COCKED when he got up to ride . . . The man could ride as well half-drunk as sober.

TO GO OFF AT HALF-COCK (or HALF-COCKED), *verb. phr.* 1. (sporting).—To fail through hasty and ill considered endeavours; and 2. (venery) = to ejaculate before completing erection.

1848. LOWELL, *Biglow Papers* [Wk. 1891], p. 231. Now don't GO OFF HALF-COCK: folks never gains By usin' peppersarse instid o' brains.

HALF-CRACKED, *adv.* (common).—Lacking in intelligence. *See* APARTMENTS and TILE LOOSE.

1887. W. P. FRITH, *Autobiog.*, i., 129. Who was what is vulgarly called HALF-CRACKED.

HALF-CROWN WORD, *subs. phr.* (common).—1. A difficult or uncommon vocable; a JAW-BREAKER (*q.v.*) or crack-jaw. Also (tailors') = a SLEEVEBOARD (*q.v.*).

HALF-CROWNER, *subs.* (booksellers').—A publication costing 2*s.* 6*d.*

HALF-CUT, *adv.* (common).—Half-drunk. For synonyms, *see* DRINKS and SCREWED.

HALF-FLY FLAT, *subs. phr.* (thieves').—A thief's jackal; a man (or woman) hired to do rough or dirty work.

HALF-GROWN SHAD, *subs. phr.* (American).—A dolt. For synonyms, *see* BUFFLE and CABBAGE-HEAD.

1838. NEAL, *Charcoal Sketches.* No more interlect than a HALF-GROWN SHAD.

HALF LAUGH AND PURSER'S GRIN, *subs. phr.* (nautical).—A sneer; a half-and-half meaning.—CLARK RUSSELL.

HALFLINGS, *adj.* (Scots').—Betwixt and between. [Usually said of a boy or girl just leaving childhood.]

1818. SCOTT, *Heart of Midlothian*, xi. In my youth, nay, when I was a HAFFLINS callant.

HALF-MAN, *subs.* (nautical). — A landsman rated as A.B.

HALF-MARROW, *subs.* (old Scots').—1. A faithless spouse; also a parcel husband or wife.

1600-61. RUTHERFORD, *Letters*, i., 123. Plead with your harlot-mother, who hath been a treacherous HALF-MARROW to her husband Jesus.

2. (nautical).—An incompetent seaman.

HALF-MOON, *subs.* (old). — 1. A wig; and (2) the female *pudendum*. For synonyms, *see* PERIWINKLE and MONOSYLLABLE.

1611. LODOWICK BARRY, *Ram Alley* (DODSLEY, *Old Plays*, vii., 326, ed. 1875). Is not her HALF-MOON mine?

HALF-MOURNING, *subs.* (common).—A black eye. FULL-MOURNING = two black eyes or DEEP GRIEF.

HALF-NAB (or **NAP**), *adv.* (old).—*See* quot.

1791. BAMPFYLDE-MOORE CAREW, *Life.* HALF-NAB—at a venture, unsight unseen, hit or miss.

HALF-ON, *adj.* (colloquial).—Half-drunk.

HALF-ROCKED, *adv.* (common).—Half-witted; silly. [From a West Country saying that all idiots are nursed bottom upwards.] *See* APARTMENTS and TILE LOOSE.

HALF-SAVED, *adv.* (common).—Weak-minded; shallow-brained. *See* APARTMENTS and TILE LOOSE.

1834. SOUTHEY, *The Doctor*, ch. x. William Dove's was not a case of fatuity. Though all was not there, there was a great deal. He was what is called HALF-SAVED.

1874. M. COLLINS, *Frances*, ch. xlii. This groom was what they call in the west country HALF-SAVED.

HALF-SCREWED, *adj.* (common).—More or less in liquor. *See* DRINKS and SCREWED.

1839. LEVER, *Harry Lorrequer*, ch. ii. He was, in Kilrush phrase, HALF-SCREWED, thereby meaning more than half tipsy.

HALF-SEAS OVER, *adv. phr.* (colloquial).—Loosely applied to various degrees of inebriety. Formerly = half way on one's course, or towards attainment. For synonyms, *see* SCREWED.

[In its specific sense Gifford says, "a corruption of the Dutch *op-zee zober*, 'over-sea beer,' a strong heady beverage intoduced into Holland from England." 'Up-zee Freese' is Friezeland beer. The German *zauber* means 'strong beer' and 'bewitchment.' Thus (1610) in JONSON, *Alchemist*, iv., 2. 'I do not like the dulness of your eye, It hath a heavy cast, 'tis UPSEE DUTCH.' Other nautical terms = drunk are WATER-LOGGED; SPRUNG; SLEWED; WITH ONE'S JIB WELL BOWSED; THREE SHEETS IN THE WIND; CHANNELS UNDER, but *see* DRINKS and SCREWED.]

1631-1701. DRYDEN. I am HALF-SEAS OVER to death.

1690. B. E., *Cant. Crew*, s.v. HALF-SEAS OVER, almost Drunk.

1697. VANBRUGH, *Relapse*, iii., 3. Good; that's thinking HALF-SEAS OVER. One tide more brings us into port.

1714. *Spectator*, No. 616. The whole magistracy was pretty well disguised before I gave them the slip. Our friend the alderman was HALF-SEAS OVER before the bonfire was out.

1738. SWIFT, *Pol. Convers.*, Dial 1. You must own you had a drop in your eye; when I left you, you were HALF SEAS OVER.

1751. SMOLLETT, *Peregrine Pickle*, ch. ix. Who, by this time, had entered into all the jollity of his new friends, and was indeed more than HALF-SEAS-OVER.

1785. GROSE, *Vulg. Tongue*, s.v.

1829. J. B. BUCKSTONE, *Billy Taylor.* The public-houses will not close till morn, And wine and spirituous liquors are so cheap, That we can all get nicely HALF SEAS OVER, And see no sea at all.

1839. AINSWORTH, *Jack Sheppard* [1889], p. 40. Mr. Smith, now being more than HALF-SEAS OVER, became very uproarious.

1849. THACKERAY, *Pendennis*, ch. xxx. It's pay-day with the General . . . and he's a precious deal more than HALF-SEAS OVER.

1866. G. ELIOT, *Felix Holt*, ch. xxviii. There's truth in wine, and there may be some in gin and muddy beer. . . . I've got plenty of truth in my time out of men who were HALF-SEAS-OVER, but never any that was worth a sixpence to me.

1890. *Globe*, 16 Apr., p. 2, c. 1. The familiar phrase HALF-SEAS OVER, for example, is wanting, and for this we appear to be indebted to the Dutch.

1892. *The Cosmopolitan*, Oct., p. 724. The fellow HALF-SEAS-OVER every-one excuses.

HALF-SLEWED, *adj.* (common).—Parcel drunk. For synonyms, *see* SCREWED.

HALF-SNACKS (or **HALF-SNAGS**), *adv. phr.* (colloquial). — Half-shares. *See* quots.

1683. EARL OF DORSET, *A Faithful Catalogue.* She mounts the price and goes HALF SNACK herself.

1887. *Walford's Antiquarian*, p. 252. HALF-SNAGS is a corrupted form of HALF SNACKS, *i.e.*, half shares. If one of a party of arabs finds any article it becomes his entire property unless his fellows say HALF-SNAGS, or 'Quarter-bits,' or 'Some for your neighbours.'

HALF-'UN, *subs.* (common).—Half-a glass of spirits and water; HALF-A-GO (*q.v.*).

HALF-WIDOW, *subs.* (American).—A woman with a lazy and thriftless husband.

[For Half in combination, *see* also BEAN: BORDE; BULL; CASE: CENTURY; COUTER; DOLLAR; GEORGE; GO; GRUNTER; HOG: JACK; JAMES; NED; OUNCE; QUID; SKIV; STRETCH; TUSHEROON; WHEEL.

HALIFAX. GO TO HALIFAX. *verb. phr.* (American).—Be off! GO TO HELL (*q.v.*). The full text is GO TO HELL, HULL, or HALIFAX. *Cf.*, BATH, BLAZES, HULL, PUTNEY, etc.

1599. NASHE, *Lenten Stuffe* (Grosart, 1883-84, p. 284). If frier *Pendela* and his fellowes, had any thing to say to him, in his admiral court of the sea, let them seek him, and neither in HULL, HELL, nor HALIFAX.

1875. *Notes and Queries*, 5 S., iv., p. 66. GO TO HALIFAX. This expression is sometimes used in the United States as a mild substitute for a direction to go to a place not to be named to ears polite.

HALL, *subs.* (fishmongers'). — 1. Specifically THE HALL = Leadenhall Market. *Cf.*, GARDEN, LANE, etc.

2. (Oxford Univ.).—Dinner. [Which is taken in College HALL.] To HALL = to dine.

GO AND HIRE A HALL. *phr.* (American). — A retort upon loquacious bores.

HALL BY THE SEA, *subs. phr.* (medical students').—The Examination Hall of the conjoined Board of the Royal Colleges of Physicians and Surgeons. [Situate on the Embankment at the foot of Waterloo Bridge.]

HALL OF DELIGHT, *subs. phr.* (Australian).—A music hall.

1892. HUME NISBET, *Bushranger's Sweetheart*, p. 53. I thought you coons would find your way to this HALL OF DELIGHT.

HALLAN - SHAKER (or **HALLENSHAKER**), *subs.* (old).—A vagabond or sturdy beggar. For synonyms, *see* CADGER and MUMPER.

c. 1503-4. DUNBAR, *A General Satyre* wks. (*ed.* DAVID LAING, 1834), ii., 26. Sic knavis and crakkeris to play at cartis and dyce, Sic HALLAND-SCHAKKARIS.

c. 1600. MONTGOMERIE, *Poems* (Scottish Text Soc., 1885-7), Polwart and Montgomerie's Flyting, p. 85. HALLAND-SHAKER, draught-raiker, bannock-baiker, ale-beshitten.

(?) 1642. *Old Ballad.* 'Maggie Lauder. Right scornfully she answered him, Begone, you HALLAN-SHAKER.

1724. *Journal from London*, p. 4. Had seen me than staakin about like a HALLEN-SHAKER, You wou'd hae taen me for a water-wraith.

1816. SCOTT, *Antiquary*, ch. iv. I, and a wheen HALLENSHAKERS like mysel'.

HALLIBALLO.—*See* HULLIBALLO.

HALLION (or **HALLYON**), *subs.* (old). —1. A rogue; a clod; a gentleman's servant out of livery; also (2) a shrew. *Cf.*, HELL-CAT.

1817. SCOTT, *Rob Roy*, ch. iv. This is a decentish HALLION.

1847. PORTER, *Big Bear*, etc., p. 69. The scoundrels! the oudacious little HELLIONS!

HALLOO. TO HALLOO WITH THE UNDER DOG, *verb. phr.* (American).—To take the losing side.

HALO. TO WORK THE HALO RACKET, *verb. phr.* (common).—To grumble; to be dissatisfied. [From the story of the Saint in Heaven who got dissatisfied with his nimbus.]

HALTERSACK, *subs.* (old). — A gallows-bird; a general term of reproach and contempt.

1598. FLORIO, *Worlde of Wordes*, *Bazaro*, a shifter, a conicatcher . . . a HALTERSACKE.

1619. BEAUMONT and FLETCHER, *King and no King*, ii., 2. Away, you HALTERSACK, you.

HALVES, *subs.* (Winchester College). —(pro. Hāves.) Half-Wellington boots, which were strictly *non licet* (obs.).—*Notions.*

TO GO (or CRY) HALVES, *verb. phr.* (colloquial).—To take (or claim) a half share or chance. In America, AT THE HALVES.

1831. NEAL, *Down Easters*, ch. iv., p. 45. 'Lives by preachin' AT THE HALVES a sabba'-days.' 'Preaching AT THE HALVES —how's that?' 'Why don't you know? in partnership for what's taken arter the sarmon's over.'

1851-61. MAYHEW, *Lond. Lab. and Lond. Poor*, III., 122. He'll then again ask if anybody will GO HIM HALVES.

HAM, *subs.* (old).—1. (*in. pl.*) Trousers: also HAM-CASES. For synonyms, *see* KICKS.

1725. *New Cant. Dict.*, s.v. HAMS, Breeches.

1785. GROSE, *Vulg. Tongue*, s.v.

1791. BAMPFYLDE-MOORE CAREW, *Life.* HAMS—breeches.

1859. MATSELL, *Vocabulum*, s.v. HAMS. Pants.

2. (American).—A LOAFER (*q.v.*). Also HAM-FATTER. [The *American Slang Dict.* says 'A tenth-rate actor or variety performer.]

1888. *Missouri Republican*, 27 Mar. Connelly . . . is a good fighter, but will allow the veriest HAM to whip him, if there is any money to be made by it.

1888. *New York Herald*, 29 July. The . . . more prosperous professional brother of the HAMFATTER.

NO HAM AND ALL HOMINY, *phr.* (American).—Of indifferent quality; 'no great shakes'; 'all work and no play'; 'much cry and little wool.'

HAMLET, *subs.* (old and American). *See* quots.

1690. B. E., *Cant. Crew*, s.v. HAMLET . . . a High Constable.

1725. *New Cant. Dict.* s.v. HAMLET, a High-Constable.

1785. GROSE, *Vulg. Tongue*, s.v. HAMLET, a high constable (cant).

1791. BAMPFYLDE-MOORE CAREW. HAMLET, a high-constable.

1859. MATSELL, *Vocabulum*, s.v. HAMLET. A captain of police.

HAM-MATCH, *subs.* (common).—A stand-up luncheon.

1890. *Daily Telegraph*, 4 Feb. At one o'clock they relieve their exhausted frames by taking perpendicular refreshment—vulgarly termed a HAM MATCH—at some City luncheon bar.

HAMMER, *subs.* (pugilistic).—1. A hard-hitter: especially with the right hand, like the illustrious HAMMER Lane. Also HAMMERER and HAMMER-MAN.

1819. MOORE, *Tom Crib*, p. 33. A letter written on the occasion by Henry Harmer, the HAMMERER.

1823. BEE, *Dict. of the Turf*, 93. When a man hits very hard, chiefly with a favorite hand, his blows are said to fall like those of a sledge-HAMMER. Such boxers are HAMMERING fighters, that do not defend their own vitals, cannot make sure of a blow, and are termed HAMMERERS and HAMMERMEN.

2. (common).—An unblushing lie. For synonyms, *see* WHOPPER.

Verb (pugilistic).—1. To beat; to PUNISH (*q.v.*).

1887. T. E. BROWN, *The Doctor*, p. 159. And bedad I did, and before herself too, And HAMMERED him well.

1891. GUNTER, *Miss Nobody*, ch. ii. 'HAMMER him? What with?—a club?' 'No, with my fists.'

2. (American)—To bate; to drive down (prices, etc.).

1865. *Harper's Magazine*, p. 619. The chronic bears were amusing themselves by HAMMERING, *i.e.*, pressing down the price of Hudsons.

3. (Stock Exchange). — To declare one a defaulter.

1885. *Fortnightly Review*, xxxviii., p. 578. A 'defaulter' has been declared or HAMMERED, as it is technically termed.

1888. *Echo*, 28 Dec. If any unfortunate member be HAMMERED to-day or to-morrow it will in all probability be a bear.

1890. *Daily Telegraph*, 1 Nov. This being the third day after the general settlement, a defaulter who had been unable to provide cash was HAMMERED, and private arrangements are reported in other quarters without resort to this extreme measure.

1891. *Pall Mall Gazette*, 25 July, p. 1, c. 3. But what is an 'outside broker?' some (possibly lady) reader may ask. Well, he may be, and often is, a regular, who has been HAMMERED for failing to meet his 'differences.'

1891. *Tit Bits*, 15 Aug. I need not go into the circumstances which led to my being expelled from that honourable body, or HAMMERED as it is familiarly called, owing to the taps with a hammer which the head porter gives before he officially proclaims the name of a defaulter.

DOWN AS A HAMMER, *adv. phr.* (common).—1. Wide-awake; KNOWING (*q.v.*); FLY (*q.v.*).

1819. MOORE, *Tom Crib*, p. 45. To be down to anything is pretty much the same as being up to it, and DOWN AS A HAMMER is, of course, the *intensivum* of the phrase.

2. (colloquial). — Instant; peremptory; merciless. *Cf.*, LIKE A THOUSAND OF BRICKS. Also TO BE DOWN ON . . . LIKE A HAMMER.

AT (or UNDER) THE HAMMER, *adv. phr.* (auctioneers'). — For sale at auction.

THAT'S THE HAMMER, *verb. phr.* (colloquial).—An expression of approval or assent.

TO BE HAMMERS TO ONE, *verb. phr.* (colloquial.—To know what one means.

TO HAMMER OUT (or INTO), *verb. phr.* (colloquial).—To be at pains to deceive; to reiterate; to force to hear.

1596. BEN JONSON, *Every Man in his Humour*, iii., 3. Now am I, for some five and fifty reasons, HAMMERING, HAMMERING revenge.

1719. DURFEY, *Pills*, etc., iii., 23. If any Scholar be in doubt, And cannot well bring this matter about; The Blacksmith can HAMMER IT OUT.

1888. J. MCCARTHY and MRS. CAMPBELL-PRAED, *The Ladies' Gallery*, ch. i. I think the chaps that are always HAMMERING on about repentance and atonement and forgiveness of sin have got hold of the wrong end.

HAMMER-AND-TONGS, *adv. phr.* (common). — Very violently; ding-dong.

1781. G. PARKER, *View of Society*, II., 108. His master and mistress were at it HAMMER AND TONGS.

1833. MARRYAT, *Peter Simple*, ch. xxxv. Our ships were soon hard at it, HAMMER AND TONGS.

1837. MARRYAT, *Snarleyow.* Ods bobs! HAMMER AND TONGS! long as I've been to sea.

1861. H. KINGSLEY, *Ravenshoe*, ch. lx. Mr. Malone fell upon them HAMMER AND TONGS.

1862. M. E. BRADDON, *Lady Audley's Secret*, ch. iv. 'I always said the old buffer would marry,' he muttered, after about half an hour's reverie. 'Alicia and my lady, the stepmother, will go at it HAMMER AND TONGS.

1884. JAS. PAYN, *Talk of the Town*, ch. xx. Both parties went at it HAMMER AND TONGS, and hit one another anywhere and with anything.

HAMMER-HEADED, *adj.* (common). 1. Oafish; stupid.

1600. NASHE, *Summers Last Will* (Grosart), vi., 169. A number of rude Vulcans, vnweldy speakers, HAMMER-HEADED clownes.

2. (colloquial). — Hammer-shaped: *i.e.*, long and narrow in the head.

1865. DICKENS, *Our Mutual Friend* i., 9. Mr. Boffin's equipage consisted of a long HAMMER - HEADED old horse, formerly used in the business . . . a driver being added in the person of a long HAMMER-HEADED young man.

HAMMERING, *subs.* (pugilistic and colloquial). — 1. A beating; excessive PUNISHMENT (*q.v.*).

2. (printers').—Over-charging time-work (as 'corrections').

HAMMERING-TRADE, *subs.* (pugilistic).—Pugilism.

1819. MOORE, *Tom Crib*, p. 49. The other, vast, gigantic, as if made, express, by Nature for the HAMMERING trade.

HAMMERSMITH. TO GO TO HAMMERSMITH, *verb. phr.* (common).—To get a sound drubbing.

HAMPERED, *adj.* (old: now recognised).—Let or hindered; perplexed; entangled. [From OLD. ENG., hamper = a fetter: *see* quot. 1613].

1613. BROWNE, *Britannia's Pastorals*, bk. i., s. 7. Shackles, shacklockes, HAMPERS, gives and chaines.

1690. B. E., *Cant. Crew*, s.v.

1725. *New Cant. Dict.*, s.v.

HAMPSTEAD DONKEY, *subs. phr.* (common).—*See* quot. For synonyms, *see* CHATES.

c. 1870. *Daily Paper.* The witness testified to the filthy state of the linen which she wore, and also the state of the sheets. Was told not to get into bed until she had looked for the HAMPSTEAD DONKEYS. 'Did you know what that meant?'—'No sir, not until I looked on the pillow and saw three' (loud laughter). 'Do you mean lice?'—'Yes, sir, I do.'

HAMPSTEAD - HEATH, *subs. phr.* (rhyming). — The teeth. For synonyms, *see* GRINDERS.

1887. *Referee*, 7 Nov., p. 7, c. 3. She'd a Grecian 'I suppose,' And of HAMPSTEAD HEATH two rows, In her 'Sunny South' that glistened Like two pretty strings of pearls.

HAMPSTEAD-HEATH SAILOR, *subs. phr.* (common).—A LANDLUBBER (*q.v.*); a FRESHWATER SAILOR (*q.v.*). Fr., *un marin d'eau douce* or *un amiral Suisse* (=a Swiss admiral: Switzerland having no seaboard).

HANCED, *adj.* (old).—In liquor. [From HANCE = 'to elevate.'] For synonyms, *see* DRINKS and SCREWED.

1630. TAYLOR, *Works.* I doe finde my selfe sufficiently HANCED, and that henceforth I shall acknowledge it; and that whensoever I shall offer to bee HANCED again, I shall arme my selfe with the craft of a fox, the manners of a hogge, the wisdom of an asse, mixt with the civility of a beare.

HAND, *subs.* (colloquial).—Properly a seaman; now a labourer, a workman, an agent.

1658. PHILLIPS, *New World of Words*, s.v. HAND . . . . a Word us'd among Mariners . . . . when Men are wanted to do any Labour they usually Call for more HANDS.

1632-1704. LOCKE, *Wks.* A dictionary containing a natural history requires too many HANDS, as well as too much time.

1711. *Spectator*, No. 232. The reduction of the prices of our manufactures by the addition of so many new HANDS, would be no inconvenience to any man.

1754. FIELDING, *Jonathan Wild*, i., 14. The mercantile part of the world, therefore, wisely use the term 'employing HANDS,' and esteem each other as they employ more or fewer.

1811. *Lexicon Balatronicum*, s.v. We lost a HAND, we lost a sailor.

1871. *Chambers' Miscellany*, No. 113, p. 3. He was admitted as a HAND in an establishment already numbering three hundred active workers.

1892. MILLIKEN, *'Arry Ballads*, p. 70. The HANDS has all bloomin' well struck.

1892. *National Observer*, 22 Oct., vol. viii., p. 571. The dispute in the South-East Lancashire cotton trade is like to result in the stoppage of fourteen or fifteen million spindles which will take employment from sixty thousand HANDS, a fifth of them women and children.

1893. *Fortnightly Review*, Jan., p. 62. The wages paid to the operatives in our woollen industry are, to a marked extent, lower than those received by the HANDS employed in our cotton mills.

2. (coachmen's). — *See* quot.

1856. WHYTE MELVILLE, *Kate Coventry*, ch. xv. Lady Horsingham was tolerably courageous, but totally destitute of what is termed HAND, a quality as necessary in driving as in riding, particularly with fractious or high-spirited horses.

A GOOD (or COOL, NEAT, OLD, FINE, etc.) HAND, *subs. phr.* (colloquial).—An expert.

1748. T. DYCHE, *Dictionary* (5th ed.), s.v. HAND (v.). 'He is a good HAND,' spoke of one that is an artist in some particular mechanical art or trade, etc.

1773. GOLDSMITH, *She Stoops to Conquer*, iii., 1. When I was in my best story of the Duke of Marlborough and Prince Eugene, he asked if I had not a GOOD HAND at making punch.

1854. WHYTE MELVILLE, *General Bounce*, xii. A quaint boy at Eton, COOL HAND at Oxford, a deep card in the regiment, man or woman never yet had the best of 'Uppy.'

1877. *Five Years' Penal Servitude*, i., p. 33. The new man, the GREEN HAND, takes little or no heed of the entrance of the officers. . . . Not so the OLD HAND.

1886. R. L. STEVENSON, *Kidnapped*, p. 195. Ye're a GRAND HAND at the sleeping!

1892. W. E. GLADSTONE, *Times* 'Report.' . . . . This OLD PARLIAMENTARY HAND.

1892. HENLEY and STEVENSON, *Deacon Brodie*, i., 7, p. 18. You always was a neat HAND with the bones.

A HAND LIKE A FOOT, *phr.* (common).—A large, coarse hand. Also a vulgar or uneducated handwriting.

1738. SWIFT, *Polite Conversation*, i. *Col.* Whoe'er writ it with A HAND LIKE A FOOT.

A HAND LIKE A FIST, *phr.* (gamesters'). — A hand full of trumps. Also (in derision) a hand there's no playing.

TO TAKE A HAND WITH THE OUTSIDE MUSIC, *verb. phr.* (American).—*See* quot.

1892. J. L. SULLIVAN, *A 19th Century Gladiator*, iii. After thirty-seven rounds in fifty-five minutes, the umpires and seconds got into a fight, and Sullivan felt fresh enough TO TAKE A HAND IN THE OUTSIDE MUSIC.

TO GET A HAND ON, *verb. phr.* (tailors').—To suspect; to be distrustful.

TO GET ONE'S HAND IN, *verb. phr.* (colloquial).—To practise with a view to proficiency.

TO GET ONE'S HAND ON IT, *verb. phr.* (venery).—To grope a woman.

TO BEAR A HAND, *verb. phr.* (old).—*See* quot.

1811. *Lexicon Balatronicum*, s.v. BEAR A HAND, make haste.

TO BRING UP BY HAND, *verb. phr.* (venery).—To procure erection manually.

TO BRING DOWN (OR OFF) BY HAND, *verb. phr.* (venery).—To masturbate. For synonyms, *see* FRIG.

TO STAND ONE'S HAND, *verb. phr.* (Australian). — To TREAT (*q.v.*); to STAND SAM (*q.v.*).

1892. HUME NISBET, *Bushranger's Sweetheart*, p. 58. I used to see her at some of the public-houses frequented by Mrs. Condon, STANDING HER HAND liberally to all who happened to be in the bar, and therefore being made much of by the thirsty loafers whom she treated.

TO HAND IN ONE'S CHIPS (or CHECKS). — *See* CASH ONE'S CHECKS.

TO HAVE (or GET) THE UPPER HAND, *verb. phr.* (colloquial).—To have at an advantage; to get to WINDWARD (*q.v.*).

1886. R. L. STEVENSON, *Kidnapped*, p. 173. I was growing impatient to get back and HAVE THE UPPER HAND of my uncle.

TO HAND UP, *verb.* (Winchester College). — To give information against; to betray.—*Notions.*

HANDS UP! *intj.* (common).—An injunction to desist; STOW IT! (*q.v.*). Also (police) = a command to surrender. BAIL UP (*q.v.*).

1888. J. RUNCIMAN, *The Chequers*, p. 120. HANDS UP! Jerry.

[Amongst other colloquial usages of HAND are the following:—AT HAND=readily, hard by; AT ANY HAND (Shakspeare)=on any account; AT NO HAND=on no account; FOR ONE'S OWN HAND=for one's own purpose or interest; FROM HAND TO HAND=from one to another; IN HAND=in a state of preparation, under consideration, or control; OFF ONE'S HANDS=finished; ON HAND=in possession; IN ONE'S HANDS=in one's care; OUT OF HAND=completed, without hesitation; TO ONE'S HAND=ready; HAND OVER HEAD=negligently, rashly; HAND TO MOUTH = improvident; HANDS OFF! = stand off; HEAVY ON HAND=hard to manage; HOT AT HAND=difficult to manage; LIGHT IN HAND=easy to manage; TO ASK (OR GIVE) THE HAND OF =to ask (or give) in marriage; TO BE HAND AND GLOVE WITH = to be very intimate with; TO BEAR A HAND=to help; TO BEAR IN (or ON) HAND=to cheat or mock by false promises; TO CHANGE HANDS=to change owners; TO COME TO HAND=to be received; TO GET HAND = to gain influence; TO GIVE A HAND = to applaud; TO GIVE THE HAND TO=to be reconciled to; TO HAVE A HAND IN=to have a share in; TO HAVE ONE'S HANDS FULL=to be fully occupied; TO HOLD HANDS WITH=to vie with, to hold one's own; TO LAY HANDS ON=to assault, to seize; TO LEND A HAND=to help; TO MAKE A HAND=to gain an advantage; TO PUT (or STRETCH) FORTH THE HAND AGAINST=to use violence; TO SET THE HAND TO = to undertake; TO STRIKE HANDS=to make a bargain; TO TAKE BY THE HAND=to take under one's guidance; TO TAKE IN HAND = to attempt; TO WASH ONE'S HANDS OF = to disclaim responsibility; A HEAVY HAND = severity; A LIGHT HAND = gentleness; A SLACK HAND = idleness, carelessness; A STRICT HAND = severe discipline; CLEAN HANDS=freedom from guilt; TO STAND ONE IN HAND=to concern, to be of importance to; HAND TO FIST = *tête-a-tête*, hip to haunch; HAND OVER HAND = easily; TO GET A HAND = to be applauded.]

HAND-AND-POCKET SHOP, *subs. phr.* (old).—*See* quot.

1811. *Lexicon Balatronicum*, s.v. HAND-AND-POCKET-SHOP. An eating house, where ready money is paid for what is called for.

HANDBASKET-PORTION, *subs.* (old). —*See* quot.

1811. *Lexicon Balatronicum*, s.v. HAND-BASKET-PORTION. A woman whose husband receives frequent presents from her father, or family, is said to have a HAND-BASKET-PORTION.

HANDBINDER (*in. pl.*), *subs.* (old).—Chains for the wrists. For synonyms, *see* DARBIES.

1696. RAY, *Nomenclator*, Menotes, liens à lier les mains, fers à enferrer les mains. Manicls, or HANDBINDERS.

HANDER, *subs.* (schoolboys'). — A stroke on the hand with a cane; A PALMIE (*q.v.*).

1868. JAS. GREENWOOD, *Purgatory of Peter the Cruel*, v., 149. You've been playing the wag, and you've got to take your HANDERS.

HANDICAP, *subs.* (colloquial).—An arrangement in racing, etc., by which every competitor is, or is supposed to be, brought on an equality so far as regards his chance of winning by an adjustment of the weights to be carried, the distance to be run, etc.: extra weight or distance being imposed in proportion to their supposed merits on those held better than the others. [A handicap is framed in accordance with the known performances of the competitors, and, in horse-racing, with regard to the age and sex of the entries. The term is derived from the old game of *hand-in-cap*, or handicap.]

1660. PEPYS, *Diary*, 18 Sep. Here some of us fell to HANDYCAPP, a sport that I never knew before.

1883. HAWLEY SMART, *Hard Lines* xxi. The race carried so many penalties and allowances that it partook somewhat of the nature of a HANDICAP.

Verb (colloquial). 1. To adjust or proportion weights, starts, etc., in order to bring a number of competitors as nearly as possible to an equality.

1841. LEVER, *Charles O'Malley*, ch. lxviii. Pleasant and cheerful enough, when they're HANDICAPPING the coat off your back, and your new tilbury for a spavined pony and a cotton umbrella; but regular devils if you come to cross them the least in life.

2. To make even or level; to equalise between.

3. To embarrass, burden, hinder, or impede in any way.

1883. GRENVILLE-MURRAY, *People I Have Met*, 123. He was not HANDICAPPED by a title, so that the beautiful ethics of hereditary legislation had no claim on his attention.

HANDIE-DANDIE, *subs. phr.* (old). —Copulation.

1490–1554. DAVID LYNDSAY, *Kitty's Confessioun* [LAING], i., 136. Ane plack I will gar Sandie, Gie the agane with HANDIE-DANDIE.

HANDLE, *subs.* (common).—1. The nose. For synonyms, *see* CONK.

1811. *Lexicon Balatronicum.* The cove flashes a rare HANDLE to his physog; the fellow has a large nose.

1887. *Modern Society*, 27 Aug., 864. A restless, intriguing, and busy old lady, with an immense HANDLE to her face.

2. (colloquial).—A title. Fr., *une queue*, as *Monsieur Sansqueue*=Mr. Nobody.

1855. THACKERAY *Newcomes*, xxiii. She . . . . entertained us with stories of colonial governors and their ladies, mentioning no persons but those who had HANDLES to their names, as the phrase is.

1857. DUCANGE ANGLICUS, *Vulg. Tongue.* HANDLE, *n.* Title. Oh, you want a HANDLE to your name.

1871. *London Figaro*, 17 June, 'The plaint of a poor Parson.' Neither he nor his clerical neighbours—unless they belong to county families, or have HANDLES to their names—have ever been invited by the Dean to partake of the hospitalities of the Deanery.

1886. J. S. WINTER, *Army Society*, ch. ii. That's the worst of having a HANDLE to one's name.

1891. *Licensed Vict. Gaz.*, 16 Jan. Here's the Honourable Tom Jones, and Lord Smith, and Viscount Brown—that's them, with the HANDLES knocked off their names.

1892. HENLEY and STEVENSON, *Deacon Brodie*, i., 2. He was aye ettling after a bit HANDLE to his name.

3. (colloquial). — Occasion; opportunity; means.

1753–77. MELMOTH, *Cicero*, bk. ii., let. 17 (note 5). The defence of Vatinius gave a plausible HANDLE for some censure upon Cicero.

Verb (cardsharpers').—1. To conceal cards in the palm of the hand, or up the sleeves; TO PALM (*q.v.*).

2. (colloquial).—To use; to make use of; to manage.

1606. CHAPMAN, *Gentleman Usher*, iii., 5. Now let the sport begin: I think my love will HANDLE him as well as I have done.

1811. *Lexicon Balatronicum*, s.v. HANDLE. To know how to HANDLE one's fists; to be skilful in the art of boxing.

1836. DICKENS, *Pickwick*, ii., 7. Smart chap that cabman—HANDLED his fives well.

1892. HENLEY and STEVENSON, *Admiral Guinea*, ii., 5. Commander, you HANDLED him like a babby, kept the weather gauge, and hulled him every shot.

TO HANDLE THE RIBBONS, *verb. phr.* (common).—To drive.

1857. MONCRIEFF, *Bashful Man*, ii. 4. Shouldn't have any objection in life, squire, to let you HANDLE THE RIBANDS for a stage or two, but four-in-hand, you know, requires——.

1872. *Evening Standard*, 10 Aug. The Princess of Wales is expected, and her Royal Highness has several times during the week driven through the town in an open phaeton, drawn by four beautiful ponies, and she appears TO HANDLE THE RIBBONS in a very skilful manner.

1891. N. GOULD, *Double Event*, p. 198. It was agreed Marston should HANDLE THE RIBBONS.

1892. MILLIKEN, *'Arry Ballads*, p. 32. He 'ANDLED THE RIBBINGS to rights.

TO FLY OFF THE HANDLE. *See* FLY, to which add the following earlier quot.

1825. NEAL, *Brother Jonathan*, bk. I., ch. iv. MOST OFF THE HANDLE, some o' the tribe, I guess.

HAND-ME-DOWNS (or **HAND-'EM-DOWNS**), *subs.* (common). — Second-hand clothes. HAND-ME-DOWN-SHOP, or NEVER-TOO-LATE-TO-MEND-SHOP=a repairing tailors.' Fr., *un decrochez-moi-ça.*

1878. *Notes and Queries*, 5, s. ix., 6 Apr., p. 263. HAND-'EM-DOWN—A second-hand garment (Northamptonshire).

1888. *New York World*, 5 Mar. Russell Sage, it is said, walked into a Broadway clothing store the other day and tried on and purchased a twelve-dollar suit of HAND-ME-DOWNS.

1889. *Sporting Times*, 29 June. Trousers which fit him nowhere in particular, and which all over proclaim themselves entitled to the epithet of HAND-ME-DOWN.

ENGLISH SYNONYMS.—Reach-me-downs; translations; wall-flowers.

FRENCH SYNONYMS. — *La musique* (popular); *la mise-bas* (servants': especially 'perks').

HAND-OUT, *subs.* (American).—Food to a tramp at the door.

1887. MORLEY ROBERTS, *The Western Avernus.* Some of the boys said it was a regular HAND-OUT, and that we looked like a crowd of old bummers.

HANDPIECE, *subs.* (American).—A handkerchief. For synonyms, *see* WIPE.

1852. BRISTED, *Upper Ten Thousand*, p. 67. Then . . . . he tied his white HAND-PIECES to an opening made for the purpose on one side of the dashboard.

HANDSAW, *subs.* (common).—A street vendor of knives and razors; an itinerant CHIVE-FENCER (*q.v.*).

HANDSOME, *adj.* and *adv.* (colloquial, and formerly literary).—Sharp, severe; convenient, fit; neat, graceful; dextrous, skilful, ready; ample, generous, liberal; manageable; in good or proper style; and (in America) grand or beautiful.

1553. WILSON, *Arte of Rhetorique*, p. 3. Phaourinus the Philosopher did hit a yong man ouer the thumbes very HANDSOMELY.

1553–99. SPENSER, *Wks.* For a thief it is so HANDSOME, As it may seem it was first invented by him.

1590. GOLDYNGE, *Cæsar*, p. 220. They had not so HANDSOME horses.

1593. SHAKSPEARE, *Titus Andronicus*, ii., 3. If we miss to meet him HANDSOMELY.

1600. P. HOLLAND, *Livy*, p. 255. A light footman's shield he takes with him, and a Spanish blade by his side, more HANDSOME to fight short and close.

1604. SHAKSPEARE, *Winter's Tale*, iv., 3. His garments are rich, but he wears them not HANDSOMELY.

1614. RALEIGH, *History of the World*, Bk. III., ch. viii, § 6. Playing their games HANDSOMELY against so nimble a wit.

1672-1719. ADDISON, *Wks.* An almshouse, which I intend to endow very HANDSOMELY.

1778-79. V. KNOX, *Essays*, 102. A HANDSOME sum of money.

1798. LODGE, *Illust. Brit. Hist.*, i., 178. He is very desyrus to serve your Grace, and seymes to me to be a very HANDSOME man.

1848. RUXTON, *Life in the Far West*, p. 8. He turned on his back HANDSOME.

TO DO THE HANDSOME (or THE HANDSOME THING, *verb. phr.* (common). — To behave extremely well; to be 'civil.'

1887. MANVILLE FENN, *This Man's Wife*, ii., 15. Sir Gordon's ready TO DO THE HANDSOME THING.

HANDSOME IS THAT HANDSOME DOES, *phr.* (colloquial).—'Actions, not words, are the test of merit'; also ironically of ill-favoured persons.

1811. *Lexicon Balatronicum.* HANDSOME IS THAT HANDSOME DOES: a proverb frequently cited by ugly women.

HANDSOME-BODIED IN THE FACE, *adv.* (old).—See quot.

1785. GROSE, *Vulg. Tongue*, s.v. Handsome Bodied Man in the Face, a eering commendation of an ugly fellow.

HANDSOME AS A LAST YEAR'S CORPSE, *adv. phr.* (American).—A sarcastic compliment.

HANDSOMELY! *intj.* (nautical).—Gently! A cry to signify smartly, but carefully. Also HANDSOMELY OVER THE BRICKS = Go cautiously.

HANDSOME-REWARD, *subs. phr.* (old).—See quot.

1811. *Lexicon Balatronicum.* HANDSOME-REWARD. This, in advertisements, means a horse-whipping.

HANDSPRINGS. TO CHUCK HANDSPRINGS, *verb phr.* (common).—To turn somersaults.

HANDSTAFF, *subs.* (venery).—The *penis.* For synonyms, see CREAMSTICK and PRICK. [From that member of the flail which is held in the hands].

HANDY. HANDY AS A POCKET IN A SHIRT, *phr.* (American).—Very convenient.

HANDY-BLOWS, (or CUFFS), *subs.* (old).—Cuffs with the hand; fisticuffs; hence close quarters.

1603. KNOLLES, *Hist. of the Turkes.* If ever they came to HANDY-BLOWS.

1690. B. E., *Cant. Crew*, s.v. HANDY BLOWS, Fisticuffs.

1725. *New Cant. Dict.*, s.v.

HANDY-MAN, *subs.* (colloquial).—A servant or workman doing odd jobs.

1847. DE QUINCEY, *The Spanish Military Nun* (1890), xiii., 165. She was a HANDY GIRL. She could turn her hand to anything.

1872. *Times*, 27 Aug. 'Autumn Manœuvres.' The result is he cannot be called a HANDY-MAN.

1889. *Pall Mall Gaz.*, 8 Nov., p. 2, c. i. Again did Mr. Sambourne's HANDY-MAN appear, this time clad in the real robes of the Lord Mayor.

1892. HUME NISBET, *Bushranger's Sweetheart*, p. 55. He was a HANDY-MAN.

HANG, *subs.* (colloquial).—1. The general drift, tendency, or bent: as in TO GET THE HANG OF=to get conversant with; to acquire the trick, or knack, or knowledge of.

1847. DARLEY, *Drama in Pokerville*, p. 67. The theatre was cleared in an instant . . . all running to GET THE HANG of the scrape.

1848. JONES, *Sketches of Travel*, 70. By this time I began to GIT THE HANG of the place a little better.

1851. HOOPER, *Widow Rugby's Husband*, etc., p. 64. To be efficient a solicitor must GET THE HANG OF his customers.

a. 1871. PRIME, *Hist. of Long Island.* p. 82. If ever you must have an indifferent teacher for your children, let it be after they have got a fair start and have ACQUIRED THE HANG OF the tools for themselves.

1884. MILLIKEN, *Punch*, 11 Oct. They ain't GOT THE 'ANG of it, Charlie the toffs ain't.

1890. *Daily Chronicle*, 4 Apr., p. 7 c. 2. When the Raw Cadet enters Woolwich Academy, it is sometime before he GETS what some call THE HANG OF the place.

1892. *Illustrated Bits*, Oct. 22, p. 6. c. 2. When I GET THE HANG OF them I shall be a regular dab at theosophy.

2. (colloquial).—A little bit; a bit; a DAMN. See CARE. Fr., *s'en contreficher* or *s'en tamponner le coquard* (or *coquillard*).

1861. H. KINGSLEY; *Ravenshoe*, ch. xliii. She looks as well as you by candle-light, but she can't ride a HANG.

Verb (generally HANG IT!).—An exclamation of vexation, disgust, or disappointment; also, more forcibly, a euphemism for DAMN IT! Fr., *Ah! mince alors.*

1598. SHAKSPEARE, *2 Henry IV.*, ii., 4. He a good wit? HANG HIM, baboon!

1609. JONSON, *Epicœne*, ii., 2. A mere talking mole, HANG HIM.

1614. JONSON, *Bartholomew Fair*, v. 3. Ay, and be HANGED.

1694. DUNTON, *Ladies' Dict.*, p. 229. Aristænetus telling a brisk buxom Lass of a proper fine Man that would make her a good Husband, HANG HIM [reply'd she] he has no Mony.

1772. COLES, *Eng.-Lat. Dict.*, s.v. Hanged. Go AND BE HANGED.

1780. Mrs. COWLEY, *Belle's Stratagem*, iv., 1. HANG Harriet, and Charlotte, and Maria! the name your father gave ye?

1823. W. T. MONCRIEFF. *Tom and Jerry*, ii., 5. HANG cards! bring me a bobstick of rum slim.

1836. M. SCOTT, *Cruise of the Midge*, p. 169. 'You BE HANGED, Felix,' quoth his ally, with a most quizzical grin.

1863. CH. READE, *Hard Cash*, ii., 218. HANG the grub; it turns my stomach.

1883. R. L. STEVENSON, *Treasure Island*, p. 161. You can go HANG!

1889. *Sporting Times*, 6 July. Hebrew Scholar : Rub up your Hebrew. Or GO AND HANG yourself.

1890. GRANT ALLEN, *Tents of Shem*, ch. xvii. HANG IT ALL, if that's English law, you know, I don't thing very much of the wisdom of our ancestors.

1891. N. GOULD, *Double Event*, p. 164. HANG IT ALL.

1892. MILLIKEN, *Arry Ballads*, p. 7. But 'ANG IT, I can't stand the style of the silent and the stare-me-down sort.

1892. F. ANSTEY, *Voces Populi*, 'On the Ice,' p. 122. Stick by me, old fellow, till I begin to feel my — Oh, HANG IT ALL!

TO HANG AN ARSE, *verb. phr.* (old).—To hang back; to hesitate.

1598. MARSTON, *Satyres*, 'Ad Rythmum.' But if you HANG AN ARSE like Tubered, When Chremes dragged him from his brothel bed.

1637. MASSINGER, *Guardian*, v, 5 Nay, no HANGING AN ARSE.

1639-61. *Rump Songs*, ii., 86. Nay, if it HANG AN ARSE, We'll pluck it from the stares, And roast it at hell for its grease.

1748. SMOLLETT, *Roderick Random*, ch. lxv. My lads, I'm told you HANG AN ARSE.

1780. TOMLINSON, *Slang Pastoral*, 2. My ARSE HANGS behind me as heavy as lead.

1785. GROSE, *Vulg. Tongue*, s.v.

TO HANG IN, *verb. phr.* (common).—To get to work; to do one's best; to WIRE IN (q.v.).

TO HANG IN THE BELLROPES, *verb. phr.* (common).—To defer marriage after being 'asked' in church.

TO HANG ON BY ONE'S EYE-LASHES, *verb. phr.* (colloquial).—To persist at any cost, and in the teeth of any discouragement.

TO HANG ON BY THE SPLASHBOARD, *verb. phr.* (common).—To 'catch' a tram, omnibus, etc., when it is on the move; hence to succeed by the 'skin of one's teeth.' Fr., *arcpincer l'omnibus.*

TO HANG AROUND (or ABOUT), *verb. phr.* (American). — To loiter; to loaf; to haunt.

TO HANG OUT, *verb* (common).—To live; to reside. Also (*subs.*), a residence; a lodging; and (American university) a feast; an entertainment.

1811. *Lexicon Balatronicum*, s.v. HANG OUT. The traps scavey where we HANG OUT; the officers know where we live.

1836. DICKENS, *Pickwick*, ch. xxx. 'I say, old boy, where do you HANG OUT?' Mr. Pickwick replied that he was at present suspended at the George and Vulture.

1852. BRISTED, *Five Years in an English University*, p. 80. The fourth of July I celebrated by a HANG-OUT.

1871. *City Press*, 21 Jan. 'Curiosities of Street Literature.' He HANGS OUT in Monmouth-court.

1892. MILLIKEN, *'Arry Ballads*, p. 14. I should like to go in for blue blood, and 'ANG OUT near the clubs and the parks.

TO HANG OUT A SHINGLE, *verb. phr.* (American).—To start or carry on business.

1871. *Public Opinion*, Dec. Tom Stowell HUNG OUT HIS SHINGLE as a lawyer at the Tombs, afterwards at Essex-market, and eventually in Brooklyn.

TO HANG ONE'S LATCHPAN, *verb. phr.* (common).—To be dejected; to pout. Fr., *faire son aquilin.*

TO HANG IT OUT, *verb. phr.* (common).—To skulk; TO MIKE (q.v.).

TO HANG UP, *verb. phr.* (common).—1. To give credit; to score (or chalk) up: said of a reckoning. Also 'to put on the slate' or (American) ON THE ICE (q.v.).

1725. *New Cant. Dict.*, s.v. HANG-IT-UP, speaking of the Reckoning at a Bowsing-Ken, when the Rogues are obliged, for want of Money, to run on Tick.

1785. GROSE, *Vulg. Tongue*, s.v.

2. (American).—To bear in mind; to remember.

1859. MATSELL, *Vocabulum*, s.v. HANG IT UP. Think of it, remember it.

3. (American). — To pawn, For synonyms, see POP.

4. (thieves').—To rob with violence on the street; TO HOLD UP (q.v.). Fr., *la faire au père François.*

5. (common). — To be in *extremis*; to know not which way to turn for relief: *e.g.*, A MAN HANGING=one to whom any change must be for the better.

6. (colloquial).—To postpone; to leave undecided.

1887. *Cornhill Magazine*, June, p. 624. To HANG UP A BILL is to pass it through one or more of its stages, and then to lay it aside, and defer its further consideration for a more or less indefinite period.

TO HANG ON, *verb. phr.* (colloquial). — (1) To sponge; and (2) to pursue an individual or a design.

1601. SHAKSPEARE, *Henry VIII.*, iii., 2. Oh, how wretched is that poor man that HANGS ON princes' favours!

TO HANG OFF, *verb. phr.* (printers').—To fight shy of.

TO HANG UP ONE'S FIDDLE, *verb. phr.* (American).—To retire; to desist. TO HANG UP ONE'S FIDDLE ANYWHERE=To adapt oneself to circumstances.

TO HANG UP ONE'S HAT, *verb. phr.* (common).—1. To die. For synonyms, see ALOFT.

1854. *Notes and Queries*, Vol. X., p. 203. He has HUNG UP HIS HAT. This sentence, which is sometimes used in reference to persons deceased, etc.

1882. *Punch*, lxxxii., 185, c. 1.

2. (common)—To make oneself permanently at home.

HANG-BLUFF, *subs.* (rhyming).—Snuff.

1857. DUCANGE ANGLICUS, *Vulg. Tongue*, s.v.

1859. MATSELL, *Vocabulum*, s.v.

HANG-BY, *subs.* (old).—A hanger-on; a parasite; a companion.

1598. JONSON, *Every Man in his Humour*, iv., 2. I am not afraid of you nor them neither, you HANG-BYES here.

HANG-DOG, *subs.* (old).—A pitiful rascal, only fit for the rope or the hanging of superfluous curs. *Cf.*, GALLOWS-BIRD.

1732. FIELDING, *Mock Doctor*, i., 4. Heaven has inspired me with one of the most wonderful inventions to be revenged on my HANG-DOG.

Adj. (old).—Vile, or suspicious, in aspect; GALLOWS-LOOKING (q.v.).

HANG-GALLOWS, *adj.* (old). —See quot.

1785. GROSE, *Vulg. Tongue*, s.v. HANG-GALLOWS Look, a thievish, or villainous appearance.

HANGER, *subs.* (old).—A side-arm— short sword or cutlass—hanging from the girdle. [See HANGERS, *in. pl.!*, sense I.]

1815. SCOTT, *Guy Mannering*, x. A *couteau de chase*, or short HANGER.

In. pl. (old).—1. Ornamental loops from the girdle to suspend the sword and dagger.

1596. SHAKSPEARE, *Hamlet*, v. 2. Six French rapiers and poignards, with their assigns, as girdle, HANGERS, and so on.

1596. NASHE, *Unf. Trav.* [Chiswick Press, 1891]. Huge HANGERS that have half a cowhide in them.

1599. JONSON, *Every Man out of his Humour*, iv., 4. I had thrown off the HANGERS a little before.

1610. JONSON, *Alchemist*, v., 2. Where be the French petticoats, And girdles and HANGERS?

2. (common).—Gloves; specifically gloves in the hand.

3. See POTHOOKS.

HANG-IN-CHAINS, *subs. phr.* (old). —See quots.

1785. GROSE, *Vulg. Tongue*, s.v. HANG-IN-CHAINS, a vile desperate fellow.

1811. *Lexicon Balatronicum.* HANG-IN-CHAINS. A vile, desperate fellow. Persons guilty of murder, or other atrocious crimes, are frequently, after execution, hanged on a gibbet, to which they are fastened by iron bandages; the gibbet is commonly placed on or near the place where the crime was committed.

HANGING, *adj.* (colloquial).—Fit for the halter.

HANGING-BEE, *subs.* (American).—A gathering of lynch-lawmongers, bent on the application of the rope. See BEE.

HANGING JOHNNY, *subs. phr.* (venery).—The *penis*: specifically, in a condition of impotence or disease. For synonyms, see CREAMSTICK and PRICK.

HANGMAN, *subs.* (old).—A jocular endearment.

1600. SHAKSPEARE, *Much Ado About Nothing*, iii., 2. He had twice or thrice cut Cupid's bowstring, and the little HANGMAN dare not shoot at him.

HANGMAN'S-DAY, *subs.* (old). — Monday, and (in America) Friday.

1859. MATSELL, *Vocabulum*, s.v. HANGMAN'S DAY. Friday is so calld from the custom of hanging people on a Friday.

HANGMAN'S-WAGES, *subs.* (old).—Thirteen-pence-halfpenny. [The fee for an execution was a Scots mark: the value of which piece was settled, by a proclamation of James I., at $13\frac{1}{2}$d.]

1602. DECKER, *Honest Whore*, Pt. II., in *Wks.* (1873) ii., 171. Why should I eate hempe-seed at the HANGMAN'S THIRTEENE-PENCE HALFE-PENNY ordinary?

1659. *Hangman's Last Will* (Rump Song quoted in *Notes and Queries*, 2 S. xi., 316). For half THIRTEEN-PENCE HALF-PENNY WAGES, I would have cleared out all the town cages, And you should have been rid of all the sages. I and my gallows groan.

1678. BUTLER, *Hudibras*, Pt. III., c. 2. To find us pillories and cart's-tails, Or HANGMAN'S WAGES.

1785. GROSE, *Vulg. Tongue*, s v. HANGMAN'S WAGES, thirteenpence half-penny, which according to the vulgar tradition was thus allotted, one shilling for the execution, and three halfpence for the rope.

HANG-SLANG ABOUT, *verb. phr.* (common).—To abuse; TO SLANG (*q.v.*); TO BILLINGSGATE (*q.v.*).

HANK, *subs.* (old colloquial).—1. A tie; a hold; an advantage; a difficulty. [IN A HANK = in trouble].

1690. B. E., *Dict. Cant. Crew*, s.v. He has a HANK upon him, or the Ascendant over him.

1725. *New Cant. Dict.*, s.v. He has a HANK upon him; He . . . . will make him do what he pleases.

1785. GROSE, *Vulg. Tongue*, s.v. He has a HANK on him, *i.e.*, an ascendant over him, or a hold upon him: A SMITHFIELD HANK, = An ox rendered furious by over driving and barbarous treatment.

1859. MATSELL, *Vocabulum*, s.v. HANK. To know something about a man that is disreputable. He has a HANK on the bloke, whereby he sucks honey when he chooses, he knows something about the man, and therefore induces him to give him money when he chooses.

2. (common).—A spell of rest; an easy time.

1888. *Sporting Life*, 7 Dec. So quiet was the first round that the ire of the company was raised, and they called out, 'No HANK!'

Verb (common).—To worry; to bait; to drive from pillar to post.

HANKER, *verb* (old: now recognised).—To desire eagerly; to fret after; to long or pine for: generally with 'after.' Also, HANKERING (*subs.*) = an importunate and irritating longing.

1690. B. E., *Dict. Cant. Crew*, s.v. HANKER AFTER, to Long or wish much for.

1725. *New Cant. Dict.*, s.v.

1785. GROSE, *Vulg. Tongue*, s.v. To HANKER AFTER anything, to have a longing after or for it.

1847. ROBB, *Squatter Life*, p. 98. I did see a creatur' once, named Sofy Mason . . . . that I tuk an orful HANKERIN' ARTER.

1878. WHITMAN, *Leaves of Grass*, 'Spontaneous Me,' 90 (ed. 1884). The hairy wild-bee that murmurs and HANKERS up and down.

HANKIN, *subs.* (commercial).—The trick of putting off bad work for good. [*Cf.*, TO PLAY HANKEY, or TO PLAY HANKY-PANKY.]

HANKTELO, *subs.* (old).—*See* quots.

1593. NASHE, *Strange Newes* (Grosart, *Wks.*, ii., 251). Is the Astrologicaall Discourse a better booke than Pierce Pennilesse? Gabriel HANGTELOW saies it is?

1690. B. E., *Dict. Cant. Crew*, s.v HANKTELO, a silly Fellow, a meer Codshead.

1725. *New Cant. Dict.*, s.v.

1785. GROSE, *Vulg. Tongue*, s.v.

HANKY-PANKY, *subs.* (common).—(1) Legerdemain; whence (2) trickery; UNDERHAND (*q.v.*) work; cheating; any manner of

double-dealing or intrigue. HANKY-PANKY BUSINESS = conjuring; HANKY-PANKY WORK (or TRICKS) = double-dealing. A BIT OF HANKY-PANKY = a trick; a piece of knavery.

1841. *Punch*, Vol. I., p. 88. Only a little HANKY-PANKY.

1880. G. R. SIMS, *Zeph*, ch. xiii. He knew that . . . any crime committed on his premises would tell against him on licensing day, and he kept a pretty sharp look out to see that what he was pleased to term HANKY PANKY was not carried on under his nose.

1864. E. YATES, *Broken to Harness*, ch. xxxviii. If there was any HANKY PANKY, any mystery I mean, he'd always swear he was out whenever he called, for fear it should be bullied out of him.

1877. *Five Years' Penal Servitude*, ch. v., p. 323. ——There's some HANKY PANKY business going on among the men of No. 2 prison; the Catholic side is ringing changes and it is done in this shop.

HANKY-PANKY-BLOKE, *subs. phr.* (theatrical).—A conjuror; a PILE OF MAGS (*q.v*).

HANKY-SPANKY, *adj.* (common).—Dashing; NOBBY (*q.v.*). Specifically of well-cut clothes.

HANNAH. THAT'S THE MAN AS MARRIED HANNAH, *phr.* (streets').—'That's the thing': used of a thing well begun and well ended; or as an expressive of certainty. Varied sometimes by THAT'S WHAT'S THE MATTER WITH HANNAH.

HANS CARVEL'S RING, *subs. phr.* (venery).—The female *pudendum*. For synonyms, *see* MONOSYLLABLE. [From Poggio (tit. *Annulus*); *Cent Nouvelles Nouvelles* (xi); Ariosto (*Sat.* v.); the *Nouvelle* of Malespini (89, ii.); Rabelais (*Pantagruel*, iii., 28); and Matthew Prior.]

HANSEL (or **HANDSEL**) *subs.* (common).—The first money taken in the morning; lucky money. Hence, earnest money; first-fruits, &c. HANSEL-MONDAY = the first Monday in the new year, when presents were received by children and servants. [A.S., *handselen* = to deliver into the hand.]

1587. GREENE, *Menaphon* (Arber), p. 71. He should like inough haue had first HANDSELL of our new Shepheards sheepehooke.

1614. JONSON, *Bartholomew Fair*, ii. Bring him a sixpenny bottle of ale: They say a fool's HANDSEL is lucky.

1679. HOLLAND, *Ammianus Marcellinus*. With which wofull tidings being sore astonied, as if it were the first HANSELL and beginning of evils comming toward him.

1787. GROSE, *Prov. Glossary*, etc. (1811), p. 121. It is a common practice among the lower class of hucksters, pedlars, or dealers in fruit or fish, on receiving the price of the first goods sold that day, which they call HANSEL, to spit on the money, as they term it, for good luck.

1815. SCOTT, *Guy Mannering*, ch iii. There was a whin bonnie lasses there, forbye mysel', and deil ane to gie them HANSELS. *Ibid*, ch. xxxii. Grizzy has naething frae me, by twa pair o' new shoon ilka year, and maybe a bit compliment at HANSEL MONANDAY.

1821. SCOTT, *Kenilworth*, ch. xix. 'How wears the Hollands you won of me?' 'Why, well, as you may see, Master Goldthred,' answered Mike; 'I will bestow a pot on thee for the HANDSEL.'

Verb (common).—1. To give handsel to; also (2), to use for the first time.

1599. NASHE, *Lenten Stuffe*, in *Wks.*, v., 249. And gather about him as flocking to HANSELL him and strike him good luck.

1605. CHAPMAN, etc., *Eastward Hoe*, ii. My lady . . . . is so ravished with desire to HANSELL her new coach.

1639-61. *Rump Songs*, i. [1662], 137. Belike he meant to HANSELL his New Satten.

1663. PEPYS, *Diary*, 12 Apr. Coming home to-night, a drunken boy was carrying by our constable to our new pair of stocks to HANDSEL them.

1874. [G. A. LAWRENCE], *Hagarene*, ch. xvii. The habit of stout blue cloth . . . . was Pete Harradine's last and crowning extravagance, as they passed through town on their way to Fulmerstone, and it had never been HANSELLED yet.

1881. BESANT and RICE, *Sweet Nelly*, in *Ten Years' Tenant*, etc., Vol. I., p. 200. I wanted to present her with something to HANSEL friendship.

HANSELLER, *subs.* (common).—A street vendor; a Cheap Jack.

1851-61. H. MAYHEW, *Lond. Lab. and Lond. Poor*, i., 392. The sellers of tins, who carry them under their arms, or in any way on a round, apart from the use of a vehicle, are known as HAND-SELLERS.

1876. HINDLEY, *Adventures of a Cheap Jack*, p. 10. Cheap-Jacks, as they were then as now called by the people, although the term HAN'-SELLER is mostly used by themselves.

HANS-EN-KELDER, *subs.* (old).—A child in the womb: literally, JACK-IN-THE-CELLAR (*q.v.*). [From the Dutch.]

1647. CLEAVELAND, *Character of a London Diurnall*. The originall sinner in this kind was Dutch; Galliobelgicus, the Protoplast; and the moderne Mercuries, but HANS-EN-KELDERS. The countesse of Zealand was brought to bed of an almanack; as many children as dayes in the yeare.

1648. *Mercurius Pragmaticus*, i. The birthday of that precious new government which is yet but a HANS-EN-KELDER.

*d.*1658. LOVELACE, *Poems*, p. 63. Next beg I to present my duty To pregnant sister in prime beauty, Whom [who] well I deem (ere few months elder) Will take out HANS FROM pretty KELDER.

1663. DRYDEN, *Wild Gallant*, v., *Wks.*, i. 61 (1701). Seems you are desirous I should Father this HANS EN KELDER heere.

1672. MARVELL, *Char. of Holland*, line 65. More pregnant then their Marg'ret, that laid down For HANS-IN-KELDER of a whole Hanse town.

1690. B. E., *Dict. Cant. Crew*, s.v. HANS-EN-KELDER, Jack in the Box, the Child in the Womb, or a Health to it.

1672. WYCHERLEY, *Love in a Wood*, v. Then I am as it were a grandfather to your new Wiffe's, HANS EN KELDER.

1678. T. BAKER, *Tunbridge Wells*, p. 27. Here's a health to this Lady's HANS IN KELDER!

1725. *New Cant. Dict.*, s.v.

1785. GROSE, *Vulg. Tongue*, s.v. HANS IN KELDER, a health frequently drank to breeding women, or their husbands.

HANSOM, *subs.* (coster).—A chop.

HAP-HARLOT, *subs.* (old).—A coarse stuff to make rugs or coverlets with; a rug. *Cf.*, WRAP-RASCAL = an overcoat.

1577-87. HOLINSHED, *Description of England*, bk. ii., ch. xii. A sheet vnder couerlets made of dagswain, or HAP-HARLOTS (I vse their owne termes).

HA'PORTH O' COPPERS, *subs. phr.* (legal).—Habeas Corpus.

HA'PORTH OF LIVELINESS, *subs. phr.* (Coster).—1. Music.

1851-61. H. MAYHEW, *Lond. Lab. and Lond. Poor*, i., p. 21. Or they will call to the orchestra, saying, 'Now then you catgut-scrapers! Let's have a HA'PORTH OF LIVELINESS.'

2. (common). — A loitering Lawrence; a SLOWCOACH (*q.v.*).

HAPPIFY, *verb.* (American). — To please.

1612. SYLVESTER, *Lach. Lach.*, 642. One short mishap for ever HAPPIFIES.

1848. BURTON, *Waggeries*, etc., p. 70. For eatin' and drinkin', it HAPPIFIES me to say that we bang the bush.

HAPPY, *adj.* (common).—Slightly drunk; ELEVATED (*q.v.*). For synonyms, *see* DRINKS and SCREWED.

HAPPY-DESPATCH, *subs.* (common).—Death, specifically, a sudden or violent end.

HAPPY-DOSSER. *See* DOSSER.

HAPPY ELIZA, *subs.* (common).—A female Salvationist [As in the *Broadside Ballad* (1887-8), 'They call me Happy Eliza, and I'm Converted Jane: We've been two hot'uns in our time.']

HAPPY-FAMILY, *subs.* (colloquial).—*See* quot.

1851-61. H. MAYHEW, *Lond. Lab. and Lond. Poor*, iii., p. 224. HAPPY FAMILIES, or assemblages of animals of diverse habits and propensities living amicably, or at least quietly, in one cage.

HAPPY-GO-LUCKY, *subs.* (colloquial).—Careless; thoughtless; improvident. Fr., *va comme je te pousse* and *à la flan*.

1856. READE, *Never Too Late to Mend*, ch. xv. In the HAPPY-GO-LUCKY way of his class.

1883. *Illust. London News*, 8 Dec., p. 551, c. 1. He dashes off a play in a HAPPY-GO-LUCKY style, basing it on theatrical precedent so far as certain stock situations are concerned.

HAPPY HUNTING-GROUNDS, *subs.* (American).—1. The future state; GLORY (*q.v.*). [From the North-American Indian's conception of heaven.]

1848. RUXTON, *Life in the Far West*, p. 98. After a long journey, they will reach the HAPPY HUNTING-GROUNDS.

1891. GUNTER, *Miss Nobody of Nowhere*, ch. v. Old Mescal is now keeping a sharp eye out for the child and the cowboy, that he may send them to the HAPPY HUNTING-GROUNDS also.

2. (colloquial).—A favourable place for work or play.

1892. *Cassell's Sat. Journal*, 26 Oct., p. 119. The HAPPY HUNTING-GROUND of the swell mobsman is the opening of some Exhibition.

3. (venery). — The female *pudendum*. For synonyms, *see* MONOSYLLABLE.

HAPPY-LAND, *subs.* (common).—The after life; GLORY (*q.v.*).

1893. DANVERS, *The Grantham Mystery*, ch. xiii. The old 'un will soon join the young 'un in the HAPPY LAND.

HAPPY-RETURNS, *subs.* (Australian).—Vomiting. *See* FLAY THE FOX.

HARBOUR, *subs.* (venery). — The female *pudendum*. For synonyms, *see* MONOSYLLABLE. Also HARBOUR OF HOPE.

HARD, *subs.* (prison).—1. Hard labour.

1890. *Globe*, 26 Feb., p. 1, c. 4. Monetary penalties, therefore, do not act as deterrents, but the certainty of seven days' incarceration, with or without HARD, would soon diminish the nuisance.

2. *See* HARD-SHELL.

3. (colloquial). — Third-class. As opposed to SOFT (*q.v.*). Thus: 'Do you go HARD or SOFT?' = 'Do you go Third or First?' An abbreviation of HARD-ARSE.

Adj. (American).—1. Applied to metal of all kinds: *e.g.*, HARD (COLE or STUFF) = silver or gold as compared to cheques or SOFT (*q.v.*).

1825. NEAL, *Bro. Jonathan*, ii., ch. 18. The bill . . . . amounted to one dollar and a quarter HARD MONEY.

1844. *Puck*, p. 146. That cunning old file wont let her go with the HARD CASH down.

1859. MATSELL, *Vocabulum*, s.v. HARD; metal.

1859. MATSELL, *Vocabulum*, s.v. HARD COLE. Silver or gold money.

1863. CHARLES READE, *Hard Cash*. [Title.]

2. (old: now recognised).—1. Sour or souring; as in HARD-CIDER; (2) HARD drinks (American) = intoxicating liquors, as wine, ale, etc., while lemonade, soda-water, ginger-beer, etc., are SOFT.

1690. B. E., *Dict. Cant. Crew*, s.v. HARD DRINK, that is very Stale, or beginning to Sower.

1785. GROSE, *Vulg. Tongue*, s.v. HARD, stale beer nearly sour, is said to be HARD.

1882. *Daily Telegraph*, 10 Oct., p. 5, c. 3. A fourth defendant, in pleading guilty, urged that the month of August last 'turned a lot of beer sour,' and that he had only used some sugar for the purpose of mollifying the HARD or sour porter.

HARD AS A BONE (NAILS, etc.), *adj. phr.* (colloquial).—Very hard; austere; unyielding.

1885. *Indoor Paupers*, p. 79. He stood it for a week or two without flinching—being at that date HARD AS NAILS, as he expresses it.

HARD AT IT, *adj. phr.* (colloquial).—Very busy; in the thick of a piece of work.

TO DIE HARD, *verb. phr.* (colloquial).—To sell one's life dearly; *e.g.*, The DIE-HARDS (*q.v.*), the 59th Regiment, so called from their gallantry at Albuera.

TO GIVE HARD FOR SOFT, *verb. phr.* (venery).—To copulate. *See* GREENS.

TO BE HARD HIT. *See* HARD-HIT.

[HARD, *adj.*, is used in many combinations; generally with an unpleasant intention. Thus, HARD-ARSED (or FISTED, or HANDED)=very niggardly; HARD-BIT (or HARD-MOUTHFUL)=an unpleasant experience; HARD-DRIVEN (or HARD-RUN)= sore bested; HARD-FACED (or FAVOURED, or FEATURED)=grum, shrewish, or bony; HARD-HEADED (or HARD-WITTED)=shrewd and intelligent, but unimaginative and unsympathetic; HARD-HEARTED = incapable of pity; HARD-LIPPED=obstinate, dour HARD-MASTER = a nigger-driver; HARD-NUT=a dangerous antagonist; HARD-ON= pitiless in severity; HARD-RIDING=selfish and reckless equestration; HARD-SERVICE =the worst kind of employment; HARD-WROUGHT=overworked, etc., etc.]

HARD-A-WEATHER, *adj.* (nautical).—Tough; weather-proof.

1891. W. C. RUSSELL, *Ocean Tragedy*, p. 44. They were HARD-A-WEATHER fellows.

HARD-BAKE, *subs.* (schoolboys').—A sweetmeat made of boiled brown sugar or treacle with blanched almonds.

1825. HONE, *Every-day Bk.*, I., 51. HARDBAKE, brandy-balls, and bull's-eyes.

1836. DICKENS, *Pickwick*, ii. The commodities exposed for sale in the public streets are marine stores, HARD-BAKE, apples, etc.

HARD-BAKED, *adj.* (old).—1. Constipated.

1823. JON BEE, *Dict. of Turf*, s.v.

2. (common). — Stern; unflinching; strong.

1847. ROBB, *Squatter Life*, p. 73. It's my opinion, these squirtish kind a fellars ain't perticular HARD-BAKED.

HARD-BARGAIN (or CASE), *subs.* (common).—1. A lazy fellow; a BAD-EGG (*q.v.*); a skulker. ONE OF THE QUEEN'S HARD-BARGAINS=a bad soldier.

1848. RUXTON, *Life in the Far West*, p. 71. La Bonté had lost all traces of civilised humanity, and might justly claim to be considered as HARD A CASE as any of the mountaineers then present.

1888. LYNCH, *Mountain Mystery*, ch. xliii. A fellow who comes and goes between here and Rockville, generally considered a HARD CASE, and believed to be more outlaw than miner.

2. (trade).—A defaulting debtor.

3. (nautical).—A brutal mate or officer. Also HARD-HORSE.

HARD-BIT (or BIT OF HARD), *subs.* (venery). — 1. The *penis* in erection; whence (2), for women, the act of connection.

HARD-BITTEN, *adj.* (colloquial).—Resolute; GAME (*q.v.*); desperate.

1815. SCOTT, *Guy Mannering*, liii. My sooth, they'll be HARD-BITTEN terriers will worrie Dandie.

HARD-CHEESE, *subs.* (Royal Military Academy).—Hard lines; bad luck; specifically at billiards.

HARD-COLE. *See* HARD and COLE.

HARD-DOINGS, *subs.* (American).—1. Rough fare; and (2) hard work.

1848. RUXTON, *Life in the Far West*, p. 37. HARD DOINS when it comes to that.

HARD-DRINKING, *subs.* (old: now recognized).—Drinking to excess.

1690. B. E., *Dict. Cant. Crew*, s.v. HARD-DRINKING, excessive Soking, or toping aboundance.

HARD-HEAD, *subs.* (American).—A man of good parts, physical, intellectual, or moral.

1824. R. B. PEAKE, *Americans Abroad*, i., 1. *Dou.* None of your flouting, by jumping jigs, I won't stand it—we Americans have got HARD HEADS—we warn't brought up in the woods to be scart at by an owl—you can't scare me so.

1848. DURIVAGE, *Stray Subjects*, p. 110. Most of the passengers had disappeared for the night, and only a knot of HARD-HEADS were left upon deck.

HARD-HIT. TO BE HARD HIT, *verb phr.* (colloquial).—1. To have experienced a heavy loss; as over a race, at cards, etc.

2. (colloquial).—To be deeply in love; completely GONE ON (*q.v.*).

1888. J. MCCARTHY and MRS. CAMPBELL-PRAED, *Ladies' Gallery*, ch. xxv. The wound was keen, I had been HIT HARD.

1891. M. E. BRADDON, *Gerard*, p. 312. You've been HARD HIT.

HARD-LINES, *subs.* (colloquial).—Hardship; difficulty; an unfortunate result or occurrence. [Formerly LINE=lot: *Cf.*, Bible and Prayer book version of Psalm xvi., 5, 6.]

1855. *Notes and Queries*, 1 S. xii., p. 287. HARD LINES. Whence is this expression, so common, particularly among seafaring men, derived?

1881. W. BLACK, *Beautiful Wretch*, ch. xxiii. I think it's deuced HARD LINES to lock up a fellow for merely humbugging an old parson up in Kentish Town.

1888. *Sporting Life*, 15 Dec. For the Kempton folks it was rather HARD LINES.

1888. J. MCCARTHY and MRS. CAMPBELL-PRAED, *Ladies' Gallery*, ch. xxvi. It's awful HARD LINES, Lady Star Strange, that I am only thought good enough for you Londoners in the dead season.

1892. MILLIKEN, *'Arry Ballads*, p. 3. I call it 'ARD LINES, dear old man.

HARD-MOUTHED, *adj.* (colloquial).—Difficult to deal with; wilful; obstinate. Also coarse in speech. [From the stable.]

1686. DURFEY, *Commonw. of Wordes*, i., 1. [Speaking of a girl.] I hate your young Wechees, Skitish Colts—they are so HARD MOUTH'D, there's no dealing with em.

1704. SWIFT, *Tale of a Tub*, Sect. ix. I myself, the author of these momentous truths, am a person, whose imaginations are HARD-MOUTHED, and exceedingly disposed to run away with his reason.

1704. SWIFT, *Operation of the Spir't*, Sect. ii., par. 9. The flesh . . . . when it comes to the turn of being bearer, is wonderfully headstrong and HARD-MOUTHED.

HARD-NECK, *subs.* (tailors'),—Brazen impudence, MONUMENTAL CHEEK (*q.v.*).

HARD-ON, *adj. phr.* (venery).—Prick-proud. For synonyms, *see* HORN.

HARD-PAN, *subs. phr.* (American).—The lowest point; BED-ROCK (*q.v.*).

1882. BESANT, *All Sorts and Conditions of Men*, ch. xxi. And as for business, it's got down to the HARD PAN, and dollars are skurce.

1861. HOLMES, *Elsie Venner*, ch. viii. Mr. Silas Peckham had gone a little deeper than he meant, and came upon the HARD-PAN, as the well-diggers call it, of the Colonel's character, before he thought of it.

1888. *Missouri Republican*, 2 Mar. Prices were at HARD-PAN.

TO GET DOWN TO HARD-PAN, *verb. phr.* (American).—1. To buckle to; to get to business.

HARD-PUNCHER, *subs.* (common).—The fur cap of the London rough; formerly worn by men in training; a modification of the Scotch cap with a peak. [From the nickname of a noted pugilist.]

HARD-PUSHED, *adv.* (colloquial).—In difficulties; HARD-UP (*q.v.*).

a. 1871. *Perils of Pearl Street*, p. 123. As I said, at the end of six months we began to be HARD-PUSHED. Our credit, however, was still fair.

HARD PUT TO, *adj. phr.* (colloquial).—In a difficulty, monetary or other; *e.g.*, He'd be HARD PUT TO IT to find a sovereign (or a word, or an excuse)=It would take him all his time, etc.

HARD-ROW. *See* ROW.

HARD-RUN, *adj.* (colloquial).—In want of money; HARD-UP (*q.v.*).

HARD-SHELL, *subs.* (American).—A member of an extreme section of Baptists holding very strict and rigid views. [The SOFT-SHELLS are of more liberal mind.] Also HARDS and SOFTS.

1848. JONES, *Sketches of Travel*, p. 30. The old HARD-SHELL laid about him like eath.

1888. *Baltimore Sun*. Mr. E., a regular member of the HARD-SHELL Baptist Church.

1893. STEVENSON, *Island Night's Entertainments*, p. 35. He's a HARD-SHELL Baptist is Papa.

2. (political American). — A division of the Democratic Party in 1846-48, when the HUNKERS (*q.v.*) received the name of HARDS, and their opponents, the BARN-BURNERS (*q.v.*) that of SOFTS.

1847. ROBB, *Squatter Life*, p. 91. HARDS, softs, whigs and Tylerites were represented.

Adj. (American). — Extremely orthodox; unyielding; hide-bound.

HARD-STUFF, *subs.* (American).—1. Money.

2. (Australian). — Intoxicating liquors; *see* HARD (*adj.* sense 2). For synonyms *see* DRINKS.

HARD-TACK, *subs.* (nautical).—1. Ship's biscuits; specifically, ordinary sea-fare as distingushed from food ashore, or SOFT-TOMMY (*q.v.*).

1841. LEVER, *Charles O'Malley*, ch. lxxxviii. No more HARD-TACK, thought I, no salt butter, but a genuine land breakfast.

1889. *Lippincott*, Oct., p. 476. They have feasted on salt horse and HARD-TACK many a day; but they know a good thing when they find it.

2 (common).—Coarse or insufficient fare.

HARD-UP, *subs.* (common).—1. A collector of cigar ends, a TOPPER-HUNTER. [Which refuse, untwisted and chopped up, is sold to the very poor.] Sometimes HARD-CUT. Fr., *un mégottier*.

1851-61. H. MAYHEW, *Lond. Lab. and Lond. Poor*, i., p. 5. The cigar-end finders, or HARD-UPS, as they are called, who collect the refuse pieces of smoked cigars from the gutters, and having dried them, sell them as tobacco to the very poor.

1888. *Tit Bits*, 24 March, 373. Smoking HARD-UP is picking up the stumps of cigars thrown away in the streets, cutting them up, and smoking them in the pipe.

1891. *Morning Advertiser*, 26 Mar. A constable on duty on the Embankment early in the morning saw the accused prowling about, and on asking what he was doing, received the reply that he was looking for HARD CUT.—Mr. Vaughan: Looking for what?—The Prisoner: HARD-CUT; dropped cigar-ends.

2. (common).—A poor man; a STONY-BROKE (*q.v.*).

1857. DUCANGE ANGLICUS, *Vulg. Tongue*. HARD-UP, a poor person.

Adv. phr. (colloquial).—1. Very badly in want of money; in urgent need of anything. Also HARD-RUN and HARD-PUSHED.

1809-41. TH. HOOK, *The Sutherlands*. He returned, and being HARD UP, as we say, took it into his head to break a shop-window at Liverpool, and take out some trumpery trinket stuff.

1821. HAGGART, *Life*, p. 104. There I met in with two Edinburgh snibs, who were HARD UP.

1837. BARHAM, *Ingoldsby Legends*, 'Merchant of Venice.' Who by showing at Operas, Balls, Plays, and Court, ... Had shrunk his 'weak means,' and was 'stump'd' and HARD UP.

1852. DICKENS, *Bleak House*, ch. xi. He . . . . was, not to put too fine a point upon it HARD-UP.

1865. *New York Herald*. This anxiety . . . . shows conclusively that they are HARD-UP for political capital.

1871. *Lond. Figaro*, 25 Jan. For years, England has been a refuge for HARD-UP German princelings.

1887. MANVILLE FENN, *This Man's Wife*, i., 13. I don't look HARD UP do I? No, because you've spent my money on your wretched dress.

1891. *Fun*, 25 Mar. You're HARD UP, ain't you? Stumped? Well, it's Threadneedle Street to a frying-pan, that if Popsy knew your real name, he'd lend you a thousand or two like a shot.

ENGLISH SYNONYMS.—Many under FLOORED apply equally to HARD-UP; others are:—At low water mark; cracked up; dead-broke; down on one's luck; fast; in Queer Street; in the last of pea time; in the last run of shad; low down; low in the lay; oofless; out of favor with the oof-bird; pebble-beached; seedy; short; sold-up; stony-broke; strapped; stuck; stumped; suffering from an attack of the week's (or month's) end; tight; on one's uppers; under a cloud; on one's beam ends.

FRENCH SYNONYMS.—*Se mettre dans le bœuf* (common=to go in for BLOCK ORNAMENTS (*q.v.*)); *être en brindezingue* (mountebanks = gone to smash); *être brouillé avec la monnaie* (familiar=to have had a row with one's banker); *être coupé* (printers'); *être à la côte* (familiar = on the shelf); *être fauché* (thieves' = cut down); *être dans la purée* (thieves'); *être molle* (thieves'); *être à la faridon* (popular); *être en dèche* (popular); *être désargenté* (thieves'=oofless); *être bref* (popular=short); *être à fond de cale* (popular=down to bed-rock); *être à la manque* (popular=on short commons); *manger de la misère* (popular= to sup sorrow); *être dans le lac* (popular = a hole); *être pané* (general); *panné comme la Hollande* (general=very hard up).

SPANISH SYNONYMS. — *Estar pelado* or *ser un pelado*(=skinned); *tiñoso* (=scabby).

ITALIAN SYNONYM.—*Calcare a ventun 'ora.*

2. (common). — Intoxicated. For synonyms, *see* DRINKS and SCREWED.

3. (Winchester College).—Out of countenance; exhausted (in swimming).

HARD-UPNESS or **HARD-UPPISHNESS**, *subs.* (colloquial).–Poverty; a condition of impoverishment.

1876. HINDLEY, *Adventures of a Cheap Jack.* There were frequent . . . . collapses from death or HARD-UPNESS.

1883. *Illust. London News*, 26 May, p. 519, c. 3. These I O U's . . . . do not imply, as might be supposed, common HARDUPNESS.

1891. N. GOULD, *Double Event*, p. 28. Ike's knowledge of some of the bookmakers he had met in the old land led him to believe that HARD-UPPISHNESS would scare any knight of the pencil away.

HARDWARE (or **HARD**), *subs.* (American).—Counterfeit coin.

1859. MATSELL, *Vocabulum*, s.v.

HARDWARE-BLOKE, *subs.* (thieves'). —A native of Birmingham; a BRUM (*q.v.*).

HARDY-ANNUAL, *subs.* (Parliamentary).—A bill that is brought in every year, but never passed into law. Hence (journalistic), any stock subject.

1892. *Pall Mall Gaz.*, 16 Aug., p. 4, c. 2. Signs of the so-called 'silly season' which has been somewhat delayed this year owing to the political crisis, are now beginning to appear. The readers of the *Daily Telegraph* are once more filling the columns of that journal with 'Is Marriage a Failure?' The HARDY ANNUAL is called 'English Wives' this time

HARE, *verb.* (old).—To dodge; to double; to bewilder.

1719. DURFEY, *Pills*, etc., i., 92. Running, HARING, gaping, staring.

1672. MARVELL, *Rehearsal, Tr.* (Grosart), iii, 372. They amaze, shatter and HARE their people.

TO HARE IT, *verb. phr.* (American thieves').—To retrace one's steps; to double back. [From the way of a hare with the hounds.]

TO MAKE A HARE OF, *verb. phr.* (colloquial).—To make ridiculous; to expose the ignorance of any person.

1830-32. CARLETON, *Traits and Stories*, 'The Hedge-School.' What A HARE that MADE OF him . . . . and did not leave him a leg to stand on!

1844. LEVER, *Tom Burke of Ours*, ii., 393. It was Mister Curran MADE A HARE OF your Honor that day.

TO SWALLOW A HARE, *verb. phr.* (old).—To get very drunk. For synonyms, *see* DRINKS and SCREWED.

1690. B. E., *Dict. Cant. Crew*, s.v.

1725. *New Cant. Dict.* HARE, s.v.

1785. GROSE, *Vulg. Tongue*, s.v. HE HAS SWALLOWED A HARE, he is drunk, more probably a hair which requires washing down.

1859. MATSELL, *Vocabulum*, s.v.

TO HOLD WITH THE HARE AND HUNT WITH THE HOUNDS, *verb. phr.* (colloquial).—To play a double game; to keep on good terms with two conflicting parties.

1690. B. E., *Dict. Cant. Crew*, s.v.

TO KISS THE HARE'S FOOT. *verb. phr.* (colloquial).—To be late; to be a day after the fair; to kiss the post.

HARE-BRAINED(or **HAIR-BRAINED**), *adj.* (old colloquial: now recognised).—Reckless; flighty; impudent; skittish. Also, substantively, HARE-BRAIN = a hare-brained person.

1534. N. UDAL, *Roister Doister*, I., iv., p. 27 (Arber). Ah foolish HARE-BRAINE, This is not she.

1592. NASHE, *Pierce Penilesse*, in *Wks.*, ii., 53. A HAREBRAIND little Dwarfe it is.

1621. BURTON, *Anat. of Mel.*, I., III., I., ii., 259 (1836). Yet again, many of them, desperate HARE-BRAINS.

1622. BACON, *Henry VII.* That same HAIRE-BRAINE wild fellow, my subject.

1751. SMOLLETT, *Peregrine Pickle*, ch. xliii. When the government of a nation depends upon the caprice of the ignorant, HAIR-BRAINED vulgar.

1870. *Chambers' Miscellany*, No. 53, p. 28. The Slater girls are as HARE-BRAINED as herself.

HARED, *adj.* (old).—Hurried.

HARE-SLEEP, *subs.* (old).—Sham slumber; FOXES' SLEEP (*q.v.*).

1690. B. E., *Dict. Cant. Crew*, s.v. HARE-SLEEP, with Eies a'most open.

HARKING, *subs.* (old).—*See* quots.

1690. B. E., *Dict. Cant. Crew*, s.v. HARKING, whispering on one side to borrow Money.

1725. *New. Cant. Dict.*, s.v.

1785. GROSE, *Vulg. Tongue*, s.v. HARK-YE-ING, whispering on one side to borrow money.

HARLEQUIN, *subs.* (theatrical).—1. A sovereign. For synonyms, *see* CANARY.

2. (Winchester College).—The wooden nucleus of a red india-rubber ball.

3. (old).—A patchwork quilt.

HARLEQUIN CHINA, *adj. phr.* (old).—Sets composed of several patterns and makes.

HARLOTRY, *subs.* (old).—A wanton.

d. 1529. SKELTON, *Bowge of Courte.* He had no pleasure but in HARLOTRYE.

1672. WYCHERLEY, *Love in a Wood*, iv., 1. But O the HARLOTRY, did she make that use of it then.

1695. CONGREVE, *Love for Love*, iii., 1. O you young HARLOTRY.

1893. T. E. BROWN, *Old John*, p. 205. That specious HARLOTRY from hell's black bosom spewed.

Adj. (old).—Disreputable.

1598. SHAKSPEARE, 1 *Henry IV.*, ii., 4. Oh rare! he doth it as like one of these HARLOTRY players, as ever I see.

HARMAN-BECK (or **HARMAN**), *subs.* (old).—An officer of justice. For synonyms, *see* BEAK and COPPER.

1567. HARMAN, *Caveat* (1814), p. 66. The HARMAN-BECK, the constable.

1610. ROWLANDS, *Martin Mark-All.* With the HARMAN-BEAKE out and alas to Whittington we goe.

1656. BROOME, *Jovial Crew*, ii. Here safe in our skipper let's cly off our peck, And bowse in defiance o' th' HARMAN-BECK.

1690. B. E., *Dict. Cant. Crew*, s.v. HARMAN-BECK, a Beadle.

1714. *Memoirs of John Hall* (4th ed.), p. 12. HARMINBECK, a Constable.

1785. GROSE, *Vulg. Tongue*, s.v HARMAN BECK, a beadle (*cant*).

1822. SCOTT, *Fortunes of Nigel*, ch. xvii. From the watchmen who skip On the HARMAN BECK'S errand.

1828. LYTTON, *The Disowned.* The worst have an awe of the HARMAN'S claw.

1859. MATSELL, *Vocabulum*, s.v. HARMAN BEAK. The Sheriff.

HARMANS, *subs.* (Old Cant).—The stocks. [The suffix 'MANS' is common; *Cf.*, LIGHTMANS, DARKMANS, ROUGHMANS, etc.]

1567. HARMAN, *Caveat* (1814), p. 66. The HARMANS, the stocks.

1610. ROWLANDS, *Martin Mark-All*, p. 39 (H. Club's Rept., 1874). HARMONS the stockes.

1690. B. E., *Dict. Cant. Crew*, s.v.

1714. *Memoirs of John Hall* (4th ed.), p. 12, s.v.

1725. *New Cant. Dict.*, s.v.

1785. GROSE, *Vulg. Tongue*, s.v.

HARNESS. IN HARNESS, *adj. phr.* (colloquial).—In business; at work: as, TO DIE IN HARNESS =to die at one's post; TO GET BACK INTO HARNESS=to resume work after a holiday. [HARNESS also=armour.]

1872. *Fun*, 10 Aug. 'Over.' Aye! But the sting of it's here, Just as I'm back INTO HARNESS, Others are off to sea, mountain, and mere.

1892. HUME NISBET, *Bushranger's Sweetheart*, p. 2. My father died IN HARNESS.

HARP, *interject.* (Irish).—*See* quot.

1785. GROSE, *Vulg. Tongue*, s.v. HARP . . . . HARP is also the Irish expression for 'woman' or 'tail,' used in tossing up in Ireland, from Hibernia being represented with a harp, on the reverse of the copper coins of that country, for which reason it is *in hoisting the copper, i.e.*, tossing up, sometimes likewise called music.

TO HARP ON, *verb. phr.* (old, now recognised).—To dwell persistently and at any cost upon a subject.

1596. NASHE, *Have with you to Saffron Walden.* As if I had continually HARPED UPON it in every tenth line of my book.

1596. SHAKSPEARE, *Hamlet*, ii., 2. Still HARPING ON my daughter.

1690. B. E., *Dict. Cant. Crew*, s.v. HARP-UPON a business, to insist on it.

1785. GROSE, *Vulg. Tongue*, s.v.

1886. R. L. STEVENSON, *Kidnapped*, p. 291. He was back HARPING ON my proposal.

HARPER, *subs.* (old).—A brass coin current in Ireland, *temp.* Elizabeth, value one penny. [From the Irish Harp figured upon it.]

1574-1637. BEN JONSON, *The Gipsies Metamorphosed.* A two-pence I had to spend over and above; besides the HARPER that was gathered amongst us to pay the piper.

HAVE AMONG YOU MY BLIND HARPERS, *phr.* (old).—*See* quot.

1725. *New Cant. Dict.*, s.v. HARPERS.

1785. GROSE, *Vulg. Tongue*, s.v. HAVE AMONG YOU MY BLIND HARPERS, an expression used in throwing or shooting at random among a crowd.

HARRIDAN, *subs.* (old, now recognised).—*See* quots. Also (colloquial) a disagreeable old woman. [A corruption of O. Fr. *haridelle* =a worn out horse, a jade.]

1690. B. E., *Dict. Cant. Crew*, s.v. HARRIDAN, one that is half Whore, half Bawd.

1705-7. WARD, *Hudibras Redivivus*, vol. II., pt. ii., p. 27. Old Leachers, HARRIDANS, and Cracks.

1725. *New Cant. Dict.*, s.v.

1785. GROSE, *Vulg. Tongue*, s.v. HARRIDAN, a hagged old woman, a miserable scraggy worn out harlot, fit to take her bawd's degree.

1815. SCOTT, *Guy Mannering*, ch., xxxix. 'Now what could drive it into the noddle of that old HARRIDAN,' said Pleydell.

1859. MATSELL, *Vocabulum*, s.v.

HARRINGTON, *subs.* (old).—A brass farthing. [Lord Harrington obtained a patent of manufacture under James I.]

1616. B. JONSON, *Devil is an Ass*, ii., 1. Yes, sir, it's cast to penny halfpenny farthing, O' the back side there you may see it, read; I will not bate a HARRINGTON o' the sum.

1632. B. JONSON, *Magn. Lady*, ii., 6. His wit he cannot so dispose by legacy As they shall be a HARRINGTON the better for't.

HARRY, *subs.* (old).—1. A countryman; a clown. For synonyms, *see* JOSKIN.

1811. *Lexicon Balatronicum*, s.v. HARRY. A country fellow.

2. (colloquial).—*See* 'ARRY.

OLD HARRY, *subs.* (common). —The devil. For synonyms, *see* SKIPPER.

1693. CONGREVE, *Old Bachelor*, ii., 1. By the LORD HARRY I'll stay no longer.

1811. *Lexicon Balatronicum*, s.v.

1830. LYTTON, *Paul Clifford*, ch. iv. May OLD HARRY fly off with him.

1837. BARHAM, *Ingoldsby Legends* (1865), p. 406. Shall I summon OLD HARRY himself to this spot?

HARRY OF THE WEST, *subs. phr.* (political American).—Henry Clay.

TO PLAY OLD HARRY, *verb. phr.* (common).—To annoy; to ruin; to play the devil.

1889. *Licensed Vict. Gaz.*, 18 Jan. Otherwise PLAYED OLD HARRY with the guardians of the peace.

TOM, DICK, AND HARRY, *phr.* (common).—Generic for any and everybody; the mob.

1886. R L STEVENSON, *Kidnapped*, p. 287. He rode from public house to public house and shouted his sorrows into ug of TOM, DICK, AND HARRY.

WHAT HARRY GAVE DOLL, *verb. phr.* (old venery).—The *penis*: also generic for fornication.

HARRY-BLUFF, *subs.* (rhyming).—Snuff.

HARRY-COMMON, *subs. phr.* (old). —A general wencher.

1675. WYCHERLEY, *Country Wife*, v., 4. Well, HARRY COMMON, I hope you can be true to three.

HARRY-SOPH, *subs.* (Cambridge Univ.: obsolete).—*See* quots.

1795. *Gent. Mag.*, p. 20. A HARRY, or ERRANT SOPH, I understand to be either a person, four-and-twenty years of age, and of an infirm state of health, who is permitted to dine with the fellows, are to wear a plain, black, full-sleeved gown: or, else, he is one who, having kept all the terms, by statute required previous to his law-act, is *hoc ipso facto* entitled to wear the same garment, and, thenceforth, ranks as bachelor, by courtesy.

1803. *Gradus ad Cantabrigiam.* HARRY SOPH; or HENRY SOPHISTER; students who have kept all the terms required for a law act, and hence are ranked as Bachelors of Law by courtesy. They wear a plain, black, full-sleeved gown.

HARUM-SCARUM, *adj.* and *subs.* (old colloquial).—1. Giddy; careless; wild; a thoughtless or reckless fellow.

1740. *Round about our Coal Fire*, c. i. Peg would scuttle about to make a toast for John, while Tom run HARUM SCARUM to draw a jug of ale for Margery.

1780 MAD. D'ARBLAY, *Diary*, i., 358 [ed. 1842]. He seemed a mighty rattling HAREM-SCAREM gentleman.

1785. GROSE, *Vulg. Tongue*, s.v. HARUM SCARUM, he was running HARUM SCARUM, said of any one running or walking carelessly and in a hurry, after they know not what.

1836. MARRYAT, *Japhet*, ch. xcii. I'm not one of those HARUM-SCARUM sort, who would make up a fight when there's no occasion for it.

1855. THACKERAY, *Newcomes*, ch. v. They had a quarrel with Thomas Newcome's own son, a HARUM-SCARUM lad, who ran away, and then was sent to India.

1870. *London Figaro*, 19 Oct. 'Within an inch.' Tom—that's my son—has worked with me in the mine ever since he was quite a little chap; and a HARUM-SCARUM young dog he was, when a boy.

2. (sporting).—Four horses driven in a line; SUICIDE (*q.v.*).

HAS-BEEN, *subs.* (colloquial Scots'). —Anything antiquated; specifically in commendation: as 'the good old HAS-BEENS'; *cf.*, NEVER WAS.

1891. *Sportsman*, 1 Apr. Big Joe M'Auliffe proved conclusively that he is one of the HAS BEENS or else one of the NEVER WASERS, as Dan Rice, the circus man, always called ambitious counterfeits.

HASH, *subs.* (colloquial).—1. A mess; specifically in the phrase 'to make a HASH of.' For synonyms, *see* SIXES AND SEVENS.

1747. WALPOLE, *Lett. to Mann*, 23 Feb (1833) Vol. II., p. 274. About as like it, as my Lady Pomfret's HASH of plural persons and singular verbs or infinitive moods was to Italian.

1836. MICHAEL SCOTT, *Cruise of the Midge*, p. 115 [Ry. ed.]. Listado never could compass Spanish, because, as he said, he had previously learnt French, and thus spoke a HASH of both.

1837. BARHAM, *Ingoldsby Legends*. 'M. of Venice.' Don't suppose my affairs are at all IN A HASH, But the fact is, at present I'm quite out of cash.

1843. *Punch's Almanack*, July (*q.v.*).

1845. *Punch's Guide to Servants*, 'The Cook,' Vol. IX., p. 45. He who gives a receipt for making a stew, may himself make a sad HASH of it.

1886. R. L. STEVENSON, *Kidnapped*, p. 97. Ye've made a sore HASH of my brig.

1889. *Sporting Life*, 30 Jan. Successfully negotiated the tricky entrance to the stable-yard of the hotel, at which job have been in a mortal funk many a time with poor old Jim beside me, for fear of making a HASH of it.

1890. GRANT ALLEN, *Tents of Shem*, ch. xvi. She made a HASH of the proper names, to be sure.

2. (American cadets').—Clandestine preparation for supper after hours.

3. (colloquial).—A sloven; a blockhead.

1785 BURNS, *Epistle to J. Lapraik*. A set o' dull, conceited HASHES.

Verb (colloquial).—1. To spoil; to jumble; to cook up and serve again.

1891. *Notes and Queries*, 7 S. xii., 22 Aug., p. 144. I do not think that Earle, a scholar of a high order and a man of the most keen wit and judgment, would have spoken thus of a thing HASHED UP by a hard-headed pedant, however able, such as Gauden.

2. (American). — To vomit. Also to FLASH THE HASH (*q.v.*). For synonyms, *see* ACCOUNTS and CAT.

1785. GROSE, *Vulg. Tongue*, s.v.

1859. MATSELL, *Vocabulum*, s.v.

3. (Cheltenham School).—To study hard; to SWAT (*q.v.*).

TO SETTLE ONE'S HASH, *verb. phr.* (common).—To defeat one's object; to kill. For synonyms, *see* COOK ONE'S GOOSE.

1864. BROWNING, *Dramatis Personæ*. 'Youth and Art.' You've to settle yet Gibson's HASH.

c. 1871. BUTLER, *Nothing to Wear*. To use an expression More striking than classic, it SETTLED MY HASH.

1883. *Punch*, Nov. 3, p. 208, c. 1. That one stab, with a clasp-knife, which SETTLED THE young Squire's HASH in less than two seconds.

1892. HUME NISBET, *Bushranger's Sweetheart*, p. 123. We'll keep the cops off till you SETTLE HIS HASH, the rest replied, getting round us.

TO GO BACK ON ONE'S HASH, *verb. phr.* (American).—To turn; to succumb; to WEAKEN (*q.v.*).

HASH-HOUSE, *subs.* (American).—A cheap eating-house; a GRUBBING crib (*q.v.*).

1883. *Daily Telegraph*, 10 Jan., p. 5, c. 4. There are [in New York] lunch counters, cookshops, 'penny' restaurants, fifteen-cent restaurants, commonly called HASH-HOUSES and foreign cafés.

HASLAR-HAG, *subs.* (nautical).—A nurse at the Haslar Hospital. *Cf.*, HAG.

HASTINGS. TO BE NONE OF THE HASTINGS SORT, *verb. phr.* (old colloquial). — To be slow, deliberate, or slothful.

1690. B. E., *Dict. Cant. Crew*, s.v. You are NONE OF THE HASTINGS, of him that loses an Opportunity or a Business for want of Dispatch

1785. GROSE, *Vulg. Tongue*, s.v.

1811. *Lexicon Balatronicum*, s.v. HE IS NONE OF THE HASTINGS SORT; a saying of a slow, loitering fellow: an allusion to the Hastings pea, which is the first in season.

HASTY, *adj.* (old: now recognised). —Rash; passionate; quick to move.

1690. B. E., *Dict. Cant. Crew*, s.v. HASTY, very Hot on a sudden.

1785. GROSE, *Vulg. Tongue*, s.v.

HASTY G., *subs.* (Cambridge Univ.).—*See* quot.

1883. *Daily News*, 24 Mar., p. 5, c. 2. Mr. Weller's own HASTY G (as Cambridge men say when they mean a 'hasty generalisation').

HASTY PUDDING, *subs.* (common). —1. A bastard. For synonyms, *see* BLOODY ESCAPE.

2. (old).—A muddy road; a quag.

1811. *Lexicon Balatronicum*, s.v. The way through Wandsworth is quite a HASTY PUDDING.

HAT, *subs.* (Cambridge Univ.).—1. A gentleman commoner. [Who is permitted to wear a hat instead of the regulation mortar-board.] Also GOLD HATBAND.

1628. EARLE, *Microcosmographie*. 'Young Gentleman of the Universitie' (ed., ARBER, 1868). His companion is ordinarily some stale fellow that has beene notorious for an ingle to GOLD HATBANDS, whom hee admires at first, afterwards scornes.

1803. *Gradus ad Cantabrigiam*. Hat Commoner; the son of a Nobleman, who wears the gown of a Fellow Commoner with a HAT.

1830. LYTTON, *Paul Clifford*, ch. xxxii. I knew intimately all the HATS in the University.

1841. LYTTON, *Night and Morning*, bk. I., ch. i. He had certainly nourished the belief that some one of the HATS or tinsel gowns—*i.e.*, young lords or fellow-commoners, with whom he was on such excellent terms . . . . would do something for him in the way of a living.

2. (venery). — The female *pudendum*. Generally OLD HAT. For synonyms, *see* MONOSYLLABLE.

1754. FIELDING, *Jonathan Wild*, i., 6 (note). I shall conclude this learned note with remarking that the term OLD HAT is used by the vulgar in no very honourable sense.

1760. STERNE, *Tristam Shandy*, ch. cxxvi. A chapter of chambermaids, green gowns, and OLD HATS.

1785. GROSE, *Vulg. Tongue*, s.v. ['Because often *felt*.'] *See* also TOP DIVER.

1811. *Lexicon Balatronicum*, s.v.

3. (Scots').—A prostitute of long standing. For synonyms, *ee* BARRACK-HACK and TART.

TO EAT ONE'S HAT (or HEAD), *verb. phr.* (common).—Generally, I'LL EAT MY HAT. Used in strong emphasis. *See* EAT.

1836. DICKENS, *Pickwick*, xlii., 367. 'If I knew as little of life as that, I'd EAT MY HAT and swallow the buckle whole,' said the clerical gentleman.

1837. DICKENS, *Oliver Twist*, ch. xiv. Even admitting the possibility of scientific improvements being ever brought to that pass which will enable a man to EAT HIS OWN HEAD, Mr. Grimwig's head was such a particularly large one that the most sanguine man alive could hardly entertain a hope of being able to get through it at a sitting.

1844. J. B. BUCKSTONE, *The Maid with the Milking Pail*. If you are not as astonished as I was, I'll EAT OLD ROWLEY'S HAT.

1876. HINDLEY, *Adventures of a Cheap Jack*, p. 216. I'll EAT MY HAT.

1887. E. E. MONEY, *Little Dutch Maiden*, II., viii., 148. And if you don't run up against him next day in Bond Street, you may EAT YOUR HAT!

1892. MILLIKEN, *'Arry Ballads*, p. 38. If some of the swells didn't ditto, I'll EAT MY OLD HAT, which it's tough.

TO GET A HAT, *verb. phr.* (cricketers').—*See* HAT-TRICK.

TO GET INTO THE HAT, *verb. phr.* (common). — To get into trouble.

TO HAVE A BRICK IN ONE'S HAT, *verb. phr.* (American).—To be top-heavy with drink. For synonyms, *see* DRINKS and SCREWED.

TO HANG UP ONE'S HAT.—*See* HANG.

TO PASS (or SEND) ROUND THE HAT, *verb. phr.* (colloquial).—To make a collection.

TO TALK THROUGH ONE'S HAT, *verb. phr.* (American) —To rag; to huff; to bluster.

1888. *New York World*, 13 May. Dis is only a bluff dey're makin'—see! Dey're TALKIN' TRU DEIR HATS.

ALL ROUND MY HAT, *phr.* (streets). — A derisive retort. [From a Broadside Ballad, popular *c.* 1830: 'All round my hat I wears a green willow, All round my hat for a twelvemonth and a day, And if any one should ask you the reason why I wear it, Tell them my true love is gone far away'; sung to a tune adapted from a number in *Zampa*.] Also, as in quot. = all over; completely; generally.

1892. MILLIKEN, *'Arry Ballads*, p. 54. I'm a 'ot un, mate, ALL ROUND MY 'AT.

SHOOT THAT HAT! *phr.* (streets).—A derisive retort. Also I'LL HAVE YOUR HAT! Both *circa* 1860-72.

WELL, YOU CAN TAKE MY HAT! *phr.* (American) = 'Well, that beats me,' *i.e.*, 'that is past belief.'

873. *A Yankee in a Planter's House*. 'What's yer name?' 'Name Grief, manssa.' 'Name *what?*' 'Name Grief.' 'Get out! Yew're jokin'! What's yer name, anyhow?' 'Name Grief manssa.' 'WAL, YEW KIN TAKE MY HAT.

WHAT A SHOCKING BAD HAT *phr.* (streets). — [Said to have originated with a candidate for parliamentary honours, who made the remark to his poorer constituents, and promised them new head-gear.]

1892. ANSTEY, *Model Music Hall*, 140. *Lord B.* Regular bounder! SHOCKING BAD HAT! *Ver.* Not so bad as his boots, and they are not so bad as his face.

HATCH, *verb.* (common).—To be brought to bed with child; to BUST UP (*q.v.*).

TO BE UNDER HATCHES, *verb. phr.* (colloquial).—To be in a state of trouble, poverty or depression. Also dead.

1606. MARSTON, *The Fawne*, iv. Remember hee got his elder brother's wife with child . . . . that will stow him UNDER HATCHES, I warrant you.

1632–1704. LOCKE [quoted in *Ency. Dict.*]. He assures us how this fatherhood continued its course, till the captivity in Egypt, and then the poor fatherhood WAS UNDER HATCHES.

1639-1661. *Rump Songs*, i. [1662], 260. And all her orphans bestowed UNDER HATCHES.

1690. B. E., *Dict. Cant. Crew*, s.v. UNDER THE HATCHES, in Trouble, or Prison.

1725. *New Cant. Dict.*, s.v. UNDER THE HATCHES, in Trouble, or Prison.

1785. GROSE, *Vulg. Tongue*, s.v. UNDER THE HATCHES, in trouble, distress, or debt.

1789. DIBDIN, *Tom Bowling*, For though his body's UNDER HATCHES his soul has gone aloft.

1835. BUCKSTONE, *Dream at Sea*. ., 3. Good-bye, dame, cheer up; you may not always be UNDER HATCHES.

1859. MATSELL, *Vocabulum*, s.v.

HATCHET, *subs.* (tailors'). — 1. An ill-favoured woman. For general synonyms, *see* UGLY MUG.

2. (American).—A bribe received by Customs officers in New York for permitting imported dutiable goods to remain on the wharf when they ought to go to the general store-house.

TO BURY (or DIG UP) THE HATCHET.—*See* BURY.

TO THROW (or SLING) THE HATCHET, *verb. phr.* (common). —1. To tell lies, to yarn; to DRAW THE LONG BOW (*q.v.*). Hence HATCHET FLINGING (or THROWING) = lying or yarning.

1789. GEO. PARKER, *Life's Painter*, p. 94. This is a fault, which many of good understanding may fall into, who, from giving way too much to the desire of telling anecdotes, adventures, and the like, habituate themselves by degrees to a mode of the HATCHET-FLINGING extreme.

1821. P. EGAN, *Life in London*, p. 217. There is nothing creeping or THROWING THE HATCHET about this description.

1893. EMERSON, *Signor Lippo*, ch. xx. We had to call her mother, and, if any-one stopped, she'd SLING THE HATCHET to them, and tell them she was a poor lone widow left with five children.

2. (nautical).—To sulk.

HATCHET-FACED, *adj.* (old colloquial: now recognised). — *See* quots. For synonyms, *see* UGLY-MUG.

1690. B. E., *Dict. Cant. Crew*, s.v. HATCHET-FAC'D, Hard favor'd, Homely.

1725. *New. Cant. Dict.*, s.v.

1785. GROSE, *Vulg. Tongue*, s.v. HATCHET FACE, a long thin face.

1865. SALA, *Trip to Barbary*, p. 130. The man in black baize with the felt képi, and who had a HATCHET FACE desperately scarred with the small-pox, looked from head to heel a bad egg.

1888. J. RUNCIMAN, *The Chequers*, p. 7. His HATCHET FACE with its piggish eyes, his thin cruel lips, his square jaw, are all murderous.

HATCH, MATCH, AND DISPATCH COLUMN, *subs. phr.* (journalistic). — The births, marriages, and deaths announcements. Also CRADLE, ALTAR AND TOMB COLUMN.

HATCHWAY, *subs.* (common).—1. The mouth. For synonyms, *see* POTATO-TRAP.

2. (venery). — The female *pudendum*. Also FORE-HATCH. For synonyms, *see* MONOSYLLABLE.

HATE-OUT, *verb.* (American).—To boycott; to send to Coventry.

18(?). S. KERCHEVAL, *History of Virginia*. The punishment for idleness, lying, dishonesty, and ill-fame generally, was that of HATING the offender OUT, as they expressed it. It commonly resulted in the reformation or banishment of the person against whom it was directed. If a man did not do his share of the public service, he was HATED-OUT as a coward.

HATFIELD, *subs.* (common). — A drink, whose chief ingredients are gin and ginger-beer.

1883. *Daily News*, 5 July, p. 5, c. 1 There are, we believe, all sorts of strong waters in the mild-looking and seductive HATFIELD, while the majority of 'cups' are distinctly 'mixed.'

HATFUL, *subs.* (colloquial). — A large quantity; a heap.

1859. *Punch*, lxxx., vi., 236. If they had trusted their own judgment they would have won a HATFUL.

1864. M. E. BRADDON, *Henry Dunbar*, ch. xxii. He was in a very good temper however, for he had won what his companions called a HATFUL of money on the steeple-chase.

HATPEG, *subs.* (common). — The head. For synonyms, *see* CRUMPET.

HATTER, *subs.* (Australian). — A gold-digger working alone.

1881. A. BATHGATE, *Waitaruna*, p. 88. He is what they call a HATTER, that is he works alone.

1885. *Chambers' Journal*, 2 May, p. 286. Some prefer to travel, and even to work, when they can get it, alone, and these are known to the rest as HATTERS.

1890. *Illustrations*, p. 158. The former occupant was what is known as a HATTER, *i.e.*, a digger living by himself.

1890. MARRIOTT WATSON, *Broken Billy*. He was looked upon as a HATTER, that is to say, a man who has lived by himself until his brain has been turned.

WHO'S YOUR HATTER? *phr.* (streets).—A catch-cry long out of vogue.

MAD AS A HATTER, *phr.* (colloquial).—Very mad.

1863. MARSHALL [Title of a farce]. MAD AS A HATTER.

HAT-TRICK, *subs.* (cricket).—Taking three wickets with three consecutive balls: which feat is held to entitle the bowler to a new hat at the cost of the club.

1888. *Sportsman*, 28 Nov. Mr. Absolom has performed the HAT TRICK twice, and at Tufnell Park he took four wickets with four balls.

1892. *Cassell's Sat. Jour.* 21 Sept., p. 13, c. 2. On one occasion I succeeded in doing the HAT TRICK.

1892. *Woolwich Polytechnic Mag.*, 20 May. Three of these wickets were taken in succession, thus accomplishing the HAT-TRICK.

HAT-WORK, *subs.* (journalists').—Hack work; such stuff as may be turned out by the yard without reference to quality.

1888. H. RIDER HAGGARD, *Mr. Meeson's Will*, c. 1. And five-and-twenty tame authors (who were illustrated by thirteen tame artists) sat—at salaries ranging from one to five hundred a year—in vault-like hutches in the basement, and week by week poured out that HAT-WORK for which Meeson's was justly famous.

HAULABLE, *adj.* (University).—Used of a girl whose society authorities deem undesirable for the men: *e.g.*, she's HAULABLE = a man caught with her will be proctorised.

HAUL-BOWLINE, *subs.* (nautical).—A seaman. For synonyms, *see* STRAWYARDER.

HAUL-DEVIL, *subs.* (common).—A clergyman. For synonyms, *see* DEVIL-DODGER and SKY-PILOT.

HAUL DEVIL, PULL BAKER. *See* DEVIL.

HAUT-BOY (or **HO-BOY**), *subs.* (American).—A night scavenger; a jakesman or GOLD-FINDER (*q.v.*).

HAVE, *subs.* (common).—1. A swindle; a TAKE-IN (*q.v.*); a DO (*q.v.*). For synonyms, *see* SELL.

2. *in. pl.* (common).—The moneyed classes; as opposed to the HAVE-NOTS, their antipodes.

1893. *National Observer*, Feb. 25, ix., 357. A body whose policy is to make the HAVE-NOTS as comfortable and objectionable as possible at the cost in coin and comfort of the HAVES.

3. (*in. pl.*) *subs.* (Winchester College).—Half-boots. Pronounced Hāves.

IS THAT A CATCH OR A HAVE? *verb. phr.* (vulgar).—A formula of acknowledgment that the speaker has been 'had.' [If the person addressed be unwise enough to answer with a definition, the instant retort is 'Then you CATCH (or HAVE, as the case may be) your nose up my arse.']

Verb (colloquial).—1. To cheat; TO TAKE-IN; TO DO. *See* BE.

1805. G. HARRINGTON, *New London Spy* (4th Ed.) p. 26. Ten to one but you are HAD, a cant word they make use of, instead of saying, as the truth is, we have cheated him.

1825. EGAN, *Life of an Actor*, ch. iv. 'He's not to be HAD,' said Gag, in an audible whisper.

1878. HATTON, *Cruel London*, bk. II., ch. v. 'They have HAD me, bless you,' said Brayford, 'the men who have "limbed" you.'

1889. *Licensed Vict. Gaz.*, 8 Feb. Not to be HAD so easily, my good man.

1889. *Answers*, 23 Feb., p. 196, c. 2. But even these fellows, sharp as they are, have been caught napping lately in a humorous way. Those who have HAD them have been young fellows with friends *inside the Stock Exchange*.

1891. N. GOULD, *Double Event*, p. 161. HAD me nicely once at cards.

1891. *Licensed Vict. Gaz.*, 23 Jan. I never felt so wild in my life. I'm no fool, you know, and I began to think I was being HAD a bit.

1891. J. NEWMAN, *Scamping Tricks*, p. 58. I was nearly HAD.

1892. *Illus. Bits*, 22 Oct., p. 14. c. 2. Oh, melboy, Oi wasn't t' be HAD that way. Oi always kape resates—spishully Gov'ment wans. Oi got it safe and cosy in me pocket-book.

2. (venery).—To possess carnally. [Said indifferently of, and by, both sexes.] For synonyms, *see* GREENS.

TO HAVE HAD IT, *verb. phr.* (venery).—To have been seduced.

TO HAVE (or TAKE) IT OUT OF ONE, *verb. phr.* (colloquial).—To punish; to retaliate; to extort a *quid pro quo*; to give tit for tat.

TO HAVE IT OUT WITH ONE, *verb. phr.* (colloquial).—To speak freely in reproof; to complete an explanation; to settle a dispute with either words or blows.

1886. J. S. WINTER, *Army Society*, ch. xix. Instead of going down to St. Eve's and HAVING IT OUT, he fretted, and worried, and fumed the six days away.

1888. *Daily News*, 8 Dec. There was a question as to who struck the first blow, but it seemed to him certain that a man who crossed the road to HAVE IT OUT with another was the most likely to have commenced hostilities.

TO HAVE ON, *verb. phr.* (colloquial).—To secure a person's interest, attention, sympathy: generally with a view to deceiving him (or her).

TO HAVE TOWARDS (or WITH, or AT), *verb. phr.* (old).—1. To pledge in drinking; to toast. *See* HERE.

1637. CARTWRIGHT, *Royal Slave*. Here's to thee, Leocrates. *Leoc.* HAVE TOWARDS THEE, Philotas. *Phil.* To thee, Archippus. *Arch.* Here, Molops. *Mol.* HAVE AT YOU, fidlers.

1836. M. SCOTT, *Tom Cringle's Log*, ch. ii. 'HAVE WITH YOU, boy—have with you,' shouted half-a-dozen other voices, while each stuck his oaken twig through the handkerchief that held his bundle, and shouldered it, clapping his straw or tarpaulin hat, with a slap on the crown, on one side of his head, and staggering and swaying about under the influence of the poteen.

2. (common).—To agree with

TO HAVE ON TOAST, *verb. phr.* (common).—1. To take in.

2. (common).—To worst in argument.

TO HAVE ON THE RAWS, *verb. phr.* (common).—To teaze; to touch to the quick.

TO LET ONE HAVE IT, *verb. phr.* (colloquial).—To punish severely.

1848. RUXTON, *Life in the Far West*, p. 8. 'Hurraw, Dick, mind your hair,' and I ups old Greaser and let one Injun HAVE IT, as was going plum into the boy with his lance.

HAVE UP, *verb. phr.* (colloquial).—To bring before the authorities; to SUMMONS (*q.v.*).

HAVERCAKE-LADS, *subs. phr.* (Military).—The Thirty-third Foot. [From the circumstance that its recruiting sergeants always preceded their party with an oat-cake on their swords.]

HAVEY-CAVEY, *adj.* (old).—Uncertain; doubtful; shilly-shally.

1811. *Lexicon Balatronicum*, s.v.

1859. MATSELL, *Vocabulum*, s.v.

HAVIL, *subs.* (old).—A sheep. For synonyms, *see* WOOL-BIRD.

1811. *Lexicon Balatronicum*, s.v.

1859. MATSELL, *Vocabulum*, s.v.

HAVOCK, *subs.* (old: now recognised).—Devastation; waste.

1607. SHAKSPEARE, *Julius Cæsar*, iii., 1. Cry HAVOCK, and let slip the dogs of war.

1690. B. E., *Dict. Cant. Crew*, s.v. They made sad HAVOCK, they Destroy'd all before 'em.

1725. *New Cant. Dict.*, s.v.

HAWCUBITE, *subs.* (old).—A roysterer; a street bully. [After the Restoration there was a succession of these disturbers of the peace: first came the Muns, then followed the Tityre Tus, the Hectors, the Scourers, the Nickers, the Hawcubites, and after them the MOHAWKS (*q.v.*).]

HAWK, *subs.* (common).—1. A card-sharper; a ROOK (*q.v.*).

1690. B. E., *Dict. Cant. Crew*, s.v. HAWK, *c.*, a Sharper.

1725. *New Cant. Dict.*, s.v. HAWK, a Sharper.

1785. GROSE, *Vulg. Tongue*, s.v. HAWK also signifies a sharper, in opposition to pigeon.

1859. MATSELL, *Vocabulum*, s.v. HAWK. A Confidence Man; a swindler.

1891. *New York Herald* [London ed.], 31 May. These were HAWKS and pigeons, and those who are no longer pigeons, and never had, or will have, an inclination to be HAWKS.

2. (common).—A bailiff; a constable. For synonyms, *see* BEAK.

1834. AINSWORTH, *Rookwood*, bk. I., ch. iii. 'The game's spoiled this time, Rob Rust, anyhow,' growled one, in an angry tone; 'the HAWKS are upon us, and we must leave this brave buck to take care of himself.'

Verb (old).—*See* quots.

1589. NASHE, *Anatomie*, Whereas, by their humming and HAWKING . . . they have leisure to gesture the mislike of his rudeness.

1600. SHAKSPEARE, *As You Like It*, v., 3. Shall we clap into 't roundly, without HAWKING, or spitting, or saying we are hoarse?

1604. MARSTON, *Malcontent*, ii., 2. Is he troubled with the cough of the lungs still? Does he HAWKE a night's?

1690. B. E., *Dict. Cant Crew*, s.v. . . . . Also spitting difficultly.

1785. GROSE, *Vulg. Tongue*, s.v. . . . . HAWKING, an effort to spit up the thick phlegm, called *oysters*, whence it is wit upon record, to ask the person so doing, whether he has a license, a punning allusion to the act of HAWKERS and pedlars.

1815. SCOTT, *Guy Mannering*, ch. xlvi. This tremendous volley of superlatives which Sampson HAWKED up from the pit of his stomach.

1822. BYRON, *Vision of Judgment*, xc. To cough and HAWK, and hem, and pitch His voice into that awful note of woe.

WARE HAWK! *phr.* (old).—A warning; look sharp! *See subs.* sense 2.

d. 1529. SKELTON, *Ware Hawk* (Title).

1625. JONSON, *Staple of News*, v. 2. See! the whole covey is scattered; WARE, WARE THE HAWKS!

1785. GROSE, *Vulg. Tongue*, s.v. Hawk, WARE HAWK, the word to look sharp, a bye-word when a bailiff passes.

1815. SCOTT, *Guy Mannering*, ch. iii. WARE HAWK! Douse the Glim.

TO HAWK ONE'S MEAT, *verb. phr.* (common).—To peddle one's charms, *i.e.*, to show a great deal of neck and breasts. Fr., *montrer sa viande*.

HAWK-A-MOUTHED, *adj. phr.* (old).—*See* quot.

c. 1750. *Dialogue in the Devonshire Dialect* (Palmer, 1839) s.v. One that is perpetually HAWKING and spitting; also foul-mouthed.

HAWKER, *subs.* (old: now recognized).—A pedlar.

1690. B. E., *Dict. Cant. Crew*, s.v. HAWKERS. Retail News-Sellers.

1725. *New Cant. Dict.*, s.v.

1785. GROSE, *Vulg. Tongue*, s.v. HAWKERS, licensed itinerant retailers of different commodities, called also pedlars; likewise the sellers of newspapers.

HAWKING, *verb. subs.* (old: now recognised).—Peddling; offering small wares for sale from door to door. Also see quot. 1690.

1690. B. E., *Dict. Cant. Crew*, s.v. HAWKING, going about Town and Country with Scotch-Cloth, etc., or News-Papers: also Spitting difficultly.

1725. *New Cant. Dict.*, s.v.

HAWK-EYE STATE, *subs. phr.* (American).—Iowa. [After the famous Indian chief.]

HAWSE. TO FALL ATHWART ONE'S HAWSE, *verb. phr.* (nautical).—To obstruct; to fall out with; to counter and check.

HAWSE-HOLES. TO COME (or CREEP) IN THROUGH THE HAWSE-HOLES, *verb. phr.* (nautical).—To enter the service at the lowest grade; to rise from the forecastle.

1830. MARRYAT, *King's Own*, ch. viii. His kind and considerate captain was aware that a lad who CREEPS IN AT THE HAWSE-HOLES, *i.e.*, is promoted from before the mast, was not likely to be favourably received in the midshipmen's mess.

1889. *Chambers' Journal*, 3 Aug., 495. A sailor who rose from the ranks was formerly said TO HAVE CREPT THROUGH THE HAWSE-HOLES.

HAY. TO MAKE HAY, *verb. phr.* (University).—To throw into confusion; to turn topsy-turvy; to knock to pieces in argument or single combat. Also, to kick up a row.

1861. H. KINGSLEY, *Ravenshoe*, ch. vii. The fellows were mad with fighting too. I wish they hadn't come here and MADE HAY afterwards.

TO DANCE THE HAY, *verb. phr.* (old).—*See* quot.

1690. B. E., *Dict. Cant. Crew*, s.v. To Dance the Hay. TO MAKE HAY WHILE THE SUN SHINES, or make good use of one's Time.

HAY-BAG, *subs.* (thieves').—A woman. [*I.e.*, something to lie upon.] For synonyms, *see* PETTICOAT. Fr., *une paillaisse*.

1851-61. H. MAYHEW, *Lond. Lab. and Lond. Poor*, Vol. I., p. 231, q.v.

HAY-BAND, *subs.* (common).—A common cigar. For synonyms, *see* WEED.

1864. *Glasgow Herald*, 9 Nov., q.v.

HAYMARKET-HECTOR, *subs.* (old).—A prostitute's bully. *See* HECTOR.

c. 1675. MARVELL, *Cutting of Sir John Coventry's Nose*, vi. O ye HAYMARKET HECTORS!

HAYMARKET-WARE, *subs.* (common).—A common prostitute. For synonyms, *see* BARRACK-HACK and TART.

HAY-PITCHER (or **HAY-SEED**), *subs.* (American).—A countryman. *Cf.*, GAPE-SEED.

1851. HERMAN MELVILLE, *Moby Dick*, p. 36 (ed. 1892). Ah! poor HAYSEED.

1888. *New York World*. 'I wouldn't hev come into his shop if I had known it,' protested the imitation HAY-PITCHER.

1888. *Detroit Free Press*, Sept. Al. (to HAYSEED)—Ever read Ouida? H.—No, but by golly I must get his books. The weeds in my garden are raisin' eternal tarnation.

1890. NORTON, *Political Americanisms*, p. 53. HAYSEEDS—rustics. The 'HAYSEED delegation' in a State legislature is supposed to consist of farmers or their representatives.

1890. *Judge*, 'Christmas No.' p. 31. Them two fellers . . . . has been passin' d'rog'tory remarks about that HAYSEED'S ears.

1893. CLARK RUSSELL, *Life of the Merchant Sailor*, in *Scribner's*, xiv, 8. Hired by the State to court the HAYSEED to the tenders.

HAYS! *intj.* (American).—An injunction to be gone; GIT (*q.v.*).

1851. JUDSON, *Mysteries of New York*, ch. i., p. 12. Cut and run, my darling! HAYS! is the word, and off you go.

HAZE, *subs.* (American). — Bewilderment; confusion; FOG (*q.v.*).

Verb (American). — 1. To play tricks or practical jokes; to frolic. Hence, HAZING. Also to mystify or FOG (*q.v.*).

1848. *N. Y. Com. Adv.*, 2 Dec. W. had been drinking, and was HAZING about the street at night, acting somewhat suspiciously or strangely [when the officer arrested him].

1887. *Lippincott's Mag.*, July, p. 105. This and the Dyke are the only approaches to HAZING that I have ever heard of here.

1888. *Philadelphia Bulletin*, 27 Feb. So woman is completing her conquest of the planet. She rows. She smokes. She preaches. She HAZES. She shoots. She rides.

1892. R. L. STEVENSON and L. OSBOURNE, *The Wrecker*, p. 39. In some of the studios at that date, the HAZING of new pupils was both barbarous and obscene.

2. (nautical).—To harass with overwork or paltry orders. Also to find fault.

1840. R. H. DANA, *Two Years Before the Mast*, ch. viii. HAZE is a word of frequent use on board ship, and never, I believe, used elsewhere. It is very expressive to a sailor, and means to punish by hard work. Let an officer once say 'I'll HAZE you,' and your fate is fixed. You will be 'worked up,' if you are not a better man than he is.

1852. BRISTED, *Upper Ten Thousand*, p. 205. Here I have been five days . . . . HAZING—what you call slanging—upholsterers.

1883. STEVENSON, *Treasure Island*, ch. xi., p. 89 (1886). I've had a'most enough o' Cap'n Smollett; he's HAZED me long enough, by thunder!

1889. *Notes and Queries*, 7 S. viii., 31 Aug. My old partner, who served his time at sea, always spoke of giving a man 'a good HAZING' when he meant he had been finding fault with his doings, etc.

HAZEL-GELD, *verb.*(old).—*See* quots.

1690. B. E., *Dict. Cant. Crew*, s.v. HAZEL-GELD, to Beat any one with a Hazle-Stick or Plant.

1725. *New Cant. Dict.*, s.v.

1785. GROSE, *Vulg. Tongue*, s.v. HAZLE-GILD, to beat anyone with a hazle stick.

HAZY, *adj.* (old: now recognised).—1. *See* quot.

1690. B. E., *Dict. Cant. Crew*, s.v. HAZY Weather, when it is Thick, Misty, Foggy.

2. (common). — Stupid with drink; MIXED (*q.v.*). For synonyms, *see* DRINKS and SCREWED.

1824. T. HOOK, *Sayings and Doings*, 1st. S. 'Friend of the Family,' p. 179. One night at a public-house I was foolish enough to brag. HAZY, Sir—you understand? smoking and drinking.

1837. BARHAM, *Ingoldsby Legends*. 'Lay of S. Cuthbert.' Stamp'd on the jasey As though he were crazy, And staggering about just as if he were HAZY.

HE, *subs.* (Charterhouse).—A cake. A YOUNG HE = a small cake. *See* SHE.

HEAD, *subs.* (nautical).—1. A man-of-war's privy.

2. (common).—The obverse of a coin or medal. HEADS OR TAILS? = Guess whether the coin

spun will come down with head uppermost or not. [The side not bearing the Sovereign's head has various devices: Britannia, George and the Dragon, a harp, the Royal arms, an inscription, etc.—all included in the word 'tail,' *i.e.*, the reverse of 'head.' The Romans said HEADS or SHIPS?]

d. 1680. BUTLER, *Remains* (1759), ii., 431. Let his chance prove what it will, he plays at CROSS YOU LOSE, and PILE YOU WIN.

1871. *Observer*, 16 Apr. Perhaps for the first time Parliament is asked to enjoin a settlement of public dispute by means of tossing HEADS OR TAILS, 'cross or pile.'

3. (old).—An arrangement of the hair; a coiffure.

1773. GOLDSMITH, *She Stoops to Conquer*, ii., 10. Pray how do you like this HEAD? . . . I dressed it myself from a print in the Ladies' Memorandum Book for last year.

TO HAVE AT ONE'S HEAD, *verb. phr.* (old).—To cuckold.

1640. GOUGH, *Strange Discovery*. Not if you stay at home, and warm my bed; But if you leave me, HAVE AT YOUR HEAD.

TO TAKE ONE IN THE HEAD, *verb. phr.* (old).—To come into one's mind.

1609. HOLLAND, *Amenianus Marcellinus*. Now, IT TOOKE HIM IN THE HEAD, and incensed was his desires (seeing Gaule now quited) to set first upon Constantius.

TO DO ON HEAD, *verb. phr.* (old). To act rashly.

1559. ELIOTE, *Dict. Abruptum ingenium*, a rash brayne that dooeth all thinges ON HEAD.

TO DO ON ONE'S HEAD, *phr.* (thieves').—To do easily and with joy.

TO FLY AT THE HEAD, *verb. phr.* (old).—To attack; to GO FOR (*q.v.*).

1614. *Terence in English*. Fellow servant, I can very hardly refraine my selfe, but that I must needes FLEE AT THE HEAD OF HIM.

TO EAT ONE'S HEAD. *See* HAT.

TO EAT ONE'S (or IT'S) HEAD OFF, *verb. phr.* (common).—To cost more than the worth in keep.

1703. *Country Farmer's Catechism*. My mare has EATEN HER HEAD OFF at the Ax in Aldermanbury.

1878. PARKER GILLMORE, *Great Thirst Land*, ch. vii. Our horses were EATING THEIR HEADS OFF at livery.

1893. *Cassell's Sat. Jour.*, 1 Feb. p. 384, 2. A lot of raw material in 'stock which, in local parlance, would EAT ITS HEAD OFF if kept warehoused.

TO RUN ON HEAD, *verb. phr.* (old).—To incite.

1556. HEYWOOD, *Spider and Fly*. Thirdlie, to set cocke on hope, and RUN ON HEADE.

TO GIVE ONE'S HEAD (or ONE'S BEARD) FOR WASHING, *verb. phr.* (old).—To yield tamely and without resistance. Fr., *laver la tête* = to reprimand; to admonish with point, energy, and force.

1615. BEAUMONT and FLETCHER, *Cupid's Revenge*, iv., 3. I'm resolved . . . And so am I, and forty more good fellows, That will not GIVE THEIR HEADS FOR THE WASHING, I take it.

1663. BUTLER, *Hudibras*, I., iii., 255. For my part it shall ne'er be said, I FOR THE WASHING GAVE MY HEAD, Nor did I turn my back for fear.

TO PUT A HEAD (or NEW-HEAD) ON ONE, *verb. phr.* (common).—1. To change a man's aspect by punching his head: hence, to get the better of one's opponent; to annihilate. Also TO PUT A NEW FACE ON.

1870. R. GRANT WHITE, *Words and their Uses*. But all his jargon was surpassed, in wild absurdity, By threats, profanely emphasised, TO PUT A HEAD ON ME. . . . Instead of PUTTING ON A HEAD he strove to smite off mine.

18(?). BRET HARTE, *Further Words from Truthful James*. To go for that same party for TO PUT A HEAD ON HIM.

1888. RUNCIMAN, *The Chequers*, p. 80. I'd PUT A NEW HEAD ON YER for tuppence.

2. (colloquial). — To froth malt liquors. [*E.g.*, 'Put a head on it, Miss,' addressed to the barmaid, is a request to work the engine briskly, and make the liquor take on a CAULIFLOWER (*q.v.*).]

HEADS I WIN, TAILS YOU LOSE, *phr.* (common).—A gage of certainty = In no case can I fail: I hold all the trumps.

1890. *Welfare*, Mar., p. 8., c. 1. A director holding shares to the extent of £50 will draw a yearly recognition of his patronage to the tune of £100. It is unnecessary to ask whether such a course of speculation follows the principle of TAILS YOU LOSE, HEADS I WIN.

TO GET THE HEAD INTO CHANCERY, *verb. phr.* (formerly pugilists': now common).—To get the other fighter's head under one arm and hold it there; a position of helplessness. *See* CHANCERY.

1819. MOORE, *Tom Crib*, p. 18. When Georgy, one time, got the HEAD of the Bear INTO CHANCERY.

2. (colloquial).—Hence to get, or be got, into a posture of absolute helplessness.

TO KNOCK ON THE HEAD, *verb. phr.* (common).—To kill; to destroy; to put an end to.

1871. *Weekly Dispatch*, 21 May. 'Police Report.' The magistrate (Mr. Newton) refused the application for bail, remarking that the sooner the house was done away with the better, and he would take care that it and all connected with it were KNOCKED ON THE HEAD.

TO GET (or PUT) THE HEAD IN A BAG. *See* BAG.

TO GET (or HAVE) A SWELLING IN THE (or A BIG-) HEAD, *verb. phr.* (common).—To be or become conceited; to put on airs.

1888. *Cincinnatti Enquirer*. Anna Kelly . . . . is missing from her home in Newport. Somebody has been SWELLING HER HEAD.

1890. *Star*, 27 Jan. Although he received but £100 for his share, he GOT THE BIG HEAD, went to pieces, and is now on the retired list.

TO HIT THE RIGHT NAIL ON THE HEAD, *verb. phr.* (common). To speak or act with precision and directness; to do the right thing. [The colloquialism is common to most languages. The French say, *Vous avez frappé au but* (= You have hit the mark). The Italians, *Havete dato in brocca* (= You have hit the pitcher: alluding to a game where a pitcher stood in the place of AUNT SALLY (*q.v.*)). The Latins, *Rem acu tetigisti* (= You have touched the thing with a needle: referring to the custom of probing sores.]

1719. DURFEY, *Pills*, etc., iii., 21. The common Proverb as it is read, That a Man must HIT THE NAIL ON THE HEAD.

1892. MILLIKEN, *'Arry Ballads*, p. 43. That's what I meant when I said that that josser, whose name I've forgotten 'ad 'IT THE RIGHT NAIL ON THE 'EAD.

TO ARGUE (or TALK) ONE'S HEAD OFF, *verb. phr.* (common).—To be extremely disputative or loquacious; to be all JAW (*q.v.*).

1892. MILLIKEN, *'Arry Ballads*, p. 22. ARGUE YOUR 'EAD OFF like.

TO BUNDLE OUT HEAD (or NECK) AND HEELS, *verb. phr.* (common).—To eject with violence.

TO HAVE NO HEAD, *verb. phr.* (common).—1. (of persons). To lack ballast; to be crack-brained. *See* APARTMENTS TO LET. Hence, TO HAVE A HEAD ON = to be cute, alert; TO HAVE SAND (*q.v.*).

1888. LYNCH, *Mountain Mystery*, ch. 2. Caledonia was declared to possess a Coroner with a HEAD, and a very good one ON him, and a messenger was sent to rouse him.

2. (of malt liquors).—To be flat. *See* CAULIFLOWER.

TO HAVE A HEAD, *verb. phr.* (common). — To experience the after-effects of heavy drinking (*cf.*, MOUTH); also TO HAVE A HEAD-ACHE. For synonyms, *see* SCREWED.

TO GIVE ONE HIS HEAD, *verb. phr.* (common).—To give one full and free play; to let go.

TO HAVE MAGGOTS IN THE HEAD, *verb. phr.* (common).—To be crotchetty, whimsical, freakish; TO HAVE A BEE IN ONE'S BONNET. For synonyms, *see* APARTMENTS.

TO HURT IN THE HEAD, *verb. phr.* (old).—To cuckold; to cornute.

TO LIE HEADS AND TAILS, *verb. phr.* (common).—To sleep packed sardine fashion, *i.e.*, heads to head-rail and foot-rail alternately.

OVER HEAD AND EARS (in work, love, debt, etc.), *phr.* (common).—Completely engrossed in; infatuated with; to the fullest extent.

1589. NASHE, *Pasqvill of England* (Grosart), i., 114. Presently he fetcheth his seas himselfe, and leaps very boldly OUER HEADE AND EARES.

1735. GRANVILLE (quoted in Johnson's *Dict.*, s.v. HEAD). In jingling rimes well fortified and strong, He fights intrenched o'er HEAD AND EARS IN SONG.

WITHOUT HEAD OR TAIL, *adv. phr.* (common). — Incoherent; neither one thing nor the other. *E.g.*, I can't make head or tail of it = I cannot make it out.

1728. VANBRUGH, *Journey to London*, iv. He had the insolence to intrude into my own dressing room here, with a story WITHOUT A HEAD OR TAIL.

1736. FIELDING, *Pasquin*, v. Take this play, and bid 'em forthwith act it; there is not in it either HEAD OR TAIL.

1874. MRS. H. WOOD, *Johnny Ludlow*, 1st Series, No. 12, p. 203. Mrs. Blair has been writing us a strange rigmarole, which nobody can MAKE HEAD OR TAIL OF.

1891. W. C. RUSSELL, *Ocean Tragedy*, p. 22. There is nothing to MAKE HEADS OR TAILS OF in it that I can see.

TO HAVE A HEAD LIKE A SIEVE, *verb. phr.* (common).—To be unreliable; to be forgetful.

HEADS OUT! *phr.* (American university).—A warning cry on the approach of a master.

ARSE OVER HEAD. *See* ARSE and HEELS OVER HEAD.

MUTTON-HEAD (or HEADED).—*See* MUTTON-HEAD.

FAT (or SOFT) IN THE HEAD, *adv. phr.* (common). — Stupid. For synonyms, *see* APARTMENTS.

OFF ONE'S HEAD, *adv. phr.* (common).—Stupid; crazy. For synonyms, *see* APARTMENTS.

SHUT YOUR HEAD, *phr.* (American).—'Hold your jaw.'

HEAD-BEETLER, *subs.* (workmen's).—1. A bully; and (2) a foreman; a GANGER (*q.v.*).

1886. *Chambers' Journal*, 18 Sept., p. 599. HEAD-BEETLER is used (in Ulster) in the same vulgar sense as 'Head-cook and bottle-washer' in some localities. The 'beetle' was a machine for producing figured fabrics by the pressure of a roller, and HEAD-BEETLER probably means the chief director of this class of work.

HEAD-BLOKE. *See* HEAD-SCREW.

HEAD-BULLY (or **-CULLY**). —*See* quots.

1690. B. E., *Dict. Cant. Crew*, s.v. HEAD BULLY OF THE PASS OR PASSAGE BANK. The Top Tilter of the Gang, throughout the whole Army, who Demands and receives Contribution from all the Pass Banks in the Army.

1725. *New Cant. Dict.*, s.v.

1785. GROSE, *Vulg. Tongue*, s.v.

HEAD-COOK AND BOTTLE-WASHER, *subs. phr.* (common). — I. A general servant ; in contempt.

2. (common).—One in authority; a BOSS (*q.v.*). *Cf.*, HEAD-BEETLER.

1876. HINDLEY, *Adv. of a Cheap-Jack*, p. 66. Fred Jolly being the HEAD-COOK AND BOTTLE-WASHER.

HEAD-CLERK. HEAD-CLERK OF DOXOLOGY WORKS, *subs. phr.* (American). — A parson. *See* DEVIL-DODGER.

1869. CLEMENS (Mark Twain), *Innocents at Home*, ch. ii. If I've got the rights of it, and you are the HEAD CLERK OF THE DOXOLOGY WORKS next door.

HEADER, *subs.* (tailors').—A notability ; a BIG-WIG (*q.v.*).

TO TAKE A HEADER, *verb. phr.* (colloquial).—I. To plunge, or fall, headforemost, into water : and (theatrical), to take an apparently dangerous leap in sensational drama. Hence, to go straight and directly for one's object.

1856. *Inside Sebastopol*, ch. xiv. We may surely shut the door and take a HEADER.

1863. *Fun*, 4 Apr., p. 23. Did the chairman commence the proceedings by TAKING A TREMENDOUS HEADER . . . a verbatim report might be interesting.

1884. W. C. RUSSELL, *Jack's Courtship*, ch. vii. 'Miss Hawke,' said I, plucking up my heart for a HEADER and going in, so to speak, with my eyes shut and my hands clenched.

HEAD-FRUIT, *subs.* (old).—Horns : *i.e.*, the result of being cuckolded.

1694. CONGREVE, *Double Dealer*, ii., 3. That boded horns : the FRUIT OF THE HEAD is horns.

HEAD-GUARD, *subs.* (thieves').—A hat ; specifically, a billy-cock.

1889. CLARKSON and RICHARDSON, *Police*, p. 21. A billy-cock, a HEAD-GUARD.

HEADING, *subs.* (American cowboys').—A pillow ; any rest for the head.

HEADING 'EM, *subs. phr.* (streets).—The tossing of coins in gambling. (In allusion to the head on the coin.)

HEAD-MARKED, *adj.* (venery). — Horned. TO KNOW BY HEAD-MARK = to know (a cuckold) by his horns.

HEADQUARTERS, *subs.* (racing).—Newmarket. (Being the chief racing and training centre.)

1888. *Sportsman*, 28 Nov. Of the two-year olds that ran . . . races for them are the strong point of that particular gathering at HEADQUARTERS.

HEAD-RAILS, *subs.* (old nautical). —The teeth. For synonyms, *see* GRINDERS.

1785. GROSE, *Vulg. Tongue*, s.v.

1853. BRADLEY, [Cuthbert Bede] *Verdant Green*, Pt. II., ch. iv. He had agreeable remarks for each of his opponents . . . to another he would cheerfully remark, 'your HEAD-RAILS were loosened there, wasn't they?'

HEAD-ROBBER, *subs.* (journalists'). —I. A plagiarist.

2. (popular).—A butler.

HEAD-SCREW (or **BLOKE**), *subs.* (prison).—A chief warder.

HEADY, *adj.* (old : now recognised). —I. *See* quot.

1690. B. E., *Dict. Cant. Crew*, s.v. HEADY, strong Liquors that immediately fly up into the Noddle, and so quickly make Drunk.

2. (colloquial).—Restive ; full of arrogance and airs ; opinionated.

1864. *National Review*, p. 535. I think it's the novels that make my girls so HEADY.

HEADY-WHOP, *subs.* (streets).—A person with a preternaturally large head. (A corruption of WHOPPING-HEAD (*q.v.*).)

HEALTHERIES, *subs.* (common).—The Health Exhibition, held at South Kensington. [Others of the series were nick-named The Fisheries, The Colinderies, The Forestries, etc.]

HEAP, *subs.* (colloquial).—A large number ; lots ; a great deal.

1371. CHAUCER, *Boke of the Duchesse*, iii., 295 (1888, *Minor Poems*, SKEAT, p. 23). Of smale foules a gret HEPE.

1383. CHAUCER. *Canterbury Tales*, i., 23/575 (Riverside Press). The wisdom of an HEEPE of lerned men.

1861. HUGHES, *Tom Brown at Oxford*, ch. xxxv. I sha'n't see her again, and she wont hear of me for I don't know how long ; and she will be meeting HEAPS of men.

1885. *Punch*, 4 July, p. 4. 'Splendid sight,' he goes on, 'HEAPS of people—people you don't see anywhere else—and lots of pretty girls.'

1888. *Texas Siftings*, 20 Oct. He did not encroach on the domain of familiarity, but he looked a HEAP.

1892. GUNTER, *Miss Dividends*, xi. Every one here would do a HEAP for Bishop Tranyon's darter.

Adv. (American). — A great deal.

1848. RUXTON, *Life in the Far West*, p. 223. He pronounced himself a HEAP better.

ALL OF A HEAP, *phr.* (old : now colloquial). — Astonished ; confused; taken aback; FLABBERGAST (*q.v.*); and (pugilists') 'doubled up.'

1593. SHAKSPEARE, *Titus Andronicus*, ii., 4. Lord Bassianus lies embrewed here, ALL ON A HEAP.

1775. FIELDING, *Tom Jones*, bk. VIII., ch, ii. My good landlady was (according to vulgar phrase) struck ALL OF A HEAP by this relation.

1775. SHERIDAN, *Duenna*, ii., 2. That was just my case, too, Madam ; I was struck ALL OF A HEAP for my part.

1817. SCOTT, *Rob Roy*, ch. xxiv. The interrogatory seemed to strike the honest magistrate, to use the vulgar phrase, ALL OF A HEAP.

1832. EGAN, *Book of Sports*, s.v. ALL OF A HEAP and all of a lump, unmistakably doubled up by a smasher.

1836. DICKENS, *Pickwick*. 'And what's the lady's name ?' says the lawyer. My father was struck ALL OF A HEAP. 'Blessed if I know,' said he.

1888. J. MCCARTHY and MRS. CAMPBELL-PRAED, *The Ladies' Gallery*, ch. xiv. The idea seemed to take him ALL OF A HEAP.

1891. *Scots' Mag.*, Oct., p. 321. Spinks and Durward were struck, as we may say, ALL OF A HEAP, when they fully realised that Folio had disappeared.

HEAPED, *adj.* (racing).—I. Hard put to it ; FLOORED (*q.v.*).

1884. HAWLEY SMART, *From Post to Finish*, p. 158. They've all heard of Blackton's accident, and fancy we're fairly HEAPED for someone to ride.

2. (venery).—Piled in the act.

1607. CYRIL TOURNEUR, *Revenger's Tragedy*, ii., 1. O, 'twill be glorious to kill 'em . . . when they're HEAPED.

HEAR. TO HEAR A BIRD SING (old).—To receive private communication ; in modern parlance, A LITTLE BIRD TOLD ME SO.

1598. SHAKSPEARE, 2 *Henry IV.*, v., 5. I will lay odds, that ere this year expire, We bear our civil swords and native fire As far as France. I HEAR A BIRD SO SING.

HEARING, *subs.* (common). — A scolding ; a lecture. For synonyms, *see* WIGGING.

HEARING-CHEATS, *subs.* (old cant). —The ears.

1567. HARMAN, *Caveat*, s.v.

1690. B. E., *Dict. Cant. Crew*, s.v. HEARING CHEATS, Ears.

1725. *New Cant. Dict.*, s.v.

1785. GROSE, *Vulg. Tongue*, s.v.

ENGLISH SYNONYMS.—Drums; flappers ; leathers ; lugs (Scots') ; taps ; wattles.

FRENCH SYNONYMS.—*Les plats à barbe* (popular = large ears) ; *les oches* or *loches* (thieves') ; *les isgourdes* (popular) ; *des feuilles de chou* (popular = cabbage leaves); *des écoutes* or *écoutes* (popular = hearing cheats) ; *des cliquettes* (popular).

GERMAN SYNONYMS.—*Horcher* (= the listener) ; *Linzer*, *Loser*, (Viennese: also *Losling*, *Leusling*, *Leisling*, or *Lauschling*) : *Osen*.

HEART. NEXT THE HEART, *adv. phr.* (old).—Fasting.

1592. NASHE, *Pierce Penilesse* [Grosart], ii., 37. You may command his hart out of his belly, to make you a rasher on the coales, if you will NEXT YOUR HEART.

1633. ROWLEY, *Match at Midnight*, i Made drunk NEXT HER HEART.

[Other colloquial usages are AT HEART = in reality, truly, at bottom ; FOR ONE'S HEART = for one's life ; IN ONE'S HEART OF HEARTS = in the inmost recesses of oneself ; TO BREAK THE HEART OF = (*a*) to cause great grief, or to kill by grief, and (*b*) to bring nearly to completion ; TO FIND IN ONE'S HEART = to be willing ; TO GET OR LEARN BY HEART = to commit to memory; TO HAVE AT HEART = to feel strongly about ; TO HAVE IN THE HEART = to design or to intend ; TO LAY OR TAKE TO HEART = to be concerned or anxious about ; TO SET THE HEART AT REST = to tranquilize ; TO SET THE HEART ON = to be desirous of, to be fond of ; TO TAKE HEART OF GRACE = to pluck up courage.]

HEART-AND-DART, *subs.* (rhyming). A FART (*q.v.*).

HEARTBREAKER, *subs.* (old). — A pendant curl; a LOVE-LOCK (*q.v.*). Fr., *un crèvecœur*.

1663. BUTLER, *Hudibras*, Pt. I., c. 1. Like Samson's HEARTBREAKERS, it grew In time to make a nation rue.

1694. *Ladies' Dict.* A *crevecœur*, by some called HEARTBREAKER, is the curled lock at the nape of the neck, and generally there are two of them.

1816. JOHNSON, *Eng. Dict*, s.v. A cant name for a woman's curls, supposed to break the hearts of all her lovers.

HEARTBURN, *subs.* (streets).—A bad cigar. For synonyms, *see* WEED.

HEARTSEASE, *subs.* (old).—I. *See* quot.

1690. B. E., *Dict. Cant. Crew*, s.v. HEARTSEASE. A twenty-shilling piece.

1725. *New Cant. Dict.*, s.v.

1785. GROSE, *Vulg. Tongue*, s.v.

2. (old).—Gin. For synonyms, *see* WHITE SATIN.

1690. B. E., *Dict. Cant. Crew*, s.v. HEARTS-EASE. An ordinary sort of strong water.

1725. *New Cant. Dict.*, s.v.

1785. GROSE, *Vulg. Tongue*, s.v.

HEARTY, *subs.* and *adj.* (common).—Drink ; drunk. For synonyms, *see* DRINKS and SCREWED.

MY HEARTY, *phr.* (nautical).—A familiar address.

HEARTY - CHOKE. TO HAVE A HEARTY CHOKE and CAPER SAUCE FOR BREAKFAST, *verb. phr.* (old). —To be hanged. *Cf.*, VEGETABLE BREAKFAST, and for synonyms, *see* LADDER.

1785. GROSE, *Vulg. Tongue*, s.v.

1834. AINSWORTH, *Rookwood*, 'Nix my Doly,' Who cut his last fling with great applause To a HEARTY CHOKE WITH CAPER SAUCE.

1893. DANVERS, *The Grantham Mystery*, ch. xiii, I am not particularly anxious to run the risk of being compelled to have a HEARTY-CHOKE FOR BREAKFAST one fine morning.

HEAT, *subs.* (racing and colloquial). —A bout ; a turn ; a trial ; by whose means the 'field' is gradually reduced. *Cf.*, HANDICAP.

1681. DRYDEN, *Epil. to Saunders's Tamerlane*, 25. But there's no hope of an old battered jade ; Faint and unnerved he runs into a sweat, And always fails you at the second HEAT.

1751. SMOLLETT, *Peregrine Pickle*, ch. lxxxviii. Our adventurer had the satisfaction of seeing his antagonist distanced in the first and second HEATS.

1753. *Adventurer*, No. 37. The first HEAT I put my master in possession of the stakes.

1819. SCOTT, *Bride of Lammermoor*, ch. xxii. There was little to prevent Bucklaw himself from sitting for the county—he must carry the HEAT—must walk the course.

ON HEAT, *subs. phr.* (venery). —Amorously inclined, HOT (*q.v.*). [Said of women and bitches.]

HEATHEN - PHILOSOPHER, *subs.* (old).—*See* quot.

1690. B. E., *Dict. Cant. Crew*, s.v. A sorry poor tatter'd Fellow, whose Breech may be seen through his Pocket-holes.

1725. *New Cant. Dict.* s.v.

1785. GROSE, *Dict. Vulg. Tongue*, s.v. This saying arose from the old philosophers, many of whom despised the vanity of dress to such a point, as often to fall into the excess complained of.

HEAVE, *subs.* (old).—I. An attempt to deceive or cajole : a DEAD-HEAVE = a flagrant attempt.

2. *in. pl.* (American).—An attack of indigestion or vomiting.

Verb (American). — I. To vomit.

1862. BROWNE ('Artemus Ward'), *Artemus Ward, his book*. 'Cruise of the Polly Ann.' Stickin my hed out of the cabin window, I HEV.

2. (old). — To rob : has survived, in Shropshire, as a provincialism. The heler (hider) is as bad as the HEAVER = the receiver is as bad as the thief.

1567. HARMAN, *Caveat*, p. 66. To HEUE a bough, to robbe or rifle a boweth.

1575. AWDELEY, *Fraternitye of Vacabondes*. But hys chiefest trade is to rob bowthes in a faire, or to pilfer ware from staules, which they cal HEAVING of the bowth.

1606. DEKKER, *Belman of London* in *Wks.* (Grosart) III., 102. But the end of their land-voiages is to rob Boothes at fayres, which they call HEAVING of the Booth.

1671. R. HEAD, *English Rogue*, Pt. I., ch. xlv. p. 319 (1874). I met with an old comrade that had lately HEAV'D a booth, Anglice broken open a Shop.

1690. B. E., *Dict. Cant. Crew*, s.v. HEAVE a bough. To rob a house.

1724. COLES, *Eng. Dict.*, s.v.

1725. *New Cant. Dict.*, s.v.

1748. T. DYCHE, *Dictionary*, (5th Ed.). HEAVE (v.) . . . and in the *Canting Language*, it is to rob or steal from any person or thing.

1785. GROSE, *Vulg. Tongue*, s.v.

TO HEAVE ON (or AHEAD), *verb. phr.* (old).—To make haste ; to press forward.

1833. MARRYAT, *Peter Simple*, ch. iv. Come HEAVE AHEAD, my lads, and be smart.

HEAVEN, *subs.* (venery). — The female *pudendum*. For synonyms, *see* MONOSYLLABLE. TO FEEL ONE'S WAY TO HEAVEN = TO GROPE (*q.v.*) a woman. *See* also, ST. PETER.

HEAVENLY-COLLAR, (or **LAPPEL**), *subs.* (tailors').—A collar or lappel that turns the wrong way.

HEAVER, *subs.* (old). — 1. The bosom; the PANTER (*q.v.*).

1690. B. E., *Dict. Cant. Crew*, s.v. HEAVER. A breast.

1725. *New Cant. Dict.*, s.v.

1785. GROSE, *Vulg. Tongue*, s.v.

2. (American).—A person in love: *i.e.*, sighing (= heaving the bosom, or making play with the HEAVER) like a furnace.

3. (old).—A thief: *cf.*, HEAVE (*verbal* sense 2).

HEAVY. *See* HEAVY-WET.

Adj. (American).—Large: *e.g.*, a HEAVY amount = a considerable sum of money.

TO COME (or DO) THE HEAVY, *verb. phr.* (common).—To affect a vastly superior position; to put on airs or FRILLS (*q.v.*). *See* COME and DO.

THE HEAVIES, *subs. phr.* (military).—The regiments of Household Cavalry, 4th and 5th Dragoon Guards, and 1st and 2nd Dragoons. [From their equipment and weight.]

1841. LEVER, *Chas. O'Malley*, ch. lviii. I'm thinking we'd better call out THE HEAVIES by turns.

HEAVY-ARSED (old colloquial), *adj. phr.*—Slow to move; inert; hard to stir *See* ARSE.

d. 1691. RICHARD BAXTER. *Shove to HEAVY-ARSED Christians.* [Title.]

HEAVY-CAVALRY (or **DRAGOONS**), *subs.* (common).—Bugs; LIGHT-INFANTRY = fleas. Also HEAVY HORSEMEN, the HEAVY TROOP, and THE HEAVIES.

HEAVY-GROG, *subs.* (workmen's).—Hard work.

HEAVY-GRUBBER, *subs.* (common).—1. A hearty eater; a glutton. For synonyms, *see* STODGER.

1858. DICKENS, *Great Expectations*, ch. xl., p. 190. 'I'm a HEAVY GRUBBER, dear boy,' he said, as a polite kind of apology when he had made an end of his meal, 'but I always was. If it had been in my constitution to be a lighter grubber, I might ha' got into lighter trouble.'

HEAVY-PLODDER, *subs.* (old).—A stock-broker.

1848. DUNCOMBE, *Sinks of London*, s.v.

HEAVY- (or **HOWLING-**) **SWELL**, *subs.* (common).—A man or woman in the height of fashion: a SPIFF (*q.v.*).

1892. ANSTEY, *Model Music Hall*, 74. We look such HEAVY SWELLS, you see, we're all aristo-crats.

HEAVY-WET, *subs.* (common).—1. Malt liquor; specifically porter and stout. Also HEAVY. For synonyms, *see* DRINKS and SWIPES.

1821. EGAN, *Tom and Jerry*, p. 75. The soldiers and their companions were seen tossing off the HEAVY WET and spirits.

1830. LYTTON, *Paul Clifford*, ch. vii. I had been lushing HEAVY WET.

1838. GRANT, *Sketches in London*, p. 92. If it be HEAVYWET, the favorite beverage . . . of Dr. Wade.

1849. C. KINGSLEY, *Alton Locke*, ch. ii. Here comes the HEAVY. Hand it here to take the taste of that fellow's talk out of my mouth.

1852. JUDSON, *Mysteries of New York*, bk. II., ch. x. What'll it be, my covies? HEAVY WET, cold or warm?

1888. J. RUNCIMAN, *The Chequers*, p. 86. Mother up with your HEAVY WET and try suthin' short.

2. (common).—An extraordinarily heavy drinking bout.

HEBE, *subs.* (old).—1. *See* quots.

1648–9. CRASHAW, *Poems.* 'On the Death of Mr. H.' Ere HEBE'S hand had overlaid His smooth cheeks with a downy shade.

1778. BAILEY, *Eng. Dict.*, s.v. The first Hair appearing about the genital parts; also the Parts themselves; but more specifically the Time of Youth at which it first appears.

2. (common).—A waiting maid at an inn; a barmaid.

1603. J. SYLVESTER, *Tr.* DU BARTAS, *Mag.*, p. 65 (1608). Heer, many a HEBE faire, heer more than one Quick-seruing Chiron neatly waits vpon The Beds and Boords.

1815. SCOTT, *Guy Mannering*, ch. xlix. Shortly after the same HEBE brought up a plate of beef-collops.

1886. *Athenæum*, 9 Jan., 63/2. It is not with the Colonel's HEBES, however, that the manœuvres of the military quintet are carried on.

1891. *Sportsman*, 25 Mar. Not even the kindly morning welcome of La Rærdon, most pleasant and courteous of deft-handed HEBES, could blot out the fact.

HEBREW, *subs.* (common).—Gibberish; GREEK (*q.v.*). TO TALK HEBREW = to talk nonsense or gibberish.

1705. VANBRUGH, *Confederacy*, ii., 1. *Mon.* If she did but know what part I take in her sufferings——. *Flip.* Mighty obscure. *Mon.* Well, I'll say no more; but——. *Flip.* All HEBREW.

1823. BEE, *Dict. of the Turf*, s.v. You may as well TALK HEBREW,' said of jargon.

HECTOR, *subs.* (old).—A bully; a blusterer.

1659. *Lady Alimony*, ii, 6 (DODSLEY, *Old Plays*, 4th ed., 1875, xiv., 322). HECTORS, or champion haxters, pimps or palliards. *Ibid*, iii., I., (p. 326). Levelling at honour, they declare themselves glorious HECTORS,

b. 1670. J. HACKET, *Archbp. Williams*, ii., 203. One HECTOR, a phrase at that time for a daring ruffian, had the ear of great ones sooner than five strict men.

1674. COTTON, *Complete Gamester*, p. 333. Shoals of Huffs, HECTORS, Setters, Gilts, Pads . . . . And these may all pass under the general or common appellation of Rooks.

1677. WYCHERLEY, *Plain Dealer*, iv, 1. She would rather trust her honour with some dissolute debauched HECTOR.

1679. BUTLER, *Hudibras*. iii., 2, 108. As bones of HECTORS when they differ The more th'are Cudgel'd, grow the Stiffer.

1689. LESTRANGE, *Tr. Erasmus*, p. 139. And a Ruffling HECTOR that lives upon the Highway.

1690. B. E., *Dict. Cant. Crew*, s.v. HECTOR, a Vaporing, Swaggering Coward.

1719. DURFEY, *Pills*, etc., ii., 24. I hate, she cry'd, a HECTOR, a Drone without a Sting.

1725. *New Cant. Dict.*

1750. OZELL, *Rabelais*, iv., Pref. xxiii. These roaring HECTORS.

1757. POPE, *Imit. Hor.*, ii., 1, 71. I only wear it in a land of HECTORS, thieves . . . . and Directors.

1778. BAILEY, *Eng. Dict.*, s.v.

1785. GROSE, *Vulg. Tongue*, s.v.

1826. *Congress Deb.*, ii., 1., p. 1024. He hoped it would invite . . . a reply from the Southern HECTOR . . . of this debate.

Verb (common).—To play the bully; to bluster. Also TO PLAY THE HECTOR.

1677. WYCHERLEY, *Plain Dealer*, ii., 1. No HECTORING, good Captain.

1849–61. MACAULAY, *Hist. of Eng.*, ch. xvi. TO PLAY THE HECTOR at cock-pits or hazard tables.

TO WEAR HECTOR'S CLOAK, *verb. phr.* (old).—To receive the right reward for treachery. [When Thomas Percy, Earl of Northumberland, was routed in 1569, he hid himself in the house of Hector Armstrong, of Harlaw, who betrayed him for hire, and prospered

so ill thereafter that he died a beggar by the roadside.]

HECTORING, *subs.* and *adj.* (old: now recognised). — Bullying; blustering.

1677. WYCHERLEY, *Plain Dealer*, ii., 1. Thou art soe debauched, drunken, lewd, HECTORING, gaming companion. *Ibid*, ii., 1. Every idle, young, HECTORING, roaring companion, with a pair of turned red breeches, and a broad back, thinks to carry away any widow of the best degree.

1893. *St. James's Gazette*, xxvii, 4074, p. 3. Mr. Sexton with much unnecessary outlay of HECTORING bluster, repudiates guilty knowledge.

HEDGE, *subs.* (racing).—*See verbal* sense.

1856. HUGHES, *Tom Brown*, p. 200. Now listen, you young fool, you don't know anything about it; the horse is no use to you. He won't win, but I want him as a HEDGE.

1864. *Eton Schooldays*, ch. vii. He took the precaution to take those odds five or six times by way of a HEDGE, in case anything should happen to Chorley.

Verb (racing).—1. To secure oneself against, or minimise the loss on a bet by reversing on advantageous terms; TO GET OUT (*q.v.*). [Thus, if a man backs A to win him £100 at 5 to 1, he will if possible HEDGE by laying (say) 3 to 1 to the amount of (say) £60 against him. He will then stand thus: If A wins he gains on the first bet £100, and loses on the second £60, leaving a net gain of £40; if A loses he loses on the first bet £20, and wins on the second £20, thus clearing himself.] *See* STANDING ON VELVET and GO.

1616. JONSON, *Devil is an Ass*, iii., 1. I must have you do A noble gentleman a courtesy here, In a mere toy, some pretty ring or jewel, Of fifty or threescore pound. Make it a hundred, And HEDGE in the last forty that I owe you, And your own price for the ring.

1671. BUCKINGHAM, *The Rehearsal*, Prol. Now, critics, do your worst, that here are met, For, like a rook, I have HEDG'D in my bet.

1690. B. E., *Dict. Cant. Crew*, s.v. HEDGE, to secure a desperate Bet, Wager, or Debt.

1736. FIELDING, *Pasquin*, Act iii. *Sneer*. That's laying against yourself, Mr. Trapwit. *Trap*. I love a HEDGE, sir.

1748. T. DYCHE, *Dictionary* (5th ed.). HEDGE (v.) . . . also to secure or re-insure a dangerous debt, voyage, wager, etc.

1751. SMOLLETT, *Peregrine Pickle*, ch. lxix. They changed their note, and attempted to HEDGE for their own indemnification, by proposing to lay the odds in favour of Gauntlet.

1754. *Connoisseur*, No. 15. Whatever turn things take, he can never lose. This he has effected, by what he has taught the world to call, HEDGING a bet.

1785. GROSE, *Vulg. Tongue*, s.v.

1854. WHYTE MELVILLE, *General Bounce*, ch. xii. If she says 'Yes,' sell out . . . . If she says 'No' get *second leave* . . . . So it's HEDGED both ways.

1891. N. GOULD, *Double Event*, p. 201. You'd better HEDGE some of your sweep money.

2. (common).—To elude a danger.

TO DIE BY THE HEDGE, *verb. phr.* (common). — To die in poverty.

TO HANG IN THE HEDGE, *verb. phr.* (old).—*See* quot.

1690. B. E., *Dict. Cant. Crew*. IT HANGS IN THE HEDGE, of a Law-suit or anything else Depending, Undetermined.

AS COMMON AS THE HEDGE (or HIGHWAY), *phr.* (old).—Very common.

1690. B. E., *Dict. Cant. Crew*, s.v. AS COMMON AS THE HEDGE OR HIGHWAY, said of a prostitute or Strumpet.

1725. *New Cant. Dict.* s.v.

BY HEDGE OR BY CROOK. *See* HOOK,

HEDGE-BIRD, *subs.* (old). — *See* quot.

1614. JONSON, *Bartholomew Fair*, ii., 1. Out, you rogue, you HEDGE-BIRD, you pimp, you panier-man's bastard, you.

1690. B. E., *Dict. Cant. Crew*. HEDGE-BIRD, a Scoundrel or sorry Fellow

1725. *New Cant. Dict.*

HEDGE-BOTTOM ATTORNEY (or **SOLICITOR**), *subs. phr.* (legal).—A person who, being not admitted or being uncertificated (or, it may be, admitted and certificated both, but struck off the rolls for malpractice), sets up in the name of a qualified man, and thus evades the penalties attaching to those who act as solicitors without being duly qualified. [All the business is done in another name, but the hedge-bottom is the real principal, the partner being only a dummy.]—SIR PATRICK COLQUHOUN in *Slang, Jargon and Cant.*

HEDGE-CREEPER, *subs.* (old).—A hedge-thief; a skulker under hedges; a pitiful rascal.

1594. NASHE, *Unfortunate Traveller* p. 32 (Chiswick Press, 1892). Call him a sneaking eavesdropper, a scraping HEDGE-CREEPER, and a piperley pickthanke.

1690. B. E., *Dict. Cant. Crew*, s.v. HEDGE-CREEPER; a pitiful rascal.

1725. *New Cant. Dict.*, s.v.

1785. GROSE, *Vulg. Tongue*, s.v.

HEDGE - DOCKED, *adj.* (venery).—Deflowered in the open.

HEDGE-MARRIAGE (or **WEDDING**), *subs.* (old).—An irregular marriage performed by a HEDGE-PRIEST (*q.v.*); a marriage over the broom.

HEDGE-NOTE, *subs.* (old).—Low writing. [As Dryden: 'They left these HEDGE-NOTES for another sort of poem.']

HEDGE-POPPING, *subs.* (sporting).—Shooting small birds about hedges. Whence HEDGE-POPPER = a trumpery shooter; and HEDGE-GAME = small birds, as sparrows and tits.

HEDGE-PRIEST (or **PARSON**), *subs.* (old: now recognised).—A sham cleric; a blackguard or vagabond parson; a COUPLE BEGGAR. [As Johnson notes, the use of HEDGE in a detrimental sense is common. As HEDGE-begot; HEDGE-born; HEDGE-brat; HEDGE-found; HEDGE-DOCKED (*q.v.*); HEDGE-tavern (= a low ale-house); HEDGE-SQUARE (*q.v.*); HEDGE-reared; HEDGE-mustard; HEDGE-writer (= a Grub-street author); HEDGE-BUILDING, etc. Shakspeare uses the phrase 'HEDGE-born' as the very opposite of 'gentle blooded' (1 *Henry VI.*, iv., 1).] Specifically, HEDGE-PRIESTS = (in Ireland) a cleric admitted to orders directly from a HEDGE-SCHOOL (*q.v.*) without having studied theology. [Before Maynooth, men were admitted to ordination ere they left for the continental colleges, so that they might receive the stipend for saying mass.]

1588. *Marprelate's Epistle*, p. 30 (Ed. Arber). Is it any maruaile that we haue so many swine dumbe dogs nonresidents with their iourneimen the HEDGE-PRIESTS . . . in our ministry.

1594. SHAKSPEARE, *Love's Labour Lost*, v., 2. The pedant, the braggart, the HEDGE-PRIEST, the fool, and the boy.

1598. FLORIO, *Worlde of Wordes*. *Arlotto*, the name of a merie priest, a lack-latine, or HEDGE-PRIEST.

1690. B. E., *Dict. Cant. Crew*, s.v. HEDGE PRIEST. A sorry Hackney, Underling, Illiterate, Vagabond, *see* Patrico.

1725. *New Cant. Dict.*, s.v.

1785. GROSE, *Vulg. Tongue*. s.v.

1822. SCOTT, *Fortunes of Nigel*, ch. xvii. A HEDGE-PARSON, or buckle-beggar, as that order of priesthood has been irreverently termed.

HEDGER, *See* HEDGE, sense 2.

1828-45. HOOD, *Poems* (Ed. 1846), p. 96. A black-leg saint, a spiritual HEDGER.

HEDGE-SCHOOL, *subs.* (Irish).—A school in the country parts of Ireland formerly conducted in the open air, pending the erection of a permanent building to which the name was transferred. Hence, HEDGE-SCHOOLMASTER.

HEDGE-SQUARE. TO DOSS (or SNOOZE) IN HEDGE-SQUARE (or STREET), *verb. phr.* (vagrants'). —To sleep in the open air.

ENGLISH SYNONYMS. — To skipper it; to doss with the daisies; to be under the blue blanket; to put up at the Gutter Hotel; to do a star pitch.

FRENCH SYNONYMS.—*Coucher à l'hotel de la belle étoile* (pop. = to sleep at the Star Hotel); *manger une soupe aux herbes* (popular); *fuer la comète* (popular = to nose the comet); *coucher dans le lit aux pois verts*.

1877. GREENWOOD, *Under the Blue Blanket*. The vagrant brotherhood have several slang terms for sleeping out in a field or meadow. It is called 'snoozing in HEDGE SQUARE,' etc.

HEDGE-TAVERN (or **-ALE-HOUSE**), *subs.* (old).—*See* quot.

1690. B. E., *Dict. Cant. Crew*, s.v. HEDGE TAVERN OR ALEHOUSE, A Jilting, Sharping Tavern, or Blind Alehouse.

1705. FARQUHAR, *Twin-rivals*, i., 1. That was . . . in the days of dirty linen, pit-masks, HEDGE-TAVERNS, and beef-steaks.

1725. *New Cant. Dict.*, s.v.

1785. GROSE, *Vulg. Tongue*, s.v.

HEDGE-WHORE (or **HEDGE-BIT**), *subs.* (old: now recognised).—A filthy harlot working in the open air.

1598. FLORIO, *A Worlde of Wordes*, s.v., *Zambracca*, a common - HEDGE-WHORE, strumpet, a base harlot.

1785. GROSE, *Vulg. Tongue*, s.v.

HEDGING, *subs.* (racing). — *See* HEDGE, *verbal* sense 2.

1867. A. TROLLOPE, *Claverings*, ch. xxiv. He would be lessening the odds against himself by a judicious HEDGING of his bets.

HEEL. TO BLESS THE WORLD WITH ONE'S HEELS, *verb. phr.* (old).—To be hanged. For synonyms, *see* LADDER.

1566-7. PAINTER, *Palace of Pleasure*, sign R., 8. And the next daye, the three theves were conveied forth to BLESSE THE WORLDE WITH THEIR HEELES.

TO COOL (or KICK) THE HEELS, *verb. phr.* (common).—To wait a long while at an appointed place.

1614. JONSON, *Bartholomew Fair*. Who forthwith comitted my little hot furie to the stockes, where we will leave him to COOLE HIS HEELES, whilst we take a further view of the faire.

1673. WYCHERLEY, *Gentleman Dancing Master*, iv., 1. They ne'er think of the poor watchful chambermaid, who sits KNOCKING HER HEELS IN THE COLD, for want of better exercise, in some melancholy lobby or entry.

1752. FIELDING, *Amelia*. In this parlour Amelia COOLED HER HEELS, as the phrase is, near a quarter of an hour.

1830. LYTTON, *Paul Clifford* [Ed. 1854], p 22. He expected all who KICKED THEIR HEELS at his house would behave decent and polite to young Mr. Dot.

1833. MARRYAT, *Peter Simple*, ch. xiii. Tell him that I'll trouble him to forget to go to sleep again as he did last time, and leave me here KICKING MY HEELS contrary to the rules of the service.

1879. SALA, *Paris Herself Again*, i. We COOLED OUR HEELS during the ordinary an intolerable half hour.

1888. LYNCH, *Mountain Mystery*, ch. xlvi. That young gentleman, who had been COOLING HIS HEELS for what seemed like half the night.

TO LAY BY THE HEELS, *verb. phr.* (common).—To confine; to fetter; to jail.

1601. SHAKSPEARE, *Henry VIII.*, v., 4. If the king blame me for it, I'll LAY ye all BY THE HEELS, and suddenly.

1614. JONSON, *Bartholomew Fair*, iii. Sir, if you be not quiet the quicklier, Ill have you CLAPP'D fairly BY THE HEELS, for disturbing the Fair.

1663-1678. BUTLER, *Hudibras*, i., 3. Th' one half of man, his mind, Is, *sui juris*, unconfined, And cannot be LAID BY THE HEELS.

1811. *Lexicon Balatronicum*, s.v.

1886. R. L. STEVENSON, *Kidnapped*, p. 184. If they LAY ME BY THE HEELS, Alan, it's then that you'll be needing the money.

TO LIFT ONE'S HEELS, *verb. phr.* (venery).—To lie down for copulation; to SPREAD (*q.v.*).

TO TURN (or TOPPLE) UP THE HEELS (or TOES), *verb. phr.* (old). —To die. For synonyms, *see* ALOFT.

1592. NASHE, *Pierce Penilesse* [Grosart], ii., 77. Our trust is . . . . you will TOURNE UP THEIR HEELES one of these yeares together, and prouide them of such vnthrifts to their heires, as shall spend in one weeke . . . . what they got . . . . all their lifetime.

1599. NASHE, *Lenten Stuffe*. Leaven thousand and fifty people TOPPLED UP THEIR HEELS.

TO TAKE TO (or SHOW) A PAIR OF HEELS, *verb. phr.* (colloquial). —To take to flight; to run away. For synonyms, *see* AMPUTATE.

1593. SHAKSPEARE, *Comedy of Errors*. Nay . . . Sir, I'll TAKE MY HEELS.

1864. *Chambers' Journal*, Dec. Once before he had 'found meanes yet at length to deceive his keepers, and TOOK HIM TO HIS HEELS' to the sea coast.

HIS HEELS, *verb. phr.* (gaming). —The knave of trumps at cribbage or all-fours. Hence 'TWO FOR HIS HEELS' = two points scored (at cribbage) for turning up this card.

1811. *Lexicon Balatronicum*, s.v.

TO TREAD UPON (or TO BE AT or UPON) THE HEELS, *verb. phr.* (colloquial).—To follow close or hard after; to pursue.

1596. SHAKSPEARE, *Hamlet*, iv., 7. One woe doth TREAD UPON ANOTHER'S HEELS.

TO GO HEELS OVER HEAD, *verb. phr.* (colloquial). — To turn a somersault; to be hasty; to fall violently. Also TOP OVER TAIL.

1540. LYNDSAY, *Satyre of the Thrie Estaitis*, 3744. This fals warld is turnit TOP OUIR TAILL.

TO HAVE (or GET) THE HEELS OF, *verb. phr.* (old).—To outrun; to get an advantage.

1748. SMOLLETT, *Roderick Random*. Thou hast GOT THE HEELS OF me already.

DOWN (or OUT) AT HEEL, *adv. phr.* (colloquial). — Slipshod; shabby; in decay.

1605. SHAKSPEARE, *King Lear*, ii., 2. A good man's future may grow OUT AT HEELS.

1811. *Lexicon Balatronicum*, s.v.

1851-6. MAYHEW, *Lond. Lab. and Lond. Poor*, iii., 122. He was a little DOWN AT HEEL.

HEELED, *adj.* (American).—Armed. [From the steel spur used in cock-fighting.]

HEELER, *subs.* (American).—1. Followers or henchmen of a politician or a party.

1888. *Denver Republican*, 29 Feb. The HEELERS and strikers, bummers and stuffers, otherwise known as practical

politicians, who do the work at the Democratic polls, and manipulate the primaries and local conventions.

1888. *New York Herald*, 4 Nov. A band succeeded them and preceded a lot of ward HEELERS and floaters.

2. (American).—A bar, or other loafer; anyone on the lookout for shady work.

3. (American thieves')—An accomplice in the pocket-book RACKET (*q.v.*). [The HEELER draws attention, by touching the victim's heels, to a pocket-book containing counterfeit money which has been let drop by a companion, with a view to inducing the victim to part with genuine coin for a division of the find.]

4. (Winchester College).—A plunge, feet foremost, into water. Fr., *une chandelle*.

HEEL-TAPS, *subs.* (common). —1. Liquor in the bottom of a glass. BUMPERS ROUND AND NO HEEL TAPS = Fill full, and drain dry! *See* DAYLIGHT. Fr., *la musique*.

1795. *Gent. Mag.*, p. 118. Briskly pushed towards me the decanter containing a tolerable bumper, and exclaimed, 'Sir, I'll buzz you: come, NO HEEL-TAPS!'

1836. DICKENS, *Pickwick* (Ed. 1857), p. 10. NO HEEL-TAPS, and he emptied the glass.

1838. DICKENS, *Nicholas Nickleby*, ch. xxxii. There was a proper objection to drinking her in HEELTAPS.

1841. *Punch*, i., 117. Empty them HEELTAPS, Jack, and fill out with a fresh jug.

1844. BUCKSTONE, *The Maid with the Milking Pail*. Added to which, she's a termagant, and imbibes all the HEEL-TAPS.

1855. THACKERAY, *Newcomes*, ch. xiv. The relics of yesterday's feast—the emptied bottles . . . . the wretched HEEL-TAPS that have been lying exposed all night to the air.

2. (common). — A dance peculiar to London dustmen.

HEIFER, *subs.* (common). — A woman; OLD HEIFER (in Western America) = a term of endearment. For synonyms, *see* PETTICOAT.

18(?). *In the Back Woods*, p. 71. Now, git out, I says, or the ol' HEIFER 'll show you whar the carpenter left a hole for you to mosey.

HEIFER-PADDOCK, *subs.* (Australian).—A ladies' school.

1885. MRS. CAMPBELL-PRAED, *Australian Life*. The cattle (women) hereabouts are too scattered . . . . Next year I shall look over a HEIFER-PADDOCK in Sydney, and take my pick.

HEIGH-HO, *subs.* (thieves'). — Stolen yarn. [From the expression used to apprise the fence that the speaker had stolen yarn to sell.]

HEIGHTS. TO SCALE THE HEIGHTS OF CONNUBIAL BLISS, *verb. phr.* (venery). — To copulate. For synonyms, *see* GREENS and RIDE.

HELBAT, *subs.* (back).—A table.

HELL, *subs.* (old).—1. Generic for a place of confinement, as in some games (Sydney), or a cell in a prison: specifically, a place under the Exchequer Chamber, where the king's debtors were confined.

1593. SHAKSPEARE, *Comedy of Errors*, iv., 2. A hound that runs counter, and yet draws dry-foot well, One that before the judgement, carries poor souls to HELL.

1658. *Counter-Rat*. In Wood Street's hole, or counter's HELL.

1598. FLORIO, *Worlde of Wordes*, s.v. *Secreta* . . . . Also the name of a place in Venice where all their secret records and ancient evidences be kept, as HELL is in Westminster Hall.

2. (old).—A workman's receptacle for stolen or refuse pieces, as cloth, type, etc.; ONE'S EYE. Also HELL-HOLE and HELL-BOX. *See* CABBAGE. HELL-MATTER = (printers') old and battered type.

(?). *Newest Academy of Compliments*. When taylors forget to throw cabbage in HELL, And shorten their bills, that all may be well.

1589. NASHE, *Martin's Months Minde* (Grosart), i. 185. Remember the shreddes that fall into the Tailors HELL, neuer come backe to couer your backe.

1592. *Defence of Conny Catching*, in GREENE'S *Wks.*, xi., 96. This HEL is a place that the tailors haue vnder their shopboord, wher al their stolne shreds is thrust.

1606. DAY, *Ile of Gulls*. That fellowes pocket is like a tailors HELL, it eats up part of every mans due; 'tis an executioner, and makes away more innocent petitions in one yeere, than a red-headed hangman cuts ropes in an age.

1625. JONSON, *Staple of News*, i., 1. That jest Has gain'd thy pardon, thou hadst lived Condemn'd To thine own HELL.

1663. T. KILLEGREW, *Parson's Wedding*, iii., 5., in Dodsley, *O.P.* (1780) xi., 452. *Careless* [addressing a tailor]. Why then, thou art damned. Go, go home, and throw thyself into thine own HELL; it is the next way to the other.

1663-1712. KING, *Art of Cookery*. In Covent Garden did a taylor dwell, Who might deserve a place in his own HELL.

1690. B. E., *Dict. Cant. Crew*, s.v. HELL, the Place where the Taylers lay up their Cabbage, or Remnants, which are sometimes very large.

1698. *Money Masters All Things*, p. 56. The Cheating Knave some of the clues does throw Into his HELL-HOLE; and then lets her know That he her web cannot work out o' th' Loom.

1704. SWIFT, *Tale of a Tub*, Sec. iii. The tailor's HELL is the type of a critic's common-place book.

1725. *New Cant. Dict.*, s.v.

1785. GROSE, *Vulg. Tongue*, s.v.

1814. C. LAMB, *Melancholy of Tailors* in *Poems*, etc. (Ed. Ainger), p. 333. The tailor sitting over a cave or hollow place, in the cabalistic language of his order, is said to have certain melancholy regions always open under his feet.

1853. *Notes and Queries*, 1 S., viii., 315, c. 2. The term cabbage, by which tailors designate the cribbed pieces of cloth, is said to be derived from an old word 'cablesh,' *i.e.*, wind-fallen wood. And their HELL where they store the cabbage, from *helan*, to hide.

3. (common). — A gambling house. [Whence SILVER-HELL = a gambling house where only silver is played for; DANCING-HELL = an unchartered hall; and so forth.]

1823. MONCRIEFF, *Tom and Jerry*, ii., 4. *Jerry*. A HELL, Tom? I'm at fault again! *Log.* A gambling house, Jerry!

1841. *Comic Almanack*, p. 280. A man at a HELL, Playing the part of a *Bonnetter* well.

1849. THACKERAY, *Pendennis*, ch. xxxix. He plays still; he is in a HELL every night almost.

1890. *Saturday Review*, 1 Feb, p. 134, c. 2. These private HELLS nevertheless exist, and as all money found on the premises is seized by the police, the players have to resort to all kinds of subterfuge when the three loud knocks are heard which indicate the presence of the *commissaire*.

4. (venery).—The female *pudendum*; *cf.*, HEAVEN. For synonyms, *see* MONOSYLLABLE. [*See* BOCCACCIO, *Decameron*.]

HEAVEN, HELL AND PURGATORY, *subs. phr.* (old).—Three ale-houses formerly situated near Westminster Hall.

1610. JONSON, *Alchemist*, v., 2. He must not break his fast In Heaven or HELL.

HELL BROKE LOOSE, *subs. phr.* (common).—Extreme disorder; anarchy.

1632. HAUSTED, *Rivall Friends*, v., 10. Fye, fye, HELL IS BROKE LOOSE upon me.

1672. MARVELL, *Rehearsal* (Grosart), iii, 212. War broke out, and then to be sure HELL'S BROKE LOOSE.

1703. FARQUHAR, *Inconstant*, iv., 4. HELL BROKE LOOSE upon me, and all the furies fluttered about my ears.

1719. DURFEY, *Pills*, etc., i., 96. Tho' HELL'S BROKE LOOSE, and the Devils roar abroad.

HELL OF A (LARK, GOER, ROW, and so forth), *adj. phr.* (common).—Very much of a ——; a popular intensive.

ALL TO HELL (or GONE TO HELL), *adj. phr.* (colloquial).—Utterly ruined.

TO HOPE (or WISH) TO HELL, *verb. phr.* (common).—To desire intensely.

1891. N. GOULD, *Double Event*, p. 229. I HOPE TO H—— the horse will break his neck and his rider's too.

TO PLAY (or KICK UP) HELL AND TOMMY, *verb. phr.* (common).—To ruin utterly. Also, TO PLAY HELL AND BREAK THINGS; TO RAISE HELL; TO MAKE HELL'S DELIGHT.

1837-40. HALIBURTON, *The Clockmaker*, p. 287 (Ed. 1862). And in the mean time rob 'em, plunder 'em, and tax em; hang their priests, seize their galls, and PLAY HELL AND TOMMY with them, and all because they speak French.

1859. DE QUINCEY, *Wks.* (14 vol., ed. vi., 335). About a hundred years earlier Lord Bacon PLAYED H—— AND TOMMY when casually raised to the supreme seat in the Council by the brief absence in Edinburgh of the King and the Duke of Buckingham.

1867. *Lahore Chronicle*, 20 May. The Sepoys are burning down the houses, and PLAYING H—— AND TOMMY with the station.

1879. JUSTIN M'CARTHY, *Donna Quixote*, ch. xxxii. We'll have a fine bit of fun, I tell you. I've PLAYED HELL-AND-TOMMY already with the lot of them.

TO LEAD APES IN HELL, *verb. phr.* (old).—To die an old maid. [From a popular superstition.]

1599. HENRY PORTER, *The Two Angry Women of Abingdon.* (DODSLEY, *Old Plays*, 4th ed., 1875, vii., 294-5). For women that are wise will not LEAD APES IN HELL. . . . Therefore, come husband: maidenhead adieu.

1600. SHAKSPEARE, *Much Ado about Nothing*, ii., 1. He that is more than youth is not for me, and he that is less than man I am not for him; therefore I will . . . even LEAD his APES INTO HELL.

1605. *London Prodigal*, ii. But 'tis an old proverb, and you know it well, that women, dying maids, LEAD APES IN HELL.

1611. CHAPMAN, *May-day*, v. 2. I am beholden to her; she was loth to have me LEAD APES IN HELL.

1659. *The London Chanticleers*, i., 2. I'll always live a virgin! What! and LEAD APES IN HELL?

1719. DURFEY, *Pills*, etc., i., 179. Celladon at that began To talk of APES IN HELL.

1837. BARHAM, *Ingoldsby Legends*, 'Bloudie Jacke.' They say she is now LEADING APES . . . And mends Bachelors' small clothes below.

TO PUT THE DEVIL INTO HELL, *verb. phr.* (old).—To copulate.—BOCCACCIO. [HELL = female *pudendum*.] For synonyms, *see* GREENS and RIDE.

TO GIVE HELL, *verb. phr.* (common).—To trounce; abuse; or punish severely. Also (American), TO MAKE ONE SMELL HELL (or A DAMN PARTICULAR SMELL).

HELL-FOR-LEATHER, *adv. phr.* (common). — With the utmost energy and desperation.

1892. R. KIPLING, *Barrack Room Ballads.* When we rode HELL-FOR-LEATHER, Both squadrons together, Not caring much whether we lived or we died.

LIKE HELL, *adv. phr.* (common). — Desperately; with all one's might.

1855. THACKERAY, *Newcomes*, ch. xxix. I tried every place, everything; went to Ems, to Wiesbaden, to Hombourg, and played LIKE HELL.

GO TO HELL! *phr.* (common) —An emphatic dismissal: the full phrase is, 'Go to hell and help the devil to make your mother into a bitch pie.' [A variant is,

'Go to hell and pump thunder.'] For analagous phrases, *see* OATHS.

1836. MICHAEL SCOTT, *Cruise of the Midge*, p. 72. So, good men, GO TO HELL all of you—do—very mosh go to hell—do.

1889. *Daily News*, 21 Dec., p. 7, c. 1. He was asked to see somebody about his evidence, and told him TO GO TO HELL.

1892. KIPLING, *Barrack Room Ballads.* 'Ford o' Kabul River.' Kabul town'll GO TO HELL.

HELL AND SCISSORS! *intj.* (American).—An ejaculation of surprise and ridicule. In England, SCISSORS!

HELL-BENDER, *subs.* (American).—A drunken frolic; a tremendous row. Also HELL-A-POPPING and HELL'S DELIGHT.

HELL-BROTH, *subs.* (common).—Bad liquor. For synonyms, *see* DRINKS.

HELL-CAT (-HAG, -HOUND, -KITE, etc.), *subs.* (old: now recognised).—A man or woman of hellish disposition; a lewdster of either sex; *cf.*, HALLION.

1606. SHAKSPEARE, *Macbeth*, v., 7. *Macd.* Turn, HELL-HOUND, turn! *Macb.* Of all men else I have avoided thee.

1690. B. E., *Dict. Cant. Crew*, s.v.

1725. *New Cant. Dict.*, s.v.

1785. GROSE, *Vulg. Tongue*, s.v.

HELL-DRIVER, *subs.* (old).—A coachman.

1690. B. E., *Dict. Cant. Crew*, s.v.

1725. *New Cant. Dict.*, s.v.

HELLITE, *subs.* (gaming).—A professional gambler.—DUCANGE.

1838. GRANT, *Sketches in London.* Prosecuting the HELLITES for assault.

HELLOPHONE, *subs.* (American).—The telephone. [From HALLOO! + PHONE.]

HELP, *subs.* (colloquial: once literary). — A hired assistant. LADY-HELP = a woman acting as a companion, and undertaking the lighter domestic duties with or without wages.

1824. PEAKE, *Americans Abroad*, i., 1. Have you seen my HELP—my nigger.

1839. DE QUINCEY, *Murder as one of the Fine Arts*, ii. For domestic HELPS are pretty generally in a state of transition.

1848. BURTON, *Waggeries*, p. 77. A bevy of ready HELPS rushed upon him and tore him from the seat of honour.

1861. HUGHES, *Tom Brown at Oxford*, ch. vi. 'Well, you've had a pretty good day of it,' said Tom, who had been hugely amused; 'but I should feel nervous about the HELP, if I were you.'

SO HELP (or S'ELP or S'WELP) ME GOD (BOB, NEVER, or SAY-SO, etc.), *phr.* (common).—An emphatic asseveration.

1888. J. RUNCIMAN, *The Chequers*, p. 86. I'll pay it back, S'ELP ME GORD.

1892. A. CHEVALIER, 'Mrs. 'Enery 'Awkins.' SELP ME BOB I'm crazy, Liza, you're a daisy.

1892. MILLIKEN, *'Arry Ballads*, p. 62. 'SELP ME NEVER, old pal, it's a scorcher.

1893. EMERSON, *Signor Lippo*, ch. xiv. Well, SO HELP MY BLESSED TATER, if this isn't our old Jose turned up again.

HELPA, *subs.* (back).—An apple.

HELPLESS, *adj.* (colloquial). — Drunk. For synonyms, *see* DRINKS and SCREWED.

HEMISPHERES, *subs.* (venery).—The paps. For synonyms, *see* DAIRY.

HEMP (or HEMP-SEED, STRETCH-HEMP, HEMP-STRING, or HEMPY), *subs.* (old). — 1. A rogue; a candidate fit for the gallows. Frequently used jocularly. A CRACK-HALTER (*q.v.*). Fr., *une graine de bagne.*

1532. SIR T. MORE, *Wks.* [1557], folio 715. [He] feareth [not] to mocke the Sacrament, the blessed body of God, and ful like a STRETCH HEMPE, call it but cake, bred, or starch.

1566. GASCOIGNE, *Supposes*, iv., 3. If I come near you, HEMPSTRING, I will teach you to sing sol fa.

1598. SHAKSPEARE, 2 *Henry IV.*, ii., 1. Do, do, thou rogue, thou HEMP-SEED.

1606. CHAPMAN, *Mons. D'Olive*, Act v., p. 135. (*Plays*, 1874). *Van.* A perfect young HEMPSTRING. *Va.* Peace, least he overhear you.

1659. *Lady Alimony*, iv., 6. (DODSLEY, *Old Plays*, 4th ed., 1875, xiv., p. 350). Now, you HEMPSTRINGS, had you no other time to nim us but when we were upon our visits?

1785. GROSE, *Vulg. Tongue*, s.v. HEMP, YOUNG-HEMP, An appellation for a graceless boy.

1817. SCOTT, *Rob Roy*, ch. xxxiv. She's under lawfu' authority now; and full time, for she was a daft HEMPIE.

1839. AINSWORTH, *Jack Sheppard*, [Ed. 1840], p. 139. 'We'll see that, young HEMPSEED,' replied Sharples.

2. (old).—A halter.

1754. FIELDING, *Jonathan Wild*, iv. 14. Laudanum, therefore, being unable to stop the health of our hero, which the fruit of HEMPSEED, and not the spirit of poppy-seed, was to overcome. . . .

Verb (American).—To choke or strangle.

1859. MATSELL, *Vocabulum*, s.v.

TO WAG HEMP IN THE WIND, *verb. phr.* (old).—To be hanged. *See* HEMPEN FEVER and LADDER.

1532. SIR T. MORE, *Wks.* [1557]. folio 715. Tindall calleth blessing and crossynge but wagging of folkes fingers in the æyre, and feareth not (like one yt would at length WAGGE HEMPE IN THE WINDE) to mocke at all such miracles.

HEMPEN-BRIDLE, *subs.* (old).—A ship's rope or rigging. *See* HORSE and TREE.

HEMPEN COLLAR (CANDLE, CIRCLE, CRAVAT, CROAK, GARTER, NECKTIE, or HABEAS), *subs.* (old). — The hangman's noose; a halter. Also HEMP, and the HEARTY-CHOKE. *Cf.*, ANODYNE NECK-LACE. *See* quot. 1595.

1530-95. TURBERVILE, *Of Two Desperate Men.* A man in deepe despaire, with HEMPE in hand, Went out in haste to ende his wretched dayes.

c. 1586. MARLOWE, *Jew of Malta*, iv, 4. When the hangman had put on his HEMPEN.

1594. SHAKSPEARE, 2 *Henry VI.*, iv., 7. Ye shall have a HEMPEN CANDLE then, and the pap of a hatchet.

c. 1785. WOLCOT [P. Pindar], *Rights of Kings*, Ode xviii. Your HEMP CRAVATS, your pray'r, your Tyburn miser.

1819 SCOTT, *Bride of Lammermoor*, ch. xvi. I wad wager twa and a plack that HEMP plaits his CRAVAT yet.

1823. BEE, *Dict. Turf*, s v. HEMPEN HABEAS. He will get over it by a HEMPEN HABEAS.

1830. LYTTON, *Paul Clifford*, ch. iv. If ever I know as how you makes a flat of my Paul, blow me tight, but I'll weave you a HEMPEN COLLAR: I'll hang you, you dog, I will.

1886. MISS BRADDON, *Mohawks*, ch. xxviii. A full confession were perhaps too much to expect. Nothing but the immediate prospect of a HEMPEN NECKLACE would extort that.

HEMPEN FEVER. TO DIE OF A HEMPEN FEVER, *verb. phr.* (old).—To be hanged. For synonyms, *see* LADDER.

1785. GROSE, *Vulg. Tongue*, s.v. HEMPEN FEVER, a man who was hanged, is said to have DIED OF A HEMPEN FEVER; and in Dorsetshire to have been stabbed with a Bridport dagger; Bridport being a place famous for manufacturing hemp into cords.

1839. AINSWORTH, *Jack Sheppard* [1889], p. 76. She had been married four times; three of her husbands died of HEMPEN FEVERS.

HEMPEN-FORTUNE, *subs.* (old).—Bad luck; a term for the gallows.

1705. VANBRUGH, *The Confederacy*, v., 1. If ever I see one glance of your HEMPEN FORTUNE again, I'm off your partnership for ever.

HEMPEN-SQUINCY, *subs.* (old).—Hanging. For synonyms, *see* LADDER.

1646. RANDOLPH'S *Jealous Lovers.* Hear you, tutour, Shall not we be suspected for the murder, And choke with a HEMPEN SQUINCY.

HEMPEN-WIDOW, *subs.* (old).—A woman widowed by the gallows.

1690. B. E., *Dict. Cant. Crew*, s.v. HEMPEN WIDOW, One whose Husband was Hanged.

1725. *New Cant Dict.*, s.v.

1748. T. DYCHE, *Dictionary* (5th Ed.). HEMPEN-WIDOW (s.), a woman whose husband was hanged.

1785. GROSE, *Vulg. Tongue*, s.v.

1834. HARRISON AINSWORTH, *Rookwood*, p. 89. In a box of the stone-jug I was born, Of a HEMPEN-WIDOW the kid forlorn Fake away.

HEN, *subs.* (common).—1. A woman. Specifically, a wife or mistress. For synonyms, *see* PETTICOAT.

1811. *Lexicon Balatronicum*, s.v.

1823. BEE, *Dict. Turf*, s.v. HEN. In Black-boy Alley I've a ken, A tyke and fighting cock: A saucy tip-slang mooneyed HEN, Who is oft mill-doll at block.

2. (common).—Drink money. *See* HEN DRINKING.

1892. MILLIKEN, *'Arry Ballads*, p. 20. Whenever there's HENS on the crow, 'Arry's good for a hinnings,—no fear!

Verb (Scots'). — To funk; to turn tail; TO HEN ON = to fear to attempt.

COCK AND HEN CLUB, *subs. phr.* (common).—A club composed of men and women.

1811. *Lexicon Balatronicum*, s.v.

HENS AND CHICKENS, *subs. phr.* (thieves').—Pewter measures; quarts and pints. *Cf.*, CAT AND KITTENS.

1851. H. MAYHEW, *Lond. Lab. and Lond. Poor*, Vol. i., p. 276. The HENS AND CHICKENS of the roguish low lodging-houses are the publicans' pewter measures; the bigger vessels are 'hens,' the smaller are 'chickens.'

HEN-DRINKING, *subs.* (provincial).—*See* quot.

1859. *Notes and Queries*, 2 S. viii., 239. There is yet another [Yorkshire marriage-custom], viz., the HEN-DRINKING. On the evening of the wedding day the young men of the village call upon the bridegroom for a hen—meaning money for refreshments . . . . should the hen be refused, the inmates may expect some ugly trick to the house ere the festivities terminate.

HEN FRIGATE, *subs.* (nautical).—A ship commanded by the captain's wife. *Cf.*, HEN-PECKED.

1785. GROSE, *Vulg. Tongue*, s.v.

1883. CLARK RUSSELL, *Sailors Language*, s.v.

HEN-FRUIT, *subs.* (American).—Eggs.

HEN (or CHICKEN)-HEARTED, *adj.* (old: now recognised).—Timorous; cowardly.

d. 1529. SKELTON, *Why Come Ye not to Courte.* They kepe them in their holdes Lyke HEN-HEARTED cuckoldes.

1506-56. UDAL, *James I.* He is reconed a lowte and a HENNE-HEARTED rascall.

1639-61. *Rump Songs*, i., [1662] 319. Let the HEN-HEARTED Cit drink whey.

1748. T. DYCHE, *Dictionary* (5th Ed.). HEN-HEARTED, of a cowardly, fearful, or timorous disposition.

1754. B. MARTIN, *Eng. Dict.* (2nd Ed.), s.v. 'Poltron.' A coward, or HEN-HEARTED fellow.

1762. FOOTE, *Liar*, iii., 2. Why, what a dastardly, HEN-HEARTED——But come, Papillion, this shall be your last campaign.

1785. GROSE, *Vulg. Tongue*, s.v.

1812. JOHNSON, *Eng. Dict.*, s.v. HEN-HEARTED . . . a low word.

1815. SCOTT, *Guy Mannering*, ch. xxviii. Are you turned HEN-HEARTED, Jack?

HEN-HOUSE, *subs.* (old).—*See* quot.

1785. GROSE, *Vulg. Tongue*, s.v. HEN-HOUSE, a house where the woman rules, called also a she-house.

HEN OF THE GAME. *See* GAME.

HEN-PARTY (CONVENTION- or TEA-), *subs.* (common).—An assemblage of women for political or social purposes. *Cf.*, BULL or STAG-PARTY. Also, BITCH-, TABBY-, and CAT-PARTY.

HEN-PECKED, *adj.* (old: now recognised).—Petticoat government; ruled by a woman.

1690. B. E., *Dict. Cant. Crew*, s.v. HENPECKT Friggat, whose Commander and Officers are absolutely sway'd by their Wives. *Ibid.* HENPECKT Husband, whose Wife wears the Breeches.

1695. CONGREVE, *Love for Love*, iv., 13. I believe he that marries you will go to sea in a HEN-PECKED FRIGATE.

1712. ARBUTHNOT, *History of John Bull*, Pt. I., ch. v. He had a termagant wife, and, as the neighbours said, was playing HENPECKED!

1712. *Spectator*, No. 479. Socrates, who is by all accounts the undoubted head of the sect of the HEN-PECKED.

1748. T. DYCHE, *Dictionary* (5th Ed.). HEN-PECKED, a man that is overawed by his wife, and dares do nothing disagreeable to her inclinations.

1771. SMOLLETT, *Humphry Clinker*, l. 27. I shall never presume to despise or censure any poor man for suffering himself to be HENPECKED, conscious how I myself am obliged to truckle to a domestic demon.

1785. GROSE, *Vulg. Tongue*, s.v.

1837. DICKENS, *Oliver Twist*, ch. xxxvii. He had fallen from all the height and pomp of beadleship, to the lowest depth of the most snubbed HEN-PECKERY.

1857. A. TROLLOPE, *Barchester Towers*, ch. iii. But Mrs. Proudie is not satisfied with such home dominion, and stretches her power over all his movements, and will not even abstain from things spiritual. In fact, the bishop is HEN-PECKED.

HEN'S-ARSEHOLE.—*See* MOUTH.

HEN-SNATCHER, *subs.* (American).—A chicken thief.

1888. *Bulletin*, 24 Nov. All the dead-beats and suspected HEN-SNATCHERS plead when before the Bench that they were only 'mouching round,' etc.

HENS'-RIGHTS, *subs.* (American).—Women's rights.

HEN-TOED, *adj. phr.* (common).—To turn the toes in walking like a fowl.

HERE. HERE'S TO YOU (AT YOU, UNTO YOU, NOW, or LUCK), *phr.* (common).—An invitation to drink; here's a health to you. For synonyms, *see* DRINKS.

1651. CARTWRIGHT, *Royal Slave*. HERE'S TO THEE, Leocrates.

1717. NED WARD, *Wks.* ii., 71. Then we were fain To use Hertfordshire kindness, HERE'S TO YOU again.

1853. *Diogenes* ii., 46. Each a pot in his hand . . . . Observed in a style of remarkable ease, 'Old Buck HERE'S LUCK,' And then at the pewter proceeded to suck.

HERE'S LUCK, *phr.* (tailors').—I don't believe you.

I AM NOT HERE, *phr.* (tailors').—'I don't feel inclined to work'; 'I wish to be left alone.'

HERE'S TO IT, *phr.* (common).—An obscene toast. *See* IT, sense 2.

HERE-AND-THEREIAN, *subs. phr.* (old).—A rolling stone; a person with no permanent address. *Lex. Bal.*, 1811.

HEREFORD, *adj.* (American cowboy). White. [Herefords are white-faced.]

HEREFORDSHIRE-WEED, *subs.* (old).—An oak.

HER MAJESTY'S CARRIAGE, *subs. phr.* (common).—A prison van; the Queen's 'bus. *See* BLACK MARIA. Fr., *l'omnibus à pègres*.

HER MAJESTY'S TOBACCO PIPE, *subs.* (common).—The furnace where the forfeited tobacco from the Customs House is burnt. [Now a thing of the past: the tobacco being distributed to work-houses, etc.]

1871. *Echo*, 27 Jan. All that was not sold will be burnt, according to custom, in HER MAJESTY'S TOBACCO PIPE. We cannot think such waste justifiable.

HERMIT (or BALDHEADED HERMIT), *subs.* (venery).—The *penis*. For synonyms, *see* CREAMSTICK and PRICK.

HEROD. TO OUT-HEROD HEROD, *verb. phr.* (colloquial).—To outdo; specifically (theatrical) to excel in rant.

1596. SHAKSPEARE, *Hamlet*, iii., 2. Oh, it offends me to the soul to hear a robustious, perriwig-pated fellow tear a passion to tatters, to very rags, to split the ears of the groundlings . . . . it OUT-HERODS HEROD.

HERRING. NEITHER FISH, FLESH, FOWL, NOR GOOD RED HERRING, *phr.* (old).—Neither one thing nor the other.

1682. DRYDEN, *Duke of Guise*, *Epil.* (6th line from end). Neuters in their middleway of fleering, Are NEITHER FISH, NOR FLESH, NOR GOOD RED HERRING.

TO THROW A SPRAT TO CATCH A HERRING (OR WHALE), *verb. phr.* (old).—To forego an advantage in the hope of greater profit.

1826. BUCKSTONE, *Luke the Labourer*, i., 2. I give dat like THROWING AWAY A SPRAT TO CATCH A HERRING, though I hope on this occasion to catch a bigger fish.

1890. GRANT ALLEN, *Tents of Shem*, ch. xix. He's CASTING A SPRAT TO CATCH A WHALE.

DEAD AS A HERRING (or SHOTTEN HERRING), *adv. phr.* (old).—Quite dead. [Herrings die sooner on leaving the water than most fish.] *See* DEAD.

1596. SHAKSPEARE, *Merry Wives of Windsor*, ii., 3. By gar de HERRING IS NO DEAD as I vill kill him.

1785. BURNS, *Death and Dr. Hornbook*. I'll nail the self-conceited sot As DEAD'S A HERRIN'.

1790. RHODES, *Bombastes Furioso*, Sc. 4. Ay, DEAD AS HERRINGS—herrings that are red.

LIKE HERRINGS IN A BARREL, *adv. phr.* (common).—Very crowded.

1891. N. GOULD, *Double Event*, p. 117. People jammed inside like HERRINGS IN A BARREL.

THE DEVIL A BARREL THE BETTER HERRING, *phr.* (old).—All bad alike—*Lex. Bal.* In modern American, all alike; indistinguishable. *Cf.*, SARDINE

HERRING-GUTTED, *adj.* (old).—Lanky; thin.—GROSE.

HERRING-POND, *subs.* (common).—The sea; specifically, the North Atlantic Ocean. *See* BRINY and PUDDLE. TO BE SENT ACROSS THE HERRING-POND = to be transported.

1722. *England's Path to Wealth*. 'Tis odds but a finer country, cheaper and better food and raiment, wholesomer air, easier rents and taxes, will tempt many of your countrymen to cross the HERRING-POND.

1729. GAY, *Polly*, i., 1. Bless us all! how little are our customs known on this side the HERRING POND!

1785. GROSE, *Vulg. Tongue*, s.v.

1823. BEE, *Dict. Turf*, etc., s.v. HERRING-POND—the sea, the Atlantic; and he who is gone across it is said to be lagged, or gone a Botanizing.

1830. LYTTON, *Paul Clifford*, p. 256, ed. 1854. You're too old a hand for the HERRING-POND.

1864. M. E. BRADDON, *Henry Dunbar*, ch. xxv. You're not going to run away? You're not going to renounce the pomps and vanities of this wicked world, and make an early expedition across the HERRING-POND—eh?

1884. PHILLIPPS-WOOLLEY, *Trottings of a Tenderfoot*. Everyone nowadays has read as much as he or she cares to about the voyage across the HERRING-POND.

1889. *Notes and Queries*, 7 S., vii., p. 36, c. 2. Terms which have lived in America, and again crossed the HERRING-POND with modern traffic.

1890. *Punch*, 6 Feb. *Saturday*.—My connection with war ended. Calculate I start to-morrow with the Show across the HERRING-POND, to wake up the Crowned Heads of Europe!

1891. GUNTER, *Miss Nobody*, ch. xvii. If so, I'll—I'll cut him, when I cross the—er—HERRIN' POND.

1892. HUME NISBET, *Bushranger's Sweetheart*, p. 119. I guess we have ruined one or two well-known authors, on the other side of the HERRING POND.

HERTFORDSHIRE-KINDNESS, *subs.* (old).—An acknowledgment, or return, in kind, of favours received. (But *see* quots., 1662, 1690, and 1738).

1662. FULLER, *Worthies*. This is generally taken in a good and grateful sense, for the mutual return of favours received: it being (belike) observed that the people in this county at entertainments drink back to them who drank to them.

1690. B. E., *Dict. Cant. Crew*, s.v. HERTFORDSHIRE-KINDNESS, Drinking to the same Man again.

1717. NED WARD, *Wks.*, ii., 7. Then we were fain To use HERTFORDSHIRE-KINDNESS, Here's to you again.

1725. *New Cant. Dict.*, s.v.

1738. SWIFT, *Polite Conversations*. *Neverout*. My Lord, this moment I did myself the honour to drink to your Lordship. *Lord Smart*. Why then that's HERTFORDSHIRE KINDNESS. *Neverout*. Faith, my Lord, I pledged myself: for I drank twice together without thinking.

1785. GROSE, *Vulg. Tongue*, s.v. HERTFORDSHIRE KINDNESS, drinking twice to the same person.

HEWGAG. THE HEWGAG, *subs.* (American).—A name for an undeterminate, unknown, mythical creature.—*Slang, Jargon, and Cant.*

HEY-GAMMER-COOK. TO PLAY AT HEY-GAMMER COOK, *verb. phr.* (venery).—To copulate. For synonyms, *see* GREENS and RIDE.

1720. C. JOHNSON, *Highwaymen and Pyrates*, 'Margaret Simpson' (*q.v.*).

HICCIUS DOCCIUS, *subs. phr.* (Old Cant).—A juggler; also a shifty fellow or trickster.

1676. SHADWELL, *Virtuoso*, ii., p. 19. I shall stand here till one of them has whipt away my Mistris about business, with a HIXIUS DOXIUS, with the force of Repartee, and this, and that, and Everything in the world.

1678. BUTLER, *Hudibras*, iii., 3, 579. At Westminster, and Hickses-Hall, And HICCIUS DOCKIUS play'd in all.

1688. WYCHERLEY, *Country Wife*, iii. That burlesque is a Hocus-pocus trick they have got, which by the virtue of HICTIUS DOCTIUS, topsey-turvey, etc.

1812. JOHNSON, *Eng. Dict.*, s.v. HICCIUS DOCCIUS . . . . a cant word for a juggler; one that plays fast and loose.

Adj. (old).—Drunk; slovenly. Also, HICKEY (*q.v.*). For synonyms, *see* DRINKS and SCREWED.

1733. NORTH, *Examen*, i., 3, 137 (1740). The author with his HICCIUS-DOXIUS delivery.

1785. GROSE, *Vulg. Tongue*, s.v. HICKSIUS DOXIUS, Drunk.

HIC JACET, *subs. phr.* (common).—A tombstone; also a memorial inscription. [From the opening words.]

1598. SHAKSPEARE, *All's Well*, etc., iii., 6. The merit of service is seldom attributed to the true . . . . performer. I would have that drum . . . . or HIC JACET.

1858-59. TENNYSON, *Idylls of the King* ('Vivien'). Among the cold HIC JACETS of the dead.

HICK, *subs.* (Old Cant).—1. A man; specifically a countryman; a booby. Also (American thieves') HICKJOP and HICKSAM. For synonyms, *see* JOSKIN.

1690. B. E., *Dict. Cant. Crew*, s.v. HICK, any Person of whom any Prey can be made, or Booty taken from; also a silly Country Fellow.

1720. SMITH, *Lives of Highwaymen and Pyrates*, ii., 39. Among whom was a country farmer . . . . which was not missed at all by the Country HICK.

1725. *New Cant. Dict.* Song 3. 'The Thief-catcher's Prophesy.' The Eighth is a Bulk, that can bulk any HICK.

1754. *Scoundrel's Dict.* The fourteenth, a gamester, if he sees the HICK sweet He presently drops down a cog in the street.

1785. GROSE, *Vulg. Tongue*, s.v.

HICKETY-SPLIT, *adj.* (American).—With all one's might; at top speed; HAMMER AND TONGS (*q.v.*); FULL CHISEL (*q.v.*).

HICKEY, *adj.* (old).—*See* quot.

1859. MATSELL, *Vocabulum*, s.v. HICKEY, Tipsy; not quite drunk; elated.

HICKORY-SHIRT, *subs.* (American).—A checked shirt, cotton or woollen.

HIDE, *subs.* (common).—The human skin. Once literary; now colloquial and vulgar.

1568. *Bannatyne, MSS.*, '*When Flora, etc.*' (Hunterian Club, 1879-88). Sche is so brycht of HYD and hew, I lufe bot hir allane I wene.

1607. MARSTON, *What You Will*, ii., 1. A skubbing railer, whose course harden'd fortune, Grating his HIDE, gauling his starued ribs, Sittes hauling at Deserts more battle fate.

1731. C. COFFEY, *The Devil to Pay*, Sc. 5. Come, and spin, you drab, or I'll tan your HIDE for you.

1892. KIPLING, *Barrack-Room Ballads*. 'Gunga-Din.' An' for all 'is dirty 'IDE 'e was white, clear white, inside.

Verb (common).—To flog. For synonyms, *see* TAN.

1868. *Cassell's Mag.*, May, p. 80. This was carried across the yard to Jacky as a regular challenge, and some said that Kavanagh and his friends were coming over to HIDE Jacky after dinner

1885. *Punch*, 29 Aug. p. 98. And the silver-topped rattan with which the boys I used to HIDE.

HIDEBOUND, *adj.* (old: now recognised).—Barren; intractable; niggardly; pedantic; utterly immovable.

1606. *Return from Parnassus*, ii., 4 (DODSLEY, *Old Plays*, 4th ed., 1875, ix., 125). Any of the HIDEBOUND brethren of Oxford or Cambridge.

1672. WYCHERLEY, *Love in a Wood*, i., 2. I am as barren and HIDEBOUND as one of your scribbling poets, who are sots in company for all their wit.

1690. B. E., *Dict. Cant. Crew*, s.v. HIDEBOUND HORSE, whose Skin sticks very close, and tite like a Pudding Bag, usually when very Fat. *Ibid.* HIDEBOUND MUSE, Stiff, hard of Delivery, Sir J. Suckling call'd Ben Johnson's so.

1725. *New Cant. Dict.*, s.v.

1785. GROSE, *Vulg. Tongue*. s.v.

1893. *Pall Mall Gaz.*, 24 Feb. 'High Time to Get Up.' The most dragging inertness and the most HIDE-BOUND celerity.

HIDING, *subs.* (common).—A thrashing. For synonyms, *see* TANNING.

1853. BRADLEY, *Verdant Green*, ii., p. 23. May the Gown give the Town a jolly good HIDING.

1864. MARK LEMON, *Jest Book*, p. 236. Some people have a notion that villany ought to be exposed, though we must confess we think it a thing that deserves a HIDING.

1871. *All the Year Round*, 18 Feb. p. 288. Served me right if I'd got a HIDING.

1883. *Pall Mall Gaz.*, 16 Apr., p. 7, c. 2. They should stone all boys they met who were not members of the society, or in default themselves receive a good HIDING.

1888. *Sportsman*, 22 Dec. The chairman told Deakin he could scarcely expect anything but a HIDING for being connected with such a scurrilous publication.

1891. *Licensed Vict. Mirror*, 30 Jan., p. 7, c. 1 Before Paddock could claim the victory, which cost the Redditch fighter one of the severest HIDINGS he ever had to put up with.

HIGGLEDY - PIGGLEDY, *adj.* (Old Cant: now recognised).—In confusion; topsy-turvy; at sixes and sevens.

1598. FLORIO, *Worlde of Wordes*, s.v. *Alla rappa*, snatchingly, HIGLEDIPIGLEDIE, shiftingly, rap and run.

1690. B. E., *Dict. Cant. Crew*, s.v. HIGGLEDE-PIGGLEDY, all together, as Hoggs and Piggs lie Nose in Arse.

1725. *New Cant. Dict.*, s.v.

1758. A. MURPHY, *The Upholsterer*, ii. Ambassadors and Hair-Cutters, all HIGGLEDY-PIGGLEDY together.

1785. GROSE, *Vulg. Tongue*, s.v.

1812. JOHNSON, *Eng. Dict.*, s.v. HIGGLEDY-PIGGLEDY, a cant word, corrupted from *higgle*, which denotes any confused mass, as higglers carry a huddle of provisions together.

1849. DICKENS, *David Copperfield*, ch. xxii., p. 199. His name's got all the letters in it, HIGGLEDY-PIGGLEDY.

1873. MISS BROUGHTON, *Nancy*, ch. ii We are all HIGGLEDY-PIGGLEDY—at sixes and sevens!

1876. M. E. BRADDON, *Joshua Haggard*, ch. xvi. 'If some of you will sit down,' remonstrated Judith, 'I'll pour out the tea. But I don't feel as if anybody wanted it while you're standing about HIGGLEDY-PIGGLEDY.'

HIGGLER, *subs.* (old).—A hawker.

HIGH, *adj.* (American)—Drunk. For synonyms, *see* DRINKS and SCREWED.

2. (colloquial). — Stinking; GAMEY (*q.v.*); whence, by implication, diseased (as a prostitute); obscene in intention and effect.

THE HIGH AND DRY, *subs. phr.* (clerical).—The High Church or Anglo-Catholic party in the Establishment, as opposed to the LOW AND SLOW (*q.v.*), or Evangelical section. *Cf.*, BROAD AND SHALLOW.

1854. CONYBEARE, *Church Parties*, 74. Its adherents [of the High Church] are fallen from their high estate, and are contemptuously denominated THE HIGH AND DRY, just as the parallel development of the Low Church is nicknamed 'low and slow.'

1857. ANTHONY TROLLOPE, *Barchester Towers*, ch. liii. Who belongs to THE HIGH AND DRY church, the High Church as it was some fifty years since, before tracts were written and young clergymen took upon themselves the highly meritorious duty of cleaning churches?

1886. *Graphic*, 10 Apr., 399. In the Church have we not the three schools of HIGH AND DRY, Low and Slow, and Broad and Shallow?

HIGH AND DRY, *adv. phr.* (colloquial). — Stranded; abandoned; irrecoverable.

1889. *Pall Mall Gaz.*, 18 Oct., 6, 1. It seems to me that Mr. Chamberlain must really look out or he will find himself, as the result of that insidious 'mellowing process' to which Mr. Matthews has testified, landed HIGH AND DRY in a Toryism compared to which Sir Walter Barttelot will show in Radical colours.

HIGH AND MIGHTY, *adv. phr.* (colloquial). — Arrogant; imperious; proud; 'on the high horse,' or the 'HIGH ROPES' (*q.v.*); full of SIDE (*q.v.*).

1891. N. GOULD, *Double Event*, p. 121. None of your HIGH and MIGHTY games with me.

1892. HENLEY and STEVENSON, *Deacon Brodie*, i., 2. Ye need na be sae HIGH AND MIGHTY onyway.

1892. HUME NISBET, *Bushranger's Sweetheart*, p. 49. 'MIGHTY HIGH some people are, ain't they?' the man observed loudly, straightening himself, and ordering a nobbler for himself.

TOO HIGH FOR ONE'S NUT, *adv. phr.* (American).—Out of one's reach; beyond one's capacity; OVER ONE'S BEND (*q.v.*).

YOU CAN'T GET HIGH ENOUGH, *verb. phr.* (common).—A derisive comment on any kind of failure. [Probably obscene in origin.]

HOW IS THAT FOR HIGH? *phr.* (American).—'What do you think of it?' [Once a tag universal; common wear now.]

1860. BARTLETT, *Americanisms*, s.v. HIGH. For when he slapped my broadbrim off, and asked, How's THAT FOR HIGH? It roused the Adam in me, and I smote him hip and thigh!

1872. CLEMENS (Mark Twain), *Roughing It*, 334. We are going to get it up regardless of expense. [He] was always nifty himself, and so you bet his funeral ain't going to be no slouch,—solid silver door-plate on his coffin, six plumes on the hearse, and a nigger on the box in a biled shirt and a plug hat,—HOW'S THAT FOR HIGH?

1889. *Pall Mall Gaz.*, 23 Sep., p. 2, c. 1. 'Cricket' stories are the thing just now. HOW IS THIS FOR HIGH?

HIGH-BELLIED (or **HIGH IN THE BELLY**), *adj. phr.* (colloquial).—Far gone in pregnancy. Also HIGH-WAISTED.

HIGHBINDER, *subs.* (American).—1. A Chinese blackmailer.

2. (political American).—A political conspirator.—NORTON.

HIGH-BLOKE, *subs.* (American).—1. A judge.

2. (American).—A well-dressed man; a SPLAWGER (*q.v.*).—MATSELL.

HIGHER - MALTHUSIANISM, *subs. phr.* (colloquial).—Sodomy.

HIGHFALUTE, *verb.* (American).—To use fine words. Also TO YARN (*q.v.*). *See* HIGHFALUTING. Fr., *faire l'étroite.*

HIGHFALUTING, *subs.* (formerly American: now general).—Bombast; rant.

1865. *Orchestra.* We should not think of using HIGH-FALUTIN on ordinary serious occasions, and that we never shall use it in future, unless we happen to speak of the *Porcupine* critic.

1886. *Pall Mall Gaz.*, 3 May, 6, 2. A glib master of frothy fustian, of flatulent HIGH-FALUTIN', and of oratorical bombast.

Adj. (general). — Bombastic; fustian; thrasonical.

1870. FRISWELL, *Modern Men of Letters*. A driveller of tipsy, high-flown, and HIGH-FALUTIN' nonsense.

1884. *Echo*, 17 Mar., p. 1, c. 4. It is the boast of HIGH-FALUTIN' Americans that theirs is a country 'where every man can do as he darn pleases.'

HIGH-FEATHER. IN HIGH FEATHER, *adv. phr.* (colloquial).—In luck; on good terms with oneself and the world.

HIGH-FLY. TO BE ON THE HIGH-FLY, *verb. phr.* (thieves').—Specifically, to practise the begging-letter imposture, but (generally) to tramp the country as a beggar.

1839. BRANDON, *Poverty, Mendicity, and Crime*, 163. The HIGH-FLY—beggars, with letters, pretending to be broken down gentlemen, captains, etc.

1857. SNOWDEN, *Mag. Assistant*, (3rd ed.), p. 445. Begging letters—THE HIGHFLY.

HIGHFLYER, *subs.* (old). — 1. Anything or anybody out of the common, in opinion, pretension, attire, and so forth: as a prostitute (high - priced and well - dressed); an adventurer (superb in impudence and luck). 2. A dandy, male or female, of the first water 3. A fast coach.

1690 DRYDEN. Prol. to *Mistakes* in *Wks.*, p. 473 (Globe). He's no HIGH-FLYER—he makes no sky-rockets, His squibs are only levelled at your pockets.

1690. B. E., *Dict. Cant. Crew*, s.v. HIGH-FLYERS, Impudent, Forward, Loose, Light Women. Also, bold adventurers.

1693. CONGREVE, *Old Bachelor*, i., 1. Well, as HIGH A FLYER as you are, I have a lure may make you stoop.

1706. R. ESTCOURT, *Fair Example*, Act i., p. 10. You may keep company with the HIGHEST FLYER of 'em all.

1725. *New Cant. Dict.*, s.v.

1818. SCOTT, *Heart of Midlothian*, i. Mail-coach races against mail-coach, and HIGH - FLYER against HIGH - FLYER, through the most remote districts of Britain.

1821. EGAN, *Tom and Jerry*, v. As you have your HIGH-FLIERS at Almack's, at the West End, we have also some 'choice r eatures at our All Max in the East.

1823. BEE, *Dict. Turf*, s.v. HIGH-FLYERS—women of the town, in keeping, who job a coach, or keep a couple of saddle-horses at least.

1830. LYTTON, *Paul Clifford*, (Ed. 1854) p. 75. Howsomever, the HIGH-FLYERS doesn't like him; and when he takes people's money, he need not be quite so cross about it!

1860 DICKENS, *Uncommercial Traveller*, xxii., p. 131. The old room on the ground floor where the passengers of the HIGH-FLYERS used to dine.

1864. DICKENS, *Our Mutual Friend*, i., 5. Mrs. Boffin, Wegg ... is a 'IGHFLYER at fashion.

1892. MILLIKEN, *'Arry Ballads*, p. 40. Foller yer leader, ... all who can carry sufficient skyscrapers to keep in the 'unt, with that 'IGHFLYER 'Arry.

4. (thieves').—A beggar with a certain style; a begging-letter writer; a broken swell.

1851-61. H. MAYHEW, *Lond. Lab. and Lond. Poor*, vol. I., p. 268. While pursuing the course of a HIGH-FLYER (genteel beggar)

1858. A. MAYHEW, *Paved with Gold*, bk. III., ch. iii., p. 268. He was a HIGH-FLIER, a genteel beggar.

1887. *Standard*, 20 June, p. 5, c. 2. The pretended noblemen and knights who 'say they have suffered by war, fire, or captivity, or have been driven away, and lost all they had,' are still represented by the HIGH - FLYERS or broken-down gentlemen.

5. (circus).—A swing fixed in rows in a frame much in vogue at fairs.

HIGH-FLYING, *subs.* (old).—1. Extravagance in opinion; pretension or conduct.

1689. DRYDEN, *Epil. to Lee's Princess of Cleves*, 6. I railed at wild young sparks; but without lying Never was man worse thought on for HIGH-FLYING.

2. (thieves').—Begging; THE HIGH-FLY (*q.v.*); STILLING (*q.v.*).

HIGH-GAG, *subs.* (American).—A whisperer.—MATSELL.

THE HIGH-GAG, *subs. phr.* (American).—Telling secrets.—MATSELL.

HIGH-GAME, *subs.* thieves').—*See* quot.

1889. C. T. CLARKSON and J. HALL RICHARDSON, *Police*, p. 321. A mansion .... a HIGH GAME.

HIGH-GIG. IN HIGH-GIG, *adv. phr.* (old).—In good fettle; lively. *Cf.*, GIG.

1819. MOORE, *Tom Crib*, p. 15. Rather sprightly—the Bear IN HIGH-GIG.

HIGH-GO, *subs.* (common). — A drinking bout; a frolic.

HIGH-HEELED SHOES. TO HAVE HIGH-HEELED SHOES ON, *verb. phr.* (American).—To set up as a person of consequence; to DO THE GRAND (*q.v.*).

HIGH HORSE. TO BE (or GET) ON (or RIDE) THE HIGH HORSE, *verb. phr.* (colloquial).—To give oneself airs; to stand on one's dignity; to take offence. [Fr. *monter sur ses grands chevaux.* The simile is common to most languages.]

1716. ADDISON, *Freeholder*, 5 Mar. He told me, he did not know what travelling was good for, but to teach a man to RIDE THE GREAT HORSE, to jabber French, and to talk against passive obedience.

1836. MARRYAT, *Midshipman Easy*, ch. xii. He was determined to RIDE THE HIGH HORSE—and that there should be no Equality Jack in future.

1842. *Comic Almanack*, p. 327. Yet Dublin deems the foul extortion fair, And swears that, as he's RIDDEN THE HIGH HORSE, So long and well, she now will make him mayor.

1864. *Times*, 5 July. Mr. Gladstone in the Dano-German Debate. The right hon. gentleman then GOT ON what I may call HIS HIGH HORSE, and he would not give us the slightest opinion upon any matter of substantive policy, because that, he said, would be accepting office upon conditions.

1868. WILKIE COLLINS, *The Moonstone*, 2nd Period, 3rd Narr., ch. ii. Miss Rachael has her faults—'I've never denied it,' he began. 'And RIDING THE HIGH HORSE now and then is one of them.'

HIGH-JINKS, *subs.* (old).—1. An old game variously played. [Most frequently dice were thrown by the company, and those upon whom the lot fell were obliged to assume and maintain for a time a certain fictitious character, or to repeat a certain number of fescennine verses in a particular order. If they departed from the characters assigned ... they incurred forfeits, which were compounded for by swallowing an additional bumper.—*Guy Mannering*, 1836. Note to ch. xxxii.]

1690. B. E., *Dict. Cant. Crew*, s.v. HIGHJINKS, a Play at Dice who Drinks.

1780. RAMSAY, *Maggy Johnston*, i., 25. The queff or cup is filled to the brim, then one of the company takes a pair of dice, and after crying HY-JINKS, he throws them out; the number he casts out points out the person that must drink; he who threw beginning at himself number one, and so round till the number of the person agree with that of the dice (which may fall upon himself if the number be within twelve); then he sets the dice to him, or bids him take them; he on whom they fall is obliged to drink, or pay a small forfeiture in money, then throws, and so on. But if he forgets to cry 'Hy-jinks' he pays a forfeiture into the bank. Now, he on whom it falls to drink (if there be anything in the bank worth drawing) gets it all if he drinks; then with a great deal of caution he empties his cup, sweeps up the money, and orders the cup to be filled again, and then throws; for if he errs in the articles he loses the privilege of drawing the money. The articles are—(1) Drink, (2) Draw, (3) Fill, (4) Cry 'Hy-jinks,' (5) Count just, (6) Chuse your doublet, man—viz., when two equal numbers of the dice is thrown, the person whom you chuse must pay a double of the common forfeiture, and so must you when the dice is in his hand (*sic*).

1815. SCOTT, *Guy Mannering*, ch. xxxvi. The frolicsome company had begun to practise the ancient and now forgotten pastime of HIGH JINKS.

1861. H. KINGSLEY, *Ravenshoe*, lv. He had made an engagement to drive Lord Saltire, the next morning, up to Wargrave in a pony-chaise, to look at Barrymore House, and the place where the theatre stood, and where the game of HIGH JINKS had been played so bravely fifty years before.

2. *See* quot., and *cf.* sense 1.

1785. GROSE, *Vulg. Tongue*. A gambler at dice, who, having a strong head, drinks to intoxicate his adversary, or pigeon. Under this head are also classed those fellows who keep little goes, take in insurances; also, attendants at the races, and at the E O tables; chaps always on the look out to rob unwary countrymen at cards, etc.

3. (common).—A frolic; a row. [From sense 1.]

1861. HUGHES, *Tom Brown at Oxford*, i. All sorts of HIGH JINKS go on on the grass plot.

1872. *Daily Telegraph*, 13 Sept. 'Filey the Retired.' Frisky Filey cannot assuredly be called. There are no HIGH JINKS on her jetty; and, besides, she hasn't got a jetty, only a 'Brigg.'

1890. *Pall Mall Gaz.*, 24 July, 4, 2. Yesterday and to-day there have been HIGH JINKS in Petworth Park, rich and poor for miles round being invited, and right royally feasted on the coming of age of Lord and Lady Leconfield's eldest son.

1891. *Licensed Vict. Gaz.*, 3 Apr. While Bank Holiday was being celebrated with such *éclat* at Kempton, they were carrying on HIGH JINKS over hurdles and fences at Manchester.

1892. *Sala's Journal*, 2 July, p. 223. HIGH JINKS with the telephone have been the order of the day at Warwick Castle; taps and wires have been turned on and off, and floods of melody of various kinds have delighted listening ears.

1893. *National Observer*, 25 Feb., ix., 357. Time was when there were HIGH JINKS in that vast quadrangle.

TO BE AT HIS HIGH JINKS, *phr.* (common).—To be stilted and arrogant in manner; to RIDE THE HIGH HORSE (*q.v.*). Fr., *faire sa merde* or *sa poire.*

HIGH-KICKER, *subs.* (colloquial).— Specifically, a dancer whose speciality is the high kick or the *porte d'armes*; whence, by metaphor, any desperate SPREESTER (*q.v.*), male or female.

HIGH-KILTED, *adj.* (Scots').— Obscene or thereabouts; FULL FLAVOURED (*q.v.*).

HIGHLAND-BAIL, *subs.* (Scots').— The right of the strongest; *force majeure.*

1816. SCOTT, *Antiquary*, ch. xxix. The mute eloquence of the miller and smith, which was vested in their clenched fists, was prepared to give HIGHLAND BAIL for their arbiter.

HIGH-LAWYER, *subs.* (old).—A highwayman. For synonyms, *see* ROAD AGENT.

1592. JOHN DAY, *Blind Beggar*, p. 21 (Ed. Bullen). He wo'd be your prigger, your prancer, your HIGH-LAWYER.

1610. ROWLANDS, *Martin Mark-all*, p. 50 (H. Club's Rept., 1874). He first gaue termes to robbers by the high-way, that such as robbe on horse-backe were called HIGH LAWYERS, and those who robbed on foote, he called Padders.

HIGH-LIVER, *subs.* (old).—A garretteer; a thief housed in an attic. Hence, HIGH-LIVING=lodging in a garret.—*Lex. Bal.*

HIGH-MEN, *subs.* (old). — Dice loaded to show HIGH numbers. Also, HIGH-RUNNERS. *See* FULHAMS and LOW-MEN.

1594. NASHE, *Unf. Traveller* in *Wks.* [GROSART], v., 27. The dice of late are growen as melancholy as a dog, HIGH MEN and low men both prosper alike.

1596. SHAKSPEARE, *Merry Wives*, i., 3. Let vultures gripe thy guts! for gourd and fullam holds, And HIGH and low beguiles the rich and poor.

1598. FLORIO, *A Worlde of Wordes.* *Pise*, false dice, HIGH MEN or low men.

1605. *London Prodigal*, i., 1. I bequeath two bale of false dice, videlicet, HIGH MEN and low men, fullams, stopcatertraies, and other bones of function.

1615. HARINGTON, *Epigrams*, i., 79. Your HIGH And low men are but trifles.

1657-1733. JOHN DENNIS, *Letters*, ii., 407. Shadwell is of opinion, that your bully, with his box and his false dice, is an honester fellow than the rhetorical author, who makes use of his tropes and figures, which are his HIGH and his low RUNNERS, to cheat us at once of our money and of our intellectuals.

1866. YATES, *Land at Last*, ii. He's ON THE HIGH ROPES, is Master Charley! Some of you fellows have been lending him half a-crown, or that fool Caniche has bought one of his pictures for seven-and-six!

HIGH - SEASONED (or HIGHLY-SPICED), *adj.* (colloquial). — Obscene. For synonyms, *see* SPICY.

HIGH- (or CLOUTED-) SHOON, *subs.* (old).—A countryman. For synonyms, *see* JOSKIN.

1690. B. E., *Dict. Cant. Crew*, s.v.

1725. *New Cant. Dict.*, s.v.

1785. GROSE, *Vulg. Tongue*, s.v.

HIGH-SNIFFING, *adj. phr.* (colloquial).—Pretentious; supercilious; very obviously better than one's company; HIGH-NOSED (*q.v.*).

HIGH-STEPPER, *subs.* (common).— An exemplar, male or female, of what is fashionable in conversation, conduct, or attire; a SWELL (*q.v.*). Also, a person of spirit. Whence, *adj.*, HIGH-STEPPING (or HIGH-PACING)= conspicuously elegant or gallant in dress, speech, manner, conduct, anything.

1891. GUNTER, *Miss Nobody of Nowhere*, ch. ix. From her actions and style I'm pretty certain she's English and a HIGH-STEPPER.

HIGH-STOMACHED, *adj.* (colloquial). —Proud; disdainful; very valiant.

HIGH-STRIKES, *subs.* (common).— A corruption of 'hysterics.'

1838. SELBY, *Jacques Strop*, ii., 4. Capital! . . . didn't I do the HIGH-STRIKES famously.

1860. MISS WETHERELL, *Say and Seal*, ch. vii. She wants you to come. I'm free to confess she's got the HIGH-STRIKES wonderful.

HIGH-TEA, *subs.* (colloquial).—A tea with meat, etc. In Lancashire BAGGING (*q.v.*).

1888. *Sporting Life*, 15 Dec. Following run there will be HIGH TEA and a grand smoking concert, to which visitors are cordially invited.

HIGH-TI, *subs.* (American: Williams Coll.).—A showy recitation; at Harvard=a SQUIRT (*q.v.*).

HIGH-TIDE (or WATER) *subs.* (colloquial).—Rich for the moment; The state of being FLUSH (*q.v.*). For synonyms, *see* WELL BALLASTED.

1690. B. E., *Dict. Cant. Crew*, s.v. HIGH TIDE when the Pocket is full of Money.

1725. *New Cant. Dict.*

1785. GROSE, *Vulg. Tongue*, s.v.

1823. BEE, *Dict. Turf*, s.v. HIGH-TIDE—plenty of the possibles; whilst 'low-water' implies empty clies.

UP TO HIGH-WATER MARK, *adv. phr.* (colloquial).—In good condition; a general expression of approval.

HIGH-TOBY. *See* HIGH PAD.

1834. AINSWORTH, *Rookwood*, bk. III., ch. v. Oh! the game of HIGH-TOBY for ever

HIGH-TONED, *adj.* (American).— Aristocratic; also, morally and intellectually endowed; spiritually beyond the common. HIGH-SOULED = cultured; fashionable. HIGH-TONED NIGGER = a negro who has raised himself in social position. [Once literary; now utterly discredited and never used, save in ignorance or derision.] Stokes, the maniac who shot Garfield, described himself as a 'HIGH-TONED Lawyer.'

1884. PHILLIPS WOOLLEY, *Trottings of a Tender Foot.* I never saw any so-called HIGH-TONED NIGGERS.

1822. SCOTT, *Fort. of Nigel*, ch. xxiii. Men talk of HIGH and low DICE.

HIGH-NOSED, *adj. phr.* (colloquial). —Very proud in look and in fact; supercilious in bearing and speech; SUPERIOR (*q.v.*).

HIGH- [or GAY-] OLD (TIME, GAME, LIAR, etc.], *adj. phr.* (common). —A general intensitive: *e.g.*, HIGH OLD TIME=a very merry time indeed; HIGH OLD LIAR= a liar of might; HIGH OLD DRUNK =an uncommon BOOZE (*q.v.*).

1883. *Referee*, 11 Mar., p. 3, c. 2. All the children who have been engaged in the Drury Lane pantomime took tea on the stage, and had a HIGH OLD TIME (while it lasted).

1888. J. McCARTHY and MRS. CAMPBELL-PRAED, *Ladies' Gallery*, ch. xxxv. I went down to Melbourne, intending to have a HIGH OLD TIME.

1891. *Murray's Mag.*, Aug., p. 202. There will be a Want of Confidence Motion, and a HIGH OLD debate.

1891. J. NEWMAN, *Scamping Tricks*, p. 7. You are a big fraud and a HIGH OLD liar.

1892. MILLIKEN, *'Arry Ballads*, p. 35. We'd the HIGHEST OLD game.

1892. F. ANSTEY, *Voces Populi.* 'The Riding Class,' p. 108. We've bin having a GAY OLD time in 'ere.

HIGH-PAD (or TOBY, or HIGH-TOBY-SPLICE), *subs.* (old).—1. The highway. Also, HIGH - SPLICE TOBY. For synonyms, *see* DRUM.

1567. HARMAN, *Caveat*, p. 86. *Roge.* Nowe bynge we a waste to the HYGH PAD, the ruffmanes is by.

c. 1819. *Slang Song* (quoted in notes to *Don Juan*, x., 19). On the HIGH-TOBY-SPLICE flash the muzzle In spite of each gallows old scout.

1836. H. M. MILNER, *Turpin's Ride to York*, i., sc. 2. Come, lads a stirrup-cup at parting, and then hurrah for the game of HIGH-TOBY.

1876. HINDLEY, *Adventures of a Cheap Jack*, p. 4. Halting for a few hours at mid-day during the heat in the HIGH SPICE-TOBY, as we used to call the main road.

2. (old). — A highwayman. Also, HIGH-TOBYMAN (or-GLOAK). For synonyms, *see* ROAD AGENT.

1690. B. E., *Dict. Cant. Crew*, s.v. HIGH PAD, a Highwayman, Highway Robber well Mounted and Armed.

1785. GROSE, *Vulg. Tongue*, s.v.

1823. BEE, *Dict. Turf*, s.v. HIGH TOBY-GLOAK, a highway robber well mounted.

1834. AINSWORTH, *Rookwood*, bk. IV., ch i. Tom King, a noted HIGH-TOBY GLOAK of his time.

1857. *Punch*, 31 Jan. (from slang song). That long over Newgit their Worships may rule, As the HIGH-TOBY, mob, crack, and screeve model school.

3. (old).—Highway robbery.

1819. VAUX, *Cant. Dict.* HIGH-TOBY, the game of highway robbery, that is exclusively on horseback.

HIGH-POOPED, *adj.* (colloquial).— Heavily buttocked.

HIGH-RENTED, *adj.* (popular).—1. Hot.

2. (thieves').—Very well known to the police; HOT (*q.v.*).

HIGH-ROLLER, *subs.* (American).— A GOER (*q.v.*); a fast liver; a heavy gambler; a HIGHFLYER (*q.v.*).

1887. FRANCIS, *Saddle and Moccasin.* He's a HIGH-ROLLER, by gum!

HIGH - ROPES. TO BE ON THE HIGH ROPES, *verb. phr.* (common). —To be angry or excited. Also to put on airs; to stand on one's dignity; to ride the HIGH-HORSE (*q.v.*).

1811. *Lexicon Balatronicum*, s.v. TO BE ON THE HIGH ROPES, to be in a passion.

1859. MATSELL, *Vocabulum*, s.v.

1893. *Cassell's Sat. Jour.*, 1 Feb., p. 389, 1. One day a fashionably-dressed young man, giving an address in a HIGH-TONED suburb, called upon Messrs. Glitter.

HIGHTY-TIGHTY (or HOITY-TOITY), *subs.* (old).—A wanton.

1690. B. E., *Dict. Cant. Crew*, s.v. HIGHTETITY, a Ramp, or Rude Girl.

1725. *New Cant. Dict.*, s.v.

Adj. (colloquial). — Peremptory; waspish; quarrelsome.

1848. THACKERAY, *Vanity Fair*, ch. xviii. La, William, don't be so HIGHTY-TIGHTY with us. We're not men.

HIGH WOOD. TO LIVE IN HIGH WOOD, *verb. phr.* (common).— To hide; to dissemble of purpose; to lie low and keep quiet.

HIGULCION-FLIPS, *subs.* (Texas).— An imaginary ailment.

HIKE, *verb.* (old).—To move about. Also to carry off; to arrest.

1811. *Lexicon Balrtronicum*, s.v. HIKE. To HIKE OFF; to run away.

1884. *Daily Telegraph*, 2 Feb., p. 3, c. 1. We three, not having any regler homes nor a steady job of work to stick to, HIKE ABOUT for a living, and we live in the cellar of a empty house.

HILDING, *subs.* (old).—A jade; a wanton; a disreputable slut.

1593. SHAKSPEARE, *Taming of the Shrew*, ii., 1. For shame thou HILDING of a devilish spirit.

1595. SHAKSPEARE, *Romeo and Juliet*, ii., 4. HILDINGS and harlots.

HILL. NOT WORTH A HILL OF BEANS, *phr.* (American).—Absolutely worthless.

HILLS, *subs.* (Winchester Coll.).— 1. St. Catharine's Hill.

1870. MANSFIELD, *School Life*, p. 28. Some of his principal duties were to take the boys 'on to HILLS,' call names there, etc.

2. (Cambridge Univ.).—The Gogmagog Hills; a common morning's ride. *Gradus ad Cantab.*

HILLY, *adj.* (colloquial).—Difficult: *e.g.*, HILLY READING=hard to read; HILLY GOING=not easy to do; etc.

HILT. LOOSE IN THE HILT, *adv. phr.* (old). — Unsteady; ROCKY (*q.v.*); lax in the bowels.

1639-61. *Rump Songs.* 'Bum-fodder,' ii., 56. If they stay longer, they will us beguilt With a Government that is LOOSE IN THE HILT.

HIND-BOOT, *subs.* (common).—The breech. For synonyms, *see* MONOCULAR EYEGLASS.

HIND-COACHWHEEL, *subs.* (common).—A five shilling piece. Fr., *roue de derrière, thune*, or *palet*, =a five-franc piece. For synonyms, *see* CAROON.

HINDER - BLAST, *subs.* (old).— Crepitation.

1540. LINDSAY, *Thrie Estaitis* [in *Bannatyne MSS.*, Hunterian Club, ed., 1879-88), p. 511] line 1429-30. Scho hes sic rubling in her wame, That all the nycht my hairt ouercastis With bokking and with HINDER BLASTIS.

HINDER-END, *subs. phr.* (common). —The breech. Also, HINDER-PARTS and HINDER-WORLD.

HINDER - ENTRANCE, *subs. phr.* (common).—The fundament.

HIND-LEG. TO KICK OUT A HIND LEG, *verb. phr.* (old).—To lout; to make a rustic bow.

TO TALK THE HIND LEG OFF A HORSE (or DOG). See TALK.

TO SIT UPON ONE'S HIND LEGS AND HOWL, verb. phr. (American).—To bemoan one's fate; to make a hullabaloo.

HINDOO, subs. (American). — See KNOW NOTHING.

HINDOO PUNISHMENT, subs. phr. (circus).—See quot.

1875. FROST, Circus Life, ch. xviii. The HINDOO PUNISHMENT is what is more often called the muscle grind, a rather painful exercise upon the bar, in which the arms are turned backward to embrace the bar, and then brought forward upon the chest, in which position the performer revolves.

HIND-SHIFTERS, subs. (old).— The feet. For synonyms, see CREEPERS.

1823. LAMB, Elia, Wks., (Ed. 1852), p. 311. They would show as fair a pair of HIND-SHIFTERS as the expertest loco-motor in the colony.

HINGES. OFF THE HINGES, adv. phr. (common)—In confusion; out of sorts; 'not quite the thing.'

HINTERLAND, subs. (old). — The breech.

HIP, (in. pl.), subs. (colloquial).—Conventional—as in the proverb, 'Free of her lips; free of her hips'—for the buttocks. Hence, to WALK WITH THE HIPS=to make play with the posteriors in walking; LONG IN THE HIPS; and HIPS TO SELL=broad in the beam; NIMBLE-HIPPED=active in copulation.

c. 1508. DUNBAR, Poems, 'Of a Dance in the Quenis Chalmer' (1836), i., 119. His HIPPIS gaff mony a hiddouss cry. Ibid. i., 124. 'Of Ane Blak-moir.' . . . Sall cum behind and kiss hir HIPPIS.

1540. LINDSAY, Thrie Estaits, line 3327. My craig will wit quhat weyis my HIPPIS. Ibid., line 4424. Ye wald not stick to preise my graith With hobbling of your HIPPIS.

c. 1580. Collier of Croydon, iv., I. (DODSLEV, Old Plays, 4th ed., 1875, 459). I keep her lips and her HIPS for my own use.

d. 1607. MONTGOMERIE, Poems, 'Polwart and Montgomerie's Flyting,' p. 85, line 779 (Scottish Text Soc., 1885-6). Kailly lippes, kiss my HIPS.

TO HAVE (GET, or CATCH) ON THE HIP, verb. phr. (old).—To have (or get) an advantage. [From wrestling.]

1591. HARINGTON, Orlando Furioso, bk. xlvi., st. 17. In fine he doth apply one speciall drift, Which was to GET the pagan ON THE HIP, And having caught him right, he doth him lift By nimble sleight, and in such wise doth trip That down he threw him.

1598. SHAKSPEARE, Merchant of Venice, i. 3. If I can CATCH him once UPON THE HIP. I will feed fat the ancient grudge I bear him.

1605. MARSTON, Dutch Courtezan. iii., 1. He said he had you A THE HYP.

1617. ANDREWES, Sermons ('Library of Ang.-Cath. Theology'), Vol. IV., p. 365. If he HAVE us at the advantage, ON THE HIP as we say, it is no great matter then to get service at our hands.

1635. D. DIKE, Michael and the Dragon, in Wks., p. 328. The Divell HATH them ON THE HIP, he may easily bring them to anything.

1690. B. E., Dict. Cant. Crew, s.v. UPON THE HIP . . . . at an Advantage in Wrestling, or Business.

1697. VANBRUGH, Relapse, iv., 1. My lord, she has had him UPON THE HIP these seven years.

1812. JOHNSON, Eng, Dict. HIP, s.v., A low phrase.

1836. MICHAEL SCOTT, Cruise of the Midge, p. 226. 'Ha! ha! I HAVE you ON THE HIP now, my master,' shouted Peter.

HIPE, subs. (wrestling).—A throw over the hip. Hence HIPE, verb =to get across the hip before the throw.

HIP-HOP, verb (old).—To skip or move on one leg; to hop. 'A cant word framed by the reduplication of hop.'—JOHNSON, 1812.

1670-1729. CONGREVE [Quoted in JOHNSON's Eng. Dict.]. Like Volscius HIP-HOP in a single boot.

HIP-INSIDE, subs. (thieves').—An inner pocket. HIP-OUTSIDE = an outer ditto.

1857. SNOWDEN, Mag. Assistant (3rd Ed.), p. 445, s.v.

HIPPED (or HIPPISH), adj. (common). — Bored; melancholical; out of sorts. [From HYPOCHONdria.]

1710. GAY, Wine in Wks. (1811) p. 348. By cares depress'd, in pensive HIPPISH mood.

1712. Spectator, No. 284. I cannot forbear writing to you, to tell you I have been to the last degree HIPPED since I saw you.

1837. BARHAM Ingoldsby Legends, 'Babes in the Wood.' The wicked old Uncle, they say, In spite of his riot and revel, Was HIPPISH and qualmish all day, And dreamt all night long of the devil.

1864. DICKENS, Our Mutual Friend, bk. III., ch. x. 'You are a little HIPPED, dear fellow,' said Eugene; you have been too sedentary. Come and enjoy the pleasures of the chase.'

HIPPEN, subs.(Scots': colloquial).— A baby's napkin (i.e., HIPPING cloth). Also (theatrical), the green curtain.

HIREN, subs. (old).—1. A prostitute. [A corruption of 'Irene,' the heroine in Poole's play: see quot. 1584.] For synonyms, see BARRACK-HACK and TART.

1584. POOLE, The Turkish Mahomet and Hyren the Fair Greek. Note. In Italian called a courtezan; in Spaine a margarite; in English . . . . a punk.

1598. SHAKSPEARE, 2 Henry IV., ii., 4. Have we not HIREN here?

1615. ADAMS, Spiritual Navigator. There be sirens in the sea of the world. Syrens? Hirens, as they are now called. What a number of these sirens [HIRENS], cockatrices, courteghians, in plain English, harlots, swimme amongst us!

d. 1618. SYLVESTER, Trans. Du Bartas' Week of Creation, ii., 2, pt. 3. Of charming sin the deep-inchaunting syrens, The snares of virtue, valour-softening HYRENS.

2. (old).—A sword. Also a roaring bully; a fighting hector. [From Irene = the Goddess of Peace, a lucus a non lucendo.]

HISHEE-HASHEE. See SOAP-AND-BULLION.

HIS NIBS (or NABS). See NIBS.

HISS. THE HISS, subs. phr. (Winchester College).—The signal of a master's approach.

HISTORICAL- (WROUGHT, or ILLUSTRATED-) SHIRT, subs. (old).—A shirt or shift worked or woven with pictures or texts.

1596. BEN JONSON, Every Man out of his Humour, iv., 6. I wonder he speaks not of his WROUGHT-SHIRT.

1639. MAYNE, City Match, ii., 2. My smock sleeves have such holy imbroideries, And are so learned that I fear in time, All my apparel will be quoted by Some pure instructor.

1647. BEAUMONT and FLETCHER, Custom of the County, ii., 1. Having a mistress, sure you should not be Without a neat HISTORICAL-SHIRT.

1848. Punch, XIV., 226. He never broke a bank, He shurs cross-barred trousers, His linen is not ILLUSTRATED, but beautifully clean.

1851. MAYHEW, Lond. Lab. and Lond. Poor, I., 51. Colored, or ILLUSTRATED SHIRTS, as they are called, are especially objected to by the men.

1889. Puck's Library, Apr., p. 12. Being an educated man, I feel ten thousand woes, Cavorting for the populace In ILLUSTRATED CLOTHES.

HISTORY OF THE FOUR KINGS. See FOUR KINGS.

HIT, subs. (common).—A success; e.g., TO MAKE A HIT=to score; to profit; to excel.

1602. MARSTON, Antonio and Mellida. Induction. When use hath taught me action to HIT the right point of a ladie's part.

1700. CONGREVE, Way of the World, ii., 5. A HIT, a HIT! a palpable hit! I confess it.

1821. EGAN, Tom and Jerry, bk. I., ch. i. Teach me to make a HIT of so Kean a quality that it may not only 'tell,' but be long remembered in the metropolis.

1822-36. JNO. WILSON, Noctes Amb., Wks. II., 210. Mr. Peel seems to have MADE A HIT in the chief character of Shiel's play, The Apostate.

1828-45. T. HOOD, Poems, v. , p. 197, (Ed. 1846). Nor yet did the heiress herself omit The arts that help TO MAKE A HIT.

1870. Figaro, 10 June. TO MAKE A GREAT HIT is, after all, more a matter of chance than merit.

1889. Pall Mall Gaz., 3 July. Madam Melba MAKES AN ESPECIAL HIT in the valse from Roméo et Juliette.

1889. Referee, 6 Jan. Quite a HIT HAS BEEN MADE by the clever juvenile, La Petite Bertoto.

Adj. (Old Bailey).—Convicted.

HARD-HIT, adj. phr. (colloquial).—Sore beset; HARD-UP (q.v.). Also deep in love (or grief, or anger).

1890. Licensed Vict. Gaz., 7 Nov. It was pretty generally known that he had been HARD HIT during the season.

Verb (American).—To arrive at; to light upon.

1888. Detroit Free Press, Oct. Professor Rose, who HIT this town last spring, is around calling us a fugitive from justice.

TO HIT IT, verb. phr. (colloquial).—To attain an object; to light on a device; to guess a secret.

1594. SHAKSPEARE, Love's Labour Lost, iv., 1. Thou cans't not hit IT, HIT IT, HIT IT, Thou can'st not HIT IT, my good man.

1596. SHAKSPEARE, Merry Wives. iii., 2. I can never HIT one's name.

1773. O. GOLDSMITH, She Stoops to Conquer. Ecod, I have HIT IT. It's here. Your hands. Yours and yours, my poor sulky' My boots there, ho! Meet me two hours hence at the bottom of the garden.

1880. A. TROLLOPE, The Duke's Children, ch. iii. He dressed himself in ten minutes, and joined the party as they had finished their fish. 'I am awfully sorry,' he said, rushing up to his father, 'but I thought that I should just HIT IT.'

TO HIT OFF, verb. phr. (colloquial).—To agree together; to fit; to describe with accuracy and precision.

*1857. A. TROLLOPE, Barchester Towers, ch. xxxiv. It is not always the case that the master, or warden, or provost, or principal can HIT IT OFF exactly WITH his tutor. A tutor is by no means indisposed to have a will of his own.

1880. A. TROLLOPE, The Duke's Children, ch. xxxvi. 'One gentleman with another, you mean?' 'Put it so. It don't quite HIT IT OFF, but put it so.'

1886. J. S. WINTER, Army Society. 'Sidelight,' ch. xiv. 'Hey!' said Orford. 'Didn't you and he HIT IT OFF?'

1889. Daily News, 22 Oct., p. 5. The nations that quarrel are the nations that do not HIT IT OFF ON some point of feeling or taste.

TO HIT THE FLAT, verb. phr. (American cowboy).—To go out on the prairie.

TO HIT THE PIPE, verb. phr. (American).—To smoke opium.

TO HIT ONE WHERE HE LIVES, verb. phr. (American).—To touch in a tender part; to hurt the feelings; TO TOUCH ON THE RAW (q.v.).

HIT (or STRUCK) WITH, adv. phr. (colloquial). — Taken; enamoured; prepossessed. Also, HIT UP WITH.

1891. Tales from Town Topics. 'Count Candawles,' p. 28. She is very amusing, but the Count cannot be really HIT WITH such a little mountebank.

HIT ON THE TAIL, verb. phr. (old venery).—To copulate. For synonyms, see GREENS and RIDE.

d. 1529. SKELTON, Bowge of Courte. How oft he hit Jonet on the TAYLE.

HIT IN THE TEETH, verb. phr. (old). — To reproach; to taunt; to fling in one's face.

1663. KILLIGREW, The Parson's Wedding, ii., 6 (DODSLEY, Old Plays, 4th ed., 1875, xiv., 431). They are always HITTING ME IN THE TEETH with a man of my coat.

HITCH, verb (American).—1. To marry. HITCHED = married.

1867. BROWNE, Artemus Ward's Courtship, People's ed., p. 23. If you mean getting HITCHED, I'm in.

1883. L. OLIPHANT, Altiora Peto, II., xxix., 156. 'How long is it since we parted, Ned?' 'A matter of five years; and it wasn't my fault if we didn't stay HITCHED till now.'

1892. Tit-Bits, 17 Sept., p. 419, c. 1. 'We've come to get HITCHED,' said the man, bashfully.

2. (American). — To agree. Also TO HITCH HORSES.

TO HITCH ONE'S TEAM TO THE FENCE, verb. phr. (American).—To settle down.

HITTITE, subs. (pugilists').—A prize fighter.

ENGLISH SYNONYMS. — Basher; bruiser; dukester; fistite; knight of the fist; gemman of the fancy; milling-cove; pug; puncher; scrapper; slasher; slogger; slugger; sparring-bloke.

1823. BEE, Dict. Turf, s.v. HITTITES—boxers and ring-goers assembled.

1860. THE DRUID, Post and Paddock. 'The Fight for the Belt.' And the Sherwood Ranger, bold Bendigo, Is on training no more intent; But the trout full well that ex-HITTITE know On a Summer's eve in the Trent.

HIVE, subs. (venery).—The female pudendum. Cf. HONEY. Hence, verbally, TO HIVE IT = to effect intromission.

Verb (American cadet).—To steal. For synonyms, see PRIG.

TO GET HIVED, verb. phr. (American Cadets' and popular).—1. To be caught out in a scrape. Also, to be hidden. TO BE HIVED PERFECTLY FRIGID = to be caught in flagrante delicto.

HIVER, subs. (Western American).—A travelling bawd.

HIVITE, subs. (school).—A student of St. Bees' (Cumberland).

1865. John Bull, 11 Nov. To be a HIVITE has long been considered a little worse than a 'literate' . . . . Of the value of some St. Bees testimonials we may form an estimate, etc., etc.

HOAKY. BY THE HOAKY, intj. (nautical). — A popular form of adjuration.

HOAX, *subs.* (old: now recognised).—A jest; a practical joke; a TAKE-IN. Originally (GROSE) University cant. [Probably from HOCUS (*q.v.*).]

1796. GROSE, *Vulg. Tongue* (3rd Ed.), s.v.

1811. *Lexicon Balatronicum*, s.v. HOAXING. Bantering, ridiculing. HOAXING a quiz; joking an odd fellow.—*University wit.*

1815. SCOTT, *Guy Mannering*, ch. iii. Whose humble efforts at jocularity were chiefly confined to what were then called bites and bams, since denominated HOAXES and quizzes.

1835-7. RICHARDSON, *Dict. Eng. Lang.*, s.v. HOAX. Malone considers the modern slang HOAX as derived from *hocus*, and Archdeacon Nares agrees with him.

Verb. To play a practical joke; to 'take-in'; to BITE (*q.v.*). *See subs.* sense. For synonyms, *see* GAMMON.

1812. COMBE, *Syntax, Picturesque*, xix. An arch young sprig, a banker's clerk, Resolv'd to HOAX the rev'rend spark.

1854. F. E. SMEDLEY, *Harry Coverdale*, ch. viii. I thought you were HOAXING us, and I sat down to play the duet for the amiable purpose of exposing your ignorance.

HOB (or **HOBBINOL**), *subs* (old).—A clown.—GROSE.

HOB AND NOB (or **HOB NOB**), *verb.* (old). — 1. To invite to drink; to clink glasses.

1756. FOOTE, *Englishman from Paris*, i. With, perhaps, an occasional interruption of 'Here's to you, friends,' 'HOB OR NOB,' 'Your love and mine.'

1759. TOWNLEY, *High Life Below Stairs*, ii. *Duke.* Lady Charlotte, HOB OR NOB. *Lady Char.* Done, my lord; in Burgundy, if you please.

1772. GRAVES, *Spiritual Quixote*, bk. VIII., ch. xxi. (new Ed., 1808). Having drunk HOB OR NOB with a young lady in whose eyes he wished to appear a man of consequence, he hurried out into the summer-house.

1823. BEE, *Dict. Turf*, s.v. HOB NOB—two persons pledging each other in a glass.

1836. HORACE SMITH, *Tin Trumpet*, 'Address to a Mummy.' Perchance that very hand now pinioned flat, Has HOBANNOBBED with Pharoah glass for glass.

1849. THACKERAY, *Pendennis*, ch. xxx. He would have liked to HOB AND NOB with celebrated pick-pockets, or drink a pot of ale with a company of burglars and cracksmen.

1886. R. L. STEVENSON, *Kidnapped*, p. 68. So the pair sat down and HOB-A-NOBBED.

2. (old).—To give or take; to hit or miss at random. [Saxon, *habban*, to have; *nabban*, not to have.]

1577-87. HOLINSHED, *Chroncles of Englande, Scotlande, and Irelande* (1807) p. 317. The citizens in their rage shot HABBE OR NABBE (*hit or miss*) at random.

1602. SHAKSPEARE, *Twelfth Night*, iii., 4. HOB-NOB is his word, give 't or take 't.

1615. HARINGTON, *Epigrams*, iv. Not of Jack Straw, with his rebellious crew, That set king, realm, and laws, at HAB OR NAB.

1673. *Quack Astrologer.* He writes of the weather HAB NAB, and as the toy takes him, chequers the year with foul and fair.

3. (colloquial) —To be on terms of close intimacy; to consort familiarly together.

1870. MARK TWAIN, *Innocents Abroad*, ch. i. They were to HOB-NOB with nobility and hold friendly converse with kings and princes.

1892. HUME NISBET, *Bushranger's Sweetheart*, p. 109. I had HOB-NOBBED for the last two hours with the most notorious bushranger in the colony.

1892. A. K. GREEN, *Cynthia Wakeham's Money*, p. 5. Each tree looks like a spectre HOB-NOBBING with its neighbour.

HOBBES'S-VOYAGE, *subs.* (old).—A leap in the dark.

1697. VANBRUGH, *Provoked Wife*, v., 6. So, now, I am in for HOBBES'S VOYAGE; a great leap in the dark.

HOBBINOL, *subs.* (old).—A countryman. For synonyms, *see* JOSKIN.

1663. KILLIGREW, *The Parson's Wedding*, ii., 3 (DODSLEY, *Old Plays*, 4th ed., 1875, xiv., 396). Who, Master Jeffrey? HOBBINOL the second! By this life, 'tis a very veal, and licks his nose like one.

HOBBLE. IN A HOBBLE (or HOBBLED), *adv. phr.* (colloquial).—In trouble; hampered; puzzled. Also (thieves), committed for trial. Fr., *tomber dans la mélasse* (=to come a cropper), and *faitré* (=BOOKED (*q.v.*)). HOBBLED UPON THE LEGS=transported, or on the hulks.

1777. FOOTE, *Trip to Calais* (1795), ii., p. 39. But take care what you say! you see what a HOBBLE we had like to have got into.

1789. GEO. PARKER, *Life's Painter*, p. 163. A term when any of the gang is taken up and committed for trial, to say, such a one is HOBBLED.

1811. POOLE, *Hamlet Travestie*, iii., 5. Horatio, I am sorry for this squabble; I fear 'twill get me in a precious HOBBLE.

1819. VAUX *Cant. Dict.*, s.v. HOBBLED, taken up, or in custody; to HOBBLE a plant, is to spring it.

1838. HALIBURTON, *Clockmaker*, 2nd S., ch. xvii. A body has to be cautious if he don't want to get into the centre of a HOBBLE.

1849. *Punch*, *Fortune - Tellers' Almanack.* To dream that you are lame is a token that you will get into a HOBBLE.

1892. MILLIKEN, *'Arry Ballads*, p. 44. I got into a 'OBBLE.

Verb (venery).—*See* quot.

1688. SEMPILL, 'Crissell Sandilands' in *Bannatyne MSS.* (Hunterin Club, 1879-88), p. 354, lines 21-2. Had scho bene undir, and he HOBLAND above, That were a perellous play for to suspect them.

HOBBLEDEHOY, *subs.* (old, now colloquial).—A growing gawk: as in the folk-rhyme, 'Hobbledehoy, neither man nor boy.' [For derivation, *see Notes and Queries*, 1 S., v., 468, vii., 572; 4 S., ii., 297, viii., 451, ix., 147; 7 S., iv., 523, and v., 58.]

1557. TUSSER, *Husbandrie*, ch. 60, st 3, p. 138 (E. D. S.). The first seuen yeers bring vp as a childe, The next to learning, for waxing too wilde. The next keepe vnder sir HOBBARD DE HOY, The next a man no longer a boy.

1738. SWIFT, *Polite Convers.*, Dial 1. Why, he is a mere HOBBLEDEHOY, neither a man nor a boy.

1785. GROSE, *Vulg. Tongue*, s.v.

1837. BARHAM, *Ingoldsby Legends*, 'Aunt Fanny.' At the epoch I speak about, I was between a man and a boy, A HOBBLE-DE-HOY, A fat, little, punchy concern of sixteen.

1848. THACKERAY, *Vanity Fair*, ch. iv. He remembered perfectly well being thrashed by Joseph Sedley, when the latter was a big, swaggering, HOBBADYHOY, and George an impudent urchin of ten years old.

Hence HOBBLEDEHOYISH and HOBBLEDEHOYHOOD.

1812. COLMAN, *Poetical Vagaries*, p. 12 (2nd Ed.). When Master Daw full fourteen years had told, He grew, as it is term'd, HOBBEDYHOYISH; For Cupidons and Fairies much too old, For Calibans and Devils much too boyish.

1839. THACKERAY, *Fatal Boots*, Apr. From boyhood until HOBBADYHOYHOOD (which I take to be about the sixteenth year of the life of a young man).

1848. THACKERAY, *Book of Snobs*, ch. xlii. A half-grown, or HOBBADEHOYISH footman, so to speak, walked after them.

HOBBLEDEJEE, *subs.* (old).—A pace between a walk and a run; a jog-trot.

1811. *Lexicon Balatronicum*, s.v.

HOBBLER, *subs.* (nautical). — A coast-man, half smuggler, half handyman; an unlicensed pilot. Also a landsman acting as tow-Jack.—SMYTH. ALSO (Isle of Man), a boatman.

1887. T. E. BROWN, *The Doctor*, p. 226. An' the HOBBLERS there was terr'ble divarted.

HOBBY, *subs.* (old).—A hackney; a horse in common use.

1606. *Return from Parnassus*, ii., 6 (DODSLEY, *Old Plays*, 4th ed., 1875, ix., 151). An't please you, your HOBBY will meet you at the lane's end. *Idem* (p. 154). Is not my master an absolute villain that loves his hawk, his HOBBY, and his greyhound more than any mortal creature? *Idem* (p. 145). Sirrah, boy, hath the groom saddled my hunting HOBBY?

2. (university).—A translation. TO RIDE HOBBIES=to use CRIBS (*q.v.*).

SIR POSTHUMOUS HOBBY, *subs. phr.* (old).—One nice or whimsical in his clothes.

HOBBY-HORSE, *subs.* (old: now recognised). — 1. A whim; a fancy; a favourite pursuit. Hence HOBBYHORSICAL = strongly attached to a particular fad.

1759. STERNE, *Tristam Shandy* (1793), ch. vii., p. 18. Have they not had their HOBBY-HORSES?

d. 1768. STERNE, *Letters* (1793), letter 19, p. 65. 'Tis in fact my HOBBY-HORSE.

1785. GROSE, *Vulg. Tongue*, s.v. HOBBY HORSE, a man's favourite amusement, or study, is called his HOBBY HORSE.

1893. *Westminster Gaz.*, 15 Mar., p. 9, c. 1. We quarrel a bit—he is so HOBBY-HORSICAL, you can't avoid it—and then we make friends again.

2. (colloquial).—A rantipole girl; a wench; a wanton.

1594. SHAKSPEARE, *Love's Labour Lost*, iii., 1. Call'st thou my love HOBBY-HORSE? *Moth.* No, master; the HOBBY-HORSE is but a colt, and your love, perhaps a hackney.

1604. SHAKSPEARE, *Winter's Tale*, i., 2. They say my wife's a HOBBY-HORSE.

3. (old).—A witless and unmannerly lout.

1609. JONSON, *Epicœne*, iv., 2. *Daw.* Here be in presence have tasted of her favors. *Cler.* What a neighing HOBBY-HORSE is this!

Verb (old).—To romp.

HOB-COLLINGWOOD, *subs. phr.* (North Country).—The four of hearts, considered an unlucky card.

HOB-JOBBER, *subs.* (streets).—A man or boy on the look out for small jobs—holding horses, carrying parcels, and the like.

HOB-NAIL, *subs.* (old).—A country-man. For synonyms, *see* JOSKIN.

1647. BEAUMONT and FLETCHER, *Women Pleased*, ii., 6. The HOB-NAIL thy husband's as fitly out o' th' way now.

1785. GROSE, *Vulg. Tongue*, s.v. HOBNAIL, a country clodhopper, from the shoes of country farmers and ploughmen being commonly stuck full of HOBNAILS, and even often clouted, or tipped with iron.

HOBNAILED, *adj.* (colloquial).—Boorish; clumsy; coarse; ill-done.

1599. JONSON, *Every Man out of his Humour.* *Sog.* A wretched HOBNAILED chuff.

HOBSON'S-CHOICE, *subs.* (common).—That or none: *i.e.*, there is no alternative. [Popularly derived from the name of a Cambridge livery stable keeper, whose rule was that each customer must take the horse next the door, or have no horse at all. That old Hobson existed is clear from Milton's epitaph, but Bellenden Ker (*Archæology of Popular Phrases*) affirms the story to be a Cambridge hoax, and maintains the proverb to be identical in sound and sense as the Low Saxon, *Op soens schie ho eysche*=when he had a kiss he wanted something else.]

1690. B. E., *Dict. Cant. Crew*, s.v. HOBSON'S CHOICE, that or None.

1710. WARD, *England's Reformation*, ch. iv. 'Tis HOBSON'S CHOICE, take that or none.

1712. STEELE, *Spectator*, No. 509, p. 191. I shall conclude this discourse with an explanation of a proverb [HOBSON'S CHOICE], which by vulgar error is taken and used when a man is reduced to an extremity, whereas the propriety of the maxim is to use it when you would say there is plenty, but you must make such a choice as not to hurt another who is to come after you. *Ibid* He [HOBSON] kept a stable of forty good cattle, always ready and fit for travelling; but when a man came for a horse he was led into the stable, where there was great choice, but was obliged to take the horse which stood nearest to the stable-door; so that every customer was alike well served, according to his chance, and every horse ridden with the same justice.

1717. CIBBER, *Non-Juror*, i. Can any woman think herself happy that's obliged to marry only with a HOBSON'S CHOICE?

1725. *New Cant. Dict.*, s.v.

1785. GROSE, *Vulg. Tongue*, s.v.

1820. REYNOLDS [Peter Corcoran], *The Fancy.* Black men now are HOBSON'S CHOICE.

1851. F. E. SMEDLEY, *Lewis Arundel*, ch. liii. 'When shall we go?' inquired Laura. 'Why, it's a case of HOBSON'S CHOICE,' returned Leicester.

1854. *Notes and Queries*, 21 Jan., p. 51. It was clear a choice had been given to him, but it was a HOBSON'S CHOICE.

HOCK, *subs.* (American).—1. The last card in the dealer's box at faro. [From SODA (*q.v.*) TO HOCK=from beginning to end.

2. *In. pl.* (common).—The feet. CURBY HOCKS = clumsy feet. For synonyms, *see* CREEPERS. [From the stable.]

1785. GROSE, *Vulg. Tongue*, s.v. HOCKS . . . . you have left the marks of your dirty HOCKS on my clean stairs.

1859. MATSELL, *Vocabulum*, s.v.

OLD HOCK, *subs. phr.* (common).—Stale beer; SWIPES (*q.v.*). *See* HOCKEY.

IN HOCK, *adv. phr.* (general).—Laid by the heels; fleeced; BESTED (*q.v.*).; and (thieves'), in prison.

1859. MATSELL, *Vocabulum.* 'If the cove should be caught IN THE HOCK he won't snickle,' if the fellow should be caught in the act, he would not tell.

HOCK-DOCKIES, *subs.* (old).—Shoes. For synonyms, *see* TROTTER-CASES.

1789 GEO. PARKER, *Life's Painter*, p. 173. Shoes. HOCKEY-DOCKEYS.

HOCKEY, *adj.* (old).—Drunk, especially on stale beer. For synonyms, *see* DRINKS and SCREWED.

1796. GROSE, *Vulg. Tongue* (3rd Ed.), s.v.

HOCUS, *subs.* (old: now recognised).—1. A cheat; an imposter. [An abbreviation of HOCUS - POCUS (*q.v.*).]

1654. *Witts Recreations.* Here HOCAS lyes with his tricks and his knocks, Whom death hath made sure as a juglers box; Who many hath cozen'd by his leiger-demain, Is presto convey'd and here underlain. Thus HOCAS he's here, and here he is not, While death plaid the HOCAS, and brought him to th' pot.

2. (old: now recognised).—Drugged liquor.

1823. BEE, *Dict. Turf*, s.v. HOCUS or HOCUS POCUS .... A deleterious drug mixed with wine, etc., which enfeebles the person acted upon.

Adj. (old).—*See* quots. For synonyms, *see* DRINKS and SCREWED.

1725. *New. Cant. Dict.*, s.v. HOCUS, disguised in Liquor; drunk.

1785. GROSE, *Vulg. Tongue*, s.v. HOCUS POCUS, he is quite HOCUS, he is quite drunk.

Verb (old: now recognised).—1. To cheat; to impose upon.

2. (old: now recognised).—To drug; TO SNUFF (*q.v.*).

1836. DICKENS, *Pickwick*, ch. xiii., p. 104. 'What do you mean by HOCUSSING brandy and water?' inquired Mr. Pickwick. 'Puttin' laund'num in it,' replied Sam.

1836. *Comic Almanack*, p. 1. For that we HOCUSS D first his drink.

1848. THACKERAY, *Vanity Fair*, II., ch. xxix. Mr. Frederick Pigeon avers that it was at her house at Lausanne that he was HOCUSSED at supper and lost eight hundred pounds to Major Loder and the Honourable Mr. Deucease.

54. DE QUINCEY, *Murder as one of the Fine Arts*, *Wks.*, xiii., 119. Him they intended to disable by a trick then newly introduced amongst robbers, and termed HOCUSSING, *i.e.*, clandestinely drugging the liquor of the victim with laudanum.

1859. MATSELL, *Vocabulum*, s.v. HOCUS ... 'HOCUS the bloke's lush, and then frisk his sacks,' put something into the fellow's drink that will stupify him, and then search his pockets.

1859. *The Bulletin*, 21 May. An offence which goes by the name of HOCUSSING, and which consists of an evil doer furtively introducing laudanum or some other narcotic into beer or spirits, which the victim drinks and, becoming stupified thereby, is then easily robbed.

1864. DICKENS, *Our Mutual Friend*, bk. II., ch. xii. I will not say a HOCUSSED wine, but fur from a wine as was 'elthy for the mind.

HOCUS-POCUS, *subs.* (old: now recognised). — 1. A juggler's phrase. Hence a juggler's (or impostor's) stock in trade. Also HOCUS-TRADE.

1639-61. *Rump Songs.* 'Vanity of Vanities.' A HOCUS - POCUS, juggling Knight.

1639-61. *Rump Songs*, ii., 156. 'The Rump Ululant.' Religion we made free of HOCUS TRADE.

1646. RANDOLPH, *Jealous Lovers*, If I do not think women were got with riddling, whip me! HOCAS POCAS, here you shall have me, and there you shall have me.

1654. GAYTON, *Test. Notes Don. Quix.*, 46. This old fellow had not the HOCAS POCAS of Astrology.

1675. WYCHERLEY, *Country Wife*, iii., 2. That burlesque is a HOCUS-POCUS trick they have got.

d. 1680. BUTLER, *Remains* (1759), ii., 122. With a little heaving and straining, would turn it into Latin, as Mille HOCOPOKIANA, and a thousand such.

1689. MARVELL, *Historical Poem*, line 90. With HOCUS POCUS. .... They gain on tender consciences at night.

c. 1755. ADEY, *Candle in the Dark*, p. 29. At the playing of every trick he used to say, HOCUS POCUS, tontus, talontus, vade celeriter jubeo.

1785. GROSE, *Vulg. Tongue*, s.v.

1824-28. LANDOR, *Imaginary Conversations* [2nd Ed., ii., 275]. *Torke.* What think you, for instance, of HOCUS! POCUS! *Johnson.* Sir, those are exclamations of conjurors, as they call themselves.

1883. *Daily Telegraph*, 26 Mar., p. 5, c. 3. The lock of hair, the dragon's blood, and the stolen flour were only the HOCUS-POCUS of her sham witchcraft like the transfixed waxen puppets of the sorcerers of the past.

2. (old).—A trickster; a juggler; an impostor.

1625. JONSON, *Staple of News*, ii. That was the old way, gossip, when Iniquity came in [on the stage] like HOKOS POKOS, in a juggler's jerkin, with false skirts, like the knave of clubs.

1634. HOCUS POCUS JUNIOR, *The Anatomie of Leger de main.* [Title].

1656. BLOUNT, *Glossographia*, s.v. HOCUS POCUS, a juggler, one that shows tricks by sleight of hand.

1690. B. E., *Dict. Cant. Crew*, s.v. HOCUS-POCUS, a Juggler that shews Tricks by Slight of Hand.

1725. *New Cant. Dict.*, s.v.

3. (old).—A cheat; an imposition; a juggler's trick.

1713. BENTLEY, *Free Thinking*, 12. Our author is playing HOCUS-POCUS in the very similitude he takes from that juggler.

4. (old).—*See* HOCUS, sense 2.

Adj. (old).—Cheating; fraudulent.

1715. ADDISON, *The Drummer.* If thou hast any HOCUS-POCUS tricks to play, why can'st not do them here?

1725-29. MASON, *Horace*, iv., 8. Such HOCUS-POCUS tricks, I own, Belong to Gallic bards alone.

1759. MACKLIN, *Love à la Mode*, ii., 1. The law is a sort of HOCUS-POCUS science that smiles in yer face while it picks your pocket.

Verb (old).—To cheat; to trick.

HOD (or **BROTHER HOD**), *subs.* (common).—A bricklayer's labourer.

1785. GROSE, *Vulg. Tongue*, s.v.

1859. MATSELL, *Vocabulum*, s.v.

HOD OF MORTAR, *subs. phr.* (rhyming).—A pot of porter.

HODDY-DODDY (or **HODDIE-DODDIE**), *subs.* (old).—A short thickset man or woman. The full expression is 'Hoddy Doddy, all arse and no body.'—GROSE. For synonyms, *see* FORTY-GUTS. Also a fool.

c. 1534. UDALL, *Roister Doister*, i., 1. (DODSLEY, *Old Plays*, 4th ed., 1875, iii., 58). Sometimes I hang on Hankyn HODDYDODDY'S sleeve.

1596. BEN JONSON, *Every Man in his Humour*, iv., 8. Well, good wife bawd, Cob's wife, and you, That make your husband such a HODDY-DODDY.

1639-61. *Rump Songs*, ii. [1662], 55. Every noddy .... will .... cry HODDYDODDY Here's a Parliament all arse and no body.

1723. SWIFT, *Mary the Cookmaid's Letter* (CHALMERS, *Eng. Poets*, 1810, xi., 433). My master is a personable man, and not a spindle-shanked HODDY-DODDY.

HODDY - PEAK (or **-PEKE**), *subs.* (old).—A fool; a cuckold.

d. 1529. SKELTON, *Poems*, 'Duke of Albany.' Gyue it up, And cry creke Lyke an HUDDY PEKE.

1551. *Gammer Gurton*, O. P., ii., 45. Art here again, thou HODDYPEKE?

1554. CHRISTOPHERSON, *Exh. ag. Rebel.* They counte peace to be cause of ydelnes, and that it maketh men HODIPEKES and cowardes.

d. 1555. LATIMER, *Sermons*, fol. 44, b. What, ye brainsicke fooles, ye HODDYPEAKES, ye doddy poules.

1560. *Nice Wanton* (DODSLEY, *Old Plays*, 4th ed., 1875, ii., 164). Yea, marry, I warrant you, master HODDY-PEAK.

1589. NASHE, *Anatomie of Absurdities*, b. Who, under her husband's HODDY-PEKE'S nose, Must have all the destilling dew of his delicate rose.

1594. NASHE, *Unf. Trav.*, 106 [*Chiswick Press*, 1891.] No other apte meanes had this poore shee captived Cicely to worke her HODDY PEAKE husband a proportionable plague to his jealously.

HODGE, *subs.* (colloquial).—A farm labourer; a rustic.

1589. GREENE, *Menaphon*, p. 58 [ed. Arber, 1880]. These Arcadians are giuen to take the benefit of euerie HODGE.

1675. A. MARVEL, *Satire. HODGE'S Vision from the Monument.* [Title.]

1690. B. E., *Dict. Cant. Crew*, s.v. HODGE, a Country Clown, also Roger.

1725. *New Cant. Dict.*, s.v.

1785. GROSE, *Vulg. Tongue*, s.v.

1791. SMART, *Fables*, xiii., 27. Is that the care (quoth HODGE)? O rare!

1880. RICHARD JEFFERIES, *HODGE and his Masters.* [Title.]

1884. MRS. CRAIK, in *Eng. Ill. Mag.*, Mar., p. 356. Quite different from the bovine, agricultural HODGE of the midland counties.

1893. *National Observer*, 25 Feb., ix., 358. 'Pay me an infinitesimal sum,' Lord Winchilsea says (in effect) to HODGE, 'and you shall have a weekly newspaper for nothing.'

HODGE-PODGE (or **HOTCH-POTCH**), *subs.* (old: now recognised).—A mixture; a medley. Sp., *commistrajo.* *See* HOTCH-POTCH.

1553-99. SPENSER, *State of Ireland.* They have made our English tongue a gal-imaufrey, or HODGEPODGE of all other peeches.

1719. DURFEY, *Pills*, etc., i., 199. Some Cillier-like Saint, ... Had rak'd a HODG PODG for the Devil.

1726. VANBRUGH, *Journey to London.* They were all got into a sort of HODGE-PODGE argument for the good of the nation which I did not well understand.

d. 1764. LLOYD, *Poems* (774), 'A Tale.' Was ever such an HODGE-PODGE seen.

1785. GROSE, *Vulg. Tongue*, s.v.

HODMAN, (Oxford Univ.).—A scholar from Westminster School admitted to Christ Church College, Oxford.

1728. BAILEY, *Eng. Dict.*, s.v. HODMAN.

HODMANDOD, *subs.* (old).—1. A snail in his shell—BACON. *See* DODDY.

1663. KILLIGREW, *The Parson's Wedding*, v., 4 (DODSLEY, *Old Plays*, 4th ed., 1875, xiv., 525) Painted snails with houses on their backs, and horns as big as Dutch cows. ... Can any woman be honest that lets such HODMANDODS crawl o'er her virgin breast and belly?

1690. B. E., *Dict. Cant. Crew*, s.v.

1725. *New Cant. Dict.*, s.v.

1728. BAILEY, *Eng. Dict.*, s.v.

1785. GROSE, *Vulg. Tongue.* s.v.

2. (old).—A Hottentot.

1686. CAPTAIN COWLEY in Harris *Voyages*, i., 82. We walked, moreover, without the town to the villages inhabited by the HODMANDODS, to view their nasty bodies.

HOE. To HOE IN (American Univ.).—To work with vigour; TO SWOT (*q.v.*).

To HOE ONE'S OWN ROW, *verb. phr.* (American).—To do one's own work.

HARD ROW TO HOE. *See* HARD ROW.

HOE-DOWN, *subs.* (American).—A negro dance; a BREAKDOWN (*q.v.*).

HOG, *subs.* (old).—1. A shilling: also a sixpence: and (in America) a ten-cent piece. For synonyms, *see* BLOW. HALF-A-HOG = sixpence, or five-cent piece.

1688. SHADWELL, *Squire of Alsatia*, s.v. HOG, a shilling.

1690. B. E., *Dict. Cant. Crew*, s.v. HOG, You Darkman Budge, will you Fence your HOG at the next Boozing ken?

1714. *Memoirs of John Hall* (4th Ed.), p. 12, s.v.

1725. *New Cant. Dict.*, s.v. Half a HOG, Six-Pence.

1809-12. MISS EDGEWORTH, *Ennui*, ch. vi. 'It's only a tester or a HOG they want your honour to give 'em, to drink your honour's health,' said Paddy. 'A HOG to drink my health?' 'Ay, that is a thirteen, plase your honour; all as one as an English shilling.'

1825. EGAN, *Life of an Actor*, ch. iv. You shall have .... eighteen HOG a week, and a benefit which never fails.

1842. THACKERAY, *Cox's Diary* in *Comic Almanack*, p. 237. Do you think I'm a-going to kill my horses, and break my precious back, and bust my carriage, and carry you, and your kids, and your traps, for six HOG?

1851-61. H. MAYHEW, *Lond. Lab. and Lond. Poor*, vol. i., p. 529. The slang phrases are constantly used by the street lads; thus a sixpence is a 'tanner'; a shilling a 'bob,' or a HOG .... The collections of coin dealers amply show, that the figure of a hog was anciently placed on a small silver coin.

1857. MRS. MATHEWS, *Tea Table Talk*, p. 207. The shopwoman satisfied Suett after her fashion, that his little lump of Suett had absorbed flour and lard (pastry) to the amount of what her queer customer would have termed a HOG.

1859. MATSELL, *Vocabulum*, s.v. HOG, a ten-cent piece.

2. (colloquial). — A foul-mouthed blackguard; a dirty feeder. Also, a common glutton.

1598. FLORIO, *A Worlde of Wordes*, s.v. *Ciro*, a HOGGE, a swine, a filthie fellowe.

1892. MILLIKEN, *'Arry Ballads*, p. 69. 'Arry's a HOG when he feeds.

3 (Cambridge Univ.: obsolete).—A student of St. John's. Also, JOHNIAN HOG. *See* CRACKLE, BRIDGE OF GRUNTS, and ISTHMUS OF SUEZ.

1690. *Diary of Abraham dela Pryme* (Surtees Society, No. 54), quoted in *Notes and Queries*, 6, S. xi., 328. For us Jonians are called abusively HOGGS.

1795. *Gent. Mag.*, lxv., 22. The JOHNIAN HOGS were originally remarkable on account of the squalid figures and low habits of the *students*, and especially of the *sizars* of Saint *John's* College. [Another story of how name originated is given in detail in *Gent. Mag.* (1795), lxv., 107.]

1889. WHIBLEY, *In Cap and Gown*, p. 28. An obsolete name for members of St. John's College, Cambridge.

4. (old Scots').—A yearling sheep.

1796. BURNS, *Poems.* What will I do gin my HOGGIE die, my joy, my friend, my HOGGIE.

5. (American).—An inhabitant of Chicago. [That city being a notable pig-breeding and pork-packing centre.]

6. (old).—A Hampshireman.

1770. LORD HAILES, *Ancient Scottish Poems*, 'Dance of the Seven Deadly Sins.' Note on line 115. And thus his ill-bred raillery will be like that of Essex calves, HAMPSHIRE HOGS, Middlesex mongrels, Norfolk dumplings, Welsh goats, etc.

Verb (American). — 1. To cheat; to humbug; TO GAMMON (*q.v.*).

1867. BROWNE (Artemus Ward). 'Among the Mormons, ii., 10. Go my son, and HOG the public.

2. (venery). — To copulate. For synonyms *see* GREENS and RIDE.

3. (stables).—To cut short; *e.g.*, to HOG a horse's mane.

A HOG IN ARMOUR, *subs. phr.* (old).—A lout in fine clothes. Also a JACK-IN-OFFICE; HOG-IN-TOGS = (in America) a well-dressed loafer. [HOG = HODGE (*q.v.*), a rustic.]

1785. GROSE, *Vulg. Tongue*, s.v. HOG .... an awkward, or mean looking man or woman, finely dressed, is said to look like a HOG IN ARMOUR.

HOG AND HOMINY, *subs. phr.* (American).—Plain fare; COMMON DOINGS (*q.v.*). [Pork and maize are the two cheapest food stuffs in the U.S.A.]

TO GO THE WHOLE HOG. *See* WHOLE ANIMAL.

TO BRING ONE'S HOGS (or PIGS) TO A FINE MARKET, *verb. phr.* (old).—To do well; to make a good DEAL (*q.v.*). Also, in sarcasm, the opposite.

1690. B. E., *Dict. Cant. Crew.*, s.v. HE HAS BROUGHT HIS HOGGS TO A FAIR MARKET, or he has Spun a fair Thread.

1785. GROSE, *Vulg. Tongue*, s.v. HOG. . . . HE HAS BROUGHT HIS HOGS TO A FINE MARKET, a saying of one who has been remarkably successful in his affairs, and is spoken ironically to signify the contrary.

TO DRIVE ONE'S HOGS (or PIGS) to MARKET, *verb. phr.* (colloquial).—To snore.

1738. SWIFT *Polite Conversations*, ii., 455. I'gad he fell asleep, and snored so loud that we thought he was DRIVING HIS HOGS TO MARKET.

1785. GROSE, *Vulg. Tongue*, s.v. HOG . . . . to DRIVE ONE'S HOGS, to snore, the noise made by some persons in snoring being not much unlike the notes of that animal.

HOG-AGE, *subs.* (American).—The period between boyhood and manhood. *Cf.*, HOBBLEDEHOY.

HOGAN-MOGAN, *subs.* (old).—*See* quot.

1892. AITKEN, *Satires of Andrew Marvell*, p. 128. The States General of the United provinces were officially addressed as High and Mighty Lords, or in Dutch, Hoogmogenden; hence English satirists called them HOGANS-MOGANS, and applied the phrase to Dutchmen in general. *Cf.*, *Hoganmogandes, or the Dutch Hudibras* (1694), and '*A New Song on the HOGAN-MOGANS*' in '*A Collection of the Newest Poems . . . against Popery, etc.*' (1680).

HOG-GRUBBER, *subs.* (old). — A miser; a niggard; a MEAN CUSS (*q.v.*).

1690. B. E., *Dict. Cant. Crew*, s.v. A HOG-GRUBBER, ... a narrow-soul'd sneaking Fellow.

1725. *New Cant. Dict.*, s.v.

1785. GROSE, *Vulg. Tongue*, s.v. HOG GRUBBER, a mean stingy fellow.

HOGMAGUNDY (or **HOUGHMAGANDIE**), *subs.* (Scots).—Copulation. For synonyms, *see* GREENS and RIDE.

1786. BURNS, *The Holy Fair* [last stanza]. There's some are fou o' love divine, There's some are fou o' brandy; An' mony jobs that day begin, May end in HOUGMAGANDIE Some ither day.

HOGMENAY, *subs.* (old Scots').—1. New Year's Eve, which is a national festival. [The origin has been the subject of much discussion.]

1776. BRAND, *Popular Antiquities*, p. 102. Sirs, do you what HAGMANE signifies? It is the devil be in the house.

1793. *The Bee*, 10 July, p. 17. The night preceding that festival HOGGMONAY.

1879. JAMES NAPIER, *Folk Lore*, p. 154. After the Reformation, the Scotch transferred HAGMANAY [from Xmas Eve] to the last day of December, as a preparation day for the New Year.

2. Hence a wanton. [The feast is celebrated with much drink and not a little license.]

HOGO, *subs.* (old).—A flavour; an aroma; a relish. Hence, in irony, and by corruption, a stink. *Cf.*, FOGO. [From Fr., *haut goût*.] *See* HIGH, sense 2.

1569. ERASMUS, Trans. *Praise of Folly*, p. 13 [1709]. Pleasure that HAUT-GOUST of Folly.

1639-61. *Rump Songs*. 'A Vindication of the Rump.' Oh! what a HOGO was there.

1645. HOWELL, *Letters*, V., xxxviii., p. 42. He can marinat fish, make gellies, and is excellent for a *pickant* sawce, and the HAUGOU.

1653. WALTON, *Compleat Angler*, I., ch. vii. To give the sawce a HOGOE let the dish (into which you let the Pike fall) be rubed with it [garlick].

1656. *Choyce Drollery*, p. 34. And why not say a word or two Of she that's just? witness all who Have ever been at thy HO-GO.

1663. KILLIGREW, *The Parson's Wedding*, iii., 2 (DODSLEY, *Old Plays*, 4th ed., 1875, xiv., 451). We'll work ourselves into such a sauce as you can never surfeit on, and yet no HOGOUGH.

1667. COWLEY, *Government of Oliver Cromwell*, Prose Works (Pickering, 1826), 94 Cromwell . . . . . found out the true HOGO of this pleasure, and rejoiced in the extravagance of his ways.

1672. WYCHERLEY, *Love in a Wood*, ii., 1. She has . . . . no more teeth left than such as give a HAUT GOUT to her breath.

1686. *Twelve Ingenious Characters*. A bad husband is an inconsiderate piece of sottish extravagance; for though he consist of several ill ingredients, yet still good fellowship is the *causa sine qua non*, and gives him the HO-GO.

1690. B. E., *Dict. Cant. Crew*, s.v. HOGO.

1705-7. WARD, *Hudibras Redivivus*, Vol. I., Pt. vi., p. 4. Most stinking meat, Toss'd up with leeks into *Raggoo*, To overcome the unsav'ry HOGO.

1718. DURFEY, *Pills*, iii., 177. 'Let's drink and be merry.' Your most Beautiful Bit, that hath all Eyes upon her, That her Honesty sells for a HOGO of Honour.

1785. GROSE, *Vulg. Tongue*, s.v. HOGO . . . . it has a confounded HOGO, it stinks confoundedly.

HOGSHEAD. TO COUCH A HOGSHEAD, *verb. phr.* (Old Cant).—*See* quot. For synonyms, *see* BALMY.

1567. HARMAN, *Caveat* (1814), p. 66. To COUCH A HOGSHEAD: to ly downe and slepe. *Ibid*, I COUCHED A HOGSHEAD in a skypper this darkemans.

HOG-SHEARING, *subs.* (old).—Much ado about nothing; great cry and little wool.

1690. B. E., *Dict. Cant. Crew*, s.v. HOG. Labour in vain, which the Latines express by Goats-wooll, as the English by the SHEARING OF HOGGS.

HOGS-NORTON. TO HAVE BEEN BORN AT HOGS-NORTON, *verb. phr.* (old).—To be ill-mannered.

d. 1666. HOWELL, *Eng. Proverbs*, p. 16. I think thou wast BORN AT HOGGS-NORTON, where piggs play upon the organs.

1676. MARVEL, *Mr. Smirke* [Grosart], iv., p. 89. A pair of organs of cats which he had done well to have made the pigs at HOGS-NORTON play on.

HOGSTYE OF VENUS, *subs. phr.* (venery).—*See* quot. For synonyms, *see* MONOSYLLABLE.

1598. FLORIO, *Worlde of Wordes*, s.v. *Porcile di venere*, the HOG-STYE OF VENUS, a womans privities or geare.

HOG-WASH, *subs.* (common).—1. Bad liquor; specifically, ROT-GUT (*q.v.*).

2. (journalists'). — Worthless newspaper matter; SLUSH, SWASH, and FLUB-DUB (*q.v.*).

HOI POLLOI, *subs. phr.* (university). The candidates for ordinary degrees. [From the Greek.] *Cf.*, GULF.

HOIST, *subs.* (old). — A shoplifter; also a confederate hoisting or helping a thief to reach an open window. THE HOIST = shoplifting. TO GO UPON THE HOIST = to enter a house by an open window.

1796. GROSE, *Vulg. Tongue* (3rd Ed.), s.v. HOIST. This is done by the assistance of a confederate called THE HOIST, who leans his head against the wall, making his back a kind of step or ascent.—GROSE.

1819. VAUX, *Cant. Dict.* HOIST, the *game* of shop-lifting is called THE HOIST; a person expert at this practice is said to be *a good hoist*.

1821. HAGGART, *Life*, p. 38. We were principally engaged UPON THE HOYS and coreing.

Verb (thieves').—1. To practise shop-lifting; to rob by means of THE HOIST (*q.v.*).

2. (American).—To run away; to decamp. For synonyms, *see* AMPUTATE and SKEDADDLE.

1847. PORTER, *Quarter Race*, etc., p. 174. Jist HIST, and take yourself off.

3. (common).—To drink. *E.g.*, Will you HOIST? = will you have a liquor?; HOISTING = drinking; ON THE HOIST = on the drunk. Also a HOIST IN.

TO GIVE A HOIST, *verb. phr.* (tailors').—To do a bad turn.

TO HAVE (OR DO) A HOIST IN. *verb. phr.* (venery).—To copulate. For synonyms, *see* GREENS and RIDE.

HOISTER, *subs.* (old).—1. A shoplifter; a HOIST (*q.v.*, sense 1). Also a pickpocket.

1847-50. J. H. JESSE, *London*, i., 30. He that could take out a counter without any noise was allowed to be a public HOYSTER. N.B.—That a hoyster is a pickpocket.

2. (common).—A sot. For synonyms, *see* LUSHINGTON.

HOISTING (or **HOIST-LAY**), *subs.* (thieves').—1. Shop-lifting. THE HOIST (*q.v.*). Also shaking a man head downwards, so that his money rolls out of his pockets.

1811. *Lexicon Balatronicum*, s.v.

1821. D. HAGGART, *Life*, glossary, p. 172. HOYS, shop-lifting.

1868. *Temple Bar*, xxiv., 534. She can secrete articles about her dress when in a shop looking at things, and that's one way of HOISTING.

2. (old).—*See* quot.

1785. GROSE, *Vulg. Tongue*, s.v. HOISTING, a ludicrous ceremony, formerly performed on every soldier, the first time he appeared in the field, after being married: as soon as the regiment, or company, had grounded their arms, to rest awhile; three or four men of the same company, to which the bridegroom belonged, seized upon him, and putting a couple of bayonets out of the two corners of his hat, to represent horns, it was placed on his head, the back part foremost, he was then hoisted on the shoulders of two strong fellows, and carried round the arms, a drum and fife beating and playing, the pioneers call, named *Round-heads and Cuckolds*, but on this occasion stiled the *Cuckold's March*; in passing the colours, he was to take off his hat . . . . This in some regiments was practised by the officers on their brethren.

HOIT (or **HOYT**), *verb.* (old).—To be noisily or riotously inclined.

1611. BEAUMONT and FLETCHER, *Knight of the Burning Pestle*, iv., 1. He sings, and HOYTS, and revels among his drunken companions.

HOITY-TOITY. *See* HIGHTY-TIGHTY.

HOKEY-POKEY, *subs.* (common). — 1. A cheat; a swindle; nonsense. [From HOCUS POCUS.]

2. (common).—A cheap ice-cream sold in the streets.

HOLBORN HILL. TO RIDE BACKWARDS UP HOLBORN HILL, *verb. phr.* (old colloquial).—To go to the gallows. [The way was thence to Tyburn, criminals riding backwards.—GROSE.]

1614. JONSON, *Bartholomew Fair*, ii., 1. *Urs.* Up the heavy HILL—*Kuock.* Of HOLBOURN, Ursula, mean'st thou so? for what, for what, pretty Urse? *Urs.* For cutting halfpenny purses, or stealing little penny dogs out o' the Fair.

1659. *Harry White's Humour* (Nares). Item, he loves to ride when he is weary, yet at certaine times he holds it ominous to ride up HOLBORNE.

1695. CONGREVE *Love for Love*, ii., 7. Sirrah, you'll be hanged; I shall live to see you GO UP HOLBORN HILL.

HOLD, *verb.* (old).—1. To bet; to wager. *See* DO YOU HOLD?

1534. UDALL, *Roister Doister*, i., 2 (DODSLEY, *Old Plays*, 4th ed., 1875, iii., 7). I HOLD a groat ye will drink anon of this gear.

1551. W. STILL, *Gammer Gurton's Needle*, iii., 3 (DODSLEY, *Old Plays*, 4th ed., 1875, iii., 216, and *passim*). I HOLD thee a groat I shall patch thy coat.

1697. VANBRUGH, *Provoked Wife*, ii., 1. I'll HOLD you a guinea you don't make her tell it you.

1719. DURFEY, *Pills*, etc., ii., 54. I'll HOLD ye five Guineas to four.

2. (venery) (or HOLD IT).—To be impregnated; to be got with child. [In certain parts of Scotland, it is said, a farm servant stating that she "disna HAUD" commands double wages.]

TO HOLD ON TO, *verb. phr.* (colloquial),—To apply oneself; to be persistent: generally, TO HOLD ON LIKE GRIM DEATH.

1848. RUXTON, *Life in the Far West*, p. 71. He recovered, and wisely HELD ON TO for the future.

HOLD UP, *verb. phr.* (American and Australian). — 1. To rob on the highway; TO BAIL or STICK UP (*q.v.*). Also as *subs.* = a highwayman or ROAD-AGENT (*q.v.*).

1888. *Detroit Free Press*, 8 Dec. One man HELD UP six stage passengers in Arizona the other day and robbed them of $2,000. Each was armed, but it is customary to submit out there, and so up went their hands.

1888. *Detroit Free Press*, 13 Oct. Mounted on a white horse, he started on a land-prospecting tour and ran against a party of HOLD-UPS.

1892. *Lippincott*, Oct., p. 495. Would HOLD the train UP until I had finished.

2. (thieves').—To arrest. For synonyms, *see* NAB.

TO HOLD THE STAGE, *verb. phr.* (theatrical).—To have the chief place on the boards and the eye of an audience. Fr., *avoir les planches*.

TO HOLD A CANDLE TO (THE DEVIL, etc.), *verb. phr.* (colloquial).—*See* DEVIL, and add the following quot.

1868. READE and BOUCICAULT, *Foul Play*, p. 65. But you see, sir, he has got the ear of the merchant ashore; and so I am obliged to HOLD A CANDLE TO THE DEVIL.

TO HOLD A CANDLE TO, *verb. phr.* (colloquial).—To vie with; to be comparable to; also to assist in or condone.

1886. R. L. STEVENSON, *Kidnapped*, p. 79. They had killed poor Ransome; and was I to HOLD THE CANDLE TO another murder?

TO HOLD (or HANG) ON BY THE EYELIDS, EYELASHES or EYEBROWS, *verb. phr.* (common).—To pursue an object desperately; to insist upon a point; to carry on a forlorn hope. *See* also quot. and SPLASH BOARD.

1883. CLARK RUSSELL, *Sailor's Language*, p. 69. HOLDING ON WITH HIS EYELIDS. Said of a man aloft with nothing much to lay hold of.

TO HOLD IN HAND, *verb. phr.* (colloquial). — To amuse; to possess the attention or the mind; to have in one's pocket.

TO HOLD THE MARKET, *verb. phr.* (colloquial).—To buy stock and hold it to so large an extent that the price cannot decline.

DO YOU HOLD? *phr.* (streets). —Have you money to lend? Can you stand treat? *Cf. verb.*, sense 1.

HOLD YOUR HORSES, *phr.* (American).—Go easy; don't get excited: a general injunction to calm in act and speech.

HOLD YOUR JAW, *phr.* (colloquial).—Hold your tongue; STOW YOUR GAB (*q.v.*).

HOLD HARD! (or ON)! *intj.* (colloquial).—Wait a moment! don't be in a hurry!

1761. COLMAN, *Jealous Wife*, V., in *Wks.* (1777), i., 130. HOLD HARD! HOLD HARD! you are all on a wrong scent.

1835. DICKENS, *Sketches by Boz*, p. 280. 'HOLD HARD!' said the conductor; 'I'm blowed if we ha'n't forgot the gen'lm'n as vas to be set down at Doory-lane.'

1864. E. YATES, *Broken to Harness*, ch. iv., p. 38 (1873). I told Meaburn to HOLD ON, and we'd get a rise out of Punch.

HOLD-STITCH.—*See* STITCH.

HOLD-WATER.—*See* WATER.

HOLD-OUT, *subs.* (gambling).—An old-fashioned apparatus, in poker, for 'holding out' desirable cards.

HOLE (venery).—1. The female *pudendum*. Also, HOLE OF CONTENT, and HOLE (or QUEEN) OF HOLES. For synonyms, *see* MONOSYLLABLE. TO GIVE A HOLE TO HIDE IT IN = TO GRANT THE FAVOUR (*q.v.*). [Hence, by a play upon words, HOLY OF HOLIES.]

1595. SHAKSPEARE, *Romeo and Juliet*, ii., 4. This drivelling love is like a great natural, that runs lolling up and down to hide his BAUBLE (*q.v.*) in a HOLE.

1598. FLORIO, *Worlde of Wordes*, s.v. *Carnafau*, the brat-getting place, or HOLE OF CONTENT.

1620. PERCY, *Folio MS.*, p. 197. . . . He light in a HOLE ere he was aware!

1647-80. ROCHESTER, *Poems.* Thou mighty princess, lovely QUEEN OF HOLES.

d. 1649. DRUMMOND, *Posthumous Poems*, 'The Statue of Alcides.' Fair nymph, in ancient days, your HOLES, by far, Were not so hugely vast as now they are.

1719. DURFEY, *Pills*, etc., iv., 72. It has a head much like a Mole's, And yet it loves to creep in HOLES: The fairest She that e'er took Life, For love of this became a Wife.

2. (old).—A cell; *cf.*, HELL, sense 1.

1540. LINDSAY, *Thrie Estaits*, line 1016. Wee have gart bind him with ane poill, And send him to the theifis HOILL.

1607. *Miseries of Enforced Marriage*, iii., I. (DODSLEY, *Old Plays*, 4th ed., 1875, ix., 514). If you shall think . . . it shall accord with the state of gentry to submit myself from the feather-bed in the master's side, or the flock-bed in the knight's ward, to the straw-bed in the HOLE.

1607. WENTWORTH SMITH, *The Puritan*, iii. But if e'er we clutch him again the Counter shall charm him. *Rav.* The HOLE shall rot him.

1657. *Walks of Hogsdon.* Next from the stocks, the HOLE, and little-ease.

1663. KILLIGREW, *The Parson's Wedding*, iv., 2 (DODSLEY, *Old Plays*, 4th ed., 1875, xiv., 482). Make his mittymus to the HOLE at Newgate.

3. (old).—A private printing office where unlicensed books were made; a COCK-ROBIN SHOP (*q.v.*).—MOXON, 1683.

4. (colloquial).—A difficulty; a fix; on the turf, TO BE IN A HOLE = to lose (a bet) or be defeated (of horses).

1760-61. SMOLLETT, *Sir L. Greaves*, ch. xvi. I should be in a deadly HOLE myself if all my customers should take it into their heads to drink nothing but water-gruel.

1868. OUIDA, *Under Two Flags*, ch. i. 'I am in a hole—no end of a HOLE.

5. (common). — A place of abode; specifically, a mean habitation; a dirty lodging. For synonyms, *see* DIGGINGS.

6. (common). — The *rectum*: short for ARSE-HOLE. *E.g.*, SUCK HIS HOLE = a derisive retort upon an affirmative answer to the

question, 'Do you know So-and-So?' For synonyms, *see* MONOCULAR EYEGLASS.

1383. CHAUCER, *Canterbury Tales*, 'The Miller's Tale.' And at the window she put out hir HOLE.

1540. LINDSAY, *Thrie Estaits*, line 2174. Lift vp hir clais: Kis hir HOILL with your hart.

1614. JONSON, *Bartholomew Fair*, v., 3. A pox o' your manners, kiss my HOLE here, and smell.

1649. DRUMMOND, *Madrigals and Epigrams*, 'A Jest' (CHALMERS, *English Poets*, 1810, x., 667). She turned, and turning up her hole beneath, Said, 'Sir, kiss here.'

d. 1732. GAY, *Tales* 'In Imitation of Chaucer's Style' (CHALMERS, *English Poets*, 1810, x., 504). Thou didst forget to guard thy postern, There is an HOLE which hath not crossed been.

Verb (venery).—To effect intromission; to PUT IN (*q.v.*). Hence, HOLED, *adj.* = IN (*q.v.*).

A HOLE IN ONE'S COAT, *subs. phr.* (colloquial).—A flaw in one's fame; a weak spot in one's character. TO PICK A HOLE IN ONE'S COAT = to find a cause for censure.

1789. BURNS, *Verses on Capt. Grose.* If there's a HOLE IN A' YOUR COATS, I rede you tent it.

TO MAKE (or BURN) A HOLE IN ONE'S POCKET, *verb. phr.* (colloquial).—Said of money recklessly spent.

TO MAKE A HOLE IN ANYTHING, *verb. phr.* (colloquial).—To use up largely.

1663. KILLIGREW, *The Parson's Wedding*, iii., 5 (DODSLEY, *Old Plays*, 4th ed., 1875, xiv., 456). Do it then, and make a HOLE in this angel.

TO MAKE A HOLE IN THE WATER, *verb. phr.*—(common).—To commit suicide by drowning.

1892. MILLIKEN, *'Arry Ballads*, p. 76. I should just MAKE A HOLE IN THE WATER, if 'tworn't for the wife and the kids.

TO MAKE A HOLE, *verb. phr.* (colloquial). — To break; to spoil; to upset; to interrupt. Thus to MAKE A HOLE IN ONE'S MANNERS = to be rude; to MAKE A HOLE IN ONE'S REPUTATION = to betray, to seduce; to MAKE A HOLE IN THE SILENCE = to make a noise, to RAISE CAIN (*q.v.*).

TOO DRUNK TO SEE A HOLE IN A LADDER, *phr.* (common).—Excessively intoxicated. For synonyms, *see* DRINKS and SCREWED.

HOLE-AND-CORNER, *adj.* (colloquial).—Secret; underhand; out of the way: *e.g.*, HOLE-AND-CORNER WORK = shady business. Also (venery) = copulation. [*Cf.*, HOLE, *subs.* sense 1.]

HOLER (also **HOLEMONGER**), *subs.* (colloquial). — A whoremaster (*cf.*, HOLE, *subs.*, sense 1). Also (old), a harlot; a light woman (*cf.*, HOLE, *verb.*). Hence, HOLING = whoring.

HOLIDAY, *adj.* (old).—Unskilled; indifferent; careless.

1785. GROSE, *Vulg. Tongue*, s.v. HOLIDAY, A HOLIDAY BOWLER, a bad bowler.

BLIND MAN'S HOLIDAY. *See ante.*

TO HAVE A HOLIDAY AT PECKHAM, *verb. phr.* (colloquial).—To go dinnerless. ALL HOLIDAY AT PECKHAM = no work and nothing to eat. [A play upon words.] *See* PECKISH.

1811. *Lexicon Balatronicum.* ALL HOLIDAY AT PECKHAM . . . . a saying signifying that it is all over with the business or person spoken of or alluded to.

1848. FORSTER, *Oliver Goldsmith*, bk. I., ch. vi., p. 55 (5th Ed.). 'Oh, that is ALL A HOLIDAY AT PECKHAM,' said an old friend very innocently one day.

TO TAKE A HOLIDAY, *verb. phr.* (common).—To be dismissed; to get the BAG (*q.v.*) or SACK (*q.v.*).

GONE FOR A HOLIDAY, *adv. phr.* (colloquial).—Said of a flaw, lapse, or imperfection of any kind (as dropped stitches, lost buttons, slurred painting, and so forth). *See* also quots.

1785. GROSE, *Vulg. Tongue*, s.v. HOLIDAY . . . . a holiday is any part of a ship's bottom, left uncovered in painting it.

1883. CLARK RUSSELL, *Sailors' Language*, p. 69, s.v. HOLIDAYS. Places left untarred on shrouds, backstays, etc., during the operation of tarring them.

HOLLER, *verb.* (American).—To cry enough; to give in; to CAVE IN (*q.v.*).

1847. PORTER, *Quarter Race*, etc., p. 89. The truth must come, he warped me nice, So jist to save his time I HOLLERED.

HOLLIS, *subs.* (Winchester College).—A small pebble. [Said to be derived from a boy.—*Notions.*]

HOLLOW, *adj.* (colloquial).—Complete; certain; decided. As *adv.* completely; utterly. *E.g.*, to beat or lick HOLLOW. *See* BEAT and CREATION.

1759. TOWNLEY, *High Life Below Stairs*, i., 2. Crab was beat HOLLOW.

1761. COLMAN, *Jealous Wife*, V., in *Wks.* (1777), i., 134. So, my lord, you and I are both distanced: a HOLLOW thing, damme.

1811. *Lexicon Balatronicum*, s.v. HOLLOW. It was quite a HOLLOW thing, *i.e.*, a certainty, or decided business.

1814. EDGWORTH, *Patronage*, ch. iii. Squire Burton won the match HOLLOW.

1837. BARHAM, *Ingoldsby Legends.* 'Bloudie Jack.' His lines to Apollo Beat all the rest HOLLOW And gained him the Newdegate Prize.

1852. DICKENS, *Bleak House*, ch. lxiv., p. 529. I have therefore taken a 'ouse in that locality, which, in the opinion of my friends, is a HOLLOW bargain (taxes ridiculous, and use of fixtures included in the rent).

1871. *Durham County Advertiser*, 10 Nov. 'It licks me HOLLOW, sir, as I may say,' put in the silent member.

1892. *Punch*, 9 July, p. 3. Booby-traps were beaten HOLLOW.

HOLLOWAY, *subs.* (venery).—The female *pudendum*. For synonyms, *see* MONOSYLLABLE.

HOLLOWAY, MIDDLESEX (common).—The lower bowel; the ARSE-GUT (*q.v.*).

HOLT, *verb.* (American).—To take; to take hold of.

HOLUS-BOLUS, *subs.* (nautical).—The head. Also the neck.

Adv. (colloquial). — Helter skelter; altogether; first come, first served.

1868. WILKIE COLLINS, *The Moonstone*, 1st Period, ch. xv. And, making a sudden snatch at the heap of silver, put it back, HOLUS-BOLUS, in her pocket.

HOLY. MORE HOLY THAN RIGHTEOUS, *adv. phr.* (common).—Said of a person in rags, or of a tattered garment.

HOLY-BOYS, *subs.* (military).—The NINTH FOOT. [From a trick of selling bibles for drink in the Peninsula.] Also, FIGHTING NINTH.

1886. *Tinsley's Magazine*, Apr., 322. The 9th having bartered their Bibles in Spain for wine, and having there gained a reputation for sacking monasteries, were long known as the HOLY BOYS.

HOLY-FATHER, *subs.* (Irish).—*See* quot.

1785. GROSE, *Vulg. Tongue*, s.v. HOLY FATHER, A butcher's boy of St. Patrick's Market, Dublin, or other Irish blackguard; among whom the exclamation, or oath, by the Holy Father (meaning the Pope), is common.

HOLY IRON. *See* HOLY POKER.

HOLY JOE, *subs. phr.* (colloquial).—A pious person, whether hypocritical or sincere. Also (nautical), a parson.

HOLY JUMPING MOTHER OF MOSES. *See* MOSES.

HOLY-LAMB, *subs.* (old).—A thorough-paced villain.—GROSE.

HOLY-LAND (or **GROUND**), *subs.* (old).—1. St. Giles's; PALESTINE (*q.v.*).

1819. MOORE, *Tom Crib's Memorial to Congress*, p. 7. For we are the boys of the HOLY GROUND, And we'll dance upon nothing and turn us round.

1821. *The Fancy*, i., p. 250. The HOLY-LAND, as St. Giles's has been termed, in compliment to the superior purity of its Irish population.

1821. EGAN, *Tom and Jerry*, ch. ii. At Mammy O'Shaughnessy's in the back Settlements of the HOLY LAND.

1823. W. T. MONCRIEFF, *Tom and Jerry*, ii., 5. Let's have a dive among the cadgers in the back slums, in the HOLY LAND.

1843 *Punch's Almanack*, 1 Sept. St. Giles. The Marquis of Waterford makes a pilgrimage to his shrine in the HOLY LAND.

1859. SALA, *Twice Round the Clock*, one a.m., par. 28. Unfaithful topographers may have told you that the HOLY LAND being swept away and Buckeridge Street being pulled down, St. Giles's exists no more.

1891. *Licensed Vict. Gaz.*, 3 Apr. p. 215, col. 1. It would be hard to say whether the Irishmen of the HOLY LAND or the Hebrew scum of Petticoat Lane showed the finest specimens of 'looped and windowed raggedness.'

2. (common).—Generic for any neighbourhood affected by Jews; specifically, Bayswater, and Brighton. *Cf.*, NEW JERUSALEM, and HOLY OF HOLIES.

HOLY MOSES. *See* MOSES.

HOLY OF HOLIES, *subs. phr.* (common).—1. The Grand Hotel at Brighton. [Which is largely tenanted by Jews: *cf.*, HOLY LAND (sense 2), and NEW JERUSALEM.]

2. (colloquial). — A private room; a SANCTUM (*q.v.*).

1891. N. GOULD, *Double Event*, p. 215. Fletcher did not venture into that HOLY OF HOLIES.

1893. *Westminister Gaz.*, 31 Jan., p. 3, c. 2. The Cabinet Council is the HOLY OF HOLIES of the British Constitution, and as Mr. Bagehot long ago regretted, no description of it at once graphic and authentic has ever been given.

3. (venery).—*See* HOLE, sense 1, and for synonyms, MONOSYLLABLE.

HOLY POKER (or **IRON**), *subs. phr.* (university).—The mace carried by an esquire bedel (of Law, Physic, or Divinity) as a badge of authority. [The term, which is applied to the bedels themselves, is very often used as an oath.]

1840. *Comic Almanack*, 'Tom the Devil,' p. 214. A hotel's the place for me! I've thried em all, from the Club-house at Kilkinny, to the Clarendon, and, by the HOLY POKER, never wish mysilf worse luck than such cantonments!

1870. *London Figaro*, 8 Oct., p. 2, col. 2. The bedels of a University are very important persons, although derisive undergraduates familiarly term them HOLY POKERS.

1886. R. L. STEVENSON, *Kidnapped*, p. 169. I swear upon the HOLY IRON I had neither art nor part.

2. (venery).—The *penis* (by a play upon words). *Cf.*, HOLE, sense 1, HOLY OF HOLIES, sense

3, and POKE. For synonyms, *see* CREAMSTICK and PRICK.

HOLY-WATER SPRINKLER, *subs. phr.* (old).—A mediæval weapon of offence; a MORNING STAR (*q.v.*).

HOME, *subs.* (colonial).—England.

1893. *Gentlemen's Mag.*, Jan., p. 74. And then I learnt that by HOME he meant England, which, moreover, is referred to as 'home' by dusky myriads, who have never seen her cliffs rise above the waves.

TO GET HOME, *verb. phr.* (colloquial).—1. To achieve an object; to succeed perfectly; and (athletic) to reach the winning post.

1891. *Sportsman*, 26 Mar. A close struggle for the Palace Selling Plate ended in favour of Rosefield, who just GOT HOME a head in front of Mordure.

1892. *Pall Mall Gaz.*, 23 Jan., 3, 2. It is delightful to watch Mr. Charles Hawtrey telling lie after lie to his unbelieving wife, and joyfully, in misplaced confidence, saying to himself, 'I've GOT HOME.'

2. (pugilists').—To get in (a blow) with precision and effect; TO LAND (*q.v.*). Also (old) to give a mortal wound.

1559. ELYOT, *Dictionarium*, 3rd. ed. *Aere meo me lacessis*, thou gevest me scoffe for scoffe, or as we saie, thou PAIEST ME HOME.

1631. CHETTLE. *Hoffman*. *Sax.* Not any, Austria; neither toucht I thee. *Aust.* Somebody TOUCHT ME HOME; vaine world farewell, Dying I fall on my dead Lucibell.

1698. FARQUHAR, *Love and a Bottle*, iv., 3. But hark ye, George; don't push too HOME; have a care of whipping through the guts.

1706. FARQUHAR, *Recruiting Officer*, ii., 1. That's HOME.

1888. *Sporting Life*, 10 Dec. In the next round GOT HOME several times without a return.

1891. *Licensed Vict. Gaz.*, 19 June, p. 395, c. 3. Mac GOT HOME a terrific cross-counter with the left on Bob's left eye, which seemed to split the flesh open both above and below.

3. (turf).—To recover a loss; neither to win nor lose; to come out quits. Also, TO BRING ONESELF HOME.

4. (venery). — To get with child. Also, to compel the sexual spasm.

TO MAKE ONESELF AT HOME, *verb. phr.* (colloquial).—To take one's ease; to be familiar to the point of ill-breeding.

1892. MILLIKEN, *'Arry Ballads*, p. 10. AS AT HOME as a cat in a cream-shop.

TO COME HOME TO, *verb. phr.* (colloquial).—To reach the conscience; to touch deeply.

TO GO (SEND, OR CARRY) HOME (OR TO ONE'S LAST HOME), *verb. phr.* (colloquial).—To die; to kill; to bury. [The Chinese say 'to go home horizontally.'] *See* ALOFT.

1598. FLORIO, *A Worlde of Wordes*. *Mandar 'al palegro*, to SEND TO ONES LAST HOME.

1823. BEE, *Dict. Turf*, s.v. HOME. GONE HOME, dead.

HOME-BIRD, *subs.* (colloquial).—A henpecked husband. Also, a milksop. Fr., *chauffe-la-couche* (=warming-pan).

HOME FOR LOST DOGS, *subs. phr.* (medical).—A large and well known medical school in London. [From the fact that the majority of its inmates have strayed there from the various hospital schools, as a last resource toward taking a degree.]

HOME-RULE, *subs.* (common). — Irish whiskey. For synonyms, *see* DRINKS and OLD MAN'S MILK.

HOME-SWEET-HOME, *subs.* (venery).—The female *pudendum*. For synonyms, *see* MONOSYLLABLE.

HOMO, *subs.* (old).—A man: generally OMEE (*q.v.*). [From the Latin.] For synonyms, *see* COVE.

HOMONEY, *subs.* (old).—A woman. For synonyms, *see* PETTICOAT. Also, a wife. For synonyms, *see* DUTCH and *Cf.* HOMO.

1754. *Discoveries of John Poulter*, p. 43. My HOMONEY is in quod, my wife is in gaol.

HOMO-OPATHISE, *verb.* (American).—To get bills (*i.e.*, petitions) through Legislature, Congress, or City Council, by means of bills (*i.e.*, bank-bills).

HONE, *subs.* (venery).—The female *pudendum*. For synomyms, *see* MONOSYLLABLE.

1719. DURFEY, *Pills*, etc., i., 204. So I may no more pogue the HONE of a Woman.

HONEST, *adj.* (old).—1. Chaste.

1596. BEN JONSON, *Every Man in his Humour*, ii., 1. Why't cannot be, where there is such resort, O wanton gallants, and young revellers, That any woman should be HONEST long.

1599. HENRY PORTER, *Two Angry Women of Abingdon* (DODSLEY, *Old Plays*, 4th ed., 1875, vii., 389). Is my fellow Dick in the dark with my mistress? I pray God they be HONEST, for there may be much knavery in the dark.

1600. *Look About You*, Sc. 28 (DODSLEY, *Old Plays*, 4th ed., 1875, vii., 476). What, lecher? No, she is an HONEST woman. Her husband is well known.

1602. SHAKSPEARE, *Othello*, iii., 3. I do not think but Desdemona's HONEST.

1614. JONSON, *Bartholomew Fair* v., 3. De HONEST woman's life is a dull scurvy life, indeed.

1663. KILLIGREW, *The Parson's Wedding*, iii., 2 (DODSLEY, *Old Plays*, 4th ed., 1875, xiv., 454). There's none but HONEST women.

1663. KILLIGREW, *The Parson's Wedding*, v., 4 (DODSLEY, *Old Plays*, 4th ed., 1875, xiv., 525). Crooked, dirty-souled vermin, predestined for cuckolds, painted snails with houses on their backs, and horns as big as Dutch cows . . . . Can any woman be HONEST that lets such hodmandods crawl o'er her virgin breast and belly?

1672. WYCHERLEY, *Love in a Wood*, ii., 1. A man . . . . may bring his bashful wench, and not have her put out of countenance by the impudent HONEST women of the town.

1686-7. AUBREY, *Gentilisme* (1881), p. 163. The towne is full of wanton wenches, and . . . . (they say) scarce three HONEST women in the Town.

1693. CONGREVE, *Old Bachelor*, iii., 10. *Silvia*. I'm not such a fool neither, but I can keep myself HONEST.

1695. CONGREVE, *Love for Love*, iii., 14. *Mrs. Fore.* Do you think any woman HONEST? *Scan.* Yes, several very honest; they'll cheat a little at cards sometimes; but that's nothing. *Mrs. Fore.* Pshaw! but virtuous, I mean.

2. (common).—Not positively illegal: as HONEST PENNY or SHILLING = money earned by means immoral (as by prostitution] but within the law. Also, TO TURN AN HONEST PENNY = to make a profitable deal.

1677. WYCHERLEY, *Plain Dealer*, iii., 1. You must call usury and extortion God's blessing, or the HONEST TURNING OF THE PENNY.

1886. J. S. WINTER, *Army Society*, ch. xxi. There was a chance of TURNING AN HONEST PENNY in hiring them out for the donkey-race.

TO MAKE AN HONEST WOMAN, *verb. phr.* (colloquial).—To marry a mistress.

1629. EARLE, *Microcosmographie* (5th ed.). 'A Serving Man.' The best work he does is his marrying, for he MAKES AN HONEST WOMAN, and if he follows in it his master's direction, it is commonly the best service he does him.

1672. WYCHERLEY, *Love in a Wood*, v., 6. *Dap.* Why she was my wench. *Gripe.* I'll MAKE HER HONEST then.

1750. FIELDING, *Tom Jones*, bk. XV., ch. viii. Mr. Nightingale, and his love, stepped into a hackney-coach, which conveyed him to Doctors' Commons, where Miss Nancy was, in vulgar language, soon MADE AN HONEST WOMAN.

1811. *Lexicon Balatronicum*, s.v.

1825. SCOTT, *St. Ronan's Well*, ch. xxv. My right honourable father nourished some thoughts of MAKING AN HONEST WOMAN of Marie de Martiguy, and a legitimate elder brother of Francis.

1827. EGAN, *Anecdotes of the Turf*, p. 182. She had now only to play her cards well, she was sure of winning the game, also of becoming an HONEST WOMAN.

AS HONEST A MAN AS WHEN KINGS ARE OUT, *phr.* (old).—Knavish.

HONEST AS THE SKIN BETWEEN THE BROWS (or HORNS), *phr.* (old).—As honest as may be.

1551. W. STILL, *Gammer Gurton's Needle*, (*O.P.*), ii., 67. I am as true, I wold thou knew, AS SKIN BETWENE THY BROWS.

1599. JONSON, *Every Man out of his Humour*, ii., 2. *Punt.* Is he magnanimous? *Gent.* AS THE SKIN BETWEEN YOUR BROWS, sir.

1600. SHAKSPEARE, *Much Ado*, iii., 5. An old man, sir, and his wits are not so blunt, as, God help, I would desire they were, but in faith, HONEST, AS THE SKIN BETWEEN HIS BROWS.

1614. JONSON, *Bartholomew Fair*, iv., 5. It shall be justified to thy husband's faish, now; tou shalt be as HONESHT AS THE SKIN BETWEEN HIS HORNSH, la.

HONEST INJUN! *phr.* (American).—A pledge of sincerity; HONOUR BRIGHT (*q.v.*).

1884. CLEMENS [Mark Twain], *Huckleberry Finn*. She says 'HONEST INJUN, now hain't you been telling me a lot of lies?' 'HONEST INJUN' says I.

1892. *Detroit Free Press*, 12 Aug. I'll agree not to feel hard about it. HONEST INJUN?

HONEY, *subs.* (American).—1. A good fellow.

1888. *Missouri Republican*, 24 Feb. Dave is a HONEY.

2. (rhyming slang).—Money. For synonyms, *see* ACTUAL and GILT.

3. (old colloquial).—A term of endearment.

4. (venery).—The *semen*. Also, WHITE HONEY (*q.v.*). *Cf.*, HIVE.

Verb (American).—To cajole; to exchange endearments; to deceive by soft words or promises.

1596. SHAKSPEARE, *Hamlet*, iii., 4. Stew'd in corruption; HONEYING and making love Over the nasty sty.

1602. MARSTON, *Antonio and Mellida*, A. 4. Can'st thou not HONEY me with fluent speach, And even adore my toplesse villany?

1604. MARSTON and WEBSTER, *Malcontent*, O.P., iv., 66. O unpeerable! invention rare! Thou god of policy, it HONIES me.

1631. CHETTLE, *Hoffman*. *Clo.* A pretious villaine: a good villaine too. Well if he be no worse; that is doe worse, And HONEY me in my death-stinging thoughts, I will preferre him.

1888. *Tuskaloosa News*. It is of no use to HONEY; payments must be made at least once a year.

TO SELL HONEY FOR A HALFPENNY, *verb. phr.* (old). — To rate at a vile price.

1592. NASHE, *Pierce Penilesse* [1842], p. 43. Thou that in thy dialogues SOLDST HUNNIE FOR A HALFE-PENIE, and the choysest writers extant for cues a peece.

HONEY-BLOBS, *subs.* (Scots'). — Large, ripe, yellow gooseberries.

1746. WALPOLE, *Letters*, i., 144. As he returned to the Tower, he stopped the coach at Charing Cross to buy HONEY-BLOBS, as the Scotch call gooseberries.

HONEYCOMB, *subs.* (old).—A sweetheart; a general term of endearment.

1552. HULOET, *Abcedarium*, s.v. DARLYNGE, a wanton terme used in veneriall speach, as be these: HONYCOMBE, pyggisnye, swetehert, true love.

HONEY-FOGLE (or **FUGLE**), *verb.* (American). — To cheat; to swindle; to humbug. For synonyms, *see* GAMMON.

1888. *Missouri Republican*, 20 Jan. Noonan's companion objected to this HONEY-FUGLING by knocking the demonstrative stranger down.

HONEY-POT, *subs.* (old). — The female *pudendum*. For synonyms, *see* MONOSYLLABLE.

1719. DURFEY, *Pills*, etc., iii., 342. For when you have possession got, Of Venus' Mark, or HONY-POT.

HONOUR BRIGHT! *intj.* (common).—Upon my honour.

1819. MOORE, *Tom Crib*, p. 36. At morning meet, and,—HONOUR BRIGHT,—Agree to share the blunt and tatters!

1843. SELBY, *Antony and Cleopatra Married*. *Cle.* Will you love me as dearly as ever? *Ant.* Dearer, dear Chloe, dearer! *Cle.* HONOUR? *Ant.* BRIGHT and SHINING.

1869. F. HALL, Marginal reading to LYNDSAY'S *Satire of Three Estates* [E.E. Text Soc.], p. 382. She is more than a match for twenty-four a night, HONOUR BRIGHT.

1878. HATTON, *Cruel London*, bk. VIII., ch. ii. HONOUR BRIGHT, no kid, as we say in London.

1881. W. BLACK, *Beautiful Wretch*, ch. xix. 'I do not mean to marry Mr. Jacomb, if that is what you mean.' 'No? HONOUR BRIGHT?' 'I shall not marry Mr. Jacomb.'

1892. *Cassell's Sat. Jour.*, 28 Sep., p. 29., c. 3. 'Come, come, Mr. Smith, you're drawing the long bow!' 'HONOUR BRIGHT, I'm not.'

1892. N. GOULD, *Double Event*, p. 158. 'She did, HONOUR BRIGHT,' said Smirk.

HOOD. TWO FACES UNDER ONE HOOD (or HAT), *phr.* (old).—Double-dealing.

1690. B. E., *Dict. Cant. Crew*, s.v. HOOD.

1725. *New Cant. Dict.*, s.v.

1823. BEE, *Dict. Turf*, s.v. HOOD. May the man be d—d and never grow fat, Who carries TWO FACES UNDER ONE HAT.

TO PUT A BONE IN ONE'S HOOD, *verb. phr.* (obsolete).—To cuckold.

1560. *Nice Wanton* (DODSLEY, *Old Plays*, 4th ed., 1875, ii., 169). I could tell you who putteth A BONE IN YOUR HOOD. *Ibid.* (p. 170), Then by the rood, A BONE IN YOUR HOOD, I shall put you ere long.

HOODLUM, *subs.* (American).—A boy rough. Also, a rough of either sex. Also (political), a low-class voter. Originally Californian. *Cf.*, ARAB.

1872. *Sacramento Weekly Union*, 24 Feb., p. 2. All the boys to be trained as scriveners, tape-measurers, clerk-hoppers, clerks, pettifoggers, polite loafers, street-hounds, HOODLUMS, and bummers.

1877. *Los Angeles Express*, 25 Aug. A gang of boys . . . . associated for the purpose of stealing. . . . Their words of warning were 'Huddle 'em, Huddle 'em!' . . . . soon contracted into HOODLUM.

1877. *Boston Journal*, Aug. You at the East have but little idea of the HOODLUMS of this city. They compose a class of criminals of both sexes, far more dangerous than are to be found in the Eastern cities. They travel in gangs, and are ready at any moment for the perpetration of any crime.

1877. *Congregationalist*, 26 Sep. A newspaper man attempting to coin a word to designate a gang of young street Arabs under the beck of one named 'Muldoon,' hit upon *noodlums*, simply reversing the leader's name. . . . The compositor, taking the *n* for an *h*, printed it HOODLUM.

1877. *Morning Call*, 27 Oct. The rowdy element in the city . . . . who were soon after designated as HOODLUMS.

1885. G. A. SALA, in *Daily Telegraph*, 12 Aug., p. 5, c. 5. In order to guard against the contingency of the white HOODLUMS, or roughs, coming down in force from the American quarter of the city [San Francisco], and 'going for' the Celestials.

1888. *Missouri Republican*, 31 Mar. It is conceded by all that the HOODLUMS have nominated weak men, and the citizens will have easy sailing on Tuesday.

1890. NORTON, *Political Americanisms*, s.v. HOODLUMS, A general name for roughs. It originated on the Pacific coast, as the designation of a company of young ruffians in San Francisco (about 1868). Subsequently it spread Eastward, and attained some political significance; as 'the HOODLUM element' in politics.

1892. *Pall Mall Gaz.*, 29 Feb., p. 2, c. 2. A right of public meeting dependent on the good will of the HOODLUM is not worth having.

1893. *National Observer*, 4 Mar., ix., 398. In America, home of the HOODLUM, where they turn their murderers nto mayors.

HOODMAN, *subs.* (old).—A blind man; a GROPER (*q.v.*).

Adj. (old).—1. Blind. Also HOODMAN BLIND = blind drunk; *cf.*, sense 2. Fr., *berlu* and *sans mirettes*.

2. (streets). — Drunk. For synonyms, *see* DRINKS and SCREWED.

HOOF, *subs.* (common).—A foot. For synonyms, *see* CREEPERS.

1836. M. SCOTT, *Cruise of the Midge*, p. 134. Contriving in their complex twirlifications not only to tread heavily on my toes with his own HOOFS, but to hop his partner repeatedly over the same unfortunate members.

1838. GRANT, *Sketches in London*, p. 213. He again put both his ugly HOOFS on it.

1867. BROWNE ('Artemus Ward'), *Among the Mormons* [People's ed.], p. 193. Waving their lily-white HOOFS in the dazzling waltz.

1892. SYDNEY WATSON, *Wops the Waif*, ch. iv., p. 5. Teddy, look out, yer've got yer HOOF on my trotters!'

Verb (common).—To kick; *e.g.*, TO HOOF (or TOE) ONE'S BUM; to ROOT (*q.v.* for synonyms). Hence TO HOOF OUT = to eject; to dismiss; to discharge; to decline to see.

TO HOOF IT, (OR TO PAD OR BEAT THE HOOF), *verb. phr.* (common). To walk; to 'tramp it'; to run away. For synonyms, *see* AMPUTATE and SKEDADDLE. Hence HOOF-PADDING.

1596. SHAKSPEARE, *Merry Wives*, i., 3. Rogues, hence, avaunt, vanish like hailstones, go: Trudge, plod, AWAY O' THE HOOF.

d. 1687. COTTON, *Poems*, 'Epistles' (CHALMERS *English Poets*), vi., 736. Being then on foot away I go And BANG THE HOOF incognito.

1690. B. E., *Dict. Cant. Crew.* s.v. HOOF IT or BEAT IT ON THE HOOF, to walk on Foot.

1691-2. WOOD, *Athenæ Oxonienses*, ii., 560. Landing at Liverpool, in Lancashire, they all BEATED IT ON THE HOOF thence to London.

1725. *New Cant. Dict.*, s.v.

1772. CUMBERLAND, *Fashionable Lover.* Prologue. I am a devil, so please you, and must HOOF Up to the poet yonder with this proof.

1785. GROSE, *Vulg. Tongue*, s.v. HOOF. To BEAT THE HOOF, to travel on foot; he HOOFED IT, or BEAT THE HOOF, every step of the way from Chester to London.

1813. J. and H. SMITH, *Horace in London*, 'Hurly-Burly,' p. 24. When hostile squadrons BEAT THE HOOF.

1837. DICKENS, *Oliver Twist*, ch. ix. Charley Bates expressed his opinion that it was time TO PAD THE HOOF.

1885. *Detroit Free Press*, 5 Sept., p. 1, c 1. These busted theatrical people who are HOOFING IT back to Detroit. They come along at all hours of the day and night.

1888. LYNCH, *Mountain Mystery*, ch. xviii. I s'posed he was tired out, and had got over watchin' for tricks. So I HOOFED IT in.

1892. MILLIKEN, *'Arry Ballads*, p. 70. Scenery's all very proper, but where is the genuine pot who'd PAD THE 'OOF over the moors.

TO SEE ONE'S HOOF IN (a thing), *verb. phr.* (common).—To detect personal influence or interference in a matter.

1863. THACKERAY, *Roundabout Papers*, 'On Screens in Dining Rooms' (1887, p. 58). I am informed by the same New York correspondent that . . . . I once said to a literary gentleman, who was possibly pointing to an anonymous article as his writing, 'Ah! I thought I RECOGNISED YOUR HOOF IN IT.'

HOOF-PADDER, *subs.* (common).—A pedestrian.

HOOFY, *adj.* (common).—Splay (or large).

HOOK, *subs.* (thieves').—1. A finger. (*Cf.*, CUNT-HOOKS). For synonyms, *see* FORK. In *plural* = the hands. Also, HOOKS and FEELERS.

d. 1842. MAGINN, *Vidocq Versified.* To his clies my HOOKS I throw in.

1877. *Five Years' Penal Servitude*, ch. iv., p. 259. I one day asked a man . . . . if the hard work of prison did not spoil his hands for delicate manipulations. 'Oh, bless you, no!' he replied; . . . . In a week or two a man can bring his HOOKS and feelers into full working trim again and no mistake.'

2. (thieves').—A thief. Specifically, a pickpocket; a HOOKER (*q.v.*). For synonyms, *see* THIEVES.

1562. *Jacke Juggler* (DODSLEY, *Old Plays*, 4th ed., 1875, ii., 139). So, yonder cometh that unhappy HOOK.

1887. HORSLEY, *Jottings from Jail.* Take my tip and turn square, from a HOOK who is going to be lagged, would be, in common parlance, take my advice and get your living honestly.

1892. ANSTEY, *Voces Populi* (2nd Series). 'In Trafalgar Square.' A professional HOOK.

3. (common).—A catch; an advantage; an imposture.

Verb (old).—1. To rob; to steal. Specifically, to steal watches, rings, etc., from a shop by cutting a small hole in the window, and fishing for such articles with a piece of string with a hook at the end.

1615. *Albumazar*, iii., 3. Is not this braver than sneak all night in danger, Picking of locks, or HOOKING cloths at windows.

b. 1796. BURNS, *Jolly Beggars.* For mony a pursie she had HOOKIT.

1876. CLEMENS [Mark Twain], *Tom Sawyer*, p. 34. And while Aunt Polly closed with a happy Scriptural flourish, Tom HOOKED a doughnut.

1884. M. TWAIN, *Huck. Finn*, xxx., 312. Didn't you have it in your mind to HOOK the money and hide it?

2. (colloquial).—To secure, as for marriage; to marry.

1886. J. S. WINTER, *Army Society*, ch. xviii. I wonder if Mrs. Traff has contrived to HOOK him for her sweet Laura.

1892. MANVILLE FENN, *New Mistress*, ch. xxv. Have you I will—there now. Don't you think you're going to HOOK Lambent.

Intj. (Oxford Univ.). — An expression implying doubt. [Query from the note of interrogation (?) or connected with HOOKEY WALKER (*q.v.*).]

ON THE HOOK, *subs. phr.* (common).—1. On the thieve; ON THE CROSS (*q.v.*).

2. (old).—On the HIP (*q.v.*); at an advantage.

1694. CONGREVE, *Double Dealer*, iv., 18. Consider I have you ON THE HOOK; you will but flounder yourself a-weary, and be nevertheless my prisoner.

HOOK AND EYE, *subs. phr.* (tailors').—Arm in arm.

TO TAKE (or SLING) ONE'S HOOK (OR TO HOOK IT), *verb. phr.* (common).—To decamp; to run away. For synonyms, *see* AMPUTATE and SKEDADDLE.

1851-61. MAYHEW, *Lond. Lab. and Lond. Poor*, ii., 137. He slipped from her and HOOKED IT.

1852. DICKENS, *Bleak House*, ch. xlvi. 'HOOK IT! Nobody wants you here,' he ses. 'YOU HOOK IT. You go and tramp,' he ses.

1856. BRADLEY [Cuthbert Bede], *Tales of College Life*, p. 36. HOOK IT! old 'un, HOOK IT!

1861. H. KINGSLEY, *Ravenshoe*, ch. xli. They all begins to get a bit noisy and want to fight, and so I HOOKED IT.

1891. *Licensed Vict. Gaz.*, 16 Jan., p. 43, col. 3. If you lot don't HOOK IT, I'll stave in your blooming cocoa-nuts.

1891. *Sportsman*, 2 Apr., p. 2, col. 1. Plainly the worthy magistrate laid it down that a wife may HOOK IT when and how she pleases.

1892. ANSTEY, *Model Music Hall*, 129-30. TAKE YOUR 'OOK while you can. Even now the outraged populace approaches.

1892. MILLIKEN, *'Arry Ballads*, p. 58. I went jest for a lark, and wos quietly SLINGING MY 'OOK.

1892. KIPLING, *Barrack-Room Ballads*, 'Loot.' Before you SLING YOUR 'OOK, at the 'ousetops take a look.

1892. *Globe*, 19 Oct., p. 3. Again from some neighbouring roof comes back the weird responsive cry, HOOK IT! HOOK IT.

1892. HERBERT CAMPBELL, *Broadside Ballad*, 'Then Up Comes I with My little Lot.' And the houses shook and the copper TOOK HIS 'OOK, and down come all the tiles.

TO DROP (GO, OR POP) OFF THE HOOKS, *verb. phr.* (common).—1. To die. For synonyms, *see* ALOFT.

1837. BARHAM, *Ingoldsby Legends*, 'Black Mousquetaire.' I fear by his looks, Our friend, Francis Xavier, has POPP'D OFF THE HOOKS!

1842. *Punch's Almanack*, Dec. 15. Death wandered by the sea And struck by Walton's looks Broke Isaac's line of life And TOOK HIM OFF THE HOOKS.

1872. M. E. BRADDON, *Dead Sea Fruit*, ch. iv. 'S'pose the odds are against Jerningham GOING OFF THE HOOKS between this and the first spring-meeting, so as to give a party a chance with Mrs. J. herself,' speculates young Belgravia, dreamily.

1880. GREENWOOD, *Odd People in Odd Places*, p. 37. I thought, to be sure, I was GOING OFF THE HOOKS, and it was no use talking about it.

1890. GRANT ALLEN, *Tents of Shem*, ch. xii. The old man has POPPED OFF THE HOOKS this afternoon at Aix.

2. (colloquial).—To get married.

1876. M. E. BRADDON, *Joshua Haggard*, ch. x. Some of the young chaps will be wanting her to get married. These here pretty ones GO OFF THE HOOKS so soon.

TO HOOK ON TO, *verb. phr.* (colloquial).—To attach oneself to; TO BUTTONHOLE (*q.v.*); to follow up.

1892. MILLIKEN, *'Arry Ballads*, p. 4. It's nuts to 'OOK ON TO a swell.

ON ONE'S OWN HOOK, *adv. phr.* (colloquial).—On one's own account, risk, or responsibility; for one's own sake; dependent on one's own resources or exertions.

1847. ROBB, *Squatter Life*, p. 23. The signal was given, and in poured the subscribers to the dinner, with their guest, and in poured John ON HIS OWN HOOK.

1849. THACKERAY, *Pendennis*, ch. lxix. Do we come out as Liberal Conservative, or as Government man, or ON OUR OWN HOOK?

1861. WHYTE MELVILLE, *Good for Nothing*, ch. xxvii. I worked ON MY OWN HOOK, after that, and I rather think I paid my expenses.

1869. GREENWOOD, *Seven Curses of London*, p. 409. To steal ON YOUR OWN HOOK as a bookmaker.

1889. *Answers*, iv., p. 52, c. 3. Finally Edison went to work ON HIS OWN HOOK

1893. EMERSON, *Signor Lippo*, ch. viii. We used to have to part company and go in twos and threes then ON OUR OWN HOOK.

BY HOOK OR BY CROOK, *phr.* (colloquial).—By some means or other; by fair means or foul; at al hazards. [Probably of forestal origin.]

d. 1298. THOMAS THE RHYMER, *On Parliaments.* Their work was BY HOOK OR CROOK to rap and bring all under the emperor's power.

1525. *Bodmin Register.* Dynmure Wood was ever open and common to the . . inhabitants of Bodmin . . . . to bear away upon their backs a burden of lop, crop, HOOK, CROOK, and bag wood.

d. 1529. SKELTON, *Collyn Cloute.* Nor wyll suffer this boke BY HOOKE NE BY CROOKE Prynted for to be.

1550. BACON, *Fortress of the Faithful.* Whatsoever is pleasant or profitable must be theirs BY HOOK OR BY CROOK.

1557. TUSSER, *Good Husbandrie*, 30 Mar. Watch therefore in Lent, to thy sheepe go and look, For dogs will have vittels BY HOOKE AND BY CROOKE.

1566. ARCHBP. PARKER, *Correspondence* (Parker Soc.), p. 252. To win him in time, BY HOOK OR CROOK.

1596. SPENSER, *Faery Queen*, v., 2, 27. The spoyle of people's euill gotten good, The which her sire had scrapt BY HOOKE AND CROOKE.

1598. FLORIO, *Worlde of Wordes*, s.v. *Barocco*, a shift made for good cheere, meate and drinke gotten BY HOOKE OR CROOKE.

1621. BURTON, *Anatomy of Melancholy*, xi., 186 (1836). BY HOOK AND BY CROOK he will obtain it.

1629. FONSECA [Eng. by J. M.]. *Devout Contemplations.* Bee it BY HOOKE OR BY CROOKE, by right or wrong.

1678. BUTLER, *Hudibras*, iii., 1. Which he BY HOOK, OR CROOK, had gather'd.

1690. B. E., *Dict. Cant. Crew*, s.v. By Hedge or By Style, BY HOOK OR BY CROOK.

1725. *New Cant. Dict.*, s v.

1781. COWPER, *Letter to Newton*, 12 July. And BY HOOK OR CROOK, with another book, If I live and am here, another year.

1820. REYNOLDS [Peter Corcoran]. *The Fancy.* Father, ere our purpose cool, Get down BY HOOK OR CROOK to Liverpool.

1824. HITCHINGS and DREWE, *Hist. Cornwall*, ii., 214. The prior's cross, on which is cut the figure of a hook and a crook, in memory of the privilege granted . . . to the poor . . . for gathering such boughs and branches of such trees . . . as they could reach with a hook or by a crook . . . whence . . . they will have it BY HOOK AND BY CROOK.

1836. MICHAEL SCOTT, *Cruise of the Midge*, p. 363. We must be manned BY HOOK OR CROOK, you know, however unwilling to distress running ships.

1868. READE and BOUCICAULT, *Foul Play*, p. 54. Several fellow-creatures have cheated me. Well, I must get as much back, BY HOOK OR BY CROOK, from several fellow-creatures.

1883. W. BLACK, *Yolande*, ch. xlix. I should get you a ticket BY HOOK OR BY CROOK, if I failed at the ballot; I heard that one was sold for £40 the last time.

1888. RIDER HAGGARD, 'Mrs. Meeson's Will' [in *Illustrated News*, Summer Number, p. 5, c. 1]. Somehow or other, it would go hard if, with the help of the one hundred a year that he had of his own, he did not manage, with his education, to get a living BY HOOK OR BY CROOK.

WITH A HOOK AT THE END, *phr.* (common).—A reservation of assent; OVER THE LEFT (*q.v.*); IN A HORN (*q.v.*). *Cf.*, HOOK, *intj.*: and HOOKEY WALKER.

1823. BEE, *Dict. of the Turf*, s.v. HOOKEY WALKER—and WITH A HOOK, usually accompanied by a significant upliftment of the hand and crooking of the forefinger, implying that what is said is a lie, or is to be taken contrary-wise.

1843. MONCRIEFF, *Scamps of London*, i., 1. *Bob.* Will you have some gin? *Fogg.* Gin—Yes! *Bob* (turning away). Ha—ha!—WITH A HOOK . . . I wish you may get it.

1870. TRAILL, *Saturday Songs*, p. 22. It's go and go over the left, It's go WITH A HOOK AT THE END.

OFF THE HOOKS, *phr.* (old). — Out of temper; vexed; disturbed; out of sorts. Fr., *sortir de ses gonds* = off the HINGES (*q.v.*). For synonyms, *see* NAB THE RUST.

1639-61. *Rump Songs.* 'Bum-fodder.' That's a thing would please the Butchers and Cooks, To see this stinking Rump quite OFF THE HOOKS.

1665. PEPYS, *Diary*, 26 May. In the evening by water to the Duke of Albemarle, whom I found mightily OFF THE HOOKS, that the ships are not gone out of the River; which vexed me to see.

1690. B. E., *Dict. Cant. Crew*, s.v. HOOKS. OFF THE HOOKS, in an ill Mood, or out of Humour.

d. 1704. L'ESTRANGE [quoted in *Ency. Dict.*]. Easily put OFF THE HOOKS, and monstrous hard to be pleased again.

1719. DURFEY, *Pills*, etc., iii., 22. Another that's in the Blacksmith's Books, And only to him for remedy looks, Is when a Man is quite OFF THE HOOKS.

1725. *New Cant. Dict.*, s.v.

1825. SCOTT, *St. Ronan's Well*, ch. xxx. Everybody that has meddled in this St. Ronan's business is a little OFF THE HOOKS— .... in plain words, a little crazy.

HOOK AND SNIVEY (or **HOOKUM SNIVEY**), *subs. phr.* (old).—1. An imposture; specifically, the getting of food on false pretences.

1781. G. PARKER, *View of Society*, ii., 79. 'HOOK AND SNIVEY, with Nix the Buffer' [Title].

1811. *Lexicon Balatronicum*, s.v. HOOK AND SNIVEY WITH NIX THE BUFFER. This rig consists in feeding a man and a dog for nothing. ... Three men, one of whom pretends to be sick and unable to eat, go to a public house; the two well men make a bargain with the landlord for their dinner, and when he is out of sight feed their pretended sick companion and dog gratis.

1823. BEE, *Dict. Turf.* s.v. HOOK AND SNIVVY—practised by soldiers in quarters when they obtain grub for *nix*.

1835 in *Comic Almanack* 1835-43 (Hotten), p. 17, *Zoological Society at Hookem Snivey.* A new animal has been transmitted from No-Man's Land, which has been named the Flat-Catcher.

2. (old).—An impostor as described in sense 1.

3. (streets).—A contemptuous or sarcastic affirmation, accompanied by the gesture of TAKING A SIGHT (*q.v.*) or PLAYING HOOKEY (*q.v.*).

4. (thieves').—A crook of thick iron wire in a wooden handle, used to undo the wooden bolts of doors from without.

1801. EDGEWORTH. *Irish Bulls*, With that I ranges 'em fair and even on my HOOK 'EM SNIVEY, up they goes.

HOOKED, *adj.* (old).—*See* quot.

1690. B E., *Dict. Cant. Crew*, s.v. HOOKT, over-reached, Snapt, Trickt.

1725. *New Cant. Dict.*, s.v.

1785. GROSE, *Vulg. Tongue*, s.v.

HOOKER, *subs.* (Old Cant).—1. A thief; an ANGLER (*q.v.*). Also, (modern) a watch-stealer; a DIP (*q.v.*). *Cf.*, quots. 1567 and 1888.

1567. HARMAN, *Caveat*, p. 35. These HOKERS, or Angglers, be peryllous and most wicked knaues, ... they customably carry with them a staffe of v. or vi. foote long, in which, within one ynch of *the* tope thereof, ys a lytle hole bored through, [leaf 9] in which hole they putte an yron hoke, and with the same they wyll pluck vnto them quickly any thing *that* they may reche ther with.

1610. ROWLANDS, *Martin Mark-all*, p. 8 (H. Club's Rept., 1874). They are sure to be clyd in the night by the angler, or HOOKER, or such like pilferers that liue upon the spoyle of other poore people.

d. 1626. JOHN DAVIES, *Scourge of Folly*, p. 34. [Wks., Ed. Grosart]. A false knaue needs no brokers, but a broker Needs a false knaue (a hangman or a HOOKER).

1690. B. E., *Dict. Cant. Crew*, s.v. HOOKERS, the third Rank of Canters; also Sharpers.

1725. *New Cant. Dict.*, s.v.

1834. H. AINSWORTH, *Rookwood*, bk. III., ch. v. No strange Abram, ruffler crack, HOOKER of another pack.

1888. *Tit Bits*, 17 Nov., p. 82, col. 2. There are usually three men in a gang; the HOOKER having got into conversation with his man, number two 'covers' his movements, whilst number three (on the opposite side of the

street) keeps a look-out for the 'enemy.' The HOOKER, having by careful manipulation got a hold of the desired prize, detaches it from the chain by breaking the ring and passes it to number two, who in turn passes it on to number three, from whom it is usually transferred to a receiver and melted down within a few hours of its being purloined.

2. (American).—A prostitute: *i.e.*, a fisher, angler, or HOOKER of men. For synonyms, *see* BARRACK HACK and TART.

HOOKEY. TO PLAY HOOKEY, *verb. phr.* (American). — To play truant; to do CHARLEY-WAG (*q.v.*).

1876. CLEMENS [Mark Twain], *Tom Sawyer*, p. 100. Took his flogging .... for PLAYING HOOKEY the day before.

TO DO (or PLAY) HOOKEY (or HOOKY), *verb. phr.* (common).—To apply the thumb and fingers to the nose; TO TAKE A SIGHT (*q.v.*); TO COFFEE-MILL (*q.v.*).

HOOKEY WALKER! (or **WALKER!**) *intj.* (common). — Be off! go away. Also implying doubt. *Cf.*, WITH A HOOK. [BEE: From John Walker, a hook-nosed spy, whose reports were proved to be fabrications.]

1811. *Lexicon Balatronicum*, s.v. HOOKEY WALKER, An expression signifying that the story is not true, or that he thing will not occur.

1843. DICKENS, *Christmas Carol* [1843], p. 169. 'Buy it,' said Scrooge. 'WALKER!' said the boy.

1837. BARHAM, *Ingoldsby Legends*. 'Old Woman Clothed in Grey.' For mere unmeaning talk her Parch'd lips babbled now,—such as HOOKEY!—and WALKER!—She expired, with her last breath expressing a doubt If 'his Mother were aware he was out?'

1840. 'Characters of Freshmen' (WHIBLEY, *Cap and Gown*, p. 183). The pestilent freshman .... is very pugnacious, and walking in the streets suddenly turneth and asketh a huge snob 'what the deuce he meant by that?' Whereat the snob (having done nothing at all) coolly answereth (as the Pestilent Freshman intended he should) HOOKY WALKER, provocative of a combat.

HOOKING-COW, *subs.* (Western American).—A cow that shows fight.

1887. FRANCIS, *Saddle and Mocassin*. One .... was .... a HOOKING-COW, and to escape her repeated charges tested all our ability.

HOOK-POINTED (or **HOOK-PINTLED**), *adj.* (venery). — Imperfectly erected. *Cf.*, LOB (*q.v.*).

HOOK-POLE LAY, *subs. phr.* (old).—Pulling a man off his horse by means of iron hooks at the end of a long pole, and plundering him. (SMITH, *Lives of Highwaymen*, III., 192, 1720).

HOOK-SHOP, *subs.* (American).—A brothel. [HOOKER (*q.v.*) = prostitute.] For synonyms, *see* NANNY-SHOP.

HOOP, *subs.* (American). — 1. A ring.

2. (Devon).—*See* BULLFINCH.

3. (venery).—The female *pudendum*. For synonyms, *see* MONOSYLLABLE.

Verb (old). — To beat. To WELL HOOP ONE'S BARREL = to thrash soundly. For synonyms, *see* TAN.

1785. GROSE, *Vulg. Tongue*, s.v.

TO HOOP IT (or GO THROUGH THE HOOP), *verb. phr.* (old).—1. To pass the Insolvent Debtor's Court; TO GET HOOPED UP = WHITEWASHED (*q.v.*). For synonyms, *see* DEAD-BROKE.

2. (old).—To run away. For synonyms, *see* AMPUTATE and SKEDADDLE.

1839. BRANDON, *Poverty, Mendicity, and Crime*, 116. I have heard them tell .... boys .... who have HOOPED IT from home that they had better go back whilst they had a home to go to.

HOOPER'S HIDE, *subs. phr.* (old venery).—Copulation. For synonyms, *see* GREENS.

1719. DURFEY, *Pills*, etc., i., 278. The while that his wife with Willy Was playing at HOOPER'S HIDE.

HOOP-STICK, *subs.* (common).—The arm. For synonyms, *see* CHALK FARM.

HOOSIER, *subs.* (American). — A native of Indiana. [Perhaps the most reasonable of several ingenious explanations is, that in the early days the customary challenge or greeting in that region was, 'Who's yer?' (who's here?): pronounced hoosier.—NORTON.]

1843. D. CORCORAN, *A Genuine Hoosier*. An original character is your genuine HOOSIER. By genuine, we mean such a one as has all the attributes that peculiarly belong to the back-woodsmen of the West.

1847. DARLEY, *Drama in Pokerville*, p. 197. None of them 'cotton'd' to him more kindly than an elderly HOOSIER from the innermost depths of Indiana.

1848. DURIVAGE, *Stray Subjects*, p. 79. There is a swarm of 'suckers,' 'HOOSIERS,' 'buckeyes,' 'corn-crackers,' and 'wolverines' eternally on the *qui vive* in those parts.

HOOTER, *subs.* (American).—1 A steam-whistle; an AMERICAN DEVIL (*q.v.*).

2. (colloquial). — A wooden trumpet, so contrived as to make a horrible noise.

3. (American).—A corruption of 'iota': *e.g.*, 'I don't care a HOOTER for him.'

HOOTING-PUDDING, *subs.* (provincial).—A plum-pudding with such a paucity of plums that you can hear them hooting after each other.—*Slang, Jargon, and Cant.*

HOP, *subs.* (common).—A dance. [Generally informal, as a CINDERELLA (*q.v.*).] Also, as in quot. 1579, the motions of dancing. For synonyms, *see* SKIP.

1579. GOSSON, *Schoole of Abuse*, p. 33 (Arber's Ed.). He gaue Dauncers great stipends for selling their HOPPS.

1811. JANE AUSTEN, *Sense and S.*, ch. ix. At a little HOP at the park, he danced from eight o clock till four.

1823. BEE, *Dict. Turf*, s.v. HOP—a contra-dance of ordinary persons and promiscuous company is 'a HOP' and 'a penny-HOP' from the price formerly paid for admission.

1830. LYTTON, *Paul Clifford*, iv. He gave them from time to time a very agreeable HOP.

1847. THACKERAY, *Mrs. Perkins's Ball* (*Mr. Larkins*). To describe this gentleman's infatuation for dancing, let me say, in a word, that he will even frequent boarding-house HOPS, rather than not go.

1848. RUXTON, *Life in the Far West*, p. 189. The 'temple' was generally cleared for a HOP two or three times during the week.

1850. SMEDLEY, *Frank Fairleigh*, p. 121. You'll be at old Coleman's HOP to-night, I suppose; so bye! bye! for the present.

1852. BRISTED, *Upper Ten Thousand*, p. 129. Two undress-balls—HOPS they were.

1882. *Daily Telegraph*, 13 Nov., p. 5, c. 3. At all seasons there is an immense amount of dancing; and at Washington there are continual 'hotel HOPS' in the winter.

1887. W. S. GILBERT, *Patience*, ii. Prefers suburban HOPS To all your Monday Pops.

1889. *Lippincott*, Oct., p. 447. Hang me if she isn't always on the plain, or at a HOP, with one of those twin kids!

1892. KIPLING, *Barrack Room Ballads*. 'Gentlemen Rankers.' To dance with blowzy housemaids at the regimental HOPS.

HOP-AND-GO-KICK, *subs. phr.* (tailors'). — A lameter; a HOP-AND-GO-ONE. *Cf.*, DOT-AND-CARRY-ONE.

TO HOP THE WAG, *verb. phr.* (common).—To play truant, or CHARLEY-WAG (*q.v.*).

1851-61. MAYHEW, *Lond. Lab. and Lond. Poor*, iii., 207. They often persuaded me TO HOP THE WAG, that is play truant from school.

TO HOP (or JUMP) OVER THE BROOM (or BROOMSTICK), *verb. phr.* (colloquial). — To live as husband and wife; to LIVE (or GO) TALLY (*q.v.*).

1811. POOLE, *Hamlet Travestied*, ii., 3. JUMP O'ER A BROOMSTICK, but don't make a farce on The marriage ceremonies of the parson.

1851-61. MAYHEW, *Lond. Lab. and Lond. Poor*, i., 336. There was always a BROOMSTICK wedding. Without that ceremony a couple weren't looked on as man and wife.

1860. DICKENS, *Great Expectations*, xlviii., 227. This woman in Gerrard Street, here, had been married very young, OVER THE BROOMSTICK (as we say), to a tramping man.

c. 18(79). *Broadside Ballad*, 'David Dove that Fell in Love.' By L. M. THORNTON. The girl that I had hoped to hear Pronounce my happy doom, sir, Had bolted with a carpenter, In fact HOPPED O'ER THE BROOM, sir.

TO HOP THE TWIG, *verb. phr.* (common).—1. To leave; to run away; TO SKEDADDLE (*q.v.*). For synonyms, *see* AMPUTATE.

1785. GROSE, *Vulg. Tongue*, s.v.

1789. GEO. PARKER, *Life's Painter*, p. 143. HOP THE TWIG .... means to depart suddenly.

1830. EGAN, *Finish to Life in London*, p. 217. I have lost my ticker; and all my toggery has been boned, I am nearly as naked as when I was born—and the cause—the lady bird—has HOPPED THE TWIG.

1884. *Daily News*, 31 Oct., p. 3, c. 1. They knocked the Liberals down as fast as they could until they got too numerous and strong, and then we HOPPED THE TWIG.

1888. *All the Year Round*, 9 June 543. TO HOP THE TWIG . . . and the like, are more flippant than humorous.

2. (common). — To die; to 'kick the BUCKET' (*q.v.*); to PEG OUT (*q.v.*). Also TO HOP OFF.

ENGLISH SYNONYMS. To be content; to cock up one's toes; to croak; to cut (or let go) the painter; to cut one's stick; to give in; to give up; to go to Davy Jones' locker; to go off the hooks; to go under; to go up; to kick the bucket; kickeraboo (West Indian); to lay down one's knife and fork; to lose the member of one's mess; to mizzle; to pass in one's checks; to peg out; to put on a wooden surtout; to be put to bed with a shovel; to slip one's cable; to stick one's spoon in the wall; to snuff it; to take an earth bath; to take a ground sweat.

FRENCH SYNONYMS.—*Passer l'arme à gauche* (pop.: = to ground arms); *casser sa pipe* (= to break one's pipe); *dévisser* or *décoller son billard* (= to break one's cue); *graisser ses bottes* (= to grease one's boots); *avaler sa langue* (= to swallow one's tongue); *avaler sa gaffe* (= to lower one's boat-hook); *avaler sa cuiller* or *sa fourchette* (= to swallow one's spoon or one's fork); *avaler ses baguettes* (military: = to swallow one's drum-sticks); *n'avoir plus mal aux dents* (= to get rid of the tooth-ache: *mal de dents*, also = love);

poser sa chique (pop. := to put down one's quid); *claquer* (familiar := to croak); *saluer le public* (theat. := to go before the curtain); *recevoir son décompte* (military := to get one's quietus; *décompte* = also [military] a mortal wound); *cracher son embouchure* (= to spit one's mouthpiece); *déteindre* (pop. := to wash off one's colour); *donner son dernier bon à tirer* (familiar: in American = to pass in one's checks; properly = to send one's last proof to press); *lâcher la perche* (pop. := to hop the twig); *éteindre son gaz* (pop. := to turn off one's gas. *Cf.*, to snuff it); *épointer son foret* (pop. := to blunt one's drill, as in boring); *être exproprié* (pop. := to be dispossessed); *exproprier* (= to take possession of a debtor's land); *péter son lof* (sailor's); *fumer ses terres*; *fermer son parapluie* (pop. := to close one's umbrella); *perdre son bâton* (pop. := to lose one's walking stick); *descendre la garde* (pop. := to come off guard); *défiler la parade* (military := to face about); *tortiller*, or *tourner de l'œil* (pop.); *perdre le goût du pain* (pop.: = to lose one's appetite); *lâcher la rampe* (theat.: = to chuck the footlights); *faire ses petits paquets* (pop. := to pack up one's traps); *casser son crachoir* (pop. := to break one's spittoon); *remercier son boulanger* (thieves': = to thank the baker; *boulanger* = the Devil); *canner*; *dévider à l'estorgue* (thieves'); *baiser* or *épouser la Camarde* or *camarder* (pop := to hug, or go to church with, Mother Bones [*Camarde* = Death]); *fuir* (thieves': = to flee or escape); *casser son câble* (pop. := to slip one's cable); *casser son fouet* (pop. := to break one's whip); *faire sa crêvaison* (pop.: *crêver* = to burst up); *déralinguer* (sailors' := to loose from the bolt-rope); *virer de bord* (sailors' := to tack about); *déchirer son faux-col* (pop. := to break one's collar); *dégeler* (= to thaw); *couper sa mèche* (coachman's := to cut off one's lash); *piquer sa plaqu* (sailors'); *mettre la table pour les asticots* (pop. := to lay the cloth for the worms); *aller manger les pissenlits par la racine* (pop. := to go grubbing off dandelion roots); *laisser fuir son tonneau* (familiar); *calancher* (vagrants'); *laisser ses bottes quelque part* (familiar: = to leave one's boots about); *déchirer son habit* (pop.: = to tear one's coat); *déchirer son tablier* (pop.: = to tear one's apron); *souffler sa veilleuse* (pop. := to blow out one's candle: *cf.*, to snuff it); *pousser le boum du cygne* (pop.); *avoir son coke* (familiar := to get one's cargo); *rendre sa secousse* (pop.); *rendre sa bûche* (tailors'); *rendre sa canne au ministre* (military: = to resign one's commission); *rendre sa clef* (gipsy := to give in one's key); *rendre son livret* (pop.: = to pass in one's checks); *passer au dixième régiment* (military); *s'ennuyer* (pop.: = to be at death's door); *chasser les mouches* (pop.: to go fly-catching); *ingurgiter son bilan* (popular); *resserrer son linge* (pop.); *faire sa malle* (pop. := to pack one's trunk); *avaler le goujon* (pop.); *s'habiller de sapin* (pop. := to put on a wooden surtout); *avoir son compte* (pop.); *battre de l'œil* (thieves'); *s'évanouir* (pop.: to mizzle); *machaber* (pop.: *machabre* = the Dance of Death); *glisser* (pop.); *s'en aller dans le pays des marmottes* (pop.: *marmotte* = puppet); *déménager* (pop.: = to move house).

GERMAN SYNONYMS. — *Krachen gehen*; *niftern*; *pegern* or *peigern*; *schochern* or *verschochern* (= to get black); *verschwarzen*.

ITALIAN SYNONYMS. *Sbasire* (= to faint); *sbasire su le funi* (= to faint on the rope).

SPANISH SYNONYMS.—*Hacer bodoques* (= to take an earth bath); *liarlas* (= also to run away); *obispar*; *corvado* (= bent, curved); *cierto* (= certain).

1839. DANCE, *Alive and Merry*, i., 1. Couldn't you wait a bit till she's HOPPED OFF, and then you and I could marry, and be ladies and gentlemen?

1841. *Punch*, I., 2, 2. Clare pines in secret—HOPS THE TWIG and goes to glory in white muslin.

1842. *Punch*. vol. II., p. 20, c. 2. Yet henceforth-dash my wig! I'll live with thee, with thee I'll HOP THE TWIG!

1863. *Fun*, vol. IV., p. 188. The night when Cromwell died a storm tore up many of the trees [of St. James's Park]—though what connexion there may be between the destruction of their branches and the HOPPING THE TWIG of the Protector, we leave to our philosophical readers to decide.

1870. *Chambers's Miscellany*, No. 87, p. 26. That her disease was mortal, was past a doubt, and a month or two more or less could make no difference, provided she HOPPED OFF . . . . before the year was expired.

ON THE HOP, *adv. phr.* (common). — 1. Unawares; at the nick of time; in *flagrante delicto*. Also ON THE H. O. P.

1868. *Broadside Ballad*, 'The Chickaleary Cove.' For to catch me ON THE HOP . . . . You must wake up very early in the morning.

1870. *London Figaro*, 26 Aug. If to catch any of the more ordinary folk ON THE HOP is to secure a laugh, what must it be to catch the Tycoon 'on the—top?'

1872. *Daily Telegraph*, 3 Sept. Goodbye, Johnny: before I leave you, One more kiss before I go. For to catch me ON THE HOP.

1892. ANSTEY, *Model Music Hall*, 32. I never saw a smarter hand at serving in a shop, For every likely customer she caught UPON THE 'OP.

2. (common).—On the go; in motion; unresting.

1892. MILLIKEN, *'Arry Ballads*, p. 22. A deal ON THE 'OP.

3. (colloquial). - *See* HIP.

HOPEFUL (or **YOUNG HOPEFUL**), *subs.* (colloquial). — A boy or young man; in sarcasm or contempt.

1856. BRADLEY ('Cuthbert Bede'), *Tales of College Life*, 24. He'll be no end riled at seeing his HOPEFUL play truant in this fashion.

HOP- (or **HAP-**) **HARLOT**, *subs.* (old). — A coarse coverlet; *Cf.*, WRAP-RASCAL.

1807-8. HOLLINSHED, *Chronicles of England*, ch. 12. Covered only with a sheet, under coverlets made of dag-swain, or HOP-HARLOTS.

HOPKINS (**HOPPY**, or **MR. HOPKINS**), *subs.* (old).—A lameter. For synonyms, *see* DOT-AND-GO-ONE GILES.

1785. GROSE, *Vulg. Tongue*, s.v.

DON'T HURRY, HOPKINS! *phr.* (American). — Ironical to persons slow to move or to meet an obligation.

HOP-MERCHANT (or **HOPPY**), *subs.* (common).—A dancing master; a CAPER-MERCHANT (*q.v.*). Also, a fiddler.

1690. B. E., *Dict. Cant. Crew*, s.v.

1725. *New Cant. Dict.*, s.v.

1785. GROSE, *Vulg. Tongue*, s.v.

1823. BEE, *Dict. Turf*, s.v.

1892. SYDNEY WATSON, *Wops the Waif*, ch. iii., p. 4. Who-ay, Cully, here's HOPPY with the ROZIN.

HOP-O-MY-THUMB, *subs.* (common).—A dwarf.

1599. NASHE, *Lenten Stuffe*, in *Wks.* v., 248. Though the greatnesse of the redde herring be not small (as small A HOPPE-ON-MY-THUMBE as hee seemeth).

1603. DEKKER, etc., *Patient Grissell*, IV., ii., in *Wks.* (Grosart) vi., 195. *Bab.* No; he shall not haue them [children]: knocke out his braines, and saue the little HOP-A-MY-THOMBES.

1748. SMOLLETT, *Rod. Random*, ch. xi. You pitiful HOP-O'-MY-THUMB coxcomb.

1764. O'HARA, *Midas*, i., 5. You Stump-o'-the-gutter, you HOP-O'-MY-THUMB, A husband must for you from Lilliput come.

1785. GROSE, *Vulg. Tongue*, s.v. HOP-O-MY-THUMB. She was such a HOP-O-MY-THUMB that a pigeon, on sitting on her shoulder, might pick a pea out of her a—se.

1821. SCOTT, *Kenilworth*, ch. xi. A mean-looking HOP-O'-MY-THUMB sort of person.

1837. BARHAM, *Ingoldsby Legends*. 'Account of a New Play.' A HOP-O'-MY-THUMB of a Page.

ENGLISH SYNONYMS.—Go-by-the-ground; grub; grundy; Jack Sprat; little breeches; shrimp; stump-of-the-gutter; tom-tit. *See* also, FORTY-FOOT.

HOPPER, *subs.* (colloquial).—The mouth. For synonyms, *see* POTATO-TRAP.

TO GO A HOPPER, *verb. phr.* (sporting).—To go quickly.

HOPPER-ARSED (or **HIPPED**), *adj.* (old). — Large in the breech. Also (as in quot. 1529) snaggy-boned. Also as *subs.*

d. 1529. DUNBAR, *Poems*, 'Complaint to the King' (1836, i., 144). With HOPPER-HIPPIS and hanches narrow.

1672. WYCHERLEY, *Love in a Wood*, ii., 1. Moreover, she is bow-legged, HOPPER-HIPPED, and, betwixt pomatum and Spanish red, has a complexion like a Holland cheese.

1690. B. E., *Dict. Cant. Crew*, s.v. HOPPER-ARST, when the Breech sticks out.

1704. KING, *Orpheus and Eurydice* (CHALMERS *English Poets*), vol. ix., p. 284. A lady of prodigious fame, Whose hollow eyes and HOPPER BREECH Made common people call her witch.

1719. DURFEY, *Pills*, etc., vi., 351. And there'll be HOPPER-ARSED Nancy.

1785. GROSE, *Vulg. Tongue*, s.v.

HOPPER-DOCKER, *subs.* (old).—A shoe. For synonyms, *see* TROTTER-CASES.

HOP-PICKER, *subs.* (common).—1. A prostitute; also HOPPING-WIFE. For synonyms, *see* BARRACK-HACK and TART.

1888. *Indoor Paupers*, p. 55. Numbers of them go regularly to the hop-gardens; and each man must have a female companion—a HOPPING WIFE as she is termed.

2. *in. pl.* (gaming). — The queens of all the four suits.

HOPPING-GILES, *subs.* (common).—A cripple. For synonyms, *see* DOT-AND-GO-ONE.

1785. GROSE, *Vulg. Tongue*, s.v.

1811. *Lexicon Balatronicum*, s.v.

1885. *Household Words*, 27 June, p. 180. St. Giles is the patron saint of cripples; hence a lame person is mockingly called HOPPING GILES.

HOPPING-JESUS, *subs.* (colloquial). A lameter. For synonyms, *see* DOT-AND-GO-ONE.

HOPPING-MAD, *adj.* (American).—Very angry.

HOP-POLE, *subs.* (common). — A tall, slight person, male or female. For synonyms, *see* LAMP-POST.

1850. SMEDLEY, *Frank Farleigh*, p. 5. I was tall for my age, but slightly built, and so thin, as often to provoke the application of such epithets as HOP-POLE, 'thread-paper,' etc.

HORIZONTAL-REFRESHMENT, *subs.* (venery).—1. Carnal intercourse; *cf.*, UPRIGHT. For synonyms, *see* GREENS and RIDE. [Fr., *une horizontale* = a prostitute.] Also, TO HORIZONTALISE.

2. (common). — Food taken standing; generally applied to a mid-day snack at a bar.

HORN, *subs.* (common).—1. The nose. Also, HORNEY. For synonyms, *see* CONK.

1823. BEE, *Dict. of the Turf*, s.v. HORNEY—a nose; one that resounds in expectoration.

2. (common).—A drink; a dram of spirits. For synonyms, *see* GO.

1847. PORTER, *Quarter Race*, p. 193. Go on, Venus. Take another HORN first.

1848. RUXTON, *Life in the Far West*. p. 126. They called the Scotchman to take a HORN.

3. (venery).—An erection of the *penis*. [Properly of men only; but said of both sexes. In the feminine equivalents are CUNT-ITCH and CUNT-STAND].

Hence TO GET (or HAVE) THE HORN, *verb phr.* = to achieve erection; TO CURE THE HORN = to copulate; HORNING and HORNY, in course of, or disposed to erection; HORNIFICATION, *subs.* = the state, or process, of erection; HORNIFY (*see* verb), = to get (or give) the HORN; MISS HORNER, *subs.* = the *pudendum muliebre*; OLD HORNEY (or HORNINGTON) = the *penis*.

ENGLISH SYNONYMS.—Cock- (or prick-) stand; Irish toothache; in one's Sunday (or best) clothes; the jack; hard-on (American); horn-colic; horn-mad (said also of an angry cuckold); fixed bayonets; lance in rest; the old Adam; standing; on the stand; stiffened up; the spike.

4. (old). -- The *penis*. For synonyms, *see* CREAMSTICK and PRICK.

5. (colloquial).—Also in *pl.*, *see* verb.

HORN, *verb* (colloquial). — To cuckold. [*Becco* (= a he-goat) and *cornuto* (= a horned thing) are good Italian for a cuckold; in Florio (*Worlde of Wordes*, 1598) *andar in cornouaglia senza barca* (*i.e.*, to go to Cornwall without a ship) = to win the horn; and the expression, as the example from Lydgate appears to show, may very well have been imported into English from the Italian. Also, it seems to have begun to be literary about the middle of the sixteenth century, when the Italian influence was at its height. For the rest it passed in triumph into written English, was used in every possible combination, had a run at least two centuries long, and is still intelligible, though not in common service.] *See* ACTÆON, ANTLERS, BULL'S FEATHER, FREEMAN OF BUCKS, etc.

Hence, TO HORNIFY (*see subs.*, sense 3), and TO GRAFT (or GIVE) HORNS; to WEAR HORNS = to live a cuckold; HORNER, *subs.* = a cuckold maker; HORN-MAD, *adj. phr.* (*q.v.*); HORNED, *adj.* = cuckolded; HORN-GROWER (or MERCHANT) *subs.* = a married man; HORN-FEVER, *subs.* = cuckoldry; TO EXALT ONE'S HORN, *verb. phr.* = (1) to cuckold, and (2) to rejoice in, or profit by, the condition; TO WIND THE HORN = to publish the fact of cuckoldom; HORNS-TO-SELL, *subs. phr.* = (1) a lewd wife, and (2) a wittol; TO POINT THE HORN = to fork the fingers in derision (as in Hogarth's 'Industrious and Idle Apprentice,' 1790, plate v.); HORN-WORKS = the process of cuckolding; AT THE SIGN OF THE HORN = in cuckoldom; HORN-PIPE = (*see* quot. 1602); HORNED HERD, *subs. phr.* = husbands in general (specifically, the city men, the Citizens of London (the cuckolding of whom by West-end gallants is a constant theme of seventeenth century jokes); GILT-HORN, *subs.* = a contented cuckold; SPIRIT OF HARTSHORN = the suspicion or the certainty of cuckoldom; LONG HORNS, *subs.* = a notorious cuckold; KNIGHT OF HORNSEY, also MEMBER FOR HORNCASTLE, *subs. phr.* = a cuckold, etc.

d. 1440. LYDGATE, *Falle of Prynces*, ii., leaf 56 (ed. Wayland, 1557, quoted in

DYCE'S *Skelton*, 1843, ii., 132). To speke plaine Englishe made him cokolde. Alas I was not auised wel before Vnkonnyngly to speake such language: I should haue sayde how that he had an HORNE . . . And in some land *Cornodo* men do them call, And some affirme that such folk have no gall.

c. 152(?). *Hick Scorner* (DODSLEY, *Old Plays*, 4th ed., 1875, i., 180). My mother was a lady of the stews, blood born, And (Knight of the Halter) my father wore an HORNE.

c. 1537. *Thersites* (DODSLEY, *Old Plays*, 4th ed., 1875, i., 412). Why wilt thou not thy HORNES inhold? Thinkest thou that I am a cuckold.

c. 1550. *The Pride and Abuse of Women* (176 in *Early Pop. Poetry*, ed. Hazlitt, iv., 237). And loke well, ye men to your wives . . . Or some wyll not styche . . . To HORNE you on everye side.

1568. *Bannatyne MSS.* 'The use of Court,' p. 765 (Hunterian Club, 1886). Vp gettis hir wame, Scho thinkis no schame For to bring hame The laird ane HORNE.

1574. *Appius and Virginia* (DODSLEY, *Old Plays*, 4th ed., 1875, iv., 118). A hairbrain, a hangman, or a grafter of HORNES.

1575. *Laneham's Letter* (ed. 1871). p. 40. With yoor paciens, Gentlmen, . . . be it said: wear it not in deede that HORNZ bee so plentie, HORNWARE I beleeue woold bee more set by than it iz, and yet thear in our parts, that wyll not stick too auoow that many an honest man both in citee and cuntree hath his hoous by HORNING well vpholden, and a daily freend allso at need.

c. 1580. *Collier of Croydon* (DODSLEY, *Old Plays*, 4th ed., 1875, viii., 436). My head groweth hard, my HORNS will shortly spring.

1586. LUPTON, 1,000 *Not. Things*, ed. 1675, p. 261. Take heed thou art not HORN'D, and then fetcht home.

1597. HALL, *Satires*, i., 8. Fond wittol that would'st load thy witless head, With timely HORNS before thy bridal bed. *Idem*, ii., 7. If chance it come to wanton Capricorne, And so into the Ram's disgraceful HORNE.

1598. SHAKSPEARE, 2 *Henry IV.*, Act i., sc. 2. Well, he hath the HORN OF ABUNDANCE and the lightness of his wife shines through it.

1598. JONSON, *Every Man in his Humour*, v., 1. See, what a drove of HORNS fly in the air, Winged with my cleansèd and my credulous breath.

1598. SYLVESTER, *Du Bartas*, ed. 1641, v., 41. The adulterous Sargus . . . Courting the Shee Goates on the grassie shore Would HORN their husbands that had horns before.

1599. JONSON, *Every Man Out of his Humour*, iv., 4. Now HORN UPON HORN pursue thee, thou blind, egregious, dotard.

1600. *Look About You*, Sc. 10 (DODSLEY, *Old Plays*, 4th ed., 1875, v., 415). By adding HORNS unto our falcon's head.

1600. SHAKSPEARE, *As You Like it*. iv., 2. Take thou no scorn to wear the HORN, It was a crest ere thou wast born.

1600. SHAKSPEARE, *Much Ado about Nothing*, i. Then up comes the devil with his HORNS upon his head, looking like an old cuckold. *Ibid.* v. 1. But when shall we see the savage bull's HORNS on the sensible Benedict's head.

1601. JONSON, *Poetaster*, iv., 3. And there is never a star in thy forehead but shall be a HORN if thou dost persist to abuse me.

1602. CAMPION, *English Poesy* (BULLEN, *Works*, 1889, p. 248). Mock him not with HORNS, the case is altered.

1603. *Philotus* (PINKERTON, *Scottish Poems*, 1792, iii., 17). Sen thair may be na uther buit? Plat on his heid ane HORNE.

1604. MARSTON, *Malcontent*, i., I. Mendoza is the man makes thee a HORNED BEAST: 'tis Mendoza cornutes thee.

1605. JONSON, *Volpone*, ii., 4. *Volp.*: Nay, then, I not repent me of my late disguise. *Mos.*: If you can HORNE him, Sir, you need not.

1605. CHAPMAN, *All Fools*, v., 1 (*Plays*, 1874, p. 75). And will you BLOW THE HORN yourself where you may keep it to yourself? Go to, you are a fool. *Ibid.* (p. 76.) It may very well be that the devil brought HORNS into the world, but the women brought them to the men.

1607. *How a Man May Choose a Good Wife From a Bad*, ii., I. (DODSLEY, *Old Plays*, 4th ed., 1875, ix., 28). *Quando venis aput*, I shall have two HORNS on my *caput*.

1607. DEKKER, *Northward Hoe*, Act i., p. 8. If a man be deuorst, whether may he haue an action or no, gainst those that MAKE HORNS AT HIM. *Ibid.* iv., p. 54. This curse is on all letchers throwne, They give HORNS and, at last, HORNES are their owne.

1608. ROWLANDS, *Humor's Looking Glass*, p. 22. Besides, shee is as perfect chast as faire, But being married to a jealous asse, He vowes shee HORNS him.

1609. JONSON, *Epicœne*, iii., 1. By that light you deserve to be grafted, and your HORNS reach from one side of the island to the other.

1616. JONSON, *Devil's an Ass*, v., 5. And a cuckold is, Wherever he puts his head, with a wannion, his HORNS be forth, the devil's companion.

1618. SAMUEL ROWLANDS. *The Night Raven*, p. 25. 'Tis this bad liver doth the HORNE-PLAGUE breed, Which day and night my jealous thoughts doth feed.

1623. COCKERAN, *Eng. Dict.* s.v. SARGUS, an adulterous fish which goes on the grassie shore, and HORNES the hee Goates that had horns before.

1627. DRAYTON. *Agincourt and Other Poems*, p. 174. Some made mouthes at him, others as in scorne With their forkt fingers POYNTED him THE HORN.

1629. DAVENANT, *Albovine*, ed. 1673, p. 436. 'Twas a subtle reach to tell him that the King had HORN'D his brow.

1633. ROWLEY, *Match at Midnight* (DODSLEY, *Old Plays*, 4th ed., 1875, xiii., 40). HORNING the headman of his parish and taking money for his pains.

1633. FORD, *Love's Sacrifice*, iii., 3. Fernando is your rival, has stolen your duchess's heart, murther'd friendship; HORNS your head, and laughs at your horns.

1637. BEAUMONT and FLETCHER, *Elder Brother*, iv., 4. I shall have some music yet At my making free o' th' company of HORNERS.

1640. RAWLINS, *The Rebellion*, i., I. (DODSLEY, *Old Plays*, 4th ed., 1875, xiv., 15). Fresh as a city bridegroom that has signed his wife a grant for the GRAFTING OF HORNS.

1643. BROME, *A New Diurnal.* (CHALMERS, *Eng. Poets.*, 1810, vi, 667). Prince Rupert, for fear that his name be confounded, Will saw off his HORNS, and make him a Roundhead.

1647. BEAUMONT and FLETCHER, *Women Pleased*, v. 3. I shall then be full of scorn, Wanton, proud (beware the HORN).

1653. MIDDLETON and ROWLEY, *The Spanish Gypsy*, iii., I. Beggars would on cock-horse ride, And boobies fall a-roaring, And cuckolds though no HORNS be spied, Be one another goring.

1653. DAVENANT, *The Siege of Rhodes*, p. 34. It stuffs up the marriage bed with thorns, It gores itself, it gores itself with imagined HORNS.

1657. MIDDLETON, *Women, Beware of Woman* (1657), iii., 2. Cuckolds dance the HORNPIPE, and farmers dance the hay. *Idem.*, iv., 2. Go, lie down, master; but take care your HORNS do not make holes in the pillow-beers.

1659. *Lady Alimony*, i., 2 (DODSLEY, *Old Plays*, 4th ed., 1875, xiv., 280). My scene, Trillo, is HORN ALLEY. *Ibid.*, iii., 6 (p. 340). Doubt nothing, my fellow Knights of HORNSEY.

1661. WEBSTER, *Cure for a Cuckold* (1661), v., 2. He that hath HORNS thus let him learn to shed.

1663. KILLIGREW, *The Parson's Wedding*, iv., 1 (DODSLEY, *Old Plays*, 4th ed., 1875, xiv., 473). I hope to EXALT THE Parson's HORN here. *Ibid.*, (p. 477). Only to fright the poor cuckolds and make the fools visit their HORNS. *Ibid.*, v., 4 (p. 519). Methinks my HORNS ache more than my corns. *Ibid. ib* (p. 520.) I have seen a cuckold of your complexion: if he had lent as much hoof as HORN, you might have hunted the beast by the slot.

1664. BUTLER, *Hudibras*, II., ii. For when men by their wives are cowed, Their HORNS of course are understood.

1668. L'ESTRANGE, *Visions of Quevedo*, p. 251 (ed. 1708). He that marries, ventures fair for the HORN, either before or after.

1672. RAY, *Proverbs* (in BOHN, 1889), s.v. He had better PUT HIS HORNS IN HIS POCKET than wind them. *Idem.* (p. 184). HORNS and gray hairs do not come with years. *Idem. id.*, Who hath HORNS in his pocket let him not put them on his head.

1675. WYCHERLEY, *Country Wife*, v., 4. Epilogue: Encouraged by our woman's man to-day, A HORNER'S part may vainly think to play. *Ibid*, i., 1. I make no more cuckolds, sir. [*MAKES HORNS.*] *Ibid.*, iv., 3. If ever you suffer your wife to trouble me again here, she shall carry you home a pair of HORNS.

1677. WYCHERLEY, *Plain Dealer*, iv., 1. First, the clandestine obscenity in the very name of HORNER.

d. 1680. BUTLER, *Remains* (1757), ii., 372. His own branches, his HORNS, are as mystical as the Whore of Babylon's Palfreys, not to be seen but in a vision.

1693. CONGREVE, *Old Bachelor*, iv., 15. Pox choke him. Would his HORNS were in his throat.

1695. CONGREVE, *Love for Love*, iv., 15. The clocks will strike twelve at noon, and the HORNED HERD buzz in the Exchange at two.

1698. FARQUHAR, *Love and a Bottle*, iv., 3. Should I ever be tried before this judge, how I should laugh to see how gravely his goose cap sits upon a pair of HORNS!

1700. CONGREVE, *Way of the World*, iii., 7. Man should have his head and HORNS, and woman the rest of him.

1702. STEELE, *The Funeral or Grief à la Mode*, Act. i., p. 22. This wench I know has played me false, and HORNED me in my gallants. [NOTE.—That the speaker is a female shows the word to have been transferable to the other sex.]

1708. W. KING, *Art of Love*, pt. x. (CHALMERS, *English Poets*, 1810, ix., 274). Sometimes his dirty paws she scorns, While her fair fingers show his HORNS.

1706. PRIOR, *Poems.* 'The Turtle and Sparrow,' line 302-9. 'Two staring HORNS,' I often said, 'but ill became a sparrow's head' . . . 'Whilst at the root your HORNS are sore, The more you scratch, they ache the more.'

1719. DURFEY, *Pills*, etc., i., 174. Who's the Cuckoo, Who's the Cuckold, who's the HORNER?

1728. PATRICK WALKER, *Alexander Peden*, 'Postscript' (ed. 1827, i.). A profane, obscene meeting called the HORN-ORDER.

1737. FIELDING, *Tumble-Down Dick, Works* (1718) iii., 408. Think it enough your betters do the deed, And that by HORNING you I mend the breed.

d. 1742. SOMERVILLE, *Occasional Poems* (CHALMERS, *English Poets*, 1810, xi., 238). If I but catch her in a corner, Humph! 'tis your servant, Colonel HORNER.

1759-67. STERNE, *Tristam Shandy*, ch. xxxvii. Nor have the horn-works he speaks of anything to do with the HORN-WORKS of Cuckoldom.

1765. C. SMART, *Fables*, xi., line 66. And though your spouse my lecture scorns. Beware his fate, beware his HORNS.

d. 1770. CHATTERTON, *The Revenge*, i., I. Let her do what she will, The husband is still, And but for his HORNS you would think him an ass. *Idem.*, ii., 4 Have you come HORNING.

1785. GROSE, *Dict. Vulg. Tongue*, s.v.

1786. CAPTAIN MORRIS (Collection of Songs), *The Great Plenipotentiary*, (9th ed. 1788, stanza ix., p. 43). She had HORNED the dull brows of her worshipful spouse Till they sprouted like Venus's myrtle.

d. 1796. BURNS, *Merry Muses*, 'Cuddy the Cooper,' p. 84. On ilka brow she's PLANTED A HORN, An' swears that there they shall stan', O.

1813. MOORE, *Poems*, 'Re-inforcements for the Duke,' iii., 209. Old H——df—t at HORN-WORKS again might be tried.

1816. QUIZ, *Grand Master*, canto vii., p. 199, line 10 (She) smil'd, declaring that she scorn'd him, (She might have added that she'd HORN'D him).

1822. SCOTT, *Fortunes of Nigel*, c. xxxvi. O what a generous creature is your true London husband! HORNS hath he, but, tame as a fatted ox, he goreth not.

1825. SCOTT, *The Betrothed*, ch. xvii. I ever tell thee, husband, the HORNS would be worth the hide in a fair market.

TO DRAW IN ONE'S HORNS, *verb. phr.* (colloquial).—To withdraw or to retract; to cool down.

1785. GROSE, *Vulg. Tongue*, s.v. HORNS.

TO HORN OFF, *verb. phr.* (American). = To put on one side; to shunt. [As a bull or stag with his horns.]

1851. HOOPER, *Widow Rugby's Husband*, etc., p. 69. You HORNED me off to get a chance to get gaming witnesses out of the way.

IN A HORN, *adv. phr.* (American).—A general qualification, implying refusal or disbelief; OVER THE LEFT (*q.v.*).

1858. *Washington Evening Star*, 26 Aug. I have mentioned before the innumerable comforts—IN A HORN—of the old White Sulphur Springs.

TO WIND (or BLOW) THE HORN, *verb. phr.* (old). — To break wind; TO FART (*q.v.*).

1620. PERCY, *Folio, MSS.*, 'Fryar and Boye.' Her tayle shall wind the HORNE.

TO CURE THE HORN, *verb. phr.* (venery).—To copulate. *See* HORN, *subs.*, sense 3. For synonyms, *see* GREENS and RIDE.

TO HAVE THE HORN, *verb. phr.* (venery). *See* HORN, *subs.*, sense 3.

TO COME OUT OF THE LITTLE END OF THE HORN, *verb. phr.* (common).—To get the worst of a bargain; to be reduced in circumstances. Also, to make much ado about nothing. Said generally of vast endeavour ending in failure. [Through some unexpected SQUEEZE (*q.v.*)].

1605. JONSON, CHAPMAN, and MARSTON, *Eastward Hoe*, i., 1. I had the horne of suretiship ever before my eyes. You all know the devise of the HORNE, where the young fellow slippes in at the butte-end, and comes squesd out at the buckall.

1624. FLETCHER, *Wife for a Month*, iii., 3. Thou wilt look to-morrow else Worse than the prodigal fool the ballad speaks of, That was squeezed THROUGH A HORN.

1847. PORTER, *Big Ben*, etc., p. 37. How did you make it? You didn't COME OUT AT THE LITTLE END OF THE HORN, did you?

1847. PORTER, *Quarter Race*, etc., p. 24. You never saw such a run of luck; everywhere I touched was *pizen*, and I CAME OUT OF THE LEETLE END OF THE HORN.

1891. *Pall Mall Gaz.*, 3 July, i., 2. The 'great Trek,' in that expressive transatlantic phrase, has toddled OUT OF THE LITTLE END OF THE HORN.

HORN-COLIC, *subs.* (venery).—*See* HORN, *subs.*, sense 3.

1785. GROSE, *Vulg Tongue*, s.v

HORNET, *subs.* (common).—A disagreeable, cantankerous person.

HORNIE (or HORNESS), *subs.* (old). —1. A constable or watchman; a sheriff.

1819. VAUX, *Life*, s.v. HORNEY, a Constable.

1821. HAGGART, *Life*, 51. The woman missing it immediately, she sent for the HORNIES.

1859. MATSELL, *Vocabulum*, s.v. HORNESS.

2. (Scots').—The devil; generally AULD HORNIE (*q.v.*).

1785. BURNS, *Address to the Deil.* O thou! whatever title suits thee, AULD HORNIE, Satan, Nick, or Clootie.

HORNIFY, *verb.* (colloquial).—*See* HORN, *subs.*, sense 3 and *verb.*

2. (venery).—*See* HORN, *subs.*, sense 3.

HORN-MAD *adj.* (old).—1. *See* quot. 1690.

1593. SHAKSPEARE, *Comedy of Errors*, ii., 1. Why, mistress, sure my master is HORN-MAD.

1599. HENRY PORTER, *The Two Angry Women of Abingdon* (DODSLEY, *Old Plays*, 4th ed., 1875, vii.). And then I wound my horn, and he's HORN-MAD.

1604. MARSTON, *Malcontent*, i., 7. I am HORN MAD.

1605. JONSON, *The Fox*, iii., 6. Yet I'm not mad, Not HORN-MAD, see you.

1639-61. *Rump Songs*, [1662], 293. The Country has grown sad, The City is HORN-MAD.

1647. BEAUMONT and FLETCHER, *The Woman's Prize*, ii., 6. After my twelve strong labours to reclaim her, Which would have made Don Hercules HORN-MAD.

1690. B. E., *Dict. Cant. Crew*, s.v. HORN-MAD, stark staring Mad, because Cuckolded.

1693. CONGREVE, *Old Bachelor*, iv., 22. Ay, I feel it here; I sprout; I bud; I blossom; I am ripe HORN-MAD.

1694. CONGREVE, *Double Dealer*, iv., 20. She forks out cuckoldom with her fingers, and you are running HORN-MAD after your fortune.

1695. CONGREVE, *Love for Love*, v., 8. She's mad for a husband, and he's HORN-MAD

1698. FARQUHAR, *Love and a Bottle*, iv., 3. Thou'rt HORN-MAD. Prithee, leave impertinence.

1725. *New Cant. Dict.*, s.v.

1822. SCOTT, *Fortunes of Nigel*, ch. xxvi. Ye might as well expect brandy from beanstalks, or milk from a crag of blue whunstane. The man is mad, HORN-MAD, to boot.

1825. HARRIETTE WILSON, *Memoirs*, ii. 228. The little he did say was chiefly on the subject of cuckolds and cuckolding. His lordship was HORN-MAD.

2. (venery).—Sexually excited; lecherous; MUSTY (*q.v.*). Also, HORNY.

HORNSWOGGLE, *subs.* (American).—Nonsense; HUMBUG (*q.v.*). For synonyms, *see* GAMMON.

Verb (American).—To humbug; to delude; to seduce.—*Slang, Jargon, and Cant. Cf.*, IN A HORN.

HORN-THUMB, *subs.* (old). — A pickpocket. [From the practice of wearing a sheath of horn to protect the thumb in cutting out.] *See* THIEVES.

1569. PRESTON, *Cambises* (DODSLEY, *Old Plays*, 4th ed., 1874, iv., 235). But cousin, because to that office ye are not like come, Frequent your exercises, a HORNE ON YOUR THUMBE, A quick eye, a sharp knife.

1614. JONSON, *Bartholomew Fair*, ii. I mean a child of the HORN-THUMB, a babe of booty, boy, a cut-purse.

1614. GREENE, *Looking-Glass* [Dyce], p. 138. I cut this from a new-married wife by means of a HORN-THUMB and a knife.—Six shillings, four pence.

HORRORS, *subs.* (common).—The first stage of *delirium tremens*. For synonyms, *see* GALLON-DISTEMPER. Also low spirits, or THE BLUES (*q.v.*).

1848. RUXTON, *Life in the Far West*, p. 50. Paying the penalty in a fit of HORRORS.

1857. *Philadelphia Evening Bulletin* (quoted by Bartlett). This poison (fusil oil). which acts with te rible results on the nerves; seeming like a diabolical inspiration, stirring up mania, convulsions, and the HORRORS in an incredibly short space of time.

1864. DICKENS, *Our Mutual Friend*, bk. iv., ch. viii. What are popularly called 'the trembles' being in full force upon him that evening, and likewise what are popularly called THE HORRORS, he had a very bad time of it; which was not made better by his being so remorseful as frequently to moan 'Sixty threepennorths.'

1864. F. W. ROBINSON, *Mr. Stewart's Intentions*, ch. i. 'Well, sermons always gave me THE HORRORS, and engendered a hate of the sermonizer.

1883. STEVENSON, *Treasure Island* ch. iii., p. 20 (1886). If I don't have a drain o' rum, Jim, I'll have THE HORRORS.

1889. C. HADDON CHAMBERS, *In Australian Wilds*. He's sober now, you see; but he managed to get blind drunk before eleven o'clock this morning, and last week he narrowly escaped an attack of THE HORRORS.

1892. HENLEY and STEVENSON, *Three Rags*, 'Admiral Guinea,' iv., 3. It's THE HORRORS come alive.

2. (common).—Sausages. *See* CHAMBER OF HORRORS and DOG'S-PASTE.

3. (thieves').—Handcuffs. For synonyms, *see* DARBIES.

HORSE, *subs.* (common).—1. A five-pound note. *See* FINNUP.

2. (thieves'). — Horsemonger Lane Gaol. Also THE OLD HORSE. Now obsolete.

1851-61. H. MAYHEW, *Lond. Lab. and Lond. Poor*, 1, p. 457. The only thing that frightens me when I'm in prison is sleeping in a cell by myself—you do in THE OLD HORSE and the Steel.

3. (American).—A man: generally in affection. Also OLD HOSS, or HOSS-FLY.

1838. HALIBURTON ('Sam Slick'), *The Clockmaker*, 3 S., ch. xviii. He is all sorts of a HOSS, and the best live one that ever cut dirt this side of the big pond, or t'other side either.

1847. ROBB, *Squatter Life*, p. 74. What in the yearth did you do with old Hoss on the road?—He ain't *gin out*, has he? *Ibid*, p. 70. None of your stuck-up imported chaps from the dandy states, but a real genuine westerner—in short, a HOSS!

1848 RUXTON, *Life in the Far West*, p. 5. Hyar's a HOSS as'll make fire come.

1857. GLADSTONE, *Englishman in Kansas*, p. 43. Here, boys, drink. Liquors, captain, for the crowd. Step up this way, OLD HOSS, and liquor.

Verb (venery).—1. To possess a woman. For synonyms, *see* RIDE.

1614. JONSON, *Bartholomew Fair*, iv., 3. Say'st thou so, filly? Thou shalt have a leap presently, I'll HORSE thee myself, else.

2. (workmen's). — *See* quots. *Cf.*, FLOG THE DEAD HORSE.

1857. *Notes and Queries*, 2 S., iv., p. 192. A workman HORSES it when he charges for more in his week's work than he has really done. Of course he has so much unprofitable work to get through in the ensuing week, which is called dead horse.

1867. *All the Year Round*, 13 July, p. 59. To HORSE a man, is for one of two men who are engaged on precisely similar pieces of work to make extraordinary exertions in order to work down the other man. This is sometimes done simply to see what kind of a workman a new man may be, but often with the much less creditable motive of injuring a fellow workman in the estimation of an employer.

THE GRAY MARE IS THE BETTER HORSE. *See* GRAY-MARE.

HORSE FOALED OF AN ACORN, *subs. phr.* (old).—1. The gallows. For synonyms, *see* TRIPLE-TREE.

1760-61. SMOLLETT, *Sir L. Greaves*, ch. viii. I believe as how 'tis no horse, but a devil incarnate; and yet I've been worse mounted, that I have—I'd like to have rid A HORSE THAT WAS FOALED OF AN ACORN (*i.e.*, he had nearly met with the fate of Absalom).

1785. GROSE, *Vulg. Tongue*, s v.

1827. LYTTON, *Pelham*, ch. lxxxii. The cove . . . . is as pretty a Tyburn blossom as ever was brought up to ride A HORSE FOALED BY AN ACORN.

1839. AINSWORTH, *Jack Sheppard* [1889], p. 8. . . . . As to this little fellow . . . . he shall never mount A HORSE FOALED BY AN ACORN, if I can help it.

2. (military).—The triangles or crossed halberds under which soldiers were flogged.

OLD- (or SALT-) HORSE, *subs.* (nautical). Salt beef. Also JUNK and SALT-JUNK.

1889. *Chambers's Journal*, 3 Aug., 495. Mr. Clark Russell declares that SALT-HORSE works out of the pores, and contributes to that mahogany complexion common to sailors, which is often mistakenly attributed to rum and weather.

ONE-HORSE, *adj.* (American). Comparatively small, insignificant, or unimportant.

1858. *Washington Evening Star*. On Friday last, the engineer of a fast train was arrested by the authorities of a ONE-HORSE town in Dauphin County, Pa., for running through the borough at a greater rate of speed than is allowed by their ordinances.

1871. DE VERE, *Americanisms*, p. 221. The indignant settler who has been ill-treated, as he fancies, in court, denounces his attorney as a 'miserable, ONE-HORSE lawyer;' and the Yankee newly arrived in England does not hesitate to declare that 'Liverpool is a poor ONE-HORSE kind of a place,' a term applied by Mark Twain to no less a city than Rome itself; and a witty clergyman of Boston inveighed once bitterly against 'timid, sneaking, ONE-HORSE oaths, as infinitely worse than a good, round, thundering outburst.

1891. *National Review*, Sep., p. 127. Mr. Marion Crawford's *Witch of Prague* (Macmillan & Co.) is, as his compatriots would say, rather a ONE-HORSE witch.

TO BE HORSED, *verb. phr.* (old).— To be flogged [from the wooden-horse used as a flogging-stool]; to take on one's back as for a flogging.

1678. BUTLER, *Hudibras*, pt. III., c. 1. The spirit HORS'D him like a sack Upon the vehicle his back.

1751. SMOLLETT, *Peregrine Pickle*, ch. xvii. Our unfortunate hero was publicly HORSED, *in terrorem* of all whom it might concern.

1857. THACKERAY, *Virginians*, ch. v. Serjeants, school-masters, slave-overseers, used the cane freely. Our little boys had been HORSED many a day by Mr. Dempster.

1881. *Notes and Queries*, 1 Jan., p. 18. I got well HORSED for such a breach of discipline.

TO FALL AWAY FROM A HORSE-LOAD TO A CARTLOAD, *verb. phr.* (old).—*See* quot.

1690. B. E., *Dict. Cant. Crew*, s.v. HORSEPLAY. FALLEN AWAY FROM A HORSELOAD TO A CARTLOAD, spoken ironically of one considerably improved in flesh on a sudden.

TO FLOG THE DEAD HORSE.—*See* DEAD-HORSE and HORSE, *verb.* sense 2.

TO PUT THE CART BEFORE THE HORSE, *verb. phr.* (colloquial).—To begin at the wrong end; to set things hind-side before.

1690. B. E., *Dict. Cant. Crew*, s.v. HORSE.

TO PUT THE SADDLE ON THE RIGHT HORSE, *verb. phr.* (colloquial).—To apportion accurately.

1690. B. E., *Dict. Cant. Crew*, s.v. HORSE. SET THE SADDLE ON THE RIGHT HORSE, lay the Blame where the Fault is.

TO RIDE ON A HORSE WITH (or BAYARD OF) TEN TOES, *verb. phr.* (common).—To walk; to use the MARROWBONE-STAGE. *Cf.*, SHANKS'S MARE.

1606. BRETON, *Good and Badde*, p. 14. His trauell is the walke of the woful, and his HORSE BAYARD OF TEN TOES.

1662. FULLER, *Worthies, Somerset*, ii., 291. At last he [Coryat] undertook to travail into the East Indies by land, mounted on AN HORSE WITH TEN TOES.

1785. GROSE, *Vulg. Tongue*, s.v. BAYARD.

AS GOOD AS A SHOULDER OF MUTTON TO A SICK HORSE, *phr.* (old).—Utterly worthless.

1596. BEN JONSON, *Every Man in his Humour*, ii., 1. Counsel to him is AS GOOD AS A SHOULDER OF MUTTON TO A SICK HORSE.

AS STRONG AS A HORSE, *adv. phr.* (colloquial).—Very strong: a general intensitive.

HORSE AND HORSE, *adv. phr.* (American).—Neck and neck; even.

HORSEBREAKER (or **PRETTY HORSEBREAKER**), *subs.* (colloquial).—A woman (*c.* 1860), hired to ride in the park; hence, a riding courtesan. *See* also quot. 1864. For synonyms, *see* BARRACK-HACK and TART.

1864. E. YATES, *Broken to Harness*, ch. iv., p. 33 (1873). Kate Mellor was a HORSEBREAKER, a *bonâ fide* horsebreaker; one who curbed colts, and 'took it out of' kickers and rearers.

1865. *Public Opinion*, 30 Sep. These *demi-monde* people, anonymas, HORSEBREAKERS, hetairæ . . . . are by degrees pushing their way into society.

HORSE-BUSS, *subs.* (old).—A loud-sounding kiss; a bite.

1785. GROSE, *Vulg. Tongue*, s.v.

HORSE-CAPPER (**-COPER**, **-COSER**, **-COURSER**, or **-CHAUNTER**), *subs.* (common).—A dealer in worthless or 'faked' horses. [Originally good English. To COPE = to barter.] *See* CHANTER. Hence HORSE-COPING and HORSE-DUFFING.

1616. OVERBURY, *Characters* (RIMBAULT, 9th ed., 1856, p. 120). An arrant HORSE-COURSER hath the trick to blow up horseflesh as the butcher does veal.

d. 1680. BUTLER, *Remains* (1759), ii., 458. A HORSE-COURSER is one that hath read horses, and understands all the virtues and vices of the whole species by being conversant with them, and how to take the best advantage of both.

1742-4. NORTH, *Life of the Lord Keeper* i., 271. There were HORSE-COPERS among them.

1785. GROSE, *Vulg. Tongue*, s.v. HORSE-COSER, vulgarly and corruptly pronounced horse courser, a dealer in horses. The verb to cose, was used by the Scots, in the sense of bartering or exchanging.

1863. *Sporting Life*, 29 Apr., p. 4, col. 3. COPERS and Chaunters are now in full feather.

1864. *London Review*, 18 June, p. 643. Amongst the mysteries of horse-flesh is the noble science of coping, and its practitioners the HORSE-COPERS.

1874. G. A. LAWRENCE, *Hagarene*, ch. ii. He had lived somewhat precariously by his wits; eking out the scanty allowance wrung from his miserly old sire, by betting and HORSE-COPING on a small scale.

1884. *Daily News*, 23 Aug., p. 4, c. 7. The most accomplished gipsy COPERS, if they are not belied, are not satisfied with merely doing up an unsound horse and selling him as a sound one, but frequently steal outright the subject of their scientific and often lucrative experiments.

1888. ROLF BOLDREWOOD. *Robbery Under Arms*, ch. i. Poaching must be something like cattle and HORSE-DUFFING.

1889. *Answers*, 27 July, p. 141, c. 1. Allow me to expose some more tricks of HORSE COPERS.

1893. *National Observer*, 5 Aug., p. 291, col. 1. A veracious HORSE-COPER is a monster which the world ne'er saw.

HORSE-COLLAR, *subs.* (venery).—1. The female *pudendum*. For synonyms, *see* MONOSYLLABLE.

2. (tailors'). — An extremely long and wide collar.

3. (old).—A halter. TO DIE IN A HORSE'S NIGHTCAP = to be hanged. *See* LADDER.

ENGLISH SYNONYMS. — Anodyne necklace; Bridport dagger; choker; hempen cravat; hempen elixir; horse's neckcloth; horse's necklace; neck-squeezer; neckweed; squeezer; St. Andrew's lace; Sir Tristram's knot; tight cravat; Tyburn tiffany; Tyburn tippet; widow.

FRENCH SYNONYM.—*La cravate de chanvre.*

1593. *Bacchus' Bountie* in *Harl. Misc* (ed. Park), ii., 304. Yea, his very head so heavie as if it had beene harnessed in an HORSE-NIGHTCAP.

1608. *Penniles Parliament* in *Harl. Misc.* (ed. Park), I., 181. And those that clip that they should not, shall have a HORSE NIGHT-CAP for their labour.

1681. *Dialogue on Oxford Parliament* (*Harl. Misc.*, ii., 125.). He better deserves to go up Holbourn in a wooden chariot, and have a HORSE NIGHT-CAP put on at the farther end.

1883. *Echo*, 25 Jan., p. 2, c. 4. Even an attempt is made to lighten the horror of the climax of a criminal career, by speaking of dying in a HORSE'S NIGHT-CAP, *i.e.*, a halter.

HORSE-EDITOR, *subs.* (American journalists').—A sporting editor. HORSE-COPY = sporting news.

HORSEFLESH, *See* DEAD HORSE and HORSE, *verb.* sense 2.

HORSE-GODMOTHER, *subs.* (old).—A strapping masculine woman; a virago. Fr., *une femme hommasse.*

1785. GROSE, *Vulg. Tongue*, s.v.

d. 1819. WOLCOT, *Wks.* In woman angel sweetness let me see No galloping HORSE-GODMOTHER for me.

1838. SELBY, *Jacques Strop*, iii., 1 What a couple of HORSE-GODMOTHERS.

1846-8. THACKERAY, *Vanity Fair*, ii., ch. 4. How do, my dear? Come to see the old man, hay? Gad—you've a pretty face, too. You ain't like that old HORSE-GODMOTHER, your mother.

HORSE-LATITUDES, *subs.* (nautical).—A space in the Atlantic, north of the trade-winds, where the winds are baffling.

1891. W. C. RUSSELL, *Ocean Tragedy*, p. 137. The winds even north of the rains and HORSE-LATITUDES were in a sense to be reckoned on.

HORSE-LAUGH, *subs.* (colloquial).—A loud, noisy laugh; a guffaw.

1738. POPE, *Ep. to Satires*, i., 38. A HORSELAUGH, if you please, at honesty.

HORSE-LEECH, *subs.* (colloquial).—1. An extortioner; a miser.

2. (venery).—Anything insatiable. Also a whore.

1597. HALL, *Satires*, iv., 5. An HORSE-LEECH, barren wench, or gaping grave.

1614. JONSON, *Bartholomew Fair*, ii., 1. You are one of those HORSE-LEECHES that gave out I was dead in Turnbull Street.

3. (old).—A horse-doctor; also a quack.

1594. NASHE, *Terrors of the Night* (GROSART, iii., 250). Whereas his HORSE-LEECH . . . . will give a man twenty guineas in one.

1597. HALL, *Satires*, ii., 4. No HORSE-LEECH but will look for larger fee.

HORSE-MARINES, *subs.* (common).—A mythical corps, very commonly cited in jokes and quizzies on the innocent. [THE JOLLIES (*q.v.*) or Royal Marines, being ignorant of seamanship, have always been the butt of blue-jackets.] TELL THAT TO THE MARINES (or HORSE-MARINES) THE SAILORS WON'T BELIEVE IT = a rejoinder to an attempt at imposition or credulity. Often amplified with WHEN THEY'RE RIDING AT ANCHOR. *See* also BINGHAM'S DANDIES.

1825. SCOTT, *St. Ronan's Well*, ch. xxi. 'Come, none of your quizzing, my old buck,' said Sir Bingo—'what the devil has a ship to do with horse's furniture?—Do you think we belong to the HORSE-MARINES?'

c. 1870. *Broadside Ballad*, 'Captain Jinks.' I'm Captain Jinks of the HORSE-MARINES.

1886. STEPHENS and YARDLEY, *Little Jack Sheppard*, p. 3. They may tell that yarn to the HORSE MARINES, For we bean't such fools as we looks.

1886. *Tinsley's Mag.*, Apr., 321. Owing to a singular deviation from the ordinary functions of cavalry, the 17th Lancers were once christened the HORSE MARINES.

1892. *Wops the Waif* [Horner's Penny Stories], ch. i., p. 1. Oh, nothink, eh! You'd better tell that to the HOSS MARINES; I've lived a sight too long in Shoreditch to take that in.

HORSE-MILLINER, *subs.* (common).—1. A dandy trooper.

1778. CHATTERTON, *Ballads of Charity*, ii., 113. The trammels of his palfrey pleased his sight, For the HORSE-MILLINER his head with roses dight.

1813. SCOTT, *Bridal of Triermain*, ii., 3. One comes in foreign trashery Of tinkling chain and spur, A walking haberdashery Of feathers, lace and fur; In Rowley's antiquated phrase, HORSE-MILLINER of modern days.

2. (old).—A saddler and harness-maker.

1818. SCOTT, *Heart of Midlothian*, xi. In my wretched occupation of a saddler, HORSE-MILLINER, and harness maker, we are out unconscionable sums just for barkened hides and leather.

HORSE-NAILS, *subs.* (common).—1. Money. For synonyms, *see* ACTUAL and GILT.

TO FEED ON HORSE-NAILS, *verb. phr.* (cribbage).—So to play as not so much to advance your own score as to keep down your opponent's.

TO KNOCK INTO HORSE-NAILS, *verb. phr.* (common). — To knock to pieces; to be absolutely victorious.

HORSE-NIGHTCAP, *subs.* (old).—*See* HORSE'S-COLLAR.

HORSE-POX, *subs.* (old).—A superlative of Pox (*q.v.*). Used in adjuration. *E.g.*, A HORSE-POX on you! Ay, with a HORSE-POX, etc.

HORSE-PROTESTANT, *subs.* (tailors').—A churchman.

HORSE-SENSE, *subs.* (American).—Sound and practical judgment.

1893. LIPPINCOT, Mar., p. 260. A round bullet head, not very full of brains, perhaps, yet reputed to be fairly stocked with what is termed HORSE sense.

HORSES-AND-MARES. TO PLAY AT HORSES-AND-MARES, *verb. phr.* (schoolboys').—To copulate. For synonyms, *see* GREENS and RIDE.

HORSE'S-HEAD, *subs.* (cobblers').—The boot-sole, heel, and what is left of the front after the back and part of the front have been used TO FOX (*q.v.*) other boots withal.

HORSE-SHOE, *subs.* (venery).—The female *pudendum*. [In German, *Sie hat ein Hufeisen verloren* (of women) = she has been seduced, *i.e.*, she has lost a horse-shoe.]

HORSE'S-MEAL, *subs.* (old).—Meat without drink.

1785. GROSE, *Vulg. Tongue*, s.v.

HORSE-SOVEREIGN, *subs.* (common).—A twenty-shilling piece with Pistrucci's effigies of St. George and the Dragon.

1871. *London Figaro*, 26 Jan. A number of those coins, sometimes known as HORSE SOVEREIGNS, are to be issued.

HORTUS, *subs.* (venery).—*See* quot. [*Cf.*, GARDEN.] For synonyms, *see* MONOSYLLABLE.

1728 BAILEY, *Eng. Dict.*, s.v. HORTUS [by some writers] the privy parts of a woman.

HOSE. IN MY OTHER HOSE, *subs. phr.* (old). A qualification of refusal or disbelief; IN A HORN (*q.v.*); OVER THE LEFT (*q.v.*).

1598. FLORIO. *A Worlde of Wordes*, s.v. *Zoccoli Zoccoli*, tushtush, awaie, in faith sir no, yea IN MY OTHER HOSE.

HOSS. *See* HORSE.

HOSS-FLY (or **OLD HOSS-FLY**), *subs.* (American). - A familiar address; *cf.*, HORSE, *subs.* sense 3.

HOST, TO RECKON WITHOUT ONE'S HOST, *verb. phr.* (old: now recognised).—To blunder.

1690. B. E., *Dict. Cant. Crew*, s.v. HOST. To RECKON WITHOUT ONE'S HOST, or count your Chickens before they are Hatched.

MINE HOST, *subs. phr.* (colloquial).—A taverner.

HOSTELER, *subs.* (old).—*See* quot.

1785. GROSE, *Vulg. Tongue*, s.v. HOSTELER, *i.e.*, oat stealer

HOT, *subs.* (Winchester College).—1. A mellay at football.

2. (*Ibid*).—A crowd.

1878. ADAMS, *Wykehamica*, p. 367. It would be replaced and a fresh HOT formed.

Adj. (colloquial).—1. Of persons: sexually excitable; lecherous; ON HEAT (*q.v.*); RANDY (*q.v.*). Of things (as books): obscene; BLUE (*q.v.*); HIGH-KILTED (*q.v.*); HOT MEMBER (*q.v.*) = a male or female debauchee; or (as in sense 2), a man or woman contemptuous of decorum.

HOT AS THEY MAKE THEM = exceedingly amorous or reckless. HOT-BLOODED = lecherous: as (in *Merry Wives*, v., 5) 'the HOT-BLOODED gods assist me.' HOT-HOUSE (*q.v.*) = a brothel.

1383. CHAUCER, *Canterbury Tales*. Prologue to *Canterbury Tales*, lines 97 and 98. So hote he lovede, that by nightertale, He sleep no more than doth a nightyngale.

1596. BEN JONSON, *Every Man in his Humour*, iv., 8. Dost thou not shame, When all thy powers in chastity are spent, To have a mind so HOT.

1598. SHAKSPEARE, 1 *Henry IV.*, i., 2. A fair HOT wench in flame-coloured taffeta.

1599. H. PORTER, *Two Angry Women of Abingdon* (DODSLEY, *Old Plays*, 4th ed., 1875, vii., 354. Are ye so HOT, with a pox? Would ye kiss my mistress?

1605. JONSON, *Volpone*, iii., 6. I am now as fresh, As HOT, as high, and in as jovial plight As when in that so celebrated scene At recitation of our comedy For entertainment of the great Valois, I acted young Antinous.

1608. SHAKSPEARE, *Antony and Cleopatra*, iii., 11. Besides what HOTTER hours, Unregistered in vulgar fame you have Luxuriously picked out.

1614. JONSON, *Bartholomew Fair*, ii., 1. The whelp was HOT and eager.

1693. CONGREVE, *Old Bachelor*, v., 8. If either you esteem my friendship or your own safety, come not near that house—that corner house—that HOT brothel.

1697. VANBRUGH, *Relapse*, iii., 5. Young men are HOT, I know, but they don't boil over at that rate.

1719. DURFEY, *Pills*, etc., iv., 123. He laughs to see the girls so HOT.

1892. MILLIKEN, *'Arry Ballads*, p. 37. As most of our plays are now cribbed from the French, wy they're all pooty HOT.

2. (colloquial). — Careless of decorum; boisterous; utterly reckless and abandoned.

1888. J. RUNCIMAN, *The Chequers*, p. 187. You're a RED-HOT MEMBER!

3. (thieves').—Well known to the police; dangerous; uncomfortable; *e.g.*, TO MAKE IT HOT FOR ONE.

1830. BUCKSTONE, *Wreck Ashore*, i., 4. *Mil.* This place is now too HOT for me, captain. Bills overdue, and bailiffs in full chase, have driven me to a hasty leave of my home.

1841. *Tait's Edinburgh Mag.*, viii. 217. Finding all too HOT to hold him.

1859. MATSELL, *Vocabulum*, s.v. HOT. The cove had better move his beaters into Dewsville, it is too HOT for him here.

1882. *Evening Standard*, 3 Oct., p. 5, c. 4. The Constable added that at the station the Prisoner told him that if he did not make it too HOT he would give him £5.

1888. *Tit Bits*, 24 Mar., 373. The HOTTEST suburb of London during Jubilee year was supposed to be Ealing.

1890. MARRIOTT-WATSON, *Broken Billy* (in *Under the Gum-tree*, p. 31). With a few pals, almost as brutal as himself, he made the place pretty HOT from time to time.

1891. *Morning Advertiser*, 26 Mar., p. 2, col. 4. When Baker was arrested he asked Detective-sergeant Gold not to make it too HOT for them, and tried to induce the officer to receive a sovereign.

1891. J. NEWMAN, *Scamping Tricks*, p. 36. You'll find they will make it HOT for you.

4. (colloquial).—*See* quot. 1690. Also violent; sharp; severe.

1690. B. E., *Dict. Cant. Crew*, s.v. HOT, exceeding Passionate.

1886 R. L. STEVENSON, *Kidnapped*, p. 167. 'Well,' said he, 'yon was a HOT burst, David.'

1893. EMERSON, *Signor Lippo*, ch. xvi. I started life in a training stable, and a HOT life it was for a boy.

5. (venery).—Infected; venereally diseased.

6. (colloquial).—Alive; vehement; instant.

1864. BROWNING, *Dramatic Romances* (ed. 1879, iv., 180), The Italian in England.' Breathed HOT and instant on my train.

Verb (Winchester College).—To crowd; to mob.

TO GIVE (GET, or CATCH) IT HOT, *verb. phr.* (colloquial).—To thrash or reprove soundly; to be severely beaten or taken to task.

1859. *Fast Life*, p. 54. The craters, of course, CAUGHT IT HOT, and many had the sack.

1872. *Figaro*, 22 June. The German Emperor, Bismarck, and Earl Granville also GOT IT, but not quite so HOTLY.

1877. *Five Years' Penal Servitude*, ch. iv., p. 887. A young man who . . . . had been guilty of bigamy, and to such a degree that he GOT IT HOT for such a crime—five years.

1892. ANSTEY, *Model Music-Hall*, 32. She spotted me in 'alf a jiff, and chaffed me precious HOT.

LIKE A CAT ON HOT BRICKS, *phr.* (colloquial). — Uncomfortable; restive.

1886. J. S. WINTER, *Army Society*, ch. xvi. Lady Mainwaring looked like an eel in a frying-pan, or, most of anything perhaps, LIKE A CAT ON HOT BRICKS.

HOT WITH, *phr.* (common).—Spirits with hot water and sugar. *See* CIDER AND, and COLD WITHOUT.

HOT-ARSED, *adj. phr.* (venery).—Excessively lewd. [Of women only.] *Cf.*, BITER.

HOT-BEEF. TO GIVE HOT-BEEF, *verb. phr.* (thieves' rhyming).—To cry 'Stop thief.' Also BEEF (*q.v.*).

1879. J. W. HORSLEY, in *Macm. Mag.*, xl., 506. He followed, giving me HOT BEEF (calling 'Stop thief').

HOT-CAKES. TO GO OFF LIKE HOT CAKES, *verb. phr.* (common),—To sell readily; to be in good demand.

1889. *Pall Mall Gaz.*, 11 Oct., p. 6, c. 1. Sold at one penny retail they often GO OFF LIKE HOT CAKES.

1893 EMERSON, *Signor Lippo*, ch. xii. It went off LIKE HOT CAKES.

HOT-FOOT, *adv.* (colloquial). — Instant in pursuit.

HOTCH-POTCH, *subs.* (old: now recognised).—Amedley; a HODGE-PODGE (*q.v.*).

1597. HALL, *Satires*, i., 3. A goodly HOTCH-POTCH when vile russettings are matched with monarchs and mighty kings.

1606. *Return from Parnassus*, iv., 2. (DODSLEY, *Old Plays*, 4th ed., 1875, ix., 183). This word, HOTCH-POTCH in English is a pudding; for in such a pudding is commonly not one thing only, but one thing with another.

1690. B. E., *Dict. Cant. Crew*, s.v. HOTCH-POTCH, an Oglio, or Medly of several Meats in one Dish.

c. 1709. W. KING, *Art of Cookery*, ix. (CHALMERS, *English Poets*, 1810, ix., 259). The first delighting in HODGE-PODGE, gallimaufry, forced meats . . . . and salmagundy.

1725. *New Cant. Dict.*, s.v.

1728. PATRICK WALKER, *Alexander Peden*, 'Postscript' (ed. 1827, i., 128). A HOTCH-POTCH or bagful of Arian, Arminian, Socinian, Pelagian, etc.

1892. *Pall Mall Gaz.*, 17 Oct., p. 2, c. 1. Both are a sort of HOTCHPOTCH of songs, dances, and extravaganzas.

HOT-COPPERS, *subs.* (common).—The fever and parched throat, or MOUTH (*q.v.*), attending a debauch. *See* COOL ONE'S COPPER.

1830. EGAN, *Finish to Life in London*, 156. The 'uncommonly big gentleman' in spite of swallowing oceans of soda-water, declared his COPPER to be so HOT that he thought all the water in the sea could not reduce his thirst!

1841. *Punch*, vol. I., p. 244. 'Oh blow your physiology!' says Rapp. 'You mean to say you've got a HOT COPPER—so have I. Send for the precious balm and then fire away.

1849. THACKERAY, *Pendennis*, ch. xliii. 'Nothing like that beer,' he remarked 'when the COPPERS are HOT.'

1864. *Comic Almanack*, p. 63. 'Cold Cream Internally.' Cold cream is an excellent remedy for HOT COPPERS.

1892. HUME NISBET, *Bushranger's Sweetheart*, p. 134. He came . . . . as happy-looking, and lively as if no such hing as HOT COPPERS existed.

HOTEL (also CUPID'S HOTEL and CUPID'S ARMS).—*subs.* (venery). —The female *pudendum*. *Cf.*, COCK INN. For synonyms, *see* MONOSYLLABLE.

HOTEL BARBERING, *subs.* (common).—Bilking.

1892. *Daily Chronicle*, 28 Mar., p. 5. c. 7. The inference is now fairly admissable that he may possibly have divided his time between polygamous pursuits and HOTEL BARBERING exploits.

HOTEL WARMING-PAN, *subs. phr.* (common). — A chambermaid. Also WARMING-PAN (*q.v.*). Fr., *une limogère*.

HOT-FLANNEL (or **FLANNEL**), *subs.* (old).—Gin and beer, with nutmeg, sugar, etc., made hot.

1789. GEO. PARKER, *Life's Painter*, p. 144. A mixed kind of liquor . . . . when drank in a morning it is called FLANNEL.

1858. A. MAYHEW, *Paved with Gold*, bk. III., ch. iii., p. 269. A jug of what he termed HOT FLANNEL for three—a mixture of gin, beer, and eggs.

HOT-HOUSE, *subs.* (old). — A brothel. Also (*see* quot. 1616), a public bath. For synonyms, *see* NANNY-SHOP.

1596. NASHE, *Have with You to Saffron Walden* (GROSART, iii., 106). Any HOT-HOUSE or bawdy-house of them all.

1599. JONSON, *Every Man out of His Humour*, iv., 4. Let a man sweat once a week in a HOT-HOUSE, and be well rubbed and froted with a plump juicy wench and clean linen.

1603. SHAKSPEARE, *Measure for Measure*, ii., 1. Now she professes a HOT-HOUSE, which is a very ill house too.

1606. *The Return from Parnassus*, i., 2 (DODSLEY, *Old Plays*, 4th ed., 1875, ix., 115). He cannot swagger it well in a tavern, nor domineer in a HOT-HOUSE.

1616. JONSON, *Epigrams*, 'On the New HOT-HOUSE.' Where lately harboured many a famous whore, A purging bill now fixed upon the door Tells you it is a HOT-HOUSE: So it may, And still be a whore-house. They're synonyma.

1699. GARTH, *The Dispensary*, ii., line 157. A HOT-HOUSE he prefers to Julia's arms.

HOT MEAT (or BEEF or MUTTON), *subs. phr.* (venery).—*See* BIT.

HOT-MEMBER (or **HOT 'UN**).—*See* WARM MEMBER.

HOT-MILK, *subs.* (venery). — The semen. For synonyms, see CREAM.

HOT-PLACE, *subs.* (colloquial).—Hell. For synonyms, *see* TROPICAL CLIMATE.

1891. F. H. GROOME, *Blackwood*, Mar., p. 320. A letter from her son in Hull, told the curate that 'that did give me a tarn at fust, for I thought that come from the HOT PLACE.'

HOT-POT, *subs.* (old).—Ale and brandy made hot.

1785. GROSE, *Vulg. Tongue*, s.v.

1788. G. C. STEVENS, *Adv. of a Speculist*, ii.. 56. A watchman and an old Blind Woman, troubled with the palsy, drinking HOT-POT together.

HOT-POTATO. TO DROP LIKE A HOT POTATO, *verb. phr.* (common). — To abandon (a pursuit, a person, a thing) with alacrity.

HOT-PUDDING. TO HAVE A HOT-PUDDING FOR SUPPER, *verb. phr.* (venery). — To copulate. Of women only. [PUDDING (Durfey) = the *penis*]. For synonyms, *see* GREENS and RIDE.

HOT-STOMACH. SO HOT A STOMACH AS TO BURN THE CLOTHES OFF HIS BACK, *phr.* (old).—Said of one who pawns his clothes for drink.—*Lex. Bal.*

HOTTENTOT, *subs.* (East-end). *See* quot.

1880. G. R. SIMS, *How the Poor Live*, ch. x. The cry of HOTTENTOTS went round. 'Hottentots' is the playful way in this district of designating a stranger, that is to say, a stranger come from the West.

2. (common).—A fool. For synonyms, *see* BUFFLE and CABBAGE-HEAD.

HOT-TIGER, *subs.* (Oxford Univ.). — Hot-spiced ale and sherry.— HOTTEN.

HOT-WATER. TO BE IN HOT-WATER, *verb. phr.* (colloquial).— To be in trouble, in difficulties, or worried.

1846. *Punch's Almanack*, 29 Nov. The *Times* first printed by steam, 1814, and has kept the country in HOT WATER ever since.

1864. MARK LEMON, *Jest book*, p. 238. Lord Allen, in conversation with Rogers, the poet, observed: 'I never put my razor into hot water, as I find it injures the temper of the blade.' 'No doubt of it,' replied Rogers; 'show me the blade that is *not out of temper* when plunged into HOT WATER.'

HOUND, *subs.* (Cambridge Univ.). —1. *See* quot.

1879. E. WALFORD, in *N. and Q.*, 5 S., xii., 88. In the *Anecdotes of Bowyer* . . . . we are told that a HOUND of King's College, Cambridge, is an undergraduate not on the foundation, nearly the same as a 'sizar.'

2. (colloquial). A mean, contemptible fellow; a scoundrel; a filthy sneak.

HOUNSLOW-HEATH, *subs.* (rhyming). —The teeth. For synonyms, *see* GRINDERS. Also HAMPSTEAD-HEATH.

1887. DAGONET in *Referee*, 7 Nov., p. 7, c. 3. She'd a Grecian 'I suppose,' And of HAMPSTEAD HEATH two rows.

HOURI OF FLEET-STREET, *subs. phr.* (common).—A prostitute. For synonyms, *see* BARRACK-HACK and TART.

HOUSE, *subs.* (theatrical).—1. An audience. TO BRING DOWN THE HOUSE = to elicit a general burst of applause. Fr., *avoir sa côtelette; boire du lait.*

1823. BEE, *Dict. of the Turf*, s.v. HOUSE. With them (the players) it means Covent-garden or Drury-lane, or indeed any other theatre. 'A full-HOUSE' and 'half-a-HOUSE' indicate the state of the receipts or number of the audience.

1870. *Athenæum*, 13 Aug., p. 120. 'Letter of J. O. Halliwell.' It is now certain that Shakespeare was never proprietor of either (the Globe or Blackfriars) theatre. His sole interest in them consisted in a participation, *as an actor* in the receipts of what is called the HOUSE.

1873. *Home News*, 24 Jan. I exerted myself, not for praise of that well-dressed mob they called THE HOUSE, but for very love of the congenial sport.

1892. SYDNEY WATSON, *Wops the Waif*, ch. iii., p. 4. There was tremendous enthusiasm this evening. Every scene was uproariously applauded, and at the climax the whole HOUSE rose and cheered and encored with tumultuous feeling.

THE HOUSE (colloquial).—(1) The Stock Exchange; (2) The House of Commons; (3) Christ Church, Oxford.

HOUSE UNDER THE HILL, *subs. phr.* (venery).—The female *pudendum*. For synonyms, *see* MONOSYLLABLE.

HOUSE (or APARTMENTS) TO LET, *subs. phr.* (common).—A widow.—*Lex. Bal.* Also BILL-OF-SALE and MAN-TRAP.

FATHER OF THE HOUSE, *subs. phr.* (Parliamentary).—The oldest elected member. *See* BABE.

HOUSE THAT JACK BUILT, *subs. phr.* (common).—A prison. For synonyms, *see* CAGE.

LIKE A HOUSE ON FIRE, *adv. phr.* (common).—Quickly; with energy. *See* LIKE.

1851-61. MAYHEW, *Lond. Lab. and Lond. Poor*, ii., 85. I'm getting on LIKE A regler HOUSE ON FIRE.

SAFE AS HOUSES, *adv. phr.* (common).—Perfectly safe.

1864. E. YATES, *Broken to Harness*, ch. xxxii., p. 361 (1873). I have the means of doing that, as SAFE AS HOUSES.

1874. T. HARDY, *Far from the Madding Crowd*, ch. lvii. 'The clothes will floor us as SAFE AS HOUSES,' said Coggan.

1886. GRANT ALLEN, *In All Shades*, ch. i. Why, of course, then, that's the explanation of it—as SAFE AS HOUSES, you may depend upon it.

1890. GRANT ALLEN, *Tents of Shem*, ch. xxviii. You may make your forgery itself as SAFE AS HOUSES.

HOUSE-BIT (or **-KEEPER**, or **-PIECE**), *subs.* (colloquial). — A servant-mistress.

HOUSE-DOVE, *subs.* (old).—A stay-at-home.

HOUSEHOLD-BRIGADE. TO JOIN THE HOUSEHOLD BRIGADE, *verb. phr.* (common).—To marry. For synonyms, *see* SPLICE.

1881. *Home Tidings*, April, p. 42, c. 1. Jem Ryan joined the HOUSEHOLD BRIGADE on Easter Monday, E. New acting as best man.

HOUSE OF CIVIL RECEPTION, *subs. phr.* (old).—A brothel. For synonyms, *see* NANNY-SHOP.

1785. GROSE, *Vulg. Tongue*, s.v.

HOUSE OF COMMONS (or **HOUSE OF OFFICE**), *subs. phr.* (old).—A W.C. For synonyms, *see* MRS. JONES.

1611. CHAPMAN, *May-Day*, iv., 2. No room save you turn out my wife's coal-house, and her other HOUSE OF OFFICE attached to it, reserved for her and me sometimes, and will you use it being a stranger?

1748. SMOLLETT, *Roderick Random*, c. xiii. Taking the candle in his hand, which he had left burning for the purpose, he went down to the HOUSE OF OFFICE.

d. 1780. ROBERTSON of Struan, *Poems*, 83. So to a HOUSE OF OFFICE straight a school-boy does repair, To ease his postern of its weight.

HOUSE-TAILOR, *sub.* (old). — An upholsterer.

1690. B. E., *Dict. Cant. Crew*, s.v. HOUSE-TAILERS, Upholsterers.

1725. *New Cant. Dict.*, s.v.

HOUSEWIFE (or **HUSWIFE**, or **HUSSY**), *subs.* (colloquial).—1. Primarily, a house-keeper. Hence (*a*) a domestic servant; (*b*) a wanton or a gad-about wench; and (*c*) a comic endearment. Hence, too, HOUSEWIFERY, *subs.*, and HOUSEWIFE'S TRICKS = the habit of wantonness, the practice of men.

1508. *Gawain and Gologras*, 'Ballade.' (PINKERTON, *Scottish Poems*, 1792, iii.). A gude HUSY-WIFE ay rinning in the toun.

1589. PUTTENHAM, *English Poesie*, 1589, ii., 16 (ed. ARBER, p. 148). Half lost for lack of a good HUSWIFE'S looking to.

1600. *Look about You*, sc. 28 (DODSLEY, *Old Plays*, 4th ed., 1875, vii., 476). HUSWIFE, I'll have you whipped for slandering me.

1602. SHAKSPEARE, *Twelfth Night*, i., 2. I hope to see some HOUSEWIFE take thee between her legs and spin it off.

1659. *Lady Alimony*, iii., 3 (DODSLEY, *Old Plays*, 4th ed., 1875, xiv., 331). And if the HUSSY challenge more, Charm the maundering gossip with your roar. *Idem.* iii., 6. (p. 340). If I make not these haxters as hateful to our HUSSIES as ever they were to us, their husbands, set me up for a Jack-a-Lent.

1672. RAY, *Proverbs*, s.v., CAT. Cats eat what HUSSIES spare

1673. WYCHERLY, *Gentleman Dancing Master*, iv., 1. What, HUSSY, would you not do as he'd have you?

1690. B. E., *Dict. Cant. Crew*, s.v.

1694. CONGREVE, *Double Dealer*, iv., 3. When I was of your age, HUSSY, I would have held fifty to one I could have drawn my own picture.

1697. VANBRUGH, *Æsop*, i., 1. Hark you HUSSY. You can give yourself airs sometimes, you know you can.

1708. MRS. CENTLIVRE, *The Busy-Body*, iv., 2. I'll charm you, HOUSEWIFE. Here lies the charm that conjured this fellow in.

1708. PRIOR, *Poems* (Aldine ed. ii., 270), 'The Insatiable Priest.' To suppress all his carnal desires in their birth At all hours a lusty young HUSSY is near.

1720. SWIFT, *Poems*, 'A Portrait' (CHALMERS, *English Poets*, 1810, xi., 448). A HOUSEWIFE in bed, at table a slattern.

1728. SWIFT, *Poems*, 'My Lady's Lamentations' (CHALMERS, *English Poets*, 1810, xi., 460). Consider before You come to threescore, How the HUSSIES will fleer Whene'er you appear.

1731. C. COFFEY, *The Devil to Pay*, i. Don't you know, HUSSY, that I am king in my own house.

1732. HENRY FIELDING, *The Mock Doctor*, i. Ay, HUSSY, a regular education; first at the charity-school where I learned to read.

1751. SMOLLETT, *Peregrine Pickle*, c. xviii. He supposed the object of his love was some paltry HUSSY, whom he had picked up when he was a boy at school.

d. 1764. LLOYD, *Poems* (1774), 'Chit-Chat.' Lud! I could beat the HUSSEY down, She's poured it all upon my gown.

1768. GOLDSMITH, *Good Natured Man*, ii. And you have but too well succeeded, you little HUSSY, you.

1771. SMOLLETT, *Humphrey Clinker* (ed. 1890, p. 43). And I have been twice in the bath with mistress and na'r a smock upon our backs, HUSSY.

1782. COWLEY, *Bold Stroke for a Husband*, i., 2. *Don C.* Now, HUSSY, what do you expect?

1785. GROSE, *Vulg. Tongue*, s.v.

1786. BURNS, *The Inventory*. Frae this time forth I do declare, I'se ne'er ride horse nor HIZZIE mair.

1822. SCOTT, *Fortunes of Nigel*, ch. xxii. Say nothing of that, HOUSEWIFE, ... or I will beat thee—beat thee with my staff.

1829. C. A. SOMERSET, *The Day After the Fair*, i. Oh, you HUSSY! so you were Madame Maypole!

1893. R. LE GALLIENNE, Intro. *Liber Amoris*, p. xliv. To think of poor Hazlitt gravely lavishing his choice Elizabethan quotations on the HUSSEY.

2. (venery). — The female *pudendum*. For synonyms, *see* MONOSYLLABLE.

HOUSEY, *adj.* (Christ's Hospital).— Belonging to the Hospital.

HOUSLE, *verb.* (Winchester College). —To hustle.

HOVELLER, *subs.* (nautical). — A beach-thief.

HOW. HOW CAME YOU SO? *phr.* (old). — Drunk. For synonyms, *see* DRINKS and SCREWED.

1824. T. HOOK, *Sayings and Doings*, 1st S. *Merton*, ch. xiii. Ould Mrs. Etherington was a right bad one; she used to be LORD, HOW COME YOU SO! every night, as regular as she went to bed.

HOW MUCH? *phr.* (common). —'What do you say?' 'What do you mean?' What price?— a general request for explanations.

1852. F. E. SMEDLEY, *Lewis Arundel*, ch. xxxiv. 'Then my answer must mainly depend on the exact height of the principles.' 'On the HOW MUCH?' inquired Frere, considerably mystified.

HOW ARE YOU OFF FOR SOAP, *phr.* (old).—A street catch.

1833. MARRYAT, *Peter Simple*. ch. iv. Well, Reefer, HOW ARE YOU OFF FOR SOAP?

1842. *Punch*, ii., 94, c. 2. Walker! HOW ARE YOU OFF FOR SOAP?

HOW THE BLAZES. *See* BLAZES.

HOW IS THAT FOR HIGH. *See* HIGH.

HOW'S YOUR POOR FEET, *phr.* (streets').—A street catch, of no particular meaning. *See* STREET CRIES.

1863. *All the Year Round*, x., 180. How's YOUR POOR FEET? a year ago cheated half the natives of Cockaigne into the belief that they were gifted with a special genius for repartee.

1863. G. A. SALA, *Breakfast in Bed*, p. 163 (1864). But how would you like a screeching multitude, fifty thousand strong, and with not one of whom, to the best of your knowledge, you had even a bowing acquaintance, to vociferate in your track—in the public street, mind—'Ya-a-a-h! HOW ARE YOUR POOR FEET?'

1890. *Town and Country* (Sydney), 11 Jan., p. 19, c. 4. Henry Irving's revival of 'The Dead Heart' has revived a bit of slang. . . . When the play was brought out originally, where one of the characters says, 'My heart is dead, dead, dead!' a voice from the gallery nearly broke up the drama with HOW ARE YOUR POOR FEET? The phrase lived.

HOW'LL YOU HAVE IT, *phr.* (common). — An invitation to drink. For synonyms, *see* DRINKS.

HOW WE APPLES SWIM (sometimes amplified by QUOTH THE HORSE-TURD)! *verb. phr.* (old). —Said in derision of a parvenu; of a person in better company than he (or she) has any right to keep; or of a pretender to honour or credit he (or she) does not deserve.

1670. RAY, *Proverbs*, s.v.

1697-1764. HOGARTH (Works by J. Ireland and J. Nichols, London, 1873) III., p. 29. And even this, little as it is, gives him so much importance in his own eyes, that he assumes a consequential air, sets his arms akimbo, and strutting among the historical artists cries, HOW WE APPLES SWIM.

1860. *Cornhill Mag.* (D. Mallett, *Tyburn*), Dec., p. 737. While tumbling down the turbid stream, Lord, love us, HOW WE APPLES SWIM.

HOWARD'S GARBAGE, *subs. phr.* (military).—The Nineteenth Foot. Also GREEN HOWARDS.

HOWARD'S GREENS, *subs. phr.* (military).—The Twenty-fourth Foot. [From its facings and its Colonel's name, 1717-37.]

HOW-DO-YOU-DO, *subs.* (colloquial). —A 'to do'; a 'kettle of fish'; a 'pass.'

1835. HALIBURTON, *Clockmaker*, 1 S., ch. xxvi. Thinks I, here's a pretty HOW DO YOU DO; I'm in for i now, that's a fact.

HOWLER, *subs.* (common).—An unblushing falsehood; an enormous blunder; a serious accident: and so forth. To COME (or GO) A HOWLER = to come to grief; to run amuck.

1885. *Daily News*, 16 May, p. 4, c. 8. Now, to speak respectfully of old scholars that were before us, the translators of the Bible constantly made what undergraduates call HOWLERS, or grievously impossible blunders.

1886. STEPHENS and YARDLEY, *Little Jack Sheppard*, p. 34. *Jack.* My dears, you're late. *Bess.* Our hansom came a HOWLER.

1888. *Indoor Paupers*, p. 24. As to how we are to spend the eight hours, or thereabouts, that remain after meals, church, and HOWLERS are disposed of, nobody, except ourselves and a few private friends outside, cares in the least.

1891. *Moonshine*, 14 Mar. Oh, *I* saw some piece in which a Johnnie smoked some cigarettes, and at last CAME A HOWLER, and wanted to commit suicide.

1891. *Pall Mall Gaz.*, 12 Sep., p. 2, c. 3. We wondered yesterday how many of our classical readers would see the HOWLER—or the joke.

HOWLING, *adj.* (common).—A general intensive. *E.g.*, HOWLING-SWELL = a man in the extreme of fashion; HOWLING-LIE = a gross falsehood; HOWLING-BAGS = trousers extravagant in cut or pattern; HOWLING-CAD, etc.

1865. G. A. SALA, *Trip to Barbary*, ch. vii. The hotel at Marseilles was full of our countrymen of the order known at Lane's and Limmer's as HOWLING SWELLS.

1887. *Household Words*, 11 June, 116. Let's hook it; that Jenny Morris is such an HOWLING SWELL that she won't wait for any one.

1889. *Licensed Vict. Gaz.*, 8 Feb. The Hon. Juggins was what is popularly known as a HOWLING SWELL.

1892. ANSTEY, *Model Music-Hall*, 146. And all the while your heart was given to a HOWLING CAD.

HOXTER, *subs.* (old).—1. An inside pocket.

1834. H. AINSWORTH, *Rookwood* bk. III., ch. v. No slour'd HOXTER my snipes could stay.

2. (Royal Military Academy). —Extra drill. [Corruption of extra.] Fr., *le bal.*

1887. BARRÈRE, *Argot and Slang*. The HOXTER consists in the painful ordeal of being compelled to turn out of bed at an early hour, and march up and down under the watchful eye of a corporal.

HOYS. *See* HOIST.

HOYT. *See* HOIT.

HUB, *subs.* (American).—1. Boston. Also, HUB OF THE UNIVERSE. [The description is Oliver Wendell Holmes's.] Since extended to other centres or chief cities (*see* quot. 1876).

1869. *Boston Herald*, Dec. He is to have a quintette club of amateurs with him, from THE HUB.

1872. *Daily Telegraph*, 4 July. Boston claims to be the HUB of the universe; but New York grandiloquently asserts itself to be the universal wheel itself.

1872. *Daily Telegraph*, Dec. The wealth of the HUB OF THE UNIVERSE, as Bostonians delight to call their city, is very great.

1876. *Daily News*, 18 Jan. Calcutta . . . . swaggers as if it were the HUB OF THE UNIVERSE.

1888. *Boston Daily Globe*. The typical girl of THE HUB has been much written about in the novels of the period, and without doubt she is worth all the attention bestowed upon her.

2. (colloquial).—A husband. *See* HUBBY.

HUBBLE-BUBBLE, *subs.* (colloquial). —1. *See* quots.

1748. F. DYCHE, *Dictionary* (5th Ed.). HUBBLE-BUBBLE (*s.*) a confused noise made by a talkative person, who speaks so quick, that it is difficult to understand what he says or means.

1811. *Lexicon Balatronicum*, s.v. HUBBLE-BUBBLE. Confusion. A HUBBLE BUBBLE fellow, a man of confused ideas, or one thick of speech, whose words sound like water bubbling out of a bottle.

2. (common).—A hookah; a pipe by which the smoke is passed through water.

1811. *Lexicon Balatronicum*, s.v. HUBBLE-BUBBLE . . . . Also an instrument used for smoaking through water in the East Indies, called likewise a caloon and hooker.

1868. OUIDA, *Under Two Flags*, ch. xxii. The Moor, warmly grateful, was ever ready to give him a cup of coffee and a HUBBLE-BUBBLE in the stillness of his dwelling.

1887. *Field*, 15 Oct. Off I went down the ravine, and half a mile below came to Besan quietly smoking his HUBBLE-BUBBLE.

1891. W. C. RUSSELL, *Ocean Tragedy*, p. 130. A burning atmosphere sickly with the smell of the incense of the HUBBLE-BUBBLE, with a flavour of hot curry about.

HUBBLE-DE-SHUFF, *adv.* (old).— Confusedly.—*Lex. Bal.*

HUBBUB, *subs.* (old: now recognised).—*See* quots.

d. 1639. ROBERT CAREY (Earl of Monmouth), *Memoirs*, 1759, p. 155. This made a great HUB-BUB in our Court.

1667. MILTON, *Paradise Lost*, ii., 951. A universal HUBBUB wild, Of stunning sounds.

1682. BUNYAN, *Holy War* (1893 ed. M. Peacock, p. 58). The conscience and understanding begin to receive conviction, and they set the soul in a HUBBUB.

1690. B. E., *Dict. Cant. Crew*, s.v. HUBBUB, a Noise in the Streets made by the Rabble.

1785. GROSE, *Vulg. Tongue*, s.v. HUBBUB, a noise, riot, or disturbance.

1893. *Westminster Gaz.*, 8 Aug., p. 2, col. 1. An indescribable HUBBUB of showmen's, hawkers', and children's voices from near and far.

HUBBY (or **HUB**), *subs.* (colloquial). —A husband.

1798. MORTON, *Secrets Worth Knowing*. Epilogue. The wife poor thing, at first so blithe and chubby, Scarce knows again her lover in her HUBBY.

1807. STEVENS, *Wks.*, p. 175. What could HUBBY do then, what could HUBBY do? But sympathy-struck, as she cry'd, he cry'd too.

1811. POOLE, *Hamlet Travestied*, ii., 3. Now, madam, this once was your HUBBY.

1883. *Referee*, 17 Apr., p. 3, c. 2. I did hear it whispered that her parents and guardians, or her horrified HUBBY, had turned the key on her.

HUCK, *verb.* (old).—To chaffer; to bargain.

1577. HOLINSHEAD, *Description of England*, ed. 1807, i., 315. It was his custome likewise to saie, if anie man HUCKED hard with him about the price of a gelding: 'So God helpe me . . . either he did cost me so much,' or else, 'By Jesus I stole him.'

HUCKLEBERRY. ABOVE ONE'S HUCKLEBERRY (BEND, or HOOK), *adv. phr.* (American).—Beyond one's ability; out of one's reach. *See* BEND.

1848. J. F. COOPER, *The Oak Openings*. It would be ABOVE MY BEND to attempt telling you all we saw among the red skins.

1852. '*L'Allegro*,' *As Good as a Comedy*, p. 61. Well, Squire Barry, you're a HUCKLEBERRY ABOVE MY PERSIMMON, but I reckon something can be done.

HUCKLE-MY-BUTT, *subs.* (old).— Beer, egg, and brandy made hot.

1785. GROSE, *Vulg. Tongue*, s.v.

1834. AINSWORTH, *Rookwood*, iii., 5. 'If that's a bowl of HUCKLE-MY-BUTT you are brewing, Sir William,' added he, addressing the knight of Malta, 'you may send me a jorum at your convenience.'

HUCKSTER, *subs.* (old: now recognised).—1. A retailer of small goods; a pedlar.

1690. B. E., *Dict. Cant. Crew*, s.v. HUCKSTER, the Retailers of the Market, who Sell in the Market at second Hand.

1785. GROSE, *Vulg. Tongue*, s.v. HUCKSTERS, itinerant retailers of provisions.

2. (old).—A mean trickster.

1690. B. E., *Dict. Cant. Crew*, s.v.

IN HUCKSTER'S HANDS, *adv. phr.* (old).—*See* quot.

1690. B. E., *Dict. Cant. Crew*, s.v. HUCKSTERS . . . . IN HUCKSTER'S HANDS, at a desperate Pass, or Condition, or in a fair way to be Lost.

HUCKSUM (also **HUCKLE**, or **HUCKLE-BONE**, or **HUCK-BONE**).—The hip.

c. 1508. DUNBAR, *Flyting* (*Poems*, ed. 1834, ii., 72). With HUCK-BONES harth and haw.

d. 1529. SKELTON, *Elynor Rummyn* (*Poems*, 1843, i.). The bones of her HUCKELS Lyke as they were buckels.

1575. STILL, *Gammer Gurton's Needle*, i., 3 (DODSLEY, *Old Plays*, 4th ed., 1875, iii., 180). For bursting of her HUCKLE-BONE, or breaking of her shin.

HUDDLE, *verb.* (venery).—To copulate. For synonyms, *see* GREENS and RIDE.

HUE, *verb.* (old).—*See* quot.

1690. B. E., *Dict. Cant. Crew*, s.v. The Cove was HUED in the Naskin, the Rogue was severely Lasht in Bride wel

1785. GROSE *Vulg. Tongue*, s.v.

HUEY, *subs.* (Old Cant).—A town or village.

1851-61. H. MAYHEW, *Lond. Lab. and Lond. Poor*, vol. I., p. 231. 'Where do you stall to in the HUEY?' which, fairly translated, means, 'Where do you lodge in the town?'

HUFF, *subs.* (colloquial).—1. An outburst of temper; peevishness; offence at some real or imaginary wrong or slight. Hence, TO GET (or TAKE) THE HUFF = to fly into a passion.

1599. H. PORTER, *Two Angry Women of Abingdon* (DODSLEY, *Old Plays*, 4th ed., 1875, vii., 311). And as thou say'st to me, to him I said, But in a greater HUFF and hotter blood.

1676. ETHEREGE, *Man of Mode*, *Wks.* (1704), i., 190. Tax her with the next fop that comes Into my head, and in A HUFF march away.

1688. SHADWELL, *Sq. of Alsatia*, *Wks.* (1720), iv., 63. If you were not the brother to my dearest friend, I know what my honour would prompt me to [*walks in a* HUFF].

1700. FARQUHAR, *Constant Couple*, ii., 2. I offer'd her fifty guineas, and she was in her airs presently, and flew away in A HUFF.

1705-7. WARD, *Hudibras Redivivus*, vol. II., pt. iv., p. 26. I pay'd three Shillings, in A HUFF, For my half Pint of liquid Stuff.

1759-67. STERNE, *Tristram Shandy*, ch. xxix. He left off the study of projectiles in a kind of HUFF, and betook himself to the practical part of fortification only. *Idem.* ch. c. Can I? cried Susannah, shutting the door in a HUFF.

1769. CHATTERTON, *Poems*, 'Journal' (CHALMERS, *English Poets*, 1810, xv., 495). 'Sir,' quoth the Rector in a HUFF.

1777. SHERIDAN, *Trip to Scarborough*, i., 1. The lady not condescending to give me any serious reasons for having fooled me for a month, I left her IN A HUFF.

1825. NEAL, *Bro. Jonathan*, bk. II., ch. 16. What a HUFF you're at! I only axed a question.

1855. THACKERAY, *Newcomes*, ch. xx. He is as proud as Lucifer, he is always taking HUFF about one thing or the other.

1855. BROWNING, *Men and Women* 'Fra Lippo Lippi' (Ed. 1864, p. 357) You'll not mistake an idle word Spoke in A HUFF by a poor monk?

1885. T. E. BROWN, *The Doctor*, p. 30. Already my goodness! he's TAKING THE HUFF.

1892. ANSTEY, *Model Music-Hall*, 37. Some parties IN A HUFF rage At the plea for Female Suffrage.

2. (old).—A bully; a HECTOR (*q.v.*); a sharper. Also CAPTAIN HUFF.

1569. PRESTON, *Cambises* (DODSLEY, *Old Plays*, 4th ed., 1875, iv., 177). [Enter three ruffians, HUFF, Ruff, and Snuff.]

1680. COTTON, *Complete Gamester*, p. 333. HUFFS, hectors, setters, gilts pads, biters, etc.

1690. B. E., *Dict. Cant Crew*, s.v.

1693. CONGREVE, *Old Bachelor*, iv., 9. Good, slovenly CAPTAIN HUFF, Bluffe (what is your hideous name?).

1785. GROSE, *Vulg. Tongue*, s.v.

3. (common).—A dodge; a trick.

4. (draughts').—A term in the game of draughts; the penalty for not taking a piece.

5. (Winchester College).—*See* HUFF-CAP.

Verb. (colloquial). — 1. To bluster; to bounce; to swagger.

1607. *How a Man May Choose a Good Wife*, etc., iv., 3 (DODSLEY, *Old Plays*, 4th ed., 1875, ix., 78). A HUFFING wench i' faith.

1630. TAYLOR, *Workes*. The smell is the senting bawd, that HUFFS and snuffs up and downe, and hath the game alwayes in the winde. *Ibid.* One asked a HUFFING gallant why hee had not a looking-glasse in his chamber; he answered, he durst not, because hee was often angry, and then he look'd so terribly that he was fearefull to looke upon himselfe.

d. 1631. DONNE, *Satires*, iv. (CHALMERS, *English Poets*, 1810, v., 158). To th' HUFFING, braggart, puffed nobility

1643. RANDOLPH, *Muses Looking-Glasse*, i., 1. *Flowrd.* Iniquity aboundeth, though pure zeal Teach, preach, HUFFE, puffe, and snuffe at it, yet still, Still it aboundeth.

1673. WYCHERLEY, *Gentleman Dancing Master*, v., 1. How! my surly, HUFFING, jealous, senseless, saucy master.

1675. WYCHERLEY, *Country Wife.* 'Prologue.' Well, let the vain rash fop, by HUFFING so, Think to obtain the better terms of you.

1680. DRYDEN, *Prol. to Lee's Cæsar Borgia*, p. 29. So big you look, though claret you retrench, That, armed with bottled ale, you HUFF the French.

d. 1680. ROCHESTER, *Poems*, 'Woman's Honour' (CHALMERS, *English Poets*, 1810, viii., 239). This HUFFING honour domineers In breasts when he alone has place.

1682. BUNYAN, *Holy War* (ed. M. Peacock, 1803, p. 72). He refused and HUFFED as well as he could, but in heart he was afraid.

1690. B. E., *Dict. Cant. Crew*, s.v HUFF. To HUFF AND DING, to bounce and swagger.

1690. *The Pagan Prince.* And the same threats and menaces of the palatine being carry'd to the marshal de Tonneure, notwithstanding all his former encomiums, Oh! quo he, the palatine's a young prince; give him leave to HUFF AND DING for his living; words break no bones: when all's done, 'tis the coach wheel, not the fly that raises the dust.

1699. ROBERT FRANCK, *Northern Memoirs* (quoted in *New Review*, Aug., 1893, p. 145). So HUFFED away.

1700. MRS. CENTLIVRE, *Perjured Husband.* 'Epilogue.' Let cowards cease to HUFF.

1705. WARD, *Hudibras Redivivus*, vol. I., pt. iii., p. 14. And in their frenzy, HUFF and threaten With what sad stripes we shall be beaten.

1708. PRIOR, *Poems*, 'The Mice.' (Aldine ed. ii., 244, 50). One went to Holland where they HUFF folk, T'other to vend his wares in Suffolk.

1714. *Newest Academy of Compliments.* Pray neighbour, why d'ye look awry? You're grown a wondrous stranger; You HUFF, you pout, you walk about As tho' you'd burst with anger.

1719. DURFEY, *Pills*, etc., i., 283. Thus, thus I strut and HUFF. *Idem.*, i., 154. But when the new ones did stoop, The t'other as HUFFING would be. *Idem.*, v., 99. When Bullies leave HUFFING and Cowards their Trembling.

1725. SWIFT, *Poems*, 'A New Song' (CHALMERS, *English Poets*, 1810, xi., 446). If he goes to the baker's the baker will HUFF, And twenty pence ask for a two-penny loaf.

d. 1742. SOMERVILLE, *Occasional Poems*, 'The Officious Messenger' (CHALMERS, *English Poets*, 1810, xi., 206). Her ladyship began to HUFF.

1785. GROSE, *Vulg. Tongue*, s.v.

2. To anger; TO CHEEK (*q.v.*); to get angered.

1708. MRS. CENTLIVRE, *The Busy-Body*, iii., 4. Impossible, without he HUFFS the lady, and makes love to Sir Francis.

1835. MARRYAT, *Jacob Faithful*, ch. xiii. Upon this she HUFFS outright, and tells Tom he may go about his business, for she didn't care if she never sees him no more.

1839. W. H. AINSWORTH, *Jack Sheppard*, p. 133 (Ed. 1840). If they *do*, now and then, run away with a knocker, paint a sign, beat the watch, or HUFF a magistrate.

Intj. (obsolete). — *See* quots. Also HUFFA and HUFFA-GALLANT. [Probably the oldest form of the word.]

c. 1510. RASTELL, *Four Elements* (DODSLEY, *Old Plays*, 4th ed., 1875, i., 20). With HUFFA GALLANT, tirl on the berry, And let the wide world wind.

c. 152(?). *Hick Scorner* (DODSLEY, *Old Plays*, 4th ed., 1875, i., 188). HUFF! HUFF! HUFF! who sent after me.

d. 1529. SKELTON, *Poems*, 'Against Garnesche' (DYCE, i., 118, and note ii., 181-2). HUF A GALANTE, Garneysche, loke on your comely ars.

TO STAND THE HUFF, *verb. phr.* (old).—To stand the reckoning.—*Lex. Bal.*

Also HUFFY = easily offended; HUFFED = annoyed; HUFFILY = testily; in a tantrum.

1825. NEAL, *Bro. Jonathan*, bk. II., ch. 15. A leetle on the HUFFY order, I guess! Aint you?

1852. H. B. STOWE, *Uncle Tom's Cabin*, ch. xvi. I . . . . actually was so cruel as to restrict him to one dozen of my cambric handkerchiefs. Dolph was particularly HUFFY about it, and I had to talk to him like a father to bring him round.

1853. LYTTON, *My Novel*, bk. I., ch. ix. Though the Squire was inclined to be very friendly to all his neighbours, he was, like most country gentlemen, rather easily HUFFED.

1873. MISS BROUGHTON, *Nancy*, ch. xxxvi. 'I have no doubt you would!' say I, turning sharply and HUFFILY away.

1875. OUIDA, *Signa*, vol. II., ch. xx., p. 324. 'She is a stupid little mule,' thought the old woman, angrily. 'She feels nothing, she sees no greatness in it all—she is only good to grub amongst her cabbages.' And she went away HUFFED.

1885. T. E. BROWN, *The Doctor*, p. 31. HUFFED is he, eh? And who regards him?

HUFF-CAP (or **HUFF**), *subs.* (Old Cant: still in use at Winchester College).—1. Strong ale. ['From inducing people to set their caps in a bold and HUFFING style.'—NARES.]

1579. FULWELL, *Art of Flattery.* Commonly called HUFCAP, it will make a man look as though he had seene the devil.

1586. HOLINSHED, *Description of England.* These men hale at HUFF-CAP till they be red as cockes, and little wiser than their combes.

1602. CAMPION, *English Poesy* (BULLEN, *Works*, 1889, p. 247). Hunks detests when HUFFCAP ale he tipples.

1614. GREENE, *Looking-Glass* [Dyce], p. 127. The ale is strong ale, 'tis HUFCAP; I warrant you, 'twill make a man well.

1630. TAYLOR, *Wks.* And this is it, of ale-houses and innes, Wine-marchants vintners, brewers, who much wins By others losing, I say more or lesse, Who sale of HUFCAP liquor doe professe.

1870. MANSFIELD, *School Life*, p. 180. Washed down by libations of HUFF.

1878. ADAMS, *Wykehamica*, s.v. HUFF, the strong ale brewed by the College.

2. (old).—A swaggering bully; a HECTOR (*q.v.*).

1596. NASHE, *Lenten Stuffe* (GROSART, *Works*, v., 306). The HUFF-CAPPES to drink in that house, thou shalt be sure of always.

1630. TAYLOR, *Wks.* But 'tis a maxime mortals cannot hinder, The doughty deeds of Wakefield's HUFFE-CAP Pinder Are not so pleasant as the faire Aurora, When Nimrod rudely plaid on his bandora.

1687. CLIFFORD, *Notes upon Dryden*, letter 2. Prethee tell me true, was not this HUFF-CAP once the Indian emperour, and at another time did not he call himself Maximine?

1706. FARQUHAR, *Recruiting Officer*, v., 6. You have made a fine speech good Captain HUFF-CAP.

Adj. (old). — Swaggering; blustering; rousing.

1597. HALL, *Satires*, i., 3. Graced with HUFF-CAP terms and thundering threats.

HUFFER, *subs.* (old).—A swaggerer.

1682. BANKS, *Vertue Betrayed*, Prol. lines 23-4. Welcome mask-teazer, peevish gamster, HUFFER: All fools, but politicians, we can suffer.

1770. LORD HAILES, *Ancient Scottish Poetry*, note on 'Seven Deadly Sins,' line 34. HUFFERS (or threateners), boasters, and they who pick quarrels.

HUFFLE, *verb.* (venery).—1. TO BAGPIPE (*q.v.*).

2. (colloquial).—To shift; to hesitate; to waver.

HUFF-SNUFF, *subs.* (old).—A person apt to take offence.

1592. NASHE, *Strange News*, etc. (GROSART, *Works* ii., 184). Gabriel HUFFE-SNUFFE Knowne to the world for a foole, and clapt in the Fleete for a poet.

1598. FLORIO, *A Worlde of Wordes*' s.v. *Risentito.* . . Also a HUFFE SNUFFE' one that will soone take pepper in the nose, that will revenge euerie small matter.

1750. OZELL, *Rabelais*, iv., pref. xxiii. Freebooters, desperadoes, and bullying HUFF-SNUFFS.

HUFTIE-TUFTIE, *adj.* (old).—Swaggering; gallant.

1596. NASHE, *Saffron Walden* (GROSART, *Works*, iii., 106). Came a ruffling it out, HUFTIE-TUFTIE, in his velvet suit.

1599. NASHE, *Lenten Stuffe*, (GROSART, *Works*, v., 250). HUFTIE-TUFTIE youthful ruffling comrades, wearing every one three yards of feathers in his cap for his mistres' favour.

HUG, *subs.* (thieves').—GARROTTING (*q.v.*). Also *verbally*, and TO PUT ON THE HUG.

1864. *Home Magazine*, 16 Mar. Hoax upon hoax about the putting on THE HUG was played off upon a credulous and bugbear-loving community.

2. (old).—The sexual embrace. For synonyms, *see* GREENS and RIDE. Also THE CLOSE HUG.

1659. *Lady Alimony*, ii., 'Prologue' (DODSLEY, *Old Plays*, 4th ed., 1875, xiv., 288). Apt for a spousal HUG.

1719. DURFEY, *Pills*, etc., iv., 163. They've a new drug Which is called THE CLOSE HUG.

Verb. (colloquial). — Properly to grapple with and hold the body, as a bear with his fore-paws. Hence (1) to cuddle; and (2) to perform the sexual embrace (*see subs.*, sense 2). Hence, also, TO HUG BROWN BESS (*q.v.*); TO HUG THE GUNNER'S DAUGHTER = to cuddle a gun for punishment; TO HUG THE GROUND = to fall, or be hit off one's legs; TO GIVE THE HUG (pugilists) = to close with and grapple the body; TO HUG THE SHORE (or BANK. or WALL) to keep close to; CORNISH HUG = a hold in wrestling; TO HUG A BELIEF (or DELUSION, or THOUGHT) = to cherish; TO HUG ONE'S CHAINS = to delight in captivity.

1696. LANDSDOWNE, *Poems*, 'Prologue to *The She-Gallants*' (CHALMERS, *English Poets*, 1810, xi., p. 36). Then, like some pensive statesman, treads demure, And smiles and HUGS to make distinction sure.

1602. CAMPION, *English Poesy* (BULLER, *Works*, 1889, p. 249). Changed is Helen. Helen HUGS the stranger.

1631. DRAYTON, *The Mooncalf* (CHALMERS, *English Poets*, 1810, iv., 133). HUG him, and swear he was her only joy.

1637. BEAUMONT and FLETCHER, *Elder Brother*, iv., 1. This night I'll HUG my Lilly in my arms.

d. 1649. DRUMMOND, *Posthumous Poems*, 'Of a Kiss.' Nor her who had the fate Ravis'd to be and HUGGED on Ganges' shore.

1659. *Lady Alimony*, iv. (DODSLEY, *Old Plays*, 4th ed., 1875, xiv., 288a). Shall we HUG none of our own, But such as drop from the frigid zone.

c. 1708. W. KING, *The Art of Love*, Pt. iv. (CHALMERS, *English Poets*, 1810, ix., 266). Then HUGGING her in brawny arm.

d. 1710. R. DUKE, *Poems*, 'A Song' (CHALMERS, *English Poets*, 1810, ix., 224. Close HUGS the charmer, and ashamed to yield, Though he has lost the day yet keeps the field. *Idem.* She HUGS the dart that wounded her, and dies.

d. 1742. SOMERVILLE, *Occasional Poems*, etc., 'The Fortune-Hunter,' canto iii. (CHALMERS, *English Poets*, 1810, xi., 221. Drinks double bub with all his might And HUGS his doxy every night.

1746. SMOLLETT, *Advice*, line 4. We'll HUG the curse that not one joy can boast.

d. 1764. LLOYD, *Poems* (1774), '*The Cit's County Box.*' HUGGING themselves in ease and clover.

d. 1773. G. CUNNINGHAM, *Poems*, 'Holiday-Gown' (CHALMERS, *English Poets*, 1810, xiv., 441). He HUGS me so close, and he kisses so sweet.

1791. *Antient and Modern Scottish Songs*, 'My Jockey is a Bonnie Lad,' ii., 325. And then he fa's a kissing, clasping, HUGGING, squeezing, tousling, pressing, winna let me be.

d. 1796. BURNS, *The Jolly Beggars.* And at night in barn or stable, HUG our doxies on the hay.

HUGGER-MUGGER, *subs.* (colloquial). —Muddle; confusion.

1868. C. READE, *Foul Play*, ch. vii. Why didn't you tell me, and I'd have tidied the room: it is all HUGGER-MUGGER, with miss a leaving.

1885. T. E. BROWN, *The Doctor*, p. 36. And every place as neat as a pin, And couldn't stand no HUGGER-MUGGER.

1892. *Pall Mall Gaz.*, 28 Oct., p. 2, c. 2. He wrote some lampoons in the papers at the time, in which he ridiculed the HUGGER-MUGGER of the prosecution.

Adv. (old).—*See* quots.

1690. B. E., *Dict. Cant. Crew*, s.v. HUGGER-MUGGER, Closely or by Stealth, Underboard: *To eat so*, that is, to Eat by one's self.

1785. GROSE, *Vulg. Tongue*, s.v. HUGGER-MUGGER, by stealth, privately, without making an appearance; they spent their money in a HUGGER-MUGGER way.

Adj. (common). — Confused; disorderly; hap-hazard; HAND-TO-MOUTH (*q.v.*).

1882. *Daily Telegraph*, 5 Oct., p. 2, c. 2. Nor can they be very severely blamed for this HUGGER-MUGGER, slipshod way of life.

Verb. (common).—To meet by stealth; to lay heads together.

1879. JUSTIN MCCARTHY, *Donna Quixote*, ch. xxxii. I can see already that she won't stand much more of you and me HUGGER-MUGGERING together.

IN HUGGER-MUGGER, *adv. phr.* (old).—1. In secret.

1565. STAPLETON, *Fort. of the Faith*, fol. 88. They should not have lurked all this while IN HUCKER-MUCKER.

1588. J. UDALL, *Demonstration of Discipline*, p. 30. (ed. Arber). The Byshop without any lawfull election, is chosen IN HUGGERMUGER of the canons, or prebendaries onely, without the knowledge of the people.

1594. NASHE, *Unfortunate Traveller* (GROSART, *Works*, v., 19). Myself that am but a poore childish wel-willer of yours, with the vain thought that a man of your desert and state by a number of pesants and varlets should be so incuriously abused in HUGGER-MUGGER haue wept al my vrine upward.

1596. NASHE, *Saffron Walden* (GROSART, *Works*, iii., 181). Hee sent her 18 pence IN HUGGER MUGGER, to pay the fiddlers.

1596. SHAKSPEARE, *Hamlet*, iv., 5. *King.* . . . . We have done but greenly, IN HUGGER-MUGGER to inter him.

1602. DEKKER, *Satiromastix*, iii., 133 (DODSLEY. *Old Plays*, viii., 48). One word, sir Quintilian, in HUGGER-MUGGER.

1607. TOURNEUR, *Revenger's Trag*, (DODSLEY, *Old Plays*, 4th ed., 1875), v., i. And how quaintly he died, like a politician, in HUGGER-MUGGER.

1611. CORYAT, *Crud.*, ii., p. 251, repr. So these perhaps might sometimes have some furtive conversation IN HUGGER MUGGER.

1633. FORD, *'Tis Pity She's a Whore*, ii., 1. There is no way but to clap up a marriage IN HUGGER-MUGGER.

1639-61. *Rump Songs*, i. [1662], 54. They brought me Gold and Plate in HUGGAR-MUGGAR.

1663. BUTLER, *Hudibras*, i., 3. Where'er th' in HUGGER-MUGGER lurk, I'll make them rue their handy-work.

1762. CHURCHILL, *The Ghost*, bk. iii., line 27. It must not, as the Vulgar say, Be done IN HUGGER MUGGER way.

1815. *Mirror for Mag.*, p. 457. For most that most things knew, IN HUGGER-MUGGER utter'd what they durst.

HUGGING, *subs.* (common).—GAROTTING (*q.v.*).

HUGSOME, *adj.* (colloquial).—Carnally attractive; FUCKABLE (*q.v.*).

HULK (HULKY, or HULKING Fellow), *subs.* (colloquial).—A fat person; a big lout. Generally, 'great hulk of a fellow.'

d. 1631. DRAYTON, *The Mooncalf* (CHALMERS, *English Poets*, 1810, iv., 126). Wallowing she lay, like to a boist'rous HULK Dropsied with humours.

1698. WARD, *London Spy*, Pt. xiv., p. 324. Up in the Chimney Corner sat a great HULKING Fellow.

1748. T. DYCHE, *Dictionary* (5th Ed.). HULK (s.) . . . . also a lazy, dronish fellow.

1785. GROSE, *Vulg. Tongue*, s.v. HULKEY, or HULKING, a great HULKEY fellow, an overgrown clumsy lout, or fellow.

1858. G. ELIOT, *Mr. Gilfil's Love-Story*, ch. ii. When you've got . . . . some great HULKY fellow for a husband, who swears at you and kicks your children.

1870. *Chambers's Journal*, 9 July, p. 447. He sees a slouching, shambling, HULK of a fellow standing listlessly in a doorway.

1871. G. ELIOT, *Middlemarch*, ch. lvi. I want to go first and have a round with that HULKY fellow who turned to challenge me.

1883. A. DOBSON, *Old-World Idylls*, p. 164. I'd like to give that HULKING brute a hit—Beating his horse in such a shameful way!

1893. *National Observer*, 29 July, p. 267, col. 2. The absolute ascendancy exercised by a small but brilliant member . . . . over a HULKING Junior.

Verb (colloquial). — To hang about; to MOOCH (*q.v.*).

HULL BETWEEN WIND AND WATER, *verb. phr.* (venery). — To possess a woman. For synonyms, *see* GREENS and RIDE.

HULL-CHEESE, *subs.* (Old Cant).— *See* quot. For synonyms, *see* SWIPES.

1622. TAYLOR, *A Very Merry Wherry-Ferry* (HINDLEY, *Works*, 1872), 19. Give me HULL-CHEESE, and welcome and good cheer. *Ibid.* HULL-CHEESE, is much like a loafe out of a brewers basket, it is composed of two simples, mault and water, in one compound, and is cousin germane to the mightiest ale in England.

HULVERHEAD, *subs.*, and **HULVER-HEADED**, *adj.* (old).—*See* quots. For synonyms, *see* BUFFLE and CABBAGE-HEAD.

1690. B. E., *Dict. Cant. Crew*, s.v. HULVER-HEAD, a silly Foolish fellow.

1785. GROSE, *Vulg. Tongue*, s.v. HULVER HEADED, silly, puzzle-pated.

HUM, *subs.* (Old Cant).—1. A kind of strong liquor: probably a mixture of beer and spirits, but *see* quot. 1690. Also HUM-CAP.

1616. BEN JONSON, *Devil's an Ass*, i., 1. Carmen Are got into the yellow starch, and chimney sweepers To their tobacco, and strong waters, HUM, Meath, and Obarni.

1619. FLETCHER, *Wild Goose Chase* ii., 3. Lord, what should I ail? What a cold I have over my stomach; would I'd some HUM.

1622. FLETCHER, *Beggars' Bush*, ii., 1. Except you do provide me HUM enough, And lour to bouze with.

d. 1645. HEYWOOD, *Drunkard*, p.48 [Gifford]. Notwithstanding the multiplicity of wines, yet there be stills and limbecks going, swetting out aqua vitæ and strong waters, deriving their names from cinnamon, balm, and aniseed, such as stomach-water, HUMM, etc.

1690. B. E., *Dict. Cant. Crew*, s.v. HUM-CAP, old, mellow and very strong Beer.

1785. GROSE, *Vulg. Tongue*, s.v.

2. (common). — A trick; a delusion; a cheat. Also a lie.

1756. *The World*, No. 164. Now if this be only a HUM (as I suppose it is) upon our country apes, it being blown in the *World* will put an end to it.

d. 1764. LLOYD, *Poems* (1774), 'A Tale.' There, my good critics, lies the HUM.

1806. LAMB, *Letters* in *Wks.* (Ed. 1852), ch. v., p. 81. I daresay all this is HUM!

1820. REYNOLDS (P. Corcoran), *The Fancy*, 'King Tims the First.' You or your son have told a bouncing HUM.

1823. BEE, *Dict. Turf*, s.v. HUM —a whispered lie.

1837. BARHAM, *Ingoldsby Legends*, 'Row in an Omnibus Box.' It's 'No Go!'—it's 'Gammon!'—it's 'all a HUM!'

1848. *Punch*, vol. XIV., p. 37. 'Ye Frenche Goe Uppe to London.' That ye French threats were all bouncing, That ye muster was a HUM, And they'd never dare to come.

1885. T. E. BROWN, *The Doctor*, p. 49. A HUM and a huff, And none o' the real stuff.

1892. MILLIKEN, *'Arry Ballads*, p. 76. Married life may be ticketed honey, but I know it's more of a HUM.

3. (old).—*See* quot.

1725. *New Cant. Dict.*, s.v.

1785. GROSE, *Vulg Tongue*, s.v. HUMS, persons at church; there is a great number of HUMS in the autem, there is a great congregation in the church.

Verb (old).—1. To cheat; to bamboozle; TO QUIZ (*q.v.*).

1762. GOLDSMITH, *Life of Nash*, in *Wks.*, p. 552 (Globe). Here Nash, if I may be permitted the use of a polite and fashionable phrase, was HUMM'D.

1764-1817. J. G. HOLMAN, *Abroad and at Home*, i., 3. *Ser.* It is queer enough that his father, Sir Simon Flourish, should be HUMMED so as to think he is going the tour of Europe, when, all the while, he never got a step farther than St. George's Fields.

1785. GROSE, *Vulg. Tongue*, s.v.

1811. POOLE, *Hamlet Travestied*, iii., 1. Go seek him there: I fear he's only HUMMING.

1819. MOORE, *Tom Crib*, p. 4. While you HUM the poor spoonies with speeches so pretty,

d. 1840. MAD. D'ARBLAY, *Diary*, ii., 153 [ed. 1842]. I don't mean to cajole you hither with the expectation of amusement or entertainment; you and I know better than to HUM or be HUMMED in that manner.

1856. ELLIOTT, *Carolina Sports*, p. 122. I HUMMED him, my stripping was all a feint.

2. (old).—To mumble.

d. 1842. MAGINN, *Vidocq Versified.* To hear Old Cotton HUMMING his pray.

TO HUM AND HAW, *verb. phr.* (colloquial). — To hesitate, to raise objections.

1469. *Paston Letters*, II., 347 (Ed. Gairdner). He wold have gotyn it aweye by HUMYS and by HAYS, but I wold not so be answeryd.

1594. NASHE, *Unf. Traveller* (GROSART, *Wks.*, v., 96). Hee made no more HUMMING OR HAULTING, but in despite of her husbandes kinsfolkes, gaue her her *Nunc dimittis.*

1610. JONSON, *Alchemist*, iii., 2. You may be anything, and leave off to make Long-winded exercises; or suck up Your HA! and HUM! in a tune.

1614. JONSON, *Bartholomew Fair*, i., 1. A sober-drawn exhortation of six hours, whose better part was the HUM-HA-HUM.

1620. MASSINGER, *Fatal Dowry*, iv., 1. Do you stand HUMMING and HAHING now?

d. 1680. BUTLER, *Remains* (1759), ii., 103. He HUMS AND HAHS.

1690. B. E., *Dict. Cant. Crew*, s.v. HUM AND HAW, to Hesitate in Speech; also to delay, or difficultly to be brought to Consent.

1706. MRS. CENTLIVRE, *Love at a Venture*, iv., 2, *Wks.* (1872), i., 304. That was the first excuse that came at my tongue's end—and you know there is no HUMMING AND HAWING with my old master, sir.

1729. SWIFT, *Intelligencer*, No. 14, p. 165 (2nd Ed.). If any person . . . . shall presume to exceed six minutes in a story, to HUM OR HAW, use hyphens between his words, or digressions.

1785. GROSE, *Vulg. Tongue*, s.v.

1861. H. KINGSLEY, *Ravenshoe*, ch. vi. Lord Ascot HUMMED AND HAWED, and told him to tell his father he had been a good boy.

TO MAKE THINGS HUM, *verb. phr.* (American). — To force the pace; to keep moving.

1888. *San Francisco Weekly Exam.*, 23 Feb. Ever since he has taken the newspaper reins in San Francisco he has MADE THINGS HUM.

1890. *Punch*, 22 Feb. If I was flush of the ochre, I tell you I'd make the thing HUM.

1891. *Pall Mall Gaz.*, 28 Aug., p. 2, c. 3. With their advent things begin to HUM.

1893. W. T. STEAD, *Review of Reviews*, p. 152. In the opinion of both foes and friends we make things HUM.

TO HUM AROUND, *verb. phr.* (American).—To call to account; TO CALL OVER THE COALS (*q.v.*).

HUMAN, *subs.* (old: now American).—A human being. [Also HUMAN BOAR]. For synonyms, *see* COVE.

1719. DURFEY, *Pills*, etc., ii., 332. Mongst HUMANS by Court dunning.

1783-5. COWPER, *Task*, ii., line 105. And agonies of HUMAN and of brute.

1835. HALIBURTON, *Clockmaker*, 1 S., ch. xxviii. They have little hovels for their cattle . . . . and a house for THE HUMANS as grand as Noah's Ark.

1882. *Daily Telegraph*, 13 Dec., p. 2, c. 2. In the opening pages Mr. Matthew Arnold mourns in verse over the death of 'Poor Matthias,' who is not A HUMAN but a canary.

1888. *Denver Republican.* He was only a dog . . . . but was much more useful to society than many HUMANS.

HUMBER-KEELS. *See* BILLY-BOY.

HUMBLE PIE. TO EAT HUMBLE PIE, *verb. phr.* (colloquial).—To submit; to apologise; to knock under. For synonyms, *see* CAVE IN.

1862. THACKERAY, *Philip*, xxvii. If this old chief had to eat HUMBLE PIE, his brave adversaries were anxious that he should gobble up his portion as quickly as possible, and turned away their honest old heads as he swallowed it.

1887. MANVILLE FENN, *This Man's Wife*, ch. ii., 4. Our savings are gone and we must EAT HUMBLE PIE for the future.

HUM-BOX, *subs.* (common).—1. A pulpit.

1725. *New Cant. Dict.*, s.v.

1785. GROSE, *Vulg. Tongue*, s.v.

1827. LYTTON, *Pelham*, p. 302 [Ed. 1862]. Well, you parish bull prig, are you for lushing Jacky, or pattering in the HUM-BOX?

1858. A MAYHEW, *Paved with Gold*, bk. III., ch. ix., p. 309. He was nicknamed the 'Amen bawler' (parson) and recommended to take to the HUM-BOX (pulpit) as better suited to him than cadging.

ENGLISH SYNONYMS:—Autem; cackle tub; clack loft; cowards' castle; gospel mill (also a church); wood.

2. (American).—An auctioneer's rostrum.

HUMBOX PATTERER, *subs.* (common).—A parson. For synonyms, *see* DEVIL DODGER and SKY PILOT.

1839. G. W. M. REYNOLDS, *Pickwick Abroad*, p. 223. Though the HUMBOX PATTERER talked of hell.

HUMBUG, *subs.* (old: now recognised).—1. A hoax; an imposture; a swindle.

1735-40. KILLIGREW, *The Universal Jester; or a pocket companion for the Wits: being a choice collection of merry conceits, facetious drolleries, &c., clenchers, closers, closures, bon-mots, and* HUMBUGS. [Title].

1754. *Connoisseur.* No. 14. Single words, indeed, now and then broke forth; such as — odious, horrible, detestable, shocking, HUMBUG. This last new-coined expression, which is only to be found in the nonsensical vocabulary, sounds absurd and disagreeable whenever it is pronounced.

1762. CHURCHILL, *The Ghost*, bk. I., line 72. And that Great Saint, we Whitefield call, Keeps up the HUMBUG Spiritual.

1785. GROSE, *Vulg. Tongue*, s.v.

1828. WEBSTER, *Eng. Dict.*, s.v.

2. Deceit; pretence; affectation.

1837. R. H. BARHAM, *Ingoldsby Legends.* (Ed. 1862). p. 239. That sort of address which the British call HUMBUG and Frenchmen '*Finesse.*' (It's 'Blarney' in Irish—I don't know the Scotch.)

1842. DOUGLAS JERROLD, *Bubbles of the Day*, i. Never say HUMBUG; it's coarse. *Sir P.* And not respectable. *Smoke.* Pardon me, my lord; it *was* coarse. But the fact is, HUMBUG has received such high patronage, that now it's quite classic.

3. A cheat; an impostor; a pretender. Also (old), HUMMER.

d. 1783. HENRY BROOKE, *Poems* (1776). 'On Humbugging.' (CHALMERS' *English Poets*, 1810, xvii., 428). Our HUMMERS in state, physic, learning, and law.

1823. BEE, *Dict. of the Turf*, s.v. HUM. He is a HUMBUG that has recourse to the meanness. He wishes to be a bugaboo, or most exalted fool.

1836. DICKENS, *Pickwick*, ch. xxx. 'You're a HUMBUG, sir.' 'A what?' said Mr. Winkle, starting. 'A HUMBUG, sir. I will speak plainer, if you wish it. An impostor, sir.'

Verb. To hoax; to swindle; to cajole.

1751. SMOLLETT, *Peregrine Pickle*, ch. lxxxv. He who seemed to be most afflicted of the two taking his departure with an exclamation of 'HUMBUGGED, egad!'

1785. GROSE, *Vulg Tongue*, s.v.

1826. *The Fancy*, ii., 77. We would not have the reader believe we mean to HUMBUG him—not for a moment.

1861. H. KINGSLEY, *Ravenshoe*, ch. xliii. She was always ready to help him, provided, as she told him, 'he didn't HUMBUG.'

Hence HUMBUGGING = hoaxing, swindling, or HUMBUGABLE = gullible. HUMBUGGERY = deception; imposture. HUMBUGGER = a cheat, a hoaxer.

d. 1763. HENRY BROOKE, *Poems* (1778), 'On Humbugging.' (CHALMERS, *English Poets*), 1810, xvii., 428). Of all trades or arts in repute or possession HUMBUGGING is held the most ancient profession. *Idem.* To you, . . . the HUMBUGGERS of hearts.

1822. SCOTT, *Fortunes of Nigel*, ch. xviii. The species of wit which has been long a favourite in the city, under the names of cross-biting, giving the dor, bamboozling, cramming, hoaxing, HUMBUGGING, and quizzing.

1825. SOUTHEY, *Letters*, iii., 488 [ed. Warter, 1856]. My charity does not extend so far as to believe that any reasonable man (HUMBUGGABLE as the animal is) can have been so humbugged.

1826. *The Fancy*, ii., 29. A contemporary writer of eminence some years ago termed such exhibitions HUMBUGGING.

1840. THACKERAY, *Paris Sketch Book*, p. 31. Do you not laugh, O Pharos of Bungay, at the continuance of a humbug such as this?—at the HUMBUGGING anniversary of a humbug?

1852. JUDSON, *Myst., etc., of New York* ch. iv. Oh, blast your HUMBUGGERY—talk plain English to me.

1855. THACKERAY, *Newcomes*, ch. v. When the old lady was gone, Mr. Hobson had no need of any more HUMBUGGING, but took his pleasure freely.

1883. MARK TWAIN, *Life on the Mississippi*, ch. xl., p. 369. Traces of its inflated language and other windy HUMBUGGERIES survive along with it.

HUMDRUM, *subs.* (old: now recognised).—1. A tiresome dullard; a steady-going, common-place person. *See* also quot. 1725.

1596. JONSON, *Every Man in His Humour*, i., 1. By gads-lid I scorn it, I, so I do, to be a consort for every HUMDRUM.

1725. *New Cant. Dict.*, s.v. HUMDRUMS or HUMS, a Society of Gentlemen, who meet near the *Charter-House*, or at the *King's Head* in St. *John's Street.* Less of mystery, and more of Pleasantry than the *Free Masons.*

1785. GROSE, *Vulg. Tongue*, s.v.

2. Monotony; tameness; dullness.

1823. *Hints for Oxford*, p. 63. Men of spirit must ever dislike the unleavened HUMDRUM of its monkish constitution.

1893. *The Nation*, 13 July, p. 32, col. 1. We go so far with the adorers of home and HUMDRUM.

3. (old).—The same as HUMBUG (*q.v.*).

1596. NASHE, *Saffron Walden* (GROSART, *Works*, iii., 14). Whereof generous Dick (without HUMDRUM be it spoken) I utterly despair of them.

4. (old).—A wife; also a husband.

Adj. Dull; tame; common-place; monotonous.

1702. VANBRUGH, *False Friend*, ii. A very HUMDRUM marriage this.

1705. WARD, *Hudibras Redivivus*, vol. I., pt. ii., p. 6. Tho' it is their HUMDRUM fashion To hate all musical precation.

1730. JAS. MILLER, *Humours of Oxford*, Act I., p. 7 (2nd Ed.). Your fellows of colleges are a parcel of sad, muzzy, HUMDRUM, lazy, ignorant old caterpillars.

d. 1764. LLOYD, *Poems* (1774), 'A Familiar Epistle.' So frothy, vapid, stale, HUMDRUM.

1765. C. SMART, *Fables*, xv., line 5. Content in HUMDRUM mood t'adjust Her matters to disperse the dust.

1774. FOOTE, *Cozeners*, i., 1. Not one, madam, of the HUMDRUM, drawling, long winded tribe.

1775. SHERIDAN, *Rivals*. ii., 1. Yet am I by no means certain that she would take me with the impediment of our friends' consent, a regular HUMDRUM wedding, and the reversion of a good fortune on my side.

d. 1823. BLOOMFIELD, *Poems*, 'Richard and Kate' (1825), p. 89. Come, Goody, stop your HUMDRUM wheel.

1825. HARRIET WILSON, *Memoirs*, iii., 237. You are, in fact, too constant for Paris. One has enough of all that HUM-DRUM stuff in England.

1849. THACKERAY, *Pendennis*, ch. lxi. The most fervent Liberals, when out of power, become HUMDRUM Conservatives, or downright tyrants or despots in office.

1863. ALEX. SMITH, *Dreamthorpe*, p. 23. Giddy people may think the life I lead here staid and HUMDRUM, but they are mistaken.

1893. *Standard*, 8 Aug., p. 4, col. 6. The thing, in his view, is to rattle off something pretentious, and avoid the HUMDRUM and tiresome methods which statesmanship of the pre-Home-Rule period used to respect.

HUMDURGEON, *subs.* (old).—1. An imaginary illness.—GROSE.

2. (common).—Needless noise; ado about nothing.

1815. SCOTT, *Guy Mannering*, ch. xxiii. I would never be making a HUMDUDGEON about a scart on the pow.

HUMDURGEONED, *adj.* (old). —Annoyed.

1830. LYTTON, *Paul Clifford*. Don't be HUMDURGEONED but knock down a gemman.

HUMGUFFIN (common).—A hobgoblin. Also a derisive address.

HUMGUMPTIOUS, *adj.* (obsolete).—*See* quot.

1823. BEE, *Dict. of the Turf*, s.v. HUM. A knowing sort of humbug is HUMGUMPTIOUS.

HUMMER, *subs.* (old).—1. *See* quot.

1690. B. E., *Dict. Cant. Crew*, s.v. HUMMER, a loud Lie, a Rapper.

1725. *New Cant. Dict.* s.v.

1748. T. DYCHE, *Dictionary* (5th Ed.). HUMMER (*s.*) a great, monstrous, or notorious lie.

1785. GROSE, *Vulg. Tongue*, s.v.

2. (American). — A man or woman of notable parts; a HIGH STEPPER (*q.v.*); a GOOD GOER (*q.v.*). *Cf.*, RUSTLER.

1889. *Ally Sloper*, 6 July. If Tootsie is anything as lively as the 'Gaiety Girls,' she must be a HUMMER.

1891. GUNTER, *Miss Nobody*, ch. xvii. I just wanted to see my Tillie dance once. She's a society HUMMER now.

3. (obsolete).—*See* HUMBUG, sense 3.

HUMMING, *adj.* (old). Strong—applied to drink; brisk—applied to trade; hard—applied to blows. HUMMING OCTOBER = the specially strong brew from the new season's hops; STINGO (*q.v.*).

1690. B. E., *Dict. Cant. Crew.* HUMMING *Liquor*, Double Ale, Stout, Pharoah.

1701. FARQUHAR, *Sir Harry Wildair*, iv., 2. The wine was HUMMING strong.

1736. FIELDING, *Don Quixote*, iii., 4. Landlord, how fares it? You seem to drive a HUMMING trade here.

1821. EGAN, *Tom and Jerry*, ch. vii. Let us fortify our stomachs with a slice or two of hung beef, and a horn or so of HUMMING stingo.

1822. SCOTT, *Fortunes of Nigel*, ch. xxiii. A HUMMING double pot of ale.

1837. BARHAM, *Ingoldsby Legends*. 'The Wedding Day.' A mighty magnificent tub Of what men, in our hemisphere, term 'HUMMING Bub,' But which gods—who, it seems, use a different lingo, From mortals, are wont to denominate 'Stingo.'

1864. DICKENS, *Our Mutual Friend*, bk. III., ch. vii. Wegg, in coming to the ground, had received a HUMMING knock on the back of his devoted head.

HUMP, *verb.* (common). — 1. To spoil; to botch; to do for.

1851-61. H. MAYHEW, *Lond. Lab. and Lond. Poor*, vol. i., p. 252. To HUMP in street parlance, is equivalent to 'botch,' in more genteel colloquialism.

2. (colonial).—To shoulder and carry. *E.g.*, TO HUMP ONE'S SWAG = to shoulder one's kit.

1886. *Daily Telegraph*, 1 Jan. Ladies whom I have met HUMPING their own drums.

1887. *All the Year Round*, 30 July, p. 66. A large blanket rolled up which contains the personal luggage of the man who carries or HUMPS it.

1887. G. A SALA in *Illus. Lon. News*, 12 Mar., 282/2. All kinds of luggage, generally speaking, which are manually carried, are at present said to be HUMPED. I have had to HUMP mine many a time and oft.

1888. ROLF BOLDREWOOD, *Robbery Under Arms*, ch. xxii. We HUMPED our saddles and swags ourselves.

1890. *Family Herald*, 8 Feb., p. 227. I was just debating whether I had better HUMP my drum.

3. (old).—*See* quot. For synonyms, *see* GREENS and RIDE.

1785. GROSE, *Vulg. Tongue*, s.v. HUMP, to HUMP. Once a fashionable word for copulation.

TO HUMP ONESELF, *verb. phr.* (American).—To stir; to prepare for attack; to fancy oneself.

1847. PORTER, *Quarter Race*, etc. p. 177. Ef thar are anything he HUMPS hisself on besides ugly, it is his manners among the fimmales.

1847. PORTER, *Big Bear*, etc., p. 126. He was breathin' sorter hard, his eye set on the Governor, HUMPIN' himself on politics

TO GET (or HAVE) THE HUMP, *verb. phr.* (common). — To be despondent, hurt, put out, DOWN IN THE MOUTH (*q.v.*). Also, TO HAVE THE HUMP UP or ON. For synonyms, *see* SNAGGY.

1599. NASHE, *Lenten Stuffe* (GROSART, *Works*, v., 267). So in HIS HUMPS about it . . . . that he had thought to have tumbled his hurrie-currie . . . . into the sea.

1885. *Punch*, 10 Jan., p. 24. I had GOT THE 'UMP, and no error, along o' Bill B. and that gal.

1892. ANSTEY, *Model Music-Hall*, 43. The company consume what will be elegantly referred to as 'a bit of booze.' Aunt Snapper GETS THE 'UMP.

1886. JEROME, *Idle Thoughts*, p. 14. 'Arry refers to the heavings of his wayward heart by confiding to Jimee that he has GOT THE BLOOMING HUMP!

HUMPEY, *subs.* (Australian).—*See* quot.

1893. GILBERT PARKER, *Pierre and his People*, p. 135. McGann was lying on his back on a pile of buffalo robes in a mountain hut. Australians would call it a HUMPEY.

HUMPHREY, *subs.* (American thieves').—A coat with pocket holes but no pockets.—MATSELL.

TO DINE WITH DUKE HUMPHREY. *See* DINE, SIR THOMAS GRESHAM, and KNIGHTS.

1592. NASHE, *Pierce Penilesse* [Grosart], ii., 18. I . . . . . retired me to Paules, TO SEEKE MY DINNER WITH DUKE HUMFREY.

1843. MONCRIEFF, *The Scamps of London*, i., 1. DINES oftener WITH DUKE HUMPHREY than anybody else, I believe.

HUMPTY-DUMPTY, *subs.* (colloquial).—1. A short and thick-set person; a GRUNDY (*q.v.*); a hunch-back. For synonyms, *see* FORTY GUTS.

1785. GROSE, *Vulg. Tongue*, s.v.

2. (old).—*See* quot. 1690.

1690. B. E., *Dict. Cant. Crew*, s.v. HUMPTEY DUMPTEY, Ale boild with Brandy.

1698. M. SORBIÈRE'S *Journey to London in the Year* 1698, p 135, quoted in *Notes and Queries*, 6 S., xii., 167. He answer'd me that he had a thousand such sort of liquors, as HUMTIE DUMTIE, Three Threads . . . .

1785. GROSE, *Vulg. Tongue*, s.v.

1837. DISRAELI, *Venetia*, i., 14. As for the beverage they drank HUMPTY-DUMPTY, which is ale boiled with brandy.

Adj. and *adv.* (colloquial).—Short and thick; all of a heap; all together.

HUM-STRUM. *subs.* (old). — *See* quot.

1785. GROSE, *Vulg. Tongue*, s.v. HUMSTRUM, a musical instrument made of a mopstick, a bladder, and some pack-thread, thence also called bladder and string, and hurdy gurdy; it is played on like a violin, which is sometimes ludicrously called a HUMSTRUM; sometimes instead of a bladder, a tin canister is used.

HUNCH, *verb.* (old: now colloquial). —To jostle; to shove; to squeeze. For synonyms, *see* RAMP.

1690. B. E., *Dict. Cant. Crew*, s.v. HUNCH, to justle, or thrust.

1712. ARBUTHNOT, *Hist. of John Bull*, Pt. III., App., ch. iii. Then Jack's friends began to HUNCH and push one another.

1738. SWIFT, *Polite Convers.*, Dial. 1. I was HUNCHED up in a hackney-coach with three country acquaintance.

1785. GROSE, *Vulg. Tongue*, s.v.

1847. PORTER, *Quarter Race*, etc., p. 163. I hadn't fairly got to sleep before the old 'oman HUNCHED me.

HUNG. *See* WELL-HUNG.

TO BE HUNG UP, *verb. phr.* (colloquial).—To come to a stand-still; to be in a fix.

1891. *Fun*, 10 June, p. 237. 'Ah! by Bendigo, I forgot! Grimmy's HUNG UP!' 'What, Grimmy? Never!'

HUNGARIAN, *subs.* (Old Cant).—1. A hungry man; a RARE PECKER (*q.v.*).

1608. DODSLEY, *Merry Devil of Edmonton* [*Old Plays*, v. 267]. Away, I have knights and colonels at my house, and must tend the HUNGARIANS.

1632. LUPTON, *London* ['Harl. Misc.'], ix., 314. The middle aile [of St. Paul's] is much frequented at noon with a company of HUNGARIANS, not walking so much for recreation as need.

2. (Old Cant).—A freebooter.

1608. *Merry Devil of Edmonton* [DODSLEY, *Old Plays*, v. 285]. Come, ye HUNGARIAN pilchers, we are once more come under the zona torrida of the forest.

1893. *National Observer*, 'Spoliation,' ix., 357. But, after all, it is only another note in the gamut of spoliation, whereof Mr. Gladstone's HUNGARIANS (a good old word that!) would have the mastery.

HUNK. TO BE (or GET) HUNK or ALL HUNK, *verb. phr.* (American). —1. To hit a mark; to achieve an object; to be safe. Also (2) to scheme. [From Dutch *honk* = goal or home.]

1847. DARLEY, *Drama in Pokerville*, p. 50. I'll allow you're just HUNK this time.

1893. *Detroit Free Press*, June 23, 'He Threatens to go back,' p. 3. I propose to have some of it, or I'll GET HUNK.

HUNKER (or **OLD HUNKER**), *subs.* (American).—In New York (1844) a Conservative Democrat, as opposed to the Young Democracy or BARN-BURNERS (*q.v.*). Hence, an anti-progressive in politics.

HUNKS, *subs.* (old).—A miser; a mean, sordid fellow; a curmudgeon. For synonyms, *see* SNIDE.

1602. DEKKER, *Satiro-Mastix*, in *Wks.* (1873), i., 201. *Blun.* Nay prethee deare Tucca, come you shall shake— *Tuc.* Not hands with great HUNKES there, not hands, but Ile shake the gull-groper out of his tan'd skinne.

1602. CAMPION, *English Poesy* (Works, BULLEN, 1889, p. 247). But it drinks up all: that HUNKS detestable.

1647-80. ROCHESTER, *Wks.*; p. 11. There was an old coveteous HUNKS in the neighbourhood, who had notwithstanding his age, got a very pretty young wife.

1677. WYCHERLEY, *Plain Dealer*, v., 2. Make a very pretty show in the world, let me tell you; nay, a better than your close HUNKS.

1690. B. E., *Dict. Cant. Crew*, s.v. HUNKS, a covetous Creature, a miserable Wretch.

1712. *Spectator*, No. 264. Irus has . . . . given all the intimations he skilfully could of being a close HUNKS with money.

1785. GROSE, *Vulg. Tongue*, s.v.

1837. MARRYATT, *Snarley-yow*, ch. 12. So while they cut their raw salt junks, With dainties you'll be cramm'd. Here's once for all my mind, OLD HUNKS, Port Admiral, you be dammed!

1839. BUCKSTONE, *Brother Tom* (DICK'S ed., p. 15). One calls him an OLD HUNKS, another a selfish brute.

1840. DICKENS, *Old Curiosity Shop*, ch. vii., p. 35. That you become the sole inheritor of the wealth of this rich old HUNKS.

1846. MELVILLE, *Moby Dick*, 75 (ed. 1892). Bildad, I am sorry to say, had the reputation of being an incorrigible old HUNKS.

1857. A. TROLLOPE, *Three Clerks*, ch. iii. I am sure he is a cross old HUNKS, though Mamma says he's not.

1893. THEODORE MARTIN, *Roman Elegies*, ii. (Goethe Society Trans., 1891-2, p. 72). Joys that he stints not his gold like the close HUNXES of Rome.

HUNKY, *adj.* (American).—Good; jolly; a general superlative. Also HUNKIDORUM.

d. 1867. BROWNE, 'Artemus Ward,' *The Shakers* (Railway ed.), p. 43. 'HUNKY boy! Go it my gay and festive cuss!'

1873. JUSTIN MCCARTHY. *Fair Saxon*, ch. xxxviii. The guard dies, but never surrenders! Fine, isn't it? But the HUNKY-boy that said that surrendered all the same.

1888. *Texas Siftings*, 20 Oct. Robert is all HUNKY, but he had a mighty close call the week before last.

HUNT, *verb.* (old). — To decoy a PIGEON (*q.v.*) to the tables. Hence HUNTING = card-sharping. FLAT-CATCHING (*q.v.*).

1690. B. E., *Dict. Cant. Crew*, s.v HUNTING (*c.*), decoying or drawing others into Play.

1785. GROSE, *Vulg. Tongue*, s.v.

TO HUNT FOR SOFT SPOTS, *verb. phr.* (American).—To make oneself comfortable; to seek one's ease.

1888. *San Francisco Weekly Examiner*, 22 Mar. It was demnition hot, and I commenced to HUNT FOR SOFT SPOTS in my saddle.

TO HUNT GRASS, *verb. phr.* (pugilists'). — To be knocked down; TO BE GRASSED (*q.v.*). Also, to be puzzled; to be dumfoundered.

1869. CLEMENS [Mark Twain], *Innocents at Home*, ch. ii. I HUNT GRASS every time.

TO HUNT LEATHER, *verb. phr.* (cricketers').—To field at cricket.

1892. *Cassell's Sat. Jour.*, 21 Sep. p. 13, c. 2. For nearly ten years I earned a living—and a good one—by 'wielding the willow' and HUNTING THE LEATHER.

TO HUNT THE DUMMY, *verb. phr.* (thieves').—To steal pocket books.

1878. CHARLES HINDLEY, *Life and Times of James Catnach*, p. 171. (Chorus)—Speak to the tattler, bag the swag, And finely HUNT THE DUMMY.

TO HUNT THE SQUIRREL, *verb. phr.* (old).—*See* quot.

1785. GROSE, *Vulg. Tongue*, s.v. HUNTING THE SQUIRREL, an amusement practised by post boys, and stage coachmen, which consists in following a one-horse chaise, and driving it before them, passing close to it so as to brush the wheel, and by other means terrifying any woman, or person that may be in it. A man whose turn comes for him to drink, before he has emptied his former glass, is said to be HUNTED.

IN, or OUT OF, THE HUNT, *adv. phr.* (colloquial).—Having a chance, or none; IN or OUT OF THE SWIM (*q.v.*). Admitted to, or outside, a circle or society.

HUNT-ABOUT, *subs.* (colloquial).—
1. A prying gossip.

2. (common). — A walking whore.

HUNT-COUNTER, *subs.* (old).—A beggar.

1623. SHAKESPEARE, *2 Henry IV.*, i., 2. You HUNT-COUNTER, hence! Avaunt!

HUNTERS. PITCHING THE HUNTERS, *verb. phr.* (costermongers'). See quot.

1851-61. MAYHEW, *Lond. Lab. and Lond. Poor*, i., 390. PITCHING THE HUNTERS is the three sticks a penny, with the snuff-boxes stuck upon sticks; if you throw your stick, and they fall out of the hole, you are entitled to what you knock off.

1876. HINDLEY, *Cheap Jack*, p. 235. When . . . . there was no cattle jobbing to be done, he would PITCH THE HUNTERS, that is, put up the 'three sticks a penny' business.

HURLY-BURLY, *subs.* (old: now colloquial). — A commotion; a bustle; an uproar.

c. 1509-1547. *Lusty Juventus* (DODSLEY, [*Old Plays*, 4th ed., 1874, ii., 85]. What a HURLY-BURLY is here! Smick smack, and all this gear!

1539. TAVERNIER, *Garden of Wysdom*, E. ii. verso. Thys kynge [Gelo] on a tyme exacted money of hys comons, whome when he perceuyed in a HURLY BURLY for the same, and ready to make an insurrection, he thus sodaynly appeased.

1542. UDALL, *Apophthegms of Erasmus* [1877], p. 115. The meaning of the Philosopher was, that princes for the ambition of honour, rule and dominion, being in continuall strife, and HURLEE BURLEE, are in very deede persons full of miserie and wo.

1551. MORE, *Utopia*, (Pitt Press ed., 1884, i., 52, 5). Whereby so many nations for his sake should be broughte into a troublesome HURLEI-BURLEY.

1567. FENTON, *Tragical Dicsourses*, f. 104. They heard a great noyse and HURLEYBURLEY in the street of the Guard and chief officers of the Watch.

1592. NASHE, *Pierce Penilesse* (GROSART, *Works*, ii., 53). Not trouble our peaceable Paradise with their private HURLIE-BURLIES about strumpets.

1599. NASHE, *Lenten Stuffe* (GROSART, *Works*, v., 293). Put them in feare where no feare is, and make a HURLIE-BURLIE in the realm.

1606. SHAKSPEARE, *Macbeth*, i., 1. When the HURLEY-BURLEY'S done, When the battle's lost and won.

1619. T. NORTH'S *Diall of Princes* (1557), corrected, p. 703, c. 1. Two or three dayes before you shall see such resort of persons, such HURLY BURLY, such flying this way such sending that way, some occupyed in telling the cookes how many sorts of meates they will have . . .

1690. B. E., *Dict. Cant. Crew*, s.v.

1725. *New Cant. Dict.*, s.v.

1771. SMOLLETT, *Humphrey Clinker* (ed. 1890, p. 185). As for the lawyer he waited below till the HURLY-BURLY was over, and then he stole softly to his own chamber.

1785. GROSE, *Vulg. Tongue*, s.v.

1811. J. and H. SMITH, *Horace in London*, pp. 18-25, Ode ii., 'HURLY-BURLY' (Title).

1886. MAX ADELER *Out of the HURLY-BURLY*. Title.

1893. *St. James's Gazette*, xxvii., 4076, p. 4. While all London was making holiday, Paris was engaged in a HURLY-BURLY of a very different kind.

HURRA'S-NEST, *subs.* (nautical).— The utmost confusion; everything topsy-turvy. For synonyms, *see* SIXES AND SEVENS.

1840. R. H. DANA, *Two Years Before the Mast*, ch. ii. Everything was pitched about in grand confusion. There was a complete HURRAH'S NEST, as the sailors say, 'everything on top and nothing at hand.'

1869. Mrs. STOWE, *Old Townsfolks*, ch. iv. You've got our clock all to pieces, and have been keeping up a perfect HURRAH'S NEST in our kitchen for three days. Do either put that clock together or let it alone.

HURRAH IN HELL. NOT TO CARE A SINGLE HURRAH IN HELL, *verb. phr.* (American).—To be absolutely indifferent.

1893. HAROLD FREDERIC, *National Observer*, IX., 1 Apr., p. 493, col. 2. I don't care a single HURRAH IN SHEOL.

HURRY, *subs.* (musical).—A quick passage on the violin, or a roll on the drum, leading to a climax in the representation.

1835. DICKENS, *Sketches by Boz*, p. 66. The wrongful heir comes in to two bars of quick music (technically called a HURRY).

HURRY-CURRY, *subs.* (obsolete).— *See* quot.

1599. NASHE, *Lenten Stuffe* (GROSART, *Works*, v. 267). The was so in his humps upon it . . . that he had thought to have tumbled his HURRIE CURRIE, or can, into the sea.

HURRY-DURRY, *adj.* (old).— Rough; boisterous; impatient of counsel or control.

1677. WYCHERLEY, *Plain Dealer*, i., 1. 'Tis a HURRYDURRY blade.

HURRYGRAPH, *subs.* (American).— A hastily written letter.

1861. *Independent*, 31 July. I must close this HURRYGRAPH, which I have no time to review.

HURRY-WHORE, *subs.* (old). — A walking strumpet.

1630. TAYLOR, *Wks.* And I doe wish with all my heart, that the superfluous number of all our hyreling hackney carryknaves, and HURRY-WHORES, with their makers and maintainers, were there, where they might never want continuall imployment.

HUSBAND'S-BOAT, *subs.* (common) —The Saturday boat to Margate during the summer season.

c. 1867. VANCE, *Broadside Ballad*. The HUSBAND'S BOAT.'

1887. MURRAY, in *New Eng. Dict.*, Pt. III., p. 956, c. 3. Waiting at Margate Pier for the HUSBAND'S BOAT on Saturday afternoon.

HUSBAND'S-SUPPER. TO WARM THE HUSBAND'S SUPPER, *verb. phr.* (common).—To sit before the fire with lifted skirts. Fr., *faire chapelle*.

HUSBAND'S-TEA, *subs.* (common). —Weak tea; WATER BEWITCHED (*q.v.*).

HUSH, *verb.* (old).—To kill.— GROSE.

HUSH-MONEY, *subs.* (old: now recognised). — Money paid for silence, to quash a case, or stay a witness; a bribe; blackmail.

1709. STEELE, *Tatler*, No. 26. I expect HUSH-MONEY to be regularly sent for every folly or vice any one commits in this whole town.

1713. *Guardian*, No. 26. A poor chambermaid has sent in ten shillings out of her HUSH-MONEY, to expiate her guilt of being in her mistress's secret.

1725. *New Cant. Dict.*, s.v.

1748. T. DYCHE, *Dictionary* (5th Ed.), s.v.

1785. GROSE, *Vulg. Tongue*, s.v.

1852. DICKENS, *Bleak House*, ch. xxxvii. To allow Ada to be made a bribe and HUSH-MONEY of, is not the way to bring it out.

1884. *Spectator*, p. 530. They were disappointed of their HUSH-MONEY, but he gave them an easy revenge.

HUSH-SHOP (or-CRIB), *subs.* (common).—An unlicensed tavern.

1872. *Globe*, 18 Sep. At Barrow-in Furness the new Licensing Act has had the effect of calling numerous HUSH SHOPS into existence.

HUSKY, *subs.* (Winchester College). —Gooseberry fool with the husks in it, obsolete. [*Notions.*]

1870. MANSFIELD, *School Life*, p. 145. There were two kinds [Gooseberry fool] HUSKY and non-husky.

Adj. (American).—Stout; well built.

HUSKY-LOUR, *subs.* (Old Cant).—A guinea; a JOB (*q.v.*). For synonyms, *see* CANARY.

1690. B. E., *Dict. Cant. Crew.*, s.v.

1725. *New Cant. Dict.*, s.v.

1785. GROSE, *Vulg. Tongue*, s.v.

HUSSY, *subs.* (colloquial).—A corruption of HOUSEWIFE (*q.v.*).

HUSTLE, *verb.* (venery).—1. To copulate. For synonyms, *see* GREENS and RIDE.

2. (American).—To bestir oneself; to go to work with vigour and energy. Also to HUSTLE AROUND.

HUSTLER, *subs.* (American).—An active, busy man or woman. A HUMMER (*q.v.*); a RUSTLER (*q.v.*).

1890. HAROLD FREDERIC, *Lawton Girl*. A whimsical query as to whether this calamitous boy had also been named Benjamin Franklin crossed his confused mind, and then . . . . . whether the child if so named, would be a HUSTLER or not.

HUTCH, *subs.* (common).—A place of residence or employment; one's DIGGINGS (*q.v.*).

HUTTER. See HATTER.

HUXTER, *subs.* (common).—Money. Also HOXTER. For synonyms, *see* ACTUAL and GILT.

c. 186 (?). *Broadside Ballad*. These seven long years I've been serving, and Seven I've got for to stay, All for meeting a bloke down our alley And a-taking his HUXTERS away.

HUZZY (or HUZZIE), *subs.* (old).—A case of needles, pins, scissors, bodkins, etc.; a *housewife's* companion.

HYMENEAL-SWEETS, *subs.* (venery). —Copulation.

1604. MARSTON, *Malcontent*, i., 3. True to her sheetes, nay, diets strong his blood, To give her height of HYMENEALL SWEETES.

HYPERNESE, *subs.* (Winchester College).—See quot. ZIPH (*q.v.*).

1864. *The Press*, 12 Nov. p. 1098. This dialect of school cryptoëpy was known in our youth as HYPERNESE. When spoken fast it defies an outsider's curiosity. If two consonants commence a syllable, the former is dropped, and W substituted: thus breeches would be *wareechepes*. If P commences a syllable, G is interpolated: thus penny would be *pegennepy* . . . . That Ziph and its cognate languages are well known beyond the boundaries of Winchester is certain. Bishop Wilkins described it, without mentioning it as a novelty, a couple of centuries ago.

HYPHENATED AMERICAN, *subs.* (American).—A naturalised citizen, as German-Americans, Irish-Americans, and the like. [NORTONS.]

HYPOCRITE, *subs.* (American).— A pillow slip or 'sham.'

HYPOGASTRIC-CRANNY, *subs.* (venery). The female *pudendum.*— URQUHART. For synonyms, *see* MONOSYLLABLE.

HYPS (or HYPO), *subs.* (old).—The BLUE DEVILS (*q.v.*).

1710. SWIFT, *Tatler*, No. 230. Will Hazard has got the HIPPS, having lost to the tune of five hund'rd pound.

1729. SWIFT, *Poems* (CHALMERS, *English Poets*, 1810, xi., 486). And the doctor was plaguily DOWN IN THE HIPS.

1738. SWIFT's *Polite Conversation*, Dial 1. Her ladyship was plaguily bamb'd; I warrant it put her into the HIPPS.

1811. *Lexicon Balatronicum*, s.v.

1830. C. LAMB, *Pawnbroker's Daughter*, i., 2. The drops so like to tears did drip, They gave my infant nerves the HYP.

1854. HALIBURTON, *Americans at Home*, i., 176. The old man would give up to the HYPO, and keep his bed for weeks. During this time, he wouldn't say a word, but 'I'm not long for this world.'

END OF VOL. III.

SLANG AND ITS ANALOGUES

PAST AND PRESENT.

DICTIONARY, HISTORICAL AND COMPARATIVE, OF THE
HETERODOX SPEECH OF ALL CLASSES OF SOCIETY
FOR MORE THAN THREE HUNDRED YEARS.

*WITH SYNONYMS IN ENGLISH, FRENCH, GERMAN,
ITALIAN, ETC.*

COMPILED AND EDITED BY

JOHN S. FARMER and W. E. HENLEY.

VOL. IV.—I TO MYZ.

PRINTED FOR SUBSCRIBERS ONLY.

—

MDCCCXCVI.

A · Dictionary · of Slang · and · its · Analogues.

CE. A BIG THING ON ICE, *subs. phr.* (American). — A profitable venture; a good thing; also B.T.I.

1890. GUNTER, *Miss Nobody*, xx. In the hall, prominently posted up by a wag, under new memberships, is a notice: FOR ELECTION. Gussie de P. Van Beekman, *vice* Baron Bassington, of Harrowby Castle, England. ON ICE.

ICKEN, *adj.* (American thieves').— Oak. ICKEN-BAUM = Oak-tree. [From the German].—MATSELL (1859).

ICTUS, *subs.* (legal).—A lawyer. For synonyms *see* GREEN-BAG [A corruption of *juris consultas*].

IDEA-POT (or **-BOX**), *subs.* (old).— The head. For synonyms *see* CRUMPET.—GROSE (1785); MATSELL (1859).

IDENTICAL, *subs.* (colloquial).— Generally THE IDENTICAL = the self-same; the person, point, argument, or action in question.

VOL. IV.

1664. BUTLER, *Hudibras*, pt. ii, c. i, I. 149. The beard's TH' IDENTIQUE beard you knew.

1891. N. GOULD, *Double Event*, p. 283. 'I'm THE IDENTICAL' said Jack.

I DESIRE, *subs. phr.* (rhyming).—A fire.

IGNORAMUS, *subs.* (old : now literary). —A stupid and unlettered person, male or female: first applied to ignorant lawyers. [From Latin = we ignore (it), the endorsement by which a grand jury threw out a bill].

1569. ERASMUS, *Praise of Folly.* Tr. [Reeves & Turner] p. 64. The lawyer who is so silly . . . as to be IGNORAMUS to a proverb.

1621. BURTON, *Anat. Mel.* Pt. 2. Sec. 2, Mem. 4, Vol. i, p. 425 (1827). Let them go as they are in the catalogue of IGNORAMUS.

1670. SHADWELL, *Sullen Lovers*, iv, p. 58. The greatest Owl. . . . Rascal, Oaf, IGNORAMUS.

1690. B.E. *Dict. Cant. Crew.* s.v.

*b.*1733. R. NORTH, *Examen*, I, ii. 82. If he had declared otherwise he would have been an IGNORAMUS.

1785. GROSE, *Vulg. Tongue*, s.v.

1811. *Lex. Bal.* s.v.

1883. BRADDON, *Golden Calf*, II, ch. iv, p. 140. Brian is a tremendous botanist, and Mr. Jardine is not an IGNORAMUS in that line.

IGNORAMUS-JURY, *subs. phr.* (old). —A Grand Jury.

1690. B.E., *Dict. Cant. Crew.* s.v. IGNORAMUS. . . . also, We are Ignorant, written by the Grand Jury on Bills, when the Evidence is not Home, and the Party (thereupon) Discharged.

1725. *New Cant. Dict.*, s. v.

IKEY, *subs.* (thieves').—A Jew : specifically a Jew FENCE (*q.v.*). [A corruption of Isaac]. For synonyms *see* YID. Also IKEY MO.

Adj. (common).—Smart; FLY (*q.v.*); KNOWING (*q.v.*).

1870. LEYBOURNE , *Song.* My name it is IKEY Bill, A Whitechapel Covey am I.

1892. CHEVALIER, '*The Little Nipper*'. But artful little IKEY little ways, As makes the people sit up where we stays.

ILE. *See* OIL.

ILL, *adv.* (American).—Vicious; unpleasant; ill-tempered.*Cf.* RELIGIOUS. Also ILL FOR = having a vicious propensity for anything (JAMIESON). *Cf.*, 'Neither is it ill air only that makes an ill seat, but ill ways, ill markets, and ILL neighbours' (BACON).

1887. *Trans. Am. Philol. Ass.*, xvii. 39. I heard a man in the Smoky Mountains say, 'Some rattlesnakes are ILLER'n others;' and another that 'black rattlesnakes are the ILLEST'.

1887. *Scribner's Mag.* In course the baby mus' come in the thick er it ! An't make me mad, seein' him so ILL with her.

TO DO ILL TO, *verb. phr.* (Scots' colloquial).—To have sexual commerce with : generally in negative, and of women alone.

1889. *Bird O' Freedom*, 7 Aug.s p. 1. If you say of a man he is IMMENSE, you pay him a compliment.

1891. *Tales from Town Topics*, 'Mimi & Bébé', p. 65. The love of twins is phenomenal. It is IMMENSE, pure, and heavenly.

IMMENSIKOFF, *subs.* (common).—A fur-lined overcoat. [From the burden of a song, 'The Shore-ditch Toff', sung (*c.* 1868) by the late Arthur Lloyd, who described himself as Immensikoff, and wore an upper garment heavily trimmed with fur].

1889. *Pall Mall Gazette*, 25 Sept., p. 6., col. 1. Heavy swells clad in IMMENSIKOFFS, which is the slang term, I believe, for those very fine and large fur robes affected by men about town.

IMMORTALS, *subs.* (military).—The Seventy-Sixth Foot. [Most of its men were wounded, but escaped being killed, in India in 1806]. Also THE PIGS and THE OLD SEVEN AND SIXPENNIES.

IMP, *subs.* (colloquial).—A mischievous brat; a small or minor devil: originally, a child. [TRENCH : there are epitaphs extant commencing 'Here lies that noble IMP; and Lord Cromwell writing to Henry VIII speaks of 'that noble IMP, your son'].

1771. BEATTIE, *Minstrel*, I. Nor cared to mingle in the clamorous fray Of squabbling IMPS.

2. (legal).—A man who gets up cases for a DEVIL (*q.v.*).

IMPALE, *verb.* (venery).—To possess a woman : specifically to effect intromission. For synonyms *see* GREENS and RIDE.

IMPERANCE, *subs.* (vulgar).—Impertinence; impudence; CHEEK (*q.v.*). Also, inferentially, an impudent

---

ILLEGITIMATE, *subs.* (old).—I. A counterfeit sovereign : YOUNG ILLEGITIMATE = a half sovereign. —BEE (1823).

2. (common).—A low grade costermonger.

Adj. (racing).—Applied to steeple-chasing or hurdle-racing, as distinguished from work on the flat.

1888. *Daily Chronicle*, 31 October. A much smarter performer at the ILLEGITIMATE game than she was on the flat.

ILL-FORTUNE, *subs.* (Old Cant.).— Ninepence : also THE PICTURE OF ILL-LUCK.—B.E. (1690); GROSE (1785).

ILLUMINATE, *verb.* (American).—To interline with a translation.

1856. HALL, *College Words*, p. 261. s.v. ILLUMINATED books are preferred by good judges to ponies or hobbies, as the text and translation in them are brought nearer to one another.

ILLUSTRATED CLOTHES. *See* HISTORICAL SHIRT.

I'M-AFLOAT, *subs. phr.* (rhyming).—
I. A boat.
2. (rhyming).—A coat. For synonyms *see* CAPELLA.

IMAGE, *subs.* (colloquial).—An affectionate reproof : *e.g.* 'Come out, you little IMAGE!' *See* LITTLE DEVIL.

IMMENSE, *adj.* (colloquial).—A general superlative : *cf.* AWFUL, BLOODY &c.

1771. G. A. STEVENS, *Songs Comic & Satyrical*, p. 216. Dear Bragg, Hazard, Loo, and Quadrille, Delightful ! extatic ! immense !

1884. W. C. RUSSELL, *Jack's Courtship*, xxv. 'What do you think of this, Florence darling?' I whispered. 'Is it not IMMENSE?'

1888. *Florida Times Union*, 8 Feb. The afterpiece is said to be IMMENSE.

---

person; *e.g.*, 'What's your IMPERENCE about'?

1766. COLMAN, *Cland. Marriage*, v. in *Works*, (1777) i. 274. I wonder at your IMPURENCE, Mr. Brush, to use me in this manner.

1821. EGAN, *Life in London*, ii. 2. She is blowing up the fellow for his IMPERANCE.

1836. DICKENS, *Pickwick*, ch. xiv. 'Don't go away, Mary,' said the black-eyed man. 'Let me alone, IMPERENCE,' said the young lady.

IMPERIAL, *subs.* (colloquial).—A tuft of hair worn on the lower lip. [From being introduced by the Emperor Napoleon III]. *See* GOATEE.

1892. *Tit Bits*, 19 Mar., p. 421, col. 2. An IMPERIAL, or carefully cultivated small tuft tapered down to a point from the lower lip to the chin.

IMPLEMENT, *subs.* (old).—*See* quot.

1690. B.E. *Dict. Cant. Crew.* s.v.

1725. *New Cant. Dict.*, s.v., IMPLEMENT, a Tool, a Property or Fool easily engag'd in any (tho' difficult or Dangerous) Enterprise.

IMPORTANCE, *subs.* (common).—A wife; a COMFORTABLE IMPORTANCE (*q.v.*).

1647-80. ROCHESTER, *Works* (1718), ii. 29. IMPORTANCE, thinks too, tho' she'd been no sinner To wash away some dregs he had spewed in her.

IMPOST-TAKER, *subs.* (old).—A gambler's and black-leg's money-lender; a SIXTY-PER-CENT (*q.v.*).

1690. B.E. *Dict. Cant. Crew.* s.v.

1725. *New Cant. Dict.*, s.v.

1785. GROSE, *Vulg. Tongue*, s.v.

IMPROVEMENT, *subs.* (American).— That part of a sermon which enforces and applies to every-day life the doctrine previously set forth; the application.

I

1869. *Putnam's Magazine*, August [quoted by DE VERE]. Long sermons running on to a tenthly, with a goodly number of IMPROVEMENTS appended.

IMPURE, *subs.* (common).—A harlot. For synonyms *see* BARRACK-HACK and TART.

1811. *Lexicon Balatronicum*, s. v.

1823. GROSE, *Vulg. Tongue* (3rd ed., EGAN) s. v.

IN, *subs.* (colloquial).—A person in, or holding an office; specifically, (in politics) a member of the party in office. *Cf.* OUT.

1768. GOLDSMITH, *Good Natured Man*, v. Was it for this I have been dreaded both by INS and outs? Have I been libelled in the *Gazetteer*, and praised in the *St. James's*?

1770. CHATTERTON, *Prophecy*. And doomed a victim for the sins. Of half the outs and all the INS.

1842. DICKENS, *American Notes*, ch. ii. The INS rubbed their hands; the outs shook their heads.

1857. LAWRENCE, *Guy Livingstone* (5th Ed.) p. 216. If he had backed the IN instead of the Out.

1884. *Pall Mall Gazette*, 20 March. p. 1, col. 2. When there shall be no distinction in principle between Radicals and Tories, but a mere scramble for office between INS and 'outs'.

1884. *Pall Mall Gazette*, 7 July. The pledges which the INS have to contend with in their strife with the Outs.

1888. *Boston Daily Globe*. It is the civil service that turns out all the INS and puts in the outs.

1890. NORTON, *Political Americanisms*, s. v. INS AND OUTS.

Adv. (colloquial).—Various: (cricketers') = at the wickets; (general) = in season; also, on an equality with, sharing, or intimate with, or fashionable; (political) = in office; (thieves') = in prison, or QUODDED (*q.v.*)

1851-61. H. MAYHEW, *London Lab. & Lon. Poor*, i, p. 85. During July cherries are IN as well as raspberries

1877. *Five Years Penal Servitude*, iii, p. 147. It is the etiquette among prisoners never to ask a man what he is IN for. The badge upon his left arm gives his sentence.

1883. *Punch*, 28 July, p. 38, col. 1. I was IN it, old man, and no kid.

1891. N. GOULD, *Double Event*, p. 180. You are all IN with me at this.

1892. HUME NISBET, *Bushranger's Sweetheart*, p. 311. Jenkins has been on a visit to us for the past two months, so that we are all IN it.

1894. GEORGE MOORE, *Esther Walters*, xxx. Are the 'orses he backs what you 'd call well IN?

TO BE IN (OR IN IT) WITH ONE, *verb. phr.* (common).—1. To be 'even with'; to be on guard against.

2. (colloquial).—To be on intimate terms, or in partnership with; to be in the SWIM (*q.v.*) *Cf.*, IN, *prep.*

1845. SURTEES, *Hillingdon Hall*, v. p. 22 (1888). He was IN with the players too, and had the *entrée* of most of the minor theatres.

1879. *Justin McCarthy*, *Donna Quixote*, xxxii. You have gone a great deal too far to turn back now, let me tell you. You have been IN with me from the very first.

1888. J. MCCARTHY and MRS. CAMPBELL PRAED, *The Ladies Gallery*, xxii. The love of woman, the thirst for gold, the desire for drink, the ambition of high command, are not IN it with the love of speech-making when once that has got its hold.

1892. *Ally Sloper's Half-holiday*, 27 Feb., p. 71, col. 3. Peter was fascinated all the time. Hypnotism was not IN it as compared with the effect of that . . . . umbrella.

TO BE IN FOR IT, *verb. phr.* (common).—1. To be in trouble; generally to be certain to receive, suffer, or do (something).

1668. DRYDEN, *An Evening's Love*, ii. I fear that I am IN FOR a week longer than I proposed.

1773. GOLDSMITH, *She Stoops to Conquer*, iv. I was IN FOR a list of blunders.

2. (colloquial).—To be with child.

IN FOR THE PLATE, *phr.* (old).—Venereally infected.

FOR ALL THERE'S IN IT, *phr.* (common).—To the utmost capacity (of persons and things). TO PLAY ONE'S HAND FOR ALL THERE'S IN IT = to use fair means or foul to attain an object.

1888. ROOSEVELT, *Ranch Life*. Cowboys must ride FOR ALL THERE IS IN THEM, and spare neither their own nor their horses' necks.

TO GET IT IN FOR ONE, *verb. phr.* (common).—To remember to one's disadvantage.

1864. *Derby Day*, p. 121. 'Brentford:' cried the tout. 'That was a bad job for you, guv'nor, I've GOT IT IN FOR you. I don't forget if I do look a fool.'

[For combinations *see* ALTITUDES; ARMS OF MORPHEUS; BAD WAY; BLUES; BOTTOM OF THE BAG; BUFF; BUNCH; CART; CLICK; CLOVER; CRACK; CROOK; CUPS; DEAD ERNEST; DIFFICULTY; HOLE; JIFFY; JUG; KISH; KNOW; LAVENDER; LIMBO; LIQUOR; LURCH; PATTER; POUND; PRINT; QUEER STREET; RAGS; RUNNING; SHAPE; SHELL; SKIFFLE; SLASH; STATE OF NATURE; STRAW; STRING; SUDS; SUN; SWIM; TIN-POT WAY; TOWN; TWINKLING; WATER; WIND; WRONG BOX, etc.]

IN-AND-IN. TO PLAY AT IN-AND-IN, *verb. phr.* (old).—To copulate. For synonyms *see* GREENS and RIDE. Also IN-AND-OUT (*q.v.*).

1635. GLAPTHORNE, *The Hollander*, in *Wks.* (1874), i. 127. They are sure fair gamesters. . . . especially at IN-AND-IN.

1653. BROME, *Five New Plays*, 239. The Physitian thought to have cured his patient (who has bin a notable gamester at IN-AND-IN) between my Lady's legs.

1675. COTTON, *Scoffer Scofft*, in *Works* (1725), p. 192. What with some Goddess he'd have bin. Playing, belike, at IN-AND-IN. . . . For so thy words seem to import.

1719. DURFEY, (quoted) *Pills etc.*, iv. 78. Their wives may PLAY AT IN-AND-IN, Cuckolds all-a-row.

IN-AND-OUT, *subs.* (colloquial).—The detail or intricacies of a matter; generally in pl., *e.g.*, To know all the INS-AND-OUTS of a matter.

Adv. (racing).—1. Unequal; variable: applied to the performances of a horse which runs well one day, and on another not.

1885. *Referee*, 26 April, p. 1, col. 2. Now and again IN-AND-OUT running on the part of a horse subjects his owner to considerable annoyance.

1888. *Sportsman*, 28 Nov. It is best if possible to overlook IN-AND-OUT running, or variation of form.

TO PLAY AT IN-AND-OUT, *verb. phr.* (venery).—To copulate. For synonyms *see* GREENS and RIDE.

1620. PERCY, *Folio M.S.*, p. 93. 'Walking in a Meadow Green'. Then stifly thrust . . . . and PLAY about AT IN-AND-OUT.

INCH, *verb.* (old).—To encroach; to move slowly.

1690. B. E. *Dict. Cant. Crew.* s. v. INCHING IN, Encroaching upon.

1694-6. DRYDEN, *Ænid*, ix. With slow paces measures back the field, And INCHES to the wall.

1725. *New Cant. Dict.*, s. v.

1785. GROSE, *Vulg. Tongue*, s. v.

1868. BROWNING, *Ring & Book*, i. 118. Like so much cold steel INCHED through the breast blade.

INCOG, *adv.* (colloquial).—1. Unknown; in disguise. Also as *subs.* [An abbreviation of *incognito*].

1690. B. E. *Dict. Cant. Crew*, s. v. INCOG, for Incognito, a Man of Character or Quality concealed or in disguise.

1711. *Spectator*, No. 41, 17 April, p. 69 (MORLEY). So many Ladies, when they first lay it (painting) down, INCOG in their own faces.

1739. GRAY, *Letters*, No. xxiv, Vol. 1, p. 49 (1819). He passes INCOG without the walls.

1777. SHERIDAN, *School for Scandal*, iv. 3. What! turn inquisitor, and sake evidence INCOG.

1795. BURNS, *Poems*. 'Address to the De'il.' Then you, ye auld sneck-drawing dog, Ye cam to Paradise INCOG.

1812. *Edinburgh Review*, xx. p. 113. He travels INCOG to his father's two estates.

1819. MOORE, *From the Diary of a Politician*. INCOG he (the king) was travelling about.

1826. DISRAELI, *Vivian Grey*, Bk. v, ch. v, p. 187 (1881). Whose well-curled black hair, diamond pin, and frogged coat hinted at the magnifico INCOG.

1828-45. HOOD, *Poems*, (1846) i. 215. A Foreign Count who came INCOG, Not under a cloud, but under a fog.

1836. MAHONEY, *Father Prout*, i. 319. O the vile wretch! the naughty dog! He's surely Lucifer INCOG.

1855. THACKERAY, *Newcomes*, ii. 183. 'Don't call me by my name here, please Florac, I am here INCOG.'

2. (common).—Drunk: *i.e.*, 'disguised' in liquor.

1823. BEE, *Dict. Turf.* s. v. INCOG. A man drunk is INCOG. *Ibid*, s. v. COG: COGUE, a glass of gin or rum with sugar in it . . . . COGEY = drunk.

INCOGNITA, *subs.* (obsolete).—A high-class harlot; ANONYMA, (*q.v.*). For synonyms *see* BARRACK-HACK and TART.

INCUMBRANCE, *subs.*, in pl. (common).—Children. For synonyms *see* KID.

INDENTURES, TO MAKE INDENTURES, *verb. phr.* (old).—To stagger with drink.

1622. ROWLANDS, *Good Newes and Bad Newes*, p. 43. [Hunterian Club's Rep.]. A fellow that had beene excessive trading, In taking liquor in beyond his lading, Of Claret and the Spanish Malligo, That's legs vnable were vpright to goe; But sometimes wall, and sometimes kennell taking, And as the phrase is vs'd, INDENTURES MAKING.

INDESCRIBABLES, *subs.* (common).—Trousers. For synonyms *see* BAGS and KICKS.

1835. DICKENS, *Sketches by Boz*, (C. D. Ed.) p. 67. A pair of INDESCRIBABLES of most capacious dimensions.

1836. DICKENS, *Pickwick*, ch. xvi. Mr. Trotter . . . . gave four distinct slaps on the pocket of his mulberry INDESCRIBABLES.

INDEX, *subs.* (common).—The face. For synonyms *see* DIAL and PHIZ.

1818-24. EGAN, *Boxiana*, ii. 438. The INDEX of Church was rather transmogrified.

1828. EGAN, *Finish to Tom & Jerry*, p. 48. Kind-hearted Sue! Bless her pretty INDEX.

INDIA, *subs.* (venery).—The female *pudendum*. For synonyms *see* MONOSYLLABLE.

1613. DONNE, *Elegy*, XVIII. [CHALMERS, *English Poets*, VI. 151]. And sailing towards her India in that way Shall at her fair Atlantic navel stay.

INDIAN, *verb.* (American colloquial).—To prowl about, or live like an Indian.

1869. H. B. STOWE, *Old Town Folks*, 189. Jake Marshall and me has been INDIANING round these 'ere woods more times 'n you could count.

INDIAN-GIFT, *subs.* (American).—An inadequate return or exchange; 'a sprat for a whale'. INDIAN GIVER = one who takes back a gift.

INDIA-WIPE, *subs.* (old).—A silk handkerchief.—GROSE, (3rd Ed. EGAN. 1823).

INDIES. *See* BLACK INDIES.—(Grose 1785).

INDISPENSABLES, *subs.* (common).—Trousers. *See* BAGS and KICKS.

1842. *Comic Almanack*, June. He slapped his hand against his yellow leather INDISPENSABLES.

1843. SELBY, *Anthony & Cleopatra Married & Settled.* But my love, consider, the gentleman is waiting for his INDISPENSABLES.

INDORSE, *verb.* (old).—1. To cudgel; to 'lay cane on Abel'—GROSE (1785).

2. (venery).—To practise sodomy.

INDORSER, *subs.* (venery).—A sodomite; a CHUFFER (GROSE, 1785). For synomyns *see* USHER.

INEFFABLE, *subs.* (venery).—The female *pudendum*. For synonyms *see* MONOSYLLABLE.

2. in pl. (common).—Trousers. For synonyms *see* BAGS and KICKS.

1850. L. HUNT, *Autobiography*, ch. iii. It was said, also, that during the blissful era of the blue velvet, we had roast mutton for supper; but that the small clothes not being then in existence, and the mutton suppers too luxurious, the eatables were given up for the INEFFABLES.

INEXPLICABLES, *subs.* (common).—Trousers. For synonyms *see* BAGS and KICKS.

1836. DICKENS, *Sketches by Boz*, ch. ii. (C.D.Ed.) p. 182. He usually wore a brown frock-coat without a wrinkle, light INEXPLICABLES without a spot.

INEXPRESSIBLES, *subs.* (common).—Trousers. For synonyms *see* BAGS and KICKS.

1790. WOLCOT, (P. Pindar) *Rowland for an Oliver*, in *Wks* [Dublin 1795] Vol. ii. p. 154. I've heard, that breeches, petticoats, & smock, Give to thy modest mind a grievous shock, And that thy brain (so lucky its device) Christ'neth them INEXPRESSIBLES, so nice.

1820. REYNOLDS, (Peter Corcoran), *The Fancy* 'King Tim', i. 1. That single breasted coat, that sweet snub nose, Those INEXPRESSIBLES: I know the clothes.

1830. LYTTON, *Paul Clifford*, vi. While thus musing, he was suddenly accosted by a gentleman in boots and spurs, having a riding whip in one hand, and the other hand stuck in the pocket of his INEXPRESSIBLES.

1835. BUCKSTONE, *Dream at Sea*, ii. 2. *Tom.* Body & breeches. *Bid.* Hush: you should say INEXPRESSIBLES—that's the way genteel people talk.

1836. DICKENS, *Pickwick Papers*, ch. lv, p. 483. Symmetrical INEXPRESSIBLES, and scented pocket-handkerchiefs.

183 . MICHAEL SCOTT, *Tom Cringle's Log*, xii. Whenever I get my INEXPRESSIBLES on, I will come to you there.

1837. BARHAM, *Ingoldsby Legends*, i. 39. Condescend to don at the same time an Elizabethan doublet and Bond-St. INEXPRESSIBLES.

1842. DICKENS, *American Notes*, ch. xxi., p. 100. He . . . . had grown recently, for it had been found necessary to make an addition to the legs of his INEXPRESSIBLES.

1871. *City Press*, 21 Jan. 'Curiosities of Street Literature'. The sale of a wife, and full particulars of 'Taking off Prince Albert's INEXPRESSIBLES,' done by a scamp.

INFANT. *See* WOOLWICH INFANT.

INFANTRY, *subs.* (common).—Children. In French, *entrer dans l'infanterie* = to fall with child. For synonyms *see* KID.

1623. JONSON, *Time Vindicated*. Hangs all his school with sharp sentences, And o'er the execution place hath painted, Time whipt, as terror to the INFANTRY.

1675. COTTON, *Scoffer Scoffed* [4th ed. 1725, p. 181]. Others a spirit that doth lie In wait to catch up INFANTRY.

LIGHT INFANTRY, *subs. phr.* (common).—Fleas. *Cf.* HEAVY DRAGOONS.

1894. *Westminster Gazette*, 15th Nov. p. 2, col. 1. An Irish lady of good family was remonstrated with by a guest on account of the noctural assaults of heavy cavalry, as well as LIGHT INFANTRY issuing after dark from the cracks of an old wood bedstead.

INFARE (or **INFAIR**), *subs.* (Old Scots & American colloquial).—An installation with ceremony and rejoicing; a house-warming; more particularly an entertainment given by a newly married couple on their return from the honeymoon.

1375. BARBOUR, *The Bruce*, xvi. 340 (MSS.) For he thoucht to mak an INFAR, And to mak gud cher till his men.

1847. PORTER, *Big Bear*, etc. p. 162. I hurried home to put up three shotes and some turkies to fatten for the INFARE.

1878. E. EGGLESTON, *Roxy*, xxix. There could be no wedding in a Hoosier village thirty or forty years ago without an INFARE on the following day.

INFERIOR, *subs.* (Winchester College).—Any member of the School not a PRÆFECT (*q.v.*).

1870. MANSFIELD, *School Life*, p. 28. The Præfect of hall . . . . was looked upon by the INFERIORS with something more than a becoming awe and reverence.

INFERNAL, *adj.* (colloquial).—An intensive: detestable; fit only for Hell. *Cf.* AWFUL, BLOODY. Also *adv.*

1602. COOKE, *How a Man may Choose a Good Wife* etc. [DODSLEY: *Old Plays* (1874), ix. 50]. Not these drugs Do send me to the INFERNAL bugs, But thy unkindness.

1646. LADY MARY VERNEY [in *Seventh Report Hist. MSS. Com.* 454]. Besides coaches which are most INFE(R)NELL dear.

1775. SHERIDAN, *The Duenna*, iii. 1. There is certainly some INFERNAL mystery in it I can't comprehend!

1846. THACKERAY, *Vanity Fair*, xi. Besides, he's such an INFERNAL character—a profligate in every way.

1854. WHYTE MELVILLE, *General Bounce*, xi. The nights are INFERNALLY dark, though, in this beastly country.

1855. THACKERAY, *Newcomes*, lxxv. What an INFERNAL tartar and catamaran!

1888. ROLF BOLDREWOOD, *Robbery Under Arms*, ix. It had broken her INFERNAL neck.

1891. N. GOULD, *Double Event*, 114. 'Never is any news in this INFERNAL hole,' growled Smirk.

INFRA-DIG, *adj.* (Winchester College).—Scornful; proud. *E.g.* 'He sported INFRA-DIG duck,' or 'I am INFRA-DIG to it.'

INGLE, *subs.* (old).—1. A pathic.

1593. NASHE, *Strange Newes*, in *Works* [GROSART, ii. 277]. I am afraid thou wilt make me thy INGLE.

1598. FLORIO, *Worlde of Wordes*, s. v. *Cinedo* . . . . a bardarsh a buggring boy, a wanton boy, an INGLE.

1617. MINSHEW, *Guide into Tongues*, s. v. INGLE, or a boy kept for sodomie.

1675. COTTON, *Scoffer Scoffed*, 4th ed., 1725, p. 186. Both at thy INGLES and thy jades.

2. (old).—An intimate; a dear friend.

1601. B. JONSON, *Poetaster*, i. 1. What! shall I have my son a stager now? an ENGHLE for players.

1602. DEKKER, *Honest Whore*, [DODSLEY, *Old Plays*, iii. 260]. Call me your love, your INGLE, your cousin, or so; but sister at no hand.

1609. BEN JONSON, *Silent Woman*, i. 1. Wks. (1860), p. 208. col. i. His INGLE at home.

1659. MASSINGER, *City Madam*, iv. 1. Coming, as we do, from his quondam patrons, his dear INGLES now.

1773. T.HAWKINS, *Origin of Dr.* iii. p. 118. I never saw mine INGLE so dashed in my life before.

1821. SCOTT, *Kenilworth*, iii. Ha! my dear friend and INGLE, Tony Foster.

Verb.(old).—1.To practise sodomy; TO INDORSE (*q.v.*); TO CHUFF (*q.v.*).

1598. FLORIO, *Worlde of Wordes*, s.v. *Cinedulare*, to bugger, to bardarsh, TO INGLE.

2. (old).—To caress; to make much of.

1599. NASHE, *Lenten Stuffe*, in *Works* [GROSART, v. 194]. Hug it, INGLE it, kiss it.

INGLENOOK, *subs.* (venery).—The female pudendum. For synonyms *see* MONOSYLLABLE.

INGLER, *subs.* (old.)—1. A sodomist. For synonyms *see* USHER.

1598. FLORIO, *Worlde of Wordes*, s.v. *Pedicone*, a buggrer, an INGLER of boyes.

2. (thieves').—A fraudulent horse-dealer.

1825. *Modern Flash Dict.*, s.v.

1859. MATSELL, *Vocabulum*, s.v. INGLERS. Horse-dealers who cheat those that deal with them.

INGOTTED, *adj.* (common).—Rich; WARM (*q.v.*). For synonyms *see* WELL-BALLASTED.

1864. E. YATES, *Broken to Harness*, xvii. p. 168. (1873). They are a tremendously well-timed set at Schröders; and he's safe to ask no women who are not enormously ingotted.

INIQUITY OFFICE, *subs.* (American).—A registry office. [A play upon 'inquiry' office].

INGUN. TO GET UP ONE'S INGUN, *verb. phr.* (American).—To get angry; to turn savage.

INK. TO SLING INK, *verb. phr.* (colloquial).—To make a business of writing. *See* INK-SLINGER.

INKHORN (or **INK-POT**) *adj.* (obsolete).—Pedantic; dry; smelling of the lamp.

1579. CHURCHYARD, *Choice*, sig. Ee 1. As YNKEHORNE termes smell of the schoole sometyme.

1592. NASHE, *Summer's Last Will*, [DODSLEY, *Old Plays* (1874), viii, 70]. Men that, removed from their INK-HORN terms, Bring forth no action worthy of their bread.

INKLE, *verb.* (American thieves').—To warn; to give notice; to hint at; to disclose.

1340-50. *Alesaunder of Macedoine* [E.E.T.S.] i. 615. A brem brasen borde bringes he soone, Imped in iuory, too INCLE the truthe, With good siluer & golde gailich atired.

INKLE-WEAVER, *subs.* (old).—A close companion; a CHUM (*q.v.*).

1725. *New Cant. Dict.* s.v. INKLE . . . . As great as two INKLE-WEAVERS, or As great as Cup and Can.

1785. GROSE, *Vulg. Tongue*.

INK-SLINGER, (INKSPILLER or **INK-WASTER)**, *subs.* (common).—1. A journalist or author: a BROTHER OF THE QUILL: generally in contempt of a raw hand. Fr. *un marchand de lignes*. *See* INK.

1888. *Texas Siftings*, Oct. 13. 'Who's a big gun? You don't consider that insignificant INK-SLINGER across the way a big gun, do you?'

1888. *Illustrated Bits*, 14 April. But, helas! I am but a poor INK-SLINGER.

1892. MILLIKEN, *'Arry Ballads*, p. 69. The INK-SPILLER's slate.

1894. *Tit Bits*, 7 April, p. 7, col. 3. You insulting INK-WASTER!

INK-SLINGING, *subs.* (common). Writing for the press. Fr. *scribouillage*.

1892. MILLIKEN, *'Arry Ballads*, p. 91. Wot with INK-SLINGING, hart, and all that.

INKY, *adj.* (tailors'). Used evasively: *e.g.* of a question to which a direct answer is undesirable or inconvenient.

INLAID (or **WELL-INLAID**), *adv.* (old).—In easy circumstances; with well-lined pockets; WARM (*q.v.*).

1690. B.E. *Dict. Cant. Crew.* s.v.

1785. GROSE, *Vulg. Tongue*, s.v.

1859. MATSELL, *Vocabulum*, s.v.

INNARDS, *subs.* (vulgar).—The stomach; the GUTS (*q.v.*). Also INWARDS.

1602. SHAKSPEARE, *Othello*, ii. 1. The thought whereof Doth like a poisonous mineral gnaw my INWARDS.

1653. BROME, *Five New Plays*, 347. Bestow steeping thy skin in perfumes to kill the stink of thy paintings and rotten INWARDS.

*d.*1674. MILTON [quoted in JOHNSON, Ed. 1755]. There sacrificing laid, The INWARDS and their fat. . . . on the cleft wood.

1870. WHITE, *Words and their Uses*, 387. The simple English word (guts) for which some New England females elegantly substitute IN'ARDS, would shock many.

1871. *London Figaro*, 17 March. The usual answer given to William's enquiry as to what was found in the shark is, 'his INNARDS'.

TO FILL ONE'S INNARDS, *verb. phr.* (common).—To eat.

INNER-MAN, *subs.* (common).—The appetite.

1889. *Sporting Life*, 30 Jan. Having satisfied the INNER-MAN.

ININGS, *subs.* (colloquial).—A turn; a spell; a chance: from the game of cricket

1836. DICKENS, *Pickwick Papers*, (ed. 1857) p. 103. The friends of Horatio Fizkin Esq., having had their INNINGS, a little choleric pink-faced man stood forward to propose another fit and proper person to represent the electors of Eatanswill in Parliament.

1848. THACKERAY, *Book of Snobs*, xx. The opposition wag is furious that he cannot get an INNINGS.

1883. JAMES PAYN, *Naturalness*, in *Longman's Mag.*, May, p. 67. And others consent to listen to him upon the understanding that they are presently o have their INNINGS.

TO HAVE A GOOD INNINGS, *verb. phr.* (colloquial).—To be fortunate, especially in money matters.

TO HAVE A LONG INNINGS, *verb. phr.* (colloquial). To die in the fulness of years.

INNOCENT, *subs.* (old).—1. A simpleton; an idiot.

1598. SHAKESPEARE, *All's well*, etc. iv. 3. A dumb INNOCENT that could not say him nay.

1605. JONSON, CHAPMAN, &c., *Eastward Hoe* (DODSLEY, *Old Plays*, iv. 209). Again, if you be a cuckold, and know it not, you are an INNOCENT; if you know it and endure it, a true martyr.

1609. JONSON, *Epicœne*, iii. 4. Do you think you had married some INNOCENT out of the hospital, that would stand with her hands thus, and a playse mouth, and look upon you.

1634. BEAUMONT & FLETCHER, *Two Noble Kinsmen*, iv. 1. She answered me So far from what she was, so childishly, So sillily, as if she were a fool, an INNOCENT.

1639. BEAUMONT & FLETCHER, *Wit without Money*, ii. There be three kinds of fools, mark this note, gentlemen, Mark it, and understand it. . . . An INNOCENT, a knave fool, a fool politic.

1785. GROSE, *Vulg. Tongue*, s.v. INNOCENTS, one of the INNOCENTS, a weak or simple person, man or woman.

1811. *Lex. Bal.*, s.v.

2. (American).—A corpse; a STIFF (*q.v.*).

1859. MATSELL, *Vocabulum*, s.v.

3. (American). A convict.

1859. MATSELL, *Vocabulum*, s.v.

THE MURDER (SLAUGHTER, or MASSACRE) OF THE INNOCENTS, *subs. phr.* (parliamentary). The abandonment, towards the end of a session, of measures whether introduced by the Government or by private members, when they would have no chance of passing.

1859. *Times*, 20 July, p. 7, co. 3l The Leader of the House would have to go through that doleful operation called THE MASSACRE OF THE INNOCENTS, devoting to extinction a number of useful measures which there was not time to pass.

1860. *Punch*, xxxviii. 255. I brooded o'er my discontent, saying—The Notice-paper thins: Now that with early June begins THE MASSACRE OF INNOCENTS.

1870. *London Figaro*, 6 August. So vigorously has THE SLAUGHTER OF THE INNOCENTS been proceeding that the Appropriation Bill was read a first time in the House of Commons on Wednesday.

1871. *Times*, 'Leader' 9 May. THE MASSACRE OF THE INNOCENTS has begun.

1872. *Saturday Review*, 20th July. When the proposals of a member will stand the test of being expressed in a Bill, they are often of great value, and have an effect on legislation, and on the conduct of the Government, although they are MASSACRED WITH HUNDREDS OF OTHER INNOCENTS at the end of the Session.

1879. *Graphic*, 9th July, p. 50. Formerly . . . THE MASSACRE OF THE INNOCENTS was chiefly confined to measures which owed their existence rather to individual and sectional enthusiasm than to the deliberate wishes of the nation.

INNOMINABLES, *subs.* (obsolete).—Breeches; trousers; INEXPRESSIBLES. For synonyms *see* BAGS and KICKS.

1834. SOUTHEY, *The Doctor*, p. 688. The lower part of his dress represented INNOMINABLES and hose in one.

INSIDE, *subs.* (common).—A passenger riding inside a vehicle. *See* OUTSIDE.

1816. SCOTT, *Old Mortality*, ii. A wheel carriage bearing eight INSIDES and six outsides.

*d.*1820. G. CANNING, *Loves of the Triangles*, i. 178. So down thy hill, romantic Ashbourn, glides The Derby dilly, carrying six INSIDES.

1889. *Daily Telegraph*, 5 Jan. The INSIDES were terrified.

Adj. and *adv.* (colloquial).—Trustworthy; pertinent; in touch with; BOTTOM (*q.v.*). TO KNOW THE INSIDE OF EVERYTHING = to be well informed.

1888. *Daily Inter-Ocean.* A secret service officer, who has just arrived from Washington on important business, claims to have INSIDE information as to the facts in the case.

1889. *Pall Mall Gazette*, 12 Nov., p. 6, col. 2. He saw everything and missed not the smallest incident or accident. The latter were few enough, but such as they were he was, so to speak, INSIDE OF them without a falter.

INSIDE OF, *subs.* and *adv.* (colloquial).—Within the limit; in less time than.

1888. *Missouri Republican*, 22 Feb. He is very desperate, and INSIDE OF thirty days shot at four men.

1887. *Hartford Courant*, 13 Jan. Both animals had been killed INSIDE OF five minutes.

1888. ROLF BOLDREWOOD, *Robbery Under Arms*, chap. xi. He knocked the seven senses out of him INSIDE OF three rounds.

1890. W. C. RUSSELL, *Ocean Tragedy*, 74. Tain't to be done in the INSIDE OF a month.

TO DO AN INSIDE WORRY, *verb. phr.* (venery).—To copulate. For synonyms *see* GREENS and RIDE.

TO TAKE THE INSIDE OUT OF (a glass, a book &c.), *verb. phr.* (colloquial).—To empty; to GUT (*q.v.*).

1843. W. T. MONCRIEFF, *The Scamps of London*, iii. 1. Haven't you TAKEN THE INSIDE OUT OF that quart of gatter yet?

TO BE ON (or TO HAVE) THE INSIDE TRACK, *verb. phr.* (colloquial).—To be on the safe side; to be at a point of vantage; or (of a subject) to understand thoroughly.

INSIDE AND OUTSIDE! *phr.* (old).—A toast: 'the inside of a cunt and the outside of a gaol'.—GROSE (1823).

INSIDER, *subs.* (American thieves').—1. One IN THE KNOW (*q.v.*).
2. (general).—One who has some special advantage, as in a business enterprise.

INSIDE-LINING, *subs.* (common).—Food: specifically in quot. *See* LINING. For synonyms *see* GRUB.
1851-61. H. MAYHEW, *London Lab. & Lond. Poor*, i. 20. He was 'going to get an INSIDE-LINING' (dinner).

INSIDE-SQUATTER, *subs.*(Australian). A settler within the bounds of civilization: *see* OUTSIDE-SQUATTER.

INSPECTOR OF PAVEMENTS, *subs. phr.* (old).—1. A man in the pillory.
1821. EGAN, *Life in London*, ii. 97. Having once been made INSPECTOR OF THE PAVEMENT, or in other words 'kidnapped on the stoop.'
2. (common).—A man out of work. Also INSPECTOR OF PUBLIC BUILDINGS. Fr. *Inspecteur de monuments publiques.*

INSPIRE, *verb.* (journalistic).—To impart a tone, possibly official, to the subject matter of a newspaper or magazine article.
1884. *Daily Telegraph*, 11 Sept. A paragraph obviously INSPIRED appears in a local journal this evening.
1889. *Daily Telegraph*, 14 Feb. All the INSPIRED papers keep laying stress upon this fact, which is significant.

INSPIRED, *adj.* (common).—1. Drunk. For synonyms *see* DRINKS and SCREWED.
2. (journalistic).—*See* INSPIRE.

INSTITUTION, *subs.* (colloquial).—A practice; an idea; an invention; an established custom or usage.
1851. THACKERAY, *English Humorists*, p. 207. The pillory was a flourishing and popular INSTITUTION in those days.
1858. *Times*, April. The camels form an INSTITUTION of India.

INSTRUMENT, *subs.* (old).—The female *pudendum*. For synonyms *see* MONOSYLLABLE.
1606. *Return from Parnassus* [DODSLEY, *Old Plays* (1874), ix. 165]. Her *viol-de-gamba* is her best content; For 'twixt her legs she holds her INSTRUMENT.

INT, *subs.* (old).—A sharper.
1621. BRATHWAYTE, *Clitus's Whimzies*, p. 12. His nipps, INTS, bungs and prinados.
1658. BRATHWAYTE, *Honest Ghost*, p. 231. Nips, and INTS, prinados etc.. ?

INTENSE, *adj.* (colloquial).—Serious; soulful; ÆSTHETIC (*q.v.*); YEARNEST (*q.v.*).
1879. W. D. HOWELLS, *Lady of the Aroostook*, xiv. 'Why Miss Blood you are INTENSE.' 'I dont know what you mean by that' said Lydia. 'You like to take thing seriously. You can't bear to think that people are not the least in earnest, even when they least seem so.'
1889. DU MAURIER, *English Society at Home*, plate 49. Fair Æsthetic to Smith who has just been introduced 'Are you INTENSE'?

INTIMATE, *subs.* (American thieves').—A shirt.
TO BE IMPROPERLY INTIMATE WITH, *verb. phr.* (colloquial).—To copulate outside marriage. For synonyms *see* GREENS and RIDE.

INTERCOURSE, TO HAVE IMPROPER INTERCOURSE WITH, *verb. phr.* (colloquial).—To possess a woman outside marriage. For synonyms *see* GREENS and RIDE.

Adj. (common).—(An epithet expressive of contempt and derogation: as, the IRISH-ARMS (or -LEGS) = thick legs. *See* MULLINGAR HEIFER.

NO IRISH NEED APPLY, *phr.* (American).—'You're not wanted'; GIT! (*q.v.*).

YOU'RE IRISH, *phr.* (common).—Said of any one talking unintelligibly.

IRISH-APRICOT, (APPLE or LEMON), *subs.* (old). A potato. For synonyms *see* MURPHY.
1785. GROSE, *Vulg. Tongue*, s.v.
1811. *Lex. Bal.*, s.v.
1825. *Modern Flash Dict.*, s.v.

IRISH-ASSURANCE, *subs.* (old).—See quot.
1785. GROSE, *Vulg. Tongue*, s.v. IRISH APRICOTS . . . . IRISH ASSURANCE, a bold forward behaviour; it is said a dipping in the Shannon annihilates bashfulness

IRISH-BEAUTY, *subs.* (old).—A woman with two black eyes.—GROSE.

IRISHMAN'S-DINNER, *subs.* (common).—A fast. *Cf.* DINE OUT.

IRISH-EVIDENCE, *subs.* (old.)—A false witness. GROSE (1785).

IRISH-FORTUNE, *subs.* (old).—A cunt and pattens.

IRISHMAN'S-HARVEST, *subs.* (London costers').—The orange season.

IRISHMAN'S-HURRICANE, *subs.* (nautical).—A dead calm.

IRISH-PENNANTS, *subs.* (nautical).—Fag ends of rope, rope-yarns etc.

IRISHMAN'S-REEF, *subs.* (nautical).—The head of a sail tied up.—CLARK RUSSELL.

IRISH-RIFLE, *subs.* (common).—A small tooth-comb.

IRISH-RISE (or PROMOTION), *subs.* (common).—A reduction in position or pay.

IRISH-ROOT, *subs.* (venery).—The *penis*. For synonyms *see* CREAMSTICK and PRICK.

IRISH-THEATRE, *subs.* (military).—A guard room or lock-up in barracks. For synonyms *see* CAGE. Fr. *maison de campagne.*

IRISH-TOOTHACHE, *subs.* (venery).—An erection of the *penis*. For synonyms *see* HORN.

IRISH-TOYLE, *subs.*(old).—See quots.
1690. B. E., *Dict. Cant. Crew*, s.v. IRISH TOYLES, c., the Twelfth Order of Canters: also Rogues carrying Pinns, Points, Laces, and such like Wares, and under pretence of selling them, commit Thefts and Robberies.
1785. GROSE, *Vulg. Tongue*, s.v.
1811. *Lex. Bal.*, s.v.

IRISH-WEDDING, *subs.* (old).—The emptying of a cesspool. *See* GOLDFINDER.—BEE (1823).
TO HAVE DANCED AT AN IRISH WEDDING, *verb. phr.* (common).—To have got two black eyes.

IRISH-WHIST, (WHERE THE JACK TAKES THE ACE), *subs. phr.* (venery).—Copulation. For synonyms *see* GREENS and RIDE.

IRON, *subs.* (old).—1. Money. For synonyms *see* ACTUAL and GILT.
1785. GROSE, *Vulg. Tongue*, s.v.
1811. *Lex. Bal.*, s.v.
1825. *Mod. Flash Dict.*, s.v.

INTERESTING CONDITION (or SITUATION), TO BE IN A, *verb. phr.* (colloquial).—To be with child.
1748. SMOLLETT, *Rod. Random*, lxix. So that I cannot leave her in such an INTERESTING SITUATION, which I hope will produce something to crown my felicity.
1751. SMOLLETT, *Peregrine Pickle*, lxxxi. I found myself in a fair way of being a mother; and that I might be near my own relations in such an INTERESTING SITUATION, etc.
1838. DICKENS, *Nicholas Nickleby*, xxix. Mrs. Leuville was in an INTERESTING STATE.

INTERFERE, *verb.* (Western American).—To maltreat.

INTERLOPER, *subs.* (old: now recognised).—An unlicensed trader; a smuggler; one who interferes, or intercepts unwarrantably. Also as in quot. 1690.
1627. MINSHEW, *Dict.*, INTERLOPERS in trade.
1675. SIR W. TEMPLE, *Letter*, (To the Gov. and Compt. of Merchant Adventurers) 26 March. Whatever privileges are allowed your Company at Dort will be given at the other towns, either openly or covertly, to all those INTERLOPERS who may bring their manufactures directly thither.
1690. B.E. *Dict. Cant. Crew*, s.v. INTERLOPERS, Hangers on, retainers to, or dependers upon other folks; also Medlers and Busybodies, intruders into other Men's Professions, and those that intercept the Trade of a Company, being not legally authorised.
1725. *New Canting Dict.*, s.v.

INTERCRURAL TRENCH, *subs.* (venery).—The female *pudendum*.—URQUHART. For synonyms *see* MONOSYLLABLE.

INTO. TO BE INTO A MAN, *verb. phr.* (common).—To pitch into him; to fight him.

Prep. (American).—'Short of'; wanting: *e.g.* 'I thought I did pretty well delivering all the load into one box (*i.e.*, all but one box).
TO BE (or GET) INTO A WOMAN, *verb. phr.* (venery).—To possess a woman carnally. For synonyms *see* GREENS and RIDE.

INVADE, *verb.* (venery).—To effect intromission; also, to lay hands on; TO GROPE (*q.v.*).
1684. DRYDEN, *The Disappointment* (Prologue). INVADE and grubble one another's punk.

INVITE, *subs.* (vulgar: once literary).—An invitation.
1615. SANDYS, *Relation of a Journey*, 305. The Lamprey swims to his Lord's INVITES.
1778. D'ARBLAY, *Diary*, (1876) i. 73. Everybody bowed and accepted the INVITE but me.
1836. DICKENS, *Sketches by Boz*, 'Steam Excursion.' Guest after guest arrived, the INVITES had been excellently arranged.
1837. BARHAM, *Ingoldsby Legends*, 'Merchant of Venice.' To give all his old friends that farewell INVITE.

INWARD, *subs.* (old).—1. An intimate.
1603. SHAKESPEARE, *Measure for Measure*, iii. 2. Sir, I was an INWARD of his: a shy fellow was the Duke.
1607. MIDDLETON, *Michaelmas Term*, ii. 3. He is a kind gentleman, a very INWARD of mine.
2. in pl. *See* INNARDS.

IRISH, *subs.* (colloquial).—Irish whiskey; FENIAN (*q.v.*).
1893. H. CRACKENTHORPE, *Wreckage*, 125. 'Mary, . . . a large IRISH for Mr. Hays here.'
TO GET ONE'S IRISH UP, *verb. phr.* (common).—To get angry. Also TO GET ONE'S DUTCH (or, in America, INDIAN) UP.

2. (American thieves').—Courage. For synonyms *see* SPUNK.
3. in pl. (thieves').—Fetters. For synonyms *see* DARBIES.—BEE (1823).
1888. ROLF BOLDREWOOD, *Robbery Under Arms*, xxxvii. I was kept in IRONS night and day for a month.

Verb. (old).—To flatter.
1823. BEE, *Dict. of the Turf*, s.v. IRONING, i.e. Irony *e.g.* 'Bill Noon, you are one of the best in all England, for nollidge and for larning.' *Noon.* 'Nay, my Coney, now you're IRONING me. . . . all down the back'.

BAD IRON, *subs. phr.* (workmen's).—Failure; misadventure; bad luck.

SHOOTING-IRON. See *post.*

THIEVING-IRONS. See *post.*

TO POLISH THE KING'S IRON WITH ONE'S EYEBROW, *verb. phr.* (old).—To look out of grated or prison windows.—GROSE (1785).

TO HAVE MANY IRONS IN THE FIRE (or ON THE ANVIL), *verb. phr.* (colloquial).—To carry out many projects at the same time, especially schemes for making money.
1593. G. HARVEY, *Pierces Supererog.* in *Works* ii. 330. It is some men's fortune to have their handes full of vnneedefull businesse attonce: and for miselfe, I should make no great matter of two, or three such glowing IRONS IN THE FIRE.
1614. JONSON, *Bartholomew Fair*, i. Aye, quickly, good mistress, I pray you; for I have both eggs on the spit, and IRON IN THE FIRE.
1622. CHAPMAN, *Widows Tears*, ii. 1. And you know, brother, I have other IRONS ON THE ANVIL.
1640. HOWELL, *Dodona's Grove*, p. 38. Elaiana. . . . hath divers nurseries to supplie, MANY IRONS perpetually IN THE FIRE.
1668. DRYDEN, *An Evening's Love*, iv. 1. I have more IRONS IN THE FIRE:

When I have done with you, I have another assignation.
1760-1. SMOLLETT, *Sir L. Greaves*, iii. Anthony Darnel had begun to canvass, and was putting every IRON IN THE FIRE.
1849. LYTTON, *Caxtons*, pt. VII. ii. He had other IRONS IN THE FIRE besides the 'Literary Times' and the 'Confederate Authors' Society'.

IRONBARK, *adj.* (Australian). *See* IRONCLAD.

IRON-BOUND, *adj.* (old).—1. Laced with metal. IRON-BOUND HAT = A silver laced hat.—GROSE(1785).
2. (common).—A hard-baked pie.

IRONCLAD, *subs.* (American).—1. A paragon: as a severely chaste girl, popular play, song, horse, etc.
2. (common).—An iron-cased watch.
Adj. (common).—Strong; hard; unyielding. Also IRONBARK (*q.v.*).
1888. ROLF BOLDREWOOD, *Robbery Under Arms*, chap. vi. I always thought he was IRONBARK outside and in.

IRON-COW. See COW.
1785. GROSE, *Vulg. Tongue*, s.v.
1811. *Lex. Bal.*, s.v.

IRON-DOUBLET, *subs. phr.* (old).—1. A prison. For synonyms *see* CAGE.
1779. BAMFYLDE-MOORE CAREW.
1785. GROSE, *Vulg. Tongue*, s.v.
2. (American thieves').—Innocence.

IRON-HORSE, *subs.* (common).—1. A locomotive.
2. (cyclists'). A tricycle or bicycle.
1875. *Echo*, 29 Oct. Mr. S. started on his third day's journey of the 650 miles ride on his IRON-HORSE.

IRONMONGER'S-SHOP. TO KEEP AN IRONMONGER'S SHOP BY THE SIDE OF A COMMON, WHERE THE SHERIFF SETS ONE UP, *verb. phr.* (old).—To be hanged in chains. For synonyms *see* LADDER.—GROSE (1785).

IRON-RATIONS, *subs.* (nautical).—Tinned meat: specifically boiled salt-beef. *See* BULLY-BEEF.

IRON-TOOTHPICK, *subs.* (military).—A sword. For synonyms *see* POKER.

IRRIGATE, *verb.* (common).—To take a drink; to liquor up. For synonyms *see* DRINKS. Also TO IRRIGATE ONE'S CANAL.

1708. PHILIPS, *Cyder*, ii. Their frying blood compels to IRRIGATE their dry-furred tongues.

1892. JOHN HILL, *Treason Felony*, ii. 106. They went into the Hotel de Florence in Rupert Street and ate a *seconda collazione* or *déjeuner à la fourchette*, IRRIGATED with Barolo.

ISABELLA, *subs.* (rhyming).—An umbrella. For synonyms *see* MUSHROOM.

ISLAND. TO DRINK OUT OF THE ISLAND, *subs.* (old).—*See* quot.

1811. *Lex. Bal.*, s.v. ISLAND. He drank out of the bottle till he saw the island: the ISLAND is the rising bottom of a wine bottle, which appears like an island in the centre, before the bottle is quite empty.

ISLAND OF BERMUDA.—*See* BERMUDAS.

ISLE-OF-FLING, *subs.* (East End). A coat. For synonyms *see* CAPELLA.

ISSUES. TO POOL ONE'S ISSUES, *verb. phr.* (colloquial).—To work in unison; to come to an understanding for mutual advantage.

ISTHMUS-OF-SUEZ, *subs.* (Cambridge university).—The bridge at St. John's College Cambridge, leading from the grounds to one of the Courts, familiarly known as the 'Bridge of Sighs'. Also THE BRIDGE OF GRUNTS. [From its slight similiarity to the Venetian example *Sues* = swine, in punning reference to the JOHNIAN HOGS (*q.v.*). *See* CRACKLE and HOG.

1857. *Punch*, June 20. A resident Fellowe he was, I wis, He had no cure of Soules; And across ye BRIDGE OF SUES he'd come From playinge ye game of bowles.

1885. CUTHBERT BEDE, in *N. & Q.*, 6, S. xi. 414. Another word is *Sues*, for swine. This is applied to the bridge leading from the old courts to the new, familiarly known as the BRIDGE OF SIGHS from its slight similiarity to the Venetian example, but also known as the ISTHMUS OF SUEZ. This word *Suez* was then transformed to *Suez*, swine, to adapt it to its Johnian frequenters.

I SUBSCRIBE, *phr.* (common).—A response to an invitation to drink. For synonyms *see* DRINKS.

I SUPPOSE, *subs.* (rhyming).—The nose.

1859. DU CANGE ANGLICUS, *Vulgar Tongue*, s.v. I gave him a blow with this neddy on the I-SUPPOSE.

IT, *subs.* (common).—1. A chamber-pot.

ENGLISH SYNONYMS. Bishop; chantie (Scots'); jerry; jordan; jerker; jockum-gage; lagging-gage; looking-glass; member-mug; mingo; piss-pot; po; smoker; smokeshell; tea-voider; thunder-mug; twiss.

FRENCH SYNONYMS. *Un Thomas* (popular: also *la mère* or *la veuve Thomas* = nightstool); *la cassolette* (popular = perfuming-pan); *un dépotoir*

(thieves': also a confessional or brothel); *un gare l'eau* (thieves': *cf.* GARDY-LOO); *un Jules* (popular: also *aller chez Jules* = to ease oneself: *prendre, pincer,* or *tirer les oreilles à Jules* = to carry away the privy tub: *passer la jambe à Jules* = to assist at an IRISH WEDDING (*q.v.*): *travailler pour Jules* = to eat).

2. (venery). The female *pudendum*. For synonyms *see* MONOSYLLABLE.

ITCH. TO HAVE AN ITCH IN THE BELLY, *verb. phr.* (venery).—To be sexually excited; to have a MUST (*q.v.*). Also TO ITCH.

1675. COTTON, *Scoffer, Scoffed*, 4th ed. 1725, p. 173. Why then to cure thy ITCHING, Jove, thou art now going a bitching.

1720. DURFEY, *Pills to Purge etc.*, vi, 324. Each has an ITCH IN HER BELLY. To play with the scarlet hue.

ITCHER (or ITCHING JENNY), *subs.* (venery).—The female *pudendum*. For synonyms *see* MONOSYLLABLE.

ITCH-BUTTOCKS. TO PLAY AT ITCH-BUTTOCKS, *verb. phr.* (venery).—To copulate. For synonyms *see* GREENS and RIDE.

1598. FLORIO, *Worlde of Wordes*, s.v. *Giocar' aleua culo*, to play at leuell coile or ITCH BUTTOCKES.

ITCHLAND (or SCRATCHLAND), *subs.* (old).—1. Wales (B.E. 1690); 2. Scotland (*New Cant. Dict.* and GROSE 1785). ITCHLANDER = a Scot.

ITCHING-PALM. *See* PALM.

ITEM, *subs.* (common).—A hint; a piece of news: (in gaming) a signal from a confederate; (Amer-

ican journalist) a paragraph of news; (thieves') a warning.

d.1680. GLANVIL, (quoted in *Enc. Dict.*). If this discourse have not concluded our weakness, I have one more ITEM of mine.

1823. BEE, *Dict. of the Turf*, s.v. ITEM. It was I that gave the ITEM that the traps were a coming.

1893. RUSSELL, *Current Americanisms*, s.v. ITEM. 'To give an ITEM', is to signal information to a confederate unfairly.

1864. KIMBALL, *Was He Successful?* 129. Otis is ITEM-man and reporter for the Clarion.

b.1877. *New York Spirit of the Times*, (quoted in BARTLETT). Keep your eyes skinned and your rifles clean, and the minit yer get ITEM that I'm back, set off for the cross roads.

IVORIES, *subs.* (common).—1. The teeth. For synonyms *see* GRINDERS.

1782. MRS. COWLEY, *Bold Stroke for a Husband*, ii. 2 Gas. What, Don Sancho, who, with two-thirds of a century in his face, affects . . . . to make you believe that the two rows of IVORY in his head grew there.

1811. *Lex. Bal.*, s.v. IVORIES. How the swell flashed his IVORIES: how the gentleman shewed his teeth.

1818-24. EGAN, *Boxiana*, iii. 253. So severe a blow on his mouth as to dislodge some of his IVORY.

1819. MOORE, *Tom Crib*, 22. The Adonis would ne'er flash his IVORY again.

1849. THACKERAY, *Pendennis*, lxvii. Chatter your old IVORIES at me, do you, you grinning old baboon.

1868. *Orchestra*, 20 Oct. Mr. Buckstone might let us off with what Bell's Life would designate a rattling on the IVORIES.

1882. *Punch*, lxxxii, 185, 2. I never heard of him sluicing his IVORIES with what you call S. & B.

1889. *Notes and Queries*, 7, S. vii. 13 April, p. 292. I sometimes think that the attrition in which we so joyously indulge when we 'sharpen' our IVORIES may be easily overdone.

2. (gaming).—Dice: also (cards') checks and counters.

ENGLISH SYNONYMS. (for both genuine and false pieces). Bones; cogs; fulhams; devil's teeth; devil's bones; gourds; rattlers; tats; high men; low men; uphills.

FRENCH SYNONYMS. *Les mathurins* (thieves'); *les maturbes* (thieves').

SPANISH SYNONYM. *Hormiga.*

1830. LYTTON, *Paul Clifford*, 23, (ed. 1854). Suppose we adjourn to Fish Lane, and Rattle the IVORIES. What say you, Mr. Lobkins?

1864. G. A. SALA, *Quite Alone*, vii. Yes, I will promise you I will keep my head cool, and won't touch IVORY to-night.

3. (billiards').—The balls.

1888. *Sporting Life*, 28 Nov. On new premises . . . . where erstwhile the click of IVORIES was heard.

TO FLASH THE IVORIES, *verb. phr.* (common).—1. To show the teeth.—GROSE (1785).

2. (medical).—To be dissected or 'anatomised' after execution, the skeleton being taken to the College of Surgeons; hence, to be hanged.

1830. LYTTON, *Paul Clifford*, ii. 'I want to make him an honour to his country and an ixciption to my family" 'Who all FLASHED their IVORIES at Surgeon's Hall', added the metaphorical Dummie.

TO SLUICE (WASH or RINCE) ONE'S IVORIES, *verb. phr.* (common).—To drink.

1823. MONCRIEFF, *Tom & Jerry*, ii. 6. Mr. J. Sluice your dominos vill you? *Green.* Vot! I never plays at dominos—it's too vulgar. Mr. J. Vy then, vash your IVORIES? *Green.* I've got no HIVERIES to vash. Mr. J. Drink vill you? dont you understand Hinglish?

IVORY-BOX, *subs.* (pugilists').—The mouth. For synonyms *see* POTATO-TRAP.

1888. *Sportsman*, 28 Nov. Harris countered heavily on Joseph's IVORY BOX, a compliment which he at once returned, and with considerable interest.

IVORY-CARPENTER, *subs.* (common).—A dentist. For synonyms *see* SNAG-CATCHER.

IVORY-GATE, *subs.* (venery).—The female *pudendum*. For synonyms *see* MONOSYLLABLE.

IVORY-THUMPER, (or SPANKER), *subs.* (common).—A pianist.

IVY-BUSH, *subs.* (old).—*See* quot.

1785. GROSE, *Vulg. Tongue*, s.v. Ivy-Bush. Like an owl in an IVY BUSH, a simile for a meagre, or weazle-faced man, with a large wig, or very bushy hair.

 JAB (or JOB), *subs.* (colloquial American).—A prod; a poke; a stab.

1872. C. D. WARNER, *Backlog Studies*, 279. 'Oh yes, I have,' I cried, starting up and giving the fire a JAB with the poker.

1884. *Detroit Free Press*, 3 May, p. 5, col. 4. He gave each of the Epistles a vicious JAB with the cancelling stamp, and then tossed it into the mail-bag.

Verb. (colloquial American).—To handle harshly; to hustle; to prod or poke; to stab (with a pointed weapon).

1868. *Putnam's Magazine*, Sept. (quoted by DE VERE). 'The Missouri stoker pulls and JABS his plutonic monster as an irate driver would regulate his mule.'

1885. F. R. STOCKTON, *Rudder Grange*, iv. 'Shall we run on deck and shoot him as he swims?' I cried. 'No,' said the boarder, 'we'll get the boat-hook, and JAB him if he tries to climb up.'

1888. *Denver Republican*, 6 May. When it [hair] don't twist easily she's as like to JAB at it with her scissors and shorten it herself as trust it to anybody as knows how.

1889. *Detroit Free Press*, 5 Jan. Moses JABBED at him and ran the umbrella clean through him.

1890. *Tit Bits*, 26 April, p. 55, col. 3. If you JAB that umbrella in my eye again, you'll get a broken head!

JABBER, *subs.* (old colloquial).—Chatter; incoherent or inarticulate and unintelligible speech (as a foreign language heard by one ignorant of it). See *verb.*

1706. WARD, *Hudibras Redivivus*, I, v. 5. And stopp'd their bold presumptuous labour, By unintelligible JABBER.

1726. SWIFT, *Gulliver's Travels*, 'Gulliver, to his cousin Sympson.' They use a sort of JABBER and do not go naked.

1827. JOHNSON, *Eng. Dict.* [Todd] s.v. JABBER, garrulity. . . . Bishop Fleetwood somewhere uses the word in his works; and it is still a colloquial term.

1854. *Our Cruise in the Undine*, p. 35. The JABBER began. . . . and almost distracted us.

1879. JAS. PAYN, *High Spirits (Aunt by Marriage)*. When one considers the packing, and the crossing the Channel, and the JABBER upon the other side of it, which not one in ten of us understands and the tenth only imperfectly.

1888. BOLDREWOOD, *Robbery Under Arms*, viii. Is it French or Queensland blacks' JABBER?

Verb. (old: now recognised). See quots.

1543. BALE, *Yet a Course*, fol. 43, b. Censynge, Latyne, JABBERINGE.

1690. B. E. *Dict. Cant, Crew*, s.v. JABBER, to Talk thick and fast, as great Praters do, or to Chatter, like a Magpye.

1716. ADDISON, *Tory Foxhunter*, [in *Freeholder*, No. 22, Mar. 5]. He did not know what travelling was good for but to teach a man to ride the great horse, to JABBER French &c.

1725. *New Cant. Dict.*, s.v. JABBER.

1728. POPE, *Dunciad*, ii. 237. 'Twas chatt'ring, grinning, mouthing, JABB'RING all.

d.1745. SWIFT, [quoted by JOHNSON]. We scorn, for want of talk, to JABBER Of parties.

1785. GROSE, *Vulg. Tongue*, s.v. JABBER . . . . also to speak a foreign language; he JABBERED to me in his damned outlandish parlez-vous.

1853. THACKERAY, *Barry Lyndon*, vi. p. 82. A couple more of the same nation were JABBERING oaths and chattering incessantly.

1859. MATSELL, *Vocabulum*, s.v. JABBER. To talk in an unknown language.

1884. W. C. RUSSELL, *Jack's Courtship*, xvii. We sallied forth arm in arm, he JABBERING incessantly.

1888. *Daily Chronicle*, 19 Oct. The woman said that he was a perfect stranger to her, and . . . . JABBERED something she did not understand.

JABBERER, *subs*. (old: now colloquial).—One who JABBERS (*q.v.*).

1678. BUTLER, *Hudibras*, III, c.2. T'out-cant the Babylonian labourers, At all their dialects of JABBERERS.

JABBERING, *subs*. (old: now colloquial).—Nonsense; indistinct and rapid speech; PATTER (*q.v.*).

1690. DURFEY, *Collin's Walk*, C. IV, p. 183. With which, and wild Egyptian JABBERING, She got her Living without Labouring.

1720. DEFOE, *Capt. Singleton*, I, xi. Pray what are we the wiser for all their JABBERING?

JABBERINGLY, *adv*. (old: now colloquial).—Indistinctly; nonsensically.

JABBERMENT, *subs*. (old: now colloquial).—Nonsense; gibberish; JABBER (*q.v.*).

1645. MILTON, *Colasterion* [quoted in *Enc. Dict.*]. At last, and in good hour, we are come to his farewel, which is to be a concluding taste of his JABBERMENT in law.

JABBERNOWL. *See* JOBBERNOWL.

JABERS (or **JABEZ**). BE (or BY) JABERS (or JABEZ), *intj*. (common).—An oath.

1821. HAGGART, *Life*, 118. By JAPPERS! we were tould he was the boy.

1890. HUME NISBET, *Bail up*, p. 265. A head wind, BE JABBERS!

1892. HUME NISBET, *Bushranger's Sweetheart*, p. 152. Arrah, BE JABBERS! but that's the foinest song I have listened to since I left Ould Oirland.

JACK, *subs*. (old).—1. A farthing; also (American thieves'), a small coin.

1690. B. E., *Dict. Cant. Crew*. s.v. JACK.

1714. *Memoirs of John Hall*, p. 12, s.v.

1725. *New Cant. Dict*. s.v. JACK. He wou'd not tip me a JACK, Not a farthing wou'd he give me.

1785. GROSE, *Vulg. Tongue*, s.v.

1859. MATSELL, *Vocabulum*, s.v.

2. (old).—The small bowl aimed at in the game of bowls.

1605. SHAKSPEARE, *Cymbeline*, ii. 1, 2. Was there ever man had such luck! when I kissed the JACK upon on upcast to be hit away!

1690. B. E., *Dict. Cant. Crew*. s.v. JACK.

1726. BUTLER, *Human Learning*, Pt. 2. Like bowlers strive to beat away the JACK.

d.1742. BENTLEY, [quoted by JOHNSON, 1755]. But if it, [a bowl] be made with a byass . . . . it may . . . . run spontaneously to the JACK.

1785. GROSE, *Vulg. Tongue*, s.v. JACK.

1811. *Lex. Bal*. s.v. JACK.

3. (old: now recognised).— A contrivance to assist a person in taking off his boots; a bootjack.

1690. B. E., *Dict. Cant. Crew*. s.v. JACK.

1785. GROSE, *Vulg. Tongue*, s.v. JACK.

4. (old: now colloquial).— The Knave in any of the four

suits in a pack of cards. *Fr. le galuchet*, or *le larbin savonné* or *le mistigris*.

1662. *Rump Songs*, '*Rump Carbonado'd*'. No admiral like an old Puritan JACK. A craftier knave you can't find in the pack.

1754. MARTIN, *Eng. Dict*. 2nd Ed. Knave, ... or a JACK at cards.

1860. DICKENS, *Great Expectations*, viii. He calls the Knaves JACKS.

5. (old).—A post-chaise (GROSE 3rd ed. 1823).

6. (old: now recognised).—A pitcher varying in capacity: generally made of leather; a BLACK-JACK (*q.v.*).

1592. NASHE, *Summer's Last Will* [DODSLEY, *Old Plays* (1874), viii. 59]. Rise up Sir Robert Toss-pot. [*Here he dubs Will Summer with the* BLACK-JACK.]

1606. *Return from Parnassus* [DODSLEY, *Old Plays* (1874), ix. 207]. A BLACK-JACK of beer and a Christmas pie.

1690. B. E., *Dict. Cant. Crew*. s.v. JACK.

7. (old).—A Jacobite. [In the quot. there is a punning reference to the flag, sense 13].

1723. SWIFT, *Elegy, on Judge Boat*, [*Works*, Aldine ed. iii. 96]. With every wind he sailed, And well could tack; Had many pendents, but abhorred a JACK.

8. (old).—A term of contempt. [The usage is common in most modern languages: *e.g.* Fr. *Jean-guêtré* = peasant, *Jean-bête* = 'cabbage-head', *Jean-fesse* or *Jean-foutre* = scamp; It. *Gianni*, whence ZANY; Sp. *Juan*, as *bobo Juan* = foolish John, &c.].

[See also many of the combinations following. To PLAY THE JACK = to act the fool (or GOAT (*q.v.*); CHEAP JACK = a peddling tradesman; JACK-FOOL (CHAUCER) = a thundering idiot; JACK-FRIAR = a HEDGE-PRIEST (*q.v.*); JACK-SLAVE = a vulgarian; JACK-BRAG = a boaster; JACK-SNIP = a botching tailor; JACK-STRAW = a low-born rebel; JACK-SPRAT = a mannikin; SKIP-JACK = an upstart; JACK-AT-WARTS = a little conceited fellow; JACK-IN-THE-BOX = the sacrament; JACK-UPALAND (CHAUCER) = a peasant].

1383. CHAUCER, *Canterbury Tales* [SKEAT (1894), p. 106]. 'Go fro the window, JAKKE FOOL,' she said.

1580. H. GIFFORD, *Posie of Gilleflowers* (GROSART 1875), 'A delectable dream', p. 113. I know some peppernosed dame Will term me fool and saucy JACK.

1593. SHAKSPEARE, *Taming of the Shrew*, ii. A mad-cap ruffian, and a swearing JACK, That thinks with oaths to face the matter out.

1595. SHAKSPEARE, *Romeo and Juliet*, ii. 4. *Nurse*. An a' speak any thing against me, I'll take him down, an a' were lustier than he is, and twenty such JACKS, and if I cannot, I'll find those that shall.

1596. NASHE, *Have with You, Wks*. [GROSART]. Teaching it to do tricks, Hey come aloft, JACKE, like an ape over the chain.

1597-8. HAUGHTON, *A Woman will have her Will* [DODSLEY, *Old Plays* (1874), x. 496]. Some scoffing JACK had sent thee. . . . To tell a feigned tale of happy luck.

1600. NASHE, *Summer's Last Will*, in *Works* (GROSART, vi. 107). This sawcie upstart JACKE That now doth rule the chariot of the sun.

1606. *Return from Parnassus* [DODSLEY, *Old Plays* (1874), ix. 101]. Scurvy in thy face, thou scurvy JACK.

1607. WILKINS, *Enforced Marriage* [DODSLEY, *Old Plays* (1874), ix. 488]. Shall I be crossed by such a JACK.

1611. DAVIES, *Scourge of Folly*, *Wks*. (GROSART, p. 39, Epig. 282). Such jocund JACKS as mock thee.

1621. BURTON, *Anat. of Mel.*, 291. A company of scoffers and proud JACKS are commonly conversant and attendant in such places.

1636. T. HEYWOOD, *Love's Mistress*, i. They call her Queen of Love, will know no other, And swear my Son shall kneel and call her mother. *Cup*. But Cupid swears to make the JACKS forsworn.

1647. BEAUMONT & FLETCHER, *Faithful Friend*, i. 2. A company of quarrelling JACKS. . . . They say they have been soldiers, and fall out About their valours.

1653. BROME, *Five New Plays*, 403. The frumping JACKS are gone.

1677. WYCHERLEY, *Plain Dealer*, ii. *Wid*. Marry come up, you saucy familiar JACK!

1738. SWIFT, *Polite Convers*. Dial. I. But, I swear, you are a saucy JACK to use such expressions.

9. (gaming).—A counter resembling in size and appearance a sovereign. Also HALF-JACKS. *See* quot.

1851. MAYHEW, *Lond. Lab. etc*. i. 387. They are all made in Birmingham, and are of the size and colour of the genuine sovereigns and half sovereigns. . . . Each presents a profile of the Queen; but instead of the superscription 'Victoria Dei Gratiâ' of the true sovereign, the JACK has 'Victoria Regina'. On the reverse, in the place of the 'Britanniarum Regina Fid. Def.' surrounding the royal arms and crown, is a device (intended for an imitation of St. George and the Dragon) representing a soldier on horseback—the horse having three legs elevated from the ground, while a drawn sword fills the right hand of the equestrian, and a crown adorns his head. The superscription is, 'to Hanover,' and the rider seems to be sociably accompanied by a dragon. Round the Queen's head on the HALF JACK is 'Victoria, Queen of Great Britain,' and on the reverse the Prince of Wales's feather, with the legend, 'The Prince of Wales's Model Half Sovereign.'

10. (common).—(a) A sailor: also JACK-tar, English-JACK, and Spanish-JACK. (b) An attendant at a boat-house. Also JACK-IN-THE-WATER (*q.v.*).

1788. C. DIBDIN, *Poor Jack*, 'Song'. There's a sweet little Cherub that sits up aloft, To keep watch for the life of poor JACK.

1867. *Cassell's Family Paper*, 23 Feb. The old brigadier ordered the JACKS to storm.

11. (American schools').—A stranger.

12. (old).—A male sweetheart; *cf*. GILL.

c.1500. *Babees Book*, [E.E.T.S.], 22. And aryse up soft and stylle, And iangylle nether IAK ne IYLLE.

1592. SHAKSPEARE, *Midsummer Nights Dream*, iii. 2. JACK shall have Jill.

1620. PERCY, *Folio MSS*., p. 104. Yet there is neuer a IACKE for GILL.

13. (nautical).—The Union Jack; THE RAG (*q.v.*).

1652. In PREBLE, *Hist. of the Flag*, p. 151. In a paper dated Jan. 14, 1652 . . . . it is ordered, 'all the ships to wear JACKS as formerly'.

1892. KIPLING, *Barrack Room Ballads*, '*The Rhyme of the Three Captains*'. Now he floated the Gridiron, and now he floated the JACK.

14. (Old Cant.).—A seal. *See* JARK.

15. (thieves').—A policeman. For synonyms *see* BEAK and COPPER.

1889. RICHARDSON, *Police*, p. 320, s.v.

16. (Scots').—*See* JAKES.

17. (venery).—An *erectio penis*. For synonyms *see* HORN.

18. (venery).—The *penis*. For synonyms *see* CREAMSTICK and PRICK.

19. (colloquial).—A male: as in the compounds JACK-HARE, JACK-CROW, JACK-ASS, JACK-RABBIT, etc.

1563. *Appius & Virginius* [DODSLEY, *Old Plays* (1874), iv. 151]. A gentleman?—nay, a JACK-HERRING.

1894. DE SOMERVILLE & ROSS, *The Real Charlotte*, i. 210. And I don't care a JACK-RAT what he thought, or what you think either.

20. (old).—An ape.

21. (old).—A peasant.

1513. DUNBAR, *Poems* (1883-4), i. 106. JOK that was wont to keep the stinks.

1589. NASHE, *Anatomie of Absurdity*, in *Works* [GROSART, i. 9]. They distinguish a gentleman from a . . . . JACKE.

c.1636. *London Chanticleers*, Sc. i. Thou believ'st that more may be gotten with a *Good your worship* to every JACK than a *Sirrah, deliver your purse* to the best lord i' th' land.

1678. COTTON, *Virgil Travestie*, in *Wks*. (1725), Bk. iv. p. 122. Shall I invite . . . Some saucy, proud Numidian JACK, and humbly beg of him to take Æneas' leavings.

Verb. (American).—1. To brand an unmarked yearling or MAVERICK (*q.v.*).

1871. DE VERE, *Americanisms*, 211. Any owner of a large herd considers himself authorised to brand a maverick which he finds on or near his ranche, and this operation is called TO JACK a maverick.

2. (venery).—To copulate. For synonyms *see* GREENS and RIDE.

3. (thieves'). To run away quickly. For synonyms *see* AMPUTATE.

TO LAY ON THE JACK, *verb. phr*. (old).—To thrash soundly; to scold in good round terms. For synonyms *see* BASTE and TAN.

1557-8. *Jacob & Esau* [DODSLEY, *Old Plays* (1874), ii. 253]. If I wrought one stroke to-day, LAY ME ON THE JACK.

1579. NORTH, *Noble Grecians*, p. 127. And that they should make no reckoning of all that bravery and bragges, but should stick to it like men, and LAY it ON THE JACKS of them.

TO MAKE ONE'S JACK, *verb. phr*. (American).—To succeed; to gain one's point. [From the game of faro].

TO BE COPPERED ON THE JACK, *verb. phr*. (American).—To fail; to lose one's point. [From the game of faro].

1878. J. H. BEADLE, *Western Wilds*, 46. He. . . . staked a pile of 'chips' and won; then made and lost, and made and lost alternately, selling his stock, when 'broke', and scarcely ate or drank till the tail of his last mule was COPPERED ON THE JACK.

TO PLAY THE JACK, *verb. phr*. (old).—To play the rogue.

1609. SHAKSPEARE, *Tempest*, iv. 1. Your fairy . . . . has done little better than PLAY THE JACK with us.

1612. ROWLANDS, *Knave of Hearts*, p. 20. [Hunterian Club Rept.]. Boy y'are a villaine, didst thou fill this Sacke? Tis flat, you Rascall, thou hast PLAID THE JACKE.

1668. PEPYS, *Diary*, Feb. 23. Who PLAYED THE JACKE with us all, and is a fellow that I must trust no more.

TO BE UPON THEIR JACKS, *verb. phr*. (old).—To have an advantage.

TO GET JACK IN THE ORCHARD, *verb. phr*. (venery).—To achieve intromission. For synonyms *see* GREENS and RIDE.

EVERY MAN JACK (or EVERY JACK-RAG), *phr*. (common).—Every one without exception.

1845. DISRAELI, *Sybil*, VI, vi. There is none: my missus says that NOT A MAN JOHN of them is to be seen.

1846. THACKERAY, *Vanity Fair*, viii. Sir Pitt had numbered EVERY MAN JACK of them.

1852. C. READE, *Peg Woffington*, viii. Send them (the children) to bed; EVERY MAN JACK of them.

1861. MISS BRADDON, *Trail of the Serpent*, IV, i. I knows EVERY MAN JACK of 'em, sir; and a fine staff they is.

1892. ANSTEY, *Voces Populi*, 'Free Speech', p. 103. Traitors, HEVERY MAN JACK of 'em.

JACK-AT-A-PINCH, *subs.* (old).—A person employed in an emergency; a stop-gap: specifically, a clergyman who has no cure, but on occasion officiates for a fee: *cf.* GUINEA-PIG.

1690. B. E., *Dict. Cant. Crew.*, s.v.

1725. *New. Cant. Dict.*, s.v.

1785. GROSE, *Vulg. Tongue*, s.v.

1883. WHITCHER, *Widow Bedott Papers*, p. 27. The fact is, Miss Coon feels wonderfully cut up, because she knows that her husband took her JACK-AT-A-PINCH.

JACK-IN-A(or-THE)-BOX, *subs.* (old).—1. *See* quots.

1632. DEKKER, *English Villanies*, [quoted by NARES]. This JACKE-IN-A-BOXE, or this divell in mans shape, wearing (like a player on a stage) good cloathes on his backe, comes to a goldsmiths stall, to a drapers, a habberdashers, or into any other shoppe, where he knowes good store of silver faces are to be seene.

1690. B. E., *Dict. Cant. Crew.*, s.v. JACK-IN-A-BOX, c. a Sharper or Cheat.

1725. *New. Cant. Dict.* s.v.

1785. GROSE, *Vulg. Tongue*, s.v.

1811. *Lex. Bal.* s.v.

2. (old).—A child's toy, consisting of a box out of which, on raising the lid, a figure springs.

1570. *Satirical Poems of Reformation* [S.T.S.], 1889-90, I, p. 163, l. 78. JAK-IN-THE-BOKKIS, for all thy mokkis.

1600. NASHE, *Works* [GROSART, 1885, vi. 149). Close under a hedge, or under a house wall, playing JACK-IN-A-BOX.

1702. *The Infernal Wanderer* [quoted by NARES]. As I was thus walking my rounds, up comes a brother of the quill, belonging to the office, who no sooner made his entiance amongst the equitable fraternity, but up started every one in his seat, like a JACK IN A BOX, crying out Legit aut non Legit; To which they answer'd themselves, Non legit, my lord.

1878. GRENVILLE MURRAY, *Round about France*, p. 268. With the suddenness of a JACK-IN-THE-BOX.

3. (common).—A game in which some article, of more or less value, is placed on the top of a stick standing in a hole, and thrown at with sticks. If the article be hit so as to fall clear of the hole, the thrower takes it.

4. (thieves').—A small but powerful kind of screw, used by burglars to open safes.

1848. ALBERT SMITH, *Christopher Tadpole*, ch. xiii. Take care of the JACK-IN-THE-BOX: there never was but two made.

5. (venery). The *penis.* For synonyms *see* CREAMSTICK and PRICK.

6. (old). *See* JACK-IN-THE-CELLAR.

7. (old.). A street-pedler.

1698-1700. WARD, *London Spy* [quoted in *Century*]. Here and there a JACK-IN-THE-BOX . . . . Selling Cures for your Corns, Glass-eyes for the Blind &c.

8. (old).—The sacrament.

JACK-IN-OFFICE, *subs.* (common).—An over-bearing petty official; an upstart; a JACK-IN-THE-PULPIT (*q.v.*).

1690. B. E., *Dict. Cant. Crew.* s.v. JACK IN AN OFFICE . . . . one that behaves himself imperiously in it.

1785. GROSE, *Vulg. Tongue*, s.v. JACK-IN-AN-OFFICE, an insolent fellow in authority.

1894. *St. James's Gazette*, 27 Aug. p. 13. Radical Governments and their JACKS-IN-OFFICE seem to have a happy knack of making enemies.

JACK-IN-THE-CELLAR (or BOX), *subs.* (old).—A child in the womb; a HANS-EN-KELDER (*q.v.*).

1765. SMOLLETT, *Peregrine Pickle*, i. 65. When his companions drank to HANS IN KELDER, or Jack in the Low Cellar.

JACK-IN-THE-DUST, *subs.* (nautical).—A steward's mate.

JACK-IN-THE-GREEN, *subs.* (common).—A chimney-sweep enclosed in a portable framework of boughs for the processions on the first of May: now mainly a thing of the past.

JACK-IN-THE-PULPIT, *subs.* A pretender; an upstart; a JACK-IN-OFFICE (*q.v.*).

JACK-IN-THE-WATER, *subs.* (common).—An odd or handy man at a boat-house or landing stage: also JACK (*q.v.* sense 10).

JACK-OF-ALL-TRADES, *subs.* (common).—One who can (or pretends to be able to) turn his hand to any business: now usually in contempt, as 'JACK-OF-ALL-TRADES and master of none'.

c. 1633. *Lady Alimony*, iv. 2. What else, you JACK-OF-ALL-TRADES?

c. 1636. *London Chanticleers*, Sc. ii. Any old pots or kettles to mend? Will you buy my ballads? Or have you any corns on your feet-toes? Nay, I am JACK-OF-ALL-TRADES now.

1662. *Rump Songs*, i. 193. For where Sir John with JACK-OF-ALL-TRADES joyns His finger's thicker than the prelates' loyns.

1675. COTTON, *Scoffer Scofft*, in *Wks.* (1725), p. 229. An then, thy son, that hopeful piece, Apollo, JACK-OF-ALL-TRADES is.

1698-1700. WARD, *London Spy*, III, 59. He is by his Profession a Labourer to a Physician, but has made himself, by a curious inspection into Mysteries of Universallity a JACK OF ALL TRADES.

1857. HOOD, *Pen and Pencil Pictures*, 138. A JACK-OF-ALL-TRADES and master of none was Panurgus Pebbles . . . . his shallow versatility was his bane.

1860. DICKENS, *Great Expectations*, xxv. 'I am my own engineer, and my own carpenter, and my own plumber, and my own gardener, and my own JACK OF ALL TRADES.'

JACK-OF-LEGS, *subs.* (old).—1. An extra tall man; a LAMP-POST (*q.v.*).

1785. GROSE, *Vulg. Tongue*, s.v.

1811. *Lex. Bal.* s.v.

1859. MATSELL, *Vocabulum*, s.v.

2. (old).—A large clasp knife. *See* JOCTELEG.

JACK-ON-BOTH-SIDES, *subs.* (old).—A neutral: also one who 'hunts with the hounds and runs with the hare'; a FENCE-RIDER (*q.v.*).

1594. NASHE, *Terrors of the Night*, in *Works* [GROSART, 1885, iii. 252]. Like a craftie JACKE A BOTH SIDES.

1654. *Witts Recreations* [quoted by NARES]. Reader, John Newter, who erst plaid, The JACK ON BOTH SIDES, here is laid.

1662. *Rump Songs*, i. 140. Did I a factious covenant, subscribe, Or turn a JACK-ON-BOTH-SIDES for a tribe?

JACK-OUT-OF-DOORS, *subs.* (old).—A vagrant.

1634. WITHAL, *Dict.*, p. 569. Neque pessimus neque primus: not altogether JACK OUT OF DOORES, and yet no gentleman.

JACK-OUT-OF-OFFICE, *subs.* (old).—A discharged official: in derision.

1592. SHAKSPEARE, *1 Henry VI*, i. 1. But long I will not be JACK-OUT-OF-OFFICE.

1606. RICH, *Farewell to Militarie Profession* [quoted by NARES]. For liberalitie, who was wont to be a principall officer . . . . is tourned JACKE OUT OF OFFICE, and others appointed to have the custodie.

1611. DAVIES (of Hereford), *Scourge of Folly*, in *Works* [GROSART, 1878, ii. 41]. He's IACKE OUT OF OFFICE that John was in it.

JACK-THE-PAINTER, *subs.* (Australian). A much adulterated green tea used in the bush.

1852. MUNDAY, *Our Antipodes*, [quoted in 'Slang, Jargon, & Cant.']. Another notorious ration tea of the bush is called JACK-THE-PAINTER.

JACK-THE-SLIPPER, *subs.* (thieves'). The treadmill. For synonyms *see* WHEEL OF LIFE.

TO JACK THE INTERIM, *verb.* (thieves').—To be remanded.

TO JACK UP, *verb.* (common).—To clinch; to abandon; TO CHUCK; (*q.v.*); JACKED-UP = ruined; done for.

1888. ROLF BOLDREWOOD, *Robbery Under Arms*, xix. Not but what I'd had a lot to bear, and took a deal of punishment before he JACKED UP.

1889. *Answers*, 23 March, p. 265, col. 2. When a man JACKS UP his work—will not do his tasks that is to say.

JACK ADAMS, *subs.* (old).—A fool. For synonyms *see* BUFFLE and CABBAGE-HEAD.

1690. B. E., *Dict. Cant. Crew.*, s.v.

1725. *New Cant. Dict.*, s.v. JACK ADAMS, a fool. JACK ADAMS' Parish, Clerkenwell.

1785. GROSE, *Vulg. Tongue*, s.v.

1812. *Lex. Bal.*, s.v.

1883. CLARK RUSSELL, *Sailor's Language*, s.v.

JACK-A-DANDY, *subs.* (old).—1. A little fop; a coxcomb; a DANDIPRAT (*q.v.*): also JACK DANDY. For synonyms *see* DANDY.

1632. BROME, *Northern Lass*, iii. 2. I'll throw him into the dock rather than that he shall succeed JACK-O-DANDY.

1664. ETHEREGE, *Comical Revenge*, ii. 3, [in *Works* (1704) 28]. Leave her, she's only worth the care Of some spruce JACK-A-DANDY.

1690. B. E., *Dict. Cant. Crew.* s.v. JACK-A-DANDY, a little impertinent insignificant Fellow.

1795. R. CUMBERLAND, *The Jew*, i. 'And when my monies is all gone, what shall I be then? An ass, a fool, a JACK-A-DANDY!'

1823. BEE, *Dict. of the Turf.*, s.v. JACK-O'-DANDY. . . . of Dandy manners, foolish, proud, and choleric as a turkey or *dindon.*

1839. AINSWORTH, *Jack Sheppard*, [ed. 1840], p. 141. 'Because they're in the next room, and the door's shut; that's vy, my JACK-A-DANDY!' replied Abraham, unsuspiciously.

1881. J. B. HARWOOD, in *Cassell's Mag.*, Feb. 164. 'I take it very unkind o' you, Sir, to have gone tempting and luring my hands away to your own three mills, and be hanged to you for a JACK-A-DANDY, there!'

2. (rhyming). Brandy.

JACK-A-GREEN. *See* JACK-IN-THE-GREEN under JACK.

JACK-A-LENT, *subs.* (old).—1. A dapperling; a dwarf; and (2) a simpleton: also JACK-O'-LENT.

1596. SHAKSPEARE, *Merry Wives*, iii. 3. You little JACK-A-LENT, have you been true to us?

1596. NASHE, *Have with You* etc. in *Works* [GROSART, 1882-3, iii. 78]. For his stature he is such another pretie JACK-A-LENT.

1602. COOKE, *How to Choose a Good Wife* [DODSLEY, *Old Plays* (1874), ix. 41]. That JACK-A-LENT, that ghost, that shadow, that moon in the wane.

JACKANAPES, *subs.* (old colloquial).—An absurd fop; a whipper-snapper: a general term of reproach. JACKANAPES-COAT = a dandy-coat (PEPYS). [Originally, no doubt, a gaudy-suited and performing ape (the word is still good Scots for a monkey; *cf.* SCOTT, *Redgauntlet*); and, hence, by implication anybody at once ugly (or diminutive), showy, and impudent. Also a **JACK-OF-APES**

was a man who exhibited performing apes].

*d.*1529. SKELTON, *Poems*, p. 160. He grins and he gapes, As it were JACK NAPES.

1543. BALE, *Romish Foxe*, fol. 92. He played JACK-A-NAPES swearynge by his tenne bones.

1567. EDWARDS, *Damon and Pithias* [DODSLEY, *Old Plays* (1874), iv. 60]. Away, JACKANAPES, else I will col'phise you by and by.

*c.*1590-1600. ALEX MONTGOMERIE, *Sonnets* [ed. Irving, 1821] p. 97. Blind brutal Boy, that with thy bou abuses Leill leisome Love by Lechery and Lust, Judge, JAKANAPIS and Jougler maist unjust &c.

1596. NASHE, *Have with You* etc. in *Works* [GROSART, iii. 156]. Common marks for every JACKANAPES preacher to kick, spit, or throw dirt at.

1598. SHAKSPEARE, *All's Well &c.*, iii. 5. That JACKANAPES with scarfs.

*b.*1602. *Lingua* [DODSLEY, *Old Plays* (1874), ix. 390]. This Invention is the proudest JACKANAPES. . . . that ever breathed.

1604. MARSTON & WEBSTER, *Malcontent*, i. 3. Sir Tristam Tristam come aloit, JACKE-A-NAPES, with a whim-wham.

1612-13. TAILOR, *Hog hath Lost his Pearl*, ii. Malapert, my father's butler, being a witty JACKANAPES, told me why it was.

1639. GLAPTHORNE, *Argalus and Parthenia*, in *Wks.* (1874), i. 38. Ladies shall beat thee to death . . . . thou JACKANAPES.

1653. BROME, *Five New Plays*, 200. Thou art a JACKANAPES of the basest tricks that ever I saw for a halfpenny.

1675. COTTON, *Scoffer Scofft*, in *Wks.* (1725), p. 180. Transformed myself (my pretty knave) Into these Man and Eagle's shapes, To snap my little JACK-A-NAPES.

1690. B. E. *Dict. Cant. Crew.*, s.v. JACKANAPES, a Term of Reproach, a little sorry Whipper-snapper.

1712. *Spectator*, No. 311. I have myself caught a young JACKANAPES, with a pair of silver-fringed gloves, in the very fact.

1752. FOOTE, *Taste* (5th ed.) 33. Saucy JACKANAPES.

1775. SHERIDAN, *Rivals*, ii. 1. None of your sneering, puppy! no grinning, JACKANAPES!

1785. GROSE, *Vulg. Tongue*, s.v. JACKANAPES. . . . a pert ugly little fellow.

JACKAROO, *subs.* (Australian).—A fresh arrival from England: a NEW CHUM (*q.v.*).

1887. *Chamber's Journal*, 23 April, 262. The JACKAROO . . . . is the invariable local name, or rather nickname, given to those young men who are sent out to the Australian colonies from almost every part of the United Kingdom in order to learn sheep or cattle-faming—generally the former—as carried on at the Antipodes.

1881. A. C. GRANT, *Bush Life*, i. 53. The young JACKAROO woke early next morning, and went to look around him.

1889. E. W. HORNUNG, in *London Society Holiday No* 'Bushed'. I had been in the colony but a few months, and was engaged as JACKEROO—that is, apprentice to 'colonial experience'.

JACKASS, *subs.* (colloquial). — A stupid ignoramus. For synonyms see BUFFLE, and CABBAGE-HEAD. Also JACKASSISM = stupidity.

1837. BARHAM, *Ingoldsby Legends*, II, 268. Calling names, whether done to attack or to tack a schism, Is, Miss, believe me, a great piece of JACK-ASS-ISM.

JACKASS-FRIGATE, *subs.* (nautical).—A small slow-sailing frigate.

1833. MARRYAT, *Peter Simple*, xiii. He recommended me to the Captain of a JACKASS-FRIGATE. . . . so called because there is as much difference between them and a real frigate. . . . as there is between a donkey and a race-horse.

JACK-COVE, *subs. phr.* (American thieves').—A mean low fellow; a SNIDE (*q.v.*).—MATSELL (1859).

JACK (or TOM) DRUM'S ENTERTAINMENT, *subs. phr.* (old).—Ill-treatment; ignominious dismissal: *cf.* STAFFORD LAW.

1579. GOSSON, *Schoole of Abuse*, 22 (Arber's ed.). Plato when he sawe the doctrine of these Teachers, neither for profite, necessary, nor to be wished for pleasure, gave them all DRUMMES ENTERTAINMENT, not suffering them once to shew their faces in a reformed common wealth.

1587. HOLINSHEAD, *Hist. of Ireland.* B. ii. col. i. *cit. cap.* His porter or other officer durst not for both his ears give the simplest man that resorted to his house, TOM DRUM'S ENTERTAINMENT, which is, to hale a man in by the head, and thrust him out by both the shoulders.

1592. GREENE, *Groatsworth of Wit*, in *Works*, xii, 129. And so giving him JACKE DRUMS ENTERTAINMENT, shut him out of doores.

1594. NASHE, *Unf. Traveller*, in *Wks.* v. 26. I would give him JACKE DRUMMES ENTERTAINMENT, and send him packing.

1598. SHAKESPEARE, *All's Well*, iii, 6. 41. If you give him not JOHN DRUM'S ENTERTAINMENT, your inclining cannot be removed.

1611. COTGRAVE, *Dictionarie*, s.v. *Festin. Il a esté au festin de Martin Baston.* He hath had a tryall in Stafford Court, or hath received JACKE DRUM'S ENTERTAINEMENT.

1611. T. CORYAT, *Extracts &c.* [1776] iii. C. c. 3. Not like the ENTERTAINMENT OF JACKE DRUM, Who was best welcome when he went away.

1626. *Apollo Shroving* [quoted by NARES]. It shall have TOM DRUM'S ENTERTAINMENT, a flap with a fox-tail.

1649. JOHN TAYLOR, *Wandering to see the Wonders of the West.* Where the hostess being very willing to give me the courteous ENTERTAINMENT OF JACK DRUM, commanded me very civilly to get out of doors, for there was no room for me to lodge in.

JACKED, *adj.* (old).—Spavined; lamed.

JACKEEN (or DUBLIN JACKEEN), subs. (Irish).—A Dublin 'ARRY (*q.v.*). [From JACK + EEN, a suffix expressive of contempt or inferiority; a diminutive].

1894. DE SOMERVILLE & ROSS, *The Real Charlotte*, iii. 246. Don't you remember what Mr. Baker said about me, 'that you couldn't expect any manners from a DUBLIN JACKEEN.'

JACKEN-CLOSER, *subs.* (old).—A seal.

1825. *Modern Flash Dict.*, s.v.

JACKERIES, *subs.* (Australian).—*See* quot.

1890. HUME NISBET, *Bail Up*, p. 123. The JACKERIES, *i.e.*, favored station hands, cursed him.

JACKET, *subs.* (colloquial).—1. The skin of an unpared potato: generally in phrase 'boiled in their jackets'.

1878. R. L. STEVENSON, *Inland Voyage*, p. 58. Some potatoes in their JACKETS.

2. (American).—A pinafore; a ROUNDABOUT (*q.v.*).

3. (American).—A folded paper, or open envelope containing documents, endorsed without as to the contents; a docket.

Verb. (old).—1. To cheat; to swindle; to betray.

1819. DE VAUX, *Memoirs*, s.v. JACKET .... This term is ... properly applied to removing a man by underhand and vile means from any berth or situation he enjoys, commonly with a view to supplant him.

1823. GROSE (3rd ed.), *Vulg. Tongue*, s.v.

2. (common).—To thrash; to beat. Also TO TRIM (or DUST or LACE) ONE'S JACKET. For synonyms *see* BASTE and TAN. *See* JACKETTING.

*d.*1704. LESTRANGE [quoted by JOHNSON 1755]. She FELL UPON THE JACKET of the parson, who stood gaping at her.

1845. BUCKSTONE, *Green Bushes*, i., 1. I'll DUST YOUR JACKET if you do that again.

3. (American).—To enclose (a document) after scheduling within it other papers relating to the same subject; to docket.

1888. *The American*, 16 May. Another record was made in the book of the office of letters received and JACKETTED.

4. (American thieves'). To denote; to point out.

1859. MATSELL, *Vocabulum*, s.v. JACKET. The fly cops pulled him, and allowed the flat cops TO JACKET him.

TO GIVE A RED-LACED JACKET, *verb. phr.* (old military).—To flog.

1871. *Temple Bar*, XXXI, 311. When soldiers used to be flogged more commonly than now, their commanders used to facetiously call it, GIVING THEM A RED-LACED JACKET.

TO LINE ONE'S JACKET, *verb. phr.* (old).—To eat or drink; to fill one's stomach. For synonyms *see* GRUB.

1611. COTGRAVE, *Dictionarie*, *Il s'accoustre bien.* He stuffes himselfe soundly, hee LINES HIS JACKET throughly with liquor.

PULL DOWN YOUR JACKET (or VEST), *phr.* (American).—Keep cool! don't get excited! HOLD YOUR HAIR ON (*q.v.*)!

TO SEND IN ONE'S JACKET, *verb. phr.* (jockies').—To resign; to deliver up one's badge of office.

1884. HAWLEY SMART, *From Post to Finish*, p. 222. 'I presume you know the consequences of refusing?' 'I shall have to SEND IN MY JACKET, I suppose.' The baronet nodded.

JACKETING, *subs.* (common).—A thrashing; a reprimand.

1851-61. MAYHEW, *Lond. Lab. & Lond. Poor*, i. 92. I don't work on Sundays. If I did, I'd get a JACKETING.

1862. MRS. H. WOOD, *Channings*, lvii. 'You may look Mr. Tod but I'll be after giving ye a JACKETING for ye're pains.'

1871. *Durham County Advertiser*, 10 Nov. The quiet man told him about having found it, and got a JACKETING for not having come direct and reported it at once.

1883. *Graphic*, May 26, 531, 3. Who the moment before had been administering a vigorous JACKETING to him anent her neglected wardrobe.

1893. EMERSON, *Signor Lippo*, xvi. I eased up, and he gave me a JACKETING.

JACKET-REVERSER, *subs.* (common).—A turncoat.

JACKEY, *subs.* (old).—Gin. For synonyms *see* DRINKS and SATIN.

1811. *Lex. Bal.* s.v. JACKEY, Gin.

1821. EGAN, *Life in London*, p. 179. Taking her drops of JACKEY with old Mother Brimstone.

1823. BEE, *Dict of the Turf.*, s.v.

1827. LYTTON, *Pelham*, [ed. 1864] p. 302. Well, you parish bull prig, are you for lushing JACKY, or pattering in the hum-box.

1859. SALA, *Gaslight and Daylight*, xxiii. The stuff itself, which in the western gin-shops goes generally by the name of 'blue ruin' or 'short,' is here called .... JACKY.

1878. W. S. GILBERT, *Pinafore*, i. I've snuff, and tobacky, And excellent JACKY.

JACK-FROST, *subs.* (colloquial).—A popular personification of frost; *cf.* JOHN FOG and TOMMY SNOW.

1888. *Notes & Queries*, 7, S. v. 109. This jubilee year of 1887 has not commenced very well with us sporting folk. JACK FROST, John Fog, and Tommy Snow, having formed themselves into a syndicate, spoilt all our Christmas steeplechasing and hurdle-racing.

JACK-GAGGER, *subs.* (American thieves').—A man living on his wife's prostitution; a married PONCE (*q.v.*).—MATSELL (1859).

JACK KETCH (or KITCH), *subs.* (old).—A hangman or executioner; a DANCING-MASTER (*q.v.*); A TOPSMAN (*q.v.*). [From a famous practitioner of that name (*circa* 1663-86). Before his time the office had been filled by men whose names each and all became popular colloquialisms: *e.g.* DERRICK (*q.v.*); GREGORY BRANDON (GREGORIAN TREE *q.v.*); DUN (*q.v.*).

FRENCH SYNONYMS. *L'adjoint* (thieves': the assistant); *l'aricoteur* (thieves'); *le béquillard* (thieves'); *le béquilleur* (thieves'); *le bourreau* (= the hangman); *le buteur* (thieves'); *le Charlot* (popular: *les soubrettes de Charlot* = Charley's maids: cf. *Monsieur de Paris*: *le panier à Charlot* = Charley's basket); *le faucheur* (popular: = the reaper); *le mec des gerbiers* (thieves'); *l'Haricoteur* (thieves'); *le marlou de Charlotte* (thieves': = Lottie's ponce); *le mécanicien* (pop.: = engine-driver); *Monsieur de Paris* (pop.: an official title); *le père Rasibus* (pop.: a play on *raser* = to shave); *le tolle* or *tollart* (thieves'); *le rouastre* (thieves':=('sawbones'); *le marieux*; *le lamboureur.*

ITALIAN SYNONYMS. *Cattaron; cattarone.*

SPANISH SYNONYMS. *Caffler; malvechino.*

1676. *Darkmans Budge*, verse 5. And we come to the Nubbing-Cheat, For running on the Budge, There stands JACK KITCH, that son of a Bitch.

1678. *Broadside*, 'The Plotters' Ballad, being JACK KETCH'S incomparable Receipt for the cure of Traytorous Recusants &c.

1682. DURFEY, *Butler's Ghost*, p. 54. Till KETCH observing he was chous'd, &c.

1682. DRYDEN, *Epil. to Duke of Guise*, 30. 'JACK KETCH,' says I, ''s an excellent physician.'

1690. B. E., *Dict. Cant. Crew.*, s.v. JACK KITCH, c, the Hangman of that Name, but now all his Successors.

1785. GROSE, *Vulg. Tongue*, s.v.

1849-61. MACAULAY, *Hist. Eng.* v, Note. He (Monmouth) then encountered JACK KETCH, the executioner.... whose name has, during a century and a half, been vulgarly given to all who have succeeded him in his odious office.

1856. C. READE, *Never Too Late*, lxx. 'He will come back without fear, and we will nail him with the fifty pound note upon him: and then — JACK KETCH.'

1859. MATSELL, *Vocabulum*, s.v.

1870. MANSFIELD, *School-Life at Winchester College*, p. 109. The culprit had to 'order his name to the BIBLE-CLERK,' and that individual, with the help of Ostiarius, performed the office of JACK KETCH.

Verb. (old).—To hang.

1694. *Gentlemen's Journal*, June, p. 147. JACK-KETCH thyself or cut thy throat.

JACK KETCH'S KITCHEN, *subs. phr.* (old). *See* quots.

1714. *Memoirs of John Hall* (4th ed.), p. 17. Over them is JACK KETCH his kitchen, where, in *Pitch, Tar* and *Oil*, he boils the Quarters of .... Traitors.

1882. *Fortnightly Review*, xxxi, 798. 'JACK KETCH'S KITCHEN': A room in Newgate, where that honest fellow, the hangman, boiled the quarters of those executed and dismembered for high treason.

JACK KETCH'S PIPPIN, *subs. phr.* (old).—A candidate for the gallows; a GALLOWS-APPLE: *cf.* HEMPSEED.

JACK-LEG, *subs.* and *adj.* (American).—Blackleg.

1888. *Florida Times Union*, 11 Feb. It seems that the State Bar Association is disposed to draw the line between attornies and JACK-LEG lawyers.

JACKMAN. *See* JARKMAN.

JACK-NASTY, *subs.* (common).—A sneak; a sloven: *cf.* JACK-NASTY-FACE.

1856. HUGHES, *Tom Brown's School-Days*, I. iii. Tom and his younger brothers, as they grew up, went on playing with the village boys, without the idea of equality or inequality (except in wrestling, running, and climbing) ever entering their heads, as it doesn't till it's put there by JACK NASTYS or fine ladies' maids.

JACK-NASTY-FACE, *subs.* (old).—1. A sailor; specifically a cook.

1811. *Lex. Bal.*, s.v.

1884. G. A. SALA, in *Ill. Lond. News*, April 12, p. 339, col. 3. I should be glad to learn .... why the cook's mate is called 'JACK-NASTY-FACE.'

2. (common).—A filthy or unpleasant-looking person: *cf.* JACK-NASTY.

1823. BEE, *Dict. of the Turf.*, s.v. JACK-NASTY-FACE — a dirty fellow.

JACK-PUDDING, *subs.* (old).—A serving merry-andrew; a low-class buffoon. Fr. *jean-pottage* (=jack-soup); Germ. *Hans-wurst* (= jack-sausage); Dutch, *pickel-herringe*; It. *macaroni.* Hence JACK-PUDDINGHOOD (WALPOLE) = buffoonery.

1650-51. MILTON, *Defence of People of England*, i. The extempore rhymes of some antic JACK-PUDDING may deserve printing better.

1653. ASTON COCKAINE. 'On Mr. Richard Brome's Playes.' Our theatres of lower note in those More happy daies Shall scorn the rustic prose Of a JACK-PUDDING.

1664. ETHEREGE, *Comical Revenge*, iii. 4, in *Wks* (1704), 35. He was JACK-PUDDING to a Mountebank, and turned off for want of wit.

1670. J. EACHARD, *Contempt of the Clergy*, in Arber's *Garner*, vii, p. 265. Those usually that have been Rope Dancers in the Schools, oft times prove JACK-PUDDINGS in the Pulpit.

1672. W. WYCHERLEY, *Love in a Wood*, i. 2. He is a mere buffoon, a JACK-PUDDING.

1691-2. *Gentlemen's Journal*, Jan., p. 35. All its inhabitants are JACK-PUDDINGS born.

1757. FOOTE, *The Author* [1782], 46. A JACK-PUDDING! that takes fillips on the nose for sixpence a piece.

1772. G. A. STEVENS, *Songs Comic and Satyrical*, p. 50. So JACK-PUDDINGS joke, with distorted grimace, Benetting their gudgeons, the croud.

1785. GROSE, *Vulg. Tongue*, s.v.

1795. R. CUMBERLAND, *The Jew*, iv. 2. *Sheva.* You are a saucy knave to make a joke of your master. Do you think I will keep a JACK-PUDDING in my house like you, to listen at my keyhole and betray my conversation.

1811. *Lex. Bal.*, s.v.

1825. SCOTT, *St. Ronan's Well*, iii. The JACK-PUDDING to the company, whose business it was to crack the best joke, and sing the best song, he could.

1849. MACAULAY, *Hist. of England*, vi. Booth had bitterly complained to the Commons that the dearest of his constituents were entrusted to a drunken JACK-PUDDING.

1881. BESANT & RICE. *Chap. of Fleet*, pt. 1. They were again jocund, light-hearted, the oracle of the tavern, the jester and JACK PUDDING of the Feast.

JACK RANDALL, *subs. phr.* (rhyming).—A candle. [The name of a famous pugilist].

JACK ROBINSON, *subs.* (venery).—The *penis.* For synonyms *see* CREAMSTICK and PRICK.

BEFORE ONE CAN SAY 'JACK ROBINSON', *phr.* (common).—Instantly; in the shortest possible time; IN TWO-TWO'S (*q.v.*).

1785. GROSE, *Vulg. Tongue*, s.v. JACK ROBINSON .... a saying to express a very short time, originating from a very volatile gentleman of that appellation, who would call on his neighbours, and be gone before his name could be announced.

1811. *Lex. Bal.*, s.v.

1836. M. SCOTT, *Cruise of the Midge* [ed. 18.] p. 295. BEFORE YOU COULD SAY JACK ROBINSON, the pursuer's starboard leg was whipped out of Jack Lennox's clutches.

1837. BARHAM, *Ingoldsby Legends* [ed. 1842] p. 256. I have not a doubt, I shall rout every tout, ERE YOU'LL WHISPER JACK ROBINSON.

1846. *Punch*, xi. 9. Here it was he married my mother whose name was Robinson, whose ancestor was the famous JACK ROBINSON of whom is still retained a popular proverb relating to rapidity of expression.

JACKRUM, *subs.* (old).—A marriage license.—*Modern Flash Dict.* (1825).

JACK-SAUCE, *subs.* (old).—An impudent fellow; a SAUCE-BOX (*q.v.*).

1571. EDWARDS, *Damon and Pitheas* (DODSLEY, *O. Pl.*, i. 271). Heere is a gay world! boyes now set old men to scoole: I sayd wel inough; what, JACK-SAWCE, think'st cham a fool?

1593. G. HARVEY, *Pierce's Super.* in *Wks.* (GROSART) ii. 328. A JACK-SAUCE, or vnmannerly puppy.

1597-8. HAUGHTON, *A Woman will have her Will* [DODSLEY, *Old Plays* (1874), x. 537]. Well, JACK-SAUCE, The rogue is waking yet to spoil your sport.

1599. SHAKESPEARE, *Henry V*, iv. 7. If he be perjured, see you now, his reputation is as arrant a villain, and a JACK SAUCE, as ever. . . . trod upon God's ground and his earth, in my conscience la.

1602. COOKE, *How a Man may Choose a Good Wife etc.* [DODSLEY, *Old Plays* (1874), ix. 78]. Why, you JACK-SAUCE! You cuckold! you what-not!

1612. FIELD, *Woman is a Weather-cock*, ii. 1. What say ye, JACK SAUCE.

1620. HALL, *Honour of the Maried Clergie*, ii § 12. Every JACK-SAUCE of Rome shall thus odiously dare to controll and disgrace it.

1633. JONSON, *Tale of a Tub*, iii. 1. *Dame* 7. Come up, JACK SAUCE.

1638. RANDOLPH, *Muses' Looking Glass*, iv. 4. Such a JACK-SAUCE.

1659. MASSINGER, *City Madam*, iv. 2. Do you so, JACK SAUCE! I'll keep them further off.

1702. VANBRUGH, *False Friend*, iii. 2. Why how now, JACK-SAUCE? why how now, Presumption?

1719. DURFEY, *Pills &c.* v. 287. A sword and buckler good and strong, To give JACK-SAUCE a rap.

JACK'S DELIGHT, *subs. phr.* (common).—A sea-port strumpet. For synonyms *see* BARRACK-HACK and TART.

JACK-SHAY, *subs.* (Australian).—A tin quart used for boiling tea, and contrived to hold a tin pint.

1881. GRANT, *Bush Life* [quoted in *Slang, Jargon & Cant.*]. Hobbles and JACK-SHAYS hang from the Saddle-dees.

JACK-SPRAT, *subs.* (old).—An undersized man or boy.—GROSE (1785).

1570. *Wit and Science* [DODSLEY, *Old Plays* (1874), ii. 39]. But what, no force, ye are but JACK SPRAT to me.

JACK-STRAW, *subs.* (old).—. 1. A nobody; and (2) a dwarf. For synonyms *see* HOP-O'-MY-THUMB.

1596. NASHE, *Have With You* etc. in *Works* [GROSART] iii. 158. These worthless whippets and IACKE-STRAWES.

1629. *Flyting of Polwarth and Montgomerie* (Edin. Montgomerie's *Poems*, 1885-6, i. 64]. IACSTRO, be better anes ingined.

1672. WYCHERLEY, *Love in a Wood*, i. 2. You are a saucy JACK-STRAW to question me.

1690. B. E., *Dict. Cant. Crew.* s.v.

1725. *New. Cant. Dict.*, s.v.

1785. GROSE. *Vulg. Tongue*, s.v.

1811. *Lex. Bal.*, s.v.

1859. MATSELL, *Vocabulum*, s.v.

JACK STRAW'S CASTLE, *subs. phr.* (venery).—The female *pudendum*. For synonyms *see* MONOSYLLABLE.

JACKSY-PARDY, *subs.* (common).—The posteriors: also JACKSY PARDO. For synonyms *see* MONOCULAR EYEGLASS.

JACK TAR, *subs. phr.* (old).—1. A sailor; and (2) a hornpipe.

1781. G. PARKER, *View of Society*, i. 53. Our house in this place was chiefly supported by JACK TARS.

1785. GROSE, *Vulg. Tongue*, s.v.

1811. *Lex. Bal.*, s.v.

1822. LAMB, *Elia (Some old Actors)*. Displays before our eyes a downrignt concretion of a Wapping sailor—a jolly warm-hearted JACK TAR.

JACK WEIGHT, *subs. phr.* (old).—A fat man; a FORTY-GUTS (*q.v.*).

1785. GROSE, *Vulg. Tongue*, s.v.

1811. *Lex. Bal.*, s.v.

1859. MATSELL, *Vocabulum*, s.v.

JACK-WHORE, *subs. phr.* (old).—A large, masculine, overgrown wench.—GROSE (1785).

JACOB, *subs.* (old).—1. *See* quot.

1753. *The Thief-Catcher*, p. 25. There are another sort of Rogues called JACOBS; these go with ladders in the Dead of the Night, and get in at the windows, one, two or three pair, of stairs and sometimes down the area.

2. (Old Cant.)—A ladder.

1714. *Memoirs of John Hall* (4th ed.), p. 12, s.v.

1785. GROSE, *Vulg. Tongue*, s.v.

1823. BEE, *Dict. of the Turf*, s.v. JACOB . . . . to prig the JACOB from the dunckin-drag.

1859. MATSELL, *Vocabulum*, s.v.

3. (old).—A soft fellow; a spooney; a fool.—GROSE (1785); DE VAUX (1819).

4. (venery).—The *penis*: *cf.* JACOB'S LADDER sense 2.

JACOBITE, *subs.* (old).—A sham shirt; a DICKEY (*q.v.*); a shirt-collar.—B. E. (1690), GROSE (1785), MATSELL (1859).

JACOB'S LADDER, *subs. phr.* (originally theatrical: now general).—1. A longitudinal flaw in the leg of a pair of tights; now applied to any rent of which only the woof threads are left.

1859. SALA, *Gaslight and Daylight*, xxx. Here he [a tramp] sat down on a milestone; and producing a remarkably neat housewife case, proceeded to overhaul all parts of his apparel with as much care and circumspection as if they had been of purple and fine linen, catching up any strong rents and JACOB'S LADDERS with a grave and deliberate countenance.

2. (venery).—The female *pudendum*. For synonyms *see* MONOSYLLABLE.

JADE, *subs.* (old).—1. An epithet applied to women: in contempt. [Originally a horse or man (CHAUCER): especially (1) one overridden or foundered; and (2) unsafe and full of tricks. Hence, by implication, a knavish, battered, or worn-out whore]. JADISH, *adj.* (NASHE) = malicious; tricky; untrustworthy.

1560. *Nice Wanton* [DODSLEY, *Old Plays* (1874), ii. 172]. *Iniquity*. Gup, whore; do ye hear this JADE?

1592. BRETON, *Pilgrimage to Paradise*, p. 10. Earthly joys will make him prove a JADE.

1607. WILKINS, *Enforced Marriage* [DODSLEY, *Old Plays* (1874), ix. 550]. Whore, ay, and JADE.

1611. BARRY, *Ram Alley*, iv. Does the filthy JADE send to me for money?

1614. COOK, *City Gallant* [DODSLEY, *Old Plays* (1874), xi. 226]. She's good for nothing then, no more than a JADE.

1635. BROME, *Antipodes*, iv. 2. Some cowardly JADE That dare not strike a woman.

1647-80. ROCHESTER, *Ramble in St. James's Park*, in *Wks.* (1728), 82. But to turn damned abandoned JADE, Whom neither head nor tail persuade.

1678. COTTON, *Virgil Travestie*, in *Wks* (1725), Bk. iv. p. 103. And (like a simple hair-brain'd JADE) This Youth hail Fellow with me made. *Ibid.* p. 105. At last a crew of strapping JADES, That were or should have been her Maids.

1690. B. E., *Dict. Cant. Crew.*, s.v. JADE a Term of Reproach given to Women, as Idle JADE, Lazy JADE, Silly JADE &c.

1712. STEELE, *Spectator*, No. 479. There are perverse JADES . . . . with whom it requires more than common proficiency in philosophy to . . . . live.

1714. ALLAN RAMSAY, *Elegy on John Cowper*, in *Works* (1848), i. 294. And she, poor JADE, withouten din Is sent to Leith-Wynd—fit to spin.

*d.*1719. ADDISON, [quoted in *Century*]. You now and then see some handsome young JADES.

1725. *New. Cant. Dict.*, s.v.

1770. FOOTE, *Lame Lover*, i. 1. Why, you pert JADE, do you play on my words?

1772. G. A. STEVENS, *Songs Comic* etc., 'Chastity'. Turn your face to that table, at once you will see What faces JADES wear.

1785. GROSE, *Vulg. Tongue*, s.v.

1791. BURNS, *Tam O'Shanter*. A souple JAUD she was, an' strang.

1807. CRABBE, *Parish Register*. To let an artful JADE, The close recesses of thine heart invade.

1863. LONGFELLOW, *The Musician's Tale*. A faded old woman, a heathenish JADE.

2. (American thieves').—A long term of imprisonment; a STRETCH (*q.v.*).

JAG, *subs.* (American). —A scrap; a load, parcel, or lot: *e.g.*, a fare, a catch of fish &c.

1692. HACKETT, *Life of Archbishop Williams*, 136. The latter of these two letters is come abroad; whereof, because it is in many hands, some JAGS will suffice to be recited.

1834. C. A. DAVIS, *Major Downing's Letters*, p. 168. As there was very little money in the country, the bank bought a good JAG on't in Europe.

1839. URE, *Dict.*, iv. 376. The flint is sold by the one-horse load, called a JAG (in Suffolk, Eng.) and carted to the Knapper's Shops.

1866. TROWBRIDGE, *Coupon Bonds*, p. 393. The wagon stood in the road, with the last JAG of rails still on it.

1888. *Missouri Republican*. One broker buying on a heavy order. . . . occasionally caught a JAG of 2000 or 3000 shares.

2. (American).—A whim; a fancy.

3. (American).—Intoxication: *e.g.* TO HAVE A JAG ON = to be drunk.

4. (American).—A drunkard; a LUSHINGTON (*q.v.*).

JAGGED, *adj.* (American).—Drunk. For synonyms *see* DRINKS and SCREWED.

JAGGER, *subs.* (American thieves').—1. A gentleman.

1859. MATSELL, *Vocabulum*, s.v.

1859. DU CANGE ANGLICUS, *Vulg. Tongue*, s.v.

2. (common).—A hawker.

1888. *Cassell's Sat. Journal*, 8 Dec., p. 261. He had a strong suspicion that the old coal JAGGER was an aider and abettor.

JAGUE, *subs.* (Old Cant.).—A ditch.

1622. HEAD & KIKMAN, *English Rogue*, 'Canting Song'. Let Cove bing then, Thro' Ruffmans, JAGUE or Laund.

1690. B. E., *Dict. Cant. Crew*, s.v.

1754. *Scoundrel's Dict.*, s.v.

1785. GROSE, *Vulg. Tongue*, s.v.

1859. MATSELL, *Vocabulum*, s.v.

JAIL-BIRD, *subs.* (Old Cant: now recognised).—A prisoner; a CRACK-HALTER (*q.v.*).—[*Cf.* CAGE and CANARY].

1603. DAVIES (of Hereford), *Microcosmus*, in *Works* [GROSART], i. 991. 'To the Lady Rich.' But such a IAILE-BIRDE heavenly nightingale.

1690. B. E., *Dict. Cant. Crew*, s.v. JAYL-BIRDS.

1785. GROSE, *Vulg. Tongue*, s.v.

1819. MOORE, *Tom Crib's Memorial*, 77. A new set of darbies, when first they are worn, Makes the JAIL-BIRD uneasy.

1849. MAHONY, *Reliques of Father Prout* (Bohn) p. 233. The fellow must be what Terry calls 'a bad mimber intirely,' what we English call a JAIL-BIRD; what the French denominate a '*vrai gibier de grêve*;' termed in Latin '*corvus patibularius*'; and by the Greeks, κακου κοραξος κακον ωον.

JAKES, *subs.* (old colloquial).—A privy; a house of office. [*Century*: The occurrence of dial. *johnny*, a JAKES—'also called *Mrs. Jones* by country people' (HALLIWELL), with dial. *Tom*, a close-stool, suggests that JAKES was originally Jake's or Jack's, a humorous euphemism]. Also (Scots) JACK. *See* AJAX.

*c.*1550. INGLELEND, *Disobedient Child* [DODSLEY, *Old Plays* (1874), ii. 276]. To. . . . do as poor knaves, which JAKES do scour.

1596. NASHE, *Have With You*, etc., in *Works* [GROSART], iii. 196. I worse scorne it than to have so foul a JAKES as his mouth for my groning stool.

1598. FLORIO, *Worlde of Wordes*, s.v. *Condotto*. . . . Also a conduite, a priuie, a IAKES, a sinke.

1605. CAMDEN, *Remains*, p. 307. Soloman, a Jew, fell into a JAXE at Tewkesbury on a Saturday.

1605. SHAKSPEARE, *Lear*, ii. 2. I will tread this unbolted villain into mortar, and daub the walls of a JAKES with him.

1641. MILTON, *Apology for Smectymnuus*. Christe himself, speaking of unsavory traditions scruples not to name the Dunghill and the JAKES.

1678. COTTON, *Virgil Travestie*, in *Wks* (1725), Bk. iv. p. 91. Thou here thyself most busie makes In building for the Queen a JAKES.

1690. B. E., *Dict. Cant. Crew.*, s.v. JAKES.

1728. POPE, *Dunciad*, i. 144. And 'scape the martyrdom of JAKES and fire.

1737. *The Mobiad* [quoted in *N.&Q.* 2 S. xi. 125]. Now Chiefs of haughty bosom supple stoop Ev'n to the JAKES to angle for a dupe.

1751-54. JORTIN, *Remarks on Eccl. Hist.*, an. 379. Their tenets were an horrible confusion of all sorts of impieties, which flowed into this sect as into a JAKES.

1785. GROSE, *Vulg. Tongue*, s.v.

JAKES-FARMER, *subs.* (old).—An emptier of cesspools; a GOLD-FINDER (*q.v.*). Also JAKES-RAKER (SKELTON) and JAKES-BARRELLER.

1596. NASHE, *Have With You*, in *Works* [GROSART], iii. 196. Like a JAKES-BARELLER.

1606. MARSTON, *Fawne*, ii. 1. Nay, I will embrace a JAKES-FARMER, after eleven o'clock at night.

1613. CHAPMAN, JONSON & MARSTON, *Insatiate Countess*, ii. 2. Well, what time goes the JAKES-FARMER?

1615. SYLVESTER, *Tobacco Battered* &c., *Wks*, p. 575. Not scorning scullions, coblers, colliers, JAKES-FARMERS, fidlers, ostlers, oysterers.

1647. BEAUMONT & FLETCHER, *Love's Cure*, ii. 1. Nay we are all signiors here in Spain, from the JAKES FARMER to the grandee, or adelantado.

JAM, *subs.* (common).—1. A sweetheart; a mistress: also BIT OF JAM. LAWFUL-JAM = a wife.

*c.*1880. *Broadside Ballad*. 'Just the Identical Man.' And he made this young girl feel queer When he called me his JAM, His pet and his lamb.

*c.*1886. *Broadside Ballad.* 'Up they Go.' There were three bits of JAM stepping out of the tram, So we tipped them a wink in a trice.

1889. HENLEY, *Villon's Good Night.* Gay grass-widows and LAWFUL-JAM.

2. (venery).—The female *pudendum*: whence TO HAVE A BIT OF JAM = to copulate: *cf.* TART. Fr. *sucre.*

3. (racing).—A certainty of winning; clear profit: also REAL JAM.

4. (common).—Excellence; good luck; happiness. JAM-UP (*adj.* and *adv.*) = the pink of perfection; SLAP-UP (*q.v.*); BANG-UP (*q.v.*). Also REAL JAM.

1855. HALIBURTON, *Nature & Human Nature*, p. 273. Connubial bliss, I allot, was REAL JAM UP.

1882. F. ANSTEY, *Vice-Versâ*, xiv. 'Ah!' observed Dick. 'I thought you wouldn't find it all JAM! And yet you seemed to be enjoying yourself, too,' he said with a grin, 'from that letter you wrote.'

1889. *The Mirror*, 26 Aug., p. 6, col. 2. He'll marvel at the rod you have in pickle For him who now considers you REAL JAM.

1892. MILLIKIN, *'Arry Ballads*, p. 56. Society's lions' wag their tails on the cheap, and that's JAM.

1892. KIPLING, *Barrack-Room Ballads.* 'Oonts.' It aint no JAM for Tommy.

5. (colloquial).—A crush; a crowd.

1812. J. & H. SMITH, *Rejected Addresses.* All is bustle, squeeze. . . . and JAM.

1864. LOWELL, *Fireside Travels*, p. 111. The surest eye for . . . . the weak point of a JAM.

1889. *Illustrated Bits*, 13 July. 'I knew that there would be such a JAM that I couldn't get inside the door.'

6. (American thieves').—A ring.—MATSELL (1859).

7. (gaming).—The pool at Nap, into which each dealer pays, the winner of the next nap taking the lot.

Adj. (common).—Neat; smart; spruce: *cf. subs.* sense 5.

Verb. (old).—To hang.—GROSE (1785).

JAMBOREE (or **JIMBOREE**), *subs.* (American).—A frolic; a SPREE (*q.v.*). For synonyms *see* FLARE-UP.

1872. *Scribner's Mag.*, iv. 363. There have not been so many dollars spent on any JAMBOREE.

JAMES, *subs.* (thieves').—1. A crowbar. For synonyms *see* JEMMY. Fr. *un jacques.*

1819. DE VAUX, *Memoirs*, s.v. JAMES.

1879. *Macmillan's Magazine*, 'Autobiography of a Thief,' xl. 503. I had the JAMES and screws on me.

2. (thieves').—A sovereign or twenty shillings.

1858. A. MAYHEW, *Paved with Gold*, III, xvii, 365. The firm that received most of his 'favours' was in the habit of pricing its 'half-JAMES' and JAMES (*i.e.*, half and whole sovereigns) at 2/10 and 7/-

1887. HORSLEY, *Jottings from Jail.* I put a half JAMES in the hand and said 'Guy!'

1893. EMERSON, *Signor Lippo*, xxi. He gives him the half-JAMES, and told him never to bother him more.

3. (common).—A sheep's head: more frequently, when uncooked, BLOODY JEMMY (*q.v.*).

1827. *Belcher's Every Night Book*, p. 38. Hear us, great JAMES, thou poetry of mutton; Delicious profile of the beast that bleats.

1870. *London Figaro*, 2 July. Club your pence, and you may attain to the glories of Osmazome and JAMES—that is, of baked sheep's head.

JAMIE MOORE. TO HAVE BEEN TALKING TO JAMIE MOORE, *verb. phr.* (Scots').—To be drunk. For synonyms *see* DRINKS and SCREWED.

JAMMED. TO BE JAMMED, *verb. phr.* (old).—To meet with a violent death, by accident, murder, or hanging. *See* JAM, *verb.*

1811. *Lex. Bal.*, s.v.

1859. MATSELL, *Vocabulum*, s.v.

JAMMY.—*See* JAM, *subs.* sense 4 and JAM-UP.

JAMPOT, *subs.* (Australian).—1. A high collar.

2. (venery).—The female *pudendum.* For synonyms *see* MONOSYLLABLE.

JAM-TART, *subs.* (Stock exchange).—1. Exactly the market; buyers and sellers at the same.

2. (common).—A wife or mistress; a TART (*q.v.*).

JAMS, *subs.* (common).—An abbreviation of JIM-JAMS (*q.v.*).

JAN, *subs.* (Old Cant.).—A purse. For synonyms *see* POGE.

1610. ROWLANDS, *Martin Markall*, p. 39 (H. Club's Repr. 1874) s.v.

JANE, *subs.* (thieves').—A sovereign. For synonyms *see* CANARY.

1864. *Times*, 14 April, 'Law Report.' He had told me before I went out, that I could keep half a JANE. A JANE is a sovereign.

JANE-OF-APES, *subs.* (old).—A pert forward girl; the counterpart of JACKANAPES (*q.v.*).

1624. MASSINGER, *Bondman*, iii, 3. Here's JANE-OF-APES shall serve.

JANGO, *subs.* (obsolete).—Liquor.

1721. RAMSAY, *Lusky Spence's Last Advice*, in *Wks.* (1848), ii. 302. Drive at the JANGO till he spew.

JANIZARY, *subs.* (old). *See* quots.

1684. HEAD, *Proteus Redivivus*, 238. At door is received by some half-a-dozen JANIZARIES more, of the same brotherhood.

1690. B. E., *Dict. Cant. Crew*, s.v. JANIZARIES . . . . also the Mob sometimes so called, and Bailives, Sergeants, Followers, Yeomen, Setters, and any lewd gang depending upon others.

1691-2. *Gentlemen's Journal*, March, p. 13. The aunt spied them in deep consult with all their JANIZARIES.

1785. GROSE, *Vulg. Tongue*, s.v.

1859. MATSELL, *Vocabulum*, s.v. JANIZARIES, a mob of pickpockets.

1895. H. B. MARRIOTT-WATSON, *The Lady's Chamber* in *New Review.* lxxii, 489. And was out and away upon the turnpike to Uxbridge ere ever a JANIZARY were in sight.

JANNOCK (or **JONNOCK**), *adj.* (provincial).—Sociable; fair; just; straightforward; conclusive.

1843. MONCRIEFF, *Scamps of London*, ii. 2. You'll act JANNOCK surely.

1871. *Times*, 4 Nov. When a gentleman, began by blowing his own trumpet, it was not altogether JANNOCK.

1878. HATTON, *Cruel London*, VIII, ii. 'Honour bright, no kid, as we say in London, JANAK, as we say in the North?

TO DIE JANNOCK, *verb. phr.* (old).—To die with bravado.

1882. FENNELL, *Antiq. Chronicle*, 'Collection of Old Words,' July, p. 25, s.v.

JANUSMUG, *subs.* (American thieves').—A go-between; an intermediary between a thief and a receiver.

1859. MATSELL, *Vocabulum*, s.v.

JAP, *subs.* (colloquial).—A Japanner (PURCHAS) or Japanese.

JAPAN, *verb.* (common).—1. To ordain: TO BE JAPANNED = to take orders.

1756. *Connoisseur*, 29 Jan. Jack . . . . sent me a very hearty letter, informing me that he had been double JAPANNED (as he called it) . . . . and was the present incumbent of . . . .

1811. *Lex. Bal.*, s.v. JAPANNED . . . . to put on the black cloth, from the color of the Japan ware which is black.

1819. MOORE, *Tom Crib*, 5. Lobsters will lie such a drug upon hand, That our do-nothing Captains must all get JAPANNED.

1852. BRISTED, *Five Years in an English University*, 344. Many . . . . step . . . . into the Church without any pretence of other change than in the attire of their outward man, on being JAPANNED, as assuming the black dress and white tie is called in University slang.

1879. JAMES PAYN, *High Spirits (Change of Views).* He . . . . was to be JAPANNED in a fortnight. That was the expression which, I am grieved to say, he used, in those unregenerate days, for the ceremony of ordination.

2. (American thieves').—To convert: TO BE JAPANNED = to be converted.—MATSELL (1859).

3. (common).—To black one's boots. Fr. *sabouler.* Also to JAPAN ONE'S TROTTER-CASES.

1712. GAY, *Trivia*, [quoted by JOHNSON]. And aids with soot the new JAPANNING art.

1734. POPE, *Satire*, iii, 156. Prefer a new JAPANNER to their shoes.

1755. JOHNSON, *Eng. Dict.*, s.v. JAPAN. To black and gloss shoes. A low phrase.

1772. G. A. STEVENS, *Songs Comic and Satyrical*, 171. With Courtier-like bowing the shoe-cleaners call, And offer their Brush, Stool and shining Blackball: 'JAPANNING, your Honour', these Colourists plan; And, really, some Honours may want a JAPAN.

1837. DICKENS, *Oliver Twist*, xviii. He applied himself to a process which Mr. Dawkins designated as JAPANNING his trotter-cases. The phrase, rendered into plain English, signifieth cleaning his boots.

JAPANESE KNIFE-TRICK, *subs. phr.* (common).—Eating with one's knife.

JAPPERS. *See* **JABERS.**

JAPE, *verb.* (old).—To copulate. Formerly (CHAUCER) = to trifle; to scoff. For synonyms *see* GREENS and RIDE.

1510. *Hycke Scorner* [DODSLEY, *Old Plays* (1874), i. 171]. Nay, brother, lay hand on him soon; For he JAPED my wife, and made me cuckold.

1530. PALSGRAVE. I IAPE a wench, *i.e. fout* and *ie bistocque*, it is better to IAPE a wench than to do worse.

1540. LYNDSAY, *Thrie Estaitis*, in *Works* (1879), ii. 23. line 324. There is ane hundred heir sittand by That luiffis GEAPING als weill as I.

*c.*1550. A. SCOTT, *Poems* (1821), p. 26. Sum gois so gymp in gyis Or sche war kissit plane, Sche leir be JAPIT thryis.

1568. *Bannatyne MSS.* [Hunterian Club Rept. vi. 764]. 'The Vse of Court.' His wyfe JAIPPIT, his siller spendit.

1572. GASCOIGNE, *Councell . . . to Master. . . . Withipoll* (CHALMERS, ii. 533). First, in thy journey JAPE not overmuch.

1589. *Puttenham.* Art of Eng. Poesie, B. iii, ch. 22. Such wordes as may be drawen to a foule and unshamefast sense, as one that should say to a young woman, I pray you let me JAPE with you, which is indeed no more than let me sport with you. . . . For it may be taken in another perverser sense.

1598. FLORIO, *Worlde of Wordes*, *Fottere*, to JAIPE, etc.

*b.*1600. *Grim the Collier* etc. [DODSLEY, *Old Plays* (1874), viii. 389]. Heard you not never how an actor's wife, Whom he (fond fool) lov'd dearly as his life, Coming in's way did chance to get a JAPE.

1602. SPEGHT, in *Wks.* of CHAUCER. 'Hard Words of Chaucer Explained', s.v.

JARGONELLE, *subs.* (venery).—The *penis.* For synonyms *see* CREAMSTICK and PRICK.

JARGOOZLE, *verb.* (common).—To mislead; to lead astray; TO BAMBOOZLE (*q.v.*).

JARK, *subs.*(Old Cant.).—1. *See* quot. It. *tirella.* Also JACK.

1567. HARMAN, *Caveat* (1814), p. 65. A JARKE, a seal.

1608. DEKKER, *Belman of London*, in Wks (GROSART, iii, 102). Which license they (beggars) call a gybe, and the Seales to it, JARKES.

1690. B. E., *Dict. Cant. Crew*, s.v.

1724. E. COLES, *Eng. Dict.*, s.v.

1785. GROSE, *Vulg. Tongue*, s.v.

1811. *Lex. Bal.*, s.v.

1818. SCOTT, *Heart of Midlothian*, xxv. He knows my gybe [pass] as well as the JARK [seal] of e'er a queer cuffin [justice of peace] in England.

1859. MATSELL, *Vocabulum*, s.v.

2. (common).—A watch. For synonyms *see* TICKER.

3. (Oxford University and general).—A safe-conduct pass; a JASKER (*q.v.*),

1818. SCOTT, *Heart of Midlothian*, xxix. Stay, gentlemen, ... this is a JARK from Jim Radcliffe.

TO JARK IT, *verb. phr.* (old).—To run away. For synonyms *see* AMPUTATE and SKEDADDLE.—BEE (1823).

JARKMAN, *subs.* (Old Cant).—A begging-letter writer: a fabricator of false characters, counterfeit-passes, and certificates.

1567. HARMAN, *Caveat*, p. 60. For as much as these two names, a IARKEMAN and a Patrico, bée in the old briefe of vacabonds, and set forth as two kyndes of euil doers, you shall vnderstande that a Iarkeman hathe his name of a *Iarke*, which is a seale in their Language, as one should make writinges and set seales for lycences and pasporte.

1608. DEKKER, *Belman of London*, sig. C. 3, (ed. 1608). There [are] some in this Schoole of Beggers that practise writing and reading, and those are called JARKMEN [old ed. JACKMEN]: yea, the JARKMAN is so cunning sometimes that he can speake Latine; which learning of his lifts him vp to aduancement for by that means he becomes Clarke of their Hall, and his office is to make counterfeit licenses, which are called gybes, and to which he puts Seales, and those are termed JARKES.

1622. BEAUMONT & FLETCHER, *Beggar's Bush*, ii, 1. And then, what name or title e'er they bear, JARKMAN or Patrico.

1690. B. E., *Dict. Cant. Crew*, s.v.

1785. GROSE, *Vulg. Tongue*, s.v.

1834. AINSWORTH, *Rookwood*, iii, 5. No JARKMAN, be he high or low.

1859. MATSELL, *Vocabulum*, s.v.

JARREHOE, *subs.* (Wellington College).—A man-servant. *Cf.* GYP and SCOUT.

JARVEL, *subs.* (old).—A jacket.

JARVEY (or **JARVIS**), *subs.* (old: now recognised).—1. A hackney coachman.

1811. *Lex. Bal.*, JARVIS, s.v.

1819. DE VAUX, *Memoirs*, s.v. JERVIS.

1823. BEE, *Dict. of the Turf*, s.v. JARVY.

1835. BEULER, *The Devil and the Hackney Coachman.* 'JARVIE! JARVIE!' 'Here I am your honor'.

1837. CARLYLE, *French Revolution*, II, iv. 3. The glass coachman waits, and in what mood! A brother JARVIE drives up; enters into conversation; is answered cheerfully in JARVIE dialect etc.

1845. DISRAELI, *Sybil*, V, vii. I pity them ere JARVIES a' sitting on their boxes all the night and waiting for the nobs what is dancing.

1851-61. MAYHEW, *London Lab. and Lond. Poor*, iii, 360. He didn't take the corners or the crossings careful enough for a regular JARVEY.

1882. SERJ. BALLANTINE, *Experiences*, ch. ii, p. 19 (6th ed.). The driver [of a hackney-coach] was called a JARVEY, a compliment paid to the class in consequence of one of them named Jarvis having been hanged.

1883. *Daily Telegraph*, 16 Dec. The assembled Londoners placed more faith in the real four-wheeler, the grey horse, and the loquacious JARVEY.

2. (old).—A hackney coach.

1823. MONCRIEFF, *Tom and Jerry*, II. 4. A rattler . . . . is a rumbler, otherwise a JARVEY . . . . better known perhaps by the name of a hack.

1835. T. HOOK, *Gilbert Gurney*, iii. 1. I stepped into the litter, ... at the bottom of the JARVY.

1838. GLASCOCK, *Land Sharks & Sea Gulls*, i, 203. And now . . . . was Waddy seen to enter a JARVEY, and to drive from the Temple Court.

1865. G. F. BERKELEY, *My Life*, i. 275. Dan McKinnon slipped through the windows of the first, and so on out of the others till the whole string of JARVIES were bumping in procession to the destination, having no one in them.

JASEY (or **JAZEY**), *subs.* (old).—1. A worsted wig. COVE WITH A JAZEY = judge.

1789. PARKER, *Life's Painter*, 172. Wig, JASEY.

1811. *Lex. Bal.*, s.v.

1837. BARHAM, *Ingoldsby Legends*, 'Jerry Jarvis's Wig'. With an infrenzied grasp he tore the JASEY from his head. *Ibid.* 'The Coronation'. All jools from his JASEY to his di'mond boots.

1841. *Punch*, i. 208. If you only see his big cock'd hat, Stuck up on the top of his JAZY.

1842. LEVER, *Jack Hinton*, iii. The head would have been bald but for a scanty wig, technically called a JASY, which shrunk by time, merely occupied the apex of the scalp.

1869. THACKERAY, *Lyra Hibernica*, 'Molony's Lament.' When spring with its buds and its dasies, Comes out in her beauty and bloom, Them tu'll never think of new JASIES.

1895. *Sporting Times*, No. 1653, p. 9. There is nothing to he ashamed of in wearing a JASEY.

2. (American thieves').—A man with an enormous quantity of hair upon his head and face.—MATSELL (1859).

JASKER, *subs.* (American thieves'). A seal.—MATSELL (1859). *Cf.* JARK.

JASON'S FLEECE, *subs. phr.* (Old Cant.).—A citizen cheated of his gold.—B. E. (1690); GROSE (1785).

JAUM, *verb.* (thieves').—To discover.

1821. HAGGART, *Life*, 57. McBean . . . . JAUM'D a scout on the chimney-piece.

JAW, *subs.*(vulgar).—Abuse; chatter; impudence; any sort of talk. HOLD (or STOW) YOUR JAW = hold your tongue. ALL JAW, LIKE A SHEEP'S HEAD = nothing but talk.

ENGLISH SYNONYMS. Chin-music; gab (or gob); lingo; lip lobs; patter; snaffle.

FRENCH SYNONYMS. *Le debérage* (popular); *une coup de gaffe* (general); *la jactance* (thieves'); *la jappe* (popular); *le jaspin* (thieves').

ITALIAN SYNONYMS. *Canzonamento; contrapunto* (= counterpoint).

SPANISH SYNONYMS. *Champarrado; chapurrado; dichido.*

1748. SMOLLETT, *Roderick Random*, iii. 'None of your JAW, you swab' . . . . replied my uncle.

1751. SMOLLETT, *Peregrine Pickle*, xxxii. Desiring him to do his duty without farther JAW.

1753. FOOTE, *Englishman in Paris* (1783), 15. Hold your JAW, and despatch!

1771. G. A. STEVENS, *Songs Comic and Satyrical*, p. 47. O my love, though I cannot well JAW.

1785. GROSE, *Vulg. Tongue*, s.v. JAW, speech, discourse.

1825. TODD, *Eng. Dict.*, s.v. JAW. In low language, gross abuse.

1830. LYTTON, *Paul Clifford*, xvi. Hand me the brandy and cease your JAW.

1836. M. SCOTT, *Cruise of the Midge*, 256. Bring the felt, you spalpeen, and no JAW.

1852. H. B. STOWE, *Uncle Tom's Cabin*, viii. 'Stop that ar JAW o' yourn, there' said Tom gruffly.

1859. H. KINGSLEY, *Geoffrey Hamlyn*, xxvi. Stop your JAW about him!

1874. E. LYNN LINTON, *Patricia Kemball*, xxi. 'Dora, I and my father have had a JAW', Sydney began.

1876. HINDLEY, *Adventures of a Cheap Jack*, 41. He's ALL JAW LIKE A SHEEP'S HEAD.

1883. *Daily Telegraph*, 5 Jan. 2. 2. He had audibly expressed his disgust that some fellows should have all the JAW to themselves.

1883. CLARK RUSSELL, *Sailor's Language*, s.v. JAW.

1892. S. WATSON, *Wops the Waif*, i. I'll hev yer run in . . . . if yer don't hold yer JAW.

1892. MILLIKEN, *'Arry Ballads*, 68. These stuckuppy snipsters as JAW about quiet and peace.

Verb. (vulgar).—To chatter; to abuse; to use violent language. Fr. *faire péter son grelot* or *jouer du mirliton.*

1748. SMOLLETT, *Roderick Random*, xxiv. They JAWED together fore-and-aft a good spell.

1760-61. SMOLLETT, *Sir L. Graves*, Bk. II. i. You might give good words, however: an we once fall a-JAWING, d'ye see, I can heave out as much bilge-water as another.

1825. TODD (JOHNSON, *Eng. Dict.* s.v. JAW. In low language, to abuse grossly.

1843. THACKERAY, *Irish Sketch Book*, ii. Why should four waiters stand and JAW, and gesticulate among themselves, instead of waiting on the guests?

1862. LOWELL, *Biglow Papers*, ii. p. 61. But, neighbour, ef they prove their claim at law, The best way is to settle, an' not JAW.

1883. *Daily Telegraph*, 8 Feb., p. 3, col. 1. If I was to JAW till a blue moon, I couldn't tell you more about her.

1888. *Detroit Free Press*, 8 Dec. She'll lick both of us and JAW father all the evening.

TO JAW ON THE TOBY (or DRUM) *verb. phr.* (tramps').—To go on the road.

JAWBATION, *subs.* (old).—1. A general CONFAB (*q.v.*); a JAWING-MATCH. *See* JOBATION.

2. (colloquial).—A scolding.

JAWBONE, *subs.*(American).—Credit; DAY (*q.v.*). TO CALL ONE'S JAWBONE = to live on credit, or RUN ONE'S FACE (*q.v.*).

ENGLISH SYNONYMS. To run one's face; to get a light; to give (or strike) on the mace; to mace it; to get on sock (or, on the nod), to go tick.

FRENCH SYNONYMS. *Avoir l'arche; avoir l'ardoise* (= TO CHALK IT UP); *le crôme* or *croume* (tramps'); *grésillonner* (= to ask credit); *avoir l'œil* (general); *la symbole.*

1862. *Times*, 21 Oct. (San Francisco correspondent). Individuals, who, in digger's parlance, live on JAWBONE.

JAWBREAKER (or **JAWTWISTER**) *subs.* (common).—1. A hard or many-syllabled word. JAWBREAKING = difficult.

1839. LEVER, *Harry Lorrequer*, xx. I'd rather hear the Cruiskeen Lawn. . . . as my old friend. . . . could sing [it] than a score of your high Dutch JAWBREAKERS.

1851-61. MAYHEW, *Lond. Lab.*, i. 27. 'I can't tumble to that barrikin', said a young fellow; 'it's a JAWBREAKER.'

1872. *Chambers' Miscellany*, No. 152, p. 2. The most JAWBREAKING polysyllables were cleared in a flying gallop.

1883. *Illustrated London News*, 8 Dec., p. 551, col. i. Such tedious talk, such sledge-hammer humour, and JAW-CRACKING jokes.

2. (pugilists').—A hard punch on the whisker.

JAW-COVE, *subs.* (American thieves').—1. An auctioneer; and (2) a lawyer.—MATSELL (1859).

JAWHAWK, *verb.* (American).—To abuse; to vilify; TO JAW (*q.v.*).

1890. *Scribner's Magazine*, p. 242. 'He'd ev shot him, if he hadn't skedaddled.' 'Well, *sir!* What fur?' 'Oh, jest JAWHAWKIN' a Yank and burnin' his heouse down.'

JAWING- (or **JAW-**) **TACKLE**, *subs.* (nautical).—The organs of speech. TO HAVE ONE'S JAWING TACKS ABOARD (or TO CAST-OFF ONE'S JAW-TACKLE) = to talk fluently. —CLARK RUSSELL. JAWING-MATCH = wordy warfare.

1859. C. READE, *Love me Little*, xxii. Ah! Eve, my girl, your JAWING-TACKLE is too well hung.

1819. MOORE, *Tom Crib*, xviii. Chap 6 proves from the JAWING-MATCH and set-to etc.

JAW-SMITH, *subs.* (colloquial).—An orator; also a loud-mouthed demagogue. [Originally an official 'orator' or 'instructor' of the Knights of Labor—*St. Louis Globe Democrat*, 1886].

JAY (or **J**), *subs.* (common).—1. A simpleton. For synonyms *see* BUFFLE and CABBAGE-HEAD.

1889. *Pall Mall Gazette*, 21 Sept., p. 3, col. 1. The amateur gamblers—youths of sixteen or seventeen, and flats or JAYS—are the chief patrons of faro.

1890. *Punch*, 22 Feb. She must be a fair J as a mater.

TO PLAY (or SCALP) ONE FOR (or TO FLAP) A JAY, *verb. phr.* (common).—To dupe; to swindle. *See* FLAP. Fr. *rouler dans la farine.*

1890. GUNTER, *Miss Nobody*, p. 25. Telling in broken English how he SCALPED THE Eastern JAY.

2. (old).—A wanton. It. *putta.*

1596. SHAKSPEARE, *Merry Wives*, iii, 3. Go to, then;—we'll use this unwholesome humidity, this gross watry pumpion;—we'll teach him to know turtles from JAYS!

1605. SHAKSPEARE, *Cymbeline*, iii, 4. Some JAY of Italy, Whose mother was her painting, hath betray'd him.

3. (theatrical).—An amateur; a poor actor.

JAYHAWKER, *subs.* (political American).—A freebooter; a guerilla: specifically a marauder during the Kansas troubles and since extended to all bandits.

1887. G. W. CABLE, *Century*, xxxiii, 360. He and his father are catching the horses of the dead and dying JAY-HAWKERS.

JEAMES, *subs.* (common).—1. A footman; a flunkey.

1845-6. THACKERAY, *Jeames' Diary.* [Title].

1857. THACKERAY, *Virginians*, xxxvi. That noble old race of footmen is well nigh gone . . . . and Uncas with his tomahawk and eagle's plume, and JEAMES with his cocked hat and long cane, are passing out of the world where they once walked in glory.

1876. J. GRANT, *One of the Six Hundred*, xv. Where, doubtless, she and her family would be on a Sunday, in their luxuriously-cushioned pew, attended by a tall JEAMES in plush, carrying a great Bible, a nosegay, and gold headed cane.

1891. *Licensed Victuallers' Mirror*, 30 Jan., p. 6, col. 3. The JEAMESES and Allplushes who frequent that part of the town.

1892. *Tit Bits*, 19 Mar, p. 421, col. 1. Mutton-chop whiskers . . . . are now little seen, save on the physiognomy of JEAMES Yellowplush.

2. (obsolete).—*The Morning Post* newspaper.

JEFF, *subs.* (circus).—A rope.

1854. DICKENS, *Hard Times*, vi. Tight-JEFF or Slack-JEFF, it don't much signify; it's only tight-rope and slack-rope.

Verb. (American printers').—To gamble with 'quads', as with dice.

1888. *American Humorist.* He never set any type except in the rush of the last day, and then he would smouch all the poetry, and leave the rest to JEFF for the solid takes.

JEFFY, *subs.* (American thieves').—Lightning.—MATSELL (1859).

IN A JEFFEY. *See* JIFFEY.

JEGGER.—*See* JIGGER.

JEHU, *subs.* (common).—A coachman; a driver. [From 2 *Kings* ix, 20].

1660. J. CROUCH, *Return of Chas. II*, p. 9. Now the restored Rump, JEHU-like, drives on.

1681. DRYDEN, *The Medal*, 119. But this new JEHU spurs the hot mouthed horse.

1694. CONGREVE, *Double Dealer*, iii. 10. Our JEHU was a hackny coachman, when my Lord took him.

1759. GOLDSMITH, *The Bee*, No. 5, p. 388 (Globe ed.). Our figure now began to expostulate: he assured the coachman, that though his baggage seemed so bulky, it was perfectly light . . . . But JEHU was inflexible.

1811. *Lex. Bal.*, s.v. JEHU.

1841. MACAULAY, *Comic Dramatists of the Reformation* [quoted in *Century*]. A pious man . . . . may call a keen foxhunter a Nimrod . . . . and Cowper's friend, Newton, would speak of a neighbour who was given to driving as JEHU.

1846-8. THACKERAY, *Vanity Fair*, vii. The worthy Baronet whom he drove to the city did not give him one single penny more than his fare. It was in vain that JEHU appealed and stormed.

1855. LADY HOLLAND, *Sidney Smith*, vi. She soon . . . . raised my wages, and considered me an excellent JEHU.

1860. *Punch*, iii. 177. The JEHUS who drive.

1889. *Daily Telegraph*, 5 Jan. For some time past the JEHUS of Paris have betrayed a lamentable ignorance of metropolitan topography.

JELLY, *subs.* (common).—1. A buxom, good-looking girl: also ALL JELLY. *Cf.* Scots JELLY, = excellent or worthy.—'A JELLY man well worthy of a crown'.—SHIRREFS, *Poems*, (1790) p. 33.

*d.*1758. RAMSAY, *To Lieutenant Hamilton*, in *Wks.*, iii. 47. A JELLY sum to carry on A fishery's designed.

2. (venery).—The seminal fluid. For synonyms *see* CREAM.

1622. FLETCHER, *Beggar's Bush*, iii. 1. Give her cold JELLY To take up her belly, And once a day swinge her again.

*d.*1631. DONNE, *Progress of the Soul*, st. xxiii. A female fish's sandy roe With the male's JELLY newly leaven'd was.

JELLY-BAG, *subs.* (venery).—1. The *scrotum.* For synonyms *see* PURSE.

2. (venery).—The female *pudendum.* For synonyms *see* MONOSYLLABLE.

JELLY-BELLY, subs. (common).—A fat man or woman; a FORTY-GUTS (q.v.).

JEM, subs. (Old Cant.).—A gold ring: RUM-GEM = a diamond ring.

1725. New Cant. Dict., s.v.

1785. GROSE, Vulg. Tongue, s.v.

1811. Lex. Bal., s.v.

1859. MATSELL, Vocabulum, s.v.

JEMIMA, subs. (common).—A chamber-pot; a URINAL (q.v.). For synonyms see IT.

JEMINY! (or O JEMINY!), intj. (common).—See GEMINI.

1686. DURFEY, Commonwealth of Women, Epil. OH JEMMINY! what is the cause of that?

1880. BESANT and RICE, Seamy Side, xxii. 'OH, JEMINY!' says the judge—crafty old man, that!—'here's artfulness!'

JEMMINESS. See JEMMY.

JEMMY (or JIMMY), subs. (common).—1. A short crowbar, usually made in sections screwing together, used by housebreakers. Also JAMES (q.v.).

ENGLISH SYNONYMS. Bess; betty; crow; dog; Jack-in-the-box; James; jilt; lord-mayor; persuading plate; pig's-foot; the stick; screw (also a skeleton key); tivvill; twist; twirl.

FRENCH SYNONYMS. Les agobilles (thieves' = house-breaking tools); les alènes (pop: = shoe-makers' awls); l'avant-courier (thieves'); le bataclan (= the kit); le cadet (thieves'); l'enfant; Jacques (= JEMMY); sucre de pomme (thieves'); le biribi; le rigolo; les halènes (see alènes, ante);

le monseigneur (Cf. LORD MAYOR); les outils (= tools).

SPANISH SYNONYMS. Culebra (= adder).

1752. Adventurer, No. 100. And when I went out, carried in my hand a little switch, which, as it has been long appendent to the character that I had just assumed, has taken the same name, and is called a JEMMY.

1811. Lex. Bal., s.v. JEMMY. A crow. This instrument is much used by housebreakers. Sometimes called JEMMY ROOK.

1837. DICKENS, Oliver Twist, xx. She presently returned with a pot of porter and a dish of sheeps' heads: which gave occasion to several pleasant witticisms on the part of Mr. Sikes, founded upon the singular coincidence of JEMMIES, being a cant name, common to them, and also to an ingenious implement much used in his profession.

1851. BARHAM, Ingoldsby Legends (Nell Cook), They call for crowbars—JEMMIES is the modern name they bear.

1851. H. MAYHEW, Lon. Lab. and Lon. Poor, iv, 339. Expert burglars are generally equipped with good tools. They have a JEMMY, a cutter, a dozen of betties, better known as picklocks.

1888. Saturday Review, 15 Dec, p. 719. One side of slang was illustrated by the burglar Casey in a well-known case of robbery in the City some years ago, who explained in Court that the big JEMMY with which iron shutters were prised open was called the 'Alderman,' adding, 'it would never do to be talking about crowbars in the street.'

1890. Daily Graphic, 7 Jan., p. 14, col. 4. He saw the prisoner leaving, and he detained him until a constable arrived. A JEMMY was found in the back yard.

1890. Standard, 7 Ap., p. 6, col. During the chase the Prisoner threw away a JEMMY, a lantern, and a key.

1892. Globe, 10 May, p. 2, col. 1. Opening a front door with.... a JEMMY.

1894. Westminster Gazette, 31 March, 5, 2. Police constable Skeggs said there were marks of a JEMMY on the window and the front door.

2. (common).—See quots; cf. SANGUINARY JAMES and BLOODY JEMMY.

1823. BEE, Dict. of the Turf, s.v. JEMMY (bloody)—a sheep's head; so called from a great dealer in these delicious morceaux.

1835. DICKENS, Sketches by Boz, p. 41. The man in the shop, perhaps, is in the baked JEMMY line.

1837. DICKENS, Oliver Twist, xx. [See ante, sense 1, quot. 1837].

1843. MONCRIEFF, Scamps of London, ii. I shall stand a JEMMY and sauce at Mother White's.

1851-61. MAYHEW, Lond. Lab. &c. ii, 48. They clubbed together for a good supper of tripe, or had a 'prime hot JEMMY' apiece.

1884. HENLEY & STEVENSON, Deacon Brodie, iv, 1. You're all jaw like a sheep's JIMMY.

3. (common).—A shooting coat; also a great coat.

1836. DICKENS, Pickwick ch. ii. Your friend in the green JEMMY.

4. (common).—A term of contempt. ALL JIMMY = all rot.

Adj. (common).—1. Spruce; dandified. JEMMINESS = spruceness; neatness.

1754. Connoisseur, No. 19. The JEMMY attorney's clerk, — the prim curate.

1767. Gentleman's Mag., Sept. A cute man is an abbreviation of acute.... and signifies a person that is sharp, clever, neat, or, to use a more modern term, JEMMY.

1785. GROSE, Vulg. Tongue, s.v. JEMMY-FELLOW

1800. WHITER, Etym. Magn., p. 359. To this race of words I must refer our vulgar term JEMMY.

1788. G. A. STEVENS, Adv. of a Speculist, vol. i. p. 11. He.... once was as smart a fellow as ever stood toast-master, dressed as JEMMY... as e'er a commoner in all England.

d.1800. PEGGE [quoted by TODD]. Perhaps the new word JEMMY should be GIMMY.

1825. TODD, Eng. Dict. s.v. JEMMY, spruce. A low word.

1840. CHAMBERS, Land of Burns, Div. N. I must tell you that Burns had got a pair of JEMMY boots for the journey.

2. (common).—A term of contempt. See subs., sense 4.

JEMMY DUCKS, subs. phr. (nautical).—The ship's poulterer; also BILLY DUCKS.

1860. HARWOOD, [U. S. N.] Mess Table Chat. As to chanticleer, the keeper of the live-stock, JEMMY DUCKS, had long ceased to regard him as worthy of his solicitude.

1883. CLARK RUSSELL, Sailors' Language, s.v.

JEMMY JESSAMY, subs. phr. (old).—A dandy. For synonyms see DANDY. Also as adj.

1753. Adventurer, No. 100. The scale, however, consists of eight degrees; Greenhorn, JEMMY, JESSAMY, Smart, Honest Fellow, Joyous Spirit, Buck, and Blood.

1772. G. A. STEVENS, Songs Comic and Satyrical, 139. Macaronies so neat, Pert JEMMIES so sweet, With all their effeminate brood.

1788. G. A. STEVENS, Adv. of a Speculist, i. 24. With ladies when JEMMYS and JESSAMYS mix.

1853. THACKERAY, Barry Lyndon, xiii, 180. This was very different language to that she had been in the habit of hearing from her JEMMY JESSAMY adorers.

1853. THACKERAY, Barry Lyndon, i. 19. My dear young lady readers may know.... what a courage and undaunted passion he had. I question whether any of the JEMMY-JESSAMINES of the present day would do half as much in the face of danger.

JEMMY AND JESSAMY; subs. phr. (American).—A pair of lovers.—MAITLAND

JEMMY-JOHN, subs. (common).—A demijohn.

1861. MARSH, Lectures on the English Language, (q. v. for Etymology from Damaghan a town in Khorassan, once famous for its glass works).

1873. T. B. ALDRICH, Marjorie Daw &c. p. 76 (TAUCHNITZ). 'A gill o' wather out of a JIMMY-JOHN 'd fuddle him, mum.'

JEMMY O'GOBLIN, subs. phr. (theatrical).—A sovereign. For synonyms see CANARY.

JENKINS' HEN. TO DIE LIKE JENKINS' HEN, verb. phr. (Scots').—To die unmarried.

1805. A. SCOTT, Poems, 'The Old Maid', p. 87. I ance had sweethearts nine or ten, And dearly dawted wi' the men.... But Oh! the DEATH OF JENKINS' HEN, I shudder at it.

JENNY, subs. (colloquial).—1. A she-ass.

2. (thieves').—A small crowbar; formerly BETTY or BESS (q.v.): also a hook on the end of a stick.

1690. B. E., Dict. Cant. Crew, s.v. JENNY, an instrument to lift up a grate, and whip anything out of a shop window.

1725. New. Cant. Dict. s.v.

1785. GROSE, Vulg. Tongue, s.v.

1859. MATSELL, Vocabulum, s.v.

3. (billiards').—A losing hazard into the middle pocket off a ball an inch or two from the side cushion.

4. (popular).—A hot water bottle.

JENNYLINDA, subs. (rhyming).—A window.

JEREMY DIDDLER, subs. phr. (common).—A SHARK (q.v.); a shabby swindling borrower.

1803. KENNEY, Raising the Wind. [Among the Dramatis Personæ, is JEREMY DIDDLER].

1840. LYTTON, Money, iv. 5. Blount. And he borrowed £700 of me! Gloss. And £600 of me! Sir John. And £500 of me! Stout. Oh! a regular JEREMY DIDDLER!

1843. THACKERAY, Irish Sketch Book, xiii. As for trade, there seemed to be none: a great JEREMY-DIDDLER kind of hotel stood hard by, swaggering and out-at-elbows.

1857. THACKERAY, Virginians, xxxi. Poor JEREMY DIDDLER calls about eleven o'clock for another half-sovereign.

1895. St. James's Gazette, 15 June, p. 13. Your deeply obliged, JEREMY-DIDDLER.

JERICHO, subs. (old).—1. A place of concealment or banishment; latterly and specifically, a prison: e.g. as in phr. GO TO JERICHO = Go to the devil. [Generically, a place of retirement, cf. 2 Sam. x: 4 and 5].

1635. HEYWOOD, Hierarchie, iv. p. 208. Bid such young boyes to stay in JERICHO Untill their beards were growne, their wits more staid.

1648. Mercurius Aulicus quoted in Athenæum. Nov. 14. 1874, p. 645. Let them all GOE TO JERICHO, And n'ere be seen againe.

1758. A. MURPHY, The Upholsterer, ii. He may GO TO JERICHO for what I cares.

1775. D'ARBLAY, Diary (1876), Vol. i. p. 167. I should wish all my new friends AT JERICHO.

1857. THACKERAY, Virginians, xvi. 'She may go to Tunbridge, or she may go to Bath, or she may go TO JERICHO for me.'

2. (common).—A watercloset. For synonyms see Mrs. JONES.

3. (Oxford university).—A low quarter of Oxford.

1853. REV. E. BRADLEY, ['CUTHBERT Bede'], Verdant Green, p. II. ch. iii. It was darkly whispered that the purlieus of Jericho would send forth champions to the fight.

FROM JERICHO TO JUNE, phr. (common).—A long distance.

1837. BARHAM, Ingoldsby Legends. His kick was tremendous.... he would send a man from JERICHO TO JUNE.

JERK, subs. (common).—1. In pl. = delirium tremens. For synonyms see GALLON-DISTEMPER.

2. in pl. (American).—Religious paroxysm.

1874. E. EGGLESTON, Circuit Rider, xii. These Methodis' sets people crazy with the JERKS.

3. (old).—A retort; a jest; a quirk.

1653. BROME, Mad Couple well matched [in Five Newe Playes], p. 13. I charge you meddle not with my wife: you have had two or three JERKS at her.

4. (old).—A stripe; a lash with a whip. Hence JERKING (or YERKING), adj. = lashing; stinging; JERK, verb., = to lash; and TO CLY THE JERK (Old Cant) = to be whipped at the post.

1557-8. Jacob and Esau [DODSLEY, Old Plays (1874). ii. 194]. Come on, ye must have three JERKS for the nonce.

1597. HALL, Satires, ii. 6. He must ask his mother to define, How many JERKES she would his breech should line.

1598. MARSTON, Satyres, iii. Ne'er yerking him with my satyric whip.

1609. DEKKER, Lanthorne and Candlelight (GROSART, Wks.). iii. 203, If we heave a Booth we straight CLY THE JERK.

1653. BROME, The Damoiselle, in Wks (1872), ii. 448. I' faith she JERKED that humour out of me.

5. (various).— A common verb of action, especially if rapid.

[Some conbinations are: TO JERK THE CAT = to vomit; TO JERK THE TINKLER = to ring the bell; TO JERK ONE'S JUICE or JELLY (also TO JERK OFF) = to masturbate; TO JERK CHINMUSIC = to talk; TO JERK A POEM, ARTICLE OR BOOK = to write; TO JERK A GYBE = to counterfeit a license; JERKED, or JERKED TO JESUS (American) = hanged; IN A JERK = instantly; DR. JERK = flogging schoolmaster.]

1622. HEAD & KIRKMAN, English Rogue. A Jybe well JERKED.

1651. On Dr. Gill, Master of St. Paul's School. In Paul's Churchyard in London, There dwells a noble Ferker. Take heed, you that passe, Lest you taste of his Lash, For I have found him a JERKER.

1752. FOOTE, Taste (1781). The child has been two years and three quarters at school with Dr. Jerk near Doncaster.

1755. JOHNSON, Eng. Dict. s.v. Jerk. To strike up; to accost eagerly.... is mere cant.

1772. G. A. STEVENS, Songs Comic and Satyrical, 161. Put wine into wounds You'll be cured in a JERK.

1837. DICKENS, Oliver Twist. JERK THE TINKLER.... These words in plain English conveyed an injunction to ring the bell.

1872. S. L. CLEMENS ('Mark Twain'), Roughing It, p. 332. The thing I'm now on is to roust out somebody to JERK a little chin-music for us.

JERKER, subs. (common).—1. A tippler. For synonyms see LUSHINGTON.

2. (common).—A chamber-pot. For synonyms see IT.

3. (nautical).—A steward.

4. (streets').—A prostitute. For synonyms see BARRACK-HACK and TART. [See quot., but possibly, also, from JERK OFF = to masturbate].

1887. WALFORD, Antiquarian, p. 252. A JERKER is a loose woman of the streets, and possibly comes from 'jerk' to accost eagerly.

JERKEY, *subs.* (American).—A roughly-made vehicle; a BONE-SHAKER (*q.v.*).

JEROBOAM, *subs.* (common).—1. A four-fold measure of wine; a double-MAGNUM (*q.v.*); one especially apt to 'cause Israel to sin' [*See* 1 *Kings*, xi. 28]. Also a large bowl or goblet.

1880. H. S. CUMINGS, (quoted in *Century*). The corporation of Ludlow formerly possessed a JEROBOAM which was used as a. . . . loving cup.

2. *See* JERRY sense 1.

JERRAN, *adv.* (Australian).—Concerned.

1888. ROLF BOLDREWOOD, *Robbery Under Arms*, chap. 41. When I saw the mob there was I didn't see so much to be JERRAN about.

JERRY, *subs.* (common).—1. A chamber-pot; a JEROBOAM. For synonyms *see* IT.

2. (old).—A hat: formerly TOM & JERRY HAT (*q.v.*); a hard, round hat; a POT-HAT.

1841. *Punch*, i. 98. 2. Displaying to the greatest advantage those unassuming castors designated JERRYS.

1864. LE FANU, *Uncle Silas*, viii. A rather fat and flashily equipped young man, with large, light whiskers, a JERRY HAT, green cutaway coat.

3. (printers').—A celebration of the completion of indentures. Fr. *un roulance*.

4. (thieves').—A watch. For synonyms *see* TICKER. Fr. *une babillarde*.

1889. RICHARDSON, *Police*, p. 321. .v.

5. (thieves').—A fog, or mist. —DE VAUX (1819).

Adj. (common).—As an adjectival prefix JERRY is frequently used in contempt: *e.g.* JERRY-GO-NIMBLE, JERRY-SHOP, JERRY-BUILDER (all which and others *see*). [An abbreviation of Jeremiah: perhaps a Restoration jibe upon the Puritan use of Old Testament names; but see JERRY-BUILDER].

Verb. (common).—To jibe; to chaff with malice.

JERRY-BUILDER, *subs.* (common).—A rascally speculating builder. JERRY-BUILT, *adj.* = run up in the worst materials. [The use of the term arose in Liverpool *circa* 1830].

1883. *Daily Telegraph*, 23 Mar., p. 6, col. 1. But the JERRY BUILDER is a man of enterprise and energy, and promptly showed himself equal to the occasion. *Ibid*, Ap. 5, p. 2, col. 1. 'Houses, of the JERRY-BUILT sort especially, when the builders have a difficulty in raising money to finish 'em, are singularly liable to catch fire.'

1884. *Pall Mall Gazette*, 15 Feb., Two lumps of plaster, fall from the roof of the JERRY-BUILT palace; then the curse begins to work.

1889. *Ally Sloper's Half-Holiday*, 3 Aug., p. 242, col. 3. 'Well, sir,' said a JERRY BUILDER, 'I don't think as 'ow it's right on you to be a-runnin' the house down as you do.'

1889. *Daily Chronicle*, 15. Feb. The vestries and district local boards, in fact, have been dominated too much by JERRY-BUILDERS and house-jobbers.

1891. *Sportsman*, 21 April, p. 2, col. 1. She lives in a JERRY-BUILT house.

1891. J. NEWMAN, *Scamping Tricks*, 119. It was in the days when every JERRY-BUILDER thought he was a railway and dock contractor.

1893. *St. James's Gazette*, 2 Nov., p. 4, col. 2. All this loss of life and all this fearful suffering are to be laid at the door of scamping JERRY-BUILDERS or of careless employers.

JERRYCUMMUMBLE, *verb.* (old).—To shake; to tumble about; to towzle. —GROSE (1785).

JERRY-GETTING (or NICKING, or STEALING).—Stealing watches.

1888. *Tit-Bits*, 17 Nov. Watch stealing, or JERRY GETTING, as the thieving fraternity designate the operation, is carried on to a considerable extent all the year round.

JERRY-GO-NIMBLE, *subs.* (old).—1. The diarrhœa; the BACK-DOOR-TROT (*q.v.*); the COLLYWOBBLES (*q.v.*). Formerly THOROUGH-GO-NIMBLE (*q.v.* for synonyms).

1734. CAREY, *Chrononhotonthologos*, sc. 3. Now. . . . for a swingeing lye. . . . Say she has got the THOROUGH-GO-NIMBLE.

2. (old.)—An antic; a JACK-PUDDING (*q.v.*).

1884. HENLEY & STEVENSON, *Deacon Brodie*, iii, 3. You're a man of parts, you are, you're solid, you're a true-born Englishman; you ain't a JERRY-GO-NIMBLE like him.

JERRY LYNCH, *subs.* (common)—A pickled pig's-head.

JERRYMANDER, *subs.* (political).—*See* GERRYMANDER and add following quots.

1871. *Pall Mall Gazette*, 4 Mar. Wonderful adepts in the art of JERRYMANDERING.

1872. *Globe*, 19 July. JERRYMANDERING is not to be numbered with the other novelties imported into our political system from America.

1883. *Echo*, 7 Dec., p. 1, col. 5. The Marquis of Salisbury, in a recent speech, attributed the origin of what he called JERRYMANDERING to an individual called Jeremiah Manders. This is a fair example of the Marquis's accuracy, neither one nor the other of these names being correct.

1883. H. FAWCETT, in *Daily News*, Nov. 9, p. 3, col. 2. If equal electoral districts were introduced, the success of political parties would mainly depend on skilfully manipulating, from time to time, the boundaries of boroughs. This is so well known in the United States that this manipulation has been elevated into a fine art, and is known there as JERRYMANDERING.

JERRY-SHOP, *subs.* (old).—A beer-house. Also JERRY.

1851-61. H. MAYHEW, *London Lab. & Lon. Poor*, ii. p. 255. An advance of 5/- made to him by the keeper of a beer-shop, or, as he called it, a JERRY.

JERRY-SNEAK, *subs.* (old).—1. *See* quot. 1763, the origin of the phrase.

1763. FOOTE, *Mayor of Garrett*, *Dramatis Personae*. JERRY SNEAK, a henpecked husband.

1772. G. A. STEVENS, *Songs Comic and Satyrical*, 177. He is always at home Sir John Brute to his wife, Abroad, JERRY-SNEAK to his drab.

1785. GROSE, *Vulg. Tongue*, s.v.

1821. COMBE, *Syntax, Wife*, C. I. I know, my friend, that you inherit A portion large of manly spirit. That you would ne'er be brought to speak In humble tone of JERRY SNEAK.

1845. SURTEES, *Hillingdon Hall*, ii. 6 (1888). A poor, little, henpecked, JERRY SNEAK of a husband.

1830. JOHN POOLE, *Turning The Tables*, sc. iii. A poor JERRY SNEAK, as they took me to be.

2. (thieves').—A watch thief. *Cf.* JERRY.

JERRY-WAG, *subs.* (old).—A SPREE-STER (*q.v.*) especially one half drunk.—BEE (1823). JERRY-WAG-SHOP = coffee shop.

JERSEY-LIGHTNING, *subs.* (American).—Cider brandy.

1871. DE VERE, *Americanisms*, p. 415. Known . . . . in the pretentious form of Apple-john in New England it has the terrible name of JERSEY LIGHTNING farther south.

JERUSALEM! *intj.* (common).—An exclamation of surprise. GO TO JERUSALEM! = GO TO JERICHO (*q.v.*).

JERUSALEM THE GOLDEN, *subs. phr.* (common).—Brighton; *Cf.* HOLY OF HOLIES.

JERUSALEM-PONY, *subs.* (common).—1. An ass.

1842. *Punch*, iii, p. 168, col. 2. We saw a JERUSALEM PONY in Clare market yesterday.

1846. THACKERAY, *Cornhill to Cairo*, xv. Here we alighted upon donkeys . . . . We had a JERUSALEM PONY race into Cairo.

1851. MAYHEW, *Lond. Lab.*, i. 28. Sometimes a party of two or three will be seen closely examining one of these JERUSALEM PONIES.

1876. HINDLEY, *Cheap Jack*, p. 215. The proper thing is to have a real JERUSALEM PONY, i.e. donkey.

2. (clerical).—A needy clergyman helping for hire. *Cf.* GUINEA-PIG.

JESSAMY. *See* JEMMY JESSAMY.

1684. R. HEAD, *Proteus Redivivus*, 279. That they may not poison their JISSAMY barbers.

1772. G. A. STEVENS, *Songs Comic and Satyrical*, 190. By terror of parents, or tempted by gain, The lady resigns to some JESSAMY swain.

JESSE (or **JESSIE** or **JESSY**). TO GIVE (or RAISE) JESSE, *verb. phr.* (American). To rate with vigor; to thrash. For synonyms *see* BASTE and TAN.

1847. ROBB, *Squatter Life*, p. 33. Well, hoss, you've slashed the hide off 'er that feller, touched his raw, and rumpled his feathers,—that's the way to GIVE HIM JESSY.

1854. HALIBURTON (Sam Slick), in BARTLETT. Allen was GIVING HIM PARTICULAR JESSE.

1857. *St. Louis Republican* (quoted by BARTLETT). They all say that the Mormons are going to GIVE US JESSIE.

1867. *Campaign with General Price*, p. 27. Well, gentlemen, I think we have GIVEN THEM VERY PARTICULAR JESSIE on this field.

JESTER, *subs.* (colloquial).—A general term of banter for a man; a JOKER (*q.v.*); a 'NICE UN' (*q.v.*).

2. (American).—*See* JOKER, sense 2.

JESUIT, *subs.* (Cambridge University).—1. A graduate or undergraduate of Jesus College.

1771. SMOLLETT, *Humphrey Clinker*, To Sir W. Phillips, April 20. 'Direct your next to me at Bath; and remember me to all our fellow JESUITS.'

1856. HALL, *College Words and Phrases*, p. 270, s.v.

2. (venery).—A sodomite: JESUIT'S FRATERNITY = the World of Sodomy. For synonyms *see* USHER.

1647-80. ROCHESTER, *A Ramble in St. James's Park*, in *Wks.* (1728), 84. The JESUITS' FRATERNITY Shall leave the use of buggery.

TO BOX THE JESUIT, *verb. phr.* (old). *See* quot. For synonyms *see* FRIG.

1785. GROSE, *Vulg. Tongue*, s.v. BOX THE JESUIT . . . . for masturbation . . . . A crime it is said much practised by the reverend fathers of that society.

1811. *Lex. Bal.*, s.v.

JET, *subs.* (old).—A lawyer. For synonyms *see* GREENBAG. AUTEM-JET = a parson.

1725. *New Cant. Dict.*, s.v.

1785. GROSE, *Vulg. Tongue*, s.v.

1811. *Lex. Bal.*, s.v.

1859. MATSELL, *Vocabulum*, s.v.

Verb. (old).—To strut; to walk pompously. *See* JETTER.

1537. *Thersites* [DODSLEY, *Old Plays* (1874), i. 430]. The Knave that here erewhile did JET.

1562-3. *Jack Juggler* [DODSLEY, *Old Plays* (1874), ii. 117]. She simpereth, she pranketh, and JETTETH without fail, As a peacock that hath spread and showeth her gay tail.

1594. *Look About You* [DODSLEY, *Old Plays* (1874), vii. 436]. Thus JETS my noble Skink along the streets To whom each bonnet vails, and all knees bend.

1602. SHAKSPEARE, *Twelfth Night*, ii. 5. How he JETS under his advanced plumes.

1640. RAWLINS, *The Rebellion*, ii. The proudest creatures; you shall have them JET it with an undaunted boldness.

TO JET ONE'S JUICE, *verb. phr.* (venery).—To COME (*q.v.*); to experience the sexual spasm.

JETTER, *subs.* (old).—A pompous man; a STRUT-NODDY (*q.v.*). *See* JET, *verb.*

1510. *Hycke Scorner*, [DODSLEY, *Old Plays* (1874), i. 164]. Brawlers, liars, JETTERS, and chiders.

1540. HEYWOOD, *Four P's* [DODSLEY, *Old Plays* (1874), i. 384]. What, should a beggar be a JETTER?

JEW, *subs.* (colloquial).—1. A cheat; a hard bargainer; a sharking usurer.

1659. BROME, *The English Moor*, in *Wks* (1873), ii. 45 (Act iii. 1). The best, Sir, I can tell is, the old JEW, Quicksands, hath lost his wife.

1690. B. E., *Dict. Cant. Crew.*, s.v. JEW. . . . He treated me like a JEW, he used me very barbarously.

1725. *New Cant. Dict.*, s.v.

1785. GROSE, *Vulg. Tongue*, s.v.

Verb. (colloquial).—To drive a hard bargain; to beat down. Also to cheat.

*c.*1871. *California Flush Times*, [quoted in DE VERE]. To JEW, colloquially known in England as meaning to cheat, is here often used in the sense of haggling, bargaining. 'Don't you think the old hunks wanted to JEW me down to three thousand dollars?'

1883. M. TWAIN, *Life on the Mississippi*, xliii, p. 390. There's one thing in this world which isn't ever cheap. That's a coffin. There's one thing in this world which a person don't ever try TO JEW you down on. That's a coffin.

WORTH A JEW'S EYE, *phr.* (colloquial).—Extremely valuable; 'worth its weight in gold'. [In the Middle Ages the Jews were subject to great extortions, and many stories are related of eyes put out, or teeth drawn, to enforce payment].

1593. G. HARVEY, *Pierces Super.*, in *Works*, ii. 146. Let it euerlastingly be recorded for a souerain Rule, as deare as a JEWES EYE.

1598. SHAKSPEARE, *Merchant of Venice*, ii. 5. There will come a Christian by Will be WORTH A JEWES EYE.

1785. GROSE, *Vulg. Tongue*, s.v.

1811. *Lex. Bal.*, s.v.

1838. HALIBURTON, *Clockmaker*, 2 S. xxi. 'Tho' they are no good to you they are WORTH A JEW'S EYE to us, and have 'em we will.'

JEW-BAIL, *subs.* (old).—STRAW-BAIL (*q.v.*).

1785. GROSE, *Vulg. Tongue*, s.v.

1811. *Lex. Bal.*, s.v.

1823. BEE, *Dict. of the Turf*, s.v.

JEW-BUTTER, *subs.* (American).—Goose-grease.

JEW-FENCER, *subs.* (common).—A Jew street buyer or salesman, generally of stolen goods.

JEWHILLIKENS! *intj.* (American).—A general exclamation of surprise.

*b.*1872. *Country Merchant*, p. 221, (quoted by DE VERE). Now they are coming to the rich licks! JEWHILLIKIN!

JEWLARK, *verb.* (American).—To 'fool around': a 'portmanteau' verb of action. [*See* JEW = to delude + LARK = irresponsible action].

1851. HOOPER, *Widow Rugby's Husband*, p. 59. Wonder if I'll ketch that rascal Jim Sparks JEWLARKIN' round Betsy.

JEW'S-POKER, *subs.* (common).—*See* quot.

1891. *Lloyd's Weekly*, 17 May, p. 11, col. 4. Deceased used to get her living lighting the Jews' fires on Saturdays. She was what is known as a JEWS' POKER.

JEZEBEL, *subs.* (colloquial).—1. An objectionable woman; a termagant or shrew. [From the wife of Ahab.]

1553. BRADFORD, *Writings* &c. p. 36 (1853). The papists . . . . are cast into JEZEBEL'S bed of security.

1601. SHAKSPEARE, *Twelfth Night*, ii. 5. Fie on him, JEZEBEL.

1677. BUTLER, *Hudibras* III, iii, 194. To win the JEZEBEL.

1711. *Spectator*, No. 175. My lodgings are directly opposite those of a JEZEBEL.

1751. SMOLLETT, *Peregrine Pickle*, xlvii. 'Lord curse that chattering JEZEBEL of a landlady, who advised such a preposterous disguise!'

1771. SMOLLETT, *Humphry Clinker*, L. 52. They hissed and hooted all the way; and Mrs. Jenkins was all bespattered with dirt, as well as insulted with the opprobrious name of painted JEZEBEL.

1857. A. TROLLOPE, *Barchester Towers*, xi. 'Mr. Slope,' said Mrs. Proudie, catching the delinquent at the door, 'I am surprised that you should leave my company to attend on such a painted JEZEBEL as that.'

2. (venery).—The *penis*. For synonyms *see* CREAMSTICK and PRICK.

JIB, *subs.* (colloquial).—1. The face: THE CUT OF ONE'S JIB = the peculiar or characteristic appearance of a person.

1825. SCOTT, *St. Ronan's Well*, i. 22. If she disliked what sailors call the CUT OF THEIR JIB . . . . none so likely as they to give them what in her country is called a sloan.

1833. MARRYAT, *Peter Simple*, ii. I axes you because I see you're a sailor by the CUT OF YOUR JIB.

1838-40. HALIBURTON, *Clockmaker*, 3, S. iv. For I seed by the CUT OF THE feller's JIB that he was a preacher.

1836. M. SCOTT, *Cruise of the Midge*. A good seaman evidently, by the CUT OF HIS JIB.

1881. BUCHANAN, *God & the Man*, xvi. By the voice of you, by the rigs of you, and by the CUT OF YOUR precious JIB.

1884. CLARK RUSSELL, *Jack's Courtship*, iii. 'My democratic wideawake, and the republican CUT OF MY JIB,' said he, looking down at his clothes.

2. (Dublin university).—A first-year's man.

1841. LEVER, *Charles O'Malley*, xiv. 'There [referring to Trinity College Freshmen] . . . . are JIBS, whose names are neither known to the proctor nor the police-office.'

3. (vet's.).—A horse given to shying; a JIBBER.

1851. H. MAYHEW, *London Lab. & Lon. Poor*, vol. i. p. 189. Frequently young horses that will not work in cabs—such as JIBS—are sold to the horse-slaughterers as useless.

Verb. (colloquial).—1. To shirk; TO FUNK (*q.v.*); TO CUT (*q.v.*).—*Lex. Bal.* (1811).

2. (common).—To depart; to be off. For synonyms *see* AMPUTATE and SKEDADDLE.

TO BE JIBBED, *verb. phr.* (Christ's Hospital).—To be called over the coals; to get into trouble; TO BE TWIGGED (*q.v.*).

JIB-OF-JIBS, *subs.* (nautical).—An impossible sail—a STAR-GAZER (*q.v.*) or SKY-SCRAPER (*q.v.*).

JIBB, *subs.* (Old Cant).—1. The tongue: hence (2) language; speech.

JIBBER THE KIBBER. *See* KIBBER.

JIBE, *verb.* (American).—To agree; to live in harmony; TO JUMP (*q.v.*).

1871. S. CLEMENS, *Screamers*, p. 60. The piece you happened to be playing was a little rough on the proprietors, so to speak—didn't seem to JIBE with the general gait of the picture that was passing at the time, as it were.

JICKAJOG, *subs.* (old).—A commotion; a push.

1614. JONSON, *Bartholomew Fayre, Induct.* He would ha' made you such a JICKAJOG i' the booths, you should ha' thought an earthquake had been i' the Fair.

1825. TODD, *Eng. Dict.* s.v. JICKAJOG. . . . a cant word.

JIFFY (or **JEFFEY**), *subs.* (colloquial).—The shortest possible time. Also JIFF.

1793. T. SCOTT, *Poems*, p. 365. Wad aften in a JIFFIE to auld Nick Sen' ane anither.

1811. *Lex. Bal.*, s.v. JEFFEY. It will be done in a JEFFEY; it will be done in a short space of time, in an instant.

1812. H. & J. SMITH, *Rejected Addresses* [quoted by TODD]. And then shall each Paddy. . . . dispense IN A JIFFY.

1818. E. PICKEN, *Poems*, ii. 47. An' in a JIFFIN Row'd his fecket like a clew.

1825. TODD, *Eng. Dict.*, s.v. JIFFEY. . . . Now a colloquial word in several parts of England; and sometimes used in ludicrous writing.

1836. MICHAEL SCOTT, *Cruise of the Midge*, p. 257. It is as clear as mud that we shall be *minus* your own beautiful self and the boat's crew in a JIFFEY, not forgetting Benjie there.

1837. BARHAM, *Ingoldsby Legends (Aunt Fanny)*. It *is* stain'd, to be sure; but 'grassbleaching' will bring it To rights in a JIFFY.

1842. MRS. GORE, *Fascination*, p. 33. The old lady in the brown hood told me that she was going to return here in a JIFFY.

1855. THACKERAY, *Rose & the Ring*, p. 109. The fact is, that when Captain Hedzoff entered into the court of Snapdragon Castle, and was discoursing with King Padella, the Lions made a dash at the open gate, gobbled up the six beef-eaters in a JIFFY, and away they went with Rosalba on the back of one of them.

1856. C. BRONTË, *Professor*, iii. 'I see such a fine girl sitting in the corner of the sofa there by her mamma; see if I don't get her for a partner in a JIFFY!'

1866. READE, *Griffith Gaunt*, ch. v. She said one of the gentlemen was strange to her; but the other was Doctor Islip from Stanhope town. She knew him well: he had taken off her own brother's leg in a JIFFEY.

1870. *Orchestra*. 15 July. His approach cleared in a JIFFEY a washerwoman's barge and the Austerlitz bathing establishment.

1888. ROLF BOLDERWOOD, *Robbery Under Arms*, xxxiv. Out of sight in a JIFFY.

1890. HUME NISBET, *Bail Up*, p. 178. Come along, mate; we'll have that five hundred pounds out in a JIFFEY.

1892. MILLIKEN, *'Arry Ballads*, 49. Put me at 'ome in a JIFF.

1892. G. MANVILLE FENN, *Witness to the Deed*, ii . . . . Back for you in a JIFFY.

JIFFESS, *subs.* (tailors').—An employer's wife.

JIG, *subs.* (old: now recognised).—1. A dance; GIG (*q.v.*). B. E. (1690).

2. (old).—An antic; nonsense; a GAME, OR LAY (*q.v.*).

1596. SHAKSPEARE, *Hamlet*, ii. 2. He's for a JIGG, or a tale of bawdry.

1614. COOK, *City Gallant* [DODSLEY, *Old Plays* (1874), xi. 268]. But what JIG is this?

1640. SHIRLEY, *Coronation*, v. 1. What dost think of this innovation? Is't not a fine JIGG.

1641. BROME, *Jovial Crew*, in *Wks* (1873), iii. 415. Such tricks and JIGGS you would admire.

1647. BEAUMONT and FLETCHER, *Fair Maid of the Inn*, Prol. A JIG shall be clapp'd at, and every rhyme prais'd.

1690. B. E. *Dict. Cant. Crew.*, s.v. JIG, a trick. . . . . A PLEASANT JIG = a witty, arch trick.

1725. *New Cant. Dict.*, s.v.

1785. GROSE, *Vulg. Tongue*, s.v.

1838. *Comic Almanack*. And now I'm equipped for my JIG, I'll finish my begging petition.

1848. JONES, *Sketches of Travel*, p. 14. I know'd the JIG was up.

1857-8. CHILD, *Ballads*. They will play thee anither JIGG, For they will out at the big rig.

1888. *Detroit Free Press*, 29 Dec. He knew the JIG was up.

3. (old).—*See* JIGGER.

4. (old).—Short for GIGLOT (*q.v.*).

1887. *Lippincott*, July, p. 141. Shame on thee to say't, thou bold-faced JIG.

5. (Winchester College).—A clever man: fifty years ago it meant a swindler. The word has now the meanings (i) a low joke, (ii) a swindle, (iii) an object of sport. —*Notions*.

1600. HEYWOOD, 2 *Edward IV*. i. 1. There domineering with his drunken crew Makes JIGS of us.

1652. STAPYLTON, *Herodion* (quoted in *Notions*). Devising with his mates to find a JIGG, That he thereby might make himself a king.

Verb. (old).—1. To cheat; to delude; to impose upon.

1876. HINDLEY, *Adventures of a Cheap Jack*, p. 268. The animal was JIGGED, digged and figged.

2. (old). To dance.

1719. DURFEY, *Pills etc*, iv. 124. Oh! how they do frig it, Jump it and JIGG it, Under the greenwood tree.

FEATHER-BED (also BUTTOCK- and MOLL PEATLEY'S) JIG, *subs. phr.* (venery).—Copulation. For synonyms *see* GREENS and RIDE.

JIG BY JOWL, *adv. phr.* (old).—

1719. DURFEY, *Pills to Purge*, v. 293. He with his master, JIG BY JOWL, Unto old Gillian hy'd.

JIG-A-JIG, *verb.* (American).—To copulate. For synonyms *see* GREENS and RIDE.

JIGAMAREE, *subs.* (American).—A bit of chaff; nonsense or any triviality; a THINGUMBOB (*q.v.*).

JIGGA-JOGGY, *subs.* (old).—A jolting motion. Also JIG-JOG.

1605. MARSTON, *Dutch Courtezan*, v. 1. I bid myselfe most hartily welcome to your merry nuptials, and wanton JIGGA-JOGGIES.

JIGGER, *subs.* (Old Cant).—1. A door: also JIG, JEGGER, and GYGER. Fr. *une fendante; une guimbarde; une lourde.* It. *diorta; introibo; turlante.*

1567. HARMAN, *Caveat* [E. E. T. Soc., 1869], p. 85. Dup the GYGGER, and maund that is bene shyp.

1610. ROWLANDS, *Martin Mark-all*, p. 38 (H. Club's Rept. 1874) s.v. GIGGER, a door.

1690. B. E., *Dict. Cant. Crew.*, s.v.

1724. E. COLES, *Eng. Dict.*, s.v.

1754. *Discoveries of John Poulter*, 34. Nap my kelp whilst I stall at the JEGGER.

1785. GROSE, *Vulg. Tongue*, s.v.

1821. HAGGART, *Life*, p. 83. The outer JIGGER which opens from the yard.

1839. AINSWORTH, *J. Sheppard*, p. 20. 'Help!' ejaculated Wood, renewing his cries. 'Arrest!' 'JIGGER closed!' shouted a hoarse voice in reply.

1848. DUNCOMBE, *Sinks of London Laid Open*, p. 106. Dub the JIGGER, fasten the door.

1851-61. H. MAYHEW, *London Lab. and Lond. Poor*, i. 342. 'Such men are always left outside the JIGGER (door) of the houses.'

2. (old).—A doorkeeper; a SCREW (*q.v.*); a jailor or turnkey: also JIGGER-DUBBER. Fr. *duc de guiche*. [In Hants = a policeman].

1749. *Humours of the Fleet* [quoted in ASHTON'S *The Fleet*, p. 281.] The Door-keeper, and he who opens shuts the Jigg, is call'd the JIGGER.

1781. PARKER, *View of Society*, ii. 69. JIGGER-DUBBER is a term applied to jailors or Turnkeys, JIGGER being flash or cant for door.

1823. BEE, *Dict. of the Turf*, s.v. JIGGER-DUBBER — a JIGGER is a key, and with the adjunct DUBBER, means turnkey to a prison.

1828. SMEETON, *Doings in London*. 'Humours of the Fleet.' Near Fleet's commodious market's miry verge, This celebrated prison stands compact and large, Where, by the JIGGER'S more than magic charm Kept from the power of doing good or harm.

1888. RUNCIMAN, *The Chequers*, 183. One of the JIGGERS says one thing, and one of them says another thing.

3. (old).—*See* quot.

1823. BEE, *Dict. of the Turf*, s.v. JIGGER-DUBBER—a JIGGER is a key.

4. (old).—A whipping-post.

1708. HALL, *Memoirs* etc., s.v.

1811. *Lex. Bal.* s.v.

5. (old).—A secret still. JIGGER-STUFF = illicitly distilled spirits; JIGGER-WORKER = a vendor of the same. Hence, also, a drink of whiskey.

1823. BEE, *Dict. of the Turf*, s.v. JIGGER-DUBBER . . . . The JIGGER is a private still.

1851-61. MAYHEW, *Lond Lab. etc.* i. 429. Two, and sometimes three, female lace-sellers are also 'JIGGER-WORKERS.' They carry about their persons pint bladders of 'stuff,' or 'JIGGER-STUFF' (spirit made at an illicit still). 'I used to supply them with it until lately,' one street-trader told me, 'from a friend that kept a "JIGGER," and a tidy sale some of them had.

1853. *Diogenes*, ii. 199. JIGGER-GIN will kill body and brain faster than arrack punch or Sangaree.

1886. *Judy*, 4 August, p. 58. He imbibed stupendous quantities of JIGGERED gin, dog's nose, and Paddy's eye-water.

6. (billiards).—The 'bridge' or 'rest' for the cue when a ball is beyond arm's length.

7. (theatrical).—The curtain or RAG (*q.v.*).

8. (military).—A guard-room. Fr. *la boite*. Also, specifically as in quot.

1882. *Fortnightly Review*, xxxi. 798. Communicating with the GIGGER, an interviewing chamber (in Newgate) where felons, on payment, saw their friends.

9. (old).—A fiddlestick. [JIGGER (or JIG) is also applied to many small mechanical contrivances or handy tools].

10. (venery).—The female *pudendum*. For synonyms *see* MONOSYLLABLE.

11. (venery).—The *penis*. For synonyms *see* CREAMSTICK and PRICK.

12. (old.)—A shifty fellow; a trickster.

1675. COTTON, *Scoffer Scofft*, in *Wks* (1725), p. 268. And (Paris) when thou com'st to bedding, Oh how I'll trip it at thy wedding. Nay you're a JIGGER we all know; But if you should deceive me now!

Verb. (common).—1. *See* quot.

1888. *Detroit Free Press*, 22 Dec. I'll JIGGER (bet) you 'un knows roots from tree-tops.

2. (colloquial).—To shake; to jerk.

1869. *Quarterly Rev.*, cxxvi. 350. Many is the fish who has JIGGERED himself free by this method.

NOT WORTH A JIGGER, *phr.* (common).—Valueless.

1861. *Punch*, xl. 145. The churches here AIN'T WORTH A JIGGER—nor, not half-a-JIGGER.

JIGGER-DUBBER. *See* JIGGER, sense 2.

JIGGERED. TO BE JIGGERED! *verb. phr.* (common).—Used as a mild imprecation; as BLOW IT! (*q.v*), BUST ME! (*q.v.*): also in astonishment.

1860. DICKENS, *Great Expectations*, xvii. 76. 'Well, then', said he, 'I'M JIGGERED if I don't see you home!'

1883. CLARK RUSSELL, *Sailor's Language*, s.v.

1884. *Daily Telegraph*, Feb. 2. p. 3. col. 2. 'We ain't seen the p'liceman since, and JIGGERED if we want to.'

1886. BURNETT, *Little Lord Fauntleroy*, ii. 'Well,' said Mr. Hobbs, 'I'll be JIGGERED!'

1888. *Notes and Queries*, 7 S. vi. 322. Lately, I read an article beginning with 'I'm JIGGERED if I don't love Jane.'

1892. MILLIKEN, *'Arry Ballads*, 73. Kerrectness be folly, well JIGGERED.

JIGGERED UP, *adv.* (nautical).—Used up; Exhausted.

1867. SMYTH, *Sailor's Word Book*, s.v.

1883. CLARK RUSSELL, *Sailor's Language*, s.v. JIGGERED.

JIGGERY-POKERY, *subs.* (tailors').—Humbug; nonsense.

JIGLETS. HIS JIGLETS! *phr.* (American).—A contemptuous form of address; HIS NIBS (*q.v.*).

1888. *Boston Globe*, 4 March, Ain't HIS JIGLETS pretty near ready to see de rat, Jummy.

JIG-WATER, *subs.* (American).—Bad whisky; ROT-GUT (*q.v.*). For synonyms *see* DRINKS and OLD MAN'S MILK.

1888. *Boston Globe*, March 4. A middle-aged countryman had just tottered away from the counter over which JIG-WATER is dispensed.

JIGGLE, *verb.* (venery).—To copulate. Hence JIGGLING-BONE = *penis*. For synonyms *see* CREAM-STICK and PRICK.

JIGGUMBOB (or **JIGGAMBOB**), *subs.* (common).—1. A knick-knack; a trinket: anything particular, strange, or unknown. *Cf.* THINGAMBOB.

1640. BROME, *Antipodes*, iii. 5. Kills Monster after Monster, takes the Puppets Prisoners, knocks downe the Cyclops, tumbles all Our JIGUMBOBS and trinckets to the wall.

1647. BEAUMONT & FLETCHER, *Knight of Malta*, iv. 1. More JIGGAMBOBS: is not this the fellow that swom like a duck to the shore.

1657. MIDDLETON, *Women Beware Women*, ii. 2. On with her chain of pearls, her ruby bracelets, lay ready all her tricks and JIGGEMBOBS.

1678. BUTLER, *Hudibras*, III. i. 108. He rifled all his pokes and fobs Of jimcracks, whims, and JIGGUMBOBS.

2. (venery).—The female *pudendum*. For synonyms *see* MONOSYLLABLE.

1675. COTTON, *Scarronides*, in *Wks* (1725), Bk. iv. p. 65. Were I not with my first Honey Half tyr'd as t'were with Matrimony; I could with this same Youngster tall, Find in my heart to try a fall . . . This only . . . has made my JIGGAMBOB to water.

3. in pl. (venery).—The testicles: for synonyms *see* CODS.—GROSE (1785).

JILL. *See* GILL.

JILL-FLIRT. *See* GILL-FLIRT.

JILT, *subs.* (old: now recognised).—Specifically, a woman who encourages, or solicits, advances to which she designs there shall be no practical end. But see quots. *passim*. Hence JILTED and JILT, *verb.*

1648-80. ROCHESTER, *Bath Intrigues*, in *Wks.* (1728), 87. Thither two beldams and a JILTING wife came. *Id.* The cheating JILT. . . . a dry-bob whore.

1672. WYCHERLEY, *Love in a Wood*, i. 2. How has he got his JILT here?

1681. BLOUNT, *Glossographia*, s.v. JILT is a new canting word, signifying to deceive and defeat one's expectations, more especially in the point of amours.

1684. R. HEAD, *Proteus Redivivus*, 278. I only aimed at the lascivious JILT.

1690. B. E., *Dict. Cant. Crew.*, s.v. JILT, a tricking whore. JILTED, abused by such a one; also deceived or defeated in one's expectation, especially in Amours.

1691-2. *Gentlemen's Journal*, Jan., p. 20. You all know, or have heard at least, what a JILT this same fortune is. *Ibid.* Feb., p. 11. The lewd conversation of the town-JILTS.

1691-2. T. BROWN, in *Gentlemen's Journal*, Mar. p. 10. There dwells not another such JILT in the city.

1696. CONGREVE, *Oroonoko*, Epil. She might have learn'd to cuckold, JILT and sham Had Covent Garden been at Surinam.

1714. LUCAS, *Gamesters*, 214. One, Mary Wadsworth, a JILT of the town.

1725. *New Cant. Dict.*, s.v.

1772. G. A. STEVENS, *Songs Comic and Satyrical*, 129. So here's to the girl who will give one a share; But as to those JILTS who deny, So cursedly coy though they've so much to spare.

1785. GROSE, *Vulg. Tongue*, s.v. JILT, a tricking woman, who encourages the addresses of a man whom she means to deceive and abandon. JILTED, rejected by a woman who has encouraged one's advances.

1823. BEE, *Dict. of the Turf*, s.v. JILT—a she-deceiver.

1859. MATSELL, *Vocabulum*, s.v. JILT, a prostitute who hugs and kisses a countryman while her accomplice robs him.

2. (thieves').—A crowbar; a JEMMY (*q.v.*). In pl. = housebreaking tools generally.

Verb. (thieves'). *See* quot.

1868. *Temple Bar*, xxiv. 537. JILTING is getting in on the sly or false pretences at the door, and sneaking what you can find.

JILTER, *subs.* (thieves').—Thieves who work as described under JILT (*verb.*).

1863. *Cornhill Magazine*, vii. 91. Another notable class of criminals called JILTERS or Noteblankers: they go in pairs.

JIM-BROWN, *subs. phr.* (rhyming).—Town.

1893. EMERSON, *Signor Lippo*, v. 'When did you come into . . . . JIM BROWN?' 'Oh, yesterday morning', says I, tumbling.

JIMCRACK. *See* GIMCRACK.

JIMBUGG, *subs.* (Australian squatters').—A sheep; a WOOLLY-BIRD (*q.v.*).

1854. RIDLEY, *Phil. Soc. Trans* (1855), p. 73. JIMBUGG, a slang name for sheep.

JIM CROW. *See* BILLY BARLOW.

JIMJAMS, *subs.* (common).—1. Delirium tremens; THE HORRORS (*q.v.*). Also, THE JAMS. For synonyms *see* GALLON-DISTEMPER.

1888. *Detroit Free Press*, 4 Aug. He was a character noted for going on frequent benders until he came very near having the JIMJAMS and then sobering up.

1888. *St. Louis Globe Democrat.*, 16. Febr. He had the JIM-JAMS yesterday evening.

1888. J. RUNCIMAN, *The Chequers*, 43. Our landlord of the Chequers was very funny about the JIM-JAMS.

1891. *Gentleman's Mag.*, Aug., p. 119. I thought as 'ow 'twas only the JIM-JAMS he'd got; but the doctor 'e says it's a bad job, an' 'is ribs is broke.

1891. *Punch*, 4 April. 'Look, Polly!—shee that creature long and lean, Crawling towardsh us! JIM-JAMSH are not in it With thish 'ere Bri'sh Museum! Wai' a minute!'

2. (American). Distorted views; KINKS (*q.v.*).

1888. *Cincinnatti Commercial Gazette*, 22 July. We are glad to see *Harper's Weekly* suffering the JIM-JAMS of distortion on the envenomed pencil of an extraordinary artist.

JIM-DANDY, *adj.* (American).—Superfine.

1888. *Daily Inter-Ocean*, 14 Feb. George C. Ball came upon the floor yesterday arrayed in a JIM-DANDY suit of clothes.

JIMMY, *subs.* (common).—1. *See* JEMMY.

2. (colonial). A NEW CHUM (*q.v.*). Specifically (Australian convicts), a free emigrant.

1859. H. KINGSLEY, *Geoffry Hamlyn*, xxvi. 'Why, one,' said Lee, 'is a young JIMMY (I beg your pardon, sir, an emigrant), the other two are old prisoners.'

3. (showmen's).—A contrivance; a concealed confederate; a FAKE (*q.v.*).

4. (American).—A coal waggon.

1887. N. Y. *Semi-weekly Tribune*, 18 Mar. Two JIMMIES loaded with coal.

ALL JIMMY, *adv. phr.* (Cambridge university). 1. All nonsense.

2. (American).—Exactly; fit; suitable: *cf.* JEMMY.

JIMMY SKINNER, *subs. phr.* (rhyming).—A dinner.

JIMPLECUTE (or **JIMPSECUTE**), *subs.* (American).—*See* quot.

1870. *Figaro*, 1 Dec. The JIMPLECUTE of Texas changed her name, which was a good thing to do—JIMPLECUTE being Texas vernacular for sweetheart.

JING-BANG, *subs.* (Scots').—A lot complete; BOILING (*q.v.*).

1891. STEVENSON, *Kidnapped*, 61. The men had a great respect for the chief mate, who was, as they said, 'the only seaman of the whole JING-BANG, and none such a bad man when he was sober.'

JINGLE, *subs.* (Irish).—A hackney carriage (Dublin).

1860. TROLLOPE *Castle Richmond*, vi. An elderly man was driven up to the door of the hotel on a one horse car—a JINGLE as such conveniences were called in the South of Ireland.

JINGLE-BOX, *subs.* (old).—*See* quot.

1690. B. E., *Dict. Cant. Crew.*, s.v.

1785. GROSE, *Vulg. Tongue*, s.v. JINGLE BOXES, leathern jacks tipped with silver, and hung with bells formerly in use among fuddlecaps (Cant).

JINGLEBOY. *See* GINGLE BOY.

1658. BROME, *The Weeding of Covent-Garden*, p. 16. But Mistress, here is a Gallant now below, A GINGLE-BOY indeed.

JINGLER, *subs.* (old).—*See* quot.

1690. B. E. *Dict. Cant. Crew.*, s.v.

1785. GROSE, *Vulg. Tongue*, s.v. JINGLERS, horse cosers frequenting country fairs.

JINGLEBRAINS, *subs.* (colloquial).—A wild, harum-scarum fellow.—B. E. (1690); GROSE (1785).

JINGO, *intj.* (common).—Used in mild oaths: as BY JINGO! or BY JINGS. [HALLIWELL: a corruption of St. Gingoulph or Gingulphus; by others from Basque *Jinkoa* = God. *Cf. Notes and Queries*, 2 S. xii. 272, 336; 5 S. ix. 263, 400, x. 7, 96, 456; 6 S. i. 284, ii. 95, 157, 176, 335, iii. 78, iv. 114, 179]. Also BY THE LIVING JINGO.

1691-2. *Gentlemen's Journal*, Feb., p. 24. Hye, JINGO what a deel's the matter; Do mermaids swim in Dartford water?

1764. O'HARA, *Midas*, ii. vi. BY JINGO! well performed for one of his age.

1766. GOLDSMITH, *Vicar of Wakefield*, ix. She observed, that, 'BY THE LIVING JINGO, she was all of a muck of sweat.'

1773. O. GOLDSMITH, *She Stoops to Conquer*, v. 2. BY JINGO, there's not a pond or a slough within five miles of the place, but they can tell the taste of.

1824. *Atlanta Monthly*, i. 141. He swore by George, BY JINGO and by Gemini.

1834. M. G. DOWLING, *Othello Travestie*, i. 6. It is the way, BY JINGO, you are right.

1836. MICHAEL SCOTT, *Tom Cringle's Log*, v. Dem sell a me Peter, BY JINGO.

1848. *Punch*, xiv. 172. If I kill you it's nothing; but if you kill me, BY JINGO it's murder.

1850. F. E. SMEDLEY, *Frank Fairleigh*, xxvi. There's the coach, BY JINGO!

1860. *Chambers' Jour.*, xiii. 233. 'Uncle Bob, BY JINGO!' said the boy.

1864. *Press*, November 12. JENCO is Basque for the Devil and in the Basque Provinces there were of old Manichæans, who worshipped the evil spirit and naturally swore by him, hence we think the phrase [BY JINGO] may find a much more likely explanation [than St. Gingoulph].

1871. A. H. CLOUGH, *Poems.* 'With the Lassie? with her?' the piper exclaimed undoubtedly! 'BY GREAT JINGO!'

1878. C. H. WALL, tr. *Molière*, ii. 114. Gently if you please; BY JINGO, how skilful you are in giving clean plates!

1889. DRAGE, *Cyril*, ii. 'Inez de Ribera, BY THE LIVING JINGO!' said he, half out aloud.

1892. HENLEY and STEVENSON, *Deacon Brodie*, Tab. ii, sc. 2. BY JINGO! I'll show them how we do it down South.

Subs. (political).—One of that party which advocated the Turkish cause against Russia, in the war of 1877-8. Hence, one clamorous for war; one who advocates a warlike policy. [In this sense taken directly from the refrain of a popular music-hall song (*c.* 1874), 'We don't want to fight, but BY JINGO if we do, We've got the ships, we've got the men, we've got the money too!']. Hence JINGOISM = the theory and practice of the JINGOES.

1884. *Graphic*, 22 Nov. He is a more pernicious kind of JINGO than his predecessors.

1884. *Pall Mall Gazette*, 12 June. In the days when JINGOISM had to be combatted and overcome.

1895. JOHN MORLEY, in *The Times*, 17th June, p. 7, col. 5. But then the hight honourable gentleman will ask, Have you proposed a statue to Cromwell from the point of view of JINGOISM?

JINIPER-LECTURE, *subs.* (old).—A scolding.—B. E. (1690). *Cf.* CURTAIN LECTURE.

JINK, *subs.* (old).—1. Coin; money; CHINK (*q.v.*).

2. (in pl.). *See* HIGH JINKS.

Verb. (old Scots').—To copulate; also to sport. For synonyms *see* GREENS and RIDE.

1715. ALLAN RAMSAY, *Christ's Kirk, etc.* ii. *Wks.* (1848), i. 324. Was n'er in Scotland heard or seen Sic banquetting and drinkin'—Sic revelling and battles keen, Sic dancing and sic JINKIN'.

c. 1750. ROBERTSON (of Struan), *Poems*, 86. Let pass, let pass, The naughty Glass, And wisely fall A-JINKING.

TO JINK ONE'S TIN, *verb. phr.* (common).—To pay money; to 'shell out'; to rattle or FLASH (*q.v.*) one's cash.

JINKER, *subs.* (venery).—A PERFORMER (*q.v.*).

1724-27. RAMSAY, *Clout the Caudron*, in *Wks.* (at sup.), ii, 275. Yet to yourself I'm bauld to tell, I am a gentle JINKER.

JINNY, *subs.* (thieves').—A geneva watch.

JIPPER, *subs.* (nautical).—Gravy.

JO, *See* JOE.

JOAN, *subs.* (old).—A fetter: specifically DARBY AND JOAN = fetters coupling two persons. *See* DARBIES.

HOMELY JOAN, *subs. phr.* (old).—A coarse, ordinary looking woman.—B. E. (1690).

JOAN IN THE DARK IS AS GOOD AS MY LADY, *phr.* (old).—A variant of 'When you cannot kiss the mistress kiss the maid', or 'When candles are out all cats are grey'.—B. E. (1690); *New Cant. Dict.* (1725).

1678. COTTON, *Virgil Travestie*, in *Works* (1725), Bk iv. p. 81. The Cave so darksome was that I do Think JOAN had been AS GOOD AS DIDO.

JOB, *subs.* (Old Cant: now colloquial).—1. Specifically, robbery; generally, any unfair arrangement, or effect of nepotism: *e.g.* the obtaining of an office, or a contract, by secret influence, or the undertaking of a piece of business ostensibly for public but really for private ends.

1667. PEPYS, *Diary*, April 10. And for aught I see likely only to be used as a JOBB to do a kindness to some lord, or he that can get to be governor. *Ibid.* 1665, Aug. 31. My late gettings have been very great to my great content, and am likely to have yet a few more profitable JOBBS in a little while.

1711. POPE, *Essays on Criticism*, i. 104. No cheek is known to blush or heart to throb, Save when they lose a question or a JOB.

1712. ARBUTHNOT, *Hist. of John Bull*, Pt. III. App. ch. iii. Like an old favourite of a cunning Minister after the JOB is over.

1730. JAS. MILLER, *Humours of Oxford*, iv. i. p. 54 (2nd ed.). But I have another JOB for you; and if my stratagem takes there, my fortune's made.

1788. G. A. STEVENS, *Adv. of a Speculist*, i. 67. In our august House of Parliament, the word JOB is never made use of but to express an action thoroughly base.

1815. SCOTT, *Guy Mannering*, xxxiii. 'But, Hatteraick, this,—that is, if it be true, which I do not believe,—this will ruin us both, for he cannot but remember your neat JOB.'

1819. MOORE, *Tom Crib*, p. 10. C—nn—g Came in a JOB, and then canter'd about On a showy, but hot and unsound, bit of blood.

1827. TODD, *Johnson's Dict.*, s.v. JOB. A low word now much in use, of which I cannot tell the etymology.

1848. THACKERAY, *Book of Snobs*, iii. Who shall hold the first rank, have the first prizes and chances in all government JOBS and patronages.

1859. *Political Portraits*, p. 219. His (Mr. Disraeli's) representation of the Reform Bill of 1832 as a Whig JOB is a silliness.

1859. MATSELL, *Vocabulum*, s.v. JOB. To do a JOB, to commit a robbery.

1864. THOMAS HUGHES [in *Spectator*, 26 Nov.]. The present JOB (and a very stiff one it is, though not in the *Standard's* sense) was offered to and accepted by me as a mere piece of conveyancing.

1877. *Five Years' Penal Servitude*, ii. 135. The third day after his discharge he got drunk, joined some old associates, entered with them into a JOB, and was captured 'redhanded.'

1889. *Star*, 3 Dec., 1. 5. The whole thing was probably a put-up JOB.

1889. *Daily Telegraph*, 25 Jan. JOBS abounded and contracts were corrupt.'

2. (colloquial).—A piece of work; an occurrence, fortunate or otherwise; a situation or place of employment. A BAD JOB = an unlucky occurrence, a misfortune, an unsuccessful attempt. Hence JOBBER = one who does piece or occasional work.

1658. BROME, *New Academy*, in *Wks.* 1873), ii. 97 (Act v. 2). He confest receipt of fifty pounds my wife has lent him (false woman that she is!) for horn-making, JOB journey-work.

1661. T. MIDDLETON, *Mayor of Quinborough*, iv. 1. And yet not I myself, I cannot read, I keep a clerk to do those JOBS for need.

1787. GROSE, *Prov. Glossary*. JOB, a piece of labour, undertaken at a stated price. Norf.

1857. LORD DUFFERIN, *Letters from High Latitudes*, vii. Giving it up as a bad JOB.

1895. HENLEY & STEVENSON, *Macaire* (*New Review*, June, 701) iii. 1. Blinding dark, and a good JOB.

3. (old).—A guinea: also JOBE.—B. E. (1690); *New Cant. Dict.* (1725); GROSE (1785); *Lex. Bal.* (1811).

4. (American thieves').—As *subs.* = patience; as *intj.* = take time; 'don't be in a hurry!'—MATSELL (1859).

5. (colloquial).—*See* JAB.

1827. TODD, *Johnson's Dict.*, s.v. JOB.

1885. *Eng. Ill. Mag.*, April, 505. Some say that if a fish takes fairly, he will and must hook himself. Others that it requires a good JOB to drive the point of a large hook in beyond the baib.

6. (venery).—*See* BY-JOB.

Verb. (colloquial).—1. To do work, or perform duties, ostensibly *pro bono publico* but in reality for one's private ends or advantage.

1731-35. POPE, *Moral Essays*, iii. 141. And judges JOB and bishops bite the town.

1833. MACAULAY, *Let. to Sister* [in *Life* by Trevelyan, v. 241 (1884)]. We shall be suspected of JOBBING if we proceed to extremities on behalf of one of ourselves.

1838. LYTTON, *Alice*, III. i. No JOBBING was too gross for him. He was shamefully corrupt in the disposition of his patronage.

1843. THACKERAY, *Book of Snobs*, iii. A man becomes enormously rich, or he JOBS successfully in the aid of a Minister, or he wins a great battle .... and the country rewards him for ever with a gold coronet.

2. (colloquial).—To thrust violently and suddenly; to prod; TO JAB (*q.v.*).

1557. TUSSER, *Husbandrie*, ch. 37, st. 12, p. 89 (E. D. S.). Stick plentie of bows among runcinall pease to climber thereon, and to branch at their ease. So dooing, more tender and greater they wex, If peacock and turkey leaue IOBBING their bex [See also note in E. D. Soc.'s ed. of Tusser's *Husbandrie*, p. 263].

1560. SLEIDANE *Commentaries*, Book x. fol. cxxx. Then caught he a boore speare out of a young mans hande that stode next him and as he laie JOBBED him in with the staffe heade.

1692. L'ESTRANGE, *Esop* [quoted in E. D. Soc.'s ed. of Tusser's *Husbandrie* s.v. JOB]. As an ass with a galled back was feeding in a meadow, a raven pitched upon him, and there sate JOBBING of the sore.

1843. DICKENS, *Martin Chizzlewit*, xxxiii. p. 326. He . . . was greatly beloved for the gallant manner in which he had JOBBED OUT the-eye of one gentleman.

1852. DICKENS, *Our Bore*, [in *Reprinted Pieces*, p. 298]. As if he were being stabbed—or, rather, JOBBED—that expresses it more correctly—JOBBED—with a blunt knife.

1883. *Daily Telegraph*, Jan. 11, p. 3. col. 7. There was a disturbance at his door early on Christmas morning, and on going out to see what was wrong the prisoner JOBBED a lantern into his eye.

1891. *Lic. Vict. Gaz.*, 17 Ap., 247. i. Following up his advantages, Jem JOBBED his adversary terrifically in the face with the left till Giles was bathed in blood.

1892. ANSTEY, *Voces Populi*, 60. I'll JOB the 'helliphants ribs, and make 'im gallop, I will.

3. (colloquial).—To chide; to reprimand: also JOBE.

1685. *Autobiography of Sir J. Bramston*. The king had talked earnestly to the duke and JOBED him soe that the teares stood in his eyes.

1754. B. MARTIN, *Eng. Dict.*, 2nd ed. s.v.

1785. GROSE, *Vulg. Tongue*, s.v.

1794. *Gent. Mag.*, p. 1085. I heard a lively young man assert that, in consequence of an intimation from the tutor relative to his irregularities, his own father came from the country to JOBE him.

1811. *Lex. Bal.*, s.v.

1837-40. HALIBURTON, *The Clockmaker* [ed. 1862] p. 471. I am as weak as a child, and can't stand JOBBING.

4. (venery).—To copulate. For synonyms *see* GREENS and RIDE.

1537. *Thersites*, [DODSLEY, *Old Plays* (1874), i. 422]. Jenkin Jacon, that JOBBED jolly Joan.

1786. BURNS, 'What Ails Ye?' (BOHN, 1842, p. 253), Cry'd three times, 'Robin, Come hither, lad, and answer for't, Ye're blamed for JOBBIN'.

TO BE ON THE JOB, *verb. phr.* (general).—To mean honestly; to be genuine; to 'run straight'; to work quickly and steadily; to achieve complete success; to be bent on.

1891. *Licensed Victuallers Gaz.*, 23 Jan. Of course, there was a long wrangle over the choice of referee, for no one cared to occupy that thankless post when the Lambs were ON THE JOB.

1892. MILLIKEN, *'Arry Ballads*, 3. 'Arry is fair ON THE JOB.

1892. HUME NISBET, *Bushranger's Sweetheart*, p. 64. I was ON THE JOB.

1893. EMERSON, *Signor Lippo*, ch. v. Being ON THE JOB we hoped to improve.

TO HAVE GOT THE JOB, *verb. phr.* (racing).—To have a commission to back a horse.

TO DO THE JOB FOR ONE, *verb. phr.* (common).—To 'finish' or kill.

TO DO A WOMAN'S JOB FOR HER, *verb. phr.* (venery).—To do smock-service.

JOBATION (or **JAWBATION**), *subs.* (old).—A tedious rebuke; a prolonged scolding; a dreary homily.

1746. SIR W. MAYNARD [in *G. Selwyn & his Contemp.* by JESSE i. p. 106 (ed. 1882)]. You would not commend yourself for having sent me a JORATION for not punctually answering your obliging letters.

1767. COLMAN, *Oxonian in Town*, ii. 3. And now I find you as dull and melancholy as a fresh-man at college after a JOBATION.

1785. GROSE, *Vulg. Tongue*, s.v. JOBATION, a reproof.

1803. *Gradus ad Cantab.* He recounts this JOBATION to his friends.

1811. *Lex. Bal.*, s.v.

1820. COMBE, *Syntax, Consolation*, canto 5. For Patrick, fearing a JOBATION, Said nought to forward conversation.

1859. MATSELL, *Vocabulum*, s.v.

1861. HUGHES, *Tom Brown at Oxford*, xlii. 410. But here I am at the end of my paper. Don't be angry at my JOBATION; but write me a long answer of your own free will, and believe me ever affectionately yours.

1863. H. KINGSLEY, *Austin Elliot*, xiv. Away he went, after getting a most fearful JOBATION from the Dean for daring to appear in his presence without his cap and gown.

1883. CLARK RUSSELL, *Sailor's Language*, s.v.

1884. G. A. SALA, *Ill. London News*, Sept. 6, p. 219, col. 2. 'Why,' writes 'R.R.R.' (Holloway), 'do you write the word JOBATION, and thereby upset all my preconceived notions that 'jawbation' is a mock solemnity for the vulgar 'jaw'?' My good sir, I wrote, JOBATION because the word means a long dreary homily or reprimand, and has reference to the tedious rebukes inflicted on the Patriarch Job by his too obliging friends.

JOBBERNOWL, *subs.* (old).—1. A fool's head. For general synonyms *see* CRUMPET.

1562. *Grim* [DODSLEY, *Old Plays*, xi. 241]. Now, miller, miller, dustipoll, I'll clapper-claw thy JOBBERNOUL.

1599. NASHE, *Lenten Stuffe* in *Works*, v. 293. Onely to set their wittes a nibbling, and their IOBBERNOWLES a working.

1609. DEKKER, *Guls Horne-Booke*, iii. If all the wise men of *Gotham* should lay their heades together, their JOBBERNOWLES should not bee able to compare with thine.

1638. FORD, *Lady's Trial*, iv. 2. Took a thousand Spanish JOBBERNOWLS by surprise, And beat a sconce about their ears.

1678. BUTLER, *Hudibras*, III. ii. 1007. And powder'd th' inside of his skull, Instead of th' outward JOBBERNOL.

1716. DRYDEN, *Counterscuffle*, [in *Misc.* 12mo, iii. 340]. No remedy in courts of Pauls, In common pleas, or in the rolls, For jolling of your JOBBERNOULS together.

1785. GROSE, *Vulg. Tongue*, s.v.

1791. G. HUDDESFORD, *Salmagundi*, p. 93. Crack'd ev'n the Sexton's JOBBERKNOWL, And spoil'd him for saying Amen.

1811. *Lex. Bal.*, s.v.

1834. AINSWORTH, *Rookwood*, Book iv. ch. i. 'What we now call a 'belcher' bound his throat; a spotted *fogle* bandaged his JOBBERNOWL, and shaded his right peeper.'

1837. BARHAM, *Ingoldsby Legends*, (*Lord of Thoulouse*). So find me out something new under the sun, Or I'll knock your three JOBBERNOWLS all into one!

2. (old).—*See* quot. 1690. For synonyms *see* BUFFLE and CABBAGE-HEAD.

1598. MARSTON, *Satires*, II, vi. 200. His guts are in his brains, huge JOBBERNOULE, Right gurnet's head, the rest without all soule.

1690. B. E., *Dict. Cant. Crew*, s.v. JOBBERNOLL, a very silly fellow.

1725. *New Cant. Dict.*, s.v.

1768. GAYTON, *Festiv. Notes*, iv. 17, p. 260. Thou simple animal, thou JOBBERNOLE, Thy basons, when that once they hang on pole, Are helmets strait.

JOBBER, *subs.* (old: now recognised).—1. One who purchases goods in bulk and is the medium of their distribution; a middleman.

1662. *Rump Songs*, i. 79. Weavers, Dyers, Tinkers, Cobblers, And many other such like JOBBERS.

1690. B. E., *Dict. Cant. Crew*, s.v. BADGERS, MATCHMAKERS, SALESMEN, STOCKJOBBERS.

1725. *New Cant. Dict.*, s.v.

2. (colloquial).—*See* JOB, *subs.* sense 2.

JOBBER-KNOT (or **JOBBER NUT**), *subs.* (old).—A tall ungainly fellow.

1823. *Modern Flash Dict.*, s.v.

1859. MATSELL, *Vocabulum*, s.v.

JOBBERY, *subs.* (colloquial).—The practice of political corruption; the employment of unfair means to public or private advantage.

1857. DICKENS, *Dorrit*, II. xii. 351. Mr. Merdle had decided to cast the weight of his great probity and great riches into the Barnacle scale. JOBBERY was suspected by the malicious.

JOBBING, *subs.* (venery).—Copulation. For synonyms *see* GREENS and RIDE.

1720. RAMSAY, *'Epistle to Lord Ramsay'*, in *Wks.* (1848), ii. 326. And compliment them with a clap Which by oft JOBBING grows a pox.

JOBE. *See* JOB, *verb.* sense 3.

JOB'S-COMFORT, *subs.* (old: now colloquial).—Reproof instead of consolation. Hence JOB'S-COMFORTER = a sharp-tongued friend: also = a boil (in allusion to *Job* ii, 7.). JOB'S-NEWS = bad news; JOB'S-POST = a messenger of bad news; AS POOR AS JOB'S TURKEY = (*see* quot. 1871). JOB'S-WIFE = a whoring scold. JOB'S-DOCK = a hospital; JOB'S-WARD = a ward for the treatment of venereal diseases.

1738, SWIFT, *Polite Convers.*, Dial. 3. *Lady Smart.* . . . I think your ladyship looks thinner than when I saw you last. *Miss.* Indeed, madam, I think not; but your ladyship is one of JOB'S COMFORTERS.

1811. *Lex. Bal.*, s.v. JOB'S COMFORT and JOB'S COMFORTER and JOB'S DOCK.

1837. CARLYLE, *French Revolution*, iii. 3. ch. 4. From home there can nothing come except JOB'S-NEWS. *Ibid.* This JOB'S POST from Dumouriez.... reached the National Convention.

1838. HALIBURTON, *Clockmaker*, 2. S. ch. ii. 'Well, I'm e'en a'most starved, and Captain Jack does look AS POOR AS JOB'S TURKEY; that's a fact.'

1854. F. E. SMEDLEY, *Harry Coverdale*, xxiv. The amiable and timid London butler, who had played the character of JOB'S COMFORTER to Alice's *Didone abandonata* on the memorable evening of the first of September.

1857. *Notes and Queries*, I, S. vii. 180. s.v.

1871. *Once a Week.* May (quoted by DE VERE). Intensified, in American fashion, by some energetic addition; for instance, 'AS POOR AS JOB'S TURKEY, that had but one feather in its tail,' or, 'As POOR AS JOB'S TURKEY, that had to lean against a fence to gobble.'

JOCK, *subs.* (venery).—1. *See* quot. For synonyms *see* CREAMSTICK, PRICK, and MONOSYLLABLE. JOCK-HUNTING = seeking the sexual favor; and JOCK-HUNTER = MUTTON-MONGER (*q.v.*). [Probably an abbreviation of (Old Cant) JOCKUM (*q.v.*). For synonyms *see* GREENS and RIDE.

1790. POTTER, *Dict. of Cant & Flash*, s.v. JOCK, private parts of a man or woman.

2. (colloquial).—*See* JOCKEY.

Verb. (venery).—1. *See* quot. For synonyms *see* GREENS and RIDE.

1690. B. E., *Dict. Cant. Crew*, s.v. JOCK, to copulate with a woman.

1725. *New Cant. Dict.*, s.v.

1785. GROSE, *Vulg. Tongue*, s.v. JOCK, to enjoy a woman.

1859. MATSELL, *Vocabulum*, s.v.

2. (American).—To enjoy oneself.

JOCKEY, *subs.* (old: now recognised in most senses).—1. A professional rider; also a horse-dealer. Hence (*see* quot. 1690) a sharper. Also (colloquially) JOCK and GENTLEMEN-JOCK and JOCKER.

1638. BROME, *Antipodes*, i. 5. Let my fine lords talk o' their horse-tricks, and their JOCKIES that can out-talke them.

1684. R. HEAD, *Proteus Redivivus*, 306. There are such plenty of JOCKEYS in this bungalow, they swarm everywhere.

1690. B. E., *Dict. Cant. Crew*, s.v. JOCKEYS, rank Horse-Coursers, Race Riders; also Hucksters or Sellers of Horses, very slippery Fellow to deal with.

1725. *New Cant. Dict.*, s.v.

1725. BAILEY, *Colloq. Erasmus*, i. 412. You know what cheating tricks are play'd by our JOCKEYS, who sell and let out Horses.

1815. SCOTT, *Guy Mannering*, vii. The tribes of gipsies, JOCKEYS, or cairds,—for by all these denominations such banditti were known,—became few in number.

1828-45. T. HOOD, *Poems*, vi. p. 252 [ed. 1846]. And what with keeping a hunting box Following fox.... Shooting blue rocks, Trainers and JOCKS....

*d.*1881. G. BORROW (in Annandale).—The word JOCKEY is neither more nor less than the term (chukni) slightly modified, by which they (the gypsies) designate the formidable whips which they usually carry, and which are at present in general use amongst horse-traffickers, under the title of jockey-whips.

2. in pl. (commercial).—Top-boots.

1851. *Lond. Lab. Lond. Poor*, V. II. p. 43. Top boots (they're called JOCKEYS in the trade and sold in the streets).

3. (old).—A Scot.

*d.*1529. SKELTON, *Against the Scots*, line 92. King Jamy, Jemmy, JOCKEY, my jo.

Verb. (colloquial).—1. To cheat; to ride foul. Generally, to use dishonest means to a profitable end. For synonyms *see* BAMBOOZLE.

1748. THOMPSON. *Letter to Mr. Paterson*, May. 'Coriolanus has not yet appeared on the stage, from the little dirty jealousy of Jullus (Quin) towards him (Garrick) who alone can act Co-

riolanus. Indeed the first has entirely JOCKEYED the last off the stage for this season.

1833. NEAL, *Down Easters*, VI. p. 84. Fair traders terrible scase—most every body JOCKIES for themselves now.

1839. LEVER, *Harry Lowegner*, II. He seemed to think that probably he ... might be merely JOCKEYED by some bold-faced poacher.

1840. THACKERAY, *Paris Sketch Book*, p. 173. Have we penniless directors issuing El Dorado prospectuses, and JOCKEYING their shares through the market?

1865. DUNBAR, *Social Life in Former Days.* They did not see it necessary to be JOCKEYING one another.

1890. W. C. RUSSELL, *Ocean Tragedy*, p. 3. To suffer your passion to JOCKEY your reason.

2. (Winchester College).—(i) to supplant; (ii) to appropriate; (iii) to engage: *e.g.* 'He JOCKEYED me up to books'; 'Who has JOCKEYED my baker'; 'This court is JOCKEYED'. Probably an extended use of the word borrowed from turf slang. JOCKEY NOT = the Commoner cry claiming exemption, answering to 'feign' at other schools: of which the college 'finge' seems a translation. The opposite of JOCKEY UP = to lose down.—*Notions.*

TO JOCKEY (or BAG) THE OVER, *verb. phr.* (cricketter's).—To manage the running in such a manner as to get all the bowling to oneself.

JOCK BLUNT. TO LOOK LIKE JOCK BLUNT, *verb. phr.* (old).—*See* quot.

1723. RAMSAY, 'Epistle to Lord Ramsay', in *Wks*, ii. 325. Footnote. Said of a person who is out of countenance at a disappointment.

JOCK-TE-LEEAR, *subs.* (Scots').—A small almanack, *i.e.* JOCK (or JOHN) THE LIAR [From its loose weather forecasts].

JOCTELEG (or **JACKYLEG**), *subs.* (Scots').—A large pocket-knife. [From Jacques de Liège, a famous cutler]. For synonyms *see* CHIVE.

1730. RAMSAY, *Fables and Tales*, in *Wks.* (1849), iii. 172. And lay out ony ora-bodles On sma' gimcracks that pleased their noddles, Sic as a JOCTELEG, or sheers.

1787. GROSE, *Provincial Glossary*, s.v. JOCTELEG, Liege formerly supplied Scotland with cutlery.

1791. BURNS, 'To Captain Grose'. The knife that nicket Abel's craig He'll prove ye fully, It was a faulding JOCTELEG Or lang-kail gully.

1874. E. L. LINTON, *Patricia Kemball*, xxv. A huge buckhorn-handled knife of the kind called in the north JACKYLEGS, or JOCTELEGS.

JOCKUM (or **JOCKAM**), *subs.* (Old Cant).—The *penis.* For synonyms *see* CREAMSTICK and PRICK. Hence JOCKUM-CLOY = copulation, and JOCKUM-GAGE = (literally) MEMBER-MUG (*q.v.*).

1567. HARMAN, *Caveat*, 87. He took his IOCKAM in his famble.

1690. B. E., *Dict. Cant. Crew.* s.v. JOCKUM-GAGE. RUM JOCKUM-GAGE, a silver chamberpot.

1725. *New Cant. Dict.*, s.v.

1785. GROSE, *Vulg. Tongue.*

1859. MATSELL, *Vocabulum*, s.v.

JOCKUM-GAGGER, *subs.* (old).—*See* JACK-GAGGER.—POTTER (1790); *Mod. Flash Dict.* (1825).

JOE (or **JOEY**), *subs.* (common).—1. A fourpenny piece [For derivation *see* quot. 1841 and *cf.* BOB].

1841. HAWKINS, *Hist. Silver Coinage of England.* These pieces are said to have owed their existence to the pressing instance of Mr. Hume, from whence they, for some time, bore the nickname of JOEYS.

1842. *Punch's Almanack*, Aug. Each baited with a JOEY.

1851-61. MAYHEW, *Lond. Lab.*, ii. 218. The chance hands are sometimes engaged for half a day, and, I was told, jump at a bob and a JOEY (1*s.* 4*d.*), or at a bob.

1865. H. KINGSLEY, *The Hillyars and the Burtons*, xlii. A young man as has owed me a JOEY ever since the last blessed Greenwich fair.

1869. WHYTE-MELVILLE, *M. or N.*, p. 66. 'Done for another JOEY,' replied Buster, with the premature acuteness of youth foraging for itself in the streets of London.

1883. *Antiquary*, April, p. 168, col. 2. The fourpenny piece was coined for the first time, after a lapse of two centuries, in the reign of William iv., and it owed its existence to the pressing instance of JOEY Hume, after whom it obtained the name of JOEY.

1889. *Pall Mall Gazette*, 9 Oct., p. 5, col. 3. The docker's wife was worth her JOEY, which it may be explained is 'Eastend' for fourpence.

1892. S. WATSON, *Wops the Waif*, p. 13. A bob, a tanner, a JOEY, and a brown.

2. (common).—*See* JOE MILLER.

3. (American university).—A watercloset. For synonyms *see* MR. JONES.

4. (nautical).—A marine: *see* JOSEPH.

5. (American).—A lobster too small for sale; *i.e.* one under ten inches long.

6. (old).—A gold coin. (Portu. and Braz.) = 8 to 9 dollars. Also DOUBLE-JOE.

1825. NEAL, *Bro. Jonathan*, II. xxiii. JOES to coppers that she speaks to me.

1837. BARHAM, *Ingoldsby Legends*, Preface v. The old house is full of shooting-jackets, shot belts, and DOUBLE-JOES.

7. (old).—A companion; a sweetheart.

*d.*1529. SKELTON, *Against the Scottes*, in *Wks* (DYCE), i. 185. Kynge Jamy, ... my JO.

1659. BROME, *The English Moor*, in *Wks.* (1873), i. 3. Clap him, and stroke him: Ha, my JOE.

1635. GLAPTHORNE, *The Hollander*, in *Wks.* (1874), i. 151. The Twibil Knights (confusion to them, my Jo!) had made me drunk.

1727. RAMSAY, *Bonny Tweed-side*, in *Wks.* (1848), ii. 244. I'll make it my care To secure myself a JO.

*d.*1796. BURNS, '*John Anderson, my Jo*' [Title].

Verb. (theatrical).—To deride; TO GET AT (*q.v.*); to take liberties with the text, 'business', or audience.

1865. KINGSLEY, *The Hillyards and the Burtons*, liii. Gertie adduced the fate of the children who had called after—or, as she expressed, JOED—the prophet Elisha.

1866. *Pall Mall Gazette*, 23 Jan., p. 244. There they was JOEYING away in style, making the people laugh until the house shook again.

NOT FOR JOE.—*See* JOSEPH.

JOE MANTON, *subs.* (old).—A name given to fowling-pieces made by Joseph Manton, a celebrated London gunsmith. Also MANTON.

JOE MILLER, *subs. phr.* (common). —A stale joke; a dull tale; a CHESNUT (*q.v.*). [From a collection entitled *Joe Miller's Jest book* published *circa* 1750, the term having been used to pass off not only the original stock but thousands of jokes manufactured long after]. Hence JOE-MILLERISM (*subs.*) and JOE-MILLERIZE (*verb.*).

1789. GEO. PARKER, *Life's Painter*, 96. The Narrator should not laugh immoderately, and what he delivers, should not be found in every common jest book, or a JOE MILLER, page 14.

1850. F. E. SMEDLEY, *Frank Fairlegh*, liv. 'Well, of all the vile puns I ever heard, that, which I believe to be an old JOE MILLER, is the worst.'

1859. *Times*, 'Rev. of Ramsay's Reminiscences', 25 Oct. There is more '*wit*', more mere word-flashing in one page of our familiar JOE, than in the whole of Dean Ramsay's book.

1883. *Notes and Queries*, 6 S. viii. 489. All classes are given to such repetitions, and the only differences are that every set has its own peculiar style or class of JOE MILLERS and old tales.

1885. *Punch*, August 1, p. 54. What? A weir yonder? Oh! I'm a-weir of it. There! Better old JOE MILLERS than old saws.

1890. *Speaker*, 22 Feb., p. 211, col. 2. We must not spoil any of Mr. Montagu Williams's endless laughable stories, though here and there one looks very like an old JOE with a new face.

JOE SAVAGE, *subs. phr.* (rhyming).—A cabbage.

JOEY, *subs.* (American thieves').—1. A hypocrite.—MATSELL (1859).

2. (common).—*See* JOE, *subs.* sense 1.

3. (Australian).—*See* quot. 1887.

1865. H. KINGSLEY, *Hillyars and Burtons*, lvii. He had met a grey doe kangaroo with her little ones... Then the little one, the JOEY, had opened its mother's pouch and got in.

1887. Australian Colloquialisms in *All the Year Round*, 30 July, p. 67. JOEY is a familiar name for anything young or small, and is applied indifferently to a puppy, or a kitten, or a child, while a WOOD-AND-WATER-JOEY is a hanger about hotels, and a doer of odd jobs.

4. (nautical).—A marine.

5. (theatrical).—A clown. [From JOEY Grimaldi].

Intj. (Australian).—*See* quot. Also JO!

1867. *The Victorian Song-book*, 'Where's your License,' p. 6. Diggers ain't often caught on the hop, The little word JOE! which all of you know, Is a signal the traps are quite near.

JOG, *verb.* (old venery).—To copulate. For synonyms *see* GREENS and RIDE.

1608. R. MIDDLETON, *Epigrams*, p. 18. Glabreus of late lay with a common whore, But now he swears he'll JOGGE with her no more.

1736. *The Cupid*, 20. He shou'll ken I'se nae afraid When he gangs to bed me, A' night long I'se ne'er complain, Tho' he JOG'D me sprightly.

JOGGER, *verb.* (theatrical).—To play and sing; to perform.

1893. EMERSON, *Signor Lippo*, v. I could vardy that when I heard them JOGGERING.

JOGGERING OMEY, *subs. phr.* (theatrical).—A musician. [It. *giocar* = to play + *uomo* = a man].

JOG-TROT (or **JOB-TROT**), *subs.* (old: now recognised).—A slow trot: hence a dull round; an unvarying and uninteresting method. As *adj.* monotonous; easy-going. Hence, *adv.* JOG-TROTTY.

1709. M. BRUCE, *Sermon*, p. 15. You that keeps only your old JOB-TROOT, and does not mend your pace, you will not wone at soul confirmation. There is a whine old JOB-TROOT ministers among us, a whine old JOB-TROOT professors: they have their own pace, and faster they will not go.

1756. *The World*, No. 193. They contented themselves indeed with going on a JOG-TROT in the common road of application and patience.

1766. GOLDSMITH, *Vicar of Wakefield*, xx. All honest JOG-TROT men, who go on smoothly and dully.

1811. *Lex. Bal.*, s.v. JOGG-TROT.

1852. DICKENS, *Bleak House*, xvii, p. 142. 'It's rather JOG-TROTTY and humdrum. But it'll do as well as anything else!'

1872. M. E. BRADDON, *Dead Sea Fruit*, i. There is a JOG-TROT prosperity in the place, a comfortable air, which is soothing to the world-worn spirit.

1885. JAS. PAYN, *Talk of the Town*, vii. They. . . . settled their wigs upon their foreheads and started off again at a JOG TROT in search of another mare's nest.

1890. *St. James' Gazette*, 9 Ap. p. 4, col. 1. Yet the yoke is meekly borne by the JOG-TROT undergraduates of Oxford and Cambridge.

JOGUE, *subs.* (old).—A shilling.—GROSE. For synonyms *see* BOB.

JOGUL, *verb.* (gaming).—To play up at cards, or other game.—HOTTEN.

JOHN, *subs.* (Sandhurst).—A first year's cadet. For synonyms *see* SNOOKER.

2. (old).—A priest. Also SIR JOHN and MESS- (or MASS-) JOHN (*q.v.*). For synonyms *see* DEVIL-DODGER.

1383. CHAUCER, *Cant Tales* (SKEAT) iv. 270. 4000. Com neer, thou preest, com hider, thou SIR IOHN.

c.1554. *Youth* [DODSLEY, *Old Plays* (1874), ii. 25]. What! SIR JOHN, what say ye! Would you be fettered now?

1559. PORTER, *Two Angry Women* [DODSLEY, *Old Plays* (1874), VII. 320]. Leave these considerations to SIR JOHN; they become a black-coat better than a blue.

1611. BARRY, *Ram Alley*, iv. Speak, answer we, SIR JACK: stole you my daughter?

1772. STEVENS, *Songs Comic and Satyrical* (1788), 169. The next a MESS JOHN of rank Methodist taint, Who thought like a sinner, but looked like a saint.

3. *See* POOR JOHN.

JOHN'S SILVER PIN, *subs. phr.* (old).—A piece of finery amongst sluttery and dirt.

JOHN-A-NOKES (or **JOHN-AT-THE-OAKS**), *subs.* (old).—Anyhody; MR. THINGUMBOB (*q.v.*). Also JOHN-A-STILES or JOHN-AT-THE-STYLES.

d.1529. SKELTON, *Colyn Cloute*, line 323. What care they though Gil sweate, Or JACKE OF THE NOKE.

1635. GLAPTHORNE, *Hollander*, in *Wks.* (1874), 94. 'I know not how you style him.' 'Not JOHN-A-STILES, the Knight of the Post is it?'

1772. G. A. STEVENS, *Songs Comic & Satyrical*, 246. From JOHN-A-NOKES to Tom-a-Styles What is it all but fooling?

1815. SCOTT, *Guy Mannering* (ed. 1829), ii. 13, 167. Adventures who are as willing to plead for JOHN-A-NOTES as for the first noble of the land.

JOHN-A-DREAMS, *subs.* (old).—A dreamer; a man of sentiment and fancy as opposed to action; a futile person.

1596. SHAKSPEARE, *Hamlet*, ii. 2. While I a dull, and noddy-mettled rascal, peak Like JOHN-A-DREAMS, impregnant of my Cause And can say nothing.

1876. HENLEY, *A Book of Verse*, p. 91. Kate-a-Whimsies, JOHN-A-DREAMS, Still debating, Still delay, And the world's a ghost that gleams, Hovers—vanishes away.

1878. JULIAN STURGIS, *JOHN-A-DREAMS* (Title).

1894. HADDON CHAMBERS, *JOHN-A-DREAMS* [Title].

JOHN-AMONG-THE-MAIDS, *subs. phr.* (old).—A lady's man; a CARPET-KNIGHT (*q.v.*).

JOHN-AND-JOAN, *subs. phr.* (old).—An hermaphrodite.

JOHN-AUDLEY, *subs.* (theatrical).—A signal to abridge the performance. [When another 'HOUSE', (*q.v.*) is waiting the word 'JOHN-AUDLEY' is passed round]. Also JOHN ORDERLY.

1875. *Athenaeum*, 24 April, p. 545, col. 2. When that wary son of wandering Thespis (Richardson) used to step inside from the front, and ask 'Is JOHN AUDLEY here?' the stage-manager dropped the curtain wherever the tragedy might be, and a new audience took the places of the old. Even at this day, in

dramatic slang, to JOHN AUDLEY a play means to cut it down to a comfortable brevity.

1893. EMERSON, *Signor Lippo*, v. One said, 'JOHN AUDLEY', that means leave off!

JOHN-BARLEYCORN, *subs.* (common).—Beer. For synonyms *see* DRINKS and SWIPES.

1791. BURNS, *Tam O'Shanter*. Inspiring, bold JOHN BARLEYCORN.

JOHN BLUNT, *subs. phr.* (common).—A plain-spoken man. *See* also JOCK BLUNT.

JOHN-CHEESE, *subs.* (common).—A clown. Also JOHN TROT.

JOHN COLLINS, *subs. phr.* (Australian).—*See* quot.

1865. *The Australasian*, 24 Feb. p. 8. . . . That most angelic of drinks for a hot climate—a JOHN COLLINS (a mixture of soda water, gin, sugar, lemon and ice).

JOHN CHINAMAN, *subs. phr.* (old).—A Chinaman; the Chinese collectively.

JOHN COMPANY, *subs. phr.* (old).—The Hon. East India Company.

1808. *Lord Minto in India*, 184. Preparations to save JOHNNY COMPANY'S cash.

1852. *Mem. Col. Maintain*, 293. JOHN COMPANY whatever may be his faults is infinitely better than Downing street.

1880. *Sat. Review*, Feb. 14, p. 220. Doubt as to whether there were any such person as JOHN COMPANY.

JOHN DAVIS, *subs.* (American).—Money: otherwise READY JOHN. For synonyms *see* ACTUAL and GILT.

JOHNIAN, *subs.* (Cambridge university).—A student of St. John's College: also JOHNIAN PIG or HOG—*see* HOG, *subs.* sense 3. Also as *adj.*: *e.g.* JOHNIAN blazer, JOHNIAN melody etc.

1785. GROSE, *Vulg. Tongue*, s.v. HOG . . . JONIAN HOGS an appellation given to the members of St. John's College Cambridge.

1829. PRAED, *Poems*, 'The Vicar'. Sit in the Vicar's seat: you'll hear The doctrine of a gentle JOHNIAN.

1841. *Westminster Rev.*, xxxv. 236. The JOHNIANS are always known as pigs. They put up a new organ the other day which was immediately christened 'Baconi Novum Organum.'

JOHN LONG THE CARRIER. TO STAY FOR (or SEND BY) JOHN LONG THE CARRIER, *verb. phr.* (old).—To wait a long time; to postpone for an indefinite time.

JOHNNIE (or **JOHNNY**), *subs.* (common).—1. A policeman: also JOHNNY DARBY.

1851. MAYHEW, *Lond. Lab. &c.* ii. 154. The JOHNNYS on the water are always on the look-out, and if they sees any on us about we has to cut our lucky.

1878. BESANT and RICE, *By Celia's Arbour*, vi. We might run up and down the slopes or on the ramparts . . . . without rebuke from the JOHNNIES, the official guardians of the walls.

1886. *Graphic*, Jan. 30, p. 130, col. 1. Constables used to be known as JOHNNY DARBIES, said to be a corruption of the French *gensdarmes*, and they are still occasionally called JOHNNIES.

2. (general).—An acquaintance; a young man about town. Also = a sweetheart, male or female: *e.g.* My JOHNNY.

1724-27. RAMSAY, *Bonny Tweedside*, in *Wks.* ii. 245. And let us to Edinburgh go Where she that is bonny, May catch her a JOHNNY, And never lead apes below.

1883. *Punch*, August 18, p. 84, col. 2. Ah! who is more brave than your JOHNNY

of note, With his snowy shirt-front and his dainty dust-coat.

1889. *Sporting Times*, 3 Aug. p. 1. col. 1. Well, I'll put it practically to you. A straight line is the way you JOHNNIES will go to the canteen when I've done with you.

1889. *Pall Mall Gazette*, 23 Sept. p. 2, col. 3. Now to the JOHNNY in the stalls, now to the ''Arry' in the amphitheatre flew the honeyed tokens, until the air was overcast with them.

1889. *Pall Mall Gazette*, 29 Oct. p. 7, col. 1. Mr. Blake said he was very fond of her and did not intend to leave her, as many a JOHNNY would have done.

1890. *Tit Bits*, 3 Aug. p. 332, col. 3. A microcephalous youth, whose chief intellectual relaxation consists in sucking the head of a stick, thinks that his conversational style is brilliant when he calls a man a JOHNNIE, a hero 'a game sort of a chappie,' and so on.

1890. *Daily Telegraph*, 4 Feb. The committee seriously discussed the feasibility of conferring with a high-class JOHNNIE.

1892. KIPLING, *Barrack Room Ballads*, 'The Widow's Party', 57. Where have you been this while away, . . . Johnnie, my JOHNNIE, aha!

1894. PERCY WHITE, *Mr. Bailey Martin*, p. 49. What snap your sister has got, and how she must mash all your local JOHNNIES.

3. (Irish).—A half-glass of whisky.

4. (American).—*See* JOHNNY REB.

JOHNNY-BUM, *subs.* (old).—A jack-ass.—GROSE (1785); *Lex. Bal.* (1811).

JOHNNY-CAKE, *subs.* (American).—A New-Englander.

JOHNNY-HAULTANT, *subs.* (nautical).—A merchants' sailor's name for a man-o'-war's-man—CLARK RUSSELL.

JOHNNY-BATES'-FARM.—*See* BATES' FARM.

JOHNNY-BONO, *subs.* (East-end).—Generic for an Englishman.

JOHNNY-DARBY, *subs.* (old).—(1). A policeman, (2) in pl. handcuffs.

JOHNNY NEWCOME, *subs.* (common).—A new-born child. Also (nautical) an inexperienced youngster; landsman in general.

1837. BARHAM, *Ingoldsby Legends*, [ed. 1862] p. 201. Now to young JOHNNY NEWCOME he seems to confine hers, Neglecting the poor little dear out at dry-nurse.

JOHNNY RAW, *subs.* (common).—1. A recruit; a novice.

1819. MOORE, *Tom Crib*, p. 18. A prettier treat Between two JOHNNY RAWS 'tis not easy to meet.

1825. SCOTT, *St. Roman's Well*, xxv. Well, I can snuff a candle and strike out the ace of hearts; and so, should things go wrong, he has no JACK RAW to deal with, but Jack Mowbray.

1828. JON BEE, *Picture of London*, p. 2. The designations of JOHNNY RAW, *Greenhorn* or *Youkel*, whereby they hope to lessen his pretensions to equality with themselves on the score of town-knowledge.

1837. BARHAM, *Ingoldsby Legends*, p. 258 [ed. 1862]. Antonio, like most of those sage JOHNNY RAWS.

1891. STEVENSON, *Kidnapped*, p. 39. You took me for a country JOHNNIE RAW? with no more mother-wit or courage than a porridge-stick.

1887. *Sydney* (N. S. W.) *Bulletin*, 26 Feb. p. 12. He was a new-chum—a regular JOHNNY-RAW.

2. (provincial).—A morning draught.

JOHNNY REB (or JOHNNY), *subs.* (American).—A soldier in the Confederate ranks during the civil war 1861-5. *See* BLUE-BELLIES.

JOHN ROBERTS, *subs. phr.* (Welsh).—*See* quot.

1886. J. C. SIKES in *N. and Q.* 7. S. i. 306. A new measure of drink, enough to keep a man tipsy from Saturday to Sunday night, is universally known throughout Wales as a JOHN ROBERTS. It derives its name from the author of the Sunday Closing Act. See *Standard*, March 11.

JOHN THE BAPTIST, *subs. phr.* (American).—*See* quot.

1888. *Arkansas Traveller*, Oct. Mebbe he gwine ter gimme a JOHN DE BAPTIST—dat's one cent—but mos likely he gwineter jis' give thanks.

JOHN THOMAS, *subs.* (common).—1. Generic for a flunkey.

1883. *Echo*, April 18, p. 1, col. 5. Pity the sorrows of a poor flunkey! . . . Who would have thought, to see JOHN THOMAS. . . . sunning himself on the forms provided for his use outside the shops in Regent Street, that he was a sufferer from many hours of confinement in doors.

2. (venery).—The *penis*. For synonyms *see* CREAMSTICK and PRICK.

JOHN (or **JOAN**) **THOMSON'S MAN**, *subs. phr.* (Old Scot's).—An uxorious, or faithful, husband.

d.1513. DUNBAR, 'To the King', in *Poems* (S.T.S. Edinburgh, 1884-5, ii. 318-19. God gif ye war JOHN THOMSOUNS MAN.

JOHN TROT, *subs.* (common).—A clown: also JOHN CREAM.

d.1774. GOLDSMITH, *Poems*. JOHN TROT was desired by two witty pens To tell them the reason why asses had ears.

JOIN, *verb.* (colloquial).—To marry. TO JOIN GIBLETS (venery) = to copulate.

1892. *Tit Bits*, 17 Sept. 419, 1. We've come to be JINED.

JOINT, *subs.* (American).—1. An opium den; a gambling saloon; a low class drinking house of any kind.

2. (thieves').—*See* quot.

1885. *Daily Telegraph*, August 18, p. 3, col. 2. This class of thieves, when they agree on a partnership or JOINT, as the slang phrase is, work one for the other as they best can.

TO WORK THE JOINT, *verb. phr.* (thieves').—To swindle by means of a 'faked' lottery table.

JOKER, *subs.* (common).—1. A general term of banter; a 'nice un'; as COVE, CODGER, TULIP.

1665. PEPYS, *Diary*, Feb. 15. At noon, with Creed to the Trinity-house where a very good dinner among the old JOKERS.

1833. MARRYAT, *P. Simple*, ii. 'That's what you'll learn to do, my JOKER, before you've been two cruises to sea'.

1882. *Daily News*, Oct. 4, p. 2, col. 4. Her screams brought her husband downstairs, when the prisoner said, 'My JOKER, I want you.'

1892. ANSTEY, *Voces Populi*, p. 121. No 'urry, old man—this JOKER 'aint arf finished with me yet.

2. (American).—An extra card used in certain games. It is blank or bears some special device. It is always a trump and generally the highest. Often called JOLLY JOKER.

1894. *St. James's Gazette*, 19 July [quoted in Saturday Review, July 26]. 'The game of poker is played with a pack of fifty-three cards, the fifty-third card being called the JOKER.—*Ibid.*, 'It is true that American manufacturers of playing cards are wont to include a blank card at the top of the pack; and it is, alas! true that some thrifty person suggested that the card should not be wasted. This was the origin of the JOKER.'

1885. J. B. GREENOUGH, *Queen of Hearts*, iii. The White Knight, called the JOKER, otherwise the Best Bower.

3. (American political).—*See* quot.

1895. *Review of Reviews*, 15 Jan., p. 70. The little JOKERS were used. (We have one of these JOKERS in our possession.) These little JOKERS were attached to the left thumbs of certain judges of election as the ballots were being counted. These JOKERS are made of rubber and have a cross on them. They are really rubber stamps. As these judges picked up the ballots they took hold of them in such a way that their left thumbs, with the JOKERS attached thereto, pressed upon the squares opposite the name of the candidate whom they wished to aid. By thus pressing upon said squares crosses were left in them.

JOLLOCK, *subs.* (common).—A parson. For synonyms *see* DEVIL-DODGER and SKY-PILOT.

JOLLY, *subs.* (old).—1. The head: also JOLLY NOB.

1785. GROSE, *Vulg. Tongue*, s.v.

1811. *Lex. Bal.*, s.v.

2. (nautical).—A Royal Marine: *cf.* TAME JOLLY. Fr. *un bigorneau.*

1833. MARRYAT, *Peter Simple*, v. iii. ch. 1, p. 313. I ran down to Plymouth, hoisted my pennant, drew my JOLLIES from the dock yard, etc.

1883. *Graphic*, 12 May, p. 487, col. 3. The Marine. . . . not being either a soldier or a sailor, was generally described as a joey, a JOLLY, a shellback, etc.

1884. G. A. SALA, in *Illustr. L. News*, 12 April, p. 339, col. 3. I should be glad to learn. . . . why a militiaman should be a TAME JOLLY (Admiral Smythe, in 'The Sailor's Word-Book' is my authority); and a marine a 'Royal JOLLY.'

3. (thieves').—*See* quots.

1856. H. MAYHEW, *Gt. World of London*, p. 46. The dependents of cheats; as JOLLIES and 'magsmen,' or the confederates of other cheats.

1867. JAS. GREENWOOD, *Unsent. Journeys*, xxiv. 190. The 'wheel of fortune' keepers, man and woman, attended by their JOLLIES . . . . those wonderfully lucky persons who, coming up quite promiscuously, win and carry away the sets of china and diamond earrings.

4. (thieves').—A pretence; an excuse.

1859. MATSELL, *Vocabulum*, s.v.

1879. J. W. HORSLEY in *Macm. Mag.* xl. 504. I see a reeler giving me a roasting (watching me), so I began to count my pieces for a JOLLY (pretence).

5. (general).—Praise; recommendation chaff; abuse. TO CHUCK A JOLLY = to set off an address to one or other of these ends. *See* CHUCK.

*c.*1869. VANCE. *The Chick-a-leary Cove.* Now join in a chyike, the JOLLY we all like.

1871. *Daily Telegraph*, 7 March. 'Winner of the Waterloo Cup.' The boys all turned out to see 'the illustrious stranger;' and, on a suggestion to give him a JOLLY, which appears to be the local phrase, they cheered the hero loud and long.

1891. *Licensed Victuallers Gazette*, 9 Feb. The spank, spank, could be heard distinctly all round the ring of spectators, who cheered and JOLLIED both lads vociferously.

Adj. and *adv.* (colloquial).—1. Fine; excellent; very good: very; exceedingly. *Cf.* AWFULLY, BLOODY etc.

1369. CHAUCER, *Troilus* (SKEAT), ii. 223, line 1105. Tel us your IOLY wo and your penaunce.

*d.*1529. SKELTON, *Elynour Rummyng*, line 51. And yet she will iet, Lyke a IOLLY fet.

1562-3. *Jack Juggler* [DODSLEY, *Old Plays* (1874), ii. 141]. I would he were now before your gate, For you would pummel him JOLLILY about the pate.

1579. SPENSER, *Shepheardes Calender*, Sept. Indeede thy bull is a bold bigge cur, And could make a JOLLY hole in their fur.

1590-6. SPENSER, *Fairy Queen.* Full JOLLY knight he seemed, and fair did sit.

1592. NASHE, *Pierce Penilesse* [GROSART ii. 77]. It will make them IOLLY long-winded, to trot vp and downe the Dorter staires.

1594. LODGE, *Wounds of Civil War* [DODSLEY, *Old Plays* (1874), vii. 145]. Aristion is a JOLLY-timbered man.

1597-8. *A Woman will Have her Will* [DODSLEY, *Old Plays* (1874), x. 519]. 'To bed? and what hath God sent you'. 'A JOLLY girl, sir'.

1607. MARSTON, *What You Will.* With what a JOLLY presence would he pace Round the Rialto.

1694. *Gentlemen's Journal*, Mar., p. 57. Wine alone can make us JOLLY.—*Ibid.* Among my cups I sing and roar Like JOLLY topers till I snore.

1747-8. J. TRAPP, *Notes upon the Gospels*, [ed. 1865] p. 25. All was JOLLY quiet at Ephesus before St. Paul came thither.

1750. FIELDING, *Tom Jones*, II. iii. What they call a JOLLY brisk young man.

1836. H. M. MILNER, *Turpin's Ride to York*, ii. 4. That's a JOLLY lie.

1837. DICKENS, *Oliver Twist*, ch. ix. 'He is so JOLLY green,' said Charley.

1854. *Punch*, Nov. The Russian Liprandi charged John, Pat, and Sandy, And a JOLLY good licking he got.

1856. HUGHES, *Tom Brown's School Days*, ii. 1. What a JOLLY desk!

1869. *Daily Telegraph.* He is annoyed when young ladies use slang phrases, such as awfully JOLLY! Their fresh lips should drop pearls and diamonds—not snakes and toads.

1891. *Licensed Victuallers' Gaz.*, 9 Jan. I was JOLLY glad he didn't die before.

1894. S. R. CROCKETT, *The Playactress*, p. 98. My governor 'ud he JOLLY well left if I did not turn up bright and early.

2. (common).—Slightly drunk. For synonyms *see* DRINKS and SCREWED.

1883. *Daily News*, 9 Feb., p. 3, col. 7. The prosecutor came in on Friday night with Mr. S., and had several glasses of lager beer, and all got JOLLY!

3. (racing).—Fat; with too much flesh.

1888. *Daily Chronicle*, 10 Dec. Mr. Fennick's mare stripped in JOLLY condition.

Verb. (common).—To joke; to rally; to vituperate.

1610. G. FLETCHER, *Christ's Triumph*, They JOLLY at his grief.

1876. C. HINDLEY, *Life and Adventures of a Cheap Jack*, p. 69. I can't JOLLY him down, so you must settle and do away with him, or I must 'dry up,' for the fellow's bested me.

1879. *Notes and Queries*, 5, S. xi. 406. JOLLEYING is a common term among workmen in London, and is used to express nearly every description of verbal ridicule and abuse.

1889. *Licensed Vict. Gaz.*, 8 Feb. Amidst yells, shouts, hisses, and JOLLYINGS.

1892. GUNTER, *Miss Dividends*, ch. xv. You've left her alone all day—you ain't been near to JOLLY her up.

JOLLY-BOYS, *subs.* (common).—A group of small drinking vessels connected by a tube, or by openings one from another.

JOLLY-DOG, *subs.* (common).—A boon companion.

1785. GROSE, *Vulg. Tongue*, s.v. JOLLY-DOG, a merry or facetious fellow; a bon vivant, who never flinches from his glass, nor cries to go home to bed.

1811. *Lex. Bal.*, s.v.

*c.*1867. *Broadside Ballad*, 'Slap Bang'. There is a set of JOLLY DOGS I've lately come across.

1880. *Punch's Almanack*, 13.

JOLLY-JUMPER, *subs.* (nautical).—A light sail set above a SKY-SCRAPER (*q.v.*).—CLARK RUSSELL (1883).

JOLLY-NOB.—*See* JOLLY, *subs.* sense 1.

JOLLY-ROGER, *subs.* (nautical).—A pirate's flag; A DEATH'S HEAD AND CROSS BONES (*q.v.*).

1885. STEVENSON, *Treasure Island*, xix, p. 151 (1886). There was the JOLLY ROGER—the black flag of piracy—flying from her peak.

1892. HUME NISBET, *THE JOLLY ROGER* [Title].

JOLT-HEAD (or **JOLTER-HEAD**), *subs.* (old).—A blockhead: for synonyms *see* BUFFLE and CABBAGE-HEAD.

1593. SHAKSPEARE, *Taming of the Shrew*, iv. 1. You heedless JOLTHEADS, and unmannered slaves!

1595. SHAKSPEARE, *Two Gentlemen*, iii. 1. *Launce*, Fie on thee, JOLT-HEAD! thou canst not read.

1605. B. JONSON, *Volpone*, v. 5. And your red saucy cap, that seems to me Nailed to your JOLT-HEAD.

1658. BROME, *Covent Garden Weeded*, p. 23. Sir JOLTHEAD, I do not. I'll teach you to chop logic with me.

1690. DURFEY, *Collin's Walk*, C. II, p. 79. And shall I not, with reverence low, Presume to ask who's the JOLT-HEAD now?

1690. B. E., *Dict. Cant. Crew*, s.v. JOLTER-HEAD, a vast large Head; also Heavy and Dull. To jolt or Shake, jolting or shaking of a Coach.

1691-2. *Gentlemen's Journal*, Mar., p. 14. The blows he had received on his JOLT-HEAD made him fall into convulsions.

1707. WARD, *Hudibras Redivivus*, II, pt. i, p. 6. Then looking very stern and dread, He bridles up his JOLTER HEAD.

1725. *New Cant. Dict.*, s.v.

1748. T. DYCHE, *Dictionary*, (5th ed.). JOLT or JOLTER-HEAD (S.) a large head; also a dull, stupid fellow, or blockhead.

1785. GROSE, *Vulg. Tongue*, s.v. JOLTER HEAD, a long head; metaphorically, a stupid fellow.

1811. *Lex. Bal.*, s.v.

1822. SCOTT, *Fortunes of Nigel*, viii. I should like to know whether her little conceited noddle, or her father's old crazy, calculating JOLTER-PATE, breeds most whimsies.

1825. *Mod. Flash Dict.*, s.v. JOLTERHEADS—a heavy, dull fellow; a blustering landlord.

1843 DICKENS, *Martin Chuzzlewit*, li. p. 490. It isn't hanging yet for a man to keep a penn'orth of poison for his own purposes, and have it taken from him by two old crazy JOLTERHEADS who go and act a play about it.

JOLT-HEADED (or **JOLTER-HEADED**), *adj.* (old).—Stupid; dull; CHOWDER-HEADED (*q.v.*).

1690. DURFEY, *Collin's Walk*, C. II. p. 56. Insensible JOLT-HEADED Fool.

1754. H. MARTIN, *Eng. Dict.* (2nd ed.) s.v. Chub, chub . . . . a JOLT-HEADED fellow.

1849. LYTTON, *Caxtons*, III. iv. A worthless, obscure, JOLTER-HEADED booby in mail, whose only record to men is a brass plate in a church in a village!

1877. GREENWOOD, *Dick Temple*, ch. xxiv. It might be also that in his JOLT-HEADED way he really was a 'faithful dependent.'

JOLT, *verb.* (venery).—To copulate. For synonyms *see* GREENS and RIDE.

JOMER, *subs.* (theatrical).—*See* quot., FLAME, BLOWEN, BARRACK-HACK, and TART.

1857. SNOWDEN, *Mag. Assistant*, 3rd ed. p. 445. A fancy girl—JOMER.

1859. MATSELL, *Vocabulum*, s.v.

JONAH, *subs.* (common).—A person whose presence brings bad luck; specifically a clergyman. [Of Biblical origin]. JONAH-TRIP = an unlucky undertaking.

1594. GREENE, *Looking Glasse*, *Wks* 134. 2. (1861). We heav'd the hapless JONAS overboard.

1612. T. LAVENDER, *Travels etc.*, Sig. C 1. Thought it best to make a JONAS of him, and to cast both him and his books into the sea.

1644. *Merc. Brit.*, xxii. 172. I am ashamed that these JONAHS should be sleeping thus under the deck in a storme.

JONNICK (or **JONNUK**), *adj.* (showmen's).—Right; correct; proper—HOTTEN. TO BE JONNUK = to be fair; to share equally.

JORDAN, *subs.* (old).—1. A chamber-mug. For synonyms *see* IT. [Short for JORDAN BOTTLE; a memory of the Crusades]. Hence JORDAN-HEADED (DUNBAR) an opprobrious epithet.

1383. CHAUCER, *Canterbury Tales*, 12. 240. I pray to God to saue thy gentil corps, And eke thyn urinals, and thy JORDANES.

1545. LINDSAY, *Thrie Estatis*, l. 2478. Your mouth war meit to drinke an wesche JURDEN.

1592. GREENE, *Blacke Bookes Messenger*, in *Works*, xi. 33. And so pluckt goodman IURDAINE with all his contents down pat on the curbers pate.

1598. SHAKSPEARE, 1 *Henry IV*, ii. 1. They will allow us ne'er a JORDEN.

1614. JONSON, *Bartholomew Fair*, ii. 1. Good JORDAN, I know what you'll take to a very drop.

1622. JONSON, *Masque of Augurs*, in *Wks.* (CUNNINGHAM), iii. 165. My lady will come With a bowl and a broom, And her handmaid with a JORDAN.

1658. BROME, *Covent Garden Weeded*, p. Carry up a JORDAN for the Maidenhead, and a quart of white muscadine for the Blue Boar.

1690. B. E., *Dict. Cant. Crew*, s.v. JORDAIN.

1725. *New Cant. Dict.*, s.v.

1728. POPE, *Dunciad*, ii. 190. Crown'd with the JORDAN walks contented home.

1765. GOLDSMITH, *Essays*, I. Instead of a crown, our performer covered his brows with an inverted JORDAN.

1785. GROSE, *Vulg. Tongue*, s.v.

*b.*1794. WOLCOT [P. Pindar], *Peter's Prophecy.* Who knows not JORDANS, fool! from Roman vases?

1887. DR. BREWER, in *N. and Q.*, S. iii. 79. We always called the Matula the JORDAN, and into this receptacle all the bedroom slops were emptied.

2. (old).—A stroke with a staff.

1690. B. E., *Dict. Cant. Crew*, s.v. JORDAIN. I'll tip him a JORDAIN if I transnear, I will give a blow with my staff if I get up to him.

1859. MATSELL, *Vocabulum*, s.v.

3. (journalistic).—The Atlantic; THE DITCH (*q.v.*); THE HERRING-POND (*q.v.*).

1875. *Daily Telegraph*, 10 May. No sooner does a great want of any kind make itself felt, than the means of supplying that want are discovered by our ingenuous cousins on the other side of JORDAN.

Adj. (American thieves').—Disagreeable; hard of accomplishment.

1859. MATSELL, *Vocabulum*, s.v.

JORUM, *subs.* (old).—A drinking-bowl; also a portion of liquor; a NEDDY (*q.v.*). Sp. *granizo* (= hail).

*d.*1796. BURNS, *O May, thy Morn!* And here's to them that like oursels Can push about the JORUM.

1785. GROSE, *Vulg. Tongue*, s.v. JORUM, a jug or large pitcher.

1800. C. LAMB, *Letter* to Coleridge, *Wks.* [ed. 1852], ch. v. p. 46. You, for instance, when you are over your fourth or fifth JORUM.

1804. JOHN COLLINS, *Scripscrapologia*, p. 59. And drown care in a JORUM of grog.

1811. *Lex. Bal.*, s.v.

1836. DICKENS, *Pickwick*, xxxviii. p. 333. After dinner, Mr. Bob Sawyer ordered in the largest mortar in the shop, and proceeded to brew a reeking JORUM of rum-punch therein.

*d.*1842. CUNNINGHAM, '*Newcastle Beer.*' Apply for a JORUM of Newcastle beer.

1854. MARTIN and AYTOUN, *Bon Gaultier Ballads.* 'The Lay of the Lovelorn', Hark my merry comrades call me, bawling for another JORUM.

1858. TROLLOPE, *Dr. Thorne*, xi. He contrived to swallow a JORUM of scalding tea.

1867. LATHAM, *Eng. Dict.*, s.v. JORUM. . . . slang, perhaps connected with YARRUM.

1870. MANSFIELD, *School-Life at Winchester College*, p. 85. Each end and Præfect's mess had their beer served up in a large white jug, or 'bob.' The vessel used for the same purpose in Commoners' was called a JORAM.

JOSEPH, *subs.* (old).—1. *See* quots: specifically a lady's riding habit with buttons to the skirts. In American (thieves') a patched coat. *Cf.* BENJAMIN, and for synonyms *see* CAPELLA.

1671. R. HEAD, *English Rogue*, I. v. 48 (1874). JOSEPH, a cloak.

1688. SHADWELL, *Sq. of Alsatia*, ii. in *Wks.* (1720), 4. Who's here? my father? *Lolpoop, Lolpoop*, hide me; give me my JOSEPH.

1690. B. E., *Dict. Cant. Crew*, s.v. JOSEPH, a Cloak or Coat. A Rum JOSEPH, a good Cloak or Coat. A Queer JOSEPH, a coarse ord'nary Cloak or Coat; also an old or tattered one.

1714. *Memoirs of John Hall*, (4th ed.) p. 12. JOSEPH, a close coat.

1725. *New Cant. Dict.*, s.v.

1766. GOLDSMITH, *Vicar of Wakefield*, xvi. Olivia would be drawn as an Amazon. . . . dressed in a green JOSEPH.

1785. GROSE, *Vulg. Tongue*, s.v. JOSEPH, a woman's great coat.

1811. *Lex. Bal.*, s.v.

1818. S. E. FERRIER, *Marriage*, viii. Another held up a tartan cloak, with a hood; and a third thrust forward a dark cloth JOSEPH, lined with flannel.

1823. *Modern Flash Dict.*, s.v.

1825. NEAL, *Bro. Jonathan*, III. xxvii. So as to betray, with every swing of her body, the rich dress, underneath her JOSEPH.

1847. ROBB, *Squatter Life*, p. 62. 'Well, by gunflints,' says he 'ef you ain't makin' a JOSEY.'

1859. MATSELL, *Vocabulum*, s.v. JOSEPH, a coat that's patched.

2. (colloquial). — A woman-proof male. TO WEAR JOSEPH'S COAT = to defy temptation, as Joseph with Potiphar's wife.

1785. GROSE, *Vulg. Tongue*, s.v. JOSEPH.

1811. *Lex. Bal.*, s.v.

1859. MATSELL, *Vocabulum*, s.v. JOSEPH'S COAT. It's of no use trying, he WEARS A JOSEPH'S COAT.

1870. *Reynolds's Newspaper*, 6 Feb. You appear to have been a regular JOSEPH.

NOT FOR JOSEPH, *phr.* (common).—A contemptuous refusal; a sarcastic dissent: *cf.* ALL MY EYE.

1844. C. SELBY, *London by Night*, ii. 1. *Jack.* Who's to pay? *Ned.* Whichever you please. *Jack.* Oh! in that case you may as well settle it. *Ned.* NOT FOR JOSEPH! You asked me to tea.

*c.*1867. *Broadside Ballad*, 'Not for Joe'. NOT FOR JOE . . . NOT FOR JOSEPH, if he knows it.

JOSEPH'S-COAT, *subs. phr.* (colloquial).—A coat of many colours; a dress of honour.

1892. KIPLING, *Barrack Room Ballads*, 'The Rhyme of the Three Captains'. They ha' rigged him a JOSEPH'S JURY-COAT to keep his honour warm.

JOSEY, *verb.* (American).—To go; to hasten. For synonyms *see* AMPUTATE and SKEDADDLE.

JOSH, *subs.*(colloquial).—1. A sleepy-head; a dolt.

2. (American).—An Arkansas man.

Verb. (American).—To chaff; to quiz; to make fun of.

Intj. (American).—A word shouted at the New-York Stock Exchange to wake up a slumbering member.—BARTLETT.

JOSKIN, *subs.* (common).—A bumpkin: also a dolt. For synonyms *see* BUFFLE and CABBAGE-HEAD.

1811. *Lex. Bal.*, s.v. JOSKIN. The drop-cove maced the JOSKIN of twenty quid, the ringdropper cheated the countryman of twenty guineas.

1819. CHAS. LAMB, *Letter* to Mr. Manning. I hate the JOSKINS a name for Hertfordshire bumpkins.

1828. BEE, *Living Picture of London*, p. 15. The very sight of a countryman, either yokel or JOSKIN.

1859. MATSELL, *Vocabulum*, s.v.

1865. DICKENS, *Christmas Stories (Doctor Marigold)*, p. 172 (H. ed.). They all set up a laugh when they see us, and one chuckle-headed JOSKIN (that I hated for it) made the bidding, 'Tuppence for her!'

1876. HINDLEY, *Adv. of a Cheap Jack*, p. 14. An old JOSKIN of a countryman for an ostler.

1885. HENLEY, *Ballads and Rondeaux*, p. . Dull Sir JOSKIN sleeps his fill; Hard Sir Æger dints his mail.

1889. *Sporting Life*, 3 Jan. Your true JOSKIN, if an observer at all, can pretty accurately guage the weather prospects.

1892. MILLIKIN, *'Arry Ballads*. Old JOSKINS a-sucking long churchwarden pipes.

JOSSER, *subs.* (common).—1. A simpleton; a flat; a SPONGE (*q.v.*); an old *roué*. Also as *adj.*

1886. *Broadside Ballad*, 'I took it On'. I took it on, Of course I was a JOSSER.

1889. *Ally Sloper's Half Holiday*, 6 July, 'Jury Box JOSSERS' [Title].

*c.*1890. *Music Hall Song*, 'I don't like London.' Whenever I'm near them —they always cry Ain't he a JOSSER? Ain't he a guy?

*c.*1890. *Music Hall Song*, 'I'm living with Mother Now.' As a JOSSER I think you will do.

1890. *Punch*, 22 Feb. These quality JOSSERS would spile it, if 'arf their reforms they can carry.

1892. MILLIKEN, *'Arry Ballads*, p. 58. I'd keep all sech JOSSERS in mug.

1893. *Standard*, 29 Jan. p. 2. Now suppose we are on the road . . . and we meet a JOSSER policeman? Is it fair that the JOSSER should stop us?

2. (Australian).—A parson. For synonyms *see* DEVIL-DODGER and SKY-PILOT.

JOSSOP, *subs.*(schoolboys').—Syrup; juice; gravy; sauce—HOTTEN.

JOSTLE, *verb.* (Old Cant).—To cheat.

JOTTLING. TO GO JOTTLING, *verb. phr.* (venery).—To copulate. Also TO JOTTLE, and TO DO A JOTTLE. For synonyms *see* GREENS and RIDE.

JOUNCE, *subs.* (American).—A jolt; a shake.

1876. MRS. WHITNEY, *Sights and Insights*, II. xvii. Here she. . . . sat herself down. . . . with a JOUNCE.

Verb. (American).—To jolt or shake by rough riding; to handle carelessly; to deal severely with.

1833. NEAL, *Down Easters*, ii. p. 14. Mind how ye JOUNCE that air chist about!

TO BE JOUNCED, *verb. phr.* (American).—To be enamoured of.

JOURNEY, *subs.* (colloquial).—Occasion; juncture; time.

1884. *Longman's Mag.*, v. 179. 'Well,' said the policeman, when he understood, and ceased to suspect; 'as for him, he's got safe enough off, this JOURNEY!'

JOURNEYMAN SOUL-SAVER, *subs. phr.*(common).—A scripture-reader; a 'bible-woman'. Also JOURNEYMAN-PARSON (London) = a curate.

JOVE.—*See* BY JOVE.

JOWL (or JOLE), (old: now recognised). —The cheek: CHEEK BY JOWL = close together: JOWL-SUCKING = kissing.

1592. SHAKSPEARE, *Midsummer Night's Dream*, iii. 2. Follow! nay, I'll go with you CHEEK BY JOLE.

1682. DRYDEN, Prol. to *Loyal Brother*. Sits CHEEK-BY-JOWL, in black, to cheer his heart.

1811. *Lex. Bal.*, s.v.

1830. TENNYSON, *Vision of Sin*, 84. CHEEK BY JOWL, and knee by knee.

JOYFUL. TO BE ADDICTED TO THE 'O BE JOYFUL', *verb. phr.* (common).—*See* quot.

1865. *London Jour*, 8 April. Like a great many other clever fellows, he was too much addicted to the 'O BE JOYFUL!' In fact he had done so much at the business, that a red nose, somewhat swollen, was the consequence.

JUBA, *subs.* (American).—A negro. *See* SNOWBALL.

JUBILEE, *subs.* (Winchester College). —A pleasant time: *e.g.* The town was all in a JUBILEE of feasts—*Dryden.*

1772. G. A. STEVENS, *Songs Comic and Satyrical*, p. 192. Day by day, and night by night, Joyful JUBILEES we keep.

JUDAS, *subs.*(colloquial).—1. A traitor. JUDAS-COLORED = red. [From the tradition that Judas had red hair].

*c.*1384. WYCLIF, *Of Prelates*, (in F. D. MATHEW'S, *Unprinted Wks.* of W. ch. v.) And thus the lord or the lady hireth costly a fals JUDAS to his confessour.

1597-8. MUNDAY, *Downfall of Robert etc.* [DODSLEY, *Old Plays* (1874), viii. 131]. Warman himself, That creeping JUDAS, joy'd, and told it me.

1599. JONSON, *Ev. Man out of his Humour*, iv. 1. *Fal.* Now, out upon thee, JUDAS! canst thou not be content to backbite thy friend, but thou must betray him.

1600. SHAKSPEARE, *As You Like It*, iii. 4. *Ros.* His very hair is of the dissembling colour. *Cel.* Something browner than JUDAS'S.

1604. DECKER, *Honest Wh.*, Pt. II, in *Wks.* (1873), ii. 116. Thou villaine, curb thy tongue, thou art a JUDAS, to sell thy master's name to slander thus.

1673. DRYDEN, *Amboyna*, [in *Wks.* i. 561 (1701)]. I do not like his oath, there's treachery in that JUDAS-COLOUR'D beard.

1860. THACKERAY, *Four Georges (George I)*. We think within ourselves, O you unfathomable schemer! O you warrior invincible! O you beautiful smiling JUDAS! What master would you not kiss or betray?

2. *See* JUDAS-HOLE.

JUDAS-HOLE, *subs.* (common).—A spy-hole in a door(*see* quot. 1893); also JUDAS.

1856. C. READE, *Never too Late* etc. [*Century*]. He knew the world as he had seen it through JUDAS-HOLES, chiefly in its foulness and impurity.

1883. *Century*, xxvii. 75. A JUDAS is a square iron lattice . . . all have an iron flap inside to keep inquisitive eyes from prying into the house and yard.—*Ibid.* xxxv. 522. This contrivance which is known to the political prisoners as the JUDAS enables the guard to look into the cell at any time without attracting the attention of the occupant.

JUDE, *subs.* Common.—(A harlot).

1886. W. E. HENLEY, *Villon's Good-Night.* You JUDES that clobber for the stramm.

JUDISCHE (or **JEW'S**) **COMPLIMENT**, *subs.* (venery).—Lots of PRICK (*q.v.*) but no money: *c.f.* YORKSHIRE COMPLIMENT.

JUDGE, *subs.* (American cadets').—The man most popular with his fellows.

JUDGE AND JURY, *subs. phr.* (tailors').—A mock trial, the fines being paid in beer.

JUDY (or **JUDE**), *subs.* (common).—1. A girl: a woman, especially one of loose morals: also, a sweetheart. In Anglo-Chinese circles a native courtezan.

1886. *Daily News*, 26 July, p. 6, col. 1. One man saying 'Them ere Romans was them coves as goes about with a horgan an' a JUDY' (girl).

1888. RUNCIMAN, *The Chequers*, p. 80. I done the best as I knew for you, and there ain't a bloke around as has a JUDY.

2. (common).—A simpleton; a fool: TO MAKE A JUDY OF ONESELF = to play the fool; to act the GIDDY GOAT (*q.v.*) or SAUCY KIPPER (*q.v.*).

1824. *Atlantic Magazine*, i, 346. Not are ye laughin' at, ye JUDIES.

1854. *Punch*, i, p. 208, col. 2. Making a JUDY of herself.

*b.*1877. *Boston Chronotype*, (quoted by BARTLETT). It is thought that a set of men never did make greater JUDIES of themselves.

JUFF, *subs.* (old).—1. The cheek; 2. The posteriors.

JUG, *subs.* (old).—1. A prison: also more frequently STONE-JUG (*q.v.*). For synonyms *see* CAGE. Fr. *la boite aux cailloux*; Sp. *tristura.* [SKEAT: Fr. *joug* = a yoke. The Eng. JUG, a cant term for a prison (also called jocosely a STONE-JUG) is the same word].

1834. AINSWORTH, *Rookwood*, iii. v. And thus was I bowled out at last And into the JUG for a lag was cast.

1835. DICKENS, *Sketches by Boz*, p. 157. That's better than the STONE-JUG anyhow; the mill's a deal better than the Sessions.

1837. DICKENS, *Oliver Twist*, xliii. He shall be kept in the STONE-JUG, Charlie, like a gentleman.

1839. THACKERAY, *Catherine*, i. We intend to take a few more pages from the Old Bailey Calendar to bless the public with one more draught from the STONE JUG.

1842. *Punch*, ii, 188. 'Cut like bricks, and bilk the JUG,' he cried in one of those speeches which bother the French authors so much when they try to translate our works.

1852. JUDSON, *Mysteries of New-York*, x. 'What is that place?' 'It's the JUG sir,' responded Frank—'the Tombs, I meant, sir.'

1867. *Punch*, xxxii, 49. This STONE JUG at which flats dare to rail.

1870. *All the Year Round*, 5 Mar. 'Bygone Cant'. In a box of the STONE-JUG I was born, aye, And by a tightened jugular I shall die.

1871. *Chambers' Journal*, 9 Dec. p. 771. They are no worse than the swells in the City who rob right and left, and never get in the JUG for it.

1884. R. E. FRANCILLON, *Ropes of Sand*, xxi. I've not been under a roof but the JUG'S since somewhere in old Horneds's time.

1888. BOLDREWOOD, *Robbery Under Arms*, xxii. It was no use sending it to you, old man, while you was in the JUG.

1889. *Modern Society*, 16 Feb., p. 305. I got three months in the JUG for fortune-telling.

1892. MILLIKEN, *'Arry Ballads*, 58. As for O'Brien and his britches, I'd keep all sech jossers in JUG.

1895. C. WHIBLEY, in *New Review*, May, p. 570. For thirty years his squat, stout figure was amiably familiar to all such as enjoyed the Liberties of the JUG.

2. (American thieves').—A bank: A BROKEN JUGGED ONE = a note from a broken bank. Hence, also, JUG-BREAKING = burglary at a bank.

1862. *Cornhill Mag.*, vi. 648. It's all in single pennifs on the England JUG.

3. (old).—A mistress. Hence (as in quot. 1632) a term of endearment.

1569. T. PRESTON, *Cambyses.* Dost thou think I am a sixpenny JUG?

*b.*1600. *Grim the Collier* [DODSLEY, *Old Plays* (1874), viii. 409]. The collier chooseth well; . . . . JUG shall be his. [*Aside*]. But hear'st thou, Grim, I have that in my head, To plot that how thou shall the maiden wed.

1632. W. ROWLEY, *Woman Never Vext*, i. 1. Bring him away, JUG.

1707. CENTLIVRE, *Platonic Lady.* Haste ye! don't you marry that ill tempered JUG.

4. (old).—A term of contempt applied indifferently to both the sexes: *see* JUGGINS.

1892. MILLIKEN, *'Arry Ballads*, 63. Bell's a bloomer, and, Jack thought, a bit of a JUG.

Verb.(common).—1. To imprison; to lock up; to 'run in'; hence to hide.

1852. JUDSON, *Mysteries of New-York*, iv. When I was JUGGED the last time, didn't you bring me all I wanted.

1861. ALBERT SMITH, *Medical Student*, p. 33. Poor Jones got JUGG'D by mistake, but eventually got off the next morning with a five-shilling fine.

1888. *Detroit Free Press*, 15 Dec. The police came in and JUGGED him.

1888. BOLDREWOOD, *Robbery Under Arms*, xxx. Jim and I will be JUGGED.

1889. *Cassell's Sat. Jour.*, 9 Feb. That good-looking limb of the law who went wild. . . . and got himself JUGGED.

1892. GUNTER, *Miss Dividends*, vi. Buck Powers told me I'd be JUGGED if I shot at 'em.

2. (common).—To take in; to DO (*q.v.*).

JUG-BITTEN, *subs.* (old).—Drunk. For synonyms *see* DRINKS and SCREWED.

1630. TAYLOR, *Works.* For when any of them are wounded, pot-shot, JUGBITTEN, or cup-shaken, so that they have lost all reasonable faculties of the minde, and in a manner are so mad, that they dare speake felony, whistle treason, and call any magnifico a mungrell.

JUG-FULL. NOT BY A JUG FULL, *phr.* (common).—Not by a good deal, by long chalks, by no means.

1834. DOWNING, *Mayday in New-York* (quoted by BARTLETT.) Downingville is as sweet as a rose. But 'tain't so in New-York, not by a JUG-FULL.

1838-40. HALIBURTON ('Sam Slick'), *Clockmaker*, 3 S., ch. xviii. The last mile, he said, tho' the shortest one of the whole bilin', took the longest [time] to do it by a JUG FULL.

JUGGINS (or JUG), *subs.* (common).—A fool. For synonyms *see* BUFFLE and CABBAGE-HEAD.

1886. *Punch*, 17 July, p. 25. Yah! Wot a old JUGGINS he is!

1888. RUNCIMAN, *The Chequers*, 116. Only a JUGGINS or a horse ever works, and I don't intend to do any.

1888. *Sporting Life*, 29 Dec. The JUGGINSES who pull down but never build up are clamouring just a little bit for the abolition of Christmas.

1890. *Globe*, 15 Feb., p. 2, col. 1. Among the witnesses called to speak to the character of the prisoner was the Marquis of Ailesbury, who said he did not think Benzon would do any wrong intentionally, but he was a regular JUBILEE JUGGINS.

1892. MILLIKEN, *'Arry Ballads*, p. 5. Darned Sosherlist JUGGINSES 'owl till all's blue agin Wealth.

1893. EMERSON, *Signor Lippo*, xii. He was a JUGGINS though he could write songs.

JUGGLER'S-BOX, *subs.* (Old Cant).—The branding-iron.

JUICE, *subs.* (venery).—SPENDINGS, (*q.v.*). TO GIVE JUICE FOR JELLY = to achieve the sexual spasm.

TO STEW IN ONE'S OWN JUICE (or GREASE).—*See* STEW.

JUICY, *adj.* (common).—1. Piquant; racy; bawdy.

1880. GREENWOOD, *Odd People*, p. 59. 'Let me play you a tune, then,' said the frightened lad. 'All right, then. Play us something JUICY,' exclaimed the ruffian.

2. (venery). — Amorous: Of women only.

1691-2. *Gentlemen's Journal*, Jan., p. 43. She by self-denial, . . . rich, JUICY, full of love, debarr'd herself from the man she doated on.—*Ibid*, Aug. p. 5. A JUICY young amorous creature.

1719. DURFEY, *Pills &c.*, ii. 312. Snug, rich, and fantastick, no tumbler was known, That wedded a JUICY brisk girl of the town.

JUKRUM, *subs.* (Old Cant).—A license.—B.E. (1690); *New Cant. Dict.* (1725); GROSE (1785).

JULIUS CÆSAR, *subs. phr.* (venery). The *penis*. For synonyms *see* CREAMSTICK and PRICK.

DEAD AS JULIUS CÆSAR, *phr.* (old).—Dead past doubting.

JUMBAREE, *subs.* (theatrical).—Jewellery.

JUMBO, *subs.* (old).—A clumsy, unwieldy fellow.—BEE (1823).

JUMBLE, *verb.* (old).—To copulate. For synonyms *see* GREENS and RIDE. Also TO DO A JUMBLE-GIBLETS, or a JUMBLE-UP.

1582. STANYHURST, *Virgil his Aeneis* (ARBER, 1880), iv. 100. Dick and thee Troian captayns doe JUMBLE in one den.

1595. BARNFIELD, *Poems* (ARBER, 1882), 40. Both they JUMBLE in one bed.

1618. FIELD, *Amends for Ladies*, iv. 2. I would have so JUMBLED her honesty.

1651. RANDOLPH, *Hey for Honesty*, iii. 3. The wenches will tumble and merrily JUMBLE.

1687. BROME, *The Queen's Exchange*, in *Wks.* (1875), iii. 535. The dairy maid and he were JUMBLING of A posset together.

1719. DURFEY, *Pills &c.*, iv. 100. We JUMBLE our lasses upon the grass.

JUMBLE-GUT-LANE, *subs. phr.* (old).—A bad or rough road.—B.E. (1690); GROSE (1785).

JUMBLER, *subs.* (old). A FUCKSTER or FUCKSTRESS (*q.v.*)

1618. FIELD, *Amends for Ladies*, ii. 1. She has been as sound a JUMBLER as ever paid for it.

JUMBUCK, *subs.* (Australian).—A sheep. For synonyms *see* WOOLLY-BIRD.

1851. *Chambers' Journal*, xv. 317. Mind you look out well after the men as well as the JUMBUCKS.

1889. *Pall Mall Gazette*, Feb. The process by which the JUMBUCKS are shorn.

JUMM, *verb.* (venery).—To copulate.—(URQUHART). For synonyms *see* GREENS and RIDE.

JUMMIX, *verb.* (American).—To jumble up; to mix together: a PORTMANTEAU WORD (*q.v.*)

JUMP, *subs.* (old).—1. A form of robbery. *See* JILT, *verb.*

1811. *Lex. Bal.*, s.v. JUMP. Robbery effected by ascending a ladder placed by a sham lamplighter against the house intended to be robbed. It is so called because, should the lamplighter be put to flight, the thief who ascended the ladder has no means of escaping but that of JUMPING down.

2. (thieves').—A window: *cf.* BACK JUMP.

1859. MATSELL, *Vocabulum*, s.v.

3. (in pl.).—(1) the fidgets; (2) *delirium tremens.*

1879. PAYN, *High Spirits* (Capt. Cole's Passenger). I though he had been drinking, and in fact was on the verge of THE JUMPS.

1889. *Daily Telegraph*, 7 Sep., 5, 3. Only suffering from an attack of THE JUMPS.

4. (old).—Loose raiment. *See* JUMPER, sense 4.

1752. FOOTE, *Taste* (ed. 1781), p. v. Don't mind my shape this bout, for I'm only in JUMPS.

Verb.(old).—1. To seize upon, whether forcibly or by stealth; to cheat; to supplant: *e.g.* TO JUMP A MAN = to pounce upon and rob or maltreat; TO JUMP A HOUSE = to rob it; TO JUMP A CLAIM = to take possession of a mining right in the absence of an owner. Fr. *farguer à la dure.*

1789. GEO. PARKER, *Life's Painter*, 160. They . . . pick him up and take him to the above alehouse to JUMP him, or do him upon the broads, which means cards.

1855. F. MARRYAT, *Mountains and Molehills*, 217. If a man JUMPED my claim. . . . . I appealed to the crowd.

1857. WESTGARTH, *Victoria and the Australian Goldmines.* There was for that day at any rate to be no JUMPING of claims.

1870. BRET HARTE, *Luck of Roaring Camp*, 134. The old proprietor . . . . was green, and let the boys about here JUMP him.

1879. J. W. HORSLEY, in *Macm. Mag.*, xl. 500. Who used to take me a parlour-JUMPING (robbing rooms), putting me in where the window was open.

1888. *Chicago Herald.* He arose at early dawn and JUMPED his bill.

1888. BOLDREWOOD, *Robbery Under Arms*, xxxviii. We lying down and our horses hung up not far off for fear we might be JUMPED by the police at any time.

1890. *Athenæum*, 8 Feb. p. 176, col. 2. 'How a Claim was nearly JUMPED' is the most natural and the best of the five stories.

2. (venery).—To copulate. For synonyms *see* GREENS and RIDE.

1638. RANDOLPH, *Muses' Looking-Glass*, iv. 3. Then there is JUMPING Jude . . . with bouncing Nan.

3. (medical).—To try a medicine.

FROM THE JUMP, *adv. phr.* (colloquial).—From the start.

1848. *New York Tribune*, 11 Nov. Here is a whole string of Democrats, all of whom had been going the whole hog for Cass FROM THE JUMP.

*b.*1871. *Wild Bill* [quoted by DE VERE]. I knew how it would come FROM THE JUMP, for in the man's face was written rascal.

1888. *Daily Inter-Ocean*, 3 Feb. He can depend on a big crowd and fair play FROM THE JUMP.

TO JUMP AT, *verb. phr.* (colloquial).—1. To accept eagerly.

1848. LONGSTREET, *Georgia Scenes* [quoted by DE VERE]. When I offered him that, his whole face brightened wonderfully, and he JUMPED AT the offer.

1861. HUGHES, *Tom Brown at Oxford*, iii. 1. Mary was getting on badly with her drawing, and JUMPED AT the idea of a ramble in the woods.

1882. JAMES PAYN, *Thicker than Water*, vii. His circumstances were such that, to use a homely but very significant expression, he might well have JUMPED AT such an offer.

2. (colloquial).—To guess.

1892. HUME NISBET, *Bushranger's Sweetheart*, 250. I shall only give you a little of our conversation the Sunday night before we parted, and leave you to JUMP AT what had been said before.

TO JUMP (or BE JUMP) WITH, *verb. phr.* (colloquial).—To agree; to coincide; to tally.

1567. HARMAN, *Caveat* [E. E. I. S.], 44. They mete IOMPE at night.

1584. LYLY, *Alexander and Campaspe.* And thou to be JUMP WITH Alexander.

1598. SHAKSPEARE, I *Henry IV*, i. 2. In short, it JUMPS WITH my humour.

1606. *Return from Parnassus* [DODSLEY, *Old Plays* (1874), ix. 113]. As in the first, so in the last, my censure may JUMP WITH thine.

1633. *Match at Midnight*, iii. 1. How all things JUMP in a just equivalency.

1660. *Andromana*, iii. 6. This story JUMP'D Just with my dream to-night.

1838. NEAL, *Charcoal Sketches*, [quoted by DE VERE]. On the whole it JUMPED WITH his desires, and the matter was clinched.

1841. PEAKE, *Court and City*, iv. *Hum.* What a happiness it is, when people's inclinations JUMP!

TO JUMP ONE'S HORSE OVER A BAR, *verb. phr.* (colonial). *See* quot.

1886. *Daily Telegraph*, 20 Mar. Then the unhappy man would, in bush parlance, JUMP HIS HORSE OVER THE BAR, that is to say, he would, for a paltry sum, sell his horse, saddle, bridle, and all, to the lambing-down landlord.

TO GO A JUMP, *verb. phr.* (American thieves').—To enter a house by the window.—MATSELL (1859).

TO JUMP A BILL, *verb. phr.* (common).—To dishonour an acceptance.

1892. *Pall Mall Gazette*, 17 Oct., p. 2, col. 3. Painting the town red . . . JUMPING BILLS . . . evading writters etc.

TO SEE HOW THE CAT WILL JUMP, *verb. phr.* (common).—To watch the course of events; TO SIT ON THE FENCE (*q.v.*).

1825. *Universal Songster*, i. ('The Dog's-Meat Man'). He soon saw which way the cat did JUMP, And his company he offered plump.

1827. SCOTT, in *Croker Pap.* (1884), I. xi. 319. Had I time, I believe I would come to London merely TO SEE HOW THE CAT JUMPED.

1853. BULWER LYTTON, *My Novel*, IV. p. 228. 'But I rely equally on your friendly promise.' 'Promise! No—I don't promise. I must first SEE HOW THE CAT JUMPS.'

1859. LEVER, *Davenport Dunn*, III. 229. You'll see with half an eye HOW THE CAT JUMPS.

1874. *Sat. Rev.*, p. 139. This dismays the humble Liberal of the faint Southern type, who thinks that there are subjects as to which the heads of his party need not wait TO SEE HOW THE CAT JUMPS.

1887. 'Pol. Slang,' in *Cornhill Mag.*, June, p. 626. Those who sit on the fence—men with impartial minds, who wait to SEE, as another pretty phrase has it, HOW THE CAT WILL JUMP.

TO JUMP UPON, *verb. phr.* (colloquial).—To maltreat, physically or otherwise; to criticise severely; TO TAKE IT OUT OF (*q.v.*); TO SIT UPON (*q.v.*).

1872. M. E. BRADDON, *Dead Sea Fruit*, v. When a wretched scribbler was, in vulgar phraseology, to be JUMPED UPON, honest Daniel put on his hobnailed boots, and went at the savage operation with a will.

TO JUMP BAIL, *verb. phr.* (common).—To abscond.

1859. MATSELL, *Vocabulum*, s.v.

TO JUMP THE BROOMSTICK.—*See* BROOMSTICK.

TO JUMP UP (tailors').—To get the best of one, or the reverse.—*Slang, Jargon & Cant.*

TO JUMP THE GAME, *verb. phr.* (American police).—To raid a gambling den.

TO JUMP UP BEHIND, *verb. phr.* (general).—*See* quot.

1865. *Daily Telegraph*, 9 Mar. 'Has he no friend,' he asks him, 'who will JUMP UP BEHIND, that is endorse the acceptance.'

TO JUMP OUT OF ONE'S SKIN.—*See* SKIN.

ON THE KEEN JUMP, *adv. phr.* (U. S. colloquial).—On the 'go'; violently at work.

*b.*1884. T. WINTHROP, *Saccharissa Mellasys* [in *Century*]. De tar-kittle's a-bilin' ON DE KEEN JUMP.

JUMP-DOWN, *subs.* (colonial).—*See* quot. Also JUMPING OFF PLACE; a destination.

1885. STAVELEY HILL, *From Home to Home.* Colonially known as the JUMP-DOWN, that is the last place that is in course of erection on the outskirts of what is called civilized life.

1887. *Scribner's Magazine.* It is a sort of JUMPING-OFF-PLACE.

JUMPED-UP, *adj. phr.* (common).—Conceited; arrogant: also perturbed; upset.

JUMPER, *subs.* (old).—1. *See* quot.

1821. D. HAGGART, *Life*, Glossary, p. 172. JUMPER, a tenpenny-piece.—*Ibid.* p. 114. I got three JUMPERS and a kid's-eye.

2. (thieves').—A thief who enters houses by the windows: *cf.* JILTER.

1811. *Lex. Bal.*, s.v.

1825. *Mod. Flash Dict.*, s.v.

1859. MATSELL, *Vocabulum*, s.v.

3. (colonial).—One who illegally appropriates a claim : but *see* JUMP, *verb.* sense I. *Cf.* BOUNTY-JUMPER.

1890. GUNTER, *Miss Nobody*, p. 86. Bob, the hero who saved the Baby mine from the JUMPERS got us.

4. (common).—A short slop of coarse woollen or canvas.

1877. *Five Years' Penal Servitude*, iii. p. 222. 'We weren't dressed in such togs as these 'ere, but had white canvas JUMPERS and trousers.'

1883. CLARK RUSSELL, *Sailor's Language*, s.v.

1884. A. FORBES, in *Eng. Ill. Mag.*, i. 698. He wore the long boots and the woollen JUMPER of a miner [in N.-Zealand].

1888. J. RUNCIMAN, *The Chequers*, p. 156. His huge chest is set off by a coarse white JUMPER.

JUMPING-JACK, *subs.* (American).— An antic ; a gull.

1884. HENLEY and STEVENSON, *Deacon Brodie*, ii. 3. He was my ape, my tool, my JUMPING-JACK.

1892. GUNTER, *Miss Dividends*, x. Some day, my JUMPING-JACK, your wit may cost you the little brains you have.

1895. HENLEY and STEVENSON, *Macaire* (*New Review*, June, p. 688), i. 3. With the courage of a hare . . . and the manners of a JUMPING-JACK.

JUMPING JEHOSOPHAT (JUPITER or MOSES).—*See* BY.

JUMPING CAT. THE CULT OF THE JUMPING CAT, *subs. phr.* (colloquial).—The practice of waiting to see the course of events before acting. *See* CAT.

JUMPING-POWDER, *subs.* (common). —A stimulant administered to give spirit and 'go' to a person or animal.

1840. BLAINE, *Encyc. Rural Sports*, 385. 'Had he been fortified into pursuing the 'varmint' by a certain quantum of JUMPING POWDER.'

JUNE, *verb.* (Western American).— To go [Germ. *gehen*].

JUNESEY, *subs.* (American).—A sweetheart.

1889. *Atlantic Monthly*, Oct., p. 502. De young nigger men on de plantation wuz atter Dilsey, but it did n' do no good, en none un 'em could n' git Dilsey fer dey JUNESEY, 'tel Dave 'mence fer ter go roun' Aun' Mahaly's cabin.

JUNIOR, *adj.* (Winchester College).— Applied to all comparable objects. Of two neighbouring trees, the bigger is the 'senior' : there are a 'senior' and a 'JUNIOR' end to a table, a room etc. TIGHT JUNIOR =lowest of all.

JUNIPER, *subs.* (colloquial).—Gin. For synonyms *see* DRINKS etc. Also JUNIPER-BRANDY.

1857. J. E. RITCHIE, *Night Side of London*, p. 195. The pots of heavy and the quarterns of JUNIPER are freely quaffed.

JUNIPER-LECTURE, *subs.* (old).—A round scolding bout.—*Lex. Bal.* (1811).

JUNK, *subs.* (nautical).— 1. Salt beef : also OLD (or SALT) HORSE. [From being tough as old rope].

1760-61. SMOLLETT, *Sir L. Greaves*, II. i. 'Whom I value no more than old JUNK, pork-slush, or stinking stock fish.'

1830. MONCRIEFF, '*Old Booty*'. May the swabs live upon SALT JUNK.

1836. M. SCOTT, *Cringle's Log.* viii. I thought I could eat a bit, so I attacked the salt JUNK and made a hearty meal.

1837. MARRYAT, *Snarleyow*, C. XI. So while they cut their raw salt-JUNKS, With dainties You'll be crammed.

1840. HARWOOD, *Mess Table Chat.* A dry, mahogany looking lump of salt beef, aquatic JUNK, *Gallice* 'resistance.'

1891. R. L. STEVENSON, *Kidnapped*, p. 69. The meals were either of oatmeal porridge or salt JUNK.

**AFFIR**, *subs.* (common).— 1. A prostitute's bully ; a PONCE (*q.v.*). Hence a general term of contempt.

2. in pl. (Stock Exchange).— *See* quot. 1895.

1889. *The Rialto*, 23 March. Tintos climbed to 12¼, and even KAFFIRS raised their sickly heads.

1895. *Daily Telegraph*, 1 April, p. 1, col. 6. Advt KAFFIRS, as South African Mining shares are euphemistically called by dealers in the London Stock Exchange have been the leading market for the past few months.

KAIL. KAIL THROUGH THE REEK, *phr.* (Scots').—Bitter language or hard usage. [In allusion to the unpalateableness of smoky broth. TO GIVE ONE HIS KAIL THROUGH THE REEK = to revenge violently ; to punish with severity.]

1817. SCOTT, *Rob. Roy*, iii. 75. If he brings in the Glengyle folk, and the Glenfinlas and Balquhidder lads, he may come to GIE YOU YOUR KAIL THROUGH THE REEK.

1827-30. SCOTT, *Tales of my Landlord*, iii. 12. They set till the sodgers, and I think they GAE THEM THEIR KAIL THROUGH THE REEK.

KA ME, KA THEE, *phr.* (old Scots': now general).—'One good turn deserves another'; 'scratch my back and I'll scratch yours.' Also KA and KOB.

1547. HEYWOOD, *Poems on Proverbs*, E. 1 b. KA ME, KA THEE, one good tourne asketh another.

1605. JONSON, etc., *Eastward Hoe* [DODSLEY, *Old Plays*, iv. 221]. Thou art pandar to me for my wench, and I to thee for thy cousenage. K ME, K THEE, runs through court and country.

1608. ARMYN, *Nest of Ninnies*. But KAY ME, Ile KAY THEE ; give me an inch to day, Ile give thee an ell to morrow.

1611. BARRY, *Ram Alley* [DODSLEY, *Old Plays*, v. 494]. You know the law has tricks ; KA ME, KA THEE.

*d.*1625. LODGE, *Satire*, i. To keepe this rule—KAWE ME, and I KAWE THEE ; To play the saints whereas we divels be.

1630. TAYLOR, *Works*, Ep. 6. KA ME, KA THEE. My muse hath vow'd, revenge shall have her swindge To catch a parret in the woodcocks sprindge, etc.

1634. WITHAL, *Dict.*, p. 565. Manus manum fricat ; KA ME, KA THEE, one good turne requireth another.

1653. BROME, *The City Wit*, in *Wks.* (1873), i. 444. KA ME, KA THEE : an old kind of court service.

1658. ROWLEY, *Witch of Edmonton*, ii. 1. Il you'll be so kind as to KA ME one good turn, I'll be so courteous to KOB you another.

1659. MASSINGER, *City Madam*, ii. 1. We cash-keepers Hold correspondence, supply one another On all occasions. I can borrow for a week Two hundred pounds of one, as much of a second, A third lays down the rest ; and when they want, As my master's money comes in, I do repay it. KA ME, KA THEE.

1672. RAY, *Proverbs*, p. 126, s.v. Lend me an oath or testimony ; swear for me, and I'll do as much for you ; or CLAW ME, and I'LL CLAW YOU ; commend me, and I'll commend you.

JUNKET! *intj.* (Winchester College). —An exclamation of self-congratulation : *e.g.* 'JUNKET' I've got a 'remi'.

Verb. (Winchester College).— To exult over.—*Notions*.

JUNT, *subs.* (old).—A wanton. For synonyms *see* BARRACK-HACK and TART.

1608. MIDDLETON, *Trick to Catch*, v. i. Daintily abused ! you've put a JUNT upon me ;—a common strumpet.

JUPITER, *subs.* (Fleet St.).—*The Times* newspaper ; also JUPITER TONANS, or THE THUNDERER. JUPITER JUNIOR = *The Daily Telegraph.*

JURK, *subs.* (American thieves').— A seal ; a JARK (*q.v.*).—MATSELL (1859).

JURY, *subs.* (costermongers').—An assertion ; a profession.

JUST, *adv.* (colloquial).—In truth ; really ; 'rather'.

1892. MILLIKEN, '*Arry Ballads*, 13. Wouldn't I JUST !

JUSTUM, *subs.* (venery).—The *penis*. For synonyms *see* CREAMSTICK and PRICK.—URQUHART.

JYBE.—*See* GYBE.

JUTLAND, *subs.* (old).—The posteriors. For synonyms *see* BUM.

1695. CONGREVE, *Love for Love*, i. 5. Pretty round, heaving breasts, and a JUT with her bum, would stir an anchorite.

1721. KELLY, *Scottish Proverbs*, Lett. K. 21, s.v.

KANGAROO. KANGAROO DROOP, *subs. phr.* (common).—A feminine affectation (*cf.* GRECIAN BEND and ROMAN FALL): the hands are brought close to the breast and set to droop palm downward, as if muscular action were lost.

KANGAROO VOTING, *subs. phr.* (American political).—The Australian ballot system adopted, with sundry modifications, in many of the States.—NORTON.

KANITS, *subs.* (back slang).—A stink. KANITSENO = a stinking one.

KANT, *subs.* (common).—*See* CANT, *subs.*, sense 3.

KANUCK.—*See* CANACK.

KARIMPTION, *subs.* (American).—A gang ; a mob ; a party.

KARPLUNK, *intj.* (American).—*See* CACHUNK.

KATE (or **KATEY**), *subs.* (Old Cant). — 1. A picklock : *cf.* BETTY and JENNY.

1690. B. E., *Dict. Cant. Crew*, s.v. KATE. 'Tis a Rum KATE, that is a Clever Picklock.

1725. *New Cant. Dict.*, s.v.

1785. GROSE, *Vulg. Tongue*, s.v. KATE.

1859. MATSELL, *Vocabulum*, s.v. KATEY.

2. (old).—A wanton. Dutch, *Kat.*—MATSELL (1859). *See* KITTY.

1721. RAMSAY, *Lucky Spence's Last Advice*, in *Wks.* (*ut sup.*), ii. 304. Roun'd in his lug that there was a Poor country KATE, As halesum as the well of Spa, But unco blate.

KAZE, *subs.* (venery).—The female *pudendum.*—BURTON (*Thousand Nights, passim*). For synonyms *see* MONOSYLLABLE.

1882. PAYNE, *Book of the Thousand Nights etc.* 'The Porter of the Three Ladies of Baghdad'. Thy CAZE, thy tout, thy catso, thy coney.

KECK-HANDED, *adj.* (school).—Left-handed. [Prov. Eng. KECK = wrongly.]

KEDGER, *subs.* (nautical).—A mean fellow ; CADGER (*q.v.*): 'one in everybody's mess but in no one's watch'—an old term for a fisherman.'—AD. SMYTH.

KEEK-CLOY.—*See* KICKS.

KEEKER, *subs.* (Scots').—In pl. = the eyès. For synonyms *see* PEEPERS. From KEEK = to look ; to peer. *Cf.* PINTLE-KEEK.

KEEL, *subs.* (Scots').—The posteriors. For synonyms *see* BUM.

TO KEEL OVER, *verb. phr.* (colloquial).—To come to grief.

KEELBULLY, *subs.* (Old Cant).—*See* quot.

1690. B. E., *Dict. Cant. Crew*, s.v. KEELBULLIES, Lightermen that carry Coals to and from the Ships, so called in Derision.

1725. *New Cant. Dict.*, s.v.

1785. GROSE, *Vulg. Tongue*, s.v.

KEELHAUL (or **KEELRAKE**), *verb.* (Old nautical : now recognised or colloquial).—To punish offenders by dragging them under water on one side of the ship, and up again on the other, by ropes attached to the yard-arms on either side ; or in small vessels, under the craft from stem to stern. Hence, figuratively, to treat roughly ; to chastise.

1626. CAPT. J. SMITH, *Accidence*, in *Wks.* (ARBER) p. 790. The *Marshall* is to punish offendors, and to see *Justice* executed according to directions, as ducking at yards arme, HAWLING VNDER THE KEELE.

1690. B. E., *Dict. Cant. Crew*, s.v. KEEL-HALE, to draw by a Rope tied to the Neck, and fastned to a Tackle (with a jerk) quite under the Keel or bottom of the Ship.

1710. C. SHADWELL, *Fair Quaker of Deal*, i. May I be KEEL-HAWLED, if any man in the universe has more reformed the navy than myself.

1734. C. JOHNSON, *History of Highwaymen etc.*, 349. He was often whipp'd at the cap stern, put in the Bilboes, and once KEELHAULED.

1748. SMOLLETT, *Rod. Random*, iii. Whoever told him so was a lying, lubberly rascal, and deserved to be KEELHAULED.

1785. GROSE, *Vulg. Tongue*, s.v., KEEL-HAWLING.

1836. M. SCOTT, *Cringle's Log*, xii. While the old woman KEELHAULED me with a poker on one side, he jerked at me on the other, until at length he gave me a regular cross-buttock.

1837. MARRYAT, *Snarley Yow*, x. The unfortunate Smallbones was to be KEEL-HAULED.

KEELHAULING, *subs.* (old: now recognised).—*See* KEELHAUL: hence a good rating; rough treatment.

1785. GROSE, *Vulg. Tongue*, s.v.

1838. HALIBURTON, *Clockmaker*, 2. S. xxiii. 'There's a KEEL-HAULING in store for some of you that shall be nameless, as sure as you are born.'

KEEN, *subs.* (American cadets').—A funny story; a joke: TO GET OFF A KEEN = to make a witty remark.

KEEP, *subs.* (colloquial).—1. Board and lodging.

1861. T. HUGHES, *Tom Brown at Oxford*, I. viii. I performed some services to the College in return for my KEEP.

1869. BLACKMORE, *Lorna Doone*, xlvi. Moreover, we could not bear the idea that she should labor for her KEEP.

2. (colloquial).—A salaried mistress. *See verb.* sense 3.

Verb. (old and American).—1. To abide.

1593. SHAKSPEARE, *Titus Andr.*, v. 2, 5. Knock at his study where, they say, he KEEPS.

1613. BROWNE, *Brit. Past.*, I. iv. p. 87. The high top'd firres which on that mountain KEEPE, Have ever since that time beene seene to weepe.

1626. C. MORE, *Life & Death of Sir Thomas More*.'Letter to Dean Colet'. Yff the discommodities of the cittie doe, as they may very well, displease you, yet may the countrie about your parish of Stepney afforde you the like delights which that affordes you wherein now you KEEPE.

1633. FLETCHER, *Purple Island*, v. 25. Here stands the palace of the noblest sense,Here Visus KEEPS, whose court than crystal smoother, And clearer seems.

*d.*1656. HALL, *Satires*, v. p. 86. Would it not vex thee, where thy sires did KEEP, To see the dunged folds of dag-tail'd sheep?

1742-3. POPE, *Dunciad*, iv. 307. But chief her shrine where naked Venus KEEPS, And Cupids ride the Lion of the deeps.

1785. GROSE, *Vulg. Tongue*, s.v. KEEP, to inhabit; Lord, where do you KEEP, i.e. where are your rooms (academical phrase).

1790. WINTHROP, *Hist. New England*, I. 72. The Tarentines . . . rifled a wigwam where Mr.Cradock's men KEPT.

1795. *Gentleman's Magazine*, p. 118. He said I ought to have asked for his rooms, or inquired where he KEPT.

1866. M. ARNOLD, *Thyrsis*. But yet he could not KEEP Here with the shepherds and the silly sheep.

2. (old).—*See* quot. *Cf.* Scots' HAUD.

1724-27. RAMSAY, 'O Mither Dear, I Gin to Fear,' in *Wks.* (*at sup.*), II. 281. 'I 'gin to fear, Tho' I'm baith good and bonny, I wina KEEP; for in my sleep I start and dream of Johny.

1811. *Lex. Bal.*, s.v. KEEP . . . . Mother, your tit won't KEEP; your daughter will not preserve her virginity.

3. (colloquial).—To maintain a woman for bedservice. Hence KEEPER = a man who salaries a standing mistress; TO GO INTO KEEPING = to take service as a bed-fellow; TO TAKE INTO KEEPING = TO KEEP; KEPT-WOMAN = a salaried smock-servant; HOUSE-KEEPER [or HOUSE-BIT] (*q.v.*); KEEPING-CULLY (*q.v.*); etc. [*See* also BROME (*The City Wit*), *Dramatis Personæ* for 'two KEEPING women', where it seems to stand for lodging-house keeping.]

1579. NORTH, *Noble Grecians and Romanes*, 'Fabius Maximus' (in *Tudor Translations*, 1895, ii. 78). My good sister, there was a great speache in the Romaines campe that thou wert KEPT by one of the chiefest captaines of the garrison.

1640. RANDOLPH, *Poems etc.*, in *Wks.* [HAZLITT, (1875), ii, 539]. I wonder what should Madam Lesbia mean To KEEP young Histrio?

1663. KILLIGREW, *Parson's Wedding* [DODSLEY, *Old Plays* (1875), xiv. 379]. 'Will you KEEP me then?' 'KEEP thee! I'd marry thee as soon' . . . 'no, no KEEPING, I.' *Ibid.* 438. Rather than marry, KEEP a wench.

1678. DRYDEN, *All for Love*, Prol. The KEEPING tonies of the pit.

1679. DRYDEN, *Limberham* or The Kind KEEPER [*Title*].

1721. RAMSAY, *Morning Interview* (note), in *Wks.*, i. 281. A kind KEEPER.

1732. FIELDING, *Covent Garden Tragedy*. And I will let the sooty rascals see A Christian KEEPS a whore as well as they.

1773. GOLDSMITH, *She Stoops to Conquer*, i. 2. It was a saying in the place that he KEPT the best horses, dogs, and girls in the whole county.

1895. *Times*, 19 June, p. 5, col. 6. They allow their daughter, Alma, to be KEPT by Herr Mühlink's son.

TO KEEP ONE'S EYES SKINNED (POLISHED, OR PEELED, OR ONE'S WEATHER EYE LIFTED, NOSE OPEN, OR END UP, etc.) *verb. phr.* (common).—To take care; to maintain a position; to be wide-awake, or FLY (*q.v.*).

1847. PORTER, *Big Bear etc.*, p. 134. KEEP YOUR EYE SKINNED for sign, and listen for my horn.

1848. RUXTON, *Life in the Far West*, p. 14. 'Yep, old gal! and KEEP YOUR NOSE OPEN; thar's brown-skin about.

1887. FRANCIS, *Saddle & Mocassin*, 138. If you have business to attend to, you'd best go right along and do it. KEEP YOUR EYES SKINNED of course, but don't stay home.

1888. FROUDE, *The English in the West Indies*. Americans KEEP THEIR EYES SKINNED as they call it, to look out for other openings.

1890. W. C. RUSSELL, *Ocean Tragedy*, p. 88. I bade my friend Jack KEEP HIS EYE POLISHED.

1891. *Herald*, 19 July. 'Old fellow,' he said, 'we must go with them and KEEP OUR EYES PEELED, for they don't none of 'em mean to be square any more'n I do.'

1892. R. L. STEVENSON and L. OSBOURNE, *The Wrecker*, p. 21. 'Do you think,' Loudon, 'he replied,' that a man who can paint a thousand-dollar picture has not grit enough to KEEP HIS END UP in the stock market?

1892. *Ally Sloper's Half Holiday*, 19 Mar. p. 94, col. 3. 'Don't forget it's Leap Year 'Hity; KEEP YOUR WEATHER EYE PEELED.'

TO KEEP COMPANY, *verb. phr.* (old).—1. To go into society; to entertain often and be often entertained.

1658. BROME, *Covent Garden Weeded*, p. 24. Why, Sir, did not I KEEP COMPANY, think you, when I was young?

2. (colloquial).—To sweetheart: said of both sexes.

1835. DICKENS, *Sketches by Boz*, p. 140. Mr. Wilkins KEPT COMPANY with Jemima Evans.

TO KEEP A PIG, *verb. phr.* (Oxford University).—To have a lodger. [The PIG (*q.v.*) is usually a freshman who, the college being full, is quartered on a student whose rooms include two bedchambers.]

TO KEEP A STIFF UPPER LIP (or ONE'S PECKER UP), *verb. phr.* (general).—To stand firm; to keep up a heart; TO CHUCK OUT ONE'S CHEST.

TO KEEP THE DOCTOR, *verb. phr.* (common).—To retail adulterated drinks: *Cf.* DOCTOR.

TO KEEP CHAPEL, *verb. phr.* (University).—*See* quot. 1852.

1850. *Household Words*, ii. p. 161. 'As you have failed to make up your number of chapels the last two weeks,' such were the very words of the Dean, 'you will, if you please, KEEP every CHAPEL till the end of the term.'

1852. BRISTED, *Five Years etc.*, 32. The undergraduate is expected to go to Chapel eight times, or, in academic parlance, to KEEP eight CHAPELS a week.

TO KEEP *cave*, *verb. phr.* (Eton College).—To watch and give warning on a tutor's approach.

1883. BRINSLEY RICHARDS, *Seven Years at Eton*, ch. iv. Another had to mount guard in the passage, or on the staircase, TO KEEP *cave*.

TO KEEP DOWN THE CENSUS, *verb. phr.* (common.)—To procure abortion; to masturbate. Fr. *taper un môme*.

TO KEEP DARK (or IT DARK), *verb. phr.* (colloquial).—To keep secret.

1868. READE and BOUCICAULT, *Foul Play*, vii. I always thought it was a pity she KEPT IT SO DARK.

1888. J. RUNCIMAN, *The Chequers*, p. 120. I'll KEEP DARK.

1888. ROLF BOLDREWOOD, *Robbery Under Arms*, xii. It'll give us all we know to KEEP DARK when this thing gets into the papers.

1892. HUME NISBET, *Bushranger's Sweetheart*, p. 33. 'Never mind, Moll, I'll KEEP the next time DARK, you bet.'

TO KEEP SLOOM, *verb. phr.* (tailors').—To keep quiet.

TO KEEP IT UP, *verb. phr.* (common).—To continue anything vigorously; specifically to prolong a debauch.

1773. GOLDSMITH, *She Stoops to Conquer*, iii. 1. 'He mistook you for the barmaid, Madam!' 'Did he? Then, as I live, I am resolved to KEEP UP the delusion?'

1775. SHERIDAN, *Rivals*, i. 1. Their regular hours stupefy me—not a fiddle nor a card after eleven! However Mr. Faulkland's gentleman and I KEEP IT UP a little in private parties.

1788. G. A. STEVENS, *Adv. of a Speculist*, ii. 52. Yet they were KEEPING IT UP, as they called it; singing, though they wanted spirits.

1811. *Lex. Bal.*, s.v. We KEPT IT UP finely last night: metaphor drawn from the game of shuttlecock.

1836. DICKENS, *Pickwick* [ed. 1857] p. 443. We were KEEPING IT UP pretty tolerably at the stump last night.

1857-61. MAYHEW, *Lond. Lab. and Lond. Poor*, III. 57. We KEEPS IT UP for half an hour, or an hour . . . . if the browns tumble in well.

1879. *Athenæum*, July 5, p. 13, col. 2. He puts some excellent remarks on the question of KEEPING IT UP into a conversation among some of his Roman artists.

TO KEEP DRY, *verb. phr.* (American).—To hold one's tongue; TO KEEP DARK (*q.v.*).

1887. FRANCIS, *Saddle and Mocassin*, p. 295. Never let them get a chance at your sentiment; KEEP THAT DRY.

TO KEEP ONE BACK and BELLY, *verb. phr.* (common).—To feed and clothe.

FOR KEEPS, *phr.* (schoolboys').—To keep for good.

1886. *The Advance*, 9 Dec. We, the undersigned, promise not to play marbles FOR KEEPS, nor bet nor gamble in any way.

TO KEEP THE DOOR, *verb. phr.* (old).—To play the bawd.

TO KEEP THE POT BOILING, (colloquial).—To go on with anything; to 'keep the game alive'.

TO KEEP (or HOLD) ONE'S HAIR ON. *See* HAIR.

TO KEEP OPEN HOUSE, *verb. phr.* (tramps').—To sleep in the open air; TO DO A STAR PITCH. For synonyms *see* HEDGE-SQUARE.

TO KEEP UP TO THE COLLAR, *verb. phr.* (common).—To keep hard at work.

1861. J. HUGHES, *Tom Brown at Oxford*, II. ii. Hardy KEPT him pretty well UP TO THE COLLAR.

TO KEEP SHEEP BY MOONLIGHT, *verb. phr.* (old).—To hang in chains.

AS LONG AS I CAN BUY MILK I SHALL NOT KEEP A COW, *phr.* (venery).—*See* KEEP, *verb.* sense 3.

1680. BUNYAN, *Life and Death of Mr. Badman* [ed. 1696], p. 208. When . . . asked the reason he would make this answer. 'Who would KEEP A COW of their own THAT CAN HAVE A QUART OF MILK FOR A PENNY?' Meaning, who would be at the charge to have a wife that can have a whore when he listeth?

HE CAN'T KEEP A HOTEL, *phr.* (American).—A phrase intimating lack of administrative capacity.

KEEPING-CULLY, *subs.* (old).—A man who KEEPS (*q.v. verb.* sense 3).—B. E. (1690); *New Cant. Dict.* (1725); GROSE (1785); *Lex. Bal.* (1811).

KEFFEL, *subs.* (old).—A horse. For synonyms *see* PRAD.—B.E. (1690); *New Cant. Dict.* (1725); GROSE (1785); MATSELL (1859).

KEG, *subs.* (American).—The stomach. For synonyms *see* VICTUALLING OFFICE.

1887. FRANCIS, *Saddle and Mocassin*, p. 270. We'd been having a time and my KEG was pretty full too.

KEGMEG, *subs.* (common).— *See* quot.

1883. PAYN, *Thicker than Water*, xii. It was not unusual for Mrs. Beckett to seek half an hour's intimate talk with her young companion, which she playfully termed a KEG-MEG.

KEIFER, *subs.* (venery).—Generic for MUTTON (*q.v.*). For synonyms *see* MONOSYLLABLE.

KE-KEYA, *subs.* (American thieves').—The devil.—MATSELL (1859). For synonyms *see* SKIPPER.

KELDER, *subs.* (old).—The belly. *See* HANS-IN-KELDER and JACK-IN-THE-CELLAR.

1658. BROME, *New Academy*, p. 29. By this good tongue, no more than the unbegotten Hans I mean to clap into thy KELDER.

KELP, *subs.* (old).—A hat. For synonyms *see* GOLGOTHA. TO KELP = to raise one's hat in salutation.

1754. *Discoveries of John Poulter*, p. 30. We jostle him, and one knocks his KELP off.

1819. VAUX, *Memoirs*, s.v. KELP.

KELSO-BOOTS, *subs.* (Old Scots').—Heavy shackles put on the legs of prisoners; by some supposed to be a sort of stocks.—JAMIESON.

KELTER (or **KILTER**), *subs.* (old).—1. Order; condition; FORM (*q.v.*).

1630-50. BRADFORD, *Plymouth Plantation*, 235. Ye very sight of one (a gun) though OUT OF KILTER, was a terrour unto them.

1687. BARROW, *Sermons*, i. Ser. 6. If the organs of prayer are out of KELTER, or out of time, how can we pray.

1690. B. E., *Dict. Cant. Crew*, s.v. Out of KELTER, out of sorts.

1725. *New Cant. Dict.*, s.v.

1754. MARTIN, *Eng. Dict.*, 2nd ed., s.v.

1785. GROSE. *Vulg. Tongue.*, s.v.

1811. *Lex. Bal.*, s.v.

1859. MATSELL, *Vocabulum*, s.v.

1889. C.F.WOOLSON, *Jupiter Lights*, xviii. I'm a failure because I always see double, like a stereoscope OUT OF KILTER.

2. (old).—Money. For synonyms *see* ACTUAL and GILT. [Also provincial Yorkshire(HALLIWELL); and Scots' (JAMIESON)].

1789. GEO. PARKER, *Life's Painter*, p. 143, s.v.

KELTIE (or **KELTY**), *subs.* (Scots').—A bumper, imposed as a fine, on those who do not drink fair. [Said to be so called from a famous champion drinker in Kinrosshire.]

KEMESA. *See* CAMESA.

KEN, *subs.* (Old Cant).—1. A house; a place: generally in combination; *e.g.* BOOZING-KEN = drinking house; a BOB-KEN or BOWMAN-KEN = a well-furnished house; etc. TO BITE, or CRACK, A KEN = to rob a house.

ENGLISH SYNONYMS. Carsey (or case); castle; cat-and-mouse; crack; diggings; hang-out; rootee; roost; shop; panny.

ITALIAN SYNONYMS. *Canucha; tugurio.*

1567. HARMAN, *Caveat Man*, p. 86. Stowe your bene, cofe, and cut benat whydds, and byng we to rome vyle, to nyp a bong; so shall we haue lowre for the BOUSING KEN, and when we byng back to the deuseauyel, we wyll fylche some duddes of the Ruffemans, or myll the KEN for a bagge of dudes.

1609. DEKKER, *Lanthorne and Candlelight*. If we niggle or mill a BOUSING-KEN.

1610. ROWLANDS, *Martin Mark-all*, p. 39 (H. Club's Repr. 1874). KEN, an house. STAWLING KEN, a house to receive stolne goods, or a dwelling house.

1671. R. HEAD, *English Rogue*, pt. I., ch. vi., p. 54 (1874). We straight betook ourselves to the BOOZING KEN; and having bubb'd rumly, we concluded an everlasting friendship.

1690. B. E., *Dict. Cant. Crew*, s.v. KEN. A BOB KEN, or a BOWMAN-KEN, a good or well Furnished House, full of booty, worth robbing; also a House that Harbours Rogues and Thieves. Biting the KEN, Robbing the House.

1725. *New Cant. Dict.*, s.v. KEN. When we entered the KEN we leapt up the Dancers and fagotted all there. . . . 'tis a BOB-KEN, Brush upon the sneak.

1748. DYCHE, *Dictionary*, (5th ed.). KEN (S.) a cant name for a dwelling house of any sort, but more particularly cottages.

1785. GROSE, *Vulg. Tongue*, s.v.

1830. LYTTON, *Paul Clifford*, iv. Out of my KEN, you cur of the mange.

1837. DICKENS, *Oliver Twist*, p. 260. The bar of the KEN is filled with traps.

1851. MAYHEW, *London Labour and London Poor*, I., p. 336. The old woman (who kept the KEN), when any female, old or young, who had no *tin*, came into the kitchen, made up a match for her with some men.

1856. C. READE, *Never Too Late*, xlvii. We won't all go together. . . . you two meet me at Jonathan's KEN in an hour.

1859. MATSELL, *Vocabulum*, s.v.

1889. *Answers*, 27 July, p. 136, col. 1. My associations in the fourpenny lodging KEN were such as would have degenerated a stronger character than mine.

1892. HENLEY and STEVENSON, *Deacon Brodie*, Tab. ii, Sc. 1, p. 24. I had to look into a KEN to-night about the captain.

KEN-CRACKER (or **MILLER**), *subs.* (old).—A housebreaker. B. E. (1690); *New Cant. Dict.* (1725); GROSE (1785); MATSELL (1859).

KEN-CRACK-LAY, *subs.* (thieves').—Housebreaking. *See* KEN, CRACK, and LAY.

KENNEDY, *subs.* (common). *See* quot. TO GIVE KENNEDY = to lay in with a poker.

1864. *Athenæum*, 29 Oct., p. 559. St. Giles's perpetuates the memory of a. . . . man. . . . who was killed by a poker by calling that instrument a KENNEDY.

1887. HENLEY, *Villon's Good Night.* Paste 'em, and larrup 'em, and lam; GIVE KENNEDY and make 'em crawl.

KENNEL, *subs.* (old).—The female *pudendum.* For synonyms *see* MONOSYLLABLE. [*Cf.* Kennel, O. F. *canal* = a gutter or watercourse].

1647-80. ROCHESTER, *Bath Intrigues*. Twelve times I scoured the KENNEL 'twixt her thighs.

KENNEL-RAKER, *subs.* (old).—A scavenger; one fit only for low, dirty jobs.

1647. FLETCHER, *Prophetess*, iii. 1. Give your petitions in seemly sort, and keep your hat off decently, a fine periphrasis of a KENNEL-RAKER.

1655. *Comicall History of Francion* [quoted by NARES]. They heard behind them so great a hooping and hallowing of men and boys, and an outcry of women, that they were inforced to look back, and presently they discovered a young man, who had nothing but his shirt on his back, and not so much as shoes on his feet, who was followed by a number of the KENNELRAKERS, who made a perpetual shout.

d. 1735. *Arbuthnot*, *Wks.* (1751). I. 49. You did not love cruelty, you KENNEL-RAKER, you gibbet-carrier.

KENNURD, *adj.* (back slang).—Drunk. For synonyms *see* DRINKS and SCREWED.

KENT (or **KENT-RAG**, **KENT-CLOUT** *etc.*) *subs.* (common).—A colored cotton handkerchief.

KENTISH-FIRE, *subs.* (colloquial).—A prolonged and ordered salvo of applause. [From the cheers bestowed in Kent upon the No-Popery orators in 1828-9].

1865. J. H. BUCKSTONE in letter to *Morning Post*, 22 March. During the overture that peculiar beating of the feet known to a Dublin audience as the KENTISH FIRE was heard.

KENT-STREET EJECTMENT, *subs. phr.* (old).—*See* quot.

1785. GROSE, *Vulg. Tongue*, s.v. To take away the street door, a method practised by the landlords in KENT-ST., Southwark, when their tenants are above a fortnight's rent in arrear.

KERBSTONE-BROKER, *subs.* (common).—A stock-broker doing business outside the Stock-Exchange; a GUTTERSNIPE (*q.v.*). Fr. *un courtier marron*, and (collectively) *les coulissiers.*

KERFLOP, *intj.* (American).—Onomatopœic: in imitation of the sound of a body falling flat or into water.

VARIANTS: CACHUNK (*q.v.*); Kerslap; Kesouse; Keslosh; Keswosh; Kewosh; Keswollop; Kerchunk; Kerplunk; Kerthump; Kershaw; Kerslash; Kerslosh; Kerswosh, etc.

1843. *Major Jones's Courtship*, i. KERSLASH! I went rite over Miss Stallinses spinnin' wheel onto the floor.

1848. JONES, *Sketches of Travel*, p. 64. KERSLOSH went the water all over my feet.

b. 1852. *Traits of American Hamour*, p. 59. The first thing I knowed, I went KERSWASH into the drink.

d. 1867. BROWN ('Artemus Ward'). *The Shakers.* Shakers were all goin' KERSLAP to the Promist Land.

1887. FRANCIS, *Saddle & Mocassin.* He at last brought the whole tautological string down KERFLOP, full and fairly, upon the devoted crown of his auditor.

1888. *Fostorio Democrat*, 8 March. The fence broke down, and KERCHUNK! I went right through the ice all over.

1888. *Century Mag.* [quoted in *Americanisms*]. KERTHUMP! head over heels.

KERRY-SECURITY, *subs.* (old).—*See* quot.

1785. GROSE, *Vulg. Tongue*, s.v. KERRY-SECURITY, bond, pledge, oath, and keep the money.

KETCH, *subs.* (old).—A hangman; JACK KETCH (*q.v.*).

Verb. (American thieves').—To hang.

1859. MATSELL, *Vocabulum*, s.v. KETCH, I'll KETCH you; I'll hang you.

KETTLE, *subs.* (thieves').—1. A watch: RED-KETTLE = gold watch.

2. (nautical).—An iron-built vessel; an ironclad.

3. (venery).—The female *pudendum.* For synonyms *see* MONOSYLLABLE.

1719. DURFEY, *Pills to Purge etc.*, iii. 221. The tinker too with Mettle, Said he would mend her KETTLE, And stop up every Leak. *Ibid.* iv. 62. He never clencheth home a Nail, But his Trull holds up the KETTLE.

POT CALLING THE KETTLE BLACK, *phr.* (common).—On 'all fours'; 'Six of one and half a dozen of the other.'

1890. *Tit Bits*, 30 Aug. p. 332, col. 1. It was almost a case of the POT CALLING THE KETTLE BLACK, certainly; but the rebuke lost none of its point, nevertheless.

A PRETTY (or FINE) KETTLE (or KIDDLE = basket) OF FISH, *subs. phr.* (common).—A mess or confusion of any kind; a muddle.

1750. FIELDING, *Tom Jones*, VI. x. 'There is a fine KETTLE OF FISH made o't up at our house!' 'What can be the matter, Mr. Western?' said Allworthy.

1811. *Lex. Bal.*, s.v. KETTLE-OF-FISH. When a person has perplexed his affairs in general, or any particular business, he is said to have made a fine KETTLE OF FISH of it.

1835. C. SELBY, *Catching an Heiress*, ii. La, miss, you must be joking; you can't be what you ayn't, you'd be sure to be found out, and then there'd be a pretty KETTLE OF FISH.

1849. DICKENS, *David Copperfield*, xix. I intend, Trotwood, to get that done immediately . . . and then—there'll be a PRETTY KETTLE OF FISH!

1864. *Tangled Talk*, p. 337. It is an easy thing . . . to make a KETTLE OF FISH of one's whole existence.

KETTLEDRUM, *subs.* (old).—1. In plural = a woman's breasts. Also CUPID'S KETTLEDRUM.

1785. GROSE, *Vulgar Tongue*, s.v.

2. (common).—An afternoon tea-party.

1867. LATHAM, *Dict.*, s.v. KETTLEDRUM. Either recent or revived, this word is about two years old.

1869. MRS. H. WOOD, *Roland Yorke*, ch. xiii. Mrs. Bede Greatorex had cards out for that afternoon, bidding the great world to a KETTLE-DRUM; and she was calculating what quantities of ices and strawberries to order in.

1878. HATTON, *Cruel London*, I. iii. Men are as frivolous and as full of gossip and scandal as the tabbies at a West End KETTLE-DRUM.

1888. *Detroit Free Press*, 8 Dec. 'Won't it be rather hard at first to give up all the pink suppers and KETTLEDRUMS and afternoon what-do-you-call-'ems?' with a suspicion of a grin on his face.

1890. *Daily Telegraph*, 28 Jan. The ladies' KETTLEDRUM is not to be shut against male sympathisers, and gentlemen duly provided with tickets are to be suffered to join in the festivities.

KEW, *subs.* (back slang).—A week.

KEY, *subs.* (venery).—1. The *penis*: *i.e.* THE KEY that lets a man in and the maid out. For synonyms *see* CREAMSTICK and PRICK.

1772. G. A. STEVENS, *Songs Comic & Satyrical* [1788]. Here's . . . the lock of all locks and unlocking the same . . . That lock has the casket of Cupid within it, So——here's to the KEY, lads,—the critical minute.

2. (common).—A translation; a CRIB (*q.v.*).

TO HAVE THE KEY OF THE STREET, *verb. phr.* (common).—To be locked out of doors; to have no home.

1836. DICKENS, *Pickwick*, xlvii. 'There,' said Lowten, 'it's too late now. You can't get in to-night, you've got the KEY OF THE STREET, my friend.' 'Never mind me,' replied Job. 'I can sleep anywhere.'

1843. W. T. MONCRIEFF, *The Scamps of London*, I. 1. *Char.* Left your lodgings—and why, sir? *Bob.* Why?—why because the chimney smoked, my adorable; and then the paper of my rooms wasn't fashionable enough—(*aside*)—and the landlady gave me the KEY OF THE STREET.

1888. *Daily Telegraph*, 28 Dec. Society would, perhaps, be startled and saddened to know how numerous those were upon the great holiday who had the KEY OF THE STREET for home, and a crust of bread by way of Christmas banquet.

KEYHOLE, *subs.* (venery).—The female *pudendum.* *See* KEY. For synonyms *see* MONOSYLLABLE.

TO BE ALL KEYHOLE (or KEYHOLED), *verb. phr.* (common).—To be drunk. For synonyms *see* DRINKS and SCREWED.

KEYHOLE-WHISTLER, *subs.* (tramps').—A night's lodger in a barn or outhouse; a SKIPPERBIRD (*q.v.*).

1851-61. MAYHEW, *Lond. Lab. etc.* i. 339. KEYHOLE WHISTLERS, the skipperbirds are sometimes called, but they're regular travellers.

KEYSTONE OF LOVE, *subs. phr.* (venery).—The female *pudendum.* For synonyms *see* MONOSYLLABLE.

KEYSTONE STATE, *subs. phr.* (American). — Pennsylvania. [When the names of the original Thirteen States were arranged archwise in their natural geographical order, Pennsylvania occupied the central position].

KIBOSH, *subs.* (common).—1. Nonsense; anything worthless. Also KIBOSHERY.

1885. *Punch*, Jan. 3, p. 4. Still I wish you a 'Appy New Year, if you care for the KIBOSH, old chappie.

2. (East End).—SNOT (*q.v.*).

3. (common).—Style; fashion; form; 'the thing': *e.g.*, that's the proper KIBOSH.

Verb. (common).—To spoil; TO FLUMMOX (*q.v.*), TO QUEER (*q.v.*); to bewilder or knock out of time.

1892. MILLIKEN, *'Arry Ballads*, p. 5. They KIBOSHED the power of the quid. *Ibid.* p. 50. A dig in the ribs and a 'owl, Seemed to KIBOSH the Frenchmen completely.

TO PUT THE KIBOSH ON, *verb. phr.* (common).—1. To stop; to silence. (2) To wheedle or talk over. (3) To run down.

1836. DICKENS, *Sketches by Boz*, p. 40. 'What do you mean by hussies?' interrupts a champion of the other party . . . . ('Hooroar,' ejaculates a pot-boy in parenthesis, 'put the KYE-BOSH on her, Mary!')

1856 *Punch*, vol. 31. p. 139. I ope the Assistans of your powrful Penn to put the CIBOSH upon the Siety for the Perwention of wot they calls crulety to Hanimals.

KIBSY. *See* KYPSY.

KICK, *subs.* (old).—1. The fashion.

1690. B. E., *Dict. Cant. Crew*, s.v. KICK, a High KICK, the top of the Fashion; also singularity therein.

1725. *New Cant. Dict.*, s.v.

1785. GROSE, *Vulg. Tongue*, s.v. KICK. It is all THE KICK, it is the present mode.

*d.*1814. DIBDIN [quoted in *Century*]. 'Tis THE KICK, I say, old 'un, so I brought it down.

1833. NEAL, *Down Easters*, v. p. 64. What do ye pay for sech a pair o' boots as them in Eurup? Newest fashion out here—all THE KICK, I spose, hey?

*d.*1836. GEO. COLMAN the Younger [quoted by BREWER]. I cocked my hat, and twirled my stick, And the girls they called me quite THE KICK.

2. (old).—A sixpence: of compound sums only, *e.g.* 'three and a KICK' = 3s. 6d. For synonyms *see* BENDER.

1725. *New Cant. Dict.*, s.v.

1785. GROSE, *Vulg. Tongue*, s.v.

1823. MONCRIEFF, *Tom & Jerry*, iii, 3. 'What's to pay landlord?' . . . : 'Fourteen bob and a KICK your honor.'

1834. H. AINSWORTH, *Rookwood*, III. xiii. 'Two coach-wheels [crowns], half a bull [half a crown], three hogs [shillings], and a KICK.'

1860. *Punch*, xxxix, p. 97. Moshesh is a brick; This cost but ten and a KICK.

1864. *Soiled Dove*, p. 263. 'Six bob and a KICK, if so be as the holes are mended.'

1871. *Echo*, 15 May. 'What do you mean by telling me that you will take it away for a KICK?' 'Wot do I mean? why wot I say; I'll do the job for sixpence, and me and my mate 'ull sweep up any mess we makes as well.'

1871. *Figaro*, March. Let persons addicted to the use of slang, in whose dialect two-and-a-KICK means half-a-crown, remark, if they please, that they would twelve times rather have a KICK than a half-penny.

3. (common).—A moment; a JIFFY (*q.v.*)

4. (thieves').—*See* quot. 1859. For synonyms *see* POGE.

1859. MATSELL, *Vocabulum*, s.v. KICK. The Moll stubbled her skin in her KICK, the woman held her purse in her pocket.

1869. GREENWOOD, *Night in a Workhouse*. I rifled his KICK of his shiners so fine.

5. (American).—A grudge.

1887. FRANCIS, *Saddle and Mocassin*, p. 308. I haven't got any KICK against Don Juan.

6. (trade).—The hollow in the butt of a bottle.

1851-61. MAYHEW, *Lond. Lab. etc.*, II. 511. Some bottles has great KICKS at their bottoms.

1864. *Scotsman*, 29 June, ... fraudulently manufactured bottles, which by reason of an oblong cavity in the bottom (called in London a KICK) contain from 10 to 20 per cent less than the due quantity.

1864. *Left Her Home*, p. 65. The bottle fell on the KICK, and being made of strong glass. . . . did not break.

7. *in pl.* (old).—Breeches; trousers. Also KICKSTERS and KICKSIES: *cf.* HAMS.

ENGLISH SYNONYMS. Arse-rug; bum-bags; bell-bottoms; bum-curtain; bags; calf-clingers; CANVASSEENS, (*q.v.*); continuations; don't-name-'ems; ducks; gamcases; hams; inexpressibles; ineffables; inimitables; kicks; kickseys; moles; mustn't-mention-'ems; PEG-TOPS (*q.v.*); pants; rice-bags; sit-upons; SKILTS (*q.v.*); SLACKS (*q.v.*); strides; trolly-wags; trucks; TRUNKS(*q.v.*); unhintables; unmentionables; unutterables; unwhisperables; WHISTLING BREECHES (*q.v.*).

FRENCH SYNONYMS. *Unbenard* (popular); *la braillande* or *braillarde* (thieves'); *les calinettes* (common); *la cotte* (= blue canvass working trousers); *la culbute* or *le culbutant* (thieves'); *un fourreau* (thieves' = sheath); *le fusil à deux coups* (popular = the double-barrel); *les grimpants* (popular); *les inexpressibles* (from the English); *les haut-de-tire*(thieves'); *le montant*.

PORTUGUESE SYNONYM. *Os trózes*.

1690. B. E., *Dict. Cant. Crew*, s.v. KICKS, breeches.

1714. *Memoirs of John Hall* (4th ed.) p. 12. KICKSEY, Breeches.

1725. *New Cant. Dict.*, s.v. Tip us your KICKS, we'll have them as well as your Lour.

1785. GROSE, *Vulgar Tongue*, s.v.

1811. *Lex. Bal.*, s.v.

1819. MOORE, *Tom Crib*, p. 13. That bedizen'd old Georgy's bang-up togs and KICKS.

1823. MONCRIEFF, *Tom and Jerry*, p. 6. *Reg.* Stick it into him for a new pair of KICKSES, by-and-by.

1834. AINSWORTH, *Rookwood*, iii. 5. Jist twig his swell KICKSEYS and *pipes;* if they ain't the thing, I'm done.

1859. SALA, *Gaslight and Daylight*, xxx. 'There's togs, too,' he pursued, looking with proper pride at his own attire, 'the sooner you peels off them cloth KICKSIES the better.'

1859. G. W. MATSELL, *Vocabulum, or the Rogue's Lexicon*. Kersey-mere KICKSIES, any colour, built very slap with the artful dodge, from three caroon.

*c.*1867. *Broadside Ballad*, 'The Chickaleary Bloke'. Now kool my downy KICKSIES. . . . Built upon a plan very naughty.

1883. *Daily Telegraph*, August 7, p. 6, col. 1. What he termed 'the saucy cut of his KICKSIES,' and which, rendered into intelligible English, signified the smart style of his trousers.

1885. *The Stage*, p. 129. Whitechapel costers who wore slap-up KICKSIES, with a double fakement down each side, and artful buttons at bottom.

1892. MILLIKEN, *'Arry Ballads*, 76. He'd a apron, Charlie, and KICKSIES as must ha' been cut by his wife.

1892. HUME NISBET, *Bushranger's Sweetheart*, p. 31. 'A good thing Cinderella's grand ball was a little before your time, Stringy, or she'd been out of it with these KICKSEYS,' remarked Tony Peters gravely.

8. (common).—A sudden and strong objection; unexpected resistance.

Verb.(common).—1. To borrow or beg; TO BREAK SHINS (*q.v.*). For synonyms *see* SHINS. Specifically to ask for drink money.

1858. A. MAYHEW, *Paved with Gold*, p. 254. Ned Purchase suggested that they might as well try and KICK him for some coppers.

2. (colloquial).—To protest; to resist; to resent.

1611. *Bible*, Authorised Version. 1 Sam. II. 29. Wherefore KICK ye at my sacrifice?

1847. TENNYSON, *Princess*, iv. 393. You hold that woman is the better man: A rampant heresy, such as, if it spread, Would make all women KICK against their Lords.

1871. *Daily News*, 29 Dec. The love of pleasure he's been encouraged in won't make him KICK against useful information.

1888. *Detroit Free Press*, 13 Oct. There are 10,000 baby carriages in Chicago. They obstruct the travel of 200,000 people. I KICK.

1889. *Nation*, xlviii. 137. In a late number you maintain strongly that it is the duty of persons suffering from overcharges, insolence and other forms of oppression, to KICK.

1889. *Bird O'Freedom*, 7 Aug., p. 6. When it comes to editors waking up and tackling hard-worked foremen by the neck, then I KICK.

1891. *Morning Advertiser*, 6 April. The men certainly KICKED against this increase.

1892. MILLIKEN, *'Arry Ballads*, p. 25. KICK at my lingo.

3. (common).—To recoil: of fire-arms generally.

1871. *Observer*, 24 Dec. Much calculated, when fired, to develop a quality known as KICKING.

4. (American).—To jilt; TO GIVE THE MITTEN (*q.v.*).

5. (American).—To die: an abbreviation of TO KICK THE BUCKET (*q.v.*).

6. (old).—*See* quot. For synonyms *see* AMPUTATE and SKEDADDLE. Also KICK IT.

1725. *New Cant. Dict.*, s.v. KICK'D. The Rum Cull KICK'D away, *i.e.*, The Rogue made his escape.

KICK IN THE GUTS, *subs. phr.* (old).—A dram of spirits.—GROSE (1785).

TO GET MORE KICKS THAN HA' PENCE, *verb. phr.* (colloquial). —*See* MONKEY'S ALLOWANCE.

1861. TROLLOPE, *Framley Parsonage*, xix. In all this matter I have harassed myself greatly to oblige you, and in return I have GOT MORE KICKS THAN HALFPENCE.

1824. SCOTT, *St. Ronan's*, xxxiv. 'Which is like monkey's allowance, I suppose,' said the traveller, 'MORE KICKS THAN HALFPENCE.'

1856. C. KINGSLEY, *Letter*, May [3rd abridged ed. 1579]. You fellows worked like bricks, spent money, and got midshipman's half-pay (nothing a day, and find yourself) and monkey's allowance (MORE KICKS THAN HALF-PENCE).

TO KICK OVER THE TRACES, *verb. phr.* (colloquial).—(1) To GO THE PACE (*q.v.*); and (2) to resist authority.

1861. H. KINGSLEY, *Ravenshoe*, xlii. 'I'll go about with the rogue. He is inclined to KICK OVER THE TRACES, but I'll whip him in a little.'

1892. MILLIKEN, *'Arry Ballads*, p. 10. It's a sort of KICK-OVER-THE-TRACES, a thing as all females enjoy.

TO KICK UP A BREEZE (or DUST, ROW, DIVERSION, LARK, SHINDY, etc.) *verb. phr.* (common).—To create a disturbance; TO RAISE CAIN (*q.v.*); TO PAINT THE TOWN RED (*q.v.*).

1759. SMOLLETT, *Letter to Wilkes*, quoted in D. Hannay's *Smollett* (1887), p. 132. If the affair cannot be compromised we intend to KICK UP A DUST, and die hard.

1764. O'HARA, *Midas*, I. ii. Nor doubt I, with my voice, guitar, and person, Among the nymphs to KICK UP SOME DIVERSION.

1770. COLMAN, *Oxonian in Town*, I. ii. Ten to one but there's a riot—we'll KICK UP A DUST, I warrant you.

1771. G. A. STEVENS, *Songs Comic and Satyrical*, 144. The patron of voices said 'twould go for the wench Unless that A DUST he could KICK UP.

*d.*1796. BURNS, *The Rights of Women*. Would swagger, swear, get drunk, KICK UP A RIOT.

1812. COOMBE, *Syntax, Picturesque*, C. xxii. I wish to know, Sir, what you mean, By KICKING UP, Sir, such A SCENE!

1819. MOORE, *Tom Crib*, p. 5. Something may happen to KICK UP A BREEZE.

1844. *Puck*, p. 14. The ROWS that they might KICK UP.

1871. *Louisville Courier*, 19 Mar. The ill-treatment of Mr. Sumner will not be borne patiently by his friends and the New England States; it is sure to KICK UP A ROW in the Republican party.

1878. JAS. PAYN, *By Proxy*, ii. He means that you are much too excited to be sane; that you are apt to KICK UP A ROW about nothing at all.

TO KICK THE WIND, *verb. phr.* (old).—*See* quot. For synonyms *see* ALOFT.

1598. FLORIO, *Worlde of Wordes*, *Dar de' calci a Rouaio*, to be hang'd, TO KICKE THE WINDE.

TO GET THE KICK OUT (or DIRTY KICK OUT).— To be summarily dismissed, discharged, or 'kicked out'.

TO KICK THE BUCKET, *verb. phr.* (common).—To die. For synonyms *see* ALOFT. Also KICK and TO KICK STIFF.—[TAYLOR: The allusion is to the way in which a slaughtered pig is hung up—viz., by passing the ends of a bent piece of wood behind the tendons of the hind legs, and so suspending it to a hook in a beam above. This piece of wood is locally termed a BUCKET, and so by a coarse metaphor the phrase came to signify to die. Another says: To commit suicide by hanging; from a method planned and carried out by an ostler at an inn on the Great North Road. Standing on a bucket, he tied himself up to a beam in the stable, he then KICKED THE BUCKET.] In West Indies KICKERABOO: *see* also KICK THE WIND.

1785. GROSE, *Vulg. Tongue*, s.v. KICKS. He KICKED THE BUCKET one day, he died one day.

1796. WOLCOT ('Peter Pindar'), *Tristia* (in *Wks.* 1812), v. 242. Pitt KICKED THE BUCKET.

1797. M. G. LEWIS, *Castle Spectre*, Epilogue. I drew my knife, and in his bosom stuck it; He fell, you clapped—and then he KICKED THE BUCKET!

1812. COLMAN, *Poetical Vagaries*, p. 55. Near thee doth a BUCKET dangle. Chieftain, leave me not to drown; Save a maid without a smicket. If the BUCKET come not down, Soon shall I be doom'd to KICK IT.

1836. M. SCOTT, *Tom Cringle's Log*, xvi. Dat I believe him will eat till him KICKERIBOO of sorefat (surfeit, I presumed).

1838. SELBY, *Jacques Strop*, i. 1. A narrow escape of KICKING THE BUCKET, was it not—eh, you rascal?

1849. KINGSLEY, *Alton Locke*, ii. Fine him a pot roared one, for talking about KICKING THE BUCKET.

1853. *Diogenes*, ii. It is inferrible (on account of her great dislike to the detective officer) that she, as well as Lady Dedlock, KICKED THE BUCKET.

1858. *Notes and Queries*, 1 S. ix. 107. (*q.v.*).

1859. MATSELL, *Vocabulum*, s.v.

1867. JAS. GREENWOOD, *Purgatory of Peter the Cruel*, i. Tony Warren, with tears in his honest eyes, endeavouring to pour rum down the body's throat, while in kindliest tones he begged of it to look up, or at least make some sign that he had not quite KICKED THE BUCKET.

1871. *London Figaro*, 28 Jan. Yes! I'm going to KICK THE BUCKET.

1888. J. RUNCIMAN, *The Chequers*, 48. The Ramper fawned on me, and asked me if I had heard of 'that pore bloke wot KICKED THE BUCKET upstairs.'

1890. GRANT ALLEN, *Tents of Shem*, x. I've very little doubt Sir Arthur, selfish pig though he is, will do the right thing in the end before he KICKS THE BUCKET.

1892. HUME NISBET, *Bail Up*, p. 105. Four on them sickened all at once in the camp we had struck, and after they had KICKED IT, my two mates went with me.

1892. *Ally Sloper*, 27 Feb., p. 67, col 2. But a miserly aunt KICKS THE BUCKET at last And leaves you the fortune which she has amassed.

TO KICK DOWN THE LADDER, *verb. phr.* (colloquial).—To treat with contumely one's means of advancement.

1848. THACKERAY, *Book of Snobs*, viii. She has struggled so violently for polite reputation that she has won it; pitilessly KICKING DOWN THE LADDER, as she advanced, degree by degree.

TO KICK THE CLOUDS(or WIND), *verb. phr.* (thieves').—*See* quot. For synonyms *see* LADDER.

1811. *Lex. Bal.*, s.v. KICK THE BUCKET. TO KICK THE CLOUDS before the hotel door, *i.e.* to be hanged.

TO KICK AT WAIST, *verb. phr.* (tailors').—To misfit at the waist.

TO KICK FOR THE BOOT, *verb. phr.* (tailors').—To ask for money.

TO KICK FOR TRADE, *verb. phr.* (tailors').—To ask work.

TO HAVE THE KICK, *verb. phr.* (Athletic).—To be lucky; to have COCUM (*q.v.*).—[From football].

To KICK THE STUFFING OUT OF ONE, *verb. phr.* (American).—To maltreat; to take a rise, or the wind out of; to get the better of.

TO KICK (or COOL) ONE'S HEELS.—1. *See* HEELS.

2. *verb. phr.* (old).—*See* quot. For synonyms *see* ALOFT.

1598. FLORIO, *Worlde of Wordes, Fare il pane*, to dye, TO KICK VP ONES HEELES.

TO KICK THE EYE OUT OF A MOSQUITO, *verb.phr.* (Australian).—A superlative expression of capacity.

1888. ROLF BOLDREWOOD, *Robbery Under Arms*, xi. He could KICK THE EYE OUT OF A MOSQUITO.

A KICK IN ONE'S GALLOP, *subs. phr.* (old).—A whim; a strange fancy.

KICKER, *subs.* (American).—1. An obstructionist; a protestant.

1888. *Rochester Herald.* The chronic KICKER is always on hand when any improvement is proposed.

1888. *Detroit Free Press*, 20 Oct. I really and truly believe that the day will come when the KICKER will be classed where he belongs and be entitled to the reverence due him.

.... *Eclectic Review* (Amer.), xiii. 6. There is, of course, a class of chronic KICKERS who are always finding fault.

2. in pl. (common).—The feet. For synonyms *see* CREEPERS.

3. (old).—A dancing master.

1838. SELBY, *Dancing Master*, sc. II. It is the KICKER, sure enough: what am I to do? If I go out, I shall nap it.

KICKERABOO. *See* KICK THE BUCKET.

KICKING-IN, *subs.* (Winchester College).—*See* quot.

1870. MANSFIELD, *School-Life at Winchester College*, p. 138. But football wasn't all beer and skittles to the Fags. There was an institution called KICKING IN, which, while it lasted, was much worse than 'watching out' at cricket, although it had the very great merit of not continuing so long; for, even on a whole holiday, we seldom had more than two hours of it.

KICKING-STRAP, *subs.* (tailors').—An elastic strap inside a habit.

KICKSEYS, *subs.* (old).—1. *See* KICK, *subs.* sense 7.

2. (old).—Shoes or 'highlows'. Also KICKSIES.

1823. BEE, *Dict. of the Turf*, s.v. KICKSEES.

KICKSHAW, *subs.* (old: now recognised).—A trifle; anything fanciful or unsubstantial; something fantastical or with no particular name. [SKEAT: a curious corruption of Fr. *quelque-chose* (pronounced *kick-chose*) literally, something; hence a trifle or small delicacy].

1598. SHAKSPEARE, 2 *Henry IV*, v. 1. 29. A joint of mutton, and any pretty little tiny KICKSHAWS, tell William, cook.

1601. SHAKSPEARE, *Twelfth Night*, i. 3. *Sir And.* . . . . I delight in masques and revels sometimes altogether. *Sir To.* Art thou good at these KICKSHAWES, knight?

1611. COTGRAVE, *Dictionarie*, s.v. *Fricandeaux*, short, skinlesse, and dainty puddings, or QUELKCHOSES, made of good flesh and herbs chopped together, etc.

*b.*1625. FLETCHER, *Elder Brother*, iii. 2. New KICKSHAWS and delicate made things.

1630. JOHN TAYLOR, *The Great Eater of Kent*, p. 12. All is welcome; whether it be sawsedge, mackeroone, KICKSHAW, or tantadlin.

1646. FEATLEY, *Dippers Dipt*, p. 199. I made bold to set on the board KICKCHOSES, and variety of strange fruits.

1753. *Adventurer*, No. 25. She has no taste for nicknacks, and KICKSHAWS, and whim-whams.

1822. SCOTT, *Fortunes of Nigel*, xxi. I have given up. . . . roastbeef and pudding for woodcocks and KICKSHAWS.

1830. MARRYAT, *King's Own*, xxxiv. I seldom touch anything but the joint. I hate your KICKSHAWS.

1881. BESANT and RICE, *Sweet Nelly*, in *Ten Years' Tenant etc.*, vol. i. p. 188. Falbalas for your frocks, quilted petticoats, gold KICKSHAWS, china, pet negro boys.

KICK-SHOE, *subs.* (old).—A dancer; a caperer; a buffoon.

KICKSIES. *See* KICKS.

KICKSY, *adj.* (old).—Troublesome; disagreeable.

KICKSY-WICKSY, *subs.* (old).—A term of contempt for a woman.

1598. SHAKSPEARE, *All's Well etc.* ii. 3. He wears his honour in a box, unseen, That hugs his KICKSY-WICKSEY here at home.

1658. BROME, *Covent Garden Weeded*, p. 17. This KICKSY-WINSY giddi brain will spoil all.

Adj. (old).—Fantastic; restless.

KICK-UP, *subs.* (common).—A row. Also ROWDINESS.

*b.*1794. WOLCOT ('Peter Pindar'), *Odes of Condolence*, in *Wks.* (1794), iii. 259. There'd be a pretty KICK-UP—what a squall.

1850. SMEDLEY, *Frank Fairleigh*, p. 132. 'I tell you what,' said Lawless, 'the row and bother, and the whole KICK-UP altogether, has made me alarmingly hungry.'

1864. DICKENS, *Our Mutual Friend*, III. xiii. Not at all caring for. . . . the precious KICK-UP and row that will come off.

1892. MILLIKEN, *'Arry Ballads*, p. 69. As to colour, and KICK-UP, our party was well to the front.

KID, *subs.* (old).—1. A child. Hence, TO KID = to lie in: also = to get with child; KIDDED or WITH KID = pregnant; KID-LEATHER and KID-STRETCHER (*q.v.*). Also KIDDY.

ENGLISH SYNONYMS. Brat; encumbrance; get; imp; infantry (collectively); kinchin; limb; lullaby cheat; monkey; papoose; youngster.

FRENCH SYNONYMS. *Un* or *une gosse* (general: also *gossemar*); *un gluant* (thieves': a sticker); *un loupiau* or *loupiot* (popular); *un marmousin* (popular = little monkey); *un mignard* (an endearment); *un mion* (thieves'); *un momaque* (thieves'); *un momard* or *momignard* (popular); *un môme* (popular); *un morbaque* (pop. a disagreeable child); *un moucheron* (popular); *un moufflet* (popular); *un mounin* (thieves').

ITALIAN SYNONYMS. *Fantasima; fiacco* (= weak); *cifo; cifon; pivastro; pivo; smerlo.*

1599. MIDDLETON etc., *Old Law*, iii. 2. I am old, you say; Yes, parlous old, KIDS, and you mark me well!

1690. B. E., *Dict. Cant. Crew*, s.v.

1690. D'URFEY, *Collin's Walk*, iv. And at her back a KID that cry'd Still as she pinch'd it, fast was ty'd.

1694. DRYDEN, *Love Triumphant*, Epilogue, 19. What if he taught our sex more cautious carriage, And not to be too coming before marriage; For fear of my misfortune in the play, A KID brought home upon the wedding-day?

1714. *Memoirs of John Hall* (4th ed.) p. 12. KID, A child.

1719. DURFEY, *Pills to Purge*, i. 321. And thus he to an old Midwife hied, To bring the poor KID to light, Sir.

1725. *New Cant. Dict.*, s.v.

1748. T. DYCHE, *Dictionary*, (5th ed.) KID (S.). . . . also a nickname for a child or young person.

1785. GROSE, *Vulg. Tongue*, s.v.

1811. *Lex. Bal.*, s.v. KID. The blowen has napped the KID, the girl is with child.

1819. MOORE, *Tom Crib*, 5. That KID, Master Nap.

1840. THACKERAY, *Comic Almanack*, p. 237. 'Cox's Diary'. Carry you, and your KIDS, and your traps etc.

1856. READE, *Never too Late to Mend*, xxiii. A fig for being drowned, if the KID is drowned.

1859. MATSELL, *Vocabulum*, s.v.

1865. KINGSLEY, *The Hillyars and the Burtons*, xxx. Why, that six shillings as you men are asking for, is six shillings off the KIDS' victuals.

1868. *Cassell's Mag.*, 4 Jan., p. 213. If you'd have been as full of her when she was a KID, and not have left her to us so much, it might have been sumfink to brag about.

1870. *London Figaro*, 19 Oct. 'After the Fire.' In this room, sir, said my gallant conductor, lived a bricklayer with his wife and two KIDS. *He* made that hole in the wall, and got 'em safe through—the whole caboose on 'em; and a jolly good job he did.

1871. *London Figaro*, 13 May, p. 4, col. 2. 'Yer see I knowed 'er, sir, right from a KID, Loved 'er right from a boy.

1882. JAS. PAYN, *Thicker than Water*, i. He thinks how his Missis and the KIDS would enjoy the spectacle, and is half-inclined to fetch them.

1883. *Daily Telegraph*, March 27, p. 2, col 1. They were afraid of being ridiculed and laughed at by their companions for sinking their manhood and going as KIDS to a dame school.

1889. *Time*, Aug., p. 151. A reminiscence of my father, the which, now I'm not a KID, I see the value of.

1892. KIPLING, *Barrack-room Ballads*, 'Fuzzy-Wuzzy'. Then 'ere's to you Fuzzy-Wuzzy, and the Missus and the KID.

2. (common).—A man.

1811. *Lex. Bal.*, s.v.

1830. SIR E. B. LYTTON, *Paul Clifford*, p. 28. ed. 1854. 'Vy, Paul, my KID, you looks down in the chops; cheer up, care killed a cat.'

1834. W. H. AINSWORTH, *Rookwood*. Two milling coves, each vide avake, Vere backed to fight for heavy stake; But in the mean time, so it vos, Both KIDS agreed to play a CROSS.

1892. HUME NISBET, *Bushranger's Sweetheart*, p. 118. He is like all colonial KIDS, don't know when he is well off.

3. (thieves').—*See* quot.

1879. THOR FREDUR, *Sketches from Shady Places.* Their ancient terror, the bobby, Copper, KID, a policeman.

4. (old).—A thief: specifically a young thief. Also KIDDY.—MATSELL (1859). *See* quot. 1823.

1823. BEE, *Dict. of the Turf*, s.v. KID, KIDDY, and KIDLING—implies youth; but an old evergreen chap may be dressed KIDDLY (*q.v.*). People who imagine that all KIDS are thieves, carry the joke too far.

1859. MATSELL, *Vocabulum*, s.v. KIDSMAN. The KIDSMAN accompanies the KID.

5. (American).—A kidnapper.

6. (common).—*See* quots. *Cf.* *verb.* sense 1.

1876. HINDLEY, *Cheap Jack*, p. 64. One of these brother boys was well-known for his KID, that is gammon and devilry. *Ibid.* p. 3. The rarest chaps at KID.

1883. *Punch*, 28 July, p. 38, col. 1. I was in it, old man, and NO KID, As a chap of my form *can* be in it, if ready to blue 'arf a quid.

1883. GREENWOOD, *Tag, Rag and Co.* [quoted in *Slang, Jargon, and Cant*]. In his opinion it was all KID.

1885. *Punch*, 31 Jan. p. 60. The world's coming round to my views, Charlie, fast, there's no KID about that.

7. in pl. (common).—Kid gloves: *e.g.*, 'KIDS cleaned for 2d. a pair.'

1889. *Illustrated Bits*, 13 July, p. 1. 'I want to see some gloves.' 'Certainly, miss. Can I show you some undressed KIDS?' 'Young man! I only require gloves.'

Verb. (common).—1. To quiz; to wheedle; to cheat.

1811. *Lex. Bal.*, s.v. KID, to coax or wheedle. To amuse a man or divert his attention while another robs him.

1872. *Daily News*, 5 Jan., p. 2, col. 1. A stern man and a strong, he was not to be blinded, by emphatic expostulators against KIDDING, to the fact that the clamourers against that species of throwing dust in a fellow mortal's eyes were in fact themselves KIDDING with the greatest activity. Comfort is a relative term.

1879. *Macmillan's Mag.*, xl. 505. I thought they were only KIDDING at first.

1880. JAS. GREENWOOD, *Fly Faker's Hotel*, in 'Odd People in odd Places,' p. 55. 'Why, you don't mean to say that you've been KIDDED to expect a bed for your fourpence,' said he; 'a regler turn-in, I mean, with sheets and that?'

1884. R. JEFFERIES, in *Longm. Mag.*, IV. 255. While the fisherman was telling me this woeful story, I fancied I heard voices from a crowd of the bigger boys collected under a smack, voices that said, 'Ho! ho! Go on! you're KIDDING the man!'

1889. *Answers*, 2 March, p. 218, col. 1. 'One and tuppence a day,' said the bootblack, sarcastically; ''E's on'y a KIDDIN' on yer. Arsk that there copper whether he don't take 'is four or five bob a day.'

1892. MILLIKEN, *'Arry Ballads*, 33. He wos KIDDING me.

TO KID ON, *verb. phr.* (common).—To lead on by gammon or deceit.

1851. H. MAYHEW, *London Lab. and Lond. Poor*, i. p. 473. 'At the same time he KIDS them ON by promising three times more than the things are worth.'

1888. J. RUNCIMAN, *The Chequers*, p. 186. I was KIDDIN' him ON.

1889. *Licensed Victuallers' Gazette*, 4 Jan. He KIDDED—who had just come in for his father's brass—to let him have the lot.

TO KID ONESELF, *verb. phr.* (common).—To be conceited.

HARD KID, *subs. phr.* (common).—Hard lines; bad luck; HARD CHEESE (*q.v.*).

KIDDEN (or KID-KEN or KIDDY-KEN), *subs.* (thieves').—A lodging house frequented by young thieves.

1839. BRANDON, *Poverty, Mendicity, and Crime*, pp. 74 and 90, s.v.

1859. MATSELL, *Vocabulum*, s.v.

KIDDER, *subs.* (old).—1. *See* quot. 1785.

1690. B. E., *Dict. Cant. Crew*, s.v.

1725. *New Cant. Dict.*, s.v.

1785. GROSE, *Vulgar Tongue*, s.v. KIDDER, a forestaller.

2. (common).—A glib and taking speaker; a master of chaff.

1888. *Sporting Life*, 15 Dec. Ask Mr. Baldock . . . . to whom I allude, and he will probably reply the champion KIDDER.

1891. J. NEWMAN, *Scamping Tricks*, p. 88. He was a beautiful KIDDER and could patter sweet and pretty.

KIDDIER, *subs.* (common).—A pork-butcher.

KIDDILY, *adj.* (common).—Fashionably; showily; flashily. *Cf.* KID *subs.* sense 2.—Also KIDDY, *adj.*

1828. JON BEE, *Picture of London*, p. 304 *note.* He and his brother . . . . dressed KIDDILY, kept late hours, and pilfered to support it, as usual.

KID-LAY (or RIG), *subs.* (old).—*See* quot. 1690.

1690. B. E., *Dict. Cant. Crew*, s.v. KIDLAY, one who meeting a Prentice with a Bundle or Parcel of goods, wheedles him by fair words, and whipping Sixpence into his Hand, to step on a short and sham Errand for him, in the mean time runs away with the goods.

1725. *New Cant. Dict.*, s.v.

1785. GROSE, *Vulg. Tongue*, s.v.

1811. *Lex. Bal.*, s.v.

KIDDLEYWINK, *subs.* (common).—1. A raffle.

1884. *Daily Telegraph*, 6 August, p. 3, col. 1. When it is intended to 'pull off'. . . . a KIDLIWINK, or raffle.

2. (common).—A small village shop; and, (3) specifically (in the West country), an ale-house.

4. (common).—A woman of unsteady habits.

KIDDY, *subs.* (common).—1. A man; a boy; a young fellow: a diminutive of KID (*q.v.*). Also KIDLET = a boy or girl.

1860. *Funny Fellow*, 7 May, p. 1. Hollo, my KIDDY, stir your stumps, ... Make haste, young chip, my boots to shine.

1888. BOLDREWOOD, *Robbery Under Arms*, xx. Heard all kinds of rough talk ever since they were little KIDDIES.

2. (thieves').—A flash thief: ROLLING KIDDY = a dandy thief. *See* KID, senses 2 and 4.

1780. TOMLINSON, *Slang Pastoral*, i. My time, O ye KIDDIES, was happily spent. *Idem.* x. What KIDDY'S so rum as to get himself scragg'd?

1787. GEO. PARKER. *Humorous Sketches*, p. 34. No more like a KIDDY, he'll roll the flash song.

1828. BEE, *Living Picture of London*, 255. Jockies, owners, and wagering KIDDIES.

1830. S. WARREN, *Diary of a Late Physician*, xi. 'Come, my KIDDY—caged at last, eh? . . . . Here's your passport,' said one of the officers, pointing to the warrant.

1840. LYTTON, *Paul Clifford*, iii. He merely observed, by way of compliment, that Mr. Augustus and his companion seemed to be ROLLING KIDDIES. A little displeased with this metaphorical remark—for it may be observed that ROLLING KIDDY is, among the learned in such lore, the customary expression for 'a smart thief.'

3. (common).—A dandy.

1823. BYRON, *Don Juan*, xi. 17. Poor Tom was once a KIDDY upon town, A thorough varmint and a real swell.

1823. BEE, *Dict. of the Turf*, s.v. KID, KIDDY, and KIDLING. . . . hat on one side, short collar upon high, coat cut away. . . . Belcher fogle. . . . and chitterling shirt. . . . these compounded compose the KIDDY.

1832. *Brummelliana*, p. 180. Let the garçon who is about to set up as KIDDY on his own account take the advice of one who was no mean KIDDY in his day.

4. (venery).—A prostitute's bully; a PONCE (*q.v.*).

5. (old).—A stage-coach driver.

1836. DICKENS, *Sketches by Boz*, 153. It was his ambition to do something in the celebrated KIDDY or stage-coach way.

Adj. (common).—Fashionable; SMART (*q.v.*). *See* KIDDILY.

1823. MONCRIEFF, *Tom and Jerry*, p. 5. I'll tell you; before we start on our sprees and rambles, I'll send for that KIDDY artist, Dicky Primefit, the dandy habit-maker, of Regent Street.

1848. *Punch*, x. 19. A youth there was of changefulle lotte, Now bryght, now seedie broune. Hee called hymselfe a KIDDIE swelle And lived upon ye toune.

*b.*1876. C. HINDLEY, *Life and Times of James Catnach*. So KIDDY is my famble.

KIDDYISH, *adj.* (old).—Stylish; UP TO DATE (*q.v.*).

1820. *Jack Randall's Diary.* Think of the KIDDYISH spree we had on such a day.

KIDDY NIPPER, *subs. phr.* (old).—*See* quot.

1785. GROSE, *Vulg. Tongue*, s.v. KIDDY NIPPERS, thieves who cut off the waistcoat pockets of taylors, when cross legged on the board, thereby grabbling their bit.

KID-LEATHER, *subs.* (venery).—Generic for harlotry of tender years.

KIDLET. *See* KIDDY, sense 1.

KIDLEYBENDERS, *subs.* (American).—Ice which undulates under the feet of a skater.

KIDMENT, *subs.* (common).—1. Humbug; GAMMON (*q.v.*). Also (cheap Jack's) = professional patter.

1836. BRANDON, *Poverty, Mendacity, and Crime*, p. 106.

1884. *Daily Telegraph*, 8 August, p. 3, col. 2. That depended on what a man's talents were, and how he purposed employing them. 'Employing them for KIDMENT, of course,' returned the elderly mumper. 'That's what talents is give a man for, hain't it?'

2. (thieves').—*See* quot.

1857. SNOWDEN, *Mag. Assistant*, 3rd ed., p. 445. A pocket handkerchief pinned to the pocket for a trap—KIDMENT.

Adj. (American thieves').—Comical.—MATSELL (1859).

KIDNAP, *verb.* (old: now recognised).—To steal children. [SKEAT: compounded of KID, (a child in thieves' slang) NAP, more commonly NAB, to steal]. *See* KIDNAPPER.

KIDNAPPER, *subs.* (old: now recognised).—A child-stealer. *See* quots. *Cf.* SHEEP-NAPPER.

1690. B. E., *Dict. Cant. Crew*, s.v. KIDNAPPER, one that Decoys or Spirits (as it is commonly called) Children away and Sells them for the Plantations.

1725. *New Cant. Dict.*, s.v.

1785. GROSE, *Vulg. Tongue*, s.v. KIDNAPPER, originally one who stole, or decoyed children, or apprentices from their parents or masters, to send them to the colonies. Called also spiriting, but now used for all recruiting crimps, for the king's troops, or those of the East India company, and agents for indenting servants for the plantations.

1815. SCOTT, *Guy Mannering*, xxxiv. The devil can scarce save Dirk Hatteraick from being hanged for a murderer and KIDNAPPER, if the younker of Ellangowan should settle in this country.

KIDNEY, *subs.* (colloquial).—Kind; disposition; fashion: as, 'Two of a KIDNEY' = two of a mind; 'of a strange KIDNEY' = of an odd humour; 'of a different KIDNEY' = of different habit or turn. Fr. *le bouchon*.

1596. SHAKSPEARE, *Merry Wives of Windsor*, iii. 5. Think of that, a man of my KIDNEY.

1690. B. E., *Dict. Cant. Crew*, s.v. KIDNEY, of that KIDNEY, of such a stamp.

1710. *Tatler*, No. 230. Other of that KIDNEY are very uppish, and alert upon't.

1719. DURFEY, *Pills etc.*, ii. 332. Accosting one of his own crew, Whom he of the right KIDNEY knew.

1725. *New Cant. Dict.*, s.v.

1742. FIELDING, *Joseph Andrews*, II. viii. I am heartily glad to meet with a man of your KIDNEY.

1755. JOHNSON, *Dicty*, s.v. KIDNEY. Sort; kind; in ludicrous language.

1763. *Terræ Filius* [NARES]. Attempt to put their hair out of KIDNEY.

1785. GROSE, *Vulg. Tongue*, s.v.

1830. W. T. MONCRIEFF, *Van Dieman's Land*, i. 2. I must curry favour with them, as we're going to be of a KIDNEY.

1837. BARHAM, *Ingoldsby Legends*, 'Witches Frolic.' As men of his KIDNEY are wont to snore.

1859. MATSELL, *Vocabulum*, s.v.

1871. DISRAELI, *Lothair*, i. 741. Men of their own KIDNEY.

1888. RUNCIMAN, *The Chequers*, 223. At times, like Robert Burns, George Morland, and men of that KIDNEY, he would give way to a passionate burst of repentance.

1889. *Globe*, 23 July, p. 6, col. 1. Lord Justice Lopes showed himself a paragon of patience, but it is sincerely to be hoped that there will be no more suitors in person of this KIDNEY.

1892. HUME NISBET, *Bushranger's Sweetheart*, 153. I fancy the second King of Israel must have been of the same KIDNEY, if that account is quite accurate about his merry-making on one occasion.

1894. K. GRAHAME, *Pagan Papers*, p. 129. These great Beasts [hornets] . . . were of a different KIDNEY.

2. (old).—A waiter; a GRASSHOPPER (*q.v.*).

1710. *Tatler*, No. 268. It is our custom, upon the first coming of the news, to order a youth, who officiates as the KIDNEY of the coffee-house, to get into the pulpit and read every paper with a loud and distinct voice.

(Stock Exchange).—A fractional part of a shilling. [A corruption of Cadney, the name of the first dealer known to deal under $\frac{1}{32}$].

KIDNEY-HIT, *subs.* (pugilistic).—A punch in the short ribs.

KID'S-EYE, *subs.* (old).—A fippenny piece.

1821. HAGGART, *Life*, p. 114. I got three jumpers and a KID'S-EYE.

KIDSMAN, *subs.* (thieves').—*See* quot. 1859.

1836. BRANDON, *Poverty, Mendacity and Crime*, p. 149, s.v.

1859. MATSELL, *Vocabulum.* A fellow that boards and lodges boys for the purpose of teaching them how to steal, putting them through a course of training, as a dog trainer will train dogs for the hunt. The KIDSMAN accompanies the kid, and though committing no depredations himself, he controls and directs the motions of the others.

KID-STRETCHER, *subs.* (venery).—A man addicted to the use of KID-LEATHER (*q.v.*).

KILKENNY, *subs.* (old).—A frieze coat.—GROSE (1785).

KILL *subs.* (tailors').—A garment utterly spoiled.

DRESSED TO KILL. *See* DRESSED and DEATH.

KILL-CALF (or **-COW**). *subs.* (old).—A butcher: also a murderous ruffian. Also KILL-BUCK.

. . . . *Old Ballad* [quoted by NARES]. Of all occupations that nowadays are used I would not be a butcher, for that's to be refused; For whatever is gotten, or whatever is gained, He shall be call'd KILL-COW, and so shall be named.

1628. CLAVELL, *Recantation of an Ill-bred Life* [quoted by NARES]. But in the night, yet then take heed of those Base padding rascalls, for their KILL-CALFE law.

1630. TAYLOR, *Wks.* [NARES]. They make private shambles with KIL-CALFE cruelty, and sheepe-slaughtering murther, to the abuse of Lent, the deceiving of the informers, and the great griefe of every zealous fishmonger.

*c.*1636. *London Chanticleers*, Sc. iv. I know there's never a KILL-COW i' th' city becomes a woollen apron better than I do.

KILL-DEVIL, *subs.* (old and American).—Rum: specifically new spirit.

1690. B. E., *Dict. Cant. Crew*, s.v.

1785. GROSE, *Vulg. Tongue*, s.v. KILL-DEVIL, new still-burnt rum.

1859. MATSELL, *Vocabulum*, s.v.

KILLERS, *subs.* (common).—The eyes. For synonyms *see* PEEPERS.

1780. MARSELL, in WHIBLEY, *Cap and Gown*, p. 85. Oer the poor country curate that's near How their eyes (in fine language called KILLERS).

KILLING, *adj.* and *adv.* (common).—1. Fascinating; bewitching; irresistible. Also KILLINGLY.

1619. FLETCHER, *Wild Goose Chase*, iii. As KILLING eyes as yours, a wit as poignant.

1677. WYCHERLEY, *Plain Dealer*, ii. *Nov.* Ay, ay, madam, with you ladies too, martial men must needs be very KILLING.

1700. CONGREVE, *Way of the World*, iv. 1. *L. Wish.* And—well—and how do I look, Foible? *Foi.* Most KILLING well, Madam.

1712. POPE, *Rape of the Lock*, v. 64. Those eyes were made so KILLING.

1751. SMOLLETT, *Peregrine Pickle*, lxxx. The KILLING edge of her charms was a little blunted by the accidents of time and fortune.

1765. GOLDSMITH, *Essays*, v. Your modern Briton cuts his hair on the crown, and plasters it with hog's lard and flour; and this to make him look KILLING.

1828-45. T. HOOD, *Poems*, i. 231 (ed. 1846). The crowd including two butchers in blue (The regular KILLING Whitechapel hue).

1847. THACKERAY, *Vanity Fair*, iv. Mr. Joseph Sedley . . . . was actually seated *tête-à-tête* with a young lady, looking at her with a most KILLING expression.

1883. *Saturday Review*, 21 April, p. 502, col. 2. Mr. Toole is as KILLINGLY funny in this as he is in the still and constantly popular farce of *Mr. Guffin's Elopement.*

KILL-PRIEST, *subs.* (provincial).—Port wine.

KILL-THE-BEGGAR, *subs.* (common).—Whiskey. For synonyms *see* DRINKS and OLD MAN'S MILK.

KILL-TIME, *subs.* (colloquial).—A pastime.

KILMARNOCK-COWL, *subs.* (old Scots').—1. A knitted nightcap; and (2) by inplication the wretch that wore one.

1830. SCOTT, *Bonnie Dundee.* These COWLS OF KILMARNOCK had spits and had spears And long-hafted gullies to kill Cavaliers.

KILMARNOCK-WHITTLE, *subs.* (Scots'). A person of either sex, already engaged or betrothed.—JAMIESON.

KILTER. *See* KELTER.

KILT, *adv.* (Irish).—Killed.

1836. MARRYAT, *Japhet*, iii. Sure enough, it cured me, but wasn't I quite KILT before I was cured.

KIMBAW, *verb.* (Old Cant).—1. To trick; to cheat; to cozen. Also (2), to beat; to bully.

1690. B. E., *Dict. Cant. Crew*, s.v. KIMBAW. Let's KIMBOW the Cull, Let's beat that Fellow and get his money.

1725. *New Cant. Dict.*, s.v.

1785. GROSE, *Vulg. Tongue*, s.v.

1839. AINSWORTH, *J. Sheppard*, p. 23 [ed. 1840]. 'Ay! ay!' cried several of the bystanders, 'let Jonathan KIMBAW the cove. He's got the gift of the gab.'

KIMBO (or **KIMBAW**). TO SET THE ARMS AKIMBO, *verb. phr.* (old: now colloquial).—To set hands on hips with the elbows cocked.

1606. JOHN DAY, *Ile of Guls*, ii. 4, p. 52. SET MINE ARMES A KIMBO thus, Wrethe my necke and my bodie thus.

1677. WYCHERLEY, *Plain Dealer*, ii. *Nov.* But he has no use of his arms but to SET 'EM ON KIMBOW.

1712. ARBUTHNOT, *Hist. of John Bull*, III. x. He observed Frog and old Lewis edging towards one another to whisper; so that John was forced to SIT WITH HIS ARMS AKIMBO to keep them asunder.

1748. T. DYCHE, *Dictionary* (5th ed.) [s.v.] KEMBO (v.) to set or put one's hand upon one's hip, to strut or look big.

1785. GROSE, *Vulg. Tongue*, s.v. KIMBAW. TO SET ONE'S ARMS A KIMBAW, vulgarly pronounced 'a kimbo,' is to rest one's hands on the hips, keeping the elbows square, and sticking out from the body, an insolent bullying attitude.

1837. MARRYAT, *Snarleyow*, i. ch. XII. Poll PUT HER ARMS AKIMBO; At the Admiral's house looked she.

1857. A. TROLLOPE, *Barchester Towers*, xxxiii. She tossed her head, and PUT HER ARMS A-KIMBO, with an air of confident defiance.

KINCHIN (or **KINCHEN**), *subs.* (old).—1. A child; a boy; a young man. Also KINCHEN COVE (*q.v.*).

1567. HARMAN, *Caveat.* p. 76. A KYNCHEN CO is a young boye, traden vp to suche peuishe purposes as you haue harde of other young ympes before, that when he groweth vnto yeres, he is better to hang then to drawe.

1607. DEKKER, *Jests to Make You Merie*, in *Wks.* (GROSART), II. 329. KINCHEN the coue towres, which is as much as, Fellow the man smokes or suspects you.

1608. DEKKER, *Belman of London*, in *Wks.* (GROSART), III. 105. These KINCHINS, the first thing they doe is to learne how to *cant*, and the onely thing they practise is to creepe in at windowes, or celler doores.

1690. B. E., *Dict. Cant. Crew*, s.v. KINCHIN, a little child.

1725. *New Cant. Dict.*, s.v.

1785. GROSE, *Vulg. Tongue*, s.v.

1815. SCOTT, *Guy Mannering*, XXXIV. We did the KINCHIN no harm.

1836. W. H. SMITH, *The Individual*, 13 Nov. 'The Thieves' Chaunt.' Her duds are bob—she's a KINCHIN crack, And I hopes as how she'll never back.

1837. DISRAELI, *Venetia*, Bk. i. xiv. He is no lanspresado, or I am a KINCHIN.

1837. DICKENS, *Oliver Twist*, xlii. 'The KINCHINS,' said the Jew, 'is the young children that's sent on errands by their mothers with sixpences and shillings.

1839. HARRISON AINSWORTH, *Jack Sheppard* [1889], p. 13. 'Let's have a look at the KINCHEN that ought to have been throttled,' added he, snatching the child from Wood.

1841. LEMAN REDE, *Sixteen String Jack*, i. 3. *Kit*. Peter, don't patter; you're werry good in the fancy line—in the light part of our business,—such as robbing a KINCHEN of it's coral, filching an old lady's redicule, or getting up small talk with a nursery maid, vhile you takes a vax impression of the key.

1859. H. KINGSLEY, *Geoffrey Hamlyn*, xxiii. 'So *boss*,' began the ruffian, not looking at him; 'we ain't fit company for the likes of that KINCHIN, etc.?'

1876. HINDLEY, *Adventures of A Cheap Jack*, p. 2. Nor is his crying pal the KINCHIN any more faithfully drawn.

KINCHIN-COVE, *subs.* (Old Cant).—1. A child: *see* KINCHIN.

1567. HARMAN, *Caveat*, p. 76. [See quot. under KINCHIN].

1608. DEKKER, *Belman of London*, in *Wks.* (GROSART), III. 105. The last *Ranke* of those *Runnagates* is fild vp with KINCHYN COES; and they are little boyes whose parents (hauing beene beggers) are dead, or else such as haue run away from their maisters, and in stead of a trade to liue by, follow this kinde of life to be lowsie by.

1690. B. E., *Dict. Cant. Crew*, s.v. KINCHIN-COES, the Sixteenth Rank of the Canting Tribe, being little Children whose Parents are dead, having been Beggers; as also young Ladds running from their Masters, who are first taught Canting, then thieving.

1725. *New Cant. Dict.*, s.v.

1785. GROSE, *Vulg. Tongue*, s.v. KINCHIN. KINCHIN COES, orphan beggar boys, educated in thieving.

1830. LYTTON, *Paul Clifford*, p. 25. [ed. 1854]. Look you my KINCHIN COVE.

1870. *All the Year Round*, 'Byegone Cant', 5 March. Suppose a KINCHIN COVE should hear the twittle-twattle of *cobble colter*, or the sagacious cackle of *tib of the buttery*, and the said KINCHIN COVE should think a dinner off these big birds would be delicious and should steal them for that purpose, short work would have been made of it, and KINCHIN COVE would simply have been hanged.

2. (Old Cant).—A little man.

1671. R. HEAD, *English Rogue*, I. v. 50. (1874). KINCHIN COVE, a little man.

1690. B. E., *Dict. Cant. Crew*, s.v.

1725. *New Cant. Dict.*, s.v.

1785. GROSE, *Vulg. Tongue*, s.v.

3. (Old Cant).—A man who robs or kidnaps children: *cf.* KINCHIN LAY.

KINCHIN-LAY, *subs.* (old).—*See* quot. 1838. [KINCHIN (*q.v.*) + LAY (*q.v.*)].

1836. DICKENS, *Oliver Twist*, xlii. The KINCHIN is the young children that's sent on errands by their mothers, with sixpences and shillings; and the LAY is just to take their money away—they've always got it ready in their hands.

1871. *Standard*, 13 Sept. The prisoner, it appeared, is an adept at the KINCHIN-LAY, a term known to the initiated for robbing children.

KINCHIN-MORT, *subs.* (Old Cant).—*See* quots.

1567. HARMAN, *Caveat*, p. 76. A KYNCHING MORTE is a lytle Gyrle; the Mortes their mothers carries them at their backes in their slates, whiche is their shetes, and bryngs them vp sauagely, tyll they growe to be rype, and soone rype, soone rotten.

1690. B. E., *Dict. Cant. Crew*, s.v. KINCHIN-MORTS, the Twenty-seventh and last Order of the Canting Crew, being girls of a year or two old whom the *Morts* (their Mothers) carry at their Backs in *Slates (Sheets)* and if they have no children of their own they borrow or Steal them from others.

1725. *New Cant. Dict.*, s. v.

1785. GROSE, *Vulg. Tongue*, s.v. KINCHIN. KINCHIN MORTS in slates, beggars children carried at their mothers backs in sheets.

1815. SCOTT, *Guy Mannering*, xxviii. The times are sair altered since I was a KINCHIN MORT.

KINDER, *adv.* (American colloquial). As it were. Also KINDER SORTER.

1848. DURIVAGE, *Stray Subjects*, 80. 'You're short, KINDER?' 'Wal; you 'll find me long enough prehaps.'

1848. BURTON, *Waggeries etc.*, p. 18. I'm not goin' to say that I didn't feel KINDER skeered.

KIND-HEART, *subs.* (old).—A tooth-drawer: in jest. [HALLIWELL: From an itinerant dentist so-named, or nick-named, in the time of Elizabeth].

1614. JONSON, *Bartholomew Fayre, Induction*. For KIND-HEART the tooth-drawer ... a fine oily pig-woman.

1632. ROWLEY, *New Wonder*, iii. 1. Mistake me not KINDHEART; he calls you tooth-drawer.

KINDNESS, *subs.* (common).—The sexual favour; BENEVOLENCE (*q.v.*). Fr. *des bontés*.

*c.*1728. RAMSAY, *Address of Thanks*, in *Wks. (at sup.)*, ii. 345. The fair one frighted for her fame Shall for her KINDNESS bear nae blame, Nor with kirk censure grapple.

KING COTTON, *subs. phr.* (American).—Cotton, the staple of the Southern States of America, and the chief manufacture in England. COTTON-LORD = a man enriched by cotton.

KINGDOM COME, *subs. phr.* (common).—The next life: TO GO TO KINGDOM COME = to die. Fr. *la paradouze* or *part-à-douze* (a play on *paradis*); *la parabole*. It. *soprano* = higher; Sp. *claro* = light.

1785. GROSE, *Vulg. Tongue*, s.v.

1794. WOLCOT [P. Pindar], *Br. Peter to Br. Tom*, in *Wks.*, i. p. 422. Did gentlemen of fortune die, And leave the church a good round sum; Lo! in the twinkling of an eye, The Parson frank'd their souls to KINGDOM-COME.

1836. MARRYAT, *Midshipman Easy*, xxxi. 'They will not have much mercy from the waves,' replied Gascoigne; 'they will all be in KINGDOM COME to-morrow morning, if the breeze comes more on land.'

1863. MR. NORTON, *Lost and Saved*, p. 334. Treherne *loq.* 'Well, my child, I don't mean a great dangerous storm that's to wreck the yacht and send us all to KIKGDOM COME—but a nasty tossing sea, bad for women you know; men don't mind it.'

KING JOHN'S MAN, *subs. phr.* (old).—*See* quots.

1785. GROSE, *Vulg. Tongue*, s.v. He is one of KING JOHN'S MEN, eight score to the hundred, a saying of a little undersized man.

1867. SMYTH, *Sailors' Word Book*, s.v. KING JOHN'S MEN, the Adullamites of the navy.

KING'S (or QUEEN'S) BAD BARGAIN, *subs. phr.* (old).—A malingering soldier; a deserter.—GROSE (1785).

KING'S-BENCHER, *subs.* (nautical).—The busiest of the galley orators; a GALLEY-SKULKER.—SMYTH.

KING'S BOOKS, *subs. phr.* (old).—A pack of cards; THE HISTORY (or BOOKS) OF THE FOUR KINGS; DEVIL'S BOOKS (*q.v.*).

1653. URQUHART, *Rabelais*, i. 22. After supper were brought in THE BOOKS OF THE FOUR KINGS.

1760. FOOTE, *The Minor* (ed. x, 1789), 31. Come, shall we have a dip in the HISTORY OF THE FOUR KINGS this morning?

KING'S CUSHION, *subs. phr.* (common).—A seat formed by two persons holding each other's hands crossed. Also QUEEN'S CUSHION (or CHAIR), CATS-CARRIAGE (or CRADLE) etc.

1818. SCOTT, *Heart of Midlothian*, i. 168. He was now mounted on the hands of two of the rioters clasped together so as to form what, in Scotland is called the KING'S CUSHION.

KING'S (or QUEEN'S) HEAD INN, *subs. phr.* (old).—Newgate. For synonyms *see* CAGE.

1690. B. E., *Dict. Cant. Crew.* s.v. KING'S HEAD INN, or the Chequer Inn in *Newgate* street, the prison, or Newgate.

1725. *New Cant. Dict.*, s.v.

1785. GROSE, *Vulg. Tongue.*, s.v.

1836. W. H. SMITH, *The Individual*. 'The Thieves' Chaunt'. Because she lately nimmed some tin, They have sent her to lodge at the KING'S HEAD INN.

KING'S KEYS, *subs. phr.* (old legal).—The crow-bars and hammers used by sheriffs' officers to force doors and locks. [ROQUEFORT: *faire la clef du Roy*, ouvrir les clefs et les coffres avec des instruments de serrurier].

1816. SCOTT, *Black Dwarf*, 173, 4. 'And what will ye do, if I carena to thraw the keys?' . . . . 'Force our way wi' the KINGS KEYS, and break the neck of every soul we find in the house.

KINGSMAN, *subs.* (Coster).—A handkerchief with yellow patterns upon a green ground; the favourite coloured neckerchief of the costermongers. Sometimes worn by women thrown over their shoulders: *cf.* Billy.

1851-61. MAYHEW, *Lond. Lab. etc.*, i. 53. The man who does not wear his silk neckerchief—his 'KING'S-MAN' as it is called—is known to be in desperate circumstances; the inference being that it has gone to supply the morning's stockmoney. A yellow flower on a green ground, or a red and blue pattern, is at present greatly in vogue.

2. (Cambridge university).—A member of King's College.

1852. BRISTED, *Five Years*, 127. He came out the winner, with the KINGSMAN, and one of our three.

3. in pl. (military).—The Seventy-eighth Foot. [Their motto is *Cuidich'r Rhi* = Help the King].

KING'S (or QUEEN'S) PICTURES, *subs. phr.* (common).—Money. For synonyms *see* ACTUAL and GILT.—B.E. (1690); *New Cant. Dict.* (1725); GROSE (1785). TO DRAW THE KING'S (or QUEEN'S) PICTURE = to counterfeit money.

1632. BROME, *The Court Beggar*, in *Wks.* (1873), Vol. I, (v. 2) p. 258. This picture drawer drew it, and has drawn more of the KING'S PICTURES than all the limners in the town.

KING'S PLATE, *subs. phr.* (old).—Fetters.—*Lex. Bal.* (1811). For synonyms *see* DARBIES.

KINGSWOOD LION, *subs. phr.* (old).—An ass; a JERUSALEM-PONY (*q.v.*). For synonyms *see* MOKE.

KINK, *subs.* (colloquial).—A crotchet; a whim.

1846. MARRYAT, *Peter Simple*, ch. xx. Look at your shoulders above your ears, and your back with a bow like the KINKING of a cable.

1850. H. B. STOWE, *Uncle Tom's Cabin*, ch. xii. 'Buy me too, Mas'r, for de dear Lord's sake!—buy me—I shall die if you don't!' 'You'll die if I do, that's the KINK of it, said Haley,—'no!' And he turned on his heel.

1869. H. B. STOWE, *Oldtown*, 33. The fact is, when a woman gets a KINK in her head agin a man, the best on us don't do jest the right thing.

1883. JAMES PAYN, *Thicker than Water*, ch. xxiv. The wheel of life was turning smoothly enough for Mary when there suddenly came a KINK in it.

KINKY, *adj.* (colloquial).—Eccentric; short tempered; TWISTY (*q.v.*).

1848. JONES, *Sketches of Travel*, p. 146. The KINKY-HEADED cus looked at me sidways and rolled the whites of his eyes at me like he was gwine to have a fit.

1889. *Sportsman*, 2 Jan. At the former the KINKY ones and the worthy souls who play hole-and-corner with society are made to partake of the toke of contrition and the skilly of repentance.

KIP, *subs.* (old).—A brothel. For synonyms *see* NANNY SHOP. TO TATTER A KIP = to wreck a house of ill-fame.

1766. GOLDSMITH, *Vicar of Wakefield*, xx. My business was to attend him at auctions, to put him in spirits when he sat for his picture, to take the left hand in his chariot when not filled by another, and to assist at TATTERING A KIP, as the phrase was, when we had a mind for a frolic.

2. (common).—A bed.

ENGLISH SYNONYMS. Breeding-cage; bugwalk; bunk; cage; cloth-market; dab; doss; dossing crib; downy; Feathers Inn; flea-pasture; latty; letty; libb; lypken; perch; ruggins; shake-down; snooze.

FRENCH SYNONYMS. *L'au:el de plume* (popular: = Feather's Inn); *la bâche* (thieves' = awning); *le flac* (thieves'); *le flacul* (thieves'); *le fournil* (popular = bakehouse); *la halle aux draps* (common = CLOTHMARKET); *le pagne* (thieves' from *panier* = basket); *le panier aux ordures* (popular).

1879. J. W. HORSLEY, in *Macm. Mag.* xl. 501. So I went home, turned into KIP (bed).

1891. *Answers*, 31 Jan. 'Oh yes,' said the doctor, 'this is a very decent KIP; I have tried a good many, but this is the best of the lot.

1892. *Morning Post*, 25 Oct., p. 2, col. 4. White said, 'I went in there to have a KEP' (slang term for cheap lodging).

3. (American).—A fool; a silly fellow: he's a KIP = he's dull-witted—MATSELL (1859).

Verb. (old).—1. To play truant; TO DO DOLLY: *Cf.* CHARLEY WAG.

1821. HAGGART, *Life*, p. 3. I was sometimes turned down for KIPPING.

2. (thieves').— To sleep; to lodge.

KIP-HOUSE, *subs.* (tramps').—A tramps' lodging house.

KIPPER, *verb.* (common).—*See* quot.

1885. W. H. STEVENSON, in *Notes and Queries*, 6th. S. xi. 131. On the Trent a salmon is said to be KIPPER when it is seriously out of condition and has lost about half its weight. The fish are mostly found in this condition after the spawning season, but I have not hitherto been able to learn satisfactorily whether or not there is any connexion between the spawning and KIPPERING. From this has arisen the slang KIPPER = to die.

KIPSY. *See* KYPSEY.

KIRJALIS, *phr.* (American thieves'); —'Who fears? I fear not; come on!'—MATSELL (1859).

KIRKBUZZER, *subs.* (Amer. thieves').—A thief whose speciality is to ply in churches.—MATSELL (1859).

KIRKLING, *subs.* (thieves').—Breaking into a house while the occupants are at church.

KIRK'S LAMBS, *subs. phr.* (military).—The Second Regiment of Foot. [From the name of its first colonel and the Paschal Lamb, the badge of Portugal, on its colours].

1891. *Globe*, 10 Mar. KIRKE'S LAMBS were engaged at Sedgemoor.

KISKY, *adj.* (common).—Drunk; fuddled. For synonyms *see* DRINKS and SCREWED.

KISS, *subs.* (venery).—1. The sexual favor. For synonyms *see* GREENS and RIDE.

2. (common).—*See* quot.

1856. DICKENS, *The Detective Police*, in *Reprinted Pieces*, p. 242. [*Qtly Review* xcix. 177]. I observed that on the back of the letter there was what we call a KISS—a drop of wan by the side of the seal.

3. in pl. (Stock Exchange).—Hotchkiss Ordnance Co. shares.

Verb. (old colloquial).—To touch gently; to brush. In billiards and other games the balls are said TO KISS when they barely touch.

1593. SHAKSPEARE, *Taming of the Shrew*, i. 1. When with his knees he KISSED the Cretan strand.

2. (venery).—*See* KISS, *subs.* sense 1.

1730. RAMSAY, *Fables & Tales*, in *Wks.* [1800], ii. 515. Ah me! your reverence's sister, Ten times I carnally have—KIST her.

1786. CAPT. MORRIS. 'The Plenipotentiary'. The next to be KISSED on the Plenipo's list, was a delicate Maiden of Honor.

TO KISS THE CLAWS (or HANDS), *verb. phr.* (old).—To salute.

1630. TAYLOR, *Wks.* [quoted by NARES]. These men can KISSE THEIR CLAWS, with, Jack, how is't? And take and shake me kindely by the fist, And put me off with dilatory cogges.

1630. TAYLOR, *Wks.* [quoted by NARES]. I'm glad to see thee well with all my heart. Long have I long'd to drinke with thee a quart, I have beleev'd this drosse had beene pure gold, When presently I have beene bought and sold Behind my backe (for no desert and cause), By those that kindly cap'd and KIST THEIR CLAWES.

1650. HOWELL, *Familiar Letters* [quoted by NARES]. This letter comes TO KISSE YOUR HANDS from fair Florence, a citie so beutifull.

TO KISS THE COUNTER, *verb. phr.* (old).—To be confined in the Counter prison. Also CLINK.

1618. ROWLANDS, *Night Raven*, p. 11. (Hunterian Club Repr. 1872). *Constable*:—Tell me of supper, tut a puddings end, You KISSE THE COUNTER, sirra, that is flat, Ile teach you know my place deserves a hat.

1626. *Letter* dated *idem* [quoted by NARES]. Some constables, for refusing to distrain, have KISSED THE COUNTER; and some have taken up their lodgings in Newgate, but have been since released.

TO KISS THE DUST, *verb. phr.* (colloquial).—To die. For synonyms *see* ALOFT.

TO KISS THE HARE'S FOOT, *verb. phr.* (old).—To be too late for meals; TO DINE WITH DUKE HUMPHREY (*q.v.*).

.... *Serving Man's Comfort*, Sign. C. The hall summons this consort of companions (upon payne to dyne with duke Humphfrie, or to KISSE THE HARE'S FOOT) to appeare at the first call.

1616. BROWN, *Brit. Past*, ii. 2, p. 67. 'Tis supper time with all, and we had need Make haste away, unless we meane to speed With those that KISSE THE HARE'S FOOT; rhumes are bred, Some say, by going supperlesse to bed.

1672. RAY, *Proverbs*, p. 195. To KISS THE HARE'S FOOT, *prov.* Spoken to one that comes so late that he hath lost his dinner or supper.

1677. COLE, *Dict.* You must KISS THE HARE'S FOOT, *post festum venisti*.

1851. *Notes and Queries*, 1 S. 4. p. 21. KISS THE HARE'S FOOT.—This locution is commonly used in some parts of the United Kingdom, to describe, what is expressed by the Latin proverb: '*Sero venientibus ossa*.'

TO KISS THE MASTER, *verb. phr.* (old).—To hit the JACK (*q.v.*) at bowls.

1579. GOSSON, *Schoole of Muse*, p. 60 (Arber's ed.). At Diceplay, euery one wisheth to caste well; at Bowles euery one craues, TO KISSE THE MAISTER; at running euery one starteth to win the goale.

TO KISS THE POST, *verb. phr.* (old).—To be shut out.

1600. HEYWOOD, *King Edward*, iv. [NARES]. Dost thou hear me, Ned? If I shall be thy host. Make haste thou art best, for fear THOU KISS THE POST.

1612. *Pasquils' Nightcap* [NARES]. Men of al countries travels through the same, And, if they money want, may KISSE THE POST.

1630. TAYLOR, *Wks.* [NARES]. Mars yeelds to Venus, gown-men rule the rost now, And men of war may fast, or KISSE THE POST now.

KISS MY ARSE. *See* ARSE.

TO KISS THE MAID, *verb. phr.* (old).—*See* quot.

1690. B. E., *Dict. Cant. Crew*, s.v. KISSING THE MAID, an Engine in Scotland, and at Halifax in England, in which the Head of a Malefactor is Laid to be Cut off, and which this way is done to a Hair, said to be invented by Earl Morton who had the ill Fate to Handsel it. [Also *New Cant. Dict.* (1725)].

KISS-CURL, *subs.* (common).—A small curl twisted on the cheek or temple; a BEAU-CATCHER (*q.v.*): *cf.* AGGRAWATOR and LOVE-LOCK. Also KISS-ME-QUICK.

1856. *Punch*, xxxi. 219. I declare when I read that letter in print, with a picture in the corner not the least bit in the world like me (tho' I admit rather pretty in its way) I coloured up to the tip-top of my forehead and I am sure that if I had worn those pastry-cook's girl's ornaments called KISS-CURLS the gum would have been melted off in a minute.

KISSER, *subs.* (pugilistic).—1. The mouth; the DRIPPING- or LATCH-PAN (*q.v.*). For synonyms *see* POTATO-TRAP.

1860. *Chambers' Journal*, xiii. 348. His mouth is his 'potatoe trap'—more shortly, 'tatur trap'—or KISSER.

2. in pl. (pugilistic).—The lips; LISPERS (*q.v.*); MUMS (*q.v.*). Fr. *les balots*.

KISSING, *subs.* (venery).—1. Copulation. For synonyms *see* GREENS and RIDE.

2. (billiards).—*See* KISS, *verb.* sense 1. Fr. *l'oculaire astronomique*.

KISSING-CRUST, *subs.* (colloquial).—The soft-baked surface between two loaves; also the under-crust in a pudding or pie.

1708. KING, *Art of Cookery*. These baked him KISSING-CRUSTS and those Brought him small beer.

1714. *Spectator*, No. 608. A quarrel about the KISSING-CRUST; spoiling of dinners, and coming in late at nights.

1822. LAMB, *Elia (Praise of Chimney-sweepers)*. How he would recommend this slice of white bread, or that piece of KISSING-CRUST, to a tender juvenile.

1837. BARHAM, *Ingoldsby Legends*, 'Nell Cook.' And a mouldy piece of KISSING-CRUST as from a warden pie.

1785. GROSE, *Vulg. Tongue*, s.v.

1811. *Lex. Bal.*, s.v.

KISSING-STRINGS, *subs.* (old).—Ribands hanging over the shoulders; FOLLOW-ME-LADS (*q.v.*). Fr. *Suivez-moi-jeune-homme*.

1705. *London Ladies Dressing Room* [NARES]. Behind her back the streamers fly, And KISSING-STRINGS hang dangling by.

1768. A. ROSS, *Helenore*, 34. The first time I to town or market gang A pair of KISSING-STRINGS and gloves.... shall be your due.

KISSING-TRAP, *subs.* (common).—The mouth; the WHISKER-BED (*q.v.*). For synonyms *see* POTATO TRAP.

1853. C. BEDE, *Verdant Green*, pt. 1. p. 106. His KISSING TRAP countered, his ribs roasted.

1887. ATKIN, *House Scraps*. The offside of his KISSING-TRAP Displays an ugly mark!

KISS-ME-QUICK, *subs.* (common).—1. A KISS-CURL (*q.v.*).

2. (popular).—The name of a very small, once fashionable bonnet.

1855. HALIBURTON, ('Sam Slick'), *Human Nature*, p. 131. She holds out with each hand a portion of her silk dress, as if she was walking a minuet, and it discloses a snow white petticoat. Her step is short and mincing, and she wears a new bonnet called a KISS-ME-QUICK.

1885. S. BARING GOULD, *Court Royal*, ii. Or this Dolly Varden with panniers, a little passed in style, and a KISS-ME-QUICK bonnet.

3. (American).—*See* quot.

1871. DE VERE, *Americanisms*, p. .... But of all the rare compounds known to Eastern bar-rooms, few ever reach his secluded home. Nor would he appreciate the bewitching softness of 'Long Linked Sweetness,' or the ecstacy produced by a 'KISS-ME-QUICK'—he likes to *take it* strong and hot.

KIST-O'-WHUSTLES, *subs.* (Scots').—An organ.

1640. *Lesly's March* [*Minst. Scot. Border* (1812), ii. 11]. And the KIST-FOU OF WHISTLES, That mak sic a cleiro.

1864. Letter in *Glasgow Herald*, 10 Dec. We have had, especially in our city churches, highly trained choirs, and we have now at our doors, clamouring for admission, the KIST O' WHISTLES, the horror of former generations of Scotchmen.

1870. *Orchestra*, May. By a majority of seventy-two the English Presbyterian Synod has vindicated the right of congregations to adopt the KIST FU' O' WHISTLES in their church services if they be so minded. The fight fought in Regent Square Church recently was hotly contested.

KIT, *subs.* (old).—1. A dancing master.—*New Cant. Dict.* (1725); GROSE (1785); *Lex. Bal.* (1811); [From KIT = a small violin].

2. (popular).—A person's baggage or impediments; an outfit; a collection of anything. THE WHOLE KIT = the lot; the WHOLE GRIDIRON or the whole BOILING. In American, the KIT AND BOODLE.

1785. GROSE, *Vulg. Tongue*, s.v. KIT.... likewise the whole of a soldier's necessaries, the content of his knapsack, and is used also to express the whole of different commodities; here take the WHOLE KIT, *i.e.*, take all.

1811. *Lex. Bal.*, s.v.

1815. SCOTT, *Guy Mannering*, xxxiv. 'Hush!—hush!—I tell you it shall be a joint business.' 'Why, will ye give me half the KITT?' 'What, half the estate?—d'ye mean we should set up house together at Ellangowan.'

1820. SHELLEY, *Œdipus Tyrannus*, 1. Now, Soloman, I'd sell you in a lump The WHOLE KIT of them.

1833. MARRYAT, *Peter Simple*, i. ch. XIV. I need hardly say that my lord's KIT was valuable, but what was better they exactly fitted me.

1843. DICKENS, *Martin Chuzzlewit*, XXV. 'Ah! I see 'em,' said Mrs. Gamp; 'all the WHOLE KIT of 'em numbered like hackney-coaches, ain't they?'

1846. *Punch*, ii. p. 44. 'I've got a wife—more fool I—and a KIT o' children wuss luck!'

1848. THACKERAY, *Book of Snobs*, x. He has since devoted his time to billiards, steeple-chasing, and the turf. His headquarters are Rummer's, in Conduit Street, where he keeps his KIT, but he is ever on the move in the exercise of his vocation as a gentleman jockey and gentleman leg.

1860. DICKENS, *Great Expectations*, xl. 'Blast you every one, from the judge in his wig, to the colonist a stirring up the dust. I'll show you a better gentleman than the WHOLE KIT on you put together!'

3. (venery).—The *penis* and *testes*.

KITCHEN, *subs.* (venery).—1. The female *pudendum*. For synonyms *see* MONOSYLLABLE.

2. (common).—The stomach; the VICTUALLING OFFICE (*q.v.*).

KITCHENER, *subs.* (thieves').—A thief frequenting a THIEVES' KITCHEN (*q.v.*).

KITCHENITE, *subs.* (printers').—A loafing compositor frequenting the kitchen of the Compositors' Society house: in contempt.

KITCHEN-LATIN, *subs.* (common).—Barbarous or sham Latin; DOG-LATIN (*q.v.*).

KITCHEN-PHYSIC, *subs.* (old).—1. Pot-herbs; and (2) victuals.

1592. GREENE, *Quip for Upstart Courtier* [Harl. Misc. v. 406]. For my selfe, if I be ill at ease, I take KITCHYN PHYSICKE; I make my wife my doctor, and my garden my apothecaries shop.

1641. MILTON, *Def. Humb. Remonst.*, § 2. Nothing will cure this man's understanding but some familiar and KITCHEN PHYSICK. . . . Call hither your cook!

1785. GROSE, *Vulg. Tongue*, s.v. A little KITCHEN-PHYSIC will set him up; he has more need of a cook than a doctor.

1811. *Lex. Bal.*, s.v.

KITCHEN-STUFF, *subs.* (old).—A female servant.

1658. BROME, *New Academy*, p. 44. What a bold piece of KITCHEN-STUFF is this that you have married!

KITE, *subs.* (popular).—1. A fool; a sharper; a cruel and rapacious wretch. Fr. *un buse*. For synonyms *see* BUFFLE and CABBAGE-HEAD.

1534. UDALL, *Roister Doister*, v. 5. Roister Doister, that doughtie KITE.

1605. SHAKSPEARE, *King Lear*, i. 4. Detested KITE! thou liest.

1639. FLETCHER, *Wit without Money*, i. 1. Cramming of serving-men, mustering of beggars, Maintaining hospitals for KITES and Curs.

1812. From an old Dublin *Jester*. [The story, however, with slight variations is told of other judges. See *N. and Q.*, 6 S., ix. 326, 394]. In a case before the Lord Chancellor of Ireland Mr. Curran, on behalf of the suitor, prayed to be relieved from the payment of some bills for which he had not received consideration, but only lent his name as an accommodation. Mr. Curran, in the course of his pleadings, mentioned the terms KITE and RAISING THE WIND several times, when his lordship requested to know the meaning of the words. 'My lord', Mr. Curran replied, 'in your country (meaning England) the wind generally raises the KITE, but with us,' significantly looking at the gentlemen of the bar, 'the KITE raises the wind.'

2. (commercial).—An accommodation bill; fictitious commercial paper; (in Scotland) a WIND-MILL-BILL (*q.v.*). *See* KITE-FLYING. TO FLY A KITE = to raise money or keep up credit by the aforesaid means.

1817. EDGEWORTH, *Love and Law*, i. 2. Here's bills plenty—long bills and short bills—but even the KITES, which I can fly as well as any man, won't raise the money for me now.

1823. BEE, *Dict. of the Turf*, s.v. KITE-FLYING. In Ireland FLYING THE KITE is employed to describe raising the wind.

1837. BARHAM, *Ingoldsby Legends (M. of Venice)*. In English Exchequer-bills full half a million, Not KITES, manufactured to cheat and inveigle, But the right sort of 'flimsy.'

1848. *Punch*, xiv. 226. He never does a little discounting, nor lends his hand to FLYING A KITE.

1849. *Perils of Pearl Street*, 82. FLYING THE KITE is rather a perilous adventure.

1880. SIMS, *Ballads of Babylon*, 'Little Worries.' You have a KITE you cannot FLY, and creditors are pressing.

1883. GRENVILLE-MURRAY, *People I Have Met*, p. 158. His wife, one of the better of the best society, had flown KITES to the height of twenty-five thousand pounds.

1891. *Licensed Victuallers' Gazette*, 23 Jan. .... has been, FLYING KITES and getting into trouble thereby.

3. (American).—Fancy stocks. MATSELL (1859).

4. (American thieves').—A letter.—MATSELL (1859).

5. (American thieves').—The chief of a gang of thieves.

6. (old).—A recruiting sergeant. [From Farquhar's Sergeant Kite in *The Recruiting Officer*].

1827. REYNOLDS, *The Fancy*, 'The Field of Tothill.' She was ador'd by ... sober sergeants ; privates too in drink, While pampered by those red KITES their recruiters.

7. (Old Scots').—The belly.

d.1554. LINDSAY, *Kitteis Confessioun*, Wks. (1879), i. 138, line 140. Thocht Codrus KYTE suld cleve and birst.

d.1607. MONTGOMERIE, *Flyting*, Wks. (1886-7), 85, line 754. Misly KYT! And thou flyt, I'll dryt in thy gob.

1722-30. RAMSAY, *Fables & Tales*, in Wks. (1851), iii. 165. Whose KYTES can streek out like raw plaider.

Verb. (commercial).—1. To keep up one's credit by means of accommodation bills ; to obtain money by bills. See *subs.* sense 2.

2. (American).—To speculate wildly.

3. (American).—To be restless, going from place to place ; TO SKITE (*q.v.*).—MATSELL (1859).

TO FLY A KITE.—1. See KITE, *subs.* sense 2.

2. (general).—To put out a feeler before a definite announcement.

KITE-FLYER, *subs.* (commercial).—One who raises money or sustains his credit by the use of accommodation bills.

KITE-FLYING, *subs.* (commercial).—1. The fabrication or negotiation of bills of accommodation, or bills for which no value has been received, in order to raise money.

2. (old).—Whoremongering.

1823. BEE, *Dict. of the Turf*, s.v. KITE-FLYING—said of a truant husband.

KITTEN, *subs.* (thieves').—A pint or half-pint pewter pot. See CAT *subs.* sense 5.

Verb. (colloquial).—To be brought to bed ; TO BUST UP ; TO EXPLODE.

KITTIE (also KITTOCK), *subs.* (Old Scots'). 1. Generic for a girl ; (2) a romping wench ; (3) a harlot.

d.1513. DUNBAR, *Devorit with Dreme*, in *Poems (ut supra)*, I, 83. So many ane KITTY dressed up with golden chenye.

c.1538. LYNDSAY, *Against Syde Taillis*, Wks. (1879), i. 131. I ken ane man, quchilk sevoir greit aithir. How he did lift ane KITTOKIS claithis. *Idem*, i. 135. *Kittei's Confession*. The Curate KITTIE wold have kissed.

d.1542. JAMES V, *Christ's Kirk on the Green*. There cam our KITTIES weschin clene In thair now kirtillis of gray.

KITTLE-BREEKS, *subs.* (Scots').—An irritable person.

KITTLE-PITCHERING, *subs.* (old).—See quot.

1785. GROSE, *Vulg. Tongue*, s.v. A jocular method of hobbling or bothering a troublesome teller of long stories ; this is done by contradicting some very immaterial circumstance at the beginning of the narration, the objections to which

being settled, others are immediately started to some new particular of like consequence, thus impeding, or rather not suffering him to enter into the main story. KITTLE-PITCHERING is often practised in confederacy.

KITTLER, *subs.* (American thieves').—One who tickles or pleases.

KITTY, *subs.* (old).—The Bridewell or prison at Durham : hence a prison or gaol generally. [From KIDCOTE (*q.v.*)].

1827-8. HONE, *Table Book*. He would put him in the KITTY for an impostor.

2. in pl. (old).—Effects ; furniture ; stock-in-trade ; MARBLES (*q.v.*). TO SEIZE ONE'S KITTYS = to take one's effects.—*Lex. Bal.* (1811).

3. (cards').—See quot.

1892. *Daily Chronicle*, 5 Mar. p. 9. col. 2. Two officers going into the bar parlour on Feb. 20 found five or six men playing ' Nap,' with a KITTY for drinks, KITTY being the pool and the payment to it of a half-penny.

4. in pl. (military).—The Scots' Guards.

KIVEY, *subs.* (common).—A man ; a fellow : a diminutive of COVE (*q.v.*).

1854. BRADLEY, *Verdant Green*, ii. ch. 4. That 'll stop your dancing my KIVEY.

K. LEGGED, *adj.* (printers').—Knock-kneed ; shaky on the pins.

KLOOP! *intj.* (common).—An imitation of the sound of a drawing cork.

1872. *Sunday Times*, Aug. 25, p. 2. col. 5. 'The Deserted Village.' When the sudden KLOOP of a cork has startled me.

KLEM, *verb.* (American thieves').—See quot.

1859. MATSELL, *Vocabulum*, s.v. KLEM the bloke, hit the man.

KLEP, *subs.* (popular).—A thief. For synonyms see THIEVES. [Short for kleptomaniac].

Verb. To steal. For synonyms see PRIG.

KNAB THE RUST. See RUST.

KNACK, *subs.* (venery).—1. The *penis*. For synonyms see CREAM-STICK and PRICK.

1656. FLETCHER, *Martiall*, vii. 30. Why, being a *Roman* lasse, dost do this? tell, Is't cause no Roman KNACK can please so well?

2. (old : now recognised).—1. A trick ; and (2) a trinket. [TYRWHITT : The word seems to have been formed by the KNACKING or snapping of the fingers made by jugglers].

1383. CHAUCER, *Cant. Tales*, 4099. The more queinte KNAKKES that they make (= the cleverer tricks they practise).

1611. COTGRAVE, *Dictionarie*, *Matassiner des mains*, to move, KNACK, or waggle the fingers, like a jugler.

1653. BROME, *Novella*, i. 2. Such rings, such things, such KNACKS, such knots and bobs.

1675. COTTON, *Scoffer Scofft*, in Wks. (1725), p. 163. And if they Women meet do rout 'um, For the fine KNACKS they wear about 'um.

1690. B E., *Dict. Cant. Crew*, s.v. KNACK, or Slight in any Art, the Craft or Mystery in any Trade, a petty artifice, or Trick like those upon the Cards. KNACKS, or Toies.

1731-35. POPE, *Moral Essays*, ii. 155. For how could equal colours do the KNACK?

1781. COWPER, *Table Talk*, 666. While servile tricks and imitative KNACKS.

1892. MILLIKEN, *'Arry Ballads*, p. 5. Lots of good temper and NACK.

KNACKER, *subs.* (old).—1. An old horse.

1869. W. BRADWOOD, *The O. V., H.* xii. Thoroughbred weeds, and a few thoroughbred weight-carriers ; half-bred KNACKERS, and half-bred hunters cheap at three figures.

2. (old : now recognised).—A horse-slaughterer.

1839. *Comic Almanack*, Sept. Soon they'll be senseless brutes, without a bit of feeling, Or else they'll pine away so fast, the KNACKERS scarce will skin 'em.

1851-61. H. MAYHEW, *London Lab. and Lond. Poor*, i.189. The cat and dogs-meat dealers. . . . generally purchase the meat at the KNACKERS' (horse-slaughterers') yards.

3. in pl. (venery).—The testicles. For synonyms see CODS.

4. in pl. (Stock Exchange).—Harrison, Barber, & Co. Ltd. shares. [An amalgamation of horse-slaughterers].

KNACKER'S BRANDY, *subs. phr.* (common).—A beating.

KNACK-SHOP, *subs.* (old).—See quots.

1690. B. E., *Dict. Cant. Crew*, s.v. KNACK. . . . a KNACK-shop or Toy-shop, freighted with pretty Devises to Pick Pockets.

1785. GROSE, *Vulg. Tongue*, s.v. KNICK-SHOP, a toy shop, a nick-nackatory.

KNAP, *verb.* (old).—1. To steal, receive, accept, endure, etc. Thus, TO KNAP A CLOUT = to steal a handkerchief ; TO KNAP THE SWAG = to grab the booty ; TO KNAP SEVEN OR FOURTEEN PENN' ORTH = to get seven or fourteen years' ; TO KNAP THE GLIM = to catch a clap. In making a bargain TO KNAP the sum oftered is to accept it. MR. KNAP'S BEEN THERE, is said of a pregnant woman. TO KNAP THE RUST = to fall into a rage. Originally (as in quots 1537 and 1566) KNAP = to strike : whence KNAP (theatrical) = a manual retort rehearsed and arranged ; TO TAKE (or GIVE) THE KNAP = to receive (or administer) a sham blow ; and KNAPPER = the head or RECEIVER GENERAL (*q.v.*).

1537. *Thersites* [DODSLEY, *Old Plays* (1874), i. 428]. She KNAPPETH me in the nose.

1566. KNOX, *Reformation in Scotland* I. i. 47 (Wodrow Society, 1846). And then begane no little fray, but yitt a meary game ; for rockattes were rent ; typpets were torn, crownes were KNAPPED.

1714. LUCAS, *Gamesters*, 27. He was not ignorant in KNAPPING, which is, striking one die dead, and let the other run a milstone.

1820. *London Magazine*, i. 26. It was their husband's object to KNAP their thimbles.

1821. HAGGART, *Life*, p. 51.

1839. REYNOLDS, *Pickwick Abroad*, p. 223. We'll KNAP a fogle with fingers fly.

2. (pugilists').—To be in PUNISHMENT (*q.v.*) ; to CATCH IT (*q.v.*). TO KNAP A HOT 'UN = to receive a hard blow.

3. (American thieves').—To arrest.—MATSELL (1859).

TO KNAP THE STOOP, *verb. phr.* (old).—See quot.

1822. EGAN, *Real Life*, ii. 97. 'Having once been made inspector of the pavement, or in other words KNAPP'D THE STOOP.'

TO KNAP A JACOB FROM A DANNA-DRAG, *verb. phr.* (old).—To steal the ladder from a nightman's cart, while the men are absent, in order to effect an ascent to a one-pair-of-stairs window, to scale a garden-wall, etc. — DE VAUX. See KNAP.

KNAPPER'S-POLL, *subs.* (old).—A sheep's head. For synonyms see SANGUINARY JAMES.

KNAPPING-JIGGER, *subs.* (thieves').—A turn-pike gate ; *i.e.*, a gate for the receipt of tolls. See KNAP, sense 1.

1834. H. AINSWORTH, *Rookwood*, iv. Turpin treated him as he had done the *dub* [pikeman] at the KNAPPING-JIGGER, and cleared the driver and his little wain with ease.

KNARK, *subs.* (old).—A churl ; a flint-heart ; a NARK (*q.v.*).

1851-61. MAYHEW, *London Lab. etc.*, i. 343. He couldn't refuse a dog, much more a Christian : but he had a butler, a regular NARK.

KNAT, *subs.* (tailors').—1. A difficult task ; (2) a tyrant ; and (3) one not easily hoodwinked.

KNAVE, *subs.* (Christ's Hospital).—A dunce : at Hertford, a KNACK.

KNEE. TO BREAK ONE'S KNEE, *verb. phr.* (venery).—To be deflowered, or got with child. For synonyms see DOCK, *verb.* sense 1.

TO OFFER (or GIVE) THE KNEE, *verb. phr.* (old).—To play the second in a fight.

1856. HUGHES, *Tom Brown's Schooldays*, II. v. Martin, TO GIVE HIM A KNEE, steps out on the turf.

KNEE HIGH TO A MOSQUITO (A TOAD, A CHAW OF TOBACCO etc.), *phr.* (American).—Insignificant ; of scant account.

TO SIT ON ONE'S KNEES, *verb. phr.* (colloquial).—To kneel down.

KNEE-TREMBLER, *subs.* (venery).—A standing embrace ; a FAST-FUCK (*q.v.*) ; A PERPENDICULAR.

For general synonyms see GREENS and RIDE.

KNEE-TRICK, *subs.* (old).—Kneeling.

1632. BROME, *Novella*, iv. 2. No, if I worship any of 'hem more, Than in the KNEE-TRICK, that is necessary In their true use, let me be eunuchiz'd.

KNICK-KNACK, *subs.* (venery).—1. The female *pudendum*. For synonyms see MONOSYLLABLE.

2. (old).—A trinket ; a toy. See NICKNACKS.

KNIFE, *subs.* (once literary : now military).— A sword.

c.1270. *Robert of Gloucester*, p. 104. He drow 'ys KNYF, and slow the kyng.

Verb. (colloquial).—1. To stab.

1851. F. WALPOLE, *The Ansayrii*, ii. 8. A brute who in cold blood KNIVED and tortured them with his own hand.

1862. DICKENS, *Xmas Stories (Somebody's Luggage)*, p. 132 (H. ed.). If you should even get into trouble through KNIFEING—or say, garotting—a brother artist.

1870. *Globe*, 17 Nov., i. 3. Already a too refractory sufferer has been threatened by his torturer with the not very pleasant alternative of being KNIFED if he does not submit with a better grace.

2. (American electioneering).—To plot against the candidate of one's own party.

1870. *Globe*, 17 Nov. [Leader].

TO LAY DOWN ONE'S KNIFE AND FORK, *verb. phr.* (common). —To die ; TO PEG OUT (*q.v.*) ; TO SNUFF IT (*q.v.*). For synonyms see ALOFT and HOP THE TWIG.

TO KNIFE IT, *verb. phr.* (old). —To decamp ; TO CUT IT (*q.v.*).

KNIFE IT! *intj.* (old).—Separate! leave off! go away!

TO PLAY A GOOD KNIFE AND FORK, *verb. phr.* (common).—To eat with appetite.

1837. KNOWLES, *Love Chase*, i. 3. Why shouldn't I marry? KNIFE AND FORK I PLAY Better than many a boy of twenty-five.

1846-8. THACKERAY, *Vanity Fair*, ii. viii. The Colonel PLAYS A GOOD KNIFE AND FORK at tiffin, and resumes those weapons with great success at dinner.

BEFORE ONE CAN SAY 'KNIFE'! *phr.* (common).—Instanter; IN THE TWINKLING OF AN EYE (*q.v.*). *Cf.* JACK ROBINSON.

1892. ROLF BOLDREWOOD, *Robbery Under Arms*, xxiv. She'd be off and out to sea BEFORE ANY ONE COULD SAY 'KNIFE.'

KNIFE-BOARD, *subs.* (common).—A seat for passengers running lengthwise on the roof of an omnibus: now mostly superseded by 'garden seats' Fr. *l'impératrice.*

1853. *Diogenes*, ii. 21. A 'Correspondent' calls the top of an omnibus 'the eyrie of the KNIFE-BOARD.'

1856. *Punch*, xxxi. 203. And then the KNIFEBOARD cramps you so.

1859. *Punch*, xxxvi. 51, 2. Perhaps Mum'll ride on the KNIFEBOARD.

1860. ARTHUR SMITH, *Thames Angler*, ii. 'On 'busses' KNIFEBOARDS, stretch'd, The City clerks all tongue-protruded lay.'

1882. *Daily News*, 7 Oct., p. 5, col. 7. The box, or still better the KNIFE-BOARD, of an omnibus facing the docks is the real shifting point from which to view the most superb range of docks in existence on any river but the Thames.

1889. *Daily Telegraph*, 5 Jan. The 'insides' were terrified, and clamoured loudly, so the driver left his seat, staggered up on the KNIFEBOARD, and fell asleep.

KNIFER, *subs.* (common).—A sharking sponge.

KNIFISH, *adj.* (tailors').—Spiteful.

KNIGHT, *subs.* (common).—An ironical prefix of profession or calling: generic.

[Combinations are KNIGHT OF THE BLADE = a bully (B. E. 1690); KNIGHT OF THE BRUSH = an artist or painter; KNIGHT OF THE COLLAR = a gallows-bird; KNIGHT OF THE CLEAVER = a butcher; KNIGHT OF THE CUE = a billiard-marker; KNIGHT OF THE GREEN CLOTH = a gamester; KNIGHT OF HORNSEY (or OF THE FORKED ORDER) = a cuckold; KNIGHT OF INDUSTRY = a thief; KNIGHT OF THE KNIFE = a cut-purse; KNIGHT OF LABOR = (in America) a workingman; KNIGHT OF THE LAPSTONE = a cobbler; KNIGHT OF THE NAPKIN = a waiter; KNIGHT OF THE NEEDLE = a tailor; KNIGHT OF THE QUILL = an author or journalist; KNIGHT OF THE PENCIL = a book-maker; KNIGHT OF THE PESTLE = an apothecary; KNIGHT OF THE PIT = a cocker; KNIGHT OF THE PETTICOAT = a bawdy-house bully; KNIGHT OF THE PISSPOT = a physician, an apothecary; KNIGHT OF THE POST = a knight dubbed at the whipping post or pillory, also a rogue who got his living by giving false witness or false bail; KNIGHT OF THE RAINBOW = a footman (GROSE, 1785); KNIGHT OF THE ROAD—a footpad or highwayman: also KNIGHT OF THE RUMPAD; KNIGHT OF THE SHEARS or THIMBLE = a tailor (GROSE, 1785); KNIGHT OF THE SPIGOT = a tapster, a publican; KNIGHT OF THE SUN = an adventurer, a knight-errant; KNIGHT OF THE WHEEL = a cyclist; KNIGHT OF THE WHIP = a coachman; KNIGHT OF THE YARD = a shopman or counter-jumper].

*c.*1554. *Youth* [DODSLEY, *Old Plays* (1847), ii. 15]. God's fate! thou didst enough there For TO BE MADE KNIGHT OF THE COLLAR.

1592. NASHE, *Pierce Penilesse*, in *Works*, ii. 19. A KNIGHT OF THE POST, quoth he, for so I am tearmed; a fellowe that will sweare you anything for twelue pence.

1606. *Sir Gyles Goosecappe*, I, iii. [in BULLEN'S *Old Plays*, iii. 19]. O good KNIGHT A' THE POST, heele sweare.

1614. JONSON, *Bartholomew Fayre*, ii. 1. 'Is this goodly person before us here. . . . a KNIGHT OF THE KNIFE?' 'What mean you by that?' 'I mean a child of the horn thumb. . . . a cut purse.'

1620. FORD, *Line of Life.* But is his resolution any way infracted, for that some refractaries are (like KNIGHTS OF THE POST) hired to witnesse against him?

1621. BURTON, *Anat. of Mel.*, III. xi. 187 (1836). Perjur'd knaves, KNIGHTS OF THE POST, lyers.

*c.*1633. *Lady Alimony*, i. 3. That KNIGHT OF THE SUN who employed me should have done his errand himself. *Ibid.* iii. 7. Doubt nothing, my fellow KNIGHTS OF HORNSEY.

1635. GLAPTHORNE, *The Hollander*, in *Wks.* (1874), i. 94. Not John-a-Stiles, the KNIGHT OF THE POST, is it?

1653. BROME, *The Damoiselle*, in *Wks.* (1873), Act i. 1. He takes me for a KNIGHT OF THE POST.

1662. *Rump Songs*, ii. 47. Then the KNIGHT OF THE PESTLE, King Lambert, and Vane, With a sceptre of iron did over it reign. *Ibid.*, ii. 185. A KNIGHT OF THE POST, and a cobbling lord.

1662. WILSON, *The Cheats*, v. 2. How? Stick a bull's feather in my cap! Make me a KNIGHT OF THE FORKED ORDER! *Ibid.* iv. 1.

1671. R. HEAD, *English Rogue*, I, ch. xxx. p. 246 (Repr. 1874). His investation into the honour of one of the KNIGHTS OF THE ROAD.

1691-2. *Gentlemen's Journal*, Mar. p. 2. I know some of your sturdy, stuff KNIGHTS OF THE QUILL. *Ibid.* Feb. p. 5. KNIGHTS OF THE POST, Alsatian braves.

1694. ECHARD, *Plautus*, p. 151. Whene'er we meet with fellows who hire KNIGHTS OF THE POST in law-sutes, and rascals who forswear themselves.

1709. MRS. CENTLIVRE, *Gamester* (1872), i. 162. It is a kind of KNIGHT OF THE POST.—That will swear on either side for interest.

1711. *Spectator*, No. 172. A couple of courtiers making professions of esteem, would make the same figure after breach of promise, as two KNIGHTS OF THE POST convicted of perjury.

*d.*1721. PRIOR, *Poems* (1892), i. 156. There the Squires of the Pad, and the KNIGHTS OF THE POST.

1777. FOOTE, *Trip to Calais* (1795), i. p. 23. That may be the case, Master Minnikin, with those of the trade who live in the city; but I would have you to know, the KNIGHTS OF THE NEEDLE are another sort of people at our end of the town.

1819. MOORE, *Tom Crib*, 76. Whose kiss to my lip is as sweet As the brandy and tea, rather thinnish, That KNIGHTS OF THE RUMPAD so rurally sip.

1821. SCOTT, *Kenilworth*, viii. 'When an old song comes across us merry old KNIGHTS OF THE SPIGOT, it runs away with our discretion.'

1828. JON BEE, *Picture of London*, p. 27. To the practices and necessities of the coachmen and guard's *private trade*, we owe the increasing number and fresh supply of hangers-on, whose first business has been the performing fetch-and-carry services for those KNIGHTS OF THE WHIP.

1838. JAS. GRANT, *Sketches in London*, iii. 119. 'You'll do what, Sir?' observed the 'man with the Macintosh,' eyeing the KNIGHT OF THE THIMBLE steadily. 'Just call me a tailor agin, Sir.'

1840. THACKERAY, *Catherine*, v. We did not go into the Park, but turned off and cantered smartly up towards Kilburn; and, when we got into the country, galloped as if the devil were at our heels. Bless you, my love, it was all done in a minute; and the Ensign and I found ourselves regular KNIGHTS OF THE ROAD, before we knew where we were almost.

1843. W. T. MONCRIEFF, *The Scamps of London*, ii. 2. Our hells are full of Greeks—they are the Corinthians of the order, the top sawyers—KNIGHTS OF THE POST, whom you will find in Regent-street, in the clubs, at Epsom, Ascot, Newmarket, and Doncaster.

1858. A. MAYHEW, *Paved with Gold*, III, iii. p. 267. 'It's scarcely wages for a KNIGHT OF THE RAINBOW (footman).'

1864. *Reader*, 22 Oct., p. 505. i. The best guard against any such spirit, [that of only regarding books by the light of 'will they *pay*'] is that the publisher should be a KNIGHT OF THE PEN himself.

1881. *New York Slang Dictionary.* Gamblers are called KNIGHTS OF THE GREEN CLOTH, and their lieutenants, who are sent out after greenhorns, are called decoys, cappers, and steerers.

1885. JOHN COLEMAN, in *Longm. Mag.*, VII. 78. Occasionally however, the author has his nose put out of joint by the scene-painter. I once heard a distinguished KNIGHT OF THE BRUSH exclaim, 'D-n the author and the actors! the public come to see *my* scenery!'

1885. *Punch*, 7 March, p. 109. The KNIGHTS OF THE PENCIL, Sir, hold that backers, like pike, are more ravenous in keen weather, and consequently easier to land.

1890. *Daily Telegraph*, 25 Feb. p. iv. col. 7. Meanwhile, every temptation is offered to the felonious tendencies of these KNIGHTS OF INDUSTRY. Women parade the rooms with thousands of pounds' value of jewellery on their persons.

TO BE THE GUEST OF THE CROSS-LEGGED KNIGHTS, *verb. phr.* (old).—To go dinnerless; TO DINE WITH DUKE HUMPHREY (*q.v.*); TO DINE (or SUP) WITH SIR THOMAS GRESHAM (*q.v.*). [In allusion to the stone effigies in the Round Church (Temple) at one time the *rendez-vous* of lawyers and their clients, who attracted a host of dinnerless vagabonds in the hope of picking up a job]. For synonyms *see* PECKHAM.

TO BE KNIGHTED IN BRIDEWELL, *verb. phr.* (old).—To be whipped in prison.

1592. NASHE, *Pierce Penilesse* [GROSART, ii. 57]. I knewe an odde foulemouthde knaue . . . that had . . . a backe so often KNIGHTED IN BRIDEWELL that it was impossible . . . to terrifie him from ill-speaking.

KNITTING NEEDLE, *subs. phr.* (military).—A sword. For synonyms *see* CHEESE-TOASTER.

KNOB, *subs.* (common).—1. The head; THE NOB (*q.v.*). For synonyms *see* CRUMPET. ONE ON THE KNOB = a blow on the head.—GROSE (1785).

2. (workmen's).—A KNOBSTICK (*q.v.*).

KNOBBY, *adj.* (common).—*See* NOBBY.

KNOB-OF-SUCK, *subs. phr.* (provincial).—A piece of sweetmeat.

1865. *Good Words*, Feb., p. 125. These children get an hour for dinner, and when they are 'very good' and work hard they sometimes get a KNOB-O'-SUCK on Saturday.

KNOBSTICK (or **NOBSTICK**), *subs.* (workmen's).—1. A non-society hand; DUNG (*q.v.*); a RAT (*q.v.*). Also, one who takes work under price, or continues at work while his fellows are on strike. (2) A master who does not pay his men at market rates.

1851-61. H. MAYHEW, *London Lab. & Lond. Poor*, iii. 220. I next went to work at a under-priced hatter's, termed a KNOBSTICK'S.

1855. MRS. GASKELL, *North and South*, ch. xxv. 'They would try and get speech o' th' KNOBSTICKS, and coax 'em, and reason wi 'em, and m'appen warn'em off; but whatever came, the Committee charged all members o' th' Union to lie down and die, if need were, without striking a blow; and then they reckoned they were sure o' carrying th'public with them.'

1858. *Notes and Queries*, 1 S. ix. 373. In these days of strikes, turn-outs, and lock-outs we hear. . . . much of KNOBSTICKS.

1860. SIR J. K. SHUTTLEWORTH, *Scarsdale*, ii. ch. ii. By picketing the mills, by assaults on KNOBSTICKS.

1887. *Contemporary Rev.*, li. 238. The KNOBSTICK takes away the striker's hope of bringing his employer to terms.

1887. *Daily Telegraph*, 1 July, 5. 8. Hundreds of windows at Dobson and Barlow's foundry, in which are KNOBSTICKS, or 'importations', were broken.

1891. *Pall Mall Gaz.*, 25 July, p. 2, col. 2. The fact must be borne in mind that this advocate of physical force as an argument with KNOBSTICKS is repudiated by the organization of his fellow-workers.

KNOCK, *subs.* (horse-dealers').—1. A lame horse; an incurable SCREW (*q.v.*). [The horse-dealer in JONSON'S *Bartholemew Fair* (1614), is called KNOCKEM].

1864. *London Review*, 18 June, p. 643. The KNOCK, afflicted with disease of the navicular joint, or shoulder lameness, neither of which make any outward show, is a great favourite for horse-coping purposes, as he is often a fine-looking animal.

2.—*See verb.*

Verb. (venery).—1. To copulate. Hence, KNOCK, *subs.*, (1) an act of coition, and (2) the *penis* (*see* KNACK); KNOCKING-SHOP (or -HOUSE) = a brothel; KNOCKING-JACKET = a bed-gown; and KNOCKER, (1) = the *penis*, and (2) a PERFORMER (*q.v.*) male or female. [For possible derivation *see* NOCK, *subs.*, and quot. (FLORIO), 1598]. For synonyms *see* GREENS and RIDE.

1560. *Nice Wanton* [DODSLEY, *Old Play* (1874), ii]. 170. Goldlocks She must have KNOCKS, Or else I do her wrong.

1598. FLORIO, *Worlde of Wordes*, *Cunnuta*, a woman NOCKED.

1611. BARRY, *Ram Alley*, iii. 1. Comfort her tears, and say her daughters match'd With one that has a KNOCKER to his father.

1612. FIELD, *Woman is a Weathercock*, i. 2. You should be a KNOCKER, then, by the mother's side.

1719. DURFEY, *Pills etc.*, iii. 48. Ladies, make room, behold I come, Have at your KNOCKING jackets.

1722. RAMSAY, *Fables & Tales*, in *Wks.* (1851), iii. 170. For nought delights him mair than KNOCKING.

1823. EGAN, *Vulg. Tongue*, s.v.

2. (popular). To make an impression; to be irresistible; TO FETCH (*q.v.*); TO FLOOR (*q.v.*).

1883. *Referee*, May 6, p. 3, col. 3. 'It's Never too Late to Mend,' with J. H. Clynds as Tom Robinson, is KNOCKING 'em at the Pavilion.

1892. CHEVALIER, 'KNOCKED '*em in the Old Kent Rd*' [Title of Song.]

TO KNOCK ACOCK, *verb. phr.* (colloquial).—To 'floor'; TO FLABBERGAST (*q.v.*); TO DOUBLE UP. *See* COCKED HAT.

TO KNOCK ABOUT (or ROUND), *verb. phr.* (colloquial).—To wander here and there; to lounge. Also 'to see life'; 'to go the PACE' (*q.v.*).

1851. MAYHEW, *Lond. Lab. etc.*, ii. 87. I've been KNOCKING ABOUT on the streets.

1855. W. IRVING, *Life of Washington*, i. 423. A long course of solicitation, haunting public offices, and KNOCKING ABOUT town, had taught him [General Gates], it was said, how to wheedle, and flatter, and accommodate himself to the humors of others.

1888. *Harper's Mag.*, lxxvi. 349. I have been KNOCKING ABOUT Europe long enough to learn there are certain ways of doing things.

1891. *Sporting Life*, 28 Mar. He was a truant of the first water, and after KNOCKING ROUND till sixteen years of age etc.

TO KNOCK ABOUT THE BUB, *verb. phr.* (common).—To pass round the drink. *See* BUB.

1781. G. PARKER, *View of Society*, I. 212. They went away seemingly very well satisfied, leaving master and man KNOCKING ABOUT THE BUB.

TO KNOCK (or LET) DAYLIGHT INTO ONE. *See* DAYLIGHT.

TO KNOCK ALL OF A HEAP. *See* HEAP.

TO KNOCK AT THE COBBLER'S DOOR. *See* COBBLER'S KNOCK.

TO KNOCK DOWN, *verb. phr.* (American).—1. To appropriate; to embezzle.

1882. MCCABE, *New York*, p. 158. In former days the driver of a stage was furnished with a cash-box, which was securely fastened to the roof of the coach, at his left hand, All the money received passed through his hands, and he had frequent opportunities of KNOCKING DOWN or appropriating a modest sum to his own use.

2. (colloquial).—To call upon; to select.

1758-65. GOLDSMITH, *Essays*, i. While the president vainly KNOCKED DOWN Mr. Leathersides for a song.

1773. GOLDSMITH, *She Stoops to Conquer*, i. 2. 1 Now, gentlemen, silence for a song. The 'squire is going to KNOCK himself DOWN for a song.

1789. G. PARKER, *Variegated Characters*. He was KNOCKED DOWN for the crap the last sessions. He went off at the fall of the leaf at Tuck'em Fair.

1866. C. READE, *Griffith Gaunt*, x. They KNOCKED HIM DOWN for a song; and he sang a rather Anacreontic one very melodiously.

TO KNOCK DOWN FOR A SONG etc., *verb. phr.* (colloquial).—To sell under intrinsic value.

TO KNOCK DOWN A CHEQUE (or PILE), *verb. phr.* (colonical).—To spend one's savings lavishly; TO BLEW (*q.v.*).

1885. FINCH HATTON, *Advance Australia*. A man with a cheque or sum of money in his possession, hands it over to the publican, and calls for drinks for himself and his friends, until the publican tells him he has drunk out his cheque.

TO KNOCK DOWN FARES, *verb. phr.* (American).—To pilfer fares: of conductors and guards. *See* KNOCK DOWN, sense 1.

TO KNOCK IT DOWN, *verb. phr.* (common).—To applaud by hammering or stamping.

TO KNOCK ONE DOWN TO, *verb. phr.* (American).—To introduce (to a person).

TO KNOCK IN, *verb. phr.* (Oxford University).—1. To return to college after GATE is closed.

1825. *English Spy*, I. 155. 'Close the oak Jem,' said Horace Eglantine, 'and take care no one KNOCKS IN before we have knocked down the contents of your master's musical *mélange*.'

1837. BARHAM, *Ingoldsby Legends*, p. 463 [ed. 1862]. That same afternoon Father Dick, who as soon Would KNOCK IN, or 'cut chapel', as jump o'er the moon Was missing at vespers—at complines—all night! And his monks were of course in a deuce of a fright.

1853. CUTHBERT BEDE, *Verdant Green*, I. xi. At first, too, he was on such occasions greatly alarmed at finding the gates of Brazenface closed, obliging him thereby to KNOCK IN.

1861. HUGHES, *Tom Brown at Oxford*, p. 458 [ed. 1864]. There's twelve striking. I must KNOCK IN. Good night. You'll be round to breakfast at nine?

2. (gaming).—To take a hand at cards; TO CHIP IN (*q.v.*).

TO KNOCK INTO FITS (A COCKED HAT, THE MIDDLE OF NEXT WEEK etc.), *verb. phr.* (common).—To confound; TO FLOOR (*q.v.*); to punish severely. *See* COCKED HAT, BEAT and FITS.

1892. MILLIKEN, *'Arry Ballads*, 42. KNOCKS recit-ateeves INTO FITS.

TO KNOCK (or TAKE) IT OUT OF ONE, *verb. phr.* (colloquial).—To exhaust; to empty; to punish severely.

1841. *Punch*, i. p. 265, col. 2. The uphill struggles. . . . soon KNOCK IT all OUT OF HIM.

TO KNOCK OFF, *verb. phr.* (colloquial).—1. To leave off work; to abandon. Fr. *péter sur le mastic*.

1662. FULLER, *Worthies*, x [ed. Nichols, 1811]. In noting of their nativities, I have wholly observed the instructions of Pitœus, where I KNOCK OFF with his death, my light ending with his life on that subject.

1690. B. E., *Dict. Cant. Crew*, s.v. KNOCK OFF, to give over Trading; also to Abandon or Quit one's Post or Pretensions,

1725. *New Cant. Dict.*, s.v. KNOCK-OFF, to give over Thieving.

1785. GROSE, *Vulg. Tongue*, s.v., KNOCK-OFF, to conclude.

1860. DICKENS, *Uncommercial Traveller*, v. p. 25. Jack had KNOCKED OFF work in the docks some hours.

1865. *Pall Mall Gaz.*, 4 Mar. Iron ship builders and other employers will have to KNOCK OFF.

1883. *Daily Telegraph*, 10 Aug., p. 6, col. 1. Another half-pint when he KNOCKS OFF in the evening, and before he starts for home to his late tea.

1883. GREENWOOD, *Odd People etc.*, 'Genteel Slang' . . . With your leave or without, he must KNOCK OFF at midday.

1884. W. C. RUSSELL, *Jack's Courtship*, xvii. 'Why, I heard that you had KNOCKED OFF the sea some years ago—come into an estate.'

2. (colloquial).—To dispatch with ease; to put out of hand.

1886. *Westminster Rev.*, cxxv. 292. He could KNOCK OFF a parody, a drinking song.

1891. *Pall Mall Gazette*, 29 Nov. p. 6, col. 2. Here is a specimen of the 'consumptive manner' as KNOCKED OFF by Mr. Lang.

3. (colloquial).—To deduct; to 'KNOCK so much OFF the price'.

4. (colloquial).—To die.

*d.*1704. TOM BROWN, *Works*, iv. 183. Perverse people. . . . that would not KNOCK OFF in any reasonable time but lived long on purpose to spite their relation.

TO KNOCK ONE BANDY, *verb. phr.* (tailors').—To astound; TO FLABBERGAST (*q.v.*).

TO KNOCK ON THE HEAD, *verb. phr.* (colloquial).—To frustrate; to spoil; to settle.

TO KNOCK OUT, *verb. phr.* (auctioneers').—1. *See* KNOCK-OUT.

2. (racing).—To bet so persistently against a horse that from a short price he retires to an outside place: to drive out of the quotations.

1876. HINDLEY, *Adventures of a Cheap Jack*, p. 203. The concern would either remain for a time in shares or would be KNOCKED OUT at once.

1883. *Pall Mall Gazette*, 16 April, p. 4, col. 1. Foxhall. . . . was second favourite for some time, but he has now been KNOCKED OUT to comparatively long odds.

3. (common).—To make bankrupt: KNOCKED OUT = unable to meet engagements.

4. (pugilistic).—*See subs.* sense 4 and KNOCK OUT OF TIME.

1891. *Daily Telegraph*, 21 Mar. For the third time this year, they managed, after a drawn game, to KNOCK OUT the much fancied Sunderland team.

5. (Oxford University).—To leave college after hours: of out of college men only. *See* KNOCK IN and KNOCKING OUT.

1861. H. KINGSLEY, *Ravenshoe*, vii. Five out-college men had KNOCKED OUT at a quarter to three, refusing to give any name but the dean's.

1861. HUGHES, *Tom Brown at Oxford*, xlv. p. 503 [ed. 1864]. 'Hullo!' he said, getting up; 'time for me to KNOCK OUT, or old Copas will be in bed.'

TO KNOCK OUT OF TIME, *verb. phr.* (pugilistic).—So to punish an opponent that he is not able to answer the call of 'Time'.

1884. *Saturday Review*, 16 Jan., p. 108, col. 1. A man of weak physique is apt to be KNOCKED OUT OF TIME by a more robust though less skilful adversary.

1891. *Licensed Vict. Minor*, 30 Jan., p. 7, col. 2. He had, in fact, almost played with Tom with the gloves, and once, at Jem Ward's benefit, when both were a little bit pricked, had KNOCKED the Redditch man bang off his legs, and very nearly OUT OF TIME.

TO KNOCK THE SPOTS OFF (or OUT OF), *verb. phr.* (American).—To surpass; to confound; to thrash; to excel.

1887. FRANCIS, *Saddle & Mocassin*, 152. She can KNOCK THE SPOTS OUT OF these boys at that game.

1888. *Pall Mall Budget*, 26 Ap., p. 5. An American gentleman has just sailed for Sydney TO KNOCK SPOTS OUT OF the rabbits.

TO KNOCK THE BOTTOM (STUFFING, WADDING, LINING, FILLING, or INSIDE) OUT OF, *verb. phr.* (common).—To confound; to surpass; TO FLOOR (*q.v.*); to thrash; to finish off.

1889. *Sporting Times*, 3 Aug., p. 3, col. 1. 'Hold hard—here he is. Good ev'ning, sir 'aven't the pleasure of knowing you, but saw you KNOCK THE STUFFING OUT OF the ring to-day. Done well?'

1891. BELLAMY, *Dr. Heidenhoff's Process*, p. 52. This cool ignoring of all that had happened that day in modifying their relations at one blow KNOCKED THE BOTTOM OUT OF all his thinking for the past week.

TO KNOCK SMOKE OUT OF, *verb. phr.* (colonial).—To try; to vanquish utterly.

1888. ROLF BOLDREWOOD, *Robbery Under Arms*, xi. You ought to have sense enough not to KNOCK SMOKE OUT of fresh horses before we begin. *Ibid.* xxxix. A regiment or a man-of-war's crew like him would KNOCK SMOKE OUT OF any other thousand men the world could put up.

TO KNOCK SAUCEPANS OUT OF, *verb. phr.* (colloquial).—To run amuck.

1888. ROLF BOLDREWOOD, *Robbery Under Arms*, xxvi. 'He'll begin to KNOCK SAUCEPANS OUT OF all the boys between here and Weddin Mountain.

TO KNOCK OUT THE WEDGES, *verb. phr.* (American).—To desert; to leave in a difficulty.

TO KNOCK ROUND. *See* TO KNOCK ABOUT.

TO KNOCK UNDER, *verb. phr.* (old: now colloquial).—To yield; to give out; to confess defeat.

1668. DRYDEN, *An Evening's Love*, v. KNOCK UNDER, you rogue, and confess me conqueror.

1691-2. *Gentlemen's Journal*, Mar., p. 10. He that flinches his glass, and to drink is not able, Let him quarrel no more, but KNOCK UNDER the table.

1703. *The Levellers*, in *Harl. Misc.* (ed. Park), v. 447. Now, my dear, though I must acknowledge our sex to be extraordinary vicious, we will not KNOCK UNDER-BOARD to the men.

1719. DURFEY, *Pills etc.*, i. 27. Who with Water and Cannon Mahon did take, And make the Pope KNOCK UNDER.

*c.*1730. A. RAMSAY, *Address of Thanks*, in *Wks.* (1851), ii. 347. They will be forced to thumb your belt, At last and a' KNOCK UNDER.

1782. GEO. PARKER, *Humorous Sketches*, p. 164. When fame from ministers is flown, 'Tis time they should KNOCK UNDER.

1844. *Puck*, p. 82. Says mighty Dan to the Sassenach chain, I never will KNOCK UNDER.

1851-61. MAYHEW, *Lond. Lab. etc.*, iii. 71. Several had tried it, but they had to KNOCK UNDER very soon.

1852. THACKERAY, *Esmond*, iii. 4. Colonel Esmond KNOCKED UNDER to his fate.

1866. *Argosy*, No. 2, p. 191. So the Emperor of Austria has KNOCKED UNDER, and the Hungarian Diet has met for the first time for sixteen years. They have conquered by the force of passive resistance. It is the grandest thing since our Long Parliament.

1871. *Five Years' Penal Servitude*, iii. 223. The men are drove into being reg'lar devils by being constantly down upon by the blooming officers. Them as 'as any pluck in 'em turns savage, and them as 'asn't they KNOCKS UNDER, as I did, and gets ill, and lots on 'em dies.

1872. *Daily Telegraph*, 29 Aug. Finally, he KNOCKED UNDER with an abjectness which made every true American blush from the tips of his hair to the soles of his boots.

TO KNOCK UP, *verb. phr.* (Christ's Hospital).—1. To gain a place in class: *e.g.* I KNOCKED UP and 'I KNOCKED Jones up.' The Hertford equivalent is OX UP (*q.v.*).

2. (colloquial).—To achieve; to accomplish.

1888. *Sporting Life*, 10 Dec. With only 29 to win, White at his next attempt KNOCKED UP the necessary item.

3. (colloquial).—To put together hastily, as by nailing.

1852. DICKENS, *Bleak House*, xx. KNOCKING UP apologies for shelves.

4. (colloquial).—1. To exhaust or tire.

1771. SMOLLETT, *Humphry Clinker*, L. 62. In passing the sands without a guide, his horse had KNOCKED UP; and he himself must have perished, if he had not been providentially relieved by a return post-chaise.

1814. MISS AUSTEN, *Mansfield Park*, vii. If Fanny would be more regular in her exercise, she would not be KNOCKED UP so soon.

1843. DICKENS, *Martin Chuzzlewit*, xvii. p. 187. 'I am quite KNOCKED UP. Dead beat, Mark.'

1867. *All the Year Round*, 13 July, 59. You had better go by train, and not run the risk of KNOCKING yourself UP again.

KNOCKED UP, *phr.* (American).—Pregnant.

TO GET THE KNOCK, *verb. phr.* (colloquial).—1. To drink; to get SCREWED (*q.v.*).

2. (colloquial).—To be discharged; to get the SACK or BAG (*q.v*).

TO TAKE THE KNOCK, *verb. phr.* (turf). To lose more to the bookmakers than one can pay; to be DEAD BROKE (*q.v.*).

1890. *Globe*, 21 April, p. 6, col. 1. Many a broken backer of horses who has TAKEN, what is known in the language of the turf, as THE KNOCK over the many fiascoes associated with this particular horse, etc.

TO BE KNOCKED OFF ONE'S PINS, *verb. phr.* (common).—To be FLABBERGASTED (*q.v.*).

1880. A. TROLLOPE, *The Duke's Children*, ch. xlvii. He confessed to himself that he was completely bowled over,—KNOCKED OFF HIS PINS!

THAT KNOCKS ME, *phr.* (common).—That confounds, or is too much for me.

TO BE KNOCKED INTO THE MIDDLE OF NEXT WEEK, *verb. phr.* (common).—To be astounded; to get badly beaten; 'to be knocked into a COCKED HAT' (*q.v.*).

1823. MONCRIEFF, *Tom and Jerry*, ii. 4. Up comes these young sparks, and gave me such a maulagaran, that they KNOCK'D ME INTO THE MIDDLE OF NEXT WEEK—beside tipping me this here black eye—only see how red it is!

1837. DICKENS, p. 334 [ed. 1857]. If Mr. Namby would have the goodness to put his hat on again, he would KNOCK IT INTO THE LATER END OF NEXT WEEK.

1847. PORTER, *Quarter Race etc.*, p. 105. The next moment he was KNOCKED INTO THE MIDDLE OF THE NEXT THREE WEEKS!

*b.*1852. *Traits of Amer. Humour*, p. 50. Arch would fetch him er side wipe on the head, and KNOCK HIM INTO THE MIDDLE OF NEXT WEEK.

KNOCKABOUT, *subs.* (theatrical).—An actor of violent and noisy pantomime: a special *genre*.

1891. *Sportsman*. Ap. 1. The Armstrongs maintain their position as two of the best KNOCKABOUT artistes.

KNOCK-ABOUT MAN, *subs.* (Australian).—A JACK-OF-ALL TRADES (*q.v.*); a HANDY MAN.

1881. A. C. GRANT, *Bush Life*, i. 80. KNOCKABOUT MEN: that is men who are willing to undertake any work.

Knock-down (or **Knock-me-down**), *subs.* (old).—Strong ale: STINGO (*q.v.*). Also = gin.

1515. *De Generibus Ebriosorum ect.* [J. E. Hodgkin in *Notes & Queries*, 3 S. vii. 163]. In this treatise occurs a chapter on the various kinds of beer then in use in Germany .... The catalogue which follows shows that even the names of fancy drinks are not new under the sun; and that the 'Eye-openers' and 'Cocktails' of the Yankee bars had their prototypes in the mediæval taprooms. I select a few of the most presentable: Cow's-tail, Calves-neck, Buffalo, Slip-slop, Stamp-in-the-Ashes, Knock-'em-down, Crowing-Cock, Wild-oats, Redhead, Raise-head, Swell-nose, and Gnat's-mustard.

1690. B. E., *Dict. Cant. Crew*, s.v.

1698. Sorbière, *Journey to London in the Year* 1698, p. 35 [quoted in *Notes and Queries*, 6 S. xii. 167]. He answer'd me that had a thousand such sort of liquors, as Humtie Dumtie, Three Threads, Four Threads, old Pharaoh, KNOCKDOWN . . .

1785. Grose, *Vulg. Tongue*, s.v. Knock.

1811. *Lex. Bal.*, s.v. Knock-me-down.

1859. Matsell, *Vocabulum*, s.v.

1885. *Notes and Queries*, 6th S. xii. 232. A very strong ale or beer.

Adj. (old).—Rowdy.

1760. Foote, *Minor*, i. No KNOCK-ME-DOWN doings in my house. . . . no rioters.

Knock-down and Drag-out, *subs. phr.* (pugilistic).—A free fight.

1848. *New York Spirit of the Times*, 30 Sept. There are good, quiet, easy people in the world who scarcely open their lips or raise their fingers, lest Dogberry So-and-so across the way might take it in high dudgeon, and forthwith demand an explanation or a KNOCK-DOWN AND DRAG-OUT.

1852. Judson, *Myst. etc. of New York*, xii. p. 83. 'We must have a fight!' said Butcher Bill. 'What shall it be?' asked Mr. Shorter—'a genteel knock down, or a KNOCK DOWN AND DRAG OUT?'

*b.*1852. *Traits of American Humour*, p. 48. Mike . . . in a regular KNOCK-DOWN AND DRAG-OUT row was hard to beat.

Knock-'em-down Business, *subs. phr.* (common).—Auctioneering.

Knock-'em-downs, *subs.* (common).—Skittles.

1828. Jon Bee, *Picture of London*, 263. The charms of *nine-pins*—whether this be of skittles, KNOCK-'EM-DOWNS, bowl-and-tip, dutch-pins, or the more sturdy *four-corners*.

1872. *Fun*, Sept. A man, the proud possessor of KNOCK-ME-DOWNS, was brought up at Wandsworth police-court the other day for plying his trade on Putney Common.

Knocker, *subs.* (venery).—1. The *penis* (Urquhart): *see* KNOCK, *verb.* sense 1. For synonyms *see* CREAMSTICK and PRICK.

2. (venery).—*See* KNOCK, *verb.* sense 1.

3. (common).—In pl., small flat curls worn on the temples; SIXES (*q.v.*).

Up to the knocker, *phr.* (common).—1. Completely equal to; also, perfect in appearance, condition, fitness. Also *see* quot. 1870.

1844. Selby, *London by Night*, i. 2. *Jack.* How do you feel? *Ned.* Not quite UP TO THE KNOCKER.

1864. *Derby Day*, p. 110. It's a splendid turn out. RIGHT UP TO THE KNOCKER, as they say. I don't do things by halves when I go out.

1870. Hazlewood & Williams, *Leave it to Me*, i. *Joe.* If ever there was anybody else first, you're afore 'em. I 'dores you, TO THE WERRY KNOCKER AND HALF-WAY UP THE PASSAGE.

1889. *Sporting Times*, 6 July. 'I see here's a house to let in Toboggan Terrace, jest up by Sloane Street—how 'ud that suit us?' 'UP TO THE BLOOMIN' KNOCKER, Joey,' replied Mrs. M.

1892. Milliken, *'Arry Ballads*, 23. I'm UP TO THE KNOCKER, I tell you.

2. (common).—In the height of fashion.

1877. *Five Years' Penal Servitude*, iii. p. 243. She were a fine woman, and togged like a lady right UP TO THE KNOCKER.

1885. D. C. Murray, *Rainbow Gold*, Bk. ii. ch. ii. 'He's dressed too,' he added after a pause, during which the figure drew nearer—'dressed UP TO THE KNOCKER.'

Knocker-face (or **Head**), *subs.* (common).—An ugly-faced person; UGLY-MUG (*q.v.*).

1887. A. Barrère, *Argot and Slang*, p. 272. *Monstrico, m.* (familiar), ugly person, one with a KNOCKER FACE.

Knocker-out, *subs.* (pugilistic).—*See* KNOCK-OUT, *subs.* sense 4.

Knock-in, *subs.* (common).—1. The game of loo.

2. (common).—A hand at cards.

3. (trade).—The same as KNOCK-OUT, *subs.* sense 1.

Knocking-out, *subs.* (common).—*See* KNOCK-OUT, *subs.* sense 1.

2. (Oxford University).—*See* KNOCK-OUT, *subs.* sense 5 s.v. KNOCK.

Knock-out, *subs.* (common).—1. A man frequenting auction rooms and joining with others to buy at a nominal price. One of the gang is told off to buy for the rest, and after a few small bids as blinds, the lot is knocked down to the KNOCK-OUT bidders, so that competition is made impossible. At the end of the sale the goods are taken to a near hand public-house, where they are re-sold or KNOCKED-OUT among the confederates, the difference between the first purchase and the second—or tap-room KNOCK-OUT—being divided. The lowest sort of KNOCK-OUTS, with more tongue than capital, are called BABES. Hence (2) an auction at which KNOCKING-OUT is practised. Also *verbally*, as an *adj.*, and in combination.

1823. Bee, *Dict. of the Turf*, s.v. Knock out, an illegal auction.

1856. C. Reade, *Never Too Late*, xlii. This was a KNOCK-OUT transaction; twelve buyers had agreed not to bid against one another in the auction room, a conspiracy illegal but customary.

1872. *Athenæum*, 4 May. Book KNOCK-OUT. . . . buying a rare Shakspeare for £20, and afterwards selling it at a KNOCK-OUT for £525.

1876. Hindley, *Adventures of a Cheap Jack*. The concern would either remain for a time in shares, or would be KNOCKED OUT at once, that is, resold by auction among themselves, and the profit divided.

1883. A. Lang, *A Bookman's Purgatory*, in *Longman's Mag.*, September, p. 522. The auctioneer put up lot after lot, and Blinton plainly saw that the whole affair was a KNOCK-OUT. His most treasured spoils were parted with at the price of waste paper.

1891. *Pall Mall Gaz.*, 29 Nov., p. 4, c. 3. He condemned the market 'rings,' and maintained that by the process of KNOCKING OUT the price of food was kept up.

2. in pl. (gaming).—Dice: when in the box = BABES IN THE WOOD or ROGUES IN THE STOCKS. *See* FULHAMS.

3. (common).—A man or woman: used either in eulogy or in outraged propriety: also a WARM MEMBER (*q.v.*); one who does outrageous things.

4. (pugilistic).—1. A hit out of the guard on the point of the chin, which puts the recipient to sleep, and so ends the fight. Hence, 2

(common), a champion of any sort and in any walk of life. KNOCKER-OUT = a pugilist who is an adept at PUTTING TO SLEEP (*q.v.*).

1891. *Sporting Life*, 25 Mar. The Barrier man was nearly helpless, and Choynski tried frantically to pull himself together for one good KNOCK-OUT.

1892. Chevalier, *Idler*, June, p. 549. Oh! 'e's a little champion, Do me proud, well 'e's a KNOCK OUT.

1894. *Illustrated Bits*, 7 April, 4, 2. They all called her Miss Tricky, except some of the lads who preferred to describe her with fervour as 'A fair KNOCK-OUT.'

1894. Arthur Morrison, *Tales of Mean Streets*, 134. It was a hard fight and both the lads were swinging the right again and again for a KNOCK-OUT.

1895. E. B. Osborn, in *New Review*, April, 450. The hit out of the guard to the point of the chin, which is the prettiest application of the theory of the lever—is equally dangerous when it comes from a gloved hand. Accordingly, modern boxers (so-called) will give up everything for an opportunity of striking this particular blow; and a contest with or without the gloves degenerates into a struggle of waving hands and woven paces for the one position in which 'tis possible to deliver it with a fair chance of KNOCKING-OUT.

Knocksoftly, *subs.* (old).—A fool; a SOFT (*q.v.*).

1864. *Derby Day*, p. 69. 'I say,' cried Mr. Dobson. 'What's the row now? Ain't you going to let us in?' 'What! to be larruped? Not if I know it. You must think me a jolly KNOCK-SOFTLY.'

Knot, *subs.* (old: now recognised).—A crew, gang, or fraternity.

1597. Shakspeare, *Rich. III*, iii. 3. A KNOT you are of damned blood-suckers.

1725. *New Cant. Dict.*, s.v.

1785. Grose, *Vulg. Tongue*, s.v.

Verb. (old).—To copulate. For synonyms *see* GREENS and RIDE.

1602. Shakspeare, *Othello*, iv. 2. Keep it as a cistern for foul toads To KNOT and gender in.

To knot it, *verb. phr.* (common).—To abscond. For synonyms *see* ABSQUATULATE.

To tie with St. Mary's knot, *verb. phr.* (common).—To hamstring.

To tie a knot with the tongue that cannot be untied with the teeth, *verb. phr.* (colloquial).—To get married.

Know, *verb.* (conventional).—To copulate: applied to women. Also to KNOW CARNALLY and to HAVE CARNAL KNOWLEDGE. For synonyms *see* GREENS and RIDE.

To know, one's way about, round, a thing or two, a trick worth two, the ropes, the time of day, what's o'clock, what's what, one's book, life, how many blue beans make five, *verb. phr.* (colloquial).—To be well-informed, experienced, wide-awake; to be equal to any emergency; FLY (*q.v.*).

1534. N. Udall, *Roister Doister*, i. 2, p. 17 (Arber). Have ye spied out that? Ah sir, mary nowe I see you KNOW WHAT IS WHAT.

1598. Shakspeare, 1 *Henry IV*, ii. 1. *Soft*, I pray thee: I KNOW A TRICK WORTH TWO of that.

1609. Jonson, *Silent Woman*, v. *Daw.* O, it pleases him to say so, sir; but Sir Amorous KNOWS WHAT'S WHAT as well.

1679. W. Wycherley, *Love in a Wood*, Act iii. Sc. i. But you, gossip, KNOW WHAT'S WHAT.

1711. *Spectator*, No. 132. This sly saint, who, I will warrant, UNDERSTANDS WHAT IS WHAT as well as you or I, widow, shall give the bride as father.

1773. Goldsmith, *She Stoops to Conquer*, v. 'Come, boy, I'm an old fellow, and KNOW WHAT'S WHAT as well as you that are younger.'

1792. Holcroft, *Road to Ruin*. You KNOW A THING OR TWO, Mr. Selby.

1825. Scott, *St. Ronan's Well*. I am a raw Scotchman, Captain Jekyll, it is true, but yet I KNOW A THING OR TWO.

1834. Ainsworth, *Rookwood*. A man of discernment who KNEW A THING OR TWO.

1836. Dickens, *Pickwick*, p. 364 (ed. 1857). 'Never mind, Sir,' said Mr. Weller with dignity, 'I KNOW WOT'S O'CLOCK.'

1841. Lever, *Charles O'Malley*. I thought I KNEW A THING OR TWO when I landed in Portugal; but, Lord love you, I was a babe. . . . compared to the Portuguese.

1849. Lytton, *Caxtons*, p. iv. iii. 'I am no genius, but I am a practical man. I KNOW WHAT'S WHAT.'

1849-50. Thackeray, *Pendennis*, ch. x. I KNOW WHAT'S O'CLOCK tolerably well.

1854. Whyte-Melville, *General Bounce*. The old Norman *bon-vivant* evidently KNEW A THING OR TWO.

1867. *All the Year Round*, 13 July, p. 56. The tramp who KNOWS HIS WAY ABOUT knows what to do.

1887. Baumann, *Londinismen, Slang u. Cant*, pref., vi. So from hartful young dodgers From vaxy old codgers, From the blowens we got Soon to KNOW VOT IS VOT.

1888. Rolf Boldrewood, *Robbery Under Arms*, xxiv. We KNEW A TRICK WORTH TWO of that. *Ibid.* xliv. He KNEW THE ROPES.

1889. *Pall Mall Gazette*, 9 Nov., p. 7, col. 2. Tell him frankly that you are a new reader, and would be glad of his assistance until you KNOW THE ROPES, as the sailors say.

1891. Newman, *Scamping Tricks*, 120. Now it is only fair to say the assistant KNEW HIS BOOK, and was up to snuff.

1892 *Pall Mall Gaz.*, 12 Oct., p. 5, col. 2. Mr. Asquith KNOWS, if I may use the phrase, THE TIME OF DAY.

1892. Milliken, *'Arry Ballads*, 13. He did KNOW A THING OR TWO. *Ibid.* 36. KNOWS HER WAY ABOUT well, I can tell yer. *Ibid.* 44. Alfongs KNOWS THE ROPES.

Not to know B from a battledore. *See* B.

In the know, *adv. phr.* (common).—Having special and intimate knowledge; IN THE SWIM; on the GROUND FLOOR (*q.v.*).

1883. *Referee*, 29 April, p. 3, col. 2. As they are being shown about, and as everybody immediately interested knows all about them, perhaps Refereaders would like to be IN THE KNOW likewise.

1884. *Cornhill Mag.*, June, p. 617. The half-dozen young Arabs who are IN THE KNOW as to these eating-houses, and have marked them for their own.

1888. *Sportsman*, 28 Nov. That greatly desired summit of every embryo racing man's aspirations. . . . being IN THE KNOW.

1889. *Sporting Times*, 3 Aug., p. 1, col. 2. There is somebody I wot of who is fairly IN THE KNOW.

1889. *Star*, 9 Sept., p. 4, col. 3. If he were IN THE KNOW he would be more correct in his facts.

1892. *Pall Mall Gaz.*, 31 Oct., 3, 1. Racing on the Flat. By ONE IN THE KNOW [Title].

1892. *Leisure Hour*, Jan., p. 192. It is evident to the reader who is IN THE KNOW that the miserable author will have to go round by Cape Horn to get from Greenwich to the Isle of Dogs.

1894. *Illustrated Bits*, 7 Ap., p. 4, col. 2. Harry Summers, whose father did the commissions for the stable, and whose main ambition was to be IN THE KNOW, so that he might back winners.

1894. George Moore, *Esther Waters*, xxx. 'If one was really IN THE KNOW, then I don't say nothing about it; but who of us is ever really IN THE KNOW?'

All one knows, *phr.* (common).—The utmost.

1888. Rolf Boldrewood, *Robbery Under Arms*, xxiii. A good many men tried ALL THEY KNEW to be prepared and have a show for it.

I WANT TO KNOW, *phr.* (American colloquial).—'Is it possible?' 'You surprise me.'

KNOWING, *adj.* (common).—1. Artful; FLY (*q.v.*).

1712. *Spectator*, No. 314. If this gentleman be really no more than eighteen, I must do him the justice to say he is the most KNOWING infant I have yet met with.

1752. FIELDING, *Amelia*, Bk. x. v. 'We have so much the advantage, that if the KNOWING ones were here, they would lay odds of our side.'

1819-24. BYRON, *Don Juan*. . . . 'Who, on a spree with black-eyed Sal, his blowen, So swell, so prime, so nutty, and so KNOWING?'

1821. HAGGART, *Life*, p. 11. Our first business of the day, was. . . . not very unusual among KNOWING ones.

1823. MONCRIEFF, *Tom and Jerry*, p. 6. Flash, my young friend, or slang, as others call it, is a species of cant in which the KNOWING ones conceal their roguery from the flats.

1830. SIR E. B. LYTTON, *Paul Clifford*, p. 29 (ed. 1854). 'Paul, my ben cull,' said he with a KNOWING wink.

1834. H. AINSWORTH, *Rookwood*, bk. III. v. Until at last there was none so KNOWING.

1835. SELBY, *Catching an Heiress*, sc. 1. Ho, ho! he's a KNOWING one.

1841. *Punch*, i. 29, 2. Why is a cunning man like a man in debt? — Because he's a KNOWING one (*an owing one*).

1843. DICKENS, *Christmas Carol* in Prose. To edge his way along the crowded paths of life, warning all human sympathy to keep its distance, was what the KNOWING ones call 'nuts' to Scrooge.

1845. *The late fight between the Premier (Peel) and young Ben (D'Israeli)*, v. 9, p. 163. The KNOWING ones suspect that if he comes up to the scratch again—which is doubtful—he will come off second best.

1856. WHYTE-MELVILLE, *Kate Coventry*, xviii. There was a slight bustle among the KNOWING ones.

1863. READE, *Hard Cash*, i. 214. He had a very pleasant way of conveying appreciation of an officer's zeal, by a KNOWING nod with a kindly smile on the heels of it.

1863. *Frazer's Mag.*, Dec. 'The English Spy'. Much which is unfair in ordinary life is very clever and KNOWING on the race-course.

1883. *Broadside Ballad*, 'Happy Thoughts,' st. 4. My Uncle Dowle has lots of money; He's a very KNOWING looking blade.

2. (common).—Stylish.

1811. JANE AUSTEN, *Sense and S.*, xix. Many young men, who had chambers in the Temple, made a very good appearance in the first circles, and drove about town in very KNOWING gigs.

1844. *Puck*, p. 14. With his weed in his cheek and his glass on his eye, His cut-away neat, and KNOWING tie, The milliner's hearts he did trepan My spicy swell small-college man.

1861. HUGHES, *Tom Brown at Oxford*, i. 5. Tom thought his cap a very KNOWING affair.

KNOWING BLOKE, *subs. phr.* (military).—A sponger on new recruits.

*c.*1887. BRUNLEES PATTERSON, *Life in the Ranks*. Some of the KNOWING BLOKES, prominent among whom will be the 'grousers,' will, in all probability, be chewing the rag or fat.

KNOWLEDGE, *subs.* (colloquial).—Sexual intercourse. For synonyms *see* GREENS and RIDE.

KNOWLEDGE-BOX, *subs.* (common).—The head; the NOUS-BOX, (*q.v.*). For synonyms *see* CRUMPET.

1798. *Poetry of Anti-jacobin*, xxii. 116 [ed. 1801]. Coal-black is my KNOWLEDGE-BOX.

1819. MOORE, *Tom Crib*, p. 17. Found his KNOWLEDGE BOX always the first thing.

1823. MONCRIEFF, *Tom and Jerry*, iii. 1. *Jerry*. Doctor! I touch'd your KNOWLEDGE BOX there, I think.

1840. C. BRONTE, in Mrs. Gaskell's *Life*, ch. ix. The wind. . . . has produced the same effects on the contents of my KNOWLEDGE-BOX that a quaigh of usquebaugh does upon those of most other bipeds.

1868. MISS BRADDON, *Trail of the Serpent*, Bk. VI. iii. The gentlemen of the Prize ring were prepared to fight as long as they had a bunch of fives to rattle upon the KNOWLEDGE-BOX of the foe.

KNUB, *verb.* (old).—To rub against; to tickle.

1653. BROME, *The City Wit*, in *Wks.* (1874), I. 444. As you have beheld two horses KNUBBING one another. Ka me, ka the, an old kind of court service.

KNUCK, *subs.* (old and American).—A thief. Short for KNUCKLE (*q.v.*).

1834. HARRISON AINSWORTH, *Rookwood*. The KNUCKS in quod did my schoolmen play.

1851. JUDSON, *Mysteries etc. of New-York*, ch. iv. For many a year it has been known the 'crossmen' and KNUCKS of the town, as 'Jack Circle's watering place.' *Ibid.* You're as good a KNUCK as ever frisked a swell.

Verb. (American).—To steal. For synonyms *see* PRIG.

1851. JUDSON, *Myst. etc. of New-York*, iv. It's enough to break my heart to see a man of your talent forced to prig prancers, KNUCK trikers, and go on the low sneaks!

KNUCKLE, *subs.* (old).—*See* quot.

1781. PARKER, *View of Society*. 'KNUCKLE in the flash language signifies those who hang about the lobbies of both Houses of Parliament, the Opera-House, and both Play-Houses, and in general wherever a great crowd assemble. They steal watches, snuff-boxes etc.'

Verb. (thieves').—1. To fight with fists; to pummel.

2. (thieves').—To pick pockets: applied especially to the more refined or artistic branch of the art, *i.e.* extracting notes or money from the waistcoat, or breeches pockets, whereas 'buzzing' is used in a more general sense.—DE VAUX (1819). Also TO GO ON THE KNUCKLE.

1754. PARKER, *Life's Painter*, p. 43, s.v.

TO KNUCKLE (KNUCKLE DOWN TO or KNUCKLE UNDER), *verb. phr.* (colloquial).—1. *See* quots.

1748. T. DYCHE, *Dictionary* (5th ed.). KNUCKLE-DOWN (v.) to stoop, bend, yield, comply with, or submit to.

*b.*1794. WOLCOT [P. Pindar], *Ode to Tyrants*, in *Works* (Dublin), v. ii. p. 526. To KNUCKLE DOWN to Jove, And pray the gods to send an Emp'ror down. *Ibid. Rights of Kings*. Poor gentlemen! how hard, alas! their fate, To KNUCKLE TO such nuisances of State!

1846. THACKERAY, *Vanity Fair*, II. vii. So he KNUCKLED DOWN, again to use his own phrase, and sent old Hulker with peaceable overtures to Osborne.

1860. *Chamber's Journal*, XIII. p. 289. Considering how he has talked scoffingly of Benedict's KNUCKLING UNDER and being second best and of some one having always the whiphand of him and so on.

1869. BLACKMORE, *Lorna Doone*, liv. When the upperhand is taken upon the faith of one's patience by a man of even smaller wits. . . . why it naturally happens that we KNUCKLE UNDER with an ounce of indignation.

1888. *Daily Chronicle*, 31 Dec. He KNUCKLED UNDER to the last-named at the second time of asking.

1888. ROLF BOLDREWOOD, *Robbery Under Arms*, xxxvii. I wouldn't KNUCKLE DOWN to you like some of them.

2. (colloquial).—To apply oneself earnestly; to engage vigorously.

KNUCKLE-BONE. DOWN ON THE KNUCKLE-BONE, *phr.* (thieves').—Hard-up.; STONEY (*q.v.*).

1883. *Daily Telegraph*, 4 August, p. 2, col. 1. I once had the honour of being present at a 'select harmonic' held in the shady neighbourhood of Foxcourt, in Grays Inn-lane, which, according to the card pertaining thereto, was for the benefit of someone who was DOWN ON THE KNUCKLE BONE in consequence of having been put away since the previous October (it was then the month of March), and only just now released.

KNUCKLED, *adj.* (tailors').—Handsome.

KNUCKLEDABS (or **KNUCKLE-CONFOUNDERS**), *subs.* (old).—Handcuffs.—GROSE (1785). For synonyms *see* DARBIES.

KNUCKLE-DUSTER, *subs.* (common).—A knuckle-guard of iron or brass which, in striking, protects the hand from injury and adds force to a blow.

1858. *Times*, 15 Feb. KNUCKLE-DUSTER. . . . a formidable American instrument, made of brass, which slips easily on to the four fingers of the hand, and having a projecting surface, across the knuckles, is calculated, in a pugilistic encounter to inflict serious injury on the person against whom it is directed.

1861. SALA, *Twice round the Clock*, Noon Par. 12. A bunch of skeleton keys, a KNUCKLE-DUSTER, and a piece of wax candle, all articles sufficiently indicative of the housebreaker's stock-in-trade.

1866. *Era*, 18 June. Without a moment's hesitation—except to load a six-barrelled revolver with ball cartridge and to arm himself with a pair of Yankee KNUCKLE-DUSTERS—the intrepid African opened the door of the den.

1872. *Standard*, 'Middlesex Sessions Report'. In another box he found a life-preserver, the end of it being loaded with lead, KNUCKLE-DUSTERS, and other things of the same description.

1877. E. L. LINTON, *World Well Lost*, xii. A kind of panic went through the place, and the demand for revolvers and KNUCKLEDUSTERS, iron shutters and bells. . . . surprised the tradesmen.

1883. *Daily News*, 20 March, p. 6, col. 3. He struck at him in the face with a KNUCKLE-DUSTER he had in his hand.

1887. *Daily Chronicle*, 8 Dec. Hayzeman stepped from the other side of the road, and struck prosecutor on the nose, the blow, as believed, being given with a KNUCKLE-DUSTER.

1888. J. RUNCIMAN, *The Chequers*, 84. We were a jovial company: four of us were wondering how they could rob the fifth, and that fifth resolved, quite early in this seance, to use his KNUCKLE-DUSTER promptly, and to prevent either of the male warblers from getting behind him, at any risk.

1890. *Standard*, 30 July, p. 3, col. 6. The Prisoner made no reply, but struck him with a KNUCKLE-DUSTER, which he took out of his pocket.

2. (common).—A large, heavy, or over-gaudy ring.

KNUCKLER, *subs.* (old).—A pickpocket.

1834. AINSWORTH, *Rookwood*, p. 184. A universal knocking of knuckles by the KNUCKLERS was followed by profound silence.

1843. *Punch* iv. 129. A rush,—a hustle,—merrily then Begins the KNUCKLERS' war.

KNULLER, *subs.* (old).—1. *See* quot.: also KNELLER.

1851-61. H. MAYHEW, *London Lab. and Lond. Poor*, ii. p. 405. The KNULLERS or 'queriers', that is to say, those [chimney-sweepers] who solicit custom in an irregular manner, by knocking at the doors of houses and such like.

2. (common).—A clergyman. [*Cf.* sense 1 and CLERGYMAN].

KOKUM, *subs.* (Australian prison).—Sham kindness. *See* COCUM.

KONE, *subs.* (American thieves').—Counterfeit coin. — MATSELL (1859).

KONIACKER (or **COGNIAC-ER**), *subs.* (American thieves').—A counterfeiter.—MATSELL (1859).

KOOL, *verb.* (back-slang).—To look.

*c.*1865. *Broadside Ballad*, 'The Chickaleary Cove'. Now KOOL my downy kicksies.

1892. *National Observer*, 27 Feb., p. 378. Me a Plantadgenick? Who are you a-getting at? Look at my pearlies, KOOL my 'ed of 'air.

KOTOO (or **KOTOW**), *verb.* (common).—To bow down to; to scrape to; to lickspittle.

1874. E. LYNN LINTON, *Patricia Kemball*, xlii. He had never concealed his contempt for him nor KOWTOWED to him rest had done.

1890. TRAILL, *Saturday Songs*, 'A Manly Protest', p. 70. But never for Chawles! To the traitors and plotters Whom once he denounced he would scorn to KO-TOO.

KOSH (or **KOSHER**), *subs.* (thieves').—1. A short iron bar used for purpose of assault.

2. A blow.

Adj. (common).—Fair; square. [From the Hebrew = lawful].

KROP, *subs.* (back-slang).—Pork.

KUDOS, *subs.* (now recognised).—Glory and honor. To KUDOS = to praise; to glorify. [From Gr.] KUDOS = praised.

1793. SOUTHEY, *Nondescripts*, i. Bepraised in prose it was, bepraised in verse, Lauded in pious Latin to the skies, KUDOS'D egregiously in heathen Greek.

1857. CUTHBERT BEDE, *Verdant Green*, Pt. III. ch. xi. Mr. Smalls gained KUDOS by offering to give the luncheon at his rooms.

1860. *Punch*, xxxviii. 186. Nought would serve the little man [Lord John] But his private little plan, Whereby he hoped much κῦδος he should get.

1889. DRAGE, *Cyril*, vii. I gained no small KUDOS by spotting a vintage of Léoville at dinner.

1889. *Standard*, 30 Jan. Should he, then, endeavour to gain the KUDOS of his removal by associating himself conspicuously with the decree of dismissal?

1894. *The Yellow Bk.*, I. p. 195. I return to my pearl that is to bring *me* KUDOS.

KYE, *subs.* (costers').—Eighteen pence. [Short for Heb. KYEBOSH (or KIBOSH *q.v.*); *Kye* = 18 + *bosh* = pence, originally STIVERS (*q.v.*)].

KYNCHEN. *See* KINCHEN.

KYPSEY, *subs.* (old).—*See* quots. Also KIPSEY.

1754. MARTIN, *Eng. Dict.*, 2nd ed. KIBSY, a sort of wicker basket.

1879. HORSLEY, in *Macm. Mag.*, xl. 501. I was coming home with my KIPSY (basket).

1893. EMERSON, *Signor Lippo*, XIV. After tea Blower said, 'Now you must lay in your KIPSEY.'

THE THREE L'S, *subs. phr.* (nautical).—Lead, latitude, and look-out.—CLARK RUSSELL.

LABEL, *subs.* (American).—A postage stamp: *cf.* TOADSKIN.

LABOUR, *verb.* (old).—To beat.

LABOURER, *subs.* (common).—An accoucheur; a midwife. For synonyms *see* FINGER-SMITH. [From labour = child-birth].

LABOUR-LEA, *verb.* (Scots').—To copulate. For synonyms *see* GREENS and RIDE.

LACE, *subs.* (common).—Strong waters added to coffee or tea. Also (by inference, *see verb.*) sugar.

1712. *Spectator*, No. 488. He is forced every morning to drink his dish of coffee by itself, without the addition of the *Spectator*, that used to be better than LACE to it.

Verb. (common).—1. To intermix with spirits. Fr. *consoler son café* = to brandy one's coffee. Also (*see* quot. 1690) = sugar.

1677. WYCHERLEY, *Plain Dealer*, iii. *Ald.* No, faith; prithee, captain, let's go drink a dish of LACED coffee, and talk of the times.

1690. B. E., *Dict. Cant. Crew*, s.v. LAC'D coffee, Sugar'd.

1712. *Spectator*, No. 317. Mr. Nisby of opinion that LACED coffee is bad for the head.

1725. *New Cant. Dict.*, s.v.

1815. SCOTT, *Guy Mannering*, xi. He had his pipe and his tea-cup, the latter being LACED with a little spirits.

1851-61. MAYHEW, *London Lab. etc.*, iii. 359. Breakfast 1*s.*, good tea and good bread-and-butter, as much as you liked always, with a glass of rum in the last cup for the LACING of it. Tea the same as breakfast, and LACED ditto.

1852. THACKERAY, *Esmond*, ix. 'D—n it, Polly loves a mug of ale, too, and LACED with brandy, by Jove!'

1872. *Athenæum*, 2 Nov., p. 556, col. 2. Schiller refreshed himself at the small hours of the morning with coffee LACED with old cognac.

1892. MILLIKEN, '*Arry Ballads*, 35. Talk is like tea; it wants LACING with something a little bit stronger.

2. (common).—To flog. Also TO LACE ONE'S COAT (or JACKET).

1599. PORTER, *Two Angry Women* [Dodsley, *Old Plays* (1874), vii. 359]. I do not love to be lac'd in when I go to LACE a rascal.

1665. R. HEAD, *English Rogue*, Pt. I. ch. iii. p. 27 (1874). It was not long after that I was so LACED for it, that comparatively to my punishment *Bridewell* whipping is but a pastime.

1673. COTTON, *Virgil Travestie*, in *Wks.* (1725), Bk. iv. p. 126. Then if they have a mind to LACE us, Let Carthage, if they can, come trace us.

1690. B. E., *Dict. Cant. Crew*, s.v. LACING.... I'll LACE YOUR COAT, Sirrah, I will beat you soundly.

1725. *New Cant. Dict.*, s.v.

1754. MARTIN, *Eng. Dict.*, s.v.

1785. GROSE, *Vulg. Tongue*, s.v.

1811. *Lex. Bal.*, s.v.

1830. MONCRIEFF, *Heart of London*, ii. 1. You'll make me LACE you presently, if you don't mind—go on, Sir.

1847. C. BRONTE, *Jane Eyre*, xxi. LACE my quivering palm or shaking neck.

1859. MATSELL, *Vocabulum*, s.v.

3. (colloquial).—To wear tight stays.

LACEDEMONIANS, *subs.* (military).—The Forty-sixth Foot. [From its Colonel making it a long speech under a heavy fire about the Lacedemonians and their discipline]. Also MURRAYS BUCKS, and THE SURPRISERS.

LACED MUTTON, *subs. phr.* (old).—A woman; especially a wanton: *cf.* MUTTON. For synonyms *see* BARRACK-HACK and TART.

1578. WHETSTONE, *Promos and Cas.*, 6, pl. i. p. 14. And I smealt he loved LASE MUTTON well.

1595. SHAKSPEARE, *Two Gentlemen of Verona*, i. 1. Ay, sir: I, a lost mutton, gave your letter to her, a LAC'D MUTTON; and she, a LAC'D MUTTON, gave me, a lost mutton, nothing for my labour.

1596. NASHE, *Have with You* [GROSART (1885), iii. 61]. He that wold not stick so to extoll stale rotten LAC'D MUTTON, will ... sucke figges out of an asses fundament.

1599. BRETON, *Wil of Wit* [GROSART (1879), ii. c. 62(1. 18]. If your stomache stande to flesh, eate of a little warme MUTTON, but take heede it be not LACED.

1602. MIDDLETON, *Blurt Master Constable*, sign. B. Laz. Pilcher, Cupid hath got me a stomacke, and I long for LAC'D MUTTON. Pil. Plaine mutton without a lace would serve.

1602. DEKKER, *Honest Whore* [DODSLEY, *Old Plays*, iii. 466]. The sturdy beggar, and the lazy lown, Gets here hard hands, or LAC'D correction.

1624. JONSON, *Masque of Nep. Triumph* [CUNNINGHAM, iii.]. Cook. O whom for mutton, or kid? Child. A fine LAC'D MUTTON Or two; and either has her frisking husband.

1690. B. E., *Dict. Cant. Crew*, s.v.

1725. *New Cant. Dict.*, s.v.

1785. GROSE, *Vulg. Tongue*, s.v.

1811. *Lex. Bal.*, s.v. LACED MUTTON, a prostitute.

1859. MATSELL, *Vocabulum*, s.v. LACED MUTTON, a common woman.

LACING, *subs.* (common).—1. See LACE, *verb.* sense 2.

2. (common).—See quot. 1690; flogging; a lashing.

1690. B. E., *Dict. Cant. Crew*, s.v. LACING, Beating, Drubbing.

1785. GROSE, *Vulg. Tongue*, s.v. LACING.

1835. HALIBURTON, *Clockmaker*, 1. S. ch. xiv. 'He would.... throw all the blame on him and order him to have an everlastin' LACIN' with the cowskin.'

LACH, *verb.* (American thieves').—To let in.

1859. MATSELL, *Vocabulum*, s.v. LACH. 'The cove is bene, shall we LACH him?' 'The man is good, shall we let him in.'

LACK-LATIN, *subs.* (old).—An ignoramus: specifically an unlettered priest.

*d.*1555. LATIMER, *Sermon*, p. 304. Some will say our curate is naught, an ass-head, a dodipole, a LACK-LATIN.

1598. FLORIO, *Worlde of Wordes. Arlotto*, the name of a merie priest, a LACK LATINE or ledge-priest.

1598. *Servingman's Comfort* [HAZLITT: *Roxburgh Library* (1868), Tracts, p. 103]. Hoe, syr John LACK-LATTIN, you are out of the text.

1626. BRETON, *Pasquil's Madcappe* [GROSART (1879), i. e 6/2. 24]. Sir John LACK LATINE with a face of brass.

1762. FOOTE, *The Orators*, i. I'll step to the Bull and Gate, and call upon Jerry LACK-LATIN.

LADDER, *subs.* (venery).—The female *pudendum.* For synonyms *see* MONOSYLLABLE.

TO MOUNT A LADDER (TO BED or TO REST), *verb. phr.* (common).—To be hanged.

1560. *Nice Wanton* [DODSLEY, *Old Plays* (1874), ii. 172]. Thou boy, by the mass, ye will CLIMB THE LADDER.

1578. HARMAN, *Caveat* [E. E. T. S., 1869, p. 31]. Repentance is never thought upon till they CLYME THREE TREES WITH A LADDER.

1757. RAE, *Proverbs* (3rd. ed.), p. 199, s.v.

1785. GROSE, *Vulg. Tongue*, s.v.

1811. *Lex. Bal.*, s.v.

1859. MATSELL, *Vocabulum*, s.v. He MOUNTED THE LADDER, he was hung.

ENGLISH SYNONYMS. To cut a caper upon nothing, or one's last fling; to catch, or nab, or be copped with, the stifles; to climb the stalk; to climb, or leap from the leafless, or the triple tree; to be cramped, crapped, or cropped; to cry cockles; to dance upon nothing, the Paddington frisk, in a hempen cravat, or a Newgate hornpipe without music; to fetch a Tyburn stretch; to die in one's boots or shoes, or with cotton in one's ears; to die of hemp fever or squinsy; to have a hearty choke with caper sauce for breakfast; to take a vegetable breakfast; to marry the widow; to morris (Old Cant); to trine; to tuck up; to swing; to trust; to be nubbed; to kick the wind; to kick the wind with one's heels; to kick the wind before the Hotel door; to kick away the prop; to preach at Tyburn cross; to make (or have) a Tyburn show; to wag hemp in the wind; to wear hemp, an anodyne necklace, a hempen collar, a caudle, circle, cravat, croak, garter, necktie or habeas; to wear neck-weed, or St. Andrew's lace; to tie Sir Tristram's Knot; to wear a horse's nightcap or a Tyburn tippet; to come to scratch in a hanging or stretching match or bee; to ride the horse foaled of an acorn, or the three-legged mare; to be stretched, topped, scragged, or down for one's scrag.

FRENCH SYNONYMS (*i.e.* to suffer the death penalty, formerly by hanging, now by the guillotine). *Basculer* (popular = to tip-off; to see-saw); *bénir des pieds* (thieves' = to bless with the feet, a gibbetted man being *un évéque des champs*); *être béquillé* (thieves'); *monter à la bute, butte,* or *bute à regret* (thieves'); *tirer sa crampe avec la veuve* (popular); *épouser la veuve* (thieves': to wed the widow: *veuve* = guillotine); *être fauché* (thieves' = to be scythed); *être raccourci* (popular: *raccourci* = shortened); *être buté* (thieves' = earthed up); *mettre la tête à la fenêtre* (thieves': in allusion to passing the head through the lunette or aperture); *éternuer dans le son* or *dans le sac* (thieves' = to sneeze into the sawdust); *jouer à la main-chaude* (popular: in allusion to the hands tied behind the back; literally: to play hot cockles); *embrasser Charlot* (thieves': *Charlot* = executioner); *moufionner son mufle dans le son* (thieves' = to snotter in the sawdust); *passer sa bille au glaive* (thieves': *bille* = NUT (*q.v.*); *glaive* = knife]; *aller à l'Abbaye de Monte-à-regret* (common: to go to Mount Sorrowful Church); *passer à la*

voyante (thieves'); *être mécanisé* (common = to be passed through the machine: *mécanicien* = executioner); *être glaivé* (common = to be knifed); *passer sous le rasoir national* (popular = to be passed under the national razor); *être mis à la bise* (old = to be set in the wind); *vendanger à l'échelle* (old = to go vintaging on a ladder); *avoir le collet rouge* (old = to wear the red neck-band); *croître d'un demi-pied* (old = to grow half a foot taller); *faire la longue lettre* (old = to make the long letter, *i.e.* 'I'—from the Latin); *tomber du haut mât* (old); *servir de bouchon* (common = to act as a cork); *faire le saut* (common = to take the leap); *faire un saut sur rien* (old = to jump upon nothing); *danser où il n'y a pas de plancher* (common = to dance where there isn't a floor); *donner un soufflet à une potence* (common = to cuff the gallows); *donner le moine par le cou* (common); *approcher du ciel à reculons* (common = to go to heaven backwards); *danser un branle en l'air* (old = to cut capers in the air); *avoir la chanterelle au cou* (old: *chanterelle* = first string of a violin); *faire le guet à Montfaucon* (old = to do sentry go at Mont-faucon, *i.e.*, the public gibbet); *faire le guet au clair de la lune à la cour des Monnoyes* (old = to stand sentinel by moonlight); *monter à la jambe en l'air* (old = to mount the leg-in-air); *tirer la langue d'un demi-pied* (old = to stick out one's tongue).

ITALIAN SYNONYMS. *Agguinzare* (= to SWING); *allungar la vita* (= to lengthen life); *andar* or *mandar in piccardia* (FLORIO = to go, or be sent to Picardy; also *andare a Longone* or *Fuligno*); *dar de' calci al vento,* or *a Rouiao* (FLORIO = to kick the wind); *ballare in campo azzuro* (= to dance upon nothing); *sperlungare* (*perlunga*=lengthened); *aver la fune al guindo* (=to wear a hempen collar).

TO BE UNABLE TO SEE A HOLE IN A LADDER, *verb. phr.* (common).—To be hopelessly drunk. For synonyms *see* DRINKS and SCREWED.

LADDLE, *subs.* (chimney-sweeps').—A lady.

LADIES' CAGE, *subs. phr.* (parliamentary).—That portion of the gallery in the Commons which is set apart for ladies. See CAGE, *subs.*, sense 4.

1870. *Times*, 27 May, 'Leader.' The female opponents of the Contagious Diseases Act.... filled the LADIES' CAGE on Tuesday night.

LADIES' FEVER, *subs. phr.* (common).—Syphilis; FRENCH GOUT (*q.v.*).

ENGLISH SYNONYMS. BAD (or FOUL) DISEASE (or DISORDER); Barnwell ague; the CLAP (sometimes but erroneously): coals (or winter coals); Covent Garden ague; the crinkums; fire; the Frenchman or French gout; the GLIM (*q.v.*); the Garden gout; goodyears (SHAKSPEARE); grandgore (Old Scots'); knock with a French FAGGOT (*q.v.*); malady of France (SHAKSPEARE); the marbles; the stick; the Scotch fiddle; Venus' curse.

FRENCH SYNONYMS. *La baude* (thieves'); *un coup de pied de jument* or *de Venus* (common = a mare's kick or a kick from Venus); *la goutte militaire* (military = soldiers' gout); *un gros lot* (common = a prize); *le lazzi-lof* (thieves'); *le mal de Naples* or *le mal frances*; *le naze* (thieves').

ITALIAN SYNONYMS. *Galicar; galicodo; picado; potro.*

GERMAN SYNONYMS. *Der Kleiner Franzose* (= the little French girl); *Laufer* (= running); *Türkische-musik* (= Turkish-delight).

LADIES' FINGER (or WISH), *subs. phr.* (common).—A tapering glass of spirits, especially gin.

LADIES' GROG, *subs. phr.* (common).—Grog: hot, strong, sweet, and plenty of it.—DICKENS.

LADIES' MILE, *subs. phr.* (general).—Rotten Row in Hyde Park—the principal airing ground during the London season.

1871. *Daily News*, 10 May. Why should not a handsome young Englishwoman, he may ask himself, as she canters along the LADIES' MILE, be as good to look at as a cow?

1885. J. COLEMAN, in *Longman's Mag.*, v. 494. The fashionable mob in the LADIES' MILE.

LADIES' TAILORING, *subs. phr.* (venery).—Copulation. *Cf.* STITCH. For synonyms see GREENS and RIDE.

LADIES' TREASURE (DELIGHT, or PLAYTHING), *subs. phr.* (venery).—The *penis*.

LADLE, *verb.* (theatrical).—To enun-

ciate pretentiously; to MOUTH (*q.v.*).

LAD OF (or ON) THE CROSS, *subs. phr.* See CROSS.

LAD O' WAX, *subs. phr.* (old).—I. A cobbler; a COCK O' WAX (*q.v.*). For synonyms see SNOB.

2. (old).—A boy; a doll of a man; a MAN OF WAX = a 'proper' man.

LADRON, *subs.* (old).—A thief. [From the Spanish].

1652. SHIRLEY, *The Brothers* [NARES]. *Ped.* I am become the talk Of every picaro and LADRON.

LAD'S LEAVINGS (A), *subs. phr.* (old).—A girl. For synonyms see TITTER.

1737. RAY, *Proverbs* (3rd ed.), 58. Lasses are LAD'S LEAVINGS.

LADY, *subs.* (old).—1. See quot. 1690: *cf.* LORD.

1690. B. E., *Dict. Cant. Crew*, a very crooked, deformed, and ill-shapen Woman.

1725. *New Cant. Dict.*, s.v.

1785. GROSE, *Vulg. Tongue*, s.v.

1811. *Lex. Bal.*, s.v.

1859. MATSELL, *Vocabulum*, s.v.

2. (common).—The reverse or TAIL (*q.v.*) of a coin: see HEAD, *subs.*, sense 2.

3. (common).—A quart or pint pitcher wrong side uppermost.

4. (nautical).—The keeper of the gunner's small stores: LADY'S HOLE = the place where such stores are kept.

5. (American).—A woman of any station; usually in combination, as FORE-LADY, SALES-LADY, COOK-LADY.

LADY JANE, *subs. phr.* (venery).—The female *pudendum*. For synonyms see MONOSYLLABLE.

LADY-KILLER, *subs.* (colloquial).—A male flirt; a general lover. LADY-KILLING = assiduous gallantry.

1889. LEVER, *Harry Lorrequer*, xxii. I believe your regular LADY-KILLER—yourself for instance—becomes a very quiet animal for being occasionally jilted.

1846-8. THACKERAY, *Vanity Fair*, xiii. I don't set up to be a LADY-KILLER.

1880. G. R. SIMS, *Three Brass Balls*, Pledge iii. He called himself an old fool for being frightened of a dandy—a vain, empty-headed LADY-KILLER.

LADY OF PLEASURE, *subs. phr.* (old).—A prostitute. Fr. *fille de joie*. For synonyms see BARRACK-HACK and TART.

1750. ROBERTSON (of Struan), *Poems*, 203. 'On a LADY of PLEASURE' [Title].

1767. RAY, *Proverbs* (ed. 1893), 64. A whore ... a LADY OF PLEASURE.

LADY'S HOLE. See LADY, *subs.* sense 4.

LADY'S LADDER, *subs.* (nautical).—Rattlins set too close.

LADY'S LOW TOUPÉE, *subs. phr.* (venery).—The female pubic hair. For synonyms see MERKIN.

1721. DURFEY, *Pills to Purge*, etc. ... With my curling tongs so hot, sir, So well as you may see, And so well I can dress up, A lady's LOW TOPPIE.

LADY-STAR, *subs. phr.* (venery).—The female *pudendum*. For synonyms see MONOSYLLABLE.

1598. HALL, *Satires*, IV. 1 (CHALMERS, *English Poets*, 1810, v. 273). And with her cruel LADY'STAR uproze She seeks her third roust on her silent toes.

LADY-WARE, *subs.* (old).—I. The *penis* and *testes*.

1599. *Soliman & Perseda* [DODSLEY, *Old Plays* (1874), v. 345]. The ladies of Rhodes, hearing that you have lost a capital part of your LADY-WARE have made their petition to Cupid to plague you above all other, as one prejudicial to their muliebrity.

2. (old).—Trinkets; knick-knacks, ribands.

LAG, *subs.* (old).—1. Sentence of transportation or penal servitude; transportation.

1821. HAGGART, *Life*, p. 18. Under sentence of LAG for spunk.

2. (thieves').—I. A returned transport; (2) a convict; and (3) a ticket-of-leave man. For synonyms see WRONG 'UN.

1811. *Lex. Bal.*, s.v. LAG, a man transported.

1828. BEE, *Living Picture of London*, p. 39. A few are returned LAGS.

1834. AINSWORTH, *Rookwood*, iii. 5. And thus was I bowled out at last, And into the jug for a LAG was cast.

1856. READE, *Never too Late to Mend*, ix. 'He fell in with two old LAGS who had a deadly grudge against the chaplain.'

1859. MATSELL, *Vocabulum*, s.v. LAG, a convicted felon.

1864. *Daily Telegraph*, 19 Oct. The country is so wild and unexplored, that the LAG who has traversed it, or could traverse it, might re-enter society as a hero if he would impart his adventures.

1877. *Five Years' Penal Servitude*, i. 59. The prisoner who had acted as barber, and was an old LAG, passing the door, told me, 'Never mind cleaning your cell, we are all off to-day.'

1889. *Answers*, 23 Mar., p. 265, col. 3. In the old days many escapes were made from Chatham by expert swimmers. An old LAG (the slang term for prisoner) told me that twice in his recollection had men got clean away in this manner.

1890. HUME NISBET, *Bail Up*, 248. 'Are the police coming'. 'I tinky not. Only that sundowny lun away like ol' LAG.'

1888. *Philadelphia Times*. (Scene up stairs.) Servant—Missus! missus! the BEGGAR LADY is down stairs, and I hare the ash gintleman knockin' at the gate.

6. in pl. (gaming).—Cards. For synonyms see DEVILS' BOOKS.

1890. *Standard*, 15 March, p. 3, col. 5. At Stepney Fairman entered the compartment, and stated he had been to Croydon races, and had been playing with the LADIES (cards), and offered to show them how it was done.

7. (American).—A sweetheart.

OLD LADY, *subs. phr.* (common).—The female *pudendum*. For synonyms see MONOSYLLABLE.

PERFECT LADY, *subs. phr.* (common).—A harlot. For synonyms see BARRACK-HACK and TART.

LADY OF THE LAKE, *subs. phr.* (old).—A kept mistress.

b.1660. DAVENANT, *The Siege*, v. Thou LADY of the LAKE: a pox a whispering!

1678. BUTLER, *Hudibras*, III. i. 868. All women would be of one piece But for the difference marriage makes 'Twixt wives and LADIES OF THE LAKES.

LADY OF EASY VIRTUE, *subs. phr.* (common).—A harlot; a WOMAN OF ACCOMMODATING MORALS or OF MORE COMPLAISANCE THAN VIRTUE. For synonyms see BARRACK-HACK and TART.—GROSE (1785); *Lex. Bal.* (1811), and

1890. *Standard*, 21 March, p. 3, col. 7. Some LADY OF EASY VIRTUE, about whom they knew nothing, lived in another flat, and some one proved that she was an immoral woman.

LADYBIRD, *subs.* (common).—I. A whore; and (2) a term of endearment. For synonyms see BARRACK-HACK and TART.

1595. SHAKSPEARE, *Romeo and Juliet*, i. 33. What lamb! what, LADYBIRD! God forbid!

1600. JONSON, *Cynthia's Revels*, ii. 1. Is that your new ruff, sweet LADYBIRD?

1653. BROME, *Court Begger*, i. 1. A very lime bush to catch LADY-BIRDS.

1690. B. E., *Dict. Cant. Crew*, s.v. LADYBIRDS, Light or Lewd Women.

1725. *New Cant. Dict.*, s.v.

1785. GROSE, *Vulg. Tongue*, s.v.

1811. *Lex. Bal.*, s.v.

1821. EGAN, *Life in London*, p. 173. Others of these LADY-BIRDS were offering their congratulations to him.

1823. MONCRIEFF, *Tom & Jerry*, p. 5. Here, among the pinks in Rotten Row, the LADYBIRDS in the Saloon etc.

1859. MATSELL, *Vocabulum*, s.v.

LADY-CHAIR, *subs.* (common).—See KING'S CUSHION.

1869. BEECHER-STOWE, *Old Town Folks*, 436. She insisted on being carried in a LADY-CHAIR over to our woodland study.

LADY DACRE'S WINE, *subs. phr.* (old).—Gin.—*Lex. Bal.* (1811). For synonyms see DRINKS and WHITE SATIN.

LADY-FEAST, *subs.* (old).—A bout of venery.

1653. BROME, *Mad Couple*, iii. *Al.* This kisse and name your time ... *Bel.* To morrow night. *Al.* Shall you be ready so soone thinke you after your plentifull LADY-FEAST.

LADY FENDER, *subs.* (servants').—A woman who spends her time nursing the fire.

LADY-FLOWER, *subs.* (venery).—The female *pudendum*.—WHITMAN. For synonyms see MONOSYLLABLE.

LADY GREEN, *subs.* (thieves').—A clergyman; specifically the prison chaplain. For synonyms see DEVIL-DODGER.

1890. *Answers*, 27 Dec. He 'sked-addled out of the dock as quickly as he could,' fearing that he might be recognised as an old LAG if he tarried unnecessarily.

1891. *Times*, 14 Sept. 'Capital Punishment'. 'Jack, my dear fellow,' they top a LAG out here (W. Aust.) for slogging a screw. That piece of rope is a rare check. A 'screw' means a 'policeman' as well as a 'warder'.

1892. *Tit Bits*, 19 Mar., 417, 1. Broadmoor for all LAGS as go off their chump.

3. (Old Cant).—See quots. Also LAGE.

1573. HARMAN, *Caveat* (1814), p. 65. LAG, water.

1610. ROWLANDS, *Martin Markall*, p. 39 (H. Club's Repr. 1874). LAGGE water or p—se.

1641. BROME, *Jovial Crew*, ii. I bowse no LAGE, But a whole gage Of this I bowse to you.

1665. R. HEAD, *English Rogue*, Pt. i. ch. v. p. 50 (1874). LAGE, Water.

1690. B. E., *Dict. Cant. Crew*, s.v.

1724. *New Cant. Dict.*, s.v.

1724. E. COLES, *Eng. Dict.*, s.v. LAGE.

1785. GROSE, *Vulg. Tongue*, s.v.

1811. *Lex. Bal.*, s.v.

1859. MATSELL, *Vocabulum*, s.v.

4. (Old Cant).—See quots. Also LAGE.

1567. HARMAN, *Caveat, or Warening for Commen Cursetors*, p. 86. *Man.* We wyll fylche some duddes of the Ruffemans, or myll the ken for a LAGGE of dudes.

1610. ROWLANDS, *Martin Markall*, p. 39 (H. Club's Repr. 1874). LAGGE of dudes, a bucke of clothes.

1661. FLETCHER, *Beggar's Bush*, v. I. Tell us If it be milling of a LAG of duds, The fetching-off a buck of clothes, or so?

1690. B. E., *Dict. Cant. Crew*, s.v. LAG-A-DUDDS. We cloy the LAG of Duds, Come let us steal that Buck of Cloths.

1725. *New Cant. Dict.*, s.v.

1785. GROSE, *Vulg. Tongue*, s.v.

1811. *Lex. Bal.*, s.v.

1859. MATSELL, *Vocabulum*, s.v.

5. (old).—See quots.

1690. B. E., *Dict. Cant. Crew*, s.v. LAG-A-DUDDS of the Flock, the hindmost.

1725. *New Cant. Dict.*, s.v.

1785. GROSE, *Vulg. Tongue*, s.v. LAG. Lag last, the last of a company.

6. (Westminster School).—A fag.

1881. PASCOE, *Everyday Life in our Public Schools*. Every morning the LAG junior prepares and brings to hall the list.

7. (American theatrical).—I. A dialogue or scene of extra length; also (2) a wait.

1847. DARLEY, *Drama in Pokerville*, 112. A LAG on the stage was immediately made up for by the pop of a cork.

Verb. (thieves').—I. To transport; to send to penal servitude. LAGGED = (1) sentenced; and (2) imprisoned. Fr. *aller à la grotto* = TO LUMP THE LIGHTER (*q.v.*); also *se laver les haricots*.

1819. MOORE, *Tom Crib*, p. 78. A relative of poor Crockey, who was LAGGED some time since.

1811. *Lex. Bal.*, s.v. LAG, The cove was LAGGED for a drag.

1824. SCOTT, *St. Ronan's Well*, ch. xxxi. 'I should not much like to have him LAGGED for forgery.'

1830. LYTTON, *Paul Clifford*, p. 13. Ranting Rob, poor fellow, was LAGGED for doing a panny.

1838. DICKENS, *Oliver Twist*, ch. XLIII. 'What do you mean by LAGGING and a lifer,' demanded Mr. Bolter. ... Being interpreted, Mr. Bolter would have been informed that they represented that combination of words, 'Transportation for life.'

1843. MONCRIEFF, *Scamps of London*, ii. 3. He was three times LAGGED.

1843. *Punch*, iv. p. 129. They say that a lord and a reverend were LAGGED the other day.

1853. *Diogenes*, ii. 54. Sad work when at last I was LAGGED.

1859. MATSELL, *Vocabulum*, s.v.

1869. *Daily News*, 29 July. He should then be LAGGED for another job.

1872. *Times*, 2 Oct. 'Report of Middlesex Sessions.' He had expected to be LAGGED for a pocket handkerchief.

1877. *Five Years' Penal Servitude*, iii. 93. A Welshman convicted or LAGGED for passing 'shise coin'—bad money.

1879. *Macmillan's Mag.*, XL. 503. I should have got LAGGED and my pal too.

1887. BAUMANN, *A Slang Ditty*. Rum coves that relieve us of 'chinkers' and pieces, Is gin'rally LAGGED, Or, wuss luck, they gits scragged.

1880. SIMS, *How the Poor Live*, p. 18. A day or two after Bill returns alone; the girl asks him where her sweetheart is. 'He's LAGGED,' says Bill. But the girl has a bit of newspaper, and in it she reads that 'the body of a man has been found in some woods near London;' and she has an idea it may be John.

2. (Old Cant).—To steal. For synonyms *see* PRIG.

1580. TUSSER, *Husbandrie*, ch. 20, st. 15, p. 54 (E. D. S.). Some corne away LAG in bottle and bag. Some steales for a iest, egges out of the nest.

3. (old).—To catch.

1580. TUSSER, *Husbandrie*, ch. 36, st. 25, p. 86 (E. D. S.). Poore cunnie, so bagged, is soone over LAGGED.

1858. A. MAYHEW, *Paved with Gold*, Bk. III, ch. I. p. 252. They tell him adventures of how they were nearly LAGGED by the constables.

1891. NAT. GOULD, *Double Event*, 263. You'll never LAG me alive, you cur.

4. (old).—To PISS (*q.v.*).

5. (old: now recognised).—*See* quots.

1596. SPENSER, *Fairy Queen*, VI. ii. 10. Whenso she LAGGED, as she needs mote so, He with his speare.... would thumpe her forward.

1690. B. E., *Dict. Cant. Crew*, s.v. LAG-A-DUDDS. To LAGG behind, or come after with Salt and Spoons.

1725. *New Cant. Dict.*, q.v.

1725. *Pope, Odyssey*, XIV. 245. My valour.... never LAGG'D behind.

1785. GROSE, *Vulgar Tongue*, s.v. LAG.... to drop behind, to keep back.

1811. *Lex. Bal.*, q.v.

LAGE, *see* LAG, *subs.*, senses 3 and 4.

Verb. (Old Cant).—To wash down; to drink.

1567. HARMAN, *Caveat* (1869), p. 85. The vpright cofe canteth to the Roge: 'I saye by the Salomon I will LAGE it of with a gage of Benebouse; then cut to my nose watch.'

LAGER BEER, TO THINK NO LAGER BEER OF ONE SELF, *verb. phr.* (American).—*See* SMALL-BEER.

1888. *Texas Liftings*, 23 June. John Ruskin THINKS NO LAGER BEER OF HIMSELF. He knows something about pictures and Venice stones. He is boss on these points; but when he breaks out in bursts of opinion on railroads and other modern inventions, his knowledge of the spirit of the present age turns out to be mighty small pumpkins.

LAG-FEVER, *subs.* (old).—*See* quot.

1811. *Lex. Bal.*, s.v. LAG-FEVER. A term of ridicule applied to men who being under sentence of transportation, pretend illness, to avoid being sent from gaol to the hulks.

LAGGER, *subs.* (nautical).—1. A sailor.

2. (thieves').—An informer; a witness. [*Cf.* LAG, *verb.*].

LAGGING, *subs.* (thieves').—A term of imprisonment: also LAG (*q.v. subs.* sense 1). Hence, LAGGING-MATTER = a crime rendering persons liable to transportation (GROSE, 1823).

LAGGING-DUES, *subs.* (old).—*See* quot.

1823. EGAN, *Grose's Dict. Vulg. Tongue*, s.v. LAGGING-DUES. When a person is likely to be transported, the flash people observe, LAGGING-DUES will be concerned.

LAGGING-GAGE, *subs.* (old).—A chamber-pot: for synonyms *see* IT.

1891. *Referee*, 8 March. All this storm in a LAGGING-GAGE is very absurd.

LAGNIAPPE (or **LAGNAPPE**), *subs.* (American).—*See* quot.

1877. CLEMENS ('Mark Twain'), *Life on the Mississippi*, p. 404-5. We picked up one excellent word—LAGNIAPPE.... It is the equivalent of the thirteenth roll in a baker's dozen. It is something thrown in, gratis, for good measure. The custom originated in the Spanish quarter of the city. When a child or a servant buys something.... he finishes the operation by saying, 'Give me something for LAGNIAPPE.' The shopman always responds... When you are invited to drink, and you say, I've had enough,' the other says, 'But just this one time more—this is for LAGNIAPPE.'

1884. G. W. CABLE, *Creoles of Louisiana*, XVI. The pleasant institution of *napa*—the petty gratuity added by the retailer to anything bought—grew the pleasanter, drawn out into gallicized LAGNAPPE.

LAGRANGED, adj. (American).—Vexed.

LAG-SHIP, *subs.* (old).—A convict transport.

LAID. *See* LAVENDER and SHELF.

LAKER-LADY, *subs.* (old).—An actor's harlot. [Saxon LAKER = an actor].

LALA, *subs.* (American).—A swell.

LALLY, *subs.* (old).—Linen; LULLY (*q.v.*).

1800. PARKER, *Life's Painter*, p. 157. Dabble your LALLY, wash your shirt.

LALLYCODLER, *subs.* (American).—One eminently successful in any particular line.

LAM. *See* LAMB, *verb.*

LAMB, *subs.* (common).—1. A quiet easy-going person; a simpleton; a JUGGINS (*q.v.*).

1669. *The Nicker Nicked* (*Harl. Misc.*, ii. 109) [ed. 1808-12]. When a young gentleman or apprentice comes into this school of virtue unskilled in the quibbles and devices there practised, they call him a LAMB; then a rook (who is properly the wolf) follows him close and .... gets all his money, and then they smile and say, 'The LAMB is bitten.'

1672. LACY, *Old Troop*, i. *Sisted.* Why, then, it seems we religious LAMBS may play with one another without sinning.

1851-61. MAYHEW, *Lond. Lab.*, iii. 216. Made him come three times like a LAMB.

2. (common).—Ironically used of a rough, cruel, or merciless person; specifically applied to Nottingham roughs, and hence to bludgeon men at elections. The 'head-money' given is called MINT-SAUCE (*q.v.*).

ENGLISH SYNONYMS. Barker; basher; blood-tub; bouncer; bounder; boy of the Holy Ground; bruiser; dead duck; hoodlum; larrikin: mug; plug-ugly; rabbit (or dead rabbit); ramper; roarer (or roaring-boy); rough; roustabout; rouster; rowdy; rustler; short-ear. *See* also generally FURIOSO and LOAFER.

FRENCH SYNONYMS. *Un kroumir* (popular); *un lascar* (common); *un mangeur de nez* (thieves'); *un matador; un ostrogoth.*

GERMAN SYNONYMS. *Troll* (or *Tallerwatsch*).

1849. MACAULAY, *Hist. of England*, ch. v. 'As they had been levied for the purpose of waging war on an infidel nation, they bore on their flag a Christian

VOL. IV. 10

emblem, the Paschal LAMB. In allusion to this device, and with a bitterly ironical meaning, these men, the rudest and most ferocious in the English army, were called Kirke's LAMBS.'

1891. *Lic. Vict. Gaz.*, 23 Jan. Merryman had pitched on a nice level bit of turf. It was a noisy crowd—that goes without saying—for where the Nottingnam LAMBS are you can hardly expect much peace and quietness.

3. (colloquial).—A term of endearment.

1595. SHAKSPEARE, *Romeo and Juliet*, i. 3. What, LAMB! what, ladybird!

1621. BURTON, *Anat.* (ed. 1893), iii. 183. Pleasant names may be invented, bird, mouse, LAMB, puss.

1690. DAVENANT, *Love & Honour*, v. 1. We must make haste! Farewell, LAMB!

4. (common).—An elderly person dressed or got-up young.

5. *See* PET LAMB.

6. (military).—*See* KIRKE'S LAMBS.

Verb. (old).—To beat. Also LAM, LAMBASTE, LAMBACK and LAMBEAKE. *Cf.* LAMMING.

1555. *Disc. of New World*, 115 [NARES]. While the men are faine to beare off with eares, head, and shoulders. Happy may they call that daie whereon they are not LAMBEAKED before night.

1591. NASHE, *Wond. Prog.* [GROSART (1885), ii. 159]. Tall fellows ... armed with good cudgels, shall so LAMBEAKE these stubborne huswiues, that the wind shall turn into another quarter.

1592. HARVEY, *Four Letters* [GROSART (1885), i. 183]. One, which should massacre Martin's wit, or should be LAMBACKD himself.

1600. DECKER, *Shoem. Holiday*, in *Works* (1873), i. 68. Oh if they had staid I would have so LAMB'D them with flouts.

1601. MUNDAY & CHETTLE, *Death of Rob. E. of Hunt.*, sign. K. 1. [NARES]. First, with this hand wound thus about here haire, And with this dagger lustilie LAMBACKT, I would, y faith.

1613. BEAUMONT & FLETCHER, *Honest Man's Fortune*, v. 2. If I had been acquainted with LAMMING in my youth .... I should do better.

1637. DAVENANT, *Britannia Triumphans* [PATERSON, ii. 82]. Whine not, my love; his fury streight will waste him; Stand off awhile, and see how Ile LAMBASTE him.

1690. B. E., *Dict. Cant. Crew*, s.v. LAMBASTE, to beat soundly.

1710. MISSON, *Travels in England*, p. 306. A fellow whom he LAMBED most horribly.

1725. *New Cant. Dict.*, s.v.

1731. COFFEY, *Devil to Pay*, Sc. v. Come, hussy, leave fooling ... or else I'll LAMB you.

1733. FIELDING, *Don Quixote*, ii. 6. Sirrah, I am able to beat a dozen of you.—If I don't LAMB thee!

1748. T. DYCHE, *Dictionary* (5th ed.). LAMB (v.) to thresh or beat severely.

1785. GROSE, *Vulg. Tongue*, s.v. LAMB or LAMBASTE, to beat.

1811. *Lex. Bal.*, s.v.

1812. SMITH (H. and J.), *Rejected Addresses*, XX. I would pummel and LAM her well.

b. 1852. *Traits of American Humour*, 50. If he seed er fellow he thought he could LAMM without no danger, he wouldn't make no bone, but he'd just go up to the chap and make faces at him.

1859. MATSELL, *Vocabulum*, s.v. LAMB, to beat with a club.

1864. *Eton School Days*, xxvi. 291. The partial thrashing which he had himself received only made him the more anxious for revenge on Ravenous. 'LAM into him!' said Lascelles.

1872. S. L. CLEMENS ('Mark Twain'), *Roughing It*. He could LAMM any galoot of his inches in America.

1882. F. ANSTEY, *Vice-Versâ*, iv. 'Let him undress now, and we can LAM it into him afterwards with slippers.'

1887. HENLEY, *Villon's Good Night.* Paste 'em, and larrup 'em, and LAMN.

1889. *Lic. Vict. Gaz.*, 18 Jan. Still the little 'uns LAMMED into each other.

TO SKIN THE LAMB. *See* SKIN.

LAMBACK, *subs.* (old).—A blow.

1591. GREENE, *Discov. of Cosenage* [GROSART (1881-6), x. 60]. Five or six wives... gave unto him halfe a score of sound LAMBEAKES with their cudgels.

LAMBACKER, *subs.* (old).—A bully; a HECTOR (*q.v*).

1593. HARVEY, *Pierces Superer.* [GROSART (1885), ii. 210]. Out upon thee for a cowardly LAMBACKER.

LAMB AND SALAD. TO GIVE ONE LAMB AND SALAD, *verb. phr.* (common).—To thrash soundly. For synonyms *see* WIG and TAN.

LAMBASTE. *See* LAMB, *verb.* sense 1.

LAMBASTING, *subs.* (common).—A thrashing; *cf.* LAMB and BASTING. For synonyms *see* TANNING.

1835. HALIBURTON, *Clockmaker*, I. xii. 'They put me in mind of a great big hulk of a horse in a cart, that won't put his shoulder to the collar at all for all the LAMBASTIN' in the world.'

1838. NEAL, *Charcoal Sketches*, ii. 79. 'I can't hide,' says a braggadoccio, 'when anybody owes me a LAMBASTING.'

1883. CLARK RUSSELL, *Sailor's Language*, s.v. LAMBUSTING, a rope's-ending.

LAMB-DOWN, *verb.* (Australian).—*See* quot.

1886. *Daily Telegraph*, 20 Mar. Arrived there he at once handed his cheque to the landlord, and proceeded to LAMB the amount—say five-and-forty pounds— 'DOWN'; that is to say, he got excessively drunk morning, noon, and night on the infamously bad whiskey supplied to him.

LAMB-PIE, *subs.* (old).—A drubbing.—B. E. (1690); *New Cant. Dict.* (1725); DYCHE (1748); GROSE (1785); *Lex. Bal.* (1811).

LAMBSKIN, *verb.* (old).— To beat: *see* LAMB, sense 1.

1593. HARVEY, *Pierces Superer.* [GROSART (1885), ii. 210]. Thou art too young an Artist to coniure him up, that can exercise thee downe; or to lamback him with ten years preparation, that can LAMBSKIN thee with a dayes warning.

1612. CHAPMAN, *Widow's Tears*, ii. 4. What think you of.... Hercules?.... his mistress wore his lion's skin and LAMB-SKINNED him if he did not his business.

LAMB-SKIN MAN, *subs.* (old).—A judge.—B. E. (1690); *New Cant. Dict.* (1725); GROSE (1785); *Lex. Bal.* (1811).

LAMB'S-WOOL, *subs.* (old).—Hot ale, spiced, sweetened, and mixed with the pulp of roasted apples.

c. 1189. *The King & the Miller* (PERCY, *Reliques*, iii. 184). A cup of LAMBS-WOOL they dranke unto him then.

1590. PEELE, *Old Wives' Tale*, iv. 6. Lay a crab in the fire to rost for LAMBSWOOL.

1593. NASHE, *Strange Newes*, in *Works*, ii. 198. Before I vnbowell the leane Carcase of thy book any further, Ile drinke one cup of LAMBSWOOL.

b. 1602. *Lingua* [DODSLEY, *Old Plays* (1874), ix. 424]. LAMBS-WOOL, the meekest meat in the world; 'twill let any man fleece it.

1606. DEKKER, *Newes from Hell* [GROSART (1886), ii. 124]. One of those big fellows that stand like gyants, having bellies bumbasted with ale in LAMBS-WOOL.

1621. BURTON, *Anat.* (ed. 1892), ii. 297. I find more that commend use of apples ... (LAMB'S-WOOL some call it).

1633. JOHNSON, *Gerard's Herbal*, p. 1460. The pulpe of the rosted apples, in number foure or five, according to the greatnesse of the apples (especially the pomewater), mixed in a wine quart of faire water, laboured together until it come to be as apples and ale, which we call LAMBES-WOOLL.

d. 1674. HERRICK, *Poems*, p. 376. Now crowne the bowle With gentle

LAMBS-WOOLL, Add sugar, and nutmegs, and ginger.

1690. B. E., *Dict. Cant. Crew*, s.v. LAMB'S WOOL, roasted apples and ale.

1725. *New Cant. Dict.*, s.v.

1731. C. COFFEY, *The Devil To Pay*, i. Here's sixpence for you; get ale and apples, stretch and puff thyself up with LAMB'S WOOL, rejoice and revel by thyself.

1766. GOLDSMITH, *Vicar of Wakefield*, xi. Our honest neighbour's goose and dumplings were fine, and the LAMB'S-WOOL. . . . was excellent.

1785. GROSE, *Vulg. Tongue*, s.v.

1811. *Lex. Bal.*, s.v.

1822. SCOTT, *Fortunes of Nigel*, viii. The ale, or, to speak technically, the LAMB'S WOOL, was fitted for drinking.

1883. *Notes & Queries*, 6, S. VIII. p. 482. The wassail-bowl (as Horsfield states) was compounded of ale, sugar, nutmeg, and roasted apples, the latter called LAMB'S-WOOL. The wassail-bowl is placed on a small round table, and each person present is furnished with a silver spoon to stir.

LAME-DOG. TO HELP A LAME DOG OVER A STILE, *verb. phr.* (common).—To give a hand; to help; TO BUNK UP (*q.v.*). *Fr. sauver la mise à quelqu'un.*

1605. MARSTON, *Insatiate Countess*, ii. 2. Here's a stile so high as a man cannot HELP A DOG OVER IT.

1670. RAY, *Proverbs* [BOHN (1893), 168]. Help the LAME DOG OVER THE STILE.

LAME DUCK, *subs. phr.* (common).—1. A defaulter on 'Change: who has to 'waddle out of the Alley.' *Cf.* BEAR, BULL, etc.

1766. LORD MARCH in Jesse's *Selwyn*, ii. 47 (1882). As I am very deeply engaged [in racing bets], I shall perhaps be obliged to make use of your money, that in case of the worst I may not be a LAME DUCK.

1768. FOOTE, *Devil upon Two Sticks*, Act i. A mere bull and bear booby; the patron of LAME DUCKS, brokers, and fraudulent bankrupts.

1771. GARRICK, *Prologue to The Maid of Bath*. The gaming fools are doves, the knaves are rooks, Change-alley bankrupts waddle out LAME DUCKS.

1771. WALPOLE, *Letters*, iii. 337. I may be LAME, but I shall never be a DUCK, nor deal in the garbage of the Alley.

1774. COLMAN, *Man of Business*, iv. 1. in *Wks.* (1777), ii. 179. If Mr. Beverly does not pay his differences within these four-and-twenty hours, the world cannot hinder his being a LAME DUCK.

1787. *Whitehall Evening News* [quoted in FRANCIS on Stock Exchange]. There were no less than 25 LAME DUCKS who waddled out of the alley.

1846. MARRYAT, *Peter Simple*, III. xxv. 458. He was obliged to waddle: if I didn't know much about bulls and bears, I know very well what a LAME DUCK is to my cost.

1847. THACKERAY, *Vanity Fair*, xiii. 'Unless I see Amelia's ten thousand down you don't marry her. I'll have no LAME DUCK'S daughter in my family.'

1860. PEACOCK, *Gryll Grange*, xviii. In Stock Exchange slang, Bulls are speculators for a rise, Bears for a fall. A LAME DUCK is a man who cannot pay his differences, and is said to waddle off.

1865. *Harpers' Mag.*, April, p. 616. All, or nearly all, have been LAME DUCKS at some time or other.

1890. *Standard*, 5 Aug., p. 2, col. 2. We learn that it is actionable to call a stockbroker a LAME DUCK, because on the Exchange 'the word has acquired a particular meaning.'

1891. *Pall Mall Gaz.*, 19 Jan., p. 3, col. 1. We have had applications from a good many LAME DUCKS.

2. (Australian).—A scapegrace.

1895. *Pall Mall Gaz.* 15 Aug. p. 3, col. 1. Andrew appears to have been the LAME DUCK of the family, and constantly wagged it from school to go fishing in the lagoons or wallaby-hunting in the mountains with the natives.

LAME-HAND, *subs.* (old coaching).—An indifferent driver; a SPOON (*q.v.*).

LAMMAS. AT LATER LAMMAS, *phr.* (common).—Never; at the GREEK KALENDS (*q.v.*); at TIB'S EVE (*q.v.*).

1576. GASCOIGNE, *Steele Glas* (ed. ARBER), 55. Courtiers thrive at LATTER LAMMAS DAY.

1670. RAY, *Proverbs* [BOHN (1893), 168]. AT LATER LAMMAS, *ad Græcas Calendas, i.e.*, never.

LAMMERMOOR LION, *subs. phr.* (Scots').—A sheep: *cf.* COTSWOLD LION, and ESSEX LION.

LAMMIE TODD! *phr.* (tailors').—'I would if I could'.

LAMMIKIN, *subs.* (old).—A blow.

1622. R. HAWKINS, *Observations* [Hackluyt Soc. 1878, p. 228]. Wi h a truncheon which I had in mine hand, I gave the Indians three or four good LAMMIKINS.

LAMMING, *subs.* (old).—A beating; *cf.* LAMB. For synonyms *see* TANNING.

1619. BEAUMONT and FLETCHER, *King and no King*, v. *Bes.* Gentlemen, you hear my lord is sorry. *Bac.* Not that I have beaten you, but beaten one that will be beaten; one whose dull body will require a LAMMING, as surfeits do the diet spring and fall.

LAMMY, *subs.* (nautical).—A blanket: originally a thick quilted frock, or short jumper made of flannel or blanket cloth, worn by sailors as an outside garment in cold weather.—*Gentlemen's Magazine* (1866, Oct., p. 390).

LAMP, *subs.* (common).—1. *See* quot. 1811; and (2) in pl. = spectacles; GIGLAMPS (*q.v.*). For synonyms *see* PEEPERS.

1811. *Lex. Bal.*, s.v. LAMP, the cove has a queer LAMP, the man has a blind or squinting eye.

1859. MATSELL, *Vocabulum*, s.v.

1888. *Sporting Life*, 15 Dec. Why, bruise me ef 'e ain't got his LAMPS shut.

1892. MILLIKEN, *'Arry Ballads*, 49. I lifted my LAMPS and saw Billy.

TO SMELL OF THE LAMP, *verb. phr.* (colloquial).—To show signs of labour or study.

1615. BRETON, *Characters upon Essates* [GROSART (1879), ii. *q.* 4. 1. 3, *ad authorem*]. He that shall read thy character . . . they must say they are well written. They TASTE THE LAMPE.

1625. JONSON, *Staple of News*, Prol. A work not SMELLING OF THE LAMP to-night.

1647-80. ROCHESTER, *Wks.* (1793), p. 16. Though he be very correct, and has spared no pains to dress the Satires of Horace in good French, yet it SMELLS too much OF THE LAMP.

LAMP-POST, *subs.* (common).—A tall, or lanky person.

ENGLISH SYNONYMS. Clothes-prop; daddy-longlegs, Duke of Lankester; Duke of Limbs; gawk; gas-pipe; lath-legs; long-ghost; Long-shanks; long-'un; rasher-of-wind; sky-scraper; sky-topper; spindle-shanks; split-up; tongs; matches.

FRENCH SYNONYMS. *Une asperge montée* (popular); *une brinde* (popular: of women only); *un grand cadavre* (popular: of men only); *un faucheux* (thieves' = a field spider); *une planche à pain* (military); *une canne à pêche* (= fishing rod); *une perche à houblon* (= hop-pole).

SPANISH SYNONYMS. *Cigueño; filisteo; varal; zanguayo; zangarullon.*

ITALIAN SYNONYM. *Longone* (FLORIO).

LAMP OF LIFE, *subs. phr.* (venery).—The *penis.* For synonyms *see* CREAMSTICK and PRICK.

LAMP OF LOVE, *subs. phr.* (venery).—The female *pudendum.* For synonyms *see* MONOSYLLABLE.

LANCE, *subs.* (old).—The *penis.* For synonyms *see* CREAMSTICK and PRICK.

1622. ATTY, *First Book of Airs*, in BULLEN, *Speculum Amantis* (1889), 15. And when I charge, my LANCE in rest, I triumph in delight.

1675. COTTON, *Scoffer Scofft*, in *Works* (1725), p. 208. And Mankind must in darkness languish Whilst he his bawdy LAUNCE does brandish.

LANCEMAN (LANCE-KNIGHT, or LANCEMAN-PRIGGER), *subs.* (old).—A highwayman.

1591. GREENE, *Second Part of Conny-catching* [GROSART (1881-6), x. 76]. The Priggar if he be a LAUNCE-MAN, that is one that is already horst. *Ibid.* Not long after . . . this LANCEMAN PRIGGAR was brought to Tenro gayle.

1599. NASHE, *Lenten Stuffe* [GROSART (1884), v. 278]. He fell into the thieuish hands of . . . LANCEKNIGHTS.

LANCEPRESADO, *subs.* (old).—*See* quots.

1690. B. E., *Dict. Cant. Crew*, s.v. LANSPRESADO, he that comes into Company with but Two pence in his Pocket.

1725. *New Cant. Dict.*, s.v.

1785. GROSE, *Vulg. Tongue*, s.v. LANSPRISADO, one who has only twopence in his pocket; also a lance, or deputy corporal, that is, one doing the duty without the pay of corporal; formerly a lancier, or horseman, who being dismounted by the death of his horse, served in the foot by the title of LANSPRISADO OR LANCEPESATO; a broken lance.

LAND, *verb.* (pugilistic).—1. To deliver; to GET HOME (*q.v.*).

1888. *Sporting Life*, 1 Dec. The big 'un LANDED his left straight on his opponent's dial.

1888. J. RUNCIMAN, *The Chequers*, p. 93. Their object is to LAND one cunning blow.

1891. *Gentlemen's Mag.*, Aug., p. 110. That's right, Captain Kitty! LAND him one in the eye.

1892. MILLIKEN, *'Arry Ballads*, 31. The TOFF ketched the blade of Tom's scull, dragged 'im close, and jest LANDED 'im one.

2. (colloquial).—To bring or take to a position or place; to set down; to catch; to arrive.

1850. MCCOSH, *Divine Government*, Appendix, p. 522. These rules may LAND us in mistakes.

1862. CUTHBERT BEDE, *Tales of College Life*, p. 18. That's the ticket! that will just LAND me in time for Gates.

1871. *Daily Telegraph*, 26 Dec. I've LANDED him.

1872. *Judy*, 29 May, p. 59, col. 2. He's bound to be on the grand stand before the Derby's run, and that's where we'll LAND him.

1892. MILLIKEN, *'Arry Ballads*, p. 32. The wrinkles and tips I've LANDED a-bussing it to and from town.

1892. *Pall Mall Gazette*, 17 Oct., p. 2, col. 1. The song 'If I was only long enough' LANDED me with one bound at the top of the tree.

1894. *Tit Bits*, 7 Ap., p. 8, col. 1. Mr. Jenkins had been three years in Tooting when he was finally LANDED by a bold and persistent widow.

3. (colloquial).—To set up; to make all right; to secure.

1876. HINDLEY, *Adventures of a Cheap Jack*, 33. I bought a big covered cart and a good strong horse. And I was LANDED.

1879. *Macmillan's Mag.*, xl. 502. I was LANDED this time without them getting me up a lead.

4. (sporting).—To win; to gain.

1853. WH. MELVILLE, *Digby Grand*, vi. St. Agatha clears the two with a tremendous rush, and, after one of the finest races on record, is LANDED a winner by a neck.

1854. WHYTE MELVILLE, *General Bounce*, xx. 'I LANDED a hundred gold mohurs by backing his new lot for the Governor-General's Cup.'

1865. *Daily Telegraph*, 20 June. M. Van Grootvens finished the day's sport by winning a steeplechase with Vixen—this being the second stake, together £1,000 I hear, which he has LANDED with the mare since he purchased her of Mr. Roe.

1883. *Daily Telegraph*, 29 Sept. I'd make a similar wager and be more sure of LANDING the stake.

1891. *Licensed Vict. Gaz.*, 20 March. Had the French filly LANDED, what a shout would have arisen from the ring!

TO LAND OUT, *verb. phr.* (American).—To decamp.

1882. MCCABE, *New York*, XXIII. 393. When he was tired of me he LANDED OUT, an' I've never seen him since.

TO SEE HOW THE LAND LIES, *verb. phr.* (colloquial).—To see how matters stand. *See* quot. 1690.

1690. B. E., *Dict. Cant. Crew*, s.v. LANDLORD. How LIES THE LAND? How stands the reckoning?

1725. *New Cant. Dict.*, s.v.

1785. GROSE, *Vulg. Tongue*, s.v.

WHO HAS ANY LAND IN APPLEBY, *phr.* (old).—*See* quot.

1690. B. E., *Dict. Cant. Crew*, s.v. LANDLORD, WHO HAS ANY LANDS IN APPLEBY? a Question askt the Man at whose Door the Glass stands long. [Also GROSE (1785)].

LAND-BROKER, *subs.* (American thieves').—An undertaker.—MATSELL (1859).

LAND-CARACK, *subs.* (old).—A mistress.

1629. DAVENANT, *Albovine*, iii. *Grim.* I must be furnished too. *Cuny.* With a mistress? *Grim.* Yes, enquire me out some old LAND-CARACK.

LAND-CRAB, *subs.* (American).—A landsman.

LANDED ESTATE, *subs. phr.* (common).—1. The grave; DARBY'S DYKE (*q.v.*).

2. (common).—Dirt in the nails.

LANDIES, *subs.* (Winchester College).—Gaiters. [From tradespeople—Landy and Currell—who supplied them.—*Notions*].

LANDLADY. TO HANG THE LANDLADY, *verb. phr.* (common).—To decamp without payment; TO MOONSHINE; TO STAND OFF THE TAILOR.

LANDLUBBER (also **LAND-LEAPER** and **LAND-LOPER**), *subs.* (old).—A vagabond; one who fled the country for crime or debt: also (nautical) a landsman, in varying degrees of contempt, for incapacity in general or uselessness as sailors in particular. Fr. *un jus de cancre; un terrien;* or *un failli chien de terrien.*

1362. LANGLAND, *Piers Plowman*, B, xv. 207 (. . .). For he ne is no3te in lolleres, ne in LANDE-LEPERES hermytes.

1592. NEWTON, *Tryall of a Man's owne Selfe* [NARES]. Whether the governors of the commonwealth have suffered palmesters, fortune-tellers, stage-players, sawce-boxes, enterluders, puppit players, loyterers, vagabonds, LANDLEAPERS, and such like cozening make-shifts.

1606. LYTE, *Dodoene*, 348. Wherfore these LANDLEAPERS, koges etc.

1621. BURTON, *Anatomy* (ed. 1893), i. 367. Let Mariners learn Astronomy; Merchants' Factors study Arithmetick . . . LANDLEAPERS Geography.

1622. BACON, *Henry VII.* [ed. Spedding], vi. 133. Thirdly he had been from his childhood such a wanderer or (as the King called it) such a LANDLOPER, as it was extreme hard to hunt out his nest and parents.

1650. HOWELL, *Familiar Letters* [NARES]. You are sure where to find me, wheras I was a LANDLOPER as the Dutchman saith, a wanderer, and subject to incertain removes, and short sojourns in divers places before.

1671. SHADWELL, *Fair Quaker of Deal*, i. And the LANDLUBBER (for he is no sailor) had the impudence to tell me he would not be etc.

1690. B. E., *Dict. Cant. Crew*, s.v. LAND-LOPERS or LAND-LUBBERS, Freshwater Seamen so called by the true Tarrs; also Vagabonds that Beg and Steal through the Country.

1696. *Nomenclator.* Erro ... Rodeur, coureur, vagabond. A roge: a LAND LEAPER: a vagabond: a runagate.

1725. *New Cant. Dict.*, s.v.

1785. GROSE, *Vulg. Tongue*, s.v. LAND LOPERS or LAND-LUBBERS, vagabonds lurking about the country, who subsist by pilfering.

17[?]. *Ballad*, 'One Fine Morning' (*The Mermaid*), *Refrain.* Three jolly sailor boys up on the mast, And the LAND-LUBBERS down below.

1811. *Lex. Bal.*, s.v.

1884. *Graphic*, April 5. p. 338, col. 2. The veriest LAND-LUBBER cannot fail to become something of a sailor after reading it.

LAND OF NOD, *subs. phr.* (common). —Sleep. TO GO TO THE LAND OF NOD = to go to bed; to fall asleep. For synonyms *see* BALMY.

1818. SCOTT, *Heart of Mid-Lothian*, xxx. There's queer things chanced since ye hae been in the LAND OF NOD.

1828. HOOD, *Poems*, i. 205 [ed. 1846]. To the happy [bed is] a first class carriage of ease To the LAND OF NOD, or where you please.

1892. HUME NISBET, *Bushranger's Sweetheart*, p. 275. Saying which he led the way back to our hut, where we flung ourselves down on our blankets, and were soon in the LAND OF NOD.

LAND OF PROMISES, *subs. phr.* (University).—*See* quot.

1823. GROSE, *Vulg. Tongue*, s.v. LAND OF PROMISES the fair expectation cherished by a steady novice at Oxford.

LAND OF STEADY HABITS, *subs. phr.* (American).—Connecticut.

LAND OF SHEEPISHNESS, *subs. phr.* (old University).—*See* quot.

1823. GROSE, *Vulg. Tongue*, s.v. LAND OF SHEEPISHNESS, schoolboy's bondage.

LAND-PACKET, *subs.* (American).— *See* quot.

1847. PORTER, *Quarter Race*, 115. Known as the Captain of a LAND-PACKET, in plain terms, the driver of an ox-team.

LAND-PIRATE (or **LAND-RAT**), *subs.* (old).—1. *See* quot. 1690. For synonyms *see* ROAD-AGENT.

1598. SHAKSPEARE, *Merchant of Venice*, i. 3. There be LAND-RATS and water-rats, land thieves and water thieves.

1609. DEKKER, *Gul's Horn-booke* [GROSART (1885), ii. 233]. The Dukes tomb is a sanctuary, and will keep you alive from LAND-RATS. *Ibid.* iii. 262. These LAND-PYRATES lodge in ... the out-barnes of farmers.

1690. B. E., *Dict. Cant. Crew*, s.v. LAND-PIRATES, Highwaymen or any other robbers. [Also *New Cant. Dict.* (1725) and GROSE (1785)].

2. (nautical). — *See* LAND-SHARK.

LAND-RAKER, *subs.* (old).—A vagabond; a LAND-LUBBER (*q.v.*).

1598. SHAKSPEARE, *1 Henry IV*, ii. 1. I am joined with no foot LAND-RAKERS, no long-staff sixpenny strikers.

LAND SECURITY. *See* LEG-BAIL

LAND-SHARK, *subs.* (nautical).—1. A boarding-house keeper; a runner; a crimp; anyone living by the plunder of seamen. Fr. *une vermine.*

1838. GLASCOCK, *Landsharks and Seaguls* [Title].

1857. KINGSLEY, *Two Years Ago*, ch. iv. These LAND-SHARKS. . . . 'll plunder even the rings off a corpse's fingers.

1888. *Notes and Queries*, 7 S. v. 4 Feb., p. 83. Honest Jack, may he ever be kept from LAND-SHARKS. [An old Toast].

2. (common).—A usurer.

3. (common).—A landgrabber; one who seizes land by craft or force.

c.1824. *The American*, VIII. 68. There will be evasion of our laws by native and foreign LAND-SHARKS.

4. (common).—A custom-house officer.

1815. SCOTT, *Guy Mannering*, xxxiv. 'Lieutenant Brown gave him to his cousin that's in the Middleburgh house of Vanbeest and Vanbruggen, and told him some goose's gazette about his being taken in a skirmish with the LAND-SHARKS.'

LAND-SWAB, *subs.* (common).—A LANDLUBBER (*q.v.*); a GRASS-COMBER (*q.v.*).

LAND-YARD, *subs.* (American).—A cemetery.

LANE, *subs.* (old).—1. The throat. For synonyms *see* GUTTER ALLEY. Also RED LANE and RED LION LANE.

1534. UDALL, *Roister Doister*, i. 3. Good ale for the nones, Whiche will slide downe the LANE without any bones.

1818. COLMAN, *Poetical Vagaries*, 75. O butter'd egg, best eaten with a spoon, I bid your yelk glide down my throat's RED LANE.

1865. *London Soc.*, Jan., p. 13. I eat the macaroon. You see it's all gone down RED LION LANE.

2. (nautical).—The course laid out for ocean steamers between England and America. [There are two *lanes*, or *lane-routes* both narrowly defined: the northern for westward bound, and the southern for easterning bottoms].

THE LANE, *subs. phr.* (various). —1. (theatrical) Drury Lane Theatre; 2. (colonial brokers') Mincing Lane; 3. (corn factors') Mark Lane; 4. (legal) Chancery Lane; 5. (thieves') Petticoat Lane, and 6. (*ibid.*) the old Horsemonger Lane Jail, now demolished. *Cf.* CADE, HOUSE, GARDEN etc.

1856. H. MAYHEW, *Gt. World of London*, p. 82 *note*. Horsemonger Lane jail—THE LANE.

1880. G. R. SIMS, *Ballads of Babylon* (*Forgotten*). Whenever THE LANE tried Shakespeare, I was one of the leading men.

1893. EMERSON, *Signor Lippo*, iii. I started off for THE LANE, the professionals' emporium.

HARRIETT LANE, *subs. phr.* (military).—Tinned or preserved meat.

LANGOLEE, *subs.* (venery).—The *penis.* For synonyms *see* CREAM-STICK and PRICK.

LANGRET, *subs.* (old).—In pl. dice loaded so as to show 4 or 3 more often than any other number. [The opposite is BARDQUATER-TRAY.]

1591. GREENE, *Notable Discovery* [GROSART (1881-6), x. 12]. The cheter, with a LANGRET, cut contrary to the vantage. *Ibid.* 37. Cheats . . . flats, forgers, LANGRETS, gourds.

1594. NASHE, *Unfort. Traveller* [GROSART (1884), v. 27]. LANGRETS, fullams, and all the whole fellowship of them will not afoorde a man his dinner.

1600. ROWLANDS, *Letting of Humours Blood*, p. 59. His LANGRETS with his Hie men and his low.

1612. *Art of Juggling*, C, 4. 'A LANGRET. . . . is a well-favoured die and seemeth good and square, yet it is forged longer upon the cater and trea than any other way, and therefore it is called a LANGRET.'

LANK, *adj.* (old: now recognised).—*See* quot.

1590. SPENSER, *Faery Queen*, III, vi. 18. Her LANCK loynes ungirt.

1690. B. E., *Dict. Cant. Crew*, s.v. LANK, Gaunt, Thin, Hollow, Lean, Meager, Slender, Weak. Lank Ears of Corn, very thin Ears.

1725. *New Cant. Dict.*, s.v.

AFTER A LANK COMES A BANK, *phr.* (old).—Said of breeding women.

1767. RAY, *Proverbs* [BOHN (1893), 109]. s.v.

LANK SLEEVE, *subs. phr.* (old).— *See* quot.

1811. *Lex. Bal.*, s.v. LANK SLEEVE. The empty sleeve of a one armed man. A fellow with a LANK SLEEVE; a man who has lost an arm.

LANSPRESADO (or **LANSPRISADO**), *subs.* (old).—*See* LANCEPRESADO.

LANT, *verb.* (old).—To make water; to STALE (*q.v.*). Also, *subs.* = urine.—COTGRAVE.

LANTERN, *verb.* (American).—To hang from a lamp-post. Fr. *à la lanterne.* See LANTHORN.

LANTERN-JAWS, *subs.* (old: now recognised).—*See* quots.

1690. B. E., *Dict. Cant. Crew*, s.v. LANTERN-JAW'D, a very lean, thin-faced fellow.

1725. *New Cant. Dict.*, s.v.

1753. FOOTE, *Englishman in Paris*, i. I lent him a lick in his LANTHORN-JAWS.

1765. FOOTE, *Commissary*, i. This here LANTHORN-JAW'D rascal won't give me an answer.

1785. GROSE, *Vulg. Tongue*, s.v. LANTHORN JAWED, thin visaged, from their cheeks being almost transparent, or else lenten jawed, *i.e.* having the jaws of one emaciated by a too rigid observance of lent.

1811. *Lex. Bal.*, s.v.

1859. MATSELL, *Vocabulum*, s.v.

LANTHORN. DARK LANTHORN, *subs. phr.* (old).—*See* quots.

1690. B. E., *Dict. Cant. Crew*, s.v. A DARK LANTHORN, the Servant or Agent that Receives the Bribe (at Court).

1725. *New Cant. Dict.*, s.v.

1785. GROSE, *Vulg. Tongue*, s.v. DARK LANTHORN, a servant, or agent at Court, who receives a bribe for his principal or master.

1811. *Lex. Bal.*, s.v.

LAP, *subs.* (old).—1. Any sort of potable; (among ballet-girls) gin. Also LAPPER. *See* quots.

1573. HARMAN, *Caveat* (1814), p. 65. LAP, butter mylke or whey.

1609. DEKKER, *Lanthorne and Candle-light*, in *Wks.* (GROSART), III.200. LAP, Butter Milke, or Whaye. *Ibid.* 'Gypsy Song.' The Ruffin cly the nab of the Harman beck. If we mawnd Pannam, LAP or Ruff-peck.

1630. TAYLOR, *Works* [NARES]. They will make a mans belly like a sowse-tub, and inforce mee to drinke, as if they had a commission under the divels great seale, to murder men with drinking, with such a deale of complemental oratory, as, off with your LAP.

1656. BROME, *Jovial Crew* [DODSLEY (1874), *Old Plays*, x. 367]. Here's pannam, and LAP, and good poplars of yarrum.

1665. R. HEAD, *English Rogue*, Pt. I. ch. v. p. 50 (1874). LAP, Pottage.

1690. B. E., *Dict. Cant. Crew*, Pottage, Butter-milk, or Whey. 'Tis rum LAP, this is excellent Soupe.

1724. COLES, *Eng. Dict.*, s.v.

1725. *New Cant. Dict.*, s.v. LAP .... also strong Drink of any kind.

1785. GROSE, *Vulg. Tongue*, s.v. LAP, butter milk or whey.

1789. PARKER, *Life's Painter*, p. 119. To have a dish of LAP Prepar'd for those who like it. *Ibid.* p. 165. Dish of LAP, a dish of tea.

1811. *Lex. Bal.*, s.v.

1815. SCOTT, *Guy Mannering*, xxviii. I would have given baith LAP and pannel to ony puir gipsy.

1886. W. H. SMITH, *The Individual*, Nov. 15. She never lushes dog's soup or LAP.

1859. MATSELL, *Vocabulum*, s.v. LAP, Drink; butter milk.

2. (athletes').—One round of a course.

1861. *Chambers' Journal*, XVI. 333. They had gone fourteen LAPS (as these circuits are called).

1884. *Daily Telegraph*, 27 Nov. Added seven miles and eight LAPS to their score.

1885. *Daily News*, 1 Sept. 2. 5. At half-distance the positions remained unaltered, and, as they began the last LAP, it appeared to be any one's race.

Verb. (common).—1. To drink. Also, TO GO ON THE LAP.

1819. MOORE, *Tom Crib*, p. 21. Up he rose in a fuuk, LAPP'D a toothful of brandy.

1869. W. BRADWOOD, *The O. V. H.* xix. As the latter LAPPED his third go of cold gin at the bar of the Greyhound.

1886. *Punch*, 25 Sept. p. 145. Grinds 'ard, never GOES ON THE LAP, Reads Shakspeare instead o' the *Pink' Un.*

1892. MILLIKEN, *'Arry Ballads*, 62. I LAP lemon-squash.

2. (athletes').—In running a race in laps, to overtake: as, to be one or more laps ahead.

3. (American thieves').—To pick up; to take; to steal.—MATSELL (1859).

4. (American).—To seat a girl on one's knees.

5. (American).—To throw candy, papers, etc. into the laps of passengers.

TO LAP THE GUTTER. *See* GUTTER.

TO LAP UP, *verb. phr.* (American thieves').—To wipe out; to put out of sight.

CAT-LAP. *See* Ante.

LAP-CLAP, *subs.* (old).—1. An act of coition. *Cf.* BELLY-BUMPING. Also (2) the condition of pregnancy. TO GET A LAP-CLAP = to be got with child.

1606. *Wily Beguiled* [DODSLEY, *Old Plays* (1874), ix. 252]. A maid cannot love, or catch a lip-clap or a LAP-CLAP.

1707. *Poor Robin* [quoted by NARES]. Some maids will get a lip-clip, but let

them beware of a LAP-CLAP; for fear of maids they become mothers, and sing the doleful lullaby.

LAP-EAR, *subs.* (American University).—1. A student of a religious turn of mind.

2. (American).—A donkey.

LAP-FUL, *subs.* (venery).—1. A lover or husband; and (2) an unborn child.

LAPLAND, *subs.* (common).—1. The society of women.

2. (venery).—The female *pudendum.* For synonyms *see* MONO-SYLLABLE.

LAPPER, *subs.* (thieves').—1. Drink; LAP (*q.v.*). Hence, RARE-LAP-PER = a hard drinker.

LAP-FEEDER, *subs.* (common).—A silver table-spoon.

LAPPEL. TO SHIP THE WHITE LAPPEL, *verb. phr.* (nautical).—To be raised from the ranks.

LAP-PRIEST, *subs.* (old).—A clerical APPLE-SQUIRE (*q.v.*); a SERVANT (*q.v.*).

1690. CROWNE, *English Friar*, ii 1. I know him, he's a LAP-PRIEST indeed ! .... and, being of a tender constitution, ... he lies between their sheets.

LAP-TEA, *subs.* (American).—An informal afternoon meal.

LARDY, *adj.* (common).—Grand; rich; SWELL (*q.v.*). LARDY-DARDY = affected; effeminate: LARDY-DAH (or LA-DI-DA) = a swell or fop. TO DO OR COME THE LARDY-DAH = to dress for the public.

1861. MISS BRADDON, *Trail of the Serpent*, Bk. IV. ch. vi. 'You're not much good, my friend, says I, with your LARDY-DARDY ways and your cold-blooded words, whoever you are.'

1870. *London Figaro*, 8 June. The fast young men among the natives—called in their favourite slang LARDY-DARDY coves—affect a pronunciation in which the 'v's' are substituted for the 'w's,' and *vice versa*.

1871. ATKINS, *House Scraps*, p. 166. The young 'un goes to music-halls. And does the LA-DI-DA.

c.1876. *Broadside Ballad*, 'Tiddy Fol Lol.' He's no LARDY DARDY swell, Though he looks and dresses well, For he lives at an hotel, Tiddy fol lol, tiddy fol lol.

1879. MRS. B. H. BUXTON, *Nell*, XXV. p. 280 (1884). 'Not one of your haw-haw, LARDY-DARDY, eye-glass simpletons.'

1890. *Punch*, 22 Feb. The skim-milk of life's for the many, the LARDY few lap up the cream.

1892. MILLIKEN, *'Arry Ballads*, 25. See LARDY toffs.

LAREOVER, *subs.* (old). – *See* quots.

1690. B. E., *Dict. Cant. Crew*, s.v. LARE-OVER, said when the true name of the thing must (in decency) be concealed.

1725. *New Cant. Dict.*, s.v.

1785. GROSE, *Vulg. Tongue*, s.v. LAREOVERS FOR MEDLERS, an answer frequently given to children, or young people, as a rebuke for their impertinent curiosity, in enquiring what is contained in a box, bundle, or any other closed conveyance.

LARGE, *adj.* and *adv.* (colloquial).—A vulgarism expressive of excess. Thus, TO DRESS LARGE = (1) to dress showily, and (2) to flash one's PACKET (*q.v.*); TO GO LARGE = to go noisily; TO PLAY LARGE = to play high; TO TALK LARGE = to brag, etc.

1852. JUDSON, *Mysteries of New York*, ii. ch. 4, p. 29. The eyes of the gamblers sparkled all the brighter, when they noted the hundred marks upon the bills and saw that he intended to 'play LARGE.'

1891. *Globe*, 17 Sept., col. 2, p. 2. This is indeed ALL VERY FINE AND LARGE, but can it be that instead of 'which' we ought to read 'who'?

1892. KIPLING, *Barrack-Room Ballads*. Tommy. An' hustlin' drunken soldiers when they're GOIN' LARGE a bit Is five times better business than paradin' in full kit.

LARGE BLUE KIND, *phr.*(American).—A general intensitive; *e.g.* a monstrous lie; a bad headache; an interesting book and so forth.

LARGE HOUSE, *subs.* (common).—A workhouse.

ENGLISH SYNONYMS. Bighouse; grubbing-ken; lump; Lump-Hotel; pan; spinniken; wool-hole.

LARGE ORDER, *subs.* (common).—A difficult undertaking; something exaggerated; extensive, or big.

1890. *Pall Mall Gazette*, 17 Feb., p. 7, col. 1. A LARGE ORDER [Title].

1891. *Tit Bits*, 8 Aug., 274, 1. In asking me to tell you about my clients and their wills, you give a pretty LARGE ORDER.

1892. *Illustrated Bits*, Oct. 22, 10, 1. Well, sir, that's a LARGISH ORDER.

LARK, *subs.* (colloquial).—1. *See* quot. 1811. [A corruption of M. E. *lak*, *laik*, from A. S. *lác* = game, sport; cogn. with Icl. *leikr* = game; Sw. *lek*; Dan. *leg*; Goth. *laiks*]. *Cf.* LARKING, *subs.*, sense 1.

1811. *Lex. Bal.*, s.v. LARK. A piece of merriment. People playing together jocosely.

1819. MOORE, *Tom Crib*, 37. Is any spark Among you ready for a LARK?

1823. MONCRIEFF, *Tom & Jerry*, p. 46.

1829. BUCKSTONE, *Billy Taylor*, We've had a LARK ourselves.

1836. DICKENS, *Pickwick*, p. 5. 'Here's a LARK!' shouted half a dozen hackney coachmen.

1838. THOMAS HAYNES BAYLY. *The Spitalfields Weaver*. Don't offer me money, I warn you of that; no, no, when we're out on a LARK, if you wish to treat me, well and good, but no money given.

1856. WHYTE MELVILLE, *Kate Coventry*, i. I like Cousin John's constant good-humour, and the pains he takes to give me a day's amusement whenever he can, or what he calls 'have Cousin Kate out for a LARK.'

1870. *Saturday Review*, 21 May. But it is time that all vulgar habits of outrage and LARK should be put a stop to, and, however inclined grown up men may be to look indulgently on mere boyish follies, we must have these offenders treated as a gang of 'snobs' would be who should smash busts in the Crystal Palace.

1877. *'Scribner's Monthly*, Aug., p. 469. He dusted 'em reg'lar, an' wound 'em up an' set 'em goin' accordin' to rules; but he never tried no LARKS on 'em.

1882. *Punch*, vol. LXXXII, p. 69, col. 1. A fine young London gentleman, quite up to any LARK.

1884. HENLEY and STEVENSON, *Deacon Brodie* ['Three Plays', p. 61]. Fen LARKS. No rotten shirking, mind.

1888. J. RUNCIMAN, *The Chequers*, 121. I was only having a LARK.

1893. *Chambers's Journal*, 25 Feb., p. 128. Somebody's been having a LARK with you, old lady.

2. (old).—A boat.—*Lex. Bal.* (1811); GROSE (1823); MATSELL (1859).

Verb. (common).—1. To sport; to tease; to SPREE (*q.v.*).

1836. BARHAM, *Ingoldsby Legends*, ii. 200. Don't LARK with the watch, or annoy the police.

1847. THACKERAY, *Vanity Fair*, II. xxxi. Payne was a staid English maid and personal attendant upon Mrs. Osborne, to whom the courier, as in duty bound, paid court, and whom Georgy used to LARK dreadfully with accounts of German robbers and ghosts.

2. (old).—*See* LARKING, sense 1.

3. (old).—*See* LARKING, sense 2.

4. (American thieves').—A boy who steals newspapers from door-steps.

LARKER, *subs.* (old).—One given to LARKING; *see* subs., sense 2.

1856. WHYTE MELVILLE, *Kate Coventry*, xii. 'Who's that girl on the chestnut?' I again heard asked by a slang-looking man, with red whiskers meeting under his chin; 'looks like a LARKER—I must get introduced to her.'

LARKING, *subs.* (venery).—1. Irrumation.

1785. GROSE, *Vulg. Tongue*, s.v. LARKING a lascivious practice that will not bear explanation.

2. (sporting).—1. To clear a jump; to go over like a bird. Also (2) *see* quot. 1825.

1815. BYRON, *Letters* (to MOORE, July 7). If so, you and I (*without* our wives) will take a LARK to Edinburgh.

1825 *Nimrod's Hunting Tour*, p. 227. 'Exclusive of work for horses when hounds are running, there is another way of making use of horse-flesh in Leicestershire; and that is, in coming home from hunting, or what in the language of the day is called LARKING. One of the party holds up his hat, which is a signal for the start; and, putting their horses' heads in a direction for Melton, away they go, and stop at nothing till they get there.'

1834. AINSWORTH, *Rookwood*, p. 294. Dick Turpin, meanwhile, held bravely on his course. Bess was neither strained by her gliding passage down the slippery hill-side, nor shaken by LARKING the fence in the meadow.

3. (common).—Frolicking: also horse-play and rowdyism.

1851-61. MAYHEW, *Lond. Lab. etc.*, ii. 325. There never had been more street LARKING, or street gambling.

1888. *Indoor Paupers*, p. 13. There was no hurry over the job—very much the contrary—but plenty of chatter and LARKING when the taskmaster was out of sight.

Adj. (common).—*See* LARKISH.

LARKISH (LARKY or LARKING), *subs.* (common).—Frolicsome: also rowdy.

1855. THACKERAY, *The Rose and the Ring*, p. 19. . . . He was neither more nor less than a knocker! . . . . and some LARKING young men tried to wrench him off, and put him to the most excruciating agony with a turn-screw.

1863. H. KINGSLEY, *Austin Elliot*, iv. Austin, expressing himself in that low, slangy way which the young men of the present day seem so conscious to adopt, said that my Lords were 'uncommonly LARKY.'

1886. MACDONALD, *What's Mine's Thine*. The girls felt LARKY. . . . they tripped gayly along.

1891. *Licensed Victuallers Gazette*, 3 April. A LARKY youngster who loved his wine and women.

1892. HUME NISBET, *Bushranger's Sweetheart*, 247. The landlady was a free-and-easy, buxom, and LARKY woman, who made us all feel at home in the place.

LARKY SUBALTERN'S TRAIN. *See* COLD MEAT TRAIN.

LARRENCE. *See* LAZY LAURENCE.

LARREY, *adj.* (American thieves').—Artful.—MATSELL (1859).

LARRIKIN, *subs.* (Australian).—A rough; *cf.* ARAB, CABBAGE-TREE MOB, HOODLUM, etc. [For probable derivation *see* quot. 1884; and for further details, *Notes and Queries*, 7, S. VII. 344].

1872. *The Age* (Melbourne), 15 July. The accused was at the head of a gang of LARRIKINS, who on the previous night paid a visit to Hill's Hotel, Clarendon-street.

1884. SALA, 'Echoes of the Week' in *Illus. London News*, 4 April. 'It was in a Sydney newspaper that I read about LARRIKINS, but the term would appear to have spread throughout Australia. 'H. de S.' tells me that LARRIKIN was originally Melbourne slang, applied to rowdy youngsters, who, in the early days of the gold fever, gave much trouble to the police. 'An Australian Born' spells the word LARAKIN. . . . Finally, Archibald Forbes tells me: 'A LARRIKIN is a cross between the street Arab and the hoodlum, with a dash of the rough thrown in to improve the mixture. It was thus the term had its origin. A Sydney policeman of the Irish persuasion brought up a rowdy youngster before the local beak. Asked to describe the conduct of the misdemeanant, he said, 'Av if it plase yer honnor, the blaggard wor a LARRAKIN' (larking) all over the place.' The expression was taken hold of and applied.'

1888. *Bulletin*, 24 Nov. Sergeant Jem Dalton, whose rich brogue originated the term LARRIKIN passed out of Melbourne history last week. Dalton was a born policeman, and after his friends had persuaded him to send in his resignation he turned gently over on his sick bed and died forthwith. He had nothing else to live for.

1892. *Pall Mall Gaz.*, 29 Feb., p. 2, col. 2. That is to say, the disturbance was caused not by the meeting but by the police and LARRIKINS.

1892. HUME NISBET, *Bushranger's Sweetheart*, 30. He was a LARIKIN of the LARIKINS, this tiny Stringy Bark, who haunted my thoughts, waking and sleeping.

Adj. (Australian).—Rowdy.

1883. *Saturday Review*, 10 Nov., p. 614. 'In Melbourne the LARRIKIN element is becoming a danger and a nuisance to decent people.'

LARRIKINISM, *subs.* (Australian).—*See* quot.

1884. SALA, *Echoes of the Week*, in *Illus. Lond. News*, 4 April. 'From the Australian Club, Cambridge, yet another correspondent writes: 'LARRIKINISM is a purposeless, destructive rowdyism, which finds expression, from my own experience, in knocking off the heads of statues in a mason's yard, and knocking out the eyes of Chinamen with a shanghai (*anglicè*, catapult).'

LARRUP, *subs.* (colloquial).—To flog. Fr. *coller du rototo.*

1824. PEAKE, *Americans Abroad*, i. 1. I'll LARRUP you till you can't stand, if you hang chattering and stickling behind after this fashion.

1841. *Punch*, 17 July, p. 5. 'Toby,' says she, 'go and see the old gentleman; perhaps it might comfort him to LARRUP you a little.'

1847. LYTTON, *Lucretia*, II. xx. 'I wanted sum un to take care of the childern, so I takes Peg into the 'ouse. But Lor! how she LARRUPPED 'em—she has a cruel heart.'

1854. DICKENS, *Hard Times*, v. 'There was no rope-dancing for me! I danced on the bare ground, and was LARRUPED with the rope.' *Ibid.* He tries to coax her into the stall to LARRUP her.

1867. SMYTHE, *Sailor's Word Book*, s.v. LARRUP, An old word, meaning to beat a rope's end, strap, or colt.

LARRUPING, *subs.* (colloquial).—A thrashing. Fr. *la schlague.*

1844. PEAKE, *Court and City*, i. 3. I've a great mind to give you a good LARRUPPING in the open park!

1860. *Punch* xxxix. p. 181. Ain't a cove just a LARRUPIN' his wife up the court.

1888. ROLF BOLDREWOOD, *Robbery Under Arms*, xxi. 'Your father 'll give you a fine LARRUPIN' if he comes home and there's that cow lost.'

LARRY DUGAN'S EYE-WATER, *subs. phr.* (old).—*See* quot.

1785. GROSE, *Vulg. Tongue*, s.v. LARRY DUGAN'S EYE-WATER, blacking. Larry Dugan was a famous shoe-black at Dublin.

1811. *Lex. Bal.*, s.v.

LASH, *verb.* (Blue Coat School).—To envy. Usually used in the imperative as a taunt.—BLANCH (1877).

LASHINGS (or LASHINS), *subs.* (common).—Plenty; abundance. Also LASHIN'S AND LAVIN'S—plenty and to spare.

1841. LEVER, *Charles O'Malley*, lxvii. I'd as soon be myself as Lord Mayor, With LASHINGS of drink on the table.

1850. F. E. SMEDLEY, *Frank Fairlegh*, ch. xxii. 'A taste for, that is, an unbounded admiration of, the sublime and beautiful, as exemplified under the form of—' 'Rum punch, and LASHINGS of it,' chimed in Archer.

1855. THACKERAY, *Lyra Hibernica*, 'Mr. Malony's Account of the Ball.' A rare buffet before them set Where LASHINS of good dhrink there was.

1892. MILLIKEN, *'Arry Ballads*, 18. Men patter in pubs about Jack, over LASHING o' lugs.

LASK, *subs.* (old).—*See* quot.

1621. BURTON, *Anatomy* (ed. 1893), i. 304. A grave and learned Minister, and an ordinary Preacher . . . was (one day as he walked in the fields for his recreation) suddenly taken with a LASK or looseness, and thereupon compelled to retire to the next ditch.

LASS IN A RED PETTICOAT, *subs. phr.* (old).—*See* quot.

1767. RAY, *Proverbs* (ed. 1893), 59. The LASS IN THE RED PETTICOAT shall pay for all . . . meaning a wife with a good portion.

LAST COMPLIMENT, *subs. phr.* (common).—1. Burial.

1780. LEE, *Chapter of Accidents*, i. 2. *Lord G.* Why, then, does not Hardy bring her up to you? *Gov. H.* Why, for two very sufficient reasons. In the first place, that identical parson PAID HIM THE LAST COMPLIMENT—that is, buried him a twelvemonth ago.

2. (venery).—The sexual embrace. Also LAST FAVOUR.

1694. CROWNE, *Married Beau*, ii. I own common favours; that's no matter, But if she ever grants me the LAST FAVOUR,—I give her leave to cast me off for ever.

LAST-FEATHER, *subs.* (old.)—The latest fashion.

1607. *The Puritan*, ii. 1. A fine gallant Knight of the LEAST FEATHER.

LATCH, *verb.* (old).—To let in.—*New Cant. Dict.* (1725); GROSE (1785) and *Lex. Bal.* (1811).

LATCH-DRAWER, *subs.* (old).—A thief who stole into houses by drawing the latch.

1362. LANGLAND, *Piers Plowman*, p. 143. Thank lyers and LATCHE-DRAWERS and tolleres knocke, Let hem abyde tyl the bord be drawe.

LATCH-PAN, *subs.* (common).—The under-lip: TO HANG ONE'S LATCH-PAN = to pout; to be sulky.

LATE-PLAY, *subs.* (Westminster School).—A half-holiday or holiday beginning at noon.

LATH-AND-PLASTER, *subs.* (rhyming).—A master.

LATHER, *subs.* (venery).—The sexual secretion, male and female. *Cf.* LETCH-WATER. Hence, LATHER-MAKER = the female *pudendum*. For synonyms *see* CREAM.

Verb. (common).—To beat; to thrash. Also LEATHER (*q.v.*).

1849. *Punch's Almanack*. To dream of soap betokens a combat in which you may expect to get LATHERED.

LATHY, *adj.* (colloquial).—Thin.

1748. WEST, *Abuse of Travelling*, The which he tossed to and fro amain, And eft his LATHY falchion brandished.

1785. GROSE, *Vulg. Tongue*, s.v. LATHY. . . . a LATHY wench, a girl almost as slender as a lath.

1811. *Lex. Bal.*, s.v.

1858. B. TAYLOR, *Northern Travel*, 204. A LATHY young man. . . . was struggling. . . . to right himself.

1859. MATSELL, *Vocabulum*, s.v.

LATITAT, *subs.* (old).—An attorney.—GROSE (1785); *Lex. Bal.* (1811); MATSELL (1859). [From an obsolete form of writ].

1771. FOOTE, *Maid of Bath*, i. I will send for Luke LATITAT and Codicil, and make a handsome bequest to the hospital.

LATTER-END, *subs.* (common).—The breech. For synonyms *see* MONOCULAR EYEGLASS.

LATTICE. *See* RED LATTICE.

LATTY. *See* LETTY.

LAUGH. TO LAUGH ON THE WRONG (or OTHER) SIDE OF ONE'S MOUTH (or FACE), *subs. phr.* (colloquial).—To cry.

1811. *Lex. Bal.*, s.v. LAUGH.

1823. GROSE, *Vulg. Tongue*, s.v. LAUGH.

1826. BUCKSTONE, *Death Fetch*, i. 4. *Snapsch. (Aside.)* And have a pretty family of them about my ears the first time I'm left alone in the dark, who would soon make me LAUGH ON THE OTHER SIDE OF MY MOUTH, I fancy.

1837. CARLYLE, *Diamond Necklace*, iii. By and bye thou wilt LAUGH ON THE WRONG SIDE OF THY FACE.

LAUNCH, *subs.* (old).—A lying-in; BUST-UP; EXPLOSION.—GROSE (1823).

Verb. (old: public school).—*See* quot.

1865. G. J. BERKELEY, *My Life*, etc., i. 129. I had [at Sandhurst about 1815] to undergo the usual torments of being LAUNCHED, that is having my bed reversed while I was asleep; of being thrown on the floor on my face, with the mattress on my back and all my friends or foes dancing on my prostrate body.

LAUNDRESS, *subs.* (old).—1. A bed maker in chambers; and hence (2) a SMOCK SERVANT (*q.v.*).

1611. BARRY, *Ram Alley* [DODSLEY, *Old Plays* (1874), x. 275]. She is my LAUNDRESS, And by this light, no puisne Inn-a-Court But keeps a LAUNDRESS at his command To do him service.

1614. BRETON, *I would &c.* [GROSART (1879), i. *s.* 9. st. 61]. Some odde ladde or LANDRESSE find me out.

1621. BURTON, *Anatomy*, ed. 1893, i. Thou shalt have (Tamerlane-like) Kings to draw thy coach, Queens to be thy LAUNDRESSES, Emperors thy footstools.

1636. DAVENANT, *Platonic Lovers*, iii. 1. He . . . . Commits Idolatry to Euery LAUNDRESS in the house.

1639. MAYNE, *City Match*, ii. 3. From country madams to your glover's wife, Or LAUNDRESS.

LAURENCE. *See* LUSTY LAURENCE.

LAVENDER. TO LAY (or PUT) IN LAVENDER, *verb. phr.* (common).—1. To lay up or put aside carefully; as linen among lavender. Hence (1) to pawn; (2) to leave in lodging for debt; (3) to hide from the police; and (4) on the turf, to be ill or out of the way.

1592. GREENE, *Quip*, in Harl. Misc., v. 405. But the poore gentleman paies so deere for the LAVENDER IT IS LAID UP IN, that if it lie long at a broker's house, he seems to buy his apparell twice.

1593. FLORIO, *Worlde of Wordes*. To lay to pawne, as we say, TO LAY IN LAVENDER.

*b.*1593. *Six Old Plays (on which Shakspeare founded his Measure for Measure etc.* 1779. i.*)*, 186. *Sander*. The ostler will not let me have him, you owe tenpence for his meate, and sixpence for stuffing my mistriss saddle. *Fer*. Here, villaine, goe pay him strait. *Sander*. Shall I give them another pecke of LAVENDER? *Fer*. Out, slave, and bring them presently to the dore.

1599. JONSON, *Every Man out of His Humour*, iii. 3. And a black sattin suit of his own to go before her in; which suit (for the more sweet'ning) now LIES IN LAVENDER.

1605. CHAPMAN, JONSON etc., *Eastward Hoe* (DODSLEY, *Old Plays*, IV. 279), v. 1. Good faith, rather than thou shouldst pawn a rag more, I'll LAY my ladyship IN LAVENDER, if I knew where.

1628. EARLE, *Micr.*, Char. 2d. He takes on against the pope without mercy, and has a jest still IN LAVENDER for Bellarmine.

1655. COTGRAVE, *Eng. Treas.*, p. 34 [NARES]. A broaker is a city pestilence, A moth that eats up gowns, doublets, and hose, One that with bills loads smocks and shirts together, To Hymen close adultery and upon them Strews LAVENDER so strongly that the owners Dare never smell them after.

*d.*1673. BRATHWAITE, *Strappado for the Devil*, p. 154. 'Upon a Poet's Palfrey LYING IN LAVENDER, for the discharge of his Provender' [Title of Epigram].

1684. R. HEAD, *Proteus Redivivus*, 255. These men, who have LAID UP their estates in LAVENDER, that they may the more freely follow their Recreations.

1686. *Twelve Ingenious Characters* [NARES]. Hither all sorts of garments resort in pilgrimage, whilst he playing the pimp, lodges the tabby petticoat and russet breeches together in the same bed of LAVENDER.

1690. B. E., *Dict. Cant. Crew*, s.v. LAYD UP IN LAVENDER, when any Cloaths or other Moveables are pawn'd or dipt for present Money; also Rods in Pickle, of Revenge in reserve, till an opportunity offers to show it.

1725. *New Cant. Dict.*, s.v.

1772. COLES, *Eng.-Lat. Dict.*, s.v. . . . . To LAY IN LAVENDER, *pignori opponere*.

1785. GROSE, *Vulg. Tongue*, s.v. LAVENDER.

1811. *Lex. Bal.*, s.v.

1822. SCOTT, *Fortunes of Nigel*, xxii. 'The Marshalsea! . . . What of the Marshalsea?' 'Why, sir,' said the man, 'the poor gentleman is LAID UP there IN LAVENDER.'

1830. W. T. MONCRIEFF, *The Heart of London*, ii. 1. You have had a decent swing of it the last twelvemonth, while your pals have been LAID UP IN LAVENDER.

LAVENDER-COVE, *subs.* (common).—A pawnbroker; UNCLE (*q.v.*).—MATSELL (1859).

VOL. IV. 11

LAW, *subs.* (old sporting: now recognised).—A time allowance: hence a preliminary notice; a chance of escape.

1785. GROSE, *Vulg. Tongue*, s.v.

1811. *Lex. Bal.*, s.v.

1847. SHIRLEY BROOKS, *The Wigwam*, i. *Min.* Ow—ow—don't—don't! Give us ten yards' LAW—ow—[*He runs off*].

1855. *Philol. Trans*, p. 279. In making a running match one boy is said to GIVE as many yards' LAW as he allows his competitor to be in advance.

1859. MATSELL, *Vocabulum*, s.v. LAW. GIVE the cove LAW, give the fellow a chance to escape.

1883. HAWLEY SMART, *Hard Times*, xxii. 'Calvert's very late; but I suppose we must GIVE him a few minutes' more LAW!'

TO STAB THE LAW, *verb. phr.* (American).—To rail against authority.

1888. *Nevada City Journal*, Feb. These speakers were as violent as ever, and gave no evidence of having relinquished their favorite plan of STABBING THE LAW.

LAWFUL BLANKET (or **JAM**), *subs. phr.* (common).—A wife. For synonyms *see* DUTCH.—*Lex. Bal.* (1811); GROSE (1823).

1887. HENLEY, *Villon's Good-Night*. Gay grass-widows and LAWFUL JAM.

LAWFUL PICTURES, *subs. phr.* (old).—Money. *See* KING'S PICTURES.

1607. *The Puritan*, iii. 4. At this instant I have no LAWFUL PICTURE about me.

LAWK! (or **LAWKS!**) *intj.* (colloquial).—An exclamation of surprise.

1836. DICKENS, *Pickwick*, xxxix. LAWK, Mr. Weller. . . . how you do frighten me.

*d.*1845. HOOD, *Lost Heir* [*Century*]. LAWK, help me, I don't know where to look.

1860. G. ELIOT, *Mill on the Floss*, Bk. I. ch. vii. 'LAWKS! what have you been a-doing? I niver see such a fright.'

1886. BARING-GOULD, *Golden Feather*, p. 27 (S.P.C.K.). 'Going to remain here?' he asked. 'LAWK, no! only come over with the 'oss,' replied Joe Marriage.

1886. *Pioneer* (N.Y.), Oct. 'LAWKS!' exclaimed Mrs. Partington.

LAWFUL TIME, *subs.* (Winchester College).—Recess; playtime.

LAWN, *subs.* (colloquial).—A handkerchief.—GROSE (1823).

THE LAWN, *subs.* (racing).—The lawn on the course at Ascot: *cf.* HOUSE; LANE, etc.

LAWRIE (or **LAURIE**), *subs.* (old Scots').—A fox.

1567-83. SEMPILL, *Tulchene Bishop*, line 8. Ane lewrand LAURIE lickerous.

LAWYER. HIGH (or HIGHWAY) LAWYER, *subs. phr.* (thieves').—A mounted robber or highwayman. *See* also SCRIPPER, OKE, MARTIN, and STOOPING.

1592. GREENE, *Groats worth of Wit* (ed. DYCE), Int. p. xxix. The legerdemains of. . . . HIGH LAWYERS.

1608. DEKKER, *Belman of London* [GROSART (1885), iii. 151]. The thiefe that commits the robbery, and is cheife clerke to Saint Nicholas, is called the HIGH LAWYER.

LAY, *subs.* (old).—1. A pursuit; a scheme; a device; A LURK.

Also in combination, KINCHIN-LAY, (*q.v.*); AVOIRDUPOIS-LAY (*q.v.*); KEN-CRACK-LAY = housebreaking; FANCY-LAY = pugilism.

ENGLISH SYNONYMS. Dodge; game; huff; job; knack; lay-out; line; lurk; lug; move; outfit; racket; shake; show; swim.

FRENCH SYNONYMS. *La balle* (thieves': also secret); *un truc* (popular: any kind of small trade: *le truc* = thieving; *le grand truc* = murder; *des trucs* = things. From Provençal *tric* = deceit); *le pégrage* or *pégrasse* (thieves'): *le grinchissage* (thieves': specifically theft).

SPANISH SYNONYMS. *Alicantina* (= stratagem); *amaño* (= intrigue); *andromina* (also = trick or fraud); *barrabasada* (also = plot or intrigue); *brega* (also = pun or jest); *engañifa* (also = catch-penny); *gatada* (also = scurvy trick); *pega* or *pegata* (also = imposition).

*c.*1520. *Boke of Mayd Emlyn*, in RIMBAULT, *Antient Poetical Tracts* (Percy Society, 1841), 25. 6. For he used his playce—With maydens, wyves or nonnes; None amysse to him comes, Lyke they be of LAYES.

1647. BEAUMONT & FLETCHER, *Bonduca*, i. 2. I have found you Your LAYS, and out-leaps.

1703. FARQUHAR, *Inconstant*, i. 1. We fancy he must have something extraordinary about him to please us, and that we have something engaging about us to secure him; so we can't be quiet, till we put our selves upon the LAY of being both disappointed.

1706. BURTON, *Hist. of the Reign of Queen Anne* (1880), Vol. ii. p. 159. After having reconnoitred it [Alicant], I would have given something to have been off of the LAY, having found it quite another sort of a place than what it was represented to me to be.

1713. WODROW, *Analecta* (Maitland Club), ii. 357. He an' the Treasurer have been at much pains to break steele off the LAY he is upon.

1725. *New Cant. Dict.*, s.v. LAY, an Enterprise, or Attempt; *To be sick of the Lay*, To be tir'd in waiting for an opportunity to effect their Purposes. Also an Hazard or Chance; as, *He stands a queer Lay;* He stands an odd Chance, or is in great Danger.

1779. R. CUMBERLAND, *Wheel of Fortune*, iii. 2. *Livery Serv.* No offence to you, Mr. Weazel, but we would fain know what LAY we are to be upon; and whether the strange gentleman will be agreeable to allow us for bags, canes, and nosegays.

1785. GROSE, *Vulg. Tongue*, s.v.

1811. *Lex. Bal.*, s.v.

1819. MOORE, *Tom Crib*, p. 36. We who're of the FANCY-LAY, As dead hands at a mill as they.

1836. DICKENS, *Oliver Twist*, ch. xliii. The LAY is just to take that money away.

1852. DICKENS, *Bleak House*, He's not to be found on his old LAY.

1859. MATSELL, *Vocabulum*, s.v. LAY, A particular kind of rascality, trade or profession. . . . What's the cove's LAY? Why. . . . he's on the KEN-CRACK [LAY]—housebreaking.

1862. H. KINGSLEY, *Ravenshoe*, ch. xli. One on 'em plays the bagpipes with a bellus against the waterbutt of a Sunday evening when they're off the LAY.

1865. *Daily Review*, Feb. Captain Corbett said the vessel was going on the same LAY that the Alabama had gone. I afterwards went back in the Laurel to Teneriffe.

1877. *Five Years' Penal Servitude*, iii. p. 144. His peculiar LAY or line of business, which always brought him into trouble, was the stealing of pewter pots.

1888. J. RUNCIMAN, *The Chequers*, 82. Blakey's found out as you've got respectable relations as wouldn't like to see your name in the papers, and he's goin' to 'ave a new LAY on.

1889. *Answers*, 27 July, p. 136, col. 2. The secret marks have considerable significance. They briefly tell the begging-letter writer what sort of LAY to come for. Each charitable person has his, or her, particular soft spot, and it is this which the begging-letter writer endeavours to ascertain.

1892. KIPLING, *Barrack Room Ballads*, 'The Widow's Party.' Out with the rest on a picnic LAY.

1895. H. B. MARRIOTT WATSON, in *New Review*, July, p. 2. For it was his aim to stand in security somewhere half-way 'twixt us fellows and the Law, and squeeze the both; and but that he had the lives of scores upon his tongue, and was very useful withal at a pinch, both to us on the LAY and to the traps, he would have been hanged or pistolled for his pains long since.

2. (common).—A wager

1591. GREENE, *Second Part Conny-catching*, in *Works*, vol. x. p. 83. These fellows will refuse no LAY if the ods may grow to their aduantage.

1602. SHAKSPEARE, *Othello*, ii. 8. My fortunes to any LAY worth naming.

1606. JOHN DAY, *Ile of Guls*, ii. 5, p. 57. *Lis.* Badd's the best. I winne her for ten crownes; and there they be. *Vist.* I take your LAY.

1630. MASSINGER, *Renegado*, iii. 4. It is an even LAY, but that you had A courtier to your father.

1672. LACY, *Old Troop*, v. 1. It's an even LAY whether this farce be a comedy or a tragedy.

1735. OLDYS, *Life of Sir W. Raleigh.* Looked upon it as an uneven LAY to stake himself against Sir Amias.

3. (old).—A quantity.

1821. HAGGART, *Life*, p. 49. We had a weighty LAY of them that same evening.

4. (old).—Goods.

1821. HAGGART, *Life*, p. 8. Flash-kanes where I might fence my snib'd LAYS.

5. (American).—*See* quot.

1883. GEORGE, *Progress and Poverty*, Bk. I. ch. iii. On American whaling ships the custom is not to pay fixed wages, but a LAY, or proportion of the catch, which varies from a sixteenth to a twelfth to the captain down to a three-hundredth to the cabin-boy.

Verb. (colloquial).—1. To wager. TO LAY ONE'S SHIRT = to stake one's all.

ENGLISH SYNONYMS. To lump on; to plank down; to do a flutter; to wire; to slant; to snap; to tot.

*c.*1563. *Jacke Jugeler*, p. 73 [ed. GROSART]. I durst. . . . a wager LAYE That thou laiest downe and sleppest by the waie.

1591. GREENE, *Second Part Conny-catching* [GROSART, vol. x. p. 84]. I take six to one saies the Gripe, I LAY it saies the Vincent, and so they make a bet.

1597-8. MUNDAY and CHETTLE, *Playe of Robin Hode.* 'I will LAI with the Litel John, twenti pound so read.'

1601. SHAKSPEARE, *Twelfth Night*, iii. 4. *Fab.* Come, let's see the event. *Sir To.* I dare LAY any money 'twill be nothing yet.

1751. FIELDING, *Amelia*, Bk. x. ch. v. 'If the knowing ones were here, they would LAY odds of our side.'

1754. MARTIN, *Eng. Dict.*, s.v. 2nd ed.

1844. MORRIS, *Lyra Urbanica* [*N. & Q.*, 7 S. vi. 40]. His father allows him two hundred a year And he'll LAY you a thousand to ten.

1851. F. E. SMEDLEY, *Lewis Arundel*, xxxiii. 'Your sister's been five minutes already, and I'd LAY a bet we don't see her for five more.'

1864. *Derby Day*, p. 50. Now I'll bet the Littl'un would pay delicate attention to anyone who might come unawares into the stable without any right to do so. I'll LAY you an even pony, he'd help 'em out of the door in a manner more forcible than pleasant.

1892. ANSTEY, *Voces Populi*, p. 72. I'll LAY you can't knock a rabbit down.

2. (old).—To watch; to search; to lie in wait. ON THE LAY = on the alert; at work. Also TO LAY FOR and TO LAY BY.

1603. KNOLLES, *Hist. of the Turkes* [*Enc. Dict.*]. He embarked, being hardly LAID FOR at sea.

1605. MARSTON, JONSON & CHAPMAN, *Eastward Hoe*, iv. 1. *To.* Where are they? Let's go presently and LAY FOR them. *Go.* I have done that already, sir, both by constables and other officers.

1608. MIDDLETON, *Trick to Catch the Old One*, i. 2. I have been LAYING all the town for thee.

1859. MATSELL, *Vocabulum*, s.v. LAY. . . . also on the look out; watching for something to steal.

1884. M. TWAIN, *Huck. Finn*, v. 32. 'I'll LAY for you, my smarty; and if I catch you about that school I'll tan you good.'

TO LAY ABOUT, *verb. phr.* (colloquial).—To strike on all sides; to fight vigorously.

TO LAY AT, *verb. phr.* (colloquial).—To attempt to strike; to aim a blow.

TO LAY BY THE HEELS, *verb. phr.* (colloquial). — To put in prison or the stocks: *see* HEELS.

TO LAY DOWN, *verb. phr.* (thieves').—To play cards.

TO LAY DOWN ONE'S KNIFE AND FORK, *verb. phr.* (common).—To die; TO GO ALOFT (*q.v.*); to HOP THE TWIG (*q.v.*).

1888. *All the Year Round*, 9 June, p. 543. To 'hop the twig', to 'peg out', to LAY DOWN ONE'S KNIFE AND FORK, & the like [phrases for dying], are more flippant than humorous.

TO LAY A DUCK'S EGG, *verb. phr.* (common).—*See* DUCK'S EGG and CROCKETTS.

TO LAY IN, *verb. phr.* (colloquial).—To attack with vigor.

1888. ROLF BOLDREWOOD, *Robbery Under Arms*, VII. The eggs and bacon, my word! how Jim did LAY IN.

TO LAY IN ONE'S DISH, *verb. phr.* (old).—To object a thing to a person; to make an accusation against him.

1615. SIR JOHN HARRINGTON, *Epigrams*, i. 27. Last night you LAY IT, madam, IN OUR DISH, How that a maid of ours (whom we must check) Had broke your bitches leg.

1663. BUTLER, *Hudibras*, I. iii. 209. Think'st thou 'twill not be LAID I' TH' DISH, Thou turn'dst thy back? quoth Echo, *pish.*

TO LAY INTO, *verb. phr.* (colloquial).—To thrash.

1838. D. JERROLD, *Men of Character*, xiii. I shall be very happy . . . . to go and hold the door while you LAY INTO the ruffian.

TO LAY IT ON (and superlatively, TO LAY IT ON THICK) *verb. phr.* (colloquial).—To exceed—in speech, splendour, expense, charges, praise, etc.; TO EMBROIDER (*q.v.*).

1560. *Nice Wanton* [DODSLEY, *Old Plays* (1874), ii. 167]. When they come home, Your mistress-ship would have me LAY ON.

1609-10. SHAKSPEARE, *Tempest*, iii. 2. I would I could see this taborer: he LAYS IT ON.

1611. SHAKSPEARE, *Winter's Tale*, iv. 3. I cannot do 't without counters. Let me see; what am I to do for our sheep-shearing feast? *Three pounds of sugar; five pounds of currants;—rice*—What will this sister of mine do with rice? But my father hath made her mistress of the feast, and she LAYS IT ON.

1821. COMBE, *Syntax; Wife*, c. 1. That in the pulpit you're a rare one, And LAY IT ON, and never spare one.

1832-53. *Whistle-Binkie* (Sc. Songs), Ser. II. 68. He could LAY ON the cadge better than ony walleteer.

1891. *Tit Bits*, 15 Aug., p. 296, col. 1. Mr. Draper is compelled to LAY IT ON THICK.

TO LAY OFF, *verb. phr.* (colloquial).—To give over.

1888. *Detroit Free Press*, 20 Oct. Then the Governor of Michigan had to embarrass me by proclaiming a state holiday of some brand or other, and my hired man said he guessed he'd have to LAY OFF that day.

TO LAY ONESELF FORTH (or OUT), *verb. phr.* (colloquial).—To exert oneself rigorously and earnestly.

TO LAY ONESELF OPEN, *verb. phr.* (colloquial).—To expose oneself.

TO LAY ONESELF OUT FOR, *verb. phr.* (colloquial).—To be ready and willing to take part in anything.

TO LAY OUT, *verb. phr.* (colloquial).—1. To get the better of;

to disable (as with a blow); to kill; to COOK ONE'S GOOSE (*q.v.*).

2. (colloquial).—To intend; to purpose; to propose.

TO LAY OVER, *verb. phr.* (colloquial).—1. To excel.

1870. BRET HARTE, *Luck of Roaring Camp.* A street that would LAY OVER any street in Red Dog.

A GOOD LAY, *subs. phr.* (tailors').—An economical method of cutting; anything beneficial.

LAYCOCK. *See* MISS LAYCOCK.

LAYER, *subs.* (racing).— A bookmaker; a betting man.

LAY-OUT, *subs.* (American).—A company; an OUTFIT (*q.v.*); a SPREAD (*q.v.*).

1869. MCCLURE, *Rocky Mountains*, 219. A most expensive LAY-OUT.

LAYOVER. *See* LAREOVER.

LAYSTALL (LEYSTALL, or LAYSTON), *subs.* (old).—*See* quots.

1590. SPENSER, *Faerie Queene*, I. v. 53. Scarce could he groping find in that fowle way, For many corses like a great LAYSTALL lay, Of murdred men, which therein strowed lay.

1690. B. E., *Dict. Cant. Crew*, s.v. LEYSTALL, a Dunghill.

1725. *New Cant. Dict.*, s.v.

1785. GROSE, *Vulg. Tongue*, s.v. LAYSTALL a dunghill on which the soil brought from necessary houses is emptied. *Idem*, 3rd ed., s.v. LAYSTALL a dunghill about London, on which the soil brought from necessary houses is emptied; or in more technical terms where the old gold, collected at weddings by the Tom turdman is stored.

LAY-UP, *subs.* (common).—A drink; a GO (*q.v.*).

1891. NEWMAN, *Scamping Tricks*, 84. I would have given just then some one else's gold-mines for a strong LAY-UP of something neat.

LAZY. LAZY AS LUDLAM'S (or DAVID LAURENCE'S) DOG, *phr.* (old).—Excessively indolent; *see* quots. Also 'Lazy as Joe the marine who laid down his musket to sneeze.'

1670. RAY, *Proverbs*, s.v.

1678. COTTON, *Scarronides*, *Note.* 'Tis a proverb, Ludlam's dog leaned his head against a wall when he went to bark.

1811. *Lex. Bal.*, s.v. LAZY. As LAZY AS LUDLAM'S DOG who leaned against the wall to bark. As lazy as the tinker, who laid down his budget to f—t.

LAZY-BONES, *subs.* (common).—1. A loafer; also LAZY-BOOTS. Fr. *une loche.*

1593. HARVEY, *Pierces Superer.* [GROSART (1885), ii. 283]. Was legierdemane a sloweworme, or viuacitie a LASIE-BONES.

1596. NASHE, *Have With You etc.* [GROSART (1885), iii. 62]. Tell me was euer . . . Viuacitie a LAZY-BONES?

1626. BRETON, *Pasquil's Madecapp* [GROSART (1869), i. *e*, 12, 2. 31.]. Go tell the labourers, that the LAZIE BONES That will not worke, must seeke the beggars gains.

1860. GASKELL, *Sylvia's Lovers*, ch. xxxv. Like a LAZY-BOOTS as she is.

1877. *Scribner's Monthly*, p. 526. Sharp at ten o'clock, snow-shoes are strapped on again, and Indian file homeward they go, some novices and LAZY-BONES walking home *sans* shoes by the road.

LAZY-LAWRENCE (or LARRENCE).—An incarnation of laziness. *See* quot.

1655. PRIDEAUX, *Readings in History* [*N. and Q.* 7, S. xi. 212]. St. Lawrence suffered martyrdom about the middle of the third century, 250 to 260 A.C. A traditional tale has been handed down from age to age that at his execution he

bore his torments without a writhe or groan, which caused some of those standing by to remark, 'How great must be his faith!' But his pagan executioner said, 'It is not his faith, but his idleness; he is too LAZY to turn himself.'

LAZY-MAN'S LOAD, *subs.* (old).—*See* quot.

1811. *Lex. Bal.*, s.v. LAZY-MAN'S LOAD. Lazy people frequently take up more than they can safely carry, to save the trouble of coming a second time.

LAZY-TONGS, *subs.* (old).—*See* quot.

1785. GROSE, *Vulg. Tongue*, s.v. An instrument like a pair of tongs for old or very fat people, to take anything off the ground without stooping.

1811. *Lex. Bal.*, s.v.

LEAD, *subs.* (theatrical).—(1) A leading or principal part; (2) the person who plays it.

FRIENDLY LEAD, *subs.* (thieves').—An entertainment—sing-song, dance, or drinking party—got up to assist a friend IN TROUBLE (*q.v.*). Fr. *une bouline.*

1851-61. H. MAYHEW, *London Lab. & Lon. Poor*, vol. iii. p. 164. 'We went to a public-house where they were having a LEAD, that is a collection for a friend who is ill, and the company throw down what they can for a subscription, and they have in a fiddle and make it social.'

1871. *Daily Telegraph*, 4 Dec. They distribute tickets for a FRIENDLY LEAD, for the benefit of Bill, who is 'just out of his trouble.'

1889. *Cassell's Saturday Journal*, 5 Jan. The men frequently club together in a FRIENDLY LEAD to help a brother in distress.

1892. *Ally Sloper*, 2 Ap., p. 106, col. 3. My father takes the chair at FRIENDLY LEADS.

TO LEAD APES IN HELL, *verb. phr.* (old).—The employment jocularly assigned to old maids in hell.

1575. GASCOGNE, *Adv. Master F. J.* [HAZLITT (1869), *Poems*, i. 463]. I am afrayde my marryage will be marred, and I may go LEAD APES IN HELL.

1581. LYLY, *Euphues* (Arb.), 87. Rather thou shouldest leade a lyfe to thine owne lyking in earthe, than. . . LEADE APES IN HELL.

1600. SHAKSPEARE, *Much Ado etc.*, ii. 1. Therefore I will even take sixpence in earnest of the bear-herd, and LEAD HIS APES INTO HELL.

1605. *Lond. Prodigal*, i. 2. 'Tis an old proverb, and you know it well, That women dying maids LEAD APES IN HELL.

1670. RAY, *Proverbs* [BOHN (1893), 45]. Old maids LEAD APES IN HELL.

1717. MRS. CENTLIVRE, *Bold Stroke*, ii. 1. Poor girl; she must certainly LEAD APES, as the saying is.

1830. GENERAL P. THOMPSON, *Exerc.* (1842), I. 198. Joining with other old women, in LEADING THEIR APES IN TARTARUS.

1837. BARHAM, *Ingoldsby Legends*, 'Bloudie Jacke.' So they say she is now LEADING APES . . . below.

LEADING ARTICLE, *subs. phr.* (common).—1. The nose. For synonyms *see* CONK.

1886. *Chambers's Journal*, 3 July, p. 428. Men of note almost invariably possess decided and prominent LEADING ARTICLES, whilst an insufficient nasal accompaniment not unfrequently denotes inanity.

2. (venery).—The female *pudendum.* For synonyms *see* MONOSYLLABLE.

LEAF, *subs.* (American thieves').—*See* quot.

1859. MATSELL, *Vocabulum*, s.v. LEAF. . . . 'I will be out in the LEAF,' 'I will be out in the autumn.'

TO GO OFF WITH THE FALL OF THE LEAF, *verb. phr.* (Irish).—*See* quot.

1785. GROSE, *Vulg. Tongue*, s.v. LEAF, TO GO OFF WITH THE FALL OF THE LEAF, to be hanged; criminals hanged in Dublin, being turned off from the outside of the prison, by the falling of a board, propped up, and moving on a hinge like the leaf of a table.

LEAFLESS-TREE, *subs.* (Old Cant).—The gallows. For synonyms *see* NUBBING CHEAT. Fr. *la sans-feuille*.

1830. LYTTON, *Paul Clifford*. . . . Oh! there never was life like the robber's . . . . And its end—why, a cheer from the crowd below, And a leap from a LEAFLESS TREE.

LEAK, *subs.* (venery).—The female *pudendum*. For synonyms *see* MONOSYLLABLE.

1720. GAY, *Tales*, 'Work for a Cooper'. Her coats rose high, her master saw—I see—he cries—(then claspt her fast) The LEAK through which my wine has past.

Verb. (American thieves').—1. To impart a secret.—MATSELL (1859).

2. (old).—To make water.—GROSE (1823). Hence TO SPRING A LEAK = to piss.

LEAKY, *adj.* (old).—*See* quots.

d.1704. LESTRANGE [*Century*]. Women are so LEAKY that I have hardly met with one that could not hold her breath longer than she could keep a secret.

1785. GROSE, *Vulg. Tongue*, s.v. LEAKY. . . . One who cannot keep a secret is said to be LEAKY.

1859. MATSELL, *Vocabulum*, s.v.

2. (old).—Incontinent of urine.

LEAN, *adj.* (printers').—Unremunerative; the reverse of FAT (*q.v.*). Also as *subs.* = unprofitable work.

LEAN-AND-FAT, *subs.* (rhyming).—A hat. For synonyms *see* GOLGOTHA.

LEAN-AND-LURCH, *subs.* (rhyming).—A church.

LEAN-AWAY, *subs.* (Australian).—A drunkard. For synonyms *see* LUSHINGTON.

LEAP, *verb.* (venery).—To copulate. For synonyms *see* GREENS and RIDE. Hence LEAP IN THE DARK (or UP A LADDER) = the act of copulating; copulation. Also TO DO A LEAP.

1599. SHAKSPEARE, *King Henry V*, v. ii. 145. If I could win a lady . . . . by vaulting into my saddle . . . I should quickly LEAP into a wife.

1600. SHAKSPEARE, *Much Ado etc.*, v. 4. l. Bull Jove, Sir, had an amiable low, And some such strange bull LEAPED your father's cow, And got a calf.

1614. JONSON, *Bartholomew Fair*, IV. iii. (CUNNINGHAM, II. 191). How now, Whit! close vapours! stealing your LEAPS! covering in a corner. *Idem, idem, idem*. Sayst thou so, filly? Thou shalt have a LEAP presently, I'll horse thee myself else.

1623. WEBSTER, *Duchess of Malff*, ii. 5. Till I know who LEAPS my sister, I'll not stir.

1662. *Rump Songs*, i. 289. And to their children's credits and their wives, Be it still said, they LEAP fair for their lives.

1662. WILSON, *The Cheats*, v. 5. Your daughter has married a gentleman. It this not better than a Smithfield bargain—give me so much money, and my horse shall LEAP your mare.

1694. DRYDEN, *Virgil*, Georgic iii. 328. Whether the bull or courser be thy care, Let him not LEAP the cow, nor mount the mare.

Adv. (old).—All safe.—*New Cant. Dict.* (1725).

TO TAKE A LEAP AT TYBURN (or IN THE DARK), *verb. phr.* (old).—To be hanged.

*c.*1600-62. *Common Cries of London* [COLLIER, *Roxburghe Ballads* (1847),

215]. For many a proper man, . . . Doth LEAP A LEAP AT TYBURN which makes his neck to crack.

1720. DURFEY, *Pills to Purge*, vi. 327. All you that must take a LEAP IN THE DARK, Pity the fate of Lawson and Clark.

TO LEAP (or JUMP) THE BOOK (or BROOMSTICK, BROOM, BESOM, or SWORD), *verb. phr.* (common).—*See* quots.; TO DAB IT UP (*q.v.*); TO LIVE TALLY. *Cf.* RUSH-RING.

1811. POOLE, *Hamlet Travestied*, ii. 3. JUMP O'ER A BROOMSTICK, but don't make a farce on The marriage ceremonies of the parson.

1823. GROSE, *Vulg. Tongue*, 3rd ed. s.v. LEAPING OVER THE SWORD, an ancient ceremonial, said to constitute a military marriage. A sword being laid down on the ground, the parties to be married join hands when the corporal or sergeant of the company repeated these words: Leap rogue, and jump whore, And then you are married for ever more.

1851. MAYHEW, *London Labour and London Poor*, I. p. 336. The old woman when any female, old or young, who had no tin, came into the kitchen, made up a match for her with some men. Fellows half-drunk had the old women. There was always a BROOMSTICK wedding. Without that ceremony a couple weren't looked on as man and wife.

1859. MATSELL, *Vocabulum*, s.v. LEAP THE BOOK. A false marriage.

1860. DICKENS, *Great Expectations*, ch. xlviii. p. 227. 'They both led tramping lives, and this woman in Gerrard St. here, had been married very young, OVER THE BROOMSTICK (as we say), to a tramping man, and was a perfect fury in point of jealousy.'

1868. *Cassell's Mag.*, 4. Jan., p. 222. I dare say that most . . . have laughed at the old joke about getting married by jumping over a broomstick, and have always thought that it was a sheer joke, and nothing else; but this is a great mistake: the ceremony—so to dignify it—of the couple LEAPING OVER A BROOMSTICK, held by the man's mates a little way from the ground, was the essential and generally recognised rite of most navvy marriages, and was held to be binding so long as both parties were agreed—a very important qualification. There is reason to believe that this grotesque ceremony is of very ancient date.

*c.*18(79). *Broadside Ballad*, 'David Dove that Fell in Love.' The girl that I had hoped to hear Pronounce my happy doom, sir, Had bolted with a carpenter, In fact HOPPED O'ER THE BROOM, sir.

LET THE BEST DOG LEAP THE STILE FIRST, *phr.* (old).—Let the worthiest take precedence.

TO LEAP OVER THE HEDGE BEFORE YOU COME AT THE STILE, *verb. phr.* (old).—To be in a violent hurry.

1670. RAY, *Proverbs* [BOHN (1893), 168], s.v.

TO BE READY TO LEAP OVER NINE HEDGES, *verb. phr.* (old).—Exceeding ready.

1767. RAY, *Proverbs* [BOHN (1893), 168], s.v.

LEAPING-HOUSE, *subs.* (old).—A brothel.

1598. SHAKSPEARE, *I Hen. IV*, i. 2. What a devil hast thou to do with the time of the day? unless hours were cups of sack, and minutes capons, and clocks the tongues of bawds, and dials the signs of LEAPING HOUSES.

LEA-RIGS, *subs.* (Scots').—The female *pudendum*: generic. For synonyms *see* MONOSYLLABLE.

LEARY (or **LEERY**), *adj.* (common).—1. Artful; DOWNY (*q.v.*).

1823. GROSE, *Vulg. Tongue*, 3rd ed. s.v.

1841. LEMAN REDE, *Sixteen String Jack*, i. 3. The dashy, splashy, LEARY little stringer.

1857. DUCANGE ANGLICUS, *Vulgar Tongue*. For blokes to see That you're a LEARY man.

1859. MATSELL, *Vocabulum*, s.v. LEERY. On guard; look out; wide awake.

1877. *Five Years' Penal Servitude*, iii. p. 146. A LEARY look, in which fear, defiance, and cunning are mixed up together.

1888. J. RUNCIMAN, *The Chequers*, 85. The bastard gipsy smiled in LEARY fashion.

2. (American).—Drunk. For synonyms *see* DRINKS and SCREWED.

LEARY-CUM-FITZ, *subs.* (theatrical).—A vulgarian amongst actors.

LEAST. LEAST IN SIGHT, *phr.* (old).—*See* quots.

1785. GROSE, *Vulg. Tongue*, s.v. LEAST IN SIGHT, to play least in sight, to hide, keep out of the way, or make oneself scarce.

1859. MATSELL, *Vocabulum*, s.v. LEAST. Keep out of the way; hide; out of sight.

LEATHER, *subs.* (American thieves').—1. A pocket book. For synonyms *see* READER.

1859. MATSELL, *Vocabulum*, s.v. LEATHER. The bloke lost his LEATHER, the man lost his pocket book.

1881. *New York Slang Dict.*, '*On the Trail*.' We touched his LEATHER too, but it was very lathy.

1883. CLEMENS ('Mark Twain'), *Life on the Mississippi*, p. 459. When we got to Chicago on the cars from there to here, i PULLED OFF an old woman's LEATHER,: i hadn't no more than got it off when i wished i hadn't donn it, for awhile before that i made up my mind to be a square bloke.

2. (venery).—The female *pudendum*. Hence, TO LABOUR LEATHER (old) = to copulate; LEATHER-STRETCHER = the *penis*: *cf.* KID-LEATHER; and NOTHING LIKE LEATHER (*q.v.*). For synonyms *see* MONOSYLLABLE.

1540. LINDSAY, *Thrie Estaitis* [LAING (1879), ii. 72. 1332]. It is half ane yeir almaist, Sen ever that loun laborde my LEDDER.

1678. COTTON, *Virgil Travestie*, in *Wks.* (1725), Bk. iv. p. 74. At that Queen Juno smil'd and said . . . . if they once do come together, He'll find that Dido's reaching LEATHER.

d.1796. BURNS, *Court of Equity*. Hunter, a willing, hearty brither, weel skilled in dead and living LEATHER.

3. in pl. (common).—The ears; LUGS (*q.v.*). For synonyms *see* HEARING CHEATS.

4. (sporting).—A cricket-, or foot-ball. TO HUNT LEATHER (cricket) = to field. LEATHER-HUNTING (*subs.*) fielding.

1883. *Graphic*, 11 August, p. 138, col. 1. The giants of the past who handled so efficiently the 'willow' and the LEATHER.

1884. *Daily News*, 12 April, p. 5, col. 2. A man has Morley's genius with the LEATHER, combined with Morley's deficiencies as a fielder and bat.

1886. G. SUTHERLAND, *Australia*, p. 178. In most parts of Australia cricket can be played with tolerable comfort all the year round. Occasionally, in summer, there are days when the heat is unusually oppressive, and the pastime of LEATHER HUNTING becomes somewhat tiresome.

1890. *Palace Journal*, 4 Aug. Our fellows were kept LEATHER-HUNTING pretty well the whole innings.

Verb. (common).—To beat; TO TAN (*q.v.*); TO DUST (*q.v.*).

1763. FOOTE, *Mayor of Garratt*, i. Now, if you think I could carry my point, I would so swinge and LEATHER my lambkin.

1785. GROSE, *Vulg. Tongue*, s.v. To LEATHER also means to beat, perhaps originally with a strap. I'll LEATHER you to your heart's content.

1858. G. ELIOT, *Janet's Repentance*, ch. xxi. 'He'll want to be LEATHERIN' *us*, I shouldn't wonder. He must hev somethin' t'ill-use when he's in a passion.'

1892. G. M. FENN, *The New Mistress*, xxii. Please, teacher, mother LEATHERS the boys if they don't get home in time for dinner.

1892. ANSTEY, *Voces Populi*, 'The Travelling Menagerie,' p. 61. Bain't she a LEATHERIN' of 'un too!

TO GO TO LEATHER, *verb. phr.* (American).—*See* quot.

1882. DODGE, *Ranch Life in the Far West*. After a few jumps, however, the average man grasps hold of the horn of the saddle—the delightful onlookers meanwhile earnestly advising him not TO GO TO LEATHER—and is contented to get through the affair in any shape, provided he can escape without being thrown off.

TO LOSE LEATHER, *verb. phr.* (colloquial).—To be saddle-galled.—GROSE (1785).

LEATHERS, *subs.* (common).—A postboy.

1849. THACKERAY, *Pendennis*, ch. xx. 'Come along; jump in, old boy—go it, LEATHERS!' and in this way Pen found himself in Mr. Spavin's postchaise.

LEATHERHEAD, *subs.* (old).—1. A swindler. For synonyms *see* ROOK.

1690. B. E., *Dict. Cant. Crew*, s.v.

1884. PHILLIPS WOOLLEY, *Trottings of a Tenderfoot*. Now the Senator is only a LEATHERHEAD who made his pile by such and such a swindle.

2. (old: American).—A policeman or watchman.

1882. MCCABE, *New York*, xxiii. 369. During the British occupation of the city, in the war of Independence, military patrols kept the streets at night . . . . After the close of the war a patrol of civilians was appointed. . . . They wore a leather hat with a wide brim, something like a fireman's hat, and this won for them the name of LEATHERHEADS.

1888. *New York Mercury*, 21 July. Here the old police or LEATHERHEADS tried to restrain them, but in vain. Hostilities took place, several of the police were killed and several mortally wounded.

LEATHER-HUNTING. *See* LEATHER, *subs.*, sense 4.

LEATHERING, *subs.* (common).—A thrashing.

LEATHER-LANE, *subs.* (venery).—The female *pudendum*. For synonyms *see* MONOSYLLABLE.

Adj. (old).—Paltry; bad.—GROSE (1823); DE VAUX (1823).

LEATHERN-CONVENIENCE, *subs.* (old).—A stage-coach; a carriage.

1690. B. E., *Dict. Cant. Crew*, s.v.

1703. WARD, *London Spy*, vii. p. 144. Our LEATHERN CONVENIENCY being bound in the Braces to its Good Behaviour had no more Sway than a Funeral Herse.

1725. *New Cant. Dict.*, s.v.

1782. CENTLIVRE, *Bold Stroke for a Wife*, v. 1. *Col. F.* Ah! thou wicked one. Now I consider thy face, I remember thou didst come up in the LEATHERN CONVENIENCY with me.

1785. GROSE, *Vulg. Tongue*, s.v. LEATHER . . . . LEATHERN CONVENIENCY, term used by quakers for a stage coach.

1801. C. K. SHARPE, in *Correspondence* (1888), i. 102. I left Oxford with Stapleton in his mama's LEATHERN CONVENIENCY.

1824. SCOTT, *St. Ronan's Well*, xx. At the duly appointed hour, creaked forth the LEATHERN CONVENIENCE, in which, carefull screened by the curtain . . . sat Nabob Touchwood, in the costume of an Indian merchant.

LEATHERNECK, *subs.* (nautical).—A soldier. For synonyms *see* MUD-CRUSHER and FLY-SLICER.

LEATHERNLY, *adj.* (old).—Clumsily; sordidly; poorly.

1594. NASHE, *Unf. Traveller* [GROSART (1883-4), v. 71]. So filthily acted, so LEATHERNLY set forth.

LEATHER-STRETCHER, *subs.*(venery).—The *penis*. For synonyms *see* CREAMSTICK and PRICK. To GO LEATHER-STRETCHING = to copulate.

LEAVE, *subs.* (billiards').—A favorable position for a stroke.

TO TAKE FRENCH LEAVE. *See* FRENCH LEAVE.

TO LEAVE IN THE AIR. *See* AIR.

TO LEAVE IN THE LURCH. *See* LURCH.

LEAVING-SHOP, *subs.* (common).—1. An unlicensed pawn-brokery; a DOLLY-SHOP (*q.v.*). For synonyms *see* UNCLE.

1857. *Morning Chronicle*, 21 Dec. Proprietress of one of those iniquitous establishments called LEAVING-SHOPS.

1867. JAS. GREENWOOD, *Unsentimental Journeys*, II. 15. I no longer wondered to find my friend a pawnbroker! He had a hankering for it at the pig's head period, and kept, besides the sausage-shop, a LEAVING-SHOP, in Brick-lane, St. Luke's.

1871. *Daily Telegraph*, 10 Oct. A large portion of the least valuable was received in 'dolly' or LEAVING-SHOPS. The parties carrying them on purchased goods from whoever brought them, upon an understanding that they might be repurchased within a week or a month.

1880. JAS. GREENWOOD, *Odd People in Odd Place*, p. 37. There's a little shop in the second-hand clothes line, a LEAVING-SHOP, I think they call it, in —— Street. There's a parcel there that belongs to me, and which it will cost one and eightpence to redeem; at least, the woman promised I might redeem it in a month if I paid double what she gave me for what's in it.

1893. *Daily Chronicle*, 9 Jan., p. 9, col. 1. Two pawnbrokers, who appeared to have acted in a most reckless manner, and to a Mrs. Waldey, who kept what was known as a LEAVING SHOP.

2. (venery).—The female *pudendum*. For synonyms *see* MONOSYLLABLE.

LECHER, *verb.* (venery).—To copulate. For synonyms *see* GREENS and RIDE.

1594. NASHE, *Unf. Traveller* [GROSART (1883-4), v. 29]. He must be familiar with all, and trust none, drink, carouse, and LECHER with him.

1611. COTGRAVE, *Dictionarie*, passim.

LED-CAPTAIN, *subs.* (old).—A toady; a SPONGE (*q.v.*); a pimp.

1672. WYCHERLEY, *Love in a Wood*, i. 1. *Wks.* (1713), 349. For every wit has his culley, as every squire his LED CAPTAIN.

1749. FIELDING, *Tom Jones*, Bk. xi. ch. ix. Two LED CAPTAINS, who had before rode with his lordship, and who . . . . were ready at any time to have performed the office of a footman, or indeed would have condescended lower, for the honour of his lordship's company, and for the convenience of his table.

1816. SCOTT, *Antiquary*, ch. xxxix. Petrie . . . . recommends, upon his own experience, as tutor in a family of distinction, this attitude to all LED-CAPTAINS, tutors, dependents and bottle-holders of every description.

LED-FRIEND, *subs.* (old).—A parasite.

1710. STEELE, *Tatler*, No. 208. There is hardly a rich man in the world who has not such a LED-FRIEND.

LEEDS, *subs.* (Stock Exchange).—Lincolnshire and Yorkshire ordinary stock.

LEEK, *subs.* (common).—*See* quot.

1851-61. H. MAYHEW, *London Lab. & Lon. Poor*, vol. ii. p. 425. The LEEKS are men who have not been brought up to the trade of chimney sweeping, but have adopted it as a speculation, and are so called from their entering *green*, or inexperienced into the business.

LEEKSHIRE, *subs.* (common).—Wales.

LEER, *subs.* (Old Cant).—*See* quot.

1789. GEO. PARKER, *Life's Painter*, p. 178. LEER is cant for a newspaper.

LEERY, *adj.* (old).—'On one's guard.'—GROSE (1823).

LEFT. OVER THE LEFT (or LEFT SHOULDER), *adv. phr.* (common).—Used in negation of a statement, and sometimes accompanied by pointing the thumb over the left shoulder: in FLORIO 'in my other hose'. It. *zòccoli.* The expression occurs also in *le Parnasse Satyrique* (1611). *Cf.* LEFT-HANDED.

1682. *Preface to Julian the Apostate* (London, printed for Langley Curtis). What benefit a Popish successor can reap from lives and fortunes spent in defence of the Protestant religion he may put in his eye; and what the Protestant religion gets by lives and fortunes spent in the service of a Popish successor will be OVER THE LEFT SHOULDER.

1705. *Record of Country Court held in Hartford (U.S.A.)*, 4 Sept. The said Waters, as he departed from the table, said, 'God bless you OVER THE LEFT SHOULDER.' The court ordered a record thereof to be made forthwith. A true copie.

1748. RICHARDSON, *Clarissa Harlowe*, I. 242. You will have an account to keep too; but an account of what will go OVER THE LEFT SHOULDER; only of what he squanders, what he borrows, and what he owes and never will pay.

1836. DICKENS, *Pickwick*. Each gentleman pointed with his right thumb over his left shoulder. This action imperfectly described in words by the very feeble term of OVER THE LEFT . . . . its expression is one of light and playful sarcasm.

1841. *Punch*, i. 37, col. 2. I am thine, and thine only! *Thine!*—OVER THE LEFT.

1843. W. T. MONCRIEFF, *The Scamps of London*, i. 1. I think she will come. *Ned.* Yes, OVER THE LEFT—ha, ha, ha!

1870. H. D. TRAILL, *Saturday Songs*, 'On the Watch,' p. 22. Eh, waddyer say? Don't go? Ho yes! my right honnerble friend, It's go and go OVER THE LEFT. . . . it's go with a hook at the end.

TO GET (OR BE) LEFT, *verb. phr.* (common).—1. To fail; and (2) to be placed in a difficulty.

1892. GUNTER, *Miss Dividends*, ch. iv. Making the agreement for the return or the books on arrival at Ogden, much to the delight of the news agent, who remarks oracularly, 'Buck Powers is never quite LEFT.'

1894. GEORGE MOORE, *Esther Waters*, xii. I would not go out with him or speak to him any more; and while our quarrel was going on Miss Peggy went after him, and that's how I GOT LEFT.

TO BE LEFT IN THE BASKET. *See* BASKETTED.

LEFT-FOREPART, *subs.* (common).—A wife. For synonyms *see* DUTCH.

LEFT-HANDED, *adj.* (old).—Sinister; untoward; evil. Ger. *link.*

1620. JONSON, *Silent Woman*, iii. 2. It shows you are a man. . . . that would not be put off with LEFT-HANDED cries.

LEFT-HANDED WIFE, *subs. phr.* (common).—A concubine. For synonyms *see* TART. *Cf.* Fr. *mariage de la main gauche.*

1663. KILLIGREW, *The Parson's Wedding* [DODSLEY, i. 1]. Do you not know he's married according to the rogue's liturgy? a LEFT-HANDED bridegroom.

1823. GROSE, *Vulg. Tongue*, 3rd ed. s.v. LEFT-HANDED WIFE. A concubine: an allusion to an ancient German custom, according to which when a man married his concubine, or a woman greatly his inferior, he gave her his left hand.

LEFT-HANDER, *subs.* (pugilistic).—A blow delivered with the left hand.

1861. *Macmillan's Mag.*, Feb., p. 273. He let fly a terrific LEFT-HANDER at the doctor.

LEG, *subs.* (common).—1. A swindling gamester.

1836. DICKENS, *Pickwick*, xlii. 365. 'He *was* a horse-chaunter: he's a LEG now.'

1840. THACKERAY, *Character Sketches (Capt. Rook and Mr. Pigeon)*. As for Tom, he is a regular LEG now—leading the life already described. When I met him last it was at Baden, where he was on a professional tour, with a carriage, a courier, a valet, a confederate, and a case of pistols.

1843. W. T. MONCRIEFF, *The Scamps of London*, i. 1. He's your brother, Mr. Frank; but there isn't a bigger LEG on the whole pavement.

1851-61. MAYHEW, *Lond. Lab.*, i. 501. Now and then a regular LEG, when he's travelling to Chester, York, or Doncaster, to the races, may draw other passengers into play, and make a trifle, or not a trifle, by it; or he will play with other LEGS; but it's generally for amusement, I've reason to believe.

1859. MATSELL, *Vocabulum*, s.v. LEG, a gambler.

1866. *London Miscellany*, 5 May, p. 201. The two who were not of their race were of the genus LEG.

1882. THORMANBY, *Famous Racing Men*, p. 75. He [John Gully] worked on gradually as a layer of odds—a 'bettor round,' or LEG, as he was called in those days. [*c.* 1820.]

1884. HAWLEY SMART, *From Post to Finish*, p. 172. The world regards me as a compound of LEG and money-lender.

2. (cards').—A 'chalk' or point scored in a game.

3. in pl. (common).—A lanky-built man or woman; a LAMPPOST (*q.v.*).

4. (old).—A bow: *see* MAKE A LEG.

1596. NASHE, *Have With You, etc.* [GROSART (1885), iii. 146]. Whither. . . . haue you brought mee? To Newgate, good Master Doctour, with a LOWE LEG they made answer.

1598. SHAKSPEARE, *I Henry IV*, i. Well, here's my LEG.

1602. COOKE, *How to Choose a Good Wife etc.* [DODSLEY, *Old Plays* (1874), ix. 18]. With LEGS, with curtsies, congees, and such like.

1603. DEKKER, *Wonderful Yeare* [GROSART (1886), i. 83]. Janus. . . . made a very mannerly LOWE LEGGE.

1663. KILLIGREW, *Parson's Wedding*, ii. 7. Then a stranger. . . . beats about with three graceful LEGS.

Verb. (common).—1. To trip up.

1882. *Sat. Review*, 22 April. Presently they LEGGED the copper, and he fell to the ground.

2. (common). *See* LEG IT.

TO MAKE (or SCRAPE) A LEG, *verb. phr.* (old and colloquial).—To bow; to curtsey. Also TO LEG IT.

1592. NASHE, *Pierce Penilesse* [GROSART (1885), ii. 63]. How much better is it then to haue an eligant Lawier to plead ones cause, than a stuttring Townsman, that loseth himselfe in his tale, and dooth nothing but MAKE LEGS.

1603. DEKKER, *Wonderful Yeare* [GROSART (1886), i. 91]. He calls forth one by one, to note their graces, Whilst they MAKE LEGS he copies out their faces.

1606. CHAPMAN, *Mons. D'Olive*, i. p. 117 (*Plays*, 1874). Pages and parasites [live] by MAKING LEGS.

1616. JONSON, *Devil is an Ass*, ii. 3. I learned in it myself, To MAKE MY LEGS, and do my postures.

1633. SHIRLEY, *Bird in a Cage*, v. 1. He'll kiss his hand and LEG IT.

1662. *Rump*, ii. p. 192. Shall's ask him, what he means to do?—Good faith, with all my heart; Thou MAK'ST THE better LEG o'th' two.

1670. J. EACHARD, *Contempt of the Clergy*, in Arber's *Garner*, vol. vii. p. 264. He comes to the end of the table . . . having MADE A submissive LEG.

1673. DAVENANT, *Playhouse to Let*, Epilogue. Female fishes never MAKE A LEG.

1714. LUCAS, *Gamesters*, 25. The prentice MAKES A handsome LEG and bow.

1785. GROSE, *Vulg. Tongue*, s.v. LEG.

*b.*1796. WOLCOT [P. Pindar], *Rights of Kings*, Ode xii. To Thrones, with due decorum, MAKE A LEG.

1852. DICKENS, *Bleak House*, liii. p. 443. 'Mr. Bucket, my Lady.' Mr. Bucket MAKES A LEG, and comes forward.

TO LEG IT, *verb. phr.* (common).—1. To run away. *Cf.* LEG-BAIL and TO GIVE LEGS.

1859. MATSELL, *Vocabulum*, s.v.

1878. BESANT and RICE, *By Celia's Arbour*, xlviii. Whatever the werdict, you up and LEG IT, and then bring in an alibi.

2. *See* MAKE A LEG.

TO BREAK A LEG, *verb. phr.* (venery).—*See* quot. 1737.

1684. R. HEAD, *Proteus Redivivus*, 153. Though she hath BROKEN HER LEG, she is sound enough for a Drawer, newly out of his time, who, having credit for wine, his house is furnish't with the money that did set his wife's BROKEN LEG.

1737. RAY, *Praverbs* (3rd ed.), p. 200. She hath BROKEN HER LEG above the knee, *i.e.* had a bastard.

1785. GROSE, *Vulg. Tongue*, s.v. LEG.

TO CUT ONE'S LEG, *verb. phr.* (old).—To get drunk. For synonyms *see* DRINKS and SCREWED.

1767. RAY, *Proverbs* [BOHN (1893), 63]. s.v.

TO LIFT (or LAY) A LEG ON (or OVER), *verb. phr.* (venery).—To possess a woman. Hence, TO LIFT ONE'S LEG OR TO PLAY AT LIFT-LEG = to copulate (of both sexes); LEG-LIFTER = whoremaster; and LEG-LIFTING = fornication. For synonyms *see* GREENS and RIDE.

1719. DURFEY, *Pills to Purge etc.*, v. No snarling rebel shall e'er LAY LEG o'er me.

17[?]. *Old Song* [quoted by BURNS], 'Duncan Davidson'. She feed'a lad TO LIFT HER LEG.

*c.*1787. BURNS, *Holy Willie's Prayer*. I'll ne'er LIFT A lawless LEG Again UPON her.

2. (old).—To piss.

1595. SHAKSPEARE, *Two Gentlemen*, IV. 2. *Launec.* When didst thou see me HEAVE UP MY LEG and make water on a gentle woman's farthingale?

1606. *Return from Parnassus* [DODSLEY, *Old Plays* (1874), ix. 116]. What, Monsieur Kinsayder, LIFTING UP YOUR LEG, and pissing against the world.

1887. HENLEY, *Villon's Good-Night*. At you I merely LIFT MY gam, I drink your health against the wall!

3. (old).—To walk.

1791. BURNS, *Tam O'Shanter*. Weel mounted on his grey mare, Meg, A better never LIFTED LEG.

TO GET A LEG IN, *verb. phr.* (common).—To obtain one's confidence.

1891. N. GOULD, *Double Event*, p. 207. He felt exceedingly comfortable now they had GOT A LEG IN.

A LEG (or LEG UP), *subs. phr.* (colloquial).—Help.

1836. DICKENS, *Pickwick*, ch. xvi. Your servant will GIVE YOU A LEG UP.

1871. *Figaro*, 9 Oct. There are authors who require a LEG-UP before starting, and who do well to explain, and argue, and appeal, and declare beforehand what very clever authors they are.

1876. HINDLEY, *Cheap Jack*, 171. All the. . . . cheap Johnny coves. . . . promised to come. . . . just to GIVE YOU A LEG UP.

TO HAVE A BONE IN ONE'S LEG (or ARM, or THROAT), *verb. phr.* (colloquial).—To be incapable of action: a playful refusal.

1542. NICHOLAS UDALL, *Erasmus's Apophthegmes* (1877, Reprint of Ed. 1562), p. 375. He refused to speake, allegeing that HE HAD A BONE IN HIS THROTE, and he could not speake.

1738. SWIFT, *Polite Conversation* (Conv. iii.). *Nev.* Miss, come, be kind for once, and order me a dish of coffee. *Miss.* Pray go yourself; let us wear out the oldest first; besides, I can't go, for I HAVE A BONE IN MY LEG.

1767. RAY, *Proverbs* [BOHN (1893), 50]. I have A BONE IN MY ARM. This is a pretended excuse, with which people amuse young children when they are importunate to have them do something, or reach something for them, that they are unwilling to do, or that is not good for them.

1830. W. T. MONCRIEFF, *The Heart of London*, ii. 1. GOT A BONE IN MY LEG felt rather indisposed.

TO SHAKE A FREE (or A LOOSE) LEG, *verb. phr.* (colloquial).—To live as one likes; to go on tramp.

1834. AINSWORTH, *Rookwood*, iii, ch. 9. While luck lasts the highwayman SHAKES A LOOSE LEG.

1851. MAYHEW, *Lond. Lab. etc.*, i. 453. I longed for a roving life and to SHAKE A LOOSE LEG.

1856. H. MAYHEW, *Gt. World of London*, p. 87. Those who love to SHAKE A FREE LEG, and lead a roving life, as they term it, rather than settle down to any continuous employment.

TO GIVE (or SHOW) LEGS (or A CLEAN PAIR OF LEGS), *verb. phr.* (colloquial).—To decamp; to run away.

1883. *Daily News*, 15 May, p. 7, col. 2. 'The best way is to make a snatch and GIVE LEGS for it; it's better than loitering.'

1892. MILLIKEN, *'Arry Ballads*, p. 30. We bunked off in the scurry, and SHOWED 'EM A CLEAN PAIR O' LEGS.

NOT A LEG (or A LEG TO STAND ON), *subs. phr.* (colloquial).—At the end of one's resources.

IN HIGH LEG, *subs. phr.* (colloquial).—In high feather.

ON ONE'S LAST LEGS, *subs. phr.* (colloquial).—On the verge of ruin; at the end of one's tether.

1763. FOOTE, *Mayor of Garratt*, ii. *Mrs. Sneak.* Miss Molly Jollup to be married to Sneak! *Sneak.* Ay, and glad enough you could catch me: you know, you was pretty near YOUR LAST LEGS.

1767. RAY, *Proverbs* (3rd ed.), p. 200. He's ON HIS LAST LEGS.

1782. D'ARBLAY, *Cecilia*, vii. ch. 5. She can't possibly last long, for she's quite ON HER LAST LEGS.

TO BE (or GET) ON ONE'S LEGS, *verb. phr.* (colloquial).—To rise to speak; to be speaking.

TO STAND ON ONE'S OWN LEGS, *verb. phr.* (colloquial).—To depend on oneself.

TO SET ONE (or GET) ON ONE'S LEGS, *verb. phr.* (colloquial).—To restore or attain to good circumstances.

1888. *Century Mag.*, xxxvii. p. 305. When the paper GETS UPON ITS LEGS.

TO SHOW A LEG, *verb. phr.* (colloquial).—To get out of bed.

TO HAVE THE LEGS OF ONE, *verb. phr.* (colloquial).—To outrun.

1861. *Macmillan's Mag.*, Mar., p. 357. The beggar HAD THE LEGS OF ME.

TO FIGHT AT THE LEG, *verb. phr.* (old).—*See* quot.

1785. GROSE, *Vulg. Tongue*, s.v. LEG. To fight at the leg, to take unfair advantages, it being held unfair by backsword players to STRIKE AT THE LEG.

TO FALL ON ONE'S LEGS, *verb. phr.* (colloquial).—To prosper.

1841. LYTTON, *Night and Morning*, III. 3. A man who has plenty of brains generally FALLS ON HIS LEGS.

1861. JAMES CONWAY, *Forage among Salmon and Deer*, p. 155. And this inborn self-possession tends greatly to the advantage of the people who are so constituted. Hence it is that a Scotchman put him where you will, almost invariably FALLS ON HIS LEGS.

TO HAVE LEGS, *verb. phr.* (colloquial).—To be reputed fast (as a ship, a horse, a runner).

TO FEEL ONE'S LEGS, *verb. phr.* (colloquial).—To be sure of one's ground.

1846. DICKENS, *Cricket on the Hearth*, i. Remarkably beautiful child .... May seem impossible to you, but FEELS HIS LEGS ALREADY.

TO PUT ONE'S BEST LEG FOREMOST, *verb. phr.* (colloquial).—1. To make haste; and (2) to exert oneself.

1599. NASHE, *Lenten Stuffe* [GROSART (1885), v. 277]. Well, thither our Fisherman SET THE BEST LEG BEFORE, and vnfardled to the King his whole sachel of wonders.

AS RIGHT AS MY LEG, *phr.* (colloquial).—As right as may be. But *see* quot. 1767.

1719. DURFEY, *Pills to Purge etc.*, i. 93. Jolly Ralph was in with Peg, Though frekl'd like a Turkey Egg, And she AS RIGHT AS IS MY LEG, Shee gave him leave to towze her.

1762. WILSON, *The Cheats*, ii. 4. Fear nothing. All's well, and AS RIGHT AS MY LEG.

1767. RAY, *Proverbs* [BOHN (1893), 64]. A whore, she's AS RIGHT AS MY LEG.

TO PUT THE BOOT ON THE OTHER LEG, *verb. phr.* (colloquial).—To 'turn the tables.'

1850. *New York Herald*, 24 May. The Eternal City is in a very curious position. The Pope has returned to his ancestral home; but he has nothing in his pocket, and Rothschild refuses to let him have any more money. A thousand years ago, and the BOOT would have been ON T'OTHER LEG.

1890. *Pall Mall Gaz.*, 22 Feb., p. 2, col. 2. The *Times* correspondent at Durban alludes to a rumour which at the first blush seems to PUT THE BOOT quite ON THE OTHER LEG.

TO STRETCH ONE'S LEGS, *verb. phr.* (common).—To take a walk. Hence, LEG-STRETCHER (*q.v.*) = a drink.

TO MAKE INDENTURES WITH ONE'S LEGS, *verb. phr.* (old).—To be drunk. For synonyms *see* DRINKS and SCREWED.—RAY (1767).

MORE BELONGS TO MARRIAGE THAN FOUR BARE LEGS IN A BED, *phr.* (old).—Said of the engagement or wedding of a portionless couple. Ital. *Inanzi il maritare, abbi l'habitare.*—RAY (1670).

LEG-AND-LEG, *adv. phr.* (cards').—The state of the game when each player has won a 'LEG' (*q.v.*); HORSE-AND-HORSE (*q.v.*).

LEG-BAGS, *subs.* (common).—1. Stockings; and (2) trousers.

LEG-BAIL (or LEG BAIL AND LAND SECURITY), *subs. phr.* (common).—Escape from custody. Fr. *lever le pied.* *See* BAIL.

1767. RAY, *Proverbs* [BOHN (1893), 55]. He has given him LEG-BAIL; *i.e.*, decamped.

1774. FERGUSON, *Poems*, ii. 10. They TOOK LEG-BAIL and ran awa'.

1775. ADAIR, *American Indians*, 277. I had concluded to use no chivalry, but GIVE THEM LEG-BAIL instead of it, by .... making for a deep swamp.

1816. SCOTT, *Antiquary*, ch. xxxix. I wad gie them LEG-BAIL to a certainty.

1823. GROSE, *Vulg. Tongue* (3rd ed.), s.v. LEG. LEG-BAIL AND LAND SECURITY, to run away.

1823. MONCRIEFF, *Tom and Jerry*, ii. 4. 'Tis my painful duty to commit you, unless you can find good bail. *Tom.* We'll give you LEG BAIL.

1838. DICKENS, *Oliver Twist*, ch. xix. He has us now if he could give us LEG-BAIL again.

1848. MARRYAT, *Poacher*, xxii. GIVEN THEM LEG-BAIL, I swear.

1870. WILKIE COLLINS, *Man and Wife* (in Cassell's Mag., p. 309). 'Ow! ow! that's bad. And the bit husband-creature danglin' at her petticoat's tail one day, and awa' wi' the sunrise next mornin'—have they baith taken LEG-BAIL together?'

LEG-BUSINESS, *subs.* (common).—1. *See* LEG-SHOP.

2. (venery).—Copulation. For synonyms *see* GREENS and RIDE.

LEG-DRAMA (or PIECE).—*See* LEG-SHOP.

LEGEM PONE, *subs. phr.* (old).—Money: generic. [NARES: The origin of the phrase is doubtless this: The first psalm for the twenty-fifth day of the month has the title LEGEM PONE, being the first words of the Latin version. This psalm is the fifth portion of the 119th psalm, and, being constantly used on the first great pay day of the year, March 25, was easily connected with the idea of payment, while the laudable practice of daily attendance on the public service was continued].

1557. TUSSER, *Good Hus. Lessons*, 29. Use LEGEM PONE to pay at thy day, But use not Oremus for often delay.

1611. RUGGLE, *Ignolamus*, ii. 7. Hic est LEGEM PONE: hic sunt sexcentæ coronæ.

1618. G. MINSHUL, *Essayes in Prison*, p. 26. But in this, here is nothing to be abated, all their speach is LEGEM PONE, or else with their ill custome they will detaine thee.

*d.*1662. HEYLIN, *Voy.*, p. 292. In bestowing of their degrees here they are very liberal, and deny no man that is able to pay his fees. LEGEM PONERE is with them more powerful than legem dicere.

1737. OZELL, *Rabelais*, iv. 12. They were all at our service for the LEGEM PONE.

LEGER, *subs.* (Old London Cant).—*See* quot. 1822. Also LEGERING = the practice of cheating in the sale of coals.

1591. GREENE, *Discovery of Coosnage* [GROSART (1881-6), x. 51]. The law of LEGERING, which is a deceit that colliers abuse the commonwelth withall, in having unlawfull sackes.

1591. GREENE, *Notable Discovery* [GROSART (1881-6), x. 52]. The LEGER, the crafty collier I mean. *Ibid.* 51. There be. . . . in and about London certaine caterpillars (colliers I should say) that terme themselves (among themselves) by the name of LEGERS.

1822. NARES, *Glossary*, s.v. LEGER. A cant term for a Londoner who formerly bought coals of the country colliers at so much a sack, and made his chief profit by using smaller sacks, making pretence he was a country collier. This was termed LEGERING.

LEGERDEMAIN, *subs.* (old: now recognised).—Sleight of hand.

*d.*1535. SIR T. MORE, *Works*, p. 813. Perceive theyr LEYGIER DEMAINE, wyth which they would ingle forth thir falshood and shift the trouth asyde.

1592. NASHE, *Pierce Penilesse* [GROSART (1883-4), ii. 108]. Making their eyes and eares vassailes to the LEGERDEMAINE of these ingling mountebankes.

1596. SPENSER, *Faery Queene*, v. ix. 13. He in slights and jugling feates did flow, And of LEGIERDEMAYNE the mysteries did know.

1653. WALTON, *Complete Angler*, p. 112. All the money that had been got that week .... by fortune telling or LEGERDEMAIN.

1684. R. HEAD, *Proteus Redivivus*, 238. What trick they play, what LEIDGER-DE-MAIN they use.

1690. B. E., *Dict. Cant. Crew*, s.v.

1725. *New Canting Dict.*, s.v.

LEGGED, *adj.* (old).—In irons.

1859. MATSELL, *Vocabulum*, s.v.

LEGGER, *subs.* (old).—*See* quot.

1823. GROSE, *Vulg. Tongue* (3rd ed.), s.v. LEGGER. Sham LEGGERS, cheats who pretend to sell smuggled goods, but in reality only deal in shop-keepers old and damaged wares.

LEGGINGS, *subs.* (common).—Stockings.

LEGGISM, *subs.* (common).—The character, practices, or manners of a LEG (*q.v.*).

LEGGY, *adj.* (colloquial).—Long-legged.

1848. THACKERAY, *Book of Snobs*, ch. x. You behold Slapper's long-tailed, LEGGY mare.

1884. *Field*, Dec. 6. Her colour and markings are capital, in expression and style fair, but she is LEGGY and light in bone.

LEGITIMATE, *adj.* (racing).—1. Flat-racing as distinguished from steeplechasing or hurdle-racing; and (2) drama—especially the Shaksperean—as opposed to burlesque.

1888. *Sportsman*, 28 Nov. It was certainly a change from the bustle and excitement connected with the winding-up of the LEGITIMATE season.

LEGLIN-GIRTH. TO CAST A LEGLINGIRTH, *verb. phr.* (Scots').—To be got with child. [LEGLIN = milkpail + GIRTH = hoop].

*d.*1758. RAMSAY, *Poems* (1800), i. 274. Or bairns can read, they first maun spell, I learn'd this frae my mammy, And COOST A LEGLEN GIRTH mysel, Lang or I married Tammie.

LEG OF MUTTON, *subs. phr.* (common).—A sheep's trotter.

Adj. (common).—Leg-of-mutton shaped; as in the case of sleeves, whiskers, sails, etc.

1866 W. D. HOWELLS, *Venetian Life*, xx. With their honest, heavy faces comically anglicised by LEG-OF-MUTTON whiskers.

LEG OF MUTTON FIST. *See* MUTTON FIST.

LEG OF THE LAW, *subs. phr.* (common).—A lawyer. Also LIMB OF THE LAW.

LEGS-AND-ARMS, *subs.* (tailors').—Bodiless beer. For synonyms *see* DRINKS and SWIPES.

LEG-SHAKER, *subs.* (common).—A dancer. Fr. *un gambilleur.*

LEGSHIRE, *subs.* (common).—The Isle of Man. [In allusion to the heraldic bearings].

LEG-SHOP, *subs.* (common).—1. A theatre whose speciality is the display of the female form. Hence, LEG-PIECE = a play contrived to that end; LEG-BUSINESS = the condition of a woman whose chief work is to show her legs; and LEG-SHOW = the *personnel* of a LEG-SHOP in action.

1871. A. E. EDWARDS, *Ought We to Visit Her*, p. . 'She was,' says Adonis, 'in the LEG BUSINESS.'

1875. CLEMENS ('Mark Twain'), *Screamers*, p. 15. 'Nothing, sir,' was the reply; 'only they're playing 'Undine' at the Opera House, and some folks call it the LEG-SHOP.'

1882. MCCABE, *New York*, 206. They are liberal patrons of the drama, especially the ballet and the LEG-BUSINESS.

LEG-STRETCHER, *subs.* (American).—A drink: *i.e.*, an inducement or a pretext for going out. *See* TO STRETCH ONE'S LEGS. For synonyms *see* GO.

LEMON. TO SQUEEZE THE LEMON, *verb. phr.* (common).—To urinate. For synonyms *see* PISS.

LEMON JOLLY. *See* COLLY MOLLY.

LEND, *subs.* (old colloquial).—A loan: *e.g.* 'For the LEND of the ass you might give me the mill' (*Old Ballad*).

LENGTH, *subs.* (thieves').—1. Six months' imprisonment. For synonyms *see* DOSE.

2. (theatrical).—*See* quot. 1781.

1781. G. PARKER, *View of Society*, I. 43. It being one of the usual enquiries made by Managers of the candidates for country engagements, 'How many lengths can you study from night to night?' A LENGTH is forty two lines.

1838. DICKENS, *Nicholas Nickleby*, ch. xxiii. I've a part of twelve LENGTHS here which I must be up in by to-morrow night.

1871. *Edinburgh Review*, 'Lord Brougham's Recollections of a Long Life.' Keen said that Iago was three LENGTHS longer than Othello.

1885. *Household Words*, 22 Aug., p. 328. All they knew or cared to know was that they had to get into their heads certain LENGTHS of a certain drama to be produced that very night.

TO GET THE LENGTH OF ONE'S FOOT, *verb. phr.* (common).—To fascinate; to understand how to manage a person.

LENTEN-FACED, *adj.* (old).—Starved- or sad-looking.

1621. BURTON, *Anatomy* (ed. 1893), iii. 220. Howsoever they put on LENTEN FACES, and whatsoever they pretend.

LENTEN-FARE, *subs.* (old). — *See* quot.

1823. GROSE, *Vulg. Tongue* (3rd ed.), s.v. LENTEN FARE, spare diet.

LER-AC-AM, *subs.* (back slang).—Mackarel.

LERICOMPOOP (LERIPUP, LERIPOOP, or LURIPUP), *subs.* (old).—Originally an academical scarf or hood. Hence, (1) knowledge or acuteness; (2) a man or woman of parts; (3) a swindle, jest, or trick; and (4) a cheat, buffon, or jester. Thence, TO PLAY ONE'S LIRIPUPS = (1) to undergo examination for a degree; and (2) to play the fool (from the contempt into which scholastic subtleties had in the end to fall). Also as *verb* = to deceive, to cheat.

1584. *Sapho and Phaon*, i. 3. Thow maist be skilled in thy logic, but not in thy LERYPOOPE.

1593. HARVEY, *Pierces Superer*. [GROSART (1885), ii. 78]. Nash is learned, and knoweth his LERIPUP. *Ibid.* 278. Be no niggard of thy sweet accents. . . . but reach the antike muses their right LERIPUP.

1594. J. LYLY, *Mother Bombie*, i. 3. There's a girl that knows her LERRIPOOP.

1594. NASHE, *Unf. Traveller* [GROSART (1885), v. 159]. Heere was a wily wench had her LIRIPOOP without book.

1603-37. BRETON, *Packet of Letters* [GROSART (1870), ii. *h.* 34, 10, line 4]. I see you haue little to doe that haue so much leisure TO PLAY YOUR LURIPUPS.

1605. *London Prodigal*, iv. 1. Well cha' a bin zarved many a sluttish trick, but such a LERRIPOOP. . . . was never yzarved.

1611. COTGRAVE, *Dict.*, s.v. *Qui sçait bien son roulet*, one that knows his LIRIPOOPE.

1621. BEAUMONT & FLETCHER, *Pilgrim*, ii. 1. Keep me this young LIRRYPOOP within doors.

1719. DURFEY, *Pills to Purge*, i. 186. And all the day long, This, this was her song, Was ever poor Maiden so LERICOMPOOP'D.

LESBIAN, *subs.* (venery).—A fellatrix of women. [From the legend of Sappho and the women of Lesbos].

LESSON. *See* SIMPLE ARITHMETIC.

LET. LET ALONE, *adv. phr.* (colloquial).—Much less; not mentioning.

1837. BARHAM, *Ingoldsby Legends*, ... I have not had, this livelong day, one drop to cheer my heart, Nor brown to buy a bit of bread with—LET ALONE a tart.

1851. F. E. SMEDLEY, *Lewis Arundel*, i. 'You have brought a wild beast with you, which has eaten up all the tea-cakes.' 'LET ALONE fright'ning the blessed cat so that she's flowed up the chimley.'

1857. C. READE, *Never Too Late*, xxxvi. The wind emptied a glass of the very moisture, LET ALONE the liquid in a moment.

TO LET THE CAT OUT OF THE BAG, *verb. phr.* (colloquial).—To reveal a secret; to put one's foot in it. *See* CAT, and add following quots.

1888. ROLF BOLDREWOOD, *Robbery Under Arms*, xxiv. 'I'm most afraid of your father, though, LETTING THE CAT OUT OF THE BAG; he's such an old duffer to blow.'

1892. *Ally Sloper's Half Holiday*, 27 Feb., p. 67, col. 3. Cats, however, possess an exceptional faculty FOR LETTING THINGS OUT OF THE BAG, and Guy's and Violet's feline made its appearance.

TO LET DAYLIGHT INTO, *verb. phr.* (colloquial).—To stab or shoot; to kill. *See* SECOND-HAND DAYLIGHT and DAYLIGHT.

TO LET DOWN GENTLY (or EASY), *verb. phr.* (colloquial).—1. To be lenient.

1836. M. SCOTT, *Cruise of the Midge* [Ry. ed. 1840, p. 140]. I did not know it, nor did I believe it, but, by way of LETTING HIM DOWN GENTLY, I said nothing.

1888. *New York Sunday Despatch*. If the royal parents wish to see their offsprings LET DOWN EASY from their high estate, they will adopt this course.

2. (common).—To disappoint; to rebuff. *Cf.* LET-DOWN.

TO LET DRIVE, *verb. phr.* (colloquial).—To aim a blow; to attack.

1593. NASHE, *Strange Newes*, in *Works* [GROSART], ii. 224. If he . . . LET DRIVE at him with a volley of verses.

1753. FOOTE, *Englishman in Paris*, i. But I LET DRIVE at the monk, made the soup-maigre rumble in his bread-basket, and laid him sprawling.

1838. HALIBURTON, *Clockmaker*, 2nd S. ch. xiv. 'Now,' says I, 'my hearties, up and LET DRIVE at 'em, right over the wall!'

TO LET FLY, *verb. phr.* (common).—To aim at; also to strike.

1647. FLETCHER, *Sea Voyage*, ii. 2. Speak, or . . . I'll LET FLY at you all.

1671. BUCKINGHAM, *The Rehearsal*. And at that word, at t'other's head LET FLY a greasy plate.

1678. BUNYAN, *Pilgrim's Progress*, 156. They, therefore, in angry manner, LET FLY at them again.

1719. DURFEY, *Pills to Purge*, iii. 14. By cock, quote hee, Say you so, do you see, And then at him LET FLIE.

1817. C. LAMB, *Letters*, 17 May. 'To Wm. Ayton Esq.' There'd be many a damme LET FLY at my presumption.

1860. *Morning Post*, 30 Jan. 'The Wit of Extravaganza.' He has been assaulted by another *indewiddle*, who 'At his physiognimy LET FLY, Gave him in fact a oner in the eye!'

1876. HINDLEY, *Life and Adventures of a Cheap Jack*, p. 115, s.v.

1889. *Sporting Times*, 29 June. 'Another Turf Dispute.' Now, Maud was quite the 'lidy', but she LET the language FLY.

1891. W. C. RUSSELL, *Ocean Tragedy*, 42. Sir Wilfrid really means to LET FLY at the shark.

TO LET GO, *verb. phr.* (venery).—To achieve emission. *See* COME.

TO LET GO THE PAINTER. *See* PAINTER.

TO LET IN, *verb. phr.* (colloquial).—1. To deceive; to victimize; to cheat.

1855. THACKERAY, *Newcomes*, lxxii. Affairs had been going ill with that gentleman: he had been LET IN terribly, he informed me, by Lord Levant's insolvency.

1887. *Nineteenth Century*, xxii. 262. The farmer . . . persists in trying to convince himself that he was LET IN when he made himself liable for the tithes.

1887. *Field*, 25 June. An owner may be LET IN for a fine.

2. (University).—*See* quot.

1861. HUGHES, *Tom Brown at Oxford*, i. He has also been good enough to recommend to me many tradesmen . . . . but, with the highest respect for friend Perkins (my scout) and his obliging friends, I shall make some inquiries before LETTING IN with any of them.

TO LET INTO, *verb. phr.* (colloquial).—To attack; to beat; to abuse.

1851-61. H. MAYHEW, *London Lab. & Lon. Poor*, vol. iii. p. 148. 'They got from six to nine months' imprisonment; and those that LET INTO the police, eighteen months.'

TO LET OFF STEAM. *See* STEAM.

TO LET ON, *verb. phr.* (colloquial).—To betray; to admit; to seem.

1725. RAMSAY [*Poems* (1800), ii. 100]. LET na ON what's past.

*d.*1796. BURNS, *Last May a Braw Wooer*. 'I never LOOT ON that I ken'd it or car'd, But thought I might hae waur offers.'

1835. HALIBURTON, *Clockmaker*, 1st S. ch. x. 'I'll tell you the secret, but you needn't LET ON to no one about it.'

1838. NEAL, *Charcoal Sketches*, 74. But a man can't rise, after a royal hyst, without LETTING ON he feels flat.

1843. *Major Jones's Courtship*, p. 84. The tears were runnin' out of my eyes; but I didn't want to LET ON, for fear it would make her feel bad.

1858. DEAN RAMSAY, *Reminiscences*. I saw Mr. —— at the meeting, but I never LET ON that I knew he was present.

1860. BOUCICAULT, *Colleen Bawn*, i. 3. Don't LET ON to mortal that we're married.

1864. E. YATES, *Broken to Harness*, ch. iv. p. 38 (1873). 'Never LET ON that he didn't know what it was; never changed a muscle of his face.'

1871. *Binghamton Journal*, April [quoted by DE VERE]. 'Although the visitors, the gentlemanly keeper, and the prison-chaplain, all tried in every conceivable way to induce him to make a confession, he would never LET ON how the murder was committed, and all agree that Ruloff is the greatest mystery of the age.'

1879. JUSTIN MC. CARTHY, *Donna Quixote*, ch. xxxiii. 'I knew it, though she wouldn't LET ON even to me.'

1888. ROLF BOLDREWOOD, *Robbery Under Arms*, xi. He LET ON once to me—that he was awfully cut up about my changing.

1892. MILLIKEN, *'Arry Ballads*, 52. 'Arry never LET ON to them Swiss as he felt on the swivel,—no fear!

TO LET ONESELF LOOSE, *verb. phr.* (colloquial).—To speak, or launch out, without restraint.

TO LET OUT, *verb. phr.* (colloquial).—1. To disclose.

1878. BEADLE, *Western Scenes*. 'You bile the pot, and when I have had a smoke I'll LET OUT, but not afore.'

2. (colloquial).—To speak strongly.

1840. H. COCKTON, *Valentine Vox*, xxxix. 'Does he marry her because he believes her to be engaging, and sweet tempered? A month after marriage she begins to LET OUT in a style of which he cannot approve, by *any* means.'

1847. ROBB, *Squatter Life*, p. 80. After dilating at some length on the imported candidate, who was his antagonist, he LET himself OUT, on some of the measures he advocated.

1888. ROLF BOLDREWOOD, *Robbery Under Arms*, ix. Jim was just going to LET OUT when he looked up and saw Miss Falkland looking at him.

3. (colloquial).—To strike out.

1869. H. J. BYRON, *Not Such a Fool as He Looks*, p. 8. *Mur.* What did he do? *Mou.* Well, he LET OUT. *Mur.* What! his language? *Mou.* No,

his *left*. His aim was straight at the tip of my nose.

4. (common).—A general verb of action; to do.

1888. ROLF BOLDREWOOD, *Robbery Under Arms*, ix. Jim's horse was far and away the fastest, and he LET OUT to head the mare off from a creek that was just in front and at the end of the plain.

TO LET OUT A REEF, *verb. phr.* (common).—To loosen one's clothes after a meal. Fr. *lâcher un cran.*

SHE LIES BACKWARDS AND LETS OUT HER FORE-ROOMS, *phr.* (old).—Said of a whore.—RAY (1767).

TO LET RIP. *See* RIP.

TO LET SLIDE. *See* SLIDE.

TO LET UP, *verb. phr.* (colloquial).—To stop. Also (as *subs.*) LET UP (*q.v.*).

1888. *San Francisco Weekly Examiner*, 22 March. When every rabbit is killed, the coyotes sit down on their haunches to a very comfortable banquet, and never LET UP until they have taken aboard so much rabbit-meat that they can hardly stir.

1892. A. K. GREEN, *Cynthia Wakeham's Money*, 141. 'We have talked well into the night,' he remarked; 'supposing we LET UP now, and continue our conversation to-morrow.'

TO LET THE FINGER RIDE THE THUMB TOO OFTEN, *verb. phr.* (American).—To get drunk. For synonyms *see* DRINKS and SCREWED.

[For other combination *see* DISINFECT — FLICKER — IN — MARKS — MONKEY — PLAY — POCKETS — SLIDE — STIMULATE — TUCKS — UP, etc.]

LETCHWATER, *subs.* (venery).—The sexual secretion, male and female: specifically the concomitant of desire.

LET-DOWN, *subs.* (colloquial).—A decline in circumstances; a come-down.

1866. *London Miscellany*, 3 Mar., p. 57. Bug-hunting (robbing drunken men) was about the best game out, and he added, 'I don't think that's no little LET-DOWN for a cove as has been tip-topper in his time, and smelt the insides of all the coops in the three kingdoms.'

LETS. NO LETS, *subs. phr.* (schoolboys').—No hindrances.

LETTER, *subs.* (venery).—An abbreviation of FRENCH LETTER (*q.v.*).

LETTER-IN-THE-POST-OFFICE. *See* FLAG.

TO GO AND POST A LETTER, *verb. phr.* (venery).—To copulate. For synonyms *see* GREENS and RIDE.

TO GO ON THE LETTER Q, *verb. phr.* (old).—*See* quot.

1823. DE VAUX, *Memoirs*, p. 185, s.v. LETTER Q, the mace or billiard slum, is sometimes called going on the Q, or the letter Q, alluding to an instrument used in playing billiards.

LETTERED, *adj.* (old).—Branded; burnt in the hand.

LETTER-RACKET, *subs.* (vagrants').—*See* quot.

1823. GROSE, *Vulg. Tongue* (3rd ed.), s.v. LETTER RACKET, men or women of genteel address, going about to respectable houses with a letter or statement, detailing some case of extreme distress, as shipwreck, sufferings by fire, etc. by which many benevolent, but credulous, persons are induced to relieve the fictitious wants of the impostors.

LETTY, *subs.* (common).—A bed; a lodging. For synonyms *see* KIP. Also verbally = to lodge.

1875. J. FROST, *Circus Life*, p. 279. LETTY is used both as a noun and as verb signifying 'lodging' and 'to lodge'.

1893. EMERSON, *Signor Lippo*, xiv. 'Blower, how about LETTY?' 'Kip for you two, eh? I'll just go and see the under-sheriff.'

LET-UP, *subs.* (common).—1. A pause; a breach.

1888. *Troy Daily Times.* . . . It rained for three days, almost without a LET UP, after we reached our destination. *Ibid.* The stable hymn, as the boys called it, was sung in some companies where there was a little LET-UP on discipline.

1888. *Spirit of the Times.* There will be a LET UP of a few days, maybe a week, between the close of the Winter Meeting and the opening of the Spring Meeting.

2. (Stock Exchange).—A sudden disappearance of artificial causes of depression.

LEVANT, *verb.* (common).—To abscond. TO DO (or THROW or RUN) A LEVANT (gaming) = to stake and SKIP (*q.v.*). Fr. *faire voile en Levant;* It. *andare in Levante. See* quots. 1714 and 1823.

1714. LUCAS, *Gamesters*, III. He hath ventur'd to come the LEVANT over gentlemen; that is, to play without any money at all in his pocket.

1729. VANBRUGH and CIBBER, *Provoked Husband*, i. Crowd to the Hazard table, THROW A familiar LEVANT upon some sharp lurching man of quality, and if he demands his money, turn it off with a loud laugh.

1749. FIELDING, *Tom Jones*, Bk. VIII. ch. 12. Never mind that, man! E'en RUN A LEVANT.

1788. G. A. STEVENS, *Adv. of a Speculist*, i. 96. This [cheating described] at Hazard-table is called LEVANTING.

1823. GROSE, *Vulg. Tongue* (3rd ed.). LEVANTING, or RUNNING A LEVANT, an expedient practised by broken gamesters to retrieve themselves, and signifies to bet money at a race, cock-match, etc., without a shilling in their pocket to answer the event. The punishment . . . . is curious: the offender is placed in a large basket . . , hoisted up to the ceiling . . . and . . . then kept suspended . . . exposed to derision, during the pleasure of the company.

1837. BARHAM, *Ingoldsby Legends*, i. 244. When he found she'd LEVANTED, the Count of Alsace, At first turned remarkably red in the face.

1880. A. TROLLOPE, *The Duke's Children*, ch. xlix. Was it not clear that a conspiracy might have been made without his knowledge;—and clear also that the real conspirators had LEVANTED?

1883. *Referee*, 25 March, p. 3, col. 2. The late manager of the 'Vic.', it appears, LEVANTED with over £100 of the money belonging to the committee.

1887. *Daily Telegraph*, 12 March. Whom he would compel to lodge a considerable sum as caution money, so that in the event of one of the body LEVANTING, there would be wherewithal to pay his creditors.

1892. *Globe*, 2 April, p. 2, col. 1. If he could only lay his hands on LEVANTING Brown!

LEVANT ME! *intj.* (common).—Used as an imprecation: *cf.* BLOW ME.

1760. FOOTE, *The Minor*, i. LEVANT ME, but he got enough last night to purchase a principality amongst his countrymen.

LEVANTER, *subs.* (common).—A defaulting debtor; a WELSHER.

1598. FLORIO, *Worlde of Wordes.* LEVANTE . . . A limlifter, a shifter, an uptaker, a pilfrer.

1781. G. PARKER, *View of Society*, II. 168. LEVANTERS. These are of the order and number of *Black-Legs*.

1823. MONCRIEFF, *Tom and Jerry*, p. 5. Here, among the pinks in Rotten-row, the lady-birds in the Saloon, the angelics at Almack's, the-top-of-the-tree heroes, the legs and LEVANTERS at Tattersal's, nay, even among the millers at the Fives, it would be taken for nothing less than the index of a complete flat.

1826. HOOD, *Whims and Oddities*, 1st S. (*Backing the Favourite*). But she wedded in a canter, And made me a LEVANTER, In foreign lands to sigh for the Favourite!

LEVEL. TO WORK (or ACT) ON A BROAD LEVEL, *verb. phr.* (American).—To be stable and trustworthy. BROAD-LEVEL PRICE = the lowest fixed price.

LEVEL-BEST, *adj. phr.* (colloquial).—The best one can do; the utmost of one's power.

1879. E. E. HALE, *His Level Best* [*Century*]. I said, 'I'll do my LEVEL BEST,' Doctor.

1882. McCABE, *New York*, p. 217. I was listening to the aged cove, and trying to do my LEVEL BEST in replying to him.

1889. *Ally Sloper's Half Holiday*, 1 June. When that core of my heart does her LEVEL BEST to send the toe of her satin boot through the ceiling, then I somehow think the word Daisy is misapplied, however well it may look on a playbill.

1890. *Sporting Life*, 8 Nov. Both tried their LEVEL BEST.

1892. R. L. STEVENSON and L. OSBOURNE, *The Wrecker*, p. 154. But you'll do your LEVEL BEST, Loudon; I depend on you for that. You must be all fire and grit and dash from the word 'go.'

1892. HUME NISBET, *Bushranger's Sweetheart*, p. 106. I have done my LEVEL BEST to cater for them.

LEVEL-COIL. TO PLAY LEVEL-COIL, *verb. phr.* (old).—To copulate. For synonyms *see* GREENS and RIDE.

1662. WILSON, *The Cheats*, iv. 2. *Mop.* She is the Constable's wife, whom, to be short, the Alderman cuckolds. *Jol.* Hah! Are you sure of it? *Mop.* I made her confess that the Alderman and one Bilboe play LEVEL DE COILE with her.

LEVEL-HEADED, *adj.* (American).—Well-balanced; steady; judicious.

1870. *Golden City* (San Francisco: quoted in *Orchestra*), 12 Aug. Miss Markham is rather quiet off the stage, agreeable in conversation, and doesn't care much what the censorious world says about her—and herein her HEAD IS LEVEL!

1870. *Orchestra*, 12 Aug. To tell a woman her HEAD is LEVEL is apparently a compliment in America, though to call a man a 'square head' is to insult him in France.

1879. BRET HARTE, *Gabriel Conroy*, xxxix. A strong suspicion among men whose HEADS are LEVEL.

1895. *N. Y. Press*, in *Pall Mall Gazette*, Sept. 13. p. 7. This people had taken him for a gallant, persistent, even-tempered LEVEL-HEADED gentleman.

LEVITE, *subs.* (old).—1. A parson. For synonyms *see* DEVIL-DODGER.

1663. KILLIGREW, *Parson's Wedding*, ii. 4. You uncivil fellow, you come hither to tell my lady of her faults, as if her own LEVITE could not discern 'em.

1690. B. E., *Dict. Cant. Crew*, s.v.

1725. *New Cant. Dict.*, s.v.

1785. GROSE, *Vulg. Tongue*, s.v.

1849. MACAULAY, *Hist. Eng.*, ch. iii. A young LEVITE—such was the phrase then in use—might be had for his board, a small garret, and ten pounds a year.

2. (old).—A fashionable dress for women (*c.* 1780). [HORACE WALPOLE: 'a man's bed-gown bound round with a belt'].

LEVY, *subs.* (common).—1. A shilling.

2. (American).— *See* quot.

1834. *Atlantic Club-book*, II. 120. How is flour up country? They say it is six and four LEVIES, and corn seven and a fip.

1848. BARTLETT, *Dict. of Am.*, s.v. LEVY. Elevenpence. In the State of Pennsylvania, Maryland, and Virginia, the Spanish real, or eighth part of a dollar, or twelve and a half cents. Sometimes called an *elevenpenny bit*.

1848. JONES, *Sketches of Travel*, p. 76. 'How much do you ax for 'em?' ses I. 'Eight boxes for a LEVY,' ses he.

LEWD INFUSION, *subs. phr.* (venery).—The semen. For synonyms *see* SPENDINGS.

LEYSTALL. *See* LAYSTALL.

LIAR. I'M SOMETHING OF A LIAR MYSELF, *phr.* (American).—A retort upon Munchausen.

LIB, *subs.* (old).—1. Sleep. LONG LIB = death.

1622-65. HEAD & KIRKMAN, *English Rogue.* 'Bing Out etc.' By Rum-coves dine For his LONG LIB at last.

2. (common).—A bank-note. For synonyms *see* FLIMSY.

Verb. (Old Cant).—1. *See* quots. Also LYP.

1573. HARMAN, *Caveat* (1814), p. . . LYP, to lie down.

1611. MIDDLETON & DEKKER, *Roaring Girl*, v. 1. I would LIB all the darkmans.

1690. B. E., *Dict. Cant. Crew*, s.v. LIB, c, to tumble and lie together.

1725. *New Cant. Dict.*, s.v.

1785. GROSE, *Vulg. Tongue*, s.v. LIB, to lie together.

1859. MATSELL, *Vocabulum*, s.v. LIB. The coves LIB together, the fellows sleep together.

2. (old).—To castrate.

1590. FLORIO, *Worlde of Wordes*, s.v. *Castrare* . . . . to LIB.

LIBBEG (or LYBBEG), *subs.* (Old Cant).—*See* quots. [Gael. *leabadh* or *leabaidh*].

1573. HARMAN, *Caveat* (1814), 65. LYB BEGE, a bed.

1610. ROWLANDS, *Martin Markall*, p. 39 (H. Club's Repr., 1874). LYBBEG, a bedde.

1665. R. HEAD, *English Rogue*, Pt. I. ch. v. p. 50 (1874). LIBEDGE, a Bed.

1690. B. E., *Dict. Cant. Crew*, s.v.

1725. *New Cant. Dict.*, s.v.

1785. GROSE, *Vulg. Tongue*, s.v.

1859. MATSELL, *Vocabulum*, s.v.

LIBBEN, *subs.* (Old Cant).—A private house. *Cf.* LIBKEN.

1690. B. E., *Dict. Cant. Crew*, s.v.

1725. *New Cant. Dict.*, s.v.

1823. GROSE, *Vulg. Tongue* (3rd ed.), s.v.

1859. MATSELL, *Vocabulum*, s.v.

LIBERTY-HALL, *subs.* (colloquial).—A house where every one can do his pleasure.

1773. GOLDSMITH, *She Stoops to Conquer*, ii. Gentlemen, pray be under no restraint in this house; this is LIBERTY HALL, gentlemen; you may do just as you please here.

1890. HUME NISBET, *Bail Up*, p. 75. They did not bother with dressing for supper in this LIBERTY HALL.

LIB-KEN (or LYPKEN), *subs.* (Old Cant).—*See* quots.

1573. HARMAN, *Caveat* (1814), p. 65. A LYPKEN, a house to lye in.

1610. ROWLANDS, *Martin Markall*, p. 39 (H. Club's Repr., 1874). LYBKIN a house to lodge people.

1621. JONSON, *Gipsies Metamorphosed.* To their LIBKINS at the crackmans.

1690. B. E., *Dict. Cant. Crew*, s.v. LIBKEN, c, a House to lye in; also a Lodging.

1725. *New Cant. Dict.*, s.v.

1785. GROSE, *Vulg. Tongue*, s.v.

1815. SCOTT, *Guy Mannering*, xliv. These are the fees I always charge a swell that must have his LIB-KEN to himself—thirty shillings a week for lodgings, and a guinea for garnish; half-a-guinea a week for a single bed.

1858. A. MAYHEW, *Paved with Gold*, III. Bk. ch. i. p. 256. 'We can sel-'em to the 'mot' (landlady) of the LIBB-KEN (lodging-house) for a good deal.'

1859. MATSELL, *Vocabulum*, s.v.

LICK, *subs.* (old).—1. A blow. Hence, HIS LICKS = a thrashing. For synonyms *see* WIPE.

d. 1701. DRYDEN [quoted by JOHNSON]. He gave me a LICK across the face.

1753. FOOTE, *Englishman in Paris*, i. I lent him a LICK in his lanthorn-jaws.

1755. JOHNSON, *Eng. Dict.*, s.v. LICK. A low word.

b. 1785. FORBES, *Dominie Deposed*, 28. He committed all these tricks, For which he well deserv'd his LICKS.

1785. GROSE, *Vulgar Tongue*, s.v. LICK. . . . I'll give you a good LICK o' the chops, I'll give you a good stroke, or blow on the face.

1786. BURNS, *Epistle to W. Simpson*, 'Postcript.' Frae les. to mair it gaed to sticks; Frae words and aiths to clours and nicks, And mony a fallow gat his LICKS, Wi' hearty crunt.

1821. PIERCE EGAN, *Tom and Jerry* [ed. 1890], p. 78. Oh I took him such a LICK of his mummer.

1840. BARHAM, *Ingoldsby Legends*, 'Ingoldsby Penance.' I gave him a LICK With a stick, And a kick.

1851-61. MAYHEW, *London Lab. and Lon. Poor*, i. 41. If a cove was to fetch me a LICK of the head, I'd give it him again.

2. (American).—A stroke; hence, an effort; BIG LICKS = hard work.

1847. PORTER, *Quarter Race*, p. 128. When he returned we were running a twenty-five knot LICK. *Ibid.* p. 104. He went up the opposite bank at the same LICK, and disappeared. *Ibid.* p. 94. I struck a LICK back to the log and looked over.

1848. JONES, *Sketches of Travel*, 189. He could not swim a LICK.

1851. HOOPER, *Widow Rugby's Husband*, etc. 62. I can't swim a LICK—how deep is it.

1863. BRYANT, *Comic Songs* [quoted by BARTLETT]. At length I went to mining, put in my BIGGEST LICKS, Went down upon the boulders just like a thousand bricks.

1873. *Americans at Home*, i. 276. Molly war the most enticin', gizzard-ticklin', heart-distressin' feline creatur that ever made a fellar get owdacious; and I seed Tom Seller cavertin' round her, and puttin' in the BIGGEST kind a LICKS in the way of courtin'.

1882. MISS BRADDON, *Mount Royal*, xiii. Then I coiled up, and made up my mind to stay in America, till I'd done some BIG LICKS in the sporting line.

1888. ROLF BOLDREWOOD, *Robbery Under Arms*, xii. It'll be a short life and a merry one, though, dad, if we go on BIG LICKS like this.

1892. MILLIKEN, *'Arry Ballads*, 36. Stage LICKS.

3. (common).—A drinking bout.

1886. *Daily Telegraph*, 3 March. More frequently the 'sowker' wound up his big LICK in an attack of delirium tremens.

Verb. (common).—1. *See* quot. 1573.

1573. HARMAN, *Caveat*, s.v. LYCKE, to beate.

1732. FIELDING, *Mock Doctor*, Sc. ii. Suppose I've a mind he should drub, Whose bones are they, sir, he's to LICK?

1733. FIELDING, *Don Quixote*, II. vii. Stand away, landlord, stand away—If I don't LICK him!

1749. FIELDING, *Tom Jones*, Bk. XV. v. 'I'll teach you to father-in-law me. I'll LICK thy jacket.'

1785. GROSE, *Vulg. Tongue*, s.v. LICK, to beat: also, to wash, or to paint slightly over. I'll give you a good LICK of the chops; Ill give you a good stroke or blow on the face. Jack tumbled into a cow-turd, and nastied his best clothes, for which his father stepped up and LICKED him neatly. I'll LICK you! the dovetail to which is, If you LICK me all over you won't miss my arse.

1786. BURNS, 'Second Epistle to Davie.' I'm tauld the Muse ye ha'e negleckit; An gif it's sae, ye sild be LICKET.

b. 1794. WOLCOT ('Peter Pindar'), 305. And oft. . . . the gentleman would LICK her.

1840. BARHAM, *Ingoldsby Legends* (*The Cenotaph*). Chasing him round, and attempting to LICK The ghost of poor Tray with the ghost of a stick.

1843. HALIBURTON ('Sam Slick'), *Sam Slick in England*, xxii. I would like to LICK him. . . . round the park . . . . to improve his wind, and teach him how to mend his pace.

1846. THACKERAY, *Jeames's Diary* (in *Punch*, x. p. 13). It was Mary Hann who summind the House and p't an end to my physty coughs with Fitz warren. I LICKED him and bare him no mallis.

1870. *Daily News*, 25 Nov. 'Leader.' 'We ought to believe,' says the Bishop of Carlisle 'that an Englishman can LICK a Frenchman, a German or any body else.'

1888. *Missouri Republican*, 2 Feb. I'm a terror from Philadelphia, and I can LICK any man in the world.

1892. *Lippincott's Mag.*, Oct., p. 500. Till Big-Foot Zekel, who used to laff At his genteel manners, quit his chaff, An' give out the statement, cold an' chill, He'd LICK the duffer as used Hank ill.

2. (colloquial).—1. To surpass; to vanquish; and (2) to puzzle or astound. Fr. *bouler*. [*Cf.* CREATION, HOLLOW, SHINE etc.].

1864. *Derby Day*, 39. 'As sure as the sun shines, Askpart 'll LICK 'em; if so be,' he added significantly, 'as there ain't no CROSS.' *Ibid.* 79. 'Don't you know Little un?' 'They LICK me,' answered the trainer.

1871. *Durham County Advertizer*, 10 Nov. 'By G—, chum, it LICKS me how the bottom itself did not tumble clean away from the ship.'

1888. ROLF BOLDREWOOD, *Robbery Under Arms*, xxxi. But in his own line you couldn't LICK him. *Ibid.* xxiv. It LICKED me to think it had been hid away all the time.

1891. N. GOULD, *Double Event*, 108. 'Lets hope you'll draw the winner, Ike,' said Kingdon. 'If you do, and Caloola gets LICKED, you can pull us through,' he laughed.

3. (old).—1. To sleek; (2) to TITTIVATE (*q.v.*); (3) to smooth over, with varnish, rouge, and so forth; to fashion.

1594. NASHE, *Have With You, etc.* [GROSART, iii. 99]. Spending a whole forenoone euerie daie in spunging and LICKING himselfe by the glasse.

1690. B. E., *Dict. Cant. Crew*, s.v. LICKT. Pictures new varnished, Houses new whitened, or Women's faces with a wash.

1785. GROSE, *Vulg. Tongue*, s.v. LICK.

1853. TAYLOR, *Life of Haydon*, p. 212. Modern cartoons with few exceptions are LICKED (smoothed) and polished intentionally.

4. (American).—To coax.

1859. MATSELL, *Vocabulum*, s.v.

TO LICK INTO SHAPE, *verb. phr.* (colloquial).—To fashion; to train. [From the popular idea that the bear's young are born shapeless and are licked into shape by the dam].

1663. BUTLER, *Hudibras*, i. 3, 1308. A bear's . . . most ugly and unnatural . . . until the dam has LICKED IT INTO SHAPE and form.

1870. *Figaro*, 6 July. My essay on 'The Busy Bee' Wants LICKING INTO FASHION.

TO LICK SPITTLE, *verb. phr.* (colloquial).—To fawn upon. Hence, LICKSPITTLE, *subs.* = a parasite or talebearer.

A LICK AND A PROMISE, *subs. phr.* (common).—A piece of slovenliness.

TO LICK THE EYE, *verb. phr.* (colloquial).—To be well-pleased.

A LICK AND A SMELL, *subs. phr.* (common).—A DOG'S PORTION (*q.v.*).

TO LICK THE TRENCHER, *verb. phr.* (old).—To play the parasite.

1608. WITHAL, *Dictionarie*, 263. A fellow that can LICKE his lordes or his ladies TRENCHER in one smooth tale or merrie lye, and picke their purses in another.

TO LICK ONE'S DISH, *verb. phr.* (old).—To drink.—RAY (1767).

LICK-BOX (-DISH, -FINGERS, -PAN, -POT, -SAUCE, or -TRENCHER), *subs.* (old).—*See* quot. 1598; a general epithet of abuse.

1571. GOLDING, *Calvin on Ps.* (To Reader), p. 9. Not onely LICKTRENCHERS but claw backs, which curry favour with great men by their false appeachings.

1575. *Gammer Gurton's Needle*, v. 2. Thou lier LICKDISH, didst not say the neele wold be gitton?

1594. *Lochrine*, iii. 3. You slop-sauce, LICKFINGERS, will you not hear?

1598. FLORIO, *Worlde of Wordes*, s.v. *Leccapiatti*, a LICKE-DISH, a scullion in a kitching, a slouen. *Ibid.* s.v. *Leccapignatte*, a LICK-POT, scullion. . . . a slouenly greasie fellow.

1602. DECKER, *Satiro-mastix*, in *Works* (1873), i. 234. Art hardy, noble Huon? art Magnanimious, LICKE-TRENCHER?

1631. CHETTLE, *Hoffman*, I. ii. Liar, liar, LICK-DISH.

1653. URQUHART, *Rabelais*, ii. ch. xxx. Agamemnon is a LICK-BOX.

1785. GROSE, *Vulg. Tongue*, s.v.

*b.*1794. WOLCOT ['P. Pindar'], *Ode upon Ode*, in *Works* (Dublin 1795), vol. i. p. 321. A cobbler, baker, chang'd to a musician, Butlers, LICK-TRENCHERS! my reader roars.

1853. LYTTON, *My Novel*, Bk. VI. ch. xxiii. He had a passion for independence, which, though pushed to excess, was not without grandeur. No LICK-PLATTER, no parasite, no toad-eater, no literary beggar, no hunter after patronage and subscriptions.

LICKER, *subs.* (common).—Anything monstrous, excessive, or unusual; A WHOPPER (*q.v.*); A THUMPER (*q.v.*); A SPANKER (*q.v.*).

LICKETY-SPLIT, *adv.* (American).—Headlong; violently; FULL CHISEL (*q.v.*).

1869. H. B. STOWE, *Old Town Folks*, 358. If they didn't whip up and go LICKITY-SPLIT down that 'ere hill.

LICKING, *subs.* (common).—A thrashing. For synonyms *see* TANNING.

1820. COMBE, *Syntax, Consolation*, C. III. In vulgar terms, he'd had his LICKING, Not with Ma'am's cuffs, but by her kicking.

1837. BARHAM, *Ingoldsby Legends*, II. 320. What still at your tricking? I see you won't rest until you've got a good LICKING.

1838. C. SELBY, *Hunting a Turtle*, I owes you a LICKING, so I'll pay you.

1871. *Figaro*, 22 April, 'Public School' etc. Various punishments that, in schoolboy language, are called 'woppings,' LICKINGS, and 'spankings,' may be received by the sufferers with a grim John Bullish resolve to endure the pain with a martyr's fortitude.

1882. F. ANSTEY, *Vice-Versâ*, v. If I hear of her favouring you more than any other fellows, I'll give you the very best LICKING you ever had in your life. So look out!

1889. *Polytechnic Magazine*, 24 Oct. 264. The Wanderers journeyed down to Tottenham, to play the above club, half anticipating a LICKING.

LICK-PENNY, *subs.* and *adj.* (old).—An extortioner.

*d.*1450. LYDGATE, *London* LICK-PENNY (Title).

1825. SCOTT, *St. Ronan's Well*, XXVIII. Law is a LICK-PENNY Mr. Tyrell—no counsellor like the pound in purse.

LICK-SPIGOT, *subs.* (old).—1. A tapster.

1599. NASHE, *Lenten Stuffe* [GROSART (1885), v. 300]. Let the cunningest LICKE-SPIGGOT swelt his heart out.

1703. WARD, *London Spy*, Pt. XV. p. 346. He that Salutes the old LICKSPIGGOT with other Title than that of Mr. Church-Warden, runs the hazard of paying double Taxes.

2. (venery).—A *fellatrix*; a COCK-SUCKER (*q.v.*).

LICK-SPITTLE, *subs.* (old).—A toady. Fr. *un lèche-bottes*. For synonyms *see* SNIDE. Also as *verb*.

1629. DAVENANT, *Albovine*, iii. LICK her SPITTLE From the ground. This disguised humility Is both the swift, and safest way to pride.

1729. SWIFT, *Libel on Delany and Carteret*. His (Pope's) heart too great, though fortune little, To LICK a rascal statesman's SPITTLE.

1855. THACKERAY, *Newcomes*, xvii. Averring that they were a parcel of sneaks, a set of LICKSPITTLES, and using epithets still more vulgar.

1856. C. BRONTE, *Professor*, v. You mean, whining LICKSPITTLE!

1857. THACKERAY, *Shabby Genteel Story*, iii. We call him tuft-hunter, LICKSPITTLE, sneak, unmanly.

1887. HANNAY, *Smollett*, p. 96. No surgeon was ever quite such a fool, coward, figurant LICK-SPITTLE as Mackshane.

LICK-TWAT, *subs.* (old).—A *fellator*; a CUNNILINGIST (*q.v.*).

1656. FLETCHER, *Martiall*, xi. 67. A LICK-TWAT and a fencer too.

LIE, *subs.* (common).—*See* WHOLE CLOTH and WHITE LIE.

Verb. (old).—To be in pawn. For synonyms *see* POP.

1609. *Man in the Moon* [quoted by NARES, s.v. LIE]. Sir, answered the begger, I have a good suite of apparell in the next village which LIETH not for above eightpence, if you will helpe me to that first I shall thinke myselve beholding unto you.

TO LIE LOW, *verb. phr.* (colloquial). — To conceal one's thought, or one's intentions. Also to keep to one's bed.

1847. PORTER, *Big Bear etc.*, p. 129. 'LAY LOW and keep dark,' says I.

1884. F. ANSTEY, *Giant Robe*, xxxviii. So you've very prudently been LYING LOW till you could get Master Mark off his guard, or till something turned up to help you.

1890. *Athenæum*, 22 Feb., 241. 2. It becomes clear in the first chapter, or at any rate in the second, that John Ardell's intended heir is only suppressed, that he is LYING LOW only in a metaphorical sense.

TO LIE OFF, *verb. phr.* (turf).—To make a waiting race. TO LIE OUT OF ONE'S GROUND = to 'lie off' too long, so as to be unable to recover lost ground.

TO LIE AROUND LOOSE, *verb. phr.* (American).—To loaf; to be out of employment.

TO LIE FLAT, *verb. phr.* (common).—*See* TO LIE LOW.

TO LIE LIKE TRUTH, *verb. phr.* (common).—To lie with verisimilitude and propriety.

1876. HINDLEY, *Cheap Jack*, 3. The fraternity. . . . are always supposed, and by common consent allowed, to LIE LIKE TRUTH.

TO LIE DOWN, *verb. phr.* (old).—To be brought to bed.

1582. LYLY, *Euphues and his England* [quoted by NARES]. I have brought into the world two children: of the first I was delivered before my friends thought me conceived; of the second, I went a whole yeere big, and yet when every one thought me ready to LIE DOWN, I did then quicken.

1720. *The Hartlepool Tragedy* [quoted by NARES]. I promis'd her fair, that I would take care Of her and her infant, and all things prepare At Hartlepool town, where she should LIE DOWN; Poor soul she believ'd me, as always she'd done.

TO LIE IN, *verb. phr.* (Royal Military Academy).—To keep one's room when supposed to be out on leave.

TO LIE IN STATE, *verb. phr.* (venery).—To lie between two women.

LIE WITH A LATCHET (or LIE MADE OF WHOLE CLOTH) (common).—An out-and-out falsehood. Also LIE LAID ON WITH A TROWEL.

1653. URQUHART, *Rabelais*, v. ch. 30. If you hearken to those who will tell you the contrary, you'll find yourselves damnably mistaken, for that's a LIE WITH A LATCHET; though 'twas Ælian, that long-bow man, that told you so, never believe him, for he lies as fast as a dog can trot.

1672. RAY, *Proverbial Phrases*, 200. That's a LIE WITH A LATCHET, All the dogs in the town cannot match it.

A LIE NAILED TO THE COUNTER, *subs. phr.* (common).—A detected falsehood or slander.

1888. *Texas Siftings*, 20 Oct. 'That LIE WAS NAILED a good while ago.' 'I know it,' chuckled the C. L., 'but it is easy enough to pull out the nail.'

1888. *Denver Republican*, 6 May. The La Junta *Tribune* has scooped all the papers in the State by NAILING THE first campaign LIE this season.

LIE-ABED, *subs.* (colloquial).—A sluggard.

1763. FOOTE, *Mayor of Garratt*, i. If you had got up time enough, you might have secured the stage, but you are a lazy LIE-A-BED.

1859. READE, *Love Me Little &c.*, x. David was none of your LIE-A-BEDS. He rose at five in summer, six in winter.

LIFE. *See* BET and DEATH.

LIFE-PRESERVER, *subs.* (American thieves').—1. A slung shot.—MATSELL (1859).

2. (venery).—The *penis*. For synonyms *see* CREAMSTICK and PRICK.

LIFER, *subs.* (thieves').—1. *See* quot. 1838. Also, a LAG (*q.v.*) for life. Fr. *un fagot à perte de vue; un bonnet vert à perpète.*

1838. DICKENS, *Oliver Twist*, xliii. 'If they don't get any fresh evidence, it'll only be a summary conviction, and we shall have him back again after six weeks or so; but, if they do, it's a case of lagging. They know what a clever lad he is; he'll be a LIFER. They'll make the Artful nothing less than a LIFER.' 'What do yer mean by lagging and a LIFER?' demanded Mr. Bolter . . . Being interpreted, Mr. Bolter would have been informed that they represented that combination of words, 'transportation for life.'

1885. *Ency. Brit.*, xix. 756. LIFERS cannot claim any remission, but their cases are brought forward at the end of twenty years.

1892. HUME NISBET, p. 266. 'He has money enough, I am sure, raking in the thousands as he does.' 'So he has, and so have many old LIFERS.'

2. (thieves').—Penal servitude for life.

LIFT, *subs.* (old).—1. A thief. Also LIFTER.

1592. GREENE, *Quip*, in *Works*, xi. 243. A receiver for LIFTS, and a dishonorable supporter of cut purses.

1600. *Sir John Oldcastle*, ii. 2. I'se poor Irishman; I'se a LEAFTER.

1602. SHAKSPEARE, *Troilus and Cressida*, i. 2. Is he so young a man and so old a LIFTER.

1608. DEKKER, *Belman of London*, in *Works* (GROSART), III. 146. He that first stealeth the parcell is called the LIFT.

1608. *Penniless Parliament*, in *Harl. Misc.* (ed. PARK), I. 182. To the great impoverishing of all nimmers, LIFTERS, and cut-purses.

1669. *Nicker Nicked*, in *Harl. Misc.* (PARK), ii. 108, s.v.

1781. G. PARKER, *View of Society*, II. 138, s.v.

1785. GROSE, *Vulg. Tongue*, s.v.

2. (thieves').—A theft; plunder; SWAG (*q.v.*). Also LIFTING.

1592. GREENE, *A Disputation* [GROSART (1881-6), x. 227]. We practise . . . . among merchaunt taylors. . . . getting much gains by LIFTING.

1852. JUDSON, *Mysteries etc. of New York*, ch. IV. When I hear of the boys making a large LIFT, I always envy them.

3. (colloquial).—Assistance in general: as, a LIFT in a vehicle; a LIFT in life. Also LIFTING.

1711. SWIFT, *Journal to Hella*, 5 April, Letter 20. I. . . . then took a coach and got a LIFT back for nothing.

1759. STERNE, *Tristram Shandy*, I. vii. Whose distress, and silence under it, call out the louder for a friendly LIFT.

1785. GROSE, *Vulg. Tongue*, s.v. LIFT. To give one a LIFT, to assist; a good hand at a dead LIFT, a good hand on an emergency.

1796. J. G. HOLMAN, *Abroad and at Home*, i. 1. *Young T.* Yes, Sir Simon, so they tell me; but for all that, don't d— trade; for I don't think as how you'd ha' been a gentleman and a knight if the money you got by the warehouse had not given you a bit of a LIFT.

1836. DICKENS, *Pickwick*, xxxv. p. 307. There was a constant succession of Christian names in smock frocks and white coats, who were invited to have a LIFT by the guard, and who knew every horse and hostler on the road and off it.

1856. J. HUGHES, *Tom Brown's School-Days*, Pt. I. v. You know my old aunt, Miss East, she lives somewhere down your way in Berkshire. She wrote to me that you were coming to-day, and asked me to give you a LIFT.

1873. *Notes and Queries*, 4 S. xii. 16 Aug. p. 128. As she was toiling along the high-road to Oxford, she was overtaken by a student of the University on horseback. He offered her a LIFT, which she accepted.

1888. ROLF BOLDREWOOD, *Robbery Under Arms*, xl. Grateful to Maddie for giving him this LIFT.

1892. S. WATSON, *Wops the Waif*, p. 9. Glad of the LIFT Tickle stood on the edge of a broad ledge at the side of the pavement.

4. (football).—A kick.

Verb. (old).—1. To steal; TO CONVEY (*q.v.*); specifically to steal cattle and horses.

1591. GREENE, *Second Part Conny-catching* [GROSART, vol. x. p. 118]. Some base roges that LIFT when they come into Alehouses quart potts, platters. . . . or any such paltrie trash, which commonly is called pilfering.

1600. JONSON, *Cynthia's Revels*, i. 1. One other peculiar virtue you possess in LIFTING, or leiger-du-main.

1817. SCOTT, *Rob. Roy*, xxvi. Live by stealing, reiving, LIFTING cows.

1852. JUDSON, *Mysteries etc. of New York*, iii. ch. 7, p. 47. Well, old gal, wot's the swag! Wot 'ave you LIFTED.

1863. *Fun*, iv. 34. Mosstroopers bold did horses LIFT at some fierce Baron's order.

1883. G. A. SALA, in *Ill. L. News*, Nov. 24, p. 499, col. 1. 'Paley's Natural Theology' is, from beginning to end, based on the lines of the Dutchman, whose very language has, in many instances, been coolly LIFTED by the English Church dignitary.

1890. *Pall Mall Gazette*, 19 April, p. 6, col. 1. The pushing and struggling of all this miscellaneous mass at bushy parts of the road, where it got mixed up with the eighty head of cattle which Mr. Stanley had LIFTED.

1892. KIPLING, *Barrack Room Ballads*, 'The Lament of The Border Cattle Thief.' And heaved me into the central jail For LIFTING of the kine.

2. (printers').—To transfer.

1891. *Answers*, 28 March. One of the first journalistic duties I ever had to perform was that of replying to the 'Correspondents' on a new weekly newspaper attached to a daily, from which nearly all the matter was LIFTED.

3. (American thieves').—*See* quot.

1859. MATSELL, *Vocabulum*, s.v. LIFT. LIFT the poor cove, he is almost lenten, help the poor fellow, he is almost starved.

4. (sporting).—To break (in a walking race) into an unfair pace.

TO LIFT ONE'S HAND (ELBOW, LITTLE FINGER, etc.), *verb. phr.* (common).—To drink. Also *see* LEG, *ante.* For synonyms *see* DRINKS.—GROSE (1823).

TO LIFT HAIR, *verb. phr.* (American).—To scalp.

1848. RUXTON, *Life in the Far West*, 23. LIFT as much HAIR as they could.

1868. *Congressional Report*, 17 Aug. The Arrapahoes were not after stealing cattle but after LIFTING HAIR.

On THE LIFT, *adv. phr.* (American).—On the move; ready to depart.

LIFTER, *subs.*(old).—1. A thief. *See* LIFT, *subs.*, sense 1.

2. in pl. (old).—A crutch.

1690. B. E., *Dict. Cant. Crew*, s.v.

1785. GROSE, *Vulg. Tongue*, s.v.

1859. MATSELL, *Vocabulum*, s.v.

LIFT-LEG, *subs.* (old).—Strong ale; STINGO (*q.v.*).

LIG, *subs.* (old).—1. A bed.—*New Cant. Dict.* (1725); GROSE (1785). (2) A bedstead.—MATSELL (1859). *See* LIB.

2. (provincial).—A lie.

LIGBY, *subs.* (old).—A bedfellow: specifically a concubine. *Cf.* LUDBY and LOTEBY.

1632. BROME, *Northern Lass. Con.* He is wed already, sir. Another wife would gar him be put down at gallows; and I would not be she for all the worldly good that e're I saw with both mine eyen. And o' my conscience I'll be none of his LIGBY, for twise so mickle.

1684. LACY, *Sauny the Scot*, ii. 1. He means to make one of your lasses his wench—that is, his love and his LIGBY.

LIGHT, *subs.* (common).—1. Credit. TO GET A LIGHT = to get credit; TO HAVE ONE'S LIGHT PUT OUT = to exhaust one's credit; to go STONY (*q.v.*).

2. (colloquial).—A model; an example: generally SHINING LIGHT.

1871. *Figaro*, 15 April. 'A Lay of a Chelsea Bus.' And still the LIGHT seemed ill at ease, And knocked his fists upon his knees. *Ibid.* 'Another' was a SHINING LIGHT; His tie was limp, and once was white.

3. *in. pl.* (pugilistic).—The eyes. Also DAYLIGHTS (*q.v.*) and TOP-LIGHTS (*q.v.*).

1820. J. H. REYNOLDS ('P. Corcoran'), *The Fancy*, 72. She knew a smart blow, from a handsome giver Could darken LIGHTS.

4. *in pl.* (common).—A fool. For synonyms *see* BUFFLE and CABBAGE-HEAD.

Adj. (old).—Wanton. Hence, LIGHT-GIVEN (BURTON, *Anat.*) = lewd of habit; LIGHT-HEELED (*q.v.*); LIGHT-O'-LOVE (*q.v.*); LIGHT-SKIRTS, (*q.v.*); and so forth.

1538. ELYOT, *Dictionary*, s.v. *Meretrix*, An harlot, a brothel, an hoore, a strompet, a LIGHT housewyfe.

1567. EDWARDS, *Damon & Pithias* [DODSLEY, *Old Plays* (1874), iv. 50]. Believe her not, she is a LIGHT goddess; she can laugh and low'r.

1594. BARNFIELD, *Hellen's Rape or a* LIGHT *Lanthorne for* LIGHT *Ladies* (ed. ARBER), p. 38, in title.

1594. NASHE, *Dido, Queen of Carthage* [GROSART (1885), VI. 33]. I feare me, Dido hath been counted LIGHT, In being too familiar with Iarbas.

1598. SHAKSPEARE, *Second Henry IV*, i. 1. He hath the horn of abundance, and the LIGHTNESS of his wife shines through it. *Idem*, i. 2. Not so, my lord; your ill angel is LIGHT.

1598. FLORIO, *Worlde of Wordes*, s.v. *Femina red monate*, A bad LIGHT woman.

1599. PORTER, *Two Angry Women* [DODSLEY, *Old Plays*, vii. 367]. Hark ye, maid, if [a] maid, are ye so LIGHT, That you can see to wander in the night?

1621. BURTON, *Anatomy* (ed. 1893), i. 479. I write not this to patronize any wanton idle flirt, lascivious or LIGHT

housewives, which are too forward many times.

1669. DAVENANT, *Man's the Master*, iv. i. I'm a very LIGHT hus-wife.

1690. B. E., *Dict. Cant. Crew*, s.v.

1694. CROWNE, *Married Beau*, i. 1. Here's my wife! see! she is no LIGHT piece.

1855. BROWNING, *Men and Women*, Vol. i. A 'LIGHT Woman' (Title).

TO PUT OUT ONE'S LIGHT, *verb. phr.* (common).—To kill. Also *see subs.*, sense 1.

1602. SHAKSPEARE, *Othello*, v. 2. Yet she must die, else she'll betray more men. Put out the light, and then—PUT OUT THE LIGHT?

1619. BEAUMONT and FLETCHER, *Maid's Tragedy*, iv. 1. *Evad.* You will not murder me? *Mel.* No; 'tis a justice, and a noble one, To PUT THE LIGHT OUT of such base offenders.

1868. *Temple Bar*, xxiv. 539. Hocussing is putting a chap to sleep with chloroform, and bellowing is PUTTING HIS LIGHT OUT.

1884. *Graphic*, 27 Sept., p. 315, col. 2. So now, the malefactor does not murder, he 'pops a man off', or PUTS HIS LIGHT OUT.

1891. *Morning Advertizer*, 3 April. The prisoners called him a 'blackleg,' and a O'Connor said if he went to work again he would PUT HIS LIGHT OUT.

1891. *Star*, 10 Feb., p. 3, col. 6. He had been heard to say, 'I should like to PUT HER LIGHT OUT,' and had fired at her bed-room window.

TO HOLD A LIGHT (or CANDLE) TO THE DEVIL. *See* DEVIL.

TO LIGHT THE LUMPER. *See* LUMPER.

TO LIGHT OUT, *verb. phr.* (American).—*See* quot. 1882.

1882. *Notes and Queries*, 6 S. v. 65. 'Words & Phrases in Use in the Far West.' LIGHT OUT, same as 'Skin out' . . . To leave secretly and hastily as when pursued by an enemy.

1884. M. TWAIN, *Huckleberry Finn*, ch. i. p. 2. So when I couldn't stand it no longer, I LIT OUT.

1890. GUNTER, *Miss Nobody*, p. 34. LIGHT OUT as if hell were behind you.

1890. *Scribner's Magazine*, Feb., p. 493. I want to jes turn in And take and LIGHT right OUT o' here and get back West ag'in.

LIGHT-BLUE, *subs.* (old).—Gin. For synonyms *see* DRINKS and SATIN.

1820. REYNOLDS ('Peter Corcoran'), *The Fancy*. . . Never again I'll cultivate LIGHT-BLUE or brown inebriety.

1822. *Randall's Scrapbook* . . . My brain-box is airy with Deady's LIGHT-BLUE.

1823. GROSE, *Vulg. Tongue* (3rd ed.), s.v.

LIGHT-BOB, *subs.* (military).—1. A light infantry soldier. For synonyms *see* MUD-CRUSHER.

1785. GROSE, *Vulg. Tongue*, s.v.

1846. THACKERAY, *Vanity Fair*, xxiv. Mr. Stubble, as may be supposed from his size and slenderness, was of the LIGHT-BOBS.

1854. WHYTE MELVILLE, *General Bounce*, xi. 'A LIGHT-BOB on each side, with his arms sloped.'

1870. *Daily Telegraph*, 27 Sept. 'On the Superior Education of the German Soldier.' It was true that the German LIGHT-BOB was an assistant judge in the Berlin Court.

2. *in pl.* (military).—The Forty-third Foot.

LIGHTER. *See* LUMP.

LIGHT-FANTASTIC, *subs.* (common).—Dancing; *e.g.*, 'To work THE LIGHT FANTASTIC'. [*Cf.* MILTON, *l'Allegro:* Come and trip it as you go On the LIGHT FANTASTIC TOE]. Fr. *la sauterie.*

1843. STIRLING COYNE, *Binks the Bagman*, i. 1. Then you're fond of sporting on THE LIGHT FANTASTIC.

1848. RUXTON, *Life In The Far West*, 47. Sport a figure on THE LIGHT FANTASTIC TOE.

1855. STRANG, *Glasgow and its Clubs*, 150. In evening dress, muslins, which were then expensive, were much patronised by those who tripped on the LIGHT FANTASTIC TOE.

1892. GUNTER, *Miss Dividends*, ix. 'You dance very nicely;' she murmurs. 'Yes, for a man who has not tripped THE LIGHT FANTASTIC for years.'

LIGHT-FEEDER, *subs.* (thieves').—A silver spoon.

LIGHT-FINGERED, *adj.* (colloquial).—Dextrous in stealing; given to thieving.

1560. *Nice Wanton* [DODSLEY, *Old Plays* (1874), ii. 167]. I must say more, Your son is suspect LIGHT-FINGERED to be.

1592. GREENE, *Defence of Conny-catching* [GROSART (1881-6), xi. 97]. A . . . . Taylor, famous for his art, but noted for his filchinge, which although he was LIGHT-FINGERD, yet. . . . he was much sought.

1607-9. DAMPIER, *Voyages*, ii. 1. 14. The Tonguinese being very LIGHT-FINGERED.

1630. THOS. ADAMS, *Workes*, 170. 'The Fatal Banket! Is any tradesman LIGHT-FINGERED, and lighter conscienced? Here [Stolen waters are sweet] is a whole feast of Fraudes, a table furnished with Trickes, conveyances, glossings, perjuries, cheatinges.

1690. B. E., *Dict. Cant. Crew*, s.v.

1785. GROSE, *Vulg. Tongue*, s.v. LIGHT-FINGERED, thievish, apt to pilfer.

*c.*1868-9. W. S. GILBERT, *Bohemian Girl.* And yet I've heard you called LIGHT-FINGERED gentry.

LIGHT-FRIGATE, *subs.* (old).—A woman of loose morals.—B.E.(1690); *New Cant. Dict.* (1725).

LIGHT-HEELED, *adj.* (old).—1. Wanton.

*c.*1633. *Lady Alimony*, ii. 6. Lose a LIGHT-HEELED trull—That in my judgment's nothing.

1640. *The Bride*, Sig G. She is sure a LIGHT-HEELD wench.

1661. DAVENPORT, *City Nightcap*, ii. Who have heavier heads than those whose wives have LIGHT HEELS.

1785. GROSE, *Vulg. Tongue*, s.v. LIGHT-HEELED . . . a LIGHT-HEELED wench, one who is apt by the flying up of her heels, to fall flat on her back—a willing wench.

2. (old).—*See* quot.

1670. RAY, *Proverbs* [BOHN (1893), 47]. A LIGHT-HEELED mother maketh a heavy-heeled daughter. Because she doth all her work herself, and her daughter meantime sitting idle, contracts a habit of sloth. *Mère piteuse fait sa fille rogneuse* = a tender mother breeds a scabby daughter.

LIGHT-HEELS. *See* LIGHT-SKIRTS.

LIGHT-HOUSE, *subs.* (old).—A red-nosed man.—GROSE (1823). [*Cf.* SHAKSPEARE, *I Henry IV*, iii. 3. 'Thou art our Admiral, thou bearest the lantern in the poop,' etc.].

LIGHT-INFANTRY, *subs.* (common).—Fleas; F SHARPS (*q.v.*). *Cf.* HEAVY DRAGOONS. Fr. *la sauterelle* and *la sauteuse.*

LIGHTMANS, *subs.* (Old Cant).—*See* quots. *Cf.* DARKMANS = night. Fr. *le matois;* It. *specchio.*

1573. HARMAN, *Caveat* (1814), 65. The LIGHTMANS, the day.

1609. DEKKER, *Lanthorne and Candlelight.* If we. . . . dup but the gigger of a country-cove's ken, from thence at the chats we trine in the LIGHTMANS.

1610. ROWLANDS, *Martin Markall*, p. 39 (H. Club's Repr. 1874). LIGHTMANS, the day.

1611. MIDDLETON and DEKKER, *Roaring Girle*, v. 1. Oh, I would lib all the LIGHTMANS.

1663. R. HEAD, *English Rogue*, Pt. I. v. 50 (1874). LIGHTMANS, Morning or Day.

1690. B. E., *Dict. Cant. Crew*, s.v.

1724. E. Coles, *Eng. Dict.* Lightmans, (break of) day.

1785. Grose, *Vulg. Tongue*, s.v.

1859. Matsell, *Vocabulum*, s.v.

Lightness, *subs.* (old).—Wantonness: *see* Light, *adj.*

1614. Cook, *City Gallant* [Dodsley, *Old Plays* (1874), xi. 254]. Kindness is termed lightness in our sex.

Lightning, *subs.*(old).—Gin. Flash of lightning (or clap of thunder) = a glass of gin. For synonyms *see* Drinks and Satin.

1789. Geo. Parker, *Life's Painter*, 154. Noggin of lightning. A quartern of gin.

1823. Grose, *Vulg. Tongue* (3rd ed.), s.v.

1838. T. E. Wilks, *John Smith*, i. 2. Sometimes we have a little bet as well, but nothing to speak of—some heavy or a flash of lightning.

1851. Mayhew, *Lond. Lab.*, i. 160. He would. . . . express his desire to add. . . . the stimulant of a flash of lightning.

Light-o'-love, *subs.* (colloquial).—A wanton.

1589. Nashe, *Anat. of Absurditie*, in *Wks.* (Grosart), i. 14. As there was a loyall *Lucretia*, so there was a light a love *Lais*.

1592. Greene, *Quip for Up. Courtiers*, Bz. 6. Next them grew the dissembling daisie, to warn such light o' love wenches, not to trust every faire promise that such amorous bachelors make them.

1599. Porter, *Two Angry Women* [Dodsley, *Old Plays* (1874), vii. 295]. Foul strumpet, light-a-love, short-heels.

1605. *London Prodigal*, ii. i. I hate a light o' love, as I hate death.

1620. Beaumont and Fletcher, *Chances*, i. 4. Sure he has encountered Some light o' love or other, and there means To play at in and in for this night.

1652. Fletcher, *Wild-Goose Chase*, iv. i. One of your London light o' loves, a right one! Came over in these pumps, and half a petticoat.

1840. Mark Lemon, *Lost And Won*, i. 2. Now though Mistress Leyton never oversteps the bounds of modesty, yet it does look so much like what they would do were she a light of love.

1874. Ouida, *Two Wooden Shoes*, xxiii. You were spared a bad thing, lad; the child was that grand painter's light-o'-love, that is plain to see.

Light-skirts, *subs.*(old).—A strumpet. For synonyms *see* Barrack-hack and Tart. Also Light-heels.

1602. Cooke, *How[to] Choose a Good Wife etc.* [Dodsley, *Old Plays* (1874), ix. 53]. I'll tell my mistress as soon as I come home That mistress light-heels comes to dinner tomorrow.

1606. *Return from Parnassus* [Dodsley, *Old Plays* (1874), ix. 118]. Hath not Shore's wife, although a light-skirts she, Giv'n him a chaste, long-lasting memory? *Ibid.* 127. You light-skirt stars. . . . By gloomy light perk out your doubtful heads.

1612. *Passenger of Benvenuto* [quoted by Nares]. *F.* The purse serves for an art; but if I should briefly tell thee, what punkish art derived from her progenitors this light-skirts used towards me, thou wouldest laugh.

c.1633. *Lady Alimony*, ii. 6. That light-skirt, with impetuous heat, Sometimes pursu'd me.

1767. Ray, *Proverbs* [Bohn (1893), 64]. A whore, a light-skirts.

1834. Taylor, *Ph. van Art.*, pt. II. iii. 3. Oh, she's a light skirts! yea, and at this present A little, as you see, concern'd with liquor.

Light-troops, *subs.* (old).—Lice.

1823. Grose, *Vulgar Tongue* (3rd ed.), s.v. The light-troops are in full march.

Light-weight, *adj.* (American).—1. Of little importance; weak.

2. (pugilists').—Under twelve stone.—Grose (1823).

Light-wet, *subs.* (old).—Gin. For synonyms *see* Drinks and Satin.

1822. *Randall's Scrap-book.* Pure and clear rose the beads on the glass of light-wet.

Like. This word enters into numerous combinations indicating energetic, rapid, or intense action, motion, and thought. The chief are:—

Like (or as) anything; a basket of chips; beans; billy-ho; a bird; blazes; boots, or old boots; bricks, or a thousand, or a cart-load, of bricks; a dog in a fair; fun; a house on fire; hell; hot cake; mad; one o'clock; shit to a shovel; a shot; a streak; thunder; the very devil; a tom-tit on a horse-turd; winkey or winky. (Fr. *comme la bourrique à Robespierre*).

1542. Udall, *Erasmus Apoph.*, p. 32. The young maiden, where the lokers on quaked and trembled for feare, daunced without any feare at all emong sweardes and kniues, beyng as sharpe as anythyng.

1690. *The Pagan Prince* [quoted by Nares]. So that the Belgians, hearing what a clutter the Albionians made of their victory which they had got but by one spot of a die, they fell a making a bonfires and fire-works like mad, and rejoicing and triumphing for the great victory.

1690. Crowne, *English Friar*, iii. As soon as ever the stop of coaches is over, my lady will drive like mad.

*d.*1703. Pepys, *Diary*, ii. 6. A mad coachman that drove like mad.

*d.*1704. Lestrange [*Century*]. A bear, enraged at the stinging of a bee, ran like mad into the bee-garden, and overturned all the hives.

1716. Croker, *Suff. Cor.*, i. 8. [Tell] dear Molly I like her like anything.

1740. Richardson, *Pamela*, ii. 57. O my dear father and mother, I fear your girl will grow as proud as anything.

1819. Moore, *Tom Crib*, 23. But a pelt in the smeller . . . set it going like fun. *Ibid.* 25. The whole populace flashed the white grin like a basket of chips.

1835. Dickens, *Sketches*, 139. Bump they cums agin the post, and out flies the fare like bricks.

1836. M. Scott, *Tom Cringle's Log*, 2. The breeze struck us, and it came on to blow like thunder. *Ibid.* We were bowling along right before it, rolling like the very devil.

1837. Barham, *I. L.* (*Jackdaw of Rheims*). That little Jackdaw kept hopping about, Here and there, Like a dog in a fair, Over comfits and cakes, And dishes and plates. (*Ibid. Witches' Frolic*). Old goody Jones All skin and bones, Follows like winking. *Ibid.* (*Misadv. at Margate*). The tear-drop in his little eye again began to spring, His bosom throbb'd with agony, he cried like anything. *Ibid.* (*Ingoldsby Penance*). For the Friar to his skirts closely sticks, 'Running after him,'—so said the Abbot,—like bricks!

1845. B. Disraeli, *Sybil or The Two Nations*, 330. Syllabubs like blazes, and snapdragon as makes the flunkeys quite pale.

1847. Robb, *Squatter Life*, 37. He lit upon the upper town and its member like a thousand of brick!

1850. Smedley, *Frank Fairlegh*, 204. Tapping his claret for him, as the pugilists call it, and sending him down like a shot.

1851. Mayhew, *London Labour and London Poor*, iii. p. 159. She liked this very much, in fact so much, that the other little ones used to cry like blazes because I wouldn't let them have a turn at them [the stilts]. *Ibid.* i. 29. He trotted on like one o'clock.

*d.*1859. De Quincey, *Spanish Nun*, sect. 24. The horse was so maddened by the wound, and the road so steep, that he went like blazes.

1860. *New Orleans Picayune*, 27 April (Police Report). When it came to the breakdown, Your Honor, he kicked up a row like a drove of contrary mules, and when we wanted to

turn him out, he fell upon us like a thousand of bricks, and threatened to make minced meat of the police and every one of us.

1864. *Western World*, 5 March. 'When Mr. Nye had finished, Mr. Stewart rose, and with his irresistible logic and impressive language came down upon him like a thousand of bricks, till he was utterly crushed and demolished.'

1868. Miss Braddon, *Sir Jasper*, xxvii. p. 282. I'll stick to you like old boots.

1869. W. S. Gilbert, *Bab Ballads*, 'Captain Reece.' If ever they were dull or sad, The Captain danced to them like mad.

1873. Carroll, *Through a Looking Glass*, iv. 73. They wept like anything to see such quantities of sand.

1874. *Saturday Review*, Jan., 55. An Oxford man, nay even a Balliol man. . . . introduced in the story a pleasing change by such a phrase as jawing away like old boots.

1883. *Graphic*, 17 March, 287, i. Nevertheless, this solid fare disappeared, with the beer, like winking.

1888. *Puck's Library*, 15. 'Will go like hot cakes.' *Book Seller* (to Clerk). 'Haven't we an overstock of 'Jack, the Giant Killer,' on hand, James?' *Clerk.* 'Yes, sir.' *Book Seller.* 'Well, take 'm up to the Polo Grounds this afternoon; they'll sell fast enough there.'

1890. Gunter, *Miss Nobody*, 153. 'Second National Bank like a streak,' screams the new-made lord to the driver.

1891. Mrs. Lovett-Cameron, in *Lippincott*, Aug., p. 142. 'He's as fit as a fiddle, miss,' said Griggs, admiringly, as Susan kissed her old friend's satin coat with enthusiasm, 'and he'll carry you like a bird to-morrow.'

1892. Milliken, *'Arry Ballads*, 57. I'd be there, like a shot. *Ibid.* 33. I jest blew away like old boots.

Like one o'clock half struck, *phr.* (common).—Hesitatingly.

1876. Hindley, *Adventures of a Cheap Jack*, p. 19. He stands like one o'clock half-struck.

Like a whale. *See* Whale.

Like Christmas beef. *See* Beef.

Like a birch-broom in a fit. *See* Birch-broom.

I like that! *phr.* (common).—A derisive answer to a questionable statement: *e.g.* 'I am a capital pedestrian.' 'I like that!'

You talk like a halfpenny book (or penny book), *adv. phr.* (common).—Said in derision of a fluent or affected speaker.

Likeness, *subs.* (thieves').—*See* quot.

1823. Grose, *Vulg. Tongue* (3rd ed.), s.v. likeness, a phrase used by thieves when the officers. . . . are examining their countenances; as, 'the traps are taking our likeness.'

Lil (or **Lill**), *subs.* (common).—A book; a document of any kind; a five pound note. In America a dollar. [Gypsy: *cf.* Borrow, *Romano-lavo-lil* = Gypsy Word Bk.]. *See* quots.

1821. D. Haggart, *Life's Glossary*, 172. Lil, a pocket-book.

1851. G. Borrow, *Lavengro*, xvii. p. 63 (1888). The more shame for you—a snake-fellow—a horse witch—and a lil reader—yet you can't shift for yourself.

1859. Matsell, *Vocabulum*, s.v. Lil, a pocket-book. Lill, a bad bill.

Lilliputian, *subs.* (colloquial).—A dwarf.

1823. Grose, *Vulg. Tongue* (3rd ed.), s.v.

Lily-Benjamin, *subs.* (common).—A white great coat. *See* Benjamin.

Lily-liver, *subs.* (common).—A coward.

1863. Thackeray, *Roundabout Papers*, xii. When people were yet afraid

of me, and were taken in by my swagger, I always knew that I was a lily-liver, and expected that I should be found out some day.

Lily-livered, *adj.* (old).—cowardly; dastardly.

1605-6. Shakspeare, *King Lear*, ii. 2. *Osw.* What dost thou know me for? *Kent.* A knave; a rascal; a lily-livered, action-taking knave.

1857. A. Trollope, *Barchester Towers*, xiv. You will not be so lily-livered as to fall into this trap which he has baited for you.

Lily of St. Clements. *See* St. Clements.

Lily-shallow, *subs.* (common).—A white driving hat.—Grose (1823).

Lilywhite, *subs.* (old).—1. A negro; a chimney-sweep.

1690. B. E., *Dict. Cant. Crew*, s.v.

1785. Grose, *Vulg. Tongue*, s.v. Lilly white, a chimney sweep.

1819. Moore, *Tom Crib*, 45. Show the lilywhites fair play.

2. *in pl.* (military).—The Seventeenth Foot [from its facings]. Also, Bengal Tigers (*q.v.*). Also, the Fifty-ninth Foot.

Lillywhite groat, *subs.* (common).—A shilling. For synonyms *see* Bob.

1894. *Daily Bourse*, 13 Sept., p. i. For instance, a 'man,' starting with 6s. a week, and, after six years, finding himself in possession of weekly wages amounting to 19s., say nineteen shillings, can assuredly have no legitimate cause for complaint. . . . Fancy nineteen 'Lillywhite groat' a week, and not to be satisfied!

Limb, *subs.* (old).—1. A mischievous child; an imp. Also (in depreciation to older persons) Limb of Satan &c.

1589. Nashe, *Martin's Month's Mind* [Grosart (1883-4), i. 155]. He that is termed Satan. . . . and a very limm of him.

1625. Jonson, *Staple of News*, iii. 2. She had it from a limb o' the school, she says, a little limb of nine year old.

1706. R. Estcourt, *Fair Example*, iii. 2. p. 34. Blood and thunder! I'll broil ye, you limb of Satan.

1815. Scott, *Guy Mannering*, xxxiv. Meg Merrilies, the old devil's limb of a gipsy witch.

1862. Calverley, *Verses & Translations*, p. 7. He was what nurses call a limb.

1864. *Derby Day*, p. 68. You limb of brimstone; just let me get hold of you.

1880. G. R. Sims, *Ballads of Babylon (Little Jim)*. Our little Jim Was such a limb His mother scarce could manage him.

1892. Anstey, *Model Music Hall Songs*, p. 94. Now I've grown into an awful young limb.

2. (American colloquial).—A leg.

1720. Ramsay, *The Scribbler's Lashed*, p. 8. If Nellie's hoop be twice as wide As her two pretty limbs can stride.

1857. Rev. A. C. Geikie, *Canadian Journal*, Sept. If we know anything of English conversation or letters, we speedily find out, even if stone blind, that British men and women have arms and legs, But in Canada. . . . he would learn that both sexes have limbs of some sort. . . . but he could not tell whether their limbs were used to stand on or hold by.

1858. *Pittsburg Chronicle*, June. The poor brute [a horse] fell . . . . fracturing his limb.

1861. O. W. Holmes, *Elsie Venner*, vii. 'A bit of the wing, Rovy, or of—the under limb?' The first laugh broke out at this.

1867. Upham, *Witchcraft*, ii. 248. One of her lower limbs was fractured in the attempt to rescue her from the prison walls.

1870. R. G. White, *Words & their Uses*, s.v. Limb for leg. Perhaps these persons think that it is indelicate for women to have legs.

1872. DE VERE, *Americanisms.* LIMB, instead of LEG, one of the ludicrous evidences of the false prudishness prevailing in certain classes of American society.

3. in pl. (common).—A gawk. Also DUKE or DUCHESS OF LIMBS.

1785. GROSE, *Vulg. Tongue*, s.v. LIMBS.

1859. MATSELL, *Vocabulum*, s.v.

Verb. (common).—To cheat.

1878. HATTON, *Cruel London*, Bk. II. ch. v. 'They have had me, bless you,' said Bragford, 'the men who have LIMBED you and cursed the hand that fed them.'

LIMB OF THE LAW, *subs. phr.* (old).—A lawyer or lawyer's clerk. Also LIMB.

1762. SMOLLETT, *Sir L. Greaves*, I. ii. Then fixing his eyes upon Ferret, he proceeded—'An't you a LIMB OF THE LAW, friend?'

1770. FOOTE, *Lame Lover*, iii. *Sir Luke.* Well said, my young LIMB OF THE LAW.

1785. GROSE, *Vulg. Tongue*, s.v.

1786-1805. HORNE TOOKE, *Div. of Purley*, ii. ch. 4. LIMB is from the A.S. verb *Limpian*, pertinere. . . . 'Limb of the Body, LIMB OF THE LAW,' etc.

1818-24. EGAN, *Boxiana*, iii. 210. Jack and his pal, a LIMB OF THE LAW, were screwed up the whole of the darkey in the compter.

1836. DICKENS, *Pickwick*, xliii. p. 377. 'Now, Sammy, I know a gen'l'm'n here, as'll do the rest o' the bisness for us, in no time—a LIMB O' THE LAW, Sammy, as has got brains like the frogs, dispersed all over his body . . . . a friend of the Lord Chancellorship's, Sammy.'

1889. *Cassell's Saturday Journal*, 9 Feb., p. 471. That good-looking LIMB OF THE LAW who went wild over you.

TO MINGLE LIMBS, *verb. phr.* (old).—To copulate.

1629. DAVENANT, *Albovine*, iv. I'st fit I proffer her TO MINGLE LIMBS?

LIMBO, *subs.* (old).—1. A prison; a place of confinement. [From *limbus patrum* = purgatory]. *See* CAGE and SLOWED.

1553. LINDSAY, *The Dreme* [LAING (1879), i. 14. 360]. That was the LYMBE in the quhilk did remaine.

1592. GREENE, *Quip*, in *Works*, xi. 253. That reprobate is the vserers executioner, to bring such gentlemen to LIMBO, as he hath ouerthrowne with his base brocage.

1653. BROME, *Damoiselle*, iii. 1. Had I raked LIMBO as I did the compter.

1664. ETHEREGE, *Comical Revenge*, v. 4, in *Wks.* (1704), 78. *Sir Fred.* No consideration; dispatch, or to LIMBO. *Whead.* Was there ever such a dilemma? I shall rot in prison.

1785. GROSE, *Vulg. Tongue*, s.v. LIMBO.

1796. J. G. HOLMAN, *Abroad & at Home*, ii. 3. *Har.* Captain O'Neill, my friend, Jack Flourish, is a very whimsical fellow. If he had been out of LIMBO, you would have seen him earlier.

1823. MONCRIEFF, *Tom & Jerry*, iii. 5. Never desert an old pal in LIMBO, Bob.

1836. MARRYAT, *Japhet*, lxviii. Who would soon have found out that I had two legs, and have put me into LIMBO as an impostor.

1877. *Five Years' Penal Servitude*, iv. 263. It was a heartless, cruel robbery on his part, and had brought ill-luck on him ever since. Before that occurred he had never been in LIMBO.

2. (old).—A pawnshop; UNCLE'S (*q.v.*): IN LIMBO = in pawn.

1693. CONGREVE, *Old Batchelor*, ii. 1. I let him have all my ready money, to redeem his great sword from LIMBO.

1754. D. MARTIN, *Eng. Dict.*, 2nd ed. s.v.

3. (venery).—The female *pudendum.* For synonyms *see* MONOSYLLABLE.

LIMBURGER. *See* CHEESE.

LIME-BASKET. TO BE DRY AS A LIME-BASKET, *verb. phr.* (common).—To be very dry; TO SPIT SIXPENCES (*q.v.*). Also to have HOT COPPERS (*q.v.*).

1838. DICKENS, *Oliver Twist.* He wished he might be basted if he warn't AS DRY AS A LIMEBASKET.

1892. HUME NISBET, *Bushranger's Sweetheart*, 136. 'That infernal swanky has left me AS DRY AS A LIME KILN,' cried out my companion.

LIME-JUICE, *subs.* (Australian). *See* quots.

1886. E. WAKEFIELD, in *Nineteenth Century*, August, 173. In these Colonies [Australia], where pretty nearly every one has made several sea voyages, that subject is strictly tabooed in all rational society. To dilate upon it is to betray a 'new chum'—what they call in Australia a LIME JUICE.

1887. *All the Year Round*, 30 July, 66. A young man newly arrived in the Colonies from the old country is styled a new Chum or a LIME-JUICE.

LIMEJUICER, *subs.* (American nautical).—A British ship or sailor. [In allusion to the lime-juice served out as an anti-scorbutic].

1881. *International Rev.*, xi. 525. You LIMEJUICERS have found that Richmond is taken.

1884. *Pall Mall Gazette*, 26 Aug. They would not go on a LIMEJUICER, they said, for anything.

LIMETWIG, *subs.* (old).—1. A snare; a trick. Hence (2) any means of swindling. Also as *adj.*

1592. NASHE, *Pierce Penilesse* [GROSART (1885), ii. 24]. Thus walks he vp and downe. . . . and. . . . busies himselfe in setting siluer LIME TWIGS to entangle young gentlemen.

1592. GREENE, *Black Books Messenger* [GROSART (1881-6), xi. 7]. The cards to be called . . . the LIME TWIGS.

1606. *Return from Parnassus* [DODSLEY, *Old Plays* (1874), ix. 125]. Let us run through all the lewd forms of LIME-TWIG, purloining villanies.

1670. RAY, *Proverbs* [BOHN (1893), 160]. His fingers are LIMETWIGS, spoken of a thievish person.

LIMLIFTER, *subs.* (old).—A LANDLUBBER (*q.v.*).

1598. FLORIO, *A Worlde of Wordes*, *Levantino*, a lifter, a shifter, a LIMLIFTER, a pilferer, etc. *Ibid. Cefalù*, a scornefull nickname, as we say a LIMLIFTER.

LIMPING-JESUS, *subs.* (common).—A lameter; a DOT-AND-CARRY-ONE (*q.v.*).

LINDABRIDES, *subs.* (old).—A harlot. For synonyms *see* BARRACK-HACK and TART.

1663. KILLIGREW, *Parson's Wedding*, iv. 1. Such a woman is my wife, and no LINDABRIDES.

LINE, *subs.* (colloquial).—A calling; a profession; a LAY (*q.v.*).

1655. FULLER, *Church Hist.*, II. ix. 23. If I chance to make an excursion into the matters of the Commonwealth, it is not out of curiosity, or busy-bodinesse, to be medling in other men's LINES.

1803. KENNEY, *Raising the Wind*, i. 1. *Waiter* . . . The fellow lives by spunging—gets into people's houses by his songs and his bon-mots. At some of the squires' tables he's as constant a guest as the parson, or the apothecary. *Sam.* Come, that's an odd LINE to go into, however.

1836. DICKENS, *Sketches by Boz*, 41. The man in the shop, perhaps is in the baked 'jemmy' LINE, or the firewood and hearth-stone LINE, or any other LINE which requires a floating capital of eighteen-pence or thereabouts.

1888. ROLF BOLDREWOOD, *Robbery Under Arms*, xxiv. Our first try on in the coach LINE was with the Goulburn mail.

1891. N. GOULD, *Double Event*, 177. It's out of my LINE.

1892. MILLIKEN, *'Arry Ballads*, 52. Halpine Club bizness is oko, and not in my LINE.

2. (common).—A hoax; a fool-trap.

3. *in pl.* (colloquial).—A marriage certificate.

1847. *Chronicles of Pineville*, 64. One of the women, not the one who held the LINES.

18[?]. *Fast Life; an Autobiography*, p. 170. Those good-natured ladies who never had their LINES.

1862. THACKERAY, *Phillip*, XII. 'How should a child like you know that the marriage was irregular?' 'Because I had no LINES,' cries Caroline.

4. *in pl.* (common).—Reins; RIBBONS (*q.v.*).

1852. BRISTED, *Upper Ten Thousand*, 67. Handing the LINES to Ashburner, as he stopped his team.

ON THE LINE, *subs. phr.* (common).—Hung on the line at the Royal Academy.

1865. *Fortnightly Review*, ii. p. 28. Every picture should be hung at that height which in the Royal Academy Exhibition is known as THE LINE.

Verb. (venery).—1. Properly, to impregnate a bitch; hence, to copulate. For synonyms *see* GREENS and RIDE.

1601. P. HOLLAND, *Plinie*, VIII. ch. XI. The Indians take great pleasure to have their salt bitches LINED with tigres.

1725. N. BAILEY, *Erasmus*, II. 160. He would with the utmost diligence look for a dog that was on all accounts of a good breed, to LINE her, that he might not have a litter of mongrels.

1785. GROSE, *Vulg. Tongue*, s.v.

2. (colloquial).—To fill: as TO LINE ONE'S STOMACH = to eat; TO LINE ONE'S POCKETS = to take money.

1837. DICKENS, *Oliver Twist*, 43. 'A couple of pocket-books,' replied that young gentleman. 'LINED?' enquired the Jew.

A LINE OF THE OLD AUTHOR, *subs. phr.* (old).—A dram of brandy. For synonyms *see* GO.

1690. B. E., *Dict. Cant. Crew*, s.v.

1785. GROSE, *Vulg. Tongue*, s.v.

TO GET INTO (or ON) A LINE, *verb. phr.* (old).—*See* quot. *Cf.* STRING and GAMMON.

1819. DE VAUX, *Memoirs*, s.v. LINE. To GET a person IN A LINE, or IN A STRING, is to engage them in a conversation, while your confederate is robbing their person or premises; to banter or jest with a man by amusing him with false assurances or professions, is also termed *stringing* him, or *getting* him *in tow;* to keep any body in suspense on any subject without coming to a decision, is called KEEPING him IN *tow*, *in a string*, or *in* A TOW-LINE. To CUT THE LINE, or *the string*, is to put an end to the suspense in which you have kept any one, by telling him the plain truth, coming to a final decision, &c. A person, who has been telling another a long story, until he is tired, or conceives his auditor has been all the while secretly laughing at him, will say at last, I've just *dropped down*, you've had me in a fine *string*, I think it's time to *cut* it. On the other hand, the auditor, having the same opinion on his part, would say, Come, I believe you want to *string* me all night, I wish you'd *cut it;* meaning, conclude the story at once.

TO LINE ONE'S JACKET. *See* JACKET.

THE DEVIL'S REGIMENT OF THE LINE, *subs. phr.* (common).—Felons; convicts; THE POLICE-VAN CORPS.

LINE-AGE, *subs.* (journalistic).—Payment by line.

LINEN. THE LINEN, *subs. phr.* (common).—The stage curtain: THE RAG (*q.v.*).

TO WRAP UP IN CLEAN LINEN, *verb. phr.* (old).—To deliver sor

did or SMUTTY (*q.v.*) matter in decent language.—RAY (1767).

TO COOL IN ONE'S LINEN, *verb. phr.* (old).—To die.

d. 1796. BURNS, *Poems.* 'O Merry Hae I Been.' Blessed be the hour she COOLED IN HER LINENS.

LINEN-ARBOR, *subs.* (American cadets').—A dormitory.

LINEN-ARMOURER, *subs.* (common).—A tailor. For synonyms *see* SNIP.

1690. B. E., *Dict. Cant. Crew*, s.v.

1785. GROSE, *Vulg. Tongue*, s.v.

LINEN-DRAPER, *subs.* (rhyming).—Paper.

LINENOPOLIS, *subs.* (common).—Belfast: *cf.* COTTONOPOLIS.

1886. *The State*, 20 May, p. 210. There is no town of any dimensions in all Ireland more charmingly situated than LINENOPOLIS.

LINER, *subs.* (journalistic).—1. A casual reporter, paid by LINEAGE (*q.v.*). Short for PENNY-A-LINER.

1861. DUTTON COOK, *Paul Foster's Daughter*, xix. Because now and then a LINER is found in the gutter, it doesn't do to cry shame on every man that wields a pen.

1864. J. H. BURTON, *Scot Abroad*, ... The most fashionable PENNY-A-LINER of the *Morning Post.*

2. (artistic).—A picture hung ON THE LINE (*q.v.*).

1887. W. P. FRITH, *Autobiog.*, i. 114. The work advanced rapidly and I thought successfully, and in due time made its appearance in Trafalgar Square, where it was amongst the fortunate LINERS.

LING-GRAPPLING, *subs. phr.* (venery).—Groping a woman; BIRD'S-NESTING (*q.v.*). *Cf.* STINK-FINGER.

LINGO, *subs.* (colloquial).—A foreign language; unintelligible speech.

1699. CONGREVE, *Way of the World*, iv. 4. I shall understand your LINGO one of these days, Cousin: in the mean while I must answer in plain *English.*

1719. DURFEY, *Pills to Purge etc.*, iii. 100. We teach them their LINGUA, to crave and to cant.

1749. FIELDING, *Tom Jones*, Bk. VI. ch. ii. I have often warned you not to talk the court gibberish to me. I tell you, I don't understand the LINGO; but I can read a journal, or the 'London Evening Post.'

1775. SHERIDAN, *St. Patrick's Day*, i. 1. He's a gentleman of words; he understands your foreign LINGO.

1785. GROSE, *Vulg. Tongue*, s.v.

1839. AINSWORTH, *Jack Sheppard*, Pt. i. ch. 2. It's plain he don't understand our LINGO.

1846. MARRYAT, *Peter Simple*, xviii. Recollect that I cannot speak a word of their LINGO.

1857. THACKERAY, *Four Georges (George I).* He recited a portion of the Swedish Catechism to his Most Christian Majesty and his Court, not one of whom understood his LINGO.

1859. MATSELL, *Vocabulum*, s.v.

1883. CLARK RUSSELL, *Sailor's Language*, s.v. LINGO.—Sailor's name for a language he does not understand.

1888. ROLF BOLDREWOOD, *Robbery Under Arms*, viii. Droll LINGO, wasn't it?

1892. MILLIKEN, *'Arry Ballads*, 60. I can't git the 'ang of his LINGO.

LINGUA FRANCA, *subs. phr.* (colloquial).—Specifically the corrupt Italian (dating from the period of the Genoese and Venetian supremacy) employed as the language of commercial intercourse with the Levant. [Other examples are Hindustani in India, Swahilli and Houssa in Africa, Pidgin in China, and Chinook in America].

1619. WILSON, *Belphegor*, iii. 5. *Mat.* What kind of people are ye? *Rod.*

A hotch-potch of all tongues, nations, and languages. We speak the LINGUA FRANCA, keep open house, etc.

1675. DRYDEN, *Kind Keeper*, i. 1. English! away you fop! 'tis a kind of LINGUA FRANCA, as I have heard the merchants call it.

1684. E. EVERARD, Tr. *Tavernier's Japan*, ii. 41. He spoke half Portuguese, half Italian, which being a kind of LINGUA FRANCA.

1755. LORD CHESTERFIELD, *Letters* (1777), Bk. ii. No. xcviii, *Misc. Wks.*, Vol. ii. p. 431. How does my godson go on with his little LINGUA FRANCA, or jumble of different languages?

1787. BECKFORD, *Italy*, ii. (1834), 246. Talking a strange LINGUA FRANCA, composed of three or four different languages.

1825. SCOTT, *Talisman*, xiii. The LINGUA FRANCA mutually understood by Christians and Saracens.

1860. W. H. RUSSELL, *Diary in India*, i. 28. Men . . . talking in LINGUA FRANCA.

1877. F. BURNABY, *Through Asia Minor* (1878), vi. 34. 'What do you want'—he asked in LINGUA FRANCA, that undefined mixture of Italian, French, Greek and Spanish, which is spoken throughout the Mediterranean.

LINING. *See* INSIDE LINING.

1632. W. ROWLEY, *Woman Never Vext*, iv. 1. This lean gentleman looks as if he had no LINING in's guts.

TO GET WITHIN THE LINING OF ONE'S SMOCK, *verb. phr.* (venery). *See* quot.

1577. STANIHURST, *Ireland*, p. 26. The pretty poplet, his wife began to be a fresh occupieing giglot at home, and by report fell so farre acquainted with a religious cloisterer of the towne, as that he GAT WITHIN THE LINING OF HIR SMOCKE.

LINK, *verb.* (old).—To turn out a pocket.

1821. D. HAGGART, *Life Glossary*, p. 172, s.v.

1823. GROSE, *Vulg. Tongue* (3rd ed.), s.v.

LINSEY-WOOLSEY, *adj.* (old).—Neither one thing nor the other.

1592. GREENE, *Greenes Vision* [GROSART (1881-6), xii. 235]. Thou hast writ no booke well but thy *Nunquam fera est* and that is indifferent LINSEY WOOLSEY.

1593. HARVEY, *Pierces Superer.* [GROSART (1885), ii. 317]. A LINSEY-WOOLSIE wit.

1594. NASHE, *Terrors of the Night* [GROSART (1883), iii. 229]. A man must not . . . have his affections LINSEY WOLSEY, intermingled with lust, and things worthy of liking.

1609. DEKKER, *Work for Arm.* [GROSART (1886), iv. 158]. Iackes on both sides . . . a LINSEY-WOOLSEY people, that took no part, but stood indifferent between money and poverty.

1613. PURCHAS, *Pilgrimage*, 38. And Baalam's wages doe moue many still to make such LINSEY-WOOLSEY marriages.

1647-80. ROCHESTER, *A Satire on Marriage.* But if he must pay nature's debt in kind, To check his eager passion let him find Some willing female out . . . . Tho' she be LINSEY-WOOLSEY, Bawd or Whore.

1653. BROME, *City Wit*, i. 1. Venerable Mr. LINSIE-WOOLSIE; to weare satin sleeves, and whip beggars.

1662. *Rump Songs*, 'A Litany for the New-Year,' ii. 94. From LINSY-WOOLSEY Lords, from Town betrayers, From apron Preachers, and extempore Prayers, Good Lord deliver us!

1664. BUTLER, *Hudibras*, i. c. 3. A lawless LINSEY-WOOLSEY brother.

LINT-SCRAPER, *subs.* (common).—A young surgeon. For synonyms *see* CROCUS and SQUIRT. Also LINT.

1763. FOOTE, *Mayor of Garratt, Dramatis Personæ*, LINT, a surgeon.

1861. THACKERAY, *Lovel*, vi. 'If Miss Prior,' thought I, 'prefers this LINT-SCRAPER to me, ought I to baulk her? . . . . Take the vaccinator, girl, if thou preferrest him!'

LION, *subs.* (old).—1. *See* quots.

1713. *The Guardian*, No. 71. This town is, of late years, very much infested with LIONS . . . . there are many of these beasts of prey who walk our streets in broad day-light, beating about from coffeehouse to coffeehouse, and seeking whom they may devour. To unriddle this paradox, I must acquaint my rural reader, that we polite men of the town give the name of a LION to any one that is a great man's spy.

2. (colloquial).—An object (animate or inanimate) of interest. TO SEE THE LIONS = to go sight-seeing.

1590. GREENE, *Never Too Late* [GROSART, viii. 68]. This country Francesco was no other but a meere nouice, and that so newly, that to use the old proverb, he had scarce SEENE THE LIONS.

1785. GROSE, *Vulg. Tongue*, s.v. LION . . . . to SHOW THE LIONS and tombs, to point out the particular curiosities of any place, an allusion to Westminster Abbey and the Tower where the tombs and lions are shown. . . . It is a standing joke among the city wits to send boys and county-folks on the first of April to the Tower ditch to see the lions washed.

1822. LAMB, *Elia (Decay of Beggars).* The Mendicants of this great city were so many of her sights, her LIONS. I can no more spare them than I could the Cries of London.

1837. DICKENS, *Pickwick*, iv. But more than these, there were half a dozen LIONS from London—authors, real authors, who had written whole books, and printed them afterwards—and here you might see 'em, walking about, like ordinary men, smiling, and talking.

1839. MISS MARTINEAU, 'Literary Lionism,' in *London & Westm. Review*, April. In one crowded room are three LIONS,—a new musical composer, an eminent divine who publishes, and a lady poet.

1849. WASHINGTON IRVING, *Goldsmith*, xviii. He had suddenly risen to literary fame, and become one of the LIONS.

1855. THACKERAY, *Newcomes*, viii. Doctor McGuffog, Professor Bodgers, Count Poski, and all the LIONS present at Mrs. Newcome's *réunion* that evening, were completely eclipsed by Colonel Newcome.

1864. *Glasgow Herald*, 23 April. They saw only the danger of losing the LION that they hoped to show about the country in leading-strings.

1888. *Daily Telegraph*, 6 Jan. The comic LION commenced, but hardly were the first lines out of his mouth when a furious tempest of hisses, cat-calls, and whistling arose.

3. (University).—*See* quot.

1785. GROSE, *Vulg. Tongue*, s.v. LION. . . . also the name given by the gownsmen of Oxford, to inhabitants or visitors.

4. (old).—*See* quots.

1825. *English Spy*, i. 156. I'll thank you for a cut out of the back of that LION tittered a man opposite with all the natural timidity of the hare whom he thus particularised.

1828. LYTTON, *Pelham*, p. 112 [ed. 1864]. 'A LION is a hare, Sir.' 'What!' 'Yes, Sir, it is a hare, but we call it a LION because of the game laws.'

1872. *Court Journal*, 29 June. It was often impossible to get game for the table, and at dinner it was usual to ask for LION, and LION was entered in the bill of fare.

5. *in pl.* (military).—The Fourth Foot. [From its ancient badge].

Verb. (American thieves').—*See* quot.

1859. MATSELL, *Vocabulum*, s.v. LION. Be saucy; LION the fellow; make a loud noise; substitute noise for good sense; frighten; bluff.

COTSWOLD LION, *subs.* (old).—A sheep. *See* COTSOLD and LAMMERMOOR LION.

1537. *Thersites* [DODSLEY, *Old Plays* (1874), i. 400]. Now have at the LIONS ON COTS'OLD!

1600. *Sir John Oldcastle*, i. 2. You old stale ruffian, you LION OF COTSWOLD.

1659. HARRINGTON, *Epigrams*, B. iii. Ep. 18. Lo then the mystery from whence the name, Of COTSOLD LYONE first to England came.

1672. RAY, *Proverbs* [BOHN (1893), p. 204], s.v.

TO TIP THE LION, *verb. phr.* (old).—*See* quot.

1785. GROSE, *Vulg. Tongue*, s.v. LION, TO TIP THE LION, to squeeze the nose of the party tipped, flat to his face with the thumb.

TO PUT ONE'S HEAD INTO THE LION'S MOUTH, *verb. phr.* (colloquial).—To put oneself into a desperate position.

AS VALIANT AS AN ESSEX LION, *phr.* (old).—As valiant as a calf.—RAY (1767).

LION-DRUNK, *adj. phr.* (old).—*See* quot.

1582. NASHE, *Pierce Penilesse*, in *Wks.* (GROSART), ii. 81-2. Now have we not one or two kinde of drunkards onely, but eight kinde . . . The second is LION-DRUNK, and he flings the pots about the house, calls his Hostesse whore, breakes the glasse windows with his dagger, and is apt to quarrele with any man that speaks to him.

LIONESS, *subs.* (common).—1. A female celebrity; a woman of note.

1825. SCOTT, *St. Ronan's Well*, vii. All the lions and LIONESSES.

1837. DICKENS, *Pickwick*, xv. Mr. Tupman was doing the honours of the lobster salad to several LIONESSES.

1855. THACKERAY, *Newcomes*, xli. For the last three months Miss Newcome has been the greatest LIONESS in London; the reigning beauty.

2. (University).—A lady visitor to Oxford, especially at Commemoration.

1861. HUGHES, *Tom Brown at Oxford*, xxv. The notion that any of the fraternity who had any hold on LIONESSES, particularly if they were pretty, should not use it to the utmost for the benefit of the rest, and the glory and honour of the college, was revolting to the undergraduate mind.

3. (old).—A harlot. For synonyms *see* BARRACK-HACK and TART.

1596. JOHN DAVIES, *Epigrams*, 'In Faustum,' xvi. But when he lost his hair where he had been, I doubt me he had seen a LIONESS.

LION- (or LEO-) HUNTER, *subs.* (colloquial).—One who runs after celebrities. [Popularised by DICKENS in the Mrs. Leo Hunter of *Pickwick*].

1862. *Round Table*, 10 Aug. Mr. Alfred Tennyson, fleeing from the bores and LEO-HUNTERS, has bought an estate called Greenhill, near Blackdown-Hill, Haslemere.

1878. *Athenæum*, 19 Jan., p. 81, col. 2. Keats, the obscure medical student, who died before a single LION-HUNTER had found him out.

1889. *Harper's Mag.*, lxxviii. 417. One of the greatest dangers to all genius is that of being robbed of its vital strength by velvety-pawed LION-HUNTERS.

LIONISM, *subs.* (colloquial).—Attracting attention as a LION (*q.v.*); also, sight-seeing.

1839. MISS MARTINEAU, article 'Literary LIONISM' in *London & Westm. Review* of April 1839.

1851. CARLYLE, *John Sterling*, Pt. III. ch. i. Its Puseyisms, Liberalisms, literary LIONISMS, or what else the mad hour might be producing.

LIONIZE, *verb.* (colloquial).—1. To go sight-seeing. Also, TO PLAY THE LION (*q.v.*).

1838. WILBERFORCE, *Life*, ii. 12. We came on to Oxford, LIONIZED it, and on to Cuddesdon.

1852. BRISTED, *Five Years*, 129. For eight days I had been LIONIZING Belgium under the disadvantages of continual rain.

2. (colloquial).—To make much of; to treat as a LION (*q.v.*).

1843. CARLYLE, *Past & Present*, iv. 6. Can he do nothing for his Burns but LIONIZE him?

1860. CAROLINE FOX, *Journal*, ii. p. 237. Tennyson hates being LIONIZED.

1882. *Literary World*, 3 Feb. Rushing off. . . . from the splendour and LIONIZING of a London season.

1886. *Fortnightly Rev.*, xl. 357. [Liszt] allowed himself . . . . to be LIONIZED.

3. (colloquial).—To show the sights of a place; to play the cicerone.

1871. DISRAELI, *Lothair*, ch. xxiv. He had LIONIZED the distinguished visitors during the last few days over the University.

4. (colloquial).—To go sight-seeing.

1825. *English Spy*, i. 137. After partaking of some refreshment and adjusting my dress, we sallied forth to LIONISE as Tom called it, which is the Oxford term for gazing about, usually applied to strangers.

1849. THACKERAY, *Pendennis*, xviii. He would ogle the ladies who came to LIONISE the University.

LION'S PROVIDER, *subs. phr.* (colloquial).—A sycophant; a JACKAL (*q.v.*).

LION'S SHARE, *subs. phr.* (colloquial).—The bigger part.

LIP, *subs.* (common).—Impudence; SAUCE (*q.v.*). TO GIVE LIP = to CHEEK (*q.v.*).

1821. D. HAGGART, *Life*, p. 20. Giving him plenty of LIP. *Ibid.*, p. 172. LIP, abuse.

1877. *Five Years' Penal Servitude*, iv. p. 285. He looked out for a 'cheeky answer,' a 'bit of LIP,' and had I given it to him he would have reported me without fail.

1884. M. TWAIN, *Huck. Finn*, v. p. 31. 'Don't you give me none o' your LIP,' says he . . . . 'I'll take you down a peg before I get done with you.'

1888. F. R. STOCKTON, *Rudder Grange*, 99. I told him that I didn't want none of his LIP.

Verb. (colloquial).—1. To sing. For synonyms *see* WARBLE. Fr. *rossignoler.* (2) To speak.

1789. GEO. PARKER, *Life's Painter*, 124. But come, I'll LIP ye a chaunt.

1841. LEMAN REDE, *Sixteen String Jack*, ii. 3. So thus I'll trip it, LIP it.

1885. *Punch*, 10 Jan., p. 21. I had great power, millions LIPPED my name.

TO BUTTON UP THE LIP (or MOUTH), *verb. phr.* (common).—To silence. BUTTON YOUR LIP! = hold your tongue; STOW IT (*q.v.*).

1747-8. TRAPP, *Explanatory Notes on the Gospels.* Mathew xxii. 46. How easily can God BUTTON UP THE MOUTHS of our busiest adversaries.

1868. *Notes & Queries*, 4 S. i. 603. At school it was thought quite an accomplishment in the young gentlemen who were fast of tongue to be able to silence a talkative comrade with the phrase 'BUTTON YOUR LIP.'

TO FALL BETWIXT CUP AND LIP. *See* SLIP.

TO KEEP (or CARRY) A STIFF UPPER LIP, *verb. phr.* (common).—To be self-reliant under difficuities; to be unflinching in the attainment of an object.

1833. NEAL, *Down Easters*, ii. 15. KEEP A STIFF UPPER LIP; no bones broke—don't I know?

1835. HALIBURTON, *Clockmaker*, 1st S. xxxii. He was well to do in the world once, CARRIED A STIFF UPPER LIP, and keered for no one.

1847. *Chronicles of Pineville*, 150. Tut, tut, major, KEEP A STIFF UPPER LIP, and you'll bring him this time.

1850. H. D. STOWE, *Uncle Tom's Cabin*, xii. I hope you keep up good heart, and are cheerful. Now, no sulks, ye see; KEEP A STIFF UPPER LIP, boys; do well by me, and I'll do well by you.

TO MAKE A LIP, *verb. phr.* (colloquial).—To mock; to grimace.

1610. SHAKSPEARE, *Coriolanus*, ii. 1. I will MAKE A LIP at the physician.

LIP-CLAP, *subs.* (old).—A kiss. Also LIP-FAVOR.

1592. GREENE, *Philomela* [GROSART (1881-6), xi. 150]. *Lutesio.* Kinde gaue the gentlewoman a kisse: for he thought she valued a LIP FAVOUR more than a piece of gold.

1693. *Poor Robin* [quoted by NARES]. Now the spring coming on, young wenches will grow wanton, and rather than live under a mothers nose, and a granams tongue, will venture a LIP-CLAP and a lap-clap to get them a husband, when a little while after the cuckow sings at their door.

LIPEY, *subs.* (common).—A mode of address: *e.g.* 'Whatcher, LIPEY!'

LIP-LABOUR (or **-WORK**), *subs.* (common).—1. Talk; JAW (*q.v.*). Also flattery.

1575. GASCOIGNE, *Steel glas* [HAYLITT (1869), *Poems*, ii. 205]. My priests haue learnt to pray vnto the Lord, and yet they trust not in their LYPLABOUR.

1577-87. HOLINSHED, *Chronicles*, ed. I. Being but a little LIP-LABOUR.

1592. NASHE, *Pierce Penilesse* [GROSART (1883), ii. 135]. Words.... that are the vsual LIP-LABOUR of euerie idle discourser.

1630. TAYLOR, *Works* [quoted by NARES]. In briefe, my fruitlesse and worthy LIP-LABOUR, mixt with a deale of ayrie and non-substantiall matter, I gave his lordship, and the like requitall I bestowed on the right worshipfull Mr. Thomas Squibb, maior of Sarum.

1653. BROME, *Novella*, iii. 1. Meere noyse and LIP-LABOUR, with loss of time, I think with scorne upon such poore expressions.

2. (common).—Kissing.

1582. STANYHURST, *Virgil, etc.*, 'Of Tyndarus' (ed. ARBER), p. 145. Syth my nose owtpeaking, good syr, your LIPLABOR hindreth, Hardlye ye may kisse mee where no such gnomon appeareth.

LIP-SALVE (or **-WASH**), *subs.* (common).—Flattery.

1594. NASHE, *Unf. Traveller* [GROSART (1885), v. 92]. What ist? what ist for a mayde fayre and freshe to spend a little LIP SALUE on a hungrie louer.

1680. E. FANNANT, *Hist. Ed. II*, 91. Spencer . . . finds here a female wit that . . . taught him not to trust a woman's LIP-SALVE.

1891. HERMANN, *Scarlet Fortune*, vi. Oily flattery . . . termed in Western phraseology, chin-music and LIP-WASH.

LIQUID-FIRE, *subs.* (common).—Bad whiskey. For synonyms *see* DRINKS and OLD MAN'S MILK.

LIQUOR, *subs.* (common).—A drink.

1882. *Punch*, LXXXII. 193. 2. These nips and pegs and LIQUORS at all hours of the day were unknown to us.

Verb. (common).—To drink; to treat: generally TO LIQUOR UP. Also (old)—TO LIQUOR ONE'S BOOTS (*q.v.*).

1607. W. S., *Puritan.* Oh, the musicians Master Edward, call 'em in, and LIQUOR them a little.

1682. DRYDEN, *Absalom etc.*, ii. 461. Round as a globe, and LIQUORED every chink.

1699. *London Spy*, p. 15. When we had LIQUORED our throats.

1838. NEAL, *Charcoal Sketches*, i. 36. Come, boys, let's LIQUOR—what'll you have?

1847. PORTER, *Big Bear*, p. 31. Jumping up, he asked all present to LIQUOR before going to bed.

1850. TENSAS, *Odd Leaves*, p. 175. Doe, les LICKER, it's a dry talk.

1852. BRISTED, *Upper Ten Thousand*, p. 57. The very necessity of LIQUORING so often in our warm weather obliges us to weaken our liquor.

1853. HALIBURTON ('Sam Slick'), *Wise Saws*, p. 34. Come in here to the hotel, and let's LIQUOR, for I am nation dry.

1870. E. HINTON, *Plutarch's Morals*, 'Apothegms' etc. i. 268. 'If the Athenians,' said he, 'deal severely with us, let them execute *thee* snivelling and gutfoundered; I'll die WELL LIQUORED, and with my dinner in my belly.'

1872. *Daily Telegraph*, 18 Sept. All five then went into the refreshment bar, and—as a *bonâ fide* traveller has a right to do—LIQUORED UP, clinking their glasses merrily together.

1872. *Echo*, 23 Aug. He joined them, and accepted the general invitation given by De Castro to have a 'shout,' or, as the Americans would say, a LIQUOR-UP, at the hotel on the opposite side of the way.

1882. *Daily Telegraph*, 13 Nov., p. 5, col. 3. Who gobbled their food, LIQUORED UP repeatedly, smoked or chewed to excess, and expectorated incessantly.

1888. E. EGGLESTON, *The Graysons*, xix. Come boys, LIQUOR UP!

TO LIQUOR ONE'S BOOTS, *verb. phr.* (old).—*See* quot.

1785. GROSE, *Vulg. Tongue*, s.v. LIQUOR, To LIQUOR ONE'S BOOTS, to drink before a journey, among Roman Catholicks to administer the extreme unction.

IN LIQUOR, *phr.* (colloquial).—The worse for drink. For synonyms *see* DRINKS and SCREWED.

1756. *The World*, No. 186. It was her misfortune over-night to be a little IN LIQUOR.

1766. COLMAN, *Cland. Marriage*, in *Works* (1777), i. 274. And now you are a little IN LIQUOR, you fear nothing.

1883. JAMES PAYN, *Thicker than Water*, xv. For her reflection, when all was said, had been similar to that indulged in by the gentleman IN LIQUOR, 'too much, yet not enough.'

LIQUORPOND STREET. TO COME FROM LIQUOR-POND STREET, *verb. phr.* (common).—To be drunk.

1828. BUCKSTONE, *23 John St., Adelphi*, i. *Snatch.* I don't know where you are, sir; but you seem to have just COME FROM LIQUORPOND STREET.

LISPERS, *subs.* (old).—The teeth. For synonyms *see* GRINDERS.

1800. PARKER, *Life's Painter*, p. 151, s.v.

LIST. *See* ADD.

LISTENERS, *subs.* (common).—The ears.

1827. EGAN, *Anecdotes of the Turf*, 7. Hooper planted another under Wood's LISTNER.

LISTMAN, *subs.* (turf).—A ready-money bookmaker, betting according to prices on a list exhibited beside him.

1887. *Daily Telegraph*, 12 March. M. Berthaudin would also extend to the LISTMEN the same rule which is in force among the brokers and agents on the Paris Stock Exchange, all the members of which are jointly and severally responsible for the debts of any one of their number.

LISTS-OF-LOVE, *subs.* (literary).—Copulation. For synonyms *see* GREENS and RIDE.

1593. SHAKSPEARE, *Venus and Adonis.* Now are they in the very LISTS OF LOVE.

1633. FORD, *Loves' Sacrifice*, iv. 1. A prince whose eye is chooser to his heart, Is seldom steady in the LISTS OF LOVE.

LITTER, *subs.* (old: now recognised).—A muddle.—B.E. (1690); *New Cant. Dict.* (1725).

LITTLE, *adj.* (old: now colloquial).—Mean; paltry; contemptible.—B. E. (1690); *New Cant. Dict.* (1725).

LITTLE ALDERMAN, *subs. phr.* (thieves').—A JEMMY (*q.v.*) made in sections. *See* ALDERMAN.

1889. *Daily News*, 19 Oct., p. 5, col. 1. The LITTLE ALDERMAN or 'sectional jemmy,' must be condemned by virtue of the word sectional.

LITTLE BARBARY, *subs. phr.* (old).—Wapping.—B. E. (1690); *New Cant. Dict.* (1725); GROSE (1785).

LITTLE BEN, *subs. phr.* (thieves').—A waistcoat. *See* BENJAMIN.

LITTLE BIRD. *See* BIRD

LITTLE BREECHES, *subs.* (old).—*See* quot.

1785. GROSE, *Vulg. Tongue*, s.v. LITTLE BREECHES, a familiar appellation used to a boy.

LITTLE CHURCH AROUND THE CORNER, *subs. phr.* (America).—A drinking saloon. For synonyms *see* LUSH-CRIB.

LITTLE CLERGYMAN, *subs.* (old).—A young chimney-sweep.—GROSE (1823).

LITTLE DAVY, *subs. phr.* (venery).—The *penis.* For synonyms *see* CREAMSTICK and PRICK.

LITTLE DEVIL. *See* DEVIL.

LITTLE-EASE, *subs.* (old).—The pillory, stocks, or any similar mode of punishment; a prison-cell: *see* quots.

*d.*1555. LATIMER, *Sermons*, fol. 105, b. Was not this a seditious fellow? was not this fellow's preaching a cause of all the trouble in Israel? was he not worthy to be cast in *bocardo*, or LITTLE-EASE?

1586. FLEMING, *Nomencl.*, 196, b. *Nervus*—a kind of stockes for the necke and the feete: the pillorie, or LITTLE-EASE.

1688. HOLME, *Academy of Armory & Blazon.* III. cvii. No. 91, p. 312. 'Like to this [the Stocks of which he has just given a description] there is another like place of Punishment in our House of Correction in Chester (the like to it I have not heard in any other place) it is called the LITTLE EASE, a place cut into a Rock, with a Grate Door before it; into this place are put Renegadoes, Apprentices, &c. that disobey their Parents and Masters, Robbers of Orchards, and such like Rebellious Youths; in which they can neither Stand, Sit, Kneel, nor lie down, but be all in a ruck, or knit together, so and in such a Lamentable Condition, that half an hour will tame the Stoutest and Stubbornest Stomach, and will make him have a desire to be freed from the place.'

1733. *Abstract of the Sufferings of the People called Quakers etc.....* Footnote. 'This LITTLE EASE was a hole hewed out in a rock; the breadth and cross from side to side is 17 inches, from the back to the inside of the great door; at the top, 7 inches; at the shoulders, 8 inches; and the breast, 9½ inches; from the top to the bottom, 1 yard and a half, with a device to lessen the height as they are minded to torment the person put in, by drawboards which shoot over across the two sides, to a yard in height, or thereabouts.'

1738. *The Curiosity*, p. 60. LITTLE-EASE . . . . a place of punishment in Guildhall, London for unruly apprentices.

1796. GROSE, *Vulg. Tongue* (2nd ed.), s.v.

1819-30. LINGARD, *Hist. of Eng.*, viii. note G. p. 424 (4th ed.). 'A fourth kind of torture was a cell called LITTLE EASE. It was of so small dimensions and so constructed that the prisoner could neither stand, sit, nor lie in it at full length. He was compelled to draw himself up in a squatting posture, and so remained during several days.'

1871. *Daily Telegraph*, 25 Jan., p. 5, col. 2. We should see a hideous dark den . . . . apparently capable of containing about one-fourth of the prisoners with which it is commonly filled . . . . Every now and then one dies . . . . after a temporary sojourn in one of these chapels of LITTLE-EASE at the Acton Police Station.

1895. H. B. MARRIOTT WATSON, in *New Review*, July, p. 47. 'I think,' he says, 'my good highwayman, that the LITTLE-EASE in Dartford Compter is the place for you,' and chuckled as if he had made a jest.

LITTLE ENGLAND, *subs. phr.* (West Indian).—Barbadoes: *see* BIM.

LITTLE ENGLANDER, *subs. phr.* (political).—An anti-JINGO (*q.v.*); an opponent of the Imperial idea.

LITTLE FIGHTING FOURS, *subs. phr.* (military).—The Forty-fourth Foot. [From the prowess of its men, who are of small stature].

LITTLE-FINGER. TO COCK ONE'S LITTLE FINGER, *verb. phr.* (common).—To drink much and often. For synonyms *see* DRINKS and SCREWED.

LITTLE-GO, *subs.* (University).—The public examination which students at the English Universities have to pass in the second year of residence: also called the 'previous examination' (as preceding the final one for a degree), and, at Oxford, SMALLS (*q.v.*).

1841. THACKERAY, *King of Brentford's Testament*, 86, 7. At college, though not fast, Yet his LITTLE-GO and great-go He creditably pass'd.

1849. THACKERAY, *Pendennis*, iii. A tutor, don't you see old boy? He's coaching me, and some other men, for the LITTLE-GO.

LITTLE-GO-VALE, *subs.* (old).—Orderly step to the first examination.—GROSE (1823).

LITTLE-GUID, *subs.* (Scots').—The devil. For synonyms *see* SKIPPER.

LITTLE-JOKER, *subs.* (sharpers').—The pea under the thimble in the thimble-rigging game. *See* also JOKER, sense 3.

LITTLE MAN, *subs.* (Eton College).—*See* quot.

*c.*1880. *Sketchy Memoirs of Eton*, p. 16. He called the footman (or LITTLE MAN . . .) and bade him reach down the obnoxious placard.

LITTLE MAN IN THE BOAT. *See* BOAT.

LITTLE-SIDE, *subs.* (Rugby).—A term applied to all games, organised between houses only.

LITTLE-SISTER, *subs.* (venery).—The female *pudendum.* For synonyms *see* MONOSYLLABLE. Ger. *Schwesterlein.*

LITTLE-SNAKESMAN, *subs.* (thieves').—A young thief passed into a house through a window so that he may open the door to the gang.

1781. G. PARKER, *View of Society*, II. 82, s.v.

1785. GROSE, *Vulg. Tongue*, s.v.

LITTLE SPOT. *See* SPOT.

LITTLE WILLIAM, *subs. phr.* (American).—A bill.

LIVE, *adj.* (American).—Energetic; active; intelligent.

1892. *Pall Mall Gaz.*, 1 Nov., p. 6, col. 1. At a private muster the other night they came up in good force, decided to organize the party by wards, to maintain a LIVE association, and to find the money to keep it going.

TO LIVE UNDER THE CAT'S-PAW. *See* CAT'S-PAW.

TO LIVE TO THE DOOR, *verb. phr.* (common).—To live up to one's means.

LIVE-EELS, *subs.* (rhyming).—The fields.

1859. MATSELL, *Vocabulum*, s.v. LIVE EELS. Bell has gone to LIVE EELS, to 'read' and write with Joe.

LIVE-HORSE, *subs.* (workmen's).—Work done over and above that included in the week's bill: *cf.* DEAD-HORSE.

LIVE-LUMBER, *subs.* (nautical).—Landsmen on board ship.

1785. GROSE, *Vulg. Tongue*, s.v.

LIVENER, *subs.* (common).—A morning dram; a PICK-ME-UP (*q.v.*). For synonyms *see* GO.

LIVER. *See* CURL.

LIVERPOOL-BUTTON, *subs.* (nautical).—A kind of toggle used by sailors when they lose a button.

LIVERPOOL BLUES, *subs. phr.* (military).—The Seventy-ninth Foot.

LIVERPOOL TAILOR, *subs. phr.* (tailors').—A tramping workman; one who sits with his coat and hat on, ready for the road.

LIVERPUDLIAN, *subs.* (colloquial).—A native or inhabitant of Liverpool.

1884. *Graphic*, 12 April, p. 346, col. 3. Its last match was with Liverpool and it had to accept defeat at the hands of the LIVERPUDLIANS.

LIVE-SAUSAGE. *See* SAUSAGE.

LIVE-STOCK, *subs.* (common).—Fleas, bugs and lice,—all body vermin.

1785. GROSE, *Vulg. Tongue*, s.v.

LIVING FOUNTAIN, *subs. phr.* (venery).—The female *pudendum*.

1648. HERRICK, *Hesperides*, 404. Show me that hill where smiling love doth sit, Having a LIVING FOUNTAIN under it.

LIZA. OUTSIDE LIZA! *phr.* (common).—Be off!

LOAD, *subs.* (colloquial).—1. An excess of food or drink. *Cf.* JAG. LOADED = drunk: also LOADED FOR BEARS, OR TO THE GUNWALES.

1767. RAY, *Proverbs* [BOHN (1893), 63]. He has a jag or LOAD, drunk.

Verb. (horse-copers').—1. To introduce well-greased shot into the throat of a 'roaring' or broken-winded horse. This conceals the defect for a few hours, during which a sale is effected.

1890. *Answers*, 6 July, p. 81, col. 1. The process of LOADING a horse, as it is called, is one adopted by 'horse-copers'—gentry who make a living by selling patched-up horses.

2. (Stock Exchange).—To buy heavily: TO UNLOAD = to sell freely.

LOAD OF HAY, *subs. phr.* (rhyming).—A day.

LIKE A LOAD OF BRICKS. *See* LIKE.

TO LAY ON LOAD, *verb. phr.* (old).—To thrash.

1537. *Thersites* [DODSLEY, *Old Plays* (1874), i. 406]. I will search for them both in bush and shrub, And LAY ON A LOAD with this lusty club.

*c.*1550. INGLELEND, *Disobedient Child* (DODSLEY, *Old Plays* (1870), ii. 305]. [*Here the wife* must LAY ON LOAD upon her husband]—Stage direction.

*b.*1553. WEVER, *Lusty Juventus* [DODSLEY, *Old Plays* (1874), ii. 87]. But LAY LOAD on the flesh, whatsoever befall, You have strength enough to do it with all.

LOAF, *subs.* (common).—1. A lounge; dawdle; idling: *e.g.*, 'to do a LOAF'.

2. *See* LOAVES AND FISHES.

Verb. (common).—1. To lounge; to idle; TO MIKE (*q.v.*). Fr. *louper* and *gouspiner*.

FRENCH SYNONYMS. *Avoir les côtes en long* (popular); *balocher* (thieves'); *louper; trainer sa peau* (thieves'); *n'en pas foutre une*

secousse (popular); *prendre le train d'onze heures* (commercial); *traîner ses guêtres*.

1838. NEAL, *Charcoal Sketches*, III. ii. One night, Mr. Dobbs came home from his LOAFING-place, for he LOAFS of an evening like the generality of people.

1843. NORMAN, *Yucatan*, p. 88. We arrived at the town of Tincenn; the sun being exceedingly hot, we waited till evening. The Casa Real in this as in other towns of the province was the LOAFERING place of the Indians.

1843. DICKENS, *Martin Chuzzlewit*, xvi. p. 170. Just now, Mrs. Pawkins kept a boarding-house, and Major Pawkins rather LOAFED his time away, than otherwise.

1845. *New York Commercial Advertizer*, Dec. The Senate has LOAFED away the week in very gentlemanly style.

1857. BORTHWICK, *California*, p. 118. The street [in Hangtown, California] was crowded all day with miners LOAFING about from store to store, making their purchases and asking each other to drink.

1861. KINGSLEY, *Ravenshoe*, II. xv. Shoe-blacks are compelled to a great deal of unavoidable LOAFING, but certainly this one LOAFED rather energetically.

1862. LOWELL, *Biglow Papers*, 2nd S., Int. To LOAF, this, I think, is unquestionably German. *Laufen* is pronounced *lofen* in some parts of Germany, and I once heard one German student say to another 'Ich lauf (lofe) hier bis du wiederkehrest', and he began to saunter up and down—in short, TO LOAF.

1872. *Daily News*, 29 Jan., 'America in Paris.' Its glass-roofed courts are filled with men of few words and long purses, whose chief mission in life seems to be that of LOAFING ROUND, and paying the endless bills which their wives send in to them. Diving into newspapers is comprised in the verb TO LOAF.

1872. BLACK, *Princess of Thule*, ch. xiv. Amongst all those LOAFING vagabonds.

1878. WALT WHITMAN, *Leaves of Grass*, 29. I lean and LOAFE at my ease.

1880. SEEBOHM, *Siberia in Europe*, ch. xx. Gipsy emigrants who perpetually LOAF about on the outskirts.

1892. ANSTEY, *Model Music Hall Songs*, 134. I'm LOAFING about and I very much doubt If my excellent Ma is aware that I'm out.

2. (American University).—To borrow, especially with no intention of return.

TO BE IN BAD LOAF, *verb. phr.* (old).—To be in a disagreeable situation or in trouble.—GROSE (1785).

LOAFER, *subs.* (colloquial).—An idler.

ENGLISH SYNONYMS. Baker; beat; bummer; crow-eater; draw-latch; flunk; ham-fatter; hayseed; heeler; inspector of pavements; lamb; Laurence (or lazy Laurence); lazybones; miker; moucher; practical politician; Q.H.B; raff; scow-banker; striker; wood-and-water Joey. *See* CADGER.

FRENCH SYNONYMS. *La cagne* (popular: also generally in contempt); *un balochard* or *balocheur* (popular); *un batteur de flemme* (= Old Fr. *flegme* = idleness); *une baladeuse* (= a female loafer); *un gratte-pavé* (popular = scratch-pavement); *un marpant* or *marpeau* (whence *morpion* = crab louse); *un omnibus* (in allusion to slowness of pace); *un batteur de pavé* (popular: *cf.* INSPECTOR OF PAVEMENTS); *un petrouskin* (popular); *un vachard* (popular); *un chevalier de la loupe* (popular: *camp de la loupe* = an idlers' rendez-vous; *loupeur* = a Saint Mondayite); *un grand dependeur d'andouilles* (= one who prefers good cheer to work: *andouilles*=chitterlings); *un dort-dans-l'auge* (pop.: also *un dort-en-chiant*); *une fenasse* (O. FR. *fen* = hay); *un faignant* (from *fainéant*); *un cul de plomb* (= heavy-arse); *un rossard* (popular); *un fourrier de la loupe* (familiar); *un galapiat, galapian*, or *galapiau* (popular); *un las-de-chier* (common); *Madame milord quépète* or *quépette* (= a LADY FENDER); *un gouapeur* (thieves').

SPANISH SYNONYMS. *Zanguango, zangandongo*, or *zanguayo*.

GERMAN SYNONYMS. *Schallef.*

1840. R. H. DANA, *Two Years before the Mast*, vii. There are no people to whom the newly-invented Yankee word of LOAFER is more applicable than to the Spanish Americans.

1842. DICKENS, *American Notes*, xiv. p. 111. When we stop to change, some two or three half-drunken LOAFERS will come loitering out with their hands in their pockets.

1865. LADY DUFF GORDON, in *Macmillan's Mag.*, 368. One of the regular LOAFERS who lurk about the ruins to beg and sell water or curiosities and who are all a lazy, bad lot, of course.

1866. W. D. HOWELLS, *Venetian Life*, iii. I permit myself, throughout this book, the use of the expressive American words loaf and LOAFER, as the only terms adequate to the description of professional idling in Venice.

1872. BLACK, *Adv. of a Phaeton*, XVIII. The LOAFER in moleskin stood at some little distance.

1888. J. RUNCIMAN, *The Chequers*, 2. I am a LOAFER.

1892. F. ANSTEY, *Voces Populi*, 'In the Mall on Drawing Room Day,' 80. *A Sardonic* LOAFER. 'Ullo, 'ere's a 'aughty one!

LOAFERISH, *adj.* (colloquial).—Lounging.

1866. W. D. HOWELLS, *Venetian Life*, xix. The four pleasant ruffians in the LOAFERISH postures which they have learned as facchini waiting for jobs.

LOAFING, *subs.* (colloquial).—Aimless lounging. Fr. *la loupe*.

1866. W. D. HOWELLS, *Venetian Life*, iii. At night men crowd the close little caffè . . . . and beguile the time with solemn LOAFING, and the perusal of dingy little journals.

Adj. (colloquial).—Lounging.

1856. J. HUGHES, *Tom Brown's School-Days*, pt. I. ch. ii. Then follows the greasy cap lined with fur of a half-gipsy, poaching, LOAFING fellow, who travels the Vale not for much good, I fancy.

LOAVER, *subs.* (common).—*See* quot. *Cf.* LOUR, and for synonyms *see* ACTUAL and GILT.

1851-61. H. MAYHEW, *London Lab. & Lon. Poor*, i. 472. That's the time you get them to rights, when they're old and ugly, just by sweetening them, and then they don't mind tipping the LOAVER (money).

LOAVES and FISHES, *subs. phr.* (colloquial).—Emolument; profit; temporal benefits [From *John* vi. 26].

*c.*1787. JOHN ADAMS, *Works*, v. 18. These four orders must be divided . . . into factions for the LOAVES AND FISHES.

1830. J. B. BUCKSTONE, *The Cab-driver*, Act i. Do you think the gentlemen are to have all the LOAVES AND FISHES?

1841. *Punch*, i. p. 18, col. 1. I only know that I am mortal by two sensations—a yearning for LOAVES AND FISHES and a love for Judy.

LOB (or **LOBB**), *subs.* (old).—1. *See* quots. Fr. *la grenouille*. *Cf.* DAMPER.

1718. C. HIGGIN, *True Discovery*, 15. Either by a sint, alias gold watch . . . . or by a wedge LOBB, alias gold or silver snuff-box.

1754. *Discoveries of John Poulter*, p. 42. A LOBB full of glibbs, a box full of ribbons.

1857. SNOWDEN, *Mag. Assistant*, 3rd ed., p. 445. A till—a LOB.

1859. MATSELL, *Vocabulum*, s.v.

2. (old).—A blockhead; a lubber. For synonyms *see* BUFFLE and CABBAGE-HEAD.

1577. WHETSTONE, *Remembraunce* [of Gascoigne]. But as the drone the honey hive doth rob, With woorthy books so deals this idle LOB.

1592. SHAKSPEARE, *Midsummer Night's Dream*, ii. 1. Farewell, thou LOB of spirits, I'll begone.

*b.*1600. *Grim the Collier &c.* [DODSLEY, *Old Plays* (1874), viii. 443]. Well, here in Croydon will I first begin To frolic it amongst the country LOBS.

1661. GAUDEN, *Anti-Baal-Berith*, 12. This is the wonted way for quacks and cheats to gull country LOBS.

3. (colloquial).—A large lump.

1863. *Once a Week*, iii. 535. Well instead of about a pennyweight, as Joe had expected, the old fellow washed out a good half-ounce at least, so he must have a regular LOB of gold stowed away somewhere.

4. (cricket).—A slow underhand ball; delivered low and falling heavily, its course a decided curve. At Winchester LOB = YORKER (*q.v.*).

[See also SNORTER—UNDERGROUNDER — TRIMMER — TEAPOT — SWIPER — STRINGER—GRUBBER—YORKER.]

1892. *Cassell's Saturday Journal*, 21 Sept., p. 13, col. 3. I would have to try all sorts of bowling—right and left hand, fast and slow, LOBS, yorkers, and every other variety.

5. (pugilists').—The head. For synonyms *see* CRUMPET.

6. (venery).—A partial erection: *e.g.*, a urinary LOB.

TO FRISK (DIP, PINCH, or SNEAK) A LOB, *verb. phr.* (old).—To rob a till. TO GO ON THE LOB = to go into a shop for change and to steal some. Hence LOB-SNEAKING = robbing tills; LOB-CRAWLER = a till-thief.

1742. C. JOHNSON, *Highwaymen & Pyrates*, 252. He was also very good for the LOB.

1868. *Temple Bar*, xxiv. 537. Stealing the till and opening the safe is what we call LOB-SNEAKING and Peter-screwing.

1877. HORSLEY, *Jottings from Jail*. Poor old Tim, the LOB-CRAWLER fell from Racker and got pinched.

Verb. (old).—1. To droop; to sprawl.

1599. SHAKSPEARE, *Henry V.*, iv. 2. Their poor jades LOB down their heads.

1821. EGAN, *Real Life in London*, i. 187. The dancing party . . . . were LOBBING their lolleys on the table.

2. (cricketers').—To bowl a ball as a LOB (*q.v.*).

LOBCOCK, *subs.* (old).—1. A blockhead. Also *adj.*

1534. UDALL, *Roister Doister*, iii. 3. Such a calfe, such an asse, such a blocke . . . such a LOBCOCKE.

1557. BRETON, *Fancy* [GROSART (1876), i. *a*. 15, 2, 37]. The LOBCOKE lust, from thriflesse thick, both bring the in his lap.

1567. EDWARDS, *Damon & Pithias* [DODSLEY, *Old Plays* (1874), iv. 75]. In faith, ere you go, I will make you a LOB-COCK.

1575. GASCOIGNE, *Supposes* [HAZLITT (1869), *Poems*, i. 218]. I will laugh a little at this LOBCOCKE.

1594. NASHE, *Unf. Traveller* [GROSART (1883-4) v. 157]. Seneca and Lucan were LOBCOCKES to choose that death.

1606. *Wily Beguiled* [DODSLEY, *Old Plays* (1874), ix. 241]. Your lubberly legs would not carry your LOB-COCK body.

1690. B. E., *Dict. Cant. Crew*, s.v.

1719. DURFEY, *Pills etc.*, iv. 171. That ev'ry LOBCOCK hath his wench, And we but one betwixt us.

1785. GROSE, *Vulg. Tongue*, s.v.

2. (venery).—A large relaxed *penis*.—GROSE (1785).

LOBKIN, *subs.* (old).—A house; a lodging: *see* LIPKEN.

1662. BRETON, *Strange Newes* [GROSART (1876), ii. *s.* 10, 2, 27]. In a country village called LOBKIN the large.

LOBLOLLY, *subs.* (old).—1. A lubber; a lout; a fool.

1604. BRETON, *Grimello's Fortunes*, p. 9 [ed. GROSART, 1879]. This LOB-LOLLIE with slauering lips would be making loue.

1680. COTTON, *Scoffer Scofft*, in *Wks.* (1725), p. 209. Whilst he not dreaming of thy Folly, Lies gaping like a great LOB-LOLLY.

2. (nautical).—Water-gruel; spoon-meat.

1621. BURTON, *Anatomy* (ed. 1852), ii. 178. There is a differencc (he grumbles) between LAPLOLLY and pheasants.

1690. B. E., *Dict. Cant. Crew*, s.v.

1703. WARD, *London Spy*, Pt. xii. 289. Considering *Coffee* to be a liquor that sits most easie upon *Wine*, we thought it the best way to check the aspiring Fumes of the most Christian Juice by an *Antichristian Dose* of *Mahometan* LOBLOLLY.

1725. *New Cant. Dict.*, s.v.

1748. F. DYCHE, *Dictionary* (5th ed.). LOBLOLLY (S.) any uncouth, strange, irregular mixture of different things together to compose pottage or broth.

1767. GARRICK, *Peep behind the Curtain*, i. 2. My ingenious countrymen have no taste now for the high seasoned comedies; and I am sure that I have none for the pap and LOPLOLLY of our present writers.

1787. GROSE, *Prov. Glossary*. LOBLOLLY, an odd mixture of spoon-meat.

LOBLOLLY-BOY, *subs.* (nautical).—*See* quots. In America a BAYMAN or NURSE (*q.v.*). *See* quots.

1617. SHADWELL, *Fair Quaker of Deal*, i. [sailor *loq.*] Our rogue of a LOBLOLLY doctor, being not satisfied with his twopences, must have a note for ten months' pay for every cure.

1748. SMOLLETT, *Rod. Random*, xxvii. The rude insults of the sailors and petty officers, among whom I was known by the name of LOBLOLLY BOY.

1776. *The Patent, a Poem* [Note]. LOB-LOLLY-BOY is a person who on board of a man-of-war attends the surgeon and his mates, and one who knows just as much of the business of a seaman as the author of this poem.

1785. GROSE, *Vulg. Tongue*, s.v. On board of the ships of war, water-gruel is called LOBLOLLY, and the surgeon's servant or mate, the LOBLOLLY BOY.

1846. ROBERT BELL, *Ballads & Songs of the Peasantry of England*, p. 182. Jack Rider of Linton was LOBLOLLEY BOY aboard the Victory.

1883. CLARK RUSSELL, *Sailors' Language*, s.v.

1885. *Punch*, 11 July, p. 18. Lor' bless yer, a LOBLOLLY BOY can tell old hands how *not* to steer.

LOBS, *subs.* (common).—1. An assistant watcher; an under-game-keeper.

2. (common).—An abbreviation of LOBSTER (*q.v.*).

Intj. (schoolboys').—A signal of a masters' approach.

LOBSCOUSE, *subs.* (nautical).—A hash of meat and vegetable; an olio; a GALLIMAUFREY (*q.v.*); *see* SOAP-AND-BULLION.

[Other nautical food names, mostly derisive, are CHOKE-DOG; DADDY FUNK; DEAD HORSE; DOGBODY; DOUGH JEHOVAHS; HISHEE-HASHEE; MEASLES; SEA-PIE; SOFT TACK; SOAP-AND-BULLION; TOMMY; TWICE-LAID.]

1751. SMOLLETT, *Peregrine Pickle*, ix. This genial banquet was entirely composed of sea-dishes . . . . the sides being furnished with a mess of that savoury composition known by the name of LOB'S-COURSE.

1785. GROSE, *Vulg. Tongue*, s.v.

1840. R. H. DANA, *Two Years before the Mast*, v. The cook had just made for us a mess of hot SCOUSE—that is, biscuit pounded fine, salt beef cut into small pieces, and a few potatoes, boiled up together and seasoned with pepper.

1884. W. C. RUSSELL, *Jack's Courtship*, i. It takes a sailor a long time to straighten his spine and get quit of the bold sheer that earns him the name of shell-back. That is not all. LOBSCOUSE eats into the system.

LOBSCOUSER, *subs.* (nautical).—A sailor [An eater of LOBSCOUSE (*q.v.*)].

1884. W. C. RUSSELL, *Jack's Courtship*, xix. 'And besides, how many bunks does an old LOBSCOUSER like you want to sleep in?'

1891. W. C. RUSSELL, *Ocean Tragedy*, 148. 'He is superstitious, like most old LOBSCOUSERS, no doubt.'

LOBSNEAK (or **-CRAWLER**), *subs.* (common).—1. A till-robber; a TILL-SNEAK (*q.v.*).

1859. MATSELL, *Vocabulum*, s.v.

2. (cricketers').—A LOB (*q.v.*).

LOBSNEAKING, *subs.* (common).—Till-robbing. Fr. *un coup de radin.*

LOB'S-POUND, *subs.* (old).—1. A prison; a pound; the stocks: generic for any place of confinement.

1603. DEKKER, *Batchelor's Banquet* [GROSART (1886), i. 156]. He ran wilfully . . . . into the perill of LOB'S POUND.

1663. BUTLER, *Hudibras*, i. 3, 909. Crowdero whom, in irons bound, Thou basely threwst into LOB'S POUND.

1671. CROWNE, *Juliana*, i. 1. Between 'um both he's got into LOBB'S POUND. [*Note* (MAIDMENT, 1870)]. Jocularly, a prison or place of confinement. The phrase is still used and applied to the prison made for a child between the feet of a grown-up person.

1690. B. E., *Dict. Cant. Crew*, s.v. LOBCOCK, In LOB'S POUND, Laid by the Heels, or clap'd up in Jail.

1694. *Plautus, made English* [NARES]. But in what a fine pickle shou'd I be, if Mr. constable and his watch shou'd pick m' up and in wi' me to LOBS-POUND? Out o' which damn'd kitchin, to morrow must I be dish'd up for the whipping post; and not ha' the benefit o' the layety to plead i' m' own defence.

1785. GROSE, *Vulg. Tongue*, s.v.

1819. MOORE, *Tom Cribb.*, p. 18. The cull broke away, as he would from LOB'S POUND.

2. (old).—The female *pudendum.* For synonyms *see* MONOSYLLABLE.

1623. MASSINGER, *Duke of Milan*, iii. 2. Who forced the gentleman, to save her credit, To marry her, and say he was the party Found in LOB'S POUND.

LOBSTER, *subs.* (old).—A soldier. [*See* quots.]. Also BOILED LOBSTER in contradistinction to RAW LOBSTER (*q.v.*) which formerly = a sailor. UNBOILED-LOBSTER (*q.v.*) also = a policeman. For synonyms *see* MUDCRUSHER.

*c.*1642. SOMERS, *Tracts* (1811), v. 289. The nickname of LOBSTERS now *mis*applied to soldiers seems to have been first applied to Sir A. Hazilrigg's regiment of cavalry, completely armed with corslets—the first body of cavalry on that side which would be brought to stand the shock of the king's horse.

1662. *Rump Songs*, ii. 70. Sir William on Run-away-downs had a bout, Which him and his LOBSTERS did totally rout, And his Lady the conqueror could not help him out.

1690. B. E., *Dict. Cant. Crew*, s.v. A red coat, a soldier.

1748. F. DYCHE, *Dictionary* (5th ed.). LOBSTER (S.) . . . also a mock name for a foot-soldier.

1785. GROSE, *Vulg. Tongue*, s.v. LOBSTER, a nickname for a soldier, from the colour of his clothes. . . . 'I will not make a LOBSTER kettle of my ——': a reply frequently made by nymphs of the Point at Portsmouth, when requested by a soldier to grant him a favour.

1803. T. BROWN, *Works*, i. 73. The women exclaim against LOBSTERS.

1819. MOORE, *Tom Crib*, 5. LOBSTERS will be such a drug upon hand.

1829. BUCKSTONE, *Billy Taylor*, i. 1. I . . . am no more a dull drab-coated watchman . . . *Mary* . . . Thou UNBOILED LOBSTER, hence!

1839. THACKERAY, *Fatal Boots* (*April*). I don't think in the course of my whole military experience I ever fought anything, except an old woman, who had the impudence to hallo out, 'Heads up, LOBSTER!'

1845. BUCKSTONE, *Green Bushes*, i. 1. *Geo.* You must lead the soldiers to the very door . . . *Mur.* And where am I to meet the LOBSTERS?

1848. *Punch*, xiv. 256. He (a soldier) avoids a LOBSTER-shop, for fear of vulgar companions.

3. (cricket).—A bowler of LOBS (*q.v.*).

1890. E. LYTTELTON, *Cricket*, p. 36. The gentle and sensitive LOBSTER, whose success depends so largely on facts he is ignorant of and conditions he cannot control.

Verb. (Winchester College).—To cry. [*Notions:* Probably a variation of 'lowster' or 'louster' = (Hants) to make any unpleasant noise].

TO BOIL ONE'S LOBSTER, *verb. phr.* (old). *See* quot. 1819: of churchmen only. *Cf.* JAPAN.

1785. GROSE, *Vulg. Tongue*, s.v. LOBSTER.

1819. MOORE, *Tom Crib*, 5. To BOIL ONE'S LOBSTER means for a churchman to turn soldier; lobsters which are of a bluish-black, being made red by boiling. Butler's ingenious simile will occur to the reader:—When, like a LOBSTER BOILED, the morn From black to red began to turn.

LOBSTER-BOX, *subs.* (common).—A barrack. Also a transport.

1836. M. SCOTT, *Tom Cringle's Log*, ii. We landed in the LOBSTER-BOX as Jack loves to designate a transport.

LOBSTER-CART. TO UPSET ONE'S LOBSTER-CART. To knock one down. *See* APPLE-CART.

1824. MACK, *Cat-fight* [N. Y.], p. 153. Ready up to take his part, I'd soon UPSET HIS LOBSTER-CART; Make his bones ache, and blubber smart.

LOBSTER-POT, *subs.* (venery).—The female *pudendum.* For synonyms *see* MONOSYLLABLE.

LOBTAIL, *verb.* (nautical).—To sport or play: as a whale, by lifting his flukes, and bringing them down flat on the water.

LOCAL, *subs.* (American).—In pl.: an item of news of local interest; a CHIP (*q.v.*).

LOCK, *subs.* (old).—1. *See* quot. 1690.

1690. B. E., *Dict. Cant. Crew*, s.v. LOCK-ALL-FAST. . . . The LOCK, the magazine or Warehouse whither the thieves carry stolen goods to be secur'd.

1727. GAY, *Beggar's Opera*, iii. 3. At his LOCK, Sir, at the *Crooked Billet.*

1785. GROSE, *Vulg. Tongue*, s.v.

2. (old).—*See* quots. 1690 and 1718; a FENCE (*q.v.*). Also LOCK-ALL-FAST.

1690. B. E., *Dict. Cant. Crew*, s.v. LOCK-ALL-FAST, one that buys and conceals stolen goods.

1714. *Memoirs of John Hall*, 13, s.v.

1718. HIGGIN, *True Discovery*, p. 16. That woman they spoke to as they passed by is a LOCK, alias Receiver and Buyer of stolen goods.

1859. MATSELL, *Vocabulum*, s.v.

3. (old).—A line of business or conduct. *Cf.* LURK.

[?]. [NARES], *Trum s.* Why look you, colonel, he's at OLD LOCK, he's at's May-bees again.

1800. PARKER, *Life's Painter*, p. 116. What LOCK do you cut now?

1823. GROSE, *Vulg. Tongue*, s.v.

4. (old).—*See* quots.

1725. *New Cant. Dict.*, s.v. LOCK, as He stood a queer LOCK; *i.e.*, He stood an indifferent chance.

1748. T. DYCHE, *Dictionary* (5th ed.). LOCK (S.) . . . . also a cant word . . . . He stood a queer LOCK or bad chance.

1785. GROSE, *Vulg. Tongue*, s.v. LOCK, He stood a queer LOCK; *i.e.* he bore but an indifferent character.

1859. MATSELL, *Vocabulum*, s.v.

5. (venery).—The female *pudendum.* For synonyms *see* MONOSYLLABLE. Also LOCK OF ALL LOCKS: *cf.* KEY = *penis.*

1772. G. A. STEVENS, *Songs Comic and Satyrical*, 88. Here's the LOCK OF ALL LOCKS, and unlocking the same.

6. *See* LOVELOCK.

LOCKEES, *subs.* (Westminster School).—Lockhouse.

LOCKER, *subs.* (old).—1. A thieves' middleman.

1718. C. HIGGIN, *True Discovery*, ... I am a LOCKER, I leave goods at a house and borrow money on them, pretending that they are made in London.

2. (venery).—The female *pudendum.* For synonyms *see* MONOSYLLABLE.

3. (nautical).—A bar-room or GROGGERY (*q.v.*).

TO BE LAID IN THE LOCKER, *verb. phr.* (common).—To die. For synonyms *see* ALOFT.

1815. SCOTT, *Guy Mannering*, xxxiii. Brown's dead—shot—LAID IN THE LOCKERS, man.

DAVY JONES' LOCKER. *See* DAVY JONES.

SHOT IN THE LOCKER. *See* SHOT.

LOCKERAM-JAW'D (or **LOCKRAM-JAWED**), *adj.* (old).—Thin faced, or LANTHORN-JAW'D (*q.v.*).—B. E. (1690); *New Cant. Dict.* (1725); GROSE (1785).

LOCK-HOSPITAL, *subs.* (common).—A hospital for the treatment of veneral diseases.

LOCKSMITH'S DAUGHTER, *subs.* (old).—A key. Also BLACKSMITH'S DAUGHTER.—GROSE (1785).

ENGLISH SYNONYMS. Betty; blacksmith's daughter (or wife); gilkes (= skeleton keys); Jack-in-the box; screw; sket; twirl. *See* JEMMY and THIEVES.

FRENCH SYNONYMS. *Une aiguille* (popular); *un bouton* (= master-key); *un débridoir* (thieves'); *un frou-frou* (thieves' = master-key); *une Josephine* (*cf.* BETTY); *un luctrême* (thieves'); *un peigne* (thieves'); *une penne* (*une plume* = a false key).

GERMAN SYNONYMS. *Bua* (Viennese thieves': Heb. *bube*); *Dalme* or *Dalmer* (*Dalmerei* = lock; *Dalmernekef* = keyhole); *Echeder* or *Echoder* (Heb. *echod: zarfes Echeder* = French skeleton key); *Haupter* (= a master-key); *Hinterschieber; Posschener maphteach; Kleinpurim* (=skeleton keys); *Schasklamonis* (= a set of skeleton keys).

DUTCH SYNONYMS. *Draaier; klanker; tantel; troetel.*

ITALIAN SYNONYM. *Ingegnosa* (= witty or possessed of genius).

LOCK-UP-CHOVEY, *subs.* (old).—A covered cart.—GROSE (1823).

LOCK-UP HOUSE, *subs. phr.* (old).—*See* quot.

1785. GROSE, *Vulg. Tongue*, s.v. LOCK UP HOUSE, a spunging house, a public-house kept by sheriff's officers, to which they convey the persons they have arrested, where they practise every species of imposition and extortion, with impunity; also houses kept by agents or crimps, who inlist, or rather trepan men to serve the East India or African company as soldiers.

LOCK-UPS, *subs.* (Harrow School).—Detention in study.

LOCO-FOCO, *subs.* (American).—1. A self-lighting match or cigar.

2. (American).—A nickname of the Democratic party (1834-5). [At a meeting held in Tammany Hall the chairman left his seat and the lights were suddenly extinguished with a view to breaking up the meeting. Thereupon a section of the audience relighted the lights by means of their LOCO-FOCOS and continued the meeting]. Also as *adj.* = Democratic; belonging to the LOCO-FOCO party.

1843. DICKENS, *Martin Chuzzlewit*, ch. xvi. p. 162. Here's full particulars of the patriotic LOCO-FOCO movement yesterday, in which the Whigs was so chawed up.

1852. BRISTED, *Upper Ten Thousand*, p. 98. The driver was a stubborn LOCO-FOCO.

LOCOMOTE, *verb.* (American).—To walk.

1847. PORTER, *Quarter Race*, 83. He throws the galls in, and a bed too in the hay, if you git too hot to LOCOMOTE.

LOCOMOTIVE, *subs.* (common).—1. A mixed hot drink: of Burgundy, curaçoa, yolks, honey, and cloves.

2. *in pl.* (common).—The legs. For synonyms *see* PINS.

1843. W. T. MONCRIEFF, *The Scamps of London*, i. 1. *Char.* Will you listen to me, sir? *Bob.* Will I? To be sure I will. I will stop my LOCOMOTIVES directly. So now you may set your's agoing as soon as you like.

1870. *Sheffield Times*, Mar. Having regained his freedom he again made good use of his LOCOMOTIVES.

LOCOMOTIVE TAILOR, *subs.* (tailors').—A tramping workman.

LOCUST, *subs.* (thieves').—1. Laudanum.

1851-61. MAYHEW, *Lond. Lab.*, iii. 397. Some of the convicts would have given me some lush with a LOCUST in it.

2. (American thieves').—A truncheon.

1882. M'CABE, *New York*, xxiii. 383. 'Give them the LOCUSTS, men,' came in sharp ringing tones from the captain.

Verb. (thieves').—*See* quot.

1868. *Temple Bar*, xxiv. 539. LOCUSTING is putting a chap to sleep with chloroform and bellowing is putting his light out.

LODGER, *subs.* (prison).—1. A convict waiting for his discharge.

1889. *Answers*, 25 May, p. 412. We were delicately termed LODGERS, not prisoners, by the authorities.

2. (common).—A person of no account: *e.g.* 'only a LODGER.' *Cf.* HOG.

LODGING-SLUM, *subs. phr.* (thieves').—Hiring furnished lodgings and robbing them of all portable articles of value.—GROSE (1823).

LOG, *subs.* (public school).—The last boy of his 'form' or 'house.'

LOGE, *subs.* (old).—*See* quots. For synonyms *see* TURNIP.

1690. B. E., *Dict. Cant. Crew*, s.v.

1725. *New Cant. Dict.*, s.v. LOGE, a watch. I suppose from the French *horloge*, a watch or clock.

1785. GROSE, *Vulg. Tongue*, s.v. LOGE . . . he filed a cloy of a LOGE . . . he picked a pocket of a watch.

LOGES, *subs.* (old).—*See* quot.

1610. ROWLANDS, *Martin Mark-all*, p. 39 (H. Club's Repr. 1874). LOGES a passe or warrant. A Feager of LOGES, one that beggeth with false passes.

LOGGERHEAD, *subs.* (old).—A blockhead. For synonyms *see* BUFFLE and CABBAGE-HEAD.

1589. SHAKSPEARE, *Love's Labour Lost*, iv. 3, 207. Ah, you whoreson LOGGERHEAD! you were born to do me shame.

1597. SHAKSPEARE, *1 Henry IV*, ii. 4. 4. *Poins.* Where hast been, Hal? *Prince.* With three or four LOGGERHEADS amongst three or four score hogsheads.

1599. NASHE, *Lenten Stuffe* [GROSART (1883-4), v. 281]. A sweaty LOGGERHEAD.

1609. DEKKER, *Gul's Horn-booke* [GROSART (1886), ii. 204]. In defiance of those terrible blockhouses, their LOGGERHEADS make a true discovery of their wild country.

1667. DRYDEN, *Sir Martin Mark-all*, i. *Warn.* Pray, sir, let me alone: what is it to you if I rail upon myself? Now could I break my own LOGGER-HEAD.

1672. C. COTTON, *Scarronides*, Bk. i. p. 44 (ed. 1725). At last his Friend jog'd him with's Hand, How like a LOGGER-HEAD you stand!

1690. B. E., *Dict. Cant. Crew*, s.v.

1704. SWIFT, *Battle of the Books*, in *Prose Wks.* (Camelot). A pack of rogues, and fools . . . . and confounded LOGGERHEADS.

1777. SHERIDAN, *Trip to Scarborough*, i. 2. *Lory.* Here comes a head, sir, would contrive it better than both our LOGGERHEADS, if she would but join in the confederacy.

1785. GROSE, *Vulg. Tongue*, s.v. LOGGERHEAD s.v.

1815. SCOTT, *Guy Mannering*, ii. ch. vii. 'What plea, you LOGGERHEAD,' said the lawyer.

Adj. (old).—Stupid. Also LOGGERHEADED (*q.v.*).

1596. NASHE, *Saffron Walden*, in *Works*, iii. 104. For the printing of this LOGGER-HEAD Legend of lyes.

1711. SWIFT, *Journal to Stella*, 22 August, Lett. 28. Pretty, dear, little, naughty, saucy M.D. Silly, impudent, LOGGERHEAD Presto.

TO BE AT (or COME TO) LOGGERHEADS, *verb. phr.* (old).—To quarrel; to come to blows.

1678. COTTON, *Virgil Travestie*, in *Wks.* (1725), Bk. iv. p. 90. He was . . . . ready . . . . To fall to LOGGERHEADS . . . . with a few saucy Carpenters.

1688. SHADWELL, *Sq. of Alsatia*, in *Works* (1720), iv. 19. GO TO LOGGERHEADS with the constable and the watch.

1690. B.E., *Dict. Cant. Crew*, s.v.

1701. FARQUHAR, *Sir Harry Wildair*, i. They FELL TO LOGGERHEADS about their playthings.

1751. SMOLLETT, *Peregrine Pickle*, xxxix. Who having driven their carts against each other, quarrelled, and WENT TO LOGGERHEADS on the spot.

1828. SMEATON, *Doings in London*, 'The Humours of the Fleet.' Disputes more noisy now a quarrel breeds, And fools on both sides FALL TO LOGGERHEADS.

1846. *Punch* x. 46. The Queen's Speech, xxx. 'F. M. the Duke of Wellington will let Mr. Punch have the earliest intimation of anything definite being come to.' As we have not heard from his grace. . . . we can only presume that the ministers were, up to the last moment, AT LOGGERHEADS.

1876. C. H. WALL, trans. *Molière*, i. 199. You see that without my help you would still all be AT LOGGERHEADS.

LOGGERHEADED, *adj.* (old).—Blockheaded. Also LOG-HEADED.

1567. EDWARDS, *Damon & Pithias* [DODSLEY, *Old Plays* (1874), iv. 65]. For well I knew it was some mad-headed child That invented this name, That the LOG-HEADED knave might be beguiled.

1596-7. SHAKSPEARE, *Taming of the Shrew*, iv. 1. You LOGGER-HEADED and unpolish'd grooms.

1626. BRETON, *Pasquil's Mad-cappe* [GROSART (1876), i. *e.* 6, 1, 8]. Who hath not seene a LOGGER-HEADED Asse.

1672. C. COTTON, *Scarronides*, Bk. iv. p. 102 (ed. 1725). But like a LOGGER-HEADED Lubber, Thou grinning stand'st, and seest me Blubber.

1684. LACY, *Sauny the Scot*, iii. 1. Here, here, you LOGGERHEADED curs.

LOGIE, *subs.* (theatrical).—Sham jewellery. [From David Logie the inventor].

1883. SALA, *Living London*, 483. The plastering of girdles with zinc LOGIES.

2. (Winchester School).—Sewage.

LOG-ROLLER, *subs.* (colloquial).—1. A conditional ally in passing a bill through the Legislature without reference to the merits or demerits of the measure so advanced; and (2) a venal critic assistant or friend. *See* LOG-ROLLING.

1885. *Field*, 19 Dec. But some very good contracts can be made, so that the LOGROLLERS are pleased, and also the ignorant, to whose folly the defences are ostensibly a tribute.

1890. BLACK (in *Notes & Queries*, 7th S. ix. 106). Dryden presents the alternatives very clearly. If the literary friend does not praise his comrade's work, he must, of course, be dumb with envy; if he does praise it, then he is a LOG-ROLLER.

1895. *Star*, LOGROLLER (a constant signature).

LOG-ROLLING, *subs.* (colloquial).—Co-operation in the pursuit of money, business, or praise. *See* quots.

1848. BARTLETT, *Dict. of Americanisms*, s.v. LOG-ROLLING. For instance, a member from St. Lawrence has a pet bill for a plank road which he wants pushed through; he accordingly makes a bargain with a member from Onondaga, who is coaxing along a charter for a bank, by which St. Lawrence agrees to vote for Onondaga's bank, provided Onondaga will vote in turn for St. Lawrence's plank road.

1855. *Washington Union*, 10 Feb. The legislation of Congress is controlled by a system of combination and LOG-ROLLING.

1872. DE VERE, *Americanisms*, p. 260, 1. Vote for my bill and I will vote for your bill; and this is called LOG-ROLLING.

1875. *American English*, in *Chamb. Journal*, 25 Sept., p. 610. When a group of members supports a bill in which they have no direct interest, in order to secure the help of its promoters for a bill of their own, they are said to be LOG-ROLLING, a term taken from the backwoods, where a man who has cut down a big tree gets his neighbours to help him in rolling it away, and in return helps them with their logs.

1887. *Lippincott's Mag.*, July, p. 162. And first as to that question of literary LOG-ROLLING which has of late been harped upon so much.

1888. *Globe*, 17 Oct. One has always a suspicion that LOG-ROLLING is at work.

1889. *Town and Country*, 14 Dec., p. 18, col. 4. Votes which have been obtained by no end of trouble, and Heaven knows how much of LOG-ROLLING, will disappear as a dream.

LOGY, *adj.* (American).—Dull. [*Cf.* Du. *log* = heavy; slow; unwieldy].

LOLL, *subs.* (old).—1. A favorite child.—GROSE (1785); MATSELL (1859).

2. *See* LOLLPOOP.

Verb. (old colloquial).—To lounge; to lie lazily; to sprawl.

1362. LANGLAND, *Piers Plowman* (C), x. 215. He that LOLLETH is lame other his leg out of ioynte.

1602. SHAKSPEARE, *Othello*, IV. 1, l. 137. So hangs, and LOLLS, and weeps upon me.

1609. SHAKSPEARE, *Troilus and Cressida*, i. 3. At this fustie stuffe, The large *Achilles* on his prest bed LOLLING, From his deepe chest laughes out a lowd applause.

1640. T. HEYWOOD, *Love's Mistress*, i. Juno lay LOLLING in my Uncle's lap.

1676. ETHEREGE, *Man of Mode*, in *Wks.* (1704); i. 194. And his looks are more languishing than a lady's when She LOLLS at stretch in her coach.

1690. B. E., *Dict. Cant. Crew*, s.v. LOLPOOP. . . . LOLL, to Lean on the Elbows; also to put out the Tongue in derision.

1693. DRYDEN, *Juvenal*, I. 204. Meantime his lordship LOLLS within at ease.

1711. *Spectator*, No. 187. Hyæna can LOLL in her coach, with something so fixed in her countenance, that it is impossible to conceive her meditation is employed only on her dress and her charms in that posture.

1725. *New Cant. Dict.*, s.v.

1727. GAY, *Beggar's Opera*, i. Air 14. Fondly let me LOLL, Pretty, pretty Poll.

1753. *Adventurer*, No. 96. I found him in full health, LOLLING in an easy chair.

1754. *Connoisseur*, No. 11. The genuine careless LOLL and easy saunter.

1864. DICKENS, *Our Mutual Friend*, Bk. iv. ch. XVI. 'I wish to goodness, Ma,' said Lavvy . . . 'that you'd LOLL a little.'

1872. *Figaro*, 22 June, 'Lay of the Gallant Yachtsman.' You may see me here, upon the pier, LOLL lazily to and fro.

1876. M. E. BRADDON, *Joshua Haggard*, x. 'I don't see any harm in a good novel once in a way, if you take your time over it, and don't LOLL by the fireside half the day, poking your nose into a book and letting your house go to rack and ruin.'

1893. HENLEY, *London Voluntaries*, 10. Lingers and LOLLS, loth to be done with day.

LOLLER. *See* LOLLPOOP.

LOLLIPOP (or **LOLLYPOP**), *subs.* (colloquial).—1. A sweetmeat. Also LOLLY.

1823. GROSE, *Vulgar Tongue*, 3rd ed., s.v.

1838. C. SELBY, *Catching an Heiress*, Sc. 2. Our hearts we cheer, with LOLLYPOPS.

1844. DISRAELI, *Coningsby*, ix. The . . . . hopeless votary of LOLLYPOP—the opium eater of schoolboys.

1851-61. MAYHEW, *Lond. Lab.*, i. 215. Hard-bake, almond-toffy, half-penny LOLLYPOPS.

1861. THACKERAY, *Lovel the Widower*, i. I would . . . . never give these children LOLLYPOP.

1876. C. HINDLEY, *Life and Adventures of a Cheap Jack*, p. 101. William Carrol was his partner, or butty, in the LOLLIPOP business.

1885. G. A. SALA, in *Daily Telegraph*, 3 Sept., 5/5. From a perambulator to a packet of LOLLIES or sugarplums.

2. (venery).—The *penis*. Also LADIES' LOLLIPOP. For synonyms *see* CREAMSTICK and PRICK.

LOLLOP, *verb.* (colloquial).—To lounge about; TO LOAF. Hence, LOLLOP, *subs.* = a lazybones or LOAFER; and LOLLOPY, *adj.* = lazy.

1745. C. H. WILLIAMS, *Place-book*, quoted in *Notes & Queries*, 7 S. iv. 425. Next in LOLLOP'D Sandwich, with negligent grace.

1748. SMOLLETT, *Rod. Random*, xxxiv. 'You are allowed, on pretence of sickness, to LOLLOP at your ease, while your betters are kept to hard duty!'

1859. MATSELL, *Vocabulum*, s.v.

1865. MASSON, *Inaugural Address*, 13 Nov. What matters it to our judgment of a beautiful poem, it is asked, what was the appearance and personal character of the author—whether he was laborious and independent in his habits, or LOLLOPED on the surface of society, accepting all he could get and paying nobody? With all deference to those who think otherwise I say that it matters a great deal.

1878. LADY BRASSEY, *Voy. of Sunbeam*, I. i. For four long hours . . . . we LOLLOPPED about in the trough of a heavy sea.

1883. *Daily Telegraph*, 26 Jan., p. 5, col. 3. She LOLLOPS about in a loose dressing-gown, and he is seduced into the carelessness of carpet slippers.

LOLLOP-FEVER, *subs.* (American).—Laziness.

1859. MATSELL, *Vocabulum*, s.v.

LOLLOPING, *adj.* (colloquial).—Idle; lounging; slovenly.

1819. MOORE, *Tom Crib*, xvi. Turier. . . . made a heavy LOLLOPING hit.

1844. STEPHENS, *Adv. of a Gentleman*, iii. Horses having long pasterns, have usually a lumbering LOLLOPING action, neither fast nor pleasant.

LOLLPOOP (LOLL, or LOLLER), *subs.* (old).—*See* quots.

1600. BRETON, *Pasquils' Madcappe*, p. 10. A lobbe, a lovte, a heavy LOLL, a logge.

1690. B. E., *Dict. Cant. Crew*, s.v.

1785. GROSE, *Vulg. Tongue*, s.v. LOLLPOOP, a lazy, idle drone.

LOLL-TONGUE. TO PLAY A GAME AT LOLL-TONGUE, *verb. phr.* (old).—To be salivated for syphilis.—GROSE (1796).

LOLLY, *subs.* (pugilists').—1. The head. For synonyms *see* CRUMPET.

2. *See* LOLLIPOP.

LOLLYBANGER, *subs.* (nautical).—A ships' cook. *See* LOBLOLLY.

LOMBARD-FEVER, *subs.* (old).—The 'idles'; loafing.

1767. RAY, *Proverbs* [BOHN (1893), 55], s.v.

1785. GROSE, *Vulg. Tongue*, s.v.

LOMBARD ST. ALL LOMBARD STREET TO A CHINA ORANGE, *phr.* (old).—Said of a certainty; the longest possible odds.

1819. MOORE, *Tom Crib*, 38. ALL LOMBARD STREET TO NINEPENCE on it. *Note*. More usually LOMBARD ST. TO A CHINA ORANGE. There are several of these fanciful forms of betting—Chelsea College to a sentry-box; Pompey's pillar to a stick of sealing-wax, etc. etc.

1849. BULWER, *Caxtons*, iv. 3. 'It's LOMBARD ST. TO A CHINA ORANGE,' quoth uncle Jack. 'Are the odds in favor of fame against failure really so great?' answered my father.

1892. *Evg. Standard*, 9 Nov. i. 1. We describe the betting upon a moral certainty as being ALL LOMBARD-STREET TO A CHINA ORANGE.

LONDON. TO TURN (or PUT) THE BEST SIDE TO LONDON, *verb. phr.* (common).—To show one's best: *cf.* HUMPHREY'S TOPPERS.

1873. *Cassell's Mag.*, Jan., p. 248, col. 2. This placing the goods in alternate rows of large and small was followed until the top of the box was gained, and then a row of very fine fish indeed crowned the whole. Venturing a remark upon this, the packer grinned as he returned, 'Allays PUT THE BEST SIDE TO LONDON, gov'nor. Wouldn't do to shove the big uns underneath. People wouldn't b'lieve they was there, not if yer swore it. And when we tells 'em up for sale, we allays picks 'em up in double rows, takin' care to keep the big fish uppermost.'

LONDON-IVY (or LONDON PARTICULAR), *subs.* (common).—A thick fog.

1852. DICKENS, *Bleak House*, ch. iii. I asked him whether there was a great fire any-where . . . . 'O dear no, miss,' he said. 'This is a LONDON PARTICULAR.'

1889. *Sporting Life*, 4 Jan. A very severe cold caught by him during a nine hours' contact with LONDON IVY.

1890. *Sportsman*, 13 Dec. If only from the question of cost it is clear that a clean sweep should be made of LONDON PARTICULAR.

LONDON ORDINARY, *subs.* (common).—The beach at Brighton. [Where trippers feed].

LONE-DUCK (or -DOVE), *subs.* (common).—A woman out of keeping; also a prostitute, who works away from home by means of houses of accommodation. Also QUIET MOUSE (*q.v.*).

LONE-STAR STATE, *subs. phr.* (American).—Texas. [From the flag with a single star in the centre].

LONG, *subs.* (Stock Exchange).—1. A BULL (*q.v.*); *cf.* SHORT.

1888. *Daily Telegraph*, 19 Nov. The ramket continued somewhat depressed on LONGS selling.

2. (Fenian).—A rifle: *cf.* SHORT = a revolver.

3. *See* JOHN LONG.

Adj. (once literary: now colloquial or humorous).—Tall.

*c.*1189. *Destruction of Troy* [E. E. T. S.], 1. 3805. Off Duke Nestor to deme, doughty in werre, He was LONG and large, with lemys full grete.

*c.*1440. *Isumbras*, line 258. For he es bothe LANGE and heghe, The faireste mane that ever I seghe.

1888-9. *Broadside Ballad.* 'If only I were LONG enough.'

THE LONG (University).—The summer vacation.

1852. BRISTED, *Five Years in an English University*, p. 37. For a month or six weeks in THE LONG they rambled off to see the sights of Paris.

1863. READE, *Hard Cash*, i. 17. 'I hope I shall not be ['ploughed for smalls'] to vex you and puss.' . . . . ' . . . Puss? that is me [sister Julia] How dare he? Did I not forbid all these nicknames and all this Oxfordish, by proclamation, last LONG.' 'Last LONG?' [remonstrates mamma]. 'Hem! last protracted vacation.'

THE LONGS, *subs.* (Oxford University).—The latrines at Brasenose. [Built by Lady Long].

Adj. (colloquial).—Heavy; great: as a 'LONG price', 'LONG odds' etc. etc.

1850. AYTOUN, *Dreepdaily Burghs*, 10. If we look sharp after it, I bet THE LONG ODDS you will carry it in a canter.

1854. WHYTE MELVILLE, *General Bounce*, xiii. Now for good information, LONG odds, a safe man, and a shot at the favourite!

1892. MILLIKEN, *'Arry Ballads*, 63. Too LONG in the purse to let slip.

THE LONG AND THE SHORT OF IT, *phr.* (common).—The sum of a matter; the whole. *See* LONG ATTACHMENT.

*d.*1845. HOOD, *Paired not Matched.* For I am small, My wife is tall, And that's THE SHORT AND THE LONG OF IT.

LONG IN THE MOUTH, *adj. phr.* (common).—Tough.

LONG IN THE TOOTH, *adj. phr.* (common).—Elderly.

LONG ACRE, *subs. phr.* (rhyming).—A baker; a BURN-CRUST (*q.v.*).

LONG-ATTACHMENT, *subs.* (common).—A tall man and short woman walking together, or *vice versâ*: also THE LONG AND THE SHORT OF IT.

LONG-BILL, *subs.* (thieves').—A long term of imprisonment. SHORT-BILL = a short term.

LONG-BIT, *subs.* (old American).—A defaced 20 cent piece (MATSELL); also 15 cents in Western U. S. (*Century*). SHORT-BIT = 10 cents (*Century*).

LONG-BOW. TO DRAW (or PULL) THE LONG-BOW, *verb. phr.* (colloquial).—To tell improbable stories. Hence, LONG-BOW MAN = a liar.

1653. URQUHART, *Rabelais*, v. ch. 30. 'Twas Ælian, that LONG-BOW man, that told you so, never believe him, for he lies as fast as a dog can trot.

1767. RAY, *Proverbs* [BOHN (1893), 64], s.v.

1819-24. BYRON, *Don Juan*, xvi. 1. At speaking truth perhaps they are less clever, But DRAW THE LONG-BOW better now than ever.

1849. THACKERAY, *Pendennis*, xxx. What is it makes him PULL THE LONG BOW in that wonderful manner?

1871. *Daily News*, 29 Dec. If now and then he appears to DRAW THE LONG BOW, or rather to shoot with an extraordinary rifle, he does not abuse the reader's faith unmercifully.

1883. A. DOBSON, *Old-World Idylls*, p. 134. The great Gargilius, then, behold! His LONG BOW hunting tales of old Are now but duller.

ENGLISH SYNONYMS. To climb a steep hill; to come (or cut) it strong (or fat, or THICK); to embroider; TO GAMMON (*q.v.*); to lay it on thick; to put on the pot; to pull a leg; to slop over.

FRENCH SYNONYMS. *La faire à l'oseille; en voilà une sévère; c'est plus fort que de jouer au bouchon.*

SPANISH SYNONYM. *Jacarear.*

ITALIAN SYNONYM. *Spalare.*

LONG CHALK. BY A LONG CHALK, *phr.* (colloquial).—By far; in a large measure.

1837. R. H. BARHAM, *Ingoldsby Legends* (ed. 1862), 447. Still Sir Alured's steed was BY LONG CHALKS the best.

1838-40. HALIBURTON, *The Clockmaker*, p. 26 (ed. 1826). 'Yes,' says he, 'your factories down East beat all natur; they go ahead on the English a LONG CHALK.'

1844. CHARLES SELBY, *London by Night*, ii. 2. *Jack.* Yes, and I opine which will come off second best BY LONG CHALKS.

1848. RUXTON, *Life In The Far West*, 2. Not a hundred years ago BY A LONG CHALK.

1856. C. BRONTË, *Professor*, iii. 'You are not as fine a fellow as your plebeian brother BY A LONG CHALK.'

1883. GRENVILLE MURRAY, *People I Have Met*, 133. The finest thing in the world; or. . . . 'the best thing out BY MANY CHALKS.'

1888. ROLF BOLDREWOOD, *Robbery Under Arms*, v. 'Isn't it as easy to carry on for a few years more as it was twenty years ago?' 'Not BY A LONG CHALK.'

1892. HUME NISBET, *Bushranger's Sweetheart*, 209. 'Oh, everyone to their taste, of course; she's not mine BY A LONG CHALK.'

LONG-CROWN, *subs.* (old).—A clever fellow: as in the proverb, 'That caps LONG-CROWN, and he capped the Devil.'

LONG-DISPAR, *subs.* (Winchester College).— *See* quot.

1866. MANSFIELD, *School Life*, 84. There were six of these [DISPARS (*q.v.*) or portions] to a shoulder, and eight to a leg of mutton, the other joints being divided in like proportion. All these 'dispars' had different names; the thick slice out of the centre of the leg was called a 'middle cut,' . . . the ribs 'Racks,' the loin LONG DISPARS.

LONG DRINK, *subs. phr.* (common).—A considerable quantity, as compared to a NIP (*q.v.*), *i.e.*, a drop of SHORT (*q.v.*).

1883. *Daily Telegraph*, 2 July, p. 5, col. 3. The list of LONG DRINKS which may be imbibed with deliberation and through the medium of a couple of straws.

LONG-EAR, *subs.* (American University).—1. A reading man; a sober student. *See* SHORT-EAR.

2. *in pl.* (common).—A donkey. For synonyms *see* MOKE.

LONG ELIZA, *subs.* (trade).—*See* quot.

1884. *Pall Mall Gazette*, 4 Dec. LONG-ELIZAS (the trade term for certain blue and white vases ornamented with figures of tall thin china-women) is a name derived undoubtedly from the German or Dutch. Our sailors and traders called certain Chinese vases from the figures which distinguished them, *lange Lischen* (= tall Lizzies) and the English sailors and traders promptly translated this into LONG ELIZAS.

LONG-EYE, *subs. phr.* (pidgin).—The female *pudendum.* For synonyms *see* MONOSYLLABLE.

LONG-FACED ONE, *subs. phr.* (military).—A horse. For synonyms *see* PRAD.

LONG-FEATHERS, *subs.* (military).—Straw; STROMMEL (*q.v.*). Fr. *piausser sur plume de Beauce* = to sleep in the straw.

1879. Correspondent of *Notes & Queries*, 5 S. xii. 246. Is this bit of ironical slang worth preserving? An old man, lately emerged from what we North-countrymen call the 'Bastile,' objected in my hearing to that institution, because, *inter alia*, 'you had to sleep there on LONG FEATHERS,' that is, upon bedding stuffed with straw.

LONG-FIRM, *subs.* (common).—*See* quot. 1869. Fr. *la bande noire.* A somewhat similar mode of swindling is described in PARKER'S *View of Society* (ii. 33. 1781).

1869. *Orchestra*, 2 Jan., 235, i. Dismal records of the doings of the LONG FIRM, a body of phantom capitalists who issue large orders to supply an infinite variety of goods—from herrings to harmoniums, from cotton-twist to pictures; the ledger of the LONG FIRM has room for the most multifarious transactions. The rule of procedure with the LONG FIRM is simple: a noble order, a moderate sum paid on account, bills for the remainder, an order to deliver the goods at some country warehouse or depository—and exit Montague Tigg. In the next town he changes his name and his partner's, and repeats the operation. From Liverpool and Manchester he flings the bait to London tradesmen, and now and then a fish is hooked.

1886. *Daily News*, 20 Sept., 7, 1. This was the usual case of what is termed LONG FIRM swindling. The prisoner pretended to carry on business in the city, and ordered goods of all descriptions, which were never used for legitimate purposes, but which were immediately pawned or otherwise disposed of.

1892. *Pall Mall Gazette*, 17 Oct., p. 5, c. 2. Not a few of the most dangerous of the LONG FIRM class (and there are some about at the present time) haunt the locality, as our criminal courts of justice revealed only a few months ago.

LONG-FORK, *subs.* (Winchester College).—*See* quot.

1866. MANSFIELD, *School Life*, 80. We had not proper toasting forks, but pieces of stick called LONG FORKS.

LONG-GALLERY, *subs.* (old).—*See* quot.

1823. GROSE, *Vulg. Tongue* (3rd ed.), s.v. LONG-GALLERY. Throwing, or, rather, trundling, the dice the whole length of the board.

LONG-GHOST, *subs.* (common).—A gawk. For synonyms *see* LAMP-POST.

LONG-GLASS, *subs.* (Eton College).—*See* quot.

1883. BRINSLEY-RICHARDS, *Seven Years at Eton*, 321. A glass nearly a yard long, shaped like the horn of a stage-coach guard, and with a hollow globe instead of a foot. It held a quart of beer, and the ceremony of drinking out of it constituted an initiation into the higher circle of Etonian swelldom. There was LONG-GLASS drinking once or twice a week during the summer half. The *invités* attended in an upper room of Tap after two, and each before the long glass was handed to him had a napkin tied round his neck. It was considered a grand thing to drain the glass without removing it from the lips, and without spilling any of its contents. This was difficult, because when the contents of the tubular portion of the glass had been sucked down, the beer in the globe would remain for a moment as if congealed there: then if the drinker tilted the glass up a little, and shook it, the motionless beer would give a gurgle and come with a sudden rush all over his face. There was a way of holding the long glass at a certain angle by which catastrophes were avoided. Some boys could toss off their quart of ale in quite superior style, and I may as well remark that these clever fellows could do little else.

LONG-HAIRED CHUM, *subs. phr.* (tailors').—A female friend; a sweetheart.

LONG-HEADED, *adj.* (old: now colloquial).—Shrewd; far-seeing; clever. Also LONG-HEADEDNESS.

1690. B. E., *Dict. Cant. Crew*, s.v.

1711. *Spectator*, No. 52. But being a LONG-HEADED gentlewoman, I am apt to imagine she has some further design than you have yet penetrated.

1725. *New Cant. Dict.*, s.v.

1840. DICKENS, *Old Curiosity Shop*, lxvi. Many distinguished characters, called men of the world, LONG-HEADED customers, knowing dogs, shrewd fellows.

1871. LOWELL, *Study Windows*, 126. Ulysses was the type of LONG-HEADEDNESS.

LONG-HOGS, *subs.* (old).—The first growth of wool on a sheep.

1841. *Punch*, i. 85. The tailor clips the implicated LONG-HOGS from the prolific backs of the living mutton.

LONG-HOME, *subs.*(old colloquial).—The grave.—WRIGHT and HALL.

1701. *Harl. MSS.*, fol. 61. And thy traveyle shalt thou sone ende, For to thy LONG-HOME sone shalt thou wende.

1843. DICKENS, *Martin Chuzzlewit*, I. 2. Following the order book to its LONG 'OME in the iron safe.

LONG-HOPE, *subs.* (old).—*See* quot.

1823. GROSE, *Vulg. Tongue* (3rd ed.), s.v. LONG-HOPE . . . At Oxford, . . . the symbol of long expectations in studying for a degree.

LONG-LADY, *subs.* (old).—A farthing candle.

LONG-LANE, *subs.* (common).—The throat. For synonyms *see* GUTTER-ALLEY.

FOR THE LONG-LANE, *adv. phr.* (old).—Said when a thing is borrowed without intention of repayment.

LONG-LEGS (or **LONG-'UN**), *subs.* (common).—A tall man or woman. For synonyms *see* LAMP-POST.

LONG-MEG, *subs.* (old).—A very tall woman. For synonyms *see* LAMP-POST.—B. E. (1690); *New Cant. Dict.* (1725); GROSE (1785).

LONG-OATS, *subs.* (military).—A broom or fork-handle used to belabour a horse: *cf.* THORLEY'S FOOD FOR CATTLE.

LONG-ONE, *subs.* (poachers').—A hare: *cf.* LONG-TAIL.

LONG-PAPER, *subs.* (Winchester).—Paper for writing tasks on.

LONG-PIG, *subs.* (nautical).—*See* quots.

1883. ST. JOHNSTON, *Camping amongst Cannibals* [*Century*]. The expression LONG PIG is not a joke, nor a phrase invented by Europeans, but one frequently used by the Fijians, who looked upon a corpse as ordinary butcher meat, and called a human body *puaka balava*, LONG PIG, in contradistinction to *puaka dina*, or real pig.

1893. *Fortnightly Review*, Jan., p. 37. I cannot find it in my heart to condemn them for trying to get a little LONG PIG whenever an opportunity presents itself.

LONG-ROBE, *subs.* (old).—A lawyer.

1611. BARRY, *Ram Alley* [DODSLEY, *Old Plays* (1874), x. 355]. What would you, sir? I guess your LONG profession By your scant suit.

1662. *Adv. Five Hours* [DODSLEY, (*Old Plays* (1874), xv. 230]. And, having been affronted by the sword, To pray the aid of the LONG ROBE, and take An advocate for second.

1694. *Gentlemen's Journal*, Mar., p. 49. The third was of the LONG ROBE.

LONG-ROW. *See* HOE.

LONGS AND SHORTS (also **LONGS AND BROADS**), *subs. phr.* (card-sharpers').—Cards so manufactured that all above the eight are a trifle longer than those below it: nothing under an eight can be cut, and the chances against turning up an honour at whist are reduced to two to one. *Cf.* BRIEF and CONCAVE.

LONG-SAUCE, *subs.* (American).—Beets, parsnips, or carrots, in contradistinction to SHORT-SAUCE (*q.v.*) = onions, turnips, etc. [An old English usage].

LONG-SHANKS, *subs.* (old).—A tall man. For synonyms *see* LAMP-POST.—B.E. (1690); *New Cant. Dict.* (1725); GROSE (1785).

LONG-SHORE BUTCHER, *subs. phr.* (nautical).—A coastguardsman; a SHINGLE-TRAMPER (*q.v.*).

LONG-SHOT, *subs.* (racing).—A bet made at large odds: as 100 to 1 on anything not in favour.

1869. *Leisure Hour*, May. Will teach the tyro when to take a LONG SHOT . . . when to save himself by timely hedging.

1888. *Sporting Life*, 10 Dec. Bachelor was next in demand at 5 to 1, and LONG SHOTS were forthcoming about either of the others.

1892. MILLIKEN, *'Arry Ballads*, 16. A jolly LONG SHOT.

LONG-SLEEVED TOP, *subs.* (thieves').—A silk hat.—RICHARDSON (1889).

LONG-SLEEVED 'UN, *subs. phr.* (Australian).—A long glass. Fr. *un wagon*.

LONG-STOMACH, *subs.* (old).—A voracious eater; a WOLFER (*q.v.*).—GROSE (1785).

LONG-TAIL, *subs.* (sporting).—1. A greyhound: hence, as dogs unqualified to hunt were curtailed, gentlefolk.

1596. SHAKSPEARE, *Merry Wives*, iii. 4. Come cut and LONGTAIL under the degree of a squire.

1662. *Rump Songs*, ii. 126. But LONG-TAIL and bob-tail can never agree.

1885. *Graphic*, 17 Oct. 427/2. Greyhounds, as all coursers know, are often designated as LONG-TAILS.

2. (sporting).—A pheasant.

1854. F. E. SMEDLEY, *Harry Coverdale*, ch. xxiii. In the meantime, Harry and the Colonel were blazing away at the LONG-TAILS most unmercifully.

1871. *Standard*, 6 Nov. The period of the year at which we have now arrived is quite as important as the advent of the month sounding the note of war against the 'birds,' or initiating the campaign against the LONG-TAILS.

3. (old).—A native of Kent.

1628. *Robin Goodfellow* [HALLIWELL & WRIGHT], s.v. Truly, sir, sayd my hoastesse, I think we are called LONGTAYLES, by reason our tayles are long, that we use to passe the time withall, and make ourselves merry.

1662. *Rump Songs*, ii. 47. I shall not dispute whether LONG-TAILS of Kent.

1701. *Broadside* (in Dulwich College Library), 'Advice to the Kentish LONG-TAILS by the Wise Men of Gotham'. [Title].

4. (old).—*See* quot.

1755. JOHNSON, *Dict.*, s.v. LONGTAIL, a canting term for, one or another.

LONG-TAILED, *adj.* (old).—Of gentle birth; of good standing.

1662. *Rump Songs*, i. 195. She blushing said, that LONG-TAILED men would tell, Quoth I, I'll be as silent as the night.

LONG-TAILED BEGGAR, *subs. phr.* (common).—A cat.

1834. MARRYAT, *Peter Simple*, ii. 'You must larn to chaw baccy, drink grog, and call the cat a BEGGAR, and then you knows all a midshipman's expected to know nowadays.'

1874. HOTTEN, *Slang Dict.*, s.v. LONG-TAILED BEGGAR. 'A boy, during his first, and a very short voyage, to sea, had . . . entirely forgotten the name of the cat, and was obliged, pointing to puss, to ask his mother what she called that 'ere LONG-TAILED BEGGAR?' Sailors when they hear a freshwater tar discoursing largely are apt to say, 'But how mate about that LONG-TAILED BEGGAR?'

ENGLISH SYNONYMS. Baudrons (Scots'); gib; grimalkin; masheen; nimshod; puss; Thomas; Tyb.

FRENCH SYNONYMS. *Un lapin de gouttière* (familiar = rabbit of the tiles); *un greffier*, *griffard* or *griffon* (griffe = claw); *un gaspard* (popular).

ITALIAN SYNONYMS. *Laffaro; gulfo*.

SPANISH SYNONYMS. *Estafion*, *estaffin*, or *estaffier*.

LONG-TAILED FINNIPS (or **LONG-TAILED 'UNS**), *subs. phr.* (thieves').—Banknotes for high amounts.

1857. SNOWDEN, *Mag. Assist.*, 3rd ed., 144, s.v.

LONG-TEA, *subs.* (schoolboys').—1. Tea poured from a pot held high; and (2) LANT (*q.v.*).

LONG-TONGUE, *subs.* (old).—A tale-bearer; a chatterbox.

*c.*1550. INGLELEND, *Disobedient Child* [DODSLEY, *Old Plays* (1874), ii. 282]. What banging, what cursing. LONG-TONGUE, is with thee.

1886. BARHAM, *Ingoldsby Legends*, 'Grandmother's Clock.' Very short legs and a very LONG TONGUE.

LONG-TONGUED, *adj.* (old).—Talkative.

1593. SHAKSPEARE, *T. Andron.*, IV. 2. 150. 'Tis a deed of policy: Shall she live to betray this guilt of ours, A LONG-TONGUED babbling gossip?

1823. GROSE, *Vulg. Tongue* [3rd ed.], s.v. LONG-TONGUED. Loquacious, not able to keep a secret, He is as LONG-TONGUED as Granny; Granny was an idiot who could lick her own eye.

LONG-TOGS, *subs.*(nautical).—Shore-going clothes in general, and dress-clothes in particular.

1833. MARRYAT, *Peter Simple*, III. ii. May I be so bold as to ask, Captain O'Brien, whether I must wear one of them LONG-TOG, swallow-tailed coats—because if so I prefer being a quarter-master.

1834. MARRYAT, *Jack Faithful*, xxix. I had fitted on what are called at sea, and on the river, LONG TOGS; *i.e.*, I was dressed as most people are on shore.

1883. CLARK RUSSELL, *Sailor's Language*, s.v.

LONG-TOT, *subs.* (common).—A long set of figures for addition: as in examinations.

LONGWINDED, *adj.* (old: now recognised).—Diffuse; protracted; loquacious. *See* quots. 1690 and 1796.

1592. NASHE, *Pierce Penilesse* [GROSART (1883-4), ii. 77]. It will make them iolly LONG-WINDED.

1635. DAVENANT, *News from Plymouth*, ii. 1. I never read of such a LONG-WINDED monster.

1690. B. E., *Dict. Cant. Crew*, s.v. LONG-WINDED Paymaster, one that very slowly, heavily, or late Paies.

1725. *New Cant. Dict.*, s.v.

1796. GROSE, *Vulg. Tongue* (3rd ed.), s.v. LONG-WINDED, A LONG-WINDED parson, one who preached long, tedious sermons. A LONG-WINDED paymaster, one who takes long credit.

1871. CLARK RUSSELL, *Book of Authors*. Sir Walter Scott said Lord Clarendon's style was a little LONGWINDED.

LONSDALE'S NINEPINS, *subs. phr.* (old Parliamentary).—The nine boroughs for which Lord Lonsdale used to send up members to St. Stephens. A repartee connected with them is attributed to Burke.—H. J. BYRON (M.S.S. note in HOTTEN).

LOO, *subs.* (old).—1. *See* quot.

1785. GROSE, *Vulg. Tongue*, s.v. LOO, FOR THE GOOD OF THE LOO, for the benefit of the Company or Community.

2. (old).—*See* quot.

1839. AINSWORTH, *Jack Sheppard* [1889], p. 13. Blueskin . . . . turning . . . . beheld a young female, whose features were partially concealed by a LOO, or half mask, standing beside him.

Verb.(common).—To vanquish. [From the game of loo].

LOOBY, *subs.* (old: now recognised).—A fool; an idle dullard. For synonyms *see* BUFFLE and CABBAGE-HEAD.

1362. *Piers Ploughman*, A. i. 6. Great LOUBIES and long, that loth were to swinke.

1399. *Richard the Redeless*, ii. 170. This lorell that ladde this LOBY awey.

1529. S. FISH, *A Supplicacyon for the Beggers*, p. 13 (Arber's ed.). Set those sturdy LOBIES abrode in the world to get. . . . theire liuing with their laboure in the swete of theire faces.

1609. DEKKER, *Gul's Horne-Booke* [GROSART (1886), ii. 207]. And how to munch so like LOOBIES, that the wisest Solon in the world, shall not be able to take them for any other.

1690. B. E., *Dict. Cant. Crew*, s.v. LOOBY, a lazy dull Fellow.

1725. *New Cant. Dict.*, s.v.

*d.*1731. NED WARD, *Works*, ii. 20. 'Reflections on a country corporation.' Honest men precious as Rubies; Their May'rs successively are Boobies; And Aldermen great brawny LOOBIES.

1754. *Connoisseur*, No. 22. The country squire seldom fails of seeing his son as dull and awkward a LOOBY as himself.

1775. SHERIDAN, *Rivals*, ii. 1. I must leave you—I own I am somewhat flurried—and that confounded LOOBY has perceived it.

1776. FOOTE, *Bankrupt*, ii. How the LOOBIES must look.

1785. GROSE, *Vulg. Tongue*, s.v.

1815. SCOTT, *Guy Mannering*, ii. Now, you LOOBY, said the lawyer.

1845. DISRAELI, *Sybil*, Bk. IV. xi. 'I went once and stayed a week at Lady Jenny Spinner's to gain her LOOBY of a son and his eighty thousand a year.'

LOOK. TO LOOK A GIFT-HORSE IN THE MOUTH, *verb.phr.*(colloquial).—To criticize a present or favour. [From ascertaining the age of horses by looking at their teeth].

1663. S. BUTLER, *Hudibras*, I. i. 490. He ne'er consider'd it, as loth to LOOK A GIFT-HORSE IN THE MOUTH.

TO LOOK ALIVE, *verl. phr.* (colloquial).—To bestir oneself; to be on the alert. Also; TO LOOK SLIMY.

TO LOOK AS IF BUTTER WOULD NOT MELT IN ONE'S MOUTH.—*See* BUTTER.

TO LOOK AT THE MAKER'S NAME, *verb. phr.* (colloquial).—To drain (a glass) to the bottom; 'to bite one's name in the POT '(*q.v.*)

TO LOOK BABIES (or FOR CUPIDS) IN THE EYES, *verb. phr.* (old colloquial).—To look closely and amorously into the eyes for the reflected figures.

1593. *Tell-trothes N. Y. Gift*, 39. That BABIE which lodges IN womens EIES.

1607. BEAUMONT & FLETCHER, *Woman Hater*, iii. 1. I cannot think I shall become a coxcomb, To ha' my hair curl'd by an idle finger. . . . Mine EYES LOOKED BABIES IN.

1613. DRAYTON, *Polyolbion*, Song xi. While in their chrystal eyes he doth FOR CUPIDS LOOK.

1618. BEAUMONT and FLETCHER, *Loyal Subject*, iii. 2. Can ye LOOK BABIES, sister, IN THE young gallants' EYES, and twirl their bandstrings? *Ibid*. ii . 6. *Viol*. Will he play with me too? *Alin*. LOOK BABIES IN YOUR EYES, my pretty sweet one; There's a fine sport!

1621. BURTON, *Anat. Mel.*, III. ii. VI. v. (1651)576. They may kiss and coll, lye and LOOK BABIES IN one another's EYES.

1624. MASSINGER, *Renegado*, ii. 5. When a young lady wrings you by the hand,—thus; Or with an amorous touch presses your foot; LOOKS BABIES IN YOUR EYES, plays with your locks, etc.

1636. DAVENANT, *Platonic Lovers*, ii. 1. You may beget REFLECTIONS IN EACH OTHERS EYES.

1657. POOLE, *English Parnassus*, 420. [Among the phrases expressing the ways of lovers, is set down], 'LOOKING OF BABIES IN EACH OTHER'S EYES.'

1672. MARVELL, *Reher. Transp.*, i. 66. Only to speculate his own BABY IN THEIR EYES.

1682. MRS. BEHN, *City Heiress*, iii. 1. Sigh'd and LOOKT BABIES IN HIS gloating EYES.

1690. WILSON, *Belphegor*, ii. 3. What would I care for a man should court my little finger, LOOK BABIES IN MY EYES. . . . That was not the fashion of my time. Men were men then.

1692. *Gentlemen's Journal*, July, p. 9. Ten thousand CUPIDS wanton IN HER EYES.

1802. MOORE (LITTLE), *Poems*, 'Impromptu.' Thus in our looks some propagation lies, For we MAKE BABIES IN each other's EYES.

TO LOOK BIG. *See* BIG.

TO LOOK BLUE. *See* BLUE.

TO LOOK BOTTY. *See* BOTTY.

TO LOOK DOWN ONE'S NOSE, *verb. phr.* (colloquial).—To look glum; to have the BLUES (*q.v.*).

TO LOOK LIVELY, *verb. phr.* (common).—To be drunk. For synonyms *see* DRINKS and SCREWED.

TO LOOK FOR A NEEDLE IN A BOTTLE OF HAY (or IN A HAY-STACK), *verb. phr.* (colloquial). —To seek what it is impossible to find. [BOTTLE = a quantity of hay or grass, tied or bundled up. Fr. *botte*].

1592. GREENE, *Upstart Courtier* (1871), 4. b. He. . . . gropeth in the dark TO FIND A NEEDLE IN A BOTTLE OF HAY.

*c.*1845. HOOD, *Lost Heir*, ii. A child as is lost about London streets . . . . is A NEEDLE IN A BOTTLE OF HAY.

*c.*1880. W. M. BAKER, *New Timothy*, 200. How in the world will we manage to find you afterwards? After we get into the thick of the bush, it'll be like LOOKIN' FOR A NEEDLE IN the biggest sort of A HAYSTACK.

TO LOOK PRICKS, *verb. phr.* (venery).—To look lecherously; to leer an invitation to coition: *cf.* PINTLE-KEEK.

TO LOOK SHARP, *verb. phr.* (colloquial).—1. To exercise great vigilance; to be extremely careful.

1711. STEELE, *Spectator*, No. 132. The captain . . . ordered his man TO LOOK SHARP that none but one of the ladies should have the place he had taken fronting the coach-box.

2. (colloquial).—To be quick; to make haste.

1840. DICKENS, *Old Curiosity Shop*, xxxix. Kit told this gentleman TO LOOK SHARP, and he said he would not only LOOK SHARP, but he actually did, and presently came running back.

TO LOOK THROUGH A GLASS, *verb. phr.* (common).—To get drunk. For synonyms *see* DRINKS and SCREWED.

TO LOOK TOWARDS ONE, *verb. phr.* (common).—To drink one's health.

1847-8. THACKERAY, *Vanity Fair*, liii. The ladies drank to his 'ealth, and Mr. Moss, in the most polite manner, LOOKED TOWARDS him.

1890. FARJEON, *Felix*, I. i. 26. 'You know where the bottle is, and per'aps Mr. Wigg will jine you.' 'Mrs. Middlemore,' said Constable Wigg, 'you're a lady after my own heart . . . Here's LOOKING TOWARDS you.'

1892. HENLEY and STEVENSON, *Deacon Brodie*. Tableau III. Sc. 1, p. 31. Deacon, I LOOKS TOWARDS you.

TO LOOK UP, *verb. phr.* (colloquial).—1. To show a tendency to improvement; to recover.

1850. AYTOUN, *Dreepdaily Burghs*, 6. 'Suppose I were to start as a Peelite?' 'Something may be said in favour of that view, but on the whole, I should rather say not. That party may not LOOK UP for some little time, and then the currency is a stumbling block in the way.'

2. (colloquial).—To pay a visit.

1836. DICKENS, *Pickwick*, xlix. He used to go back for a week, just TO LOOK UP his old friends.

1859. *Punch*, xxxvi. 177. 1. When you hung out in Soho, old cock, one could often LOOK YOU UP.

LOOK-IN, *subs.* (colloquial). — A chance of success.

1870. *Bell's Life*, 12 Feb. If Fawcett imagines he has got a LOOK-IN, young Mullins will fight him for all the money he can get together in the London district.

1883. *Daily Telegraph*, August 7, p. 6, col. 2. Four had been examined, and he had expressed his belief that neither of them had a LOOK-IN as regarded the prizes.

1884. *Referee*, 23 March, p. 1, col. 4. Easter fought with great gameness, but he never had a LOOK-IN from the commencement.

1888. *Sporting Life*, 28 Nov. This athlete is stated to have run through the distance from the 15 yards mark in 10 min. 2⅘ sec., which did not give much of a LOOK-IN to the scratch man.

1891. *Licensed Vict. Gaz.*, 20 Mar. He will have a good LOOK-IN at Epsom if he goes for the City and Suburban.

1891. *Lic. Vict. Gaz.*, 17 April, p. 247, c. 1. It was not until the 15th round that Terry had a LOOK-IN—in a rapid exchange of counters, he got home a terrific blow on Forster's Roman nose, which smashed the nasal bone.

1892. MILLIKEN, *'Arry Ballads*, p. 28. They didn't get arf a LOOK-IN 'long o' me.

LOOKING-GLASS, *subs.* (old).—*See* quot. 1690. For synonyms *see* IT.

1690. B. E., *Dict. Cant. Crew*, s.v. LOOKING-GLASS, a Chamber-pot.

1725. *New Cant. Dict.*, s.v.

1785. GROSE, *Vulg. Tongue*, s.v.

TO LOOK ON, *verb. phr.* (turf). —Said of a horse not meant to do its best.

TO LOOK NINE WAYS FOR SUNDAYS, *verb. phr.* (nautical). —To squint. Fr. *vendre des guignes*.

LOON (LOUN or LOWN), *subs.* (old: now recognised).—A lout; a varlet; a rogue.

*c.*1500. *Babees Book* [E. E. T. S.], 291. And take it backe with manlike cheere, not like a Rusticke LOWNE.

15[?]. *Old Ballad* (quoted in *Othello*, ii. 3, 1608), 'King Stephen.' With that he called the tailor LOWN.

1602. DEKKER, *Honest Wh.*, Pt. II, in *Wks.* (1873), ii. 167. The sturdy begger, and the lazy LOWNE, Gets here hard hands, or laced correction.

1606. SHAKSPEARE, *Macbeth*, v. 3. ii. The devil damn thee black, thou cream-faced LOON.

1690. B. E., *Dict. Cant. Crew*, s.v. LOONSLATT . . . A false LOON, a true Scotchman, or Knave of any Nation.

1697. VANBRUGH, *Provoked Wife*, iii. 2. Then away John Thompson ran, And, egad! he ran with speed, But before he had run his length The false LOON had done the deed.

1725. *New Cant. Dict.*, s.v.

1771. FOOTE, *Maid of Bath*, iii. 2. I got acquainted with Maister Foote, the play-actor: I will get him to bring the filthy LOON on the stage.

1785. GROSE, *Vulg. Tongue*, s.v.

1798. COLERIDGE, *Ancient Mariner*, i. Hold-off; unhand me, gray-haired LOON.

1822. SCOTT, *Fortunes of Nigel*, xxx. It might be worth your lordship's while to have the LOON sent to a barber-surgeon's to learn some needful scantling of anatomy.

TO PLAY THE LOON, *verb. phr.* (Scots').—To play the whore.

1568. SEMPILL, *Ballats* (ed. 1878), p. 232. 'Being in ward for PLAYING OF THE LOUN With every ane list geif hir half a croun.' [Title].

*c.*1776. HERD, *Ancient & Mod. Scottish Songs*, ii. 7. I am o'er low to be your bride, Your LOWN I'll never be, Sir.

17[?]. *Old Scots Ballad* [quoted by BURNS], 'My Wife's a Wanton Wee Thing.' She PLAY'D THE LOON or she was married.

*c.*1802-5. *Minstrelsy Border*, ii. 75. I trow some may has PLAID THE LOWN, And fled her ain countree.

LOONSLATE (or LOONSLATT), *subs.* (old).—Thirteen pence halfpenny. *Cf.* HANGMAN'S WAGES.—B. E. (1690); *New Cant. Dict.* (1725); GROSE (1785).

LOONY (or LUNY), *adj.* (colloquial).—Crazy. [Short for 'lunatic']. Also as *subs.* = a fool; a natural. For synonyms *see* BUFFLE and CABBAGE-HEAD.

1883. E. C. MANN, *Psychol. Med.*, 424. He had frequent LUNY spells, as he called them.

LOOSE, *adj.* (old).—1. Wanton; BLUE (*q.v.*). Hence, LOOSE-LEGGED, *adj.* = LIGHT-HEELED (*q.v*); LOOSE IN THE HILTS (or HAFT) = incontinent; LOOSE-GIRDLED (or GOWNED) = approachable; LOOSE-WOMAN = a harlot; LOOSE-LIVER = a whoremaster, etc.

1595. SHAKSPEARE, *Two Gentlemen*, ii. 7, 41. I would prevent The LOOSE encounters of lascivious men.

1633. MASSINGER, *New Way to Pay Old Debts*, v. I had a reputation, but 'twas lost In my LOOSE course.

1636. DAVENANT, *The Wits*, iii. 3. This mansion is not her's, but a concealed retirement . . . To hide her LOOSE love.

1711. ADDISON, *Spectator*, No. 262. I have shown in a former Paper with how much Care I have avoided all such Thoughts as are LOOSE, obscene, or immoral.

1756. *The World*, No. 182. Apollo obeyed, and became a wit. He composed LOOSE sonnets and plays.

1783-85. COWPER, *Task*, iii. 692. No LOOSE, or wanton, though a wandering Muse.

2. (common).—Dissipated.

1864. DICKENS, *Our Mutual Friend*, II. iv. They were all feverish, boastful, and indefinably LOOSE; and they all ate and drank a great deal; and made bets in eating and drinking.

ON THE LOOSE, *adv. phr.* (common).—1. On the town.

2. On the drink; on the SPREE (*q.v.*).

1848. RUXTON, *Life In The Far West*, 85. They quickly disposed of their peltries, and were once more ON THE LOOSE.

1848. JAS. HANNAY, *King Dobbs*, iv. p. 63 (1856). One evening, when they were at Gibraltar, on the look-out for amusement—in modern parlance, ON THE LOOSE.

1859. *Punch*, vol. XXXVII. p. 22. Our friend prone to vices you never may see, Though he goes ON THE LOOSE, or the cut, or the spree.

1871. *All the Year Round*, Sept. He lives by anything rather than by steady work, though sometimes, when a virtuous fit is on him, and he is not out ON THE rampage, the LOOSE, or the spree, as the vernacular of the place may have it.

1871. *Daily Telegraph*, 26 Dec. When a labouring man falls into the state which is indifferently termed being tight, or being ON THE LOOSE, he is only taking a coarse but natural revenge for the previous neglect of the better things in his nature.

1876. HINDLEY, *Adventures of a Cheap Jack*, 70. Been out ON THE LOOSE all the morning.

1884. *Cornhill Mag.*, Dec., p. 607. Then presently, from the effect of alcohol and the sense of other relief, Sir Samuel went off again ON THE LOOSE for about ten days.

TO PLAY FAST AND LOOSE. *See* FAST.

TO RUN LOOSE, *verb. phr.* (racing).—*See* quot.

1884. HAWLEY SMART, *Post to Finish*, 115. He was much more prudent in his speculations than his partner, and did not at all like the idea of letting a dangerous horse what is termed RUN LOOSE, that is, unbacked, which might cost him a deal of money.

1891. *Lic. Vict. Gaz.*, 3 April. But the wise will eschew the youngsters, and seek for the winner among the older horses. Of whom the slashing Lord George must assuredly not be allowed to RUN LOOSE.

TO HAVE A SCREW LOOSE. *See* SCREW.

TO SHAKE A LOOSE LEG, *verb. phr.* (colloquial).—1. To whoremonger; and (2) to whore.

LOOSE IN THE HAFT (or HILT), *phr.* (colloquial).—1. Wanton; (2) diarrhœic; (3) untrustworthy.

1662. *Rump Songs*, ii. 56. A government that is LOOSE IN THE HILT.

1767. RAY, *Proverbs* [BOHN (1893), 54]. To be LOOSE IN THE HILTS. *Tentennar nel manico*—Ital. To be fickle, not to be relied upon.

TURNED LOOSE, *phr.* (racing). —Handicapped in a race at a very low rate.

AT LOOSE ENDS, *adv. phr.* (colloquial).—Neglected.

LOOSE-BODIED (or LOOSE-ENDED), *adj.* (old).—Lewd.

1667. SHIRLEY, *Love Tricks*, ii. 1. Be wise, and take heed of him; he's giddy-headed and LOOSE-BODIED.

LOOSE-BODIED GOWN, *subs. phr.* (old).—A harlot. For synonyms *see* BARRACK-HACK and TART.

1602. DEKKER, *Honest Whore* [DODSLEY, *Old Plays*(1874), iii. 479]. Yet if I go among the citizens' wives, they jeer at me; if I go among the LOOSE-BODIED GOWNS, they cry a pox on me, because I go civilly attired; and swear their trade was a good trade, 'till such as I am took it out of their hands.

LOOSE-BOX, *subs.* (common).—A brougham or other vehicle kept for the use of a mistress; a MOT-CART (*q.v.*).

LOOSE-COAT GAME, *subs.* (old).—Copulation. —URQUHART. For synonyms *see* GREENS and RIDE.

LOOSE-FISH, *subs.* (common).—1. A dissipated character; a BAD-EGG (*q.v.*).

1827. EGAN, *Anecdotes of the Turf*, 72. A game known among the LOOSE-FISH who frequent races by the name of thimble-rig.

1849. THACKERAY, *Pendennis*, lxii. 'Our friend Clavering . . . . who, between you and me . . . , we must own is about as LOOSE A FISH as any in my acquaintance.'

1856. C. READE, *Never Too Late*, xliv. In short Mr. Mills was a LOOSE FISH; a bachelor who had recently inherited the fortune of an old screw his uncle, and was spending thrift in all the traditional modes.

2. (parliamentary).—*See* quot.

1864. *Saturday Review*, July, 'Stray Votes.' The game he has in view is that peculiar variety of Parliamentary species known as an outsider or a LOOSE FISH, but described by itself under the more flattering title of 'an independent member.'

LOOSE-HUNG, *adj.* (common).—Unsteady.

LOOSE-KIRTLE, *subs.* (old).—A wanton: *cf.* LOOSE-BODIED GOWN.

LOOSE-LEGGED, *adj.* (old).—Incontinent.

1598. MARSTON, *Scourge of Villanie* .... 'Twas LOOSE-LEGGED Lais, that same common drab, For whom good Tubias took the mortal stab.

LOOT, *subs.* (common).—Plunder. *See* quots. 1798 and 1840.

1788. STOCKDALE, *Ind. Vocab.* [YULE], s.v. LOOT, plunder, pillage.

1791. *Gentlemen's Mag.*, p. 78, col. 2. They had orders to burn and plunder several large villages .... this former part of their instructions the LOOTIES said they had followed.

1798. WELLINGTON, *Sup. Desp.*, i. 60 (1858). Nine parts in ten of the native armies are LOOTIES or bad cavalry.

1840. FRASER, *Koordistan*, ii. Let. xiv. p. 283. The LOOTIES—that is, the rogues and vagabonds of the place.

1842. C. CAMPBELL, in *Life of Lord Clive*, i. 120. I believe I have already told you that I did not take any LOOT—the Indian word for plunder.

1875. G. CHESNEY, *Dilemma*, xxxvi. It was the Colonel Sahib who carried off the LOOT.

1893. KIPLING, *Barrack-room Ballads*. 'Loot.' [Title].

LOP, *verb.* (colloquial).—To lounge; to flop.

1852. H. B. STOWE, *Uncle Tom's Cabin*, viii. 'She .... cried about it, she did, and LOPPED round, as if she'd lost every friend she had.'

1881. BESANT & RICE, *Chap. of the Fleet*, I. x. Some debauched, idle fellow who lies and LOPS about all day, doing no work and earning no money.

1881. *Century*, XXIII. 652. The senora .... could only LOP about in her saddle.

LOPE, *verb.* (old).—1. *See* quot.

1785. GROSE, *Vulg. Tongue*, s.v. LOPE. To leap, to run away. He loped down the dancers, he ran down stairs.

2. (old).—To steal.

LOPLOLLY, *subs.* (old).—A servant who makes himself generally useful, and is always at the beck and call of his employer. *See* LOBLOLLY.

LORD, *subs.* (common).—1. *See* quots.: *cf.* LADY.

FRENCH SYNONYMS. *Un bombé* (= a crump); *une bobosse* (popular: *bosse* = hump); *porter sa malle; une boulendos* (= hunchback); *un bosmar* (popular); *un Mayeux; un moule-à-melon* (popular); *un amoureux* (popular); *un porte-balle* (popular); *un loucheur de l'épaule* (= *i.e.*, a person who squints with his shoulder).

GERMAN SYNONYMS. *Asterwitz; Pienk* (Bavarian: *Pünk* = a bundle or protruberance).

SPANISH SYNONYMS. *Brijindobio* (Sp. gypsy); *paldumo* (Sp. gypsy); *brijibio*.

1690. B. E., *Dict. Cant. Crew*, s.v. LORD, a very crooked, deformed, or ill-shapen Person.

1725. *New Cant. Dict.*, s.v.

1751. SMOLLETT, *Peregrine Pickle*, xxviii. Who ... was ... on account of his hump, distinguished by the title of My LORD.

1785. GROSE, *Vulgar Tongue*, s.v. LORD.

1820-33. LAMB, *Essays of Elia*. A deformed person is a LORD ... we do not find that that monarch [Richard III] conferred any such lordships as here pretended.

1827. TODD, *Johnson's Dicty*, s.v. LORD. A ludicrous title given by the vulgar to a hump-backed person; traced, however, to the Greek λορδος, crooked.

1864. *Athenæum*, 29 Oct., No. 1931. On the Greek origin of LORD, as applied to those who are vulgarly called 'hunchbacks,' Mr. Hotten is silent.

1886. W. BESANT, *World Went Very Well Then*, iii. He was, in appearance, short and bent, with rounded shoulders, and with a hump (which made the boys call him My LORD).

2. *in pl.* (Winchester College).—The first eleven.

3. *See* LORD OF THE MANOR.

DRUNK AS A LORD (PRINCE, or EMPEROR), *phr.* (common).—Very drunk.

1653. MIDDLETON, *Sp. Gipsy*, iv. 1. Water thy wine—*Sam.* [*sings*] And DRINK LIKE A LORD.

1678. COTTON, *Virgil Travestie*, in *Works* (1725), Bk. iv. p. 72. Trojans round beseige her Boards, Merry as Greeks, and DRUNK AS LORDS.

1719. DURFEY, *Pills to Purge*, iv. 17. For our Squire, we fear, is AS DRUNK AS A LORD.

1731. C. COFFEY, *The Devil to Pay*, Scene 2. I'm always sharp set towards punch; and am now come with a firm resolution, though but a poor cobbler, to be as richly DRUNK AS A LORD; I am a true English heart, and look upon drunkenness as the best part of the liberty of the subject.

1734. FIELDING, *Intriguing Chambermaid*, ii. 6. You dare disturb gentlemen, who are getting as DRUNK AS LORDS.

1853. THACKERAY, *Barry Lyndon*, xviii. 252. She ran screaming through the galleries, and I, as TIPSY AS A LORD, came staggering after.

THE LORD KNOWS WHAT, *phr.* (colloquial).—'Heaps'; plenty more; all sorts of things.

1691-2. *Gentlemen's Journal*, Mar., p. 3. Here's novels, and new-town adventures ... and the LORD KNOWS WHAT not.

LORD-BALDWIN. *See* QUEEN ANNE.

LORD-HARRY. *See* OLD HARRY.

LORD-JOHN-RUSSELL, *subs. phr.* (rhyming).—A bustle; a BIRD-CAGE (*q.v.*).

LORD-LOVEL, *subs. phr.* (rhyming).—A shovel.

LORD-MANSFIELD'S-TEETH, *subs. phr.* (old).—The spikes round the wall of the Kings' Bench.—GROSE (1796).

LORD-MAYOR, *subs. phr.* (thieves').—A large crowbar; a JEMMY (*q.v.*).

LORD-MAYOR'S-COAL, *subs. phr.* (old).—*See* quot.

1837. BARHAM, *Ingoldsby Legends*, 2nd Series (ed. 1851), 144. Had the coal been a LORD MAYOR'S COAL—viz., a slate.

LORD-MAYOR'S-FOOL, *subs. phr.* (old).—*See* quot.

1859. H. KINGSLEY, *Geoffry Hamlyn*, xxxii. Burnside was in the habit of saying that he was like the LORD MAYOR'S FOOL—fond of everything that was good.

LORD-OF-THE-MANOR, *subs. phr.* (rhyming).—A TANNER (*q.v.*). For synonyms *see* BENDER.

LOSE.—*See* COMBINATION; HAIR; MESS; SHIRT.

LOSER, *subs.* (billiards).—A stroke in which the player pockets his own ball, after striking either his opponent's or the red.

1888. *Sporting Life*, 10 Dec. At last brought a run of 87 to a close with a break-down at a white LOSER.

LOST-CAUSE, *subs.* (colloquial American).—Secessionism.

LOT, *subs.* (colloquial).—A person, male or female: mostly in sarcasm or contempt; as, 'a BAD LOT', 'a NICE LOT', etc.

1846-8. THACKERAY, *Vanity Fair*, I. vii. 'You'll get no good out of 'er,' continued John, pointing with his thumb towards Miss Sharp: 'a BAD LOT, I tell you, a BAD LOT.'

1878. JAS. PAYN, *By Proxy*, ix. 'So that's your young friend, is it!' said he, rattling the loose silver in his capacious pocket with one hand, and laying the other lightly upon Nelly's head. 'She's a very NICE little LOT.'

1888. *Pall Mall Gaz.*, 20 Nov., p. 2, col. 2. He is a thorough BAD LOT.

1889. C. HADDON CHAMBERS, 'Ne'er-do-well,' in *Australian Wilds*. 'I'm afraid he's a very BAD LOT,' I said. 'I wonder that you have kept him on so long.'

LOTEBY (or **LUDBY**), *subs.* (old).—A concubine. *See* LIGBY.

1360. CHAUCER, *Rom. of the Rose*, I. 6339. And with me folwith my LOTEBY To done me solas and company.

*c.*1426. AUDELEY, *Poems*, 5. Now ȝif that a man he wed a wyfe, And hym thynke sche plese hym noȝt, Anon ther rysis care and stryfe; He wold her selle that he had boȝt, And schenchypus here that he had soȝt, And takys to him a LOTEBY.

1701. *Harl. MSS.* (1809-13), fol. 20. For almost hyt is every whore, A gentyl man hath a wyfe and a hore; And wyves have now comunly Here husbondys and a LUDBY.

1701. *Harl. MSS.* (1809-13), fol. 12. But there the wyfe haunteth foly Undyr here husbunde a LUDBY.

LOTHARIO, *subs.* (colloquial).—A seducer of married women.

1630. DAVENANT, *The Cruel Brother, Dramatis Personæ*. LOTHARIO, a frantic young gallant.

1703. ROWE (& MASSINGER), *Fair Penitent, Dramatis Personæ*. LOTHARIO, a gallant.

1756. *The World*, No. 202. Proud of the summons to display his might, The gay LOTHARIO dresses for the fight.

1818. MOORE, *Fudge Family*, 87. If some who are LOTHARIOS in feeding should wish Just to flirt with a luncheon.

1849. LYTTON, *Caxtons*, XVIII. ch. vi. No woman could have been more flattered and courted by LOTHARIOS and lady-killers.

1876. *Times*, 2 Nov. Maurice, a most inflammable LOTHARIO, catches fire at her charms.

1882. COWPER, *Hope*, 28. LOTHARIO cries, 'What philosophic stuff.'

LOTHBURY. TO GO BY WAY OF LOTHBURY, *verb. phr.* (old).—To be loth. [A pun: *cf.* NEEDHAM SHORE, PECKHAM, etc.].

*d.*1580. TUSSER [p. 146, quoted by NARES]. Though such for woe, by LOTHBURY go, For being spide about Cheapside.

LOTION, *subs.* (common).—Drink.

1876. HINDLEY, *Adventures of a Cheap Jack*, 82. Try to make each other drunk, so that the one who could take the most LOTION without being so, might get the best of it by having the place to himself.

1883. *Daily Telegraph*, 13 April, p. 2, col. 7. In his evidence he said that the testator took his LOTION (liquor) 'according to his troubles.'

1888. J. RUNCIMAN, *The Chequers*, 85. You squat still, now, and git through that there LOTION.

1892. MILLIKEN, *'Arry Ballads*, 62. The 'ole thing seemed swell, with good grubbing and lots o' prime LOTION chuck-ed in.

1892. ANSTEY, *Model Music Hall Songs*, 119. What do you all say to goin' inside, and shunting a little garbage, and shifting a drop or so of LOTION?

LOUD, *adj.* (common).—1. Showy; RAFFISH (*q.v.*): applied to dress or manners. Also as *adv. Cf.* HOWLING.

1847. ALBERT SMITH, *Nat. Hist. of the Gent*, vi. 42. They were all dressed nearly alike; hats with narrow brims, coats with large buttons, staring shawls, and trousers of the most prominent style—very LOUD patterns, as a friend appropriately called them.

1849. THACKERAY, *Pendennis*, XXX. Rakish young medical students, gallant, dashing, what is called LOUDLY dressed.

1851. CARLYLE, *Life of Sterling*, I. ch. 2. In a much LOUDER style than is freely patronised on this side of the Channel.

1853. E. BRADLEY ['Cuthbert Bede'], *Verdant Green*, II. p. 7. And as Mr. Fosbrooke was far too politic a gentleman to irritate the examiners by appearing in a LOUD or sporting costume, he had carried out the idea of clerical character by a quiet, gentlemanly suit of black.

1864. *Eton School Days*, xxiii. Butler Burke made his appearance in a Jersey, which was decidedly LOUD; and some of the lookers-on exclaimed, 'By Jove! that's a LOUD shirt playing in Wynne's.'

1871. *Figaro*, 4 Jan. At the last moment Mrs. Tripp, terribly flustered, and also shiny, with a very LOUD shawl on, suggestive of an amalgamation of the brightest Scotch plaids, just popped in.

1885. *Truth*, 26 March, p. 502, col. 2. I saw a good frock of this kind with stripes of cardinal, navy blue, and amber. That sounds LOUD does it not?

1889. OUIDA, *Moths*, XV. Her own daughter ... had LOUD costumes with wonderful waistcoats.

2. (colloquial).—Strong-smelling.

1887. *Fisheries of U. S.*, vol. ii. 473. They prefer to have the meat tainted rather than fresh, declaring that it is most tender and toothsome when decidedly LOUD.

LOUD ONE, *subs. phr.* (old).—A big lie.

1767. RAY, *Proverbs* [BOHN (1893), 64], s.v.

LOUNCE, *subs.* (nautical).—A drink: specifically a pint of beer. [From 'allowance'].

LOUNGE, *subs.* (Eton and Cambridge).—1. A treat; a chief meal.

1864. *The Press*, 12 Nov. By the way, we miss the Etonian word, LOUNGE, for which there is classic authority. 'I don't care for dinner,' said Harry Coningsby at his grandfather's table; 'Breakfast is my LOUNGE.'

2. (old: now recognised).—A loitering place, or gossiping shop.—GROSE (1785).

3. (American thieves').—The dock in a criminal court.

LOUR (LOURE or LOWRE), *subs.* (old).—Money. Fr. *louer* = to hire: 'It was granted him in LOWER of his servyse' (*Merlin*, E. E. T. S. i. 59).

1568. *Colkelbie Sow*, I. 148 (Bann. MSS.). A lass that luvis bot for LOUR.

1573. HARMAN, *Caveat* (1814), p. 65. LOWRE, money.

1610. ROWLANDS, *Martin Markall*, p. 39 (H. Club's Repr. 1874). LOWER, money.

1622. FLETCHER, *Beggar's Bush*, ii. 1. A very tyrant I, an arrant tyrant, If e'er I come to reign (therefore look to 't!) Except you do provide me hum enough, and LOUR to bowze with!

1632. DEKKER, *English Villanies*, sig. M. What are they, but drunken Beggers? All that they beg being either LOWRE or Bowse.

1670. COTTON, *Scoffer Scofft*, in *Wks.* (1725), p. 280. But ere this life I'll longer lead, I'll stroll for LOWER, or beg my bread.

1671. RICHARD HEAD, *The English Rogue*. Bing out, bien morts and toure. The bien cove hath the LOURE.

1724. E. COLES, *Eng. Dict.*, s.v.

1725. *New Cant. Dict.*, s.v. LOUR, money.

1785. GROSE, *Dict. Vulg. Tongue*, s. v. CLOY. To cloy the LOUR, to steal money.

1834. W. H. AINSWORTH, *Rookwood*, p. 315 (ed. 1864). 'Well, say no more about it, Sir Luke,' said Jem, fawningly; 'I knows I owes you my life, and I thank you for it. Take back the

LOWRE. He should not have shown it me—it was that as did all the mischief.'

1889. RICHARDSON, *Police*, 321, s.v. Bad money, gammy LOWER.

LOUSE. TO CARE NOT A LOUSE, *verb. phr.* (old).—To be utterly indifferent.

1719. DURFEY, *Pills etc.*, iv. 38. For any Ale-house We CARE NOT A LOUSE.

NOT WORTH A LOUSE, *adj. phr.* (common).—Utterly worthless.

1617. GREENE, *Metamorph.* [GROSART (1881-6), ix. 97]. Lest thy ... Logike prooue NOT WORTH A LOWSE.

1786. BURNS, *Address to the De'il.* Is instant made NO WORTH A LOUSE, Just at the bit.

LOUSE-BAG, *subs.* (old).—A black bag worn to the hair or wig.—GROSE (1785).

LOUSE-HOUSE, *subs.* (old).—The round-house or cage. — GROSE (1785).

LOUSE-LADDER, *subs.* (old).—'A stitch fallen in a stocking'; a JACOB'S-LADDER (*q.v.*).—GROSE (1785).

LOUSELAND, *subs.* (old).—*See* quot. 1690. *Cf.* ITCHLAND.

1690. B. E., *Dict. Cant. Crew*, s.v. LOUSELAND, Scotland.

1725. *New Cant. Dict.*, s.v.

1785. GROSE, *Vulg. Tongue*, s.v.

LOUSE-TRAP, *subs.* (common).—*See* quots. Ital. *galletto* (= little cock).

1690. B. E., *Dict. Cant. Crew*, s.v. LOUSELAND .... A Scotch LOUSE-TRAP, a comb.

1725. *New Cant. Dict.*, s.v.

1748. T. DYCHE, *Dictionary* (5th ed.). LOUSE-TRAP (S.) a small-toothed or fine comb.

1785. GROSE, *Vulg. Tongue*, s.v.

LOUSE-WALK, *subs.* (common).—A back-hair parting.—GROSE.

LOUSY, *adj.* (painters').—1. Paint which from keeping has become full of skin.

2. (old).—Filthy; contemptible.

1690. CROWNE, *English Friar*, iv. He forgot he was a LOUSEY friar.

LOUT, *subs.* (old: now recognised). —1. *See* quots.

1577-82. BRETON, *Floorish vpon Fancie* [GROSART (1879), I. *a.* 4, 1, 12]. He that thinkes to be a lorde, first day, Will misse a lorde, and prooue a LOUTE straight way.

1583. GREENE, *Mamillia* [GROSART (1881-6), ii. 6]. Then may I well be dubbed a dolt, which dare take in hand to decipher the substaunce of loue, that am but a LOUT.

1690. B. E., *Dict. Cant. Crew*, s.v. LOUT, a heavy idle Fellow.

1725. *New Cant. Dict.*, s.v.

1785. GROSE, *Vulg. Tongue*, s.v. LOUT, a clumsey stupid fellow.

2. (Rugby school).—Anyone of the poorer classes: not necessarily an awkward, lubberly individual.

LOVE, *subs.* (common).—No score: LOVE-ALL = no points on either side. Fr. *cherche; baiser le cul de la vieille* = to make no score.

1780. *Gentlemen's Mag.*, L. 322. We are not told how, or by what means six LOVE comes to mean six to nothing.

1791. *Gent. Mag.*, lxi. 16. At the game of whist, when one of the parties reckons six, for instance, or any other number, and the other none, why is it usual to say six LOVE?

1821. LAMB, *Elia (New Year's Eve)*. I play over again for LOVE, as the gamesters phrase it, games for which I once paid so dear.

1868. *Chambers's Encyclopædia*, s.v. Whist. We will suppose ourselves to be A, the score to be LOVE-ALL, and D to have turned up the four of hearts.

1883. *Field*, 27 Oct. . . . won the game by two sets to LOVE.

1885. *Times*, 1 April, p. 6, col. 5. Both had an innings [at racquets], but did not score, and consequently the game was called 13 to LOVE.

CUPBOARD-LOVE, *phr.* (colloquial).—Interested love.

*c.*1688. *Poor Robin.* A CUPBOARD LOVE is seldom true, A love sincere is found in few.

LOVEAGE, *subs.* (common).—Taplashes; ALLS (*q.v.*); ULLAGE (*q.v.*).

LOVE-APPLES, *subs.* (venery).—The *testes*. For synonyms *see* CODS.

LOVE-CHILD (or LOVE-BRAT), *subs.* (common).—A bastard.

[?]. *Old Chap book* [NARES]. Now by this four we plainly see, Four LOVE BRATS will be laid to thee: And that she that draws the same shall wed Two rich husbands, and both well bred.

1849. KINGSLEY, *Alton Locke*, xxviii. Unless we all repent of ... LOVE-CHILDREN.

1864. DICKENS, *Our Mutual Friend*, I. xvi. 'A LOVE-CHILD,' returned Betty Higden, dropping her voice; 'parents never known; found in the street.'

LOVE-DART (or DART OF LOVE), *subs.* (venery).—The *penis*. For synonyms *see* CREAMSTICK and PRICK.

LOVE-FLESH, *subs. phr.* (colloquial). —The *pudenda*.—WHITMAN.

LOVE-JUICE, *subs.* (venery).—The sexual secretion. For synonyms *see* CREAM.

LOVE-LADDER, *subs. phr.* (old).—A laced petticoat.

1667. HEAD, *Proteus Redivivus* (1684), XII. They will make their husbands pawn their consciences, as well as their credits, . . . for another story of lace more upon their petty-coats; as if women thought men's fancies did not climb fast enough, without such a lecherous LOVE-LADDER.

LOVE-LANE, (venery).—The female *pudendum*. Hence A TURN (or AN EJECTMENT) IN LOVE-LANE = an act of coition. For synonyms *see* GREENS and RIDE.

LOVE-LIQUOR, *subs.* (venery).—The semen. For synonyms *see* CREAM.

LOVELOCK (or LOCK), *subs.* (old).— A falling curl by the ear: fashionable more or less from the time of Elizabeth to Charles I.; worn on the left side, and hanging by the shoulder, sometimes even to the girdle. Also HEART-BREAKERS (*q.v.*).

1592. LYLY, *Mydas*, iii. 2. How, sir, will you be trimmed? will you have your beard like a spade or a bodkin? . . . your LOVE-LOCKES wreathed with a silken twist, or shaggie to fall on your shoulders?

1592. GREENE, *Quip for an Upstart Courtier*, D2, b. Will you be *Frenchified*, with a LOVE-LOCK down to your shoulders, wherein you may hang your mistres' favour?

1592. NASHE, *Pierce Penilesse* [GROSART (1885), ii. 28]. Yet cannot his stabbing dagger, nor his nittie LOUE-LOCKE, keep him out of the legend of fantastical cox-combs.

1594. BARNEFIELD, *Affectionate Shepherd* [NARES]. Why should the sweet LOVE-LOCKE hang dangling downe, Kissing thy girdle-stead with falling pride?

1600. SHAKSPEARE, *Much Ado About Nothing*, iii. 3. And one Deformed is one of them: I know him, he wears a LOCK.

1615. BEAUMONT and FLETCHER, *Cupid's Revenge*, ii. He lay in gloves all night, and this morning I Brought him a new periwig, with a LOCK at it.

1633. PRYNNE, *Histriomastix*, 209. And more especially in long, unshorne, womanish, frizled, love-provoking haire, and LOVELOCKES, growne now too much in fashion with comly pages, youthes, and lewd, effeminate, ruffianly persons.

1640. SHIRLEY, *Coronation*, i. And who knows but he May lose his ribband by it, in his LOCK Dear as his saint?

1649. DAVENANT, *Love & Honour*, ii. 1. A LOCK for the left side, so rarely hung with ribbanding of various colours.

1663. BUTLER, *Hudibras*, I. i. 253. Like Samson's HEART-BREAKERS it grew In time to make a nation rue.

1821. *Blackwood's Mag.*, x. 267. Pretty little fantastic chignons and LOVE-LOCKS.

1836. MICHAEL SCOTT, *Tom Cringle's Log*, ii. The outlandishness of the fashion was not offensive, when I came to take into the account the beauty of the plaiting, and of the long raven LOVE-LOCKS that hung down behind each of his small transparent ears.

1868. BREWER, *Phrase and Fable*, s.v. LOVE LOCK. When men indulge in a curl in front of their ears, the LOVE-LOCK is called a bell-rope—*i.e.*, a rope to pull the belles after them.

LOVELY, *adj.* (colloquial).—Attractive; alluring.

1653. WALTON, *Complete Angler*, 85. This trout looks LOVELY.

LOVE-POT, *subs.* (old).—A drunkard. For synonyms *see* LUSHINGTON.

LOVER'S-KNOT. TO TIE THE TRUE LOVER'S KNOT, *verb. phr.* (venery). — To copulate. For synonyms *see* GREENS and RIDE.

LOVE'S CHANNEL (-HARBOUR, -PARADISE, -FOUNTAIN, or -PAVILLION), *subs.* (venery).—The female *pudendum*. For synonyms *see* MONOSYLLABLE.

1598. JOHN MARSTON, *Pigmalion*. Until his eye discended so far downe That it descried LOVES PAVILLION, Where Cupid doth enjoy his onely crowne, And Venus hath her chiefest mention.

*d.*1639. CAREW [ANDERSON, *Poets*, .689]. Thou shalt steer and guide . . . into LOVE'S CHANNEL.

*c.*1727. *Old Ballad* [B. M. Cat 11621, l/1. 46]. Each night when sport's over, and LOVE'S FOUNTAIN's dry, She, weary with stitching contented does lie.

LOVE'S PICKLOCK, *subs.* (venery).— The *penis*. For synonyms *see* CREAMSTICK and PRICK.

LOVEY (or LOVEY-DOVEY), *subs.* (common).—A term of endearment.

1763. FOOTE, *Mayor of Garratt*, i. I go, LOVY.

1796. HOLMAN, *Abroad & at Home*, i. 1. If I am ever so little a while away from you, my darling, it appears a long, tedious age. How does my LOVEY do? Do look tender—'tis so becoming to you; and besides, if you don't, you know you break my heart.

1837. C. DICKENS, *Pickwick Papers*, p. 385 (ed. 1857). 'Who else is a goin', LOVEY?' said Mrs. Cluppins in an insinuating manner.

1841. *Punch*, i. 226. 'The Prince's Title.' LOVEY-DOVEY has been spoken of; but it is not likely that His Royal Highness will assume the style and dignity of LOVEY-DOVEY for a considerable period.

LOW. TO LIE LOW, *verb. phr.* (colloquial).—To keep quiet; to bide one's time.

LOW IN THE LAY, *phr.* (thieves'). —In straits; HARD-UP (*q.v.*).

1830. LYTTON, *Paul Clifford*, 'Song.' As, just at present, I'm LOW IN THE LAY, I'll borrow a 'quid' if you please.

LOW-COUNTRIES, *subs.* (venery).— The female *pudendum*. For synonyms *see* MONOSYLLABLE.

LOW-DOWN, *adj.* (colloquial).— Vulgar.

1888. EGGLESTON, *The Graysons*, XVIII. Her archaic speech was perhaps a shade better than the LOW-DOWN language of Broad Run.

LOWDOWNER, *subs.* (American).— *See* quots.

1871. DE VERE, *Americanisms*, 45. So low a person . . . . he appears as Conch or LOWDOWNER in North Carolina.

1883. STEVENSON, *The Silverado Squatters*, 151. They are at least known by a generic byword, as poor whites or LOW-DOWNERS.

LOWER, *verb.* (common).—To drink. For synonyms *see* LUSH.

LOWER REGIONS, *subs. phr.* (colloquial).—Hell. Fr. *le pacquelin du raboin.*

LOWING-CHEAT (or -CHETE), *subs.* (old). —*See* quot.

1573. HARMAN, *Caveat* (1814), 65. A LOWTING CHETE, a cowe.

LOWING-LAY (or -RIG), *subs. phr.* (old).—Stealing oxen or cows.— GROSE (1823); MATSELL (1859).

LOWLANDS, *subs.* (venery).—The female *pudendum*. For synonyms *see* MONOSYLLABLE.

LOW-LIVED, *adj.* (colloquial).—Mean; shabby; vulgar.

1766 GOLDSMITH, *Vicar of W.*, XIII. She shall choose better company than such LOW-LIVED fellows as he.

LOW-MAN, *subs.* (Cambridge University).—A Junior Optimé as compared to a Senior Optimé or a Wrangler.

LOW-MEN, *subs.* (gaming).—False dice; so loaded as to show low numbers. For synonyms *see* FULHAMS. Also LOW-RUNNERS.

1594. NASHE, *Unf. Traveller*, in *Wks.* (GROSART, v. 27). The dice of late are growen as melancholy as a dog, high men and LOW MEN both prosper alike.

1596. SHAKSPEARE, *Merry Wives*, i. 3. Let vultures gripe thy guts! for gourd and fullam holds, And high and LOW beguiles the rich and poor.

1598. FLORIO, *Worlde of Wordes*, *Pise*. False dice, high men or LOW MEN.

1605. *London Prodigal*, Supp. to Sh. ii. 456. Item, to my son Mat Flowerdale I bequeath two bale of false dice, videlicet, high men and LOW MEN, fulloms, stop-cater-traies, and other bones of function.

1615. HARRINGTON, *Epigrams*, i. 79. Then play thou for a pound or for a pin, High men or LOW MEN still are foisted in.

1647. CARTWRIGHT, *The Ordinary* (DODSLEY, *Old Plays*, x. 238]. Your high And LOW MEN are but trifles; your pois'd dye, That's ballasted with quick-silver or gold, Is gross to this.

1674. COTTON, *Compl. Gamester*, p. 9. This [cheating] they do by false dice, as high-fullams, 4, 5, 6; LOW-FULLAMS, 1, 2, 3. *Ibid.* Bristle-dice are fitted for their purpose, by sticking a hog's-bristle so in the corners, or otherwise in the dice, that they shall run high or LOW as they please; this bristle must be strong and short, by which means, the bristle bending, it will not lie on that side, but will be tript over.

1714. LUCAS, *Gamesters*, 27. The high ones would run 4, 5, and 6; the LOW FULHAMS 1, 2, and 3.

1822. SCOTT, *Fort. of Nigel*, xxiii. Men talk of high and LOW dice.

LOW-PAD, *subs.* (old).—*See* quot. 1690.

1690. B. E., *Dict. Cant. Crew*, s.v. LOW-PAD, a foot-pad.

1725. *New Cant. Dict.*, s.v.

1785. GROSE, *Vulg. Tongue*, s.v. LOW-PAD.

1834. AINSWORTH, *Rookwood* (1864), p. 180. High-pads and LOW-PADS.

LOWRE. *See* LOUR.

LOW-WATER (or -TIDE). TO BE IN LOW-WATER (or AT LOW-TIDE), *verb. phr.* (colloquial).—To be in difficulties, or penniless.

1690. B. E., *Dict. Cant. Crew*, s.v. LOW-TIDE, when there's no Money in a Man's Pocket.

1725. *New Cant. Dict.*, s.v.

1785. GROSE, *Vulg. Tongue*, s.v.

1837. DICKENS, *Oliver Twist*, viii. I'm at LOW-WATER MARK, only one bob and a magpie.

1885. *Chamb. Journal*, 21 Feb., p. 125. Or who, having been 'put away', and done their time, found themselves in LOW WATER upon their return to the outer world.

1886. Miss Braddon, *Mohawks*, ch. iv. Then came talk of ways and means. His lordship was in LOW WATER financially.

L. S. D., *subs.* (colloquial).—Money.

1891. *Referee*, 8 Mar. I meet the folks who used to flee To Southern France and Italy; In London now they gladly stay, In London spend their L. S. D.—Where are the fogs of yesterday?

LUBBER (or LUBBARD), *subs.* (old: now recognised).—A hulking lout; a lumpish oaf: specifically (nautical) a bad seaman.

1362. Langland, *Piers Plowman* (A), Prol. I. 52. Gret LOBRES and longe.

1534. N. Udall, *Roister Doister*, iii. 3, p. 44 (Arber). For the veriest dolte that euer was borne, And veriest LUBBER sloven and beast.

1537. *Thersites* [Dodsley, *Old Plays* (1874), i. 404]. Come hither, Cacus, thou LUBBER and false knave!

1567. Edwards, *Damon & Pithias* [Dodsley, *Old Plays* (1874), iv. 63]. Beaten with a cudgel like a slave, a vacabone, or a lazy LUBBER.

1570. *Wit & Science* [Dodsley, *Old Plays* (1874), ii. 387]. These great LUBBERS are neither active nor wise.

1573. Harman, *Caveat*. Sturdy LUBBARES.

1580. Tusser, *Husbandrie*, ch. 57, st. 22, p. 131 (E. D. S.). For tempest and showers deceiueth a menie, And lingering LUBBERS loose many a penie.

1590. Nashe, *Pasquils Apologie* [Grosart (1885), i. 241]. Will he neuer leaue to play the LUBBER?

1590. Greene, *Neuer too Late* [Grosart (1881-6), viii. 199]. Leauing this passionate LUBBER to the conceipt of his loues.

1600. *Liberality & Prodigality* [Dodsley, *Old Plays* (1874), viii. 340]. Look forth and see: a LUBBER, fat, great, and tall. *Ibid.* 370. A luskish LUBBER, as fat as a log.

1605-6. Shakspeare, *King Lear*, i. 4. *Kent.* If you will measure your LUBBER'S length again, tarry.

1621. Burton, *Anatomy* (ed. 1892), ii. 156. The rest ot these great Zanzummins, or gigantical Anakims, heavy, vast, barbarous LUBBERS.

1662. *Rump Songs* ii. 38. If he had but the life And spirit of his Wife, He would not lye still like a LUBBER.

1671. Crowne, *Juliana*, iii. 1. Lo, blunderbuss, my lord, grand LUBBER.

1684. Lacy, *Sauny the Scot*, v. 1. Go, swagger at your greasy LUBBER there; your patient wife will make you no more sport.

1690. B. E., *Dict. Cant. Crew*, s.v. LUBBER, LUBBERLY, a heavy, dull Fellow.

1700. Congreve, *Way of the World*, iv. 7. How can you name that superannuated LUBBER? foh!

1725. *New Cant. Dict.*, s.v.

1748. Smollett, *Rod. Random*, xxiv. And called him . . . swab, and LUBBER.

1785. Grose, *Vulg. Tongue*, s.v.

1836. M. Scott, *Cringle's Log*, x. Confound the LUBBERS! Boatswain's mate, call the watch.

1837. R. H. Barham, *The Ingoldsby Legends* (ed. 1862), p. 350. Of course in the use of sea-terms you'll not wonder If I now and then should fall into a blunder For which Captain Chamier or Mr. T. P. Cooke Would call me a LUBBER and son of a sea-cook.

Adj. (old: now recognised).—Clumsy; clownish. Also LUBBERLY.

1580. Tusser, *Husbandrie*, ch. 9, st. 16, p. 17 (E. D. S.). To raise betimes the LUBBERLIE, Both snorting Hob and Margerie.

1594. Greene, *Frier Bacon* [Grosart (1881-6), xiii. 45]. This LUBBERLY lurden, ill-shapte, and ill-faced.

1596. Nashe, *Saffron Walden*, in *Works*, iii. 125. Lamely and LUBBERLY hee striues to imitate and bee another English Lipsius.

1596. Shakspeare, *Merry Wives*, v. 5. I came yonder at Eton to marry mistress Anne Page, and she's a great LUBBERLY boy.

1597-8. Haughton, *A Woman will have her Will* [Dodsley, *Old Plays* (1874), x. 533]. What shall we do with this LUBBER-lover.

1598. Florio, *A Worlde of Wordes*. *Homaccione*, a great euill fauored man, a LUBBARLY man, a loggarhead.

1606. *Wily Beguiled* [Dodsley, *Old Plays* (1874), ix. 241]. Your LUBBERLY legs would not carry your lobcock body.

1645. Milton, *L'Allegro*. Then lies him down, the LUBBAR fiend.

1673. Dryden, *Amboyna*, Epilogue, 14. Venetians do not more uncouthly ride, Than did their LUBBER state mankind bestride.

1706. Farquhar, *Recruiting Officer*, v. 4. Me for a soldier! send your own lazy, LUBBERLY sons at home.

1759. Goldsmith, *The Bee*, No. 6, p. 395 (Globe ed.). Those modest LUBBERLY boys who seem to want spirit generally go through their business with more ease to themselves and more satisfaction to their instructors.

1856. Miss Yonge, *Daisy Chain*, xxxvii. 'Poor George had been so spoiled by three aunts, and was so big, and so old that my mother did not know what to make of him.' 'A great LUBBERLY boy,' Ethel said, rather repenting the next moment.

LUBBERLAND, *subs.* (old).—The Paradise of indolence.

1767. Ray, *Proverbs* [Bohn (1893), 56]. You'd do well in LUBBERLAND, where they have half a crown a day for sleeping.

LUBBER'S-HOLE, *subs.* (nautical).—An opening in the maintop, preferred before the shrouds by raw hands and timid climbers.

*b.*1794. Wolcot ['P. Pindar'], *Peter's Prophecy*, in *Wks.*, vol. i. p. 446. And yet, Sir Joseph, Fame reports, you stole To Fortune's topmast through the LUBBERHOLE.

1822. D. Jerrold, *Black Ey'd Susan*, ii. 2. Go up the futtock-shrouds like a man—don't creep through LUBBER'S-HOLE.

1833. Marryat, *Peter Simple*, ch. vii. I was afraid to venture, and then he proposed that I should go through LUBBER'S HOLE, which he said had been made for people like me. I agreed to attempt it, as it appeared more easy, and at last arrived, quite out of breath, and very happy to find myself in the main-top.

1836. Michael Scott, *Cruise of the Midge* (ed. 18 . .), p. 363. Why, captain, I have paid great attention since we embarked, and really I have become a very capital sailor, sir. Do you know I have been twice through the LUBBER'S HOLE?

LUBRICATE, *verb.* (common).—To drink.

LUCK. DOWN ON ONE'S LUCK, *adj. phr.* (common).—Unlucky; in trouble; 'hard up'.

1846-8. Thackeray, *Vanity Fair*, lxiv. They say that when Mrs. C. was particularly DOWN ON HER LUCK, she gave concerts and lessons in music here and there.

1885. *Eng. Illustrated Mag.*, p. 638. A fellow who's DOWN ON HIS LUCK now.

1891. *Fun*, 25 Mar. Now, the real, genuine, unadulterated nob—be he ever so DOWN ON HIS LUCK—always tends his nails to the last.

1892. *St. James's Gaz.*, 29 Oct., 5, 1. Sir Harry Golightly was DOWN ON HIS LUCK. He confided his woes to Mrs. FitzHarris.

GREASY-LUCK, *subs.* (whalers').—A full cargo of oil.

FISHERMAN'S LUCK, *subs. phr.* (common).—Wet, cold, hungry, and no fish.

SHITTEN LUCK, *subs. phr.* (old).—Good luck.

1670. Ray, *Proverbs* [Bohn (1893), 131], s.v.

LUCKY, *subs.* (thieves').—Plunder.

1852. Judson, *Mysteries of New York*, iv. Ve might as vel count up the week's earnins and divide the LUCKY.

Adj. (old colloquial).—Handy.

1703. Centlivre, *Love's Contrivance*, i. 'You used to be a LUCKY rogue upon a pinch.' 'Ay, master, and I have not forgot it yet.'

TO CUT (or MAKE) ONE'S LUCKY, *verb. phr.* (common).—To decamp. For synonyms *see* AMPUTATE and SKEDADDLE.

1834. M. C. Dowling, *Othello Travestie*, i. 2. You'd better CUT YOUR LUCKY.

1835. Dickens, *Sketches by Boz*, 266. 'Let me alone,' replied Ikey, 'and I'll ha' vound up, and MADE MY LUCKY in five seconds.'

1837. Dickens, *Oliver Twist*, l. 'When was Fagin took then?' 'Just at dinner-time—two o'clock this afternoon. Charley and I MADE OUR LUCKY up the wash'us chimney.'

1839. Reynolds, *Pickwick Abroad*, p. 223. At dusk we'll MAKE OUR LUCKY.

1882. McCabe, *New York*, xxxiv. 509. (In list of slang terms).

LUCKY-BAG, *subs.* (venery).—The female *pudendum*. For synonyms *see* MONOSYLLABLE.

LUCKY-BONE, *subs.* (thieves').—*See* quot.

1883. G. A. S[ala], in *Ill. L. News*, Nov. 10, p. 451, col. 3. The detective who took him into custody found upon him when searching him 'the small bone of a sheep's head, which he understood, was known among beggars as the LUCKY BONE,' as its possession was supposed to bring good luck to the beggar during the day.

LUDBY. *See* LOTEBY.

LUDLAM'S DOG, *subs.* (old).—A culmination of laziness. *See* quot. Sailors say: 'as lazy as Joe the Marine, who laid down his musket to sneeze.'

1824. T. Fielding, *Select Proverbs*, p. 154. As lazy as LUDLAM'S DOG, that leaned his head against a wall to bark.

LUD'S-BULWARK, *subs.* (old).—Ludgate Prison.

1690. B. E., *Dict. Cant. Crew*, s.v.

1725. *New Cant. Dict.*

1785. Grose, *Vulg. Tongue*, s.v.

LUFF, *subs.* (old).—1. Speech.

1821. Egan, *Real Life*, i. 454. 'Poll,' says I, 'hold your LUFF, give us no more patter about this here rum gig.'

2. (nautical).—A lieutenant.

1848. Burton, *Waggeries etc.*, p. 12. The second LUFF, who was in the cutter, ordered us to 'go ahead.'

LUG, *subs.* (old).—1. The ear. Fr. *isgourde*.

1592. Lyly, *Midas*, ii. 5. Dare you think your clumsy LUGS so proper to decide, as the delicate ears of Justice Midas.

1592. Greene, *Defence of Conny catching*, in *Works*, xi. 62. Then the gentlewoman let loose his eares, and let slip his head, and away went he home with his bloody LUGGES.

1610. Rowlands, *Martin Markall*, p. 39 (H. Club's Repr. 1874). LUGGES, eares.

1625. Ben Jonson, *Staple of News*, v. 1. A fine round head when those two LUGS are off.

1651-57. Ray, *Cleaveland's Poems*, With hair in characters, and LUGS in texts.

1652. Tatham, *Scotch Figgaries*, v. Come, lend y'ar LUGS.

1653. Brome, *Mad Couple*, iv. 1. Take her at her word again, sir, and I shall take you by the LUGGS.

1675. Cotton, *Scoffer Scofft*, in *Wks.* (1725), p. 150. Those large LUGS of yours will crack for't.

1684. Lacy, *Sauny the Scot*, ii. 1. Gin I had yea in Scotland, I'se nea give yea a bawbee for your LUGS.

1690. B. E., *Dict. Cant. Crew*, s.v. LUGGS: hence 'to lugg by the ears.'

1725. *New Cant. Dict.*, s.v.

1762. Foote, *The Orators*, i. Satan. . . . whispers a fast speech in her LUG.

1785. Grose, *Vulg. Tongue*, s.v.

1819. Moore, *Tom Crib*, p. 7. Round LUGS and ogles flew the frequent fist.

1822. Scott, *Fortunes of Nigel*, xxxiii. A lurking place called the King's LUGG or ear, where he could sit undescried, and hear the converse of his prisoners.

1823. Moncrieff, *Tom and Jerry*, ii. 4. He napp'd it under the LUGS, too.

2. (common).—Affected manners; 'airs': *e.g.* TO PUT ON LUGS = to be conceited.

Verb. (once literary: now colloquial).—1. To drag; also to take by the ears.

*d.*1189. *Destruction of Troy* [E. E. T. S.], 1, 6663. With myche wepyng and wo, weghis of his aune LUGGIT hym out to the laund.

1609. Shakspeare, *Timon of Athens*, iv. 3, 31. Why, this Will LUG your priests and servants from your sides.

1726. Swift, *Gulliver*, 'Laputa', vi. To tread on his corns, or LUG him twice by both ears.

2. (old).—To drink steadily.

IN LUG, *phr.* (old).—In pawn; in pledge; up the SPOUT (*q.v.*).

TO LUG IN, *verb. phr.* (colloquial).—To include; to insert unnecessarily or unexpectedly.

1762. Churchill, *The Ghost*, Bk. iv. Physic and divinity are LUGGED IN by the head and shoulders.

1830. Greville, *Memoirs*, 27 Feb. He could not tell that story which I begged him to do, and which would not have been LUGGED IN neck and shoulders, because every body was telling just such stories.

1864. A. Trollope, *The Small House at Allington*, x. Joseph Cradell Esqre to John Eames Esqre. . . . 'I want you to write me at once, saying what you know about the matter. I ask you as I dont want to LUG IN any of the other people at Roper's.'

TO LUG OUT, *verb. phr.* (old).—To draw (as a sword).

1688. T. Shadwell, *Squire of Alsatia*. The Prigster LUGG'D OUT in defence of his natural, the Captain whipt his Porker out, and away rubb'd Prigster and call'd the watch.

1690. B. E., *Dict. Cant. Crew*, s.v.

1690. Dryden, *Don Sebastian*, iv. 1. They will be heard, or they LUG OUT and cut.

TO BLAW IN ONE'S LUG, *verb. phr.* (Scots').—To cajole; to flatter. Hence, BLAW-IN-MY-LUG = a flatterer; a wheedler.

IF WORTH HIS LUGS (he would do such a thing), *phr.* (Scots').—Used in approbation, or the reverse. [From the mediæval punishment of lopping the ears].

1362. Langland, *Piers Plowman*, A. ii. a. Were the bishop blessed and WORTH both HIS EARES His seale shold not be sent to deceyue the people.

TO HAVE A FLEA IN ONE'S LUG. *See* EAR.

TO LAY ONE'S LUGS, *verb. phr.* (Scots').—To wager.

LUG-CHOVEY, *subs.* (thieves').—A pawnbroker's shop.

LUGGER, *subs.* (American thieves').—A sailor.—Matsell (1859).

LUG-LOAF, *subs.* (old).—A blockhead.

1606. *Wily Beguiled* [Dodsley, *Old Plays* (1874), ix. 275]. She had little reason to take a cullion LUG-LOAF, milksop slave, when she may have a lawyer, a gentleman.

LUKE, (old).—Nothing.—Haggart (1821).

LULL, *subs.* (old).—Ale.

*c.*1636. *London Chanticleers*, Sc. 9. Mine host, Welcome, has a cup of blessed LULL.

LULLABY, *subs.* (venery).—The *penis*. For synonyms *see* CREAMSTICK and PRICK.

LULLABY-CHEAT, *subs.* (old).—A baby.

1671. Head, *English Rogue*. Carried at her back a LULLABY-CHEAT.

1690. B. E., *Dict. Cant. Crew*, s.v. LULLABY-CHEAT.

1725. *New Cant. Dict.*, s.v.

1785. Grose, *Vulg. Tongue*, s.v.

1839. W. H. Ainsworth, *J. Sheppard*, p. 25 (ed. 1840). 'Let's have a look at the kinchen that ought to have been throttled,' added he, snatching the child from Wood. 'My stars! here's a pretty LULLABY-CHEAT to make a fuss about—ho! ho!'

Lully, *subs.* (old).—*See* quot. 1785. Hence LULLY-prigger = a filcher of wet or drying linen. Fr. *défleurir la picouse* = LULLY-PRIGGING.

1754. *Discoveries of John Poulter*, p. 40. They are great priggers of LULLY.

1785. Grose, *Vulg. Tongue*, s.v. Lulleys, wet linen.

1789. Parker, *Life's Painter*, p. 120. Upon the old slang, and sometimes a little LULLY-prigging.

Lumb, *adv.* (old).—Too much.—*New Cant. Dict.* (1725); Grose (1796).

Lumber, *subs.* (thieves').—1. A room. [From the Lombard Room in which the mediæval pawnbrokers and bankers stored their pledges].

1789. Parker, *Life's Painter*, 117. Have you any-body in the LUMBER behind the bar?

1819. Vaux, *Memoirs*, s.v., p. 188.

2. (old).—A prison; QUOD (*q.v.*).

Verb. (old).—(1) To pawn; (2) to imprison.

1819. Vaux, *Memoirs*, s.v. Lumber (p. 188). to LUMBER any property is to deposit it at a pawnbroker's, or elsewhere for present security; to retire to any house or private place for a short time, is called lumbering yourself. A man apprehended, and sent to gaol, is said to be LUMBERED, to be in lumber, or to be in Lombard Street.

1830. W. T. Moncrieff, *The Heart of London*, ii. 1. They LUMBERED him for a few moons.

Live lumber, *subs. phr.* (old).—Soldiers or passengers on board a ship are so called by the sailors.—Grose (1785).

Lumberer, *subs.* (turf).—1. A swindling 'tipster'.

2. (American thieves').—A pawnbroker; UNCLE (*q.v.*).

Lumberer-crib, *subs.* (American thieves').—A pawnbroker's shop.

Lumber-house, *subs.* (thieves').—A house for storing stolen property.

1889. *Ally Sloper's Half-holiday*, 4 May. For instance, one day, when he was drinking in a LUMBER-HOUSE, near Billingsgate, 'Joe Haynes, the comedian, and a broken officer came raking thither, too, without a farthing in either of their pockets.'

Lumber-state, *subs.* (American).—Maine.

Lummoking, *adj.* (colloquial).—Heavy; awkward.

*b.*1852. *Traits of American Humour*, II. 10. What, the ensign of the Dogtown Blues? that great LUMMOKIN' feller.

Lummy, *adj.* (common).—First-rate.

1843. Dickens, *Martin Chuzzlewit*, xiii. 'Ah!' said Bill .... 'Lummy Ned of the Light Salisbury, *he* was the one for musical talents.'

1883. *Punch*, 28 July, p. 38, col. 1. London's gettin' more LUMMY each day; there's sech oshuns to see and enjoy!

1892. Milliken, *'Arry Ballads*, p. 4. 'Ardly know which is LUMMIEST.

Lump, *subs.* (colloquial).—1. Anything exceptional: *e.g.* 'a LUMP of a man'; 'I like that a LUMP'; 'that's a LUMP'.

2. (vagrants').—The workhouse; the PAN (*q.v.*). Also LUMP HOTEL.

3. (colloquial).—A party; an association.

Verb. (old).—1. To beat. For synonyms *see* Tan.

1785. Grose, *Vulg. Tongue*, s.v.

1811. *Lex. Bal.*, s.v.

2. (colloquial).—1. To dislike: 'If he does not like it he may LUMP it' = if he isn't satisfied he may do the other thing. Also, (2) to take without choice (*i.e.* to swallow 'whole').

1833. Neal, *Down Easters*, vii. Let 'em LUMP it if they don't like it.

1837-40. Haliburton, *The Clockmaker*, p. 6, preface (ed. 1862). A man that would be guilty of such an action is no gentleman, that's flat, and if you don't like it you may LUMP it.

1864. Dickens, *Our Mutual Friend*, Bk. IV, ch. iii. If you don't like it, it's open to you to LUMP it.

1878. H. B. Stowe, *Poganuc People*, xi. And if anybody don't like it, why they may LUMP it, that's all.

1887. F. R. Stockton, *The Hundredth Man*, ch. xv. If old Stull didn't like it, he could LUMP it. And to know that he LUMPED it would be a rare joy to Mrs. People.

1888. Bret Harte, *Five O'clock in the Morning*. And I told him, if he didn't like it he might LUMP it, and he travelled off on his left ear, you bet.

1888. *Detroit Free Press*, 20 Oct. If the white folks didn't like it they could LUMP it.

3. (colloquial).—To take off at a draught.

4. (racing).—To stake heavily; TO PLUNGE (*q.v.*).

1864. *Derby Day*, 12. Acting upon the gamblers' favourite axiom, that if you venture nothing you win nothing, he LUMPED it all upon an outsider, and backed him to win the Chester Cup.

1891. *Licensed Vict. Gaz.*, 3 April. Had laid against Cortolvin for the Grand National while LUMPING it down on Lecturer had not done much to repair his losses.

To knock lumps out of, *verb. phr.* (theatrical).—To command a great deal of applause.

1885. Coun, *Nutts about the Stage*, p. 12. We KNOCK LUMPS OUT OF them in these parts, don't we Mac?

To lump the lighter, *verb. phr.* (old).—To be transported.

1785. Grose, *Vulg. Tongue*, s.v.

1811. *Lex. Bal.*, s.v.

Lumper, *subs.* (old).—1. A riverside labourer; (2) a riverside thief, and (3) a contractor in a small way for labour and materials for unloading and loading ships. *See* quots.

1781. G. Parker, *View of Society*, II. 78. They then commence LUMPERS, which is skulking about ships, lighters, etc. hanging about quays, wharfs, etc. stealing old iron, fruit, sugar, or whatever comes to hand.

1796. Colquhoun, *Police of the Metropolis*, p. 57. The prevailing practice of discharging and delivering the cargoes of ships by a class of aquatic labourers, known by the name of LUMPERS.

1851-61. H. Mayhew, *London Lab. & Lon. Poor*, ii. 374. 'The men to whom it is sublet only find labour, while the LUMPER, or first contractor, agrees for both labour and materials.' *Ibid.* ii. p. 107. Then the LUMPERS, or those engaged in discharging the timber ships.

1853. Dickens, *Down with the Tide*, in *Reprinted Pieces*, p. 268. Then there were the LUMPERS, or labourers employed to unload vessels. They wore loose canvas jackets with a broad hem in the bottom, turned inside, so as to form a large circular pocket in which they could conceal, like clowns in pantomimes, packages of surprising sizes.... The LUMPERS dispose of their booty easily to marine store dealers. . . . LUMPERS also smuggle goods ashore for the crews of vessels.

2. (thieves').—*See* quot.

1851-61. Mayhew, *Lond. Lab.*, i. 413. A LUMPER would sell linens, cottons, or silks, which might be really the commodities represented; but which, by some management or other, were

made to appear new when they were old, or solid when they were flimsy.

3. (common).—A militia-man.

1869. Blackmore, *Lorna Doone*, xxxviii. He was going to bring the LUMPERS upon us.

4. *in pl.* (Irish).—Potatoes; MURPHIES (*q.v.*)

1846. *Punch*, x. 170. 'Twill tache him to be cuffin' at me with his ridin' whip when he rode over my acre and ruined my LUMPERS for me.

5. (scientific).—One who lumps together several species: as opposed to a SPLITTER (*q.v.*).

1888. *Nature*, xxxix. 156. The happy medium between LUMPERS and splitters.

Lump hotel. *See* Lump, sense 2.

Lumping, *adj.* (old: now colloquial).—Heavy; bulky; awkward.

1678. *Four for a Penny*, in *Harl. Misc.* (ed. Park), iv. 148. Their chief customers that bring the LUMPING bargains.

*d.*1735. Arbuthnot (in Johnson).—Nick, thou shalt have a LUMPING pennyworth.

1755. Johnson, *Dict.*, s.v. Lumping, large, heavy, great. A low word.

1796. Grose, *Vulg. Tongue*, s.v. . . . . He has got a LUMPING pennyworth; frequently said of a man who marries a fat woman.

1851. H. Mayhew, *Lon. Lab. and Lon. Poor*, i. 163. He gives what is called the LUMPING hap'orth, that is seven or eight pieces [of hot eel with the soup].

1887. *Boys Own Paper Xmas No.*, p. 3. Slick's Welsh cow-boy (a LUMPING yokel of forty summers and as many winters).

Lumpish, *adj.* (old).—Melancholy; dull; dispirited and heavy.

1592. Nashe, *Pierce Penilesse* [Grosart (1885), ii. 82]. Heavy, LUMPISH, and sleepie.

1621. Burton, *Anatomy* (ed. 1852), i. 169. We call him melancholy that is dull, sad, sour, LUMPISH, ill-disposed, solitary.

1664. Wilson, *Projectors*, i. 1. At home you're as sad and LUMPISH as a gibb'd cat.

Lump of coke, *subs. phr.* (rhyming).—A BLOKE (*q.v.*); a man.

Lump of lead, *subs. phr.* (rhyming).—The head; the CRUMPET (*q.v.*).

Lumpshious, *adv.* (common).—Delicious: *cf.* SCRUMPTIOUS.

1844. Buckstone, *The Maid with the Milking-pail. Milly.* What, paint me? Paint me on a board and hang me up against a wall! Oh, that will be LUMPSHIUS! And then I can sit and look at myself all day long.

Lumpy, *adj.* (common).—1. Drunk. For synonyms *see* Drinks and Screwed.

2. (common).—Pregnant.

English synonyms. To be awkward; bellied-up, big; big-bellied, on the bones; bow- (or bay-) windowed, cocked-up, double-ribbed, in an interesting condition, in for it, in pod, in the pudding-club, jumbled-up, knocked-up, loaded; on the bones; sewed-up, short-skirted, trussed-up, or wedged-up. To have one's apron up; a belly-ful, or a belly-ful of bones; one's cargo aboard; a nine months' dropsy (or a dropsy that will drop into the lap); one's fairing; fallen; got it; a hump in front (or on one's belly); an inside worry; a kick in the back; a lap-clap; more in one's belly than ever got there through one's mouth; young; a white swelling.

French synonyms. *Avoir le ventre* or *le sac plein* (= to be bellied-up); *avoir un arlequin dans la soupente* (of harlots: *arlequin* = a prostitute's brat;

soupente = loft); *avoir un polichinelle dans le tiroir* (= to have a Jack-in-the-box in the drawer); *en avoir dans le ventre* (= to have a belly-ful); *avoir son tablier lève* (= to have got one's apron up); *avoir le mou enflé* (= to be swelled in the soft); *avoir avalé un pépin* (= to have swallowed a seed); *entrer dans l'infanterie* (popular); *avoir un député dans l'urne* (popular); *avoir une affaire cachée sous la peau* (common); *avoir mal au genou* (= *cf.* TO BREAK ONE'S KNEES); *s'être fait arrondir le globe* (popular); *avoir un fédéré dans la casemate* (common); *se gâter la taille* (= to spoil one's figure); *avoir la maladie de neuf mois* (common: *cf.* NINE MONTHS' DROPSY). Also *une couleuvre* or *un chef-lieu d'arrondissement* (= a pregnant woman).

German synonyms. *Schwor* or *schwar* (*schwer* = heavy).

Spanish synonyms. *Arari; avari; barriga 'a boca; cambri; cambrobi; desembarcar; embarago.*

3. (booksellers').—Costly.

4. (cricketers').—Rough; uneven: as applied to the ground.

Lumtum, *subs.* (American thieves').—A fashionable thief.

1882. McCabe, *New York*, 221. Altogether my first evening among the LUMTUMS panned out well.

Lun, *subs.* (old).—(1) A harlequin.—Grose (1785). (2) A clown.—Matsell (1859).

Lunan, *subs.* (vagrants').—A girl. For synonyms *see* Titter. [From the Romany].

Luncheon reservoir, *subs. phr.* (common).—The stomach. For synonyms *see* Victualling Office.

Lung-box, *subs.* (common).—The mouth. For synonyms *see* Potato-trap.

Lungis, *subs.* (old).—An idle, lazy, fellow.

1592. Nashe, *Summer's Last Will* [Dodsley, *Old Plays* (1874), viii. 53]. There is not, goodman LUNGIS.

1602. Dekker, *Satiro-mastix* [Nares]. Knaves, varlets! What LUNGIS! give a dozen of stools there.

Lungs, *subs.* (old).—*See* quot. 1755.

1610. Jonson, *Alchemist*. That is his fire-drake, his LUNGS, his zephyrus, he that puffs his coals.

1755. Johnson, *Dicty.*, s.v. Lungs. Formerly a cant term for a person denoting a large and strong-voiced man, as Coles has observed; and also a chymical servant, a sort of underworkman in the art.

Lunkhead, *subs.* (American).—An ill-bred, ill-looking horse; a SCREW (*q.v.*).

Lunk-headed, *adj.* (American).—Senseless.

Luny. *See* Loony.

Lurch, *subs.* (old).—A cheat.

*d.*1597. Peele, *Jests*, 619. The tapster having many of these LURCHES fell to decay.

1606. Dekker, *Seven Deadly Sins* [Grosart (1886), ii. 52]. Betting, LURCHES, rubber, and such tricks.

1604. Middleton, *Black Book* [in *Century*]. All such LURCHES, gripes, and squeezes, as may be wrung out by the fist of extortion.

1626. BRETON, *Pasquil's Mad-cappe* [GROSART (1869), I. *e.* 6, 2, 27]. Howere his wit may GIUE the foole THE LURCH, He is not fit to gouerne in the church.

Verb. (old).—To steal; to cheat; to trick.

1563. *Appius and Virginius* [DODSLEY, *Old Plays* (1874), iv. 150]. Then—gallop to see where her father doth LURCH.

1592. GREENE, *Defence of Conny catching*, in *Works*, xi. 58. Was not this an old conny catcher M. R. G. that could LURTCH a poore conny of so many thousands at one time?

1593. NASHE, *Christe's Teares* [GROSART (1885), IV. 228]. Laughing at the Punies they haue LURCHED.

1596. SHAKSPEARE, *Merry Wives*, ii. 1. I . . . am fain to shuffle, to hedge, and to LURCH.

1598. FLORIO, *A Worlde of Wordes. Imbolare* to filch, to steale, to purloine, LURCHE, to pilfer, to prowle.

1609. JONSON, *Silent Woman*, v. You have LURCHED your friends of the better half of the garland, by concealing this part of the plot.

1662. *Rump Songs*, i. 210. Our gossips' spoons away were LURCHT, Our feasts and fees for women churcht.

TO LEAVE IN THE LURCH, *verb. phr.* (colloquial).—*See* quot. 1690. Fr. *laisser quelqu'un béar.* [From cribbage].

[?]. *Robin Hood and the Tinker* [CHILD, *Ballads*, v. 233]. Robin made them haste away, And LEFT the tinker IN THE LURCH, The great shot for to pay.

1594. NASHE, *Have with You* [GROSART (1885), iii. 150]. He . . . LEFT both of them IN THE LURTCH.

1606. *Return from Parnassus* [DODSLEY, *Old Plays* (1874), ix. 178]. 'Sblood, a while ago, before he had me IN THE LURCH, who but my cousin Prodigo?

1611. COTGRAVE, *Dictionarie*, s.v. *Il demeura lourche*, he was LEFT IN THE LURCH.

1662. *Rump Songs*, i. 9. And LEAVE us IN THE LURCH.

1690. B. E., *Dict. Cant. Crew'* s.v. LURCHED . . . LEFT IN THE LURCH' Pawned for the Reckoning or left at Stake to Smart for any Plot.

1725. *New Cant. Dict.*, s.v.

1763. *North Briton*, No. 41, Mar. [quoted in *Notes and Queries*, 7 S. iv. 48]. When John LEAVES Margaret IN THE LURCH, And Presbyterians head the Church.

1785. GROSE, *Vulg. Tongue*, s.v.

1785. BURNS, *Jolly Beggars*, ii. But the godly old chaplain LEFT him IN THE LURCH.

1827. TODD, *Johnson's Dicty*, s.v. LURCH. TO LEAVE IN THE LURCH, a ludicrous phrase.

1858. LADY HOLLAND, *Sydney Smith*, xcv. Weary will be the latter half of my pilgrimage, if you LEAVE me IN THE LURCH.

1888. ROLF BOLDREWOOD, *Robbery Under Arms*, v. It won't do to LEAVE old dad IN THE LURCH.

TO GIVE A LURCH, *verb. phr.* (old).—To tell a lie; to deceive.

LURCHER, *subs.* (common).—1. A rogue.

1603-35. BRETON, *Mad World* [GROSART (1869), ii. *i.* 12, 2, 50]. But these may rather be called LURCHMEN than Churchmen, who as they are not troubled with much learning, so they have no more honesty.

1888. *Daily News*, 4 Dec. After that shall try on the lazy LURCHERS who live on unfortunates.

1891. *Morning Advertizer*, 3 April. It was quite time that the honest and respectable drivers sat down on the LURCHERS once and for all, and when they knew that there were 7,000 of them in London they should think of their power and demand better conditions.

2. (old).—*See* quot. Also LURCHER OF THE LAW.

1785. GROSE, *Vulg. Tongue*, s.v. LURCHER, a LURCHER OF THE LAW, a bum bailiff, or his setter.

1839. HARRISON AINSWORTH, *Jack Sheppard* [1889], p. 12. 'But where are the LURCHERS?' 'Who?' asked Wood. 'The traps!' responded a bystander.

LURDEN, *subs.* (old).—A rogue. Hence LURDENRY = roguery.

1513. GAWIN DOUGLAS, *Eneados*, viii. Prol. l. q. Leis, LURDANRY, and lash.

1540. LINDSAY, *Satyre Thrie Estaitis* [E. E. T. S.], l. 2474. Thou links evin lyke ane LURDEN.

1562-3. *Jack Juggler* [DODSLEY, *Old Plays* (1874), ii. 135]. Avoid, thou lousy LURDEN and precious stinking slave.

*c.*1587. GREENE, *Follie and Loue* [GROSART (1881-6), iv. 206]. Instead of some braue gentleman, I strike some filthie LURDEN.

1606. *Wily Beguiled* [DODSLEY, *Old Plays* (1874), ix. 288]. If I had been such a great, long, large, lob-cocked, losellel LURDAN, as Master Churms is. . . . I should never have got Peg as long as I had lived.

LURK, *subs.* (vagrants').—*See* quots.

1829. *A Laconic Narrative of the Life and Death of James Wilson.* That awful monster, William Burke. Like Reynard sneaking on the LURK, Coyducked his prey into his den And then the woeful work began.

1851-61. MAYHEW, *Lond. Lab.*, i. 403. Many kinds of thieving as well as begging are termed LURKING—the dead LURK, for instance, is the expressive slang phrase for the art of entering dwelling-houses during divine service. The term LURK, however, is mostly applied to the several modes of plundering by representations of sham distress.

1889. *Answers*, 27 July, 137, 1. Begging of all kinds is divided into LURKS, or branches.

Verb. (vagrants').—To beg with false letters.

1851-61. MAYHEW, *Lond. Lab.*, i. 462. We'll LURK on your trade.

LURKER, *subs.* (vagrants').—1. A begging imposter; a SILVER BEGGAR (*q.v.*). *See* DEMAUNDER FOR GLYMMAR. Also LURKSMAN.

1851-61. H. MAYHEW, *London Lab. & Lon. Poor*, i. 233. In every large town sham official documents, with crests, seals, and signatures, can be got for half-a-crown. Armed with these, the patterer becomes LURKER,—that is, an imposter.

2. (thieves').—A JACK-OF-ALL-TRADES (*q.v.*).

LURRIES, *subs.* (old).—*See* quot. 1690. For synonyms *see* ACTUAL and GILT. Also LURRY.

1674. *The Canting Academy* (ed. 20). 'The Budge it is a Delicate Trade.' But if the cully nab us and The LURRIES from us takes, O then he rubs us to the whit.

1676. *The Twenty Craftsmen.* The fifth was a glazier, who, when he creeps in, To pinch all the LURRY he thinks it no sin.

1690. B. E., *Dict. Cant. Crew*, s.v. LURRIES, Money, Watches, Rings, or other Moveables.

1725. *New Cant. Dict.*, s.v.

1754. *Scoundrel's Dicty.* If he sees but the LURRY his hooks he will bait.

1785. GROSE, *Vulg. Tongue*, s.v.

LURRY, *subs.* (old colloquial).—1. Gabble.

1649. MILTON, *Eikonoklastes*, XVI. To turn prayer into a kind of LURREY.

2. *See* LURRIES.

LUSH, *subs.* (common).—1. Drink. [LUSHINGTON = a once well-known London brewer]. For synonyms *see* DRINKS.

1819. VAUX, *Memoirs*, p. 188, s.v. LUSH, beer or liquor of any kind.

1830. SIR E. B. LYTTON, *Paul Clifford*, ch. xvi. 'Bring the LUSH and the pipes, old bloke!' cried Ned, throwing himself on a bench; 'we are never at a loss for company!'

1841. *Comic Almanack*, 270. They are identified equally with the LUSH and the literature of the land; for he is prepared to contend that whatever has been great in literature is deducible from LUSH.

1841. LEVER, *Charles O'Malley*, XX. The Bursar of Trinity shall be a proverb for a good fellow that loveth his LUSH.

1843. W. T. MONCRIEFF, *The Scamps of London*, ii. 3. Dispose of your LUSH, and play out your game.

1851. H. MAYHEW, *Lon. Lab. and Lon. Poor*, i. 25. 'Cruickshank's 'Bottle' was very much admired. I heard one man say it was very prime, and showed what LUSH did; but I saw the same man,' added my informant, 'drunk three hours afterwards.'

1892. HUME NISBET, *Bushranger's Sweetheart*, 201. Stand me a LUSH and go back again.

2. (common).—A drinking bout.

1891. *Licensed Victuallers' Gaz.*, 16 Jan. To have a supper and a good LUSH.

3. (Eton College).—A dainty.

Verb. (common).—1. To drink; and (2) to stand treat.

ENGLISH SYNONYMS. To barley-bree; to beer; to bend; to blink; to boose; to bub; to budge; to cover; to crack (or crush) a bottle (a quart, or cup); to crook; to crook (lift, or tip) the elbow (or little finger); to damp; to damp one's mug; to dip; to dip one's beak (or nose); to disguise oneself; to do a dram (or wet); to drown the shamrock; to flicker; to flush; to fuddle; to gargle; to give a bottle a black eye; to guttle; to guzzle; to go and see a man (or—of women—one's pa); to grog; TO HAVE, or GET, or TAKE an ante-lunch, a little anti-abstinence, an appetiser, a ball, a bead, a bit of tape, a bosom friend, a bucket, a bumper, a big reposer, a chit-chat, a cheerer, a cinder, a cobbler, a corker, a cooler, some corn-juice, a damp, something damp, a damper, a dannie, a drain, a dram, a doch-an-dorroch, a digester, an eye-opener, an entr'acte, a fancy smile, a flash, a flip, a forenoon, a go, a hair of the dog that bit one, a heeltap, an invigorator, Johnny, a jorum, a leaf of the old author, a morning rouser, a modicum, a nip, or nipperkin, a night cap, a nut, one's medicine, a pistol shot, a pony, a piil, a quantum, a quencher, a refresher, a revelation, a rouser, a reposer, a smile, a swig, a sleeve-button, a something, a slight sensation, a shant, a shout, a sparkler, a settler, a shift, a stimulant, a sneaker, a snifter, a soother, a thimbleful, a tift, a taste, a toothful, a Timothy, a warmer, a willy-wacht; to huff; to irrigate; to knock about the bub; to lap; to lap the gutter; to liquor; to liquor up; to load in; to look thro' a glass; to lower; to lug; to make fun; to malt; to moisten (or soak) the chaffer (clay, or lips); to mop; to mop-up; to mug; to peg; to potate; to prime oneself; to pull; to put (or drive) another nail in one's coffin; to read the maker's name; to revive; to rince; to rock; to save a life; to scamander; to shed a tear; to shake a cloth; to sherry-fog; to shift; to shout; to slosh; to sluice (or wet) the bolt, gob, or ivories; to soak; to splice the mainbrace; to squiff; to stab; to suck the monkey; to swill; to swig; to swipe; to swizzle; to take the pin out; to take a drop in the eye; to take in some O-be-joyful; to tiff; to tipple; to toddy; to wet; to wet one's whistle; to wine.

FRENCH SYNONYMS. *Absorber* (familiar); *s'affûter le sifflet* (common); *arroser ses galons* (= to pay one's footing); *asphyxier* (= to nip); *bidonner* (= to swig: *bidonner à la cambuse* = to splice the mainbrace); *bocker* (popular); *boire une chifferlinde* (= to take a nip); *se rincer le bocal* (= to sluice one's

gob); *boissonner* (popular); *se rafraîchir les barres* (popular); *buvailler* (popular); *chauffer le four* (= to guzzle); *se dessaler* (specifically to take an EYE-OPENER); *écoper* (= to bale a boat); *écraser une bouteille* (= to crack a bottle: *écraser un grain* = to drink a dram); *s'enflaneller* (= to take a night-cap); *s'éclairer le fanal* (= to light-up); *se machaber* (popular); *étouffer une mitrailleuse* (popular: *cf. boire un canon*); *se mouiller* (RABELAIS); *se rincer le moule à blagues* (= to moisten the chaffer); *étouffer, éreinter une*, or *éternuer sur, une negresse* (= to crack a bottle); *se passer quelque chose sous le nez* (= to crook the elbow); *s'humecter le pavillon* (= to dip one's flag: also *pavillonner*); *s'en pousser dans le battant, le cornet, le fusil*, etc. (common); *s'humecter le pectoral* (familiar); *picter* (*cf.* Gr. πιεῖν); *pier* (old); *pitancher* (popular); SE RINCER or SE GARGARISER *l'avaloir, le bec, le bocal, la gargoine, la corne, la cornemuse, le cornet, la dalle, la dalle du cou, la dent, le fusil, le goulot, le gaviot, le sifflet, le tube, la trente-deuxième, la gargarousse* (popular); *fioler* (familiar); *flûter* (popular); *s'en fourrer dans le gilet* (= to line one's waistcoat); *se rincer la gargoine* (thieves'); *se gargariser le rossignolet* (= to gargle one's nightingale); *prendre un coup de gaz* (common); *se laver le gosier* (popular); *s'emplir le gilet* (popular); *sucer un glace* (= to take an ice); *glouglouter* (popular); *jouer du*, or *se rincer, le goulot* (= to wash one's throat); *se graisser les roues* (= to grease one's wheels); *siffler le guindal* (common); *pomper les huiles* (*huile* = wine; *huile blonde* = beer); *s'humecter les amygdales* (popular); *s'imbiber le jabot* (popular); *faire jambe de vin* (old); *se laver les yeux* (= to take an eye-opener); *se laver le tuyau* (popular); *licher* (familiar = to swill); *litronner* (of wine only); *renifler* (popular); *sabler* (common = to shift); *sécher* (popular); *se calfater le bec* (common); *se blinder* (popular); *se suiver; sucer* (popular); *siroter* (common); *soiffer* (popular = to load in); *s'en taper; téter; zinguer* (= to drink at a bar).

GERMAN SYNONYMS. *Ausschassjenen* (Heb. *schoso*); *bacheln* (Fr. *bocal;* also *pecheln* and *picheln*); *bafen* (from Lat. *bibere*); *schasjenen* (Heb. *schoso:* also *schaskenen*); *schöchem.*

ITALIAN SYNONYMS. *Tirar l'alzana; stibbiare; scabbiare; ventare; chiarire.*

SPANISH SYNONYMS. *Echar una limpia* (= to take a peg); *champurrar; churrupear: palabrar; remojar.*

PORTUGUESE SYNONYM. *Piar.*

1819. VAUX, *Memoirs*, p. 188, s.v. LUSH, to drink; speaking of a person who is drunk they say, Alderman Lushington is concerned, or he has been voting for the Alderman.

1821. HAGGART, *Life*, 18. We had LUSHED the coachman so neatly that Barney was obliged to drive.

1830. SIR E. B. LYTTON, *Paul Clifford*, p. 47, ed. 1854. 'Vy, I had been LUSHING heavy vet—' 'Till you grew light in the head, eh and fell into the kennel.' 'Yes.'

1837. DICKENS, *Oliver Twist*, XXVI The richest sort you ever LUSHED.

1851-61. H. MAYHEW, *London Lab. & Lon. Poor*, i. 187. I was out of work two or three weeks, and I certainly LUSHED too much.

1864. *Eton School Days*, viii. 'Gents, will yer please to LUSH?' inquired Bird's-eye, with a suavity of manner peculiar to himself.

1888. J. RUNCIMAN, *The Chequers*, 80. Ain't I LUSHED you?

1891. J. NEWMAN, *Scamping Tricks*, 94. I had a lot of militia chaps, and well paid and LUSHED them.

1892. MILLIKEN, *'Arry Ballads*, p. 17. A workman well LUSHED shies his 'at for the Queen.

LUSHBOROUGH, *subs.* (old).—See quots.

1362. LANGLAND, *Piers Plowman*, xv. 342. In LUSSHEBORWES is a lyther alay, and yet loketh he lyke a sterlynge.

1383. CHAUCER, *Cant. Tales* [SKEAT (1894), iv. 243, 3152]. God wood, no LUSSHEBORGHES payen ye!

1661. BLOUNT, *Nomolexicon*, s.v. A brass coyn in the days of Edward III.

1894. SKEAT, *Chaucer*, v. 225. Note to line 3152. LUSSHEBURGHES, light coins . . . spurious coins imported into England from Luxembourg, whence the name. The importation of this false money was frequently forbidden, viz. in 1347, 1348, and 1351.

LUSH-CRIB (or KEN), *subs.* (common). —See quot. 1819.

ENGLISH SYNONYMS. Ale draper's; black-house; boozer; budging-ken; church; cold-blood house; confectionery; cross-dram; devil's-house; dive; diving-bell; drum; flash-case (-drum, -ken, or -panny); flat-iron; flatty-ken; gargle-factory; gin-mill; grocery; groggery; grog-shop; guzzle-crib; jerry-shop; hash-shop; hedge-house; kiddly-wink; little church round the corner; lush-house (-panny, or -ken); lushery; mop-up; mug-house; O-be-joyful works; panny; patter-crib; piss-factory; pot-house; pub (or public) red-lattice; roosting-ken; rum-mill; shanty; shebeen; side-pocket; sluicery; suck-casa; tippling-shop; Tom-and-Jerry-shop; whistling-shop; wobble-shop.

FRENCH SYNONYMS. *Un abreuvoir* (= a watering-place); *un assommoir* (= a knock-me-down shop); *une bibine* (rag-pickers' shop); *une bouffardière* (common: *bouffard* = pipe or WEED [q.v.]); *un bousin* (also = shindy); *un bousingot* (popular); *une buverie* (Old Fr.); *un cabermon* (thieves': from *cabaret*); *un caboulot* (popular); *une cambuse* (nautical = store-room); *une chapelle* (popular: *cf.* CHURCH); *une goguette* (common); *une guinche* (common); *un malzingue* (thieves'); *une mine à poivre* (*poivre* = brandy); *un mintzingue* (popular); *le notaire* (= also taverner); *une piolle* (also = KEN [q.v.]); *une filature à poivrots* (= a manufactory of LUSHINGTONS [q.v.]); *un rideau rouge* (*cf.* RED-LATTICE).

GERMAN SYNONYMS. *Aules* (also = pitcher); *Baisel* (also = brothel and pitcher); *Chessenkitt, Chessenpenne, Chessenspiesse* (thieves'); *Finkel* (also = thieves' kitchen); *Kessefinkel* (thieves'); *Katschäume* (trom gypsy *tschemika*); *Molun* or *Maline* (Heb. *lun: Chessenmaline* = common lodging-house); *Spiese* (from *Ospes* = Lat. *hospes*); *Penne* (Heb. *pono*); *Plattpenne, Platt-spiesse, Plattebajis, Plattbes* (also = intercourse with thieves'); *Serafbajis* (Heb. *soraf*); *Scho-cherskitt* (Heb. *schechor* from *schochar*); *Schlederhaus* (from

schlodern or *schlottern* = to totter); *Schwäche, Schwächaules,* or *Schwächkitt* (Heb. *sewach* = to sacrifice, to kill); *Eintippel* or *Intippel* (*tippen* or *tippeln* = to dip).

ITALIAN SYNONYMS. *Bruzza; calda; cerchiosa; scabbiosa.*

SPANISH SYNONYMS. *Alegria* (= pleasure or joy); *aduana* (= custom-house); *percha* (= perch or pole); *puerto* (= port).

1819. VAUX, *Memoirs*, 188, s.v. LUSH-CRIB or LUSH-KEN, a public house, or gin-shop.

1820. *Randall's Diary*, 'Farewell to the King.' Then blame me not kids, swells, or lads of the fancy, For opening a LUSH-CRIB in Chancery Lane.

LUSHING-MUZZLE, *subs.* (pugilistic). —A blow on the mouth.—GROSE (1823).

LUSHINGTON, *subs.* (common).—A sot. Also LUSHING MAN and LUSHY-COVE.

ENGLISH SYNONYMS. Admiral of the Red; after-dinner man; ale-knight; ale-wisp; artilleryman; bang-pitcher; beer-barrel; belch-guts; bencher; bench-whistler; bezzle; bibber; blackpot; bloat; blomboll; boozer; boozington; borachio; bottle-sucker; brandy-face; brewer's-horse; bubber (or bubster); budge (or budger); bung-eye; burster; common sewer; coppernose; drainist; drainpipe; dramster; D-T-ist; elbow-crooker; emperor; ensign-bearer; fish; flag-of-distress; fluffer; fuddle-cap (or fuddler); full-blown angel; gargler; gin-crawler (or -slinger); ginnums; gravel-grinder; grog-blossom; guttle (or guttle-guts); guzzler (or guzzle-guts); high-goer; jolly-nose; lapper; love-pot; lowerer; lug-pot; moist-'un; mooner; mop (or mopper-up); nazie-cove (or -mort); nipster; O-be-Joyfuller (or O-be-Joyful-merchant); pegger; piss-maker; potster; pot-walloper; pub-ornament; sapper; shifter; sipster; soaker; sponge; swallower; swill-pot (or -tub); swigsby; swigster; swipester; swizzle-guts; Thirstington; tipple-arse; toddy-cask; toss-pot; tote; tut; wet-subject; wetster.

FRENCH SYNONYMS. *Un bec-salé; un louave* (thieves'); *un litronneur* (popular); *une grosse culotte* (popular = fat-arse); *un gavé* (thieves': *gaver* = to stuff); *une lampe-à-mort* (pop. *lamper* = to swill); *un zingueur* (popular); *un boyau rouge; un marquant* (thieves'); *un canonneur* (pop. = an artilleryman: *canon* = long glass); *un camphrier* (popular); *un fioleur* (popular: *fiole* = phial: *cf.* TOSS-POT and BOTTLE-SUCKER); *une éponge* (popular = a SOAKER); *un bibard* (thieves'); *un buvard* (popular = blotting book); *un pochard* (colloquial); *un adroit du coude* (pop. = ELBOW-CROOKER); *un artilleur* (pop. *cf.* ARTILLERY-MAN); *un boissonneur* (pop. = a BOOZER); *un buvailleur* or *buvaillon* (pop. = LUSHINGTON); *un chocaillon* (pop. a female tippler); *un poivrot* (familiar: also *poivreau*); *un sac-à-vin* (pop.); *un pompier* (popular); *un soiffeur* (*soiffeuse* [fem.], or *soiffard* = THIRSTINGTON); *un schniqueur* (= NIPSTER); *un ventre d'osier; un siroteur* (= a SIPSTER); *un*

pion (VILLON); *un pilier de cabaret* (= a PUB-ORNAMENT); *un pictonneur* (*picton* = wine); *un mannezingueur; un marchand d'eau chaude* (= PISS-MAKER); *un marchand d'eau de javelle.*

GERMAN SYNONYM. *Mattobolo* (= a drunken pig: from the Gypsy *matto* = drunk).

ITALIAN SYNONYMS. *Fransoso* (= a Frenchman); *chiaritore; chiaristante.*

SPANISH SYNONYMS. *Cucro* (= a goat-skin bottle); *colodra* (= a wooden pail in which wine is measured and retailed); *cuba* (= a measure for wine); *difunto de taberna* (lit., a public-house corpse); *odre* (= a wine-skin); *pellejo* (= a wine-skin); *peneque; potista; odrina* (= an ox-hide bottle).

DUTCH SYNONYMS. *Buisbalk; buiskinne* or *buizerik.*

1826. *The Fancy*, i. 31. He is reported not to take sufficient care of himself: LUSHINGTON is evidently his master.

1840. *Comic Almanack*, 239. A blessed school of physic—half-and-half! The LUSHINGTON of each young Doctor's Commons.

1851-61. MAYHEW, *Lond. Lab.*, i. 68. They sell it at the public houses to the LUSHINGTONS.

1859. MATSELL, 'A hundred stretches hence.' With all the prigs and LUSHING-MEN, A hundred stretches hence.

LUSHY, *adj.* (common).—Drunk. For synonyms *see* DRINKS and SCREWED.

1819. VAUX, *Memoirs*, 188, s.v.

1821. HAGGART, *Life*, 33. We met with a drover, quite LUSHY.

1821. *The Fancy*, I, p. 303. At the Goat, as aforementioned, Ben Burn and Randall being both a little LUSHY.

1828. MAGINN, from VIDOCQ, *The Pickpocket's Chaunt*. A regular swell cove LUSHY lay. To his clies my hooks I throw in, Tol, lol, etc.

1836. DICKENS, *Pickwick*, xx. I was so uncommon LUSHY, that I couldn't find the place where the latch-key went in, and was obliged to knock up the old 'ooman.

1876. HINDLEY, *Adventures of A Cheap Jack*, 57. A LUSHY cove.

LUSK, *subs.* (old).—An idler. Also, LUSKISH; as *adj.* = idle.

1531-47. COPLAND, *Hye Way to the Spyttel Hous*, l. 40. Boyes, gyrles, and LUSKISH strong knaues.

b.1602. *Lingua* [DODSLEY, *Old Plays* (1874), ix. 462]. Up, with a pox to you; up you LUSK. [Note: LUSK = idle, lazy, slothful. Minshew derives it from the French *lasche, desidiosus*].

LUST-PROUD. See PRICK-PROUD.

LUSTRES, *subs.* (American thieves'). —Diamonds.—MATSELL (1859).

LUSTY-LAWRENCE, *subs.* (old).— A good wencher; a PERFORMER (q.v.). Also LUSTY-GUTS.

1599. PORTER, *Two Angry Women* [DODSLEY, *Old Plays* (1874), vii. 295]. Well, LUSTY-GUTS, I mean to make ye stay.

1603-37. BRETON, *Mad Letters*, [GROSART (1869), h. 33, 7, 12]. While LUSTIE-GUTS and his best beloued were casting sheepes eyes at a cods head.

1621. BURTON, *Anat.* (ed. 1892), ii. 40. Well fed like Hercules, Proculus . . . . and LUSTY LAURENCE.

LUTE, *subs.* (venery).—The female *pudendum*. For synonyms *see* MONOSYLLABLE.

1719. DURFEY, *Pills to Purge*, ii. 312. Her face like an angel, fair, plump, and a Maid, Her LUTE well in Tune too, could he but have plaid. *Ibid.* v. 4. Her white belly'd LUTE she set to his flute.

LUX, *subs.* (Blue-coat School).—A good thing; 'a splendid thing; *e.g.*, My knife is wooston a LUX.

Probably short form of luxuriant. Hertford word.'—BLANCH.

LUXER, *subs.* (Winchester College). —See quot.

1878. ADAMS, *Winchester College*, s.v. LUXER. A handsome fellow, I presume from luxuries, it being a pleasure to look at him?

LUXURIES. See BAR.

LYB-BEG, *subs.* (old).—A bed.

LYERBY (or LIG-BY), *subs.* (old).— A KEEP (q.v.).

LYP, *verb.* (old).—To lie down.— HARMAN (1567).

LYPKEN. See LIBKEN.

LYRIBLIRING, *subs.* (Old Cant).— Warbling or singing.

1580. PHILIP SIDNEY, *Arcadia*, iii. p. 395. So may her ears be led, Her ears where musike lives, To heare and not despise Thy LYRIBLIRING cries.

M

To have an M under (or by) the girdle, *verb. phr.* (old).—To have a courteous address. [By using the titles Mr., Mrs., Miss, etc.]. *See* quot. 1850.

1597-8. Haughton, *A Woman will have her Will* [Dodsley, *Old Plays* (1874), x. 531]. Hark ye . . . methinks you might do well to have an M under your girdle.

1605. Jonson, Chapman, etc., *Eastward Hoe*, iv. 1. You might carry an M under your girdle.

1738. Swift, *Polite Conversation*, i. The devil take you Neverout . . . . What plain Neverout! methinks you might have an M under your girdle, Miss.

1850. Halliwell, *Dict. Arch. & Prov. Words*, s.v. M . . . To keep the term 'Master' out of sight, to be wanting in proper respect.

Mab, *subs.* (old).—1. *See* quot.

1823. Moncrieff, *Tom & Jerry*, i. 7. *Tom.* But if you dislike going in a hack, we'll get you a mab. *Jerry.* A mab? I'm at fault again—never shall get properly broken in. *Tom.* A mab is a jingling jarvy!—a cabriolet, Jerry.

2. (old).—A slattern. *See* verb.

1690. B. E., *Dict. Cant. Crew*, s.v.

1725. *New Canting Dict.*, s.v.

3. (American).—A prostitute. For synonyms *see* Barrack-hack and Tart.

1859. Matsell, *Vocabulum*, s.v.

Verb. (old).—*See* quots.

1596. Shakspeare, *Hamlet*, ii. 2. But who, O! who had seen the mobled queen Run bare-foot up and down . . . .

1672. Ray, *Proverbs*, 'North Country Words,' s.v. To mab [pronounced *mob*], to dress carelessly. Mabs are slatterns.

1690. B. E., *Dict. Cant. Crew*, s.v. Mab . . . Mab'd up, Drest carelessly, like a Slattern.

1725. *New Cant. Dict.*, s.v.

*d.*1728. Kennett, *MS. Lansd.* 1033, Mobb'd up, dresst in a coarse clownish manner.

Macaroni, *subs.* (old).—1. *See* quot. 1711. [It. *maccarone*, now *maccherone*, a blockhead: *cf.*, Ger. *Hanswurst;* Fr. *Jean-farine;* and Jack-pudding].

1711. Addison, *Spectator*, No. 47, Ap. 24. 'In the first Place I must observe that there is a Set of merry Drolls whom the Common People of all Countries admire, and seem to love so well that they could eat them, according to the old Proverb: I mean those circumforaneous Wits whom every Nation calls by the Name of that Dish of Meat which it loves best. In Holland they are termed Pickled Herrings; in France Jean Pottages; in Italy Maccaronies; and in Great Britain Jack Puddings. These merry Wags, from whatsoever Food they receive their Titles, that they may make their Audiences laugh, always appear in a Fool's Coat, and commit such Blunders and Mistakes in every Step they take, and every Word they utter, as those who listen to them would be ashamed of.'

2. (old). — A dandy from 1760—75. [From the Macaroni Club, which introduced Italian macaroni at Almack's].

1764. Walpole, *To Hertford*, 27 May. Lady Falkener's daughter is to be married to a young rich Mr. Crewe, a macarone, and of our loo.

1768. Hall Stevenson, *Makarony Fables* (addressed to the Society of Macaronies) *Title.*

1770. *Oxford Magazine*, iv. 228, 2. There is indeed a kind of animal, neither male nor female, a thing of the neuter gender, lately started up amongst us. *It* is called a macaronie. *It* talks without meaning, *it* smiles without pleasantry, *it* eats without appetite, *it* rides without exercise.

1770. Foote, *Lame Lover*, i. 1. Frederick is a bit of macaroni, and adores the soft Italian termination in *a*.

1772. G. A. Stevens, *Songs Comic & Satyrical*, 139. Macaronies so neat, Pert Jemmies so sweet.

1773. Fergusson, *Auld Reekie* (*Poems*, 1851, p. 130). Close by his side, a feckless race O' macaronies show their face.

1774. Burgoyne, *Maid of the Oaks*, ii. 1. All the macaronies passed by, whistling a song through their toothpicks, and giving a shrug.

1776. Garrick, *High Life above Stairs*, i. 1. *Sir T.* This fellow would turn rake and macaroni if he were to stay here a week longer. Bless me, what dangers are in this town at every step!

1779. Mrs. Cowling, *Who's the Dupe?* ii. 2. You! you for to turn fop and macaroni!

1785. Grose, *Vulgar Tongue*, s.v.

1790. *The Busy Bee* (quoted in), ii. 248. Some macaronies there came in, All dressed so neat, and looked so thin.

1805. G. Barrington, *New London Spy* (4th ed.), p. 53. The present degenerate race of macaronies, who appear to be of a spurious puny breed.

1820. C. Lamb, *Elia*, 'South Sea House,' in *Works* [1852], p. 316. He wore his hair, to the last, powdered and frizzed out, in the fashion which I remember to have seen in caricatures of what were termed, in my young days, maccaronies.

1834. Ainsworth, *Rookwood*, i. ix. Though a Frenchman he was a deuced fine fellow in his day—quite a tip-top maccaroni.

1883. A. Dobson, *Hogarth*, p. 56. A slim macaroni, with his hair in curl papers, and his *queue* loose like a woman's tresses.

1885. *Daily Telegraph*, 14 Aug., p. 5, col. 1. The hat of the maccaroni has gone out as surely as the lights at Ranelagh, or the masquerades in Soho.

3. (American).—A Maryland regiment noted for its smartness, which took part in the Revolution.—'Stuck a feather in his cap, and called it macaroni'.—*Yankee Doodle.*

4. (rhyming).—A pony.

Adj. (old).—1. Foppish; affected; and (2) *see* quot. 1742. Also macaronian and macaronical.

1596. Nashe, *Have With You* [Grosart, iii. 47]. One Dick Litchfield . . . who hath translated my Piers Pennilesse into the macaronicall tongue.

1742. Cambridge, *The Scribleriad*, b. ii. note 16. The macaronian is a kind of burlesque poetry, consisting of a jumble of words of different languages, with words of the vulgar tongue latinized, and latin words modernized.

1773. Goldsmith, *She Stoops to Conquer*, Epil. Ye travelled tribe, ye macaroni train.

1806. J. Dallaway, *Obs. Eng. Arch.*, 222. Travellers who have seen . . . will look on the architecture of Bath as belonging to the macaronick order.

Macaroni-stake, *subs.* (old).—A race ridden by a gentleman-jock (*q.v.*).—Bee (1823).

Macaroon, *subs.* (old).—An affected blockhead.

1650. *Elegy on Donne* [Nares]. A macaroon, And no way fit to speak to clouted shoon.

1662. Donne, *Satires*, Sat. 4. 116, 117. I sigh and sweat To hear this makaron talke, in vaine.

Mace, *subs.* (old).—*See* quots.

1785. Grose, *Vulgar Tongue*, s.v. Mace, the mace is a rogue assuming the character of a gentleman, or opulent tradesman, who under that appearance defrauds workmen, by borrowing a watch or other piece of goods, till one he bespeaks is done.

1821. Egan, *Life in London*, 287. Mace . . . which is a slang term for imposition or robbery.

1887. W. E. Henley, *Villon's Straight Tip*, ii. Fiddle, or fence, or mace, or mack.

Verb. (common).—To defraud. *See* quot. 1868. Also on the mace, and to strike the mace. To mace the rattler = to travel by rail without paying the fare.

1821. Egan, *Life in London*, p. 320. He laughed heartily at their being maced.

1827. Lytton, *Pelham*, lxxxiii. To swindle a gentleman did not sound a crime when it was called macing a swell.

1830. W. T. Moncrieff, *The Heart of London*, ii. 1. He's been working on the mace.

1868. *Temple Bar*, xxiv. 535. Macing means taking an office, getting goods sent to it, and then bolting with them; or getting goods sent to your lodgings and then removing.

1885. *Daily Telegraph*, 18 Aug., p. 3, col. 2. Fancy him being so soft as to give that jay a quid back out of the ten he'd maced him of!

On the mace, *adv. phr.* (common).—1. *See verb.;* and (2) on credit; on tick (*q.v.*).

1893. Emerson, *Signor Lippo*, 100. Letting 'em have the super and slang on mace, for he gets to know their account, and he puts the pot on 'em settling day.

Maceman (Mace-cove, Mace-gloak, or Macer), *subs.* (thieves').—A general swindler. But *see* quots. 1879 and 1884.

1781. G. Parker, *View of Society*, ii. 34, s.v.

1823. Bee, *Dict. of the Turf*, s.v. Mace. The mace-cove is he who will cheat, take in, or swindle as often as may be.

1828. G. Smeeton, *Doings in London*, p. 39. It is a game in very great vogue among the macers, who congregate nightly at the flash-houses.

1859. Matsell, *Vocabulum*, s.v.

1861. Sala, *Twice Round the Clock*, 2 p. m. Par. 10. The turf has its blacklegs and touts; the nightside of London is fruitful in macemen, 'mouchers', and 'go-alongs'.

1879. J. W. Horsley, in *Macm. Mag.*, xl. 502. The following people used to go in there—toy-getters (watch-stealers) . . . men at the mace (sham loan offices).

1883. G. A. S[ala], in *Illustr. L. News*, 28 April, p. 407, col. 2. The lovely and loving spouse of an abandoned macer, named Brabazon Sikes—to further whose villainous ends she consents to 'nobble' Damozel in his stable.

1884. *Daily News*, 5 Jan., p. 5, col. 2. The victim appears to have entered an omnibus and to have been at once pounced upon by two macemen, otherwise 'swell mobsmen'.

Machine, *subs.* (venery).—1. The female *pudendum*. For synonyms *see* Monosyllable. (2) The *penis*. For synonyms *see* Creamstick and Prick.

3. (common).—A bicycle or tricycle; a carriage; (Scots') and (in America) a fire-engine.

*d.*1797. Walpole, *Letters*, iv. 12. Will set out tomorrow morning in the machine that goes from the Queen's Head in the Gray's Inn Lane.

1871. De Vere, *Americanisms*, p. 325. A special kind of rowdy known only in America is the b'hoy that runs wid de machine . . . the fire-engine.

1884. *Field*, 6 Dec. As we proceeded the machine became more of an encumbrance.

4. (old).—A cundum; a French letter (*q.v.*).

1811. *Lex. Bal.*, s.v.

5. (American politics). — A party; a party organization.

Machiner, *subs.* (old coaching).—A coach-horse.

1859. Lawrence, *Sword and Gown*, xi. Steady old machiners, broken for years to don the harness.

Mack, *verb.* (common).—*See* Mackerel.

1887. W. E. Henley, *Villon's Straight Tip*, ii. Fiddle, or fence, or mace, or mack.

Mackerel, *subs.* (old).—1. A pander; and (2), a bawd. [Skeat: O. Fr. *maquereau* = pandar, from Teut. source preserved in Du., *makelaar* = broker, pandar, from Du. *makelen* = to procure].

1483. Caxton, *Cato Magnus.* Nighe his house dwellyd a maquerel or bawde.

1513. Gavin Douglas, *Eneados*, 'Prolog' (Book iv), (*Edinburgh*, 1874, ii. 170, l. 30). Sic poyd makrelles for Lucifer bene leche.

1615. Overbury, *New & Choice Characters* [Nares]. A maquerela, in plain English, a bawd, is an olde charcole that hath beene burnt herselfe, and therefore is able to kindle a whole greene coppice.

1630. Taylor, *Wks.* [Nares]. As some get their living by their tounges, as interpreters, lawyers, oratours, and flatterers; some by tayles, as maquerellaes, concubines, curtezanes, or in plaine English, whores.

*c.*1633. *Lady Alimony*, ii. 2. The only safe way for these gamesome macquerellas is to antedate their conception before their separation.

1633. Shirley, *Triumph of Peace* [Nares]. After these, a maquerelle, two wenches, two wanton gamesters.

1650. Howell, *Familiar Letters* [Nares]. The pandar did his office, but brought him a citizen clad in damoisells apparell, so she and her maquerell were paid accordingly.

1690. B. E., *Dict. Cant. Crew*, s.v.

1725. *New Cant. Dict.*, s.v.

1785. Grose, *Vulgar Tongue*, s.v.

Adj. (printers'). — Smeared; blurred and indistinct.

Mackarel-back, *subs.* (old).—*See* quots.

1690. B. E., *Dict. Cant. Crew*, s.v. Mackarel-back, a very tall, lank Person.

1725. *New Cant. Dict.*, s.v.

1785. Grose, *Vulg. Tongue*, s.v. Mackerel-backed, long backed.

Mad, *adj.* (Old English and American).—Angry; vexed. To get one's mad up = to get angered. Also as *verb.*

1369. Chaucer, *Troilus* [Skeat, 1894], line 479. Ne made him thus in armes for to madde.

1593. Shakspeare, *Titus And.*, iii. 1. 104. Had I but seen thy picture in this plight, It would have madded me. *Ibid.* iii. 1. 223. If the winds rage doth not the sea wax mad.

1596. Jonson, *Every Man in His Humour*, iv. 1. You'd mad the patient'st body in the world.

1607. Middleton, *Your Five Gallants* [De Vere]. They are mad; she graced me with one private minute above their fortunes.

1611. *Acts XXVI. 11* [Authorised Version].—And being exceeding mad against them, I persecuted them even unto strange cities.

1667. Pepys, *Diary*, iv. 482 [Bickers, 1875]. The King is mad at her entertaining Jermin, and she is mad at Jermin's going to marry from her, so they are all mad; and so the kingdom is governed.

1816. Pickering, *Collection of Words etc.*, s.v. Mad, in the sense of 'angry,' is considered as a low word in this country, and at the present day is never used except in very familiar conversation.

1824. R. B. PEAKE, *Americans Abroad*, i. 1. I guess—I'm MADDED, but I'll bite in my breath a bit—not that I'm sitch a tarnation fool as to believe all you tell me.

1848. RUXTON, *Life in the Far West*, p. 167. That nation is MAD.

1871. *New Era*, April [DE VERE]. The Squire's MAD riz.

1891. N. GOULD, *Double Event*, p. 189. My eye! won't he be just MAD.

LIKE MAD. *See* LIKE.

MAD AS A HATTER, *phr.* (colloquial).—Violently angry; crazy. [HATTER = atter = adder].

MAD AS A MARCH HARE, *phr.* (colloquial).—As mad as may be.

*d.*1535. MORE, *Supplycacion of Soulys*, C. ii. As MAD not AS MARCHE HARE, but as a madde dogge.

1597. HEYWOOD, *Epig.*, 95. AS MAD AS A MARCH HARE; where madness compares, Are not Midsummer hares as MAD AS MARCH HARES?

1609. FLETCHER, *Wild-Goose Chase*, iv. 3. They are all, all mad: I came from a world of mad women, MAD AS MARCH HARES.

1651. TATHAM, *Distracted State*, iv. 1. My lord, 'tis done! I am as MAD AS A MARCH HARE upon 't.

1665. *Homer à la Mode* [NARES]. Therefore, ere since this cunning archer Has been AS MAD AS any MARCH HARE.

1678. COTTON, *Virgil Travestie*, in *Wks.* (1725), Bk. iv. p. 73. Thy little Archer Has made our Dido MAD AS MARCH-HARE.

1754. FOOTE, *The Knights*, i. Mother's as MAD AS A MARCH HARE about it.

1760. GEORGE COLMAN, *Polly Honeycombe*, i. 4. She's downright raving—MAD AS A MARCH HARE.

*d.*1796. BURNS, *Ep. to J. R.*, 13. It pits me ay AS MAD'S A HARE.

1841. *Comic Almanack*, p. 260. Vell, I've heard of MAD AS A MARCH AIR, and precious mad I find it is, still I can't say as I care: as long as I get home safe.

1851. *Notes and Queries*, 20 Sept., p. 208. Perhaps the allusion to the well-known saying, AS MAD AS A MARCH HARE, on this occasion was made without the collector of hareskins being aware of the existence of such a saying.

MADAM, *subs.* (old).—1. A pocket-handkerchief; a WIPE (*q.v.*). Fr. *une fassollette.*

1879. *Macmillan's Mag.*, 'Autobiography of a Thief,' xl. 503. I tore up my MADAM, and tied the wedge in small packets.

2. (old).—A mistress.

*d.*1634-5. RANDOLPH, *In Lesbiam, etc.*, in *Wks.* (London: 1875), p. 539. And yet has no revenues to defray These charges but the MADAM; she must pay His prodigal disbursements. MADAMS are To such as he more than a treble share.

1719. DURFEY, *Pills, etc.*, iv. 139. Hide-Park may be called the market of MADAMS.

1785. GROSE, *Vulg. Tongue*, s.v.

1811. *Lex. Bal.*, s.v.

1859. MATSELL, *Vocabulum*, s.v.

3. (colloquial).—A bold girl; an artful woman.

4. (old).—An ironical address.

1726. GAY, *Beggar's Opera*, ii. Air xx. Why, how now, MADAM flirt.

1790. *The Busy Bee* (quoted in), iii. 59. Every bush beat, And no signs of MADAM, no trace of her feet.

MADAM VAN, *subs. phr.* (old).—*See* quot. For synonyms *see* BARRACK-HACK and TART.

1690. B. E., *Dict. Cant. Crew*, s.v. MADAM VAN, a whore. The cull has been with MADAM VAN, the fellow has enjoyed such a one.

1725. *New Cant. Dict.*, s.v.

1785. GROSE, *Vulg. Tongue*, s.v.

1811. *Lex. Bal.*, s.v.

1859. MATSELL, *Vocabulum*, s.v.

MADCAP, *subs.* (old: now recognised).—A whimsical humourist; a rashling. Fr. *un lanturlu.* As *adj.* = wild; freakish.

1594. *Look About You* [DODSLEY, *Old Plays* (1874), vii. 420]. But pray have a care of this MADCAP.

1595. SHAKSPEARE, *Two Gentl. of Verona*, ii. 5, 8. Come on, you MADCAP, I'll to the ale-house.

1597-8. HAUGHTON, *A Woman will have her Will* [DODSLEY, *Old Plays* (1874), x. 498]. You madman, MAD-CAP, wild-oats.

1609. FLETCHER, *Wild-Goose Chase*, iv. 1. If any of the MAD-CAP gentlemen should come by, That take up women on special warrant, you were in a wise case now.

1639. GLAPTHORNE, *Wit in a Constable* [PEARSON (1874), i. 199]. Pray be you Sir Timothy, know his entrance: 'Tis such another MAD-CAP.

1658. *Wit Restored* [HOTTEN], 147. Two MADCAPS were committed late, For treason, as some say.

1678. COTTON, *Virgil Travestie*, in *Wks.* (1725), Bk. iv. p. 95. Her grace finds me amongst a Crew Of MAD-CAPS.

1690. B. E., *Dict. Cant. Crew*, s.v.

*d.*1796. BURNS, *To R.G. of F.*, 8. Not so the idle Muses' MAD-CAP train.

1823. BEE, *Dict. of the Turf*, s.v. MAD-CAP a frisky, wild lass, full of fun.

1831. LYTTON, *Eugene Aram*, Bk. 4, ch. xi. I could not a-think what could make so shy an' resarved a gentleman as Mr. Aram admit these 'ere wild MAD-CAPS at that hour.

MAD-DOG, *subs.* (Old Cant).—Strong ale. For synonyms *see* DRINKS and SWIPES.

1586. HARRISON, *England*, 202. There is such headie ale. . . . Commonly called huffe-cappe, the MAD DOG, father-whore-sonne, angel's-food, dragon's-milk, go-by-the-wall, stride-wide, and lift-leg.

MADE. *See* MAKE, *verb.* sense 1.

MADE-BEER, *subs.* (Winchester College).—College swipes bottled with rice, a few raisins, sugar, and nutmeg to make it 'up'.—MANSFIELD.

MADGE, *subs.* (American thieves').—1. *See* quot. 1882.

1859. MATSELL, *Vocabulum*, s.v.

1882. MCCABE, *New York*, xxxiv. 510 (in list of slang terms). MADGE, private places.

2. (venery).—*See* quots. For synonyms *see* MONOSYLLABLE. Also MADGE-HOWLET.

1785. GROSE, *Vulg. Tongue*, s.v.

1811. *Lex. Bal.*, s.v. MADGE. The private parts of a woman.

1850. HALLIWELL, *Archaic and Provincial Words*, s.v. MADGE (3). The *pudendum muliebre.* South.

3. (Scots').—A woman: partly in sport, and partly in contempt.—JAMIESON.

MADGE-CULL, *subs.* (Old Cant).—*See* quot. *Cf.* MARY-ANN.

1785. GROSE, *Vulg. Tongue*, s.v. MADGE CULLS, sodomites *(Cant).*

1811. *Lex. Bal.*, s.v.

MAD-PASH, *subs.* (provincial).—*See* quot.

1850. HALLIWELL, *Archaic & Provincial Words*, s.v. MAD-PASH. A mad fellow.

MAD-TOM, *subs. phr.* (old).—*See* quots.: a TOM OF BEDLAM (*q.v.*).

1811. *Lex. Bal.*, s.v. MAD TOM . . . a rogue that counterfeits madness.

1859. MATSELL, *Vocabulum*, s.v. MAD TOM. A fellow who feigns to be foolish.

MAD-WOMAN, *subs.* (old coaching).—An empty coach.

MADZA, *adj.* (theatrical).—Half. MADZA-CAROON = half a crown; MADZA-SALTEE = a halfpenny. [It. *mezza*]. MEDZA-BEARGERED = half-drunk.

1893. EMERSON, *Signor Lippo*, xiv. They come at MADZA nova butchers to inspect and see all is bona.

MAG, *subs.* (old).—1. Talk; chatter; JAW (*q.v.*). Also a jabberer. Fr. *un caquet-bon-bec.*

1778. DARBLAY, *Diary*, i. 100. If you have any MAG in you, we'll draw it out.

1874. E. LYNN LINTON, *Patricia Kemball*, xviii. 'Don't be a fool, woman, and hold your MAG on things you don't understand,' said Mr. Simpson coarsely.

1892. MILLIKEN, *'Arry Ballads*, p. 20. Tipped the MAG with as much bellows-blowing as though he'd two tongues in his cheeks.

2. (thieves').—*See* quots. Also MAKE and MAGPIE. *In pl.* (in Scotland) = a gratuity expected by servants. *Cf.* MEG = a guinea.

1567. HARMAN, *Caveat* (1814), p. 65. A MAKE, a halfepenny.

1610. ROWLANDS, *Martin Mark-all*, p. 39 (H. Club's Repr. 1874). MAKE, an halfpenny.

1676 *Warning for Housekeepers*, 'Song.' But if the cully nap us . . . it is hardly worth a MAKE.

1690. B. E., *Dict. Cant. Crew*, s.v. MAKE.

1748. T. DYCHE, *Dictionary* (5th ed.). MAKE (S.) a cant name for a half-penny.

1785. GROSE, *Vulg. Tongue*, s.v. MAKE.

1789. GEO PARKER, *Life's Painter*, p. 124. Bless you eyes and limbs, lay out a MAG with poor chirruping Joe.

1823. MONCRIEFF, *Tom and Jerry*, 6. If any body offers you less nor a MAG, or a duce, vy, you may say with the poet, Who vou'd his farthings bear? ven he himself might his quivetus make vith a bare bodkin.

1830. W. T. MONCRIEFF, *The Heart Of London*, ii. 1. I haven't a MAG.

1838. DICKENS, *Oliver Twist* viii. 'But come,' said the young gentleman, you want grub, and you shall have it. I'm at low-water-mark myself—only a bob and a MAGPIE, but as it goes Ile fork out and stump.'

1840. LYTTON, *Paul Clifford*, xvi. You care not a MAG if our party should fall.

1842. *Comic Almanack*, 29 Aug. 'La Fontaine's Homeric Exhibition.' It's a science; methinks—tho' La Fontaine may brag That in language of slang, sir, is not worth a MAG.

1843. W. T. MONCRIEFF, *The Scamps Of London*, ii. 3. I'll play you three times round the board for a MAG a turn, and a pint to come in—the first five out of nine.

1852. DICKENS, *Bleak House*, ch. liv. p. 451. If he don't keep such a business as the present as close as possible it can't be worth a MAG to him.

1861. WHYTE MELVILLE, *Good for Nothing*, ch. xliv. 'I've kept this safe for many a long day. I've held on to it when I hadn't a MAG in my pocket, nor a crust in my wallet.'

1864. *Standard*, 13 Dec. We do not find the word MAKE (a halfpenny) used by boys in Ireland and extensively among the Irish labouring people settled in London.

1876. HINDLEY, *Adventures of a Cheap Jack*, 64. We should not have taken a MAG, as we left the place in the morning.

3. (American).—A half-cent.

1859. MATSELL, *Vocabulum*, s.v.

4. (shooting).—The same MAGPIE.

5. (common).—A magazine.

1796. WOLCOT, *Peter Pindar*, p. 309 [ed. 1830]. And now of Hawkesbury they talked, who wrote in MAGS for hire.

1837. *Comic Almanack*, 92. At least 'twas so Some years ago, Ere wisdom oped our eyes; And farthing folks, with penny MAGS, Made people penny wise.

1869. *Chamb. Journal*, 8 May, p. 303. 'Why don't you fellows write something for the MAGS?' said Tom.

1882. MRS. E. R. ALEXANDER, *The Freres*, 45. He . . . is on the staff of I don't know how many papers and MAGS.

Verb. (old).—1. To talk.

1836. *Comic Almanack*, October. Just stow your MAGGING, for you've piped enough.

1843. W. T. MONCRIEFF, *The Scamps of London*, i. 2. Stow MAGGING—here's more coves coming.

1885. G. A. SALA, in *Daily Telegraph*, 26 Sept., 5-6. Who hangs for hours about the Piazza Colonna at Rome, chattering and scandal-MAGGING.

2. (thieves').—To steal.

1818. SCOTT, *Heart of Midlothian*, xliii. And loot the carters MAGG the coals.

3. (American thieves').—*See* quot.

1859. MATSELL, *Vocabulum*, s.v. MAGGING. Getting money by cheating countrymen with balls, patent safes, etc.

MAG'S DIVERSION. *See* MEG.

MAGA, *subs.* (literary).—*Blackwood's Magazine.*

MAGDALENE, *subs.* (colloquial).—A reformed prostitute.

1693. CONGREVE, *Old Batchelor*, iv. 6. You don't love mutton, you MAGDALEN unconverted?

1818. LADY MORGAN, *Fl. Macarthy*, II. ii. 79 [1819]. I will not have my house made a MAGDALEN Asylum to a parcel of canting methodistical thieves.

1873. WILKIE COLLINS, *The New* MAGDALENE [Title].

1883. TROLLOPE, *Autobiography*, p. 239. Very little of the MAGDALENE about her—because though there may be many MAGDALENES they are not often found.

MAG-FLYING, *subs.* (thieves').—*See* quot. *Cf.* MAG = halfpenny.

1883. *Daily Telegraph*, 26 March, p. 2, col. 8. Of the twenty-nine 'night charges', by far the greater number were of . . . boys for MAG FLYING, *i.e.*, 'pitch and toss'.

MAGGIE, *subs.* (Scots').—A harlot. *Cf.* KITTY.

1603. *Philotus*, S. P. R. [1792], iii. 50. Ye trowit to get ane burd of blisse, To have ane of thir MAGGIES.

MAGGIE RAB (or ROBB), *subs. phr.* (Scots').—1. A bad half-penny.

2. (Scots').—A bad wife.

MAGGING, *subs.* (colloquial).—Talking.

1864. E. YATES, *Broken to Harness*, xxx. I can understand it all, you've been worked upon by the chatter and MAGGING of these silly women until you've lost your own calm common sense.

MAGGOT, *subs.* (common).—1. A whim; a crotchet; a FAD (*q.v.*). *Cf.* (Scots') 'bee in bonnet'; (Fr.) *aes rats dans la tête.*

1655. MASSINGER, *Very Woman*, v. 1. Now I dare swear Thou hast MAGGOTS in thy brains, thou wouldst not else, Talk of impossibilities.

1678. BUTLER, *Hudibras*, iii. 2, 1375. To reconcile our late dissenters, Our breth'ren though by other venters; Unite them and their different MAGGOTS, As long and short sticks are in faggots.

1685. CROWNE, *Sir Courtly Nice*, ii. 1. The beef o' the nation breeds all the MAGGOTS in the people's heads.

1701. FARQUHAR, *Sir Harry Wildair*, iii. 1. Some time ago he had got the travelling MAGGOT in his head, and was going to the Jubilee upon all occasions.

1706. FARQUHAR, *Recruiting Officer*, iii. 1. Pride possesses their hearts, a MAGGOT fills their heads.

1712. ARBUTHNOT, *History of John Bull*, Pt. I. ch. x. John heard all this while, with patience, till she pricked his MAGGOT, and touched him in the tender point.

1719. DURFEY, *Pills to Purge*, IV. 77. Not long ago as all alone I lay upon my Bed, 'Twixt sleeping and waking, this MAGGOT came in my Head.

1822. SCOTT, *The Fortunes of Nigel*, iii. 'The King is a weel-natured and just man of his ain kindly nature, but he has a wee MAGGOTS that maun be cannily guided.'

1843. JOHN STERLING, in *Life* by CARLYLE, Pt. III. ch. vi. The thing is not bad; but will require great labour. Only it is labour that I thoroughly like; and which keeps the MAGGOTS out of one's brain, until their time.

1855. TENNYSON, *Maud*, XXVII. 3. To tickle the MAGGOT born in an empty head.

2. (old).—*See* quots.

1690. B. E., *Dict. Cant. Crew*, s.v. MAGGOT, a whimsicall Fellow, full of strange Fancies and Caprichio's. MAGGOTTY, Freakish.

1725. N. BAILEY, *Erasmus*, 177. You were as great a MAGGOT as any in the world.

1748. T. DYCHE, *Dictionary* (5th ed.) MAGGOT (S.) . . . also a whimsical fellow that is full of strange freakish fancies.

MAGGOT-BOILER, *subs.*(old).—A tallow chandler.—GROSE (1796).

MAGGOTY (MAGGOT-HEADED or **-PATED)**, *adj.* (common).—Fanciful; eccentric; full of whimsies.

1687. BISHOP, *Marrow of Astrology*, 60. A fantastick man wholly bent to fool his time and estate away in . . MAGGOT-PATED whimsies, to no purpose.

1690. B. E., *Dict. Cant. Crew*, s.v. MAGGOT.

1706. FARQUHAR, *Recruiting Officer*, ii. 2. I should have some rogue of a builder . . . transform my noble oaks and elms into cornices, portals, sashes . . . to adorn some MAGOTTY, new-fashioned bauble upon the Thames.

1748. T. DYCHE, *Dictionary* (5th ed), s.v.

1785. GROSE, *Vulg. Tongue*, s.v.

1811. *Lex. Bal.*, s.v.

1817-26. KIRBY and SPENCE, *Int. to Entomology*, 85. The common saying that a whimsical person is MAGGOTY, or has got maggots in his head, perhaps arose from the freaks the sheep have been observed to exhibit when infested by bots.

1882. REV. J. PICKFORD, in *Notes and Queries*, 6. S. v. 238. Be it observed that MAGGOTY is a Cheshire provincialism for 'crotchety', like the expression used in other parts, 'a bee in the bottom.'

MAGISTRAND, *subs.* (Aberdeen University).—A student in arts of the last year: *cf.* BEJAN.

MAGISTRATE, *subs.* (Scots').—A herring. For synonyms *see* GLASGOW MAGISTRATE.

MAGNET, *subs.*(venery).—The female *pudendum*. For synonyms *see* MONOSYLLABLE.

MAGNIFICENT, *subs.* (colloquial).—High and mighty. In *pl.* = a state of dignified resentment.

1886. MARRYAT, *Midshipman Easy*, ch. xxvii. Nevertheless, Jack walked his first watch in the MAGNIFICENTS, as all middies do when they cannot go on shore, and turned in at twelve o'clock, with the resolution of sticking to his purpose, and quitting his Majesty's service.

MAGNIFY. IT DOESN'T MAGNIFY, *phr.* (common).—'It doesn't signify.'

MAGNUM, *subs.* (colloquial).—A double quart. *Cf.* JEROBOAM, REHOBOAM etc.

1796. BURNS, *Election Ballads*, VI. High-wav'd his MAGNUM-BONUM round With Cyclopean fury.

1811. *Lex. Bal.*, s.v. MAGNUM BONUM. A bottle containing two quarts of wine. *See* Scotch pint.

1815. SCOTT, *Guy Mannering*, XXXVI. Discussing the landlord's bottle, which was, of course, a MAGNUM.

1829. *Edinburgh Review*, XL. 378. Daily washing down turtle and venison with quarts of sherry and MAGNUMS of claret.

1837. DICKENS, *Pickwick*, xix. They . . . ordered a glass of brandy and water . . . with a MAGNUM of extra strength.

1850. THACKERAY, *Pendennis*, xxxi. They had a MAGNUM of claret at dinner at the club that day.

1888. *Athenæum*, 21 April, 449. I. Your noble MAGNUM of Lafitte, E'en Rothschild would have deemed a treat.

MAGPIE, *subs.* (old).—1. A bishop. [From his vestments of black and white].

1663. KILLIGREW, *Parson's Wedding* [DODSLEY, *Old Plays*(1874), xiv. 459]. In pure charity laid with him, and was delivered, of a MAGPIE . . . for the midwife cried out 'twas born a bishop, with tippet and white sleeves.

1707. F. BROWN, *Works*, i. 107. Let not those silkworms and MAGPIES have dominion over us.

2. (thieves').—*See* MAG, *subs.* sense 2.

3. (common).—A pie; pastry. Fr. *parfond.*

4. (military).—A shot striking a target, divided into four sections, in the outermost but one. [It is signalled with a black and white disk]. *Cf.* BULL'S-EYE.

1884. *Times*, 23 July. Running through the scoring gamut with an outer, a MAGPIE, and a miss.

MAGPIE'S-NEST, *subs.* (venery).—The female *pudendum*. For synonyms *see* MONOSYLLABLE.

*c.*1720. *Ballad* [Brit. Mus. Cat. 11621, i. 1. 75]. I heard the merry wag protest, The muff between her haunches, Resembled most a MAGPIE's nest, Between two lofty branches.

*d.*1796. *Old Ballad*, 'Ken ye Na Our Lass, Bess?' [quoted by BURNS in *Merry Muses*]. Between her lily-white thies She's biggit a MAGPIE'S-NEST.

MAGSMAN, *subs.* (thieves').—A street swindler, a CONFIDENCE-TRICK MAN. [From MAG = to talk + man]. For synonyms *see* THIEVES. Fr. *un chevalier de la retourne.*

1838. *The Town*, 'The Swell Mob,' 27 Jan. A MAGSMAN must, of necessity be a great actor, and a most studious observer of human nature . . . Without [these attributes] a man might as well attempt to fly as to go out for a 'mag-stake.'

1856. H. MAYHEW, *Gt. World of London*, p. 46. The dependents of cheats; as 'jollies' and MAGSMEN, or the confederates of other cheats.

1859. MATSELL, *Vocabulum*, s.v. MAGSMEN. Fellows who are too cowardly to steal, but prefer to cheat confiding people by acting on their cupidity.

1864. *Leeds Mercury*, 7 June. The case we now report is one in which an Englishman—a Yorkshireman too—was swindled by two MAGSMEN.

1887. W. E. HENLEY, *Villon's Good Night.* You MAGSMEN bold that work the cram.

1888. G. R. SIMS, in *Cassell's Sat. Journal*, 31 March, p. 7. The MAGSMAN earns his living by what is called the confidence trick.

MAHOGANY, *subs.* (common).—1. A dining-table. Also MAHOGANY-TREE.

1840-1. DICKENS, *Master Humphrey's Clock.* I had hoped to have seen you three gentlemen with your legs under the MAHOGANY in my humble parlor in the Marks.

1847. THACKERAY [in *Punch*, vol. XII, p. 13]. The MAHOGANY TREE [Title].

1847. THACKERAY, *Vanity Fair*, Vol. II. ch. vii. 'I . . . can show a handsomer service of silver, and can lay a better dinner on my MAHOGANY, than ever they see on theirs.'

1856. STRANG, *Glasgow & its Clubs*, 102. With his legs below the tavern MAHOGANY, etc.

1889. *Licensed Victuallers' Gaz.*, 18 Jan. The men who had so constantly had their legs under his MAHOGANY.

1892. HENLEY and STEVENSON, *Deacon Brodie*, Tableau III. Sc. I. p. 30. Why man, if under heaven there were but one poor lock unpicked, and that the lock of one whose claret you've drunk, and who has babbled of woman across your own MAHOGANY—that lock, sir, were entirely sacred.

2. (nautical).—Salt beef; OLD HORSE (*q.v.*).

3. (common).—*See* quot.

1791. BOSWELL, *Johnson* (1835), viii. 53. Mr. Elliot mentioned a curious liquor peculiar to his country which the Cornish fishermen drink. They call it MAHOGANY; and it is made of two parts gin, and one part treacle, well beaten together.

1855. STRANG, *Glasgow & its Clubs*, 102. With his legs below the tavern mahogany, and with his own tankard of MAHOGANY before him.

TO HAVE ONE'S FEET UNDER ANOTHER MAN'S MAHOGANY, *verb. phr.* (common).—To live on someone else.

TO AMPUTATE ONE'S MAHOGANY, *verb.phr.* (common).—To run away; to CUT ONE'S STICK (*q.v.*).

MAHOGANY-FLAT, *subs.* (common).—A bug: *cf.* HEAVY CAVALRY. For synonyms *see* NORFOLK HOWARD.

MAHOMETAN-GRUEL, *subs.*(common).—Coffee.—GROSE (3rd ed., 1796).

MAID. NEITHER WIFE, WIDOW, NOR MAID, *phr.* (old).—*See* MAIDEN-WIFE-WIDOW.

MAIDEN, *subs.*(Old Scots' colloquial).—1. A decapitating machine.

1715. PENNECUIK, *Descr. of Tweeddale*, pp. 16-17. Which fatal instrument, at least the pattern thereof, the cruel Regent [Earl Morton] had brought from abroad to behead the Laird of Pennecuik of that ilk, who notwithstanding died in his bed, and the unfortunate Earl was the first himself that handselled that merciless MAIDEN.

1849. MACAULAY, *Hist. Eng.*, v. The rude, old guillotine of Scotland, called the MAIDEN.

1890. *Pall Mall Gaz.*, 7 Mar., p. 2. col 1. A young Scotch gentleman of good birth, named 'A. Balfour,' was executed by an instrument called the MAIDEN.

2. (colloquial).—In cricket, an over with no runs; in racing, a horse which has never run. Also as *adj.*: as, a MAIDEN-speech, a MAIDEN-attempt etc.

1690. B. E., *Dict. Cant. Crew*, s.v. MAIDEN-SESSIONS, when none are hanged.

1785. GROSE, *Vulg. Tongue*, s.v.

1882. *Daily Telegraph*, 2 Jan. The conditions contain no allowance for MAIDENS.

MAIDEN-GEAR, *subs.* (old).—The virginity. Fr. *côte de tribulation.*

1719. DURFEY, *Pills to Purge*, i. 130. My father takes me for a Saint, Tho' weary of my MAIDEN GEER, That I may give you full content, Pray look, Sir Knight, the coast be clear.

MAIDENHEAD, *subs.* (vulgar: once literary).—'Newness; freshness; uncontaminated state. This is now become a low word.'—JOHNSON (1755).

1594. NASHE, *Unf. Traveller* [GROSART, v. 114]. He would let Florence his mistres natiue citie have the MAIDENHEAD of his chiualrie.

1598. SHAKSPEARE, *Henry IV*, I. 59. The devil and mischance look big Upon the MAIDENHEAD of our affairs.

1694. CROWNE, *Married Beau*, ii. 1. I'll give your ladyship the MAIDENHEAD of a new song of mine.

*d.*1726. WOTTON [JOHNSON]. Some . . . have stained the MAIDENHEAD of their credit with some negligent performance.

MAIDEN-TOWN, *subs.* (Old Scots').—Edinburgh; AULD REEKIE. [From a tradition that the maiden daughters of a Pictish King sought protection there during a time of civil war].

MAIDEN-WIFE-WIDOW, *subs. phr.* (old).—1. *See* quot.; and (2) a whore [RAY (1767)].

1688. RANDAL HOLMES, *Academy of Armory*, 404. A MAIDEN-WIFE-WIDOW, one that gave herself up to a man that could never enjoy her maidenhead.

MAID MARIAN, *subs. phr.* (old).—A wanton. [The character in the old morris-dance was taken by a loose woman].

1598. SHAKSPEARE, *Henry IV*, *Falstaff.* And for chastity MAID MARIAN is deputy's wife of the wand to thee.

MAIDS-ADORNING, *subs.* (rhyming).—The morning.

MAIDSTONE-JAILER, *subs.* (rhyming).—A tailor. For synonyms *see* PRICK-LOUSE.

MAIL, *subs.* (Stock Exchange).—In *pl.* = Mexican railway shares.

TO GET UP THE MAIL, *verb. phr.* (thieves').—To find money to defend a prisoner.

MAIN, *subs.* (gaming).—The averages of the number to be thrown at dice; at (cock-fighting) the advantage on a series of battles.—BEE (1823).

TO TURN ON THE MAIN, *verb. phr.* (common).—To weep. For synonyms *see* NAP A BIB.

1853. BRADLEY (Cuthbert Bede), *Verdant Green*, Part 3, p. 90. The Mum cut up doosid this last time; You've no idea how she TURNED ON THE MAIN and did the briny.

MAIN-AVENUE, *subs.* (venery).—The female *pudendum*. For synonyms *see* MONOSYLLABLE.

MAIN-BRACE. TO SPLICE THE MAIN-BRACE, *verb. phr.* (nautical).—To serve an allowance of gr hence to drink.

1834. MARRYAT, *Peter Simple*, ch. xv. With a bottle of rum, procured at the time they SPLICED THE MAINBRACE.

1877. HARRIET MARTINEAU, *Autobiography*, vol. ii. Appendix p. 480. Yesterday the captain shouted, for the first time, SPLICE THE MAIN-BRACE (give out grog).

MAIN-CHANCE. *See* CHANCE.

MAIN-SHEET, *subs.* (common).—Drink: specifically (in quot.) brandy.

1886. GRANT ALLEN, *In All Shades*, ch. vii. 'In Trinidad! Well, well, beautiful island, beautiful, beautiful! Must mind they don't take too much MAINSHEET, or catch yellow Jack, or live in the marshes, that's all.'

MAIN-TOBY, *subs.* (old).—The highway, or main road. *See* TOBY.

MAJORITY. TO GO OVER TO (or JOIN) THE MAJORITY (or GREAT MAJORITY), *verb. phr.* (old).—To die. For synonyms *see* HOP THE TWIG. [The expression ἐς πλεόνων ἱκέσθαι is found in Crinagoras (*Anthol. Palat.* 11, 42), and *penetrare ad plures* in Plautus (*Trin.*, ii, 2, 14). A correspondent of the *Illustrated London News* ('Echoes,' Sept. 9, 1883) writes: 'The phrase JOINING THE MAJORITY is a free translation of the sepulchral formula, *Abierunt ad multos*, used by the Roman legionaries in Britain'; but in all probability the English use of the expression comes from quot. 1721].

1721. YOUNG, *Revenge*, iv. 1. Life is the desert, life the solitude; Death JOINS US TO THE GREAT MAJORITY.

1891. *Licensed Victuallers' Mirror*, 30 Jan., p. 1, col. 3. Henry Saffrey, the Paris Leviathan, has JOINED THE ever-increasing MAJORITY. 'Lucky Saff' was very popular in the French capital.

MAKE, *subs.* (old).—1. *See* MAG.

2. (thieves').—*See* quot.

1748. T. DYCHE, *Dictionary*(5th ed.). MAKE (A.) done, performed, produced; also a cant word for theft.

Verb. (thieves').—1. To steal. For synonyms *see* PRIG.

1690. B. E., *Dict. Cant. Crew*, s.v. MAKE . . . I MADE this knife at a heat, I stole it cleaverly.

1785. GROSE, *Vulg. Tongue*, s.v. MADE.

1859. MATSELL, *Vocabulum*, s.v. MADE.

1877. J. GREENWOOD, *Dick Temple*, ch. vi. Ten or twelve pounds per week! There are hundreds of London thieves, who are known and branded as such, who do not MAKE twice as many shillings.

2. (Winchester College).—To appropriate.

1866. MANSFIELD, *School Life*, 46. In the matter of certain articles.... supplied by the College, we used to put a liberal interpretation on the eighth commandment.... and it was considered fair to MAKE them if you could.

3. (colloquial).—To earn.

1873. JAS. GREENWOOD, *In Strange Company*. But what one in vain looked for was the 'jolly beggar,' the oft-quoted and steadfastly believed-in personage who scorns work because he can MAKE in a day three times the wages of an honest mechanic by the simple process of cadging.

ON THE MAKE, *adv. phr.* (common).—Intent on (1) booty, or (2) profit.

TO MAKE UP ONE'S MOUTH, *verb. phr.* (colloquial).—To get one's living.

TO MAKE HORNS, *verb. phr.* (old).—1. To reproach with cuckoldom by forking two fingers from the brows. *See* HORNS.

2. (colloquial).—*See* FACES.

TO MAKE AWAY (WITH ONESELF), *verb. phr.* (colloquial).—*See* quot. 1836.

1633. SPENSER, *Ireland* [Ency. Dict.]. Clarence... soon after, by sinister means, was clean MADE AWAY.

1836. C. DICKENS, *Pickwick Papers*, p. 65 (ed. 1857). 'Perhaps he may hang himself.' 'Very good,' rejoined Mr. Simmery, pulling out the gold pencil-case again. 'I've no objection to take you that way. Say—MAKES AWAY with himself.' 'Kills himself in fact' said Wilkins Flasher Esquire.

TO MAKE DAINTY, *verb. phr.* (colloquial).—To scruple.

TO MAKE NICE, *verb. phr.* (old colloquial).—To scruple or object.

TO MAKE UP, *verb. phr.* (theatrical and common).—1. To dress: as an actor for a part. *See* MAKE-UP.

1602. DECKER, *Satiro-mastix* in *Works* (1873), i. 253. Wat Terrill, th'art ill suited, ill MADE VP, In Sable collours, like a night piece dyed, Conn'st thou the Prologue of a Maske in blacke.

1633. JONSON, *Tale of a Tub*, i. 3. I would have him The bravest, richest, and the properest man A tailor could MAKE UP; or all the poets, With the perfumers.

1655. MASSINGER, *Very Woman*, i. 1. *Pedro*. Morrow, sister! Do I not come unseasonably? *Alm*. Why, good brother? *Pedro*. Because you are not yet fully MADE UP, Nor fit for visitation.

1844. *Puck*, p. 30. Feeling convinced that lovers were my line I once tried Romeo, but was hissed; since then My young ambition, sadly I resign,—My mind and face MADE UP for first old men.

1869. MRS. H. WOOD, *Roland Yorke*, xxv. That lady . . . had absolute need of artistic aid in the matter of MAKING-UP; face and shape and hair and attire alike requiring daily renovation.

1883. D. COOK, *Nights at the Play*, vol. I. ch. xv. The actor had taken exceeding pains with the part. His face had been carefully MADE UP, and every detail of his dress and deportment elaborately studied.

2. (common).—To get up, or invent: as a catch or 'take in'.

TO MAKE (or TAKE) IT UP, *verb. phr.* (colloquial).—To be reconciled after a quarrel.

1598. SHAKSPEARE, *Merchant of Venice*, v. 4, 103. I knew when seven justices could not MAKE UP a quarrel.

TO MAKE MOUTHS, *verb. phr.* (colloquial).—To jeer; to grin.

TO MAKE ENDS MEET, *verb. phr.* (venery).—To copulate. For synonyms *see* GREENS and RIDE.

TO MAKE HAY, *verb. phr.* (common).—To tumble; to confuse; to disorder.

1863. H. KINGSLEY, *Austin Elliot*, ch. xiii. His usual holiday amusements were these—to interrupt his sister's lessons as much as possible, and in the absence of the governess, to (as he called it) MAKE HAY in the school-room.

TO MAKE MEAT OF, *verb. phr.* (American).—To kill.

1841. RUXTON, *Life in the Far West*, p. 3. Poor Bill Bent! them Spaniards MADE MEAT of him.

TO MAKE A HOUSE, *verb. phr.* (Parliamentary).—To gather a quorum (40 members).

1864. *The Spectator*, p. 529. Nobody played marplot, but the division revealed the absence of a quorum, and a bill which interests all capitalists, and will before long interest every taxpayer, was interrupted by mere official carelessness as to MAKING A HOUSE.

AS GOOD (BAD, HOT, DRUNK, etc.) AS THEY MAKE THEM, *phr.* (common).—As good, bad, etc. as may be.

187[?]. *Broadside Ballad*, 'AS GOOD AS THEY MAKE 'EM' [Title].

1889. *Modern Society*, 12 Oct., p. 1265, col. 2. About a dozen yards in, I think you said, and the tide coming in about AS FAST AS THEY MAKE IT. *Ibid.* p. 1267, col. 2. The couple were engaged to be married, and Miss King, who seems to be AS SENTIMENTAL AS AMERICANS ARE MADE, suggested that they should carry out the marriage ceremony in Greenwood Cemetery.

1889. *Bird o' Freedom*, 7 Aug., p. 3. On reaching the party it was evident that one of the Frenchmen was, not to put too fine a point on it, about AS DRUNK AS THEY MAKE 'EM. He opened the campaign by asking us to have a drink with him. Of course, he spoke in French.

1890. G. ALLEN, *The Tents of Shem*, iii. I like them; thorough ladies, and well brought up, and AS CLEVER AS THEY MAKE THEM.

1894. GEORGE MOORE, *Esther Waters*, xvii. You are AS STRONG AS THEY MAKE 'EM.

MAKE HIM SWIM FOR IT, *phr.* (American thieves').—*See* quot.

1859. MATSELL, *Vocabulum*, s.v. MAKE HIM SWIM FOR IT. Cheat him out of his share.

See also BACK; BACON; BATES; BEEF; BLUE; BONES; BOOKS; BUTTONS; CHILDREN'S SHOES; CLEAN BREAST; CLEAN SWEEP; CLINK; CRIMSON; DUCKS-AND-DRAKES; FACE; FEATHER; FIGURE; FISH; FLASH; FOOL; FUN; FUR; GOOD; HAIR; HAND; HARE; HASH; HAY; HONEST WOMAN; KISS; LEG; LIP; LONG-ARM; LUCKY; MAN; MEAL; MEAT; MOUTH; NIGHT; PILE; PLAY; POINT; QUEEN ANNE'S FAN; RAISE; RUNNING; SCARCE; SHOW; SPLASH; SPLIT; STAND; THINGS; TRACKS; TURKEY-MERCHANT; TWO COME; VIRGINIA FENCE; WATER; WHACK; WHOLE CLOTH; WOMAN; etc. etc.

MAKEPEACE, *subs.* (old).—*See* quot. For synonyms *see* TOKO.

1657. COLE, *Adam in Eden*. It [the birch] is useful for the punishment of children, both at home and at school, for it hath an admirable influence on them when they are out of order, and therefore some call it MAKEPEACE.

MAKER, *subs.* (American).—A tailor; a PRICKLOUSE (*q.v.*). For synonyms *see* SNIP. Span. *picapiojos*.

1833. NEAL, *Down Easters*, v. 63. 'Who's your MAKER?' 'My MAKER!—Oh! I understand you, my tailor you mean?' 'Yes—who made your coat?'

MAKESHIFT, *subs.* (old).—A thief. For synonyms *see* THIEVES.

1584. *A Mirour for Magistrates of Cyties*, fol. 33 (back). London is sore charged with these MAKESHIFTES.

MAKESURES, *subs.* (potmen's).—Petty pilferings; FLUFF (*q.v.*); CABBAGE (*q.v.*). Fr. *la gratte*.

VOL. IV. 18

MAKE-UP, *subs.* (theatrical).—1. The arrangement of an actor's face and dress. *See* TO MAKE UP, sense 1. MAKE-UP BOX = a box of materials—rouge, sponges, grease-paint, and the like—used in making-up.

1870. *Figaro*, 25 Nov. 'A Dream of the Kow.' An elderly gentleman—who is seventy if he is a day, but wishes to pass himself off for—let us be charitable and say—half his real age. Certainly, his MAKE-UP is wonderfully good.

1876. G. ELIOT, *Daniel Deronda*, iii. The sort of professional MAKE-UP which penetrates skin, tones, and gestures, and defies all drapery.

1879. DICKENS, *Dict. of London*, s.v. 'Private Theatricals'. For wigs and MAKE-UP the amateur may depend upon Mr. Clarkson, of Wellington-street.

1882. *Daily Telegraph*, 22 Feb. 'The success of the idea was prejudiced by the MAKE-UP, for though there was hideousness in the eyes, the lower part of the face of the new Caliban was anything but unprepossessing.'

1883. G. A. SALA, *Echoes of the Year*, 362. Her MAKE-UP was so terrifically weird and ghastly.

1889. *Academy*, 6 July, p. 14. Mr. Somerset, who makes up badly for the part of the father, unless it is, as it may be, very clever to suggest by MAKE-UP, a character wholly artificial etc.

1889. *Globe*, 11 Feb. The arrangement of paunch and limb and the MAKE-UP of the face are perfect.

1891. *Sporting Life*, 25 Mar. No more a type than those two comedians at the Opera Comique are—thanks to the MAKE-UP and the words they speak and warble.

2. (common).—A piece of deception; a BARNEY (*q.v.*); GAMMON (*q.v.*); HUMBUG (*q.v.*); a TAKE-IN (*q.v.*).

MAKE-WEIGHT, *subs.* (old).—1. A small candle.—GROSE (1785).

2. (old).—A short slender man.—GROSE (1785).

MAKINGS, *subs.* (colloquial).—1. Material for anything.

1836. DICKENS, *Pickwick*, xxxvii. 324. He seemed to have the MAKINGS of a very nice fellow about him.

1858. *Frazer's Mag.*, Aug., 220. Men who have in them the MAKINGS of better preachers.

1876. G. ELIOT, *D. Deronda*, Bk. II. ch. xvi. 'You've not the MAKINGS of a Porson in you, or a Leibnitz either.'

1885. *World*, 1 April, p. 18, col. 2. If I mistake not, he has the MAKINGS of a first-class steeplechaser about him.

2. (common).—(1) Profits; (2) earnings. Fr. *le jus*.

1892. *Cassell's Saturday Jl.*, 21 Sept., p. 13, col. 3. Of course my MAKINGS varied considerably, and to some extent depended on the success of my particular patrons at batting in the college matches.

MALADY OF FRANCE, *subs. phr.* (old).—Syphilis. For synonyms *see* LADIES' FEVER.

1599. SHAKSPEARE, *Henry V*, v. 1. 87. News have I that my Nell is dead i' th' spital Of MALADY OF FRANCE.

MALINGER, *verb.* (old: now recognised).—To sham illness; to shirk duty.

1890. *Century Dict.*, s.v. MALINGER .... from F. malingrer, a slang word meaning 'suffer' .... formerly applied to beggars who feigned to be sick or injured in order to excite compassion.

1895. *Pall Mall Gaz.*, No. 9542, p. 1. 'Administering Angels.' The answer is comparatively simple: because the Shadow understands English politics, and thought to gain by MALINGERING.

MALINGERER, *subs.* (old: now recognised).—A shirker under pretence of sickness.

1785. GROSE, *Vulg. Tongue*, s.v.

1811. *Lex. Bal.*, s.v. MALINGEROR. A military term for one who, under pretence of sickness, evades his duty.

MALKIN (MAUKIN or MAWKIN), *subs.* (old).—1. Originally (JOHNSON) a kitchen-wench (MOLL for Mary + KIN). Hence, a dish-clout; a scarecrow; a wisp: and so, a slattern.

1579. GOSSON, *Schoole of Abuse*, p. 37 (ARBER). There are more houses then Parishe Churches, more maydes then MAULKIN, more wayes to the woode than one.

1596. NASHE, *Have With You etc.* [GROSART, iii. 169]. He makes a MAULKIN and a shoo-clout of her.

1606. DEKKER, *Newes from Hell* [GROSART, ii. 130]. Filthyer than a Baker's MAWKIN that hee sweeps his ouen with.

1610. SHAKSPEARE, *Coriol.*, ii. 1. The kitchen MALKIN pins Her richest lockram round her reechy neck.

1629. DAVENANT, *Albovine*, iv. 'Las poor MAULKIN! she's caught.

1690. B. E., *Dict. Cant. Crew*, s.v. MALKIN or MAUKIN, a Scare-crow, Drest and Set up to fright the birds .... Hence MALKIN-TRASH, for one in a rueful Dress, enough to fright one. There are more Maids than MALKINS. MAWKS, the same abbreviated. Mawkish, a Wallowish, ill Tast.

1693. CONGREVE, *Old Bachelor*, iii. 2. Thou MAUKIN, made up of the shreds and parings of his superfluous fopperies.

1728. SWIFT, *Ballyspellin* (Answer), [CHALMERS, *English Poets*, xi. 525]. Your MAWKINS there smocks hempen wear. Of holland not an ell in.

1785. GROSE, *Vulg. Tongue*, s.v.

1847-50. TENNYSON, *Princess*, v. 25. Or a draggled MAWKIN, thou.

1872. *Gardener's Chronicle*, 22 Nov. Our old friend of the hat and coat all stuffed with straw (in some districts called a MAWKIN) is in nine cases out of ten useless.

2. (Scots').—A hare; also (old) a cat.

1787. BURNS, *Tam Samson's Elegy*. Ye maukins, cock your fuds fu' braw.

3. (Scots').—The female *pudendum*: *i.e.*, PUSSIE (*q.v.*). Also ROUCH-MAWKIN.

1540. LYNDSAY, *Thrie Estaitis*, line 1924. And ye Ladies, that list to pisch, Lift up your taill plat in ane disch; And gif that your MAWKINE cryis quhisch, Stap in ane wusp of strae.

MALKIN-TRASH, *subs.* (old).—*See* quot.

1690. B. E., *Dict. Cant. Crew*, s.v.

1785. GROSE, *Vulg. Tongue*, s.v. MALKIN-TRASH. One in dismal garb.

MALMSEY-NOSE, *subs.* (old).—*See* quot. *Cf.* GROG-BLOSSOM.

1785. GROSE, *Vulg. Tongue*, s.v. MALMSEY-NOSE. A red-pimpled snout, rich in carbuncles and rubies.

MALT, *verb.* (common).—To drink beer.

1828-45. T. HOOD, *Poems*, i. p. 148 (ed. 1846). She drank nothing lower than Curaçoa, Maraschino, or pink Noyau, And on principle never MALTED.

1835. MARRYAT, *Jacob Faithful*, xxii. Well, for my part I MALT.

TO HAVE THE MALT ABOVE THE WHEAT (WATER, or MEAL), *verb. phr.* (Scots' colloquial).—To be drunk. For synonyms *see* DRINKS and SCREWED.

1767. RAY, *Proverbs* [BOHN (1893), 63]. 'Proverbial Periphrases of one Drunk', The MALT IS ABOVE THE WATER.

1816. SCOTT, *Old Mortality*, iv. Aweel,—when the MALT BEGINS TO GET ABOON THE MEAL . . . then Jenny, they're like to quarrel.

MALTOOLING, *subs.* (thieves').—*See* quot. *Cf.* MOLLTOOLER.

1862. H. MAYHEW, *Lon. Lab. & Lon. Poor*, iv. 324. Which she does by shoplifting, and picking pockets in omnibuses, the latter being termed MALTOOLING.

MALTOUT, *subs.* (old).—*See* quot.

1785. GROSE, *Vulg. Tongue*, s.v. MALTOUT, a nickname . . . used by soldiers and sailors of other corps, probably a corruption of *matelot* . . . a sailor.

MALT-WORM (-BUG or -HORSE), *subs.* (old).—A tippler; a LUSHINGTON (*q.v.*).

1551. STILL, *Gammer Gurton's Needle* [DODSLEY, *Old Plays*, ii. 21]. Then doth she trowle to me the bowle, Even as a MAULT-WORME shold.

1586. HARRISON, *England*, p. 202. It is incredible to say how our MALT-BUGS lug at this liquor.

1591. NASHE, *Prognostication* [GROSART, ii. 147]. If violent death take not away such consuming MAULT WORMS.

1593. SHAKSPEARE, *Comedy of Errors*, iii. 1. 32. MALT-HORSE . . . . Coxcomb, idiot!

1593. *Life & Death of Jack Straw* [DODSLEY, *Old Plays* (1874), v. 403]. You shall purchase the prayers of all the alewives in town, for saving a MALT-WORM and a customer.

1598. SHAKSPEARE, *1 Hen. IV*, ii. 1. None of these mad, mustachio, purple-hued MALT-WORMS.

1889. AUSTIN DOBSON, *Poems on Several Occasions*, II. 209. 'The MALT-WORM's Madrigal.' [Title].

MAMMET, *subs.* (old).—A puling girl.

1595. SHAKSPEARE, *Romeo & Juliet*, iii. 5. And then to have a wretched puling fool, A whining MAMMET, in her fortunes tender, To answer I'll not wed—I cannot love.

1610. JONSON, *Alchemist*, v. 5. 'Slight! you are a MAMMET! O I could touse you now.

MAMMY, *subs.* (colloquial).—1. Mother: an endearment.

1560. *Nice Wanton* [DODSLEY, *Old Plays* (1874), ii. 180]. Cards, dice, kiss, clip, and so forth; All this our MAMMY would take in good worth.

*d.*1796. BURNS, *There Was a Lass*. An' aye she wrought her MAMMIE'S waik, An' aye she sang sae merrilie.

2. (obsolete American).—A negro nurse; MAUMER.

MAN, *subs.* (once literary: now vulgar).—1. A husband; a lover: generally 'my MAN'.

*c.*1369. CHAUCER, *Troilus*, iv. 447. I wol nat ben untrewe for no wight, But as hire MAN I wol ay lyve and sterve, And nevere noon other creature serve.

*d.*1437. JAMES I (of Scotland), *King's Quhair*, ii. 44. Quhen sall your merci rew upon your MAN, Quhois seruice is yet uncouth to yow?

*d.*1719. ADDISON, *The Ladies' Association*. In the next place, every wife ought to answer for her MAN.

1788. R. GALLOWAY, *Poems*, p. 124. 'Twas thus he left his royal plan, If Mar'gret cou'd but want a MAN; But this is more than Mar'gret can.

2. (common).—The 'head' or obverse of a coin used in tossing: *cf.* WOMAN.

1828. BEE, *Living Picture of London*, 241. The person calling for MAN or 'woman'.

3. (old university).—*See* quot.

1811. *Lex. Bal.*, s.v. MAN (Cambridge). Any undergraduate from fifteen to thirty. As, a MAN of Emanuel—a young member of Emanuel.

Verb. (venery).—To possess a woman. For synonyms *see* GREENS and RIDE.

DEAD MAN, *subs. phr.* (old).—A supernumery.

1659-60. PEPYS, *Diary*, 8 Mar. Philip Holland . . . told me to have five or six servants entered on board as DEAD MEN, and I to give them what wages I pleased, and so their pay to be mine.

MAN ALIVE! *phr.* (common).—A mode of salutation. Used in remonstrance or surprise.

MAN OF MANY MORNS, *subs. phr.* (Scots').—A procrastinator.

MAN OF THE WORLD, *subs. phr.* (old: now colloquial).—*See* quot.

1811. *Lex. Bal.*, s.v. MAN OF THE WORLD. A knowing man.

MAN-FRIDAY, *subs.* (common).—A factotum. [From the character in *Robinson Crusoe*].

MAN-A-HANGING, *subs.* (old).—A man in difficulties.

THE MAN IN THE MOON, *subs. phr.* (political).—1. A mythical personage who finds money for electioneering, and for such electors as vote straight.

1866. *Totness Election Petition*, 'Evidence of Mr. Rob. Harris.' I have had to deal with unknown gentlemen in Totnes before. A MAN IN THE MOON is the natural consequence of a Totnes election.

1881. *Contemporary Review*, xxxix. 869. My labourers were paid in a public-house in the town by a man from behind a screen, who was invisible; after the fashion of the MAN IN THE MOON, who pays bribes at elections.

1884. *Graphic*, 9 August, p. 123, col. 1. What would Mr. Schnadhorst and the Six Hundred say if they were deprived of their favourite occupation because a few weak-kneed fellow-townsmen had been caught pocketing the guineas of some MAN IN THE MOON.

1889. *Daily Telegraph*, 25 Nov. Formerly bribery and corruption were personal. On or before the election day a mysterious stranger descended on the town, and took up his abode in a retired chamber of a private inn. The word was sent round, and there repaired to his presence quietly, and one by one, those undecided electors who were reported to have an itching palm. In many boroughs this stranger was called The MAN IN THE MOON, perhaps on account of the 'silver lining' to the voters' pockets which resulted from his hidden rays.

2. (old).—A dolt. For synonyms *see* BUFFLE and CABBAGE-HEAD.

1621-3. ARCHBP. LAUD, *Sermons*, p. 17 (ed. 1847). 'And all the Kings of the gentiles shall do homage to their King.' Good God, what a fine people have we here? MEN IN THE MOON.

IF MY AUNT HAD BEEN MY UNCLE SHE'D HAVE BEEN A MAN (or HAD A PAIR OF BALLS UNDER HER ARSE), *phr.* (old).—Said in derision of a ridiculous surmise: —'If wishes were horses, beggars would ride;' 'If pigs had wings, what lovely birds they'd make!'

1767. RAY, *Proverbs* [BOHN (1893), 167], s.v.

HE'LL BE A MAN BEFORE HIS MOTHER. *See* MOTHER.

TO GO OUT AND SEE A MAN, *verb. phr.* (common).—To drink: an excuse for a glass.

THE MAN IN THE STREET, *phr.* (common).—Everybody.

1868. WHYTE MELVILLE, *White Rose*, ch. xlvii. The moment the door closed, Burton's face assumed an expression of deep and friendly concern. 'Jerry,' said he, 'I didn't come here at early dawn only to tell you what the MAN IN THE STREET says.'

1889. *Pall Mall Gaz.*, 6 Nov., p. 1, col. 3. The Swaziland question, which has been smouldering in Government offices and between the covers of Bluebooks for the last twelve years, has reached the flaming point when THE MAN IN THE STREET begins to turn round and look and wonder what is the matter in Swaziland.

1892. *National Observer*, 20 Aug., p. 355, c. 1. He tells you little or nothing that is not familiar to THE MAN IN THE STREET.

TO GET BEHIND A MAN, *verb. phr.* (common).—To endorse a bill.

THE FRUIT THAT MADE MAN WISE, *phr.* (old).—Copulation.

1605. MARSTON, *Insatiate Countess*, iii. I'll lead the way to Venus's paradise, Where thou shalt taste that FRUIT THAT MADE MAN WISE.

OLD MAN, *subs. phr.* (common).—An employer; a chief; the GOVERNOR (*q.v.*); the father of a family. Also, a husband.

1847. HOWITT, *Journal*, p. 187. To begin with the captain. He was a first-rate OLD MAN as far as good treatment and good living went.

THE SICK MAN, *subs. phr.* (literary).—Turkey.

MAN ABOUT TOWN, *subs. phr.* (colloquial).—*See* quot.

1690. B. E., *Dict. Cant. Crew*, s.v. MAN O' TH' TOWN, a Lew'd Spark, or very Debaushe.

1785. GROSE, *Vulg. Tongue*, s.v.

MAN OF KENT, *subs. phr.* (common).—*See* quot. 1787.

1787. GROSE, *Prov. Glossary etc.* (1811), p. 72. All the inhabitants of Kent, east of the river Medway, are called MEN OF KENT, from the story of their having retained their ancient privileges, particularly those of gavel-kind, by meeting William the Conqueror at Swanscomb-bottom; each man, besides his arms, carrying a green bough in his hand; by this contrivance concealing their number under the appearance of a moving wood. The rest of the inhabitants of the county are stiled Kentish-men.

1861. CUTHBERT BEDE, *Our New Rector*, ch. x. p. 104. 'And the MEN OF KENT, you know, were never conquered!—ar'n't we just proud of that!'

A MAN OR A MOUSE, *phr.* (old).—Something or nothing (FLORIO); one on the other.

1541. *Schole House of Women* [HAZLITT, *Early Pop. Poetry* (1866), iv. 111]. Fear not, she saith unto her spouse, A MAN OR A MOUSE whether ye be.

NINE TAILORS MAKE A MAN. *See* NINTH.

THE LITTLE MAN IN THE BOAT, *subs. phr.* (venery).—The clitoris. *See* BUTTON.

MANABLINS, *subs.* (old).—Broken victuals. Fr. *arlequin*, and *le bijou*. Also MANAVILINS.

1888. ROLF BOLDREWOOD, *Robbery Under Arms*, xxii. No end of MANAVILINS either.

MANARVEL, *verb.* (nautical).—To pilfer small stores.

MAN-BOX, *subs.* (old).—A coffin.

1820. REYNOLDS ('Peter Corcoran'), *The Fancy*, 'King Tims the First.' Mr. Munster Hatband, when shall I have a long MAN-BOX bespoke?

MANCHESTER, *subs.* (common).—The tongue. For synonyms *see* PRATING-CHEAT.

1819. VAUX, *Memoirs*, s.v.

1820. *London Magazine*, i. 26. Bidding her hold her MANCHESTER.

1823. GROSE, *Vulg. Tongue* (3rd ed.), s.v.

MANCHESTER-SILK, *subs.* (common).—Cotton.

MANCHESTER SOVEREIGN, *subs. phr.* (common).—A shilling. For synonyms *see* BOB.

MANCHET. *See* BREWER'S-BASKET.

MAN-CHOVEY. *See* CHOVEY.

MANDER, *subs.* (thieves').—*See* quot.

1877. J. GREENWOOD, *Dick Temple*, ch. xvi. A couple of MANDERS (the slang phrase amongst this callow brood of young gaol-birds for 'remands').

MANDOZY, *subs.* (old).—1. A telling hit; and (2) term of endearment among East-end Jews. [Both from the fighter, Mendoza].

MANG, *verb.* (Scots').—To talk; to brag; to boast.

1819. VAUX, *Memoirs*, s.v.

1821. D. HAGGART, *Life*, 'Glossary', p. 172. MANG, to boast; to talk of.

MANGER. *See* DOG.

MANGLE, *subs.* (venery).—The female *pudendum*. For synonyms *see* MONOSYLLABLE.

MANHANDLE, *verb.* (common).—To maltreat; to handle roughly; to thrash. For synonyms *see* TAN.

1886. *Century*, XXXI. 905. In two minutes they were so mauled and MANHANDLED that it was reported aft.

MANHOLE, *subs.* (venery).—The female *pudendum*. For synonyms *see* MONOSYLLABLE.

MAN-IN-BLACK, *subs. phr.* (old).—A parson. For synonyms *see* DEVIL-DODGER and SKY-PILOT.

1691-2. *Gentlemen's Journal*, May, p. 5. The MAN IN BLACK makes . . . one of two in less than half an hour.

MAN-IN-BLUE, *subs. phr.* (old).—A policeman. For synonyms *see* BEAK.

MANNERS. AFTER YOU IS MANNERS, *phr.* (old).—A jocular implication of inferiority.

1659. BROME, *Queen & Concubine* [1873], p. 61. *Cur.* Wilt thou be a scholar? *Andr.* AFTER YOU IS MANNERS.

MANNISH, *adj.* (old).—Amorous.

1383. CHAUCER, *Merchant's Tale*, i. 292. A childstere or wastour of thy good, Or riche or poore, or elles MANNYSH wood.

MANOEUVRE. *See* APOSTLE.

MAN-OF-STRAW. *See* STRAW.

MAN (or LAD) OF WAX, *subs. phr.* (old).—A sharp, clever fellow; a model man.

1595. SHAKSPEARE, *Romeo & Juliet*, i. 3. Why, he's a MAN OF WAX . . . Nay, he's a flower, i' faith; a very flower.

1612. FIELD, *Woman is a Weather-cock* [DODSLEY, *Old Plays* (1874), XI. 19]. By Jove! it is a little MAN OF WAX.

1823. W. T. MONCRIEFF, *Tom and Jerry*, ii. 3. A glass of good max, had they twigg'd it, Would have made them, like us, LADS OF WAX.

MAN-ROOT, *subs.* (venery).—The *penis* [WHITMAN]. For synonyms *see* CREAMSTICK and PRICK.

MAN'S MEAT. *See* MEAT.

MAN-THOMAS, *subs. phr.* (venery).—The *penis*. For synonyms *see* CREAMSTICK and PRICK.

MAN-TRAP, *subs.* (common).—1. A widow; HOUSE TO LET (*q.v.*).

1773. GOLDSMITH, *She Stoops to Conquer*, iii. *Y. M.* There's Mrs. MAN-TRAP.

1785. GROSE, *Vulg. Tongue*, s.v.

1859. MATSELL, *Vocabulum*, s.v.

2. (old).—A lump of excrement; a QUAKER (*q.v.*).

3. (venery).—*See* quot. For synonyms *see* MONOSYLLABLE.

1785. GROSE, *Vulg. Tongue*, s.v.

1811. *Lex. Bal.*, s.v. MANTRAP. A woman's commodity.

MANUAL-COMPLIMENT (or SUBSCRIPTION), *subs.* (colloquial).—A blow; a SIGN-MANUAL (*q.v.*).

1750. FIELDING, *Tom Jones*, XVI. 2. These he accompanied with some MANUAL REMONSTRANCES, which no sooner reached the ears of Mr. Western than that worthy squire began to caper very briskly about the room.

MANUFACTURE, *subs.* (old).—*See* quot.

1811. *Lex. Bal.*, s.v. MANUFACTURE. Liquors prepared from materials of English growth.

MAP, *subs.* (printers').—A dirty proof.

MARBLE (or **MARVEL**), *verb.* (American).—To move off; TO ABSQUATULATE (*q.v.*).

MARBLE-ARCH, *subs.* (venery).—The female *pudendum.* For synonyms *see* MONOSYLLABLE.

MARBLES, *subs.* (common).—1. Furniture; moveables. MONEY AND MARBLES = cash and effects. [From Fr. *meubles*]. Hence, any substantial *quid pro quó.*

ENGLISH SYNONYMS. Belongings; household gods; lares and penates; moveables; sticks; sprats; slows; traps.

FRENCH SYNONYMS. *Le bahut* (popular = large dresser); *le bazar* (prostitutes'); *du fourbi* (popular).

1867. A. TROLLOPE, *Claverings*, ch. xxx. And you may be sure of this, she won't get any money from me, unless I get the MARBLES for it.

2. (old).—Syphilis; FRENCH GOUT (*q.v.*).

1592. R. GREENE, *Theeves Falling Out* [Harl. Misc., viii. 392]. Look into the spittle and hospitalls, there you shall see men diseased of the French MARBLES, giving instruction to others.

1592. GREENE, *Quip for Upstart Courtier* [Harl. Misc., vi. 406]. Neither do I frequent whore-houses to catch the MARBLES, and so grow your patient.

3. (venery).—The *testes.* For synonyms *see* CODS.

MARCH. *See* DIRTY-SHIRT MARCH.

MARCHING-REGIMENT, *subs.* (military).—An infantry regiment of the line: in disparagement.

MARCHIONESS, *subs.* (common).—A slatternly maid-of-all-work; a SLAVEY (*q.v.*). [From the character in *The Old Curiosity Shop*, by C. DICKENS].

1883. G. A. SALA, in *Ill. L. News*, 24 Nov., p. 499, col. 1. I light upon the London papers, containing alarming statements about a little bit of a maid-of-all-work . . . This MARCHIONESS down in Shrewsbury Vale has, it would appear, been the object of the most astounding 'manifestations.'

1885. J. S. WINTER, *Bootles' Baby*, ch. ii. p. 36. To develop into the unnaturally widened and unkempt hand of a MARCHIONESS.

MARE, *subs.* (common).—A woman; a wife. THE GREY MARE IS THE BETTER HORSE = the wife rules the husband.

TO WIN THE MARE OR LOSE THE HALTER, *verb. phr.* (old).—To play double or quits.

MONEY MAKES THE MARE GO, *phr.* (common).—Money does anything you will.

1605. BRETON, *An Old Man's Lesson* [GROSART, ii. *l*, 7, 2, line 32]. Money is a matter of more moment than you make account of; why MONEY MAKES THE medicine for the sick, pleads the client's cause, maintains the merchant's trade, makes the soldier fight, and the craftsman work, and the traveller tread lightly, and THE OLD MARE TROT, and the young tit amble.

1662. *Rump Songs*, i. 232. 'The Power of Money.' Furr'd Aldermen too, and Mayors also; This makes the old wife trot, and MAKES THE MARE TO GO.

1728. BAILEY, *Eng. Dict.*, s.v. MONEY.

1857. KINGSLEY, *Two Year's Ago*, Introd. I'm MAKING THE MARE GO here in Whitford, without the money too, sometimes.

1886. GREGO, *Parl. Elections*, 9. The proverb still remains, a relic of the days in which it had its origin, 'MONEY MAKES THE MAYOR TO GO.'

SHANKS'S MARE. *See* SHANKS.

MARINE (or **DEAD MARINE**), *subs.* (common).—1. *See* quot. 1864; a CAMP-CANDLESTICK (*q.v.*). Also (GROSE) MARINE OFFICER.

1864. MARK LEMON, *Jest Book*, p. 161. William IV seemed in a momentary dilemma one day, when, at table with several officers, he ordered one of the waiters to 'take away that MARINE there,' pointing to an empty bottle. 'Your majesty!' inquired a colonel of marines, 'do you compare an empty bottle to a member of our branch of the service?' 'Yes,' replied the monarch, as if a sudden thought had struck him; 'I mean to say it has *done its duty* once, and is ready to do it again.'

1865. G. F. BERKELEY, *My Life etc.*, II. 302. It was just as he said; our host did wake, but seeing a bottle with wine in it, closed his eyes, and Loraine soon made another MARINE.

2. (nautical).—*See* quot.

1840. R. H. DANA, *Two Years before the Mast*, ch. xvii. MARINE is the term applied more particularly to a man who is ignorant and clumsy about seaman's work—a green-horn—a landlubber.

TELL THAT TO THE MARINES. *See* HORSE MARINES, and add following quots.

1830. W. T. MONCRIEFF, 'Old Booty,' *A Sailors Tale*, p. 31. 'So luff there with your death-bed scenes And TELL THAT tale TO THE MARINES; Those lubbers may perhaps receive it, But sailors never will believe it.'

1836. M. SCOTT, *Cringle's Log*, ch. vii. I told them who I was, and that curiosity alone brought me there. 'Gammon, TELL THAT TO THE MARINES; you're a spy.'

1846. *Punch*, v. p. 3. *A New National Drama. Admiral.* But I've bad news for you, my boy. The Admiralty has forbidden smoking on board . . . . except in the galley. *Tom.* TELL THAT TO THE MARINES. What! your Honour, forbid a sailor his pipe!

MARK, *subs.* (colloquial).—1. A preference; a fancy.

1760. FOOTE, *Minor*, ii. Did I not tell you old Moll was your MARK? Here she has brought a pretty piece of man's meat already.

1887. HENLEY, *Culture In The Slums.* My MARK's a tidy little feed, And 'Enery Irving's gallery.

1883. MISS BRADDON, *Golden Calf*, ch. xxv. Vernon was what Rogers the butler called a MARK ON strawberries and cream.

2. (thieves').—A person; a PIG (*q.v.*); a RAW (*q.v.*). OLD MARK = a lady.

3. (common).—*See* quot.

1823. BEE, *Dict. of the Turf*, s.v. MARK—(ring). The pit of the stomach is termed THE MARK, and 'Broughton's MARK.' It was Bill Warr's favourite hit; also, had been Dick Humphries's.

1859. MATSELL, *Vocabulum*, s.v.

4. *See* MARK OF THE BEAST.

5. (thieves').—A victim.

1885. *Pall Mall Gaz.*, 6 July. The girl, a likely MARK, was a simple country lass.

6. (American).—A streetwalker.

Verb. (thieves').—To watch; to pick out a victim. *See* MARKING, sense 2.

TO TOE THE MARK. *See* TOE.

THE MARK OF THE BEAST, *subs. phr.* (venery).—The female *pudendum.* Also MARK. For synonyms *see* MONOSYLLABLE.

1719. DURFEY, *Pills etc.*, iv. 116. Now all my Friends are laid in grave, And nothing they have left me But a MARK a Year my mother gave, By which for to protect me. Yet I live . . . As brave as any Lady, And all is with a MARK a year, The which my mother gave me.

TO MARK UP, *verb. phr.* (tailors').—To know all about (*cf. verb.*) persons,

TO GO BEFORE THE MARE TO MARKET, *verb. phr.* (old).—To do preposterous things.—RAY (1767).

MARE'S-NEST, *subs.* (common).—A supposed discovery; a hoax; a delusion. Also TO FIND A MARE'S NEST AND LAUGH AT THE EGGS.

1647. BEAUMONT and FLETCHER, *Bonduca*, v. 2. Why dost thou laugh? What MARE'S NEST hast thou found?

1764. O'HARE, *Midas*, i. 3. Heyday! What MARE'S NEST'S found?

1767. RAY, *Proverbs* [BOHN (1893), 56], s.v.

1785 and 1823. GROSE, *Vulg. Tongue* (1st and 3rd eds.), s.v. MARE'S. NEST. He has found a MARE'S NEST, and is laughing at the eggs; said of one who laughs without any apparent cause.

1859. LEVER, *Davenport Dunn*, i. 206. He's always MARE'S NESTING.

1861. *Cornhill Magazine*, iv. 105. 'A Cumberland MARE'S NEST.' In short you Lorton wiseacres, on coming to examine it, Have found a regular MARE'S NEST, and 'stead of eggs, a *lamb* in it.

1864. *The Spectator*, p. 355. It would not do for Englishmen to be ticketted as Englishmen all over the Continent, for they are recognised easily enough by that dialect of French which Mr. Kinglake once called Continental English—he has exchanged *mots* since then for MARES' NESTS.

1870. LOWELL, *Among my Books*, 1st Ser., p. 292. It [the average German mind] finds its keenest pleasure in divining a profound significance in the most trifling things, and the number of MARE'S NESTS that have been stared into . . . passes calculation.

1873. *Notes and Queries*, 4 S. XII. 136. Each, in his endeavour to correct me, actually justifies my doubt, and their united criticisms prove that the stumbling-block which I have found, be it what it may, is not a MARE'S NEST.

1883. JAMES PAYN, *Thicker than Water*, ch. xlvii. 'Dr. Bilde and the rest discovered something wrong and hoped for the worst, whereas they've only found a MARE'S NEST.'

THE MARE WITH THREE LEGS, *subs phr.* (old).—The gallows; THE TRIPLE TREE (*q.v.*).

1834. AINSWORTH, *Rookwood*, 'The game of High toby.' For the MARE WITH THREE LEGS, boys, I care not a rap.

MARE'S-TAILS, *subs.* (nautical).—Feather-like clouds indicative of wind.

MARGERY-PRATER, *subs.* (Old Cant). —*See* quot.; a CACKLING CHEAT (*q.v.*).

1573. HARMAN, *Caveat* (Repr. 1814), p. 65. A MARGERI PRATER, a hen.

1609. DEKKER, *Lanthorne and Candlelight*, in *Wks.* (GROSART), III. 201. MARGERY PRATER, a Henne.

1652. R. BROME, *A Jovial Crew.* Here's grunter and bleater, with tib-of-the-buttry, And MARGERY PRATER all dress'd without slutt'ry.

1665. R. HEAD, *English Rogue*, Pt. i. ch. v. p. 50 (1874), s.v.

1690. B. E., *Dict. Cant. Crew*, s.v.

1712. T. SHIRLEY, *Triumph of Wit*, 'The Maunder's Praise of His Strowling Mort.' When the Lightman up does call, MARGERY PRATER from her nest.

1724. E. COLES, *Eng. Dict.*, s.v.

1785. GROSE, *Vulg. Tongue*, s.v.

MARIA. *See* BLACK MARIA.

MARIGOLD (or **MARYGOLD**), *subs.* (common).—1. One million sterling.

2. (old).—A gold coin. [From the color].

1663. COWLEY, *Cutter of Coleman St.* I'l write it an'you will, in short-hand, to dispatch immediately, and presently go put five hundred MARIGOLDS in a purse for you.

MARINATED, *adj.* (obsolete).—Transported over sea.—GROSE (1785).

MARK OF MOUTH, *subs. phr.* (colloquial).—The tale told by the teeth. (Originally horse-copers'). *Cf.* the proverb :—'You mustn't look a gift horse in the mouth.'

1857. G. A. LAWRENCE, *Guy Livingstone*, VIII. From a distant corner two ancient virgins, long past MARK OF MOUTH.

MARKER, *subs.* (Cambridge University).—A person employed to walk up and down chapel during a part of the service, pricking off the names of the students present.

1849. *Blackwood's Mag.*, May. His name, pricked off upon the MARKER'S roll, No twinge of conscience racks his easy soul.

MARKET, *subs.* (racing).—The betting ring.

TO DRIVE PIGS TO MARKET. *See* PIGS.

MARKET-DAME, *subs.* (old).—A strumpet. For synonyms *see* BARRACK-HACK and TART.

1705-7. E. WARD, *Hudibras Rediv.*, II. ii. (1715), 25. Punks, Strolers, MARKET DAMES, and Bunters.

MARKETEER, *subs.* (racing).—A betting man who devotes himself, by means of special information, to the study of favourites and their diseases : the principal agent in all MILKING (*q.v.*) and KNOCKING-OUT (*q.v.*) transactions.

1847. ROBB, *Squatter Life*, 116. The MARKETEER started a few rods with him.

MARKET-FEVER. *See* PENCIL-FEVER.

MARKET-HORSE, *subs.* (racing).—A horse kept on the lists for the sake of the betting.

MARKET-PLACE, *subs.* (provincial).—The front teeth.

MARKING, *subs.* (thieves').—1. A watcher; a STALL (*q.v.*).—MATSELL.

2. (thieves').—*See* quot.

1859. MATSELL, *Vocabulum*, s.v. MARKING. Observing; taking notice.

MARLEY-SLOPPER, *subs.* (street).—*See* quot.

1887. *Walford's Antiquarian*, 252. A MARLEY-SLOPPER is a splay-footed person. MARLEY is a corruption of marble . . . . In playing it is common for a boy to put his heels together, and turn out his toes . . . . to stop an eccentric marble.

MARMALADE. TRUE MARMALADE, *subs. phr.* (common).—A variant of 'real JAM' (*q.v.*).

MARMOZET, *subs.* (old).—An endearment; also in jocular contempt, as MONKEY (*q.v.*).

1607. *Puritan*, i. 3. Why, do't now then, MARMOZET.

MARM-PUSS, *subs. phr.* (tailors').—A wife.

MAROON, *verb.* (nautical).—*See* quot. Hence, MAROON, *subs.* = a man MAROONED.

1862. MAYNE REID, *The Maroon* [Title].

1892. *Leisure Hour*, Jan., p. 172. Stealing was punished with great severity, generally by MAROONING—*i.e.* abandonment on a desert isle, with a little powder and shot and a flask of water.

MARPLOT, *subs.* (old; now recognised).—An officious bungler; a SPOIL-SPORT (*q.v.*). [From a character in *The Busybody*; see quot. 1709].

1709. CENTLIVRE, *Busybody*, iii. 5. That unlucky dog MARPLOT . . . is ever doing mischief, and yet (to give him his due) he never designs it. This is some blundering adventure, wherein he thought to show his friendship, as he calls it.

1764. A. MURPHY, *No One's Enemy but his Own*, i. You are the very sieve of your own intentions; the MARPLOT of your own designs.

1785. GROSE, *Vulg. Tongue*, s.v.

1844. THACKERAY, *Barry Lyndon*, ch. ii. p. 32. 'You great blundering MARPLOT—you silly beggarly brat. . . . hold your tongue!'

1848. EMERSON, *Spiritual Laws*, 'Essays,' 1 S. p. 125. If we will not be MARPLOTS with our miserable interferences, the work . . . would go on far better than now.

MARQUIS OF GRANBY, *subs.* (common).—A bald-head; a BLADDER OF LARD.

MARQUIS OF MARROWBONES. *See* MARROWBONE.

MARRIAGE-MUSIC, *subs.* (old).—*See* quot.

1690. B. E., *Dict. Cant. Crew*, s.v. MARRIAGE-MUSIC, Childrens Cries.

1785. GROSE, *Vulg. Tongue*, s.v.

MARRIED, *adj.* (old).—Chained or handcuffed together.—GROSE (1785).

MARRIED ON THE CARPET AND THE BANNS UP THE CHIMNEY, *phr.* (common).—Living as man and wife; TALLY (*q.v.*).

MARRIED MAN'S COTILLION, *subs. phr.* (venery).—Copulation. For synonyms *see* GREENS and RIDE.

MARROW, *subs.* (old).—1. A partner; an equal. Specifically (Old Scots') a lover or spouse. Amongst colliers = MATE (*q.v.*).

1513. GAVIN DOUGLAS, *Virgil*, 183, 3. The tyme complete was for thare jornay grant: Bot sone him warnis Sibylla the sant, His trew MARROW, gan schortly to him say.

1538. LYNDSAY, *Complaynt to the King* [LAING i. 54, 307]. For every lord, as he thocht best, Brocht in ane bird to fyll the nest; To be ane wacheman to his MARROW.

1578. WHETSTONE, *I Prom. & Cassand*, ii. 4. Birds of a fether, best flye together; Then like partners about your market goe; MARROWES adew: God send you fayre wether.

1580. TUSSER, *Husbandrie*, ch. 57, st. 40, p. 134 (E. D.S.). Yet chopping and changing I cannot commend, With theefe and his MARROW, for feare of ill end.

1621. BEN JONSON, *Metam. Gipsies*. Oh, my dear MARROWS! No shooting of arrows Or shafts of your wit, Each other to hit.

1630. DRAYTON, *Muses' Elys. Nym.*, ii. 1459. Cleon, your doves are very dainty, Tame pigeons else are very plenty. These may win some of your MARROWS, I am not caught with doves and sparrows.

1677. COLES, *Eng.-Lat. Dict.* The gloves are not MARROWS; chirotheæ non sunt pares.

1728. LINDSAY of Pitscottie, *Hist. of Scotland*, p. 78. This Cochran was so proud in his conceit, that he counted no Lords to be MARROWS to him.

1778. GROSE, *Prov. Glossary*, s.v. MARROW, a fellow, or companion. Exm. This pair of gloves or shoes are not MARROWS, *i.e.* are not fellows. N.

1818. SCOTT, *Rob. Roy*, xxxv. He saw that he wasna to get Die Vernon for his MARROW.

1822. NARES, *Glossary*, s.v. MARROW. The word is often used for things of the same kind, and *(sic)* of which there are two; as of shoes, gloves, stockings: also eyes, hands, feet, &c. Either from the French *camerade*, Angl. *camrad* (*i.e.*, comrade), socius, sodalis, by an aphæresis; or from the French *mari*, Latin *maritus* in which sense the word is also taken. Thus Scot, a husband or wife is called *half* MARROW, and such birds as keep chaste to one another are called MARROWS.

1852. *Lloyd's Paper*, 31 Oct. 'Northumberland'. Afraid to face the angry

frowns of their grieving MARROWS, they determined, like desperate men, to stay where they were. Great was the consternation and mourning at Hylton, and, bent on knowing the worst, the forsaken wives set forth on a voyage in search of the lost husbands.

2. (venery).—The semen. For synonyms *see* SPENDINGS, and *cf.* MARROWBONE, *subs.* sense 2.

1598. *All's Well etc.*, ii. 3, 298. Spending his manly MARROW in her arms.

MARROWBONE, *subs.* (old).—1. *In pl.* = the knees. Ital. *devoti* = worshippers.

*a.*1553. N. UDALL, *Roister Doister*, I. iv. p. 29 (ARBER). Couche on your MARRYBONES whooresons, down to the ground.

1567. THOS. DRANT, *Horace his Epistles*, fo E iiij. Ep. 12. 'To Iccius' Phraates tooke his mace Kneeling upon his MARRIBONES, to Cesar's aufull grace.

1594. NASHE, *Unf. Traveller* [GROSART, v. 23]. My welbeloued Baron of double beere got him humbly on his MARYBONES to the King.

1603. DEKKER, *Wonderful Yeare* [GROSART, i. 141]. At these speeches my tender-hearted hoste, fell downe on his MARIBONES, meaning indeede to entreate his audience to bee good to him.

1665. *Homer à la Mode* [NARES]. Some more devout clownes, partly guessing When he's almost come to the blessing, Prepare their staves, and rise at once, Say'ng Amen, off their MARYBONES.

1667. DRYDEN, *Sir Martin Markall*, ii. Down on your MARROW-BONES, and confess the truth.

1672. C. COTTON, *Scarronides*, Bk. i. p. 36 (ed. 1725). Upon a Stool set for the nonce, She went to rest her MARROW-BONES.

1700. DRYDEN, *Wife of Bath Her Tale*, l. 192. On her majestic MARY-BONES she kneeled.

1714. *Spectator*, 5 Nov. The mob drank the kings health on their MARROWBONES.

1721. N. AMHERST, *Terræ Filius*, p. 33. The [Oxford] scholars, in most of their disputes and quarrels with the townsmen or aliens, usually came off the best at last, and brought their adversaries down upon their MARROWBONES to them.

1760. GEORGE COLMAN, *Polly Honeycombe*, i. 3. I'll carry her off to-day, if possible, clap up a marriage at once, and then down upon our MARROW-BONES, and ask pardon and blessing of papa and mama.

1777. ISAAC JACKMAN, *All the World's a Stage*, i. 2. When I come down, you are all to fall upon your MARROW-BONES.

1785. GROSE, *Vulg. Tongue*, s.v.

1840. BARHAM, *Ingoldsby Legends (Merchant of Venice)*. So down on your MARROWBONES, Jew, and ask mercy! Defendant and Plaintiff are now *wisy wersy*.

1869. THACKERAY, *The White Squall*. And they call in their emergence Upon countless saints and virgins; And their MARROWBONES are bended And they think the world is ended.

2. (venery).—The *penis*. For synonyms *see* CREAMSTICK and PRICK. Also MARROWBONE-AND-CLEAVER.

MARQUESS OF MARROWBONES, *subs. phr.* (old).—A lackey.

1592. NASHE, *Pierce Penilesse* [GROSART, ii. 33]. Poor scullians, that, from turning spit in the chimney corner, are on the sodaine hoisted vp from the Kitchin into the waiting chamber, or made Barons of the beanes, and MARQUESSES OF THE MARY-BOANES.

MARROWBONES AND CLEAVERS, *subs. phr.* (common).—Butcher's music to new-married couples: formerly there was a regular peal in every parish.

1785. GROSE, *Vulg. Tongue*, s.v.

1789. G. PARKER, *Life's Painter*, 'The Happy Pair.' Ye butchers bring your CLEAVERS too, Likewise your MARROW-BONES.

1844. J. B. BUCKSTONE, *The Maid with the Milking Pail*. Of course; all in honour, church, parson, MARROWBONES AND CLEAVERS, and all that! Now, as I'm a man o' my word, I ask your hand in mattermony.

MARROWBONE- (or MARYLEBONE) STAGE (or COACH). TO RIDE IN (or GO BY) THE MARROWBONE-STAGE, *verb. phr.* (common).—To go on foot. *See* BAYARD OF TEN TOES and SHANKS' MARE.

MARROW-PUDDING, *subs.* (venery).—The *penis*. Hence, A BELLY-FULL OF MARROW-PUDDING = the condition of pregnancy.

MARROWSKYING, *subs.* (general).—At the London University they had a way of disguising English (described by Albert Smith, in *Mr. Ledbury*, 1848, as the 'Gower-street dialect'), which consisted in transposing the initials of words: as 'poke a smipe' = smoke a pipe; 'flutter-by' = butterfly; 'stint of pout' = pint of stout; *etc.* This is often termed MARROWSKYING. *See* MEDICAL (or HOSPITAL) GREEK.

1883. SALA, *Living London*, p. 491. On the whole, the *Kaukneigh Awlminek* seems to consist in pretty equal proportions of the vocabulary of Tim Bobbin, Josh Billings, Joe Scoap, the 'Fonetik Nuz', and the MARROWSKY language.

MARSHALL, *subs.* (obsolete).—A five pound Bank of England note: *cf.* ABRAHAM NEWLAND.

*c.*1870. *Newspaper Cutting*. To the Yankee I'm partial, and those who see far shall, Impounding each MARSHALL, so smooth and so crisp.

MARTEXT, *subs.* (common).—A clergyman: specifically a blundering or ignorant preacher. For synonyms *see* SKY-PILOT.

1600. SHAKSPEARE, *As You Like It*, iii. 3, 43. I have been with Sir Oliver MARTEXT, the vicar of the next parish. *Idem* v. 1. 5. A most vile MARTEXT.

1663. KILLIGREW, *Parson's Wedding* [DODSLEY, *Old Plays* (1874), xiv. 385]. Adieu, heir-apparent to Sir Oliver MARTEXT.

MARTIN, *subs.* (old).—1. *See* quot.

1612. ROWLANDS, *Hist. of Rogues* [Century]. I have heard and partly know a highway lawyer rob a man in the morning, and hath dined with the MARTIN or honest man so robbed the same day.

2. (tramps').—A boot.

1893. EMERSON, *Signor Lippo*, 55. A pair of turtles on his MARTINS finished him.

3. *See* ST. MARTIN.

MARTIN-DRUNK, *adj.* (old). — *See* quot. For synonyms *see* DRINKS and SCREWED.

1592. NASHE, *Pierce Penilesse* [GROSART, ii. 82]. The sixt is MARTIN DRUNKE, when a man is drunk, and drinkes himselfe sober ere he stirre.

MARTINET, *subs.* (old: now recognised).—*See* quot.

1785. GROSE, *Vulg. Tongue*, s.v.

1811. *Lex. Bal.*, s.v. A military term for a strict disciplinarian: from the name of a French general, famous for restoring military discipline to the French army. He first disciplined the French infantry, and regulated their method of encampment; he was killed at the siege of Doesbourg in the year 1672.

MARTINGALE, *subs.* (gaming).—Doubling a stake at every loss. [From the fact that, as in all fair games, a player must win once, there is a safe hold of fortune. The difficulty is to command a big enough bank, or, having the bank, to find some one to follow in a fair game].

1823. BEE, *Dict. of the Turf*, s.v. MARTINGALE—at play, to double stakes constantly, until luck taking one turn only, repays the adventurer all.

1855. THACKERAY, *Newcomes*, xxviii. You have not played as yet? Do not do so; above all, avoid a MARTINGALE if you do.

1874. MORTIMER COLLINS, *Frances*, ix. 'This is my cousin, Dick Wyldote. You ought to know *him*. He's got an infallible MARTINGALE—breaks the bank everywhere.'

1887. *Science*, x. 44. The fallacy of those who devise sure methods of defeating the bank (MARTINGALES as they are termed), etc.

MARTIN'S-HAMMER. MARTIN'S-HAMMER KNOCKING AT THE WICKET, *subs. phr.* (old).—Twins.

MARVEL, *verb.* (American).—To walk; TO BE OFF: *e.g.* 'He MARVELLED for home'. Also MARBLE (*q.v.*).

MARY! *intj.* (printers').—No score or love in JEFF-ING (*q.v.*) with quads.

TO TIE WITH ST. MARY'S KNOT, *verb. phr.* (Scots').—To hamstring.

1784. *Poetical Museum*, 'Dick o' the Cow,' p. 27. Then Dickie into the stable is gane,—Where there stood thirty horses and three; He has TIED THEM A' WI' ST. MARY'S KNOT, A' these horses but barely three.

MARY-ANN, *subs.* (obsolete).—1. The *dea ex machinâ* evolved from trades-unionism at Sheffield, to the utter destruction of recalcitrant grinders. *Cf.* MOLLY MAGUIRES.

2. (dressmakers').—A dress stand.

3. (common). — A sodomite. For synonyms *see* USHER. Sp. *manflorito*.

1895. *Reynolds's Newsp.*, 2 June, p. 1, col. 4. I remember when residing in Oxford having pointed out to me in 'the High' more than one professional catamite; just as waiting for a 'bus at Piccadilly-circus a few years later I heard prostitutes jocosely apostrophizing the MARY-ANNS who plied their beastly trade upon the pavement beside the women.

MARYGOLD. *See* MARIGOLD.

MARY-JANE, *subs. phr.* (venery).—The female *pudendum*. For synonyms *see* MONOSYLLABLE.

MARYLAND-END, *subs.* (American).—The hock of a ham: *cf.* VIRGINIA-END.—BARTLETT.

MARYLEBONE STAGE. *See* MARROWBONE-STAGE.

MARY-WALKERS, *subs. phr.* (American).—Trousers. For synonyms *see* KICKS. [After Dr. Mary Walker, who adopted Turkish trousers].

MASCOT, *subs.* (common).—A luck-piece, or talisman; somebody, or something, which ensures good fortune to the owner. Fr. *la mascotte*. [If the luck-piece be alive, the master-quality disappears with the loss of his (or her) virginity].

1886. *Popular Science Monthly*, xxx. 121. It is even fashionable to talk about MASCOTS—a MASCOT being an object, animate or inanimate, that contributes to the good fortune of its possessor.

1888. *Lippincott*, Jan., p. 137. What is the origin of the term MASCOT?

MASH, *subs.* (common).—1. A sweetheart. Also MASHER.

1883. *Illustrated London News*, 9 June, p. 563, col. 3. He appears to be the MASH (if it is permissible to quote the cant phrase of the day) at one and the same time of Queen Anne, the Duchess of Marlborough, and his own legitimate sweetheart.

1889. *The Mirror*, 26 Aug., p. 6, col 2. For whom, dear Mabel, do you dye your wig-hair, And paint and powder?—Who is this new MASH?

2. (common).—ON THE MASH, *see* MASHER.

1888. *Daily Telegraph*, 15 Nov. An impecunious fellow who was always ON THE MASH.

1892. *Idler*, June, p. 550. I loves to see 'im cuttin' of a dash, A walkin' down our alley ON THE MASH.

Verb. (common).—To court; to ogle; to lay oneself out for the practical approval of the other sex.

1883. *Referee*, 30 Sept., p. 2, col. 4. And looks so handsome that were he not so wicked he would be likely to MASH all the ladies who see him.

1891. *Licensed Vict. Gaz.*, 9 Jan. But only fancy what a fellow with my taste for seeing life and MASHING the girls must have suffered!

1892. *Illustrated Bits*, 22 Oct., p. 4, col. 2. Successfully MASH a girl by reciting poetry to her.

MASHED, *adj.* (common).—Amorous; SPOONY (*q.v.*).

1883. *Graphic*, 17 March, p. 287, col. 3. There is always a certain amount of flirtation carried on at the half-crown ball.... There are nooks and passages which give sufficient cover for the smitten (or the MASHED, as, alas! the current slang is) to exchange their confidences, as they flatter themselves unobserved.

MASHED-ON, *adj. phr.* (common).—In love.

1886. *Philadelphia Times*, 19 Febr. He was MASHED ON fair Finette.

1892. MILLIKEN, *'Arry Ballads*, p. 66. Bell Bonsor is MASHED ON me.

MASHER, *subs.* (common).—1. *See* quots. 1883, and—especially—1890. A species of Don Juan in a small way of business: specifically among choristers and actresses. Hence (2) a dandy.

1883. T. A. GARTHAM, in *Pall Mall Gaz.*, 11 Oct. The participle MASHED was in use, in America, before the substantive. A person who was very 'spooney' on another was said to be MASHED. Then came the verb TO MASH, and latterly the noun MASHER; *i.e.* he who produces the effect, or at least who imagines himself a 'lady-killer.' Need I say that men of this calibre are often fops or dandies? Hence, the word MASHER as now understood here.

1883. *Athenæum*, 10 Feb., p. 181, col. 1. One poem, indeed, called 'A Cry from the Stalls,' presents our poet in the strange guise of the laureate of the MASHERS—we apologize humbly for employing a detestable phrase with which America has enriched (?) our vocabulary significatory of the worshippers of actresses.

1883. *Daily Telegraph*, 10 Oct. The talk around them will fairly match in mental vigour the ejaculations of the gaming table or the race-course, or the prattle of the MASHER between the acts.

1884. A. LANG, *Much Darker Days*, p. 24. That mass, once a white hat, had adorned the brows of that MASHER!

1885. *Sporting Times*, 23 May, 'The Chorister's Promise.' She sat disconsolate, musing, sad, ... For times were deucedly awful bad, As MASHERS were close with what chips they had (And alas for the chips she owed!).

1890. *Standard*, 11 Febr., p. 3, col. 1. There were specimens of tramps and beggars, of fortune-tellers and hawkers, of village musicians and MASHERS, called in Vienna '*Gigerls*,' which every good painter or sculptor would be delighted to have as models—better specimens of the picturesque, in fact, than can be found in Rome or Naples.

1890. *Slang, Jargon, & Cant*, s.v. MASH. About the year 1860 MASH was a word found only in theatrical parlance in the United States. When an actress smiled at.... a friend in the audience she was said to MASH him... It occurred to the writer [C. G. LELAND] that it must have been derived from the gypsy *mash (masher-ava)* to allure, to entice .... Mr. Paluez a well-known impresario said.... he could confirm [the suggestion] for the term had originated with the C— family, who were all actors and actresses, of Romany stock, who spoke gypsy familiarly among themselves.

1895. *Sporting Times*, 23 Nov. 'Nothing to Do.' There's the MASHER, the great unemployed of the day.

Adj. (common).—Smart.

1890. *Globe*, 7 Feb., p. 1, col. 4. What are umbrellas or MASHER canes to students immersed in Mill or Emerson, or the latest shilling dreadful?

MASHERDOM, *subs.* (common).—The world of MASHERS (*q.v.*).

1883. *Referee*, 6 May, p. 7, col. 3. In the smoking-rooms of the best club, in the haunts of MASHERDOM.

MASH-TUB, *subs. phr.* (colloquial). —A brewer. Hence (Fleet St.) *The Morning* MASH-TUB = *The Morning Advertiser.*

MASKIN, *subs.* (Old Cant).—Coal.

MASON, *subs.* (old).—*See* quot.

1754. POULTER, *Discov.*, p. 30. One who swindled farmers etc. by giving worthless notes for horses etc. bought by them. The Dealers, called MASONS.... giving Notes for Money, and never to pay it.

Verb. (old).—*See* quot.

1754. *Discoveries of John Poulter*, p. 9. If we could not get any Money at the Nobb we would buy a Horse or two, and give our Notes for our Money, telling our Dealer we lived at a Town where we did not. This is called MASONING.

MASONRY, *subs.* (colloquial).—Secret signs and passwords.

1841. LYTTON, *Night and Morning*, Bk. III. ch. viii. I was one of them, and know the MASONRY.

MASON'S-MAWN'D, *subs.* (old).—*See* quot.

1690. B. E., *Dict. Cant. Crew*, s.v. MASON'S-MAWN'D, a Sham sore above the Elbow, to counterfeit a broken Arm, by a Fall from a Scaffold, expos'd by subtil Beggers, to move Compassion, and get Money.

1785. GROSE, *Vulg. Tongue*, s.v.

MASSACRE. *See* INNOCENTS.

MASSE-STAPLER, *subs.* (Old Cant). —A rogue disguised as a woman.

MASTER-CAN (or MORE), *subs. phr.* (Old Scots').—A chamber-pot.— FERGUSSON.

1776. HERD, *Collection*, ii. 214. She hae dung the bit fish off the brace, An' it's fallen i' the MAISTER-CAN.

MASTER-OF-THE-BLACK-ART, *subs.* (old).—A beggar. For synonyms *see* CADGER.

MASTER-OF-THE-MINT, *subs.* (common).—A gardener. *Cf.* BURNCRUST and CORKS.

1785. GROSE, *Vulg. Tongue*, s.v.

MASTER-OF-THE-ROLLS, *subs.* (common).—A baker.

1641. H. PEACHAM, *Worth of a Penny*, in Arber's *English Gamer*, Vol. vi. p. 272. For a Penny, you may search among the ROLLS, and withal give the MASTER good satisfaction. I mean, in a baker's basket.

*c.*1762. DERRICK in FOSTER'S *Goldsmith*, Bk. III. ch. vi. p. 167 (5th ed.). 'No, no,' whispered Derrick, who knew him to be a wealthy baker from the city, 'only for a MASTER OF THE ROLLS.'

1785. GROSE, *Vulg. Tongue*, s.v.

1826. *The Fancy*, i. 123. Martin is the only baker who has appeared in Chancery Lane lately without insult; but they possess, generally, so little of the retiring modesty of their MASTER OF THE ROLLS, that they deserve all they catch in that way.

ENGLISH SYNONYMS. Burncrust; doughy; dough-puncher; crumbs; fourteen-to-the-dozen.

MASTER-OF-THE-WARDROBE, *subs. phr.* (old).—One who pawns his clothes to buy liquor. — GROSE (1785).

MASTERPIECE, *subs.* (venery).—1. The female *pudendum.* For synonyms *see* MONOSYLLABLE.

2. (colloquial).—A culmination: the best that can be.

1715. PENNECUIK, *Poems* (1815), 338. Callit the MASTERPIECE of George's reign.

VOL. IV. 19

MATCH, *subs.* (Stock Exchange).—1. In *pl.* Bryant and May Limited Stock.

2. (American cadets').—A stripling. For synonyms *see* LAMP-POST.

3. (old).—*See* quot.

1821. BEE, *Dict. of the Turf*, s.v. MATCH—persons nearly of a size are said to 'make a good match,' (ring). Horses' MATCH consists in colour and size. A two-horses' race, is a MATCH, when specially agreed upon. The agreement for a man-fight, is 'making a MATCH.' Young folks are said to 'make a MATCH of it,' when they marry; they do the same when they do not *wed* frequently, but bring gyblets together *sans ceremonie.*

TO LOSE THE MATCH AND POCKET THE STAKES, *verb. phr.* (venery).—To copulate: of women only. For synonyms *see* GREENS and RIDE.

MATE, *subs.* (colloquial).—A companion; a partner; a PAL (*q.v.*). Also MATEY.

1580. TUSSER, *Husbandrie*, ch. 113, st. 30, p. 212 (E. D. S.). As for such MATES, as vertue hates, ... small matter it is.

1630. MASSINGER, *Renegado*, iv. 1. Come, my MATES, I hitherto have lived an ill example, And, as your captain, led you on to mischief.

1859. H. KINGSLEY, *Geoffry Hamlyn*, ch. xxxi. I took him for a flash overseer, sporting his salary, and I was as thick as you like with him. And, 'MATEY,' says I, (you see I was familiar, he seemed such a jolly sort of bird), 'MATEY, what station are you on?'

1864. H. KINGSLEY, *The Hillyars and the Burtons*, chap. xxx. 'Well, then, I'll tell you where it is,' said Jack Marton [Blacksmith] 'me and my MATES must look to ourselves'...

1874. Mrs. H. WOOD, *Johnny Ludlow*, 1 S. No. XXII. p. 403. ''Twasn't me that originated the strike. I but joined in it with the rest of my MATES.'

1892. SYDNEY WATSON, *Wops the Waif*, ch. i. p. 2. 'I say, Tickle MATEY, wot's all them a-readin' of on that bill over there?' interrupted Wops.

1892. ANSTEY, *Model Music Hall Songs*, 119. Way-oh ole MATEY, I don't bear no malice.

MATER, *subs.* (colloquial).—A mother; THE OLD WOMAN (*q.v.*). Fr. *la maternelle.*

1859. MATSELL, *Vocabulum*, s.v.

1883. BRADDON, *Golden Calf*, vi. The pater and MATER are away... So we can have things all our own way.

MATIN-BELL, *subs.* (thieves'). — A thieves' rendezvous; an EVENING-CHIMES (*q.v.*).

MATRIARCH, *subs.* (American). — An old dowager.

MATRIMONIAL, *subs.* (venery).—The act of kind in the natural position. Also MATRIMONIAL POLKA. For synonyms *see* GREENS and RIDE.

MATRIMONIAL PEACEMAKER, *subs. phr.* (venery).—*See* quot. For synonyms *see* CREAMSTICK and PRICK.

1796. GROSE, *Vulg. Tongue* (3rd ed.), s.v. MATRIMONIAL PEACEMAKER. The sugar stick or *arbor vitæ.*

MATTER. AS NEAR AS NO MATTER, *phr.* (colloquial).—Very nearly; as near as may be.

1892. MILLIKEN, *'Arry Ballads*, p. 69. I've reported as NEAR AS NO MATTER.

MATTRESS-JIG, *subs. phr.* (venery). — Copulation. For synonyms *see* GREENS and RIDE.

MAUKES (MAUX, or MAWKES), *subs.* (old).—*See* MAWKES.

MAUKIN. *See* MALKIN.

MAULED, *adj.* (common).—*See* quot. For synonyms see DRINKS and SCREWED.

1690. B. E., *Dict. Cant. Crew*, s.v. MAUL'D, swingingly Drunk, or soundly Beat.

1785. GROSE, *Vulg. Tongue*, s.v.

1859. MATSELL, *Vocabulum*, s.v. MAULD.

MAULEY (MORLEY or MAWLEY), *subs.* (common).—1. A fist; a hand. TO TIP A MAULEY = to give a hand. FAM THE MAWLEY = shake hands.

1800. PARKER, *Life's Painter*, 139. The key of the street-door in her MAULEY. *Ibid.* 144. When one asks the other to shake hands, that is, sling us your MAULY.

1821. EGAN, *Life in London*, 207. Learn the use of your MORLEYS.

1823. MONCRIEFF, *Tom and Jerry*, ii. 6. *Mr. J.* It was but t'other day they took'd me up; slapp'd a pick-ax into one of my MAULEYS, and shov'd a shovel into t'other, and told me to vork.

1852. JUDSON, *Mysteries of New York*, iv. Ello, Charley, my kid! tip us your MAWLEY.

1857. CUTHBERT BEDE, *Verdant Green*, pt. II. ch. iii. 'I couldn't use my MAWLEYS no how!' and the Pet illustrated his remark in a professional manner, by sparring at an imaginary opponent in a feeble and unscientific fashion.

1859. MATSELL, *Vocabulum*, s.v.

1861. MISS BRADDON, *Trail of the Serpent*, Bk. IV. ch. v. 'Let the man as murdered your uncle keep clear of my left MAWLEY, if he wants to preserve his beauty.'

1870. *London Figaro*, 2 July. 'Milling Ancient and Modern.' We think MAWLEYS is the correct sporting term for 'bunches of fives.'

1888. ROLF BOLDREWOOD, *Robbery Under Arms*, i. It takes a good man to put me on my back, or stand up to me with the gloves, or the naked MAULEYS.

1888. *Sporting Life*, 11 Dec. Lambert ducked and the MAWLEY flew over his head.

1890. *Lic. Vict. Gaz.*, 31 Jan. TIP US YOUR MAWLEYS, old pal!

2. (common). — A signature; handwriting; a FIST (*q.v.*).

1851-61. MAYHEW, *Lond. Lab.*, i. 340. One of those specious but deceitful 'fakements' upon which the 'swells,' (especially those who have 'been in the service,') 'come down with a *couter*' (sovereign) if they 'granny the MAULEY' (perceive the signature) of a brother officer or friend.

MAUND (or MAUNDER).—1. To beg. TO MAUND UPON THE PAD (or ON THE FLY) = to beg in the highway or the street. MAUNDING = begging. [From MAUND = a basket: *cf.* BEG from bag].

1531-47. COPLAND, *Hye Way to the Spyttel House*, line 1046. With bowsy Cove MAUND Nace, Tour the Patring Coue inthe darkeman Case.

1607. DEKKER, *Jests to Make You Merie*, in *Wks.* (GROSART), II. 322. In her MAWND or basket which she beares on her arme, lapt in a pure white cloth, some fine tidy pig.

1610. ROWLANDS, *Martin Mark-all*, p. 39 (H. Club's Repr. 1874). What MAUND doe you beake = what kind of begging use you? Ile myll your MAUND = Ile spoyle your begging.

1611. MIDDLETON, *Roaring Girl*, v. 1. I instructed him in the rudiments of roguery, and by my map made him sail over any country you can name, so that now he can MAUNDER better than myself.

1621. FLETCHER, *Thierry & Theodoret*, v. 1. Keep constables waking, wear out stocks and whipcord, MAUNDER for buttermilk, etc.

1622. BEAUMONT and FLETCHER, *The Beggar's Bush*, ii. 1. And every man to keep In his own path and circuit. *Hig.* Do you hear? You must hereafter MAUND on your own pads, he says.

1625. JONSON, *Staple of News*, ii. A rogue, A very canter, I, sir, one that MAUNDS Upon the pad.

1665. R. HEAD, *English Rogue*, pt. i. ch. v. 'p. 44 (1874). Having sufficiently warm'd our brains with humming liquor, which our *Lower* (money) shall procure ; if our deceitful MAUNDING (Begging) cannot.

1724. E. COLES, *Eng. Dict.*, s.v. MAUNDING, begging.

1748. T. DYCHE, *Dictionary* (5th ed.). MAUNDER(s). . . . also the cant word for to beg.

1785. GROSE, *Vulg. Tongue*, s.v.

1859. MATSELL, *Vocabulum*, s.v.

1876. M. E. BRADDON, *Joshua Haggard*, ch. vii. Who [a Devonshire lad]. . . had already unpacked the basket, or MAUND, as he called it.

2. (Old Cant).—To ask.

1567. HARMAN, *Caveat*, p. 86. MAUNDE of this morte what bene pecke is in her ken, Aske of this wyfe what good meate shee hath in her house.

MAUNDER. See MAUND, sense I.

Subs. (old).—A beggar ; a CADGE-GLOAK (*q.v.*). Also MAUNDERER and MAUNDING-COVE.

1611. MIDDLETON, *Roaring Girl* [DODSLEY, *Old Plays* (1825), vi. 108]. I am no such nipping Christian, but a MAUNDERER upon the pad, I confess.

1622. BEAUMONT and FLETCHER, *The Beggar's Bush*, ii. 1. Our king and sovereign, monarch o' the MAUNDERS.

1656. BROME, *Jovial Crew* (PEARSON, iii. 377). My noble Springlove, the great commander of the MAUNDERS, and king of canters.

*c.*1660. *Bagford Ballads* [EBSWORTH, i. 195]. A Craver my Father, a MAUNDER my Mother.

1665. R. HEAD, *English Rogue*, pt. i. ch. v. p. 50 (1874), s.v.

1690. B. E., *Dict. Cant. Crew*, s.v.

1712. SHIRLEY, *Triumph of Wit*, The MAUNDER's Praise of his Strowling Mort [Title].

1785. GROSE, *Vulg. Tongue*, s.v.

1823. W. T. MONCRIEFF, *Tom and Jerry*, ii. 6. Cadgers make holiday, Hey, for the MAUNDER's joys, Let pious

---

ones fast and pray, They save us the trouble, my boys.

1834. W. H. AINSWORTH, *Rookwood*, p. 183 (ed. 1864). Rogue or rascal, frater, MAUNDERER.

MAUNDERING, *subs.* (old).—See quot. Also MAUNDING and as *adj.*

*c.*1603. *Sack for my Money* [COLLIER, *Roxbughe Ballads* (1847), 180]. A MAUNDING cove that doth it love.

1610. ROWLANDS, *Martin Markall*, p. 39 (H. Club's Repr.1874). MAUNDING = begging.

1630. TAYLOR, *Works* [quoted by NARES]. As for example, suppose a begger be in the shape or forme of a MAUNDRING, or wandering souldier, with one arme, legge, or eye, or some such maime.

1690. B. E., *Dict. Cant. Crew*, s.v.

MAUNDRING-BROTH, *subs.* (old).—A scolding.—B. E. (1690) ; GROSE (1785).

MAVERICK, *subs.* (Texan).—An unbranded yearling. [From one Maverick].

MAW, *subs.* (old).—The mouth.

1592. GREENE, *Quip*, in *Works*, xi. 236. That pinch their bellies to polish their backs, that kepe their MAWES emptie, to fill their pursses.

1599. SHAKSPEARE, *Henry V*, ii. 1. And in thy hateful lungs,—yea, in thy MAW, perdy.

1603. SHAKSPEARE, *Measure for Measure*, iii. 2. Do thou but think What 'tis to cram a MAW, or clothe a back.

1654. CHAPMAN, *Revenge for Honour*, i. 1. Here men o' th' shop can gorge their musty MAWS With the delicious capon.

HOLD YOUR MAW ! *verb. phr.* (old).—Stop talking.

MAWKES, *subs.* (old).—1. A vulgar slattern.—GROSE (1785).

1859. MATSELL, *Vocabulum*, s.v.

1819. MOORE, *Tom Crib*, 14. The Porpus kept guard O'er bis beautiful mug, as if fearing to hazard One damaging touch in so dandy a MAZZARD.

1823. BEE, *Dict. of the Turf*, s.v. MAZZARD—the face, or perhaps the whole head. 'Tis Irish, and mostly confined to Dublin. 'Toss up the coppers now Thady,' 'head or harp?' 'Harp!' cried Paddy, 'and down came three black MAZZARDS.' 'Chop his MAZZARD,' a cut in the face.

1833. CRUIKSHANK, *Sunday in London*, p. 63. Knocking each other over the MAZZARD for a *qvort'n* of gin !

1834. W. H. AINSWORTH, *Rookwood*, p. 312 [ed. 1864). 'Here is that shall put fresh marrow into your old bones,' returned Jem, handing him a tumbler of brandy ; 'never stint it. I'll be sworn you'll be the better on't, for you look desperate queer, man, about the MAZZARD.'

1859. MATSELL, *Vocabulum*, s.v.

Verb. (old).—To knock on the head.

M.B.COAT (or WAISTCOAT), *subs.* (clerical).—A long coat worn by some clergymen. [M.B. = Mark of the Beast]. *See* CAPELLA.

1853. DEAN CONYBEARE, in *Edin. Rev.*, Oct., p. 315. Who does not recognise . . . the stiff and tie-less neckcloth, the M.B.COAT and cassock waistcoat, the cropped hair and un-whiskered cheek?

1884. *Graphic*, 20 Sept., p. 307/2. He has begun to affect the strictest clerical garb—M.B.WAISTCOAT, hard felt hat with band and tassels.

MEACOCK, *subs.* (old colloquial).—1. *See* quots. 1581, 1584-7, 1590, and 1610 ; and (2), a hen-pecked husband. (COLES : '*uxorius, uxori nimium deditus et obnoxius*').

1563. *Appius & Virginius* [DODSLEY, *Old Plays* (1874), iv. 118]. As stout as a stockfish, as meek as a MEACOCK.

1581. LYLY, *Euphues*, 109. I shall be compted a MECOCKE, a milksop.

1584-7. GREENE, *Carde of Fancie* [GROSART (1881-6), iv. 47]. Shall I then . . . . proue such a MEACOCKE, or a milkesoppe.

1590. *Newes out of Purgatorie* (HALLIWELL). She found fault with him because he was a MEACOCKE and milk-soppe.

1593. NASHE, *Strange Newes* [GROSART (1885), ii. 245]. Meere MEACOCKS and ciphars in comparison of thy excellent out-cast selfe.

1593. HARVEY, *Pierce's Supererogation* [GROSART (1884), ii. 49]. Martin himselfe but a MEACOCKE ; and Papphatchet himself but a milkesop.

1603. DEKKER, *The Batchelars Banquet* [GROSART (1886), i. 274]. The poore MEACOCK . . . . hauing his courage thus quailed, wil neuer afterwards fal at ods with her.

1610. *Mir. for Magistrates*, 418. A MEACOCK is he who dreadth to see bloud shed.

1619. FLETCHER, *Wildgoose Chase*, v. 2. Fools and MEACOCKS, To endure what you think fit to put upon 'em.

1635. GLAPTHORNE, *Hollander* [PEARSON (1874), i. 98]. They are like my husband, meere MEACOCKS, verily : and cannot lawfully beget a childe once in seaven yeares.

Adj. (old colloquial).—Cowardly.

1593. SHAKSPEARE, *Taming of the Shrew*, ii. 1. 315. 'Tis a world to see How tame, when men and women are alone, A MEACOCK wretch can make the curstest shrew.

1593. HARVEY, *Pierces Supererog.* [GROSART (1885), ii. 17]. The MEACOCK Verse that dares not sing.

MEAL. See SQUARE-MEAL.

MEALER, *subs.* (teetotallers').—1. A partial abstainer : pledged to take intoxicants only at meals.

2. (colloquial).—One who lodges at one place and boards elsewhere.

1887. *Christian Union*, 11 Aug. One of those cheap boarding-houses . . . . where humanity is resolved into two classes only . . . . roomers and MEALERS,

---

2. (old).—A whore.

172[?]. *Street Robberies Considered*, 25. I had the clever'st MAUX in town.

MAWLEY. See MAULEY.

MAW-WALLOP, *subs.* (old).—A filthy composition, sufficient to provoke vomiting.—GROSE (1785).

MAWWORM, *subs.* (common).—A hypocrite. [From Bickerstaff's play, *The Hypocrite*]. Also as *adj.*

1823. GROSE, *Vulg. Tongue* (3rd ed.), s.v.

1866. SALA, *Trip to Barbary*, p. 130. There was a sanctified MAWWORM expression, too, about this fellow, which filled you with a strong desire to fling him overboard.

1871. G. ELIOT, *Middlemarch*, Bk. I. ch. ii. A man naturally likes to look forward to having the best. He would be the very MAWWORM of bachelors who pretended not to expect it.

1891. *Lic. Vict. Gaz.*, 17 April. Superintendent S— is no MAWWORM, And it must have gone very much against the grain.

MAWPUS. See MOPUS.

MAWTHER, *subs.* (old).—1. A girl (JONSON) ; and (2), an old drudge (DICKENS).

MAX, *subs.* (old).—Gin. For synonyms *see* DRINKS and WHITE SATIN. [From *maxime* and so properly applied only to the best quality spirit].

1823. BYRON, *Don Juan*, C. xi. st. 16. The dying man cried, 'Hold ! I've got my gruel, Oh ! for a glass of MAX.'

1837. R. H. BARHAM, *Ingoldsby Legends (Bagman's Dog)*. Who, doffing their coronets, collars, and ermines, treat Boxers to MAX at the Old Inn in Jermyn Street.

1851-61. H. MAYHEW, *London Lab. & Lon. Poor*, v. 8, i. p. 168. The

---

stimulant of a 'flash of lightning,' a 'go of rum,' or a 'glass of MAX,'—for so a dram of neat spirit was then called.

1859. MATSELL, *Vocabulum*, s.v.

Verb. (United States military). —At West Point to gain the maximum of marks ; hence, to do well.

MAY, *subs.* (Cambridge University).—The Easter Term examination.

1852. BRISTED, *Five Years etc.*, 70. As the MAY approached I began to feel nervous.

MAY-GATHERING, *subs.* (thieves').—Sheep-stealing ; FLEECY CLAMMING (*q.v.*) ; BLEAT-MARCHING (*q.v.*).

MAZARINE, *subs.* (common).—1. A Common Councilman of the City of London. [From the robe of mazarine blue].

1761. *Chronicle*, 'Annual Reg.' 238. I had procured a ticket through the interest of Mr.— who was one of the committee for managing the entertainment, and a MAZARINE.

2. (theatrical). — A platform under the stage.

MAZZARD (MAZARD, or MAZER), *subs.* (common).—The head ; the face.

1602-3. SHAKSPEARE, *Hamlet*, v. 1. Ham. Chapless, and knocked about the MAZZARD with a sexton's spade.

1602. DEKKER, *Honest Whore* [DODSLEY, *Old Plays*, iii. 329]. Break but his pate, or so ; only his MAZER, Because I'll have his head in a cloth as well as mine.

1605. CHAPMAN, *All Fools*, iv. 1. But in thy amorous conquests, at the last, Some wound will slice your MAZER.

1639. FLETCHER, *Wit Without Money*, ii. 3. The pint-pot has so belaboured you with wit, your brave acquaintance, that gives you ale, so fortified your MAZARD, that now there's no talking to you.

MEAL-MOUTH, *subs.* (old).—See quot.

1690. B. E., *Dict. Cant. Crew*, s.v. MEAL-MOUTH, a sly sheepish Dun, or Sollicitor for Money. *Cf.* MEALY-MOUTHED.

MEAL-TUB (or -SACK), *subs.* (clerical).—The stock of sermons. 'I've nothing in my MEAL-TUB'= I've no sermon ready.

MEALY- (or MEAL-) MOUTHED, (or MEALY), *adj.* (old : now recognised).—Fluent ; plausible, persuasive. *See* also quot. 1748. *Cf.* MEAL-MOUTH.

1587. HARMAR, *Beza's Sermons*, 315. Ye whited walls and painted sepulchres, ye MEAL-MOUTHED counterfeits, ye devourers of widows.

1598. MARSTON, *Sat.*, ii. Who would imagine yonder . . . MEALE-MOUTHED precisian... is a vile, sober, damn'd politician.

1600. DEKKER, *Skom. Holiday* [GROSART (1873), i. 13]. This wench with the MEALY MOUTH that wil neuer tire, is my wife I can tel you.

1606. JOHN DAY, *Ile of Guls*, iv. 4. p. 93. *Wife.* Tho I may not scold I may tel em roundly out I hope . . . and Ile not be MEALLY MOUTHD, I warrant em.

1631. SHIRLEY, *Love Tricks*, i. A very crazy, old, MEAL-MOUTH'D gentleman ; you are younger at least by thirty years.

1639. FLETCHER, *Bloody Brother*, iii. 2. A place too good for thee, thou MEAL-MOUTH'D rascal !

1748. DYCHE, *Dictionary* (5th ed.). MEALY-MOUTHED, one that is fainthearted, bashful, or afraid to speak his mind freely.

1759. TOWNLEY, *High Life below Stairs*, ii. Out, you MEALY-MOUTHED cur !

1785. GROSE, *Vulg. Tongue*, s.v.

1854. WHYTE MELVILLE, *General Bounce*, ix. 'We might get money—ay, plenty of it—if you were only like the rest : you're too MEALY-MOUTHED, Mrs. Blacke, that's where it is.'

1854. DICKENS, *Hard Times*, ... I didn't mince the matter with him. I'm never MEALY with 'em.

1886. *Edinburgh Review*, clxiii. 425. Angry men hotly in earnest are not usually MEALY-MOUTHED.

MEAN, *adj.*(colloquial).—1. Disobliging ; petty ; STINGY. TO FEEL MEAN = to feel guilty.

2. (old : now American).—A general epithet of disparagement : MEAN night = a bad night ; MEAN horse = a sorry screw ; MEAN crowd = a man of no account ; MEAN bit = a worn-out whore.

1848. *Georgia Scenes*, 27. He'll cut the same capers there as here. He's a monstrous MEAN horse.

1887. FRANCIS, *Saddle & Mocassin*, p. 146. There ain't a drop of MEAN blood in him.

1888. *Century Mag.*, Oct. There can be no greater provocation than is given by a MEAN horse, or a refractory steer.

MEAN ENOUGH TO STEAL ACORNS FROM A BLIND HOG, *phr.* (American).—As mean as may be.

MEAN WHITE, *subs. phr.* (American negro).—*See* quots. ; poor WHITE TRASH (*q.v.*).

1837. H. MARTINEAU, *Soc. in America*, ii. 311. There are a few, called by the slaves MEAN WHITES, signifying whites who work with the hands.

1873. JUSTIN MCCARTHY, *Fair Saxon*, xix. That despised and degraded class, the MEAN WHITES—the creatures who had neither the social position and property that seemed essential to freedom in the South, nor the protected comfort of slavery.

MEASLY, *adj.* (vulgar).—Contemptible. [*Cf.* var. dial. MEASLED = diseased].

1864. M. E. BRADDON, *Henry Dunbar*, xxviii. 'And to think that the government of this country should have the audacity to offer a MEASLY hundred pounds or so for the discovery of a great crime !'

1884. HENLEY & STEVENSON, *Admiral Guinea* ('Three Plays', p. 203). Now in my blind old age I'm to be sent packing from a MEASLY public 'ouse.

MEASURE, *subs.* (old).—*See* quot.

1690. B. E., *Dict. Cant. Crew*, s.v. MEASURE, the Distance of Duellers. To BREAK MEASURE, to be out of the Adversaries reach.

TO MEASURE OUT, *verb. phr.* (common).—To knock down flat; to kill.

1891. *Morning Advertiser*, 3 April. The witness went to Martin's assistance, and became engaged in a tussle with the prisoner Tounsel, who took an empty lemonade bottle from his pocket and said, 'Look out, or I'll MEASURE you OUT.'

TO TAKE (or GET) ONE'S MEASURE, *verb. phr.* (old).—1. To marry; and (2) to copulate.

1684. LACY, *Sir Hercules Buffoon*, v. 3. Gin I'd let him alane, he had TAKEN MEASURE o' th' inside of me as well as o' th' out.

1771. FOOTE, *Maid of Bath*, i. She is a tight bit of stuff, and I am confident will turn out well in the wearing. I once had some thoughts myself of TAKING MEASURE of Miss.

2. (colloquial).—To appreciate; to SIZE UP.

1859. MATSELL, *Vocabulum*, s.v. MEASURE. To examine closely.

1872. *Derby Mercury*, 1 May, 'Freemasonry in New Zealand.' He became thin and haggard, and afraid to meet any of his former companions for fear that they should say they would TAKE HIS MEASURE.

1891. N. GOULD, *Double Event*, 215. Fletcher did not venture into that 'holy of holies'; there were too many men there had GOT HIS MEASURE.

TO BE MEASURED [for a part &c.] *phr.* (theatrical).—To get a part written to one's liking or capacity; to be exactly suited.

1859. BLANCHARD JERROLD, *Life of Douglas Jerrold*, vi. p. 94. Even the pig was to be MEASURED FOR HIS PART.

TO HAVE BEEN MEASURED FOR A NEW UMBRELLA, *verb. phr.* (American).—(1) To appear in new but ill-fitting clothes; whence (2) to pursue a policy of doubtful wisdom.

TO BE MEASURED FOR A SUIT OF MOURNING, *verb. phr.* (pugilistic).—*See* quot.

1819. MOORE, *Tom Crib*, xix. No pugilist can be considered worth anything, till he has had his peepers TAKEN MEASURE OF FOR A SUIT OF MOURNING, or in common language, has received a pair of black eyes.

MEASURED FOR A FUNERAL SERMON, *adv. phr.* (American).—At death's door.

MEAT, *subs.* (venery).—Generic for (1) the female *pudendum*, and (2) the *penis*: *cf.*, BEEF, FISH, FLESH, GAME, GREENS, MUTTON, &c. Hence, A BIT OF MEAT = the sexual favour; FOND OF MEAT = amorous; MEATY = enjoyable; FRESH MEAT = a new PIECE (*q.v.*); RAW MEAT = a nude PERFORMER (*q.v.*); MEAT-HOUSE = a brothel; MEAT-MARKET = (1) the female *pudendum*, (2) any *rendezvous* of public women, and (3) the paps; MEAT-MERCHANT = a bawd; MEAT-MONGER = a whoremaster; the PRICE OF MEAT = the cost of an embrace; MEAT-AND-DRINK = an amorous carouse; TO FLASH MEAT = to expose the person. Fr. *la viande*.

1595. GOSSON, *Quippes, etc.* [HAZLITT, *Early Pop. Poetry* (1866), iv. 259]. That you should coutch your MEAT in dish, And others feel it is no fish.

1597-8. HAUGHTON, *A Woman will have her Will* [DODSLEY, *Old Plays*

(1874), x. 498]. I am no MEAT for his mowing.

1611. *Ram Alley* [DODSLEY, *Old Plays* (1874), x. 369]. Faith, take a maid, and leave the widow, master: Of all MEATS I love not a gaping oyster.

1664. FALKLAND, *Marriage Night*, i. 1. But is she man's MEAT? I have a tender appetite, and can scarcely digest one in her teens.

1668. KILLIGREW, *Parson's Wedding*, v. 2. Your bed is big enough for two, and my MEAT will not cost you much.

1684. LACY, *Sir Hercules Buffoon*, iii. 3. I am so plagued with citizens that I cannot have a deer that's man's MEAT, but they steal it out of my park, my Lord.

1760. FOOTE, *Minor*, ii. Did I not tell you old Moll was your mark? Here she has brought a pretty piece of man's MEAT already; as sweet as a nosegay, and as ripe as a cherry.

1856. WHITMAN, *Leaves of Grass*, Children of Adam (1891-2, ix. 87). The naked MEAT of the body.

TO CHEW ONE'S OWN MEAT, *verb. phr.* (American).—To do a thing oneself; hence, to CHEW MEAT FOR ONE = to do another's work for him.

MEAT-AND-DRINK, *subs.* (common).—1. Strong drink; also liquor thickened with yolk of eggs, etc.

2. (old colloquial).—Delight.

1600. SHAKSPEARE, *As you Like it*, v. 1. It is MEAT-AND-DRINK to me to see a clown.

3. (venery).—*See* MEAT.

MEAT-AXE. SAVAGE AS A MEAT-AXE, *phr.* (American).—Extremely hungry.

1843. CARLTON, *New Purchase* [BARTLETT]. It would be a charity to give the pious brother some such feed as chicken fixins and doins, for he looks half-starved and as SAVAGE AS A MEAT AXE.

1852. KIRKLAND, *Forest Life*, i. 103. 'Why, you don't eat nothing!' he exclaimed; 'ridin' don't agree with you, I guess! Now, for my part, it makes me as SAVAGE AS A MEAT-AXE.'

MEAT-BAG (or **-SAFE**), *subs.* (American).—The stomach. For synonyms *see* VICTUALLING-OFFICE.

1848. RUXTON, *Life In The Far West*, p. 8. Well, Dick was as full of arrows as a porkypine; one was sticking right through his cheek, one in his MEAT-BAG, and two more 'bout his hump-ribs.

MEAT-FLASHING, *subs.* (common).—Exposure of the person. Hence, MEAT-FLASHER = a public offender in this line.

MEAT-IN-THE-POT, *subs.* (Western American).—A revolver.

ENGLISH SYNONYMS. Barker; barking iron; black-eyed Susan; blazer; bulldog; Colt; the democratiser (American: as making all men equal); unconverted friend; pop, or pop-gun; persuader; shooting-iron; shot-gun; six-shooter; stick; towel; two-pipe scatter-gun.

FRENCH SYNONYMS. *Un bayafe* (thieves'); *un blavin* (also = pocket handkerchief); *les burettes* (= phials); *un crucifix* or *crucifix à ressorts* (thieves'); *un mandolet* (thieves'); *un mouchoir de poche (Cf. blavin)*.

MEATY, *adj.* (common).—1. Plump; and (2) enjoyable. *See* MEAT.

1851-61. MAYHEW, *London Lab.*, iii. 210. I'm just MEATY enough for my profession.

MECHANIC, *subs.* (old: now recognised).—*See* quot. 1690. As *adj.* = common; vulgar; mean.

1599. SHAKSPEARE, *Henry V*, i. 2. 200. The poor MECHANIC porters crowding in.

1690. B. E., *Dict. Cant. Crew*, s.v. MECHANIC, a Tradesman; also a mean, inconsiderable, contemptible Fellow.

MED (MEDIC, MEDICAL, or MEDICO), *subs.* (medical).—A medical man. Also a student.

1823. *The Crayon* (Yale Coll.), p. 23. Who sent The MEDIC to our aid!

1850. *Yale Banger* [HALL], Nov. Seniors, Juniors, Freshmen blue, And MEDICS sing the Anthem too.

1853. *Songs of Yale*, p. 16. Take .... Sixteen interesting MEDS, With dirty hands and towzeled heads.

1864. D. MASSON, in *Macm. Mag.*, Dec., p. 124. Those minute physiognomic differences, which enable an expert to distinguish a jolly young MEDICAL from a prematurely-sharp *leguleian*.

1885. B. G. WILDER, *Journal Nervous Diseases*, xii. MEDIC is the legitimate paronym of *medicus*, but is commonly regarded as slang.

1889. *Lancet*, 13 July [No. 3437], p. 96. The London MEDICALS were quite as popular.

1890. *Answers*, 25 Dec. She did her exercise and work and had her meals alone, and during the whole of that period the only persons she spoke to were the governor (known in prison as the 'boss'), the chaplain (in prison parlance 'sky pilot'), the MEDICO (doctor), and the 'screw' (female warder).

MEDDLER. LAY-OVERS FOR MEDDLERS. *See* LARE-OVER.

MEDES AND PERSIANS, *subs. phr.* (Winchester College).—Jumping on a MAN (*q.v.*) when in bed.

MEDICAL GREEK, *subs. phr.* (common).—*See* MARROWSKYING.

1885. *Household Words*, 20 June, p. 155. Medical students have liberally assisted in the formation of slang, their special department thereof being known as MEDICAL GREEK.

MEDICINE, *subs.* (common).—1. Liquor; and (2) GREENS (*q.v.*). To TAKE ONE'S MEDICINE = (1) to drink; and (2) to copulate. For synonyms *see* DRINKS and RIDE.

MEDIUM, *subs.* (Australian).—A person engaged by a squatter, part of whose 'run' is offered by Government at a land lottery. The MEDIUM takes lot-tickets, as if bent upon cultivation, attends the drawing, and, if his ticket be drawn before his principal's land is gone, selects it, and hands it over on payment of the attendance fee.

MEDLAR, *subs.* (venery).—1. The female *pudendum*. *Cf.* OPEN-ARSE. For synonyms *see* MONOSYLLABLE. Hence, a harlot.

1603. SHAKSPEARE, *Measure for Measure*, iv. 3. Else they would have married me to the rotten MEDLAR.

2. (American thieves').—A dirty person.

1859. MATSELL, *Vocabulum*, s.v.

MEECH, MEECHING. *See* MIKE.

MEERSCHAUM, *subs.* (pugilistic).—The nose. For synonyms *see* CONK.

1891. *Sporting Life*, 25 March. At the call of 'Time' ending in favour of Burford, Phillips being very weak, and his MEERSCHAUM beautifully painted. *Ibid.*, 3 April. Determined left-handed exchanges, Macdonald standing over Harland, who made the most of the ring, but coloured Mac's MEERSCHAUM in the last minute.

MEETINGER, *subs.* (Nonconformist).—A chapel-goer.

1885. *Notes and Queries*, 11 April, p. 297. Those who attend the meeting are called MEETINGERS.

MEG, *subs.* (old).—1. *See* quots. For synonyms *see* YELLOW-BOYS and CANARY. *Cf.* MAG, *subs.*, sense 2.

1688. SHADWELL, *Sq. of Alsatia*, i. in *Wks.* (1720), iv. 18. *Sham.* No, no; MEGGS are guineas, smelts are half guineas.

1690. B. E., *Dict. Cant. Crew*, s.v. MEGGS .... We fork'd the Rum Culls MEGGS to the tune of Fifty, We pickt the Gentleman's Pocket of full Fifty Guineas.

1725. *New Cant. Dict.*, s.v.

1785. GROSE, *Vulg. Tongue*, s.v.

2. in *pl.* (Stock Exchange).—Mexican Railway First Preference Stock.

3. (Old Scots').—A wench. MEG DORTS = a pert girl. MEG-HARRY (Lanc.) = a hoyden.

1538. LINDSAY, *Syde Taillis* [CHALMERS, ii. 201]. Ane muirland MEG, that milkes the yowis, Claggit with clay abone the howis.

1725. RAMSAY, *The Gentle Shepherd*. She scour'd away, and said——'What's that to you?' 'Then fare ye weel MEG DORTS, and e'en's ye like.'

ROARING MEG, *subs. phr.* (old).—A monster piece of ordnance; hence, an unfailing antidote.

1624. BURTON, *Anat. Melan.*, Pt. II. ii. 6. 3. *Musica est mentis medecina mœstæ*, a ROARING MEG against melancholy.

MEGRIM, *subs.* (old colloquial).—1. A crotchet; and (2) a headache. Fr. *une migraine*.

*d.*1520(?). DUNBAR, *My Heid did Yak*, in *Poems* (Scottish Text Society Edition, 1888-9), p. 254. So sair the MEGRYM dois me menzie.

1609. DEKKER, *Almanacke* [GROSART, iv. 185]. But shall be strucke with such MEGRIMS and turnings of the braine, that instead of going to church, they will (if my Arte faile me not) stumble into a Tauerne.

1639. BEAUMONT & FLETCHER, *Wit without Money*, i. 1. He had never Left me the misery of so much means eke, Which, till I sold, was a mere MEGRIM to me.

1673. DRYDEN, *The Assignation*, iii. 3. Now will I have the headach, or the MEGRIM, or some excuse.

1795. R. CUMBERLAND, *The Jew*, ii. 2. *Dorcas.* How you ramble, Sirrah! What MEGRIMS you have in your head!

1866. G. ELIOT, *Felix Holt*, xi. 'Can't one work for sober truth as hard as for MEGRIMS?'

MEG'S DIVERSIONS, *subs. phr.* (common).—1. Whimsical pleasantry; and (2) OLD HARRY (*q.v.*).

1834. M. G. DOWLING, *Othello Travestie*, i. 3. The galley slaves Are playing MEG'S DIVERSION on the waves.

1850. CRAVEN, *Meg's Diversions* [Title].

MEGSMAN. *See* MAGSMAN.

MEJOGE, *subs.* (old).—A shilling; a BOB (*q.v.*).—*Discoveries of John Poulter* (1754).

MELL, *subs.* (Old Cant).—The nose. For synonyms *see* CONK.

Verb. (venery).—To copulate. For synonyms *see* GREENS and RIDE. Also MEDDLE.

*d.*1450. LYDGATE (HALLIWELL). Like certeyn birdes called vultures, Withouten MELLYNG conceyven by nature.

*b.*1468. *Ludus Coventriæ* [Shaks. Soc. 1841], p. 215. And a talle man with her dothe MELLE ... We xul take them both togedyr Whylle that thei do that synful dede.

1541. *Schole House of Women* [HAZLITT, *Early Pop. Poetry* (1866), iv. 133]. Made him drunk, and so at last MEDLED with him.

1598. SHAKSPEARE, *All's Well etc.*, iv. 3. Men are to MELL with, boys are not to kiss.

MELLOW, *adj.* (common).—*See* quot. 1690.

1690. B. E., *Dict. Cant. Crew*, s.v. MELLOW, a'most Drunk; also smooth, soft Drink.

1725. *New Cant. Dict.*, s.v.

1774. GARRICK, *Epitaph on Goldsmith*, 'Here Hermes,' says Jove, who with nectar was MELLOW.

1785. GROSE, *Vulg. Tongue*, s.v.

1821. BYRON, *Don Juan*, Cant. iii. St. 82. Had been the favourite of full many a mess Of men and made them speeches when half-MELLOW.

1859. MATSELL, *Vocabulum*, s.v.

MELON, *subs.* (Royal Military Academy).—A new cadet. For synonyms *see* SNOOKER.

MELT, *verb.* (old).—1. *See* quots.; TO BLEW (*q.v.*).

1690. B. E., *Dict. Cant. Crew*, s.v. MELT . . . Will you MELT a Bord? Will you spend your Shilling? The Cull MELTED a couple of Decuses upon us, the Gentleman spent ten Shillings upon us.

1714. *Memoirs of John Hall* (4th ed.), p. 19. And if any of their Acquaintances gives them *l'argent*, then they jump into their Cellar to MELT it.

1725. *New Cant. Dict.*, s.v.

1748. DYCHE, *Dictionary* (5th ed.). MELT (VI) . . . also a cant word for extravagantly spending any considerable sum of money.

1765. FOOTE, *Commissary*, i. 1. Give him the sixpence, then, there lay it out as you will. *Coachm.* It will be to your health, mistress; it shall MELT at the Mews, before I go home.

1785. GROSE, *Vulg. Tongue*, s.v.

1843. MONCRIEFF, *The Scamps of London*, i. 1. What did you do with the tin? *Bob.* MELTED it, of course, in less than a month.

1859. MATSELL. *Vocabulum*, s.v.

1869. C. READE, *Foul Play*, lii. I had him arrested before he had time to MELT the notes.

1880. JAMIESON, *Dict. Scott. Lang.*, s.v. MELT, to spend money on drink; a low term, but much used; as, 'I've jist ae saxpence left, let's MELT it.'

1887. W. E. HENLEY, *Villon's Straight Tip*, How do you MELT the multy-swag?—Booze and the blowens cop the lot.

2. (venery).—To SPEND (*q.v.*). Fr. *fondre*.

1629. CAREW, *Poems* (1772), 'Second Rapture,' p. 174. In whose sweet embraces I, May MELT myself to lust and die.

TO LOOK AS IF BUTTER WOULD NOT MELT IN THE MOUTH. *See* BUTTER.

'TWILL CUT BUTTER WHEN IT'S MELTED (or HOT). *See* BUTTER.

MELTED-BUTTER, *subs.* (venery).—The semen; CREAM (*q.v.*).

MELTING, *subs.* (pugilistic).—*See* quot.

1823. BEE, *Dict. of the Turf*, s.v. MELTING—a sound drubbing, all one way. A *melter* is he who punisheth, and the thing administered is a MELTING—a corruption of malletting.

MELTING MOMENTS, *subs. phr.* (old).—*See* quot.

1823. GROSE, *Vulg. Tongue* (3rd ed.), s.v. MELTING MOMENTS, a fat man and woman in the amorous congress.

MELTING-POT, *subs.* (venery).—The female *pudendum*. For synonyms *see* MONOSYLLABLE.

MELTON, *subs.* (tailors').—Dry bread.

MEMBER, *subs.* (conventional).—1. The *penis*. For synonyms *see* CREAMSTICK and PRICK. Also UNRULY MEMBER, PRIVY-MEMBER and MEMBER FOR COCKSHIRE.

1356. MANDEVILLE, *Travels*, p. 197. Thei gon all naked, saf a litylle Clout, that thei coveren with here knees and hire MEMBRES.

1611. *Deut.* XXIII. 1 [Authorised Version]. He that hath his privy MEMBER cut off.

1639. GLAPTHORNE, *Argalus*, i. 2. Leg neatly made. . . . thigh proportionable. . . . a back that can bear any weight. . . . full limbs. . . . a lusty chine . . . . rump so well made, and firmely knit, The nymphs are all stark mad for it, Because they think the rest of my MEMBERS proportionable.

1647-80. ROCHESTER, *A Satire on the King*. E'er she can raise the MEMBER she enjoys.

*d.*1796. BURNS, *Epistle to a Tailor*. An' whatfor no Your dearest MEMBER.

3. (common).—A person: almost exclusively with qualifying terms, as HOT (*q.v.*); RUM (*q.v.*); WARM (*q.v.*) and the like.

1891. *Sporting Life*, 28 Mar. Accordingly Jem was put to work, but, WARM A MEMBER as our hero was, standing in front of a blazing furnace for hours and pushing in and pulling out huge bars of iron was too hot even for Jem's *sanguinary* temperament.

MEMBER-MUG, *subs.* (common).—1. A chamber-pot. For synonyms *see* IT.

1690. B. E., *Dict. Cant. Crew*, s.v.

1725. *New Cant. Dict.*, s.v.

1785. GROSE, *Vulg. Tongue*, s.v.

2. (Westminster School).—An out-of-door boy.

MEN. *See* MAN for all senses.

MENAGERIE, *subs.* (theatrical).—The orchestra.

MENAVELINGS, *subs.* (railway clerks').—Odd money in the daily accounts; FLUFF (*q.v.*); OVERS AND SHORTS. *Cf.* MANABLINS.

MEND. TO MEND FENCES, *verb. phr.* (American).—To mind one's own business; to attend to one's interest.

TO CORRECT (or MEND) THE MAGNIFICAT, *verb. phr.* (old).—To correct that which is faultless.—RAY (1670).

MENTOR, *subs.* (American).—*See* quot.

1859. MATSELL, *Vocabulum*, s.v. MENTOR. A second in the ring.

MEPHISTO, *subs.* (tailors').—A foreman.

MERCHANT, *subs.* (old).—A term of abuse.

*d.*1555. LATIMER, *Sermons*, 115. b. [NARES]. The crafty MERCHANT that will set brother against brother meaneth to destroy them both.

1557-8. *Jacob & Esau* [DODSLEY, *Old Plays* (1874), ii. 253]. What, ye saucy MERCHANT, are ye a prater now?

1595. SHAKSPEARE, *Romeo & Juliet*, ii. 4. 153. I pray you, sir, what saucy MERCHANT was this that was so full of his ropery?

1633. *Match at Midnight*, v. 1. I knew you were a crafty MERCHANT.

TO PLAY THE MERCHANT, *verb. phr.* (old).—*See* quot. 1593.

1593. NASHE, *Christ's Teares* [GROSART (1885), iv. 240]. Is it not a common proverb amongst us, when any man hath cosened or gone beyonde us, to say, Hee hath PLAYDE THE MERCHANT with us.

1632. W. ROWLEY, *Woman Never Vext*, iv. 1. I doubt, Sir, he will PLAY THE MERCHANT with us.

MERCURY, *subs.* (old: now recognised).—1. *See* quots.

1690. B. E., *Dict. Cant. Crew*, s.v. MERCURY . . . . and a Courant or News-letter.

1725. *New Cant. Dict.*, s.v.

1755. JOHNSON, *Eng. Dict.*, s.v. MERCURY . . . . it is now applied in cant phrase to the carriers of news and pamphlets.

1827. TODD, *Johnson's Dict.*, s.v. MERCURY . . . it had been a cant phrase more than a century before Dr. Johnson's time; and was used generally for a messenger.

2. (old).—*See* quot. 1690. MERCURIAL = witty.

1690. B. E., *Dict. Cant. Crew*, s.v. MERCURY, Wit. *Ibid.* s.v. MERCURIAL, witty.

1725. *New Cant. Dict.*, s.v.

3. (old).—A thief; a trickster.

1599. JONSON, *Every Man Out of His Humour*, i. 2. I would ha' those MERCURIES should remember they had not their fingers for nothing.

MERCURY-WOMEN, *subs.* (old).—*See* quot.

1690. B. E., *Dict. Cant. Crew*, s.v. MERCURY WOMEN, Wholesale Newssellers who retail to the Hawkers.

1725. *New Cant. Dict.*, s.v.

MERIDIAN, *subs.* (old).—Refreshment taken at noon. ANTE-MERIDIAN = a morning dram: POST-MERIDIAN = an appetizer before dinner.

1818. SCOTT, *Heart of Midlothian*, iv. Plumdamas joined the other two gentlemen in drinking their MERIDIAN (a bumper-dram of brandy).

MERKIN, *subs.* (old).—1. *See* quots. 1736 and 1796.

1620. PERCY, *Folio MS.*, p. 508. A health to all Ladyes that neuer used MERKIN.

16[?]. JONSON, *A Song of the Moon* [CUNNINGHAM and BELL (1870), iii. 465]. The moon commends her to the merry beards in hall . . . Morts and MIRKINS that wag all, Tough, foul, or tender.

1647-80. ROCHESTER, *To the Author of a Play called 'Sodom'*. Or wear some stinking MERKIN for a beard.

167[?]. COTTON, *Voyage to Ireland*, iii. 26. By these the true colour one can no more know Than by mouse-skins above-stairs the MERKIN below.

1688. RANDAL HOLME, *Academy of Armoury*, 389. Some term it . . . MERKIN when set about the lower parts.

1720. PHILLIPS, *New World of Words*, s.v.

1724. E. COLES, *Eng. Dict.*, MERKIN (f. la mère, *matrix*) *pubes* (eminentia) *mulieris*.

1736. BAILY, *Engl. Dict.*, s.v. MERKIN . . . . counterfeit hair for the privities of women.

1796. GROSE, *Vulg. Tongue* (3rd ed.), s.v. MERKIN, counterfeit hair for the private parts of a woman.

1873. HOTTEN, *Slang Dict.*, s.v.

1890. BARRÈRE and LELAND, *Slang, Jargon, and Cant*, s.v.

2. (obsolete).—Fur.

1678. COTTON, *Virgil Travestie*, in *Wks.* (1725), Bk. iv. p. 90. Upon his back he had a Jerkin Lin'd through, and through with sable MERKIN.

3. (venery).—The female *pudendum*. For synonyms *see* MONOSYLLABLE.

1656. R. FLETCHER, *Martiall*. Why dost thou reach thy MERKIN now half dust?

1661. *Merry Drollery*, 'A Puritan' [EBSWORTH (1876), p. 196]. Her zeal was in a sound. He edified her MERKIN Upside down.

1719. A. SMITH, *Higwaymen*, ii. 6. A strange whim . . . which was to get the hairy circle of her MERKIN. This he dried well, and combed out.

4. (American thieves').—Hair dye.

1859. MATSELL, *Vocabulum*, s.v.

MERMAID, *subs.* (old).—A strumpet. For synonyms *see* BARRACK-HACK and TART.

1599. MIDDLETON, ROWLEY, and MASSINGER, *Old Law*, iv. 1. What, a MERMAID? No, but a maid.

MERRY (or **MERRY-ARSED**), *adj.* (venery).—Wanton. Hence, MERRY-ARSED CHRISTIAN = a whore (GROSE, 1823); MERRY-BEGOT (*q.v.*); MERRY-BIT = a willing wench; MERRY-MAKER = the *penis*; MERRY-LEGS = a LIGHT-SKIRTS (*q.v.*) or QUICUNQUE-VULT (*q.v.*).

1610. BEAUMONT and FLETCHER, *Maid's Tragedy*, iii. 1. *Diph.* What odds, he has not my sister's maidenhead to-night? . . . . She's MERRY enough of herself; she needs no tickling.

*c.*1800. BURNS, *The Merry Muses of Caledonia* [In title, and *passim*].

1887. HENLEY, *Book of Verses*, 'Ballade of a Toyokuni Colour-Print' When MERRY maids in Miyako.

MERRY-ANDREW, *subs.* (common).—*See* quot. 1785. Also MR. MERRYMAN.

1682. DRYDEN, *Epil. to Univ. of Oxford*. 'Th'Italian MERRY-ANDREWS took their place. And quite debauch'd the Stage with lewd grimace.'

1710. ROCHESTER, *Poems*, p. 56. They ne'er had sent to Paris for such fancies, As monster's heads and MERRY-ANDREW'S dances.

1732. HENRY FIELDING, *The Mock Doctor*, i. 1. I waited on a gentleman at Oxford, where I learned very near as much as my master; from whence I attended a travelling physician six years, under the facetious denomination of a MERRY ANDREW, where I learned physic.

1770. ST. FOIX, *Essays upon Paris*, ii. 64, ii. cap. 6. The MERRY-ANDREWS told stories.

1785. GROSE, *Vulg. Tongue*, s.v. MERRY ANDREW or MR. MERRYMAN, the jack-pudding, jester, or zany of a mountebank, usually dressed in a party-colored coat.

1785. BURNS, *Jolly Beggars*, R. iii. Poor MERRY-ANDREW in the neuk Sat guzzling with a tinkler-hizzie. *Ibid.* S. iii. Poor ANDREW that tumbles for sport.

1842. C. LEVER, *Jack Hinton*, . . . I wonder how a Christian would make a MERRY-ANDREW of himself by wearing such clothes.

MERRY-BEGOT (or **-BEGOTTEN**), *subs.* (old).—A bastard: *cf.* quot. 1377.—GROSE (1785). For synonyms *see* BLOODY ESCAPE, etc.

*c.*1377. LANGTOFT, *Chronicle* [BRUNNE (1725), p. 50]. Knoute of his body gate sonnes thre, Tuo bi tuo wifes, the thrid in jolifte [in jollity].

1890. HALL CAINE, *The Bondman*, i. ch. 6. Maybe you think it wise to bring up your daughter with the MERRY-BEGOT of any ragabash that comes prowling along.

MERRY-CAIN. *See* CAIN, RAISE and JESSE.

MERRY-DANCERS, *subs.* (colloquial).—The Northern Lights. [From their motion]. Fr. *chèvres dansantes* (= dancing goats).

MERRY-DOG, *subs.* (common).—A boon companion; a JOLLY-DOG (*q.v.*).

1891. W. C. RUSSELL, *Ocean Tragedy*, p. 18. He was a MERRY-DOG enough when Wilfrid was out of sight.

MERRY DUN OF DOVER, *subs.* (nautical).—A ship so large that, passing through the Straits of Dover, her flying jib-boom knocked down Calais steeple; while the fly of her ensign swept a flock of sheep off Dover Cliff. She was so lofty that a boy who went to her mast-head found himself a grey old man when he reached the deck again. [This yarn is founded on a story in Scandinavian mythology].

MERRY-GO-DOWN, *subs.* (Old Cant).—Strong ale; STINGO (*q.v.*). For synonyms *see* DRINKS and SWIPES.

*c.*1530. *Hoow Gossip Mine* [in *Neuenglische Lesebuch* (1895), p. 154]. I know a draught of MERRY-GO-DOWN, The best it is in all the town.

1599. NASHE, *Lenten Stuffe*, Ded. [*Harl. Misc.* vi. 145]. I present you with meate, and you. . . . can do no less than present mee with the best morning's draught of MERRY-GO-DOWNE in your quarters.

MERRY-GO-SORRY, *subs.* (old colloquial).—Hysteria.

1600. BRETON, *Fortunes of Two Princes*, 25. The ladie with a MERRIE-GO-SORRIE.

MERRY-GO-UP, *subs.* (old).—Snuff.

1821. EGAN, *Real Life*, ii. 90. Short but pungent like a pinch of MERRY-GO-UP.

MERRY GREEK, *subs. phr.* (old).—A jolly companion.

1602. SHAKSPEARE, *Troilus and Cressida*, i. 2. Then she's a MERRY GREEK indeed.

1647. BEAUMONT and FLETCHER, *Woman's Prize*, ii. 2. Go home, and tell the MERRY GREEKS that sent you, Ilium shall burn, etc.

d.1669. PRYNNE, *Hedlthes Sicknesse*, fol. B 2, b. Open, liberall, or free housekeepers, MERRY GREEKS, and such like stiles and titles.

1820. *Barn. Journ.*, i. p. 54. A true Trojan, and a mad MERRY grig, though no GREEK.

MERRYMAN. See MERRY-ANDREW.

MERRY-MEN-OF-MAY, *subs.* (nautical).—Currents formed by the ebb-tides.

MERRY-PIN, *subs.* (old).—A happy chance; a jolly time; a gay mood. IN A MERRY PIN = jovially inclined. [See quot.1655.]

1560. *Nice Wanton* [DODSLEY, *Old Plays* (1874), ii. 166]. I will set my heart On a MERRY-PIN, Whatever shall befall.

1655. FULLER, *Church History*, iii. 17. The Dutch, and English in imitation of them, were wont to drink out of a cup marked with certain pins, and he accounted the man who could nick the pin; whereas, to go above or beneath it, was a forfeiture.

1670. RAY, *Proverbs* [BOHN (1893), 174]. To be in A MERRY-PIN.

1715. PENNECUIK, *Poems* (1815), 332. Finding the brethren IN A MERRY PIN.

1719. D'URFEY, *Pills etc.*, i. ... Well, since you're ON THE MERRY PIN And make so slight the counter-gin, I'll do't.

d.1774. FERGUSSON, *Poems* (1851), 'A Drink Eclogue,' 114. And set the saul upon a MERRY PIN.

MERRY THOUGHT, *subs.* (colloquial).—The furcula or forked bone of a fowl's breast.

1598. FLORIO, *A Worlde of Wordes*, s.v. *Catriosso*, the bone called the MERIE THOUGHT.

1694. ECHARD, *Plautus* [*Ency. Dict.*]. 'Let him not be breaking MERRY-THOUGHTS under the table with my cousin.'

d.1719. ADDISON, *Omens* [*Century*]. I . . . have seen a man in love grow pale, and lose his appetite upon the plucking of a MERRY THOUGHT.

MESOPOTAMIA, *subs.* (obsolete).—1. Belgravia; CUBITOPOLIS (q.v.). Cf. ASIA MINOR, NEW JERUSALEM etc.

1864. E. YATES, *Broken to Harness*, xv. p. 143 (1873). A house in Great Adullam Street, Macpelah Square, in that district of London whilom known as MESOPOTAMIA.

2. (Oxford University). — See quot.

1886. *Pall Mall Gazette*, 23 June, p. 13. Every Oxford man has known and loved the beauties of the walk called MESOPOTAMIA

THE TRUE MESOPOTAMIA RING, *phr.* (common).—High-sounding and pleasing, but wholly past comprehension. [In allusion to the story of the old woman who told her pastor that she found great support in that blessed word MESOPOTAMIA].

MESS, *subs.* (colloquial).—1. A difficulty; a fiasco; a muddle. TO MAKE A MESS OF IT = to fail utterly or permanently.

1851-61. MAYHEW, *Lond. Lab. etc.*, ii. 193. They make it a rule when they receive neither beer nor money from a house TO MAKE AS GREAT A MESS AS possible the next time they come.

1880. *Life in a Debtor's Prison*, 77. Contemptuous pity due to a poor devil who has MADE A MESS OF IT.

c.1884. J. W. PALMER, *After His Kind*, p. 91. What A MESS they MADE OF IT!

2. (Winchester College).—See quot.

1866. MANSFIELD, *School Life*, 219. The Præfects' tables in Hall were called 'Tub, Middle, and Junior MESS' respectively. The boys who dined at each were also so named. Any number of boys who habitually breakfasted together were so called, with some distinguishing prefix, as Deputy's MESS. In Chambers tea was called MESS; as was also the remains of a joint of meat. Lest the reader should make a MESS of all these different meanings, I will give a sentence in which they shall all figure, 'Look. . . . Junior MESS has sat down at Tub MESS, but as they will find nothing left but a MESS, they had better go down to chambers as MESS is ready.'

TO MESS ABOUT, *verb. phr.* (venery).—1. To take liberties; to FIRKYTOODLE (q.v.).

2. (common).—To play fast and loose; to swindle; to put off.

TO LOSE THE NUMBER OF ONE'S MESS, *verb. phr.* (military and nautical).—To die. For synonyms see HOP THE TWIG.

1834. MARRYAT, *Peter Simple*, ch. xxxiii. 'I can't say, Mr. Simple,' said Mr. Chucks to me in an under tone, 'that I think well of this expedition; and I have an idea that some of us will LOSE THE NUMBER OF OUR MESS.'

1881. T. F. KEANE, *Six Months in Meccah*, p. 60. Another followed, fetching me one on the skull, that would have 'SETTLED THE NUMBER OF MY MESS' but for the thickness of my too attractive head-dress.

MESSEL, *subs.* (old).—A partner; an associate.

1605. *London Prodigal*, ii. 1. I defy thee; press scoundrells, and thy MESSELS.

MESS-JOHN, *subs.* (old).—A clergyman : in contempt. [*Mass-JOHN*]. See JOHN, sense 2.

1772. STEVENS, *Songs Comic and Satyrical* (1788), 169. The next a MESS JOHN of rank methodist taint, Who thought like a sinner, but looked like a saint.

1785. *Poems in the Buchan Dialect*, ii. 42. This breeds ill wills, ye ken fu' aft, In the black coat, Till poor MASS-JOHN and the priest-craft Goes ti' the pot.

1785. GROSE, *Vulg. Tongue*, s.v. MESS-JOHN, a Scotch Presbyterian teacher or parson.

c.1786. BURNS, *To a Tailor*. An' syne MESS-JOHN, beyond expression, Fell foul o' me.

MESS-MATE, *subs.* (old: now recognised).—See quot. 1785.

1772. G. A. STEVENS, *Songs Comic and Satyrical*, 'The Storm.' MESS-MATES, hear a brother sailor Sing the dangers of the sea.

1785. GROSE, *Vulg. Tongue*, s.v. MESS-MATE, one who eats at the same mess, companion, or camerade.

MESTING, *subs.* (American thieves').—See quot.

1859. MATSELL, *Vocabulum*, s.v. MESTING. Dissolving; melting.

MET, *subs.* (American).—A member of the Metropolitan (or New York) Base-Ball Club.

2. in *pl.* (Stock Exchange).—Metropolitan Railway Shares.

THE MET, *subs. phr.* (London).—The Metropolitan music-hall.

METAL, *subs.* (common).—1. Money. For synonyms see ACTUAL and GILT.

2. See METTLE.

METALLICIAN, *subs.* (obsolete racing).—A bookmaker. [From the use of metallic books and pencils].

1887. *Lic. Vict. Gazette*, 2 Dec., 359. 2. He may, like Jem Smith, have three big METALLICIANS quarrelling for the honour of being his 'Captain.'

1887. *Daily Telegraph*, 12 Mar. As for the long-suffering Australian public, they are mulcted, except in the colony of Victoria, as heavily as the much-taxed METALLICIAN.

METAL-RULE, *subs.* (printers').—An oath; an obscenity. 'You be metal-ruled' = 'You be damned.' [From the use of '—' in print].

METTLE, *subs.* (venery).—The semen. For synonyms see CREAM and SPENDINGS. METTLED = amorous.

1612. FIELD, *Woman is a Weathercock*, i. 2. What a sin were it in me . . . to marry a man that wants the METTLE OF GENERATION.

1649. DAVENANT, *Love & Honour*, ii. 1. I must provide her . . . . broths That may stir METTLE in her . . . . I find Her no more fit for the business of increase Than I am to be a nun.

1672. HOWARD, *All Mistaken*, iii. The very same, my METTLED female.

1785. GROSE, *Vulg. Tongue*, s.v.

TO FETCH METTLE, *verb. phr.* (venery).—To masturbate.—GROSE (1785). For synonyms see FRIG.

METTLESOME, *adj.* (old : now recognised).—Bold; spirited.—GROSE (1785). [Cf. METTLE].

MEW-MEW! *intj.* (tailors').—In sarcasm: 'tell that to the MARINES' (q.v.).

MICE-FEET. TO MAKE MICE-FEET o', *verb. phr.* (old Scots').—To destroy wholly.

MICH, MICHER, MICHERY, MICHING. See MIKE, MIKER, MIKERY, and MIKING.

MICHAEL, *subs.* (old).—A man.

1647. FLETCHER, *Woman's Prize*, i. 4. There are more maids than Maudlin. And more men than MICHAEL.

1785. GROSE, *Vulg. Tongue*, s.v. MICHAEL. Hip, MICHAEL, your head's on fire. See HYP.

MICK (MIKE or MICKY), *subs.* (American).—1. An Irishman. Cf. MIKER.

1869. S. L. CLEMENS ('Mark Twain'), *Innocents at Home*, 22. The MICKS got to throwing stones.

2. (Australian).—A young wild bull.

1881. GRANT, *Bush-life*, i. 227. There were two or three MICKIES and wild heifers.

MID (or MIDDY), *subs.* (common).—A midshipman.

1812. SOUTHEY, *Letters* [ed. WARTER, 1856], ii. 315. I have written to Bedford to learn what MIDS of the Victory fell in that action.

1886. M. SCOTT, *Tom Cringle's Log*, xii. The purser and doctor, and three of the MIDDIES forward, Thomas Cringle, gent., pulling the stroke-oar.

1847. LYTTON, *Lucretia*, pt. II. ch. I. Percival was meant for the navy, and even served as a MID for a year or so.

MIDDEN, *subs.* (Scots').—A foul slattern; a HEAP (q.v.). [MIDDEN = dunghill].

AN EATING MIDDEN, *subs. phr.* (Scots').—A glutton; a belly-god.

MIDDIES, *subs.* (Stock Exchange).—Midland Railway Ordinary Stock.

MIDDLE, *subs.* (venery).—1. The waist.

1640. *Wit's Recr.* [HOTTEN], 136. I care not, let my friend go fiddle; Let him mark her end, I'll mark her MIDDLE.

1719. T. D'URFEY, *Pills to Purge*, v. 79. In troth sweet Robin, I cannot, He hath got me about the MIDDLE.—*Ibid.* VI. 31. He took her by the MIDDLE, and taught her by the flute.

2. (Fleet St.).—See quot.

1887. *Walford's Antiquarian*, Ap., 283. The writer of social, literary and scientific articles for the press is said to be a writer of MIDDLES, or a Middleman.

3. (Old Cant).—A finger.

MIDDLE-CUT, *subs.* (Winchester College).—See quot. and DISPAR.

1866. MANSFIELD, *School Life*, p. 84. There were . . . eight [portions] to a leg of mutton . . . the thick slice out of the centre of the leg was called a MIDDLE CUT.

MIDDLE-FINGER (or LEG), *subs.* (venery).—The *penis*. For synonyms see CREAMSTICK and PRICK.

MIDDLE-GATE, *subs.* (venery).—1. The female *pudendum*. For synonyms see MONOSYLLABLE.

1692. *Gentlemen's Journal*, Aug., p. 8. You must as cautionary [an earnest] give a gate—that MIDDLE GATE which leads to th' seat of bliss.

MIDDLE-KINGDOM, *subs.* (venery).—The female *pudendum*. For synonyms see MONOSYLLABLE.

MIDDLE-MATCH. See MATCH.

MIDDLE-MESS, *subs.* (Winchester College).—See MESS.

MIDDLE-PIECE, *subs.* (common).—The stomach. For synonyms see VICTUALLING-OFFICE. Also MIDDLE-PIE and MIDDLE-STOREY.

1675. CROWNE, *Country Wit*, iv. 1. I'll lodge a cudgel in your MIDDLE-STOREY backward.

1859. MATSELL, *Vocabulum*, s.v.

MIDDLING, *adv.* (colloquial).—Tolerably; moderately.

1869. H. B. STOWE, *Oldtown*, p. 31. Wal, I don't jedge him nor nobody . . . Don't none on us do more than MIDDLIN' well?

Phr. (tailors').—'I don't think so.' 'I don't believe what you say.'

MIDDY. See MID.

MIDGE, *subs.* (provincial).—A small one-horse carriage used in the Isle of Wight.

MIDGE-NET, *subs.* (common).—A lady's veil.

MIDGET, *subs.* (colloquial).—Anything small of its kind; *e.g.*, a sprightly child.

1869. H. B. STOWE, *Oldtown*, p. 177. Now you know Parson Kendall's a little MIDGET of a man.

MIDLANDS, *subs. phr.* (venery).—The female *pudendum*. For synonyms see MONOSYLLABLE.

MIDNIGHT, *subs.* (American).—Sarsparilla. MIDNIGHT WITHOUT = sarsparilla without ice.

AS WHITE AS MIDNIGHT'S ARSE-HOLE, *phr.* (old).—As black as may be.

1557-8. *Jacob & Esau* [DODSLEY, *Old Plays* (1874), ii. 253]. As WHITE AS MIDNIGHT'S ARSE-HOLE or virgin pitch.

MIDSHIPMAN'S-HALF-PAY, *subs.* (nautical).—See quot. and MONKEY'S ALLOWANCE.

1856. C. KINGSLEY, *Letters* [3rd abridged ed. 1879], May. You fellows worked like bricks, spent money, and got MIDSHIPMAN'S HALF-PAY (nothing a-day and find yourself) and monkey's allowance (more kicks than halfpence).

MIDSHIPMAN'S-NUTS, *subs.* (nautical).—Broken biscuit, eaten by way of dessert.

MIDSHIPMAN'S WATCH AND CHAIN, *subs. phr.* (old).—See quot.

1785. GROSE, *Vulg. Tongue*, s.v. . . . . a sheep's heart and pluck.

MIDSHIPMITE, *subs.* (colloquial).—A diminutive midshipman.

1833. MARRYAT, *Peter Simple*, I. p. 56. 'Clap on here Peg,' cried the woman to another, 'and lets have this little MIDSHIPMITE, I wants a baby to dry nurse.'

1877. W. S. GILBERT, *Bab Ballads*, 'Yarn of the Nancy Bell.' A bosun tight and a MIDSHIPMITE.

MIFF, *subs.* (old).—A petty quarrel; a tantrum.

1623. BUTLER, *Feminine Monarchy*, c. 5. Fol. L. 4. Your remedy is to knocke out the bees upon the mantle between two single Rests, and to set a fitter Hive over them; but this is not to be done before the swarming hours be fast, lest some of the bees take a MIFF.

1749. FIELDING, *Tom Jones*, Bk. III. ch. vi. When a little quarrel, or MIFF, as it is vulgarly called, arose between them.

1768. GOLDSMITH, *Good-Natured Man*, iv. It's the worst luck in the world, in anything but white. I knew one Bett Stubbs, of our town, that was married in red; and, as sure as eggs is eggs, the bridegroom and she had a MIFF before morning.

1816. SCOTT, *Antiquary*, v. In accomplishing an arrangement between tendencies so opposite, little MIFFS would occasionally take place.

Verb. (old).—1. To offend; and (2) to fall out.

Adj. (old).—Angered; MIFFED.

1802. W. TAYLOR, in *Robberds's Memoir*, i. 447. You are right about Burnett, but being MIFF with him myself, I would not plead against him in the least particular.

1825. SCOTT, *Diary*, in *Life*, VIII. 133. This is not the way to make her pluck a bawbee and Lord M—, a little MIFFED in turn sends the whole correspondence to me.

MIFF-MAFF, *subs.* (provincial).—Nonsense; ROT (*q.v.*).

MIFFY, *subs.* (common).—The devil; OLD SCRATCH (*q.v.*).

MIFTY, *adv.* (old).—*See* quot. *Cf.* MIFF.

1690. B. E., *Dict. Cant. Crew*, s.v. MIFTY, apt to take Pet, or be out of Humour.

MIGHTY (or **MIGHTILY**), *adj.* and *adv.* (colloquial).— *See* quot. 1755. Also MIGHTILY.

1596. SHAKSPEARE, *Merry Wives*, iii. 3. 221. You do yourself MIGHTY wrong, Master Ford.

1609. FLETCHER, *Wild-Goose Chase*, iv. 2. This is some MIGHTY dairy-maid in man's clothes.

1668. PEPYS, *Diary*, 26 Sept. To my house, where D. Gauden did talk a little, and he do MIGHTILY acknowledge my kindness to him.

1693. CONGREVE, *Old Bachelor*, i. 1. Your son's MIGHTY like his Grace, has just his smile and air of's face.

1695. CONGREVE, *Love for Love*, iii. 4. *Scan.* Your lady says your sleep has been unquiet of late. . . . *Mrs. Fore.* O MIGHTY restless.

1712. STEELE, *Spectator*, No. 438. This gentleman deals MIGHTILY in what we call the irony.

*d.*1721. PRIOR, in *Wks.* [quoted in *Ency. Dict.*]. He reigns: How long? Till some usurper rise, And he too MIGHTY thoughtful, MIGHTY wise: Studies new lines.

1738. POPE, *Epilogue to Sat.*, ii. 133. But let me add, Sir Robert's MIGHTY dull.

1755. JOHNSON, *Eng. Dict.*, s.v. MIGHTY. In a great degree. Not to be used but in very low language.

1775. SHERIDAN, *The Rivals*, iv. 3. There is a probability of succeeding about that fellow that is MIGHTY provoking.

1780. CHASTELLUX, *Travels in N. Am.*, ii. 14. On my asking him the next morning how he found himself, he answered, MIGHTY weak. *Ibid.* [Note by translator]. MIGHTY little, MIGHTY few, MIGHTY weak, &c., are favorite expressions in America.

1793. LD. H. SPENCER, in *Auckland Correspondence*, III. 83 (1862). Madame Bosset is arrived, and MIGHTY plain.

1793. BURNS, *Impromptu on Mrs. ——'s Birthday*. Now, Jove, for once be MIGHTY civil.

1802. C. K. SHARPE, in *Correspondence* (1882), i. 152. He is a MIGHTY neat, pretty little, fiddling fellow, and exceedingly finely bred.

1844. KENDALL, *Santa Fé Expedition*, i. 32. You'll be MIGHTY apt to get wet, said a thorough-bred Texan, who stood watching our movements.

1846-7. DICKENS, *Dombey and Son*, xi. The Doctor's was a MIGHTY fine house, fronting the sea.

1847. HALLIWELL, *Archaic and Provincial Words*, etc., s.v. MIGHTY, fine, gay.

1848. *Georgia Scenes*, 84. His face is MIGHTY little for his body.

1892. GUNTER, *Miss Dividends*, iii. I am MIGHTY glad.

HIGH AND MIGHTY, *phr.* (common).—Consequential; full of 'airs'.

1892. HENLEY and STEVENSON, *Deacon Brodie*, Act.Sc.2,p.10. Ye needna be sae HIGH AND MIGHTY, onyway.

MIKE, *subs.* (common).—1. An Irishman.

2. *See* MIKER.

3. *See* MICKY.

Verb. (common).—1. To lurk; to skulk; to hang about: also TO DO A MIKE (or MOUCH). Also MICH, MICHE, MOOCH, or MOUCH. For synonyms *see* LOAF.

149[?]. *Towneley Mysteries* ('Judicium'), *Surtees Soc. Pub.* (1835), p. 320. The negons thai MOWCHID, and hadde no wile.

1598. FLORIO, *A Worlde of Wordes*, s.v. *Fare a chetichegli* . . . . to sneake or MICH about lurkingly.

*d.*1599. SPENSER, *View of the State of Ireland* [*Ency. Dict*]. 'Straggle up and down the country, or MICH in corners amongst their friends idlely.'

1612. CHAPMAN, *Widow's Tears* [DODSLEY, *Old Plays*, vi. 212]. Not for this MICHING base transgression Of truant negligence.

1613. BEAUMONT and FLETCHER, *Hon. Man's F.*, v. 1. Say we should all MEACH here, and stay the feast now, What can the worst be? we have plaid the knaves, That's without question.

1825. EGAN, *Life of an Actor*, p. 28. MIKE or *Shammock*. Technical or cant phrases amongst printers. To have a MIKE is to loiter away the time, when it might be more usefully or profitably employed.

1851-61. H. MAYHEW, *London Lab.*, i. p. 472. These hedge fellows are slow and dull; they go MOUCHING along as if they were croaking themselves.

1876. HINDLEY, *Adventures of a Cheap Jack*, p. 59. When not employed MOUCHED about.

1887. W. E. HENLEY, *Villon's Good Night*. You spongers MIKING round the pubs.

1888. *Cornhill Mag.*, Febr., p. 178. The poacher is a product of sleepy village life, and usually MOUCHES on the outskirts of country towns.

1888. ROLF BOLDREWOOD, *Robbery Under Arms*, xxii. MOOCHING about cattle.

2. (old).—To play truant; to CHARLEY-WAG (*q.v.*).

1581. LYLY, *Euphues*, 29. What made the gods so often to trewant from heaven, and MICH here on earth.

1787. GROSE, *Prov. Glossary*, s.v. MOOCH.

3. (tramps').—To hang about: for alms, a job, or a chance to pilfer. Also ON THE MOUCH.

1888. *Daily Telegraph*, 27 Nov. Yet it might safely be wagered that, while the poor street folk who pick up a precarious livelihood in this way would not resent being called costermongers, they would be bitterly offended at being stigmatised as mouchers, and would hotly assert that they never MOUCHED a penny from anybody.

1888. *Indoor Paupers*, i. Most of these people knew how to MOUCH or beg with skill and effect, while I could not beg at all.

1888. *Bulletin*, Nov. 24. All the dead-beats and suspected hen-snatchers plead when before the Bench that they were 'only MOUCHING ROUND to find out whether the family neglected its religious dooties, yer washup.'

4. (old).—To steal.

1655. *History of Francion* [NARES]. The eagle more mindfull of prey than honour, did one day MOOTCH from the thunder which lame Vulcan had made, as crooked as himself, for almighty Jupiter.

1862. H. MAYHEW, *Lon. Lab.*, iv. 418. I don't mean to say that if I see anything laying about handy that I don't MOUCH it (*i.e.*, steal it).

MIKER (**MOUCHER**, or **MOOCHER**), *subs.* (common).—A skulker; a petty thief; a beggar. Also, a truant. Also MICH and MICHER. *See* quots. *passim*. For synonyms *see* LOAFER.

1360. CHAUCER, *Rom. of Rose* [SKEAT (1894), i. 241. 6541]. Unne the that he nis a MICHER.

1450-1500. *Gesta Roman.* I. ch. 28, 94. The first [duty] is to wake in goode werkes, when othere men slepithe in synne, and for to slepe, when othere men wakithe, dothe thevis and MYCHERS.

149[?]. *Towneley Mysteries* [*Surtees Soc.'s Pub.* (1835), p. 216]. Thefes and MYCHERS keyn.

15[?]. *Babees Book* [E. E. T. S.], 401. Chyld, be thou lyer nother no theffe: Be thou no MECHER for myscheffe.

*c.*1520. *Hycke Scorner* [DODSLEY, *Old Plays* (1874), i. 164]. Wanton wenches, and also MICHERS.

1590. GREENE, *Mourning Garment* [GROSART (1881-6), ix. 133]. If Aristotle had still, like a MICHER been stewed up in Stagyra.

1592. NASHE, *Summer's Last Will* [DODSLEY, *Old Plays* (1874), viii. 57]. I know thou art but a MICHER, and dar'st not stand me.

1598. FLORIO, *A Worlde of Wordes*, s.v. *Pillucone*, a sot, a coxcombe, a dodger, a wrangler, a MICHER.

1598. SHAKSPEARE, *1 Henry IV*, ii. 4. Shall the blessed sun of heaven prove a MICHER and eat blackberries?

1611. COTGRAVE, *Dict.*, s.v. *Caqueraffe*, a base MICHER, scurvie hagler, lowsie dodger, etc.

1755. JOHNSON, *Eng. Dict.*, s.v. MICHER. A lazy loiterer, who skulks about in corners and by-places, and keeps out of sight; a hedge-creeper. *Mich* or *mick* is still retained in the cant language for an indolent, lazy fellow. It is used in the western counties for a truant boy.

1775. ASH, *Eng. Dict.*, s.v. MICH (a local word). An indolent lazy fellow.

1847. HALLIWELL, *Archaic and Provincial Words*, s.v. MICH. MICHER . . . may be explained, a sly thief, one who steals things of small value, or more usually, a truant or skulking fellow . . . . It was often used as a term of contempt; Hollyband gives it as the translation of *Caignard*, and Cotgrave has, '*Chiche-face*, a chichiface, MICHER, sneake-bill, wretched fellow.'

1867. *London Herald*, 23 Mar., p. 221. If . . . asked . . . . what he was doing, he would have said he was ON THE MOUCH, which being interpreted—French, *mouchard*, a spy; English MOUCHER, to be on the look-out for something.

1888. *Indoor Paupers*, 33. Another and about as numerous a class of Ins and Outs, whose members come and go and come again even more frequently than the tiptop-spree fellows, are the MOUCHERS or cadgers.

1888. *Cornhill Mag.*, Feb., p. 182. It has been already remarked that the poacher is nothing if not a specialist. As yet we have spoken only of the MOUCHER, who directs his attention to fur.

1888. *Daily Telegraph*, 27 Nov. [A MICHER is] one who lives a semi-vagabond life, selling watercresses, wild flowers, blackberries, and other things that may be obtained in country places for the gathering. He is a vendor, too, of dandelion leaves, parsley, sow-thistle, clover, and so forth, as food for the myriads of tame rabbits kept in towns.

MIKING (**MOOCHING** or **MOUCHING**), *subs.* (common).—1. Prowling; (2) pilfering; and (3) playing-truant. Also MICHERY and MIKERY.

1393. GOWER, *Conf. Amant*, v. Nowe thou shalt fall sore able That like stelthe of MICHERIE. *Ibid.* For no man of his counsaile knoweth What he maie gette of his MICHYNGE.

*c.*1420-80. HENRYSON, *Fables*, 'The Fox and the Wolf' l. 5. That durst no more with MICHING intermell.

1596. SHAKSPEARE, *Hamlet*, iii. 2, 147. Marry, this is MICHING mallecho; it means mischief.

1603. DEKKER, *Wonderful Yeare*, [GROSART (1886), i. 113]. Yet went they (most bitterly) MICHING and muffled vp and downe.

1892. HUME NISBET, *Bushranger's Sweetheart*, p. 115. Sandy Macintosh looked fit for anything, from MOUCHING up to murder, so long as not too much courage was required.

Adj. (common).—1. Skulking; (2) lurking; (3) mean.

15[?]. *Songs & Poems on Costume* [Percy Soc.], 687. Nothinge so fearde we are of theves Which ofte are layde in jayles, As now we are of MYCHING knaves, That cut off horses tayles.

1616. BEAUMONT & FLETCHER, *Scornful Lady*, v. 1. Some MEECHING rascal in her house.

1648. HERRICK, *Hesp.*, II. 67. A cat I keep That plays about my house, Grown fat With eating many a MICHING mouse.

1822. SCOTT, *Fortunes of Nigel*, xxiii. To mingle the soul of martial honour with thy thieving, MICHING, petty-larceny blood.

1862. LOWELL, *Biglow Papers*, 2nd Ser. p. 13. But I ain't o' the MEECHIN' kind, thet sets an' thinks fer weeks The bottom's out o' th'univarse coz their own gill-pot leaks.

1890. S. O. JEWETT, *Deephaven*, p. 159. 'How came the ship to run up a tailor's bill?' 'Why, them's mine,' said the captain, very MEECHING.

MILCH-COW, *subs.* (colloquial).—*See* quot. 1785. Hence any living source of alms or revenue.

1690. B. E., *Dict. Cant. Crew*, s.v. MILCH-KINE.

1785. GROSE, *Vulg. Tongue*, s.v. MILCH-COW. One who is easily tricked out of his property: a term used by gaolers, for prisoners who have money, and bleed freely.

1859. MATSELL, *Vocabulum*, s.v.

MILD, *adj.* (common).—Second-rate; feeble; inefficient.

1885. *Sat. Review*, 7 Feb., p. 166. Most of us have no wish to cheat railway companies by travelling first class at third-class prices, but there are ingenious adventurers who practise this MILD swindle.

DRAW IT MILD! *See* DRAW.

MILD-BLOATER. *See* BLOATER.

MILER (or **MYLA**), *subs.* (vagrants').—An ass. *See* MOKE.

MILES'S BOY. *See* RALPH.

MILESTONE, *subs.* (old).—A country booby.—VAUX (1823).

MILESTONE-MONGER, *subs.* (common).—A tramp.

MILK, *subs.* (venery).—SPENDINGS (*q.v.*).

1669. JOHN AUBREY, *MS. Aubr.*, 21. Her breath is sweet as the rose in June Her skin is as soft as silk And if you tickle her in the flank She'll freely give down her MILK.

Verb. (venery).—1. To cause ejaculation. *Cf.* MILKMAN.

1610. JONSON, *Alchymist*, iii. 2. For she must MILK his epididimis.

1719. DURFEY, *Pills to Purge*, iii. 108. May teach her how to sleep all Night, And take a great deal more Delight, To MILK the cows than thee.

2. (old).—To plunder.

*d.*1536. TYNDALL, *Workes*, p. 365. 'And to ayd the kynge in hys right must the commons be MILKED till they bleede agayne.'

1605. JONSON, *Volpone*, i. 1. This three year I have MILKED their hopes.

1808. JAMIESON, *Dict. Scot. Lang.*, s.v. MILK.

3. (old racing).—To bet against a horse, which is one's own pro-

perty but is not meant to win; to keep him a favourite, at short odds, for a race in which he has no chance whatever, or in which he will not be run.

1862. *Times*, 2 Jan., p. 8, col. 6. If men of fortune and honour will permit their pastime to be sullied by such tricks as MILKING—by keeping a horse a favorite at short odds for a race in which he has no chance whatever, only to lay against him—etc.

1863. *Fraser's Mag.*, Dec. 'The English Turf.' MILKING then is an expressive term for getting as much as possible out of a horse.

1869. W. BRADWOOD, *The O.V.H.* xx. They'll accuse you—or rather me, for he's entered in my name and colours—of MILKING right and left. . . . It's far simpler to let him run for the public money, and save a jaw and a long explanation.

1870. *Field*, 14 May, 'The Present Condition of the Turf.' We are not in the habit of producing examples of the proceedings at our race meetings, which are in vulgar language described as MILKING and roping, because we believe them to be so common that it would be unjust to select any one in particular for animadversion.

1871. *Fun*, 4 Nov. MILKING we fear is inseparably connected with the turf; we noted that sporting journals of the highest class picked 'the cream' of the autumn handicaps.

1888. *Referee*, 11 Oct. The assumption that no horse other than Paradox has ever been MILKED in open market, and many thousands of pounds made out of the transaction, is a trifle too utopian for present emergencies.

4. (general).—To get possession by artifice: as, TO MILK a telegram = to get access to it before the addressee. *Cf.* MILKER, sense 1.

1860. PRESCOTT, *Electrical Invent.*, p. 108. The rapidity and simplicity of the means by which a wire could be MILKED without being cut, or put out of circuit struck the whole of the party.

1869. *Times*, 14 August [quoted in BREWER'S *Phrase & Fable*, s.v. 'Telegram']. They receive their telegrams in cipher to avoid the risk of their being MILKED by rival journals.

1871. *Milk Journal.* MILKING the wires is telegraphic slang for tapping the wires. . . . In India wires have been MILKED for fraudulent commercial purposes.

1884. *Saturday Review*, 10 May, p. 607. The Central News telegram, if it was MILKED at all, was MILKED through the medium of Sir C. Wilson's, etc.

5. (old).—To exhaust; to drain.

1642. SYMMONS, *Vindication*, 175. Tho' perhaps they have been pilled and MILK'D a few years longer by these new-states-men it will be confessed that the old government [that of the king] was far the better and more easie.

TO GIVE DOWN MILK, *verb. phr.* (old).—To pay.

1655. R. LESTRANGE, *The Reign of King Charles*, p. 187. The City was sullen, would not GIVE DOWN THEIR MILK, and pleaded want of trade and poverty.

TO MILK THE PIGEON, *verb. phr.* (common).—To attempt impossibilities: *cf.* PIGEON'S MILK.

1785. GROSE, *Vulg. Tongue*, s.v.

TO MILK THE STREET, *verb. phr.* (American).—To hold stock so well in hand as to make it fluctuate as you will.

1870. MEDBERY, *Men and Mysteries of Wall St.*, 336. There is a distinction between the cliques and brokers . . . . Great operators rob the brokers by destroying their customers. To use the slang of the financial quarter, they MILK THE STREET.

1876. *New York Tribune* [BARTLETT]. The majority of stocks are still blocked, and the market, so far as possible, worked entirely upon the MILKING process.

TO MILK OVER THE FENCE, *verb. phr.* (common).—*See* quot.

1871. *Milk Journal*, Sept. Stealing milk from neighbours' cows is . . . known as MILKING OVER THE FENCE.

NO MILK IN THE COCOA-NUT, *adj. phr.* (common).—Silly or crazed. For synonyms *see* APARTMENTS TO LET.

BRISTOL-MILK. *See* BRISTOL.

MILK-AND-MOLASSES, *subs.* (American).—*See* quot.

1833. NEAL, *Down Easters*, VII. p. 96. The people of this country are of two colours, black and white . . . or half-and-half sometimes at the south, where they are called MILK-AND-MOLASSES.

MILK-AND-WATER, *subs.* (old).—1. A stuff under this strange designation appears in 16th century inventories, but we have no guide as to what determined its title.—*Draper's Dict.*

1555. *Inventory* of Richard Gurnell, a Kendal clothier, xj. Yards of MYLKE AND WATTER, 18s.

1571. *Inventory* of John Wilkenson, of Newcastle, j. Piece of MYLK AND WATTER.

2. (venery).—*See* quot.

1785. GROSE, *Vulgar Tongue*, s.v. MILK-AND-WATER. Both ends of the busk. [An old world toast].

Adj. (colloquial).—Insipid: undistinguished; harmless.

1823. BYRON, *Don Juan*, C. VIII. stanza 80. And one good action in the midst of crimes Is 'quite refreshing,' in the affected phrase Of these ambrosial Pharisaic times, With all their pretty MILK-AND-WATER ways.

1847. THACKERAY, *Vanity Fair*, iv. Simple appeals to the affections, which people understood better than the MILK-AND-WATER *lagrime, sospiri*, and *felicità* of the eternal Donizettian music with which we are favoured now-a-days.

1861. C. READE, *Cloister and the Hearth*, XXVI. A MILK-AND-WATER bourgeois.

1889. *Star*, 12 Dec., p. 7, col. 1. The giant will be no MILK-AND-WATER giant, as young Mr. Geo. Conquest will represent him.

MILKER, *subs.* (common).—1. *See* quot. and MILK, *verb.* sense 4.

1891. *Cassell's Sat. Jour.*, Sept., p. 1036, col. 2. When a telegram sent to a specific person is surreptitiously made use of or drawn from by others, it is said to have been 'milked;' and those who thus steal are called MILKERS. To guard, as far as possible, against this being done, important special and press messages from abroad, and sometimes home telegrams also, are written in cipher.

2. (venery).—The female *pudendum*. Also MILKING-PAIL, MILK-JUG, and MILK-PAN. For synonyms *see* MONOSYLLABLE.

3. (colloquial).—A milk-giver.

1854. *Quarterly Rev.*, cxlv. 292. One individual, several years ago, possessed 1500 MILKERS.

MILKER'S-CALF, *subs.* (Australian).—A calf yet with the cow; hence, a mother's boy or girl.

1888. ROLF BOLDREWOOD, *Robbery Under Arms*, i. I used to laugh at him, and call him a regular old crawler of a MILKER'S CALF in the old days.

MILK-FEVER. *See* PENCIL-FEVER.

MILK-HOLE, *subs.* (Winchester College).—The hole formed by the ROUSH (*q.v.*) under a POT (*q.v.*).—*Notions.*

MILKING-PAIL. TO WORK (or CARRY) THE MILKING-PAIL, *verb. phr.* (old racing).—*See* MILK, *verb.*, sense 3.

*c.*186[?]. *Baily's Magazine.* These *al fresco* speculators have their 'dead uns' and carry MILKING-PAILS like their more civilized brethren privileged with the *entrée* to the clubs and the Corner.

MILK-LIVERED, *adj.* (old colloquial).—Timid; cowardly.

1605-6. SHAKSPEARE, *King Lear*, iv. 2. *Gon.* MILK-LIVER'D man! That bear'st a cheek for blows, a head for wrongs.

MILKMAN (MILKER, or MILK-WOMAN), *subs.* (venery).—A trader in masturbation; a SHAGSTER (*q.v.*).

MILK-SHOP (MILK-WALK, or MILKY WAY), *subs.* (common).—The paps. For synonyms *see* DAIRIES.

1640. *Wit's Recr.* [HOTTEN], 363. Her breast. . . . Bears up two globes. . . . Which headed with two rich round Rubies, show Like wanton Rose-buds. . . . And in the MILKY-VALLEY that's between, sits Cupid.

MILK-SOP, *subs.* (old: now recognised).—A coward; a ladified man; a novice; a MEACOCK (*q.v.*).

1390. CHAUCER, *Monkes Tale*, b. 15396. 'Allas!' sche saith, 'that ever I was i-schape, To wedde a MYLK-SOP or a coward ape.'

1590. GREENE, *Mourning Garment* [GROSART (1881-6), ix. 173]. What is it for mee to pinne a fayre meacocke and a witty MILKSOP on my sleaue who dare not answere with their swords in the face of the enemy?

1593. HARVEY, *Pierces Supercr.* [GROSART (1885), ii. 17]. Are MILKSOP Muses such whiteliuer'd Trontes?

1598. FLORIO, *Worlde of Wordes*, s.v. *Biancone*, a goodly, great MILKE-SAPPE, a fresh-water soldier.

1600. SHAKSPEARE, *Much Ado*, v. 1. Boys, apes, braggarts, Jacks, MILK-SOPS.

1603. DEKKER, *Patient Grissill* [GROSART (1886), v. 167]. Fye, Signior; no musicke in your mouth but battles, yet a meere MILKESOP?

1618. FIELD, *Amends for Ladies*, iv. 2. Thou art a faint-hearted fellow, a MILK-SOP.

1621. BURTON, *Anat.*, p. 143. 'Tis now come to that pass that he is no gentleman, a very MILK-SOP, a clown.

1660. TATHAM, *The Rump*, i. [MAIDMENT (1873), p. 202]. A meer MILK-SOP . . . A wheybrain'd fellow.

1892. *Evening Standard*, 25 Nov. p. 4, c. 5. Everyone knows how boys dread being set down as MILKSOPS.

MILK-WOMAN, *subs.* (Scots' colloquial).—1. A wet-nurse. GREEN MILK-WOMAN = a woman recently delivered.

2. (venery).—*See* MILKMAN.

MILKY ONES, *subs. phr.* (common).—White linen rags. MILKY-DUDS = white clothes. — MATSELL (1859).

MILL, *subs.* (pugilistic).—1. A fight; a SET-TO (*q.v.*).

1785. GROSE, *Vulg. Tongue*, s.v.

1819. MOORE, *Tom Crib's Memorial*, p. 36. We, who're of the fancy-lay, As dead hands at a MILL as they.

1823. W. T. MONCRIEFF, *Tom & Jerry*, ii. 1. *Cribb.* Thank'ye, gentleman, thank'ye—but as I see by our sporting oracle, 'The Dispatch,' there's a MILL on foot—I'll give you, '*May the best man win.*'

1834. AINSWORTH, *Rookwood*, 'The Double Cross.' The MILL is o'er, the crosser crost, The loser's won, the winner's lost!

1843. *Comic Almanack*, 378, 'Stoppage of the Mills.' Indeed, I never saw the like, Our minds with wonder it must fill, Though MILLS ensue when people strike, The strikes have stopp'd full many a mill.

1853. *Diogenes*, ii. p. 134. *Bell's Life* the other day told us of two noted pugilists who (we quote the very words), 'had a MILL for 200*l*.' When the decimal coinage is established, they will be able to have no less than five 'mils' for a penny.

1856. T. HUGHES, *Tom Brown's School-Days*, Pt. II. ch. v. A champion was picked out on each side tacitly, who settled the matter by a good hearty MILL.

1860. THE DRUID, *Post and Paddock*, 'The Fight for the Belt.' By sea and by land, in village and town, Nothing whatever seemed to go down, Save the latest *on dit* of the MILL.

1862. *The Cork Examiner*, 28 March. Since this little event there have been . . . . some very exciting little MILLS.

1883. *Saturday Review*, 31 March, p. 398, col. 1. This apparently harmless elderly victim was a retired light-weight prize-fighter, and so, with the ready consent of everybody, a MILL was arranged.

2. (thieves').—1. The treadmill; (2) a prison.

1837. BARHAM, *Ingoldsby Legends*, 2nd Ser., p. 156 (ed. 1851). A landsman said, 'I twig the chap—he's been upon the MILL.'

1838. DICKENS, *Oliver Twist*, viii. 'Was you never on the MILL?' 'What MILL?' inquired Oliver. 'What MILL!—why, *the* MILL—the MILL as takes up so little room that it'll work inside a stone jug, and always goes better when the wind's low with people than when it's high, acos then they can't get workmen.'

1851-61. MAYHEW, *Lond. Lab. etc.*, i. 390. A few weeks after I was grabbed for this, and got a month at the MILL.

1853. WH. MELVILLE, *Digby Grand*, x. The latter worthy... gave a policeman such a licking the other night, that he was within an ace of getting a month at the MILL.

3. (obsolete).—The old Insolvent Debtors' Court. Hence, TO GO THROUGH THE MILL = to be adjudicated bankrupt.

4. (military).—A guard-room in barracks; a JIGGER (*q.v.*).

5. (venery).—The female *pudendum*. For synonyms *see* MONOSYLLABLE. *Cf.* GRIND.

1719. DURFEY, *Pills etc.* (quoted in), v. 139. For Peggy is a bonny lass, and grinds well her MILL, For she will be Occupied when others they lie still.

6. (old).—A chisel.—GROSE (1785); MATSELL (1859).

Verb. (pugilistic).—1. To fight; to pummel; to kill: *see* quot. 1748. TO MILL THE NOB = to punch the head.

1748. T. DYCHE, *Dictionary* (5th ed.). MILL . . . . in the *Canting Language*, means to beat, thresh, maul, or kill a person.

1785. GROSE, *Vulg. Tongue*, s.v.

1818. P. EGAN, *Boxiana*, i. 10. When his Lordship, instead of redressing, set about MILLING him for his insolence.

1840. THACKERAY, *Shabby Genteel Story*, viii. He had MILLED a policeman.

1840. BARHAM, *Ingoldsby Legends (The Ghost)*. Boxing may be a very pretty *Fancy*, When Messrs. Burke or Bendigo engage:—'Tis not so well in Susan, Jane, or Nancy:—To get well MILL'D by any one's an evil, But by a lady—'tis the very Devil.

1864. *Eton School Days*, iii. 38. Science, you know, is better than brute force, and although Chorley is older and bigger than me, if I knew how to MILL I wouldn't stand still to be licked.

2. (old).—To rob. Also to break or force. MILL-LAY (GROSE, 1785) = burglary.

1567. HARMAN, *Caveat* (1869), p. 86. Yonder dwelleth a quyere cuffen, it were beneship to MYLL him.

1598. STOW, *Survey of London* (ed. 1754, vol. II. p. 543). Add one phrase more in those times used among this sort, MYLKEN, which is to commit a robbery, or Burghlary in the night in a dwelling house.

1609. DEKKER, *Lanthorne & Candlelight* [GROSART, iii. p. 203], 'The Beggar's Curse.' The Ruffin cly the ghost of the Harman-beck . . . . If we niggle or MILL but a poor Boozing-KEN . . . . Straight we're to the Cuffin Queer forced to bing.

1611. MIDDLETON and DEKKER, *Roaring Girl*, v. 1. A gage of ben Rom-bouse . . . is benar than a Caster, Peck, pennam, lay, or popler, Which we MILL in deause-a-vile.

1621. JONSON, *Gipsies Metamorphosed.* Can they cant or MILL? Are they masters in their art?

1622-65. HEAD and KIRKMAN, *English Rogue*, 'Bing out, bien Morts.' To MILL each KEN let cove bing then Thro' Ruffmans, Jague, or Laund.

1661. FLETCHER, *Beggar's Bush*, v. 1. Tell us If it be MILLING of a lag of duds, The fetching-off a buck of clothes, or so?

1690. B. E., *Dict. Cant. Crew*, s.v.

1712. T. SHIRLEY, *Triumph of Wit*, 'The Maunder's Praise of His Strowling

Mort.' If Lour we want; I'll MILL A gage, or nip for thee a bung.

1724. E. COLES, *Eng. Dict.*, s.v.

1754. *Disc. John Poulter*, 14. While we went a MILLING that swag.

1785. GROSE, *Vulg. Tongue*, s.v. MILL. To rob; also to break, beat out, or kill. I'll MILL your glaze; I'll beat out your eye. To MILL a bleating cheat; to kill a sheep. To MILL a ken; to rob a house.

1790. A. WILSON, *Poems*, 73. His dearie glad of siccan routh, To MILL a note was aye right ready.

1829. SCOTT, *Mid-Lothian*, xxx. Rot me, one might have MILLED the Bank of England and less noise about it.

3. (thieves').—To send to the tread-mill.

1838-9. DICKENS, *Oliver Twist*, p. 122 (ed. 1859). 'So I *do* do as she bids me,' replied Mr. Chitling; 'I shouldn't have been MILLED if 't hadn't been for her.'

TO GO THROUGH (or BE ON) THE MILL, *verb. phr.* (common). —1. To go through the Bankruptcy Court; to be WHITEWASHED (*q.v.*). *See* MILL, *subs.* sense 3.

2. (colloquial).—To pass through a more or less severe course of discipline, experience, or training.

1829. SCOTT, *Heart of Midlothian*, xxxi. 'She [Jeanie Deans] 's got a jark from Jim Ratcliffe' said the short fellow 'and Frank won't hear of our PUTTING HER THROUGH THE MILL.

1858. W. W. PRATT, *Ten Nights in a Bar-room*, ii. 1. P'raps you have BEEN THROUGH THE MILL.

1872. *Fun*, 10 Aug. 'Over.' One more year ON THE MILL, Twelve months more at the pen, Ere I of respite again have my fill—

1883. *Referee*, 1 July, p. 2, col. 4. He hinted at the hardships which many actors and actresses have to endure, and did not disguise the fact that he had himself BEEN THROUGH THE MILL.

1887. *Contemp. Rev.*, li. 10. Certain persons who have GONE THROUGH THE MILL of what is known as our 'higher education.'

3. (thieves').—*See* MILL, *verb.* 3.

1889. *Daily News*, 4 July. He had BEEN THROUGH THE MILL, and could do it again.

TO BRING GRIST TO THE MILL, *verb. phr.* (colloquial).—To be a source of profit.

1726. AYLIFFE, *Parergon [Century]*. The computation of degrees, in all matrimonial causes, is wont to be made according to the rules of that law, because it BRINGS GRIST TO THE MILL.

TO PUT THROUGH THE MILL, *verb. phr.* (common).—To put to trial: as a horse before a race.

1872. *Morning Post*, 7 Nov. Totally disregarding the horse's retrogression in the betting after he was PUT THROUGH THE MILL I advised my readers to make him a winner.

1888. *Daily Telegraph*, 24 Dec. The number of yearlings PUT THROUGH THE MILL before Christmas is fewer than usual.

MILL-CLAPPER, *subs.* (common).—The tongue: specifically of women.

1690. B. E., *Dict. Cant. Crew*, s.v.

MILL-DOLL, *subs.* (obsolete).—The Bridewell, once situate in Bridge Street Blackfriars.

1781. MESSINK, in *Choice of Harlequin*, 'The Keeper of Bridewell's Song.' I'm Jigger Dubber here, and you are welcome to MILL DOLL.

1785. GROSE, *Vulg. Tongue*, s.v.

1823. BEE, *Dict. Turf*, s.v.

Verb. (old).—To beat hemp in Bridewell; to do work on the treadmill. *See* MILL-DOLLY.

1751. FIELDING, *Amelia*, I. x. I am sent hither to MILL DOLL.

1780. R. TOMLINSON, *Slang Pastoral*, vi. When sitting with Nancy, what sights have I seen! . . . But now she MILLS DOLL.

1785. GROSE, *Vulg. Tongue*, s.v.

MILL-DOLLY, *subs.* (thieves').—*See* quot.

1719. SMITH, *Lives of Highwaymen*, i. 108. 'Punisht at hard labour in Bridewell, which beating of hemp, the thieves call MILL DOLLY.'

MILL-DOSE, *subs.* (American thieves').—Prison labour.—MATSELL (1859).

MILL-LAY, *subs.* (old).—*See* quot.

1785. GROSE, *Vulg. Tongue*, s.v. MILL LAY. To force open the doors of houses in order to rob them.

MILLER, *subs.* (pugilistic).—1. A pugilist.

1823. BEE, *Dict. Turf*, s.v. MILLERS—second-rate boxers, whose arms run round in rapid succession, not always falling very hard, or with determinate object.

1837. S. WARREN, *Diary of a Late Physician*, vii. The captain. . . . being a first-rate MILLER, as the phrase is. . . . let fall a sudden shower of blows about Mr. Marningham's head and breast.

*c.*1840. HOOD, *Miss Kilmansegg*. Because she wouldn't go to a mill, She didn't know when but remembered still, That the MILLER's name was Mendoza.

2. *See* JOE MILLER.

3. (old).—A vicious horse.

1825. *The English Spy*, i. 236. The horse shewed symptoms of being a MILLER. The Baronet, nothing daunted, touches him smartly under the flank, when up he goes in his forequarters, smashes the tilbury into ten thousand pieces, bolts away with the traces and shafts, and leaves the baronet with a broken head.

4. (old coaching).—A white hat.

5. (Old Cant).—*See* quot.

1690. B. E., *Dict. Cant. Crew*, s.v. MILLER, a Killer or Murderer.

1785. GROSE, *Vulg. Tongue*, s.v.

TO GIVE THE MILLER, *verb. phr.* (common).—*See* quot.

1876. HINDLEY, *Adventures of a Cheap Jack*, p. 193. Some of his pals GAVE HIM THE MILLER, that is a lot of flour is wrapped up in thin paper about the size of a fist, and when thrown, the first thing it comes in contact with, breaks and smothers the party all over.

TO DROWN THE MILLER, *verb. phr.* (common).—1. To water overmuch. Originally TO DROWN THE MILLER'S THUMB, *i.e.*, the thumb-mark on the glass.

1767. RAY, *Proverbs* [BOHN (1893), 171]. TO PUT OUT THE MILLER'S THUMB. Spoken by good housewives, when they have wet their meal for bread or paste too much.

1821. SCOTT, *The Pirate*, ii. 64. 'He shall drink off the yawl full of punch.' 'Too much water DROWNED THE MILLER,' answered Triptolemus.

1834. MARRYAT, *Jacob Faithful*, ch. xii. Old Tom put the pannikin to his lips. 'DROWNED THE MILLER, by heavens!' said he; 'what could I have been about?' ejaculated he, adding more spirits to his mixture.

1886. MISS HUME, *Shrops. Folk Lore*, p. 597. To DROWN THE MILLER = to add too much water to the flour in bread-making; also frequently applied to tea-making, when it is of course meaningless.

2. (Scots').—To go bankrupt. [JAMIESON].

1805. A. SCOTT, *Poems*, 34. Honest men's been ta'en for rogues, When bad luck gars DROWN THE MILLER, Hunted 'maist out o' their brogues, Fortune-smit for lack o' siller.

MILLER'S-EYE, *subs.* (common).—A lump of flour in a loaf.

TO PUT THE MILLER'S-EYE OUT, *verb. phr.* (common).—To be sparing of flour.

MILLER'S-THUMB. *See* COBBLER'S-THUMB.

MILLINER'S-SHOP, *subs.* (venery).—The female *pudendum*. For synonyms *see* MONOSYLLABLE.

MILL-KEN, *subs.* (thieves').—A housebreaker. *See* AREA-SNEAK, and (for synonyms) THIEVES.

1665. R. HEAD, *English Rogue*, Pt. I. ch. v. (Repr. 1874), p. 50. MILKEN, one that breaks houses.

1669. *Nicker Nicked*, in *Harl. Misc.* (ed. PARK), ii. 108. MILL-KEN [in list of names of thieves].

1724. E. COLES, *Eng. Dict.* MILKEN, a house breaker.

1725. *Old Ballad* (in *New Cant. Dict.*), 'The Twenty Craftsmen.' The fourth was a MILL-KEN, to crack up a door, He'd venture to rob both the rich and the poor.

1754. FIELDING, *Jonathan Wild*, bk. I. ch. v. The same capacity which qualifies a MILL-KEN, a bridle-cull, or a buttock-and-file to arrive at any degree of eminence in his profession would likewise raise a man in what the world esteem a more honourable calling.

1859. MATSELL, *Vocabulum*, s.v.

MILLING, *subs.* (common).—1. A beating. Also fighting.

1810. COMBE, *Dr. Syntax*, ii. 2. One blood gives t'other a MILLING.

1819. MOORE, *Tom Crib*, iv. The champion of England stands unrivalled for his punishment, game, and MILLING on the retreat.

1841. MRS. GORE, *Cecil*, 158. Put myself in a Cribb-like attitude for a MILLING-match.

2. (old).—Stealing.

MILLING IN THE DARKMANS, *subs. phr.* (Old Cant).—Murder by night. *See* MILL, *verb.* 1.

1815. SCOTT, *Guy Mannering*, xxviii. Men were men then, and fought each other in the open field, and there was nae MILLING IN THE DARKMANS.

MILLING-COVE, *subs. phr.* (pugilists').—A pugilist.

1785. GROSE, *Vulg. Tongue*, s.v. MILLING COVE. How the MILLING COVE served the cull out; how the boxer beat the fellow.

1819. VAUX, *Memoirs*, s.v.

1834. W. H. AINSWORTH, *Rookwood*, p. 250 (ed. 1864). Zoroaster, who was not merely a worshipper of fire, but a thorough MILLING-COVE, had engaged to some purpose in a pugilistic encounter with the rustics.

MILL-ROUND, *subs.* (common).—Routine: *see* GO THROUGH THE MILL, sense 2.

1892. M. E. BRADDON, *Gerard*, p. 4. 'What have you been doing with yourself?' 'Nothing beyond the usual MILL-ROUND.'

MILLSTONE. TO SEE (or LOOK) THROUGH A MILL-STONE (or BRICK WALL), *verb. phr.* (common).—To be well-informed; to judge with precision; to be quick of perception.

1582. LYLY, *Euphues and His England* [NARES]. Then, Fidus, since your eies are so sharp that you cannot onely LOOKE THROUGH A MILSTONE, but cleane through the minde, and so cunning that you can levell at the dispositions of women whom you never knew.

1767. RAY, *Proverbs* [BOHN (1893), 171], s.v.

1782. MRS. CENTLIVRE, *Bold Stroke for a Wife*, iii. 1. I'm sorry such a well-invented tale should do you no more service. We old fellows can SEE AS FAR INTO A MILLSTONE as them that pick it.

TO WEEP MILLSTONES, *verb. phr.* (old).—Said of a person not likely to cry.

1597. SHAKSPEARE, *Rich. III*, i. 3. Your eyes DROP MILL-STONES when fools' eyes drop tears. *Ibid.* i. 6. *Cl.* Bid Glo'ster think on this, and he will weep. *1 M.* Aye, MILL-STONES, as he lesson'd us to weep.

1607. *Cæsar & Pompey* [NARES]. He, good gentleman, Will weep when he hears how we are used. *1 Serj.* Yes, MILL-STONES.

TO RUN ONE'S HEAD AGAINST A MILLSTONE (MILESTONE, or BRICK WALL), *verb. phr.* (common).—1. To resist mulishly; to attempt impossibilities.

1837. C. DICKENS, *Pickwick Papers*, p. 129 (ed. 1857.) 'All them old cats will RUN THEIR HEADS AGIN MILESTONES.'

TO RUN A MILESTONE, *verb. phr.* (old dicing).—*See* quot. and KNAP.

1714. LUCAS, *Gamesters*, 27. He was not ignorant of knapping, which is, striking one die dead, and let the other run a MILESTONE.

MILL-TOG (TAG or TWIG), *subs.* (old).—A shirt. For synonyms *see* CAMESA.

1821. HAGGART, *Life*, 133. Few had either a MILL-TWIG, toper, or crabs.

1823. GROSE, *Vulgar Tongue* (3rd ed.), s.v.

1851-61. MAYHEW, *Lond. Lab. and Lon. Poor*, Vol. i. p. 231, s.v. MILL TAG—A shirt.

1859. MATSELL, *Vocabulum*, s.v.

1888. *Temple Bar*, XXIV. 536. I've known him to get thirty MILL-TOGS in one day.

MILL-WASH, *subs.* (tailors').—Vest canvas.

MILT, *subs.* (venery).—The semen; Hence, MILT-MARKET (or -SHOP) = the female *pudendum* ; TO DOUBLE ONE'S MILT (old) = to ejaculate twice without removal.

MILTON, *subs.* (common).—An oyster.

1841. THACKERAY, *Comic Tales and Sketches*, ii. p. 175. Mrs. Grampus herself operated with the oyster-knife, and served the MILTON morsels to the customers.

1854. AYTOUN and MARTIN, *Bon Gualtier Ballads* [14th ed. (1884), p. 180]. These mute inglorious MILTONS are divine.

MILVADER, *verb.* (old).—*See* quot.

1821. D. HAGGART, *Life*, 'Glossary,' p. 172, s.v. MILVAD, a blow. MILVADERING, boxing.

1823. GROSE, *Vulgar Tongue* (3rd. ed.), s.v.

MINCE, *verb.* (medical students').—To dissect.

MINCE-PIES, *subs.* (rhyming).—The eyes. Also MUTTON-PIES (*q.v.*).

1892. *Sporting Times*, 29 Oct. 'The Rhyme of the Rusher.' And I smiled as I closed my two MINCE-PIES.

1894. CHEVALIER, *Jerusalem's Dead*, i. My MINCE-PIES are waterin' jes like a pump, and they're red as a ferrit's.

MINCKINS. *See* MINX.

MIND. *See* P'S AND Q'S.

MIND YOUR EYE, *phr.* (common).—Be careful. Also (nautical) MIND YOUR HELM.

MINDEN BOYS, *subs. phr.* (military).—The Twentieth Foot. [From their bravery at Minden, 1759].

MINDER, *subs.* (common).—A child put out to nurse.

MINE-ARSE. *See* BANDBOX.

MINE-OF-PLEASURE, *subs.* (venery).—The female *pudendum*. For synonyms *see* MONOSYLLABLE.

17[?]. *Old Ballad* [quoted by BURNS in *Merry Muses*], 'O Saw Ye my Maggy?' A HIDDEN MINE OF PLEASURE.

MINE UNCLE. *See* UNCLE.

MINGLE-MANGLE, *subs.* (old).—A hotch-potch.

1550. *Apol. of Johan Bale*, fo. 25. Al thys have I wrytten afore leaste we shulde take euyll for good, and couple sower wyth swete, making of the a MINGLE-MANGEL, for pigges of the pope's old puddel.

1600. HOOKER, *Sermons*, v. 7. He cannot love the Lord Jesus with his heart . . . which can brook to see a MINGLE-MANGLE of religion and superstition.

MINIKIN (or **MINNIKON**), *subs.* (old).—*See* quots. Also as *adj.* = diminutive; dainty; delicate.

1598. FLORIO, *Worlde of Wordes*, s.v. *Mingherlina*, a daintie lasse, a MINNIKIN, smirking wench.

1605. SHAKSPEARE, *Lear*, iii. 6, 45. Sleepest, or wakest thou, jolly shepherd, Thy sheep be in the corn; And for one blast of thy MINIKIN mouth, Thy sheep shall take no harm.

1606. DEKKER, *Newes from Hell* [GROSART (1886), ii. 146]. Tickle the next MINKIN.

1611. COTGRAVE, *Dictionary*, s.v. *Mignonnet*. A prettie, or young minion; a MINIKIN.

1635. GLAPTHORNE, *Hollander*, ii. 1. Surely the MINIKIN is enamoured of me.

1656. *Muses' Recr.* [HOTTEN], 71. I should begin to call my strings My catlings, and my MINIKINS.

1667. PEPYS, *Diary*, 18 March. Angling with a MINNIKIN, a gut string varnished over, which keeps it from swelling, and is beyond any hair for strength or smallness.

1785. GROSE, *Vulg. Tongue*, s.v. MINIKIN, a little man or woman; also the smallest sort of pin.

1823. BEE, *Dict. Turf*, s.v. MINIKIN . . . 'What a MINIKIN mouth she has.'

1859. MATSELL, *Vocabulum*, s.v., MINNIKON.

MINOR, *subs.* (Eton College).—1. A younger brother.

1864. *Eton School Days*, vii. 'Let my MINOR pass, you fellows!' exclaimed Horsham.

2. (old).—A water-closet.

1785. GROSE, *Vulg. Tongue*, s.v.

MINOR CLERGY, *subs. phr.* (old).—Young chimney-sweeps.

1811. *Lex. Bal.*, s.v.

MINT, *subs.* (Old Cant).—Money: also MINT-SAUCE or MINT-DROPS.

*c.*1420. PALLADIUS, *Husbondrie* [E. E. T. S.], p. 99. Thees if me spende, or MYNT for them receyve.

1573. HARMAN, *Caveat* (1814), p. 65, s.v.

1610. ROWLANDS, *Martin Mark-all*, p. 39 (H. Club's Repr. 1874), s.v.

1621. JONSON, *Metam. Gipsies*. Strike fair at some jewel, That MINT may accrue well.

1665. R. HEAD, *English Rogue*, Pt. I. ch. v. p. 50 (1874), s.v.

1690. B. E., *Dict. Cant. Crew*, s.v.

1724. E. COLES, *Eng. Dict.*, s.v.

1785. GROSE, *Vulg. Tongue*, s.v.

1828. EGAN, *Finish to Tom and Jerry*, 53. I not only hope that he gets lots of MINT-SAUCE, etc.

1867. JAS. GREENWOOD, *Unsent. Journeys*, xxx. 230. The requisite MINT SAUCE (as that horribly vulgar and slangy B. P. terms money).

1871. DE VERE, *Americanisms*, p. . . When the Hon. T. H. Benton, of Missouri, put his whole strength forward on the floor of Congress and through the press to introduce a gold currency, he accidentally called the latter MINT-DROPS.

Adv. (colloquial).—Plenty of money.—*Lex. Bal.* (1811); MATSELL (1859). Also A MINT OF MONEY = a big sum.—GROSE.

MINX, *subs.* (old).—1. A woman: in contempt; and (2) a harlot. Also MINCKINS.

*d.*1593. MARLOWE, *Doctor Faustus*, vi. What are you, Mistress MINX.

1597-8. HAUGHTON, *A Woman will have her Will* [DODSLEY, *Old Plays* (1874), x. 509]. How now, you unreverent MINX.

1598. FLORIO, *A Worlde of Wordes*, s.v. *Magalda*, a queane, a harlot, a strumpet, an old trot, a trull or MINXE, a gixie.

*b.*1600. *Grim the Collier etc.* [DODSLEY, *Old Plays* (1874), viii. 436]. Come hither, MINX!

1602. SHAKSPEARE, *Othello*, iii. 3, 475. Lewd MINX! Come, go with me apart.

1605. *London Prodigal*, iii. 3. MINCKINS, look you do not follow me!

1635. GLAPTHORNE, *Hollander* [PEARSON (1874), i. 129]. Well said, MINX!

1678. BUTLER, *Hudibras* [JOHNSON]. Some torches bore, some links, Before the proud virago MINX.

1690. B. E., *Dict. Cant. Crew*, s.v. MINKS, a proud Flirt.

1691-2. *Gentlemen's Journal*, May, p. 3. 'Twas there this precious MINX agreed to betray this young innocent.

1775. SHERIDAN, *St. Patrick's Day*, i. 2. Why, you little provoking MINX.

MIRACULOUS-CAIRN, *subs.* (venery). —The female *pudendum*. For synonyms *see* MONOSYLLABLE.

MISCHIEF, *subs.* (colloquial).—1. A vexatious person; and (2) ruin. TO GO TO THE MISCHIEF = to go to the bad. Hence, WHAT, WHO, or WHERE THE MISCHIEF = what, who, or where the hell, or the devil; TO PLAY THE MISCHIEF = to play havoc; to disorder; WITH A MISCHIEF = with a vengeance.

1614. JONSON, *Bartholomew Fair*, i. WHAT THE MISCHIEF do you come with her? or she with you?

1630. JOHN TAYLOR, *Wks.* [NARES]. Will in a little time make her encrease with a vengeance, and multiply WITH A MISCHIEFE.

1818. S. E. FERRIER, *Marriage*, xv. Boys may GO TO THE MISCHIEF, and be good for something—if girls go, they're good for nothing I know of.

1822. SCOTT, *Fortunes of Nigel*, xxvii. Bide down, WITH A MISCHIEF TO YE, bide down!

1885. *Morning Post*, 5 Febr. These move slowly through the camp, their centrifugal force PLAYING THE MISCHIEF, blowing everything to pieces, knocking down tents, carrying them off 100 yards, and generally causing a good deal of bad language.

1892. *Tit-Bits*, 17 Sept., p. 19, col. 3. 'What will our wives say when we get home?' 'Let them say what they want to; mine will tell me to GO TO THE MISCHIEF,' responded number two.

1892. KIPLING, *Barrack-Room Ballads*, 'Gunga Din.' You 'eathen, WHERE THE MISCHIEF 'ave you been?

3. (old).—*See* quot.

1785. GROSE, *Vulg. Tongue*, s.v. MISCHIEF. A man loaded with mischief, *i.e.*, a man with his wife on his back.

MISERY, *subs.* (common).—Gin. For synonyms *see* DRINKS and WHITE SATIN.

MISFIT, *subs.* (tailors').—An awkward man.

MISH, *subs.* (old).—A shirt or chemise; *cf.* CAMESA. [An abbreviation of COMMISSION (*q.v.*)].

1665. R. HEAD, *English Rogue*, Pt. I. ch. v. p. 48 (1874), s.v.

1712. T. SHIRLEY, *Triumph of Wit*, 'The Maunder's Praise of his Strowling Mort.' What though I no Togeman wear, Nor Commission, MISH or Slate.

1714. *Memoirs of John Hall* (4th ed.), p. 13, s.v.

1785. GROSE, *Vulg. Tongue*, s.v.

1859. MATSELL, *Vocabulum*, s.v.

MISHMASH, *subs.* (old).—*See* quots.

1598. FLORIO [HALLIWELL], p. 95. A chaos, a confused lump, a formelesse mass, a MISH-MASH.

1609. HOLLAND, *Ammianus Marcellinus* [NARES]. And these are so full of their confused circumlocutions, that a man would thinke he heard Thersites with a frapling and bawling clamor to come out with a MISHMASH and hotchpotch of most distastfull and unsavorie stuffe.

1638. SIR T. HERBERT, *Travels in Africa*, p. 27. Their language . . . [is] a MISH-MASH of Arabic and Portuguese.

1755. JOHNSON, *Eng. Dict.*, s.v. MISHMASH. A low word. A mingle or hotch-potch.

MISH-TOPPER, *subs.* (old).—A coat or petticoat.

1785. GROSE, *Vulg. Tongue*, s.v.

1859. MATSELL, *Vocabulum*, s.v.

MISS, *subs.* (old).—1. *See* quot. 1662.

1662. EVELYN, *Diary*, 9 Jan. She being taken to be the Earle of Oxford's MISSE, as at this time they began to call lewd women.

1675. COTTON, *Scoffer Scofft*, in *Wks.* (1725), p. 268. It is mettle carries MISSES.

1675. *The Character of a Town Miss*, 3. 'A MISS is a new name which the civility of this age bestows on one that our unmannerly ancestors called whore and strumpet.'

1678. BUTLER, *Hudibras* [JOHNSON]. All women would be of one piece, The virtuous matron and the MISS.

1690. B. E., *Dict. Cant. Crew*, s.v. MISS, a Whore of quality.

1691-2. *Gentlemen's Journal*, Jan. p. 37. As subject to mistake an affected sorrow for a real grief, as our cullies, the fawnings of their MISSES for a true passion.

*d.*1701. DRYDEN, in *Wks.* [JOHNSON]. This gentle cock, for solace of his life, Six MISSES had besides his lawful wife.

1714. LUCAS, *Gamesters*, 197. Not sufficient to support his extravagancy in keeping several MISSES.

1719. DURFEY, *Pills to Purge*, i. 174. Then bring the MISS for Morning Bliss.

1729. GAY, *Polly*, i. xix. Abroad after MISSES most husbands will range.

1775. ASH, *Eng. Dict.*, s.v. MISS . . . . a strumpet, a prostitute, a concubine.

1785. GROSE, *Vulg. Tongue*, s.v.

1786. BURNS, *The Inventory*. I hae nae wife, an' that my bliss is. An' ye hae laid nae tax on MISSES.

1859. MATSELL, *Vocabulum*, s.v.

2. (old).—A very young girl.

1695. CONGREVE, *Love for Love*, ii. 2. Madam, you are too severe upon MISS; you must not find fault with her pretty simplicity.

1712. SWIFT, *Corinna* [CHALMERS, *English Poets* (1810), XI. 386]. She made a song how little MISS Was kissed and slobbered by a lad.

1785. GROSE, *Vulg. Tongue*, s.v. MONEY.

3. (dressmakers').—A girl from about 10 to 15 years of age. Before and after, a 'child' and a 'young lady' respectively.

A MISS IS AS GOOD AS A MILE, *phr.* (colloquial).—A narrow escape is as good as an easy one.

TO MISS THE CUSHION, *verb. phr.* (old).—*See* quot.

1598. FLORIO, *Worlde of Wordes*, s.v. *Armeggiare* . . . to raue or commit some foolish part, to MISSE THE CUSHION, or to be wide from the purpose.

TO MISS ONE'S TIP. *See* TIP.

TO MISS THE FIGURE. *See* COMBINATION and SLUMP.

MISS BROWN, *subs. phr.* (venery).—The female *pudendum*. For synonyms *see* MONOSYLLABLE.—GROSE (1785).

MISS LAYCOCK, *subs.* (venery).—*See* quot. For synonyms *see* MONOSYLLABLE.

1785. GROSE, *Vulg. Tongue*, s.v. MISS LAYCOCK. The monosyllable.

1811. *Lex. Bal.*, s.v.

MISS-NANCY, *subs.* (colloquial).—An affectedly prim person: male or female. Hence, MISS-NANCYISM = affected nicety; effeminacy.

1883. *Philadelphia Times*, 2 July. The milksops and MISS-NANCYS among the young men, etc.

1886. *Harper's Weekly*, 20 March. Ineffable silliness, sneering at the demand for honesty in politics as MISS-NANCYISM.

MISSUS (THE), *subs.* (vulgar).—1. A wife: sometimes written as in quot. 1864; and (2), among servants, a mistress.

1846-8. THACKERAY, *Vanity Fair*, xxv. So he altered these words, bowing to the superior knowledge of his little MISSIS.

1857. TROLLOPE, *Barchester Towers*, xxxii. Mr. Harding and Mr. Arabin had all quarrelled with MISSUS for having received a letter from Mr. SLOPE.

1864. *Glasgow Herald*, 11 Nov. 'Bankruptcy Examinations.' I did not buy the property in Crown Street. THE MRS. bought a property in Rosehall Street.

MIST. SCOTCH MIST, *subs. phr.* (colloquial).—Rain.

MISTAKE. AND NO MISTAKE, *phr.* (colloquial). — Unquestionably; without fail.

MISTRESS, *subs.* (old).—The mark in the game of bowls; the JACK (*q.v.*, sense 2).

1580. SIDNEY, *Arcadia*, p. 281. Zelmane using her own byas, to bowl near the MISTRESSE of her own thoughts.

1600. *Weakest goes to the Wall*, 4to. G. 3. I hope to be as near the MISTRESSE as any of you all.

1602. SHAKSPEARE, *Troilus & Cressida*, iii. 2. So, so, rub on, and kiss the MISTRESS.

1632. W. ROWLEY, *Woman Never Vext*, ii. 1. Everyone strives to lie nearest the MISTRESS. *Ibid.* iv. 1. This city bowler has kissed the MISTRESS at first cast.

1653. BROME, *Queen and Concubine*, ii. 3. Rather than to have my head bowl'd at her, though I were sure it should kiss the MISTRESSE.

1655. FANSHAW, *Lusiad*, ix. 71. Like one That rubs the MISTRESS when his bowl is gone.

1657. MIDDLETON, *No Wit like a Woman's*, ii. 3. There's three rubs gone, I've a clear way to the MISTRESS.

MISTRESS ROPER, *subs. phr.* (nautical).—A marine. [Because he handles the ropes awkwardly].

MITE (or **MITEY**), *subs.* (common).—A cheesemonger; *cf.* BURNCRUST, CORKS, etc.

1765. FOOTE, *Commissary*, iii. 1. There liv'd Miss Cicely MITE, the only daughter of old MITE the cheesemonger.

1785. GROSE, *Vulg. Tongue*, s.v.

1811. *Lex. Bal.*, s.v.

MITRE, *subs.* (University).—A hat. *See* TUFTS. For synonyms *see* GOLGOTHA.

MITTEN, *subs.* (common).—1. A hand. For synonyms *see* BUNCH OF FIVES.—GROSE (1823).

1819. VAUX, *Memoirs*, s.v.

2. (pugilistic).—A boxing glove; a MUFFLER (*q.v.*). Also MITTS.

1859. MATSELL, *Vocabulum*, s.v.

1887. *Lic. Vict. Gazette*, 2 Dec., 359/2. I'll get him to put the MITTENS on vid your friend, and have three rounds.

1888. GREENWOOD, *Odd People in Odd Places*, p. 56. You see them two there, sitting on t'other end of the table and eating fried fish and bread. That's their MITTENS they've got tied up in that hankercher. They're fighting coves.

Verb. (common). — To jilt. Also TO GIVE THE MITTEN. In Devonshire TO GIVE ONE TURNIPS.

1838. NEAL, *Charcoal Sketches* [BARTLETT]. Young gentlemen that have GOT THE MITTEN, or young gentlemen who think they are going to GET THE MITTEN, always sigh. It makes them feel bad.

1848. LOWELL, *Fable for Critics*, p. 43. Here comes Dana, abstractedly loitering along Involved in a paulo-post-future of song Who'll be going to write what'll never be written Till the Muse, ere he thinks of it, GIVES HIM THE MITTEN.

1855. HALIBURTON ('Sam Slick'), *Human Nature*, p. 90. There is a young lady I have set my heart on; though whether she is a-goin' to give me hern, or GIVE ME THE MITTEN, I ain't quite satisfied.

1868. O. W. HOLMES, *Guardian*

Angel, ch. xxxiii. p. 264 (Rose Lib.). Some said that Susan had GIVEN her young man THE MITTEN, meaning thereby that she had signified that his services as a suitor were dispensed with.

1871. DE VERE, *Americanisms*, s.v. More ungracefully still, an unfortunate lover, who is simply 'jilted' at the North, is more violently 'kicked' at the South—a phrase marking most characteristically the contrast between the free and easy manners of our day with those of past days, when the strongest term used for the painful occasion WAS TO GIVE and TO GET THE MITTEN. The latter word ought, however, always to be MITTENS, as the phrase is derived from the same use made of the French *mitaines*, which had to be accepted by the unsuccessful lover instead of the hand, after which he aspired.

1873. CARLETON, *Farm Ballads*, 19. Once, when I was young as you, and not so smart, perhaps, For me she MITTENED a lawyer, and several other chaps.

1884. *Punch*, 1 March, p. 108, col. 2. Lifeboat hands who are found shrinking, Or with fear of danger smitten, GET, not medals, but THE MITTEN.

1887. *Lippincott's Magazine*, Aug., p. 241. Ah, I see. Popped the question, and GOT THE MITTEN. Oh, well you mustn't let that discourage you.

1888. *Notes & Queries*, 7 S. vi. 126. TO GET THE MITTEN . . . Without doubt the Latin *mitto*, to send (about your business), to dismiss, is the *fons et origo* of the word.

1890. E. BELLAMY, *Dr. Heidenhoff's Process*, p. 42. 'After all,' she said, suddenly, 'that would be taking a good deal of trouble to GET A MITTEN. If you are so anxious for it, I will give it to you now;' and she held out the glove to him with an inscrutable face.

TO HANDLE WITHOUT MITTENS, *verb. phr.* (common).—*See* quot.

1755. JOHNSON, *Eng. Dict.*, s.v. MITTENS. TO HANDLE WITHOUT MITTENS. To handle roughly. A low phrase.

EASY AS MITTENS, *phr.* (common).—Free.

1892. MILLIKEN, *'Arry Ballads*, p. 22. The ladies was EASY AS MITTENS.

MITTEN-MILL, *subs.* (American).—A glove-fight.

1859. MATSELL, *Vocabulum*, s.v.

MIVVY, *subs.* (common).—1. A woman: in contempt. Hence (2) a lodging-house landlady; a CAT (*q.v.*).

1887. *Punch*, 10 Sept., p. 111. Talk about stodge! Jest you arsk the old MIVVY as caters for me at the crib where I lodge.

1892. MILLIKEN, *'Arry Ballads*, p. 13. Bare-armed old MIVVIES you meet spread out pink in a theatre stall.

2. (schoolboys').—A marble.

1856. *Notes & Queries*, 2 S. i. 283. s.v.

MIX, *subs.* (colloquial).—A muddle; a mess.

1882. W. D. HOWELLS, *A Likely Story*, iii. What a fatal, fatal MIX.

Verb. (colloquial).—1. To confuse; and (2) to involve or implicate. Also TO MIX UP (*see* quot. 1823).

1823. BEE, *Dict. Turf*, s.v. MIX IT UP—to agree secretly how the parties shall make up a tale, or colour a transaction in order to cheat or deceive another party, as in case of a justice-hearing, of a law-suit, or a *cross* in a boxing-match for money.

1879. E. DICEY, *Victor Emanuel*, p. 53. An Italian exile, who in his hot youth had been MIXED UP, very much against the grain, in an abortive plot for the assassination of the late king.

TO MIX (or JOIN) GIBLETS. *See* quots.

1823. GROSE, *Vulg. Tongue*, s.v. GIBLETS.

1823. BEE, *Dict. Turf*, s.v. MIX GIBLETS—to intermarry—naturally or legally.

1887. *Notes and Queries*, 7 S. iv. 511. TO JOIN GIBLETS. This expression may occasionally be heard . . . and has a very offensive meaning.

MIXED, *adj.* (colloquial).—1. Confused; muddled; bewildered.

1880. *Punch*, 4 Sept., 106. 'Tomkins's First Session.' Rather MIXED after twenty-one hours' continuous sitting.

2. (old: now American).—Foul; bad; inferior.

*c.*1280. *Havelok the Dane*, l. 2533, p. 88 (Roxb. A). Of Cornwayle that was erl, That fole traytour, that MIXED cherl.

3. (common).—Slightly drunk. For synonyms *see* DRINKS and SCREWED.

1872. *Leeds Mercury*, 29 Aug. 'NottinghamPolice Report.' 'Was defendant drunk?' 'No, Sir, he was not drunk, and he wornt sober.' 'You say he wasn't drunk?' 'No, Sir, he was MIXED.'

MIX-METAL, *subs.* (old).—A silversmith.

1785. GROSE, *Vulgar Tongue*, s.v.

1811. *Lex. Bal.*, s.v.

1859. MATSELL, *Vocabulum*, s.v.

MIXUM, *subs.* (old).—An apothecary.

1635. GLAPTHORNE, *Hollander*, i. 1. Sir, I am sent from Mr. MIXUM, your apothecary.

MIZMAZE, *subs.* (old).—*See* quot. 1755.

1706. LOCKE, *Conduct of the Understanding*, § 20. Those who are accustomed to reason have got the true key of books, and the clue to lead them through the MIZMAZE of variety of opinions and authors to truth.

1755. JOHNSON, *Eng. Dict.*, s.v. MIZMAZE. A cant word, formed from *maze* by reduplication. A maze; a labyrinth.

1875. PARISH, *Sussex Glossary* [DAVIES]. I was all of a MIZMAZE—I was all in a bewilderment.

1883. *American*, viii. 308. Unless he had repeated that verbal MIZ-MAZE of the Convention.

MIZZARD, *subs.* (tramps').—The mouth: *cf.* MAZZARD.

1893. EMERSON, *Signor Lippo*, xiv If the beds ain't all made . . . . and everything fat and lean in the kitchen, they open their MIZZARDS and slam I can tell you.

MIZZLE, *verb.* (common).—To decamp; TO AMPUTATE (*q.v.*); to SKEDADDLE (*q.v.*).

1781. G. PARKER, *View of Society*, II. 231. He preferred MIZZLING off to France.

1789. GEO. PARKER, *Life's Painter*, p. 143, s.v.

1821. EGAN, *Real Life*, i. 224. He tipp'd the slavey a tanner and MIZZLED.

1823. GROSE, *Vulg. Tongue* (3rd ed.), s.v.

1823. BEE, *Dict. Turf*, s.v.

1823. MONCRIEFF, *Tom and Jerry* p. 6. *Tom.* That will do—now then Dicky, MIZZLE!—be scarce!—broom! *Prince.* Wouldn't intrude a moment, gentlemen, good morning—order my carriage.

1830. T. HOOD, *On a Royal Demise.* How monarchs die is easily explained, And thus it might upon their tombs be chiselled: As long as George IV. could reign, he reigned, And then he MIZZLED.

1830. DICKENS, *Pickwick*, p. 74 (ed. 1847). 'How you run on,' said Rachael. 'Run on—nothing to the hours, days, weeks, months, years, when we're united—*run* on—they'll fly on—bolt,—MIZZLE—steam—engine—thousand-horse-power—nothing to it.'

1840. BARHAM, *Ingoldsby Legends (Lay of S. Cuthbert).* 'Cut your stick, sir—come, MIZZLE! be off with you! go!'

1841. HOOD, in *Comic Almanack*, 256. But, oh! pride, pride must have a fall; Her cash he soon got through: And then, one mizzling Mich'lmas day, The Count he MIZZLED too.

1843. S. COYNE, *Binks the Bagman*, i. *Binks.* Sanguinary scoundrel! you have murdered that angelic woman. Begone—abscond—dissolve—MIZZLE!

1844. CHARLES SELBY, *London by Night*, i. 1. *Jack.* Hawkhurst! (*Aside.*) I'd better MIZZLE.

1849. DICKENS, *David Copperfield*, p. 202. Now you may MIZZLE, Jemmy, and if Mr. Copperfield will take the chair I'll operate on him.

1851-61. H. MAYHEW, *London Lab.*, iii. 154. Of course I MIZZLED, for fear of a stone or two.

1853. *Comic Almanack*, p. 52. 'The Vulture.' 'Smith!' I cried, 'your horrid smoking, Irritates my cough to choking. Having mentioned it before, Really, you should not compel one—will you MIZZLE—as before?' Quoth the Vulture 'Never more.'

1853. SURTEES, *Mr. Sponge's Sporting Tour*, i. Soapey Sponge, as his good natured friends called him, was seen MIZZLING along Oxford St., wending his way to the west.

1857. *New York Herald*, 17 June. They say the treasurer has MIZZLED, and as there is a small sum of a hundred thousand dollars missing, the presumption is not a very violent one.

1859. MATSELL, *Vocabulum*, s.v.

1863. C. READE, *Hard Cash*, III. 77. 'How dare you eat it there,' said Hayes brutally: 'take it to your own crib: come, MIZZLE.' And with that he lent him a contemptuous kick behind.

MIZZLER *subs.* (common).—A fugitive. RUM MIZZLER = a good hand at dodging or getting off.

1834. W. H. AINSWORTH, *Rookwood*, p. 180 (ed. 1864). From the Arch-cove to the needy MIZZLER.

MOAB, *subs.* (obsolete University).—1. A hat: specifically, the turban-shaped hat fashionable among ladies 1858-9. [From the Scripture phrase, 'MOAB is my washpot' (Ps. lx. 8)].

1864. *Reader*, 22 Oct. MOAB, a . . . hat. . . . University it is all over. We feel sure we know the undergraduate who coined the expression; he is now a solemn don delivering lectures in Cambridge.

1884. *Graphic*, 20 Sept., p. 307/2. The third, with his varnished boots, his stiff brown MOAB of the newest fashion, his well-displayed shirt-cuffs.

2. (Winchester College).—*See* quot.

1866. MANSFIELD, *School Life*, 190. On the west side of School court, a spacious room, nicknamed MOAB, has been erected, with numerous marble basins, and an unlimited supply of fresh water.

MOABITE, *subs.* (old).—A bailiff; a PHILISTINE(*q.v.*).—GROSE (1785).

1811. *Lex. Bal.*, s.v.

1859. MATSELL, *Vocabulum*, s.v. MOABITE, a constable.

MOB, *subs.* (old: now recognised).—1. The populace; the crowd. [A contraction of *mobile vulgus*]. Also MOBILITY and MOBOCRACY.

1686. DURFEY, *Common. of Women*, 'Dedication.' The MOBILE being all poison'd with the pernitious Tenets of a misled, ungrateful Usurper.

1688. SHADWELL, *Sq. of Alsatia* I, in *Wks.* (1720), iv. 15. This morning your cloaths and liveries will come home, and thou shalt appear rich and splendid like thy self, and the MOBILE shall worship thee.

1690. DRYDEN, *Don Sebastian*, iv. 1. She singled you out with her eyes, as commander-in-chief of the MOBILITY.

1694. *Country Conversations* [*Notes and Queries*, 7 S.vi.126]. 'I cannot approve of the word MOB, in these verses, which though significant enough, yet is a word but of Late Use, and not sufficiently Naturalized to appear in a serious Poem: Besides I esteem it a kind of Burlesque word and unsuitable to the Dignity of Horace.'

1702. MRS. CENTLIVRE, *Beau's Duel*, ii. 1. If so, you'll have both the MOB and the law on your side.

1703. WARD, *London Spy*, pt. VI. p. 140. The House was surrounded with the MOBILITY, that it look'd like the *Welsh-Cow-keepers-camp*, consisting of a number of both Sexes, of all sorts and sizes.

1711. *Spectator*, No. 135. It is perhaps this humour of speaking no more words than we needs must which has so miserably curtailed some of our words,

that in familiar writings and conversation they often lose all but their first syllables, as in MOB., red., pos., incog., and the like.

1719. DURFEY, *Pills to Purge*, v. 308. Damsel with squire, and MOB in the Mire.

1740. NORTH, *Examen*, p. 574. I may note that the rabble first changed their title, and were called the MOB, in the assemblies of this club (the Green Ribbon club 1680–82), first *mobile vulgus*, then contracted in one syllable.

1755. JOHNSON, *Eng. Dict.* [1815], s.v. MOBILITY. . . . In cant language, the populace.

1780. LEE, *Chapter of Accidents*, ii. 1. *Brid.* I don't love to go much among the MOBILITY, neither.

1785. GROSE, *Vulgar Tongue*, s.v.

1811. *Lex. Bal.*, s.v.

1822. SCOTT, *Fortunes of Nigel*, ix. The court-yard for the MOBILITY, and the apartments for the nobility.

1859. MATSELL, *Vocabulum*, s.v.

1878. GREEN, *Short Hist. Eng. People*, ch. x. § 1. p. 729. When MOBS were roaring themselves hoarse for 'Wilkes and liberty.'

2. (common).—*See* quots. and SCHOOL; *Cf.* SWELL-MOB.

1851-61. H. MAYHEW, *London Lab.*, i. p. 234. Some classes of patterers, I may here observe, work in schools or MOBS of two, three, or four.

1859. MATSELL, *Vocabulum*, s.v. MOBS. A number of thieves working together.

3. (Australian).—A number of horses, or cattle; part of a flock of sheep: a flock is the total number of fleeces tended by one shepherd; any portion of it being a MOB.

1885. MRS. CAMPBELL PRAED, *The Head Station*, p. 2. I wonder whether there will be a MOB of fat cattle ready for the butcher next month.

4. (common). — A strumpet (also MAB).

1785. GROSE, *Vulg. Tongue*, s.v.

1811. *Lex. Bal.*, s.v.

Verb. (old: now recognised).—To crowd; to hustle; to annoy. Hence MOBBING.

1741. H. WALPOLE, *Letters*, No. 9, 12 Nov. The city-shops are full of favours, the streets of marrowbones and cleavers, and the night will be full of MOBBING, bonfires, and lights.

1754. MARTIN, *Eng. Dict.*, 2nd ed. s.v.

1759. TOWNLEY, *High Life below Stairs*, i. 2. Ay, let us begone; for the common people do so stare at us—we shall certainly be MOBBED.

1884. BURROUGHS, *Birds and Poets*, p. 41. They swarm about him like flies, and literally MOB him back into his dusky retreat.

SWELL-MOB. *See* SWELL-MOB.

MOBILITY, (or **MOBOCRACY**). *See* MOB, *subs.*, sense 1.

MOBSMAN, *subs.* (thieves').—A pickpocket: *i.e.*, a member of the SWELL-MOB (*q.v.*).

1851-61. H. MAYHEW, *Lon. Lab.*, iv. 25. MOBSMEN, or those who plunder by manual dexterity.

MOCKERED, *adj.* (common).—Full of holes: *e.g.*, a ragged handkerchief, or a blotched or pitted face.

MOCTEROOF, *verb.* (Covent Garden).—To doctor or FAKE (*q.v.*) damaged produce: *e.g.*, pines are washed with a solution of gum; chesnuts shaken in a bag with bees-wax, *etc.*

MODEL (THE), *subs.* (old).—*See* quot.

1856. H. MAYHEW, *Gt. World of London*, p. 113. This is Pentonville Prison, vulgarly known as THE MODEL.

MODERN BABYLON, *subs.* (common).—London. MODERN ATHENS = Edinburgh.

MODEST, *adj.* and *adv.* (colloquial).—A vulgarism expressive of moderation; the reverse of LARGE (*q.v.*). Hence, MODEST QUENCHER = a small drink.

MODICUM, *subs.* (venery).—The female *pudendum*. For synonyms *see* MONOSYLLABLE.

1675. COTTON, *Scoffer Scofft*, in *Works* (1725), p. 258. Such knees, such thighs, and such a bum And such a, such a MODICUM.

MODS, *subs.* (Oxford University).—The first public examination for degrees. [An abbreviation of 'Moderations'].

1887. *Chambers' Journal*, 14 May, 310. MODS cannot be attempted until the end of one year from matriculation, and need not be tackled until the expiration of two.

MOEY, *subs.* (common).—1. The mouth. For synonyms *see* POTATO-TRAP.

2. (American thieves').—*See* quot.

1859. MATSELL, *Vocabulum*, s.v. MOEY, a petition.

MOFFLING-CHETE, *subs.* (old).—*See* MUFFLING-CHEAT.

MOFUSSIL, *subs.* and *adj.* (Anglo-Indian).— Any part of India except the three capitals, Calcutta, Bombay, and Madras: specifically rural; provincial.

1772. *Order of Council of H. E. I. C. in Claim of Roy Rada Churn*. 13. 2. In each district shall be established two Courts of Judicature: one by the name of the MOFUSSIL Audauler or Provincial Court of Dewannee.

1845. *The Mofussilite* [Title]. Published in Calcutta.

1863. G. A. SALA, *Breakfast in Bed*, Essay I. p. 11 (1864). 'The conduct of the Indian government with reference to the Gwalior bungalows, the farming of MOFUSSILS to Kansamahs.'

MOGGY, *subs.* (old).—1. A badly-dressed woman; a GUY (*q.v.*).

2. (old).—A calf.

MOGUE, *verb.* (common).—To gammon; to throw dust in one's eyes.

1870. *Bell's Life*, 19 June. If Mr. Milsom means business and not MOGUING let him cover my deposit.

1893. EMERSON, *Signor Lippo*, 60. Sometimes we MOGUE 'em by pulling 'em a bit, but those bookies are fly to the game.

MOHAIR, *subs.* (old).—1. An upholsterer. *Cf.* BURN-CRUST.

1811. *Lex. Bal.*, s.v.

1859. MATSELL, *Vocabulum*, s.v.

2. (old).—*See* quot.

1785. GROSE, *Vulgar Tongue*, s.v. MOHAIR, a man in the civil line, a townsman, or tradesman, a military term, from the mohair buttons worn by persons of those descriptions, or any others not in the army; the buttons of military men being always of metal; this is generally used as a term of contempt.

MOHAWK (or **MOHOCK**), *subs.* (old).—A ruffian who infested the streets of London at the beginning of the eighteenth century. At the Restoration, the street bullies were called Muns and Tityre-Tus; then Hectors and Scourers; then, Nickers and Hawcubites; and lastly, MOHOCKS or MOHAWKS. Also as *verb.*

1711. SWIFT, *Journal to Stella*, 8 March. Did I tell you of a race of rakes, called the MOHAWKS that play the devil about this town every night?

1712. STEELE, *Spectator*, No. 324. The MOHOCK-club, a name borrowed, it seems, from a sort of cannibals in India, who subsist by plundering and devouring all the nations about them.

1712. GAY, *Trivia*, iii. 326. Who has not trembled at the MOHOCK'S name?

1717. PRIOR, *Alma*, iii. Give him port and potent sack; From a milksop he starts up MOHACK.

1719. T. DURFEY, *Pills to Purge*, vi. 336. There's a new set of Rakes, Entitled MOHACKS, Who infest Her Majesties subjects.

1755. *Gentlemen's Mag.*, xxv. 65. The MOHOCKS and Hell-Fire-Club, the heroes of the last generation.

1825. NEAL, *Bro. Jonathan*, I. ch. viii. Some loitering rascal who has been out a MOHAWKING to-day.

1839. AINSWORTH, *Jack Sheppard* [DICK'S ed.], p. 58. He's the leader of the MOHOCKS.

1861. SALA, *Twice Round the Clock*, 4 a. m. Par. 9. A Billingsgate fish-fag, was more than a match for a MOHOCK.

1882. *Punch*, lxxxii. 83. 'The MOHOCK Revival.' That ancient form of ruffianism known as MOHOCKISM.

1889. CLARKSON and RICHARDSON, *Police*, 7. These were the Muns . . . the Hectors . . . and the MOHOCKS.

MOHICAN, *subs.* (obsolete).—*See* quot.

1848. *Tait's Mag.*, 2 S. xv. 309. A MOHICAN, in Cadonian phraseology, is a tremendously heavy man, who rides five or six miles [in an omnibus] for sixpence.

MOIETY, *subs.* (old).—1. *See* quots.

1785. GROSE, *Vulg. Tongue*, s.v.

1811. *Lex. Bal.*, s.v.

1859. MATSELL, *Vocabulum*, s.v. MOIETY, fifty.

2. (colloquial).—A wife.

MOISTEN, *verb.* (common).—To drink; TO LUSH (*q.v.*). Also TO MOISTEN ONE'S CHAFFER (or CLAY).

MOKE, *subs.* (common).—1. An ass.

ENGLISH SYNONYMS. Baldwin; cuddy (Scots'); donkey; Dick; Edward; Issachar; Jack; Jenny; Jerusalem; Jerusalem pony; King of Spain's trumpeter; long-ears; myla; Neddy.

1851. MAYHEW, *Lond. Lab.*, ii. 85. I had a good MOKE, and a tidyish box of a cart.

1855. THACKERAY, *Newcomes*, xxx. The one who rides from market on a MOKE.

1856. *Punch*, xxxi. 218. We understand that the directors have been actually challenged by a sporting minded costermonger who has offered to back his MOKE against the fastest engine.

1866. G. A. SALA, *Trip to Barbary*, iii. As one out of every three Bedouins you meet in the country is mounted on a meek little MOKE . . . I should put down the number of Arab asses at about one million.

1888. ROLF BOLDREWOOD, *Robbery Under Arms*, viii. I am regular shook on this old MOKE, I believe.

1888. J. RUNCIMAN, *The Chequers*, 85. I got to go to market, and we ain't no bloomin' MOKE.

1889. *Illustrated Bits*, 13 July. Billy Skipper once came to Ben Bouncer to ask for the loan of his MOKE.

1894. *Sketch*, 28 March, 458, col. 2. ''E wants a barrer an' a MOKE of 'is 'hown,' said Nan. ''E's tired of a barsket.'

2. (common).—A dolt. *See* quot. 1871.

1871. DE VERE, *Americanisms*, s.v. MOKE, possibly a remnant of the obsolete *moky*, which is related to 'murky,' is used in New York to designate an old fogy or any old person, disrespectfully spoken to.

1871. *Galveston News*, 4 May. See here, my lively MOKE, said he, you sling on too much style.

3. (theatrical).—A variety artist who plays on several instruments.

4. (American).—A negro; a SNOWBALL (*q.v.*).

1859. MATSELL, *Vocabulum*, s.v.

1871. DE VERE, *Americanisms*, p. 617. s.v.

MOKO, *subs.* (sportsmen's).—A pheasant shot by mistake before the end of the close time. The tail

feathers are pulled out. *Cf.* LION, *subs.*, sense 4.

MOLE, *subs.* (venery).—The *penis*. For synonyms *see* CREAMSTICK and PRICK. *See* MOWDIWARK.

MOLECATCHER, *subs.* (venery).—The female *pudendum*. For synonyms *see* MONOSYLLABLE.

MOLL, *subs.* (common).—1. A girl; and (2) a female companion. [From MOLLESHER (*q.v.*)]

1823. BEE, *Dict. Turf*, s.v. MOLLS—are the female companions of low thieves, at bed, board, and business.

1859. MATSELL, *Vocabulum*, s.v.

3. (common).—A prostitute; a MOLLY (*q.v.*). For synonyms *see* BARRACK-HACK and TART.

1785. GROSE, *Vulg. Tongue*, s.v.

1811. *Lex. Bal.*, s.v.

1877. *Five Years' Penal Servitude*, iii. p. 245. She went up to some of the swell streets at the West End to see another MOLL, a pal of hers.

1887. W. E. HENLEY, *Villon's Good Night*. Likewise you MOLLS that flash your bubs For swells to spot.

MOLLED UP, *adj. phr.* (thieves').—1. *See* quot.

1851-61. MAYHEW, *Lond. Lab. etc.*, i. 336. Furnished cribs let to needys (nightly lodgers) that are MOLLED UP (that is to say, associated with women in the sleeping rooms).

2. (colloquial).—Arm-in-arm with, or accompanied by, a woman.

MOLL-BLOOD, *subs.* (old Scots').—The gallows. For synonyms *see* LADDER.

1818. SCOTT, *Heart of Midlothian*, xx. Three words of your mouth would give the girl the chance to nick MOLL BLOOD.

MOLL-BUZZER, *subs.* (thieves').—*See* quot.

1859. MATSELL, *Vocabulum*, s.v. Moll . . . MOLL-BUZZER a thief that devotes himself to picking the pockets of women.

MOLLIE, *subs.* (nautical).—*See* quot.

1885. SCHLEY and SOLEY, *Rescue of Greely*, p. 183. Whenever the whaling fleet is stopped for a number of days in the ice, it is the practice for the captains to assemble on board one or other of the ships to discuss the prospects of the season's catch. These interviews are called MOLLIES and are announced by a bucket hoisted as a signal at the fore-royal mast-head . . . Generally speaking a MOLLIE means making a night of it.

MOLLISHER, *subs.* (thieves').—A thief's mistress; a MOLL (*q.v.*).

1819. VAUX, *Memoirs*, s.v.

1851-61. H. MAYHEW, *London Lab. etc.*, i. p. 472. One old MOLLESHER . . . brought out 8lbs. of white rags.

MOLL PEATLEY'S GIG, *subs. phr.* (old).—Copulation. For synonyms *see* GREENS and RIDE.

1785. GROSE, *Vulg. Tongue*, s.v.

1811. *Lex. Bal.*, s.v.

MOLL-SACK, *subs.* (thieves').—A lady's hand-bag; a market basket.

1859. MATSELL, *Vocabulum*, s.v.

MOLL-THOMPSON'S MARK (or **M.T.**), *subs. phr.* (old).—Empty packages are said to be so marked: as *adj.* = empty.

1785. GROSE, *Vulg. Tongue*, s.v.

1811. *Lex. Bal.*, s.v.

MOLL-TOOLER, *subs.* (thieves').—A female pick-pocket. For synonyms *see* THIEVES.

MOLL-WIRE, *subs.* (thieves').—*See* MOLL-BUZZER. For synonyms *see* THIEVES.

MOLLY (**MISS MOLLY**, or **MOLLY-CODDLE**), *subs.* (common). — 1.

An effeminate person; a MILK-SOP (*q.v.*).

1811. *Lex. Bal.*, s.v.

1849. THACKERAY, *Pendennis*, xxxi. You have been bred up as a MOLLY-CODDLE, Pen, and spoilt by the women.

1859. MATSELL, *Vocabulum*, s.v.

1860. G. ELIOT, *Mill on the Floss*, ix. Such a thin-legged silly fellow as his uncle Pellet—a MOLLY-CODDLE in fact.

1864. HAMILTON AÏDÉ, *Mr. & Mrs. Faulconbridge*, I. 279. You young men are such a set of MOLLY-CODDLES.

1883. *Daily News*, 2 July, p. 5, col. 2. Attempts are sometimes made to dismiss as MOLLY-CODDLES those who protest against the mania for indiscriminate mountaineering.

2. (old).—A prostitute; a MOLL (*q.v.*). For synonyms *see* BARRACK-HACK and TART.

1719. DURFEY, *Pills to Purge*, i. 5. Town follies and cullies, and MOLLEYS and Dolleys.

3. (old).—A sodomite; a MARY-ANN (*q.v.*).—GROSE (1785).

1811. *Lex. Bal.*, s.v.

4. (old).—A country wench.

MOLLY-CODDLE, *verb.* (common).—To pamper. Also MODDLEY-CODDLEY.

1870. DICKENS, *Mystery of Edwin Drood*, ii. Don't MODDLEY-CODDLEY, there's a good fellow. I like anything better than being MODDLEY-CODDLEYED.

1895. *Referee*, 29 Dec., p. 5, col. 2. Who treats of MOLLY-CODDLING regulations.

MOLLY-CODDLISH, *adj.* (common).—Effeminate. Also MOLLYISH.

1801. DIBDIN, *The Frisk*. 'Jack at the Opera.' If it wan't for the petticoat gear, With their squeaking so MOLLYISH, tender, and soft, One should scarcely know ma'am from mounseer.

1883. *Referee*, 25 March, 7, 4. I daresay to make even such remarks as I have is only the sign of a MOLLY-CODDLISH mind.

MOLLYGRUBS. *See* MULLIGRUBS.

MOLLY MAGUIRES, *subs.* (obsolete).—1. An Irish secret society (*c.* 1843) formed to intimidate bailiffs and process-servers.

1868. TRENCH, *Realities of Irish Life*, VI. 'These MOLLY MAGUIRES were generally stout active young men, dressed up in women's clothes, with faces blackened or otherwise disguised; sometimes they wore crape over their countenances, sometimes they smeared themselves in the most fantastic manner with burnt cork about their eyes, mouth, and cheeks. In this state they used suddenly to surprise the unfortunate grippers, keepers, or process-servers, and either duck them in bog-holes, or beat them in the most unmerciful manner, so that the MOLLY MAGUIRES became the terror of all our officials.'

2. (American).—A secret society formed in 1877 in the mining districts of Pennsylvania. The members sought to effect their purpose by intimidation, carried in some cases to murder. Several were brought to justice and executed.

1867. HEPWORTH DIXON, *New America*, ii. 28. The judge who tried the murderer was elected by the MOLLY MAGUIRES; the jurors who assisted him were themselves MOLLY MAGUIRES. A score of MOLLY MAGUIRES came forward to swear that the assassin was sixty miles from the spot on which he had been seen to fire at William Dunn . . . . and the jurors returned a verdict of Not Guilty.

MOLLY-PUFF, *subs.* (old).—A gamblers' decoy.

1629. SHIRLEY, *Wedding*, iv. 3. Thou MOLLY-PUFF, were it not justice to kick thy guts out?

MOLLY'S-HOLE, *subs.* (venery).—The female *pudendum*. For synonyms *see* MONOSYLLABLE.

MOLOCKER, *subs.* (common).—*See* quots. Also as *adj.* and *verb.*

1863. G. A. SALA, *Breakfast in Bed*, 'On Things Going,' Essay v. p. 105 (1864). 'Tis like an old hat that has been MOLOKERED, or ironed and greased into a simulacrum of its pristine freshness.

1892. *Westminster Gaz.*, 4 Aug., p. 3. Even our beth customerth—vorking men ath likth a good MOLOCKER (MOLOCKER, it appears, is the trade term for renovated old chapeaux).

MOLROWER, *subs.* (common).—A whoremonger. For synonyms *see* MUTTON-MONGER.

MOLROWING, *subs.* (common).—1. Whoring. *Cf.* sense 2. *See* GREENS and RIDE.

2. (common).—Caterwauling.

1892. MILLIKEN, *'Arry Ballads*, p. 42. Beats 'Andel's MOLROWINGS a buster.

MOME, *subs.* (old).—A blockhead. For synonyms *see* BUFFLE and CABBAGE-HEAD.

*c.*1550. INGLELEND, *Disobedient Child* [DODSLEY, *Old Plays* (1874), ii. 315]. Me her husband, as a stark MOME, With knocking and mocking she will handle.

1557-8. *Jacob & Esau* [DODSLEY, *Old Plays* (1874), ii. 208]. Or whether Jacob have any, that peakish MOME.

1560. *Nice Wanton* [DODSLEY, *Old Plays* (1874), ii. 165]. I would sit quaking like a MOME for fear.

1562-3. *Jack Juggler* [DODSLEY, *Old Plays* (1874), ii. 138]. But if I were a wise woman as I am a MOME, I should make myself, as good cheer at home.

*b.*1583. *Flodden Field* [CHILD, *Ballads*, vii. 73]. Away with this foolish MOME.

1593. SHAKSPEARE, *Comedy of Errors*, iii. 1. 32. MOME, malt-horse, capon. . . . idiot, patch.

1606. DRAYTON, *Skeltoniad* [CHALMERS, iv. 428]. Parnassus is not clome By every such MOME.

1661. BROME, *Songs*, p. 105. Words are but wind, but blows come home, A stout-tongu'd lawyer's but a MOME.

MONARCH, *subs.* (thieves').—1. A name. Also MONEKER, MONIKER, MONARCHER, and MONICK.

1851. MAYHEW, *Lond. Lab.*, i. 232. What is your MONEKEER?

1859. MATSELL, *Vocabulum*, s.v.

1879. *Macmillan's Mag.*, XL. 502. At the station they asked me what my MONARCH was.

1891. *Sporting Life*, 1 April. Then came Perrin (otherwise 'Curley') and 'The Pocket Knifton' (whose real MONIKER did not transpire).

1893. EMERSON, *Signor Lippo*, 83. I go by the MONARCHER of North Eye ever since. *Ibid.* 93. I can't read or write my MONARCHER.

1895. *Times*, 11 Nov., p. 3, col. 5. 'Silver Robbery'. The van is all right. I have had the MONNICK taken off.

2. (Eton College).—The ten-oared boat.

3. (old).—Formerly a guinea; now a sovereign. For synonyms *see* CANARY.

BIG MONARCHER (tramps').—A person of note; a BIG-BUG (*q.v.*).

1893. EMERSON, *Signor Lippo*, 84. It's always a bad day for me if a BIG MONARCHER preaches.

MONAS, *subs.* (Stock Exchange).—Isle of Man Railway shares.

MONDAY. *See* ST. MONDAY.

MONDAY, *subs.* (common).—An intensive. *Cf.* AWFUL, BLEEDING, BLOODY, *etc.*

1892. KIPLING, *Barrack-Room-Ballads*, 'Snarleyow.' An' if one wheel was juicy, you may lay your MONDAY head 'Twas juicier for the niggers when the case began to spread.

MONDAYISH (or MONDAYFIED), *adj.* (common).—*See* quots.

1864. *Fraser's Magazine*, March, p. 382. Sunday is not a day of rest to him [the clergyman]; it is a day of grateful work, in which many week duties are laid aside; but it is a day of work, the reaction from which has created the clerical slang word MONDAYISH.

1885. *Ill. Lon. News*, 26 Sept., p. 331. When one feels fagged and wearied, with nerves overstrained, and altogether in that used-up condition that a parson, after a hard Sunday's work, terms MONDAYISH.

ENGLISH SYNONYMS. In the Idles; not-up-to-work; run down; seedy; off colour; off it; off the spot; out of it; shilly-shally; soft in the back; stale.

FRENCH SYNONYMS. *Etre carne* (popular); *s'engrouillé* (popular); *s'enrossé* (popular); *être un Flémard*: also *avoir la flème* or *flemme; n'en pas foutre un clou, un coup*, or *une secousse* (= to be superlatively idle); *malade du pouce; mou comme une loche; un Saint-lâche* (= a MONDAYISH workman).

MONDONGO. *See* MUNDUNGUS.

MONEY, *subs.* (colloquial).—1. Money's worth; a way or line of investing money.

1851-61. MAYHEW, *London Lab.*, i. 95. I sell dry fruit, sir, in February and March, because I must be doing something, and green fruit's not my MONEY then.

2. (venery).—*See* quot. For synonyms *see* MONOSYLLABLE.

1785. GROSE, *Vulg. Tongue*, s.v. MONEY. A girl's private parts, commonly applied to little children: as: Take care, Miss, or you will show your MONEY.

1811. *Lex. Bal.*, s.v.

1859. MATSELL, *Vocabulum*, s.v.

EGGS FOR MONEY, *subs. phr.* (old).—An excuse; a trick.

1604. SHAKSPEARE, *Winter's Tale*, i. 2. Mine honest friend, Will you take eggs for MONEY.

HARD-MONEY, *subs.* (colloquial). —Coin. SOFT MONEY = notes.

1848. LOWELL, *Biglow Papers*, 1st Ser. vi. I du believe hard coin the stuff, For 'lectioneers to spout on; The people's 'ollers soft enough. To make HARD MONEY out on.

MONEY MAKES THE MARE TO GO. *See* MARE.

POT OF MONEY, *subs. phr.* (common).—A large amount.

MONEY-BAGS, *subs.* (common).—A miser; a usurer; a man of means.

MONEY-BOX (MAKER, or SPINNER). The female *pudendum*. For synonyms *see* MONOSYLLABLE.

MONEY-DROPPER, *subs.* (thieves'). —A swindler who lets money drop before some 'flat', and, offering to share it with him, passes off counterfeit coin in return for good 'change'.

1748. SMOLLETT, *Roderick Random*, A rascally MONEY-DROPPER.

1785. GROSE, *Vulg. Tongue*, s.v.

1811. *Lex. Bal.*, s.v.

MONEY-GRUBBER, *subs.* (colloquial). —A miser.

MONGREL, *subs.* (old).—*See* quot. 1785.

1785. GROSE, *Vulg. Tongue*, s.v. MONGREL, a hanger on amongst cheats, a spunger; also a child, whose father and mother are of different countries.

1811. *Lex. Bal.*, s.v.

MONIKER. *See* MONARCH.

MONK, *subs.* (common).—1. A term of contempt.

2. (printers').—An over-inked spot in a printed sheet; a dark patch; a blackened or wasted impression. *See* FRIAR.

1811. *Lex. Bal.*, s.v.

1868. BREWER, *Phrase and Fable*, s.v. MONK. Caxton set up his printing press in the *scriptorium* of Westminster Abbey; and the associations of this place gave rise to the slang expressions MONK and *friar* for black and white defects.

MONKERY, *subs.* (tramps').—1. The country; DAISYVILLE (*q.v.*).

1819. VAUX, *Memoirs*, s.v.

1820. EGAN, *Boxiana*, iii. 18. Having a snooze and blowing a long one in the MONKERY.

1823. GROSE, *Vulg. Tongue* (3rd. ed.), s.v.

1851. MAYHEW, *Lond. Lab.*, i. 266. 'Well,' said he, 'I don't know what this ere MONKRY will come to, after a bit.'

1893. EMERSON, *Signor Lippo*, v. 'Do you belong to the start or the MONKERY?' they asked. 'London,' says I. *Ibid.* 58. The boss had training quarters in the MONKERY for racers and hunters.

2. (tramps').—Tramps; vagrants: collectively.

1851-61. MAYHEW, *Lond. Lab.*, i. 336. The place was well-known to the MONKRRY.

ON THE MONKERY, *phr.* (tramps').—On tramp.

1851-61. MAYHEW, *Lond. Lab.*, i. 344. Thirty years ON THE MONKERY.

MONKEY, *subs.* (colloquial).—1. A term of real or affected displeasure. Also, an endearment.

1602. SHAKSPEARE, *Othello*, iv. 1. 'This is the MONKEY'S own giving out; She is persuaded that I will marry her.'

1606. *Return from Parnassus* [DODSLEY, *Old Plays* (1874), ix. 206]. My mistress is so sweet . . . she never goes to the stool. O she is a most sweet little MONKEY.

1639. GLAPTHORNE, *Wit in a Constable* [PEARSON (1874), i. 219]. *Clar. Grace.* Ha, ha, ha. *Free.* What doe the MONKYES laugh at?

1786. BURNS, *Address to the Deil.* The bleezin', curst, mischievous MONKEYS.

1879. RUSKIN, *Letter to Young Girls [Century].* Serve the poor, but, for your lives, you little MONKEYS, don't preach to them.

1895. IOTA, *A Comedy in Spasms*, vii. That MONKEY there might be a countess in her own right.

2. (racing).—Five hundred pounds sterling; also (in America) $500. *See* RHINO.

1856. THE DRUID, *Post and Paddock*. 'Voltigeur's Derby-day.' 'Our Jim' is 'up', triumphant over surgeon, drugs, and nurse, And he hopes to see Newmarket with a MONKEY in his purse.

1861. WHYTE-MELVILLE, *Good for Nothing [Century].* A MONKEY at least to the credit side of your own book landed in about a minute and a half.

1864. *Derby-day*, 132. 'In that case, I'll lay you two to one in MONKEYS.' The Duke took out his book, and made an entry.

1882. *Punch*, LXXXII. 69. 1. He'll bet in MONKEYS, ponies, though he has seldom ready cash.

1883. *Graphic*, 13 Jan., p. 39, col. 2. Notwithstanding the increase of 'added' money from 200 sovs. to a MONKEY, which, as every one knows, is the turf parlance for 500 sovs.

1885. *Daily Chronicle*, 3 Feb. The Grand Hurdle Handicap, the added money to which is a MONKEY.

1890. *Globe*, 13 Feb., p. 5, col. 5. The amount of the Slavin testimonial subscribed by the sporting public was £500, which was given to him at his wedding breakfast yesterday. Slavin is indeed a lucky fellow to have a MONKEY and a charming wife presented to him on one day.

1891. *Lic. Vict. Gaz.*, 9 Jan. Keen, yet honest and business-like, he soon got on, and took a place inside the ring, and worked his way up until he disdained to lay odds to anything under a MONKEY, and had some £30.000 depending upon the great events of the year.

1892. N. GOULD, *Double Event*, p. 101. He had bought a couple of horses with Lord Mayfield's MONKEY, and was preparing them for a selling race.

3. (bricklayers').—A hod.

4. (prison).—A padlock.

1819. VAUX, *Memoirs*, s.v.

5. (military).—A rocket-driving instrument.

6. (nautical).—A vessel in which a mess receives its full allowance of grog.

7. (old).—*See* quot.

1889. *Notes & Queries*, 7 S. vii. 22 June, p. 498. The MONKEY was a small 'bustle', which in the days of very short waists was worn just below the shoulder blades.

8. (American).—The female *pudendum*. For synonyms *see* MONOSYLLABLE.

Verb. (common).—To trifle; to play; to fool about.

1887. FRANCIS, *Saddle & Mocassin*, 143. It is just possible that I may have been MONKEYING with the cards a little.

1889. *Harper's Mag.*, lxxix. 465. I hope he'll fetch money. I've had enough o' MONKEYING 'long o' checks.

MONKEY ON HORSEBACK, *subs. phr.* (old).—*See* quot.

1785. GROSE, s.v. Who put that MONKEY ON HORSEBACK without tying his legs? Vulgar wit on a bad horseman.

1811. *Lex. Bal.*, s.v. MONKEY.

MONKEY ON A WHEEL, *subs. phr.* (common).—A bicyclist. Fr. *un imbécile à deux roues.*

MONKEY WITH A LONG TAIL, *subs. phr.* (legal).—*See* quot. A MONKEY UP THE CHIMNEY = a mortgage on one's house.

1886. *Graphic*, 10 April, p. 399. To a lawyer . . . a mortgage is a MONKEY WITH A LONG TAIL.

TO GET ONE'S MONKEY UP, *verb. phr.* (common).—1. To get angry. Hence, his MONKEY IS UP (or he has A MONKEY ON HIS BACK) = he is angry. Fr. *reniquer.*

1877. *Five Years' Penal Servitude*, iii. p. 229. My MONKEY WAS UP, and I felt savage.

1888. ROLF BOLDREWOOD, *Robbery Under Arms*, ix. The mare, like some women when they GET THEIR MONKEY UP, was clean out of her senses.

1891. *Lic. Vict. Gazette*, 23 Jan. Each man's MONKEY WAS UP.

TO SUCK THE MONKEY, *verb. phr.* (nautical).—1. To drink rum out of cocoa-nuts, emptied of milk and filled with spirits; (2) to liquor from a cask through a gimlet-hole and a straw (called TAPPING THE ADMIRAL, which *see*); and (3) to drink from the bottle.

1811. *Lex. Bal.*, s.v. MONKEY.

1833. MARRYAT, *Peter Simple*, lvii. I didn't peach at Barbados, when the men SUCKED THE MONKEY.

1837. BARHAM, *Ingoldsby Legends*, 'The Black Mousquetaire.' What the vulgar call SUCKING THE MONKEY, Has much less effect on a man when he's funky.

1864. *Daily Telegraph*, 26 July. Behind and in front of the bourgeois warriors, who, standing or sitting at ease, were smoking or taking a SUCK AT THE MONKEY, otherwise the whisky flask, there marched another dress parade.

MONKEY WITH A TIN TOOL, *subs. phr.* (common).—A phrase expressive of impudence or self-content: *e.g.*, O, they're as cocky as MONKEYS WITH TIN TOOLS.

MONKEY-BOARD, *subs.* (obsolete).—The conductor's place on an old-style omnibus.

1860. *Punch*, xxxviii. p. 186. I was on the MONKEY-BOARD behind.

1883. JAS. GREENWOOD, *Tag, Rag, & Co.*, p. 27. The omnibus conductors . . . the ill-paid and hard-worked drudges of the MONKEY-BOARD.

MONKEY-BOAT, *subs.* (nautical).—A long, narrow, canal boat. Also a small boat used in the docks.

MONKEY-CAGE, subs. (common).—The grated room in which a convict sees his friends. Fr. *le parloir des singes.*

MONKEY-COAT (or -JACKET). subs. (nautical).—A short, close-fitting jacket: a coat 'with no more tail than a monkey.' See CAPELLA.

MONKEY-PUMP, subs. (nautical).—The straw used in 'sucking the MONKEY' (q.v.).

MONKEY'S-ALLOWANCE, subs. (common).—'More kicks than half-pence.'

1785. GROSE, *Vulg. Tongue,* s.v.
1811. *Lex. Bal.,* s.v. MONKEY.
1823. BEE, *Dict. Turf,* s.v.
1833. MARRYAT, *Peter Simple,* ii. When you get on board you'll find MONKEY'S ALLOWANCE.
1856. C. KINGSLEY, *Letter* [3rd abridged ed. 1879], May. You fellows worked like bricks, spent money, and got midshipman's half-pay (nothing a-day and find yourself) and MONKEY'S ALLOWANCE (more kicks than halfpence).

MONKEYSHINES (MONKEYTRICKS or MONKEYINGS), subs. (common).—1. Antics ; and (2) tricks.

1830. BUCKSTONE, *Wreck Ashore,* i. Take care, young woman, you can't tell what MONKEY TRICKS she may have been up to in foreign parts.
1878. A. R. GROTE, *Pop. Sic. Monthly,* XIII. 435. You may have noticed bare-footed boys cutting up MONKEY-SHINES on trees with entire safety to themselves.
1887. *Lippincotts' Mag.,* Aug. 'A Land of Love,' p. 231. Such MONKEY-SHINES ! It proves that you have no serious interest in science.
1888. ROLF BOLDREWOOD, *Robbery Under Arms,* xi. Don't get up to any MONKEY TRICKS.
1892. MILLIKEN, *'Arry Ballads,* p. 6 . Your MONKEYINGS mar every pageant.

MONKEY'S-MONEY, subs. (old).—1. Goods; (2) labour; and (3) words. Fr. *monnaie des singes.*

1653. URQUHART, *Rabelais,* iv. 3. It was an original by Master Charles Charmois, principal painter to king Megistus (*of France*), paid for in court fashion with MONKEY'S MONEY.

MONKEY'S-TAIL, subs. (old nautical).—*See* quot.

1823. MARRYAT, *Peter Simple,* p. 28 [ed. 1863]. 'Youngster, hand me that MONKEY'S TAIL !' I saw nothing like a MONKEY'S TAIL, but I was so frightened that I snatched up the first thing that I saw which was a very short bar of iron, and it so happened that it was the very article wanted.

MONMOUTH-STREET FINERY, subs. phr. (old).—*See* quot. [Monmouth-Street (now Dudley-Street) was long a mart for second-hand clothes]. *Cf.* WARDOUR-STREET ENGLISH.

1851. MAYHEW, *Lond. Lab.,* etc. ii. 25. MONMOUTH-STREET FINERY was a common term to express tawdriness and pretence.

MONNIKER (or MONICK). *See* MONEKER.

MONOCULAR-EYEGLASS, subs. (common).—The breech. For synonyms *see* BUM.

MONOSYLLABLE, (also DIVINE MONOSYLLABLE) subs. (venery).—The female *pudendum;* CUNT (q.v.).

ENGLISH SYNONYMS. A.B.C.; Abraham's bosom (generic) ; ace ; ace of spades ; Adam's own ; agility ; agreeable ruts of life ; alcove ; alley ; almanack ; Alpha and Omega ; altar ; altar of Hymen ; altar of love ; altar of pleasure ; amulet ; antipodes ; aphrodisaical tennis court (URQU-

HART) ; arbour ; attic ; Aunt Maria ; axis.

Baby-maker ; bag of tricks ; bank ; basket-maker ; bath of birth (WHITMAN) ; bazaar ; beauty ; beauty-spot ; bed-fellow ; bee-hive ; belle chose (CHAUCER) ; Belly Dale ; Belly Dingle ; belly-entrance ; Berkeley-Hunt (rhyming) ; best (DORSET) ; best in Christendom (ROCHESTER) ; best-worst part (DONNE) ; bird's nest ; bit ; bite (GROSE) ; bit of fish, of jam, of meat, of mutton, of pork, of rough, or of skate ; bit on a fork ; Black (WILL. CAVENDISH) ; Black Bess ; black hole ; black (or brown, or grey) jock ; black ring ; blind eye ; Bluebeard's closet ; boat ; bob-and-hit ; bonne-bouche ; bore ; Botany Bay ; book-binder's wife ('manufacturing in sheets': G. A. STEVENS) ; Bottomless Pit ; bower ; bower of bliss (CAREW and HERRICK) ; box ; brat-getting place (FLORIO) ; breach ; bread-winner (prostitutes') ; broom ; brown madam (GROSE) ; bucket ; Buckinger's boot (GROSE) ; budget ; bull's eye (ROCHESTER) ; bumbo (negro) ; bun ; bung-hole ; busby ; Bushey Park ; butcher's shop ; butter-boat ; button-hole.

Cabbage ; cabbage-field, -garden, or -patch ; cab-mat ; caldron (RAMSAY) ; callibistry (URQUHART) ; can ; candlestick ; canister (BURNS) ; Cape Horn ; Cape of Good Hope ; carnal-trap (URQUHART) ; case ; cat (DURFEY) ; catch-'em-alive-o ; cat's-meat; catherine wheel ; cauliflower ; cave of harmony ; caze (BURTON) ; cellar (R. BROME) ; cellarage ; cellar-door ; central furrow (CLELLAND) ; central office ; centre of attraction ; centre-of-bliss ; centrique part (DONNE) ; certificate of birth ; chat ; chink ; chum ; churn ; circle (SHAKSPEARE and CONGREVE) ; civet ; claff (LYNDSAY);clap-trap ; cleft of flesh (CLELLAND); clock ; cloth (generic); the clouds ; cloven spot (CLELLAND) ; cock ; Cock-Alley ; cock-chafer ; cock-holder ; Cock-Inn ; Cock-Lane ; cockloft ; cockpit ; Cockshire ; cockshy ; coffee-shop ; cogie (Scots) ; commodity (SHAKSPEARE, etc.) ; concern ; coney ; confessional ; conjuring-book (DURFEY) ; contrapunctum (URQUHART) ; conundrum ; cookie ; copy-hold (DURFEY) ; corner-cupboard ; cornucopia ; County-Down ; coupler ; covered way (STERNE) ; coynte (BURTON) ; coyote ; crack ; cradle ; cranny ; cream-jug ; crevice ; crinkum-crankum ; crooked way ; crown of sense (ROCHESTER) ; cuckoo's nest ; cunnie (DURFEY) ; cunnikin ; cunny-burrow (URQUHART) ; cunt-kin ; cuntlet ; Cupid's-Alley, (-anvil, -arbour, -cave, -cloister, -corner, -cupboard, -highway, -ring, or -pincushion) ; cushat ; cushion ; custom-house ; custom-house goods (a harlot's: 'because fairly entered': GROSE) ; cut-and-come-again ; Cyprian-arbour, -cave, or -strait (CAREW).

Daisy ; dark, or dark-hole ; dearest bodily part (SHAKSPEARE); diddle ; diddly-pout ; dimple ; doodle-case ; doodle-sack ; dormouse ; down bed of beauty (STEVENS) ; Downshire ; downstairs; downy-bit ; drain ; dripping-pan ; duck pond ; dumb-glutton ; dumb-, or -hairy-, oracle ; dumb-

squint ; duster ; Dutch clock ; dyke.

Eel-pot (or -trap) ; eel-skinner ; End of the Sentimental Journey (STERNE) ; entrance ; Et-cetera (ROCHESTER and CLELLAND) ; evergreen ; everlasting wound ; Eve's custom-house ('where Adam made the first entry': GROSE) ; exchequer (DONNE) ; Exeter-hall ; eye that weeps most when best pleased (STEVENS).

Factotum ; fancy bit ; Fanny ; Fanny-Artful ; Fanny-Fair ; faucett ; fiddle (BURNS) ; fie-for-shame (schoolgirls') ; fig ; firelock ; fireplace ; firework ; fish (generic) ; fish-market ; flap ; flapdoodle ; fleshly-idol (BROWN); fleshly-part ; flower ; flower of chivalry ; flower-pot ; fly-by-night ; fly-cage ; fly-trap ; forecaster ; forecastle ; fore-hatch ; fore-room ; forewoman ; forge ; fort ; fortress ; fountain of love ; free fishery ; front-garden ; front-gut ; front-parlor ; fruitful vine (' which bears flowers every four weeks, and fruit every nine months': GROSE) ; Fumbler's-Hall ; funniment ; furrow (BURNS).

Gallimaufry ; gap (DURFEY) ; garden ; Garden of Eden ; gash ; Gate of Horn ; Gate of Life (BURNS) ; G.C. ; gentleman's pleasure garden ; garrison (CROWNE) ; gear (FLORIO) ; gigg (GROSE) ; goatmilker ; goldfinch's nest ; gravy-giver ; greens (generic) ; green meadow ; grotto ; Grove of Eglantine (CAREW) ; grummett ; gully ; gut-entrance ; gutter ; gymnasium ; gyvel (BURNS).

Hair-court ; Hairyfordshire ; hairy ring ; half-moon (KILLIGREW) ; Hans Carvel's ring (URQUHART and PRIOR) ; happy hunting-grounds ; harbour ; harbour of hope ; hatchway ; heaven ; hell ; hole of content (FLORIO) ; hole of holes ; Holloway ; home-sweet-home ; horse-collar ; hotel ; house under the hill ; housewife ; hypogastrian cranny(URQUHART).

India (DONNE) ; ineffable ; in-glenook ; intercrural trench(URQUHART) ; It ; itcher ; Itching Jenny ; Ivory Gate.

Jacob's Ladder ; Jack Straw's Castle ; jam-pot ; jelly-bag ; jewel ; jigger ; jock ; justum (URQUHART).

Kaze ; keifer (generic) ; kennel (ROCHESTER) ; kettle (DURFEY, etc.) ; kitchen;Kitty;knick-knack.

Ladder ; Lady Berkeley ; lady-flower (WHITMAN) ; Lady Jane ; lady-star (HALL) ; lamp of love ; Lapland ; lather-maker ; leading article ; lea-rigs (generic: BURNS) ; leather (generic: URQUHART, LYNDSAY,BURNS) ; Leather-Lane ; leavingshop ; Life's Dainty (G. A. STEVENS) ; ling ; little sister ; little spot where uncle's doodle goes ; living fountain (HERRICK) ; lobster-pot ; lock ; locker ; lock of all locks (STEVENS) ; Love-lane ; Love's harbour (CAREW) ; Love's Paradise (MARSTON) ; Lowlands ; Low Countries ; lucky-bag.

Machine ; maddikin ; Madge (GROSE) ; Madge Howlett ; magnet ; main avenue (CLELLAND) ; malkin (LYNDSAY) ; mangle ; man-hole ; man-trap ; Marble Arch ; mark (DURFEY) ; mark-of-the-beast ; Mary-Jane ; masterpiece ; meat (generic) ; meat-market ; medlar ; melting-pot ; merkin (R. FLETCHER,and A. SMITH);Middle Kingdom ; Midlands ; milker ; milking-pail ; milk-pan ; milt-market ; mill (DURFEY, BURNS, etc.);milliner's shop; mine of pleas

ure ; miraculous cairn;Miss Brown (GROSE) ; Miss Laycock (GROSE) ; modicum (COTTON) ; money (GROSE) ; money-box ; money-maker ; money-spinner ; monkey (American);mole-catcher; Molly's Hole· Mons Meg ; mortar ; moss-rose ; mossy bank ; mossy cell ; mossy-face ; mother of all saints, all souls, or St. Patrick ; Mount-Faulcon (FLORIO) ; Mount Pleasant ; mouse ; mouser ; mouse-trap ; mouth thankless ; (Old Scots': KENNEDY, LYNDSAY, SCOTT) ; mouth that says no word about it (G. A. STEVENS) ; muff (BURNS) ; mumble-peg ; mushroom ; mustard-pot ; mutton (generic and universal).

Naggie ; name-it-not; nameless ; nature ; nature's tufted treasure ; naughty ; needle-case;nest (American) ; nest in the bush ; nether eye, or lips (CHAUCER) ; never-out ; niche ; niche-cock ; nick-in-the-notch ; nonny-nonny ; non-such ; notch ; novelty ; Number-Nip ; nursery.

Old Ding ; old hat (FIELDING and STERNE) ; old woman ; omnibus ; open C ; oracle ; orchard ; ornament ; orifice ; open charms (LITTLE) ; oven ; oyster (KILLIGREW) ; oyster-catcher.

Palace of pleasure ; pancake ; parenthesis (JON BEE) ; parsley-bed (DURFEY) ; parts of shame (POPE) ; patch ; peculiar river (SHAKSPEARE) ; penwiper ; periwinkle ; pfotz (HALL STEVENSON) ; pincushion ; pintle-case ; pipe ; pisser ; pit (HERRICK) ; pitcher ; pit-mouth ; pit of darkness ; place ; placket-box (DURFEY) ; pleasure-boat ; pleasure ground ; pleasure's place (DAVIS) ; plum-tree (COTGRAVE) ; p-maker ; portal to the bower of bliss (HERRICK) ; postern gate to the Elysian fields (HERRICK) ; pouter ; premises ; pretty ; prick-holder ; prick-skinner ; princock (DUNBAR) ; privates; privities; privy-hole; privy Paradise ; pudend (URQUHART) ; punse (YIDDISH) ; pulpit (old) ; purse (DONNE) ; puss (DURFEY and COTTON) ; pulse ; pussy-cat.

Quaint ; quarry ; quaver-case (A. SCOTT) ; Queen of Holes (ROCHESTER) ; quem ; queynte (CHAUCER and FLORIO) ; quim ; quimsby ; quivive.

Rasp ; rattle-ballocks ; receipt of custom; red ace ; Red-C.; regulator (BURNS) ; rest-and-be-thankful ; ring ; road to a christening ; roasting jack ; rob-the-ruffian ; rooster ; rose ; rough-O ; rough malkin ; rough-and-ready ; rough-and-tumble ; rufus.

Sack (DURFEY) ; saddle ; salt-cellar ; sampler ; scabbard ; scuttle ; seal ; sear ; secret parts (SHAKSPEARE) ; seed-plot ; seminary ; sex ; shake-bag ; sharp-and-blunt (rhyming) ; sheath ; shell (LYNDSAY and DUNBAR) ; skin-coat (URQUHART) ; skin-the-pizzle ; slipper ; slit ; slot ; Smock-Alley ; snatch (American) ; snatch-blatch (MOTTEUX) ; snatch-box ; socket (JONSON) ; solution of continuity (URQUHART) ; South Pole ; spender ; sperm-sucker ; spit-fire ; spinning-jenny ; split-apricot ; split-fig ; split-mutton (generic) ; spleuchan (BURNS) ; sporran ; Sportsman's Gap ; Sportsman's Hole ; spot of Cupid's archery (ROCHESTER) ; square push (American) ; standing room for one; star; star over the garter (LORD CORK); Stream's Town (Irish: GROSE); suck-and-swallow; sugar-basin.

Tail (general); target; teazle (RAMSAY); temple of Venus; tench; tenuc (back-slang); that; Thatched House; thing; thingamy; thingumbob; tickler; tickle-Thomas; tickle-toby; tile; tirly-whirly (BURNS); tit-mouse; toll-dish (DURFEY); tool-chest; touch-'em-up; touch-hole; towdie (DUNBAR); tow-wow (A. SMITH); towsy-mowsy (DORSET); toy (ETHEREGE); toy-shop; treasure; treasury of love (CLELLAND); tu quoque (GROSE); turnpike; tuzzi-muzzy; twat (DURFEY); twachylle; twittle; tunnel.

Under-belongings; under-dimple; under-entrance; under-world; undeniable; Upper Holloway; upright wink; undertaker.

Vacuum; vade-mecum; Venus's Secret Cell, Highway, Honey pot, or Mark; vessel (SEMPLE); vestry; vineyard.

Wame (BURNS); wanton ace; ware; waste-pipe; water-box (FLORIO); water-gap (URQUHART); water-gate (DURFEY); water-mill (GROSE); way-in; wayside-fountain; wayside-ditch; weather-gig (DURFEY); what-do-you-call-it; whim-wham; wicket; wonderful lamp; workshop.

Yoni; you-know-what; yum-yum.

FRENCH SYNONYMS. *L'abricot de la jardinière* (common: also *abricot fendu* = split-apricot); *l'affaire* (conventional = THING, q.v.); *l'amarris* (O. Fr. = matrix. Also *l'amatrix*); *l'an*gora (common = CAT, q.v.); *l'animal* (= the beast), *l'anneau* (common = ring, q.v. Also *l'anneau d'Hans Carvel* = HANS CARVEL'S RING, q.v.); *l'antre* or *l'antre à Priape* (conventional: = Priapus' lair); *les appas* (= charms); *l'argument* (= ORACLE); *l'atelier* (common = WORKSHOP, q.v. Also *l'atelier de Vénus*); *l'armoyre*(= cup board); *l'autel* (conventional = the altar: also *l'autel de Vénus* and *l'autel velu*); *l'autre* or *l'autre chose* = THING or THINGAMY); *l'avec* (= the wherewithal); *le bagage*; *la bague* (common = RING, q.v.); *le bahut* (common: = cupboard); *le baquet* (common: = pissing-tub); *le bas* (conventional = the under-world or -entrance); *la basse-cour* (= courtyard); *les basses-marches* (common = the bottom-steps); *le bassin* (= the dock); *la batterie*; *la baudrière équinoxiale* (= the equinoctial belt); *le bedon* (= drum); *la belouse*; *le beauvoire* (= BEAUTY-SPOT: also *beauvoire de Vénus*); *le bénitier* (common = font); *le bidault*; *le bijou* (literary = the jewel); *le biribi*; *le bis* (= Miss Brown); *le bissac* (common = wallet); *le blanc*; *la blouse* (billiard players' = pocket); *la boîte d'amourette* (= Love's casket); *le bonnet* (common = CAP, q.v. Also *le bonnet à poils* = hair-cap; and *le bonnet de grenadier* = BUSBY); *la bouche d'en bas* (common = under-mouth); *la bourse à vits* (RABELAIS = prick-purse); *la boussole* (= compass); *la bouteille* (= bottle); *la boutique* (common = shop); *le bouton*; *la boutonnière* (general =

BUTTON-HOLE); *le brasier* (common = MELTING-POT); *la brèche* (common = BREACH); *le brelingot*; *le bréviaire*, cf. CONJURING BOOK; *le but d'amour* (common = Love's bull's-eye: also *le but de désir* and *le but mignon de fouterie*); *Ça* (conventional = THAT, q.v.); *le cabinet* (common = the W.C.); *le cadran* (= Love's dial); *la cage* (common = CAGE, q.v.); *le canal* (= DRAIN); *le canichon* (common = poodle); *le calendrier* (common = ALMANACK); *le callibistri* (RABELAIS); *le calibre* (= BORE); *le carimara*; *le carrefour*; *le cas* (= HOLE); *le cas du devant* (= FOREHATCH); *la casemate*; *le caudet*; *la cave* (common = CELLAR); *la caverne* (= BOTTOMLESS PIT, q.v.); *ce* (= THAT); *ceci* (conventional = this: cf. THAT, q.v.); *cela* (= THAT, q.v.); *le Céleste-empire* (literary = Celestial empire); *celui qui a perdu*; *celui de l'argent* (= MONEY); *celui qui regarde*; *celui qui contrebas*; *le centre* (common = CENTREBIT); *le centre de délices* (= CENTRE OF BLISS); *la chambre*; *la chambre défendue* (= Bluebeard's closet); *le champ* (common = GARDEN); *le champ de bataille* (=battle-field); *le champ de Vénus* (= Venus's garden); *le chandelier* (common = CANDLESTICK); *le chapeau* (common: cf. OLD HAT and *le bonnet*); *la chapelle* (common: cf. HOLY OF HOLIES); *les charmes*; *le charmier* (= charmer); *le chat* (common = PUSS); *le château de gaillardin* (= Wanton Castle); *la divine cicatrice* (literary =divine scar); *le chaud*; *le chaudron* (common = KETTLE); *le chemin de Paradis* (literary = the ROAD TO HEAVEN, q.v.); *la cheminée* (= CHIMNEY); *la chose* (conventional = THING, q.v.); *la citadelle* (=FORT); *la cité d'amour* (literary = City of Love); *le clapier* (= WARREN: cf. CUNNYBOROUGH); *le cloître* (= cloister); *le cœur* (O. Fr.); *la coiffe* (common = cap); *le coin* (= nook); *le combien* (prostitutes' = 'how much?' cf. BREAD-WINNER); *le comment-à-nom* (= WHAT'S-ITS-NAME); *le con* (old and common = CUNT, q.v.: other forms, diminutive or familiar, are *concon, conil* = CUNNY, *conillon* = CUNTLET, *connin, conneau, connasse* = BUSHEL-CUNT, and *connichon* = CUNNI-KIN, *conibert, connaud*); *le concentrique* (= centrique part); *le cornet*; *le cornichon* (common); *le corps-de-garde* (= guard-room); *la coquille* (=shell); *le corbillon* (= basket); *le corridor d'amour* (literary: cf. CUPID'S ALLEY); *le creuset* (common = MELTING-POT); *le creux* (= chasm); *la crevasse* (= CHINK, or CRANNY); *le crot*; *le crot à faire bon-bon*; *la cuisine* (= KITCHEN); *le crypsimen*; *le cul* (popular: specifically, the *rectum*); *le cymbe*; *le custodinos*; *le dé*; *le dédale* (common = maze); *le dedans* (cf. HOLY OF HOLIES); *le drôle*; *le devant* (common: cf. FRONT-PARLOUR); *le dévorant* (common: cf. DUMB-GLUTTON); *l'écaille* (= SHELL); *l'écoutille* (nautical = scuttle); *l'écu*; *l'écrevisse*; *l'écuelle* (common); *l'empire du Milieu* (literary = MIDDLE KINGDOM: cf. *l'empire Céleste*);*l'emplâtre*; *l'enclume*(=

anvil); *l'endroit* (= the PLACE); *enfer*(=HELL); *l'engin*(=TOOL); *l'ennemi* (= the enemy); *l'entrée*; *l'entonnoir* (= funnel); *l'entre-deux* (popular: also *l'entremise* and *l'entre-sol*); *l'essaim*; *l'estré*; *l'étable*; *l'évier* (= SINK); *l'éteignoir* (common = the extinguisher); *l'éternelle cicatrice* (literary = the everlasting scar); *l'étoffe à faire la pauvreté* (common); *l'étui* (= NEEDLE-CASE, q.v.); *le faquin*; *le faucon*; *la fendasse* (military = GASH); *le fenil* (COCK-LOFT); *la fente* (common = SLIT); *la feuille de sauge* (= *fève*; *la figue* (common = FIG); *la figuatelle*; *le fita*; *la fontaine* (common = fountain); *la fontenelle*; *le formulaire*; *la forêt de bois-mort*; *le fort* (= FORT); *la forteresse* (= stronghold); *la fosse* (cf. HOLE); *le fossé* (= ditch); *le four* (common = OVEN); *la fourche* (= fork); *la fournaise* (= furnace); *le fracte*; *la fressure* (Old Fr.); *le frippe-lippe*; *le front*; *le fruit d'amour* (general); *la gaîne* (= SHEATH); *le gardon*; *la garenne* (cf. CUNNYBOROUGH); *la gauffrière*; *le gnomon*; *le golfe* (common: cf. BOTTOMLESS PIT); *le gouffre secret*; *la gouttière* (= GUTTER); *la grange* (common); *le grenier* (= COCKLOFT); *la grille*; *le grobis*; *la guérite* (common = sentry-box: cf. STANDING ROOM FOR ONE); *hæc*; *la hariquoque*; *le harnois* (general: cf. HORSE-COLLAR); *le haubert*; *l'hérisson* (general = urchin); *l'hiatus* (common = GAP: also *l'hiatus divin*); *l'histoire* (general: also = speci-fically the penis); *l'honneur*; *le huilhot*; *le huis*; *l'huître* (= OYSTER); *l'humanité*; *l'ignominie* (cf. FIE-FOR-SHAME); *il* (= IT); *l'instrument* (also = penis); *l'intersection du corps*; *le jardin* (= GARDEN: common to most languages: also *le jardin d'amour*); *la jolie*,or *belle chose* (= PRETTY: conventional); *la jointe*; *la jointure*; *le jouet* (= TOY); *le jou-jou* (common: cf. TOY); *le joyau* (common = *la* = THAT); *le labyrinthe de concupiscence* (RABELAIS); *la lampe amoureuse*; *la lampe merveilleuse* (= WONDERFUL LAMP); *la lanterne* (common); *le lapin* (= CONEY); *le leidesche* (RABELAIS); *la latrine* (general: cf. PRIVY-HOLE); *le lieu*; *l'autre lieu*; *lieu sacré*; *le limosin*; *le lure*; *la machine* (common); *le maljoint* (common); *le mallier*; *le manchon* (common: cf. MUFF); *la marchandise* (common: cf. GEAR or WARE); *la marmite*, or *marmotte*; *le maroquin* (cf. LEATHER); *le masteau*; *le membre*; *le ménage*; *la métaire*; *le messire Noc* (literary and anagrammatic: *Noc* = *Con*); *le mignon d'amourette* (= LOVE'S DARLING); *le milieu* (common); *le minon* (= PUSSY); *la mirely*; *le mirliton* (general); *la mitaine* (= mitten); *le mont-fendu*; *le morceau* (= BIT); *le morel*; *la mortaise*; *le mortier* (common); *le mosel*; *le moule à pine* (common = pintle-mould); *le moulin-à-eau* (common: cf. WATER-MILL); *la moniche*, or *monique* (thieves'); *la nacelle*

(= BOAT); *la nature* (conventional); *la navire*; *le noc* (anagram of con: cf. TENUC); *le noir* (common: cf. BLACK, BLACK-HOLE and MISS BROWN); *l'object* (common = CONCERN); *la petite oie*; *l'osière*; *l'outil* (= TOOL); *l'ouverture divine* (literary: cf. HOLY OF HOLIES); *l'ouvroir* (= workshop); *l'ovale*; *le panier*; *le Paradis* (= PARADISE); *le parchemin*; *les parties honteuses* (= PARTS OF SHAME); *le passage*; *les Pays Bas* (common: cf. LOWLANDS or LOW COUNTRIES); *le pelisson*; *la pénillière* (= COCK-HOLDER); *le pertuia* (BALZAC); *la petiote délectation*; *le petit je-ne-sais-quoi* (= LITTLE WHAT'S-ITS-NAME); *le petit centre* (common); *le petit lapin* (common: cf. CONEY); *le petit trou* (common); *le petit vase* (common); *la pièce du milieu* (common: cf. CENTREBIT); *la pissette* (common PISSER: cf. WATER-WORKS); *la place*; *la plaie* (= the wound); *le point conjugal*; *le pôle*; *le portail* (= FRONT-ENTRANCE); *la porte* (also *porte du devant* = FRONT-DOOR); *le port de Cythère* (literary); *la poste*; *le pot* (=PISS-POT); *les pudendes*; *le puits d'amour*; *le quartier*; *Quasi-modo*; *quelque chose de chaud* (= a bit of hot); *la queue* (common = TAIL); *le quoniam bonus*(literary); *la raie*; *la ratoire*; *le réduit* (common); *le reste*; *la rivière*; *la rose* (conventional); *le sac* (cf. BAG OF TRICKS); *le saint* (= patron saint; *le salon du plaisir* (cf. PLEASURE-PLACE, -GARDEN, and -GROUND); *le sanctuaire* (= HOLY OF HOLIES); *le sadinet* (VILLON); *le seau* (= pail); *le Sénégal* (military: cf. INDIA); *la serrure* (common: cf. LOCK); *la solution de continuité* (RABELAIS); *la souris* (= MOUSE); *la tabernacle* (literary = ARK); *la table*; *le tapecul*; *le temple de Cypris* (literary); *la terre*; *la terrier*; *la tesnière*; *le théâtre de la nature* (common: cf. NATURE'S WORKSHOP); *le thermomètre*; *le tirelire* (common: cf. MONEY-BOX); *la toison* (= FLEECE); *la tonsure*; *la tranchée* (= TRENCH); *la trappe* (= TRAP-DOOR); *le trône du plaisir* (literary); *le trou* (common = HOLE: also, *le trou de service*, *le petit trou*, *le trou charnel*, *le trou-madame*, *le trou mignon*, *le trou par où la femme pisse*, and *le trou velu*); *tu-autem*; *l'un*; *l'ustensile*; *le vagin* (conventional); *le vaisseau* (cf. BOAT); *le vaisseau charnel*; *la vallée paphienne* (=PAPHIAN VALE); *le vallon*; *le vase*; *le velu*; *le ventre* (= WAME); *le petit ventre*; *Vénus*; *la viande du devant* (= fore-meat); *la vigne du seigneur*; *le zin-zin*; *le verger de Cypris* (literary = the Cyprian orchard).

GERMAN SYNONYMS. *Busche* (Hebrew = modesty); *Haar-truhe* (Old. Ger. *truhe* = HAIR TRUNK); *Kuttoch* (also = pocket handkerchief, pocket, and sweetheart); *Pfotze*; *Schmu*; *Schema*; *Schmalle*; *Schummel* (also = hawker); *Schwesterlein* (= LITTLE SISTER); *Weiberscham* (= PRIVITIES): *Weiblichescham* or *Weiblichkeit* (= womanhood).

ITALIAN SYNONYMS. *Bisti;* or *bistolfo* (Fr. *bis*); *baschiera;* *bécchina* (TORRIANO - FLORIO: = 'a woman's quaint or gear'; *bacchi* = 'certain blazing stars all shaggie, compassed with a long main or hairy fringe'); *bella bellina* (cf. PRETTY); *cioncia* (FLORIO: = 'a woman's free quaint'); *carnafau* (FLORIO: = 'the brat-getting place, or hole of content'); *cioncia* (FLORIO); *cionno* (TORRIANO-FLORIO: = 'gullish, silly-witted'; cf. BIT OF FOOLISH-NESS); *connino* (cf. CUNNY); *conno* (FLORIO: = 'a woman's privy parts, or quaint, as Chaucer calls it.'); *cotale* (= WHAT'S-ITS-NAME); *cotalina* (= THING-AMY); *facende; ferne; ferale; femora* (FLORIO); *fessa* (= CLEFT); *fica* (= a fig); *firiende; forame; fregna* or *fringa; gabbia,* or *gaggia* (= a cage); *golfo di fetalio* (FLORIO: = 'a rugged and bristlie gulf'); *grignapolla* (used of both sexes); *horto de venere* (Venus' garden); *malforo* (FLORIO: = 'a mischievous hole'); *menchia* (= sport: cf. FUNNY BIT); *mentole* (used of both sexes); *monina* (= MONKEY); *monte di Venere* (= Venus' Hill); *monte di ficcule* (TORRIANO-FLORIO: = 'a woman's Mount-falcon'); *mortaio* (= mortar); *mozza* (FLORIO: = 'a wench, a lass, a girl. Also a woman's gear or cunnie'); *moneta* (= MONEY); *natura* (FLORIO: = 'the privie parts of man, woman, or beast'); *pettinale* (FLORIO: = 'the privities that have haires upon them'); *pinca* (feminine of *pinco*=PRICK); *porcile di venere* (Venus' Pig-sty); *potta* (FLORIO: = 'a wom-

an's commodity; whence, *potissiare* = 'to use or play with'—*idem* 'roundlie'); *pottaccia* (FLORIO: = 'a filthy great cunt'); *San Giovanni Bocca d'Oro* (used of both sexes); *sermolina; serpolina; val cava* (BOCCACCIO: = a cave); *val costura; valle di Acheronte* (cf. BOTTOMLESS PIT); *valle satalio* (FLORIO: = 'a brizlie, buskie, brackish, hairie, gloomie, cloudie, duskie place; Boccace doth use it for a woman's privie parts'); *vergogne* (cf. PARTS OF SHAME).

SPANISH SYNONYMS. *Aceitero* (= oil-flask); *aduana* (= CUSTOM-HOUSE); *camino oscuro* (= COVERED-WAY); *camino real* (= highway); *changa* (= joke); *Chocho* (common); *chumino* (rare); *cicople* (= CYCLOPE); *ciega* (= blind woman); *cimenterio* (= churchyard); *conejera* (= rabbit-warren); *Conejo; confesionario* (= confessional); *coño* or *coña* (classic); *cosquillosa* (= MISS TICKLISH); *Cuba* (cf. INDIA and *la Sénégal*); *Do bemol* (= C. flat); *Doña Fulana de Tal* (= MRS. WHAT'S-HER-NAME); *espondeo* (=spondee *i.e.* two longs); *la fachada* (= façade); *foco de vida* (= Life's focus); *fogón* (= touch-hole); *fortaleza; greta* (= CRACK); *grieta* (= RIFT); *guerica; huerfana* (= orphan); *jopo; Juana la loca* (= Crazy Jane); *lesma; lonja* (= Exchange); *Madre Eterna* (= Eternal Mother); *Madre Soledad* (= Mother Lonely); *mata* (= bush); *miriñaque* (= toy); *mocosa* (= SNOTTY); *mofa* (= flirt); *ostra; paca; Paises Bajos* (= Low

COUNTRIES or *Les Pays bas*); *pan; papo; periquito; perra* (= bitch); *piadosa* (= MISS PRIMSY); *posada general* (= common inn); *pozo nupcial* (= nuptial well); *propriedad; raja* (= SLIT); *regalona* (= pet); *Señora López* (cf. MISS BROWN); *semana santa* (= holy week); *sierra* (= mountain: cf. MOUNT PLEASANT and *le mont fendu); superiora* (= abbess); *tienda* (=shop); *tranvía* (= tram-car); *tronera* (= loophole); *vaina* (= scabbard); *vasija morena* (= brown jug).

PORTUGUESE SYNONYMS. *Abbadessa* (= abbess); *aranha caranguegeira; as* (= ACE); *asbeiras; assoadouro do caralho; boceta* (classical); *cabra* (= goat); *cadinho* (= MELTING-POT or CRUCIBLE); *lagea; lanha; mata dos chatos* (= crab-walk: also = MOTTE); *papudo* (of a stout woman); *passarinho; pinto; poço sem fundo* (= BOTTOMLESS PIT); *registro de bacalháo* (cf. FISHMARKET).

VARIOUS. *Kut* (Dutch); *gatte* (Walloon).

1714. LUCAS, *Gamesters*, 186.. They [girls] all at once set up a laughing ... occasion'd by some silly naughty word they have got by the end; perhaps a bawdy MONOSYLLABLE, such as boys write upon walls.

1785. GROSE, *Vulg. Tongue*, s.v.

1786. PINKERTON, *Ancient Scottish Poems*, 384. Addison, the best instructor of the small morals who ever lived, yet thought nothing, in papers designed for the breakfast table, and the ladies, as he says himself, to tell us that a MONOSYLLABLE was his delight.

1788. G. A. STEVENS, *Songs Comic & Satyrical*, p. 88. But why from this round-about phrase must be guessed, What in ONE single SYLLABLE's better

expressed; That SYLLABLE then I my sentiment call, So here's to that WORD, which is ONE WORD for all.

1811. *Lex. Bal.*, s.v. MONOSYLLABLE. A woman's commodity.

1823. BEE, *Dict. Turf*, s.v. MONOSYLLABLE—(the); feminine only, and described by Nat Bailey as *pudenda muliebris*. Of all the thousand monosyllables in our language, this *one* only is designated by the definite article—THE MONOSYLLABLE; therefore do some men call it 'the article,' 'my article,' and 'her article,' as the case may be.

MONS, *subs.* (Winchester College).—A crowd. Also as verb: *e.g.,* 'Square round there, don't MONS.' —*Notions.*

MONS MEG, *subs.* (venery).—1. The female *pudendum.* For synonyms see MONOSYLLABLE.

MONSTROUS, *adv.* (colloquial).—A general intensitive. See AWFUL, BLOODY, LARGE etc.

1619. FLETCHER, *Wild-Goose Chase*, ii. 2. She is MONSTROUS proud, then.

1635. GLAPTHORNE, *Hollander*, ii. 1. The very scraping of our Galley-pots performes more MONSTROUS wonders.

1693. CONGREVE, *Old Batchelor*, iv. 4. O MONSTROUS filthy fellow.

1843. *Maj. Jones Courtship*, viii. That makes mother MONSTROUS jealous.

MONS VENERIS, *subs. phr.* (venery). —See quot. cf. MOUNT PLEASANT.

1728. BAILEY, *Eng. Dict.* (1778), s.v. MONS VENERIS is that plump part of the female privities which covers the *os pubis.*

MONTEM, *subs.* (Eton College).—An Eton custom up to 1847, which consisted in the scholars going in procession on the Whit-Tuesday of every third year to a mound (Lat. *ad montem*), near the Bath Road, and exacting a gratuity from persons present or passing by. The collection was

given to the captain or senior scholar, and helped to defray his expenses at the University.

MONTH, *subs.* (old conventional).—In *pl.* = *menses.* For synonyms see FLAG. Also MONTHLIES.

1611. COTGRAVE, *Dictionarie*, s.v. MONETH ... Woemens MONETHS, Menstruæ, les mois des femmes.

1617. MINSHEU, *Guide into Tongues*, s.v. A Woman's MONTHES, or Monthlie Termes. *Vide* Flowers.

1664. PEPYS, *Diary* (1894), 27 Sept. So home, where my wife having. . . her MONTHS upon her is gone to bed.

A BAD ATTACK OF THE END OF THE MONTH, *phr.* (common).—Impecuniosity.

MONTH-OF-SUNDAYS, *subs.* (common).—An indefinitely long time: cf. GREEK KALENDS.

1850. C. KINGSLEY, *Alton Locke*, xxvii. I haven't heard more fluent or passionate English this MONTH OF SUNDAYS.

1888. ROLF BOLDREWOOD, *Robbery Under Arms*, XL. 'I ain't been out of this blessed hole,' he says, 'for a MONTH OF SUNDAYS.'

1892. HENLEY and STEVENSON, *Deacon Brodie*, Sc. 2. p. 7. A MONTH OF SUNDAYS.

MONTH'S MIND, *subs. phr.* (old colloquial).—Longing. [From the cravings of pregnant women.]

1596. HALL, *Satires*, B. 4. s. 4. And sets a MONTH'S MIND upon smiling May.

1598. SHAKSPEARE, *Two Gentlemen*, i. 2. I see you have a MONTH'S MIND to them.

1605. *London Prodigal*, i. 2. He hath a MONTH'S MIND here to Mistress Frances.

1636. DAVENANT, *Platonic Lovers*, ii. 1. Belike then, you have a MONTH'S MIND to her.

1655. FULLER, *Church Hist.*, B. 4. § 23. The king had more than a

MONTH'S MIND to procure the pope to canonize Henry VI for a saint.

1663-78. BUTLER, *Hudibras* [quoted by JOHNSON]. For if a trumpet sound, or drum beat, Who has not a MONTH'S MIND to combat?

1670. RAY, *Proverbs* [Bohn (1893), 171]. To have a MONTH'S MIND to a thing.

1700. CONGREVE, *Way of the World*, iii. 1. She has a MONTH'S MIND; but I know Mr. Mirabell can't abide her.

1847. HALLIWELL, *Archaic and Provincial Words*, s.v. MONTH'S-MIND . . . a strong inclination. A common phrase in our early dramatists, and still in use.

MOOCH. See MIKE.

MOOCHER. See MIKER.

MOOCHING. See MIKING.

MOOER, *subs.* (common).—A cow; a WET-UN. Also MOO-COW.

1810. COMBE, *Dr. Syntax*, i. 14. The MOO-COW low'd, and Grizzle neigh'd.

MOON, *subs.* (common).—1. A month: specifically (thieves') a term of imprisonment, *e.g.,* ONE, TWO, or THREE MOONS; LONG MOON = a calendar month or CALLINGDER. See DRAG.

1823. J. F. COOPER, *Pilot*, iv. If you wait, sir, till the land-breeze fills your sails, you will wait another MOON, I believe.

1830. W. T. MONCRIEFF, *The Heart of London*, ii. 1. Mr. S.—Excuse my freedom but his modesty wouldn't permit him to tell you himself—he's been working on the mace—doing it up very blue, and so they've lumbered him for a few MOONS, that's all.

1848. RUXTON, *Life in the Far West*, 22. They would return to their village, and spend a MOON relating their achievements.

1859. MATSELL, *Vocabulum*, s.v. MOON. One month; thirty days' imprisonment.

1879. J. W. HORSLEY, in *Macm. Mag.*, xl. 501. I went on all straight the first few MOONS (months) at costering.

1893. EMERSON, *Signor Lippo*, 48. The quilts have to be changed once a MOON.

2. (American).—A large, round biscuit.

1883. S. CLEMENS ('Mark Twain'), *Life on the Mississippi*, 460. I spent my last ten cents for two MOONS and cheese.

3. (old).—A wig. Also HALF-MOON.

1608. MIDDLETON, *Mad World*, iii. 3. To wear HALF-MOONS made of another's hair.

1663. KILLIGREW, *The Parson's Wedding* [DODSLEY, *Old Plays* (1874), xiv. 456]. Score a Sack of Score in the HALF-MOON, *i.e.,* put a quart of sack into your head at my expense].

Verb. (colloquial).—To wander or lounge as in a dream.

1856. MISS YONGE, *Daisy Chain*, XXI. 'There! that bet is lost!' exclaimed Larkins. 'I laid Hill half-a-crown that you would not see me when you were MOONING over your verses!'

1863. C. READE, *Hard Cash*, i. 39. The silence continued till it was broken by—a fish out of water. An undergraduate in spectacles came MOONING along all out of his element.

1871. *Standard*, 14 April. 'Italy.' The press in vain raised its voice against this tomfoolery, which gives us an excuse for indulgence in our favourite occupation of MOONING at street corners, and of losing as much time as we can.

1871. *London Figaro*, 6 Mar. 'French Refugees in London.' Some of the Frenchmen still look wretched. The other day I saw two of them in blouses, mopingly MOONING along Broad-street.

1873. BLACK, *Princess of Thule*, xxvii. Spend their time in MOONING up in that island of theirs.

1877. BESANT and RICE, *Golden Butterfly*, xvi. I might have MOONED away the afternoon in the Park and dined at the club.

1884. W. C. RUSSELL, *Jack's Courtship*, xiii. All this hoping and moping and MOONING has made your heart too battered a thing to offer to the next peerless creature ye may happen to light on.

1888. ROLF BOLDREWOOD, *Robbery Under Arms*, xli. Well, I kept dark, you be sure, and MOONED about.

1889. MRS. OLIPHANT, *Poor Gentleman*, xliv. He went MOONING along with his head down in dull and hopeless despondency.

TO MAKE BELIEVE THE MOON IS MADE OF GREEN CHEESE, *verb. phr.* (common).—To hoax.

1562-3. *Jack Juggler* [DODSLEY, *Old Plays* (1874), ii. 154]. TO BELIEVE AND SAY THE MOON IS MADE OF A GREEN CHEESE Or else have great harm, and percase their life lese.

1640. *Wit's Recr.* [HOTTEN], 114. The way to make a Welch-man thirst for blisse, ... Is, to perswade him, that most certain 'tis, THE MOON IS MADE OF nothing but GREEN CHEESE.

1670. RAY, *Proverbs* [Bohn (1893), 171]. Tell me the MOON'S MADE OF GREEN CHEESE.

1846. T. MILDENHALL, *Sister and I*, sc. ii. Aye, you'd better ASK WHY THE MOON IS MADE OF GREEN CHEESE?

A BLUE MOON, *subs. phr.* (common).—An indefinite time; never; GREEK KALENDS (q.v.); TIB'S EVE (q.v.).

1528. ROY and BARLOW, *Rede me and Be nott Wroth*, p. 114. Yf they saye the MONE is BELEWE, We must beleve that it is true, Admittynge their interpretacion.

1876. B. H. BUXTON, *Jennie of the Prince's*, ii. 140. 'Does he often come of an evening?' asks Jennie. 'Oh, just once in a BLUE MOON, and then always with a friend.'

MINIONS OF THE MOON. See MOONMAN.

MAN IN THE MOON. See MAN.

TO SHOOT (or BOLT) THE MOON, *verb. phr.* (general).—To clear a house by night to evade distraint or payment of rent; TO DO A MOONLIGHT flitting. Hence MOONSHOOTERS.

1825. *Universal Songster*, i. 70. She wished to gammon her landlord, and likewise BOLT THE MOON.

1842. *Comic Almanack*, 18 June. Now prepare for LUNAR SHOOTING, and hunt out Huntley's vans. Convert your intimate friends after dark into light porters of household furniture.

1885. *Sporting Times*, 23 May. 'The Chorister's Promise.' The landlady woke next day at noon, And was thinking of getting her rent full soon, When she found that her lodger had SHOT THE MOON And gone with the chips she owed.

1891. *Morning Advertiser*, 27 Mar. It was proved that the goods were removed after eleven o'clock on the nights of the 2nd and 3rd of March—a process described as SHOOTING THE MOON.

1892. *Globe*, 2 April, p. 1, c. 5. The MOON-SHOOTERS sometimes have lodgers in their abodes. Not always do they think it worth while to inform them of their intended journeying, and this may be awkward for the lodger. *Ibid.* Who shall say that our popular phraseology is not occasionally picturesque when we describe the flight of impecunious tenants as SHOOTING THE MOON, or 'a midnight flit?'

TO CRY FOR THE MOON, *verb. phr.* (common).—To crave for the impossible. Fr. *Vouloir prendre la lune avec les dents.*

TO CAST BEYOND THE MOON, *verb. phr.* (common).—To make extravagant conjectures.

1606. *Wily Beguiled [Orig. Eng. Drama*, iii. 329]. Why, master gripe, he CASTS BEYOND THE MOON.

TO LEVEL AT THE MOON, *verb. phr.* (common).—To be very ambitious.

TO FIND AN ELEPHANT IN THE MOON, *verb. phr.* (old).—To find a mare's nest. [Sir Paul Neal, a seventeenth century virtuoso, gave out that he had discovered an elephant in the moon. It turned out that a mouse had crept into his telescope. *See* BUTLER, *The Elephant in the Moon*].

MOON-CALF, *subs.* (old).—1. A monster.

1609. SHAKSPEARE, *Tempest*, ii. 2. How, now, MOON-CALF? how does thine ague.

1620. BEN JONSON, *News from the New World, Print.* O, ay, MOON-CALVES! what monster is that, I pray you? 2 *Her.* Monster! none at all, a very familiar thing, like our fool here on earth.

2. (old).—A false conception.

1598. FLORIO, *A Worlde of Wordes*, s.v. *Mola*, . . . Also a lump of flesh in women's bellies which they call a tympanie or a MOONE CALFE.

1601. HOLLAND, *Pliny*, viii. ch. 15. A false conception, called MOLA, *i.e.*, a MOONECALFE.

1611. COTGRAVE, *Dictionarie* . . . . A MOONECALFE, a hard swelling or shapelesse peece of flesh in the wombe which makes women beleeve they are with child when they are not.

3. (colloquial).—A blockhead. For synonyms *see* BUFFLE and CABBAGE-HEAD. Also as *adj.* MOONCALFY.

1693. DRYDEN, *Journal*, vi. 798. The sotted MOON-CALF gapes, and staring on, Sees his own bus'ness by another done.

1858. DICKENS, *Great Expectations*, vii. 29—30. 'And Lor-a-mussy me!' cried my sister, casting off her bonnet in sudden desperation, 'here I stand talking to mere MOONCALFS, with Uncle Pumblechook waiting.'

1891. R. L. STEVENSON, *Kidnapped*, p. 44. 'No,' said the poor MOON-CALF, changing his tune at once.

1892. MILLIKEN, *'Arry Ballads*, 4. Look at the MOON-CALFY mash.

MOON-CURSER, *subs.* (old).—A linkboy; a GLIM-JACK. [His services were not required on moon-light nights].

1690. B. E., *Dict. Cant. Crew*, s.v.

*c.*1750. [quoted in ASHTON'S *Eighteenth Cent. Waifs*, 1887, p. 234]. Otherwise call'd *Glym Jack* from his having been a MOON CURSER, or Link Boy.

1786. GROSE, *Vulg. Tongue*, s.v.

1881. *Lex. Bal.*, s.v.

MOONER, *subs.* (common).—An idler; a GAPE-SEED (*q.v.*).

MOON-EYED, *adj.* (old). —*See* quots.

1785. GROSE, *Vulg. Tongue*, s.v. MOON-EYED HEN. A squinting wench.

1792. A. YOUNG, *Travels in France* (1787-9), p. 75. The English mare that carries me . . . is going rapidly blind. She is MOON-EYED.

1811. *Lex. Bal.*, s.v.

1859. MATSELL, *Vocabulum*, s.v. MOON-EYED HEN. A squinting prostitute.

MOONFLAW. MOONFLAW IN THE BRAIN, *verb. phr.* (old).—An idiosyncrasy; a craze. *See* BEE IN THE BONNET.

1659. BROME, *Queen and Concubine.* I fear she has a MOONFLAW in her brains; She chides and fights that none can look upon her.

MOONLIGHT (or **MOONSHINE**), *subs.* (old).—1. Smuggled spirits. [From the night-work of smugglers].

Verb. (Irish).—*See* quot.

1888. *Daily Telegraph*, 21 Nov. Colletty, the rent-warner, was a witness of a very unsatisfactory sort, and after he had deposed to his experience of being MOONLIGHTED in the thigh—Moonlighters, it appears, generally giving a grain or two, as another witness put it, in the legs of their victims.

MOONLIGHT ON THE LAKE, *subs. phr.* (American).—Sarsaparilla. *See* DRINKS.

A RUSH FOR MOONLIGHT, *subs. phr.* (American University).—An attempt at the prize for elocution.

MOONLIGHTER, *subs.* (common).—1. A prostitute. For synonyms *see* BARRACK-HACK and TART.

2. in *pl.* (Irish).—Men (*c.* 1880) enforcing the decrees of secret societies by violence. Their action was chiefly confined to the western counties, and their raids were nocturnal, whence the name. Their notices were signed 'Captain Moonlight.'

1882. *Saturday Review*, 30 Sep., p. 422. Taking MOONLIGHTERS under his direct protection.

3. The same as MOONSHINER (*q.v.*).

MOONLIGHT-FLITTING, *subs.* (common). *See* SHOOTING THE MOON (*q.v.*). Also LONDON-FLITTING.

1802. CAMPBELL, *Journey*, ii. 1. He made what is termed a MOON-LIGHT FLITTING.

1892. *Cassell's Sat. Jl.*, 28 Sep., p. 26, col. 3. He had done what is known in Lancashire as a MOONLEET FLIT, or, in other words, removed quietly in the dead of night, that nobody knew where he had gone.

MOONLIGHTING, *subs.* (Irish).—Playing the MOONLIGHTER (*q.v.*).

1888. *Daily Chronicle*, 17 Jan. The prisoners, with two other men, were arrested on a charge of MOONLIGHTING in county Clare.

MOON-MAN, *subs.* (old).—*See* quots.

1603-8. DEKKER, *Lanthorne and Candlelight*, viii. A MOONEMAN signifies in English a madman . . . By a byname they are called gypsies, they call themselves Egiptians, others in mockery call them MOONEMEN.

1690. B. E., *Dict. Cant. Crew*, s.v.

1785. GROSE, *Vulg. Tongue*, s.v. MOON-MEN. Gypsies.

1811. *Lex. Bal.*, s.v.

3. (old).—A nocturnal robber. Also MINIONS OF THE MOON.

1597. SHAKSPEARE, *1 Henry IV*, i. 2. The fortune of us that are MOON'S MEN doth ebb and flow like the sea.

MOON-RAKER, *subs.* (nautical).—1. An imaginary sail above the SKY-SCRAPER (*q.v.*); a MOON-SAIL (*q.v.*).

2. (common).—A Wiltshire man. [*See* quots.]. Hence, a smuggler.

1767. RAY, *Proverbs* [BOHN (1893), 223], s.v.

1787. GROSE, *Prov. Glossary* (1811), p. 93. Wiltshire MOON-RAKERS. Some Wiltshire rustics, as the story goes, seeing the figure of the moon in a pond, attempted to rake it out.

1811. *Lex. Bal.*, s.v.

1865. OUIDA, *Strathmore*, ch. xiv. 'It was fine moonlight, last night, my dear fellow, and Hampshire MOONRAKERS do go fishing after contraband goods, *au clair de la lune*, but I didn't know *you* belonged to the fraternity!'

1887. JAS. PAYN, *Glow-Worm Tales*, i. 182. In Wiltshire we are not fond of strangers; we are a simple race —some people even call us MOON-RAKERS.

1889. HUNTER, *Ency. Dict.*, s.v. MOON RAKER. Another version is, that some countrymen, raking for kegs of smuggled spirits which had been sunk in a pond, on being questioned by a revenue-officer, told him they were trying to rake that great cheese (the reflection of the moon) out of the water.

3. (common).—A blockhead. For synonyms *see* BUFFLE and CABBAGE-HEAD.

MOON-RAKING, *subs.* (common).—Wool-gathering.

1869. BLACKMORE, *Lorna Doone*, xvii. It irked me much that any one should take advantage of me; yet everybody did so as soon as ever it was known that my wits were gone MOON-RAKING.

MOONSHINE, *subs.* (common).—1. Anything unreal or unsubstantial; HUMBUG (*q.v.*); ROT (*q.v.*).

1593. HARVEY, *Pierces Superer.* [GROSART (1884), ii. 63]. You may discourse . . . I wott not what marvelous egges in MOONSHINE.

*d.*1667. JER. TAYLOR [in *Wks.* (1835), ii. 126]. Labouring for nothings, and preaching all day for shadows and MOONSHINE.

1785. GROSE, *Vulg. Tongue*, s.v. MOONSHINE. A matter or mouthful of MOONSHINE, a trifle, nothing.

2. (common).—*See* quots.

1785. GROSE, *Vulg. Tongue*, s.v. MOONSHINE. The white brandy smuggled on the coasts of Kent and Sussex, and the gin in the north of Yorkshire, are also called MOONSHINE.

1819. SCOTT, *Bride of Lammermoor* [Saunders MOONSHINE, a smuggler].

1884. *Notes & Queries*, 24 May., p. 401. MOONSHINE signifies smuggled spirits, which were placed in holes or pits and removed at night. *Ibid.* At Piddinghoe they dig for MOONSHINE.

3. (old).—A month.

1605. SHAKSPEARE, *Lear*, i. 2. 5. I am some twelve or fourteen MOONSHINES Lag of a brother.

4. (old).—A dish of poached eggs served with a sauce.

1605. SHAKSPEARE, *Lear*, ii. 2. 35. Draw, you rogue; for, though it be night, yet the moon shines; I'll make a sop o' th' MOONSHINE of you.

Adj. (colloquial).—1. Nocturnal; (2) empty; and (3) trivial.

1596. SHAKSPEARE, *Merry Wives*, v. 5. 42. You MOONSHINE revellers.

GILDED MOONSHINE, *subs. phr.* (old).—*See* quot.

1823. BEE, *Dict. Turf*, s.v. GILDED MOONSHINE—sham bills of exchange; 'no effects.'

MOON-SHINER, *subs.* (American).—1. *See* quots.

1877. *N. Y. Evening Post*, 16 June. Nelson County, Kentucky, is the home of the MOONSHINER; that is, the manufacturer of illicit whiskey . . . . The MOONSHINER regards the revenue officer as a being to be extinguished, and favorable opportunity is the only thing he asks for putting his belief into practice.

1885. *Saturday Review*, 7 Nov., p. 615. Old Layce, a MOONSHINER—that is to say, a maker of untaxed whiskey.

1891. *Daily Telegraph*, 23 Mar. A desperate and fatal encounter took place early on Saturday morning between a posse of Revenue officers and a party of MOONSHINERS, by which name the illicit distillers of the mountain districts are known.

2. (common).—*See* quot. and MOON.

1823. BEE, *Dict. Turf*, s.v. MOONLIGHT WANDERERS; or 'fly-by-night' persons, who cheat their landlords and run away by night; when 'tis illegal to detain the goods.

MOONSHINING, *subs.* (American).—Illicit distilling.

MOONSHINY, *adj.* (common).—Unreal.

MOONSHOOTER. *See* TO SHOOT THE MOON.

MOON'S-MINION, *subs.* (old).—1. A watchman; a CHARLEY (*q.v.*).

1828. LYTTON, *Pelham*, p. 142, ed. 1864. This action was not committed with impunity; in an instant two of the MOON'S MINIONS, staffs, lanterns, and all, were measuring their length at the foot of their namesake of royal memory: the remaining Dogberry was however a tougher assailant.

2. (old).—*See* MOON-MAN, sense 2.

MOONY, *subs.* (common).—A noodle. For synonyms *see* BUFFLE and CABBAGE-HEAD.

Adj. (common).—1. Silly. Also MOONISH.

1600. SHAKSPEARE, *As You Like It*, iii. 2. 430. Being but a MOONISH youth.

1861. G. MEREDITH, *Evan Harrington*, xxv. p. 293 (1885). Rose gave him no time for reflection, or the MOONY imagining of their raptures lovers love to dwell upon.

1876. GEORGE ELIOT, *Daniel Deronda*, xxii. Violent and capricious, or MOONY and insipid.

1890. G. ALLEN, *The Tents of Shem*, xxx. You've seemed preoccupied and absorbed and MOONY and distracted.

1892. MILLIKEN, *'Arry Ballads*, p. 16. MOONEY young women in grey.

2. (common).—Drunk. For synonyms *see* DRINKS and SCREWED.

MOOSE-FACE, *subs.* (common).—*See* quot.

1859. MATSELL, *Vocabulum*, s.v. MOOSE-FACE. A rich ugly-faced man.

MOP, *subs.* (common).—1. *See* quots.

1787. GROSE, *Prov. Glossary*. MOP, a statute fair for hiring servants.

1811. *Lex. Bal.*, s.v. MOP. A kind of annual fair in the west of England where farmers usually hire their servants.

1860. MRS. GASKELL, *Sylvia's Lovers*, i. Many a rustic went to a statute fair or MOP, and never came home to tell of his hiring.

1874. MRS. H. WOOD, *Johnny Ludlow*, 1. S. No. xvi. p. 269. 'There are as good servants to be picked up in a MOP as out of it; and you get a great deal better choice,' said he. 'My mother has hired many a man and maid at the MOP: first-rate servants too.'

2. (common).—A confirmed drunkard; a LUSHINGTON (*q.v.*).

3. (common).—A drinking bout: ON THE MOP = on the drink.

*c.*1860. *Newspaper Cutting.* 'It was all along of Bill Jones the printer, as keeps comp'ny with me,' she muttered. 'He'd been having a MOP, as he called it, because he was on piecework, and the author—oh! he did go on! and call him names such as I shouldn't like to repeat—hadn't sent the copy; whatever that may mean.'

4. (old).—An endearment. Also MOPPET and MOPSY.

*c.*1388. *Townely Mysteries, ut sup*, 'Prima Pastorum,' p. 96. Hayllé, lytylle, tyne MOP.

1589. PUTTENHAM, *Arte of Engl. Poes.*, p. 184. As in our triumphals, calling familiarly upon our muse, I called her MOPPE, But will you weet, My little muse, my prettie MOPPE, If we shall algates change our stoppe, Chose me a sweet. Understanding by this word MOPPE a little pretty lady, or tender young thing.

1598. FLORIO, *Wordle of Wordes*, s.v. *Pupo*, . . . a daintie MOP, a playing babie.

1680. DRYDEN, *Spanish Friar*, i. 1. A globe in one hand, and a sceptre in t'other? A very pretty MOPPET!

1690. B. E., *Dict. Cant. Crew*, s.v.

1706. *Hudibras Redivivus*, x. These mix'd with brewers, and their MOPSIES, Half dead with timpanies and dropsies.

1706. VANBRUGH, *The Mistake*. *Leon.* Ah woman! foolish, foolish woman! *San.* Very foolish indeed. *Jacin.* But don't expect I'll follow her example. *San.* You would, MOPSIE, if I'd let you.

5. (old).—A grimace.

1609. SHAKSPEARE, *Tempest*, iv. 1. Each one, tripping on his toe, Will be here with MOP and mow.

1621. FLETCHER, *Pilgrim*, iv. 2. What MOPS and mows it makes!

6 (old).—A fool.

*c.*1399. *Depos. Richard II* [WRIGHT (1838), 24]. Daunsinge to pipis, In myrthe with MOPPIS, myrrours of sin.

*c.*1430. *York Plays*, 299. This MOP meynes that he may marke men to ther mede He makis many maistries and mervayles emange.

Verb. (common).—1. *See* quot. 1811. Also MOP UP.

1675. COTTON, *Scoffer Scofft*, in *Works* (1725), p. 261. I'll stand, or lie as thou dost pray me, And MOPPE too, if thou'lt not betray me.

1811. *Lex. Bal.*, s.v. To MOP UP. To drink up. To empty a glass or pot.

1851-61. H. MAYHEW, *London Lab.*, iii. 260. I have seen the youngest MOP UP his half-quartern as well as I did.

1868. WHYTE MELVILLE, *White Rose*, xxix. He MOPPED UP his champagne, though, pretty freely. Do you suppose now, he could have been drunk?

2. (colloquial).—To collect. Also MOP UP.

1851-61. H. MAYHEW, *London Lab.*, iii. 213. If I gets inside, I'll MOP UP 1/- if it's good company, or perhaps 3d. or 4d., and always plenty to drink.

TO MOP UP, *verb. phr.* (common).—1. *See verb.*, senses 1 and 2.

2. (common).—*See* quot.

1887. WALFORD, *Antiquarian*, April, 250. MOP UP means 'Stop your talk,' and is another form of 'dry up.'

TO MOP (or WIPE) THE FLOOR (GROUND, or EARTH) WITH ONE, *verb. phr.* (common).—To knock one down.

1887. HENLEY & STEVENSON, *Deacon Brodie*, I. iii. 1. Muck that's my opinion of him . . . I'll MOP THE FLOOR UP with him any day.

1888. *Detroit Free Press*, 25 Aug. 'I told him that I could MOP THE EARTH with him, but had been careful not to use provoking language!'

TO BE MOPPED (or WIPED) OUT, *verb. phr.* (common).—To be ruined; FLOORED (*q.v.*); or killed.

1892. MILLIKEN, *'Arry Ballads*, 53. They say he's MOPPED OUT; I dunnow.

MOPS AND BROOMS, *adj. phr.* (common).—Drunk. For synonyms *see* DRINKS and SCREWED.

1828. EGAN, *Finish to Tom and Jerry*, 135. Jerry declared himself to be quite MOPS AND BROOMS.

1840. H. COCKTON, *Valentine Ven*, xviii. He did mix, but scarcely took the rawness off the brandy . . . . 'The governor's GETTING MOPS AND BROOMS,' whispered Horace to his amiable spouse.

1858. SHIRLEY BROOKS, *The Gordian Knot*, p. 173. If I had married a wife, I don't think I should go home to her in a state of MOPS AND BROOMS, after offering to fight a fishmonger in the Haymarket because he had arranged his lobsters and prawns in a way displeasing to my bewildered eye.

IN THE MOPS, *adv. phr.* (common).—Sulky.

MOPE, *subs.* (colloquial).—1. A dullard. For synonyms *see* BUFFLE and CABBAGE-HEAD.

1621. BURTON, *Anat. Mel.*, 149. 'They will be scoffing, insulting over their inferiours, till they have made by their humoring or gulling, *ex stulto insanum*: a MOPE, or a noddy.'

1726. POPE, *Dunciad*, ii. No meagre, Muse-rid MOPE, adust and thin, In a dun night-gown of his own loose skin.

1861. DICKENS, *Tom Tiddler's Ground* [Mr. MOPES, a hermit].

2. in *pl.* (colloquial).—Low spirits; THE HUMP (*q.v.*); THE BLUES (*q.v.*).

Verb. (colloquial).—To despond.

1596. SHAKSPEARE, *Hamlet*, iii. 4. 81. Or but a sickly part of one true sense. Could not so MOPE.

1635. QUARLES, *Emblems*, i. 8. One's MOP'D, the other's mad.

1667. MILTON, *Paradise Lost*, xi. 485. MOPING melancholy and moon-struck madness.

1749. GRAY, *Elegy*. The MOPING owl doth to the moon complain.

*d.*1792. HORNE, *Works*, v. 23. It directs him not to shut himself up in a cloister, alone, there to MOPE and moan away his life.

1888. ROLF BOLDREWOOD, *Robbery Under Arms*, li. You'd better think over your situation and don't MOPE.

MOPED, *adj.* (colloquial).—*See* quots. 1690 and 1785. Also MOPISH, MOPING and MOPE-EYED.

1621. FLETCHER, *Pilgrim*, iii. 3. What a MOPE-EY'D ass was I.

1640. *Wit's Recr.* [HOTTEN], 465. MOP-EY'D I am, as some have said, Because I've liv'd so long a Maid.

1647. BEAUMONT and FLETCHER, *Humourous Lieutenant*, iv. 6. He is bewitched, or MOPED, or his brains melted.

*d.*1656. BP. HALL, *Spirituale Bedleem*, 29. 'Here one MOPISHLY stupid, and so fixed to his posture, as if he were a breathing statue.'

1690. B. E., *Dict. Cant. Crew*, s.v. MOP-EIED, one that can't see well, by living too long a maid. *Ibid.* MOP'D, maz'd.

1717. KILLINBECK, *Sermons*, 348. [They are] generally traduced as a sort of MOPISH and unsociable creatures.

1785. GROSE, *Vulg. Tongue*, s.v. MOPED. Stupid, melancholy for want of society.

1880. RHODA BROUGHTON, *Second Thoughts*, viii. 'She sits drearily stitching, absently reading, MOPINGLY thinking.'

MOPPET. *See* MOP, *subs.* sense 4.

MOPPY, *adj.* (common).—Drunk. For synonyms *see* DRINKS and SCREWED.

MOP-SQUEEZER, *subs.* (common).—A housemaid.

1785. GROSE, *Vulg. Tongue*, s.v.

MOPSY, *subs.* (old).—1. A familiar term for a woman: specifically a young girl; a MOP (*q.v.* sense 4).

2. (common).—*See* quots.

1690. B. E., *Dict. Cant. Crew*, s.v.

1785. GROSE, *Vulg. Tongue*, s.v. MOPSEY. A dowdy, or homely woman.

1859. MATSELL, *Vocabulum*, s.v. MOPSY. A short dowdy woman.

MOPUS, *subs.* (old).—*See* quot. 1755.

*d.*1745. SWIFT, *Miscellanies*, 'The Grand Question Debated.' I'm grown a mere MOPUS; no company comes But a rabble of tenants.

1755. JOHNSON, *Eng. Dict.* (1814), s.v. MOPUS . . . a cant word from 'mope'. A drone, a dreamer.

2. (common).—A small coin. [Said to be a corruption of the name of Sir Giles Mompesson, a monopolist notorious in the reign of James I].

1690. B. E., *Dict. Cant. Crew*, s.v.

1841. *Tait's Edinburgh Rev.*, viii. 222. Slily to my fob repair, And leave me not a MOPUS there.

3. in *pl.* (MOPUSSES).—Money.

1785. GROSE, *Vulg. Tongue*, s.v.

1811. *Lex. Bal.*, s.v. MOPUSSES Money.

1824. EGAN, *Boxiana*, iv. 443. Ned not having the MOPUSSES to spare.

1834. AINSWORTH, *Rookwood*, I. ix. p. 55. Then whose inclinations are so uncontrolled as the highwayman's, so long as the MOPUSES last?

1842. *Punch*, 'Prolusiones Etymoligiere,' p. 16. He that has the MOPUSSES May buy diamonds and topazes.

1844. CHARLES SELBY, *London by Night*, ii. 1. *Ned.* I see an improvement in the financial position—lucky, like myself. *Jack.* (Aside.) Lots of MOPUSSES.

1859. MATSELL, *Vocabulum*, s.v.

1883. *Punch.* 3 Nov., p. 210, col. 1. But what's that to us, so's we pull in the MOPUSSES.

MORAL, *subs.* (colloquial).—1. An exact counterpart.

1590. H. CONSTABLE, *Sonnets*, Decade 4. Fooles be they that inveigh 'gainst Mahomet who's but a MORRAL of loves monarchie.

1726. SWIFT, *Gulliver's Travels*, v. 'I have seen the MORAL of my own behaviour very frequent in England.'

1771. SMOLLETT, *Humphrey Clinker*, 385. The long chin is the very MORAL of the governor's.

1789. G. PARKER, *Life's Painter*, 'The Bunter's Christening.' A chopping boy; Which was, as one might say, The MORAL of his dad, Sir.

1851. DOUGLAS JERROLD, *St. Giles and St. James*, 110. She's the very pictur—yes, the very MORAL of Dick Turpin's Bess.

1882. *Graphic*, 9 Dec., p. 643, col. 2. They are, for the most part, very dungeon-like rooms; and the ventilation of the ordinary prison cell—yes, we have tried it—is a MORAL by comparison.

2. (racing).—*See* quot. 1869. [Abbreviation of 'moral certainty:' *see* CERT].

1869. GREENWOOD, *Seven Curses of London*, 397. Everything that is highly promising becomes, in the slang of the advertising tipster, a MORAL.

1877. *Belgravia*, xxxii. 241. To invest a sovereign or two for her on what they may consider a MORAL.

1879. JAS. PAYN, *High Spirits (Number Forty-seven)*. 'Come, Bob,' said my master, 'that disposes of your friend Adamson's having had anything to do with it, which you thought such a MORAL.'

1880. A. TROLLOPE, *The Duke's Children*, lxxiv. 'I think that we shall beat Cambridge this year to a MORAL,' said Gerald.

1883. *Referee*, 25 March, p. 1, col. 1. She landed the stake with much ease, and thereby upset what at first appeared one of the biggest coursing MORALS upon record.

1888. N. GOULD, *Double Event*, p. 178. Lord Mayfield went into ecstasies over him, and said the double looked a MORAL.

1889. *Ally Sloper's Half-Holiday*, 6 July. Cucumber was, to use the words of a sporting friend of Pottle's, a MORAL.

1891. *Lic. Vict. Gaz.*, 3 April. An idea of the strength of the MORAL may be gathered when it is stated that in a field of fifteen 6 to 4 was freely taken about the Danebury horse.

1892. MILLIKEN, *'Arry Ballads*, p. 62. Hangling isn't my mark, that's a MORAL, and fishermen mostly is fools.

MORAL-SHOCKER, *subs.* (Fleet St.).—A novel dealing with sex. Also HILL-TOPPER.

MORAY-COACH, *subs.* (Scots').—*See* quot.

1808-25. JAMIESON, *Dict.*, s.v. MORAY-COACH, a cart. A cant term, used in ridicule. . . ; like the phrase, a Tyburn coach.

MORE. *See* ELBOW, POWER, SACKS, SEVEN, TWELVE.

MORE SO, *adv.* (common).—A general intensitive: *see* quots.

1892. HUME NISBET, *Bushranger's Sweetheart*, viii. But that distant production of Australia, the larikin, is still very much to the fore, as spry, active, and wicked as he ever was, perhaps rather MORE SO.

1892. MILLIKEN, *'Arry Ballads*, p. 38. Pink Dominos style, only MORE so, but blowed if 't was up to that mark.

MOREISH, *adj.* (colloquial).—*See* quots. 1847 and 1864.

1738. SWIFT, *Polite Conversation* (Conv. 1). *Lady S.* How do you like this tea, Colonel! *Col.* Well enough, madam, but methinks it is a little MORISH. *Lady S.* Oh Colonel, I understand you; Betty, bring the canister.

1847. HALLIWELL, *Arch. & Provin. Words*, s.v. MOORISH . . . wishing for more.

1864. HOTTEN, *Slang Dict.*, s.v. MORE-ISH. When there is scarcely enough of an eatable or drinkable, it is said to taste MORE-ISH; as, 'This wine is very good, but it has a slight MORE-ISH flavour.'

MORGAN, *subs.* (American).—A bare-faced imposture.

1826. WEED [in *Auto.*, i. 319]. [In 1826 American masons were accused of murdering *Morgan*, a renegade. Popular feeling ran high, and a violent anti-masonry crusade resulted, national politics being considerably influenced. Mr. Thurlow Weed, one of the chief figures of the episode, says:—] The election of 1827 elicited an accusation against me, which assumed proportions not dreamed of by those with whom it originated . . . . Ebenezer Griffin, Esq., one of the council of the 'kidnappers,' who was going to Batavia to conduct the examination, observed laughingly to me, 'After we have proven that the body found at Oak orchard is that of Timothy Monroe, what will you do for a *Morgan?*' I replied in the same spirit, '*That is a good enough Morgan* for us until you bring back the one you carried off.'

MORK, *subs.* (thieves').—A policeman. For synonyms *see* BLUE.

1889. CLARKSON and RICHARDSON, *Police*, 346. To hear if there are any MORKS or any one in the way.

MORNING, *subs.* (common).—An early dram; an EYE-OPENER (*q.v.*). Also MORNING-ROUSER.

1814. SCOTT, *Waverley*, XVIII. Of this he took a copious dram, observing he had already taken his MORNING with Donald Bean Lean.

1854. R. W. VAN DER KISTE, *The Dens of London*, p. 268. On rising to attend his work, according to his custom, he first went to a certain gin-shop in T—street for his MORNING.

1872. *Globe*, 12 Mar. That species of 'refresher' which in some parts of our country is known as a MORNING is also a German institution.

THE TOP OF THE MORNING, *phr.* (Irish).—A cheery greeting.

MORNING-DROP, *subs.* (old).—1. The gallows. For synonyms *see* NUBBING-CHEAT.

1811. *Lex. Bal.*, s.v. MORNING DROP. He napped the king's pardon and escaped the MORNING DROP; he was pardoned, and was not hanged.

1859. MATSELL, *Vocabulum*, s.v.

MORNING-HILLS, *subs.* (Winchester College).—*See* quot.

1866. MANSFIELD, *School Life*, 52. On holidays and Remedies we were turned out for a couple of hours on to St. Catherine's Hill . . . . once before breakfast, (MORNING HILLS), and again in the afternoon, (MIDDLE HILLS).

MORNING-ROUSER. *See* MORNING.

MORNING-SNEAK, *subs.* (old).—*See* quot.

1819. VAUX, *Memoirs*, 'Glossary,' s.v. MORNING-SNEAK, going out early to rob private houses or shops by slipping in at the door unperceived, while the servant or shopman is employed in cleaning the steps, windows, etc.

MORNING-STAR, *subs.* (old).—A weapon used as late as by the London train-bands, *temp.* Henry VIII. It consisted in a spiked ball chained to a staff. Called also HOLY-WATER SPRINKLER.

MOROCCO-MAN, *subs.* (old).—*See* quot.

1868. BREWER, *Phrase & Fable*, s.v. MOROCCO MEN, agents of lottery assurances. In 1796, the great State lottery employed 7500 MOROCCO MEN. Their business was to go from house to house among the customers of the assurances, or to attend in the back parlours of public-houses, where the customers came to meet them.

MORPHEUS. IN THE ARMS OF MORPHEUS, *phr.* (colloquial).—Asleep. *See* MURPHY.

MORRIS (or **MORRICE**), *verb.* (old).—To decamp. *See* quot. 1785.

1773. GOLDSMITH, *She Stoops to Conquer*, iii. *Tony*, I don't value her resentment the bounce of a cracker; zounds, here they are! MORRICE! Prance! (*Exit Hastings*).

1785. GROSE, *Vulg. Tongue*, s.v. MORRIS. Come, MORRIS OFF; dance off or get you gone; allusion to morris, *i.e.*, *morisco*, or Moorish dancing.

1811. *Lex. Bal.*, s.v.

1835. *Comic Almanack*, 34. Being naturally desirous of recovering his footing, a messenger was MORRISSED OFF for a supply.

1838. DICKENS, *Oliver Twist*, p. 37 (ed. 1850). Up with you on your pins. There! Now then! MORRICE.

1859. MATSELL, *Vocabulum*, s.v.

1883. GRENVILLE MURRAY, *People I Have Met*, p. 69. The fellows dine with them, flirt with them, and MORRIS OFF to town in spring for better amusement.

MORSEL, *subs.* (old).—1. A person; (2) hence, a harlot, a BIT (*q.v.*) a PIECE (*q.v.*).

*d.*1529. DUNBAR, *Woving of the King*, in *Wks.* (Scot. Text, Soc., Edinburgh, 1883-4). Scho was ane MORSALE of delight.

1609. SHAKSPEARE, *Tempest*, ii. 1. 286. To the perpetual wink for aye might put This ancient MORSEL, this Sir Prudence. *Ibid.* (1603) *Measure for Measure*, iii. 2. 57. How doth my dear MORSEL, thy mistress.

1641. MARMION, *Antiquary*, iv. 'Tis your own leman, your own dear MORSEL.

DEAREST MORSEL (or BODILY PART), *subs. phr.* (old).—The female *pudendum.* For synonyms *see* MONOSYLLABLE.

1605. SHAKSPEARE, *Cymbeline*, i. 5. I have enjoyed the DEAREST BODILY PART of your mistress.

MORT, *subs.* (Old Cant).—1. A woman, chaste or not. *See* quots. *passim.* And (2) a yeoman's daughter. Also MOT. Hence, AUTEM-MORT = a married woman; WALKING (or STROLLING) MORT = a female tramp; KINCHIN-MORT = a little girl; DIMBER-MORT = a pretty wench.

1567. HARMAN, *Caveat* (1814), p. 49. These AUTEM MORTES be maried women, as there be but a fewe: For Autem in their language is a church, so shee is a wyfe maried at the church, and they be as chaste as a cowe I have, that goeth to bull eury moone, with what bull she careth not. *Ibid.* 'Glossary.' MORTES, harlots.

1597-8. MUNDAY, *Downfall of Robert, etc.* [DODSLEY, *Old Plays* (1874), viii. 156]. If I can get the girl to go with me Disguis'd in habit like a pedlar's MORT.

1607. DEKKER, *Jests to Make You Merie*, in *Wks.* (GROSART), ii. 308. He is not worthy of the name of notable theefe among theeues, which is without his MORT or punck.

1610. ROWLANDS, *Martin Mark-all*, 'The Maunder's Wooing.' O Ben Coue that may not be, For thou hast an AUTUM-MORT who euer that is she.

1611. MIDDLETON, *Roaring Girl* [DODSLEY, *Old Plays*, vi. 110]. Marry, this, my lord, says he: Ben MORT (good wench), shall you and I heave a bough, etc.

1611. COTGRAVE, *Dictionarie*, s.v. *Belistresse* .... a doxie, MORTE.

1621. B. JONSON, *Maske of Gipsies*. Male gypsies all, not a MORT among them.

1622. BEAUMONT and FLETCHER, *Beggar's Bush*, ii. 1. Each man shall eat his own stol'n eggs and butter In his own shade, or sun-shine, and enjoy His own dear dell, doxy, or MORT at night.

1640. *Wit's Recr.* [HOTTEN], 441. And for the *Rome*-MORTS ... They are of the sorts That love the true sports.

1656. *Muses Recr.* [HOTTEN], 48. A Lord of this land that lov'd a Bum well, Did lie with this MORT one night in the Strummel.

1690. B. E., *Dict. Cant. Crew*, s.v. MORTS. . . . Yeoman's daughters; also a Wife, Woman, or Wench.

1712. T. SHIRLEY, *The Triumph of Wit*, 'The Maunder's Praise of His STROWLING MORT.' Doxy oh! thy glaziers shine, As Glimmar by the Salomon, No GENTRY-MORT hath parts like thine, No Cove e'er wap'd with such a one.

1785. GROSE, *Vulg. Tongue*, s.v. MORT. A woman or wench; also a yeoman's daughter.

1811. *Lex. Bal.*, s.v.

1822. SCOTT, *Fortunes of Nigel*, ch. xvii. 'Tour out,' said the one ruffian to the other; 'tour the bien MORT twiring at the gentry cove.'

1834. H. AINSWORTH, *Rookwood*, bk. III. ch. v. MORTS, AUTEM-MORTS, WALKING MORTS, dells, doxies, with all the shades and grades of the canting crew, were assembled.

1837. DISRAELI, *Venetia*, ch. xiv. Tip me the clank like a DIMBER MORT, as you are.

1859. MATSELL, *Vocabulum*, s.v.

1885. BURTON, *Arabian Nights*, iii. 302. Nor MOTT nor maid from thee my heart shall spell.

2. (colloquial).—A large quantity; a great number.

1694. *Plautus made English* [NARES]. Then they had a MORT of prisoners, with boys and girls.

1740. RICHARDSON, *Pamela* [quoted by HALLIWELL]. He gave her a MORT of good things at the same time, and bid her wear them in remembrance of her good friend, my lady, his mother.

1775. SHERIDAN, *Rivals*, i. 1. Here's a MORT o' merry-making, hey?

*d.*1823. BLOOMFIELD, *The Horkey*. And sitch a MORT of folks began To eat up the good cheer.

ALL AMORT. *See* AMORT.

MORTAL, *adj.* (vulgar).—1. Extreme. *Cf.* AWFUL, JOLLY, etc.

1679. DRYDEN, *Ovid*, i. 733. The nymph grew pale, and in a MORTAL fright.

*d.*1704. LESTRANGE [quoted by JOHNSON]. The birds were in a MORTAL apprehension of the beetles, till the sparrow reasoned them into understanding.

2. (common).—*See* quot. 1808. For synonyms *see* DRINKS and SCREWED.

1808-25. JAMIESON, *Dict.*, s.v. MORTAL, ... dead drunk.

1889. STEVENSON and OSBOURNE, *The Wrong Box*, vi. His men were all as MORTAL as himself.

3. (colloquial).—Expletive and intensitive.

1755. JOHNSON, *Eng. Dict.*, s.v. MORTAL. Extreme, violent. A low word. *Ibid.* MORTALLY ... a low ludicrous word.

*d.*1832. SCOTT [quoted in *Century*]. Six MORTAL hours did I endure her loquacity.

1837. DICKENS, *Oliver Twist*, xviii. Forty-two MORTAL long hard-working days.

1852. DICKENS, *Bleak House*, xiv. I go there a MORTAL sight of times.

1878. STEVENSON, *Inland Voyage*, 255. They performed a piece ... in five MORTAL acts.

Adv. (colloquial).—Extremely. Also MORTALLY.

1625. BACON, *Essays*, 'Of Envy.' 'Adrian the Emperour MORTALLY envied poets and painters.'

*d.*1735. GRANVILLE [quoted by JOHNSON]. Know all, who would pretend to my good grace, I MORTALLY dislike a damning face.

1838. D. JERROLD, *Men of Character*, iii. I was MORTAL certain I should find him here.

1840. HALIBURTON, *Sam Slick*, 3, Ser. 102. It was a MORTAL hot day, and people actually sweated to that degree it laid the dust.

MORTAR, *subs.* (common).—1. The same as MORTAR-BOARD (*q.v.*).

2. (venery).—The female *pudendum.* For synonyms *see* MONOSYLLABLE.

MORTAR-BOARD (or **MORTAR**).—The trencher-cap worn at certain public schools and at the Universities.

1600. KEMP, *Nine Days' Wonder*, 'Ded. Ep.' So that methinkes I could flye to Rome ... with a MORTER on my head.

*d.*1635. BP. CORBET to T. Coryate. No more shall man with MORTAR on his head Set forward towards Rome.

1647 FLETCHER, *Fair Maid of the Inn*, v. 2. He ... may now travel to Rome with a MORTAR on's head.

1857. CUTHBERT BEDE, *Verdant Green*, Pt. II. ch. iii. 'I don't mind this 'ere MORTAR-BOARD, sir,' remarked the professor of the noble art of self-defence, as he pointed to the academical cap which surmounted his head.

1864. *Fun*, 21 May, p. 96. Anon I saw a gentle youth (no '*sub fusc*' under-grad.) '*Toga virilis*' he had none, no MORTAR-BOARD he had.

1881. PASCOE, *Every-day Life*, 147. On admission ... a boy provides himself with a MORTAR or college-cap.

MORTGAGE-DEED, *subs.* (common).—A pawnticket. For synonyms *see* TOMB-STONE.

MOSES. TO STAND MOSES, *verb. phr.* (old).—*See* quots.

1611. COTGRAVE, *Dictionarie* .... HOLIE MOYSES, whose ordinarie counterfeit having on either side of the head an eminence, or luster, arising somewhat in the forme of a horne, hath imboldened a prophane author to stile cuckolds *parents de Moyse*.

1785. GROSE, *Vulg. Tongue*, s.v.

1811. *Lex. Bal.*, s.v. MOSES. A man is said TO STAND MOSES when he has another man's bastard child fathered upon him, and he is obliged by the parish to maintain it.

1859. MATSELL, *Vocabulum*, s.v. MOSES. A man that fathers another man's child for a consideration.

BY THE PIPER THAT PLAYED BEFORE MOSES, *phr.* (common).—An oath. Also BY THE HOLY JUMPING MOTHER OF MOSES. *See* OATHS.

1855. STRANG, *Glasgow and Its Clubs*, 243. But, HOLY MOSES! what a rear?

1876. HINDLEY, *Adventures of a Cheap Jack*, p. 109. Screw your courage to the sticking place and BY THE HOLY-JUMPING-MOTHER-OF-MOSES—who was my uncle—we'll not fail.

1890. HUME NISBET, *Bail Up!* 212. 'And, BY THE PIPER THAT PLAYED BEFORE MOSES, so they did, replied her companion coolly.

1892. HUME NISBET, *Bushranger's Sweetheart*, p. 153. 'Did I spake concerning the stable and a wisp of straw, me boy, for you and your friend? No, BY THE PIPER WHICH PLAYED BEFORE MOSES, ye shall have our best bedroom this night to lie in, and be carried up to it also.'

MOSEY, *verb.* (American).—To decamp. For synonyms *see* AMPUTATE and SKEDADDLE.

1838. NEAL, *Charcoal Sketches*, i. If your tongue wasn't so thick, I'd say you must MOSEY: but MOSEYING is only to be done when a gemman's half shot.

18[?]. *N. Y. Family Companion* [quoted by BARTLETT]. After I left you, or rather after you left me, when them fellows told you to MOSEY OFF before the boat went to sea.

1848. BARTLETT, *Americanisms*, s.v. MOSEY. The following is said to be the origin of the word: A postmaster in Ohio by the name of Moses ran away with a considerable sum of money belonging to the government. To MOSEY OFF, or to run away, as Mr. Moses had, then became a by-word in Ohio, and, with its meaning somewhat extended, has spread over the Union.

1857. *Louisville Journal*, 9 Oct. My friend, let me tell you, if you do not MOSEY this instant, and clear out for good, you'll have to pay pretty dear.

1871. DE VERE, *Americanisms*, s.v. This mysterious word MOSEY is, probably correctly, said to be nothing more than a mere variety of the Americanized verb *vamose*, with the final vowel sounded, and the first syllable lost. It certainly has the same meaning, of leaving suddenly, and generally involuntarily.

1888. *Daily Inter-Ocean*, 6 Feb. But the bullets and their own fighting began to tell pretty soon, even on grizzlies. First one rolled over and stretched out, then another sat down on his haunches and dropped his head and finally sprawled out, a third MOSEYED OFF some distance to sit down and lick his wounds.

TO MOSEY ALONG, *verb. phr.* (American).—1. To jog along.

18[?]. *New York Tribune* [quoted by BARTLETT]. I'll get a room nicely furnished, and my wife and I will jes MOSEY ALONG till the election trouble is over, an' den dere'll be a powerful sight of whitewashin' to be done.

2. (American).—To bustle about.

1885. M. N. MURFREE, *Prophet of Gt. Smoky Mountains*, xiii. Hurry 'long, D'rindy, you-uns ain't goin' ter reel a hank ef ye don't MOSEY.

MOSH, *verb.* (thieves').—To leave a restaurant without paying. A corruption of 'mouch' (MIKE, *q.v.*).

MOSKENEER, *verb.* (common).—To pawn for more than the pledge is worth: MOSKERS (*q.v.*) = men who make MOSKENEERING a profession. Also as *subs.* = the agent.

1887. W. E. HENLEY, *Villon's Straight Tip*. Fiddle, or fence, or mace, or mack; Or MOSKENEER, or flash the drag.

1893. EMERSON, *Signor Lippo*, 100. He MOSKENEERS from twenty to thirty supers a week. *Ibid.* p. 99. As we were talking in came Johnson, a fair MOSKENEER.

MOSKER, *subs.* (common).—*See* quot. and MOSKENEER.

1883. *Daily Telegraph*, 9 July, p. 3, col. 1. The MOSKER .... is, in slang vernacular, one who makes a living by taking advantage of the business incapacity of persons engaged in the pawnbroking trade, and by subtle wiles and subterfuge imposes on their credulity and weak good nature. [From long article on The MOSKER].

MOSQUE, *subs.* (old).—A church or chapel.—PARKER, *Life's Painter*, 120 (1800).

MOSS, *subs.* (thieves').—1. *See* quot. and BLUE PIGEON.

1811. *Lex. Bal.*, s.v. MOSS. A cant term for lead, because both are found on the tops of buildings.

2. (American).—Money. For synonyms *see* ACTUAL and GILT.

1859. MATSELL, *Vocabulum*, s.v.

MOSS-ROSE, *subs.* (venery).—The female *pudendum.* For synonyms *see* MONOSYLLABLE.

MOSSYBACK, *subs.* (American).—1. A man hiding in woods or swamps — ('till the moss grew on his back') — to escape the conscription for the Southern army. Also MOSSBACK.

2. (American political).—An extreme conservative in politics.

3. (common).—An old fashioned person; a BACK-NUMBER (*q.v.*).

MOSSY-CELL (**FACE** or **VALE**), *subs. phr.* (venery).—The female *pudendum.*—GROSE. For synonyms *see* MONOSYLLABLE.

MOSSYFACE (or **OLD MOSSYFACE**), *subs.* (common).—The ace of spades.

MOST, *verb.* (American thieves').—See quot.

1859. MATSELL, *Vocabulum*, s.v. MOST. Dining at an eating-house and leaving without making payment.

ALL THERE, BUT THE MOST OF YOU ! *phr.* (venery).—Copulation.

MOT (MOTT) or MORT, (*q.v.*) *subs.* (old).— 1. See quots. 1785, 1851, and MORT.

1785. GROSE, *Vulg. Tongue*, s.v. MOT. A girl, or wench.

1811. *Lex. Bal.*, s.v.

1823. BEE, *Dict. Turf*, s.v.

1851-61. MAYHEW, *Lond. Lab.*, i. 266. The MOT of the ken (nick-name for matron of the establishment).

2. (common).—See quot. 1819. For synonyms *see* BARRACK-HACK and TART.

1819. VAUX, *Memoirs*, 189. MOTT, a blowen, or woman of the town.

1821. EGAN, *Life in London*, i. 223. The Hon. Tom Dashall. . . . was in close conversation with his MOTT.

1828. MAGINN, *Vidocq Versified*. With the MOTS their ogles throwing.

1887. W. E. HENLEY, *Villon's Good Night*. A MOT's good night to one and all.

MOT-CART, *subs.* (common).— 1. A brougham; a LOOSE-BOX (*q.v.*). (2) A mattress.—BARRÈRE and LELAND.

MOTH, *subs.* (common).—A prostitute; a FLY-BY-NIGHT (*q.v.*). For synonyms *see* BARRACK-HACK and TART.

MOTHER, *subs.* (old).— 1. A bawd. Also MOTHER-ABBESS, MOTHER MIDNIGHT, and MOTHER DAMNABLE. *See* ABBESS.

1690. B. E., *Dict. Cant. Crew*, s.v.

1785. GROSE, *Vulg. Tongue*, s.v.

1811. *Lex. Bal.*, s.v. MOTHER, or THE MOTHER, a bawd. MOTHER ABBESS, the same.

2. (common).—A familiar mode of address.

1647. FLETCHER, *The Chances*, i. 8. Good MOTHER.

1847. C. BRONTË, *Jane Eyre*, XIX. But, MOTHER, I did not come to hear Mr. Rochester's fortune, I came to hear my own.

3. (old colloquial).—Hysteria.

1605. SHAKSPEARE, *Lear*, ii. 4, 56. O, how this MOTHER swells up toward my heart.

1662. MIDDLETON, *Mayor of Queensborough* [DYCE (1840), i. 186]. I'm so troubled with the MOTHER too.

1662. *Rump Songs*, i. 161. From Damnable Members, and fits of the MOTHER, Good Lord, deliver us.

DOES YOUR MOTHER KNOW YOU'RE OUT ? *phr.* (common).— A derisive street catch-phrase. *See* DOES.

1836. BARHAM, *Ingoldsby Legends, Misadventures at Margate*. He smiled and said, 'Sir, DOES YOUR MOTHER KNOW, THAT YOU ARE OUT ?'

1840. *Sporting Review*, III. 2. Has he no friends to look after him? 'DOES HIS MOTHER KNOW HE'S OUT?'

1841. *Punch*, i. p. 6, col. 2. In this darkling hour of doubt—DOES YOUR MOTHER KNOW YOU'RE OUT ?

1844. *Puck*, 134. Tailors or cobblers, both, I trow, From board or stall ye roam, And DO YOUR ANXIOUS MOTHERS KNOW THAT YE ARE OUT? Go home !

1895. *Chatham & Rochester News*, 'Political News' . . . . *A Voice*. DOES YOUR MOTHER KNOW YOU'RE OUT? *Ald. Davies*. Yes! and next week she'll know that I'm in as well.

HAS YOUR MOTHER SOLD HER MANGLE ? *phr.* (streets').—A catch phrase: *see* DOES.

TEACH YOUR MOTHER (or

GRANDMOTHER) TO ROAST (or SUCK) EGGS, *verb. phr.* (common).—A derisive retort upon a piece of information or an offer of help. Fr. *les oisons veulent mener les oies paître* = the goslings want to drive the geese to pasture.

1670. RAY, *Proverbs* [BOHN (1893), 7]. Teach your father to get children.

HE'LL BE A MAN BEFORE HIS MOTHER, *phr.* (common).—A derisive retort.

MOTHER-AND-DAUGHTER, *subs.* (rhyming).—Water.

MOTHER-CAREY'S CHICKENS, *subs. phr.* (nautical).— 1. Snow; GOOSE-FLUFF (*q.v.*). Fr. *les mouches d'hiver*.

2. (old).—See quot.

1823. BEE, *Dict. Turf*, s.v. MOTHER CARY'S CHICKENS—to fare alike and pay the same.

MOTHER-IN-LAW, *subs.* (common).— A mixture of 'old' and 'bitter' ales.

1884. *Daily Telegraph*, 3 July, p. 5, col. 4. Others incline towards MOTHER-IN-LAW, otherwise 'old-and-bitter.'

MOTHER-IN-LAW'S BIT, *subs. phr.* (old).—See quot.

1785. GROSE, *Vulg. Tongue*, s.v. MOTHER. MOTHER IN LAW'S BIT ; a small piece, mothers-in-law being supposed not apt to overload the stomachs of their husband's children.

1811. *Lex. Bal.*, s.v.

MOTHER-MIDNIGHT, *subs.* (common). — 1. A midwife; a FINGERSMITH (*q.v.*) and (2) a bawd.

1690. B. E., *Dict. Cant. Crew*, s.v. MOTHER-MIDNIGHT, a midwife (often a Bawd).

1785. GROSE, *Vulg. Tongue*, s.v.

1811. *Lex. Bal.*, s.v. MOTHER.

MOTHER MOREY. I'LL TELL YOU A STORY OF OLD MOTHER MOREY, *phr.* (American).—In derision of an inconsequent yarn. [In allusion to the nursery rhyme].

MOTHER-OF-ALL-SAINTS (ALL SOULS, MASONS, ST. PATRICK), *subs.* (venery).—The female *pudendum*. For synonyms *see* MONOSYLLABLE.

1785. G. A. STEVENS, *Songs Comic and Satyrical*, p. 88. Lads pour out libations from bottles and bowls, THE MOTHER OF ALL SAINTS is drunk by *all souls*.

1788. GROSE, *Vulg. Tongue*, s.v. MOTHER OF ALL SAINTS. The Monosyllable. *Ibid.* MOTHER OF ALL SOULS. The same. *Irish. Ibid.* MOTHER OF ST. PATRICK. The same. *Irish.*

1823. BEE, *Dict. Turf*, s.v. MOTHER OF MASONS—a toast—not among their secrets in lodge, whatever it be at home.

MOTHER-OF-THE-MAIDS, *subs. phr.* (old).—See quot.

1785. GROSE, *Vulg. Tongue*, s.v.

1811. *Lex. Bal.*, s.v. MOTHER OF THE MAIDS. A bawd.

MOTHER'S-MILK, *subs.* (common).— Gin. For synonyms *see* DRINKS and WHITE-SATIN. Also = spirits of any kind (quot. 1860).

1823. MONCRIEFF, *Tom & Jerry*, iii. 3. *Log*. What, my lily! here, take a drop of MOTHER'S MILK. *(Gives black child gin out of measure he has received from Landlord)*.

1860. DION BOUCICAULT, *Colleen Bawn*, i. 3. *Sheelah*. Here's the hot water. *Myles*. Lave it there till I brew Father Tom a pint of MOTHER'S MILK.

MOTHER'S-SON, *subs.* (old colloquial).—A man.

[?]. *M.S. Cantab.* Ff. v. 48. f. 127 [HALLIWELL]. Woundyt many a MODUR SONE, and xij he slew that day.

[?]. *M.S. Linc.* A. i. 17. f. 19 [HALLIWELL]. Perischte ilk a MODER SONE, and drownede in the water.

MOTTE, *subs.* (venery).—The *mons veneris*. *See* FLEECE and MONOSYLLABLE.

MOTTING, *subs.* (venery).—Wenching; also GROUSING (*q.v.*). For synonyms *see* GREENS and RIDE.

MOTTOB, *subs.* (back slang).—Bottom.

MOUCH. *See* MIKE.

MOUCHER. *See* MIKER.

MOUCHEY, *subs.* (common).—A Jew. For synonyms *see* YID.

MOUCHING. *See* MIKING.

MOULDER, *subs.* (pugilists').—See quot.

1823. BEE, *Dict. Turf*, s.v. MOULDER—a lumbering boxer, one who fights as if he were moulding clay.

MOULDY, *subs.* (nautical).—A purser's steward.

Adj. (common).— 1. Grey-headed. MOULDY-PATE = a lackey in powder.

2. (colloquial). — Worthless: *e.g.*, a MOULDY offer.

MOULDY-GRUBS, *subs.* (common).—Travelling showmen ; mountebanks who work in the open without tent or covering. MOULDY-GRUBBING = working as described.

MOULDY-'UN, *subs.* (common).—A copper.

MOUNCH-PRESENT, *subs.* (old).— 1. See quot.; (2) a glutton; and (3) one who takes bribes. Also MUNCH-PRESENT.

1530. PALSGRAVE, MAUNCHE PRESENT, *briffault*.

1560-1. AWDLEY, *Fraternitye of Vacabondes*. MOUNCH PRESENT is he that is a great gentleman, for when his mayster sendeth him with a present, he wil take a tast thereof by the way. This is a bold knave, that sometyme will eate the best and leave the worst for his mayster.

MOUNSEER, *subs.* (colloquial).—A Frenchman.

1627. DRAYTON, *Battle of Agincourt*. A shoeless soldier there a man might meet Leading his MOUNSEER by the arms fast bound.

1719. DURFEY, *Pills*, i. 98. The next a Nymph who to be Queen Her *Monsieur* was engaging.

1755. *Gent. Mag.*, xxv. 229. And now, thus ballasted—what course to steer ! Shall I again to sea—and bang MOUNSEER.

1887. W. S. GILBERT, *Savoy Songs*, p. 14. Though he's only a darned MOUNSEER, d'ye see?

MOUNT, *subs.* (common).— 1. A saddle-horse.

1856. WHYTE MELVILLE, *Kate Coventry*, i. We ride many an impetuous steed in safety and comfort that a man would find a dangerous and uncontrollable MOUNT.

1873. MISS BROUGHTON, *Nancy*, vi. 'His horses would certainly carry me: I wonder would he give me a MOUNT now and then.'

2. (venery).— 1. A wife or mistress; and (2) an act of coition. [*Cf.* Mrs. MOUNT in *Richard Feverel*].

3. (Old Cant).—A bridge.

Verb. (common).— 1. To wear; to carry as an equipment.

1822. MOORE, *Life*, 26 Mar. Weather like midsummer: the dandies all MOUNTING their white trousers.

1847. THACKERAY, *Vanity Fair*, viii. One is bound to speak the truth as far as one knows it, whether one MOUNTS a cap and bells or a shovel-hat.

2. (theatrical).—To prepare for representation on the stage.

1880. *Athenæum*, 6 March, p. 322. As regards MOUNTING and general decorations the revival is superior to any previous performance of *As You Like It*.

3. (old).—To swear falsely ; to give false evidence: for money.

1789. GEO. PARKER, *Life's Painter*, p. 159, s.v.

1819. VAUX, *Memoirs*, s.v. MOUNT, to swear, or give evidence falsely for the sake of a gratuity. To MOUNT FOR a person is also synonymous with *bonnetting for* him.

1859. MATSELL, *Vocabulum*, s.v. MOUNT. To give false testimony.

4. (venery).—To copulate. For synonyms *see* GREENS and RIDE.

1593. SHAKSPEARE, *Venus and Adonis*. Her champion MOUNTED for the hot encounter . . . . He will not manage her although he MOUNT her.

1620. MIDDLETON, *Chaste Maid*, v. 4. A woman may be honest according to the English print, when she's a whore in the Latin ; so much for marriage and logic : I'll love her for her wit, I'll pick out my runts there ; and for my mountains, I'll MOUNT—[So in original, but the play on words is clear].

1629. JONSON, *The New Inn* [CUNNINGHAM, ii. 344], i. 1. Instead of backing the brave steed o' mornings, My copy has, to MOUNT the chambermaid.

1662. *Rump Songs*, i. p. 358. He caught a Foal and MOUNTED her (O base !) below the crupper.

1668. ETHEREGE, *She Would if She Could*, iii. 2. How she'd curvet and frisk, If a man were once MOUNTED upon her.

1715. PENNECUIK, *Poems* (1815), p. 363. To see old Cuff upon young Helen MOUNTED.

1847. HALLIWELL, *Arch. & Prov. Words*, s.v. MOUNT. *Futuo.*

TO MOUNT THE ASS, *verb. phr.* (old).—To go bankrupt. [In

France it was customary to mount a bankrupt on an ass, face to tail, and ride him through the streets].

MOUNTAIN-DEW, *subs.* (common).—Scotch whiskey. [From the secret hill-side stills.] For synonyms *see* DRINKS and OLD MAN'S MILK.

1821. *Edinburgh Evening Courant*, 22 Jan. Bread, cheese, and MOUNTAIN-DEW were liberally provided.

1841. LEVER, *Charles O'Malley*, xxviii. Nor quit the land where whiskey grew, To wear King George's button, Take vinegar for MOUNTAIN DEW, And toads for mountain mutton.

MOUNTAIN-PECKER, *subs.* (common).—A sheep's head. *See* JEMMY.

MOUNTER, *subs.* (old).—See quot. 1859.

1781. G. PARKER, *View of Society*, II. 23; s.v.

1819. VAUX, *Memoirs*, s.v.

1859. MATSELL, *Vocabulum*, s.v. MOUNT. . . MOUNTER. Men who give false bail ; or who, for a consideration, will swear to anything required. Fellows who hire clothes to wear for a particular occasion ; those who wear second-hand clothes.

MOUNT-FAULCON, *subs.* (venery).—See quot. 1850. For synonyms *see* MONOSYLLABLE.

1593. FLORIO, *Worlde of Wordes*, s.v.

1850. HALLIWELL, *Archaic and Provincial Words*, s.v. MOUNTFALCON. The female *pudendum*. Apparently from the Italian. It occurs in Florio and is still in use.

MOUNT OF VENUS, *subs. phr.* (venery).—The *mons veneris* ; the MOTTE (*q.v.*).

1750. STRUAN, *Poems*, 'Horace,' iii. 13. By this lov'd spot*, I'd live and die with thee. [* Note. Clapping her hand on the MOUNT OF VENUS].

MOUNT-PLEASANT, *subs. phr.* (venery).—The *mons veneris*. *Cf.* SHOOTERS-HILL. For synonyms *see* MOTTE.

MOUNTS-OF-LILIES, *subs.* (old).—The paps. For synonyms *see* DAIRY.

1694. CROWNE, *Married Beau*, iii. 1. Who would not, to ascend these MOUNTS OF LILIES, Leave for a while religion at the bottom.

MOURNER, *subs.* (American).—One taking a drink; a SPREESTER (*q.v.*).

1847. PORTER, *Quarter Race etc.*, p. 126. The cards were dropt instanter . . . . and the MOURNERS were soon distributed in knots upon the promenade deck.

1848. DURIVAGE, *Stray Subjects*, p. 110. By common consent the MOURNERS settled themselves down into comparative quiet.

MOURNING. FULL MOURNING, *subs. phr.* (pugilists').—Two black eyes: HALF-MOURNING = one black eye or a MOUSE. Fr. *œufs sur le plat; yeux au beurre noir; yeux pochés.*

Adj. (old).—Bruised. Also IN MOURNING.

1708. MRS. CENTLIVRE, *The Busy-Body*, i. 1. *Mar.* I would give ten guineas, I say, to be ranked in his acquaintance. But, pr'ythee, introduce me. *Chas.* Well on condition you'll give us a true account how you came by that MOURNING nose, I will.

1820. REYNOLDS, *The Fancy*, 'King Tims'. Her eyes were all sweetly IN MOURNING.

1821. EGAN, *Anecdotes of the Turf*, 67. Never again would he put the ogles of the ring IN MOURNING.

1828. BEE, *Living Picture of London*, 283. To send him before his betters with his peepers IN MOURNING.

1837. S. WARREN, *Diary of a Late Physician*, xii. His left eye was sent INTO DEEP MOURNING, which threatened to last for some weeks.

MOURNING-SHIRT, *subs.* (old).—An unlaundered shirt: *cf.* BILED-RAG.

1650. FULLER, *Pisgah Sights*, 98. We say MOURNING SHIRTS, it being customary for men in sadnesse to spare the pains of their laundresses.

MOUSE, *subs.* (pugilistic).—1. *See* quots. 1860 and 1895. *Cf.* BLACKWALL.

1857. CUTHBERT BEDE, *Verdant Green*, pt. II. ch. iv. 'That'll raise a tidy MOUSE on your ogle, my lad!'

1860. W. E. HOLMES, *The Professor at the Breakfast Table*, xi. 354. MOUSE is a technical term for a bluish, oblong rounded elevation occasioned by running one's forehead or eyebrow against another's knuckles.

1887. ATKIN, *House Scraps*. His dexter ogle has a MOUSE; His conk's devoid of bark.

1888. *Sporting Life*, 10 Dec. Bringing his right into play with extreme force, caused a MOUSE to appear on his opponent's left peeper.

1895. *Westminster Gazette*, . . . A black eye in true cockney slang is known as a MOUSE, and this accounts for the fact that a cockney near his platform on Sunday shouted out, 'Jack, where is your rat-trap?' Mr. Burns was rather astounded. 'Why a rat-trap?' he said, thinking vaguely of 'black-legs' and Liberal Unionists. 'For that big MOUSE on yer eye,' cried the delighted cockney.

2. (venery).—The *penis*. For synonyms *see* CREAMSTICK, and PRICK. *Cf.* MOUSER.

3. (old).—A term of endearment.

1593. ALLEYN, ... [in COLLIER, *Memoirs*, 25]. My good, sweete MOUSE [of his wife].

1594. SHAKSPEARE, *Love's Lab. Lost*, v. 2. What's your dark meaning, MOUSE?

1594. *Look About You* [DODSLEY, *Old Plays* (1874), vii. 463]. Sweet MOUSE, the hermit bids you stay here.

1611. BEAUMONT and FLETCHER, *Knight of the Burning Pestle*, i. 2. *Wife.* Stay. . . . till I question my husband. *Cit.* What is it, MOUSE.

1656. *Muses Recr.* [HOTTEN], p. 33. Even Mopsa, pretty MOUSE.

4. (common).—The face.

5. (old).—The mouth. Also as *verb.* = to bite. *Cf.* MOUSLE.

1557. TUSSER, *Husbandie* [E.E. T.S. 91, 38, 3]. If foxes MOUSE them, then watch or house them.

1596. SHAKSPEARE, *King John*, ii. 1. line 354. And now he feasts, MOUSING the flesh of kings.

1675. WYCHERLEY, *Country Wife*, ii. 1. He told me none but naughty women sat there whom they tous'd and MOUS'D.

6. (common).—The same as MOUSE-PIECE (*q.v.*).

1888. N. GOULD, *Double Event*, p. 223. He's turned MOUSE, has he?

Verb. (American).—To go mouse-like: *i.e.*, as in depreciation of one's self. [A variant of MOUCH].

1871. S. L. CLEMENS ('Mark Twain'), *Screamers*. The poor blunderer MOUSES among the sublime creations of the old masters.

Intj. (old).—*See* quot.

1859. MATSELL, *Vocabulum*, s.v. MOUSE. Be quiet; be still; talk low; whisper; step light; softly.

TO SPEAK LIKE A MOUSE IN A CHEESE, *verb. phr.* (old).—*See* quot.

1811. *Lex. Bal.*, s.v. MOUSE. To SPEAK LIKE A MOUSE IN A CHEESE; *i.e.*, faintly or indistinctly.

AS DRUNK AS A MOUSE, *phr.* (old).—Very drunk. *See* DRINKS and SCREWED.

*c.*1508[?]. *Colin Blowbol's Testament*, line 141. Oft hath made me DRONKE AS ANY MOUSE.

153[?]. *Doctour Doubble Ale* [quoted by HALLIWELL]. Then seke another house, This is not worth a louse; As DRONKEN AS A MOUSE.

MOUSE-DIGGER, *subs.* (Winchester College).—*See* quot.

1866. MANSFIELD, *School Life*, 150. Plying the MOUSE DIGGER (a kind of diminutive pick-axe) in search of mice.

MOUSER, *subs.* (venery).—The female *pudendum*; the CAT (*q.v.*). For synonyms *see* MONOSYLLABLE. *Cf.* MOUSE, *subs.* sense 2.

MOUSE-FOOT, *subs.* (old).—An oath.

1563. *Appius & Virginius* [DODSLEY, *Old Plays* (1874), iv. 151]. Yet, by the MOUSE-FOOT, I am not content.

1601. A. DENT, *Pathway*, 142. I know a man that will never sweare but by Cocke, or Pie, or MOUSE FOOT. I hope you will not say these be oathes.

1605. *London Prodigal*, ii. 2. I'll come and visit you: by the MOUSE-FOOT I will.

MOUSE-HUNT, *subs.* (old colloquial).—A wencher; a GROUSER (*q.v.*).

1595. SHAKSPEARE, *Romeo & Juliet*, iv. 4. Aye, you have been a MOUSE-HUNT in your time, But I will watch you from such watching now.

MOUSEPIECE (MOUSE-BUTTOCK, or MOUSE), *subs.* (colloquial).—A piece of beef or mutton below the round; the part immediately above the knee joint.

1591. LYLY, *Sappho and Phaon*, i. 3. Aptly understood, a MOUSE of beef.

MOUSETRAP, *subs.* (common).—1. The mouth; the potato-trap (*q.v.*).

2. (venery).—The female *pudendum*. For synonyms *see* MONOSYLLABLE. *Cf.* MOUSE, *subs.* sense 2.

3. (common).—A sovereign; a CANARY (*q.v.*). [From a fancied resemblance of the crown and shield to a set trap].

THE PARSON'S MOUSETRAP, *subs. phr.* (common).—*See* quot. 1785.

1690. B. E., *Dict. Cant. Crew*, s.v.

1785. GROSE, *Vulg. Tongue*, s.v. MOUSETRAP. The PARSON'S MOUSETRAP; the state of matrimony.

1811. *Lex. Bal.*, s.v.

MOUSLE, *verb.* (old).—1. To nibble. Hence (2) to tongue a woman: *cf.* MOUSE, sense 5; TO TIP THE VELVET (*q.v.*).

1672. MARVELL, *Rehearsal* [GROSART (1873), iii. 152]. The poor word is sure to be mumpled and MOWSLED to purpose.

1675. WYCHERLEY, *Country Wife*, v. 1. He put the lip of his tongue between my lips, and so MOUSLED me—and I said I'd bite it.

1695. CONGREVE, *Love for Love*, iii. 4. Ben's a brisk boy . . . he'll touzle her and MOUZLE her; . . . if he shou'd not stay for saying grace . . . but fall to without the help of a parson, ha?

1762. WILSON, *The Cheats*, ii. 4. *I.I.* Dear Mopus! *[He hugs her]. Mr. Mop.* Away, Captain! You do so MOUSLE one.

MOUTH, *subs.* (common).—1. *See* quots. Also MOUTH-ALMIGHTY. For synonyms *see* CLACK-BOX and FURIOSO.

1596. SHAKSPEARE, *King John*, ii. 1, line 397. Large MOUTH indeed!

1690. B. E., *Dict. Cant. Crew*, s.v.

1748. T. DYCHE, *Dictionary* (5th ed.) MOUTH (S.). . . . also a cant word for a noisy, silly, ignorant, prating, scolding fellow.

1785. GROSE, *Vulg. Tongue*, s.v. MOUTH. A noisy fellow. MOUTH half cocked; one gaping and staring at every thing he sees.

1811. *Lex. Bal.*, s.v.

1859. MATSELL, *Vocabulum*, s.v. MOUTH. A noisy fellow; a silly fellow.

2. (old).—*See* quot.

1754. *Discoveries of John Poulter*, 34. Another shall look out for a MOUTH that has a horse to sell or change.

1811. *Lex. Bal.*, s.v. MOUTH. A silly fellow. A dupe. To stand MOUTH; *i.e.*, to be duped.

1819. VAUX, *Memoirs*, s.v. MOUTH, a foolish silly person; a man who does a very imprudent act, is said to be A RANK MOUTH.

3. *See* CHEEK.

4. (common).—The after-effects of a debauch; HOT COPPERS (*q.v.*).

Verb. (colloquial).—To rant.

1596. SHAKSPEARE, *Hamlet*, iii. 2. If you MOUTH it as many of your players do.

1759. GOLDSMITH, *Citizen of the World*, x[?]. I hate to hear an actor MOUTHING trifles.

1871. LOWELL, *Study Windows*, 180. In his pompous, MOUTHING way of saying it.

TO GIVE MOUTH, *verb. phr.* (common).—1. To put into words; and (2) to speak loudly and distinctly. Also MOUTH IT. It. *dar la bocca.*

1840. DICKENS, *Barnaby Rudge*, lxv. 'What I say in respect to the speeches always is, GIVE IT MOUTH. That's my maxim. GIVE IT MOUTH.'

1850. MATSELL, *Vocabulum*, s.v. MOUTH IT. Speak loudly.

1861. DICKENS, *Our Mutual Friend*, Bk. II. ch. vii. 'I have an opinion of you, sir, to which it is not easy to GIVE MOUTH.'

1883. *Daily Telegraph*, 4 Sep., p. [?], col. 2. 'Black Bess,' they said, was nothing unless you GAVE IT MOUTH, and the two remaining verses, with the chorus, were rendered with unabated vigour.

1892. MILLIKEN, *'Arry Ballads*, p. 42. GIVE IT MOUTH!

DOWN IN THE MOUTH, *verb. phr.* (common).—Dejected.

1608-11. BISHOP HALL, *Epistles*, i. 6. The Roman orator was DOWN IN THE MOUTH; finding himself thus cheated by the money-changer.

1693. CONGREVE, *Old Batchelor*, iv. 9. *Sir. J. Witt.* Now am I slapdash DOWN IN THE MOUTH, and have not one word to say!

1751. SMOLLETT, *Peregrine Pickle*, xlix. He . . . told the physician that he was like the root of the tongue, as being cursedly DOWN IN THE MOUTH.

1864. EDMUND YATES, *Broken to Harness*, x. What won't do? asked Prescott, with flaming face. Why, this Kate Mellon business, Jim. It's on hot and strong, I know. You've been DOWN IN THE MOUTH all the time she was away.

1880. A. TROLLOPE, *The Duke's Children*, xlvii. I'm sorry you're so DOWN IN THE MOUTH. Why don't you try again?

1888. ROLF BOLDREWOOD, *Robbery Under Arms*, xxxiii. Poor Old Jim looks dreadful DOWN IN THE MOUTH.

1894. GEORGE MOORE, *Esther Waters*, xxx. I'm a bit DOWN IN THE MOUTH.

TO LAUGH ON THE WRONG (or OTHER) SIDE OF ONE'S MOUTH (or FACE), *subs. phr.* (colloquial).—To cry.

1714. LUCAS, *Gamesters*, 65. But tho' he laugh; 'twas on the WRONG SIDE OF HIS MOUTH.

1811. *Lex. Bal.*, s.v. LAUGH.

1823. GROSE, *Vulg. Tongue*, s.v. LAUGH.

1826. BUCKSTONE, *Death Fetch*, i. 4. *Snapsch. (Aside.)* And have a pretty family of them about my ears the first time I'm left alone in the dark, who would soon make me LAUGH ON THE OTHER SIDE OF MY MOUTH, I fancy.

1837. CARLYLE, *Diamond Necklace*, iii. By and bye thou wilt LAUGH ON THE WRONG SIDE OF THY FACE.

MOUTH THAT SAYS NO WORDS ABOUT IT (or CANNOT BITE), *subs. phr.* (old).—The female *pudendum.*

1719. DURFEY, *Pills etc.*, IV. 71. That feeds the MOUTH THAT CANNOT BITE.

See also, ALL MOUTH; BIG-MOUTH; BONE; CAT; SILVER-SPOON; LION; WATER.

MOUTH-BET, *subs.* (racing).—A verbal bet.

MOUTHER, *subs.* (pugilists').—A blow on the mouth.

1821. *The Fancy*, Vol. I. p. 254. The Jew brought first blood by a MOUTHER.

MOUTH-GLUE, *subs.* (old).—Speech.

160[?] DAVIES OF HEREFORD, *Wittes Pilgrimage* (GROSART, 1878, II. *h*). 'In Praise of Poesie.' And Iudgement ioyne them fast with Art's MOUTH-GLUE.

1688. CROWNE, *City Politics*, ii. 1. As for marriage-promises, they are but church MOUTH-GLUE, they won't hold a couple together three days.

MOUTHING, *subs.* (common).—*See* quot.

1859. MATSELL, *Vocabulum*, s.v. MOUTHING. Crying.

MOUTHPIECE, *subs.* (thieves').—*See* quot. Fr. *un lessiveur* (thieves' = whitewasher); *un médecin* (= doctor: *cf. malade* = prisoner; *l'hôpital* = prison); *un parrain.*

1888. GREENWOOD, *Old People etc.*, 18. It was for the benefit of a man, whose name I needn't mention, who was 'in trouble' and in need of a bit of money, the card said, to procure him a MOUTHPIECE,—which, perhaps you might not be aware, is another word for a defending counsel among those sort of characters.

MOUTH-THANKLESS, *subs. phr.* (Old Scots').—The female *pudendum*. For synonyms *see* MONOSYLLABLE.

1460-1505. KENNEDY, *Ane Aigit Man* (Bannantyne *MSS.* Hunt. Soc. Publications, p. 780-82). That ewir I scherwit MOWTH THANKLESS.

*d.*1555. LYNDSAY, *Answer to the King's Flyting*, in *Wks.* (Edinburgh, 1873), I. 106, l. 33. Sae sair I rew That ewir I did MOUTH-THANKLESS so persew.

15?-15?. A. SCOTT, *Of May*, in *Wks.* (Edinburgh, 1826). For helth of body now have e Nocht oft to mell with THANKLESS MOWTH.

MOVE, *subs.* (common).—*See* quots. TO BE UP (or FLY) TO A MOVE OR TWO (or EVERY MOVE ON THE BOARD) = to be wide-awake.

1819. VAUX, *Memoirs*, s.v. MOVE, any action or operation in life; the secret spring by which any project is conducted, as, There is a MOVE in that business which you are not *down to*. To be FLASH TO EVERY MOVE UPON THE BOARD, is to have a general knowledge of the world, and all its numerous deceptions.

1853. WH. MELVILLE, *Digby Grand*, xiii. The champion glared . . . . putting in play all the different manœuvres of the King, which the initiated call MOVES.

1891. *Lic. Vict. Gaz.*, 16 Jan. He said he had as good as given me a fortune, for he had made me a tip-top player, put me UP TO EVERY MOVE UPON THE BOARD, and the next time I played I should sweep it clean.

MOVEABLES, *subs.* (thieves').—1. Furniture; and (2) *see* quots.

1599. SHAKSPEARE, *Henry V.* ii. 8. 50. Look to my chattels and my MOVABLES.

1607. MIDDLETON, *Trick to Catch the Old One*, iii. 1. He's rich in money, MOVABLES, and land.

1690. B. E., *Dict. Cant. Crew*, s.v. MOVEABLES . . . . We bit all the Cull's cole and MOVEABLES, we won all the man's money, rings, watches etc.

1785. GROSE, *Vulg. Tongue*, s.v. MOVEABLES. Rings, watches, or any toys of value.

1811. *Lex. Bal.*, s.v.

MOVED, *adv.* (American thieves').—*See* quot.

1859. MATSELL, *Vocabulum*, s.v. MOVED. Bowed to.

MOW, *verb.* (American).—1. To kiss.

1859. MATSELL, *Vocabulum*, s.v. Mow. To kiss.

2. (venery).—*See* quots. For synonyms *see* GREENS and RIDE. Also MOWE.

*d.*1554. LYNDSAY, *Kitteis Confessioun*, l. 16. Quod scho, Will Leno MOWIT me.

1597-8. HAUGHTON, *A Woman will have her Will* [DODSLEY, *Old Plays* (1874), x. 493]. I am no meat for his MOWING.

1719. DURFEY, *Pills to Purge*, v. 18. For when at her Daddy's Ise gang to Bed, Ise MOW'D her without any more to do.

1785. GROSE, *Vulg. Tongue*, s.v. To Mow. A Scotch word for the act of copulation.

1793. BURNS, (In Title) *Poor Bodies do Nothing but* MOW. May the deil in her arse Ram a huge prick of brass, An' damn her to hell wi' a MOW.

1808-25. JAMIESON, *Dict.*, s.v. Mow . . . to copulate.

1811. *Lex. Bal.*, s.v.

1850. HALLIWELL, *Archaic & Provincial Words*, s.v. Mow . . . Futuo.

MOWDIWORT (or MOWDIWARK), *subs.* (venery).—The *penis*. For synonyms *see* CREAMSTICK and PRICK.

17[?]. *Old Song* [quoted by BURNS in *Merry Muses*], 'The MODIEWARK.' The MODIWARK has done me ill, And under my apron has biggit a hill.

MOWER, *subs.* (Old Cant).—A cow.

1690. B. E., *Dict. Cant. Crew*, s.v.

1728. BAILEY, *Eng. Dict.*, s.v. MOWER . . . *Cant.*

1785. GROSE, *Vulg. Tongue*, s.v.

1811. *Lex. Bal.*, s.v.

MOW- (or MOO-) HEATER, *subs.* (old).—*See* quot.

1690. B. E., *Dict. Cant. Crew*, s.v.

1811. *Lex. Bal.*, s.v. MOW HEATER. A drover: from their frequent sleeping on hay mows. *Cant.*

1870. *All the Year Round*, 5 Mar. 'Bye-gone Cant,' s.v.

MOZZY, *subs.* (showmen's).—Judy. SWATCHELL = Mr. Punch.

M. P., *subs. phr.* (common).—A policeman. For synonyms *see* BEAK.

MR. FERGUSON, MR. KNAP, MR. NASH, MR. PALMER, MR. PULLEN. *See* FERGUSON, KNAP, NASH, PALM, and PULL.

MRS. GOFF, *subs. phr.* (American University).—A woman. For synonyms *see* PETTICOAT.

MRS. GRUNDY, *subs. phr.* (common).—A personification of respectability. *See* quots. 1849 and 1855. [From a character in *Speed the Plough*, *see* quot. 1798].

1798. J. MORTON, *Speed the Plough*, i. 1. Be quiet woolye? always ding, dinging DAME GRUNDY into my ears—What will MRS. GRUNDY say? What will MRS. GRUNDY think?

1849. LYTTON, *Caxtons*, Pt. xv. ch. iii. I have hit upon a mode of satisfying the curiosity of our friend MRS. GRUNDY—that is, 'the World'—without injury to any one.

1855. THACKERAY, *Newcomes*, li. 'What will Richmond, what will society, what will MRS. GRUNDY in general say to such atrocious behaviour?'

1891. *Tales from Town Topics*, 'How a Shell Broke the Ice,' p. 39. Come in; MRS. GRUNDY has run away from Paris long ago.

MRS. HARRIS and MRS. GAMP, *subs. phr.* (Fleet St.).—*The Morning Herald* and *The Standard* under the proprietorship of Mr. Baldwin. [*Cf.* DICKENS, *Martin Chuzzlewit*, *passim*].

1846. *Punch*, x. p. 11. It is a fact—and as the evening MRS. HARRIS says, we will stake our reputation upon it—that MRS. GAMP of the *Herald* did, one day last week, write, that is scold, a leader about Lord John Russell, and did *not* quote Sydney Smith!

1885. *Punch*, 8 August. *The Standard* figures as 'Sairey Gamp' scolding—in allusion to a recent article in the *S.* abusing Lord Randolph Churchill.

MRS. JONES, *subs. phr.* (common).—A water-closet.

ENGLISH SYNONYMS. Bog; bog-shop (or -house); cacatorium; chapel (or chapel-of-ease); coffee-shop (or -house); colfabias; crapping-castle (-case, -casa, -house, or -ken); draught-chapel; dunnakin; Forty-two; fourth; gong; House of Commons; house-of-office; jakes; letter-box; the Long (University); my aunt's; necessary-house; quaker's burying-ground; place (or house)-of-ease; rear; shit-house; Sir Harry; the West Central; where the Queen goes on foot (or sends nobody).

FRENCH SYNONYMS. *Madame Bernard* (*cf.* MRS. JONES); *le buen-retiro* (popular); *chez Jules*; *le goguenau* (*gogueno* or *goguenot*—military); *le gras* (thieves': *cf.* BOG); *le longchamps* (*cf.* LONG); *la mousserie* (thieves'); *le numbro cent* (popular: a play on *sent*); *le restaurant à l'envers* (common); *la sacristie* (*cf.* CHAPEL).

MRS. LUKEY PROPS, *subs.* (tramps').—A bawd.

MRS. PARTINGTON, *subs. phr.* (colloquial).—A personification of impotent and senile prejudice. Also, a kind of Malaprop.

1831. SYDNEY SMITH, 'Speech at Taunton.' I do not mean to be disrespectful; but the attempt of the lords to stop the progress of reform reminds me very forcibly of the great storm of Sidmouth, and the conduct of the excellent Mrs. Partington on that occasion. In the winter of 1824, there set in a great flood upon that town; the tide rose to an incredible height; the waves rushed in upon the houses; and everything was threatened with destruction. In the midst of this sublime storm, Dame Partington, who lived upon the beach, was seen at the door of her house with mop and pattens, trundling her mop, squeezing out the sea-water, and vigorously pushing away the Atlantic Ocean. The Atlantic was roused; Mrs. Partington's spirit was up; but I need not tell you that the contest was

unequal. The Atlantic beat Mrs. Partington. She was excellent at a slop or puddle, but should never have meddled with a tempest.

1872. BESANT and RICE, *Ready-Money Mortiboy*, xxx. As MRS. PARTINGTON would say, they might all three have been twins.

MR. SPEAKER, *subs.* (America).—A revolver. For synonyms *see* MEAT-IN-THE-POT.

MRS. SUDS, *subs.* (common).—A laundress.

1757. FOOTE, *Author*, i. MRS. SUDS, your washerwoman, makes the three half crowns.

M'S AND W'S, TO MAKE M'S AND W'S, *verb. phr.* (printers').—To be drunk.

M. T., *subs. phr.* (railway).—1. Empties, or empty carriages: *see* MOLL THOMPSON'S MARK.

2. (common).—An empty bottle; a DEAD-MAN (*q.v.*).

1859. MATSELL, *Vocabulum*, s.v.

MUBBLEFUBBLES, *subs.* (Old Cant).—Low spirits. *Cf.* MULLIGRUBS.

1592. LYLY, *Mydas*, v. 2. Melancholy is the creast of courtiers armes, and now every base companion, being in his MUBLEFUBLES, says he is melancholy.

1654. GAYTON, *Festiv. Notes*, 46. Whether Jupiter was not joviall, nor Sol in his MUBBLEFUBBLES, that is long clouded, or in a total eclipse. *Ibid.* 145. Our Mary Gutierez, when she was in the MUBBLEFUBLES, do you think I was mad for it?

[?] *Misc. Antiq. Angl. in X. Prince*, 55. And when your brayne feeles any payne, With cares of state and troubles, We'll come in kindnesse to put your highnesse Out of your MUMBLE-FUBBLES.

1847. HALLIWELL, *Archaic Words*, s.v. MUBBLE-FUBBLES . . . . depressed in spirits without any serious cause. A cant term.

MUCH, *subs.* (colloquial).—An expression of quality, *e.g.*, 'Not MUCH of a lawyer' = not a very good lawyer.

MUCH OF A MUCHNESS, *phr.* (colloquial).—Very much the same thing.

1837. S. WARREN, *Diary of a Late Physician*, xxi. 'The people I want are very, *very* poor!' 'Oh! oh! oh! I'm thinking they're all MUCH OF A MUCHNESS for the matter of that, about here,' he replied.

1840. HALIBURTON, *Clockmaker*, 3. S. ii. It is MUCH OF A MUCHNESS, sir,—six of one, and half a dozen of the other.

1860. *Punch*, v. 28, p. 135. The two are MUCH OF A MUCHNESS.

1870. DICKENS, *Mystery Ed. Drood*, iv. p. 27. 'Surely this key is the heaviest of the three,' 'You'll find 'em MUCH OF A MUCHNESS, I expect,' says Durdles 'They all belong to monuments.'

1876. G. ELIOT, *Daniel Deronda*, xxxi. Gentle or simple, they're MUCH OF A MUCHNESS.

1891. *Sportsman*, 2 April. The sport was MUCH OF A MUCHNESS with that usually seen there of recent years.

NOT MUCH! (or NOT MUCHLY!), *adv.* (colloquial).—Not likely; certainly not! in derision.

1598. SHAKSPEARE, *2 Hen. IV*, ii. 4. What with two points on your shoulder? MUCH!

1599. JONSON, *Ev. Man Out of His Humour*, i. 3. To charge me bring my grain into the markets, Aye, MUCH! when I have neither barn nor garner.

MUCH CRY AND LITTLE WOOL. *See* CRY.

MUCHLY, *adv.* (common).—A great deal.

[?]. *M. S. Bibl. Reg.*, 17 B, 15 [HALLIWELL]. Went gravelie dight to entertaine the dame, They MUCHLIF lov'd, and honour'd in her name.

MUCK, *subs.* (old: now colloquial).—1. A dripping, or oozing, mass of filth. Hence, MUCK-CHEAP = very cheap; MUCK-HEAP, or MUCK-SCUTCHEON = a foul sloven: *cf.* MIDDEN; MUCK-GRUBBER = a miser; MUCK-HILL = a dunghill; MUCK-SPOUT = a foul-mouthed talker; MUCK-SUCKLE = a filthy woman; MUCKY-WHITE = sallow in complexion; MUCK OF SWEAT = a violent perspiration, etc.

1766. GOLDSMITH, *Vicar of Wakefield*, ix. She was all of a MUCK OF SWEAT.

2. (common).—Anything vile.

1884. HENLEY and STEVENSON, *Deacon Brodie*, I. iii. 1. MUCK: that's my opinion of him.

1888. *Sportsman*, 28 Nov. 'Yuss,' quoth somebody else, 'and a precious little luck he'll get a drinking sech like MUCK.'

1892. MILLIKEN, *'Arry Ballads*, p. 28. Up to now it's bin MUCK and no error, fit only for fishes.

3. (old).—Money. For synonyms *see* ACTUAL and GILT.

1393. GOWER, *Confessio Amantis*, v. 'For to pinche, and for to spare, Of worlds MUCKE to gette encres.'

1587. TURBERVILLE, *Tragicall Tales* [NARES]. Not one in all Ravenna might compare With him for wealth, or match him for his MUCK.

1592. NASHE, *Summer's Last Will* [DODSLEY, *Old Plays* (1874), viii. 29]. St. Francis a holy saint and never had any money. It is madness to doat upon MUCK.

1603. DAVIES OF HEREFORD, *Microcosmos* [GROSART (1878), i. *c*], 70. Our MUCKE and Earthly Mammon's continent.

1611. DAVIES, *Scourge of Folly* [NARES]. He married her for MUCKE, she him for lust; The motives fowle, then fowlly live they must.

1624. MASSINGER, *Bondman*, i. 3. Do you prize your MUCK Above your liberties.

1655. MASSINGER, *Guardian*, v. 4. Deliver such coin as you are furnish'd with . . . . *Dur.* When we have thrown down our MUCK, what follows? *Sev.* Liberty, with a safe convoy, To any place you choose.

1748. T. DYCHE, *Dictionary* (5th ed). MUCK (S.) . . . also a cant name or money hoarded up.

1754. B. MARTIN, *Eng. Dict.*, s.v. MUCK . . . . pelf, which a miser scrades.

1785. GROSE, *Vulg. Tongue*, s.v.

1859. MATSELL, *Vocabulum*, s.v.

4. (common).—A heavy fall. Also MUCKER.

5. (common).—A coarse brute.

Verb. (common).—1. To spend; and (2) to ruin.

1851-61. MAYHEW, *Lond. Lab.*, i. 20. He'd MUCK a thousand!

1892. MILLIKEN, *'Arry Ballads*, p. 75. Wot MUCKS me, old man. *Ibid.* p. 70. I'm MUCKED, that's a moral.

2. (racing).—*See* quot.

1865. *Sporting Gazette*, 1 April. If this letter had not already reached a considerable length, I would discourse upon the probability that to RUN A MUCK, and to GO A MUCKER, which Mr. Hotten treats as synonymous, are in reality unconnected. The meaning and derivation of to RUN A MUCK are no doubt correctly given; but to GO A MUCKER as men frequently do on the Turf, seems to be connected with muck, to clean out, and perhaps with muckinger, a pocket handkerchief.

TO GO (or RUN) A MUCK (or A MUCKER), *verb. phr.* (common).—To go headlong; also to be recklessly extravagant; to run AMOK (*q.v.*). [*Stanford Dict.* The homicidal frenzy (of a Malay), used originally in Port. forms *amouca*, *amuco*; hence, in a homicidal frenzy, furiously, viciously; metaphorically, headlong. Rare as *adv.* except with 'run.' Sometimes used as if it were the indef. art. 'a' with *subs.* 'muck'].

1588. J. Hickock, *Tr. C. Frederick's Voyage*, fol. 13, r8. This King of Cochine . . . hath a great number of gentlemen which he calleth Amochy, and some are called *Nayry;* these two sorts of men esteeme not their lives any thing. They will thrust themselves forward in every danger, although they knowe they shall dye.

1613. Purchas, *Pilgrimage* [1626], ii. 557. There are also certaine people called Amorichi, otherwise *Chiani*, which perceiving the end of their life approach, lay hold on their weapons . . . and going forth kill every man they meet with, till somebody (by killing them) make an end of their killing.

1665. Head, *English Rogue*, Sig. Hhh, 2 v°. A great crew of Indians and Chineses. . . . fell upon them, killing whom they could, not directing their revenge on any particular person, (which they call a muck).

1684. J. P., *Tr. Tavernier's Travels*, I. ii. iii. 202. Which the Java lords seeing . . . Cried a mocca on the English, killing a great number of them.

1687. Dryden, *Hind and Pauth*, iii. 1188. He scours the streets And runs an Indian muck at all he meets.

1754. Smollett, *Ferd. Ct. Fathom*, l. The Malays never run a muck, but in consequence of misery and despair.

1821. De Quincey, *Confessions* (1823), ii. 135. Brought other Malays with him . . . that ran amuck at me.

1866. Lowell, *Biglow Papers*, viii. The late muck which the country has been running.

To go a muck (or mucker), *verb. phr.* (common).—To go to smash. Also, to risk one's all; to put on one's shirt (*q.v.*).

1877. C. Kingsley, *Life*, 275. Only four more doing it and one receiving a mucker.

To muck about, *verb. phr.* (coster).—To fondle; to mess about (*q.v.*).

Muckcook, *verb.* (common).—To laugh behind one's back.

Muckender (Muckinder, Mucking-er, or Mucketer), *subs.* (Old Cant).—A handkerchief. [From Sp. *mocadero*, (influenced by muck) from *muco* = mucus]. For synonyms *see* Wipe.

1468. *Cov. Mysteries*, 'Christ in the Temple' p. 190. Goo hom lytyl babe, and sytte on the moderes lappe And put a mokador upon thi brest: And pray thi modyr to fede the with the pappe.

1598. Florio, *Worlde of Wordes*, s.v. *Bavaro*, a bib or muckender.

1600. *Weakest goes to Wall*, sign. I. 2 b. Onely upon his muckiter and band he had an F, By which I did suppose his name was Ferdinand.

1607. Marston, *What You Will*, ii. 1. Wipe your nose: fie on your sleeve! where's your muckender your grandmother gave you?

1608. Middleton, *Trick to Catch the Old One*, iv. 5. One must wipe his mouth for him with a muckinder.

1612. Chapman, *Widow's Tears*, iv. 1, p. 327 (*Plays*, 1874). To which all the Paphian widows shall after their husbands' funerals offer their wet muckinders, for monuments of the danger they have passed.

1633. Jonson, *Tale of a Tub*, iii. 1. Take my muckinder, And dry thine eyes.

1658. *On Dr. Corbet's Marriage* [Nares]. You knew her little, and when her Apron was but a muckender.

1668. Wilkins, *Real Char. Alph. Dict.* Mucketer, wiping thing.

1719. Durfey, *Pills to Purge*, v. 220 . . . . And now and then with a greasy muckender wipe away the dripping that bastes their foreheads.

1785. Grose, *Vulg. Tongue*, s.v.

1830. C. Lamb, *Pawnbroker's Daughter*, i. 2. Scarce three clean muckingers a week Would dry the brine that dew'd my cheek.

1847. Halliwell, *Arch. & Prov. Words*, s.v. Muckinder . . . The term is still in use, but generally applied to a dirtied handkerchief.

Mucker, *subs.* (common).—*See* to go a muck: also to come a cropper.

2. (common).—*See* muck, sense 4.

3. (military).—A commissariat officer.

Verb. (colloquial).—To blunder badly; to come to grief; to fail.

1861. H. Kingsley, *Ravenshoe*, xiv. Welter has muckered . . . but worse than that, they say that Charles Marston's classical first is fishy.

Muckerer (or Mokerer), *subs.* (old).—A miser.

c.1381. Chaucer, *Boethius*, Bk. ii. Auarice maketh alwaie muckerers to be hated.

Muck-fork, *subs.* (common).—A hand; a finger.

Muckibus, *adj.* (old).—*See* quot. For synonyms *see* Drinks and Screwed.

1756. Walpole, *Letters*, i. 498. She said in a very vulgar accent, if she drank any more she should be muckibus. 'Lord,' said Lady Mary Coke, 'what is that?' 'Oh, it is Irish for sentimental!'

Muckingtogs (or Muckintogs).—A mackintosh.

1851-61. Barham, *Ingoldsby Legends*, ii. 137. With a carpet-swab and muckingtogs.

Muckrake, *subs.* (American).—*See* quot.

1871. De Vere, *Americanisms*, s.v. Muckrakes, a slang term in politics for persons who 'fish in troubled waters,' from the idea of their raking up the muck to see what valuable waifs and strays they may find in it. The term is generally used in the form of muckrakes and placemongers.

Mucks. *See* mux.

Muck-snipe, *subs.* (common).—A ruined gambler. *Cf.* Muck, *verb.*, sense 2.

1851-61. H. Mayhew, *London Lab. & Lon. Poor*, i. 279. I was a muck-snipe when I was there—why, a muck-snipe, sir, is a man regularly done up, coopered, and humped altogether.

Muck-train, *subs.* (military).—A commissariat train.

Muck-worm, *subs.* (old).—A miser; [*Cf.* Muck = money]. Also an upstart.

1665. Howard, *The Committee*, ii. Come, pr'y thee let's go; these muckworms will have earth enough to stop their mouths with one day.

1670. J. Eachard, *Contempt of the Clergy* [Arber, *Garner*, Vol. vii. p. 298]. It is a great hazard if he be not counted a caterpillar! a muckworm! a very earthly minded man!

1695. Congreve, *Love for Love*, ii. 1. 'Oons, whose son are you? how were you engendered, muckworm?

1748. Thomson, *Castle of Indolence*, i. 50. Here you a muckworm of the town might see.

1785. Grose, *Vulg. Tongue*, s.v.

1795. R. Cumberland, *The Jew*, i. Here comes one that supersedes all other visitors—old Sheva, the rich Jew, the merest muck-worm in the city of London.

1811. *Lex. Bal.*, s.v.

1859. Matsell, *Vocabulum*, s.v.

1895. H. B. Marriott-Watson, in *New Review*, July, p. 7. 'You muck-worm, you——I'll slit your gizzard, you——.'

Mud, *subs.* (old).—1. *See* quots. For synonyms *see* Buffle and Cabbage-head.

1714. *Memoirs of John Hall* (4th ed.), p. 13. Mud, a Fool, or Thick-scull Fellow.

1748. T. Dyche, *Dictionary* (5th ed.). Mud(s) . . . . also a dull, heavy-headed fellow is called a mud.

1823. Bee, *Dict. Turf*, s.v. Mud—a stupid twaddling fellow. 'And his name is mud!' ejaculated upon the conclusion of a silly oration, or of a leader in the Courier.

1836. W. H. Smith, *The Individual*, 'The Thieves' Chaunt.' There is a nook in the boozing-ken, Where many a mud I fog.

1859. Matsell, *Vocabulum*, s.v.

2. (printers').—A non-society man; dung (*q.v.*).

1811. *Lex. Bal.*, s.v.

As clear as mud, *phr.* (common).—Very obscure. Also the reverse: as plain as may be.

1837-40. Haliburton, *The Clockmaker*, p. 480 (ed. 1862). Well, I get her to set down and go over it all ever so slow, and explain it all as clear as mud, and then she says,—Now do you see, Sam, ain't it horrid pretty?

1890. G. Allen, *The Tents of Shem*, vi. I'll explain the whole thing to you, as clear as mud, in half a second.

1892. Milliken, *'Arry Ballads*, p. 75. Clear as mud, my dear feller.

His name is mud! *phr.* (American political).—Said in cases of utter defeat; sent up Salt River (*q.v.*).

Mud-cat, *subs.* (American).—A Mississippi man.

Mudcrusher, *subs.* (military).—An infantryman. Fr. *pousse-caillou*.

English synonyms. Beetle-crusher (or -squasher); blanket-boy (a volunteer); boiled lobster; brother-blade; caterpillar; cat-shooter (volunteer); coolie; flat-foot; fly-slicer (a cavalryman); grabby; jolly gravel-grinder (a marine, *see* Royal Jolly); leather-neck; light-bob; lobster; mud-major (*q.v.*); mud-plunger; plunger; prancer (a cavalryman); Q.H.B. (= Queen's Hard Bargain = a malingerer); raw lobster (*see* lobster); red-coat; red-herring; Saturday-soldier (a volunteer); scarlet-runner; skid; snoddy; swaddy; tame jolly (*see* jolly); toe-footer (or bloody toe-footer); Tommy Atkins; tow-pow; wobbler; worm-crusher (or -squasher).

French synonyms. *Un allumeur de gaz* (= a lancer: in allusion to the weapon and a lamp-lighter's rod); *un barbe-à-poux* (= a sapper: they wear long beards); *un bibi* (popular); *un biffin*, or *bifin* (the knapsack is likened to a rag-picker's basket); *un bouffeur de kilomètres* (the Chasseurs de Vincennes; a picked corps of skirmishers and scouts); *un briscard* (= an old soldier with long-service stripes); *un cabillot* (sailors'); *un camisard* (a military convict who serves his time in Africa: also *un camisard en bordée*); *un centrier* or *centripète* (popular); *un chacal* (= a Zouave); *une citrouille* or *un citrouillard* (= a dragoon); *les clous* (the infantry *en masse*); *un court-à-pattes* (a foot artilleryman); *un cul rouge* (in allusion to the red trousers: *cf.* cherry-bum); *Dumanet* (= Tommy Atkins: from a character in a play); *une écrevisse de rempart* (cavalrymen's); *un fiferlin* (popular); *un fiffot* (popular); *un griffeton* or *grivier* (popular); *un homard* (= a spahi: *cf.* lobster); *un hussard à quatre roues* (= an army-service man); *un lascar* (= a malingerer); *un lignard* (= a linesman); *un marche à terre*

(*cf.* mud-crusher); *une marionette* (popular); *un méfiant* (military); *un mousse-caillou* (popular); *les mutilés* (= soldiers drafted to Africa for self-mutilation); *officier de guérite* (military); *un Parisien* (military: a crack soldier); *un pied de banc* (= a sergeant); *un pousse-caillou* (popular = gravel-grinder).

Italian synonyms. *Burasco; formigotto; foco* or *fuoco*.

Mudding-face, *subs.* (common).—A fool; a muff or muffin-face (*q.v.*).

Muddle, *subs.* (colloquial).—A state of confusion.

1854. Dickens, *Hard Times*, *passim*.

1882. E. J. Worboise, *Sissie*, xxv. 'There is no management in our house; there is nothing but muddle.'

Verb. (common).—1. To stupefy with liquor. For synonyms *see* Drinks and Screwed.

1712. Arbuthnot, *Hist. of John Bull* [*Ency. Dict.*]. 'I was for five years often drunk, always muddled.'

1834. Ainsworth, *Rookwood*, iii. ii. I must not muddle my brain with any more Pharaoh.

1872. *Daily Telegraph*, 5 Jan. 'The Clerical Scandal.' The vicar had a pocket handkerchief in his hand, and was wiping his face. He appeared to be muddled.

2. (colloquial).—To bungle.

3. (old Scots').—To copulate. For synonyms *see* Greens and Ride.

To muddle away, *verb. phr.* (colloquial).—To squander aimlessly; to waste one knows not how.

Muddle-head, *subs.* (common).—A fool. Hence muddle-headed, *adj.* (colloquial).—Doltish.

1837. Dickens, *Oliver Twist*, xxx. What a precious muddle-headed chap you are.

1856. Reade, *Never too Late to Mend*, vi. They are muddle-heads.

Muddler, *subs.* (racing).—A clumsy horse.

Mud-fog Association, *subs. phr.* (obsolete).—*See* quots.

1838. Dickens in *Bentley's Mag.*, iv. 209-227. Full Report of the Second Meeting of the Mudfog Association for the Advancement of Everything [Title].

1886. C. Dickens, Junior, in *Household Words*, 1 May, p. 13. Many critics have derided as a gross exaggeration a very early skit of my father's which satirised the proceedings of a certain Mudfog Association, but some recent meetings of the Social Science Association were quite as ridiculous.

Mudge, *subs.* (thieves').—*See* quot. For synonyms *see* Golgotha.

1888. *Sportsman*, 22 Dec. The judge said that he had noticed that one of the witnesses had referred to the hat as a mudge, a word which he had not heard of before. One had always to learn, and for the future he should be able to add mudge to his vocabulary. The gangs of Liverpool are clever at 'bashing mudges,' 'slipping wipes,' and 'catching a Waterbury wind-for-ever.'

Mudger, *subs.* (old).—A milk-sop.

1830. Sir E. B. Lytton, *Paul Clifford*, xxii. Ah, he *was* a fellow! none of your girl-faced mudgers, who make love to ladies, forsooth—a pretty woman need not look far for a kiss when he was in the room, I warrant, however coarse her duds might be.

Mud-hen, *subs.* (American Stock Exchange).—A female gambler.

1876. *San Francisco Post*, Nov. The average mud-hen is middle-aged, rather stout in person, as voluble in conversation as a stump-speaker, and possessed of an inordinate desire to become a 'stock-sharp.' She has a wonderful amount of gossip and 'dead-sure points' to communicate, and is by no means unwilling to reveal all she knows to any one who is supposed to have information relative to any stock, and in return can give her a point.

MUD-HOLE, *subs.*(whalers').—A salt-water lagoon in which whales are captured.

MUD-HONEY,*subs.*(common).—Mud; street slush.

MUD-HOOK, *subs.* (nautical).—An anchor.

MUD-LARK, *subs.* (common).—1. *See* quots.

1796. COLQUHOUN, *Police of the Metropolis*, p. 60. These aquatic plunderers. . . . practise another device, by connecting themselves with men and boys, known by the name of MUD-LARKS, who prowl about, and watch under the ship when the tide will permit, and to whom they throw *small parcels of sugar, coffee*, and other articles of plunder, which are conveyed to the receivers by the MUD-LARKS, who generally have a certain share of the booty.

1811. *Lex. Bal.*, s.v.

1823. BEE, *Dict. Turf*, s.v. MUD-LARKS—fellows who scratch about in gutters for horsenails, and other fragments of scrap-iron; also women who go into the Thames, at low-water, to pick from the mud bits of coal, which are spilled from the barges along-shore.

1851-61. MAYHEW, *Lond. Lab.*, ii. 173. There is another class who may be termed riverfinders, although their occupation is connected only with the shore; they are commonly known by the name of MUD-LARKS, from being compelled, in order to obtain the articles they seek, to wade sometimes up to their middle through the mud left on the shore by the retiring tide. The MUD-LARKS collect whatever they happen to find, such as coals, bits of old-iron, rope, bones, and copper nails that drop from ships while lying or repairing along shore.

1871. *Daily News*, 26 Dec. 'Workhouse Xmas. Depravity.' Why, there's Jemima Ann . . . has . . . been bleeding me of a fiver to send to some Christmas Dinner Fund for juvenile MUDLARKS.

2. (old).—A duck.

1785. GROSE, *Vulg. Tongue*, s.v.

3. (City).—Any one with outdoor duties.

4. (common).—A street-Arab (*q.v.*).

5. (old).—A hog. — GROSE (1785).

MUD-MAJOR, *subs.* (military).—An infantry major: *i.e.*, one who, on parade, commands a company on foot.

MUD-PICKER, *subs.* (military).—A garrison policeman.

MUD-PLAYER, *subs.* (cricketers').—A batsman partial to a soft wicket.

MUD-PLUNGING, *subs.* (tramps').—Tramping through slush in search of sympathy.

1883. *Daily Telegraph*, 8 Feb., p. 3, col. 1. 'The bitterest sort of weather is their [cadgers'] weather, and it doesn't matter if it's house-to-house work or chanting, or MUD-PLUNGING, it's cold work.'

MUD-SALAD MARKET, *subs. phr.* (common).—Covent Garden.

1880. *Punch*, 14 Aug., p. 71. MUD-SALAD MARKET belongs to His Grace the Duke of Mudford. It was once a tranquil Convent Garden.

MUD-SILL, *subs.* (American).—1. A low-born, ignorant,contemptible wretch.

2. (obsolete American).—A Southerner: *circa* 1861-4.

MUD-SLINGER, *subs.* (common).—A slanderer.

MUD-STUDENT, *subs.* (*see* def.).—A student at the Agricultural College, Cirencester.

1856. *Notes & Queries*, 2 S. ii. 198. A young friend of mine . . . . a MUD-STUDENT.

MUFF, *subs.* (old).—1. A milksop; a bungler; a dolt. *See* quots. 1598, 1648, 1862 and 1879. Also MUFFIN.

1586-1606. WARNER, *Albion's England*. 'Those stiles to him were strange, but thay Did feofe them on the baceborne MUFFE, and him as king obay.'

1598. FLORIO, *Worlde of Wordes*. *Pupo*, a pigsneye, a sweet-hart, a prettie MUFFE, a daintie mop etc. *Ibid. Stiticozzie*, swearing or swaggring MUFFS or dutchmen.

c.1610. CHAMBERLAIN, *Letters*, 159. More than beseemed the King to give to such MUFFES.

1648. *Travels of Sir John Reresby* [quoted in *Notes and Queries*, 2 S. ix. 402]. The Low Dutch call the High MUFFES, that is *étourdis* as the French have it, or blockheads.

1830. W. T. MONCRIEFF, *The Heart of London*, act. ii. sc. i. A visitor? hurrah: some MUFFIN, I daresay.

1837. R. H. BARHAM, *The Ingoldsby Legends* (ed. 1862), p. 437. If any young man, though a snubb'd younger brother When told of her faults by his father or mother Runs restive, and goes off to sea in a huff, Depend on't, my friends, that young man's a MUFF!

1843. W. T. MONCRIEFF, *The Scamps of London*, ii. sc. 1. I'm a ruined homo—a MUFF.

1845. DISRAELI, *Sybil*, p. 146 [ed. 1863]. 'I came about him. I wished to know whether he were alive, and that you have been able to inform me and where he was; and that you have not been able to inform me.' 'Why you're a regular MUFF!'

1849. THACKERAY, *Hoggarty Diamond*, xi. Another called me a MUFF (which means, in the slang language, a very silly fellow).

1850. SMEDLEY, *Frank Fairleigh*, 26. 'Put on the gloves!' repeated I; 'how do you mean?—what has that to do with Lawless?' 'Oh, you MUFF! don't you understand?—of course, I mean the boxing-gloves.'

1857. G. A. LAWRENCE, *Guy Livingston*, XII. I heard him growl out, 'That there MUFF's enough to spile one's taste for a fortnit.'

1857. HOOD, *Pen and Pencil Pictures*, p. 144. Awful MUFF! Can't pull two strokes without catching as many crabs; he'd upset the veriest tub on the river.

1862. *Notes and Queries*, 3 S. i. 56. MUFF is the nickname applied by the natives of the Low Countries to all foreigners . . . . the term will have passed the Channel with the motley troops of William III.

1866. MANSFIELD, *School Life*, 136. I must now proceed to football, a game I like. . . . far more than cricket. The reason is simple: I was a tolerably good hand at the former, and rather a MUFF at the latter.

1869. *Daily Telegraph*, 2 Sept. Boys do not generally like to be considered MUFFS. What but a MUFF—a MUFF of the most hopeless, helpless sort—is a young fellow who cannot manage, by motions which Nature herself almost indicates in such a crisis, to keep himself afloat?

1879. *Notes and Queries*, 5 S. XII. 16. MUFF = a stupid person may have been introduced into England from the Netherlands, probably in the reign of Queen Elizabeth. In Dutch, *Mof* = (1) a clown, a boor; (2) as a nickname, a German and particularly a Westphalian. *Moffenland* = Germany, Westphalia. This *muf* (2) occurs in MARLOWE, *Tamburlane*, i. 1. Sclavonians . . . MUFFS and Danes.

1888. ROLF BOLDREWOOD, *Robbery Under Arms*, xliii. What a MUFF Sir Ferdinand must be.

2. (common).—Anything badly bungled.

3. (old).—*See* quot. 1607.

1607. DEKKER, *Northward Ho*, iv. 3. Marry, MUFF, sing thou better, for I'll go sleep my old sleeps. [Dyce in note in Webster's *Wks.*, p. 274 (1859)

says:—'A not uncommon expression in our old writers (equivalent, I believe, to stuff, nonsense).']

1620. SHELTON, *Don Quixote*, Pt. II. x. Marry, MUFF (quoth the Countrey-Wench), I care much for your courting.

4. (venery).—*See* quot. 1785. [*Cf.* the old equivocal wheeze:—'Lost, lost, and can't be found; A lady's thing with hair all round.']

c.1720. *Ballad* [Brit. Mus. Cat. 11621, i. 1. 75]. I heard the merry wagg protest, The MUFF between her haunches, Resembled most a Mag-pies nest, Between two lofty branches.

17[?]. *Old Ballad* [quoted by BURNS in *Merry Muses*], 'Duncan Davidson.' Meg had a MUFF, and it was rough, 'Twas black without and red within.

1785. GROSE, *Vulg. Tongue*, s.v. MUFF, the private parts of a woman; to the well wearing of your MUFF, mort; to the happy consummation of your marriage, girl, a health.

1811. *Lex. Bal.*, s.v.

5. (old).—*See* quot.

1819. VAUX, *Memoirs*, s.v. MUFF, an epithet synonymous with *mouth*. *Ibid.* s.v. MOUTH, a foolish silly person.

Verb. (common).—1. To bungle: *e.g.*, to MUFF a catch.

1857. G. H. LAWRENCE, *Guy Livingstone*, vi. *I don't* see why you should have MUFFED that shot.

2. (Eton College).—To fail in an examination; TO BE SPUN (*q.v.*) or PLUCKED (*q.v.*); TO SKIP A COG (*q.v.*).

1884. JULIAN STURGIS, in *Longm. Mag.*, III. 617. Freddy and Tommy and Dicky have all MUFFED for the army. It's really dreadful!

MUFFIN, *subs.* (American).—1. *See* quot.

1870. JOHN WHITE, *Sketches from America* [BARTLETT]. When a man, availing himself of the custom of the country, has secured a young lady for the season, to share with him his sleigh-driving and other of the national amusements, in Canadian phrase she is called his MUFFIN. Her status is a sort of temporary wifehood, limited, of course, by many obvious restrictions, but resembling wifehood in this, that, though a close and continuous relationship, it has nothing in it which shocks, and much in it which allures, the Canadian mind. Among the British commodities exported to our colonies, 'la pruderie Anglaise' does not find a place. The origin of the term MUFFIN seems to be wrapped in obscurity.

2. *See* MUFF, *subs.* sense 1.

COLD MUFFIN, *phr.* (common).—Poor; of no account.

1892. MILLIKEN, *'Arry Ballads*, p. 36. I thought the theayter COLD MUFFIN.

MUFFIN-BAKER, *subs.* (rhyming).—A QUAKER (*q.v.*).

MUFFIN- (or MUFF-)CAP, *subs.* (common).—The flat woollen cap worn by charity-boys.

1837. R. BARHAM, *The Ingoldsby Legends* (ed. 1862), p. 9. Mr. Peters, though now a wealthy man, had received a liberal education at a charity-school and was apt to recur to the days of his MUFFIN-CAP and leathers.

1838. DICKENS, *Oliver Twist*, vi. His jealousy was roused by seeing the new boy promoted to the black stick and hatband, while he, the old one, remained stationary in the MUFFIN-CAP and leathers.

1872. *Daily Telegraph*, 4 July. The Americans, indeed, appear to have a peculiar fondness for the 'busby' and the MUFF-CAP as items of military headgear, distinctly preferring them to the helmet.

MUFFIN-FACE, *adj.* and *subs.* (common).—A hairless countenance. *See* quot. 1823.

1777. ISAAC JACKMAN, *All the World's a Stage*, i. 2. Master Charles, who is that gentleman? He's acting, isn't he? Has he a MUFFIN-FACE?

1823. BEE, *Dict. Turf*, s.v. MUFFIN-FACED—one who has large protruding muscles on his phiz, which is pale withal, is 'a MUFFIN-FACED son of a——;' mostly cooks, idle gourmands, &c. who delight in fat, soups, and slip-slops, evolve mutton-faces.

MUFFING, *adj.* (common).—Bungling; clumsy.

1851-61. H. MAYHEW, *London Lab.*, iii. 62. 'You can pick out a good many Punch performers, without getting one so well versed as I am in it; they in general makes such a MUFFING concern of it.'

MUFFIN-WORRY, *subs.* (common).—A tea-party.

1864. *Derby Day*, p. 16. There are men who do not disdain MUFFIN-WORRIES and crumpet-scrambles.

MUFFLE, *subs.* (pugilistic).—1. A boxing-glove. Also MUFFLER.

1755. *Connoisseur*, No. 52. He has the shape and constitution of a porter, and is sturdy enough to encounter Broughton without MUFFLERS.

1811. MOORE, *Tom Crib*, xix. Chap. 7. . . . shows that the Greeks, for mere exercise of sparring, made use of MUFFLES or gloves.

1819. BYRON, *Don Juan*, ii. 92. For sometimes we must box without the MUFFLE.

1823. BEE, *Dict. Turf*, s.v. MUFFLERS—gloves with wool stuffed upon the knuckles, for boxers to spar withal, and not hurt each other too much; claret comes sometimes.

1827. REYNOLDS, *The Fancy*, 'Stanzas to Kate.' Forgive me—and MUFFLERS I'll carefully pull O'er my knuckles hereafter.

1859. MATSELL, *Vocabulum*, s.v.

1891. *Licensed Victuallers' Mirror*, 30 Jan. p. 7, c. There were few, if any, men of about his height and weight who could stand before him with the MUFFLERS.

2. (pugilistic).—A stunning blow.

3. (thieves').—A crape mask: once a kind of vizard or veil worn by women (STOW, 1539).

1838. GLASCOCK, *Land Sharks and Sea Gulls*, ii. 126. The dark lanterns —the MUFFLERS—and the jemmy.

MUFFLING-CHEAT, *subs.* (old).—*See* quots.

1573. HARMAN, *Caveat* (1814), p. 65, s.v. A MOFLING CHETE, a napkin.

1777. BAILEY, *Eng. Dict.*, s.v.

1785. GROSE, *Vulg. Tongue*, s.v. MUFFLING CHEAT. . . . a towel.

MUFTI, *subs.* (military colloquial).—*See* quots. 1834 and 1836. Fr. *en pékin*.

1834. MARRYAT, *Peter Simple*, xxxi. The governor's aide-de-camps, all dressed in MUFTI (*i.e.*, plain clothes).

1836. M. SCOTT, *Tom Cringle's Log*, ii. The company was composed chiefly of naval and military men, but there was also a sprinkling of civilians, or MUFTEES, to use a West India expression.

1854. THACKERAY, *Newcomes*, VII. He has no MUFTI-coat, except one sent him out by Messrs. Stulty, to India in the year 1821.

1857. A. TROLLOPE, *Three Clerks*, xxxviii. He was dogged at the distance of some thirty yards by an amiable policeman in MUFTI.

1865. *A Son of the Soil*, in *Macmillan's Mag.*, March, p. 389. He had still a stolen inclination for MUFTI and wore his uniform only when a solemn occasion occurred like this, and on grand parade.

1876. GRANT, *One of Six Hundred*, i. I relinquished my gay lancer-trappings, and resumed the less pretentious MUFTI of the civilian.

1884. *Notes and Queries*, 6 S. IX. 398. MUFTI . . . the well-known title of a Mahommedan high-priest . . . officers in India, on returning from their duties . . . don pyjamas and loose white jackets, and when so arrayed bear a resemblance to the white-robed priests of Islam.

1888. *Athenæum*, 27 Oct., p. 554, col. 3. An elderly gentleman in MUFTI.

MUG, *subs.* (common).—1. The face; the mouth.

1789. GEO. PARKER, *Life's Painter*, p. 166. Face. MUG.

1818. EGAN, *Boxiana*, ii. 41. A slight tint of the claret appeared upon both their MUGS.

1819. MOORE, *Tom Crib's Memorial*, p. 21. 'Twas all dicky with Georgy, his MUG hung so dead.

1823. BEE, *Dict. Turf*, s.v.

1830. W. T. MONCRIEFF, *The Heart of London*, ii. 1. But how's he to disguise his MUG from the turnkey?

1836. MICHAEL SCOTT, *Cruise of the Midge*, p. 305. 'And you have said it with your own beautiful MUG, Benjie Brail,' quoth Dennis Donovan.

1855. THACKERAY, *Newcomes*, LVI. 'Clive has just inherited the paternal MUG.'

1855. *Punch*, xxix. p. 3. Then I did the meek and lowly, Pullin' sitch a spoony MUG.

1857. O. W. HOLMES, *Autocrat of the Breakfast Table*, iii. The smile they carry has a quiet assertion in it, such as the champion of the Heavy Weights . . . . wears upon what he very inelegantly calls his MUG.

1859. MATSELL, *Vocabulum*, s.v.

1860. *Chamber's Journal*, xiii. 348. His face as a whole is termed his MUG.

1877. GREENWOOD, *Dick Temple*, Downy-looking Cove, the fair 'un; a MUG like that ought to be worth a fortune to him.

1883. *Referee*, 1 April, p. 2, col. 4. He is a low comedian . . . . and has an awfully funny MUG.

1892. MILLIKEN, *'Arry Ballads*, p. 10. The face of a cad with the MUG of a terrier pup.

2. (common).—A dolt. Also, a raw, or clumsy hand. *See* quots. 1851 and 1879.

1851-61. H. MAYHEW, *London Lab. & Lon. Poor*, iii. p. 203. 'We sometimes have a greenhorn wants to go out pitching with us—a MUG, we calls them.'

1859. MATSELL, *Vocabulum*, s.v.

1879. *Auto. of Thief*, in *Macm. Mag.*, XL. 500. One being a MUG at the game.

1888. J. RUNCIMAN, *The Chequers*, p. 4. Many eager souls were longing for a chance to plunder such an obvious MUG.

1889. *Sporting Times*, 3 Aug., p. 3, col. 1. The method of plucking the MUG varies according to circumstances.

1890. *Pall Mall Gaz.*, 8 Feb., p. 7, col. 1. 'Look here,' said another, 'if you offer me a tip, do you suppose I'm going to be MUG enough to refuse it?'

1891. *Morning Advertiser*, 30 Mar. There was no doubt that these men stole the orders from the office, and that Woodman and the females had been used as what the police termed MUGS in assisting to dispose of the property.

1891. *Lic. Vict. Gaz.*, 23 Jan. He was stopped by a policeman and asked who the horse belonged to, and he gave the young MUG'S name and address.

1895. *Pall Mall Gaz.*, 22 Jan., p. 2, col. 2. He expects the MUG to bet on his hand and to win the wager with the last trump.

3. (common).—A cooling drink; a 'cup'.

1883. *Daily Telegraph*, 2 July, p. 5, col. 3. Anglo-Indian manuals of domestic economy give the formulas for such beverages as . . . . cool tankard, or MUG, into the composition of which beer as well as wine or spirits enters.

Verb. (common).—1. To strike (or catch it) in the face.

1821. *The Fancy*, i. p. 261. Madgbury showed game, drove Abbot in a corner, but got well MUGG'D.

1857. DUCANGE ANGLICUS, *Vulg. Tongue*, 'The Leary Man.' And if you come to fibbery You must MUG one or two.

1866. *London Miscellany*, 5 May, p. 102. 'Suppose they had MUGGED you?' 'Done what to me?' 'MUGGED you. Slogged you, you know.'

2. (common).—To grimace.

1762. COLLINS, *Miscellanies*, p. 122. Wit hung her blob, ev'n Humour seem'd to mourn, And silently sat MUGGING o'er his urn.

1857. DICKENS, *Little Dorrit*, i. 20. The low comedian had MUGGED at him in his richest manner fifty nights for a wager.

1879. *Macmillan's Mag.*, XL. 479. He [C. J. Mathews] never MUGGED at the pit, as we once heard him warn Whiskerandos against doing in the second act of *The Critic*.

3. (common).—To rob; to swindle.

4. *See* MUG UP.

5. (Winchester College).—1. To study: *e.g.*, I MUGGED all the morning, and shall thoke this afternoon; and (2) to take pains; *e.g.* 'He has MUGGED his study, and made it quite cud.'

1866. MANSFIELD, *School Life*, 122. The præfects would. . . . set to work MUGGING.

1890. G. ALLEN, *The Tents of Shem*, xxiv. 'Miss Knyvett,' and he paused with his brush upturned, 'you're a sight too clever for me to talk to.' 'Not clever,' Iris corrected; 'only well read. I've MUGGED it up out of books, that's all.' *Ibid.* ii. Instead of reading her 'Odyssey' and her 'Lucretius,' and MUGGING up amusing works on conic sections.

TO CUT MUGS, *verb. phr.* (theatrical).—To grimace.

TO MUG ONESELF, *verb. phr.* (common).—1. To get drunk.

2. (common).—To make oneself cosy or comfortable.

TO MUG UP, *verb. phr.* (theatrical).—1. To paint; to MAKE UP (*q.v.*)

1851-61. MAYHEW, *Lond. Lab.*, iii. 203. He underwent the operation of MUGGING him UP with oil-color, paint, black, and not forgetting the lips, red.

1876. HINDLEY, *Adventures of a Cheap Jack*, p. 193. He put on the clown's dress, got MUGGED UP, and went into the ring.

1882. *Chambers's Journal*, 19 Aug., p. 530. He drew a long breath and repeated his ejaculation; 'My eye! How you do MUG UP, Charley! You might go through this town, ah! if you owed money in every shop, and I don't believe a soul would know you.'

1892. MILLIKEN, *'Arry Ballads*, p. 59. You're MUGGED UP to rights.

2. (common).—To cram for examination. Also TO MUG.

MUGGARD, *adj.* (old).—Sullen; displeased.

MUGGER, *subs.* (provincial).—1. A gipsy.

1861. *Cornhill Magazine*, iv. 102. 'A Cumberland Mare's Nest.' The scourge of tramp and MUGGER, he Commanded the intruder to be shown into his snuggery.

1871. *London Figaro*, 1 April. But the English gipsy is another character; although the members of the Lees, Jones, Hernes, and other families proudly hold their heads as being many grades above the travelling MUGGERS and tramping vagabonds who mend pots and kettles and re-seat old chairs.

2. (public schools').—*See* quot.

1883. JAMES PAYN, *The 'Canon's Ward*, viii. 'A MUGGER, that's what he is,' said the other, contemptuously; a MUGGER—a comprehensive term understood to include all persons with an ambition for University distinction.

3. (theatrical).—A comedian whose best point is grimace. Also MUG-FAKER.

1892. *National Observer*, 27 Feb., p. 379. None had ever a more expressive viznomy than this prince of MUGGERS. He can say more with his eyebrow than the common tragedian with the full resources of his double-bass.

4. (Anglo-Indian).—A crocodile.

1895. KIPLING, *Second Jungle Book*, 'The Undertakers,' 106. The MUGGER of Ahmedmugger Ghaut.

MUGGILL, *subs.* (old).—*See* quot.

1610. ROWLANDS, *Martin Markall*, p. 39 (H. Club's Repr. 1874). The MUGGILL, the Beadle.

MUGGING, *subs.* (pugilistic).—1. A thrashing. *See* MUG, *verb.*, sense 1.

2. (public schools').—Hard work.

3. (theatrical).—*See* MUG, *verb.*, sense 2.

1871. *London Figaro*, 17 Mar. A collection of judicious and injudicious gags might prove as edifying as a selection of good and bad performances; although, on the whole, it is a dangerous custom, and one which is assuredly 'more honoured in the breach than the observance.' Judicious MUGGING is, perhaps, the more harmless of the two.

MUGGINS, *subs.* (common).—1. A fool. For synonyms *see* BUFFLE and CABBAGE-HEAD.

2. (common).—A borough-magnate; a local leader.

MUGGLED, *adj.* (thieves').—A term applied to 'cheap' trash offered for sale as smuggled goods.

1851-61. MAYHEW, *Lond. Lab.*, ii. 44. Another ruse to introduce MUGGLED or 'duffer's' goods.

MUGGLES, *subs.* (old).—Restlessness; THE FIDGETS (*q.v.*).

1750. ROBERTSON OF STRUAN, *Poems*, 96. Push till the MUGGLES seize the Fair, And the unruly breaks his Bridle.

MUGGY, *adj.* (common).—1. Tipsy. For synonyms *see* DRINKS and SCREWED.

2. (vulgar).—Stifling and damp: of the weather. Also MUGGINESS.

1865. G. F. BERKELY, *Life etc.*, ii. 120. I shall never forget a still hot day, or what would vulgarly be called a MUGGY lazy day in June at the fullest time of the Park.

1871. *London Figaro*, 27 Jan. Here a north-east aspect means exposure to the keenest winds that blow, to the sharpest frosts that occur, to the most damp and dismal atmosphere whenever the weather happens to be MUGGY in winter.

1873. MISS BROUGHTON, *Nancy*, ch. xliv. 'Nice and fresh! Much better than one of those MUGGY days, when you can hardly breathe!'

1883. G. A. S[ALA], in *Illustr. London News*, 30 June p. 647, col. 1. A temperature varying between raw chilliness one day and oppressive MUGGINESS the next.

MUGHOUSE, *subs.* (old).—An alehouse. For synonyms *see* LUSHING-CUB.

1710. *Tatler*, No. 180. There is a MUGHOUSE near Long Acre.

MUG-HUNTER. *See* POT-HUNTER.

MUGSTER, *subs.* (Winchester College).—One who MUGS (*q.v.*). [*Notions:* STER is generally the termination of the agent, as in 'Brockster', 'Thokester', etc. *Cf.* Harrow termination ER as in 'footer' = a footballer; loather = one to be loathed. So REVOLTER (*q.v.*); DISGUSTER (*q.v.*). *Cf.* MUGGER.

1888. *Times*, 1 Feb., p. 12. col. 2. Remember the many epithets applied to those who, not content with doing their work, commit the heinous offence of being absorbed in it. Every school, every college has had its choice nickname, for this unfortunate class . . . such as a 'sap', a 'smug', a 'swot', a 'bloke', a MUGSTER.

MUG-TRAP, *subs.* (common).—A fool-catcher.

1892. MILLIKEN, *'Arry Ballads*, 75. The 'D. T.' is a regular MUG-TRAP.

MUGWUMP, *subs.* (American).—1. A man of consequence. Hence (2) one who sets himself up as better than his fellows; (3) an independent Republican, who, in 1884 openly refused to vote for the party nominee; and (4) a citizen who declines to take any part in politics. *See* quots. 1887 and 1896.

1840. *Great Western*, 4 July, 'Leader'. Then the great MUGWUMP was delivered of a speech which the faithful loudly applauded.

1887. *Cornhill Mag.*, June, p. 626. MUGWUMP . . . . is now generally applied to those who profess to study the interests of their country before those of their party.

1888. NORTON, *Political Americanisms*, s.v. After the Independent movement was started, the word was launched on its career of popularity. *The Critic* of September 6th, 1884, contained a note to the effect that the word was of Algonquin origin, and occurred in Elliott's Indian Bible, being used to translate such titles as lord, high-captain, chief, great man, leader, or duke. In Matthew vi. 21, it occurs as MUKXUOMP; and again in Genesis xxxvi. 40-43, and several times in II. Samuel xxiii. As is frequently the case in American politics, the word was used as a term of derision and reproach by one section, and accepted with a half-humorous sense of its aptness by the other.

1896. MORTON FREWIN, in *National Review*, Jan., p. 600. A nucleus of pretentious political thinkers who get together to discuss counsels of perfection. These superior beings. . . . are described in the latest editions of American dictionaries as MUGWUMPS.

Verb. (American).—To abstain from politics.

Also MUGWUMPERY and MUGWUMPISM = the habit of MUGWUMPING.

1896. MORTON FREWIN, in *National Review*, Jan., p. 600. I fear, however, that the warm heart of MUGWUMPERY will no longer follow that idol which had been shattered prematurely in 1884 but for this handful of its votaries.

MULE, *subs.* (colloquial).—1. An obstinate person, male or female.

1891. W. C. RUSSELL, *Ocean Tragedy*, 131. I saw that he was a MULE of a man.

2. (colloquial).—An impotent man.

3. (printers').—A day hand in the composing-room.

TO SHOE ONE'S MULE, *verb. phr.* (old).—To embezzle.

1655. *History of Francion* [NARES]. He had the keeping and disposall of the moneys, and yet SHOD NOT HIS MULE at all.

MULL, *subs.* (old).—1. A cow.

1689. *Satyr against Hypocrites* [NARES]. Tedious have been our fasts, and long our prayers; To keep the Sabbath such have been our cares, That Cisly durst not milk the gentle MULLS, To the great damage of my lord mayor's fools.

2. (colloquial).—A muddle: a result of mismanagement.

1821. EGAN, *Real Life*, i. 606. Somebody must make a MULL.

1839. CHARLES DANCE, *Alive & Merry*, i. 2. Mr. Patrick Day, it strikes me, with the greatest respect, that you have made a MULL of your fortunes.

1844. *Puck*, p. 14. He tried his *dos* and *ras* and *mes* But floundering in his *A's* and *B's* He *made* among his bunch of keys As great a MULL as The class of Dons in Trinity With Mr. Hullah's.

1858. SHIRLEY BROOKS, *The Gordian Knot*, p. 14. If that woman had anything to do with the dinners, one can see what a MULL they must have been.

1860. BINNEY, *Church Life in Australia*, App. No. viii. 59. The whole thing is a MULL.

1874. JOS. HATTON, *Clytie*, II. ch. xii. And look what a MULL you made of the old Earl business! Why, the examination upon that point damns your whole case.

3. (colloquial).—A simpleton. Generally OLD MULL or REGULAR MULL.

Verb. (colloquial).—1. To spoil to muddle; TO MUFF (*q.v.*).

2. (American thieves').—*See* quot.

1859. MATSELL, *Vocabulum*, s.v. MULL. To spend money.

MULLER. TO MULLER A HAT, *verb. phr.* (obsolete).—To cut down a chimney-pot hat into the low-crowned MULLER. [From Müller, who murdered Mr. Briggs on the Brighton Railway, and tried to disguise himself by this means].

1864. *Builder*, November. One murderer gave us the word 'burke;' a second appears likely to add to the vocabulary of trade. In a small shop not far from Sloane-square, Chelsea, may be seen the following tasteful announcement: Hats MULLER'D here!

MULLIGRUBS (or **MOLLYGRUBS**), *subs.* (colloquial).—1. Colic; the COLLYWOBBLES (*q.v.*).

1619. BEAUMONT and FLETCHER, *Monsieur Thomas*, ii. 2. 'Whose dog lies sick o' th' MULLIGRUBS?'

1634. S. ROWLEY, *Noble Souldier*, iv. 2. *Cor.* The Divell lyes sicke of the MULLIGRUBS.

1719. DURFEY, *Pills to Purge*, v. 311. The pox, the MULLIGRUBS.

1738. SWIFT, *Polite Convers.*, Dial. I. What! you are sick of the MULLIGRUBS with eating chopt hay?

1837-40. HALIBURTON, *The Clockmaker*, p. 388 (ed. 1862). It draws the cold out, and keeps it from flyin' to the stomack, and saves you a fit of the MULLIGRUBS p'raps.

1887. HENLEY, *Villon's Good-Night*. You coppers, narks, and dubs.... Who gave me mumps and MULLIGRUBS.

2. (colloquial).—MUBBLE-FUBBLES (*q.v.*). *See* quot. 1748.

1599. NASHE, *Lenten Stuffe*, in *Works*, v. 280. Wherwith Peters successour was so in his MULLIEGRUMS that he had thought to have buffeted him, and cursed him with bell book and candle.

1748. T. DYCHE, *Dictionary* (5th ed.). MULLIGRUBS (S.) a pretended or counterfeit sullenness, a resolute, and fixed, and artificial displeasure, in order to gain some point desired.

1785. GROSE, *Vulg. Tongue*, s.v.

1811. A. SCOTT, *Poems*, p. 19. Waes me, the MULLIGRUMPHS she's ta'en An' toss'd him wi' a vengeful wap Frae out her silk-saft downy lap.

1822. SCOTT, *Fortunes of Nigel*, xxi. Repeating as the rich cordial trickled forth in a smooth oily stream—'Right Rosa Solis, as ever washed MULLIGRUBS out of a moody brain

1823. BEE, *Dict. Turf*, s.v.

1895. H. B. MARRIOTT-WATSON, in *New Review*, July, p. 6. But what's gone is gone, and to curl up with the MULLYGRUBS because the milk is a trifle sour, is neither to your credit nor to mine. And that's plain, I says.

MULLINGAR HEIFER, *subs. phr.* (Irish).—A girl with thick ankles.

MULTICATTIVO, *phr.* (theatrical). —Very bad. [*Italian*, MOLTO CATTIVO].

1887. *Sat. Review*, 14 May, p. 700. To theatrical slang belong a good many terms that are now either introduced into familiar and slangy talk or are familiar; we know how to make the ghost walk when biz is rumbo, and what it is that makes the company MULTICATTIVO.

MULTY, *adj.* (common).—An expletive. *Cf.* MONDAY, *etc.*

1887. HENLEY, *Villon's Straight Tip*. How do you melt the MULTY swag? Booze and the blowens cop the lot.

MUM, *subs.* (old).—1. in *pl.* The lips; more frequently MUNS (*q.v.*).

Adj. (old).—Silent; also as *adv.* MUM! as *intj.* and in *phr.*, MUM'S THE WORD! KEEP MUM! MUM YOUR DUBBER = Silence! Also MUM-CHANCE and MUM-BUDGET! *See* quots. 1611, 1660, and 1811.

1557-8. *Jacob & Esau* [DODSLEY, *Old Plays* (1874), ii. 191]. But peace, MUM, no more: I see Master Esau.

1563. *Appius & Virginius* [DODSLEY, *Old Plays* (1874), iv. 131]. But peace, for man's body! Haphazard be MUM.

1567. EDWARDS, *Damon & Pithias* [DODSLEY, *Old Plays* (1874), iv. 38]. Bah, MUMBUDGET, for Carisophus I espy.

1588. *Jeronimo* [DODSLEY, *Old Plays* (1874), iv. 376]. Peace; no words: I'll get thy pardon: Why, MUM, then.

1594. *Look About You* [DODSLEY, *Old Plays* (1874), vii. 420]. MUMBUDGET, not a word, as thou lovest thy life.

1594. SHAKSPEARE, *Richard III*, iii. 7. *Glo.* How now, how now? what say the citizens? *Buck.* Now, by the holy mother our Lord, The citizens are MUM, say n a word.

1596. SHAKSPEARE, *Merry Wives*, v. 2. I come to her in white, and cry MUM; and she cries BUDGET, and by that we know one another.

1599. PORTER, *Two Angry Women* [DODSLEY, *Old Plays* (1874), vii. 327]. Hush then; MUM, mouse in cheese, cat is near.

1607. *Puritan*, ii. 1. MUM! Mary's a good wench still.

1611. COTGRAVE, *Dictionarie*, s.v. *Avoir le bec gelé*, to hold MUMBUDGET, to be tongue-tyed, to say never a word.

1611. BARRY, *Ram Alley*, iv. Will Small-shanks has your daughter—no word but MUM.

1615. COTTON, *Scoffer Scofft*, in *Works* (1725), p. 273. But should another chance to come, Of Mavors not a word, but MUM.

1660. HOWELL, *Lexicon*, s.v. To play at MUM-BUDGET, *demurer court, ne sonner mot*.

1660. TATHAM, *The Rump*, i. 1. Odd, ... they are here. I cry MUM.

1663. BUTLER, *Hudibras*, I. iii. v. 207. Nor did I ever wince or grudge it, For thy dear sake: quoth she, MUM BUDGET.

1664. WILSON, *Projectors*, i. 1. Farewell! but MUM.

1672. W. WYCHERLEY, *Love in a Wood*, iii. 2. MUM, MUM, make no excuses man; I would not Ranger should have known me for five hundred kicks.

1766. KENRICK, *Falstaff's Wedding*, i. 1. He stood MUMCHANCE, and spoke never a living syllable.

1773. O. GOLDSMITH, *She Stoops to Conquer*, i. 2. 'I'll just step myself, and show you a piece of the way. (*To the Landlord*). MUM!'

1785. GROSE, *Vulg. Tongue*, s.v.

1789. GEO. PARKER, *Life's Painter*, p. 150. Dubber MUM'D. To keep your mouth shut, or be obliged to hold your tongue.

1811. *Lex. Bal.*, s.v. MUM. An interjection directing silence. MUM FOR THAT: I shall be silent as to that. As mute as MUMCHANCE, who was hanged for saying nothing; a friendly reproach to any one who seems low-spirited and silent.

*d.*1817. HOLMAN, *Abroad and at Home*, iii. 2. You know, one should not brag of one's connexions, so MUM'S THE WORD before my father; I must pass off for a foreign count; so mind your hits, Dicky.

1820. SCOTT, *The Abbot*, ch. xv. 'We grow older every moment we stand idle, and life is too short to be spent in playing MUMCHANCE.'

1837. THEODORE HOOK, *Jack Brag*, ii. 3. I could tell you such a story—but, MUM, for the present.

1847. HALLIWELL, *Archaic and Provincial Words*, s.v. MUMBUDGET, a cant word inplying silence.

1855. THACKERAY, *Newcomes*, xxi. The boys are always MUM under the eyes of the usher.

1859. MATSELL, *Vocabulum*, s.v. MUM. Say nothing; nothing to say.

1863. H. KINGSLEY, *Austin Elliot*, ch. vi. This man could talk to her and amuse her, when he sat MUMCHANCE.

1869. C. READE, *Foul Play*, ch. l. To use her own words, she was one as couldn't abide to sit MUMCHANCE.

1893. MILLIKEN, *'Arry Ballads*, p. 35. A fig for sech MUMCHANCE old mivvies.

1895. H. B. MARRIOTT-WATSON, in *New Review*, July, p. 4. But when the Law says MUM, why I says MUM, too, as in duty bound.

Verb. (theatrical).—To act.

1569. PRESTON, *Cambyses* [DODSLEY, *Old Plays* (1874), iv. 231]. Running at tilt, justing, with running at the ring, Masquing and MUMMING, with each kind of thing.

1598. FLORIO, *Worlde of Wordes*, *Mascarare*, to maske... to MUM, to cloke, to hide.

1606. *Return from Parnassus* [DODSLEY, *Old Plays* (1874), ix. 190]. And all the grisly sprights of griping hell With MUMMING look hath dogg'd thee since thy birth.

1851-61. MAYHEW, *Lond. Lab.*, iii. 149. We call strolling acting, MUMMING and the actors mummers.

MUMBLE-CRUST, *subs.* (old).—A toothless man or woman.

1623. MIDDLETON and ROWLEY, *Spanish Gypsy*, ii. 1. Farewell, old greybeard;—adieu mother MUMBLE-CRUST.

MUMBLE-MATINS, *subs.* (old).—A priest.

*d.*1576. BISHOP PILKINGTON, *Wks.*, 26. How can they be learned having none to teach them but Sir John MUMBLE-MATINS?

MUMBLE-NEWS, *subs.* (old colloquial).—A tale-bearer.

1594. SHAKSPEARE, *Love's Labour Lost*, v. 2. Some MUMBLE-NEWS, some trencher-knight, some Dick.

MUMBLEPEG, *subs.* (venery).—The female *pudendum*. For synonyms *see* MONOSYLLABLE.

MUMBLE-SPARROW, *subs.* (old).—*See* quot.

1785. GROSE, *Vulg. Tongue*, s.v. MUMBLE SPARROW. A cruel sport practised at wakes and fairs, in the following manner: A cock sparrow whose wings are clipped, is put into the crown of a hat; a man having his arms tied behind him, attempts to bite off the sparrow's head, but is generally obliged to desist, by the many pecks and pinches he receives from the enraged bird.

MUMBO-JUMBO, *subs.* (common).—1. An African deity.

1831. T. CARLYLE, *Sartor Resartus*, p. 137, ed. 1858. So likewise a day comes when the Runic Thor with his Eddas, must withdraw into dimness and many an African MUMBO-JUMBO and Indian Pawaw be utterly abolished.

1864. *The Times*, 2 Nov. And MUMBO-JUMBO will not be put off with inferior articles—the slightest blemish in colour or inferiority in cloth is instantly detected and rejected by these semi-savages, hence the greatest care is necessary in catering for their wants.

2. (colloquial). — Unmeaning jargon.

MUM-BUDGET. *See* MUM.

MUM-GLASS, *subs.* (old).—The Monument on Fish St. Hill.

1760. DYCHE & PARDON, *Dict.*, s.v.

1785. GROSE, *Vulg. Tongue*, s.v.

1811. *Lex. Bal.*, s.v.

MUMMER, *subs.* (theatrical).—1. A player.

1599. *Solyman and Perseda* [DODSLEY, *Old Plays* (1874), v. 309]. I was one of the MUMMERS myself, simple as I stand here.

1605. MARSTON, *Insatiate Countesse*, iii. Dost make a MUMMER of me, oxe-head? Make answer gentleman.

1610. SHAKSPEARE, *Coriolanus*, ii. 1. If you chance to be pinched with the cholick, you make faces like MUMMERS.

1772. COLES, *Dict.*, s.v.

1821. EGAN, *Tom & Jerry*, p. 78.

1851-61. H. MAYHEW, *London Lab.*, iii. 141. 'They talk of strolling actors living so jollily and well, but I never knew it fall to my share. What we call a MUMMER'S feed is potatoes and herrings.'

1871. *Newark Advertiser*, 18 Jan. A party of MUMMERS visited the towns and villages of North Notts during the past fortnight, and highly diverted the inhabitants by their dancing, singing of old songs, and the play of the *Hobby Horse*. The latter play was in existence in the days of the Plantagenets, and probably the song and tune which they sang, viz., 'When Joan's ale was new.'

1886. *Fun*, 4 August, p. 44. Now is the witching hour when country companies are formed, and MUMMERS go on tour.

1893. *Daily Telegraph*, 30 March. Mr. J. L. Toole has humorously described how at the outset of his career he once took lodgings in a house, the proprietor of which, when the popular comedian went away, cordially shook hands with him, and said how delighted he should be to see him again, although he was a MUMMER; for, the prudent man added, 'the last MUMMERS took away the chairs and tables.'

2. (pugilistic).—The mouth. For synonyms *see* POTATO-TRAP.

1785. GROSE, *Vulg. Tongue*, s.v.

1818. EGAN, *Boxiana*, ii. 559. Then he hit him on the MUMMER, and on the ropes he dropped.

1859. MATSELL, *Vocabulum*, s.v.

MUMMERY-COVE, *subs.* (old).—An actor. For synonyms *see* CACKLING-COVE.

MUMMING-SHOW, *subs.* (theatrical). —A travelling entertainment; a strolling company.

1871. *London Figaro*, 7 Oct. A scenic artist and actor in Theatres Royal at some goodly 3/- per week, and the same in a travelling MUMMING SHOW, sharing at the drum-head my 4d. per night.

MUMMY. TO BEAT TO A MUMMY, *verb. phr.* (old).—To beat severely.

MUMP, *verb.* (old).—1. To beg.

1624. MASSINGER, *Parliament of Love*, ii. 1. And, when she finds she is of all forsaken, Let my lady Pride repent in vain, and MUMP, And envy others' markets.

1633. *Match at Midnight*, ii. 1. Remember that you do not MUMP, as if you were chewing bacon.

1673. DAVENANT, *Playhouse to Let*, v. Of MUMPING minx would we were fairly out.

1678. COTTON, *Virgil Travestie*, in *Works* (1725), Bk. iv. p. 72. Then she begins to MUMP and smatter.

*d.*1680. ROCHESTER, *A Dream*. To see it MUMP, and wagg its upper lip.

1728. BAILEY, *English Dictionary*, s.v. MUMP .... to spunge upon, to beg.

1755. JOHNSON, *Eng. Dict.* (1814), s.v. MUMP. In cant language. To go a begging.

1820. LAMB, *Elia (Two Races of Men)*. To say *no* to a poor petitionary rogue (your bastard borrower), who, by his MUMPING visnomy, tells you that he expects nothing better.

1849-61. MACAULAY, *Hist. Eng.* xix. 'One prince came MUMPING to them annually with a lamentable story about his distresses.'

1866. *Temple Bar*, xvii. 183. Having MUMPED a small shop and several private houses.

1883. G. A. S[ALA], *Ill. London News*, 17 Nov., p. 475, col. 3. Although the tramp when hard pressed solicits alms or food, he is not a MUMPING or professional beggar.

1887. W. E. HENLEY, *Villon's Straight Tip*. Bonnet, or tout, or MUMP and gag.

2. (old).—To overreach.

1671. BUCKINGHAM, *Rehearsal*, p. 23. I'm resolv'd to MUMP your proud players.

1673. WYCHERLEY, *Gentleman Dancing Master*, iii. 1. You will MUMP the poor old father.

MUMPER, *subs.* (old).—*See* quots. 1665, 1748, 1755, 1785 and 1876.

ENGLISH SYNONYMS. Abram-man (or -cove); bawdy-basket; Bedlam-beggar; blue-gown (old Scots'); cadator; cadger; canter; croaker; curtail; durry-nacker; dry-land sailor; filer; frater; goose-shearer; Irish toyle; key-hole whistler; master of the black art; maunder; milestone-monger; moucher; mud-plunger; mugger; mumper; munger; needy-mizzler; niffler; overland-mailer (or -man); palliard; paper-worker; pikey; ruffler; scoldrum; shivering James (or Jemmy); shyster; skipper-bird; skitting-dealer; silver-beggar; street-ganger; strolling-mort; sundowner; swag-man; tinkard; Tom of Bedlam; traveller; turn-pike; uhlan; upright man; wash-man; whip-jack.

For foreign synonyms *see* SHYSTER.

1665. R. HEAD, *English Rogue*, Pt. I. ch. v. p. 50 (1874). MUMPERS gentile [genteel] beggars.

1690. DURFEY, *Collin's Walk*, C. I. p. 27. That even Vagabonds and MUMPERS, Have from my bounty had full Bumpers.

1690. CROWNE, *English Friar*, ii. 1. My lady is . . . rather a MUMPER; she has begg'd the backhouse, the gardens, to lay herself and her goods in.

1693. CONGREVE, *Old Batchelor*. *Lucy*. Hang thee—Beggar's cur!—Thy master is but a MUMPER in love, lies canting at the gate.

1694. *Poor Robin* [NARES]. Since the king of beggars was married to the queen of sluts, at Lowzy-hill, near Beggars-bush, being most splendidly attended on by a ragged regiment of MUMPERS.

1703. WARD, *London Spy*, pt. I. p. 7. He is one of those gentile MUMPERS, we call Cadators; he goes a Circuit round England once a year, and under Pretence of a decay'd gentleman, gets both Money and Entertainment at every good House he comes at.

1705. *Hudibras Redivivus*, pt. 4. Here, said I, take your MUMPER'S fee, Let's see one; thank you, sir, said she.

1712. *Spectator*, No. 509. The MUMPERS, the halt, the blind, and the lame.

1748. T. DYCHE, *Dictionary* (5th ed.) MUMPERS (S.) among the *Gipsy Crew*, is called the 47th order of canters or genteel beggars, who will not accept of victuals, but only money or cloaths.

1754. *The World*, No. 64. I was at his door by nine; where, after the fashion of MUMPERS, I gave but one single knock for fear of disturbing him.

1755. JOHNSON, *Eng. Dict.* (1814), s.v. MUMPER. In cant language. A beggar.

1777. BAILEY, *Eng. Dict.*, s.v. MUMPER, a genteel beggar.

1785. GROSE, *Vulg. Tongue*, s.v. MUMPER, originally beggars of the genteel kind, but since used for beggars in general.

1830. SCOTT, *Doom of Devorgoil*, ii. 2. The courtier begs a riband or a star, And like our gentler MUMPERS, is provided With false certificates of health and fortune Lost in the public service.

1834. W. H. AINSWORTH, *Rookwood*, p. 130 (ed. 1864). 'Ha, ha! Are you there, my old death's head on a mop-stick?' said Turpin, with a laugh. 'Ain't we merry MUMPERS, eh? Keeping it up in style. Sit down, old Noah; make yourself comfortable, Methusalem.'

1849. MACAULAY, *Hist. Eng.*, iii. A Lincoln's Inn MUMPER was a proverb.

1859. MATSELL, *Vocabulum*, s.v.

1868. *Temple Bar*, xxiv. 537. When he can't go on in that racket he'll turn MUMPER.

1876. HINDLEY, *Adventures of a Cheap Jack*, p. 64. A big MUMPER, that is a half-bred gipsey.

MUMPER'S-HALL, *subs.* (old).—A hedge tavern; a beggar's alehouse.

1785. GROSE, *Vulg. Tongue*, s.v.

MUMPING, *subs.* and *adj.* (old).—Begging.

1820-33. LAMB, *Elia*, *Works* (ed. 1852), p. 389. When they come with their counterfeit looks and MUMPING tones.

MUMPINS, *subs.* (old).—Alms.

c.1460. *Towneley Mysteries*, *Primus Pastorum*, p. 89. 2d Pastor. . . . let us go foder Our MOMPYNS.

MUMPISH, *subs.* (colloquial).—Dull; dejected.

MUMPLE-MUMPER. *See* MUMMER.

MUMPS, *subs.* (common).—Low spirits. *See* quot. 1754.

1599. NASHE, *Lenten Stuffe*, in *Wks.* (GROSART). v. 267. The sunne was so in his MUMPS vppon it, that it was almost noone before hee could goe to cart that day.

1754. B. MARTIN, *Eng. Dict.* (2nd ed.). MUMPS. . . . flouts, or ill humour.

MUMPSIMUS, *subs.* (old).—*See* quot.

1847. HALLIWELL, *Archaic & Provincial Words*, s.v. MUMPSIMUS. An old error in which men obstinately persevere: taken from a tale of an ignorant monk, who in his breviary had always said MUMPSIMUS instead of *sumpsimus*, and being told of his mistake, said, 'I will not change my old MUMPSIMUS for your new *sumpsimus*'.

MUNCH-PRESENT (or **MOUNCH-PRESENT**), *subs.* (old).—*See ante.*

MUND. *See* MUNS.

MUNDUNGUS, *subs.* (old).—Bad tobacco.

c.1633. *Lady Alimony*, ii. 2. Sir Gregory Shapeless, a MUNDUNGO monopolist.

1665. HOWARD, *The Committee*, ii. A pipe of the worst MUNDUNGUS.

1671. SHADWELL, *Humorists*, iii. 41. A glass of Windy-Bottle-Ale in one hand, and a pipe of MUNDUNGUS in the other.

d.1680. BUTLER, *Remains* [1759, ii. 107]. Spoiled the tobacco for it presently became MUNDUNGUS.

1689. J. PHILLIPS, *Satyr against Hypocrites*, 13. Now steams of garlick whiffing thro' the nose Stank worse than Luther's socks, or foot-boy's toes. With these MUNDUNGOS, and a breath that smells Like standing pools in subterranean cells.

1691-2. *Gentlemen's Journal*, Mar., p. 10. To nasty MUNDUNGUS, and heath 'nish small beer.

1703. WARD, *London Spy*, Part IV. p. 80. The mixtures of scents that arose from MUNDUNGUS-TOBACCO.

1755. JOHNSON, *Dict.*, s.v. MUNDUNGUS, *n. f.* Stinking tobacco. A cant word.

1811. *Lex. Bal.*, s.v.

1824. SCOTT, *St. Ronan's Well*, xxxii. Her jet-black cutty pipe, from which she soon sent such clouds of vile MUNDUNGUS vapour as must have cleared the premises of Lady Penelope.

Adj. (old).—Stinking.

1750. ROBERTSON of Struan, *Poems*, 50. To drink MUNDUNGUS ALE.

1859. MATSELL, *Vocabulum*, s.v. MONDONGO. Filthy; full of stench; it stinks beyond the power of endurance.

MUNG, *subs.* (American).—News; MUNG-NEWS = false news.

1849. *New York Express*, 17 Feb. As many of our citizens who intend to go to California may base their arrangements upon the MUNG NEWS of some of the papers, we conceive it to be our duty to state that most of these letters are fictions.

Verb. (tramps').—*See* quots.

1811. *Lex. Bal.*, s.v.

1851-61. MAYHEW, *Lond. Lab.*, i. 265. I sold small articles of Tunbridge ware, perfumery, &c., &c., and by MUNGING (begging) over them—sometimes in Latin—got a better living than I expected, or probably deserved.

1859. MATSELL, *Vocabulum*, s.v. MUNG. To solicit; to beg.

1893. EMERSON, *Signor Lippo*, 52. Many's the time you've been waiting on me coming home to give you some of the grub I've MUNGED.

MUNGARLY (MUNJARI, or MUNGARE), *subs.* (strollers' and tramps').—*See* quots.

1851-61. H. MAYHEW, *London Lab. and Lon. Poor*, iii. 149. We [strolling actors] call breakfast, dinner, tea, supper, all of them MUNGARE.

1876. HINDLEY, *Adventures of a Cheap Jack*, p. 170. Help you and your school to some dinarly and MUNGARLY, *i.e.*, money and food.

1889. *Answers*, 11 May, p. 374. The 'clobber' (old clothes) which have been presented by charitable persons are exchanged and sold, broken meat and scraps of bread ('Bull and MUNJARI' they are called) are given out liberally, and the blind men and cripples are the jolliest crowd imaginable.

1893. EMERSON, *Signor Lippo*, x. I . . . went to one of my regular padding-kens to sell the MUNGARLY to some of the needies there for nova soldi. *Ibid.* 12. Chuck it, we'll go and have a bit of MUNGARLY now.

MUNGARLY-CASA, *subs.* (thieves').—*See* quot.

1864. *Times*, 18 Oct. Another curious instance of the prevalence of this *Lingua Franca* is the word *Mungarly*, as representing bread or food. MUNGARLY CASA is a baker's shop, evidently a corruption of some *Lingua Franca* phrase for an eating-house. The well-known *Nix Mangiare* stairs at Malta derive their name from the endless beggars who lie there and shout 'Nix Mangiare,' *i.e.*, 'Nothing to eat,' to excite the compassion of the English who land there—an expression which exhibits remarkably the mongrel composition of the *Lingua Franca*, *mangiare* being Italian, and *nix* an evident importation from Trieste or other Austrian seaport.

MUNPIN, *subs.* (old).—In *pl.* = the teeth. For synonyms *see* GRINDERS.

d.1450. LYDGATE, *Minor Poems*, p. 30. Thy MONE-PYNNES bene lyche old yuong.

MUNS, *subs.* 1. (old).—The mouth. *See* quot. 1665. Also MUND.

1665. R. HEAD, *English Rogue*, Pt. I. ch. v. p. 50 (1874). MUNNS. The Face.

1724. COLES, *Eng. Dict.*, s.v.

1760. FOOTE, *Mirror*, i. Why, you jade, you look as rosy this morning, I must have a smack at your MUNNS.

1789. G. PARKER, *Life's Painter*, 'The Bunter's Christening'. The first thing that was done, Sir, Was handling round the kid, That all might smack his MUNS, Sir.

1811. *Lex. Bal.*, s.v.

1819. T. MOORE, *Tom Crib's Memorial*, p. 16. While Sandy's long arms . . . Kept *paddling* about the poor Porpus's MUNS, Till they made him as *hot* and as *cross* as *lent* Buns!

1823. BEE, *Dict. Turf*, s.v. MUNS—the mouth. 'One a penny, two a penny, hot cross buns, If you have no daughters give them to your sons: If you have no sons, stuff them in your MUNS.'

1859. MATSELL, *Vocabulum*, s.v. MUND. The mouth. *Ibid.* MUNDS, the face.

2. in *sing.* (obsolete).—A MOHAWK (*q.v.*).

MUNSTER-HEIFER, *subs.* (old).—*See* quot.

1785. GROSE, *Vulg. Tongue*, s.v. MUNSTER HEIFER. An Irish woman. A woman with thick legs is said to be like a MUNSTER HEIFER; *i.e.*, beef to the heels.

1811. *Lex. Ball.*, s.v.

MUNSTER-PLUMS, *subs.* (common).—Potatoes; MURPHIES (*q.v.*).

1785. GROSE, *Vulg. Tongue*, s.v.

1811. *Lex. Bal.*, s.v.

MUR, *subs.* (back slang).—Rum. NETTOCK OF MUR = quartern of rum.

MURDER. *See* BLUE MURDER.

THE MURDER IS OUT, *phr.* (colloquial).—The mystery is displayed.

MURERK, *subs.* (tramps').—The mistress of the house. *See* BURERK.

MURKAUKER, *subs.* (obsolete).—A monkey. [Jacko Macauco, or Maccacco, who was a famous fighting monkey, who used some fifty years ago to display his prowess in the Westminster Pit].

MURPHY, *subs.* (common).—1. A potato: *cf.* DONOVAN. Also MURPH.

ENGLISH SYNONYMS. Bog-orange; Donovan; Irish apricot; Munster-plum, or orange; murph; ruggin; spud; tatur.

1811. *Lex. Bal.*, s.v.

1821. EGAN, *Anecdotes of the Turf*, 154. Mathews relished the Irish stews and MURPHIES.

1839. *Comic Almanack*, 199. Having well roasted my MURPHY, I take him *cum grano salis*.

1842. *Punch*, ii. 214, col 2. A story that Raleigh first introduced the potato—meaning the MURPHY—into this country.

1856. J. HUGHES, *Tom Brown's School-Days* Pt. I. vi. 'That's our School-house tuck-shop—she bakes such stunning MURPHIES, we'll have a penn'orth each for tea; come along, or they'll all be gone.'

1856. *Leisure Hour*, 3 Jan., p. 12, col. 2. Past the potato and coal shed, well known to the Irish labourer, who for twopence can get three pounds of MURPHIES.

1869. THACKERAY, *Peg of Limavaddy*. Playing round the fire, which of blazing turf is, Roaring to the pot which bubbles with the MURPHIES.

1888. *Sporting Life*, 10 Dec. Surround him with a stack of bottles of ale and a dish of MURPHIES.

2. (American).—An Irishman.

3. (colloquial). — Morpheus, *i.e.*, sleep.

1748. SMOLLETT, *Roderick Random*. What time MURPHY sends his slipping puppies to the heyes of mortals.

MURPHY'S-FACE, *subs.* (Irish).—A pig's head.

1819. VAUX, *Memoirs*, s.v. MURPHY'S COUNTENANCE.

MUSH (MUSH-TOPPER or MUSH-ROOM), *subs.* (common).—1. *See* quots.

1821. HAGGART, *Life*, 62. In one shop they robbed two MUSH-TOPERS.

1856. H. MAYHEW, *Gt. World of London*, p. 6, *note*. Fanciful metaphors contribute largely to the formation of slang. It is upon this principle that the mouth has come to be styled the 'tater-trap'; . . . . umbrellas, 'MUSHROOMS' (or, briefly 'MUSH').

1859. MATSELL, *Vocabulum*, s.v. MUSH. An umbrella; the mouth, in pugilism.

1870. *London Figaro*, 15 June. What pretty faces, MUSH of mine, I've sheltered 'neath thy shade! What jolly walks in 'auld lang syne' Beneath thy ribs I've made!

2. (old).—The mouth.

1785. GROSE, *Vulg. Tongue*, s.v.

1811. *Lex. Bal.*, s.v.

1859. MATSELL, *Vocabulum*, s.v.

1887. WALFORD, *Antiquarian*, 252. s.v.

MUSH- (or MUSHROOM-) FAKER (or MUSH-TOPPER-FAKER). — *See* quot. 1851. MUSHFAKING = mending umbrellas.

1821. HAGGART, *Life*, 56. Tommy Twenty, a MUSH-TOPER-FAKER.

1851-61. H. MAYHEW, *London Lab.*, ii. 28. In *Umbrellas* and *Parasols* the second-hand traffic is large, but those vended in the streets are nearly all 'done up' for street-sale by the class known as MUSH or more properly MUSHROOM FAKERS. *Idem.*, ii. 127. The umbrella-menders are known by an appellation of an appropriateness not uncommon in street language. They are MUSHROOM-FAKERS. The form of the expanded umbrella resembles that of a mushroom, and it has the further characteristic of being rapidly or suddenly raised, the MUSHROOM itself springing up and attaining its full size in a very brief space of time. The term, however, like all street or popular terms or phrases, has become very generally condensed among those who carry on the trade—they are now MUSH-FAKERS, a word which, to any one who has not heard the term in full, is as meaningless as any in the vocabulary of slang.

1893. EMERSON, *Signor Lippo*, 91. My old man . . . got his dudder by chinay-faking and MUSH-FAKING.

MUSHROOM, *subs.* (common).—1. A hat.

2. (venery).—The female *pudendum*. For synonyms *see* MONOSYLLABLE.

3. (old).—*See* quots.

1622. BACON, *Nat. Hist. [Enc. Dict.]*. MUSHROOMS come up in a night, and yet they are unsown; and therefore such as are upstarts in state, they call in reproach MUSHROOMS.

1811. *Lex. Bal.*, s.v. MUSHROOM. A person or family suddenly raised to riches and eminence: an allusion to that fungus which starts up in a night.

1859. MATSELL, *Vocabulum*, s.v.

MUSIC, *subs.* (American).—1. Fun; frolic.

2. (American).—*See* quot.

1859. MATSELL, *Vocabulum*, s.v. MUSIC. The verdict of a jury when they find not guilty.

3. (old).—*See* quot.

1785. GROSE, *Vulg. Tongue*, s.v. MUSIC. The watchword among highwaymen, signifying the person is a friend, and must pass unmolested.

1811. *Lex. Bal.*, s.v.

4. (old).—*See* quot.

1811. *Lex. Bal.*, s.v. MUSIC . . . . is also an Irish term, in tossing up, to express the harp side, or reverse, of a farthing or halfpenny opposed to the head.

TO FACE THE MUSIC. *See* FACE.

MUSIC-BOX, *subs.* (common).—A piano.

1863. C. READE, *Hard Cash*, i. 178. But just you hear her sing, that is all . . . Just smiles and sits down to the MUSIC-BOX.

MUSICIANER, *subs.* (American).—A musician.

1848. BURTON, *Waggeries etc.*, p. 186. The landlord cursed the MUSICIANER who paid his rent in such uncurrent notes.

MUSLIN (or **A BIT OF MUSLIN**), *subs.* (common).—A woman. For synonyms *see* PETTICOAT.

1823. MONCRIEFF, *Tom and Jerry*, i. 1. A BIT OF MUSLIN on the sly.

1828. G. GRIFFIN, *Collegians*, x. Captain, I see you laugh a great deal, but you mustn't laugh at our girls, though, there are sume pretty BITS O' MUSLIN there, I can tell you.

1843. W. T. MONCRIEFF, *The Scamps of London*, i. 1. I came up to town to see life, leaving behind me as pretty a PIECE OF MUSLIN as you'd wish to see.

1849. THACKERAY, *Pendennis*, l. 'That was a pretty BIT OF MUSLIN hanging on your arm—who was she?'

1884. HAWLEY SMART, *Post to Finish*, 128. One thing more: take my advice, and keep clear of MUSLIN for the next six or seven years. It's brought as many of your profession to grief as spirits.

MUSN'T-MENTION-EMS, *subs.* (common).—Trousers. For synonyms *see* BAGS and KICKS.

MUSS, *subs.* (American).—1. Confusion; a fuss. *See* quot. 1859.

1848. BURTON, *Waggeries etc.*, p. 25. They soon raised a pretty MUSS, and kept on tearin' at each other like a pack o' wolves.

1848. DURIVAGE, *Stray Subjects*, p. 138. You're eternally kicking up A MUSS with somebody.

1848. JONES, *Sketches of Travel*, p. 9. We're all in a MUSS now gettin' ready for the journey.

1859. MATSELL, *Vocabulum*, s.v. MUSS. A quarrel; a row.

1888. *Texas Siftings*, 18 Aug. 'Raw oysters for two, mister.' 'Yes, sir—have 'em in the shell?' 'Yes, John, if you think you kin open 'em 'thout makin' A MUSS.'

2. (old).—A term of endearment. [Probably from MOUSE].

1596. JONSON, *Every Man in His Humour*, ii. 3. What ails you, sweetheart? Are you not well? Speak, good MUSS.

Verb. (American).—To confuse; to disorder; to mess-up.

MUSSY, *adj.* (American).—Disordered. Also MUSSED-UP.

1888. *Detroit Free Press.* Neither of us got two winks of sleep during the night on the car, and Mr. Bowser narrowly escaped coming into deadly conflict with conductor and porter. We reached Chicago in a MUSSED-UP condition.

MUSTANG, *subs.* (American).—An officer entering the U. S. navy from the merchant service, after serving through the Civil War.

MUSTARD-POT, *subs.* (venery).—The female *pudendum*. For synonyms *see* MONOSYLLABLE.

MUTCHER, *subs.* (thieves').—*See* quot.

1862. H. MAYHEW, *Lon. Lab.*, iv. 282. They loiter about the streets and public-houses to steal from drunken persons, and are called 'Bug-hunters' and MUTCHERS.

MUTE, *subs.* (old: now recognised).—*See* quot.

1785. GROSE, *Vulg. Tongue*, s.v. MUTE. An undertaker's servant, who stands at the door of a person lying in state: so named from being supposed mute with grief.

MUTTON (or **LACED MUTTON**).—1. A loose woman. Generic for the sex.

1569. BRACTON, *De Legibus*, ii. Courtisans. . . . *oves*.

1578. WHETSTONE, *Promos and Cas.*, 6, pl. i. p. 14. And I smealt he loved LASE MUTTON well.

1594. GREENE, *Frier Bacon*, in *Wks.* (GROSART), xiii. 94. The old lecher hath gotton holy MUTTON to him, a Nunne my lord.

1595. SHAKSPEARE, *Two Gentlemen of Verona*, i. 1. Ay, sir: I, a lost mutton, gave your letter to her, a LAC'D MUTTON; and she, a LAC'D MUTTON, gave me, a lost mutton, nothing for my labour.

1596. NASHE, *Have with You*, [GROSART (1885), iii. 61]. He that wold not stick so to extoll stale rotten LAC'D MUTTON, will . . . . sucke figges out of an asses fundament.

1599. BRETON, *Wil of Wit* [GROSART (1879), ii. *c.* 62/1. 18]. If your stomache stande to flesh, eate of a little warme MUTTON, but take heede it be not LACED.

1602. MIDDLETON, *Blurt Master Constable*, sign. B. *Laz.* Pilcher, Cupid hath got me a stomacke, and I long for LAC'D MUTTON. *Pil.* Plaine MUTTON without a lace would serve.

1602. DEKKER, *Honest Whore* [DODSLEY, *Old Plays*, iii. 365]. Baa, lamb, there you lie, for I am MUTTON.

1604. MARLOW, *Doctor Faustus* [NARES]. I am one that loves an inch of raw MUTTON, better than an ell of dride stockfish; and the first letter of my name begins with letchery.

1606. *Return from Parnassus* [DODSLEY *Old Plays* (1874), ix. 180]. But there's no pleasure always to be tied to a piece of MUTTON . . . For mine own part . . . I am well-provided of three bouncing wenches.

1608. MACHIN, *Dumb Knight* [DODSLEY, *Old Plays* (1874), x. 134]. 'She is meat for your master.' 'And your man, sir, may lick your foul trencher.' 'Ay, but not eat of his MUTTON.'

1614. COOK, *City Gallant* [DODSLEY, *Old Plays* (1874), xi. 279]. More villany; there's another goodly MUTTON going.

1620. MIDDLETON, *Chaste Maid*, ii. I'll tender her a husband; I keep of purpose two or three gulls in pickle To eat such MUTTON with, and she shall choose one.

1624. JONSON, *Masque of Nep. Triumph* [CUNNINGHAM, iii]. *Cook.* O whom for mutton, or kid? *Child.* A fine LAC'D MUTTON Or two; and either has her frisking husband.

1633. ROWLEY, *Match at Midnight*, ii. 1. Say she be young . . . If, like an old cock he with young MUTTON meet He feeds like a cuckold.

1640. RAWLINS, *The Rebellion*, iv. No more, I say, it is a parcel of excellent MUTTON. I'll cut it up myself.

1640. J. HEYWOOD, *Love's Mistress*, ii. [Cupid described as] Lord of lamentations, and Monsieur of MUTTON-LAC'D.

1690. B. E., *Dict. Cant. Crew*, s.v.

1719. DURFEY, *Pills to Purge*, i. p. 353. I'm a loyn of MUTTON plainly dress'd, And those nice volk, love all their MUTTON LAC'D.

1725. *New Cant. Dict.*, s.v.

1785. GROSE, *Vulg. Tongue*, s.v.

1811. *Lex. Bal.*, s.v. LACED MUTTON, a prostitute.

1859. MATSELL, *Vocabulum*, s.v. LACED MUTTON, a common woman.

2. (venery).—*See* quots. 1811 and 1864. For synonyms *see* MONOSYLLABLE.

*d.*1680. ROCHESTER, *Epitaph on Chas. II.* Here lies our MUTTON-eating king, Whose word no man relies on; He never *said* a foolish thing, And never *did* a wise one.

1693. CONGREVE, *Old Batchelor*, iv. 6. You don't love MUTTON, you Magdalen unconverted?

1697. VANBRUGH, *The Provoked Wife*, iv. And I hope your punks will give you sauce to your MUTTON.

1811. *Lex. Bal.*, s.v. MUTTON. In her MUTTON, *i.e.*, having carnal knowledge of a woman.

1864. HOTTEN, *Slang Dict.*, s.v. MUTTON. In that class of English society which does not lay any claim to refinement, a fond lover is often spoken of as being 'fond of his MUTTON,' which, by the way, in this place does not mean the woman so much as something else.

3. in *pl.* (Stock Exchange).—The Turkish loans of 1865 and 1873. [From being in part secured on the sheep-tax].

4. (colloquial).—A sheep.

1595. SHAKSPEARE, *Two Gentlemen*, i. 1. 106. Here's too small a pasture for such store of MUTTONS.

1598. SHAKSPEARE, *Merchant of Venice*, i. 3. Flesh of MUTTONS, beefs, or goats.

*d.*1626. BACON [quoted by JOHNSON]. The flesh of MUTTONS is better tasted where the sheep feed upon wild thyme and wholesome herbs.

*d.*1627. HAYWARD [quoted by JOHNSON]. Within a few days were brought out of the country two thousand MUTTONS.

1755. JOHNSON, *Eng. Dict.*, s.v. MUTTON. (2) A sheep. Now only in ludicrous language.

1860. THACKERAY, *Philip*, ch. xx. The appetites of those little ones were frightful, the temper of Madame la Générale was almost intolerable, but Charlotte was an angel, and the General was a MUTTON—a true MUTTON. . . . The brave are often MUTTONS at home.

BOW-WOW MUTTON. *See* BOW-WOW.

TO CUT ONE'S MUTTON, *verb. phr.* (common).—To dine.

DEAD AS MUTTON, *phr.* (common).—*See* DEAD.

1835. C. SELBY, *The Widow's Victim.* I'm caught in a trap—DEAD AS MUTTON!

MUTTON DRESSED LAMB-FASHION, *subs. phr.* (common).—An old woman dressed young.

TO RETURN TO ONE'S MUTTONS, *verb. phr.* (colloquial).—To hark back to the point at issue.

1868. BREWER, *Phrase & Fable*, s.v. MOUTONS. The phrase is taken from an old French play, called *l'Avocat Pathelin*, in which a woollen-draper charges a shepherd with stealing sheep. In telling his grievance he kept for ever running away from his subject; and to throw discredit on the defendant's attorney, accused him of stealing a piece of cloth. The judge had to pull him up every moment with 'Mais, mon ami, REVENONS À NOS MOUTONS.'

1889. *Pall Mall Gaz.*, 8 Nov., p. 2, col. 1. 'Now to RETURN TO OUR MUTTONS. Here is a drawer full of M.P.'s, Liberals, Radicals, Conservatives.'

1890. G. ALLEN, *The Tents of Shem*, chap. xi. I desire to live and die a humble Christian, in complete ignorance of that hard-hearted science. Let's RETURN TO OUR MUTTONS.

WHO STOLE THE MUTTON, *phr.* (obsolete).—*See* quot.

1868. BREWER, *Phrase & Fable*, s.v. MUTTON. *Mutton (Who Stole the)?* This was a common street jeer flung on policemen when the force was first organized, and rose thus: The first case the force had to deal with was the theft of a leg of mutton; but they wholly failed to detect the thief, and the laugh turned against them.

MUTTON-CHOPS, *subs.* (common).—1. A sheep's head.

2. (common).—*See* quot. Also MUTTON-CHOP WHISKERS.

1865. *Evening Citizen*, 28 July. Mr. Steinmetz shaved close, leaving no hair on his face save a short pair of MUTTON-CHOP whiskers.

1878. BESANT & RICE, *By Celia's Arbour*, ii. His whiskers, equally white, were cut to the old-fashioned regulation MUTTON-CHOP, very much like what has now come into fashion again. They advanced into the middle of the cheek, and were then squared off in a line which met the large stiff collar below at an angle of forty-five.

1880. *Life in a Debtor's Prison*, 62. The equally well-trained whiskers, which were of the old military style, known as MUTTON-CHOPS.

1892. MILLIKEN, *'Arry Ballads*, p. 53. White aprons, and trim MUTTON-CHOPPER each side.

MUTTON-COVE, *subs.* (old).—1. The Coventry-Street end of Windmill Street. [Once a notorious resort of harlots]. *Cf.* MUTTON, senses 1 and 2.

2. (common).—A man addicted to women; a MUTTON-MONGER (*q.v.*). For synonyms *see* MOLROWER.

MUTTONER, *subs.* (obsolete Winchester College).—A blow on the knuckles from a cricket-ball.

2. (old).—A MUTTON-MONGER (*q.v.*).

MUTTON-EYED. *See* SHEEP'S-EYED.

MUTTON-FIST (or **-HAND**), *subs.* (common).—A hand large, bony, and coarse.

1672. C. COTTON, *Scarronides*, Bk. i. p. 10 (ed. 1725). With woful Heart and blubber'd Eyes, Lifting his MUTTON-FISTS to th' Skies.

1693. DRYDEN, *Juvenal*, XVI. 45. Will he, who saw the soldier's MUTTON-FIST, And saw thee maul'd, appear within the list To witness truth?

1706. WARD, *Hudibras Redivivus*, Vol. 1. pt. vii. p. 25. Attended by a Rogue, design'd To guard and vindicate his Jewel With MUTTON FIST and Oaken Towel.

1719. DURFEY, *Pills to Purge*, i. 92. But when plump Ciss got the Ball in her MUTTON FIST, once fretted, she'd hit it farther than any.

1812. H. AND J. SMITH, *Rejected Addresses* ('Punch's Apotheosis'). See she twists her MUTTON FISTS like Molyneux or Beelzebub, And t'other's clack, who pats her back, is louder far than Bell's hubbub.

1819. MOORE, *Tom Crib*, 34. By showing such a FIST of MUTTON, As.... Would take the shine from Speaker Sutton.

1836. M. SCOTT, *Cringle's Log*, viii. But Paul, with his shoulder of MUTTON FIST, gave me a very unceremonious rebuff.

1836. BARHAM, *Ingoldsby Legends*, 'The Bagman's Dog.' At each twist of her wrist, and her great MUTTON-FIST.

1846. *Punch*, x. 163. Ruggins of the MUTTON-FIST.

1876. HINDLEY, *Adventures of a Cheap Jack*, 190. The big fellow's MUTTON-FIST dropping him a hot 'un.

MUTTON-HEADED, *adj.* (old).— Stupid.

1785. GROSE, *Vulg. Tongue*, s.v.
1811. *Lex. Bal.*, s.v.

MUTTON-MONGER, *subs.* (old).—A whoremonger.

ENGLISH SYNONYMS. Ballocks (or ballocker); beard-splitter; belly-bumper; bird (or cock) of the game; bird's-nester; Bluebeard; bull; bum-faker (-tickler, -ranger, or -worker); button-hole-worker; carrion-hunter; cavaulter; chau-vering-cove (or chauverer); chim-ney-sweep; cock-fighter; Corin-thian: Don Juan; fish- (flesh- or meat-) monger; fuckster; game-cock; goat; high priest of Paphos; horseman; hot- (or warm-) mem-ber; hot-'un; jumbler; king of clubs; knocker; ladies' tailor; leather-stretcher; leg-lifter; ling-grappler; miller; molrower; Mor-mon; Mr. Horner; muttoner; per-former; petticoal-merchant; prick-scourer; quim-sticker; rattle-cap; rifle-man; rump-splitter; sharp-shooter; smell-smock; Solomon; sports-man; stallion; striker; thrumster; town- (or parish-) bull;

twat-faker; tummy-tickler; wench-er; woodman.

FRENCH SYNONYMS. *Un abat-teur de bois* (popular); *un acteur* (general); *un ami* (prostitutes') *un Anglais; un bébé; un bobosse* (common); *un boche* (popular); *un bordelier* (ge-neral); *un boucaneur* (popu-lar); *un boxonneur* (*boxon* = brothel); *un cascadeur* (theatri-cal); *un chaud de la pince* (po-pular); *un chevaucheur* (popular); *un courasson* or *vieux courasson* (familiar); *un coureur* (popular); *un cousin; un couvreur; un dénicheur de fauvettes; un en-filé à la rigolade* (thieves'); *un étalon* (= STALLION); *un fou-ailleur* (popular); *un godilleur* (popular); *un goteur* (popular); *un gourgandin* (popular); *un Hercule* (common); *un homme à femmes* (common: also, *un homme ardent, un homme à ressorts*); *un juponnier; un larcottier* (Old French); *un leveur de femmes* (common); *un amant de la lune* (popular); *un matou* (= molrower); *un menin* (Old French); *un miché, michet,* or *micheton* (popular: from *michon* = money); *un milord; un noctambule* (popu-lar); *un novateur des plaisirs* (popular); *un paillard* (old); *un paillasson* (= mattress); *un porté sur l'article* (popular); *un roumard* (thieves').

1594. *Look About You* [DODSLEY, *Old Plays* (1874), vii. 473]. Ah ! old MUTTON-MONGER, I believe here's work.

1598. FLORIO, *Worlde of Wordes*, s.v. *Feminiére*, a whore-monger, a frequenter of women, a MUTTON MONGER. Also belonging or pertaining to women.

1600. *Sir J. Oldcastle*, ii. 1. [MALONE, *Suppl.* ii. 294]. You whor-son bawdy priest ! You old MUTTON-MONGER.

1602. DEKKER, *Honest Whore* [DODSLEY, *Old Plays*, iii. 406]. Is 't possible that the lord Hipolito, whose face is as civil as the outside of a dedicatory book, should be a MUTTON-MONGER ?

1611. CHAPMAN, *May-day*, ii. p. 38. As if you were the only noted MUTTON-MONGER in all the city.

1611. COTGRAVE, *Dictionarie*. A noteable smel-smocke, or MUTTONMON-GER, a cunning solicitor of a wench.

1654. WEBSTER, *Appius & Virg.* [*Ancient Drama*, v. 400], iii. MUTTON'S MUTTON now. *V.* Why, was it not so ever ? *C.* No, madam, the sinners i' th' suburbs had almost ta'en the name quite away from it, 'twas so cheap and common ; but now 'tis at a sweet reckoning ; the term time is the MUTTON-MONGER in the whole calendar.

1677. COLES, *Dictionary*, s.v. MUTTON-MONGER, *scortator*.

1811. *Lex. Bal.*, s.v.

1847. HALLIWELL, *Arch. & Pro-vin. Words*, s.v. MOTONER. A wencher.

MUTTONOUS, *adj.* (common).—Slow; monotonous. Fr. *guitare*.

MUTTON-PIES, *subs.* (rhyming).— The eyes. For synonyms *see* PEEPERS.

1887. *Referee*, 7 Nov., p. 7, col. 3. Bright as angels from the skies Were her dark-blue MUTTON-PIES.

MUTTON-THUMPER, *subs.* (book-binders').—A bungling workman.

MUTTON-WALK, *subs.* (old).—1. The saloon at Drury Lane theatre.

1821. EGAN, *Real Life*, Tally-ho ... had not yet learned to trip it lightly along the MUTTON-WALK.

2. (common).—Any resort fre-quented by women of the town; specifically Piccadilly; *cf.* FLESH-MARKET.

MUX, *verb*. (American).—To muddle

1869. BLACKMORE, *Lorna Doone*, lxii. Nicholas ... had thoroughly MUXED up everything.

1872. J. M. BAILEY ('Danbury Newsman'), *They all do it*, 22. Stop MUXIN' that bread ! one would think you were a drove of young hogs to see you at the table. You've eaten enough for twenty people. I shan't have you MUXING and *gauming* up the victuals.

MUZZ, *verb.* (common).—1. To intoxicate.

1836. *Comic Almanack*, 48. While Harlequin half-MUZZ'D with wine, Don't care a rush for Columbine.

2. (Westminster School).—To read.

MUZZLE, *subs.* (common).—1. The mouth.

1821. *The Fancy*, Vol. I. p. 260. He ... got hit anywhere and every-where, about the MUZZLE particularly.

1828. JON. BEE, *Picture of London*, p. 113. Barbers .... having nought more in view than to plenish the MUZZLES of bristly handicraftsmen.

1836. M. SCOTT, *Cringle's Log*, xiii. With which the worthy lady painted our friend's face and MUZZLE in a most ludicrous manner.

2. (old).—A beard.

1785. GROSE, *Vulg. Tongue*, s.v.
1811. *Lex. Bal.*, s.v.

Verb. (pugilistic).—1. To strike in the mouth.

1851-61. MAYHEW, *Lond. Labour*, I. 233. Razor George and his moll slept here the day afore Christmas; just out of 'stir' (jail), for MUZZLING a peeler.

2. (common).—To drink.

3. (old).—To kiss. *Cf.* MOUSLE.

1697. VANBRUGH, *The Relapse*, i. 2. Ah, you young, hot, lusty thief, let me MUZZLE you. (*Kisses him*).

MUZZLED BULL-DOG, *subs. phr.* (nautical).—See quot.

1867. SMYTH, *Sailor's Word Book*. Bull-dog or MUZZLED BULL-DOG, the great gun which stands housed in the officer's ward-room cabin. General term for main-deck guns.

MUZZLER, *subs.* (pugilists').—1. See quot. 1811.

1811. *Lex. Bal.*, s.v. MUZZLER ... The milling cove tipped the cull a MUZZLER; the boxer gave the fellow a blow on the mouth.

1818. EGAN, *Boxiana*, ii. 459. He gave Dick a precious MUZZLER.

1821. EGAN, *Real Life*, i. 350. He saluted poor Pat with a MUZZLER.

2. (common).—A dram of spi-rits; a GO (*q.v.*).

MUZZY, *adj.* (common).—Half-tipsy ; dull with drink. For syno-nyms *see* DRINKS and SCREWED.

1730. JAS. MILLER, *Humours of Oxford*, Act I. p. 7 (2nd ed.). Your fellows of colleges are a parcel of sad, MUZZY, humdrum, lazy, ignorant, old caterpillars.

1770. FOOTE, *Lame Lover*, i. Pick-ing our teeth, after a damned MUZZY dinner at Boodle's.

1789. G. PARKER, *Life's Painter*, 'The Bunter's Christening.' Long Ned, and Dust-Cart Chloe, ... With whom came MUZZY Tom.

1829. BUCKSTONE, *Billy Taylor*, i. The constable of the night is at a ball, The keeper of the watchhouse down at Brighton, And all our brethren MUZZY.

1849. THACKERAY, *Pendennis*, v. The captain was not only unaccustomed to tell the truth,—he was unable even to think it—and fact and fiction reeled together in his MUZZY, whiskified brain.

1889. *Lic. Vict. Gaz.*, 18 Jan. My little game was very simple—just to sham being MUZZY and sulky.

MY AUNT (AUNT JONES or MRS. JONES), *subs. phr.* (common).— The W.C.; MRS. JONES (*q.v.*).

MY BLOATER. See BLOATER.

MY EYE! *intj.* (common).—An ex-clamation of surprise. See ALL MY EYE.

1819. MOORE, *Tom Crib*. 36. My eyes ! how prettily Tom writes.

1847. HALLIWELL, *Arch. & Prov. Words*, s.v.

1876. M. E. BRADDON, *Joshua Haggard*, ch. vii. 'Such juicy steak, and lots of potato ! ... MY EYE, ain't I hungry ! '

1892. F. ANSTEY, *Voces Populi*, 'In the Mall on Drawing-Room Day,' p. 82. Look at the dimonds all over 'er bloomin' old nut. MY EYE !

MYLA, *subs.* (tramps').—See MILER.

MYLL. See MILL.

MY LORD. See LORD.

MY NABS. See NABS.

MYNT. See MINT.

MY PIPPIN. See PIPPIN.

MYRMIDON, *subs.* (old).—See quot. 1811.

1809. BYRON, *English Bards and Scotch Reviewers*. 'When Little's lead-less pistol met his eye And Bow Street MYRMIDONS stood laughing by.'

1811. *Lex. Bal.*, s.v. The consta-ble's assistants, watchmen etc.

MY STARS AND GARTERS. See STAR.

MYSTERY, *subs.* (common).—A sau-sage. Also MYSTERY-BAG.

ENGLISH SYNONYMS. Bags of mystery ; chambers of horrors ; darbies ; dogs (dog's meat or dog's body); mystery-bags; Sharps-Alley blood-worms ; sore-leg ?

1887. HENLEY, *Culture in the Slums*. 'O crikey, Bill!' she ses to me, she ses. 'Look sharp,' ses she, 'with them there sossiges. Yea! sharp with them there BAGS OF MYSTEREE !'

1889. *Sportsman*, 2 Feb. But the MYSTERY-BAGS of Sieur X, if we are to believe the common report, were far from being fragrant. This gentleman has been sentenced to six months' imprisonment for 'making sausages of tainted meat.'

MY TULIP. See TULIP.

MY UNCLE. See UNCLE.

MY UNCONVERTED FRIEND. See UNCONVERTED FRIEND.

MY WIG. See WIG.

SLANG AND ITS ANALOGUES

PAST AND PRESENT

A DICTIONARY HISTORICAL AND COMPARATIVE OF THE HETERODOX SPEECH OF ALL CLASSES OF SOCIETY FOR MORE THAN THREE HUNDRED YEARS

WITH SYNONYMS IN ENGLISH FRENCH GERMAN ITALIAN ETC.

COMPILED AND EDITED BY

JOHN S. FARMER & W. E. HENLEY

VOL. V.—N. TO RAZZLE-DAZZLE

A Dictionary of Slang and its Analogues.

**AB** (or **NAP**), *subs.* (Old Cant.)—1. The head: also NAPPER. *See* TIBBY.— B. E. (*c.* 1696); COLES (1706); BAILEY (1728); GROSE (1785); JAMIESON (1880).

1567. HARMAN, *Caveat*, (E. E. T. S.), 86. Now I tower that bene bouse makes nase NABES.

1609. DEKKER, *Lanthorne and Candlelight* [GROSART, *Wks.* (1886), iii., 203]. The Ruffin cly the NAB of the Harman beck.

1610. ROWLANDS, *Martin Mark-all* p. 39 [Hunt. Club. Repr.]. *s.v.*

1611. MIDDLETON and DEKKER, *Roaring Girl*, v. 1. So my bousy NAB might skew rome bouse.

1622. FLETCHER, *Beggar's Bush*, 'The Maunder's Initiation.' I crown thy NAB with a gage of ben bouse.

1632. DEKKER, *English Villanies* [GROSART, *Wks.* (1886), iii]. He carries a short staff . . . having in the NAB or head of it a ferme.

1671. R. HEAD, *English Rogue* (1874), I., v., 50, *s.v.*

1893. EMERSON, *Signor Lippo*, xiv. A long-sleeve cadi on his NAPPER, and a pair of turtles on his martins finished him.

2. (old).—A hat ; a cap: also NAB-CHEAT and NAPPER. *See* GOLGOTHA.—B. E. (*c.* 1696); COLES (1708); BAILEY (1728); DYCHE (1748); GROSE (1785); MATSELL (1859).

1531-47. COPLAND, *Hey-way to the Spyttel-hous* [HAZLITT, *Early Popular Poetry*, iv.]. His watch shall feng a prounces NAB-CHETE.

1567. HARMAN, *Caveat* [E. E. T. S. (1869), 85]. I toure the strummel upon thy NABCHET and Togman.

1622. FLETCHER, *Beggar's Bush*, i., 1. We throw up our NAB-CHEAT, first for joy, And then our filches.

1671. R. HEAD, *English Rogue*, i., v. 51 (1874), *s.v.*

1688. SHADWELL, *Sq. of Alsatia*, ii. [*Works* (1720), iv., 47]. *Belf. Sen.* . . . Here's a NABB ! you never saw such a one in your life. *Cheat.* A rum NABB : it is a beaver of £5.

1706. FARQUHAR, *Recruiting Officer*, ii., 3. Ise keep on my NAB.

1754. FIELDING, *Jonathan Wild*, ii., vi. Those who preferred the NAB, or trencher-hat with the brim flapping over their eyes.

3. (old).—A fop : *see* DANDY. —MATSELL (1859).

4. (American).—*See* quot., BEAK, and COPPER.

1852. JUDSON, *Mysteries of New York*, iv. I don't know nothin' about no persuits, 'cept the NAB's persuits. *Ibid.*, *s.v.* NAB, an officer or constable.

Verb. (Old Cant.)—1. Primarily, to catch ; but also a general verb of action. *E.g.*, To NAB THE RUST=(1) to take offence, to turn rusty ; (2) to receive punishment unexpectedly ; TO NAB THE SNOW=to steal hedge-linen ; TO NAB THE STIFLES= to be hanged ; TO NAB THE STOOP=to stand in the pillory ; TO NAB THE TEIZE=to be whipped ; TO NAB IT ON THE DIAL= to get a blow in the face ; TO BE NABBED=to be arrested ; TO NAP A COG=to cheat (at dice) ; TO NAP THE BIB=to cry ; TO NAB THE REGULARS=to divide a booty ; TO NAP A WINDER=to be hanged ; TO NAP IT AT THE NASK=to be lashed at Bridewell ; etc. *See* BIB, REGULARS, and RUST.

ENGLISH SYNONYMS (*see* also COP and PRIG when=to take or receive). To bag ; to bone ; to box ; to claw ; to collar ; to cop ; to grab ; to nail ; to nap ; to nibble ; to nick ; to nim ; to nip ; to pinch ; to pull over ; to rope in ; to scoop ; to smug ; to snabble ; to snaffle ; to snake ; to snam ; to sneak ; to snitch.

FRENCH SYNONYMS. *Aganter* (popular : *agenter une claque*= to warm the wax of the ear) ; *agrafer* (=to hook) ; *arcpincer* (or *arquepincer*) ; *attrimer* (thieves') ; *cintrer en pogne* (thieves') ; *colletiner* (thieves') ; *coltiger* (thieves') ; *enflaquer* (thieves') ; *graffinger* (common) ; *griffer* (a falconry term=to claw) ; *grifler* (thieves') ; *gripper* (RABELAIS) ; *harper* (popular) ; *harponner* (= to harpoon) ; *pagourer* (thieves')

1609. DEKKER, *Lanthorne and Candlelight* [GROSART, *Wks.* (1886) iii. 233]. This hearbe being chewd downe by the Rabbit-suckers almost kils their hearts, and is deerer to them than NABBING on the neckes to Connies.

1676. *Warning for Housekeepers* [FARMER, *Musa Pedestris* (1896), 30]. But if the cully NAP us, And the lurries from us take.

1688. SHADWELL, *Squire of Alsatia*, iii. [*Works* (1720), iv., 56]. Our Suffolk heir is NABBED, for a small business ; and I must find him some sham-bail.

c. 1696. B. E., *Dict. Cant. Crew*, s.v. NAP and NASK.

1708. *Memoirs of John Hall*, s.v. NAP and Nask.

1723. CAPT. ALEX. SMITH, *Lives of Bailiffs*, 5. The bailiff, though he had long waited for him, could not nap him.

1728. BAILEY, *Eng. Dict.*, s.v. NAB . . . . to surprise, to take one NAPPING ; also to cog a dice.

1733. FIELDING, *Tom Thumb*, ii., 1. Were he a bully, a highwayman, or a prizefighter I'd NAB him.

1748. SMOLLETT, *Rod. Random*, xxiii. They embraced the prisoner . . . and asked how long she had been NABBED, and for what.

1754. *Discoveries of John Poulter*, 37. NAP my kelp (hold my hat) whilst I stall at the jigger.

1755. JOHNSON, *Eng. Dict.*, s.v. NAB. To catch unexpectedly ; to seize without warning. A word seldom used but in low language.

1785. GROSE, *Vulg. Tongue*, s.v. NAB. TO NAB THE RUST. A jockey term for a horse that becomes restive. *Ibid.* (1796). TO NAB THE SNOW ; to steal linen left out to bleach or dry. TO NAB THE STOOP ; to stand in the pillory.

1789. G. PARKER, *View of Society*, ii., 30, note. NAP THE STOOP, pilloried. *Ibid.*, ii., 75. TO NAP THE TEIZE is to receive this correction (whipping) privately.

1789. GEO. PARKER, *Life's Painter*, 153. NAPT a couple of bird's eye wipes. *Ibid.*, 163. NAP THE BIB, a person crying.

*d.*1817. HOLMAN, *Abroad and Home*, iii., 2. Bravo ! NAB 'em, have 'em tight, Merry then we'll be at night.

1819. VAUX (J. H.), *Memoirs*, I., 190. s.v. NAP THE BIB, to cry ; as, the mollisher NAP'D HER BIB, the woman fell a crying.

1821. EGAN, *Life in London*, 227. Dirty Suke began now to NAP HER BIB. *Ibid.*, *Boxiana* (1824), iv., 145. Josh NAPPED again on the other eye.

1830. LYTTON, *Paul Clifford*, xvi., NABBING, grabbing all for himself.

1833. MARRYAT, *Peter Simple*, I., x. Well, cried she, they've NABBED my husband.

1837. BARHAM, *Ingoldsby Legends*, 'The Black Mousquetaire.' Once he prevail'd . . . On the bailiff who NABB'D him, himself to ' go bail ' for him.

1838. *Comic Almanac*, April. Don't NAB THE BIB, my Bet, this chance must happen soon or later.

1851-61. MAYHEW, *Lond. Lab.*, iii., 139. I give him the NAP and knock him on the back.

1859. MATSELL, *Vocab.*, 'Hundred Stretches.' Some rubbed to wit had NAPPED a winder.

1867. *London Herald*, 23 Mar., 221, 3. We're safe to NAB him ; safe as houses.

1885. *Bell's Life*, 3 Jan., 8, 4. Johnny led off with his left, but NAPPED IT in return from Bungaree's left on the temple, which raised a bump.

1886. *Daily News*, 3 Nov., 5, 6. In one corner, four boys are learning how to KNAP a fogle fly.

1888. *Sporting Life*, 1 Dec. In endeavouring to reach his opponent's ribs with the right, NAPPED it on the dial.

1892. MILLIKEN, '*Arry Ballads*, 21. He NAPPED me.

2. (old).—*See* quot.

1775. ASH, *Dict.*, s.v. NAB (a *colloquial word*). To bite, to bite with repeated quick but gentle motion.

HIS NABS. *See* NIBS.

NABALL, *subs.* (old).—A fool : *see* BUFFLE and CABBAGE-HEAD.

1612. ROWLANDS, *More Knaves Yet*, 'Epig.' To all London's NABALLS.

NABBER (or **NABBLER**), *subs.* (Scots').—A thief. Whence NABBERY = theft. — JAMIESON (1808) ; MATSELL (1859).

NABBING-CULL, *subs.* (old).—A bailiff ; a constable. Also NABMAN.

1780. TOMLINSON, *Slang Pastoral*, st. x. Will no blood-hunting footpad, that hears me complain, Stop the whine of that NABBING-CULL, constable Payne?

1816. TERRY, *Guy Mannering*, ii. 3. Old Donton has sent the NABMAN after him at last.

NABBY. *See* NOBBY.

NAB-CHEAT. *subs.* (old).—1. *See* NAB, *subs.*, sense 2.

NAB-GIRDER, *subs.* (Old Cant.)— A bridle : also NOB-GIRDER.— B. E. *c.* 1696) ; BAILEY (1728) ; GROSE (1785) ; MATSELL (1859).

NABOB, *subs.* (Anglo-Indian : now colloquial).—1. *See* early quots. ; and (2) a rich man. Hence NABOBBERY = the class of nabobs.

1612. R. COVERTE, *Voyage*, 37. An Earle is called a NAWBOB.

1625. PURCHAS, *Pilgrims*, I., iv., 467. The NABOB with fifty or 60 thousand people in his campe.

1665. SIR TH. HERBERT, *Travels* (1677), 99. Nobleman, NABOB.

1764. WALPOLE, *Lett.* (1857), iv., 222. Mogul Pitt and NABOB Bute.

1772. FOOTE, *The Nabob* [Title].

1784. BURKE on *Fox's E. I. Bill* [*Works* (1852), III., 506]. He that goes out an insignificant boy in a few years returns a great NABOB.

1786. H. MORE, *Florio*, 272. Before our tottering castles fall And swarming NABOBS seize on all !

*d.*1796. BURNS, *Election Ballads*, III. But as to his fine NABOB fortune We'll e'en let this subject alane. *Ibid.*, ' Ded. to G. H.' 2. And there will be rich brother NABOBS, Though NABOBS, yet men o' the first.

1815. SCOTT, *Guy Mannering*, xix. (1852), 170. He resolved . . . to place himself upon the footing of a country gentleman of easy fortune, without assuming . . . any of the *faste* which was then considered as characteristic of a NABOB.

1834. *Baboo*, I., vii., 18. Though no king, I wait for no man, not even for a NUWAB.

1848. THACKERAY, *Van. Fair* (1867), i. They say all Indian NABOBS are enormously rich.

1852. SAVAGE, *R. Medlicot*, II. x. [1864]. 'How particularly great he is to-night; he reminds me of a NABOB!' 'NABOBBERY itself,' said Hyacinth.

1862. THACKERAY, *Philip*, xiv. The days of NABOBS are long over, and the General had come back . . . with only very small means for the support of a great family.

1872. E. BRADDON, *Life in India*, i., 4. The English flag was raised over the kingdom once ruled by Mogul, Rajah, and NUWAUB.

1878. LECKY, *Eng. in 18th Cent.*, xiii. The Indian adventurer, or, as he was popularly called, the NABOB, was now a conspicuous . . . figure in Parliament.

NABS ON, *subs. phr.* (thieves').—A hall-mark.

1889. RICHARDSON, *Police*, 320, s.v. WATCH.

NACE.—*See* NASE.

NACK.—I. *See* KNACK.

2. (thieves').—*See* quot. and *cf.* NAG.

1889. RICHARDSON *Police*, 320. A horse. A prad, NACK, four-runner.

NACKERS, *subs. pl.* (common).—The *testes*: *see* CODS.—JAMIESON (1880).

NACKY, *adj.* (old).—Ingenious; full of KNACKS (*q.v.*) or dexterity. Also NACKIE.—GROSE (1785); JAMIESON (1808); MATSELL (1859).

*d.*1758. RAMSEY, *Elegy on John Cowper* [JAMIESON] He was right NAIKIE in his way.

NAF, *subs.* (back-slang). — The female *pudendum*: *see* MONOSYLLABLE and FANNY.—HALLIWELL (1847).

NAG, *subs.* (colloquial). — I. A horse; a MOUNT (*q.v.*): *see* PRAD. Also NAGGON, NAGGIE or NAGGY, and (Scots') = a horse of blood.

*c.*1189. *Destruction of Troy* (E. E. T. S.), I., 7727. He neyt as a NAGGE at his nosethrilles!

*c.*1596. *Dick o' the Cow.* [CHILD, *Ballads*, VI., 80]. Yet here is a white-footed NAGIE, I think he'll carry both thee and me.

1598. SHAKESPEARE, I *Hen. IV.*, iii., I, 135. Like the forced gait of a shuffling NAG.

1611. CORYAT, *Crudities*, I, 287. I saw but one horse in all Venice . . . and that was a little bay NAGGE.

1624-45. Spalding, *Troubles in Scotland* (1850), ii., 183. [JAMIESON]. The ladies came out with two grey plaids, and gat two work NAIGS, which bore them into Aberdeen.

1630. TAYLOR, *Workes* [NARES]. My verses are made, to ride every jade, but they are forbidden, of jades to be ridden, they shall not be snaffled, nor braved nor baffled, wert thou George with thy NAGGON, that foughtst with the draggon.

1692. L'ESTRANGE, *Fables*. A hungry lion would fain have been dealing with good horseflesh; but the NAG was too fleet.

*d.*1721. PRIOR [JOHNSTON]. Thy NAGS, the leanest things alive, So very hard thou lov'st to drive.

1755. JOHNSTON, *Eng. Dict.*, s.v. NAG. A horse in familiar language.

*d.*1796. BURNS, *Tam o' Shanter*, 3. That every NAIG was ca'd a shoe on The smith and thee gat roaring fou on

1836 H. M. MILNER, *Turpin's Ride to York*, i., 3. If your mistress is only as true to you as my NAG is to me.

1864. E. YATES, *Broken to Harness*, xxxviii. Old boy was splendacious, did everything one wanted—good NAG to ride, good shooting, capital cellar—let you smoke where you like—no end!

1887. HENLEY, *Villon's Straight Tip*, i. Or fake the broads, or fig a NAG.

2. (venery).—The *penis*: *see* CREAMSTICK and PRICK.

1675. COTTON, *Scoffer Scofft* [*Works* (1725), p. 174]. Let her alone, and come not at her, But elsewhere, lead thy NAG to water.

*c.*1707. *Old Ballad*, 'The Trooper Watering His Nag' [FARMER, *Merry Songs and Ballads* (1896), i., 192]. When Night came on to Bed they went, . . . What is this so stiff and warm, . . . 'Tis Ball my NAG—he will do you harm.

3. in *pl.* (venery).—The *testes*: *see* CODS. Span., *angle*.

4. (common).—A whore; a JADE (*q.v.*).

1598. MARSTON, *Scourge of Vill.* vi., 64. Gull with bombast lines the witless sense of these odd NAGS.

1608. SHAKESPEARE, *Antony and Cleopatra*, iii., 10, 10. You ribaudred NAG of Egypt.

1775. ASH, *Dict.*, s.v. NAG . . . a paramour.

Verb. (colloquial).—To scold, or fault-find persistently; to tiff. Whence NAGGER = a persistent scold; NAGGING (*subs.* and *adj.*) = fault-finding; and NAGGY = shrewish; irritable.

1846. *Notes and Queries*, x., 89. NAGGING—whence is this word derived?

1861. THACKERAY. *Lovell the Widower*, iii. Is it pleasing to . . . have your wife NAG-NAGGING you because she has not been invited to the Lady Chancelloress's soirée, or what not.

1869. *Orchestra*, Mar. 14, 'Reviews.' Don't NAG. I know the expression is vulgar, and not in the dictionaries.

*c.*1870. DICKENS, *Ruined by Railways*. You always heard her NAGGING the maids.

1872. *Daily News*, 10 Aug. Harvey pleaded in his defence that his wife was a NAGGER.

1880. W. D. HOWELLS, *The Undiscovered Country*, ii. The . . . sparrows . . . quarrelled about over the grass, or made love like the NAGGING lovers out of a lady's novel.

1882. *Athenæum*, 25 Feb. Describes Agnes as having NAGGED the painter to death.

1884. BESANT, *Julia*, ii. Where there would be no old grandmother to beat and NAG at her.

TO WATER THE NAG (or DRAGON), *verb. phr.* (common).—To urinate: *see* DRAGON.

TO TETHER ONE'S NAG, *verb. phr.* (Scots').—To copulate: *see* GREENS and RIDE.

NAG-DRAG, *subs. phr.* (thieves').—A term of three months' imprisonment: *see* DRAG.

NAGGIE, *subs.* (venery).—I. The female *pudendum*: *see* MONOSYLLABLE.

2. *See* NAG, *subs.*, sense I.

NAGGLE, *verb.* (colloquial).—To toss the head in a stiff and affected manner.—HALLIWELL (1847).

NAIL, *subs.* (Winchester College).—I. *See* quots. and BIBLING UNDER NAIL.

1866. MANSFIELD, *Sch. Life Winchester*, s.v. NAIL. TO STAND UP UNDER THE NAIL. The punishment inflicted on a boy detected in a lie; he was ordered to stand up on Junior Row, just under the centre sconce, during the whole of school time. At the close of it he received a 'Bibler.'

1887. ADAMS, *Wykehamica*, s.v. NAIL, the central sconce at the east and west ends of the school were so-called. A boy who had committed some unusually disgraceful offence, was placed there during school, previously to being 'bibled.'

2. (Old and Scots').—Disposition; spirit; nature. THE AULD NAIL = original sin; A BAD NAIL = a bad disposition; A GUID NAIL = a good disposition. Also as in quot. 1819.

1819. VAUX, *Memoirs*, I., 190, s.v. NAIL. A person of an over-reaching, imposing disposition, is called a NAIL, a dead NAIL, a NAILING rascal, a rank needle or a needle pointer [also (1823), GROSE].

Verb. (common).—I. To catch: like NAB (*q.v.*) and COP (*q.v.*), a general verb of action. Whence NAILING = thieving.

1383. CHAUCER, *Cant. Tales*, Clerkes Tale' 1184 (SKEAT, 425). Let noon humilitee your tongë NAILLE.

1760. FOOTE, *Minor*, ii. Some bidders are shy, and only advance with a nod; but I NAIL them.

1766. GOLDSMITH, *Vicar of Wakefield*, xii. When they came to talk of places in town you saw at once how I NAILED them.

1875. GROSE, *Vulg. Tongue*, s.v. NAILED. He offered me a decus and I NAILED him.

*d.*1796. BURNS, *Death and Dr. Hornbook*. Ev'n Ministers, they ha'e been kenn'd . . . A rousing whid . . . to vend, An' NAIL 't wi' Scripture, *Ibid.* I'll NAIL the self-conceited sot As dead's a herring.

1819. VAUX (J. H.) *Memoirs*, I., 190, s.v. NAIL. To NAIL is to rob or steal; as, I NAIL'D him for (or of) his reader, I robbed him of his pocket-book; I NAIL'D the swells montra in the push, I picked the gentleman's pocket in the crowd. To NAIL a person, is to overreach, or take advantage of him in the course of trade or traffic.

1823. BEE, *Dict. Turf*, s.v. NAIL . . . The man is NAILED who is laid hands upon.

1836. M. SCOTT, *Tom Cringle*, viii. This is my compact—if he NAILS you, you will require a friend at court, and I will stand that friend.

1840. BARHAM, *Ingoldsby Legends*, I., 25. Mrs. Ogleton had already NAILED the cab.

1850. *Lloyd's Weekly*, 3 Feb. 'Low Lodging-houses of London.' Now I'll have money, NAILED or not NAILED. I can pick a woman's pocket as easy as a man's, though you wouldn't think it.

1851-61. MAYHEW, *Lond. Lab.*, ii., 57. At last he was bowled out in the very act of NAILING a yack. *Ibid.*, i., 457. At Maidstone I was NAILED and had three months of it.

1857. LAWRENCE, *Guy Livingstone*, xxxiv. Get him to talk . . . he's safe to commit himself, and we'll NAIL him at the first word.

1877. *Five Years' Penal Servitude*, iv., 270. He listened to the tempter, 'filched the ticker,' and was NAILED almost immediately.

1883. STEVENSON, *Treasure Island*, (1886), iii., 21. Lubbers as couldn't keep what they got, and want to NAIL what is another's.

1888. BOLDREWOOD, *Robbery Under Arms*, xxiv. I'll give you and Bell a pair each, if you're good girls, when we sell the horses, unless we're NAILED at the Turon.

1889. RICHARDSON, *Police*, 322. Stealing Horses. NAILING hacks.

1892. MILLIKEN, *'Arry Ballads*, 16. It NAILED her. *Ibid.*, 46. You haven't quite NAILED.

*b.*1893. Sir S. W. BAKER, *Heart of Africa*, xxii. We had lost the boats at Gondokoro, and we were now NAILED to the country for another year.

2. (American).—*See* quot.

1885. *North American Review*, cxli., 434. What did you do before you was a snatcher? . . . NAILED [*i.e.*] I worked as a carpenter.

3. (printers').—To back-bite. Also TO BRASS NAIL. *See* NAIL-BOX.

4. (Winchester College).—To impress for any kind of fagging. Also, to detect.—*S.J.C.* (1889).

1808. JAMIESON, *Dict.*, s.v. NAIL. To strike smartly, to beat, a cant use of the term.

5. (Scots).—*See* quot.

ON THE NAIL, *phr.* (old).—At once; on the spot; instanter.

1596. NASHE, *Saffron Walden*, [*Works*, iii., 59]. Tell me, haue you a minde to aine thing in the Doctors Booke? speake the word, and I will help you to it VPON THE NAILE.

1622. FLETCHER, *Spanish Curate*, v., 2. Pay it ON THE NAIL to fly my fury.

1663. DRYDEN, *Wild Gallant*, iv. A waiter's place at Custom-House, that had been worth to him an £100 a year UPON THE NAIL.

1733. SWIFT, *On Poetry*, [*Works* (1824), xiv., 334]. He pays his workmen ON THE NAIL.

1798. COLMAN (the Younger), *Blue Devils*, i. I. I will make the proposal, pay down all the money that's wanted, ON THE NAIL.

1834. AINSWORTH, *Rookwood*, II., vi. A thousand pounds for his life. UPON THE NAIL? asked Rust.

1845. DISRAELI, *Sybil*. You shall have ten thousand pounds ON THE NAIL, and I will . . . teach you what is your fortune.

1859. *Punch*, xxxvii., 51, I. I must have money *now*. I cannot wait. The word must be—fork out UPON THE NAIL.

1872. BRADDON, *Dead Sea Fruit*, vii. He does a bad adaptation of a French vaudeville, and gets twenty pounds down ON THE NAIL for his labour.

1889. *Century Dict.*, s.v. NAIL (ON THE). This phrase is said to have originated in the custom of making payments, in the exchange of Bristol, England, and elsewhere on the top of a pillar called THE NAIL.

1898. BRADDON, *Rough Justice*, 38. And paid him half a sovereign for it ON THE NAIL.

TO HIT THE NAIL (or THE RIGHT NAIL) ON THE HEAD (or TO DRIVE THE NAIL HOME,) *verb. phr.* (colloquial). — To succeed; to come to the point. Fr. *toucher au blanc* (= to hit the white).

1574. WITHALS, *Dict.* (1608), 460. You HIT THE NAILE ON THE HEAD, *rem tenes*.

1654. *Witts Recreations* [NARES]. Venus tels Vulcan, Mars shall shooe her steed, For he it is that HITS THE NAILE O' THE HEAD.

1670. RAY, *Proverbs* [BOHN], 165, s.v.

1675. COTTON, *Scoffer Scofft* [*Wks.* (1725), 151]. Ha! ha! old Smutty-face, well said, Th'ast HIT THE NAIL (i' faith) O'TH' HEAD.

1719. DURFEY, *Pills to Purge*, iii., 21. The common proverb as it is read, That a man must HIT THE NAIL ON THE HEAD.

1892. *Illustrated Bits*, 22 Oct., 6, 2. I have DRIVEN THE NAIL HOME.

1897. BARRETT, *Harding Scandal*, xiv. He must DRIVE THE NAIL HOME, and clench it on the other side, by leaving no doubt in the minds of Denise and Thrale.

1897. KENNARD, *Girl in Brown Habit*, ii. "In other words," said I, with a broad smile, "he goes a-courting against his master's wishes and advice." Exactly; you've HIT THE RIGHT NAIL ON THE HEAD.

TO PUT (OR DRIVE) A NAIL IN ONE'S COFFIN, *verb. phr.* (colloquial).—To do anything that shortens life: specifically, to drink. Hence, as *sub.* = a drink.—GROSE (1823).

1836. FONBLANQUE, *Eng. Under Seven Adm.* (1837), III., 321. A dram which . . . DRIVES NAILS INTO THE VICTIM'S COFFIN, according to the expressive vulgar expression.

1874. M'CARTHY, *Linley Rockford*. Every dinner eaten under such conditions is A NAIL DRIVEN INTO ONE'S COFFIN.

1888. *Fun*, 4 April, 148. Silently they walked into the Gaiety bar just as though they were going to order a couple of coffins instead of only two more NAILS.

1897. MITFORD, *Romance of Cape Frontier*, I., iii. Every moment lost is A NAIL IN HIS COFFIN.

2. (colloquial).—To hasten an end; to advance a business by a step.

1884. *Ill. Lond. News*, 29 Nov., 526, 3. The great value of 'The Candidate' to the contemporary stage is that it is one more NAIL IN THE COFFIN of slow acting.

1885. *Society*, 7 Feb., 8. This dispelling of the illusion of cheapness should prove a NAIL IN THE COFFIN of Co-operative Stores.

1897. *Daily Mail*, 26 Oct., 4, 3. With the occupation of this important post another NAIL will be DRIVEN INTO THE COFFIN of Dervish tyranny.

HARD AS NAILS, *adj. phr.* (colloquial).—1. In good condition.

1891. *Sportsman*, 25 Mar. Neither Rathbeal, who struck me AS HARD AS NAILS not long since.

2. (colloquial).—Harsh; unyielding; pitiless.

1888. BOLDREWOOD, *Robbery Under Arms*, xxxvii. HARD AS NAILS.

TO NAIL TO THE COUNTER, *verb. phr.* (colloquial).—To expose as false: as a lie. [From putting a counterfeit coin out of circulation by fastening it with a nail to the counter of a shop.]

1883. O. W. HOLMES, *Med. Essays*, 67. A few familiar facts . . . have been suffered to pass current so long that it is time they should be NAILED TO THE COUNTER.

1888. *Texas Siftings*, 20 Oct. That LIE WAS NAILED a good while ago. I know it, chuckled the C. L., but it's easy enough to pull out the NAIL.

1888. *Denver Republican*, 6 May. The La Junta *Tribune* has scooped all the papers in the State by NAILING THE first campaign LIE this season.

1898. *Referee*, 18 Sep., 2, 1. How often this particular falsehood has been NAILED TO THE COUNTER I don't know; more than once I have done it myself. Still, it obtains currency.

1900. *Daily Telegraph*, 20 Mar., 9, 3. That truth, sooner or later, will out is an accepted maxim among many of us; and it is, therefore, with a peculiar satisfaction that I am able to announce that the champion LIE of this campaign HAS, without doubt, BEEN securely NAILED TO THE COUNTER of public judgment.

NAKED AS MY NAIL, *phr.* (old colloquial).—Stark-naked.

1605. DRAYTON, *Man in the Moone*, 510. And tho' he were as NAKED AS MY NAIL, Yet would he whinny then, and wag the tail.

1633. HEYWOOD, *Eng. Trav.*, ii., 1. Did so towse them and . . . plucke them and pull them, till he left them as NAKED AS MY NAILE.

OFF AT THE NAIL, *phr.* (Scots').—1. *See* quot.

1808. JAMIESON, *Dict.*, s.v. NAIL. It is conceivable, that the S. phrase . . . might originate in family and feudal connexion. . . . When one acted as an alien, relinquishing the society, or disregarding the interests of his own tribe, he might be said to GO OFF AT THE NAIL; as denoting that he in effect renounced all the ties of blood. But this is offered merely as a conjecture.

2. (Scots').—Mad.

3. (Scots'). — Tipsy: *see* DRINKS and SCREWED.

1822. *The Steamboat*, 300. When I went up again intil the bedroom, I was what you would call a thought OFF THE NAIL; by the which my sleep wasna just what it should have been.

NAILS ON THE TOES, *phr.* (old).—*See* quot.

1602. SHAKESPEARE, *Troi. and Cress.*, ii., 1. Whose wit was mouldy ere your grandsires had NAILS ON THEIR TOES.

TO EAT ONE'S NAILS, *verb. phr.* (colloquial). *See* quot.

1708-10. SWIFT, *Polite Conversation*, i. Indeed, Mr. *Neverout*, you should be cut for Simples this morning: Say a word more, and you had as good EAT YOUR NAILS.

Also *see* DEAD; DOWN.

NAIL-BEARERS, *subs. phr.* (old). The fingers: *see* Fork.

NAIL-BOX, *subs. phr.* (printers').—A centre of back-biting: *see* NAIL, *verb.*, sense 3.

NAILER, *subs.* (colloquial).—1. An extortioner.

1888. *Illustrated London News*, Summer Number, 26, 3. The Stomach of the Bar, collective and individual, is revolted and scandalised at the idea of one of its members doing anything for nothing. Yes, put in Eustace, I have always understood that they were regular NAILERS.

2. (common).—Something out of the common; a CLIPPER (*q.v.*). A general term of excellence: *e.g.*, a handsome woman; a clever student; a fast horse, and so forth.

1886-96. MARSHALL, '*Pomes' from the Pink 'Un*, 88. At guzzling the whole lot were NAILERS.

NAILING, *subs.* (common).—1. *See* NAIL, *verb*.

2. (common).—Excellent; almost beyond comparison.

1894. GEORGE MOORE, *Esther Waters*, xxxvi. A NAILING good horse once.

NAILROD, *subs.* (Australian). *See* ROD.

NAIR, *subs.* (back-slang). Rain.

NAKED, *subs.* (common). — Raw spirit; NEAT (*q.v.*).

NAKEDNESS, *subs.* (conventional).—The privy parts: *see* PRICK and MONOSYLLABLE.

1613. *Bible* (Authorised Version), Gen. ix., 22. And Ham . . . saw the NAKEDNESS of his father.

NALE, *subs.* (old Scots'). — *See* quot.

1808. Jamieson, *Dict.*, s.v. NALE. This, I suspect, is a cant term used as an abbreviation, *an ale*, for 'an ale-house.' I observe no similar word.

NAM, *subs.* (back-slang).—A man. NAM ESCLOP = a policeman.

NAMASE. *See* NAMMOUS.

NAMBY-PAMBY, *adj.* (old colloquial).—Affected; effeminate; overnice. [Swift's invention, and first applied to the affected short-lined verses addressed by Ambrose Philips to Lord Carteret's infant children]. Also as *subs.* and *verb.* = to flatter; to pamper.

1781. JOHNSON. *Lives of the Poets* [A. PHILLIPS], iv., p. 173 (ed. 1793.) The pieces that please best are those which, from Pope to Pope's adherents, procured him the name of NAMBY PAMBY, the poems of short lines, by which he paid his court to all ages and characters.

1812. MARIA EDGWORTH, *Absentee*. xvi. A lady of quality . . . sends me Irish cheese and Iceland moss for my breakfast, and her waiting gentlewoman to NAMBY-PAMBY me.

1823. BEE, *Dict. Turf*, s.v. NAMBY-PAMBY—verse, ill-composed, unmeaning.

1857. BELL, *Ballads and Songs of Peasantry*, Intro., p. 8. Resisting everywhere the invasion of modern NAMBY-PAMBY verse.

1862. THACKERAY, *Philip*, ix. That NAMBY-PAMBY ballet and idyll world, where they tripped up to each other in rhythm, and talked hexameters.

NAME. HIS NAME IS DENNIS (or MUD), *phr.* (American).—A phrase indicative of collapse or defeat; TO BE SENT UP SALT RIVER (*q.v.*); TO BE PLAYED OUT (*q.v.*).

TO TAKE ONE'S NAME IN VAIN, *verb. phr.* (colloquial).—To mention by name: the person spoken of having unexpectedly or accidentally overheard.

1708-10. SWIFT, *Polite Conversation*, *Neverout* . . . . Smoke Miss yonder biting her lips . . . . (*Miss*). Who's that TAKES MY NAME IN VAIN?

TO PUT ONE'S NAME INTO IT, *verb. phr.* (tailors'). To get a thing well forward; to greatly advance a matter.

NAMELESS, THE (or **NAME-IT-NOT**), *subs.* (venery). — The female *pudendum*: *see* MONOSYLLABLE.

*c.*1674. *Bristol Drollery* [FARMER, *Merry Songs and Ballads* (1897), v., 50], 89. Such delicate Thighs, And that shall be NAMELESS between.

NAMELESS CREEK (THE), *subs. phr.* (anglers')—A lucky place whose whereabouts is for that reason untold.

NAMMOUS (NAMASE, NOMMUS or **NAMOUS)**, *verb.* (thieves').—*See* quots., and SKEDADDLE.

1857. J. E. RITCHIE, *Night Side of London*, p. 193. NOMMUS (be off), I am going *to do the tightner*.

1859. MATSELL, *Vocabulum*, s.v.

1866. *London Miscellany*, 3 Mar., p. 57. It was a regular trosseno (bad one). If it went on that always, he said, he should precious soon NOMMUS (cut it).

NAMMOW, *subs.* (back-slang).—A woman; DELO NAMMOW = an old woman.

NAMURS (THE), *subs. phr.*, (military). — The Royal Irish Regiment, formerly The 18th Foot. Also "Paddy's Blackguards."

NAN, *subs.* (colloquial).—A maid.

1596. SHAKSPEARE, *Merry Wives*, i., 4, 160. Good faith, it is such another NAN.

NAN-BOY, *subs.* (common).—An effeminate man; a MISS NANCY (*q.v.*)

1691. *Merry Drollery*, 'Jovial Lover,' p. 12. The Pipe and the Flute are the new Alamode for the NAN-BOYS.

1898. *Sporting Times*, 19 Feb., 1., 3. But do you think we enjoyed these superfine MISS NANCIES a quarter as much as we did the daring darlings who subsequently lured them down the Madeira Drive?

2. (venery).—A catamite.

NANCY, *subs.* (common).—1. The breech.—VAUX (1823). *See* BUM and MONOCULAR EYEGLASS. ASK MY NANCY, *see* quot.

1823. BEE, *Dict. Turf*, s.v. ASK MY NANCY, a very vulgar recommendation, seeing that it is a mute.

ALSO *see* NANBOY.

NANNY, *subs.* (colloquial).—1. A goat.

2. (common).—A whore: *see* BARRACK-HACK and TART.

NANNY-GOAT, *subs.* (colloquial).—

1. An anecdote.

1860. HALIBURTON (SAM SLICK), *The Season Ticket*, No. 11. I'll swop NANNY GOATS with you, and give you best when you tell the best one.

2. (military).—In *pl.* = The Royal Welsh Fusiliers, formerly the Twenty-third Foot: the regiment has a pet goat which is led with garlanded horns and a shield at the head of the drums—how the custom arose is unknown. Also "The Royal Goats."

NANNY-HEN, AS NICE AS A NANNY-HEN, *phr.* (old).—Very affected; delicate. *Cf.* NUN'S HEN.

[?] *M.S. Lambeth*, 306, f. 135. Women, women, love of women Make bare purs with some men. Some be NYSE AS A NANNE HEN, . . . Some be lewde, some all be shreude, Go schrewes where thei goo.

1611. COTGRAVE, *Dictionarie* [HALLIWELL]. . . . AS NICE AS NUNNES HENNE.

NANNY-SHOP (or **-HOUSE**), *subs.* (common).—A brothel: in quot. 1836 the cottage of a planter's smock-servant.—B. E. (*c.* 1696); GROSE (1785).

ENGLISH SYNONYMS. Academy; badger-crib; bawdy-house; bed-house; bread-and-butter-warehouse (specifically Ranelagh Gardens: *cf.* BREAD AND BUTTER-FASHION); bum-shop; buttocking-shop (*cf.* Fr. *magasin de fesses*); cab (*cf.* Fr. *un bordel ambulant*); button-hole factory; case (Old Cant); cavaulting school; Corinth; coupling-house; Covent Garden nunnery; cunt-shop; cunny-warren; disorderly-house; fancy-house; finishing-academy; fish-market; fish-pound; flash-drum (-house, or -ken); flesh-market; fuckery; garden-house; goal; green-grocery; hook-house (or -shop); also hock-house: hooker in America =

prostitute); house of accommodation; House of Civil Reception; knocking-shop; ladies' college; leaping-house; meat-fancier's (-market, or -house); molly-shop; mot-case; naughty-house; Number 9; nunnery; occupying-house; (FLORIO); panel-crib; pushing-school; stews; touch-crib; trugging-ken; vaulting house (or -school); vrow-case; warren; whore-house (or -shop).

FRENCH SYNONYMS. *Une abbaye des s'offre à tous* (RABELAIS); *une academie d'amour*; *un autel de besoin*; *un bazar*; *un boc*, *bocan*, *bocson*, *boucan*, or *bocard* (LA FONTAINE); *un bordeau*, or *bordel* (RABELAIS and VILLON); *une boucherie* (*cf.* MEAT-MARKET); *une boui* (popular); *une bousin* or *bousingot* (also disorder, or disturbance); *un boxon*; *les carreaux brouillés*; *un clapoire* (RABELAIS); *un claque-bosse*; *un claquedent*; *un couvent*, *un couvent de Venus*, or *un couvent laique* (VOLTAIRE); *un curatrie* (RABELAIS); *la cythère* (generic); *un dépotoir* (also chamber-pot and confessional); *un foutoir* (generic); *une gantière* (Parisien); *un gros numéro*; *une laure* (thieves'); *lieu d'honneur* (generic); *un lupinar*, or *une lupinaire* (RABELAIS, *un magasin de blanc*, or *de fesses* (*cf.* BUTTOCKING-SHOP); *une maison à gros numéro*, *de tolérance*, *de sociétié*, *parties*, or *de passe*; *un manufacture de bouchon* (RABELAIS); *un montretout* (generic); *un pailloire* (RABELAIS); *un peautre* (RABELAIS); *une petite maison* (COLLÉ); *un pince-cul* (generic, but specifically a low public-house given over to sexual debauchery); *un poulailler* (generic); *un putefy* (RABELAIS); *un serail* (generic); *un trucsin*.

GERMAN SYNONYMS. *Baisel* (also = inn and pitcher); *Kandich*; *Kitt*; *Knalhutte* (*knallen* = (1) to shoot; (2) to copulate); *Kuwo* (also *Kubbe*, *Kowe*, *Kauwo*); *Puff* (also = the act of kind); *Schofelbajis* (Heb. *schophal* = bad, common, low).

SPANISH SYNONYMS. *Aduana*; *casa llana*, *de putas*, *de tapadillo*; *cerco*; *comejera*; *conventillo*; *cortejo*; *guanta*; *guisado*; *mancebia*; *manfla*; *manflota*; *montana*; *montaña de pinos*; *pifla*; *pisa*; *puteria*; *rameria*; *vulgo*.

DUTCH SYNONYMS. *Poetkeete*; *sonnenkeete*; *trankeete*.

1836. M. SCOTT, *Cruise of Midge*, p. 166. A nest of NANNY HOUSES, as they are called, inhabited by brown free people.

NANTEE, *adv.* (Lingua Franca).—Nor any; 'I have none;' also 'shut up!' or 'leave off!' NANTEE PALAVER = hold your tongue! NANTY DINARLY = no money; NANTY PARNARLY = be careful! [Ital. *niente* = nothing].

1851-61. H. MAYHEW, *London Lab.*, iii., 136. He had NANTI VAMPO, and your NABS must FAKE it; which means,—we have no clown, and you must do it.

NANTZ, *subs.* (old).—Brandy.

1691-2. *Gentlemen's Journal*, Feb., 24. Our jovial crew there made a halt To drink some NANTZ or what-d'ye call-'t.

*c.*1817. KEATS, *A Portrait*. He sipped no olden Tom or ruin blue, or NANTZ or cherry brandy.

1821. SCOTT, *Pirate*, xxix. What a leer the villain gave me as he started the good NANTZ into the salt water.

1884. HENLEY and STEVENSON, *Deacon Brodie*, 1., i. 7. G. S. and Co's. celebrated NANTZ.

NAP. 1. *See* NAB, *subs.* and *verb.* in all senses.

2. *subs.* (common).—'A short sleep.'—B. E. (*c.* 1696).

1600. *The Maydes Metamorphosis*, I'll take a NAP and come annon.

1625. MASSINGER, *Parliament of Love*, ii., 3. I here shall take a NAP.

1664. COTTON, *Scarronides*, 102. And whilst he taking was a NAP, She layed him neatly in her Lap.

*d.*1796. BURNS, *Awa, Whigs, Awa.* Grim Vengeance lang has ta'en a NAP.

1842. TENNYSON, *Day Dream*, 156. 'Twas but at after dinner NAP.

3. (colloquial).—*See* quot. 1867.

1858. LYTTON, *What Will He Do With It*, 309. He would not have crossed a churchyard alone at night for a thousand NAPS.

1867. LATHAM, *Dict.*, s.v. NAP. Abbreviation for Napoleon, *i.e.*, the coin so called.

4. (Scots').—*See* quot. 1808; an abbreviation of NAPPY (*q.v.*).

1804. TARRAS, *Poems*, p. 24. Nor did we drink o' gilpin water; But reemin NAP, wi' houp weel heartit.

1808. JAMIESON, *Dict.*, s.v. NAP. A cant term for ale, or a stronger kind of beer. Aberd.

5. (old).—*See* quots. Also as *verb*.

*c.*1696. B. E., *Dict. Cant. Crew*, s.v. NAP, a clap or pox.

1785. GROSE, *Vulg. Tongue*, s.v. NAP. You have NAPT it, you are infected.

Verb. (old).—1. *See* quots.

*c.*1996. B. E., *Dict. Cant. Crew*, s.v. NAP. By cheating with the Dice to secure one chance.

*d.*1704. TOM BROWN, *Works*, III., 60. Assisting the frail square die with high and low fullams, and other NAPPING tricks.

1728. BAILEY, *Eng. Dict.*, s.v. NAP, to cheat at dice.

1785. GROSE, *Vulg. Tongue*, s.v. NAP.

TO CATCH (or TAKE NAPPING. *verb. phr.* (colloquial).—1. To take unawares; to take in the act.

1587. GREENE, *Tritameron*, II. [GROSART, Works (1886), iii.]. With that Panthia, & the rest, TOOKE THEM NAPPING.

1593. SHAKSPEARE, *Taming of the Shrew*, iv., 2. Nay, I have TA'EN YOU NAPPING, gentle love.

1606. *Ret. fr. Parnassus*, iii., 5 [DODSLEY, *Old Plays*, ix., 286]. Now may it please thy generous dignity To TAKE this vermin NAPPING, as he lies In the true lap of liberality.

1663. BUTLER, *Hud.*, I., iii. I TOOK THEE NAPPING unprepared.

*c.*1696. B. E., *Dict. Cant. Crew*, s.v.

*d.*1727. DEFOE, *Tour through Gt. Brit.*, III., 143. HAND-NAPPING—that is when the criminal was taken in the very act of stealing cloth.

1785. GROSE, *Vulg. Tongue*, s.v. NAP. He caught him NAPPING as Morse caught his mare.

1847. PORTER, *Quarter Race*, 120. They'd caught the old man NAPPING once.

TO GO NAP, *verb. phr.* (colloquial).—To risk everything on a single point; 'to go the WHOLE HOG' (*q.v.*) [From the game of cards].

1860. GLOVER, *Racing Life*, 38. Look here, you GO NAP—now, hear that? NAP—on Royal Angus.

1883. W. BLACK, *Yolande*, xxxix. After dinner the familiar and innocent sixpenny nap was agreed upon. But even at this mild performance you can lose a fair amount if you persistently GO NAP on almost any sort of a hand that turns up.

1888. *Barnet Press*, 1 Dec. He could say that Elstree and Shenley would GO NAP for Mr Todhunter.

1891. *Answers*, 28 Mar. In the innocence of my heart, I adjured all readers of the paper to GO NAP on Nostrils for the 2.30 race!

1898. *Pall Mall Gaz.*, 20 Sep., 2., 2. It is permissible to doubt whether it was wise to GO NAP—if an Orleans can GO NAP—on Dreyfus's guilt and the infallibility of the court-martial which condemned him.

TO NAP TOCO FOR YAM, *verb. phr.* (old).—*See* quot.

1823. BEE, *Dict. Turf*, s.v. NAP . . . to get more beating than is given.

See also REGULARS, SLAP, and TEIZE.

NAPKIN. *See* DISH-CLOUT.

TO BE BURIED IN A NAPKIN, *verb. phr.* (common).—1. To be asleep; and (2) to be half-witted.

KNIGHT OF THE NAPKIN, *subs. phr.* (common).—A waiter; a GRASSHOPPER (*q.v.*)

NAPKIN-SNATCHING, *subs. phr.* (old).—*See* quot. Also NAPKIN-SNATCHER.

1823. GROSE, *Vulg. Tongue* [EGAN], s.v. NAPKIN-SNATCHING, or Fogle-hunting. Sneaking pocket-handkerchiefs.

NAP-NIX, *subs. phr.* (theatrical).—An amateur player of minor parts for the sake of experience.

NAPPER, *subs.* (common).—1. *See* NAB, *subs.*, senses 1 and 2.

2. (old).—A cheat or thief. Whence NAPPER (or NAPER) OF NAPS = a sheep-stealer. — B. E. (*c.* 1696); BAILEY (1728); GROSE (1785); JAMIESON (1880).

*c.*1712. *Old Ballad*, 'The Black Procession' [FARMER, *Musa Pedestris* (1896), 39]. The sixteenth a sheep-NAPPER.

3. (old).—A false witness.

4. (old).—*See* RAIN-NAPPER.

NAPPY, *subs.* (old).—Strong ale: also NAPPING-GEAR. Hence as *adj.* (1) strong or heady; and (2) drunk.

1593. HARVEY, *Pierces Super.* [GROSART, *Works*, II., 51]. The nippitaty of the NAPPIEST grape; that infinitely surpasseth all the Invention . . in the world.

1593. HARVEY, *New Lett. Notable Contents* [GROSART, *Works*, i., 283]. The very steame of the NAPPY liquor will lullaby thy fine wittes.

1594. *Lochrine*, ii. 1. The can stands full of NAPPY ALE.

*c.*1600. *My Wife Will Be My Master* [COLLIER, *Roxburghe Ballads* (1847), 87]. A cup of NAPPY ALE and spice of which she is first taster.

1602. COOKE, *How a Man may Choose a Good Wife* [DODSLEY, *Old Plays* (1874), ix., 64]. And from the pond and river clear Mak'st NAPPY ale and Good March beer.

*c.*1630. PARKER, *Harry White, his Humour*. M. P. wisheth happy Successe and ale NAPPY, That with the one's paine He the other may gaine.

1662. *Rump Songs*, ii., 59. The body being eaten, we strive for the Tayl, Each man with his Kanikin of NAPPY brown Ale, Doth box it about for the Rump.

*b.*1685. *The King and the Miller of Mansfield.* NAPPY ale, good and stale, in a browne bowle.

*c.*1696. B. E., *Dict. Cant. Crew*, s.v. NAPPY ALE. Very strong, heady.

17 [?] *Old Ballad, Pattie's Wedding* HERD, ii., 191]. The auld wives sat and they chew'd, and when that the carles grew NAPPY, they danc'd as weel as they dow'd, Wi' a crack o' their thumbs and a kappie.

1714. GAY, *Shepherd's Week.* Tues. In misling days, when I my thresher heard, With NAPPY beer I to the barn repair'd.

1762. WILSON, *The Cheats*, i. 5. This is NAPPING GEAR . . . . but pray no more of this bowl.

1785. GROSE, *Vulg. Tongue*, s.v.

*d.*1796. BURNS, *Twa Dogs*, 18. An' whyles twa pennie worth o' NAPPY Can mak the bodies unco happy. *Ibid.*, *Tam o' Shanter.* While we sit bousing at the NAPPY.

1867. LATHAM, *Dict.*, s.v. NAPPY Old epithet applied to ale: (this is the entry in the previous editions, and the present editor is unable to give greater definitude to it.)

NARE. *See* NEVER.

NARK (or **COPPER'S-NARK**), *subs.* (common).—A police spy; a common informer.

ENGLISH SYNONYMS (*See* also BEAK and COPPER). Buz-man; D; dee; deeker; fox; marker; nose; noser; peach (omnibus spy); pig; piper (omnibus spy); queer-rooster; rat; rosser (or rozzer); setter; shadow; shepherd; snitcher; split; spotter; squealer; stag (or stagger); tec; teck; worm.

FRENCH SYNONYMS. *Un arnacq* (also *arnache*); *une bourrique* (= an ass); *le cadratin* (generic); *une casserole*; *un charieur*; *un contre-allumeur* (= spy engaged by thieves to counteract the machinations of the police); *un coqueur* (also *coqueur mouton*, or *musicien* = a prison-informer); *un co uin* (= knave); *un correcteur* (a prison-spy); *un cuisinier*; *un diable*; *un fileur*; *un flancheur*; *un friquet* (= tree-sparrow); *un gobemouches* (= gull trap); *un grand meudon*; *un gaffeur*; *un indicateur*; *un larnac* (see *arnacq*: *also rousse à larnac*); *un macaron*; *un mireur*; *un mouchard*; *une mouche* (= FLY [*q.v.*]); *un mouton* (a prisoner-spy); *un bourgeois de nuit*; *un rousse* (also *roussin* and *une rousselette*); *une vache*; *un vesto de la cuisine*.

1879. HORSLEY in *Macm. Mag.*, XL., 505. He had a NARK (policeman's spy) with him.

1887. HENLEY, *Villon's Good Night.* Likewise you COPPER'S NARKS and dubs What pinched me when upon the snam.

1888. *Daily Chronicle*, 29 Dec. Take that, you COPPER'S NARK!

1889. *Daily Telgraph*, 11 Sept. You are what is known as a COPPER'S NARK, are you not?

1892. MILLIKEN, *'Arry Ballads*, 60. I once knew a COPPER'S NARK, as earned many a quid.

1895. *Daily Telegraph*, 26 Feb., 3. Is not a COPPER'S NARK an associate of thieves, who gives information against his companions to assist the police? Certainly not. A COPPEP'S NARK would not go amongst thieves.

1898. *Pall Mall Gaz.*, 19 Jan., 2, 3. The NARKS may light upon that swag even yet.

Verb. (thieves').—To see; to watch; to spy.

ENGLISH SYNONYMS. To buz; to castell; to dick; to fox; to lay; to mark; to nose; to ogle; to pipe; to quiz; to roast (or roast-brown); to shadow; to shepherd; to skin; to snitch; to spot; to stag; to tout; to twire; to be on the beefment; to be on the pounce.

FRENCH SYNONYMS. *Etre à l'affut* (colloquial); *battre l'antif* (also = to pad the hoof); *borgner*; *coquer*; *donner la chasse à la rousse* (thieves': = to watch the police); *faire le gaf*; *filer un sinve*; *faire la filature* (or *lâcher de la filature*) *à quel-qu'un*; *exhiber*; *gaffer* (also *gaffiner*); *allumer son gaz*; *surbiner*.

1886-9. MARSHALL, *Honest Bill* ['Pomes,' 49]. You'd be sure to NARK the ruby round his gill.

1889. *Sporting Times*, 29 June. And as terseness of expression was an art she'd studied well, She determined that her lady friend should NARK it.

NARP, *subs.* (Scots).—A shirt: *see* FLESH-BAG.—DUCANGE (1857).

NARRISH, *adj.* (colloquial).—Thrifty: *see* NARROW.

1889. *London Society*, Oct., p. 367. I have been told that he is very NARRISH. . . . He has always paid his debts very scrupulously, lived within his income, and certainly I saw no signs of undue economy.

NARROW, *adv.* (old colloquial).—1. Ne'er a; not one.

1750. FIELDING, *Tom Jones*, VIII., ii. I warrants me there is NARROW a one of all those officer fellows but looks upon himself to be as good as arrow a squire of £500 a year.

1711. SMOLLETT, *Hump. Clink.*, 186. As for master and the young squire, they have as yet had NARRO glimpse of the new light.

Adj. (colloquial).—1. *See* quot., and NEAR.

*c.*1696. B. E., *Dict. Cant. Crew*, s.v. NARROW. A NARROW-SOUL'D Fellow, poor or mean-spirited, stingy.

2. (common).—Stupid; foolish the reverse of FLY (*q.v.*) or WIDE-AWAKE (*q.v.*).

3. (bowlers').—*See* quot.

*c.*1696. B. E., *Dict. Cant. Crew*, s.v. NARROW. When the Bias of the Bowl holds too much.

4. (old).—*See* quot.

*c.*1696. B. E., *Dict. Cant. Crew*, s.v. NARROW. NARROW or NEAR search, Watch him narrowly or nearly. *Ibid.* Of a NARROW or slender Fortune.

ALL NARROW, *adv. phr.* (old).—*See* quot.

*c.*1696. B. E., *Dict. Cant. Crew*, s.v. NARROW. 'TIS ALL NARROW. Said by the Butchers one to another when their meat proves not so good as expected.

NARROWDALE NOON, *subs. phr.* (provincial).—*See* quot.

1868. BREWER, *Phrase and Fable*, s.v. NARROWDALE NOON. One o'clock. The top of Narrowdale Hills, in Staffordshire, is so high that the inhabitants under it never see the sun for one quarter of the year, and when it reappears they do not see it till one o'clock, which they call NARROWDALE NOON. A thing long deferred.

NARROW - GAUGE, *adj. phr.* (American). — Inferior; small: *e.g.*, a NARROW-GAUGE mule = a worthless beast.

NARROW-SQUEAK. *See* SQUEAK.

NARY, *adj.* (American). — Not one [ne'er a]. *See* NARROW, NARY RED = not a red cent. Also as an emphatic negative.

1848. LOWELL, *Biglow Papers* [BARTLETT]. It's a good way, though, come to think, coz ye enjoy the sense o' lendin' lib'rally to the Lord, an' NARY red o' expense.

1850. SEAWORTHY, *Nag's Head*, xix., 162. There shan't NARY drop on't go into him.

1857. *Philadelphia Bulletin*, May, As regards the old cents, there will be NARY RED to be seen, except such as will be found in the cabinets of coin collectors.

1858. *New York Evening Post*, 1 Sept. The Atlantic Cable and the White Mountains—both monuments of God's power, but NARY one alike.

NASAL, *subs.* (pugilists').—The nose: *see* CONK.

1888. *Sporting Life*, 21 Nov. Planted a couple of well-delivered stingers on Harris's NASAL.

NASE, *adj.* (old). — Drunken. Also NACE, NAZE, and NAZY. *See* quots. — B. E. (*c.* 1696); BAILEY (1728); MATSELL (1859).

1536. COPLAND, *Spittel-hous* [HAZLITT, *Early Pop. Poet.* (1866), iv. 69]. With bousy cove maimed NACE.

1567. HARMAN, *Caveat*, p. 86. Now I tower that bene bouse makes NASE nabes.

1785. GROSE, *Vulg. Tongue*, s.v. NAZIE, drunken: NAZIE COVE or MORT, a drunken rogue or harlot; NAZIE NABS, drunken coxcombs.

NASH, *verb.* (old).—1. *See* quot. 1819.—GROSE (1823); BEE (1823).

1819. VAUX, *Memoirs*, I, 191, s.v. NASH, to go away from, or quit, any place or company; speaking of a person who is gone, they say, he is NASH'D, or MR. NASH is concerned.

2. (old). — To throw away: *e.g.*, 'NASH your leading-strings' = throw off all restraint.

NASH-GAB, *subs. phr.* (common). —Insolent language; impertinence.

NASK (or **NASKIN**), *subs.* (old). —*See* quots. and CAGE.

1686. HIGDEN, *On Tenth Satire of Juv.*, p. 38. Each heir by dice, drink, whores, or masking, Or, Stistead brought into the *NASKIN. [* Note.—The cant word for a Prison.]

*c.*1696. B. E., *Dict. Cant. Crew*, s.v. NASK. THE OLD NASK, the City Bridewell. THE NEW NASK, Clerkenwell Bridewell. TUTTLE NASK, The Bridewell in Tuttle-Fields.

1775. ASH, *Dict.* s.v. NASKIN (*a Cant word*), a jail, a bridewell.

1785. GROSE, *Vulg. Tongue*, s.v.

1859. MATSELL, *Vocabulum*, s.v.

See also NAB.

NASTY, *adj.* (colloquial). — Ill-tempered; disagreeable; cutting: *e.g.*, NASTY JAR, a stinging retort; NASTY KNOCK (or ONE), a disagreeable experience; NASTY ONE IN THE EYE = a telling blow.

1874. E. L. LINTON, *Patricia Kemball*, iii. He would have thought her temper had turned NASTY, though that was not her way.

1878. TROLLOPE, *Is he Popenjoy?* ix. She is a NASTY hateful creature; and I do hate her . . . How a woman can be so NASTY I can't imagine.

1880. OUIDA, *Moths*, xv. The lovely Fuschia possessed in reserve an immense relating power of being NASTY were she displeased

1881. R. G. WHITE, *Eng. Without and Within*, xvi. Lady A—said . . . to her husband . . . Do take some, [soup] A—, it's not at all NASTY. *Ibid.* A stormy day in England is called a NASTY day.

1886-96. MARSHALL, *Honest Bill*, ['Pomes,' 50]. They called him Captain Chickweed, and he'd planned a NASTY KNOCK.

1891. *Harry Fludyer*, 84. Then he said . . . one idle son in a family was more than enough (that's a NASTY ONE for you, Pat, my boy).

CHEAP AND NASTY, *adv. phr.* (colloquial).—Pleasing to the eye, but worthless in fact.

1864. *Athenæum*, 29 Oct. CHEAP AND NASTY, or, in a local form, 'CHEAP AND NASTY, LIKE SHORT'S IN THE STRAND,' a proverb applied to the deceased founder of cheap dinners.

NASTY-MAN, *subs.* (thieves').—*See* GARROTTE, *verb.*

NATION, *subs.* and *adv.* (old colloquial).—*See* quot. 1785.

1759-67. STERNE, *Trist. Shandy*, v., 21. The French have such a NATION of hedges.

1765. *Moving Times* [BARTLETT], 4. I believe, my friend, you're very right: They'll get a NATION profit by 't

1775. *Yankee Doodle.* And every time they shoot it off, It takes a horn of powder, And makes a noise like father's gun, Only a NATION louder.

1785. GROSE, *Vulg. Tongue*, s.v. NATION, an abbreviation of damnation, a vulgar term used in Kent, Sussex, and the adjacent counties, for very; NATION good, a NATION long way, a very long way.

1805. J. REYNOLDS, *Blind Bargain*, i., 1. There it be—there be the old fire-side, and NATION glad I am to clap eyes on't.

1824. PEAKE, *Americans Abroad*, i., 1. I have no doubt he will push his fortune, as he is a NATION deal of the gentleman. *Ibid.*, ii., 2. It's NATION lonesome to sit by one's self.

1835. HALIBURTON, *Clockmaker*, 1st S., xix. There was a NATION sight of folks there.

1848. BURTON, *Waggeries, etc.*, p. 20. As much as you say, 'What the NATION are you at?'

1854. AINSWORTH, *Flitch of Bacon*, pt. i., v. We're 'NATION fond of old brandy.

1868. C. READE, *Foul Play*, ix. Don't be in such a NATION hurry: for, if you do, it will be bad for me, but worse for you.

NATIONAL INTELLIGENCER. UNABLE TO SAY NATIONAL INTELLIGENCER, *phr.* (American).—Drunk: *see* DRINKS and SCREWED. *Cf.* BRITISH CONSTITUTION.

NATTY, *adj.* (colloquial).—Neat; tidy; spruce. Hence NATTILY, nattiness.

1557. TUSSER, *Husbandrie*, ch. 68, st. i, p. 159 (E.D.S.). Concerning how prettie, how fine and how NETTIE, Good huswife should iettie, from morning to night.

1789. GEO. PARKER, *Life's Painter*, p. 149. A kind of fellow who dresses smart, or what they term NATTY.

1819. MOORE, *Tom Crib's Mem.*, 10. From NATTY barouche down to buggy precarious.

1823. BEE, *Dict. Turf*, s.v.

1849. C. BRONTE, *Shirley*, xv. Sweeting alone received the posy like a smart, sensible little man as he was, putting it gallantly and NATTILY into his button-hole.

1860. G. ELIOT, *Mill on the Floss*, ii., 7. A connoisseur might have seen 'point' in her which had a higher promise for maturity than Lucy's NATTY completeness. *Ibid.*, *Silas Marner* (1861), xi. Everything belonging to Miss Nancy was of delicate purity and NATTINESS . . . as for her own person it gave the same idea of perfect unvarying neatness as the body of a little bird.

1867. LATHAM, *Dict.*, s.v., NATTY, Smart, spruce [colloq.].

1872. *Figaro*, 22 June. A NATTIER rig you'll hardly twig.

1875. OUIDA, *Signa*, III., x., p. 221. It seems a nice easy trade, said Nita, tempted; and lying must be handy in it; that would suit him. No one lies so NATTILY as Toto.

1889. *Harper's Mag.*, LXXIX., 819. A very NATTY little officer, whose handsome uniform was a source of great pride and a matter of great pride to him.

1892. MILLIKEN, *'Arry Ballads*, p. 24. NATTY cove.

NATTY-LAD, *subs.* (thieves').—A young thief or pickpocket.—GROSE (1785); HALLIWELL (1847).

NATURAL, *subs.* (old).—1. A mistress: *see* TART.—B. E. (*c.* 1696); GROSE (1785).

1688. SHADWELL, *Sq. of Alsatia*, ii. [*Wks.* (1720), iv., 47]. But where's your lady, captain, and the blowing, that is to be my NATURAL, my convenient, my pure? *Ibid.*, I., iv., *Shamwell.* Thou art i' th' right; but, captain, where's the convenient, the NATURAL?

2. (colloquial).—An idiot; a simpleton. — B. E. (*c.* 1696); GROSE (1785).

1595. SHAKSPEARE, *Romeo and Juliet*, ii., 4. This drivelling love is like a great NATURAL, that runs lolling up and down to hide his bauble in a hole. *Ibid.*, *Tempest* (1609), iii., 2, 37. That a monster should be such a NATURAL.

1609. DECKER, *Guls Horne-booke*, ii. [GROSART, *Works* (1886), ii., 216]. They which want sleepe . . . become either mere NATURALS or else fall into the Doctor's hands.

1614. ROWLANDS, *A Fooles Bolt is Soone Shott*, I. p. 22 (H. Club's Repr., 1873). The Duke of *Brunswicke* had a NATURALL, Whom all the Court did sotton *Joris* call.

1722. STEELE, *Consc. Lovers*, ii., 1. I own the man is not a NATURAL; he has a very quick Sense, tho' a slow Understanding.

1766. COLMAN, *Cland. Marriage*, i. [*Works* (1777), i., 177]. This ridiculous love! we must put a stop to it. It makes a perfect NATURAL of the girl.

1825. NEAL, *Bro. Jonathan*, ii., 15. He's your brother, I guess?—ain't he?—sort of a NATTERAL, too, I guess?

1874. MRS. H. WOOD, *Johnny Ludlow*, 1st S., No. xvi., p. 287. The man opened his mouth and closed it again; like, as Molly put it, a born NATURAL.

3. (old).—A bastard. — B. E. (*c.* 1696); GROSE (1785).

4. (American thieves'). — A clever, quick-witted, generous man.—MATSELL (1859).

5. (obsolete).—*See* quot.

1888. *Encycl. Brit.* XXIV., 560 s.v. Wig. In 1724 the peruke-makers advertised full bottom tyes, full bobs, minister's bobs, NATURALS, half naturals . . . among the variety of artificial head gear which they supplied.

Adj. (American). — Not squeamish.—MATSELL (1859).

NATURE, *subs.* (venery). — 1. The generative organs: male or female; and (2) the semen (quot. 1547). Hence NATURE'S PRIVY-SEAL (TREASURY, or TUFTED-TREASURE) = the female *pudendum*; NATURE'S SCYTHE = the *penis*; NATURE'S DUTY = copulation; NATURE'S FOUNTS = the paps. *See* CREAM, CREAMSTICK, DAIRIES, GREENS, MONOSYLLABLE, PRICK, and RIDE.

1547. BOORDE, *Seconde Booke of the Breviary of Health*, Fol. XXII. back. I had two lordes in cure that had distyllacion like to NATURE.

1635. GLAPTHORNE, *The Lady Mother*, i., 1. *Lovell.* The totall some of my blest deity Is the magazine of NATURE'S TREASURY.

*c.*1661. *Old Song*, 'The Maid a Bathing' [FARMER, *Merry Songs and Ballads* (1895), ii., 41]. Her legs she opened wide, My eyes I let down steal, Until that I espy'd Dame NATURE'S PRIVY-SEAL.

*c.*1707. DURFEY, *Pills to Purge*, iii., 213. I am rashly bent, To subject your Beauty To kind NATURE'S DUTY.

1766. RATTLE, 33. Love's meadow, happy Dick, With NATURE'S SCYTHE was mowing.

1827. *The Merry Muses*, 75. What words can paint the pleasure, That springs from love's soft powers, When NATURE'S TUFTED TREASURE Pours sweets in spermy showers.

NATURE'S GARB, *subs.* (common).—Nakedness.

ENGLISH SYNONYMS. To be abram; all face; in one's birthday suit; in buff; to cast one's skin; peeled; on the SHALLOW (*q.v.*).

FRENCH SYNONYMS. *Etre en couennes; s'habiller en sauvage.*

SPANISH SYNONYMS. *Pelota; poseta; en cuero.*

NAUGHTY, *adj.* (common).—1. Loose; obscene. Hence TO DO THE (GO, OR BE) NAUGHTY = to play the whore: shop and working girls in large towns sometimes say they work for their living, but DO THE NAUGHTY for their clothes; NAUGHTINESS = lewdness; THE NAUGHTY = the female *pudendum*; NAUGHTY-PACK (or DICKY-BIRD) = a wanton; NAUGHTY-HOUSE = a brothel; NAUGHTY-MAN = a whoremonger; NAUGHTY-DREAM = a lascivious dream.

1550. BANSLEY, *Pride of Women* [HAZLITT], *Early Pop. Poetry*, iv., 232. For wanton lasses and gallant women, And other lewde NOUGHTY PACKES.

[?]. *Apprehen, Three Witches.* Having two lewde daughters, no better than NAUGHTY PACKS.

1588. R. B[ERNARD], *Terence*, in English. Dost thou still speake ambiguously to me, thou NAUGHTY PACKE?

1603. SHAKSPEARE, *Measure for Measure*, ii., 1, 77. It is a NAUGHTY HOUSE.

1611. MIDDLETON and DECKER, *Roaring Girl* [DODSLEY, *Old Plays* (1874), vi., p. 20). She's a varlet—a NAUGHTY PACK.

1638. ROWLEY, *Shoemaker a Gent.* G. 4. Got a wench with childe, Thou NAUGHTY PACKE, thou hast undone thyself for ever.

1632. NABBES, *Covent Garden*, iii., 1. *Susan.* If ever I lie under any of them for the greene sickness. *Dorot.* Fie upon thee. *Susan.* Why, I doe not meane NAUGHTINES.

1673. WYCHERLEY, *The Gentleman Dancing Master*, i., 1. Ay; but to be delighted when we wake with a NAUGHTY DREAM, is a sin, aunt; and I am so very scrupulous, that I would as soon consent to a NAUGHTY MAN as to a NAUGHTY DREAM.

1675. CROWNE, *Country Wit*, i., 1. Most severely censuring all that are young and handsome TO BE NAUGHTY.

1708-10. Swift, *Polite Conversations*, i. *Miss.* She's no better than she should be. *Lady Smart.* Well . . . the world is very censorious: I never heard that she was a NAUGHTY-PACK.

1772. COLES, *Eng.-Lat. Dict.*, s.v

1869. HALL [LYNDSAY, *Satyre of the Three Estaitis* (E. E. T. S.), 498, Note]. The wealth of the prelates keeps our daughters unwedded. And some of them go NAUGHTY.

1891. N. GOULD, *Double Event*, p. 118. Lady Mayfield's history was pretty well-known, and the NAUGHTINESS surrounding her past life added a piquant flavour of excitement to the curiosity manifested on the occasion.

1896. COTSFORD DICK, *Ways of the World*, 12. J. is the juvenile maiden of forty, Who hopes it's not wrong, but she longs to be NAUGHTY. *Ibid.*, 18. French songs, that are *tant soit peu* NAUGHTY.

1898. LE QUEUX, *Scribes and Pharisees*, iv. If a poet isn't NAUGHTY now-a-days, nobody reads him.

2. (old).—Flash.

1864. VANCE, *Chickaleary Cove.* My downy kicksies . . . Built on a plan werry NAUGHTY.

NAUGHTY-PACK, *subs.* (old colloquial).—1. *See* NAUGHTY.

2. (modern).—A half reproving endearment of children.

NAVEL, *subs.* (old colloquial)—Combinations are: PROUD BELOW THE NAVEL = amorous, or wanton; NAVEL-TIED = inseparable; TO GALL ONE'S NAVEL = to wax wanton; TO WRIGGLE NAVELS = to copulate. See CUNTITCH; GREENS; PRICK-PROUD; RIDE.

1629. DAVENANT, *Albovine*, i. When I see her I grow PROUD BELOW THE NAVEL.

1767. RAY, *Proverbs* [BOHN], 52. They have tied their navels together, *i.e.*, they are inseparable companions.

NAVIGATOR, *subs.* (rhyming slang).—A potato; 'tatur. NAVIGATOR SCOT = a hot baked potato. Also NAV.

1893. EMERSON, *Signor Lippo*, XIV. As we were dining, in came North Eye carrying a dish from the bake-house, a sheep's knock over a dollop of NAVS.

NAVVY, *subs.* (old: now recognised).—An abbreviation of 'navigator': a term humorously applied to excavators employed in cutting and banking canals, making dykes to rivers, &c.

1848. C. KINGSLEY, *Yeast*, xl. There's enough of me to make a good NAVIGATOR if all trades fail.

1863. FAWCETT, *Pol. Econ.*, II., v. It was proved that one English NAVVY would do as much work as two French labourers.

1865. M. E. BRADDON, *Henry Dunbar*, xxvi. Great wooden barricades and mountains of uprooted paving-stones, amidst which sturdy NAVIGATORS disported themselves with spades and pickaxes . . . blocked the way.

1872. *Builder*, Aug. The class of men employed in earthwork were very peculiar, and very unlike the ordinary labourers of the country. They were called NAVVIES, from having been employed originally upon works of internal navigation, and they came from the Northern counties, especially Lancashire.

NAVY-OFFICE, *subs.* (old). — *See* quot.

1823. GROSE, *Vulg. Tongue* [EGAN], s.v. NAVY OFFICE. The Fleet Prison. Commander of the Fleet: the warden of the Fleet prison.

NAVY-SHERRY, *subs.* (American).—Man-of-war grog.

NAWPOST. MR. NAWPOST, *subs. phr.* (old).—'A foolish fellow.'—B. E. (*c.* 1696); GROSE (1785).

NAY, *verb.* (old colloquial).—To deny.

1589. GREENE, *Tullies Love*, Shepherd's Ode [GROSART, *Works* (1886), VII., 183]. Shee nise, Following fashion, NAYED him twise.

NAY-WORD, *subs.* (old).—'A common By-word or Proverb.'—B. E. (*c.* 1696); GROSE (1785).

NAZOLD, *subs.* (old colloquial).—A vain fool.

1629. *Optick Glasse of Humors*, 160. I know some selfe-conceited NAZOLD, and some jaundice-fac'd ideot, that uses to deprave and detract men's worthinesse, by their base obloquy.

NAZY, *See* NASE.

N.C. *phr.* (common).—'Enough said' (nuf ced); *Cf.* O.K.

NEAR (also **NIGH** and **NARROW**), *adj.* and *adv.* (colloquial).—1. Formerly careful, now (contemptuously) = stingy; 'close-fisted.' Fr. *serré*. Thus NEARNESS (*subs.*) = a parsimonious habit.

1591. SAVILE, *Tacitus*, Hist., I., 11. Now for NEARENESS Galba was noted extremelie.

1603. DEKKER, *Batchelors Banquet*, vii. The good man he goes euery way as NEERE as he can, and warilie containes himselfe within his bounds, casting vp what his yearely reuenues are, or what his gaime is by his profession, be it merchandize or other, and then what his expenses be.

1616. *The Merchants' Avizo* (quoted in *Notes and Queries*, 7 S., vi., 504). Also to be circumspect and NIGH in all his expenses.

1712. *Spectator*, No. 350. I have a very good affectionate father; but though very rich, yet so mighty NEAR, that he thinks much of the charges of my education. *Ibid.*, No. 402. I always thought he lived in a NEAR way.

1816. SCOTT, *Antiquary*, xi. I'll rather deal wi' yourself; for, though you're NEAR enough, yet Miss Grizel has an unco close grip.

1847. E. BRONTE, *Wuthering Heights*, xv., iii. The villagers affirmed Mr. Heathcliff was NEAR, and a cruel hard landlord to his tenants.

1849. DICKENS, *David Copperfield*, x. Mr. Barkis was something of a miser, or, as Peggotty dutifully expressed it, 'was a little NEAR.'

2. (colloquial). — On the left side: *cf.* OFF.

1823. BEE, *Dict. Turf*, s.v. NEAR. Postillions ride on the NEAR horse in England—the Russians drive on the off horse. *Ibid.* The left kidney being nearer the heart than the right one is called THE NEAR, the melt interposing between it and the ribs.

1859. *Art of Taming Horses*, 77. The motion will draw up the off leg into the same position as the NEAR leg.

NEARDY, *subs.* (provincial: North). —A person in authority—master, parent, foreman [HOTTEN].

NEAT, *adj.* (colloquial).—Unmixed with water; NAKED (*q.v.*); SHORT (*q.v.*); STRAIGHT (*q.v.*)

ENGLISH SYNONYMS. Aboriginal; 'ah! don't mingle'; as it came from its mother; bald-faced; bare-footed; clean from the still; cold-without; *in puris naturalibus*; in a state of nature; naked; neat as imported; neat; *simplex munditiis*; out of the barrel; plain; primitive; pure; raw; raw recruit; reverend; stark-naked; straight; stripped; unalloyed; unmarried; unsophisticated; uncorrupted; untempered; virgin; without a shirt.

1596. JONSON, *Every Man in his Humour*, iv., 4. We'll go to the Windmill; there we shall have a cup of NEAT grist, we call it.

1653. URQUHART, *Rabelais*, I., iii. [BOHN, I., 106]. He loved to drink NEAT, as much as any man that then was in the world.

1711. STEELE, *Spect.*, No. 264. The hogsheads of NEAT port came safe.

1742. FIELDING, *Joseph Andrews*, III., iii. My wines, which I never adulterated after their importation, and were sold as NEAT as they came over.

1751. SMOLLETT, *Peregrine Pickle*, viii. He . . . judged the cordial to be no other than NEAT Cogniac.

1851-61. MAYHEW, *Lond. Lab., etc.*, i., 397. I was obliged to drink rum; it wouldn't ha' done to ha' drunk the water NEAT, there was so many insects in it.

1876. BESANT and RICE, *Golden Butterfly*, i. I should take a small glass of brandy NEAT. Mind, no spoiling the effect with water.

AS NEAT AS (A BANDBOX, A NEW PIN, WAX, NINEPENCE), *phr.* (colloquial).—As neat as may be.

1884. HENLEY and STEVENSON, *Deacon Brodie*, iii., 3 (Three Plays, 36). We've nobbled him, AS NEAT AS NINEPENCE.

NEAT, BUT NOT GAUDY: AS THE DEVIL SAID WHEN HE PAINTED HIS BOTTOM RED, AND TIED UP HIS TAIL WITH SKY-BLUE RIBBON, *phr.* (common).—Spick and span; 'fresh as a daisy.'

1887. *Lippincott's Mag.*, July, p. 116. I have sent, I say, just such manuscript as editors call for, fair, clean, written on one side, not with a pencil, but with a good gold pen, stamps enclosed for return if declined; the whole thing 'NEAT, BUT NOT GAUDY, as the monkey said' on the memorable occasion 'when he painted his tail sky-blue.'

1892. *Society*, 6 Aug., p. 757, col. 1. Tennyson when in a rage is NEAT AND NOT GAUDY.

NEB (or **NIB**), *subs.* (old colloquial: now recognised).—1. Originally the bill of a bird; hence the face, mouth, or nose: specifically [B.E. (*c.* 1696), GROSE (1785), and MATSELL (1859)] of a woman.

*c.*1225. *Ancren Riwle*, 90. Scheau thi leoue NEB to me.

*c.*1696. B. E., *Dict. Cant. Crew*, s.v. NEB. She holds up her NEB: she turns up her mouth to be kissed.

2. (old colloquial: now recognised).—A pen.—B. E. (*c.* 1696); GROSE (1785).

3. (old).—The neck.

1535. COVERDALE, *Bible*, Gen. viii., 11. Beholde she had broken of a leaf of an olyue tre and bare it on her NEBB.

*d.*1622. BACON, *Nat. Hist.* Take a glasse with a belly and a long NEB.

NEBUCHADNEZZAR, *subs.* (venery). —1. The *penis*. [From its taste for GREENS (*q.v.*)]. *See* PRICK. TO TAKE NEBUCHADNEZZAR OUT TO GRASS = to copulate. *See* GREENS and RIDE.

2. (common).—A vegetarian.

NECESSARY, *subs.* (old).—1. A bedfellow. *See* TART.

2. (old colloquial).—A privy. Also NECESSARY HOUSE (or VAULT).

1609. FIELD, *Woman is a Weathercock*, iv., 2. She showed me to a NECESSARY VAULT. Within a closet in the chamber too.

1611. FIELD, *Amends for Ladies*, ii., 4. I met her in the NECESSARY HOUSE i' th' morning.

*c.*1786. MORRIS, *The Plenipotentiary*. For fancied delight . . . To frig in the school NECESSARY.

NECK, *verb* (old).—1. To hang: *see* LADDER. Whence, NECK-CLOTH (NECKINGER, NECKLACE, NECK-SQUEEZER, or NECKTIE) = a halter; NECKTIE-SOCIABLE = a hanging done by a Vigilance Committee; NECK-QUESTION = a hanging matter. something vital; NECK-VERSE, *see* quot, 1696; NECK-WEED = hemp, or GALLOWS-GRASS (*q.v.*); TO WEAR A HEMPEN NECKTIE, etc. = to be hanged.

*d.*1536. TYNDALE, *Workes*, 112. Yea set foorth a NECKEUERSE to saue all maner of trespassers, fro the feare of the sword.

1578. WHETSTONE, *Promos and Cass.*, iv., 4. And it behoves me to be secret, or else my NECK-VERSE cun [con].

1578. LYTE, Transl. of DODOEN'S *Hist. of Plantes*, fol. 72. Hempe is called in . . . English, NECKE-WEEDE, and Gallows grasse.

1578. *Hist. of K. Lier* [*Six Old Plays*, ii., 410]. Madam, I hope your grace will stand Betweene me and my NECK-VERSE, if I be Call'd in question for opening the king's letters.

1586. MARLOWE, *Jew of Malta*, iv., 4. Within forty foot of the gallows conning his NECK-VERSE.

1587. GREENE, *Menaphon* [GROSART, *Works* (1886), vi., 15]. A sort of shifting companions, that . . . busie themselues with the indeuors of Art, that could scarcelie latinize their NECKE-VERSE if they should haue neede.

1593. HARVEY, *Pierces Supererogation* [GROSART, *Works* (1884-5), ii., 281]. Thy penne is as very a Gentleman Foist, as any pick-purse liuing; and, that which is most miserable, not a more famous NECK-VERSE, than thy choice.

1630. TAYLOR, *Works* [NARES]. Some call it NECK-WEED, for it hath a tricke To cure the necke that's troubled with the crick.

1637. MASSINGER, *Guardian*, iv., 1. Have not your instruments To tune, when you should strike up, but twang it perfectly, As you would read your NECK-VERSE.

1647. BEAUMONT and FLETCHER, *Bonduca*, iv., 1. What's the crime committed That they wear NECKLACES?

1655. FULLER, *Ch. Hist.* These words, 'bread and cheese,' were their NECK-VERSE or shibboleth to distinguish them.

1659. *Clobery Div. Glimpses* [quoted in *Slang, Jargon, and Cant*]. The judge will read thy NECK-VERSE for thee here.

1662. *Rump Songs*, 'The Rump Dock't,' ii., 45. Instead of NECK-VERSE, Shall have it writ on his Herse, There hangs one of the King's Fryers.

1664. COTTON, *Virgil Travestie* [*Wks.* (1725), Bk. iv., p. 133]. Seeing the Rope Ty'd to the Beam i' th' Chamber-top, With neat alluring Noose, her sick grace E'en long'd to wear it for a NECKLACE.

1696. B. E., *Dict. Cant. Crew*, s.v. NECK-VERSE. A Favor (formerly) indulged to the Clergy only, but (now) to the Laity also, to mitigate the Rigor of the Law, as in Man-slaughter, etc. Reading a verse out of an old Manuscript Latin Psalter (tho' the Book now used by the Ordinary is the same Printed in an Old English Character) save the Criminal's Life. Nay now even the Women (by a late Act of Parliament) have (in a manner) the benefit of their Clergy, tho' hot so much as put to Read; for in such cases where the men are allow'd it; the Women are of course sizz'd in the Fist, without running the risque of a Halter by not Reading.

1710 *Old Song* (in *British Apollo*). If a clerk had been taken For stealing of bacon, For burglary, murder, or rape. If he could but rehearse (Well prompt) his NECK-VERSE, He never could fail to escape.

1725. *New Cant. Dict.*, s.v.

1755. JOHNSON, *Eng. Dict.*, s.v.

1785. GROSE, *Vulg Tongue*. The . . . NECK VERSE . . . was the first verse of the fifty-first psalm, *Miserere mei, etc.*

c. 1816. *Old Song*, 'The Night Before Larry was Stretched,' [Farmer, *Musa Pedestris* (1896), 79]. For the NECKCLOTH I don't care a button.

1823. GROSE, *Vulg. Tongue* [EGAN], s.v.

1859. MATSELL, *Vocabulum*, s.v.

1877. J. H. BEADLE, *Western Wilds* [BARTLETT]. He joined the Vigilantes, and had the pleasure of presiding at a NECKTIE SOCIABLE where two of the men who had robbed him were hanged.

1886. *Notes and Queries*, 7 S., ii., 98. NECKINGER is nothing more than neckerchief, but implies, I think, its proximity to a place of execution, the 'Devil's Neckerchief on the way to Redriffe,' which sign would further imply that it was euphemistic or slang for the gallows, the rope, or the hempen collar.

2. (old colloquial). — To swallow. Also TO WASH THE NECK.—BEE (1823).

NECK AND CROP, *adv.* (colloquial).—*See* quot., 1823.

1823. BEE, *Dict. Turf, etc.*, s.v. NECK AND CROP. Turn him out NECK AND CROP, is to push one forth all of a heap, down some steps or stairs being understood, so that the patient may pitch upon his neck (or head).

1836. DICKENS, *Pickwick* (1857), 125. When I was first pitched NECK AND CROP into the world to play at leap frog with its troubles, replied Sam.

1847. LYTTON, *Lucretia*, II., xx. I was a-thinking of turning her out NECK AN' CROP.

NECK OR NOTHING, *adv.* (colloquial).—At every risk; desperately.

1708-10. SWIFT, *Polite Conversations*, I. NECK OR NOTHING; come down or I'll fetch you down.

1731. FIELDING, *Grub Street Opera*, ii. 4. It is always NECK OR NOTHING with you.

1747. *Gentleman Instructed*, 526. The world is stock'd with NECK OR NOTHING; with men that will make over by retail an estate of a thousand pound per annum to a lawyer in expectation of being pleaded into another of two hundred.

1766. GARRICK, *Neck or Nothing* [Title].

1842. DICKENS, *American Notes*, iv., 38. And dashes on haphazard, pell-mell, NECK-OR-NOTHING, down the middle of the road.

1870. *Daily News*, 31 Mar. 'On Acrobats.' It must be literally NECK OR NOTHING with him, neck or 35s. per week.

1896. SALA, *London Up to Date*, 39. We resolved for once on a NECK-OR-NOTHING outing.

NECK AND NECK, *adv.* (colloquial.—Close; almost equal: as horses in a race.

1861-2. EARL STANHOPE, *Life of Pitt*, xxii. After two NECK AND NECK votes the same evening, the final numbers were 54 against 54.

1864. *London Society*, Oct., 389. Number 1 waltzes all round her affections, but No. 2 sings like 'ten cherubs,' and he finds her out at concerts, and comes to five o clock tea. It is NECK-AND-NECK between Nos. 1 and 2.

ON (or IN) THE NECK OF, *phr.* (colloquial).—Close upon, or behind.

1598. SHAKSPEARE, 1 *Henry IV.*, iv., 3. And IN THE NECK OF that tasked the whole state.

1775. ASH, *Dict.*, s.v., NECK . . . ON THE NECK, immediately after.

TO WIN (or LOSE) BY A NECK, *verb. phr.* (colloquial).—To win (or lose) by next to nothing.

TO BREAK THE NECK OF ANYTHING, *verb. phr.* (colloquial). —To get the worst part done: *see* quot.

1775. ASH, *Dict.*, s.v. NECK . . . TO BREAK THE NECK, to do more than half, to hinder from being done.

TO BE SHOT IN THE NECK, *verb. phr.* (American). — To be drunk. *See* DRINKS and SCREWED.

1855. *Brooklyn Journal*, 18 April. Mr. Schumacher defended his client by observing that some of the prisoners' attorneys got as often SHOT IN THE NECK as the Under-Sheriff did in the head.

UNABLE TO NECK IT, *phr.* (colloquial). — Lacking moral courage.

Also *see* SHUT.

NECK-BEEF. AS COARSE AS NECK-BEEF, *phr.* (common). — Very coarse; of the poorest quality. As *subs.* = a general synonym for coarseness.

NECK-OIL, *subs.* (old). — Drink; LAP (*q.v.*).

NECK-STAMPER, *subs. phr.* (old).—*See* quots.

*c.*1696. B. E., *Dict. Cant. Crew*, s.v. NECK-STAMPER. The Pot-Boy at a Tavern or Ale-house.

1785. GROSE, *Vulg. Tongue*, s.v. NECK-STAMPER, the boy who collects the pots belonging to an ale-house, sent out with beer to private houses.

NECTAR, *subs.* (common).—Drink ; LAP (*q.v.*).

NED, *subs.* (old). — A guinea : America a 10 dollar piece. HALF A NED = half a guinea or 5 dollar piece. Also NEDDY. *See* CANARY.

1754. *Discoveries of John Poulter*, 41. They ask change for a NED or six.

1789. PARKER, *Life's Painter*, 'The Happy Pair.' With spunk let's post our NEDDIES.

1859. MATSELL, *Vocabulum*, s.v. HALF A NED. A 5 dollar gold piece.

1882. MCCABE, *New York*, xxxiv., 509, s.v.

2. *See* NEDDY.

NEDASH, *phr.* (old).—*See* quot., 1823.

1819. VAUX, *Memoirs*, s.v.

1823. GROSE, *Vulg. Tongue* [EGAN], s.v. NEDASH, of no use. *Ibid.* Nothing.

NEDDY, *subs.* (colloquial).—1. An ass ; a MOKE (*q.v*). Also NED ; *see* MOKE.

1658. ROWLEY, TOURNEUR, etc., *Witch of Edmonton* [SOUTHEY'S *Commonplace Book*, ii., 447]. The ass was called *Tom*, as well as *Jack* and NEDDY.

1790. WOLCOT [P. Pindar], *Rowland for an Oliver* [*Wks.* (Dublin, 1794), ii., 412.] But, Peter, thou art mounted on a NEDDY : Or, in the London phrase—thou Dev'nshire Monkey, Thy Tegasus is nothing but a Donkey.

1818. EGAN, *Boxiana*, I., 35. Costermongers, in droves, were seen mounting their NEDDIES.

2. (colloquial). — A fool ; a DONKEY (*q.v.*). *See* BUFFLE and CABBAGE-HEAD.

1823. BEE, *Dict. Turf*, s.v. NEDDY —sometimes Ass-neger, other names for jackass—the living emblem of patience and long suffering.

1855. THACKERAY, *Newcomes*, i. All types of all characters march through all fables ; tremblers and boasters ; victims and bullies ; dupes and knaves ; long-eared NEDDIES, giving themselves leonine airs.

3. (Irish)—A large quantity ; plenty. Fr. *hugrement ; la foultitude* (*subs.*) ; and *gourdement*.

4. (thieves').—*See* quots. Fr. *un tourne-clef*.

ENGLISH SYNONYMS. Billy ; cosh ; colt.

1864. *Cornhill Mag.*, vi., 647. Pistols are seldom carried by them ; the weapon is generally a NEDDY or life-preserver.

1879. J. W. HORSLEY [*Macm. Mag.*, XL., 503]. He said, We shall want . . . the stick (iron-bar), and bring a NEDDIE (life-preserver) with you.

1884. *Referee*, 21 Dec., 1, 2. If husbands left off kicking their wives to death . . . and if the NEDDY and knuckle-duster went suddenly out of fashion.

1897. BREWER, *Phrase and Fable*, s.v. NEDDY. A life-preserver ; so called from one *Kennedy*, whose head was broken in St. Giles's by a poker.

5. *See* NED.

NED-FOOL, *subs.* (old). — A noisy idiot. *See* JACK (*subs.*, sense 8).

1600. NASHE, *Summer's Last Will* [DODSLEY, *Old Plays* (1874), viii., 61]. NED FOOL'S clothes are . . . perfumed with the beer he poured on me.

NED STOKES, *subs.* (old provincial). *See* quot.

1791. *Gent. Mag.*, lxi., 141. The Queen of Clubs is here [Lincs.] called *Queen Bess* . . . the Four of Spades, NED STOKES, for why I don't know.

NEEDFUL (THE), *subs.* (common).—Money. *See* RHINO.

1771. FOOTE, *Maid of Bath*, ii. Then I will straight set about getting THE NEEDFUL.

1821. EGAN, *Life in London*, I., iv. The diamond necklace . . . did not operate more strongly . . . than the poor woman's flat-iron to raise THE NEEDFUL.

1836. *Comic Almanack*, 45, 'Transfer day.' Needy men THE NEEDFUL need.

1836. DICKENS, *Pickwick*, xxxviii. I *passed*, soon after that precious party, and my friends came down with THE NEEDFUL for this business.

1857. HOOD, *Pen and Pencil Pictures*, 153. Let me have the pleasure of lending an old college-mate some of THE NEEDFUL !

1864. *Eton School Days*, i., 3. Good-bye. Here's a supply of THE NEEDFUL.

1889. *Lic. Vict. Gaz.*, 8 Feb. Searching for THE NEEDFUL to satisfy so just a demand.

1900. *Free Lance*, 6 Oct., 20, 1. I am glad to take anything that comes along, even if it is only ten per. Someone had to get THE NEEDFUL, you know.

NEEDHAM. ON THE HIGH-ROAD to NEEDHHAM, *phr.* (old). —*See* quot. *Cf.* PECKHAM, LAND OF NOD, BEDFORDSHIRE, Etc.

1670. RAY, *Proverbs* [BOHN], 221. You are ON THE HIGH-WAY TO NEEDHAM. Needham is a market-town in this county [Suffolk] ; according to the wit of the vulgar, they are said to be in the highway thither which do hasten to poverty.

NEEDLE, *subs.* (old). — 1. A sharper ; a thief.

1821. EGAN, *Life in London*, 138. Amongst the NEEDLES at the West end of the town.

2. (venery).—The *penis : see* PRICK. Whence NEEDLE-WOMAN = a harlot (*see* quot. 1849).

1632. NABBES, *Covent Garden*, i., 6. *Susan.* The loadstone of my heart . . . pointing still to the North of your love. *Jeffery.* Indeed, mistris, 'tis a cold corner ; pray turne it to the South, and let my NEEDLE run in your DIALL.

*c.*1680. EARL OF DORSET, *Poems*, 'On Dolly Chamberlain.' In revenge I will stitch Up the hole next her breech, With a NEEDLE as long as my arm.

*d.*1680. ROCHESTER, *Poems*, 'A Satire which the King took out of his Pocket.' The seaman's NEEDLE nimbly points the pole ; But thine still turns to ev'ry craving hole.

*c.*1720. DURFEY, *Pills to Purge*, vi., 91. But if by chance a Flaw I find, In dressing of the Leather ; I straightway whip my NEEDLE out, And I tack 'em close together.

1849. CARLYLE, *Nigger Question* [Cent. ed. xxix. 366]. We have thirty thousand distressed NEEDLEWOMEN . . . who cannot sew at all . . . on the street with five hungry senses.

Verb. (common).—1. To annoy ; to irritate ; TO RILE (*q.v.*). TO GIVE (or GET) THE NEEDLE = to annoy (or be annoyed).

1881. G. R. SIMS, *Dagonet Ballads* (*Polly*). There, he's off ! the young warmint, he's NEEDLED.

1884. *Daily Telegraph*, 4 Sept., 2, 2. I felt a bit NEEDLED at the sort of sneering way Teedy had spoken.

1887. *Punch*, 30 July, 45. It GIVE 'im THE NEEDLE in course, being left in the lurch in this way.

1889. *Sporting Times*, 3 Aug., 3, 1. He's seen a girl, one of his old flames, pass the door. He doesn't want to NEEDLE her, as she's a good little sort.

1891. *Lic. Vict. Gaz.*, 3 April. This seemed to NEEDLE Gideon, who, determined not to be outdone, offered 900 to 100 on the field.

1897. *Evening Standard*, 24 Dec., 4, 5. When one, or both, of two proficient antagonists at any sport have TAKEN THE NEEDLE . . . the result, nine times out of ten, is an improvement in the exhibition.

1898. *Illustrated Bits*, Xmas No., 50. Then Maudie GETS THE NEEDLE, and she jumps across the floor, And ketches me a fair ole rousin' socker on the jore.

2. (old).—To haggle over a bargain.—VAUX (1819).

Also *see* SPANISH NEEDLE; ST. PETER'S NEEDLE, Knight.

NEEDLE-AND-THREAD, *subs. phr.* (rhyming).—Bread.

NEEDLE-BOOK (or -CASE), *subs.* (venery).—The female *pudendum: see* MONOSYLLABLE.

NEEDLE-DODGER, *subs.* (common). —A dress-maker.

NEEDLE - POINT, *subs.* (old).— A sharper : also NEEDLE-POINTER.—B.E. (*c.* 1696); GROSE (1785) ; VAUX (1819) ; *Ency. Dict.* (1885).

NEEDY - MIZZLER (or **NEEDY**), *subs.* (tramps').—*See* quot. 1823. Hence NEEDY-MIZZLING.

1819. VAUX, *Memoirs*, s.v.

1823. GROSE, *Vulg. Tongue* [EGAN], s.v. NEEDY MIZZLER. A poor ragged object of either sex.

1834. AINSWORTH, *Rookwood*, III., v. Though a NEEDY MIZZLER mysel, I likes to see a cove vot's vel dressed.

1868. *Temple Bar*, xxiv., 536. His game is NEEDY-MIZZLING. He'll go without a shirt, perhaps, and beg one from house to house. *Ibid.* NEEDY-MIZZLERS, mumpers, shallow-coves.

1893. EMERSON, *Signor Lippo*, XIV. All I get is my kip and a clean mill tog, a pair of pollies and a stoock, and what few medazas I can make out of the lodgers and NEEDIES.

NEEL, *adj.* (back - slang). — Lean.

NE'ER - BE - LICKIT, *subs.* (colloquial Scots).—*See* quot.

1885. *Encycl. Dict.*, s.v. NE'ER-BE-LICKIT. Nothing which could be licked by a dog or cat ; nothing whatever.

NE'ER - DO - WELL, *subs.* (colloquial.—*See* quot.

1885. *Encycl. Dict.*, s.v. NE'ER-DO-WELL. One who is never likely to do well.

Adj. (colloquial).—Incorrigible.

1898. LE QUEUX, *Scribes and Pharisees*, v. His two cousins . . . looked on the NE'ER-DO-WELL student as an interloper.

NEERGS, *subs.* (back - slang). — Greens.

NEGGLEDIGEE, *subs.* (old). — *See* quot.

1823. GROSE, *Vulg. Tongue*, [EGAN], s.v. NEGLIGEE. A woman's undressed gown, vulgarly termed a NEGGLEDIGEE.

NEGOTIATE, *verb.* (colloquial).— To contrive ; to accomplish.

1891. *Sporting Life*, 18 Mar. They pulled themselves together, and ultimately NEGOTIATED Hammersmith Bridge in better style.

1891. *Daily Chronicle*, 20 Mar. The other two—who also NEGOTIATED the same distance, namely, a mile and a half—went together as usual.

1892. MILLIKEN, *'Arry Ballads*, 32. To see him NEGOTIATE corners was one of the loveliest sights.

1897. KENNARD, *Girl in Brown Habit*, ii. She had NEGOTIATED the obstacle all right, but if we had happened to come to grief, I should have blamed myself a little.

NEGRO, *subs.* (old : now recognised).—A black man ; a slave.— GROSE (1785).

NEGRO-HEAD, *subs.* (nautical).— A brown loaf.—GROSE (1796).

NEGRO - NOS'D, *adj.* (old : now recognised).—Flat-nosed.—B. E. (*c.* 1696).

NEIGHBOURLY, *adj.* (old : now recognised).—Friendly; obliging. —*Dict. Cant. Crew* (1696).

NEMAN, *subs.* (American thieves'). —Stealing.—MATSELL (1859).

NENTI, *adv.* (circus).—Nothing : *cf.* NANTIE.

1893. EMERSON, *Signor Lippo*, XX. I gets sixteen bob a week . . . and I get my kip for NENTI here for helping old Blower tidy up.

NEPHEW, *subs.* (common). — The illegitimate son of a priest : *see* NIECE.

1847. RUXTON, *Far West*, 145. They were probably his nieces and NEPHEWS— a class of relations often possessed in numbers by priests and monks.

NEPTUNE'S BODYGUARD, *subs. phr.* (military). — The Royal Marines. Also "The Little Grenadiers," "The Jollies," "The Globe Rangers," and "The Admiral's Regiment."

NERVE, *subs.* (old). — 1. *See* quot.

1753. *Adventurer*, No. 98. I am, in short, one of those heroic Adventurers, who have thought proper to distinguish themselves by the titles of Buck, Blood, and NERVE.

2. (common). — Impudence ; cheek.

1899. *Critic*, 21 Jan., 12, 2. How Messrs Gordon and Levett can have the NERVE to refer to the evidence given at the Royal Commission on Money-lending in one sentence and in the other boldly proclaim that they charge from 60 to 108 per cent. per annum interest to borrowers, passes my comprehension.

NERVOUS-CANE, *subs. phr.* (venery). —The *penis* (URQUHART). For synonyms, *see* CREAMSTICK, PRICK.

NESCIO. TO SPORT A NESCIO. *verb. phr.*, 1823 (old University). —*See* quot.

*b.*1670. J. HACKET, *Abp. Williams*, II., 94, 97 (1693) But as our Cambridge term is, he was staid with NESCIO'S.

1823. GROSE, *Vulg. Tongue* [EGAN], s.v. NESCIO. He SPORTS A NESCIO ; he pretends not to understand anything. After the senate-house examination for degrees, the students proceed to the schools to be questioned by the proctor. According to custom immemorial the answers must be NESCIO. The following is a translated specimen : *Q.* What is your name? *A.* I do not know. *Q.* What is the name of this University? *A.* I do not know. *Q.* Who was your father? *A.* I do not know. The last is probably the only true answer of the three.

NEST, *subs.* (venery : American).—1. The female *pudendum :* also THE NEST IN THE BUSH : *see* MONOSYLLABLE. Hence, TO HAVE AN EGG IN THE NEST = to be pregnant; NEST-HIDING = illicit intercourse (attributed to Henry Ward Beecher); NEST-HUNTING = GROUSING (*q.v.*) or fornicating.

1782. STEVENS, *Songs Comic and Satyrical*, 124. Here's the NEST in that bush, and the bird-nesting lover.

*d.*1796. BURNS, *The Court of Equity*, [FARMER, *Merry Songs and Ballads* (1897), iv., 284]. And yet, ye loon, ye still protest, Ye never herried Maggy's NEST.

2. in *pl.* (thieves').—*See* quot.

1851-61. H. MAYHEW, *London Lab.*, *etc.*, i., 231. List of patterer's words. NESTS—Varieties.

3. (colloquial).—A place : as of residence ; a centre : as of activity ; a gang : as of thieves.

1595. SHAKSPEARE, *Romeo and Juliet*, v., 3. Come from that NEST of death.

1596. SPENSER, *Fairie Queene*, IV., v., 32. They spied a little cottage, like some poor man's NEST.

1604. SHAKSPEARE, *Winter's Tale*, ii., 3. A NEST of traitors.

1728. BAILEY, *Dict.*, NEST . . . an Harbour for Thieves and Pirates.

1847. TENNYSON, *Princess*, v., 416. We seem a NEST of traitors—none to trust.

Verb. (old).—To defecate.

1670. *Mod. Act. Scotland.* TO NEST upon the stairs.

See also FEATHER.

NEST-COCK (NESCOCK or NESTLE-COCK), *subs.* (colloquial).—*See* quot. 1775.

1662. FULLER, *Worthies*, ii., 55. One . . . made a wanton or a NESTLE COCK of.

1775. ASH, *Dict.*, s.v. NESTCOCK (*a Cant word*). A tenderling, a fondling.

1859. MATSELL, *Vocabulum*, s.v.

NEST-EGG, *subs.* (colloquial). — Money saved ; a little hoard.

NESTLING, *subs.* (old: now recognised).—*See* quot. 1696.

*c.*1696. B. E., *Dict. Cant. Crew*, s.v. NESTLING, Canary-Birds brought up by Hand.

1728. BAILEY, Dict., s.v.

TO KEEP A NESTLING, *verb. phr.* (old).—*See* quot.

*c.*1696. B. E., *Dict. Cant. Crew*, s.v. NESTLING. What a NESTLING you keep, how restless and uneasy you are.

NESTOR, *subs.* (Winchester College).—An undersized boy.

NET. ALL IS FISH THAT COMES TO NET, *phr.* (colloquial).—All serves the purpose.

1670. RAY, *Proverbs* [BOHN], 160, s.v.

1830. BUCKSTONE, *Wreck Ashore*, ii., 4. We are not on one of our Spanish Islands, where ALL'S FISH THAT COMES TO NET.

NETGEN, *subs.* (back-slang).—Half a sovereign: *see* RHINO [NET=ten+GEN (*q.v.*)=a shilling].

NETHER-END (or -EYE), *subs.* (venery).—The female *pudendum*: *see* MONOSYLLABLE. Whence NETHER-EYEBROWS (WHISKERS or LASHES)=the pubic hair; NETHER-LIPS=the *labia majora*; NETHER-WORK=groping or copulation.

1383. CHAUCER, *Cant. Tales*, Miller's Tale, 666 [SKEAT (1895), I., v., 111]. Thus swyved was the carpenteres wyf, For al his keping and his Ialousye; and Absolon hath kist hir NETHER YE.

*d.*1749. ROBERTSON OF STRUAN, *Poems*, 126. At th'upper End she Cracks her Nuts, While at the NETHER END her Honour.

NETHERLANDS (THE), *subs.* (venery).—A man's or woman's underparts.

NETTLE, *verb.* (common).—To annoy; to provoke; TO RILE (*q.v.*); TO NEEDLE (*q.v.*). TO HAVE PISSED ON A NETTLE=to be peevish or out of temper; NETTLED=(1) annoyed, and (2) afflicted (Amer. MATSELL, 1859); NETTLER=a SPOIL-TEMPER (*q.v.*).—B.E. (*c.* 1696); GROSE (1785).

*a.*1592. GREENE, *George a Greene*, 397 [GROSART, *Works* (1886), xiv., 139]. There are few fellowes in our parish so NETTLED with loue as I haue bene of late.

1625. MASSINGER, *Parliament of Love*, iii., 1. *Nov.* We have NETTLED him. *Peri.* Had we stung him to death, it were but justice.

1641. MILTON, *Animad. upon the Remons. Def., etc.* But these are the NETTLERS, these are the blabbing books that tell.

1767. FAWKES, *Theocritus*, Idyl 5. I've NETTLED somebody full sore.

1847. TENNYSON, *Princess*, i., 161. I, tho' NETTLED that he seem'd to slur . . . Our formal compact.

1851-61. MAYHEW, *Lond. Lab.*, iii., 221. Of course he was NETTLED.

1895. MARRIOTT-WATSON [*New Review*, July 2]. As for that, I said, for I was NETTLED at his sneering.

NETTLE IN, DOCK OUT, *phr.* (old).—Fickleness of purpose; thing after thing; place after place.

1369. CHAUCER, *Troi. and Cres.*, v. NETTLE IN, DOCK OUT, now this, now that, Pandare?

*c.*1696, B. E., *Dict. Cant. Crew*, s.v. NETTLED. IN DOCK, OUT NETTLE, upon the change of Places, when one is no sooner out, but another is in his Place.

Also *see* ROSE.

NETTLE-BED, *subs.* (children's).—*See* quot.: *cf.* PARSLEY-BED and GOOSEBERRY-BUSH: *see* MONOSYLLABLE.

1875. *Notes and Queries*, 5 S., iii., 'Babies in Folk-lore.' In England every little girl knows that male babies come from the NETTLE-BED, and the female ones from the parsley-bed.

NEVELE, *adj.* (back-slang).—Eleven. Thus, NEVELE GEN, eleven shillings; NEVELE YANNEPS, elevenpence.

NEVER. NEVER- (or -NARE) -A-FACE-BUT-HIS-OWN, *phr.* (old).—*See* quot.

*c.*1696, B. E., *Dict. Cant. Crew*, s.v. NARE-A-FACE-BUT-HIS-OWN, Not a Penny in his Pocket.

NEVER-FEAR, *subs. phr.* (rhyming).—Beer: *see* DRINKS and SWIPES.

NEVER-NEVER COUNTRY, *subs. phr.* (Australian).—The confines of civilization: specifically (in Queensland) the occupied pastoral land furthest from the more settled districts.

1890. NISBET *Bail up!* An Australian hot wind in the great NEVER-NEVER LAND.

1895. *Pall Mall Gaz.*, 15 Aug. 3, 1. 'Yarns' about traces of the party have often been told by bushmen from the NEVER-NEVER COUNTRY, but nothing has ever been recovered from the wide wastelands of the interior to back up the romantic stories.

2. (Australian).—The future life; heaven.

1888. BOLDREWOOD, *Robbery Under Arms*, 2. I want to die and go with him to the NEVER-NEVER COUNTRY parson tells us about up there!

NEVER-OUT (THE), *subs.* (venery).—The female *pudendum*: *see* MONOSYLLABLE.

NEVER-TOO-LATE-TO-MEND-SHOP, *subs. phr.* (tailors').—A repairing tailor's.

NEVER-WAG MAN-OF-WAR, *subs. phr.* (old).—The Fleet Prison: *see* CAGE.

1821. EGAN, *Life in London*, II., viii. Bob Logic . . . will be happy to see them in Freshwater Bay, on board the NEVER-WAG MAN-OF-WAR, on the homeward-bound station.

NEVER-WASER, *subs.* (circus).=*See* quot.

1891. *Sportsman*, 1 April. He is one of the 'has beens' or else one of the NEVER WASERS as Dan Rice, the circus man, always called ambitious counterfeits.

NEVIS, *adj.* (back-slang).—Seven. Thus, NEVIS-GEN=seven shillings; NEVIS-STRETCH=seven year's hard; NEVIS-YANNEPS=sevenpence.

NEW. TO NEW COLLAR AND CUFF *verb. phr.* (clerical).—To furbish up an old sermon.

NEW-BILLINGSGATE, *subs. phr.* (Stock Exchange).—*See* GORGONZOLA HALL.

1887. ATKIN, *House Scraps*. Gorgonzola Hall got changed into NEW BILLINGSGATE.

NEW-BUG, *subs. phr.* (Marlborough School).—A new boy.

NEWCASTLE. TO CARRY (or SEND) COALS TO NEWCASTLE, *verb. phr.* (colloquial).—To undertake a work of supererogation; *see* OWL. [Newcastle is a large coal centre].

1662. *Arsy Versy*, x. Stanza [*Rump songs* (1874), II., 48]. So that their fewel upon him to spend, What was it but COALS TO NEWCASTLE TO SEND.

1670. RAY, *Proverbs* [BOHN], 154, s.v.

1813. BYRON, *Occasional Verses* [HENLEY, Works, I. 434]. When COALS TO NEWCASTLE ARE CARRIED, and owls sent to Athens as wonders.

NEW-CHUM, *subs.* (Australian).—A new arrival: *cf.* CURRENCY, STERLING and LIME-JUICE.

1887. *All the Year Round*, 30 July, 66. The NEW CHUM generally betrays his character by the newer cut of his clothes, the shape and brilliance of his hat . . . and by the topics of his conversation.

1889. *Star*, 2 Jan. We quickly rolled up our blankets into swags, somewhat 'tokening' of the NEW CHUM, and started on the road to Castlemaine.

NEWCOME, *subs.* (common).—A new arrival; a fresh face: as a freshman at college; a new midshipman; a new baby. Also JOHNNIE NEWCOME.

1821. EGAN, *Life in London, Nocturnal Hells*. There were some NEWCOMES. [The name given to any new faces or persons among the usual visitants in a gambling house].

1823. BEE, *Dict. Turf, etc.*, s.v. NEWCOME JOHNNY.

NEW-DROP, *subs.* (old).—*See* quot.

1788. GROSE, *Vulg. Tongue*, s.v. NEW DROP. The scaffold used at Newgate for hanging criminals; which dropping down, leaves them suspended. By this improvement, the use of that vulgar vehicle, a cart, is entirely left off.

NEW ENGLAND OF THE WEST, *subs. phr.* (American).—The State of Minnesota. [Many New Englanders settled there].

NEWGATE, *subs.* (old).—A gaol: specifically the prison for the City of London: *see* quots. 1592 and 1823. Also NEWMAN'S HOTEL (or TEA-GARDENS: MAN'S (Old Cant.)=a place). Hence, NEWGATE-BIRD (or NEWGATE-NIGHTINGALE = a thief, sharper, or gaol-bird; NEWGATE (or TYBURN) COLLAR, FRINGE, or FRILL=a collar-like beard worn under the chin; NEWGATE-FRISK = a hanging; NEWGATE-KNOCKER = a lock of hair like the figure 6, twisted from the temple back towards the ear (chiefly in vogue 1840-50—*see* AGGERAWATORS); NEWGATE-RING = moustache and beard as one, without whiskers; NEWGATE-SAINT = a condemned criminal; TO DANCE THE NEWGATE-HORNPIPE=to be hanged; NEWGATE-SOLICITOR= a pettifogging attorney; BORN ON NEWGATE-STEPS=of thievish origin; AS BLACK AS NEWGATE = very black; NEWGATE SEIZE ME= 'the gaol be my portion'; NEWMAN'S-LIFT=the gallows.

*c.*1531. COPLAND, *Hyeway to Spyttelhous* [HAZLITT, *Pop. Poet*, iv., 41]. By my fayth, NYGHTYNGALES OF NEWGATE: These be they that dayly walkes and jettes.

1592. NASH, *Pierce Penilesse* . . . NEWGATE . . . a common name for all prisons as *homo* is a common name for a man or woman.

1598. SHAKSPEARE, I *Henry IV.*, iii., 3. Must we all march? Yes, two and two, NEWGATE FASHION.

1607. DEKKER, *Jests* [GROSART, *Works* (1886), ii., 343]. Our NEWGATE-BIRD . . . spreading his Dragon-like wings, . . . beheld a thousand Synnes.

1677. THOMAS OTWAY, *Cheats of Scapin*, i., 1. NEWGATE-BIRD . . . what a trick hast thou played me in my absence.

1732. OZELL, *Miser*, i., 3. Out of my House, thou sworn Master-Catpurse, true NEWGATE-BIRD.

1823. GROSE, *Vulg. Tongue* [EGAN], s.v. NEWMAN'S-HOTEL.

1823. BEE, *Dict. Turf, etc.*, s.v. NEWGATE. A house of entertainment for rogues of every description. . . . The name itself has been . . . naturalized in Dubliu, as also in Manchester, where the sessions-house is modernized into New Bailey. The old building . . . stood across the entrance to Newgate Street; and probably had its name from . . . having been the newest of all the gates that then choked up the accesses to the metropolis. *Ibid.* NEWGATE STEPS, figurative for a low or thievish origin. Before 1780, these steps . . . were much frequented by rogues and w—s connected with the inmates of that place: some might be said to have received their education there, if not their birth. *Ibid.* AS BLACK AS NEWGATE is said of a street Lady's lowering countenance, or of her muslin-dress, when either is changed from the natural serene. *Ibid.* NEWGATE SEIZE ME IF I DO, THERE NOW! is an asseveration of the most binding nature, when both parties may be following the same course of life.

1829. MAGINN, *The Pickpocket's Chaunt* [FARMER, *Musa Pedestris* (1896), 105], xiii. And we shall caper a-heel and toeing A NEWGATE HORNPIPE some fine day.

1851-61. MAYHEW, *Lon. Lab.*, I., 36. As for the hair, they [coster-lads] say it ought to be long in front, and done in figure-six curls or twisted back to the ear, NEWGATE KNOCKER style.

1867. SMYTH, *Word Book*, 497, s.v. NEWGATE BIRD. The men sent on board ships from prisons; but the term has also been immemorially used, as applied to some of the *Dragon's* men in the voyage of Sir Thomas Roe to Surat, 1615.

1868. BRADDON, *Trail of the Serpent*, VI., vi. Two greasy locks of hair carefully twisted into limp curls . . . known to his poetically and figuratively-disposed friends as NEWGATE KNOCKERS.

1871. *Echo*, 11 Dec. The greasy and begrimed wide-awake, which they wear pushed back, for the display of a philosopher's brow, and a NEWGATE KNOCKER of ambitious dimensions and oleaginous rigidity.

1885. *Cornhill Mag.*, Sept., 259. Some of them beardless, others with a fringe of hair around their faces, such as the English call a NEWGATE FRILL.

1888. *Daily News*, 1 Dec. Visions of Bill Sykes, with threatening look and carefully-trained NEWGATE KNOCKERS, are almost inevitably suggested in the mind of the recipient.

1892. *Tit Bits*, 19 March, 421, 2. The frill round the chin . . . called the NEWGATE FRILL, and the *sweep's frill*, would, I imagine, have made the Antinous, or the Apollo Belvedere, look undignified and slovenly.

Verb. (old).—To imprison.

1740. NORTH, *Exam.*, 258. Soon after this he was taken up and NEWGATED.

NEW GUINEA, *subs. phr.* (Oxford Univ.).—*See* quot.

1823. GROSE, *Vulg. Tongue* [EGAN], s.v. NEW GUINEA. First possession of income.

NEW-HAT, *subs.* (cheap-jacks').—*See* quot.

1876. HINDLEY, *Adventures of a Cheap Jack*, 104. I'll lay you a NEW HAT (*i.e.*, a guinea).

NEW JERUSALEM. *See* CUBITOPOLIS.

NEWLAND. *See* ABRAHAM NEWLAND.

NEW LIGHT, *subs. phr.* (old).—1. *See* quot.

1823. GROSE, *Vulg. Tongue* [EGAN], s.v. NEW LIGHT. One of the NEW LIGHT; a methodist; [one] who attends the gaols to assist villains in evading justice.

2. (American thieves').—New money.—MATSELL (1859).

NEWMARKET, *subs.* (tossing).—*See* quots. 1823 and 1842: *cf.* SUDDEN DEATH.

1823. BEE, *Dict. Turf, etc.*, s.v. NEWMARKET; best two in three as a phrase is erroneous; races are not decided there by the best in three, as prevails elsewhere.

1840. DICKENS, *Old Curiosity Shop*, xxxvi. He imparted to her the mystery of going the odd man or plain NEWMARKET for fruit, ginger-beer, baked potatoes, or even a modest quencher.

*b.*1842. MAGINN, *Bob Burke's Duel*. . . . Which is it to be—two out of three, as at NEWMARKET, or the first toss to decide? Sudden death, said I, and there will soon be an end of it.

NEWMARKET-HEATH COMMISSIONER, *subs. phr.* (old).—A highwayman; a ROAD-AGENT (*q.v.*).

NEW PIN. SMART (BRIGHT, NEAT, or NICE) AS A NEW PIN, *phr.* (colloquial).—First-class.

1893. EMERSON, *Signor Lippo*, xxii. One day when I came into the kitchen, there sat Jack looking as SMART AS A NEW PIN.

NEW PLATES. *See* PLATES.

NEWS. TELL ME NEWS! *phr.* (colloquial).—A retort to a stale jest or CHESTNUT (*q.v.*); usually preceded by 'that's ancient history': *cf.* QUEEN ANNE.

1708-10. SWIFT, *Polite Conversations*, i. *Miss.* Lord! Mr. *Neverout*, you are as pert as a Pearmonger this Morning. *Neverout.* Indeed, Miss, you are very handsome. *Miss.* Poh! I know that already; TELL ME NEWS.

NEW SETTLEMENTS, *subs. phr.* (old Oxford Univ.).—*See* quot.

1823. GROSE, *Vulg. Tongue* [EGAN], s.v. NEW SETTLEMENTS, Final reckoning.

NEWTOWN-PIPPIN, *subs.* (common). —A cigar: *see* WEED.

NEWY, *subs.* (Winchester College). —The 'cad' paid to look after the canvas tent in 'Commoner' field.

NEW YORK GRAB, *subs. phr.* (American).—

1858. W. W. PRATT, *Ten Nights in a Bar-room*, i., 1. First throw, or NEW YORK GRAB?

N.F., *subs.* (printers').—A knowing tradesman. [An abbreviation of 'no flies'].

N.G., *phr.* (common).—'No go'; 'no good'; of no avail.

1888. *Cincinnatti Weekly Gazette*, 22 Feb. His claim was N.G.

N.H. (That is, NORFOLK HOWARD), *subs. phr.* (common).—A bug. [From one Bugg who, it is said, so changed his name in 1863].

NIAS, *subs.* (old).—A simpleton. [From the Fr. *niais*].

1616. BEN JONSON, *The Devil's an Ass*, i., 3. Laugh'd at, sweet bird! Is that the scruple? come, come, Thou art a NIAISE.

NIB (or **NIB-COVE**), *subs.* (beggars'). —1. A gentleman. Whence HALF-NIBS = one who apes gentility (Fr. *un herz*); NIBLIKE (or NIBSOME) = gentlemanly; NIBSOMEST-CRIBS = the best houses. —VAUX (1819); GROSE (1823). *Cf.* NIBS.

1834. AINSWORTH, *Rookwood*, III., v. He's a rank NIB. *Ibid.* And ne'er was there seen such a dashing prig, . . . All my togs were SO NIBLIKE.

1839. REYNOLDS, *Pickwick Abroad*, 223. Betray his pals in a NIBSOME game.

2. *See* NEB.

3. (printers').—A fool.

Verb. (old).—1. To catch; to arrest; to NAB (*q.v.*). —VAUX (1819); GOOSE (1823).

2. *See* NIBBLE.

NIBBLE, *verb.* (old).—1. To catch; to steal. Also to cheat. Whence NIBBLER (or NIBBING-CULL) = a petty thief or fraudulent dealer: *see* quot., 1819.

1608. MIDDLETON, *Trick to Catch the Old One*, i., 4. The rogue has spied me now: he NIBBLED me finely once.

1775. *Old Song* [FARMER, *Musa Pedestris* (1396), 54]. For NIBBING CULLS I always hate.

1819. VAUX, *Memoirs*, s.v. NIBBLE, to pilfer trifling articles, not having spirit to touch anything of consequence.

1823. BEE, *Dict. Turf, etc.*, s.v. NIBBLE. I only NIBBLED half a bull for my regulars [=I only got a half-crown for my share]. There now I feel you NIBBLING: said by thieves when they are teaching each other to pick pockets.

1823. GROSE, *Vulg. Tongue* [EGAN], s.v. NIBBLER. A pilferer, or petty thief.

1843. W. T. MONCRIEFF, *The Scamps of London*, iii., 1. You are spliced—NIBBLED at last—well, I wish you joy.

2. (venery).—To copulate. Also TO DO A NIBBLE. *See* GREENS and RIDE.

3. (colloquial).—To consider a bargain, or an opportunity, eagerly but carefully: as a fish considers bait.

TO GET A NIBBLE, *verb. phr.* (tailors').—To get an easy job.

NIBS (or **NABS**), *subs.* (colloquial).— Self: HIS NIBS = the person referred to; YOUR NIBS = yourself; MY NIBS = myself—'dis child.' Also = 'friend,' 'boy,' &c., in addressing a person. Also NIBSO. *Cf.* WATCH.

1819. VAUX, *Memoirs*, s.v. YOUR NABS, yourself; an emphatical term used in speaking to another person.

1821. D. HAGGART, *Life*, 'Glossary,' p. 172, s.v.

1851-61. H. MAYHEW, *London Lab.*, iii. 136. He had nanti-vampo, and YOUR NIBS must fake it; which means,—We have no clown, and you must do it.

1890. *Punch*, 22 Feb. So Robert, MY NABS, it's no go.

1892. *Sporting Times*, 29 Oct. For out of HIS NIBS I had taken a rise.

1893. MILLIKEN, *'Arry Ballads*, 23. That nicked 'er, MY NIBS.

1893. CHEVALIER, 'Our Little Nipper.' So in we goes, followed by 'IS NIBS.

NICE, *adj.* and *adv.* (old: still colloquial).—1. Simple; witless.

1297. *Robert of Gloucester*, 106. He was NYCE and knowthe no wisdome.

1350. *William of Palerne* (E. E. T. S.), i., 491. Now witterly ich am vn-wis wonderliche NYCE.

1383. CHAUCER, *Wife of Bath's Tale*, i., 82. But seye that we be wyse, and no-thing NYCE.

1430. *Ye Develis Perlament and Hymns to Virgin* (E. E. T. S.), 54. Whi were thou so NYCE to leete him go?

*c.*1696. B. E., *Dict. Cant. Crew*, s.v. NICE. More NICE than wise; a Sir Courtly NICE, a silly, empty, gay, foolish Fellow.

1725. *New Cant. Dict.*, s.v.

2. (old: still colloquial).—*See* quot., 1696, and *cf.* Swift's definition of a 'NICE man' as 'a man of nasty ideas.'

1543. *Book of Precedence* (E. E. T. S., extra series), i., 66. Be not to noyous, to NYCE, ne to nefangle.

*c.*1696. B. E., *Dict. Cant. Crew*, s.v. NICE; squeamish, precise.

1775. SHERIDAN, *Rivals*, ii., 2. Nay, Sir Lucius, I thought you wa'n't rich enough to be so NICE.

1818. GREVILLE, *Memoirs*, 15 Aug. I have seen her . . . much amused with jokes, stories, and allusions which would shock a very NICE person.

1895. IOTA, *A Comedy in Spasms*, 1. Fine blend of Henry Fairchild, Pelham, and John Halifax, all NICE books to think of in connection with boys.

3. (colloquial). — Pleasant; agreeable: *e.g.*, a NICE woman or a NICE fellow; *cf.* the satirical extension: as in 'a NICE young man for a small tea-party.'

NICHE (or **NICHE - COCK**), *subs.* (venery).—The female *pudendum*: *see* MONOSYLLABLE.

NICHOLAS (SAINT), *subs. phr.* (old). —The devil: *see* OLD NICK.

1822. NARES, *Glossary*, s.v. NICHOLAS, SAINT. But a very different person was also jocularly called ST. NICHOLAS, now converted into OLD NICK; the same person whom Sir James Harrington has called *saunte Satan*, in his introduction to the Blacksaunt.

SAINT NICHOLAS'S CLERK, *subs. phr.* (old).—A highwayman. Also KNIGHT OF ST. NICHOLAS, and ST. NICHOLAS CLERGYMAN. [St. Nicholas was the patron saint of thieves].

1595. SHAKSPEARE, *Two Gent. Ver.*, iii., 1. *S.* Come, fool, come try me in this paper. *L.* There, and ST. NICHOLAS be thy speed.

1598. R. HARVEY, *Pl. Perc.*, i., A quarrel, by the highway side, between a brace of SAINT NICHOLAS CLARGIE MEN.

1598. SHAKSPEARE, *1 Henry IV.* ii., 1. *G.* Sirrah, if they meet not with SAINT NICHOLAS'S CLERKS, I'll give thee this neck.

1598. SHAKSPEARE, *1 Henry IV.* ii., 1. I prythee keep that for the hangman; for I know thou worships't SAINT NICHOLAS as truly as a man of falsehood may.

1611. COTGRAVE, *Dictionarie*, s.v. *Compter.* One of SAINT NICHOLAS CLERKS, or an arrant theefe.

1633. ROWLEY, *Match at Midnight* [DODSLEY, *Old Plays* (1874), vii., 353]. I think yonder come prancing down the hills from Kingston a couple of hur tother cozens SAINT NICHOLAS'S CLERKS.

1662. WILSON, *The Cheats*, i. I was t'other night upon the randan, and who should I meet with but our old gang, some of ST. NICHOLAS' CLERKS?

NICK, *subs.* (American).—1. A five-cent piece. [Abbreviation of 'nickel'].

2. (venery).—The female *pudendum*. Also NICK IN THE NOTCH. *See* MONOSYLLABLE.

*c.*1720. *Old Song* [FARMER, *Merry Songs and Ballads* (1897), iii., 223]. And in the NICK he seiz'd her, She trembled, blush'd, and hung her head.

1736. *The Cupid*, p. 129. So in the NICK the Nymph was finely fitted.

*d.*1749. ROBERTSON OF STRUAN, *Poems*, 186. And as one guides me to the NICK, The other cries—Put up thy——

1782. STEVENS, *Songs Comic and Satirycall*, 'The Sentiment Song.' The NICK makes the tail stand, the farrier's wife's mark!

3. *See* OLD NICK.

4. (old).—A dent, or island, in the bottom of a beer can: *cf.* KICK. Hence NICK AND FROTH = (1) false measure; and (2) a publican.

*d.*1529. SKELTON, *Elynour Rummynge.* Our pots are full quarted, We were not thus thwarted With froth-canne and NICK POT.

1612. ROWLAND, *Knave of Hearts*, 13. We must be tapsters running up and downe With cannes of beere (malt sod in fishes broth) And those they say are fil'd with NICK AND FROTH.

*a.*1625. FLETCHER, *Poems*, 133. From the NICK AND FROTH of a penny pothouse.

1628. *Life of Robin Goodfellow.* There was a tapster, that with his pots smalnesse, and with frothing of his drinke, had got a good summe of money together. This NICKING of the pots he would never have.

1661. *Poor Robin.* All we know of the matter is, that she [a conscientious hostess] still continues the NICK AND FROTH trade as usual.

1696. B. E., *Dict. Cant. Crew*, s.v. NICKUM. NICK AND FROTH built the Pye at Aldgate, sharping in the Reckonings and cheating in the measure built that (once) Noted House.

1822. NARES, *Glossary*, s.v. NICK. A deceptive bottom in a beer can, by which the customers were cheated, the NICK below AND the FROTH above filling up part of the measure.

5. (colloquial). — The exact or critical instant.

1594. *Look About You* [DODSLEY, *Old Plays* (1874), vii., 459]. Come they in the NICK To hinder Reynard of his fox's trick?

1611. BARRY, *Ram Alley* [DODSLEY, *Old Plays* (1874), x., 286]. I have a trick, To second this beginning, and in the NICK To strike it dead.

1621. BEAUMONT and FLETCHER, *Pilgrim.* Now ye have hit the NICK.

1633. FORD, *Love's Sacrifice*, ii., 2. Most fit opportunity! her grace comes just i' th' NICK.

1655. *Phillis of Scyros.* And see when Nerea comes just in the NICK.

1664. WILSON, *Andronicus*, v., i. Drama. Rest. (1874), i. 94. He catches at anything. This is our NICK.

1708. CENTLIVRE, *Busie Body*, ii., Sir *Geo.* Ads-heart, Madam, you won't leave me just in the NICK, will you? Sir *Fran.* Ha, ha ha, She has NICK'D you, Sir *George*, I think, Ha, ha, ha.

*d.*1716. SOUTH, *Sermons*, ix., ser. 4. God delivered them at the very NICK of time.

1823. BEE, *Dict. Turf, &c.*, s.v. NICK. You are arrived in the NICK of time, is addressed to one who comes in at the critical minute.

6. (gaming).—A winning throw at dice.

*d.*1721. PRIOR, *Cupid and Ganymede.* The usual trick, Seven, slur a six, eleven a NICK.

Verb. (old).—1. To steal; and (2) to cheat. Fr. *rifler.*

1617. FLETCHER, *Mad Lover*, i., 1. You men of wares, the men of wars will NICK ye: For starve nor beg they must not.

1677. WYCHERLEY, *Plain Dealer*, iii. *Free.* I ventured my last stake upon the squire to NICK him of his mother.

1727. GAY, *Beggar's Opera*, ii., 4. She rivetted a linen-draper's eye so fast upon her, that he was NICK'D of three pieces of cambric before he could look off.

1750. FIELDING, *Tom Jones*, VII., xii. Thinks I to myself. I'll NICK you there, old cull; the devil a smack of your nonsense shall you ever get into me.

1752-1840. DARBLAY, *Diary.* I entirely depended upon it, and for four mornings was up at 7 o'clock and all the trouble and fatigue of washing face and hands quite clean, putting on clean linnen, a tidy gown and smug cap, and after all we were *choused*, for he NICKED us entirely and never came at all.

1817. SCOTT, *Rob Roy*, iii. The polite and accomplished adventurer, who NICKED you out of your money at White's.

1823. BEE, *Dict. Turf, &c.*, s.v.

1834. HARRISON AINSWORTH, *Rookwood*, IV., ii. I NICK the broads.

1869. *Temple Bar*, xxvi., 75. I bolted in and NICKED a nice silver tea-pot.

1869. *Echo*, 9 Sept. 'Life of London Boys.' They climbed up there as they would climb anywhere—in at your window, over your hedges, where they would NICK the taters, or apples, or onions, or anything else, and waste them in the kiln.

1871. *Standard*, 8 Sept. 'Bow St.' Shannon confessed that he himself was as big a thief as any one in London, and asked him (witness) to NICK a watch, pledge it at Morris's, and give him (Shannon) the ticket, as he was determined to have Morris convicted.

1880. *Punch's Almanack*, 9. *The Cad's Calendar.* 'Ot July, just NICKED a handy fiver.

1889. *Sporting Times*, 6 July. 'The Shah at Fleet St.' The well-known diamond aigrette and the celebrated emerald were also left behind, to the intense disgust of the staff, who had calculated on NICKING out a few stones from the former.

1897. *Ally Sloper's Half Holiday*, 23 Oct., 342, 2. Even down to her Sunday stays, Which she calmly NICKS from missus's box.

3. (old).—*See* quot.

1808. JAMIESON, *Dict.*, s.v. NICK. A cant word signifying, 'to drink heartily; as, he NICKS fine.'

4. (old).—To break windows with copper coins. Hence, NICKER = a person addicted to the practice.

1712. GAY, *Trivia*, iii., 313. His scattered pence the flying NICKER flings.

[17?] *Martinus Scriblerus* [*Century*]. Your modern musicians want art to defend their windows from common NICKERS.

1714. LUCAS, *Gamesters*, 203. Called by the NICKERS and sharpers little Dick-Fisher.

1717. PRIOR, *Alma*, iii. Break watchmen's heads and chairmen's glasses, And thence proceed to NICKING sashes.

1886. BRADDON, *Mohawks*, ix. The *Flying Post* described how the NICKERS had broken all Mr. Topsparkle's windows with halfpence.

5. (old).—To fool.

1593. SHAKSPEARE, *Com. Errors*, v., 1. His man with sissors NICKS him like a fool.

1683. BEAUMONT and FLETCHER, *Little Thiefs.* NICK him home, thou knowest she dotes on thee.

6. (old).—To score at dice.— B. E. (*c.* 1696); GROSE (1785).

1598. FLORIO, *Worlde of Wordes*, p. 280. To tye or NICKE a caste at dice.

1677. WYCHERLEY, *Plain Dealer*, ii., 1. Thou art some debauch'd drunken, leud, hectoring, gaming companion, and want'st some Widow's old gold to NICK upon.

1773. GOLDSMITH, *She Stoops to Conquer*, iii. My old luck; I never NICKED seven that I did not throw ames ace three times following.

7. (old).—To hit the mark.— B. E. (*c.* 1696); GROSE (1785).

1690. *Pagan Prince* [NARES]. She NICKT it, you'l say, exactly.

1696. AUBREY, *Miscel.*, 50. This dream . . made him get up very early; he NICKED the time, and met with the waggoner just at the very door, and asked him what he bad in his cart.

1691-2. *Gentlemen's Journal*, Jan., p. 39. It seems he NICK'D the critical moment.

1714. LUCAS, *Gamesters*, 62. He conjur'd that Beldam to NICK the opportunity.

1823. MONCRIEFF, *Tom & Jerry* [DICK], p. 6. *Tom.* You've NICKED it; the fact is this, Dicky—you must turn missionary. Here is a young native from the country, just caught, whom you must civilize.

1831. C. LAMB, *Satan in Search of a Wife*, I., xii. 'I wish my Nicky is not in love'—'O mother, you have NICKED it'—And he turn'd his head aside with a blush.

1883. *Field*, 21 Jan. The white [greyhound] NICKED up on the inside for two or three wrenches.

1891. *Sporting Life*, 26 March. As he interfered with Innisheen, it perhaps saved an objection when the latter just NICKED the verdict by the shortest of heads.

8. (old).—To nickname.

1634. FORD, *Perkin Warbeck*, iv., 3. Warbeck, as you NICK him, came to me.

1689. *Princess of Cleve.* Believe me, sir, in a little time you'll be NICK'D the town-bull.

9. (old).—To catch; to arrest.

1700. CIBBER, *Love Makes a Man*, v., 3. Well, madam, you see I'm punctual—you've NICK'D your man, faith.

1759. TOWNLEY, *High Life Below Stairs*, ii., 1. You have just NICKED them in the very minute.

*d.*1817. HOLMAN, *Abroad and at Home*, ii., 3. He had NICKED his man, and accosted me accordingly. We lost one another in the crowd, and he departed in his error.

1835. SELBY, *Catching an Heiress*, I. I've NICKED it!

1836. MARRYAT, *Japhet*, lvii. That is the other fellow who attacked me, and ran away. He has come to get off his accomplice, and now we've just NICKED them both.

1841. LYTTON, *Night and Morning*, II., iv. I must be off—*tempus fugit*, and I must arrive just in time to NICK the vessels. Shall get to Ostend or Rotterdam, safe and snug; thence to Paris.

1893. EMERSON, *Signor Lippo*, xvii. I found my way back to Vestminster, got palled in with a lot more boys, done a bit of gonoffing or anything to get some posh, but it got too hot, all my pals got NICKED, and I chucked it and done a bit of costering and that's how I lost my eye.

1896. FARJEON, *Betray. of John Fordham*, III. 279. Louis had plenty of money to sport; e'd been backin' winners. Maxwell 'ad been NICKED the other way through backin' losers.

10. (common).—To compare or jump with.

1887. BURY and HILLIER, *Cycling*, 227. Only one sport NICKS with cycling.

11. (old).—To indent a beer can; to falsify a measure by indenting and frothing up.

1628. *Life of Robin Goodfellow* [HALLIWELL]. There was a tapster, that with his pots smallnesse, and with frothing of his drinke, had got a good somme of money together. This NICKING of his pots he would never leave.

*c.*1636. *London Chanticleers*, Sc. 5. The sleights of NICKING and frothing he scorns as too common.

12. (venery).—To copulate: *see* GREENS and RIDE.

TO NICK THE PIN, *verb. phr.* (old).—To drink fairly.—B. E. (*c.* 1696).

TO KNOCK A NICK IN THE POST, *verb. phr.* (old).—*See* quot.

1847. HALLIWELL, *Archaic & Prov. Words*, s.v. NICK. TO KNOCK A NICK IN THE POST, *i.e.*, to make a record of any remarkable event. This is evidently an ancient method of recording.

OUT OF ALL NICK, *adv. phr.* (old).—Past counting.

1595. SHAKSPEARE, *Two Gent.*, iv., 2. I tell you what Launce, his man, told me, he lov'd her OUT OF ALL NICK.

OUT ON THE NICK, *phr.* (thieves').—Out thieving; ON THE PINCH (*q.v.*).

TO NICK WITH NAY, *verb. phr.* (old).—To deny.

1350. *William of Palerne*, (E. E. T. S.), 4145. Zif sche NICKES WITH NAY & nel nouzt com sone.

[?]. *Romance of Athelstone.* On her knees they kneleden adoun, And prayden hym off hys benysoun: he NYKKYD HEM WITH NAY.

1820. SCOTT, *Abbot*, xxxviii. As I have but one boon to ask, I trust you will not NICK me WITH NAY.

NICKS. *See* NIX.

NICKEL, *subs.* (American).—A five-cent piece.

1857. *New York Herald*, 27 May. The new cent creates quite a *furor*. It is a neat, handy coin, and will soon supplant the cumbersome copper one. 'Nary red' will soon be an obsolete phrase among the boys, and 'nary NICKEL' will take its place.

NICKER, *subs.* (old).—A DANDY (*q.v.*).

NICKERERS, *subs. pl.* (Scots').—'A cant term for new shoes.'—JAMIESON (1808).

NICKERIES, *subs. pl.* (old).—'NICKERIES are the same [as Nicknames] applied to actions and things. or *quid pro quo*.'—BEE (1823).

NICKEY. *See* NIKIN and OLD NICK.

NICK-NACK, *subs.* (old: now recognised).—1. A trifle; a toy; a curio. Also KNICK-KNACK. *See* KNACK. sense 2. Hence, NICK-NACKATORY, NICK-NACKERY and NICK-NACKY.—GROSE (1785).

1580. G. HARVEY, *Two Other Letters, &c.*, in *Wks.* (GROSART), i., 80. Jugling castes and KNICKKNACKES, in comparison of these.

1618. BEAUMONT and FLETCHER, *Loyal Subject*, ii., 1. But if ye use these KNICK-KNACKS, This fast and loose, with faithful men and honest, You'l be the first will find it.

*d.*1682. T. BROWN, in *Works* (1760), ii., 15. For my part, I keep a KNICK-NACKATORY or toy-shop.

1726. *Terræ Filius*, No. 34, ii., 183. I went with two or three friends, who were members of the University, to the museum, vulgarly called the NICK-NACKATORY.

1750. FIELDING, *Tom Jones*, VIII., x. Besides the extraordinary neatness of the room, it was adorned with a great number of NICKNACKS, and curiosities, which might have engaged the attention of a virtuoso.

1753. RICHARDSON, *Grandison*, v., 71 (ed. 1812). I know he has judgement in NICK-KNACKATORIES, and even as much as I wish him in what is called taste.

1790. MORISON, *Poems*, 458. And in the kist, twa webs of wholesome claith; Some ither NICK NACKS, sic as pot and pan, Cogues, caps, and spoons, I at a raffle wan.

1824. MISS FERRIER, *Inheritance*, i., 86. His dressing-room is a perfect show, so neat and NICK-NACKY.

1849. LYTTON, *Caxtons*, I., iv. One of those fancy stationers common in country towns, and who sell all kinds of pretty toys and NICK-NACKS.

1876. HINDLEY, *Adventures of a Cheap Jack*, 7. Chimney ornaments and her sideboard NICK-NACKERY on the Pembroke table.

2 (venery).—The female *pudendum*: *see* MONOSYLLABLE.

3. in *pl.* (venery).—The *testes*; CODS (*q.v.*).

NICKNAME, *subs.* (old: now recognised).—A name invented in derision, contempt, or reproach. [M. E. *an ekename* = an agnomen].—GROSE (1785); BEE (1823).

1836. DICKENS, *Pickwick*, xvi. A very good name it [Job] is; only one I know that aint got a NICKNAME to it.

Verb. (colloquial).—To miscall in contempt, derision, or reproach.

NICK-NINNY, *subs. phr.* (old).—A flat-catcher.—B. E. (*c.* 1696); GROSE (1785).

NICK-POT, *subs.* (old).—A stealer of publican's pots.

1602. ROWLANDS, *Greene's Ghost*, 22. A necessarie caveat for victuallers and NICK-POTS.

NICKUM, *subs.* (old).—*See* quot.

*c.*1696. B. E., *Dict. Cant. Crew*, s.v. NICKUM. A sharper; also a Rooking Ale-house or Innkeeper, Vintner, or any Retailer.

NICKUMPOOP. *See* NINCUMPOOP.

NIDDICOCK, *subs.* (old).—A fool.

1587. HOLINSHED, *Disc. of Ireland*, G. 3, col. 1 *a*. They were never such fond NIDDICOCKES as to offer any man a rodde to beate their owne tayles.

1654. GAYTON, *Festivous Notes*, p. 61. Oh, Chrysostome, thou . . . deservest to be stak'd as well as buried in the open fields, for being such a goose, widgeon, and NIDDECOCK, to dye for love. *Ibid.* Shee was just such another NIDDECOOK as Joan Gutierez.

NIDDIPOL, *subs.* (old).—A fool.

1583. STANYHURST, *Vigil: Æneid*, iv., 110. What NIDDIPOL hare brayne.

NIDGET. *See* NIGIT.

NIECE, *subs.* (common).—A priest's illegitimate daughter, or concubine: whence the expression, 'No more character than a priest's NIECE.'

1848. RUXTON, *Life in the Far West*, p. 145. They were probably his NIECES.

NIFFNAFFY, *adj.* (old).—Fastidious; trifling.—GROSE (1785).

1815. SCOTT, *Guy Mannering*, xliv. NIFF-NAFFY gentles that gae sae muckle fast wi' their fancies.

NIFTY, *adj.* (American).—Conspicuous: smart.

1869. S. L. CLEMENS ('Mark Twain'), *The Innocents at Home*, ii. He was always NIFTY himself, and so you bet his funeral ain't going to be no slouch.

NIG, *subs.* in *pl.* (old).—1. The clippings of money. Also NIG, *verb.* = to clip money.—B. E. (*c.* 1696); GROSE (1785).

2. (American).—A negro. [Abbreviation of 'nigger']. *See* SNOWBALL.

1889. *Harper's Mag.*, lxxviii., 248. Some of the little NIGS have no clothes at all.

3. (back-slang).—Gin. *See* DRINKS and WHITE SATIN.

Verb. (old).—1. To catch. *See* NAB and NICK.

1754. *Scoundrel's Dict.* Tho' he tips them the Pikes they NIG him again.

2. (venery).—*See* NIGGLE.

3. (American).—To revoke: at cards. Also RE-NIG.

NIGGER. NIGGER IN THE FENCE, *subs. phr.* (American).—An underhand design, motive, or purpose.

NIGGER-BABY, *subs. phr.* (American Civil War).—A monster projectile: as used at the siege of Charleston. [Attributed to General Hardie of the Confederate Army]. *See* SWAMP ANGEL.

NIGGER-DRIVING, *subs.* (colloquial).—Exhausting with work.

1880. G. R. SIMS, *Three Brass Balls*, Pledge xiv. In the worst days of American slavery never was there such NIGGER-DRIVING as that practised systematically by the wholesale drapery trade.

NIGGER-LUCK, *subs. phr.* (American).—Very good fortune.

1888. *The Critic*, 14 Ap. I am cussed, he howled to a crowd of his own stripe, if any darned rebel can have such NIGGER LUCK and enjoy it while I live. You can bet I'll soon settle that.

NIGGER-SPIT, *subs. phr.* (popular).—The half-candied lumps in cane sugar.

NIGGLE (or **NIG**), *verb.* (old).—1. *See* quots., GREENS and RIDE. Also NIGGLING, *subs.* = Copulation.—B. E. (*c.* 1696); GROSE (1785).

1567. HARMAN, *Caveat* (1814), p. 66. To NYGLE, to have to do with a woman carnally.

1608. DEKKER, *Lanthorne and Candlelight* [GROSART, *Works* (1886), iii., 203]. If we NIGGLE, or mill a bowzing Ken.

1610. ROWLANDS, *Martin Mark-all*, p. 39 (H. Club's Rept. 1874). NIGLING, company keeping with a woman: this word is not used now, but *wapping*, and thereof comes the name wapping morts, Whoores.

1612. DEKKER, '*Bing out, bien Morts*,' v. [FARMER, *Musa Pedestris* (1896), 11]. And wapping Dell that NIGGLES well, and takes loure for her hire.

1641. BROME, *Jovial Crew* [FARMER, *Musa Pedestris* (1896), 25]. The autum-mort finds better sport In bowsing than in NIGLING.

2. (common).—To trifle. Also NIGGLING = trifling.—GROSE (1785).

1632. MASSINGER, *Emperor of the East*, v., 3. Take heed, daughter, You NIGGLE not with your conscience.

3. (artists').—To attend excessively to detail; to work on a small scale, with a small brush, to a small purpose.

1883. W. BLACK, *Yolande*, ch. xlix. Do you think Mr. Meteyard could get that portrait of you finished off to-day? Bless my soul, it wasn't to have been a portrait at all!—it was only to have been a sketch. And he has kept on NIGGLING and NIGGLING away at it—why?

NIGHT, *subs.* (old).—Combinations are NIGHT-BIRD (*q.v.*); NIGHT-CAP (*q.v.*); NIGHT-FOSSICKER (Australian mining) = a nocturnal thief of quartz or dust: whence NIGHT-FOSSICKING; NIGHT-GEAR (or -PIECE) = a bedfellow, male or female; NIGHT-HAWK (-HUNTER, -SNAP, or -TRADER) = NIGHT-BIRD (*q.v.*); NIGHT-HOUSE = (1) a public-house licensed to open at night, and (2) a brothel; NIGHT-HUNTER = (1) a poacher, and (2) a NIGHT-BIRD (*q.v.*); NIGHT-JURY = a band of night brawlers; NIGHT-MAGISTRATE = (1) the head of a watch-house, whence (2) a constable; NIGHT-MAN = *see* quot., 1785, and GOLD-FINDER; NIGHT-PHYSIC (or -WORK) = copulation: NIGHT-RALE (or -RAIL) = (1) night apparel, and (2) a combing-cloth; NIGHT-SHADE = NIGHT-BIRD, 2 (*q.v.*); NIGHT-SNEAKER = *see* quot., 1598; NIGHT-WALKER = NIGHT-BIRD (*q.v.*), whence NIGHT-WALKING = prowling at night for robbery, prostitution, etc.

1598, FLORIO, *Worlde of Wordes*, p. 105. Wanton or effeminate lads, NIGHT SNEAKERS.

1598. SHAKSPEARE, 2 Hen. IV., iii., 2. *Shallow.* And is Jane NIGHTWORK alive? . . . She was a bona-roba . . . certain she's old, and had Robin NIGHTWORK by old NIGHTWORK before I came to Clement's Inn.

*b.*1600. *Grim the Collier* [DODSLEY, *Old Plays* (1874), viii., 463]. Except my poor Joan here, and she is my own proper NIGHT-GEAR.

1632. MASSINGER, *Maid of Honour*, ii., 2. Which of your grooms, Your coachman, fool, or footman, ministers NIGHT-PHYSIC to you?

1637. MASSINGER, *Guardian*, iii., 5. Now I think I had ever a lucky hand in such smock NIGHT-WORK.

1639. MAYNE, *City Match*, v., 7. Panders, avoid my house! O devil! are you my wife's NIGHT-PIECES.

*c.*1696. B. E., *Dict. Cant. Crew*, s.v., NIGHT-RALE. A woman's combing cloth, to dress her head in. *Ibid.* NIGHT-MAGISTRATE.

1725. *New Cant. Dict.*, s.v. NIGHT-MAGISTRATE.

1785. GROSE, *Vul. Tongue*, s.v. NIGHTMAN, one whose business it is to empty necessary houses in London, which is always done in the night, the operation is called a wedding. *Ibid.* NIGHT-MAGISTRATE.

1835. DICKENS, *Sketches by Boz*, i. The NIGHT-HOUSES are closed.

TO MAKE A NIGHT OF IT, *verb. phr.* (common).—To spend the night in drinking, whoring, gaming, etc.

NIGHT-AND-DAY, *subs. phr.* (rhyming).—The play.

NIGHT-BIRD (-CAP, -HAWK, -HUNTER, -POACHER, -SNAP, -TRADER, or **-WALKER),** *subs.* (old).—1. A thief working by night.—B. E. (*c.* 1696); *New Cant. Dict.* (1725).

1544. ASCHAM, *Toxophilus.* Men that hunt so be privy stealers, or NIGHT WALKERS.

1620. BEAUMONT and FLETCHER, *Chances*, ii. 1. Sure these fellows Were NIGHT SNAPS. *Ibid. The Night walker, or the Little Thief* [Title].

1623. WEBSTER, *Duchess of Malfi*, ii., 1. If you hear the common people curse you, be sure you are taken for one of the prime NIGHT-CAPS.

1637. MASSINGER, *Guardian*, v., 2. *Ador.* You have been, Before your lady gave you entertainment, A NIGHT-WALKER in the streets. *Mirt.* How, my good lord! *Ador.* Traded in picking pockets.

*c.*1819. *Old Song* [FARMER, *Musa Pedestris* (1896), 83]. A NIGHT BIRD oft I'm in the cage.

2. (old).—A harlot. Also NIGHT-PIECE (or -SHADE): *see* NIGHT.—B. E. (*c.* 1696); *New Cant. Dict.* (1725).

1612. BEAUMONT and FLETCHER, *Coxcomb*, ii., 2. Here comes a NIGHT-SHADE.

1630. MASSINGER, *Picture*, i., 2. All kinds of females, from the NIGHT-TRADER, in the street.

*c.*1707. DURFEY, *Pills to Purge*, iii., 99. Now Miss turn NIGHT-WALKER.

3. (common). — A bully; a street brawler. Also (in bands), NIGHT-JURY.

1664. ETHEREGE, *Comical Revenge*, iv., 2. *Grace.* Do you take me for a NIGHT-WALKER, Sir?

1693. CONGREVE, *Old Batchelor*, i., 5. The knight was alone, and had fallen into the hands of some NIGHT-WALKERS, who, I suppose, would have pillaged him.

1708. HATTON, *New View of London* [quoted in ASHTON'S *Soc. Life in Reign of Q. Anne*], vii., 238. Loose and disorderly Servants, NIGHT-WALKERS, Strumpets, etc.

4. (old).—A bellman; a watchman.—B. E. (*c.* 1696); *New Cant. Dict.* (1725).

NIGHT-CAP, *subs.* (common).—1. The last drink; a DODGER (*q.v.*).

1840. HALIBURTON, *Clockmaker*, 3rd S., xi. Suppose we have brandy cocktail, it's as 'bout as good a NIGHT-CAP as I know on.

1843. MONCRIEFF, *The Scamps of London*, i., 2. You've had your NIGHT-CAP, a little daffy.

1843. *Handley Cross*, xxiv. Mr. Jorrocks celebrated the event with . . . a NIGHT-CAP of the usual beverage.

1883. GREENWOOD, 'Seaside Insanity' in *Odd People in Odd Places*, p. 51. Who would begrudge them their pilfered repast, or the stiff glass of gin or brandy and water on which their parents and the maid-of-all-work regale after supper, and by way of a NIGHTCAP.

2. (old).—The cap pulled over the face before execution. *See* HORSE'S NIGHT-CAP.

1681. *Dialogue on Oxford Parliament* [*Harl. MSS.*, II., 125]. He better deserves to go up Holbowrn in a wooden chariot and have a horse NIGHT-CAP put on at the further end.

1851-61. MAYHEW, *Lon. Lab.*, &c., iii., 153. I always come on to that scene with a white NIGHT-CAP and a halter on my arm.

1884. HENLEY and STEVENSON, *Deacon Brodie*, iv., 9. [*Three Plays*, 62]. The gallows . . . How's a man to die with a NIGHT-CAP on.

3. (old).—*See* NIGHT-BIRD.

4. (common). — A wife: *see* DUTCH.

NIGHTINGALE, *subs.* (military).—1. *See* quot.

1785. GROSE, *Vulg. Tongue* [EGAN], s.v. NIGHTINGALE. A soldier who, as the term is, sings out at the halberts. It is a point of honour in some regiments, among the grenadiers never to cry out, or become NIGHTINGALES, whilst under the discipline of the cat of nine tails; to avoid which, they chew a bullet.

2. (common).—A prostitute. *See* BARRACK-HACK and TART.

3. *See* SPITHEAD, CAMBRIDGESHIRE, and ARCADIAN NIGHTINGALE.

NIGHT-LINER, *subs. phr.* (American).—A night-walking cab: *cf.* OWL-TRAIN.

NIGHTY (or **NIGHTIE**), *subs.* (colloquial).—A night-dress.

NIGIT (or **NIDGET**), *subs.* (old).—A fool. *See* BUFFLE, and CABBAGE-HEAD.—B. E. (*c.* 1696); *New Cant. Dict.* (1725); BAILEY (1728); MATSELL (1859).

*d.*1623. CAMDEN, *Works* [JOHNSON]. There was one true English word of greater force than them all, now out of all use; it signifieth no more than abject, base-minded, false-hearted, coward, or NIDGET.

1785. GROSE, *Vulg. Tongue*, s.v. NIGIT, a fool, seemingly a corruption and contraction of the words *an idiot.*

1867. SMYTH, *Sailors' Word-book*, 497, s.v. NIDGET. A coward. A term used in old times for those who refused to join the royal standard.

NIGLER (or **NIGGLER**), *subs.* (old).—1. A clipper of money; a SWEATER (*q.v.*). *See* NIG.—B. E. (1696); GROSE (1785).

2. (venery). — A practical amorist: *cf.* NIGGLE, sense 1; a PERFORMER (*q.v.*).

1659. *Lady Alimony*, ii., 5. This was a bold-faced NIGGLER.

3. (old).—*See* quot.

1796. GROSE, *Vulg. Tongue*, s.v. NIGLER. One who is clever and dextrous.

NIHIL-AD-REM, *adj. phr.* (Winchester College).—Vague; unconscious: *e.g.*, 'He sported NIHIL-AD-REM duck.'

NIKIN, *subs.* (old).—*See* quots.

1725. *Dict. Cant. Crew*, s.v. NIKIN. A Natural, or very soft creature; also Isaac.

1785. GROSE, *Vulg. Tongue*, s.v. NICKIN, NIKEY or NIZEY.

NIL, *adj.* (common).—Half; half profits, etc.

NILLY-WILLY, *adv.* (old).—NILL YE, WILL YE, whether you will or no. [A familiar version of the *Latin*, NOLENS-VOLENS, Generally written now, WILLY-NILLY].

NIM, *verb* (old).—To seize, take, or steal; TO NAB (*q.v.*). [A. S., *niman* = to take]. Whence NIMMER = a thief, and NIMMING = theft, robbery.

1350. *Will. of P.* [E. E. T. S., 51, 1364]. How William went to here foos, & dede deliuerly NYM the duk.

1369. CHAUCER, *Troilus*, i., 242. Men reden not that folk han gretter witte Than they that han ben most with love YNOME.

[?]. *Harl. MS.*, 1701, f. 44. Goddes aungeles the soule NAM And bare hyt ynto the bosum of Abraham.

[?]. *MS. Trin. Coll. Oxon.*, 57. NYM, he seyde, this thief Faste in alle wyse, And wyn of him the tresour, And make him do sacrifyse.

1586. *The Booke of Hunting* [quoted by HALLIWELL]. Then boldly blow the prize thereat, Your play for to NIME or ye come in.

*c.*1600-62. *Common Cries of London* [COLLIER, *Roxburghe Ballads* (1847), 213]. And some there be . . . That pinch the countryman With NIMMING of a fee.

1606. JOHN DAY, *Ile of Guls*, iii., p. 67. As I led him to his Chamber I NIMDE his Chayne and drew his Purse, and next morning perswaded him he lost it in the great Chamber at the Reuels.

1608. *Penniles Parl.* in *Harl. Misc.* (ed. PARK), I., 182. To the great impoverishing of all NIMMERS, lifters, and cutpurses.

1634. T. TOMKIS (?), *Albumazar*, iii., 7. Met you with Ronca? 'tis the cunning'st NIMMER Of the whole company of Cut-Purse Hall.

1637. MASSINGER, *Guardian*, v., 2. I am not good at NIMMING.

1640. RAWLINS, *The Rebellion*, iii. If our hell afford a devil, but I see none, unless he appear in a delicious remnant of NIM'D satin.

1663. BUTLER, *Hudibras*, I., i., 598. Examine Venus, and the Moon, VVho stole a thimble or a spoon . . . They'l question Mars, and by his look Detect who 'twas that NIMM'D a Cloke.

1664. BUTLER, *Hud.*, II., iii., 209. *Booker's*, *Lilly's*, *Sarah Jimmers* And *Blank-Schemes* to *dis-cover* NIMMERS.

*c.*1696. B. E., *Dict. Cant. Crew*, s.v. NIM. NIM a togeman—to steal a cloak. NIM a cloak, To cut off the buttons in a crowd, or whip it off a man's shoulders.

*d.*1704. LESTRANGE, *Works* [JOHNSON]. They could not keep themselves honest of their fingers, but would be NIMMING something or other for the love of thieving.

1727. GAY, *Beggar's Opera*, ii., 2. I must now step home, for I expect the gentleman about this snuff-box that Filch NIMMED two nights ago in the park.

1728. BAILEY, *Eng. Dict.*, s.v.

1785. GROSE, *Vulg. Tongue*, s.v.

1823. BEE, *Dict. Turf*, &c., s.v.

1831. C. LAMB, *HerculesPacificatus*, in *Englishman's Mag.* And whatsoe'er they NIMM'D, she hid it.

1836. SMITH, *The Individual*, 'The Thieves' Chaunt,' 5. But because she lately NIMM'D some tin, They have sent her to lodge at the King's Head Inn.

NIMBLE, *adj.* (colloquial).—Easy-got; quickly 'turned-over': of money. *Cf.* NINEPENCE.

1898. LE QUEUX, *Scribes and Pharisees*, viii. The baronet was not very wealthy, and allowed his name to appear as director of certain companies, and pocketed fees ranging from the NIMBLE half-sovereign to the crisp and respectable five-pound note.

NIMBLE AS A CAT ON A HOT BAKESTONE (or HOT BRICKS), *phr.* (common).—As nimble as may be; in a hurry to get away; alert; on the *qui-vive.* Also AS NIMBLE AS AN EEL IN A SAND-BAG, AS A NEW-GELT DOG, AS A BEE IN A TAR-BARREL, AS A COW IN A CAGE, or AS NINEPENCE.—RAY (1676).

NIMENOG, *subs.* (old).—A fool. Also NIGMENOG.—B. E. (1696).

NIMGIMMER, *subs.* (old).—*See* quot.—GROSE (1785 and 1823).

1696. B. E., *Dict. Cant. Crew*, s.v. NIM-GIMMER. A Doctor, Surgeon, Apothecary or any one that cures a Clap or the Pox.

NIMROD, *subs.* (colloquial).—1. A hunting-man; a sportsman.

1599. HAKLUYT, *Voyages*, II., i., 309. These mighty NIMRODS fled, some into holes and some into mountaines.

1765. BLACKSTONE, *Comm.*, IV., 416. The game laws have raised a little NIMROD in every parish.

1823. BEE, *Dict. Turf*, s.v.

1887. *Athenæum*, 13 Aug., 208, 1. To the former (old sportsmen) he will recall events almost forgotten concerning the NIMRODS of a past generation.

2. *subs.* (venery).—The *penis.* [Because 'a mighty hunter']. *See* CREAMSTICK and PRICK.

NIMSHI, *subs.* (American).—A nincompoop; a conceited fellow.—DE VERE (1872).

NIMSHOD, *subs.* (common).—A cat.

NINCOMPOOP (or **NICKUMPOOP**), *subs.* (common).—An impotent ass.—B. E. (*c.* 1696); *New Cant. Dict.* (1725).

1673. SHADWELL, *Epsom Wells*, II., in *Wks.* (1720), ii., 217. Yes, you NICOMPOOP! you are a pretty fellow to please a woman indeed!

1677. WYCHERLEY, *Plain Dealer*, ii. *Wid.* Thou senseless, impertinent, quibbling, drivelling, feeble, paralytic, NINCOMPOOP!

1706. WARD, *Hudibras Redivivus*, I., x., p. 9. Thus did the sundry Female Troops, Conducted by their NINCOMPOOPS, In scatt'ring Numbers, jostling meet.

1764. FOOTE, *Mayor of Garratt*, i. I come, lovy. Trot, NINCOMPOOP.

1785. GROSE, *Vulg. Tongue*, s.v. NICKUMPOOP, or NINCUMPOOP, one who never saw his wife's ——

1821. SCOTT, *Kenilworth*, xi. Wayland Smith expressed . . . his utter scorn for a NINCOMPOOP who stuck his head under his wife's apron-string.

1823. BEE, *Dict. Turf*, &c., s.v. NINCUM-POOP, a term of derision, applied by a young lass to her lover, who presses not his suit with vigour enough.

1837. BARHAM, *Ingoldsby Legends*, ii., 367. Ackland would have called him a snob, and Buckland a NINCOOMPOOP.

1855. *Punch's Almanack*, 'A Farmer's opinion of Conscience Money.' Wha-at? send more income payments oop? You think I bees an INCOOMPOOP?

1883. GREENWOOD, *Odd People*, 101. His behaviour is that of the most consummate NINCOM, that ever was led with an apron-string.

NINE. NINE TAILORS MAKE A MAN. *See* NINTH.

NINE-BOB-SQUARE, *adv.* (obsolete).—Out of shape.

NINE CORNS, *subs. phr.* (obsolete).—A pipeful of tobacco.

NINE-EYED, *adj.* (old).—Observant.

1694. *Plautus made English*, Pref. A damnable, prying, NINE EY'D witch.

NINEPENCE, *subs.* (common).—The female *pudendum*: *see* MONOSYLLABLE. [An echo, on a liberal display of leg or underclothing, of the old alliterative retort, "Up to the Knees and NINEPENCE,"] *Cf.* MONEY.

NEAT (NICE, or RIGHT) AS NINEPENCE, *phr.* (common).—All right; correct to a nicety. Also *cf.* alliterative proverb, 'A nimble ninepence is better than a slow shilling']. *Cf.* NIMBLE.

1850. F. E. SMEDLEY, *Frank Fairlegh*, li. Well, let her say 'no' as if she meant it, said Lawless; women can, if they like, eh? and then it will all be as RIGHT AS NINEPENCE.

1864. DICKENS, *Our Mutual Friend*, I., ix. And with you and me leaning back inside, as GRAND AS NINEPENCE!

1882. *Daily Telegraph*, 7 Oct., 3, 1. When asked how he was getting on . . . he replied that he was 'RIGHT AS NINEPENCE, 'cepting a bit of rheumatism in his left shoulder.'

1884. T. ASHE, in *Temple Bar*, August, 525. The trick of alliteration is often useful to give point to old proverbs. In such familiar sayings as 'fine as fivepence,' NICE AS NINEPENCE, 'to lie by the legend,' its importance is most curious.

1886. R. A. KING, in *Household Words*, 19 June, 147. She . . . sent her children, NEAT AS NINEPENCE, to school and church on Sunday.

NINEPINS, *subs.* (common).—Life in general.

1879. SIMS, *Dagonet Ballads*, 'Told to the Missionary.' It's a cold I caught last year, as has tumbled my NINEPINS over, and left me a-dyin' here.

NINES. UP TO THE NINES, *phr.* (common).—To perfection.

*d.*1796. BURNS (attributed to), *Pastoral Poetry.* Thou paints auld nature TO THE NINES In thy sweet Caledonian lines.

1820. *London Mag.*, i., 25. He was always TOGGED OUT TO THE NINES.

1821. GALT, *Ayrshire Legatees*, viii. He's such a funny man, and touches off the Londoners TO THE NINES.

1822. WILSON, *Noctes Ambrosianæ*, i., 315. That young chiel Gibb hits off a simple scene o' nature TO THE NINES.

1856. READE, *Never too Late*, lxv. Bran-new, polished TO THE NINE.

1879. HOWELLS, *Lady of the Aroostook*, xxvii. I'd know as I see anything wrong in his kind of dressin' UP TO THE NINES, as you may say. As long's he's got the money, I don't see what harm it is.

1891. GOULD, *Double Event*, 31. You do things UP TO THE NINES here.

NINE-SHILLINGS, *subs. phr.* (rhyming).—Nonchalance.

NINE-SPOT. ONLY A NINE-SPOT, *phr.* (American).—Indifferent; of small account. [The nine at cards rarely counts for a trick].

NINE-TAIL BRUISER (or **MOUSER**), *subs. phr.* (prison).—The cat-o'-nine-tails.

NINEWAYS. TO LOOK NINE WAYS (or NINE WAYS FOR SUNDAYS), *verb. phr.* (common).—To squint.

1542. UDALL, *Apopth. of Erasmus*, 203 (Note). Squyntyied he was and looked NYNE WAYES.

NINE WINKS, *subs. phr.* (old).—A short nap: *cf.* FORTY-WINKS.—BEE (1823).

NINGLE. *See* INGLE.

NING-NANG, *subs.* (veterinary).—A worthless thoroughbred.

NINNY, *subs.* (old).—1. A fool: *see* BUFFLE and CABBAGE-HEAD. Also NINNY-HAMMER, and hence NINNY-HAMMERING = foolishness.—B. E. (*c.* 1696); *New Cant. Dict.* (1725); GROSE (1785).

1593. NASHE, *Strange Newes*, in *Works*, ii., 253. Whoreson NINIHAMMER, that wilt assault a man and have no stronger weapons.

1598. FLORIO, *Worlde of Wordes*, *Fagnone* . . . an idle loytring gull, a NINNIE.

1606. MARSTON, *The Fawne*, ii., 1. A foole? A coxecombe? A NINNY-HAMMER?

1604. *Yorkshire Trag.*, i., 2. Why the more fool she; Ay, the more NINNY-HAMMER she.

1609. SHAKSPEARE, *Tempest*, iii., 2. What a pied NINNY'S this.

1609. FIELD, *Woman is a Weathercock* [DODSLEY, *Old Plays* (1874), xi., 24]. My father is a NINNY; and my mother was a HAMMER.

1698-1700. *London Spy*, VII. (1706), i., 154. You cuckoldy company of Whissling, Pedling, Lying, Over-reaching NINNY-HAMMERS.

1712. ARBUTHNOT, *History of John Bull*, I., xii. Have you no more manners than to rail at my husband, that has saved that clod-pated, numskulled, NINNY-HAMMER of yours from ruin?

1719. DURFEY, *Pills to Purge*, ii., 2. A Senator some say He made his dapple grey For his Italian Neigh A crack-brain'd NINNY.

1725. *New Cant. Dict.*, s.v.

1753. *Adventurer*, No. 25. The words NINNY-HAMMER, noodle, and numscull, are frequently bandied to and fro betwixt them.

1763. FOOTE, *Mayor of Garratt*, ii., 2. This whey-faced NINNY, who is but the ninth part of a man.

1811. JANE AUSTIN, *Sense and Sensibility*, xl. The Colonel is a NINNY, my dear; because he has two thousand a-year himself, he thinks that nobody else can marry on less.

1838. *Comic Almanack* [HOTTEN], p. 159. We're not such NINNIES as to stand in all this riot.

1847. LYTTON, *Lucretia*, II., ii. If she's a good girl, and loves you, she'll not let you spend your money on her. I haint such a NINNY as that, said Beck, with majestic contempt.

1882. H. W. LUCY, in *Harper's Mag.*, April, 747. Any bore or NINNY-HAMMER who cared to invest a penny in a postage stamp could draw from the great man a post-card written in the well-known handwriting.

1892. HUME NISBET, *Bushranger's Sweetheart*, 64. Who would have thought the old duffer such a NINNY?

2. (Old Cant). — A whining beggar.—B. E. (*c.* 1696); *New Cant. Dict.* (1725); DYCHE (1748).

NINNY-BROTH, *subs.* (old).—*See* quot., 1696.

1696. *Poor Robin* [NARES]. How to make coffee, alias NINNY BROTH.

1698-1700. WARD, *London Spy*, I. (1706), i., 15. Being half choak'd with the Steem that arose from their Soot-colour'd NINNY-BROTH, their stinking Breaths, and suffocating Fumes.

1708. *Hudibras Redivivus*, pt. I. Their wounded consciences they heal With NINNY-BROTH, o'er which they seek Some new religion ev'ry week.

NINTH. NINTH (or TENTH*) PART OF A MAN, *subs. phr.* (common). A tailor. *See* SNIP. [From the proverb 'Nine tailors make a man': whence Queen Elizabeth's traditional address to a deputation of eighteen tailors:—'God save you, gentlemen both.']

[*There exists literary usage for this form. Unfortunately, however, the quotation, which ante-dated the first authority *infra* by fifty years or more, has been mislaid, and memory, though judicially certain as to its existence, fails as regards the reference.—J. S. F.]

1763. FOOTE, *Mayor of Garratt*, ii., 30. A journeyman taylor . . . This cross-leg'd cabbage-eating son of a cucumber, this whey-fac'd ninny, who is but the NINTH PART OF A MAN.

1767. RAY, *Proverbs* [BOHN], 135. NINE TAILORS MAKE but ONE MAN.

1838. DESMOND, *Stage Struck*, I. The most savage of hoaxes! instead of gallanting a goddess to our shores, I had the felicity to usher from the boat the NINTH PART OF A MAN.

NIP, *subs.* (colloquial). — 1. A pinch.

2. (old).—A thief: specifically a cut-purse.—B. E. (*c.* 1696); GROSE (1785).

1592. GREENE, *Third Part Conny-catching*, in *Works*, x., 174. Away goes the young NIP with the purse he got so easily.

1608. DEKKER, *Belman of London*, in *Wks.* (GROSART), III., 154. He that cuts the purse is called the NIP . . . The knife is called a cuttle-bung. *Ibid.*, Sig. H. 3. They allot such countries to this band of foists, such townes to those, and such a city to so many NIPS.

1611. MIDDLETON, *Roaring Girle* [DODSLEY, *Old Plays*, vi., 113]. One of them is a NIP, I took him in the twopenny gallery at the Fortune. *Ibid.*, vi., 115. Of cheaters, lifters, NIPS, foists, puggards, curbers, With all the devil's black guard.

1658. *Honest Ghost*, p. 231. Pimps, NIPS, and tints, prinados, highway standers, All which were my familiars.

3. (colloquial).—(*a*) *See* quot. 1808: hence (*b*) a sip; a small drink; a GO (*q.v.*). Also NIPPER.

1606. ROLLOCK, on 2 *Thes.* 140. If thou hast not laboured . . . looke that thou put not a NIP in thy mouth. *Ibid.*, 150. The Lord vouchsafes not a NIP on them unless they worke.

1788. GROSE, *Vulg. Tongue*, s.v. NYP or NIP. A half pint, a nip of ale; whence the nipperkin, a small vessel. *Ibid.* NYP-SHOP. The Peacock, in Gray's-Inn-lane, where Burton ale is sold in NYPS.

1808. JAMIESON, *Dict.*, s.v. NIP. A small quantity of spirits; as a NIP of whiskey.—generally half a glass. *Ibid.* A small bit of anything, as much as is NIPPED or broken off between the finger and thumb.

1848. LOWELL, *Biglow Papers* [BARTLETT]. Then it waz, 'Mister Sawin, sir, you're middlin' well now, be ye? Step up an' take a NIPPER, sir; I'm dreffle glad to see ye.'

1855. *Harper's Mag.*, May. One of our Western villages passed an ordinance forbidding taverns to sell liquor on the Sabbath to any persons except travellers. The next Sunday every man in town, who wanted a NIP, was seen walking around with a valise in one hand and two carpet-bags in the other.

1861. JAMES CONWAY, *Forays Among Salmon and Deer*, 71. Having discussed a Scotch breakfast . . . preceded by a NIP of bitters as a provocative of the appetite.

1868. COLLINS, *Moonstone*, I., 15. Mrs. Yolland . . . gave him his NIP.

1873. BLACK, *Princess of Thule*, xxiii. Young Eyre took a NIP of whiskey.

1888. RUNCIMAN, *The Chequers*, 86. The missus 'll fetch me some corrfee, and, hear you, put a NIP o' that booze in.

4. (old).—A hit; a taunt.

1556. HEYWOOD, *Spider and Flie* [NARES]. Wherwith, thought the flie, I have geven him a NYP.

1567. EDWARDS, *Damon & Pithias* [DODSLEY, *Old Plays* (1876), iv., 27]. From their NIPS shall I never be free?

1581. LYLY, *Euphues*, D 3 b. Euphues, though he perceived her coie NIP, seemed not to care for it.

1589. PUTTENHAM, *Art of Eng. Poesie*, 43. The manner of Poesie by which they vttered their bitter taunts and priuy NIPS.

Verb. (colloquial). — 1. To pinch. *See* quot. 1696.

[16 ?]. *Little John and the Four Beggars*, 49 [CHILD, *Ballads*, v. 327]. John NIPPED the dumb, and made him to rore.

*c.*1696. B. E., *Dict. Cant. Crew*, s.v. NIP. To Press between the Fingers and Thumb without the Nails, or with any broad Instrument like a pair of Tongs as to squeeze between Edged Instruments or Pincers.

1859. TENNYSON, *Merlin and Vivien*, 200. May this hard earth cleave to the Nadir hell, Down, down, and close again and NIP me flat.

1886. GREELY, *Arctic Service*, 73. The launch . . was NIPPED between two floes of last year's growth.

1887. HENLEY, *Villon's Straight Tip to all Cross Coves* [FARMER, *Musa Pedestris* (1896), 177]. It's up the spout and CHARLEY-WAG With wipes and tickers and what not. Until the squeezer NIPS your scrag, Booze and the blowens cop the lot.

2. (old).—To steal: specifically, to cut a purse.

1567. EDWARDS, *Damon & Pithias* [DODSLEY, *Old Plays*, I. (1874), iv., 19]. I go into the city some knaves to NIP For talk, with their goods to increase the kings treasure.

1573. HARMAN, *Caveat* (1814), p. 66. To NYP a boung, to cut a purse.

1592. GREENE, *Third Part Conny-catching*, in *Works*, x., 157. Oft this crew of mates met together, and said there was no hope of NIPPING the boung [purse] because he held open his gowne so wide, and walked in such an open place.

1600. *Sir John Oldcastle*, v., 2. Be lusty, my lass; come, for Lancashire: we must NIP the bung for these crowns.

1608. DEKKER, *Lanthorne and Candlelight* [GROSART, *Works* (188 .), iii., 203]. Or NIP a boung that has but a win.

1610. ROWLANDS, *Martin Markall*, p. 39 (H. Club's Rept. 1874). To NIP a Ian, to cut a purse.

1620. *Descr. of Love* [FARMER, *Musa Pedestris* (1896), 15]. Then in a throng, I NIP his bung.

*c.*1636. *London Chanticleers*, Sc. i. I mean to be as perfect a pick pocket, as good as ever NIPPED the judge's bung while he was condemning him.

*d.*1658. CLEVELAND, *Works* [NARES]. Take him thus and he is in the inquisition of the purse an authentick gypsie, that NIPS your bung with a canting ordinance; not a murthered fortune in all the country, but bleeds at the touch of this malefactor.

*c.*1696. B. E., *Dict. Cant. Crew*, s.v.

1712. SHIRLEY, *Triumph of Wit*, '*The Black Procession*,' 4. If a cull be does meet, He NIPS all his cole.

1714. *Memoirs of John Hall* (4th ed.), p. 13. NIP, to pick.

1736. Ramsay, *Scotch Proverbs*, 87 [JAMIESON]. Yet was set off frae the oon for NIPPING the pyes.

1740. *Poor Robin.* Meanwhile the cut-purse in the throng, Hath a fair means to NYP a bung.

1768. ROSS, *Helenore*, 126. Frae your ain uncle's gate was NIPT awa' That bonny bairn, 'twas thought by Junky Fa.

3. (common).—To go. To NIP ALONG = to move with speed; TO NIP IN = to slip in, etc.

1885. *Daily Telegraph*, 2 Jan., 2, 2. I NIPPED OUT of bed.

1892. MILLIKEN, *'Arry Ballads*, 66. Managed to NIP IN first-class.

1892. F. ANSTEY, *Voces Populi*, 'At the Tudor Exhibition.' Jove—my Aunt! NIP OUT before she spots me.

4. (common).—To take a dram.

1888. ROLF BOLDREWOOD, *Robbery Under Arms*, xxiv. You never saw a man look so scared as the passenger on the box-seat, a stout, jolly commercial, who'd been giving the coachman Havana cigars, and yarning and NIPPING with him at every house they passed.

1896. *The Lancet*, No. 3452, 863. In the homes alike of rich and poor the women have learned the fatal habit of NIPPING, and slowly but surely become confirmed dipsomaniacs.

5. (old).—*See* quot., NIP, *verb.*, sense 1, NIP-CHEESE, and NIP-LOUSE.

*c.*1696. B. E., *Dict. Cant. Crew*, s.v. NIP. To pinch or sharp anything.

6. (old).—To taunt; to wring.

1599. STOWE, *Hist. Lond.*, 55. There were some, which on the other side, with epigrams and rymes, NIPPING and gripping their fellowes.

1581. RICHE, *Farewell.* These cogitations did so NIPPE him, that he could not so well dissemble his grief.

7. (thieves').—To arrest; TO PINCH (*q.v.*).

1851-61. MAYHEW, *Lon. Lab.*, iii., 147. They'd follow you about, and keep on NIPPING a fellow.

NIP AND TUCK, *adv. phr.* (common).—Touch and go; neck and neck; equality or thereabouts. Also NIP AND TACK, NIP AND CHUCK, &c.

1847. PORTER, *Quarter Race, &c.*, 17. It will be like the old bitch and the rabbit, NIP AND TACK every jump.

1869. *Putnam's Mag.*, Jan. It was NIP AND TUCK all along, who was to win her.

1888. *Detroit Free Press*, 20 Oct. We had some pretty running. It was NIP AND TUCK. We kept about an equal distance apart.

TO NIP IN THE BUD, *verb. phr.* (old: now recognised).—*See* quot.

*c.*1696. B. E., *Dict. Cant. Crew*, s.v. NIP. TO NIP IN THE BUD. Of an early Blast or Blite of Fruit; also to crush anything at the beginning.

1725. *New Cant. Dict.*, s.v.

NIP-CHEESE, *subs.* (old).—1. A miser. Also NIP-SQUEEZE and NIP-FARTHING.—GROSE (1785).

1566. DRANT, *Horace*, Sat. I. I would thee not a NIP-FARTHING, Nor yet a niggard have.

2. (nautical).—*See* quots. 1785, 1842, and 1867.

1785. GROSE, *Vulg. Tongue*, s.v. NIP CHEESE, a nickname for the purser of a ship, from those gentlemen being supposed sometimes to NIP, or diminish the allowance of the seamen, in that and every other article.

1834. MARRYAT, *Jacob Faithful*, xx. (1873), 156. It's some of old NIPCHEESE'S eights, that he has sent on shore to bowse his jib up with, with his sweetheart.

1842. MARRYAT, *Percival Kerne*, xiii. 'That's a NIPCHEESE.' 'NIPCHEESE!' 'Yes; NIPCHEESE means purser of the ship.'

1867. SMYTH, *Sailors' Word Book*, 477, s.v. NIPCHEESE. The sailors' name for a purser.

NIP-LOUSE, *subs.* (common).—A tailor. Also PRICKLOUSE. *See* SNIP.

NIP-LUG, *subs.* (Scots').—A teacher; a schoolmaster.

AT NIP-LUG, *adv. phr.* (Scots').—At loggerheads; on the point of collision.

NIPPENT, *adj.* (American).—Impudent.

NIPPER, *subs.* (common).—1. A lad.

1851-61. MAYHEW, *London Lab. and Lond. Poor*, i., p. 37. Such lads, however, are the smallest class of costermongering youths; and are sometimes called 'cas'alty boys,' or NIPPERS.

1888. RUNCIMAN, *Chequers*, 54. They calls it a stream, but I dussn't say wot I thinks it is afore the NIPPER.

1888. *Referee*, 11 Nov. Other NIPPERS—the little shrimps of boys—were sometimes the best part of an hour at a stretch, from the time they left till they returned to the paddock to weigh in.

1892. CHEVALIER, *Idler*, June, p. 549. I've got a little NIPPER, when 'e talks I'll lay yer forty shiners to a quid You'll take 'im for the father, me the kid.

2. (old thieves').—*See* quot. 1785.

1659. JOHN DAY, *Mind Beggar*, I., 3, p. 21. *Had.* Your NIPPER, your foyst, your rogue, your cheat, your pander, your any vile thing that may be.

1785. GROSE, *Vulg. Tongue*, s.v. NYPPER, a cut purse, so called by one Wotton, who in the year 1585, kept an academy for the education and perfection of pick-pockets and cut purses; his school was near Billinsgate, London. As in the dress of ancient times many people wore their purses at their girdles, cutting them was a branch of the light fingered art, which is now lost, though the name remains . . there was a school house set up to learn young boys to cut purses: two devices were hung up, one was a pocket, and another was a purse, the pocket had in it certain counters, and was hung about with hawks bells, and over the top did hang a little sacring bell. The purse had silver in it, and he that could take out a counter, without noise of any of the bells, was adjudged a judicial NYPPER, according to their terms of art; a foyster was a pickpocket; a NYPPER was a pick purse, or cut purse.

3. (navvys').—The serving lad attached to a gang of navvies, to fetch water and carry tools.

4. in *pl.* (thieves').—Handcuffs or shackles.—HAGGART (1821); GROSE (1823); MATSELL (1859).

5. in *pl.* (thieves').—A burglar's instrument used from the outside on a key. Also AMERICAN TWEEZERS.

6. (Marlborough School).—A boy or 'cad.'

Verb (old).—To arrest; to catch. *See* NAB, and NIP.

1823. BEE, *Dict. Turf, &c.*, s.v. NIPPERED. What d'ye think? My eyes, if Bill Soames warnt NIPPERED only for a fogle little better than a wipe; and he was there upon transported.

1824. EGAN, *Boxiana*, iv., 150. The Pope being NIPPERED and brought to face the Beak.

NIPPERKIN, *subs.* (old).—A small measure: *see* quot. 1696; a stone jug.

c. 1696. B. E., *Dict. Cant. Crew*, s.v. NIPPERKIN. Half a pint of Wine, and but half a Quartern of Brandy, strong waters, &c.

1608-1700. WARD, *Lond. Spy*, II. (1706), i., 31. By that time we had sip'd off our NIPPERKIN of my Grannums *Aqua Mirabilis*.

1707. DURFEY, *Pills to Purge* . . . Quart-pot, pint-pot, NIPPERKIN, &c.

1785. GROSE, *Vulg. Tongue*, s.v.

1832. *Noctes Ambrosianæ*, Sept. William III., who only snoozed over a NIPPERKIN of Schiedam with a few Dutch favourites.

1882. J. ASHTON, *Social Life in Reign of Q. Anne*, i., 197. [Beer] was of different qualities, from the 'penny NIPPERKIN of Molassas Ale' to 'a pint of Ale cost me five-pence.'

NIPPING, *adj.* (old).—Sharp; cutting.—B. E. (*c.* 1696).

1596. SHAKSPEARE, *Hamlet*, i. 4. It is a NIPPING and an eager air.

NIPPING CHRISTIAN, *subs. phr.* (old).—A cut-purse: *see* NIPPER, sense 2.

NIPPING-JIG, *subs.* (old).—Hanging.

NIPPITATE, *subs.* and *adj.* (Old Cant).—Strong drink, especially ale. Also NIPPITATO and NIPPITATUM.

c. 1575. LANEHAM, *Letter* [NARES]. And ever quited himself with such estimation, az yet too tast of a cup of NIPPITATI, hiz judgement will be taken above the best in the parish, be hiz nose near so read.

1583. STUBBES, *Anat. of Abuses* [NARES]. Then when this NIPPITATUM, this huffe cappe, as they call it, this nectar of life, is set abroach, well is he that can get the soonest to it, and spend the most upon it.

1592. NASHE, *Summer's Last Will* [DODSLEY, *Old Plays* (1874), viii., 60]. Never cap of NIPITATY in London come near thy niggardly habitation.

1593. HARVEY, *Pierce's Supererogation*. The NIPITATY of the nappiest grape.

1594. *Look About You* [DODSLEY, *Old Plays* (1874), vii., 445]. He was here to-day, Sir, And emptied two bottles of NIPPITATE sack.

1600. OLIFFE, *Weakest Goes to Wall*, B. 2. Well fare England, where the poore may have a pot of ale for a penny, fresh ale, firme ale, nappie ale, NIPPITATE ale.

1611. BEAUMONT and FLETCHER, *Knight of Burning Pestle*, iv. *R.* Lady, 'tis true, you need not lay your lips To better NIPPITATO than there is.

1654. CHAPMAN, *Alphonsus*, iii., 1. 'Twill make a cup of wine taste NIPPITATE.

1891. FENNELL, *Stanford Dict.*, s.v. NIPPITATUM, *quasi*-Lat.; NIPPITATO, quasi-It. . . . possibly connected with the Eng. vb. *nip*, = Du. *nippen*, 'to take a dram.'

NIPPS, *subs.* (old).—Shears for clipping money.—B. E. (*c.* 1696): GROSE (1785).

NIPPY, *subs.* (children's).—The *penis*: *see* CREAMSTICK and PRICK.

Adj. (common).—Mean; stingy; curt; snappish.

NIPSHOT. TO PLAY NIPSHOT, *verb. phr.* (old).—To fail; to decamp: *see* ABSQUATULATE and SKEDADDLE.

1775. BAILLIE, *Letters*, ii., 108. Our great hope on earth, the City of London has played NIPSHOT; they are speaking of dissolving the assembly.

NIQUE, *subs.* (American thieves').—Contemptuous indifference.—MATSELL (1859).

NISEY. *See* NIZEY.

NIT, *subs.* (old).—1. *See* quot.

c. 1696. B. E., *Dict. Cant. Crew*, s.v. NIT. Wine that is brisk, and pour'd quick into a glass.

2. (old: now recognised).—The egg of a louse.—B. E. (*c.* 1696); *New Cant. Dict.* (1725).

1598. FLORIO, *Worlde of Words* (1611). *Zeiche* NEETS in the eie lids. Also tikes that breed in dogs.

1698-1700. WARD, *London Spy*, I. (1706), i., 12. [He] has as many *Maggots* in his *Noddle*, as there are . . . NITS in a *Mumpers Doublet*.

3. (Scots').—A wanton: *see* BARRACK-HACK and TART [JAMIESON].

NITS WILL BECOME LICE, *phr.* (old).—*See* quot.

1725. *New Cant. Dict.*, s.v. NITS WILL BECOME LICE; of small matters that become important.

NIT-SQUEEZER, *subs.* (common).—A hair-dresser.—GROSE (1788).

NIX (or **NICKS**), *adv.* (common).—Nothing. Also NIX MY DOLL, and (American), NIXY and NIXYCULLY. SYNONYMS. Ack (Christ's Hospital); love; *nib*, *niberque*, *niberte*, *nif*, *nisce*, *nix* (French); *niba*, *niberto* (Italian); *nexo* (Spanish).

1789. GEO. PARKER, *Life's Painter*, p. 143. NICKS. How they have brought a German word into cant. I know not, but NICKS means *nothing* in the cant language.

1819. VAUX, *Memoirs*, s.v.

1824. EGAN, *Boxiana*, iv., 444. Men who can be backed for large stakes do seldom fight for NIX (comically called 'love').

1852. *Old Song*, 'The Cadger's Ball' [FARMER, *Musa Pedestris* (1896), 147]. Old Mother Swankey, she consented to lend her lodging-house for NIX.

1858. A. MAYHEW, *Paved with Gold*, III., I, p. 254. Do you see all this land? said he . . . well, the grandfather of this here Lord Southwark got it for NIX.

1887. HENLEY, *Villon's Straight Tip*, 3. For NIX, for NIX the dibbs you bag.

1892. *Ally Sloper*, 19 Mar., 90, 3. When death of Uncle John bereft us, We said we mourned because he'd left us; Our mourning was a lot profounder To find he'd left us NIX—the bounder!

2. (American).—*See* quot.

1885. *W. S. Official P.O. Guide*, Jan., 685. NIXES is a term used in the railway mail service to denote matter of domestic origin, chiefly of the second and first class, which is unmailable because addressed to places which are not post-offices, or to States, etc., in which there is no such post-office as that indicated in the address.

Intj. (common).—*See* quot.

1883. *Indoor Paupers*, 45. So the thing goes on until some one on the watch cries, 'NIX lads, buttons!'—the warning that the taskmaster is at hand.

NIX MY DOLL, *phr.* (common).—Never mind! [Popularised by Ainsworth's song]. Also (VAUX) = nothing.

1819. VAUX, *Memoirs*, s.v.

1834. AINSWORTH, *Rookwood* . . . . And my old dad, as I've heard say, Was a famous merchant in capers gay; NIX MY DOLLY, pals, fake away!

1846. *Punch Almanack*, 'Song of September' (after AINSWORTH) . . What ho! my gun, my gallant boys, September's always jolly; I love the sportsman's pleasant noise Yoicks! Forward! NIX MY DOLLY.

NIZ-PRIZ, *subs.* (legal).—A writ of nisi-prius.

NIZZIE, *subs.* (old).—1. A fool: *see* BUFFLE and CABBAGE-HEAD. Also NIKIN.—B. E. (*c.* 1696); COLES (1724).

1755. JOHNSON, *Eng. Dict.*, s.v. NI'ZY [from *niais*]. A dunce; a simpleton. A low word.

b. 1755. ANON [quoted by JOHNSON]. True critics laugh, and bid the trifling NISY Go read Quintilian.

2. (old).—A coxcomb.—B. E. (*c.* 1696).

NO. NO BATTLE, *phr.* (printers').—No good; not worth while.

NO CHICKEN, *phr.* (common). Getting on in years: usually of women.

1889. DRAGE, *Cyril*, iv. I dont think that Miss Vera is ANY CHICKEN.

NO END, *adv. phr.* (colloquial).—Extremely; a great many. A general intensive.

1861. HUGHES, *Tom Brown at Oxford*, xiii. (1864), 141. The black and yellow seems to slip along so fast. They're NO END of good colours. I wish our new boat was black.

1863. READE, *Hard Cash*, I. 325. They drifted past a Revenue Cutter, who was lying to with her head to the Northward. She howled NO END of signals, but they understood none of them.

1876. GRANT, *One of the Six Hundred*, xiv. We were beset by London Jews and army contractors, and I had, as the phrase goes, NO END of unsuspected things to provide.

NO FEAR. *See* FEAR.

NO-FLIES, *adv.* (printers').—Artful; designing. Also N.F. (*q.v.*)

NO FOOL, *adv. phr.* (common).

—An ironical intensive: *cf.* NO SLOUCH.

1888. BOLDREWOOD, *Robbery Under Arms*, xix. It was thirty feet high—NO FOOL of a drop.

NO GO, *adv. phr.* (common).—No use; impossible. Fr. *zut!* and *ça ne mord pas*.

1830. MONCRIEFF, *Heart of London*, i. 1. I'm much obliged to you: it's NO GO.

1836. MARRYAT, *Midshipman Easy*, xix. But it's NO GO with old Smallsole, if I want a bit of caulk.

1848. RUXTON, *Life in Far West*, 146. Outside is NO GO.

1852. *Notes and Queries*, 17 Jan. Ser. I. v. 55. My publisher coolly answered that it was NO GO.

1871. *Daily News*, 17 April, p. 2. col. 2. How many beyond those mentioned in the foregoing remarks have been backed in earnest, I should not like to say; and it strikes me that it is a case of NO GO with Autocrat, Sarsfield . . . .

1893. EMERSON, *Signor Lippo*, viii. Well, I tried to get some banjo pupils—NO GO; no testimonials.

1896. FARJEON, *Betray. John Fordham*, III., 281. But it was NO GO; them as gathered round wouldn't part.

NO KID, *adv. phr.* (common).—No mistake.

1893. EMERSON, *Signor Lippo*, xx. I was knocked silly and taken to the same 'orspital, and when I woke I was in bed, my boko all plastered up like a broken arm, and a gal in a white hat and blue dress a-waiting on me—a real lady, NO KID.

NO MOSS, *phr.* (tailors').—No *animosity*.

NO NAME, NO PULL, *phr.* (tailors').—If I name no names there can be no libel = if I do not mention his name he cannot take offence, unless he likes to apply the remarks to himself.

NO ODDS, *adv. phr.* (colloquial).—No matter; of no consequence.

1855. DICKENS, *Little Dorrit*, I. ch. xix. 'How vexatious, Chivery?' asked the benignant father. 'NO ODDS,' returned Mr. Chivery. 'Never mind.'

NO REPAIRS. *See* REPAIRS.

NOAH'S ARK, *subs.* (common).—1. A long closely-buttoned overcoat. [A coinage of *Punch*: from a similarity to the wooden figures in a toy ark.]

2. (nautical).—*See* quot.

1867. SMYTH, *Sailors' Word-book*, 498, s.v. NOAH'S ARK, Certain clouds elliptically parted, considered a sign of fine weather after rain.

3. (rhyming slang).—A LARK (*q.v.*).

1887. SIMS, *Referee*, Nov. 7. Tottie She cried, What a NOAH'S ARK.

NOAKES. *See* JOHN O' NOAKES.

NOB, *subs.* (common).—1. The head: *see* CRUMPET.—B. E. (*c.* 1696); GROSE (1785).

1733. KANE O'HARA, *Tom Thumb*, i. 4. Do pop up your NOB again, And egad I'll crack your crown.

1782. PARKER, *Humorous Sketches*, 155. Here no despotic power shews oppression's haughty NOB.

1819. MOORE, *Tom Crib's Mem.*, p. 23. With daddles high uprais'd, and NOB held back, In awful prescience of th' impending thwack.

1823. BEE, *Dict. Turf, etc.*, s.v. NOB. 'Josh paid his respects pretty plentifully to the Yokel's NOB.' 'His NOB was pinked all over,' *i.e.* marked in sundry places.

1834. DOWLING, *Othello Travestie*, i. 3. A thought has crossed my NOB.

1837. DICKENS, *Pickwick Papers* (1857), 360. Leave off rattlin' that 'ere NOB o' yourn, if you don't want it to come off the springs alltogether, said Sam impatiently, and behave reasonable.

1840. BARHAM, *Ingoldsby Leg.* (*Black Mousquetaire*). Whom I once saw receive, such a thump on the NOB From a fist which might almost an elephant brain.

1845. *Punch*, ix. 9. Getting the NOB into chancery is a fine achievement, I once got several NOBS into chancery; and I certainly gave several of them severe punishment.

1851-61. MAYHEW, *London Lab.*, i. 341. These he would engage at a bob a NOB.

1856. *Punch*, xxx. 241. *Mary Ann's Notions.* Vulgar, dear. You might as well have written one for his NOB—you meant it.

1892. MILLIKEN, *'Arry Ballads*, 40. Why shouldn't her stage trotter-out take his perks too at so much a NOB.

2. (common).—A person of rank or position. [From Nobility: *cf.* MOB, Fr. *mobile vulgus*]. Hence TO COME THE NOB=to put on airs.—GROSE (1823). *See* DANDY.

1703. *English Spy*, 255. Be unto him ever ready to promote his wishes, whether for spree or sport, in term and out of term . . . against dun or don—NOB or big-wig—so may you never want a bumper of bishop.

1823. BEE, *Dict. Turf*, s.v. NOB. A . . . NOB . . . differs from *swell*, inasmuch as the latter makes a show of his finery; whereas the NOB, relying upon intrinsic worth, or bona-fide property, or intellectual ability, is clad in plainness.

1837. DICKENS, *Pickwick Papers*, (ed. 1857), 12. 'Wait a minute,' said the stranger, 'fun presently—NOBS not come yet—queer place. Dock-yard people of upper rank don't know Dock-yard people of lower rank—small gentry don't know tradespeople—Commissioner don't know any body.'

1840-45. BARHAM, *Ingoldsby Legends* (1862), 70. No! no!—The Abbey may do very well For a feudal NOB, or poetical 'swell.'

1843. DICKENS, *Martin Chuzzlewit*, vii. The high principle that Nature's NOBS felt with Nature' NOBS.

1849. THACKERAY, *Hoggarty Diamond*, iv. He was at the West End on Thursday, asked to dine, ma'am, with the tip-top NOBS.

1851-61. MAYHEW, *Lon. Lab.*, II., 56. I may observe that the NOBS is a common designation for the rich among these sporting people.

1855. THACKERAY, *Newcomes*, II., 58. Sherrick *loq.* Capital house, Mr. Newcome, wasn't it? I counted no less than fourteen NOBS.

1863. READE, *Hard Cash*, I., 228. Once more, [1846 Railway Mania] . . . a motley crew of peers and printers, etc. . . . ; in a word, of NOBS and snobs, fought and scrambled pell mell for the popular paper; and all to get rich in a day.

1870. *Figaro*, 18 July. Is it more cruel for a snob to shoot a sea-bird in the breeding season than it is for a NOB to shoot pigeons in the breeding season, thereby starving all their young?

1888. BOLDREWOOD, *Robbery Under Arms*, xli. He was introduced to all the NOBS.

1892. ANSTEY, *Voces Populi*, '*In the Mall on Drawing Room Day*,' p. 84. All I was goin' to see was a set o' blanky NOBS shut up in their blankdash kerridges.

3. (Oxford University).—*See* quot.

1825. *The English Spy*, i. 136. We must find you some more tractable personage; some good-humoured NOB.*

[NOTE. * A fellow of a college].

4. (workmen's). — A KNOBSTICK (*q.v.*).

5. (old).—The game of prick- (or cheat-) the-garter.

1754. *Discoveries of John Poulter*, 10. We got about three pounds from a butterman at the Belt or NOBB.

6. (old).—A sovereign; 20s.

Verb. (pugilists'). — 1. To strike; to get home a blow (specifically on the head): *cf.* NOBBER.

1821. MONCRIEFF, *Tom and Jerry*, ii., 5. *Tom.* I've NOBB'D him on the canister.

2. (showmen's).—To collect money; to take round the hat. Fr. *faire la manche.*

1851-61. MAYHEW, *London Lab.*, III., 145. When we go about the streets with tumblers . . . we also NOB or gather the money.

1890. *Spare Moments*, 23 Aug. A good nobber or collector—always a very gentlemanly fellow—is worth every penny of his share for NOBBING alone.

1893. EMERSON, *Signor Lippo*, vi. At Chichester we opened up opposite the George Hotel, and I NOBBED half a sovereign from a young visitor, besides a lot of small money.

NOB IN THE FUR TRADE, *subs. phr.* (old).—A judge.

*c.*1838. REYNOLDS, *Pickwick Abroad*, 'The Housebreaker's Song.' Let NOBS IN THE FUR TRADE hold their jaw.

TO NOB IT, *verb. phr.* (old).—*See* quot.

1819. VAUX, *Memoirs*, s.v. NOB IT. To act with such prudence and knowledge of the world, as to prosper and become independent without any labour or bodily exertion; this is termed NOBBING IT, or FIGHTING NOB WORK. To effect any purpose or obtain anything by means of good judgment and sagacity, is called NOBBING IT for such a thing.

1823. GROSE, *Vulg. Tongue* [EGAN], s.v.

ONE FOR HIS NOB, *subs. phr.* (pugilists').—1. A blow on the head.

2. (gamesters').—A point in cribbage for holding the knave of trumps. *Cf.* TWO FOR HIS HEELS.

1888. *Notes and Queries*, 7th S. v., 28th April, 340. The old name of cribbage was 'noddy.' 'Noddy,' being the name for the knave, has been contracted into NOB. As NOB=head, the antagonism of 'heels' is obvious.

TO PITCH THE NOB. *See* PRICK-THE-GARTER.

NOB-A-NOB.—*See* HOB-NOB (q.v.). Probably a corruption.

1834. AINSWORTH, *Rookwood* (ed. 1864), 192. We must have a NOB-A-NOB glass together, for old acquaintance sake.

NOBBA, *adj.* (common). — Nine [Italian, *Nove*; Spanish, *Nova*; the *b* and *v* being interchangeable, as in sa*b*e and sa*v*vey].

NOBBER, *subs.* (pugilists'). — See NOB, sense 1.

1819. MOORE, *Tom Crib*, 40. For, though, all know, that flashy spark From C—st—r—gh received a NOBBER.

2. (showmen's).—*See* quots.

1890. *Echo*, 30 Oct. NOBBER is beach slang for financial agent, and indicates the gentleman who goes round with the plate or box. Great care is always bestowed upon the selection of the NOBBER. He is really the most important member of the troupe, and must be an artist of the first water if he is to get any money . . . Only a NOBBER can know the extraordinary meanness of the British public, the reluctant way in which it doles out its coppers, and its refusal to donate silver on any terms.

1893. EMERSON, *Signor Lippo*, vi. I have often met honourable NOBBERS since like the poller, that poor honest artiste, who was far too honourable to allow any slur to be cast upon his character.

NOBBILY, *adj.* (common).—Showily; smartly: *cf.* NOBBY.

NOBBING, *subs.* (pugilists').—1. The administration of blows on the head.

1825. JONES, *True Bottomed Boxer* [FARMER, *Musa Pedestris* (1896), 92]. With flipping and milling, and fobbing and NOBBING.

2. in *pl.* (showmen's).—Money collected: *see* NOBBER.

1851-61. MAYHEW, *London Lab. and Lond. Poor*, III. 118. After him I began my performance, and he went round for the NOBBINGS.

NOBBING-CHEAT, *subs.* (old).—*See* NUBBING-CHEAT.

NOBBING-SLUM, *subs. phr.* (showmen's).—The bag for collecting money: *see* NOBBER, sense 2.

NOBBLE, *verb.* (pugilists').—1. To strike on the head; to stun.

2. (racing).—*See* quot. 1882; TO GET AT (*q.v.*).

1868. *Pall Mall Gaz.*, 4 May. Buccaneer underwent the same fate as Old Calabar, and was NOBBLED, *i.e.* maimed purposely, before the Two Thousand in which he was engaged, and this rascally proceeding drove Lord Portsmouth, from the turf in disgust.

1882. *Saturday Review*, 25 Mar. In the elegant dialect of sporting novelists to NOBBLE is a stronger term for to 'get at' a horse, or his owner or his jockey, and to 'get at' means secretly to frustrate, spoil, lame, dose, drug, or otherwise prevent the horse from 'doing his level best,' or for that matter his best across hurdles, or in a steeple-chase.

1888. GOULD, *Double Event*, 145. Found out who tried to NOBBLE the horse?

1892. *Evening Standard*, 11 May, 4, 4. A very sensible suggestion has been made with reference to the NOBBLING of horses. It is extremely improbable that there would be any attempt to injure a horse except for the purpose of winning bets of one sort or another about him.

3. (common).—To circumvent; to cheat; TO DO (*q.v.*); TO SQUARE (*q.v.*).

1877. GREENWOOD, *Dick Temple* [*Slang, J. & C.*]. There's a fiver in the puss, and nine good quid. Have it. NOBBLE him, lads, and share it betwixt you.

1883. *Punch*, 2 June, 264, 1. Never have anything to do with the Turf. They are all scamps alike, and would sell their own fathers to gain their ends. But if you can't resist it, like me, there's only one chance for you, and that is, to NOBBLE the jockey!

1886. *Fortnightly Rev.*, xxxix. 136. It was never certain whether he was going to NOBBLE the Tories, or square the Radicals.

1890. GRANT ALLEN, *The Tents of Shem*, xii. I've NOBBLED her, he thought to himself, with a triumphant smile.

1896. SALA, *London up to Date*, 67. The proposers and seconders of the various candidates have warily ranged themselves on guard . . . . and remain there hour after hour, skilfully NOBBLING members as they enter.

4. (common).—To appropriate; to catch; TO NAB (*q.v.*).

1855. THACKERAY, *Newcomes*, xxv. I don't know out of how much the reverend party has NOBBLED his poor old sister at Brighton.

1860. THACKERAY, *Philip*, xvi. The old chap has NOBBLED the young fellow's money, almost every shilling of it, I hear.

1888. BOLDREWOOD, *Robbery Under Arms*, xi. We're bound to be NOBBLED some day.

NOBBLER, *subs.* (pugilists').—1. A blow on the head; and 2 (common), a finishing stroke; A SETTLER (*q.v.*). In rod-fishing = the gaff (that kills).

18[?]. SIR HARRY POTTINGER, *Trout Fishing.* Then after one alarming flurry on the top of the water, my left hand slips the landing-net under him and his final struggles are shortly ended with a single tap of the NOBBLER.

3. (sharpers').—A confederate of thimble-riggers and card-sharpers; BONNET (*q.v.*); BEARER UP (*q.v*); also: NOB PITCHER. [The NOBBLER plays as if a stranger to the RIG (*q.v.*), to draw unsuspecting persons into play.]

1854. WHYTE-MELVILLE, *General Bounce*, vii. NOBBLERS and noblemen—grooms and gentlemen—betting-house keepers and cavalry officers—apparently all layers and no takers.

1876. HINDLEY, *Cheap Jack*, 261. In my young days there used to travel about in gangs, like men of business, a lot of people called NOBBLERS, who used to work the 'thimble and pea rig' and go buzzing, that is, picking pockets, assisted by some small boys.

4. (North country).—A pettifogging lawyer.

5. (Australian).—A drink: A GO (*q.v.*); specifically of spirits.

1759. FOWLER, *Southern Lights ana Shadows*, p. 53. To pay for liquor for another is to 'stand,' or to 'shout,' or to 'sacrifice.' The measure is called a NOBBLER, or a break-down.

1859. KINGSLEY, *Geoffrey Hamlyn* xxxi. I had two NOBBLERS of brandy and one of Old Tom.

1860. *Chambers' Jl.* xiii. 154. On the banks of the winding but now streamless creeks, . . . there was generally a solitary inn or squatter's hut, where the universal NOBBLER of brandy and a snack of food were to be procured.

1870. AMPHION, in *Baily's Mag.*, xix. 172. Who hit his leg for Spite or for pelf, Was it the NOBBLER, or Was it himself?

1873. BRADDON, *To the Bitter End*, xliv. He had eaten nothing since yesterday, but he did not get through these dismal hours of suspense without an occasional NOBBLER.

1881. GRANT, *Bush Life*, I. 243. He must drink a NOBBLER with Tom, and be prepared to 'shout' for all hands at least once a day.

1888. BOLDREWOOD, *Robbery Under Arms*, iii. We used to make it a point of drinking our NOBBLER, and sometimes treating the others twice, if we had cash.

NOBBLE-TREE, *subs. phr.* (provincial).—The head; the NOB (*q.v.*).

NOBBY, *subs.* (provincial).—A fool. *See* BUFFLE and CABBAGE-HEAD.

Adj. (colloquial).—1. Smart; elegant; fashionable. Also NOBBISH, NOBBILY, and NABBY.

1808. JAMIESON, *Dict. Scot. Lang.*, s.v. NOBBY. Neat, trim, well dressed; hence applied to a person who dresses above his position.

*c.*1810. *Broadside Ballad* . . . And all the coves said, what around did stan', That he were a werry NOBBY dog's meat man.

1844. SELBY, *London by Night*, ii. 1. My togs being in keeping with this NOBBY place.

1847. ALBERT SMITH, *Nat. Hist. of the Gent*, x. 67. He would think that he was not NOBBY if he did not have some wretched champagne.

1852. DICKENS, *Bleak House*, liv. The NOBBIEST way of keeping it quiet.

*d.*1870. DICKENS, *Our English Watering-Place*, in *Reprinted Pieces*, 167. So far from being at a discount as to company, we are in fact what would be popularly called rather a NOBBY place. Some tip-top NOBBS come down occasionally—even Dukes and Duchesses.

1897. *Sporting Times*, 13 Mar. 1. 1. Who says a GO O' NOBBY whelks?

NOBLE. TO BRING A NOBLE TO NINE-PENCE, *verb. phr.* (old).—To decline in fortune.—B. E. (*c.* 1696).

1725. N. BAILEY tr. *Erasmus, Colloquies*, I. 348. *En.* Have you given over study then! *Po.* Altogether; I have BROUGHT A NOBLE TO NINEPENCE, and of a master of seven arts I am become a workman of but one art.

See BEGGAR'S NOBLE.

NOBLE ART, *subs. phr.* (common).—Pugilism; boxing.

NOB-PITCHER, *subs.* (old). — *See* quot. 1819, and NOB, sense 3.

1819. VAUX, *Memoirs*, s.v. NOB-PITCHERS: A general term for those sharpers who attend at fairs, races, etc. To take in the flats at prick-in-the-garter, cups and balls, and other similar artifices.

1823. GROSE, *Vulg. Tongue* [EGAN], s.v.

NOBS-HOUSES, *subs. phr.* (old).—The Houses of Parliament.—BEE (1823).

NOB'S-NOB, *subs. phr.* (old).—King George IV.—BEE (1823).

NOB-STICK.—*See* KNOBSTICK.

NOB-THATCH, *subs.* (common).—The hair.

1865. YATES, *Land at Last*, vii. You look, tho' you've got a paucity of NOB-THATCH, and what 'air you 'ave is gray.

NOB-THATCHER, *subs. phr.* (common).—A wig-maker; a STRUMMEL-FAKER (*q.v.*). Also a straw-bonnet maker.—GROSE (1823).

1823. MONCRIEFF, *Tom and Jerry*, i. 5. Now you can make an assignation with some of our dashing straw-chippers and NOB-THATCHERS in Burlington Arcade.

NOB-WORK, *subs.* (common). — Mental occupation.

NOCKANDRO (or **NOCK**), *subs.* (old). —1. The posteriors; THE BUM (*q.v.*). [NOCK = notch + Gr. *andros* = a man].—GROSE (1785); NARES (1822).

1632. COTGRAVE, *Dict.*, s.v. *Cul.* An arse, bumme, tayle, NOCKANDRO, fundament.

1653. URQUHART, *Rabelais*, i. 194. My foul NOCKANDROW all bemerded.

1654. GAYTON, *Fest. Notes*, 14. Blest be Dulcinea, whose favour I beseeching, Rescued poor Andrew, and his NOCK-ANDRO from breeching.

1662. *Rump Songs*, ii. 85. *The Rump Carbonado'd*, 41. Lenthall now Lords it though the Rabble him mock, In calling him Speaker, and Speaker to the Dock, For an hundred pound more hee'l kiss their very NOCK.

1663. BUTLER, *Hudibras*, I. i. 285. But when the date of NOCK was out, Off drop't the sympathetic snout.

1775. ASH, *Dict.*, s.v. NOCK. . . . the aperture of the fundament.

2. (venery).—The female *pudendum*: *see* MONOSYLLABLE.

1598. FLORIO, *Worlde of Wordes*, *Cunno* a womans NOCKE.

1675. COTTON, *Scoffer Scofft*, in *Works* (1725), p. 278. It being pretty coldish weather, He needs must have us lie together; And so we did . . . When . . . Twixt some twelve and one o'clock, He tilts his tantrum at my NOCK.

Verb. (venery). — *See* quot. 1775. *Cf.* KNOCK, *verb.* *See* GREENS and RIDE.

1568. FLORIO, *Worlde of Wordes*, s.v. *Cunnata*, a woman NOCKED.

1775. ASH, *Dict.*, s.v. NOCK, to perform the act of generation on a female.

NOCKY, *subs.* (old).—A simpleton; a dullard. Also NOCKY-BOY, and as *adj.*—B. E. (*c.* 1696); GROSE (1785); MATSELL (1859).

NOCTURNE, *subs.* (venery). — A prostitute; a NIGHT PIECE (*q.v.*): *see* BARRACK-HACK and TART.

NOD, *verb.* (colloquial). — To be stupid or dull.

THE LAND OF NOD, *subs. phr.* (colloquial). — Sleep. [*Cf.* 'the LAND of NOD on the East of the JORDAN' (*q.v.*), *Gen.* iv. 16.]

1608-10. SWIFT, *Polite Conversation*, iii. *Col.* I'm going to the LAND of NOD. *Neverout.* Faith, I'm for Bedfordshire.

1819. SCOTT, *Tales of my Landlord*, III. 124. And d'ye ken, lass, said Madge, there's queer things chanced since ye hae been in THE LAND OF NOD.

1823. GROSE, *Vulg. Tongue* [EGAN], s.v.

1828. HOOD, *Miss Kilmansegg.* A first-class carriage of ease, In the LAND OF NOD, or where you please.

1889. *Detroit Free Press*, 16 Feb. So he waked it up, and all baby did was to open its little eyes, sniff, smile sleepily, and go right off again to the LAND OF NOD.

1892. HUME NISBET, *Bushranger's Sweetheart*, 275. We flung ourselves down on our blankets, and were soon in the LAND OF NOD.

A NOD IS AS GOOD AS A WINK TO A BLIND HORSE, *phr.* (colloquial).—Said of a covert hint—an allusion not put into plain words.

1831. BUCKSTONE, *Beggar Boy*, i. 1. *Jean* (*laughing.*) You understand him by that? *Bart.* To be sure I do! A NOD'S AS GOOD AS A WINK FOR A BLIND HORSE, you know, master.

1837. RICHARD BRINSLEY PEAKE, *A Quarter To Nine*, ii. A NOD'S AS GOOD AS A WINK TO A BLIND HORSE.

1889. *Evg. Standard*, 25 June. A WINK WAS AS GOOD AS A NOD, and trainers and jockeys . . . . easily gathered whether a particular horse was only out for an airing, &c.

1893. *Nineteenth Century*, July, 6. A NOD IS AS GOOD AS A WINK TO A BLIND HORSE; and there are certain understandings, in public as well as in private life, which it is better for all parties not to put into writing.

ON THE NOD, *phr.* (common). —On credit.

1882. *The Rag*, 30 Sept. [FARMER, *Musa Pedestris* (1896), 163.] A PAY-ON-THE NOD, An always-in-quod young man.

1889. *Bird o' Freedom*, 7 Aug., 1. The next book you make, take a Gentile's advice, It's safer to bet ON THE NOD.

1889. *Daily Telegraph*, 23 Oct., 5, 5. The defendant deposed that he lost over £30 by taking the bank, and that then the players agreed that he might go ON THE NOD, which meant that he might owe what he lost.

1891. *Standard*, 25 Aug., 3, 6. When Witness asked where he got them from; he said, ON THE NOD, meaning that he did not intend to pay for them.

1894. MOORE, *Esther Waters*, xxxi. He didn't suppose the guv'nor would take him ON THE NOD, but he had a nice watch which ought to be good for three ten.

1897. *Daily Telegraph*, 15 March, 8, 4. The old idea of the law was that betting on credit—or, as it is vulgarly called, betting ON THE NOD—was not illegal.

NODCOCK, *subs.* (old).—A simpleton: *see* BUFFLE and CABBAGE-HEAD.

NODDIPOL. *See* NODDY.

NODDLE, *subs.* (old).—The head: *see* CRUMPET. B. E. (*c.* 1696); *New Cant. Dict.* (1725); GROSE (1785).

1593. SHAKSPEARE, *Taming of the Shrew*, i. 1. Doubt not her cares should be to comb your NODDLE with a three-legg'd stool, And paint your face, and use you like a fool.

1596. NASHE, *Saffron Walden*, in *Works*, III. 149. No roofe had he to hide his NODDLE in.

1598. FLORIO, *A Worlde of Wordes*, s.v. *Occipute*, the hinder part of the head, the nape of the necke, the NODDLE.

1611. BARRY, *Ram Alley*, iv. 1. You say very right, Sir Oliver, very right; I have't in my NODDLE i' faith.

1620. SHELTON, *Don Quixote*, III. iii. 21. Let every Man looke how he speakes or writes of Men, and set not downe each thing that comes into his NODDLE in a mingle-mangle.

1645. HOWELL, *Letters*, II. 43. I could tell you how, not long before her Death, the late Queen of Spain took off one of her Chapines, and clowted Olivares about the NODDLE with it.

1662. *Rump Songs*, I. iii. God blesse Ruperte and Maurice withall, Tha' gave the Roundheads a great downfall, And knockt their NODDLES 'gainst Worcester wall.

1663. BUTLER, *Hudibras*, I. iii. 123. He'l lay on Gifts with hands, and place On dullest NODDLE light and grace.

1675. COTTON, *Scoffer Scofft*, in *Wks.* (1725), 164. And could I in ingenuous NODDLE, Have chosen out a fitter Model.

1683. EARL OF DORSET, *A Faithful Catalogue.* O sacred James! may thy dread NODDLE be As free from danger, as from wit 'tis free,

1690. *Mundus Muliebris* [NARES]. Behind the NODDLE every baggage, Wears bundle 'choux,' in English cabbage.

1692. L'ESTRANGE, *Æsop.*, Come, master, I have a project in my NODDLE.

1705. WARD, *Works* (ed. 1717), ii. 3. When ready we adjourned to an Alehouse . . . And there I made the Bumkin fuddle Till muddy ale had seized his NODDLE.

1709. STEELE, *Tatler*, No. 178. These reflections, in the writers of the transactions of the times, seize the NODDLES of such as were not born to have thoughts of their own.

1719. DURFEY, *Pills to Purge Melancholy*, i. 154. The New with false, sham storys of which each NODDLE was full.

1749. ROBERTSON OF STRUAN, *Poems*, '*The Wheel of Life.*' Then fill about a Bumper to the Brim, Till all repeat it round, and ev'ry NODDLE swim.

1825. *The English Spy*, I. 188. Old dowagers, their *fubsy* face, Painted to eclipse the Grace, By their NODDLES out In some old family affair That's neither chariot, coach, or chair, Well known at every rout.

1834. DOWLING, *Othello Travestie*, i. 1. For fear old Drab, when he comes back, should take it in his NODDLE To march me to the Duke with him.

1864. DICKENS, *Our Mutual Friend*, II. ii. There's something in that, replied Miss Wren; you have a sort of an idea in your NODDLE sometimes.

NODDLE-CASE, *subs.* (old).—A wig.

*d.*1680. T. BROWN, *Works*, ii. 197. Next time you have occasion for a NODDLE-CASE.

NODDY (NOD, NODDIE-NODDIPOLE, NODDY-POLE, NODDY-PATE, or **NODDY-PEAKE)**, *subs.* (old).—1. A simpleton: *see* BUFFLE and CABBAGE-HEAD. Also TOM NODDY.—GROSE (1785).

1540. HEYWOOD, *Four P's* [DODSLEY, *Old Plays* (1874), i. 360]. If I denied, I were a NODDY.

1557. SIR THOS MORE, *Works*, 709. Or els so foolyshe, that a verye NODY-POLL nydote myght be ashamed to say it.

1562-63. *Jack Juggler* [DODSLEY, *Old Plays* (1874), ii. 130]. It would grieve my heart, so help me God, To run about the streets like a masterless NOD.

1567. EDWARDS, *Damon and Pithias* [DODSLEY, *Old Plays* (1874), iv. 17]. Ere you came thither, poor I was somebody; The King delighteth in me, now I am but a NODDY.

1589. PUTTENHAM, *Arte of Eng. Poesie*, B. I. xx. As we find of Irus the beggar, and Thersites the glorious NODDIE, whom Homer makes mentions of.

1598. FLORIO, *A Worlde of Wordes. Coglione*, a NODDIE, a foole.

1606. *Return from Parnassus* [DODSLEY, *Old Plays* (1874), ix. 102]. You that can play at NODDY, or rather play upon NODDIES.

1610. JONSON, *Alchemist*, iv. 2. Nay, see; she will not understand him! Gull, NODDY!

1611. COTGRAVE, *Dict.*, s.v. *Benet.* A simple, plaine, doltish fellow; a NODDI-PEAKE, a ninny-hammer, a pea-goose, a cox, a sillie companion.

1614. *Terence in English. Vix tandem sensi stolidus.* I now yet scarse perceive it, foole that I am; I now at length hardly understand with much adoe, whorson NODIPOL that I am.

1662. *Rump Songs*, ii. 55. There is another Proverb which every NODDY, Will jeer the Rump with, and cry hodd-doddy, etc.

1675. COTTON, *Scoffer Scofft* [*Works* (1725), 203]. What would'st thou have me such a NODDY.

1691-92. *Gentlemen's Journal*, Feb., p. 24. Diana, whom poetic NODDIES Would have us think to be some goddess.

1852. JUDSON, *Myst. of New York*, IV. Open a jewelry store, you NODDY, 'ow 're you goin' to do that?

2. (old).—*See* quots.

1785. GROSE, *Vulg. Tongue*, s.v. NODDY a kind of buggy or one horse chaise, with a seat before it for a driver, used in and about Dublin in the manner of a hackney coach.

1847. *Sketches of Ireland* [quoted by BREWER]. The 'Set-down' was succeeded by the NODDY, so called from its oscillating motion backwards and forwards.

*d.*1894. STEVENSON, *Treasure of Franchard.* Jean-Marie led forth the doctor's NODDY.

Adj. (old).—Simple; foolish.

1598. SHAKSPEARE, *Two Gentlemen*, i. 1. *S.* She did nod, and I said, I. *P.* And that set together is NODDY. *S.* Now you have taken the pains to set it together, take it for your pains.

KNAVE NODDY, *subs. phr.* (old).—The knave of trumps.—B. E. (*c.* 1696); GROSE (1823).

1757. FOOTE, *Author*, ii. 1, *Mod. Brit. Dram.* (1811), V. 281. You want four, and I two, and my deal: now KNAVE NODDY—no, hearts be trumps.

NODDY-HEADED, *adj.* (common).—1. Witless.

2. (common). — Drunk: *see* DRINKS and SCREWED.

NODGECOCK, *subs.* (old).—A simpleton.

1566-7. PAINTER, *Pal. Pleas.*, i. E and 5. This poore NODGECOCK contriving the time with sweete and pleasaunt woordes with his dareling Simphorosia.

NOFFGUR, *subs.* (popular). — A prostitute: *see* BARRACK-HACK and TART.

18 [?]. *Bird o' Freedom* [quoted in *S. J. & C.*]. Wrong 'uns at the Wateries, NOFFGURS at the Troc, Coryphées by Kettner, Tartlets anywhere.

NOG. *See* NOGGIN.

NOGGIN (NOG or **KNOGGIN)**, *subs.* (old).—1. A small measure of spirits; a GO (*q.v.*). — B. E. (*c.* 1696).

1719. SWIFT, *To Dr. Sheridan*, 14 Dec. For all your colloguing, I'd be glad of a KNOGGIN.

1789. PARKER, *Life's Painter*, 154, s.v.

1860. MRS. GASKELL, *Sylvia's Lovers*, XXIV. The sergeant . . . brought up his own mug of beer, into which a NOGGIN of gin had been put.

2. (old).—A mug.

1635. HEYWOOD, *Drunkard Opened*, 45. Mazers, broad mouth'd dishes, NOGGINS, whiskins, piggins, etc.

*c.*1720. *Virgin Sacrifice*, Song [FARMER, *Merry Songs and Ballads* (1897), iii. 221]. When merrily jogging, Home to the Brown NOGGIN.

*c.*1816. MAHER, *Song*, 'The Night before Larry was Stretched' [FARMER, *Musa Pedestris* (1896), 79]. 'Pon my conscience, dear Larry,' says I, 'I'm sorry to see you in trouble, And your life's cheerful NOGGIN run dry.'

1818. LADY MORGAN, *Fl. Macarthy* (1819), I. iii. 161. Repeatedly drank from a NOGGIN of water beside him.

1833-34. CARLYLE, *Sart. Resar.* 196. The furniture of this caravansera consisted of a large iron Pot, two oaken Tables, two Benches, two Chairs, and a Potheen NOGGIN.

3. (old).—The head: *see* CRUMPET.

NOGGY, *adj.* (provincial).—Intoxicated: *see* DRINKS and SCREWED.

NO-HOW, *adv.* (colloquial).—1. Upset; out of sorts.

1868. DICKENS, *Dr. Marigold's Prescription.* Ain't Mr. B. so well this morning? You look all NOHOW.

2. (old colloquial).—Out of countenance.

*c.*1840. D'ARBLAY, *Diary*, I. 161. I could not speak a word; I dare say I looked NO-HOW.

NOISE, *subs.* (old colloquial).—1. A band of musicians.

1598. SHAKSPEARE, *2 Henry IV.* ii. 4. And see if thou canst find Sneak's NOISE; mistress Tear-sheet would fain hear some music.

1608. DEKKER, *Belman of London* [HALLIWELL]. Those terrible NOYSES, with thredbare cloakes.

1614. BEAUMONT and FLETCHER, *Wit at Several Weapons*, iii. 1. Have you prepared good music? *G.* As fine a NOISE, uncle, as heart can wish.

1632. HEYWOOD, *Iron Age* [NARES]. We shall have him in one of Sneak's NOISE,—with—will you have any music, gentlemen?

1633. JONSON, *Tale of a Tub*, i. 4. Press all NOISES of Finsbury in our name.

2. (old).—*See* quot.

*c.*1696. B. E., *Dict. Cant. Crew*, s.v. NOISE. Used either of Harmonious or confused Sounds, NOISE of Thunder, or of a Mill, NOISE of the Hounds, A NOISE of Fiddles, of Trumpets and Drums, A NOISE of Swords, or clashing.

TO MAKE A NOISE AT ONE, *verb. phr.* (colloquial).—To scold.

TO NOISE ONE, *verb. phr.* (colloquial).—To tell tales of; TO SPLIT (*q.v.*).

NOISY-DOG-RACKET, *subs. phr.* (old). —*See* quot.

1823. GROSE, *Vulg. Tongue* [EGAN], s.v. NOISY DOG RACKET. Stealing Brass knockers from doors.

NOKES, *subs.* (old).—*See* quots., and JOHN-A-NOKES.

*c.*1696. B. E., *Dict. Cant. Crew*, s.v. NOKES. A Ninny or Fool; also a noted Droll lately Dead.

1785. GROSE, *Vulg. Tongue*, s.v. NOKES; JOHN-A-NOKES and Tom-a-Stiles, two honest peaceable gentlemen, repeatedly set together by the ears by lawyers of different denominations. Two fictitious names commonly used in law proceedings.

NOLI-ME-TANGERE, *subs. phr.* (Scots').—1. The itch; the pox: any disgusting contagious disease: *cf.* SCOTCH FIDDLE.

1626. COCKERAM, Pt. I. (2nd Ed.). NOLI-ME-TANGERE, The French disease.

1676. COLES, *Eng. Dict.* (1732) (Touch me not) . . . The French disease.

1728. BAILEY, *Eng. Dict.*, s.v.

1755. JOHNSON, *Eng. Dict.*, s.v. NOLI ME TANGERE. A kind of cancerous swelling, exasperated by applications.

2. (old colloquial).—A repellant, person, attitude, or occurrence. Also as *adj.* = repellant, forbidding. [Lat. 'touch-me-not'.]

1591. PEELE, *Speeches*, iii. [*Works* (1861) 579, 2]. NOLI ME TANGERE; I let go my hold and desire your majesty that you will hold yours.

c. 1630. R. NAUNTON, *Frag. Reg.* (1870) 18. He was wont to say of them that they were of the tribe of Dan, and were NOLI ME TANGERE'S.

1634. W. WOOD, *New England's Prosp.*, 22. The Porcupine is a small thing not unlike a Hedgehog; something bigger, who stands upon his guard and proclaims a NOLI ME TANGERE, to man and beast that shall approach too neare him.

1692. WATSON, *Body of Div.* (1858), 460. Herod could not brook to have his incest meddled with—that was a NOLI ME TANGERE.

1791. C. SMITH, *Desmond*, I. 248 (1792). Every attempt at redress is silenced by the NOLI ME TANGERE which our constitution has been made to say.

1806. BERESFORD, *Miseries*, I. 219. Every dish, as it is brought in, carrying a NOLI ME TANGERE on the face of it.

1817. BYRON in MOORE'S Life (1875), 605. I used to think that I was a good deal of an Author in . . . NOLI ME TANGERE.

1821. DE QUINCEY, *Confess.* (1823,) I. 29. A sort of NOLI-ME-TANGERE manner.

1828. LYTTON, *Pelham*, iii. The NOLI ME TANGERE of literary lions.

1832. *Edin. Rev.*, LV. 520. Under less restraint from the NOLI ME TANGERE etiquettes of conventional good breeding.

1877. READE, *Woman Hater*, x. A trick of putting on NOLI ME TANGERE faces amongst strangers.

NOLL (or **NOLE**), *subs.* (old).—The head: *see* CRUMPET.

c. 1400. *Arthur* [E. E. T. S.], line 211. How darst now any wyse Azenst the *Emperour nus* aryse? And make kynge to be obey? *nu* art wood on the NOLLE!

2. (old).—A simpleton.

1587. HIGGINS, *Mir. for Mag. K. Chirinnus*, 20 *Brit. Bibl.* (1814), iv. A drousy NOLE that lyes On drinke a sleepe so long, May pardon craue, although His tongue trip twifold wrong.

OLD NOLL, *subs.* (old).—*See* quot. 1696.

c. 1696. B. E., *Dict. Cant. Crew*, s.v. NOL Oliver. OLD NOL, the late Vsurper, Cromwell.

1785. GROSE, *Vulg. Tongue*, s.v.

NO-MAN'S-LAND, *subs. phr.* (common).—Waste ground; an unsettled acreage; a barren or broken stretch between two provinces or kingdoms: *cf.* TOM TIDDLER'S GROUND.

NOMINATE. *See* POISON.

NOMMUS. *See* NAMMOUS.

NON-COM, *subs.* (common). — A non-commissioned officer.

1885. J. S. WINTER, *In Quarters*, viii. Well-tipped quartermasters and their favourite tools among the NON-COMS.

NON-CON, *subs. phr.* (old).—A nonconformist: *see* quots. 1696 and 1823.

c. 1696. B. E., *Dict. Cant. Crew*, s.v. NON-CON, one that don't conform to the Church of England.

c. 1707. DURFEY, *Pills to Purge, &c.* (1707), ii. 226. The Niece of a Canting, Bleer-Ey'd NON-CON.

1748. DODSLEY, *Collection of Poems*, I. 66. Said a formal NON-CON, whose rich stock of grace Lies forward expos'd in shop-window of face, Ah! pity your soul, come, be of our sect, For then you are safe, and may plead you're elect.

1785. GROSE, *Vulg. Tongue*, s.v.

1823. BEE, *Dict. Turf*, s.v. NON-CONFORMIST—a discontented person, who will think and act differently from all others.

1843. CRABB ROBINSON, in *Diary*, 7 April, ii. 239 (3rd ed. 1872). So it is that extremes meet, and that we NON-CONS are in accord with the High Church divines.

NON-EST-INVENTUS, *phr.* (popular).—Absent.—DE QUINCEY, *Murder as one of the Fine Arts.*

NON-LICET, *adj. phr.* (Winchester College).—Illegal; unbefitting a Wykehamist: *e.g.* Don't sport NON-LICET notions.

NONNY (NONINO, or HEY, NONNY, NONNY), *subs.* (old).—1. A refrain once used to cover indelicate allusions.

1593. DRAYTON, *Eccl.* These NONINOS of beastly ribauldry.

c. 1620-50. *Percy Folio MS.*, 201. Cupid bidds itt shold bee soe, because all men were made for her HINONONINO.

c. 1625. BEAUMONT and FLETCHER, *Hum. Lieut.*, iv. 2. That noble mind to melt away and moulder For a HEY NONNY, NONNY.

2. (old).—A simpleton: *see* BUFFLE and CABBAGE-HEAD.

NONPLUST, *adv.* (old).—At the end of one's tether. Also AT POINT NONPLUS.

1708-10. SWIFT, *Polite Conversation*, ii. Faith, Tom is NONPLUST; he looks plaguily down in the mouth.

1821. EGAN, *Life in Lond.*, II. i. 147. Remember that he is not yet out of Pupil's Straits, and must not, as you say, be blown up at POINT NONPLUS.

NONSENSE, *subs.* (old).—1. Money: *see* ACTUAL and GILT.

1821. EGAN, *Life in London.* Shell out the NONSENSE: half a quid Will speak more truth than all your palaver.

2. (old).—*See* quot.

1823. GROSE, *Vulg. Tongue* [EGAN], s.v. NONSENSE. Melting butter in a wig. Also, fastening the door with a boiled carrot.

3. (Eton College).—A small division of the Third Form.

NONSUCH, THE, *subs.* (venery).—1. The female *pudendum*: *see* MONOSYLLABLE.

2. (old colloquial).—*See* quot. 1785. Ital. *una coppa d'oro.*

1767. RAY, *Proverbs* [BOHN], 172, s.v.

1785. GROSE, *Vulg. Tongue*, s.v. NONE-SUCH, one that is unequalled; frequently applied ironically.

NONJUROR, *subs.* (old).—*See* quot.

c. 1696. B. E., *Dict. Cant. Crew*, s.v. NONJURORS. Clergymen and others (Officers in the Army, Navy, etc.) That refus'd to take the Oaths to King William and Queen Mary, and were turn'd out of their Livings and Employments.

NOODLE, *subs.* (common). — A simpleton. Also BILLY NOODLE. *See* BUFFLE and CABBAGE-HEAD.—ASH (1775); BEE (1823).

1843. MONCRIEFF, *The Scamps of London*, ii. 3. Half-and-half know-nothing NOODLE.

c. 1845. SYDNEY SMITH *Review of Bentham on Fallacies.* The whole of these fallacies may be gathered together in a little oration which we will denominate the NOODLES' oration.

1864. FORSYTH, *Life of Cicero*, xi. He was such a NOODLE he did not know the value of what he had bought.

1892. G. M. FENN, *The New Mistress*, xv. Making a great NOODLE of yourself.

THE HOUSE OF NOODLES, *subs. phr.* (old).—*See* quot.

1823. BEE, *Dict. Turf*, s.v. NOODLE. The HOUSE OF NOODLES, the Upper Nobs' house at Palace Yard, Westminster.

Verb. (common).—To fool.

1829. *The Lag's Lament* [FARMER, *Musa Pedestris* (1896), 111]. He so prewailed on the treach'rous varmint That she was NOODLED by the Bow St. sarmint.

NOODLEDOM, *subs.* (colloquial).—The world of fools.

NOOKERY, *subs.* (colloquial).—A snug corner; a place of hiding.

1857. *Old Song*, 'The Leary Man' [FARMER, *Musa Pedestris* (1896), 154]. Then go to St. Giles's Rookery, And live up some strange NOOKERY . . . To be a Leary Man.

NOOM, *subs.* (back-slang).—The moon; OLIVER (*q.v.*).

NOOSE (or **NOOZE**), *verb.* (common).—1. To hang.—B. E. (*c.* 1696); GROSE (1785).

1676. *Warning for Housekeepers* [FARMER, *Musa Pedestris* (1896), 32]. And when that he hath NOOSED us.

c. 1712. *Old Ballads*, 'The Twenty Craftsmen' [FARMER, *Musa Pedestris* (1896), 37]. None shall be NOOZ'D if you find but one true.

1754. *Scoundrel's Dict.* If they catch him horse-stealing he's NOOZ'D for all.

1809. SCOTT, *The Poacher.* Our buckskinn'd justices expound the law, Wire-draw the acts that fix for wires the pain, And for the netted partridge NOOZE the swain.

2. (old).—To marry. Whence NOOSING = a wedding; NOOSE (or MARRIAGE-NOOSE) = the nuptial knot.—B. E. (*c.* 1699); GROSE (1785); MATSELL (1859).

1617. C. SHADWELL, *Fair Quaker of Deal*, iv. I'll take the freedom of sending for our noble commodore and his lady too, who are by this time NOOZED.

1693. DRYDEN, *Juvenal*, VI. 59. To thrust his neck in the MARRIAGE-NOOSE!

1694. CROWNE, *Married Beau*, i. I. *Works* (1874), iv. 258. I'm loth to NOOSE myself in marriage.

1748. DYCHE, *Dictionary* (5th ed.). NOOZE (V.) . . . in the *Cant Language*, it means both to marry and to hang.

1751. SMOLLETT, *Peregrine Pickle*, xxix. The lieutenant, with a sly regard, pronounced, 'Tunley, warn't you NOOZED by the curate?'

1771. SMOLLETT, *Humphry Clinker*, Letter 52. His indefatigable rival ordered a post-chaise, and set out with the lady for Coldstream, a few miles up the Tweed, where there was a person who dealt in this branch of commerce, and there they were NOOSED.

1821. COMBE, *Syntax, Wife*, v. Nay, on the third or fourth day after: They were both NOOS'D in Hymen's garter.

1828-45. T. HOOD, *Poems*, i. 22 (ed. 1846). Next to that interesting job The hanging of Jack, or Bill, or Bob, There's nothing do draws a London mob As the NOOSING of very rich people.

1901. *St. James's Gaz.*, 7 Feb., 8, 5. The attendant announced that the bride and bridegroom were at the altar. "Oh, if that's so," said the Bishop to Wesley, "let's go and tie the NOOSE"!

NOPE, *subs.* (old). — A blow.—GROSE (1785); MATSELL (1859).

NOPE, *intg.* (American).—' No.'

NORAS, *subs. pl.* (Stock Exchange).—Great Northern Railway Deferred Ordinary Stock.

1887. ATKIN, *House Scraps.* For we have our Sarahs and Claras, Our NORAS and Doras for fays.

NORFOLK-CAPON, *subs.* (common).—A red herring: *see* GLASGOW MAGISTRATE.—GROSE (1785).

1836. SMITH, *The Individual*, 4. A NORFOLK CAPON is jolly grub.

NORFOLK-DUMPLING, *subs. phr.* (old).—*See* quot. 1785.

1670. RAY, *Proverbs*, 245. NORFOLK DUMPLINGS. This referres (*sic*) not to the stature of their bodies; but to the fare they commonly feed on and much delight in.

1785. GROSE, *Vulg. Tongue*, s.v. NORFOLK DUMPLING, a nick name or term of jocular reproach to a Norfolk man, dumplings being a favourite food in that country.

NORFOLK HOWARD, *subs. phr.* (common).—A bug.

[From (says John Camden Hotten) an advt. in *Times*, 23 June 1862, as follows:—I, Norfolk Howard, heretofore called and known by the name of Joshua Bug, late of Epsom, in the county of Surrey, now of Wakefield, in the county of York, and landlord of the Swan Tavern, in the same county, do hereby give notice that on the 20th day of this present month of June, for and on behalf of myself and heirs, lawfully begotten, I did wholly abandon the use of the surname of Bug and assumed, took, and used, and am determined . . . to be called and known by the name of Norfolk Howard only . . . duly enrolled by me in the High Court of Chancery.—Dated this 23 day of June, 1862.—NORFOLK HOWARD, late JOSHUA BUG.—Diligent search in the *Times* of the date mentioned has failed to unearth the document. At the same time it is certain that a Joshua Bug lived at Epsom about the date mentioned.]

1870. *Figaro*, 19 Oct. Those entomological pests that are euphemistically called NORFOLK HOWARDS. *Ibid.* 1871, 26 Dec. A traveller at a hotel, while registering his name, saw a lively NORFOLK HOWARD making his way briskly across the page. In consternation he declared that he had . . . never before stopped at a place where a NORFOLK HOWARD looked over the hotel register to see where his room was.

1872. *Era*, 27 July. Negligent domestic servants, lodging-house keepers, bathing arrangements, bad drainage, NORFOLK HOWARDS, careless boatmen, and a thousand other topics will be seized upon as pegs on which to hang a series of grumblings.

1885. SALA, in *Daily Telegraph*, 14 August, 573. 'Bed bugs,' the convertible term for which is 'chintzes,' are the disagreeable insects known in modern polite English as NORFOLK HOWARDS.

1892. *Society*, 6 Aug., 757/1. Such writers as this, says the lord of verse, are the lice on the locks of literature. Also I should presume they are the flea down the back of Poetry, and the NORFOLK HOWARD in the shirt of Art.

2. In pl. (military).—The Norfolk Regiment, formerly the 9th Foot.

NORFOLK-NOG, *subs. phr.* (old).—A kind of strong ale.

1726. VANBRUGH, *Journey to London*, i. 2. Here's NORFOLK NOG to be had at next door.

c. 1745. SWIFT, *Upon The Horrid Plot.* Dog Walpole laid a quart of NOG on't He'd either make a hog or dog on't.

NOR-LOCH TROUT, *subs. phr.* (Scots').—*See* quot.

1808. JAMIESON, *Dict.* s.v. A cant phrase formerly denoting a joint or leg of mutton, ordered for a club of citizens who used to meet in one of the *closes* leading down to the North loch. The invitation was given in these terms: Will ye gang and eat a NOR LOCH TROUT? The reason of the name is obvious. This was the only species of *fish* which the North Loch, on which the shambles were situated, could supply.

NORP, *verb.* (theatrical).—To put in phrases that will 'fetch' the gallery; to PILE IT UP (*q.v.*).

NORTH, *adj.* (nautical).—1. Strong; good; well fortified; usually of grog. Hence DUE NORTH = neat; TOO FAR NORTH = drunk.

1864. *Glasgow Herald*, 9 Nov. 'Review of Hottens' Slang Dict.' An old salt delights to order his steward to make his grog 'a little more NORTH,' 'another point, steward;' and so on he may go until the beverage is DUE NORTH as the needle.

2. (common). — Intelligent; FLY (*q.v.*); UP TO SNUFF (*q.v.*). *Cf.* Fr. *perdre le nord* = to be confused.

1700. *Step to the Bath* [quoted in ASHTON, *Social Life in Reign of Q. Anne*, v. ii. p. 168]. I ask'd what Countrey-man my Landlord was? answer was made, Full NORTH; and Faith 'twas very Evident, for he had put the *Yorkshire* most damnably upon us.

1859. SALA, *Gaslight and Daylight*, iii. p. 39. Her husband—who, however far gone he may be in liquor, is a long way too FAR NORTH to 'list in reality.

NORTHALLERTONS. *See* quot.

1823. GROSE, *Vulg. Tongue* [EGAN], s.v. NORTHALLERTONS. Spurs; that place, like Rippon, being famous for making them.

NORTH COUNTRY COMPLIMENT, *subs. phr.* (common).—A gift not wanted by the giver nor valued by the receiver.

NORTH-EASTER, *subs.* (old American).—A New England sixpence or shilling *temp.* Charles I. [On one side were the letters N.E.]

NORTH-EYE, *subs. phr.* (showmen's).—[As in quot., but failure has followed all attempts to ascertain the meaning].

1893. EMERSON, *Signor Lippo*, xiv. Don't get your back up only having a bit of chaff with your NORTH EYE.

NORTHUMBERLAND, LORD NORTHUMBERLAND'S ARMS, *subs. phr.* (old).—*See* quot.

1823. GROSE, *Vulg. Tongue* [EGAN], s.v. NORTHUMBERLAND. LORD NORTHUMBERLAND'S ARMS; a black eye: so called in the last century.

NORWAY NECKCLOTH, *subs. phr.* (old).—*See* quot.

1785. GROSE, *Vulg. Tongue*, NORWAY NECKCLOTH, the pillory, usually made of Norway fir.

NORWICHER, *subs.* (old).—An unfair drinker: *i.e.*, a man who, taking first pull at a tankard, does not draw breath till he has pretty well emptied the pot.

1896. *Athenæum*, 15 Aug., p. 168. Thirsty souls! there was no resisting it. Half-a-dozen old NORWICHERS, after a bout of this sort, would become as hilarious and would dance as uproariously as half-a-dozen Egyptians, full of the barleywine of Memphis.

NOSE, *subs.* (old).—1. An informer. Fr., *une riflette*; *une tante*; *une soulasse*, and *une sondeur*.

1789. PARKER, *Life's Painter*, 167, s.v. NOSE. Snitch.

1819. VAUX, *Memoirs*, s.v.

1823. GROSE, *Vulg. Tongue* [EGAN], s.v.

1828. BEE, *Living Picture of London*, 286. They are frequently made use of as NOSES by the officers.

1836. BARHAM, *Ingoldsby Legends* (ed. 1862), 356. Now Bill, . . . Who as his last speech sufficiently shows Was a 'regular trump'—did not like to turn NOSE?

1838. REYNOLDS, *Pickwick Abroad*, 223. I was never a NOSE for the regulars came Whenever a pannie was done.

2. (police).—A paid spy; A SHADOW (*q.v.*); a NARK (*q.v.*). Also NOSER.

1819. VAUX, *Memoirs*, s.v. A person who, seeing one or more suspicious characters in the street, makes a point of watching them, in order to frustrate any attempt they may make, or cause their apprehension.

1823. GROSE, *Vulg. Tongue* [EGAN], s.v. NOSE.

1851-61. MAYHEW, *Lond. Lab. and Lond. Poor*, i. 391. I live in Westminster, at a padding-ken. I'd rather not tell you where, not I've anything to fear, but people might think I was a NOSE, if anybody came after me.

1862. *Cornhill Mag.*, ii. 336. There are a few men and women among thieves called NOSERS. They are so called because they are in the secret pay of the police, giving information when the information will not lead to the crimination of themselves.

1877. J. GREENWOOD, *Dick Temple.* How could they know that there wasn't a NOSE—that is a detective p'lceman—there in disguise?

1884. *Saturday Review*, 9 Feb., 178. To bring a hidden crime to light by means of the policeman's NOSE.

Verb. (old).—1. *See* quots. 1598 and 1785.

1596. SHAKSPEARE, *Hamlet*, iv. 3. You shall NOSE him as you go up the stairs into the lobby.

1598. FLORIO, *Worlde of Wordes*, *Nasare*, to smell, to scent, TO NOSE.

1728. BAILEY, *Eng. Dict.*, s.v.

1785. GROSE, *Vulg. Tongue*, s.v. NOSE, TO NOSE a stink, to smell it.

2. (common).—To pry; to suspect; to discover.

1651. CARTWRIGHT, *Ordinary*, v. 5. NOSING a little treason 'gainst the King.

1662. *Rump Songs*, i. 60. We will thrust them out of the Main-yard, If they do but NOSE us.

1664. COTTON, *Virgil Travestie* (1st ed). Must these same *Trojan* Rascals NOSE me, Because the *Fates* (forsooth) oppose me?

1819. VAUX, *Memoirs*, s.v.

1821. EGAN, *Life in London*, II. v. You are determined no one shall NOSE your ideas. *Ibid.* Their ogles were on the roll, under an apprehension that the beaks were "on the NOSE."

1830. *Westminster Rev.*, April, *The Six Acts.* The public that NOSED the 'Six Acts' gave the title that has stuck by them; and condemned them to everlasting remembrance by the energy of its simplicity.

1830. MONCRIEFF, *The Heart of London*, ii. 1. I NOSE: up to snuff.

1838. GLASCOCK, *Land Sharks and Sea Gulls*, ii. 103. Go to the landlord an' ax if he knows the cove:—'t won't do to be NOSED, you know.

1889. *Detroit Free Press*, 16 Feb. He said he didn't like one NOSING around downstairs.

3. (thieves').—To inform.

1821. EGAN, *Life in London*, 278. No, no, no! no NOSING.

1823. GROSE, *Vulg. Tongue* [EGAN], s.v. NOSE. His pall NOSED, and he was twisted for a crack; his confederate turned king's evidence, and he was hanged for burglary.

1829. *The Lag's Lament* [FARMER, *Musa Pedestris* (1896), III.]. I adwise you TO NOSE on your pals.

1834. AINSWORTH, *Rookwood*, v. i. Nor was he ever known to NOSE upon any of his accomplices; or in other words to betray them.

4. (old).—*See* quot. 1775.

1775. ASH, *Dict.*, s.v. NOSE. To bluster, to look big.

1785. GROSE, *Vulg. Tongue*, s.v.

5. (old).—*See* quot.

1819. VAUX, *Memoirs*, s.v. NOSE.. To NOSE UPON any one, is to tell of anything he has said or done with a view to injure him, or to benefit yourself.

[Many colloquialisms are here conveniently grouped: *e.g.*, TO PUT ONE'S NOSE OUT OF JOINT = to supplant; TO WIPE ONE'S NOSE = (1) to cozen; (2) to affront; and (3) in medicine, to discover an error in diagnosis and alter treatment (the mistaken practitioner is said to have his NOSE WIPED); TO PUT ONE'S NOSE IN THE MANGER = to eat; TO FOLLOW ONE'S NOSE = to go straight forward; TO LEAD BY THE NOSE = to govern; TO PAY THROUGH THE NOSE = to pay extravagantly; TO PUT ONE'S NOSE INTO ANYTHING = to meddle; TO TURN UP ONE'S NOSE = to disdain; TO CAST IN (or TO PLAY WITH) ONE'S NOSE = to twit, or to ridicule; TO HAVE ONE'S NOSE ON THE GRINDSTONE = to be held at a disadvantage; TO BE BORED THROUGH THE NOSE = to be cheated; IN SPITE OF YOUR NOSE = in your teeth; TO BITE (or TO CUT OFF) ONE'S NOSE TO SPITE ONE'S FACE = to be revenged to one's own detriment; TO TELL (or TO COUNT) NOSES = to appeal to numbers; TO MAKE A PERSON'S NOSE SWELL = to make jealous; TO MEASURE NOSES = to meet; TO TAKE PEPPER IN THE NOSE = (1) to take offence; and (2) to mistrust; AS PLAIN AS THE NOSE ON ONE'S FACE = beyond argument; A GOOD NOSE = a smell-feast; TO MAKE A BRIDGE OF SOMEONE'S NOSE = to pass in drinking, also to supersede; TO HOLD UP ONE'S NOSE = to be proud; A NOSE OF WAX = a complaisant or accommodating disposition; CANDLES (or DEWDROPS) IN THE NOSE = snots; ON THE NOSE = on the look out; A NOSE TO LIGHT CANDLES AT = a drunkard's nose, a poop-lantern; YOUR NOSE UP MY ARSE = an expression of supreme contempt; A LONG NOSE IS A LADY'S LIKING (length above being held to indicate length below); TO SEE THE NOSE CHEESE FIRST = to refuse contemptuously; MY NOSE ITCHES! = a jocular invitation to kiss, the retort being 'I knew I was going to sneeze, be cursed, or kissed by a fool,' but *see* quot. 1708-10; and so forth].

1542. UDALL, tr. of *Apopht. of Erasmus*, p. 65. A feloe had CAST HIM IN THE NOSE, that he gave so large monie to soche a naughtie drabbe.

1570. ELDERTON, *Lenten Stuffe.* Pepper ys come to a marvelus pryse, Som say, thys Lenton season; And every body that ys wyse May soone perceve the reson; For every man takes PEPPER IN THE NOSE For the waggynge of a strawe, God knowse.

1580. TARLTON, *Newes out of Purg.*, 10. Myles, hearing him name the baker, took straight PEPPER IN THE NOSE, and, starting up . . . swore I by cockes-bread, the baker; and he that saies to the contrary, heere stand I, Myles, the bakers man, to have the proudest cardinall of you all by the eares.

1581. RICHE, *Farewell* [NARES]. Who . . . was verie well assured that it could bee no other than his owne manne that had thrust HIS NOSE SO FARRE OUT OF JOYNTE.

1591. NASHE, *Prognostication* [GROSART (1883-4), ii. 167]. Some shal be so sun burnt with sitting in the Alehouse, that their NOSES SHALL BEE ABLE TO LIGHT A CANDLE.

1598. FLORIO, *Worlde of Wordes*, s.v. *Montare su la Bica*, to TAKE PEPPER IN THE NOSE, to be sore angrie.

1602. DECKER, *Satiromastix*, in *Wks.* (1873), i. 216. Yonder bald Adams, is PUT MY NOSE FROM HIS IOYNT; but Adam I will be even to you.

1604. SHAKSPEARE, *Winter's Tale*, iv. 4, 832. Though authority be a stubborn bear, yet he is oft LED BY THE NOSE with gold.

1606. *Wily Beguiled* [DODSLEY, *Old Plays* (1874), ix. 242]. There is one Sophos, a brave gentleman; he'll WIPE YOUR son Peter's NOSE of Mistress Lelia.

1607. MARSTON, *What You Will*, Induction. He's a chollerick gentleman: he will TAKE PEPPER IN THE NOSE instantly.

1607. *Puritan*, v. 1. Now all the Knights NOSES ARE PUT OUT OF JOINT.

1608. ARMIN, *Nest of Ninnies* [NARES]. Standing on tip-toe, looking toward the door to behold a rivall, that he would PUT HIS NOSE OUT OF JOINT.

1612. *Passenger of Benvenuto* [NARES]. Strange children, TO WIPE HER HUSBANDS OWNE CHILDRENS NOSE of their share in his goods.

1614. BERNARD, *Terence in English* [NARES]. And why so, I pray you, but that you love him better than me? And fearing now least this wench which is brought over hither should PUT YOUR NOSE OUT THE JOYNT, comming betweene home and you, and so have such a trimme fellow her selfe.

1614. BERNARD, *Terence in English* [NARES]. But loe, nowe comes forth the very destruction of our substance: WHO WIPES OUR NOSES of all that we should have. *Ibid.* I'VE WIPED THE OLD MEN'S NOSES of their money.

1639. *Optick Glasse of Humors* [NARES]. A man is teisty, and anger wrinckles his nose, such a man takes PEPPER IN THE NOSE.

1639. MASSINGER, *Unnat. Combat*, v. 2. But vows with you being like To your religion, a NOSE OF WAX, To be turned every way.

1642. HOWELL, *Forreine Travell*, p. 44. I have known divers Dutch Gentlemen grosly guld by this cheat, and som English BOR'D also THROUGH THE NOSE this way.

1646. RANDOLPH, *Jealous Lovers* [NARES]. Shee was soe NOSE-WIP'T, slighted, and disdain'd, Under honour's cloak soe closely muffled, And in my rare projects soe shuffled.

1660. HOWELL, *Parl. of Beasts*, p. 35. Those fears and jealousies appeared afterwards to every common man AS PLAIN AS THE NOSE ON HIS FACE to bee but meer forgeries and suppositious things.

d. 1660. BP. GAUDEN, *Teares of the Church*, p. 105. The polle and number of the names . . . I think to be but the number of the Beast, if we onely TELL NOSES, and not consider reasons.

1662. PEPYS, *Diary*, 31 May. The King is pleased enough with her: which I fear, will put Madam Castlemaine's NOSE OUT OF JOYNT.

1662. *Rump Songs* [NARES]. Alas, what take ye PEPPER IN THE NOSE To see king Charles his colours worne in pose?

1664. COTTON, *Virgil Travestie* (1st ed.), 60. There lies your way, FOLLOW YOUR NOSE.

1675. COTTON, *Scoffer Scofft*, in *Wks.* (1725), p. 182. SPIGHT OF YOUR NOSE, and will ye, nil ye, I will go home again, that will I.

1693. WOOD, *Fasti Oxon.*, ii. Too easy, like A NOSE OF WAX, to be turned on that side.

c. 1696. B. E., *Dict. Cant. Crew*, s.v. NOSE. FOLLOW YOUR NOSE, said in a jeer to those that know not the way, and are bid to smell it out, as we say to smell a post. *Ibid.* He is LED BY THE NOSE. Of one that is easily imposed upon. *Ibid.* AS PLAIN AS THE NOSE in your face. *Ibid.* He has a good NOSE. Of a Smell Feast. *Ibid.* You MAKE A BRIDGE OF HIS NOSE. When you pass your next Neighbor in Drinking or one is preferr'd over another's head. *Ibid.* He HOLDS UP HIS NOSE, of one that is Haughty, and carries his Head high.

1708-10. SWIFT, *Polite Conversations*, I. FOLLOW YOUR NOSE; go, enquire among the Servants. *Ibid. Neverout.* Pray, my Lord, don't MAKE A BRIDGE OF MY NOSE. *Ibid. Miss.* Anything for a quiet life; MY NOSE ITCH'D, and I knew I should drink wine, or kiss a fool.

1720. *New Cant. Dict.*, s.v. NOSE.

d. 1745. SWIFT, *To Gay.* Nor think yourself secure in doing wrong By TELLING NOSES with a party strong.

1731. *Windsor Medley*, 13. If you FOLLOW YOUR NOSE, you're as sure as a Gun.

1764. O'HARA, *Midas*, i. 4. Aye, Pol, the hind, PUT OUT OF JOINT OUR NOSES.

1767. RAY, *Proverbs* [BOHN], 151, s.v. TO MAKE A BRIDGE OF ONE'S NOSE. *i.e.* To intercept one's trencher, cup, or the like; or to offer or pretend to do kindnesses to one, and then pass him by, and do it to another; to lay hold upon and serve himself of that which was intended for another.

1781. COWPER, *Truth.* . . With slipshod heels & DEWDROP AT HIS NOSE.

1785. GROSE, *Vulg. Tongue*, s.v. NOSE; TO PUT ONE'S NOSE OUT OF JOINT, to rival one in the favor of any person. *Ibid.* TO FOLLOW ONE'S NOSE, to go straight forward. *Ibid.* He is LED BY THE NOSE, he is governed. *Ibid.* AS PLAIN AS THE NOSE ON YOUR FACE, evidently to be seen. *Ibid.* TO MAKE A BRIDGE OF ANYONE'S NOSE, to pass by him in drinking.

1833. LYTTON, *Godolphin*, II. iii. To find their NOSES PUT OUT OF JOINT by that little mischief-making interloper!

1838. NEAL, *Charcoal Sketches* [DE VERE]. At all events he had his NOSE TO THE GRINDSTONE, an operation which should make men keen.

1844. BUCKSTONE, *The Maid with Milking Pail.* Now MY NOSE IS PUT COMPLETELY OUT OF JOINT. No niceties—no pudding—no fresh salt butter—no cabbage soup—no nothing!

1859. KINGSLEY, *Geoffry Hamlyn*, xxxiii. Lesbia gave herself the airs, and received the privileges of being the handsomest woman in those parts, till Alice came, and PUT HER NOSE OUT OF JOINT, for which she never forgave her.

1860. GEO. ELIOT, *Mill on the Floss*, iii., 5. To TURN UP HIS NOSE at his father's customers, and to be a fine gentleman.

1861. HUGHES, *Tom Brown at Oxford*, vi. I like to see a fellow an honest grubber at breakfast and dinner; but you've always got YOUR NOSE IN THE MANGER.

1869. YEATS, *Fairy Tales of the Irish Peasantry*, 237. From this. . . he KEPT BILL'S NOSE TO THE GRINDING-STONE.

1870. *Figaro*, 26 Oct. The Prussians, to whom an immediate supply of these is necessary, have to pay what is vulgarly called THROUGH THE NOSE.

1872. DE VERE, *Americanisms*, 620, s.v. NOSE TO THE GRINDSTONE, a very expressive phrase, denoting the ill-treatment received at the hands of a successful adversary who takes full advantage of his triumph.

1888. ROLF BOLDREWOOD, *Robbery under Arms*, xxiii. These sort of men PAY THROUGH THE NOSE for everything.

NOSE-AND-CHIN, *subs. phr* (rhyming).—A penny: a WIN (*q.v.*).

NOSEBAG, *subs.* (waiters').—1. A sea-side visitor who carries his own victuals with him.

2. (common).—A veil.

3. (old: now recognised).—A bag of provender fastened to a horse's head.—GROSE (1788).—Whence (colloquial) a hand-bag.

1887. *Cornhill Mag.*, April, 370. So I yesterday packed up my NOSEBAG, and away I posted down to Aldgate.

TO HAVE THE NOSE-BAG IN ONE'S FACE. *See* quot.

1788. GROSE, *Vulg. Tongue*, s.v. NOSE-BAG. I see the NOSE-BAG IN HIS FACE; *i.e.*, he has been a private man, or rode private.

TO PUT ON THE NOSE-BAG, *verb. phr.* (colloquial).—To eat hurriedly, or whilst at work.

NOSEGENT, *subs.* (Old Cant).—*See* quot. 1785.

1573. HARMAN, *Caveat* (Repr. 1814), p. 87. There was a proude patrico and a NOSEGENT.

*c.*1696. B. E., *Dict. Cant. Crew*, s.v.

1720. *New Cant. Dict.*, s.v.

1785. GROSE, *Vulg. Tongue*, s.v. NOSE-GENT, a nun.

NOSE'M, *subs.* (common).—Tobacco; FOGUS (*q.v.*).

NOSENDER (NOSER or NOSEGAY), *subs.* (pugilists').—A bloody blow on the nose.

1823. GROSE, *Vulg. Tongue* [EGAN], s.v. NOSE-GAY. A blow on the nose. Pugilistic cant.

1851-61. MAYHEW, *London Lab.*, I. 14. A bloody nose however is required to show that the blow was veritably a NOSER.

1860. BRADLEY ('Cuthbert Bede'), *Verdant Green*, II. p. 25. You see, Sir, said the Pet, I ain't used to the feel of it, and I couldn't go to business properly, or give a straight NOSENDER, nohow.

1868. WHYTE MELVILLE, *White Rose*, xxxvi. He told his neighbour at the Blues Mess how it was a regular NOSE-ENDER for the Dandy, and he was glad of it.

1876. HINDLEY, *Adventures of a Cheap Jack*, 190. Giving the man such a NOSE-ENDER that sent him all abroad.

NOSER-MY-KNACKER, *subs. phr.* (rhyming). — Tobacco; FOGUS (*q.v.*)

NOSE-WARMER. *subs.* (common).—A short pipe. Fr., *un brûle-gueule*.

NOSE-WATCH, *phr.* (Old Cant).—*See* quot. and WATCH.

1573. HARMAN, *Caveat* (E. E. T. S. Rept.), 85. I will lage it of with a gage of benebouse; then cut to my NOSE WATCH. I wull washe it off with a quart of good drynke; then say to me what thou wylt.

NOSE-WIPE, *s. phr.* (vulgar).—A handkerchief: *see* FOGLE.

NOS-RAP, *subs. phr.* (back-slang).—A parson; a DEVIL-DODGER (*q.v.*).

NOSTRUM, *subs.* (old: now recognised).—*See* quot.

1785. GROSE, *Vulg. Tongue*, s.v. NOSTRUM, a medicine prepared by particular persons only, a quack medicine.

NOT. *See* BAKER; CARE; CARROT; CURSE; DAM; DEVIL; FEATHER; FIG; FIT; FLY; HALF BAD; IN IT; JOE (or JOSEPH); LONG SHOT (or SIGHT); MUCH; SHOWER; RAP; TO-DAY; WORTH; YESTERDAY.

NOTCH, *subs.* (venery).—*See* quot., and MONOSYLLABLE.

1785. GROSE, *Vulg. Tongue*, s.v. NOTCH, the private parts of a woman.

Verb. (cricketers'). — 1. To score; and (2—common) to denote an advantage: *e.g.*, 'Notch me another.'

1836. DICKENS, *Pickwick*, vii. In short, when Dumkins was caught out, and Podder stumped out, All-Muggleton had NOTCHED, some fifty-four, while the score of the Dingley Dellers was as blank as their faces.

NOTE, *subs.* (American).—1. A bon-bon.

2. (American). — A singer.—MATSELL (1859).

NOTER, *subs.* (Harrow School).—A notebook.

NOTE-SHAVER, *subs. phr.* (American).—A usurer; a usurious compositor: specifically a WILD-CAT BANK (*q.v.*) purchasing notes of hand at excessive rates of discount. [Obsolete since the regulation of banks by Congress.] *See* PAPER.

NOTHING. *See* DANCE, NECK, and SAY.

NOTICE TO QUIT, *subs. phr.* (old).—*See* quot.

1823. GROSE, *Vulg. Tongue* [EGAN], s.v. NOTICE TO QUIT. A cant phrase. When a person is in danger of dying from bad health, it is said, he has received A NOTICE TO QUIT.

NOTION, *subs.* (Winchester College).—1. A word, usage, or phrase peculiar to Winchester College.

1891. *Notions* [Title].

2. (American).—A trifle; a nick-nack: specifically (in *pl.*) = wares in general.

1719. WARD, *London Spy*, i. 2. s.v.

1825. NEAL, *Bro. Jonathan*, II. 22. The tallow, corn, cotton, hams, hides, and so forths, which we had got in exchange for a load of Yankee NOTIONS.

1836. MICHAEL SCOTT, *Cruise of Midge*, 300. A cargo of flour and NOTIONS, consigned to Macal, Walker, and Co.

1840. DANA, *Two Years before the Mast*, xxxv. A cargo of fresh provisions, mules, tin bake-pans, and other NOTIONS.

1846. MARRYAT, *Peter Simple*, III. iii. [1846], 325. Her cargo consisted of what the Americans call NOTIONS: that is in English an assorted cargo.

1866. HOWELLS, *Venetian Life*, ix. Fruitstands, and stands for the sale of crockery, and—as I must say for want of a better word, if there is any—NOTIONS, were in a state of tasteful readiness.

1867. SMYTH, *Sailor's Word Book*, 501, s.v. NOTIONS. An American sea-term for a cargo in sorts; thus a NOTION vessel on the west coast of America is a perfect bazaar: but one, which sold a mixture—logwood, bad claret, and sugar—to the priests for sacrament wine had to run for it.

1884. C. KENNAN, in *The Century*, xxxviii. 82. American goods of all kinds bought from California, suddenly made their appearance in the village shops; and . . . I saw the American tin-ware, lanterns, and YANKEE NOTIONS.

1888. *St. Louis Globe-Democrat*, 21 Jan. Thursday, January 26, regular auction sale of dry goods, furnishing goods, NOTIONS, hats and caps, etc.

1891. *Sportsman*, 1 April. To examine the remedies which came from the land of the Stars and Stripes, the home of Colonel Buncombe and of innumerable NOTIONS.

NOTIONAL, *adj.* (colloquial).—Imaginative; whimsical; sentimental. Also NOTIONATE.

1691-92. *Gentlemen's Journal*, Mar., 5. The lady tip'd (perhaps) out of her NOTIONAL love, was downright bent for a more substantial one.

1728. BAILEY, *Eng. Dict.*, s.v.

1881. HOWELLS, *Dr. Breen's Practice*, ix. She's been a little NOTIONAL, she's had her head addled by women's talk, and she's in a queer freak.

NOTTAMIZER, *subs.* (old).—A dissecting surgeon.

1828. SMEATON, *Doings in London*. At length his affectionate rib acknowledged that she had sold the corpse saying she had no idea the NOTTAMIZERS would have given so much for poor John's body.

NOTTINGHAM LAMB. *See* Lamb, *subs.*, sense 2.

NOUS, *subs.* (literary). — Sense; shrewdness. [From the Greek *nous*].

1678. CUDWORTH, *Intell. System*, Bk. I. iv. 406. But in other places of his Writings he frequently asserts, above the self-moving Psyche an Immovable and standing NOUS or Intellect, which was properly the Demiurgus, or Architectonic Framer of the whole World.

1729. POPE, *Dunciad*, iv. 244. Terine is the genuine head of many a house, And much Divinity without a NOUS.

*a.*1796. WOLCOT ('Peter Pindar'), i. 229. Oh! aid, as lofty Homer says, my NOUSE To sing sublime the Monarch and the LOUSE.

1800. R. POLWHELE, in *Biogr. Sk. in Cornwall*, ii. App. p. 37. In admiration of my own keen NOUS That framed the model of so fine a house.

1819. BYRON, *Don Juan*, II. cxxx. The good old man had so much NOUS.

1823. BEE, *Dict. Turf*, s.v. NOUS—uppishness; 'to be up,' is to be NOUS; but this latter is chiefly confined to the gambling-houses—hells.

1827. REYNOLDS, *The Fancy*, 'The Fields of Tothill.' Most men of any NOUS will tell you this.

1838. *Comic Almanack*, 133. No doubt it's very wrong, and shows but little NOUS, To go a tea-drinking, and making merry.

1839-47. TODD, *Cyc. Anat. and Phys.*, iii. p. 144/2. Aristotle regarded the NOUS or reasoning faculties as separable from the remainder of the *psyche*.

1840-45. BARHAM, *Ingoldsby Legends*, II. 247. Dont . . . fancy, because a man's NOUS seems to lack, That whenever you please, you can give him the sack.

1846. HOOD, *Poems*, 92. But where's the reverence or where the NOUS, To ride on one's religion thro' the lobby.

1862. THACKERAY, *Phillip*, ii. ch. xvii. (1887), p. 244. The fellow has not NOUS enough to light upon any scientific discovery more useful than a new sauce for cutlets.

1870. *London Figaro*, 26 Oct. A Bab Ballad.' When burglars came to rob his house, He never failed their chief to thank; And, to reward their skilful NOUS, Would hand them cheques upon his bank.

1877. READE, *Woman Hater*, xiv. (1883), p. 136. It is only of late I have had the NOUS to see how wise she is.

*c.*1880. J. G. SAXE, *Wife's Revenge*. The literal Germans call it Mutterwiss, The Yankees gumption, and the Grecians NOUS. A useful thing to have about the house.

NOUS-BOX, *subs.* (common).—The head. *Cf.* KNOWLEDGE-BOX: *see* CRUMPET. — GROSE (1823); MATSELL (1859).

NOVA, *adj.* (showmen's).—Nine.

1893. EMERSON, *Signor Lippo*, xiv. There I bought the lot from big-headed Tom for NOVA SOLDI, and as you are gen-a-men you can have it for the same.

NOVELTY, THE, *subs. phr.* (venery).—The female *pudendum*: *see* MONOSYLLABLE.

NOWHERE, *adv.* (common).—Not in the reckoning; so far behind as not to be. [A reminiscenee of that 'Eclipse first, and the rest nowhere,' which described the victory of a famous horse].

1852. MISS WETHERELL, *Queechy*, x. All start alike, or there's no fun in the race. You've fairly distanced us—left us NOWHERE.

1859. *Spirit of the Times* [DE VERE, 620]. Where was Flora? Flora? why, she was NOWHERE—came in last but one.

1869. J. GREENWOOD, *Seven Curses of London*. The brave Panther when he has once crossed the threshold of that splendid damsel (who, by the way, is a thief, and addicted to drinking brandy by the 'bumper') is, vulgarly speaking, NOWHERE.

1872. DE VERE, *Americanisms*, 620, s.v. NOWHERE, to be, denotes utter failure or complete ignorance.

1884. MRS. OLIPHANT, *Madam*, xxvii. You are kept in such a state till the last moment, not knowing which is to win. Sometimes the favourite is simply NOWHERE.

NOZZLE, *subs.* (pugilists'). — The nose: *see* CONK.—GROSE (1785).

1871. G. MEREDITH, *Harry Richmond*, vii. 79 (1886). Fight, my merry one; she takes punishment, the prize-fighter sang out. First blood to you, Kiomi; uncork his claret, my duck; straight at the NOZZLE, he sees more lamps than shine in London, I warrant.

Verb. (tailors').—1. To shrink: *e.g.*, TO NOZZLE THE BOTTOMS = to shrink the fronts of trousers. Also (2), to pawn.

NTH (or **NTH PLUS ONE**), *subs.* (University).—*See* quot.

1864. BREWER, *Phrase and Fable*, s.v. . . . NTH, to the utmost degree. Thus *Cut to the Nth* means wholly unnoticed by a friend. The expression is taken from the index of a mathematical formula, where *n* stands for any number, and *n plus* 1 more than any number.

NUB, *subs.* (Old Cant).—1. The neck. —B. E. (*c.* 1696); BAILEY (1728); GROSE (1785); MATSELL (1859).

2. (old). — Copulation: *see* GREENS and RIDE. — GROSE (1785).

3. (Old Cant).—A husband.

Verb. (Old Cant).—To hang: *see* LADDER.

*c.*1712. *Budg and Snudg Song* [FARMER, *Musa Pedestris* (1896), 32]. When that he hath NUBBED us.

1743. FIELDING, *Jonathan Wild*, IV. ii. I am committed for the filing lay, man, and we shall be both NUBBED together.

NUBBIN, *subs.* (American).—A remnant; a small remainder.

NUBBING, *subs.* (Old Cant).—1. Hanging.—B. E. (*c.* 1696); *New Cant. Dict.* (1725); GROSE (1785).

2. (Old Cant).—Copulation: *see* GREENS and RIDE.

NUBBING-CHEAT (or **NUBBLING-CHIT**), *subs.* (Old Cant).—The gallows, whence NUBBING = a hanging; NUBBING-COVE = the hangman; and NUBBING-KEN = the Sessions House. — B. E. (*c.* 1696); *New Cant. Dict.* (1725); GROSE (1785).

ENGLISH SYNONYMS. Abraham's balsam (in botany = a species of willow); Beilby's ball-room; Chates (chattes or chats); City stage (formerly in front of Newgate; crap; deadly nevergreen; derrick; forks; government sign-post; hanging-cheat; horse foaled by an acorn; hotel door-posts; the ladder; leafless-tree; mare with three legs; Moll Blood (old Scots'); morning-drop; prop (Punch and Judy); the queer-'em (queer-'un queer-'um); scrag; scrag-squeezer; sheriff's picture-frame; squeezer; stalk (Punch and Judy); the stifler; the swing; three-legged mare; three trees; topping cheat; Tower-hill vinegar (the swordsman's block); tree that bears fruit all the year round; tree with three corners; treyning-cheat; triple-tree; Tuck'em Fair; Tyburn cross; widow; wooden-legged mare.

FRENCH SYNONYMS. *L'abbaye de Monte-à-regret* (= Mount Sorrowful Church: also *l'abbaye de Monte-à-rebours*, and *l'abbaye de Saint-Pierre* = *cinq pierres*, the five flag-stones in front of La Roquette); *la bascule; le béquille* (= crutch); *la béquillarde; la butte-à-regret* (= Heavy - Arse-Hill); *les deux mâts*, or *le haut mât* (old); *l'échelle* (= LADDER, *q.v.*); *la fenetre* (in allusion to the aperture into which falls the knife); *le géant; la jambe; la louisette* (old); *la lune à douze quartiers* (=the wheel on which criminals were broken); *la lunette d'approche* (specifically, the knife); *la Marianne; la mécanique; la mère*, or *la mère au bleu; le monde renversé; le Monte-à-regret* (= Mount Sorrowful: also *monte-à-rebours*); *la passe; le rasoir national* (so named in'93: also *le rasoir à Roch*, or *de la Cigogne —Roche*=a one-time executioner, and *la Cigogne*=the Préfecture of Police); *la sans-feuille* (=the LEAFLESS TREE, *q.v.*); *la veuve* (=the WIDOW, *q.v.*); *la voyante*.

1712. *The Black Procession* [FARMER, *Musa Pedestris* (1836) 37]. Up to the NUBBING CHEAT where they are nubb'd.

1714. JOHN HALL, *Memoirs* (4th ed.), 13, s.v.

1749. FIELDING, *Tom Jones*, xii. NUBBING CHEAT, cries Partridge, pray, sir, what is that? Why that, sir, said the stranger, is a cant phrase for the gallows.

*c.*1812. MAHER, *The Death of Socrates* [FARMER, *Musa Pedestris* (1896)], . . . When he came to the NUBBING-CHIT, He was tucked up so neat and so pretty.

1821. MARTIN and AYTOUN ('BON GUALTIER'), in *Tait's Edinburgh Mag.*, viii. 223. The faking boy to the crap has gone, at the NUBBLING-CHIT you'll find him.

1834. AINSWORTH, *Rookwood* (ed. 1864), 313. I fear Dick will scarce cheat the NUBBING-CHEAT this go. His time's up, I calculate.

NUDDIKIN [or **NODDLEKEN**], *subs.* (common).—The head.

NUFF, *adj.* and *adv.* (soldiers').—Enough. TO HAVE HAD ONE'S NUFF = to be 'elevated' or drunk: *cf.* N. C.

NUG, *verb.* (old).—1. To fondle; to grubble; and (2.) TO SWIVE (*q.v.*). Whence MY NUG = 'My dear': a general endearment. *Cf.* NUGGING DRESS and NUGGING HOUSE.—B. E. (*c.* 1696); *New Cant. Dict.* (1725); GROSE (1785); MATSELL (1859).

NUGGET, *subs.* (common).—In *pl.* = money: *see* ACTUAL and GILT.

1892. MILLIKEN, *'Arry Ballads*, 53. Keep check on the NUGGETS you spend.

NUGGETY, *adj.* and *adv.* (Australian).—*See* quot.

1887. *Daily News*, April 9, 5/4. The sort of man we call 'cobby,' the Americans designate 'stocky,' and the Australians style NUGGETTY.

NUGGING-DRESS, *subs. phr.* (old).—*See* quots. 1696 and 1823, NUG, *verb.* and NUGGING-HOUSE.

*c.*1696. B. E. *Dict. Cant. Crew*, s.v. NUGGING-DRESS. An odd or particular way, out of the Fashion.

1785. GROSE, *Vulg. Tongue*, s.v.

1823. GROSE, *Vulg. Tongue* [EGAN], s.v. NUGGING-DRESS. . . A loose kind of a dress, denoting a courtezan.

NUGGING-HOUSE, *subs.* (old).—A brothel: *see* NANNY-HOUSE.—GOOSE (1823); HALLIWELL (1847).

'NUITY. *subs.* (American). — *See* quots.

1872. DE VERE, *Americanisms*, 620, s.v. 'NUITY, a word believed by some writers to be derived from annuity, and by others to be an absurd form of knew, is thus explained.

18[?]. CHARLES NORDHOFF [DE VERE, 620]. Tom had what the capemen call 'NUITY, which means what the rest of Americans call go-aheaditiveness—a barbarous word, which no nation could coin, that did not find it easier to coin money than words.

NULL, *verb.* (old).—To beat: *see* TAN.—GROSE (1785); MATSELL (1859).

NULL-GROPERS, *subs. phr.* (old).—*See* quot.

1823. GROSE, *Vulg. Tongue* [EGAN], s.v. NULL GROPERS. Persons who sweep the streets, in search of old iron, nails, etc.

NULLING-COVE, *subs.* (pugilists').—A pugilist. — VAUX (1819); GROSE (1823).

NULLI SECUNDUS CLUB, *subs. phr.* (military). — The Coldstream Guards. Also known as "The Coldstreamers."

NUMANS, *subs.* (Old Cant).—Newgate.

1610. ROWLANDS, *Martin Mark-all* (H. Club's Repr. 1874), 39, s.v.

NUMBER. *See* MESS.

TO CONSULT THE BOOK OF NUMBERS, *verb. phr.* (old Parliamentary).—To call for a division; to put the matter to the vote.—GROSE (1785).

NUMBER 9, *subs. phr.* (old).—The Fleet Prison. [No. 9, Fleet Market].—BEE (1823).

NUMBER NIP, *subs.* (venery).—The female *pudendum*: *see* MONOSYLLABLE.

NUMBER ONE, *subs.* (colloquial).—1. Self. TO TAKE CARE OF NUMBER ONE = to look after one's own interests.

1838. DICKENS, *Oliver Twist*, xlii. Some conjurors say that number three is the magic number, and some say number seven. It's neither, my friend, neither. It's NUMBER ONE. Ha! ha! cried Mr. Bolter. NUMBER ONE for ever.

1848. LOWELL, *A Fable for Critics*, 48. Like most fathers, Bull hates to see NUMBER ONE Displacing himself in the mind of his son.

1871. *Judy*, 29 July. If a man doesn't TAKE CARE OF No. 1, he will soon have O to take care of!

1873. *Spectator*, 22 Mar., 379, col. 1. It is in the early chapters, too, that the author speaks of himself, seldom referring to NUMBER ONE afterwards—for a less egotistical book we have seldom seen.

1886. KENNARD, *Girl in Br. Habit*, xi. I was just beginning to find NUMBER ONE remarkably bad company, and am most grateful to you for your visit. It will do me an immensity of good.

2. (nursery).—Urination; also a chamber-pot.

3. (prison).—The cat-o'-nine-tails.

1889. *Answers*, 9 March, 233, 3. Punishment was ordered by the Directors—the Governor has no power to order flogging—and took the shape of two dozen of No. 1.

To be at NUMBER ONE, LONDON, *verb. phr.* (common).—To have the menstrual discharge: *see* FLAG.

NUMBER SIX. *See* NEWGATE KNOCKER.

NUMBER TWO, *subs. phr.* (prison).—1. The birch.

1889. *Answers*, 9 Mar., 233, 3. No. 2, by the way, is the birch.

2. (nursery).—Evacuation.

NUMPS, *subs.* (old).—A dolt; a fool: *see* BUFFLE and CABBAGE-HEAD.

1614. JONSON, *Bartholomew Fair*, s.v.

1673. PARKER, *Reproof of Rehearsal Trans*, p. 85. Take hearts, NUMPS! here is not a word of the stocks.

NUMS (or **NUMMS**), *subs.* (Old Cant).—A clean collar on a dirty shirt. *Cf.* DICKEY. — B. E. (*c.* 1696); *New Cant. Dict.* (1725); GROSE (1785). Also as *adj.* = sham.—MATSELL (1859).

NUMSKULL, *subs.* (old: now colloquial).—A simpleton: *see* BUFFLE and CABBAGE-HEAD.—B. E. (*c.* 1696); *New Cant. Dict.* (1725); GROSE (1785).

1712. ARBUTHNOT, *John Bull Still in his Senses*, III. i. Arber's *Garner*, vi. 614. D— this NUMBED SKULL of mine, quoth he, that I could not light on it sooner.

1728. VANBRUGH, *Journey to London*, i. 2. Thou art a NUMSKULL I see already.

1742. FIELDING, *Joseph Andrews*, III. xii. His wife . . . told him he would never leave following the nonsensical dictates of his own NUMSKULL, till she and her family were ruined.

1773. GOLDSMITH, *She Stoops to Conquer*, ii. 1. You NUMSKULLS! and so while like your betters, you are quarrelling for places, the guests must be starved.

1859. DICKENS, *Tale of Two Cities*, II. iv. I dined, myself, while those NUMSKULLS were deliberating which world you should belong to—this, or some other.

NUMSKULLED, *adj.* (old).—Foolish; silly.

1712. ARBUTHNOT, *History of John Bull*, I. xii. Have you no more manners than to rail at my husband, that has saved that clodpated, NUMSKULLED, ninny-hammer of yours from ruin.

1856. *Punch's Ess. of Parliament*, xxx. 61. Such blockheads as Vincent Scully ruin whatever cause they advocate. Mr. Punch means to get Vincent the Royal licence to call himself, as other people call him, NUM SCULLY.

NUN, *subs.* (old).—A prostitute: *cf.* ABBESS. Also COVENT GARDEN NUN. *See* BARRACK-HACK and TART. Hence NUN'S FLESH=a cold temperament.

1608-10. SWIFT, *Polite Conversation*, i. *Col.* Faith, you'll never lead Apes in Hell. *Neverout.* No, no, I'll be sworn Miss has not an Inch of NUN'S Flesh about her.

1777. RANDALL, *Excursion round London*, 33. A couple of NUNS out of Hedge-lane, Bet Brazer and Charlotte Cheap.

1770. FOOTE, *Lame Lover*, i. Last night . . . who should trip by but an abbess, well known about town with a smart little NUN in her suite.

1821. EGAN, *Life in London*, II. 1. Those three nymphs . . . are three NUNS; and the plump female is of great notoriety and generally designated the abbess.

NUNKY (**NUNKS** or **NUNCLE**), *subs.* (colloquial).—An uncle [NUNCLE =mine uncle: once the customary address of the licensed fool to his superiors].

1599. PORTER, *Two Angry Women* [DODSLEY (*Old Plays*), vii. 381]. I' faith, I should be glad To have myself called NUNCLE, and thou dad.

1684. LACY, *Sir Hercules Buffoon*, ii. 3. Now good my Hony NUNCLE, let us not gea to France, but send me back to my Naunt at York again.

1760. FOOTE, *Minor*, ii. p. 57. I suppose this is a spice of your foreign breeding, to let your uncle kick his heels in your hall . . . *Sir George.* Oh, a proof of my respect, dear NUNCLE.

1841. *Comic Almanack*, 291. But where's the stoic can resist When pretty lips so sweetly coax? Come, NUNKS, one game at Blindman's-buff.

1888. *Sporting Life*, 10 Dec. Wallace now fought him with both hands and got all the best of the exchanges. Mr. Bull, Good, my little NUNKY!

1892. HENLEY and STEVENSON, *Deacon Brodie*, I. vii. p. 16. I don't mind telling you that NUNKEY Lawson's a customer of George's.

NUNNERY, *subs.* (old).—A brothel; *cf.* ABBESS and NUN. *See* NANNY-HOUSE.—GROSE (1785); HALLIWELL (1847).

1822. EGAN, *Real Life*, II. 182. Having visited a certain NUNNERY in the precincts of Pall-Mall.

NUNQUAM, *subs.* (old).—*See* quot. [From the Latin].

1560-1. AWDELEY, *Fraternitye of Vacabondes*, leaf 9. NUNQUAM is he that when his Maister sendeth him on his errand he wil not come againe of an hour or two.

NUNYARE, *subs.* (showmen's).—*See* quot.

1851-61. MAYHEW, *London Lab.*, vol. III. 201. [Ethiopian serenader *loq.*] We could then, after our NUNYARE and buvare (that's what we call eat and drink, and I think it's broken Italian), carry home our 5/- or 6/- each, easy. *Ibid.*, 149. We [strolling actors] call breakfast, dinner, tea, supper, all of them NUNYARE; and all beer, brandy, water, or soup, are beuvare.

NUP (or **NUPSON**), *subs.*—A fool: *see* BUFFLE and CABBAGE-HEAD.

1580. *Lingua* [DODSLEY, *Old Plays*, v. 150]. 'Tis he indeed, the vilest NUP; yet the fool loves me exceedingly. *Ibid.*, v. 238. I say Phantastes is a foolish transparent gull; a mere fanatic NUPSON.

1596. B. JONSON, *Every Man in his Humour*, iv. 4. O that I were so happy as to light upon a NUPSON now.

1616. BEN JONSON, *Devil is an Ass*, ii. 2. Who having matched with such a NUPSON.

1785. GROSE, *Vulg. Tongue.*, s.v.

NUPPENCE, *subs.* (American).—Nothing. [From 'no pence,' on the model of 'tuppence'=2d.]

1886. A. LANG, in *Longmans' Mag.*, VII. 551. The Americans can get our books, and do get them, and republish them and give us nothing—that awful minus quantity, NUPPENCE!

NUPTIATE, *verb.* (American).—To marry; TO GET HITCHED (*q.v.*).

NUREMBURG-EGG, *subs. phr.* (old).—An early kind of watch, oval in shape. [Invented, *c.* 1500, in Nuremburg].

NURLY, *adj.* and *adv.* (American).—Ill-tempered; cross-grained. [From 'gnarly']. — DE VERE (1872).

NURSE, *subs.* (common).—1. An old man's maid, frequently doing double duty—nurse and SMOCK SERVANT (*q.v.*).

2. (nautical).—*See* quot.

1867. SMYTH, *Sailor's Word-Book*, 502, s.v. NURSE. An able first lieutenant, who in former times had charge of a young boy-captain of interest, but possessing no knowledge for command.

3. *See* WET-NURSE.

Verb. (Old Cant).—1. To cozen.—GROSE (1785).

2. (billiards').—To keep the three balls close in play so as to score successive cannons. Hence, NURSERY-BUSINESS (*q.v.*).

3. (omnibus drivers').—To cheat an opposition bus of passengers by driving close in front or behind; two vehicles are generally employed TO NURSE the victim.

1858. *Morning Chronicle*, 8 Mar. The cause of the delay was that defendant was waiting to NURSE one of their omnibuses.

1863. The DEAN OF CANTERBURY, in *Good Words*, p. 197. Many words are by rule hitched off with two commas; one before and one behind; NURSED, as the Omnibus Company would call it.

1884. *Echo*, 7 May, 1, 4. Another phenomenal witness, a 'bus conductor, did not even know what NURSING rivals meant.

1893. EMERSON, *Signor Lippo*, xvi. Some of 'em wanted to NURSE me, but I managed to give the mare a touch of the spur and she flew out, the starter calling me to account.

1889. *Man of the World*, 29 June. Only a fortnight ago I witnessed an elderly man run over and killed in Qneen Victoria Street through this very cause. Surely a man's life is worth more than the gratification of the ambition of a NURSING omnibus driver.

1900. *Daily Telegraph*, 22 Mar., 4, 6. A case of alleged NURSING by rival omnibuses occupied a large part of the afternoon sitting.

TO BE AT NURSE, *verb. phr.* (old).—To be in the hands of trustees.—GROSE (1785).

NURSERY, subs. (racing).—A race for two-year-olds; almost always a handicap. Also as adj.

1883. *Daily Telegraph*, 26 Oct. Winning three NURSERIES off the reel.

THE NURSERY, subs. (venery).—The female *pudendum*: see MONOSYLLABLE.

NURSERY-BUSINESS (or CANNON), subs. (billiards').—Playing the three balls close together and so scoring successive cannons.

1891. *Licensed Victuallers' Mirror*, 30 Jan., 3. Richards, too, is a demon on the NURSERY BUSINESS, some of his breaks being extremely interesting.

NURSE'S-VAIL, subs. phr. (common).—A nurse's petticoats when they are wet with urine.

NUSH, subs. (American).—The mouth: see POTATO-TRAP.—MATSELL (1859).

NUT, subs. (common).—1. The head. [Hence, as in quots. 1888 and 1889=intelligence, brains]. See CRUMPET.

1858. A. MAYHEW, *Paved with Gold*, II. xii. The first round was soon terminated, for Jack got a cracker on his NUT.

1860. *Chambers's Journal*, xiii. 348. He no longer a head, but a NUT: his hair is 'wool.'

1879. *Mac. Mag.*, xl. 501. He rammed my NUT against the wall.

1888. J. RUNCIMAN, *The Chequers*, 106. It's Tom Tiddler's ground if you've got a NUT on you.

1889. *Sporting Times*, 3 Aug, 1, 2. They gave Gladstone a portico on his golden wedding day. A few tiles to repair deficiencies in the old 'un's NUT would have been better while they were at building materials.

1892. ANSTEY, *Voces Populi*, 'In the Mall on Drawing-Room Day,' 82. Look at the diamonds all over 'er bloomin' old NUT.

1892. KIPLING, *Barrack-Room Ballads*, 'Gonga Din.' If we charged or brike or cut, You could bet your bloomin' NUT, 'E'd be waiting fifty paces right flank rear.

2. (common).—The core of fat in a leg of mutton; the POPE'S-EYE (q.v.).

1611. COTGRAVE, *Dict.*, s.v. *Nuguette de Mouton*, The NUT of a leg of mutton.

3. (provincial). — A harum-scarum ass.

4. in pl. (venery).—The *testes*: see CODS.

5. in pl. (common).—Small round coals.

6. in pl. (common).—A delightful practice or experience.

1678. COTTON, *Scarronides*, p. 15. It will be NUTS, if my case this is, Both Atrides and Ulysses.

1712. SWIFT, *Journal to Stella*, Jan. 8, Letter 38. Lord-keeper and Treasurer teazed me for a week. It was NUTS to them.

1744. NORTH, *Life of Lord Guilford*, i. 37 [2nd ed. 1808]. This was NUTS to the old Lord, who thought he had outwitted Frank.

1785. GROSE, *Vulg. Tongue*, s.v. NUTS. It was NUTS for them, i.e. it was very agreeable to them.

1805. C. LAMB, *Letter*, in *Wks.* (1852), v. 72. But 'tis NUTS to the adept.

1840. DANA, *Two Years before the Mast*, xxv. He . . . found them waiting on the beach, and a little afraid about going off, as the surf was running very high. This was NUTS to us; for we liked to have a Spaniard wet with salt water.

1843. DICKENS, *Christmas Carol*, STAVE 1. To edge his way along the crowded paths of life, warning all human sympathy to keep its distance, was what the knowing ones call NUTS to Scrooge.

1884. HAWLEY SMART, *Post to Finish*, 223. Yes, it was NUTS to me to find I had just done Phaeton, and hit my black-blooded cousin in his only vulnerable spot—the pocket. But why should Cuthbert detest me.

1887. HENLEY, *Culture in the Slums*, 'Ballade,' iii. The Grosvenor's NUTS—it is, indeed.

1893. MILLIKEN, *'Arry Ballads*, 4. It's NUTS to 'ook on to a swell.

7. in pl. (Stock Exchange).—Barcelona Tramway Shares.

8. (common).—A drink; a GO (q.v.): see DRINKS.

Verb. (old).—1. To fondle; to ogle; to SPOON (q.v.).—VAUX (1819).

1820. *London Mag.*, i. 26. Always NUTTING each other.

1823. GROSE, *Vulg. Tongue* [EGAN], s.v. NUTS. The cove's NUTTING the blowen; the man is trying to please the girl.

2. (pugilists'). — To strike on the head.

TO BE NUTS (or DEAD NUTS) ON, verb. phr. (common). — 1. See quot. 1819.

1819. VAUX, *Memoirs*, s.v. NUTS UPON IT, to be very much pleased or gratified with any object, adventure, or overture; so a person who conceives a strong inclination for another of the opposite sex, is said to be quite NUTTY, or NUTS UPON him or her.

1823. GROSE, *Vulg. Tongue* [EGAN], s.v. NUTS. She's NUTS UPON her cull; she's pleased with her cully.

1853. *Diogenes*, ii. 30. It's rich nutty flavour I'm NUTS on no more.

1860. *Punch's Book of British Costumes*, xxxviii. p. 219. Or cowls, but left their heads with nothing but their hair to cover them. The fact was that the dandies were so NUTS UPON their 'nuts' that they did not like to hide their fair (or dark) proportions.

1873. BLACK, *Princess of Thule*, xi. My aunt is awful NUTS on Marcus Aurelius; I beg your pardon, you don't know the phrase; my aunt makes Marcus Aurelius her Bible.

1882. *Punch*, LXXXII. 177. I am NUTS UPON Criminal Cases, Perlice News, you know, and all that.

1893. MILLIKEN, *'Arry Ballads*, 10. I'm not NUTS ON Bohea.

2. (common). — To be very skilful or dexterous.

3. (common).—To be particular; to detest.

1890. *Punch*, 22 Feb. He's NUTS on Henery George.

TO CRACK A NUT (Old Scots').—See quot.

1889. *Notes and Queries*, 7 S. viii. 437. In country gentlemen's houses [in Scotland] in the olden time, when a fresh guest arrived he was met by the laird, who made him CRACK A NUT—that is, drink a silver-mounted cocoa-nut shell full of claret.

THE NUT, subs. phr. (nautical).—See quot.

1891. *Daily Telegraph*, 27 Mar. Other notes and time-honoured hostelries of Portsmouth town are affectionately commemorated, if not by absolute reproduction, by borrowing their signs. Thus, in one corner, may be discovered the KEPPEL'S HEAD, known to all her Majesty's navy as the NUT, but perhaps hardly to be recognised in its Chelsea guise—a temperance café.

A NUT TO CRACK, phr. (colloquial).—A problem to solve; a puzzle to explain; a difficulty to overcome.

1843. LONGFELLOW, *Spanish Student*. I've NUTS TO CRACK, but where shall I find almonds.

1849. LYTTON, *Caxtons*, I. i. To others this NUT of such a character was hard TO CRACK.

1897. *Daily Mail*, 26 Oct., 4, 3. The information gained by the recent gun-boat reconnaissance up river . . . shows that this position will be a hard NUT TO CRACK.

OFF ONE'S NUT, phr. (common).—1. Crazy.

1876. SIMS, *Dagonet Ballads* (*Polly*). Or to go OFF THEIR NUTS about ladies as dies for young fellers as fights.

2. (common).—Drunk; in liquor: see DRINKS and SCREWED.

NUT-CRACKER, subs. (pugilists').—1. The head; (2) a sharp blow on it; and (3) in pl. the fists.

4. in pl. (old).—See quot. 1696:—HALL, *Memoirs* (1708); GROSE (1785).

c.1696. B. E., *Dict. Cant. Crew*, s.v. NUT-CRACKERS. The cull looked through the NUT CRACKERS, the rogue stood in the pillory.

5. in pl. (common).—A curving nose and protruding chin.

6. (common).—The teeth: see GRINDERS.

7. (military).—The Third Foot. See BUFF HOWARDS.

1871. *Chambers's Journal*, 23 Dec., 802. The 3rd Foot, best known as the 'Old Buffs,' their accoutrements having been the first that were made of buffalo leather, possess two other sobriquets, the NUT-CRACKERS and the 'Resurrectionists.'

NUT-HOOK, subs. (old).—See quot. 1755.

1598. SHAKSPEARE, *Henry IV.*, NUTHOOK, NUTHOOK, you lie.

1755. JOHNSON, *Eng. Dict.*, s.v. NUTHOOK . . . anciently, I know not why, a name of contempt.

NUTMEGS, subs. (venery).—The *testes*; THE CODS (q.v.).—GROSE (1785); HALLIWELL (1847).

16 [?]. *Hist. of Jack Horner* (1697), p. 13. My precious NUTMEGS doe not wound, For fear I should not live.

WOODEN NUTMEGS, subs. phr. (American).—See quot. 1872.

1871. *Congress-Globe*, March [DE VERE, 620]. I leave the honorable gentleman from Massachusetts to his WOODEN NUTMEGS and silver spoons; he will receive his deserts before the people are done with him.

1872. DE VERE, *Americanisms*, 620, s.v. NUTMEGS, when made of wood, as were those immortalized by Sam Slick, have become so familiar to the public mind, that they have passed into a slang term for any cunning deception. Not only is Connecticut called the NUTMEG State—although a factious native says the true reason is 'because you will have to look for a grater,'—but in the press and in Congress WOODEN NUTMEGS have to answer for forged telegrams, political tricks and falsified election-returns.

NUTMEG-STATE, subs. phr. (American).—Connecticut. [A nick name of Judge Haliburton's].

1851. ALLIN, *Home Ballads*, 19. Still give me the NUTMEG STATE—Where shall we find a *grater?*

NUTSHELL. IN A NUTSHELL, phr. (colloquial).—In small compass. Condensed; 'boiled down.'

1622. FLETCHER, *Spanish Curate*, ii. 1. All I have to lose, Diego, is my learning; And, when he has gotten that, he may put it in a NUT-SHELL.

a.1745. SWIFT, *Tale of a Tub*, vii. I have sometimes heard of an Iliad in a NUT-SHELL.

1866. W. COLLINS, *Armadale*, iii. A nervous patient who is never worried is a nervous patient cured. There it is in a NUTSHELL.

NUTTED, adj. (common).—Deceived by a false friend.

NUTTY, adj. and adv. (common).—1. See quot. 1823. Also = fascinating.

1821. EGAN, *Life in London*, 230. He was so NUTTY upon the charms of his fair one.

1823. BEE, *Dict. Turf*, s.v. NUTTY—sweet, amatory; bestowed by bucks upon buxom landladies, and spruce barmaids.

1827. EGAN, *Anecdotes of the Turf*, 183. Jemmy became quite NUTTY, and often repeated his visits.

1834. AINSWORTH, *Rookwood*, 116 (ed. 1864). But my NUTTIEST blowen, one fine day, To the beaks did her fancy-man betray.

2. (common). — Fruitful of details; SPICY (q.v.).

1894. SALA, *London up to date*, 329. The case, he incidentally adds, promises to be a NUTTY one.

3. (common).—Smart; DOGGY (q.v.); SWAGGER (q.v.); NOBBY (q.v.); NICE (q.v.).

1823. BYRON, *Don Juan*, XI . . . . So prime, so gay, so NUTTY and so knowing.

1839. REYNOLDS, *Pickwick Abroad*, 223. And the beak wore his NUTTIEST wig.

1841. MARTIN and AYTOUN, *Bon Gaultier Ballads*, The NUTTY Blowen [Title].

1842. *Punch*, iii. 126. Colin Youth's most NUTTY son.

1893. MILLIKEN, *'Arry Ballads*, 75. Life goes on NUTTY and nice.

NUX, subs. (thieves').—The object in view; THE PLANT (q.v.); THE LAY (q.v.).

NYMPH OF DARKNESS (or THE PAVEMENT), subs. phr. (colloquial).—A prostitute: see BARRACK-HACK and TART.

NYP. See NIP.

OAF, *subs.* (old).—1. A loutish simpleton: *see* BUFFLE and CABBAGE-HEAD. Hence OAFDOM = the world of louts; OAFISH = stupid.—B. E. (*c.* 1696); GROSE (1785).

1621. BURTON, *Anat. of Mel.*, I. II. IV. vi. 229 (1836). Though he be an AUFE, a ninny, a monster, a goos-cap.

1627. DRAYTON, *Nymphidia*, 79. The fairy left this OAF, And took away the other.

1633. FLETCHER and SHIRLEY, *Night Walker*, i. 4. The fear of breeding fools and OAFS.

1668. DRYDEN, *An Evening's Love*, ii. This master of mine, that stands before you, without a word to say for himself, so like an OAF, as I might say.

1693. CONGREVE, *Old Batchelor*, v. 6. *Sharp.* Death! it can't be—an OAF, an ideot, a wittal.

1700. CONGREVE, *Way of the World*, Prologue. With Nature's OAFS, 'tis quite a diff'rent Case. For Fortune favours all her Idiot-race.

1706. FARQUHAR, *Recruiting Officer*, iii. 1. What's that to you, OAF?

1773. GOLDSMITH, *She Stoops to Conquer*, IV. You great ill-fashioned OAF, with scarce sense enough to keep your mouth shut.

18[?]. BYRON, *Verses left in a Summerhouse.* This guiltless OAF his vacancy of sense Supplied, and amply too, by innocence.

1853. THACKERAY, *Barry Lyndon*, iii. 45. Her chair had been stopped by a highwayman; the great OAF of a servant-man had fallen down on his knees armed as he was.

1883. A. DOBSON, *Old-World Idylls*, 34. We have passed from *Philosophe*-dom Into plainer modern days,—Grown contented in our OAFDOM, Giving grace not all the praise.

1892. MILLIKEN, *'Arry Ballads*, 68. I'll 'owl at sich OAFS till I'm 'oarse.

2. (old).—*See* quot.

1696. B. E., *Dict. Cant. Crew*, OAF, a Wise-acre.

OAK. *subs.* (old).—1. A man of substance and credit.—B. E. (*c.* 1696); GROSE (1785); MATSELL (1859).

2. (University). — An outer door. TO SPORT ONE'S OAK = to be 'not at home': indicated by closing the outer door.

1785. GROSE, *Vulg. Tongue*, s.v.

1845. *The Collegian's Guide*, 14. In college each set of rooms is provided with an OAK or outer door, with a spring lock, of which the master has one key, and the servant another.

1853. BRADLEY ('Cuthbert Bede'), *Verdant Green*, I. viii. Mr. Verdant Green had, for the first time, SPORTED HIS OAK.

1861. HUGHES, *Tom Brown at Oxford*, vii. One evening he found himself as usual at Hardy's door about eight o'clock. The OAK was open, but he got no answer when he knocked at the inner door.

Adj. (American). — Strong; rich; in good repute.—MATSELL (1859).

FELLING OF OAKS, *subs. phr.* (old).—Sea-sickness.

1608. WITHAL, *Dict.*, 39. The word signifieth to be provoked, or to have appetite or desire to vomit properly upon the sea, or in a ship. They call it FELLING OF OAKS merilie.

OAKEN-TOWEL, *subs. phr.* (old).—A cudgel; a PLYMOUTH CLOAK (*q.v.*).—Whence TO RUB DOWN WITH AN OAKEN TOWEL = to thrash.—GROSE (1785); MATSELL (1859).

OAR, *subs.* (old).—1. A busy body: hence, TO PUT (or SHOVE) ONE'S OAR IN = to interfere; to meddle officiously.—GROSE (1785).

1596. FLORIO, *Worlde of Wordes*, 37. A busie-body, medler in other's matters, one that hath an OARE IN other's boates.

1597. G. HARVEY, *Trimming of Nashe*, in *Wks.* (GROSART), III. 33. Think not that I thinke all those to haue good wits, that will talke of euerie subiect, and HAVE AN OARE (as we say) IN euerie mans boate: for manie fooles doo so, and so doost thou.

1606. *Return from Parnassus.* [NARES]. Lodge for his OARE IN every paper boate, He that turnes over Galen every day, To sit and simper Euphues legacie.

1614. JONSON, *Bartholomew Fair*, iii. Pray thee mind him not, fellow; he'll HAVE AN OAR IN everything.

1659. HOWELL, *Dict.* He loves to HAVE AN OAR IN every one's boat, he likes meddling with other people's business.

1731. COFFEY, *Devil to Pay*, i. 2. I say, meddle with your own affairs; I will govern my own house, without your PUTTING IN AN OAR.

1843. MONCRIEFF, *The Scamps of London*, iii. 1. I'll thank you not to PUT YOUR OAR IN my private affairs.

1874. Mrs. H. WOOD, *Johnny Ludlow*, 1st S. No. III. 41. If you SHOVE IN YOUR OAR, Johnny Ludlow, or presume to interfere with me, I'll pummel you to powder.

1892. GUNTER, *Miss Dividends*, ix. Mr. Kruger thinks to himself, 'Time for Lot to PUT HIS OAR IN.'

2. (colloquial).—(1) In *pl.* = a waterman: *i.e.*, OARS (= two men) as opposed to SCULLS, *q.v.* = one man); and (2) an oarsman.

1611. *Tarleton's Jests* [Halliwell]. Tarlton being one Sunday at court all day, caused a paire of OARES to tend him, who at night called on him to be gone. Tarlton, being a carousing, drunk so long to the watermen, that one of them was bumpsie; and so, indeede, were all three for the most part.

FIRST-OARS, *subs. phr.* (common).—A favorite; a person or thing holding the first or highest place.

1774. DIBDIN, *The Waterman* . . . 'The Jolly Young Waterman.'—He was always FIRST OARS with the fine City ladies.

1836. DICKENS, *Pickwick*, xxxiii. But was it the maidens of humble life only who soothed, consoled, and supported him? No! He was always FIRST OARS with the fine City ladies.

TO LIE (or REST) ON ONE'S OARS, *verb. phr.* (colloquial).—To rest; to take things easy.

1889. *Pall Mall Gaz.*, 3 Aug., 3, 2. The Jacobyns, who were not present in force, and who have rested on their OARS since the famous muster of 116, were not at all sorry that the division was decently let slip.

OAT, *subs.* (common).—An atom; a particle: *e.g.* 'I've not an OAT' = I'm penniless.

WILD OATS, *subs. phr.* (old).—A rake; a debauchee: hence, TO SOW ONE'S WILD OATS = to indulge; TO HAVE SOWN ONE'S WILD OATS = to have reformed.

d. 1570. BECON, *Works* (1843), 240. The tailors now-a-days are compelled to excogitate, invent, and imagine diversities of fashions for apparel, that they may satisfy the foolish desire of certain light brains and WILD OATS, which are altogether given to new fangleness.

1576. *Touchstone of Complexions*, 99. We meane that wilful and unruly age, which lacketh rypeness and discretion, and (as wee saye) hath not SOWED ALL THEYR WYELD OATES.

1602. *How a Man may Chuse a Good Wife* [NARES]. Well, go to, WILD OATS! spendthrift, prodigal.

1670. RAY, *Proverbs* [BOHN (1893), 178], s.v.

1696. B. E., *Dict. Cant. Crew*, s.v. OATS. One that has SOLD HIS WILD OATS, or one having run out of all, begins to take up and be more staied.

b. 1707. DURFEY, *Pills to Purge*, &c. (1707), ii. 276. Sow your WILD OATS, And mind not her wild Notes.

1785. GROSE, *Vulg. Tongue*, s.v. OATS, HE HAS SOWED HIS WILD OATS, he is staid, or sober, having left off his wild tricks.

1858. LYTTON, *What Will He Do With It?* VIII. v. Poole had picked up some WILD OATS—he had SOWN them now.

FEED OF OATS, *subs. phr.* (common).—1. A whip; and (2) a beating.

TO EARN A GALLON OF OATS, *verb. phr.* (provincial).—Of horses: to fall on the back rolling from one side to the other [HALLIWELL].

TO FEEL ONE'S OATS, *verb. phr.* (American).—To get bumptious. *Cf.* BEANS.

1888. *St. Paul and Minneapolis Pioneer*, 22 July. The Kentuckians have certainly brought Little Falls to the front durng the past year, and Little Falls FEELS HER OATS, and will undoubtedly expand under her new name of Falls City.

OATH.—TO TAKE AN OATH, *verb. phr.* (common).—To drink; TO LIQUOR UP (*q.v.*).—MATSELL (1859).

HIGHGATE OATH, *subs. phr.* (old).—A jocose asseveration which travellers towards London were required to take at a certain tavern at Highgate. They were obliged to swear that they would not prefer small beer before strong, unless indeed they liked the small better; never to kiss the maid if they could kiss the mistress, unless the maid was prettier; with other statements of a similar kind.

OATMEAL, *subs.* (old).—A roystering profligate: *see* ROARING BOY and DANDY.

1656. FORD, *Sun's Darling*, I. i. Swagger in my pot-meals, D—n—me's rank with, Do mad pranks with Roaring boys and OATMEALS.

ALL THE WORLD IS NOT OATMEAL, *phr.* (old colloquial).—*See* quots. *Cf.* BEER AND SKITTLES.

1542. *Apoph. of Erasmus* (Rept.), 329. When Leosthenes had perswaded the citee of Athenes to make warre *beeyng set agog to thinke* ALL THE WORLDE OTEMELE, and to imagin the recouering of an high name of freedome and of principalitee or soueraintee.

1615. *Araignment of Lewde, Idle Wowen*, cap. iii. par. 1. THE WORLDE IS NOT ALL MADE OF OTEMEALE, nor all is not golde that glisters.

1673. *Vinegar and Mustard*, 'Wednesday's Lecture.' Now you are come ashore, you think the world runs on wheels, and that ALL THE WORLD IS OATMEAL; but you'll find it to the contrary.

OATS-AND-BARLEY, *subs. phr.* (rhyming).—Charley.

1898. *Pink 'Un and Pelican*, 149. Bob and his particular chum OATS (which is short rhyming slang for Charley. "OATS-AND-BARLEY" it is in full, but the true art of it lies in the abbreviation).

OATS-AND-CHAFF, *subs. phr.* (rhyming).—A footpath.

OAT-STEALER, *subs. phr.* (common).—An ostler.

OB, *subs.* (Winchester College).—A contraction of '*obit.*'

OBADIAH, *subs.* (obsolete).—A Quaker.

OB-AND-SOLLER, *subs. phr.* (old).—A scholastic disputant. [From 'Objection' and 'Solution' used in the margin of books.]

1638. WHITING, *Albino and Bellama* [NARES]. Minerva does not all her treasures rivet Into the scrues of OBS AND SOLS.

1678. BUTLER, *Hud.*, III. ii. 1241. To pass for deep and learned scholars, Although but paltry OB-AND-SOLLERS: As if th' unseasonable fools Had been a coursing in the schools.

O-BE-EASY. TO SING 'O BE EASY,' *verb. phr.* (old).—*See* quot.

1823. GROSE, *Vulg. Tongue* [EGAN], s.v. O BE JOYFUL. TO SING O BE EASY: to appear contented when one has cause to complain.

O-BE-JOYFUL, *subs. phr.* (old).—*See* quot. Whence O-BE-JOYFUL WORKS = a drinking shop.

1823. GROSE, *Vulg. Tongue* [EGAN], s.v. O BE JOYFUL, good liquor; brandy.

TO MAKE ONE SING 'O BE JOYFUL' ON (or WITH) THE OTHER SIDE OF THE MOUTH, *verb. phr.* (old).—To make one cry: *see* MOUTH.—GROSE (1785).

OBEUM, THE, *subs. phr.* (University).—The name for a water-closet building at Cambridge. [Attributed by the Undergraduates to the energy of O(scar) B(rowning)].

OBFUSCATED, *adj.* (common).—Drunk: *see* DRINKS and SCREWED. Also OBFUSCATION.

1861. H. KINGSLEY, *Ravenshoe*, xxi. In a general state of OBFUSCATION, in consequence of being plied with strange liquors by their patrons.

1869. BRADWOOD, *The O. V. H.* xxviii. Whose ignorance or temporarily OBFUSCATED brain caused him to mistake his employer for Mr. Blake.

1872. *Standard*, 30 Dec. He then missed three shillings from his pockets, and a knife. Witness added that he was very much OBFUSTICATED at the time, but he was sure there was no other man in the room.

OBIT, *subs.* (journalists').—An obituary notice.

1874. W. BLACK, in *Athenæum*, 12 Sept., 353. Some little time ago, the sub-editor of a New York daily newspaper wrote to me begging me to send him the proper materials for the construction of an OBIT. He said it was the custom of his journal to keep OBITS in readiness.

OBJECT, *subs.* (colloquial).—1. A laughing-(or gazing-) stock. LITTLE OBJECT (of children) = a half-playful half-angry endearment. Also (2) a sweetheart (*i.e.* the OBJECT of one's affections).

1824. LOCKHART, *Reginald Dalton*, III. 119. What, roars Macdonald—You puir shanglin' in-kneed scray of a thing! Would ony Christian body even you bit OBJECT to a bonny sonsie weel-faured young woman like miss Catline?

OBIQUITOUS, *adj.* and *adv.* (American).—Innocence of right and wrong. [From *oblivious* and *obliquity*].

OBSCUTE, *adj.* (American). — Under-handed; 'crooked.'

OBSERVATIONIST, *subs.* (thieves').—*See* quot.

1889. BARRERE and LELAND, *Slang, Jargon, and Cant*, s.v. OBSERVATIONIST, one who looks out tempting objects for the skilful thief to steal, etc. Generally pedlars, hawkers, etc.

OBSTROPULOUS, *adj.* (vulgar).—A corruption of 'obstreperous.'

1748. SMOLLETT, *Roderick Random*, viii. I heard him very OBSTROPOLOUS in his sleep.

1762. SMOLLETT, *Sir L. Graves*, II. iv. He has been mortally OBSTROPULOUS, and out of his senses all this blessed day.

1773. GOLDSMITH, *She Stoops to Conquer*, iii. 1. I'm sure you did not treat Miss Hardcastle, that was here awhile ago, in this OBSTROPOLOUS manner.

1785. GROSE, *Vulg. Tongue*, s.v. OIL.

1847. HALLIWELL, *Archaic Words and Phrases*, s.v. OBSTROPOLOUS. I was going my rounds and found this here gemman very OBSTROPOLOUS . . . Genuine London dialect.

1876. SIMS, *Dagonet Ballads* (*Miss Jarvis*). But their minds is so awful perverted—they're such an OBSTROPOLOUS pack.

OCCABOT, *subs.* (back-slang). — Tobacco; TIB FO OCCABOT = bit of tobacco.

OCCASION. TO IMPROVE THE OCCASION, *verb. phr.* (colloquial).—To make the most of a chance.

1860. DICKENS, *Uncommercial Traveller*, II. 6. This serene avoidance of the least attempt to IMPROVE AN OCCASION which might be supposed to have sunk of its own weight into my heart.

1865. G. MACDONALD, *Alec Forbes*, lxii. The faces of the congregation wore an expectant look, for they knew Mr. Turnbull would IMPROVE THE OCCASION.

1867. A. TROLLOPE, *Claverings*, xliv. He IMPROVED THE OCCASION by telling those around him that they should so live as to be ever ready for the hand of death.

1869. FREEMAN, *Norm. Conq. III.*, xii. 159. His next thought was how TO IMPROVE THE OCCASION.

1883. G. A. S[ALA], in *Illustr. London News*, 27 Oct., 395, 2. I am obliged to 'Nominis Umbra' for his information; but I IMPROVE THE OCCASION by observing that I am resolved for the future not to take the slightest notice of anonymous communications.

OCCUPANT, *subs.* (old).—1. A prostitute; *cf.* OCCUPY. *See* BARRACK-HACK and TART.

1598. MARSTON, *Satires* [NARES]. He with his OCCUPANT Are cling'd so close, like dew-wormes in the morn, That he'll not stir.

2. (old).—A bawdy-house; a brothel. *See* NANNY-HOUSE.

OCCUPY, *verb.* (old).—1. To copulate: *see* GREENS and RIDE.

1598. SHAKSPEARE, *2 Henry IV.*, ii. 4. These villains will make the word captain as odious as the word OCCUPY.

1598. FLORIO, *A Worlde of Wordes. Negotiare* . . . . to OCCUPIE a woman. *Ibid.* . . . . a good wench, one that OCCUPIES freely.

1620-50. *Percy Folio MS.*, 104. I bluntlye asket pro to OCCUPYE her; but first shee wold know wherfore that was good.

1640. BEN JONSON, *Epigr.*, 117. Groyne, come of age, his state sold out of hand For's whore: Groyne still doth OCCUPY his land.

1648. BEN JONSON, *Discoveries*, VII. 119. Many, out of their own obscene apprehensions, refuse proper and fit words, as OCCUPY, nature, and the like.

1656. FLETCHER, *Martiall*, xi. 98. I can swive four times in a night: but thee Once in four years I cannot OCCUPIE.

d. 1680. ROCHESTER, *B's Answer.* The only bawd that ever I, For want of whore, could OCCUPY.

1719. DURFEY, *Pills to Purge*, v. 139. For she will be OCCUPIED when others lay still.

1811. *Lex. Bal.*, s.v.

1785. GROSE, *Vulg. Tongue*, s.v. OCCUPY. To occupy a woman, to have carnal knowledge of her. *Ibid.* Now all good men upon your lives, Turn round and OCCUPY your wives, And when that you have done your best, Turn arse to arse and take your rest.

2. (American thieves').—To wear.—MATSELL (1859).

OCCUPYING-HOUSE, *subs. phr.* (old). —*See* quot. and NANNY-HOUSE.

1598. FLORIO, *A Worlde of Wordes*, s.v. *Chiausterio*, an OCCUPYING HOUSE, a bawdy house.

OCEAN, *subs.* (colloquial).—In *pl.* = a very large quantity: *e.g.* OCEANS of drink, of coin, of 'notices,' and the like.

OCEAN-GREYHOUND, *subs. phr.* (common).—A swift steamer: specifically one running between England and America. Also ATLANTIC GREYHOUND. Mr. T. Dykes (*Glasgow Mail*, 28 May, 1900), says that in 1882 three great shipbuilding yards—Barrow, Dalmuir, and Fairfield—

had each on hand a new steamer that was to beat the record, at that time held by the Arizona. He was commissioned by Mr. Gordon Bennett to write an article on the subject, and, as an old 'coursing' correspondent, was called upon to name the winner. He interviewed men best qualified to give an opinion, amongst others Mr. G. L. Watson, who plumped for the Fairfield boat as 'likely to prove THE GREYHOUND OF THE ATLANTIC.' The Alaska, therefore, was named the 'Greyhound of the Atlantic' before she was launched.

1891. *Daily Chronicle*, 24 Mar. Another is an unarmoured cruiser, a 'commerce destroyer,' to make a minimum of 21 knots an hour, and capable of catching any of the great OCEAN GREYHOUNDS.

OCHIVE, *subs.* (Old Cant).—A knife. [From the gypsy *o chif* = the knife]. Also OSCHIVE.—*Lex. Bal.* (1811); MATSELL (1859).

OCHRE, *subs.* (thieves').—Money: specifically gold. [From the colour]. *See* ACTUAL and GILT.

1854. DICKENS, *Hard Times*, I. vi. If you want to cheek us, pay your OCHRE at the doors, and take it out.

1880. *Punch's Almanack*, 12. Lor', if I'd the OCHRE, make no doubt I could cut no end of big-pots out. Call me a cad: When money's in the game, Cad and swell are pooty much the same.

1890. *Punch*, 22 Feb. If I was flush of the OCHRE, I tell yer I'd make the thing hum.

O'CLOCK. TO KNOW WHAT'S O'CLOCK, *verb. phr.* (popular). — To be alert; TO BE PUT UP TO THE TIME OF DAY. *See* KNOW.

1835. DICKENS, *Sketches by Boz.* Our governor's wide awake, he is. I'll never say nothin' agin him, nor no man; but he KNOWS WHAT'S O'CLOCK, he does, uncommon.

1849. THACKERAY, *Pendennis*, x. I'm not clever, p'raps: but I *am* rather downy; and partial friends say I know WHAT'S O'CLOCK tolerably well.

1888. BOLDREWOOD, *Robbery Under Arms*, xxvii. As for old Mullockson, he used to take a drive to Sawpit Gully, or Ten-Mile, as soon as ever he saw WHAT O'CLOCK it was—and glad to clear out, too.

LIKE ONE O'CLOCK, *phr.* (common).—Quickly; readily; in 'a JIFFY' (*q.v.*). *See* LIKE.

1851-61. MAYHEW, *London Lab.*, &c. I. 29. He trotted on LIKE ONE O'CLOCK.

1852. DICKENS, *Bleak House*, xx. He has seen him through the shop-door, sitting in the back premises, sleeping LIKE ONE O'CLOCK.

1876. BRADDON, *Dead Men's Shoes*, xx. I declare this den of yours swarms with reptiles. I saw a toad under the bench yesterday. Toads are valuable animals, answers Jane. They eat the snails LIKE ONE O'CLOCK.

O CRIMINY. *See* CRIMES.

OCTOBER, *subs.* (old). — 1. *See* quot. Specifically ale or cider brewed in October.

1869. *Sporting Life*, 1 Oct. OCTOBER . . . is a synonym for the best ale.

2. (pugilists').—Blood.

1853. BRADLEY ('Cuthbert Bede'), *Verdant Green.* While to another he would mention as an interesting item of news, Now we'll tap your best OCTOBER.

ODD, *adj.* and *adv.* (once literary: now colloquial).—Strange; peculiar; difficult.

1602. SHAKSPEARE, *Troilus and Cressida*, iv. 5. You're an ODD man.

1711-2. ADDISON, *Spectator.* Mr. Locke's Essay would be a very ODD book for a man to make himself master of.

ODD-COME-SHORTLY, *subs. phr.* (old).—Some day. Also ODD-COME-SHORT, which likewise = odds and ends or fragments.

1738. SWIFT, *Polite Conversation*, i. *Col.* Miss, when will you be married? *Miss.* One of these ODD-COME-SHORTLY'S, Colonel.

1785. GROSE, *Vulg. Tongue*, s.v.

1825. SCOTT, *St. Ronan's Well*, xvii. They say she is to be . . . off to England ane of thae ODD-COME-SHORTLYS.

1879. J. C. HARRIS, *Uncle Remus*, vii. Note. Run fetch me de ax, en I'll wait on you one er deze ODD-COME-SHORTS.

ODD FISH, *subs. phr.* (colloquial).—An eccentric: *see* QUEER CARD.

1771. FRANKLIN, Auto. [*Works* (1887) I. 137]. He was an ODD FISH.

1820. LAMB, *Elia*, 'South Sea House.' Humourists, for they were of all descriptions . . . ODD FISHES.

1837. DANCE, *The Country Squire*, i. 3. *Hor.* (Crossing behind, to George-going). He's a devilish ODD FISH.

ODDITY, *subs.* (colloquial).—A singularity.

1813. AUSTEN, *Pride and Prejudice*, 54. He must be an ODDITY, I think, said she. I cannot make him out.

1882. HOWELLS, *Modern Instance*, iv. The mother (who remained in the room when her daughter had company) was an ODDITY almost unknown in Equity.

ODD MAN OUT, *subs. phr.* (common).—A mode of tossing for drinks by three or more. Each spins a coin, and if two come up 'head' and one 'tail,' the 'tail,' or 'odd-man' is out, *i.e.* has not to pay. Should all three coins be alike, they are 'skied' again.

1840. DICKENS, *Old Curiosity Shop*, xxxvi. He imparted to her the mystery of going THE ODD MAN, or plain Newmarket for fruit, ginger-beer, baked potatoes, or even a modest quencher.

1861. ALBERT SMITH, *Medical Student*, 23. He purposes at lunch-time every day that he and his companions should go THE ODD MAN for a pot.

ODDS, *subs.* (colloquial). — The probabilities for or against; the chance of something occurring; that which justifies the attributing of superiority to one of two or more persons or things: specifically, in betting, the excess of the amount of a bet made by one party over that of another: as 'the ODDS against the favourite were 3 to 1.'

1591. GREENE, *Second Part Conny-catching*, in *Works*, vol. x. p. 83. These fellows will refuse to lay if the ODS may grow to their aduantage.

1598. SHAKSPEARE, *2 Henry IV*, v. 5, 3. I will lay ODDS that ere this year expire We bear our civil swords and native fire As far as France.

1602-3. SHAKSPEARE, *Hamlet*, v. 2. *King.* You know the wager? *Ham.* Very well, my lord; Your grace hath laid the ODDS o' the weaker side.

1704. CIBBER, *Careless Husband*, iv. *Lady Betty.* There's no standing against two of you. *L. Toppington.* No faith, that's ODDS at tennis.

1751. FIELDING. *Amelia*, x. v. If the knowing ones were here, they would lay ODDS of our side.

1754. *Connoisseur*, No. 15. He has so contrived the bets on his own life, that, live or die, the ODDS are in his favour.

1818. SCOTT, *Rob Roy*, vi. Rashleigh alone possessed more arithmetic than was necessary to calculate the ODDS on a fighting-cock.

WHAT'S THE ODDS? *phr.* (colloquial).—'What does it matter': an intensive of recklessness and good-fellowship.

1840. DICKENS, *Old Curiosity Shop*, ii. WHAT IS THE ODDS so long as the fire of soul is kindled at the taper of conviviality, and the wing of friendship never moults a feather?

1880. A. TROLLOPE, *The Duke's Children*, xvii. If they do send me down, WHAT'S THE ODDS? said the younger brother, who was not quite as sober as he might have been.

ODLING, *subs.* (old).—Cheating.

1599. BEN JONSON, *Every Man out of his Humour.* A thread bare shark; one that never was a soldier, yet lives upon lendings. His profession is skeldering and OLDING.

ODNO, *phr.* (back-slang).—'No do.' RIDING ON THE ODNO = travelling by rail without payment.

1889. *Sporting Times.* Doin' a duck, macin' the rattler, ridin' on the cheap, on the ODNO, under the bloomin' seat.

ODOUR, *subs.* (colloquial).—Repute: as 'good' or 'bad' ODOUR, the ODOUR of sanctity, &c.

1853. THACKERAY, *Barry Lyndon*, ix. As the Chevalier de Balibari was in particular GOOD ODOUR at the court of Dresden . . . . I was speedily in the very best society of the Saxon capital.

1858. GEO. ELIOT, *Amos Barton*, vi. He got into rather BAD ODOUR there, through some scandal about a flirtation, I think.

ODS, *subs.* (old). — A wilful attenuation of 'God's': common in 17th and 18th Century oaths; *e.g.*, ODS-BODKINS = God's little body, ODS-BOBS, ODS-FISH, etc.

1695. CONGREVE, *Love for Love*, iii. 5. ODSBUD, Madam, have no more to say to him.

1705. MRS. CENTLIVRE, *Gamester*, v. 1 (1892), i. 184. ODSBUD, sir, go to Angelica, this minute.

1782. CENTLIVRE, *Bold Stroke for a Wife. Free.* ODSO! 'tis Miss Anne Lovely.

1812. COMBE, *Dr. Syntax, Picturesque*, C. xi. O! were she in coal-pit bottom, And all such jades, 'OD ROT 'em! My cares would then be over, And I should live in clover.

1813. MOORE, *Twopenny Post-bag*, Letter 4. These Papist dogs—hiccup—'OD ROT 'em!

1844. BUCKSTONE, *The Maid with the Milking Pail. Lord P.* ODS FISH, why this interest in poor Lady Lucy?

OFF, *subs.* (cricketers').—The field of the wicket-keeper.

1856. HUGHES, *Tom Brown at Rugby*, ii. 8. Johnson, the younger bowler, is getting wild, and bowls a ball almost wide to THE OFF.

Adv. (colloquial).—1. Out-of-date. [Originally waiters': *e.g.* 'Chops is HOFF' = 'there are no more chops to-day'].—2. Stale; in bad condition: *e.g.* Smells a little bit OFF, don't it?

1892. *Illustrated Bits*, 22 Oct., 6, 2. Theosophy is OFF—decidedly off.

1892. *Tit-Bits*, 17 Sept., 417, 3. If the leopard's tail is not spotted to the root this conundrum is declared OFF.

TO BE OFF, *verb. phr.* (colloquial).—To depart; to run away. *See* AMPUTATE and SKEDADDLE.

1892. *Ally Sloper*, 27 Feb., 66, 2. Will you allow me to offer you a glass of ale? I'm afraid it's a little off. Is it? then, I'm OFF too.

OFF BAT, *phr.* (Winchester College).—*See* quot.

1866. MANSFIELD, *School Life at Winchester*, 222. OFF BAT. The station of one of the field in a cricket match, called by the outer world 'Point.'

OFF THE HORN, *phr.* (common).—Said of very hard steak.

OFF THE HINGE, *phr.* (common).—Out of work.

1853. *Fun*, iv. 58, A Song About Centralization. We've rights within our city bounds which no one should infringe And if those rights were broken down 'twould chuck us OFF THE HINGE.

Also *see* BASE; BAT; CHUMP; COCOANUT; COLOUR; DOT; FEED; HEAD; HOOK; KADOOVA; NUT; ONION; REEL; ROCKER; SAUCER; SONG; SPOT.

OFF-CHANCE, *subs. phr.* (colloquial).—A doubtful hazard.

1880. N. GOULD, *Double Event*, 105. He didn't think Caloola would win, but he took £50 to £5 on the OFF CHANCE, 'just to have an interest in the brute,' he said.

OFFICE, *subs.* (old).—*See* quot. 1819. Fr. *donner un tuyau.*

1818. EGAN, *Boxiana*, II. 436. Reynolds observed to his seconds that if he could but see his man he certainly must win. The OFFICE was immediately given, when a farmer jumped into the ring, and lanced his eyes.

1819. VAUX, *Memoirs*, ii. 193. OFFICE, a hint, signal, or private intimation, from one person to another; this is termed OFFICEING him, or GIVING HIM THE OFFICE; to TAKE THE OFFICE, is to understand and profit by the hint given.

1830. BUCKSTONE, *A Dead Shot*. I, understanding the game, soon discovered a crack player—went up to him—GAVE THE OFFICE—he was on his mettle.

1836. DICKENS, *Pickwick*, xlii. Mivins! said Mr. Smangle, with a passionate air. What's THE OFFICE; replied that gentleman from his couch. Who the devil is this fellow?

1843. MONCRIEFF. *The Scamps of London*, iii. 1. GIVE THE OFFICE to the waiter.

1864. BRADDON, *Henry Dunbar*, xxxix. I GAVE YOU THE OFFICE just now, he said, because I thought if you spoke to me, that old chap would leave off talking, and I might miss something that was on the tip of his tongue.

1875. GREENWOOD, *Low Life Deeps* [*Slang, Jargon, and Cant.*]. And then, in a word or two which none of the outsiders can understand, the conductor GIVES THE OFFICE to his driver, who sits the picture of good behaviour . . . . till the point of danger is passed.

1888. BOLDREWOOD, *Robbery Under Arms*, xxxii. How the deuce did you GET THE OFFICE.

1891. NEWMAN, *Scamping Tricks*, 70. I GAVE THE OFFICE.

Verb. (old).—To give notice or information.

1819. MOORE, *Tom Cribb's Memorial*, 19. To OFFICE with all due dispatch through the air, To the Bulls of the Alley the fate of the Bear.

COOK'S OFFICE, *subs. phr.* (nautical).—The galley.

JACK IN OFFICE. *See* JACK.

OFFICE - SNEAK, *subs. phr.* (common).—A stealer of office overcoats and umbrellas.

OFFISH, *adv.* (colloquial).—Distant.

1842. *Betsy Bobbet*, 289. I am naturally pretty OFFISH and retirin' in my ways with strange men folks. I think it is becoming in a woman to be so, instead of bold.

1883. *Century*, XXXVI. 35. She was rather OFFISH, but really would have been glad to make up.

1883. L. OLIPHANT, *Altiora Peto*, II. xxxii. 202. You did not know that your husband . . . married my niece before he married his other wives, or you wouldn't ha' been so OFFISH when we first met over in Paris.

1892. GUNTER, *Miss Dividend*, vi. You make me feel as if you were OFFISH, says the youthful news-agent.

OFF-OX, *subs. phr.* (American).—An unmanageable, cross-grained fellow.

1862. LOWELL, *Biglow Papers*, 2nd Series, s.v.

OGGING OT TEKRAM, *phr.* (back-slang).—Going to market.

OGLE, *subs.* (old).—1. In *pl.* the eyes. Also OGLERS. Hence, QUEER-OGLED = squinting; RUM-OGLES = bright or piercing eyes.

1696. B. E., *Dict. Cant. Crew*, s.v. OGLES. The Gentry Mort has rum OGLES, that Lady has charming black eyes.

1706. CENTLIVRE, *Love at a Venture*, iv. 1. [*Works* (1872), i. 295.] *Flor.* Why, what do you fear? *Rob.* Those pinking OGLES of thine.

1706. WARD, *Hudibras Redivivus*, I. pt. vi. 25. He rowl'd his OGLES with a grace Becoming so a zealous face.

1748. DYCHE, *Dictionary*. OGLES in the *Cant. Language*, are the eyes.

1785. GROSE, *Vulg. Tongue*, s.v.

1819. MOORE, *Tom Cribb's Memorial*, 51. Round lugs and OGLES flew the frequent fist.

1821. HAGGART, *Life Glossary*, 172. s.v. OGLERS.

1827. EGAN, *Anec. Turf*, 67. Never again would he put the OGLES of the ring in mourning.

1839. AINSWORTH, *Jack Sheppard*, I. ii. It does sparkle almost as brightly as your OGLES.

1846. *Punch's Almanac*, November. Remarks. Fiery links gleam through the unfiltered air, and in their transit sputter hot pitch on the fog-bound traveller! Let Snodgrass beware! An Adverse torch threatens his dexter OGLE.

1853. BRADLEY, ('Cuthbert Bede'), *Verdant Green*. That'll raise a tidy mouse on your OGLE, my lad.

1853. THACKERAY, *Barry Lyndon*, vi. A little brown, bright-eyed creature, whose OGLES had made the greatest impression upon all the world.

2 (common).—An ocular invitation or consent, side glance, or amorous look. Whence OGLING = an amorous look.

1704. CIBBER, *The Careless Husband*, iii. 1. Nay, nay, none of your parting OGLES. Will you go?

1710. CONGREVE, *Song to Celia*. Those OGLINGS that tell you my passion.

*d.*1719. ADDISON, *The Fortune Hunter*. When an heiress sees a man throwing particular graces into his OGLE . . . she ought to look to herself.

1719. DURFEY, *Pills to Purge, &c.*, i. 43. To OAGLE there a Tory tall, or a little Whig, Defying the Pretender.

1751. FIELDING. *Amelia*, XI. iii. He immediately laid siege in form, setting himself down in a lodging directly opposite to her, from whence the battery of OGLES began to play the very next morning.

1818. BYRON, *Beppo*, XVI. For glances beget OGLES, OGLES sighs.

*c.*1820. MAHER, *Death of Socrates*. With the mots their OGLES throwing.

1892. MILLIKEN, *'Arry Ballads*, 37. They ain't in it with OGLES and antics and 'ints.

Verb. (common).—1. To look amorously; to make SHEEP'S EYES (*q.v.*).—B. E. (*c.* 1696).

1712. POPE, *Rape of the Lock*, v. 23. To patch, to OGLE, may become a saint.

1719. DURFEY, *Pills to Purge, &c.*, ii. 97. When Tiptoes are in fashion, and Lovers will jump and play, Then he too takes occasion to leer and OGLE me.

1775. SHERIDAN, *The Rivals*, ii. 1. I will make you OGLE her all day, and sit up all night, to write sonnets on her beauty.

*d.*1800. COWPER, *Pairing Time Anticipated*. Dick heard, and tweedling, OGLING, bridling.

1834. DOWLING, *Othello Travestie*, i. 3. She first began To throw sheep's eyes, and OGLE at the man.

2. (colloquial).—To examine; to consider.

1836. MICHAEL SCOTT, *Tom Cringle's Log*. I perceived that she first OGLED the superscription, and then the seal, very ominously.

3. (thieves').—To look.

1821. HAGGART, *Life*, 62. Seeing a cove OGLING the yelpers.

1842. EGAN, *Captain Macheath*, 'The By-blow of the Jug.' Jack had a sharp-looking eye to OGLE, And soon he began to nap the fogle.

OGLER, *subs.* (old).—1. *See* OGLE, *subs.*, sense 1.

2. (common). — One who OGLES (*q.v.*).

1702. STEELE, *Grief-a-la-Mode*, iii. 1. Oh! that Kiggle, a pert OGLER.

1710. *Tatler*, 145. A certain sect of professed enemies to the repose of the fair sex, called OGLERS.

OH. *See* AFTER YOU; DUMMY; JUPITER; MOSES; MY; SWALLOW.

OIL, *subs.* (various).—1. Used in humorous or sarcastic combination: *e.g.*, OIL OF ANGELS = a gift or bribe (in allusion to the coin); OIL OF BARLEY = beer; OIL OF BASTON (BIRCH, GLAD-

NESS, HAZEL, HOLLY, ROPE, STIRRUP, STRAPPEM, or WHIP) = a beating; OIL OF GIBLETS (or HORN) = a woman's spendings (BUTTER, *q.v.*; LETCHWATER, *q.v.*); OIL OF MAN (COTGRAVE) = the semen; OIL OF PALMS (or PALM-OIL) = a bribe; OIL OF TONGUE = flattery.

1592. GREENE, *Repentance, etc.* Sig C. My Mother pampered me so long, and secretly helped mee to the OYLE OF ANGELS, that I grew thereby prone to all mischefs.

1608. WITHAL, *Dict.*, 308, s.v. OIL OF BASTON.

1608. *Penniles Parl.*, in *Harl. Misc.* (PARK), i. 183. The OIL OF HOLLY shall prove a present remedy for a shrewd housewife.

1609. DEKKER, *Ravens Almanacke*, in *Wks.* (GROSART), iv. 202. To apply . . the OILE OF HOLLY to her shoulders, I heatherto was affraide, because I had no warrant that a man might lawfullye beate his wife.

1623. MASSINGER, *Duke of Milan*, iii. 2. His stripes wash'd off With OIL OF ANGELS.

*c.*1650. *Bad Husband* [COLLIER, *Roxburghe Ballads* (184), 300]. She'd tell me it was too early, Or else it was too late, Until by the OYLE OF BARLEY They had gotten my whole estate.

1662. FULLER, *Hist. Worthies of England*, 'The Beggars of Bath.' And although OIL OF WHIP be the proper plaister for the cramp of laziness, yet some pity is due to impotent persons.

1693. *Poor Robin* [NARES]. Now for to cure such a disease as this, The OYL OF WHIP the surest medicine is.

*c.*1696. B. E., *Dict. Cant. Crew*, s.v. OYL OF BARLEY, Strong Drink.

1715. CENTLIVRE. *Wife Well Managed*, sc. 5. When wives, like mine, gives inclination scope, No cure for cuckoldom like OYL OF ROPE.

1785. GROSE, *Vulg. Tongue*, s.v. OIL OF BARLEY, barley broth, strong beer. —*Ibid.* OIL OF GLADNESS, I will anoint you with the OIL OF GLADNESS, ironically spoken for, I will beat you.—*Ibid.* OIL OF STIRRUP, a Dose the cobler gives his wife, when ever she is Obstropulus.

1819. MOORE, *Tom Crib's Memorial*, 81. OIL OF PALM'S, the thing that flowing Sets the naves and felloes going.

1823. GROSE, *Vulg. Tongue* [EGAN], s.v. OIL OF PALMS. Money.

1840. LYTTON, *Paul Clifford*, viii. I dare say you may manage to soften the justice's sentence by a little OIL OF PALMS.

1854. *Punch*, ii. 168. OIL OF PALMS. —Metaphora vetustissima. A specific much in vogue for rigid fingers and horny fistedness; though strange to say, it only serves to augment the itch which so often affects the hand.

1879. DICKENS, *Dict. of London*, s.v. SIGHT-SEEING. The enterprising sight-seer who proceeds on this plan, and who understands the virtues of PALM OIL, is sure to see everything he cares to see.

2. (venery).—The semen: *see* CREAM.

1647-80. ROCHESTER, *The Imperfect Enjoyment*. Too hasty zeal my hopes did spoil, Pressing to feed her lamp, I spilt my OIL.

Verb. (common).—To flatter; to bribe.

1616. JONSON, *Devil is an Ass*, iii. 1. They'll part, sir, with no books, without the hautgout He OILED: and I must furnish.

1877. W. THORNBURY, in *Gent. Mag.*, Jan., 85. Passed my things through the Custom-house quickly, having first OILED the douanier's hands.

1881. DORAN, *In and About Drury Lane*, ii. 62. Sir Edward had OILED the palms of men-servants and clerks to the tune of eighty shillings.

1891. NEWMAN, *Scamping Tricks*, 95. After OILING him a little and pleasing him in the old-fashioned way, we managed to overcome the natural dulness of his mind.

TO STRIKE OIL (or ILE), *verb. phr.* (American).—To meet with a stroke of good luck; to be successful. [From the financial advantage accruing from the discovery of the Pennsylvanian and other mineral oil springs.]

1866. *Sat. Review*, 6 Jan. Here the ingenious and industrious explorer constantly STRIKES ILE, and of the very best quality.

1894. *Sketch*, 28 March, 462, 1. You were speaking just now of 'Babil and Bijou' having been a financial failure, but I suppose you have STRUCK ILE sometimes?

TO OIL THE WIG, *verb. phr.* (provincial).—To make tipsy: *see* DRINKS and SCREWED.

TO OIL THE KNOCKER, *verb. phr.* (common).—To fee the porter. Fr. *graisser le marteau.*

OINER, *subs.* (University).—A cad.

OINTMENT, *subs.* (medical students').—1. Butter; CART-GREASE (*q.v.*).

2. (old).—Money. [From the 13th Century *Fabliau*, '*De la Vieille qui Oint la Palme au Chevalier*'].

3. (venery).—The semen: *see* SPENDINGS.

O.K., *phr.* (originally American: now universal).—*See* quot. 1871.

1847. ROBB, *Squatter Life*, 72. His express reported himself after his night ride, assured Allen that all was O.K., and received his dollar.

1852. JUDSON, *Mysteries of New York*, iv. 'Tis one of us; it's O.K.

1871. DE VERE, *Americanisms*. General Jackson, better known . . as *Old Hickory*, was not much at home in the art of spelling, and his friend and admirer, Major Jack Downing, found therefore no difficulty in convincing the readers of his 'Letters,' that the President employed the letters O.K. as an endorsement of applications for office, and other papers. They were intended to stand for 'All Correct,' which the old gentleman preferred writing *Oll Korrect*.

1883. *Graphic*, 17 March, 287, 1. It was voted O.K., or all correct, whereas the other was pronounced only a one-horse affair.

1889. *Answers*, 56, 1. John Jenkins . . . . was O.K. with Matilda Ann at Williams Street.

1889. *Pall Mall Gazette*, 12 Nov., 3, 1. If a stock has been falling and a sudden rise of 1 comes over there is an immediate inquiry, to make sure that there is no mistake. The reply O.K. no doubt comes back, and the price goes out.

1891. *Sporting Times*, 11 Ap. There can be no doubt that it was all O.K., for your insistence upon strict veracity is well known to all readers of the *Pink 'Un.*

Verb. (American).—To signify that all is right.

1888. *Missouri Republican*, 25 Jan. Please O.K., and hurry the return of my account.

OLD, *subs.* (common).—Money: *see* RHINO.

1900. SIMS, *In London's Heart*, 10. "Perhaps its somebody you owe a bit of the OLD to, Jack" . . . "No, I don't think so," he replied. "Most of the people I owed money to turned up, my dear, when I married you."

Adj. (old colloquial). — 1. Crafty; cunning; experienced.

2. (old literary: now colloquial).—Great; famous; grand; once a common intensitive; now only in combination with 'high,' 'good,' 'gay,' etc.

1590. TARLTON, *Newes out of Purgatorie*. On Sunday, at masse, there was an OLDE ringing of bells.

1596. SHAKSPEARE, *Merry Wives*, i. 4. There will be an OLD abusing of God's patience, and the king's English.

1600. SHAKSPEARE, *Much Ado*, v. 2, 98. Madam, you must come to your uncle. Yonder's OLD coil at home.

1603. TOMKIS, *Lingua*, ii. 6. Imagine there is OLD moving amongst them.

1611. MIDDLETON and DEKKER, *Roaring Girl (Century)*. Here's OLD cheating.

1612. DEKKER, *If it be not Good, etc.* We shall have OLD breaking of neckes.

1621. FLETCHER, *Pilgrim*, iii. 7. Strange work at sea; I fear me there's OLD tumbling.

1624. MIDDLETON, *Game at Chess*, iii. 1. Mass, here will be OLD firking.

1664. COTTON, *Vergil Travestie* (1st ed.), 104. There was OLD drinking and OLD singing.

1883. *Referee*, 11 Mar., 3, 2. All the children who have been engaged in the Drury Lane Pantomime took tea on the stage, and had a HIGH OLD TIME (while it lasted).

1888. J. McCARTHY, and MRS. CAMPBELL-PRAED, *Ladies' Gallery*, xxxv. I went down to Melbourne, intending to have a HIGH OLD TIME.

1891. J. NEWMAN, *Scamping Tricks*, 7. You are a big fraud and a HIGH OLD liar.

1892. F. ANSTEY, *Voces Populi*, 'The Riding Class,' 108. 'We've bin having a GAY OLD time in 'ere.

1899. GUNTER, *Florida Ench.*, 86. Well, my boy, did you have a HIGH OLD time last evening with that pretty widow.

3. (Old Cant).—*See quot.*

1811. *Lex. Bal.* OLD, ugly.

4. (old literary: now colloquial).—A general term of endearment or cordiality: *e.g.*, OLD CHAP; OLD FELLOW; OLD BOY; OLD HOSS; OLD MAN; OLD GAL; etc. *See* BOY.

1598. SHAKSPEARE, *1 Henry IV.*, ii. 4. Go thy ways, OLD Jack.

1696. B. E., *Dict. Cant. Crew*, s.v. OLD CUFF, a frolicksome old Fellow. *Ibid.* OLD TOAST, a brisk old Fellow.

1740. RICHARDSON, *Pamela*, III. 380. Never fear, OLD BOY, said Sir Charles, we'll bear our parts in conversation.

1785. GROSE, *Vulg. Tongue*, s.v. OLD TOAST, a brisk old fellow.

1823. GROSE, *Vulg. Tongue* [EGAN]. OLD CHAP, a good-natured flash phrase.

1854. *Our Cruise in the Undine*, 142. Here's a go, Bill! said the Doctor. Never mind, OLD BOY, replied the Captain; we'll get the other side of him yet.

1871. *The Echo*, 16 March. You are going to have a wet, OLD BOY? one familiarly remarked.

1889. *Illus. London News Summer Number*, 26, col. 2. You are right there, OLD BOY, said Eustace.

1892. HUME NISBET, *Bushranger's Sweetheart*, p. 165. Now for business, OLD BOY.

5. (common).—A general disparagement: as in OLD BLOKE; OLD BUFFER; OLD CAT; OLD COCK; OLD CODGER; OLD COON; OLD CRAWLER; OLD CURMUDGEON; OLD DOG; OLD FILE; OLD FIZ-GIG; OLD GEEZER; OLD HUDDLE AND TWANG; OLD IMAGE; OLD POT-AND-PAN; OLD SHAVER; OLD SQUARE-TOES; OLD STAGER; OLD STICK; OLD STICK-IN-THE-MUD.

1600. *Sir John Oldcastle*, i. 2. If ever wolf were clothed in sheep's coat, Then I am he; OLD HUDDLE AND TWANG.

1760. GEORGE COLMAN, *Polly Honeycombe*, i. 3. The OLD CODGER's gone, and has locked me up with his daughter.

1823. MONCRIEFF, *Tom and Jerry*, ii. 4. *Tom.* Good night, OLD STICK-IN-THE-MUD.

1836. LEMAN REDE and R. BRINSLEY PEAKE, *The Middle Temple*, 3. *Bru.* Thank you, ma'am; there was an OLD FIZGIG told me to bring that card here. Mrs. M. OLD FIZGIG! (*Aside*) Does not speak quite respectful of his parent.

1838. SELBY, *The Dancing Master*, 2. Hard-hearted OLD CODGER, he'd see me killed with as much unconcern as he would a sucking-pig.

1846. PLANCHE, *Court Favour*, i. Duke. (*Aside*) Tiresome OLD CAT! Madam—(*aloud*)—permit me.

1864. *Sun*, 28 Dec., Review of HOTTEN'S *Slang Dict.* We look in vain here for any mention of OLD SQUARE-TOES.

1867. MARK LEMON, *Golden Fetters*, ii. p. 74. Mr. Clendon did not call Mr. Barnard OLD COCK, OLD FELLOW, or OLD BEESWING.

1870. HAYLEWOOD and WILLIAMS, *Leave it to Me*, i. Jos. (*aside*) Blowed if I know what to say. (*Aloud to* Quince) My worthy OLD Cockalorum!

1888. BOLDREWOOD, *Robbery Under Arms*, xxxvi. You're a regular OLD IMAGE, Jim, says she. *Ibid.*, i. I used to laugh at him, and call him a regular OLD CRAWLER.

1892. MILLIKEN, *'Arry Ballads*, 17. Life don't want lifting, OLD OYSTER.

1895. H. B. MARRIOTT-WATSON, in *New Review*, 4 July. He was a comfortable OLD COCK, of an affluent habit, and pretty well to do, as I suspected.

AS OLD AS CHARING CROSS (or AS PAUL'S), *phr.* (old).—Of ripe age.—RAY (1676).

OLD ADAM, *subs. phr.* (venery).—The *penis*: see CREAMSTICK and PRICK.

OLD AGAMEMNONS, *subs. phr.* (military).—The 69th Foot, now the 2nd Batt. of the Welsh Regiment: bestowed by Nelson at St. Vincent in 1769, when the regiment were serving as marines. Also "The Ups and Downs."

OLD AND BOLD, *subs. phr.* (military). — The Prince of Wales's Own (West Yorkshire Regiment), formerly The 14th Foot. Also "Calvert's Entire," "The Powos," and "The Fighting Brigade."

OLD BAILEY UNDERWRITER, *subs. phr.* (old).—See quot.

1830. MONCRIEFF, *Van Dieman's Land*, i. 1. An OLD BAILEY UNDERWRITER—forgery on a small scale.

OLD BENDY, *subs. phr.* (old).—The devil: see SKIPPER.

OLD BIRD, *subs. phr.* (thieves').—1. An experienced thief. Also OLD HAND.

1877. *Five Years' Penal Servitude*, i. 32. In nine cases out of ten an OLD BIRD would betray himself.

1899. *Star*, 3 Jan. Only the cook was there; but a right good fellow was he, though an OLD HAND of very questionable antecedents.

2. (common).—An expert. Also OLD HAND and OLD DOG. Hence OLD DOG AT IT = expert.

1785. GROSE, *Vulg. Tongue*, s.v. OLD HAND, knowing, or expert in any business.

1889. *Daily News*, 9 Nov., 5, 2. Was the interest in Jane wearing off, or was Bysshe TOO OLD A BIRD to praise one lady in the hearing of another?

1892. *Ally Sloper's Half Holiday*, 19 Mar., 90, 3. I'm TOO OLD A BIRD to be had on toast like that.

OLD BLAZES (common). — The devil: see SKIPPER.

1849. *Southern Literary Messenger*, June. He looked, upon my word, like OLD BLAZES himself, with his clothing all on fire, and rage and despair in his face.

OLD BLOCK. See CHIP.

OLD BOLD, *subs. phr.* (military).—The 29th Foot, now the 1st Batt. Worcestershire Regiment. Also "The Ever-Sworded 29th."

OLD BOLD FIFTH, *subs. phr.* (military). — The Northumberland Fusiliers: formerly The 5th Foot. Also "The Shiners," "The Fighting Fifth," and "Lord Wellington's Bodyguard."

OLD BOOTS. LIKE OLD BOOTS, *phr.* (common).—A general and irrelevant comparison. *See* LIKE.

1850. SMEDLEY, *Frank Fairleigh*, xxv. He . . . drove his heels into 'Tom Trot'—that's the new grey horse, sir, if you please—and was out of sight LIKE OLD BOOTS.

1864. HOTTEN, *Slang Dict.*, s.v. OLD BOOTS . . . 'As cheeky as OLD BOOTS'; 'As quick as OLD BOOTS,' seem a little more reasonable, new boots being somewhat unfavourable to speedy locomotion.

1868. MISS BRADDON, *Sir Jasper*, xxvii. I'll stick to you LIKE OLD BOOTS.

1874. *Saturday Review*, Jan., 55. An Oxford man, nay even a Balliol man . . . introduced in the story a pleasing change by such a phrase as jawing away LIKE OLD BOOTS.

1892. MILLIKEN, *'Arry Ballads*, 33. I jest blew away LIKE OLD BOOTS.

OLD BRAGGS, *subs. phr.* (military).—The 28th Foot, now the 1st Batt. Gloucestershire Regiment: from its Colonel's name, 1734-51. Also "The Slashers."

OLD BUCKS, *subs. phr.* (military).—The Bedfordshire Regiment, formerly The 16th Foot. Also "The Peacemakers" and "The Feather-beds."

OLD BUFFS, *subs. phr.* (military).—The Third Foot, now The Buffs (East Kent Regiment). Also NUT-CRACKERS and RESURRECTIONISTS.

OLD-CROW, *subs. phr.* (American).—A drink; a dram. [In the United States OLD CROW = a choice brand of Bourbon or corn whiskey.]

c.1860. *Broadside Ballad* [quoted in *Slang, Jargon and Cant*]. Life seems a bit to soften when I try a good OLD CROW.

OLD-DING, *subs. phr.* (venery).—The female *pudendum*: see MONOSYLLABLE. — *Lex. Bal.* (1811); GROSE (1823).

OLD-DOG, *subs. phr.* (common).—1. A half-burnt plug of tobacco left in the bowl of a pipe.

2. (colloquial).—A lingering antique.

1846. DICKENS, *Dombey*, x. 79. An old campaigner, sir, said the Major, a smoke-dried, sun-burnt, used-up, invalided OLD DOG of a Major, sir.

Adj. phr. (old).—Particularly good.

1596. NASHE, *Have with you*, Epis. Ded. par. 5. O, he hath been OLDE DOGGE at that drunken, staggering kinde of verse.

1664. BUTLER, *Hudibras*, II. iii. 5, 208. He (Sidrophel) was OLD DOG at physiology.

1696. B. E., *Dict. Cant. Crew*, s.v. OLD-DOG-at-it, good or expert. *Ibid.* OLD-DOG-AT-COMMON-PRAYER, a poor Hackney that cou'd Read, but not Preach well.

1785. GROSE, *Vulg. Tongue*, s.v.

OLD DONAH (or OLD WOMAN), *subs. phr.* (tramps').—A mother.

1893. EMERSON, *Signor Lippo*, xvi. Well my old pot switched with the cook, my OLD DONAH, and . . . I was born a twelvemonth afterwards.

OLD DOSS, *subs. phr.* (thieves').—See quots. and CAGE.

1823. GROSE, *Vulg. Tongue* [EGAN]. s.v. OLD DOSS, Bridewell.

1859. MATSELL, *Vocabulum*, s.v. OLD DOSS, The Tombs [the New York City gaol].

OLD DOZEN, *subs. phr.* (military).—The Suffolk Regiment, formerly the 12th Foot.

OLD DRIVER, *subs. phr.* (common).—The devil: see SKIPPER.

OLD EBONY, *subs.* (literary).—*Blackwood's Magazine*. Also MAGA.

OLD EYES, *subs. phr.* (military).—The Grenadier Guards; also known as "The Sand Bags," "The Coalheavers," "The Housemaids' Pets," and "The Bermuda Exiles."

OLD FILE, *subs. phr.* (common).—A miser; a SKINFLINT (*q.v.*). Also see OLD, *adj.* sense 5.

OLD FIVE AND THREEPENNIES, *subs. phr.* (military).—The Fifty-third Foot. [From its number and (formerly) the daily pay of an ensign]. Also BRICKDUSTS.

OLD FLOORER, *subs. phr.* (common).—Death.

OLD FOGS, *subs. phr.* (military).—The 87th Foot, now the Royal Irish Fusiliers. [From their battle-cry, 'Fag-an-Bealach' = 'Clear the Way']. Also "Blayney's Bloodhounds" and "The Rollickers."

OLD GENTLEMAN, *subs. phr.* (card-sharpers').—1. See quot.

1828. G. SMEETON, *Doings in London*, 77. An OLD GENTLEMAN (a card somewhat larger and thicker than the rest of the pack, and now in considerable use amongst the 'legs').

2. (common).—The devil: see SKIPPER.

1727. DE FOE, *Hist. App.* [1729], 364. The devil is not so black as he is painted, but that you may form such images of THE OLD GENTLEMAN [etc.]. M.

1836. BUCKSTONE, *Marana*, ii. 1. They do say, if he's not THE OLD GENTLEMAN himself he is a very near relation. . . . *Gil.* And as true as you stand there, only two evenings ago I saw his Satanic Majesty.

1840. BARHAM, *Ingoldsby Legends* (*Lay of St. Nicholas*). And how, to the day of their death, THE OLD GENTLEMAN Never attempted to kidnap them more.

OLD GLORY, *subs. phr.* (American).—The United States' flag (1770-1844).

OLD GOOSEBERRY, *subs. phr.* (common).—The devil: see SKIPPER.

1861. H. KINGSLEY, *Ravenshoe*, xxxvii. Hornby (who would, like Faust, have played chess with OLD GOOSEBERRY) allowed himself to be taken into a skittle-ground.

TO PLAY OLD GOOSEBERRY, *verb. phr.* (common).—To play the devil.—GROSE (1785); BEE (1823).

1819. MOORE, *Tom Crib*, 22. Will PLAY UP OLD GOOSEBERRY soon with them all.

1835. SELBY, *Catching an Heiress*, 1. Go to the fair, get jolly, and PLAY UP OLD GOOSEBERRY.

1843. BARHAM, *Ingoldsby Legends* (*Bloudie Jack*). There's a pretty to do! All the people of Shrewsbury Playing OLD GOOSEBERRY, With your choice bits of taste and virtù.

1843. DICKENS, *Martin Chuzzlewit*, xxxviii. I'll PLAY OLD GOOSEBERRY with the office.

1865. H. KINGSLEY, *Hillyars and the Burtons*, lxii. LAY ON LIKE OLD GOOSEBERRY.

1892. *Globe*, 12 July, 2, 2. We all know his capacity for PLAYING OLD GOOSEBERRY with things in general.

OLD GOWN, *subs.* (common).—Smuggled tea.

OLD HAND. See OLD BIRD.

OLD HARRY, *subs. phr.* (common).—The devil. Also THE LORD HARRY. See SKIPPER.—GROSE (1785).

1687. CONGREVE, *Old Bach.*, ii. 2. By THE Lord Harry he says true.

1744. O'HARE, *Midas*, ii. 1. I swear by THE LORD HARRY, The moment madam's coffined—Her I'll marry.

1810. POOLE, *Hamlet Travestie*, i. 1. I'll speak to it, should even OLD HARRY dare me.

1849. LYTTON, *Caxtons*, VIII. ch. ii. By THE LORD HARRY! muttered the policeman, if he ben't going to sleep again!

1866. MAHONY, *Reliques of Father Prout*, 'Vert-Vert.' Nay sometimes, too, by THE LORD HARRY! He'd pull their caps and 'scapulary.'

2. (old).—See quot. 1696.

1696. B. E., *Dict. Cant. Crew*, s.v. OLD HARRY, a composition used by Vintners, when they bedevil their Wines.

1785. GROSE, *Vulg. Tongue*, s.v.

TO PLAY OLD HARRY, *verb. phr.* (common).—To play the devil: see PLAY.

1837. MARRYAT, *Dog Friend*, xlvii. They've PLAYED OLD HARRY with the rigging.

1884. W. C. RUSSELL, *Jack's Courtship*, xii. I'm afraid he'll now take such steps to stop all chance of my meeting or communicating with his daughter as will PLAY OLD HARRY with my hopes.

OLD HARVEY, *subs. phr.* (nautical).—The large boat (the launch) of a man-of-war.

OLD HAT, *subs. phr.* (venery).—*See* quots. and MONOSYLLABLE.

1754. FIELDING, *Jonathan Wild*, I. vi. (note). I shall conclude this learned note with remarking that the term OLD HAT is used by the vulgar in no very honourable sense.

1760. STERNE, *Tristram Shandy*, cxxvi. A chapter of chambermaids, green gowns, and OLD HATS.

1785. GROSE, *Vulg. Tongue*, s.v. HAT. OLD HAT, a woman's privities: because frequently felt.

OLD HORNEY (or **HORNINGTON**), *sub. phr.* (venery).—The *penis*: *see* PRICK. *Cf.* MISS HORNER = the female *pudendum*.

OLD (or **SALT**) **HORSE**, *subs. phr.* (nautical).—1. Salt junk. Fr. *souspied*, and *tire-fiacre*.

1889. *Chambers's Journal*, 3 Aug., 495. Mr. Clark Russell declares that SALT-HORSE works out of the pores, and contributes to that mahogany complexion common to sailors, which is often mistakenly attributed to rum and weather.

2. (American).—An endearment: a familiar address. *See* OLD, *adj.*, sense 4. Also OLD HOSS.

1884. S. L. CLEMENS ('M. Twain'), *Huckleberry Finn*, xvii. Are you all ready? All right—come olong, OLD HOSS.

1888. GUNTER, *Mr. Potter of Texas*, 123. Lubbius, OLD OS, is that ere lunch ready?

1893. EMERSON, *Signor Lippo*, xiv. Well, OLD HOSS, how are you, and how's the world been playing on yer since I last vardied yer? Alright, mate.

OLD INNISKILLINGS, *subs. phr.* (military).—The 6th (Inniskilling) Dragoons. Also "The Skillingers."

OLD IRON, *subs. phr.* (nautical).—Shore clothes. TO WORK UP OLD IRON = to go ashore.

OLD LADY, *subs. phr.* (card-sharpers').—1. *See* quot. and *cf.* OLD GENTLEMAN, sense 1.

1828. G. SMEETON, *Doings in London*, 78. There is not only an old gentleman, but an OLD LADY (a card broader than the rest) amongst them.

2. (venery).—The female *pudendum*: *see* MONOSYLLABLE.

THE OLD LADY OF THREADNEEDLE ST., *subs. phr.* (common).—The Bank of England.

1797. GILRAY, *The Old Lady in Threadneedle Street in Danger* [Title of Caricature, the reference being to the temporary stopping of cash payments 26th February, 1797, and the issue of pound bank-notes 4th March the same year.]

1859. *Punch*, xxxvi. 174. The girl for my money. The OLD LADY OF THREADNEEDLE STREET.

1864. BRADDON, *Henry Dunbar*, xxv. The . . . . convenient and flimsy paper circulating medium dispensed by the OLD LADY IN THREADNEEDLE STREET.

1871. *Chambers's Journal*, 9 Dec., 773. The OLD LADY IN THREADNEEDLE STREET can always take care of herself: if a note is stolen, *she* don't suffer; while, if it is lost, it is just so much in her own pocket, unless you can get a justice of the peace to swear it's burned.

1889. *Tit Bits*, 30 Nov., 119, 1. From seven o'clock in the evening until seven o'clock in the morning the OLD LADY OF THREADNEEDLE STREET is as well protected by Her Majesty's soldiers as Her Majesty in her palace.

1894. *Pall Mall Gazette*, 28 July. In its infancy there were only fifty-four persons employed in the service of the OLD LADY OF THREADNEEDLE STREET; now the staff numbers nearly a thousand employees.

OLD LAG. *See* LAG.

OLD LINE STATE, *subs. phr.* (American).—Maryland. [From the OLD LINE regiments contributed to the Continental army in the War of the Revolution].

OLD MAN, *subs. phr.* (venery).—1. The *penis*: *see* CREAMSTICK and PRICK.

2. (Australian).—A full-grown male kangaroo.

18[?]. *Bush Wanderings of a Naturalist* . . . . Some of the OLD MEN reach to an immense size, and I have often killed them over 2 cwts.

1873. J. B. STEPHENS, *Mis. Poems* [1880] 'Brisbane Reverie.' Where the Kangaroo gave hops, the OLD MAN fleetest of the fleet.

1897. *Pall Mall*, 23 Sep., 9, 2. Almost the first kangaroo put up was an OLD MAN, and the pack bustled him through a patch of heavy timber, into a bog and out of it again.

3. (common).—A familiar mode of address. *See* OLD, *adj.*, sense 4.

4. (common).—A master; a GOVERNOR (*q.v.*); a BOSS (*q.v.*).

1899. GUNTER, *Florida Ench.* 9. 'One would think you like to frighten people.' 'So I does,' grins the youth solemnly, 'when the OLD MAN's out.'

5. (common).—A husband: *cf.* OLD WOMAN. Fr. *le géniteur*.

1856. WHYTE MELVILLE, *Kate Coventry*, xvi. Aunt Deborah only stipulating that there should be no male addition to the party, except Mr. Lumley himself, or, as the lady of the house termed him, her OLD MAN.

1883. STEVENSON, *The Silverado Squatters*, 98. When her OLD MAN wrote home for her from America.

6. (American).—The captain of a merchantman.

1823. FENIMORE COOPER, *Pilot*, vi. We must get them both off . . . before the OLD MAN takes it into his head to leave the coast.

1847. HOWITT, *Journal*, 187. To begin with the captain. He was a first-rate OLD MAN as far as good treatment and good living went.

1850. SEAWORTHY, *Nag's Head*, viii. 66. Land O! Where away? shouted the OLD MAN.

1883. W. CLARK RUSSELL, *Sailor's Language*, preface, xi. But the lack of variety is no obstruction to the sailor's poetical inspiration when he wants the OLD MAN to know his private opinions without expressing them to his face, and so the same chantey, as the windlass or halliard chorus is called, furnishes the music to as many various indignant remonstrances as Jack can find injuries to sing about.

7. (common).—The ridge between two sleepers in a feather bed.

8. (nurses').—A blanket used to wrap a young child in.

9. (common).—A father.

OLD MAN'S MILK, *subs. phr.* (common).—Whiskey: *see* DRINKS. In Scotland a mixture of cream, eggs, sugar and whiskey.

18 [?]. *Saxon and Gael*, ii. 78, 79. Flora made me a bowl of OULD MAN'S MILK, but nothing would bring me round.

OLD MR. GORY, *subs. phr.* (old).—'A piece of gold.'—B.E. (*c.*1696); GROSE (1785).

OLD MR. GRIM, *subs. phr.* (old).—Death: *see* OLD FLORER (*q.v.*).—GROSE (1785); *Lex Bal.* (1811).

OLD NICK, *subs. phr.* (common).—The devil: *see* SKIPPER. Also NICKIE and NICKIE-BEN.—B. E. (*c.*1696); GROSE (1785).

1662. *Rump Songs*, ii. 43. In this prodigal trick They have outdone OLD NICK For what he did give he did show.

1678. BUTLER, *Hudibras*, III. i. 1313. NICK Machiavel had no such trick, Though he gave's name to our OLD NICK.

1706. WARD, *Hudibras Redivivus*, I. v. 14. In painful fury roaring out, I wish your patterns at OLD NICK.

1719. DURFEY, *Pills to Purge, &c.*, i. 264. The God of Love, or else OLD NICK, Sure had design'd this Devilish trick.

1720. SWIFT, *Apollo to the Dean* [*Works* (1824), xiv. 134]. For I think in my conscience he deals with OLD NICK.

*a.*1796. BURNS, *Tam o' Shanter*, II. There sat AULD NICK, in shape o' beast. *Ibid. Add. to the Devil.* But fare-you-weel, AULD NICKIE-BEN.

1829. BUCKSTONE, *Billy Taylor*, NICK or Belzebub, Or as our children call thee, black old Bogey, Appear!

1835. HALIBURTON, *Clockmaker*, I S. x. And kick like mad, and then OLD NICK himself wouldn't start 'em.

1855. *Notes and Queries*, I S. xii. 228. All over the North a demon bearing this designation, slightly modified by dialectic variations, is commonly acknowledged. He is the Anglo-Saxon Nicer; Dan. Nöecke or Nökke (Nikke); Swedish Neck, Necken ('ejusdem significationis' as Finn Magnusen observes, 'ut et Anglorum Nick—Old Nick; Belgarum, Nicker—qui, jam nune diabolum indicant'); Fennish Næki; Esthonian Nack; Scotch Nicneven; German Nichs, Nicks, Nichse, the Nickar of the people of the Feroës, and the Nikel of those of the Rügen.

1870. MONCRIEFF, *Giovanni in London*, i. 2. And, pray, what were you sent to OLD NICK for, my love?

1884. CLARK RUSSELL, *Jack's Courtship*, xvi. I knew you'd do it—it's the Seymour spirit—a fair grip, and OLD NICK may shriek for mercy.

1892. MILLIKEN, *'Arry Ballads*, 38. In that Gallery, Charlie, OLD NICK would have found it too warm.

OLD ONE (or **OLD 'UN**), *subs. phr.* (common).—1. The devil: *see* SKIPPER.—GROSE (1785).

2. (common).—A father.

1836. DICKENS, *Pickwick*, xx. It's the OLD 'UN. OLD ONE, said Mr. Pickwick, What OLD ONE? My father, sir, replied Mr. Weller.

3. (racing).—A horse more than three years old.

4. (theatrical).—The pantaloon; the FOOL'S FATHER (*q.v.*).

OLD PEGG, *subs. phr.* (old).—'Poor Yorkshire cheese, made of skimmed milk.'—GROSE (1785).

OLD PELT, *subs. phr.* (printers').—An old pressman. [In allusion to the ink pelts formerly in use for distributing the ink].

OLD POD (or **OLD POT-AND-PAN**), *subs. phr.* (rhyming).—1. An old man; a father. Also (2) a wife; a woman.

1893. EMERSON, *Signor Lippo*, xvi. You must know that my OLD POT was a bark.

OLD POGER, *subs. phr.* (old).—The devil: *see* SKIPPER.—GROSE.

OLD PROBABILITIES, *subs. phr.* (American).—The Superintendent of the United States' weather bureau. Sometimes OLD PROB.

1888. *New York Herald*, 4 Nov. When you come to think of the sort of weather we have had in New York upon the occasions of great popular political turnouts . . . . you will find that as a rule OLD PROBABILITIES has been rather kindly disposed to both parties.

OLD RED-EYE, *subs. phr.* (American).—Whiskey. *See* OLD MAN'S MILK.

OLD RIP. *See* RIP.

OLD ROGER, *subs. phr.* (old).—The devil: *see* SKIPPER.—GROSE (1785); *Lex. Bal.* (1811).

OLD SALT, *subs. phr.* (nautical).—An experienced sailor.

OLD SAUCY SEVENTH, *subs. phr.* (military).—The 7th (The Queen's Own) Hussars: in Peninsula times. Also "The Lily-White Seventh," "Young Eyes," "Old Strawboots" and "Straws."

OLD SCRATCH, *subs. phr.* (common).—The devil: *see* SKIPPER.

1762. SMOLLETT, *L. Greaves*, II. x. He must have sold himself to OLD SCRATCH; and, being a servant of the devil, how could he be a good subject to his Majesty.

1780. LEE, *Chapter of Accidents*, v. 2. I be sick enough of passing for a lady; but if OLD SCRATCH ever puts such a trick again in my head, I hope—your lordship will catch me, that's all.

1857. A. TROLLOPE, *Three Clerks*, xx. He don't mean anything, and I said he didn't all along. He'd have pitched me to OLD SCRATCH, while I was sitting there on his knee, if he'd have had his own way.

OLD SEVEN AND SIXPENNIES, *subs. phr.* (military).—The 76th Foot, now the 2nd Batt. Duke of Wellington's (West Riding Regiment): from its former number and the amount of a lieutenant's pay. Also "The Immortals" and "The Pigs."

OLD SHELL, *subs. phr.* (nautical).—A sailor.

OLD SHOE, *subs. phr.* (common).—A portent (or augury) of good fortune.

*d.*1892. TENNYSON, *Will Waterproof.* And wheresoe'er thou movs't good luck Shall fling her OLD SHOE after.

TO WEAR (or RIDE IN) ANOTHER MAN'S OLD SHOES (or BOOTS), *verb. phr.* (colloquial).—To marry or keep another man's woman.

OLD SOLDIER, *subs. phr.* (common).—A cigar end or old quid.

1901. *People*, 7 Ap., 18, 2. An OLD SOLDIER—both in the literal and metaphorical sense—down to every move on the board, suspicious and even touchy, he forms a genuine friend, ever ready to do his comrade a good turn.

TO COME THE OLD SOLDIER. *See* COME.

OLD SONG, *subs.* (common).—A trifle; a nominal sum or price.

OLD SPLIT-FOOT, *subs. phr.* (common).—The devil: *see* SKIPPER.

1848. LOWELL, *Biglow Papers*, . . . They go it like an Ericsson's ten-hoss-power coleric ingine, An' make OLE SPLIT-FOOT winch an' squirm, for all he's used to singein'.

OLD STAGER, *subs. phr.* (common).—A person of experience; an OLD DOG (*q.v.*).

OLD STICK, *subs. phr.* (common).—1. A disparagement: *cf.* OLD, *adj.*, sense 5.

2. (old).—A complimentary mode of address to an old man, signifying he is a capital fellow [HALLIWELL].

OLD STUBBORNS, *subs. phr.* (military).—The Forty-fifth Foot, now THE SHERWOOD FORESTERS.

OLD STRAWBOOTS (or **STRAWS**), *subs. phr.* (military).—The 7th (The Queen's Own) Hussars: for substituting at Warbourg (1760) strawbands for worn-out boots. Also "The Old Saucy Seventh" and "The Lily-White Seventh."

OLD TIMER, *subs. phr.* (colloquial).—1. A *laudator temporis acti*; and (2) one who has grown old in a place or profession.

1860. *Music and Drama*, XIII. ix. 14. OLD TIMERS unanimously declared that in the new-comer had indeed arisen another Tausig.

1866. *New Princetown Rev.*, v. 122. Most of us OLD TIMERS . . . are poor now.

OLD TOAST, *subs. phr.* (common).—1. The devil: *see* SKIPPER. Also OLD TOASTER.—MATSELL (1859).

2. (old).—'A brisk old fellow.' GROSE (1785); *Lex. Bal.* (1811).

OLD TOM, *subs. phr.* (common).—Gin: *see* WHITE SATIN.

1823. BEE, *Dict. Turf*, s.v.

1832. EGAN, *Book of Sports*, 268. When Love turns his back, and old friendships are failing, And the spirits are sinking therefrom—The only receipt, that is ne'er unavailing, Is a jolly stiff glass of OLD TOM.

1837. LYTTON, *Ernest Maltravers*, IV. i. OLD TOM, he is the best of gin: Drink him once, and you'll drink him *agin!*

1851-61. MAYHEW, *London Lab.* ii. p. 256. Rum he preferred to gin, only it was dearer, but most of the scavengers, he thought, liked OLD TOM (gin) best.

1854. *Punch*, xxxvii. 75. Mr. Stuggers was promptly thrust into a cell into which five of his companions followed him, and their united consolations, and those of a bottle of the ANCIENT THOMAS Vintage which was speedily produced, restored the Varmint to something of his habitual placidity.

1868. BREWER, *Phrase and Fable*, s.v. OLD TOM. Thomas Norris, one of the men employed in Messrs. Hodges' distillery, opened a gin palace in Great Russell Street, Covent Garden, and called the gin concocted by Thomas Chamberlain, one of the firm of Hodges, OLD TOM, in compliment to his former master.

1892. SYDNEY WATSON, *Wops the Waif*, i. 2. And a-slides along from 'shampain' to brandy, and from that to OLD TOM.

OLD TOUGHS, *subs. phr.* (military).—The One Hundred and Third Foot, now the 2nd Batt. Royal Dublin Fusiliers. [For long and arduous service in India].

OLD TROT. *See* TROT.

OLD 'UN. *See* OLD ONE.

OLD WHALE, *subs. phr.* (nautical).—A sailor.

OLD WOMAN, *subs. phr.* (venery).—1. The female *pudendum*: *see* MONOSYLLABLE.

2. (prison).—A prisoner who, unfit for physical hard work, is set to knitting stockings.

3. (common).—A man with the character and habits of a woman. Also, OLD WIFE.

4. (colloquial).—A wife or mother: *cf.* OLD MAN. *See* DUTCH.

1892. *Idler*, June, p. 550. As we was a-comin' 'ome I says to the OLD GAL, Let's pop into the Broker's Arms and 'ave a drop o' beer.

OLIVE-BRANCHES, *subs. phr.* (colloquial).—Children. [In allusion to Psalm cxxviii. 4, in Book of Common Prayer].

1688. PRIOR, *The Mice.* May you ne'er meet with Tends or Babble, May OLIVE-BRANCHES crown your Table.

1888. *Harper's Mag.*, lxxvi. 791. There were hardly quarter's enough for the bachelors, let alone those blessed with wife and OLIVE BRANCHES.

OLIVER, *subs.* (old).—The moon; the SKY-LANTERN. OLIVER WHIDDLES (or IS UP) = the moon shines; OLIVER IS IN TOWN = the nights are moonlight.

1781. G. PARKER, *View of Society*, II. 133, *note.* OLIVER DON'T WIDDLE. The Moon not up.

1819. VAUX, *Memoirs*, ii. 193, s.v.

1834. AINSWORTH, *Rookwood*, III. v. Now OLIVER puts his black nightcap on And every star its glim is hiding. *Ibid.* IV. vi. OLIVER WHIDDLES—the tatler old! Telling what best had been left untold, OLIVER ne'er was a friend of mine; All glims I hate that so brightly shine. Give me a night black as hell, and then See what I'll show to you, my merry men.

1837. LYTTON, *Ernest Maltravers*, IV. i. In half an hour OLIVER puts on his nightcap, and we must then be off.

1895. H. B. MARRIOTT-WATSON, in *New Review*, 7 July. There's a moon out, The better for us to pick 'em off, Dan, I returned, laughing at him. What—OLIVER? damn OLIVER! said Zacchary. Let's push forward and come to quarters.

TO GIVE A ROWLAND FOR AN OLIVER. *See* ROWLAND.

OLIVER'S SKULL, *subs. phr.* (old).—A chamber-pot: *see* IT.—B. E. (*c.* 1696); GROSE (1785); MATSELL (1859).

OLLAPOD, *subs.* (old).—An apothecary. [From George Coleman's comedy (1802) *The Poor Gentleman.*] Sp. *olla podrida* = putrid pot.

OLLI COMPOLLI, *subs. phr.* (Old Cant).—'The by-name of one of the principal Rogues of the Canting Crew.'—B. E. (*c.* 1696); GROSE (1785); MATSELL (1859).

OMEE, *subs.* (thieves' and theatrical). A man: specifically, a master. [Fr. It. *uomo*]. Fr. *le pilier du creux.* Also OMER and HOMEE.

1864. HOTTEN, *Slang Dict.*, s.v. OMEE ... the OMEE of the Carsey's a nark on the pitch, the master of the house will not let us perform.

1883. *Echo*, 25 Jan., 2, 3. From the Italian we got the thieves' slang terms casa for house ... and OMEE for man (nomo).

1893. EMERSON, *Signor Lippo*, xiii. When I got back the cullies said, Well, cully, how did you get on with the OMER? Bono, about sa rounds of fine blocks.

OMNIBUS, *subs.* (venery).—1. The female *pudendum*: *see* MONOSYLLABLE.

2. (venery).—A prostitute: *see* BARRACK-HACK and TART.

3. (common).—A man of all-work; a handy man.

1894. *Pall Mall Gaz.*, 7 Dec., 8, 2. One of the OMNIBUSES employed at the café says that he saw a man in one of the upstairs lavatories after the café had been closed.

OMNIUM, *subs.* (Stock Exchange).—The aggregate value of the different stocks in which a loan is funded.

OMNIUM GATHERUM, *subs. phr.* (old: now recognised).—A medley; a Jack-of-all-trades. [Lat. *Omnium*, genit. plural of *omnis* = all, and Eng. *gather.*] GROSE (1785).

1576. DEE [ARBER, *English Gamer* (1879), ii. 63]. A fortnight in providing a little company of OMNI GATHARUMS taken up on a sudden to sewe at sea.

1592. G. HARVEY, *Foure Letters* [GROSART, *Wks.* i. 190]. A Player, a Coosener, a Rayler, a beggar, an OMNIGATHERUM, a Gay nothing.

1596. NASHE, *Saffron Walden*, in *Works*, iii. 46. Shew vs some of them, that like a great Inquest, we may deliuer our verdit before it come to the OMNIGATHERUM of Towne and Countrey.

1610. ROWLANDS, *Martin Markall*, p. 24 (H. Club's Repr. 1874). They haue a language among themselues, composed of OMNIUM GATHERUM.

1689. SELDEN, *Table-Talk*, p. 62 (Arber's ed.). So in our Court in Queen *Elizabeth's* time Gravity and State were kept up. In King *James's* time things were pretty well. But in King *Charles's* time, there has been nothing but *French*-more and the Cushion Dance, OMNIUM GATHERUM, tolly, polly, hoite come toite.

18[?]. D. OF BUCKINGHAM, *Court of William IV. and Victoria*, ii. ch. v. Our meeting ... was merely an OMNIUM-GATHERUM of all the party.

1855. THACKERAY, *Newcomes*, lxiii. She ... gave me to understand that this party was only an OMNIUM GATHERUM, not one of the select parties.

ON, *adv.* (back-slang).—1. No.

1874. HOTTEN, *Slang Dict.*, *Back Slang*, 355. ON DOOG, no good.

2. (common).—Tipsy: *see* DRINKS and SCREWED.

1882. JAS. PAYN, *For Cash Only*, xxii. I was no more ON at the Crown that night than I am at this blessed moment of time.

1888. *Cornhill Mag.*, March, 227. I wasn't drunk, only ON, but if she had given me another bumper I should have gone clean off my head.

3. (once literary: now vulgar).—Used for 'of'.

1657. MIDDLETON, *Women Beware Women*, I. ii. *Ward.* Many, that I am afraid ON.

d. 1625. FLETCHER, *Elder Brother*, IV. iii. We have no quarrel to you, that we know ON, sir.

1836. DICKENS, *Pickwick*, ii. 3. Come on! said the cab-driver, sparring away like clockwork. Come on—all four ON you.

4. (Winchester College).—*See* quot.

1866. MANSFIELD, *School Life at Winchester*, 222. ON—The word given by the Præfect of Hall for the boys to start to or from Hills, or to Cathedral. When any person or thing of importance was known to be likely to meet the boys when on Hills, the word was passed that he, she, or it was ON,—*e.g.*, RIDSWORTH ON, SNOBS ON, BADGER ON, etc.

5. (venery).—Carnally minded; concupiscent: ON IT (in America), said of a woman willing to copulate unlawfully.

1847. HALLIWELL, *Archaic Words*, *etc.*, s.v.

TO BE (or GET) ON, *verb. phr.* (racing).—1. To make a bet: generally TO HAVE A BIT ON.

1872. *Standard*, 23 Oct. Everyone ... HAD SOMETHING ON.

1881. W. BLACK, *Beautiful Wretch*, xxiv. I'll bet you five sovereigns to one that they let him out ... are you ON?

1883. HAWLEY SMART, *Hard Lines*, ix. In the mean time you are ON at 100 to nothing about your own horse.

1891. *Answers*, 28 Mar. Thanks to the eagerness of some small local bookmakers to let people GET ON late.

1894. GEORGE MOORE, *Esther Waters*, ii. Oh, we did have a fine time then, for we all had a bit ON.

2. (common).—Ready and willing; good at; fond of.

1872. S. L. CLEMENS ('Mark Twain'), *Innocents at Home*, ... Pard, he was ON it! He was ON it bigger than an Injun! ON it! ON what? ON the shoot. ON the shoulder. ON the fight, you understand.

1883. *Referee*, 6 May, 3, 3. If the directors should think fit to offer me £200 a night to warble, you may depend upon it I shall be ON at that figure.

1888. BOLDREWOOD, *Robbery Under Arms*, xi. I'm half a mind to tell Warrigal to go back and say we're not ON, I said.

1891. N. GOULD, *Double Event*, 124. Make it a hundred, and I'm ON, said Bandy.

1893. EMERSON, *Signor Lippo*, xiv. One day he meets an old college pal and off they go on the booze, and when he got the flavour of it he was ON TO IT and the old man chucked him.

TO TRY IT ON. *See* TRY.

[See also BACK; BALLOT; BAT; BATTER; BEAM-ENDS; BEER; BEND; BOARD; BONE; BOOT-LEG; BOUNCE; BOX; BURST (or BUST); CARDS; CHAIN; CHEAP; CROOK; CROSS; DEAD; DEAD BROKE; DEAD QUIET; DEE; FLY; FORTY-NINTH; FOURTH; FUDDLE; GRASS; GROUND-FLOOR; HALF-SHELL; HEAD; HIP; HOP; ICE; JOB; LAY; LEDGE; LOOSE; MAKE; MUDDLE; NAIL; NOD; NOSE; ONE'S P'S AND Q'S; POUNCE; PRAIRIE; PROMOTION; QUIET; Q.T.; RAMBLE; RAMPAGE; RAN-TAN; READY; REERAU; ROAD; RAILS; SCENT; SCOOT; SCOUT; SENTRY; SHALLOW; SHARP; SHELF; SHOVE; SHUNT; SKYTE; SLATE; SLY; SNAP; SPREE; SPOT; SQUARE; STAIRS; STRAIGHT; STRETCH; STRING; SWING; TAILBOARD; TAKE; TAPPY; TILES; TIME; TICK; TRAMP; TOAST; TOP; UPPERS; VELVET; WALLABY; WARPATH; WIN, etc.].

ONCE. IN ONCE, *phr.* (common).—First time.

1900. SIMS, *In London's Heart*, 72. "Meaning, Jim," he said ... "you found something in the cab as is of a private natur'?" "You've guessed it IN ONCE, father."

1900. *Free Lance*, 6 Oct., 16, 1. You've hit it IN ONCE.

ONE, *subs.* (common).—1. A lie: *see* WHOPPER.

2. (general).—A blow; a grudge; a score. Also ONE IN THE EYE.

1839. O'CONNELL, in *O'Connell Correspondence* (1888), ii. 168. I owe Brougham ONE, and I intend, if I can, to pay him.

1856. T. HUGHES, *Tom Brown's School Days*, II. vii. If we can slip the collar and do so much less without getting caught, that's ONE to us.

1883. J. H. WILSON, in *Longman's Mag.*, Nov., 103. But you know, Cap'n, you ain't a man to be trusted. I owe you ONE already for stealing my silver.

1892. *Ally Sloper*, 27 Feb., 67, 2. On his wife on one occasion saying to him, 'I wish you would reform, Bill, yourself,' he was much enraged, and gave her ONE for herself—not a Reform Bill, but IN THE EYE.

1900. SIMS, *In London's Heart*, 25. The girl took the money and went downstairs three at a time. She felt that it was, in the outdoor language of Exeter Street, ONE IN THE EYE for her aunt.

ONE IN, *phr.* (tailors').—Hearing another's good fortune and wishing the same to oneself.

ONE OUT, *phr.* (tailors').—Congratulating oneself on a fortunate escape.

ONE OF MY COUSINS, *phr.* (old).—A harlot.—B. E. (*c.* 1696); GROSE (1785).

ONE OF US (or THEM), *phr.* (old).—'A woman of the town.'—RAY (1767); GROSE (1785).

ONE UNDER THE ARM, *phr.* (tailors').—An extra job.

ONE OUT OF IT, *phr.* (tailors').—'I don't want to be mixed up with it.'

ONE OF THE LORD'S OWN, *subs. phr.* (American).—A dandy.

ONE WITH T'OTHER, *phr.* (venery).—Copulation: *see* GREENS and RIDE.

1661. *Old Song*, 'Maidens Delight' [FARMER, *Merry Songs and Ballads* (1897), i. 137]. Quoth she, my friend, let kissing end, Where with you do me smother, And run at Ring with t'other thing; A little o' th' ONE WITH T'OTHER.

TO BE ONE UPON ANOTHER'S TAW, *verb. phr.* (old).—*See* quot.

1819. VAUX, *Memoirs*, ii. 193. ONE UPON YOUR TAW, a person who takes offence at the conduct of another, or conceives himself injured by the latter, will say, never mind I'll be ONE UPON YOUR TAW; or, I'll be a MARBLE ON YOUR TAW; meaning I'll be even with you some time.

ONE AND THIRTY, *adj. phr.* (old).—Drunk: *see* DRINKS and SCREWED.—RAY (1767).

ONE FOR HIS NOB, *phr.* (common).—1. A blow on the head.

2. (cards').—*See* NOB.

See THREE OUT.

ONE-A-PIECE. TO SEE ONE-A-PIECE, *verb. phr.* (common).—To see double: *see* DRINKS and SCREWED.

1842. *Punch*, ii. 21. Our head swims, and our eyes SEE ONE A-PIECE.

ONEE, *adj.* (theatrical).—One: *e.g.* ONEE SOLDI (or WIN) = one penny.

ONE-EYED SCRIBE, *subs. phr.* (American).—A revolver: *see* MEAT-IN-THE-POT.

ONE-HORSE (or -EYED), *adj.* (formerly American; now general).—Petty; insignificant; of no account. Also ONE-GOAT.

1858. *Washington Star* [quoted by BARTLETT]. On Friday last, the engineer of a fast train was arrested by the authorities of a ONE-HORSE town in Dauphin County, Pa., for running through the borough at a greater rate of speed than is allowed by their ordinances. Having neglected, however, to give publicity to these ordinances, they could not impose any fine; and their discomfiture was aggravated by the malicious excuse of the engineer, that 'he didn't know there was a town there!'

d. 1877. MOTLEY, *Letters*, II. 334. Any other respectable, ONE-HORSE New England city.

1884. CLEMENS, *Huckleberry Finn*, xx. 195. There was a little ONE-HORSE town about three mile down the bend.

1886. GOLDWIN SMITH, *Nineteenth Century*, July, p. 21. The provincial University of Toronto was thrown open to Nonconformists, unluckily not before the practice of chartering sectarian institutions had been introduced, and Canada had been saddled with ONE-HORSE universities.

1888. *Boston Weekly Globe*, 28 Mar. It seems a shame to let a petty ONE-GOAT power kingdom insult our citizens.

ONE-IN-TEN, *subs. phr.* (old).—A parson. [In allusion to tithes].

ONE NITCH (or **NICK**), *subs. phr.* (printers').—A male child: TWO NITCH = a baby girl.

ONE O'CLOCK. *See* LIKE.

ONE-ER, *subs.* (common).—A person or thing of great parts: as a very successful play; an exceedingly pretty woman; a crushing blow, a 'monumental' lie, etc. Also WUNNER.

1840. DICKENS, *Old Curiosity Shop*, lviii. Do they often go where glory waits 'em and leave you here? Oh, yes; I believe you they do, returned the small servant. Miss Sally's sich a ONE-ER for that, she is.

1861. DUTTON COOK, *Paul Foster's Daughter*, x. Oh, I've got it at last—such a ONENER—clean off my legs—first blood—first knock down—everything.

1869. GREENWOOD, *Seven Curses of London*, . . . The watcher is generally hanging about, and he'll 'down' you with a ONER in the back or side (he won't hit you in the face, for fear of spoiling it).

1871. HAMILTON, *Parodies*, part 71, p. 269. Before a-inviting of you to enter, and taste the joys of Elysium to be 'ad at the small charge of one penny, I will exhibit to your astonished and admiring gaze a few pictorual illustrations of the wonders to be shortly disclosed to you. Give the drum a ONE-ER!

1893. EMERSON, *Signor Lippo*, xi. Well, pal, forgive me, I always was a ONE-ER for the gab. Here's off or the missus will be waiting. When you're off the pitch there's a bite and a sup at Duke's cottage, Lea, for you. So 'long!

1895. F. BOYLE, in *Idler*, Aug. Mrs. Mumson is a ONER.

2. (common).—A shilling: *see* BLOW.

ONE'S EYE, *subs. phr.* (tailors' and dressmakers'). — A hiding-place for CABBAGE (*q.v.*); HELL (*q.v.*).

ONE TWO, *phr.* (pugilists').—*See* quot. 1823.

1823. GROSE, *Vulg. Tongue* [EGAN], s.v. ONE TWO. In boxing, two blows rapidly put in after each other. Jem Belcher was distinguished for his ONE TWO.

ONICKER, *subs.* (streets').—*See* quot.

1887. *Walford's Antiquarian*, 252. A mot and ONICKER are also terms for fallen women.

ONION, *subs.* (common).—1. The head. Hence, OFF HIS ONION = off his wits. *See* TIBBY.

2. (thieves').—A seal: generally in plural: *e.g.* BUNCH OF ONIONS.

1811. *Lex. Bal.* s.v. ONION HUNTERS, a class of young thieves who are on the look out for gentlemen who wear their seals suspended on a ribbon, which they cut, and thus secure the seals or other trinkets suspended to the watch.

1819. VAUX, *Memoirs*, ii. 193, s.v.

18[?]. MAGINN, *Vidocq's Slang Song* [FARMER, *Musa Pedestris* (1896) . . .] When his ticker I set a-going, With his ONIONS, chain, and key.

1834. H. AINSWORTH, *Rookwood*, IV. i. A handsome gold repeater . . . with a monstrous bunch of ONIONS (*anglice*, seals) depending from its massive chain. *Ibid.* 'Nix my doll.' My fawnied famms and my ONIONS gay.

ODDISH, *adv.* (popular).—Tipsy: *see* DRINKS and SCREWED.

OODLES, *subs.* (American).—*See* quot. 1869.

1869. *Overland Monthly*, iii. 131. A Texan never has a great quantity of any thing, but he has 'scads' of it or OODLES or DEAD OODLES or SCADOODLES or 'swads.'

1886. *Century Magazine*, xxxiii. 846. All you lack's the feathers, and we've got OODLES of 'em right here.

OOF (or **OOFTISH**), *subs.* (popular).—Money. Hence OOF-BIRD = the goose that lays the golden eggs, the source of supply; the FEATHERED OOF-BIRD = money in plenty; TO MAKE THE OOF-BIRD WALK = to circulate money; OOFLESS = poor. *See* quot. 1870.

c. 1870. *Sporting Times*, 26 Dec., 1891. 1. OOFTISH was, some twenty years ago, the East End synonym for 'money,' and was derived from *auf tische*, 'on the table'—the aristocracy of Houndsditch being in the habit of refusing to play cards, even with their best friends, unless the money were down 'on the table.' Hence OOFTISH, a word which was freely used by the late Mr. Benson and his companions in the De Goncourt frauds. We—that is to say Gub—met OOFTISH at a thieves' supper in Little Wylde Street, took the animal home, cut his tail off, and turned him loose. So that OOF now swaggers about the mansions of the aristocracy.

1888. *Sportsman*, 27 Dec. It is a sad and weary time for many, for when the dustman, the man who blacks the boots, and he with the grog-blossom on his nose who does nothing but hold cab-doors open when nobody asks him to have all been paid, the OOF BIRD takes unto itself wings and flies away.

1889. *Daily News*, 27 Aug., 7, 1. Henry Smith, her coachman, next gave evidence. He said he heard King say he had come after some OOFTISH.

1897. *Pall Mall Gazette*, 8 Mar., 7, 3. No splosh, no OOF-BIRD from those blokes.

O.P., *phr.* (theatrical).—1. *See* quot. 1823.

1823. GROSE, *Vulg. Tongue* [EGAN], s.v. O.P. and P.S. Theatrical cant, for Opposite the Prompter and Prompt Side.

1836. DICKENS, *Sketches by Boz*, p. 69. That gentleman . . . lounging behind the stage-box in the O.P. side.

1885. *Sportsman*, 23 June, 2, 1. The limelight mechanic made a gorgeous full moon in a convenient position on the O.P. side.

2. (booksellers'). — 'Out of print.'

OPEN. TO OPEN THE BALL, *verb. phr.* (colloquial).—To start or begin anything.

1812. BYRON, *Waltz*, xiii. [Note]. Waltz and the battle of Austerlitz are . . . said to have OPENED THE BALL together.

1876. *Eton Chronicle*, 20 July. He who OPENED THE BALL and who saw them all fall, Scarce deserved that defeat in one innings.

1887. HAGGARD, *Allan Quatermain*, xi. When the advancing boats were about five hundred yards away, Sir Henry OPENED THE BALL by firing at the three-parts grown young one.

TO OPEN ONE'S MOUTH TOO WIDE, *verb. phr.* (Stock Exchange). — To bid for larger amounts of stock than one can pay for.

TO OPEN UP, *verb. phr.* (venery).—TO SPREAD (*q.v.*).

OPEN-ARSE, *subs. phr.* (old).—1. A medlar.

1383. CHAUCER, *Prol. to Reeve's Tale*, i. 17. I fare as doth an OPENERS; That ilke fruyt is ever leng the wers Til it be roten in mullok or in stre.

1530. PALSGRAVE, *Les Clar. Langue Fran*, s.v. OPYNARS.

1595. SHAKSPEARE, *Romeo and Juliet*, ii. 1. Now will he sit under a medlar-tree, And wish his mistress were that kind of fruit, As maids call medlars, when they laugh alone—Oh, Romeo, that she were, oh, that she were An OPEN-ARSE.

1598. FLORIO, *A Worlde of Wordes*, s.v. *Nespola*, the fruit we call a Meddler or an OPEN-ARSE.

1696. B. E., *Dict. Cant. Crew*, s.v.

1785. GROSE, *Vulg. Tongue*, s.v. MEDLAR. A fruit vulgarly called an OPEN-A—E, of which it is more truly than delicately said, that it is never ripe till it is rotten as a t—d, and then it is not worth a f—t.

2. (old).—A wench: *see* BAR-RACK-HACK and TART.—B. E. (*c.* 1696).

OPEN C, *subs. phr.* (venery).—The female *pudendum*: *see* MONOSYLLABLE.

OPEN HOUSE, *subs. phr.* (colloquial).—Hospitality for all comers.—B. E. (*c.* 1696).

1530. PALSGRAVE, 597, 1. The Kyng is determyned to kepe house or OPEN HOUSE this Christmas.

1891. *Daily Chronicle*, 23 Mar. Mr. Verburgh, M.P., again played the part of host, and kept OPEN HOUSE in a large marquee near the winning-post.

OPERA BUFFER, *subs. phr.* (theatrical).—An actor in opera bouffe.

OPERA HOUSE, *subs. phr.* (old).—A workhouse. [Fr. Latin *opera* = work].

OPERATOR, *subs.* (old).—A pickpocket.

O-PER-SE-O, *subs. phr.* (Old Cant).—A Cryer.

1612. DEKKER, O PER SE O, or a new crier of lanterne and candle-lights [*Title*].

O.P.H., *phr.* (common).—'Off': *e.g.* 'Demme, I'm O.P.H.'

OPPIDAN, *subs.* (Eton College).—A boy who boards in the town, as distinguished from a **King's** Scholar.

OPINIATOR, *subs.* (old colloquial).—*See* quot.

1696. B. E., *Dict. Cant. Crew*, s.v. OPINIATOR, an Assuming positive Fellow, an obstinate self-conceited Cox-comb.

OPIUM-JOINT, *subs. phr.* (American).—An opium den.

OPTIC, *subs.* (once literary: now chiefly colloquial).—1. An eye. For synonyms *see* GLIMS.

1600. B. JONSON, *Cynthia's Revels*, i. 3. Whose OPTIQUES haue drunke the spirit of beautie.

1782. COWPER, *Hope*, 494. From which our nicer OPTICS turn away.

1821. EGAN, *Life in London*, [DICK'S], 56. Those three nymphs who have so much dazzled your OPTICS . . .

1836. MICHAEL SCOTT, *Cruise of the Nudge*, 187. I distinctly saw, either with my bodily OPTIC, or my mind's eye, I am not quite certain which to this hour, a dark figure standing on the long-yard.

1842. THOMAS EGERTON WILKS, *Bamboozling*. I've got a pain in my OPTICS.

1851. HAWTHORNE, *Seven Gables*, xvi. She screwed her dim OPTICS to their acutest point.

1888. *Daily Telegraph*, 15 Nov. I've got my OPTIC on 'em and shall have 'em by-and-by.

1891. *Lic. Vict. Gaz.*, 10 Ap. A deep cut under the dexter OPTIC.

2. (old).—An optic-glass; a spy-glass.

d. 1721. PRIOR, *Celia to Damon*. When you Love's Joys through Honour's OPTIC view.

OPTIME, *subs.* (University).—*See* quot.

1823. GROSE, *Vulg. Tongue* [EGAN]. OPTIME. The senior and junior OPTIMES are the second and last classes of Cambridge honours conferred on taking a degree. That of wranglers is the first. The last junior OPTIME is called the Wooden Spoon.

ORACLE, *subs.* (Old Cant). — A watch: *see* TICKER.

1708-10. SWIFT, *Polite Conversations*, 1. Pray, my lord, what's o'clock by your ORACLE?

2. (venery).—The female *pudendum*: *see* MONOSYLLABLE.

TO WORK THE ORACLE, *verb. phr.* (common).—To plan; to succeed by stratagem: specifically to raise money.

1863. *All the Year Round*, 10 Oct., 168. He has a double, who . . . WORKED THE ORACLE for him.

1888. BOLDREWOOD, *Robbery Under Arms*, xii. They fetched a rattling price through Starlight's WORKING THE ORACLE with those swells.

1891. NEWMAN, *Scamping Tricks*, 116. Well, what with, so they told me, big local loan-mongers to WORK THE ORACLE and swim with them, etc.

TO WORK THE DUMB (DOUBLE, OR HAIRY) ORACLE, *verb. phr.* (venery). — To copulate: *see* GREENS and RIDE.

ORANGE. TO SUCK THE ORANGE DRY, *verb. phr.* (colloquial).—To exhaust; to deplete.

1888. HAWLEY SMART, *From Post to Finish*, 47. It is rather rough on the boy, I admit, to suddenly discover that his father has SUCKED THE ORANGE, and that he has merely inherited the skin; but it is so.

ORANGE LILIES, *subs. phr.* (military). — The Thirty-fifth Foot. [From the facings till 1832 and the plumes awarded for gallantry at Quebec in 1759]. Now the 1st Batt. Royal Sussex.

ORATE, *verb.* (American). — To make a speech.

1877. BESANT & RICE, *Golden Butterfly*, xxvi. I am not, he said, going to ORATE. You did not come here, I guess, to hear me pay out chin-music.

1883. *Referee*, 15 July, 2, 4. There was a panic among the two thousand people who were being ORATED by Mr. Ballington Booth, the general's son.

1888. *Fortnightly Review*, N.S. xliii. 848. Men are apt . . . to ORATE on any topic that chances to be uppermost.

ORATOR, *subs.* (old).—*See* quot. [*Cf.* oration, dialectical for 'noise' or 'uproar'].

1696. B. E., *Dict. Cant. Crew*, s.v. ORATOR TO A MOUNTEBANK, the Doctor's Decoy who in conjunction with Jack Pudding, amuses, diverts and draws in the Patients.

ORCHARD, *subs.* (venery).—The female *pudendum*: *see* MONOSYLLABLE. TO GET JACK IN THE ORCHARD = to effect intromission.

ORCHID, *subs.* (Stock Exchange).—A titled member.

1871. ATKINS, *House Scraps* . . . A young sprig of nobility . . . was once heard to tell a friend that when he was in the house he felt like an 'orchid' in a turnip field . . . ORCHID has become the nickname for any member who has a 'handle' to his name.

1890. *Cassell's Saturday Journal*, 26 Ap. All members [of the Stock Exchange] who have handles to their names are described as ORCHIDS.

ORDER. A LARGE ORDER, *subs. phr.* (common).—Something excessive.

1890. *Pall Mall Gazette*, 17 Feb., 7, 1. A LARGE ORDER [Title].

1891. *Tit Bits*, 8 Aug., 274, 1. In asking me to tell you about my clients and their wills, you give a pretty LARGE ORDER.

1892. *Illustrated Bits*, 22 Oct, 10. Well, sir, that's a LARGISH ORDER.

TO ORDER ONE'S NAME, *verb. phr.* (Winchester School): obsolete).—*See* quots,

1866. MANSFIELD, *School Life at Winchester*, 223. ORDER YOUR NAME. An order given to a delinquent by the Head or Second Master, which was carried out by the boy requesting the Ostiarius to do so, the consequence of which was, that at the end of school that officer presented to the Master the victim's name on a Roll who forthwith received a Scrubbing. When the words "to the Bible Clerk" were added, the business was confided to that officer, who, with the Ostiarius, officiated at the subsequent ceremony, which in this case was called a Bibler.

1878. ADAMS, *Wykehamica*, xxiii. 429. ORDER YOUR NAME, the direction given to an offender by any of the authorities. The boy so directed, if he was in College, or if the order was given in school, had to go to the Ostiarius—or to the Præfect in course, if the offence was committed in commoners—and give information of the order, and the reason why it had been given. The Ostiarius, or the Præfect in course, wrote down the culprit's name, together with that of the Master, and the offence, and carried it up to the Head or Second Master, when due execution was done.

ORDER-RACKET, *subs. phr.* (old).—*See* quot.

1819. VAUX, *Memoirs*, ii. 193. ORDER-RACKET, obtaining goods from a shopkeeper, by means of a forged order or false pretence.

ORDINARY, *subs.* (common). — A wife: *see* DUTCH.

ORGAN, *subs.* (Scots servants').—1. A clothes' trunk.

2. (old).—A pipe.

1785. GROSE, *Vulg. Tongue*, s.v. ORGAN, WILL YOU COCK YOUR ORGAN, will you smoke your pipe.

3. (printers'). — A workman who lends money to his fellows at exorbitant interest. TO PLAY THE ORGAN = to apply for such a loan.

TO CARRY THE ORGAN, *verb. phr.* (military).—To shoulder the pack or valise at defaulters' or marching order drill.

ORGAN-PIPE, *subs.* (colloquial).—1. The throat; the wind-pipe; the voice.

2. (dressmakers': obsolete).—In pl. = a fulness in skirt-backs created by folds of starched muslin.

ORIFICE, *subs.* (venery).—The female *pudendum*: *see* MONOSYLLABLE.

ORIGINAL GO, *subs. phr.* (American) —A novel predicament.

1854. T. W. N. BAYLEY, *New Tale of a Tub*. Excellent! marvellous! beautiful! O! Is'n't it now an ORIGINAL GO?

ORINOKO, *subs.* (rhyming). — *See* quot.

1874. HOTTEN, *Slang Dict.*, *Rhyming Slang*, 367. ORINOKO (pronounced Orinoker), a poker.

ORNAMENT, *subs.* (venery).—The female *pudendum*: *see* MONOSYLLABLE.

ORNYTHORHYNCHUS, *subs.* (Australian).—A creditor; 'a beast with a bill.'

ORPHAN COLLAR, *subs. phr.* (American).—One that does not match the shirt in colour or material.

OSCHIVE. *See* OCHIVE.

OSTIARIUS, *subs.* (Winchester College: obsolete).—*See* quots.

1866. *Wykehamist*, No. 1, Oct. We know of nothing more which calls for notice, except the revival of Dr. Moberley of the OSTIARIUS—an office which had been discontinued for many years, but was revived by the Head Master on account of the great increase in the number of the School.

1866. MANSFIELD, *School Life at Winchester*, 223. OSTIARIUS—An office held by the Præfects in succession. The duties were, to keep order in school, collect the Vulguses, and prevent the boys from shirking out. It is also the official title for the Second Master.

1878. ADAMS, *Wykehamica*, xxiii. 429. OSTIARIUS, the Præfect in charge of school.

OSTLER, *subs.* (old).—1. An oat-stealer; and (2) in America, a horse-thief.—MATSELL (1859).

OTTER, *subs.* (common).—A sailor.

Adj. (costermongers').—Eight. [It. *otta*]. Also OTTO.

1893. EMERSON, *Signor Lippo*, xiv. I'll take OTTO soldi, that's due soldi for baking and six soldi for navs.

OTTOMY, *subs.* (old).—A skeleton; a BAG OF BONES (*q.v.*); an ATOMY (*q.v.*). OTTOMISED=anatomised.

1738. SWIFT, *Polite Conversation* (Conv. i). *Lady Answ.* Why, my lord, she was handsome in her time; but she can't eat her cake and have her cake. I hear she grown a meer OTOMY.

1785. GROSE, *Vulg. Tongue*, s.v. OTTOMY. You'll be scragged, OTTOMISED, and grin in a glass case, You'll be hanged, anatomised, and your skeleton kept in a glass case.

1834. H. AINSWORTH, *Rookwood*, III. ii. Is that Peter Bradley? asked Sybil. Ay, you may well ask whether that old dried-up OTOMY . . . be kith and kin of . . . Luke, said Turpin.

OUNCE, *subs.* (old).—*See* quots.

1725. *New Cant. Dict.*, s.v. Half an OUNCE, Half-a-crown.

1785. GROSE, *Vulg. Tongue*, s.v. Half an OUNCE, half a crown, silver being formerly estimated at a crown or five shillings an ounce.

OUT, *subs.* (old).—1. A dram-glass: they are made '*two-out*' (= half-quartern), '*three-out*,' and '*four-out*.' When a man wants to 'treat' a couple of friends he asks for 'a quartern of gin and three-out,' meaning, a quartern of gin and three glasses, which together will exactly hold that quantity.

1836. DICKENS, *Sketches by Boz*, 40. Having imbibed the contents of various 'three-outs' of gin and bitters in the course of the morning.

2. (colloquial).—One out of employment or office; specifically (in politics) a member of the party in 'opposition'. *Cf.* IN.

1768. GOLDSMITH, *Good Naturea Man*, v. Was it for this I have been dreaded both by ins and OUTS? Have I been libelled in the *Gazetteer*, and promised in the *St. James's*?

1770. CHATTERTON, *Prophecy*. And doomed a victim for the sins. Of half the OUTS and all the ins.

1842. DICKENS, *American Notes*, ii. The in's rubbed their hands; the OUT'S shook their heads; the Government party said there never was such a good speech; the opposition declared there never was such a bad one.

1857. LAWRENCE, *Guy Livingstone* (5th ed.), 216. If he had backed the in instead of the OUT.

1884. *Pall Mall Gazette*, 7 July. The pledges which the ins have to contend with in their strife with the OUTS.

1888. *Boston Daily Globe*. It is the civil service that turns out all the ins and puts in the OUTS.

1890. NORTON, *Political Americanisms*, s.v. Ins and OUTS.

3. (colloquial).—Leave to go out; an OUTING (*q.v.*); a holiday.

1847. HALLIWELL, *Archaic Words, etc.*, s.v.

1852. DICKENS, *Bleak House*, vii. Us London lawyers don't often get an OUT.

1855. MRS. GASKELL, *North and South*, xiii. When I have gone for an OUT, I've always wanted to go high up and see far away, and take a deep breath o' fulness in that air.

1862-5. SHIRLEY BROOKS, *Naggletons* (1875), p. 202. We have had three pleasant days, Maria, and I think you need not have finished the OUT with a row.

4. (American).—A discarded mistress.—MATSELL (1859).

Verb. (thieves').—1. To kill. Whence OUTING-DUES.

1898. *Pink 'Un and Pelican*, 279. It was a dire calamity for a Cohen to handle the dead. "He is OUT," gasped the Jew.

1900. SIMS, *In London's Heart*, 294. He glanced contemptuously at the prostrate form of his accomplice. "Looks like I've OUTED him," he said, "Good job if I have—he'll never blab again." *Ibid.* 123. "I'm hanged if I haven't done for him. It's OUTING DUES this time if we're copped." "Dead!" exclaimed Joe.

2. (pugilists').—To knock out an opponent so that he fails to respond at the call of time.

1898. *Pink 'Un and Pelican*, 86. 'Gently, my lad, gently . . . yer don't want to knock 'im out yet; give us a little show o' yer quality afore you OUTS him.'

Adv. (old).—1. Tipsy: *see* DRINKS and SCREWED.

2. (colloquial).—General (society)=just presented; (cricketers')=sent from the wickets; (politicians')=not in office; (thieves')=released from gaol; (market-men's=not on sale; (popular)=(1) having a tendency to lose, (2) wrong, inaccurate, and (3) unfashionable.

1660. PEPYS, *Diary*, 7 Oct. Calling at my father's to change my long black cloake for a short one (long cloakes being now quite OUT).

1877. *Belgravia*, August, 189. This young lady is only just OUT. She lacks the ease, the imperturbability, the *savoir-vivre* of her elder sister.

1877. *Five Years' Penal Servitude*, iii. 223. Oh, that's one of the cleverest gentlemen cracksmen OUT.

1885. DICKENS, *Dorrit*, I. xvi. 123. They were all so easy and cheerful together (Daniel Doyce either sitting OUT like an amused spectator at cards, or coming in with some shrewd little experiences of his own, when it happened to be to the purpose).

TO LIVE OUT, *verb. phr.* (American).—To be in domestic service: *i.e.* as living from home.

*b.*1860. *New York Tribune* [BARTLETT]. She came to this city and LIVED OUT as a cook.

18 [?]. TERHUNE, *Hidden Path*, 78. She has never LIVED OUT before [*Century*].

OUT OF IT (THE HUNT, or THE RUNNING), *adj. phr.* (colloquial). 1. Debarred from participation; having no chance or share; completely ignorant.

1889. *Echo*, 9 Feb. For example—respecting 'the reversion' to the Laureateship—we were informed a day or two back that Mr. Browning was OUT OF THE RUNNING.

TO STAND OUT, *verb. phr.* (common).—To take no part.

OUT OF TWIG, *adj. phr.* (old).—1. *See* quot.

1819. VAUX, *Memoirs*, ii. 194. To put any article OUT OF TWIG, as a stolen coat, cloak, etc., is to alter it in such a way that it cannot be identified. *Ibid.* To put yourself OUT OF TWIG, is to disguise your dress and appearance, to avoid being recognised, on some particular account.

2. (old).—*See* quot.

1819. VAUX, *Memoirs*, ii. 149. A man reduced by poverty to wear a shabby dress is said by his acquaintances to be OUT OF TWIG.

TO PLAY AT IN AND OUT. *See* IN AND IN and IN AND OUT.

OUT OF GOD'S BLESSING INTO THE WARM SUN, *phr.* (old).—From better to worse.

1581. LYLY, *Euphues*, Z. 3, b. Therefore if thou wilt follow my advice, and prosecut thine owne determination, THOU SHALT COME OUT OF A WARME SUNNE INTO GOD'S BLESSING.

1605. SHAKSPEARE, *Lear*, ii. 2. Good King, thou must approve the common saw; Thou OUT OF HEAVEN'S BENEDICTION comest TO THE WARME SUN.

1608. SIR JOHN HARINGTON, *Catal. of Bishops*, *Carlyle*. Marks—removed from Carlisle to Lamos in Greece; viz. OUT OF GOD'S BLESSING INTO A WARME SUNNE, as the saying is.

1615. HARRINGTON, *Epigrams*, ii. 56. Pray God they bring us not, when all is done, OUT OF GOD'S BLESSING INTO THIS WARM SUN.

1660. HOWELL, *Eng. Proverbs*, 5. s.v.

1760. RAY, *Proverbs*. s.v.

OUT FOR AN AIRING, *phr.* (racing).—Said of a horse not meant to win.

1889. *Sporting Times*, 29 June. But while Isabel, in racing slang, was fairly 'on the job,' Her friend was only OUT FOR AN AIRING.

1889. *Standard*, 25 June. Trainers and jockeys, from various trivial circumstances, very easily gathered whether a particular horse was only OUT FOR AN AIRING, or whether it was on the job.

[Other colloquial combinations are TO BE AT OUTS=to quarrel; TO MAKE NO OUTS (of a person)=to misunderstand; OUT OF COUNTENANCE=confounded; OUT OF HAND=(1) immediately, without delay, (2) ungovernable; OUT OF CRY=out of measure; OUT OF FRAME = out of order; OUT OF HEART = worn out (of land), down hearted (of persons); OUT (or DOWN) AT HEEL (or AT ELBOWS)=shabbily dressed; OUT AT LEG=feeding in hired pastures (of cattle); OUT-OF-POCKET=a loser: OUT OF TEMPER=too hot, or too cold; OUT OF PRINT=*see* quot.; OUT OF THE WAY=uncommon, etc., etc. Also *see* BARREL; COLLAR; FUNDS; HARNESS; HAVE; KELTER; LOOSE; LUG; PICAROON; POCKET; PUFF; REGISTER; SORTS; WOOD.

*d.*1555. LATIMER [*Century*]. The King's majesty when he cometh to age, will see a redress of those things so OUT OF FRAME.

1605. SHAKSPEARE, *King Lear*, ii. 2. A good man's future may grow OUT AT HEELS.

1696. B. E., *Dict. Cant. Crew*, s.v. OUT AT HEELS.

1785. GROSE, *Vulg. Tongue*, s.v. OUT AT HEELS.

1811. *Lexicon Balatronicum*, s.v.

1819. VAUX, *Memoirs*, ii. 194. OUT OF THE WAY, a thief who knows that he is sought after by the traps on some information, and consequently goes out of town, or otherwise conceals himself, is said by his pals to be OUT OF THE WAY FOR SO AND SO, naming the particular offence he stands charged with. [*See* WANTED].

1823. GROSE, *Vulg. Tongue* [EGAN]. OUT OF PRINT. Slang made use of by booksellers. In speaking of any person that is dead, they observe, HE IS OUT OF PRINT.

1851-6. MAYHEW, *Lond. Lab. and Lond. Poor*, iii. 122. He was a little DOWN AT HEEL.

OUT-AND-OUT, *adj.* and *adv.* (colloquial). — Thorough; PRIME (*q.v.*); 'far and away.'

. . . . *Rawlinson MS.*, C. 36. The kyng was good alle aboute, And she was wyckyd OUTE AND OUTE, For she was of suche comforte, She lovyd mene ondir her lorde.

1819. VAUX, *Memoirs*, ii. 193. OUT-AND-OUT, quite; completely; effectually.

1837. THACKERAY, *Yellow Plush Papers*, in *Fraser's Mag.*, 10 Oct. Skelton's Anatomy is a work which as been long wanted in the littery world A reglar, slap up, no mistake, OUT-AN'-OUT account of the manners of gentele society.

1843. DICKENS, *Martin Chuzzlewit*, vii. 71. A quarrelsome family, or a malicious family, or even a good OUT-AND-OUT mean family, would open a field of action as I might do something in.

1874. E. L. LINTON, *Patricia Kemball*, vii. You are OUT-AND-OUT the most independent radical for a lady I have ever seen.

1897. KENNARD, *Girl in Brown Habit*, ii. That's the way with them OUT-AND-OUT sportsmen. They're always the first to come to a comrade's assistance.

OUT-AND-OUTER, *subs. phr.* (colloquial). — A person or thing, superlative.

1819. VAUX, *Memoirs*, ii. 194. OUT AND OUTER, an incorrigible depredator, who will rob friend or stranger indiscriminately. *Ibid.* A person of a resolute determined spirit, who pursues his object without regard to danger or difficulties.

1821. EGAN, *Life in London* [DICK], 95. Logic . . . was considered an OUT-AND-OUTER.

1829. *Old Song* [FARMER, *Musa Pedestris* (1896), 107]. Are they OUT-AND-OUTEPS, dearie?

1836. DICKENS, *Pickwick*, xl. p. 354. It was discovered that one of the turnkeys had a bed to let . . . If you'll come with me, I'll show it you at once, said the man. It ain't a large 'un, but it's an OUT-AND-OUTER to sleep in.

1838. DICKENS, *Nicholas Nickleby*, lx. I am the man as is guaranteed . . . . to be an OUT-AND-OUTER from this.

1855. THACKERAY, *Newcomes*, xvii. Master Clive was pronounced an OUT-AND-OUTER, a swell, and no mistake.

1877. *Five Years' Penal Servitude*, iii. She were an OUT-AND-OUTER in going into shops on the filch.

1888. BOLDREWOOD, *Robbery Under Arms*, xx. Isn't he a regular OUT-AND-OUTER to look at?

1893. MILLIKEN, *'Arry Ballads*, 37. Now one twigs OUT-AND-OUTERS take down wots too spice a'most for the Pis.

OUTER, *subs.* (shooting).—1. That part of a target used in rifle-shooting, which is outside the circles surrounding the bull's-eye; and (2) a shot which strikes the outer part of a target.

1884. *Times*, 23 July. Running through the scoring gamut with an OUTER, a magpie, and a miss.

OUTFIT, *subs.* (colonial).—*See* quot. 1840.

d. 1840. MCCLURE, *Rocky Mountains*, 211. In the Far West and on the Plains, every thing is an OUTFIT, from a railway train to a pocket-knife. It is applied indiscriminately,—to a wife, a horse, a dog, a cat, or a row of pins.

1889. O'REILLY, *Fifty Years on the Trail* . . . The wagon master had the presence of mind to gallop his team out into the prairie, whilst the entire OUTFIT made for the best cover it could find.

1888. *St. Louis Globe-Democrat*, 16 Feb. The fortune we had longed for lay at our feet . . . That night we let three of the most reckless devils in the OUTFIT into the secret, and the next morning I started for San Francisco.

1888. *Missouri Republican*, 1 Ap. I returned to Las Vegas with a freighter, whose OUTFIT consisted of six horses and two wagons, one of the latter being a trail vehicle.

OUT-HEROD. To OUT-HEROD HEROD, *verb.* (colloquial).—To exceed in excess.

1596. SHAKSPEARE, *Hamlet*, iii. 2, 15. I would have such a fellow whipped for o'er-doing Termagant; it OUT-HERODS HEROD: Pray you, avoid it.

1821. EGAN, *Life in London* [DICK'S], 23. The author . . . intends to do a great deal, but he does not mean to OUT-HEROD HEROD.

1845. POE, *Prose Tales*, I. 343. The figure in question had OUT-HERODED HEROD, and gone beyond the bounds of even the prince's indefinite decorum.

d. 1859. DE QUINCEY, *Essenes*, i. Yet another and a very favourite emperor OUT-HERODS even this butcher [Gallienus].

OUTING, *subs.* (colloquial).—1. A holiday; an OUT (*q.v.*).

1860. HALIBURTON ('Sam Slick'), *The Season Ticket*, No. vii. I once gave her an OUTING to London, and when she returned, I asked her how she liked it.

1864. *Sun*, 28 Dec., *Review of Hotten's Sl. Dict.* There is no mention of a holiday term in very common use that we ought to have found here alphabetically recorded in 'The Slang Dictionary'—meaning the phrase of an OUTING.

1879. JAS. PAYN, *High Spirits (Adventure in a Forest)*. I only knew Epping Forest as a spot rarely visited save by the wild East Enders on their Sunday OUTINGS.

1885. *Field*, 4 Ap. They got their OUTING which is a great deal.

2. (provincial).—*See* quot.

1847. HALLIWELL, *Arch. Words, etc.*, s.v. OUTING. A feast given to his friends by an apprentice, at the end of his apprenticeship: when he is *out* of his time. In some parts of the kingdom, this ceremony is termed by an apprentice and his friends 'burying his wife.'

OUTRIDER, *subs.* (old).—A highwayman: *see* ROAD-AGENT.

1600. HEYWOOD, *1 Edward IV.* [PEARSON, *Works* (18 . .), I. 43]. I fear thou art some OUTRIDER that lives by taking of purses.

OUTRUN. *See* CONSTABLE.

OUTS. GENTLEMEN OF THE THREE OUTS, *subs. phr.* (old).—*See* quots.

1785. GROSE, *Vulg. Tongue*, s.v. GENTLEMAN — without money, without wit, and without manners.

1830. LYTTON, *Paul Clifford*, iv. Paul became A GENTLEMAN OF THREE OUTS—out of pocket, out of elbows, and out of credit.

1834. H. AINSWORTH, *Rookwood*, III. v. Jerry Juniper was what the classical Captain Grose would designate A GENTLEMAN WITH THREE OUTS, and, although he was not entirely without wit, nor his associates avouched, without money, nor certainty, in his own opinion, had that been asked, without manners.

OUTSIDE, *subs.* (common). — An outside passenger. Fr. *un voyageur à quinze francs le cent. See* INSIDE.

1798. CANNING, *Anti-Jacobin*, 163 [1890]. So down thy hill, romantic Ashbourn, glides The Derby dilly carrying three insides.

1816. SCOTT, *Old Mortality*, ii. A wheel carriage bearing eight insides and six OUTSIDES.

1836. DICKENS, *Pickwick*, . . . The OUTSIDES did as OUTSIDES always do. They were very cheerful and talkative at the beginning of every stage.

Adj. (old colloquial):—1. The utmost.—B. E. (*c.* 1696).

OUTSIDE 'LIZA, *intj.* (common).—'Get out of this.'

TO GET OUTSIDE OF, *verb. phr.* (common).—1. To eat or drink; as, to get outside of a pint of beer, or a chop; (2) to understand; and (3) *see* quot.

1888. BOLDREWOOD, *Robbery Under Arms*, xiv. He looked better OUTSIDE of a horse than on his own legs.

2. (venery).—To copulate: of women only: *see* GREENS and RIDE.

OUTSIDER, *subs.* (thieves').—1. In *pl.* A pair of nippers with semi-tubular jaws which can be inserted in a keyhole from the outside to turn the key.

2. (common).—An ignoramus. Also, a person unattached. Also, an incompetent, doubtful, or unknown champion or competitor in any walk of life or sport. Also, a DUFFER (*q.v.*), moral, physical or social.

1864. *Saturday Review*, July, 'Stray Votes.' The game he has in view is that peculiar variety of Parliamentary species known as an OUTSIDER or a loose fish, but described by itself under the more flattering title of 'an independent member.'

1877. W. MACK, *Green Past. and Piccadilly*, xxvii. Of course it was as a mere pleasure excursion that we OUTSIDERS were permitted to speak of this long journey.

1880. HAWLEY SMART, *Social Sinners*, xxxiii. That fellow Hainton, has beat the lot of us. I never was more than quite an OUTSIDER myself, still I feel so bad about it, that really I must . . . have something to drink!

1884. HAWLEY SMART, *Post to Finish*, xvii. For the stable to follow up last year's successes by taking the first great three-year-old event of the season, with an OUTSIDER, ridden by a Riddleton lad, was something to boast of.

1885. *Morning Post*, 5 Feb. So far as OUTSIDERS can see there is always the same cheerfulness.

1890. GRANT ALLEN, *The Tents of Shem*, x. Nobody, and especially not a peppery old General who's served more than half his life in India likes to have it dictated to him by RANK OUTSIDERS what disposition he's to make of his own money.

1901. *M. A. P.*, 2 Feb., 113, 2. As he has already some connection with the music halls, he must have more opportunities of learning the ropes than an OUTSIDER.

3. (racing).—A person who fails to gain admission to the 'ring' from pecuniary or other causes.

OVEN, *subs.* (old).—1. A large mouth.—GROSE (1785); MATSELL (1859).

2. (venery).—The female *pudendum*: *see* MONOSYLLABLE.

c. 1720. DURFEY, *Pills to Purge, &c.* (1720), vi. 91. 'The Jolly Tradesmen.' But if my OVEN be over-hot, I dare not thrust it in, Sir; For burning of my Wrigling-Pole, My Skill's not worth a Pin, Sir.

IN THE SAME OVEN, *adj. phr.* (common).—In the same plight.

OVER, *subs.* (commercial).—In *pl.* A surplus on the day's accounts; FLUFF (*q.v.*); MENAVELINGS (*q.v.*).

TO COME OVER (or THE OLD SOLDIER OVER) ONE. *See* COME OVER and COME THE OLD SOLDIER.

TO GET OVER, *verb. phr.* (common).—To get the better; TO BEST (*q.v.*).

1870. HAZLEWOOD and WILLIAMS, *Leave it to Me*, i. She'll soon GET OVER her foolish attachment, but whether or no she don't GET OVER me.

TO CALL (or FETCH) OVER THE COALS, *verb. phr.* (common).—To reprimand.

1719. DURFEY, *Pills to Purge, &c.*, iii. 22. Yet your Blacksmith can FETCH THEM OVER THE COALS.

TO DO OVER, *verb. phr.* (venery).—To possess a woman: *see* GREENS and RIDE.

OVER THE BAY, *phr.* (American).—Drunk: *see* DRINKS and SCREWED.

OVER THE STILE, *phr.* (rhyming).—Sent for trial. (HOTTEN).

TO PUT OVER THE DOOR, *verb. phr.* (old colloquial).—To turn out; TO GIVE THE KEY OF THE STREET (*q.v.*).

OVER AT THE KNEES, *phr.* (stable).—Weak in the knees.

OVER-SHOES, OVER BOOTS, *phr.* (old).—*See* quot.

c. 1696. B. E., *Dict. Cant. Crew.* OVER-SHOES OVER BOOTS, or to go through-stitch.

See also BENDER; BROOMSTICK; and LEFT.

OVER-DAY TARTS, *subs. phr.* (Billingsgate).—*See* quot.

1889. *Tit Bits*, 17 Aug., 298, 2. About 24 hours after capture the herring is liable to the pouring out of extravasation of blood about his gills and fins, which darkened and damaged or bruised appearance is quaintly called in the fish trade OVER-DAY TARTS.

OVERDO, *verb.* (old: now recognised).—*See* quot. *c.* 1696.

1614. JONSON, *Bartholomew Fair*, Justice OVERDO, &c.

c. 1696. B. E., *Dict. Cant. Crew*, s.v. OVERDO, double diligence.

OVERDRAW. TO OVERDRAW THE BADGER. *See* BADGER.

OVERFLOW AND PLUNDER, *subs. phr.* (theatrical).—*See* quot.

1890. COLEMAN [*Slang, Jargon, and Cant*], s.v. OVERFLOW and PLUNDER. The unsuspecting auditor has an order for the pit; he goes there, and finds the pit crammed to suffocation by people who have not paid. Upon payment of sixpence he goes to the upper boxes, they are also crowded; sixpence more takes him to the dress circle. Before he can obtain a seat he is bled of another sixpence for his greatcoat, another for his umbrella, and another for a programme. The performances in these places were as disreputable as the management, and, as a rule, would disgrace a show at a country fair.

OVERLANDER, *subs.* (Australian).—A tramp; a SUNDOWNER (*q.v.*). Also OVERLAND MAN and OVERLAND-MAILER.

OVERLAND-TROUT, *subs. phr.* (American).—Bacon.

OVERRUN. *See* CONSTABLE.

OVERSCUTCHED (OVERSWITCHED or **OVERWHIPPE) - HOUSEWIFED**, *subs. phr.* (old).—*See* quots., BARRACK-HACK and TART.

. . . . *Kennett MS.* [HALLIWELL]. An OVERSWITCHT HOUSWIFE, a loose wanton slut, a whore.

1598. SHAKSPEARE, *2 Henry IV*, iii. 2. He came ever in the rear-ward of the fashion; and sung those tunes to OVERSCUTCHED HUSWIFES that he heard the carmen whistle, and sware—they were his fancies, or his good-nights.

1675. RAY, *North-Country Words.* OVERSWITCHED housewife. A whore; a ludicrous word.

OVERSEEN, *adj.* (old).—More or less in liquor: *see* DRINKS and SCREWED.

1611. COTGRAVE, *Dict.* Well nigh whittled, almost drunke, somewhat OVERSEENE.

d. 1654. L'ESTRANGE [THOMS. (1838), *Anecd. and Trad.*, p. 54.] He heard he tooke a Cuppe too much at Ipswich, and was sorry . . . he should be so much OVERSEENE.

1847. HALLIWELL, *Arch. Words, etc.*, s.v.

OVERSEER, *subs.* (old).—A man in the pillory.—GROSE (1785).

OVERSHOT, *adj.* (common). — Drunk: *see* DRINKS and SCREWED.

OVERSPARRED, *adj.* (nautical).—Top-heavy; drunk: *see* DRINKS and SCREWED.

1891. CLARK RUSSELL, *Ocean Tragedy*, 4. I believe he could have carried a whole bottle in his head without exhibiting himself as in the least degree OVERSPARRED.

OVERTAKEN, *adj.* (common).—Drunk: *see* DRINKS and SCREWED.

1655. MASSINGER, *Very Woman*, iii. 5. And take heed of being O'ERTAKEN with too much drink.

1692. HACKET, *Life of Williams*, ... He was temperate also in his drinking . . . . but I never spake with the man that saw him OVERTAKEN.

1699. CONGREVE, *Way of the World*, iv. 10. My nephew's a little OVERTAKEN, cousin—but 'tis with drinking your health.

1712. *Spectator*, No. 450. I do not remember I was ever OVERTAKEN in drink.

1847. HALLIWELL, *Arch. Words, &c.*, s.v.

1871. MRS. S. C. HALL, in *Chambers's Misc.*, No. 122, 11. I'm sure Murphy must have been OVERTAKEN, or he'd never dare to propose such a thing.

OVERTOYS BOX, *subs. phr.* (Winchester College).—A box like a cupboard to hold books: *see* TOYS.

OWL, *subs.* (common).—1. A prostitute: *see* BARRACK-HACK and TART.

2. (University).—A member of Sidney Sussex College, Cambridge: obsolete.

3. (general).—A person much about at night.

Verb. (common).—1. To sit up at night; and 2 (obsolete) to carry on a contraband night-trade; to smuggle. *Cf.* OWLER.

TO CATCH THE OWL, *verb. phr.* (old).—See quot.

1785. GROSE, *Vulg. Tongue*, s.v. OWL, TO CATCH THE OWL, a trick practised on ignorant country boobies, who are decoyed into a barn under pretence of catching an owl, where after divers preliminaries, the joke ends in their having a pail of water poured upon their heads.

TO TAKE THE OWL, *verb. phr.* (old).—To get angry.

TO LIVE TOO NEAR A WOOD TO BE FRIGHTENED BY AN OWL, *verb. phr.* (old).—Not easy to alarm.

1708-10. SWIFT, *Polite Conversations*, 1. What, do you think I was born in a wood, TO BE AFRAID OF AN OWL?

TO BRING (or SEND) OWLS TO ATHENS, *verb. phr.* (common).—To undertake a work of supererogation; TO TAKE COALS TO NEWCASTLE (*q.v.*). [Gr. *Noctuas Athénas*: owls abounded in Athens].

DRUNK AS A BILED OWL, *phr.* (American).—Very drunk: *see* DRINKS and SCREWED.

LIKE AN OWL IN AN IVY-BUSH, *phr.* (old).—See quot. 1823.

1708-10. SWIFT, *Polite Conversations*, 1. Lord Sparkish. How did the Fool look? Col . . . Egad, he look'd for all the world LIKE AN OWL IN AN IVY BUSH.

1767. RAY, *Proverbs* [BOHN], 57, s.v.

1823. GROSE, *Vulg. Tongue* [EGAN], s.v. He looks LIKE AN OWL IN AN IVY BUSH; frequently said of a person with a large frizzled wig, or a woman whose hair is dressed a-la-blouze.

OWL-CAR (or TRAIN), *subs. phr.* (American).—A late tram-car, or train.

1882. MCCABE, *New York*, 100. The Third avenue line runs its trains all night . . . These are the OWL-TRAINS, and carry home the late workers in the great newspaper offices, belated travelers, and the 'b'hoys' who have been making a night of it.

OWLER, *subs.* (old).—See quot. [At one time it was illegal to carry wool or sheep out of the country: OWLING was repealed by 3 Geo. IV. c. 107].

c.1696. B. E., *Dict. Cant. Crew*, s.v. OWLERS, those who privately in the Night carry Wool to the Sea-Coasts, near Rumney-Marsh in Kent, and some Creeks in Sussex, etc. and Ship it off for France against Law.

1785. GROSE, *Vulg. Tongue*, s.v.

OWL-LIGHT, *subs. phr.* (old).—Dusk. Hence, TO WALK BY OWL-LIGHT = to skulk from arrest. Fr. *Entre chien et loup.*

1610. *Letter* [quoted by NARES]. Ned Wimarke appears not in Paul's, but ever since before Christmas hath taken a toy to keep in, saving that now and then he STEALS OUT BY OWL-LIGHT to the Star and to the Windmill.

1625. MASSINGER, *Parliament of Love*, ii. 1. To have it order'd, All women that have stumbled in the dark, Or given, by OWL-LIGHT, favours, should complain, Is most intolerable.

1675. COTTON, *Scoffer Scofft* [*Works* (1725) 207]. A great-design. He has, that won't endure the Sun, But is by OWL-LIGHT to be done.

1767. RAY, *Proverbs* [BOHN], 57, s.v.

OWN. ON ONE'S OWN, *phr.* (common).—On one's own account.

1897. *Daily Mail*, 25 Sep., 2, 6. I came to Europe ON MY OWN, and I only got about £400 from Mr. Hoffmeyer.

TO OWN UP, *verb.* (colloquial).—To confess; to 'make a clean breast.'

1880. A. TROLLOPE, *The Duke's Children*, xxxv. The fact is if you OWN UP in a genial sort of way the House will forgive anything.

OWNED, *verb.* (obsolete ecclesiastical).—See quot.

1853. DEAN CONYBEARE, in *Edin. Rev.*, Oct., 295 *note*. A preacher is said in this phraseology to be OWNED when he makes many converts and his converts are called his 'seals.'

OWT, *adj.* (back-slang).—Two: *e.g.* OWT-YANNEP-FLATCH = twopence-halfpenny; OWT-GENS = two shillings.

OX. THE BLACK OX HAS TROD ON HIS FOOT, *phr.* (old colloquial).—To know decay, misfortune, or old age.—B. E. (*c.* 1696).

1537. TUSSER, *Wiving and Thriving* [BREWER]. Why then, do folk this proverb put, THE BLACK OX NEAR TROD ON THY FOOT, If that way were to thrive?

1581. LYLY, *Euphues*, E 1. When the black crowe's foote shall appeare in their eie, or the BLACK OXE TREAD ON THEIR FOOTE—who will like them in their age who liked non in their youth.

1646. HEYWOOD [BREWER]. THE BLACK OXE HAD NOT TRODE ON HIS OF HER FOOTE; But ere his branch of blisse could reach any roote, The flowers so faded, that in fifteen weekes a man might copy the change in the cheekes Both of the poore wretch and his wife.

1670. RAY, *Proverbial Phrases*, 205. THE BLACK OX NEVER TROD ON HIS FOOT, *i.e.*, he never knew what sorrow or adversity meant.

1850. LEIGH HUNT, *Autobiography*, iv. THE BLACK OX TROD ON THE fairy FOOT of my Cousin Fan.

OXER, *subs.* (sporting).—An ox-fence.

1879. *Cornhill Mag.*, v. 722. Across the road, over, an OXER, "like a bird."

1886. KENNARD, *Girl in Brown Habit*, ix. Good mare that, Sir, you are on. That double OXER has choked most of them off.

OXFORD, *subs.* (common).—A crown piece; HALF-OXFORD = half-a-crown: *see* Bull.

1898. *Pink 'Un and Pelican*, 65. In peacocked the little man with the long chain, the 'wine-steward' who chucked away Ernest's HALF-OXFORD.

OXFORD BLUES, *subs. phr.* (military).—The Royal Horse Guards. [From their facings, 1690].

OXFORD CLINK, *subs. phr.* (old).—1. A play upon words.

2. (theatrical).—A free pass.

OXFORD GROVE, *subs. phr.* (old).—See quot.

1608. DEKKER, *Dead Tearme* [NARES]. Conscience goes like a fool in pyed colours, the skin of her body hanging so loose, that like an OXFORD GLOVE, thou wouldst swear there wer a false skin within her.

OX-HOUSE. TO GO THROUGH THE OX-HOUSE TO BED, *verb. phr.* (old).—To be cuckolded; to wear HORNS (*q.v.*).

c.1696. B. E., *Dict. Cant. Crew*, s.v. OX-HOUSE . . . of an old Fellow that marries a young woman.

1785. GROSE, *Vulg. Tongue*, s.v.

OX-POP, *subs.* (old).—A butcher.

OYL-OF-BARLEY. See OIL.

OYSTER, *subs.* (common)—1. Profit or advantage: because it has a beard.

2. (old).—See quot.

1785. GROSE, *Vulg. Tongue*, s.v. OYSTER, a gob of thick phlegm, spit by a consumptive man, *unum viridum gobbum* (law Latin).

3. (venery).—The female *pudendum*: *see* MONOSYLLABLE.

4. (common).—A gob of spittle.

A CHOKING OYSTER, *subs. phr.* (old).—A reply that leaves one nothing to say.

d.1556. UDALL, *Apoph.*, 61. At another season, to a feloe laiyng to his rebuke that he was over deintie of his mouthe and diete, he did with this reason give a STOPPING OISTRE.

1547. HEYWOOD, *Proverbs*, xi. [She] therefore deviseth to cast in my teeth checks and CHOKING OYSTERS.

OLD OYSTER, *subs. phr.* (common).—A vulgar, playful endearment.

1892. MILLIKEN, *'Arry Ballads*, 17. Life don't want lifting, OLD OYSTER.

THE OYSTER, *subs.* (venery).—The semen. Whence OYSTER CATCHER = the female *pudendum*; and OYSTER-CATCHING = whoring.

OYSTER-FACED, *adj.* (streets').—In need of shaving. [In allusion to the oyster's beard].

P AND Q. TO BE P AND Q, *verb. phr.* (old colloquial).—To be of the first quality, or good measure.

1612. ROWLANDS, *Knaue of Harts*, 20 (Hunterian Club's Repr.). Boy y'are a villaine. didst thou fill this Sacke? Tis flat you Rascall, thou hast plaid the Iacke, Bring in a quart of Maligo, right true: And looke, you Rogue, that it be PEE and KEW.

TO MIND ONE'S P'S AND Q'S, *verb. phr.* (colloquial).—To be careful or circumspect in behaviour; to be exact. [Of uncertain origin; amongst suggested derivations are (1) the difficulty experienced by children in distinguishing between 'p' and 'q'; and (2) the old custom of alehouse tally, marking 'p' for pint, and 'q' for quart, care being necessary to avoid over- or under-charge. Probably both, in combination with the phrase TO BE P AND Q (*q.v.*), have helped to popularise the expression].—GROSE (1785).

1779. COWLEY, *Who's the Dupe?* i. 1. You must MIND YOUR P'S AND Q'S with him, I can tell you.

1821. EGAN, *Life in London*, v. I must once more remind you, my dear Jerry, said Tom, that we must BE ON OUR P'S AND Q'S.

1826. BUCKSTONE, *Luke the Labourer*, i. 1. Now, lad, MIND THY P'S AND Q'S, and you're a made man!

1840. BARHAM, *Ingoldsby Legends* Wedding-day). Gently! gently, Miss Muse! MIND YOUR P'S AND YOUR Q'S!

1861. TROLLOPE, *Framley Parsonage*, xlv. But the Archdeacon was not quite at ease. KEEP Dumbello UP TO HIS P'S AND Q's, you know, a friend had whispered to him at his club.

1864. *Essays on Social Subjects* [*Saturday Review*, 265.] A chiel's among us takin' notes. Virtue is put upon its P'S AND Q'S.

1881. JAMES, *Washington Square*, xix. He hoped very much that, as regarded this affair of Catherine's, she would MIND HER P'S AND Q'S.

1892. FENN, *New Mistress*, xxxv. If you don't MIND YOUR P'S AND Q'S. You hold your tongue.

1894. MOORE, *Esther Waters*, i. My mother's the cook here; you'll have to MIND YOUR P'S AND Q'S or else you'll be dropped on.

1896. COTSFORD DICK, *Ways of World*, 25. Thus our letters we learn, with their P'S AND their Q's, From some pseudonym sexual transgressions.

PAC, *subs.* (back-slang).—A cap.

PACE. TO GO THE PACE, *verb. phr.* (common).—To live a fast life; to be extravagant.

c.1710. STEELE, *Tatler* [*Slang, Jargon and Cant*]. He is the son of a famous racing man, who WENT THE PACE, and cut his throat in Newmarket.

1869. *Daily News*, 8 Nov. 'Leader.' GOING THE PACE and taking a cropper are gradually being admitted into small talk.

1890. *Lic. Vict. Gaz.*, 5 Dec. Fresh from Oxford Arthur had been GOING THE PACE.

ALDERMAN'S PACE, *subs. phr.* (common).—A slow and stately gait. Fr. *pas d'Abbé.*

1611. COTGRAVE, *Dict.*, s.v. Abbe. ALDERMAN'S PACE a leasurely walking, slow gate.

1629. GAULE, *Holy Madn.*, 94. What an ALDERMAN'S PACE he comes.

TO SHOW ONE'S PACES, *verb. phr.* (colloquial). — To exhibit one's capability; to show what one can do.

PACER, *subs.* (colloquial).—Primarily a fast horse; hence anything of great speed or activity.

PACK, *subs.* (old).—A prostitute: *see* TART. Also a general term of reproach with no reference to sex. *See* NAUGHTY.

Adj. (Scots': colloquial). — Intimate; familiar.

d. 1795. BURNS, iii. 3. Nae doubt but they were fain o' ither; An' unco' PACK an thick the gither.

1805. NICOL, *Poems*, ii. 89. They war auld comrades, frank an' free, AN' PACK an' thick as tods cou'd be.

1808. JAMIESON, *Dict.*, s.v. PACK. Probably a cant word from English PACK, a number of people confederated.

Verb. (also PACK OFF, SEND PACKING, GIVE A PACKING-PENNY TO, etc.) (old colloquial). —1. To dismiss without ceremony; to send about one's business; to discharge summarily: also, to depart hurriedly.—B. E. (*c.* 1696).

1540. LYNDSAY, *Satyre of the Thrie Estaitis* [E. E. T. S. (1869) line 975] Suyith! hursun Carle: gang, PAK the hence.

1580. BARET, *Alvearie* [HALLIWELL]. Make speede to flee, be PACKING awaie.

1593. SHAKSPEARE, *Taming of the Shrew*, ii. 1. If she do bid me PACK, I'll give her thanks, As though she bid me stay by her a week. *Ibid. Richard III.* (1597) i. 1. He . . . must not die, Till George be PACK'D with post horse up to Heav'n.

1603. TOMKIS, *Lingua* [BREWER]. Roses and bays, PACK hence! This crown and robe . . . How gallantly it fits me!

1608. DAY, *Law Trickes*, iii. Win, prethee give the Fidler a testar and SEND HIM PACKING.

1609. JONSON, *Case is Altered*, iii. 3. Will you GIVE A PACKING-PENNY to virginity?

1629. *Descr. of Love* [FARMER, *Musa Pedestris* (1896) 15]. Without delay, poore wretches they will set their Duds A PACKING.

1641. BAKER, *Chronicles*, 106. So once again is Gaveston SENT PACKING out of the Kingdom.

1659. DAY, *Blind Beggar*, i. 2. *Tudy.* Do you but send away Sir Walter Playnsey, Let me alone to PACK the Cardinal.

1662. *Rump Songs*, i. 59. And so we'll banish Popery, And SEND IT PACKING hence.

1664. COTTON, *Virgil Travestie*, 78. And if that he shall still be lacking, Then back again we'll straight be PACKING.

1667. DRYDEN, *Sir Martin Markall*, iv. One word more of this gibberish, and I'll SET YOU PACKING from your new service.

1656. *Muses Recr.* [HOTTEN], 31. We must all PACK into the North.

1728. BAILEY, *Eng. Dict.*, s.v. PACK. To PACK UP HIS AWLS . . . to march off, to go away in haste.

1730. MILLER, *Humours of Oxford*, iv. 2. I have SENT HIM A PACKING as conjurors do a ghost.

1766. GOLDSMITH, *Vicar of Wakefield*, xxi. Gentle or Simple out she shall PACK.

1815. SCOTT, *Guy Mannering*, xxxiv. I believe he would have PACKED him back here, but his nephew told him it would do up the free trade for many a day, if the youngster got back to Scotland.

18.6. PLANCHE, *Court Favour*, i. *Lucy.* It would be so charming to SEND all the Dutch PACKING . . . and for you to be made generalissimo!

1884. WOOD, *Johnny Ludlow*, 1st S. No. VI. 94. I'll send you back to school: you shall both PACK OFF this very hour.

2. (American).—To drink: *see* DRINKS and SCREWED.

1847. PORTER, *Quarter Race, &c.*, 103. The captain used to boast that he could PACK a gallon without its setting him back any.

TO EAT THE PACK (or PACKIE), *verb. phr.* (Scots').—To waste one's substance; to spend all. EAT-THE-PACK = a spendthrift. *Cf.* PACT.

PACKET, *subs.* (provincial).—A hoax; a false report. PACKETS = an expression of incredulity.—GROSE (1785).

PACK-THREAD, *subs.* (old).—Covert obscenity.—GROSE (1785).

PACT. TO SPEND THE PACT, *verb. phr.* (Scots').—To waste one's substance: also TO PERISH THE PACT.

PAD, *subs.* (Old Cant).—1. A path; a road or highway. Also HIGH-PAD.

1573. HARMAN, *Caveat* (1814), 66. The HYGH PAD, the high way.

1610. ROWLANDS, *Martin Markall*, 40 (H. Club's Repr. 1874), s.v.

1611. MIDDLETON and DEKKER, *Roaring Girl*, v. 1. Avast, to the PAD, let us bing.

1622. FLETCHER, *Beggar's Bush.* To maund on the PAD.

1625. JONSON, *Staple of News*, ii. A rogue, a very canter I, sir, one that maunds upon the PAD.

d. 1721. PRIOR, *Thief and Cordelier.* The squire of the PAD and the knight of the post.

1724. COLES, *Eng. Dict.*, s.v.

1818. SCOTT, *Rob Roy*, iv. Gentlemen of the PAD, as they were then termed.

2. (old colloquial).—An easy-paced horse; an ambler. Also PAD-NAG.—B. E. (*c.* 1696).

1717. CIBBER, *Nonjuror*, i. 1. I was about buying a PAD-NAG for your sister.

1770. FOOTE, *Lame Lover*, i. 1. He would not sample to break an appointment . . . in order to buy a PAD-NAG for a lady.

d. 1892. TENNYSON, *Lady of Shalot*, ii. 20. An abbot on an ambling PAD.

3. (old).—A highway robber; a foot-PAD; a tramp: also PADDER and (Scots') PADDIST.

1610. ROWLANDS, *Martin Markall*, p. 40 (H. Club's Repr. 1874), s.v.

1665. R. HEAD, *English Rogue*, I. v. p. 51 (1874), s.v.

1625. MASSINGER, *New Way to Pay Old Debts*, ii. 1. Are they PADDERS or Abram-men that are your consorts?

1668. DRYDEN, *Albumazar*, *Prol.* 19. Who, like bold PADDERS, scorn by night to prey, But rob by sunshine, in the face of day.

1671. ANNAND, *Mysterium Pietatis*, 85. A PADDIST or highwayman, attempting to spoil a preacher, ordering him to stand . . . was answered, etc.

1672. SHADWELL, *Epsom Wells*, III. [*Wks.* (1720), ii. 245]. Bribes received from PADS, pick-pockets, and shop-lifts.

1678. BUTLER, *Hudibras*, III. 1. He spurr'd as jockies use to break, Or PADDERS to secure a raik.

1680. COTTON, *Gamester*, 333. Gilts, PADS, biters, etc. . . . may all pass under the general appellation of rooks.

1683. CROWNE, *City Politics*, v. 1. Such rogues as you, who abuse your trade, and like so many PADDERS, make all people deliver their purse that ride in the road of justice.

c. 1696. B. E., *Dict. Cant. Crew*, s.v. PAD . . . RUM PAD, a daring or stout Highwayman.

1707. WARD, *Hudibras Redivivus*, II. iv. 22. Since the Ladder Has turn'd off many a handsom PADDER.

1708. *London Bewitched*, 6. This month hedges . . . will be the leacher's bawdy-house; the PADDER'S ambuscade; . . . and the farmer's security.

1712. SHIRLEY, *Triumph of Wit* [FARMER, *Musa Pedestris* (1896), 37]. The third was a PADDER, that fell to decay, Who used for to plunder upon the highway.

1746. *Poor Robin* [NARES]. Mercury, What does that thief Mercury do with Venus? Why even the very same that hectors and PADDERS do with ladies of pleasure.

1781. MESSINK, *Song* [*Choice of Harlequin*]. Ye scamps, ye PADS, ye divers, and all upon the lay.

1818. SCOTT, *Heart of Midlothian*, xxv. A gude fellow that has been but a twelvemonth on the lag, be he ruffler or PADDER.

1819. BYRON, *Don Juan*, II. 11. These freeborn sounds proceeded from four PADS In ambush laid.

4. (old).—*See* quot. 1823.

1664. ETHEREDGE, *The Comical Revenge*, I. 2. *Palmer* . . . I am grown more than half virtuous of late. I have laid the dangerous PAD now quite aside.

c. 1819. *Song of the Young Prig* [FARMER, *Musa Pedestris* (1896), 83]. The cleanest angler ON THE PAD.

1823. BEE, *Dict. Turf*, s.v. PAD (the)—highway robbery, forcibly. *Foot-pads*—dismounted highwaymen. Pads—are also street-robbers.

c. 1824. EGAN, *Boxiana*, iii. 621-2. For Dick had beat the hoof UPON THE PAD.

1892. HENLEY and STEVENSON, *Deacon Brodie*, II. i. 23. He's a light hand on the PAD, has Jemmy, and leaves his mark.

5. (old).—A bed: also POD. [POD = a bundle (*Dict. Cant. Crew*), often used as a pillow or bed]. *See* LETTY.

Verb. (Old Cant). — 1. To travel on foot; to tramp: also TO PAD (PLOD, BANG, or BEAT) THE HOOF (*q.v.*). Fr. *fendre l'ergot* (= to split the spur).

1598-9. SHAKSPEARE, *Merry Wives of Windsor*, i. 3. Trudge, PLOD, away, O' THE HOOF.

1610. ROWLANDS, *Martin Mark-All*, 'The Maunder's Wooing.' O Ben mort wilt thou PAD with me.

1644-55. HOWELL, *Letters*, I. i. 17 [1726]. The Secretary was put to BEAT THE HOOP himself, and foot it home.

d. 1659. BRADFORD, *Letters* [Parker Soc. (1858), ii. 46]. Though the weather be foul . . . yet go not ye alone . . . your brothers and sisters PAD the same path.

1684. BUNYAN, *Pilgrim's Progress*, II. A lion . . . came a great PADDING pace after.

1665. HEAD, *Eng. Rogue*, I. vi. 59. BEATING THE HOOF we overtook a Cart.

1687. BROWN, *Saints in Up.*, 82 [*Wks.* (1730), i. 78.] We BEAT THE HOOF as pilgrims.

1748. DYCHE, *Dict.*, s.v. Hoof. To BEAT THE HOOF (V.) to walk much up and down, to go a-foot.

1788. PICKEN, *Poems*, 37, 85. Fareweel, ye wordiest pair o' shoon, On you I've PADDED, late an' soon.

1789. PARKER, *Life's Painter* [FARMER, *Musa Pedestris* (1896), 69]. Ere they to church did PAD, To have it christen'd Joe, sir.

1859. MATSELL, *Vocab.* I must PAD like a bull or the cops will nail me.

1868. BROWNING, *Ring and Book*, II. 277. The muzzled ox . . . gone blind in PADDING round and round one path.

1880. SOMERVILLE, *Fables*, I. Two toasts, with all their trinkets gone, PADDING the streets for half-a-crown.

1883. *Daily News*, 22 June, 3, 2. As the child of Seven Dials walks the streets, PADDING THE weary HOOF . . . . he sees plenty of street sights.

1887. HENLEY, *Fillon's Straight Tip*, 2. PAD with a slang, or chuck a fag.

2. (old).—To rob on foot, or on the highway: also TO GO ON THE PAD.—B. E. (*c.* 1696); GROSE (1785).

1639. FORD, *Lady's Trial*, v. i. One can . . . pick a pocket, PAD for a cloak, or hat, and, in the dark, Pistol a straggler for a quarter-ducat.

1685. COTTON MATHER, *Discourse on Witchcraft* (1689), 7. As if you or I should say: We never met with any robbers on the road, therefore there never was any PADDING there.

d. 1745. SWIFT, to Mr. Congreve [*Century*]. These PAD on wit's high-road, and suits maintain, with those they rob.

ON THE PAD, *phr.* (common).—On the tramp.

1851. MAYHEW, *Lond. Lab.* I. 462. Her husband was ON THE PAD in the country.

TO STAND PAD, *verb. phr.* (vagrants')—To beg by the wayside.

1862. H. MAYHEW, *Lond. Lab.* IV. 24. Beggars . . . who STAND PAD with fakement and pretend to hide their faces.

1875. *Letter* [RIBTON-TURNER, *Vagrants and Vagrancy*, 642]. I obtained three children . . . for three shilling, . . to STAND PAD with me . . . on a Saturday.

TO PAD ROUND, *verb. phr.* (tailors').—To pay great attention to a customer; to cringe; TO CRAWL.

GENTLEMEN OF THE PAD. *See* PADDER.

PAD IN THE STRAW, *subs. phr.* (old colloquial).—Anything amiss; danger concealed; 'a snake in the grass.'

1551. STILL, *Gammer Gurton's Needle*, v. 2. Ye perceive by this lingring there is a PAD IN THE STRAW.

15 [?] COLLIER, *Old Ballads* [HALLIWELL]. Here lyes in dede the PADDE WITHIN THE STRAWE.

PAD-BORROWER, *subs. phr.* (old). A horse thief.—GROSE (1785).

PAD-CLINKING, *subs. phr.* (Old Cant).—Hobnobbing with foot-pads.

1865. KINGSLEY, *Hillyars and Burtons*, xix. My PAD-CLINKING . . . bucks, Good day.

PADDED, *subs.* (old).—1. *See* PAD; *subs.* sense 3.

2. *in pl.* (common). — Feet; boots, or shoes; *see* CREEPERS.

1828. EGAN, *Finish to Tom and Jerry*, 309. My PADDERS, my stampers, my buckets, otherwise my boots.

PADDING-CRIB (or -KEN), *subs. phr.* (Old Cant).—A lodging house: *cf.* DOSS-HOUSE.

1851. H. MAYHEW, *London Lab.* i. 261. Others resort to the regular PADDING-KENS, or houses of call for vagabonds.

1857. SNOWDEN, *Mag. Assist.* 444, s.v.

1866. *Temple Bar*, xvi. 184. Let the spikes be what they may they were a great deal better than the PADDING-KENS.

1883. *Referee*, 25 March, 1, 4. The hotel and lodging-house keepers, the proprietors of PADDING-KENS, ... expect to make profit out of the race being held where it is to be held.

1889. *Answers*, 11 May, 374. Not long ago considerable disturbances took place at this very PADDEN KEN.

1893. EMERSON, *Signor Lippo*, xiv. Before you can open a PADDIN-KEN, you must get a licence from the charpering carsey which lasts for a stretch.

PADDINGTON-FAIR, *subs.* (old).—A hanging. [Tyburn being in Paddington Parish]. TO DANCE THE PADDINGTON FRISK = to be hanged: *see* LADDER. — *Dict. Cant. Crew* (1696); GROSE (1785).

PADDINGTON - SPECTACLES, *subs. phr.* (old).—The cap pulled over the eyes of a criminal on the scaffold: *see* PADDINGTON-FAIR.

PADDLE, *subs.* (common). — The hand: *see* DADDLE.

Verb. (common).—1. To drink: hence TO HAVE PADDLED = to be intoxicated: *see* DRINKS and SCREWED.

2. (venery).—To play with a woman; TO MESS ABOUT: *see* FIRKYTOODLE.

1604. SHAKSPEARE, *Winter's Tale*, i. 7. PADDLING palms and pinching fingers.

1847. HALLIWELL, *Dict.*, s.v. PADDLE . . . *etiam designat molliter manibus tractare aliquid et agitare*, as to PADDLE in a ladies neck or bosom.

3. (American).—To go or run away.

See CANOE.

PADDY, *subs.* (common).—1. An Irishman: also PADDY-WHACK and PADDYLANDER. Hence, PADDY-LAND = Ireland.—GROSE (1785).

ENGLISH SYNONYMS. Bog-trotter; Emeralder; Mick, mike or micky; paddylander; paddy-whack; Pat; patent Frenchman; patlander; shirt.

1801. SHARPE [*Correspondence* (1888), i. 113]. You would be much surprised to see these cronies of mine . . . they are all there PADDIES.

1817. SCOTT, *Search after Happiness*, xxii. The odds that foil'd Hercules foil'd PADDY WHACK. . . . Alack! Ubbubboo! PADDY had not—a shirt to his back!!!

1850. SMEDLEY, *Frank Fairlegh*, lx. After I had had a good laugh . . . I . . . 'discoorsed' 'em, as PADDY calls it.

1874. LINTON, *Patricia Kemball*, xii. He once went over on business to what he always called PADDY-LAND.

18 [?]. *Irish Song* [HOTTEN]. I'm PADDY WHACK, from Ballyhack.

2. (common).—A rage; a passion: also PADDY-WHACK.

TO COME PADDY OVER, *verb. phr.* (American).—To bamboozle; to humbug.

PADDY QUICK, *subs.* and *adj.* (rhyming slang).—1. A stick; and (2) thick.

PADDY'S BLACKGUARDS, *subs. phr.* (military). — The Royal Irish Regiment, formerly The 18th Foot. Also "The Namurs."

PADDY'S HURRICANE, *subs. phr.* (nautical).—No wind at all; a 'breeze up and down the mast.'

PADDY-WACK (PADDY, or PADDY'S WATCH), *subs. phr.* (common).—*See* quot

1886. *Notes and Queries*, 7th S., i. 478. Before the tax on almanacs . . . a class of printers [sold] an almanack unstamped, and this was often called PADDY'S WATCH. They were hawked about, . . . sold at 3d., and often for less, when a stamped almanac cost 1s. 9d. or 2s. I have often heard . . . 'Have you an almanac?' and the answer has been, 'We have a PADDY.'

2. *See* PADDY, *subs.* 1 and 2.

PADDYWESTER, *subs.* (nautical).—*See* quot.

1892. PERRY, *Voyage of Boadicea* [*Boy's Own Paper*, 28 May, 649]. PADDY WESTERS . . . Incompetent, worthless, or destitute sailors or landsmen masquerading as seamen.

PADLOCK. *See* PLEASURE-BOAT.

PAD-NAG. *See* PAD, *subs.* sense 2.

PADRE, *subs.* (services).—A clergyman: *see* DEVIL-DODGER. [From the Portuguese].

1888. *Chamb. Journal*, 14 Jan., 18. The chaplain, who on board ship is known by a a thousand more or less irreverent names—PADRE, sky-pilot, etc.

PAFF, *intj.* (colloquial). — An interjection of contempt; bosh! Hence PIFF-PAFF = jargon.

1851. LONGFELLOW, *Golden Legend*. These beggars . . . lamed and maimed, and fed on chaff, chanting their wonderful PIFF AND PAFF.

1897. *Pall Mall*, 28 Sept., 2, 3. The combatants used their fists only . . . PAF! PAF! one for you, and PAF! PAF! for your opponent.

PAGAN, *subs.* (old).—A prostitute: *see* BARRACK-HACK and TART.

1659. MASSINGER, *City Madam*, ii. 1. I have had my several PAGANS billeted for my own tooth.

PAGET'S IRREGULAR HORSE (military). — The Fourth Hussars. [From its loose drill after return from India].

PAID, *adj.* (old).—Intoxicated: *see* DRINKS and SCREWED.

PAIKER (PAIKIE or CALSAY PAIKER). *subs. phr.* (Old Scots'). — A prostitute: *see* BARRACK-HACK and TART.

PAINT, *subs.* (common).—Money: *see* ACTUAL and GILL.

1866. HARRIS [*Evidence before Totness Election Commission*]. The voters ask for 'sub,' which is the term used here for money, as 'sugar' and PAINT are used elsewhere.

Verb. (common).—To drink. PAINTED = DRUNK. [*Cf. Macbeth*, ii. 3].

1853. WHYTE MELVILLE, *Digby Grand*, ii. Each hotel we passed . . . called forth the same observation, 'I guess I shall go in and PAINT.'

1857. KINGSLEY, *Two Years Ago*, xxiv. The muse is dry and fain would PAINT—imbibe the vulgar call.

See RED, and FRESH.

PAINTED-BOX, *subs. phr.* (American).—A coffin.

1888. *Point Pleasant Register*. We give such creatures timely and due notice to have a PAINTED BOX prepared.

PAINTED MISCHIEF, *subs. phr.* (old).—Playing cards; the HISTORY OF THE FOUR KINGS (*q.v.*).

1879. *Daily News*, 8 Mar. There are plenty of ways of gambling . . . without recourse to the "painted mischief."

PAINTER. TO CUT THE PAINTER, *verb. phr.* (colloquial).—To send away; to cut adrift; to interfere to prevent mischief: also *see* CUT.

*c.*1696. B. E., *Dict. Cant. Crew*, s.v. PAINTER. I'll CUT YOUR PAINTER for ye, I'll prevent ye doing me any Mischief; the Tar-Cant when they quarrel one with another.

1785. GROSE, *Vulg. Tongue*, s.v. PAINTER. I'll CUT YOUR PAINTER for you; I'll send you off; the painter being the rope that holds the boat fast to the ship.

PAIR, *subs.* (colloquial).—A flight of stairs; *e.g.*, TWO-PAIR back = the room at the back of the second flight of stairs.

PAIR OF SHEARS. *See* SHEARS.

PAIR OF SPECTACLES. *See* SPECTACLES.

PAIR OF WINGS, *subs. phr.* (old).—Oars.—GROSE (1785).

PAL, *subs.* (common).—A chum; a friend; a partner; an accomplice. [Probably from the Gypsy.]

1785. GROSE, *Vulg. Tongue*, s.v. PALL. A companion. One who generally accompanies another, or who commit robberies together.

1789. PARKER, *Life's Painter*, 150. PAL. When highwaymen rob in pairs, they say such a one was his or my PAL.

1821. HAGGART, *Life*, 172, s.v.

1821. EGAN, *Life in London* [DICK], p. 60. Jem is so cut up, that all his old PALS have turned their backs upon him.

1830. MONCRIEFF, *Heart of London*, ii. 1. Your PALS have been laid up in lavender.

1836. MILNER, *Turpin's Ride*, i. 3. A further reward . . . for the apprehension of his PAL, the gentleman highwayman.

1838. REYNOLDS, *The Housebreaker's Song* [FARMER, *Musa Pedestris* (1896) 123]. But if ever a PAL in limbo fell, He'd sooner be scragg'd at once than tell.

1839. AINSWORTH, *Jack Sheppard*, (1889), 15. It's all right, PALS, cried Baptist.

1841. *Comic Almanac*, 260. I can't even svear; my PALS u'd hardly know me.

1840-1845. BARHAM, *Ingoldsby Legends* (1862), 267. Highborn Hidalgos With whom e'en the King himself quite as a PAL goes.

1843. MONCRIEFF, *Scamps of London*, i. 2. Our young PAL.

1844. SELBY, *London by Night*, i. 2. I see you are not too proud to shake hands with an old PAL.

1858. MAYHEW, *Paved with Gold*, III. v. Ned and Phil, mutually agreed that their PAL was 'a born genius.'

1871. *Standard*, 26 Dec. Their PALS outside, the gentry who hocus Jack ashore in the east, pick the pockets of Lord Dundreary in the west.

1879. MCCARTHY, *Donna Quixote*, xxxvii. A coward like that couldn't even be true to his PAL.

1882. *Daily Telegraph*, 7 Oct., 6, 1. The witness added that the parties were very good friends; in fact, they were PALS together.

1891. NEWMAN, *Scamping Tricks*, 70. I had an old PAL with me.

1892. CHEVALIER, *The Little Nipper* [FARMER, *Musa Pedestris* (1896), 192]. 'E call 'is mother 'Sally,' and 'is father 'good old PALLY,' and 'e only stands about so 'igh, that's all!

1893. EMERSON, *Signor Lippo*, v. His PALS didn't seem to take notice.

Verb. (common).—1. To make friends with; to chum.

1879. *Autobiography of a Thief*, in *Macmillan's Mag.*, XL. 500. I PALLED in with some older hands at the game.

1892. MILLIKEN, *'Arry Ballads*, 7. We'll PALL OFF to Parry.

1893. EMERSON, *Signor Lippo*, xvii. I PALLED IN with a lot more boys, done a bit of gonoffing or anything to get some posh, but it got too hot, all my pals got nicked, and I chucked it.

1898. *Cigarette*, 26 Nov., 13, 1. It's their weddin' day on Toosday; Married fifty year ago. That's a TIDY time to PAL it! More than I could do, I know!

2. (thieves').—*See* quot.

1851. MAYHEW, *London Lab.* ix. 768. It was difficult to PALL him upon any racket (detect him in any pretence).

PALACE, *subs.* (police).—A police-station.

PALARIE, *verb.* (vagrants').—To talk: *cf.* PALAVER.

1893. EMERSON, *Signor Lippo*, xvi. Though they offered me lots of money to blow the gaff, I felt afraid to PALARIE a dickey for fear of being trapped. *Ibid.* She knew all the cant, and used to PALARIE thick to the slaveys.

PALATIC, *adj.* (theatrical).—Drunk: *see* DRINKS and SCREWED.

1885. *The Stage*, 28. Sandy told me he last saw him dreadfully PALATIC.

PALAVER, *subs.* (colloquial Scots').—1. A fussy and ostentatious person: generally OLD PALAVER.

2. (general). — Conversation; discussion: specifically idle talk, flattery, or cajolery: also as *verb.* Hence, PALAVERER = a flatterer. [From Port. *palavra* (= talk)].—GROSE (1785); BEE (1823).

1748. SMOLLETT, *Rod. Random*, xli. None of your PALAVER.

1763. FOOTE, *Mayor of Garratt*, ii. 2. Have a good caution that this Master Mug does not cajole you; He is a damned PALAVERING FELLOW.

1822. DOUGLAS JERROLD, *Black Ey'd Susan*, ii., 2. *Wil.* No PALAVER; tell it to the marines.

1838. BAYLY, *Spitalfields Weaver*. Hang it! he'll see through all that PALAVER the way you say it.

1838. DESMOND, *Stage Struck*, 2. No more of your PALAVER—I'll not be made a Jerry Sneak.

1858. G. ELIOT, *Janet's Repentance*, xxv. I used to think there was a great deal of PALAVER in her, but you may depend upon it there's no pretence.

1864. MISS WETHERELL, *Melbourne House*, v. Come . . . don't PALAVER.

1866. HOWELL'S, *Venetian Life*, xxii. There hang their mighty works for ever, high above the reach of any PALAVERER.

1883. PAYN, *Canon's Ward*, xv. You have deceived him long enough with PALAVER, now you'll have to undeceive him with PALAVER.

1884. SMART, *Post to Finish*, 193. Have a PALAVER with your father.

1888. RUNCIMAN, *Chequers*, 107. I liked to hear Jowett PALAVER.

1892. *Illustrated Bits*, 22 Oct. 14, 2. She can't get the comehither over me for all her PALAVER.

Verb. 1. *See subs.* 2.

2. (colloquial Scots').—To fuss.

PALE. TO LEAP THE PALE, *verb. phr.* (old colloquial).—To break bounds; to exceed.

1593. SHAKSPEARE, *Com. Errors*, ii. 1, 100. But, too unruly deer, he BREAKS THE PALE And feeds from home.

1609. *The Man in the Moone*, sig. C. 4. If you proceede as you have begune . . . your LEAPING THE PALE will cause you looke pale.

1847. TENNYSON, *Princess*, ii. Deep, indeed, Their debt of thanks to her who first had dared TO LEAP THE rotten PALES of prejudice.

PALEFACE, *subs.* (American colloquial).—A white: in poetry and fiction, as from an Indian dialect.

18 [?] G. H. COLTON, *Tecumseh*, ii. 18. [F]. Then shall the PALEFACE sink to-night.

1826. COOPER, *Last of Mohicans*, xxxiii. The hunting grounds of the Lenape contained vales as pleasant, streams as pure, and flowers as sweet as the heaven of the PALE-FACES.

18 [?] DURFEE, WHATCHER, IV., xxxv. The PALEFACED strangers came.

PALESTINE IN LONDON, *subs. phr.* (old).—*See* quot. and HOLY LAND.

1821. EGAN, *Real Life*, II. 165. PALESTINE IN LONDON, or the *Holy Land*, includes that portion of the parish of St. Giles, Bloomsbury, inhabited by the lower Irish.

PALETTE, *subs.* (old).—A hand: *see* DADDLE.

PALLIARD, *subs.* (Old Cant.).—1. A born beggar; a tramp; primarily a vagabond who lies on straw. [From. Fr. *paillard*].—AWDELEY (1567); COLES (1724); *New Cant. Dict.* (1725); GROSE (1785); *Lex. Bal.* (1811).

1573. HARMAN, *Caveat* (1814), 26. These PALLIARDS be called also Clapperdogens, these go with patched clokes, and haue their morts with them which they cal wiues.

1608. DEKKER, *Belman of London*, [GROSART, *Wks.*, III. 99]. A PALLIARD carryes about him (for feare of the worst) a *Certificate* . . . where this Mort and he were marryed, when all is but forged.

1611. MIDDLETON and DEKKER, *Roaring Girl*, v. 1. And couch till a PALLIARD docked my dell.

1616. BEAUMONT and FLETCHER, *Monsieur Thomas*, ii. 2. No, base PALLIARD, I do remember yet.

1687. DRYDEN, *Hind and Panther*, II. 563. Thieves, panders, PALLIARDS, sins of every sort.

*c.*1696. B. E., *Dict. Cant. Crew*, s.v. PALLIARDS, *c.* the Seaventh Rank of the Canting Crew, whose Fathers were Born Beggers, and who themselves follow the Same Trade, with Sham Sores, making a hideous Noise, Pretending grievous Pain, do extort Charity.

1707. SHIRLEY, *Triumph of Wit* [FARMER, *Musa Pedestris* (1896), 35]. PALLIARDS all thou didst excel.

1748. DYCHE, *Dict.* A cant name for wretched men and women, who live by begging, thieving—anything but honest industry. The women go with one, or more small children, in a dirty, ragged condition, who cry, as though starved, the women making a doleful tale. Her male companion lies begging in fields, streets, &c., with cleymes or artificial sores, the flesh raw and shocking to the sight; the impostor pretending great pain, deceives the compassionate, charitable, and well-disposed passengers, whom, when opportunity presents, he can recover his limbs to rob, and even murder, if resisted. [Condensed].

1834. AINSWORTH, *Rookwood*, III. v. Adjoining him was the PALLIARD, a loathsome tatterdemallion, his dress one heap of rags, and his discoloured skin one mass of artificial leprosy and imposthumes.

2. (old).—A lecher; a WOMANIZER (*q.v.*). Hence PALLIARDISE = fornication; and PALLIARDY = whoredom.

1512-13. DOUGLAS, *Virgil*, Prol. 96. 41. Eschame ye not rehers and blaw on brede Your awin defame? hawand of God na drede, Na yit of hell, prouokand vtheris to syn, Ye that list of your PALYARDRY neuer blyn.

*d.*1555. LYNDSAY, *Works*, 76. That blind gat sicht, and cruikit gat their feit; The quhilk the PALYARD na way can appreue.

1598. FLORIO, *Worlde of Wordes*, sig. a 6 vo. Whose Communication is Atheisme, contention, detraction, or PAILLARDISE.

1604. DIGGES, *Foure Parad*, i. 4. PALLARDIZE, Murder, Treachery, and Treason are their Attendants.

1728. BAILEY, *Eng. Dict.*, s.v. PALLIARDISE, Whoredom, Fornication.

PALLIASSE, *subs.* (common).—A harlot: *see* TART.

PALM, *verb.* (old).—1. To bribe; TO TIP (*q.v.*): also TO GREASE (ANOINT, or GILD) THE PALM (or HAND): *cf.* sense. 2. Hence (1) AN ITCHING PALM = a hand ready to receive bribes: *cf.* the old superstition that money is about to be received if the palm itches; and (2) PALM-OIL (GREASE or SOAP, or OIL OF PALMS or ANGELS, *q.v.*) = a bribe, whence also = money: Fr. *huile* and *graisse* (GROSE, 1785); MR. PALMER IS CONCERNED, of a person bribed or bribing (VAUX, 1819). *See* GREASE.

*c.*1513. SKELTON [DYCE, *Works* (1843), ii.]. GRESE MY HANDES with gold.

*d.*1572. KNOX, *Hist. of Reformation*, [*Works* (1846) I. 102.] Yea, the HANDIS of our Lordis so liberallie were ANOYNTED.

1592. GREENE, *Repentance, etc.* Sig C. My Mother pampered me . . . and secretly helped mee to the OYLE OF ANGELS, that I grew . . . prone to all mischefs.

1607. SHAKSPEARE, *Jul. C.* iv. Let me tell you, Cassius, you . . . Are much condemned to have AN ITCHING PALM.

1623. MASSINGER, *Duke of Milan*, iii. 2. His stripes wash'd off With OIL OF ANGELS.

1678. COTTON, *Virgil Travestie* [Works (1725) 71]. She conjures, prays, . . . GREASES HIS FIST.

17 [?] [quoted in ASHTON, *Social Life in Reign of Q. Anne*, II. 220]. He accounts them very honest Tikes, and can with all safety trust his Life in their Hands, for now and then GILDING THEIR PALMS for the good services they do him.

1819. MOORE, *Tom Crib*, 81. OIL OF PALM's the thing, that flowing, Sets the naves and felloes going.

1840. LYTTON, *Paul Clifford*, viii. I dare say you may manage to soften the justice's sentence by a little OIL OF PALMS.

1854. *Punch*, ii. 168. OIL OF PALMS. —*Metaphora vetustissima.* A specific much in vogue for rigid fingers and horny fistedness; though, strange to say, it only serves to augment the itch which so often affects the hand.

1858. *Morning Chronicle*, 10 Feb. It is not an unusual thing in our trade to PALM the police.

1879. DICKENS, *Dict. of London*, s.v. SIGHT-SEEING. The enterprising sight-seer who proceeds on this plan, and who understands the virtues of PALM OIL, is sure to see everything he cares to see.

1898. *Saturday Review*, 3 Sep., 298, 1. It was suggested . . . that one of the reasons for the failure of British diplomacy in China was that we did not rightly appreciate the uses of PALM OIL.

1900. OUIDA, *Massarenes*, 32. I think she'll take us up, William, . . . but she will want a lot of PALM-GREASE.

2. (colloquial).—To conceal in the palm of the hand; to swindle; to misrepresent. Whence PALMING (PALMISTRY or PALMING-RACKET) = trickery (by secreting in the palm of the hand): specifically shop-lifting, the thieves hunting in pairs, one bargaining, the other watching opportunities: *see* quots. 1714 and 1755. Also TO PALM OFF = to beguile; TO GAMMON (*q.v.*); PALMER = a trickster: specifically at cards and dice. — DYCHE (1748); VAUX (1819).

1601. BEN JONSON, *Poetaster*, v. Well said, this CARRIES PALM with it.

1698. FARQUHAR, *Love and a Bottle* [Old Dram. 492]. [He will] PALM letters on you.

1700. *Step to the Bath* [ASHTON, *Soc. Life in Reign of Q. Anne*, ii. 111]. . . . There was PALMING, Lodging, Loaded Dice, Levant, and Gammoning, with all the Speed imaginable.

1704. SWIFT, *Tale of a Tub*, Sect. VI. A rogue that . . . . PALMED his damned crusts upon us for mutton.

1711. *Spectator*, No. 117. She . . . has made the country ring with several imaginary exploits which are PALMED UPON her. *Ibid.*, 130. He found his pocket was picked; that being a kind of PALMISTRY at which this race of vermin [gypsies] are very dexterous.

1714. LUCAS, *Gamesters*, 27. PALMING the die; that is, having the box in hand, he nimbly takes up both dice as thrown within the hollow of his hand, puts but one into the box, reserving the other in the PALM, and observing with quick eye what side was upward, he accordingly conforms the next throw to his purpose, delivering that in the box, and the other in his hand smoothly together.

1755. *Connoisseur*, No. 68. The dexterity . . . TO PALM an ace, or cog a die.

1811. AUSTEN, *Sense and S.*, xx. Don't PALM all your abuses . . . UPON me.

1818. SCOTT, *Rob Roy*, xxxvii. A foundered blood-mare, which he wished to PALM UPON a Manchester merchant.

1826. LAMB, *Elia* (*Popular Fallacies*, xi.). A horse-giver, no more than a horse-seller, has a right to PALM his spavined article UPON us for good ware.

1857. SNOWDEN, *Mag. Assistant*, 445. Robbing in shops by two—PALMING.

1877. *Five Years' Penal*, ii. 119. The warder . . . watches that the prisoner does not PALM anything—in other words, practise some legerdemain trick to conceal any contraband article.

TO BEAR THE PALM, *verb. phr.* (colloquial).—To excel; to be first or best. [The Romans gave branches of palm to a victorious gladiator.]

PALM-ACID (or **OIL**) *subs. phr.* (schoolboys').—1. A caning: on the hand.

2. *See* PALM, *verb.* 1.

PALMER, *subs.* (Durham School).—1. A shy fellow.

2. *See* PALM, sense 2.

PALMERSTON, *subs.* (pugilists').—*See* quot.

1865. *Field.* Feb. Bottle-Holder . . . Slang term for Lord Palmerston . . . . He described himself as acting the part of a judicious bottle-holder among the foreign Powers. A lately-invented instrument to hold a bottle has thus received the name of a PALMERSTON.

PALMETTO STATE, *subs. phr.* (American). — South Carolina. [From the arms of the State: a variety of dwarf palm or palmetto is abundant therein.] Whence PALMETTO FLAG, PALMETTO CITY, and PALMETTO BOYS.

1861. *Charleston Mercury*, 'War Song.' March, march on, brave PALMETTO BOYS, Sumter and Lafayette, forward in order.

PALM-OIL.—*See* PALM, and PALM-ACID.

PALSY, *subs.* (old colloquial).—1. Generic for weakness. PALSY IN THE HAND (old) = the habit of dicing.

1608. *Yorkshire Tragedy*, i. 4. What is there . . . to make a man . . . with the gentleman's PALSY in the hand shake out his posterity, thieves or beggars?

1623. MASSINGER, *Duke of Milan*, iv. 3. Lock up thine own wife, fool, that must take physic From her young doctor, physic upon her back, Because thou hast the PALSY in that part That makes her active.

PALTOCK'S INN, *subs. phr.* (old).—A poverty-stricken place.

1579. GOSSON, *School of Abuse*, 52. Comming to Chenas, a blind village, in comparison of Athens a PALTOCKES INNE, he found one Miso well governing his house.

1582. STANIHURST, *Æneid*, iii. 65. Swiftlye they determind too flee from a countrye so wycked, PALTOCKS INNE leauing, too wrinche thee nauye too southward.

PAM, *subs.* (old gaming).—1. The Knave of Clubs. [SKEAT: A contraction of Pamphillion (Fr.) = the Knave of Clubs: *see* LITTRE].—B.E. (*c.*1696); GROSE (1785); *Lex. Bal.* (1811).

1706. ESTCOURT, *Fair Example*, i. Scandal is the very PAM in conversation.

1712. POPE, *Rape*, III. 61. Ev'n mighty PAM that kings o'erthrew.

1713. *Guardian*, 120. Play . . . . engrosses the whole woman. She quickly grows . . . more fond of PAM, than of her husband.

1745. WALPOLE, *Letters* (1833), II. 74. One gets PAM, the other gets PAM, but . . . no conclusion of the game, till one side has never a card left.

1777. COLMAN, *School for Scandal. Epil.* That spirit-stirring drum!—odd trick—PAM—basto—king and queen!

1810. CRABBE, *Borough*, 9, *Amusements.* Faint in the morn, no powers could she exert; at night with PAM delighted and alert.

2. (literary).—Lord Palmerston.

1854. SMEDLEY, *Harry Coverdale*, xxxvii. I just scribbled off a line to Palmerston . . . It's very jolly to be on those terms with a man like PAM.

PAN, *subs.* (tramps'). — 1. The workhouse: *see* PANNY, *subs.* 2.

1893. EMERSON, *Signor Lippo*, xx. Next day all us kids were sent to the PAN, and she got two months' hard.

2. (old).—A bed: *see* KIP.—HALL (1708).

3. (Old Cant). — Money: *see* RHINO.—HALLIWELL (1847).

TO PAN OUT, *verb. phr.* (American).—To yield; to give a result or return: originally a mining term; 'gold dust' being put with water in a pan and shaken, when gold sinks to the bottom.

1882. MCCABE, *New York*, 221. Altogether, my first evening among the 'lumtums' PANNED OUT well.

1888. *Providence Journal.* A penniless young man, with nothing to back him but a dream, had secured almost unlimited credit and a rich heiress in the bargain. Dreams don't PAN OUT in that way, said one.

1888. *Detroit Free Press*, 25 Aug. They got to blows, but things didn't PAN OUT as I thought they would.

1894. *To-day*, 21 Ap., 317, 1. Hereupon the current of criticism takes a turn . . . 'Ought ter PAN OUT well.'

1901. *Referee*, 7 Ap. 1. 1. We do not want to know about repairs to the M.C.C.'s big roller, or the plumbing account, or how the members' luncheon PANS OUT as a commercial speculation.

TO HAVE A PAN ON, *verb. phr.* (printers').—To have a fit of 'the blues'; to be 'down in the dumps.'

TO SAVOR OF THE PAN (or FRYING-PAN), *verb. phr.* (colloquial).—To betray origin; to smell of the lamp (*q.v.*) Also (old literary) to savour of heresy: cf. *Sentir le fagot*, from which there would appear to be a reference to the ancient punishment for heresy.]

*d.*1555. RIDLEY [BRADFORD *Letters*, Parker Society, 1853, II. 160]. Although there be many things that SAVOURETH OF THE PAN, and also he himself was afterward a Bishop of Rome, yet, I dare say, the papists would glory but a little to see such books go forth in English.

1824. SOUTHEY, *Book of the Church*, XI. Bishop Nix of Norwich, one of the most infamous for his activity in this persecution, used to call the persons whom he suspected of heretical opinions men SAVOURING OF THE FRYING-PAN.

See CAT, FLUFF and FLASH.

PANCAKE, *subs.* (venery).—The female *pudendum*: *see* MONOSYLLABLE.

PAN-CAKE TUESDAY, *subs. phr.* (colloquial).—Shrove Tuesday. [By ancient custom pancakes are then eaten.]

PANDY (or **PANDIE**), *subs.* (schools' and nursery). A stroke from a cane, strap, or tawse on the palm of the hand by way of punishment. Also (Scots) PAUMIE. [From the order in Latin '*Pande* palmum' (or manum) = 'Hold out your hand.'] Also as *verb* = to cane or strap.

1832. SCOTT, *Redgauntlet*, i. You taught me . . . to . . . obey the stern order of the *Pande manum*, and endure my pawmies without wincing.

1863. KINGSLEY, *Water-Babies*, 187. And she boxed their ears, and thumped them over the head with rulers, and PANDIED their hands with canes.

PANEL (PARNEL or PERNEL), *subs.* (old).—An immodest woman; a prostitute: *see* TART.—BAILEY (1728); GROSE (1785).

1362. LANGLAND, *P. Plowman's Vision*, 2313. Til PARNELLS purfille be put in hire hucche. *Ibid.* 2790. Dame PERNELE a priestes fyle.

1560. PILKINGTON, *Works*, 56. But these tender PERNELS must have one gown for the day, another for the night.

1560. BECON, *Prayers* [Parker Soc. *Works*], 267. Pretty PARNEL [= a nickname for a priest's mistress].

PANEL-CRIB (-DEN, or -HOUSE), *subs. phr.* (common).—A brothel specially fitted for robbery. A woman picking up a stranger takes him to a PANEL-HOUSE, known also as a BADGER or TOUCH-CRIB, or a SHAKEDOWN. The room has means of secret ingress—door frames, moveable *panels*, and the backs of wardrobes—swinging noiselessly on oiled hinges. The woman engages her victim, an accomplice enters the room, rifles his pockets, and retires. Then, coming to the door he knocks, and demands admission. The victim hastily dresses, leaves by another exit, and discovers that the whole thing is a PLANT (*q.v.*). Hence PANEL-GAME and PANEL-DODGE: *cf.* PANNY. For syns. *see* NANNY-SHOP.—BARTLETT (1848); FARMER (1888).

1882. MCCABE, *New York*, XXX. 187. Many of the street walkers are in the regular employ of the PANEL-HOUSES.

1885. BURTON, *Thousand Nights*, i. 323. The PANEL-DODGE is common throughout the East—a man found in the house of another is helpless.

1899. *Reynolds*, 22 Jan., 8, 3. PANEL Robberies. [Title.]

PANJAMDRUM (THE GREAT), *subs. phr.* (common).—A village potentate; a Brummagem magnate. [From Foote's nonsense lines, written to test Macklin's memory: *see* quot.].

*d.*1777. FOOTE [*Quarterly Review*, XCV. 516-7]. So she went into the garden to cut a cabbage leaf to make an apple pie; and at the same time a great she-bear, coming up the street, pops its head into the shop. "What! no soap?" So he died, and she very imprudently married the barber; and there were present the Picninnies, and the Joblillies, and the Garyulies, and the GRAND PANJANDRUM himself, with the little round button at top, and they all fell to playing the game of catch as catch can, till the gunpowder ran out at the heel of their boots.

1883. H. JAMES, in *Harper's Mag.*, LXXVII. 86. 'Well, no, not exactly a nobleman.' 'Well, some kind of a PANJANDRUM. Hasn't he got one of their titles?'

PANNICKY, *adj.* (colloquial).—Given to panic.

1886. *New Princeton Review*, v. 206. Our national party conventions have come to be PANNICKY hordes.

PANNIER. TO FILL A WOMAN'S PANNIER, *verb. phr.* (common).—*See* quot. 1611.—HALLIWELL (1847).

1611. COTGRAVE, *Dict.*, s.v. *Emplir une femelle*, TO FILL HER PANNIERS to get her with yong.

See WEAR.

PANNIER-MAN, *subs. phr.* (old).—A servant of an inn of court: his office is to announce dinner.—GROSE (1785).

1654. *Witts Recreation* [NARES]. On T. H. the PANNIER MAN of the Temple. [Title.]

1712. *Great Britans Honycombe*, MSS. [NARES]. The PANYER MAN, whose office is to lay the cloths on the tables in the hall, set saltsellers, cut bred, whet the knifes, and wait on the gentlemen, and fetch them beer and other necessaries when they are in commons in term time. He also blows the great horn between twelve and one of the clock at noon at most of the corners in the Temple three times presently one after another to call the gentlemen that are in commons to dinner.

PANNIKIN. TO ROLL ONE'S PANNIKIN INTO ANOTHER SHED (Australian). To leave one man's service for another.

PANNUM (PANUM, or PANNAM), *subs.* (Old Cant).—Bread; food. [Latin *panis*]. Hence PANNUM-BOUND = (prison) cut of one's allowance; PANNUM- (or COKEY-) FENCE = a street pastry cook; PANNUM-STRUCK = starving.—HARMAN (1567); B. E. (*c.*1696); HALL (1714); COLES (1724); GROSE (1785). For synonyms *see* STAFF-OF-LIFE.

1608. DEKKER, *Lanthorne and Candlelight* [FARMER, *Musa Pedestris* (1896), 3]. The Ruffin cly the nab of the Harmanbeck, If we mawnd PANNAM, lap, or Ruff-peck.

1611. MIDDLETON and DEKKER, *Roaring Girl*, v. 1. [FARMER, *Musa Pedestris* (1896), 10]. A gage of ben Rombouse. . . . Is benar than a Caster, Peck, PENNAM, lap, or popler.

1641. BROME, *Jovial Crew* [FARMER, *Musa Pedestris* (1896), 23]. Here's PANNAM . . . To fill up the Crib, and to comfort the Quarron.

1823. BEE, *Dict. Turf*, s.v. PANUM. "Mat de dem div, me Middery?" asks the gipsey child. Nonarem PANUM.

1837. DISRAELI, *Venetia*, xiv. Beruna flick the PANEM.

1844. SELBY, *London by Night*, i. 2. As far as an injun, PANNUM, and cheese, and a drop of heavy goes, you are perfectly welcome.

1867. VANCE, *Chickaleary Cove*. Some PANNUM for my chest.

PANNY, *subs.* (old).—1. The highway.

1754. *Discoveries of John Poulter*, 42. I'll scamp on the PANNEY.

2. (Old Cant). — A house, public or otherwise; also apartments, rooms, lodgings. Hence FLASH-PANNY = (1) a brothel; and (2) a public-house used by thieves.

1785. GROSE, *Vulg. Tongue*, s.v. PANNY. The pigs frisked my PANNEY and nailed my screws.

1819. VAUX, *Memoirs*, s.v.

1821. EGAN, *Life in London*, II. ii. To send them to their PANNIES full of spirits.

1823. BEE, *Dict. Turf*, s.v. PANNY —a small house, or low apartment; a dwelling-shed, or gipsey *building* without stairs.

1827. EGAN, *Anec. of Turf*, 183. He never called at her PANNY now without invitation.

3. (thieves'). — A burglary: also PANNY-LAY. Hence, PANNY-MAN = a housebreaker; TO DO A PANNY = to rob a house.—GROSE (1785); SNOWDEN (1857).

1830. LYTTON, *Paul Clifford*, ii. Ranting Rob, poor fellow, was lagged for DOING A PANNY.

*c.*1838. REYNOLDS, *Pickwick Abroad* [FARMER, *Musa Pedestris* (1896), 122]. The reg'lars came Whenever a PANNIE was done.

PANTABLES. TO STAND UPON ONE'S PANTABLES, *verb. phr.* (old colloquial).—To stand upon dignity; to assert one's position. [PANTABLES = pantoufle = slipper].

1580. SAKER, *Narbonus*, II. 99. Hee STANDETH UPON HIS PANTABLES, and regardeth greatly his reputation.

1647. BEAUMONT and FLETCHER, *Faithful Friend*, iii. 2. Then comes a page: the saucy jacket-wearer STOOD UPON'S PANTABLES with me, and would in: But, I think I took him down ere I had done with him.

1734. COTTON, *Works*, 85. Is now, forsooth, so proud, what else! And STANDS SO ON HER PANTABLES.

PANTAGRUELIAN, *subs.* (literary).—An artist in life. [From Pantagruel, the title character of Rabelais.]

PANTER, *subs.* (Old Cant).—1. The hart. [Because said (in Psalms) to pant after the fresh water brooks].—B. E. (*c.*1696); GROSE (1785).

2. (common). — The heart. Also, in *pl.* = the paps. Fr. *le Saint-ciboire*; *le battant* (= the beater); *la fressure* (= the pluck or fry); *le palpitant*. It. *la salsa* (= sauce).

*c.*1725. *Old Song* [FARMER, *Musa Pedestris* (1896), 44]. Didst thou know, my dear doxy, but half of the smart Which has seized on my PANTER, since thou didst depart.

PANTS, *subs.* (vulgar).—Short for 'pantaloons.' Also PANTEYS, and (colloquial) PANTALETTES [= a school-girl's breeches].

1870. WHITE, *Words and their Uses*, 211. Gent and PANTS—Let these words go together like the things they signify. The one always wears the other.

1847. PORTER, *Big Bear*, 104. If I hadn't a had on PANTALETS I reckon somebody would of knowd whether I gartered above my knees or not.

1848. BURTON, *Waggeries*, 95. I've a colt's revolver in each PANTEY'S pocket.

1851. WENDELL HOLMES, *Poems*, 217. The thing named PANTS in certain documents, A word not made for gentlemen, but gents.

1852. WETHERELL, *Queenie*. Miss Letitia Ann Thornton, a tall grown girl in PANTALETTES.

1853. WHYTE MELVILLE, *Digby Grand*, xx. Wonderfully-fitting continuations, PANTS he calls them.

1878. YATES [*World*, 16 Jan.]. Sterry, the pet of PANTALETTES, the laureate of frills.

1883. CLEMENS, *Life on Mississippi*, xxxviii. The young ladies, as children, in slippers and scalloped PANTELETTES.

PANTILE *subs.* (common).—1. A hat.

2. (schoolboys').—A flat cake covered with jam.

3. (nautical).—A biscuit.

Adj. (old colloquial).—Dissenting. [*See* PANTILER.]

1715. CENTLIVRE, *Gotham Election*, sc. ii. Mr. Tickup's a good churchman, mark that! He is none of your hellish PANTILE crew.

PANTILER, *subs.* (common).—A Dissenter—minister or layman: *see* DEVIL-DODGER. Hence PANTILE, *adj.* (*q.v.*), and PANTILE-SHOP (*see* quot. 1785).

1785. GROSE, *Vulg. Tongue*, s.v. PANTILE-SHOP. A presbyterian, or other dissenting meeting house, frequently covered with pantiles: called also a Cock-pit.

1856. MAYHEW, *World of London*, 249. The officers used to designate the extraordinary religious convicts as PANTILERS.

1863. KNIGHT, *Pass. of a Working Life* (1873), i. 217. This vulgar term of opprobrium for sectaries in the palmy days of 'Church and King' was PANTILERS.

PANTLER, *subs.* (literary: perhaps obsolete).—A butler; a pantryman.—B. E. (*c.*1696); GROSE (1785).

1598. SHAKSPEARE, *2 Henry* ii. 4. A good shallow young fellow; he would have made a good PANTLER, he would have chipped bread well.

1604. SHAKSPEARE, *Winter's Tale*, IV. 4. My old wife . . . was both PANTLER, butler, cook; Both dame and servant; welcom'd all; serv'd all.

1605. *Mis. of Inf. Marr.* [DODSLEY, *Old Plays* (REED), v. 26.] A rogue that hath fed upon me—like pullen from a PANTLER'S chippings.

1656. BROME, *Jovial Crew* [DODSLEY, *Old Plays* (REED), x. 338]. But I will presently take order with the cook, PANTLER, and butler, for my wonted allowance to the poor.

PANUPETASTON *subs.* (obsolete, University).—A loose overcoat with wide sleeves.

PAP, *subs.* (common).—1. The emoluments of office—salaries, fees, perquisites.

1880. *Nation*, xlviii. 379. At the end of four years, not only should an officer make an accounting and submit to an audit, but should vacate his place, so that somebody else might get some of the PAP he had enjoyed during this period.

2. (thieves').—Paper: specifically paper money, or SOFT (*q.v.*)

1877. HORSLEY, *Jottings from Jail*. Come on, we have had a lucky touch for half-a-century in PAP.

3. (literary: perhaps obsolete).—(*a*) A nipple; (*b*) a breast.

1390. MANDEVILLE, *Travels*, 154. Zif it be a female, thei don away that on PAPPE, with an hote Hiren; and zif it be a Womman of gret Lynage, thei don awey the left PAPPE, that thei may the better beren a Scheeld.

1592. SHAKSPEARE, *Mid. Night's Dream*, v. 1, 303. Ay, that left PAP, Where heart doth hop.

1594. LYNDSAY, *Squyer Meldrum* [E. E. T. S. 945]. Hir PAPPIS wer hard, round, and quhyte, Quhome to behald wes greit delyte.

1603. CHAPMAN, *Homer*, 'Iliad,' iv. He strooke him at his breastes right PAPPE, Quite through his shoulder bone.

1612. DRAYTON, *Polyolbion*, i. Nourish'd and bred up at her most plenteous PAP.

4. (American).—Father: POP (*q.v.*)

1892. GUNTER, *Miss Dividends*, iii. Your PAP has had too much railroad and mine on his hands.

5 (old).—Bread sauce.—GROSE (1785).

TO GIVE PAP WITH A HATCHET, *verb. phr.* (old). — To chastise; to do an unkindness, or treat unhandsomely.

1589. NASH, *Pappe with a Hatchet* [Title].

1594. SHAKSPEARE, *2 Henry VI.*, iv. 7. Ye shall have a hempen caudle then, and the PAP [now read *help*] OF A HATCHET.

. . . . *Disc. of Marr.* [*Harl. MS.* (PARK), ii. 171]. He that so old seeks for a nurse so young, shall have PAP WITH A HATCHET for his comfort.

1623. LYLY, *Court Comedy*, Z. 12b. They give us pap with a spoone before we can speake, and when we speake for that wee love, PAP WITH A HATCHET.

MOUTH FULL OF PAP, *phr.* (old).—Still childish. — GROSE (1785).

PAPAW, *subs.* (American). A bushwhacker. [*Century*: with reference to possible subsistence on the fruit].

PAPER, *subs.* (theatrical).—1. Free passes of admission to a place of entertainment; also (collectively) recipients of such passes; also OXFORD CLINK and STATIONERY. Hence, PAPERY = occupied by persons admitted with free tickets; and, as *verb* = to issue free passes. Fr. *une salle de papier* = a house filled with PAPER.

1870. MRS. JOHN WOOD [*Figaro*, 15 July]. I have abolished the free order system from a firm belief that the best sort of PAPER for a theatre is Bank of England notes.

1880. SIMS, *Zeph*, 84. The house was only half full and there were whispers that a good deal of PAPER was about.

1885. *Referee*, 8 Nov. The stalls were partly PAPERY, and partly empty.

1890. *Figaro*, 1 June. A box now and then, or *carte-blanche* in the way of PAPERING a theatre, will go far to wring from them profuse admiration of everything and everybody.

2. (commercial).—Negotiable instruments: as promissory notes, bills of exchange, &c.

1837. DICKENS, *Pickwick*, xl. Ah, said Mr. Smangle, PAPER has been my ruin. A stationer, I presume, sir? said Mr. Pickwick . . . No, no. When I say PAPER, I mean bills.

1849. THACKERAY, *Pendennis*, lxiv. It was whispered . . . that the Captain's PAPER was henceforth of no value.

1891. STEVENSON, *Kidnapped*, 185. For I'll have TO PAPER your friend from the lowlands too.

3. (old).—Broadsides and similar literature: hence PAPER WORKER = a vendor of street literature: a RUNNING STATIONER (*q.v.*).

1851. MAYHEW, *Lond. Lab.* I, 234. The best known publisher of the PAPER in demand for street sale, was the late 'Jemmy Catnach,' who is said to have amassed upwards of 10,000*l* in the business.

TO EAT PAPER, *verb. phr.* (American).—*See* quot.

*c.*1852. *American Humour*, I., 200. He . . . took a very long sight—fired, and didn't even EAT PAPER.

TO READ THE PAPER, *verb. phr.* (common).—To excuse oneself for taking a nap: *see* DOSS.

See SHAVE and SPOT.

PAPER-BUILDING, *subs.* (old).—*See* quot. and *cf.* House of Cards.

*c.*1696. B. E., *Dict. Cant. Crew*, s.v. PAPER-BUILDINGS, Slight, Wooden, or old.

PAPER-MAKER, *subs. phr.* (common).—A rag-gatherer; a gutter-raker. Fr. *un chiffortin.*

PAPER-MAN, *subs. phr.* (military). *See* quot.

1892. *Standard*, 24 Oct. The practice of retaining on the strength . . . . PAPER MEN; that is to say, officers who, being employed on the staff, are not available for regimental duty.

PAPER-MARRIAGE, *subs. phr.* (common).—A Society wedding. [The fees are paid in bank notes.]

PAPER-MILL, THE, *subs. phr.* (old legal).—The Record Office of the Court of Queen's Bench.

PAPER-SCULL, *subs.* (old).—A fool: hence PAPER-SCULLED = foolish; silly: *see* BUFFLE. — B. E. (*c.*1696); GROSE (1785).

PAPER-STAINER, *subs. phr.* (common).—An author, or clerk: in contempt.

PAP-FEEDER, *subs.* (old).—A spoon.

1858. A. MAYHEW, *Paved with Gold*, III. iii. 268. In the hopes of purloining a silver PAP FEEDER.

PAP-HEAD, *subs.* (old).—A woman's nipple; the CHERRYLET (*q.v.*).—PALSGRAVE (1530).

PAPHIAN, *subs.* (literary).—A prostitute. [Paphos a city in Cyprus sacred to Venus]. *See* TART.

PAPLER. *See* POPLAR.

PAP-MOUTH, *subs. phr.* (old).—An effeminate man.

PAPOOSE, *subs.* (colloquial). — A child; a KID (*q.v.*). [Of Indian origin.]

1634. W. WOOD, *New England's Prosp.*, 96. This little PAPPOUSE travells about with his bare footed mother to paddle in the Icie Clammbankes.

1677. MATHER, *New England* (1864), 197. To make the English believe those base PAPOOSES were of royal Progeny.

1683. ROGER WILLIAMS [BARTLETT]. PAPOOSE . . . among the native Indians of New England, a babe or young child.

18 [?]. DOW, *Sermons* [BARTLETT] Where the Indian squaw hung her young PAPPOOSE upon the bough, and left it to squall at the hush-a-by of the blast, the Anglo-Saxon mother now rocks the cradle of her delicate babe.

PAR, *subs.* (old colloquial: now recognised).—1. *See* quot.

*c.*1696. B. E. *Dict. Cant. Crew*, s.v. PAR, gold and silver at a like Proportion.

2. (colloquial).—An abbreviation of 'paragraph.'

1885. *Sat. Review*, 7 Feb., 163. It is natural that the reporter should want news. PARS are as much his quarry as dynamiters are that of the police.

1891. *Morning Advertiser*, 28 Mar. I cannot give the wording of the PAR, but here is a faithful digest of it.

PARADE, TO BURN THE PARADE, *verb. phr.* (old).—*See* quot.

1785. GROSE, *Vulg. Tongue*, s.v. Warning more men for a guard than were necessary, and excusing the supernumeraries for money. . . . A practice formerly winked at in most garrisons, a perquisite to the adjutants and sergeant majors; the pretence for it was to purchase coal and candle for the guard, whence it was called BURNING THE PARADE.

PARADER, *subs.* (old).—1. A person of good figure and address employed to walk up and down in front of, or inside a shop; a shop-walker: *cf.* BARKER. Hence (2) a person or thing that by challenging attention acts as a foil or set-off.

1748. RICHARDSON, *Clarissa*, ii. 3. What think you . . . of rejecting both your men and encouraging my PARADER.

1821. EGAN, *Anec. of Turf*, 179. His fine figure obtained him employment as a PARADER to Richardson.

PARADISE, *subs.* (popular).—1. The gallery of a theatre; THE GODS (*q.v.*). Fr. *le paradis.*

2. (University).—A grove of trees outside St. John's College, Oxford.

3. (venery).—The female *pudendum*: *cf.* THE WAY TO HEAVEN: *see* MONOSYLLABLE.

*d.*1638. CAREW, *A Rapture*, 59. So will I rifle all the sweets that dwell In thy delicious PARADISE.

1640. HERRICK, *Disc. of a Woman*, 72. This loue-guarded PARRADICE.

*c.*1697. APHRA BEHN, *Poems* (2nd ed.), 70. His daring Hand that Altar seiz'd, Where Gods of Love do Sacrifice: That Awful Throne, the PARADISE.

FOOL'S PARADISE, *subs. phr.* (colloquial).—A state of fancied security, enjoyment, &c.

1528. ROY, *Rede Me, &c.* [OLIPHANT, *New Eng.*, i. 446]. A FOLES PARADYSE.

1591. SHAKSPEARE, *Romeo and Juliet*, ii. 4. If ye should lead her into a FOOL'S PARADISE, as they say, it were a very gross kind of behaviour.

1607. DEKKER, *Westward Hoe*, v. 1. Since we ha' brought 'em thus far into a FOOL'S PARADISE, leave 'em in't.

1733. BAILEY, *Erasmus Coll.* (1900), ii. 173. The designing courtier had been for a long time kept in FOOL'S PARADISE.

1896. COTSFORD DICK, *Ways of World*, 20. So she dreamt of a PARADISE (fool so fair!) Whose glories she now is allowed to share.

1898. BRADDON, *Rough Justice*, 22. She had exchanged a wretched wandering Life with her father for a FOOL'S PARADISE at the West End of London.

TO HAVE (or GET) A PENN'ORTH OF PARADISE, *verb. phr.* (common).—To take drink, esp. gin: *see* SCREWED.

PARALYSED, *subs.* (common).—Drunk: *see* DRINKS and SCREWED.

PARALYTIC-FIT (or **-STROKE**), *subs. phr.* (tailors').—A badly fitting garment — that 'fits where it touches.'

PARAM, *subs.* (Old Cant).—Milk: also YARUM.—HARMAN (1573).

PARCEL, *subs.* (racing). — The day's winnings; a pocket-book.

1898. *Pink 'Un and Pelican*, 227. Here it was that Exile No. 1 made the painful discovery that he'd lost his PARCEL. His pocket-book and all it contained had vanished.

1901. *Sporting Times*, 6 Ap., 1, 3. No less than four winners did the wily one back. "My word!" he cried, "I shall have a pretty little PARCEL in my kick."

PARCEL-BAWD, *subs. phr.* (old).—One whose employment was partly that of bawd. [PARCEL = part: as 'parcel-gilt' = partly gilt.]

1603. SHAKSPEARE, *Meas. for Meas.*, i. 2. A tapster, sir! PARCEL-BAWD; one that serves a bad woman.

PARD, *subs.* (chiefly American).—A partner; a CHUM (*.v*).

1872. CLEMENS, *Roughing It*, ii. He was the bulliest man in the mountains, PARD.

1882. MCCABE, *New York*, xxiii. 398. Let's have a shake-down for me and my PARD, for the night.

1889. *Mod. Society*, 19 Oct., 1296. We got such a strain, me and my PARD, starting the car, that we ought to have been entitled to a lay-off for a week.

PARENTHESIS, *subs.* (printers').—*In pl.* = a pair of bandy legs.

WOODEN PARENTHESIS, *subs. phr.* (old).—A pillory.—GROSE (1785).

IRON PARENTHESIS, *subs. phr.* (old).—A prison: *see* CAGE and STIR.—GROSE (1785).

TO HAVE ONE'S NOSE (or BOWSPRIT) IN PARENTHESIS, *verb. phr.* (old).—To have it pulled.—GROSE (1785). Also *see* quot.

1823. BEE, *Dict. Turf*, s.v. PARENTHESIS (a)—it is this thing, itself ( ); and when a man's nose, or any prominent part of him, may get irrevocably between the thing—he is in a bad way: some few novices have died of it.

PARINGS, *subs.* (Old Cant).—Clippings of money. — B. E. (*c.*1696).

PARISH. HIS STOCKINGS BELONG TO TWO PARISHES, *phr.* (old).—Odd; mis-paired.—GROSE (1785).

PARISH-BULL (**-PRIG**, or **-STALLION**), *subs. phr.* (thieves').—1. A parson: *see* DEVIL-DODGER.—GROSE (1785). Also (2) *see* MUTTON-MONGER.

PARISH-LANTERN, *subs. phr.* (old).—The moon; OLIVER (*q.v.*); NOOM (*q.v.*). Fr. synonyms are *la cafarde* (= the tell-tale); *la cymbale*; *la luisante* (or *luisarde*); *la grosse lentille*; *la moucharde*; *la pâlote*; and *le pair*.

1847. HALLIWELL, *Arch. Words*, s.v.

1887. J. ASHTON, *Eighteenth Cent. Waifs*, 235 *note*. The link-boy's natural hatred of the PARISH LANTERN which would deprive him of his livelihood.

PARISH-SOLDIER, *subs. phr.* (old).—*See* quot. and MUDCRUSHER.

1785. GROSE, *Vulg. Tongue*, s.v. PARISH SOLDIER. A jeering name for a militia-man: from substitutes being frequently hired by the Parish.

PARK, *subs.* (common).—1. A prison: *see* CAGE and STIR. Also as in quot. 1823.

1823. BEE, *Dict. Turf*, s.v. PARK. . . . The PARK is also the rules or privileged circuit round the king's bench or fleet. 'The PARK is well stocked,' when many prisoners have obtained the rules.

1847. HALLIWELL, *Arch. Words*, s.v.

2. (common).—A back yard; a strip of town-garden.

PARKER, *verb.* (tramps').—*See* quot.

1893. EMERSON, *Signor Lippo*, xiv. Have you PARKERED to the omer for your letties? *Ibid.* I get no regular PARKERING-ninty. *Ibid.* xx. She had to PARKER letty every darkie, and PARKER for someone to look arter me.

PARKEY (or **PARKY**), *adj.* and *adv.* (tramps').—Cold; uncomfortable: as when sleeping in the open.

1898. *Pink 'Un and Pelican*, 273. 'Morning, William; cold s'morning?' remarked the victualler patronisingly. 'It is a bit PARKY,' assented William.

PARK-RAILINGS (or **-PALINGS**), *subs. phr.* (common).—1. The teeth: *see* GRINDERS.—GROSE (1785).

2. (common). — The neck of mutton.

PARLEYVOO, *sub.* (school).—The conventional school study and use of the French language: hence, as *verb* = to speak French; to talk gibberish.

1837. BARHAM, *Ingoldsby Legends*, 'Bagman's Dog.' Grimacing and what sailors call PARLEYVOOING.

1843. MACAULAY, *St. Dennis and St. George*. He kept six French masters to teach him PARLEYVOO.

*d.*1891. LOWELL, *Oracle of the Goldfishes*. No words to spell, no sums to do, No Nepos and no PARLYVOO.

PARLIAMENTARY-PRESS, *subs. phr.* (tailors').—*See* quot.

1889. *Slang, Jargon, and Cant.* s.v. PARLIAMENTARY PRESS . . . an old custom of claiming any iron, which happens to be in use, for the purpose of opening the collar seam.

PARLOUR (or FRONT PARLOUR, *subs. phr.* (venery).—The female *pudendum*: *see* MONOSYLLABLE.

1823. BEE, *Dict. Turf*, s.v. PARLOUR—may be a room as well as some other thing. Mrs. Fubb's FRONT PARLOUR is no part of any building . . . she who is said to let out her PARLOUR and lie backward, cannot be supposed to repose with her face downwards.

OUT OF THE PARLOR INTO THE KITCHEN, *phr.* (old).—From better to worse; 'out of God's blessing into the warm sun.'

1598. FLORIO, *Worlde of Wordes*, s.v. *Da baiante a ferrante* . . . OUT OF THE PARLOR INTO THE KITCHEN.

PARLOUR FULL OF RAZORS, *subs. phr.* (American).—Claret with seltzer or lemonade: *see* DRINKS.

PARLOUR-JUMPING, *subs. phr.* (thieves').—Robbing rooms: specifically by window-entry: *see* JUMP.

1879. *Autobiography of a Thief* [*Macmillan's Mag.* xl. 500.] I palled in with some older hands at the game, who used to take me PARLOUR-JUMPING.

PARNEL. *See* PANEL.

PARNEE (or **PAUNEE**), *subs.* (theatrical).—Rain. DOWRY OF PARNEY = plenty of rain. PAWNEE-GAME = water-drinking. [Hindoo *pani* = water: *cf.* BRANDY-PAWNEE; Gipsy *pane*.]

1851. MAYHEW, *London Lab.*, iii. 149. PARNI is rain [among strolling actors].

1893. EMERSON, *Signor Lippo*, xiv. Arter a bit the old man gets him a berth . . . So he sticks to the PAWNEE GAME . . . long enough to learn the graft.

PARROT (or **PARROTEER**), *subs.* (colloquial).—A talkative person, esp. one given to mechanical repetition. Whence, as *verb* = to chatter; to repeat mechanically. Also PARROTRY = servile imitation; PARROT-LAWYER = a solicitor obsequious to a client's Yea and Nay.

1612. CHAPMAN, *Widow's Tears*, v. 5. If you PARROT to me long—go to.

16 [?]. T. ADAMS, *Works*, I. 16. They have their bandogs, corrupt solicitors, PARROT LAWYERS that are their properties and mere trunks.

*d.*1859. DE QUINCEY, *Style*, iii. Passages of great musical effect . . . vulgarised by too perpetual a PARROTING.

18 [?]. HALL, *False Philol.* 31. The verb experience is, to Mr. White, PARROTING Dean Alford, altogether objectionable.

1873. MILL, *Autobiog.*, 31. Mere PARROTEERS of what they have learnt.

See ALMOND.

PARSLEY, *subs.* (venery). — The pubic hair: *see* FLEECE. Hence PARSLEY-BED = the female *pudendum*: *see* MONOSYLLABLE; TO TAKE A TURN AMONG THE PARSLEY = to copulate.

1707. *Old Song* [FARMER, *Merry Songs and Ballads* (1897), I S. III. 131]. It was said, that one Mr. Ed—mond, Did both dig and sow in her PARSLY-BED.

1719. WARD, *London Spy*, I. 36. I am very glad it's no worse; I was never so scar'd since I pop'd out of the PARSLEY BED.

1851. *Notes and Queries*, 1, S. vi. 517. I was told that little girls came out of a PARSLEY-BED, and little boys from under a gooseberry bush. *Ibid.* 5 S. iii. (1875) 'Babies in Folk-lore.' In England every little girl knows that the male babies come from the NETTLE-BED, and the female ones from the parsley-bed.

PARSON, *subs.* (old).—A wayside SIGN-POST (*q.v.*).—GROSE (1785).

Verb. (colloquial). — 1. To marry; and (2) to church (after child-delivery). Whence PARSONED = married or churched; MARRIED AND PARSONED = duly and legally married.

TO KISS THE PARSON'S WIFE, *verb. phr.* (old).—To be lucky in horse-flesh.—GROSE (1785).

REMEMBER PARSON MALLUM! *intj. phr.* (old).—'Pray drink about Sir.'—B. E. (1696).

MARYLAND PARSON, *subs. phr.* (American). — A disreputable cleric.

PARSON PALMER, *subs. phr.* (old).—*See* quot.

1785. GROSE, *Vulg. Tongue*, s.v. PARSON PALMER. One who stops the circulation of the glass, by preaching over his liquor, as it is said was done by a parson of that name whose cellar was under his pulpit.

PARSON'S BARN, *subs. phr.* (old).—A barn never so full but there is room for more.

PARSON'S-JOURNEYMAN, *subs. phr.* (common).—A curate. — GROSE (1785).

PARSON'S-NOSE, *subs. phr.* (common).—A chicken's rump: *cf.* POPE'S NOSE and POPE'S-EYE: Fr. *le bonnet d'évêque*.

PARSON'S LEMAN. *See* TENDER.

PARSON'S WEEK, *subs. phr.* (clerical).—The period from Monday to Saturday.

1800. PRICE, *Life of H. F. Carey*, i. 144. Get my duty done for a Sunday, so that I may be out a PARSON'S WEEK.

PART, *verb.* (colloquial).—To pay; to restore; to give: hence PARTER = a paymaster, good or bad. *Cf.* 'a fool and his money are soon parted' (TUSSER, 1573, and HOWELL, 1617).

1670. *Old Ballad*, 'Seaman's Adieu.' Some . . . Have PARTED with their ready rino.

1880. SIMS, *Three Brass Balls*, xix. The top floor rarely PARTED before Monday morning.

1888. RUNCIMAN, *Chequers*, 106. If I could get the mater to PART.

1892. *Ally Sloper*, 2 April, 107, 2. 'Hand over the other tenner.' Miss Mudge PARTED cheerfully.

1896. FARJEON, *Betray. John Fordham*, III. 281. But it was no go; them as gathered round wouldn't PART.

PARTS BELOW (PARTS MORE DEAR, OF SHAME, OF CARNAL, OF OTHER PARTS).—1. The female *pudendum: see* MONOSYLLABLE; and (2) the *penis* and *testes: see* PRICK: also OTHER PARTS = the paps; PARTS BEHIND = the buttocks.

1620-50. *Percy Folio MS.*, f. 480 [FARMER, *Merry Songs and Ballads* (1897), iii. 31]. Yett, for her PARTS BELOW, there's not a woman ffairer to the showe.

1656. *Muses Recr.* [HOTTEN], 33. Forehead, eyes . . . Breast . . . Neck . . . And OTHER PARTS not evident.

*b.*1683. *Roxburghe Ballads*, i. 66-7. Skinne white as snow . . . brest soft as doune, . . . PARTS BELOW . . . all firme and sound.

1731-5. POPE, *Moral Essays*, II. 67. A very heathen in the CARNAL PART, Yet still a sad, good Christian at her heart.

PARTICULAR, *subs.* (old).—A favorite mistress: Fr. *une particulière: see* TART. Also (generally) a special choice: *e.g.*, to 'ride one's own PARTICULAR,' to 'a glass of one's PARTICULAR,' &c.: *see* SPECIAL.

PARTICULAR JESSE. *See* JESSE.

LONDON PARTICULAR (or LONDON IVY), *subs. phr.* (common).—A thick yellow or black fog, the product of certain atmospheric conditions and carbon: formerly peculiar to London, now common in most large manufacturing cities situated near water and lying low.

1852. DICKENS, *Bleak House*, iii. 'Was a great fire any-where?' 'O dear no, miss,' he said. 'This is a LONDON PARTICULAR.'

1889. *Sport. Life*, 4 Jan. A cold caught by contact with LONDON IVY.

1890. *Sportsman*, 13 Dec. From the question of cost . . . a clean sweep should be made of LONDON PARTICULAR.

1891. *Belfort's Magazine*, Sep., 29. But the crowning masterpiece of the climate is a London fog, locally known as a LONDON PARTICULAR.

1896. SALA, *London Up to Date*, 86. It happens to be a LONDON PARTICULAR foggy morning.

1897. *Daily Chronicle*, 20 Dec., 6, 4. The real LONDON PARTICULAR . . . played sad havoc with the traffic arrangements.

PARTLET, *subs.* (old colloquial).—A woman.

1598. SHAKSPEARE, *1 Henry IV.*, iii. 3. How now, Dame PARTLET. *Ibid. Winter's Tale* (1604), ii. 3. Thou dotard, thou art woman tyr'd, unroosted By thy dame PARTLET here!

PARTNER. *See* SLEEPING PARTNER.

PARTRIDGE, *subs.* (old).—A whore: *cf.* PLOVER.

*c.*1700. *Old Song.* [FARMER, *Merry Songs and Ballads* (1897), iv. 247.] Go home, ye Fop . . . And for half Crown a Doxey get, But seek no more a PARTRIDGE here.

PARTY, *subs.* (once literary: now vulgar).—A person; an individual. *See* COVE.—BAILEY (1744).

1542. UDALL, *Apoph. of Erasmus* [ROBERTS, 1877], 325. To please all PARTIES [PARTY = *homo* occurs *passim*].

1596. JONSON, *Every Man in Humour*, iv. 9. See when the PARTY comes you must arrest . . . him quickly.

1538. FLORIO, *Worlde of Wordes*, s.v. *Zuccoli.* We vse also to say so, when speaking of anybody in secrecie, and the PARTIE comes in.

1609. SHAKSPEARE, *Tempest*, iii. 2. Canst thou bring me to the PARTY?

1837. *Comic Almanack*, 103. A werry slap-up PARTY, I assure you.

1852. DICKENS, *Bleak House*, xxii. My little woman . . . attends the Evening Exertions . . . of a reverend PARTY of the name of Chadband.

1864. YATES, *Broken to Harness*, xxxiii. Mr. Schröder . . . a good old cock, sir; a worthy old PARTY; kind-hearted, and all that.

1885. *Daily Telegraph*, 25 Aug. The seedy-looking old PARTY . . . may be worth a million of money.

1895. IOTA, *Comedy in Spasms*, I. He had dropped into the nursery shortly after luncheon, and . . . stumbled on an ecstatic PARTY, nearly naked.

PARTY-ROLL, *subs. phr.* (Winchester College).—A list of boys going home together: *see* PEAL.

PASS, *verb.* (colloquial).—To fail to understand; to have no concern in: *e.g.*, I PASS=I don't know what you are driving at. [From euchre.]

TO PASS (or HAND) IN ONE'S CHIPS (or CHECKS), *verb. phr.* (American).—To die: *see* ALOFT. [From adjusting one's accounts at poker.]

1872. CLEMENS, *Roughing It*, 332. One of the boys has PASSED IN HIS CHECKS, and we want to give him a good send-off.

1892. NISBET, *Bushranger's Sweetheart*, 310. Money-lending Mortimer . . . PASSED IN HIS CHECKS quite unexpectedly, without leaving a will.

TO PASS THE TIME OF DAY, *verb. phr.* (colloquial).—To salute.

1851-6. MAYHEW, *Lond. Lab.*, II. 489. The police . . . are very friendly. They'll PASS THE TIME OF DAY with me.

1900. SIMS, *London's Heart*, 4. I thought it was only right to PASS THE TIME O' DAY to an old pal.

TO PASS THE COMPLIMENT, *verb. phr.* (common).—To offer (or give) a douceur; to tip.

PASSAGE-AT-ARMS, *subs. phr.* (colloquial).—A squabble; a row.

PASSENGER, *subs.* (rowing).—An oar who, from incompetence or accident, is unable to do his share of the work.

TO WAKE UP THE WRONG PASSENGER, *verb. phr.* (American).—To 'mistake one's man'; to commit an error of judgment in regard to character, action, or motive. [From transcontinental travel.]

1855. HALIBURTON, *Human Nature*, 289. 'Poor, ignorant wretch!' 'Massa,' replied the negro, 'you have WAKED UP DE WRONG PASSENGER dis time. I isn't poor. I ab plenty to eat and plenty to drink.'

1871. *Ev. Post* (Chicago), 21 Ap. He had clearly found out that in making the attack he had WAKED UP THE WRONG PASSENGER.

PASSIONS. *See* POCKET.

PASSY, *adj.* (Christ's Hospital).—Severe: of a master. [That is 'passionate'—BLANCH.] Now obsolete; the modern equivalent is VISH (*q.v.*)

1844. *Remin. Ch. H.* [*The Blue*, Aug. 1874]. Punishment depended less on correctness than on temper. Anxiously the question was asked, 'Is he PASSY this morning?' and of a new master our first queries were of his manners and temper [abridged].

PAST. PAST COMPLAINING, *phr.* (old).—*See* quot.

1785. GROSE, *Vulg. Tongue.* The man is PAST COMPLAINING, saying of a person murdered for resisting the robbers.

TO BE PAST DYING OF A FIRST CHILD, *verb. phr.* (old).—To have had a bastard. RAY (1767).

[COLLOQUIALISMS are: PAST BELIEVING = incredible; PAST PRAYING FOR = hopeless; PAST-MASTER (or -MISTRESS) = an adept; PAST WHOOPING = undeniable, beyond question; PAST-PRICE = invaluable. *See* also MARK OF MOUTH.]

1602. DAVIES, *Mirum in Modum* [GROSART, *Works*, i. 6]. The Soule is such a precious thing As costs the price of PAST-PRICE deerest bloud.

PASTE, *subs.* (printers').—Brains. [From 'paste-and-scissors': in sarcasm.]

Verb. (common).—To beat; to thrash: specifically to slap the face right and left. [From bill-sticking]. Hence PASTING = a drubbing.

1851. MAYHEW, *London Lab.*, I. 461. He . . . gave me a regular PASTING.

1882. *Daily Telegraph*, 6 Oct. 2, 2. No matter how he punches her and PASTES her, she won't give in about that.

1887. HENLEY, *Villon's Good Night.* PASTE 'EM, and larrup 'em, and lamm! Give Kennedy, and make 'em crawl!

1888. *Sport. Life*, 11 Dec. Set to work in earnest, and, driving his man round the ring, PASTED him in rare style.

1896. CRANE, *Maggie*, iii. I'll PASTE yeh when I ketch yeh!

PASTE-AND-SCISSORS, *subs. phr.* (journalistic).—Extracts; 'padding': as distinguished from original matter.

PASTEBOARD, *subs.* (common).—1. A playing card.

1857. THACKERAY, *Virginians*, xv. The company voted . . . three honours in their hand, and some good court cards, more beautiful than the loveliest scene of nature; . . . hour after hour delightfully spent over the PASTEBOARD.

1896. FARJEON, *Betrayal of John Fordham*, III. 277. I might 'ave done well among the swells, I'm that neat with the PASTEBOARDS. I can shuffle 'em any way I want, kings at top, aces at bottom, in the middle, anywhere you like.

2. (common).—A visiting card. Also as *verb* (or TO SHOOT, or DROP, ONE'S PASTEBOARD) = to leave a visiting card at a person's house.

1849. THACKERAY, *Pendennis*, xxxvi. We shall only have to leave our PASTEBOARDS.

1861. HUGHES, *Tom Brown at Oxford*, xxv. I shall just leave a PASTEBOARD.

1886. KENNARD, *Brown Habit*, x. I told my missus to drop a card on you to-day. You see . . . we hunting men have not much time for that sort of thing; and PASTEBOARD leaving is quite out of my line.

1891. *Ally Sloper*, 3 Jan. Then his PASTEBOARD he presented—puffed a cigarette, contented.

1897. MITFORD, *Romance Cape Frontier*, ii. 'Engaged,' said the sharp boy. . . . 'Take that PASTEBOARD in.'

PASTEBOARD-CUSTOMER, *subs.phr.* (trade).—A customer taking long credit.

PASTE-HORN, *subs.* (shoemakers').—The nose: *see* CONK: hence OLD PASTE-HORN = a large-nosed man.

1856. MAYHEW, *World of London*, 6, *note.* Upon this principle the mouth has come to be styled the 'tater-trap'; . . . the nose, the PASTE-HORN.

PASTERN, *subs.* (common).—In *pl.* = the feet: *see* CREEPERS. Hence, FULL IN THE PASTERNS = thick-ankled.

1700. DRYDEN, *Wife of Bath's Tale*, 32. So straight she walked on her PASTERNS high.

PASTY, *subs.* (common).—A bookbinder.

Adj. (colloquial).—Out of sorts; angry; OFF COLOUR (*q.v.*).

1885. *Daily Telegraph*, 25 Aug. A mealy-faced, at least a PASTY-FACED boy.

1891. NEWMAN, *Scamping Tricks*, 2. I feel PASTY, but am better now.

1892. MILLIKEN, *'Arry Ballads*, 65. Miss Bonsor went PASTY, and reared.

PAT, *subs.* (common).—An Irishman. Also PATLANDER.

1828. BEE, *Picture of London*, 170. Mild rebuke is little calculated to cool a PATLANDER.

1836. SCOTT, *Tom Cringle.* The officer was a PATLANDER.

Adj. and *adv.* (old: now recognised).—Apt, convenient, suitable; timely; exactly to the purpose.—B. E. (*c.*1696); GROSE (1785).

1592. SHAKSPEARE, *Mid. Night's Dream*, v. 1. It will be full PAT as I told you.

1612. BEAUMONT and FLETCHER, *Coxcomb*, iii. 2. This falls out PAT.

1678. BUTLER, *Hudibras*, III. iii. I thank you, . . . 'tis to my purpose PAT.

1838. *Comic Almanack*, 137. 'Tis a matter, I know, that you're PAT in.

1869. BLACKMORE, *Lorna Doone*, lvii. You are very PAT with my grand-daughter's name, young man.

1895. MARRIOTT-WATSON [*New Review*, 16 July]. A . . . brave bold tongue you ply . . . You have it all PAT.

PATCH, *subs.* (old colloquial).—1. A saucy fellow; a fool. Primarily, the domestic jester. Hence CROSS-PATCH = an ill-natured fool: as in the children's rhyme:—CROSS-PATCH, draw the latch, Sit by the fire and spin.

1579. LYLY, *Euphues, England*, 296. When I heard my Physition so PAT to hit my disease I could not dissemble with him.

1588. *Marprelate's Epistle* (ARBER), 3. Bridges was a verie PATCH and a dims when he was in Cambridge.

1592. SHAKSPEARE, *Mids. Night's Dream*, iii. 2. A crew of PATCHES . . . That work for bread upon Athenian stalls.

1595. *Menæchmi* [HALLIWELL]. Why doating PATCH, didst thou not come with me . . . from the ship?

1598. FLORIO, *Worlde of Wordes. Coticone*, a great gull, sot, PATCH, lubbar.

1619. FLETCHER, *Wild Goose Chase*, iv. 2. Call me PATCH and puppy, And beat me if you please.

1633. MASSINGER, *Old Debts*, v. The ideot, the PATCH, the slave, the booby.

1830. SCOTT, *Doom of Devorgoil*, ii. 1. Thou art a foolish PATCH.

1840. CUNNINGHAM [Glossarial Index to GIFFORD'S *Massinger*, s.v.]. PATCH was the cant name of a fool kept by Cardinal Wolsey . . . transmitting his appellation to a very numerous body of descendants.

2. (venery).—The female *pudendum: see* MONOSYLLABLE.

NOT A PATCH UPON, *phr.* (common).—Not to compare to.

1861. READE, *Cloister and Hearth*, xxxvii. NOT A PATCH UPON you for looks.

1884. RUSSELL, *Jack's Courtship*, xvii. Is Wellington a PATCH UPON the living splendid generals?

1888. BOLDREWOOD, *Robbery under Arms*, xxviii. There isn't a woman here that's a PATCH ON her for looks.

1897. MITFORD, *Romance Cape Frontier*, I. xv. I don't think she's A PATCH ON Miss Brathwaite; but there's something awfully fetching about her.

PATCHEY, *subs.* (theatrical).—The harlequin; SPANGLE-MAKER (*q.v.*)

PATE, *subs.* (old colloquial).—The head: almost always in derision: *see* CRUMPET.—GROSE (1785).

1604. SHAKSPEARE, *Winter's Tale*, i. 2. Was this taken By any understanding PATE but thine?

1622. FLETCHER, *Sp. Curate*, iii. 4. She gave my PATE a sound knock that it rings yet.

1825. JONES, *True-Bottom'd Boxer* [*Univ. Songst.* ii. 96.] Shaking a flipper, and milling a PATE.

1836. BARHAM, *Ingoldsby Legends*, I. 54. The thin grey locks of his failing hair Have left his little bald PATE all bare.

PATENT-COAT, *subs. phr.* (obsolete).—*See* quot.

1857. SNOWDEN, *Mag. Assist.* 446. Inside skirt coat pocket—PATENT COAT.

PATENT-DIGESTER, *subs.* (common).—*See* quot)

1836. DICKENS, *Pickwick*, xxxviii. Ben . . . bring out the PATENT DIGESTER. Mr. Benjamin Allen smiled . . . and produced . . . a black bottle half full of brandy.

PATENT FRENCHMAN, *subs. phr.* (tailors').—An Irishman.

PATENT-INSIDE (or **-OUTSIDE**), *subs. phr.* (journalistic).—A newspaper printed on the inside (or outside) only, the unprinted space being intended for local news, advertisements, &c.

PATENT SAFETIES (THE), *subs. phr.* (military).—The First Life Guards. Also "The Cheeses"; "The Piccadilly Butchers"; and "The Tin Bellies."

PATER-COVE. *See* PATRICO.

PATERNOSTER, *subs.* (anglers').—A fishing-line with hooks and shot at regular intervals. [As beads on a rosary.]

1849. C. KINGSLEY, *Yeast*, iii. Here's that PATERNOSTER as you gave me to rig up.

DEVIL'S PATERNOSTER, *subs. phr.* (old). — A muttering or grumbling; a profane expletive.

1383. CHAUCER, *Canterbury Tales* (1856), 540. Grutche and murmure prively for veray despit; which wordes they call THE DIVELS PATER NOSTER, though so be that the divel had never Pater noster but that lewed folke yeven it swiche a name.

1614. TERENCE in English [NARES]. What DEVILLS PATERNOSTER is this he is saying?

APE'S PATERNOSTER. *See* APE.

IN A PATERNOSTER WHILE, *phr.* (old).—Quickly; in a JIFFEY (*q.v.*). [While one could say a paternoster.]

1362. LANGLAND, *Piers Plowman*, 3169. He pissed a potel IN A PATERNOSTER WHILE.

1422-1509. *Paston Letters*, i. 74. All . . . don . . . in a PATERNOSTER WYLE.

1597. LANGHAM, *Garden of Health* [SMYTHE-PALMER]. [A direction to boil onions] WHILE one may say three PATERNOSTERS.

[?]. FARINDON, *Sermons* [JACKSON, iv. 241]. Indeed, there is nothing sooner said, we may do it IN A PATER-NOSTER-WHILE.

PATHIC, *subs.* (old).—A pederast; an INGLE (*q.v.*): *see* USHER.

1603. JONSON, *Sejanus*, I. 2. The noted PATHIC of his time.

1748. SMOLLETT, *Roderick Random*, li. His valet-de-chambre, who, it seems, had been the favourite PATHIC of his lord.

1750. ROBERTSON, *Poems*, 56. Your PATHICK cannot boast an A— so fair as I.

PATIENCE ON A MONUMENT, *subs. phr.* (colloquial).—A long-suffering person.

1892. HENLEY and STEVENSON, *Three Plays* ['Beau Austin,' i. 2]. Dolly, I must insist on your eating a good breakfast: I cannot away with your pale cheeks and that PATIENCE-ON-A-MONUMENT kind of look.

PATRICO, *subs.* (Old Cant).—A vagabond, or unfrocked priest; a HEDGE-PRIEST (*q.v.*): *also* PATRIARCK-CO, PATRICOVE, PATTERING-COVE and PATER-COVE. [Suggested derivations are: (1) PATER = father + COVE = a man; *cf.* PATRIARCK-CO; (2) PATTER (or PATTERING) = talk + COVE, *i.e.*, a patterer or mutterer of paternosters = a priest.]—B. E. (*c.*1696); GROSE (1785).

1536. COPLAND, *Spyttel-hous* [FARMER, *Musa Pedestris* (1896), 1]. Teare the PATRYNG COUE in the darkeman cace Docked the dell.

1565. AWDELEY, *Vacabondes* [E. E. T. S. (1896), 6]. A PATRIARKE-CO doth make marriages . . . untill death depart . . . after this sort: when they come to a dead horse or any dead catell, then they shake hands, and so depart every one of them a severall way.

1567. HARMAN, *Caveat* [E. E. T. S. (1896), 89]. There was a proude PATRICO and a nosegent, He tooke his Iockam in his Famble, and a wappinge he went.

1610. ROWLANDS, *Martin Markall*, 40 (H. Club's Repr. 1874), s.v.

1614. JONSON, *Bartholomew Fair*, ii. You are the PATRICO, are you? the patriarch of the cut-purses? *Ibid. Staple of News* (1625), iv. 1. *Alm.* A supercitious rogue! he looks as if He were the PATRICO. *Mad.* Or archpriest of Canters.

1622. BEAUMONT and FLETCHER, *Beggar's Bush*, ii. 1. What name or title e'er they bear, Jarkman, or PATRICO, Cranke, or Clapper-dudgeon.

1725. *Old Song* [FARMER, *Musa Pedestris* (1896), 45]. But alas! 'tis my fear that the false PATRI-COE Is reaping those transports are only my due.

1749. *Old Song* [FARMER, *Musa Pedestris* (1896), 51]. No whip-jack, palliard, PATRICO; No jarkman, be he high or low.

1791. CAREW, *Bamphylde-Moore Carew*. Cadge-cloak, curtal, or curmudgeon; no Whip-Jack, palliard, PATRICO.

1827. LYTTON, *Pelham*, lxxx. My idea at the moment was to disguise myself in the dress of the PATER COVE and perform the double job.

1834. AINSWORTH, *Rookwood*, III. iv. This venerable personage was no other than the PATRICO . . . or hierophant of the canting crew.

1892. HENLEY and STEVENSON, *Deacon Brodie*, iii. 2. He's a PATTER-COVE from Seven Dials.

PATTENS. TO RUN ON PATTENS *verb. phr.* (common).—To clatter; 'to talk nineteen to the dozen.'

1575. STILL, *Gammer Gurton's Needle*, ii. 4. The tongue it WENT ON PATINS, by him that Judas sold!

[?]. *Taming of a Shrew* [CHILD, *Ballads*, VIII. 185.] Stil hir tongue ON PATTENS RAN Though many blowes she caught.

PATTER, *subs.* (common).—1 Originally muttering (of paternosters): hence, talk of any kind, but specifically (1) the inconsequent orations of CHEAP JACKS (*q.v.*), BUSKERS (*q.v.*), or showmen; and (2) the dialect or cant of a class. Hence also PATTER = a piece of street literature; a PIN-UP (*q.v.*); a SLUM (*q.v.*). Hence, PATTERER = a vendor of street literature: with RUNNING-PATTERER (or STATIONER): obsolete since police control of traffic. Also as *adj.* and *verb*, whence TO PATTER FLASH = to talk slang or cant; TO FLASH THE PATTER = to talk, or to talk slang; to STAND (OR BE IN FOR) THE PATTER = (thieves') to stand for trial (VAUX, 1819, and HAGGART, 1821), HUMBOX-PATTERER = a parson. [Conjecturally from *Pater noster*: *see* quots. 1590 and 1864.] Also GAMMON AND PATTER.

ENGLISH SYNONYMS. To cackle; to cant; to chin; to chinwag; to chip; to chirp; to chow; to chuck it out; to clack; to confab; to crack; to cut; to Duke of York (rhyming = talk); to flam; to flummox by the lip; to gabble; to give lip; to jabber; to jaw; to jaw-hawk; to jerk chin-music; to ladle; to lip; to lip-labour; to mag; to mang; to pipe; to rap; to slam; to slang; to voker; to waffle; to wag the red rag; to warble.

FRENCH SYNONYMS. *Arçonner; arsouiller; bajoter; balancer la rouscaillante* (also *balancer son chiffon rouge* = 'to wag the red rag'); *baver; jaspiner bigorne* (= 'to patter flash': also *rouscailler bigorne*); *blaguer* (specifically to chaff); *bonir; bouffeter; cabasser; casser un mot; chamberter* (= to talk indiscreetly); *lever son copeau; cracher* (also *jouer du crachoir*); *débagouler; dégueularder; dépenser sa salive; dévider* (= 'to patter'; *dévider à l'éstorgue* = to flam; *dévider le jars* = 'to patter flash'; *dévider son peloton* = 'to clack'); *engueuler; gazouiller* (= 'warble'); *pousser sa glaire; glousser; faire peter*

son grelot; faire la jactance; jarguer (= to patter flash; also *jaspiner le jars*); *jarviller; javoter; radouber la lanterne; lantenni* (Breton cant.); *limer* (= 'to stutter'); *mouliner* (= to prattle: specifically of women); *pallasser; papoter; parlotter; rouscailler.*

*c.*1360. *Alliterative Poems* [MORRIS, p. 15, l. 485]. Thou coutheg neuer god nauther plese ne pray Ne neuer nawther PATER ne crede.

*c.*1394. *Piers Plowman's Creed*, 5. A, and all myn a b c, After have I lerned, And PATRED in my pater-noster Iche poynt after other.

1500. *How the Ploughman learned his Paternoster* [HALLIWELL]. Ever he PATRED on theyr names faste; Than he had them in ordre at the laste.

*d.*1536. TYNDALE, *Works*, 232. How blind are they which thinke prayer to be the PATTERING of many words.

1546. HEYWOOD, *Wit and Folly* [Percy Soc.], p. xxxvii. Lorde! how my husbande nowe doth PATTER, And of the pye styl doth clatter.

1561. *Godly Queene Hester* [GROSART], 22. By his crafti PATTERING, hath turned law into flattering.

1589. NASHE, *Month's Mind* [*Works*, i. 173]. See how like the old Ape this young Monkey PATTERETH.

*c.*1648. *Knaves No Honest Men, &c.* [COLLIER, *Roxburghe Ballads* (1847), xxi]. Marry, they say that the RUNNING STATIONERS of London, I mean such as used to sing ballads, and those that cry malignant pamphlets in the streets.

*c.*1696. B. E., *Dict. Cant. Crew*, s.v., PATERING.

1781. PARKER, *View of Society*, I. 200. I could PATTER him on the Cant Universities of Newgate, Bedlam, and Bridewell.

1785. GROSE, *Vulg. Tongue*, s.v., PATTERING. The maundering or pert replies of servants: also talk or palaver . . . to amuse one intended to be cheated. PATTERING of prayers; the confused sound of . . . praying together. *Ibid.* PATTER. How the blowen lushes jackey, and PATTERS FLASH.

1789. PARKER, *Life's Painter*, 150. GAMMON AND PATTER is the language of cant.

1819. SCOTT, *Bride of Lammermoor*, i. Your characters . . . PATTER too much.

1821. HAGGART, *Life*, 88. It was shown upon my PATTER that I had the dub in my fam.

*c.*1838. REYNOLDS, *The Housebreaker's Song* [FARMER, *Musa Pedestris* (1896), 125]. Though the HUM-BOX PATTERER talked of hell.

1841. LEMAN REDE, *Sixteen String Jack*, i. 6. Stash your PATTER and come along!

1851. MAYHEW, *London Lab.*, 228-51. The pattering genus known as RUNNING PATTERERS, or FLYING STATIONERS, from the fact of their being continually on the move . . . Contradistinguished from them, however, are the STANDING PATTERERS, [who] require, a 'pitch' . . . where they can hold forth . . . The long-song sellers did not depend upon PATTER—though some of them PATTERED a little. . . . The parsons came out as stunning patrons of the PATTER. . . . He PATTERS very little in the main drag. *Ibid.* i. 253. One quick-witted Irishman, whom I knew to be a Roman Catholic, was working a PATTER against the Pope.

1852. JUDSON, *Myst., &c., of New York*, iv. Nothin' much worth PATTERING about. *Ibid.* iv. PATTER FLASH, my lucky, you're as used to it as I am.

1853. DICKENS, *Bleak House*, xxxix. PATTER allusions to the subject, [are] received with loud applause.

1856. MAYHEW, *World of London*, 6, *note*. PATTER, . . . is borrowed merely from the PATER-NOSTERS that the old-established mendicants delighted to mumble.

1863. *Story of a Lancashire Thief*, 9. Joe was . . . a PATTERER; and could screeve a fakement with any one.

1864. HOTTEN, *Slang Dict.*, s.v. PATTER. . . . Probably from the *Latin*, PATERNOSTER . . . said, before the Reformation, in a 'low voice' by the priest, until he came to 'and lead us not into temptation,' to which the choir responded, 'but deliver us from evil.' In the reformed Prayer Book this was altered, and the Lord's Prayer directed to be said 'with an *loud voice.*' Dr. Pusey takes this view of the derivation in his *Letter to the Bishop of London*, 78, 1851.

1864. *Derby Day*, 155. She had finished the PATTER she had learnt by heart.

1877. *Five Years' Penal Servitude*, ii. 244. Well she could do the French's PATTER, as she'd been there afore, when she was living on the 'square.'

1880. SIMS, *Three Brass Balls*, xvii. It is thieves' PATTER, but someone in the crowd understands it well enough and answers him.

1883. *Daily News*, 26 March, 2, 4. A PATTER song . . . was twice redemanded.

1889. *Answers*, 11 May, 374. Beggars who cannot read are being taught hymns or doleful songs, PATTER as it is called professionally.

1891. NEWMAN, *Scamping Tricks*, 61. Pay me and I'll PATTER pretty; but no pay, no PATTER is my motto.

1897. *Sporting Times*, 13 Mar., 1, 3. She did it in a sort of "it's of no consequence" way that fairly amazed the learned counsel who was PATTERING on her behalf.

2. *Verb.* (common). — 1. *See subs.* 2. (Australian).—To eat.

1833. C. STURT, *Southern Australia*, II., vii. 223. He himself did not PATTER any of it.

1881. GRANT, *Bush Life*, I. 236. 'You PATTER potehuni.' 'Yohi,' said John, doubtful . . . how his stomach will agree with the strange meat.

PATTERAN, *subs.* (vagrants').—*See* quots.

1864. HOTTEN, *Slang Dict.*, s.v. PATTERAN, a gipsy trail, made by throwing down a handful of grass.

1877. BESANT and RICE, *Son of Vulcan*, I. xi. Maybe it's the gipsy's PATTERAN they mean.

PATTER-COVE. *See* PATRICO.

PATTER-CRIB, *subs.* (thieves').—A lodging-house or inn frequented by thieves; a FLASH-PANNY (*q.v.*).

PAUL. TO GO TO PAUL'S (or WESTMINSTER) FOR A WIFE, *verb. phr.* (old colloquial).—To go whoring: TO MOLROW (*q.v.*). [HALLIWELL: Old St. Paul's was in former times a favorite resort for purposes of business, amusement, lounging, or assignations; bills were fixed up there, servants hired, and a variety of matters performed wholly inconsistent with the sacred nature of the edifice.] Hence PAUL'S-WALKERS = loungers; AS WELL-KNOWN AS PAUL'S = notorious.

1598. SHAKSPEARE, *1 Henry IV.*, ii. 4. This oily rascal is KNOWN AS WELL AS PAUL'S.

1598. SHAKSPEARE, *2 Henry IV.*, i. 2, 58. I bought him in PAUL'S, and he'll buy me a horse in Smithfield: an I could get me but a wife in the stews, I were manned, horsed, and wived.

1670. RAY, *Proverbs*, 254. Who goes to Westminster for a wife, to ST. PAUL'S for a man, and to Smithfield for a horse, may meet with a whore, a knave, and a jade.

1807. MOSER, *European Magazine*, July. The young gallants . . . used to meet at the central point, St. Paul's; and from this circumstance obtained the appellation of PAUL'S WALKERS, as we now say *Bond Street Loungers.*

See also OLD; PETER; PIGEON.

PAUL PRY, *subs. phr.* (colloquial).—An inquisitive man. [From Poole's comedy.]

1825. POOLE, *Paul Pry* [Title].

1864. SALA, *Quite Alone*, i. I asked him one day who she was, and he called me PAUL PRY.

1901. *Referee*, 7 April, I. 1. No one except, perhaps, the PAUL PRY'S of the press . . . desire to publish what is of private concern only.

PAUNCH, *verb.* (old colloquial).—To eat.

1564. UDAL, *Erasmus*, 382. Now ye see him fed, PAUNCHED as lions are.

1612. *Pass. of Benvenuto* [NARES]. If you did but see . . . how negligent he is in my profit, and in what sort he useth to glut and PANCHE himself.

TO JOIN PAUNCHES, *verb. phr.* (venery).—To copulate; TO JOIN GIBLETS (*q.v.*): *see* GREENS and RIDE.

1656. *Muses Recr.* [HOTTEN], 48. My Father and Mother when first they JOIN'D PAUNCHES.

PAUNCH-GUTS, *subs. phr.* (common).—A fat-bellied man; a JELLY-BELLY (*q.v.*): *see* FORTY-GUTS.

PAV, *subs.* (London).—The Pavilion Music Hall: *cf.* MET.

PAVED. TO HAVE ONE'S MOUTH PAVED, *verb. phr.* (old).—To be hard of mouth.

1708-10. SWIFT, *Polite Conversations*, i. How can you drink your Tea so hot? Sure your MOUTH'S PAV'D.

PAVEMENT. *See* NYMPH.

PAVIOR'S-WORKSHOP, *subs. phr.* (old). — The street. — GROSE (1785).

PAW, *subs.* (common).—The hand: *see* BUNCH OF FIVES and DADDLE. Hence FOREPAW = the hand; HIND-PAW = the foot; PAW-CASES = gloves; and as *verb* = to handle roughly or obscenely. — B. E. (*c.*1696); DYCHE (1748); GROSE (1785).

1605. CHAPMAN, *All Fools*, ii. I . . . laid these PAWS Close on his shoulders, tumbling him to earth.

*d.*1637. JONSON (attributed to) [FARMER, *Merry Songs and Ballads* (1897), iii. 13]. Then with his PAWE . . . hee puld to a pye of a traitor's mumbles.

*d.*1701. DRYDEN [*Century*]. Be civil to the wretch imploring And lay your PAWS upon him without roaring.

1753. FOOTE, *Englishman in Paris*, i. How do'st, old buck, hey? Give's thy PAW!

1836. SCOTT, *Cruise of Midge*, 137. He held out him's large PAW.

1840. THACKERAY, *Paris Sketch Book*, 107. The iron squeeze with which he shook my passive PAW.

1848. RUXTON, *Far West*, 164. Ho, Bill! . . . not gone under yet? . . . Give us your PAW.

1891. *Sporting Life*, 3 Ap. In less than a minute he held out his PAW, to the surprise of the company.

PAWN, *verb.* (old).—*See* quot.

*c.*1696. B. E., *Dict. Cant. Crew*, s.v. PAWN. To PAWN ANYBODY, to steal away and leave him or them to Pay the Reckoning.

PAWNEE. *See* PARNEY.

PAW-PAW, *adj.* (old).—Naughty. Hence PAW-PAW WORDS = obscene expressions; PAW-PAW TRICKS = (1) masturbation; and (2) (of children, by nurses) = tiresome pranks, etc. — GROSE (1785).

PAX, *subs.* (Winchester College).—An intimate friend. [WRENCH: Possibly the plural of *pack*, which word has an extended use in reference to friendship . . . as adj., subs., and vb. . . . This seems a more likely origin than the *Pax* of the Church.]

Intj. (school).—Keep quiet! Hands off! Also HAVE PAX! [WRENCH: Almost the pure Latin use of the word.]

1900. KIPLING, *Stalky & Co.*, 4. 'I'm an ass, Stalky!' he said, guarding the afflicted part. 'PAX, Turkey, I'm an ass.'

PAY, *verb.* (colloquial).—To beat; to punish; to 'serve out'; to 'pitch into': generally with *out*: also TO PAY HOME (or AWAY). Hence PAYMENT = chastisement. —GROSE (1785).

1592. GREENE, *Blacke Bookes Messenger*, in *Works*, xi. 34. Though God suffer the wicked for a time yet hee PAIES HOME at length.

1595. SHAKSPEARE, 3 Hen. VI., i. 4. To such mercy as his ruthless arm, With downright PAYMENT, showed unto my father.

1614. TERENCE in *English* [NARES]. To conclude, be sure you crosse her, PAY HER HOME with the like.

1620. *Robin Goodfellow* [HALLIWELL]. If they uncase a cloven and not unty their points, I so PAY their armes that they cannot sometimes untye them, if they would.

*d.*1631. CAPT. JOHN SMITH, *Works*, I. 140. Defending the children with their naked bodies from the vnmercifull blowes, that PAY them soundly.

1631. CHETTLE, *Hoffman. Luc.* Well farewell fellow, thou art now PAID HOME For all thy councelling in knavery.

1640. *King and poore Northerne Man* [HALLIWELL]. They with a foxe tale him soundly did PAY.

1711. *Spectator*, No. 174. Sir Roger . . . thinks he has PAID me OFF, and been very severe upon the merchant.

1748. DYCHE, *Dict.* PAY . . . also to thrash, beat, or whip a boy, *i.e.*, for a fault.

1785. GROSE, *Vulg. Tongue*, s.v. PAY. I will PAY you as Paul paid the Ephesians, over the face and eyes and all your d—d jaws.

*d.*1796. BURNS, *Poems.* An' wi' a mickle hazel rung, She made her a weel PAYED daughter.

1849. THACKERAY, *Dr. Birch.* You see if I don't PAY you OUT after school—you sneak you!

1871. MEREDITH, *Harry Richmond*, xlv. Now they had caught me, now they would PAY me, now they would pound me.

1884. RUSSELL, *Jack's Courtship*, xxiv. Were he not so cruelly ill I should say he was being well PAID OUT.

TO PAY AWAY, *verb.* (colloquial). —1. To go on; to proceed: as with a narration or action. 2. *See* quot. 1785.

1670. EACHARD, *Contempt of Clergy* [ARBER, *Garner*, vii. 308]. Who . . . think, had they but licence and authority to preach, O how they could PAY IT AWAY! and that they can tell the people such strange things, as they never heard before, in all their lives.

1785. GROSE, *Vulg. Tongue*, s.v. PAY. TO PAY AWAY, to fight manfully, also to eat voraciously.

1887. BESANT, *World Went Very Well Then*, xxviii. Ay, ay, my girl; PAY IT OUT. I am a sailors' apothecary. I am old and envious. PAY IT OUT. I value not thy words—no, not even a rope's yam.

TO PAY WITH A HOOK, *verb. phr.* (Australian thieves'). — To steal; *cf.* HOOK: *see* PRIG.

1873. STEPHENS, *My Chinee Cook.* . . . You bought them? Ah, I fear me John, You PAID them WITH A HOOK.

COLLOQUIALISMS are: — TO PAY OLD SCORES = to get even; TO PAY ONE IN HIS OWN COIN = to give tit for tat; TO PAY THE LAST DEBT (or THE DEBT OF NATURE) = to die; 'WHAT'S TO PAY?' = 'what's the matter'; TO PAY UP AND LOOK PRETTY (or BIG) = to accept the inevitable with grace. *See* also DEUCE, DEVIL, FOOTING, FIDLER, NOSE, PEPPERIDGE, PIPER, RENT, SCORES, SHOT, and WHISTLE.

1633. FORD, *'Tis Pity*, iv. 1. I was acquainted with the danger of her disposition; and now have fitted her a just PAYMENT IN HER OWN COIN.

1678. COTTON, *Virgil Travestie* [*Works* (1725) 74]. *Venus* . . . Like cunning Quean in Smiles array'd her, And in HER OWN COIN thus SHE PAID HER.

1687. PRIOR, *The Mice.* The Sire of these two Babes (poor Creature) PAID HIS LAST DEBT TO HUMAN NATURE.

1894. SALA, *London Up to Date*, 297. The Hon. Plantagenet PAID UP AND LOOKED PRETTY.

P. D., *subs. phr.* (trade).—A mixture used in adulterating pepper. [A contraction of 'pepper-dust.']

P. D. Q., *phr.* (common).—'Pretty damned quick.'

1900. *Free Lance*, 6 Oct., 20, 1. It looked as if I'd be on my uppers if I didn't get something to do P. D. Q.

PEA, *subs.* (common).—The favourite; the choice. [From thimble-rigging: *e.g.*, 'This is the pea I choose.']

1888. *Sport. Life*, 11 Dec. Sweeny forced the fighting, and was still the PEA when 'Time!' was called.

1891. *Lic. Vict. Gaz.*, 20 Mar. Well, Albert, now what is the PEA? we asked, hurrying towards the paddock. How much do you want on? he queried. Oh, a fiver is quite enough.

TO PICK (or DO) A SWEET PEA, *verb. phr.* (common).—To urinate; *cf.* TO GATHER VIOLETS, and TO PLUCK A ROSE.

PEACEMAKER, *subs.* (venery).—1. The *penis*: also MATRIMONIAL PEACEMAKER: *see* PRICK.

1796. GROSE, *Vulg. Tongue* (3rd ed.), s.v. MATRIMONIAL PEACEMAKER. The sugar stick, or arbor vitæ.

2. in *pl.* (military).—The Bedfordshire regiment, formerly The Sixteenth Foot. [From Surinaam in 1804 to Chitral in 1895 the Bedfordshires missed all chances of active service.]

3. (American).—A revolver: *see* MEAT IN THE POT.

PEACH, *subs.* (old).—1. A detective: specifically one employed by omnibus and (formerly) by stage-coach proprietors to check receipts. [*See verb.*]

2. (common).—A girl or young woman of pleasing parts; *cf.* PLUM.

Verb. (once literary: now colloquial or slang).—To inform; to betray; TO SPLIT (*q.v.*): TO ROUND ON (*q.v.*). [From 'impeach.'] Hence PEACHER = an informer.—GROSE (1785).

ENGLISH SYNONYMS. To bust; to blow the gaff; to cast up accounts; to cackle; to castell; to crab; to crack; to clipe; to chirp; to come it; to hedgehog; to dick; to inkle; to leak; to let on; to let out; to lip; to make a song; to nose; to give the office; to put away; to put up: to put a down on; to be rusty; to ruck on; to round on; to scream; to snap; to snitch; to stag; to squeal; to squeak; to split; to tip; to tip the wink; to whiddle; to whittle. [For other synonyms *see* SPLIT.]

*c.*1362. *York Plays*, 429. For-thy as wightis that are will thus walke we in were, For PECHYNG als pilgrymes that putte are to pees.

1554. FOX, *Martyrs.* Accusers or PEACHERS of others that were guiltless.

1598. SHAKSPEARE, *I Henry IV.*, ii. 2. If I be ta'en, I'll PEACH for this. *Ibid. Measure for M.* (1603), iv. 3. Then is there here one master Caper, at the suit of master Three-pile the mercer, for some four suits of peach-colour'd satin, which now PEACHES him a beggar.

1607. *Puritan*, iv. 3. George, look to't; I'll PEACH at Tyburn else.

1607. MIDDLETON, *Phænix*, v. 1. Let me have pardon . . . and I'll PEACH 'em all.

1632. JONSON, *Magnetic Lady*, iv. 2. Go PEACH, and cry yourself a fool.

1639. BEAUMONT and FLETCHER, *The Bloody Brother*, iii. 2. "You PEACHING rogue, that provided us These necklaces."

1641. EVELYN, *Diary* [*Century*]. I, I did not amidst all this PEACH my liberty.

1663. BUTLER, *Hudibras*, I. i. Make *Mercury* confesse and PEACH Those thieves which he himself did teach.

1713. ARBUTHNOT, *Hist. of John Bull*, III. i. Your Ptschirnsooker came off, as rogues usually do upon such occasions, by PEACHING his partner.

1731. FIELDING, *Letter Writers*, ii. 11. It were good for you to resolve on being an evidence, and save your own neck at the expence of his. *Risq.* Well, sir, if I must PEACH, I must, I think.

1830. LYTTON, *Paul Clifford*, xxxi. You will not PEACH, I suppose! I PEACH! devil a bit!

1839. AINSWORTH, *Jack Sheppard* [1889], 31. He . . . only escaped the gallows by IMPEACHING his accomplices.

1849. KINGSLEY, *Alton Locke*, x. Now . . . no PEACHING. If any man is scoundrel enough to carry tales, I'll——

1857. HUGHES, *Tom Brown at Rugby*, I. 8. He . . . used to toady the bullies by offering to fag for them, and PEACHING against the rest of us.

1884. *Sat. Review*, 9 Feb. 178. Known to the police, as likely to PEACH.

1890. *Pall Mall Gaz.*, 8 Feb., i. If some fellow was to go and PEACH, how would he prove the case?

1901. *Sporting Times*, 27 Ap., 1, 4. A sea-green, incorruptible navvy was offered half a sovereign for his vote, which he accepted. At the same time, he felt that it was an outrage on his honour and integrity, so he PEACHED, and became a valuable witness in the unseating of Mr. Barker.

PEACOCK, *subs.* (old).—1. A gull; and (2) (racing) a horse with action: *cf.* PEACOCK-HORSE = (undertakers') a horse with a showy mane and tail. Hence PEACOCKY = showy; as *verb* = (1) to display (as a peacock its tail), to put on 'war-paint,' or 'side'; and (2—Anglo-Indian) = to make a formal call (*see* quots. 1883 and 1893).

1580. SIDNEY, *Arcadia*, i. That love which in haughtie hearts proceeds of a desire onely to pleas, and as it were PEACOCK themselves.

1596. SHAKSPEARE, *Hamlet*, iii. 2. And now reigns here A very, very—PAJOCK.

1598. FLORIO, *Worlde of Wordes*, s.v. *Zazzeare.* To play the simple selfe-conceited gull, to go ietting or loytring vp and downe PEACOCKISING and courting of himself.

1869. *Telegraph*, 5 Ap. Speculators . . . were fairly disgusted with the flash PEACOCK, with his bumble foot and 'threadleing' action.

1872. TENNYSON, *Gareth and Lynette.* PEACOCKED up with Lancelot's noticing.

1883. *Graphic*, 17 Mar., 286, 3. Another curious custom of Indian hospitality which extended to a late period—not longer than thirty years ago—was that of inviting visitors, or 'callers,' to take beer at eleven o'clock in the forenoon. . . . The quantity of bottled ale which a gentleman of the period out PEACOCKING, as it was called, could put inside him may be calculated when it is said that a visit never extended beyond ten minutes, and he had three hours in which to make the most of his time.

1884. SMART, *Post to Finish*, xvi. Bushranger was pronounced PEACOCKY, a three-cornered brute, and was very generally disliked.

1893. *Life of Sir R. Burton*, I. 136. Few preferred PEACOCKING, which meant robing in white grass clothes and riding . . . to call upon regimental ladies.

1898. *Pink 'Un and Pelican*, 65. In PEACOCKED the little man with the long chain.

PEACOCK-ENGINE, *subs. phr.* (railway).—A locomotive with a separate tender for coals and water.

PEA- (or PEAK-) GOOSE, *subs. phr.* (old).—A silly fellow: a general term of reproach: *see* BUFFLE.—COTGRAVE (1611); B.E. (*c.*1696).

1570. ASCHAM, *Scholemaster*, 48. If thou be thrall to none of these, Away, good PEAKGOOSE, away, John Cheese.

1606. CHAPMAN, *Mons. d'Olive*, iii. Respect's a clowne supple-jointed, courtesie's a very PEAGOOSE.

1622. FLETCHER and MASSINGER, *Prophetess*, iv. 3. 'Tis a fine PEAK-GOOSE.

1653. URQUHART, *Rabelais*, III. xii. The phlegmatic PEAGOOSE Asopus.

PEAK, *subs.* (old).—1. Lace.—B. E. (*c.*1696); GROSE (1785).

2. (common).—The nose: *see* CONK.

PEAK-GOOSE. *See* PEA-GOOSE.

PEAKING, *subs.* (trade).—Remnants of cloth: *cf.* MAKINGS and CABBAGE.

PEAL, *subs.* (Winchester: obsolete).—(1) A custom in Commoners of singing out comments on Præfects at CLOISTER-TIME (*q.v.*); (2) cheers given on the last three Sundays of the Half for articles of dress, &c., connected with going home, such as "GOMER HATS" (*q.v.*), PARTY ROLLS (*q.v.*), &c.; and (3) Chapel bells which were divided into PEALS. [HALLIWELL = a noise or uproar: *cf.* M. E. *apel* = an old term in hunting music consisting of three long moots.]

*c.*1840. MANSFIELD, *School Life*, 62. The Junior in chamber . . . had to keep a sharp ear on the performance of the chapel bell, and to call out accordingly, 'first PEAL!' 'second PEAL!' 'bells down!'

Verb. (old). — To scold.—GROSE (1785).

PEALER, *subs.* (American).—A very energetic person; a RUSTLER (*q.v.*); a HUMMER (*q.v.*).

1869. STOWE, *Old Town Folks*, 117. She was spoken of with applause under such titles as 'a staver,' a PEALER, 'a roarer to work.'

See PEELER.

PEANUT-POLITICS, *subs. phr.* (American).—Secret tactics. [The pea-nut buries its pods after flowering, a process by which the nuts are ripened.]

1887. *New York Mail*, 27 May. Governor Hill to-day said what he thought of Quarantine Commissioner T. C. Platt's letter, offering to resign his post, if the Governor would consent not to play PEANUT POLITICS, and would appoint Colonel Fred Grant in his stead.

PEAR, *verb.* (thieves').—To draw supplies from both sides: as from the police for information, and from thieves for a warning: *cf.* PEAR-MAKING = bounty jumping.

1785. GROSE, *Vulg. Tongue*, s.v. PEAR-MAKING. The Cove was fined in the steel for PEAR MAKING; the fellow was imprisoned in the house of correction for taking bounties from different regiments.

PEA-RIGGER (or **PEA-MAN**). *See* THIMBLE-RIGGER.

PEARL. TO MAKE A PEARL ON THE NAIL, *verb. phr.* (old).—To drink.—RAY (1767).

PEARLIES, *subs.* (costers').—*In pl.* = pearl buttons: sewn down the sides of the trousers.

1886-96. MARSHALL, '*Pomes' from the Pink 'Un* ('Bleary Bill'), 60. Oh! why are your PEARLIES so bright, bleary Bill?

1892. *National Observer*, 27 Feb., p. 378. Look at my PEARLIES, Kool my 'ed of 'air.

1894. CHEVALIER, *The Coster's Serenade* [FARMER, *Musa Pedestris* (1896), 196]. Me in my PEARLIES felt a toff that day.

1900. *Daily Mail*, 23 Mar., 4, 5. Had the soldier had as many buttons to his tunic as the average London coster has PEARLIES on his holiday inexpressibles, he could speedily have realised a small fortune.

1901. HENLEY, *Hawthorn and Lavender*, 78. With PEARLIES and a barrer and a Jack.

PEAS. AS LIKE AS TWO PEAS, *phr.* (common).—As like as may be.

1765. WALPOLE, *Letters*, 13 Oct. Yes, yes, Madam, I am AS LIKE the Duke de Richelieu AS TWO PEAS; but then they are two old withered grey peas.

PEASE-KILL. TO MAKE A PEASE-KILL, *verb. phr.* (Scots' colloquial).—To squander lavishly: *e.g.* when a man's affairs go wrong and interested persons get the management of his property it is said 'They're makin' a bonny PEASE-KILL o't.' A law-suit is said to be a PEASE-KILL for the lawyers. [JAMIESON.]

PEAS-FIELD. TO GO INTO THE PEAS-FIELD, *verb. phr.* (old).—To fall asleep: *see* BALMY.—RAY (1670).

PEAT, *subs.* (old).—A delicate person: esp. a young girl. Also = (ironically) a spoilt favourite.

1578. *King Lear* [NARES]. To see that proud pert PEAT, our youngest sister.

1593. SHAKSPEARE, *Taming of Shrew*, I. 1. A pretty PEAT! 'tis best Put finger in the eye.

1605. JONSON, CHAPMAN, &c.. *Eastward Hoe* [*Old Plays* (REED), iv. 279. God's my life, you are a PEAT indeed.

1632. MASSINGER, *Maid of Honour*, ii. 2. You are a pretty PEAT, indifferent fair too.

PEA-TIME. IN THE LAST of PEA-TIME (or -PICKING), *phr.* (American colloquial).—In decline of years; 'hard-up'; *passé*. PEA-TIME IS PAST = dead; ruined; gone beyond recall.

1848. LOWELL, *Biglow Papers* . . . There's oller's chaps a-hangin' roun' that can't see PEA-TIME'S PAST.

PEBBLE, *subs.* (venery).—*In pl.* = the *testes*: *see* CODS.

MY PEBBLES, *phr.* (old).—A familiar address.

1843. MONCRIEFF, *Scamps of London*, iii. 1. Dick, MY PEBBLE. *Ibid.* Now, MY PEBBLES, I'll give you a toast.

PEBBLY-BEACHED, *adv. phr.* (common).—Without means; STONY-BROKE (*q.v.*); HIGH-AND-DRY (*q.v.*). Hence TO SIGHT (or LAND ON) a PEBBLY BEACH = to be face to face with ruin; TO PEBBLE BEACH = to suck dry, to clean out: *see* DEAD-BROKE.

1886-96. MARSHALL, *Age of Love* ['*Pomes*,' 26]. Yiffler could see himself stranded, for he could SIGHT A PEBBLY BEACH. *Ibid.* (*Beautiful Dreamer*), 65. I was able to see that my beautiful dreamer had PEBBLE-BEACHED me.

1889. *Lic. Vict. Gaz.*, Jan. One of those mysteries which only those who have been PEBBLY-BEACHED can reveal.

1898. *Pink 'Un and Pelican*, 278. Fleet St. can possibly 'give a bit of weight' to most places as a 'run' for the utterly wagless, rapless, and PEBBLE-BEACHED.

1901. *Referee*, 21 Ap., 9, 2. In the slang of the day a gentleman who is "stony broke" describes himself as PEBBLY BEACH. With a deficit of fifty-three millions to warrant the change, "Hicks Beach" may now be fairly substituted.

PEC, *subs.* (Eton College: obsolete). Money: *see* RHINO. [From Latin *pecunia.*]

PECCAVI, *intj.* (colloquial). — An acknowledgment of offence, mistake, or defeat. TO CRY PECCAVI = to confess to wrong-doing or failure. [Latin = 'I have sinned.'] —GROSE (1785).

1578. WHETSTONE, *Promos and Cassandra*, 32.

1611. BEAUMONT and FLETCHER, *Knight of the Burning Pestle*, iv. 1. Make him sing PECCAVI ere I leave him.

PECK (or **PEK**), *subs.* (Old Cant).—1. Food of any kind; GRUB (*q.v.*); a meal; a feed: also PECKAGE. Hence RUFF-PECK (*q.v.*) = bacon; GERE-PECK = a turd; PECK AND BOOZE = meat and drink; RUM-PECK (*q.v.*) =

good eating; GRUNTING-PECK = pork; OFF ONE'S PECK = without appetite, 'off one's feed.'—HARMAN (1567); HEAD (1665); B. E. (*c.*1696); DYCHE (1748); GROSE (1785).

1610. ROWLANDS, *Martin Mark-all* [FARMER, *Musa Pedestris* (1896), 8]. A GERE PECK in thy gan. *Ibid.* [Hunt. Club Rept. (1874), 40]. PECKAGE meat or *Scroofe* scraps.

1611. MIDDLETON and DEKKER, *Roaring Girl*, v. 1. A gage of ben Rombouse . . . Is benar than a Caster, PECK, pennam, lap, or popler.

1621. JONSON, *Metam. Gipsies*. With the convoy, cheats [goods] and PECKAGE, Out of clutch of Harman Beckage.

1641. BROME, *Jovial Crew* [FARMER, *Musa Pedestris* (1896), 23]. Here safe in our Skipper let's cly off our PECK.

1706. CENTLIVRE, *Basset Table*. Prologue, Free from poor housekeeping; where PECK is under locks, Free from cold kitchens, and no Christmas-box.

1821. EGAN, *Life in London*, vii. The PECK and booze are lying about in such lots that it would supply numerous poor families.

1836. SMITH, *The Thieves' Chaunt* [FARMER, *Musa Pedestris* (1896), 121]. Oh! GRUNTING PECK in its eating Is a richly soft and savoury thing.

1843. MONCRIEFF, *The Scamps of London*, i. 2. Hurrah:—the PECK. *Ibid.* iii. 1. I don't care how soon after this walk I bite my name in for a PECK.

1884. *Daily Telegraph*, 30 July, 2, 1. A pint of cocoa, five slices of thick bread and butter, and a bloater! Or a fair PECK without the relish—a pint of cocoa or coffee, and as much bread and butter as you can eat, for the same money!

1892. MILLIKEN, *'Arry Ballads*, 71. Gives yer the primest of PECKS.

2. *See* RACING-PECK.

Verb. (Old Cant: now colloquial).—1. To eat.

*c.*1536. COPLAND, *Spyttel-hous* [FARMER, *Musa Pedestris* (1896), 2]. Thou shalt PEK my jere In thy gan.

1610. ROWLANDS, *Martin Mark-all*, p. 39. (H. Club's Repr. 1874.) PECKE is taken to eate and byte: *as the Buffa peckes me by the stampes*, the dogge bites me by the shinnes.

1665. HEAD, *English Rogue*, I. iv. 36 (1874). The night we spent in Boozing, PECKING rumly.

1703. *Levellers* [*Harl. Misc.* (PARK), v. 454]. So they all fell heartily to PECKING till they had consumed the whole provision.

1821. EGAN, *Life in London*, vii. Jerry . . . Complained that he could not PECK as he wished.

1867. DICKENS, *No Thoroughfare*, i. But if you wish to board me and to lodge me, take me. I can PECK as well as most men.

2. (colloquial).—To pitch; to throw.

1856. HUGHES, *Tom Brown's Schooldays*, II. iv. I've been longing for some good honest PECKING this half hour.

PECK-ALLEY, *subs. phr.* (common).—The throat; GUTTER-ALLEY (*q.v.*).

PECKER, *subs.* (common).—1. The appetite. Hence, a GOOD (or RARE) PECKER = a hearty eater. [*Cf.* PECK.]

2. (common).—Courage; spirits; good cheer: *e.g.* KEEP YOUR PECKER UP = 'be of good heart.'

1853. BRADLEY, *Verdant Green*, I. 114. KEEP UP YOUR PECKER, old fellow . . . and don't be down in the mouth.

1861. *Punch*, xl. 205. The times were bad, and Gladstone looked sad, . . . And puzzled to KEEP UP HIS PECKER.

1866. *London Miscellany*, 3 Mar. 57. You'll be better for something cheering, sir, said he, just to KEEP YOUR PECKER UP.

1869. *Standard*, 31 Aug. When a crew is taking very hard and rapid work, some slight stimulant is absolutely necessary; it KEEPS UP THE PECKER, and gives the digestion a timely fillip.

18[?]. GILBERT, *The Haughty Actor*. Dispirited because our friend Depressed his moral PECKER.

1880. SIMS, *Zeph*, 86. KEEP YOUR PECKER UP, old-man, and I'll pull you through.

1892. WATSON, *Wops the Waif*, 16. Since that I've been a-trying to KEEP MY PECKER UP and git a honest livin'.

3. (venery).—The *penis*: *see* PRICK.

PECKHAM. TO HAVE (or SPEND) A HOLIDAY AT PECKHAM, *verb. phr.* (old).—To have nothing to eat. GOING TO PECKHAM = going to dinner.—HALLIWELL (1847).

1823. BEE, *Dict. Turf*, s.v. PECKHAM . . . 'No PECKHAM for Ben, he's been to Clapham,' *i.e.*, is indisposed, in a certain way.

PECKISH, *adj.* (common).—Hungry.—GROSE (1785); BEE (1823). For synonyms *see* WOLF.

1837. HALIBURTON, *Clockmaker* (1862), 167. I don't care if I stop and breakfast with you for I feel considerably PECKISH this mornin'.

1845. DISRAELI, *Sybil*, VI. iii. When shall I feel PECKISH again?

1847. THACKERAY, *Vanity Fair*, xxix. Seeing these nobs grubbing away has made me PECKISH too.

1860. *Chambers' Journal*, xiii. 212. There's the tea on the hob, brewing like mad. Are you PECKISH?

1887. HENLEY, *Culture in Slums*, 'Rondeau' 1. For lo, old pal, says she, I'm blooming PECKISH.

1894. MOORE, *Esther Waters*, xli. I feel a bit PECKISH, don't you? We might have a bit of lunch here.

PECNOSTER, *subs.* (venery.)—The *penis*: *see* PRICK.

PECULIAR, *subs.* (old).—1. A belonging; and (2) a mistress: *see* TART.—B. E. (1696); GROSE (1785).

1647-8. HERRICK, *Hesperides*, 'Larr's Portion.' A Holy-cake: Part of which I give to Larr, Part is my PECULIAR.

PECULIAR RIVER (THE), *subs. phr.* (venery).—The female *pudendum*: *see* MONOSYLLABLE.

1603. SHAKSPEARE, *Meas. for Meas.*, ii. 1. *Ov.* What's his offence? *Pom.* Groping for trouts in a PECULIAR RIVER. *Ov.* What, is there a maid with child by him?

PECULIAR INSTITUTION, *subs.* (American). — Negro slavery—'the peculiar domestic institution of the Southern States.'

PED, *subs.* (Old Cant).—1. A basket.—B. E. (*c.*1696); GROSE (1785).

1579. SPENSER, *Shepheards Calender*, Nov. A hask in a wicker PED, wherein they use to carry fish.

2. (common).—A professional walker or runner.

1884. *Sat. Review*, 21 June, 810, 1. Running paths, except for the use of professional PEDS, were then unknown.

1888. *Sportsman*, 28 Nov. The six PEDS turned out to fight their way through the roaring and raging wind.

PED-BELLY, *subs.* (provincial).—A fat man or woman; a CORPORATION (*q.v.*). [PED = basket.]

PEDESCRIPT, *subs.* (old).—Bruises from kicks.

1659. SHIRLEY, *Hon. and Mammon* [NARES]. I have it all in PEDESCRIPT.

PEDESTRIAN DIGITS, *subs. phr.* (schoolboys').—The legs.

PEDLAR'S FRENCH, *subs. phr.* (old).—1. Cant, or the language of thieves and vagabonds; and (2) any unintelligible jargon; also ST. GILES' GREEK (*q.v.*). ['French' and 'Greek' here = 'unintelligible.']—B. E. (*c.*1696); GROSE (1785).

1530. PALSGRAVE, *Lang. Françoyse*, 368. S.V. SPEKE. They speke a PEDLARS FRENCHE amongst themselfe.

*c.*1536. COPLAND, *Spyttel-hous* [FARMER, *Musa Pedestris* (1896), 2]. And thus they babble . . . I wote not what with their PEDLYNG FRENCHE.

1567. HARMAN, *Caveat* (1841). vi. Their language which they terme PEDDELERS FRENCHE or canting.

1595. FLORIO, *Worlde of Wordes*, s.v. *Gergare*, to speake fustian, PEDDLERS FRENCH, or rogues language, or gibbrish.

1611. MIDDLETON and DEKKER, *Roaring Girl*, v. 1. I'll give a schoolmaster half-a-crown a week, and teach me this PEDLER'S FRENCH.

1622. MASSINGER, *Virgin Martyr*, ii. 1. Why, fellow Angelo, we were speaking in PEDLAR'S FRENCH, I hope.

1640. [SHIRLEY], *Captain Underwit*, [BULLEN, *Old Plays*, ii. 351]. *Gis.* One rime more and you undoe my love for ever. Out upon't! PEDLARS FRENCH is a Christian language to this.

1647. BEAUMONT and FLETCHER, *Faithful Friend*, i. 2. 'Twere fitter Such honest lads as myself had it, that instead Of PEDLAR'S FRENCH gives him plain language for his money.

1834. AINSWORTH, *Rookwood*. Preface. Its meaning must be perfectly clear and perspicuous to the practised patterer of Romany, or PEDLER'S FRENCH.

PEDLAR'S-NEWS, *subs. phr.* (common).—State news; 'stereo.' Also PIPER'S (MUNG- or TINKER'S) NEWS.

PEDLAR'S-PONY (-HORSE or -PAD), *subs. phr.* (common).—A walking-stick; a PENANG-LAWYER (*q.v.*); a WADDY (*q.v.*).

PEE, *verb.* (chiefly nursery).—To urinate; TO PUMP SHIP (*q.v.*).

1788. PICKEN, *Poems*, 'The Favourite Cat,' 47. He never stealt though he was poor, He never PEE'D his master's floor.

PEEL, *verb.* (common).—To undress; to strip.—GROSE (1785). Hence PEELED = naked: *see* NATURE'S GARB.

1811. MOORE, *Tom Crib*, 13.

1823. MONCRIEFF, *Tom and Jerry*, i. *Tom.* Come Jerry, cast your skin—PEEL—slip into the swell case at once.

1827. CORCORAN, *The Fancy*, Note, 89. Randull's figure is remarkable when PEELED for its statue like beaty.

1827. SCOTT, *Two Drovers*, ii. Robin had not art enough even to PEEL before setting to, but fought with his plaid dangling about him.

1830. LYTTON, *Paul Clifford* (1854), 256. You may call me an apple if you will, but I take it, I am not an apple you'd like to see PEELED.

1834. AINSWORTH, *Rookwood*, 'The Double Cross.' They PEELED in style, and bets were making.

1857. HOLMES, *Autocrat of Breakfast Table*, i. What resplendent beauty that must have been which could have authorised Phryne to PEEL in the way she did!

1885. *Field*, 4 Ap. I got into bed, and under cover PEELED off, one by one, those pieces of clothing.

1888. *Detroit Free Press*, 20 Oct. She PEELED OFF her wedding dress and boots, . . . and threw them at him.

TO PEEL IT, *verb. phr.* (American).—To run at full speed.

TO PEEL ONE'S BEST END, *verb. phr.* (venery).—To effect intromission: *see* GREENS and RIDE.

TO PEEL EGGS, *verb. phr.* (common).—To stand on ceremony.

See KEEP.

PEELER, *subs.* (common).—1. A policeman: *see* BEAK. [First applied to the Royal Irish Constabulary established by Sir Robert Peel, when Irish Secretary (1812-18), and subsequently, for similar reasons (1828-39), to the Metropolitan Police: *see* quot. 1889 and *cf.* BOBBY.]

1842-3. *Dublin Monthly Mag.* [*Notes and Queries*, 7th S. vii. 392], 'The PEELER and the Goat.' As some Bansha PEELERS were out wan night On duty and pathrollin, O.

1843. THACKERAY, *Irish Sketch Book*, xiv. Half-a-dozen PEELERS . . . now inhabit Bunratty.

1846. *Punch*, x. 163. And forth three PEELERS rushing Attempt to storm the Pass; Truncheons are thick, but fists are quick, and down they go to grass!

1850. KINGSLEY, *Alton Locke*, xxxv. He's gone for a PEELER and a search warrant to break open the door.

1851. MAYHEW, *Lond. Lab.*, I. 22. As regards the police, the hatred of a costermonger to a PEELER is intense.

1857. LAWRENCE, *Guy Livingstone*, iv. Six or seven PEELERS and specials.

1889. *Encyclo. Brit.*, xviii. 453. His [Sir Robert Peel] greatest service to Ireland as secretary was the institution of the regular Irish constabulary, nicknamed after him PEELERS.

1886-96. MARSHALL, *Word of a Policeman* ['*Pomes*,' 73]. The other PEELER had a cut at him as well.

1889. *Daily News*, 24 July, 6, 1. The PEELERS seized it.

1892. NISBET, *Bushranger's Sweetheart*, 64. When I heard him shout thieves, I thought it was the PEELER, and knew it was time to walk.

1897. *Punch*, 23 Oct., 191, 1. He goes his way escorted by A single mounted PEELER.

2. (pugilistic).—One ready to strip for the combat.

1852. *L'Allegro*; *As Good as a Comedy*, 56. Just you try it, then, with another sort of look in your face, and see if I ain't a PEELER.

3. (American).—A very energetic person; a RIPPER (*q.v.*).

1869. H. B. STOWE, *Oldtown Folks*. She was spoken of with applause as a staver, a PEELER, 'a roarer to work.'

SIR PEELER, *subs. phr.* (old).—A poverty-striking crop.

1557. TUSSER, *Husbandrie*, xviii. 12. Wheat doth not well, Nor after SIR PEELER he loveth to dwell.

PEEP, *verb.* (colloquial).—1. To speak.

2. (Old Cant).—To sleep.—B. E. (*c.*1696).

PEEPER, *subs.* (common).—1. A spy-glass; (2) the eye; and (3), *in pl.* = a pair of spectacles. Hence PAINTED PEEPERS (or PEEPERS IN MOURNING) = black eyes.—B. E. (*c.*1696); DYCHE (1748); GROSE (1785).

ENGLISH SYNONYMS. Blinkers; daylights; glaziers; glims; mutton-pies (rhyming); ogles; optics; sees; winkers.

1656. FLETCHER, *Martiall*, I. 51. Thy PEEPERS more than active friends delight.

1707. WARD, *Hudibras Redivivus*, II. iv. 4. No sooner had they fix'd their PEEPERS Upon the lifeless Whipper-Snappers.

1795. GROSE, *Vulg. Tongue*, s.v. PEEPER. A spying glass.

1808. JAMIESON, *Dict.*, s.v. PEEPERS . . . a cant term for spectacles.

1818. EGAN, *Boxiana*, II. 43. His PEEPERS were taken measure of for a suit of mourning.

1821. EGAN, *Life in London*, II. v. If you have even the good fortune to keep your PEEPERS from being measured for a suit of mourning, you are perhaps . . . in more real danger among the refined heroes.

1822. SCOTT, *Fortunes of Nigel*, xvi. Chalk him across the PEEPERS with your cheery.

1831. ALMAR, *Pedlar's Acre*, ii. 3. There's something to open your aged PEEPERS.

1852. JUDSON, *Myst. of New York*, x. You just keep cool, and say nothing, but use your PEEPERS.

1857. THACKERAY, *Virginians*, xvi. Keep on anointing my mistress's dainty PEEPERS with the very strongest ointment, so that my noddle may ever appear lovely to her.

1861. PENNELL, *Puck on Pegasus*, 16. Slave! (I said) base Kitchen-creeper! (said I) I will stop your PEEPER! I will tap your claret.

1864. *Times*, 18 Oct. Which will at least, my gentle friends, open your PEEPERS for the rest of time.

1891. *Lic. Vict. Mirror*, 30 Jan., 7, 3. Jones had one of his PEEPERS . . . ornamented with a fringe of black.

4. (old).—A looking-glass.—B. E. (*c.*1696); DYCHE (1748); GROSE (1785).

SINGLE PEEPER, *subs. phr.* (common).—A one-eyed man.—GROSE (1785).

PEEPING. A PEEPING TOM, *subs. phr.* (common).—An inquisitive person; a PAUL PRY (*q.v.*). [From the Coventry legend.]—GROSE (1785).

PEEP-O'-DAY BOY, *subs. phr.* (old).—A street roister [Regency].

1821. EGAN, *Life in London*, II. vi. Jerry and Bobby, . . . With the PEEP-O'-DAY BOYS, Hunting after wild joys.

PEEPSIES, *subs.* (street performers').—The pan-pipes.

PEEPY, *adj.* and *adv.* (old).—Drowsy; sleepy. TO GO TO PEEPY (or PEEP-) BY = to sleep.—B. E. (1696); GROSE (1785).

PEERY (or PEERIE), *adj.* (old: now recognised).—Suspicious; knowing; sly; sharp-looking: also as *verb.* = to look about suspiciously.—HEAD (1665); B. E. (*c.*1696); GROSE (1785).

1703. WARD, *London Spy*, xi. 259. Another . . . look'd as PEERY as if he thought every fresh Man that came in a Constable.

1751. FIELDING, *Amelia*, II. ix. You are so shy and PEERY, you would almost make one suspect there was more in the matter.

1758. CIBBER, *Refusal*, iii. Are you PEERY, as the Cant is?

1819. MOORE, *Tom Crib*, 20. Fixing his eye on the Porpus's snout, Which he knew that Adonis felt PEERY about.

PEETY, *adj.* and *adv.* (Old Cant).—Cheerful.—BAILEY (1726).

PEE-WEE, *subs. phr.* (nursery).—(1) The *penis* and (2) the female *pudendum*. *See* PRICK and MONOSYLLABLE. Also as *verb.* = to urinate. *See* PEE.

3. (school).—A small marble.

PEG, *subs.* (common).—1. A dram; a 'drink'; a GO (*q.v.*): specifically (in India), a 'brandy-and-soda.' In the 16th century 'peg-tankards' held two quarts, divided by seven pegs or pins, one above the other, into eight equal portions. Hence, TO DRINK TO PEGS = to drink the draught marked in a peg tankard; TO ADD (OR DRIVE) A PEG (or NAIL) INTO ONE'S COFFIN = to drink hard; TO GO A PEG LOWER = to drink to excess; A PEG TOO LOW = (1) drunk, and (2) low-spirited; PEGGER = a persistent drinker, or NIPSTER (*q.v.*).

1821. EGAN, *Life in London*, II. ii. To chaff with the flash Mollishers, and in being home to a PEG in all their various sprees and rambles.

1871. *Figaro*, 15 Oct. A man who, in the days of PEG TANKARDS, would have got on PEG BY PEG, marvellously rapidly to the state of the 'much-loved intemperance of the Saxons'—as the old chronicler, Brady, has it.

1871. SALA [*Belgravia*, April]. Ensign Plume of the 200th Foot, at present languishing obscure at 'Gib' and taking too many PEGS of brandy and soda when on guard.

1883. *Graphic*, 17 March, 286, 3. The dispensation of food and liquor, however, never entered into the calculations of the Anglo-Indian of the last generation. Even the shopkeepers used to think nothing of giving their customers PEGS.

1884. *World*, 16 April, 18, 2. And then he took to play and PEGS, and his naturally excitable disposition did the rest.

1894. *Illustrated Bits*, 31 Mar., 7, 1. Come and have a PEG, be cried.

1898. *Pink 'Un and Pelican*, 35. Just as we were all taking a PEG at the bar . . . a local postman delivered that letter.

2. (old).—A blow: spec. (old boxers') a straight drive in the pit of the stomach: *see* DIG and WIPE. Whence PEGGING = a beating.—GROSE (1785).

*c.*1600. [COLLIER, *Dram. Poet.* (1831), ii. 198]. Strike a PEGGE into him with a club.

1748. SMOLLETT, *Roderick Random*, xxviii. PEGS on the stomach without number.

3. (common).—A foot or leg: CRIBBAGE-PEGS: *see* CREEPERS.

1841. *Punch*, i. 243. You'll not STIR A PEG out of where you are untill you pay me for my throwble.

1851-61. MAYHEW, *Lond. Lab.* III. 221. The donkey stopt short and wouldn't move a PEG.

1862. LOWELL, *Biglow Papers*, II. 99. To rise a PEG an' jine the crowd that went for reconstruction.

*d.*1874. HOOD, *Faithless Nelly Gray*. The army-surgeons made him limbs; said he, 'They're only PEGS; But there's as wooden members quite As represent my legs.

1887. SIMS, *Referee*, 7 Nov. A bow-wow . . . right through my 'rank-and-riches' Did my CRIBBAGE-PEGS assail.

4. (common).—A tooth.

5. (thieves').—A shilling; a BOB (*q.v.*).

1857. DUCANGE ANGLICUS, *The Vulgar Tongue*, 39. Lawyer Bob draws fakements up; he's tipped a PEG for each.

6. (colloquial).—A step; a degree: *cf.* sense 1. Hence TO TAKE DOWN A PEG = to humiliate; TO HOIST A PEG HIGHER = to advance.

1625. *Court and Times*, Chas. I. i. 58. Two maids . . . fell a-talking together of the brave times that would be shortly . . . when . . . the Bishop of Chester that bore himself so high should be HOISTED A PEG higher to his little ease.

*d.*1677. BARROW, *Pope's Supremacy* (*Encyclopædic Dict.*). To screw papal authority to the highest PEG.

1664. BUTLER, *Hudibras*, II. 2. Trepanned your party with intrigue, And TOOK your grandees DOWN A PEG.

1834. DOWLING, *Othello Travestie*, i. 4. I'll TAKE YOU DOWN A PEG, and stop your music.

1848. JONES, *Sketches of Travel*, 163. If they didn't get their nations TUCK DOWN A PEG or two, then I'm terribly mistaken.

1869. *Daily Telegraph*, 6 Sept. It was her duty to bring him DOWN A PEG or two. She did her duty.

1882. *Literary World*, 3 Feb. The brilliant young athlete wanted TAKING DOWN A PEG.

1888. *Detroit Free Press*, 1 Sep. It was Hallam who . . . not liking a certain condescension in his manner, resolved to TAKE him DOWN A PEG or two.

1891. GOULD, *Double Event*, 195. You TOOK me DOWN A PEG, Jack, and I deserved it.

1892. NISBET, *Bushranger's Sweetheart*, 85. We were regarded . . . as blooming swells, who wanted TAKING DOWN A PEG or two.

1900. *Free Lance*, 6 Oct., 8, 1. 'TAKING him DOWN A PEG' [Title].

7. (colloquial).—A text; an excuse.

1791-1823. DISRAELI, *Curiosities of Literature*. His successors now only made use of the sentences as a row of PEGS to hang on their fine-spun metaphysical questions.

1871. *Globe*, 22 Sep. Given a PEG—that is to say, some scrap of news or incident of passing interest—upon which to hang a string of historical, argumentative, or moral reflections.

1885. *Field*, 17 Oct. A PEG whereon to hang an account of a hunt breakfast.

8. (colloquial).—A diminutive of Margaret: also PEGGY.

Verb. (old).—1. To drive.

1819. MOORE, *Tom Crib*, 80. I first was hired TO PEG a hack.

2. (old).—*See* quot.

*c.*1696. B. E., *Dict. Cant. Crew*, s.v. PEG AT COCKS, to throw at them at Shrovetide.

3. (old).—To beat.

4. (common).—To drink frequently; to tipple.

1883. MISS BRADDON, *Golden Calf*, xxv. There is a great deal of what is called PEGGING—an intermittent kind of tippling which goes on all day long.

5. (Stock Exchange).—To fix a market price, and prevent fluctuation by buying all that is offered at it, thus debarring lower quotations; or, selling all that the market will take at it, thus preventing higher quotations.

1891. *New York Herald*, 31 May, 6, 2. Portuguese have also been well PEGGED, but other 'Internationals' have been featureless.

6. (old).—To run: *cf.* TO PEG AWAY.

1884. LE FANU [*Temple Bar*, August, 484]. Away with me out of the hall-door, that chanced to be open, and down the street I PEGGED like a madman.

7. (venery).—To copulate: also TO PEG UP (or DOWN): *see* GREENS and RIDE.

TO PEG AWAY (AT or ON), *verb. phr.* (colloquial).—1. To work persistently; TO PUT IN LICKS (*q.v.*). *Cf.* Fr. *aller son petit bonhomme de chemin.* Hence PEGGING = plodding.

1749. SMOLLETT, *Gil Blas* [ROUTLEDGE], 167. Large pieces of bread and good substantial slices of roast meat, AT which we began PEGGING with all possible pertinacity.

1837. DICKENS, *Pickwick Papers*, xxx. PEG AWAY, Bob, said Mr. Allen to his companion, encouragingly. *Ibid.*, *Bleak House* (1852), xvii. 143. I should PEG AWAY at Blackstone and all those fellows with the most tremendous ardour.

1856. BRET HARTE, *Dow's Flat.* But Dow in his well kept a PEGGIN', in his usual ridiculous way.

1862. THACKERAY, *Philip*, vii. He's been . . . PEGGING AWAY at the olives and maceroons.

1864. *Daily Telegraph*, 19 Oct. The plan of PEGGING AWAY must end either in the capture of Richmond, or in the utter discomfiture of the attacking force.

1864. *Glasgow Herald*, 10 Dec. In all . . . I find only an echo of the words of their chief, to KEEP PEGGING AWAY till the end comes.

1873. *Pall Mall Gazette*, Jan. To PEG AWAY continually is, as we well know, the loftiest idea of modern statesmanship, but it is necessary to find something to PEG AT, as even a statesman PEGGING AWAY at nothing, and beating the air with vain motions may become ridiculous.

1879. LELAND, *Abraham Lincoln*, xi. President Lincoln, when asked what we should do if the war should last for years, replied, "We'll keep PEGGING AWAY."

1888. BLACK, *House-boat*, vii. The rain KEEPS PEGGING AWAY in a steady, unmistakeable, business-like fashion.

18 [?]. *American Hebrew*, xxxix. 52. We have gradually worked and PEGGED ALONG year by year.

2. (colloquial).—To fight.

TO PEG INTO, *verb. phr.* (colloquial).—To hit; to 'let drive.'

1834. DOWLING, *Othello Travestie*, ii. 5. You PEG it INTO him, and pray don't spare him.

1889. *Lic. Vict. Gaz.*, 18 Jan. PEG INTO him, snacks.

TO PEG OUT, *verb. phr.* (colloquial).—1. To die: *see* HOP THE TWIG.

1870. *Echo*, 10 Mar. Then . . . the heart-broken man exclaimed, Oh, George, George, why did you PEG OUT?

1884. *Daily Telegraph*, 9 Oct., 2. 3. He . . . was told that it was so bad that it might PEG-OUT any minute.

1892. *Daily Chronicle*, 28 Mar., 5, 6. I thought . . . I was going to PEG OUT last night.

1897. MITFORD, *Romance Cape Frontier*, II. xv. Better fun than PEGGING OUT with only the sooty-faced niggers prodding away at you.

2. (colloquial).—To be ruined; QUISBY (*q.v.*)

TO BE PEGGED OUT, *verb. phr.* (common).—*See* quot.

1886. *Tit-bits*, 31 July, 252. Being PEGGED OUT (*i.e.* too notorious) in the neighbourhood, he begged by proxy.

ON THE PEG, *phr.* (military).—1. Under arrest; ROOSTED (*q.v.*).

2. (military).—Under stoppage of pay; fined.

TO PUT ON THE PEG, *verb. phr.* (military).—To pull oneself up (or together); to be careful: as of drink, behaviour, etc.

TO PEG UP. *See verb.*, sense 7.

THERE ARE ALWAYS MORE ROUND PEGS THAN ROUND HOLES, *phr.* (colloquial).—There are always more candidates than places.

OLD PEG, *subs. phr.* (old).—*See* quot.

1785. GROSE, *Vulg. Tongue*, s.v. PEG. OLD PEG, poor hard Suffolk or Yorkshire Cheese.

PEGASUS. TO BREAK PEGASUS'S NECK, *verb. phr.* (old).—To write halting verse.

1728. POPE, *Dunciad*, iii. 161. Some, free from rhyme or reason, rule or check, BREAK Priscian's head, and PEGASUS'S NECK.

PEGGY, *subs.* (common).—A slender poker, disposedly bent at right angles for the purpose of raking the fire: *cf.* RECTOR and CURATE.

PEG-LEG, *subs. phr.* (common).—A wooden legged man or woman.

PEGO, *subs.* (venery).—The *penis*: *see* PRICK. [Gr. *pege* = a fountain.]—GROSE (1785); HALLIWELL (1847).

1709. WARD, *London Spy*, ii. 8. PEGO like an upstart Hector . . . Would fain have rul'd as Lord Protector, Inflam'd by one so like a goddess, I scarce cou'd keep him in my codpiece.

PEG PUFF, *subs. phr.* (Scots').—An old young woman: *cf.* OLD EWE DRESSED LAMB-FASHION.

PEGTOPS, *subs.* (obsolete).—*In pl.* = Trousers: very wide at the hips and narrowing down to a tight-fit at the ancles.

1859. FARRAR, *Julian Home*, xx. His . . . tailor . . . produced . . . the cut-away coat, and mauve-coloured PEGTOPS.

1861. KINGSLEY, *Ravenshoe*, lxvi. PEGTOPS, and a black bowler hat.

1864. LE FANU, *Uncle Silas*, xlvi. Dudley, in a flagrant pair of cross-barred PEGTOPS . . . approaching our refined little party with great strides.

1892. MILLIKEN, *'Arry Ballads*, 24. 'Im with the PEG-TOPS and pipe.

1892. GUNTER, *Miss Dividends*, iii. Trousers that are cut in what was then called the PEG-TOP pattern.

PEG TRANTUM. GONE TO PEG TRANTUM'S, *phr.* (old).—Dead: *see* HOP THE TWIG. [PEG TRANTUM (provincial) = a wild romping girl.]—GROSE (1785).

PEK. *See* PECK.

PELICAN STATE, *subs. phr.* (American).—Louisiana. [From its armorial bearings, the bird being common in the State.]

PELL-MELL, *adv.* (old: now recognised).—In confusion; 'higgledy-piggledy.'—B. E. (*c.* 1696); GROSE (1785). Also as *subs.* and *verb.*

1591. GARRARD, *Art Warre*, 299. That either they may enter PESLE MESLE, or kill some Chiestana, or make such a slaughter of Soldiours.

1663. BUTLER, *Hudibras*, I. 3. To come PELL-MELL to handy blows.

1664. COTTON, *Virgil Travestie* (1st ed.), 109. Too't they fell, Roaring and Swaggering PELL MELL.

*c.*1709. *The Female Scuffle* [DURFEY, *Pills to Purge* (1709), iv. 18]. Both PELL-MELL fell to't, and made this uproar, With these Compliments, th'art a Baud, th'art a Whore.

bef. 1733. NORTH, *Examen* (1740), I. iii. 48, 151. He falls in PESLE-MESLE.

1764. W. TAVERNIER, *Trav.*, II. 16. They fought hand to hand with their sables, PESLE MESLE.

1767. STERNE, *Tristam Shandy* [*Works* (1839), IX. xxvi. 386.] To attack the point of the advancing counterscarp, and PELE MELE with the Dutch, to take the counterguard.

1837. COOPER, *Europe*, II. 188. The revolution has made a PELE MELE in the Salons of Paris.

1850. LYTTON, *Harold*, VII. iii. For some minutes the PELE MELE was confused and indistinct.

1865. OUIDA, *Strathmore*, I. iii. They fell PELE MELE one on another.

1892. FENNELL, *Stanford Dict.*, s.v. PELE-MELE . . . The form PESLE MESLE is earlier Fr. (Cotg.). Early Anglicised as PELLE(y) MELLE(y).

PELT, *subs.* (old).—1. A hurry: hence TO PELT (or GO FULL PELT) = to go as hard or as fast as may be.

1843. DICKENS, *Christmas Carol.* The clerk . . . ran home to Camden Town as hard as he could PELT.

2. (common).—A rage; a passion; a blow: also PELTER. As *verb.* = to be violently angry; PELTING (or OUT FOR A PELTER) = very angry, passionate.—B. E. (*c.* 1696); GROSE (1785).

1594. SHAKSPEARE, *Lucreece* [MALONE, *Supp.* i. 554]. Another smother'd seems to PELT and swear.

1608. TOPSELL, *Hist. Serpents*, 250. In a PELTING chafe she brake all to peaces the wenches imagery worke.

1632. VICARS, *Virgil* [NARES]. Troyes Illioneus brave With a huge stone a deadly PELT him gave.

1677. *Wrangling Lovers* [NARES]. That the letter, which put you into such a PELT, came from another.

1688. GRUBB, *British Heroes* [PERCY, *Reliques*], line 99. George hit th' dragon such a PELT.

1697. *Unnatural Brother.* Which put her ladyship into a horrid PELT.

1819. MOORE, *Tom Crib*, 23. A PELT in the smellers . . . set it going like fun.

1865. KINGSLEY, *Hillyars and Burtons*, iii. I wasn't really in a PELTER.

3. (colloquial).—The skin.

1694-6. DRYDEN, *Virgil*, Georgic, iii. 672. A scabby tetter on their PELTS will stick.

4. (old).—A miser; a stingy fellow: also PELTER.

1552. HULOET, *Dict.* s.v. A PELT or pinchbecke.

1577. KENDALL, *Flowers of Epigrammes.* The veriest PELTER pilde maie seme To have experience thus.

1587. GASCOIGNE, *Works* [NARES]. Yea let such PELTERS praite, Saint Needam be their speed, We need no text to answer them but this, the Lord hath neede.

5. (old).—Clothes; sometimes *in pl.*: spec. garments made of 'peltry' = the furs of beasts.

1567. HARMAN, *Caveat* [E. E. T. S. (1869), 76]. Many wyll plucke of their smockes, and laye the same vpon them in stede of their vpper sheete, and all her other PELTE and trashe vpon her also.

1585. *Nomenclator* [NARES]. A PELT, or garments made of wolves and beares skin, which nobles in old time used to weare.

1630. TAYLOR, *Works* [NARES]. For they from sundry men their PELTES can pull, Whereby they keepe themselves as warme as wooll.

Verb. 1. *See subs.*, sense 2.

2. (tailors').—To sew thickly.

PELTER, *subs.* (colloquial).—1. A heavy shower: hence, a rain of missiles.

1837. BARHAM, *Ingoldsby Legends*, 'Dead Drummer.' The lightning kept flashing, the rain too kept pouring . . . what I've heard term'd a regular PELTER.

1887. *Religious Herald*, 24 Mar. Presently, another shower came. . . . She shrugged up her shoulders and shut her eyes during the PELTER.

2. (colloquial).—Anything large; a WHOPPER (*q.v.*).

1892. MILLIKEN, *'Arry Ballads*, 70. Down upon Sport, now, a PELTER.

3. (tramps').—A whore-monger; a MUTTON-MONGER (*q.v.*).

4. *See subs.*, senses 2 and 4.

5. (obsolete).—*See* quot.

1827. J. BARRINGTON, *Personal Sketches* (3rd Edition, 1869), i. 274-275. Every family then had a case of hereditary pistols, which descended as an heirloom . . . for the use of their posterity. Our family pistols, denominated PELTERS, were brass.

PELTING, *adj.*—1. *See* PELT, *subs.*, sense 2.

2. (obs.).—Mean; paltry; contemptible.—B. E. (*c.* 1696).

1570. ASCHAM, *Scholemaster*, 191. Packing up PELTING matters, such as in London commonly come to the hearing of the masters of Bridewell.

1578. NORTH, *Plutarch*, 458. Hybla being but a PELTING little town. *Ibid.*, 69. My mind in PELTING prose shall never be exprest, But sung in verse heroical, for so I think it best.

1581. LYLY, *Alexander* [DODSLEY, *Old Plays* (1874), ii. 140]. Good drink makes good blood, and shall PELTING words spill it?

1597. SHAKSPEARE, *Richard II.*, ii. 1. This land—Is now leas'd out . . . Like to a tenement or PELTING farm.

1605. SHAKSPEARE, *Lear*, ii. 3. From low farms, Poor, PELTING villages, sheepcotes, and mills.

*d.*1616. BEAUMONT and FLETCHER, *Bloody Brother*, iii. 2. Your penny-pot poets are such PELTING thieves.

PELTIS-HOLE, *subs. phr.* (Old Scots').—A term of reproach: of women: *cf.* PELT, *subs.*, sense 4. [That is 'tan-pit.']

15[?]. *Aberdeen Register* [JAMIESON]. Maly Awaill was conwickit . . . for myspersonyng of Besse Goldsmycht, calling her PELTIS HOYLL.

PEMPE, *subs.* (Winchester).—An imaginary object in search of which a new comer is sent: *cf.* PIGEON'S MILK, STRAP-OIL, THE SQUAD UMBRELLA, &c. [From *pempe moron proteroy* = 'Send the fool farther.']

PEN, *subs.* (old).—1. A prison; a penitentiary: *see* CAGE.

2. (Scots').—A saucy man with a sharp nose—[JAMIESON].

3. (colonial).—A three-penny piece.

4. (venery).—The female *pudendum*: *see* MONOSYLLABLE. [Properly of sows.]

TO HAVE NO INK IN THE PEN, *verb. phr.* (old).—*See* quot.

*b.*1547. WEVER, *Lusty Juventus* [DODSLEY, *Old Plays* (1874), ii. 97]. When there is NO MORE INK IN THE PEN*, I will make a Shift as well as other men. [* Note by Hazlitt: 'an indelicate figure, which occurs in jest-books and other early literature.']

KNIGHT OF THE PEN, *subs. phr.* (common).—An author or journalist.

1864. *Reader*, 22 Oct., 505. 1. The best guard against any such spirit, is that the publisher should be a KNIGHT OF THE PEN himself.

PENANCE-BOARD, *subs. phr.* (old).—The pillory.—B. E. (*c.* 1696); GROSE (1785).

PEN-AND-INK, *subs. phr.* (rhyming).—A stink. Also as *verb.*

1892. *Sporting Times*, 29 Oct., 'Rhyme of Rusher,' 6. The air began . . . to PEN-AND-INK.

PENANG-LAWYER, *subs. phr.* (common).—*See* quot. [Probably a corruption of *Penang liyar*, the wild areca.]

1865. *Chambers's Encyclopædia*, VII. 371. PENANG LAWYERS, the commercial name for the stems of a species of palm imported from Penang for walking sticks. They are small and hard, and have a portion of the root-stock attached, which is left to form the handle.

PENBANK, *subs.* (Old Cant).—A beggar's can.—BAILEY (1728).

PENCIL-FEVER, *subs. phr.* (racing).—A 'disease' amongst racehorses, generally preceded by MILKING (*q.v.*). When a horse has been MILKED to the utmost, and can no longer, in spite of MARKETEERS (*q.v.*), be kept at a short price, his true condition gets known, PENCIL-FEVER sets in, and every layer is anxious to PENCIL his name in his betting-book, *i.e.* lay against him as a SAFE or STIFF-'UN (*q.v.*). Also MILK-FEVER and MARKET-FEVER. Whence PENCILLER = a bookmaker: also KNIGHT OF THE PENCIL; and PENCILLING FRATERNITY = the world of bookmakers.

1885. *Punch*, 7 March, 109. The KNIGHTS OF THE PENCIL, Sir, hold that backers, like pike, are more ravenous in keen weather, and consequently easier to land.

1886-96. MARSHALL, *'Pomes' from the Pink 'Un* ('The Merry Stumer'), 8. The KNIGHT OF THE PENCIL was wide awake.

1887. *Field*, 31 Dec. The race proved a busy one for the PENCILLERS, the greater part of the runners being backed.

1888. *Sporting Life*, 13 Dec. The defeat of the favourite could not have brought much grist to the mill of the PENCILLERS.

1891. *Lic. Vict. Gaz.*, 20 Mar. Last year some of the shrewdest of the PENCILLING FRATERNITY were had over Theodolite when he won the Champion Hurdle-race at Sandown.

PEN-DRIVER, *subs. phr.* (common).—A clerk or writer: *cf.* QUILL-DRIVER.

1888. *Century*, xxxvii. 580. She . . . looked round on the circle of fresh-faced PEN-DRIVERS for explanation.

PENDULUM, *subs.* (venery).—The *penis: see* PRICK.

PEN-GUN (or **PENGUIN**), *subs.* (Scots').—A talkative person: esp. of small stature. TO CRACK LIKE A PEN-GUN = to chatter.

PENINSULAR, *subs.* (old colloquial).—A veteran of the Peninsular war.

1845. *Quarterly Review*, clxvi. He speaks of the ruffling captain, who was, no doubt, an old PENINSULAR.

PENNIF, *subs.* (back-slang).—A five pound note; a FINNUP (*q.v.*).

1862. *Cornhill Mag.*, vi. 648. It is all in single PENNIFS on the England jug.

PENNILESS BENCH, *subs. phr.* (Old Cant).—Poverty. ON THE PENNILESS BENCH = poverty stricken; PIERCE PENNILESS = an embodiment of impecuniosity: *cf.* POVERTY CORNER.

1579. LYLY, *Euphues*, D. 3. That everie stoole he sate on was PENNILESSE BENCH, that his robes were rags.

1630. TAYLOR, *Works* [NARES]. I entred like PIERCE PENNILESSE, altogether monyles.

*d.*1640. MASSINGER, *City Madam*, iv. 1. Bid him bear up, he shall not Sit long on PENNILESS BENCH.

PENNY, *subs.* (old).—1. Money in general; OOF (*q.v.*). Hence 'A PRETTY PENNY' = a large sum.

See RHINO.

1362. LANGLAND, *Piers Plowman*, xiii. 246. Lo, how PANE purchasede faire places and drede.

1596. SHAKSPEARE, *Merry Wives*, ii. 2. 1. I will not lend thee a PENNY.

1596. SHAKSPEARE, *King John*, v. 2. What PENNY hath Rome borne, what men provided?

1887. *Contemporary Review*, li. 17. Shah Sujah and Shere Ali cost India a PRETTY PENNY.

*d.*1892. TENNYSON, *Will Waterproof.* That eternal want of PENCE Which vexes public men.

2. (American).—A cent.

[Various colloquial usages obtain: *e.g.* A PENNY FOR YOUR THOUGHTS = a call to persons in a BROWN STUDY (*q.v.*); AT FIRST PENNY = at first bid or offer; CLEAN AS A PENNY = (1) very clean, and (2) completely; NOT A PENNY TO BLESS ONESELF WITH = very poor; PENNY OR PATERNOSTER = pay or prayers, love or money: *cf.* MONEY OR MARBLES (GASCOIGNE); TO THINK ONE'S PENNY SILVER = to have a good opinion of one's self; TO TURN A HONEST PENNY = to earn money honestly; TO TURN (or GET) A PENNY = to make money, to endeavour to live (DRYDEN); PENNY WISE AND POUND FOOLISH = careful in small matters and extravagant in large ones (GROSE); PENNY PLAIN OR TWO-PENCE COLOURED = said of things varying in quality.]

1510. FOXE, *Acts and Monuments* [Cattley], iv. TO TURN A PENY.

*c.*1520. *Maid Emlyn* [HAZLITT, *Early Pop. Poet.* iv. 85]. His wyfe made hym so wyse, That he wolde TOURNE A PENY TWYSE, And then he called it a ferthynge.

1546. HEYWOOD, *Proverbs*, s.v. He had NOT ONE PENY TO BLISSE HIM. *Ibid.* A PENY FOR YOUR THOUGHT. *Ibid.* NO PENY NO PATERNOSTER.

1566. GASCOIGNE, *Supposes*, i. 1. Pity nor pension, PENNY NOR PATERNOSTER should never have made nurse once to open her mouth in the cause.

1594. GREENE and LODGE, *Looking Glass for London and England*, 123. Believe me, though she say that she is fairest, I THINK MY PENNY SILVER, by her leave.

1594. GREENE, *Friar Bacon and Friar Bungay* [*Century*]. How cheer you, sir? A PENNY FOR YOUR THOUGHTS.

*d.*1631. CAPT. JOHN SMITH, *Works*, ii. 219. Her fraught, which she sold AT THE FIRST PENNY.

1641. PEACHAM, *Worth a Penny*, 267. PENNY WISE AND POUND FOOLISH.

*c.*1696. B. E., *Dict. Cant. Crew*, s.v. PENNY-WHITE. PENNY-WISE AND POUND-FOOLISH, Sparing in a little and Lavish in a great Deal, save at the Spiggot and let it out at the Bung-hole. *Ibid.* TO GET A PENNY, to endeavour to Live. *Ibid.* TO TURN AND WINDE THE PENNY, to make the most of one's Money.

*d.*1701. DRYDEN, *Works* [*Century*]. Be sure to TURN THE PENNY.

1708-10. SWIFT, *Polite Conversations*, i. *Neverout.* . . . Come; A PENNY FOR YOUR THOUGHTS. *Miss.* It is not worth a Farthing; for I was thinking of you.

1740. RICHARDSON, *Pamela*, II. 56. I am AS CLEAN AS A PENNY, though I say it.

1885. *Daily Telegraph*, 23 Sep. Override any arguments advanced by the supporters of a PENNY-WISE and POUND-FOOLISH policy.

PENNY-A-LINER, *subs. phr.* (journalists').—A writer of paragraphs at the rate of a penny a line, or some such small sum; a literary hack. Fr. *un écrivain de ferblanc.* Hence, PENNY-A-LINERISM.

1840. THACKERAY, *Paris Sketch Book*, 232. As inflated as a newspaper document, by an unlimited PENNY-A-LINER.

1845. *Punch*, viii. 190. If the paper were limited in its knowledge to facts, what on earth would become of the PENNY-A-LINERS.

1853. *Diogenes*, ii. 21. An idea worth, we should say, a very great deal more than a PENNY A LINE.

1857. BRADLEY, *Verdant Green*, II. viii. Young ladies, moreover, who, as PENNY-A-LINERS say, are possessed of considerable personal attractions.

1865. *Atlantic Monthly*, June, 711. There must be an end to all temporal things, and why not to books. The same endless night awaits a Plato and a PENNY-A-LINER.

1872. KINGTON OLIPHANT, *Standard English*, 244. The PENNY-A-LINERS now write about a splendid shout.

PENNY-BOY, *subs. phr.* (old).—A boy who haunted the cattle markets on the chance of driving beasts to the slaughter-house, an ANKLE-BEATER (*q.v.*). [They were paid a penny per head.]

PENNY-DREADFUL (or **-AWFUL**), *subs. phr.* (colloquial).—A sensational story, newspaper, or print. [Published at a penny.] *See* AWFUL, BLOOD-AND-THUNDER, and SHILLING SHOCKER.

1883. *Daily News*, 30 Jan., 5, 2. Persons of culture are apt to speak harshly of PENNY DREADFULS, as they call the novels which appear in cheap weekly journals.

1885. *Daily Telegraph*, 3 Oct. From whatever PENNY DREADFUL she had got the chloroform incident.

1891. *Morning Advertiser*, 18 Mar. The chairman said he must have been reading some PENNY DREADFULS or other low literature.

1892. *Pall Mall Gaz.*, 17 Nov., 7, 2. A victim of the PENNY DREADFUL [Title].

PENNY-FATHER (or PENI-FATHER), *subs. phr.* (old).—A miser; a niggard.

1551. MORE, *Utopia*, II. vi. And yet knowing them to be such niggish PENY-FATHERS, that . . . as long as they live, not the worth of one farthing of that heap of gold shall come to them.

1594. DRAYTON, *Idea*, x. 1262. To nothing fitter can I thee compare Than to the son of some rich PENNY-FATHER.

1595. FLORIO, *Worlde of Wordes*, s.v. *Ghiarone*, old gold laide vp by mizers, . . . or PENNIE-FATHERS.

1607. TOPSELL, *Beasts*, 262. The great men, the rich mysers and PENNY-FATHERS.

*d.*1612. HARRINGTON, *Epigrams*, ii. 21. Alas, this reconfirms what I said rather, Cosmus has ever been a PENNY-FATHER.

*d.*1627. MIDDLETON, *Father Hubbert's Tales* [*Century*]. Illiterate hinds, rude boors, and hoary PENNY-FATHERS.

1629. *Pasquil's Jests* [HALLIWELL]. Hee (good old PENNY-FATHER) was glad of his liquor, and beganne to drinke againe.

*d.*1693. MORGAN, *Phoenix Brit.*, 33. Ranck PENNY-FATHERS scud, with their halfe hammes Shadowing their calves, to save their silver dammes.

PENNY-GAFF, *subs.* (obsolete).—A low-class theatre or music-hall. [The charge for admission being a penny or two.] *See* quot. 1851. Also PENNY-ROOM and DUKEY: *cf.* PENNY-HOP.

1851. MAYHEW, *Lond. Lab.*, I. 42. In many of the thoroughfares of London shops have been turned into a kind of temporary theatre . . . Rude pictures of the performers are arranged outside, to give the front a gaudy and attractive look, and at night-time coloured lamps and transparencies are displayed to draw an audience. These places are called by the costers PENNY-GAFFS; and on a Monday night as many as six performances will take place, each one having its two hundred visitors.

1866. ANNIE THOMAS, *Walter Goring*, II. 131. The difference between a PENNY-GAFF and a fair, or, as we call it, a canvas-clown.

PENNY-HOP, *subs. phr.* (old).—A country dancing club. [Each person paid a penny to the fiddler.]

PENNY-LATTICE-HOUSE, *subs. phr.* (old).—A low ale-house: *see* LUSH-CRIB and RED-LATTICE.

PENNY-POET, *subs. phr.* (old).—A reproach; a gutter rhymester.—KEMP, *Dance to Norwich* (1601).

PENNY-POTS, *subs. phr.* (common).—Pimples on the face of a hard drinker.

PENNY-ROYAL, *adj.* (American).—Poor; common; inferior.

PENNY-STARVER (or **-BUSTER**), *subs. phr.* (common).—A penny roll, or bun.

PENNY-WEDDING, *subs. phr.* (Old Scots').—*See* quot. 1897.

1822. SCOTT, *Fortunes of Nigel*, xxvii. We'll have a' to pay . . . a sort of PENNY-WEDDING it will prove, where all men contribute to the young folks' maintenance.

1897. BREWER, *Phrase and Fable*, s.v. PENNY-WEDDING. Wedding banquets in Scotland, to which a number of persons were invited, each of whom paid a small sum of money not exceeding a shilling. After defraying the expenses of the feast, the residue went to the newly-married pair, to aid in furnishing their house. Abolished in 1645.

PENNY-WEIGHT, *subs.* (American).—*See* quot.

1890. *Daily Chronicle*, 1 Dec. Wright and two American women . . . had pleaded guilty to . . . stealing . . . jewellery from the shops of jewellers in the City and the West-end. . . . Wright was well known as a PENNY-WEIGHT thief in America, which was explained as a thief who devoted his attention to robberies of this description.

PENNY-WHITE, *adj.* (old). — *See* quot.

*c.*1696. B. E., *Dict. Cant. Crew*, s.v. PENNY-WHITE, said of her to whom Fortune has been kinder than Nature.

PENNYWORTH (or **PENN'ORTH**), *subs.* (colloquial).—One's money's-worth; a right equivalent; what's owing and more: A GOOD PENNYWORTH = a royal bargain: *cf.* ROBIN HOOD'S PENNYWORTH; TO CAST PENNYWORTHS = to count the cost.—B. E. (*c.*1696); GROSE (1785).

1534. UDALL, *Roister Doister*, IV. vii. 75 [ARBER]. I will haue some PENYWORTH, I will not leese [lose] all.

1588. *Marprel. Epistle*, 27 [ARBER]. If you deny me this request I will . . . haue my PENIWORTHS of them for it.

1600. SHAKSPEARE, *Much Ado*, ii. 3. We'll fit the kid fox with a PENNYWORTH.

1605. CHAPMAN, *All Fools*, ii. I do not doubt, But t'have my PENNYWORTHS of these rascals one day.

1678. DRYDEN, *Prol. to Œdipus*, 33. You needs will have your PENN'ORTHS of the play, And come resolved to damn, because you pay.

1695. LOCKE, *Reas. of Chr.* [*Ency.*]. The priests sold the better PENNYWORTHS, and therefore had all the custom.

1713. SWIFT, *Journal to Stella*, 25 March, 62. The bishop . . . has bought abundance of pictures, and Dr. Pratt has got him very good PENNYWORTHS.

1717. CIBBER, *Non-Juror*, iv. *Col.* One would think the villain suspects his footing . . . is but short-lived: he is in such haste to have his PENNYWORTHS out on't.

1724. DEFOE, *Tour thro' East. Counties*, 21. It is very good farming in the marshes, because the landlords let good PENNYWORTHS.

1748. MONTAGUE [DODSLEY, *Poems*, III. 287]. Behold this equipage by Mathers wrought, With fifty guineas (a good PEN'ORTH!) bought!

1757. FRANKLIN, *Poor Richard's Almanac*, f. 1758. Many have been ruined by buying good PENNYWORTHS.

1771. SMOLLETT, *Humph. Clinker* [GIBBINGS (1900), i. 54]. Mistress said, if I didn't go, I should take a dose of bum-taffy; and so remembering how it worked Mrs. Gwyllim a PENN'ORTH, I chose rather, &c.

1860. ELIOT, *Mill on Floss*, III. vi. My mother gets a good PENN'ORTH in' picking feathers an' things.

PENSIONER, *subs.* (venery).—1. A prostitute's bully; FANCY-MAN (*q.v.*): *see* PETTICOAT.—VAUX (1819).

1887. A. BARRERE, *Argot and Slang*, 272. Prostitute's bully, or PENSIONER.

2. (University: Cambridge).—One who pays a 'pensio' or rent for rooms in College: at Oxford a COMMONER (*q.v.*).

1780. MANSEL [WHIBLEY, *Cap and Gown*]. At Cambridge Commencements the time When gentlemen come for degrees, And with wild-looking cousins and wives Through a smart mob of PENSIONERS squeeze.

PENT (THE), *subs.* (old).—Pentonville prison: *see* CAGE.

1857. *Punch*, 31 Jan., 49. For if Guv'ment wos here, not the Alderman's Bench, Newgit, soon 'ud be bad as THE PENT, or 'the Tench.'

PENTHOUSE-NAB, *subs. phr.* (old).—A broad-brimmed hat: *see* GOLGOTHA. — B. E. (1696); GROSE (1785).

PENWIPER, *subs.* (venery).—1. The female *pudendum*: *see* MONOSYLLABLE.

2. (common).—A handkerchief: *see* FOGLE.

PEOPLE, *subs.* (colloquial). — Any sort of allies or connections—racial, parental, hired, voluntary: with or without the possessive. At Harrow = relations or visitors: 'I've got PEOPLE coming down.'

13 [?]. *English Gilds* [E. E. T. S.], 332. Where-thurgh the Kynges lege PEOPELL scholde be disceuyd.

1440. *Generydes* [E. E. T. S.], 1, 1967. And what PEOPVLL they brought among them three, Mynne Auctour seith it is a wonder to see.

1474. CAXTON, *Game of the Chesse* [KINGTON-OLIPHANT, *New English*, i. 331. Caxton is fond of using PEPLE for *homines*; a queen should spring *of* (from) *honest* PEPLE, p. 27 (ed. Axon); we now often use *my* PEOPLE for *my family*].

1602. SHAKSPEARE, *Twelfth Night*, iii. 3. You slew great number of his PEOPLE.

1743. POCOCKE, *Description of the East*, I. 33. A stranger . . . being conducted . . . to the Pacha's coffee-room, is civilly entertained by his PEOPLE with sweetmeats and coffee.

1790. BRUCE, *Source of the Nile*, I. 141. Some of our PEOPLE had landed to shoot.

1841. LEVER, *Charles O'Malley*, xxxvi. Our PEOPLE have not been engaged.

PEPPER, *subs.* and *verb.* (old).—1. Vigorous or persistent action. Thus PEPPER, *verb.* = (1) to chastise desperately by word or deed; and (2) to pain or inconvenience or punish: as a pugilist by blows, cannon by shot, or a whore by infection. Whence (3) violent and ardent motion: *e.g.* pelting rain, heavy betting, or (in skipping) when the turn of the rope is increased from a slow pace to SALT (*q.v.*), and then to the quickest possible or PEPPER (Fr. *du vinaigre*). Derivatives are PEPPERER = (1) forcible or rigorous attack, and (2) a hot-tempered, active, or violent person; PEPPERING = a fierce attack. As *adj.* (PEPPERING or PEPPERY) = angry; and PEPPERED = badly hurt, or hurt to the death (*see* PIPPED): usually with a hint at pox or clap.

1589. NASHE, *Returne of Pasquill*, [*Works*, i. 97]. *Mar.* It is a common reporte that the faction of *Martinisme* hath mightie freends. *Pas.* Thats a bragge *Marforius*: yet if there be any such . . . I wyll picke out a time to PEPPER them.

1595. SHAKSPEARE, *Romeo and Juliet*, iii. 1. I am PEPPERED, I warrant, for this world.

1598. SHAKSPEARE, *1 Hen. IV.*, ii. 4. 'Pray God you have not murdered some of them.' 'Nay, that's past praying for: I have PEPPERED two of them.'

1607. DEKKER, *Northward Hoe*, ii. 1. *Hor.* Hold up, my fine girl—what ghosts haunt thy house? *Doll.* I have a clothier's factor or two, a grocer that would fain PEPPER me . . . a Dutch merchant that would spend all . . . to take measure of my Holland sheets when I lie in 'em.

1615. STEPHENS, *Essays and Characters* [NARES]. You snarle . . . As if you had beene PEPPERD with your wench.

1622. MASSINGER, *Virgin Martyr*, iv. 1. Gone, gone; he's PEPPERED. It is thou Hast done this act infernal.

1652. SHIRLEY, *Brothers*, v. 3. I have made him sure too, I have PEPPER'D him . . . I have cut his throat.

c. 1696. B. E., *Dict. Cant. Crew*, s.v. PEPPERD OFF, Damnably Clapt or Poxt. *Ibid.* PEPPER proof, not CLAPT or POXT.

c. 1707. DURFEY, *Pills to Purge, &c.* (1707), ii. 211. Their *Tails* are PEPPER'D with the *Pox*, And that you're welcome to.

1712. SWIFT, *Journ. to Stella*, Feb. Letter 20, 41. Sir Thomas Hamner is . . . drawing up a representation of the state of the nation to the queen . . . I believe it will be a PEPPERER.

1764. HARA, *Midas*, ii. 4. And I'll warrant we'll PEPPER his jacket.

1785. GROSE, *Vulg. Tongue*, s.v.

1819. MOORE, *Tom Crib*, . . . Showers of Randall's shot . . . fell PEPPERING hot.

1836. M. SCOTT, *Tom Cringle*, i. The French, . . . are . . . sufficiently strong to PEPPER us very decently in the outgoing.

1851. MAYHEW, *London Lab.*, III. 109. I felt it when the doctor dressed it, for it gave me PEPPER taking the plaster off.

1856. HUGHES, *Tom Brown's School-days*, I. iv. What do they do with the pea-shooters? inquires Tom. Do wi'em! Why, PEPPERS every one's faces as we comes near.

1856. C. READE, *Never Too Late*, xxxiv. Now don't you be so PEPPERY, father, said she. There is nothing to make a quarrel about.

1863. *Literary Times*, 14 Mar. There were several shops, where, under pretence of a small purchase, you could get PEPPER to a 'pony' on any pending race.

1865. DICKENS, *Mutual Friend*, I. vi. It's my way to make short cuts at things. I always was a PEPPERER.

1868. OUIDA, *Under Two Flags*, iii. Some PEPPERING one or other of the favorites, hotly.

1882. *Athenæum*, 28 Nov. The PEPPERY governor promptly refused to see such people.

1884. *Field*, 6 Dec. The PEPPERING of the rain on the tent.

1885. *Cassell's Sat. Journal*, 19 Sep. The vessel at which we were now PEPPERING away.

1891. GOULD, *Double Event*, 135. It seemed to be an understood thing that the horse was a 'dead un,' and they PEPPERED him accordingly. *Ibid.* 183. Messrs. Isaacs and Moss PEPPERED Caloola to their heart's content.

1888. *Sporting Life*, 15 Dec. Gower sent his man down twice, and, following up, administered PEPPER. *Ibid.* 6 Dec. Continued to PEPPER his canister with his left.

1891. RUSSELL, *Ocean Tragedy*, 23. Will she be armed, I wonder. It would then make the oddest of all PEPPERING matches.

1892. ANSTEY, *Voces Populi*, 'At the Military Exhibition,' 72. Never mind. You PEPPERED 'im. I sor the feathers floy!

1897. MITFORD, *Romance Cape Frontier*, II. xii. Twenty of the best shots are told off to PEPPER the retreating enemy.

2. *Verb.* (University). — To mark-in the accents of a Greek exercise.

3. *Verb.* (common).—To humbug; TO GAMMON (*q.v.*). Also TO THROW PEPPER IN THE EYES (or TO USE THE PEPPER-BOX).

TO HAVE (or TAKE) PEPPER IN THE NOSE, *verb. phr.* (old).—1. To be testy; to offend quickly; to get angry. Fr. *la moutarde lui monte au nez.*

1362. LANGLAND, *Piers Plowman*, xv. 197. There are ful proude-herted men paciente of tonge, And boxome as of berynge to burgeys and to lordes, And to pore peple hav PEPER IN THE NOSE.

d. 1529. SKELTON [DYCE, *Works*, ii. 38]. For drede of the red hat TAKE PEPER IN THE NOSE.

1547. HEYWOOD, *Dialogues*, sig. G. Hee TAKETH PEPPER IN THE NOSE, that I complayne Vpon his faultes.

1570. ELDERTON, *Lenton Stuffe* [HALLIWELL]. For every man takes PEPPER I' THE NOSE For the waggynge of a strawe.

1578. NORTH, *Plutarch*, 173. Wherewith enraged all (with PEPPER IN THE NOSE) The proud Megarians came to us, as to their mortal foes.

1590. TARLETON, *Newes out of Purgatorie* [HALLIWELL]. Myles, hearing him name the baker, TOOK straight PEPPER IN THE NOSE, and, starting up, threw of his cardinals roabes.

1595. FLORIO, *Worlde of Wordes*, s.v. *Montare su la Bica*, to TAKE PEPPER IN THE NOSE, to be sore angrie.

1607. MARSTON, *What you Will*, Induction. He's a chollerick gentleman: he will TAKE PEPPER IN THE NOSE instantly.

1611. CHAPMAN, *May-Day*, iii. Because I entertained this gentleman . . . he TAKES PEPPER I' THE NOSE.

1639. *Optic Glasse of Humors* [NARES]. A man is teisty, and anger wrinckles his nose, such a man TAKES PEPPER IN THE NOSE.

1653. MIDDLETON and ROWLEY, *Spanish Gipsy* [*Anc. Dr.*, iv. 190] Take you PEPPER IN YOUR NOSE, you mar our sport.

c. 1662. *Rump Songs* [NARES]. Alas, what take ye PEPPER IN THE NOSE To see king Charles his colours worne in pose?

1670. RAY, *Proverbs* [BOHN (1883), 174]. s.v.

PEPPER-AND-SALT, *adj.* (common).—Light grey; mingled black and white: applied to fabrics.

1843. DICKENS, *Chuzzlewit*, xxvii. A short-tailed PEPPER-AND-SALT coat.

1876. ELIOT, *Daniel Deronda*, xlii. A man in a PEPPER-AND-SALT dress.

PEPPER-BOX, *subs. phr.* (old).—A revolver.

THE PEPPER-BOXES (or CASTORS), *subs. phr.* (common).—Domes or cupolas: specifically the National Gallery in Trafalgar Square, but applied to any dome-shaped building: *cf.* BOILERS.

1855. THACKERAY, *Newcomes*, xxii. Think of half a mile of pictures at the Louvre! Not but that there are a score under the old PEPPER-BOXES in Trafalgar Square as fine as the best here.

1887. FRITH, *Autobiog.*, i. 56. What the students called the PEPPER-BOX, namely, the centre cupola of the new National Gallery in Trafalgar Square.

1901. *Daily Telegraph*, 2 Feb., 10, 5. Godalming's PEPPERBOX is to be preserved. This is the local appellation by which the old market house and former town hall is known, and the title was bestowed on it because the shape of the structure, which stands in the middle of the main street, is more like that article of domestic use than anything else.

See PEPPER, *verb.* 3.

PEPPERIDGE. TO PAY THE PEPPERIDGE, *verb. phr.* (provincial).—To pay one's FOOTING (*q.v.*): as a schoolboy has to PEPPERIDGE his mates when he puts on a new suit of clothes.

PEPPER'S DRAGOONS, *subs. phr.* (military).—The Eighth Hussars.

PEPST, *adj.* (old).—Drunk: *see* DRINKS and SCREWED.

1577. KENDALL, *Flowers of Epigrammes* [NARES]. Thou drunken faindst thyself of late; Thou three daies after slept: How wilt thou slepe with drinke in deede, When thou art thoroughly PEPST?

PERAMBULATOR, *subs.* (streets').—*See* quot.

1870. HAZLEWOOD and WILLIAMS, *Leave it to Me*, i. Joe's a PERAMBULATOR; . . . a perambulating greengrocer, called by vulgar people a costermonger.

PERCH, *subs.* (colloquial).—A high seat; a resting place.

TO DROP (HOP or FALL) OFF (or TIP OVER) THE PERCH, *verb. phr.* (common).—To die: *see* HOP THE TWIG. Also TO PERCH.

1594. NASHE, *Nuf. Traveller* [GROSART, *Works*, v. 41]. It was inough [in the time of the 'sweating sickness'] if a fat man did but trusse his points, to TURNE him OUER THE PEARCH.

1653. URQUHART, *Rabelais*, III. Prol. Through negligence, or want of ordinary sustenance, they both TIPT OVER THE PERCH.

1748. RICHARDSON, *Clarissa*, vi. 350. Her late husband . . . TIPT OFF THE PERCH in it, neither knowing how to yield, nor knowing how to conquer.

1821. SCOTT, *Pirate*, xl. He . . . expired without a groan. I always thought him a d—d fool . . . but never such a consummate idiot as to HOP THE PERCH SO sillily.

1886. *Sporting Times*, 3 Aug. 1, 3. Well, s'pose I PERCHED first? Well, replied Pitcher, I should just come in where you were lying in the cold-meat box, and I should whisper in your ear, etc.

TO KNOCK OFF THE PERCH, *verb. phr.* (common).—To upset; to defeat: TO DO FOR (*q.v.*).

PERCHER, *subs.* (Winchester College).—A Latin cross laid horizontally against the name of an absentee on any roll.

PERFECT-LADY, *subs. phr.* (common).—A prostitute: *see* TART.

PERFECTLY DEMMY, *adj.* (American cadet).—Stylishly dressed.

PERFORATE, *verb.* (venery).—1. To take a maidenhead: *see* GREENS and RIDE.

PERFORM, *verb.* (colloquial).—1. To carry out a design: generally a dishonest one; to play; to work. TO PERFORM ON A FLAT = to cozen a fool.

2. (venery).—To copulate: *see* GREENS and RIDE. Hence, PERFORMER = a whoremonger.

PERGER. *See* PURGER.

PERICRANIUM (or **PERICRANE**), *subs.* (old: now recognised). — The head or skull. [Properly the lining membrane of the bones of the skull.].—B. E. (*c.* 1696).

1690. DURFEY, *Collin's Walk*, i. Attempt to storm thy PERICRANE.

PERIODICITY-RAG, *subs. phr.* (common).—The menstrual cloth; THE FLAG (*q.v.*).

PERISHED, *adj.* (colloquial). — Starved with cold: hence, collapsed, as from fear or pain.

1888. BOLDREWOOD, *Robbery under Arms*, xli. Says Aileen, looking regularly PERISHED, You don't mean to say they've taken him?

PERISHER, *subs.* (common).—1. A short-tailed coat; a jacket: also BUM- (or ARSE-) PERISHER.

2. (common). — A consummation; an extreme.

1888. BOLDREWOOD, *Robbery under Arms*, xli, Then he most times went in an awful PERISHER—took a month to it, and was never sober day or night the whole time.

1890. *Lic. Vict. Gaz.*, 7 Nov. He went in a PERISHER last night, laying against Sir Tatton Sykes for the Derby with a half-a-dozen thousand pound notes in his hands, all of which he will lose.

PERIWINKLE (or **PERRIWINKLE**), *subs.* (old).—1. A wig. [A corruption of periwig]. Fr. *une panoufle*, *un gazon*, and (thieves') *un boubane*.—B. E. (1696).

2. (venery).—The female *pudendum* : *see* MONOSYLLABLE.

PERKS, *subs.* (vulgar).—Perquisites.

1887. *Fun*, 30 March, 138. The PERKS, etc., attached to this useful office are not what they were in the 'good old times.'

1889. *Pall Mall Gaz.*, 27 Sep., 2, 2. How incorrigible the City Corporation is, to be sure, in a matter of its PERKS.

1890. TRAILL, *Saturday Songs*, 68. The position ain't high, and the PERKS isn't weighty.

1897. *Sporting Times*, 13 Mar., 1, 2. She's of value in a thousand ways, she never looks for PERKS, Even when she takes a holiday she stops at home and works.

TO PERK UP, *verb. phr.* (old colloquial).—1. To plume oneself; to adorn.

1601. SHAKSPEARE, *Henry VIII.*, ii. 3. 'Tis better to be lowly born . . . Than to be PERKED up in a glistering grief, And wear a golden sorrow.

2. (colloquial). — To recover from sickness.—B. E. (*c.*1696).

BOARD OF PERKS, *subs. phr.* (common).—Board of Works.

1889. *Pall Mall Gaz.*, 27 Sep. Provincial BOARDS OF PERKS. [Title.]

PERKIN, *subs.* (old).—1. Weak cider or perry.—GROSE (1785).

2. (obsolete). — Beer. [From Barclay, Perkin & Co.]

PERKING, *subs.* (old).—*See* quot. *c.*1696: as *adj.* = peering; inquisitive.

*c.*1696. B. E., *Dict. Cant. Crew*, s.v. PERKING, the late D of M. Also any pert, forward, silly Fellow.

1835. DICKENS, *Sketches by Boz*, iv. He is a tall, thin, bony man with . . . little restless, PERKING eyes.

PERNEL. *See* PANEL.

PERNICATED, *adj.* (American).—Swaggering; full of SIDE (*q.v.*).

PERNICKITY (or **PERNICKETTY**), *adj.* (Scots').—Fastidious; over-particular.—JAMIESON.

1886. *Pop. Sci. Monthly*, xxvi. 52. This I say for the benefit of those who otherwise might not understand what PERNICKITY creatures astronomers are.

1888. *Harper's Mag.*, Eng. ed. viii. 875. Any white man . . . grows lame and impatient at such confining and PERNICKETY work.

PERPENDICULAR, *subs.* (common).—1. A stand-up lunch; an evening party where the majority of the guests stand; an upright position.

1888. *Sporting Life*, 10 Dec. He soon resumed the PERPENDICULAR, and went for his antagonist, who evaded him easily.

1882. EDNA LYALL, *Donovan*, ix. I duly attended my mother to three fashionable crowds, PERPENDICULARS is the best name for them, for there is seldom more than standing room.

2. (venery). — Coition taken standing: *cf.* HORIZONTAL. Also UPRIGHT and KNEE-TREMBLER.

PERSIMMON, *subs.* (American colloquial).—[A species of wild plum; in America as common, south of latitude 42°, as is the blackberry in England. Its fruit and hard wood are much esteemed. The huckleberry is akin to the whortleberry.] Among popular phrases are: TO RAKE UP THE PERSIMMONS = to pocket the stakes or spoils, TO RAKE (or PULL) IN THE PIECES (*q.v.*); THE LONGEST

POLE GETS (or KNOCKS) THE MOST PERSIMMONS = the best man wins, the strongest party gains the day [the persimmon tree sometimes attains to 60 ft.]; THE PERSIMMON IS ABOVE THE HUCKLEBERRY = a confession of inferiority; NOT A HUCKLEBERRY TO ONE'S PERSIMMON = not comparable; THAT'S PERSIMMON (or ALL PERSIMMON) = 'That's fine.'

PERSPIRE, *verb.* (colloquial).—To melt away; to vanish.

1897. MAUGHAM, *'Liza of Lambeth*, iii. The money's PERSPIRED like . . . It got less.

PERSUADER, *subs.* (common).—A pistol or revolver; a spur or DIGGER (*q.v.*); a JEMMY (*q.v.*) or other burglar's tool; the tongue.

1785. GROSE, *Vulg. Tongue*, s.v. PERSUADERS . . . The kiddey clapped his PERSUADERS to his prad, but the traps boned him.

1841. LEMAN REDE, *Sixteen String Jack*, ii. 4. *Dra* (*showing pistols*). I came in with my PERSUADER.

1886-96. MARSHALL, *Une Affaire d'Honneur* ['*Pomes*,' 110]. With finger nails she soon was going strong; As PERSUADERS they were nobby, for it seems it was her hobby To invariably wear them rather long.

PERSUADING-PLATE, *subs. phr.* (thieves').—An iron disk used in forcing safes: it revolves on a pivot, and is fitted with a cutting point.

PERT, *adj.* (colloquial).—Impudent. PERT END UP (American) = in good spirits; cheerful.

PERTHSHIRE GREYBREEKS (THE), *subs. phr.* (military).—The 2nd Batt. Cameronian (Scottish Rifles): formerly the 90th (Perthshire Volunteers) Regiment of Foot.

PER USUAL. *See* USUAL.

PESKY, *adj.* (American colloquial).—Troublesome; plaguy: also, as *adv.* = excessively.

1843-4. HALIBURTON, *Attache*, viii. He might have known how to feel for other folks, and not funkify them so PESKILY. *Ibid.* xxviii. I'm PESKILY sorry about that mare.

1869. H. B. STOWE, *Oldtown Folks*, 66. I got caught in those PESKY blackberry-bushes.

1881. *Harper's Monthly*, May, 872. I'm fishin' for pickerel, 'n I vaow they're PESKY scarce.

PESTER, *subs.* (American colloquial).—A trouble; a bother.

1869. H. B. STOWE, *Oldtown Folks*, 119. The PESTER on't was they allers lost.

PESTLE, *subs.* (venery).—1. The *penis*: *see* PRICK: *cf.* MORTAR = female *pudendum*. Also, as *verb.* = to copulate: *see* RIDE.

2. (old).—A constable's staff.

3. (old).—A leg: *cf.* 'PESTLE of pork,' long and still in vogue.

*d.*1529. SKELTON, *Elynour Rummyng* [Dyce, i. 108]. Her kyrtell she did vptucke An ynche aboue her kne, Her legges that ye might se . . . Myghty PESTELS . . . As fayre and as whyte As the fote of a kyte.

See KNIGHT.

PESTLE-HEAD, *subs.* (old). — A blockhead: *see* BUFFLE.

PET, *subs.* (colloquial). — 1. An angry mood; a tantrum; a fling of temper. — B. E. (*c.*1696); BAILEY (1748); GROSE (1785). Hence, TO BE PETTED = to take offence.

1548. BARCLAY, *Eclogue*, iv. Of rascolde poetes yet is a shamfull rable . . . Though all their cunning be scantly worth a PET.

1634. MILTON, *Comus* [Aldine], 721. Should in a PET of temperance feed.

1685. SIR P. HUME, *Narrative*, 42. As we were to goe, several gentlemen inclined to have gone with us, but the Erle PETTING at it, forbare and stayed there.

1749. SMOLLETT, *Gil Blas* [ROUTLEDGE], 109. They may take themselves off in a PET sometimes, the itch of writing brings them back again.

1766. BROOKE, *Fool of Quality*, i. 193. I would have sent to enquire after them, but I was PETTED at their neglect of us during our long illness.

2. (old: now recognised).—A darling: also in sarcasm. [In quot. 1607 = a delicate young thing.] Also PEAT. Whence, as *verb.* = to fondle.

*d.*1529. DUNBAR [KINGTON-OLIPHANT, *New English*, i. 361-3. Dunbar wrote . . . in Northern English . . . There are the Celtic words tartan . . . PET (darling) . . . tedder (tether), brat].

1562-77. GASCOIGN [CHALMERS, *Eng. Poets*, ii. 485.] I grooped in thy pocket pretty PEATE, And found a Lemman which I looked not.

1578. *King Lear* [NARES]. To see that proud pert PEAT, our youngest sister.

1581. RICHE, *Farewell to Mil. Prof.* [*Shakspeare Soc.*, 63]. Have you founde your tongue, now pretie PEATE? then wee most have an almon for parrat. How durst thou, strompette, chalenge me to bee thy father.

1593. SHAKSPEARE, *Taming of Shrew*, i. 1. A pretty PEAT! 'tis best Put finger in the eye.

1605. JONSON, CHAPMAN, &c., *Eastward Hoe* [*Old Plays* (REED), iv. 279.] God's my life, you are a PEAT indeed.

1607. DEKKER and WEBSTER, *Westward Hoe*, ii. 2. *Mon.* She's not troubled with the green sickness still, is she? *Bird.* The yellow jaundice . . . Troth she's as good a PEAT!

1629. BOYD, *Last Battell*, 324. Grosse euill thoghts fedde and PETTED with yeelding and consent.

*d.*1631. DONNE, *Poems*, 90. The wench a pretty PEAT, And (by her eye) well fitting for the seat.

1632. MASSINGER, *Maid of Honour*, ii. 2. You are a pretty PEAT, indifferent fair too.

1749. SMOLLETT, *Gil Blas* [ROUTLEDGE (1866), 168]. I was her PET, and came in for the caresses of all the men that frequented the house.

PETARD. HOIST WITH A PETARD (or PETAR), *phr.* (old).—Caught in one's own trap; involved in danger meant for others.

1596. SHAKSPEARE, *Hamlet*, iii. 4, 207. For 'tis the sport to have the engineer HOIST WITH HIS OWN PETAR.

PETE JENKINS, *subs. phr.* (circus).—An auxiliary clown. [The original Pete Jenkins (*c.*1855) had a line of BUSINESS (*q.v.*): he planted 'rustics' in the audience, and played them thence.

PETER, *subs.* (Old Cant).—1. A portmanteau, box, trunk, bag, or purse: generic for any parcel, bundle, or package, large or small. Whence PETER-BITER (-CLAIMER, or -MAN) = a carriage thief (*see* DRAG); PETER-DRAG (-HUNTING, or -LAY) = robbery from vehicles of all kinds; PETER-HUNTING JEMMY = a small crowbar used in smashing the chains securing luggage to a vehicle.—GROSE (1785); VAUX (1819); BEE (1823).

1724. HARPER, *Frisky Moll's Song* [FARMER, *Musa Pedestris* (1896), 41]. To you of the PETER LAY.

1728. *Street Robberies Consider'd*, 'Glossary,' s.v. PETER.

1752. SMOLLETT, *Faithful Narrative* [HENLEY, *Works* (1901), xii. 184]. For snabbling his PETER and queer Joseph.

1830. LYTTON, *Paul Clifford*, x. If so be as your name's Paul, may you always rob PETER [a portmanteau] in order to pay Paul.

1863. *Story of a Lancashire Thief*, 9. Sometimes he'd turn PETERMAN, and he had been generally lucky at it.

1879. HORSLEY, in *Macmillan's Mag.*, Oct. While I was looking about I piped a little PETER (parcel). *Ibid.* After we left the course we . . . got a PETER (cash-box) with very near a century of quids in it.

2. (Australian prison). — A punishment cell: *see* BOX.

3. (poachers').—A partridge.

4. (venery).—The *penis*: also ST. PETER (*q.v.*): *see* PRICK.

5. *Intj.* (old).—An oath: *cf.* MARY!

6. *See* PETER-SEE-ME.

7. (old gaming).—*See* quot.

1762. WILSON, *The Cheats*, iv. 1. Did not I . . . teach you . . . the use of up-hills, down-hills, and PETARS.*

[* Note. Terms applicable to false or loaded dice, or to the knavish mode of handling them.]

Verb. (gaming).—1. To call (in whist) for trumps by discarding an unnecessarily high card: *see* BLUE-PETER.

1887. *Notes and Queries*, 7 S. iv. 356. The Blue Peter . . . is always used when a ship is about to start. . . . Calling for trumps, or PETERING, is derived from this source.

2. (old).—To cease word or deed; TO STOW IT (*q.v.*).—VAUX (1819).

3. (auctioneers').—To run up prices: *see* PETER FUNK.

TO PETER OUT, *verb. phr.* (colloquial).—To fail; to become exhausted.

1876. *Boston Post*, 5 May. The speculator recommended a gentleman . . . to sell out at any sacrifice, as the mines were PETERED OUT.

1877. *New York Tribune*, 28 Feb. The influence of the Hon. ——, formerly a Democratic politician of some prominence, seems to have quite PETERED OUT.

1888. *Missouri Republican*, 15 Feb. The *Boston Herald* thinks the Hill boom is PETERING OUT.

1893. BRET HARTE, *Dow's Flat.* Then the bar PETERED OUT, And the boys wouldn't stay.

1899. *M. A. P.*, 8 Ap., 315, 2. In 1869 rumours went abroad that the Comstock mines were PETERING OUT.

TO GO (or PASS) THROUGH ST. PETER'S NEEDLE, *verb. phr.* (old).—To be severely disciplined: of children.

TO ROB (or BORROW FROM) PETER TO PAY (or CLOTHE) PAUL, *verb. phr.* (old).—To take of one to give to another; TO MANŒUVRE THE APOSTLES (*q.v.*).—GROSE (1785). [John Thirleby, the first and only bishop of Westminster (1541-50), 'having wasted the patrimony allotted by the King (Hen. VIII.) for the support of the see was translated to Norwich, and with him ended the bishopric of Westminster.'—HAYDN, *Dignities*: *see* quot. 1661.]

1548. BARCLAY, *Eclogues* [Percy Soc., xxii. p. xvii.] They ROBBE ST. PETER TO CLOTH ST. PAUL.

1653. URQUHART, *Rabelais*, III. iii. You may make a shift by BORROWING FROM PETER TO PAY PAUL ['*fa ez versure*' = Lat. *versurum facere*], and with other folks earth fill up his ditch.

1661. HEYLIN, *Hist. Ref. Ch. Eng.*, i. 256. The lands of Westminster so delapidated by Bishop Thirlby that there was almost nothing to support the dignity . . . Most of the lands invaded by the great men of the Court, the rest laid out for reparation to the Church of St. Paul, pared almost to the very quick in those days of rapine. From hence came first that significant byeword (as is said by some) of ROBBING PETER TO PAY PAUL.

PETER COLLINS (theatrical).—*See* quot.

1889. J. C. COLEMAN [S. J. & C., s.v. PETER COLLINS.] A gentleman never to be found . . . [on whom] young aspirants . . . are told to call. . . . The youth is sent from roof to cellar, and, finally, is generally let down a trap and left to get out as best he can. The password at circuses is the "green-handled rake," which the youth is requested to ask for. He is generally settled with a pill of horse-dung when they have had enough of him.

PETER FUNK, *subs. phr.* (American).—1. A decoy at a mock auction; also, at genuine but petty sales, a runner-up of prices; a PUFFER (*q.v.*). Hence (2) the personification of petty deceit and humbug.

PETER-GRIEVOUS, *subs. phr.* (common).—A fretful child.

PETER-GUNNER, *subs. phr.* (old).—An amateur gun; a PLASTERER (*q.v.*).—GROSE (1785).

1614. *The Cold Year* [NARES]. It was a shame that poore harmlesse birds could not be suffered to save themselves under a bush . . . but that every paltrie PETER-GUNNER must shoote fire and brimstone at them.

1633. SHIRLEY, *Witty Fair One*, ii. 2. I smell powder . . . this PETER-GUNNER should have given fire.

PETER LUG, *subs. phr.* (old).—A laggard in drinking.—B. E. (*c.*1696); GROSE (1785).

PETER-MAN, *subs. phr.* (old).—1. A fisherman: specifically 'those who formerly used unlawful engines in catching fish in the river Thames.'—BAILEY (1728). Whence, PETER-BOAT = a fishing-boat: specifically one built sharp, bow and stern, for quick handling. [In allusion to Math. iv. 18.]

1605. MARSTON, JONSON, and CHAPMAN, *Eastward Hoe*, ii, 3. Yet his skin is too thick to make parchment; 'twould make good boots for a PETERMAN to catch salmon in.

1607. DEKKER, *Northward Hoe*, ii. 1. If we have but good draughts in my PETER-BOAT, fresh salmon, you sweet villains, shall be no meat with us.

1657. HOWELL, *Londinop.*, 14. There are a great number of other kind of fishermen—belonging to the Thames, called Hebber-men, PETERMEN, and Trawlermen.

2. (thieves').—*See* PETER.

PETER-SEE-ME, *subs. phr.* (old).—A Spanish wine. [From Sp. 'Pedra Ximenes,' the famous cardinal.] Also PETER, PETER-SA-MENE, and PETER-SEMINE.

1617. BRATHWAITE, *Vandunk's Four Humours* [PALMER in *Stanford*]. I am phlegmaticke as may be, PETER SEE ME must inure me.

1620. BEAUMONT and FLETCHER, *Chances*, v. 3. By Canary thus I charge thee, By Britain metheglin, and PEETER, Appear and answer me in meeter.

1623. MIDDLETON, *Spanish Gypsy*, iii. 1. PETER-SEE-ME shall wash thy noul, And malaga glasses for thee.

1630. TAYLOR, *Works*, sig. 2 Fff 4 r. 1. PETER-SEE-MEA or head strong Charnico.

PETMAN, *subs.* (provincial).—The smallest pig in a litter; a TANTONY-PIG (*q.v.*).

PETRONEL. SIR PETRONEL FLASH, *subs. phr.* (old).—A swaggerer; a penniless ruffler; *see* quot. 1595.

1595. FLORIO, *Worlde of Wordes*, 585. SIR PETRONEL FLASH, a boasteing fellowe, a braggadochio.

1605. JONSON, CHAPMAN, and MARSTON, *Eastward Hoe*, Dram. Pers. SIR PETRONEL FLASH.

[?]. *Brit. Bibl.*, ii. 167. Give your scholler degrees, and your lawyer his fees, And some dice for SIR PETRONELL FLASH.

PETTICOAT, *subs.* (colloquial).—A woman: also as *adj.* Hence, PETTICOAT-AFFAIR = a matter with a woman in it; PETTICOAT-GOVERNMENT = female home-rule; PETTICOAT-HOLD = a life interest in a wife's estate (GROSE, 1785); PETTICOAT-MERCHANT = a whoremonger (*see* MOLROWER); PETTICOAT-PENSIONER (SQUIRE, or -KNIGHT, or SQUIRE OF THE PETTICOAT) = a male KEEP (*q.v.*); PETTICOAT-HUNTING = whoring; PETTICOAT-LED = infatuated of a woman; PETTICOAT-LOOSE (of women) = 'always ready'; UP ONE'S PETTICOAT = unduly intimate, &c.—B. E. (*c.*1696); GROSE (1785).

1607. DEKKER, *Northward Hoe*, v. 1. Where's this wench to be found? here are all the moveable PETTICOATS of the house.

1662. *Rump Songs*, ii. 41. The late PETTICOAT SQUIRE From his shop mounted higher.

1690. DRYDEN, *Amphitryon*, i. 1. Venus may know more than both of us, For 'tis some PETTICOAT AFFAIR.

1690. WILSON, *Belphegor*, iv. 2. Thou shalt supply my place—all PETTICOATS are sisters in the dark.

*c.*1707. *Old Song*, 'The Irish Jigg' [FARMER, *Merry Songs and Ballads* (1897), iv. 181]. In short I found it was one of the PETTICOAT sort . . . And then I went to her, resolving to try her.

1717. PRIOR, *Lucius* [Epilogue]. Fearless the PETTICOAT contemns his Frowns; The Hoop secures whatever it surrounds.

1725. BAILEY, *Coll. Erasmus*, 186. What does this PETTICOAT-PREACHER do here? Get you in and mind your kitchen.

1749. SMOLLETT, *Gil Blas* [ROUTLEDGE], 356. This . . . made me suspect that he was tied to the string of some PETTICOAT in the hamlet.

1766. BROOKE, *Foot of Quality*, 1. 199. I am quite impatient to be instructed in the policies and constitution of this your PETTICOAT GOVERNMENT.

1830. BUCKSTONE, *Cabdriver*, i. Do you think the gentlemen are to have all the loaves and fishes? PETTICOATS must be provided for.

1834. AINSWORTH, *Rookwood*, II. 6. Disarmed—defied by a PETTICOAT . . . What! afraid of a woman?

1849. KINGSLEY, *Alton Locke*, xxvii. Out came the very story which I had all along dreaded, about the expurgation of my poems, with the coarsest allusions to PETTICOAT INFLUENCE.

1897. MITFORD, *Romance of Cape Frontier*, I. i. There was a PETTICOAT in the case.

See SMOCK.

PETTICOAT LANE, *subs. phr.* (common).—Middlesex Street, E.: a well-known rendezvous of old-clothes dealers, mostly Jews. [In Yiddish = PILOMET = the initials (in Hebrew) P. L. Also Dover-street, Piccadilly, the seat of the Court milliner.

1887. *I. D. B.*, 251. 'What do you think?' ejaculated Soloman, falling back on PILOMET for his expletives.

1901. *D. Telegraph*, 9 Nov., 5, 5. The dovecotes of PETTICOAT-LANE, as Dover-street is now called, and its vicinity are fluttered by rumours of a great invasion of London during the Coronation festivities by representatives of French firms.

PETTIFOGGER, *subs.* (old: now recognised).—An attorney of the baser sort; a sharking lawyer. Hence (generally) = one given to mean or underhand practices, and as *verb.* = to conduct business in a sharp or paltry way. Whence derivatives: PETTIFOGGERY, PETTIFOGGING, and PETTIFOGULISE.—GROSE (1785).

1576. FLEMING, *Panopl. Epist.*, 320. As for this PETTIE FOGGER, this false fellowe that is in no credite or countenance.

1577. HARRISON, *Desc. of Eng.* [HOLINSHED'S *Chron.* (Shakspeare Soc.), i. 206]. Brokers betweene the PETTIE FOGGERS of the lawe, and the common people.

1588. M. KYFFIN, *Terence's Andria*, iv. 5. I should be exclaimed vpon to bee a beggerly FOGGER, greedily hunting after heritage.

*c.*1600. NORDEN, *Spec. Brit. Cornw.* (1728), 27. The baser sorte . . . verie litigious . . . whereof the FOGERS and Petie Lawiers . . . gett . . . great advauntage.

1604. MARSTON, *Malcontent*, i. 6. *Pas.* You will know me again, Malvole. *Mal.* O ay, by that velvet. *Pas.* Ay, as a PETTIFOGGER by his buckram bag.

1610. WEBSTER, *Devil's Law Case*, iv. 1. *Ari.* Are you her knave. *San.* No, sir, I am a clerk *Ari.* You whoreson FOGGING rascal.

1618. ROWLEY and MIDDLETON, *Cure for a Cuckold*, Dram. Pers. PETTIFOG, an Attorney.

1627. MINSHEU, *Guide to Tongues*, . . . A PETTIE FOGGER, a sillie aduocate or lawyer, rather a trouble-Toune, having neither law nor conscience.

1709. WARD, *London Spy*, i. 191. It may not be improper to conclude our Remarks of this Place with the Character of a PETTYFOGGER [then follows a description of upwards of two pages].

1749. SMOLLETT, *Gil Blas* [ROUTLEDGE], 138. A plodding PETTIFOGGER'S worthless brood might have gorged . . . on the love of a young nobleman . . . like yourself. *Ibid.*, 193. He practised as an attorney at Valencia, and bore his faculties in all the infamy of PETTIFOGGING.

1837. DICKENS, *Pickwick*, xxxi. 'Ah, they're smart fellows; very smart indeed' . . . Messrs. Dodson and Fogg. 'They are great scoundrels,' said Mr. Pickwick.

1886. OLIPHANT, *New English*, i. 596. PETTIE FOGGER of the law; this strange word is the Dutch *fokker*, a monopolist.

PETTY, *subs.* (old).—A scholar low in the school.

1692. HACKET, *Archb. Williams*, I. 37. Mr. Lamb . . . came, by holding fast to Fortunes' middle finger, from a schoolmaster that taught PETTIES, to a proctor in a Christian Court, and so to an official.

PEW, *subs.* (colloquial).—A place of abode, or business; a crib: *see* DIGGINGS. Formerly a box at a theatre: *see* ROOM. In quot. 1659 = a sheep-pen.

1605. SHAKESPEARE, *Lear*, iii. 3. Poor Tom whom the foul fiend . . . hath laid knives under his pillow, and halters in his PEW; set ratsbane by his porridge.

1613. WEBSTER, *Devil's Law Case*, iv. 1. In a PEW of our office . . . I have been dry-founder'd . . . this four years, Seldom found non-resident from my desk.

1659. MILTON, *Means to Remove Hirelings.* His sheep oft-times sit the while to as little purpose of benefitting, as the sheep in their PEWS at Smythfield.

PEW-OPENER'S MUSCLE, *subs. phr.* (medical).—A muscle in the palm of the hand. [SIR BENJAMIN BRODIE: 'because it helps to contract and hollow the palm for the reception of a gratuity.']

PEWTER, *subs.* (nautical).—Generic for money: specifically prize-money: *see* RHINO.

1842. EGAN, *Macheath*, 'The Bould Yeoman,' v. Hand up the PEWTER, farmer, you shall have a share.

1857. WHITTY, *Fr. of Bohemia*, 9. In these days it's the PEWTER makes the rank—and no mistake. By PEWTER Dwyorts meant gold.

1888. *Academy*, 24 Mar., 202. Another trifle to be noticed is the anxiety for PEWTER or prize-money which . . . animated our officers and men.

PEWY, *adj.* (sporting).—Enclosed by fences so as to form small fields.

1885. *Daily Telegraph*, 11 Dec. Sixty or seventy years since the fences were stronger, the enclosures smaller, the country more PEWY, and the hedges rougher and hairier than is now the case.

PFOTZE, *subs.* (venery).—The female *pudendum*: *see* MONOSYLLABLE.—J. HALL STEVENSON, *Crazy Tales* (1762).

PHALLUS, *subs.* (literary).—The *penis*: *see* PRICK. [Latin.]

PHARAOH, *subs.*—1. A corruption of 'faro.'

*d.*1732. GAY, *To Pulteney* [DAVIES]. Nanette last night at twinkling PHARAOH play'd, The cards the Talliers sliding hand obeyed.

1748. WALPOLE, *Letters*, II. 105. We divert ourselves extremely this winter; plays, balls, masquerades, and PHARAOH are all in fashion.

1760. MURPHY, *Way to Keep Him*, i. May I never taste the dear delight of breaking a PHARAOH bank, &c.

*c.*1796. WOLCOT, *Peter Pindar*, 249. Behold a hundred coaches at her door, Where PHARO triumphs in his mad career.

2. (old).—A strong ale or beer: also OLD PHARAOH: *see* SWIPES.—B. E. (*c.*1696); GROSE (1785).

1685. *Praise of Yorkshire Ale*, 3. Lac'd Coffee, Twist, OLD PHARAOH, and Old Hoc.

*d.*1704. T. BROWN [*Works*, ii. 286]. Ezekiel Driver, of Puddle-dock, carman, having disorder'd his *pia mater* with too plentiful a morning's draught of three threads and OLD PHARAOH, had the misfortune to have his cart run over him.

1839. AINSWORTH, *Jack Sheppard* [1889], 39. Don't muddle your brains with any more of that PHARAOH.

ONE OF PHARAOH'S LEAN KINE, *subs. phr.* (common).—A thin, spare person: one who looks (1) as though he'd run away from a bone-house; or (2) as if he were walking about to save his funeral expenses.

1598. SHAKSPEARE, *1 Hen. IV.*, ii. 4. If to be fat be to be hated, then PHARAOH'S LEAN KINE are to be loved.

1708-10. SWIFT, *Polite Conversation*, iii. *Lady Smart.* . . . The Man and his Wife are coupled like Rabbets, a fat and a lean; he's as fat as a Porpus, and she's ONE OF PHARAOH'S LEAN KINE.

PHEASANT, *subs.* (common).—1. A wanton. Hence PHEASANTRY = a brothel.

2. *See* BILLINGSGATE-PHEASANT.

PHEEZE (**PHEAZE**, **FEAZE**, or **FEIZE**), *verb.* (old).—To chastise; *see* TAN.

1579. PUTTENHAM, *Partheniades*, 180. Your pride serves you to FEAZE them all alone.

1593. SHAKSPEARE, *Taming of Shrew*, Induct. I'll PHEESE you, i'faith.

1602. SHAKSPEARE, *Troilus and Cr.*, ii. 3. An he be proud with me, I'll PHEEZE his pride.

1610. JONSON, *Alchemist*, v. 5. Come, will you quarrel? I will FEIZE you, sirrah.

PHILADELPHIA-CATECHISM, *subs. phr.* (American nautical).—The couplet:—'Six days shalt thou labour, and do all thou art able, And on the seventh —— holystone the decks and scrape the cable.'

PHILADELPHIA-LAWYER, *subs. phr.* (common).—A smart attorney: hence, TO PUZZLE (BE AS SMART AS, BEAT, or KNOW AS MUCH AS) A PHILADELPHIA-LAWYER = to be a paragon of shrewdness: *see* GREENBAG.

1876. HINDLEY, *Cheap Jack*, 128. In that style he'd hammer out all the old and usual 'whids' which, to persons away south of his country, . . . to use a modern metaphor, would PUZZLE HALF-A-DOZEN PHILADELPHIA-LAWYERS to understand.

188[?]. HAMILTON, *Men and Manners*, xi. 203. It is not unusual among the lower orders in England, when any knotty point is proposed for discussion, to say it would PUZZLE A PHILADELPHIA-LAWYER.

1901. *Daily Telegraph*, 6 Nov., 'Racing in the Fog.' Racing by electric light is better, all the same, than racing by no light at all, and what entertainment is afforded by a horse-race run "in camera," ONLY A PHILADELPHIA LAWYER WOULD BE ABLE TO EXPLAIN.

PHILANDER, *verb.* (old colloquial: now recognised).—To flirt; TO SPOON (*q.v.*); to wanton: of both sexes. Hence, as *subs.* (or PHILANDERER) = a lover: specifically a dangler after women.

1619. MASSINGER and FLETCHER, *Laws of Candy. Dram. Pers.* PHILANDER, Prince of Cyprus, passionately in love with Erota.

1700. CONGREVE, *Way of the World*, v. 1. I'll couple you; I'll baste you together, you and your PHILANDER.

1709. STEELE, *Tatler*, 10 May. PHILANDER . . . the most skilful of all men in an address to women.

1749. SMOLLETT, *Gil Blas* [ROUTLEDGE], 113. Tired of waiting . . . she had gone back . . . and the happy moment of PHILANDERING was over. *Ibid.*, 364. In a PHILANDERING tone of voice.

1800. EDGEWORTH, *Castle Rackrent*, II. Sir Kit was too much taken up PHILANDERING to consider the law in this case.

1827. LYTTON, *Pelham*, iii. Sir Lionell Garrett . . . the favourite of the old ladies, the PHILANDER of the young.

1852. THACKERAY, *Esmond*, III, iv. 'Tis no question of sighing and PHILANDERING between a nobleman of his Grace's age and a girl who hath little of that softness in her nature.

1857. KINGSLEY, *Two Years Ago*, xix. A phenomenon which . . . perturbed . . . the spirits not only of the Oxford PHILANDERERS, but also those of Elsley Vavasour.

1870. HALL, *Modern English*, 275. Who in Queen Anne's time ever heard . . . of the verbs cede, olden, PHILANDER? This verb not impossibly did not see the light till after Mr. Thackeray (*b.*1812) himself.

1876. ELIOT, *Deronda*, xxv. You can't go PHILANDERING after her again for six weeks.

PHILIP, *subs.* (thieves').—A policeman: *see* BEAK.

Intj. (thieves').—A warning. Hence, PHILIPER = a thief's accomplice. [Who watches and cries PHILIP!]

PHILIP AND CHEINEY, *subs. phr.* (old). —Any, and every one; 'TOM, DICK, and HARRY' (*q.v.*).

1542. UDALL, *Apop. of Erasmus*, 311. It was not his entent to bryng unto Sylla PHILIP AND CHEINEY, mo than a good meiny, but to bryng hable souldiours of manhood approued and well tried to his handes.

1557. TUSSER, *Good Husby.* [E. E. D. S. (1878), 8]. Loiterers I kept so meanie, Both PHILIP, HOB, and CHEANIE.

1563-4. BECON, *Workes*, iii. 276. Ye pray for PHILIP AND CHENY more than a good meany.

PHILIPPI. TO MEET AT PHILIPPI, *verb. phr.* (old).—To keep an appointment without fail. [*Cf. Julius Cæsar*, iv. 3, where the ghost of J. C. so delivers itself to Brutus.]

1782. COWLEY, *Bold Stroke for a Husband*, i. 1. *Car.* At seven, you say? *Jul.* Exactly. *Car.* I'll MEET THEE AT PHILIPPI!

PHILISTIA, *subs.* (literary).—The region of the unenlightened or commonplace: specifically (MATHEW ARNOLD) the English middle-class—'ignorant, narrow-minded, and deficient in great ideas.' Whence (generally) PHILISTINE = an unlettered BARBARIAN (*q.v.*); a person, male or female, who has never read Mathew Arnold. [Orig. German students' = anybody not belonging to a university.]

1857. KINGSLEY, *Two Years Ago*, x. Yet have PHILISTIA and Fogeydom neither right nor reason to consider him a despicable or merely ludicrous person.

1886. MCCARTHY and CAMPBELL-PRAED, *Rt. Hon.*, I. iii. Aristocratic PHILISTIA and Upper Bohemia.

1900. KIPLING, *Stalky & Co.*, 209. Vile bad form to turn your back on the audience! He's a PHILISTINE—a Bopper—a Jebusite an' a Hivite?

1901. *Daily Telegraph*, 25 Ap., 8, 7. We . . . have always had a reputation on the Continent for an almost brutal vitality and vigour, combined with a PHILISTINE deficiency in all matters concerning the delicate and the beautiful.

PHILISTINE, *subs.* (old).—1. Generic for a representative of authority: a sheriff's officer, a bailiff, a revenue officer, a watchman, and (in *pl.*) the press-gang [Judges xvi.].—B. E. (*c.*1696); GROSE (1785); BEE (1823).

1751. FIELDING, *Amelia*, v. vi. She was too ignorant . . . to know that if he had fallen into the hands of the PHILISTINES he would hardly have been able so soon to recover his liberty.

1771. SMOLLETT, *Humphrey Clinker*, ii. 191. I must make an effort to advance what further will be required to take my friend out of the hands of the PHILISTINES.

2. (old).—A drunkard: *see* LUSHINGTON.

1708-10. SWIFT, *Polite Conversation*, i. *Lady Answ.* But, Colonel, they say, you went to Court last Night very drunk: Nay, I'm told for certain you had been among PHILISTINES.

3. (provincial).—'Earwigs and such like insect tormentors.'—B. E. (*c.*1696).

4. *See* PHILISTIA.

PHIZ (PHYZ or PHYSOG), *subs.* (old).—The face: *see* DIAL.—B. E. (*c.*1696); GROSE (1785).

1693. CONGREVE, *Old Bachelor*, iv. 8. What a furious PHIZ I have.

1702. STEELE, *Grief a-la-Mode*, i. 1. Who can see such a horrid ugly PHYZ as that Fellow's and not be shock'd?

1708-10. SWIFT, *Polite Conversations*, Intro. Abbreviations exquisitely refined; as, . . . PHIZZ for Phisiognomy.

1725. BAILEY, Fr. of *Colloquies of Erasmus*, I. 51. Why, truly a Body would think so by thy slovenly Dress, lean Carcass, and ghastly PHYZ.

1785. *Poems in Buchan Dial*, 33. Can Ajax count his sculls wi' me? Fan I brought Priam's sin, And Pallas' PHIZ, out through my face.

1789. PARKER, *Song*, 'The Masqueraders' [FARMER, *Musa Pedestris* (1896), 73]. Twig methodist PHIZZES, with mask sanctimonious, Their rigs prove to judge that their PHIZ is erroneous.

1828. SMEATON, *Doings in London*. There is an odious harmony between his glossy garment and his smooth and senseless PHIZ.

1841. REDE, *Sixteen String Jack*, 'Song.' Says he, with his knowing PHIZ, I ain't very pertic'lar who it is!

1886-96. MARSHALL, '*Pomes' from the Pink 'Un*, 76. He'd his right mince in mourning, which so worried Liz That she bung'd up his left, just to steady his PHIZ.

1894. EGERTON, *Keynotes*, 87. It was so jolly to see the quaint little PHIZ smile up.

PHIZ-GIG, *subs.* (old).—1. An extravagantly dressed old woman; 'an old ewe dressed lamb-fashion.'

2. (school).—A pyramid of moistened gunpowder, which, on ignition, fuses but does not flash.

PHŒNIX-MAN, *subs. phr.* (old).—*See* quot. — BAILEY (1726); GROSE (1785).

*c.*1696. B. E., *Dict. Cant. Crew*, s.v. FIRE-DRAKES, Men with a Phenix for their Badge, in Livery, and Pay from the Insurance-Office, to extinguish Fires, Covering their Heads with an Iron-pot, or Head-piece.

PHŒNIX-NEST, *subs. phr.* (venery). —The female *pudendum*: *see* MONOSYLLABLE.

1619. MASSINGER and FIELD, *Fatal Dowry*, iii. 1. He toil'd to climb up to the PHŒNIX' NEST, And in his prints leaves your ascent more easy. I do not know, you that are perfect critics, In women's books, may talk of maidenheads.

*c.*1620-44. HERRICK, *Hesperides*, 'Love perfumes all Parts.' If I kisse Anthea's brest, There I smell the PHENIX NEST . . . Hands, and thighs and legs, are all Richly Aromaticall.

PHYSIC, *subs.* (venery).—1. Copulation: *see* GREENS and RIDE.

1623. MASSINGER, *Bonduca*, i. 2. You are no sooner out of sight, but she Does feel strange qualms; then sends for her young doctor, Who ministers PHYSIC to her on her back, Her ladyship lying as she were entranced. *Ibid.*, *Duke of Milan*, iv. 3. Lock up thy own wife, fool, that must take PHYSIC from her young doctor, PHYSIC upon her back Because thou hast the palsy in that part that makes her active.

*c.*1707. *Old Ballad* [DURFEY, *Pills* (1707), ii. 160]. For in your warm Beds Your PHYSICK works best; And tho' in the taking Some stirring's required, The motion's so pleasant You cannot be tir'd.

2. (common).—Strong drink; MEDICINE (*q.v.*); LUSH (*q.v.*): *see* DRINKS and SCREWED.

3. (pugilists').—Hard hitting; PUNISHMENT (*q.v.*): also as *verb.*

4. (gaming).—Losses: wagers, points, and so forth. Also as *verb.*—BEE (1823).

1821. EGAN, *Life in London*, II. v. If you do not get punished in your person, yet you may be most preciously PHYSICKED in your clie.

PHYZ. *See* PHIZ.

PI (or PIE), *subs.* (printers').—1. Type, jumbled and mixed. [Ordinarily a compositor, when distributing type, reads a line or sentence and is enabled to return it to 'case' with expedition: with PI, however, each 'stamp' has to be recognised separately.] Fr. *le pâté*: *faire du pâté* = to distribute PI; German, *zwiebelfisch* (= 'fish with onions').—BAILEY (1728). Also as *verb.*

*d.*1790. FRANKLIN, *Autobiog.*, 176. One night, when, having impos'd my formes, I thought my day's work over, one of them by accident was broken, and two pages reduced to PI.

1837. CARLYLE, *Fr. Revol.*, II. ii. iv. Your military ranked arrangement going all (as the typographers say of set types in a similar case) rapidly to PIE.

2. (booksellers').—A miscellaneous collection of books out of the ALPHABET (*q.v.*).

Adj. (general.) — Virtuous; sanctimonious: *e.g.*, 'He's very PI now, he mugs all day'; 'He PI-JAWED me for thoking.' Whence, PI-JAW (or GAS) = a serious admonition; PI-MAN = SIM (*q.v.*).

1901. *To-Day*, 22 Aug., 124, 2. The one blot on her staircase was an individual who . . . had turned ostentatiously pious. "I 'ates them PI-MEN," Mrs. Moggs was wont to say, "as often as not it's sheer 'ypocrisy."

PIAZZAS. TO WALK THE PIAZZAS, *verb. phr.* (old).—To quest for men; now 'to walk the streets.' —BEE (1823). [The PIAZZAS were those in Covent Garden, only a portion of which now (1901) remain.]

PICAROON (PICKAROON or PICARO), *subs.* (old).—A rogue; a shabster: also as *verb.* = to rob; to prowl in quest of plunder.—B. E. (*c.*1696); GROSE (1785). Also, ON THE PICARO = on the MAKE (*q.v.*). *See* PICK, *verb.* 1.

*c.*1617. HOWELL, *Letters*, I. iii. 30. I could not recover your diamond Hatband, which the PICAROON snatched from you in the Coach, tho' I used all Means Possible.

1653. MIDDLETON, *Spanish Gypsy*, ii. 1. The arts . . . used by our Spanish PICAROES—I mean filching, foisting, nimming, jilting.

1675. CROWNE, *Country Wit*, iii. 1. These night-corsairs and Algerines call'd the Watch, that PICAROON up and down the streets.

1749. SMOLLETT, *Gil Blas*, VII. ii. Monsieur de Santillane . . . I see you have been in your time a little ON THE PICARO.

1821. SCOTT, *Kenilworth*, xx. Notwithstanding thy boasted honesty, friend . . . I think I see in thy countenance something of the pedlar, something of the PICAROON.

PICAYUNE, *subs.* (American).—Formerly the Spanish half-real in Florida, Louisiana, &c.: now a five cent. piece or any small coin. Also (generic) money; RHINO (*q.v.*). Whence PICAYUNE (or PICAYUNISH) = small; mean; of little value. [*Cf.* Title of a famous journal, *The New Orleans Picayune* (the price of which is five cents).]

*b.*1848. *New York Herald* [BARTLETT]. There is nothing PICAYUNE about the members of St. George's Club; for the love of sport they will . . . enter upon matches that other clubs would not accept.

18 [?]. *The Writer* [*Century*], III. 112. If only two cents are required, you will have prevented a PICAYUNE waste.

PICCADILL (or PICCADILLO), *subs.* (old).—1. *See* quot. 1892. Also (2) the ornamental border of a broad collar worn by women early in 17th century, as in quot. 1607.

1607. DEKKER and WEBSTER, *Northward Ho*, iii. 1. A short Dutch waist with a round Catherine-wheel fardingale, a close sleeve with a cartouse collar, and a PICKADIL.

1611. COTGRAVE, *Dict.*, s.v. PICCADILLES . . . the seuerall divisions or peeces fastened together about the brimme of the collar of a doublet.

1616. JONSON, *Devil is an Ass*, ii. 1. I am not . . . the man . . . of that truth of PICARDIL in clothes, To boast a sovereignty o'er ladies.

1621. FLETCHER [? and another], *Pilgrim*, ii. 2. Do you want a band, Sir? This is a coarse wearing. 'Twill sit but scurvily upon this collar, But patience is as good as a French PICKADEL.

1670. R. LASSELS, *Voy. Ital.*, ii. 117 (1698). One half of his band about his neck, was a broad bone lace, starched white, the other half was made of coarse Lawn, starched blew, and standing out upou a PICKYDILLY of wire.

1892. FENNELL, *Stanford Dict.*, s.v. PICCADILL . . . A stiff collar over which an ornamental fall or collar was arranged, worn first at the close of the 16th century. Perhaps the spelling PICCADIL was suggested by the Italian use of *Picardia* for 'hanging,' 'place where persons are hanged.'

PICCADILLY BUTCHERS (THE), *subs. phr.* (military).—The First Life Guards. [Having been called out to quell the Piccadilly riots in 1810.] Also "The Cheeses"; "The Tin Bellies"; and "The Patent Safeties."

PICCADILLY-CRAWL, *subs. phr.* (obsolete).—A walk: modish in the Eighties. *Cf.* ALEXANDRA LIMP, GRECIAN BEND, ROMAN FALL, &c.

PICCANINNY (PICKANINNY, PINKANINNY, &c.), *subs.* (colloquial).—A baby; a child: specifically (modern) a child of negro parents. [Originally from PINK (an endearment) = small: *see* PIGSNEY.] —GROSE (1785).

1696. DURFEY, *Pills to Purge* (1719), i. 283. Dear Pinckaninny, if half a guinea, To Lord will win ye, I lay it here down.

1855. HALIBURTON, *Nature and Human Nature*, 59. Let me see one of you dare to lay hands on this PICKANINNY.

1865. H. KINGSLEY, *Hillyars and Burtons*, xxviii. Five-and-forty black fellows, lubras, PICANINNIES, and all, at my heels.

1879. F. LOCKER, *The Old Cradle*. You were an exceeding small PICANINNY, Some nineteen or twenty short summers ago.

1883. *Harper's Mag.* [*Century*], lxxvi. 809. A poor puny little PICKANINNY, black as the ace of spades.

PICK, *verb.* (old colloquial: now wrestlers').—1. To shoot; to fling.—BEE (1823).

1530. PALSGRAVE, *Lang. Francoyse* [HALLIWELL]. I holde a grote I PYCKE as farre with an arrowe as you.

1610. SHAKSPEARE, *Coriolanus*, i. 1. Il'd make a quarry With thousands of these quarter'd slaves, as high As I could PICK my lance.

2. (old: now colloquial).—To pilfer; to choose thievishly: also PICKEER, but, usually TO PICK AND CUT or TO PICK POCKETS. Also as *subs.* (or PICKING) = petty larceny (GROSE, 1785): *cf.* (Prayer Book) 'Keep my hands from PICKING and stealing.' Hence PICKER (PICKER-UP or PICKEERER) = (1) a petty thief;

and (2, *in pl.*) = the fingers (B. E., *c.*1696). The same idea (stealthy, underhand) occurs in PICKPENNY, PICKTHANK, PICK-PURSE, &c. (all of which *see*). *See* PRIG.

*d.*1400. CHAUCER, *Leg. Good Women*, 2456. He PIKED of her all the good he might.

1440. *Prompt Parv.*, s.v. PYKARE, lytylle theef, *furculus*.

1503. *Acts of Parliament* [quoted by OLIPHANT]. Theves and PIKARS.

*d.*1529. SKELTON, *Bowge of Courte*, 236. To kepe him from PYKYNGE it was a grete payne. *Ibid.*, *Maner of the World*, 130. PICKERS OF PURSES and males [bag or wallet]. *Ibid.*, *Garlande of Laurell*, 184. Some be called crafty that can PYKE A PURSE.

1550. T. LEVER, *Sermons* [ARBER], 38. PICKINGE theft is lesse than murtheryng robrye.

[?]. URE, *Hist. Rutherglen* [Act Counc.] (1793). Whaevir beis found out sheiring, leiding, &c., before the bell ringing in the morneing, and efter the ringing thairof at night shall—be repute and holden as a PYCKER, and one that wrongeth there neighbours.

*d.*1555. LATIMER, *Sermons* [Parker Soc.], 452. I had of late occasion to speak of PICKING and stealing.

1577. HOLINSHED, *Chronicles* [NARES]. Thefte and PICKERIE were quite suppressed.

1582. HAKLUYT, *Voyages*, I. 241. If he be a PICKER or a cutpurse . . . the second time he is taken he hath a piece of his Nose cut off.

1596. SHAKSPEARE, *Hamlet*, iii. 2. By these PICKERS and stealers. *Ibid.*, *Merry Wives*, i. I. Pistol, did you PICK Master Slender's PURSE.

1604. SHAKSPEARE, *Winter's Tale*, iv. iv. In this time of lethargy I PICKED AND CUT most of their festival purses.

1611. COTGRAVE, *Dict.*, s.v. *Picoree*, PICCORY, forraging, ransacking. *Ibid.* *Picorer*, to forrage, rifle, rob, or prey upon the poor husbandman.

1660. HOWELL, *Lex. Tetra*, s.v. PICAROON.

1749. SMOLLETT, *Gil Blas* [ROUTLEDGE], 55. They PICKED MY POCKET of my ring. *Ibid.*, 173. Moralez . . . had conned over the pretty PICKINGS to be made out of this juggle.

1754-64. ERSKINE, *Instit.*, B. iv., Tit. 4, s. 50. The stealing of trifles, which in our law language is styled PICKERY, has never been punished by the usage of Scotland, but by imprisonment, scourging, &c.

1808. JAMIESON, *Dict.* Scot. Proverb. It is ill to be called a thief and aye found PIKING.

1878. STEVENSON, *Edinburgh* (1894), I. 29. Slinking from a magistrates' supper-room to a thieves' ken, and PICKEERING . . . by the flicker of a dark lamp.

Expressions more or less colloquial are: TO PICK A BONE (CROW OR MATTER) = to seek a quarrel: *see* BONE, CROW, and PLUCK; TO PICK UP = (1) to improve gradually: as from illness or failure; (2) to make acquaintance with, or accost: usually in disparagement of the person accosted—sharpers, street walkers, and such like PICK UP 'flats' or 'culls; (3) to get casually; and, generally, (4) to impose upon or take an advantage in a contract or bargain (BEE, 1823); TO PICK FLIES OFF (tailors') = to fault-find; TO PICK OUT ROBINS' EYES (tailors') = to side-stitch black cloth or fine material; TO PICK OFF (general) = (1) to aim with effect, and (2) to wound or kill; TO PICK ON = to disturb, to nag; TO PICK UP = to put in order: as a room; TO PICK A BIT = to eat mincingly; TO PICK AND CHOOSE = to select with discrimination; TO PICK THE BRAINS (or MIND) = to steal ideas; to plagiarise; TO PICK HOLES (or A FAULT) = to fault-find: hence PICK-FAULT = a censorious fault-finder; TO PICK A QUARREL = to make offence: hence PICK-QUARREL =

a cantankerous person; TO PICK AT = to nag; and so forth. *See* also PICK-THANK and PICK-PURSE.

1321. *Old Poem* [Camden Soc., *Political Songs*, 334, line 238]. The best he PIKETH UP himself, and maketh his mawe touht; And zeveth the Gode man soupe, the lene broth that nis noht for seke.

1448-60. *Paston Letters* [OLIPHANT, *New English*, i. 288-90. In the *Paston Letters* we mark the lingering traces of the Norfolk dialect soon to vanish from the correspondence of the educated. Among the (new) verbs may be remarked *go lose* (loose), PEKE A QUARRELL, &c.].

*d.*1529. SKELTON, *Ag. Comely Coystrowne*, 35. A bungler, a brawler, a PYKER OF QUARELLYS. *Ibid.*, *Bowge of Courte*, 314. Fyrste PYCKE A QUARRELL, and fall oute with hym then.

1530. TYNDALE, *Works* [OLIPHANT, *New English*, i. 427. Tyndale talks of A PICK-QUARREL].

15[?]. HYRDE, Tr. *Christian Woman* (1541), fol. 138b. They medle with other folkes busines . . . exhort and give preceptes, rebuke and correcte, PYKE FAUTES.

1579. LYLY, *Euphues* [ARBER], 246. Men PICKE THY MINDE out of thy hands.

1581. LYLY, *Euphues*, 'Anat. of Wit,' 107. As I am not minded to PICKE A THANK with the one, so am I not determined to PICKE A QUARRELL with the other.

1598. SHAKSPEARE, *All's Well*, iv. 5. We may PICK a thousand salads ere we light on such another herb. *Ibid.*, *1 Hen. IV.*, iii. 3. You owe me money, Sir John; and now you PICK A QUARREL to beguile me of it.

1609. SHAKSPEARE, *Pericles*, iv. 2. Therefore, if in our youths we could PICK UP some pretty estate, 'twere not amiss to keep our door hatched.

1612. BEAUMONT and FLETCHER, *Coxcomb*, iii. 3. She'll PICK A QUARREL with a sleeping child, Ere she fall out with me.

1673. WYCHERLEY, *Gent. Dancing Master*, ii. 2. Since we poor slavish women know Our men we cannot PICK AND CHOOSE.

1680. NORTH, *Lives of the Norths* [Oliphant: There are the verbs *take fire*, *go to the expence*, PICK HOLES, *kidnap*].

1709. DAMPIER, *Voyages*, II. i. 167. By this trade the Freemen of Malacca PICK UP a good livelihood.

*d.*1719. ADDISON, *Vision of Mirza*. When I was at Grand Cairo, I PICKED UP several oriental manuscripts which I have still by me.

1730. VANBRUGH, *Provoked Husband*, iv. Feyther, an you doan't come quickly the meat will be coaled; and I'd fain PICK A BIT with you.

1749. SMOLLETT, *Gil Blas* [ROUTLEDGE (1866), 169]. I halted . . . to recruit a little under the trees. At one of these baits I PICKED UP two young gentlemen who were chatting at their ease. *Ibid.*, 375. As long as I had money . . . my landlord was cap in hand; but . . . the funds low he became high and mighty, PICKED A German QUARREL with me, and . . . begged . . . me to march out of his house.

1767. RAY, *Proverbs* [BOHN], 25. Children and chickens must be always PICKING.

1786. CAPT. MORRIS, *Lyra Urban.* (1848), I. 80-2. For me, I protest, if it wasn't for shame, I could PICK till to-morrow at dinner. *Ibid.* I hope from their budget they'll PICK OUT a song, While I PICK a little more dinner.

*b.*1790. *Busy Bee*, 'Flash Man of St. Giles's.' She PICK'D UP the flats as they passed by.

1790. BRUCE, *Source of the Nile*, I. 195. I PICKED UP courage, and . . . said, without trepidation, 'What men are these before?'

1855. BROWNING, *Men and Women*, 'An Epistle.' Karshish the PICKER-UP of learning's crumbs.

1888. *Texas Siftings*, 7 July. The act closes by the party PICKING OFF 200 Indians with unerring aim.

1892. MILLIKEN, *'Arry Ballads*, 23. I'm just tidy myself, flush of tin, with no end of a thunderin' PICK.

PICK-A-BACK (PICKBACK, PICK-A-PACK, or PICKPACK), *adv.* (colloquial).—On the back or shoulders: as a pack.

1558. FOXE, *Acts and Mon.* [Cattley (1843), i. 30]. Carried PICK-BACK on men's shoulders.

1598. FLORIO, *Worlde of Wordes*, *Disdossa, alla disdossa*, loosely on ones backe, a PICK-A-PACK.

1663. BUTLER, *Hudibras*, I. ii. 72. Mounted a PICK-BACK.

1665. *Homer-a-la-mode* [NARES]. Some two or three meet in a hole Together, their state to condole, Yet none of them knowes what they lack Unlesse they'd be brought home PICK-PACK.

1677. *Wrangling Lovers* [NARES]. Ile have her to him, tho it be on PICK-PACK.

1678. COTTON, *Virgil Travestie* [*Works* (1725), 129]. And through the Fire A-PICK A-PACK, Bore the old Sinner on his Back.

*d.*1704. L'ESTRANGE [*Century*]. In a hurry she whips up her darling under her arms, and carries the other A PICKAPACK upon her shoulders.

PICK-AND-DAB, *subs. phr.* (Scots').—A meal of potatoes and salt; POTATOES-AND-POINT (*q.v.*).

PICKERS. *See* PICK, *verb.* 2.

PICKER-UP, *subs. phr.* (Stock Exchange).—A dealer buying on quotations trickily obtained from a member trapped into giving a wrong price.

PICKLE, *subs.* (colloquial).—1. A difficult or disagreeable position; a plight. Hence, A CASE OF PICKLES = a bad breakdown; a serious quandary.

1609. SKAKSPEARE, *Tempest*, v. I. How camest thou in this PICKLE?

1614. *Time's Whistle* [E. E. T. S.], 60. But they proceed till one drops downe dead drunke, . . . And all the rest, in a sweet PICKLE brought, . . . Lie downe beside him.

1633. JONSON, *Tale of a Tub*, iii. 5. I am now in a fine PICKLE.

1694. CROWNE, *Married Beau*, iv. I. Oh! pox! IN WHAT A PICKLE am I!

1697. VANBRUGH, *Provoked Wife*, iv. 6. *Sir J.* [*covered with dirt and blood*]. What the plague does the woman squall for? Did you never see a man IN A PICKLE before?

1749. SMOLLETT, *Gil Blas*, IV. vi. Gentlemen, I know this epicure; it is . . . the . . . rector of our university; notwithstanding THE PICKLE yon see him in now, he is a great man . . . a little addicted to lawsuits, a bottle, and a wench.

2. (colloquial).—A wag: specifically, a troublesome child: *cf.* PEREGRINE PICKLE (1751), *Title*. Hence PICKLED = roguish; waggish.—B. E. (*c.*1696); GROSE (1785).

1706. FARQUHAR, *Recruiting Officer*, v. 4. His poor boy Jack was the most comical bastard . . . a PICKLED dog; I shall never forget him.

1883. *Harper's Mag.*, lxxvi. 140. Tummas was a PICKLE—a perfect 'andful.

3. (medical students').—In *pl.* = specimens for dissection direct from the subject.

Verb. (common).—To humbug; TO GAMMON (*q.v.*).

IN PICKLE, *adv. phr.* (old).—Poxed or clapt.—B. E. (*c.*1696); GROSE (1785).

A ROD IN PICKLE (or PISS), *subs. phr.* (colloquial).—A flogging or scolding in reserve; 'a revenge in lavender.'—B. E. (*c.*1696); GROSE (1785). [As in the old school rhyme:—'ROD IN PICKLE, Rump to tickle.' In the days of authority rods were pickled in urine or in brine, which elements, it was held, imparted toughness.]

1678. COTTON, *Virgil Travestie* [Works (1725), 126]. Therefore I think it not amiss for's To launch, for there are RODS IN PISS for's.

PICKLE-HERRING (or **PICKLED-HERRING**), *subs. phr.* (old).—A buffoon: *see* BUFFLE.—GROSE (1785).

1602. SHAKSPEARE, *Twelfth Night*, i. 5. A plague o' these PICKLE-HERRING! How now, sot.

1694. CROWNE, *Married Beau*, iv. I. I don't know what I am now; a PICKLE-HERRING I think. I'd be loath to meet with a hungry Dutch seaman.

1711. ADDISON, *Spectator*, No. 47. There is a set of merry drolls . . . whom every nation calls by the name of that dish of meat which it loves best. In Holland they are termed PICKLED HERRINGS, &c. [*See* JACK PUDDING.]

PICKLE-JAR, *subs. phr.* (common).—A coachman in yellow.

PICKLE-ME-TICKLE-ME. TO PLAY AT PICKLE-ME-TICKLE-ME, *verb. phr.* (venery).—To copulate.—URQUHART (1653). *See* GREENS and RIDE.

PICKLOCK, *subs.* (venery).—The *penis*; THE KEY (*q.v.*): *see* PRICK.—URQUHART (1653); CLELLAND.

PICK-ME-UP, *subs. phr.* (common).—A stimulant.

1901. *Free Lance*, 11 May, 123, 2. The doctors are said to frown upon the new PICK-ME-UP, and to threaten serious consequences from its use.

PICK-PENNY, *subs.* (old).—1. *See* PINCHFIST.

2. (old).—A sharper.

PICK-PIE. TO TURN A PICK-PIE, *verb. phr.* (old).—To make a somersault.

PICK-PURSE, *subs.* (old).—A thief: also as *adj.* = mercenary; fraudulent.

*d.*1529, DUNBAR [LAING, *Works*, 161]. Be I ane lord, and not lord like, Than every pelour and PURSE-PIKE.

1555. [MAILLAND, *Reformation* (1849), 529]. Such PICK-PURSE matters is all the whole rabble of your ceremonies; for all is but money matters that ye maintain.

1594. LYLY, *Mother Bombie*, v. 3. This is your old trick, to PICK one's PURSE, and then to picke quarrels.

15[?]. *Reasoning betw. Crossraguell and J. Knox*, B. iii, b. They affirmed—Purgatorie to be nothing but a PYKEPURS.

1598. SHAKSPEARE, *1 Hen. IV.*, ii. 1, 54. At hand, quoth PICK-PURSE. *Ibid.* (1600), *As You Like it*, iii. 4. I think he is not a PICK-PURSE nor a horse-stealer.

1767. RAY, *Proverbs* [BOHN], 69. A good bargain is a PICK-PURSE.

PICKSOME, *adj.* (colloquial).—Fastidious; particular; given to 'picking and choosing.'

1888. BESANT, *Fifty Years Ago*, 136. We were not quite so PICKSOME in the matter of company as we are now.

PICK-THANK, *subs.* (old).—A toady: also as *adj.* and *verb.*—AWDELEY (1567); B. E. (*c.*1696); GROSE (1785).

1412. OCCLEVE, *De Reg. Prin.* [Roxburgh Club], 110. He never denyethe His lordes resons, but a THANKE TO PIKE.

1512-13. DOUGLAS, *Virgil*, Prol. 238, b.55. Sum prig penny, sum PYKE THANK with preuy promit.

1513-25. SKELTON [DYCE, *Works*, ii. 60]. There be two tyther, rude and ranke, Symkyn Tytyuell and PERS PYKTHANKE.

1516. MORE, *Utopia*, i. He is ashamed to say that which is said already, or else to PICK A THANK with his prince,

*d.*1577. GASCOIGNE [ARBER. *English Garner*, I. 63]. A pack of PICK-THANKS were the rest, Which came false witness for to bear.

1580. LYLY, *Euphues*, A4, b. Fine heads will PICK a quarrell with me, if all be not curious, and flatterers A THANKE if anie thing be currant.

1598. SHAKSPEARE, *1 Henry IV.*, iii. 2. Which oft the ear of greatness needs must hear, By smiling PICK-THANKS and base newsmongers.

1603. KNOLLES, *His. Turks*, 108. Whereunto were joined also the hard speeches of her PICKTHANKE favourites, who to curry favell spared not, &c.

*d.*1612. HARRINGTON, *Epigrams*, 55. Or doth he mean that thou would'st PICK A THANK. No sure, for of that fault I count thee frank.

1628. WITHER, *Brit. Rem.*, 89. By slavish fawning or by PICKING THANKS.

*d.*1682. SIR T. BROWNE, *Christ. Mor.*, i. 20. Be deaf unto the suggestions of . . . PICK-THANK or malevolent delators.

*d.*1688. BUCKINGHAM, *Works* (1705), ii. 118. They . . . insinuated themselves into the familys of the poor good natured tenants; then they carry'd PICKTHANK stories from one to another.

1740. NORTH, *Examen*, 278. He did it to PICKTHANK an opportunity of getting more money.

PICKT-HATCH TO GO TO THE MANOR OF PICKT-HATCH (or TO PICKT-HATCH GRANGE), *verb. phr.* (old). — To whore: *see* GREENS and RIDE. [The PICKT-HATCH—a hatch with pikes—was a common brothel sign: specifically in Shakspeare's time a notorious tavern-brothel in Turnbull St., Clerkenwell].—GROSE (1785).

1596. SHAKSPEARE, *Merry Wives*, ii. 2. Go—a short knife and a thong—TO YOUR MANOR OF PICKT-HATCH.

1596. JONSON, *Ev. Man in his Humour*, i. 2. From the Bordello it might come as well, The Spittle, or PICT-HATCH.

1610. JONSON, *Alchemist*, ii. 1. The decay'd vestals of PICT-HATCH would thank you That keep the fire alive there.

*d.*1618. SYLVESTER, *Du Bartas*, 576. Borrow'd and brought from loose Venetians, Becomes PICKT-HATCH and Shoreditch courtizans.

1630. *Optick Glasse of Humours*, 89. These be your PICKT-HATCH Curtezan wits that merit after their decease to bee carted in Charles waine.

1630. *Cupids' Whirligig* [NARES]. Set some PICKES upon your HATCH, and I pray profess to keep a bawdy-house.

*d.*1635. RANDOLPH (?) *Muses' Looking Glass* [REED, *Old Plays*, ix. 244]. The lordship of Turnbal so—which with my PICKT-HATCH GRANGE, And Shoreditch farm, and other premises Adjoining—very good—a pretty maintenance.

1638. RANDOLPH, *Hey for Honesty*, B. 3b. Why the whores of PICT-HATCH, Turnbull, or the unmerciful bawds of Bloomsbury.

PICK-TOOTH, *adj. phr.* (old colloquial).—Leisurely.

1726. VANBRUGH and CIBBER, *Provoked Husband*, iii. My lord and I . . . sat us down by the fireside in an easy, indolent, PICK-TOOTH way.

1749. SMOLLETT, *Gil Blas* [ROUTLEDGE], 155. With the PICK-TOOTH carelessness of a lounger.

PICK-UP, *subs. phr.* (common).—A carnal acquaintance, male or female: whence, a whoremaster. *Adj.* (colloquial).—Composed of what is at the moment available: as a PICK-UP dinner; a PICK-UP crew, or team. *Cf.* SCRATCH and POT-LUCK.

1840. *Betsy Bobbet*, 302. She needn't make no fuss about dinner at all. I will eat a PICKED-UP dinner.

PICKWICKIAN SENSE, *subs. phr.* (colloquial).—A technical or constructive sense. [*See* quot. 1837.]

1837. DICKENS, *Pickwick*, i. The chairman felt it his imperative duty to demand . . . whether he had used the expression . . . in a common sense. Mr. Blotton had no hesitation in saying he had not—he had used the word in its PICKWICKIAN SENSE.

18[?]. H. JAMES, *Substance and Shadow*, 199 [*Century*]. Unitarianism and Universalism call themselves the church in an altogether PICKWICKIAN SENSE of the word, or, with pretensions so affable as to offend nobody.

PICNIC, *subs.* (common).—A mellay; a rough-and-tumble.

1898. *Pink 'Un and Pelican*, 177. He asked me if I'd "yeared" what a PICNIC old Ben Harrity had had with his missis.

PICTURE, *subs.* (colloquial). — A model; a pattern; a beau-ideal: as 'a PICTURE of health,' 'a

perfect PICTURE'—child, horse, and so forth: also ironically, *e.g.*, a pretty PICTURE = a strange figure.

NOT IN THE PICTURE, *phr.* (colloquial).—Strange; inappropriate; better away; and (racing) unplaced.

See also LAWFUL PICTURES.

PICTURE-FRAME. *See* SHERIFF'S PICTURE-FRAME.

PICTURE-HAT, *subs. phr.* (common). —*See* quot.

1901. *Referee*, 14 Ap., 5. 3. The lady who is the subject of the picture [the Gainsborough Duchess of Devonshire] set a fashion in hats which women continue to wear up to the present style. Even the Parisian ladies affected the style. And nowadays no suburban wedding is complete if the bridesmaids do not wear PICTURE HATS, the usual but very foolish description of the articles under discussion. *Ibid.*, 9, 3. The return of the Gainsborough will, we are told, revive the big hat. The amiable "Gainsborough" of South Molton-street assures me that the PICTURE HAT has never really gone out of fashion.

PIDDLE, *subs.* (nursery). — LANT (*q.v.*). Also as *verb.* = RACK OFF (*q.v.*); STROAN (*q.v.*). — GROSE (1785).

2. (common). — To do languidly or to little purpose; TO NIGGLE (*q.v.*). Hence, PIDDLER = a trifler; and PIDDLING = mean, of small account, squeamish.—GROSE (1785).

1544. ASCHAM, *Toxophilus* [Arber], 117. And so . . . auoyde bothe greate trouble and also some cost whiche you cunnynge archers . . . put your selues vnto . . . neuer ceasynge PIDDELYNGE about your bowe and shaftes when they be well, but eyther with . . . newe fetheryng, &c.

*c.*1622. MIDDLETON, *Mayor of Quinborough* (1661), v. 1. Nine geese, and some three larks for PIDDLING meat.

1629. MASSINGER, *Picture*, iii. 6. My lord Hath gotten a new mistress. *Ubald.* One! a hundred . . . They talk of Hercules' fifty in a night, 'Twas well; but yet to yours he was a PIDDLER.

1632. SHIRLEY, *The Changes*, ii. 2. Let children, when they versify, stick here and there these PIDDLING words for want of matter. Poets write masculine numbers.

1690. CROWNE, *English Friar*, ii. He has a weak stomach and cant make a meal, unless he has a dozen pretty dishes to PIDDLE upon.

1733. POPE, *Horace*, II. ii. 137. Content with little I can PIDDLE here, On brocoli and mutton round the year.

*d.*1745. SWIFT [quoted by Maidment]. From stomach sharp, and hearty feeding, To PIDDLE like a lady breeding.

*d.*1774. GOLDSMITH, *Criticisms* [*Century*]. A PIDDLING reader . . . . might object to almost all the rhymes of the above quotation.

1902. HENLEY, *Views and Reviews*, II. 10. Though the Castle of Otranto is a PIDDLING piece of super-nature.

PIE, *subs.* (colloquial).—(1) A magpie; and (2) a prating gossip. WILY PIE = a sly rogue.

1369. CHAUCER, *Troilus*, iii. 527. Dredeles it clere was in the wynde Of every PIE, and every lette-game.

*d.*1529. SKELTON, *Balletys and Dyties* [DYCE, i. 24, 34]. By theyr consusaunce knowing how they serue a WILY PY.

1577. STANIHURST, *Desc. of Ireland*, 13. Howbeit in the English pale to this day they use to tearme a slie cousener a WILIE PIE.

*c.*1580. *Ballad of Troilus* [HALLIWELL]. Then Pandare, lyke a WYLY PYE . . . Stept to the tabell by and by, And forthe he blewe the candell.

[?]. M. S. Rawlinson, C 258. The PYE hathe pecked you.

3. *See* PI, *subs.*, sense 1.

[More or less colloquial are:—TO HAVE A FINGER IN THE PIE (or, indeed, any matter) = to meddle, to join in: *cf.* BOAT; TO MAKE A PIE = to combine with a view to profit; LIKE PIE = with

N

zest: *cf.* JAM; IN SPITE OF THE PIE = obstinately (PIE = the Book of the Offices of the Church); NOT TO COOK ANY OF THE PIE (American) = to abandon an enterprise, to take no further interest (MARK TWAIN).

1601. SHAKSPEARE, *Henry VIII.*, i. 1. No man's PIE IS FREED FROM HIS ambitious FINGER.

1603-15. *Court Jas. I.* (1848), I. 37. If this earl should be found hereafter anyways privy thereto, it cannot be but that Beaumont's HAND WAS IN THE PIE.

1608. WITHAL, *Dictionarie*, 390. Pertinax in rem aliquam, that is fully bent to doe a thing, that will doe it, yea marie will he, maugre or IN SPIGHT OF THE PIE.

1749. SMOLLETT, *Gil Blas* [ROUTLEDGE], 169. It was but fair I should have A FINGER IN THE EARNINGS. *Ibid.*, 297. I was entitled to have A FINGER IN THE DISSIPATION.

1767. RAY, *Proverbs* [BOHN], 159. He had A FINGER IN THE PIE when he burnt his nail off.

1842. EGAN, *By-blow of the Jug*, ii. She taught him soon to swear and lie, And to HAVE A FINGER IN EVERY PIE.

1887. HENLEY, *Culture in Slums*, 'Ballade' 3. I goes for 'Olman 'Unt LIKE PIE.

PIECE, *subs.* (old).—1. A person, male or female: often in contempt. Also (of women) PIECE (or BIT) OF MUTTON, MUSLIN, or GOODS.

1290. *Cursor Mundi*, 634. A wel godd PECE [of St. John].

1574. R[ICHARD] B[OWER], *Appius and Virginia* [DODSLEY, *Old Plays* (Hazlitt), iv. 125]. O passing PIECE.

1604. SHAKSPEARE, *Winter's Tale*, v. 1. 'His princess say you?' . . . 'Ay, the most peerless PIECE.' *Ibid.*, v. 3. O royal PIECE.

1606. CHAPMAN, *Monsieur D'Olive*, v. 1. She's but a sallow, freckle-faced PIECE when she is at the best.

1607. DEKKER, *Northward Hoe*, iv. 1. 'S blood, I was never cozened with a more rascal PIECE of mutton, Since I came out a' the Lower Countries.

1614. JONSON, *Bartholomew Fair*, i. 1. He is another manner of PIECE than you think for.

1629. MASSINGER, *Picture*, iii. 6. *Ubald.* This ring was Julietta's, a fine PIECE, But very good at the sport.

1633. NABBES, *Totenham-Court*, ii. 2. She seems a handsome PIECE. That opportunity Would play the Bawd a little!

1635. GLAPTHORNE, *The Lady Mother*, i. 3. She is . . . a corrupted PEICE, A most lascivious prostitute.

1655. STRODE, *Floating Island*, E 1. This lewde crack'd abominable PEICE.

1673. WYCHERLEY, *Gentleman Dancing Master*, v. 1. I am thinking . . . what those ladies who are never precise but at a play would say of me now:—that I were a confident coming PIECE, I warrant, and they would damn the poor poet for libelling the sex.

1678. COTTON, *Scoffer Scoft* [*Works* (1725), 227]. But each one must not think to bear So fine a PIECE as *Mulciber*.

1688. CROWNE, *City Politics*, i. 1. Since she is so weak a PIECE I'll fortify her.

1749. SMOLLETT, *Gil Blas* [ROUTLEDGE (1866), 4]. She seemed a pretty PIECE OF GOODS enough, and such a stirring body. *Ibid.*, 80. Keeping open house . . . for the votaries of pleasure . . . She had always two or three other PIECES of damaged goods in the house.

1785. GROSE, *Vulg. Tongue*, s.v. PIECE . . . A damned good or bad PIECE; a girl who is more or less active and skilful in the amorous congress. Hence the (*Cambridge*) toast, May we never have a PIECE (peace) that will injure the Constitution.

1823. BEE, *Dict. Turf*, s.v. PIECE—a soldier calls his musket his PIECE, and so he calls his trull; but highflyers are so termed—behind their backs.

2. *in pl.* (common).—Money; RHINO (*q.v.*). [From the old Spanish 'pieces of eight.']

1558. FOXE, *Martyrs* [Catley (1843), 473]. The maid . . . having a PIECE of money lying by her, given unto her by the death of a kinsman of hers . . . brought unto him thirty pounds.

1886-96. MARSHALL, '*Pomes' from the Pink 'Un* ['Boycotting the Author'], 45. So he added two 'oughts,' and got cash for it too, And promptly, proceeded the PIECES to 'blew.'

1887. BAUMAN, *Londonismen*, 'Rum Coves.' Rum coves that relieve us Of chinkers and PIECES, Is gin'rally lagged.

TO GO (or FALL) TO PIECES, *verb. phr.* (colloquial).—To be brought to bed.

TO GO ALL TO PIECES, *verb. phr.* (colloquial).—To collapse; to become exhausted; to be ruined.

1667. PEPYS, *Diary*, 29 Aug. I find by all hands that the Court is at this day ALL TO PIECES, every man of a faction of one sort or other.

1672. RAY, *Proverbs* [BOHN], 64. s.v. A Bankrupt. He's ALL TO PIECES.

1811. AUSTEN, *Sense and S.*, xxx. 'Fifty thousand pounds! and by all accounts it won't come before its wanted; for they say he is ALL TO PIECES.'

1882. *Punch*, LXXXII., 185, 2. 'These pals will be all right after dinner.' 'Let us hope they will,' said the Corinthian, 'for they look ALL TO PIECES now.'

1884. *Echo*, 7 April, 3, 1. The Oxford men were now ALL TO PIECES! their boat was full of water.

TO EAT A PIECE, *verb phr.* (U. S. colloquial).—To eat between meals. Also TO PIECE.

See also FLESH, MUSLIN, PUDDING, THICK, and TOP.

PIECE-OF-ENTIRE, *subs.* (old).—A jolly fellow.

PIECE-OUT, *subs.* (tailors').—Employment; a loan.

PIEMAN, *subs.* (streets').—The one in hand at PITCH-AND-TOSS (*q.v.*).

2. *See* PI, *adj.*

PIERCER, *subs.* (common).—A squinteye; one looking nine ways for SUNDAYS (*q.v.*).

PIFFING. *See* SPIFF.

PIFFLE, *subs.* (colloquial).—Twaddle: esp. mincing, pretentious, affected twaddle. Hence as *verb* (colloquial) = to trifle pretentiously; to twaddle with a purpose and an air. PIFFLER = an earnest futility, *i.e.*, a person with a moral end in view, and nothing to back it but a habit of talking, or writing sentimental rubbish. [In JAMIESON, 'Piffer' = to do peevishly,' or 'in a feeble or trifling way'; while 'pifferin' = 'trifling, insignificant.']

Verb (old).—2. To filch; and 3 (old) = to be squeamish.—BAILEY (1728); HALLIWELL (1847).

PIG, *subs.* (colloquial).—1. An epithet of disparagement or abuse. Thus, A DIRTY PIG = a person unclean in word or deed (GROSE); AN OLD PIG = an ill-natured boor; A LEARNED PIG = a bombastic shallow-pate; as *verb.* (or TO PIG IT, GROSE) = to herd as pigs; TO PIG TOGETHER = to lie (or sleep) two (or more) in a bed (GROSE); PIGGERY = a squalid or untidy room; PIG-EYED = small-eyed; PIG-FACED = heavy jowled; PIGGISH = greedy; PIG-HEADED = obstinate (GROSE); AS HAPPY AS A PIG IN MUCK (or SHIT) = contented but filthy; LIKE A PIG, NO GOOD ALIVE = selfish; TO LONG FOR PIG (or A BARTHOLOMEW PIG) (*q.v.*) = to show signs of, or presume upon, pregnancy; TO BLEED LIKE A PIG = to bleed copiously, like a pig under the knife; TO STARE LIKE A STUCK PIG = to look fixedly or terrifically.

*d.*1529. SKELTON, *Elynour Rummyng*, 233. Then swetely together we ly, As two PYGGES IN A STY.

1621. JONSON, *News from the New World* [*Century*]. You should be some dull tradesman by your PIG-HEADED sconce now.

1607. DEKKER and WEBSTER, *Westward Hoe*, v. 3. He BLEEDS LIKE A PIG, for his crown's crack'd.

1678. COTTON, *Scoffer Scoft* [*Works* (1725), 185]. *Gan.* But when I PIG'D with mine own *Dad*, I us'd to make him hopping mad.

1697. VANBRUGH, *Provoked Wife*, iv. 6. Now, you being as dirty and as nasty as myself, we may go PIG TOGETHER.

1698. *Unnatural Mother* [NARES]. By the zide of the wood there is a curious hansom gentlewoman lies as dead as a herring, and BLEEDS LIKE ANY STUCK PIG.

1704. *Gentleman Instructed*, 537. When reason sleeps extravagance breaks loose; quality and peasantry PIG TOGETHER.

1749. SMOLLETT, *Gil Blas* [ROUTLEDGE], 373. He STARED LIKE A STUCK PIG at my equipment.

*c.*1780. TOMLINSON, *Flash Pastoral.* And Nancy PIGGED with me wherever I went.

*d.*1845. HOOD, *Tale of a Trumpet.* How the Smiths contrived to live and whether The fourteen Murphies all PIGG'D TOGETHER.

1857. WHITTY, *Fr. of Bohemia*, 86. What narrow stairs! How dreadful it is that grandfather will stick to this PIGGY street.

*d.*1859. MACAULAY, *Sir Wm. Temple.* But he hardly thinks that the sufferings of a dozen felons PIGGING together on bare bricks . . . suited to the dignity of history.

18 [?]. *West. Review* [*Century*]. To PIG IT like the prodigal son.

18 [?]. *The Engineer* [*Century*]. The working man here is content to PIG it, to use an old-country term, in a way that an English workman would not care to do.

1860. GEORGE ELIOT, *Mill on the Floss*, i. 3. A thoroughly PIG-HEADED fellow.

1888. HENLEY and STEVENSON, *Deacon Brodie*, ii. 4, 1. *Brodie* (*searching*). Where's a hat for the Deacon? where's a hat for the Deacon's headache? This place is a PIGGERY.

2. (old). — A policeman, or detective. Also GRUNTER: *see* BEAK. CHINA STREET PIG = a Bow St. officer.—GROSE (1785); VAUX (1819).

1821. EGAN, *Life in London*, I. i. Do not frown upon me, but stretch out thine hand to my assistance, thou bashaw of the PIGS, and all but beak!

3. (military). — In *pl.* = The Seventy-Sixth Foot, now the 2nd Batt. West Riding Regiment. [From its badge.] Also THE IMMORTALS (*q.v.*) and THE OLD SEVEN AND SIXPENNIES (*q.v.*).

4. (printers'). — A pressman: *cf.* DONKEY.

1841. SAVAGE, *Dict.* s.v.

5. (common).—Sixpence: *see* BENDER, HOG, and RHINO.—B. E. (*c.*1696); GROSE (1785).

6. (Cambridge University).—*See* HOG, *subs.*, sense 3.

7. (tailors').—An utterly spoiled garment. Also PORK.

COLLOQUIAL PHRASES are:—A PIG IN A POKE = a blind barbargain: Fr. *acheter chat en poche* (B. E., *c.*1696; GROSE, 1785; BEE, 1823); TO STUFF A FAT PIG IN THE TAIL = to give unnecessarily: TO TAKE ONE'S PIGS (or HOGS) TO MARKET = to deal, or do business: generally with PRETTY, FAIR, FINE, or BAD, when = a good or bad bargain, to succeed or fail (B. E., *c.*1696; GROSE, 1785); TO DRIVE ONE'S PIGS (or HOGS) TO MARKET = to snore (GROSE, 1785); TO FOLLOW LIKE AN ANTHONY PIG = to beg, to hang on (GROSE, 1785); TO GET THE WRONG SOW BY THE EAR (or, Am., THE WRONG PIG BY THE TAIL) = to make a mistake; WHEN PIGS FLY = Never:

see QUEEN DICK; COLD PIG = (1) see *ante* and add 'GROSE, 1785'; (2) goods on sale when returned (BEE, 1823); and (3, medical) = a corpse, DEAD-MEAT (*q.v.*); TO HAVE BOILED PIG AT HOME = to be master in one's house (GROSE: an allusion to a well-known poem and story); BRANDY IS LATIN FOR PIG AND GOOSE = an excuse for a dram after either (GROSE); PLEASE THE PIGS = 'If circumstances permit,' '*Deo volente*'; LONG (or -MASKED) PIG = human flesh: exposed openly for sale in Hayti under this name; TO TEACH A PIG TO PLAY ON A FLUTE = to attempt the absurd or impossible; 'WHEN A PIG IS PROFFERED, HOLD UP THE POKE' = 'Never refuse a good offer'; 'YOU CAN'T MAKE HORN OF PIG'S TAIL' (*see* SOW'S EAR); TO MISTAKE A PIG FOR A DOG = to act stupidly; CHILD'S PIG BUT FATHER'S BACON = a pretended benefit: as when a pet animal is sold; TO GREASE A FAT PIG (or SOW) ON THE ARSE (RAY) = to be insensible of a kindness.

1383. CHAUCER, *Reeves Tale*, l. 358. And in the floor, with nose and mouth to broke, They walwe as doon two PIGGES IN A POKE.

14 [?]. *Douce MS.* 52. When me profereth THE PIGGE, open THE POGHE.

1546. HEYWOOD, *Proverbs*, s.v. To PULL THE WRONG PIG BY THE EAR.

1634. WITHAL, *Dict.*, 583. *Terra volat*, PIGS FLIE in the ayre with their tayles forward.

1678. COTTON, *Scoffer Scoft* [*Works* (1725) 257]. He will not BUY A PIG A POKE IN: But wisely will bring all things out, And see within doors and without.

1678. COTTON, *Virgil Travestie* [*Works* (1725) 122]. Thou hast of Hope not one Spark left, Th' hast BROUGHT THY HOGS TO A FAIR MARKET.

*d.*1682. T. BROWN, *Works*, ii. 198. I'll have one of the wigs to carry into the country with me, and PLEASE THE PIGS.

1708-10. SWIFT, *Polite Conversations*, ii. 455. I'gad he fell asleep, and snored so loud that we thought he was DRIVING HIS HOGS TO MARKET.

1748. SMOLLETT, *Roderick Random*, xv. Strap with a hideous groan observed that we had BROUGHT OUR PIGS TO A FINE MARKET. Ibid., *Hump Clinker* (1771). Roger may CARRY HIS PIGS TO ANOTHER MARKET.

*d.*1819. WOLCOT ('Peter Pindar')[BEE]. 'And then for why, the folk do rail; To STUFF AN OLD FAT PIG I' TH' TAIL,—Old gripus of Long-Leat.'

1853. LYTTON, *My Novel*, v. xvii 'PLEASE THE PIGS,' then said Mr. Avenel to himself, 'I shall pop the question.'

1890. BOLDREWOOD, *Squatter's Dream*, 50. Of course I must see them . . . I never BUY A PIG IN A POKE.

1896. STEVENSON, *South Seas* [Edin. xx. 84]. While the drums were going twenty strong . . . the priests carried up the blood-stained baskets of LONG PIG.

1900. NISBET, *Sheep's Clothing*, 201. He felt that he had SOLD HIS PIGS IN A BAD MARKET. If he had waited he might have met the right woman with even a larger dower.

PIG AND TINDER-BOX, *subs. phr.* (old).—The Elephant and Castle.

1821. EGAN, *Life in London*, II. iii. Toddle to the PIG AND TINDER-BOX, they have got a drap of comfort there.

PIG AND WHISTLE LIGHT INFANTRY (THE), *subs. phr.* (military).—The Highland Light Infantry, formerly the 71st and 74th Regiments of Foot.

PIG-EATER, *subs.* (old).—An endearment.

PIGEON (or **STOOL-PIGEON**), *subs.* (old).—1. A dupe; a GULL (*q.v.*); a FLY (*q.v.*): *cf.* ROOK and SPIDER [*cf.* Thackeray's title, *Captain Rook and Mr. Pigeon*]. Hence, as *verb.* (or TO PLUCK A PIGEON = to swindle.) Fr. *un*

pigeon, un dindon, or *un tordu*; Sp. *palamo* (= pigeon), or *sangrado* (= subject for bleeding); It. *un spagnuolo*.—GROSE (1785); BEE (1823).

1585. *Les Dialogues de Jacques Tahureau.* Je me deffieroy tantost que tu serois un de ceux qui ne se laissent si facilement PIGEONNER à telles gens.

1720. *Observer*, No. 27. He's PIGEON'D and undone.

1749. SMOLLETT, *Gil Blas* [ROUTLEDGE (1866), 146]. A flatterer may play what game he likes against the PIGEONS of high life! They let you look over their hand, and then wonder that you beat them.

1821. EGAN, *Life in London*, II. i. Always on the look out for a 'good customer.' He, however, prefers PIGEONS.

1831. DISRAELI, *Young Duke*, IV. vi. Lord Castlefort was the jackal to these prowling beasts of prey; looked out for PIGEONS, and got up little parties to Richmond or Brighton.

1871. *Levant Herald*, 22 Feb., 'Gambling Table at Constantinople.' The police agents . . . made a sudden *razzia* . . . Catching some of the croupiers, bonnets, and PIGEONS *in fragrante delicto*.

1888. HENLEY and STEVENSON, *Deacon Brodie*, i. 1, 7. *Smith.* I've trapped a PIGEON for you. *Brodie.* Can't you PLUCK him yourself?

1897. *Referee*, 14 Mar., 1, 1. These senators could differentiate between the claimants and debtors who knew the ropes, the hawks who harried PIGEONS, and, generally speaking, the straight and the crooked.

1901. *Pall Mall Gaz.*, 13 May, 7, 3. A plaintiff objected to the description of "moneylender," and explained that he had many other interests besides the lending of money—for instance, he was devoted to birds. "PIGEONS?" asked the judge.

2. (old).—*See* quots. and *cf.* sense 1.

1785. GROSE, *Vulg. Tongue*, s.v. PIGEONS. Sharpers, who, during the drawing of the lottery, wait ready mounted near Guildhall, and, as soon as the first two or three numbers are drawn, which they receive from a confederate on a card, ride with them full speed to some distant insurance office, before fixed on, where there is another of the gang, commonly a decent-looking woman, who takes care to be at the office before the hour of drawing: to her he secretly gives the number, which she insures for a considerable sum: thus biting the biter.

1823. BEE, *Dict. Turf*, s.v. PIGEON . . . 'To pigeon the news' is to send information by carrier pigeon. So fellows, who ran or rode with news surreptitiously obtained, received the name of PIGEONS from their occupation.

3. *See* BLUE PIGEON.

4. (colonial). — Business: *see* PIGEON ENGLISH. [The Chinese pronunciation of the English word.]

PAUL'S PIGEONS, *subs. phr.* (school).—The scholars of St. Paul's school.

1662. FULLER, *Worthies* (London), i. 65. St. Anthonie's Pigs (so were the scholars of that School [City of London] commonly called, as those of St. Paul, PAUL'S PIGEONS). [Fuller refers to STOWE'S *Survey* as his authority.]

TO MILK THE PIGEON, *verb. phr.* (old).—'To attempt impossibilities, to be put to shifts for want of money.'—GROSE (1785). *Cf.* PIGEON'S-MILK.

PHRASES more or less colloquial are:—PIGEON-BREASTED = with protruding breast; PIGEON-HEARTED (or LIVERED) = timid; PIGEON-TOED = with turned-in toes; PIGEON-WING = (1) a late 18th century mode of dressing the side hair: now American, (2) a wig so called, and (3) a brisk step or caper in dancing, skating; TO SHOOT AT A PIGEON AND KILL A CROW = to blunder wilfully; TO CATCH TWO PIGEONS WITH ONE BEAN (*see* STONE).

1596. SHAKSPEARE, *Hamlet*, ii. 2. I am PIGEON-LIVER'D, and lack gall To make oppression bitter.

1621. FLETCHER, *Pilgrim*, iii. 4. I never saw such PIGEON-HEARTED people.

1749 SMOLLETT, *Gil Blas* [ROUTLEDGE], 328. Yet he was not so PIGEON-LIVERED as to surrender without an effort in my favour.

1836. CLARKE, *Ollapodiana Papers.* One haw-buck dancer—a fellow whom I caught in several vulgar attempts to achieve a PIGEON-WING—came up to me with an impudent air.

1837. BARHAM, *Ingoldsby Legends*, 'Dead Drummer,' II. 171. The PIGEON-TOED step and the rollicking motion, Bespoke them two genuine sons of the ocean.

PIGEON ENGLISH (or **PIDGIN**), *subs. phr.* (colonial).—A jargon serving as a means of inter-communication between the Chinese and the English-speaking races all over the world: alike in Shanghai and San Francisco. [A corruption of 'business-English'—business—bidginess—bidgin—pidgin—pigeon.]

PIGEON-HOLE, *subs. phr.* (printers').—1. An over-wide space between printed words; a RAT-HOLE (*q.v.*).

2. (Winchester College). — A small study.

3. (venery).—The female *pudendum*; the BREADWINNER (*q.v.*): *see* MONOSYLLABLE.

PIGEON-HOLE SOLDIERS, *subs. phr.* (military).—Clerks and orderlies.

1871. *Echo*, 1 July, 'The Guards' Review.' Now and then I observed a little confusion, but this was caused by a number of PIGEON-HOLE SOLDIERS who scarcely ever do any duty in the ranks.

PIGEON-PAIR, *subs. phr.* (old).—Twins of opposite sex. [Pigeons lay two eggs which usually hatch as a pair.]

PIGEON'S-MILK, *subs. phr.* (common).—An imaginary product in quest of which fools are sent: *cf.* STRAP-OIL, SQUAD UMBRELLA, &c.—GROSE (1785). Hence TO MILK THE PIGEON = to attempt impossibilities. [The idea is old: *cf.* Aristophanes in *Aves* (line 1672).]

1883. FRERE, *Birds of Aristophanes*, iii. p. 75. Here you shall domineer and rule the roast, With splendour and opulence and PIGEON'S MILK.

PIGGOT, *verb.* (political: obsolete).—To forge. [A reminiscence of the Parnell Commission: the expression was born in the House of Commons, 28th Feb., 1889.] *Cf.* SALISBURY; BURKE; BOYCOTT; MAFFICK, &c.

PIGGY-WIGGY (**PIGWIGGIN** or **PIGGY-WHIDDEN**), *subs. phr.* (familiar).—A pet pig: hence, a comic endearment (*see* DRAYTON, *Nymphidia*, where it is used as the name of a kind of Puck). [From PIGGY = a diminutive + WHIDDY = white.]

1678. COTTON, *Scoffer Scofft* [*Works* (1725), 197]. *Vulc.* What such a nazardly PIGWIGGEN, A little Hang-strings in a Biggin?

PIG-POKER, *subs.* (old).—A swineherd.

PIG-RUNNING, *subs. phr.* (old).—*See* quot.

1785. GROSE, *Vulg. Tongue*, s.v. PIG RUNNING. A piece of game frequently practised at fairs, wakes, &c. A large pig, whose tail is cut short, and both soaped and greased, being turned out, is hunted by the young men and boys, and becomes the property of him who can catch and hold him by the tail, above the height of his head.

PIGS-AND-WHISTLES. TO GO TO PIGS-AND-WHISTLES, *verb phr.* (Scots).—To be ruined.

1801. *The Har'st Rig*, 48. The back-ga'en fell ahint, And couldna stand; So he TO PIGS-AND-WHISTLES WENT, And left the land.

1822. GALT, *Entail*, i. 9. I would be nane surprised the morn to hear that the Nebuchadnezzar was a' GANE TO PIGS AND WHISTLES, and driven out wi' the divors bill to the barren pastures of bankruptcy.

PIG-SCONCE, *subs.* (old).—A lout; a dullard: *see* BUFFLE.

1659. MASSINGER, *City Madam*, iii. 1. *Ding.* He is no PIG-SCONCE mistress. *Secret.* He has an excellent headpiece.

1879. MEREDITH, *Egoist*, xxxvii. These representatives of the PIG-SCONCES of the population.

PIG'S-EAR (or **-LUG**), *subs. phr.* (tailors').—A very large lappel collar or flap.

PIG'S-FOOT, *subs. phr.* (American).—A short cloven crowbar; a JEMMY (*q.v.*).

PIGSKIN, *subs.* (racing).—A saddle. Hence KNIGHT OF THE PIGSKIN = a jockey.

*d.*1870. DICKENS [quoted in *Century*]. He was my governor, and no better master ever sat in PIG-SKIN.

1898. *Sporting Times*, 26 Nov., 3, 3. After a few days' rest he was in the saddle and has again electrified English turf followers by riding rings around their crack KNIGHTS OF THE PIGSKIN.

PIGSNEY, *subs. phr.* (old).—A girl: an endearment: *see* TITTER. Hence (2), a woman's eye.—B. E. (*c.*1696); GROSE (1785).

13 [?] CHAUCER, *Remedie of Loue* [Ency. Dict.]. Come hither, ye PIGGESNYE, ye little babe.

*d.*1529. SKELTON [DYCE, *Works*, i. 20, 19]. Good mastres Anne . . . What prate ye, praty PYGGSNEY.

1534. UDALL, *Roister Doister* [ARBER, i. 4, p. 27]. Then ist mine oune PYGS NIE, and blessing on my hart.

1580. SIDNEY, *Arcadia*, 277. Miso, mine own PIGSNIE, thou shalt have news of Dametas.

*d.*1588. TARLETON, *Horse Loade of Fooles* [HALLIWELL]. The player fooles deare darling PIGSNIE.

1594. LYLY, *Mother Bombie*, ii. 2. PIGSNIE is put up, and . . . I'le let him take the aire.

1621. BURTON, *Anat. Melan.* III., ii. 4, 1. All the pleasant names may be invented; bird . . . lamb, puss . . . PIGSNEY, hony, love, dove . . . he puts on her.

1665, *Homer-a-la-Mode* [NARES]. As soon as she close to him came, She spake and call'd him by his name . . . PIGSNY, Quoth she, tell me who made it cry.

PIG-STICKER, *subs.* (common).—1. A pork-butcher.

2. (common).—A long-bladed pocket-knife; and (3) a sword.

PIG-STY, *subs. phr.* (printers').—1. The press-room. *See* PIG, *subs.* sense 4.

2. (common). — A place of abode or business: *see* DIGGINGS.

PIG'S-WHISPER, *subs. phr.* (common) = 1. A grunt.

2. (common).—A very short space of time [*i.e.*, as brief as a grunt]. BEE (1823). Also (American), PIG'S-WHISTLE.

1836. DICKENS, *Pickwick*, xxxii. You'll find yourself in bed in something less than A PIG'S WHISPER.

PIG-TAIL, *subs.* (colloquial).—1. A Chinaman.

2. (Stock Exchange).—*In pl.* = the Shares of the Chartered Bank of India, Australia, and China: *see* STOCK EXCHANGE.

PIG-YOKE, *subs. phr.* (nautical).—A quadrant.

1836. MARRYAT, *Midshipman Easy*, xiv. Mesby agreed with Jack that this was the 'ne plus ultra' of navigation; and that old Smallsole could not do better with his PIG-YOKE and compasses.

PIKE, *subs.* (common).—1. A turnpike road; and (2) = a tramp, a gypsy (also PIKEY and PIKER): as *verb* = to walk (also TO PIKE OFF, and TO TIP A PIKE): whence TO PIKE ON THE BEEN = to hook it for all one's worth. Hence PIKE-KEEPER (or PIKEMAN) = a toll-keeper; TO BILK A PIKE = to cheat a toll-gate.

15 [?]. *Parlament of Byrdes* [HAZLITT, *Early Pop. Poet.* iii. 180]. When his fethers are pluked he may him GO PIKE.

*c.*1570. *Ane Ballat of Matrymonie* [LAING, *Pop. Poet. Scotland*, ii. 77]. He bad them then GO PYKE them home.

1712. SHIRLEY, *Triumph of Wit*, 'Budg and Snudg Song,' 2. We file off with his cole As he PIKES along the street. *Ibid.*, 'The Black Procession.' Tho' he TIPS THEM A PIKE, they oft nap him again.

*c.*1789. PARKER, *Sandman's Wedding* [FARMER, *Musa Pedestris* (1896), 65]. Into a booze-ken they PIKE IT.

1826. MORLEY, *Song*, 'Flashey Joe' FARMER, *Musa Pedestris* (1896), 97]. So I'll PIKE OFF with my mack'ral And you may bolt with your salt cod.

1837. DICKENS, *Pickwick*, xxii. 'What do you mean by a PIKE-KEEPER?' enquired Mr. Peter Magnus. 'The old 'un means a turn-pike keeper' . . . observed Mr. Weller.

1857. HUGHES, *Tom Brown's Schooldays*, I. iv. Then there was . . . the cheery toot of the guard's horn to warn some drowsy PIKEMAN, or the ostler at the next change.

1874. BORROW, *Wordbook*, . . . The people called in Acts of Parliament, sturdy beggars and vagrants in the old cant language Abraham men, and in the modern PIKERS.

1888. BESANT, *Fifty Years Ago*, 42. The turnpike has gone, and the PIKEMAN . . . has gone . . . and the gates have been removed.

3. (American: Southern States).—A poor white.

1873. NORDHOFF, *California*, 137. The true PIKE . . . is the wandering, gipsy-like southern poor white.

4. (venery).—The *penis*: *see* PRICK.

1600. SHAKSPEARE, *Much Ado*, v. 2. You must put in the PIKES with a vice; and they are dangerous weapons for maids.

Verb. (old). — 1. *See* subs., sense 1.

2. (old). — To die: also TO PIKE OFF: *see* HOP THE TWIG.

3. (American gaming). — To play cautiously and for small stakes. Hence PIKER = a moderate punter.

TO PASS THE PIKES, *verb. phr.* (old).—To be out of danger.—B. E. (*c.*1696).

1648. HERRICK, *Hesperides*, 'His Cavalier.' This a virtuous man can doe, Saile against Rocks, and split them too: I! and a world of PIKES PASSE THROUGH.

*d.*1663. SANDERSON, *Works*, ii. 45. Neither John's mourning nor Christ's piping can PASS THE PIKES.

1675. HACKET, *Transfig.* (3rd Ser.). There were many PIKES TO BE PASSED THROUGH, a complete order of afflictions to be undergone.

TO GIVE THE PIKE, *verb. phr.* (old).—To dismiss: *see* BAG and SACK.

PIKE I (or **PRIOR PIKE**), *intj.* (schools').—An assertion of prior claim or privilege; BAGS (or BAGS I).

PIKER, *subs.* (common).—1. *See* PIKE, *subs.* 1 and *verb.* 3.

2. (Australian).—Wild cattle.

PIKESTAFF, *subs.* (venery).—The *penis*: *see* PRICK.

See PLAIN.

PILATE-VOICE, *subs. phr.* (old).—A big ranting voice. [BREWER: In the old mysteries all tyrants were made to speak in a rough ranting manner. Thus Bottom the Weaver, after a rant "to show his quality," exclaims, "That's 'Ercles' vein, a tyrant's vein;" and Hamlet describes a ranting actor as "out-heroding Herod."]

1383. CHAUCER, *Canterbury Tales*, 3126. In PILATE VOYS he gan to cry, And swor by armes, and by blood and bones.

1530. PALSGRAVE, *Lang. Francoyse*, 442. *A haulte* voyx . . . A PYLATE'S VOYCE.

1564. UDALL, *Apophth.*, 382. He heard a certain oratour speaking out of measure loude and high, and altogether in PILATE'S VOICE.

PILCH, *verb.* (American thieves').—To pilfer: *see* PRIG.

1557. TUSSER, *Husbandrie*, 33. Some steale, some PILCH, Some all away filch.

PILCHER, *subs.* (Old Cant).—A scabbard. [The word is used nowhere in English save in *Romeo and Juliet.* It seems to be a 'literal' due to an Elizabethan 'comp.' Perhaps Shakspeare wrote 'pilch, Sir'; perhaps he didn't. Anyhow 'pilch' = a leathern coat, or overall, and was good enough business for a leathern sheath.]

1595. SHAKSPEARE, *Romeo and Juliet*, iii. 1. Will you pluck your sword out of his PILCHER by the ears?

PILE, *subs.* (American and colonial).—A large sum of money; a fortune: *see* RHINO. Hence, TO MAKE ONE'S PILE = to make a fortune; TO GO THE WHOLE PILE = to stake everything.

1732-57. FRANKLIN, *Poor Richard's Almanack*, Ap. Rash mortals, ere you take a wife, Contrive your PILE to last your life.

1858. *New York Tribune*, 25 Oct. I dug 25 dollars worth of gold dust, and my expenses were about 300 dollars; however, I have clung to the PILE, and intend to keep it as a memorial of my trip. *Ibid.* (Dec., 1861). The jobber has MADE HIS PILE, and what does he care?

1877. BLACK, in *North Am. Rev.*, July, 8. While the carpet-baggers . . . were MAKING enormous PILES, petty larceny ruled supreme.

1888. BRYCE, *American Commonwealth*, II. 704. Great fortunes grow with the growing prosperity of the country, and the opportunity it offers of amassing enormous PILES by bold operations.

1897. MITFORD, *Romance Cape Frontier*, I. xxi. Didn't care what they did, so they MADE THEIR PILE quickly.

TO PILE ON. *See* AGONY.

TO PILE IN, *verb. phr.* (American).—(1) To take part; (2) to eat.

1887. ROBERTS, *Western Avernus* [S. J. and C.]. They . . . asked up to sit down with them and PILE IN.

TO PILE OUT, *verb. phr.* (American).—To come forth.

PILE-DRIVER, *subs. phr.* (venery).—The *penis*: *see* PRICK. Whence PILE-DRIVING = copulation: *see* GREENS and RIDE.

PILGARLICK, *subs.* (old).—1. An outcast; *see* quot. 1785.

1483. *Cath. Anglicum* [E. E. T. S.], s.v. *Vellicare* . . . PILLE GARLEKE.

*d.*1529. SKELTON [DYCE, *Works*, i. 122, 68]. Your PYLLED GARLEKE hed.

1619. FLETCHER, *Humourous Lieutenant*, ii. 2. And there got he a knock, and down goes PILGARLICK.

1708-10. SWIFT, *Polite Conversation*, i. *Col.* Was your Visit long, Miss? *Miss.* Why, truly, they went all to the Opera; and so poor PILGARLICK came home alone.

1785. GROSE, *Vulg. Tongue*, s.v. PILL, or PEELE GARLICK. Said originally to mean one whose skin or hair had fallen off from some disease, chiefly by the venereal one; but now commonly used by persons speaking of themselves; as, there stood poor PILL GARLICK: *i.e.*, there stood I.

2. (old).—A person of ripe age: *see* ANTIQUE.

*d.*1605. STOW [*Century*]. He will soon be a PEELED GARLIC like myself.

PILGRIM, *subs.* (American).—1. *See* quot.

1875. L. SWINBURNE [in *Scribner's Monthly*, II. 508]. PILGRIM and 'tender-foot' were formerly applied almost exclusively to newly imported cattle, but by a natural transference they are usually used to designate all new-comers, tourists, and business-men.

2. (Western American). — In *pl.* = cattle on the drive.

1889. ROOSEVELT, *Ranch Life.* PILGRIMS . . . that is animals driven up on the range from the South, and therefore in poor condition.

PILGRIM'S-SALVE, *subs. phr.* (old).—Excrement; SHIT (*q.v.*).—GROSE (1785).

1670. *Mod. Account of Scotland* [*Harl. Misc.*, vi. 137]. The whole pavement is PILGRIM-SALVE, most excellent to liquor shoes withal, and soft and easy for the bare-footed perambulators.

PILGRIM'S-STAFF, *subs. phr.* (venery).—The *penis*: *see* PRICK.

PILL, *subs.* (common).—1. A black balloting ball: *see* BLACKBALL. Also as *verb.* = to reject by ballot.

1855. THACKERAY, *Newcomes*, XXX. He was coming on for election at Bays, and was as nearly PILLED as any man I ever knew in my life.

1901. *Free Lance*, 27 Ap., 74, 1. The ex-acrobat, as every one knows, was badly PILLED—some people being malicious enough to say that, although he had a proposer and a seconder, there was not a single white ball!

2. (common).—A disagreeable or objectionable person; a BORE (*q.v.*): also of events—'a BITTER PILL.'

*a.*1556. UDALL, *Luke IV.* [*Century*]. Yet cannot thei abyde to swallow down the holsome PILLE of viritie, being bitter in their mouths.

1580. LYLY, *Euphues*, 468. Thinking . . . that the time was past to wo[o]e hir . . . I digested the PILL which had almost [choakt] me.

1595. SHAKSPEARE, *Two Gentlemen*, ii. 4. *Val.* O, flatter me; for love delights in praises. *Pro.* When I was sick you gave me BITTER PILLS, And I must minister the like to you.

1749. SMOLLETT, *Gil Blas* [ROUTLEDGE], 191. This decision was a BITTER PILL for me to swallow.

*c.*1801. JEFFERSON, *To Madison* [BANCROFT, *Hist. Const.*, I. 430. He said the renunciation of this interest was a BITTER PILL which they could not swallow.

1897. MAUGHAM, *'Liza of Lambeth*, iii. Well, you are a PILL.

3. (common).—A drink; a GO (*q.v.*): *see* DRINKS.

4. (American).—A bullet: also BLUE-PILL (*q.v.*).

18 [?]. *Drake's Mag.*, 'He Died Game' [S. J. and C.]. He had always told him he'd run plumb ag'in' a PILL some day if he wan't blanked careful like.

Verb. 1. See *subs.* 1.

2. (University).—To twaddle; to talk platitudes.

THE PILLS, *subs. phr.* (military).—The Royal Army Medical Corps. Also "The Licensed Lancers"; "The Poultice Wallopers"; and "The Linseed Lancers." Also (generally) PILLS = a doctor or surgeon.

1899. *Cassell's Saturday Journal*, 15 March, 1, 1. "PILLS, are they all mad on board that vessel, or merely drunk, as usual?"

TO GILD THE PILL, *verb. phr.* (colloquial).—To sweeten a bitter thing, soften a hard thing, beautify an ugly thing, explain away a sure thing; to present the inevitable as though it were optional: TO GAMMON (*q.v.*). Also PILL.

1612. WEBSTER, *White Devil*, iii. 2. I discern poison under your GILDED PILLS.

1749. SMOLLETT, *Gil Blas*, IV. iii. I . . . began to GILD THE PILL, and . . . prove that this mad project was no more than an agreeable frolic. *Ibid.* IV. vii. The good old man . . . GILDED THE PILL I was to swallow with a present of fifty ducats.

1899. *Critic*, 8 Ap., 3, 2. He quotes Goldsmith, then himself; his desire being to GILD THE PILL.

TO PILL AND POLL, *verb. phr.* (old). — To pillage and strip: specifically in modern usage (thieves'), to cheat a comrade of his REGULARS (*q.v.*): Fr. *faire l'ésgard.* Whence (POLL-THIEF, or POLLER) = (1) a thief; and (2) an informer.

*d.*1529. SKELTON [DYCE, *Works*, ii. 29]. With POLLYNG and shaving. *Ibid.* [i. 204]. Like voluptuous harlottes, that . . . to haue their goodes, presenteth to them their beddes, for to take their carnall desires, and after they haue taken all their disportes, they PILL them as an onion. Ibid., *Maner of World*, 147. So many baudes and POLLERS, Sawe I never. Ibid., *Colin Clout*, 362. By POOLYNGE and PYLLAGE In cytyes and vyllage.

1548. HALL, *Union* [HALLIWELL]. And have wynked at the POLLYNG and extorcion of hys unmeasureable officiers.

*d.*1577. GASCOIGNE, h. 3 b. [NARES]. Bicause they PILL AND POLL, because they wrest.

1587. HOLLINSHED, *Hist. Ireland*, F7, col. 2a. Kildare did use to PILL AND POLL his friendes, tenants, and reteyners.

1596. SPENSER, *Faerie Queene*, v. ii. 6. Which POLS and PILS the poor in piteous wise.

1597. SHAKSPEARE, *Rich. II.*, ii. 1. The Commons he hath PILL'D With grievous taxes, and quite lost their hearts. *Ibid.*, *Rich. III.*, 1. Hear me, you wrangling pirates, that fell out In sharing that which you have PILL'D from me.

1600. W. KEMP, *Nine Days' Wonder* [ARBER, *English Garner*, vii. p. 37]. One that . . . would POL his father, Derick his dad! do anything, how ill soever, to please his apish humour!

1610. *Mirr. for Magistrates*, 279. The prince thereby presumed his people for to PILL. *Ibid.* 467. Can PILL, AND POLL, and catch before they crave. *Ibid.* They would not bear such POLLING.

1621. BURTON, *Anatomy of Mel.*, 41. Great man in office may securely rob whole provinces, undo thousands, PILL AND POLL.

*d.*1626. BACON, *Judicature* [quoted in *Century* from edition 1887]. Neither can justice yield her fruit with sweetness among the briars and brambles of catching and POLLING clerks and ministers.

1648. HERRICK, *Hesperides*, 'Duty to Tyrants.' Doe they first PILL thee? next, pluck off thy skin?

1675. CROWNE, *Country Wit*, ii. . . . 'Tis a rare thing to be an absolute Prince, and have rich subjects. Oh, how one may PILL 'em and POLL 'em.

1893. EMERSON, *Lippo*, v. I spose he wants to accuse us of POLLING—a thing I never done in my life, and I know my other pals are as straight as darts. *Ibid.*, vi. I have often met honourable robbers since like the POLLER.

PILLAR. *See* POST.

PILL-BOX, *subs. phr.* (common).—A small brougham.

1857. DICKENS, *Little Dorrit*, xxviii. She drove into town in a one-horse carriage, irreverently called at that period of English history, a PILL-BOX.

2. (common).—A soldier's cap.

3. (American).—A revolver or gun. Also PILL-BOTTLE. *See* MEAT-IN-THE-POT.

PILL-DRIVER (**-MONGER** or **-PEDDLER**).—An itinerant apothecary: *see* TRADES and PROFESSIONS.

1763. FOOTE, *Mayor of Garret*, i. There has, Major, been here an impudent PILL-MONGER, who has dar'd to scandalise the whole body of the bench.

PILLICOCK (**PILLOCK** or **PILICOCK**), *subs.* (venery).—1. The *penis*: *see* PRICK. Hence PILLICOCK-HILL = the female *pudendum.* Also (BURNS and JAMIESON) PILLIE.

[?]. *Reliq. Antiq.*, ii. 211. Ye ne may no more of love done, Mi PILCOC pisseth on my schone.

1539. LYNDSAY, *Thrie Estaitis*, l. 4419. Methink my PILLOCK will nocht ly doun.

1598. FLORIO, *Worlde of Wordes*, *Dolcemelle* . . . Also taken for a mans PILICOCK.

1605. SHAKSPEARE, *King Lear*, iii. iv. *Edg.* PILLICOCK sat on Pillicock-hill.

1611. COTGRAVE, *Dict.*, s.v. *Turelurean* and *Vitault*, a PILLICOCK, a man's yarde.

1653. URQUHART, *Rabelais*, I. xi. Very pleasantly would pass their time in taking you know what between their fingers and dandling it . . . One of them would call it her PILLICOCK, her fiddle-diddle, her staff of love, &c.

1719. DURFEY, *Wit and Mirth*, Song. When PILLICOCK came to his lady's toe.

*d.*1796. BURNS, *Merry Muses* . . . He followed me baith out and in, Wi' a stiff standin' PILLIE.

1879. DAVENPORT ADAMS, *Shakspeare's Works* [Howard ed., p. 1216]. Note on PILLICOCK . . . Lear's mention of his *pelican* daughters suggests this word—a cant term of familiar licentiousness—to Edgar.

2. (obs.).—An endearment.

1598. FLORIO, *Worlde of Wordes*, 382. A prime-cocke, a PILLICOCKE, a darlin, a beloved lad.

1611. COTGRAVE, *Dict.*, s.v. *Vitault.* A great toole, or one that has a good toole, also a flattering word for a young boy like our my pretty PILLICOCKE.

1653. URQUHART, *Rabelais*, I. xli. By my faith, saith Ponocrates, I cannot tell, my PILLICOCK, but thou art more worth than gold.

PILLORY, *subs.* (old).—1. A baker: *see* TRADES and PROFESSIONS.—B. E. (*c.*1696).

2. (old: now recognised).—*See* quot.

*c.*1696. B. E., *Dict. Cant. Crew*, s.v. PILLORY . . . also a Punishment mostly heretofore for Beggers, now for Perjury, Forgery and suborned Persons.

PILLOW-MATE, *subs. phr.* (common). —1. A wife; and (2) a whore: *see* DUTCH and TART.

PILL-PATE, *subs.* (old).—A friar; a shaveling.

*d.*1570. BECON, *Works*, ii. 315. These smeared PILL-PATES, I would say prelates, first of all accused him, and afterward pronounced the sentence of death upon him.

PI-MAN. *See* PI, *adj.*

PIMGINNIT, *subs.* (old).—'A large, red, angry Pimple.'—B. E. (*c.*1696). *Cf.* Old Saying, 'Nine PIMGENETS make a pock royal.'

1694. DUNTON, *Ladies Dict.* [NARES]. Is it not a manly exercise to stand licking his lips into rubies, panting his cheeks into cherries, parching his PIMGINITS, carbuncles, and buboes.

PIMP, *subs.* (common).—1. A pander; a cock-bawd: also PIMP-WHISKING (*see* quot. 1696). Hence as *verb.* = to procure.—B. E. (*c.*1696); GROSE (1785).

1638. FORD, *Fancies*, i. 2. 'Tis a gallant life to be an old lord's PIMP-WHISKIN: but beware of the porter's lodge for carrying tales out of the school.

1681. DRYDEN, *Absolam and Achit.*, i. 81. But when to sin our biassed nature leans, The careful Devil is still at hand with means, And providently PIMPS for ill desires.

*c.*1696. B. E., *Dict. Cant. Crew*, s.v. PIMP. *Ibid.* PIMP-WHISKING, a Top Trader that way; also a little mean-spirited narrow-soul'd Fellow.

*d.*1742. BAILEY, *Erasmus*, 'The Profane Feast.' Go hang yourself, you PIMP.

1890. *Century Dict.*, s.v. PIMP. This explanation [Skeats] is, however, inadequate; the word is apparently of low slang origin, without any recorded basis.

2. (old).—*See* quots.

1724-7. DEFOE, *Tour through Gt. Britain*, i. 138. Here they make those faggots . . . used in taverns in London to light their fagots, and are called . . . by the woodmen PIMPS.

1785. GROSE, *Vulg. Tongue*, s.v. PIMP . . . also a small faggot used about London for making fires, named from introducing the fire to the coals.

3. (University). — To act meanly; to curry favour. Whence PIMPING (*adj.*) = small, feeble; perhaps well-meaning, but in every way inconsiderable.

1749. SMOLLETT, *Gil Blas* [ROUTLEDGE], 32. They only care for PIMPING sycophants.

*d.*1832. CRABBE [quoted in *Century*]. He had no paltry arts, no PIMPING ways.

1890. S. JUDD, *Margaret*, i. 4. 'Was I so little?' asked Margaret. 'Yes, and PIMPING enough.'

PIMPLE, *subs.* (old).—1. A boon companion.

1700. CONGREVE, *Way of the World*, iv. 10. The Sun's a good PIMPLE, an honest Soaker, he has a Cellar at your Antipodes.

2. (common).—The head: *see* TIBBY. — GROSE (1785); BEE (1823). Hence, PIMPLE-COVER = a hat: *see* GOLGOTHA.

PIMPLE IN A BENT, *subs. phr.* (old).—Something very minute: *cf.* KNOT IN A RUSH.

1582. STANYHURST, *Ænid.*, Dedic. I could lay down heere sundrye examples, were yt not I should bee thoght ouer curious by prying owt a PIMPLE IN A BENT.

PIN, *subs.* (common).—*In pl.* = the legs. Hence, ON ONE'S PINS = (1) alive; (2) faring well; and (3) in good form.—GROSE (1785); VAUX (1819).

1520. *Hick Scorner* [HAWKINS, *Eng. Drama*, i. 102]. Than wolde I renne thyder on MY PYNNES As fast as I might goe.

1628. EARLE, *Microcos.* [Downe-right scholler]. His body is not set upon nice PINNES . . . but his scrape is homely and his nod worse.

1783. BURGOYNE, *Lord of the Manor*, iii. 3. I never saw a fellow better set upon his PINS.

1821. EGAN, *Life in London*, Intro. Therefore he must get upon his PINS how he can.

1842. *Song*, 'By-blow of the Jug' [FARMER, *Musa Pedestris* (1896), 144]. Scarcely had Jack got ON HIS YOUNG PINS, When his mammy . . . taught him soon to swear and lie, And to have a finger in every pie.

1889. *Harper's Mag.*, LXXX. 269. Glad to hear that he is ON HIS PINS yet; he might have pegged out in ten years, you know.

2. (venery).—The *penis*: *see* PRICK: *cf.* PINCUSHION = female *pudendum*; and PUSH-PIN = copulation.

1635. GLAPTHORNE, *The Lady Mother*, i. 1. *Lovell.* Her Belly a soft Cushion where no sinner But her true love must dare stick a PIN in her. *Grimes.* That line has got the prick and prayse from all the rest.

3. (common).—A trifle: the lowest standard of value: also PIN-HEAD. *See* BUTTON, CENT, FIG, POINT, RAP, RUSH. STRAW, &c.—B. E. (*c.*1696). [In quots. 1470 and 1592 PREIN = pin, but is derived [JAMIESON] from Su-G. Dan, *pren* = a graving tool or any sharp instrument.]

1433. *Babees Book* [E. E. T. S.], 93. But when he is to highest power, Yet he is not worth a PIN.

1470. WALLACE, vii. 910, MS. Quhat gentill man had nocht with Ramsay beyne; Off courtlynes thai cownt him nocht a PREYNE.

*c.*1540. *Doctour Doubble Ale* [HAZLITT, *Early Pop. Poet*, iii. 306]. He CARETH NOT A PYN, How much ther be wythin, So he the pot may wyn.

1550. BANSLEY, *Abuse of Women* [HAZLITT, *E. Pop. Poet*, iv. 233]. And therefore your fonde blynd skuses wyl not serve; They are not worth a PYN.

*d.*1555. LYNDSAY, S. P. K., ii. 29. Thocht I ane servand long hes bene, My purchess is nocht worth ane PRENE.

*c.*1555. *A Pore Helpe* [quoted in DYCE, *Skelton*, i. cxiv.]. If she were suppress, A PYN for all the rest.

1596. SHAKSPEARE, *Hamlet*, i. 4. I do not set my life at a PIN'S fee.

[?]. *Sir Andrew Barton* [CHILD, *Ballads*, VII. 206]. And tho' he cared not a PIN For him and his company.

1633. MARMYON, *Fine Compan.*, II. i. 68. I do not care a PIN for her.

1678. COTTON, *Virgil Travestie* [*Works* (1725), 90]. But neither by the Nap, nor Tearing, Was it a PIN the worse for wearing.

*c.*1707. DURFEY, *Pills* (1707), ii. 112. For her Favour I CARE NOT A PIN.

1708-10. SWIFT, *Polite Conversation*, i. Here's a PIN for that Lye; I'm sure Lyars had need of good Memories.

*d.*1796. BURNS, *Poems* (*Globe*), 80. My memory's no worth a PREEN.

1886-96. MARSHALL, '*Pomes' from the Pink 'Un* [' Boycotting the Author '], 44. Not caring a PIN if the lotion was whiskey or unsweetened gin.

1887. STEVENSON, *Underwoods*, 'The Scotsman's Return.' A bletherin' clan, no worth a PREEN, As bad as Smith o' Aiberdeen.

1890. BOLDREWOOD, *Squatter's Dream*, 157. For two PINS I'd put a match in every gunyah on the place.

4. (old: now recognised).—A measure containing four-and-a-half gallons, or the eighth part of a barrel.—B. E. (*c.*1696).

Verb. (thieves').—To steal; TO NAB (*q.v.*).

PHRASES:—TO BE DOWN PIN = to be out of sorts; TO PUT IN THE PIN = to stop, arrest, or pull up: as a habit or indulgence; TO PIN ONESELF ON ANOTHER = to hang on; TO PIN DOWN (or TO THE GROUND) = (1) to secure, (2) to make sure, and (3) to attack with no chance of escape; PINNED TO A WIFE'S TAIL = petticoat-led; TO PIN ONE'S FAITH TO (or UPON ONE'S SLEEVE) = to trust implicitly: *see* also BOTTLE; MERRY-PIN; NICK.

PIN-BASKET, *subs. phr.* (old).—The youngest child.—GROSE (1785).

PIN-BUTTOCK, *subs. phr.* (old).—A bony rump: with bones like pins pricking: the reverse of BARGE-ARSE (*q.v.*).

1598. SHAKSPEARE, *All's Well*, ii. 2, 18. It is like a barber's chair that fits all buttocks, the PIN-BUTTOCK, the quatch-buttock, the brawn-buttock, or any buttock.

PIN-CASE (or **-CUSHION**), *subs. phr.* (venery).—The female *pudendum*: *cf.* PIN, *subs.* 2: *see* MONOSYLLABLE.

PINCH, *subs.* (common).—1. A dilemma; a critical situation; a scrape. Whence, TO COME TO THE PINCH = to face the situation; AT A PINCH = 'upon a push or exigence.'—B. E. (*c.*1696); GROSE (1785).

*d.*1486. BERNERS, *Froiss. Chron.*, II. cxviii. AT A PYNCH a frend is knowen.

1607. DEKKER, *Westward Hoe*, iii. 1. O, the wit of a woman when she is put TO THE PINCH.

1613. SELDEN, *Drayton's Polyolb.*, xviii. 735. The Norman IN THIS narrow PINCH, not so willingly as wisely, granted the desire.

1647. FLETCHER, *Hum. Lieut.*, iv. 4. I can lie yet, And swear, too, AT A PINCH.

1704. SWIFT, *Tale of a Tub*, i. Where THE PINCH lay I cannot certainly affirm.

1749. SMOLLETT, *Gil Blas* [ROUTLEDGE], 433. If you want my purse, come and take it: it will not fail you AT A PINCH.

1880. GLOVER, *Racing Life*, 38. It's one of the deadest PINCHES ever known. I guy or hook it, skedaddle or absquatulate.

2. (racing).—A certainty.

1886-96. MARSHALL, '*Pomes' from the Pink 'Un* [' Honest Bill'], 50. The race would be a PINCH, Sir, barring accident or spill.

Verb. (thieves').—1. To steal: formerly, encroach little by little; to appropriate. THE PINCH (or PINCHING LAY) = (1) pilfering while purchasing, (2) exchanging bad money for good: RINGING THE CHANGES (*q.v.*). Hence PINCHER (or PINCH-GLOAK) = a shop-lifter. Also, TO PINCH ON THE PARSON'S SIDE = 'to sharp him of his tithes'; and PINCHED TO THE BONE = robbed of all.—B. E. (*c.*1696); GROSE (1785); VAUX (1819).

1362. LANGLAND, *Piers Plowman* [WRIGHT, vii. 267]. Yf ich zede to the plouh ich PYNCHEDE on hus half-acre.

1712. SHIRLEY, *The Black Procession*, ii. To PINCH all the lurry he thinks it no sin.

1749. SMOLLETT, *Gil Blas* [ROUTLEDGE], 378. The old codger will be PINCHED TO THE BONE and left penniless.

1842. EGAN, *Captain Macheath* (Song, 'Miss Dolly Trull.') She runs such precious cranky rigs With PINCHING wedge and lockets.

1859. *A Hundred Stretches Hence* [FARMER, *Musa Pedestris* (1896), 159]. And where the swag so bleakly PINCHED?

1886-96. MARSHALL, '*Pomes' from the Pink 'Un* ['The Luxury of Doing Good'], 41. He charged the barmaid's mash with the PINCHING of the cash.

1898. *Pink 'Un and Pelican*, 227. He was convinced, from the instant he discovered his boodle was gone, that it had been PINCHED.

2. (thieves').—To arrest.

*c.*1600-62. *Common Cries of London* [COLLIER, *Roxburghe Ballads* (1847), 213]. And some there be . . . That PINCH the countryman With nimming of a fee.

1851. MAYHEW, *Lond. Lab.*, III. 397. He got acquitted for that there note after he had me PINCHED.

1886-96. MARSHALL, '*Pomes*,' 72. And she was PINCHED for loitering with felonious intent.

1887. HENLEY, *Villon's Good Night*, iii. For you, you copper's-narks, and dubs, Who PINCHED me when upon the Snam.

1900. SIMS, *London's Heart*, 284. Her husband had been PINCHED, and these were his pals who were going to try . . . to get a lawyer to defend him.

3. (old).—'To cut the Measures of Ale, Beer,' &c.—B. E. (*c.*1696).

TO PINCH AT, *verb. phr.* (old).—To demur; to fault-find.

1383. CHAUCER, *Manciples' Tale*, Prol. He speke wol of smale thynges As for to PYNCHEN AT thy rekenynges, That were not honeste, if it came to pruf.

See NAB, NICK, and SHOE.

PINCHBECK, *adj.* (common).—Showy; meretricious; sham. [In the 18th century Christopher Pinchbeck, a London watchmaker, invented an amalgam much used in cheap jewellery.]

1782. WALPOLE, *Letters*, viii. 310. The highwayman . . . insisted on more. The poor girl, terrified, gave him not only her own PINCHBECK watch, but her grandmother's gold one.

1886. *West. Rev.*, Oct., 795. Most of these men were of the school of Molyneux, and theirs was PINCHBECK patriotism.

1901. *Punch*, 25 Dec., 452, 1. The Irish Party, under the leadership of a PINCHBECK Parnell, have given themselves away.

PINCH-BELLY (-BACK, -COMMONS, -FIST, -GUTS, -PENNY, or -PINCHER,, *subs. phr.* (old).—A miser; a niggard in food, dress, or money: *see* SKINFLINT.

1412. OCCLEVE, *De. Reg. Princip.* [OLIPHANT, *New English*, i. 210]. He [Occleve] uses many phrases seldom repeated before Barclay's time, a hundred years later, such as . . . *shepes skyn* (parchment) . . . PYNCHEPENY (niggard).

1440. *Prompl. Parv.* s.v. *Cupidinarius* . . . PYKEPENY . . . PINCHER.

1579. LYLY, *Euphues*, 'Anat. of Wit, p. 109. They accompt one . . . a PYNCH PENNY if he be not prodygall.

1593. HOLLYBAND, *Dict.*, s.v. *Chiche* . . . PINCHPENNY.

1653. URQUHART, *Rabelais*. I. xlvii. PINCHPENNY said to him . . . we are here very ill provided of victuals.

1690. CROWNE, *Eng. Friar*, ii. 1. 'We are my Lady PINCH-GUT'S men Sir.' . . . 'Her men? no, her mice. We live on crumbs.'

1821. SCOTT, *Pirate*, VI. If this house be strewed in ruins before morning where would be the world's want in the . . . niggardly PINCHCOMMONS by which it is inhabited.

1883. CLARK RUSSELL, *Sailor's Language*, s.v. PINCHGUT. A mean purser.

PINCH-BOARD, *subs. phr.* (American).—A swindling roulette table: *see* PINCH, *verb.*

PINCH-BOTTOM (-BUTTOCK, or -CUNT), *subs. phr.* (venery).—A whoremaster: *see* MUTTON-MONGER.

PINCHER, *subs. phr.* (political American).—A legislative measure calculated to secure a pecuniary reward to those interested in its rejection.

See PINCH, *verb.*, and PINCH-BELLY.

PINCH-GUT-MONEY, *subs. phr.* (old).—*See* quot.

*c.*1696. B. E., *Dict. Cant. Crew*, s.v. PINCH-GUT-MONEY, allowed by the King to the Seamen, that Serve on Bord the Navy Royal, when their Provision falls Short; also in long Voyages when they are forced to Drink Water instead of Beer.

PINCH-PRICK, *subs. phr.* (venery).—1. A whore; and (2) a wife that insists on her dues.

PINCH-WIFE, *subs. phr.* (venery).—A vigilant and churlish husband.

PINCUSHION. *See* PIN-CASE.

PINEAPPLE, *verb.* (American).—To close-shave; to 'county-crop'; TO SHINGLE (*q.v.*).

PINE-TOP, *subs. phr.* (American).—Common whiskey: *see* OLD MAN'S MILK.

PINE-TREE MONEY, *subs.* (old American).—Money coined in Massachusetts in 17th century: as bearing a figure resembling a pine-tree.—BARTLETT.

PINE-TREE STATE, *subs. phr.* (American).—Maine. [From its extensive pine forests.]

1888. *Boston Transcript*. The good old PINE-TREE STATE is pretty well represented . . . scarcely a town of any size . . . but what contains one or more Maine men.

PINK, *subs.* (old).—1. A beauty: hence (2) a pattern or model: as a woman of fashion, a well-groomed man, the pick of the litter, a champion at sport, &c.—GROSE (1785).

1595. SHAKSPEARE, *Romeo and Juliet*, ii. 4, 4. I am the very PINK of courtesy.

1602. BRETON, *Wonders*, 7. He had a pretty PINCKE to his own wedded wife.

1621. FLETCHER, *Pilgrim*, 1, 2. This is the prettiest pilgrim, The PINK of pilgrims.

1693. CONGREVE, *Old Batchelor*, ii. 1. I am happy to have obliged the Mirrour of Knighthood and PINK of Courtesie in the age.

1708-10. SWIFT, *Polite Conversation*, i. *Miss*. Oh! Mr. *Neverout*; every body knows that you are the PINK of Courtesy.

1821. EGAN, *Life in London*, II. i. The lady and her scullion—the PINK of the ton and his "rain-bow"— . . . they are "all there."

1827. LYTTON, *Pelham*, xl. Now, reely, Mr. Ritson, you, who are the PINK of feeshion, ought to know better than I can.

3. (American cadet).—A bad report, *e.g.*, 'There are several PINKS against you.' Also as *verb*.

4. (hunting).—A hunting coat: commonly SCARLET (*q.v.*). Also a hunting man (as wearing PINK).

1857. HUGHES, *Tom Brown's School-days*, I. iv. The PINKS stand about the inn door lighting cigars and waiting to see us start.

1860. *Macm. Mag.*, 16. With pea-coats over their PINKS.

Verb. (old).—1. To put home a rapier's point. Also, as *subs.* = a wound so made.—B. E. (*c.*1696); GROSE (1785).

1598. JONSON, *Ev. Man in His Humour*, iv. 1. I will PINK your flesh full of holes with my rapier for this.

1607. MIDDLETON, *Five Gallants*, iii. 5. A freebooter's PINK, sir, three or four inches deep.

1778. DARBLAY, *Evelina*, lxxxiii. Lovel . . . you must certainly PINK him; you must not put up with such an affront.

1823. BEE, *Dict. Turf, etc.*, s.v. NOB. 'Josh paid his respects . . . to the Yokel's nob.' 'His nob was PINKED all over,' *i.e.* marked in sundry places.

2. (American thieves').—To convict: as a result of perjury or cross-examination to one's prejudice.

3. (tailors').—To make carefully, even exquisitely.

4. (pugilists').—To get home easily and often.

1819. MOORE, *Tom Cribb*, 'The Milling Match.' And muns and noddle PINK'D in every part.

1823. BEE, *Dict. Turf*, s.v. PINK [of Jim Belcher's method]. I felt myself suddenly PINKED all over . . . no blow of finishing importance, to be sure, but all conducing toward victory.

DUTCH PINK, *subs. phr.* (pugilists').—Blood: *cf.* CLARET.

1853. BRADLEY, *Verdant Green*, II. 31. That'll take the bark from your nozzle, and distill the DUTCH PINK for you, won't it?

PINKING-DINDER, *subs. phr.* (old).—*See* quot.

1785. GROSE, *Vulg. Tongue*, s.v. PINKING-DINDER. A sweater or mohawk. *Irish.*

PINK-SPIDERS, *subs. phr.* (common).—Delirium tremens; GALLON-DISTEMPER (*q.v.*).

PINKY, *subs.* (Scots' and American).—The little finger: also anything little; the smallest candle, the weakest beer, etc.

PIN-MONEY, *subs. phr.* (old colloquial).—An allowance to a woman for pocket expenses: originally to a married woman by her husband, either by settlement or gift [GROSE, 1785]. Also (modern) the proceeds of adultery or occasional prostitution.

1673. WYCHERLEY, *Gentleman Dancing Master* [LEIGH HUNT, *Old Dramatists*, 67]. 'But what allowance?' . . . 'Stay let me think! first for advance MONEY, five hundred pounds for PINS.'

1703. STEELE, *Tender Husband*, i. 1. The main article with me is, that foundation of wives' rebellion, and husbands' cuckoldom—that cursed PIN-MONEY.

1705. VANBRUGH, *Confederacy*, iv. But then, sir, her coach-hire, her chair-hire, her PIN-MONEY, her play-money, her china, and her charity would consume peers.

1718. HEARNE, *Diary*, 29 Aug. Mr. Calvert tells me, that the late princess of Orange (wife of him that they call King William III.) had fifty thousand pounds per annum for PIN MONEY (as they commonly call ordinary pocket-money).

*d.*1719. ADDISON, *Ladies Association* [*Century*]. They have a greater interest in property than either maids or wives, and do not hold their jointures by the precarious tenure of portions or PIN-MONEY.

1901. *D. Telegraph*, 13 Nov., 6, 3. I was to take a profit of 2s. or 3s., his explanation being that he would like to give his wife a little 'PIN' MONEY.

PINNACE, *subs.* (old).—A bawd; a prostitute: *see* TART. Also (quots. 1607 and 1693) = a woman; a PIECE (*q.v.*).

[?]. *Songs of the London Prentices*, 66. For when all the gallants are gone out o' th' town, O then these fine PINNACES lack their due lading.

1607. DEKKER and WEBSTER, *Northward Hoe*, v. 1. There is as pretty a little PINNACE struck sail hereby, and come in lately!—she's my kinswoman . . . her portion three thousand . . . her hopes better.

1614. *Bartholomew Fair*, i. 1. She hath been before me—punk, PINNACE and bawd—any time these two and twenty years, upon record in the Pie-Poudres.

1693. CONGREVE, *Old Bachelor*, v. 7. A goodly PINNACE, richly laden . . . Twelve thousand pounds and all her rigging, besides what lies concealed under hatches.

PINNER (or PINNY), *subs.* (old colloquial).—A pinafore.

1672. WYCHERLEY, *Love in a Wood*, iii, 2. Pish! give her but leave to gape, rub her eyes, and put on her day PINNER.

[?]. *The Crafty Miller* [NARES]. With a suit of good PINNERS pray let her be drest, And when she's in bed let all go to rest.

1681. RADCLIFFE, *Ovid Travestie*, 5. My hair's about my ears, as I'm a sinner He has not left me worth a hood or PINNER.

1705. *The London Ladies Dressing Room* [NARES]. The cinder wench, and oyster drab, With Nell the cook, and hawking Bab, Must have their PINNERS brought from France.

1886. F. LOCKER, *Piccadilly* [quoted in *Century*]. When, poor bantling! down she tumbled, daubed her hands, and face, and PINNY.

1901. *Referee*, 14 Ap., 9, 2. Hundreds of tiny toddles in their white PINNIES and their little bows of pink and blue were dancing together to a piano-organ.

PINNER-UP, *subs. phr.* (tramps').—A vendor of broadside songs and ballads. [They are usually PINNED-UP on canvas against a wall.]

PINNIPE, *subs.* (American thieves').—A crab. Hence PINNIPED = sideways; crab fashion. [The Pinnipedia are fin-footed animals.]

PINNOCK. TO BRING PINNOCK TO PANNOCK, *verb. phr.* (old colloquial).—*See* quot.

1552. HULOET . . . . Brynge somethynge to nothynge, as the vulgare speache is, TO BRYNGE PYNNOCK TO PANNOCK.

PIN-PANNIERLY-FELLOW, *subs. phr.* (old).—*See* quot.

. . . . *Kennett MS.* [HALLIWELL]. A PIN-PENNIEBLE fellow, a coveteous miser that pins up his baskets or panniers, or that thinks the loss of a pin to be a pain and trouble to him.

PINS-AND-NEEDLES, *subs. phr.* (common).—The tingling which accompanies the recovery of circulation in a benumbed limb.

1876. G. ELIOT, *Deronda*, lxiii. A man . . . may tremble, stammer, and show other signs of recovered sensibility no more in the range of his acquired talents than PINS AND NEEDLES after numbness.

PIN'S-HEAD. TO LOOK FOR A PIN'S-HEAD IN A CARTLOAD OF HAY, *verb. phr.* (old).—To attempt the impossible. Whence TO FIND A PIN'S-HEAD, &c. = to achieve wonders. *See* BOTTLE.

1565. CALFHILL, *Martialls Tr. of Cross* [Parker Soc.], 173.

PINSRAP, *subs.* (back slang).—A parsnip.

PINT, *subs.* (tailors').—Recommendation; praise.

PINTS ROUND! *intj.* (tailors').—A fine imposed upon a cutter for dropping his shears: nearly obsolete.

PINTLE, *subs.* (venery).—The *penis*: *see* PRICK. Whence PINTLE-BIT (or -MAID) = a mistress or KEEP (*q.v.*); PINTLE-BLOSSOM = a chancre; PINTLE-FEVER = a clap or pox; PINTLE-MERCHANT (or -MONGER) = a harlot; PINTLE-RANGER (or -FANCIER) = a wanton; PINTLE-CASE = the female *pudendum*: *see* MONOSYLLABLE.—BAILEY (1728); HALLIWELL (1844). Also PINTLE-KEEK (Scots') = a leer of invitation.

13 [?]. *Sloane MS.*, 2584, 50. [A receipt] ffor bolnyng of PYNTELYS.

14 [?]. *MS. Med. Rec.*, xv. century. For sore PYNTULLES Take lynschede . . . with sweet mylke . . . make a plaster, and ley to, and anoynte . . . till he be whole.

1598. FLORIO, *Worlde of Wordes*, s.v. *Cazzomarino*, a PINTLE-FISH.

1749. ROBERTSON of Struan, *Poems*, 83. So to a House of Office streight A School-Boy does repair, To ease his Postern of its Weight, And fr— his P—— there.

1785. C. HANBURY WILLIAMS, *Odes*, To L—d L—n,' 112. With whores be lewd, With Whigs be hearty, And both in (PINTLE) and in party, Confess your noble race.

*c.*1786. CAPTAIN MORRIS, *The Plenipotentiary*. She spread its renown through the rest of the town, As a PINTLE past all understanding.

*d.*1796. BURNS, *Merry Muses*, 'Nine Inch Will Please a Lady.' We'll add two thumb-breads to the nine And that's a sonsie PINTLE. *Ibid.*, BURNS, *Godly Girzie*. But ay she glowr'd up to the moon, And ay she sigh'd . . . I trust my heart's in Heaven aboun, Where 'er your sinful PINTLE be. *Ibid.* (old), *For a' That and a' That*. A PINTLE like a rolling-pin: She nicker'd when she saw that.

PIONEER-OF-NATURE, *subs. phr.* (venery).—The *penis*: *see* PRICK.

1653. URQUHART, *Rabelais*, I. xi. And some . . . women . . . give these names, my Roger, my . . . PIONEER . . . lusty live sausage . . . my rump-splitter.

PIP, *subs.* (gaming).—1. A spot on dice or playing cards.—BAILEY (1728). [A corruption of *picks* = (O.E.) 'diamond' and (sometimes) 'spade': from old Fr. *picque* = a spade.]

2. (old). — The pox: *see* FRENCH DISEASE: hence PIPPED = poxed.

1584. MONDAY, *Weakest to the Wall*, iii. 5. Do not you pray that the PIP may catch the people, and that you may earn many groats for making graves?

1622. DEKKER and MASSINGER, *Virgin Martyr*, ii. 1. Therein thou shewed'st thyself a perfect demi-christian too, to let the poor beg, starve, and hang, or die of the PIP.

1670. RAY, *Proverbs* [BOHN], 172. As much need of it as he has of the PIP, or a cough.

Verb. (club).—To blackball; TO PILL (*q.v.*).

1880. HUTH, *Buckle*, I. 252. If Buckle were PIPPED, they would do the same to every clergyman.

1892. *Punch's Model Music-hall Songs*, 20. And what his little game is, he'll let us perceive, And he'll PIP the whole lot of 'em, so I believe.

2. (gaming).—To take a trick from an opponent.

TO HAVE (or GET) THE PIP, *verb. phr.* (colloquial).—To be depressed, or out of sorts: *see* HUMP.

1886-96. MARSHALL, '*Pomes' from the Pink 'Un* ['The Luxury of Doing Good'], 41. It cost a bit to square up the attack; For the landlord HAD THE PIP.

PIPE (or **PIPERS**), *subs.* (old).—1. Generic for the vocal organs; and (2) the voice: *in pl.* = the lungs. Hence as *verb.* = (1) to talk; and (2) to cry: also TO PIPE UP, TO TAKE A PIPE, TO

TUNE ONE'S PIPES, and TO PIPE ONE'S EYE. Hence, TO SHUT (or PUT) UP THE PIPES = to be silent. Also, PIPER = a broken-winded horse; a ROARER (*q.v.*).

1383. CHAUCER, *Canterbury Tales* [SKEAT], l. 2752. The PYPES of his longes gonne to swelle.

*c.*1400. *Towneley Myst.* [Camden Soc.], 103. Who is that PYPYS so poore?

1560. PILKINGTON, *Sermons* [Parker Soc.], 601. If that were true, physicians might put up their PIPES.

1579-80. LYLY, *Euphues*, 278. Hee also strayned his olde PYPE, and thus beganne . . .

*d.*1663. SANDERSON, *Works*, ii. 45. Neither John's mourning nor Christ's PIPING can pass the pikes.

1749. SMOLLETT, *Gil Blas*, I. v. I happened one day to scratch myself, upon which, SETTING UP MY PIPES, as if he had flayed me my mother . . . turned my master out of doors.

1772. *Burlesque Trans. Homer*, IX. 392. His wife came last, and rubbed her eye, Then TUN'D HER PIPES. *Ibid.*, II., 72. Sink me, says one, there hardly PIPES A braver fellow than Ulysses.

1790. DIBDIN, *Song*. Why, what's that to you if my eyes I'm a PIPING, A tear is a comfort, d'ye see, in its way.

[?]. *Brownie of Bodsbeck*, ii. 155. He's coming, poor fellow—he's TAKIN A PIPE to himsel at the house-end—his heart—is as soft as a snaw-ba'.

1825. JONES, *Song*, 'True Bottom'd Boxer' [FARMER, *Musa Pedestris* (1896), 93]. With ogles and smellers, no PIPING and chiming.

1829. *The Prigging Lay* [*Vidocq's Mem.*, iv.]. There's a time to PIPE, and a time to snivel.

1843. DICKENS, *Martin Chuzzlewit*, xxxii. He had got it into his head that his own peculiar mission was TO PIPE HIS EYE; which he did perpetually.

*d.*1845. HOOD, *Faithless Sally Brown*. He heav'd a bitter sigh, And then began to eye his pipe, And then TO PIPE HIS EYE.

1899. WHITEING, *John St.*, 88. Nance is called to oblige with a song. She is shy . . . But the Amazon brings her forward with a stern 'PIPE UP, yer blessid little fool.'

3. (Scots').—*In pl.* = the bagpipes. Hence TO TUNE ONE'S PIPES = to talk or write.

4. (old).—A boot: *see* TROTTER-CASES.—VAUX (1819).

5. (venery).—The female *pudendum*: *see* MONOSYLLABLE.

Verb. (old).—*See subs.* 1 and 2. 3. (American). — To waylay; to intercept.

4. (thieves'). — To watch; to spy. Also TO PIPE OFF. Fr. *allumer*. *See* NARK. Whence PIPER = a spy.

1886-96. MARSHALL, '*Pomes' from the Pink 'Un* ['Nobbled'], 115. I waited to PIPE OFF the fun.

1898. *Pink 'Un and Pelican*, 87. His mission up there on the roof was to exclude . . . any who sought TO PIPE OFF the contest through the skylight.

1888. SIMS [*Referee*, 12 Feb.]. If I PIPE a good chat, why I touch for the wedge.

1899. *Daily Telegraph*, 7 Ap., 8, 3. Then, King Kid. You PIPED him. There's a child o' sin, now.

THE QUEEN'S PIPE, *subs. phr.* (common). — The kiln in the great East Vault of the Wine-Cellars of the London Docks, where useless and damaged goods that have paid no duty are burnt: as regards tobacco a thing of the past, stuff of this kind being distributed to workhouses, &c.

1871. *Echo*, 27 Jan. All that was not sold will be burnt, according to custom, in HER MAJESTY'S TOBACCO PIPE. We cannot think such waste justifiable.

1899. *Daily Mail*, 21 Mar., 3, 3. Tea for the QUEEN'S PIPE. Five hundred and eighty-two half-chests of tea were seized by the sanitary authorities of the Port of London.

TO PUT ONE'S PIPE OUT, *verb. phr.* (common). — 1. To spoil sport or a chance; 'to take the shine out'; and (2) to kill: *see* LIGHT. Fr. *casser sa pipe.*

PUT THAT IN YOUR PIPE AND SMOKE IT, *phr.* (common).—A straight rebuke; 'digest that if you can.' Fr. *mets ça dans ta poche et ton mouchoir par dessus*. *See* TAKE.

1824. PEAKE, *Americans Abroad*, i. 1. *Dou. (writes.)* "No tobacco allowed in England." There—(*shuts book.*) PUT THAT IN YOUR PIPE AND SMOKE IT. There's another slap at 'em!

1836. DICKENS, *Pickwick* (1857), p. 6. Pull him up—PUT THAT IN HIS PIPE—like the flavour—dammed rascals! And with a lengthened string of similar broken sentences . . . the stranger led the way to the travellers' waiting room.

1840. BARHAM, *Ingoldsby Legends* (*Lay of S. Odille*). For this you've my word, and I never yet broke it, So PUT THAT IN YOUR PIPE, my Lord Otto, AND SMOKE IT!

1883. MISS BRADDON, *Golden Calf*, ch. xix. Ah, then he'll have to PUT HIS LOVE IN HIS PIPE AND SMOKE IT! That kind of thing won't do out of a French novel.

TO PIPE ANOTHER DANCE, *verb. phr.* (old). — To change one's means, or one's course of action or attack.

*d.*1529. SKELTON, *Colyn Clout* [BREWER]. They would PYPE YOU ANOTHER DAUNCE.

1544. KNOX, *Godly Letter* [MAITLAND, *Ref.*, 88]. Nowe they haue . . . lerned amongst ladyes TO DAUNSE AS THE DEUILL LYST TO PYPE.

1749. SMOLLETT, *Gil Blas* [ROUTLEDGE], 112. How do I know but my young mistress may caper to a TUNE OF MY PIPING.

TO PIPE IN (or WITH) AN IVY-LEAF, *verb. phr.* (old).—To busy oneself to no purpose: as a consolation for failure; 'to go whistle,' or 'to blow the buck's horn.' [IVY-LEAF = a thing of small value, as FIG, RUSH, STRAW, &c.].

*c.*1374. CHAUCER, *Troilus*, v. 1433. But Troilus thou mayst now east and west PIPE IN AN IVIE LEAFE, if that thee lest.

1383. CHAUCER, *Cant. Tales*, I. But on of you, al be him loth or lefe, He mot GON PIPEN IN AN IVY LEFE.

1387-8. [T. USK], *Test. Love*, III. vii. [SKEAT], l. 50. Far wel the gairdiner, he may PIPE WITH AN YUE LEAFE, his fruite is failed.

1390. GOWER, *Conf. Aman.*, II. 21. That all nis worth an YVY LEFE.

PIPECLAY, *subs.* (colloquial).—Routine; RED-TAPE (*q.v.*).

Verb. (colloquial).—1. To wipe out; to settle: as accounts.

1853. DICKENS, *Bleak House*, xvii. You . . . would not understand allusions to their PIPE-CLAYING their weekly accounts.

2. (tailors').—To hide faults of workmanship; or defects in material.

PIPE-LAYER, *subs. phr.* (American).—A political intriguer; a schemer. Hence PIPE-LAYING = scheming or intriguing for political purposes. [BARTLETT: *circa* 1835, a traitorous New York Whig election agent concocted a plot to throw odium on the party, supporting it by correspondence in the form of bogus business letters relating to the Croton water supply then in progress, the number of men hired to vote being spoken of as so many yards of pipe.—*Abridged.*]

1848. *New York Tribune*, 30 Oct. The result of the Pennsylvania election would not be in the least doubtful, if we could be assured of fair play and no PIPE-LAYING.

1856. *New York Herald*, Sep. There is a magnificent scheme of PIPE-LAYING and log-rolling going on in Pennsylvania.

1883. THURLOW WEED, *Autobiography*, 493. Among the Glentworth papers was a letter in which he said that the men sent from Philadelphia were to be employed in laying the pipes for the introduction of Croton water. The Whig leaders were immediately stigmatised as PIPE-LAYERS, a term persistently applied to them for several years.

1888. *San Francisco Weekly Examiner*, 22 Mar. There are not a few who are PIPE-LAYING and marshalling forces for the fray.

PIPE-MERRY, *adj.* and *adv.* (old).—Merry: as from wine [Which is stored in pipes].

1564. UDAL, *Eras. Apophth.*, 159. Wine deliuereth the harte from all care and thought when a bodie is PIPE MERIE.

PIPER, *subs.* (common).—1. A detective: specifically (in England) an omnibus spy: *see* NARK.

2. *See* PIPE, subs. 1.

DRUNK AS A PIPER, *phr.* (old).—Very drunk: also PIPER-FOU: *see* FOU and SCREWED.

1772. GRAVES, *Spiritual Quixote*, X. xxix. Jerry . . . proceeded so long . . . in tossing off horns of ale, that he became AS DRUNK AS A PIPER.

TO PAY THE PIPER (or FIDDLER), *verb. phr.* (colloquial).—To pay expenses; to assume responsibility. Fr. *payer les violons.*

1695. CONGREVE, *Love for Love*, ii. I warrant you, if he danced till doomsday, he thought I were TO PAY THE PIPER.

1749. SMOLLETT, *Gil Blas* [ROUTLEDGE], 69. We will make Doctor Oloroso PAY THE PIPER. . . . There is no reason why the forehead of a physician should be smoother than the brow of an apothecary.

1819. SCOTT, *Ivanhoe*, I. 267. 'I like not that music, father Cedric' . . . 'Nor I either,' said Wamba, 'I greatly fear we shall have TO PAY THE PIPER.'

*d.*1868. BROUGHAM [quoted in *Century*]. They introduce a new tax, and we shall have TO PAY THE PIPER.

1881. CARLYLE, *Miscell.*, iv. 89. Negotiation there now was . . . Dupont de Nemours as daysman between a Colonel and a Marquis, both in high wrath;—Buffière TO PAY THE PIPER.

PIPER'S-CHEEKS, *subs.* (old).—Swollen or puffed cheeks.

1608. WITHAL, *Dictionarie*, 286. That hath bigge or great cheekes, as they tearme them, PIPER'S CHEEKES.

PIPER'S-NEWS, *subs. phr.* (Scots').—Stale news.

18 [?]. *Perils of Man*, i. 29. 'I came expressly to inform you'—'Came with PIPER'S NEWS,' said the lady; 'which the fidler has told before you.'

PIPER'S-WIFE, *subs. phr.* (old).—A whore: *see* TART.

PIPING HOT, *adv. phr.* (colloquial).—Very hot.

1383. CHAUCER, *Cant. Tales*, 'Miller's Tale,' 193. Wafres PIPYNG HOOT, out of the glede.

1530. PALSGRAVE, *Lang. Francoyse*, s.v.

*c.*1600. *London Cries*, 12 [HALLIWELL]. PIPING HOT, smoking hot! What have I got? You have not; Hot grey pease, hot! hot! hot!

1618. MAINWARING, *Letter* [LODGE, *Illus. Brit. Hist.*, iii. 403]. Foure huge brawnie piggs, PIPEING HOTT, bilted and harnised with ropes of sausages.

1678. COTTON, *Virgil Travestie* [*Works* (1725), 103]. Yet having now fall'n to his Lot, A good rich Farm lies PIPING HOT.

1698. CONGREVE, *Old Bachelor* [*Old Dramatists* (1880), 163], iv. 8. She thanked me, and gave me two apples, PIPING HOT out of her under-petticoat-pocket.

1759. GOLDSMITH, *Citizen of the World*, lxv. A nice pretty bit of ox-cheek, PIPING-HOT, and dressed with a little of my own sauce.

1821. EGAN, *Life in London*, II. iii. In rushed Chaffing Peter . . . the oracle of the dustmen, PIPING HOT from the Old Bailey, with an account of one Lummy.

PIPKIN (THE), *subs. phr.* (venery).—The female *pudendum*: *see* MONOSYLLABLE. Hence, TO CRACK A PIPKIN = to deflower.—GROSE (1785).

1709. WARD, *London Spy*, i. 16. He became one of her earliest suitors, and was very importunate with her to have the CRACKING OF HER PIPKIN.

2. (pugilists').—The head: *see* TIBBY.

1825. JONES, *True Bottom'd Boxer* [*Univ. Songst.*, ii. 96]. At the PIPKIN to point.

PIPPIN. MY PIPPIN, *subs. phr.* (common).—An endearment.

1892. MILLIKEN, *'Arry Ballads*, 23. Take the shine out of some screamers, I tell yer, MY PIPPIN, would Loo.

PIPPIN-SQUIRE. *See* APPLE-SQUIRE.

PIRATE, *subs.* (literary).—1. An infringer of copyright: specifically of publishers, print-sellers, and booksellers, who, without permission, appropriate the work or ideas of an author or artist; a FREEBOOKER. Also as *verb.*: *cf.* BARABBAS, GHOST, JACKAL, &c.

1703. W. KING, *Art of Cookery*, vii. I am told that, if a book is anything useful, the printers have a way of PIRATING on one another, and printing other persons copies: which is very barbarous.

1729. HEARNE, *Diary*, 23 Sep. The said Davis . . . makes it his business to PYRATE books, and hath reprinted something from mine without acknowledgment.

*d.*1744. POPE [quoted in *Century*]. They advertised they would PIRATE his edition. Ibid., *Letters*, Pref. The errors of the press were . . . multiplied . . . by the avarice and negligence of PIRATICAL printers.

1887. *Shakespeariana*, VI. 105. Meres refers to them [Shakspere's 'Sonnets'] in 1598 . . . and in 1599 two of them were printed by the PIRATE Jaggard.

1888. *New Princeton Review*, v. 50. We are doing all the PIRATING in these days; the English used to be in the business, but they dropped out of it long ago.

*d.*1891. LOWELL, *Coleridge* [*Century*]. It was a PIRATED book, and I trust I may be pardoned for the delight I had in it.

2. (venery).—An adulteress: one who chases other women's men: also, conversely, of men.

1749. SMOLLETT, *Gil Blas* [ROUTLEDGE], 222. Lorenza . . . smuggles the surgeon . . . Every evening into her apartment . . . the PIRATE generally stays pretty long upon his cruise.

3. (common).—*See* quot. Now (1902), thanks to police regulations and the imposition of heavy penalties, almost a thing of the past: chiefly applied, without depreciation, to any non "Company" or "Association" vehicle.

1897. *Pall Mall Gaz.*, 31 Dec., 5, 3. In 1829 George Shillibeer introduced omnibuses into London, and . . . took care to impress upon every man he employed the importance of politeness towards all passengers. But in 1832 it was noticed that this high standard . . . was not maintained by . . . conductors of the new 'buses running from Paddington to the Bank via Oxford-street. They overcharged passengers, and met protests with abuse. Frequently, when females only were in the 'bus, they brought their journey to an end long before they reached their advertised destination, compelling the passengers to walk a considerable distance after paying their fares. . . . These were the first PIRATE omnibuses. To let the public know which really were his vehicles Shillibeer at once had painted on them "Shillibeer's Original Omnibus." In a few days the same inscription appeared on some of the pirates with the word "not" in very small letters preceding it.

PISHERY-PASHERY, *subs.* (old).—Gabble.

1621. *Shoe-maker's Holy-day* [NARES]. Peace, my fine Firke! stand by with your PISHERY-PASHERY! Away!

PISS, *subs.* (vulgar).—Urine. Also as *verb.* = to urinate. Combinations are many: thus, PISSER = (1) the *penis*, and (2) the female *pudendum*; PISS-BOWL (or POT) = a chamber pot; PISS-BURNT = stained with urine; PISS-MAKER = one given to much liquor; PISS-PROPHET (or KNIGHT OF THE PISS-POT = a pot-inspecting physician; PISS-POT HALL = (*see* quot. 1785); PISS-FACTORY = a

public house; PISSING-POST (or PISS-DALE) = a urinal; PISS-FIRE = a blusterer; PISS-KITCHEN = a kitchen-maid; PISS-PROUD = of a false *erectio penis*; PISS-QUICK = hot gin-and-water (BEE, 1823); PISSING-CLOUT = a napkin; PISSING = small, mean, brief, as in PISSING-WHILE = a very short time; PISSING-CONDUIT = a conduit with a flow of water like a stream of urine: specifically one near the Royal Exchange set up by John Wels (Lord-mayor, 1430); PISSING-CANDLE = a small make-weight candle; RODS IN PISS = a reckoning in store; TO PISS PURE CREAM (or PINS AND NEEDLES) = to be clapped (GROSE); TO PISS WHEN ONE CAN'T WHISTLE = to be hanged (GROSE); TO PISS MONEY AGAINST THE WALL = to spend money in drink (GROSE); TO PISS DOWN THE BACK = to flatter (GROSE); TO PISS ON A NETTLE = to be peevish or angry; WHEN THE GOOSE PISSETH = never; AS GOOD AS EVER PISSED = as good as may be; TO PISS IN A QUILL = to agree on a course of action; PISS-A-BED = a dandelion: with reference to its diuretic properties; "SO DRUNK THAT HE OPENED HIS SHIRT COLLAR TO PISS" = blind drunk; "the tin-whiffin" = when you cannot sh-t for PISSING; TO PISS HARD (BONES, or CHILDREN) = to be brought to bed; TO PISS BLOOD (URQUHART) = to bleed; TO PISS ONE'S TALLOW = to sweat. Also not a few saws and proverbs —'As easy PISSING a bed as to lick a dish'; 'As good (or, as very a knave) as ever PISSED'; 'As surly as if he had PISSED on a nettle'; 'By fits and starts as the hog PISSETH'; 'Every little helps as the old woman said when she PISSED in the sea'; 'Fire! quoth the fox, when he PISSED on the ice'; 'He did me as much good as if he had PISSED in my pottage'; 'He who once a good name gets, May PISS a bed and say he sweats'; 'Let her cry, she'll PISS the less'; 'PISS clear and defy the physician'; 'PISS not against the wind,' or 'He that PISSETH against the wind wets his shirt'; 'He'd have died had he never PISSED or shit'; 'Money will make the pot boil though the devil PISS in the fire'; 'Many excuses PISSES the bed'; 'My horse PISSETH whey, My man PISSETH amber: My horse is for my way, My man is for my chamber'; 'The devil shits and PISSES on a great heap'; 'Such a reason PISSES my goose'; 'You'll be good when the goose PISSETH'; 'He that's afraid of every grass must not PISS in a meadow.' *See* RACK-OFF.

1356. MANDEVILLE, *Travels*, 242. The moste Synne that ony man may do is to PISSEN in hire Houses that thei dwellen in.

1362. LANGLAND, *Piers Plowman's Vision*, l. 3169. He PISSED a potel in a paternoster-while.

1383. CHAUCER [SKEAT, *Works*, 3798]. This Nicholas was risen for to PISSE. *Ibid.*, 4215. Sone after this the wyf hir routing leet, An gan awake, and wente hir out to PISSE. *Ibid.*, 729. That Socrates had with hise wyes two How Xantippa caste PISSE up-on his heed.

1440-99. BLIND HARRY, *Maner of Crying* [LAING, *Scot. Poet*, ii. 14]. Scho PISCHIT the mekle matter of Forth; Sic tyde ran efter hendir.

1525. TYNDALE, Tr. *Bible*, 1 Sam. xviii. 22. If I leave by the morning light any that PISSETH against the wall.

*d.*1529. SKELTON, *Elynour Rummyng*, 370. And as she was drynknge . . . She PYST where she stood.

1539. LYNDSAY, *Thrie Estaitis*, II. 98. And ye ladies that list to PISCH, Lift up your taill plat in ane disch.

1539. PALSGRAVE, *Lang. Francoyse*, . . . But a PYSSYNGE WHYLE, *tant quon auroyt pisse*, or *ce pendant*. *Ibid.*, subst. f. 66. Stale, PYSSE, *escloy*.

*c.*1541. *Scholehouse of Women* [HAZLITT, *E. Pop. Poet.*, iv. 113]. He would not once turn me for to kisse; Every night he riseth for to PISSE. *Ibid.*, 121. A PISSEPOT they brake vpon his pate.

1551. STILL, *Gammer Gurton* [DODSLEY, *Old Plays*, ii. 50]. He shall never be at rest one PISSING-WHILE a day.

1554. UDALL, *Apoph. of Erasmus*, 25. She, beyng moche the more incensed by reason of her husbandes quietnesse and stillnesse, powred doune a PISSEBOLLE upon hym out of a windore.

*c.*1555. *Vpcheringe of the Messe*, 96. Alacke, for payne I PYSSA.

1575. *Touchstone of Complexion*, 99. Manye men . . . take the matter in as greate snuffe, as they would to be crowned with a PYSSEBOLLE.

1594. SHAKSPEARE, *1 Hen. VI.*, iv. 6. I charge and command, that, of the cities cost, The PISSING-CONDUIT run nothing but claret wine, The first year of our reign.

1595. SHAKSPEARE, *Two Gentlemen*, iv. 3. He had not been there a PISSING-while but all the chamber smelt him.

1598. FLORIO, *Worlde of Wordes*, s.v. *Ciangola* . . . Also a PISSE-POT. Ibid., *Pisciatoio*, a PISSING place . . . Also a PIS-POT.

1598. STOWE, *London*, 144. Some distance west is the Royal Exchange—and so downe to the little conduit, called the PISSING-CONDUIT by the stockes market.

1620. FLETCHER, *Women Pleas'd*, i. 2. I shall turn PISSING-CONDUIT shortly [quoth a servant drenched with water].

1623. MABBE, *Guzman* (1630), 240. Master Nicolas hath RODS IN PISSE for you . . . and is plotting how he may be reuenged of thee.

1623. WEBSTER, *Devil's Law Case*, ii. 1. When that your worship has BEPIST yourself, Either with vehemency of argument, Or, being out from the matter.

1630. TAYLOR, *Works* [NARES]. On every PISSING-POST their names I'll place.

1632. JONSON, *Magnetic Lady*, i. 7. I shall entreat your mistress . . . to have patience but a PISSING-WHILE.

1653. URQUHART, *Rabelais*, I. v. The PISSING TOOL and urinal vessels shall have nothing of it. *Ibid.*, xi. He PISSED in his shoes, shit in his shirt, and wiped his nose on his sleeve.

1672. LACY, *Dumb Lady*, v. 1. The household . . . paid my worship with their PISSE-POTS out of the garret.

1672. WYCHERLEY, *Love in a Wood*, i. 2. That spark, who has his fruitless designs upon the bed-ridden rich widow, to the sucking heiress in her PISSING-CLOUT.

1672. RAY, *Proverbs*, 206. To stay a PISSING-WHILE.

1676. ETHEREDGE, *Man of Mode*, ii. 1. *Old Bell.* Out, A PISE of their Breeches. *Idem*, v. 2. *Old Bell.* Out, A PISE! (*et passim*).

1678. COTTON, *Virgil Travestie* [*Works* (1725), 137]. All at the first that they amiss thought, Was that her Grace had mist the PISS-POT. *Ibid.*, 126. Therefore I think it not amiss for's To launch, for there are RODS IN PISS for's.

*d.*1678. MARVELL, *Poems* [MURRAY], 188. I'll have a council shall sit always still, And give me a license to do what I will; and two secretaries shall PISS THROUGH A QUILL.

1682. A. RADCLIFFE, *The Ramble*, 86. I roused my doe, and laced her gown, I pinn'd her whisk, and dropt a crown, She PISS'D, and then I drove her down, Like thunder.

1694. *Poor Robin* [NARES]. Each PISSING-POST will be almost pasted over with quacks bills.

1706. WARD, *Wooden World*, 67. He crawls up upon Deck to the PISS-DALE. *Ibid.* (1709), *London Spy*, i. 64. He had provided them a plentiful bowl of PISS.

1714. LUCAS, *Gamesters*, 71. As he was PISSING at Temple Bar.

1740. NORTH, *Examen*, 70. So strangely did Papist and Fanatic or . . . the Anti-court Party PISS IN A QUILL; agreeing in all things that tended to create troubles and disturbances.

*d.*1745. SWIFT, *Miscellanies*, "On the Discovery of the Longitude." Now Ditton and Whiston may both be BE-PISSED on. [*Et passim.*]

1749. ROBERTSON of Struan, *Poems*, 259. Thou drunken sot, go Home and spue, And PISS a Bed, as thou art wont.

1772. *Burlesque Trans. Homer*, III. 181. But what I mostly fear is this, Some God has steep'd a ROD IN PISS.

1785. GROSE, *Vulg. Tongue*, s.v. PISS-PROUD. . . . The old fellow thought he had an erection, but his prick was only PISS-PROUD: said of any old fellow who marries a young wife. *Ibid.* PISS-BURNED, PISS-MAKER, and PISS-PROPHET. *Ibid.* PISS POT HALL. A house at Clapton, near Hackney, built by the potter chiefly out of the profits of chamber pots, in the bottom of which the portrait of Dr. Sacheverel was depicted.

1821. BYRON, *Occasional Pieces* (ed. 1840), p. 574. Posterity will ne'er survey a nobler grave than this: Here lie the bones of Castlereagh; stop, traveller, P— !

PISTOL, *subs.* (venery).—1. The *penis*: *see* PRICK.

1598. SHAKSPEARE, *2 Hen. IV.*, ii. 4. *Fal.* Here Pistol . . . do you discharge upon mine hostess. *Pistol.* I will discharge upon her, Sir John, with two bullets. *Fal.* She is PISTOL-PROOF, sir. . . . *Pist.* Then to you Mistress Dorothy. . . . *Dol.* Charge me! . . . you lack-linen mate! Away . . . I am meat for your master.

1623. WEBSTER, *Duchess of Malfi*, ii. 2. *Serv.* There was taken even now a Switzer in the duchess' bed-chamber . . with a PISTOL in his great cod-piece.

2. (old).—A swaggering bully: *see* FURIOSO.

1596. SHAKSPEARE, *Merry Wives*, Dram. Pers. *Bardolph*, PISTOL, *Nym*, sharpers attending on Falstaff. *Ibid.* (1598), *2 Hen. IV.*, ii. 4. *First D.* Sir, Ancient PISTOL's below. *Dol.* Hang him, swaggering rascal! . . . it is the foul-mouthed'st rogue in England.

1598. FLORIO, *Worlde of Wordes*, s.v. *Pistolfo* . . . a roguing begger, a cantler, an upright man that liveth by cosenage.

1748. SMOLLETT, *Rod. Random*, xlvi. He snatched his hat and hanger, and assuming the looks, swagger, and phrase of PISTOL, burst out, &c.

Also *see* POCKET-PISTOL.

PISTOL-SHOT, *subs. phr.* (common).—A drink; a GO (*q.v.*): *see* DRINKS and *cf.* POCKET-PISTOL.

PIT, *subs.* (old).—1. A breast pocket in a coat. Also, a fob. —GROSE (1785); VAUX (1819). Hence PITMAN = a pocket-book.

2. (venery).—The female *pudendum*: also BOTTOMLESS PIT, PIT-HOLE, PIT-MOUTH, and PIT OF DARKNESS: *see* MONOSYLLABLE. Hence, TO LAY PIT AND BOXES (or BACK AND FRONT SHOPS) INTO ONE (*see* quot. 1785).

*d.*1674. HERRICK, *Poems*, 'Cherry-pit.' Julia and I . . . playing for sport at Cherry-pit: . . . I got the PIT, and she the stone.

1785. GROSE, *Vulg. Tongue*, s.v. PIT. To lay pit and boxes into one; an operation in midwifery or copulation, whereby the division between the anus and vagina is cut through, broken, and demolished: a simile borrowed from the playhouse, when, for the benefit of some favourite player, the pit and boxes are laid together.

3. (old).—*See* quot. 1696.—GROSE (1785).

*c.*1696. B. E., *Dict. Cant. Crew*, s.v. PIT, the hole under the gallows into which those that Pay not the Fee, viz., 6s. 8d., are cast and Buried.

KNIGHT OF THE PIT, *subs. phr.* (old).—A cocker.

TO SHOOT (or FLY) THE PIT, *verb. phr.* (old).—To turn tail [Cocking].

1740. NORTH, *Examen*, 327. The whole nation . . . expressing utmost detestation and abhorence of the Whig principles, which made the whole party SHOOT THE PIT and retire.

1740. RICHARDSON, *Pamela*, ii. 308. We were all to blame to make madam here FLY THE PIT as she did.

PIT-A-PAT, *verb.* (colloquial).—To walk lightly and quickly: as with a quick succession of sounds; to palpitate. Also *adj.* and *subs.* [The same word as 'prittle-prattle' (or 'pittle-pattle' = to chatter): *see* quot. 1555.]

*d.*1555. LATIMER, *Remains* [Parker Soc. (1844-5), i. 106]. In our deeds I fear me too many of us deny God to be God, whatsoever we PITTLE-PATTLE with our tongues. Ibid., *Sermons*, 306 verso. She doth not as our Papistes doe, which PRITTLE PRATTLE a whole day uppon theyr Beades.

1601. JONSON, *Poetaster*, iv. 1. You shall have kisses from them go PIT-PAT, PIT-PAT, PIT-PAT upon your lips as thick as stones out of slings at the assault of a city.

1605. SYLVESTER, *Du Bartas*, ii. Run bow'd with burthens to the fragrant Fat, Tumble them in and after PIT-A-PAT Vp to the Waste.

1618. FLETCHER, *Loyal Subject*, ii. 2. 'Lord, how my heart leaps' . . . 'Twill go PIT-A-PAT shortly.

1690. DRYDEN, *Don Sebastian*, iii. 2. Now again I hear the PIT-A-PAT of a pretty foot through the dark alley.

1693. CONGREVE, *Old Batchelor*, ii. 2. Agad, my heart has gone a PIT PAT for thee.

1711. STEELE, *Spectator*, 503. She immediately stepped out of her pew, And fell into the finest PITTY-PAT air.

*d.*1891. LOWELL, *Courtin'* [*Century*]. His heart kept going PITY-PAT, But hern went pity Zekle.

PITCH, *subs.* (showmen's and tramps').—(1) A place: of sale or entertainment. Also (2) a performance or sale. Hence, TO PITCH (or DO A PITCH) = to do business; TO QUEER A PITCH = to spoil a performance or a sale; to mar one's plans.

1851-6. MAYHEW, *Lond. Lab.*, i. xii. In consequence of a new Police Regulation 'stands' or PITCHES have been forbidden.

*c.*1864. VANCE, *The Chickaleary Cove*, 3. At Groves's you're safe to make a sure PITCH.

1876. HINDLEY, *Adv. of a Cheap Jack.* When I had DONE MY PITCH, and got down from the stage.

1887. HENLEY, *Villon's Good Night*, 2. You swatchel-coves that PITCH and slam. Ibid., *A Book of Verses*, 'Hospital Outlines.' A conjuror DOING HIS PITCH in the street.

1899. *Pall Mall Gaz.*, 21 Ap., 8, 1. Lord Rosebery and his sons had come out evidently to enjoy a brief spell of the bright sunshine. When they came to the crossing-sweeper's PITCH there was a cheery word with a smile, and something bright and yellow changed hands.

1901. *St. James's Gaz.*, 10 Ap., 3, 1. The Russian Squadron, by a timely appearance at Villefranche, followed by a visit of its chiefs to President Loubet at Nice, has at once testified to the solidarity of the Franco-Russian alliance, and avoided QUEERING THE PITCH of the Italians at Toulon.

3. (common).—A short sleep; a nap.

Phrases: TO PITCH THE HUNTERS = to set up the three-sticks-a-penny business; TO PITCH IT STRONG = to exaggerate, overdo, or EMBROIDER (*q.v.*): TO PITCH AND PAY = to pay on the nail (at Blackwell Hall it was enacted that a penny be PAID by the owner of every bale of cloth for PITCHING); TO PITCH IN = (1) take a hand; (2) to start; and (3) to work hard; TO PITCH INTO = to attack; TO PITCH A TALE (or FORK) = to tell a story, romantic, playful, or pitiful; TO PITCH ON = to select at random.

*d.*1580. TUSSER, 145 [NARES]. Where strangers well may seem to dwell That PITCH AND PAY.

1599. SHAKSPEARE, *Henry V.*, ii. 3. Let senses rule; the word is 'PITCH AND PAY'; Trust none.

1610. *Mirror for Magistrates*, 374. No creditor did curse me day by day, I used plainnesse, ever PITCH AND PAY.

1651. BARLOW, *Remains* (1693), 'To Rev. J. Goodwin.' It is this argument of yours I shall PITCH ON, And the rather because it hath been cry'd up.

1810. EVANS, i. 23, 'Yorkshire Song.' And there was neither fault nor fray, Nor any disorder any way, But every man did PITCH AND PAY.

1851-61. MAYHEW, *Lond. Lab.*, i. 390. PITCHING THE HUNTERS is the three sticks a penny, with the snuff-boxes stuck upon sticks; if you throw your stick, and they fall out of the hole, you are entitled to what you knock off.

1863. *Story of a Lancashire Thief*, Brummagem Joe, a cove as could patter and PITCH THE FORK with any one.

1867. *London Herald*, 23 March, 222, 2. If he bad had the sense to appeal for help, and PITCH THEM A TALE, he might have got off.

1876. HINDLEY, *Cheap Jack.* When Elias was at a pleasure fair, he would PITCH THE HUNTERS, that is, put up the three sticks a penny business.

1901. *Punch*, 25 Dec., 461, 1. We were PITCHING INTO the umpire.

PITCH-AND-FILL, *subs. phr.* (rhyming).—Bill.

PITCHED, *adj.* and *adv.* (tailors').—CUT (*q.v.*).

PITCHER, *subs.* (venery).—1. The female *pudendum.* Also THE MIRACULOUS PITCHER ('that holds water with the mouth downwards'). Whence, CRACKED-PITCHER = a harlot with a certain pretension to repute; TO CRACK A PITCHER = to deflower. *See* MONOSYLLABLE.—GROSE (1785).

1672. WYCHERLEY, *Love in a Wood*, iii. 2. My daughter is a girl of reputation, though she has been seen in your company; but . . . she is resolved never more to venture her PITCHER to the well.

1771. SMOLLETT, *Humph. Clinker* [*Works* (1899), III. 92]. Though my being thought capable of making her a mother might have given me some credit, the reputation of an intrigue with such a CRACKED PITCHER does me no honour at all.

2. (old).—Newgate prison: also the STONE PITCHER or (JUG): *see* CAGE.—VAUX (1819).

3. (thieves').—*See* SNIDE-PITCHER.

PITCHERS HAVE EARS! *phr.* (colloquial).—'Listeners may overhear': also (of children) LITTLE PITCHERS HAVE LONG (or GREAT) EARS = What children hear at home soon flies abroad: Fr. *Ce que l'enfant oit au foyer, est bientôt connu jusqu'au Monstier.*—HEYWOOD (1546); BAILEY (1728).

1593. SHAKSPEARE, *Taming of the Shrew*, iv. 4. Not in my house, Lucentio, for, you know PITCHERS HAVE EARS, and I have many servants.

Other colloquialisms are:—TO GET THE SHEARDS AFTER THE PITCHER IS BROKEN (RAY, 1760) = to receive a kindness after others have no need of it, or to get the refuse; TO BANG A PITCHER = to drain a pot. *See* also CROCUS-PITCHER.

PITCHER-BAWD, *subs. phr.* (old).—*See* quot.

*c.*1696. B. E., *Dict. Cant. Crew*, s.v. PITCHER-BAWD. The poor Hack that runs of Errands to fetch Wenches or Liquor.

PITCHER-MAN, *subs. phr.* (old).—A drunkard; a TICKLE-PITCHER. *See* LUSHINGTON.

1738. *Poor Robin* [NARES]. For not one shoemaker in ten But are boon blades, true PITCHER-MEN.

PITCH-FINGERS, *subs. phr.* (colloquial).—A pilferer: also TAR-FINGERS (*q.v.*). Whence PITCH-FINGERED = thievishly inclined.

PITCHFORK, *subs.* (common).—A tuning-fork.

Verb. (colloquial).—To thrust into a position; to toss, or settle carelessly.

1708-10. SWIFT, *Polite Conversation*, i. She wears her Cloaths as if they were thrown on her with a PITCHFORK.

1879. *Nineteenth Century*, 277. Your young city curate PITCHFORKED into a rural benefice . . . is the most forlorn . . . of all human creatures.

PITCH-KETTLED, *adj. phr.* (old).—Puzzled; stuck fast; confounded.—GROSE (1785).

*d.*1800. COWPER, *Ep. to Lloyd*, 32. I fairly find myself PITCH-KETTLED, And cannot see . . . How I shall hammer out a letter.

PITCHPOLE, *verb.* (old colloquial).—1. To sell for double the cost.

2. (schoolboys').—To turn a somersault.

PITCH-UP, *subs. phr.* (Winchester School).—One's home circle; a crowd or knot of people; a set of chums. Hence, TO PITCH UP WITH = to associate with.

PIT-HOLE (or **PIT**), *subs.* (colloquial).—A grave. Hence, as *verb.* = to bury.

1607. *Puritan*, i. 2. All my friends were PIT-HOLED, gone to graves.

2. (venery).—*See* PIT.

PITMAN. *See* PIT.

PIT-OF-DARKNESS, *subs. phr.* (venery).—The female *pudendum*: *see* MONOSYLLABLE. Also PIT-MOUTH, and PIT-HOLE.

PITTER-PATTER, *verb.* (common).—To palpitate; to 'go PIT-A-PAT.'

PITTLE-PATTLE. *See* PIT-A-PAT.

PITT'S-PICTURE, *subs. phr.* (old political).—A bricked-up window. [To save Pitt's Window-tax].—GROSE (1785).

PIZZLE, *subs.* (venery).—1. The *penis*: *see* PRICK. Also, as *verb.* = to copulate: *see* RIDE.—BAILEY (1728). Whence (2) a scourge: as made of bull's pizzles.

1607. DEKKER, *Northward Hoe*, iv. 1. *Doll.* This goat's-PIZZLE of thine —. *Bell.* Away! I love no such implements in my house.

1749. SMOLLETT, *Gil Blas*, I. vi. I felt across my shoulders five or six hearty thwacks with a bull's PIZZLE.

PLACE, *subs.* (colloquial).—(1) An abode; a place of business: *see* DIGGINGS. (2) A jakes, or HOUSE OF EASE (*q.v.*): *see* MRS. JONES.

THE PLACE, *subs. phr.* (venery).—The PRIVITIES (*q.v.*): *see* MONOSYLLABLE and PRICK: also PLACE OF EASE.

1759-67. STERNE, *Tristram Shandy*, IX. xx. You shall see THE very PLACE, said my uncle Toby. Mrs. Wadman blushed.

PLACE OF SIXPENNY SINFULNESS, *subs. phr.* (old).—The suburbs: specifically a bawdy-house so situated.

1607. DEKKER, *Westward Hoe*, v. 3. 'Go, sail with the rest of your bawdy-traffickers to THE PLACE OF SIXPENNY SINFULNESS . . .' 'I scorn the sinfulness of any suburbs in Christendom.'

See SPOT.

PLACEBO, *subs.* (medical and general).—1. A pacifying dose: hence (2) a sop of placation. Whence, TO SING (or HUNT, or GO TO THE SCHOOL OF) PLACEBO = to be servilely complaisant, or time-serving; to 'hold with the hare and hunt with the hounds.'

1362. LANGLAND, *Piers Plowman's Vision*, l. 1991. Preestes and persons With PLACEBO TO HUNT.

*c.*1383. WYCLIF (?) *Leaven of Pharisees*, iv. [MATHEW, *Unpr. Eng. Wks. of Wyclif* (1880), 15]. Zif thei visyten not pore men in here sikenesse but riche men with preue massis and PLACEBOES and diriges.

1383. CHAUCER, *Summoner's Tale*, I. 367. Beth ware, therefore, with lordes how ye pleye, SYNGETH PLACEBO—and I shal if I kan.

1481. CAXTON, *Reynard the Fox* (1880), xxvii. 65. Ther ben many that PLAY PLACEBO.

1508. SKELTON, *Phyl Sparowe*, 466. At this PLACEBO We may not well forgo The countrynge of the coe.

1544. KNOX, *Godly Letter* [MAITLAND, *Reformation*, 88]. Nowe they haue BENE AT THE SKOOLE OF PLACEBO, and ther they haue lerned amongst ladyes daunse as the deuill lyst to pype.

1591. SIR J. HARRINGTON, Pref. to ARIOSTO'S *Orlando Furioso.* Of which comedie . . . when some (TO SING PLACEBO) aduised that it should be forbidden, because it was somewhat too plaine, . . . yet he would haue it allowed.

1625. BACON, *Ess.* xxvi. And in stead of giuing Free Counsell SING him a Song of PLACEBO.

1819. SCOTT, *Bride of Lammermoor*, i. I made my bow in requital of the compliment, which was probably thrown in by way of PLACEBO.

18 [?]. *American Jour. Psychol.* [*Century*]. Physicians appeal to the imagination in desperate cases with bread pills and PLACEBOS.

1890. *Microcosm* (New York), Mar. Delight at the temporary effects of such a PLACEBO hypodermically administered.

1892. FENNELL, *Stanford Dict.*, s.v. PLACEBO . . . Lat. PLACERE = to please: the opening antiphon of the vespers for the office of the dead in the Latin church, named from the first word of the Vulgate version, *Placebo Domino in regione vivorum*, 'I will walk before (please) the Lord in the land of the living' . . . hence phrases TO SING PLACEBO, TO PLAY PLACEBO = 'to be complacent,' 'to be obsequious'; also an useless medicine intended merely to gratify and conciliate a patient.

PLACER, *verb.* (American).—To live in concubinage; TO LIVE TALLY (*q.v.*); to DAB IT UP (*q.v.*).

PLACKET (or **PLACKET-HOLE**), *subs.* (old).—(1) A petticoat-slit or pocket-hole; (2) a woman: *cf.* PETTICOAT; (3) the female *pudendum* (also PLACKET-BOX): *see* MONOSYLLABLE; and (4) a petticoat. Whence PLACKET-RACKET = the *penis*: *see* PRICK; TO SEEK A PLACKET = to whore; PLACKET-STUNG = infected (RAY). Occasionally PLACKET = shift.

1594. SHAKSPEARE, *Love's Lab.*, iii. 1. Liege of all loiterers and malcontents, Dread prince of PLACKETS, King of codpieces.

1594. TYLNEY, *Locrine*, iii. 3. My first wife was a loving quiet wench; but this, I think, would weary the devil . . . O Codpiece, thou hast done thy master; this it is to be meddling with warm PLACKETS.

1604. SHAKSPEARE, *Winter's Tale*, iv. 3. Is there no manners left among maids? will they wear their PLACKETS where they should bear their faces?

1605. SHAKSPEARE, *Lear*, iii. 4. Keep thy foot out of brothels, thy hands out of PLACKETS.

*c.*1608. BEAUMONT and FLETCHER, *Love's Cure*, i. 2. That a cod-piece were far fitter here than a pinn'd PLACKET. *Ibid.* (1619), *Humourous Lieut.*, iv. 3. Was that brave heart made to pant for a PLACKET?

1623. WEBSTER, *Duchess of Malfi*, iv. 2. A snuffling knave, that while he shows the tombs, will have his hand in a wench's PLACKET.

1653. URQUHART, *Rabelais*, I. xi. One would call it her pillicock . . . another her touch-trap . . . Another again her PLACKET-RACKET.

1654. GAYTON, *Fest. Notes*, 170. Just like a plow-boy tir'd of a broune jacket, And breeches round, long leathern point, no PLACKET.

1665. *Sel. Coll. Epigrams* [HALLIWELL]. Deliro playing at a game of racket Far put his hand into Florinda's PLACKET; Keep hold, said shee, nor any further go, Said he, just so, the PLACKET well will do.

*d.*1674. HERRICK, *Works* [1897], ii. 160. If the maides a spinning goe, Burn the flax, and fire their toe, Scorch their PLACKETS, But beware that ye singe no maiden-haire.

PLAGUY (or **PLAGUILY**), *adj.* and *adv.* (colloquial).—Troublesome; annoying; 'deuced'; very.

1580. SIR P. SIDNEY, *Arcadia*, iii. Most wicked woman, that hast so PLAGUILY a corrupted mind as thou . . . must most wickedly infect others.

16[?]. *Sir Eglamour* [CHILD, *Ballads*, VIII. 197]. The dragon he had a PLAGUY hide, Which could both sword and spear abide.

1601. WEBSTER, *Cure for Cuckold*, ii. 3. What PLAGUY boys are bred now-a-days.

1602. SHAKSPEARE, *Troilus*, ii. 3, 187. He is so PLAGUY proud that the death-tokens of it cry 'No recovery.'

*c.*1608. FLETCHER, *Humourous Lieutenant*, ii. 2. I am hurt PLAGUILY. *Ibid.* (1617), *Mad Lover*, v. 4. Oh, 'twas a PLAGUY thump, charg'd with a vengeance.

1709. STEELE, *Tatler*, No. 55. He looked PLAGUY sour at me.

1711. SWIFT, *To Stella*, xxxi. He was PLAGUILY afraid and humbled.

1768. GOLDSMITH, *Good Natured Man*, ii. You're so PLAGUY shy that one would think you had changed sexes.

1843-4. HALIBURTON, *Attache*, xix. 'Squire,' said Slick, 'I'd a PLAGUY sight sooner see Ascot than anything else in England.

PLAIN, *adj.* (colloquial).—Watered; NEAT (*q.v.*).

PLAIN AS A PIKESTAFF (or PACKSTAFFE), *phr.* (colloquial).—Beyond argument: also PACK-STAFF (*adj.*) = plain. Also PLAIN AS THE NOSE ON YOUR FACE.

1546. BECON [Parker Soc., *Early Works*, 276]. He is no dissembler, his heart and tongue goeth together, He is as PLAIN AS A PACKSTAFF.

1598. J. HALL, *Virgid.*, III., Prol., l. 4. Not riddle-like obscuring their intent, But PACK-STAFFE PLAINE, uttering what things they meant.

1599. MARSTON, *Scourge of Villanie*, I. [HALLIWELL, *Works*, iii. 249]. His honestie Shall be as bare as his anatomie, To which he bound his wife. O, PACK-STAFFE rimes! Why not, when court of stars shall see these crimes?

1641. BERNARD, *Terence in Eng.*, 89. You make a doubt, where all is PLAINE AS A PIKE STAFFE.

*d.*1656. HALL, *Satires*, vii. Prol. Not riddle-like, obscuring their intent, But PACK-STAFFE PLAINE, uttering what thing they ment.

*d.*1657. J. BRADFORD, *Works* [Parker Soc., 1853, II. 319]. To make all AS PLAIN AS A PACK-STAFF.

1695. CONGREVE, *Love for Love*, iv. 'As witness my hand' . . . in great letters. Why, 'tis AS PLAIN AS THE NOSE ON ONE'S FACE.

1749. SMOLLETT, *Gil Blas* [ROUTLEDGE], 409. Continual intercourse gave me an opportunity of prying into the duke's inmost soul, . . . a masked battery to all mankind beside, but PLAIN AS A PIKESTAFF to me.

PLAIN-STATEMENT, *subs. phr.* (tailors').—1. An indifferent meal; COMMON-DOINGS (*q.v.*); and (2) a simple straight-forward piece of work.

PLANK, *subs.* (political). — *See* PLATFORM.

Verb. (common).—To deposit: as money; to pay: also to PLANK UP (or DOWN).

1843-4. HALIBURTON, *Attache* [BARTLETT]. I've had to PLANK DOWN handsome . . . *Ibid.* 'Why,' says he, 'shell out and PLANK DOWN a pile of dollars.'

1856. *Southern Sketches*, 163. Come, PLANK UP the tin.

1886-96. MARSHALL, '*Pomes' from the Pink 'Un* ('The Merry Stumer'), 8. He PLANKED DOWN a stumer bob.

PLANT, *subs.* (thieves').—(1) Plunder; (2) a swindle or robbery; (3) a decoy; and (4) a place of hiding. Whence as *verb.* = (1) to conceal; (2) to select a person

or house for swindling or robbery; (3) to utter base coin; (4) in mining, to SALT (*q.v.*); (5) to humbug, TO GAMMON (*q.v.*); and (6) to prepare cards for unfair play. Also IN PLANT = in hiding; TO SPRING A PLANT = to unearth.—B. E. (*c.*1696); GROSE (1785); VAUX (1819); MATSELL (1859). Hence (conjurors') = to prepare a trick by depositing an object in charge of a conscious or unconscious confederate.

1610. ROWLANDS, *Martin Mark-all*, E 4. To PLANT, to hide.

1612. DEKKER, *O per se O* [FARMER, *Musa Pedestris* (1896), 12]. When they did seeke, then we did creepe, and PLANT in ruffe-mans low.

*c.*1819. *Song*, 'The Young Prig' [FARMER, *Musa Pedestris* (1896), 82. I have a sweet eye for a PLANT.

1838. DICKENS, *Oliver Twist*, xxxix. 'I was away from London a week and more, my dear, on a PLANT,' replied the Jew.

1853. READE, *Gold*, iv. 1. *Levi.* This dust is from Birmingham, and neither Australian nor natural. *Rob.* The man PLANTED it for you.

*d.*1870. DICKENS [quoted in *Century*]. It wasn't a bad PLANT, that of mine, on Filey, the man accused of forging the Sou' Western Railway Debentures.

1886-96. MARSHALL, '*Pomes' from the Pink 'Un* ['Honest Bill'], 50. For PLANTS he always hated, 'cept the plants upon his sill.

1889. *Notes and Queries*, 7 S. ix. 50. Such-and-such an author says that so-and-so was 'burnt alive,' followed by . . . righteous indignation at what never happened, while the dispassionate scholar finds the whole thing a PLANT.

1892. PERCY CLARKE, *New Chum in Australia*, 72. A salted claim, a pit sold for a £10 note, in which a nugget worth a few shillings had before been PLANTED.

5. (old).—*In pl.* = the feet.

Verb. (thieves').—1. *See* subs. 1.

2. (old: now mostly colloquial).—To post, set, or fix in position.

1555. CAVENDISH, *Wolsey* [OLIPHANT]. [He PLANTS himself near the King.]

1600. JONSON, *Cynthia's Revels*, ii. 1. PLANT yourself there, sir: and observe me.

1602. SHAKSPEARE, *Twelfth Night*, ii. 3. I will PLANT you two, and let the fool make a third, where he shall find the letter.

1837. BARHAM, *Ingoldsby Legends*, I. 148. He PLANTED himself with a firm foot in front of the image.

3. (old).—To bury. — GROSE (1785).

1872. CLEMENS ('Mark Twain'), *Innocents at Home*, 20. 'Now, if we can get you to help PLANT him —.' 'Preach the funeral discourse?'

4. (footballers').—To drive the ball into another player: hence PLANTER = a blow so given: specifically one delivered in the face.

5. (venery).—To achieve (or assist) intromission; also TO PLANT A MAN (old) = to copulate: *see* GREENS and RIDE.

TO PLANT WHIDS AND STOW THEM, *verb. phr.* (old).—To be wary of speech.—B. E. (*c.*1696); GROSE (1785).

1610. ROWLANDS, *Maunder's Wooing* [FARMER, *Musa Pedestris* (1896), 8]. STOW YOUR WHIDS & PLANT, and whid no more of that.

TO PLANT HOME, *verb. phr.* (common).—(1) To deliver (as a blow); (2) to make a point (as in argument); and (3, general) to succeed.

1886. *Phil. Times*, 6 May. Cleary PLANTED two rib-roasters.

1899. *Daily Telegraph*, 7 Ap., 8, 3. See over there! Opposition in the crowd. That roar means the opposition 's PLANTED one 'OME.

TO WATER ONE'S PLANTS, *verb. phr.* (old).—To shed tears: *see* BIB.

PLASTER, *verb.* (common). — To flatter.

PLASTER OF WARM (or HOT) GUTS, *subs. phr.* (venery).—Copulation; 'one warm Belly clapt to another.'—B. E. (*c.*1696); GROSE (1785): *see* GREENS and RIDE.

PLASTERER, *subs.* (sporting).—An amateur gun: *see* quot. and *cf.* PETER GUNNER.

1885. BROMLEY-DAVENPORT, *Sport*. The PLASTERER is one who thinks nothing of the lives and eyes of the men who surround him on all sides, and blows his pheasant to a pulp before the bird is seven feet in the air.

PLATE (**PLATE-FLEET** or **FAMILY PLATE**), *subs.* (common). — 1. Generic for money: formerly a piece of silver: also (HALLIWELL) = 'illegal silver money': *see* RHINO. Hence TO MELT THE PLATE = to spend lavishly; WHEN THE PLATE-FLEET COMES IN = money in plenty.—B. E. (*c.*1696); GROSE (1785).

1586. MARLOW, *Jew of Malta* [DODSLEY, *Old Plays* (REED), viii. 335]. He's worth three hundred PLATES.

1608. SHAKSPEARE, *Antony and Cleopatra*, v. 2. In his livery Walk'd crowns and crownets; realms and islands were AS PLATES dropt from his pocket.

1624. BEAUMONT and FLETCHER, *Rule a Wife*, ii. 2. 'Tis such a trouble to . . . have a thousand things of great importance, Jewels and PLATES.

1749. SMOLLETT, *Gil Blas*, VII. vii. I left [Phenicia] busy in MELTING THE PLATE of a little merchant goldsmith, who, out of vanity, would have an actress for his mistress.

2. (rhyming).—*In pl.* = the feet: originally PLATES OF MEAT: *see* CREEPERS. Whence TO PLATE IT = to walk. Also (American thieves') PLATES OF MEAT = a street.

1886-96. MARSHALL, *Pomes from the Pink 'Un* ['Some Object Lessons'], 108. He is rocky on his PLATES, For he has forced them into 'sevens.' *Ibid.* ('Nobbled), 114. A cove we call Feet, sir, on account of the size of his PLATES.

1887. SIMS, in *Referee*, 7 Nov. 'Tottie.' As she walked along the street With her little PLATES OF MEAT.

OLD PLATES, *subs. phr.* (Stock Exchange).—The shares of the London and River Plate Bank. NEW PLATES = shares of the English Bank of the River Plate: *see* STOCK EXCHANGE.

TO BE IN FOR THE PLATE AND WIN THE HEAT, *verb. phr.* (old). —To get pox or clap.—GROSE (1785).

TO FOUL A PLATE, *verb. phr.* (old).—To dine or sup.—GROSE (1785).

PLATFORM, *subs.* (colloquial).—Formerly a plan, design, or model: now a declaration of principles or doctrines (chiefly religious and political) governing organised public action, each section or paragraph of which is called a PLANK. Also, as *verb.* = to draft or publish such a declaration of principles or doctrines. [*See* the earlier quots. for an inkling of the modern usage.]

1555. FOXE, *Acts and Monuments*, vi. 25. If my lord of St. Davids . . . have their head encumbered with any new PLATFORM. *Ibid.*, 592. The bishop had spent all his powder in casting such a PLATFORM to build his policy on as he thought should stand for ever and a day.

1605. BACON, *Adv. of Learning*, ii. 355. The wisdom of a lawmaker consisteth not only in a PLATFORM of justice, but in the application thereof.

1641-2. MILTON, *Reas. Ch. Government*, i. Some . . . do not . . . grant that church discipline is PLATFORMED in the Bible.

*d.*1732. BISHOP ATTERBURY, *Sermons*, II. xiii. Every little society . . . imposed the PLATFORM of their doctrine, discipline, and worship as divine.

1848. *New York Herald*, 6 May. The Whigs, whether on the Lexington PLATFORM, or some other non-committal PLATFORM, will be and must be at once known as the party that opposed their country in her just and generous war.

*d.*1865. LINCOLN [in *Raymond*, p. 86]. In the Chicago PLATFORM there is a PLANK on this subject.

*d.*1878. S. BOWLES [MERRIAM, I. 291]. We want two PLANKS—non-extension of slavery, and state reform.

1888. *Louisville Courier Journal*, Feb. Mr. Cleveland will be re-nominated by acclamation. His message will be his PLATFORM.

PLATTER-FACE, *subs.* (old). — A broad or flat face: also as *adj.*: *see* DIAL.—B. E. (*c.*1696); GROSE (1785).

PLAUSIBLE, *adj.* (recognised). — Specious; persuasive. — B. E. (*c.*1696).

PLAY, *subs.* (venery).—Copulation: *see* GREENS and RIDE. Hence, FOUL PLAY = adultery; FAIR PLAY = fornication; PLAYFELLOW = a lover, mistress, husband, or wife; PLAYTHING = (1) a mistress, and (2) the *penis* (as in the proverb, 'A fool's BAUBLE (*q.v.*) is a lady's PLAYTHING': *cf.* TOY); LOVE'S PLAYGROUND = (1) the female *pudendum*, and (2) a bed: *see* MONOSYLLABLE and KIP. As *verb.* = (1) to wanton (BAILEY), and (2) to copulate: also TO PLAY WITH; TO PLAY THE WOMAN (THE WANTON, THE FOOL, or THE ACE AGAINST THE JACK) = to grant the favour; TO PLAY THE GOAT = to fornicate hard; TO PLAY OFF (or WITH ONESELF) = to masturbate: *see* FRIG; PLAYSOME (BAILEY) = wanton. *See* BEAST, WILY-BEGUILED, TAIL, &c.

1383. CHAUCER, *Miller's Tale*, l. 87. On a day this hende Nicholas Fil with this yonge wyf to rage and PLEYE. *Ibid.*, 13,352. Let us laugh and PLAY, Ye shal my joly body han to wedde: By God I n'ill not pay you but a-bedde.

1393. GOWER, *Confess. Aman.*, i. She bygan to PLAIE and rage, As who saith, I am well enough.

*c.*1520. *Mayd Emlyn* [HAZLITT, *E. Pop. Poetry*, iv. 94]. To ease her louer She toke another, That lustely conde do . . . With her lusty PLAYE.

*d.*1529. SKELTON, *Elynour Rummyng*, 219. Ich am not cast away, That can my husband say, Whan we kys and PLAY In lust and in lykyng. *Ibid.* [DYCE, *Works*, i. 24, 37]. For your jentyll husband sorowfull am I; . . . he is not the first hath had a loss . . . warke more secretly . . . PLAYE FAYRE, madam . . . Or with gret shame your game wylbe sene.

*d.*1549. BORDE, *Mylner of Abyngton* [HAZLITT, *Early Pop. Poet.*, iii. 109]. Of her he had his will ynough, And PLAIDE them togyther. When the clarke had done his will, By the damosell he lay full stil.

1603. SHAKSPEARE, *Meas. for Meas.*, i. 4. He hath got his friend with child . . . I would . . . PLAY WITH all virgins so.

1608. SHAKSPEARE, *Pericles*, i. [GOWER]. The beauty of this sinful dame made many princes thither frame, To seek her as a bedfellow: In marriage-pleasures PLAYFELLOW.

1612. WEBSTER, *White Devil*, iv. 4. I do suspect my mother PLAYED FOUL PLAY, When she conceiv'd thee.

1749. SMOLLETT, *Gil Blas* [ROUTLEDGE], 93. The favours which my goddess winked at my snatching . . . fell short of the only perfect issue . . . Said I, this lady . . . thinks it beneath her quality TO PLAY THE very WOMAN at the first interview. *Ibid.*, 190. Though noblemen . . . attach themselves to pretty PLAYTHINGS like yourself, it is highly unbecoming in you to forget your proper distance.

*d.*1796. BURNS, *Merry Muses*, 'They Took Me,' &c. They took me to the Holy Band For PLAYING by [= away from] my wife, Sirs.

PHRASES:—TO PLAY ARTFUL = to feign simplicity, to keep a card or two up one's sleeve; TO PLAY BOOTS (THE DEVIL, THE MISCHIEF, NED, &c.) = to thrust, to spoil, to ruin; TO PLAY OFF = (1) to simulate, and (2) to expose to merriment, and (3) to make an end; TO PLAY ON (or UPON) = to trifle with; TO PLAY UP = (1) to do one's best, and (2) to be troublesome; TO PLAY UP TO = to take one's cue from another; PLAYED UP (or OUT) = used up, or ruined; TO PLAY WITH ONE'S BEARD = to deceive; TO PLAY IT LOW = to take advantage; TO PLAY LIGHT = (1) to take it easy, and (2) to keep one's temper; TO PLAY FOR = to deal with generally; TO PLAY DARK = to conceal one's character or motive; TO PLAY THE WHOLE GAME = to cheat; TO PLAY LEAST IN SIGHT = to hide; TO PLAY TO THE GAS (theatrical) = to play to small audiences (*see* quot. 1899); TO PLAY TO THE GALLERY (theatrical) = to rant, to gag, to use the coarsest and cheapest means; TO PLAY IT OFF = to cheat; TO PLAY THE SOVEREIGN = to flatter an inferior; TO MAKE GOOD PLAY = to work to advantage, or with execution; TO COME INTO PLAY = to take one's turn, or share; TO PLAY FAIR (or FALSE) = to act or deal honestly (or the reverse); TO PLAY ONE'S CARDS WELL = to advance one's interests; TO PLAY INTO ONE'S HANDS = to advantage; TO KEEP (or HOLD) IN PLAY = to retain control, keep things going, or to engage; TO PLAY THE GIDDY GOAT = to behave like a fool; TO PLAY WITH = to trifle; TO PLAY UPON ADVANTAGE = to cheat; TO PLAY IN AND OUT = to trifle; PLAYED OUT = exhausted, ruined, done for; TO PLAY A GOOD KNIFE AND FORK (*see* KNIFE, and add quot. 1749); TO PLAY THE GAME = to do honestly at whatever cost; TO PLAY DIDDLE-DIDDLE = to trick, to cajole; TO PLAY THE DUCK = (1) to go contrary, or against the grain: as ducks are plucked, and (2) to prove a coward; TO PLAY OFF ONE'S DUST = to drink. Other proverbial sayings are: 'She's like a cat, she'll PLAY with her tail,' of a wanton; 'The PLAY won't pay the candles' (or 'the acting is not worth the lights') = the end is not worth the means or risk; 'He'll PLAY a small game rather than stand out,' of a meddler or busybody. Also *see* BEAR; BEARD; BOB-FOOL; BOOTY; DEUCE; DEVIL; DICKENS; DUCKS; FAST; FATHERS-AND-MOTHERS; FIDDLE; GOOSEBERRY; HARRY; HELL; HOB; HOOKY; IN-AND-IN; IN-AND-OUT; KNIFE; LOVE; MISCHIEF; POSSUM; SECOND FIDDLE; SCHOOLMASTER; TAIL; UGLY; UPTAILS-ALL; VELVET; WAG; WAGTAIL.

1383. CHAUCER, *Cant. Tales*, l. 13,163. Til we be ded, or else that we PLAY a pilgrimage [*i.e.*, to play off or pretend to go a pilgrimage].

1400. *York. Myst.* [OLIPHANT, *New English*, i. 194. There are the new phrases . . . spille sport, PLAY FAIR, &c.].

1525. TYNDALE, *Works* [Parker Soc.], ii. 35. As soon as he hath PLAYED OUT all his lusts . . . he cometh again with his old profession.

1530. SKELTON [DYCE, *Works*, ii. 203]. What blunderer is yonder that PLAYTH DIDIL-DIDDIL.

1544. ASCHAM, *Toxophilus* [ARBER], 97. Men PLAY WITH laws.

1566. R. EDWARDS, *Damon and Pythias* [NARES]. Yet have I PLAY'D WITH HIS BEARD, in knitting this knot I promist friendship, but . . . I meant it not.

1596. SHAKSPEARE, *Hamlet*, iii. 2. Though you can fret me you cannot PLAY UPON me.

1598. SHAKSPEARE, *1 Hen. IV.*, v. 4. Art thou alive? Or is it fantasy that PLAYS UPON our eyesight? I prithee, speak. *Ibid.*, ii. 4. They call drinking deep, dyeing scarlet; and when you breathe in your watering, they cry 'hem!' and bid you PLAY IT OFF.

1600. JONSON, *Cynthia's Revels*, iv. 1. If she hath PLAYED LOOSE with me, I'll cut her throat.

1609. JONSON, *Case is Altered*, iv. 5. Is't not enough That you have PLAYED UPON me all this while, But still to mock me, still to jest at me.

1610. BEAUMONT and FLETCHER, *Maid's Tragedy*, iv. 1. Do not PLAY WITH mine anger.

1653. URQUHART, *Rabelais*, I. xlii. By God! whoever of our party shall offer TO PLAY THE DUCK . . . I give myself to the devil if I do not make a monk of him.

1705. VANBRUGH, *Confederacy*, iii. *Flip.* Brass, the game is in our hands if we can but PLAY THE CARDS.

1749. SMOLLETT, *Gil Blas* [ROUTLEDGE (1866), 14. Domingo, after PLAYING A GOOD KNIFE AND FORK, and getting gloriously muddled, took himself off to the stable. *Ibid.*, 143. Ortiz . . . was determined TO PLAY UP TO my mistress. *Ibid.*, 108. The little fellow . . . was but just COMING INTO PLAY. *Ibid.* (1812), iii. 83. 'What dost thou think of my lodging and œconomy?' 'Thou must have certainly PLAYED THY CARDS well at Madrid, to be so well furnished.

1778. SHERIDAN, *Rivals*, ii. 1. You rely upon the mildness of my temper . . . you PLAY UPON the meekness of my disposition. *Ibid.*, ii. 2. You PLAY FALSE with us, madam—I saw you give the baronet a letter.

1842. MACAULAY, *Horatius*, xxix. Hew down the bridge, Sir Consul, With all the speed ye may; I with two more to help me, Will HOLD the foe IN PLAY.

1868-9. BROWNING, *Ring and Book*, vi. Why PLAY . . . INTO THE DEVIL'S HANDS Dy dealing so ambiguously.

186[?]. BRET HARTE, *Further L. from Truthful James*. Is our investigation a failure, or is the Caucasian PLAYED OUT?

1882. *Fortnightly Review*, 88. After all there is some refreshing sense of the primæval about this PLAYED-OUT country.

1888. HENLEY and STEVENSON, *Deacon Brodie*, i. You PLAY FALSE, you hound!

1888. MILLIKEN, *'Arry Ballads* . . . Bin PLAYING SOME dark LITTLE GAME?

1892. ZANGWILL in *Idler*, Feb., 62. I think it's PLAYING IT TOO LOW upon a chap. It's taking a mean advantage of my position.

1895. POCOCK, *Rules of the Game*, ii. You can ride on the waggon if you are too PLAYED OUT for a saddle horse.

1898. NEWBOLT, *Admirals All*, 21. The word that, year by year, While . . . School is set . . . her sons must hear, And none . . . forget. This, they all, with joyful mind, Bear through life like a torch in flame, And falling, fling to the hosts behind, PLAY UP, PLAY UP, and PLAY THE GAME!

1899. *Daily Mail*, 16 Mar., 7, 1. PLAYING TO THE GAS is used in the general sense in reference to small audiences, but strictly it means that an audience was only large enough to render receipts sufficient to pay the bill for the evening's lighting.

PLEASURE, *subs.* (venery).—The sexual spasm: Fr. *le plaisir*. Hence, THE ART OF PLEASURE = the practise of love; THE DEED OF PLEASURE = the act of kind; PLEASURE-BOAT (-GARDEN, -GROUND, or -PLACE) = the female *pudendum*: also THE PALACE OF PLEASURE: *see* MONOSYLLABLE; PLEASURE-GARDEN PADLOCK = the menstrual cloth; PLEASURE-LADY (or LADY OF PLEASURE) = a harlot: Fr. *fille de joie*; A VOTARY OF PLEASURE = a whoremonger (BAILEY, 1748); TO PLEASURE (or PLEASE) A WOMAN = to give her an orgasm (as the Duchess of Marlborough wrote in her diary that the Duke had PLEASURED her thrice 'in his boots').

*c.*1500. *Roberte the Deuyll* [HAZLITT, *Early Pop. Poetry*, i. 223]. He toke her in hys armes, and her kyste; And of that Lady he had all hys PLEASURE, And so begate a chylde.

*d.*1529. SKELTON, *Phyllyp Sparowe*, 1194. Her kyrtell so goodly lased, And vnder that is brased [ready] Such PLASURES that I may Neyther wryte nor say.

1594. LYLY, *Mother Bombie*, iii. 4. *Rix.* If you take your PLEASURE of me, I'le in and tell your practises against your masters. *Half.* In faith, soure hart, he that takes his PLEASURE on thee, is very PLEASURABLE.

1596. DAVIES, *Epigrams*, 'In Katam,' viii. Kate being PLEASED, wished that her PLEASURE could Endure as long as a buff jerkin would: Content thee, Kate, although thy PLEASURE wasteth, Thy PLEASURE'S PLACE like a buff jerkin lasteth.

1605. CHAPMAN, *All Fools*, i. 1. All day in ceaseless uproar with their households, If all the night their husbands have not PLEASED them.

1608. SHAKSPEARE, *Pericles*, i. 1. Untimely claspings with your child (Which PLEASURE fits a husband, not a father); And she an eater of her mother's flesh.

1623. WEBSTER, *Duchess of Malfi*, v. 2. We that are great WOMEN OF PLEASURE . . . join the sweet delight and the pretty excuse together.

*c.*1640-2. SHIRLEY, *Captain Underwit*, i. Custome and nature make it less offence In women to commit THE DEED OF PLEASURE Than men to doubt their chastity.

1663-85. *Old Ballad*, 'Poor Robin's Prophesie.' Your LADY OF PLEASURE . . . will then become modest, and . . . live like a Nun in a Cloyster all day.

1681. RADCLIFFE, *Ovid Trav.*, 30. When first with PLEASURE I lay under you, Would yo'd been lighter by a stone or two.

1736. JACOB, *Rape of the Smock*, 21. And ardently round Celia's waist he twines . . . Soft PLEASURE now succeeds an age of pain.

1749. SMOLLETT, *Gil Blas* (1812), ii. 77. Is it possible that a person of such delicacy can be a LADY OF PLEASURE? *Ibid.* [ROUTLEDGE], 89. A celebrated wanton . . . keeping open house night and day for the VOTARIES OF PLEASURE. She was . . . so perfect a mistress in the ART OF PLEASURE that she sold the waste and refuse of her beauty at a higher price than the first sample of the unadulterated article. *Ibid.*, 286. Whether pimping was a virtue or a vice . . . what a promotion for me to be the provider of PLEASURE to a great prince. *Ibid.*, 222. You cannot help admitting, that where a young man does insinuate himself slily into a girl's bedchamber, he takes better care of his own PLEASURE than of her reputation.

1754. EARL OF CORK, *Connoisseur* [*England in 18th Century*, i. 47]. I was present at an entertainment where a celebrated LADY OF PLEASURE was one of the party; her shoe was pulled off . . . filled . . . with champagne and drank off to her health.

1772. BRIDGES, *Burlesque Homer*, 97. A fine long nose, and proper measure . . . to give the fair ones PLEASURE. *Ibid.*, 244. He'd done his best to PLEASE. *Ibid.*, 399. Patroclus' bed was warm'd the last, And he his nights in PLEASURE past By a fair maiden's side.

*d.*1796. BURNS, *Merry Muses*, 'O, Saw Ye my Maggie?' My Maggie has a treasure, A hidden MINE O' PLEASURE, I'll heuk it at my leisure, It's a' alane for me. *Ibid.*, 'Nine-Inch,' &c. I learned a sang in Annandale, Nine-inch will PLEASE a lady.

1827. LYTTON, *Pelham*, xlix. The rest were made up of unfortunate women of the vilest . . . decrepit, but indefatigable VOTARIES OF PLEASURE.

1866. SWINBURNE, *Poems and Ballads*, 'In the Orchard.' The PLEASURE lives there, when the sense has died. 'Dolores.' PLEASURE more salt than the foam of the sea, Now felt as a flame, now at leisure, As wine shed for me. *Et passim.*

PLEB, *subs.* (Westminster School).—A tradesman's son.

PLEBE, *subs.* (American Collegiate).—A freshman; specifically one in the lowest class at West Point. Hence PLEBESKIN = a freshman's tunic.

1888. *New York World*, 22 July. West Point, N.Y., July 21.—The fourth class entered camp on Monday, but are still wearing their PLEBESKINS.

PLEDGE, *subs.* (colloquial). — A baby.

1622. FLETCHER, *Sp. Curate*, i. 3. 'Tis the curse Of great estates to want those PLEDGES which The poor are happy in.

1751. SMOLLETT, *Per. Pickle* (1895), iii. 122. In a few hours a living PLEDGE of my love and indiscretion saw the light.

Verb. (Winchester School).—To give away. 'PLEDGE ME' = 'After you'; 'I'll PLEDGE it you when I have done with it: *cf.* POSTE TE.

PLENIPO, *subs.* (old colloquial).—1. A plenipotentiary.

1697. VANBRUGH, *Provoked Wife*, iii. 1. I'll . . . say the PLENIPOS have signed the peace, and the Bank of England's grown honest.

1740. NORTH, *Examen*, 297. Whiteacre . . . was the treason PLENIPO at that time.

1815. D'ARBLAY, *Diary*, 329. We were buoyed up . . . with the hope that G neral Laurington was gone to England as PLENIPO.

2. (venery).—The *penis*: *see* PRICK.

*c.*1786. CAPT. MORRIS, THE PLENIPOTENTIARY [Title and *passim*].

PLIER, *subs.* (common).—The hand: *see* DADDLE.

PLOLL-CAT, *subs.* (old).—A whore: *see* TART.

PLOUGH, *verb.* (University).—1. To reject in an examination. [See *infra* Smyth-Palmer on PLUCK.]

1863. READE, *Hard Cash*, Prol. Gooseberry pie . . . adds to my chance of being PLOUGHED for smalls.

1877. *Driven to Rome*, 68. These two promising specimens were not PLOUGHED, but were considered fit to teach that . . . of which they were so lamentably ignorant themselves.

1895. POCOCK, *Rules of the Game*, i. I knew one of that lot at Corpus; in fact, we were crammed by the same Tutor for 'smalls,' and both got PLOUGHED.

1900. WHITE, *West End*, 148. 'I'll pay you back directly I have passed' . . . 'But suppose you're PLOUGHED.' 'Well, then, I suppose you'll have to wait.'

Verb. (venery).—To copulate: *see* GREENS and RIDE.

1608. SHAKSPEARE, *Pericles*, vi. 6. *Bawd.* Take her . . . use her . . . crack the glass of her virginity . . . *Boult.* She shall be PLOUGHED. Ibid., *Ant. and Cleop.*, ii. 2, 232. Royal wench! She made great Cæsar lay his sword to bed: He PLOUGH'D her and she cropped.

TO PLOUGH THE DEEP, *verb. phr.* (rhyming).—To sleep.

TO PUT THE PLOUGH BEFORE THE OXEN, *verb. phr.* (old).—To reverse; 'to put the cart before the horse.'

1653. URQUHART, *Rabelais*, I. He would PUT THE PLOUGH BEFORE THE OXEN, and claw where it did not itch.

PROVERBIAL PHRASES are:—TO PLOUGH WITH ASS AND OX = to sort or do things ill; TO LET THE PLOUGH STAND TO CATCH A MOUSE = to neglect weighty matters for small; TO PLOUGH THE AIR (or A ROCK) = to attempt the absurd or impossible.

PLOUGHED, *adj.* and *adv.* (common).—Drunk: *see* SCREWED.

PLOUGHSHARE, *subs.* (venery).—The *penis*: *see* PRICK.

1865. SWINBURNE, *Atalanta*, &c., 107. Thou, I say Althea, since my father's PLOUGHSHARE, drawn Through fatal seedland of a female field, Furrowed thy body.

PLOVER, *subs.* (old).—A wanton: *cf.* PARTRIDGE, PHEASANT, and GROUSE: *see* TART.

1614. JONSON, *Bartholomew Fair*, iv. 3. Here will be Zekiel Edgworth, and three or four gallants with him at night, and I have neither PLOVER nor quail for them; persuade this . . . to become a bird of the game.

PLOWTER, *verb.* (venery). — To copulate: *see* GREENS and RIDE.

PLUCK, *subs.* (colloquial).—Courage; SPUNK (*q.v.*): also PLUCKINESS. — GROSE (1785). Hence PLUCKED = valiant: usually with 'good,' 'well,' 'rare,' &c.; HARD-PLUCKED (*see* quot. 1857); PLUCKY = bold, spiritedly, or indomitable; PLUCK-LESS = fainthearted.

1821. EGAN, *Life in London*, I. i. My hand . . . possesses not weight enough to combat with thee, although the PLUCK, perhaps, attached to it may be always gay.

1837. BARHAM, *Ingoldsby Legends*, II. 146. If you're PLUCKY, and not over-subject to fright.

1854-5. THACKERAY, *Newcomes*, lix. 'Shall I break off with the finest girl in England, and the BEST-PLUCKED one, and the cleverest and the wittiest?' . . . 'By Jove, you are a GOOD-PLUCKED fellow, Farintosh.'

1857. HUGHES, *Tom Brown's School-days*, I. vii. The BAD-PLUCKED ones thinking that after all it isn't worth while to keep it up.

1857. KINGSLEY, *Two Years Ago*, iv. A terrible HARD-PLUCKED one . . . hanged if I don't think he has a thirty-two pound shot under his ribs instead of a heart.

1858. TROLLOPE, *Dr. Thorn*, xxix. 'No,' said Frank, PLUCKILY, as he put his horse into a faster trot.

1860-3. THACKERAY, *Roundabout Papers*, 'On a Peal of Bells,' Note. I wish I was such a GOOD-PLUCKED one as you, Miss Anville.

1863. *Story of a Lancashire Thief*, 8. We prigs liked to see the RARE PLUCKED 'uns as much as decent folk hanker after Barnum and Blondin.

1883. MAX MULLER, *Biog. Essays*, 289. He set to work digging at Nineveh with that PLUCK . . . which he has since shown on other occasions.

1889. MRS. WHITNEY, *Leslie Goldthwaite*, vi. [*Century*]. Her quaint, queer expression, in which curiosity, PLUCKINESS, and a foretaste of amusement mingled.

Verb. (University).—To reject at an examination. [Suggested derivations are (1) the analogy between PLUCKING, or divesting a bird of plumage, as the magpie in the fable (*see* quot. 1360); and (2) as given in quot. 1853. As regards PLOUGH (*q.v.*) Smyth-Palmer says (*Folk Etymology*) it seems a wilful perversion of PLUCK, . . . the Germ. *pflücken* having been sportively confounded with *plough*, Ger. *pflügen*, from *pflug*, a plough].—GROSE (1785). Also as *subs.*

1360. CHAUCER, *Romaunt of the Rose*, 5983. I shall so pulle him, if I can That he shall in a fewe stoundes Lese all his markes and his poundes, . . . Our maidens shall eke PLUCKE him so, That he shall neden fethers mo.

1749. SMOLLETT, *Gil Blas* [ROUTLEDGE (1866), 146]. I had attended an experimental course among the actresses; and had always found that the elderly candidates had been PLUCKED in their amours.

1847. C. BRONTE, *Jane Eyre*, x. He went to college, and he got PLUCKED, as I think they call it.

1849-50. THACKERAY, *Pendennis*, xix. Pendennis of Boniface was PLUCKED. *Ibid.*, xx. 'Was it done in public,' the Major said. 'What?' 'The —— the PLUCKING,' asked the guardian.

1849. KINGSLEY, *Alton Locke*, xx. He had been a medical student, and got PLUCKED, his foes declared, in his examination.

1853. BRADLEY, *Verdant Green*, xi. [Note]. When the degrees are conferred, the name of each person is read out before he is presented to the Vice-Chancellor. The proctor then walks once up and down the room, so that any person who objects to the degree being granted may signify the same by pulling or PLUCKING the proctor's robes. This has been occasionally done by tradesmen, in order to obtain payment of their 'little bills,' but such a proceeding is very rare, and the proctor's promenade is usually undisturbed.

1855. BRISTED, *Eng. Univ.*, 258. If a man is PLUCKED—that is, does not get marks enough to pass—his chance of a Fellowship is done for.

1886. STUBBS, *Medieval and Mod. History*, 386. I trust that I have never PLUCKED a candidate . . . without giving him every opportunity of setting himself right.

2. (venery).—To deflower: *see* DOCK.

1608. SHAKSPEARE, *Pericles*, vi. 5. Never PLUCKED yet, I can assure you. Is she not a fair creature.

AGAINST THE PLUCK, *adv. phr.* (old).—Against the inclination.—GROSE (1785).

TO PLUCK THE RIBAND, *verb. phr.* (old).—*See* quot.—GROSE (1785).

*c.*1696. B. E., *Dict. Cant. Crew*, s.v. PLUCK THE RIBAND, or PLUCK SIR ONION, ring the Bell at the Tavern.

See CROW; PIGEON; NOSE; ROSE.

PLUCK-PENNY, *subs. phr.* (old).—*See* quot.

1643. *Theeves, Theeves*, 2. He that is once so skilled in the art of gaming as to play at PLUCK PENNY, will quickly come to sweepstake.

PLUG, *subs.* (common).—1. A silk hat: also PLUG-HAT: *see* GOLGOTHA.

1872. CLEMENS, *Innocents at Home*, . . . A nigger in a biled shirt and a PLUG-HAT.

1888. *Eclectic Mag.* Cæsar was the implacable foe of the aristocracy, and refused to wear a PLUG-HAT up to the day of his death.

2. (common).—A man or beast, short and thick-set: *see* FORTY-GUTS.

1872. CLEMENS, *Innocents at Home.* An old PLUG-HORSE, that eat up his market value in hay and barley in seventeen days by the watch.

1888. *Brooklyn Daily Eagle*, 22 April. Some . . . screamed with delight, and others . . . anathemised the jockey who rode the PLUG they had backed.

3. (artisans'). — A workman whose apprenticeship has been irregular; a TURN-OVER (*q.v.*): specifically (in America) a craftsman who has learned his business in casual or evening classes. Such teaching is called PLUG-TEACHING.

4. (common). — Anything damaged or deteriorated: as an unsuccessful book; an old horse; coins bored full of holes and PLUGGED with base metal; a shop-soiled bicycle; and so forth. Also OLD PLUG. Hence (generally) PLUG = any defect—moral, physical, or otherwise.

1888. *Texas Siftings*, 3 Nov. Can't sell you a ticket for that quarter; it's PLUGGED.

5. (schools').—A translation; a CRIB (*q.v.*); a PONY (*q.v.*).

1853. BRADLEY, *Verdant Green.* Getting up his subjects by the aid of those royal roads to knowledge, variously known as cribs, crams, PLUGS, abstracts, analyses, or epitomes.

6. (American).—A loafer, well-dressed or other: *see* PLUG-UGLY.

Verb. (Western States). — 1. To hit with a bullet.

2. (venery).—To copulate: *see* GREENS and RIDE.

PLUG-HAT. *See* PLUG, *subs.* 1.

PLUG-TAIL, *subs. phr.* (old).—The *penis*: *see* PRICK.—GROSE (1785).

PLUG-UGLY, *subs. phr.* (American).—A Baltimore street rowdy, *circa* 1860-80. Hence any loafer or ROUGH (*q.v.*).

1876. *Providence Journal*, 30 Sep. The Democrats are getting up a soldiers' convention at Indianapolis. As Union soldiers are scarce in the Democrat ranks, many are recruited from the PLUG-UGLIES of Baltimore.

1891. *Daily Telegraph*, 13 July, p. 5, col. 1. The PLUG-UGLY, the 'dead rabbit,' and the Californian 'hoodlum' are as racy of the soil of America as the 'larrikin' is of that of Australia.

1896. CRANE, *Maggie*, xiv. And she goes off with that PLUG-UGLY, who looks as if he had been hit in the face with a coin die.

PLUM (or PLUMB), *subs.* (common).—1. £100,000; a fortune: *see* RHINO. Hence, a rich man.—GROSE (1785).

1709-11. STEELE, *Tatler*, No. 244. An honest gentleman who sat next to me, and who was worth half a PLUMB, stared at him.

*d.*1721. PRIOR, *The Ladle*, Moral. The Miser must make up his PLUMB, And dares not touch the hoarded Sum.

*c.*1719. *Vision of Justice* [quoted in *Century*]. Several who were PLUMS, or very near it, became men of moderate fortunes.

1766. COLMAN, *Clandestine Marriage*, iii. My brother Heidelberg was a warm man, a very warm man; and died worth a PLUMB at least.

1821. EGAN, *Life in London*, II. v. Then your visit to Almack's will be at least worth a PLUM to you.

1844. THACKERAY, *Barry Lyndon*, xiii. An English tallow-chandler's heiress, with a PLUM to her fortune.

1890. BOLDREWOOD, *Squatter's Dream*, 104. Twenty years on the Warroo with the certainty of a PLUM and a baronetcy at the end.

1899. BESANT, *Orange Girl*, 56. You the only son of Sir Peter Halliday . . . the heir to a PLUM—what do I say? Three or four PLUMS at the least.

2. (common).—A good thing; a tit-bit: also as *adj.* (*q.v.*).

1889. *Academy*, 2 Nov., 280. The reviewer who picks all the PLUMS out of a book . . . is regarded with . . . terror . . . by both authors and publishers.

1892. *The Writer*, 120 [*Century*]. Often, indeed, the foot-note contains the very PLUM of the page.

Adj. (old). — A general appreciative: good; desirable; exactly; quite; dextrously; thorough-going. Whence also PLUMB-CENTRE = exactly at the centre: as a plummet hangs.—GROSE (1785); VAUX (1819). Also PLUMMY.

1667. MILTON, *Paradise Lost*, ii. 933. He meets a vast vacuity, all unawares, Fluttering his pennons vain, PLUMB down he falls.

1748. RICHARDSON, *Clarissa*, iv. 262. Neither can an opposition, neither can a ministry be always wrong. To be a PLUMB man therefore with either is an infallible mark that the man must mean more and worse than he will own he does mean.

1819. *Song*, 'The Young Prig' [FARMER, *Musa Pedestris* (1896), 82]. Frisk the cly, and fork the rag, Draw the fogles PLUMMY.

1830. BARRINGTON, *Personal Sketches* [BARTLETT]. The best way to avoid danger is to meet it PLUMB.

1859. REID, *Osceola*, 415. We seed 'em both fire across the gleed, an' right PLUM-CENTRE at young Randolph.

1867. *London Herald*, 23 March, 222, 1. Ain't this ere PLUMMY.

1876. GEORGE ELIOT, *Daniel Deronda*, xvi. The poets have made tragedies enough about signing oneself over to wickedness for the sake of getting something PLUMMY.

1883. *Century Magazine*, xxxvi. 900. O Sal, Sal, my heart ar' PLUM broke.

1888. *San Francisco Weekly Examiner.* I'm awful fond o' po'try—jus' PLUMB crazy ovah it.

1895. POCOCK, *Rules of the Games*, II. 10. But, doc, he ain't PLUMB stove up; He ain't going to die here in this goal 3.

1898. WINTHROP, *Cecil Dreeme*, vi. How refreshing to find such a place and such a person PLUMP in the middle of New York.

Verb. (common).—To deceive: *see* GAMMON.

See BLUE PLUM.

PLUM-DUFF, *subs. phr.* (nautical).—Plum-dumpling; SPOTTED-DOG (*q.v.*).

PLUMP, *subs.* (old).—A blow.—GROSE (1785). Also PLUMPER.

1772. BRIDGES, *Burlesque Homer*, 378. Gave me a PLUMPER on the jaw, And cry'd: Pox take you!

Adj. and *adv.* (old: now recognised).—1. Exactly; downright; quite. Also as *verb.* = to meet in more or less violent contact; and PLUMPLY (or PLUMP AND PLAIN) = without reserve, roundly.

1535. COVERDALE, *Trans. Bible* [OLIPHANT, *New English*, i. 441. We see 'The waters PLUMPED together'; hence our 'going PLUMP INTO a thing.']

1614. BEAUMONT and FLETCHER, *Wit at Several Weapons*, i. 1. The art of swimming he that will attain to't, Must fall PLUMP and duck himself at first.

1778. BURNEY, *Evelina*, lv. PLUMP we comes against a cart, with such a jog it almost pulled the coach-wheel off.

2. (old: now recognised).—Fat, full, fleshy.—GROSE (1785). Hence, PLUMP IN THE POCKET = with plenty of money; WARM (*q.v.*).

Verb. (political).—1. To record a whole- (*i.e.*, an unsplit-) vote. Whence PLUMPER = (1) the voter and (2) the vote. Also (racing) = to back one horse; and (general) = 'to put all one's eggs in one basket.'—GROSE (1785).

1871-2. G. ELIOT, *Middlemarch*, li. Mr. Brooke's success must depend either on PLUMPERS, or on the new minting of Tory votes into reforming votes.

1885. *Westminster Rev.* [*Century*]. They refused to exercise their right of electing local members, and PLUMPED for Earl Grey himself in 1848.

2. (old).—To strike; to shoot.—GROSE (1785).

3. *See adj.* and *adv.*, sense 1.

PLUMPER, *subs.* (common).—1. An unqualified falsehood: *see* WHOPPER.

2. (common). — A device for puffing out to smoothness the wrinkles of the cheeks.—GROSE (1785). Also a false bosom.

16 [?]. *London Ladies Dressing Room* [NARES]. And that the cheeks may both agree Their PLUMPERS fill the cavity.

*d.*1745. SWIFT, *Young Nymph.* Now dextrously her PLUMPERS draws, That serve to fill her hollow jaws.

1772. BRIDGES, *Burlesque Homer*, 123. Unless I dress your PLUMPERS out . . . Then you'll . . . be willing To earn a sixpence or a shilling.

3. (political and general).—*See* PLUMP, *verb.*—GROSE (1785).

4. *See* PLUMP, *subs.*

PLUMP-CURRANT, *adj.* and *adv.* (old). — In good condition; in fettle; in high spirits.—GROSE (1785).

PLUM-PORRIDGE, *subs. phr.* (old). — A term of contempt: *cf.* PUDDING-HEAD.

1634. SHAKSPEARE and FLETCHER, *Two Noble Kinsmen*, ii. 2. I'll be hanged though If he dare venture; hang him, PLUM-PORRIDGE! He wrestle? he roast eggs.

PLUMP-PATE, *subs.* (old).—A blockhead: *see* BUFFER.

PLUM-PUDDINGER, *subs. phr.* (American). — A small whaler making short voyages. [*Century*: the crew is dieted on fresh provisions and an abundance of plum-pudding.]

18 [?]. SCAMMON, *Marine Mammals*, 241. Provincetown has ever been foremost with her numerous fleet of PLUM-PUDDINGERS.

PLUM-TREE, *subs.* (venery).—The female *pudendum*: *see* MONOSYLLABLE. Whence HAVE AT THE PLUM-TREE, a proverbial phrase, or the burden of a song.

*c.*1547. *Mariage of Witt and Wisdome*, 16. I was neuer stained but once falling out of my mother's PLUMTRE.

1594. SHAKSPEARE, *2 Henry VI.*, ii. 1. *Suf.* How camest thou so? [lame]. *Simp.* A fall off of a tree. *Wife.* A PLUM-TREE, master. *Glou.* How long hast thou been blind? *Simp.* O, born so, master.

1611. COTGRAVE, *Dict.*, s.v. *Hocheprunier.* A PLUM-TREE shaker, a man's yard.

PLUNDER, *subs.* (American).—1. Household goods; personal effects; baggage. [M. D. *plunder* = household effects.]

*d.*1834. COLERIDGE, *Letters*, 214. They [Americans] had mistaken the English language for baggage (which is called PLUNDER in America), and had stolen it.

1846. *Major Jones's Courtship*, 165. Old Bosen was going to have more'n his match to pull us, they'd put in so much PLUNDER, Two trunks, handboxes, &c.

1859. HOFFMAN, *Winter in the West*, xxxiii. 'Help yourself, stranger,' added the landlord, 'while I tote your PLUNDER into the other room.'

1873. *Lynch Law in the Sucker State.* On Sunday afternoon, two long dug-outs, loaded with PLUNDER, stopped at the cabin . . . This was the family and property of Hank Harris.

2. (common).—Profit; MAKINGS (*q.v.*).

PLUNGE, *verb.* (racing).—To bet recklessly. Hence A PLUNGE = a reckless bet; PLUNGING = gambling for high stakes; PLUNGER = a reckless gambler. [*E.g.*, the Marquis of Hastings, the first so-called. One night he played three games of draughts for £1000 a game and lost all three. He then 'cut' for £500 a 'cut' and lost £5000 in less than two hours. Benzon (the Jubilee Plunger) lost £250,000 in little more than twelve months.]

1880. *Fortnightly Review*, 319. PLUNGING was the order of the day.

1890. SIMS, in *Referee*, 20 Ap., 'Rondeau of the Knock.' One PLUNGER more has had his little flare, And then came Monday when he couldn't 'square.'

1891. *Lic. Vict. Gaz.*, 3 Ap. The Squire of Kingscote took to PLUNGING and shaking his elbow at baccarat nearly every night.

1901. *Free Lance*, 9 Feb., 471, 1. Sponging on their friends in order to settle their Stock Exchange "differences" . . . Husbands are ruined in a day by the secret PLUNGING of their wives.

PLUNGER, *subs.* (military).—1. A cavalry man.

1857. KINGSLEY, *Two Years Ago*, xvi. It's an insult to the whole Guards, my dear fellow, after refusing two of us, to marry an attorney, and after all to bolt with a PLUNGER.

2. *See* PLUNGE, *verb.*

3. (clerical).—A Baptist.

PLUSH, *subs.* (nautical).—1. *See* quot.

1867. SMYTH, *Sailors' Word Book*, s.v. PLUSH . . . The overplus of the gravy, arising from being distributed in a smaller measure than the true one, and assigned to the cook of each mess, becomes a cause of irregularity.

2. (venery).—The pubic hair: *see* FLEECE.

JOHN PLUSH, *subs. phr.* (common).—A footman: *cf.* THACKERAY, *The Yellowplush Correspondence*, by Charles YELLOWPLUSH, Esq.

PLYER, *subs.* (old).—A crutch.—B. E. (*c.*1696); GROSE (1785).

2. (old).—A trader.—GROSE (1785).

PLYMOUTH (or **DUNKIRK**) **-CLOAK,** *subs. phr.* (old).—A cudgel.

1602. DEKKER, *Honest Whore*, ii. Shall I walk in a PLYMOUTH CLOAK (that's to say) like a rogue, in my hose and doublet, and a crab-tree cudgel in my hand.

1626. OWEN, *Spec. Jesuit* (1629), 10. I would haue soone recall'd him with a PLYMOUTH CLOAKE (*margin* Cudgell).

[?]. LENTON, *Characterismi*, Char. 30. Reserving still the embleme of a souldier (his sword) and a PLIMOUTH CLOAKE, otherwise called a battoone.

1628. MASSINGER, *New Way to Pay Old Debts*, i. 1. *Wellborn.* How, dog? *(Raising his cudgel.) Tapwell.* Advance your PLYMOUTH CLOAK, There dwells, and within call . . . A potent monarch, called the constable, That doth command a citadel, called the stocks.

*d.*1668. DAVENANT [NARES], fol. p. 229. Whose CLOAK (at PLIMOUTH spun) was crabtree wood.

*d.*1668. DENHAM, *Works*, 75, 'Ballad on Sir J. Mennis.' He being proudly mounted Clad in CLOAK of PLYMOUTH.

1742. RAY, *Proverbs*, 238. That is a cane, a staff; whereof this is the occasion. Many a man of good extraction, coming home from far voyages, may chance to land here, and being out of sorts, is unable for the present time and place to recruit himself with clothes. Here (if not friendly provided) they make the next wood their draper's shop, where a staff cut out serves them for a covering. For we use, when we walk *in cuerpo*, to carry a staff in our hands, but none when in a cloak.

P-MAKER, *subs. phr.* (venery).—1. The *penis*: *see* PRICK; and (2) the female *pudendum*: *see* MONOSYLLABLE.

POACH, *subs.* (colloquial).—1. To steal; to SNEAK (*q.v.*): *see* PRIG. Hence (venery) = to steal a man's wife or mistress—generally TO POACH UPON ANOTHER MAN'S PRESERVES: *cf.* PIRATE 2. Also (racing) = to get the best of a start: esp. by unsportsmanlike methods.—GROSE (1785); BEE (1823).

*c.*1531. COPLAND, *Spyttel Hous* [HAZLITT, *E. Pop. Poet*, iv. 41]. Prolyng and POCHYNG to get somwhat.

1611. COTGRAVE, *Dict.*, s.v. *Pocher de labeur d'autruy*, to POCH into, or encroach upon, another man's employment, practice in trade.

1620. BEAUMONT and FLETCHER, *Philaster*, iv. 1. His greatest fault is he hunts too much in the purlieus; would he leave off POACHING.

1821. EGAN, *Life in London*, II. iv. You shall be admitted into the PRESERVE; but remember, no POACHING.

1862. *Cornhill Mag.*, vi., 651. In their wanderings they fall in with other shoals, and some get lost, and some are famished to death, and some are POACHED, and some get hooked.

1891. *Lic. Vict. Gaz.*, 20 Mar. Seward maintained that the start was a false one, and that his opponent POACHED full five yards before he (Seward) moved.

2. (old).—To blacken the eyes. Fr. *les yeux pochés au beurre noir.*

1819. MOORE, *Tom Crib*, 23. With grinders dislodg'd and with peepers both POACH'D.

POACHER, *subs.* (Stock Exchange).—A jobber or broker who deals out of, or is continually changing, his market.

POACHER-COURT, *subs. phr.* (Scots').—The Kirk-Sessions.

*d.*1796. BURNS, *Ep. to J. Rankine.* Ae night lately in my fun, I brought a paitrik to the grun, . . . But, deil-ma care! Somebody tell't the POACHER-COURT The hale affair.

POCKET, *subs.* (colloquial).—1. Money; means; resources: also POCKET-BOOK and POCKET-LINING. Hence, TO BE IN POCKET = to profit; TO BE OUT OF POCKET = to lose; POCKETS TO LET = penniless, BROKE (*q.v.*); TO PUT ONE'S HAND IN ONE'S POCKET = (1) to give money (as in charity), and (2) to spend; TO

HAVE (or CARRY) IN ONE'S POCKET = to control; TO PICK POCKETS = to steal from the person (hence PICK-POCKET = a thief from the person: *cf.* PICK-PURSE); POCKET-PIECE = (1) a show coin, whence (2) anything meretricious or unreal: *see* RHINO.

1598. SHAKSPEARE, *1 Hen. IV.*, iii. 3. I'll be sworn my POCKET was PICKED. *Ibid.* (1603), *Meas. for Meas.*, iii. 2. Is there none . . . to be had now for PUTTING THE HAND IN THE POCKET and extracting it clutched? *Ibid.* (1604) *Winter's Tale*, iv. 3. *Aut.* [PICKING HIS POCKET]. Softly, good sir!

1693. CONGREVE, *Old Batchelor*, ii. 1. *Sir Jo.* But, agad, I'm a little OUT OF POCKET at present. *Sharp.* Pshaw, you can't want a hundred pound. Your word is sufficient anywhere.

1709. DAMPIER, *Voyages*, II. i. 93. For tho there were Fowls to be bought at every house where I lay, yet my POCKET would not reach them.

1738. *Lady's Decoy*, 4. My money is spent; Can I be content With POCKETS depriv'd of their LINING?

1749. SMOLLETT, *Gil Blas* [ROUTLEDGE], 191. As long as his POCKETS were LINED his reception was warm: empty purses meet with fastened doors. *Ibid.*, 216. Not only did we LINE OUR POCKETS with ducats, &c.

1823. MONCRIEFF, *Tom and Jerry*, ii. 5. *Tom.* Clean'd out! both sides; look here—POCKETS TO LET!— . . . and we have stood the nonsense in prime style.

1836. DICKENS, *Pickwick* (1857), 380. This is rayther a change for the worse, Mr. Trotter, as the gen'l'm'n said, wen he got two doubtful shillin's and six penn'orth o' POCKET-PIECES for a good half-crown.

1846. *Punch*, x. 272. It is the work of one moiety of the world to put off certain POCKET-PIECES as though they were sterling coin. *Ibid.*, 268. Cannot see the brassy POCKET-PIECE under the thin wash of a 'Gentleman exterior.'

1856. *Quarterly Review*, CXLV. 315. They . . . have more than once again glutted our markets, and been punished in POCKET.

1857. TROLLOPE, *Barchester Towers* [*Century*]. Dr. Proudie had interest with the government, and the man CARRIED, as it were, Dr. Proudie IN HIS POCKET.

1885. *Queen*, 26 Sep. It is entirely a question of position, POCKET, and inclination.

Adj. (colloquial).—Small: *e.g.*, POCKET-HERCULES = a sturdy dwarf; POCKET-VOLUME = a portable book; POCKET-VENUS (or -PIECE) = a diminutive whore or mistress; POCKET-PARLIAMENT = a town-council, or debating society; POCKET-HELL = a Tartarus of one's own, a Tophet on a minor scale; and so forth.

Verb. (colloquial).—1. To endure; to submit: as to ridicule, insult, or wrong. Hence, TO POCKET ONE'S HORNS = to play the wittol; TO PUT ONE'S PRIDE IN ONE'S POCKET = to suppress one's pride; TO CARRY ONE'S PASSIONS IN ONE'S POCKET = to smother one's feelings; TO POCKET AN AFFRONT = to submit and say nothing.—RAY (1670); B. E. (*c.*1696); GROSE (1785).

1592. HARVEY, *Foure Letters* [GROSART, *Works*, i. 166]. Patience hath trained mee to POCKET-VP more hainous indignities.

1596. SHAKSPEARE, *K. John*, iii. 1. Well, ruffian, I must POCKET-UP these wrongs.

1600. JONSON, *Cynthia's Revels*, iv. When they come in swaggering company, and will POCKET UP anything, may they not properly be said to be white-livered?

1607. HEYWOOD, *Woman Killed*, ii. 3. My master shall not POCKET UP this wrong.

1630. MABBE, *Guzman* [OLIPHANT, ii. 85. We are paid in our own coyne; . . . wrongs are POCKETED].

1659. DAY, *Blind Beggar*, i. 2. Yet the worst boy that feeds on Glosters beef Hold it high scorn to POCKET UP the lye.

1700. FARQUHAR, *Constant Couple*, iii. 1. What! Wear the livery of my king, and POCKET an affront.

1749. SMOLLETT, *Gil Blas* [ROUTLEDGE], 235. Take my advice . . . and POCKET the affront.

1759. GOLDSMITH, *Citizen of the World*, xix. If I calmly POCKET the abuse, I am laughed at.

1772. BRIDGES, *Burlesque Homer*, 72. Like the bold blust'ring Dickey Hunt, He POCKETED THE whole AFFRONT.

1869. *Gent. Mag.*, July, 195. The member had sense enough to POCKET the rebuke, and sat down quietly to enjoy the remaining convivial hours.

2. (common).—To embezzle or steal.

1851. SPENCER, *Social Statics*, 463. They seized the goods of traders, sold them, and POCKETED a large part of the proceeds.

1885. *Daily Telegraph*, 9 Nov. She appears to have been POCKETING money from her employer.

3. (colloquial).—To win.

IF NOT PLEASED PUT HAND IN POCKET AND PLEASE YOURSELF, *phr.* (old).—A retort on grumblers.—RAY (1760).

HE PLAYS AS FAIR AS IF HE'D PICKED YOUR POCKET, *phr.* (old).—Said of rooking gamblers.

POCKET-BOOK DROPPER. *See* DROP-GAME.

POCKET-BOROUGH, *subs. phr.* (political).—A constituency in which votes are controlled by one man: theoretically, since the Reform Act of 1832, a thing of the past; TO POCKET A BOROUGH = to control votes.

1872. ELIOT, *Middlemarch*, xlvi. "When I think of Burke I can't help wishing somebody had a POCKET-BOROUGH to give you, Ladislaw." . . . "POCKET-BOROUGHS would be a fine thing," said Ladislaw, "if they were always in the right pocket, and there were always a Burke at hand."

1882. SCHOULER, *Hist. U. States*, i. 10. He was . . . loyal to some one of the blood families who contended for the honour of POCKETING the borough in which he voted.

POCKETED, *adj.* (racing).—Said of a runner so surrounded that he cannot possibly get out of the press, and push to the front.

POCKET-PISTOL, *subs. phr.* (common).—*See* quots.

1598. SHAKSPEARE, *1 Hen. IV.*, v. 3. *Fal.* But take my PISTOL if thou wilt . . . [*The Prince draws it out and finds it to be a bottle of sack.*]

1834. AINSWORTH, *Rookwood*, IV. viii. He had conveyed a thimbleful of the liquid to his own parched throat, and replenished what Falstaff calls a POCKET-PISTOL which he had about him.

1847. THACKERAY, *Vanity Fair*, I. xxx. A wicker-covered flask or POCKET-PISTOL, containing near a pint of a remarkably sound Cognac brandy.

1861. G. ELIOT, *Silas Marner*, iv. The inclination for a run, encouraged by . . . a draught of brandy from his POCKET-PISTOL at the conclusion of the bargain, was not easy to overcome.

18 [?]. NAYLOR, *Reynard the Fox*, 42. He . . . swigged his POCKET-PISTOL.

1864. BABBAGE, *Life of a Philosopher*, 218. A glass bottle enclosed in a leather case, commonly called a POCKET-PISTOL.

1870. *Orchestra*, 7 Jan. My friend was only saved from fainting by a little sherry which I had happily brought in a POCKET PISTOL.

POCKET-THUNDER, *subs. phr.* (vulgar).—A fart.

POCK-NOOK. TO COME IN ON ONE'S OWN POCK-NOOK, *verb. phr.* (Scots').—*See* quot.

1821. SIR A. WYLIE, *Works*, iii. 61. I CAME IN ON MY OWN POCK-NOOK; as we say in Scotland when a man lives on his own means.

POCK-PUDDING, *subs. phr.* (old Scots').—A bag-pudding: hence, by force of metaphor, a glutton: especially an Englishman: whose appetite the Scotchman affected to despise, even as he hated and envied him for its manifold opportunities.

1730. BURT, *Letters*, i. 13, 138. 'Tis from this notion of the people, that my countrymen not only here, but all over Scotland, are dignified with the title of POKE-PUDDING, which, according to the sense of the word among the natives, signifies a glutton.

.... HERD, *Scot. Songs* (1776), i. 118. They'll fright the fuds of the POCK-PUDS, For mony a buttock bare's coming.

POCKY. *See* POX.

POD, *subs.* (colloquial).—1. A foot: specifically of children. Hence, TO POD = to toddle.

2. A protuberant belly; a CORPORATION (*q.v.*): also POD-BELLY. Hence, POD-BELLIED (PODDY, or IN POD) = (1) fat or stout: of men; and (2) pregnant, LUMPY (*q.v.*): of women. Hence. too, PODGY, PUDGY, and PUDSEY, *See* POT.

1753. RICHARDSON, *Grandison*, vii. 232. He . . . kissed its forehead, its cheek, its lips, its little PUDSEY hands, first one, then the other.

1836. DICKENS, *Boz*, I. The vestry clerk, as everybody knows, is a short, PUDGY, little man in black.

1845. THACKERAY, *Cornhill to Cairo*, iii. The good old man! I wish I had had a shake of that trembling PODGY hand somehow before he went. *Ibid.* (1854), *Newcomes*, vii. She . . . with infinite grace put forward one of the PUDGY little hands, in one of the dirty gloves.

1871. MATHEW ARNOLD, *Friendship's Garland*, v. A blond and disorderly mass of tow-like hair, a PODGY and sanguine countenance.

1885. *Field*, 17 Oct. A good little spaniel if she was not shown so fat and PODGY.

3. (Scots').—A louse: *see* CHATES.

PODGE, *subs.* (colloquial).—1. A fat man or woman.

2. (old).—An epaulette.

1834. MARRYAT, *Peter Simple*, . . . To put it into the wame of yon man with the gold PODGE on his shoulder, who has dared to affront the bluid of McFay.

PODDY, *adj.* (colloquial).—1. Drunk: *see* DRINKS and SCREWED.

2. *See* POD, sense 2.

PODUNK, *subs.* (American).—An imaginary place: in burlesque.

POEM, *subs.* (colloquial).—A foolish appreciative: as a well-cooked dish; a pretty dress; a smart-cut coat, and so forth.

1898. *Pelican*, 19 Feb., 17. Certain newly-shaped pieces, which, instead of being called by old-time English names are now referred to as bifurcated "Watteau visions"—"dreams"—"creations"—POEMS.

1899. *Illustrated Bits*, 25 Mar., 15, 2. Your dress is charming—a perfect POEM in curves.

POET-SUCKER, *subs. phr.* (old colloquial).—A budding poet: *cf.* RABBIT-SUCKER.

1625. JONSON, *Staple of News*, iv. 2. What says my POET-SUCKER? He's chewing his muse's cud.

POET'S-WALK, *subs. phr.* (Eton).—The tea served to Upper Club, on half holidays, in RIVER-WALK.

POGE (POGUE, or POGH). *See* POKE.

POGRAM, *subs.* (old).—A Dissenter; a formalist; a puritanical starch maw-worm; a CREAK-SHOES (*q.v.*).—HOTTEN (1864).

POGY, *adj.* (old).—Drunk. *See* DRINKS and SCREWED.—GROSE (1785); HALLIWELL (1847). [*Cf.* (BEE, 1823) 'POGEY-AQUA—long-shore for—make the grog strong.']

1881. *New York Slang Dict.*, 42. Without his bloss to prevent him from getting POGY.

POINT, *subs.* (colloquial).—In *pl.* = Beauties: of women or children: accepted as applied to the characteristics of animals.

1370. *Torrent of Portugal* [HALLIWELL], 1910. This lady . . . delyvered were, Of men children two. In POYNTES they were gent, And like they were to Ser Torent.

POSSESSION IS NINE (or ELEVEN) POINTS OF THE LAW, *phr.* (colloquial).—Said in deprecation of any attempt to change things as they are, or to seek redress.

1749. SMOLLETT, *Gil Blas* [ROUTLEDGE], 368. At least she had POSSESSION, and that IS NINE POINTS OF THE LAW, though scarcely one of honesty.

PHRASES, more or less colloquial, are numerous. They mostly centre on a figurative use of POINT = (1) a sharp end, or (2) a small but well-defined spot: as a dot, a speck, a hole, a moment, &c. TO SEE (TELL, or MAKE PLAIN) A POINT = to understand (narrate or explicate) the drift, or application of a thing: as an argument, a narrative, a detail; TO CARE (or BE WORTH) BUT A POINT = to esteem lightly; POINT (like PIN, RAP, CENT, &c.) = the smallest standard of value; TO UNTRUSS A POINT = (1) to take down one's breeches, and hence (2) to ease one's bowels; POINT = a tagged lace, used of old to keep doublet and hose together; TO GIVE POINT TO (or BRING A POINT TO BEAR ON) = to emphasise: also TO POINT; TO COME TO THE POINT = to go to the root of a matter; TO BOIL DOWN (or CLOSE) TO A POINT = (1) to condense: as a paragraph, and (2) to balance: as an account; TO STRETCH (or STRAIN) A POINT = to exceed a limit (GROSE); TO MAKE A POINT OF = (1) to strive (or insist) to an end, and (2) to elicit a detail or make a desired impression (also TO PROVE ONE'S POINT); TO GAIN ONE'S POINT = to effect a purpose; TO STAND ON POINTS = to be punctilious; TO BE AT A POINT = to be determined; TO COME TO POINTS = to fight: with swords; TO GIVE POINTS TO = (1) to have (or give) an advantage, and (2) to impart exclusive or valuable information, TO TIP (*q.v.*): also POINTERS; AT ALL POINTS = completely; AT (or IN) THE POINT = (1) ready, and (2) in the act of; IN GOOD POINT = in good condition (Fr. *embonpoint*); IN POINT = apropos; IN POINT OF = as regards; POINT FOR POINT = exactly; TO POINT = completely; BEYOND A POINT = in excess; A POINT IN FAVOUR = an advantage in hand; FULL OF POINT = epigrammatic, effective; THE POINT OF A MATTER = its end or purpose; AT POINT NONPLUS = hard up, IN QUEER ST. (*q.v.*); AT POINT BLANK = immediately, direct. *See* also CUCKOLD'S POINT; POTATO; SPEAR; and V.

1350. *William of Palerne* [E. E. T. S.], 107. Armed AT ALLE POYNTES.

1358. CHAUCER, *Parliament of Fowls* [Chaucer Soc.], 76. [OLIPHANT, *New Eng.*, I. 112. Another verb is dropped in TO THE POYNTE.]

1359. GAYTRIGG [*Relig. Pieces* (E. E. T. S.), 29]. And PROVE HIS POYNT [purpose].

1362. LANGLAND, *Piers Plowmans Crede* [WRIGHT], l. 1676. But for I am a lewed man, Paraunter I myghte Passen par adventure, And in some POYNT erren.

.... *Rom. of Partenay* [E.E.T.S.], 3392. Where she no POINT had of diffame no dais.

.... PALLADIUS, *Husbondrie* [E. E. T. S.], 154. And over yere thai wol been IN GOODE POINTE.

1383. CHAUCER, *Cant. Tales*, Prol., 136. He was a lord ful fat and IN GOOD POYNT. Ibid., *Man of Lawes Tale*, 232. Lordes . . . ye knowen everich on, How that my sone IN POINT is for to lete The holy lawës of our Alkaron. Ibid., *Monkes Tale.* He can al devyse FRO POINT TO POINT, nat o word wol he faille.

*c.*1400. *The Smyth and his Dame* [HAZLITT, *Early Pop. Poet.* iii. 219]. But here A POYNT I GYUE THE, The mayster shalt thov yet be Of all thy craft trvely.

*c.*1440. MERLIN [E. E. T. S.], ii. 350. Amaunt be-thought hym that he myght come neuer IN BETTER POYNT to conquere his Castell. *Ibid.*, i. 106. Thei cowde not in hym espie no POYNTE of covetise. *Ibid.*, iii. 562. The thirde was Monevall, that was a noble knyght, and richely armed OF ALLE POINTES.

*d.*1529. SKELTON, *Bowge of Courte*, 246. But TO THE POYNTE shortely to procede.

1564. UDALL, *Apoph. Eras.*, 8. In matters NOT WORTH A BLEWE POINCT . . . we will spare for no cost.

1580. SIDNEY, *Arcadia*, i. But in what particular POINTS the oracle was, in faith I know not.

1587. HARRISON, *Desc. of England* [OLIPHANT, *New Eng.*, II. 3. Among the Romance words are . . . AT POINT BLANK, &c.].

1590. SPENSER, *Faerie Queene*, I. ii. 12. Full large of limbe and every joint He was, and CARED NOT for God or man A POINT.

1592. SHAKSPEARE, *Mid. Night's Dream*, v. 1, 118. This fellow doth not STAND UPON POINTS. *Ibid.* (1594), *Henry VI.*, iv. 7. Now art thou within POINT-BLANK of our jurisdiction legal. *Ibid.* (1596), *Hamlet*, i. 2. A figure like your father, Armed AT POINT exactly, Cap-a-pe, Appears before them. *Ibid.* (1598), *2 Hen. IV.*, ii. 4. Give me some sack: and, sweetheart, lie thou there. [*Laying down his sword.*] Come we to FULL POINTS here, *Ibid.* (1601), *Henry VIII.*, i. 2. I'll hear him his confessions justify; And POINT BY POINT the treasons of his master he shall again relate. *Ibid.* (1602). *Twelfth Night*, v. 1. Like to the Egyptian thief AT POINT OF DEATH. *Ibid.* (1603), *Measure for Measure*, i. 2. No, indeed, sir . . . you are therein in the right: but TO THE POINT. *Ibid.* (1609), *Tempest*, i. 2, 194. Hast thou . . . Performed TO POINT the tempest that I bade thee.

1611. CHAPMAN, *May-day*, i. 2. I'll to the enemy POINT BLANK; I'm a villain else.

1611. *Bible* [Auth. Ver.], Gen. xxv. 32. And Esau said, Behold, I am AT THE POINT to die.

1616. JONSON, *Devil is an Ass*, iii. 1. If I transgress IN POINT OF manners, afford me Your best construction.

1637. FLETCHER, *Elder Brother*, iii. 1. Young Eustace is a gentleman AT ALL POINTS. *Ibid.* (1647), *Knight of Malta*, i. 1. Thou hurriest me beyond mine honour's POINT.

1648. SUCKLING, *Letters*, 86. A pretty POINT of security, and such a one as all Germany cannot afford.

*d.*1657. BRADFORD, *Letters* [Parker Soc. (1853), ii. 120]. Be AT A POINT with yourselves, to follow not your will but God's will.

1713. STEELE, *Guardian*, 42. There is a kind of drama in the forming of a story, and the manner of . . . POINTING it is the same as in an epigram.

*d.*1732. GAY, *Poems* [*Century*]. Beauty with early bloom supplies Her daughter's cheek, and POINTS her eyes.

*d.*1745. SWIFT, *To a Young Clergyman.* The constant design of both these orators, in all their speeches, was to DRIVE SOME one particular POINT.

1749. JOHNSON, *Human Wishes*, 222. He left the name at which the world grew pale To POINT a moral, or adorn a tale.

1749. SMOLLETT, *Gil Blas* [ROUTLEDGE], 110. Set their faces POINT-BLANK against the tastes of the public; and as a proof of this there were a thousand cases IN POINT. *Ibid.*, 120. Blanche . . . was armed AT ALL POINTS with the weapons of a most perfect beauty.

1759. STERNE, *Tristam Shandy*, i. 9. Every author has a way of his own in BRINGING HIS POINTS TO BEAR.

1760. SMOLLETT, *Greaves*, iii. They would have COME TO POINTS immediately had not the gentlemen interposed.

1779. SHERIDAN, *Critic*, ii. 1. When history . . . furnishes anything like A CASE IN POINT . . . an author will take advantage of it . . . It is a received POINT among poets that . . . you may fill up with a little love at your own discretion.

1790. BRUCE, *Source of Nile*, I. 371. Many disadvantages IN POINT OF climate.

1814. WORDSWORTH, *Excursion*, vi. Our Swain, A very hero till his POINT WAS gained.

1819. GRENVILLE, *Memoirs*, 3 Feb. Both her letters and her conversation are FULL OF POINT.

1830. SOUTHEY, *Bunyan*, 42. He maintained, which indeed was THE POINT AT ISSUE, that the opinions held that day by the Quakers were the same that the Ranters had held long ago.

*d.*1832. CRABBE, *Works*, I. 93. Not one grief was POINTED by remorse.

1841. D'ISRAELI, *Amen. of Lit.*, II. 352. An epigram now is a short satire, Closing with a POINT of wit.

1843. MACAULAY, *Clive* [*Century*]. Shah Alum had invested Patna, and was ON THE POINT OF proceeding to storm.

1847. TENNYSON, *Princess*, iii. I . . . found her there AT POINT to move.

1847. BRONTE, *Jane Eyre*, xi. I suppose the POINT of the exhibition lay in hearing the notes of love and jealousy warbled with the lisp of childhood; and in very bad taste that POINT was.

1870. MEDBERY, *Men and Mysteries of Wall St.*, 83. If the operator has a good POINT, he has a sure thing . . . In other words, . . . a bit of secret information concerning a stock, whether an extra dividend to be declared, a bull movement organizing, an emission of new shares to take place, or some other cause at work, or likely to be at work, which will seriously affect prices.

1883. *American*, vi. 383 [*Century*]. Any average Eton boy could GIVE POINTS TO his Holiness in the matter of Latin verses.

1884. *New York Herald*, 4 Nov. I will give him a POINTER that will be of great benefit to you in your business.

1888. *New York Mercury*, 7 Aug. All things taken into consideration, there never was a bolder voyage over the Atlantic than this made by the 'Romer,' all for the sake of a few POINTS in news.

1888. *Denver Republican* [*Americanisms*]. There is a big POINTER for those gentlemen who cannot restrain their sporting proclivities in these sentences.

1888. *Pittsburg Times*, 26 Jan. BOILED DOWN TO A fine POINT, bondsmen are in demand.

1889. *Pall Mall Gaz.*, 23 Sep., 2, 1. The smallest chit of a dressmaker's apprentice could give her POINTS about modern dress and its present rational tendency.

1892. *Ally Sloper's Half Holiday*, 19 Mar., 94, 2. Harry Payne is a clown of the old school, 'tis true, but still he can give POINTS and an easy licking to most, if not all, of his modern rivals.

1901. *Daily Tel.*, 19 Oct., 7, 1, 2. Would any person who was not mad say he was not himself? I have MADE MY POINT.

POINTER, *subs.* (American).—1. *See* POINT.

2. (venery).—The *penis*: *see* PRICK, and *cf.* SPORTSMAN'S TOAST.

POINT-OF-ATTRACTION, *subs. phr.* (venery).—The female *pudendum*: *see* MONOSYLLABLE.

1782. STEVENS, *Songs Comic and Satyrical*, 184. Beneath, where in centre Love buckles her Zone, The POINT OF ATTRACTION we place.

POISON, *subs.* (common).—1. Drink; TIPPLE (*q.v.*). NOMINATE YOUR POISON = 'What will you drink?': *cf.* quot. 1362, where POYSON = a draught, a drink.

1362. LANGLAND, *Piers Plowman*, C. xxi. 52. And with a pole POYSON putten to hus lippes, And beden hym drynke.

*d.*1641. SUCKLING, *Brennoralt*, ii. 1. *Mar.* Come, your liquor and your stanzas . . . *Vil.* Since it must be, Give me the POISON then. [*Drinks and spits.*]

1827. LYTTON, *Pelham*, xlix. Champagne with the taste of a gooseberry, and hock with the properties of a pomegranate . . . young men . . . purchase POISON at a dearer rate than the most medicine-loving hypochondriac in England.

*c.*1863. ARTEMUS WARD [*Works* (1890) 160]. I found Dr. Schwazey, a leadin citizen, in a state of mind which showed that he'd bin histin in more'n his share of PIZEN.

1867. PINKERTON, *Great Adams Express Robbery*, 41. It's a cold day when Barney O'Hara will let a bog-trotter go dry. Name your POISON.

1886-96. MARSHALL, '*Pomes' from the Pink 'Un* ['The Garret'], 20. 'My favourite POISON,' murmurs she, 'Is good old gin.'

1888. MILLIKEN, *'Arry Ballads*, 50. Wot's yer PISON, old pal?

2. (common).—Anything unpleasant. Whence TO HATE LIKE POISON = to detest.

1530. PALSGRAVE, *Lang. Fran.*, 259. HATE me LIKE POYSON.

1837. BARHAM, *Ingoldsby Leg.* 'Knight and the Lady.' And both HATING brandy, LIKE what some call PISON.

1847. ROBB, *Squatter Life*, 60. It got to be parfect PIZEN to hear.

POISONED, *adj.* (old).—Pregnant; LUMPY (*q.v.*).—B. E. (*c.*1696); GROSE (1785).

POISON-PATED, *adj. phr.* (old).—Red-haired.—GROSE (1785).

POJAM, *subs.* (Harrow).—A poem: set as an exercise: a PORTMANTEAU-WORD (*q.v.*).

POKE (POGE, POGH, or POGUE), *subs.* (common).—1. A pocket; a bag; a sack; a pouch; a purse: generic: *cf.* PETER.—B. E. (*c.*1696); MARTIN (1754); GROSE (1785); VAUX (1819). Also (corrupt) PALKE and PAKKE.

ENGLISH SYNONYMS.—Bounge; brigh; bung; busy-sack; carpet-swab; cly; cod; haddock; hoxter; kick; peter; pit; roger (also = portmanteau); roundabout; skin; sky (or skyrocket = rhyming); slash; suck.

FRENCH SYNONYMS. — *Une baguenaude; une balade* (*ballade*, or *valade*: *avaler* = to swallow); *un bouchon; une felouse (felouze, filoche, fouille*, or *fouillouse*); *une fondrière; un four* (or *un four banal*); *une grande; un gueulard* (or *une gueularde*); *une louche; une morlingue; une parfonde* (or *profonde*); *une prophête; un porte-morningue* (or *porte-mornif*).

ITALIAN SYNONYMS.—*Fegatello; figadelto; foglia* (= Fr. *fouillouse*: MICHEL); *santa; scarsello* (= Fr. *escarcelle*); *scarpa; tuosa; zavatta* (= Fr. *savate*).

1362. LANGLAND, *Piers Plowman Creed* [WRIGHT (1847), line 791]. Trewely, frere, quath I tho, To tellen the the sothe, There is no peny in my PAKKE To payen for my mete. Ibid., *Vision*, l. 165. A POKE full of pardons.

1383. CHAUCER [SKEAT, *Works* (1894), 'Reeves Tale,' l. 358]. And in the floor, with nose and mouth to-broke, They walwe as doon two pigges in a POKE.

14 [?]. *Douce MS.*, 52. When me profereth the pigge, opon the POGHE.

1514. MORE, *A Sergeaunt wold lerne*, &c. [HAZLITT, *Early Pop. Poet.*, iii. 128]. They roule and romble, they turne and tumble, as pygges do in a POKE.

d. 1529. SKELTON, *Bowge of Courte* [DYCE, i. 48]. I have a stoppynge oyster in my POKE.

*d.*1549. BORDE [?], *Mylner of Abyngton* [HAZLITT, *Early Pop. Poet.*, iii. 106]. Me thinke our POKE is waxen light.

1600. SHAKSPEARE, *As You Like It*, ii. 7. And then he drew a dial from his POKE.

1662. FULLER, *Worthies*, 63. Some will have the English so called from wearing a pouch or POAKE (a bag to carry their baggage in) behind their backs.

1678. BUTLER, *Hudibras*, III. i. Had rifled all his POKES and fobs.

1868. *Temple Bar*, xxiv. 538. I prigged an old woman's POKE on the fly.

1879. HORSLEY, *Macm. Mag.*, xl. 504. A POGE, with over five quid in it.

1883. *Echo*, 25 Jan., 2, 3. The POKE, which a pickpocket glories in having appropriated, is the Saxon bag or purse.

1888. *Echo*, 18 Dec. He heard a woman demanding money of the accused, who replied, "What have you done with the £2 I gave you out of the POGE?"

2. (thieves').—Stolen property.

3. (colloquial).—A thrust or push; a dig with the fingers; 'a blow with the fist' (GROSE, 1785). As a *verb.* POKE has always been literary.

1849. BULWER, *Caxtons*, xvii. I. 'But,' concluded Uncle Jack, with a sly look, and giving me a POKE in the ribs.

4. (venery).—(1) An act of coition, and (2) a mistress: a GOOD (or BAD) POKE = an expert (or the reverse) at the game. Also as *verb* = to copulate: *cf.* PUSH and *see* GREENS and RIDE. Whence POKE- (or POKING-) HOLE = the female *pudendum. See* POKER.

1709. DURFEY, *Pills to Purge Melancholy* . . . May I never more POGUE the hone of a woman.

5. (colloquial). — A poke-bonnet.

1876. G. ELIOT, *Daniel Deronda*, xxiv. A grey frieze livery, and a straw POKE.

6. (American).—A dawdler; a LAZY-BONES (*q.v.*).

*d.*1891. LOWELL, *Fitz Adam's Story* [*Century*]. They're only worn by some old-fashioned POKES.

COLLOQUIALISMS are: — TO POKE ABOUT (or ONE'S NOSE INTO) = (1) to meddle, and (2) to busy oneself aimlessly or officiously; whence POKE-NOSE = a meddler, and as *adj.* = offensively intrusive; TO POKE FUN = to ridicule; TO POKE BOGEY = to humbug; TO BUY A PIG IN A POKE (*see* PIG); TO POKE FLY (tailors') = to show how; TO POKE A SMIPE (old: *cf.* MEDICAL GREEK) = to smoke a pipe: *see* MARROW-SKYING; TO POKE BORAK (*see* BORAK).

1837. BARHAM, *Ingoldsby Legends*, I. 280. POKING YOUR FUN at us plain-dealing folks.

1838. NEAL, *Charcoal Sketches*, III. 124. Don't you be POKING FUN at me now, Judge; this is too serious a matter.

1853. THACKERAY, *Barry Lyndon*, i. 'What's the Latin for gooseberry, Redmond?' says she. She was always POKING her FUN, as the Irish phrase it.

1857. KINGSLEY, *Two Years Ago*. POKING ABOUT where we had no business.

1862. *New York Tribune*, 7 June. The Senate refused to tax watches, plate, and dogs. The main reason for this refusal is the large expense of collecting, and the POKE-NOSE scrutiny involved in levying such taxes.

*d.*1865. *Life of Abraham Lincoln*, 137. It was often said of Mr. Lincoln that he liked nothing so much as to POKE FUN at his advisers in the Cabinet, but those who could appreciate him knew very well, what a depth of wisdom and earnest lay under the slight drapery of jest.

POKER, *subs.* (old).—1. A sword; a CHEESE-TOASTER (*q.v.*).—B. E. (*c.*1696); GROSE (1785).

2. (venery).—The *penis*: *see* PRICK. Hence, TO BURN ONE'S POKER = to get a pox or clap, GROSE (1785); and POKER-BREAKER = a married woman.

3. (Oxford).—A BEDEL (*q.v.*) carrying a silver mace before the Vice-Chancellor; also the mace itself: also HOLY POKER. Frequently used as an oath.

1841. *Rime of the New-Made Baccalere.* Around, around, all, all around, On seats with velvet lined, Sat Heads of Houses in a row, And Deans and College Dons below, With a POKER or two behind.

1853. BRADLEY, *Verdant Green*, vii. A sort of young procession—the Vice-Chancellor and Yeoman-bedels. The silver maces carried by the latter gentlemen, made them by far the most showy part of the procession. *Ibid.* Tom is the bell that you hear at nine each night; the Vice has to see that he is in proper condition, and, as you have seen, goes out with his POKERS for that purpose.

1865. *Cornhill*, Feb., 225. The heads of houses and university officers attend [St. Mary's] in their robes, and form a stately procession to and from the church. The Vice-Chancellor is escorted by his mace-bearers, familiarly called POKERS, to and from his residence.

1870. *London Figaro*, 8 Oct., 2, 2. The bedels of a University are very important personages, although derisive undergraduates familiarly term them HOLY POKERS.

4. (old).—A single-barrelled gun.

5. (fencing).—A rough fencer.

6. (old).—'One that conveys coals (at Newcastle) in sacks, on Horseback.'—B. E. (*c.*1696).

OTHER COLLOQUIAL USAGES: —FORE-POKERS (old) = 'Aces and kings at cards' (GROSE, 1785); OLD POKER = the devil: *see* SKIPPER; BY THE HOLY POKER (or IRON) = an oath: also, BY THE HOLY POKER AND TUMBLING TOM: *cf.* POKER, *subs.* 3; JEWS-POKER (*q.v.*), and add quot. 1899; TO CHANT THE POKER = to exaggerate, to swagger, 'to put on SIDE' (*q.v.*): Fr. *se gonfler le jabot*, and *faire son lard*.

*d.*1797. WALPOLE, *Letters*, iv. 359. As if OLD POKER was coming to take them away.

1836. MARRYAT, *Midshipman Easy*, xxvii. "BY DE HOLY POKER, Massa Easy, but that terrible sort of gale the other day, anyhow."

1840. *Comic Almanack*, 'Tom the Devil,' 214. A hotel's the place for me! I've thried em all, from the Club-house at Kilkinny, to the Clarendon, and, BY THE HOLY POKER, never wish mysilf worse luck than such cantonments!

1886. R. L. STEVENSON, *Kidnapped*, 169. I swear UPON THE HOLY IRON I had neither art nor part.

1897. MITFORD, *Romance Cape Frontier*, I. viii. "I never saw anything to beat that—BY THE HOLY POKER I never did."

1899. WHITEING, *John St.*, 210. 'Does the JEW'S POKER, Saturdays,' says Low Covey, 'tho' it's a poor lay summer-time' . . . 'A JEW'S POKER is a Christian person who attends to Jewish fires on the Sabbath-day.

POKERISH, *adj.* (colloquial).—1. Stiff; reserved: hence POKERISHLY.

1867. BROUGHTON, *As a Flower*, xxxvi. I'm afraid I'm interrupting a pleasant tête-a-tête,' says the old lady POKERISHLY.

1883. *Century Mag.*, xxxvi. 35. Stiff and POKERISH, Ella called her.

2. (American). — Frightful: *cf.* OLD POKER.

1864. LOWELL, *Fireside Travels*, 144. There is something POKERISH about a deserted dwelling, even in broad daylight.

POKER-TALK, *subs. phr.* (common).—Gossip; fireside chit-chat.

1885. MRS. EDWARDES, *Girton Girl*, ii. Gaston rattled forth this specimen of POKER-TALK lightly.

POKY (or POKING), *adj.* (colloquial).—Cramped; stuffy; shabby; stupid: a general depreciative. Also POKE-HOLE.

*d.*1771. GRAY, *Works*, II. Letter 36. Bred to some POKING profession.

1850. KINGSLEY, *Alton Locke*, xxiv. I shall be shoved down into some POKING little country-curacy, without a chance of making play before the world.

1855. THACKERAY, *Newcomes*, lvii. The ladies were in their POKIEST old head-gear.

1856. BEECHER-STOWE, *Dred*, I. 138. That's the way we girls studied at school, except a few POKEY ones, who wanted to be learned.

1864. *Studies for Stories*, I. 67. Amelia made me believe that there was plenty of property in ther family, but that her sisters had a natural liking for living in that POKEY way, and for having no footman.

1882. ANSTEY, *Vice-Versa*, iv. They've a POKY little house in Brompton somewhere, and there was no dancing.

POLE, *subs.* (printers').—1. The weekly account for wages.

2. (venery). — The *penis.* Hence POLING (or POLE-WORK) = copulation.

Verb. (American University).—To study hard.

UP THE POLE, *phr.* (military).—In good report: also goody-goody; strait-laced.

2. (common).—Over-matched; in difficulty.

1886-96. MARSHALL, '*Pomes' from the Pink 'Un* ['The Word of a Policeman'], 73. But, one cruel day, behind two slops he chanced to take a stroll, And . . . he heard himself alluded to as being UP THE POLE.

1899. *Daily Mail*, 29 March, 5, I. When there are nineteen Frenchmen to four Englishmen they were slightly UP THE POLE. Nineteen, you know, were rather too many for them.

LIKE A ROPE-DANCER'S POLE, *phr.* (old).—'Lead at both ends; a saying of a stupid sluggish fellow.'—GROSE (1785).

POLE-CAT, *subs. phr.* (old).—A whore: also a general reproach.

1596. SHAKSPEARE, *Merry Wives*, iv. 2. You witch! you hag! you POLECAT!

1607. DEKKER, *Northward Hoe*, i. I. Your captains were wont to take their leaves of their London POLE-CATS (their wenches I mean, sir), at Dunstable.

POLE-WORK, *subs.* (colloquial).—A long, tedious business; COLLAR-WORK (*q.v.*).

See POLE.

POLICEMAN, *subs.* (common).—1. A fly: esp. a BLUE-BOTTLE (*q.v.*), which (in turn) = a constable.

1864. E. D. FORGUES, *Revue des deux Mondes*, 15 September, 470. Quand celui-ci [un *prig* de Londres] appelle un mouche un POLICEMAN, et quand celui—là qualifie de "mouche" un sergent de ville, l'un et l'autre font même rapprochement, bien qu'en seus inverse.

2. (thieves').—A mean fellow; a spy.

POLICE-NIPPERS, *subs. phr.* (common).—Handcuffs or leg-irons: *see* DARBY'S BANDS.

POLICY, *verb.* (American). — To gamble in lottery numbers: *see* quot. Also as *subs.*: whence POLICY-SHOP = a lottery office.

1882. MCCABE, *New York*, xxxix. POLICY-DEALING is one degree lower in infamy than the lottery business . . . The game consists in betting on certain numbers within the range of the lottery schemes being drawn at the noon or night drawing. Seventy-eight numbers usually make up the lottery-scheme, and the policy player can take any three of these numbers and bet that they will be drawn, either singly, or in such combinations as he may select. The single numbers may come out anywhere in the drawing, but the combination must appear as he writes it in making his bet. He pays one dollar for the privilege of betting, and receives a written slip containing the number or numbers on which he bets. If a single number is chosen and drawn, he wins 5 dollars; two numbers constitute a 'saddle,' and if both are drawn the player wins from 24 to 32 dollars; three numbers make a 'gig,' and win from 150 to 225 dollars; four numbers make a 'horse,' and win 640 dollars. A 'capital straddle' is a bet that two numbers will be among the first three drawn, and wins 500 dollars.

POLISH, *verb.* (common).—To thrash; TO PUNISH (*q.v.*).

TO POLISH OFF, *verb. phr.* (colloquial).—To finish out of hand; to get rid of summarily: as a dinner, or an adversary.

1834. DOWLING, *Othello Travestie*, i. 6. Just wait awhile, And may be I won't POLISH you OFF in style.

1836. DICKENS, *Pickwick*, xxvi. "Mayn't I POLISH that ere Job OFF, iu the front garden?" said Mr. Weller. "Certainly not," replied Mr. Pickwick.

1847. THACKERAY, *Vanity Fair*, xxxiv. 246. Bob had his coat off at once —he stood up to the Banbury man for three minutes, and POLISHED HIM OFF in four rounds easy. *Ibid.* (1855), *Newcomes*, II. 252. He expressed repeatedly a desire that some one would speak ill of the Colonel, so that he might have an opportunity of POLISHING THAT INDIVIDUAL OFF in about two seconds.

1862. *Cornhill Mag.*, vi. 643. I used to steal something and take it to the marine-store dealers. . . . As I got on in thieving, I left home, and was soon POLISHED OFF into a first-class wire.

1870. *Sunday Times*, 21 May. If you keep a sharp look-out you may perchance see a critic, for, unfortunately, the Royal Academy cannot be POLISHED OFF at a private view like other exhibitions.

1888. BOLDREWOOD, *Robbery Under Arms*, i. He rolled into a man big enough to eat him, and POLISHED him OFF.

TO POLISH (PICK, or EAT) A BONE, *verb. phr.* (common).—To make a meal.—GROSE (1785).

TO POLISH THE KING'S IRON WITH THE EYEBROWS, *verb. phr.* (old).—'To look through the iron-grated windows of a prison.' —GROSE (1785).

POLITE. See DO, *verb.*, sense 4.

POLKA. THE MATRIMONIAL POLKA, *subs. phr.* (venery).— Copulation: *see* GREENS and RIDE.

POLL, *subs.* (Cambridge University). —1. The ordinary examination for the B.A. degree: as distinguished from the Honours examination. Whence (2) a student taking the "pass" degree without "Honours." [Gr. *Hoi polloi* = the many.] Hence, TO GO OUT IN THE POLL = to take an ordinary degree. Also POLL-MAN and POLL-DEGREE.

1855. BRISTED, *Five Years in an English University*, 62. Several declared that they would GO OUT IN THE POLL.

1884. PAYN, *Cornhill*, Ap., 370. I took my degree, however—a first-class POLL; which my good folks at home believed to be an honourable distinction.

1889. *Academy*, 2 Mar. It is related of some Cambridge POLL-MAN that he was once so ill-advised as to desert a private tutor.

3. (nautical).—A woman: generic. Hence (specifically) = a prostitute. POLLY-HOOD = a state of wantonness (Walpole accused the ladies of his day of POLLY-HOOD, 'more fond than virtuous'); TO POLL UP = (1) to court; and (2) to live in concubinage.

1893. EMERSON, *Lippo*, ix. They began to give him money . . . a POLL gave him a bob.

4. (old).—A wig.—HALL (1708); GROSE (1785).

5. (thieves').—A decoy bitch. *See* PILL AND POLL.

Verb. 1. *See* PILL AND POLL.

2. (sporting).—To beat; to distance.

3. (common).—To snub.

TO POLL OFF, *adj. phr.* (common). — To get drunk: *see* DRINKS and SCREWED.

POLLARD, *subs.* (old).—A counterfeit coin, worth about a halfpenny, made abroad, and smuggled into England, *temp.* Ed. I. [Said to be named after the original maker.]

c.1350. FABYAN, *Chronicle*, ii. He sodeynly dampned certayne coynes of money, called POLLARDES.

POLLER. 1. *See* PILL AND POLL. 2. (old).—*See* quot.

1676. *Warning for Housekeepers*, 4. They carry in one hand a dark Glim, and in the other a POLLER, which is a dark Lanthorn and a Pistol.

POLL-PARROT, *subs. phr.* (common). —A talkative woman: also POLL and POLLY.

1865. DICKENS, *Our Mutual Friend*, xii. If it warn't wasting good sherry wine on you, I'd chuck this at you for POLL PARROTING with this man.

POLLRUMPTIOUS, *adj.* (colloquial). —Restive; unruly; foolishly confident.

POLLY, *subs.* (tramps').—1. Used as in quot.

1893. EMERSON, *Signor Lippo*, XIV. All I get is my kip and a clean mill tog, a pair of POLLIES and a stoock, and what few medazas I can make out of the lodgers and needles.

2. (common).—Apollinaris water.

1894. G. EGERTON, *Keynotes*, 59. The draught is transformed into lukewarm water, or POLLY without the 'dash' in it.

1894. *Illustrated Bits*, 31 Mar., 10, 3. What is more gratifying—he could drink. Not sips of weak tea, or "POLLY," but the Extra Sec of the right year, and plenty of it.

TO DO POLLY, *verb. phr.* (American prison).—To pick oakum; TO MILL DOLL (*q.v.*).— MATSELL (1859).

POLLYCON, *subs. phr.* (American students').—Political economy.

POLT, *subs.* (old). — A blow; a stroke.—B. E. (*c.*1696); GROSE (1785).

1782. D'ARBLAY, *Cecilia*, II. ix. Give me a good POLT of the head.

POLTROON, *subs.* (old: now recognised). — A coward. — B. E. (*c.*1696).

1595. SHAKSPEARE, *3 Henry VI.*, i. 1. Patience is for POLTROONS such as he.

1778. SHERIDAN, *The Rivals*, iv. 1. Out, you POLTROON!—you ha'n't the valour of a grasshopper.

POLTY (or **DOLTY**), *adj.* (cricketers'). —Easy.

POLYPHEMUS, *subs.* (venery).— The *penis: see* PRICK. [The MONOPS, the ONE-EYED ONE.]

POMMEL. *See* PUMMEL.

POMPADOURS (THE), *subs.* (military).—The late 56th Regiment of Foot, now the 2nd Batt. Essex Regiment. [Tradition relates that, when facings were changed in 1764, the crimson not wearing well, the Colonel desired Blue. The authorities, however, objected, and he chose purple, a favourite colour of Madame de Pompadour, the mistress of Louis XV. of France.] Also "THE SAUCY POMPADOURS."

POMPAGINIS. AQUA POMPAGINIS, *subs. phr.* (old). — Pure water: *see* AQUA.—GROSE (1785).

POMPEY'S - PILLAR. POMPEY'S - PILLAR TO A STICK OF SEALING-WAX, *phr.* (old).—A fanciful bet: *cf.* ALL LOMARD-STREET TO A CHINA ORANGE, and CHELSEA-COLLEGE TO A SENTRY-BOX.

POMPKIN. *See* PUMPKIN.

POM-POM, *subs.* (military).—A quick-firing gun, of light construction, much used in South Africa 1899–190[?]. [Onomatopeia.]

PONCE (POUNCEY or **POUNCE-SHICER)**, *subs.* (common). — A harlot's KEEP (*q.v.*), or bully. Hence PONCESS = a woman supporting another woman by prostitution.

ENGLISH SYNONYMS. — Abbot (croziered abbot, or abbot on the Cross); apple-knight (-monger or -squire); apron-knight (or -squire); bouncer; brother of the gusset; bruiser; buck; bully; captain; carpet - knight; cock-bawd (or -pimp); cunt-pensioner; faker; family-man; fancy-bloke (-cove or -man); fancy-Joseph; fish; fucker; gamester; jack-gagger; kaffir; kiddy; knight of the petticoat; lap-priest; mack (or mackerel); mash; meat-merchant; pensioner; petti-coat-pensioner; prosser; smock servant; servant; squire of the body (or the petticoat); stallion; Sunday-man (-cove, or -bloke); twat-faker.

FRENCH SYNONYMS. — *Un adonis; un advocatière* (RABE-LAIS); *un Alphonse* (generic: hence *Alphonsisme* = the calling of a cunt-pensioner (*cf.* DUMAS FILS, who classicised the term in his *M. Alphonse*); *un amant de cœur* (RABELAIS); *un aqua-rium* (*de poissons : un maquereau, &c.*); *un architriclin* (DE NERCIAT); *un Arthur* (generic); *un baigne-dans-le-beurre* (deriv. = CREAM, *q.v.*); *une barbe; un barbeau* (deriv. are *une barbille* and *un barbillon*); *un barbise; un bébé; un bichon; un bonneau;*

un bordelier (RABELAIS); *un bouffeur de blanc* (*blanc* = CREAM, *q.v.*); *un boxonneur; un bras-de-fer; un brochet; un caprice; une casquette à trois ponts* (in allusion to the tall three-storied silk cap of the French ponce); *un chalant* (RABELAIS); *un chasseur* (DE NEUVILLE); *un chevalier de bidet* (or *de guiche*); *un chiquette de blanc; un con-combre; un coquardeau; un costel; un courratier* (RABE-LAIS); *un cousin; un cousin de Moïse* (spec. a man who marries a whore); *un dauphin; un Désgrieux* (PREVOST); *un des-sons; un dos* (*un dos vert*, or *un dos azur*, BRUANT); *un dresseur de femmes; un écaillé* (*i.e.,* scaled like a fish: cf. *poisson*); *un embaucher; un entremetteur; un faraud; un farfadet* (XVIII. Century); *un fish* (cf. *poisson*); *un foulard rouge; un gandelin* (RABELAIS); *un gentilhomme sous-marin = macquereau* or *dos vert; un goujon; un goyer* (RABELAIS); *un greluchon* (= half ponce, half client); *un guiche; un lacro-muche; un mac* (*macque, mac-quet = maquereau*); *un mac-choux; un machabé; un macro-tin; un mangeur de blanc; un maquereau* (VILLON, RABELAIS, VOLTAIRE); *un maquignon bidoche; un marcheur; un marlou* (*marloupatte, marloupin,* or *marlousier;* JEAN RICHEPIN); *un marquant; un mec* (also *un mec de la guiche: les guiches* = kiss-curls worn by fancy men); *un meublant; un monsieur à nageoires* (or *à ronflaquettes*); *un neg à viande chande* (= meat merchant); *un patenté; un poisson* (*un poisson d'Avril* or *un poisson frayeur*); *un porte - nageoires; un qui va à*

épinards (cf. GREENS); *un rele-veur de fumeuse; un rétrousseur; un roi de la mer; un rouflaquette* (in allusion to the kiss-curl); *un roule-en-cul* (= CUNT-PEN-SIONER); *un rufien* (old); *un sacristain* (see ABBESS); *un servi-teur; un soixante-six; un soute-neur; un tête de patère; un trimbaleur de rouchies* (or *de carne pour la sèche*); *un valet de cœur; un visqueux.*

1851-61. MAYHEW, *Lond. Lab., &c*, III. 364. They are a queer set we have to do with in the ranks. The 'POUNCEYS' (the class I have alluded to as fancy-men, called 'POUNCEYS' by my present informant) are far the worst.

1887. HENLEY, *Villon's Good Night*, 1. You PONCES good at talking tall.

POND (THE), *subs.* (common).— The sea: spec. the North Atlantic Ocean: also HERRING-POND (*q.v.*); THE BIG (or GREAT) POND (*q.v.*); and THE PUDDLE (*q.v.*).—GROSE (1785); BEE (1823).

1722. *England's Path to Wealth*. A finer country, cheaper and better food . . . easier rents and taxes, will tempt many . . . to cross the HERRING-POND.

1729. GAY, *Polly*, i. 1. Bless us all! how little are our customs known on this side the HERRING-POND.

1838. HALIBURTON, *Clockmaker*, 3 S. xviii. He is . . . the best live one that ever cut dirt this side of the BIG POND, or t'other side either.

1863. *Story of a Lancashire Thief*, 8. A swell prig who had hooked it from London to escape being slowed, and maybe sent over the HERRING-POND.

1883. SALA, *Living London*, 204. Next time Miss Ward crosses the BIG POND, I . . . hope that she will cross the Rockies.

1890. *Tit-Bits*, 29 Mar., 388, 3. I may tell you that I came over the BIG POND for poisoning from jealousy. It wasn't for petty thefts

1901. *D. Telegraph*, 7 Oct., 3, 5. Two gentlemen who betrayed a strong American accent . . . offered to buy the house as it stood in order "to lift it bodily across THE POND."

PONG, *subs.* (common).—Beer: also PONGELOW or PONGELLORUM: as *verb.* (1) = to drink: *see* SWIPES.

Verb. (theatrical).—2. To vamp a part, or (circus) = to perform; and (3) to talk, TO GAS (*q.v.*).

PONGO, *subs.* (showmen's). — A monkey.

PONIARD (or **PONYARD**), *subs.* (old: long recognised).—A dagger.— B. E. (*c.*1696).

PONTE, *subs.* (showmen's).—Twenty shillings. [It. *pondo* = pound.]

PONTIE, *adv.* (common). — On credit; 'on TICK' (*q.v.*).

PONTIUS PILATE, *subs. phr.* (common).—A pawn-broker.—GROSE (1785).

PONTIUS PILATE'S BODY-GUARD, *subs. phr.* (military).—The late 1st Regiment of Foot, now The Royal Scots, the oldest regiment in the service. [When the *Régiment de Douglas*, and in the French service [1633-78], the officers disputed with the Picardy regiment about the antiquity of their corps. The Picardy men declared they were on duty on the night of the Crucifixion, when the colonel of the 1st Foot replied, "If we had been on guard, we should not have slept at our posts."—BREWER.] — GROSE (1785).

PONTIUS PILATE'S COUNSELLOR, *subs. phr.* (legal).—A briefless barrister: Fr. *avocat ae Pilate.* [Who, like Pilate, 'can find no (just) cause.']

PONTO, *subs.* (school).—New bread-crumbs kneaded into a pellet.

1900. *St. James's Gazette*, 15 Mar., 'Arnoldiana.' He [Mathew Arnold] was placed at the end of the great school, and, amid howls and jeers, pelted with a rain of PONTOS for some time.

PONY, *subs.* (old).—1. A bailiff: spec. an officer accompanying a debtor on a day's liberty.

2. (common).—Money. Hence, as *verb.* (TO POST THE PONY or TO PONY UP) = to pay; to settle. *See* POST, *verb.*—GROSE (1785); VAUX (1819); BEE (1823).

1823. MONCRIEFF, *Tom and Jerry* [DICK], 6. It's every thing now o'days—to be able to flash the screens—sport the rhino—show the needful—POST THE PONY—nap the rent—stump the pew.

1824. *Atlantic Mag.*, I. 343. Every man . . . vociferously swore that he had PONIED UP his 'quarter.'

1834. AINSWORTH, *Rookwood* (1864), 240. I shan't let you off so easily this time, depend upon it. Come, POST THE PONY, or take your measure on that sod.

1838. J. C. NEAL, *Charcoal Sketches* [BARTLETT]. It was my job to pay all the bills. "Salix, PONY UP at the bar, and lend us a levy."

*c.*1861-5. *Song*, 'A Portland Conscript' [B]. We hadn't no rich parients to PONY UP the tin, So we went unto the Provost, and there were mustered in.

1876. *New York Herald*, 16 Mar. General Rice is a bachelor of expensive habits . . . you must PONY UP and keep him going, for he can't live on less than 10,000 dollars a year.

3. (common). — Twenty-five pounds sterling: *see* RHINO.

1818. GREVILLE, *Memoirs*, 15 Aug. He is equally well amused whether the play is high or low, but the stake he prefers is fives and PONIES.

1837. DANCE, *The Country Squire*, i. 3. *Geo.* Look here, old man! (*Holding up note.*) *Hor.* Well, to be sure a fifty is two PONIES; and the hair will grow again.

1842. *Comic Almanack*, 327. A Mayor who, though he makes of Fifties—cronies, Yet has a most maternal love for PONIES.

1849. THACKERAY, *Pendennis*, lxi. The five-and-twenty pounds, or PONY, which the exemplary Baronet had received.

1857. KINGSLEY, *Two Years Ago*, xviii. The bet of a PONY which he offers five minutes afterwards.

1870. *Figaro*, 1 June. I have pulled off a couple of PONIES on the event.

1880. SIMS, *Three Brass Balls*, Pledge xv. "Here's a PONY for the young 'un, and directly I get a bit straight I'll send you some more."

1883. BRADDON, *Phantom Fortune*, xli. Sheafs of bank notes were being exchanged for counters which represented divers values, from the respectable PONY to the modest chip.

1892. *Pall Mall Gaz.*, 23 Mar., 6, 3. Mr. Kisch said the bets were two PONIES The Master of the Rolls: What? Two what? Mr. Kisch said a PONY was £25.

1898. *Pink 'Un and Pelican*, 155. He would write a long letter . . . and reproach him for not sending the PONY he had been three times asked for.

4. (American school).—A translation; a BOHN (*q.v.*); a CRIB (*q.v.*): also as *verb.*

1832. *Tour Through College*, 30. Their lexicons, PONIES, and text-books were strewed round their lamps on the table.

1852. *Yale Tomahawk*, May. We learn that they do not PONY their lessons.

1854. *New England Mag.*, 208. In the way of PONY or translation to the Greek of Father Griesbach, the New Testament was wonderfully convenient.

1856. HALL, *College Words*, s.v. PONY. So-called, it may be, from the fleetness and ease with which a skilful rider is enabled to pass over places which to a common plodder may present obstacles.

5. (common).—A generic diminutive, prob. of turf origin: as PONY = a very small horse, and PONY-STAKES = an insignificant event. Whence (generally).in comparison, anything of small size, stature, or value. Hence, PONY = (1) a small glass ('a PONY of ale, or stout'), containing a gill, or (of wines and spirits) a mouthful; (2) a woman of very small stature. Also PONY-BRANDY = the best brandy: as served in a PONY-GLASS; PONY-PURSE = an impromptu collection: of small contributions. The word is becoming recognised: as in PONY-SAW, PONY-ENGINE, and PONY-TRUCK.

1885. *New York Journal*, Aug. 'I'm on the inside track,' said a PONY of beer as it went galloping down a man's throat.

1896. CRANE, *Maggie*, vii. Bring d'lady a big glass! What use is dat PONY?

6. (venery).—The *penis*: *see* PRICK.

*d.*1796. BURNS, *Merry Muses*, 'Ye Hae Lien Wrang, Lassie.' Ye've let THE POUNIE o'er the dyke, And he's been in the corn.

7. (common). — A GAFFING-coin (*q.v.*); a piece showing either two heads or two tails. Whence, TO SELL THE PONY (or LADY) = to toss for drinks: certain coins, say twelve, are placed one on top of another, all, save one, being turned the same way; the coins are cut, as at cards, and he who cuts the single piece has to pay, having BOUGHT THE PONY.

See JERUSALEM.

POODLE, *subs.* (common).—A dog: in sarcasm, without reference to breed.

POON, *verb.* (Winchester College).—To prop a piece of furniture with a wedge.—WRENCH.

POONA, *subs.* (costermongers').—A sovereign: *cf.* PONTE.

POONA GUARDS, *subs. phr.* (military).—The East Yorkshires, formerly the 15th Regiment of Foot: also "The Snappers."

POONT, *subs.* (common).—*In pl.* = the paps: *see* DAIRY.

POOP, *subs.* (old).—1. A worthless creature, a weakling, a NINCUMPOOP (*q.v.*); (2) the posteriors: *see* STERN and *verb.* sense 3; and (3) the face (*cf.* SHAKSPEARE, 1 Henry IV., *Falstaff to Bardolph, &c.*, 'Thou art our admiral, thou bearest the lantern in the POOP, but 'tis in the nose of thee').

1598. SHAKSPEARE, 1 *Hen. IV.*, iii. 4. *Fals.* Thou art our admiral, thou bearest the lantern in the POOP, but 'tis in the nose of thee.

1706. WARD, *Wooden World*, 67. He crawls up upon Deck, to the Piss-dale, where, while he manages his Whip-staff with one hand, he scratches his POOP with the other.

Verb. (old).—1. To overcome; to be set down.

1551. STILL, *Gammer Gurton's Needle*, ii. 1. But there ich was POWPTE indeed.

1609. SHAKSPEARE, *Pericles*, iv. 2. She quickly POOPED him, she made him roast meat for worms.

2. (venery).—To copulate: *see* GREENS and RIDE. Hence POOP-NODDY = copulation.

1606. *Wily Beguiled* [HAWKINS, *Eng. Drama*, III. 310]. I saw them close together at POOP-NODDY.

3. (vulgar).—To break wind: also as *subs.*—BAILEY (1728).

POOP-DOWNHAUL, *subs. phr.* (nautical).—An imaginary rope, a seaman's jest: *cf.* 'clapping the keel athwart-ships,' &c.—CLARK RUSSELL.

POOP-ORNAMENT (old nautical).—An apprentice.

*c.*1855. [*Athenæum* (1902), 8 Feb., 177, 1, 'Rev. of School and Sea Days']. [For the rest, he was and is emphatically the ship's loblolly-boy and "rouse-about," miscalled "a blarsted POOP ORNAMENT," the drudge even of ordinary seamen.]

POOPSTER (or **POOPER**), *subs.* (venery).—A fornicator; a MUTTON-MONGER (*q.v.*).

POOR. TO SERVE THE POOR, WITH A THUMP ON THE BACK WITH A STONE, *phr.* (colloquial). — To shark the needy.—RAY (1670).

POOR-MAN, *subs.* (Scots').—1. A heap of corn-sheaves: four set upright and one above.

2. (Scots').—*See* quot.

1819. SCOTT, *Bride of Lammermoor*, xix. I should like well would my wife and family permit me to return to my sowens and my POOR-MAN-OF-MUTTON. [SCOTT: 'The blade-bone of a shoulder of mutton is called in Scotland "a POOR MAN," as in some parts of England it is termed a "poor knight of Windsor," in contrast, it must be presumed, to the baronial' Sir Loin. A Scotch laird was once asked by an English landlord what he would have for dinner. He replied, "I think I could relish a morsel of a POOR MAN."]

POOR MAN'S BLESSING, *subs. phr.* (venery). — The female *pudendum*: *see* MONOSYLLABLE.

POOR MAN'S OYSTER, *subs. phr.* (common).—*See* quot.

1891. *Tit-Bits*, 8 Aug., 277, 2. There are thousands of costers who earn a livelihood by the sale of . . . mussels, which are regarded as the POOR MAN'S OYSTER.

POOR-MAN'S TREACLE, *subs. phr.* (common).—An onion.—*Century.*

POOR MOUTH. TO MAKE A POOR MOUTH, *verb. phr.* (Scots').—To whine; to make the worst of things.

1822. *Blackwood*, Sep., 307. It's no right o' you to be aye making a PUIR MOUTH.

POOR ROBIN, *subs. phr.* (old).—An almanack. [Robert Herrick, in the 17th century, issued a series of almanacks so-called.]

*b.*1704. DARRELL, *Gentleman Instructed*, 120. I was informed she discern'd by the beat of the pulse a Feast from a Feria without the help of POOR ROBIN.

POP, *subs.* (American).—1. A father; 'papa': also POPPA and POPPER.

1888. *Detroit Free Press*, 22 Dec. Jerry wants a new POP right bad.

1899. *Sporting Times*, 15 Ap., 2, 1. Say, Van, why should we fret? It was POPPA'S house.

1901. *Free Lance*, 16 Nov., 171, 2. The young lady has an independent fortune, and POPPER happened to be at the other end of a cable, three thousand miles away, at the moment she was getting married!

2. (common).—A popular concert: as 'The Saturday (or Monday) POPS.'

1869. *Orchestra*, 19 Nov. How beautiful is the behaviour of our eminent artists at the Monday POPS!

1891. GILBERT, *Patience*, ii. Who thinks suburban hops more fun than Monday POPS.

1898. *D. Telegraph*, 13 Dec., 7, 5. Probably never before did the experienced director of the POPS. give a special concert on account of a particular artist.

3. (Eton College). — A club chiefly confined to Oppidans though Collegers are sometimes elected: otherwise "The Eton

Society" for reading and debates. [Supposed to be a contraction of 'Popina,' the rooms having been for many years over a cook-shop or confectioner's. — *See Public School Word Book.*]

1865. *Etoniana*, 207. The chief attraction of POP lies in its being a sort of social club . . . and as the members are strictly limited (originally twenty-two, since increased to twenty-eight), to be elected into the society gives a boy a certain degree of prestige in the school.

Verb., with *subs.* and *adv.* (old).—Generic for more or less quick, unexpected, and explosive action. Whence, (1) = to shoot: as *subs.* (or POPPER) = (1) a shop, and (2) a firearm: spec. a pistol, but in quot. 1383, a dagger (HALL, 1714; GROSE, 1785; VAUX, 1819; and BEE, 1823); (2) = to crack—as a whip; (3) = to explode—as a hat when sat on, or a cork when drawn: as *subs.* = (a) a drink which fizzes from the bottle when opened—spec. ginger-beer, but in quot. 1836 = champagne (GROSE, 1785; BEE, 1823), and (b) the noise made in drawing a cork; and (4) = to rap out one's words: whence POPPING = babbling. Also, as *adv.* = suddenly or unexpectedly. *See* also many allied colloquialisms *infra.*

1383. CHAUCER, *Canterbury Tales*, 3929. A joly POPPERE baar he in his pouche.

1621. FLETCHER, *Pilgrim*, iii. 2. Into that bush POP goes his pate, and all his face is comb'd over.

1724. HARPER, 'Frisky Moll's Song' [*Harlequin Jack Sheppard*]. Two POPPS Had my Boman when he was ta'en.

1748. SMOLLETT, *Roderick Random*, viii. A pair of POPS silver mounted . . . I took them from the captain. *Ibid.* (1749), *Gil Blas* [ROUTLEDGE], 345. We were startled out of our sleep by the report of musketry POPPING so near.

1821. HAGGART, *Life*, 98. I plunged my fam into my sack, as if for a POP.

1829. MONCRIEFF, *Giovanni in London*, ii. 1. Made up your mind to have a POP at him.

1830. LYTTON, *Paul Clifford* (1854), 296. Lord love ye, they says as 'ow you go to all the fine places in ruffles, with a pair of silver POPS in your waistcoat pocket!

1834. AINSWORTH, *Rookwood*, III. v. His crape-covered vizard drawn over his eyes, His tol by his side and his POPS in his pocket.

1834. BUCKSTONE, *Agnes de Vere*, ii. 3. I've an excellent case of POPPERS here that I always keep loaded for such occasions.

1836. MILNER, *Turpin's Ride to York*, i. 3. It is not even safe to hunt without POPS in your pocket. *Ibid.* Damn the POPPER! we must be off to Yorkshire now.

1836. HOOD, *Miss Kilmansegg* [*Works* (1846), i. 246]. Home-made POP that will not foam.

1837. BARHAM, *Ingoldsby Legends*, I. 277. With wine and naygus and imperial POP.

1844. MARRYAT, *The Settlers*, I. vi. 103. "Fowling-pieces,—they are birdguns, I believe,—no use at all; muskets are soldiers' tools,—no use; pistols are POPS, and nothing better."

1845. BROWNING, *Englishman in Italy*. And all around the glad church lie old bottles With gunpowder stopped, Which will be, when the Image re-enters, Religiously POPPED. *Ibid.* More POPPERS bang.

1847. PORTER, *Quarter Race, &c.*, 95. He'd POP his whip, and stretch his chains, and holler 'wo, gee!'

1848. JONES, *Sketches of Travel*, 150. The rascal went to his coach, jumped on the box, POPPED his whip and wiggled his fingers at me as he drew off.

1848. LOWELL, *Biglow Papers*, Intro. Past noontime they went trampin' round An' nary thing to POP at found.

1851-61. MAYHEW, *Lond. Lab., &c.*, I. 187. Not above one-eighth . . . but sell with their POP some other article.

1857. HOLMES, *Autocrat of Breakfast Table*, viii. A hat which has been POPPED, or exploded by being sat down upon, is never itself again afterwards.

1863. ALEX. SMITH, *Dreamthorp*, 133. In the pit, sober people relax themselves, and suck oranges, and quaff ginger-POP.

1871. *Morning Advertiser*, 11 Sept. Shall the Admirals of England now their former prowess drop, All courage ooze from tarry hands, like fiz from uncorked POP?

1872. *Standard*, 29 Aug. 'Autumn Manœuvres.' Buying POP in the cheapest and selling it in the dearest market is his trade.

1876. GEORGE ELIOT, *Daniel Deronda*, xxxix. I cannot bear people to keep their minds bottled up for the sake of letting them go off with a POP.

1884. HAWLEY SMART, *Post to Finish*, 228. I went for this Dancing Master myself, and he don't warrant my calling for POP (Champagne).

1893. EMERSON, *Signor Lippo*, xiv. Well, I don't mind if I do, and old Teapot here can come and have POP, like the little boys.

1887. HENLEY and STEVENSON, *Three Plays*, 69. Another illusion gone POP.

1893. MILLIKEN, *'Arry Ballads*, 71. I 'm horf for a POP at the birds.

5. (common).—To pawn; 'to put away': whence POP-SHOP = a pawnbroker.—GROSE (1785); BEE (1823). *See* SPOUT.

1837. LYTTON, *Maltravers*, IV. I. As to the other cloak and shawl, don't be afraid; they shan't go to the POP-SHOP.

1841. *Punch*, I. 77. The eight waistcoats wanted for dinner. Peter ordered to POP accordingly—proceeds 7s. 6d. Invested in a small leg of mutton and half and half.

1851-61. MAYHEW, *Lond. Lab.*, &c., I. 530. Knew of such a book to a sartinty, because a young 'oman took one to POP for an old 'oman what was on the spree.

1866. *Orchestra*, 10 Nov. The next day the gentleman transports it to a pawnbroker's, and, as cognoscenti have it, POPS it.

1880. G. R. SIMS, *Three Brass Balls*, Pledge x. I am not at all sure that all congregations would act so kindly and thoughtfully as did the Bishop Ortonites if they found out that their parson was in the habit of POPPING his surplice.

1886-96. MARSHALL, *'Pomes' from the Pink 'Un* ['Nixes in the Kick'], 63. With his nibs the luck was out, for he POPPED it up the spout.

1889. *Answers*, 13 July, 105, 1. Having, unfortunately, a very extended acquaintance with the POP SHOP, my account . . . may be relied upon as being accurate.

1891. *Harry Fludyer*, iii. When your aunt Sophia was with us last week it kept on yelling something about 'the POP-SHOP round the corner' and 'paying your uncle a visit,' which I did not understand.

1898. HUME, *Hagar*, 54. Rosa, to get rid of the necklace until the affair of the murder was blown over, might pawn it . . . so I sent a printed slip to all the POP-SHOPS in London.

1900. KIPLING, *Stalky & Co.*, 44. 'Confound you! You haven't been POPPING my Sunday bags, then?' 'Keep your hair on. It's only your watch . . . got 13s. 7d. Here's the ticket.'

6. (American University).—To get an advantage.

OTHER COLLOQUIALISMS, mostly with the same root-idea, are:—TO POP OFF SAWS = to babble; TO POP UPON (IN, INTO, ABOVE or OUT) = (1) to come, put, spring, or thrust suddenly into view or place, and (2) to offer abruptly; TO POP WITH THE MOUTH = to smack the lips; TO POP ONE OUT (or OFF) = to deprive, with little or no warning; TO POP OFF WITH = to put off (or aside); TO POP THE QUESTION (or TO POP) = to offer marriage; TO POP UP (or DOWN) = to appear (or disappear) suddenly; TO POP OFF = (1) to die (also TO POP OFF the hooks—*see* POP and HOOK), and (2) to make a sudden exit; TO POP IT IN = to effect intromission; TO POP IT ON = to increase a demand: as chance offers.

1513-25. SKELTON [OLIPHANT, *New Eng.*, i. 394. We see the phrase TO POP FORTH saws; at p. 235, POPPING means *babbling*; our POP still implies noise, as *pop-gun*].

1575. *Touchstone of Complexions*, 124. Still to dilate and open his breaste with coughing, hawking, neesing and POPPING or smacking with the mouth.

1596. SHAKSPEARE, *Hamlet*, v. 2. He that hath killed my king, and whored my mother, POPPED IN between the election and my hopes. Ibid., *King John*, i. That is my brother's plea . . . The which if he can prove, a' POPS ME OUT at least from fair five hundred pounds a year. *Ibid.* (1602), *Troilus and Cressida*, iv. 5. That's no argument for kissing now; for thus POPPED Paris in his hardiment, and parted thus you and your argument.

1600. HEYWOOD, *1 Ed. IV.* [PEARSON, *Works* (1874), I. 47]. My daughter Nell shall POP a posset VPON thee, when thou goest to bed.

1626. FLETCHER, *Noble Gent.*, i. 1. And do you POP me OFF with this slight answer.

d. 1631. DONNE, *Sermons*, iv. So, diving in a bottomless sea, they POP some times ABOVE the water to take breath.

d. 1674. MILTON, *Def. Humb. Remonst.* [*Century*]. These our Prelates, who are the true successors of those that POPT them INTO the other world.

1706. WARD, *Wooden World*, 'To Reader.' Finding . . . the air begin to change apace, and wet, thick, cloudy weather POP IN at once upon us.

d. 1745. SWIFT [quoted in *Century*]. Others have a trick of POPPING UP AND DOWN every moment from their paper to their audience, like an idle schoolboy.

1749. SMOLLETT, *Gil Blas* [ROUTLEDGE], 113. I know how to tickle a girl in a stiff gown, or an actress. You swagger . . . with an easy, impudent assurance, and POP THE QUESTION without making any bones about it. *Ibid.*, I. 3. When they had been together long enough, IN POPPED I, with a message to the enamoured spark.

1753. RICHARDSON, *Grandison*, vi. 103. Afraid he would . . . POP OUT THE QUESTION which he had not the courage to put.

1764. FOOTE, *Patron*, i. O fie! what chance have I there? Indeed, if Lady Pepperpot should happen to POP OFF—

1773. GOLDSMITH, *Stoops to Conquer*, ii. When company comes you are not to POP OUT and stare, and then run in again.

1773. THOMPSON, *Fair Quaker of Deal* [Shadwell's comedy recast], ii. 3. If I could get a lover upon the first POPPING OF THE QUESTION.

1835. DICKENS, *Sketches by Boz*, 'Watkins Tottle.' I suppose you POPPED THE QUESTION more than once.

1837. BARHAM, *Ingold. Legends* (1862), 249. His abruptness in POPPING THE QUESTION So soon after dinner disturbed her digestion. *Ibid.* (1857), 2 S. 29. I fear by his looks Our friend, Francois Xavier, has POPPED OFF THE HOOKS. *Ibid.* (1900), 141. On the fire, too, she POPS some nice mutton-chops.

1841. *Punch*, I. 153. A considerate old aunt, who had kindly POPPED OFF in the nick of time.

1851. SMEDLEY, *Lewis Arundel*, iii. Some of the fools about here wanted me to put up for the county if he POPPED OFF.

1853. LYTTON, *My Novel*, v. xvii. 'Please the pigs,' then said Mr. Avenel to himself, 'I shall POP THE QUESTION.'

1855. TAYLOR, *Still Waters*, i. I'll deposit my carpet-bag in my dressing room, and then POP IN on Emmy.

1855. THACKERAY, *Newcomes*, l. She was so handsome, and so clever . . . that he had been on the point of POPPING THE fatal QUESTION ever so many times. *Ibid.* (1862), *Philip*, xvi. Eat your porridge now, little ones. Charlotte, POP a bit of butter IN Carrick's porridge.

1869. STOWE, *Oldtown Folks*, 37. One of the sort that might POP OFF any time.

1871. *Figaro*, 18 Mar., The Penalty for POPPING. To Bachelors and Widowers: If you are about to POP THE QUESTION, think of Breach of Promise at Nisi Prius, and don't. He who POPS and does not wed, By a jury will be punished.

1876. HINDLEY, *Cheap Jack*, 313. Travellers well know how they must put the price when doing business with Cheap John now that he is keeping a shop. It's no use for them TO POP IT ON.

1888. BLACK, *Houseboat*, viii. While some of the small fry POPPED OUT their heads to have a look.

1892. CHEVALIER, *Little Nipper*. Let's POP INTO the 'Broker's Arms' and 'ave a drop o' beer. Ibid., *Wot Cher!* Your rich Uncle Tom of Camberwell, POPPED OFF recent, which it ain't a sell.

POPE, *subs.* (old: now provincial).—A term of contempt: *e.g.*, 'What a POPE of a thing!' Also, DRUNK AS A POPE = very drunk (Benedict XII., a glutton and a wine-bibber gave rise to the expression, *Bibamus papaliter*): *see* DRINKS and SCREWED; TO BE (or PLAY) POPE-HOLY = to be sanctimonious; to play the PRIG (*q.v.*) or hypocrite; TO KNOW NO MORE THAN THE POPE OF ROME = to know nothing.—RAY (1670). Ray also gives, 'If you would be a POPE, you must think of nothing else.'

1360. CHAUCER, *Rom. of Rose* [*Works* (1662), III.]. Another thing was doen . . . That seemed like an ipocrite, And it was cleped POPE HOLY.

1362. LANGLAND, *Piers Plowman*, sig. T, ii. (1561). And none so singuler by himselfe, nor so POPE HOLY.

d. 1460. LYDGATE, *Prohemy of a Mariage* [*MS.*, Harl., 372, 51]. And for POPHOLY and nyce loke wel aboute.

1509. BARCLAY, *Ship of Fooles* (1570), 57. Ouer sad or proude, disceitfull and POPE HOLY.

d. 1529. SKELTON, *A Replycation* [DYCE, i. 208]. POPHOLY and penysshe presumpcion. Ibid., *Garlande of Laurell*, 611. Fals forgers of mony, for kownnage atteintid, POPE HOLY ypocrytis.

d. 1536. TYNDALE, *Ans. Sir T. More* [Parker Soc. (1850), 36]. There be POPE-HOLY, which . . . resist the righteousness of God in Christ.

1620. *Westward for Smelts* [HALLIWELL]. He, having no answere, began to curse and ban, bidding a POPE on all women.

1706. *Oxford Jests*, 93. They bid him read. 'Read! truly, my Lord,' says he, 'I can read NO MORE THAN THE POPE OF ROME.'

POPE-OF-ROME, *subs. phr.* (rhyming).—Home

POPERINE-PEAR, *subs. phr.* (venery).—The *penis*: *see* PRICK.

1595. SHAKSPEARE, *Romeo and Juliet*, ii. 1. Oh, Romeo! that she were, oh, that she were an open arse, thou a POPERIN PEAR!

1632. ROWLEY, *Woman Never Vexed* [DODSLEY, Old Plays (HAZLITT), xii.]. I requested him to pull me A Katherine pear, and had I not look'd to him, He would have mistook and given me a POPPERIN.

1822. NARES, *Glossary*, s.v. POPERIN . . . In the quarto edition of Romeo and Juliet was a passage, afterwards very properly omitted, containing a foolish and coarse quibble on the name.

POPE'S-EYE, *subs. phr.* (common).—The thread of fat in a leg of mutton.

1852. SHIRLEY BROOKS, *Miss Violet*. The oratorical undertaker having made a most successful joke about the POPE'S-EYE on a leg of Protestant mutton.

1869. BLACKMORE, *Lorna Doone*, ii. You should have . . . the POPE'S-EYE from the mutton.

POPE'S- (or TURK'S-) HEAD, *subs. phr.* (common).—A round broom, of bristles or feathers, with a long handle.

d. 1849. EDGEWORTH, *Love and Law*, I. v. You're no witch if you don't see a cobweb as long as my arm. Run, run, O child, for the POPE'S-HEAD.

1852. SAVAGE, *Reuben Medlicott* (1864), I. iii. You are not going to send the boy to school with this ridiculous head of hair; why, his schoolfellows will use him for a POPE'S HEAD.

POPE'S-NOSE, *subs. phr.* (common).—A chicken's rump: also PARSON'S-NOSE.—GROSE (1785).

POPE'S-SIZE, *subs. phr.* (trade).—*See* quot.

1888. *Notes and Queries*, 7 S. vii. 225. A year or two ago I bought a merino vest. On the bill I noticed P.S. after it, and by enquiry elicited that P.S. stood for POPE'S SIZE, and that POPE'S SIZE meant short and stout.

POP-GUN. *See* POT-GUN.

POPINJAY, *subs.* (old).—A general term of contempt: specifically (1) a chatterer; and (2) a fop.

1598. SHAKSPEARE, *1 Hen. IV.*, i. 3. "I then, all smarting with my wounds being cold, To be so pestered with a POPINJAY, Answered neglectingly I know not what."

1599. JONSON, *Every Man Out of His Humour*, ii. 2. A number of these POPINJAYS there are.

1620. MASSINGER and FIELD, *Fatal Dowry*, iii. 1. *Nov. jun.* What have I done, sir, To draw this harsh unsavoury language from you? *Rom.* Done, POPINJAY! why, dost thou think.

POPLARS (POPPELARS, POPLER, or PAPLAR), *subs.* (Old Cant).—Porridge: spec. milk-porridge.—HARMAN (1576); HEAD (1665); B. E. (*c.* 1696); COLES (1724); GROSE (1785).

1608. DEKKER, *Lanthorne and Candlelight* [FARMER, *Musa Pedestris* (1896), 3]. The Ruffin cly the nab of the Harmanbeck, If we maund . . . POPLARS of yarum, he cuts, bing to the Ruffmans.

1611. MIDDLETON and DEKKER, *Roaring Girl*, v. 1. A gage of ben Rombouse . . . Is benar than . . . Peck, pennam, lap, or POPLER.

1641. BROME, *Jovial Crew*, ii. Here's Pannam and Lap, and good POPLARS of Yarrum.

1707. SHIRLEY, *Triumph of Wit* [FARMER, *Musa Pedestris* (1896), 36]. With lap and POPLARS held I tack.

POPLET (POPELET or POPPET), *subs.* (old).—*See* quot. 1694: also as an endearment.

1694. DUNTON, *Ladies Dict.*, s.v. POPELET. A puppet, or young wench.

1843. SELBY, *Antony and Cleopatra Married and Settled*. There, there's a POPPET; hush, hushaby—hush! it's very like me—very, just the same interesting twist of the eyes, and insinuating turn of the nose.

2. (old).—A corpulent person.—CHAUCER (*d.* 1400).

POP-LOLLY, *subs. phr.* (cheap-jacks').—A sweetmeat: *i.e.*, LOLLIPOP.

1860. HINDLEY, *Cheap-Jack*, 100. Ever and anon bawling out in a Billingsgate voice, 'Two ounces a penny again—lollipop and POP-LOLLY.

POPPED, *adj.* (tailors').—Annoyed. POPPED AS A HATTER = very angry.

POPPER. *See* POP, *subs.* 1.

POPPY-COCK, *subs. phr.* (American).—Nonsense; BOSH (*q.v.*). Also POPPY-COCK RACKET.

POP-SHOP. *See* POP, *verb.* 5.

POP-SQUIRT, *subs. phr.* (American).—A jackanapes.

POPSY-WOPSY, *subs. phr.* (common).—A foolish endearment.

1892. *Ally Sloper's Half-Holiday*, 19 Mar., 90, 3. Bless me if the little POPSY-WOPSY hasn't been collecting all the old circus hoops and covering them with her old muslin skirts.

POPULAR, *adj.* (colloquial American).—Conceited.

1862. LOWELL, *Biglow Papers*, 2 S. Int. POP'LAR as a hen with one chicken.

P.P. *See* PLAY OR PAY.

PORK, *subs.* (old).—1. A pig-headed one: *cf.* PIG, *subs.* 1.

1645. MILTON, *Colasterion* . . . I mean not to dispute philosophy with this PORK.

2. (tailors').—A garment spoiled in cutting or making; goods returned on hand: also PIG: *cf.* COLD PIG.

3. (venery).—MUTTON (*q.v.*): *cf.* FLESH, MEAT, GREENS, BEEF, FISH, &c.

TO CRY PORK, *verb. phr.* (old).—To act as undertaker's tout.—GROSE (1785).

PORKER, *subs.* (common).—1. A young hog.—GROSE (1785).

1725. POPE, *Odyssey*, xiv. 86. Where the fat PORKERS slept beneath the sun.

2. (old).—A Jew.—GROSE (1785).

3. (old).—A sword.—B. E. (*c.*1696).

1688. SHADWELL, *Sq. of Alsatia*, i. [*Works* (1720), iv. 18]. The captain whipt his PORKER out.

PORKOPOLIS, *subs.* (American).—Chicago: formerly Cincinnati: *cf.* COTTONOPOLIS.

1888. *American Humourist*, Aug. Since Cincinnatti ceased to be PORKOPOLIS.

1901. *Daily Telegraph*, 7 Jan., 8, 4. The firm of Armour and Co. is one of the chief of those huge meat-packing concerns which have given to Chicago its epithet of "PORKOPOLIS."

PORK-PIE, *subs. phr.* (obsolete).—A hat: modish in the Sixties. [In shape resembling a pork-pie, or the Spanish 'toreador,' fashionable in the Nineties.]

186[?]. *Music Hall Song*, 'In the Strand.' A PORK-PIE hat with a little feather.

1860. *Punch*, xxxix. 118. 'O, look here, Bill; here's a swell with a PORK-PIE on his head!"

1863. BRADDON, *Aurora Floyd*, xii. She rode across country, wearing a hat which provoked considerable criticism,—a hat which was no other than the now universal turban, or PORK PIE, but which was new to the world in the autumn of fifty-eight.

1869. C. READE, *Foul Play*, xxxii. She made herself a sealskin jacket and PORK-PIE hat.

1883. BRET HARTE, *In the Carquinez Woods*, iv. The hat thus procured a few days later became, by the aid of a silk handkerchief and a blue-jay's feather, a fascinating PORK-PIE.

PORPOISE, *subs.* (common).—A stout man; FORTYGUTS (*q.v.*) = Fr. *Saint-Lichard*, or *Saint-Pansart.*

PORRIDGE. TO COOK THE PORRIDGE, *verb. phr.* (Scots').—To contrive and execute a design.

1814. SCOTT, *Waverley*, iii. 354. 'But wha COOKIT THE PARRIDGE for him?' exclaimed the Bailie, 'I wad like to ken that:—wha, but your honour's to command.'

See BREATH.

PORRIDGE-BOWL, *subs. phr.* (common). The stomach; the BREAD-BASKET (*q.v.*); *see* VICTUALLING OFFICE.

PORRIDGE-DISTURBER, *sub. phr.* (pugilistic).—A drive in the pit of the stomach.

PORTABLE, *adv.* (old).—'Pocketable.'—B.E. (*c.*1696).

PORTAGE, *subs.* (old: now recognised).—'Carriage of anything, whether by land or water.'—B.E. (*c.*1696).

PORTAL TO THE BOWER OF BLISS, *subs. phr.* (literary).—The female *pudendum: see* MONOSYLLABLE.

1647-8. HERRICK, *Poems* [HAZLITT, *Works*, ii. 273]. This loue-guarded parradice—Above the entrance there is written this, This is THE PORTAIL TO THE BOWER OF BLISSE.

PORTCULLIS (or **PORTCULLIS MONEY**), *subs. phr.* (old colloquial).—Money, of various values, *temp.* Elizabeth, struck for the East India Company (est. 1599): also INDIA MONEY [it bore a PORTCULLIS *verso*].

1599. JONSON, *Every Man Out of Humour*, iii. 6. It comes well, for I had not so much as the least PORTCULLICE of coyn before.

PORTER, *subs.* (old: long recognised).—'Hirelings to carry Burthens, Beasts of Burthen, or else Menial Servants set to guard the gates in a great Man's House.'—B.E. (*c.*1696).

PORTERHOUSE-STEAK, *subs. phr.* (American).—A chop from the middle of the sirloin—with upper and undercut: occasionally, but improperly, from the wing-rib.

1870. CLEMENS, *Innocents Abroad*, xiii. One would not be at all surprised to hear him say: 'A mutton-roast to-day, or will you have a nice PORTERHOUSE-STEAK?'

PORTER'S-KNOT, *subs. phr.* (obsolete).—A large bob of hair, with a hanging curl: fashionable with women in the Sixties: also WATERFALL, CATARACT, &c.

PORT-HOLE, *subs.* (venery).—(1) The fundament: *see* BUM; and (2) the female *pudendum: see* MONOSYLLABLE.

1664. COTTON, *Virgil Travestie* (1st ed.) 15. Bounce cries the PORT-HOLE, out they fly, And make the world dance Barnaby.

PORTIONIST, *subs.* (University).—*See* POSTMASTER.

PORTMANTLE (**PORTMANTICK** or **PORTMANTUA**), *subs.* (once literary: now vulgar).—A corruption of 'portmanteau.'

[?] *Robin Hood and the Butcher* [CHILD, *Ballads*, v. 38]. And out of the sheriff's PORTMANTLE He told three hundred pounds.

1617-30. HOWELL, *Letters*, 127 [OLIPHANT, *New English*, ii. 79. Buckingham, in his Spanish journey carries a PORTMANTLE under his arm; our form of the word was to come seven years later.]

1623. MABBE, *Guzman* (1630) 158 [OLIPHANT, *New English*, ii. 86. We see PORTMANTEAU in page 158, and the form PORTMANTUA in the Index; our mantua-maker is a relic of this confusion].

1690. HACKET, *Life of Williams*, i. 160. He would linger no longer, and play at cards in King Philip's palace till the messenger with the PORT-MANTICK came from Rome.

1726. VANBRUGH, *Provoked Husband*, i. 1. My lady's gear alone were as much as filled four PORTMANTEL trunks.

1753. MRS. LENNOX, *Henrietta*, v. x. He sent orders to a servant to bring his PORTMANTUA.

PORTMANTEAU-WORD, *subs. phr.* (common).—A made vocable packed with two or more meanings: *e.g.*, slithy = lithe + slimy; torrible = torrid + horrible; SQUARSON = squire + parson; SQUIRSHOP = squire + bishop. [The name was Lewis Carrol's, the method Bishop Sam. Wilberforce's.]

1876. LEWIS CARROL, *Hunting of the Snark*, Preface. [Concerning] PORTMANTEAU-WORDS—take the two words 'fuming' and 'furious.' Make up your mind that you will say both words, but leave it unsettled which you will say first . . . if you have that rarest of gifts, a perfectly balanced mind, you will say 'frumious.'

1892. *Globe*, 12 Oct., 1. 4. In these circumstances it is really surprising that so few of these PORTMANTEAU WORDS, as Lewis Carroll called them, are perpetrated.

PORTRAIT.—*See* QUEEN'S PICTURES.

TO SIT FOR ONE'S PORTRAIT, *verb. phr.* (prison).—*See* quot.

1837. DICKENS, *Pickwick* (1857) 339. Here they stopped, while the tip-staff delivered his papers; and here Mr. Pickwick was apprised that he would remain until he had undergone the ceremony known to the initiated as SITTING FOR YOUR PORTRAIT. . . . Mr. Pickwick complied with the invitation, and sat himself down: when Mr. Weller, who stationed himself at the back of the chair, whispered that the sitting was merely another term for undergoing an inspection by the different turnkeys, in order that they might know prisoners from visitors.

PORTUGUESE MAN-OF-WAR, *subs. phr.* (nautical).—A nautilus.

POS (**POSS** or **POZ**), *adj.* and *adv.* (common).—Positive.

1708-10. SWIFT, *Polite Conversation. Lady Smart.* What! . . . Do you say it upon Rep? *Neverout.* Poz, I saw her with my own Eyes.

1711. *Spectator*, No. 135. It is perhaps . . . speaking no more than we needs must which has so miserably curtailed some of our words, that . . . they often lose all but their first syllables, as in mob, rep, POS, incog, and the like.

1715. ADDISON, DRUMMER, iii. I will be flattered, that's POS.

1719. DURFEY, *Pills to Purge*, v. 329. Drunk I was last night, that's POSS, my wife began to scold.

1839-40. THACKERAY, *Catherine* [*Century*]. I will have a regiment to myself, that's POZ.

1853. *Diogenes*, II. 46. But the crier said, POZ, They were fresh as it was.

1886-96. MARSHALL, '*Pomes' from the Pink 'Un* ['The Dolls'], 24. While the public morals-shaper Thinks of writing to the paper To upset the show, if POS.

POSE, *verb.* (old colloquial).—1. To puzzle; and (2) to posture, to pretend, to feign. [Sense 1 has been chiefly influenced by the scholastic M.E. *posen* (*Prompt. Parv.*) = to examine, whence to puzzle; whilst sense 2 owes more to *posture*, which again is from the same Latin root.] Whence POSER (1) = an unanswerable question or argument; and (2) an impostor, a pretender: also TO PUT A POSER. Also (3) POSER [APPOSER, OPPOSER or OPPOSITOR] (old) = a bishop's examining chaplain; (in modern schools) = an examiner—at Eton for King's College, and at Winchester for New College scholarships and exhibitions.

1387. TREVISA, *Higden*, iv. 291. The childe Jesus . . . sittynge and APPOSYNGE the doctours.

1574. QUEEN ELIZABETH, *Endorsement on Recommendation of Candidates for College Election*, 8 May. To our trustie and welbeloved, the wardens of the new Colledges in Oxford and nere Winchester and others of them and to the OPPOSITORS and others having interest in the election of scollers.

1577-87. HARRISON, *England*, I. II. iii. 84. In those [Windsor, Wincester, Eaton, Westminster schools] . . . the triall is made by certeine APPOSERS yearlie appointed to examine them.

1603. BACON, *Discourse* [1887]. Let his questions not be troublesome, for that is fit for a POSER.

1662. FULLER, *Worthies*, Norfolk, II. 462. The university [of Cambridge] . . . appointed Dr. Cranmer . . . to be POSER-general of all candidates in Divinity.

1647-8. J. BEAUMONT, *Psyche*, i. 110 I still am POS'D about the case, But wiser you shall judge.

1662. DONNE, *Satires* [1819]. A thing which would have POS'D Adam to name.

1807. CRABBE, *Parish Register* [*Works* (1823)], i. 62. Then by what name th' unwelcome guest to call Was long a question, and it POSED them all.

1820. LAMB, *South Sea House* [*Century*]. A sucking babe may have POSED him.

1838. W. DESMOND, *Stage Struck*, I. My own aunt by the mother's side—but how to find her out will be a POSER, for we never could learn the name of the great man she caught.

1867. COLLINS, *The Public Schools*, 61. 'Winchester.' Two POSERS (or at one time supervisors) arrive at the college, where they are received with a Latin oration 'ad portas' by the senior scholar.

1872. C. D. WARNER, *Backlog Studies*, 161. 'What do you think women are good for?' 'That's a POSER!'

POSH, *subs.* (thieves').—1. Money: generic, but specifically, a halfpenny or other small coin: *see* RHINO.

1888. PAGE'S *Eavesdropper*, II. ii. They used such funny terms: 'brads,' and 'dibbs,' and 'mopusses,' and 'POSH' . . . at last it was borne in upon me that they were talking about money.

1891. *Ally Sloper's Half Holiday*, 4 April. I am authorized by the executive council . . . to send you an invitation . . . to take care of the POSH.

1893. EMERSON, *Lippo*, xx. She'd always get some POSH from them.

2. (society).—A dandy.

POSSE MOBILITATIS, *subs. phr.* (old).—The mob.—GROSE (1785).

POSSESS, *verb.* (conventional).—To HAVE (*q.v.*): *see* GREENS and RIDE.

1620. MASSINGER and FIELD, *Fatal Dowry*, iii. 1. To set down to a lady of my rank Limits of entertainment? *Rom.* Sure a legion Has POSSEST this woman!

*c.*1707. *Old Ballad*, 'Wooburn Fair' [FARMER, *Merry Songs and Ballads* (1897), 1 S. iv. 179]. And tho' I let Loobies Oft finger my Bubbies: Who think when they kiss me, That they shall POSSESS me.

1749. SMOLLETT, *Gil Blas* [ROUTLEDGE], 209. The four cut-throats all avowed a like desire of POSSESSING the female who had fallen into their hands; and they were proposing to draw lots for her.

POSSIBLE, *adv.* (old).—*See* quot.

1823. EGAN, *Dict. Turf*, s.v. HIGH-TIDE. —— plenty of the POSSIBLES; whilst 'low-water' implies empty clies.

POSSUM, *verb.* (American).—*See* quots.: also TO PLAY POSSUM.

1828. FLINT, *Geog. of the Mississippi Valley.* As one who counterfeits sickness, or dissembles strongly for a particular purpose, is said to be POSSUMING.

1855. HALIBURTON, *Human Nature*, 14. I will PLAY POSSUM with these folks, and take a rise out of them that will astonish their weak nerves.

1877. BARTLETT, *Americanisms*, s.v. POSSUM. The expression alludes to the habit of the opossum, which throws itself on its back, and feigns death on the approach of an enemy.

1886. *Scribner's Mag.*, Jan., 436. It's almost time for Babe to quit PLAYING POSSUM.

POSSOM-GUTS, *subs. phr.* (colonial).—A term of reproach.

1859. H. KINGSLEY, *Geof. Hamlyn* [S. J. & C.]. I'll teach you to whistle when a gentleman comes into the hut, you POSSUM-GUTS.

POST, *subs.* (old: now recognised or colloquial).—1. 'Employment, Office, Station; also an advanced or advantageous piece of ground: a Pillar in the Way or Street.'—B.E. (*c.*1696).

2. (venery).—An act of coition.

Verb. (University).—1. To reject; TO PLUCK (*q.v.*): also as *subs.* At Eton = to put down for bad work in 'Collections': the penalty is a holiday-pœna or a swishing.

1855. BRISTED, *Eng. Univ.*, 74. Should a man be POSTED twice in succession, he is generally recommended to try the air of some other college, or devote his energies to some other walk of life.

2. (common).—To publish: by exposing a list of nominations or defaulters: spec. (Univ.) to publish a list of those in debt for College rations; and (3) to hold up to ridicule or contempt, as (*see* quot. 1882) a coward. Whence, TO POST UP (or BE WELL POSTED) = to keep one (or be) well informed.

1731. HEARNE, *Diary*, 13 Ap. The Royal Society sinks every day in its credit . . . try its new statues for election of foreigners and natives, by POSTING UP their names . . . for ten weeks together, and . . . with much difficulty electing them.

1860. *Chambers'*, XIII. 22. But there is no occasion for us to say, with the Americans, that a man is well POSTED UP on a subject, while we can say that he is well informed on it.

1861. *Blackwood*, April, 429. We hear often enough in passable London Society of a man who is well POSTED UP on any special subject, or on the general topics of the day.

1861. KINGSLEY, *Ravenshoe*, lv. We are now POSTED UP well enough in the six weeks which preceded the arrival of the mysterious Archer.

1863. READE, *Hard Cash*, I. 191. He will say to himself, 'She can—POST me, I think these people call it—this afternoon for not cashing her cheque, and she can turn me and my bank into the street to-morrow.'

1864. *Spectator*, 455. The reader is POSTED carefully in the latest news about uncial fragments and Biblical MSS.

1882. *Harper's Monthly*, June. The fiery young midshipman POSTED him in the streets of Baltimore.

1884. W. C. RUSSELL, *Jack's Courtship*, xviii. Where I could have kept myself POSTED in all the latest news about the Hawkes' movements.

1885. *D. Telegraph*, 13 Nov. Nor may the merest schoolboy be POSTED UP in the dates.

4. (old).—To pay: *cf.* COLE, PONY, and TIP.—GROSE (1785); VAUX (1819).

1789. PARKER. *Happy Pair* [FARMER, *Musa Pedestris* (1896), 68]. With spunk let's POST our neddies.

1854. MARTIN and AYTOUN, *Bon Gualtier Ballads.* 'The Knyghte and the Taylzeour's Daughter.' Once for all, my rum 'un, I expect you'll POST the tin.

1885. *D. Telegraph*, 7 Sep. He must to-day POST the final deposit.

1891. *Lic. Vict. Gaz.*, 3 Ap. 'Done! POST the money.'

5. (nautical).—To raise to the rank of post-captain.

1818. AUSTIN, *Persuasion*, xxiii. Tell me . . . when I . . . was POSTED into the Laconia, if I had then written to you, would you have answered my letter?

1833. MARRYAT, *Peter Simple*, lv. Whispers were afloat which . . . prevented him from being POSTED.

FROM PILLAR TO POST, *phr.* (old).—Hither and thither; with aimless effort or action. [Lit. from the same to the same—PILLAR = Lat. *columna* = POST]. —B. E. (*c.* 1696); GROSE (1785).

1340. *Ayenbite of Inwyt* [OLIPHANT, *New English*, i. 30. A good man becomes a POST in God's temple; this explains our phrase, 'FROM PILLAR TO POST'].

1509. BARCLAY, *Eclogues* [Percy Soc.], XXII., lvii. From POST UNTO PILLAR tosseth.

1531-47. COPLAND, *Spyttel Hous* [HAZLITT, *Pop. Poet*, iv. 56]. And auentreth, tyll them haue all lost, And turmoyleth alway FRO PYLER TO POST.

1537-50. *Vox Populi, Vox Dei* [HAZLITT, *Early Pop. Poet.*, iii. 274]. That FROM PILLER VNTO POST The powr man he was tost.

1582. STANIHURST, *Æneid*, iv. 296. FROM thee POAST TOE PILER with thoght his rackt wyt he tosseth.

1607. MARSTON, *What You Will*, iv. 1. Come you; you prate: yfaith He tosseth you FROM POST TO PILLER.

*c.*1611. SHAKSPEARE and FLETCHER, *Two Noble Kinsmen*, iii. 5. And, dainty duke, whose doughty dismal fame From Dis to Dædalus, FROM POST TO PILLAR, Is blown abroad.

*d.*1624. BRETON, *Character of Elizabeth*, 5. In the tyme of her sister Queene Marie's raigne, how was she handled? tost FROM PILLAR TO POST, imprisoned, sought to be put to death.

1678. COTTON, *Scarronides*, 62. Our guards FROM PILLAR banged TO POST, He kicked about till they were lost.

1749. SMOLLETT, *Gil Blas* [ROUTLEDGE], 86. He threw his arms about the old man's neck; and these two . . . began sending him backwards and forwards . . . After they had tossed him about FROM PILLAR TO POST they suffered him to depart.

1767. RAY, *Proverbs* [BOHN], 175. To be tost FROM POST TO PILLORY.

1898. BRADDON, *Rough Justice*, 18. Hunted from PILLAR TO POST.

Other COLLOQUIALISMS are:—TO RUN (or KNOCK) THE HEAD AGAINST A POST = to go blindly; STIFF AS A POST = unyielding: as a gatepost in the ground; TO TALK (or PREACH) TO A POST = to talk to deaf ears: hence DEAF AS A POST = as deaf as may be; TO RIDE A POST = to copulate; TO GO TO THE POST = to visit a woman; TO TALK POST = to speak hastily; POST ALONE = solitary; TO KISS THE POST = (*see* KISS, and *add* quots. 1529 and 1548); TO HOLD UP A POST (or THE WALL) = to cling for support when drunk. *See* also BEDPOST; KNIGHT; NICK.

1400. *Hymns to Virgin and Christ* [E. E. T. S.], 61. [Here conscience is scornfully told] TO PRECHE TO THE POST.

*d.*1529. SKELTON, *Phyllyp Sparowe*, 715. Troylus also hath lost On her moch loue and cost, And now must KYS THE POST.

1548. BARCLAY, *Eglogues* (1570), ii. sig. B iiii. Yet from beginning absent if thou be, Eyther shalt thou lose thy meat and KISSE THE POST.

1582. STANIHURST, *Œnid*, iv. 492. Her self left also she deemed POST ALOAN, and soaly from woonted coompanye singled.

1599. SHAKSPEARE, *Hen. V.*, iii. 2. A' never broke any man's head but his own, and that was AGAINST A POST when he was drunk.

*d.*1608. SACKVILLE, *Stafford D. of Buck.*, st. 49. She chang'd her cheer, and left me POST ALONE.

1632. SHIRLEY, *The Changes*, i. 1. 'Twere no good manners to speak hastily to a gentlewoman, TO TALK POST (as they say) to his mistress.

POST-AND-RAIL, *subs. phr.* (Australian).—A wooden match; POST-AND-RAIL TEA = ill-made tea, with floating stalks and leaves.

1851. *Australasian*, 298. Hyson-skin and POST-AND-RAIL TEA have been superseded by Mocha, claret, and cognac.

1855. MUNDY, *Our Antipodes*, 163. A hot beverage in a tin pot, which richly deserved the colonial epithet of POST-AND-RAIL TEA, for it might well have been a decoction of 'split stuff,' or 'ironbark shingles,' for any resemblance it bore to the Chinese plant.

1870. BRAIM, *New Homes*, i. The shepherd's wife kindly gave us the invariable mutton-chop and damper, and some POST-AND-RAIL TEA.

1883. KEIGHLEY, *Who are You?* 36. Then took a drink of tea . . . Such as the swagmen in our goodly land Have with some humour named the POST-AND-RAIL.

POSTERIORS, *subs.* (old colloquial).—1. The buttocks; and (2) the after part.

1594. SHAKSPEARE, *Love's Lab. Lost*, v. 1, 94. It is the King's . . . pleasure . . . to congratulate the princess at her pavilion in the POSTERIORS of this day, which the rude multitude call the afternoon.

POSTERN, *subs.* (venery).—1. The fundament; also POSTERN-DOOR: *see* MONOCULAR-EYEGLASS; (2) the female *pudendum*; also POSTERN GATE TO THE ELYSIAN FIELDS (HERRICK): *see* MONOSYLLABLE.

1678. COTTON, *Virgil Travestie* [*Works* (1725), 139]. And thrice her latest breath did roar, In hollow Sound at POSTERN-DOOR. *Ibid.* (1st ed., p. 8). Whom Jove observing to be so stern, In the wise conduct of his POSTERN.

1719. DURFEY, *Pills to Purge*, i. 264. So Sissly shone with Beauty's rays Reflecting from her POSTERN grace.

1749. ROBERTSON of Struan, *Poems*, 83. So to a House of Office streight A School-Boy does repair, To ease his POSTERN of its Weight.

POST-HORN, *subs. phr.* (common).—The nose: also PASTE-HORN: *see* CONK.

POSTILLION. *See* ST. GEORGE.

POSTILLION OF THE GOSPEL, *subs. phr.* (old).—A gabbling parson.—GROSE (1785).

POSTMAN, *subs.* (obsolete legal).—*See* quot. [The old Court of Exchequer is now merged in the High Court of Justice.]

1765-9. BLACKSTONE, *Com.*, III. iii. Note. In the courts of exchequer, two of the most experienced barristers, called the POST-MAN and the tub-man (from the places in which they sit), have also a precedence in motions.

POSTMASTER, *subs.* (University).—An exhibitioner of Merton College: also PORTIONIST.

1853. BRADLEY, *Verdant Green*, vii. I remember Mr. Larkyns . . . telling us that the son of one of his old friends had been a POSTMASTER of Merton.

1886. *Oxford Guide* [S. J. & C.]. The POSTMASTERS anciently performed the duties of Choristers, and their payment for this duty was six shillings and fourpence per annum.

POSTMASTER GENERAL, *subs. phr.* (old).—The prime minister: 'who has the patronage of all posts and places.'—GROSE (1785).

POST-MORTEM, *subs. phr.* (Cambridge).—The examination after failure.

1844. *Puck*, 13. I've passed the POST-MORTEM at last.

POST-ANOINTER, *subs. phr.* (old).—A house painter.—GROSE (1785).

POST-OFFICE. A LETTER IN THE POST-OFFICE, *subs. phr.* (American).—A flying shirt-tail.

POST-OFFICE BIBLE, *subs. phr.* (Post-office).—The London Delivery Book.

POST-OFFICE PRAYER-BOOK, *subs. phr.* (Post-office).—The Post-office Guide.

POT, *subs.* (old colloquial).—A quart: the quantity contained in a POT. Whence as *verb.* = to drink: also (American) TO POTATE; POTTING = BOOZING (*q.v.*); POTATIONS (recognised) = a drinking-bout; POT-HOUSE (or SHOP) = a beer-shop, a LUSH-CRIB (*q.v.*); POT-HOUSE (or COFFEE-HOUSE) POLITICIAN = an ignorant, irresponsible spouter of politics; POT-COMPANION = (1) a cup-comrade, and (2) an habitual drunkard: as also = POT-FURY (also = drunkenness), -KNIGHT, -HEAD, -LEACH, -MAN, -POLISHER, -SUCKER, -WALLOPER, POTATOR, POTSTER, TOSS-POT, and ROB-POT; POT-PUNISHMENT = compulsory tippling; POT-QUARREL = a drunken squabble; POT-SICK (or -SHOT) = drunk; POT-SURE (-HARDY, or -VALIANT) = emboldened by liquor: *cf.* DUTCH COURAGE (B. E., *c.* 1696, and GROSE, 1785); POT-BELLIED = fat, bloated in stomach as from guzzling: also POT-BELLY (or GUTS) = a big-bellied one; POT-REVEL = a drunken frolic; POT-MANIA (or POTOMANIA) = dipsomania; SIR (or MADAM) PINT-POT = a host (or hostess); POT-BOY (or -MAN) = a bar-scullion: whence POT-BOY-DOM.

1560. BECON, *Works* [Parker Soc.], 276. Good wife PINT-POT.

1584. [? MONDAY], *Weakest to Wall*, iii. 4. Now, mine host ROB-POT, empty-can, beer-barrel.

1594. LYLY, *Mother Bombie*, iii. 2. *Dro.* How sped'st thou after thy POTTING? *Ris.* Nay, my master rung all in the taverne, and thrust all out.

1597. HALL, *Satires*, I. iii. With some POT-FURY . . . they sit and muse.

1598. *Lomatius on Painting* [NARES]. But these base fellowes I leave in their ale-houses, to take POT-PUNISHMENT of each other once a day, till, &c.

1598. SHAKSPEARE, *1 Hen. IV.*, ii. 4, 438. Peace, good PINT-POT: peace, good tickle-brain. Ibid., *2 Henry VI.*, ii. 3. And here's a POT of good double beer. *Ibid.* (1602), *Othello*, ii. 3. I learned it in England, where, indeed, they are most potent in POTTING: your Dane, your German, and your swag-bellied Hollander . . . are nothing to your English.

1614. *Time's Whistle* [E. E. T. S.], 59. One POT-COMPANION and his fashion I will describe.

1620. FELTHAM, *Resolves*, 84. It is less labour to plow than TO POT IT.

1630. TAYLOR, *Works* [NARES]. And being mad perhaps, and hot POT-SHOT, A crazed crowne or broken pate hath got. *Ibid.* This valiant POT-LEACH that upon his knees Has drunke a thousand pottles up-se-freese.

*c.*1650. BRATHWAYTE, *Barnaby's J.* (1723), III. 119. Kindly drink to one another Till POT-HARDY. *Ibid.*, 167. If thou dost love thy flock, leave off TO POT.

1651. CARTWRIGHT, *Royal Slave* [NARES]. *Arc.* Faith, landlord. *Mol.* I'd have sworn thou hadst bin of a better nature, than to remember POT-QUARRELS.

1653. WALTON, *Complete Angler*, 181. Let's each man drink a POT for his morning's draught.

1653. URQUHART, *Rabelais*, I. xl. Well-antidoted with POT-PROOF armour.

1659. *Legend of Captain Jones* [NARES]. When these rough gods beheld him thus secure, And arm'd against them like a man POT-SURE.

1703. WARD, *London Spy*, xv. 366. He had made himself POT VALIANT with his Countryman's Liquor.

*d.*1704. L'ESTRANGE, *Quevado* [Latham]. For fuddling they shall make the best POT-COMPANION in Switzerland knock under the table.

1715. HEARNE, *Diary*, 11 Oct. Tho' he [a posture-master] is a well-growu fellow yet he will appear . . . as hunchtback'd, POTT-BELLYD, sharp-breasted.

1729. SWIFT, *Directions to Servants*, iv. They will wait until you slip into a neighbouring ale-house to take a POT with a friend.

*b.*1744. ARBUTHNOT and POPE, *Martin Scriblerus* [Ency. Dict.]. He will find himself a forked stradling animal, and a POT-BELLY.

1749. SMOLLETT, *Gil Blas* [ROUTLEDGE], 179. A long bench, such as usually graces a POT-HOUSE porch. *Ibid.*, 266. He told me . . . they could only be COFFEE-HOUSE POLITICIANS. *Ibid.* (1771), *Humphrey Clinker*, l. 30. Like a man who has drunk himself POT-VALIANT, I talked to her in such a style of authority and resolution, as produced a most blessed effect.

1772. GRAVES, *Spiritual Quixote*, IV. viii. You POT-GUTTED rascal.

1803. LAMB, *To Coleridge*, 13 Ap. Last night . . . a pipe, and some generous Port, and *King Lear* had their effects as solacers. I went to bed POT-VALIANT.

18[?]. GRAY, *To Mason* [LATHAM]. He appears to be near forty; a little POT-BELLIED and thick-shouldered, otherwise no bad figure.

1834. SOUTHEY, *The Doctor*, xliv. Barnabee, the illustrious POTATOR, saw there the most unbecoming sight that he met with in all his travels.

1836. M. SCOTT, *Tom Cringle*, xii. The little POT-VALIANT master, primed with two tumblers of grog, in defiance of the Captain's presence, fairly fastened on him.

1837. DICKENS, *Pickwick*, li. 'Perhaps we had better retire,' whispered Mr. Pickwick. 'Never, sir,' rejoined Pott, POT-VALIANT in a double sense, 'never.' *Ibid.*, lii. A sequestered POT-SHOP on the remotest confines of the Borough.

1849. KINGSLEY, *Alton Locke*, xiii. It is a part of his game to ingratiate himself with all POT-BOY-DOM.

1849. MACAULAY, *Hist. Eng.*, v. The coarse dialect which hé had learned in the POT-HOUSES of Whitechapel.

1851. S. JUDD, *Margaret*, iii. The old man is still mecurial; but his POT-VALIANTRY is gone.

1851. MAYHEW, *Lond. Lab.*, II. 17. I could get a POT-BOY'S place again, but I'm not so strong as I were, and its slavish work in the place I could get.

1855. KINGSLEY, *Westward Ho*, xv. She was too good for a poor POT-HEAD like me.

1860. DICKENS, *Uncommercial Traveller*, xiii. The POTMAN thrust the ast brawling drunkards into the street.

1864. *Eton School Days*, viii. Bird's-eye's patrons would . . . sit in his cottage and smoke and drink beer, for they were potent at POTTING.

1876. S. DOWELL, *Taxes in England*, I. 200. The increase in drinking . . . carried your English in potency of POTTING above even your Dane, your German, and your swag-bellied Hollander.

1899. WHITEING, *John St.*, xiv. I have contracted fatal habits . . . one . . . is that I want a nip in a POT-HOUSE before retiring to rest. *Ibid.*, xxiv. You could never git through it if you paid a quid for every POT o' beer.

2. (sporting).—A large sum; the collective amount of money staked; the pool. Hence (racing) = a horse backed for a large amount, a favourite; TO POT, or TO PUT ON THE POT = to wager large sums (BEE, 1823); and TO UPSET THE POT = to beat the favourite.

1840. *Sporting Review*, iv. 119. It needed only to lay against all, to insure a prize proportioned to the POT put on.

1859. LEVER, *Davenport Dunn* [TAUCHNITZ], I. 191. The horse you have backed with a heavy POT.

1864. *Derby-day*, 2. The knowing ones . . . POTTED their money on him without hesitation. *Ibid.*, 170. The trainer of course found the ready money to buy a share in the 'Horse and Jockey,' but that's not to be wondered at considering the POT he made when Ascapart won the Derby.

1868. OUIDA, *Under Two Flags*, v. All them fiddlers have lost such a sight of money by you; them bookmakers have had such a lot of POTS UPSET by you.

1870. L. OLIPHANT, *Piccadilly*, v. 196. "Harrie . . . went down to the Derby on Helter's drag, and won a POT on the French horse under his judicious advice."

1883. *Graphic*, 17 Nov., 494. 2. Medicus, the great Cambridgeshire POT, and Thebais, who showed well in that race, were among the runners.

1887. HENLEY, *Villon's Straight Tip*, 1. Suppose . . . you land your POT . . . Booze and the blowens cop the lot.

1891. *Sportsman*, 28 Feb. Homeward Bound, the medium of a plunge here last week, was the POTTED article for the United Service Selling Hunters' Steeplechase.

1894. MOORE, *Esther Waters*, vi. My great-grandfather had a POT of money, but it all went.

3. (sporting).—A prize. [Usually given in cups, mugs, or pots.] Whence POT-HUNTER (or -FISHER) = (1) a professional athlete of the baser sort—one who, of good quality, enters for events he is sure to win for the sake of the POTS offered as prizes; and (2) = a man who seeks a large BAG (*q.v.*) without regard to the rules and usages of sport. Also POT-HUNTING = going in for sport for profit alone.—GROSE (1785).

1879. *Scribner's Mag.*, Aug., 506. With no other let or hindrance than those which the gory POT-HUNTERS compel.

1882. W. W. GREENER, *The Gun*, 570. Poachers and POT-HUNTERS are encouraged that they may keep the tables of their friends in office well-supplied with game. *Ibid.*, 575. The Chinese have an original and effective manner of POT-HUNTING after Wild-fowl.

1884. *Daily News*, 9 Feb., 5, 3. Common birds are better off in England than abroad where they are shot by way of sport, and POTTED by pot-hunters.

1885. *Field*, 12 Dec. Some protection should be taken against POT-HUNTING.

1889. SIR H. POTTINGER, *Trout-Fishing*. But ordinary mortals have a natural dislike to returning with empty baskets, and some people not necessarily POT-HUNTERS like to eat trout.

1891. *National Observer*, 14 Feb., 332. But does Mr. Everard seriously pretend . . . he was contemplating the rivalry of the two in a gigantic POT-HUNTING 'competeetion'?

4. (common).—A person of importance; an adept: also BIG POT.

1892. MILLIKEN, *'Arry Ballads*, 70. The genuine POT.

1891. *Licensed Victualler's Gaz.*, 9 Feb. Dick pointed out some of the BIG POTS of the day, but there did not seem much union of hearts among them.

1899. WHITEING, *John St.*, 150. Grandfather sold things over the counter. The father's some tremendous POT in the financial way, and got his baronetcy for a Royal visit.

1900. NISBET, *Sheep's Clothing*, 131. He is rather a BIG POT as a preacher I hear.

5. (nautical).—A steward.

6. (medical students').—Sixpence: FIVE-POT PIECE = 2s. 6d.

1885. *Household Words*, 20 June, 155. To many drinkers the coin . . . was known as a POT, because it was the price of a POT [*q.v.*, sense 1], or quart of 'half-and-half.'

7. (Stock Exchange).—*In pl.* = North Staffordshire Railway Ordinary Stock. [The railway serves the Potteries.]

8. (Winchester College).—The POT = the Canal. POT-CAD = a workman at the saw mills; POT-GATES = lock-gates; POT-HOUSER = a jump into the canal from the roof of a house called POT-HOUSE.—MANSFIELD (*c.* 1840).

9. (venery).—The female *pudendum*: *see* MONOSYLLABLE.

1678. COTTON, *Scoffer Scofft* [*Works* (1725), 260]. In Love I'm not so simple, But to observe she has a Dimple, And such a one, as who would not Put all his Flesh into the POT?

10. (old).—A urinal; a chamber. Hence AS GOOD A PIECE AS EVER STRODE A POT = as good a girl as ever pissed.

Adj. (back slang).—Top.

Verb. (old colloquial).—1. To kill: specifically (modern) to shoot from cover: also TO POT-SHOT. Hence POT-SHOT, *subs.* = (1) a shot so made; (2) a shot made for the sake of a BAG (*q.v.*) without regard to the rules and usages of sport; and (3) a shot at random, as into a flight of birds without definite aim: *cf.* SNIPE. Whence TO POT AWAY = to keep up a rain of shot.

1858. *Edinburgh Courant*, 2 Sep. All . . . were firing POT-SHOTS at him, while he was rushing about with a tulwar determined to sell his life dearly.

1860. RUSSELL, *Diary in India*, II. 327. Taking POT-SHOTS at their sentries and pickets.

1860. *Chambers' Jl.*, xiii. 90. A few . . . amuse themselves by POTTING at us, but they are in too great a state of fear to make good practice.

1861. HUGHES, *Tom Brown at Oxford*, xl. My gracious sovereign pays me seven and sixpence a day: for which sum I undertake to be shot at on certain occasions and by proper persons . . . But that doesn't include turning out to be POTTED AT like a woodcock.

1861. READE, *Cloister and Hearth*, viii. Martin had been in a hurry TO POT her, and lost her by an inch.

1866. G. A. SALA, *Trip to Barbary*, xv. Tourists . . . are in the habit of bringing Devisme's fowling-pieces with them, and POTTING the monkeys by way of a *chasse-cafe*.

1883. *Daily Telegraph*, 23 Mar., 5, 3. The English father of a family has not yet taken to the evil course of waiting for the tax-collector behind a stone wall and POTTING him with a blunderbuss.

1884. *Sat. Rev.*, 15 Mar. All the pretty shy beasts . . . are POTTED by cockneys.

1888. GREENER, *The Gun*, 531. The desire of puntsmen TO POT as many birds as possible by one shot.

1888. BOLDREWOOD, *Robbery Under Arms*, xxiii. He and old Crib were a stunning pair for POT-SHOOTING. *Ibid.*, xvi. Take a cool POT at him with a revolver.

1889. PHILLIPPS-WOLLEY, *Trottings of a Tenderfoot* [S. J. and C.]. There is none of the credit due to the quiet POT-SHOT which a quick snap-shot at a buck on the jump might earn.

1889. *Time*, Aug., 151. The proper thing for men, with their powerfuller brains, is not to set on to a woman as though they despise her, but just to POT away at her, unless she carries it too far, when it is necessary to go for her.

1891. *Murray's Mag.*, Aug., 211. I came here about a week ago TO POT at the pigeons, and I've done very well, so far.

1900. NISBET, *Sheep's Clothing*, 26. 'He'll carry the trade mark of Elola . . . for the rest of his life.' 'Serve him jolly well right for not shooting straight. However, he is in with us now since he has POTTED the girl.

2. See *subs.*, senses 1 and 2.

3. (billiards).—To pocket a ball.

1885. *Ev. Standard*, 18 Dec. After making three he POTTED his opponent's ball.

1891. *Sportsman*, 26 Mar. Roberts, opening with a fluke by POTTING the red, ran up in his best style a capital 132.

4. (common).—To 'take a rise out of'; TO DO (*q.v.*); to be revenged; TO LAND (*q.v.*).

1855. TAYLOR, *Still Waters*, ii. A greater flat was never POTTED.

1880. MILLIKIN, *Punch's Almanack*, St. Valentine's Day. Crab your enemies,—I've got a many, You can POT 'em proper for a penny.

5. (old).—To excel: as TO POT verses = to cap them.

1599. STOWE, *Survey*, 53. The boies of different schooles did cap or POTTE verses.

TO GO TO POT, *verb. phr.* (common).—To perish; to be done for: as by death, bad seasons, pecuniary difficulties, and so forth.—RAY (1670). [SMYTH-PALMER, *Folk Etymology*, thinks POT = a pit (*i.e.*, of destruction): An alternative suggestion, apparently supported by most of the (especially the earlier) quotations, is that POT = a cooking, or a refiner's melting pot]. Whence GO TO POT! = 'Go to the devil'; 'Go hang yourself': Fr. *Sucré*! and *Va-te-faire-suer*! POTTED-OUT = buried. *See* HOP THE TWIG and QUISBY.

1394. LANGLAND, *Piers Ploughman*, 627. Vnder A POT he schal be put in a pryvie chambre.

1512-3. DOUGLAS, *Eucados* (1710), 108, 16. And vthir sum thare with gan schete ful hot Deip in the sorowfull grisle hellis POT.

1525. TYNDALE, *Ans. to Sir T. More* [Parker Soc. (1850), 110]. Then GOETH a part of little flock TO POT, and the rest scatter.

1552. LATIMER, *Sermons*, 183. The more wicked, the more lucky: but they that pertaine to God . . . must GO TO THE POT, they must suffer here according to the Scriptures.

1563. HAKLUYT, *Voyages*, 'Ballad of R. Baker.' If Cannibals they be In kind we doe not know; And if they be, then welcome we, To POT straightway we goe.

1573. *New Custom*, ii. 3. *Crew.* Thou wouldest not sticke to bringe thine owne brother to payne. *Avar.* No, nor father and mother, if there were ought to be got, . . . if I could I would bring them TO THE POT.

1601. *Jack Drum's Ent.* (1616), i. 218. *Flawn.* Why, the weakest GOE TO THE POT still. *Mam.* That jest shall saue him.

1610. SHAKSPEARE, *Coriolanus*, i. 4. *First sold.* See they have shut him in. *All.* To THE POT, I warrant him.

1611. COTGRAVE, *Dict.*, s.v. *Aussitost meurt vache comme veau.* As soon the young, as old, GOES TO THE POT.

1612. WEBSTER, *White Devil*, iv. 4. Pigeons though they destroy never so much corn, the farmer dare not present the fowling-piece to them . . . because they belong to the lord of the manor; whilst your poor sparrows, that belong to the lord of heaven, they GO TO THE POT for't.

1648. *Life of A. a Wood* [BLISS], 39. He was conniv'd at and kept in his place, otherwise he had infallibly GON TO THE POT.

1662. *Rump Songs*, ii. 44. If Monesk be turn'd Scot, The Rump GOES TO POT, And the good Old cause will miscarry.

1665. HEAD, *English Rogue* (1874), I. x. 77. We will make his Till spring a leak for it, or his Goods GO TO POT, and break him at last.

1680. DRYDEN, *Prol. to Univ., Oxford*, 15 (Globe, 443). Then all you heathen wits shall GO TO POT For disbelieving of a Popish plot.

1686. HIGDEN, *On Tenth Satire of Juvenal*, 13. The Founder's fournace grows red-hot—Sejanus Statue GOES TO POT.

1712. ARBUTHNOT, *Hist. of John Bull*, I. vi. John's ready money, book debts, bonds, mortgages, all went into the lawyers' pockets. Then John began to borrow money on *Bank Stock*, *East India Bonds*: and now and then a farm WENT TO POT.

1771. SMOLLETT, *Humphry Clinker*, 61. We went by sea to another kingdom, called Fife, and, coming back, had like to have GONE TO POT in a storm.

1772. BRIDGES, *Burlesque Homer*, 31. Mother, since I'm to GO TO POT, And must be either hang'd or shot.

1840. BARHAM, *Ingoldsby Legends*, 'Merchant of Venice.' "In the first place you know all the money I've got, Time and often, from now has been long GONE TO POT."

1889. *Cornhill Mag.*, July, 46. For the potato is really GOING TO POT . . . Constitutional disease and the Colorado beetle have preyed too long upon its delicate organism.

COLLOQUIALISMS are:—A POT (or PITCHER) OFT SENT TO THE WELL IS BROKEN AT LAST = the inevitable must happen: *see* PITCHER, *subs.* 1; TO AGREE LIKE POT AND KETTLE = to wrangle: *see* BLACK-ARSE; AS LIKE AS ONE POT'S LIKE ANOTHER = very like indeed; A LITTLE POT IS SOON HOT = (1) a little suffices, and (2) little people (or minds) are soon angered (B. E., *c.* 1696); TO MAKE THE POT BOIL (or KEEP THE POT BOILING) = (1) to provide necessaries, and (2) to keep things going: Fr. (artists') *faire du métier*: *see* POT-BOILER; TO MAKE A POT WITH TWO EARS = to set the arms akimbo; TO PUT ON THE POT = (1) *see* POT, *subs.*, (2) = to overcharge, (3) = to exaggerate, (4) = to bully, (5) = to snub, or patronise (also TO PUT ON THE BIG POT): *see* POT, *subs.* 4, and (6) = to provide the necessaries of life; TO PUT ON THE POT = to banish, to extinguish; TO MAKE A POT AT = to grimace; TO MAKE POTS AND PANS = 'to spend freely, then beg' (BEE, 1823); TO GIVE MOONSHINE IN A MUSTARD-POT = to give nothing (RAY, 1670); 'IF YOU TOUCH POT, YOU MUST TOUCH PENNY = 'You must pay for what you have.' Also *see* PISS, POT-AND-PAN, OLD POD, POT-SHOT, POT-HAT, HONEY-POT, &c.

1481. *Reynard the Foxe* [Percy Soc.]. A POT MAY GOO SO LONGE TO WATER THAT AT LAST IT COMETH TO-BROKEN HOOM.

1535. COVERDALE, *Bible*, Eccles. xiii. HOW AGREE THE KETELL AND THE POT TOGETHER.

1546. HEYWOOD, *Proverbs*, s.v. LITTLE POT, SOONE HOT.

1593. SHAKSPEARE, *Tam. of Shrew*, iv. 1, 5. Now, were I not A LITTLE POT AND SOON HOT.

1661. HEYLIN, *Hist. Reformation*, 212. So poor that it is hardly able to KEEP THE POT BOILING for a parson's dinner.

1678. COTTON, *Scarronides*, 236. See what a goodly port she bears, MAKING THE POT WITH THE TWO EARS.

1812. COOMBE, *Dr. Syntax*, I. xxiii. No fav'ring patrons have I got, But just enough TO BOIL THE POT.

1836. DICKENS, *Pickwick*, xxx. Mr. Pickwick . . . went slowly and gravely down the slide . . . "KEEP THE POT A BILIN', sir!" said Sam; and down went Wardle . . . Mr. Pickwick, and then Sam, . . . following closely upon each other's heels.

1837. MARRYAT, *Snarley-Yow* (1897), 52, 4. Smack! crack! This is our jubilee! Huzza, my lads, we'll KEEP THE POT BOILING.

1847. BUCKSTONE, *Nine too Many*, i. Well, then, I was saying that I furnish the means to KEEP THE POT BOILING, therefore it only remains to distribute the different employments of our little household!

1858. G. ELIOT, *Amos Barton*, vi. "The poor fellow must have a hard pull to get along, with his small income and large family. Let us hope the Countess does something towards MAKING THE POT BOIL."

1869. *Fun*, 29 May, '*A Double Event.*' The Treasurer and the Box Book-keeper take their benefits . . . heavily backed by the two companies, and we trust the public will PUT ON A POT for them.

1888. BOLDREWOOD, *Robbery Under Arms*, i. There were other chances and pickings which helped to MAKE THE POT BOIL.

1893. EMERSON, *Lippo*, xxii. He gets to know their account, and he PUTS THE POT ON 'em settling day. *Ibid.*, viii. I found at last I must go on pitch by myself, to KEEP THE POT BOILING, as many a true artiste has too.

1898. *Cigarette*, 26 Nov., 13, 3. Now then, KEEP THE POT A-BILING, Mister Graydon down below!

POTATO, *subs.* (common). — *See* quot.: used esp. for a heel through an undarned sock or stocking.

1885. BARING-GOULD, *Eng., Ill. Mag.*, June, 616. The gladiators wore pasteboard helmets . . . and fleshings for legs and arms, with—what are vulgarly termed POTATOES, that is, holes in the fleshings perceptible in many places.

SMALL POTATOES, *adv. phr.* (American).—Petty; mean; contemptible: also as *adj.* and *subs.*

1846. *New York Herald*, 13 Dec. SMALL POTATO politicians and pettifogging lawyers.

1855. HALIBURTON, *Human Nature*, 38. It's SMALL POTATOES for a man of war to be hunting poor game like us little fore-and-aft vessels.

18 [?]. WHITCHER, *Widow Bedott Papers*, 188. The Presbyterian minister here is such SMALL POTATOES.

1891. *Morning Advertiser*, 20 April. The Hardwicke Plate dwindled down to very SMALL POTATOES.

THE POTATO (or CLEAN POTATO), *subs. phr.* (common).—The best; THE WHITEST (*q.v.*); the tip-top: *see* A 1.

1849. AINSWORTH, *Rookwood*, Pref. xxxvi. Of all rhymesters of the 'road,' however, Dean Burrowes is as yet most fully entitled to the laurel. Larry is quite THE POTATO.

1880. R. M. JEPHSON, *Pink Wedding*, 235. "I am convinced he is a first-rate one—quite THE CLEAN POTATO, in fact."

1899. *Sporting Times*, 15 Ap., 2, 4. Mr. Pinero has . . . pulled his play out from the oven absolutely the CLEAN POTATO.

POTATOES AND POINT, *subs. phr.* (common).—Potatoes without salt: POINT = an imaginary seasoning, as in POINTING, to bacon, cheese, anything: *cf.* 'Eat your bread and smell your cheese!'

1834. CARLYLE, *Sartor Resartus* [*Century*]. Their universal sustenance is the root named POTATO, . . . generally without condiment or relish of any kind, save an unknown condiment named POINT.

POTATO-BOGGLE, *subs. phr.* (common).—A scarecrow.

POTATO-FINGER, *subs. phr.* (old colloquial). — 1. A long thick finger. Whence (2) a *penis* of dimensions; and (3) a DILDO (*q.v.*).

1602. SHAKSPEARE, *Tr. and Cress.*, v. 2, 56. How the devil Luxury, with his fat rump and POTATO-FINGER, tickles these together.

POTATO-TRAP (or **-JAW**), *subs. phr.* (common).—The mouth: hence, 'Shut your POTATO-TRAP and give your tongue a holiday' = Be

silent!—GROSE (1785), BEE (1823); 'to make full use of one's POTATO-TRAP = to scold roundly.

ENGLISH SYNONYMS.—Beak; blabber; blubber; bone-box; box of dominoes (or wories); chaffer; chirper; chops; clacker (or clack-box); clams (or clam-shells); coffee-mill; coffer; dining-room; domino-box; dribbler; dubber; East-and-south (rhyming); flatter-trap; fly-trap; gab; gan; gash; gig; gills; gin-lane (or trap); gob; gobbler; gob-box; grave-yard; grog-shop; grub-trap (-shop, or -box); grubbery; hatchway; hopper; ivory-box; jug; kisser; kissing-trap; lung-box; maw; mizzard; moey; mouse (or mouse-trap); mug; muns; mush; muzzle; neb; prater; prattler; prattle-box; rattler; rattle-trap; rat-trap; respirator; sauce-box; sewer; sink; sluice-house (or -mill); sluicery; trumpeter; yob (or yop).

FRENCH SYNONYMS. — *Abajoues* (= the chops); *angoulême* (thieves': *engouler* = to swallow. *se caresser l'angoulême* = to eat and drink); *babines* (popular); *babouines* (also = little hussy); *badigoinces* (popular); *barres* (popular); *bavarde* (= the prater or blab-box); *bécot*; *caisse d'épargne* (also = Savings-bank); *cassolette* (= the stinkpot); *couloir* (popular); *crachoir* (also = spittoon); *égout* (= the sewer); *gargoine* (formerly *gargamelle* = the gargler); *gaviot* (popular); *gargouille* (*gargouine, or gargue*); *goule*; *goulot*; *guadeloupe*; *menteuse*; *mornos*; *moule à blagues* (= chaffer); *mouloir*; *pampine* (specficially a thick-lipped coarse mouth); *pantière* (= bread-basket, which in English = stomach); *plomb*; *respirante* (*bâche, ta respirante* = Shut up!); *ruette* (popular); *salle à manger* (= dining-room); *tinette*; *triangle* (artists'); *trompette* (= trumpeter); *trou aux pommes de terre* (= potato-trap).

1791. DARBLAY, *Diary*, v. 209. 'Hold you your POTATO-JAW, my dear,' cried the Duke, patting her.

1836. M. SCOTT, *Cruise of the Midge*, xv. Hold your tongue, and give your POTATO-TRAP a holiday.

1853. DODGSON, *Verdant Green*, II. iv. That'll damage your POTATO-TRAP.

1856. MAYHEW, *World of London*, 6, *note*. Fanciful metaphors contribute largely to the formation of slang. It is upon this principle that the mouth has come to be styled the 'TATER-TRAP'; the teeth, dominoes.

POT-BELLY (or **-GUTS**).—*See* POT, *subs.*

POT-BOILER, *subs. phr.* (artists').—1. A piece of work done for money: *i.e.*, TO BOIL THE POT (*q.v.*); also as *adj.* Hence, POT-BOILING, and TO POT-BOIL.

1870. *Daily Telegraph*, 10 Feb. Even those who buy pictures and art-objects merely out of vanity would prefer good work for their gold if they only knew how to choose it; and consequently Professor Ruskin cast upon the artists the great responsibility for the eccentric, superficial, or POT-BOILING qualities which degrade much of what is manufactured and sold.

1879. LINDSAY, *Mind in the Lower Animals*, i. 20. What are vulgarly known as POT-BOILER books or articles.

1880. HOWELLS, *Undiscovered Country*, xx. They write for pleasure and from duty. I am sorry to say that my work is mostly for the pay it brings . . . I write and sell my work. It's what they call POT-BOILING.

1882. *Athenæum*, 1 April. A mere POT-BOILER, though it is marked by much of the ability of the artist. *Ibid.* (1883), 17 Mar., 340, 2. "The Captain's Room" is, in fact, a POT-BOILER.

1885. *D. Telegraph*, 28 Dec. Below the composer's mark, and distinctly of the POT-BOILING order.

1887. *Lippincott's Mag.*, July, 160. Colonel Higginson, for example—advises a connection with a newspaper. Doubtless as a POT-BOILER that would be a good thing.

1888. *Globe*, 17 Oct. It is quite impossible for an author to produce a level series of books . . . First there is a good book, then a POT-BOILER, perhaps two POT-BOILERS, perhaps more, and then a return to the old form.

1892. *Sala's Journal*, 2 July, 239. Between the ages of eighteen and twenty-three I must have produced myself many scores of POT-BOILERS.

2. (provincial).—A house-keeper.

3. (scientific).—*See* quot.

1874. DAWKINS, *Cave Hunting*, iii. Among the articles of daily use were many rounded pebbles, with marks of fire upon them, which had probably been heated for the purpose of boiling water. POT-BOILERS, as they are called, of this kind are used by many savage peoples at the present day, and if we wished to heat water in a vessel that would not stand the fire, we should be obliged to employ a similar method.

POTCHING, *subs.* (waiters?).—*See* quot. [*Century*: POTCH = an obsolete form of 'poach.']

1883. *Graphic*, 17 March, 283, 3. Good-natured customers may imagine that if they have given a fee to the waiter who presents the bill, they may hand another to the usual man who has attended upon them; but head-waiters are alive to the perils of this practice, which they call POTCHING (probably from poaching), and dismissal will be the punishment of the waiter who is caught taking vails on the sly.

POT-FAKER, *subs. phr.* (common).—A hawker; a CHEAP-JACK (*q.v.*): spec. one dealing in crockery.

POT-GUN, *subs. phr.* (old).—1. A toy gun: POP-GUN is a later form: *see* POP, *verb*.

1550. UDAL, *Roister Doister* [ARBER], 73. Bryng with thee my POTGUNNE hangyng by the wall.

1585. *Nomenclator*, s.v. *Sclopus, &c.* A POT-GUN made of an elderne sticke, or hollow quill, whereout boyes shoote chawen paper.

1610. HALL, *Married Clergy*, 148. They are but as the POTGUNS of boys.

d. 1637. JONSON [MOXON, *Works*, 719]. The ratling pit-pat noise Of the less poetic boys, When their POTGUNS aim to hit With their pellets of small wit.

1707. WARD, *Hudibras Redivivus*, I. xii. 16. Such dreadful POT-GUNS of Correction, That threaten'd nothing but Destruction.

1899. WHITEING, *John St.* [1901], 80. Pigeons may be killed, of course, with a POP-GUN IN a back-yard.

2. (old).—A reproach.

1623. WEBSTER, *Duch. of Malfi*, iii. 3. I saw a Dutchman break his pate once For calling him POT-GUN.

1693. CONGREVE, *Old Bachelor*, iii. 8. That sign of a man there—that POT-GUN charged with wind.

POT-HAT, *subs. phr.* (common).—*See* quot. 1891.

1869. BRADWOOD, *O. V. H.*, xi. Jemmy . . . securing a POT-HAT, pea-jacket, and double-thong as precaution, went to the servants' hall.

1889. *Sporting Times*, 3 Aug., 3, 1. A gentlemanly young fellow in a tweed suit and a POT HAT.

1891. *Notes and Queries*, 7 S. xii. 48. . . . The term POT-HAT . . . until lately I always thought was short for 'chimney-pot hat,' less reverently known as a 'tile'; but at the present time it is often applied to a felt hat.

1896. SALA, *London Up to Date*, 62. I should respectfully advise him . . . not to be in the habit of perambulating Pall Mall in a suit of dittoes and a POT HAT.

POTHEEN, *subs.* (Irish). — Illicit whiskey. Also POTSHEEN.

c. 1809. EDGEWORTH, *Absentee*, x. 'A glass of what?' 'POTSHEEN, plase your honour; beca-ase it's the little whiskey that's made in the private still or *pot*; and *sheen* it's a fond word for whatsoever we'd like, and for what we have little of, and would make much of.

1836. M. SCOTT, *Tom Cringle's Log*, ii. Staggering and swaying about under the influence of the POTEEN.

POT-HOOKS, *subs. phr.* (military).—The Seventy-seventh Foot, now the 2nd Batt. Duke of Cambridge's Own (Middlesex Regiment). [From the resemblance of the two sevens in the old regimental number to POT-HOOKS.]

POT-HOOKS AND HANGERS, *subs. phr.* (colloquial).—1. The elementary characters formed by children when learning to write. Hence, a scrawl, or bad writing.—B. E. (*c.* 1696); GROSE (1785). [*Cf.* FLESH-HOOKS (*c.* 1321, *Rel. Antiq.* i.) = notes of music.]

1690. DRYDEN, *Don Sebastian*, ii. 2. I long to be spelling her Arabick scrawls and POT-HOOKS.

1772. BRIDGES, *Burlesque Homer*, 469. If ever . . . I such a pack of POT-HOOKS saw. What language does he write?

1821. EGAN, *Life in London*, II. v. Whose to understand it? Vy it's full of POTHOOKS AND HANGERS.

2. (old).—Shorthand.

POT-HOUSE (THE), *subs. phr.* (Cambridge). — St. Peter's College: formerly Peterhouse.

1891. *Harry Fludyer*, 85. I made a shot and said 'POTHOUSE.' He said, 'I suppose you mean St. Peter's College.'

See POT, *subs.* 1.

POTION. *See* BITTER PILL.

POT-HUNTER. *See* POT, *verb* 3, and POT-LUCK.

POTLE-BELL. TO RING THE POTLE-BELL, *verb. phr.* (Scots').—To confirm a bargain by linking the little fingers of the right hand.

POT-LUCK, *subs. phr.* (old colloquial).—Whatever is going in the way of food and drink; an impromptu invitation; whence, a hearty welcome: TO TAKE POT-LUCK = to take the hazard of a meal. Hence POT-HUNTER = a self-invited guest.

1593. NASHE, *Strange Newes* [GROSART, *Works*, ii. 242]. This . . . greedy POTHUNTER after applause, is an apparent Publican and sinner; a selfe-loue surfetted sot. *Ibid.* (1600), *Summers Last Will* [GROSART, *Works*, VI., 131]. We had but even POT-LUCK, a little to moysten our lips, and no more.

1749 SMOLLETT, *Gil Blas* [ROUTLEDGE], 71. He then offered us his crusts, and asked with a smile if we would TAKE POTLUCK with him.

1772. GRAVES, *Spiritual Quixote*, XIX. xii. He should be very welcome to TAKE POT-LUCK with him.

1814. *Saxon and Gael*, i. 55. If you . . . and my Leddy Mary, wad come in a canny way, and tak PAT-LUCK wi' Jean and me . . . I gie nae dinner ae day but what I can gie ilka day in the year.

1837. BARHAM, *Ingoldsby Legends* (1862), 248. Quoth the Lady, 'Dear Sir, no apologies, pray, You will TAKE our POT-LUCK in the family way.'

1857. THACKERAY, *Virginians*, lxxvi. "What! come to TAKE POT-LUCK with us, Brown my boy? Betsy! put a knife and fork for Mr. Brown. Eat! Welcome! Fall to! It's my best!"

1858. G. ELIOT, *Amos Barton*, i. He never contradicted Mrs. Hackit, a woman whose POT-LUCK was always to be relied on.

1870. *Chambers's Miscellany*, No. 87, 6. "I'm going home to dinner, and you must TAKE POT-LUCK with us."

1891. *Harry Fludyer at Cambridge* . . . 38. I decided to accept a very kind invitation from Blofield to TAKE POT-LUCK with him and Mrs. Blofield yesterday in Grosvenor Gardens.

1898. *Sat. Rev.*, 19 Nov., 657, 1. Whilst rival nations have been taking 'POT-LUCK' and helping themselves freely to whatever happened to be going.

1899. WHITEING, *John St.*, xxv. He leaves the meeting, and accepts an invitation to POT-LUCK for the remainder of the revel from one of the Bacchanalian floors.

POT-OF-WINE, *subs. phr.* (old).—A bribe. Fr. *pot-de-vin.*

POT-SHOT. *See* POT, *subs.* and *verb.* 1.

POTTAGE. *See* BREATH and PISS; besides which there are proverbial sayings:—'With cost one may make POTTAGE of a joint-stool'; 'Scald not your lips in another man's POTTAGE'; 'Like a chip in a POTTAGE-pot, neither good nor harm.'

POTTED-FUG, *subs. phr.* (Rugby).—Potted meat.

POTTER, *verb.* (colloquial).—1. To walk aimlessly and listlessly; (2) to make a pretence of work; and (3) to dawdle: usually with *about.* Hence as *subs.* = a saunter, a slow pace: also POTTERER.

1854. MARTIN and AYTOUN, *Bon Gualtier Ballads*, 'The Lay of the Lover's Friend.' He waxes strong upon his pangs, And POTTERS o'er his grog.

1857. T. HUGHES, *Tom Brown's Schooldays*, I. 2. Past the old church and down the footpath, POTTERED the old man and the child, hand-in-hand.

1859. GEORGE ELIOT, *Adam Bede*, xvii. His servants stayed with him till they were so old and POTTERING he had to hire other folk to do their work.

1868. COLLINS, *Moonstone*, I. xxiii. I . . . was POTTERING ABOUT the grounds, when I heard my name called.

1870. *Bell's Life*, 29 July. It was a day of POTTERING ABOUT—no run worthy of the name, and no kill.

1878-80. MCCARTHY, *Hist. Own Times*, xvii. Lord John Russell's Government POTTERED with the difficulty rather than encountered it.

1884. H. JAMES, JR., *Little Tour*, 252. I . . . POTTERED ABOUT Beaune rather rather vaguely for the rest of my hour.

1886. *Field*, 27 Feb. The run . . . degenerated into a POTTER.

1898. BOLDREWOOD, *Robbery Under Arms*, v. You haven't got to do with the old-fashioned mounted police as was POTTERING ABOUT.

POTTERY, *subs.* (common).—Poetry.

POT-WALLOPER (-WABBLER, -WALLONER, or **-WALLER)**, *subs. phr.* (political: was obsolete).—1. *See* quots. [The qualification was abolished by the Reform Bill of 1832.] Hence POT-WALLOPING, and also *subs.* and *adj.*—GROSE (1785).

1724-7. DE FOE, *Tour thro' Great Britain*, II. 18. The election of members here [Taunton] is by those whom they call POT-WALLONERS—that is to say, every inhabitant, whether housekeeper or lodger, who dresses his own victuals; to make out which, several inmates or lodgers will, some little time before the election, bring out their pots, and make fires in the street, and boil victuals in the sight of their neighbours, that their votes may not be called in question.

1787. GROSE, *Prov. Glossary*, s.v. "Walling." *Walling*, i.e., boiling . . . Perhaps the same as *wallopping*; whence in some boroughs, persons who boil a pot there are called POT-WALLOPPERS, and entitled to vote for representatives in Parliament.

1807. SOUTHEY, *Letters*, iv. 39. A POT-WALLOPING borough like Taunton.

1857. TROLLOPE, *Three Clerks*, xxix. "I am once more a constituent part of the legislative wisdom of the United Kingdom, thanks to the patriotic discretion of the POT-WALLOPERS, burgage-tenants, and ten-pound freeholders of these loyal towns."

2. (common).—A scullion; a kitchen-maid; and (nautical) a cook, esp. on board a whaler: also POT-WRESTLER.

3. (common).—A tap-room loafer; a spouter: esp. (theatrical) a PROSSER (*q.v.*).

POUCH (or POUCH UP), *verb.* (colloquial).—1. To pocket.

1567. EDWARDS, *Damon and Pythias* [DODSLEY, *Old Plays* (1874), iv. 40]. [OLIPHANT, *New English*, i. 565. In p. 40 stands TO POUCH UP money (for his own use); in our time a liberal friend POUCHES schoolboys.]

1635. QUARLES, *Emblems*, i. 9. Come, bring your saint POUCH'D in his leathern shrine.

1821. SCOTT, *Pirate*, vi. And for the value of the gowden piece, it shall never be said I POUCHED her siller.

1881. *Sci. Amer*, 55. They [the letters] have next to be POUCHED.

1886-96. MARSHALL, '*Pomes' from the Pink 'Un* ['Parkey'], 90. He POUCHED the change.

1889. *Licensed Victuallers' Gaz.*, 4 Jan. Two hundred solid quids he POUCHED, And then he slid.

2. (common).—To eat.

1892. MILLIKEN, *'Arry Ballads*, 49. Fancy POUCHING your prog on a terrace.

3. (common).—To tip; to provide with money.

1844. DISRAELI, *Coningsby*, i. 11. He had been loaded with kindness, . . . and, finally, had been POUCHED in a manner worthy of a Marquess and of a grandfather.

1864. *Eton School Days*, i. 4. "Did your governor POUCH you," asked Purefoy, as they were going towards the Station. "Yes," replied Butler Burke, "and so did the mater."

POUCHET, *subs.* (old).—A pocket.

1682. RADCLIFFE, *Rambler, &c.*, 44. 'Upon a Bowl of Punch.' Did out of his POUCHET three nutmegs produce.

POUCH-MOUTH, *subs. phr.* (old).—A ranter. Also as *adj.* = ranting.

1600. DEKKER, *Satiro-Mastix* [HAWKINS, *Eng. Dr.*, iii. 172]. Players, I mean, theaterians, POUCH-MOUTH stage-walkers.

POUDERING- (or **POWDERING-**) **TUB**, *subs. phr.* (old).—The salivating cradle or pit formerly used in cases of *lues venerea*; the pickling tub.—GROSE (1785), and HALLIWELL (1847). Also 'The Pocky Hospital at Kingsland, near London.'—B. E. (*c.* 1696).

1599. SHAKSPEARE, *Henry V.*, ii. 1. "From the POWD'RING-TUB of infamy Fetch forth the lazar kite Doll Tearsheet."

1611. CHAPMAN, *May-day*, ii. 5. How mean you that? d'ye think I came lately ath' POWDERING TUB.

c. 1697. T. BROWN, *Comical View* [*Works* (1715), I. 182]. As fair as a sinner newly Come out of the POWDERING TUB.

POUF, *subs.* (theatrical).—A would-be actor.

POULAIN, *subs.* (venery).—A bubo; a WINCHESTER-GOOSE (*q.v.*).—GROSE (1785). Fr. *poulain.*

POULDERLING, *subs.* (obs. University).—*See* quot.

1607. *Christmas Prince* (1816), 1. The whole companye, or most parte of the students of the same house mette toogeher to beginne their Christmas, of wch some came to see sports, to witte the seniors as well graduates as vnder-graduates. Others to make sports, viz., studentes of the seconde yeare, whom they call POULDERLINGS.

POULTERER, *subs.* (old).—A thief who stole and gutted letters.—GROSE (1785); MATSELL (1859).

POULTICE WALLAH, *subs. phr.* (military).—A surgeon's assistant.

POULTICE-WALLOPPERS, *subs. phr.* (military).—The Royal Army Medical Corps. Also "The Licensed (or Linseed) Lancers"; "The Pills."

POULTRY, *subs.* (old).—Women-kind: generic: *cf.* HEN, PLOVER, PHEASANT, PARTRIDGE, &c. CELESTIAL POULTRY = angels.

1611. CHAPMAN, *May-Day*, i. 2. If I do not bring . . . at least some special favour from her . . . then never trust my skill in POULTRY whilst thou livest again.

POUNCE, *verb.* (American).—To thrash: *see* TAN.

1847. PORTER, *Big Bear, &c.*, 146. He did then and there . . . most wantonly POUNCED his old wife.

POUNCEY. *See* PONCE.

POUND, *subs.* (old).—A prison: *see* CAGE and LOB'S POUND. Hence POUNDED = imprisoned.—GROSE (1785).

Verb. (colloquial).—To HAMMER (*q.v.*): *see* TAN.—GROSE (1785). Whence POUNDING-MATCH = a fight. Also PUN.

1596. SPENSER, *Fairy Queen*, IV. iv. 31. A hundred knights had him enclosed round, . . . All which at once huge strokes on him did POUND, in hope to take him prisoner.

1598. FLORIO, *Worlde of Wordes*, 6. To stampe or PUNNE in a mortar.

1602. SHAKSPEARE, *Troilus*, ii. 1. He would PUN thee into shivers with his fist, as a sailor breaks a biscuit.

1859. WHITBY, *Political Portraits*, 206. The Crimean War was at best a POUNDING-MATCH; the result proved nothing but that Russia, single-handed, could not hope to keep its ground against united France and England.

1888. *Sportsman*, 28 Nov. To see the men POUND each other.

2. (colloquial).—To move forward, steadily and with more or less noise: generally with 'along,' or 'up and down.'

1884. *Century Mag.*, XXXVII. 900. He's POUNDED up and down across this Territory for the last five years.

1885. *Daily Telegraph*, 3 Oct. POUNDING ALONG a dusty high road.

1894. *Yellow Book*, I. 196. We can't escape her . . . she POUNDS ALONG untiringly.

3. (hunting).—To get caught, or left in a field with no easy means of egress save a fence your horse won't take: stuck as in a pound.

1884. *Saturday Review*, 5 Jan. He jumps a little and I see him POUNDED every day.

1885. *Daily Telegraph*, 27 Oct. Any fence which would be likely to POUND or give a fall to his rival.

4. (old).—*See* quot.

1821. EGAN, *Life in London*, II. ii. This feature is what the *bon vivants* term being POUNDED; *i.e.*, being caught "astray" from propriety.

5. (American).—To copulate: *see* GREENS and RIDE.

TO POUND IT, *verb. phr.* (old).—1. *See* quot. 1819. Hence POUNDABLE = certain, inevitable; and (2) to wager in pounds (BEE, 1823).

1819. VAUX, *Memoirs*, s.v. POUND IT. To ensure or make a certainty of any thing; thus, a man will say, I'll POUND IT to be so; taken, probably, from the custom of laying, or rather offering ten pounds to a crown at a cock-match, in which case if no person takes this extravagant odds, the battle is at an end. This is termed POUNDING A cock.

1828. BEE, *Living Picture of London*, 44. You'll soon be bowled out, I'll POUND IT.

1838. DICKENS, *Oliver Twist*, xxxix. I'll POUND IT that you ban't.

TO GO ONE'S POUND, *verb. phr.* (military).—To eat a thing out. [The weight of a soldier's ration of bread and meat is 1 lb.]

IN FOR POUND, *adv. phr.* (thieves').—Committed for trial.

SHUT IN THE PARSON'S POUND, *phr.* (old).—Married; SPLICED (*q.v.*).—GROSE (1785).

POUNDERS, *subs.* (old).—The *testes*: *see* CODS.

1693. DRYDEN, *Juvenal*, vi. (3rd ed.), 114. Their solid joy, Is when the Page, already past a boy, Is caponed late, and to the guelder shown, With his two POUNDERS to perfection grown.

POUNDREL, *subs.* (old).—1. The head.

1734. COTTON, *Works*, 14. So nimbly flew away these scoundrels, Glad they had 'scap'd, and sav'd their POUNDRELS.

POUND-TEXT, *subs. phr.* (common).—A parson: *see* SKY-PILOT.

POUPE (or **POOP**), *subs.* (vulgar).—A noisy vent; a FART (*q.v.*): also as *verb.*

POUT, *subs.* (Scots').—A sweetheart. [O. E. *pult* = a yong henne, *Prompt. Parv.*]

1768. ROSS, *Helenore*, 93. The Squire—returning mist his POUT, . . . And for her was just like to burn the town.

POUTER, *subs.* (venery).—The female *pudendum*: *see* MONOSYLLABLE, and *cf.* DIDDLY-POUT.

POVERTY-BASKET, *subs. phr.* (old).—A wicker cradle.—BEE (1823).

POVERTY-JUNCTION (or **-CORNER**), *subs. phr.* (variety artists').—The corner of the York and Waterloo Roads, London. *See* quot. In New York that portion of 14th Street, opposite the Washington Statue, is known as 'The Slave Market' for similar reasons.

1890. *Tit-Bits*, 29 Mar., 390, 3. Any Monday, between eleven and three, may be seen a hundred or more persons of both sexes outside [the York Hotel] waiting in the hope of obtaining engagements in music-halls or variety theatres—"lion comiques," "serio-comics," "character comedians," in fact, every variety of music-hall artiste. Anyone wishing to see faces beaming with joy and prosperity [or] worn pale and thin by privation, care, and anxiety, will not find any better opportunity than by paying a visit on a Monday morning to POVERTY JUNCTION.—[*Abridged.*]

POWDER, *subs.* (old: now pugilists').—Strength; vigour; inspiration; BEANS (*q.v.*); DEVIL (*q.v.*): hence, as *verb.* = to be all over an adversary; TO POWDER ONE'S JACKET = to swinge 'like hell.'

1664. COTTON, *Virgil Travestie* (1st ed.), 19. The Windes grew louder still and louder, And play'd their gambals with a POWDER.

d. 1704. SIR R. L'ESTRANGE [*Century*]. Whilst two companions were disputing it at sword's point, down comes a kite POWDERING vpon them, and gobbets up both.

d. 1870. DICKENS [*Century*]. He had done wonders before, but now he began to POWDER away like a raving giant.

1889. *Licensed Victualler's Gaz.*, 18 Jan. Peg into him, Snacks—put more POWDER in 'em.

POWDER AND SHOT, *subs. phr.* (colloquial).—Cost; effort; labour. NOT WORTH POWDER OR SHOT = not worth trouble or cost.

POWDER-MONKEY, *subs. phr.* (formerly naval).—A boy employed to carry gunpowder from magazine to gun. Fr. *moussaillon.*—B. E. (*c.* 1696); GROSE (1785).

1682. RADCLIFFE, *Rambler, &c.*, 68. 'Call to the Guard.' To be near him the next takes care not to fill, POWDER-MONKEY by name.

d. 1704. T. BROWN, *Works* (1760), ii. 212. Lucifer . . . would not . . . have listed them; they would not have been fit for so much as POWDER-MONKEYS.

1787. SIR J. HAWKINS, *Johnson*, 195. One poet feigns that the town is a sea, the playhouse a ship, the manager the captain, the players sailors, and the orange-girls POWDER-MONKIES.

1815. SCOTT, *Guy Mannering*, lii. Ellangowan had him placed as cabin-boy or POWDER-MONKEY on board an armed sloop.

1870. *Chambers's Mis.*, No. 77, 4. The boy is employed in handing the cartridges, for which he is honoured with the name of POWDER-MONKEY.

POWER, *subs.* (old: now colloquial).—A large number or quantity: also POWERATION. Whence POWERFUL, *adj.* and *adv.* = extremely; also (quot. 1847) eloquent.

[?]. *MS. Cotton*, Vespas. A, xxv. Then came into Inglond kynge Jamys of Skotland, with a POUAR of men, after Alhalow tide.

1675. WYCHERLEY, *Country Wife*, iii. 2. Lord, what a POWER of brave signs are here.

1740. RICHARDSON, *Pamela*, ii. 389. I am providing a POWER of pretty things for her.

1751. SMOLLETT, *Peregrine Pickle*, ii. "He has a POWER of money, and spends it like a prince."

1777. SHERIDAN, *Trip to Scarborough*, iv. 1. These lords have a POWER of wealth indeed.

1847. DARLEY, *Drama in Poterville*, 94. Mr. Gwie, a 'POWERFUL man,' was expected to make a 'great effort.'

1848. BURTON, *Waggeries*, 23. He felt it tickle POWERFUL from the top of his head to the end of his starn-fin.

1851. HOOPER, *Dick McCoy's Sketches*, 36. "Is he lazy much?" 'POWERFUL.'

*d.*1869. CARLTON, *New Purchase*, II. 8. This piano was sort o' fiddle like,—and with a POWERFUL heap of wire strings. *Ibid.*, 74. Yes, Mr. Speaker, I'd a POWERFUL sight sooner go into retiracy among the red, wild aborigines of our wooden country, nor consent to that bill.

1872. *Chambers's Miscellany*, No. 152, 3. 'Was there a good fair to-day?' 'There was, ma'am, a POWER and all of people in it.'

1876. CLEMENS, *Tom Sawyer*, 34. You can work when you're a mind, Tom . . . But it's POWERFUL seldom you're a mind to, I'm bound to say.

1892. *Tit-Bits*, 17 Sep., 419, 2. He's POWERFUL bad, miss.

POWOS (THE), *subs.* (military).—The Prince of Wales's Own (West Yorkshire Regiment), formerly The 14th Foot. Also "The Old and Bold"; "Calvert's Entire."

POW-WOW, *subs. phr.* (American).—Noise: hence (political) = a noisy meeting, and as *verb.* = to take part in such: also to frolic. [From N.A. Indian POW-WOW = a council.]

1825. NEAL, *Bro. Jonathan*, III. 37. Off she goes; and if all they say's true, turned witch herself, an' cussed poor Bet with sich a POW-WOW. *Ibid.* (1833). *Down Easters*, vii. 105. Glancing at the ladies' cabin, where a tremendous POW WOW had just broken out. Such a screaming of mothers! and such a squalling of babies!

1885. *New York Herald*, 22 June. The Know-Nothings were holding their grand national POW-WOW . . . and laying it on thick that "Americans shall rule America."

POX, *subs.* (old).—Syphilis: sometimes qualified as FRENCH-(ITALIAN-, GERMAN-, or INDIAN-) POX, for which, and other synonyms *see* FRENCH-GOUT and LADIES'-FEVER. Whence, *verb.* = to syphilize; and POCKY, or POCKIFIED (*adj.*) = syphilized. Used vulgarly and popularly as a petty oath or common malison (*e.g.*, Pox! POX ON'T! POX TAKE YOU! WHAT A POX! WITH A POX! &c.: *see* the Elizabethan drama *passim*). Hence POXTER = a syphilist; POXOPHOLIT = an opponent of the Contagious Diseases Acts; POXOLOGY = the study of SIPH. (*q.v.*); and POXOLOGIST = a pox-doctor, a SIPHOPHIL (*q.v.*).—B. E. (*c.* 1696); GROSE (1785). [Originally and occasionally as in quots. 1594 and 1631, the small-pox; but for some three centuries specialized as above.] *See* HORSE-POX.

1522-3. SKELTON, *Why Come ye not to Courte*, 1167. Men wene that he [Wolsey] is POCKY, Or els his surgions they lye. *Ibid.*, Balthasor, they helyd Domingo . . . From the puskylde POCKY nose . . . Hath promised to hele our cardinals eye: Yet sum surgions put a dout, Lest he will put it clene out, And make him lame of his neder limmes.

1528. ROY, *Rede me, &c.* [*Harl. Mis.* [PARK], ix. 32]. He [Wolsey] had the POCKES, without fayle, Wherefore people on hym did rayle.

1584. [MONDAY?], *Weakest to Wall*, i. 2. These Frenchmen's feet have a POCKY strong scent.

1588. LYLY, *Endimion*, iv. 1. A POXE of all false proverbs.

1594. SHAKSPEARE, *Love's Lab. Lost*, v. 2. *Ros.* O that your face were not so full of O's! *Kath.* A POX of that jest! *Ibid.* (1598), 2 *Hen. IV.*, i. 2. A man can no more separate age and covetousness than a' can part young limbs and lechery: but the gout galls the one, and the POX pinches the other. . . . A POX of this gout! or, a gout of this POX! for the one or the other plays the rogue with my great toe. *Ibid.* (1609) *Pericles*, iv. 6. *Pand.* Now a POX on her green sickness for me. *Bawd.* Faith there's no way to be rid on't, but by the way to the POX.

1598. FLORIO, *Worlde of Wordes*, s.v. *Varolare*, to infect, or to be infected with the POXE. Ibid., *Varole*, the GREAT or FRENCH POXE. Ibid., *Varoloso*, POCKIE, full of the POXE, botches, or blanes.

1599. T. HALL, *Virgid.*, III. i. When ech brasse-basen can professe the trade Of curing POCKIE wenches from their paine.

1599. JONSON, *Ev. Man Out of His Humour*, iv. 4. *Carlo.* Let a man sweat once a week in a hot-house and be well rubbed and froted, with a good plump juicy wench, and sweet linen, he shall ne'er have the POX. *Punt.* What, the FRENCH POX? *Car.* The FRENCH POX! our POX: we have them in as good a form as they. What? *Ibid.* (1613), *Epigrams*, xii. But see! the old bawd hath served him in trim, Lent him a POCKY whore—— She hath paid him. Ibid., *Underwoods*, lxii. Pox on thee, Vulcan! thy Pandora's POX, And all the ills that flew out of her box Light on thee! or if those plagues will not do, Thy wife's POX on thee, and Bess Broughton's too.

1605. CHAPMAN, *All Fools*, iii. 1. *Da.* I know a doctor of your name, master POCK. *Po.* My name has made many doctors. sir.

1613. WEBSTER, *Devil's Law Case*, ii. 1. *Ari.* Incontinence is plagued in all the creatures of the world! *Jul.* When did you ever hear that a cock-sparrow Had the FRENCH POX. *Ibid.*, iii. 3. The scurvy, or the INDIAN POX, I hope, Will take order for their coming back.

1619. FLETCHER, *Humorous Lieut.*, i. 2. *Celia.* Pox on these bawling drums! I'm sure you'll kiss me.

1631. MASSINGER, *Emp. of East*, iv. 4. *Surg.* An excellent receipt! . . . 'tis good for . . . the gonorrhœa, or, if you will hear it In a plainer phrase, the POX.

*d.*1631. DONNE, *Letters* [NARES]. At my return from Kent, I found Peggy had the POXE—I humbly thank God it has not much disfigured her.

1653. URQUHART, *Rabelais*, I. xlv. Let me be peppered with the POX if you find not all your wives with child at your return . . . for the very shadow . . . of an abbey is fruitful.

1662. *Rump Songs*, i. 28. Pox take dem all, it is (Mort-Dieu) Not à la mode de France.

1668. ETHERIDGE, *She Would, &c.*, i. 1. *Sir Oliv.* Well, A POX OF this tying men and women together, for better or worse. *Ibid.*, iii. 2. *Sir John.* A POX UPON these qualms.

1675. WYCHERLEY, *Country Wife*, i. 1. A POX ON'T! the jades would jilt me. *Ibid.* ii. 1. *Mrs. Pinch.* He says he won't let me go abroad for fear of catching the POX. *Alitha.* Fy! The small POX, you should say.

*d.*1680. ROCHESTER, *Works*, 63. But punk-rid Ratcliffe's not a greater cully, Nor taudry Isham, intimately known To all POX'D whores.

*d.*1680. BUTLER, *Dildoides.* By dildo Monsieur sure intends For his FRENCH POX to make amends.

1680. DORSET, *Poems*, 'On the Countess of Dorchester.' Can't thou forget thy age and POX? *Ibid.* (1686), *Faithful Catalogue.* With Face and Cunt all martyred with the POX. *Ibid.* Thou wondrous POCKY art, and wondrous poor.

1682. RADCLIFFE, *Ramble*, 88. With mangled fist he grasp'd the box, Giving the table BLOODY knocks, He throws —— and calls for plague and POX T'assist him. *Ibid.*, 34. What a POX of these fellowes' contriving.

16[?]. T. BROWN, *Horace*, I. xxvii. What a POX should we fight for? *Ibid.* The arms of a POCKIFIED whore.

1693. CONGREVE, *Old Bachelor*, iii. 6. The POX light upon thee for a contemplative pimp. *Ibid.* (1694), *Double Dealer*, iii. 3. Pox, I have lost all appetite to her; yet she's a fine woman.

1693. URQUHART, *Rabelais*, III. Prol. As for Hypocrites, much less; altho' they were all of them unsound in Body, POCKIFY'D, scurfie, furnish'd with unquenchable Thirst.

1697. VANBRUGH, *Provoked Wife*, ii. 1. *Heart.* Why, there's no division, I hope. *Sir John.* No; but there's a conjunction: and that's worse. A POX o' the parson.

1705. HEARNE, *Diary*, 17 Nov. The duke of Buckingham . . . whilst he was there [Spain] happened to receive a POX, by lying with a Spanish beauty . . . so violent that he could not rid himself of it before he was obliged to return to England.

1706. WARD, *Wooden World*, 9. He epicurizes his POCKY Carcass for ever after. *Ibid.*, 45. One POCKY Whore brings the Surgeon more grist in than a thousand French cannon. *Ibid.*, 67. A POX ON it, cries he.

1714. POPE, *Rape of the Lock*, iv. 128. 'Nay, prithee, POX! Give her the hair'—he spoke and rapped his box. *Ibid.* (1733). *Imitations of Horace*, I. 83-4. From furious Sapho scarce a milder fate, POX'D by her love, and libell'd by her hate.

1772. BRIDGES, *Burlesque Homer*, 12. Pray, WHO THE POX made you a witch?

POZ. *See* POS.

PRACTICAL-POLITICIAN, *subs. phr.* (common).—A pot-house spouter.

PRACTISE. TO PRACTISE IN THE MILKY WAY, *verb. phr.* (venery).—To handle a woman's breasts.

1633. CAREW, *Cœlum Brit.* [EBSWORTH], 139. Jupiter too begins to learn to lead his own wife: I left him PRACTISING IN THE MILKY WAY.

PRACTITIONER, *subs.* (thieves').—*See* quot.

1869. GREENWOOD, *Seven Curses of London* [S. J. & C.]. He had them from a PRACTITIONER: from a thief that is to say.

PRAD, *subs.* (Old Cant).—A horse. Hence PRAD-COVE = a horse-dealer; PRAD-NAPPER = a horse-thief; THE PRAD-LAY = the theft of bridles, saddle-bags, and the like; PRAD-HOLDER = a bridle.—HALL (1714); GROSE (1785).

ENGLISH SYNONYMS.—Bit of blood; Charing-cross (rhyming); crock; crocodile; daisy-kicker (or -cutter: also = an ostler); gee; gee-gee; ginger; grogham; jade; jib (or jibber); high-stepper; knacker; long-faced 'un; lunk-head; macaroni; mount; muddler; nag (naggie or naggon); ning-nang; pinto; prancer; roarer; screw; scrub; star-gazer; tit; undergraduate; weaver; whistler; wind-sucker; wobbler.

FRENCH SYNONYMS.—*Bique*; *canard* (tram drivers'); *canasson* (= gee-gee); *carcan*; *carne* (= screw); *gail*; *galier*; *gaillon*; *gayet*; *maître d'école* (horse-breakers'); *parisien* (= screw); *rase-tapis* (= high-stepper); *trottin*.

1819. MOORE, *Tom Crib*, 8. Long before daylight gigs, rattlers, and PRADS.

1821. EGAN, *Life in London*, II. iv. I am going to Tattersall's, to purchase a PRAD.

1837. BARHAM, *Ingoldsby Legends*, I. 93. It would never do To go to the wars on a rickety PRAD.

1841. LEMAN REDE, *Sixteen String Jack*, 'The High-pad's Frolic.' Coaches and PRADS, lasses and lads.

1846. DICKENS, *Dombey*, xlvi. How can a cove stand talking in the street with his master's PRAD a wanting to be took to be rubbed down?

1851-61. MAYHEW, *London Lab.*, iii. 143. Veal's was the best circus I was at; there they had six PRADS and two ponies.

1854. AINSWORTH, *James the Second*, I. ii. It may be, young squire, you'll have to go forth afoot, instead of on your PRAD.

1893. EMERSON, *Signor Lippo*, xvi. We moved to some new stables, where there was stalls for eight PRADS, four each side, besides a loose box.

1895. MARRIOTT-WATSON, *New Review*, July, 9. Creech . . . swerved out of line and ran his mare full face upon the struggling PRADS.

PRAIRIE. ON THE PRAIRIE, *phr.* (Western American).—*See* quot.

1848. RUXTON, *Far West*, 127. Presented to them ON THE PRAIRIE, or "gift-free."

PRAIRIE-DEW, *subs. phr.* (American).—Whiskey: *cf.* MOUNTAIN-DEW (Scots').

1848. DURIVAGE, *Stray Subjects*, 81. Jest fetch on your PRARY DEW for the hull lot, and d—— the expense.

PRAIRIE-OYSTER (or **-COCKTAIL**), *subs. phr.* (American).—A raw yolk dropped into spirits, flavoured with Worcester or cayenne, and gulped.

1898. *Sporting Times*, 19 Feb., i. 5. "Take anything?" "Yes, I'll have a PRAIRIE OYSTER." "Hedge! hedge!" cried the young 'un, "I don't mean *lunch* . . . have a *drink*?"

PRAIRIE-SCHOONER, *subs. phr.* (American).—An emigrant waggon.

1887. STEVENS, *Around the World* [S. J. & C.]. Meeting PRAIRIE-SCHOONERS will now be a daily incident of my Eastward journey.

1888. *Daily Inter-Ocean*, 14 April. The old PRAIRIE-SCHOONER . . . is now mainly a thing of the past.

PRAIRIE STATE, *verb. phr.* (American).—Illinois.

PRAM, *subs.* (vulgar).—A perambulator.

1891. *Notes & Queries*, 7 S. xi. 104. May we not hope that the odious and meaningless vulgarism of PRAM, for perambulator, will be exploded from popular use.

PRANCER, *subs.* (Old Cant).—1. A horse: *see* PRAD; and (2) a horse-thief. Hence PRANCER'S-NAB = a horse's head: as a seal to a counterfeit pass; THE SIGN OF THE PRANCER = The Nag's Head.—ROWLANDS (1610); B.E. (*c.*1696); HALL (1714); GROSE (1785).

1567. HARMAN, *Caveat* (1869), 85. A BENE MORT hereby at THE SIGN OF THE PRAUNCER.

1591. GREENE, *Second Part Conny-catching* [GROSART, *Works*, x. 76]. They . . . take an especiall and perfect view where PRANCERS or horses be.

1622. FLETCHER, *Beggar's Bush*, v. 2. Higgen hath prigged the PRANCERS in his day.

1712. *The Twenty Craftsmen* [FARMER, *Musa Pedestris* (1896), 37]. The fifteenth a PRANCER, whose courage is small, If they catch him horse-coursing, he's nooz'd once for all.

1749. *Oath of Canting Crew* [FARMER, *Musa Pedestris* (1896), 51]. Prig of cackler, prig of PRANCER.

1834. AINSWORTH, *'The Game of High Toby'* [FARMER, *Musa Pedestris* (1896), 115. His matchless cherry-black PRANCER riding.

1843. DICKENS, *Martin Chuzzlewit*, xix. 203. My four long-tailed PRANCERS, never harnessed under ten pound ten!

1852. JUDSON, *Mysteries of New York*, iv. I prigged two PRANCERS and sold 'em.

3. (old).—A dancer: also as *verb.* = to dance. Also PRANKER.

1621. BURTON, *Anat. Melan.*, III. ii. If she be a noted reveller, a gadder, a singer, a PRANKER or dancer, then take heed of her.

4. (military).—A cavalry officer.

Prank, *subs.* (old: now recognised).—A trick.—B. E. (*c.* 1696).

Prat, *subs.* (old).—1. Usually *in pl.* = the buttocks or thighs.—HARMAN (1573); ROWLAND (1610); HEAD (1665); B. E. (*c.* 1696); COLES (1724); GROSE (1785). Hence, as *verb* = to beat; to swish.

1596. SHAKSPEARE, *Merry Wives*, iv. 2. *Mrs. Page.* Come, Mother PRAT; . . . *Ford.* I'll PRAT her [*Beating him*].

1610. ROWLANDS, *Martin Mark-all* (H. Club's Rept. 1874), 3. And tip lowr with thy PRAT.

1641. BROME, *Jovial Crew*, ii. Fiddle' Patrico, and let me sing. First set me down here on both my PRATS.

1707. SHIRLEY, *Triumph of Wit* [FARMER, *Musa Pedestris* (1896), 33]. No gentry mort hath PRATS like thine.

1895. MARRIOTT-WATSON [*New Review*, July, 8]. We ain't to do nothing, Dick Ryder, but to set down upon our PRATS and see 'em put up their hands and cry for mercy to this fire-eater here.

2. (old).—A tinder-box.—B. E. (*c.* 1696); GROSE (1785).

3. (venery).—The female *pudendum*: *see* MONOSYLLABLE.

4. (old).—A trick.

Verb. (thieves').—*See* quot. Fr. *entauler*, and *enquiller*.

1879. HORSLEY [*Macm. Mag.*, xl. 501]. I piped a slavey (servant) come out of a chat (house), so when she had got a little way up the double (turning), I PRATTED (went) in the house.

Pratie (or **Praty**), *subs.* (Irish).—A potato: *see* MURPHY.

1834. MARRYAT, *Peter Simple*, xii. In future you must do something to get your own dinner; there's not PRATIES enow for the whole of ye.

1857. C. READE, *Never Too Late*, lxv. I wish it was PRATEES we are digging, I'd may be dig up a dinner any way.

Prating (prattling- or prattle-) cheat, *subs. phr.* (Old Cant).—The tongue: *see* CLACK, where add to syns. 'Manchester' (Eng.), and *la rouscaillante* (Fr.). [PRITTLE or PRATTLE = diminutives of 'prate': and from PITTLE-PATTLE the weakened reduplication of PRITTLE-PRATTLE comes PIT-A-PAT (*q.v.*).] Whence, PRATING (PRATTLE or PRITTLE-PRATTLE) = talk, esp. gabble; TO PRATTLE (PRITTLE or PRITTLE-PRATTLE) = to chatter or CLACK (*q.v.*); PRATTLE-BASKET (-BOX, PRATE-ROAST, PRATTLER, or PRATE-APACE) = a chatterbox; PRATTLE-BROTH = tea: *cf.* CHATTER (or SCANDAL-) BROTH (*q.v.*); PRATTLING-BOX = a pulpit, or HUM-BOX (*q.v.*); PRATTLING-PARLOUR = a private apartment, or SNUGGERY (*q.v.*); PRATY (*adj.*) = talkative.—HARMAN (1567); B. E. (*c.* 1696); GROSE (1785).

1520. *Schole House of Women* [HAZLITT, *Early Pop. Poet*, iv. 129]. No remedy for to discontent, To PRATTLE to them of reason or lawe.

1528. ROY, *Rede me, &c.* [Arber (1871), 43]. Nevertheless amonge this arraye, Was there not . . . A littell PRATYE foolysshe poade?

1548. LATIMER, *Sermons and Remains* [Parker Soc.]. To PRITTLE-PRATTLE prayers. *Ibid.* To PITTLE-PATTLE.

1577. BELLOWES, *Guevara Letters*, 161. The office of the woman is to spin and PRATTLE, and the office of the man is to hold his tongue and talk.

1594. LYLY, *Mother Bombie*, iv. 2. I see my daughter hath PRATTLED with Accius, and discovered her simplicity.

1598. FLORIO, *Worlde of Wordes*, s.v. *Cianfrogna*, gibrish, pedlars french, roguish language, fustian toong, PRITTLE-PRATTLE.

1598. SHAKSPEARE, *All's Well*, iv. 1, 46. Tongue, I must put you into a butter-woman's mouth, and buy myself another of Bajazet's mule, if you PRATTLE

me into these perils. *Ibid.* (1602), *Othello*, i. 1, 26. Mere PRATTLE without practice Is all his soldiership. *Ibid.* (1606) *Macbeth*, iv. 2, 64. Poor PRATTLER, how thou talk'st.

d. 1626. BRETON, *Mother's Blessing*, lxxiv. A PRATTLE-BASKET or an idle slut.

1636. HEYWOOD, *Love's Mistress*, 26. Prince of passions, PRATE-APACES, and pickl'd lovers . . . admiral of ay-mes! and monsieur of mutton lac'd. *Ibid.* (1637), *Royall King*, Sig. B. You PRITTLE AND PRATTLE nothing but leasings and untruths.

1638. FORD, *Lady's Trial*, i. 2. Now we PRATTLE of handsome gentlemen.

1659. BRAMHALL, *Church of England Defended*, 46. It is plain PRITTLE-PRATTLE.

1673. WYCHERLEY, *Gentleman Dancing Master*, ii. 2. Y'fackins but you shant ask him! if you go there too, look you, you PRATTLE-BOX you I'll ask him.

1693. CONGREVE, *Old Bachelor*, iv. 9. Nay, now I'm in, I can PRATTLE like a magpie.

1697. VANBRUGH, *Provoked Wife*, ii. 1. By your ladyship's leave we must have one moment's PRATTLE together.

1720. DURFEY, *Pills to Purge*, vi. 11. Her PRITTLE-PRATTLE, little tattle.

1725. BAILEY, *Erasmus* (1900), i. 78. Don't be a PRITTLE PRATTLE, nor PRATE APACE, nor be a minding anything but what is said to you.

1749. SMOLLETT, *Gil Blas* [ROUTLEDGE], 261. These two noblemen . . . were listening with admiration to his PRATTLE.

1757. [PALTOCK], *Peter Wilkins*, I. ii. The old PRATTLE-BOX made a short pause to recover breath.

1783. COWPER, *Task*, ii. 382. Frequent in park with lady at his side, Ambling and PRATTLING scandal as he goes.

1821. MONCRIEFF, *Tom and Jerry* [DICK], 5. *Jerry.* Chaffing crib! I'm at fault, coz, can't follow. *Tom.* My PRATTLING PARLOUR—my head quarters, coz, where I unbend with my pals.

1836. *The Thieves' Chaunt* [FARMER, *Musa Pedestris* (1896), 121.] She's wide-awake, and her PRATING CHEAT, For humming a cove was never beat.

Prayer, *subs.*—Common colloquial expressions are: TO SAY PRAYERS = to stumble: of horses: *cf.* DEVOTIONAL HABITS; TO SAY PRAYERS BACKWARDS = to blaspheme (RAY); TO PRAY WITH KNEES UPWARDS (GROSE) = to copulate: of women; AT HER LAST PRAYERS = of an old maid (RAY); PRAYER-BONES = the knees.

1706. WARD, *Wooden World*, 42. All the Ship's Company daily pray for him, but they PRAY as they row, BACKWARDS.

1725. BAILEY, *Erasmus* (1900), i. 73. *Ra.* Sirrah! did I not hear you mutter? *Sy.* I was SAYING my Prayers. *Ra.* Ay, I believe so, but it was THE LORD'S-PRAYER BACKWARDS then.

Prayer-book, *subs. phr.* (gaming).—1. A pack of cards.

2. (nautical).—A small holystone; a BIBLE (*q.v.*).—CLARK RUSSELL (1883).

1840. DANA, *Before the Mast*, xxiii. Smaller hand-stones, which the sailors call PRAYER-BOOKS, are used to scrub in among the crevices and narrow places, where the arge holystone will not go.

See POST-OFFICE PRAYER-BOOK.

Prayer-book Parade, *subs. phr.* (common).—A promenade in fashionable places of resort, after morning service on Sundays.

Prayer-powder, *subs. phr.* (American).—*See* quot.

1825. NEAL, *Bro. Jonathan*, II. xiv. With a silver bullet—a leaf o' the Bible for wadding—and a charge of PRAYER-POWDER—powder, over every 365 grains of which the Lord's prayer has been said.

Pray-pray fashion, *adv. phr.* (old).—Imploringly.

1753. RICHARDSON, *Grandison*, ii. 183. 'Pray, sir, forgive me;' and she held up her hands PRAY-PRAY fashion thus.

Preach, *verb.* (colloquial).—To moralise out of season; TO CANT (*q.v.*): as *subs.*—(1) a sermon; and (2) canting talk. Hence PREACHING-SHOP = a church (or chapel); PREACHIFYING = tiresome moralising; PREACHY-PREACHY = long-windedly moral; PREACHMAN = a clergyman; PREACHMENT = affectedly solemn cackle.

1592. MARLOWE, *Edward II.*, iv. 6. Come, come, keep these PREACHMENTS till you come to the place anointed.

1595. SHAKSPEARE, *3 Henry VI.*, i. 4. Was't you that revell'd in our parliament, And made a PREACHMENT of your high descent?

1597. HOOKER, *Eccles. Polity*, v. 28. No sermon, no seruice. Which ouersight occasioned the French spitefully to terme religion in that sort exercised a mere PREACH.

1644-5. HOWELL, *Letters*, II. 33. Some of our PREACHMEN are grown dogmad.

1795. BURNS, *Spoken at the Theatre, Dumfries* [*Century*]. Old Father Time deputes me here before ye, Not for to PREACH but tell his simple story.

1822. DOUGLAS JERROLD, *Black Ey'd Susan*, i. 2. Tut! if you are inclined to PREACH, here is a mile-stone—I'll leave you in its company.

1847. THACKERAY, *Vanity Fair*, I. x. 'Shut up your sarmons, Pitt, when Miss Crawley comes down,' said his father; 'she has written to say that she won't stand the PREACHIFYING.' *Ibid.* (18 . .), *Ballads of Policeman X* (*A Woeful New Ballad*). And them benighted Protestants, on Sunday they must go Outside the town to the PREACHING-SHOP by the gate of Popolo.

1889. *Academy*, 19 Oct., 260. She has the art of making her typical good women real and attractive . . . never . . . prudish or PREACHY.

1894. MOORE, *Esther Waters*, xvii. I don't 'old with all them PREACHY-PREACHY brethren says about the theatre.

TO PREACH AT TYBURN-CROSS, *verb. phr.* (old).—To be hanged: *see* LADDER.

Precious, *adj.* and *adv.* (colloquial).—Worthless; great; overnice: as PRECIOUS little = very little; a PRECIOUS humbug = an eminent rascal, and so forth.

1383. CHAUCER, *Cant. Tales*, Prol. to Wife of Bath's Tale [TYRWHITT], line 5659. In swiche estat as God hath cleped us, I wol persever, I n'am not PRECIOUS.

1535. COVERDALE, *Trans. of Bible*, Ezek. xvi. 30. Thou PRECIOUS whore.

1605. JONSON, *Volpone*, i. 1. Your worship is a PRECIOUS ASS.

1612. WEBSTER, *White Devil*, iv. 4. Now my PRECIOUS gypsy . . . We have many wenches about the town heat too fast.

c. 1616. FLETCHER, *Bonduca*, iv. 2. Run, run, ye rogues, ye PRECIOUS rogues, ye rank rogues. *Ibid.* (1617), *Mad Lover*, iii. 3. Oh, you're a PRECIOUS man! two days in town, and never see your old friend.

1749. SMOLLETT, *Gil Blas* [ROUTLEDGE], III. This PRECIOUS abigail . . . was just as young, just as pretty, and just as loose as her mistress.

1784. *Connoisseur*, No. 7. This PRECIOUS fooling, though it highly entertained them, gave me great disgust.

1777. SHERIDAN, *School for Scandal*, v. 2. A PRECIOUS couple they are.

c. 1790. *Song*, 'The Flash Man of St. Giles' [FARMER, *Musa Pedestris* (1896), 74]. For we have mill'd a PRECIOUS go.

1792. LORD THURLOW, *Lett. to Cowper* [*Cowper's Letters* (1834), ii. 318]. PRECIOUS limbs was at first an expression of great feeling, till vagabonds, draymen, &c., brought upon it the character of coarseness and ridicule.

1821. EGAN, *Life in London*, II. ii. Suke swears by her PRECIOUS sparklers that she will have a fight.

1837. DICKENS, *Pickwick Papers* (1857), 443. PRECIOUS warm walking, isn't it? said Lowden, drawing a Bramah key from his pocket, with a small plug therein to keep out the dust.

1857. HUGHES, *Tom Brown's Schooldays*, I. v. PRECIOUS little good we get out of that. *Ibid.*, II. vii. It's a PRECIOUS sight harder than I thought.

1869. BLACKMORE, *Lorna Doone*, xxvii. A PRECIOUS heavy book it was.

1881. BLACK, *Beautiful Wretch*, xix. 'She might as well try to leave off her affectations as her clothes. She couldn't go about without any.' 'She goes about with PRECIOUS little,' said Mr. Tom.

Precisian, *subs.* (old: now recognised).—A stickler: spec. (17th century) = a PURITAN (*q.v.*) in depreciation: also as *adj.* = punctillious, rigidly exact.—B. E. (*c.* 1696).

1596. JONSON, *Ev. Man in his Humour*, iii. 2. He's no PRECISIAN, that I'm certain of.

1607. DEKKER, *Westward Hoe*, i. 2. We have the finest schoolmaster, a kind of PRECISIAN, and yet an honest knave too.

1615. HARINGTON, *Epigrams*, i. 20. The man, affrighted at this apparition, Upon recovery grew a great PRECISIAN.

1612. DRAYTON, *Polyolbion*, vi. 301. These men . . . like our PRECISIANS be, Who for some Cross or Saint they in the window see Will pluck down all the Church.

1614. *Time's Whistle* [E. E. T. S.], 10. Hypocriticall PRECISIANS, By vulgar phrase entitled Puritanes.

1619. FLETCHER, *Custom of the Country*, iv. 1. He was of Italy, and that country breeds not PRECISIANS that way, but hot libertines.

1625. MASSINGER, *New Way*, i. 1. Verity, you brach, The devil turn'd PRECISIAN.

1628. EARLE, *Micro-cosmog*, 2. His fashion and demure Habit gets him in with some Town-PRECISIAN, and maks him a Guest on Fryday nights.

d. 1655. REV. T. ADAMS, *Works*, II. 465. If a man be a Herod within and a John without, a wicked politician in a ruff of PRECISIAN set, God can distinguish him.

1694. GILDON, *Mis. Let. and Essays*, Pref. I hope too the graver gentlemen, the PRECISIANS will not be scandaliz'd at my zeal for the promotion of poetry.

1821. SCOTT, *Kenilworth*, ii. Tony married a pure PRECISIAN . . . as bitter a PRECISIAN as ever eat flesh in Lent, and a cat-and-dog life she led.

1822. BYRON, *Vision of Judgment*, cv. As Wellborn says—'the devil turn'd PRECISIAN.'

1864. ALFORD, *Queen's English*, 78. This pronunciation in the mouth of an affected PRECISIAN is offensive.

1888. STEVENSON, *Inland Voyage*, Epilogue. He is no PRECISIAN in attire.

Preeze, *verb.* (provincial).—To urinate; TO PISS (*q.v.*).

Premises, *subs.* (venery).—The female *pudendum*; *cf.* LODGER and LODGINGS TO LET: *see* MONOSYLLABLE.

Presbyteress, *subs.* (old colloquial).—*See* quot.

d. 1563. BALE, *English Votaries*, i. Marianus sayth she was a PRESBYTERESSE, or a priestes leman.

Presbyterian, *adj.* (old).—An epithet of ridicule or contempt.

16[?]. *Broadside Ballad* [Title]. A PRESBYTERIAN TRICK.

1706. WARD, *Hudibras Redivivus*, v. 26. But, Lord, I pray thee, by the bye, Look down and cast a jealous Eye Upon our cunning Elder Brethren, Call'd by the name of PRESBYTERIAN.

1772. BRIDGES, *Burlesque Homer*, 117. For the right PRESBYTERIAN breed Always coin pray'rs in time of need.

1847. HALLIWELL, *Archaic Words and Phrases*, s.v. PRESBYTERIAN-TRICK. A dishonest bargain; a knavish trick.

Prescott, *subs.* (rhyming).—A waistcoat: also CHARLEY PRESCOTT.

Present, *subs.* (colloquial).—1. A white spot on the finger nail: supposed to augur good fortune.

2. (common).—A baby.

1749. SMOLLETT, *Gil Blas* [ROUTLEDGE], 13. Three months after marriage . . . as . . . I had no particular wish for the PRESENT my wife was likely to make me, I joined issue with some desperate blades.

PRESENTERER, subs. (old).—A whore: see TART.

PRESERVE, subs. (old University).—A collection of outstanding bills.—GROSE (1785).

PRESS, subs. (American sporting).—A winning bet added to the original stake.

PRETTIFY, verb. (colloquial).—To adorn; to decorate. Whence PRETTIFICATION = the process of adornment; PRETTIFIED = the fact (or condition) of being adorned.

PRETTY, subs. (venery).—The female *pudendum*: also PRETTY-PRETTY: see MONOSYLLABLE. PRETTY DEAR = a mistress.

1749. SMOLLETT, *Gil Blas* [ROUTLEDGE], 372. Who pamper up their PRETTY DEARS.

Adj. and adv. (literary and colloquial).—A generic intensive: ironical or complimentary at occasion or will: see quot. 1814.

c.1500. *How a Sergeaunt, &c.* [HAZLITT, *Early Pop. Poet*, iii. 122]. First faire and wele a PRETIE deale, he hyd it in a potte.

1530. PALSGRAVE, *Langue Fran.*, 453. A PREATY whyle ago, *ung peu de temps passe.*

1537-40. *Supp. of Monasteries* [Camden Soc.], 198. PRATY besynes [of some monkish crimes].

1550. UDAL, *Roister Doister* [ARBER], 37. My PRETTY maid [an ironical address by a mistress to a servant].

15[?]. *Political Poems* [FURNIVALL], 244. A bok hym is browt Naylyd on a brede of tre, That men callyt an abece, PRATYLYCH I-wrout.

1594. SHAKSPEARE, *Lucreece*, 1233. A PRETTY while these pretty creatures stand.

1596. JONSON, *Ev. Man in His Humour*, i. 2. *Know.* Is the fellow gone that brought this letter? *Brai.* Yes, sir, a PRETTY while since.

1611. CORYAT, *Crudities*, i. 6. It is a PRETTY way distant from the town.

1628. EARLE, *Micro-cosmog*, 'A Weake Man.' A great affecter of wits and such PRETTINESSES.

1630. CAPT. JOHN SMITH, *True Travels*, i. 26. Meldritch ... was advised of a PRETTY stratagem by the English Smith.

d.1657. BRADFORD, *Plymouth Plantation*, 235. Aboute some 3. or 4. years before this time ther came over one Captaine Wolastone (a man of PRETIE parts).

1678. BUNYAN, *Pilgrim's Progress*, 208. You are PRETTY near the business.

1714. LUCAS, *Gamesters*, 143. He ... being no bad player won a PRETTY deal of money.

1726. VANBRUGH, *Provoked Husband*, ii. 1. A PRETTY sort of a young woman.

1763. FOOTE, *Mayor of Garratt*, i. 1. I believe things are PRETTY secure. *Ibid.* 'A PRETTY son you have provided' ... 'I hope all for the best.'

1772. BRIDGES, *Burlesque Homer*, 96. You then will find, tho' now you pish on't You've made a PRETTY kettle of fish on't.

d.1774. GOLDSMITH, *Reverie at Boar's-Head Tavern* [Century]. The gallants of these times PRETTY MUCH resembled the bloods of ours.

1814. SCOTT, *Waverley*, xvii. He even mentioned the number of recruits ... and observed that they were PRETTY men, meaning not handsome, but stout warlike fellows.

1777. SHERIDAN, *School for Scandal*, i. 1. Egad! ma'am, he has a PRETTY wit, and is a PRETTY poet too. *Ibid.* (1778), *The Rivals*, iv. 3. The quarrel is a very PRETTY quarrel as it stands.

1870. HAWTHORNE, *Eng. Note Books*, ii. 306. Suburban villas, Belgrave terraces, And other such PRETTINESSES.

1874. J. A. SYMONDS, *Italy and Greece*, 76. The painter ... was forced ... to perpetuate pious PRETTINESSES long after he had ceased to feel them.

1891. STEVENSON, *Kidnapped*, 73. "There are some PRETTY men gone to the bottom."

1892. ANSTEY, *Voces Populi*, 'At the Military Tournament,' 97. Cost a PRETTY SIGHT o' the People's MONEY.

1899. WHITEING, *John St.*, ix. PRETTY child you must ha' been ... Oh my! *Ibid.* Was you knocked about much when you was a young 'un? PRETTY tidy, only I alwiz stepped it when it got too 'ot.

TO DO THE (or TALK) PRETTY, verb. phr. (colloquial).—To affect amiability or obsequiousness.

1891. J. NEWMAN, *Scamping Tricks*, 2. We can talk PRETTY to each other. *Ibid.*, 46. I saw they were started on the road of mutual admiration, and travelling PRETTY, and that he meant calling again.

1902. *Free Lance*, 5 April, 8, 2. They must be spoken PRETTY to, caressed, humoured, coaxed.

See also WAY and HORSE-BREAKER.

PRETTY- (or MERRY-) DANCERS, subs. phr. (Scots').—The Aurora Borealis.

PRETTY-PRETTY, subs. (common).—1. A knick-knack; and (2) see PRETTY.

1887-9. TROLLOPE, *What I Remember*, 21. My mother ... had contrived to keep a certain number of PRETTY-PRETTIES which were dear to her heart.

PREVIOUS, adv. (colloquial).—See quot. 1885.

1885. *D. Telegraph*, 14 Dec. "He is a little before his time, a trifle PREVIOUS, as the Americans say, but so are all geniuses."

1890. *Pall Mall Gaz.*, 23 June, 4, 2. Next year his term of service expires, and then we shall both be ... But to state that now is what the Americans would call a little PREVIOUS. *Ibid.* (1901), 10 Ap., 1, 3. So there it is—an object-lesson in the inadvisability of the too PREVIOUS.

PREY, subs. (old).—Money.—B. E. (c.1696).

PRIAL, subs. (old gaming).—Three cards of a sort (at commerce, cribbage, &c.): DOUBLE-PRIAL = four of a kind: whence also, of persons and things. [A corruption of *pair-royal*: in quot. 1608 is seen a step towards PRIAL, whilst in quot. 1680 'pair-royal' rhymes with 'trial.']

1608. DAY, *Humour out of Breath*, sig. C2. *Fl.* Why two fooles? *Fr.* Is it not past two, doth it not come neere three, sister [meaning, to call her one]. *Pa.* Shew PERRVALL at tale.

a.1680. BUTLER, *Ballad on Parl.* But when they came to trial, Each one prov'd a fool, Yet three knaves in the whole, And that made up a PAIR-ROYAL.

PRIAP (or PRIAPUS), subs. (venery).—1. The *penis*: see PRICK; (2) = a DILDO (q.v.); and (3) = a STALLION (q.v.).

1672. BUTLER, *Dildoides*. Who envying their curious frame Expos'd their PRIAPS to the flame. *Ibid.* PRIAPUS thus, in Box opprest, Burnt like a Phœnix in his Nest.

d.1680. ROCHESTER [*Works* (1718), 87]. Saying if one PRIAPUS I could shew, One holy relic of kind pearly dew. *Ibid.* PRIAPUS squeez'd, one Snowball did emit.

1692. DRYDEN, *Juvenal* (1702), 114, Seen from afar and famous for his ware, He struts into the bath among the fair; Th' admiring crew to their devotion fall; And, kneeling, on their new PRIAPUS call.

PRICE, verb. (colloquial).—To enquire the cost of.

1837. BARHAM, *Ingoldsby Legends*, ii. 261. If you PRICED such a one in a drawing-room here, And was asked fifty pounds, You'd not say it was dear.

1886-96. MARSHALL, '*Pomes from the Pink 'Un* [' The Age of Love '], 26. They PRICED him at fifty to one.

WHAT PRICE——? phr. (racing and common).—How's that? What do you think? How much? What odds?

1893. EMERSON, *Signor Lippo*, xiv. What PRICE you, when you fell off the scaffold.

1895. POCOCK, *Rules of the Game*, ii. 10. WHAT PRICE Mr. Jack Hayles, eh, boys? That proves he's a thief.

1898. *Cigarette*, 26 Nov., 13, 1. Ain't he gone on saucy colours, Eh? WHAT PRICE the green and red?

1899. WHITEING, *John St.*, i. ix. WHAT PRICE grammar? It don't seem to teach people to keep a civil tongue in their head.

1901. *Free Lance*, 13 Ap., 28, 2. "It is all very well," writes a traveller, "to legislate with regard to pure beer, but WHAT PRICE pure wine?"

PRICK (or PRICKLE), subs. (common).—1. The *penis*; and (2) a butcher's skewer (see quot. 1622, with a pun on both senses of the word). Hence PRICK-HOLDER (-PURSE, -SCOURER, or -SKINNER) = the female *pudendum*; PRICK-SCOURING = copulation; PRICK-PRIDE = an *erectio penis*, a PRICK-STAND; PRICK-PROUD = 'satyrical, lustful' (FLORIO: also cf. PRIDE); PRICK-HUNTING = GROUSING (q.v.); PRICK-CHINKING = copulating; TO LOOK PRICKS = to challenge with the eye; TO KNOCK DOWN A PRICK = to abate an erection; cf. also BEGGAR'S BENISON (q.v.) = 'May your PRICK and your purse never fail you.'

ENGLISH SYNONYMS.—Aaron's-rod; Abraham; Adam (The old); Adam's-arsenal (*penis and testes*); affair (CLELLAND); angle (ROCHESTER); arbor-vitæ; arse-opener; arse-wedge; aspersing-tool (URQUHART); Athenæum.

Baby-maker; bag-of-tricks (*penis and testes*); bald-headed hermit; battering-piece (CLELLAND); bauble (SHAKSPEARE); bayonet; beak; bean-tosser; beard-splitter; bed-fellow; belly-ruffian; best-leg-of-three; Billy-(or Bob) my-nag; bird; bit of hard; blade (DAVIES); bludgeon; Bluebeard; blueskin; bodkin; bonfire; bow; bracmard (URQUHART); brat-getter; broom-handle; bum-tickler; bush-beater; bush-whacker; busk; butcher (butcher's-shop = female *pudendum*); butter-knife (BUTTER = SPENDINGS q.v.).

Candle (CANDLESTICK = female *pudendum*); Captain Standish (*Merry Drollery*: EBSWORTH); catso; child-getter; chink-stopper; claw-buttock; clothes-prop; club; cock (SHAKSPEARE); concern; copper-stick; coral-branch (URQUHART); crack-hunter; cracksman; cranny-haunter; creamstick; crimson-chitterling (URQUHART); cuckold-maker (MARSTON); cuckoo; cunny-burrow ferret (URQUHART); cunny-catcher; Cupid's-torch; custom's-officer; cutlass; cutty-gun (Scots').

Dagger; dearest member (BURNS); dibble (old Scots'); dick; dicky (nursery); diddle (nursery); dingus (American); dirk (Scots'); dolly; Don Cypriano (URQUHART); Don Orsino (URQUHART); Dr. Johnson; down-leg; dropping-member; drumstick.

Engine (CLELLAND); enemy; eye-opener.

Father Abraham; father-confessor; father-of-all; fiddle-bow; fiddle-diddle; fiddle-stick; firebrand; flap-doodle; flapper; flesh (generic); flip-flap (URQUHART); floater; fork; fornicating member; fornicator; flute (DURFEY).

Gadso; gap-stopper; garden-engine (GARDEN = female *puden-*

dum); gardener; gaying-instrument (GROSE); gear (SHAKSPEARE, FLORIO, BURNS); generation-tool (C. JOHNSON, URQUHART); gentle-tittler (URQUHART); girl-catcher; girlometer; goat; gooser; goose's-neck; gravy-maker; gristle (CLELLAND); gully-raker; gut-stick.

Hair-divider; hair-splitter; handstaff; hanging-Johnny; hard-bit (= the *penis* in erection); hermit; hunter.

Intercrural-pudding (URQUHART); Irish-root; It (generic).

Jack (an erection); Jack-in-the-box; Jack Robinson; Jacob; jargonelle; Jezabel; jigger; jiggling-bone (Irish); JOCK (q.v.); jockam (Old Cant); John Thomas; jolly-member (URQUHART); Julius Cæsar.

Kennel-raker; key; king-member; kit (= *penis and testes*); knack (FLETCHER); knocker.

Ladies'-delight; ladies'-plaything; ladies'-treasure; lady-ware (= *penis and testes*); lamp-of-life; lance-of-love; Langolee (Irish); leather-dresser; leather-stretcher; life-preserver; lingam; little-Davy (Scots'); liver-turner; live-sausage (URQUHART); lobster; lodger; lollipop; love-dart; love's-picklock; luggage (= *penis and testes*); lullaby.

Machine; man-root (WHITMAN); man-Thomas; marrowbone; marrowbone-and-cleaver; Master John Goodfellow (URQUHART); Master John Thursday (URQUHART); master-member (CLELLAND); master of the ceremonies; Master Reynard; matrimonial-peacemaker (GROSE); meat (generic); meat-skewer; member (conventional); member-for-Cockshire; mentule; merry-maker; merry-man; middle; middle-leg; milkman; mole; mouse; mowdiwart (Scots').

Nag; nakedness; nature's-scythe; Nebuchadnezzar (cf. GREENS); needle (DORSET); nervous cane (URQUHART); nil-nisitando (URQUHART); Nimrod; nocker (or nine-inch-nocker, URQUHART); nippy.

Old-Adam; old man; old-Slimy; old Rowley.

Partner; peacemaker; pecker; pecnoster; pee-wee; pego (A. RADCLIFFE); pendulum; pestle; peter; phallus; picklock (CLELLAND); pike (SHAKSPEARE); pike-staff; pile-driver; pilgrim's-staff; pillicock (SHAKSPEARE, FLORIO, DURFEY); pillock (LYNDSAY); pin; pintle (FLORIO, BURNS, DORSET, MORRIS); pioneer-of-nature; pisser; pistol; pizzle; placket-racket (URQUHART); plenipo; ploughshare; plug (BURNS); plug-tail (GROSE); P-maker; pointer; Polyphemus; pond-snipe (WHITMAN); pony; poperine-pear (SHAKSPEARE); priap; priapus (ROCHESTER); prick (SHAKSPEARE, FLETCHER *et passim*); prickle (FLETCHER, CLELLAND, R. BURTON); private-property (= *penis and testes*); privates (= *penis and testes*); privities; privy-member (Biblical); pudding (DURFEY).

Quarter-master; quim-stake; quickening-peg (URQUHART).

Radish; ramrod; ranger; raw-meat; rector-of-the-females (ROCHESTER); rod; Robin (GASCOIGNE); Roger; rolling-pin; root; rubigo; rudder; ruffian; rump-splitter.

Saint Peter (who keeps the keys of PARADISE [*q.v.*]); sausage (STERNE); sceptre; schnickel (Yiddish); sensitive-plant (CLELLAND); sensitive truncheon (CLELLAND); shaft of delight; shove-straight (URQUHART); Sir Martin Wagstaff (URQUHART) sky-scraper; snapper; solicitor-general; spike-faggot; spigot; spindle; split-rump (URQUHART); sponge (*cf.* RAMROD); staff-of-life; stern-post; sugar-stick; sweet-meat.

Tail; tail-tree; tallywag (schoolboys'); tantrum; tarse (DORSET); tenant-in-tail; that; tent-peg; thing; thingamy; thingumbob; thorn-in-the-flesh; thumb-of-love (WHITMAN); thyrsus; tickle-faggot; tickle-gizzard (URQUHART); tickle-toby; Timothy-tool; tool (FLORIO); toy; touch-her-home (URQUHART); touch-trap (URQUHART); trifle; trouble-giblets (URQUHART); tug-mutton; twanger (FLORIO).

Uncle; unruly-member.

Vestry-man.

Wand (DENHAM); ware (DRYDEN); watch-and-seals (= *penis* and *testes*); weapon; wedge; wepene (HALLIWELL); What Harry gave Doll (DURFEY); whore-pipe (ROCHESTER); winkle (nursery); wimble; worm (nursery).

Yard (FLORIO, &c.); yum-yum.

Zadkiel (ALMANACK = female *pudendum*).

FRENCH SYNONYMS.—*Acteur*; *affaire* (also *affaire avec quoi l'homme pisse*); *agréments naturels*; *aiguille* (also *aiguillon*, and *aiguillette*: = needle: RABELAIS); *allumelle* (RABELAIS); *allumette*; *anchois* (RABELAIS); *andouille* (= chitterling: also *andouille des carmes*: RABELAIS); *animal*; *antenne*; *arbalète* (RABELAIS); *arc* (also *arc-boutant*); *ardillon*; *argument*; *arme*; *asperge*; *aspersoir* (= 'aspersing-tool': RABELAIS); *astic* (= glazing-stick); *asticot* (= slug); *autre-chose* (also = female *pudendum*); *avance*.

Badinage d'amour (RABELAIS); *bagage* (= LUGGAGE = *penis* and *testes*); *baguette* (RAMROD [*q.v.*]); *balancier*; *ballestrou* (RABELAIS); *bandage*; *batail* (Old Fr. = bell-clapper); *baton* (also *baton de lit*, *baton à un bout*, *baton de sucre de pomme*, *baton de chair*, and *baton pastoral*); *battant*; *béquille*; *berlingot* (RABELAIS); *bête* (cf. *animal*); *bibite*; *bichette* (= PRETTY, *q.v.*); *bidault*; *bidet* (= pony); *bijou* (RABELAIS, DIDEROT: also *bijou de famille*); *billart* (RABELAIS); *bistoquette* (RABELAIS); *bon-bon*; *bondon* (= BUNG); *bonhomme*; *bouchon* (RABELAIS); *boudin* (= PUDDING: RABELAIS: also *boudin blanc*); *bougeoir*; *bougie* (= CANDLE: RABELAIS); *bourdon* (RABELAIS); *bourse* (= *penis* and *testes*); *bout* (also *bout de viande*); *boute-feu* (= firebrand: also *boute-joie* = pleasure-maker); *boutique* (= WARE [*q.v.*]); *boyau* (RABELAIS); *braguette* (RABELAIS); *branche* (also *branche de corail*); *brandon* (firebrand: RABELAIS); *braquemard* (= cutlass); *bras*; *brèviare*; *briche*; *brichouard*; *broche* (= SPIT); *broque* (also *broquette*: of children).

Ça (= THAT); *canal*; *canon à pisser* (RABELAIS); *carotte*; *catze* (= CATZO: RABELAIS); *cauda* (= TAIL: RABELAIS); *ceci* (= THIS: RABELAIS); *cela* (= THAT: RABELAIS); *cerkos* (RABELAIS);

cervelas (= the SAUSAGE); *chair* (= flesh: generic); *chalumeau* (RABELAIS); *chameau*; *champignon*; *chandelle* (= CANDLE: RABELAIS); *chanterelle* (RABELAIS); *charrue* (*cf.* PLOUGHSHARE); *chenille* (= WORM); *cheval* (*cf.* RIDE); *cheville* (= PIN [*q.v.*]: also *cheville ouvrière* and *cheville d'Adam*: RABELAIS); *chevillot* (= belaying-pin: RABELAIS); *chibre*; *chiffe* (specifically = LOBCOCK [*q.v.*]); *Chinois* (*cf.* CELESTIAL EMPIRE = female *pudendum*); *chose* (= THING); *chouart*; *cierge* (= CANDLE and TORCH: RABELAIS); *cigarette*; *clavis* (RABELAIS); *clé* (*cf.* LOCK = female *pudendum*: RABELAIS); *clou*; *clysoir galant* (= the lover's clyster-pipe); *cognoir* (printers' = shooting-stick); *coin* (= PIN and WEDGE: also *petit coin*); *colonne*; *compagnon* (also *compagnon fidèle*); *corde sensible*; *cordon de saint François* (RABELAIS); *corne* (= MR. HORNER); *cornichon* (RABELAIS); *cotal* (RABELAIS); *coue* (RABELAIS); *coursier* (*cf.* BILLY-MY-NAG); *courte* (also *plus courte*); *courtaud* (= PONY: RABELAIS); *couteau* (also *couteau naturel*: *cf.* BUTTER-KNIFE); *crête de coq d'Inde*; *criquet* (= 'the little man'); *cyclope*; *cylindre* (*cylindre consolateur* = a dildo).

Dard (RABELAIS); *dardillon* (RABELAIS); *dauphe*; *degré de longitude*; *denrée* (*cf.* COMMODITY: also *denrée d'aventure*); *diable* (BOCCACCIO and LA FONTAINE: *cf.* HELL = female *pudendum*); *dille* (RABELAIS); *dispensateur des plaisirs* (= MERRY-MAKER); *docteur*; *doigt* (RABELAIS: also *petit doigt*, *doigt de milieu*, and *doigt qui n'a point d'ongle*); *don* (LA FONTAINE); *douzil* (= SPIGOT: RABELAIS): *dressouer* (RABELAIS); *droit* (also *droit d'homme*); *drôle* (RABELAIS).

Echalas; *écluse* (= SLUICE, *écureuil* (O. Fr., also = fem. *pud.*); *écuvillon*; *égout*; *élytroïde* (MUSSET); *endure* (= the sufferer); *enflure* (= the bloated); *engenreure* (RABELAIS); *engin* (= TOOL); *ennemi*; *epée* (RABELAIS); *éperon*; *épervier*; *épine* (= THORN-IN-THE-FLESH: RABELAIS); *espadon*; *esprit*; *et cætera* (= MR. WHAT'S-ITS-NAME); *étendard* (also *étendard d'amour*); *éteuf*; *étrille*; *étui* (also = female *pudendum*); *exécuteur de la basse justice*.

Fascinum (RABELAIS); *fax* (RABELAIS); *ferrement* (= TOOL: RABELAIS); *fétu*; *fifre*; *flageolet* (RABELAIS); *flambeau* (= torch: BERANGER); *flamberge*; *fléau*; *flèche* (RABELAIS: also *flèche d'amour*); *flûte* (= FLAGEOLET and FLUTE: RABELAIS: also *flûte à bec*: cf. SILENT-FLUTE); *fouet* (sportmen's = 'dog-tail'); *fourrier de nature* (= Nature's-quartermaster: RABELAIS); *frappart*; *friandise* (= SWEET-MEAT: RABELAIS); *fruit de caspendu*; *furon*; *fuseau*; *fusil* (= cutty-gun).

Gaule; *gibre* (also *chibre*); *gland*; *gluant* (OLD SLIMY); *gogotte*; *goujon* (also *gougon*); *goupillon* (= 'holy-water sprinkler: RABELAIS); *gouvernail*; *grand-maître des cérémonies*; *grimaudin* (RABELAIS); *gros boyau*; *grosse corde*; *guigui* (also [nursery] *guiguitte*).

Haire (RABELAIS); *hameçon*; *harnais* (RABELAIS); *hasta* (RABELAIS); *herbe qui croit dans la main* (= GREENS [*q.v.*] that grow in the hand: RABELAIS);

hic (RABELAIS); *histoire* (RABELAIS); *hochet* (= TOY [*q.v.*]: also *hochet de Vénus*).

Il (= IT); *inconvénient*; *instrument* (RABELAIS: also *instrument de musique*).

Jacquemard (RABELAIS); *Jacques* (RABELAIS: also *Jacquot*); *jambe* (RABELAIS); *jambot* (VILLON); *Jean Chouart*; *Jean Jeudi* (RABELAIS); *joie*; *joujou*; *joyau* (also = female *pudendum*).

Kapros (RABELAIS).

Laboureur (RABELAIS: also *laboreur de nature*: *cf.* NATURE'S WORKSHOP = the female *pudendum*); *lacet*; *lance* (= LANCE-OF-LOVE: also *lance à deux boulets* and *lance gaie*: RABELAIS); *lancette*; *lard*; *lavette*; *le* (cf. *la* = female *pudendum*); *limace*; *lingot d'amour* (RABELAIS); *longon* (RABELAIS); *lourdois* (Old Fr.).

Machin (LA FONTAINE); *Mahomet*; *petite majesté* (RABELAIS); *manche* (= BROOM-HANDLE: also *manche de gigot*: RABELAIS); *marque de la vaisselle* (RABELAIS); *mât*; *mèche*; *membre* (RABELAIS: also *membre viril*); *mentule* (RABELAIS); *mirliton* (RABELAIS); *misère*; *mistigouri* (RABELAIS); *moignon*; *moineau* (also *moineau de Lesbie*: RABELAIS); *Monsieur le Fils*; *Monsieur la Pine*; *morceau* RABELAIS: also *morceaux honteux*; *moule*; *muscle*; *mutinum* (RABELAIS); *muto* (RABELAIS).

Nature de l'homme; *navette*; *nerf* (RABELAIS: also *nerf caverneux*); *nervus* (RABELAIS); *nez*; *n'importe quoi* (= THINGUMBOB); *nipleseth* (RABELAIS: from the Heb.); *noctuinus* (RABELAIS); *nœud* (= *penis* and *testes*).

Obélisque; *objet* (= THING); *oiseau* (RABELAIS); *onzieme doigt* (*cf.* MIDDLE-LEG); *organe*; *os à moelle* (= MARROW-BONE); *outil* (= TOOL: also *outil priapesque*, *outil à faire la pauvreté*, and *outil à faire la belle joie*: RABELAIS); *ouvrier de nature*.

Pacquet de mariage (= *penis* and *testes*: also *pacquet d'amour*: RABELAIS); *paf*; *paille*; *pain* (cf. *devorant* = female *pudendum* = DUMB GLUTTON); *palette*; *palus* (RABELAIS); *partie* (also, in pl. *parties casuelles*, and *parties honteuses* = the *penis* and *testes*); *Pascal*; *pasnaise* (O. Fr.); *pastenade* (O. Fr.); *pâte*; *pauvre cas* (RABELAIS); *pauvre marchandise* (RABELAIS); *pauvreté* (RABELAIS); *pauvre petit*; *paxillus* (RABELAIS); *peculium* (RABELAIS); *pelée* (cf. PRICK-SKINNER); *penart* (RABELAIS); *pendeloche* (RABELAIS); *penis* (RABELAIS); *perchaut*; *Perrin-boute-avant* (RABELAIS); *perroquet* (RABELAIS); *persuasif* (RABELAIS); *pestel* (RABELAIS); *petit* (*cf.* GRAND = female *pudendum*); *petit pauvre* (also *petit bonhomme*, *petit caporal* [*cf.* DR. JOHNSON and JULIUS CÆSAR], *petit jeune homme*, and *petit bout*); *petite flûte*; *petit frère* (*cf.* SCHWESTERLEIN = female *pudendum*); *petit voltigeur*; *phalle* (RABELAIS); *pible* (nautical: RABELAIS: also *pibol*); *piche*; *pièce* (RABELAIS: also *pièce de génération* and *pièce du milieu*); *pied de roi*; *pierre à casser les œufs* (RABELAIS: also *pierre de touche*); *pieu*; *pignon* (RABELAIS); *pilon* (= pestle: RABELAIS); *pilum* (RABELAIS: classical); *pine* (= PRICK: RABELAIS, &c.); *pinette* (= PRICKLE: also *pinoche*); *pique* (RABELAIS);

pis (RABELAIS); *pissot* (RABELAIS: *pissotière* = f.p.); *pistolandier*; *pistolet*; *piston*; *pivot*; *plume charnelle*; *poignard*; *poinçon* (RABELAIS = PUNCH); *poinil* (also *poinille*); *pointe* (LA FONTAINE); *poireau*; *poisson*; *polichinelle*; *pommeau*; *pompe aspirante* (also *pompe foulante*); *pomus* (RABELAIS); *potence* (RABELAIS); *poulain*; *poupignon*; *poussouer* (RABELAIS); *précurseur*; *premier rôle*; *Priape* (RABELAIS, &c.); *proportion*; *provision*; *pyramide*.

Quelque chose de chaud (also *quelque chose de court* = SOMETHING WARM and SOMETHING SHORT); *uenouille* (RABELAIS); *quéquette*; *queue* (RABELAIS = TAIL); *quille* (RABELAIS).

Racine (= ROOT); *radis* (*radis noir* = negro's *penis*); *raquette*; *rat* (also *raton*); *rélique* (BERANGER); *rène*; *rien*; *robinet de l'âme* (RABELAIS); *roide*; *rossignol* (LA FONTAINE); *rubens*; *rubiscabochon*.

Sacrement (BERANGER); *Saint-Agathon*; *Saint-Esprit de la culotte*; *Saint-Pierre*; *salsifis*; *sangsue*; *sannion* (RABELAIS: from the Gr.); *sansonnel*; *saucisse* (= LIVE SAUSAGE: also *saucisson*); *scapus* (RABELAIS); *sceptre*; *schtiv* (*sch* + anagram of *vit*); *sentinelle*; *serin*; *seringue* (also *seringue à peruque*, and *seringue à poil*: RABELAIS); *sexe* (RABELAIS); *sifflet*; *simulacre d'amour*; *sixième sens*; *soulier*; *sous-préfet*; *sucre d'orge*.

Taurus (RABELAIS); *tétin* [RABELAIS]; *thermomètre*; *timon* (LA FONTAINE); *tirliberly*; *tiv* (anagram of *vit*); *torche*; *toton*; *totoquini* (RABELAIS); *touche d'alemant*; *trabes* (RABELAIS); *train*; *trait*; *tréhans* (RABELAIS); *trépignoir*; *triquebille*; *troisième jambe* (*cf.* MIDDLE-LEG); *truelle*; *tube*; *turlututu*.

Utensile (RABELAIS).

Vélu; *verge* (= YARD: RABELAIS: also *verge de saint-Benôit*); *verpe* (RABELAIS); *veretille* (RABELAIS); *verêtre* (RABELAIS); *viande de devant* (also *viande crue*); *vibrequin*; *viçon* (RABELAIS); *violon*; *vireton* (RABELAIS); *virgule* (RABELAIS); *virolet* (O. Fr.); *vit* (= PRICK); *vitault* (RABELAIS); *vivandier de nature* (RABELAIS).

Zèbre; *zist*.

GERMAN SYNONYMS.—*Bletzer* (= wedge); *Breslauer* (Viennese); *Bruder* (*cf. Schwesterlein* = little sister = female *pudendum*); *Butzelmann*; *Fiesel*; *Dickmann*; *Pinke*; *Schmeichaz*; *Schwanz*.

ITALIAN SYNONYMS.—*Anguisigola* (FLORIO = NEEDLE); *barbagianni*; *bestia* (FLORIO); *cazzo*; *coda* (= TAIL); *cotale* (FLORIO); *cucitusa* (FLORIO); *destriere*, or *destriero* (FLORIO) *dolcemelle* (FLORIO); *erpice* (FLORIO, 'a harow to breake clods of earth'); *facende* (FLORIO); *grignappola* (FLORIO); *mentole* (FLORIO); *natura* (FLORIO); *naturale* (FLORIO); *nervo* (FLORIO); *occhello*; *pastinaca* (FLORIO: '*pastinaca muranese*, a dildoe of glasse'); *pastorale*; *pestello* (FLORIO: 'a pestle'); *pinchino*; *pinco* (FLORIO); *pina* (FLORIO: *cf.* Fr. *pine*); *rilla* (FLORIO); *robinetto* (FLORIO: 'a little rubie . . . also a dildoe'); *rozzone* (FLORIO); *San Cresci-in-Mano* (FLORIO: 'because it grows in one's hand'); *San Giovanni bocco d'oro* (FLORIO); *tempella* (FLORIO: 'a great swaggring twanger, a horse-toole, a great dildo, or good pricke'); *tincone* (FLORIO); *vergogne* (FLORIO); *verpa* (FLORIO); *vieto* (FLORIO); *vitto* (FLORIO: 'victuals . . . vsed in iest for a man's priuie member'); *vómere* (FLORIO: 'the iron of the plough that pierceth the ground').

SPANISH SYNONYMS.—*Berga; bergajo; capullo; carajo; mague; maquilen* (Sp. gypsy); *menina; monda; nabo; picha; pijote; pinga; pitilén; poya; quile* (Sp. gypsy).

PORTUGUESE SYNONYMS.—*A parario; bacamarte* (= CREAM-STICK); *badalo; baioneta; banana; bimba; capitão; caralho; chico; chinguiço; chunço; deabrete; Don Cipriano; espadão* (augmentative); *espada; espiga; formigão; fumo; largato; linguiça; macacheira; malho; minhoca; maranhão; marsapo; nabo; Philippe; paosinho da matrimonio; pão de Leite; pão de todos* (= FATHER-OF-ALL); *pão magico; porra* (classic); *pica; pica* (classic); *pomba; paio; pichota; quiabo; rolla; sulipa; tromba; vergalho; virgolleiro; vara; zé-caitano.*

DUTCH SYNONYM.—*Pit.*

WALLOON SYNONYM.—*Bock.*

1595. SHAKSPEARE, *Romeo and Juliet*, ii. 4. *Mer.* 'Tis no less, I tell you, for the bawdy hand of the dial is now on the PRICK of noon. *Nurse.* Out upon you! what a man are you?

[?]. *The Wyll of the Devill* [HALLIWELL]. I geve to the butchers PRICKES inoughe to sette up their thinne meat that it may appeare thick and well fedde.

1598. FLORIO, *Worlde of Wordes*, *Coglinto*, a man that hath a good PRICKE. *A conscienza vitta* . . . with a stiffe standing PRICKE. *Ibid. Priapismo* . . . the standing of a man's yard which is when the yard is stretched out in length and breadth . . . If it come with a beating and panting of the yard the phisicians call it then Satiriasi. Called also in English . . . PRICK-PRIDE, or lust-pride (*et passim*).

1605. JONSON, MARSTON, &c., *Eastward Ho!* iii. 2. *Gert.* May one be with child afore they are married, mother? *Mistr. T.* Ay, by'r lady, madam; a little thing does that; I have seen a little PRICK no bigger than a pin's head swell bigger and bigger till it has come to an ancome; and e'en so 'tis in these cases [*see* sense 4].

1608. HEYWOOD, *Rape of Lucrecce*, iii. 5. I would wish all young maids, before they be sick, To enquire for a young man that has a good PRICK.

*c.*1610-20. *Rawl. MS.*, B 35, 54 back He shall not do so that I love, But so soone as I am sick, Shall never faile me in the nick, To give me proof of his good ——.

1611. BEAUMONT and FLETCHER, *Kn. of Burning Pestle*, v. 3. With hey, trixy, tirlery-whiksin, The world goes round on wheels. When the young man's PRICK's in, Up go the maiden's heels.

*c.*1613. FLETCHER, *Nice Valour*, v. 1. As nightingales, And things in cambric rails, Sing best against a PRICKLE.

1622. DEKKER and MASSINGER, *Virgin Martyr*, ii. 1. Bawdy Priapus, the first schoolmaster that taught butchers to stick PRICKS in flesh, and make it swell, thou know'st, was the only ningle that I cared for under the moon.

1656. FLETCHER, *Martiall*, x. 63. One PRICK was privy to my chastitie.

1672. BUTLER, *Dildoides.* Women must have both youth and beauty, Ere PRICK, damn'd Rogue will do his duty. *Ibid.* Are you afraid lest merry Griggs Will wear false PRICKS like Perriwigs? *Ibid.* He paus'd, another stepp'd in With limber PRICK and grisly chin.

1678. COTTON, *Virgil Travestie* [*Works* (1725) 74]. ('Twixt you and me) I'm sore afraid, My son's so big (which rarely falls) About his ——, and Genitals, That I am half afraid lest he Should chance to spoil her Majesty. *Ibid.* And quickly The Trojan does with the great P——K lie.

*d.*1680. ROCHESTER, *Satire on the King.* His sceptre and his PRICK are of a length. *Ibid.* (*Works*, 1718). Here walks Cuff and Kick, With brawny back and legs, and potent PRICK.

1681. JOHN AUBREY, *Life of Selden*, MS. He told me that Mr. Selden had got more by his PRICK than by his practice.

1682. A. RADCLIFFE, *The Ramble*, 85. While duns were knocking at my door, I lay in bed with reeking whore, With back so weak and PRICK so sore, You'd wonder.

*d.*1694. ETHEREDGE [ROCHESTER and ROSCOMMON, *Works* (1718), I. 159]. A Band of naked Cupids draws With PRICKS no bigger than Wheatstraws. *Ibid.* One figures Love's Hieroglyphic, A couchant Cunt and rampant PRICK.

*c.*1698. DURFEY, *Tom Tinker* [*Pills to Purge* (1719), VI. 265]. I met with a Butcher a killing a Calf, I then stepp'd to him and cryed out half: At his first denial I fell very sick, And he said it was all for a touch of his ——.

1749. ROBERTSON, of Struan, *Poems*, 256. My Lord had but one P——K To satisfy my Lady's C—ny. *Ibid.*, 186. And as one guides me to the NICK, The other cries—Put up thy ——.

17 [?]. EARL OF CORK, *The Bumper Toast.* In a lovely field argent, crown sable she glows, And two rampant P——s as supporters we fix, Here's C—— in a bumper wherever she goes.

1760-7. STERNE, *Tristram Shandy*, VIII. xx. 'I can honestly say, an' please your honour—that ** ***** ***** ***** once.' 'That was very odd, Trim,' quoth my uncle Toby.' 'I think so too,' said Mrs. Wadman. 'It never did,' said the corporal.

1785. HANBURY WILLIAMS, *Odes*, 'To L—d L——n.' Oh, Lincoln! joy of womankind, To you this humble ode's designed; Let (PRICK) inspire my song: Gods! with what powers you are endu'd! Tiberius was not half so lewd, nor Hercules so strong.

*c.*1786. CAPT. MORRIS, *The Plenipotentiary.* 'Christ Jesus,' she said, 'what a PRICK for a maid.

*d.*1796. BURNS, *The Merry Muses of Caledonia*, 'Act Sederunt o' the Court o' Session' [FARMER, *Merry Songs and Ballads* (1897) v. 215]. In Embrugh town they've made a law, In Embrugh, at the Court o' Session, That stanin' PRICKS are fau'tors a', An' guilty o' a high transgression. Ibid. *We're a' Gaun Southie, O.* Kind kimmer Kirsty, I loe wi' a' my heart, O; An' whaur there's ony PRICKS gaun, She'll ay get a part, O.

17 [?]. *Old Song*, 'The Highland Laddie.' The gayest girl in Embro's town, With paint and clothes made ready, Can't knock a PRICK so sweetly down As bonny, buxom Peggy Brady.

*b.*184 [?]. *Old Country Side Doggrel* [quoted by HALLIWELL]. Now if Steenie Smith don't mend his manners The skin of his —— shall go to the tanners.

1885. BURTON, *Thousand Nights*, III. 302. My PRICKLE is big.

3. (old).—A term of endearment. — PALSGRAVE (1540); HALLIWELL (1847).

4. (old colloquial).—A pimple: *see* sense 1, quot. 1605.

PRICK-EARS, *subs. phr.* (old cavalier). — A Roundhead. [The Puritan head-gear was a black skull-cap, drawn down tight, leaving ears exposed].—GROSE (1785). Also PRICK-EARED (or LUGGED) *adj.* = a general term of contempt.

1599. SHAKSPEARE, *Hen. V.*, ii. 1, 44. Pish for thee, Iceland dog! thou PRICK-EAR'D cur of Iceland.

PRICKED, *adj.* (costermongers').—'Sour; acid.'—B. E. (*c.*1696).

1851-61. MAYHEW, *Lond. Lab.*, I. 68. It [salmon] is usually bought for 1s. a kit, a little bit PRICKED.

PRICKER (old military).—*In pl.* = a Cavalry regiment. [That is a light horseman: *cf.* PRICK = to ride: *e.g.*, 'A gentle knight was PRICKING o'er the plain.']

PRICKET, *subs.* (auctioneers').—A fictitious bidder; a PETER FUNK (*q.v.*); a PUTTER-UP (*q.v.*).

PRICKING ÆGER. *See* ÆGER.

PRICK-LOUSE (NIP-LOUSE, or **PRICK-THE-LOUSE)**, *subs. phr.* (common).—A tailor: *see* SNIP.—B. E. (*c.*1696); GROSE (1785).

1590. TARLETON, *Purgatorie* [HALLIWELL]. She would in brave termes abuse him, and call him rascall, and slave, but above all PRICKLOUSE, which he could not abide. *Ibid.* The more she beat her, the more she calde him PRICKLOUSE.

1592. GREENE, *Defence of Conny-catching* [*Works*, xi. 96]. Even the poore PRICKLOUSE the country taylor.

*c.*1603. *Sack for my Money* [COLLIER, *Roxburghe Ballads* (1847), 178]. Rich Malligo is pure, I know, And bravely can compose a man Of a very PRICK-LOWS taylor.

1607. DEKKER and WEBSTER, *Northward Hoe*, ii. 1. If I take master PRICK-LOUSE ramping so high again . . . I'll make him know how to kiss your blind cheeks sooner.

1620. ROWLANDS, *Night Raven*, 9 (Hunterian Club's Repr., 1872). My choller tells thee, th'art a botching slaue, Thy Journy-man a very PRICKLOWSE knave.

1625. JONSON, *Staple of News*, i. 1. Tailor, thou art a vermin, Worse than the same thou prosecut'st, and PRICK'ST in subtle seam.

*c.*1700. THOMAS BROWN, *Paneg. on a Louse* [*Works* (1715), i. 145]. No wonder then . . . such sturdy Valour Against thy Enemy, the PRICK-LOUSE Taylor, To take him every Moment by the Collar.

*d.*1704. LESTRANGE [*Century*]. A taylour and his wife quarrelling, the woman in contempt called her husband PRICK-LOUSE.

1720. DURFEY, *Pills to Purge*, vi. 293. Says PRICK LOUSE, my Jewel I love you most dearly, My breast every minute still hotter does grow.

*d.*1796. BURNS, *To a Tailor*, st. 2. Gae mind your seam, ye PRICK THE LOUSE, An' jag the flae.

PRICKMEDENTY (PRICK-ME-DAINTY or **PRICK-MA-DAINTY)**, *subs.* (old).—A finical person. Also, as *adj.* = over-precise; affected.

*d.*1529. SKELTON, *Elynour Rummyng*, 582. There was a PRYCKMEDENTY, Sat lyke a seynty, And began to paynty, As thoughe she would faynty.

1534. UDALL, *Roister Doister*, ii. 3. Mary, then PRICK-ME-DAINTY, come toste me a fig.

1822. GALT, *Provost*, xxxi. Bailie Pirlet, who was naturally a gabby PRICK-ME-DAINTY body.

PRICK-THE-GARTER, *subs. phr.* (old).—1. *See* quot. 1762. Also PITCH THE NOB, PRICK THE BELT (or LOOP), and FAST AND LOOSE.

1762. GOLDSMITH, *Life of Nash* [*Works* (*Globe*), 545]. The manner in which country men are deceived by gamblers, at a game called PRICKING IN THE BELT, or the old Nob. This is a leathern strap folded up double, and then laid upon a table: if the person who plays with a bodkin pricks into the loop of the belt, he wins, if otherwise he loses. However, by slipping one end of the strap, the sharper can win with pleasure.

1776. BRAND, *Popular Antiquities.* This was, doubtless, originally a gipsy game, and was much practised by the gipsies in the time of Shakespeare. In those days it was termed PRICKING AT THE BELT, or fast and loose.

1788. G. A. STEVENS, *Adv. of a Speculist*, i. 69. This is the cant of those who go about the country defrauding the unwary with the game called, PRICKING AT THE BELT.

1840. COCKTON, *Valentine Vox*, lx. They were standing at a PRICK-IN-THE-GARTER table, at which a gentleman had a long piece of list, which he wound round and offered any money that no man could prick in the middle.

1892. SYDNEY, *Eng. and English in 18th Century*, i. 83. One class of gamblers cheated passers-by . . . by inviting them to PRICK IN THE BELT, OR THE GARTER for a wager.

TO PLAY AT PRICK-THE-GARTER, *verb. phr.* (venery).—To copulate: *see* GREENS and RIDE.

PRIDE, *subs.* (conventional).—Sexual appetite: hence PROUD = amorous; lustful.—B. E. (*c.*1696); GROSE (1785). *See* PRICK.

. . . . *Arthur and Merlin* [Edinburgh Auchinleck MS., 11]. Yong man wereth jolif, And than PROUDETH man and wiif.

1598. FLORIO, *Worlde of Wordes*, s.v. *Esser in frega*, to be PROUD . . . as a bitch or a caterwalling as cats.

1602. SHAKSPEARE, *Othello*, iii. 3, 402. It is impossible you should see this, Were they as prime as goats, as hot as monkeys, As salt as wolves in PRIDE.

1629. DAVENANT, *Albovine*, i. When I see her I grow PROUD below the navel.

*d.*1680. ROCHESTER, *Ramble in St. James's Park* [*Works* (1718), i. 82]. So a PROUD Bitch does lead about Of amorous Curs the humble Rout.

PRIDE-AND-POCKETS, *subs. phr.* (common).—*See* quot.

1893. EMERSON, *Lippo*, xiii. The place, too, was what we call 'shabby genteel'—a lot of retired tradesmen and half-pay officers . . . PRIDE-AND-POCKETS as we called them.

PRIDE-OF-THE-MORNING (THE), *subs phr.* (Irish).—A shower of rain.

PRIEST, *subs.* (Irish). — A short bludgeon: used to administer the 'last rites' to a landed fish.

TO BE ONE'S PRIEST, *verb. phr.* (Scots').—To kill.

1810. *Homespun Lays*, 135. An' wi' an awfu' shak, Swore he wad shortly BE HIS PRIEST, An' threw him on his back Fu' flat.

A GREAT PRIEST, *subs. phr.* (Scots'). — A strong but ineffectual inclination to stool.—JAMIESON.

TO LET THE PRIEST SAY GRACE, *verb. phr.* (old).—To marry: hence PRIEST-LINK'D = married. — B. E. (*c.*1696); GROSE (1785).

PRIEST OF THE BLUE-BAG, *subs. phr.* (common).—A barrister: *see* GREENBAG.

1849. KINGSLEY, *Alton Locke*, xx. "He . . . showed himself as practised in every law quibble . . . as if he had been a regularly ordained PRIEST OF THE BLUE BAG."

PRIEST'S NIECE, *subs. phr.* (old).—A cleric's illegitimate daughter, or concubine: whence 'No more character than a PRIEST'S NIECE.'

1663. KILLIGREW, *Parson's Wedding* [1827], i. 3, p. 471.

1848. RUXTON, *Far West*, 145. They were probably his NIECES.

PRIG, *subs.* (Old Cant).—1. A thief: also PRIGGER and PRIGMAN; as *verb.* = to steal. Whence PRIGGER OF PRAUNCERS (or PALFREYS) = a horse-thief; PRIGGER OF CACKLERS = a poultry-thief; PRIG-NAPPER = a thief-taker; PRINCE PRIG (or (PRIG-STAR) = 'a King of the Gypsies, also a Top Thief, or Receiver General' (B. E.); TO WORK ON THE PRIG (or PRIGGING-LAY) = to thieve; TO PRIG AND BUZ = to pick pockets; PRIGGISH = thievish; PRIGGERY (or PRIGGISM) = thievery. — AWDELEY (1560); HARMAN (1563); DEKKER (1608); HEAD (*c.*1665); B. E. (*c.*1696); HALL (1714); GROSE (1785).

ENGLISH SYNONYMS. — To angle; to annex; to bilk; to bite; to bone; to bounce; to bunco; to bust; to buz; to cabbage; to chouse; to claim; to clift; to clink-rig; to cloy (cligh or cly); to collar; to collect; to convey; to cop; to crack; to crib; to cross-fam; to curb; to cut; to dip; to dive; to drag; to draw; to ease; to fake; to filch; to file; to find; to flap; to fleece; to flimp; to fop; to fork; to fraggle; to free; to frisk; to glean; to haul; to hook; to jump; to klep; to knap; to knuckle; to lag; to lap; to lurch; to mag; to make; to maltool (or moll tool); to manarvel; to mill; to mug; to nab; to nail; to nap; to nibble; to nick; to nim; to nip; to palm; to parlor-jump; to pay with a hook; to pinch; to poach; to poll; to pug; to pull; to purchase; to ramp; to rent; to respun (tinker); to ring; to shake; to shark; to shoulder; to smouch; to smug; to snabble; to snaggle; to snake; to snam; to snap; to snatch; to sneak; to snipe; to speak; to spice; to swipe; to tool; to touch; to trot; to wolf; to work.

FRENCH SYNONYMS.—*Agripper; aquiger* (or *quiger*); *aumôner* (or *roler à l'aumône*, giving small articles stolen from counters as alms to a confederate); *barboter* (= to TURN OVER [*q.v.*]); *barboter les poches; barboter la caisse; bijouter* (= to purloin jewels); *faire le bobe; cabasser; rincer une cambriole* (= 'to clean out a crib'); *caribener; casser la hane* (= 'to buz a skin'); *chambrer; chaparder* (military); *grincher à la chicane* (= picking pockets with your back to the pocket picked); *choper* (or *faire un chopin*); *comprendre; décrasser; décrocher; défleurir la picouse; dégauchir; dégraisser; dégringoler* (also *dégringoler à la carre* = to shoplift); *doubler; faire en douceur; entiffler; fabriquer* (also *fabriquer un gas à la flan. fabriquer à la rencontre*, or *fabriquer à la dure* = to rob with violence); *fabriquer un poivrot* (= to 'jump a lushington'); *faire; faire le bobe; faire la bride* (= 'to buz slangs'); *faire la retourne des baguenaudes* (= 'to fake a cly'); *faire la souris* (= to do the mouse); *faire la tire* (= 'to cut a bung'); *faire le barbot dans une cabriolle* (= 'to crack a crib'); *faire le saut; faire le morlingue* (= 'to cut a bung'); *faire le mouchoir* (= 'fogle-hunting'); *faire un coup à l'esbrouffe* ('to flimp'); *faire un coup d'étal* (= to shoplift); *faire un coup de fourchette* (= to fork); *faire un coup de radin; faire un coup de roulette* (= 'to claim a peter'); *faire grippe-cheville; faire la soulasse sur le grand trimar* (= HIGH-TOBY); *faucher; filer; acheter à la foire d'empoigne* (= buying at Pinching-Fair); *fourliner; fourlourer; fourmiller* (= 'to cross-fam'); *goupiner; graisser* (also *gressier*); *gratter* (= 'to cabbage'); *greffer* (= 'to nip'); *griffer; grinchir; tirer la laine* (Old Fr.); *lever* (= LIFT); *marner; matriculer* (military: *le numero matricule* = a soldier's mess number, his sole proof of ownership); *mettre de la paille dans ses souliers; mettre la pogne dessus; taper un mome; pagoure; pegrer; piger; poisser* (also *poisser les philippes* or *poisser l'auber; ramastiquer; retirer l'artiche; ribler; sauter; savonner* (also *savonner une cambuse* (= 'to mill a ken'); *faire la savoyarde* (= 'to claim a peter'); *secouer la perpendiculaire* (= 'to snatch a slang'; also *secouer un chandelier* = 'to rob with violence at night'); *solicer* (also *sollicer*); *soulever; travailler* (= 'to work').

1591. GREENE, *Second Part Conny catching* [*Works*, x. 78]. He bestrides the horse which he PRIGGETH, and saddles and bridles him as orderly as if he were his own.

1610. ROWLANDS, *Martin Mærkall* [FARMER, *Musa Pedestris* (1896). 5. That did the PRIGG good that bingd in the kisome.

1611. SHAKSPEARE, *Winter's Tale*, iv. 3. *Clo.* Out upon him! PRIG, for my life, PRIG: he haunts wakes, fairs, and bear-baitings.

1612. DEKKER, *O per se O* [FARMER, *Musa Pedestris* (1896), 11]. And PRIG and cloy so benshiply, All the dewsea-vile within.

1622. FLETCHER, *Beggar's Bush*, v. 2. Higgen hath PRIGGED the prancers in his days.

[?]. DRANT, *Horace*, 'To Julius Florus.' A PRIDGEMAN from him pryuillie his money did purloyne.

1712. SHIRLEY, *Triumph of Wit*, 'The Black Procession.' The nineteenth's a PRIGGER OF CACKLERS who harms, The poor country higlers, and plunders the farms.

1724. J. HARPER, 'Frisky Moll's Song' in *Harlequin Jack Sheppard*. From PRIGGS that snaffle the prancers strong.

1743. FIELDING, *J. Wild* (1893), 17. The PRIG . . . the vulgar name for thief. *Ibid.*, 28. An undeniable testimony of the great antiquity of PRIGGISM. *Ibid.* Without honour PRIGGERY was at an end.

1749. GOADBY, *Bamfylde Moore-Carew*, 'Oath of Canting Crew.' PRIG of cackler, PRIG of prancer.

1772. BRIDGES, *Burlesque Homer*, 160. A staring, gaping, hair-brain'd PRIG, Came up to steal his hat and wig.

1789. PARKER, *Life's Painter*, 158. In order to give them an opportunity of working upon the PRIG and buz, that is, picking of pockets.

1821. EGAN, *Life in London*, II. iii. Cadgers; . . . fish-fags; . . . and the PRIGS, spending the produce of the day; and all . . . happy and comfortable.

1827. LYTTON, *Pelham*, lxxx. Well, you parish-bull PRIG, are you for lushing jackey, or pattering in the hum box?

1828-9. H. T. R., *Vidocq's Memoirs*, Tr. of *Un Jour a la Croix Rouge*. When twelve bells chimed, the PRIGS returned.

1829. MAGINN, *The Pickpocket's Chaunt*, i. As from ken to ken I was going, Doing a bit on the PRIGGING LAY.

1834. AINSWORTH, *Jack Sheppard* (1889), 20. I'll give him the edication of a PRIG—teach him the use of his forks . . . make him . . . as clever a cracksman as his father.

1838. DICKENS, *Oliver Twist*, xviii. I suppose you don't even know what a PRIG is? said the Dodger mournfully. 'I think I know that,' replied Oliver, looking up. 'It's a th—; you're one, are you not?' inquired Oliver, checking himself.

1840. BARHAM, *Ingoldsby Legends*, '*Jackdaw of Rheims*.' They can't find the ring! And the Abbot declared that, "when nobody twigg'd it, Some rascal or other had popp'd in, and PRIGG'D IT!"

1841. HEWLETT, PETER PRIGGINS [Title].

1850. THACKERAY, *Policeman X* [*Misc.* (1899), 213]. PRIGS their shirts and umbrellers, PRIGS their boots and 'ats and clothes.

1851. BORROW, *Lavengro*, xxxi. We never calls them thieves here, but PRIGS and fakers.

1864. *Glasgow Daily Mail*, 9 May. All kinds of cheats, and thimble-riggers, and PRIGS.

1870. *London Figaro*, 19 Feb. They came and PRIGG'D my stockings, my linen, and my store; But they couldn't PRIG my sermons, for they were PRIGG'D before.

1891. CLARK RUSSELL, *Ocean Tragedy*, 87. She PRIGGED the furniture.

2. (old colloquial).—A superior person, *i.e.*, a person esteeming himself superior; in dress, morals, social standing, anything; and behaving as such. [The connotation is one of deliberate and aggressive superiority: you must get that, or you get no PRIG: *see* quot. 1836.] Also a bore. Whence PRIGDOM, PRIGGERY, PRIGGISHNESS, and PRIGGISM.—B. E. (*c.*1696); DYCHE (1748); GROSE (1785).

1676. ETHERIGE, *Man of Mode*, iii. 3. What spruce PRIG is that?

1686. DORSET, *Faithful Catalogue*. Her Court (the Gods be prais'd) has long been free From Irish PRIGGS, and such dull Sots as he.

1688. SHADWELL, *Sq. of Alsatia*, i. Thou shalt shine, and be as gay as any spruce PRIGG that ever walked the street. *Ibid.* If you meet either your father, or brother, or any from those PRIGSTERS, stick up thy countenance.

1695. CONGREVE. *Love for Love*, v. What does the old PRIG mean? I'll banter him, and laugh at him.

*c.*1697. TOM BROWN, *Satire on the French King* [*Works* (1715), i. 66. Thou that hast look'd so fierce, and talk'd so big, In thy old Age to dwindle to a Whigg, By Heaven, I see thou'rt in thy Heart a PRIGG.

1702. STEELE, *Funeral*, iv. Trim sounds so very short and PRIGGISH—that my name should be a monosyllable! Ibid. *Tatler*, No. 77. A cane is part of the dress of a PRIG.

1714. *Spectator*, No. 556. His companion gave him a pull by the sleeve, begging him to come away, for that the old PRIG would talk him to death.

1749. ROBERTSON of Struan, *Poems*, 83. T'other unperforming puny PRIG Could only with his Page retire and f——.

1749. SMOLLETT, *Gil Blas* [ROUTLEDGE], 265. He is a young barrister, with more of the PRIG than the lawyer about him.

1752. *Adventurer*, No. 12. He placed more confidence in them, than he would in a formal PRIG, of whom he knew nothing but that he went every morning and evening to prayers.

1752. FOOTE, *Taste*, ii. How I adore the simplicity of the antients! How unlike the present PRIGGISH, prick-eared puppets!

1836. DICKENS, *Sketches*, 23. Little spare PRIGGISH men, who are perfectly satisfied wilh their own opinions, and consider themselves of paramount importance.

1849. THACKERAY, *Dr. Birch* (*The Doctor*). A more supercilious little PRIG . . . a more empty, pompous little coxcomb I never saw.

1851. BORROW, *Lavengro*, lxvii. The subjects being, if I remember right, college education, PRIGGISM, church authority, tomfoolery. and the like.

1857. TROLLOPE, *Three Clerks*, xlvii. I think I'll take out that about official PRIGGISM—hadn't I better?

1857. HUGHES, *Tom Brown*, i. 2. Your great Mechanic's Institutes end in intellectual PRIGGISM.

1861. KINGSLEY, *Ravenshoe*, lv. Lord Hainault, who was accused by some people of PRIGGISHNESS, was certainly not PRIGGISH before Lord Saltire. He was genial and hearty.

1884. STEVENSON [*Eng. Illustr. Mag.*, Feb., 303]. One is even stirred to a certain impatience with a character so destitute of spontaneity, so passionless in justice, and so PRIGGISHLY obedient to the voice of reason.

1871. GEO. ELIOT, *Middlemarch*, xi. A PRIG is a fellow who is always making you a present of his opinions.

*d.*1882. EMERSON, *Clubs*. One of those conceited PRIGS who value nature only as it feeds and exhibits them.

1884. OXENHAM, *Short Studies*, 150. There is a deficiency, a littleness, a PRIGGISHNESS, a set of vulgarity.

1885. *Notes & Queries*, 7 S. II. 438. All but the . . . very PRIGGISH admit that the folk-lore of the people can teach us several things . . . not to be learned in any other manner.

1892. MCCARTHY and CAMPBELL-PRAED, *Ladies' Gallery*, 53. Fancy a fellow studying Homer when he was camping out in the bush! Not that he is a PRIG. It slipped out quite naturally when we were talking.

1898. *Saturday Review*, 10 Dec., 769, 2. Courteous even at the risk of being branded as PRIGGISH.

3. (Old Cant).—A tinker.

1567. HARMAN, *Caveat* (1876), 59. These droncken Tynckers, called also PRYGGES.

Verb. I. See *subs.* I.

2. (old).—To ride.—HARMAN (1573); DEKKER (1608); ROWLANDS (1610); HEAD (1665); B. E. (*c.*1696); COLES (1724); GROSE (1785).

3. (venery).—To copulate: *see verb.*, sense 2, and RIDE.—B. E. (*c.*1696); GROSE (1785). Whence, as *subs.* = a fornicator. —BEE (1823).

1707. SHIRLEY, *Triumph of Wit*, 'Maunder's Praise of Strowling Most.' Wapping thou I know does love . . . then remove, Thy drawers, and let's PRIG in sport.

4. (Scots'). —To haggle; to cheapen. Hence PRIGGER and PRIGGING.

1512-3. DOUGLAS, *Virgil*, Prol. 238, b. 55. Sum treitcheoure crynis the cunye, and kepis corne stakkis; Sum PRIG penny, sum pyke thank with preny promit.

1623. WEBSTER, *Devil's Law-Case*, i. 2. The wafer-woman that PRIGS abroad With musk-melons and malakatoones.

1765. RUTHERFORD, *Letters*, II, II. The frank buyer—cometh near to what the seller seeketh, useth at last to refer the difference to his will, and so cutteth off the course of mutual PRIGGING.

*d.*1796. BURNS, *Briggs of Ayr*, *New Brig*. Men wha grew wise PRIGGIN' owre hops an' raisins.

1800. RAMSAY, *Poems*, i. 439. In comes a customer, looks big, Looks generous, and scorns to PRIG.

1818. SCOTT, *Heart of Midlothian*, xxiv. Took the pains to PRIGG for her himself.

PRIG-STAR, *subs. phr.* (old).—I. *See* PRIG, *subs.* I.

2. (old).—'A rival in love.'—B. E. (*c.*1696); GROSE (1785).

1725. *New Canting Dictionary*, 'When my Dimber Dell I Courted,' ii. Her glaziers too are quite benighted Nor can any PRIG-STAR charm.

PRIM, *subs.* (old).—I. A wanton: *see* TART.

1509. BARCLAY, *Ship of Fooles* [JAMIESON (1874), i. 250]. [KINGTON OLIPHANT (i. 379): 'The French had a phrase *cheveux primes*, delicate hair; a PRYME means a paramour: our adjective *prim* has now a very different sense; but we still talk of a *prime* cut.']

*c.*1520. *Mayd Emlyn* [HAZLITT, *Pop. Poet*, iv. 84]. The yonge lusty PRYMME She coude byte and whyne . . . And with a pretty gynne Gyue her husbande an horne.

1548. BARCLAY, *Fyfte Eclog.* [NARES]. Aboute all London there was no propre PRYM, But long tyme had ben famylyer with hym.

2. (old).—'A very neat or affected person.'—B. E. (*c.*1696).

PRIME, *adj.* (venery).—Sexually excited; PROUD (*q.v.* PRIDE).—GROSE (1785).

1602. SHAKSPEARE, *Othello*, iii. 3. Were they as PRIME as goats, as hot as monkeys, as salt as wolves in pride.

2. (colloquial).—(1) Eager; more than ready. Whence (2) = of the first quality (esp. butchers': as in PRIME joints, PRIME American, &c.); BANG-UP (*q.v.*).—GROSE (1785). Hence, *verb.* = to fortify, to invigorate, to inspire, bring to the height of a situation: with liquor, information, counsel.

1637. JONSON, *Sad Shepherd*, I. ii. *Rob.* Had you good sport i' your chase to-day? *John.* O PRIME!

1819. VAUX, *Memoirs*, s.v. . . . Any person who is found an easy dupe to the designs of the family is said to be a PRIME flat.

1815. MOORE, *Tom Crib to Big Ben* [*Works* (1854), 401]. Having conquered the PRIME one that milled us all round. *Ibid.* (1819), *Tom Crib's Memorial* . . . What madness could impel So rum a Flat to face so PRIME a Swell. *Ibid.* (183 [?]), *Grand Dinner, &c.* [*Works* (1854), 575]. Joints of poetry—all of the PRIME.

1821. EGAN, *Life in London*, II. ii. Tom and Jerry have just dropped in, . . . quite PRIME for a lark.

1823. *Hints for Oxford*, 73. They [young Oxonians] for a determination when they sit down to table to have a row as soon as they are PRIMED, and often before they rise they commence the work of destruction on glasses and plates and decanters.

1823. BYRON, *Don Juan*, XI. 19. So PRIME, so swell, so nutty, and so knowing.

1827. LYTTON, *Pelham*, lxxxiii. You are going to stall off the Daw's baby IN PRIME TWIG.

1836. DICKENS, *Pickwick*, xxx. Capital! said Mr. Benjamin Allen. PRIME! ejaculated Mr. Bob Sawyer.

1837. BARHAM, *Ingoldsby Legends*, ii. 8. Your thorough French Courtier . . . thinks it's PRIME fun to astonish a citizen.

1854. WHYTE MELVILLE, *General Bounce*, viii. PRIMED with such sage counsel, his lordship determined to lose no time in "opening the trenches." *Ibid.*, xii. A fat little man, PRIMED with port.

*c.*1886. *Music Hall Song*, 'They're all very Fine and Large.' They're all very fine and large, they're all very fine and large, they're all very fresh and PRIME.

1887. HENLEY, *Culture in Slums.* Was it not PRIME—I leave you all to guess How PRIME! to have a jude in love's distress Come spooning round.

1899. WHITEING, *John St.*, ix. It's PRIME, jest when you are goin' off, and jest when you're coming to.

PRIME-COCK-BOY. *See* PRINCOCK.

PRIMITIVE, *adj.* (colloquial).—Unmixed: as spirits with water; NEAT (*q.v.*).

PRIMO, *subs.* (friendly societies').—The chairman or master of a lodge of Buffaloes.

PRINADO, *subs.* (old).—A sharper.

1631. *Clitus's Whimzies*, 12. His nipps, ints, bungs, and PRINADOS, of whom he holds in fee, ofttimes prevent the lawyer by diving too deep into his client's pocket.

16[?]. *Honest Ghost*, 231. Pimps, nips, and ints, PRINADOS, &c.

PRINCOCK (PRINCOX, PRIMCOCK, or PRINCYCOCK), *subs.* (old).—1. A pert youth.—Also as *adj.* = saucy; conceited. — B. E. (*c.* 1696); GROSE (1785). PRIME-COCK-BOY also = (FLORIO), 'a freshman, a novice, a milkesop, a boy new come into the world.'

1573. *New Cust.* [DODSLEY, *Old Plays* (REED), i. 264]. Yes, PRINKOCKES, that I have; for fortie yeares agoe, I could smatter in a Duns—Better I am sure then an hundred of you.

1592. NASHE, *Pierce Pennilesse* (Shaks. Soc.), 52. You shall heare a caualier of the first feather, a PRINCOCKES that was but a page the other day in the court, and is now all to be frenchified in his souldiours sute.

1592. GREENE, *Quip for Up. Courtier*, B. 4. I will teach thee a lesson worth the hearing, proud PRINCOCKS, how gentility first sprung up.

1594. LYLY, *Mother Bombie*, i. 3. I have almost these two yeares cast in my head, how I might match my PRINCOCKS with Stellio's daughter.

1595. SHAKSPEARE, *Romeo and Juliet*, i. 5. You are a saucy boy . . . You are a PRINCOX, go.

1595. TYLNEY, *Locrine*, ii. 4. "Naught reek I of thy threats, thou PRINCOX boy."

1596. GOSSON, *Quippes for Up. Gentlewomen* [HAZLITT, *Pop. Poet*, iv. 250]. And when proud PRINCOKS, rascals bratte, In fashion will be princes mate.

1598. FLORIO, *Worlde of Wordes*, s.v. *Pinchino.* A pillicock, a PRIMCOCK, a prick, a prettie lad, a gull, a noddie.

1611. CORYAT, *Crudities*, ii. 255 [Reprint]. To teach many proud, PRINCOCKE scholars, that are puffed up with the opinion of their learning, to pull downe the high sailes of their lofty spirits.

1611. CHAPMAN, *May-Day*, i. 1. I have love to employ thee in as well as the proudest young PRINCOCK.

1615. DANIEL, *Hymen's Triumph*, 313. Ah, sirrah, have I found you? are you heere, You PRINCOCK boy?

2. (venery).—The female *pudendum*: *see* MONOSYLLABLE.—[DUNBAR.] Also the *penis*: *see* PRICK.

PRINCOD, *subs.* (old). — 1. 'A round, plump man or woman.'—GROSE (1785).

2. (old). — A pincushion.—GROSE (1785).

PRINK (or PRINCK), *verb.* (old).—To dress for show; to adorn fantastically; to 'put on airs': *see* quot. *c.* 1696.—GROSE (1785). Hence PRINCUMS = high-sniffing niceties, and fads, scruples; MRS. PRINCUM PRANCUM (B. E. and GROSE) = 'a nice, precise, formal madam'; PRINKER = a JETTER (*q.v.*).

[?]. *Lansdowne MS.*, 1033. To be PRINKT up, to be drest up fine or finical like children or vain women.

1576. GASCOIGNE, *Philomene* [CHALMERS, ii. . . .]. Enflamede hir haughtie harte To get more grace by crummes of cost, And PRINCKE it out hir parte.

1614. TOMKIS, *Albumazar*, ii. 5. "Just Æsop's crow, PRINK'D up in borrow'd feathers."

1690. DURFEY, *Collins Walk*, i. My behaviour may not yoke With the nice PRINCUMS of that folk.

c. 1696. B. E., *Dict. Cant. Crew*, s.v. PRINKING . . . PRINKT-UP, set up on the Cupboards-head in their best Cloaths, or in State, Stiff-starched. MISTRESS PRINCUM-PRANCUM, such a one.

1753. JANE COLLIER, *Art of Tormenting* [*Ency. Dict.*]. "She was every day longer PRINKING in the glass than you was."

1820. SCOTT, *Monastery*, xxiv. Ay, prune thy feathers, and PRINK thyself gay.

PRINT. IN PRINT, *adv. phr.* (colloquial).—Exactly in order. OUT OF PRINT = disordered; tumbled. QUITE IN PRINT = formal and precise: *see* TALK. — GROSE (1785).

1621. BURTON, *Anat. Melan.*, 539. He must speak IN PRINT, walk IN PRINT, eat and drink IN PRINT.

1625. JONSON, *Staple of News*, i. 1. *P. jun.* Fits my ruff well? *Lin.* IN PRINT.

1851. *Notes and Queries*, 1 S. IV. 12. Take care, Sir, you'll put your hair OUT OF PRINT.

PRINTER'S-DEVIL. *See* DEVIL, *subs.*, sense 2.

PRINTED-CHARACTER, *subs. phr.* (common). — A pawn-ticket; a MORTGAGE-DEED (*q.v.*).

PRIORESS. *See* BETTER HORSE.

PRISCIAN'S-HEAD. TO BREAK PRISCIAN'S-HEAD, *verb. phr.* (literary).—To use bad grammar. [Lat. *diminuēre Prisciani caput.* Priscian a famous grammarian of the 5th century.]—GROSE (1785).

1527-37. ELLIS, *Orig. Letters* . . . [The well-known Father Forrest being ungrammatical is said to] BREKE MASTER PRECYENS HEDE.

1664. BUTLER, *Hudibras*, II. ii. 219. And hold no sin so deeply red As that of BREAKING PRISCIAN'S HEAD.

1728. POPE, *Dunciad*, iii. 161. Some, free from rhyme or reason, rule or check, BREAK PRISCIAN'S HEAD, and Pegasus's neck.

1819. BYRON [*Life*, 'To Moore']. Also if there be any further BREAKING OF PRISCIAN'S HEAD, will you supply the plaster.

PRITTLE-PRATTLE. *See* PRATING-CHEAT.

PRIVATES, *subs.* (conventional).—The organs of generation, male or female. Also PRIVITY (of women), PRIVITIES, and PRIVY MEMBER. Analogous terms (venery) are PRIVATE PROPERTY = (1) *penis*, and (2) the female *pudendum*; PRIVY-HOLE (-COUNCIL or -PARADISE, or PRIVY) = the female *pudendum*.

1598. FLORIO, *Worlde of Wordes*, s.v. *Capocchio.* A woman's PRIVITIE.

1620. PERCY, *Folio MS.*, 'Fryar and Boye.' The thornes this while were rough and thicke, and did his PRIVY MEMBERS pricke.

1678. COTTON, *Virgil Travestie* [*Works* (17..), 21]. When on Grounsel He firkt her Mother's PRIVY-COUNSEL.

TO PRIVATE STITCH, *verb. phr.* (tailors').—To conceal the thread in stitching.

PRIVATE-BUSINESS, *subs. phr.* (Eton).—Extra work done with a tutor.

PRIVY, *subs.* (colloquial).—An outdoor cesspool.

1647. FLETCHER, *Noble Gent.*, v. 1. Lay all night for fear of puirsuivants In Burgundy PRIVY-HOUSE.

1662. *Rump Songs*, i. 104. I hid myself i' the PRIVY.

1746. T. WARTON, *Prog. of Discontent.* This awkward hut, o'ergrown with ivy, We'll alter to a modern PRIVY.

See PRIVATE.

PRIZE-PACKET, *subs. phr.* (theatrical).—1. A novice who pays to go on the boards.

1899. *Globe*, 27 July, 7, 1. Another man spent a happy holiday as a strolling player, having got an engagement through an agent in a small company as a PRIZE PACKET.

PRO, *subs.* (theatrical).—1. An actor: *i.e.*, one who belongs to '*The* Profession' = acting. Hence, PRO'S-BIBLE = *The Era* newspaper; PRO'S-TESTAMENT = *The Sunday Times.*

c. 1860. *Music Hall Song*, 'Oh She was such a Beautiful Girl.' Oh, why did she bolt with another PRO.

1880. SIMS, *Ballads of Babylon*, 'Forgotten.' And the quiet PRO.'s pass onward To the stage-door up the court.

1886-96. MARSHALL, '*Pomes' from the Pink 'Un* ('The Merry Stumer'), 8. It was told me by Tinribs, a Fleet-street PRO.

1893. MILLIKEN, *'Arry Ballads*, 38. All our PROS. felt their nose out of joint when this Comerdee Frongsay lot came.

2. (University).—A pro-proctor: a second in command in the proctorial police.

1823. *Hints for Oxford*, 10. They [Freshmen] cap the PRO.'s too in the street. . . .

1869. BRADWOOD, *O. V. H.*, x. The proctor (more strictly a PRO.) backed out of the room with wholesale apologies.

PROBOSCIS, *subs.* (common).—The nose: *see* CONK.

1888. *Sporting Life*, 10 Dec. Atford again became the aggressor, and landing very heavily on the PROBOSCIS again drew copious supplies of claret.

PROCESSION (or PROCESH), *subs.* (colloquial).—1. A matter of following. Hence, TO GO ON WITH THE PROCESSION = to maintain continuity; TO STAND AT THE HEAD OF THE PROCESSION = to lead.

1883. *Graphic*, 24 March, 303, 1. The [boat] race can hardly be spoken of as a PROCESSION, which is a title only applicable to an ignominious defeat.

1891. *Daily Chronicle*, 23 Mar. The feeling seemed to be general that nothing better than a PROCESSION could be looked for.

1899. *Daily Telegraph*, 7 Ap., 8, 2. "A reg'lar PROCESSION o' the proprieties!" said Perce.

2. (circus).—A street parade.

PROCLAMATION. TO HAVE ONE'S HEAD FULL OF PROCLAMATIONS, *verb. phr.* (old).—'To be much taken up to little purpose.'—B. E. (*c.* 1696); RAY (1760).

PROCTOUR, *subs.* (old).—(1) *See* quot. Also (2, HALLIWELL) = one who collected alms for lepers, or other incapables. Also (KENNETT) beggars of any kind.

1560-1. AWDELEY, *Fraternitye of Vacabondes*, 'XXV. Orders of Knaues,' 12. PROCTOUR is he, that will tary long, and bring a lye, when his Maister sendeth him on his errand. This is a stibber gibber knaue, that doth fayne tales.

PRODIGIOUS, *adj.* and *adv.* (colloquial). — Very; exceedingly; immensely: *cf.* AWFUL.

d. 1744. POPE [quoted by TODD]. I am PRODIGIOUSLY pleased by this joint volume.

PROFESSION (THE). *See* PRO.

PROG, *subs.* (common).—Food.—B. E. (*c.* 1696); DYCHE (1748) 'a cant word for provisions, goods, or money laid up in store'; JOHNSON (1755) 'a low word'; GROSE (1785). Also as *verb.* = to beg; PROG-BASKET = a beggar's wallet; PROG-SHOP = an eating-house: *see* GRUB.

1440. *Prompt. Parv.*, 414. PROKKYN or styfly askyn, procor, procito.

1622. FLETCHER, *Spanish Curate*, iii. 3. That man in the gown, in my opinion, Looks like a PROGUING rogue.

1655. FULLER, *Ch. Hist.*, v. 290. The Abbot also every Saturday was to visit their beds, to see if they had not shuffled in some softer matter or purloyned some PROGGE for themselves. *Ibid.* Pandulf, an Italian and Pope's legate, a perfect artist in PROGGING for money.

1688. SHADWELL, *Sq. of Alsatia*, II. So, here's the PROG, here's the dinner coming up.

1730. SWIFT, *Directions to Servants*, ii. You can junket together at nights upon your own PROG, when the rest of the house are a-bed.

1795. CUMBERLAND, *Jew*, ii. 2. *Jabal.* I have not had a belly-full since I belong'd to you. You take care there shall be no fire in the kitchen, master provides no PROG upon the shelf, so between you both I have plenty of nothing but cold and hunger.

1818. MOORE, *Fudge Family* [*Works* (1854), 406]. There's nothing beats feeding, And this is the place for it, Dicky, you dog, Of all places on earth—the head-quarters of PROG.

1837. BARHAM, *Ingoldsby Legends* (1862), 191. Och! the Count Von Strogonoff, sure he got PROG enough.

1845. DISRAELI, *Sybil*, III. vii. Ayn't you lucky, boys, to have reg'lar work like this, and the best of PROG!

1871. *Morning Advertiser*, 11 Sep. So we'll cut down their full rations, and knock off all their grog, Whilst I feast at home with sleek lord mayors on aldermanic PROG.

1893. MILLIKEN, *'Arry Ballads*, 18. See old mivvies with PROG-BASKETS prowling about. *Ibid.*, 27. Lots o' prime PROG in the bag.

Verb. (printers').—To prognosticate.

See PROG, *subs.*

PROGGER (or PROGGINS), *subs.* (University).—A proctor: whence TO BE PROGGED = to be proctorised; and PROGGING = a proctorial discipline.

PROGNOSTIC, *subs.* (literary).—An artistic feeder. [PROG (*q.v.*) + Gr. *gnosis.*]

PROJECT, *verb.* (American).—To play tricks; TO MONKEY (*q.v.*).

1847. *Chronicles of Pineville*, 181. I'll blow 'em all to everlastin' thunderation, if they come a PROJECTIN' about me.

PROM, *subs.* (common).—A promenade concert: *cf.* POP.

1902. *Free Lance*, 4 Jan., 358, 1. Musically speaking, there is never one of the programmes at the PROMS. that is unworthy of the attendance of the most cultured music lover.

PROMOTER, *subs.* (old).—*See* quot. 1509, and PUTTER-ON.

1509. BARCLAY [JAMIESON (1874), ii. 50], *Ship of Fools.* [OLIPHANT, *New English*, i. 378. There is the word PROMOTER used for a lawyer; fifty years later it was degraded to mean an informer.]

1563. FOXE, *Acts and Monuments* [CATTLEY]. [OLIPHANT, *New English*, i. 550. Barclay had used PROMOTER for a lawyer; Foxe constantly uses the word to signify an *informer*, and this last word is also employed.]

1608. *Yorkshire Tragedy*, i. 2. My second son must be a PROMOTER; and my third a thief.

2. (colloquial).—A fool-catcher.

PROMOSS, *verb.* (Australian).—To talk rubbish; to play the fool; TO GAMMON (*q.v.*).

PROMOTION. ON PROMOTION, *adv.* (common).—1. On approval; (2) unmarried.

1848. THACKERAY, *Vanity Fair*, xliv. 'You want to smoke those filthy cigars,' replied Mrs. Rawdon. 'I remember when you liked 'em, though,' answered the husband . . . 'That was when I was ON MY PROMOTION, Goosey,' she said.

PROMPTER, *subs.* (Merchant Taylors' School).—One of the second form.

PROOF, *subs.* (University).—The best ale at Magdalen, Oxford.

PROP (or **PROPERTY**), *subs.* (theatrical).—1. Generally in *pl.*: *e.g.*, MANAGER'S-PROPS = stuff for stage use; ACTORS-PROPS = acting material provided by himself. Fr. *accessoires.*

*c.*15 [?]. *Tam. Shr.* [*Old Play*, Act i., p. 164]. My lord, we must Have a shoulder of mutton, for a PROPERTIE.

1596. SHAKSPEARE, *Merry Wives*, iv. 4. Go get us PROPERTIES and trickings for our fairies.

1845. *Punch*, ix. 60. "Well covered in With a lot of PROPERTY snow."

1871. *Standard*, 8 Sep., 'The Campaign.' Officers are buying the PROPERTIES necessary—camp beds, canteens, and pocket-flasks are at a premium.

1883. *Referee*, 6 May, 3, 2. The Theatre Royal scenery and PROPS were sold by auction.

1893. MILLIKEN, *'Arry Ballads*, 78. Names and metres is any one's PROPS; but one thing they don't 'ave the 'ang.

2. (thieves').—A breast-pin: whence PROP-NAILER (*see* quot. 1856).

185 [?]. DICKENS, *Reprinted Pieces* (*Three 'Detective' Anecdotes, The Artful Touch*). In his shirt-front there's a beautiful diamond PROP.

1856. MAYHEW, *Gt. World of London*, 46. Those who plunder by *stealth*, as . . . PROP-NAILERS, who steal pins or brooches.

1863. *Story of a Lancashire Thief*, 8. Lucky Middlesex's best was, of how he had nailed a diamond PROP only the week before.

1879. HORSLEY, *Auto. of Thief* [*Macmillan's Mag.*, xl. 506]. Pipe his spark PROP.

1888. SIMS, *Plank Bed Ballad* [*Referee*, 12 Feb., 3]. A spark PROP a pal . . . and I Had touched.

1891. *Sporting Times*, 11 Ap. But he is proudest of all of the pin, set with diamonds and rubies, presented to him by the Heir to the Throne . . . John was wearing this PROP in the Paddock at Epsom.

3. (pugilistic).—A straight hit: *see* WIPE.

1887. *Lic. Vict. Gazette*, 2 Dec., 358/3. Ned met each rush of his enemy with straight PROPS.

4. (Punch and Judy).—The gallows.

5. (common).—In *pl.* = the legs.

1891. *Sportsman*, 20 Ap. There are those amongst his detractors who assert that with such PROPS he will never successfully negociate the Epsom gradients.

6. (common).—In *pl.* = crutches.—GROSE (1785).

7. (theatrical).—*See* quot: also PROPSTER.

1889. *New York Tribune*, 14 July. The property-man, or, as he is always called, PROPS for short.

8. (common).—In *pl.* = the arms.

1869. *Temple Bar*, xxvi. 74. Take off your coat and put up your PROPS to him.

Verb. (pugilists').—To hit; to knock down. Hence, TO PUT THE PROP ON = to seize an adversary's arm, and so prevent him from hitting.

1851. MAYHEW, *Lond. Lab.*, &c., III. 397. If we met an old bloke (man) we PROPPED him.

1853. BRADLEY, *Verdant Green*. His whole person put in Chancery, slung, bruised, fibbed, PROPPED, fiddled, slogged, and otherwise ill-treated.

1887. *Lic. Vict. Gazette*, 2 Dec., 358/3. Ned . . . stopped Smith's blows neatly, and PROPPED his man right and left as he came in.

1892. *National Observer*, 27 Feb., p. 378. Give me a snug little set-to down in Whitechapel: Nobody there that can PROP you in the eye!

TO KICK AWAY THE PROP, *verb. phr.* (old).—To be hanged: *see* LADDER.

P.P. *See* PLAY OR PAY.

PROPER, *adj.* and *adv.* (old colloquial).—An ironical inversion or perversion of a popular epithet of commendation and approval.

1600. SHAKSPEARE, *Much Ado*, iv. 1. Talk with a man out at a window! A PROPER saying!

1664. PEPYS, *Diary*, 24 June. I was PROPERLY confounded. *Ibid.*, 14 July. All . . . was most PROPERLY false, and nothing like it true.

1843-4. HALIBURTON, *Attache*, xxvi. Father . . . gave me a wipe . . . that knocked me over and hurt me PROPERLY.

TO MAKE ONESELF PROPER, *verb. phr.* (colloquial).—To adorn; to TITTIVATE (*q.v.*).

PROPERTY. TO MAKE PROPERTY OF ONE, *verb. phr.* (old).—To use as a convenience, tool, or cat's-paw.—GROSE (1785); BEE (1823).

1596. SHAKSPEARE, *K. John*, v. 2, 79. I am too high-born to be PROPERTIED.

PROPHET, *subs.* (Fleet St.).—A sporting tipster.

PROPSTER and **PROP-NAILER.** *See* PROP.

PROS, *subs.* (Cambridge).—A W.C.: hence the old undergrad wheeze:—When is *pote* put for *pros*? When the nights are dark and dreary, When our legs are weak and weary, When the quad we have to cross, Then is *pote* put for *pros*.

Adv. (streets').—*See* quot.

1887. *Walford's Antiquarian*, April, 250. PROS means proper. Nothing but the word prosperous offers in explanation.

PROSE, *subs.* (Winchester).—A lecture: also as *verb.*

PROSIT, *intj.* (academical).—A salutation in drinking: 'Your health!' [*Ut tibi prosit meri potio.*] Fr. *Ut!*

PROSS, *subs.* (streets').—1. A prostitute: *see* TART: also PROSSY.

2. (theatrical).—A cadged drink: also as *verb.* (or *adv.*, ON THE PROSS) = (1) to spunge, and (2) to instruct or break in a stage-struck youth; PROSSER = (1) a cadger of drinks, dinners, and small monies (but *see* quot. 1851), and (2) a PONCE (*q.v.*). PROSSER'S AVENUE = the Gaiety bar.

1851. MAYHEW, *Lond. Lab.*, iii. 145. The regular salary [of strolling player] doesn't come to more than a pound a-week, but then you make something out of those who come up on the parade, for one will chuck you 6d., some 1s. and 2s. 6d. We call those parties PROSSES.

*c.*1876. *Song*, 'I Can't Get at it.' I've PROSSED my meals from off my pals, ofttimes I've badly fared.

1883. *Referee*, 18 Nov., 3, 4. For he don't haunt the Gaiety Bar, dear boys, A-standing (or PROSSING FOR) drinks.

1885. *Saturday Review*, 15 Aug., 218. Accept his decision and neither thunder against him in PROSSER'S AVENUE (as it is called), nor encourage young journalists to state your views upon him in print.

1886. *Cornhill Mag.*, Nov., 559. Gradually, he became what is known as a PROSSER—a loafer, a beggar of small loans, a respectful attendant outside the circle of other men's merriment, into which for charity's sake he was sometimes invited.

1893. EMERSON, *Signor Lippo*, xiv. He started walking about clamming, getting a few middays as from one and another, fairly ON THE PROSS and glad to put up with a quatro soldi kip, like the rest of us.

PROTECTED-MAN, *subs. phr.* (old naval).—A merchant seaman unfit for the Royal Service and therefore free of the press-gang.

PROTECTION. UNDER PROTECTION, *phr.* (conventional).—In KEEPING (*q.v.*); living TALLY (*q.v.*); DABBED-UP (*q.v.*).

PROUD, *adj.* (common).—1. Pleased; gratified. Hence, TO DO ONE PROUD = to flatter; to honour; TO DO ONESELF PROUD = to be pleased.

1836. CLARK, *Ollapodiana Papers.* With my brain reeling with fancies of wine and women, I really thought, for the moment, that 'she DID ME PROUD.'

1838. SELBY, *Jacques Strop*, i. 2. *Flon.* Certainly! how can we refuse? especially as he is so pressing. *Ber.* YOU DO ME PROUD.

1887. SIDNEY LUSKA, *Land of Love* [*Lippincott's Mag.*, 241]. Ah? So? The frank confession DOES YOU PROUD.

1892. CHEVALIER, 'The Little Nipper.' And 'e's a little champion, Do ME PROUD, well, 'e's a knock out!

1900. KIPLING, *Stalky & Co.*, 4. 'Beetle, give me the hammer.' 'All right. I'm not PROUD. Chuck us down that net on top of the lockers, Stalky.'

2. *See* PRIDE.

PROV. ON THE PROV, *phr.* (workmen's).—Out of work and on the Provident Fund of a trade society.

PROVENDER, *subs.* (Old Cant).—'He from whom money is taken on the highway: perhaps provider, or provider.'—GROSE (1785).

PROVOST, *subs.* (military).—A garrison or other cell for prisoners whose sentences are for a week or less.

PROW, *subs.* (old naval).—A bumpkin: *see* BUFFLE.

PROWL, *subs.* and *verb.* (old).—(1) (HUGH PROWLER) = a thief or highwayman; (2) PROWLING (or PROWLERY) = robbery; (3) to womanize; to GROUSE (*q.v.*); to go after MEAT (*q.v.*), B. E. (*c.*1696); (4, theatrical) = to wait for the GHOST (*q.v.*) to walk.

1557. TUSSER, *Husbandry*, xxxiii. 25. For fear of HUGH PROWLER get home with the rest.

1635. QUARLES, *Emblems*, ii. 2. We pry, we PROWL . . . we prog from pole to pole.

1692. HACKET, *Life of Williams*, I. 51. Thirty-seven monopolies, with other shocking PROWLERIES.

1885. *Daily Telegraph*, 4 Sep. There are so many young PROWLERS on the look-out that they'd precious soon empty a bin.

PROX, *subs.* (American).—A proxy: specifically a ticket or list of candidates at elections, presented to voters for their votes.

PRUFF, *verb.* (Winchester School).—Sturdy; 'proof' against pain.

1881. PASCOE, *Public Schools.* Deprive a Wykehamist of words . . . such as quill . . . PRUFF . . . spree . . . cad . . . And his vocabulary becomes limited.

PRUGGE, *subs.* (old).—'A partner or doxy.'—NARES (1822); HALLIWELL (1847).

1631. *Clitus's Cater-Char.*, 32. If his PRUGGE aspire to so much stock, or so great trust, as to brew to sell, he will be sure to drinke up all the gaines.

PRUNELLA, *subs.* (old).—A clergyman: *see* SKYPILOT. Also MR. PRUNELLA.—GROSE (1785). [Clerical gowns were largely made of this material.]

1838. JERROLD, *Men of Character* (John Applejohn), viii. The finest lawn [bishop] makes common cause with any linen bands—the silken apron shrinks not from poor PRUNELLA.

PRUNES. *See* STEWED PRUNES.

TO HAVE PRUNES IN THE VOICE, *verb. phr.* (American).—To speak huskily; from emotion.

1888. St. Louis *Globe-Democrat.* There seemed TO BE PRUNES IN MY VOICE, and it seemed strange to me.

PRUSSIAN-BLUE, *subs. phr.* (obsolete).—*See* quot. 1868.

1837. DICKENS, *Pickwick*, xxxiii. 'Vell, Sammy,' said the father. 'Vell, MY PROOSHAN BLUE,' responded the son.

1868. BREWER, *Phrase & Table*, s.v. PROOSHAN BLUE (*My*). A term of great endearment. After . . . Waterloo the Prussians were immensely popular, and in connection with the Loyal True Blue Club gave rise to the toasts, "The True Blue" and the "PRUSSIAN BLUE."

PRY, *subs.* (old: now recognised as *verb.*).—A busybody; a 'peeping Tom': now PAUL PRY (*q.v.*): from Poole's farce.—B. E. (*c.* 1696); GROSE (1785).

PRYGGE. *See* PRIG.

PSALM-SMITER, *subs. phr.* (common).—A ranting dissenter.

PUB (or **PUBLIC**), *subs.* (colloquial).—A tavern; IN THE PUBLIC LINE = engaged as a licensed victualler.

1816. SCOTT, *Old Mortality*, xli. This woman keeps an inn, then? interrupted Morton. A PUBLIC, in a prim way, replied Blane.

1840. LYTTON, *Paul Clifford*, xxii. Ascertaining the topography of the PUBLIC at which he spake.

1866. ELIOT, *Felix Holt*, xxviii. The Cross-Keys was a very old-fashioned PUBLIC.

*c.*1871. *Siliad*, 16. All the great houses and the minor PUBS. *Ibid.* Peelers . . . watch PUBLICS with a jealous eye.

1883. PAYN, *Thicker than Water*, xxxv. One doesn't expect to see . . . the inevitable hanger-on of PUBS outside, waiting for a job.

1884. *Good Words*, June, 400, 1. He had done twelve months for crippling the chucker-out of one of these PUBS.

1885. *D. Telegraph*, 31 Oct. The difficulty will be to persuade him to come out of the domestic paradise into a world without PUBS.

1886-87. MARSHALL, '*Pomes*' [It's a Sad Heart that never Rejoices'], 76. The bloke at the PUB.

1887. HENLEY, *Villon's Good-Night*, i. You sponges miking round the PUBS.

1893. MILLIKEN, *'Arry Ballads*, 3. No PUB but a sand-parloured shanty.

1899. WHITEING, *John St.*, vii. Waiting for the opening of the PUBS.

PUBLIC-BUILDINGS. INSPECTOR OF PUBLIC BUILDINGS, *subs. phr.* (common).—(1) An idler: from choice or necessity: a loafer or a man seeking work.

PUBLIC-LEDGER, *subs. phr.* (common).—A prostitute: *see* TART. ['Because (GROSE), like that paper, open to all parties.']

PUBLIC-MAN, *subs. phr.* (old).—A bankrupt.—GROSE (1785).

PUBLIC-PATTERER, *subs. phr.* (obsolete).—*See* quot.

1866. HOTTEN, *Slang Dict.*, s.v. PUBLIC PATTERERS, swell mobsmen who pretend to be Dissenting preachers, and harangue in the open air to attract a crowd for their confederates to rob.

PUCK, *subs.* (old).—The devil: *see* SKIPPER.

1362. LANGLAND, *Piers Plowman*, xix. 282. Fro the POUKES poundfalde no maynprise may ous fecche.

PUCKER, *verb.* (showmen's).—*See* quot.

1851. MAYHEW, *Lond. Lab.*, i. 269. The trio at this stage of the performances began PUCKERING (talking privately) to each other in murdered French, dashed with a little Irish.

IN A PUCKER, *phr.* (colloquial).—Anxious; agitated; angry; confused: *cf.* PUDDER.—DYCHE (1748); GROSE (1785). Whence TO PUCKER UP = to get angry.

1751. SMOLLETT, *Peregrine Pickle*, ii. The whole parish was in a PUCKER: some thought the French had landed.

1825. NEAL, *Bro. Jonathan*, I. vii. Miriam [was] IN A PLAGUY PUCKER.

1888. HOWELLS, *Annie Kilburn*, xxix. He was IN such A PUCKER about her.

1883. PAYN, *Thicker than Water*, xiii. Mary's letters, therefore, were among the few things that did not agitate Mrs. Sotheran, or, to use her own homely phrase, put her INTO A PUCKER—a moderately cold perspiration.

PUCKER-WATER, *subs. phr.* (old).—An astringent: used to counterfeit virginity.—GROSE (1785).

PUCK-FIST (or **PUCK-FOIST**), *subs. phr.* (old).—A braggart. [NARES: equivalent to 'vile fungus,' 'scum of the earth.']

1601. JONSON, *Poetaster*, iv. 4. Valiant? so is mine arse. Gods and fiends! . . . he dares not fight with a PUCK-FIST. *Ibid.* (1630), *New Inn.* Oh, they are pinching PUCK-FISTS.

1607. DEKKER, *Northward Hoe*, i. 2. Do you laugh, you unseasonable PUCK-FIST?

1608. MIDDLETON, *Epigrams* [HALLIWELL]. Old father PUCKFIST knits his arteries, First strikes, then rails on Riot's villanies. *Ibid.* (1657), *More Dissemb. than Women*, iv. 3. What pride Of pampered blood has mounted up this PUCK-FOIST?

1619. FLETCHER, *Cust. of Country*, i. 2. But that this PUCK-FIST, This universal rutter.

1630. TAYLOR, *Works* [NARES]. These PUCKFOYST cockbrain'd coxcombs, shallow pated, Are things that by their taylors are created.

1633. FORD, *Love's Sacrifice*, ii. 1. Sanazar a goose, Ariosto a PUCK-FIST to me.

PUD (or **PUDSEY**), *subs.* (colloquial).—A hand; a fist.

1823. LAMB, *Distant Correspondents.* Those little short . . . PUDS.

Verb. (colloquial).—To greet affectionately or familiarly.

PUDDER, *subs.* (old colloquial).—Confusion; bother: *cf.* PUCKER. Also as *verb.* = to bustle; to search; to dabble; to POTTER (*q.v.*).

[?]. *Harl. MS.*, 388 [HALLIWELL]. My Lorde Willoughbie's counsell, though to little purpose, made a great deale of PUDDER.

1605. SYLVESTER, *Du Bartas*, i. 5. Some almost always PUDDER in the mud Of sleepy pools.

1609. BEAUMONT and FLETCHER, *Scornful Lady*, ii. 2. Some fellows would have cried out now . . . and kept a PUDDER.

1642. MILTON, *Apol. for Smeet* [*Works* (1806), i. 211]. Able enough to lay the dust and PUDDER in antiquity, which he and his, out of stratagem, are wont to raise.

1663. DRYDEN, *Wild Gallant*, i. You need not keep such a PUDDER about eating his words.

1664. COTTON, *Virgil Travestie*, 19. Then, then indeed began the PUDDER.

*c.*1670. LOCKE, *Understanding*, 13. Contrary observations that . . . perplex and PUDDER him if he compares them.

1674. FAIRFAX, *Bulk and Selvedge* [HALLIWELL]. So long as he who has but a teeming brain may have leave to lay his eggs in his own nest, which is built beyond the reach of every man's PUDDERING-POLE.

*d.*1731. WARD, *Simple Cobbler*, 2. Such as are least able are most busie to PUDDER in the rubbish, and to raise dust.

1759. STERNE, *Tristram Shandy*, II. ii. What a PUDDER and racket!

1840. JUDD, *Margaret*, i. 16. Parkins's Pints has been making a great PUDDER over to England.

PUDDING, *subs.* (thieves').—1. Drugged liver: used by burglars to silence house-dogs.

1877. HORSLEY, *Jottings from Jail.* When I opened a door there was a great tyke lying in front of the door, so I pulled out a piece of PUDDING and threw it to him, but he did not move.

2. (venery).—Coition: *see* GREENS. Also the *penis*: *see* PRICK. IN THE PUDDING CLUB (or WITH A BELLY-FUL OF MARROW PUDDING) = pregnant.

1682. *Wit and Mirth* ('From Twelve Years Old'), 18. He Rumbl'd and Jumbl'd me o'er, and o'er, Till I found he had almost wasted the store Of his PUDDING.

1719. DURFEY, *Pills to Purge*, vi. 301. Quoth he, my dear Philli, I'll give unto thee, Such PUDDING you never did see.

3. (old).—The guts.—GROSE (1785). Hence PUDDING-HOUSE = the belly; PUDDING-KEN = a cook-shop; PUDDING-SNAMMER = a cook-shop thief; PUDDING-FILLER (old Scots') = a glutton.

1503-8. DUNBAR [*Bannatyne Club*], 44 st., 14. Sic PUDDING-FILLARIS, descending doun from millaris, Within this land was nevir hard nor sene.

1596. SHAKSPEARE, *Merry Wives*, ii. 1. As sure as his guts are made of PUDDINGS.

1596. NASHE, *Saffron Walden* [*Works*, iii. 148]. What a commotion there was in his entrayles or PUDDING-HOUSE, for want of food. *Ibid.* (1599), *Lenten Stuffe* [*Harl. Misc.*, vi. 166]. He . . . thrust him downe his PUDDING-HOUSE at a gobbe.

1607. ROWLANDS, *Diogenes Lanthorne*, 7 (Hunterian Club's Repr., 1873). All the guttes in his PUDDING-HOUSE rumble and grumble at their slender alowance.

1772. BRIDGES, *Burlesque Homer*, 206. As on the ground his bum came smash His PUDDINGS jumbled with a swash.

1857. SNOWDEN, *Mag. Assistant* (3rd ed.), 446. One who steals food. A PUDDING SNAMMER.

1893. EMERSON, *Lippo*, x. I just went to one of my regular PUDDING-KENS to sell the mungarly to some of the needies there.

4. (common).—Good luck.

COLLOQUIALISMS, mostly contemptuous are:—PUDDING-BELLIED = big-stomached; PUDDING-FACED = fat, round, and smooth in face; PUDDING-HEAD = a fool: whence PUDDING-HEADED (GROSE) = stupid; PUDDING-HEART = a coward; PUDDING-HOSE = baggy breeches; PUDDING-SLEEVES = (1) large baggy sleeves as in the full dress clerical gown; whence (2) a parson: *see* SKY-PILOT; IN PUDDING TIME (GROSE) = in the nick of time, opportunely; PUDDINGY = fat and round; PUDDING ABOUT THE HEELS = slovenly, thick-ankled; TO RIDE POST FOR A PUDDING = to exert for little cause; TO GIVE THE CROWS A PUDDING (GROSE) = (1) to hang on a gibbet, and (2) to die: *see* HOP THE TWIG. Also proverbs and sayings:—'The proof of the PUDDING is in the eating'; 'Hungry dogs will eat dirty PUDDINGS'; 'Cold PUDDING will settle your love (GROSE)'; 'Better some of a PUDDING than none of a pie'; 'There is no deceit in a bag-PUDDING'; 'PUDDINGS and paramours should be hastily handled'; 'PUDDINGS an' wort are hasty dirt'; 'It would vex a dog to see a PUDDING creep'; 'Be fair conditioned and eat bread with your PUDDING.'

1594. TYLNEY, *Locrine*, iii. 3. You come IN PUDDING TIME, or else I had dress'd them.

1599. SHAKSPEARE, *Hen. V.*, ii. 1, 91. By my troth he'll YIELD THE CROW A PUDDING one of these days.

1608. WITHAL, *Dict.*, 3. I came in season, as they say IN PUDDING TIME, tempore veni.

1614. *Terence in English* [NARES]. *Per tempus advenis*, you come IN PUDDING TIME, you come as well as may be.

1630. TAYLOR, *Works* [NARES]. Our land-lord did that shift prevent, Who came IN PUDDING TIME, and tooke his rent.

1663. BUTLER, *Hudibras*, i. 2. Mars that still protects the stout, IN PUDDING TIME came to his aid.

1707. WARD, *Hud. Red.*, II. ii. 25. Sweethearts aft'r 'em will be crowding Like HUNGRY DOGS TO DIRTY PUDDING.

1708-10. SWIFT, *Polite Conversation*, ii. Sir John, . . . will you do as we do? You are come IN PUDDEN-TIME. *Ibid.*, ii. *Miss.* This Almond Pudden was pure good, but it is grown quite cold. *Neverout.* So much the better, Miss; COLD PUDDEN WILL SETTLE YOUR LOVE. *Ibid.*, iii. SCORNFUL DOGS WILL EAT DIRTY PUDDENS. *Ibid.*, ii. Madam, I'm like all Fools, I love everything that is good; but THE PROOF OF THE PUDDEN IS IN THE EATING. Ibid., *Baucis and Philemon.* About each arm a PUDDING SLEEVE.

1720. HEARNE, *Diary*, 8 Feb. The whiggs and the enemies of the universities . . . all go in PUDDING-SLEEVE gowns.

*c.*1750. *Old Song*, 'Vicar of Bray.' When George IN PUDDING TIME came o'er, &c.

1749. SMOLLETT, *Gil Blas* [ROUTLEDGE], 344. THE PROOF OF THE PUDDING IS IN THE EATING; so I will . . . give you a specimen of my talent.

1759. STERNE, *Tristram Shandy*, II. ii. Such a confused, PUDDING-HEADED, muddle-headed fellow.

1772. BRIDGES, *Burlesque Homer*, 140. The horns! . . . Became this Scotchman's lawful plunder, Who just IN PUDDING TIME came in.

1777. JACKMAN, *All the World's a Stage*, i. 2. How can you extort that d—d PUDDING FACE of yours to madness?

1822. SCOTT, *Fortunes of Nigel*, xxvi. A purse-proud, PUDDING-HEADED, fat-gutted, lean-brained Southron.

1833. CARLYLE, *Cagliostro* [*Fraser*, viii.]. Stupid, PUDDING-FACED as he looks.

1834. TAYLOR, *Ph. van Artevelde*, II. iii. 1. Go, PUDDING-HEART! Take thy huge offal and white liver hence.

1851-61. MAYHEW, *Lond. Lab.*, III. 65. A limpness and roundness of limb which gave the form a PUDDINGY appearance.

PUDDLE, *subs.* (old).—1. A term of contempt: also as *adj.* Whence PUDDLE-POET = a gutter rhymester; a PUDDLE OF [a man, &c.] = a blundering fool.

1665. FULLER, *Church Hist.*, I. iii. 1. It seems the PUDDLE-POET did hope that the jingling of his rhymes would drown the sound of his false quantity.

1782. DARBLAY, *Cecilia*, VII. v. I remember, when I was quite a boy, hearing her called a limping old PUDDLE.

1834. CARLYLE [FROUDE, *Life in London*, I. 16]. A foot which a PUDDLE OF a maid scalded three weeks ago.

2. (venery).—The female *pudendum*: *see* MONOSYLLABLE.

Verb. (common).—To tipple: *see* DRINKS and SCREWED.

2. (old).—To muddy; to turbidize.

1602. SHAKSPEARE, *Othello*, iii. 4, 143. Hath PUDDLED his clear spirit.

THE PUDDLE, *subs. phr.* (common).—1. The Atlantic Ocean: *see* BIG POND, HERRING-POND, and POND; also (2), in Cornwall, the English Channel.

1889. *Half-Holiday*, 6 July. There seems to be no end to the chaff which the downy dandies across THE PUDDLE have to bear.

PUDDLE-DOCK. THE DUCHESS (or COUNTESS) OF PUDDLEDOCK, *subs. phr.* (old).—1. An imaginary dignitary. [PUDDLEDOCK = an ancient pool in Thames Street, not of the cleanest description.]

1708-10. SWIFT, *Polite Conversation*, i. *Neverout.* . . . I'll go to the Opera to-night, . . . for I promised to squire the Countess to her Box. *Miss.* The COUNTESS OF PUDDLEDOCK, I suppose.

PUDEND, *subs.* (venery).—The female *pudendum*: *see* MONOSYLLABLE.—URQUHART (1653).

PUDSEY, *subs.* (common).—1. A foot: *see* CREEPERS.

2. *See* POD and PUD.

PUDGY. *See* POD.

PUFF, *subs.* (old: now colloquial).—1. A sham; an impostor; (2) false praise: also PUFFING and PUFFERY (*see* quots. 1732 and 1779). Whence (3) a decoy: as a critic who extols a book or a play from interested motives; a mock-bidder, or RUNNER-UP (*q.v.*) of prices at auctions; or a gambler's confederate or BONNET (*q.v.*): also PUFFER (BAILEY, 1728); (GROSE, 1785). As *adj.* (also PUFFED) = fat; and as *verb.* (also PUFF UP) = to blow, to bloat, to fill with wind, falsehood, conceit: whilst PUFF-WORKER (American) = a penny-a-liner making a speciality of theatrical paragraphs.

1596. SHAKSPEARE, *Merry Wives*, v. 5. What . . . a PUFFED man. *Ibid.* (1598), 2 *Hen. IV.*, v. 3. I think a' be, but goodman PUFF of Barson.

1610. JONSON, *Alchemist*, ii. 1. *Mam.* That is his fire-drake, His Lungs . . . he that PUFFS his coals . . . *Ibid.* Lungs . . . I will restore thee thy complexion, PUFFE.

1647. FLETCHER, *Nice Valour*, iv. 1. Why I confess at my wife's instigation once (As women love these herald's kick-shaws naturally) I bought em; but what are they, think you? PUFFS.

1729. HEARNE, *Diary*, 7 Sep. I remember Bale's book is PUFF'D with other lyes.

1731. *St. James's Evg. Post*, 'List of Officers attached to Gaming-houses' . . . 4. Two PUFFS, who have money given them to play with. 5. A 'Clerk' who is a check upon the PUFFS to see that they sink none of the money given them to play with. 6. A "Squib" who is a PUFF of a lower rank, who serves at half salary while he is learning to deal.

1732. *Weekly Register*, 27 May. PUFF has become a cant word, signifying the applause set forth by writers . . . to increase the reputation and sale of a book, and is an excellent stratagem to excite the curiosity of gentle readers.

1749. SMOLLETT, *Gil Blas* [ROUTLEDGE], 79. If I had a mind to PUFF my vices into virtues, I might call this sloth of mine a philosophical indifference. *Ibid.* (1751), *Peregrine Pickle*, xciii. This science, which is known by the vulgar appellation of PUFFING, they carried to such a pitch of finesse, that an author very often wrote an abusive answer to his own performance, in order to inflame the curiosity of the town, by which it had been overlooked.

1754. *The World*, No. 100. I hope that none . . . will . . . suspect me of being a hired and interested PUFF of this work.

1772. BRIDGES, *Burlesque Homer*, 157. Tho' we, by Jove, and I'm no PUFFER, By the comparison can't suffer.

1779. SHERIDAN, *Critic*, i. 2. *Puff.* I am, sir, a practitioner in panegyric, or, to speak more plainly, a professor of the art of PUFFING . . . 'Twas I first taught [auctioneers] to crowd their advertisements with panegyrical superlatives, each epithet rising above the other, like the bidders in their own auction rooms . . . PUFFING is of various sorts; the principal are the PUFF direct, the PUFF preliminary, the PUFF collateral, the PUFF collusive, and the PUFF oblique, or PUFF by implication.

1806. ELDON, '*Mason v. Armitage*,' 13 Ves., 25, 37. Upon the suspicion that the plaintiff was a PUFFER, the question was put whether any PUFFERS were present.

1833. CARLYLE, *Sartor*, I. ii. At an epoch when PUFFERY and quackery have reached a height unexampled in the annals of mankind.

1836. MARRYAT, *Japhet*, xxxiv. They were very pretty, amiable girls, and required no PUFFING on the part of her ladyship.

1839. MARTINEAU, *Literary Lionism* [*London and Westminster Review*, April]. Like newspaper PUFFERY, which is an evidence of over population.

1850. KINGSLEY, *Alton Locke*, v. They wouldn't go home from sermon to sand the sugar, and put sloe-leaves in the tea, and send out lying PUFFS of their vamped-up goods.

1866. *London Miscellany*, 5 May, 201. He said he had been in the habit of frequenting mock auctions . . . They had a barker to entice people in, and then confederates or PUFFERS would say to the person looking at the article for sale, "Ah! that is a fine watch (or whatever it might be); I should think that is worth a good deal; if I were you I'd buy it."

1870. L. OLIPHANT, *Piccadilly*, v. 188. Is it not enough to PUFF your dinner-parties in the public journals at so much a 'notice.'

1872. *D. Telegraph*, 30 Nov. Cicero lays it down that a seller has no right to employ a PUFFER to raise prices. *Ibid.* With very few exceptions, the *bona-fide* private bidder has not the slightest chance in a sale-room against the PUFFER and the dealers.

1876. HINDLEY, *Cheap Jack*, 217. We . . . often acted as PUFFERS or bonnets, to give him a leg up.

1884. *Graphic*, 27 Dec., 659, 1. It is rather surprising that PUFFERY as a fine art should have made so little progress.

1888. *New York Mercury*, 21 July. Every professional . . . is afflicted with an unquenchable thirst for newspaper publicity, hence press paragraphers, or . . . PUFF-WORKERS . . . do a thriving trade.

1893. *Westminster Gaz.*, 20 Feb., 3, 1. He is one of our finest actors, yet has never reached the prominence of his rivals, because he has been almost quixotish in avoiding the PUFF direct or indirect.

1899. WHITEING, *John St.*, v. It ain't worth while to PUFF 'er UP abaht it.

3. (tramps').—A sodomist.

4. (common).—The breath: whence TO PUFF AND BLOW = to gasp; OUT OF PUFF = winded; PUFF-GUTS = a fat man; a JELLY-BELLY (*q.v.*).—GROSE (1785). Also (tailors') = life; existence: *e.g.*, 'Never in one's PUFF'; THE COP OF ONE'S PUFF = the copestone of one's life.

*c.*1777. *Kilmainham Minute* [*Ireland Sixty Years Ago*, 88]. You'd bring back de PUFF to my belows, And set me once more on my pins.

1886-96. MARSHALL, '*Pomes*' ['The Age of Love'], 26. He's the winner right enough! It's the one sole snip of a lifetime—simply THE COP OF ONE'S PUFF.

TO PUFF THE GLIM, *verb. phr.* (horse-copers').—*See* quot.

1891. *Tit-bits*, 11 Ap. Old horses are rejuvenated [by] PUFFING THE GLIM, that is, filling up the hollows . . . found above all old horses' eyes, by pricking the skin and blowing air into the loose tissues underneath.

PUFFER, *subs.* (common).—1. A locomotive; PUFFING-BILLY; and (2) a small river tug or launch: also PUFF-PUFF.

1899. *D. Telegraph*, 29 March, 7, 1. The wonderful PUFF-PUFF [which] breathed smoke and spat fire and screamed if it saw a station or another train.

1901. *Troddles*, 143. Down went Wilks with a blare . . . broken by lamentation for his PUFF-PUFF.

See PUFF, *subs.* 1.

PUG, *subs.* (old).—1. An endearment; and (2) a whore.

1567. DRANT, *Horace*, II. iii. Call it PUGGES and pretye peate.

1602. MARSTON, *Antonio and Mellida*, ii. 1. Good PUG, give me some capon.

1607. DEKKER and WEBSTER, *West ward Hoe*, ii. 2. The lob has his lass . . . the western-man his PUG, the serving-man his punk . . . the puritan his sister.

1611. COTGRAVE, *Dict.*, s.v. *Gouge.* A Souldier's PUG or punke, a wh—— that followes the camp.

1660. HOWELL, *Lex. Tetra.* My pretty PUG, *ma belle, m'amie.*

1653. URQUHART, *Rabelais*, I. iii. A jolly PUG, and well-mouthed wench.

1678. DRYDEN, *Kind Keeper*, Epil. 18. In all the boys their father's virtues shine, But all the female fry turn PUGS, like mine.

3. (pugilists').—A pugilist: also PUGIL (old). Hence PUG'S-ACRE = a corner of Highgate cemetery where Tom Sayers and other pugilists lie buried.

1692. HACKET, *Life of Williams*, i. 37. He was no little one, but *saginati corporis bellua*, as Curtius says of Dioxippus the PUGIL.

1858. MAYHEW, *Paved with Gold*, II. xii. 184. He was known by his brother PUGS to be one of the gamest hands in the ring.

1882. "THORMANBY," *Famous Racing Men*, 75. John Gully . . . retired from the Ring, and like most of his brother PUGS, took a public-house.

1887. HENLEY, *Villon's Good-Night*, 2. You bleeding bonnets, PUGS, and subs.

1888. *Referee*, 21 Oct. The sporting papers always kept the PUGS in their proper place, and scarcely contemplated they would have to do lip and lackey service to them.

1891. *Lic. Vict. Gaz.*, 20 Mar. A posse of PUGS guarded the course.

4. (domestics').—An upper servant: hence PUG'S-HOLE = the housekeeper's room.—HALLIWELL (1847).

5. A dog: with no reference to breed.

6. (sporting).—A fox.

1809. EDGEWORTH, *Absentee*, vii. There is a dead silence till PUG is well out of cover.

1849. KINGSLEY, *Yeast*, i. Some well-known haunts of PUG.

PUGGARD, *subs.* (old).—A thief: hence PUGGING = thievish.

1604. SHAKSPEARE, *Winter's Tale*, iv. 2. The white sheet bleaching on a hedge . . . Doth set my PUGGING tooth an edge.

1611. MIDDLETON, *Roaring Girl* [DODSLEY, *Old Plays* (REED), vi. 115]. Lifters, nips, foists, PUGGARDS.

PUKE, *subs.* (American).—1. A term of contempt: *cf.* PUKER (Shrewsbury) = a good-for-nothing.

1847. ROBB, *Squatter Life*, 152. Captain and all hands are a set of cowardly PUKES.

2. (American).—An inhabitant of the State of Missouri (*Century Dict.*).

Verb. (old).—To vomit: still in use at Winchester.—B. E. (*c.*1696).

1600. SHAKSPEARE, *As You Like It*, ii. 7. The infant Mewling and PUKING in the nurse's arms.

1734. POPE, *Satires of Donne*, iv. 153. As one of Woodwards patients, sick and sore, I PUKE.

1893. MILLIKEN, *'Arry Ballads*, 78. People PUKE at the shams till they think the originals ain't no great shakes.

PULING, *adj.* and *adv.* (old: now recognised).—Sickly: hence PULER = a weakling.—B. E. (*c.*1696).

1608. *Yorkshire Tragedy*, i. 1. My young mistress keeps such a PULING for a lover.

1609. *Man in the Moone*, Sig. G. If she be pale of complexion, she will prove but a PULER; is she high coloured, an ill cognizance.

*c.*1617. FLETCHER and others, *Knight of Malta*, ii. 3. Come . . . put this PULING passion out of your mind.

1820. LAMB, *New Year's Eve* [GIBBINGS, *Works*, iii. 181]. Where be those PULING fears of death?

PULL, *subs.* (old and still colloquial).—1. A drink; a GO (*q.v.*): as *verb.* = to drink; TO LUSH (*q.v.*). PULLER-ON = an appetiser: of liquids only: *cf.* DRAWER-ON.

1436. *Political Songs* ['Master of the Rolls,' ii. 169]. [OLIPHANT, *New Eng.*, i. 249. The verb PULLE takes the sense of *bibere*].

1469. *Coventry Myst.* [HALLIWELL], 142. I PULLE oo draught.

1600. DECKER, *Sho. Holiday* [*Works* (1873), i. 22]. O heele give a villanous PULL at a can of double beere.

1748. SMOLLETT, *Rod. Random*, lvi. The vessel being produced, I bade him decant his bottle into it . . . and said, "Pledge you." He stared . . . "What! all at one PULL, measter Randan?"

1760. FOOTE, *Minor*, i. *Mrs. Cole.* I won't trouble you for the glass; my hands do so tremble and shake, I shall but spill the good creature. *Load.* Well PULLED.

1772. BRIDGES, *Burlesque Homer*, 246. When my landlord does not nick me . . . But very fairly fills it full, I just can swigg it at one PULL.

1820. *The Fancy.* We'll PULL a little deady.

1825. SCOTT, *Talisman*, xxvi. Wash it down with a brimming flagon, man, or thou wilt choke upon it.—Why so—well PULLED!

1836. DICKENS, *Pickwick*, lii. Taking a long and hearty PULL at the rum-and-water.

1857. TROLLOPE, *Three Clerks*, xlv. A deep PULL at the pewter.

1868. WHYTE-MELVILLE, *White Rose*, II. ii. The other . . . sucked in a long PULL of his hot coffee.

1888. *Century Mag.*, xxxviii. After a long PULL at the pitcher of persimmon beer.

1891. NEWMAN, *Scamping Tricks*, 49. I went straight away and had a PULL of rum.

2. (colloquial).—An advantage; a hold; power: *e.g.*, TO HAVE A PULL OVER ONE = to have at an advantage, in one's power, or under one's thumb.—GROSE (1785); VAUX (1819).

*c.*1500. MEDWALL, *Interlude of Nature*, sig. C ii. It cost me a noble . . . The scald capper sware, That yt cost hym euen as myche But there Pryde had a PULL.

1783. BURGOYNE, *Lord of the Manor*, iii. 1. You'll have quite the PULL of me in employment.

1821. EGAN, *Life in London*, II. ii. [The watchmen,] besides having THE PULL in their favour, in opening the charge, and colouring it as they think proper. . . .

1855. THACKERAY, *Newcomes*, xli. They know . . . who naturally have the PULL over them.

1856. HUGHES, *Tom Brown's School-Days*, I. vii. What a PULL, said he, that it's lie-in-bed, for I shall be as lame as a tree, I think.

1868. WHYTE-MELVILLE, *White Rose*, II. 24. It's a great PULL not having married young.

1885. *D. Telegraph*, 21 Dec. The PULL in the weights alone enabled Ivanhoe to win by a length.

1886-96. MARSHALL, '*Pomes*' ['Her Sunday Clothes'], 105. She'd also a PULL o'er those well-dressed elves.

1888. BOLDREWOOD, *Robbery Under Arms*, xxiii. We had twice the PULL now, because so many strangers, that couldn't possibly be known to the police, were straggling over all the roads.

1892. *Half-Holiday*, 19 Mar., 91, 2. I had all the advantage of having a better case than he. I had that PULL on him.

1892. GUNTER, *Miss Dividends*, xi. Don't this give the Church a PULL upon the daddy?

3. (old).—*See* quot.

1819. VAUX, *Memoirs*, s.v. PULL. . . . A person speaking of any intricate affair, or feat of ingenuity, which he cannot comprehend, will say, There is some PULL at the bottom of it, that I'm not fly to.

4. (common).—An attempt to extort something from another; a GO (*q.v.*).

1749. SMOLLETT, *Gil Blas* [ROUTLEDGE], 74. Relations and strangers were all for having a PULL at him.

5. (colloquial).—Rowing exercise: also as *verb.* = to row.

1841. HOOK, *Fathers and Sons*, xvii. To PULL Lady Cramly and her daughters down the river.

Verb. 1. *See* subs. 1.

2. (cricketers').—To strike a ball from the 'off' to the 'leg' side of the wicket. TO TAKE A PULL = to drive a straight ball.

3. (thieves').—To arrest; to raid: *see* NAB and COP. Whence PULLED UP = brought before a magistrate.—GROSE (1785).

*c.*1811. *Broadside Ballad* [FARMER, *Musa Pedestris* (1896), 77]. He had twice been PULL'D, and nearly lagg'd, but got off by going to sea.

1819. VAUX, *Memoirs*, s.v. PULL . . . TO PULL a man, or have him PULLED is to cause his apprehension for some offence; and it is then said that MR. PULLEN is concerned.

1836. DICKENS, *Sketches by Boz*, 82. The loquacious little gentleman . . . finding that he had already paid more than he ought, avowed his unalterable determination to PULL UP the cabman in the morning.

1871. *Figaro*, 15 April. The police PULLED every Keno establishment in the city. PULLING is the slang for seizing the instruments, and arresting the players and proprietors.

4. (racing).—To slow a horse, while seeming to ride one's best.

1868. OUIDA, *Two Flags*, x. They . . . had broken down like any . . . jockey bribed to PULL at a suburban selling-race.

1889. *Evening Standard*, 25 June. [Sir Chas. Russell's speech in Durham-Chetwynd case]. Sir G. Chetwynd never did anything so gross and vulgar as that [tell the jockey to PULL horses], and that if horses were PULLED, that was not the way in which in any class of turf society instructions were given.

1890. *Sat. Rev.*, 1 Feb., 134, 1. They all bet, and when they lose of course it is the fault of the jockey, or of the trainer, or of the owner, who gave instructions to have his horse PULLED.

1891. GOULD, *Double Event*, 102. Wells had PULLED horses when no one but a thorough judge could have seen the game.

5. (old).—To steal; to cheat.

1383. CHAUCER, *Cant. Tales*, Prologue, 654. Ful prively a finch [= novice] eke coude he PULL.

1625. JONSON, *Staple of News*, ii. 1. What plover's that they've brought TO PULL.

1821. HAGGART, *Life*, 63. I PULLED a scout, and passed it to Graham.

1851-61. MAYHEW, *Lond. Lab.*, I. 460. We lived by thieving and I do still—by PULLING flesh

THE LONG PULL, *subs. phr.* (licensed victuallers').—*See* quot.

1901. *D. Telegraph*, 24 Dec., 3, 4. The attempt to abolish the LONG PULL made by the Birmingham brewers has ended in failure. . . . The result was seen in decreased profits. Customers left their houses and patronised others where over-measure was given.

COLLOQUIALISMS are:—TO PULL DOWN, 1, (thieves': *see* quot. 1857); (2) to destroy, to depress, to endanger chances; TO PULL IN THE PIECES = to make money: Fr. *faire son beurre*; TO PULL IT (or FOOT) = to decamp: *see* AMPUTATE and SKEDADDLE; TO PULL THROUGH = to succeed, to get out of a difficulty; TO PULL TOGETHER = to co-operate; TO PULL UP = (1) to take to task, to arrest, to stop; (2) to exert oneself, to make a special effort; TO PULL FACES = to grimace; TO PULL A LONG FACE = to look BLUE (*q.v.*); TO PULL OFF = to succeed; TO GET THERE (*q.v.*); TO PULL ONESELF TOGETHER = to rouse oneself; to rally; TO PULL (or DRAW) IN ONE'S HORNS = to retract; to cool down (GROSE, 1785); TO PULL DOWN A SIDE = to spoil all; TO PULL BY THE SLEEVE = to remind; TO PULL OUT (American) = (1) to CHUCK (*q.v.*); 2 (athletic) = to strive to the utmost, to EXTEND (*q.v.*), usually by means of a friendly pace-maker; 3 (common) = to run away; 4 (tailors') = to hurry, to get on with work in hand; TO PULL UP A JACK (*see* quot. 1819); TO PULL A KITE = to be serious, to LOOK STRAIGHT (*q.v.*); TO PULL ONE'S (or DRAW) THE LEG = to impose upon, to BAMBOOZLE (*q.v.*), TO CHAFF (*q.v.*); TO PULL ABOUT = (1) to masturbate: *see* FRIG, and (2) to essay a woman, TO MESS ABOUT (*q.v.*), to PADDLE (*q.v.*); TO PULL OVER = to catch, to arrest: a general verb of action, *see* NAB; TO PULL ABOUT ONE'S EARS = to ruin, to chastise. *See* BACON; BAKER; CAP; CROW; DEAD HORSE; DEVIL; FOOT; HORNS; LONGBOW; STAKES; STRING; VEST; WIRES; WOOL.

1589. PUTTENHAM, *Art of Eng. Poes.*, 34. Nothing PULLETH DOWNE a man's heart so much as aduersitie and ack e.

1596. SPENSER, *Faerie Queene*, v. ii. 41 [TWYRHITT, 252]. He PULLETH DOWNE, He setteth up on hy.

1610. SHAKSPEARE, *Coriolanus*, iii. 2. Let them PULL ALL ABOUT MINE EARS . . . yet will I still be thus to them.

1616-25. *Court James I.* [OLIPHANT, *New Eng.*, 70. As to the verbs we see PULL IN HIS HORNS].

1625. MASSINGER, *Duke of Florence*, iv. 2. If I hold your cards I shall PULL DOWN THE SIDE; I am not good at the game.

1640. HOWELL, *Vocall. Forrest*, 104. In political affairs as well as mechanical, it is farre easier TO PULL DOWN then build up.

1749. FIELDING, *Tom Jones*, XII. xiii. As the vulgar phrase is, [he] immediately DREW IN HIS HORNS.

17 [?]. FESSENDEN, *Yankee Doodle* [BARTLETT]. And then she flew straight out of sight As fast as she could PULL IT.

1818. SCOTT, *Midlothian*, iv. 51. Jeanie Deans is no the lass to PU' him BY THE SLEEVE, or put him in mind of what he wishes to forget.

1819. VAUX, *Memoirs*, s.v. PULL or PULL UP, to accost; stop. *Ibid.* To PULL UP A JACK, is to stop a post-chaise on the highway.

1825. MACAULAY, *Gladstone on Church and State* The world is full of institutions, which . . . never ought to have been set up, yet, having been set up, ought not to be rudely PULLED DOWN.

1849. *Punch's Almanack*, 'Fortune Tellers Almanack.' You are going too fast, and . . . you ought to PULL UP.

1853. DICKENS, *Bleak House*, xxxvii. I shall be all right! I shalll PULL THROUGH, my dear.

1855. BROWNING, *Fra. Lippo Lippi.* The Prior and the learned PULLED A FACE.

1857. HUGHES, *Tom Brown's School-days*, I. v. The Slogger PULLS UP at last . . . fairly blown.

1857. SNOWDEN, *Mag. Assistant* (3rd ed.), 446. To steal from shop doors—TO PULL DOWN.

1867. ANDERSON, *Rhymes*, 17. He preached, an' at last DREW THE auld BODY'S LEG, Sae the kirk got the gatherins o' our Aunty Meg.

1868. *Trip through Virginia* [DE VERE]. Driver, when will you PULL UP? I don't PULL UP at no tavern till I gets home.

1870. *Figaro*, 9 Nov. These sweep-stakes, in which the commissioners are always to PULL OFF the money, may help to lessen the figures in the Parliamentary estimates.

1871. *Globe*, 12 May. Colonel Corbett was about to speak, but he was PULLED UP by the Speaker.

1877. *Five Years' Penal Servituae*, iii. He occasionally took what required a little screw in the morning to counteract and enable him to PULL HIMSELF TOGETHER before going his rounds with the doctor.

1882. *D. Telegraph*, 9 Nov. Before the train PULLS UP at the next station.

1882. *Field*, 28 Jan. All equal to the work put in their hands, and helped to PULL THE AUTHOR THROUGH. *Ibid.* (1886), 27 Feb. The Middlesex men now PULLED THEMSELVES TOGETHER.

1888. *Cornhill Mag.*, Oct. 'Phantom Picquet.' I am very hopeful of your regiment arriving in time to PULL us THROUGH.

1888. *Missouri Republican*, 24 Feb. He knows that if he keeps his money in the show business any longer he will lose it all, and so he has PULLED OUT.

1888. CHURCHWARD, *Blackbirding*, 216. Then I shall be able to PULL THE LEG of that chap . . . He is always trying to do me.

1889. FRANCIS, *Saddle and Mocassin* [Slang, Jargon and Cant]. For a minute or two they stood looking at one another, and then Doc PULLED OUT.

1891. *Lic. Vict. Gaz.*, 3 Ap. The chief bank official . . . told him pretty plainly that he must now PULL UP, and arrangements made in regard to certain over-due acceptances.

1896. CRANE, *Maggie*, xiv. 'She was PULLING M' LEG, That's the whole amount of it,' he said.

1898. WHITEING, *John St.*, xxix. I am working up a little affair of my own just now . . . but I'm not sure I shall be able TO PULL IT OFF.

1901. *Troddles*, 38. He certainly didn't perceive that Wilks was PULLING HIS LEG, and he stammered out expressions of gratitude.

PULLED-TRADE, *subs. phr.* (tailors'). —Secured work.

PULLET (POULET or PULLEY), *subs.* (colloquial).—(1) A girl of tender years. Hence PULLET-SQUEEZER = an amateur of young girls; a CHICKEN-FANCIER (*q.v.*); VIRGIN-PULLET = 'a young woman . . . who though often trod has never laid.'—BEE (1823). Also 2 (thieves') = a female confederate.

PULLING-TIME, *subs. phr.* (provincial).—*See* quot.

1847. HALLIWELL, *Arch. and Prov. Words*, s.v. PULLING-TIME. The evening of a fair-day, when the wenches are pulled about.

PULLMAN-PUP, *subs. phr.* (railway). —*See* quot.

1890. *Tit-Bits*, 1 Nov. The Midland night Scotch train from Leeds runs in front of the London Scotch train, and is therefore nicknamed the PULLMAN PUP.

PULLY-HAULY, *adj. phr.* (colloquial). — Rough - and - tumble: HAUL DEVIL, PULL BAKER (*q.v.*). TO PLAY AT PULLY-HAULY, *verb. phr.* (venery).—To copulate: *see* GREENS and RIDE.—GROSE (1785).

PULPIT, *subs.* (venery).—The female *pudendum*: *see* MONOSYLLABLE.

1656. *Choice Drollery*, 44. Quoth she, the Son is prov'd a Daughter. But be content, if God doth blesse the Baby, She has a PULPIT where a Preacher may be.

*c.*1685-95. *Broadside Ballad* [*Roxburghe Ballads* (Brit. Mus.), ii. 73] 'The Country Parson's Folly.' He pitch'd on a subject was hard by the rump, And into her PULPIT he straightways did jump, Where all the night long he her cushion did thump.

PULPIT-CUFFER (DRUBBER, DRUMMER, SMITER, or THUMPER), *subs. phr.* (common).—A ranting parson; a CUSHION-THUMPER (*q.v.*). Whence PULPIT-CUFFING (&c.) = violent exhortation.

1699. BROWN [*Works* (1715), i. 209]. A PULPIT-DRUBBER by profession, who knows all the witches forms in the kingdom.

1706. WARD, *Hud. Redivivus*, vi. 10. Thought I, for all your PULPIT-DRUMMING, Had you no Hose to hide your Bum in.

PULPITEERS, *subs.* (Winchester College).—*See* quot.

1891. WRENCH, *Winchester Word Book*, s.v. PULPITEERS. An arrangement during Cloister-time of Sixth Book and Senior Part V. going up to books together . . . Middle and Junior Part taken together were called Cloisters.

PULSE. TO FEEL ONE'S PULSE, *verb. phr.* (colloquial).—1. To gauge opinions, views, feelings, &c.; TO SOUND (*q.v.*); TO TAKE ONE'S MEASURE (*q.v.*).

*d.*1843. SOUTHEY, *Letters*, iv. 139. So much matter has been ferretted out that this Government wishes to tell its own story, and MY PULSE WAS FELT.

2. (venery). — To grope a woman.

1648-50. BRATHWAYTE, *Barnaby's Jl.* (1723), 50, 51. Thence to Meredin did steer I, Where grown foot-sore and sore weary, I repos'd where I chuck'd Joan-a, FELT HER PULSE (*Hopitem in genu cepi*).

PUMMEL (PUMBLE or POMMEL), *subs.* (old).—A drubbing: amongst pugilists, a CRIPPLER (*q.v.*). Also as *verb.* = to beat; TO TAN (*q.v.*): also PUM.—B. E. (*c.* 1696); GROSE (1785).

1515. [HALL, *Henry VIII.*, an. 6]. Ye duke by pure strength tooke hym about the necke, and POMELED so about the hed that the bloud yssued out of his nose.

1530. PALSGRAVE, *Lang. Fran.*, s.v.

*d.*1556. UDAL, *Luke*, iii. They turne him cleane out of his owne doores, and PUMBLE him about the pate in stede.

1713. *Observer*, No. 95. I was PUMMELLED to a mummy by the boys, showed up by the ushers, &c.

1772. BRIDGES, *Burlesque Homer*, 96. But I . . . Go quite upon another plan, And sleep UNPUMMEL'D when I can.

1819. BYRON, *Don Juan*, I. 184. Alphonso PUMMELLED to his heart's desire Swore lustily.

1858. DICKENS, *Great Expectations*, xii. I used to want . . . to . . . fly at Pumblechook, and PUMMEL him all over.

1890. MILLIGAN, *Groves of Blarney.* But Oliver Cromwell he did her PUMMEL, And made a breach in her battlement.

PUMP, *subs.* (common).—1. *In pl.* = dancing shoes. Also occasionally as *verb.* = to don dancing shoes.—GROSE (1785).

1592. NASH, *Piers Penniless* [COLLIER, xxv.]. [OLIPHANT, *New English*, ii. 10. We hear of PUMPS, opposed to commoner shoes; this is from *pomp* and luxury].

1592. SHAKSPEARE, *Mid. Night's Dream*, iv. 2. Get your apparel together, good strings to your beards, new ribbons to your PUMPS. *Ibid.* (1593) *Taming of Shrew*, iv. 1. And Gabriel's PUMPS were all unpink'd i the heel.

1601. JONSON, *Poetaster*, iii. 1. Thou shalt not need to travel with thy PUMPS full of gravel any more.

1664. COTTON, *Virgil Travestie* (1st ed.), 59. You might have walkt your PUMPS apieces, Ere light on such a Place as this is.

1840. BARHAM, *Ingoldsby Legends* (Sir Rupert). When a gentleman jumps In the river at midnight for want of the dumps He rarely puts on knee-breeches and PUMPS.

1845. BUCKSTONE, *Green Bushes*, i. 2. When, to step a lady of high degree, You put on your PUMPS and are happy indeed.

1848. THACKERAY, *Book of Snobs*, i. The usual attire of a gentleman, *viz.*, PUMPS, a gold waistcoat, a crush hat, a sham frill, and a white choker.

1848. DICKENS, *Dombey & Son*, xiv. All the young gentlemen tightly cravatted, curled and PUMPED.

1857. MONCRIEFF, *Bashful Man*, i. 2. Go and dress at once; your PUMPS are all ready.

2. (common). — *In pl.* = the eyes: *see* GLIM.

1825. BUCKSTONE, *Bear Hunters*, i. 2. Your PUMPS have been at work—you've been crying, girl.

3. (venery).—1. The female *pudendum*: also PUMP-DALE: *see* MONOSYLLABLE; (2) = the *penis*: also PUMP-HANDLE: *see* PRICK; and (3, Scots') = a FART (*q.v*). As *verb.* (1) = to copulate: *see* RIDE; (2) = TO PISS (*q.v.*): also TO PUMP SHIP (or WATER); and (3) = TO FART (*q.v.*); TO PUMP OFF = to masturbate: *see* FRIG.—GROSE (1785).

1706. WARD, *Wooden World*, 3. That sage hit it best . . . who compared a ship to a Woman . . . her PUMP-DALE smells strongest when she has the soundest bottom.

1730. *Broadside Song*, 'Gee ho, Dobbin' [FARMER, *Merry Songs and Ballads* (1897), ii. 204]. I worked at her PUMP till the sucker grew dry, And then I left PUMPING a good Reason why. *Ibid.* Then Roger's PUMP-HANDLE ran the Devil knows where.

4. (Scots').—A public house: *see* LUSH-CRIB.

5. See *verb*, sense 1.

6. (common). — A solemn noodle.

Verb. (colloquial). — 1. To question artfully; to make one tell without knowing he's telling; TO SOUND (*q.v.*). Hence, as *subs.* = an indirect question; 'Your PUMP is good but the sucker's dry!' = a retort or an attempt TO PUMP.—B. E. (*c.* 1696); GROSE (1785).

1633. JONSON, *Tale of a Tub*, IV. iii. I'll stand aside whilst thou PUMP'ST out of him His business.

*d.*1635. RANDOLPH, *Muses' Looking Glass*, ii. 4. I'll in to PUMP my dad, and fetch thee more.

1668. DRYDEN, *An Evening's Love*, iii. Markall, PUMP the woman; and see if you can discover anything to save my credit.

1693. CONGREVE, *Old Batchelor*, v. 4. She was PUMPING me about how your worship's affairs stood.

1740. RICHARDSON, *Pamela*, I. 208. For all her PUMPS, she gave no hint.

1749. FIELDING, *Tom Jones*, XI. vi. She therefore ordered her maid to PUMP out of him by what means he had become acquainted with her person.

1826. BUCKSTONE, *Death Fetch*, ii. 2. She wants to PUMP me, but two words to that bargain.

1837. DICKENS, *Pickwick*, xvi. Undergoing the process of being PUMPED.

1847. THACKERAY, *Vanity Fair*, vii. But old Tinker was not to be PUMPED by this little cross-questioner.

1886-96. MARSHALL, *'Pomes' from the Pink 'Un* ['The Age of Love'], 26. So she sought him and gently PUMPED him.

1893. MILLIKEN, *'Arry Ballads*, 32. I've parted so free to the coachies, and artfully put on the PUMP.

2. (old colloquial).—To duck under the pump: also TO GIVE A TASTE OF THE PUMP (B. E., *c.*1696, and GROSE, 1785); 'CHRISTENED WITH PUMP-WATER,' said of a red-faced boy or girl (RAY, 1760, and GROSE, 1785).

1839. AINSWORTH, *Jack Sheppard* [1889], 13. If he don't tip the cole without more ado, GIVE HIM A TASTE OF THE PUMP, that's all.

3. (colloquial).—To go breathless; TO WIND (*q.v.*); PUMPED OUT (or DRY) = completely blown.—B. E. (*c.*1696). Hence PUMPER = anything that PUMPS: as counsel, a race, a course, a spurt, &c.

1860. RUSSELL, *Diary in India*, II. 370. Darkness began to set in, the artillery horses were PUMPED OUT, and orders were given to retire.

1882. *Field*, 28 Jan. Tiger . . . had all the best of a long PUMPING course.

1888. *Sportsman*, 28 Nov. She came on the scene when Bismarck was quite PUMPED out.

5. (common).—To vomit; to CAST UP ACCOUNTS (*q.v.*).—GROSE (1785).

6. (American).—To steal.

1824. *Atlantic Mag.*, I. 344. Vot I vants to show is the vay in which she PUMPED my fob this ere mornin'.

7. (common).—To cry.

1837. MARRYAT, *Snarley-Yow.* And she did PUMP While I did jump In the boat to say, Good bye.

PUMP-AND-TORTOISES (THE), *subs. phr.* (military).—The late 38th Regiment of Foot, now the 1st Batt. South Staffordshire Regiment.

PUMPKIN, *subs.* (old).—1. *See* quot.

1785. GROSE, *Vulg. Tongue*, s.v. "POMPKIN, a man or woman of Boston, America, from the number of POMPKINS raised and eaten by the people of that country. POMPKINS-HIVE, for Boston and its dependencies."

2. (common).—The head: *see* CRUMPET and TIBBY.

3. (American). — The female *pudendum*: *see* MONOSYLLABLE: whence PUMPKIN-COVER = the pubic hair: *see* FLEECE. [From the shape of a pumpkin seed.]

SOME (or BIG) PUMPKINS (or AS BIG AS PUMPKINS), *phr.* (American).—A high appreciation: *cf.* SMALL POTATOES (*q.v.*).

18[?]. *Pickings from the Picayune*, 237 [DE VERE]. I swow, my son Fred is a fine fellow; you may axe every rouster on the levee, and I'll be hanged if they don't tell you he is SOME PUMPKINS to hum.

1848. RUXTON, *Far West*, 178. Afore I left the settlements I know'd a white gal, and she was SOME PUNKINS. *Ibid.*, 41. The biggest kind of PUNKIN at that.

1852. BRISTED, *Up. Ten Thousand*, 216. We being PUNKINS were of course among the invited. *Ibid.*, Note. A slang expression of young New York for people of value and consequence.

1855. HALIBURTON, *Human Nature* [DE VERE]. Franklin was a poor printer-boy and Washington a land-surveyor, yet they growed to be SOME PUMPKINS.

1871. DE VERE, *Americanisms*. Bostonians are said to have derived, from their attachment to this vegetable, and the esteem in which it is universally held among them, the phrase SOME PUMPKINS, expressive of high appreciation. . . *Ibid.* It is stated, however, by one high in authority among New Englanders, that this explanation of the term is not the true one, although the latter cannot well be stated, because it would offend ears polite.

PUMPKIN-HEAD, *subs. phr.* (American).—A fool: *see* BUFFLE.

PUMP-SUCKER, *subs. phr.* (common).—A teetotaller.

PUMP-THUNDER, *subs. phr.* (common).—A blusterer: *see* FURIOSO. Also as *verb*. *See* HELL.

PUM-PUM, *subs. phr.* (old).—A fiddler.

PUMPWATER. *See* AQUA and YARD.

PUN, *subs.* (old: now recognised).—1. A play upon words, similar in sound but different in meaning: also as *verb*.—B. E. (*c.*1696).

2. (Harrow school).—Punishment. Hence PUN-PAPER = specially ruled paper for PUNS and impositions.

TO PUN OUT, *verb. phr.* (Christ's Hospital).—To inform against: *e.g.*, 'I'll PUN OUT'; 'I'll PUN you OUT': exclusively a London expression; at Hertford, TO PUN or PUN OF.

PUNCH, *subs.* (old).—1. *See* quots. 1669 and 1870: hence, PUNCHY = fat-bellied: *cf.* PAUNCH.—B. E. (*c.*1696). PUNCHINESS = stoutness of build.

1669. PEPYS, *Diary*, 30 Ap. I . . . did hear them call their fat child PUNCH, which pleased me mighty, that word being become a word of common use for all that is thick and short.

1707. WARD, *Hud. Rediv.*, II. iv. 24. Two PUNCHES next, with wond'rous Vigour, Perform'd a Dance in double Figure.

1837. BARHAM, *Ingoldsby Legends*, I. 119. A stout Suffolk PUNCH. *Ibid.*, II. 124. A fat, little, PUNCHY concern of sixteen.

1850. LEIGH HUNT, *Autobiog.*, iii. A short, stout man, inclining to PUNCHINESS.

1870. *Farrier's Dict.* [*Ency. Dict.*]. "PUNCH is a horse that is well-set and well-knit, having a short back and thin shoulders, with a broad neck, and well lined with flesh."

2. (colloquial).—A blow; also as *verb.*: *e.g.*, 'to PUNCH one's head.'

1603. CHAPMAN, *Iliad*, vi. 126. With a goad he PUNCH'D each furious dame.

1837. DICKENS, *Pickwick Papers*, ii Smart chap that cabman . . . but . . . PUNCH HIS HEAD.

Verb. (venery).—1. To deflower: hence PUNCHABLE = ripe for man, COMING (*q.v.*).—GROSE (1785).

2. (Western American).—To drive and brand cattle. Whence PUNCHER (BULL or COW-PUNCHER) = a cowboy.

1889. FRANCIS, *Saddle and Moccasin* [*Slang, Jargon, and Cant*]. The title 'cow-servants' so delighted the gentle PUNCHER that it has become a standing quotation in New Mexico.

18[?]. H. KENDALL, *Billy Vickers*. At PUNCHING oxen you may guess There's nothing out can camp him.

3. (old).—To walk: *see* ABSQUATULATE.—GROSE (1785). Hence TO PUNCH OUTSIDES = to go out of doors.—GROSE (1785); HAGGART (1821).

1780. TOMLINSON, *Slang Pastoral*, vii. Now she to Bridewell has PUNCH'D it along.

COBBLER'S-PUNCH, *subs. phr.* (old).—'Urine with a cinder in it.'—GROSE (1785).

PUNCHABLE, *subs.* (old).—'Old passable money, anno 1695.'—B. E. (*c.*1696).

See PUNCH, *verb.*, sense 1.

PUNCH-AND-JUDY, *subs. phr.* (common).—Lemonade.

1885. *Eng. Illus. Mag.*, June, 604. I'd drink a pennorth of gingeret, or a glass of PUNCH AND JUDY.

PUNCHER, *subs.* (sporting).—1. A pugilist.

2. *See* PUNCH, *verb.*

PUNCH-CLOD, *subs.* (provincial).—A farm-laborer; a clod-hopper.

PUNCH-HOUSE, *subs. phr.* (old).—'A bawdy house.'—B. E. (*c.*1696).

PUNCHY, *subs.* (American).—A house of entertainment.

See PUNCH, *subs.*

PUNCTURE, *verb.* (cyclists').—To deflower; to PRICK (*q.v.*). [An allusion to pneumatic tyres.]

PUNISH, *verb.* (sporting and general).—A strong verb of action: thus (in boxing) TO PUNISH = to hit hard, to handle severely; (in cricket) TO PUNISH THE BOWLING = to hit freely; (general) TO PUNISH THE BOTTLE = to drink hard; TO PUNISH THE SPREAD = to eat much and heartily; and so forth. Hence PUNISHING = exhausting, fatiguing; PUNISHER = a glutton for work; PUNISHMENT = a severe beating, complete exhaustion, &c.

1819. MOORE, *Tom Crib*. An eye that plann'd PUNISHING deeds. *Ibid.* If to level, to PUNISH, to ruffian mankind.

1821. EGAN, *Life in London*, II. iii. What a PUNISHER, too!

1831. EGAN, *Finish Life in London*, 221. Blacky PUNISHED the steaks.

1848. THACKERAY, *Vanity Fair*, liii. He PUNISHED my champagne. *Ibid.* (1862), *Philip*, iv. Tom Sayers could not take PUNISHMENT more gaily.

1857. *Barton Experiment*, xiv. After we'd PUNISHED a couple of bottles of old Crow whisky . . . he caved in all of a sudden.

1882. *Field*, 28 Jan. Each course to-day was of the most PUNISHING KIND.

1886. *D. Telegraph*, 5 Mar. Afterwards PUNISHED his opponent very scientifically.

1886. *Cassell's Saturday Journal*, 6 Mar., 359. I shall . . . PUNISH the old gentleman's sherry.

1891. *Lic. Vict. Gaz.*, 3 April. M'Carthy put in a lot of clinching to save himself from PUNISHMENT.

PUNK (or **PUNQUETTO**), *subs.* (old).—1. A harlot: *see* TART: also as *verb.* = to procure. Hence, PUNKER = a wencher; and PUNKISH = meretricious.—B. E. (*c.*1696); GROSE (1785).

*c.*1575. *Old Ballad*, 'Simon the King' [FARMER, *Merry Songs and Ballads* (1897), iii. 1]. Soe fellowes, if you be drunke, of ffrailtye itt is a sinne, as itt is to keepe a PUNCKE.

1600. JONSON, *Cynthia's Revels*, ii. 1. Marry, to his cockatrice, or PUNQUETTO, half a dozen taffata gowns or satin kirtles in a pair or two of months—why, they are nothing.

1603. SHAKSPEARE, *Measure for Measure*, v. 1. She may be a PUNK, for many of them are neither maid, widow, nor wife.

1607. DEKKER, *Westward Hoe*, ii. 2. The sewing-man [has] his PUNK, the student his nun in White-Friars. *Ibid.*, iv. 1. Thou hast more tricks in thee than a PUNK has uncles, cousins, brothers, sons or fathers.

1611. CHAPMAN, *May-day*, iv. 4. She was Some stale PUNK I warrant you.

1614. JONSON, *Bartholomew Faire*, ii. 1. Here you may have your PUNK and your pig both in state, sir, piping hot.

1620-55. *Broadside Ballad* [Roxburghe Coll. (Brit. Mus.), i. 46, 47]. A woman that will be drunk, Will eas'ly play the PUNCK.

1630. TAYLOR, *Works*, i. 110. His pimpship with his PUNKE, despight the horne, Eate gosling giblets in a fort of corne.

1632. MASSINGER, *City Madam*, ii. 2. I'll wed a pedlar's PUNK first.

*c.*1650. *Drunken Barnaby's Jl.* (1723), II. 50. Hence to Dunchurch where report is Of pimps and PUNKS a great resort is.

*d.*1655. ADAMS, *Works* [Nichols', 1861-2]. These PUNKISH outsides beguile the needy traveller.

1670. COTTON, *Scoffer Scofft* [*Works* (1725), 249]. He is a very honest Younker, A bonny Lad, and a great PUNKER.

1672. WYCHERLEY, *Love in a Wood*, ii. 1. Are you not a fireship, a PUNK, madam?

1687. CLEVELAND, *Works*. Among the roaring PUNKS and dammy-boys.

1695. CONGREVE, *Love for Love*, i. 1. A worn-out PUNK . . . without a whole tatter to her tail.

1697. VANBRUGH, *Provoked Wife*, iii. 4. What, a pox! . . . two whores, egad! . . . Have you never a spare PUNK for your friend.

1706. WARD, *Wooden World*, 15. Some snotty-nosed Letter-man, the Product of some quondam PUNK.

1772. BRIDGES, *Burlesque Homer*, 20. If you're not mad you must be drunk, To drub your gen'ral for a PUNK.

Verb. (cyclists').—2. To puncture a tyre: also, as *subs.* = a punctured tyre.

PUNSE, *subs.* (Yiddish).—The female *pudendum*: *see* MONOSYLLABLE.

PUNSH. *See* PUNCH, *verb.*

PUNT, *verb.* (colloquial).—1. To gamble: formerly generic, but mostly confined to small or 'chicken' stakes. Hence, PUNTER = a gambler; PUNTING-SHOP = a hell.

17[?]. POPE, *Basset Table*. How often have I sworn . . . I could PUNT no more.

1714. LUCAS, *Gamesters*, 230. PUNTER, a Term for every one of the Gamesters that play.

1754. *The World*, No. 69. To cut in at whist, . . . to PUNT at faro, or to sit down at a hazard-table.

*d.*1817. HOLMAN, *Abroad and at Home*, ii. 4. You who so kindly took me by the hand, taught me to PUNT at faro.

1855. THACKERAY, *Newcomes*, xxviii. A crowd of awestruck amateurs and breathless PUNTERS. *Ibid.*, xxxvi. The idea . . . of his PUNTING for half-crowns at a neighbouring hell in Air Street.

1886-96. MARSHALL, *'Pomes'* ['Nobbled'], 114. There was only one horse in the Derby at which heavy PUNTERS would look.

1889. *Sporting Times*, 3 Aug., 4, 4. If the banker deals to both sides without dealing any to himself, the PUNTERS can allow the coup to stand.

1898. *Referee*, 4 Sep., 11, 4. While Paul is PUNTING with the outside bookmakers, Virginia may listen to the artless prattle of the Silver Ring.

1899. *Critic*, 11 Mar., 2, 1. A gentleman . . . whose face is familiar in the neighbourhood of Capel-court, has been PUNTING in maximums in the private club at Monte Carlo.

2. (Rugby footballers').—To kick the ball before it touches the ground. Hence PUNT-ABOUT = a practice-ball or -game.

1856. HUGHES, *Tom Brown*, I. v. Hurra! here's the PUNT-ABOUT—come along and try your hand at a kick.

3. (auctioneers').—To act as decoy: also PUNTER.

1891. *Answers*, 4 Ap. When visiting a small place the auctioneer usually takes his PUNTERS with him, as the faces of local men might be known. A well-dressed PUNTER earns five or six shillings a day, and . . . are expected to appear in tall hats, gloves, sticks, big brass chains and button-holes.

PUNY, *subs.* (old).—1. A freshman; (2) a student at the Inns of Court; (3) a junior. Hence, PUNYSHIP = youth. Also (4) = a puisne judge or bencher.

1548. PATTEN, *Somerset's March* [OLIPHANT, *New Eng.*, i. 520. We see the phrases *good literature* (scholarship) . . . PUNIES (juniors)].

15[?]. *Christmas Prince at St. John's College* i. Others to make sporte . . . were they whom they call freshmenn, PUNIES of the first yeare.

15[?]. *Ulysses upon Ajax*, B8. A PUNEY of Oxford.

1593. NASHE, *Christ's Teares* [GROSART, *Works*, iv. 228]. Laughing at the PUNIES they have lurched. *Ibid.* (1598), *Lenten Stuffe* [*Harl. Misc.*, vi. 171]. In the PUNIESHIP or nonage of Cerdicke Sandes.

1607. DEKKER, *Westward Hoe*, i. 2. There is only in the amity of women an estate at will, and every PUNY knows that is no certain inheritance. *Ibid.*, v. 3. The PUNIES set down this decree.

1634. MARSTON, in *Lectores, &c.* [NARES]. Each odd PUISNE of the lawyer's inne.

*c.*1640. [SHIRLEY], *Capt. Underwit* [BULLEN, *Old Plays*, ii. 340]. Preach to the PUISNES of the Inne sobriety.

Adj. (old: now recognised).—Weak; small.—B. E. (*c.*1696); GROSE (1785).

PUP, *subs.* (colloquial).—1. A PUPPY (*q.v.*).

2. (colloquial).—A pupil.

Verb. (colloquial).—To be brought to bed. [As a bitch with puppies.] IN PUP = pregnant.

TO SELL A PUP, *verb. phr.* (thieves').—To swindle a greenhorn; TO FLAP A JAY (*q.v.*).

PUPE, *subs.* (Harrow school).—A pupil room.

PUPIL-MONGER, *subs. phr.* (old).—A tutor: specifically at the universities.—B. E. (*c.*1696); GROSE (1785).

1662. FULLER, *Worthies*, Northampton, II. 517. John Preston . . . was the greatest PUPIL-MONGER in England.

PUPPY (**PUP**, or **PUPPY-DOG**), *subs.* (colloquial).—1. A vain or unmannerly fool; a fop; a coxcomb.—GROSE (1785). Hence PUPPYISM = conceit or affectation; PUPPYISH (or PUPPILY) = impertinent; PUPPY-HEADED = stupid.

1593. HARVEY, *Pierce's Super.* [*Wks.* (GROSART), ii. 328]. A Jack-sauce, or vnmannerly PUPPY.

1598. CHAPMAN, *Blind Beggar* [SHEPHERD (1874), 3]. Who could have picked out three such lifeless PUPPIES, Never to venture on their mistresses.

1609. SHAKSPEARE, *Tempest*, ii. 2, 159. I shall laugh myself to death at this PUPPY-HEADED monster.

*c.*1620. FLETCHER and MASSINGER, *Little French Lawyer*, ii. 3. Go, bid your lady seek . . . Some unexperienced PUPPY to make sport with.

1639. CHAPMAN and SHIRLEY, *The Ball*, iv. Oh, my soul, How it does blush to know thee! bragging PUPPY!

*d.*1680. ROCHESTER, *From Art. to Chloe.* The unbred PUPPY, who had never seen A creature look so gay or talk so fine.

1690. CROWNE, *Eng. Friar*, ii. 1. My Lord, prithee marry thy daughter to my PUPPY.

1697. VANBRUGH, *Provoked Wife*, i. The surly PUPPY! Yet he's a fool for it.

1703. STEELE, *Tender Husband*, v. 2. What does the PUPPY mean? His wife under a hat?

1740. FIELDING, *Wedding Day*, ii. 13. Your master is a negligent PUPPY, and uses me doubly ill.

1749. SMOLLETT, *Gil Blas* [ROUTLEDGE], 104. A PUPPY of fashion, and a she-wolf of the stage. *Ibid.*, 155. The affectation of a PUPPY, and the pertness of a wit.

177[?]. R. CUMBERLAND, *The Jew*, v. 1. I knew your honour at the length of the street, and saw you turn into this tavern: the PUPPILY waiter wou'd have stopt me from coming up to you.

1775. SHERIDAN, *Rivals*, ii. 1. None of your sneering, PUPPY! no grinning, jackanapes!

1778. BURNEY, *Evelina*, lxxvi. I am by no mean such a PUPPY as to tell you I am upon sure ground.

1811. AUSTEN, *Sense and S.*, xxxiii. The PUPPYISM of his manner.

1836. DICKENS, *Pickwick*, xxxv. Silly young men, displaying various varieties of PUPPYISM and stupidity.

1851. SMEDLEY, *Lewis Arundel*, xl. His whole demeanour blasé and PUPPYISH in the extreme.

1858. G. ELIOT, *Mr. Gilfil's Love-Story*, ii. Men . . . were inclined to think this Antinous in a pig-tail a "confounded PUPPY."

2. (common).—A blind man. Fr. *sans-mirettes*; *sans-châsses.*—MATSELL (1859). Also as *adj.* = blind.

PUPPY-SNATCH, *subs. phr.* (old).—A snare; a PLANT (*q.v.*).

1670. COTTON, *Scarronides* [1692], 10. It seem'd indifferent to him Whether he did sink or swim; So he by either means might catch Us Trojans in a PUPPY-SNATCH.

PURCHASE, *subs.* (old).—Plunder: as *verb.* (or TO LIVE ON ONE'S PURCHASE) = (1) to live by swindling, thieving, or blackmailing. TO GET IN PURCHASE = to beget in bastardy. [O. Fr. *purchacier* = to procure.]

1512-3. DOUGLAS, *Virgil*, 303, 4. And first has slane the big Antiphates,—Son to the bustuous nobyl Sarpedoun, In PURCHES get ane Thebane wensche apoun.

1590. SPENSER, *Fairy Queen*, I. ii. 16. Of nightly stelths, and pillage severall, Which he had got abroad by PURCHAS criminall.

1592. GREENE, *Disputation* [*Works*, x. 207]. But looke he neuer so narrowly to it we haue his pursse, wherein some time there is fat PURCHASE, twentie or thirtie poundes.

1597. SHAKSPEARE, *1 Henry IV.*, ii. 1, 101. *Gads.* Give me thy hand: thou shalt have a share in our PURCHASE, as I am a true man. *Cham.* Nay, rather let me have it, as you are a false thief. *Ibid.* (1599), *Henry V.*, iii. 2. They will steal anything and call it PURCHASE.

1607. *Puritan*, i. 4. The slave had about him but the poor PURCHASE of ten groats.

1610. JONSON, *Alchemist*, iv. 4. Do you two pack up all the goods and PURCHASE.

1613. WEBSTER, *Devil's Law-Case*, ii. 1. Tailors in France they grow to great abominable PURCHASE, and become great officers. *Ibid.* (1623), *Duch. of Malfi*, iii. 1. They do observe I grow to infinite PURCHASE, the left hand way.

*c.*1620. FLETCHER and MASSINGER, *False One*, iii. 2. I scorn to nourish it with such bloodly PURCHASE, PURCHASE so foully got.

*c.*1622. FLETCHER, *Chaucer*, i. 2. What have I got by this now? What's the PURCHASE? (*et passim*).

1633. ROWLEY, *Match at Midnight* [DODSLEY, *Old Plays* (Reed), vii. 355]. A bag, Of a hundred pound at least, all in round shillings, Which I made my last night's PURCHASE from a lawyer.

17[?]. HERD, *Scot. Songs* (1776), ii. 234. There dwells a Tod on yonder craig, And he's a Tod of might; He LIVES as well ON his PURCHASE As ony laird or knight.

1748. SMOLLETT, *Rod. Random*, viii. This here PURCHASE, a gold snuff-box . . . which I untied out of the tail of a pretty lady's smock.

1821. SCOTT, *Kenilworth*, ii. For even when a man hath got nobles of his own, he keeps out of the way of those whose exchequers lie in other men's PURCHASE

PURE, *subs.* (old).—1. A mistress: a KEEP (*q.v.*). Hence PUREST-PURE = 'a Top mistress or Fine Woman' (B. E., *c.*1666).

1688. SHADWELL, *Sq. of Alsatia*, ii. [*Wks.* (1720), iv. 47]. But where's your lady, captain, and the blowing, that is to be my natural, my convenient, my PURE?

2. (scavengers'). —*See* quot: also as *verb.*: hence PURE-FINDER.

1851. MAYHEW, *Lond. Lab.*, ii. 158. Dogs'-dung is called PURE, from its cleansing and purifying properties. *Ibid.* The name of PURE-FINDERS, however, has been applied to the men engaged in collecting dogs'-dung from the public streets only, within the last 20 or 30 years.

Adj. (common). —Neat; unadulterated: *see* DRINKS. Whence PURE - ELEMENT = water: *see* ADAM'S ALE.

1772. BRIDGES, *Burlesque Homer*, 61. And then we all must be content To guzzle down PURE ELEMENT.

1789. WHITE, *Selborne*, i. A fine limpid water . . . much commended by those who drink the PURE ELEMENT.

1840. BARHAM, *Ingoldsby Leg.*, 'Patty Morgan.' The PURE ELEMENT is for Man's belly meant! And Gin's but a snare of Old Nick.

2. (old and colloquial).—Used intensively: *cf.* PRIME, EXQUISITE, TIP-TOP, STUNNING = NO-END (*q.v.*); MIGHTY (*q.v.*); OUT-AND-OUT (*q.v.*), &c. Also as *adv.*

1362. LANGLAND, *Piers Plowman*, viii. 20. Godes pyne and hus passion is PURE selde in my thoubte.

1371. CHAUCER, *Blanche the Duchess*, 1251. I durst no more say thereto For PURE feare.

1390. MANDEVILLE, *Travels* [HALLIWELL], 130. Natheless there is gode Londe in sum place; but it is PURE litille, as men seyn.

1393. GOWER, *Confessio Amantis*, iii. 38. It torneth me to PURE grame [= vexation].

1592. SHAKSPEARE, *1 Hen. VI.*, ii. 4. Thy cheeks blush for PURE shame.

1601. JONSON, *Poetaster*, ii. 1. PURELY jealous I would have her.

1700. CONGREVE, *Way of the World*, ii. 5. When your laship pins it up with poetry, it fits so pleasant the next day as anything, and is so PURE and so crips.

1704. CIBBER, *Careless Husband*, iii. 1. *Mrs. E.* Ha! she looks as if my master had quarrelled with her. . . . This is PURE.

1708-10. SWIFT, *Polite Conversation*, i. *Col.* I'm like all Fools; I love everything that's good. *Lady Smart.* Well, and isn't it PURE good? 'Tis better than a worse.

*d.*1797. WALPOLE, *Letters*, II. 297. His countess . . . looks PURE awkward amongst so much good company.

1847. HALLIWELL, *Arch. and Prov. Words*, s.v. PURE. Mere; very. Still in use. A countryman shown Morland's picture of pigs feeding, corrected the artist, by exclaiming, "They be PURE loike surelye, but whoever seed three pigs a-feeding without one o' em having his foot in the trough?"

1884. HENLEY and STEVENSON, *Deacon Brodie*, I. iii. 3. O, such manners are PURE, PURE, PURE! They are, by the shade of Claude Duval.

1887. *Lippincott's Magazine*, 397. I never struck a hole yet where there was more . . . what you call PURE cussedness than in that whited sepulchre of a divinity school.

THE PURE QUILL, *phr.* (common). — The best; the 'real thing': any person or thing of superlative quality. *See* A 1 and O. K.

1888. *Detroit Free Press*, Aug. When religun is religun, an' it's THE PURE QUILL . . . there's never one of us but kin take it in large doses.

PURGE, *subs.* (common).—Beer; SWIPES (*q.v.*): as in the barrack-room wheeze—"Comrades, listen while I urge; Drink, yourselves, and pass to PURGE."

PURGER (or **PERGER**), *subs.* (common).—Primarily a teetotaller; a TEA-POT SUCKER: hence a term of contempt.

*c.*1864. VANCE, *Chickaleary Cove.* My tailor serves you well, from a PERGER to a swell.

PURITAN, *subs.* (Old Cant: now recognised).—1. A name given in contempt (*c.*1564-9) to clergymen and laymen who wanted a simpler, and what they considered a 'purer,' ceremonial than was authorised: by extension, a man or woman setting up for better (esp. chaster) and more pious than their neighbours. Hence, PURITANISM = a condition of exacerbated righteousness; "unco' guidness"; a habit of life beyond impeachment, strict, godly, and austere. Also, as *adj.* = sour, precise, malevolently and tyrannically severe. Also PRECISIAN (*q.v.*).

1567. *Three Fifteenth Century Chronicles* [Camden Soc.], 143. About that tyme were many congregations of the Anabaptysts in London who cawlyd themselves PURITANS, or Unspotted Lambs of the Lord.

1598. SHAKSPEARE, *All's Well*, i. 3. Though honesty be no PURITAN, yet it will do no hurt; it will wear the surplice of humility over the black gown of a big heart. Ibid., *Twelfth Night* (1602), ii. 3. Marry, sir, sometimes he is a kind of PURITAN. *Ibid.* (1604), *Winter's Tale.* But one PURITAN among them, and he sings psalms to horn-pipes.

1599. CHAPMAN, *Hum. Day's Mirth* [SHEPHERD (1874), 26]. Why, every man for her sake is a PURITAN. The devil I think will shortly turn PURITAN, or the PURITAN will turn devil.

1605. JONSON, CHAPMAN, &c., *Eastward Hoe*, ii. 1. Your only smooth skin is your PURITAN'S skin; they be the smoothest and slickest knaves in a country.

1607. DEKKER, *Westward Ho*, ii. 2. The serving-man has his punk, the student his nun . . . the PURITAN his sister.

1650. *Barnaby's Journal*, 5. To Banbury came I, O prophane-One! Where I saw a PURITANE-One.

*c.*1690. B. E., *Dict. Cant. Crew*, s.v. PURITANS, PURITANICAL, those of the precise Cut, strait-laced Precisians, whining (as Osborn saies) for a sanctity God never yet trusted out of Heaven.

1705. HEARNE, *Diary*, 17 Nov. Magd. hall: the chief members of which were always rigid PURITANS, for whom he could not have a very fair opinion upon account of their unmercifull usage of Archbishop Laud.

1705. WARD, *Hud. Rediv.*, I. x. 24. So PURITANS, the World to cheat, Appear in Garb precisely neat.

1902. *D. Telegraph*, 2 May, 5, 1, "Special Law Reports." Mr. Tindal Atkinson called attention to the fact that at this particular licensing meeting no fewer than twenty-three out of thirty-seven applications for music license renewals were refused. No fault was suggested, no evidence offered, and that went to show that the magistrates, perhaps owing to the particular composition of the Bench at the time, and the views they took in regard to the matter, did not decide each case upon its merits, but upon a view of their own. It was true they might become so PURITANICAL that the Legislature might think fit to say that no music license should be granted to a licensed house. The Lord Chief Justice: You must not say these magistrates have acted PURITANICALLY. I do not think they have done so. Mr. Tindal Atkinson: I only made the general observation that the Legislature might become so PURITANICAL. I was not reflecting on the justices. The Lord Chief Justice: I thought you used the word PURITANICAL in a secondary sense.

2. (old).—A whore: *see* TART. [Probably an echo of the hypocrisy imputed to the Puritans: *cf.* sense 1, esp. quot. 1607.]

PURKO, *subs.* (military).—Beer: *see* SWIPES. [Barclay, Perkins and Co.]

PURL, *subs.* (old: now recognised).—1. *See* quots. 1696 and 1851; afterwards (2) applied to beer warmed nearly to boiling point, and flavoured with gin, sugar, and ginger. Hence PURL-MAN = a boating vendor of PURL to Thames watermen.—GROSE (1785).

1680. PEPYS, *Diary*, 19 Feb. Forth to Mr. Harper's to drink a draft of PURLE.

1690. DURFEY, *Collin's Walk*, IV. Or like a Porter could Regale, With Pots of PURLE, or Mugs of Ale.

*c.*1696. B. E., *Dict. Cant. Crew*, s.v. PURL, Wormwood infus'd in Ale. *Ibid.* PURL-ROYAL, Canary with a dash of Wormwood.

1711. *Spectator*, No. 88. My lord bishop swore he would throw her out at window . . . and my lord duke would have a double mug of PURL.

1790. *Old Song*, 'Flashman of St. Giles's' [*Busy Bee*]. I call'd for some PURL, and we had it hot.

1836. DICKENS, *Sketches*, 33. Watermen . . . retire . . . to solace themselves with the creature comforts of pipes and PURL.

1841. REDE, *Sixteen String Jack*, i. 2. Long Jerry's half way down a pot of PURL; Kit's finishing a bowl of punch——.

1851. MAYHEW, *Lond. Lab.*, ii. 108. It appears to have been the practice at some time or other in this country to infuse wormwood into beer or ale previous to drinking it, either to make it sufficiently bitter, or for some medicinal purpose. This mixture was called PURL. *Ibid.* The drink originally sold on the river was PURL, or this mixture, whence the title PURL-MAN.

3. (schools').—A dive, head foremost: *cf.* sense 2.

Adj. (hunting). — Thrown; SPILT (*q.v.*); FOALED (*q.v.*): *e.g.*, 'He'll get PURLED at the rails.' Hence (as *subs.*), or PURLER = a fall; a spill.

1857. C. READE, *Never Too Late*, xxxviii. They went a tremendous pace—with occasional stoppages when a PURL occurred. *Ibid.* They commonly paddle in companies of three; so then whenever one is PURLED the other two come on each side of him.

1868. OUIDA, *Two Flags*, iii. Right in front of that Stand was an artificial bullfinch that promised to treat most of the field to a PURLER, a deep ditch dug and filled with water, with two towering blackthorn fences on either side of it.

1885. *Field*, 26 Dec. To trifle with this innovation means a certain PURLER.

PURPOSE. TO AS MUCH PURPOSE AS THE GEESE SLUR UPON THE ICE (or AS TO GIVE A GOOSE HAY), *phr.* (colloquial).—To no purpose at all. Also 'to no more PURPOSE than to beat your heels against the ground (or wind).'—RAY (1670).

PURSE, *subs.* (venery).—1. The female *pudendum*: *see* MONOSYLLABLE: Fr. *bourse-à-vits*: *cf.* PRICK-PURSE. Also (2) = the *scrotum.* Hence, NO MONEY IN HIS PURSE = impotent; PURSE-PROUD = lecherous; PURSE-FINDER = a harlot; &c.

*c.*1620. BEAUMONT and FLETCHER, *Little French Lawyer*, v. 3. And put a good speed-penny in my PURSE that has been empty these thirty years.

*c.*1720. *Broadside Song*, 'The Turnep Ground' [FARMER, *Merry Songs and Ballads* (1897), i. 224]. [When] gently down I L'ayd her, She Op't a PURSE as black as Coal, To hold my Coin.

2. (colloquial). — A sum of money: a prize, a collection, a gift. Also (generic) = money; resources.

1891. *Sporting Life*, 3 Ap. He will send a deposit as a guarantee to keep his appointment if any club or gentleman will give a PURSE for him to face the victorious one in the match referred to.

Verb. (old).—To take purses; to steal.

1609. BEAUMONT and FLETCHER, *Scornful Lady*, i. 1. Why I'll PURSE: if that raise me not I'll bet at Bowling Alleys.

One or two colloquialisms merit notice: thus, a LIGHT (or EMPTY) PURSE = poverty; a LONG (or HEAVY) PURSE = wealth; SWORD AND PURSE = the military power and wealth of a nation; TO MAKE A PURSE = to amass money; PURSE-PROUD (or FULL) = haughty, because rich (B. E., 1696); OUT OF PURSE = penniless; PURSE-PINCHED = poor; 'I've left my PURSE in my other hose (old), or on the piano' = a bald excuse for not PARTING (*q.v.*). Amongst proverbs there are:—'A full PURSE makes the mouth to speak'; 'An empty PURSE fills the face with wrinkles'; 'Ask thy PURSE what thou should'st buy'; 'An empty PURSE and a new house make a man wise, but too late'; 'An empty PURSE frights away friends'; 'A friend at Court is better than a penny in the PURSE.'

1593. SHAKSPEARE, *Taming of the Shrew*, iv. 3. Our PURSES shall be PROUD, our garments poor; For 'tis the mind that makes the body rich.

1615. *Fisheries* [ARBER, *Garner*, iii. 635]. [He was] OUT OF PURSE.

*d.*1626. DAVIES, *Microcosmus* [GROSART, *Works* (1876), 14]. Ladies and lords, PURSE-PINCHED and soule-pained.

1634. WITHAL, *Dict.*, *Zonam perdidit*: he hath LEFT HIS PURSE IN HIS OTHER HOSE.

1814. EDGEWORTH, *Patronage*, xix. Dr. Percy's next difficulty was how to supply the PURSE-FULL and PURSE-PROUD citizen with motive and occupation.

PURSE-LEECH, *subs. phr.* (old).—A money-grubber.

1648. *British Belman* [*Harl. Misc.* (PARK), vii. 625]. Golden days of peace and plenty, as we must never see again, So long as you harpyes, you sucking PURSE-LEECHES, and your implements be our masters.

PURSE-MILKING, *adj. phr.* (old).—Spendthrift; greedy.

1621. BURTON, *Anat. Melan.* [1638], Democ. to Reader, 49. A PURSE-MILKING nation, a clamorous company, gowned vultures [of lawyers].

PURSENETS, *subs.* (old).—*See* quot.

*c.*1696. B. E., *Dict. Cant. Crew*, s.v. PURSENETS, Goods taken upon Trust by young Unthrifts at treble the Value; also a little Purse.

PURSER, *subs.* (nautical).—A ship's storekeeper: used contemptuously as follows:—PURSER'S DIP (QUART, &c.) = an undersized candle, or quart short in measure; PURSER'S GRIN = a hypocritical or satirical sneer: *e.g.*, 'There are no half laughs or PURSER'S GRINS about me, I'm right up and down like a yard of pump water,' meaning that the speaker is in earnest; PURSER'S-NAME = a false name; PURSER'S SHIRT ON A HANDSPIKE (said of ill-fitting clothes); PURSER'S-GRIND (venery) = 'plenty of prick and no money': a YIDDISH COMPLIMENT (*q.v.*).

1748. SMOLLETT, *Rod. Random*, xxxiii. We had languished five weeks on the allowance of a PURSER'S QUART *per diem* for each man.

PURSER'S-PUMP, *subs. phr.* (old).—(1) A syphon; and (2) a bassoon.—GROSE (1785).

PURSY (or **PURSIVE**), *adj.* (old: now colloquial).—1. Rich; (2) fat with well-being; and (3) short-winded.—B. E. (*c.*1696); GROSE (1785).

1440. *Prompt. Parv.* [Camden Soc.] ... PURCY in wynd drawynge.

1596. SHAKSPEARE, *Hamlet*, iii. 4. The fatness of these PURSY times.

1607. [? MIDDLETON] or W [? ENTWORTH] S [? MITH], *Puritan*, i. iv. I ... by chance set upon a fat steward, thinking his purse had been as PURSY as his body; and the slave had about him the poor purchase of ten groats.

18 [?]. H. LUTTRELL, *Mayfair* (1827), II. 16. Of tedious M.P.'s, PURSY peers, Illustrious for their length of ears.

1820. IRVING, *Sketch-Book*, 264. A short, PURSY man, stooping ... so as to show nothing but the top of a round, bald head.

*d.*1832. CRABBE, *Works*, iv. 12. Slothful and PURSY, insolent and mean, Were every bishop, prebendary, dean.

*c.*1871. *The Siliad*, xiv. The PURSY man, whose Capital's his God.

PURTING-GLUMPOT, *subs. phr.* (common).—A sulker.

PUSEUM (THE), *subs.* (Oxford University).—The Pusey House in St. Giles's St.

PUSH, *subs.* (old).—1. A crowd; an assembly of any kind: *e.g.* (thieves') = a band of thieves; (prisons') = a gang associated in penal labour; (general) = a knot or party of people, at a theatre, a church, a race-meeting, &c. Fr., *abadie*, *tigne*, *vade*, *trèpe*. (It., *treppo*; O. Fr., *treper* = to press, to trample).

1672. WYCHERLEY, *Love in a Wood*, ii. 1. I will not stay THE PUSH. They come! they come! oh, the fellows come!

1718. C. HIGGIN, *True Disc.*, 13. He is a ... thieves' watchman, that lies scouting ... when and where there is a PUSH, alias an accidental crowd of people.

1754. *Disc. of John Poulter*, 30. In order to be out of the PUSH or throng.

1819. VAUX, *Memoirs*, s.v. PUSH ... When any particular scene of crowding is alluded to, they say, the PUSH ... at the spell doors; the PUSH at the stooping-match.

1830. MONCRIEFF, *Heart of London*. ii. 1. He's as quiet as a dummy hunter in a PUSH by Houndsditch.

1852. JUDSON, *Myst. of New York*, II. ii. This is one ver grand PUSH.

1877. DAVITT, *Prison Diary*. Most of these pseudo-aristocratic impostors had succeeded in obtaining admission to the stocking-knitting party, which, in consequence, became known among the rest of the prisoners as the "upper ten PUSH."

2. (thieves').—A robbery; a swindle: also as in sense 1. Thus, 'I'm in this PUSH! = 'I mean to share'—an intimation from one magsman to another that he means to STAND IN (*q.v.*).

1772. BRIDGES, *Burlesque Homer*, 248. Tho' NOW-A-DAYS So bold a PUSH Would make an honest Hebrew blush.

3. (colloquial).—Enterprise; energy: also PUSHERY = forwardness.

18 [?]. D'ARBLAY, *Diary*, iv. 45. I actually asked for this dab of preferment; it is the first piece of PUSHERY I ever was guilty of.

Verb. (venery).—To copulate: *see* GREENS and RIDE: also TO STAND THE PUSH; TO DO A RANDOM PUSH; and TO PLAY AT PUSH-PIN (PUSH-PIKE or PUT-PIN). Whence PUSHING-SCHOOL = a brothel: *see* NANNY-SHOP.—B. E. (*c.*1696); GROSE (1785).

1560. RYCHARDES, *Misogonus* [HALLIWELL]. That can lay downe maidens bedds, And that can hold ther sickly heds: That can play at PUT-PIN, Blowe-poynte, and near lin.

1623. MASSINGER, *Duke of Milan*, iii. 2. This wanton at dead midnight, Was found at the exercise behind the arras, With the 'foresaid signoir ... she would never tell Who PLAY'D AT PUSHPIN with her.

1656. *Men Miracles*, 15. To see the sonne you would admire, Goe PLAY AT PUSH-PIN with his sire.

1707. WARD, *Hudibras Redivivus*, II. vii. 10. When at PUSH-A-PIKE WE PLAY With beauty, who shall win the day?

1750. ROBERTSON of Struan, *Poems*, 96. PUSH on, PUSH on, ye happy Pair.

1772. BRIDGES, *Burlesque Homer*, 337. They star'd like honest Johnny Wade, When he one evening with the maid A game at PUSHPIN had begun, And madam came before he'd done.

COLLOQUIALISMS.—TO GET (or GIVE) THE PUSH (or THE ORDER OF THE PUSH) = to be discharged (or to reject), to be sent (or send) about one's business; PUT TO THE PUSH (or AT A PUSH) = subjected to trial, in a difficulty or dilemma (B. E., *c.*1696); TO PUSH ONE'S BARROW = to move on; AT PUSH OF PIKE = at defiance (B. E., *c.*1696). *See* also FACE.

*c.*1870. *Music Hall Song*, 'I'll say no More to Mary Ann.' The girl that stole my heart has GIVEN me THE PUSH.

1886-96. MARSHALL, '*Pomes*' ['A Meeting on the "Met"'], 126. He felt like people do who GAIN THE ORDER OF THE PUSH.

1890. SIMS, *Rondeau of the Knock* [*Referee*, 20 Ap.]. No more with jaunty air He'll HAVE THE PUSH.

1893. EMERSON, *Lippo*, xx. She was always taking on new ones, for you GOT THE PUSH in a year or two, arter you got too big.

PUSHED, *adj.* (common).—1. Drunk: *see* DRINKS and SCREWED.

2. (colloquial).—Hard up.

1827. *London Mag.*, xix. 39. He was frequently PUSHED for money.

PUSHER, *subs.* (old).—1. *See* quot.

*c.*1696. B. E., *Dict. Cant. Crew*, s.v. PUSHERS, Canary-birds new Flown, that cannot Feed themselves.

2. (common).—A woman: *see* PETTICOAT. Hence SQUARE PUSHER = a girl of good reputation.

3. (shoemakers').—A blucher boot; a high-low.

4. (nursery).—A finger of bread: used by children with a fork when feeding.

PUSHING-SCHOOL, *subs. phr.* (old).—1. A fencing-school.—B. E. (*c.*1696); GROSE (1785).

PUSHING-TOUT, *subs. phr.* (old).—*See* quot.

1718. C. HIGGIN, *True Disc.*, 13. He is a PUSHING TOUTE, alias thieves' watchman, that lies scouting in and about the City to get and bring intelligence to the thieves, when and where there is a Push, alias an Accidental Crowd of People.

PUSH-PIN. *See* PUSH, *verb*.

PUSS, *subs.* (old).—1. Sometimes complacently used of a woman suspected of loose morals (*cf.* CAT): but usually a playful endearment: *e.g.*, 'little PUSS,' 'saucy PUSS,' 'you PUSS, you.'

1583. STUBBES, *Anatomy of Abuses* [New Shaks. Soc.], 97. [OLIPHANT, *New English*, i. 614. The word PUSSIE is now used of a woman.]

1621. BURTON, *Anat. Melan.*, III. II. iii. 1. Pleasant names may be invented ... PUSS ... honey, love, dove.

1664. COTTON, *Virgil Travestie* (1st ed.), 3. That cross-grained peevish scolding Quean, That scratching cater-wawling Puss.

1761. COLMAN, *Jealous Wife*, ii. 3. Gone! what a pox had I just run her down, and is the little PUSS stole away at last.

1772. BRIDGES, *Burlesque Homer*, 101. The Rainbow-goddess flies to Helen Most modern PUSS I ever knew.

1859. ELIOT, *Adam Bede*, ix. The LITTLE PUSS seems already to have airs enough to make a husband as miserable as it's a law of nature for a quiet man to be when he marries a beauty.

1885. F. LOCKER, *Mabel.* My jealous PUSSY cut up rough The day before I bought her muff With sable trimming.

2. (sporting).—A hare, or rabbit.

1821. SCOTT, *Kenilworth*, xxix. Thou shalt not give PUSS a hint to steal away—we must catch her in her form.

1886. *Field*, 27 Feb. Dusting her hare about half a dozen times up to the fence, where PUSS escaped.

3. (venery).—The female *pudendum*: *see* MONOSYLLABLE: also PUSSY and PUSSY-CAT: Fr., *chat*; *angora*. Hence, TO FEED ONE'S PUSSY = to copulate.

1664. COTTON, *Virgil Travestie*, 107. Æneas, here's a Health to thee, To PUSSE and to good company.

4. (local Woolwich: obsolete).—A cadet of the Royal Military Academy. [The uniform was a short jacket with a pointed tail: *vide* old pictures at the R.A. Institution, Woolwich.]

PUSS-GENTLEMAN, *subs. phr.* (old).—An effeminate.

1782. COWPER, *Conv.*, 284. I cannot talk with Civet in the room, A fine PUSS-GENTLEMAN that's all perfume.

PUSSY-CAT, *subs. phr.* (clerical).—1. A Puseyite.

2. *See* PUSS, *subs.*, sense 4.

PUT, *subs.* (old).—1. A rustic; a shallowpate; also COUNTRY PUT.—B. E. (*c.*1696); GROSE (1785).

1688. SHADWELL, *Sq. of Alsatia*, i. *Belf, sen.* I always thought they had been wittiest in the Universities. *Sham.* A company of PUTTS, meer PUTTS.

1708-10. SWIFT, *Polite Conversation*, ii. He's a true COUNTRY PUT.

1772. BRIDGES, *Burlesque Homer*, 531. Orestes, last, a country PUT, Got such a cursed knock o' th' gut. *Ibid.*, 55. Just such a queer old PUT as you.

1782. CHAMBAUD, *Dict.*, II. s.v.

1847. THACKERAY, *Vanity Fair*, I. xi. The captain has a hearty contempt for his father, I can see, and calls him an old PUT.

2. (old).—A harlot: *see* TART. [Fr. *putain.*] Hence PUTAGE = fornication. Also (3, venery) = an act of coition; intromission: also TO DO A PUT, TO HAVE A PUT-IN, TO PUT IT IN, TO PUT IN ALL, and TO PLAY AT TWO-HANDED PUT: *see* GREENS and RIDE.

*c.*1720. DURFEY, *Pills to Purge*, &c., vi. 251. My skin is White you see, My Smock above my Knee, What would you more of me, PUT IN ALL?

1730. *Broadside Song*, 'Gee ho, Dobbin' [FARMER, *Merry Songs and Ballads* (1897), ii. 203]. I rumpl'd her Feathers, and tickl'd her scutt, And PLAYED the round Rubber AT TWO HANDED PUT.

3. (Stock Exchange).—*See* quot. 1884: also PUT AND CALL.

1776. CIBBER, *Refusal*, i. *Gran.* And all this out of Change-Alley? *Wit.* Every shilling, Sir; all out of Stocks, PUTTS, Bulls, Rams, Bears, and Bubbles.

1884. BISBEE and SIMONDS, *Law Prod. Ex.*, 50. A PUT is an option to deliver, or not deliver, at a future day.

1889. *Rialto*, 23 Mar. Having a pocket order from the promoters, which gives him the PUT AND CALL of as many shares as he requires for his purpose.

Phrases more or less colloquial merit a mention:—TO PUT OFF (-BY or -ON) = (1) to baffle, delay, or dismiss, (2) to foist or deceive, and (3) to get rid of or sell: whence A PUT-OFF (PUT-BY or PUT-ON), *subs.* = a shift, trick, or excuse; TO PUT TO = to ask a question, advice, &c.; TO PUT DOWN = (1) to baffle or suppress, and (2) to enter one's name, for a speech, donation, &c. ; TO PUT UPON = (1) to accuse, and (2) to inflict or oppress ; TO BE PUT UPON (or ON) = to be depressed, deceived, or blamed ; TO PUT IN FOR = to compete ; TO PUT TWO AND TWO (or THIS AND THAT) TOGETHER = to draw conclusions ; TO BE PUT UP = to be accused or PULLED UP (*q.v.*) ; TO BE PUT TO IT = (1) to be compelled, and (2) to be hard pressed or embarrassed (B. E., *c.*1696) ; TO PUT IN ONE'S HEAD = (1) to suggest, and (2) to remind ; TO PUT OUT OF ONE'S HEAD = to forget ; TO PUT UP (or PUT IT UP) WITH = (1) to submit or endure, (2) to accommodate (or be received) as a lodger or guest, (3) to nominate, and (4) to spend or bet ; TO PUT BACK = to hinder or refuse ; TO PUT A QUARREL (or RUDENESS) ON ONE = to force to anger or incivility ; TO PUT AWAY = (1) to dispose of by eating (whence PUT-AWAY, *subs.* = an appetite or TWIST, *q.v.*), sale, pawning, imprisonment, &c., and (2) to inform against, to NARK (*q.v.*) ; TO PUT A HAND TO = (1) to begin a matter, (2) to sign or endorse a document, and (3) to steal ; TO PUT FINGER IN THE EYE = to cry ; TO PUT ON = to imitate, assume a character, airs, &c. (whence A PUT-ON, *subs.* = a trick or shift), and (2) see PUT-OFF, *supra* ; TO PUT OUT = (1) to confuse or perplex, and (2) to vex ; AS MUCH AS ONE CAN PUT IN ONE'S EYE = nothing (B. E., *c.*1696) ; TO PUT A GOOD (or BAD) FACE ON = to appear pleased (or the reverse) ; PUT-UP = arranged, planned (whence A PUT-UP JOB = a concerted swindle or robbery, whence also PUTTER-UP) ; TO PUT ABOUT = (1) to

publish a rumour, lie, or statement, (2) to change one's tactics, and (3) to inconvenience, annoy, or embarrass ; TO PUT THROUGH = (1) to succeed, and (2) to swindle ; TO PUT OUT (FORTH or OFF) = to set out ; TO PUT ON = to bet : see POT ; TO PUT ONE ON = (1) to TIP (*q.v.*), (2) to bet for another, and (3) to promise a bonus if a certain horse wins ; TO PUT UP TO = (1) to explain or impart information, and (2) to suggest or incite ; TO PUT OUT = to vex ; TO PUT IN ONE'S MOTTO = (1) to enter rashly into a discussion, and (2) to ' lay down the law ' ; TO STAY PUT (American) = to remain as placed ; TO PUT IN A HOLE = (1) to inconvenience, non-plus, or get the better of (see HOLE), (2) to defraud (thieves' : see WELL), and (3) to victimize ; TO PUT ON ONE'S METTLE = to urge ; TO BE PUT TO ONE'S TRUMPS = to be forced back on one's resources ; TO PUT BY = to save ; TO PUT (or LAY) HEADS TOGETHER = to confer ; TO PUT ONE'S HEAD IN THE LION'S MOUTH = to run into danger ; TO PUT TO THE DOOR = to eject ; TO PUT OVER (Australian) = to kill ; TO PUT ON THE WOMAN = to shed tears ; TO PUT A HAT ON A HEN = to attempt the impossible (RAY, 1765) ; TO PUT TOGETHER WITH A HOT NEEDLE (or BURNT THREAD) = to fasten insecurely ; PUT UP ! = Shut your mouth ! (American). *See* also APE ; BACK ; BAG ; BALMY ; BALMY-STICK ; BASKET ; BED ; BEST-LEG ; BOOT ; BUSINESS ; CART ; CHAIR ; DOCTOR ; DOUBLE ; DOWN ; DRAG ; DUKES ; END ; FRILLS ; GRINDSTONE ; HAND ; HEAD ; HORSE ; KIBOSH ; LIGHT ; MILLER ; MILLER'S-EYE ; NAIL ; NAME ; NOSE ; OAR ;

PIN ; PIPE ; POT ; SIDE ; SPOKE ; STRONG ; TIME-O'-DAY ; TONGUE ; WAR-PAINT ; WRONG-LEG.

PUTNEY. GO TO PUTNEY ON A PIG, *phr.* (common).—*See* quot., and *cf.* BATH, HALIFAX, HONG KONG, JERICHO, &c.

1863. KINGSLEY, *Austin Elliot*, xv. Now, in the year 1845, telling a man to GO TO PUTNEY, was the same as telling a man to go to the deuce.

PUTRID, *adj.* (common).—A depreciative : *cf.* AWFUL, BLOODY, &c.

1901. *Sporting Times*, 27 April, 1, 4. All beer is PUTRID, even when it's pure.

PUTTER, *subs.* (old).—A foot : see CREEPERS.

1821. HAGGART, *Life*, 53. His ogles being darkened by the PUTTER.

PUTTER-ON, *subs. phr.* (old colloquial).—An instigator ; a prompter.

1601. SHAKSPEARE, *Henry VIII.*, i. 2, 24. They vent reproaches Most bitterly on you, as PUTTER-ON Of these exactions. *Ibid.* (1604), *Winter's Tale*, ii. 1, 140. You are abus'd, and by some PUTTER-ON That will be damn'd for it.

PUTTOCK, *subs.* (old).—1. A whore : see TART.

PUTTY, *subs.* (American).—Money : generic : see RHINO.

1848. DURIVAGE, *Stray Subjects*, 82. ' I'll take that lot.' ' You will ?' ' Yes, Mister ; and yere's yer PUTTY !'

2. (common). — A glazier or painter.

THE PUTTY AND PLASTER ON THE SOLOMON KNOB, *phr.* (masons').— An intimation that the Master is coming ; ' be silent !'

PUZZLE (or **DIRTY-PUZZLE**), *subs.* (old).—A slattern.

1583. STUBBES, *Anatomy of Abuses* [NARES]. Nor yet any droyle or PUZZEL . . . but will carry a nosegay in her hand.

1592. SHAKSPEARE, *1 Henry VI.*, i. 4. Pucelle or PUZZEL, dolphin or dog fish.

1607. STEPHANUS, *Apol. for Herod.*, 98. Some filthy queans, especially our PUZZLES of Paris.

PUZZLE-COVE (or **CAUSE**), *subs.* (old).—A lawyer.—GROSE (1785) ; MATSELL (1859).

PUZZLEDOM, *subs.* (old colloquial).—Perplexity ; bewilderment : also PUZZLEMENT. Whence, PUZZLE-HEADED and PUZZLEHEADED-NESS.

1748. RICHARDSON, *Harlowe*, VI. 367. I was resolved to travel with him unto the land of PUZZLEDOM.

1881. FREEMAN, *Venice*, 79. The wonderful interior of the double basilica opens upon us. The first feeling is simply PUZZLEDOM.

PUZZLE - HEADED - SPOON. *See* APOSTLE-SPOON.

PUZZLE-TEXT, *subs. phr.* (old).—A clergyman : see SKY-PILOT.—GROSE (1785).

PUZZLING ARITHMETIC, *subs. phr.* (old gamblers').—A statement of the odds.

1613. WEBSTER, *Devil's Law-case*, ii. 1. Studying a PUZZLING ARITHMETIC at the cockpit.

PUZZLING-STICKS, *subs.* (old). —The triangle to which culprits were tied for flagellation.—VAUX (1819).

PYGOSTOLE, *subs.* (clerical). — A M.B. WAISTCOAT (*q.v.*).

1844. *Puck*, 13. It is true that the wicked make sport Of our PYGOSTOLES, as we go by.

1886. *Graphic*, 10 April, 39. The M.B. coat, otherwise known as a PYGO-STOLE.

 **(CUE** or **KUE),** *subs.* (old).—1. See quots. 1440 and 1617. Hence (2) a score (whence a reminder : *cf.* quot. 1594 and the theatrical usage), and (3) an item of small value : see WORTH.

*c.*1440. *Prompt. Parv.*, 106. Cu, halfe a farthynge or Q.

*c.*1510. BARCLAY, *Good Manners* (1570), Bij. All these . . . are scarcely worth a KUE.

1526. SKELTON, *Magnyfycence*, 36. That lyberte was not worth a CUE.

1594. LYLY, *Mother Bombie*, ii. 3. If you be examined how we met, sweare by chance . . . Every one remember his QUE.

1617. MINSHEU, *Guide unto Tongues*, CUE, halfe a farthing, so called because they set down in the Battling or Butterie Bookes in Oxford and Cambridge the letter Q for halfe a farthing, and in Oxford when they make that CUE or Q a farthing, they say, Cap my Q, and make it a farthing thus a Q

Q IN A CORNER, *phr.* (legal). —Something not seen at once, but subsequently brought to notice.

See P's and Q's.

Q.H.B. (or **K.H.B.**), *phr.* (naval and military).—*See* quots. : also QUEEN'S (or KING'S) BAD BARGAIN (or SHILLING). — GROSE (1785).

1865. *Cornhill Mag.*, Feb., 243. This was a man of the old school. The younger Bohemians of the service of my own standing were a more polished breed. . . . They were generally indeed, what used to be called Q. H. B.'s—QUEEN'S HARD BARGAINS—from a professional point of view.

1890. *Tit-Bits*, 26 Ap., 35, 1. A worthless character such as used to be called a QUEEN'S BAD SHILLING, when men were enlisted with a shilling. . . . He schemes into hospital . . . to get off a route march, a field-day, coal-carrying.

1898. *Daily Mail*, 13 Ap., 7, 2. The Q.H.B. used to devote his attention to the Militia, but the Royal Artillery is now a favourite corps with him. . . . Sent to so many different stations, the chances of detection are less.—[Abridged.]

Q.T. ON THE Q.T., *phr.* (common).—On the QUIET : also ON THE STRICT Q.T.

*c.*1870. *Broadside Ballad*, 'Talkative Man from Poplar.' Whatever I tell you is ON THE Q.T.

1893. EMERSON, *Signor Lippo*, ix. We asked him ON THE Q.T. how it was.

QUA, *subs.* (old).—A prison : hence QUA-KEEPER = a gaoler.—*Tufts* (1798).

QUAB, *subs.* (old).—1. An unfledged bird.

1628. FORD, *Lover's Melan.*, iii. 3. A QUAB. 'Tis nothing else, a very QUAB.

QUACK, *subs.* (common).—1. A duck : also QUACKING-CHEAT and QUACKER.—HARMAN (1567); DEKKER (1616) ; B. E. (*c.*1696); GROSE (1785).

1707. SHIRLEY, *Triumph of Wit*, 'Rum-Mort's Praise,' &c. A QUACKING CHEAT, Or tib-o'-th'-buttry was our meat.

2. *See* QUACKSALVER.

Verb. (old booksellers').—*See* quot.—BAILEY (1726).

1715. CENTLIVRE, *Gotham Election*, . . . He has an admirable knack at QUACKING titles . . . they tell me when he gets an old good-for-nothing book, he claps a new title to it, and sell off the whole impression in a week.

IN A QUACK, *phr.* (Scots').— In the shortest time possible : *cf.* CRACK.

QUACKLE, *verb.* (American).—To drink ; to gobble ; to choke : BARTLETT (1847) : ' provincial in England, and colloquial in America.'

1627. REV. S. WARD, *Sermons*, 153. The drink, or something . . . QUACKLED him, stuck so in his throat so that he could not get it up nor down, but strangled him presently.

1837. CARLYLE, *Fr. Revolution*, II. i. 1. Simple ducks in those royal waters QUACKLE for crumbs from young royal fingers.

QUACKSALVER (**QUACKSALVE** or **QUACK**), *subs.* (old : now recognised).—Originally a charlatan ; a travelling empiric who cackled about his salves : shortened by Wycherley to QUACK, which now = any noisy, specious cheat. Also as *adj.* and *verb.*—B. E. (*c.*1696) ; GROSE (1785). Whence QUACK-ERY = professional humbug.

1579. GOSSON, *School of Abuse* [OLIPHANT, *New Eng.*, i. 604. He has the substantive QUACKSALVER.]

1596. JONSON, *Ev. Man in Humour*, iii. 2. All mere gulleries . . . I could say what I know . . . but I profess myself no QUACKSALVER.

1608. MIDDLETON, *Mad World*, ii. 6. Tut, man, any QUACK-SALVING terms will serve for this purpose.

1625. MASSINGER, *Parl. of Love*, iv. 5. What should a QUACKSALVE, A fellow that does deal in drugs . . . do with so fair a bedfellow.

1672. WYCHERLEY, *Love in a Wood*, iii. QUACKS in their Bills . . . do not disappoint us more than gallants with their Promises.

QUAD, *subs.* (colloquial). — 1. A quadrangle. Hence as *verb.* (Rugby) = to promenade Cloisters at 'calling over' before a football-match. Also QUOD (*q.v.*).

1840. *Collegians' Guide*, 144. His mother . . . had been seen crossing the QUAD in tears.

1855. TROLLOPE, *Warden*, v. The QUAD, as it was familiarly called, was a small quadrangle.

1884. *Daily News*, 14 Oct., 5, 1. His undignified nickname is carved in the turf of the college QUAD.

2. *See* QUOD, *subs.* and *verb.*

3. (common).—A horse ; a 'quadruped.'

1885. *Eng. Ill. Mag.*, April, 509. The second rider . . . got his gallant QUAD over, and . . . went round the course alone.

4. (cyclists').—A bicycle for four.

QUÆDAM, *subs.* (old).—A harlot : see TART.

1692. HACKET, *Life of Williams*, ii. 128. A seraglio of Quædams.

QUÆ-GEMES, *subs. phr.* (old).—A bastard : *cf.* Johnny Quæ-Genus, a character title.

QUAFF, *verb.* (old : once and still literary in the weakened sense 2).—1. To carouse (B. E., *c.*1696) : also TO QUAFF OFF ; and (2) to drink with gusto. QUAFFTIDE (STANYHURST) = the time of drinking.

QUAG, *subs.* (old).—Marsh-land ; a quagmire.—B. E, (*c.*1696) ; GROSE (1785).

Adj. (American). — Untrustworthy; unsafe.--MATSELL(1859).

QUAIL, *subs.* (old).—A harlot: *see* TART and *cf.* PLOVER, PHEASANT, &c.

1602. SHAKSPEARE, *Troilus and Cressida*, v. 1. Here's Agamemnon—an honest fellow enough, and one that loves QUAILS.

1708. MOTTEUX, *Rabelais*, Prol. to Book IV. With several coated QUAILS, and laced muttons, waggishly singing.

1640. GLAPTHORNE, *Hollander*, . . . The hot desire of QUAILS, To your's is modest appetite.

QUAIL-PIPE, *subs. phr.* (old).—1. A woman's tongue. — B. E. (*c.*1696); GROSE (1785). Also (2) the throat.

1692. DRYDEN, *Juvenal*, Satire 6. And stretch his QUAIL-PIPE till they crack his voice.

1714. POPE, *Wife of Bath*, 213. To clear my QUAIL-PIPE, and refresh my soul, Full oft I drain'd the spicy nut-brown bowl.

QUAIL-PIPE BOOTS, *subs. phr.* (old).—Boots full of plaits and wrinkles: *temp.* Chas. II.; also QUILL-PIPES.—GROSE (1785).

1602. MIDDLETON, *Blurt, Master Constable*, ii. 1. A gallant that hides his small-timbered legs with a QUAIL-PIPE boot.

QUAINT (QUEINT, QUEYNTE, QUAYNTE or **CUNT)**, *subs.* (old).—The female *pudendum*: *see* MONOSYLLABLE and CUNT.

1383. CHAUCER. *The Miller's Tale.* And prively he caught hire by the QUEINT.

1598. FLORIO, *Worlde of Wordes. Conno*, A womans privie parts or QUAINT as Chaucer calles it.

Adj. and *adv.* (old: now recognised). — 'Curious, neat, also strange.'—B. E. (*c.*1696).

QUAKE-BREACH, *subs. phr.* (old).—A coward.

1608. WITHAL, *Dict.* 338. Excors, a hartlesse, a faint-hearted fellow, a QUAKE-BREECH, without boldnes, spirit, wit, a sot.

QUAKER, *subs.* (old).—1. A member of the Society of Friends. Like PURITAN (*q.v.*), which was ultimately accepted, QUAKER originated in contempt, but it has never been accepted by the Society. Whence also QUAKERDOM = the world of Quakers; QUAKERISH = prim, demure, and so forth.

1664. BUTLER, *Hudibras*, II., ii., 219. QUAKERS that, like to lanterns, bear Their lights within 'em wfll not swear.

1677. PENN, *Travels in Holland* [*Century*]. A certain minister in Bremen . . . reproached with the name of QUAKER.

1847. BRONTE, *Jane Eyre*, xxiv. Don't address me as if I were a beauty; I am your plain QUAKERISH governess.

1876. ELIOT, *Daniel Deronda*, xviii. Her rippling hair, covered by a QUAKERISH net-cap, was chiefly grey.

2. (old).—A rope or pile of excrement; a TURD (*q.v.*), Fr. *rondin* and *sentinelle.* Hence TO BURY A QUAKER = to ease the bowels; and QUAKER'S BURYING-GROUND = a jakes: *see* MRS. JONES.

3. (naval and military).—*See* quot. 1882: also QUAKER-GUN.

1840. DANA, *Before the Mast*, xxvii. A Russian government barque, from Asitka, mounting eight guns (four of which we found to be QUAKERS).

1862. *New York Tribune*, Mar. The . . . impregnability of the position turns out to be a sham . . . QUAKERS were mounted on the bulwarks.

1882. *Daily Telegraph*, 30 Dec., 6, 1. Gangways and quarter-decks bristling with guns and lower portholes rendered formidable to the eye by those sham wooden pieces called QUAKERS, because they were never fought.

STEWED-QUAKER, *subs. phr.* (American colloquial).—A remedy for colds: composed of vinegar and molasses (or honey), mixed with butter and drunk hot.

QUAKER CITY, *subs. phr.* (American). — Philadelphia. [William Penn, its founder, belonged to the Society of Friends.]

QUAKER'S BARGAIN, *subs. phr.* (old). — A bargain 'Yea' or 'Nay'; a 'take-it-or-leave-it' transaction.

1697. VANBRUGH, *Prov. Wife*, ii. *Lady F.* At what rate would this . . . be brought off? . . . *Heart.* Why, madam, to drive a QUAKER'S BARGAIN, and make but one word with you, if, &c.

QUAKING-CHEAT, *subs. phr.* (old).—1. A calf; and (2) a sheep.—B. E. (*c.*1696); GROSE (1785).

QUALIFY, *verb.* (venery).—To copulate: *see* GREENS and RIDE.

QUALITY (THE), *subs.* (once literary, now colloquial or vulgar).—The gentry; the UPPER TEN (*q.v.*): *cf.* 'the dignity' applied (PATTEN, 1548) to nobles in the army. Whence QUALITY-AIR = a distinguished carriage.

1599. SHAKSPEARE, *Henry V.*, iv., 8, 94. The rest are princes, barons, lords, knights, squires, and gentlemen of blood and QUALITY.

1700. CENTLIVRE, *Perjured Husband*, III., ii. 'Tis an insufferable fault, that QUALITY can have no pleasure above the vulgar, except it be in not paying their debts.

1749. SMOLLETT, *Gil Blas* [ROUTLEDGE], 106. They have themselves QUALITY AIRS.

1857. A. TROLLOPE, *Barchester Towers*, XXXV. THE QUALITY, as the upper classes in rural districts are designated by the lower with so much true discrimination, were to eat a breakfast, and the NON-QUALITY were to eat a dinner.

QUALM, *subs.* (old: once, and still, literary).—'A stomack-fit; also calmness.' Also QUALMISH = 'crop-sick, queasy stomackt.'—B. E. (*c.*1696).

QUANDARY, *subs.* (colloquial).—A difficulty or doubt; 'a low word' (JOHNSON, 1755). Also as *verb.* = to hesitate; to puzzle.—GROSE (1785). [*See* quot. 1563.]

*c.*1440. *Relig. Pieces* [E. E. T. S.], II. The sexte vertue es strengthe . . . euynly to suffire the wele and the waa, welthe or WANDRETH.

1563. FOXE, *Acts and Monuments* [OLIPHANT, *New. Eng.* i. 540. The *k* is prefixed; the old *wandrethe* (turbatio) becomes QUANDARY].

1590. GREENE, *Never Too Late* [*Wks.* viii, 84]. Thus in a QUANDARIE, he sate.

*d.*1655. REV. T. ADAMS, *Works.* I. 505. He QUANDARIES whether to go forward to God, or . . . to turn back to the world.

1681. OTWAY, *Soldier's Fortune*, iii. I am QUANDARY'D like one going with a party to discover the enemy's camp, but had lost his guide upon the mountains.

1748. SMOLLETT, *Rod. Random*, liv. Throw persons of honour into such QUANDARIES as might endanger their lives.

1874. MRS. H. WOOD, *Johnny Ludlow*, 1 S., No. XXIII., 424. Sam Rimmer sat looking at her as if in a QUANDARY, gently rubbing his hair, that shone again in the sun.

QUANTUM, *subs.* (common).—As much as you want or ought to have: spec. a drink; a GO (*q.v.*). Whence QUANTUM SUFF = enough.

1772. BRIDGES, *Burlesque Homer*, 57. Juno and he have had their QUANTUM, And play no more at rantum-scantum.

*c.*1871. *Siliad*, 99. I, too, O comrade, *quantum suff.* would cry.

QUARREL. — *See* BREAD-AND-BUTTER, PICK, TAKE.

QUARREL-PICKER, *subs. phr.* (old).—A glazier. — B. E. (*c.*1696); GROSE (1785).

1676. *Warening for Housekeepers*, 4. The third sort of thieves, which are called glasiers, are the right QUARREL-PICKERS . . . they take out a pane of glass, and so go in at the window, and take what stands next them.

QUARROMS (QUARROME, or **QUARRON)**, *subs.* (Old Cant).—The body.—HARMAN (1567); DEKKER (1620); B. E. (*c.*1696).

1377. LANGLAND, *Piers Plowman*, B. xiv., 331. Ne noyther sherte ne shone To keure my CAROIGNE.

*c.*1450. *Knt. de la Tour*, xxvii (1868) 39. To adorne suche a CARION as is your body.

[?] *Colin Blowbols Testament* (HAZLITT, *E. Pop. Poetry*, i, 96]. First, I bequeath my goost that is barren, When it is depertid from the CAREYNE.

1567. HARMAN, *Caveat*, 84. Bene Lightmans to thy QUARROMES, in what lipken hast thou lypped in this darkemans, whether in a lybbege or in the strummell?

1707. *Old Song*, 'The Maunder's Praise of His Strowling Mort' [Farmer, *Musa Pedestris* (1896), 33. White thy fambles, red thy gan, And thy QUARRONS dainty is.

QUARRY, *subs.* (venery). — The female *pudendum*: *see* MONOSYLLABLE.

QUARTER, *subs.* (American). — A quarter dollar; twenty-five cents.

1824. *Atlantic Magazine*, I. 343. Every man . . . vociferously swore that he had ponied up his QUARTER.

QUARTER-DECKER, *subs. phr.* (naval).—An officer more remarkable for manners than seamanship. Hence QUARTER-DECKISH = punctilious.

QUARTEREEN, *subs.* (theatrical).—A farthing: *see* RHINO.

QUARTER-SESSIONS ROSE, *subs. phr.* (gardeners').—A 'perpetual' rose. [Fr. *rose de quatre saisons.*]

QUART-MANIA, *subs. phr.* (common).—Delirium tremens: see GALLON-DISTEMPER.

QUARTO (or **MR. QUARTO)**, *subs.* (old).—A publisher or bookseller: *see* BARABBAS.

1772. BRIDGES, *Burlesque Homer*, iv. My bookseller . . . MR. QUARTO.

QUART-POT TEA, *subs. phr.* (Australian).—*See* quot.

1885. FINCH-HATTON, *Advance Australia.* QUART-POT TEA, as tea made in the bush is always called, is really the proper way to make it. A tin quart of water is set down by the fire, and when it is boiling hard a handful of tea is thrown in, and the pot instantly removed from the fire.

QUASH, *verb.* (old: once, and still, literary).—'To annul; to overthrow; to extinguish: vulgarly pron. *squash.*'—B. E. (*c.*1696); GROSE (1785).

QUASHIE (or **QUASSY)**, *subs.* (common).—A negro; generic: *see* SNOWBALL.

1836. M. SCOTT, *Tom Cringle's Log*, xi. Half a dozen mules, accompanied by three or four negroes, but with no escort whatsoever. 'I say, QUASHIE, where are the bombardiers?'

1847. PORTER, *Big Bear*, 89. To show his gratitude invited QUASHEY to go up to the doggery and liquor.

QUAT, *subs.* (old).—A dwarfish person: also (occasionally) a SHABSTER (*q.v.*).

1602. SHAKSPEARE, *Othello*, v. 1. I have rubbed this young QUAT almost to the sense, And he grows angry.

1609. DEKKER, *Gull's Horn Book*, vii. Whether he be a young QUAT of the first yeare's revennew, or some austere and sullen-faced steward.

1613. WEBSTER, *Devil's Law Case.* O young QUAT! incontinence is plagued in all creatures in the world.

Verb. (common).—To ease the bowels: also TO GO TO QUAT.

QUATCH, *adj.* (old).—Flat.

1598. SHAKSPEARE, *All's Well*, ii. 2, 18. Like a barber's chair that fits all buttocks; the pin-buttock, the QUATCH-buttock, . . . or any buttock.

QUATRO, *adj.* (showmen's).—Four. [From the It.]

QUAVER, *subs.* (common). — A musician.

QUAVERY-WAVERY, *adj.* and *adv.* (old: dialectical).—Undecided.

1749. SMOLLETT, *Gil Blas* [ROUTLEDGE], 338. Standing . . . QUAVERY-WAVERY between life and death.

QUAY, *adj.* (American thieves').—Unsafe; untrustworthy.

QUEAN (or **QUEEN)**, *subs.* — 1. Primarily a woman: without regard to character or position. Hence (2) = a slut, HUSSY (*q.v.*), or strumpet: TO PLAY THE QUEAN = to play the whore.—B. E. (*c.*1696); BAILEY (1725); GROSE (1785). Whence QUEANRY = (1) womankind; (2) harlotry; and (3) the estate of whoredom.

1362. LANGLAND, *Piers Plowman*, ix. 46. At churche in the charnel cheorles aren yuel to knowe, Other a knyght fro a knaue other a QUEYNE fro a QUEENE.

1383. CHAUCER, *Manciple's Tale*, Prol., 18. Hastow with som QUENE al nyght yswonke.

[?] SCOTT, *Chron. S. P.*, iii. 148. Quhair hurdome ay unhappis With QUENRY, cannis and coppis.

1591. HARINGTON, *Ariost.*, XXXV. 26. Penelope was but a QUEANE.

1593. NASHE, *Christ's Teares* [GROSART, *Works* (18..), iv. 224]. Every QUEANE vaunts herselfe of some or other man of Nobility.

1596. SHAKSPEARE, *Merry Wives*, iv. 2. A witch, a QUEAN, an old cozening QUEAN.

1596. JONSON, *Ev. Man in Humour*, iv. 8. Kib. A bitter QUEAN! Come, we will have you tamed. *Ibid.* (1601), *Poetaster*, iv. 3. She's a curst QUEAN, tell him, and plays the scold behind his back.

. . . . WATKYNS in HEYWARDS *Quint.*, i. 143 [NARES]. If once the virgin conscience PLAYS THE QUEAN, We seldom after care to keep it clean.

1611. MIDDLETON, *Roaring Girl*, ii. 1. There are more QUEANS in this town of their own making than of any man's provoking.

*c.*1613. FLETCHER, *Nice Valour*, ii. 1 [DYCE, x. 316]. A man can in his lifetime make but one woman, But he may make his fifty QUEANS a month.

1614. *Times Whistle* [E. E. T. S.], 45. Flavia because her meanes are somewhat scant, Doth sell her body to relieve her want, Yet scornes to be reputed as a QUEAN.

1621. BURTON, *Anat. Melan.*, I. II. iv. 6. A base QUEAN. *Ibid.*, III. II. i. 2. Rahab, that harlot began to be a professed QUEAN at ten years of age. *Ibid.*, III. II. ii. 1. They are commonly lascivious, and if women, QUEANS. *Ibid.*, III. II. ii. 5. I perceived . . . by the naked QUEANS, that I was come into a bawdy-house.

1634. FORD, *Perkin Warbeck*, ii. 3. I never was ambitious Of using congees to my daughter-queen—A queen! perhaps a QUEAN!

1731. COFFEY, *Devil to Pay*, i. 2. Where are my sluts? Ye drabs, ye QUEANS—lights there!

1777. SHERIDAN, *School for Scandal*, iii. 3. Here's to the flaunting extravagant QUEAN.

1787. BURNS, *To the Guidwife of Wauchope House*. I see her yet, the sonsie QUEAN That lighted up my jingle. *Ibid.* (1791), *Tam O'Shanter*. Now Tam, O Tam! had there been QUEANS A' plump and strapping in their teens. *Ibid., Merry Muses* (c.1800), "Wha'll Mow Me Noo." An' I maun thole the scornful sneer O' mony a saucy QUINE.

1822. SCOTT, *Nigel*, iii. I was disturbed with some of the night-walking QUEANS and swaggering billies.

QUEASY, *adj.* (old: now recognised).—Qualmish; squeamish.—B. E. (c.1696).

QUEED, *subs.* (old).—The devil: see SKIPPER.—BAILEY (1726).

QUEEN. WHERE THE QUEEN GOES ON FOOT (or SENDS NOBODY), *phr.* (common).—A water-closet: see MRS. JONES.

QUEEN ANNE. QUEEN ANNE (QUEEN ELIZABETH, MY LORD BALDWIN (RAY, 1670)—or any personage whose decease is well-known) IS DEAD, *phr.* (old).—A retort on stale news: also QUEEN ANNE IS DEAD AND HER BOTTOM'S COLD. Whence (in quot. 1753) QUEEN ELIZABETH'S WOMEN = ensigns of antiquity. *Cf.* NEWS. Fr. *C'est vieux comme le Pont-Neuf; Henri Quatre est sur le Pont-Neuf.*

c.1619. Bp CORLET, Elegy on Death of Queen Anne [of Denmark, Consort of Jas. I.] Noe; not a quatch, sad poets; doubt you There is not griefe enough without you? Or that it will asswage ill newes To say, Shee's dead that was your muse.

1708-10. SWIFT, *Polite Conversations*, i. *Lady Smart*... What news Mr. Neverout? *Neverout*. Why, Madam, QUEEN ELIZABETH'S DEAD.

1753. RICHARDSON, *Grandison*, i. 296. We will leave the modern world to themselves, and be QUEEN ELIZABETH'S WOMEN.

1837. BARHAM, *Ingoldsby Legends*, 'Account of a New Play.' Lord Brougham, it appears, isn't DEAD, though QUEEN ANNE IS.

1859. THACKERAY, *Virginians*, lxxiii. 'He was my grandfather's man, and served him in the wars of Queen Anne.'... On which my lady cried petulantly, 'Oh Lord, QUEEN ANNE'S DEAD, I suppose, and we ain't a going into mourning for her.

QUEEN ANNE'S FAN, *subs. phr.* (old).—A SIGHT (*q.v.*): see BACON, THUMB, and FIG.

QUEEN BESS, *subs. phr.* (old).—See quot. and NED STOKES.

1791. *Gent. Mag.*, lxi. 141. The Queen of Clubs is here [Lincolnshire] called QUEEN BESS, perhaps because that Queen, history says, was of a swarthy complexion.

QUEEN CITY, *subs. phr.* (American).—Cincinnati: also PORKOPOLIS and THE PARIS OF AMERICA.

d.1882. LONGFELLOW [BARTLETT]. This song of the vine... The winds and the birds shall deliver To the QUEEN OF THE WEST.

QUEEN CITY OF THE LAKES, *subs. phr.* (America).—Buffalo.

QUEEN CITY OF THE MISSISSIPPI, *subs. phr.* (American).—St. Louis.

QUEEN DICK, *subs. phr.* (old).—Nobody. Hence, IN THE REIGN OF QUEEN DICK = Never; TO THE TUNE OF THE LIFE AND DEATH OF QUEEN DICK = no tune at all.—GROSE (1785).

ENGLISH SYNONYMS.—At Latter Lammas (*see* LAMMAS); on the GREEK CALENDS (*q.v.*); on St. Tib's Eve (*see* TIB'S EVE); on to-morrow-come-never; in the month of five Sundays; when two Fridays (or three Sundays) come together; when Dover and Calais meet; when

Dudman and Ramehead meet; when the world grows honest; when the Yellow River runs clear; on the 31st June (or some other impossible date); once in a blue moon; when two Sundays come in a week; when the devil is blind (or blind drunk); at Doomsday; one of these odd-come-shortlys; when my goose pisses; when the ducks have eaten up the dirt; when pigs fly; on St. Geoffrey's day (GROSE).

FRENCH SYNONYMS.—*Dans une semaine de trois ou quatre jeudis; Mardi s'il fait chaud* (obsolete); *Dimanche après la grande messe; quand les poules pisseront.*

1691-2. *Gentlemen's Journal*, Feb., 25. And then from QUEEN DICK got a patent On Charlton Green to set up a tent.

1864. *Standard*, 13 Dec. A bus driver in altercation with his conductor, who threatened him with paying off soon, replied, Oh yes, IN THE REIGN OF QUEEN DICK.

QUEEN ELIZABETH. 1. See QUEEN ANNE.

2. (thieves').—The street-door key: see BETTY.

QUEEN ELIZABETH'S POCKET-PISTOL, *subs. phr.* (old).—'A brass cannon of a prodigious length at Dover Castle.'—B. E. (c.1696).

1751. SMOLLETT, *Per. Pickle*, xxxiv. The company walked up hill to visit the castle, ... where they saw QUEEN ELIZABETH'S POCKET-PISTOL.

QUEENITE, *subs.* (obsolete).—A partizan of Queen Caroline. [The consort of George IV.] *Cf.* KINGITE.

1834. SOUTHEY, *The Doctor*, Interch., xvi. He thought small beer at that time of some very great patriots and QUEENITES.

QUEEN-OF-HOLES, *subs. phr.* (venery).—The female *pudendum*: see MONOSYLLABLE.

d.1680. ROCHESTER, *On the Charms of Hidden Treasure* [Works (1718), i. 91]. Thou mighty Princess, lovely QUEEN OF HOLES, Whose monarchy the bravest man controls.

QUEEN-OF-THE-DRIPPING PAN, *subs. phr.* (common).—A cook.

QUEEN'S (or KING'S) ALE, *subs. phr.* (old).—The strongest ale brewed.

1574. *Burgh Rec. Glasgow* (1876), I. 25. That thair be na derare aill sauld nor sax penneies the pynt, and that the samyn be KINGIS AILL and verraye guid.

QUEEN'S BAD-BARGAIN (or SHILLING).—See Q. H. B.

QUEEN'S BAYS (THE), *subs. phr.* (military).—The Third Dragoon Guards, now "The Bays." [The Corps were (c.1767) mounted on bay horses; the other heavy regiments (except the Scots Greys) having black.]

QUEEN'S BUS, *subs. phr.* (thieves').—A prison van: BLACK MARIA (*q.v.*); also HER MAJESTY'S CARRIAGE.

QUEEN'S (or KING'S) CARRIAGE (or CUSHION), *subs. phr.* (common).—An improvised seat: made by two persons crossing and clasping hands, the rider holding both bearers round the neck; as BANDY-CHAIR (*q.v.*).

1818. SCOTT, *Heart of Midlothian*, vii. He was now mounted on the hands of two of the rioters, clasped together, so as to form what is called ... the KING'S CUSHION.

QUEEN'S COLLEGE.—See COLLEGE.

QUEEN'S (or KING'S) ENGLISH, *subs. phr.* (colloquial).—The English language correctly written or spoken.

1593. NASH, *Strange Newes*. [GROSART, *Works*, ii. 184.] He must be running on the letter, and abusing the QUEENES ENGLISH without pittie or mercie.

c.1604. SHAKSPEARE, *Merry Wives* (played c.1600). i. 4, 6. Abusing of God's patience and the KING'S ENGLISH.

1836. E. HOWARD, *R. Reefer*, xxxv. They... put THE KING'S ENGLISH to death so charmingly.

1869. ALFORD, *Plea for the Queen's ENGLISH* [Title].

1886. OLIPHANT, *New English*, i. 212. King Henry V. comes before us, and we may now fairly begin to talk of KING'S ENGLISH.

QUEEN'S (or KING'S) HEAD, *subs. phr.* (common). — A postage-stamp.

1843. MONCRIEFF, *Scamps of London*, i. 2. On that occasion you sent me a QUEEN'S HEAD, politely inviting me ... to ... advance you a few hundreds on your personal security.

QUEEN'S-HERB, *subs. phr.* (old).—Snuff.

QUEEN'S (or KING'S) PICTURE (or PORTRAIT), *subs. phr.* (old).—1. Money: generic: see RHINO. Also (2—spec.) = a sovereign; 20/-: hence TO DRAW THE QUEEN'S (or KING'S) PICTURE (or PORTRAIT) = to coin money.—B. E. (c.1696); GROSE (1785).

1632. BROME, *The Court Beggar* [Works (1873), i. 258], v. 2. This picture drawer drew it, and has drawn more of THE KING'S PICTURES than all the limners in the town.

1706. WARD, *Hudibras Redivivus*, I. vii. 26. In short, QUEEN'S PICTURES, by their features, Charm all degrees of human creatures.

1845. DISRAELI, *Sybil*, III. i. I have been making a pound a-week these two months past, but, as I'm a sinner saved, I have never seen THE young QUEEN'S PICTURE yet.

1858. MAYHEW, *Paved with Gold*, III. iii. 265. 'I've brought a couple of bene coves, with lots of THE QUEEN'S PICTURES in their sacks.'

1887. *Judy*, 27 April, 202. While we had the QUEEN'S PORTRAIT in our pockets we were well received everywhere.

QUEEN'S (or KING'S) PIPE.—See PIPE.

QUEEN'S-STICK, *subs. phr.* (common).—A stately person.

QUEEN STREET. TO LIVE IN QUEEN STREET (or AT THE SIGN OF THE QUEEN'S HEAD), *verb. phr.* (old).—To be under PETTICOAT-GOVERNMENT (*q.v.*).—GROSE (1785).

QUEEN'S-WOMAN, *subs. phr.* (military). — A soldier's trull: see TART.

1871. *Royal Commission on Cont. Dis. Act.* [Report]. Some of them are called QUEEN'S WOMEN, and consider themselves a privileged class, and exhibit the printed order to attend the periodical examination as a certificate of health.

QUEER (QUIRE or QUYER), *subs. and adj.* (Old Cant: now in some senses colloquial or accepted).—A generic depreciative: criminal, base, counterfeit, odd (B. E., c.1696, and GROSE, 1785): *cf.* RUM. Later usages are (1) = out of sorts or SEEDY (*q.v.*) from drink, sickness, or accident; (2) unfavourable or unpropitious; and (3) strange or CRANKY (*q.v.*): whence also QUEERS (*subs.*), QUEERED, and QUEERY. Thus (old) QUEER-BAIL = fraudulent bail, STRAW-BAIL (*q.v.*); QUEER-BIRD = a jail-bird, a convict; QUEER-BITCH = 'an odd, out-of-the-way fellow' (GROSE);

QUEER-BIT (-COLE, -MONEY, -PAPER, -SCREENS, -SOFT, or QUEER) = base money, coin or notes (whence QUEER-SHOVER; TO SHOVE THE QUEER = to pass counterfeit money; and QUEER-BIT MAKER = a coiner); QUEER-BLUFFER = a cut-throat innkeeper; QUEER-BOOZE = poor lap, SWIPES (*q.v.*); QUEER-BUNG = an empty purse; QUEER-CHECKER = a swindling box-keeper; QUEER-CARD (FELLOW, or FISH) = a person strange in manner or views (also, in *pl.* = QUEER-CATTLE); QUEER-CLOUT = a handkerchief not worth stealing; QUEER-COLE-MAKER = a coiner; QUEER-COLE-FENCER = a receiver (or utterer) of base coin; QUEER-COVE (-BIRD, -CULL, or -GILL) = (1) a rogue, thief, or gaol-bird, (2) a fop, (3) a fool, and (4) a shabbily-dressed person; QUEER-CUFFIN = (1) a magistrate, a BEAK (*q.v.*), and (2) a churl; QUEER-DEGEN = a poor sword; QUEER-DIVER = a bungling pickpocket; QUEER-DOXY = (1) a jilting jade, and (2) an ill-dressed whore; QUEER-DRAWERS = old or coarse stockings; QUEER-DUKE = (1) a decayed gentleman, and (2) a starveling; QUEER-'EM (QUEER-'UN or QUEER-'UM) = the gallows; QUEER-FUN = a bungled trick; QUEER-KEN (or QUEER-KEN-HALL) = (1) a prison; and (2) a house not worth robbing; QUEER-KICKS = tattered breeches; QUEER-MORT = a dirty drab, a jilting wench, a pocky whore; QUEER-NAB = a shabby hat; QUEER-PEEPER = (1) a mirror of poor quality, and (2), in *pl.* = squinting eyes; QUEER-PLUNGER = a cheat working the drowning man and rescue dodge; QUEER-PRANCER = (1) a

foundered whore, and (2) an old screw; QUEER-ROOSTER = a police spy living among thieves; QUEER-TOPPING = a frowsy wig; QUEER-WEDGE = base gold; QUEER-WHIDDING = a scolding; QUEER-GAMMED = crippled; TO QUEER = to spoil, to get the better of; TO BE QUEERED = to be drunk; TO TIP THE QUEER = to pass sentence; TO BE QUEER TO (or ON) = (1) to rob; (2) to treat harshly; IN QUEER STREET = (1) in a difficulty, (2) = wrong, and (3) = hard-up.—AWDELEY (1560); HARMAN (1567); ROWLANDS (1610); HEAD (1665); B. E. (c.1696); COLES (1724); BAILEY (1726); PARKER (1781); GROSE (1785); VAUX (1812); BEE (1823).

1560. AWDELEY, *Fraternitye of Vacabondes*, 4. A QUIRE BIRD is one that came lately out of prison, and goeth to seeke seruice.

1567. HARMAN, *Caveat*, 85. It is QUYER BOUSE (it is small and naughtye drynke).

1592. GREENE, *Quip* [GROSART, *Works* (18..) xi. 283]. You can lift or nip a bounge like a QUIRE COUE, if you want pence.

1608. DEKKER, *Lanthorne and Candlelight* [GROSART, Works (188), iii. 203]. To the QUIER CUFFING we bing. *Ibid.* 196. In canting they terme a Justice of peace, because he punisheth them belike (by no other name than by QUIER CUFFIN, that is to say, a Churle, or a naughty man). *Ibid.* Then to the QUIER KEN, to scoure the Cramp-ring.

1610. ROWLANDS, *Martin Mark-all*. 'Towre out ben Morts.' And the QUIRE COVES tippe the lowre. *Ibid.* But if we be spid we shall be clyd, And carried to the QUIRKEN HALL.

1622. FLETCHER, *Beggar's Bush*. We the CUFFINS QUERE defy.

1707. SHIRLEY, *Triumph of Wit* [FARMER, *Musa Pedestris* (1896), 35]. Duds and Cheats thou oft hast won, Yet the CUFFIN QUIRE couldst shun.

1712. *Spectator*, No. 474. I beg you would publish this letter, and let me be known all at once for a QUEER FELLOW, and avoided.

1752. SMOLLETT, *Faithful Narrative*, *Wks.* (1901, xii. 184). The very cule who hath a warrant against me for snabbling his peeter and QUEER joseph.

1772. BRIDGES, *Burlesque Homer*, 59. Thyestes died exceeding rich, And left his staff to this QUEER bitch. *Ibid.* 103. Gods are QUEER fish as well as men.

1789. PARKER, *Happy Pair* [*in Life's Painter*]. Though fancy QUEER-GAMM'D smutty Muns Was once my fav'rite man. *Ibid. Bunter's Christening*, v. Such a QUEER procession of seedy brims and kids. *Ibid.* (1800). *Life's Painter*, 144. The QUEER-PLUNGER, the surgeon, and the landlord get upon this lock about ten guineas, and share the whack.

1818. SCOTT, *Heart of Midlothian*, xxv. "He knows my gybe [pass] as well as the jark [seal] of e'er a QUEER CUFFIN [justice of peace] in England."

1821. EGAN, *Life in London*, II. i. The duke and the dealer in QUEER—the lady and her scullion— . . . . they are "all there."

1822. SCOTT, *Fortunes of Nigel*, xxiii. "You would be QUEERED in the drinking of a penny pot of malmseys."

1824. *Sonnets for the Fancy* [*Boxiana*, iii. 622]. The QUEERUM QUEERLY smear'd with dirty black. *Ibid.* The knowing bench had TIPPED her buzer QUEER.

1825. JONES, *True Bottomed Boxer* [*Univ. Songster*, ii. 96]. Till groggy and QUEERY.

1826. BRUTON, *My Mugging Maid* [*Univ. Songster*, iii. 103] Told me, that Hodge's max had QUEERED My mugging maid.

1827. LYTTON, *Pelham*, lxxxfii. Oh, my kiddies, cried Bess . . . you are in QUEER STREET.

1829. MARRYAT, *Frank Mildmay*, xx. 'You Englishmen go to work in a QUEERISH kind of way,' said he, 'you send soldiers to live on an island where none but sailors can be of use.'

1834. AINSWORTH, *Rookwood* (1864), 180. Rum gills and QUEER GILLS. *Ibid.* 'Nix my Doll.' Readily the QUEER SCREENS I could smash.

1836. DICKENS, *Pickwick*, lv. 482. "If you had gone to any low member of the profession, it's my firm conviction . . . that you would have found yourselves IN QUEER STREET before this."

1837. BARHAM, *Ingoldsby Legends*, 'Grey Dolphin.' Things . . . were looking rather QUEERISH.

1837. DISRAELI, *Venetia*. QUEER CUFFIN will be the word yet if we don't tout.

1844. THACKERAY, *Barry Lyndon*, xvii. I could tell tales of scores of QUEER DOINGS there.

1848. DICKENS, *Dombey & Son*, xl. 'A fair friend of ours has removed to QUEER STREET.' 'What do you mean, Major?' 'I mean . . . that you will soon be an orphan-in-law.'

1855. C. KINGSLEY, *Westward Ho.* "'Go away,' I heard her say, 'there's a dear man.' And then something about a 'QUEER CUFFIN,' that's a justice in these carter's thieves' Latin." *Ibid.* (1857) *Two Years Ago*, xiv. I am very high in QUEER STREET just now, ma'am, having paid your bills before I left town.

1862. THACKERAY, *Philip*, iv. 'We've seen his name—the old man's—on some very QUEER PAPER, says B. with a wink to J.

1865. DICKENS, *Our Mutual Friend*, ii. 5. Put it about in the right quarter that you'll buy QUEER BILLS by the lump.

1866. *London Misc.*, 5 May, 202. I don't think I told you all the business. A precious QUEER START it was.

1871. *Figaro*, 20 Feb. He established a saloon in New York which became the headquarters of all the counterfeiters and SHOVERS OF THE QUEER in the country.

1876. HINDLEY, *Cheap Jack*, 218. Consumption was QUEERING him.

1886-96. MARSHALL, *Pomes* [1897], 16. It is true her descent was in some respects QUEER.

1888. *Missouri Republican*, 4 Mar. The police are looking for the QUEER-SHOVER, and are confident of effecting his capture. *Ibid.* 25 Jan. Moulds for making the QUEER having been found on his premises.

1894. MOORE, *Esther Waters*, xli. It was not his habit to notice domestic differences of opinion, especially those in which women had a share—QUEER CATTLE that he knew nothing about.

1898. *Pink 'Un and Pelican*, 240. He hardly ever uttered the spurious coins himself . . . and, consequently, seldom had any QUEER about his person.

2. (old).—*See* quot.

1818. EGAN, *Boxiana*, II. 423 [Note]. QUEER, a term made use of by the dealers in soot, signifying a substitute imposed for the original article, inferior in point of value, 4d. per bushel.

3. (common).—A QUIZ (*q.v.*); a look; a hoax: also QUEER-QUISH. As *verb.* = (1) to ridicule, and (2) to distinguish or divine, TO SPOT (*q.v.*); QUEERER = a QUIZZER (*q.v.*).

*c.*1790. *Old Song*, '*Flash Man of St. Giles's*' [*Busy Bee* . . .] And QUEER'D the flats at thrums, E, O.

1814. COLMAN, *Poetical Vagaries*, 144. A shoulder-knotted puppy, with a grin, QUEERING the thread-bare curate, let him in. *Ibid.* 150. These wooden wits, these quizzers, QUEERERS, smokers.

1818. SCOTT, *Midlothian*, xxvi. "Wha is he, Jeanie?—wha is he?—I haena heard his name yet—Come now, Jeanie, ye are but QUEERING us."

1823. BYRON, *Don Juan*, xi. 19. Who in a row like Tom could lead the van, Booze in the ken, or at the spell ken hustle? Who QUEER a flat?

1844. *Puck*, 13. I'm as happy o'er my beer as anyone that's here, And if need comes can QUEER a bargee again.

1857. *Punch*, 31 Jan., 49. 'Dear Bill, This Stone-Jug.' In the day-rooms the cuffins we QUEER at our ease.

1892. HENLEY and STEVENSON, *Deacon Brodie*, v. 15. Have a QUEER at her phiz. *Ibid.* Tab. II. 2. Let's have another QUEER at the list.

2. (old).—Cute; knowing; FLY (*q.v.*).

1789. PARKER, *Sandman's Wedding*, 'Air,' ii. For he's the kiddy rum and QUEER.

Verb. (common). — 1. *See* subs. 3.

2. (common).—To spoil; to outwit; to perplex. Hence TO QUEER A PITCH (cheap Jacks and showmen) = to spoil a chance of business; TO QUEER THE NOOSE OR STIFLER = to cheat the hangman; TO QUEER FATE = to get the better of the inevitable; TO QUEER THE OGLES = to blacken the eyes.—GROSE (1785); VAUX (1819).

1818. SCOTT, *Midlothian*, xxiii. I think Handie Dandie and I may QUEER THE STIFLER for all that is come and gone. *Ibid.* If the b—— QUEERS THE NOOSE, that silly cull will marry her.

1819. *Old Song*, 'Young Prig' [FARMER, *Musa Pedestris* (1896), 83]. There no QUEERING fate, sirs.

1836. MILNER, *Turpin's Ride to York*, i. 2. I can QUEER these brither blades of the road.

1843. MONCRIEFF, *Scamps of London*, ii. 3. I'll QUEER them yet.

1875. FROST, *Circus Life*, 278. Any interruption of their feats, such as an accident, or the interference of a policeman, is said to QUEER THE PITCH.

1886. *Referee*, 21 Feb. Endeavours made to QUEER A rival's or an antagonist's PITCH. *Ibid.* (1889), 26 May. Why should not our non-professors' little game be QUEERED?

1891. *Morning Advertiser*, 27 Mar. His PITCH being QUEERED he marched to another point, but here he found the police in possession.

1900. *Free Lance*, 6 Oct., 20, 2. That's the third show she's QUEERED this season. I believe she'd sink a ship.

QUEER (FINE, ODD, or TIGHT) AS DICK'S (or NICK'S) HATBAND, *phr.* (old).—Out of order or sorts, not knowing why: also AS QUEER AS DICK'S HATBAND THAT WENT NINE TIMES ROUND AND WOULDN'T MEET.—GROSE (1785).

QUEER-ROOST. TO DOSS (or SLEEP) ON THE QUEER-ROOST, *verb. phr.* (old).—To live as man and wife; to live TALLY (*q.v.*); TO DAB (*q.v.*) IT UP.

1800. PARKER, *Life's Painter*, 120. We DORSED some time UPON THE QUEER ROOST.

QUEINT. *See* QUAINT.

QUEME. *See* QUIM.

QUENCHER, *subs.* (common).—A drink; a GO (*q.v.*). Also MODEST QUENCHER.

1840. DICKENS, *Old Curiosity Shop*, xxxv. A MODEST QUENCHER.

1856. HUGHES, *Tom Brown's School-Days*, I. i. We must really take a MODEST QUENCHER, for the down air is provocative of thirst.

1888. *Sporting Life*, 7 Dec. Oh! the L.A.C. are jovial souls, They quaff the MODEST QUENCHER.

1901. NISBET, *Hermes*, 62. Come below and have a QUENCHER.

QUERIER, *subs.* (old).—*See* quot.

1851. MAYHEW, *Lond. Lab.*, ii. 405. The "Gumblers" or QUERIERS, that is to say, those [chimney-sweepers] who solicit custom in an irregular manner, by knocking at the doors of houses and such like.

QUESTION. TO QUESTION A HORSE, *verb. phr.* (racing).—To test a horse before a race.

1890. *Lic. Vict. Gaz.*, 7 Nov. He is a thorough judge of horses, knows what work they want, and is not afraid of ASKING THEM A QUESTION, like some trainers we know of.

See POP.

QUEYNTE. *See* QUAINT.

QUI. TO GET THE QUI, *verb. phr.* (printers').—To be dismissed; to get a *quietus*.

QUIBBLE. *See* QUIP.

QUICK. QUICK AND NIMBLE, MORE LIKE A BEAR THAN A SQUIRREL, *phr.* (old).—A jeer on leisurely movement. — GROSE (1823).

See STICKS and TRIGGER.

QUICKENING-PEG, *subs. phr.* (venery). — The *penis*: also QUICKENER: *see* PRICK.

1653. URQUHART, *Rabelais*, III. Prol. In the name of . . . the four hips that engendered you, and to the QUICKENING PEG which at that time conjoined them.

QUICUNQUE VULT. *See* ATHANASIAN WENCH.

QUID, *subs.* (common). — 1. A sovereign; 20/-: formerly a guinea. Also, in *pl.*, generic for money: *see* RHINO. — B. E. (*c.*1696); GROSE (1785); PARKER (1789); VAUX (1819). Fr. *de quoi* and *quibus*.

1819. MOORE, *Tom Crib's Memorial*, 27. If QUIDS should be wanting, to make the match good.

1834. AINSWORTH, *Rookwood*, III. ix. Zoroaster took long odds that the match was off; offering a bean to half a QUID.

1857. DICKENS, *All Year Round.* 'Take yer two QUID to one,' adds the speaker, picking out a stout farmer.

1870. HAZLEWOOD and WILLIAMS, *Leave it to Me*, i. Sarah, I'm going to be rich, I shall have money—lots of money—QUIDS, QUIDS, QUIDS!

1883. *Pall Mall Gaz.*, 27 Ap., 4, 2. £4 13s. is announced in the plate, amid cheers and exhortations to "make it up to five QUID."

1900. WHITE, *West End*, 17. 'I say, Rupert, could you lend me a couple of QUID?

2. (common).—*See* quot. 1748: as *verb.* = to chew. — GROSE (1785).

1748. DYCHE, *Dict.*, s.v. QUID, so much tobacco as a person can take between his thumb and two fore-fingers, when cut small, in order to put into his mouth to chew.

1771. SMOLLETT, *Humphry Clinker*, 57. A large roll of tobacco was presented by way of dessert, and every individual took a comfortable QUID.

1836. MICHAEL SCOTT, *Cruise of Midge*, 103. Wait until your wound gets better. Surely you have not a QUID in your cheek now?

1889. *Daily Telegraph*, 1 Jan. A deleterious custom—that of chewing QUIDS.

3. (venery).—The female *pudendum*: *see* MONOSYLLABLE.

Verb. (American).—To puzzle; to embarrass.

See QUIP.

QUIDNUNC, *subs.* (colloquial).—(1) A person curious, or professing, to know everything. [Latin = 'What now?']. Hence (2) a politician. [Popularised by a character in Murphy's *Upholsterer* (1758).]

1709. STEELE, *Tatler*, No. 10. "The insignificancy of my manners to the rest of the world, makes the laughers call me a QUIDNUNC, a phrase which I neither understand, nor shall never enquire what they mean by it.'

1729. POPE, *Dunciad*, i. 270. This the great Mother dearer held than all The clubs of QUIDNUNCS, or her own Guildhall.

1818. MOORE, *Fudge Family*, pt. 81. Or QUIDNUNCS, on Sunday, just fresh from the barber's Enjoying their news.

1886. *Athenæum*, 6 Nov. 595, 1. What the masses believed . . . and what the QUIDNUNCS of London repeated, may here be found.

QUID PRO QUO, *phr.* (colloquial).—A tit for tat; a ROWLAND FOR AN OLIVER (*q.v.*): an equivalent. Also QUID FOR QUOD. *Cf.* QUIP.

1565. CALFHILL, *Answ. to Martiall* [Parker Soc.]. [OLIPHANT, *New Eng.* i. 571. Among the Romance words are . . . QUID PRO QUO, Tom Fool . . .]

1592. SHAKSPEARE, *1 Hen. IV.* v. 3. I cry for mercy, 'tis but QUID FOR QUO.

1608. MIDDLETON, *Mad World*, ii. Let him trap me in gold, and I'll lap him in lead; QUID PRO QUO.

1611. CHAPMAN, *May-day*, i. 2. Women of themselves . . . would return QUID FOR QUOD still, but we are they that spoil 'em.

1772. BRIDGES, *Burlesque Homer*, 262. Unless she lets her conscience go, And gives the knave a QUID PRO QUO.

1820. COMBE, *Syntax*, II. iii. I shall be able With all fair reasoning to bestow What you will find a QUID PRO QUO.

1890. GRANT ALLEN, *Tents of Shem*, x. A QUID PRO QUO, his friend suggested jocosely, emphasising the QUID with a facetious stress.

QUIEN, *subs.* (common).—A dog.

1861. READE, *Cloister and Hearth* iv. 'Curse these quiens,' said he.

QUIER. *See* QUEER, *passim.*

QUIET. ON THE QUIET. *See* Q. T.

AS QUIET AS A WASP IN ONE'S NOSE, *phr.* (colloquial).—Uneasy; restless.—RAY (1670).

QUIETUS (or **QUIETUS EST**), *subs.* (colloquial).—A form of finality; a settling blow; death, &c.: originally = a quittance or pardon.

*c.*1537. LATIMER, *Remains* [Parker Soc.], 309. [You will] have your QUIETUS EST.

1596. SHAKSPEARE, *Hamlet*, iii. 1. "Who would fardels bear . . . When he himself might his QUIETUS make With a bare bodkin?"

1772. BRIDGES, *Burlesque Homer*, 317. Nestor's in danger, stop and meet us, Or Hector gives him his QUIETUS.

1891. *Lic. Vic. Gaz.*, 3 Ap. After a contest which lasted for the best part of an hour and a-half, M'Carthy received his QUIETUS.

1901. CLEMENT SCOTT [in *Free Lance*, 19 Oct., 94, 1.] What am I to do with the whisky? It may do me good, but, on the other hand, it may give me an everlasting headache, or my QUIETUS.

QUIFF, *subs.* (general).—A satisfactory result: spec. an end obtained by means not strictly conventional. As *verb.* = to do well; to jog along merrily. Also (tailors') TO QUIFF IN THE PRESS = to change a breast pocket from one side to the other; TO QUIFF THE BLADDER = to conceal baldness: *cf.* QUIFF (military) = a small flat curl on the temple.

Verb. (venery).—To copulate: *see* RIDE.—GROSE (1785).

*c.*1709. *Old Ballad* [DURFEY, *Pills* (1709), iv. 18]. By QUIFFING with Cullies three Pound she had got.

QUI-HI, *subs. phr.* (Anglo-Indian).—An English resident or official in Bengal.

1855. THACKERAY, *Newcomes*, lxii. The old boys, the old generals, the old colonels, the old QUI-HIS . . . came and paid her homage.

QUILL, *verb.* (Winchester College).—To curry favour; hence, TO BE QUILLED = to be pleased; QUILLER (or QUILSTER) = a toady (Fr. *suceur*): *cf.* SUCKER.

PHRASES.—UNDER THE QUILL = under discussion: spec. in writing; TO CARRY A GOOD QUILL = to write well; IN A QUILL = in a push; TO PISS IN A QUILL (Irish proverb: 'They pissed IN THE SAME QUILL') = to be agreed to act as one; TO PISS THROUGH QUILL = to write.

1594. SHAKSPEARE, *2 Hen. VI.*, i. 3, 1. My masters let's stand close; my lord protector will come this way by and by, and then we may deliver our supplications IN THE QUILL.

1740. NORTH, *Examen*, 70. So strangely did Papist and Fanatic or . . . the Anti-court Party PISS IN A QUILL; agreeing in all things that tended to create troubles and disturbances.

*d.*1678. MARVELL, *Poems* [MURRAY], 188. I'll have a council shall sit always still, And give me a license to do what I will; and two secretaries shall PISS THROUGH A QUILL.

1692. HACKET, *Life of Williams*, ii. 28. The subject which is now UNDER THE QUILL is the Bishop of Lincoln.

QUILL-DRIVER (-MAN, -MONGER, -MERCHANT; BROTHER, or KNIGHT OF THE QUILL), *subs. phr.* (common).—A penman—author, journalist, clerk, or (racing) bookmaker: Fr. *rond de cuir*. Also HERO OF THE QUILL = a distinguished author. Hence QUILL-DRIVING = clerking; TO DRIVE THE QUILL = to write.—GROSE (1785).

1680. *Observ. 'Curse ye Meroz,'* 7. This Aphorism is but borrowed from another BROTHER OF THE QUILL.

1691-2. *Gent. Jrnl.*, 2 Mar. I know some of your sturdy tuff KNIGHTS OF THE QUILL, your old Soakers at the Cabbaline Font.

1719. DURFEY, *Pills, &c.*, iv. 319. When Inns of Court Rakes, And QUILL-DRIVING Prigs.

*d.*1745. SWIFT, *Epil. to Play for Benefit of Irish Weavers* [DAVIES]. Their brother QUILL-MEN, workers for the stage, For sorry stuffe can get a crown a page.

1761. MURPHY, *The Citizen*, 'Dram. Pers.' QUILDRIVE, clerk to old Philpot.

1827. LYTTON, *Pelham*, xlix. Tolerably well known, I imagine, to the GENTLEMEN OF THE QUILL.

1836. M. SCOTT, *Tom Cringle*, vii. A dozen clerks were QUILL-DRIVING. *Ibid.*, *Cruise of the Midge*, 3. I had much greater license allowed me than . . . any of my fellow QUILL-DRIVERS.

1853. KINGSLEY, *Hypatia*, xii. Some sort of slave's QUILL-DRIVING.

1885. *Weekly Echo*, 5 Sep. This most eccentric of QUILL-DRIVERS gets up his facts in a slap-dash fashion.

1899. BESANT, *Orange Girl*, 25. An overwhelming disgust fell upon my soul as I thought of the . . . long hours . . . DRIVING THE QUILL all the day.

QUILL-PIPES. *See* QUAIL-PIPE BOOTS.

QUILLET. *See* QUIBBLE.

QUILT, *subs.* (old).—A fat man.

1598. SHAKSPEARE, *1 Hen. IV.*, iv. 2, 53. How now, Bloun Jack? How now, QUILT.

THE QUILT, *subs. phr.* (American).—The Union Jack: *cf.* RAG.

Verb. (common).—To beat; TO TAN (*q.v.*): hence QUILTING = a rope's-ending.—GROSE (1785).

1821. EGAN, *Real Life*, I. 351. They were a set of cowardly rascals, and deserved QUILTING.

*d.*1828. RANDALL'S *Diary*, 'To Martin.' Turn to and QUILT the Nonparel.

1840. COCKTON, *Valentine Vox*, xii. "Bless his little soul, he shall have a QUILTING yet."

QUILTING, *subs.* (obsolete American).—A patchworking-party with a spree at the end: *see* BEE.

1825. NEAL, *Bro. Jonathan*, I. 7. 'Where is Edith?' said he, at last. 'Gone to a QUILTIN.'

1843. *Maj. Jones' Courtship*, viii. My time is tuck up with so many things . . . . goin to QUILTENS and partys of one kind another.

1847. HOBB, *Squatter Life*, 94. As sharp as lightnin', and as persuadin' as a young gal at a QUILTIN'.

QUIM (QUEME, QUIMSBY, QUIMBOX, or QUIN), *subs.* (venery).—The female *pudendum*: *see* MONOSYLLABLE. Hence QUIM-STAKE (or WEDGE) = the *penis*: *see* PRICK; QUIM-STICKER = a whoremonger; *see* MUTTON-MONGER; QUIM-STICKING (QUIMMING, or QUIM-WEDGING) = copulation: *see* GREENS; QUIMBUSH (-WIG, or -WHISKERS) = the pubic hair: *see* FLEECE.—GROSE (1785).

1613. *Old Play in Rawl. MS.* (Bodleian), 'Tumult' [HALLIWELL]. "I tell you, Hodge, in sooth it was not cleane, it was as black as ever was Malkin's QUEME."

*c.*1707. *Broadside Ballad*, 'The Harlot Unmask'd' [FARMER, *Merry Songs and Ballads* (1897), iv. 111]. Tho' her Hands they are red, and her Bubbies are coarse, Her QUIM, for all that, may be never the worse. *Ibid.* On her QUIM and herself she depends for support.

1847. HALLIWELL, *Archaic . . . Words*, s.v. QUEME . . . (3) the same as the old word queint, which, as I am informed by a correspondent at Newcastle, is still used in the North of England by the colliers and common people.

QUINSEY. *See* HEMPEN-SQUINCEY.

QUIP, *subs.* (old colloquial).—1. A play upon words; a jesting or evasive reply; a retort; and (2) a trifling critic.—B. E. (*c.*1696); GROSE (1787). Also as *verb.* = (1) to trifle; to jest; to censure; and (2) to criticise. Variants more or less allied in meaning and usage are conveniently grouped: *e.g.*, QUIB, QUILL, QUIBBLE, QUIDDLE, QUIBLET (also, mod. Amer.: the patter between turns in negro minstrelsy), QUIDLET, QUILLET, QUIBLIN, and QUIDLIN; SIR QUIBBLE QUEERE (QUIBBLER, QUIPPER, or QUIDDLER) = a trifler or SHATTER-BRAIN (*q.v.*); QUIBBLING (or QUIDDLING) = uncertain, unsteady, or mincing (of gait); QUIDDIFICAL = triflingly.

1420. ANDREW of WYNTOUN, *Chronicle* [LAING (1872) . . .]. [OLIPHANT, *New English*, i. 229. There is the Celtic word QUHYPE (QUIP = a quick turn or flirt.

1571. EDWARDS, *Damon & Pitheas* [DODSLEY (Old Plays, 1744), i. 279]. Set up your huffing base, and we will QUIDDLE upon it.

1583. TARLETON, *Jests* [HALLIWELL (1844) 132]. [OLIPHANT, *New Eng.*, ii. 13. The word QUIP gets a new sense, and is used of words.]

1542. UDAL, *Erasmus's Apoth.*, 139. Diogenes, mocking soch QUIDIFICALL trifles . . . said, Sir Plato, Your table and your cuppe I see very well, but as for your tabletee and your cupitee I see none soche.

1587. NASHE, *Greene's Menaphon*, Int. And here . . . some desperate QUIPPER will canuaze my proposed comparison.

1591. LYLY, *Alex. and Campaspe* [DODSLEY, Old Plays (REED), ii. 13]. Why, what's a QUIP? We great girders call it a short saying of a sharp wit, with a bitter sense in a sweet word.

*d.*1592. R. GREENE [*Harl. Misc.* viii. 383]. Are you pleasant or peevish that you QUIP with such briefe girdes.

1594. SHAKSPEARE, *Love's Labour's Lost*, iv. 3. "Oh, some authority how to proceed; Some tricks, some QUILLETS, how to cheat the devil." *Ibid.* (1595), *Two Gentlemen*, iv. 3. Her sudden QUIPS, the least whereof would quell a lover's hopes. *As You Like It*, v. 4. If I sent him word again it was not well cut, he would send me word, he cut it to please himself. This is called the QUIP modest.

1596. SPENSER, *Fairy Queen*, VI. vii. 44. The more he laughs, and does her closely QUIP.

1605. JONSON, CHAPMAN, &c., *Eastward Ho*, iii. 2. Go to, old QUIPPER; forth with thy speech. *Ibid.* 'Tis a trick rampant—'tis a very QUIBLYN.

1609. *Man in the Moone*, sig. cii. A thing repugnant to philosophy, and working miraculous matters, a QUILLIT above nature.

1611. BARRY, *Ram Alley* [DODSLEY, *Old Plays* (REED), v. 427]. Nay, good sir Throate, forbear your QUILLETS now.

1633. FLETCHER, *Tamer Tamed*, iv. 1. Let her leave her bobs . . . and her QUILLETS, She is as nimble that way as an eel.

1637. MILTON, *L'Allegro*, 27. QUIPS and cranks and wanton wiles.

1656. GOFFE, *Careless Shepherdess*, Prel. His part has all the wit, For none speakes, carps, and QUIBBLES beside him.

1705. WARD, *Hud. Rediv.*, I. vii. 6. Such frothy QUIBBLES and cunnunders.

1805. A. SCOTT, *Poems*, 65. 'The Dutch hae taken Hollan', The other, dark anent the QUIB, Cry'd, O sic doolfu' sonnets!

1856. EMERSON, *Eng. Traits*, vi. The Englishman is very petulant and precise about his accommodation at inns, and on the roads; a QUIDDLE about his toast and his chop.

*d.*1859. MACAULAY, *Mill on Govt.* QUIBBLING about self-interest and motives . . . is but a poor employment for a grown man.

QUIRE. *See* QUEER, *passim.*

QUIRK, *subs.* (old legal: now recognised).—An evasion; a shift; a QUIP (*q.v.*). Hence QUIRKIST = shifty; quibbling (B. E., *c.*1696); QUIRKS AND QUILLETTS = tricks and devices; QUIRKLUM (JAMIESON: 'a cant term') = a puzzle; QUIRKY = sportively tricky.

1538-50. [ELLIS, *Original Letters*]. [OLIPHANT, *New English*, i. 508. There is the Celtic QUIRK, connected with law.]

1600. SHAKSPEARE, *Much Ado*, ii. 3. Some odd QUIRKS and remnants of wit. *Ibid.* (1609), *Pericles*, iv. 6. She has me her QUIRKS, her reasons.

1828. BEE, *Living Picture of London*, 251. Hear them laying QUIRKISH bets that are to take in the unwary.

QUISBY, *subs.* (old).—An eccentric; a QUEER card (*q.v.*).

1838. DESMOND, *Stage Struck*, 4. That old QUISBY has certainly contrived to slink out of the house.

Adj. and *adv.* (common).—Bankrupt; drunk; upset; out-of-sorts; wrong: generic for misadventure.

1887. *Punch*, 30 July, 45. Arter this things appeared to go QUISBY.

1888. MILLIKEN, *'Arry Ballads*, 27. There's bound to be lots on 'em QUISBY *Ibid.*, 80. Makes me feel quite QUISBY.

TO DO QUISBY, *verb. phr.* (common).—*See* quot.

1851-61. MAYHEW, *Lond. Lab.*, &c., III. 219. One morning when we had been DOING QUISBY, that is stopping idle.

QUI-TAM, *subs. phr.* (old).—*See* quot. 1864. Hence QUI-TAM HORSE = 'one that will both carry and draw' (GROSE, 1785).

1782. PARKER, *Humorous Sketches*, 189. A lawyer [speaks of] John Doe and Richard Roe, terms, vacations, QUITAMS, processes and executions.

1843. MONCRIEFF, *Scamps of London*, ii. 2. The QUITAM LAWYER, the quack doctor.

1864. HOTTEN, *Slang Dict.*, s.v. QUI-TAM, a solicitor. He who, *i.e.*, "he who, as much for himself as for the King," seeks a conviction, the penalty for which goes half to the informer and half to the Crown. The term would, therefore, with greater propriety, be applied to a spy than to a solicitor.

QUIUS-KIUS, *intj.* (theatrical).—A warning to silence.

QUIVER, *subs.* (venery).—The female *pudendum*: *see* MONOSYLLABLE.

*c.*1600-20. *Old Ballad*, 'A Man's Yard' [FARMER, *Merry Songs and Ballads* (1897), i. 11]. And every wench, by her owne will, Would keep [it] in her QUIUER still.

QUIZ (or **QUOZ**), *subs.* (colloquial).—1. A puzzle; a jest; a hoax: also QUIZZIFICATION; (2) a jesting or perplexing critic; also QUIZZER; and (3) any odd-looking person or thing. As *verb.* = to banter; to puzzle; to confound. Hence QUIZZICAL (or QUIZZICALLY) = jocose or humorous; TO QUIZZIFY = to make ridiculous.—GROSE (1785); BEE (1823).

1749. SMOLLETT, *Gil Blas* [ROUTLEDGE], 147. Women of light character . . . play the comedy of love in many masks, . . . as they fall in with the QUIZ, the coxcomb, or the bully.

1797. D'ARBLAY, *Diary*, vi. 138. I cannot suffer you to make such a QUIZ of yourself. *Ibid.*, vi. 187. These and his spout of satire are mere QUIZZINESS. Ibid., *Carmilla* (1796), VII. ix. What does the old QUOZ mean?

1797. COLMAN, *Heir at Law*, iv. 3. *Dick.* What a damn'd gig you look like. *Pangloss.* A gig! Umph; that's an Eton phrase—the Westminsters call it QUIZ.

1803. C. K. SHARPE [*Correspondence* (1888), i. 17]. Billy Bamboozle, a QUIZZER and wit.

1803. EDGEWORTH, *Belinda*, ix. You have taken a fancy to the old QUIZICAL fellow. *Ibid.*, xi. After all, my dear, the whole may be a QUIZZIFICATION of Sir Philip's.

1815. SCOTT, *Guy Mannering*, iii. What were then called bites and bams, since denominated hoaxes and QUIZZES.

1818. AUSTEN, *Northanger Abbey*, 33. Where did you get that QUIZ of a hat? it makes you look like an old witch.

1830. POOLE, *Turning the Tables*, I. I'll QUIZ his heart out.

1840. LYTTON, *Paul Clifford*, vi. Stab my vitals, but you are a comical QUIZ.

1855. THACKERAY, *Newcomes*, lix. The landlord of the "King's Arms" looked knowing and QUIZZICAL. *Ibid.*, lxii. I don't think it's kind of you to QUIZ my boy for doing his duty to his Queen and to his father too, sir.

1856. C. BRONTE, *Professor*, iii. He was not odd—no QUIZ—yet he resembled no one else I had ever seen before.

1837. CARLYLE, *Diamond Necklace*, xvi. How many fugitive leaves QUIZZICAL, imaginative, or at least mendacious, were flying about in newspapers.

1902. HENLEY [HAZLITT, *Works*, I. xxi.]. And dead is Burke, and Fox is dead, and Byron, most QUIZZICAL of lords.

2. (American students').—A weekly oral examination: also spec., notes made and passed on to another: hence QUIZ-class, SURGERY-QUIZ, LEGAL-QUIZ, &c.; QUIZ-MASTER = a tutor or COACH (*q.v.*). Also as *verb.* = (1) to attend, and (2) to conduct such a class.

3. (general).—A monocular eye-glass: also QUIZZING-GLASS.

1843. THACKERAY, *Irish Sketch Book*, xxiv. The dandy not uncommonly finishes off with a horn QUIZZING-GLASS.

Verb. (common).—1. See subs.

2. (thieves').—To watch; to NOSE (q.v.); to NARK (q.v.).

QUOCKERWODGER, subs. (common).—A puppet on strings; hence (2) a tool; an agent or âme damnée; a dependant.

QUOD (or QUAD), subs. (common).—A prison: hence QUODDED = imprisoned; QUOD-COVE = a turnkey.—B. E. (c.1696); HALL (1714); GROSE (1785); VAUX (1812).

1751. FIELDING, Amelia, I. iv. He is a gambler, and committed for cheating at play; there is not such a pickpocket in the whole QUOD.

1804. TARRAS, Poems, 97. By the cuff he's led along, An' settl'd wi' some niccum, In QUAD yon night.

1834. AINSWORTH, Rookwood, III. v. The knucks in QUOD did my schoolmen play.

1836. DISRAELI, Henrietta Temple vi. xx. Fancy a nob like you being sent to QUOD.

1855. TAYLOR, Still Waters, ii. 2 A fellow who risks ... the spinning of a roulette wheel is a gambler, and may be QUODDED by the first beak that comes handy.

d.1863. THACKERAY, Ballads of Policeman X., 'Eliza Davis.' And that Pleaseman able-bodied Took this voman to the cell; To the cell vere she was QUODDED, In the Close of Clerkenwell.

1871. M. ARNOLD, Friendship's Garland, vii. Do you really mean to maintain that a man can't put old Diggs in QUOD for snaring a hare, without all this elaborate apparatus of Roman law.

1886. BRADDON, Mohawks, ii. "I got QUODDED and narrowly escaped a rope.

1900. KIPLING, Stalky & Co., 31. You got off easy considerin'. If I d been Dabney I swear I'd ha' QUODDED you.

QUODGER, phr. (legal).—QUO JURE = by what law.

QUODLING, subs. (old).—A fledgling; a GREEN-'UN (q.v.). [GIFFORD: 'A young QUOD, alluding to the quids and quods of lawyers.' NARES: 'Dol intended to call Dapper, a young raw apple, fit for nothing without dressing: codlings are particularly so used when unripe.'] QUILL-DRIVER (q.v.): cf. QUOD.

1610. BEN JONSON Alchemist, i. 1. Dol. A fine young QUODLING. Face. O, my lawyer's clerk, I lighted on last night.

QUONIAM, subs. (old).—1. See quot.

c.1620. HEALY, Disc. of New World, 69. Out of Can, QUONIAM, or jourdain. Ibid., Marginal Note. A QUONIAM is a cup well known in Drink-allia.

2. (venery).—The female pudendum: see MONOSYLLABLE.

QUOT (QUOT- or COT-QUEAN), subs. (old).—See QUEAN.

1647. BEAUMONT and FLETCHER, Love's Cure, ii. 2. Don Lucio? Don QUOT-QUEAN, Don Spinster, wear a petticoat still.

QUOTE (or QUOT.), subs. (literary). A quotation.

1888. Sportsman, 29 Dec. Will shortly make her reappearance on the London stage, and he also sends a list of QUOTES and her portrait.

QUOZ. See QUIZ.

QUYER. See QUEER, passim.

See THREE R's.

RABBIT, subs. (old).—1. A term of contempt: hence RABBIT-SUCKER (i.e., a sucking rabbit) = an innocent fool; 'Young Unthrifts taking up Goods upon Tick at excessive Rates.'—B. E. (c.1696); GROSE (1785). Cf. POET-SUCKER.

1598. SHAKSPEARE, 1 Henry IV., ii. 4. Hang me up by the heels for a RABBIT-SUCKER. Ibid., 2 Hen. IV., ii. 2. Away you whoreson, upright RABBIT, away!

1609. DEKKER, Lanthorne and Candlelight [GROSART, Wks. (1886), iii. 233]. This hearbe being chewd downe by the RABBIT-SUCKERS almost kils their hearts, and is worse to them than nabbing on the neckes to Connies.

2. (old).—A wooden drinking can: also RABIT.—B. E. (c.1696); GROSE (1785).

1697. Praise of Yorkshire Ale, I. Strong beer in RABITS and cheating penny cans, Three pipes for two-pence and such like trepans.

3. (American).—A rowdy: also DEAD-RABBIT and DEAD-DUCK. [A gang of roughs paraded New York in 1848, carrying dead rabbits and ducks as emblems of victory.]

4. (political).—See quot.

1866. House of Commons Election Commission [Report]. Out of £50 ... he had paid a number of rooks and RABBITS. ... In general it was stated that "the RABBITS were to work in the burrow and the rooks to make a noise at the public meetings."

5. (racing).—See quot. and IN AND OUT.

1882. Standard, 3 Sep. Milan, though somewhat of a RABBIT, as a horse that runs 'in and out' is sometimes called.

6. (old).—A new-born babe. Whence RABBIT-CATCHER = a midwife.—GROSE (1785).

Verb. (old).—Usually as intj. = Confound it! Also ODSRABBIT! and DRABBIT! cf. DRAT = God, rot it! [OD, 'D = God + RABBIT = rot it!]

1742. FIELDING, Joseph Andrews. 'RABBIT the fellow!' cries he.

1748. SMOLLETT, Roa. Random, xviii. RABBIT IT! I have forgot the degree.

LIVE RABBIT, subs. phr. (venery).—The penis: see PRICK: also RABBIT-PIE = a whore: see TART. Whence to SKIN THE LIVE RABBIT (or HAVE A BIT OF RABBIT-PIE) = to copulate: see GREENS and RIDE.

PHRASES.—TO BUY THE RABBIT = to get the worst of a bargain; FAT AND LEAN, LIKE A RABBIT (see quot. 1708-10); TO GO RABBIT-HUNTING WITH A DEAD FERRET = to undertake a business with improper or useless means (RAY, 1760): also see WELSH-RABBIT.

1708-10. SWIFT, Polite Conversation, 1. Col. I am LIKE A RABBIT, fat and lean in Four-and-twenty Hours. Ibid. Lady Smart. ... The Man and his Wife are coupled LIKE RABBETS, a fat and a lean; he's as fat as a Porpus, and she's one of Pharaoh's lean kine.

1825. NEAL, Bro. Jonathan, II. xv. Keep a civil tongue in your head; or you'll BUY THE RABBITS. Ibid., xviii. If that air invoice aint ready soon, thee'll BUY THE RABBIT, I guess.

RABBIT-PIE SHIFTER, subs. phr. (streets').—A policeman: see BEAK.

c.1870. Music Hall Song [S. J. & C.]. Never to take notice of vulgar nicknames, such as "slop," "copper," RABBIT-PIE SHIFTER, "peeler."

RABBIT-SKIN (or CAT-SKIN), subs. phr. (University).—An academical hood. Hence, TO GET ONE'S RABBIT-SKIN = to win the B.A. degree. [The trimming is of rabbit's fur.]

RABITTER, subs. (Winchester College).—A blow with the side of the hand, on the back of the neck: as in killing a rabbit.

RABBLE, subs., adj. and verb. (once and still literary).—Generic for confusion.—B. E. (c.1696).

RABID-BEAST, subs. phr. (American cadets').—A new-comer who sets up against the authority of his elders: cf. REPTILE.

RABSHAKLE, subs. (old).—A profligate.

RACHEL, verb. (obsolete).—To renovate; to make young again. [From Madame Rachel, the "beautiful for ever" swindler.]

RACK, subs. (Winchester).—1. A chop from the neck or loin. [RACK (HALLIWELL) = the neck of mutton or pork; (JOHNSON) = a neck of mutton cut for the table.]

2. (slaughterers').—See quot.

1851. MAYHEW, Lond. Lab., i. 189. The bones (called RACKS by the knackers) are chopped up and boiled.

PHRASES.—TO LIVE AT RACK AND MANGER = to live on the best gratis: TO LIE AT RACK AND MANGER = (1) 'to live hard' (B. E. c.1696), and (2) 'to be in great disorder' (GROSE, 1785); TO GO TO RACK AND RUIN = to go utterly wrong; ON THE RACK = (1) in a state of tension, and (2) on the move, SHINNING ROUND (Amer. spec. for money); TO RACK OFF = (1) to relate, to tell, and (2) TO PISS (q.v.).

1586-1606. WARNER, Albion's England, viii. 4, 200. A queane corrival with a queene! Nay KEPT AT RACK AND MANGER.

1599. NASHE, Leuten Stuffe [Harl. Misc.], vi. 165]. The herring is such a choleric food that whoso ties himself TO RACK AND MANGER to it shall have a child that will be a soldier before he loses his first teeth.

1605. CHAPMAN, All Fools [REED, Old Plays (17 . .) iv. 136]. To LIE AT RACK AND MANGER with your wedlock, And brother.

1628. Life of Robin Goodfellow [HALLIWELL]. When Vertue was a country maide, And had no skill to set up trade, She came up with a carriers jade, And lay AT RACKE and MANGER.

1690. Pagan Prince [NARES]. The Palatine ... LAY AT RACK AND MANGER.

1700. CONGREVE, Way of the World, ii. 1. I wou'd have him ever to continue UPON THE RACK of Feare and Jealousy.

d.1703. PEPYS, Diary [Century]. We fell to talk largely of the want of some persons understanding to look after the business, but all GOES TO RACK.

1722. STEELE, Conscious Lovers, iv. 1. Hand and Heart are ON THE RACK about my son.

1749. SMOLLETT, Gil Blas [ROUTLEDGE], 197. I wrote down in my pocket-book such anecdotes as I meant to RACK OFF in the course of the day.

1843. CARLYLE, Past and Present, ♣. i. A blustering, dissipated human figure ... tearing out the bowels of St. Edmundsbury Convent ... in the most ruinous way by LIVING AT RACK AND MANGER there.

RACKABIMUS, subs. (Scots').—See quot.

1808. JAMIESON, Dict. s.v. Rackabimus. A sudden or unexpected stroke or fall; a cant term ... It resembles RACKET.

RACKABONES (or RACK-OF-BONES, subs. (American). — A skinny person or animal; a BAG OF BONES (q.v.); a SHAPE (q.v.).

1862. New York Tribune, 13 June. He is a little afraid that this mettlesome charger cannot be trusted going down hill; otherwise he would let go of the old RACKABONES that hobbles behind.

RACKET, subs. (old).—1. A confusion, sportive or the reverse: whence (2) generic for disorder, clamour or noisy merriment (B. E., c.1696); also (3) any matter or happening (GROSE, 1785); also = a general verb of action. Thus, to RACKET ABOUT (ROUND, THROUGH, &c.) = to go the rounds at night; TO GO ON THE RACKET = to SPREE (q.v.); TO RAISE A RACKET = to make a disturbance; 'WHAT'S THE RACKET?' = 'What's going on?'; TO BE IN A RACKET = to be part in a design; TO WORK THE RACKET = to carry on a matter (see quots. 1785 and 1851, and cf. RIG, LAY, &c.: whence RACKET-MAN [thieves'] = a thief); TO STAND THE RACKET = (1) to pay a score, and (2) to take the consequences; WITHOUT RACKET = without a murmur; TO TUMBLE TO THE RACKET = (1) to understand, for TWIG (q.v.), and (2) see quot. 1890; RACKETY (or RACKETTY) = (1) noisy, and (2) dissipated; RACKETER (or RACKAPELT) = a whoremonger or SPREESTER (q.v.).

1565. PARKER, Correspondence (Parker Soc.), 234. I send you a letter sent to me of the RACKET stirred up by Withers, of whom ye were informed, for the reformation of the university windows.

1598. SHAKSPEARE, 2 Hen. IV. ii. 2. That the tennis-court keeper knows better than I; for it is a low ebb of linen with thee when thou KEEPEST NOT RACKET there.

1609. JONSON, Case is Altered, iv. 4. Then think, then speak, then drink their sound again, And RACKET ROUND about this body's court.

1678. COTTON, Virgil Travestie [Works (1725) 100]. And leads me such a fearful RACKET.

1698. Unnatural Mother [NARES]. Yonder haz been a most heavy RACKET ... there is a curious hansom gentlewoman lies as dead as a herring, and bleeds like any stuck pig.

c.1707. Old Ballad, 'The Long Vacation' [DURFEY, Pills (1707), iii. 65]. We made such a noise, And con[found]ed a RACKET; My Landlady knew, I'd been searching the PLACKET.

1751. SMOLLETT, Pickle, ii. Goblins that ... keep such a RACKET in his house, that you would think ... all the devils in hell had broke loose upon him.

1753. RICHARDSON, Grandison, I. 117. I shall be a RACKETEER, I doubt.

1767. STERNE, Tristam Shandy, ii. 6. Pray. what's all that RACKET over our heads.

1772. BRIDGES, Homer Burl., 281. Without the least demur or RACKET.

1785. GROSE, Vulg. Tongue, s.v. RACKET. Some particular kinds of fraud and robbery are so termed, when called by their flash names ... as the Letter-RACKET; the Order-RACKET ... on the fancy of the speaker. In fact, any game may be termed a RACKET ... by prefixing thereto the particular branch of depredation or fraud in question.

1789. PARKER, Life's Painter, 'Happy Pair.' And STOOD THE RACKET for a dram.

1809. BYRON, Lines to Mr. Hodgson. Then I'd 'scape the heat and RACKET Of the good ship, Lisbon Packet.

1840. BARHAM, *Ingolds. Leg.* (*M. of Venice*). Old Shylock was making a RACKET.

1840. JUDD, *Margaret*, i. 17. The wind blazed and RACKETED through the narrow space between the house and the hill.

1843. MACAULAY, in *Trevelyan*, I. 302. I have been RACKETING lately, having dined twice with Rogers and once with Grant.

1851. LONGFELLOW, *Golden Legend*, iv. What an infernal RACKET and riot.

1851. MAYHEW, *London. Lab.*, i. 268. It was difficult to pall him upon any RACKET (detect him in any pretence). *Ibid.* iii. 264. I joined because I felt I was getting RACKETTY, and giving my mind to nothing but drink. *Ibid.* (1856), *Gt. World of London*, 46. Lady and gentlemen RACKET-MEN, who steal cocks and hens . . . Noisy RACKET-MEN, who make off with china or crockery-ware from earthenware shops.

1868. *Temple Bar*, xxiv. 538. Snide-pitching . . . is a capital RACKET.

1882. *D. News*, 27 Oct., 7. 4. Walker said, 'I will STAND THE RACKET of this. I stole it because I was hard up.'

1885. *D. Teleg.*, 16 Nov. He had been off ON THE RACKET perhaps for a week at a time. *Ibid.* (1886), 20 Feb. The unhappy dispenser of police law and his RACKETY son.

1886-96. MARSHALL, *Pomes*, 82. I'm on the POLLING-RACKET.

1888. BOLDREWOOD, *Robbery Under Arms*, i. And now—that chain rubbed a sore, curse it!—all that RACKET'S over. *Ibid.* xi. It's only some other cross CATTLE OR HORSE RACKET.

1889. *Century Mag.*, xxxix. 527. 'Lucky I learned that signal-RACKET.'

1890. *New York Evg. Post* [Century], 29 Jan. To give the name of legislation to the proceedings at Albany . . . would be an abuse of language. The proper name was "TUMBLING TO THE RACKET." The Assembly passed the bill without debate . . . much as they might pass a bill authorising a man to change his name.

1901. *Troddles*, 45. They had broken a chair and kicked up such an awful RACKET that Mrs. Bloggs had to make a reproachful request for consideration.

TO PLAY RACKET, *verb. phr.* (old).—To prove inconstant.

1369. CHAUCER, *Troilus*, IV. 461. Canst thou PLAY RAKET to and fro, Nettle in, duck out, now this, now that?

RACLAN, *subs.* (tramps'). — A married woman: [*cf.* Gipsy = a girl].

RAD, *subs.* (political).—A Radical.

1844. DISRAELI, *Coningsby*. They say the RADS are going to throw us over.

1858. TROLLOPE, *Dr. Thorne*, xxxv. He's got what will buy him bread and cheese, when the RADS shut up the Church.

18 [?]. THACKERAY, *Imitations of Beranger*, 'Jolly Jack,' st. I. And RADS attacked the throne and state, And Tories the reforming.

*c.*1871. *Giliad*, 195. The Whigs are heirless, and the RADS are mad.

RADDLED, *adj.* (old).—Drunk: *see* DRINKS and SCREWED. [Dial. (Linc.) = to do anything to excess.]—RAY (1767).

RAFE (or **RALPH**), *subs.* (common). —A pawn-ticket.

RAFF and **RAFFLE.** *See* RIFF-RAFF.

RAFFLING-SHOP, *subs. phr.* (old).— A lottery agent's: the article or lottery ticket was divided into shares, and cast for by a throw of the dice. [M. E. *raffle* = a game at dice.]

1714. LUCAS, *Gamesters*, 103. He . . . haunted all the RAFFLING-SHOPS about Town.

RAFT, *subs.* (American). — I. A whole lot; and (2) a goodly number. [The rafts of lumber on American waterways are sometimes of enormous size.]

18 [?]. *Widow Bedott Papers*, 210. The Elder's wife was a sick-lookin' woman, with a whole RAFT o' young ones Squalling round her.

*c.*1861-5. *Maj. Downing's Letters*, 93. We have killed Calhoun and Biddle; but there is a RAFT of fellows to put down yet.

1886. *Phil. Times*, 24 Oct. This last spring a RAFT of them [serving girls] was out of employment.

RAG, *subs.* (old).—Generic: (1) in *pl.* = clothes, old or new; whence (2), in sing. = a tatterdemalion, a ragamuffin, anyone despicable and despised; and (3) anything made out of textile stuff (as a handkerchief, shirt, undergrad's gown, newspaper, and exercise- [or examination-] paper). Hence TAG- (or SHAG-) RAG-AND-BOBTAIL (or FAG END) = one and all, the common people (GROSE, 1785); TAG-RAG = tattered, villainous, poor, disreputable; RAG-MANNERED = violently vulgar; RAGGERY = duds, esp. women's: Fr. *chiffons*; RAG-BAG (or RAG-DOLL) = a slattern; RAG-TRADE = (1) tailoring, (2) dressmaking, and (3) the dry-goods trade in general; RAG-STABBER = a tailor, a SNIP (*q.v.*); RAG-TACKER = (1) a dressmaker, and (2) a coach-trimmer; RAG-SOOKER (or SEEKER) = *see* quot. 1878; RAGS-AND-JAGS = tatters; TO HAVE TWO SHIRTS AND A RAG = to be comfortably off (RAY, 1760); TO TIP ONE'S RAGS A GALLOP = to move, depart, get out; TO GET ONE'S RAG (or SHIRT) OUT = (1) to bluster, and (2) to get angry; TO RAG OUT = (1) to dress, to CLOBBER UP (*q.v.*); and (2) to show the WHITE RAG: *see* WHITE FEATHER.

1535. BYGOD [OLIPHANT, *New Eng.*, i. 481. Bygod has 'your fathers were wyse, both TAGGE AND RAG'; that is *one and all*].

1542. UDALL, *Apoph. Eras.* [OLIPHANT, *New Eng.*, i. 484. Phrases like . . . not a RAG to hang about him . . .].

1582. STANYHURST, *Æneis* [ARBER], 21. Thee northen bluster aproching Thee sayls tears TAG RAG.

1597. SHAKSPEARE, *Richard III.*, v. 3. These overweening RAGS of France. *Ibid.* (1610), *Coriolanus*, iii. 4. Will you hence Before the TAG return.

1597. HEYWOOD, *Timon* [Five Plays in One, p. 10]. I am not of the RAGGS or FAGG END of the people.

1623. JONSON, *Time Vindicated.* The other zealous RAGG is the compositor.

1659-60. PEPYS, *Diary*, 6 Mar. The dining-room was full of TAG-RAG-AND-BOBTAIL, dancing, singing, and drinking.

1698. COLLIER, *Eng. Stage*, 220. This young lady swears, talks smut, and is . . . just as RAG-MANNERED as Mary the Buxsome.

16 [?]. *Nursery Rhyme.* Hark, hark! the dogs do bark, The Beggars come to town, Some in RAGS, and some in JAGS, And some in velvet gowns.

1706. WARD, *Wooden World*, 73. While he has a RAG to his Arse, he scorns to make use of a Napkin.

1708-10. SWIFT, *Polite Conversation*, i. *Lady Answ.* Pray, is he not rich? *Ld. Sparkish.* Ay, a rich Rogue, Two SHIRTS AND A RAG.

1749. SMOLLETT, *Gil Blas* [ROUTLEDGE], 166. A sorry RAG of a cassock. *Ibid.*, 173. A band of robbers . . . left us not a RAG but what we carry on our backs.

1785. WOLCOT [*Works* (1812), I. 80]. TAGRAGS AND BOBTAILS of the sacred Brush.

1800. COLQUHOUN, *Comm. Thames*, ii. 75. That lowest class of the community who are vulgarly denominated THE TAG-RAG AND BOBTAIL.

1811. MOORE, *Tom Crib*, 27. One of Georgy's bright og!es was put On the bankruptcy list, with its shop-windows shut; While the other soon made quite as TAG-RAG a show.

*c.*1819. *Old Song*, 'The Young Prig' [FARMER, *Musa Pedestris* (1896). 82. Frisk the cly, and fork the RAG.

1820. BYRON, *Blues*, ii. 23. The RAG, TAG AND BOBTAIL of those they call 'Blues.'

1840. DICKENS, *Barn. Rudge*, xxxv. We don't take in no TAGRAG AND BOBTAIL at our house.

1842. TENNYSON, *Poems*, 'The Goose.' I knew an old wife lean and poor; Her RAGS scarce held together.

1855. THACKERAY, *Newcomes*, xxxv. Old hags . . . draped in majestic RAGGERY.

*d.*1867. BROWN, *Artemus Ward* [S. J. and C.]. Wall, don't make fun of our clothes in the papers. We are goin' right straight through in these here clothes—we air. We ain't agoin' TO RAG OUT till we get to Nevady.

1869. S. BOWLES, *Our New West*, 506. A finely dressed woman RAGS OUT.

1870. HAZLEWOOD and WILLIAMS, *Leave it to Me*, i. He has forbidden me his house. *Joe.* I see; told you TO TIP YOUR RAGS A GALLOP, and you won't go.

1877. *Figaro* [reference lost]. We took a last peep, and saw the RAG-TACKER, mounted on a stool, still declaiming with an energy that argued much for his zeal.

1878. *Tramp Exposed*, 21. The RAGSOOKER, an instrument attached to the end of a long pole for removing clothes-pins from the lines, and afterwards dragging the released clothes over the fence.

1889. *Sporting Times* [S. J. & C.]. A writer in a penny RAG . . . failed far more lamentably . . . to entertain the public.

1888. HENLEY, *Book of Verses*, 'Hospital Outlines.' RAGS and TATTERS, belts and bayonets.

1900. KIPLING, *Stalky and Co.*, 228. You cut along and finish up your old RAG, and Turkey and me will help.

1895. *Pall Mall Gaz.*, 19 Sept., 2, I. I refer to the . . . yelling of a set of wretched creatures selling wretched papers, which, since the introduction of these RAGS within the last few years, has become unbearable.

1899. WHITEING, *John St.*, iii. The daily paper, now, veritably . . . a daily RAG. *Ibid.*, vi. That gal would live by a flower basket where others would starve. RAG-BAGS tied in the middle with a bit of string.

1899. *Answers*, 14 Jan., I, I. This matter of the RAG is hedged about with many unwritten laws. One who has mastered these will never go to breakfast in another man's rooms in cap and gown . . . Nor will he wear the RAG in the theatre which is strictly barred.

1901. *D. Telegraph*, 3 Oct., 9, I. There is some talk, we believe, of a prosecution; but meanwhile the scandalous RAG can be seen in the kiosks, "open pages," as our Correspondent says, "being flaunted in conspicuous positions."

4. (American). — Bank paper, bills of exchange, and so forth; SOFT (*q.v.*). Whence RAG-SHOP = a bank (*see* ante); RAG-SHOP BOSS (or COVE) = a banker; RAG-SHOP COVE = a cashier; RAG-MONEY (or CURRENCY) = SOFT (*q.v.*); TO FLASH ONE'S RAGS = to display one's notes; WITHOUT A RAG = penniless. Old Cant. = a farthing: whence in *pl.* = money (B. E. and GROSE).

1593. SHAKSPEARE, *Com. Errors*, iv. 4. Not a RAG of money.

1613. BEAUMONT and FLETCHER, *Captain*, iv. 2. *Jac.* 'Twere good she had a little foolish money To rub the time away with. *Host.* Not a RAG, Not a denier.

1826. *Old Song*, 'Bobby and His Mary' [FARMER, *Musa Pedestris* (1896), 95]. The blunt ran shy, and Bobby brushed To get more RAG not fearing.

1840. *American Song* . . . The banks are all clean broke, Their RAGS are good for naught.

1864. *Glasgow Citizen*, 19 Nov. Is not the exhilarating 'short length' of handy known beyond our own Queen Street that it is not registered here? And we miss the RAG TRADE whose worthy members *do* the above named goes.

1875. *Nation*, 29 July, 66. All true Democrats were clamorous for 'hard-money' and against RAG-MONEY.

1887. HENLEY, *Villon's Straight Tip*, I. Suppose . . . you pitch a snide, or smash a RAG.

1889. LELAND in S. J. & C.. s.v. RAGS . . . bank-bills. Before . . . uniform currency, bills of innumerable banks of the "wild cat," "blue pup," and "ees' dog" description often circulated at a discount of 50 or 60 per cent., in a very dirty and tattered condition. These were . . . RAGS, a word still used . . . for paper-money.

*c.*1879. *North Am. Rev.* [*Century*]. Fortunately the 'specie basis' of the national banks is now chiefly paper—the RAG-BABY—three hundred and forty-six millions of greenbacks.

5. (service). — A flag: spec. the Union, but also the regimental colours. Hence RAG-CARRIER = an ensign (GROSE).

186 [?]. WHITMAN [in *Century*, xxxvi. 827]. It cost three men's lives to get back that four-by-three flag—to tear it from the breast of a dead rebel—for the name of getting their little RAG back again.

*c.*1870. *Music Hall Song*, 'John Bull's Flag.' In India Nana Sahib flew, when Campbell showed the flag, At Trafalgar, too, when Nelson fell, he died before THE RAG.

1892. KIPLING, *Barrack-Room Ballads*, 'The Rhyme of the Three Captains.' Dip their flag to a slaver's RAG —to show that his trade is fair. *Ibid.*, 'The Widow at Windsor.' You won't get away from the tune that they play To the bloomin' old RAG over 'ead.

1901. HENLEY, *For England's Sake*, 'The Man in the Street.' And if it's the RAG of RAGS that calls us roaring into the fight, We'll die in a glory.

6. (actors' and showmen's).— (1) The curtain; whence (2) a *dénouement*, *i.e.*, a "curtain" = a situation on which to bring down the drop; RAGS-AND-STICKS = a travelling outfit: *see* quots. *passim.*

1875. *Athenæum*, 24 April, 545, 2. RAGS is another uncomplimentary term applied by prosperous members of circuses to the street tumblers.

1876. HINDLEY, *Cheap Jack*, 99. Sawny Williams . . . was horrified at finding his RAGS AND STICKS, as a theatrical booth is always termed, just as he had left them the overnight.

1886. *Referee*, 20 June. Poor Miss A—— was left for quite a minute before the RAG could be unhitched and made to shut out the tragic situation.

1897. MARSHALL, '*Pomes*,' 44. Which brought down the RAG on no end of a mess.

7. (military).—THE ORDER OF THE RAG = the profession of arms; RAG-FAIR = kit inspection (GROSE). *See* RAG-AND-FAMISH.

1751. FIELDING, *Amelia*, II. iv. It is the opinion which, I believe, most of you young GENTLEMEN OF THE ORDER OF THE RAG deserve.

8. (common). — The tongue: also RED-RAG, or RED-FLANNEL (B. E., *c.*1696; DYCHE, 1748; GROSE, 1785); (9) = talk, banter, abuse. As *verb.* = (1) to scold; (2) to chaff; and (3—American University) to declaim or compose better than one's class-mates: *see* RAGTIME. Whence RAG-BOX (or -SHOP) = the mouth; RAG-SAUCE = (1) chatter, and (2) CHEEK (*q.v.*); RAGSTER = a bully or scold; A DISH OF RED-RAG = abuse; TO CHEW THE RAG = (1) to scold, and (2) to sulk; TO GIVE THE RED RAG A HOLIDAY = to be silent; TOO MUCH RED RAG = loquacious.

1820. COMBE, *Syntax, Consolations*, IV. For well I know by your glib tongue, To what fine country you belong, And if your RED RAG did not show it, By your queer fancies I should know it.

1821. EGAN, *Life in London*, II. iv. 'Hang you! . . . if you don't hold that are RED RAG of yours, I'll spoil your mouth.' Ibid. *Anec. of Turf*, 183. She tipped the party such a DISH OF RED RAG as almost to create a riot in the street. *Ibid.* (1842), *Jack Flashman* [in Captain Macheath]. Here's the RAG-SAUCE of a friend.

1826. BRUTON, *My Mugging Maia* [Univ. Songst. iii. 103]. Say, mugging Moll, why that RED-RAG . . . is now so mute.

1876. W. S. GILBERT, *Dan'l Druce*, i. Stop that cursed RED RAG of yours, will you?

1882. ANSTEY, *Vice-Versa*, xiv. "You're right there, sir," said Dick; "he ought to be well RAGGED for it."

1888. *Notes and Queries*, 7 S., v. 469. "He was CHEWING THE RAG at me the whole afternoon." *Ibid.*, 7 S., vi. 38. To RAG a man is good Lincolnshire for chaff or tease. At school to get a boy into a rage was called GETTING HIS RAG OUT.

1892. KIPLING, *Barrack Room Ballads*, 'The Young British Soldier.' You shut up your RAG-BOX, an' 'ark to my lay.

1900. *Athenæum*, 31 Mar., 391, 2. There is not much sport in RAGGING a body of men some of whom were but lately rowing in the same boat with yourself or dining at the same table.

10. (common).—Generic for a jollification, a wenching- (or drinking-) bout, or (Amer. Univ.) a brilliant success in class: also RAG-TIME. [In this connexion RAG-ROWTERING = romping.] As *adj.*, RAG-TIME = merry, lively. Whence RAG-TIME GIRL = (1) a sweetheart, a 'best girl,' and (2) a harlot.

1900. *Daily Mail*, 10 Mar., 2, 4. There was keen excitement at Cambridge yesterday when the magistrates proceeded to deal with the last two prosecutions of students arising out of the notorious RAG in celebration of the relief of Ladysmith.

1902. *Sp. Times*, 1 Feb., 1, 5. It's the moosic what's a-queering your pitch! the ruddy people can't eat fried fish to RAG TIME!

Verb. (common, thieves').—To divide; to NAP THE REGULARS (*q.v.*).

THE RAG, *subs. phr.* (London).—1. *See* quot.

1869. GREENWOOD, *Seven Curses of London*. The unaristocratic establishment in the neighbourhood of the Leather Lane, originally christened the "Rag-lan," but more popularly known as the "RAG."

2. (military).—*See* RAG AND FAMISH.

TO TAKE THE RAG OFF, *verb. phr.* (America) = to surpass; to overcome; to 'take the CAKE' (*q.v.*).

1855. HALIBURTON, *Human Nature*, 28. The fun of the forecastle! I would back it for wit against any bar-room in New York or New Orleans, and I believe they TAKE THE RAG OFF all creation. *Ibid.* 218. I had an everlasting fast . . . pacer . . . He TOOK THE RAG OFF THE BUSH in great style.

RAGAMUFFIN, *subs.* (old colloquial: long recognised).—A tattered vagabond; also as *adj.* and *adv.* = beggarly, ragged, disorderly. [In quot. 1383 = the Devil.]—B. E., *c.* 1696; HALLIWELL, 1847. Also RAGABOOT, RAGSHAG, RAGABRASH, &c.

1383. LANGLAND, *Piers Plowman*, xxi. 283. Ac rys vp, RAGAMOFFIN, and reche me alle the barres.

1440. *Prompt Parv.*, 421. RAGMANN, or he that goythe wyth raggyd clothys, *pannicius vel pannicia*.

1597. SHAKES., *1 Henry IV.*, 3, 36. *Fal.* . . . I have led my RAGAMUFFINS where they are peppered.

1601. JONSON, *Poetaster*, i. Here be the Emperor's captains, you RAGAMUFFIN rascal, and not your comrades.

c. 1620. *Disc. of a New World*, 81. They are the veriest lack-latines, and the most unalphabetical RAGGABRASHES that ever bred louse.

1634. S. ROWLEY, *Noble Soldier*, iv. 2. All rent and torne like a RAGAMUFFIN.

1660. DRYDEN, *Don Sebastian*, iv. 2. Be not afraid, Lady, to speak to these RAGAMUFFINS.

1707. WARD, *Hud. Rediv.*, II. iii. 3. Autumn that RAGGAMUFFIN Thief That blows down ev'ry fading leaf.

1769-72. JUNIUS, *Sin Stigmatized*. The most unalphabetical RAGABRASHES that ever lived.

1771. SMOLLETT, *Humphry Clinker*, 29. The postilion . . . was not a shabby wretch like the RAGAMUFFIN who had driven them into Marlborough

1887. *Conn. Courant*, 7 July [Century]. While the RAGSHAGS were marching . . . [he] caught his foot in his ragged garment and fell.

RAG-AND-FAMISH (or **THE RAG**), *subs. phr.* (military).—The Army and Navy Club.

1864. YATES, *Broken to Harness*, iv. From the Doctor's I went to THE RAG and found Meaburn there.

1864. SALA, *Quite Alone*, xiii. THE RAG AND FAMISH seems to me a most palatial edifice, superb in all its exterior appointments.

1877. *Punch's Pocket-Book* (1878), 172. There's a Major I know who belongs to the RAG.

1887. LOVETT-CAMERON, *Neck or Nothing*, i. The very smartest and best-looking man to be met with between THE RAG and Hyde Park Corner.

1890. *D. Telegraph*, 19 Aug., 5, 2. The genial "RAG" welcomes the sympathetic spirits of the Naval and Military with open arms.

RAG-BABY, *subs. phr.* (American).—The policy advocated by Greenbackers; inflation of the currency as a panacea for financial ills.—BARTLETT.

RAGE, *verb.* (old: colloquial).—To wanton: hence RAGERIE = wantonness; skittishness: *cf.* RAG, *subs.* 10.

1383. CHAUCER, *Cant. Tales*, 'Miller's Tale,' l. 87. On a day this hende Nicholas Fil with this yonge wyf to RAGE and pleye. *Ibid.*, 'Merchant's Tale,' l. 603. He was al Coltissh, ful of RAGERYE.

1393. GOWER, *Confess. Aman.* i. She began to plaie and RAGE, As who saith, I am well enough.

c. 1440. *Reliq. Antiq.*, i 29. When sche seyth gallantys revell yn hall, Yn here hert she thinkys owtrage, Desyrynge with them to pley and RAGE, And stelyth fro yow full prevely.

THE RAGE (or ALL THE RAGE), *phr.* (colloquial).—The fashion; the vogue; THE GO (*q.v.*).

1785. *The New Rosciad*, 37. 'Tis THE RAGE in this great raging Nation, Who wou'd live and not be in the fashion?

1857. A. TROLLOPE, *Three Clerks*, xxxv. You don't know how charming it is, and it will be ALL THE RAGE.

1868. SPENCER, *Social Statics* 178. In our day THE RAGE for accumulation has apotheosized work.

1885. *Daily Chronicle*, 16 Sep. Criterion was ALL THE RAGE.

RAG-FAIR, *subs. phr.* (old).—1. *See* quot. 1892; and (2) *see* RAG, *subs.* 7.

1748. SMOLLETT, *Rod. Random*, xxvii. Mr. Morgan's wife kept a gin-shop in RAG-FAIR.

1772. BRIDGES, *Homer Burlesque*, 205. One kept a slop-shop in RAG FAIR.

1892. SYDNEY, *English and the English in 18th Century*, i. 32. Situated in the parish of St. Mary, Whitechapel, near the Tower of London, was the district called RAG FAIR, where old clothes and frippery were sold.

RAGGED-ARSE, *adj. phr.* (vulgar).—Disreputable; tattered; spoiled. RAGGED-ARSE BRIGADE = the baser sort; TAG-RAG-AND-BOB-TAIL; 'Tom Dick, and Harry.' RAGGED-ARSE REPUTATION (or VIRTUE) = one gone to tatters.

RAGGED, *adj.* (rowing).—Collapsed.

RAGGED-BRIGADE, *subs. phr.* (military).—Thirteenth Hussars. Also "The Green Dragons"; "The Evergreens"; and "The Great Runaway Prestonpans."

RAGGED-SOPH. *See* SOPH.

RAGGED ROBIN, *subs. phr.* (provincial).—A keeper's follower (New Forest).

RAGMAN (or **RAGEMAN**), *subs.* (old).—The devil. Also (2) *see* RIGMAROLE.

1363. LANGLAND, *Piers Plowman*, xix. 122. Filius by the faders wil flegh with Spiritus Sanctus, To ransake that RAGEMAN and reue hym hus apples, That fyrst man deceyuede thorgh frut and false by-heste.

RAGOUT, *subs.* (old: now recognised).—'A Relishing Bit, with a high Sawce.'—B. E. (*c.* 1696).

RAGS-AND-BONES, *subs. phr.* (popular).—A miserable remnant; a pell-mell of rubbish. Thus RAG AND BONE SHOP (also RAG-SHOP) = a crapulous and tumbled room; a PIGGERY (*q.v.*).

c. 1890. ELIZABETH BELLWOOD, *Music Hall Song*, 'The Man that Struck O'Hara.' RAGS AND BONES was all that was left, Of the man that struck O'Hara.

RAG-SPLAWGER (or **-GORGER**), *subs. phr.* (old).—A rich man; 'generally used in conversation to avoid direct mention of names' (GROSE): Fr. *riflard*.

RAG-WATER, *subs. phr.* (old).—1. 'Any common spirit.'—B. E. (*c.* 1696); (2) = gin (GROSE).

RAID. TO RAID THE MARKET (Stock Exchange).—To derange prices by exciting distrust or causing a panic.

RAILS, *subs.* (American).—A curtain lecture: whence, A DISH OF RAILS = a regular jobation.

FRONT (or HEAD-) RAILS, *subs. phr.* (common).—The teeth.

See RIDE.

RAILLERY, *subs.* (old).—'Drolling. To RAILLY, or Droll. A Railleur, or Droll.'—B. E. (*c.* 1696).

RAILINGS. TO COUNT THE RAILINGS, *verb. phr.* (common).—To go hungry: *see* PECKHAM.

RAILROAD, *subs.* (American).—*See* quot. and DRINKS.

18 . . NEAL, *Charcoal Sketches*, I. 117 [DE VERE]. Now he is asked to take a Stone Fence, and now a RAILROAD, but both are simple whisky, so called, in the latter case, "because of the rapidity with which it hurries men to the end of their journey."

Verb. (American).—To run a matter with all speed; TO RUSH (*q.v.*).

1889. *Sci. Am.*, N.S., lvii. 37. The Alien Act that was RAILROADED through at the close of the last session.

1889. *Pop. Sci. Monthly*, xxxii. 758. A New York daily some time ago reported that a common thief . . . was RAILROADED through court in a few days.

RAIN. PROVERBS and sayings—'It never RAINS but it pours' = misfortunes never come singly; 'If it should RAIN pottage, he would want his dish,' said of a wastrel or STAR-GAZER (*q.v.*). 'It RAINS by planets,' *i.e.*, partially; TO GET OUT OF THE RAIN = to absent oneself, to refrain from meddling. *See* also CATS-AND-DOGS, RIGHT, &c.

1749. SMOLLETT, *Gil Blas* [ROUTLEDGE], 18. AS IT NEVER RAINS BUT IT POURS, I was in the front of the battle . . . that I might lose no time in learning to stand fire.

1848. DURIVAGE, *Stray Subjects*, 95. Ham was one of 'em—he was. He 'knew sufficient TO GET OUT OF THE RAIN.'

RAINBOW, *subs.* (old).—1. A mistress; (2) a footman in livery: also KNIGHT OF THE RAINBOW; and (3) a pattern book. [Dressed in or exhibiting variety of colour.]

1821. EGAN, *Life in London*, II. i. The pink of the ton and his RAINBOW—the Whitechapel knight of the cleaver and his fat rib— . . . they are "all there." *Ibid.* II. vi. It was the custom of Logic never to permit the RAINBOW to announce him. *Ibid.* 'Now, Dicky, out with your RAINBOW.' 'Here are the patterns, gentlemen, the very latest fashions.'

3. (costers').—A sovereign; HALF-A-RAINBOW = ten shillings: *see* RHINO.

RAINBOW-CHASE, *subs. phr.* (common).—A run after a dream; a WILD-GOOSE CHASE (*q.v.*). [From the folk-story of the pot of gold found where the two points of a rainbow touch the earth.]

1886. *St. James's Gaz.*, 2 June, 10. A fact which had led Mr. Rylands off a RAINBOW-CHASE after a visionary Chancellorship.

RAIN-NAPPER, *subs. phr.* (old).—An umbrella; a MUSH (*q.v.*).

1823. MONCRIEFF, *Tom and Jerry*, iii. 4. My hat and RAIN-NAPPER there!

RAINY- (or **WET-**) **DAY**, *subs. phr.* (common).—Hard times; whence, TO LAY UP FOR A RAINY-DAY = to provide against necessity or distress.—GROSE (1785).

d. 1626. *Andrews Sermons* [Ang. Cath. Lib. (1841-3), ii. 346]. This they caught as an advantage we see, and laid it up for a RAINY DAY, and three years after, out they came with it.

1662. FULLER, *Worthies*, xi. *Ergo*, saith the Miser, part with nothing, but keep all against a WET DAY.

1836. EVERETT, *Orations*, I. 285 The man whose honest industry just gives him a competence exerts himself that he may have something against a RAINY DAY

1885. *Evening Standard*, 23 Oct. They must in prosperous times put by something for A RAINY DAY.

RAISE, *subs.* (colloquial).—An improvement in conditions.

1848. RUXTON, *Far West*, 19. If we don't make a RAISE afore long, I wouldn't say so.

1886. *Phil. Times*, 6 Ap. No further difficulty is anticipated in making permanent the RAISE of the freight blockade in this city.

Verb. (old: now American colloquial).—To rear: of human beings, crops and cattle.

1597. SHAKSPEARE, *Richard III.*, v. 3, 247. A bloody tyrant and a homicide; One RAISED in blood.

1744. MATH. BISHOP [OLIPHANT, *New Eng.*, ii. 164. A child is RAISED (bred up) . . . this is still an American phrase].

1768. FRANKLIN, *Letter to J. Alleyne*, 9 Aug. By these early marriages we are blest with more children; and . . . every mother suckling and nursing her own child, more of them are RAISED.

1851. ALLIN, *Home Ballads*, 22. Rhody has RAISED the biggest man, Connecticut, Tom Thumb.

1869. STOWE, *Oldtown Folks*, 98. Miss Asphyxia had talked of takin' a child from the poor-house, and so RAISIN' her own help.

1887. LIPPINCOTT'S, August, 398. I was born and RAISED 'way down in the little village of Unity, Maine.

1890. *Literary World*, 31 Jan., 102, 2. She was RAISED in a good family as a nurse and seamstress.

See BEAD; BILL; BOBBERY; BRISTLES; CAIN; DANDER; DASH; DEAD; DEVIL; HAIR; HATCHET; HELL; MARKET; MISCHIEF; MUSS; NED; ORGAN; RACKET; ROOF; ROW; RUMPUS; WIND.

RAISE-MOUNTAIN, *subs. phr.* (old).—A braggart.

RAKE (**RAKEHELL**, **RAKEHELLONIAN**, or **RAKESHAME**), *subs.* (old: now recognised).—A disreputable person; a blackguard, esp. a whoremonger; 'one so bad as to be found only by raking hell, or one so reckless as to rake hell' (*Century*): also 'RAKE HELL and skin the devil, and you'll not find such another.'—HARMAN (1573); COTGRAVE (1611, s.v. *garnement*); B. E. (*c.* 1696); GROSE (1785). Also, as *verb.*

= to live dissolutely. Whence RAKISH (RAKING, RAKEHELLY, RAKELY, or RAKESHAMED) = dissolute (B. E., *c.*1696); RAKERY (or RAKISHNESS) = blackguardism; RAKE-JAKES = a blackguard. [RAKE = abbrev. of RAKEHELL.]

1360. *Allit. Poems* [E. E. T. S.] [OLIPHANT, *New Eng.*, i. 64. There is the Swedish RAKEL . . . to be written RAKE-HELL in more modern times].

1542. UDALL, *Apop. Eras.* [OLIPHANT, *New Eng.*, i. 487. The old adjective *rakel* (promptus) from a mistaken analogy, gives birth to the phrase TO RAKE HELL].

1557. TOTTEL, *Misc.* [ARBER], II. The RAKEHELL lyfe that longs to loues disporte.

1573. HARMAN, *Caveat* (1814), ii. All these rowsey, ragged rabblement of RAKEHELLES.

1596. SPENSER, *Faerie Queene*, v. xi. 44. And farre away, amid their RAKEHELL bands, They spide a Lady left all succourlesse. Ibid., *Shep. Cal.*, Ded. I scorne and spue out the RAKEHELLYE route of ragged rymers.

1605. JONSON, CHAPMAN, &c., *Eastward Hoe*, ii. 1. I turn not a drunken whore-hunting RAKE-HELL like thyself.

1635. *Long Meg. of Westminster* [NARES]. Away, you foule RAKE-SHAM'D whore, quoth he, if thou pratest to mee, Ile lay thee at my foote.

*d.*1704. T. BROWN, *Dial. of Dead* [*Works*, ii. 313]. I have been a man of the town . . . and admitted into the family of the RAKEHELLONIANS.

1699. FARQUHAR, *Constant Couple*, i. 1. Whipped from behind the counter to the side-box, forswears merchandise,—where he must live by cheating,—and usurps gentility, where he may die by RAKING. *Ibid.* (1703), *Inconstant*, iii. 1. A wild, foppish, extravagant RAKE-HELL.

1709. STEELE, *Tatler*, 14. We have . . . RAKES in the habit of Roman senators, and grave politicians in the dress of RAKES. *Ibid.*, 336. These RAKES are your idle Ladies of Fashion, who, having nothing to do, employ themselves in tumbling over my Ware. *Ibid.*, No. 20. I could not but be solicitous to know of her, how she had disposed of that RAKE-HELL *Punch*.

1713. SHADWELL, *Hum. of the Army*. Our RAKELY young Fellows live as much by their Wits as ever.

*c.*1728. SWIFT, *Stella*, xx. 'Tis his own fault, that will RAKE and drink when he is but just crawled out of his grave. Ibid., *Against Abol. Christ.* A RAKE-HELL of the town . . . is rewarded with a lady of great fortune to repair his own.

1740. SHENSTONE, *Epil. to Cleone*. Women hid their necks, and veil'd their faces Nor romp'd, nor RAK'D, nor star'd at public places.

1742-4. NORTH, *Lord Guildford*, II. 300. He . . . instructed his lordship in all the RAKERY and intrigues of the lewd town.

1749. SMOLLETT, *Gil Blas* (1812), III. v. You are too forward, and have the air of a libertine; I am afraid you are no better than a downright RAKE.

1809. BYRON, *Eng. Bards and Scotch Reviewers*. And every brother RAKE will smile to see That miracle, a moralist in me.

1831. C. LAMB, *Hercules Pacificatus* in *Englishman's Mag.* A crew of RAKE-HELLS *in terrorem* Spread wide, and carried all before 'em.

1859. TENNYSON, *Merlin and Vivien*. Nor will she RAKE; there is no business in her.

1866. ELIOT, *Felix Holt*, ii. The stupid RAKISHNESS of the original heir.

1890. *Globe*, 7 Feb., 6, 3. The functions of his RAKE-HELLY associates are reduced to insignificance.

2. (common).—A comb: also GARDEN-RAKE.

Colloquialisms are:—TO RAKE AND SCRAPE = to pinch, to save, to play the miser; TO RAKE IN THE PIECES = to make money in plenty; TO RAKE THE POT = to take the stakes: *see* POT; TO RAKE OUT = to possess a woman; TO CARRY HEAVY RAKES = to put on SIDE (*q.v.*); to overbear; TO RAKE DOWN = to scold, to drub: also as *subs.* RAKEDOWN = a scolding, a beating; BETTER WITH A RAKE THAN A FORK =

(RAY) 'more apt to pull in and scrape up, than to give out and communicate: also vice versa'; LEAN AS A RAKE = as lean as may be.

1383. CHAUCER, *Cant. Tales*, Prol., 289. AS LENE was his hors AS is A RAKE.

*d.*1529. SKELTON, *Phyllyp Sparowe*, 913. His bones crake, LEANE AS A RAKE.

1582. STANYHURST, *Æneis* [ARBER], 89. A meigre LEANE RAKE with a long berd.

1611. COTGRAVE, *Dict.*, s.v. *Maigre*. Maigre comme pies, AS LEANE AS RAKES (we say).

1614. *Terence in English* [NARES]. *C.* Woe is me for you, CARRIE YOU SUCH HEAVIE RAKES, I pray you? *M.* Such is my desert.

*c.*1732. GAY, *Works* (1784), II. 115. LEAN AS A RAKE with sighs and care.

RAKER (or **RAKE-KENNEL**), *subs.* (old).—A scavenger: also JACK RAKER.

1611. TARLETON, *Jests*. When the cart came, he asked the RAKER why he did his businesse so slacklye.

*c.*1704. *Gentleman Instructed*, 445. A club of RAKE-KENNELS.

TO GO A RAKER, *verb phr.* (racing).—To bet recklessly; TO PLUNGE (*q.v.*). Hence, RAKER = a heavy bet.

1884. HAWLEY SMART, *Post to Finish*, i. If Bill Greyson takes the Leger it will be with Caterham. I am standing him a RAKER, and I mean standing him out.

1891. *Sportsman*, 25 Mar. Jennings, whose usual betting limit is very moderate, indeed, stood to win a RAKER this time over Lord George.

RALLY, *subs.* (theatrical).—The rough-and-tumble work after the transformation scene in a pantomime.

1880. SIMS, *Left*, 168. Then, when the company found out the trick, the waiters, who were all supers, started a RALLY, and threw the things at each other.

1885. *D. Telegraph*, 16 Nov. Provide comic actors, pantomimes, RALLIES, and breakdowns.

RALPH, *subs.* (American).—1. A fool: also RALPH SPOONER.—B. E. (*c.*1696); GROSE (1785).

2. (printers').—A mischief-mongering *deus ex machinâ*: the supposed author of the tricks played on a recalcitrant member of a CHAPEL (*q.v.*).

RAM, *subs.* (American University).—1. A practical joke; a hoax.

2. (venery).—An act of coition: hence, as *verb.* = to possess a woman: *cf.* RAMROD and *see* RIDE.

THE RAMS, *subs. phr.* (American).—*Delirium tremens*: *see* GALLON-DISTEMPER.

TO RAM ONE'S FACE IN, *verb. phr.* (American).—To intrude; to meddle.

RAMAGIOUS, *adj.* (old).—'Untamed, wild.'—COLES (1717).

RAM-BOOZE (or **-BUZE**). *See* RUM.

RAMBOUNGE, *subs.* (Scots').—'A severe brush of labour . . . most probably a cant term.'—JAMIESON.

RAMBUSTIOUS, RAMBUNCTIOUS, RAMBUMPTIOUS, RAMGUMPTION, RAMFEEZLED, RAMSHACKLE, RAMSTRUGENOUS, and similar words. *See* RUMGUMPTION.

RAMCAT (or **RAN-CAT COVE**), *subs. phr.* (thieves').—A man wearing furs.

RAMHEAD, *subs.* (old).—A cuckold: hence RAMHEADED = HORNED (*q.v.*).

1630. TAYLOR, *Works* [NARES]. To be cald RAMHEAD is a title of honour, and a name proper to all men.

1713. *Poor Robin* [NARES]. Listen a little to my rime, The more because 'tis cuckow time; For fear you should be this day wedded, And on the next day be RAMHEADED.

RAMJAM, *subs.* (American).—A surfeit: as *verb.* = TO STUFF (*q.v.*).

RAMJOLLOCK, *verb.* (old).—To shuffle cards.

RAMMAGED, *adj.* (Scots').—Drunk: *see* DRINKS and SCREWED.

RAMMER, *subs.* (Old Cant).—The arm.—GROSE (1785).

RAMMISH, *adj.* (colloquial).—1. Stinking, hircine, abominable to the nose: *cf.* GOATISH. Also RAMMY.

1383. CHAUCER, *Canterbury Tales*, 16,409. Her savour is so RAMMISH and so hoot.

*d.*1529. SKELTON [DYCE, *Works*, i. 124]. Thou RAMMYSCHE stynkyng gote.

1601. JONSON, *Poetaster*, iii. 1. Hang him, fusty satyr, he smells all goat; he carries a RAM under his armholes.

1607. MIDDLETON, *Phœnix*, i. 2. Whose father being a RAMMISH ploughman, himself a perfumed gentleman.

1611. COTGRAVE, *Dict.*, s.v. *Bouquin*. Ranke, RAMMISH, goatlike.

1621. BURTON, *Anat. Melan.*, III. III. iii. 1. A nasty rank, RAMMY, filthy, beastly quean.

1670. COTTON, *Scoffer Scofft* [*Works* (1725), 165]. Do you not love to smell the Roast Of a good RAMMISH Holocaust?

2. (colloquial).—Lustful; on HEAT (*q.v.*): also RAMMY and RAMMISHNESS; RAMMAKING = wantonness and RAM-SKYT (*see* quot. *c.*1400).—B. E. (*c.*1696); GROSE (1785).

*c.*1400. *Towneley Myst.* [OLIPHANT, *New Eng.*, i. 200. We see RAM-SKYT . . . applied to a woman skittish as a ram].

1635. QUARLES, *Emblems*, ii. 1. Go, Cupid's RAMMISH pander, go.

RAMNUGGAR BOYS (THE), *subs. phr.* (military).—The 14th (The King's) Hussars. [They encountered enormous odds at the battle in question.] Also "The Emperor's Chambermaids."

RAMP (*see* **ROMP**), *subs.* (old).—1. A wanton; a whore: *see* TART; and (2) = lascivious horseplay. As *verb.* = to wanton, to BACK UP (*q.v.*); and RAMPANT (or RAMPISH: PALSGRAVE, 1530) = wanton (B. E., *c.*1696). *Cf.* COTGRAVE, s.v. *Rampeau. Droict de rampe*, A priviledge, or power. A lecher.

1548. HALLE, *Henry VI.* (an. 6). Ione . . . was a RAMPE of such boldnesse, that she would . . . do thynges that other yong maidens both abhorred and wer ashamed to do.

1550. UDALL, *Roister Doister*, ii. 4. Good wenches would not so RAMPE abrode ydelly.

1551. STILL, *Gammer Gurton's Needle* [DODSLEY, *Old Plays* (REED), ii. 43]. Nay, fye on thee, thou RAMPE, thou ryg.

1591. LYLY, *Sapho and Ph.*, iii. 1. What victlers follow Bacchus campes? Fools, fidlers, panders, pimpes, and RAMPES.

1593. HARVEY, *Pierces Supererog.* [*Wks.*, II. 229]. Although she were a lustie bounsing RAMPE, somewhat like Gallemetta, or maide Marian.

1598. FLORIO, *Worlde of Wordes*, s.v. *Galluta* . . . a cockring wench, a RAMP.

1605. SHAKESPEARE, *Cymbeline*, i. 6. Should he make me Live like Diana's priest, betwixt cold sheets; Whiles he is vaulting variable RAMPS, In your despite.

1614. JONSON, *Bartholomew Fair*, iv. 3. Peace, you foul RAMPING jade!

1697. *Poor Robin*. To duei RAMPANT Miss on a soft Bed.

1732. FIELDING, *Miser*, iv. 15. The young fellows of this age are so RAMPANT that even degrees of kindred cannot restrain them.

1749. SMOLLETT, *Gil Blas* [ROUTLEDGE], 69. A charming woman . . . open to all mankind . . . Let me see how many RAMPANT chaps have been brought to their bearings . . . without the . . . husband being waked out of his evening nap.

3. (thieves').—A robbery with violence (VAUX, 1812); (4) = a swindle; whence (5) = a footpad; and (6) = a trickster: also RAMPSMAN and RAMPER: *cf.* RUSH. As *verb.* = (1) to rob with violence; (2) to blackmail; and (3, racing) to bet against one's own horse; RAMPING (*adj.*) = violent; RAMPING-MAD = noisily drunk; TO RAMP AND REAVE = to get by fair means or foul (HALLIWELL).

1830. MONCRIEFF, *Heart of London*, ii. 1. And RAMP so plummy.

1840. LYTTON, *Paul Clifford*, viii. The latter personage, giving him a pinch in the ear, shouted out, "RAMP, RAMP!" and Paul found himself surrounded in a trice by a whole host of ingenious tormentors . . . this initiatory process, technically termed "RAMPING," reduced the bones of Paul, who fought tooth and nail in his defence, to the state of magnesia.

1859. MATSELL, *Vocabulum*. It is their business to jostle or RAMP the victim, while the file picks his pocket.

1876. RUNCIMAN, *Chequers*, 7. A man who is a racecourse thief and RAMPER hailed me affably.

1880. G. R. SIMS, *How the Poor Live*, x. These . . . were mostly RAMPS, or swindles, got up to obtain the gate-money.

1883. *Punch*, 26 May, 252, 1. "Look 'ere, this hinnocent cove has been trying a RAMP on!" *Crowd.* Welsher! kill him! Welsher!

1885. *Chamb. Journal*, 28 Feb., 136. He is a RAMPER and bully to a couple of outside betting-men.

1889. KIPLING, *Cleared* [in *The Scots Observer*]. They never told the RAMPING crowd to card a woman's hide.

7. (thieves').—A hall-mark. [A 'rampant lion' forms part of the essay stamp for gold and silver.]

1879. HORSLEY, *Jottings from Jail* [*Macm.* xl. 500]. They told me all about the wedge, how I should know it by the RAMP.

RAMPAGE, *verb.* (colloquial).—To storm; also ON THE RAMPAGE = (1) in a state of excitement, from anger, lust, violent movement, or drink. Whence RAMPAGING (RAMPACIOUS or RAMPAGEOUS) = (1) furious, HOT (*q.v.*), wild, or outrageous: and (2) LOUD (*q.v.*): whence RAMPAGEOUSNESS. Also RAMPAGER (or RAMPADGEON) = (1) a Hector; (2) a vagabond; and (3) a wencher.

1722. HAMILTOUN, *Wallace*, 244. Psewart RAMPAG'D to see both man and horse So sore rebuted, and put to the worse.

1768. ROSS, *Helenore*, 64. He RAMPAGED . . And lap and danc'd, and was in unco' mood.

1816. SCOTT, *Antiquary*, v. The young gentleman was sometimes heard . . . RAMPANGING about in his room, just as if he was one o' the player folk.

1823. GALT, *R. Gilhaize*, i. 40. His present master was a saint of purity compared to that RAMPAGIOUS Cardinal.

1837. DICKENS, *Pickwick*, xxii. A stone statue of some RAMPACIOUS animal . . . distinctly resembling an insane cart-horse.

1858. DICKENS, *Great Expectations*, xv. Joe . . . followed me out into the road to say . . . ON THE RAMPAGE, Pip, and OFF THE RAMPAGE, Pip—such is Life.

1860. TENNYSON, *Village Wife*, vii. An' they RAMPAGED about wi' their grooms, and was 'untin' arter the men.

1880. *Athenæum* [*Century*]. One there is . . . who out-Herod's every-one else in RAMPAGIOUSNESS and lack of manners.

1881. BLACK, *Beautiful Wretch*, xx. If only . . . Frank got to hear of it, I suppose there would soon be a noble RAMPAGE.

1890. *Spectator*, 28 June. A diplomatist like Prince Bismarck . . . OUT for the time ON THE RAMPAGE, seems to Continental Courts a terror.

RAMPALLIAN, *subs.* (old).—A villain; a Hector: *cf.* RAMP and RAPSCALLION.

1593. NASH, *Strange News* [OLIPHANT, *New Eng.*, ii. 11. . . . stands the word RAMPALIAN, whence may have come the later RAPSCALLION.]

1598. SHAKSPEARE, *2 Henry IV.* ii. 1. Away you scullion, you RAMPALLIAN, you fustilarian!

1599. GREEN, *Tu Quoque* [DODSLEY, *Old Plays* (REED), vii. 23]. Who feeds you?—'tis not your sausage face, thick, clouted cream, RAMPALLIAN, at home.

1613. BEAUMONT and FLETCHER, *Honest Man's Fortune*, ii. 1. Out upon them, RAMPALLIONS, I will keep myself safe enough Out of their fingers.

1639. DAVENPORT, *New Trick, &c.* S.t. And bold RAMPALLION like, swear and drink drunk.

1822. SCOTT, *Fortunes of Nigel*, xxvi. I was almost strangled with my own band by twa RAMPALLIANS wha wanted yestreen . . . to harle me into a change-house.

RAM-REEL, *subs. phr.* (Scots').—A dance of men; a BULL-DANCE: *cf.* STAG-PARTY.

1813. D. ANDERSON, *Poems*, 122. The chairs they coup, they hurl and loup, A RAM-REEL now they're wantin'.

RAMROD, *subs.* (venery). — The *penis*: *see* PRICK.

*c.*1796. MORRIS, *Plenipotentiary*. The Nymphs of the Stage did his RAMROD engage.

2. (Winchester). — A ball bowled along the ground; a RAYMONDER (*q.v.*)—MANSFIELD (*c.*1840).

RAMSHACKLE. *See* RUMGUMPTION.

RANCE-SNIFFLE, *subs. phr.* (American).—*See* quot.

1869. *Overland Monthly*, III. 131. RANCE-SNIFFLE is a strange combination of words to express a mean and dastardly piece of malignity.

RANDAL'S-MAN (or **RANDLESMAN**), *subs. phr.* (pugilists').—A green handkerchief with white spots: Jack RANDAL's colours: *cf.* BELCHER, BIRD'S-EYE FOGLE, &c.

RANDAN, *adv.* (colloquial). — 1. *See* quot., and (2) *see* RANT.

18 [?]. DICKENS, *Down with the Tide* [Reprinted Pieces]. These duty boats . . . were rowed RANDAN which . . . may be explained as rowed by three men, two pulling an oar each, and one a pair of sculls.

RANDEM- (or **RANDOM-**) **TANDEM**, *subs. phr.* (University).—Three horses driven abreast: *cf.* HARUM SCARUM; SUDDEN DEATH; TANDEM; and UNICORN.

RANDLE, *verb.* (various). — *See* quots.

1847. HALLIWELL, *Archaic Words*, s.v., RANDLE. To punish a schoolboy for an indelicate bnt harmless offence.

1879. THOS. SATCHELL [*Notes & Queries*, 5th S. xi. 405]. From the evidence given in a case before the police magistrate at Birkenhead, it appeared that when any apprentice, at the Britannia Works in that town, remains at work, while the others have decided on taking a holiday, he is punished by a process known as RANDLING. He is surrounded by his companions, who seize him by the hair and pull it at intervals until his scruples are overcome.

RANDY, RAND, RANDAN. *See* RANT.

RANGE, *verb.* (old venery).—To whore; to GROUSE (*q.v.*).—B. E. (*c.*1696). Whence RANGER = (1) a whoremonger; and (2) the *penis* (*see* PRICK): *cf.* the schoolboy rhyme—'Ye bitch of brass, hold up your arse Till I get in my RANGER.

RANGER, *subs.* (old.)—1. A highwayman.

2. (old). — In pl. = mounted troops using short arms: *cf.* Connaught RANGERS (late 88th and 94th Regiments).

3. *See* RANGE, *verb.*

RANK, *adj.* (old colloquial).—1. A generic intensive: unmitigated; utter (B. E., *c.*1696; GROSE, 1785; VAUX, 1819): *e.g.*, A RANK LIE = a flat falsehood; A RANK KNAVE = a rogue of the first water; A RANK OUTSIDER (*see* OUTSIDER); A RANK SWELL = a pink of fashion; A RANK DUFFER = a downright fool; and so forth.

1465-70. MALLORY, *Morte d'Arthur* [E. E. T. S.] l.2402. The RENKE rebelle has been un-to my round Table, Redy aye with Romaynes!

*d.*1547. SURREY, *Ænid*, ii. Whose sacred filletes all besprinkled were With filth of gory blod, and venim RANK.

1596. SHAKSPEARE, *Hamlet*, iii, 4, 148. RANK corruption, mining all within, Infects unseen.

*c.*1616. FLETCHER, *Bonduca*, iv. 2. Run, run, ye rogues, ye precious rogues, ye RANK rogues.

*d.*1719. ADDISON, *Man of the Town.* What are these but RANK pedants.

1834. AINSWORTH, *Rookwood*, III. v. "A RANK scamp!" cried the upright man; and this exclamation, however equivocal it may sound, was intended to be highly complimentary.

1894. MOORE, *Esther Waters*, XXX. I saw that the favourites had been winning. But I know of something, a RANK outsider, for the Leger.

2. (American). — Eager; anxious; impatient [*Century*]: *e.g.* 'I was RANK to get back.'

Verb. (common).—To cheat.

RANK-AND-RICHES, *subs. phr.* (rhyming).—Breeches = trousers.

1887. SIMS, *Tottie* [*Referee*, 7 Nov.]. And right through my RANK-AND-RICHES Did my cribbage-pegs assail.

RANKER, *subs.* (military). — An officer risen from the ranks: *cf.* GENTLEMAN-RANKER.

1878. BESANT and RICE, *By Celia's Arbour*, xxxii. Every regiment has its RANKERS; every RANKER his story. I should be a snob if I were ashamed of having risen.

1886. *St. James's Gaz.*, 2 June, 12. The new Coast battalion, most of whose officers are RANKERS.

RANK-RIDER, *subs. phr.* (old).—1. A highwayman; and (2) a jockey. *See* RIDE, *verb.* Whence RANK-RIDING = rough-riding.—B. E. (*c.*1696); GROSE (1785).

1612. DRAYTON, *Polyolbion*, iii. 28. And on his match as much the Western horseman lays As the RANK-RIDING Scots upon their Galloways.

RANNACK (or **RANNIGAL**), *subs.* (old).—A good-for-nothing.

RANNEL, *subs.* (old Cant).—A whore: *see* TART.

1600. GAB. HARVEY, *Pierces Superer.* Although she were a lusty rampe . . . yet she was not such a roinish RANNEL, such a dissolute Gillian-flirt.

RANSACK, *verb.* (old).—To GROPE (*q.v.*); to deflower; 'to explore point by point.'—B. E. (*c.*1696).

1485. MALLORY, *Morte d'Arthur*, x. civ. And anone he RANSAKYED him.

1602. SHAKSPEARE, *Troilus and Cressida*, ii. 2. But I would have the soil of her fair rape Wip'd off, in honourable keeping her, What treason were it to the RANSACK'D queen . . . .

1605. SYLVESTER, *Du Bartas*, i. 5. With sacrilegious Tools we rudely rend her, And RANSACK deeply in her bosom tender.

RANSHACKLE, *subs.* (common).—To pillage; to ransack [On model of 'RAMSHACKLE' (*q.v.*)].

?]. *Jamie Telfer* [CHILD, *Ballads*, vi. 106]. They loosed the kye out, ane and a' And RANSHACKLED the house right well.

RANT, *verb.* (various: *see* definition).—1. 'To talk Big, High, or Boast much' (B. E., *c.*1696); to storm; to rave: in this sense RANT has always been literary, including the corresponding *subs.*, *adj.*, &c. Whence, however, many usages more or less colloquial:—RANTAN (RANDAN, RANDY, RAND, RANDYDAN, RANT, RANTY, RANTAN, or RANTYTAN) = (1) a jollification, (2) a wenching bout, (3) the sound of a drum, and (4) a drunken frolic; also as *verb.* (or TO GO ON THE RANTAN, &c.) = to go on a round of debauchery; RANTER = (1) 'Extravagants, Unthrifts, Lewd Sparks, also of the Family of Love' (B. E., *c.*1696); (2) = a noisy talker, bawling singer, or ruffian; (3) = a Primitive Methodist: often extended to Dissenters generally, and spec. to a sect dating from 1822, self-registered as such in the Census returns; (4) in pl. = idle drunken boistering; RANTING, *adj.* = (1) in high spirits; and (2) = amorous, HOT (*q.v.*); and (3) extravagant: *see* quot. 1599; RANDY (or RANTY), *subs.* = (1) a beggar, ballad singer, or tinker: espec. such as bully or menace; (2) a scold: also RANDY-DANDY (or RANTY-TANTY); (4) a ramping wanton; (4) *see* RANTAN, *supra*; as *adj.* = (1) vagrant; (2) thieving, shrewish; (3) wanton, HOT (*q.v.*); as *verb.* = (1) *see* RANTAN, *supra*; and (2) to beat continuously, as a tinker; RANTIPOLE, *subs.* = (1) a whore, and (2) a ROMP (*q.v.*), a gallant hussy; as *verb.* = to run about wildly; and as *adj.* = 'wild, rakish, jovial' (B. E., *c.*1696); TO RIDE RANTIPOLE (*see* RIDE); RANTUM-SCANTUM = copulation: *see* RIDE; RANTANKEROUS = quarrelsome; RANTALLION = (GROSE) 'One whose scrotum is so relaxed as to be longer than his *penis*.'

1596. SHAKSPEARE, *Merry Wives*, ii. 1. [OLIPHANT, *New. Eng.*, ii. 25. There is the new Dutch *verb.* RANT]. Look where my RANTING host of the Garter comes.

1599. NASHE, *Lenten Stuffe* [*Harl. Misc.*, vi. 153]. I would not . . . have it cast in my dishe that therefore I prayse Yarmouth so RANTANTINGLY, because I never elsewhere bayted my horse.

1601. JONSON, *Poetaster*, iii. 1. He was born to fill thy mouth . . . he will teach thee to tear and RAND.

1630. TAYLOR, *Workes*, 110. There is RANTAN Tom Tinker and his Tib, And there's a jugler with his fingers glib.

1662. WILSON, *Cheats*, i. I was t'other night UPON THE RANDAN, and who should I meet with but our old gang, some of St. Nicholas' clerks.

1697. *Praise of Yorkshire Ale*, 5. Mistake me not, Custom, I mean not tho, Of excessive drinking, as great RANTERS do.

1699. CONGREVE, *Way of the World*, iv. 10. What, at years of discretion, and comport yourself at this RANTIPOLE rate.

1712. ARBUTHNOT, *Hist. John Bull*, II. iii. She used to RANTIPOLE about the house. *Ibid.* III. viii. She threw away her money upon roaring swearing bullies and RANDY beggars that went about the streets.

1730. JAS. MILLER, *Humours of Oxford*, v. But couldst thou not learn, Timothy, who it is that the RANTIPOLE is going to marry?

17 [?]. P. KIRKDEN, *Statts. Ac.*, ii. 515. Many RANDIES infest this country from the neighbouring towns and the Highlands.

1772. BRIDGES, *Burlesque Homer*, 57. Juno and he have had their quantum, And PLAY no more AT RANTUM-SCANTUM.

*b.*1796. BURNS, *Jolly Beggars.* Ae night, at e'en, a merry cove O' RANDIE gangrel bodies. *Ibid.* Wi' quaffing and laughing, They RANTED and they sang. *Ibid.*, *To James Tennant.* Yours, Saint or Sinner, Rob the RANTER.

1815. SCOTT, *Guy Mannering*, III. 304. I was the mad RANDY gypsey, that had been scourged, and banished and branded. *Ibid.* (1816), *Black Dwarf*, ii. I hae a good conscience, unless it be about a RANT among the lasses, or a splore at a fair.

1822. *Steamboat*, 179. 'You are one of the protectors of innocence, I can see that!' cried a RANDY-LIKE woman.

183 [?]. CARLYLE [FROUDE, *Life in London*, xviii.]. That scandalous RANDY of a girl.

*c.*1852. *Traits of Amer. Humour*, 49. He was the darndest, RANTANKEROUS hossfly that ever clum a tree.

1871. *Figaro*, 15 Ap. We put him down near Sloane Square—There was a RANTERS' chapel there.

1885. *Punch*, 27 June, 303. The Oracle, he Talks RANTIPOLE rubbish and fiddle-de-dee!

1887. STEVENSON, *John Nicolson*, vii. [*Yule Tide*, 9]. John had been (as he was pleased to call it) visibly ON THE RANDAN the night before.

2. (streets').—*See* quot.

1887. *Walford's Antiquarian*, Ap. 253. To RANT is to appropriate anything in a forcible manner. "Lets go and RANT their marleys," says one urchin to another, and straightway the pair annex the possessions of a more respectable party. But it is also used to denote undue freedom with females, and springs, no doubt, from RANTIPOLE.

RAP, *subs.* and *verb.* (old).—Quick, forcible, explosive action: generic: *e.g.* (1) a blow; 'a Polt on the pate, and a hard knocking at a Door' (B. E., *c.*1696); (2) a FART (*q.v.*); (3) an oath or exclamation (also RAPPER); and (4) a severe reprimand: as a RAP ON (or OVER) THE FINGERS, KNUCKLES, &c. Hence, as *verb.* = (1) to strike smartly or to speak forcibly (espec. to reprimand): usually with OFF or OUT; (2) to break wind; (3) to swear; (4) to perjure oneself: to deal a blow at one's honor or another's reputation (GROSE, 1785). Also ON THE RAP = on the SPREE (*q.v.*); IN A RAP = in a moment; RAPFULLY = violently; RAPPED = (1) ruined; (2) knocked out of time; and (3) killed.

1512-3. DOUGLAS, *Virgil*, 74, 13. The broken skyis RAPPIS furth thunderis leuin.

*d.*1549. [? BORDE], *Mylner of Abington* [HAZLITT, *Early Pop. Poet.*, iii. 115]. His wife lent him suche a RAPPE, That stil on grounde he laie.

*c.*1553. UDALL, *Roister Doister*, IV. iii. To speede we are not like, Except ye RAPPE OUT a ragge of your Rhetorike.

*d.*1577. GASCOIGNE [CHALMERS, *Wks.*, ii. 486, 'In Praise of Lady Sandes']. He . . . sodainly with mighty mace gan RAP hir on the pate.

1582. STANYHURST, *Æneid*, iii. 566. And a sea-belch grounting on rough rocks RAPFULLY fretting.

1591. GREENE, *Second Part Conny-catching* [*Works*, x. 99]. He began to chafe, and to sweare, and to RAP OUT gogges Nownes.

1593. SHAKSPEARE, *Taming of Shrew*, i. 2, 12. Villain, I say, knock me at this gate, And RAP me well. *Ibid.* And RAP him soundly, sir.

1610. *Percy Folio MS.*, 'Fryar and Boye,' 104. I would shee might a RAPP let goe that might ring through the place.

1612. SHELTON, *Don Quixote*, iv. 18. He RAPPED OUT an oath or two.

1712. ARBUTHNOT, *John Bull* [OLIPHANT, *New Eng.*, ii. 155. The new substantives are . . . yellow-boy . . , RAP OVER THE FINGER ENDS . . .].

1743. FIELDING, *Jon. Wild*, I. xiii. It was his constant maxim, that he was a pitiful fellow who would stick at a little RAPPING for his friend.

1749. SMOLLETT, *Gil Blas* [ROUTLEDGE], 216. The sheepish acquiescence of a man who stood in awe of an ecclesiastical RAP ON THE KNUCKLES.

1751. FIELDING, *Amelia*, I. x. Though I never saw the lady in my life, she need not be shy of us: d—n me! I scorn to RAP* against any lady. [* A cant word meaning to swear, or rather perjure yourself.]

1768. ROSS, *Helenore*, 116. Honest Jean brings forth in a RAP The green-horn cutties rattling in her lap.

1818. SCOTT, *Midlothian*, xx. When three words of your mouth would give the girl the chance . . . you make such scruple about RAPPING [swearing] to them.

1839. THACKERAY, *Fatal Boots* (August). I RAPPED OUT a good number of oaths.

1861. ELIOT, *Silas Marner*, iv. Dunstan . . . was always RAPPING his whip somewhere.

1879. *Auto. of Thief* [*Macm. Mag.*, xl. 501]. I said, "All right," but he RAPPED "It is not all right."

1888. SIMS, *Plank Bed Ballad* [*Referee*, 12 Feb.]. And he RAPPED, I shall just turn you over.

1888. BOLDREWOOD, *Robbery Under Arms*, xxiii. If he tries to draw a weapon, or move ever so little, he's RAPPED at that second.

1893. MILLIKEN, *'Arry Ballads*, 51. The way the passengers stared at me showed I was fair ON THE RAP.

1897. MARY KINGSLEY, *W. Africa*, 390. A severe RAP ON MY moral KNUCKLES from my conscience.

5. (old).—A counterfeit Irish coin nominally worth a halfpenny, but intrinsically less than half a farthing: proclaimed May 5th, 1737. Hence (6) the smallest unit of value: *see* CARE and WORTH; and (7) a cheat (Scots'); whence RAPLESS = penniless, STONY (*q.v.*).—GROSE (1785).

1724. SWIFT, *Drapier's Letters* [FAULKNER (1735), iv. 66]. Many counterfeits passed about under the name of RAPS.

1823. MONCRIEFF, *Tom and Jerry*, i. 7. I could have betted every RAP—six quid to four——

1834. AINSWORTH, *Game of High Toby* [*Rookwood*]. For the mare-with-three-legs, boys, I care not a RAP.

1900. WHITE, *West End*, 283. 'I always thought Delane had settled a handsome sum on her.' Delane never offered her a RAP. She wouldn't accept it if he did.

1902. *Sp. Times*, 1 Feb., 1, 4. But for my point of view Susie cared not a RAP.

Verb. (old).—1. See *subs.* 1.

2. (old).—To barter; to SWOP (*q.v.*).—B. E. (*c.*1696); GROSE (1785).

RAPE, *subs.* (back slang).—A pear.

RAPPAREE, *subs.* (old).—1. An Irish robber or outlaw; whence (2) a vagabond. [MALONE: They armed themselves with a rapparee or half-pike.]—B. E. (*c.*1696); GROSE (1785).

RAPPER, *subs.* (common).—1. A lie; a WHOPPER (*q.v.*).—B. E. (*c.*1696); GROSE (1785). Also (2), *see* RAP, sense 1. Whence RAPPING = very.

*d.*1688. PARKER, *Rep. of Rehers. Transp.*, 200. Though this is no flower of the sun, yet I am sure it is something that deserves to be called a RAPPER.

RAPSCALLION (RASCALLION, RABSCALLION, RAMSCALLION, or **RASCABILIAN)**, *subs.* (old).—A worthless wretch. Hence RAPSCALLIONRY, &c. = the world of rascaldom. Also as *adj.*

1622. BRETON, *Strange Newes*, 6. Makes no little gaine of RASCABILIANS.

1663. BUTLER, *Hudibras*, I. iii. 327. Used him so like a base RASCALLION.

1703. WARD, *London Spy*, v. 110. And there we saw a parcel of Ragged RAPSCALLIONS, mounted upon Scrubbed Tits.

1733. FIELDING, *Don Quixote*, i. 1. The Don is just such another lean RAMSCALLION as his . . . Rozinante. *Ibid.* (1742), *Joseph Andrews*, IV. iii. A profession [the legal] . . . which owes to such kind of RASCALLIONS the ill-will which weak persons bear towards it.

1749. SMOLLETT, *Gil Blas* (1812), III. iv. Let us take an oath never to serve such RAPSCALLIONS, and swear to it by the river Styx.

1772. BRIDGES, *Burlesque Homer*, 216. As to that copper-nosed RABSCALLION, Venus's bully-back and stallion.

*d.*1824. BYRON, *Letter to Mr. Murray* [*Ency. Dict.*]. The pompous RASCALLION.

1847. LYTTON, *Lucretia*, I. x. But the poor RAPSCALLION had a heart larger than many honest painstaking men.

1885. *Daily News*, 29 Sept. To give no goods to those RAPSCALLION servants.

RAREE-SHOW, *subs. phr.* (old).—A peep-show: specifically one carried in a box. Hence, RAREE-SHOWMAN = 'a poor Savoyard trotting up and down with portable Boxes of Puppet-shews at their backs . . . Pedlars of Puppets.'—B. E. (*c.*1696); GROSE (1785).

1697. VANBRUGH, *Provoked Wife*, ii. 1. Your language is a suitable trumpet to draw people's eyes upon the RAREE-SHEW.

1707. WARD, *Hud. Rediv.*, II. vi. 3. The Rabble-Rout, Who move, in Tumults, to and fro, To wonder at the RAREE-SHOW.

1751. SMOLLETT, *Peregrine Pickle*, xlv. At last Pickle, being tired of exhibiting this RAREE-SHOW . . . handed her into the coach.

1837. LYTTON, *Maltravers*, v. xii. He expressed a dislike to be visited merely as a RAREE-SHOW.

1885. *Field*, 4 Ap. As though a Catholic Church were a theatre or RAREE-SHOW.

RASCAL, *subs.* (colloquial).—1. A term of (*a*) affection, and (*b*) contempt: *cf.* 'rogue,' 'scamp,' &c. (B. E., *c.*1696, and GROSE, 1785). Also (2) 'a man without genitals' (GROSE, 1785). Whence RASKABILIA = the rascal people. *See* RAPSCALLION.

1557. TUSSER, *Husbandrie*, 25. Beware RASKABILIA, slothful to worke.

RASHER-OF-WIND, *subs. phr.* (common).—1. A thin person; a LAMP-POST (*q.v.*), or YARD OF PUMP-WATER (*q.v.*).

2. (common). — Anything of little or no account.

1899. *D. Telegraph*, 7 Ap., 8, 2. Lets 'em howl, an' sweat, an' die, an' goes on all the time, as if they was jest RASHERS O' WIND.

RASP, *subs.* (venery).—The female *pudendum*: *see* MONOSYLLABLE. TO RASP (or DO A RASP) = to copulate: *see* GREENS and RIDE.

RASPBERRY, *subs.* (stable). — *See* quot.

*c.*1880. *Sporting Times* [S. J. & C.]. One gentleman I came across had a way of finding out the cussedness of this or that animal by a method that I found to be not entirely his own. The tongue is inserted in the left cheek and forced through the lips, producing a peculiarly squashy noise that is extremely irritating. It is termed, I believe, a RASPBERRY, and when not employed for the purpose of testing horseflesh, is regarded rather as an expression of contempt than of admiration.

RASPBERRY-TART, *subs. phr.* (American).—A dainty girl.

2. (rhyming).—The heart; and (3) a FART (*q.v.*).

1892. MARSHALL, *Rhyme of the Rusher* [*Sporting Times*, 29 Oct.]. Then I sallied forth with a careless air, And contented RASPBERRY-TART.

RASPER, *subs.* (various).—Anything especial: as (hunting) a bad leap; (common) a punishing blow, rank tradesman, or flat falsehood; (Stock Exchange) a big turn or large profit; and so forth. Hence RASPING-SHORTER (cricketers') = a ball which, blocked by the bat, glides swiftly along the ground instead of rebounding.

1834. AINSWORTH, *Rookwood*, IV. viii. A stiff fence, captain—a reg'lar RASPER.

1841. JOHN MILLS, *Old Eng. Gentleman*, xiv. 114 (3rd Ed.). A fence of little less than six feet in height was before their horses' heads. Straight as winged arrows they flew at the leap, and cleared the RASPER without touching a shoe.

1858. Dr. J. BROWN, *Spare Hours*, 3 S. 60. You cannot . . . make him keep his seat over a RASPING fence.

1881. *Century Mag.*, xxxii. 336. Three-fourths of our fences . . . average somewhat better than four feet in height, with an occasional RASPER that will Come well up to five.

1885. *Field*, 26 Dec. Away over some RASPING, big fences.

1888. *Sporting Life*, 10 Dec. Denny . . . occasionally got home a RASPER.

RASPIN (THE), *subs.* (Old Cant).—Bridewell.

RAT, *subs.* (common).—1. A renegade: espec. through self-interest. Whence (political), a deserter; or (trades-unionists') a workman accepting lower than the Union rate, or working when his mates have 'struck': also RATTER; as *verb.*, or TO DO A RAT, in all these senses, whence (loosely) to change one's views or tactics. Hence RATTING (RATTENING, or RATTERY) = apostacy; RAT-SHOP (HOUSE, or OFFICE) = a workshop where full rates are not paid; TO RATTEN = to destroy tools and appliances, to intimidate fellow workmen, or (masters') to lock out employees or engage non-Union (or 'free') labour.—GROSE (1785); BEE (1823).

1822. SIDNEY SMITH, *Letters* [Ency. Dict.]. The RATTERY and scoundrelism of public life.

1830. CROKER [*Croker Papers*, ii. 76]. He talked of resigning with his colleagues as a matter of course, but the knowing ones suspect that he will RAT.

1838. LYTTON, *Alice*, v. ii. Political faction loves converts better even than consistent adherents. A man's rise in life generally dates from a well-timed RAT.

1840. BARHAM, *Ingolds. Leg.* (*Lay of St. Aloys*). Don't give too much credit to people who RAT!

1847. THACKERAY, *Vanity Fair*, II. v. He might have been a Peer if he had played his cards better. Mr. Pitt had very nearly made him; but he RATTED always at the wrong time.

*d.*1859. MACAULAY [TREVELYAN, I. 275.] I am fully resolved to oppose several of the clauses. But to declare my intention publicly . . . would have the appearance of RATTING.

1863. *Notes and Queries*, 3rd S., iv. 430. We should not now call a man a RAT for accepting office under a government of which he had spoken with disapprobation at the circuit table.

1870. STANHOPE, *Hist. England*, vii. 315. The word RAT (both the noun and the verb) was just . . . levelled at the converts to the Government of George the First, but has by degrees obtained a wider meaning, and come to be applied to any sudden and mercenary change in politics.

1870. *English Gilds* [E. E. T. S.], Int. cxxvii. For enforcing payment of entrance-fees . . . as well as of fines the Craft Gilds made use of the very means of much talked of in the case of the Sheffield Trade-Unions, namely RATTENING: that is, they took away the tools of their debtors.

1878. GEORGE HOWELL, *Conflicts of Capital and Labour*, viii. 13. RATTENING, as defined by the Report of the Royal Commission, is "the abstraction of the workman's tools, so as to prevent him from earning his livelihood until he has obeyed the arbitrary orders of the union.'

1885. *Evening News*, 21 Sept., 1/6. A master baker can always get rid of an obnoxious or too outspoken unionist journeyman baker, and replace him with one of the numerous RATS ever on the look-out for a job.

1888. *Puck's Library*, Jan. 13. When the Chinaman becomes a compositor, he will most likely prefer a RAT-OFFICE.

1892. *Globe*, 2 Ap., 2, 4. He would rather like to see him brought down to this House," he said, "where he would find plenty of occupation, as on this (the Opposition) side there were a good many RATS.

2. (Old Cant).—A clergyman: *see* SKY-PILOT.—GROSE (1785).

1628. EARLE, *Microcos.* [BLISS (1811), 195]. A profane man is one that . . . nick-names clergymen with all the terms of reproach as RAT, black-coat, and the like.

3. (old).—'A drunken person when in custody.'—B. E. (*c.*1696); GROSE (1785). Whence (in pl.) = D.T.'s (*q.v.*); DRUNK AS A RAT = hopelessly drunk: *see* SCREWED.

1553. T. WILSON, *Rhet.* (1580), 128. As DRONKE AS A RATTE.

1661. *Merry Drollery*, 28. He walks about the country . . . DRUNK AS A RAT, you'd hardly wot That drinking so he could trudge it.

*c.*1685. *Roxburghe Ballads* [Brit. Mus. ii. 101]. His master one night got DRUNK RS A RAT.

4. (nautical). — An infernal machine: espec. one used to founder insured bottoms.

*c.*1880. TIMES [S. J. & C.]. There are two species of RATS. One species is intended to operate upon iron ships, the other upon wooden ones.

5. (back slang).—In *pl.* = a star.

6. (thieves').—A police spy: *see* NARK; hence (general) a term of contempt.

7. (obsolete). — A hairpad, somewhat resembling a rat in shape, *circa* 1860-70. Also as *verb.*

PHRASES.—TO SMELL A RAT = to suspect a trick or roguery (Florio; B. E.; GROSE); TO GIVE GREEN RATS = to malign or backbite; TO HAVE (or SEE) RATS = (1) to be eccentric, (2) out of sorts, (3) drunk, and (4) crazy: also RATS IN THE GARRET (LOFT, or UPPER STORY); LIKE A DROWNED RAT = sopping wet; RAT ME = a varient of ROT ME: an objurgation; RATS! = a contemptuous retort: *see* WATER.

*c.*1508. *Colyn Blowbol's Test* [HAZLITT, *Early Pop. Poetry*, i. 93, 31.]. He lokyd furyous as a wyld catt, And pale or hew LIKE A DROWNED RATT.

*c.*1529. *Image of Ipocrysy*, 51. For yf they SMELL A RATT, They grisely chide and chatt.

1630. WADSWORTH, *Pilgr.* viii., 84. I got on shore as WET AS A DROWNED RAT.

1633. JONSON, *Tale of a Tub*, iv. 3. Do you not SMELL A RAT? I tell you truth, I think ali's knavery.

1664. COTTON, *Virgil Travestie*, 23. He straight began to SMELL A RAT, And soon perceiv'd what they'd be at.

1708-10. SWIFT, *Pol. Conv.*, 17. Take Pity on poor Miss; don't throw Water on a DROWNDED RAT.

1772. BRIDGES, *Burlesque Homer*, 204. Tydides' heart went pit-a-pat, For he began to SMELL A RAT.

1830. BARRINGTON, *Personal Sketches. Sir Boyle Roche*: 'Mr. Speaker, I SMELL A RAT; I see him forming in the air and darkening the sky; but I'll nip him in the bud.'

1840. LYTTON, *Paul Clifford*, xxxiv. "Whew!" said he, lifting up his forefinger, "whew! I SMELL A RAT; this stolen child, then, was no other than Paul.'

1865. YATES, *Land at Last*, v. "Well, and now, old boy, how are you?" "Well, not very brilliant this morning, Algy. I——" "Ah, like me, GOT RATS, haven't you?"

1880. *New Virginians*, II. 229. Looking like the DROWNDEST OF DROWNED RATS.

1886-96. MARSHALL, *His Bit of Trouble* ['Pomes,' 122]. One word, and that was RATS!

1892. *Ally Sloper*, 27 Feb., 66, 3. "I had 'em again last night, old man,' . . . "The usual thing?" asked Boozer. . . . "No," said Lushington, "it was a regular mixture—RATS and skeletons . . . all sorts."

1901. *Troddles*, 46. 'What is it?' . . . 'Foot sugar, my boy.' 'What do you do with it—make it into a poultice, or use it as you do mustard, for colds?' 'RATS! . . . didn't you ever have a toffee scramble?'

1902. *D. Telegraph*, 11 Feb., 7, 2. I did not issue my writ in anticipation of one being issued by the other party. They SMELT A RAT.

RATHER! *intj.* (common).—A strong affirmative; 'yes'; 'I should think so': sometimes RAYTHER. Also RATHERISH (American) = in some degree; slightly.

1836. DICKENS, *Sketches by Boz*, 240. "Do you know the mayor's house?" inquired Mr. Trott. "RATHER," replied the boots, significantly, as if he had some good reason to remember it.

1862. *New York Trib.*, 22 April [*Century*]. Lavalette is RATHERISH against Popish temporality: Gen. Guyon is RATHER favourable to it.

RATHER OF THE RATHEREST, *phr.* (colloquial).—Said of anything slightly in excess or defect; in Norfolk of underdone meat.

RAT-HOLE, *subs. phr.* (printers').—1. An overwide space between printed words; a PIGEON-HOLE (*q.v.*). *See* also RAT, *subs.* 1.

RATIONS, *subs.* (military and naval).—A flogging.

RAT'S-TAIL, *subs. phr.* (legal).—A writ; a *capias*.

RATTLE, *subs.* (old).—1. A dice-box (B. E., *c.*1696; GROSE, 1785). Also (2 and 3) *see* verb. 1, and RATTLER, 2. Also (4) in *pl.* = (a) the croup, and (b) the throat rattle preceding death.

Verb. (colloquial). — Generic for rapid movement or noisy loquacity: hence (1) to talk or move quickly or noisily (B. E. and GROSE); (2) to censure, confuse, or irritate. Whence, as *subs.* = (1) a clamour of words; (2) a scolding; (3) a lively talker: also (senses 1 and 2) RATTLING. Derivatives are numerous: RATTLE-BABY = a chattering child; RATTLE-BAG (-BLADDER, -BRAIN, -CAP, -HEAD, -PATE, -SCULL, or RATTLER) = a flighty blab, a chatterbox (*see* RATTLE-TRAP): *cf.* SCOTT, *Redgauntlet*, xi.. "The Bishop's summoner that they called 'The Deil's RATTLEBAG'": also as *adjs.* = chattering, whimsical, giddy; RATTLED = confused or flurried; WITH A RATTLE = with a rush or spurt; TO RATTLE UP = to gather noisily; TO RATTLE DOWN = to disperse with a clatter; RATTLER = (1) a RATTLE-BAG, *supra*; (2) a smart blow or sound scolding; (3) an out-and-out lie; (4) a coach, cab, or train; (5) a rattle-snake (Amer.); (6) in *pl.*, the teeth, or GRINDERS (*q.v.*); and (7) anything extra fine in size, value, &c.; RATTLING = (1) brisk; and (2) lively and conspicuous in pace, habit, manners, &c.; RATTLING-COVE = a coachman; RATTLING-MUMPER = a carriage beggar (B. E.; HALL; GROSE; VAUX). Also *see* SHAKE, TATS.

1592. SHAKSPEARE, *Mid. Night's Dream*, v. 1, 102. The RATTLING tongue of saucy and audacious eloquence.

1596. NASHE, *Saffron Walden* [GROSART, *Works*, iii. 147]. They RATLED him vp soundly, and told him if he would be conformable to the order of the prison so it was, otherwise hee should bee forc't.

1611. COTGRAVE, *Dict.* [HALLIWELL]. Extreamely reviled, cruelly RATLED, horribly railed on.

1613. BEAUMONT and FLETCHER, *Honest Man's Fortune*, v. 3. If my time were not more precious . . . I would RATTLE thee, it may be beat thee.

1630. TAYLOR, *Works* [NARES]. If our hackney RATLERS were so drawne, With cords, or ropes, or halters.

1633. COTTINGTON, *To Strafford* [HALLAM, *Const. Hist.*, II. 89]. The King hath so RATTLED my lord-keeper that he is the most pliable man in England.

1633. PRYNNE, *1 Histrio-Matrix*, i. v. Our lascivious, impudent, RATTLE-PATED gadding females.

1636. HEYWOOD, *Love's Mistress*, 9. Boys without beards get boys, and girls bear girls; Fine little RATTLE-BABIES, scarce thus high, Are now called wives.

1644. HEYLIN, *Life of Laud*, 257. Receiving such a RATTLE for his former contempt.

*d.*1649. HAKEWELL, *Apology*. All this ado about the golden age, is but an empty RATTLE and frivolous conceit.

1669. PEPYS, *Diary*, 25 March. I did lay the law open to them, and RATTLE the master-attendants out of their wits almost.

1693. HACKET, *Williams*, i. 130. Many RATTLEHEADS as well as they, did bestir them to gain-stand this match.

1694. CONGREVE, *Double Dealer*, ii. 4. Pray your ladyship, give me leave to be angry—I'll RATTLE him up, I warrant you.

1701. FARQUHAR, *Sir Henry Wildair*, v. 3. I rather fancy that the RATTLE-HEADED fellow, her husband, has broken the poor lady's heart.

1708. SWIFT, *Agst. Abolishing Xtnty.* [*Ency. Dict.*]. He RATTLES it out against Popery. *Ibid.*, *Jour. Stella*, lx. I chid the servants and made a RATTLE.

1709. STEELE, *Tatler*, No. 2. My Lady with her tongue was still prepar'd, She RATTLED loud, and he impatient heard.

1715. HEARNE, *Reliquiæ*, 1715. Townshend, one of the secretaries of state, hath sent RATTLING letters to Dr. Charlett.

1749. FIELDING, *Tom Jones*, IV. v. Tom, though an idle, thoughtless, RATTLING rascal, was nobody's enemy but his own.

1754. *Disc. John Poulter*, 37. Go three or four miles out of Town to meet the RATTLERS.

1764. MURPHY, *No One's Enemy*, ii. This RATTLE seems to please you: but let me tell you, the man who prevails with me must have extraordinary merit.

1773. GOLDSMITH, *She Stoops to Conquer*, iii. At the Ladies' Club in town I'm called their agreeable RATTLE.

1781. MESSINK, *Choice of Harlequin*, Song. RATTLING UP your darbies, come hither at my call.

1788. STEVENS, *Adv. of a Speculist*, ii. 151. He was such a RATTLE-HEAD, so inconstant and so unthinking.

1790. SHIRREF, *Poems*, 49. Gin Geordy be the RATTLE-SCULL I'm taul', I may expect to find him stiff and baul'.

1818. AUSTEN, *Northanger Abbey*, ix. She had not been brought up to understand the propensities of a RATTLE, nor to know to how many idle assertions and impudent falsehoods the excess of vanity will lead.

1819. MOORE, *Tom Crib*, 8. And long before daylight, gigs, RATTLERS, and prads were in motion for Moulsey.

1820. LAMB, *Elia* (*South-sea House*). A little less facetious, and a great deal more obstreperous, was fine, RATTLING, RATTLE-HEADED Plumer.

1821. EGAN, *Life in London*, II. v. At length a move was made, but not a RATTLER was to be had.

1844. THACKERAY, *Barry Lyndon*, i. 21. He danced prettily, to be sure, and was a pleasant RATTLE of a man.

1848. RUXTON, *Far West*, 12. Crawled like RATTLERS along this bottom.

1854. WHYTE MELVILLE, *General Bounce*, xiii. Who would have suspected the RATTLING, agreeable, off-hand Mount Helicon of deep-laid schemes and daring ambition?

1857. KINGSLEY, *Two Years Ago*, xi. "RATTLE-PATE as I am, I forgot all about it."

1862. *Cornhill*, Nov., 648. We have just touched for a RATTLING stake of sugar at Brum.

1865. DICKENS, *Our Mutual Friend*. I should have given him a RATTLER for himself, if Mrs. Boffin had not thrown herself betwixt us.

1878. JAMES, *Europeans*, iv. Robert Acton would put his hand into his pocket every day in the week if that RATTLE-PATED little sister of his should bid him.

1879. *Macmillan's Mag.*, xl., 501. I'll go to London Bridge RATTLER, and take a dearer ride.

1885. MEREDITH, *Diana of the Crossways*, III. 367. "I RATTLED at her; and oh! dear me, she perks on her hind heels and defies me to prove."

1888. *Daily Chronicle*, 10 Dec. Bachelor came on WITH A RATTLE and won by a length and a half.

1888. BOLDREWOOD, *Robbery Under Arms*, xii. They've fetched a RATTLING price. *Ibid.* xxviii. A RATTLING good magistrate.

1892. *Pall Mall Gaz.*, 19 Mar., 7, 1. Mr. Labouchere made a RATTLING speech against the Reuter contract.

1898. *Pink 'Un and Pelican*, 58. Far be it from me to suggest . . . the painful and vulgar expedient of macing the RATTLER, but the name of the person, if any, who produced . . . twice the necessary 15s. 8d. for the tickets is not forthcoming.

RATTLE-BALLOCKS, *subs. phr.* (venery).—The female *pudendum*. *see* MONOSYLLABLE.

RATTLETRAP, *subs.* (common).—1. The mouth; hence (2) a chatterbox: *see* RATTLE.

1880, *Life in a Debtors' Prison*, 180. You're as great a RATTTETRAP as ever.

3. (colloquial). — Anything old and tumble-down: spec. a broken-down rattling conveyance; also (4) personal belongings: in jocular disparagement, and (GROSE) 'any curious, portable piece of machinery or philosophical apparatus.' As *adj.* = worn-out; crazy.

1830. LYTTON, *Clifford*, xxxiv. 299. Where poor Judy kept her deeds and RATTLETRAPS.

1857. TROLLOPE, *Barchester Towers*, xxxv. "He'd destroy himself and me too, if I attempted to ride him at such a RATTLETRAP as that." A RATTLETRAP! The quintain that she had put up with so much anxious care . . . It cut her to the heart to hear it so denominated by her own brother.

*d.*1861. MRS. GORE, *Castles in the Air*, xxxiv. Hang me if I'd ha' been at the trouble of conveying her and her RATTLE-TRAPS last year across the channel.

RAT-TRAP, *subs. phr.* (obsolete).—A bustle; a BIRD-CAGE (*q.v.*).

RAUGHTY. *See* RORTY.

RAVE, *subs.* (colloquial).—A strong liking; a craze: as 'X has a RAVE on Miss Z.'

RAVILLIAC, *subs.* (Old Cant).—'Any Assasin.'—B. E. (*c.*1696).

RAW, *subs.* (colloquial). —(1) A novice: also Johnny Raw; (2) anything uncooked, as oysters, sugar, &c.

1820. CORCORAN, *The Fancy Glossary*. RAW. An Innocent.

1868. *Chamb. Journal*, 15 Feb., 110. Soft-going RAWS an' delicate boys with romantic heads.

1886. *U.S. Cons. Rep.*, lx. 96. The stock of RAWS on hand amounted . . .

1889. *Century Dict.*, s.v. RAW, I, II. i. An oyster of a kind preferred for eating RAW: as a plate of RAWS.

2. (colloquial).—A tender point; a foible: as 'to touch on the RAWS' = to irritate by allusion or joke; to rub up the wrong way.

1837. MARRYAT, *Snarley-Yow*. This was touching up Vanslyperken ON THE RAW.

1839. *Comic Almanack*, Sept. [HOTTEN], 188. Now they're gettin' out of natur, for their RAWS is all a healing.

1868. COLLINS, *Moonstone*, I. xxii. Sergeant Cuff had hit me ON THE RAW, and, though I did look down upon him with contempt, the tender place still tingled for all that.

1882. STEVENSON, *New Arab. Nights*, 248 (1884). The pleasantry TOUCHED HIM ON THE RAW.

1900. KIPLING, *Stalky & Co.*, 65. The honour of the house' was Prout's weak point, and they knew well how to flick him ON THE RAW.

Adj. (colloquial). — 1. See *subs.* 1.

2. (common). — Undiluted; NEAT (*q.v.*); a RAW RECRUIT = a nip of unwatered spirits.

RAW-HEAD (or **RAW-FLESH**), *subs. phr.* (old).—A spectre; 'a scare-child' (B. E., GROSE): usually RAW-HEAD AND BLOODY-BONES.

1550. *Jyl of Brentford's Test.* [OLIPHANT, *New Eng.*, i. 524. The Devil's secretary bears the name of BLOODDYBONE . . . whom we now couple with RAW-HEAD.]

. . . . *Wyll of the Devyll* [HALLIWELL]. Written by our faithful secretaryes, hobgoblen, RAWHED, AND BLOODYBONE, in the spitefull audience of all the Court of hell.

1598. FLORIO, *Worlde of Wordes*, *Caccianemico*, a bragging craking boaster, a bugbeare, a RAWE-FLESH AND BLOODIE BONE.

1622. FLETCHER, *Prophetess*, iv. 4. I was told before My face was bad enough: but now I look Like BLOODYBONES AND RAW-HEAD to fright children.

1693. LOCKE, *Education*, 138. Servants . . . awe children, and keep them in subjection, by telling them of RAWHEAD AND BLOODY BONES.

1870. *Figaro*, 19 Oct. We have sometimes heard of a school of literature called "The RAW-HEAD AND BLOODYBONES School."

RAW-LOBSTER, *subs. phr.* (obsolete).—A policeman: *cf.* LOBSTER = a soldier.

RAW-MEAT, *subs. phr.* (venery).—1. The *penis*: *see* PRICK; and (2) a nude performer: *see* MEAT.

1766. *Old Song*, 'The Butcher' [*The Eattle*, 13]. All women in love never like to be stinted, Take care that her mag with RAW MEAT is well fed, Lest the horns of an ox should adorn your calves' head.

RAW-'UNS (THE), *subs. phr.* (pugilistic).—The naked fists.

1887. *Daily News*, 15 Sept., 4, 8. This encounter was without gloves, or, in the elegant language of the ring, with the RAW UNS.

1891. *Sporting Life*, 26 Mar. I will stake £1000 to £800, and fight you with the RAW-'UNS. *Ibid.* Even Jem Carney . . . has been obliged to abandon the RAW-UN'S for gloves pure and simple.

RAY, *subs.* (thieves').—*See* quot.

1862. MAYHEW, *Lon. Lab.*, IV. 319. "Joe said to him, 'There is Dick's first trial, and you must give him a RAY for it,' *i.e.*, 1/6.

RAYMONDER. *See* RAMROD, 2.

RAZOR, *subs.* (American University).—*See* quot.

18 [?]. *Yale Univ. Mag.* [S. J. & C.]. A pun in the elegant college dialect is called a RAZOR, while an attempt at a pun is styled a sick RAZOR. The sick ones are by far the most numerous; however, once in a while you meet with one in quite respectable health.

2. (common).—In *pl.* = aerated waters; SOBER-WATER (*q.v.*).

PARLOUR-FULL OF RAZORS. *See* PARLOUR.

RAZOR-STROP, *subs. phr.* (legal).—A copy of a writ.

RAZZLE-DAZZLE, *subs. phr.* (American).—A frolic.

1890. GUNTER, *Miss Nobody*, xiv. I'm going to RAZZLE-DAZZLE the boys . . . with my great lightning change act. *Ibid.*, xv. 'Little Gussie's RAZZLE DAZZLE [Title of chapter].

1901. BINSTEAD, *More Gal's Gossip*, 54. Bank-holidayites on the RAZZLE-DAZZLE.

SLANG AND ITS ANALOGUES

PAST AND PRESENT

A DICTIONARY HISTORICAL AND COMPARATIVE OF THE HETERODOX SPEECH OF ALL CLASSES OF SOCIETY FOR MORE THAN THREE HUNDRED YEARS

WITH SYNONYMS IN ENGLISH, FRENCH, GERMAN, ITALIAN, ETC.

COMPILED AND EDITED BY

JOHN S. FARMER & W. E. HENLEY

VOL. VI.—REA to STOZZLE.

PRINTED FOR SUBSCRIBERS ONLY

—

MCMIII.

Vol. VI.

A Dictionary of Slang and its Analogues.

1829. *Vidocq's Memoirs,* 'On the Prigging Lay' [FARMER, *Musa Pedestris* (1896), 107. I stops a bit : then toddled quicker, For I'd prigged his READER, drawn his ticker.

1834. AINSWORTH, *Rookwood,* III. v. None knap a READER like me in the lay.

1842. EGAN, 'Jack Flashman' (in *Capt. Macheath*). Jack long was on the town, a teazer ; Could turn his fives to anything, Nap a READER, or filch a ring.

1859. MATSELL, 'A Hundred Stretches Hence' [*Vocabulum*]. The bugs, the boungs, and well-filled READERS.

READY (THE) (**READY - STUFF, -JOHN, -GILT,** or **READY-MONEY**), *subs.* (old).—I. Money: spec. money in hand (B. E. and GROSE). Hence READY THICK-'UN = a sovereign ; 20/-: see RHINO.

c.1618. WEBSTER and ROWLEY, *Cure for a Cuckold,* ii. 2. READY MONEY is the prize I look for.

1688. SHADWELL, *Sq. of Alsatia,* I. Take up on the reversion, 'tis a lusty one ; and Cheatly will help you to THE READY.

1712. ARBUTHNOT, *History of John Bull,* I. iii. He was not flush in READY, either to go to law or to clear old debts.

1732. FIELDING, *Covent Garden Tragedy,* ii. I. Therefore, come down THE READY, or I go. *Ibid.* (1743), *Jonathan Wild* (1893), 28. Mr. Wild immediately conveyed the larger share of THE READY into his pocket.

1821. EGAN, *Life in London,* I. v. The notoriety [Logic] had obtained . . . for the Waste of READY in Hoyle's Dominions, was great indeed.

1840. BARHAM, *Ingold. Leg.* (*Merchant of Venice*). While, as for THE READY, I'm like a Church-mouse,—I really don't think there's five pounds in the house.

2. (colloquial). — Prepared. Hence, A GOOD READY = ON THE SPOT (*q.v*).

1886. ROOSEVELT, *Hunting Trips,* 119. Patiently and noiselessly from the leeward . . . his rifle at THE READY.

Verb. (racing). — To pull a horse.

1886-96. MARSHALL, *Nobbled* ['Pomes,' 114]. He made us all . . . believe he could READY his chance.

1889. *Sporting Times,* 29 June. So as not to let the favourite be READIED.

REAL, *adj.* and *adv.* (originally American : now general). — A superlative : very; quite ; really. Whence REAL FINE, GLAD, GOOD, &c. = very fine, glad, good, &c., indeed ; REAL JAM = an acme : see JAM ; REAL GRIT = 'sound to the core': see GRIT ; THE REAL (or THE REAL THING) = the genuine article.

c.1830. *American Humour,* I. I reckon the chaplain was the REAL GRIT for a parson—always doin' as he'd be done by; and practisin' a darn'd sight more than he preached.

1841. THACKERAY, *Men and Pictures,* . . . Persons who make believe that they are handing you round tokay—giving you THE REAL imperial Stuff.

1872. C. D. WARNER, *Backlog Studies,* 4. A cynic might suggest as the motto of modern life this simple legend—'Just as good as THE REAL.'

1879. JUSTIN M'CARTHY, *Donna Quixote,* xvii. But I do like her. I took to her from the first . . . REAL JAM, I call her.

1885. *Punch,* 3 Jan., 4, 2. Without REAL JAM—cash and kisses—this world is a bitterish pill.

REAM. *See* RUM.

REAM-PENNY, *subs. phr.* (old).—Peter-pence (that is 'Rome'-penny). TO RECKON ONE'S REAM PENNIES = to confess one's faults.

REAR, *subs.* (University).—A jakes : also as *verb.*

REBEC (or **REBECK**), *subs.* (old colloquial).—An old woman : in reproach : *cf.* RIBIBE.

1383. CHAUCER, *Cant. Tales,* 'Friar's Tale,' 275. Here woneth an old REBEKKE That hadde almost as lief to lese hire nekke As for to geve a peny of hir good.

RECEIPT-OF-CUSTOM, *subs. phr.* (venery).—The female *pudendum*; the Custom's-house ('where Adam made the first entry') : see MONOSYLLABLE. Hence CUSTOM'S-HOUSE OFFICER = the *penis* (GROSE).

RECEIVER - GENERAL, *subs. phr.* (old).—1. A prostitute : see TART.

2. (pugilists').—A boxer giving nothing for what he gets.

RECKER, THE (or **REKKER**), *subs.* (Harrow).—The town recreation-ground. [Where the school sports are held.]

RECKON, *verb.* (once literary : now American).— To think ; to suppose ; to consider—peculiar to the Middle and Southern States, and provincial [HALLIWELL] in England : *cf.* GUESS and CALCULATE.

1611. *Bible,* Isaiah xxxviii. 13. I RECKONED [*margin,* R.V. = thought] till morning that as a lion, so will he break all my bones. *Ibid.,* Rom. viii. 18. For I RECKON that the sufferings of this present time are not worthy, &c.

d.1745. SWIFT, *Nobles and Commons,* v. I RECKON it will appear to many as a very unreasonable paradox.

1776. FOOTE, *Bankrupt,* iii. What, you are a courtier, I RECKON?

1825. SCOTT, *St. Roman's Well,* x. I RECKON you'll be selling out the whole—it's needless making two bites of a cherry.

1889. *Century Dict.* [American]. RECKON, v. II. 6. The use of RECKON in this sense [to hold a supposition or impression] though regularly developed and found in good literature . . . has by reason of its frequency in colloquial speech in some parts of the United States, especially in the South (where it occupies a place like that of 'guess' in New England), come to be regarded as provincial or vulgar.

1892. GUNTER, *Miss Dividend,* iii. RECKON your pap has had too much railroad and mine on his hands to be able to even eat for the last month.

TO RECKON UP, *verb phr.* (colloquial).—To gauge a person ; TO MEASURE (*q.v.*) ; TO SIZE (*q.v.*). Hence, to slander ; to back-bite.

1852. DICKENS, *Bleak House,* liv. 447. Mr. Tulkinghorn employed me [Bucket, the detective] to RECKON UP her Ladyship.

1877. *Five Years' Penal Servitude,* i. 33. The officer spotted him directly, and if he could not RECKON HIM UP himself, would mark him for the attention of some one else.

See CHICKENS and HOST.

RECKONING. *See* ACCOUNTS.

RECORD. TO BEAT (BREAK, CUT, LOWER, or SMASH) THE RECORD, *verb phr.* (colloquial : chiefly athletic).—To surpass all previous performances, 'to go one BETTER' (*q.v.*).

RECORDITE, *subs.* (obsolete clerical).—The Low Church Party of the Established Church. [Their organ was *The Record.*]

1854. CONYBEARE, *Church Parties,* 16. This exaggeration of Evangelicalism, sometimes called the Puritan, sometimes, from its chief organ, the RECORDITE party. *Ibid.* It is a popular delusion that the RECORDITES are excluded from public amusements.

RECREANT, *subs.* (old : now recognised).—'A Poltron, or Coward, one that eats his Words, or unsaies what he said.'—B.E.(*c.*1696.)

RECRUIT, *subs.* (Old Cant).—In *pl.* = money in prospect : *e.g.,* 'HAVE YOU RAISED THE RECRUITS?' =

REACHER, *subs.* (pugilistic). — I. A blow delivered at long point.

2. (colloquial). —An exaggeration ; a STRETCHER (*q.v.*) : see WHOPPER.

1662. FULLER, *Worthies,* ii. 117. I can hardly believe that REACHER . . . that "with the palms of his hands he could touch his knees, though he stood upright."

REACH-ME-DOWN, *subs. phr.* (common).—In *pl.* = second-hand or ready-made clothes : also HAND-ME-DOWNS : Fr. *décrochez-moi-ça.* Also as *adj.*

1860. THACKERAY, *Philip,* xxiv. In the Palais Royal they hang out the most splendid REACH-ME-DOWN dressing-gowns, waistcoats, and so forth.

1875. BESANT and RICE, *Harp and Crown,* xv. The capitalist who can afford two new pairs of second-hand machine-made REACH-ME-DOWNS in a single winter. Where is he, I say?

1888. W. S. CAINE, *Trip Round the World,* xii. The gentlemen attire themselves in ready-made REACH-ME-DOWNS of black cloth, shiny patent-leather shoes, and round pot-hats.

READ. TO READ BETWEEN THE LINES, *verb. phr.* (colloquial).—To look into a' milestone ; to quest for hidden meanings in plain English.

1883. *Gentleman's Mag.,* June. They READ BETWEEN THE LINES, as they say, and find that two and two are intended to represent five.

TO READ THE PAPER, *verb. phr.* (common).—To take a nap : see DOSS.

READ-AND-WRITE, *subs.* (rhyming).—Flight. Also, as *verb.* = to fight.

READER, *subs.* (thieves').—I. A pocket-book ; (2) a newspaper, letter, &c. Whence TO READ = to steal ; READER-HUNTER (or -MERCHANT) = a pickpocket, a DUMMY-HUNTER (*q.v.*) ; READ-ERED = advertised in the *Police Gazette* ; WANTED (*q.v.*).—PARKER, GROSE, VAUX, BEE.

c.1819. *Song,* 'The Young Prig' [FARMER, *Musa Pedestris* (1896), 82]. And I my READING learnt betime, From studying pocket-books, Sirs.

1828. BEE, *Picture of London,* 286. For this purpose they had an old pocket-book, or READER now put into one pocket, now into another.

'Has the money come in?'—B. E. Whence (GROSE) RECRUITING SERVICE = 'robbing on the highway.'

RECTOR, *subs.* (common).—1. A poker kept for show: CURATE (*q.v.*) = the work-a-day iron; (2) the bottom half of a tea-cake or muffin (as getting more butter), the top half being the CURATE, and so forth.

RECTOR OF THE FEMALES, *subs. phr.* (venery).—The *penis*: *see* PRICK.

1647-80. ROCHESTER, *Poems*. Then pulling out the RECTOR OF THE FEMALES, Nine times he bath'd him in their piping tails.

RED, *subs.* and *adj.* (thieves').—1. Gold: also RED-UN: Fr. *jaune* (= yellow); Ital. *rossume* (= redness). RED-ROGUE (old) = a gold piece; RED-TOY (or KETTLE) = a gold watch; RED-TACKLE = a gold chain. *Cf.* RUDDOCK. RED-UN also = a sovereign.

1617. FLETCHER, *Mad Lover*, v. 4. There's a RED ROGUE, to buy thee handkerchiefs.

1879. *Macm. Mag.*, xl. 502. I touched for a RED TOY and RED TACKLE.

1888. SIMS, *Plank Bed Ballad* [*Referee*, 12 Feb.]. A toy and a tackle—both RED-'UNS.

*c.*1886. *Sporting Times* [S. J. and C.]. "There's a RED-'UN—or in other words 'a quid.'"

1901. *D. Telegraph*, 14 May, 11, 5. You have got a fine RED-'UN. *Ibid.* You just now alluded to your watch as a RED-'UN.—Cooper: I did. And then you explained that "RED-'UN" was thieves' slang.—So it is.

2. (common). — Variously applied to objects red in colour: as (1) a RED HERRING (*q.v.*); (2) in pl., the menses: whence RED-RAG = the menstrual cloth; TO FLASH THE RED RAG = to have one's courses; (3) in pl. = blushes: also RED-RAG, whence TO MOUNT THE RED RAG (or FLAG) = to blush; (4) a Red Republican: spec. (France '93) a violent revolutionary of the established order. *See* also ADMIRAL, RED-CENT, and RED-COAT.

COMBINATIONS are numerous — The RED-ACE (or C) = the female *pudendum*: *see* MONOSYLLABLE; RED-BOOK = a book of the officers of State or the Peerage: *cf.* BLUE-BOOK; RED-BREAST = a Bow-St. runner (they wore red waistcoats); also *see* infra; RED-CENT (*see* quot. 1889, NARY and NICKEL); RED-COAT = a soldier: also THE REDS; RED-COCK = an incendiary fire; RED-CROSS (*see* quot. 1626); RED-DOG (*see* SHINPLASTER); RED-EEL = a term of contempt; RED-EYE (or RED-HEAD) = fiery whiskey; RED-EYE SOUR = whiskey and lemon; RED-FLANNEL = the tongue: *see* RAG, 2; RED-FUSTIAN = (1) port, (2) claret (B. E. and GROSE), and (3) porter: also RED-TAPE; RED-GRATE (*see* RED-LATTICE); RED-HEAD = a red-haired person, a CARROTS (*q.v.*); RED-HERRING = a soldier: *cf.* SOLDIER = a red-herring; RED-HORSE = a native of Kentucky; RED-HOT (*adj.*) = violent, extreme; RED-LETTER DAY = (1) a Church festival (printed in red characters in the Calendar): hence (2) a happy day or lucky occasion (GROSE): whence RED-LETTER MAN = a Roman Catholic (B. E. and GROSE); RED-LINER (*see* quot. 1851); RED-PETTICOAT (*see* quot. 1670); RED-RAG (*see* RAG and RED), and (2) = a source of annoyance or disgust: usually 'a

RED-RAG to a mad-bull'; RED-RIBBON = brandy (GROSE): *cf.* WHITE-SATIN; RED-SAIL DOCKER = a buyer of stores stolen out of the royal yards and docks (GROSE); RED-SKIN = a North American Indian.

*c.*1485. *Lady Bessy* (Queen of Henry VII.) [Percy Soc. Pub. xx.]. [OLIPHANT, *New Eng.*, i. 396. We now first hear of READE COATES, Lord Stanley's soldiers; a well-known word in Cromwell's day, 130 years later].

1626. SMITH, *Treatise on English Sea Terms* [ARBER], 262. [OLIPHANT, *New English*, ii. 66. An English ship is called a RED CROSSE].

1662. *Rump Songs*, ii. 5. Our Politique Doctors do us teach, That a Blood-snarling RED-COAT's as good as a Leech.

1670. RAY, *Proverbs* [BELL], 59. The lass in the RED PETTICOAT shall pay for it. Young men answer so when they are chid for being so prodigal and expensive; meaning, they will get a wife with a good portion, that shall pay for it.

1707. WARD, *Hud. Rediv.*, II. iii., 24. A drum was beaten on the ground By an old RED COAT.

*c.*1720. *Old Song* [DURFEY, *Pills*, &c. (1720) vi. 324]. Old musty Maids that have Money . . . May have a Bit for their Bunny, To pleasure them in their Beds, Their hearts will turn to the RED-COATS.

1815. SCOTT, *Guy Mannering*. . . . We'll see if the RED COCK craw not in his bonny barn-yard ae morning before day dawning.

1826. COOPER, *Last of Mohicans* [BARTLETT]. What may be right and proper in a RED-SKIN may be sinful in a man who has not even a cross in his blood to plead for his ignorance.

1830. LYTTON, *Paul Clifford*, 80. A tumbler of blue ruin fill, fill for me, RED TAPE those as likes it may drain.

1834. AINSWORTH, *Rookwood*, I. ix. Famous wine this—beautiful tipple—better than all your RED FUSTIAN.

1848. RUXTON, *Far West*, 8. Jest then seven darned RED HEADS top the bluff. *Ibid.*, ii. Being as a REDSKIN, thirsting for their lives.

1848. THACKERAY, *Book of Snobs*, xxv. A woman who was intimate with every duchess in THE RED BOOK.

1851. MAYHEW, *London Lab.*, ii. 564. The RED LINERS, as we calls the Mendicity officers, who goes about in disguise as gentlemen, to take up poor boys caught begging.

*c.*1852. *Traits of Amer. Humour*, II. 114. With their furniture, and the remains of a forty-two gallon RED-HEAD.

1852. BRISTED, *Upper Ten Thousand*, 144. It was a great catch for Miss Lewison, without a RED CENT of her own.

1861. MACAULAY, *Eng. Hist.*, iii. "Oliver's REDCOATS had once stabled their horses there."

1871. DE VERE, *Americanisms*, . . . "Salted provisions and RED-EYE to boot" is the refrain of many a rude song, and if the latter is fiery and raw it is none the less welcome.

1883. C. MARVIN, *Gates of Herat*, 98. These opinions cannot but be so many RED RAGS to English Russophobists.

1889. *Century Dict.*, s.v. RED. The copper cent is no longer current, but the phrase RED CENT remains in use as a mere emphatic form of cent: 'as it is not worth a RED CENT.

1888. *Detroit Free Press*, 15 Dec. When I got up on election morning I hadn't a blamed RED in my pockets.

1892. NISBET, *Bushranger's Sweetheart*, 33. Who would take her for twenty-five, and an old traveller, to see her MOUNTING THE RED RAG like a girl of fourteen?

1896. CRANE, *Maggie*, IX. Not a cent more of me money will yehs ever get—not a RED.

1899. WHITEING, *John St.*, 217. Won't it be fine to see the sojers on 'orse-back? I hope its THE REDS.

1892. KIPLING, *Barrack-room Ballads*. 'Tommy.' The publican 'e up an' sez, 'We serve no RED-COATS here.'

1892. *Globe*, 28 Sept. 6, 1. On his journey he gathers the anathemas of those to whom the literary picture is the RED RAG.

NEITHER FISH, FLESH, FOWL, NOR GOOD RED-HERRING, *phr.* (old).—Nondescript; neither one thing nor another; neither hay nor grass.—RAY.

1528. *Rede me and be nott Wrothe*, I. iij. b. Wone that is NETHER FLESSHE NOR FISSHE.

1530. TYNDALE, *Works* [Parker Soc. i. 299]. We know not whether they be good or bad, or whether they be FISH OR FLESH.

1546. HEYWOOD, *Proverbs*, I. x. Shee is NEITHER FISH, NOR FLESH, NOR GOOD RED HERRING.

1598. SHAKSPEARE, *2 Hen. IV.*, iv. 3. She's NEITHER FISH NOR FLESH; a man knows not where to have her.

1656. *Muses Recr.* [HOTTEN], 94. They are NEITHER FISH, FLESH, NOR GOOD RED HERRING.

[?] MARSDEN, *Hist. Ch. Churches*, i. 267. "They were neither Parsons, nor Vicars, nor stipendiary curates; in fact, They were NEITHER FISH, NOR FLESH, NOR GOOD RED HERRING."

1683. DRYDEN, *Duke of Guise*, Epil. Damn'd Neuters, in their Middle way of Steering, Are NEITHER FISH, NOR FLESH, NOR GOOD RED HERRING.

TO PAINT (or VARNISH) THE TOWN RED (or CRIMSON), *verb. phr.* (American).—*See* quot.

1889. *Detroit Free Press*, 9 Mar. PAINTING THE TOWN RED undoubtedly originated among the cowboys of western Texas, who, upon visits to frontier towns, would first become very drunk, or pretend to be so, and then mount their bronchos, gallop up and down the principal street, shooting at anything, and signifying their intention to PAINT THE WHOLE TOWN RED if any opposition to their origies was attempted. It was a mere extravagant threat: one constable could usually put the whole band in the calaboose.

1891. *Harry Fludyer at Cambridge*, 105. Now, do come . . . to see us row. We've got a good chance of going head, and if we do, my eye, won't we PAINT THE WHOLE PLACE RED on Tuesday night!

1892. *Pall Mall Gaz.*, 17 Oct., 2, 3. He appears here as the typical Johnnie . . . whose aid is sought by young men who are desirous of PAINTING THE TOWN RED.

REDBREASTS (THE), *subs. phr.* (military).—1. The 5th (Royal Irish) Lancers.

2. *See* RED.

RED FEATHERS (THE), *subs. phr.* (military).—The late 46th Foot, now the 2nd Batt. Duke of Cornwall's Light Infantry. [A light company were brigaded with others in 1777 as "The Light Battalion." The Americans, harassed by the Brigade, vowed "No Quarter." In derision, to prevent mistakes, the Light Battalion dyed their feathers red.] Also "Murray's Bucks"; "The Surprisers"; "The Lacedemonians"; and "The Docs."

REDGE (or **RIDGE**), *subs.* (old).—Gold: *see* RED, *subs.* 1. Hence REDGE-CULLY = a goldsmith.

1665. HEAD, *English Rogue* (1874), I. v. 52, s.v. RIDGE-CULLY.

1741. *Kentish Post*, No. 2479, 4, 1., s.v.

1834. AINSWORTH, *Rookwood*, III. v. With my thimble [watch] of RIDGE.

RED-KNIGHTS, *subs. phr.* (military).—The Cheshire Regiment (formerly the Twenty-second Regiment of Foot). [In 1795 it was served with red jackets, waistcoats and breeches in lieu of the proper uniform.] Also THE TWO TWO'S.

RED (or **SCARLET**) **LANCERS (THE)**, *subs. phr.* (military).—The 16th (The Queen's) Lancers. [The only Lancer regiment with a scarlet tunic.]

RED-LANE (-CLOSE or **-SEA)**, *subs. phr.* (old).—The throat; GUTTER-ALLEY (*q.v.*).—GROSE.

1566. UDAL, *Roister Doister*, i. 3. *M. Mumb.* And sweete malte maketh ioly good ale for the nones. *Tib Talk.* Whiche will slide downe the LANE without any bones.

1814. COLMAN, *Poetical Vagaries* (1814), 75. O butter'd egg, best eaten with a spoon, I bid your yelk glide down my throat's RED LANE.

RED-LATTICE (or **-LETTICE**), *subs. phr.* (old).—An ale-house sign. Hence RED-LATTICE PHRASES = pothouse talk: also GREEN LATTICE; RED-GRATE = tavern or brothel, or both combined.—B. E. and GROSE.

1596. SHAKSPEARE, *Merry Wives*, ii. 2. Your cat-a-mountain looks, your RED-LATTICE phrases, and your bold beating oaths. *Ibid.* (1598), *2 Henry IV.*, ii. 1. He called me even now, my lord, through a RED LATTICE.

1596. JONSON, *Ev. Man in his Humour*, iii. 3. I dwell, sir, at the sign of the Water Tankard, hard by the GREEN LATTICE: I have paid Scot and lot there any time this eighteen years.

1602. MARSTON, *Auton. and Mellida*, v. No, I am not sir Jeffery Balurdo: I am not as well known by my wit, as an alehouse by a RED LATTICE.

*c.*1607. WILKINS, *Mis. of Inf. Marr* [DODSLEY, *Old Plays* (REED), v. 44]. Be mild in a tavern! 'tis treason to the RED-LATTICE, enemy to the sign post, and slave to humour.

1622. MASSINGER, *Virgin Martyr*, iii. 3. *Spun.* I see then a tavern and a bawdy-house have faces much alike; the one hath RED GRATES next the door, the other hath peeping-holes within-doors.

REDRAW, *subs.* (back slang).—A warder; a JIGGER-DUBBER (*q.v.*).

1875. GREENWOOD, *Low-life Deeps*. Shying a lump of wet oakum at the REDRAW.

REDSHANKS, *subs.* (old). — *See* quots.—GROSE.

*c.*1540. ELDAR [PINKERTON, *Hist. Scot.*, ii. 396]. Both summer and winter . . . going always barelegged and barefooted . . . therefore . . . as we use and delight, so to go always, the tender delicate gentlemen of Scotland call us REDSHANKS.

1542. BOORDE, *Works* [E. E. T. S.] [OLIPHANT, *New Eng.*, i. 495. We see REDSHANK (applied to the Irish)].

1565. STAPLETON, *Bede*, B iii., c 4. A priest . . . called Columban cam from Ireland into Britany to preche the woorde of God to the REDSHANKES [Picti] as dwelt in the south quarters.

1577. HOLINSHED, *Hist. Scotland*, 318. In the battle of Bannockburn were three thousande of the Irish Scots, otherwise called Kateranes or REDSHANKS.

*d.*1599. SPENSER, *State of Ireland*. He [Robert Bruce, 1306-30] sent over his brother Edward with a power of Scots and REDSHANKS unto Ireland, where they got footing.

1610. *England's Eliza*, Mirr. M. 804 [NARES]. When the REDSHANKES on the borders by.

1630. TAYLOR, *Works* [NARES]. High-land-men, who for the most part speake nothing but Irish; and in former time were . . . called the RED-SHANKES.

1730. BURT, *Letters*, i. 74 [Note]. In the lowlands of Scotland, the rough footed Highlanders were called REDSHANKS from the colour of the red-deer hair.

1809. SCOTT, *Lady of Lake*, lx. [Note]. The ancient buskin was made of the undress'd deer hide . . . which procured the Highlanders the well-known epithet of RED-SHANKS.

3. (Old Cant). — A turkey. [Properly the pool-snipe.]

1707. *Old Song*, 'Rum Mort's Praise of Her Faithless Maunder' [FARMER, *Musa Pedestris* (1896), 36]. REDSHANKS then I could not lack.

*c.*1725. *Old Song*, 'Retoure my dear dell [*New Canting Dict.*]. On REDSHANKS and tibs thou shalt every day dine.

4. (Old Cant).—A duck or drake.—HARMAN and B. E.

RED-TAPE, *subs. phr.* (common).—1. Official routine; formality. Hence, as *adj.* = formal: also RED-TAPERY or RED-TAPEISM = official routine; RED-TAPIST = (1) a government clerk; and (2) a precisian. *Cf.* BLUE-TAPE.

1775. LORD MINTO, *Letter*, 31 Aug. [*N. & Q.*, 6 S, viii. 349]. Howe gets the command. The ships are in great forwardness. I can't say so much for the army. Your old friend sticks to rules, TAPE and pack thread.

1838. LYTTON, *Alice*, III. i. The men of more dazzling genius began to sneer at the RED-TAPE minister as a mere official manager of details. *Ibid.* (1853), *My Novel*, x. xx. Throw over that stiff RED-TAPIST.

1849. KINGSLEY, *Alton Lock*, iv. Fops of RED-TAPE statesmen.

1855. DICKENS, *Prince Bull* [Rep. Pieces]. He had a tyrannical old godmother whose name was TAPE (*et passim*).

1863. BRADDON, *Aurora Floyd*, xiii. A brief respite from parliamentary minutes and RED-TAPE.

1871. *Daily News*, 29 Dec. It is more RED TAPE.

1884. SPENCER, *Man* v. *State*, 59. The press and criticisms in Parliament leave no one in ignorance of the vices of RED-TAPE routine.

1873. W. MATHEWS, *Getting on in World*, 99. In no country is the RED-TAPEIST so out of place as here. Every calling is filled with bold, keen, subtle-witted men.

1890. *Pall Mall Gaz.*, 17 Feb., 7, 1. An amusing instance of RED-TAPEISM is reported from America.

2. *See* RED.

REEB, *subs.* (back slang).—Beer: TOP OF REEB = a pot of beer.

REEF, *subs.* (thieves').—To draw up a dress-pocket until the purse is within reach of the fingers.

2. (racing).—*See* quot. [from *Century*].

1888. *Atlantic*, lxiv. 115. When the driver moves the bit to and fro in his mouth, the effect is to enliven and stimulate the horse . . . If this motion be performed with an exaggerated movement of the arm, it is called REEFING.

TO LET OUT A REEF, *verb. phr.* (common).—To unfasten a button after a meal.

TO NEED A REEF TAKEN IN, *verb. phr.* (common).—To be drunk: *see* DRINKS and SCREWED.

REEFER, *subs.* (nautical).—1. A midshipman.

1834. MARRYATT, *Peter Simple*, iv. A young lady, very nicely dressed, looked at me very hard, and said "Well, REEFER, how are you off for soap?"

1888. *Harper's Mag.* [*Century*]. The gun-room, the home of darling REEFERS.

2. (colloquial).—A short all-round jacket; an ARSE-HOLE PERISHER or BUM-FREEZER (*q.v.*).

REEK, *subs.* (Old Cant).—Money: *see* RHINO.

REEKIE. *See* AULD REEKIE.

REEL. TO REEL OFF (or OUT), *verb. phr.* (colloquial).—To speak or produce easily. OFF THE REEL = in succession; right off.

1883. *D. Telegraph*, 26 Oct. Winning three nurseries OFF THE REEL.

1888. *Elec. Rev.* [*Century*]. [They] REELED OFF exactly the same number of words.

1894. MOORE, *Esther Waters*, xxx. First five favourites STRAIGHT OFF THE REEL, three yesterday, and two second favourites the day before.

TO DANCE THE MILLER'S-REEL (REEL O' STUMPIE or REEL OF BOGIE), *verb. phr.* (venery).—To copulate: *see* RIDE.

*b.*1796. *Old Scots Song*, 'The Mill, Mill, O' [*Merry Muses* (collected by Burns)]. Then she fell o'er, an' sae did I, AD' DANC'D THE MILLER'S REEL, O.

17 [?]. *Old Song*, 'Cald Kaill of Aberdene' [SHARPE, *Ane Pleasant Garden*]. The lasses about Bogingicht, Their eens they are baith cleer and richt, And if they are but girded richt, They'll DANCE THE REEL OF BOGIE.

REELER, *subs.* (rhyming).—A policeman; a PEELER (*q.v.*).

1879. HORSLEY [*Macm. Mag.*, xl. 502. A REELER came to the cell and cross-kiddled (questioned) me.

1888. SIMS, *Plank Bed Ballad* [*Referee*, 12 Feb.]. I guyed, but the REELER he gave me hot beef.

REEL-POT, *sub. phr.* (old).—A drunkard: *see* LUSHINGTON. REELING = drunk: *see* SCREWED.

REFORMADO, *subs.* (old).—A disbanded soldier: a degraded officer. [In Sp. = an officer deprived of his command but retaining rank and pay: Fr. *reformé*.] As *adj.* = degraded.

1598. JONSON, *Ev. Man in his Humour*, iii. 2. Into the likeness of one of these REFORMADOS had he moulded himself.

1663. COWLEY, *Cutter of Coleman St.* A troop of REFORMADO officers; most of them had been under my command before.

1664. BUTLER, *Hudibras*, II. ii. 115. I grant you are a REFORMADO saint.

REENER, *subs.* (tramps').—A coin: as in quot.

1893. EMERSON, *Signor Lippo*, xx. By all that kind of cant she done a very good thing, and she had to, for the old man never give her a REENER.

REESBIN, *subs.* (tinkers').—A prison; a STIR: *see* CAGE.

REFLECTOR, *subs.* (gaming).—A prepared card: the pattern on the back is so grouped as to signalise its face value.

REFRESHER, *subs.* (legal).—1. A daily fee given to a barrister after the retainer: spec. when a case is adjourned.

1616. *Court and Times James I.* [OLIPHANT, *New Eng.*, ii. 71. A man is REFRESHED with money; a well-known legal phrase now].

1841. *Punch*, i. 33, 2, 'A barrister's card.' Mr. Briefless, feeling the injustice done to the public by the system of REFRESHERS, will take out his REFRESHERS in brandy, rum, gin, ale, or porter.

*d.*1859. DE QUINCEY, *Sketches*, I. 72. Every fortnight or so I took care that he should receive a REFRESHER.

1886. *Times*, 30 Mar. Fees had been paid and extra REFRESHERS in order to swell the bill of costs.

1887. *Fortnightly Rev.*, N.S. xl. 28. He might have attained to the dignity of the Bench, after feathering his nest comfortably with retainers and REFRESHERS.

1901. *Evening Standard*, 16 Feb., 1, 1. The late Sir Charles Russell was familiar with fees of 1000 guineas a brief and REFRESHERS of 100 guineas a day.

2. (common).—A drink; a GO (*q.v.*).

1872. *Globe*, 12 Mar. That species of REFRESHER which in some parts of our country is known as a 'morning' is also a German institution.

1889. *Ally Sloper*, 3 Aug., 242, 1. As a rule barristers don't object to REFRESHERS.

REGARDLESS. *See* GET-UP.

REGULAR, *subs.* (thieves').—In *pl.* = shares of a booty: *see* NAB.—GROSE, VAUX, and BEE.

ENGLISH SYNONYMS. — To come, or stand in; to go rags; to whack, to go whacks, or to whack up; to go snacks.

1828. BEE, *Picture of London*, 15. He who obtained what he now calls the swagg, paying to his new pal an undefined share, which the thieves persist in calling their REGULARS, though nothing can be more uncertain than such divisions.

1838. REYNOLDS, *Pickwick Abroad*, 223. I never was a nose for the REGULARS came Whenever a pannie was done.

*d.*1857. MONCRIEFF, *Scamps of London*, i. 2. What do you mean by REGULARS?

1871. *Morning Advertiser*, 11 May. He knew who had committed the robbery, and as they had not paid him £20 as his REGULARS he should round on them.

1891. CAREW, *Auto. of Gipsy*, 414. He 'cused me o' playin' Ananias and Sapphira—pinchin' the REGULARS as we call it. *Ibid.*, 418. I touched two-thirds and Nat and Alf napped their REGULARS.

2. (colloquial).—(1) A person keeping stated times or doing regular duty; (2) anything recurring periodically: as a daily passenger, a drink taken at fixed hours, &c.

1397. THIRNYNG, in *Rolls of Parliament* [OLIPHANT, *New Eng.*, i. 181. He uses rewelers for REGULARS, speaking of the clergy].

1858. PRATT, *Ten Nights in a Barroom*, ii. 1. I've been in the habit of taking my REGULARS ever since I was weaned.

1888. GOULD, *Double Event*, 23. He had his breakfast before the REGULARS came down.

Adj. (colloquial).—Thorough; out-and-out: as a REGULAR tartar = a shrew (male or female); a REGULAR sell = a consummate swindle; a REGULAR corpser = a knock-out blow; a REGULAR pelter = a cat-and-dog rain; a REGULAR crow = a person dismally garbed.

1850. SMEDLEY, *Frank Fairlegh*, 403. Our fine letter's been no go,—turned out a REGULAR sell, you see, eh?

1888. *Cornhill Mag.*, March, 228. If Joanna was ever so blessed as to hear her sing 'Hoop la!' it would be a REGULAR eye-opener to her.

REGULATOR, *subs.* (venery).—1. The female *pudendum*: *see* MONOSYLLABLE.

2. (Western American).—In *pl.* = a band of lynchers; a VIGILANCE COMMITTEE (*q.v.*). *See* RUSTLER.

1892. *Scotsman*, 7 May, 'Rustlers and REGULATORS.' By this band the REGULATORS were besieged for about three days at the "Ta" ranche, where they had strongly entrenched themselves.

REHOBOAM, *subs.* (old).—1. *See* quot.

1849. BRONTE, *Shirley*, i. The whole surmounted by a REHOBOAM, or shovel-hat, which he did not seem to think it necessary to lift.

2. (common).—A quadruple MAGNUM (*q.v.*); a double JEROBOAM (*q.v.*): usually of champagne.

REIGN, *verb.* (Australian thieves').—To be at liberty.

RELATION. *See* AVUNCULAR RELATION.

RELIEVE, *verb.* (common).—To ease, (1) the bowels, (2) the *testes*, and (3) sexual desire.

1868. HALL [LYNDESAY, *Works* (E. E. T. S.), 347, Magin]. He sees her come quietly into his bedroom, scans her unconcealed charms with great relish, and grows amorous, . . . and will die, unless she RELIEVES him.

RELIEVER, *subs.* (old).—*See* quot.

1850. KINGSLEY, *Cheap Clothes and Nasty*. In some sweating places there is an old coat kept called the RELIEVER, and this is borrowed by such men as have none of their own to go out in.

RELIEVING-OFFICER, *subs. phr.*—*See* quot.

1883. GRENVILLE-MURRAY, *People I Have Met*, 227. Now the RELIEVING OFFICER, or, for brevity's sake, the "R. O.," was a term of endearment which the Honourable Felix, in common with other young noblemen and gentlemen at Eton, applied to his father.

RELIGION. TO GET RELIGION, *verb. phr.* (American).—To be 'converted.'

RELIGIOUS, *adj.* (Western American).—1. Free from vice: specifically of horses; and (2) of a horse given to going on his knees: *see* DEVOTIONAL HABITS.

RELISH, *subs.* (old).—'Carnal connection with a woman' (GROSE): *see* GREENS and RIDE.

REMAINDER, *subs.* (booksellers').—1. The unsold part of an edition bought to be re-sold at a reduced price.

1889. *Athenæum* [*Century*]. His main dealings . . . having been in REMAINDERS, and his one solitary publication a failure.

2. (publicans').—The drainings of pots and glasses: *see* ALL NATIONS.

REMEDY, *subs.* (Winchester).—1. A holiday: *cf.* WORK (= pain) and REMI.

*d.*1519. COLET, *Statutes of St. Paul's School*. I will also that they shall have no REMEDYES . . . excepte the Kynge . . . desire it.

1530. MAGNUS, *Endowment Deed*, Newark Grammar School. Thomas Magnus ordeyneth . . . that the said maisters shall not be myche inclyned . . . to graunt REMEDY for Recreacyon.

1593. *Rites Durham Cath.* [SURTEES Soc.]. There was . . . a garding and a bowling allie . . . for the Novices sumetymes to recreate themselves when they had REMEDY of there master.

*c.*1840. MANSFIELD, *School Life*, 49. REMEDYS were a kind of mitigated whole holiday.

1891. WRENCH, *Word-Book*, s.v. REMEDY . . . *Remedium* seems to have been the original word for holiday: translated REMEDY . . . The tradition of REMEDIES being granted by *great persons* survives in the custom of the Judges on Circuit demanding a Half-REMEDY.

2. (Old Cant).—A sovereign; 20/-: *see* RHINO.

REMEDY-CRITCH, *subs. phr.* (old).—A chamber-pot: *see* IT.

REMEMBER. *See* PARSON MELDRUM.

REMI, *subs.* (Westminster School).—A holiday: *cf.* REMEDY.

REM-IN-RE, *subs. phr.* (colloquial).—The deed of kind; copulation. TO BE CAUGHT WITH REM-IN-RE = to be taken in the act.

RENOVATOR, *subs.* (tailors').—A repairing tailor: *cf.* TRANSLATOR.

RENT, *subs.* (Old Cant).—Plunder; booty. TO COLLECT RENT = to rob travellers on the highway (BEE). Hence, RENT-COLLECTOR = a highwayman: specifically one whose fancy was for money only.

RENTS COMING IN, *phr.* (old colloquial).—Dilapidated; ragged.

1708-10. SWIFT, *Polite Conversation*, I. I have torn my Petticoat with your odious Romping; my RENTS ARE COMING IN; I'm afraid, I shall fall into the Ragman's Hands.

TO PAY ONE'S RENT, *verb. phr.* (old).—TO PUNISH (*q.v.*); 'to PAY out' (*q.v.*).

1370. *Rom. Rich. Coer de Lion* [WEBER] [OLIPHANT, *New Eng.*, i. 86. Richard PAYS THE Saracens their RENT; like our "give them their bellyfull."]

REP, *subs.* (old).—1. A woman of reputation (GROSE): whence (2) a harlot: a woman of a certain reputation: also demi-rep: *cf.* RIP. Also as in quot. 1732, short for 'repute.'

1721. DURFEY, *Two Queens of Brentford*, i. Flower'd callicoes that fill our shoars, And worn by dames of REP', as well as whores.

1732. FIELDING, *Covent Garden Tragedy*, 13. Nor modesty, nor pride, nor fear, nor REP; Shall now forbid this tender, chaste embrace.

'PON (or ON) REP, *phr.* (old).—'Upon my reputation.'

1708-10. SWIFT, *Polite Conversation*, I. *Lady Smart*. What! . . . Do you say it UPON REP? *Neverout*. Poz, I saw her with my own Eyes.

1713. ADDISON, *Spectator*, 135. Some of our words . . . in familiar writings and conversations . . . often lose all but their first syllables, as in mob, REP, pos, incog, and the like.

3. (Harrow).—A repetition.

1892. ANSTEY, *Voces Populi 'At the Regent Street Tuzsand's*,' 65. It's not in *Selections from British Poetry*, which we have to get up for REP.

REPAIRS. NO REPAIRS, *phr.* (common).—Said of a reckless contest; neck or nought.

See ROAD.

REPARTEE, *subs.* (old: now recognised).—'A sudden smart Reply.' —B. E. (*c.* 1696).

REPEATER, *subs.* (American political).—An elector voting twice on the same qualification.

REPORTER, *subs.* (old Irish).—A duelling pistol: *see* MEAT-IN-THE-POT.

1827. JONAH BARRINGTON, *Personal Sketches* (1869), I. 288. A tolerable chance of becoming acquainted with my friend's REPORTERS (the pet name for hair-triggers). *Idem*, 288-9. I have this moment sent to the mail coach-office two bullet-moulds, not being certain which of them belongs to the REPORTERS.

1865. *Cornhill Mag.*, xi. 166. In those days Irish gentlemen always carried their REPORTERS or pistols with them.

REPOSER, *subs.* (common).—A final drink; a NIGHTCAP (*q.v.*).

REPTILE, *subs.* (American cadet).—1. A new cadet: *cf.* RABID-BEAST.

2. (colloquial).—A degraded wretch; a baseling. Hence REPTILE PRESS = the hireling press.

REPUBLICAN, *subs.* (old colloquial: now recognised).—'A Commonwealths-man.'—B. E. (*c.* 1696).

REPUBLIC OF LETTERS, *subs. phr.* (old).—The post-office.—BEE.

REQUISITION, *verb.* (American military).—To take by force: now recognised.

1864. SALA [*Daily Telegraph*, 2 Aug., ['America in the Midst of War']. Nothing too small to be annexed. From a hundred thousand dollar REQUISITION on the Municipality of a Country Town to a basket of eggs and a housewife's fresh butter.

1871. *Morning Advertiser*, 1 Feb. We have all heard of General Butler, We know "how Providence plesht him mit teapots and shpoons" whilst he was REQUISITIONING down south.

RE-RAW, *subs.* (common).—A drinking bout; drunk.

RESERVOIR. AU RESERVOIR, *phr.* (common).—'Au revoir.'

1897. MITFORD, *Romance of Cape Frontier*, I. v. "'AU RESEVOIR,' for your way, I believe, lies past the dam."

RESIDENTIAL-CLUB, *subs. phr.* (common).—An habitual assemblage of loafers; spec. a crew of idlers, male and female, frequenting the reading-room of the British Museum for the sake of shelter and warmth.

RESPECTABLE, *adj.* (colloquial).—Chaste; decent.

1857. DICKENS, *Little Dorrit*, I. 35. Something must be done with Maggy . . . who . . . is—ha—barely respectable.

1899. WHITEING, *John St.*, xxvii. Some . . . bear it in silence, feeling that it is the price of 'keeping RESPECTABLE.'

RESPOND, *verb.* (venery).—To share the sexual spasm; TO COME (*q.v.*).

RESPONSIONS, *subs.* (Oxford).—The first examination for candidates for the B.A. degree.

1888. LANG, *XXII. Ballades in Blue China*, 'Ballad of the Midsummer Term.' When Lent and RESPONSIONS are ended.

RESPUN, *verb.* (tinkers').—To steal: *see* PRIG.

REST. AND THE REST? *phr.* (common).—A retort to anything incomplete, or in which something is being kept back.

REST-AND-BE-THANKFUL (THE), *subs. phr.* (venery).—*See* MONOSYLLABLE.

RESTY, *adj.* and *adv.* (old).—'Head-strong, Wayward, Unruly, Masterless.'—B. E. (*c.* 1696).

RESURRECTION, *subs. phr.*—A dish made of remains: also RESURRECTION-PIE.

1884. *Cornhill Mag.*, April, 438. He gave us RESURRECTION-PIE; He called it beef-steak—O my eye!

RESURRECTIONIST (or **RESURRECTION-MAN, -COVE, -WOMAN**), *subs. phr.* (old: now rare).—1. A body-snatcher. Whence RESURRECTION-RIG = body-snatching.—PARKER, GROSE, and VAUX.

1814. SCOTT, *Guy Mannering* . . . RESURRECTION WOMEN, who had promised to procure a child's body for some young surgeons.

1821. EGAN, *Life in London*, II. i. The slavey and her master—the surgeon and the RESURRECTION-MAN— . . . they are "all there."

1859. DICKENS, *Tale of Two Cities*, II. xiv. "Father," said Young Jerry, "what's a RESURRECTION MAN?" . . . "Oh, father, I should so like to be a RESURRECTION MAN when I'm quite growed up."

1862. MAYHEW, *Lon. Lab.*, IV. 26. Those who steal dead bodies—as the RESURRECTIONISTS.

1865. MACDONALD, *Alec Forbes*, lxvii. The RESURRECTIONISTS were at their foul work, and the graveyard, the place of repose, was itself no longer a sanctuary!

1896. J. B. BAILEY, *Diary of a* RESURRECTIONIST, vii. The information concerning the RESURRECTION MEN is very scattered. *Idem*, p. 137. He continued in the RESURRECTIONIST business up to the time of the passing of the Anatomy Act. *Et passim.*

RESURRECTIONISTS (THE), *subs.* (military).—The Buffs (East Kent Regiment). [From a rally at Albuera after dispersal at the hands of the Polish Lancers.] Also "The Buff Howards"; "The Nutcrackers"; and "The Old Buffs."

RES-WORT, *subs. phr.* (back slang).—Trousers: *see* KICKS.

RETOURE. *See* TOURE.

RETURNED-EMPTY, *subs. phr.* (clerical).—A colonial missionary preferred to a place at home.

1899. *Daily Telegraph*, 27 Jan., 4, 5. There are two classes of RETURNED EMPTIES, those who are called home to receive dignities and those who are not. Taken in the lump, a returned missionary does not turn out a good parish priest, but he generally turns out an admirable dignitary.

RET-SIO, *subs. phr.* (back slang).—An oyster: RET-SIOS = oysters.

REVELATION, *subs.* (American).—A drink; a GO (*q.v.*).

18 [?]. S. COURIER, *Hard and Fast.* Will you have a REVELATION, Mr. Jones, an outpouring of the spirit—Monongahela or brandy—I've got 'em both?

1863. ARTEMUS WARD, *Brigham Young.* Smith used to have his little REVELATION almost every day—sometimes two before dinner. Brigham Young only takes one once in a while.

REVEL-DASH (or **-ROUT**), *subs. phr.* (old).—(1) A rough, noisy, and indecent gathering or carouse. REVEL-ROUT also = a company of SPREESTERS (*q.v.*).

1591. SPENSER, *Mother Hub. Tale*, i. 558. Then made they REVELL ROUTE and goodly glee.

d. 1592. GREENE, *Works*, I. 175. Have a flurt and a crash, Now play REVELDASH.

1613. PURCHAS, *Pilgrimage*, 430. Laughing, singing, dauncing in honour of that God. After all this REUEL-ROUT they demaund againe of the Demoniake if the God be appeased.

1619. FLETCHER, *Monsieur Thomas*, p. 465. There is a strange thing like a gentlewoman, Like mistress Dorothy (I think the fiend), Crept into the nunnery, we know not which way, Plays REVEL-ROUT among us.

c. 1620. *Fryar and Boye*, ii. We'll break your spell Reply'd the REVEL-ROUT.

d. 1625. ROWLANDS, *Hist. Rogues* [RIBTON-TURNER, 582]. They chose a notable swaggering rogue called Puffing Dicke to reuell over them, who plaid REVELL-ROUT with them indeede.

1632. BROME, *Queen's Exchange*, ii. 2. Wilt thou forsake us, Jeffrey? then who shall daunce The hobby horse at our next REVEL ROUT.

1707. WARD, *Hud. Rediv.*, II. v. 16. Amongst the rest o' th' REVEL ROUT, Two crazy Watchmen crawl'd about.

1713. ROWE, *Jane Shore*, i. 1. "My brother—rest and pardon to his soul—Is gone to his account: for this, his minion, The REVEL-ROUT is done."

REVENGE, *subs.* (common).—An opportunity for recouping or retaliation.

1710. SWIFT, *Pol. Conv.*, iii. *Lady Smart.* Well, Miss, you'll have a sad husband, you have such good luck at cards. *Miss.* Well, my Lady Smart, I'll give you REVENGE whenever you please.

REVENGE IN LAVENDER, *phr.* (old).—A vengeance in store; a ROD IN PICKLE (*q.v.*).—B. E. (*c.* 1696); GROSE (1785).

REVERENCE. *See* SIR REVERENCE.

REVERENT, *adj.* (American).—*See* quot.

1886. *American Slang* [*The State*, 20 May, 217]. A whisky or brandy which is held in merited respect for very superior potency is entitled REVERENT, from the same kind of fancy which led the Scotch to call a whisky-jar 'a greybeard.'

REVERSED, *adj.* (old).—'A Man set (by Bullies) on his Head, and his Money turn'd out of his Breeches.'—B. E. and GROSE.

REVIEW. REVIEW OF THE BLACK CUIRASSIERS, *subs. phr.* (old).—A visitation of the clergy.—GROSE.

REVIVER, *subs.* (common).—A drink; a PICK-ME-UP (*q.v.*); a GO (*q.v.*).

1876. BESANT and RICE, *Golden Butterfly.* It was but twelve o'clock, and therefore early for REVIVERS of any sort.

2. (common).—A mending tailor: *cf.* TRANSLATOR. Hence, as *verb.* = to mend; to patch.

1864. *The Times*, 2nd Nov. REVIVERS, who rejuvenate seedy black coats, and, for the moment, make them look as good as new.

1865. *Cassell's Paper*, Article, 'Old Clo'.' They are now past 'clobbering,' 'REVIVING,' or 'translating.'

REV-LIS, *subs.* (back slang).—Silver.

REWARD, *subs.* (kennel).—Supper: specifically the blood and entrails of the quarry.—B. E. (*c.* 1696).

REX. TO PLAY REX, *verb. phr.* (old).—To handle roughly and terribly; to PLAY HELL WITH (*q.v.*).

1586. WARNER, *Alb.*, I. vi. 22. With these did Hercules PLAY REX . . . Not one escapes his deadly hand that dares to show his head.

1599. BRETON, *Dream of Str. Effects*, 17. Love with Rage KEPT such a REAKES that I thought they would have gone mad together.

1599. BRETON, *Dream of Strange Effects*, 17. Love and Rage kept such a REAKES that I thought they would have gone mad together.

d. 1599. SPENSER, *View of Ireland*, 445. Thinke it to be the greatest indignity to the queene that may be, to suffer such a caytiffe to PLAY such REX.

1605. SYLVESTER, *Du Bartas*, 504. Then PLAIES he REX, tears, kils, and all consumes.

1611. COTGRAVE, *Dict.*, s.v. *Faire le diable de Vauvdt* To keepe an old coyle, horrible, bustling, terrible swaggering; to PLAY monstrous REAKS, or raks-jakes.

1616. *Court and Times Chas. I.*, I. 256. Then came the English ordnance, which had been brought to land, TO PLAY SUCH REAKS among the horse that they were forced to fly.

1622. FLETCHER, *Sea Voyage*, iv. II. In that rage (for they are violent fellows) they play such REAKS!

1653. URQUHART, *Rabelais*, III. ii. PLAYING REEKS with the high and stately timber, and preparing . . . for the eve of the great Day of Judgment.

1655. FANSHAWE, *Luciad*, x. 65. With fire and sword he overcomes and breaks; In Beadala shall his blade PLAY REX.

RHEUMATISM IN THE SHOULDER, *subs. phr.* (common).—Arrest.—GROSE.

RHINO, *subs.* (old).—Money: generic; specifically ready money. —B. E. (*c.* 1696); DYCHE (1748); GROSE (1785). Whence RHINO-FAT (or RHINOCERAL) = rich.

SYNONYMS.—*Generic.* Actual; ballast; beans; bit (bite or byte); blunt; brads; brass; bustle; Californians; captain (the); caravan; change; charms; checks; chink; chinkers; chips; clink; coal (or cole); COD (*q.v.*); coin; coliander-seeds; coppers; cork; corn in Egypt; crap (or crop); crisp; cuckoos; darby; delog (back slang); dibs; dimmock; dinarly (or dinarlies); dingbat; dirt; dollars; dooteroomus (or doot); dots; ducats; dues; dumps; dust; dye-stuffs; evil (the); family-plate; fat; feathers; flimsy (or flim); flour; gent; gilt (gelt, gelter, or gilt-tick); gingerbread; gingleboys; ginglers; glanthorne; goree; greed; grocery; HADDOCK (*q.v.*); hard; hardstuff; hen; honey; horsenails; hoxters (or huxters); iron; jink; John (John Davis or ready-John); kelter (or kilter); King's (or Queen's pictures); lawful pictures; legem pone; loaver; lour (or loure); £ s. d.; lurries; mammon; metal; mopusses; mouldy-'uns; moss; muck; needful; nobbings; nonsense; nuggets; ochre; oil of angels; oil of palms; ointment; old; oof (or ooftish: Yiddish); paint; palm-oil; pan; pap (*cf.* SOFT); paper; pee; penny; pewter; pieces; pile; plate; plums; pocket; pony; portcullis; posh; pot; powder; prey; PUNCHABLE (*q.v.*); purse; queer; quids; rags; ready (ready-gilt or ready-John); redge (or ridge); reek; regulars; ribbon; ring; rivets; root of all evil; rowdy; salt; sawdust; scads; screens; screeves; scuds; shadscales (or scales); shan; shekels; shells; shigs; ~~shiners~~; shot; shinplasters (or plasters); sinews of war; skin; soap; soft; soft-flimsy (base); Spanish; spanks; spankers; spondulicks; spoon; stamps; steven; stevers; stiff; stuff; stumpy; sugar; tin; teaspoons; tow; wad; wedge; wherewith (or wherewithal); yellowboys; yennoms (back slang). **£1,000,000** = marigold. **£100,000** = plum. **£1,000** = cow. **£500** = monkey. **£100** = century. **£25** = pony. **£10** = double-finnup; long-tailed finnup (also of notes of higher values); tenner. **£5** = ABRAHAM NEWLAND (*q.v.*); finnup; fiver; flimsy; lil (or lill); Marshall; pinnif. **£1 (and in many cases formerly = £1 1s)** = bean (or bien); bleeder; canary; chip; couter (or cooter); dragon; dunop; foont; George (or yellow-George); gingleboy; glistener; goblin; goldfinch; harlequin; horse-sovereign; illegitimate; Jack; James; Jane; Jemmy-o'-Goblin (rhyming); job (or jobe); meg (*cf.* mag = ½d); monarch; mousetrap; ned (or neddy); new-hat; nob; old Mr. Gory; ponte; poona; quid; red-'un; remedy; ridge (or redge); shiner; skin; skiv; stranger; strike; thick-'un (also of 5/-); yellow-boy; yellow-hammer. **10s** = half-bean; half-couter; half-Jack: half-James; half-Jane; half-ned (or -neddy); net-gen; smelt; young illegitimate. **7s** = spangle. **6s 6d** = George. **5s 3d** = whore's curse. **5s** = bull (or bull's-eye); caroon; cart-wheel; coach-wheel; case; caser; decus; dollar; hind coach (or cart) wheel; Oxford; thick-'un; tusheroon; wheel. **2s 6d** = coach-wheel; five-pot piece; flatch; fore-coach-wheel; George; half-case; half-dollar; half-Oxford; half-yenork; madza-caroon; slat. **2s** = half-dollar. **1s 6d** = hog and a kye. **1s 1½d** = loonslate (or loonslatt); hangman's wages. **1s** = Abraham's willing (rhyming); blow; bob; bobstick; borde; breaky-leg; button; deaner (or deener); gen; generalise; grunter; hog; jogue; levy; lilywhite-groat; Manchester sovereign; mejoge; north-easter; oner; peg; teviss; thirteener; touch-me; twelver. **10½d** = dacha-saltee; jumper. **9d** = ill-fortune; picture of ill-luck. **6d** = bandy; bender; cripple; croaker; crook; crook-back; deaner; downer; fiddle; fiddler; fyebuck; goddess Diana; griff-metol; grunter; half-borde; half-hog; hog; kick; kye; lord-of-the-manor; northeaster; pig; pot; sice; simon; snide; sow's-baby; sprat; syebuck; tanner; tester; tilbury; tizzy. **5d** = cinqua soldi; kid's-eye. **4d** = castle-rag; flag; groat; joe (or joey). **3d** = currants-and-plums; threps; threeswins; thrums. **2d** = dace; deuce; duce. **1d** = D; dibblish; George; harper; pollard; saltee; win; yennep. **½d** = flatch; madza-saltee; Maggie Rab (or Robb); magpie; make (magg or mec); post; rap; scurrick; tonic. **¼d** = Covent-garden; fadge; farden; fiddler; gennitraf; grig; Harrington; jig (or gigg); quartereen; scrope. **Base coin or trick pieces** = cap; cover-down; dandy; double-header; flats; fleet-note; fletch (or flatch); gaffing-coin; galley-halfpenny; gammy lour; gray; hard; hardware; kone; mopus; pony; queer; soft-flimsy; snide; stumer.

FRENCH SYNONYMS.—Generic. *Achetoires*; *affure*; *artiche*; *atout*; *bathe*; *beurre*; *bille*; *braise*; *carme*; *ce qui se pousse*; *de quoi*; *douille*; *foin*; *galette*; *galtos*; *graisse*; *graissage*; *gras*; *huile*; *huile de mains*; *jaunets*; (or *jauniau*); *métal*; *miche* (or *miche de profonde*); *monaco*; *mornifle*; *morlingue*; *morningue*; *mouscaillons*; *nerf*; *noyaux*; *oignons*; *os*; *oscille*; *patards*; *pécune*; *pépettes*; *pedzale*; *pèse* (or *pèze*); *picaillons*; *piesto*; *pimpions*; *plâtre*; *plombes*; *pognon* (or *poignon*); *pouiffe*; *poussier*; *quantum*; *quibus*;

ronds; *rouis caillons*; *rubis*; *sable*; *sauvette*; *sine quâ non*; *sitnomen*; *soldats*; *sonnettes*; *sous*; *thune* (or *tune*); *vaisselle de poche*; *zinc*.

ITALIAN SYNONYMS.—Generic. *Agresto* (= sour grapes); *albume*; *argume*; *asta* (or *asti*); *brunotti*; *contramiglia*; *cucchi*; *lugani*; *penne*; *smilzi*; *squame*.

SPANISH SYNONYMS.—Generic. *Amigos* (= friends); *caire*; *florin*; *lana*; *lozurraco*; *morusa*; *mosca*; *numerario*; *plume* (= feathers); *sangré* (= blood); *á toca teja*; *unguento* (or *unguento de Mejica*).

1670. *Old Ballad*, 'The Seaman's Adieu' [*Notes and Queries*, 7 S., v. 417]. Some as I know, Have parted with their ready RINO.

1688. SHADWELL, *Sq. of Alsatia*, i. *Cole* is, in the language of the witty, money; the ready, the RHINO. Thou shalt be RHINO-CERICAL, my lad.

1772. BRIDGES, *Burlesque Homer*, 139. For getting RHINO here's the spot.

1840. BARHAM, *Ingold. Leg.* (*Sir Rupert the Fearless*). And to sum up the whole, in the shortest phrase I know, Beware of the Rhine, and take care of the RHINO!

1848. LOWELL, *Biglow Papers*, 1 S., Intro. A gold mine . . . Containing heaps heaps of native RHINO.

1899. *Scarlet City*, 65. He added, throwing a sovereign on the table, 'Split up that bit of RHINO.'

RHODY (LITTLE), *subs. phr.* (American). — The State of Rhode Island: the smallest in the Union.

RHYME-SLINGER, *subs. phr.* (common).—A poet.

RHYMING SLANG.—A method of indicating words by a rhyming or quasi-rhyming substitute; *e.g.*, ABRAHAM'S WILLING = shilling; STAND-AND-SHIVER = river; ELEPHANT'S TRUNK = drunk; PENNY-COME-QUICK = trick; and so forth. First in vogue during the late Fifties, but artistically developed of late years by *The Sporting Times* or *Pink 'Un.* With use the rhyme has been suppressed by experts: *e.g.*, I'M-SO-FRISKY = whiskey becomes I'M-SO, while FLOUNDER-AND-DAB = cab is merely FLOUNDER.

RIB, *subs.* (common).—1. A wife: whence CROOKED RIB = a cross-grained wife. — GROSE (1785). *See* DUTCH.

1609. HALL, *Soloman's Divine Arts.* How many have we known whose heads have been broken by their own RIB.

1632. JONSON, *Magnetic Lady*, ii. 1. An ample portion for a younger brother, With a soft, tender, delicate RIB of man's flesh.

1707. FARQUHAR, *Beaux' Stratagem*, v. *Mrs. Sullen.* Spouse! *Squire Sul.* RIB.

1732. FIELDING, *Mock Doctor*, i. Go thrash your own RIB, Sir, at home.

1772. BRIDGES, *Burlesque Homer*, 133. Your dunder-pate Shan't use your RIB at such a rate.

1857. TROLLOPE, *Three Clerks*, xlvi. Half a dozen married couples all separating, getting rid of their RIBS and buckling again, helter-skelter, every man to somebody else's wife.

2. (common).—In *pl.* = a stout person.

See DEVIL'S BONES.

RIBALD (RIBOLD or RIBAUD), *subs.* (old colloquial: long recognised). —A profligate, male or female; spec. (*a*) a harlot, and (*b*) a PONCE (*q.v.*) or MUTTON-MONGER (*q.v.*). Whence RIBALDRY (RIBAUDRY, or RIBBLE-RABBLE) = (1) indecency, 'profligate talk' (GROSE), and (2) the mob, the scum of society; RIBAUDOUR = a retailer of SMUT (*q.v.*); RIBALDIST

(RIBAUDROUS, OR RIBAUDRED) = whorish, whoreson, filthy and the like; RIBBLE-ROW = (1) a list of the rabble: whence (2) an inventory.

1360. CHAUCER, *Rom. of Rose*, 5673. Many a RIBAUDE is mery and baude.

1362. LANGLAND, *Piers Plowman* (C), vii. 435. On fasting-dais by-fore noon iche fedde me with ale, Out of reson, a-mong RYBAUDES here RYBAUDRYE to huyre. *Ibid.* (A), vii. 66. Ionete of the stuyues, And Robert the RIBAUDOUR.

1376. [RIBTON-TURNER, *Vagrants, &c.*, 52]. In the last year of this reign we find the Commons petitioning the King "that RIBALDS . . . and Sturdy Beggars may be banished out of every town."

1491. *Destr. of Troy* [E. E. T. S.], 7651. Ephistafus hym presit with his proude wordes, As a RIBOLD with reueray to his roide speche.

1573. BARET, *Alvearie* [NARES]. A RIBAUDROUS and filthie tongue, *os incestum, obscœnum, impurum, et impudicum.*

1599. HALL, *Satires*, ix. Rhymed in rules of stewish RIBALDRY.

1608. SHAKSPEARE, *Ant. & Cleop.*, iii. 8. Yon RIBAUDRED nag of Egypt Whom leprosy o'ertake.

1611. COTGRAVE, *Dict.*, s.v. RIBAULD. A rogue, ruffian, rascale, scoundrele, valet, filthie fellow; also a RIBAULD fornicator, whore-munger, bawdie-house haunter. s.v. RIBAULDE. A whore, queane, punke, gill flurt, common hackney, doxie, mort. [See also, s.v. RIBAUDAILLE, RIBAUDINE, ROYAKS, RIBAULDS, RIBAULDES, &c.]

1641. MILTON, *Def. of Humb. Remons.* As for the proverb, the Bishop's foot hath been in it, it were more fit for a Scurra in Trivio, or som RIBALD upon an Ale-bench.

1630. TAYLOR, *Works* [NARES]. A RIBBLE-RABBLE of gossips.

1670. COTTON [*Works* (1734), 119]. This witch a RIBBLE-ROW rehearses, Of scurvy names in scurvy verses.

1705. WARD, *Hud. Rediv.*, I. vii. 6. Such uncouth, wretched RIBBLE-RABBLE.

1841-6. BROWNING, *Bells and Pomegranates*, 'Pied Piper.' Insulted by a lazy RIBALD.

RIBBIN (RIBBON or RIBBAND), *subs.* (old).—1. Money: generic. Hence, THE RIBBIN RUNS THICK (or THIN) = 'the breeches are well lined' (or 'there's little cash about').—B. E. (*c.*1696); GROSE (1785); VAUX (1812).

2. (common).—In *pl.* = reins: whence TO HANDLE (or FLUTTER) THE RIBBONS = to drive. *See* HANDLE and add quots. *infra.*

1837. DICKENS, *Pickwick* (1857), 36. Give the gen'l'man the RIBBINS.

1837. BARHAM, *Ingoldsby Legends*, 'St. Odille.' 'Tis the same with a lady, it once she contrives To get hold of the RIBANDS.

See BLUE RIBBON.

RIB-ROAST (-BASTE or -TICKLE), *verb.* (old). — To thrash; TO PUNISH (*q.v.*). Whence RIB-ROASTING (&c.: also RIB-BENDING OR RIBBING) = a pummelling; RIB-ROASTER (&c.: also RIB-BENDER, RIBBER, OR A RIB OF ROAST) = (pugilists') a blow on the body, or in the ribs, which brings down an opponent's guard and opens up the head.—B. E.; MARTIN (1754); GROSE.

1576. GASCOIGNE, *Steel Glass*, Ess. Ded. [ARBER]. Though the shorneful do mocke me for a time, yet in the ende I hope to giue them al a RYBBE TO ROSTE for their paynes.

1595. HALL, *Maroccus Extalicus.* Such a piece of filching as is punishable with RIB-ROAST.

1620. ROWLANDS, *Night-raven* [NARES]. Tom, take thou a cudgell and RIB-ROAST him.

1663. BUTLER, *Hudibras.* And he departs, not meanly boasting Of his magnificent RIB-ROASTING.

*d.*1704. L'ESTRANGE, *Works* [*Ency. Dict.*]. I have been . . . well RIBROASTED . . . but I'm in now for skin and all.

1762. SMOLLETT, *Sir L. Greaves*, I. v. In which he knew he should be RIBROASTED every day, and murdered at last.

1819. MOORE, *Tom Crib*, 51. While RIBBERS rung from each resounding frame.

1857. CUTHBERT BEDE, *Verdant Green*, II. iv. To one gentleman he would pleasantly observe . . . "There's a regular RIB-ROASTER for you!"

1876. HINDLEY, *Cheap Jack*, 284. It was some time before he recovered the RIB-BENDER he got from the fat showwoman.

1886. *Phil. Times*, 6 May. There was some terrible slogging . . . Cleary planted two RIB-ROASTERS, and a tap on Langdon's face.

1891. *Lic. Vict. Gaz.*, 9 Feb. Repaid the compliment with another RIB-BENDER.

RIBSTONE, *subs.* (common).—*See* PIPPIN.

1883. MILLIKEN, *'Arry Ballads* [*Punch*, 11 Oct.]. 'Ow are yer, MY RIBSTONE.

RIB-TICKLER, *subs. phr.* (colloquial).—1. Thick soup; GLUE (*q.v.*).

2. *See* RIB-ROAST.

RICE-BAGS, *subs. phr.* (common).—1. TROUSERS: *see* KICKS.

2. (American).—In sing. = a rice planter.

RICH, *adj.* and *adv.* (colloquial).—1. Outrageous; (2) ridiculous; and (3) SPICY (*q.v.*).

*c.*1350. *Turnament of Totenham* [HAZLITT, *Early Pop. Poet.*, iii. 91]. Alle the wyues of Totenham come . . . To fech home thaire husbondis . . . With wispys and kixes, that was a RICH sight.

1821. EGAN, *Life in London*, II. ii. The left-hand side of the bar is a RICH bit of low life.

1840. PORTER, *Southwestern Tales*, 57. Thar we was . . . rollin' with laughin' and liquor, and thought the thing was RICH.

1844. DISRAELI, *Coningsby*, viii. 1. 'Was Spraggs RICH?'—'Wasn't he! I have not done laughing yet . . . Killing! . . . The RICHEST thing you ever heard.'

1897. MITFORD, *Romance of Cape Frontier*, ix. The notion of Allen bothering anyone to take out a bees' nest . . . struck them all as ineffably RICH.

RICH-FACE, *subs. phr.* (old).—'A Red-face.'—B. E. (*c.*1696).

RICHARD, *subs.* (common).—A dictionary: also RICHARD SNARY and RICHARDANARY.—GROSE. Fr. *musicien.*

1622. TAYLOR (Water Poet), *Motto*, Intro., s.v. RICHARD SNARY.

RICK-MA-TICK, *subs. phr.* (Scots'). —1. A concern; a business; a thing: as 'The whole blessed RICK-MA-TICK went to smash.'

2. (school).—Arithmetic.

RICOCHET, *adj.* (American cadet). —Gay; splendid.

RID. TO RID THE STOMACH, *verb. phr.* (common).—To vomit.

RIDDLEMEREE, *subs.* (old).—*See* quot.

*c.*1772. JUNIUS, *Letters* [WOODFALL], II. 316. This style, I apprehend, Sir, is what the learned Scriblerus calls rigmarol in logic—RIDDLEMEREE amongst Schoolboys.

RIDE, *verb.* (venery).—1. To possess carnally; to SWIVE (*q.v.*). Fr. *chevaucher* (= to swive) and *chevaucherie* (= a swiving) (COTGRAVE, 1611; and GROSE, 1785).

ENGLISH SYNONYMS (also *see* GREENS). — To accommodate; Adamize; ballock; belly-bump (URQUHART); bitch (generic); block; bob (FLETCHER); bore; bounce; brush; bull; bum; bumbaste (URQUHART); bumfiddle (DAVIES of Hereford); bung; buttock; caress; caulk; cavault; chauver; chuck; clicket (FLET-

CHER, GROSE); club; cock; come about; come aloft (E. SPENSER); compress; couple with; cover; cross; cuddle; dibble; diddle; do (SHAKSPEARE, JONSON, generic); dock; dog; do over; ease (= (1) to rump, and (2) to deflower); embrace; ferret (FLETCHER); fiddle; flap; flesh (FLORIO); flimp; flourish; flutter; foin (generic); fondle; foraminate (URQUHART); frisk; fuck (LYNDSAY, FLORIO, BAILEY, BURNS); fuckle; fugle (DURFEY); fulke; fumble (FLETCHER); futter (R. BURTON); get-into; ginicomtwig (FLORIO); goose; goose-and-duck (rhyming); go through; handle; have; hog; hole; hoist; horse (JONSON); huddle; huffle; hug (FLETCHER, BURNS); hump; hustle; impale; invade; jack; jape (SKELTON, PALSGRAVE, LYNDSAY, FLORIO); jig-a-jig; jiggle; jink (RAMSAY, ROBERTSON, of Struan); job (BURNS); jock; jog (MIDDLETON); jolt; jottle; jounce; jumm (URQUHART); jumble (or jumble up: STANYHURST, DURFEY); jump (RANDOLPH); kiss (RAMSAY, MORRIS); knock (for *nock*: DURFEY, RAMSAY); know (Biblical); lay out; lard; leacher (COTGRAVE); leap (SHAKSPEARE, JONSON, DRYDEN); lerricompoop; lie with; line (SHAKSPEARE); love; man; meddle with; mell (LYDGATE, SHAKSPEARE); mount (SHAKSPEARE, JONSON); mow (Scots': LYNDSAY, DURFEY, BURNS); muddle; mump; muss; nibble; nick; nidge (Scots'); nig; niggle (DEKKER, ROWLANDS, BROME); nock (FLORIO, ASH); nodge (Scots'); nub; nug; oblige; occupy (SHAKSPEARE, FLORIO, JONSON); peg; perforate; perform on; pestle; phallicize; pizzle; please (CHAPMAN, BURNS); pleasure; plough (SHAKSPEARE); plowter; pluck (SHAKSPEARE); plug; poke (DURFEY); pole; poop; possess (MASSINGER, SMOLLETT); pound; priapize; prick; prig; push; qualify; quiff; quim; rake; rasp; relish; rig; roger; rummage; rump; rut; Saint-George; sard (LYNDSAY, FLORIO); scour; screw; see; serve; sew up; shag; shake; smock; smoke (FLETCHER); snabble; snib; solace; spike; split; stick; strike; stroke; stitch (DORSET); spread; strain; strum; swinge (FLETCHER); swive; tail; taste (FIELDING); thrum; towze; touzle (FIELDING); tread; trim (SHAKSPEARE, FLETCHER); trounce; tumble; tup (SHAKSPEARE); turn up; up; vault; wap (Old Cant); womanize; work.

FRENCH SYNONYMS [R. = RABELAIS].—*Abattre* (or *abattre du bois*); *s'aboucher*; *abuser*; *acclamper* (R.); *accointer* (*s'accointer* or *avoir des accointances*: R.); *accoler* (R.); *accommoder* (R.); *accomplir* (*accomplir son désir* or *plaisir*); *accorder sa flûte*; *accoupandir* (R.); *s'accoupler*; *accoutrer*; *accrocher* (R.); *accueillir*; *affiler le bandage* (R.); *affronter* (R.); *aforer le tonel* (O. Fr.); *agir* (LA FONTAINE); *aimer* (conventional); *ajuster* (R.); ALLER *à Cythère*, *à dame*, *à la charge*, *à pinada*, *au beurre*, *au bonheur*, *au choc*, *au ciel*, *au gratin*, *aux armes*, *aux épinards* (*cf.* GREENS), *d'attaque* (*y*), *l'amble*, and *se faire couper les cheveux*; *allumer le flambeau d'amour*; *anhaster* (R.); *apaiser sa braise* (LA FONTAINE); *appointer* (R.); *apprivoiser*; *approcher*; *approvisionner*; *arieter*

(R.); *arracher son copeau*; *arresser* (R.); *arriver à ses fins*; *arriver au but*; *assailler* (R.: also *assaillir*); *astiquer*; AVOIR *commerce*, *contentement*, *du plaisir*, *forfait*, *la cheville au trou*; *la jouissance*, *les bonnes grâces*, *le solaz*, *son plaisir*, and *une bonne fortune*. BADIGEONNER; *badiner* (= JAPE); *baguer* (STITCH, *q.v.*); *baiser* (KISS, *q.v.*); *ballotter*; *baratter*; *bâter d'âne* (R.); *battre le briquet*; *battre les cartiers* (R.); *battre la laine* (R.); *beliner* (R.); *beluter* (R.); *bistoquer*; *bistouriser* (R.); *bluter*; *bobeliner* (R.); *boire* (also *boire la coupe de plaisir*); *boudiner*; *bourrer*; *bourriquer*; *boxonner*; *branler le cul* (or *la croupière*); *braquemarder* (R.); *brecolfrétiller*; *bricoler* (R.); *brimballer* (R.); *brisgoutter* (R.); *brochier*; *brodequiner*; *broquer*; *brouiller* (= JUMBLE, *q.v.*); *brûler une cierge*; *brusquer*. CALENDOSSER (also *encaldosser*); *calfeutrer* (*cf.* CAULK); *carabiner* (R.); *caracoler* (R.); *caramboler*; *caresser* (LA FONTAINE); *carillonner* (R.); *cauquer*; *causer*; CHANTER *la messe*, *l'office de la Vierge*, *l'introit*, or *un couplet*; *charger*; *chauldronner* (R.); *cheminer autrement que des pieds*; *chevaucher* (R.: RIDE, *q.v.*); *cheviller*; *choser*; *cliqueter* (R. = CLIQUET); *cocher* (R.); *cogner* (R.); *se coller*; *combattre*; *commettre la folie* (or *le forfait*); *conailler*; *conférer*; *confesser*; *conjoindre* (also *se conjoindre*); *conjouir*; *connaître* (also *connaître au fond*: KNOW, *q.v.*); *conniller*; *conceuvrer*; *consoler*; *consommer le sacrifice*; *contenter* (CONTENT, *q.v.*: also *contenter l'envie*, *ses désirs*, or *sa flamme*); *converser*; *copuler*; *coucher* (LIE WITH, *q.v.*); *coudre* (LA FONTAINE: SEW UP, *q.v.*); *se coupler* (R.); COURIR, *un poste*, or *des postes*, *l'aiguillette*, *la lance*, *l'amble*, or *sur le ventre*; *courter*; *couvrir* (R.: COVER, *q.v.*); *cramper*; *crêver l'œil*; CUEILLIR *des lauriers*, *la fraise*, *la noisette*, or *un bouton de rose sur le nombril*; *culbuter*; *culler* (O. Fr.); *cultiver*. DANSER, *aux noces*, *la basse danse* (R.), *la basse note*, *le branle de un dedan et deux*, *dehors*, *le branle du loup*, *une bourrée*, and *une sarabande*; *darder*; *debarbouiller* (R.); *débraguetter* (R.); *décrotter*; *déduire*; *déliter*; *déniaiser*; *dépêcher*; *dépenser ses cotelettes*; *descroter* (R.); *se désennuyer*; *déshouser* (O. F. = to scour); *deviser*; *dire ses oraison*; *disposer s'en* DONNER; *se donner carrière*, *de la satisfaction*, *des leçons de droit*, *des preuves d'estime*, *des secousses*, *au bon temps*, and *du plaisir*; *donner l'aubade*, *l'avoine*, *l'assant*, *le picotin*, *un branle*, *une leçon de physique expérimentale*, *une venue*, *du contentement*, and *un clystère*; *dormir*; *doubler*. S'EBATTRE; *s'ébaudir* (R.); *s'édifier*; *s'éjouir*; *embloquer à la cupidique* (R.); *emboiter*; *emboucher*; *emboudiner*; *embourrer*; *embriconner* (also R. = to seduce); *embrocher* (R.); *emmancher*; *s'émoucheter*; *empêcher* (R. and LA FONTAINE); *enchtiver*; *enclouer*; *encocher* (R.); *enconner* (*cf.* R. BURTON'S 'encunt' = TO PUT IN); ENFERRER; *enfiler* (R.); *enfoncer*; *enfourcher* (= TO SPREAD); *enfourner*; *engaîner* (also *engaîner sa virgule*); *enjamber* (*cf.* crop); *entamer le cuir*; *entoiser*; *s'entrefaire le jeu*; *entreprendre*; ENTRER *au couple*, *en champ clos*, *en danse*, *en guerre*, *en joute*, and *en lice*; *entretenir*; *envahir*; *enviander*;

épousseter; *s'escarmoucher* (ROUSSEAU); *essayer un lit*; *estocader*; *étaller*; ÉTEINDRE *sa braise*, *sa chandelle*, and *ses feux*; *étrangler*; Y ETRE; *être aux mains*, *aux prises*, *en action*, *en œuvre*, *impertinent*, and *vainqueur*; *être de corvée à la viande*; *étriller*; *évacuer*; *exécuter*; *exercer* (R.: also *exercer les bons membres*); *expédier* (LA FONTAINE); *exploiter* (also *exploiter au Pays-bas*: R.). *Façonner*; FAIRE (= TO DO), *une barbe*, *une façon*, *bataille*, *beau bruit de culetis* (R.), *bonne chère*, *campagne*, *ça*, *cela* (VILLON), *connaissance*, *des bêtises*, *des galipettes*, *dia*, *Rue Haut*; *s'en faire donner*; *se faire donner la fessée*; *faire du bon compagnon*; *faire en levrette* (= DOG-FASHION); *se le faire faire*; *faire fête*, *folie de son corps*, *galanterie*, *la belle joir*, *la besogne*, *la bête à deux dos* (R., SHAKSPEARE), *la bonne chose*, *la cause* (or *chose*) *pourquoi* (R.), *la chasse aux conins*, *la chosette*, *le cœur*, *la culbute*, *la fête*, *la folie* (LA FONTAINE: also *la folie aux garçons*), *la grenouille*, *la guerre* (VOLTAIRE), *l'aubade*, *la pauvreté*, and *la vilenie*; *le faire*; *faire l'acte vénérien*, *l'amour*, *l'amoureux tripot*, *l'androgyne*, *le cas*, *le déduit* (TALLEMENT DES REAUX, &c.), *délit*, *désir*, *devoir*, *heurtebelin*, *jeu d'amour*, *l'œuvre de nature*, *le pagnet*, *péché*, *le petit verminage*, *le saut* (LA FONTAINE: also *le saut de Michelet*), *le reste*, *le truc*, *pénitence*, *plaisir*, *river son clou*, *sa besogne*, *sa fête*, *sa partie*, *sa volunté*, *service*, *ses besognettes* (VILLON), *ses choux gras*, *ses petites affaires*, *ses privantés*, *son bon*, *son délit*, *son devoir*, *son plaisir*, *son talent*, and *son vouloir*; *faire tort*, *tout*, *un duel*, *une charade*, *une politesse*, *un tour de cul*, *un tronçon de bon ouvrage*, *un tronçon de chière lie* (R.), *virade*, *une pirouette sur le nombril*, *compter les solives à une femme*, *chou blanc*, and *pan-pan*; *se faire dégraiser*; *faire zizi*; *fanfrelucher* (R.); *farfouiller* (R.); *fatrouiller* (O. Fr.); *favoriser*; *fergier*; *ferrer*; *festoyer* (VOLTAIRE); *fêter* (VOLTAIRE: also *fêter le Saint-Priape*); *ficher*; *flatter*; *follier* (R.); *foraminer* (R.); *se forfaire*; *forger*; *forligner* (of women: LA FONTAINE); *forriller* (R.); *fouailler* (R.); *fouiller*; *fouler*; *fourbir* (R.); *fourcher* (R.); *fourgonner* (R.); *fournir* (also *fournir la carrière*); *foutre* (= FUCK, *q.v.*); *foutriller*; *franchir le saut*; *frayer*; *frétiller* (also *frétiller-nature* and *frétinfrétailler*: R. = O. Fr. = TO FRISK); *fringoter*; *fringuer* (also *fringasser*); FROTTER *sou lard*, *la coine* and *la conenne* (R.). *Galantiser*; *galler* (O. Fr. = *s'amuser*)) *gésir* (O. Fr. = *coucher*); *gesticular*; *gimbretter* (R.); *glisser*; *goûter les ébats*, *les plaisirs* or *les joies*; *grappiller*; *greffer* (VOLTAIRE); *gribouiller* (R.); *grimper* (R.); *guerroyer*; *guincher*. *Habeloter*; *habiller*; *habiter*; *haillonner* (R.); *hanter*; *harigoter* (R.); *hennequiner*; *hocher* (R. = shake); *hoder* (R.); *hoguiner* (R.); *houbler*; *hourdebiller* (R.); *housser* (O. Fr. = to scour); *houspiller*; *hubir*; *hurter*; *hurtibiller* (R.: O. Fr. = *s'accoupler*); *hutiner* (R.). S'INCARNER; *incruster*; *inir*; *instruire* (also *s'instruire*); *instrumenter* (R.); *investir*. *Janculer*; *jaser* (also *jazer*); *iocqueter* (R.); *joindre* (also *se joindre*); JOUER (LA FONTAINE), *à la bête à deux dos*, *à la corniche*

(R.); *à cul-bas* (R.); *à la fossette* (R. *cf.* CHERRY-PIT); *à l'homme*, *au passe-temps de deux à deux*, *au piquet* (R.), *au reversis*, *aux cailles*, *aux dames rabattues* (R.), *aux quilles*, *ce jeu-là*, *de la braguette*, *de la flûte*, *de la marotte*, *de la navette* (R.), *de la saque-boute*, *des basses marches* (R.), *des cymbales*, *des gobelets*, *des mannequins*, *des reins*, *du cul*, *du serre-cropière* (R.), *du mirliton*, *du piston*, and *de l'amorabaquine*; *jouir*; *joûter* (also *joûter à la quintaine*: R.). *Labourer*; *se laisser aller* (also *laisser aller le chat au fromage*, *se le laisser faire*, and *laisser tout faire*); *larder* (R.); *lever la chemise* (*la cotte*, *le cul*, *le devant*, or *son droit*); *levretter* (R.); *lier son boudin*; *loger les aveugles* (or *les nus*); *lutter*. *Manger de la chair crue* (or *de la viande de Vendredi*); *manier*; *manipuler*; *margauder* (R.); *marjoller* (R.); *marteler*; *le* METTRE, *se mettre à la besogne*, *à la juchée*, *à l'ouvrage*, *chair vive en chair vive*; *mettre dedans*, *en besogne*, *en œuvre*, *en presse*, *andouille au pot*, *la charrue devant les bœufs*, *la queue entre les jambes*; *le corps en presse*, *ses reins en besogne*, *un membre dans un autre*; *mettre du lard en bouteille*; *monter* (also *monter à l'assant* or *sur la bête*); *moudre* (GRIND, *q.v.*); *mouvoir des reins*. *Negocier*; *niguer* (R.). *Obliger*; *officier*; *ourser*. *Paffer*; *paillarder* (VILLON); *parler*; PASSER *le pas*, *les detroits*, *par la par les mains*, *par les piques*, *par l'étamine*, *sa fantaisie*, *son appétit*, *son envie*. and *sur le ventre*; *payer la bienvenue* (also *les arrérages de l'amour*, *son écot*, or *la comédie à Ferdinand*); *pêcher*; *percer*; *piner* (*cf.* TO JOCK, TO COCK, TO PRICK); *planter* (*des hommes ou des femmes*: also *le cresson* and *le mai*); *pousser un argument naturel et irrésistible* (also *sa pointe*, *l'aventure à bout*, or *une moulure*); *polluer*; *pomper* (R.); *ponifler*; *pourvoir*; PRENDRE *charnelle liesse*, *le déduit*, *le pâture*, *le passe-temps*, *le provande*, *ses ébats* (LA FONTAINE), *ses rafraichissements*, *son déduit*, *son délit*, *son plaisir*, *soulas*, or *une poignée*; *prier*; *promiscuiter*; *putasser*. *Quiller* (R.); *quouailler* (R.). *Raccointer* (R.); *racoutrer*; *ralentir sa braise*; *ramoner* (R.); *rataconniculer* (R.); *ratisser*; *reçevoir un clystère* (also *une leçon*, or *l'assaut*: of women or pathics); *recogner* (also *recoigner*); *recueillir la jouissance* (also *le fruit d'amour*); *régaler*; *rehausser le linge* (LA FONTAINE); *se rejouir*; *rembourrer*; *remuer le croupion* (R.); *rempeller*; *remuer* (BÉRANGER: also *remuer les fesses*, or *les reins*); *rendre le devoir*; *repasser*; *retaper*; *retour de matines* (LA FONTAINE); *ribauder*; *rire*; *river le bis*; *rompre un lance*; *rouscailler* (R.); *roussiner* (R.). *Sabouler* (R.); *saccader* (R.); *sacrificier* (of women); *saigner entre deux orteils* (R.); *saillir* (R.); *sangler* (R.); *se satisfaire* (also *satisfaire à son plaisir*); *se faire sauter*; *sauter*; *savonner* (also *donner une savonnade*); *secouer* (= TO SHAKE: also *secouer le pélisson*); *seutir douceur* (also *sentir de la volupté*); *séringuer*; *serrer*; *servir* (LA FONTAINE: also *se servir*); *solacier*; *sonder*; *sonner l'antiquaille*; *souffler en cul*; *soûler la volonté*; *soumettre* (also *soumettre à ses désirs*); *supposer*. *Tabourer* (also *tabourder*: O. Fr. = *battre du tambour*: R.); *tâcher* (BÉRANGER); *talocher* (R.);

tamiser (R.); *tantarer* (R.); *tarabuster; tâter* (also *tâter de la chair* or *la sauce*); *têter; thermométriser;* TIRER *à la cordelle, au blanc, au naturel, sa lance, son plaisir, du nerf, une venue* (R.); TOMBER, *à la renverse*, and *sur le dos; toucher* (LA FONTAINE); *tracasser; trafarcier; travailler* (also *travailler à la vigne* or *du cul*); *trousser* (BÉRANGER). *User. Vendanger;* VENIR (*en*); *venir à l'abordage, au choc; en venir au fait*, or *aux prises; venir la; ventouser; ventrouiller; verger; verminer* (R.); *vervignoler* (R.); *vétiller* (R.); *vitœuvrer; voir. Ziguer.*

*c.*1520. *Mayd Emlyn* [HAZLITT, *Pop. Poet.*, iv. 96]. And bycause she loued RYDYNGE, At the stewes was her abydynge.

[. . . .]. *MS.* [*Bodleian*, 548]. The hares haveth no seson of hure love, that as I sayde is clepid RYDYNG-TYME.

*d.*1529. SKELTON, *Bowge of Courte*, 400. I let her to hyre, that men maye on her RYDE.

*c.*1542. D. LYNDSAY, *On Jas. V. his Three Mistresses.* RYD not on your Olifauntes, For hurting of thy Geir.

1598. FLORIO, *Worlde of Wordes*, s.v. *Baiarda*, a common, filthie, ouer-RIDDEN whore.

1599. SHAKSPEARE, *Henry V.*, iii. 7, 60. They that RIDE so and RIDE not warily.

1607. WEBSTER and DEKKER, *Westward Hoe*, ii. 2. You know gentlewomen used to come to lords' chambers, and not lords to the gentlewomen's: I'd not have her think you are such a rank RIDER.

1611. CHAPMAN, *May-Day*, i. 1. I have heard of wenches that have been won with singing and dancing, and some with RIDING, but never heard of any that was won with tumbling in my life.

*c.*1618-19. FLETCHER, *Mad Lover*, iv. 5. He RIDES like a nightmare, all ages, all conditions. *Ibid.*, 1637 [?], *Elder Brother*, iv. 4. He'll RIDE you the better, Lily.

*c.*1620-50. *Percy Folio MS.*, 200, 'Lye Alone.' If dreames be true, then RIDE I can: I lacke nothing but a man, for tis onlye hee can ease my moane.

1621. BURTON, *Anat. Melan.*, III. III. i. 2. The adulterer sleeping now was RIDING on his master's saddle.

1653. URQUHART, *Rabelais*, I. iii. If you find any . . . females worth the pains . . . get up, RIDE upon them.

1656. FLETCHER, *Martiall*, xi. 105. The Phrygian Boyes in secret spent their seed As oft as Hector's wife RID on his steed.

1656. *Muses Recr.* [HOTTEN], 74. A smooth and gentle hand keeps women more in awe of due command Than if we set a ganneril on their Docks, RIDE them with bits, or on their Geer set locks.

1692. DRYDEN, *Juvenal*, 'Tenth Satire' (Ed. 3, 1702, p. 218). How many Boys that Pedagogue can RIDE.

17 [?]. *Old Scots' Song*, 'Heigh for Bread and Cream.' She poppit into bed, And I popp't in beside her; She lifted up her leg, And I began to RIDE her.

1772. BRIDGES, *Homer Burlesque*, 127. More than nine long tedious years Paris has RODE my brother's gear.

1786. BURNS, *The Inventory.* Frae this time forth I do declare, I'se ne'er RIDE horse nor hizzie mair.

*c.*1796. MORRIS, *Plenipotentiary*, 13. She had been well RID.

*b.*1796. *Old Scots' Song*, 'Ye'se get a Hole to Hide it in.' [FARMER, *Merry Songs and Ballads* (1897), iv. 269]. O haud it in your hand, sir, Till I get up my claes, Now RIDE me, as you'd ride for life.

2. (old).—To rob on the highway.

1605. *London Prodigal*, v. 1. It is well known I might have RID out a hundred times if I would

PHRASES.—TO RIDE AND TIE *see* quot. 1742); TO RIDE THE FRINGES (*see* quot. *c.*1787); TO RIDE AS IF FETCHING THE MIDWIFE = to go post haste; TO RIDE OUT = to adopt the profession of arms. *See* BACK; BLACK DONKEY; BODKIN; BROSE; COWLSTAFF; GRUB;

HOLBORN HILL; HIGH-HORSE; HOBBY-HORSE; MARYLEBONE STAGE; ROMFORD; ROUGH-SHOD; SPANISH MARE; STANG; WILD-MARE.

1383. CHAUCER, *Cant. Tales*, Gen. Prol., 45. A knight ther was . . . That fro the time that he firste began To RIDEN out, he loved chevalrie.

1737. BOSWELL, *Johnson*, I. v. note. Both used to talk pleasantly of this their first journey to London. Garrick . . . said one day in my hearing, 'We RODE AND TIED.'

1742. FIELDING, *Joseph Andrews*, ii. 2. They . . . agreed TO RIDE AND TIE . . . The two . . . set out together, one on horseback, the other on foot: he on horseback . . . when he arrives at the distance agreed on . . . is to dismount, TIE his horse to some gate, tree, post . . . and then proceed on foot; when the other comes up to the horse, he unties him, mounts, and gallops on; till having passed by his fellow traveller, he likewise arrives at the place of TYING.

*c.*1787. *Ireland Sixty Years Ago* (1847), 51. To guard themselves from encroachment, the citizens from time immemorial perambulated the boundaries of their chartered district every third year, and this was termed riding their franchises, corrupted into RIDING THE FRINGES.

RIDER, *subs.* (common).—A question or clause added to a geometrical problem, an Act of Parliament, an examination paper, &c.

1852. DICKENS, *Bleak House*, xxxix. Vholes finally adds, by way of RIDER to this declaration of his principles . . . perhaps Mr. C. will favour him with an order on his agent.

1885. *Report of Com. of Council on Education in Scotland for 1884*, 285. They showed a very satisfactory knowledge of Euclid's propositions, and a very creditable porportion of students worked a considerable number of the RIDERS.

2. *See* RIDE, *verb.* 1.

3. (old).—A Dutch coin with a man on horseback, worth about twenty-seven shillings: also a Scots gold piece issued by James VI.

1647. FLETCHER, *Woman's Prize*, I, 2. His mouldy money! Half a dozen RIDERS, That cannot sit, but stampt fast to their saddles.

4. (old).—A commercial traveller; a BAGMAN (*q.v.*).

1810. CRABBE, *Borough*, iv. The come to us as RIDERS in a trade.

1825. LAMB, *Letters*, cxii. A RIDER in his youth, travelling for shops.

RIDGE (or **REDGE**), *subs.* (old).—Gold: manufactured or specie: in latter case specifically = a guinea. Whence, RIDGE-MONTRA = a gold watch; CLY FULL OF RIDGE = a pocket-full of money; RIDGE-CULLY = a goldsmith.—B. E. (*c.*1696); PARKER (1781); GROSE (1785); VAUX (1812).

RIDICULOUS, *adj.* (provincial).—*See* quot. 1847.

1847. HALLIWELL, *Archaic . . . Words, &c.*, s.v. RIDICULOUS . . . Something very indecent and improper is understood; as, any violent attack upon a woman's chastity is called "very RIDICULOUS behaviour:" a very disorderly, and ill-conducted house, is also called a "RIDICULOUS one."

1889. *Notes and Queries*, 7 S., ix. 453. A man once informed me that the death by drowning of a relative was most RIDICULOUS.

RIDING-HAG, *subs. phr.* (colloquial).—The night-mare: also THE RIDING OF THE WITCH.

RIFF-RAFF (**RAFF** or **RAFFLE**), *subs.* (old).—1. Refuse, lumber; (2) the mob: spec. (Oxford Univ.) TOWN (*q.v.*) as opposed to GOWN (*q.v.*), or *vice versâ*; and (3) booty: as *adj.* = worthless. Whence RAFF-MERCHANT = a marine-store dealer; RAFFISH = disreputable; RAFFISHNESS = scampishness. As *verb.* RAFF (or RAFFLE) = to live filthily, to PIG IT (*q.v.*). RAFFLE-COFFIN = 'a ruffian, ribald fellow.'—B. E. (*c.*1696); GROSE (1785).

*d.*1210. MAPES, *Appendix*, 340. Maken of the rym and RAFF Suche gylours for pompe and pride.

*c.*1337. MANNING, *Tr. French Poem* [OLIPHANT, *New Eng.*, i. 21. The French words are quash . . . RIFF AND RAFF].

14 [?]. *MS.* [Lincoln, A. i. 17, fol. 148]. Ilk a manne agayne his gud he gaffe, That he had tane with RYFE AND RAFFE.

1531-47. COPLAND, *Spyttel Hous* [HAZLITT, *Pop. Poet.*, iv. 41]. And euer haunteth among such RYF RAF.

1611. FLORIO, *Ital. Dict. Gentaglia*, common or base, RIFFE-RAFFE, the scum of the earth, the base multitude of common people. Ibid. *Ciarpance*, RIFF-RAFF, luggage, trash.

*d.*1677. BARROW, *Unity of the Church.* The synod of Trent was convened to settle a RAFF of errors and superstitions.

1709. HEARNE, *Diary*, 10 Sept. He has his RIFF-RAFF notes upon Lycophron.

1847. THACKERAY, *Vanity Fair*, xxix. There is no town of any mark in Europe but it has its little colony of English RAFFS.

1851. MAYHEW, *Lond. Lab.*, I. 325. 'People, you see,' he said, 'wont buy their "accounts" of RAFF; they won't have them of any but respectable people.'

1884. CLARK RUSSELL, *Jack's Courtship*, xvii. Her main deck was a surface of straw, dirt, wet, and what sailors call RAFFLE.

1886. *D. Tel.*, 1 Ap. Shipping all sorts of sea-faring RIFF-RAFF.

1888. KIPLING, *Departmental Ditties*, 'The Galley.' And the topsmen clear the RAFFLE.

RIFLE, *verb.* (venery).—To grope or possess a woman: *see* RIDE.

1620. PERCY, *Folio MS.*, p. 194. Then lets imbrace and RIFFLE and trifle.

RIG, *subs.*, *adj.*, and *verb.* (old).—1. Generic for wantonness. As *subs.* = (1) a wanton (also RIG-MUTTON and RIGSBY); (2) a drinking or wenching bout; (3) anything dubious, as a knock-out, a cross fight, a cheat; (4) an unscrupulous person; and (5) a half or whole gelding (*see* quots. 1647 and 1678). As *verb.* = (1) to play the wanton; (2) TO SPREE (*q.v.*); (3) to trick, to steal; and (4) to ride pick-a-back. Hence RIGGISH = wanton; RIGOLAGE = wantonness; TO RUN (PLAY or CARRY) A RIG = to play fast-and-loose; TO RIG THE MARKET = to raise or depress prices for one's private advantage: hence to swindle; UP TO THE RIGS = expert, wide-awake, FLY (*q.v.*).—GROSE (1785).

*c.*1320. *Cursor Mundi*, MS. Coll. Trin., Cantab., f. 1. In ryot and in RIGOLAGE Spende mony her youthe and her age.

1551. STILL, *Gammer Gurton's Needle* [DODSLEY, *Old Plays* (REED), ii. 43. Nay, fy on thee, thou rampe, thou RYG, with al that take thy part.

1557. TUSSER, *Husbandrie*, Sept., 39. Some prowleth for fewel, and some away RIG Fat goose and the capon.

1570. LEVINS, *Manip. Vocab.*, 119. To RIGGE, *lasciuire puellam.*

1598. FLORIO, *Worlde of Wordes*, s.v. *Galluta*, a cockish, wanton, or RIGGISH wench. Ibid. *Mocciacca* . . . a RIGGE, a harlot.

1608. SHAKSPEARE, *Antony and Cleopatra*, ii. 2. For vilest things Become themselves in her; that the holy priests Bless her when she is RIGGISH.

1647. FLETCHER, *Women Pleased*, ii. 6. A pox o' yonder old RIGEL.

1650. FULLER, *Pisgah Light*, IV. vi. Let none condemn them [the girls] for RIGS because thus hoyting with the boys.

1653. URQUHART, *Rabelais*, III. ix. The mad-pate REEKS of Bedlam.

1678. COTTON, *Virgil Travestie* [*Works* (1725), 64]. I hate a base cowardly Drone, Worse than a RIGIL with one Stone.

1739. DUKE OF MONTAGUE [quoted by Theodore Hook in *Odd People*, 'An Honest Practical Joke']. "Now all my wig-singeing, and nose-blacking exploits, will be completely outdone by the RIG [that was the favorite word in the year 1739] I shall run upon this unhappy devil with the tarnished lace."

1775. *Old Song*, 'The Potato Man' [FARMER, *Musa Pedestris* (1896), 55]. I'm up to all your knowing RIGS.

1782. COWPER, *John Gilpin*, 25. He little dreamt when he set out Of RUNNING such a RIG.

1823. MONCRIEFF, *Tom and Jerry*, ii. 6. We haven't had a better job a long vile nor the shabby genteel lay. That, and the civil RIG told in a pretty penny.

1836. MARRYAT, *Japhet*, ii. Sometimes I carry on my RIGS a little too far.

1837. DICKENS, *Pickwick* (1857), 351. One expressed his opinion that it was "a RIG," and the other his conviction that it was "a go."

1848. LOWELL, *Biglow Papers*, . . . Who ever'd ha' thought sech A pisonous RIG Would be RUN by a chap thet wuz chose fer a Wig?

1857-61. MAYHEW, *London Lab.*, iii. 144. You're up to the RIGS of this hole; come to my hole—you can't play there!

1851. *Chamber's Journal*, xv. 103. A pawnbroker contributes the linen, an exuberant quantity of which is generally one of the characteristics of the RIG Sale.

1855. TOM TAYLOR, *Still Waters* [DICKS], 13. We must RIG THE MARKET. Go in and buy up every share that's offered.

1892. *Pall Mall Gaz.*, 28 Oct., 6, 2. Mr. Burr, without the knowledge of Mr. Westmacott, issued underwriting agreements, and proceeded to . . . RIG THE MARKET.

1892. HENLEY and STEVENSON, *Deacon Brodie*, I. vii. That's the RIG, Deacon.

1901. *D. Telegraph*, 29 April, 4, 4. He never thought of RUNNING such A RIG as that which caused his appearance before Mr. Sheil, at Westminster Police-court, on Saturday. *Ibid.*, 21 Dec., 2, 7. Yesterday the RIG in Scotch pig-iron collapsed.

2. (common).—Dress; style: whence = a turn-out, or outfit: also RIG-OUT and RIGGING. As *verb* = to equip; RIGGED = dressed; TO RIG A BLOSS = to strip a wench; RUM RIGGING = fine clothes.—B. E. (*c.*1696); GROSE (1785).

1594. NASHE, *Unf. Traveller* [*Wks.* v. 164]. Her wardrop was richly RIGD.

1625. JONSON, *Staple of News*, ii. 1. She is not RIGGED, sir; setting forth some lady Will cost as much as furnishing a fleet.

1639. MASSINGER, *Unnatural Combat*, iv. 2. But if you will look on the malecontent Belgarde, newly RIGG'D UP, with the train that follows him, 'twill be an object worthy of your noting.

1677. WYCHERLEY, *Plain Dealer*, iv. 1. You shall see how I RIGGED my 'squire OUT, with the remains of my shipwrecked wardrobe.

1709. CENTLIVRE, *Busie Body*, ii. Buy a Lady's Favour at the Price of a thousand Pieces, to RIG OUT an Equipage for a Wench.

1729. GAY, *Polly*, i. 2. She is in most charming RIGGING; she won't cost you a penny, Sir, in cloaths at first setting out.

1757. FOOTE, *Author*, i. He's very young, and exceedingly well RIGGED.

1789. PARKER, *Life's Pain er*, 62. We shortly after RIGGED her with an entire new and very neat change of wearables.

1818. BYRON, *Beppo*, v. Such as in Monmouth Street, or in Rag Fair, would RIG you OUT in seriousness or joke.

1823. MONCRIEFF, *Tom and Jerry*, 5. This toggery will never fit—you must have a new RIG-OUT.

1878. BESANT & RICE, *By Celia's Arbour*, ch. ix. I was saluted in the street—it was on the Hard—by a tall and good-looking young sailor, in his naval RIG, the handiest ever invented.

1899. WHITEING, *John St.*, xvii. A fad every week at the 'osiers shops . . . and . . . a new RIG-OUT for every fad.

RIGGEN. TO RIDE THE RIGGEN, *verb. phr.* (provincial).—To be very intimate.

RIGGER, *subs.* (Durham School).—A racing boat.

RIGHT, *adj.* and *adv.* (old colloquial).—Very; just; quite. COLLOQUIALISMS are numerous: RIGHT AS RAIN (AS NINEPENCE, MY LEG, ANYTHING, A FIDDLE, TRIVET, &c.) = absolutely dependable; TO RIGHTS = completely to one's satisfaction; RIGHT THERE = on the spot; RIGHT GREAT = very much; RIGHT NOW = instanter; RIGHT SO = just so; TO DO ONE RIGHT (or REASON) = (1) to do justice, and (2) to pledge in drinking; RIGHT OUT = to a finish; RIGHT DOWN = downright; RIGHT SMART = extremely clever; RIGHT AWAY (OUT, or STRAIGHT), RIGHT OFF (HERE or OUT) = immediately; TO TURN (or SEND) TO THE RIGHT-ABOUT = to dismiss; RIGHT YOU ARE = a complete acquiescence; ALL RIGHT = certainly, O. K. (GROSE); A BIT OF ALL RIGHT = extremely good; RIGHT ALONG = at these presents; RIGHT UP TO THE HANDLE = excellent; TO DO (or HAVE) ONE TO RIGHTS = to serve one out; TO SET TO RIGHTS = to put in order; RIGHT ON = entirely, straightforward; RIGHT FORTH = straight; BY GOOD RIGHTS = it should be so; RIGHT ROYAL = drunk. *See* LEG.

*c.*1307. *Rel. Antiq.*, ii. 19. AS RYT AS RAMIS ORN.

1340. *Gamelyn* [OLIPHANT, *New Eng.*, i. 39. Men dress (set) things TO-RIGHTES; this adverb (few recognise it) is the source of our setting things TO RIGHTS].

1350. *William of Palerne* [E.E.T.S.], 3066. The quen er the day was dight wel TO RIGHTES Hendli in that hynde-skin as swiche bestes were. *Ibid.*, 4268. Sche swelt for sorwe and swoned RIT THERE.

1356. MANDEVILLE, *Travels*, 181. And he hem turnethe alle the Firmament RIGHTE as dothe a Wheel that turneth be his Axille Tree.

1383. CHAUCER, *Cant. Tales*, 3629 [OLIPHANT, *New Eng.*, i. 127. There are new phrases like RIGHT (just) NOW . . .].

*c.*1440. *Merlin* [E. E. T. S.], ii. 129. Thei asked yef thei hadde grete haste; and thei ansuerde, 'Ye, RIGHT GRETE.'

*c.*1450. *Knight of La Tour-Landry* [OLIPHANT, *New Eng.*, i. 284. We have RIGHT SO . . . where we now say *just so*].

*d.*1460. LYDGATE [*MS. Harl.*, 172, 71]. Conveyde by lyne RYGHT AS A RAMMES HORNE.

*d.*1529. SKELTON, *Why Come Ye Not, &c.*? 86. Do ryght and doe no wronge, As RYGHT AS A RAMMES HORNE. Ibid., *Speke Parrot*, 498. So myche raggyd RYGHTE OF A RAMMES HORNE. Ibid., *Colyn Cloute*, 1200. They say many matters ar born Be hyt RYGHTE AS A RAMBES HORN.

1598. SHAKSPEARE, *2 Henry IV.*, v. 3. Why now you have DONE ME RIGHT. *Ibid.* (1609), *Tempest*, iv. i. 101. And be a boy RIGHT OUT.

1605. SYLVESTER, *Du Bartas*, ii. I doo adiure thee (O great King) by all That in the World we sacred count or call, TO DOE ME RIGHT.

1607. W[ENTWORTH] S[MITH], *Puritan*, i. 1. He was my brother, as RIGHT AS RIGHT.

1612-5. HALL, *Contemp.* [TEGG], v. 176. A prudent circumlocution which RIGHT DOWN would not be digested.

1622. FLETCHER, *Beggar's Bush*, ii. 3. 'Tis freely spoken, noble burgomaster I'll DO YOU RIGHT.

1624. MASSINGER, *Bondman*, ii. 3. These glasses contain nothing; DO ME RIGHT As e'er you hope for liberty.

1663. TUKE, *Adv. Five Hours* [DODSLEY, *Old Plays* (REED), xii. 26]. Your master's health, sir—I'LL DO YOU REASON, sir.

1703. FARQUHAR, *Inconstant*, ii. 2. Oh, pardon me, sir, you shall DO ME RIGHT . . . Now, sir, can you drink a health.

1726. SWIFT, *Gulliver's Travels*, II. viii. They let the hulk drop into the sea, which by reason of many breaches made in the bottom and sides, sunk TO RIGHTS.

1749. SMOLLETT, *Gil Blas* [ROUTLEDGE], 26. God knows if his heart lay in the RIGHT place.

18[?]. HUMPHREYS, *Yankee in England. Aunt.* Bring back an answer,—quick. *Doolittle.* In a jiffing, I'll be back TO RIGHTS.

1842. DICKENS, *American Notes*, ii. I now saw that "RIGHT AWAY" and "directly" meant the same thing. *Ibid.* (1854), *Hard Times*, iv. TURN this girl TO THE RIGHT-ABOUT, and there's an end of it.

1855. TAYLOR, *Still Waters*, ii. 2. 'How are you?' . . . 'RIGHT AS A TRIVET, my prince of prospectus mongers.

1856. STOWE, *Dred*, I. 209. She had RIGHT SMART of life in her, and was always RIGHT BUSY 'tending to something or other. *Ibid.*, I. Get the carriage out for me RIGHT AWAY.

1856. WEBSTER, *Correspondence*, I. 339. We will shut ourselves up in the office and do the work RIGHT OFF.

1857. OLMSTED, *Texas*, 301. Each man's ration consisting of a pint of mouldy corn and a RIGHT SMART chunk of bacon.

1876. MACAULAY, *Life and Letters*, I. 235. I guess I must answer him RIGHT slick AWAY.

1882. MCCABE, *New York*, xliii. 570 Take hold of it, my boy, RIGHT NOW.

1883. HAWLEY SMART, *At Fault*, III. viii. 125. "RIGHT YOU ARE, Dickinson," replied Mr. Usher, rubbing his hands softly.

1899. WHITEING, *John Street*, ix. If yer want to get it TO RIGHTS. *Ibid.*, xviii. He is simply 'RIGHT' from top to toe.

RIGHT-ABOUTS (THE), *subs.* (military).—The Gloucestershire Regiment. Also "The Old Braggs"; "The Slashers"; and "The Whitewashers."

RIGHT-EYE (or HAND). MY RIGHT-EYE ITCHES, *phr.* (old colloquial). —*See* quot.

1708-10. SWIFT, *Polite Conversation*, iii. *Lady Answ.* And MY RIGHT EYE ITCHES; I shall cry. *Ibid. Lady Smart.* And MY RIGHT HAND ITCHES; I shall receive Money.

RIGHT-HANDER, *subs. phr.* (pugilists').—A hit with the right hand.

1857. HUGHES, *Tom Brown's School-days*, ii. 5. Tom gets . . . deposited on the grass by a RIGHT-HANDER from the Slogger.

RIGHT-SIDE. TO RISE ON THE RIGHT-SIDE, *verb. phr.* (old).—A happy augury: *cf.* WRONG SIDE (*q.v.*) of the bed.

1607. MARSTON, *What you Will* [*Works* (1633), sig. Rb]. You RISE ON YOUR RIGHT SIDE to-day, marry.

1614. *Terence in English* [NARES]. *C.* What doth shee keepe house alreadie? *D.* Alreadie. *C.* O good God: WE ROSE ON THE RIGHT SIDE to-day.

*c.*1620. FLETCHER, *Women Pleased*, i. [end of act].

1633. MACHIN, *Dumb Knight*, iv. 1. Sure I said my prayers, RIS'D ON MY RIGHT SIDE . . . No hare did cross me, nor no bearded witch, Nor other ominous sign.

RIGHT-SORT, *subs. phr.* (old).—Gin: *see* WHITE SATIN.—*The Fancy* (1820).

RIGHTEOUS, *adj.* (colloquial).—An inverted appreciation: *e.g.*, a RIGHTEOUS (*i.e.*, fine) as distinguished from a WICKED (*q.v.*) day, &c.: *cf.* RELIGIOUS.

MORE HOLY THAN RIGHTEOUS, *phr.* (common).—Applied to a tattered garment or person.

RIGMAROLE, *subs.* (colloquial).—A tedious story; twaddle; a rambling statement: also RAGMAN ROLL, RIG-MY-ROLL, and RIG-MAROLE. As *adj.* = roundabout, nonsensical (GROSE). [A corruption of RAGMAN ROLL—*i.e.*, the Devil's Roll: *cf.* RAGEMAN—applied apparently to any document containing many details; also to an old game in which a parchment roll played a part.]

*d.*1529. SKELTON, *Garlande of Laurell* [DYCE, i. 420], 1490. I did what I cowde to scrape out the scrollis, Apollo to rase out of her RAGMAN ROLLIS.

1533. *Pardoner and Frere* [HALLIWELL]. Myster parson, I marvayll ye wyll gyve lycenc To this false knave . . . To publish his RAGMAN ROLLES with lyes.

*d.*1556. UDALL [SMYTH PALMER]. A RAGMAN'S REWE . . . we call a long geste that railleth on any person by name or toucheth a bodyes honesty somewhat near.

1753. RICHARDSON, *Sir Chas. Grandison*, IV. iv. You must all of you go in one RIG-MY-ROLL way, in one beaten track.

1757. FOOTE, *Author*, ii. You are always running on with your RIGGMON-ROWLES, and won't stay to hear a body's story out.

1874. MRS. H. WOOD, *Johnny Ludlow*, 1st S., No. xii., 203. Mrs. Blair has been writing us a strange RIGMAROLE, which nobody can make head or tail of.

RIGOL (or RIGIL).—*See* RIG, *subs.* 1.

RILE (ROIL or ROYLE), *verb.* (old). —To vex; to irritate; to disturb. Hence RILY = cross-grained; RILEMENT = ill temper. [Originally = to make turbid.] Fr. *cavaler* (or *courir*) *sur le haricot.*

1656-8. GURNALL, *Christian in Armour*, III. 296. There are dregs enough within to ROYLE and distemper the spirit.

1740. NORTH, *Examen*, 359. The lamb down stream ROILED the wolf's water above. Ibid., *Lives of the Norths*, I. 415. He took a turn or two in his dining room and said nothing, by which I perceived that his spirits were very much ROILED.

1843. DICKENS, *Chuzzlewit*, xxi. My feller critters . . . RILE up rough, along of my objecting to their selling Eden off too cheap.

1847. ROBB, *Squatter Life*, 64. I gin to git RILEY. *Ibid.*, 31. RILE him up, and sot his liver workin?

1848. LOWELL, *Biglow Papers*, . . . We begin to think it's natur To take sarse and not be RILED.

1849. THACKERAY, *Pendennis*, lxiv. What vexed and "RILED" him (to use his own expression) was the infernal indifference and cowardly ingratitude of Clavering.

1883. *Sat. Rev.*, 13 Jan., 42, 2. It is not surprising that . . . they [his speeches] "RILED" some of Sir Charles's political friends not a little. But it was perhaps a little surprising that the RILEMENT was so little manifested among Sir Charles's audiences.

RIMBLE-RAMBLE, *subs. phr.* (old). —Nonsense: as *adj.* = nonsensical.

1690. *Pagan Prince* [NARES]. The greatest part of the task was only RIMBLE-RAMBLE discourse.

RINDER, *subs.* (Queen's University). —An outsider.

RINER. TO SHED RINERS WITH A WHAVER, *verb. phr.* (old).—To cap; to surpass.

RING, *subs.* (venery).—1. The female *pudendum*: also HAIRY RING, HANS CARVELS RING (*q.v.*) and BLACK-RING. Hence CRACKED (or CLIPPED) IN THE RING = seduced.

1597. LYLY, *Woman in Moon*, iii. 2. *Lear.* Will Pandora be thus light? *Gun.* If she were twenty graines lighter I would not refuse her, provided alwayes She be CLIPT WITHIN THE RING.

1613. BEAUMONT and FLETCHER, *Captain.* Come to be married to my lady's woman, After she's CRACK'D IN THE RING.

1622. ATLEY, *Book of Airs*, s.v.

1653. URQUHART, *Rabelais*, III. xxviii. Never fail to have continually the RING of thy wife's Commodity upon thy finger.

1660. WATSON, *Cheerful Airs*, s.v.

*c.*1700. PRIOR, *Hans Carvel.* Hans took the RING . . . And, thrusting it beyond his joint, 'Tis done, he cry'd' . . . 'What's done, you drunken bear, You've thrust your finger God knows where!'

2. (colloquial).—A place set apart for, or a concourse engaged in, some specific object: as (racing) = (1) an enclosure used for betting, and (2) the bookmakers therein; (pugilists') = (3) the circle, square, or parallelogram within which a fight takes place: hence THE PRIZE RING = the world of pugilists; (horse-

dealers') = (4) the space within which horses are exhibited at fair, market, or auction; (general) = (5) a combination for controlling a market or political measure; in America a TRUST.—B. E. (*c.* 1696); GROSE (1785). Hence RINGMAN = a BOOKMAKER (*q.v.*).

1705. FARQUHAR, *Twin Rivals*, i. 1. I fly at nobler game; THE RING, the Court, Pawlett's and the Park.

1819. MOORE, *Tom Crib*, 57. Ruffian'd the reeling youngsters round the RING.

1822. SCOTT, *Fortunes of Nigel*, ii. Cold water and . . . vinegar applied . . . by the bottle-holders in a modern RING.

1845. DISRAELI, *Sybil*, I. ii. 'Will any one do anything about Hybiscus?' sang out a gentleman in the RING at Epsom.

1848. THACKERAY, *Vanity Fair*, xix. One day, in THE RING, Rawdon's Stanhope came in sight.

1855. TAYLOR, *Still Waters*, ii. 1. I should have done better to have stuck by Tattersall's and the Turf. The RING are sharp fellows.

1857. LAWRENCE, *Guy Livingstone*, ix. No RINGMEN to force the betting and deafen you with their blatant proffers.

1871. *Manchester Guardian*, 23 Dec. 'American RINGS and Lobbyists.' The modern political RING he described as a combination of selfish bad men, formed for their own pecuniary advancement.

1877. *Nation*, xiii. 333 [*Century*]. A [political] RING is, in its common form, a small number of persons who get possession of an administrative machine, and distribute the offices or other good things connected with it among a band of fellows, of greater or less dimensions, who agree to divide with them whatever they make.

1888. *D. Chronicle*, 12 July. The victory was very popular, and by the success of Satiety the RING sustained a severe blow.

3. (old).—'Money extorted by Rogues on the High-way, or by Gentlemen Beggers.'—B. E. (*c.*1696); GROSE (1785).

Verb. (common).—1. To manipulate; spec. to change: *e.g.*, TO RING CASTORS = to exchange hats (GROSE); TO RING THE CHANGES = (1) to substitute bad money for good; and (2) so to bustle that change is given wrong.—GROSE (1785); VAUX (1812).

1678. BUTLER, *Hudibras*, III. iii. The skill To wind and manage it at will . . . And RING THE CHANGES upon cases.

1749. SMOLLETT, *Gil Blas* [ROUTLEDGE], 4. The CHANGES were just beginning TO RING upon some new subject.

1828. BEE, *Liv. Pict. London*, 45. Jarvis . . . after turning your money over and over . . . declares they ring bad, and you must change them for good ones. If you appear tolerably 'soft,' and will 'stand it,' he perhaps refuses these also, after having RUNG THE CHANGES once more. This is called a double do.

2. (thieves').—*See* quot.

1863. *Cornhill Mag.*, vii. 91. When housebreakers are disturbed and have to abandon their plunder they say that they have RUNG themselves.

3. (Australian).—To patrol cattle by riding round and round them. Also TO RING UP.

4. (American).—To create a disturbance; TO RACKET (*q.v.*).

5. (old).—To talk: spec. to scold: of women.—GROSE.

PHRASES.—TO RING THE HORSESHOES (tailors') = to welcome a man returning from a drinking bout; TO GO THROUGH THE RING = to go bankrupt, to be WHITEWASHED (*q.v.*); TO RING IN (American) = (1) to quote; to implicate, (2) to get the better of, (3) in gaming, to add to (or substitute) cards in a pack surreptitiously: whence TO RING IN A COLD DECK = to substitute a prepared pack of cards; CRACKED IN THE RING = (1) flawed; (2) see *subs.*, sense 1; TO COME ON THE RING = to take one's turn; TO TAKE THE MANTLE AND RING = to vow perpetual widowhood. Also *see* BALL.

*d.*1400. CHAUCER, *Good Women*, 1887. Judge infernal Mynos . . . Now cometh thy lotte! now COMESTOW ON THE RYNGE.

[. . . .]. *Gesta Grayorum*, 'Progr. of Eliz.,' ii. 54. His highness' master of the ordnance claimes to have all peeces gul'd in the touch-hole or broken WITHIN THE RINGE.

1596. SHAKSPEARE, *Hamlet*, ii. 2, 448. Pray God your voice, like a piece of uncurrent gold, be not CRACK'D WITHIN THE RING.

1632. JONSON, *Magnetic Lady*. Light gold, and CRACK'D WITHIN THE RING. [This quot. also illustrates sense 1.]

1887. FRANCIS, *Saddle and Mocassin*. Between them they RUNG IN A COLD DECK in a faro-box.

1889. LESTER WALLACK, *Memories* [*Scribner*, iv. 723]. They want TO RING me INTO it, but I do not see anything in it I can do.

RING-DROPPER (or -FALLER), *subs. phr.* (thieves').—*See* quot. 1851-61: hence RING-DROPPING: *see* FAWNEY-DROPPER.—AWDELEY (1567); PARKER (1781).

1843. DICKENS, *Martin Chuzzlewit*, xxxvii. Tom's evil genius did not . . . mark him out as the prey of RING-DROPPERS . . . or any of those bloodless sharpers.

1849. MACAULAY, *Hist. of Eng.*, xviii. The crowd of pilferers, RING-DROPPERS, and sharpers who infested the capital.

1851-61. MAYHEW, *London Lab.*, i. 389. In RING-DROPPING we pretend to have found a ring, and ask some simple-looking fellow if it's good gold, as it's only just picked up [they then get the fellow to buy].

RINGER, *subs.* (common).—A bell; a tinkler. Fr. *battante; brandillante.*

RING-MAN, *subs. phr.* (old).—The middle, or ring finger: *cf.* DARKMANS; RUFF-MANS, &c.

1544. ASCHAM, *Toxophilus*, 137. When a man shooteth, the might of his shoote lyeth on the foremost finger, and on the RING-MAN.

2. *See* RING, *subs.* 1.

RING-TAIL, *subs.* (military).—A recruit: *see* SNOOKER.

RING-TAILED ROARER, *subs. phr.* (American).—The nonsense name of some imaginary beast.—*Century*.

RINK. TO GET OUT OF ONE'S RINK, *verb. phr.* (old colloquial).—To sow wild oats. [RINK = a course, a race, ring, or circle.]

RINSE, *subs.* (common).—Any sort of potable; LAP (*q.v.*). Hence as *verb.* = to drink; TO LUSH (*q.v.*).

RIOT ACT. TO READ THE RIOT ACT, *verb. phr.* (colloquial).—To administer a jobation; to reprove.

RIOTOUS-LIVING, *subs. phr.* (colloquial).—Luxuries. [*Cf.* Luke xv. 13.]

RIP, *subs.* (common).—A reprobate; a RAKE (*q.v.*). Hence anything censurable: as a SCREW (*q.v.*) of a horse (GROSE), 'a shabby mean fellow' (GROSE): sometimes in jest.

1827. PEAKE, *Comfortable Lodgings*, i. 2. *Roue.* So, at last at Paris; and I'll be bound I'm the greatest RIP in it.

1853. DICKENS, *Bleak House*, lv. If it's ever broke to him that his RIP of a brother has turned up I could wish . . . to break it myself.

1892. *Pall Mall Gaz.*, 20 Oct., 6, 1. The prisoner said a RIP (an Americanism for low woman) has told him that she had been employed by the police to track him.

1900. KIPLING, *Stalky & Co.*, 25. 'Hold on, till King loses his temper,' said Beetle. 'He's a libellous old RIP, an' he'll be in a ravin' paddywhack.'

Verb. (old: now chiefly American).—1. To take one's own course; to go as one will: to tear along; to drive furiously:

usually in *phr.* LET HER RIP: also TO RIP AND STAVE. Whence RIPPER = a tearer; TO RIP AND TEAR = to be furious; TO RIP OUT = to explode; also as an oath, RIP ME! = BLAST ME! (*q.v.*).

1600. DECKER, *Shom. Holiday* [*Works* (1873), i. 29]. Auaunt kitchin-stuffe, RIPPE, you browne bread tannikin, out of my sight.

1848. JONES, *Sketches of Travels*, 78. He RIPPED OUT an oath that made the hair stand on my head.

1869. H. B. STOWE, *Old Town Folks*, 607. If she don't do nothing more . . . why, I say, let 'er RIP.

1877. *Temple Bar*, May, 209. It has its drawbacks, the principal of which is a growing tolerance of misrule and misconduct in office. "Let him RIP," is a common verdict; "we can turn him out when his time is up."

1885. STEVENSON, *Prince Otto*, ii. 7. 'You may leave the table,' he added, his temper RIPPING OUT.

1895. MARRIOTT-WATSON [*New Review*, 2 July]. "RIP ME," says he, starting up, "d'ye think I could not ha' been in the job myself?"

2. (old).—To search; to rummage: espec. with a view to plunder; hence (3) to steal. RIPPER = a robber.

[. . . .]. *Ormulum*, 10,212. To RIPPENN hemm and ræfenn.

*c.*1388. *Towneley Myst.*, 112. Com and RYPE oure howse, and then may ye se Who had hir.

[. . . .]. *Robin Hood and Beggar* [CHILD, *Ballads*, v. 190]. And loose the strings of all thy pocks, I'll RIPE them with my hand.

1816. SCOTT, *Old Mortality*, xxiii. I e'en RIPED his pouches, as he had dune mony an honester man's.

RIPE, *adj.* and *adv.* (common).—1. Drunk; and (2) ready.

1609. SHAKSPEARE, *Tempest*, v. 1. Trinculo is reeling RIPE: where should they find this grand liquor that hath gilded 'em?

*c.*1615. FLETCHER, *Woman's Prize*, i. 1. Do all the ramping, roaring tricks a whore, Being drunk and tumbling-RIPE.

*d.*1704. BROWN, *Works*, i. 272. To show you how soon the Women of this age grow RIPE . . .

1821. EGAN, *Life in London*, 178. Jerry was now RIPE for anything.

1842. TENNYSON, *Poems*, 'Will Water-proof.' Half mused or reeling-RIPE.

RIPON (or RIPPON), *subs.* (old).—1. A spur; and (2) a sword. [The Yorkshire City was formerly famous for its fine steel.]—GROSE (1785).

1625. JONSON, *Staple of News*, i. 3. Why there's an angel, if my SPURS Be not right RIPPON.

1636. WITS [DODSLEY, *Old Plays* (REED), viii. 501]. Whip me with wire, headed with rowels of Sharp RIPPON SPURS.

RIPPER, *subs.* (colloquial).—Anything especial: a good ball (cricket); a knock-down blow (pugilistic); a fine woman; an outrageous lie, &c. Hence RIPPING = great, excellent, STUNNING (*q.v.*).

1851. MAYHEW, *Lond. Lab.*, i. 237. The . . . battle between the two young ladies of fortune is what we call a RIPPER.

1877. *Belgravia*, xxxii. 241. Mr. Wilkie Collins's last novel is a RIPPING book.

1881. HOWELLS, *Dr. Breen's Practice*, ii. Barlow says it's the hottest day he's ever seen here. . . . "It's a RIPPER."

1884. HAWLEY SMART, *Post to Finish*, i. What a RIPPING race it was.

1892. NISBET, *Bushranger's Sweetheart*, 209. 'How are you getting on with her?' 'RIPPINGLY as far as she is concerned.'

1896. COTSFORD DICK, *Ways of World*, 53. He calls the sunrise a 'RIPPIN show.'

RIPPING, *subs.* (Eton College).—A ceremony incidental to the departure of a Senior Collegér for King's College, Cambridge: when

he has 'got King's' his gown is stitched up that it may be RIPPED afterwards.

Adj. *See* RIPPER.

RISE, *subs.* (colloquial).—An advance: in salary, price, betting, status, rank, &c. *See* RAISE.

1837. DICKENS, *Pickwick*, liii. Eighteen bob a-week, and a RISE if he behaved himself.

1851-61. MAYHEW, *Lond. Lab.*, ii. 42. A friend or two in London . . . gave me a bit of a RISE, so I began as a costermonger.

1864. TENNYSON, *Aylmer's Field*. Wrinkled benchers oft talk'd of him Approvingly, and prophesied his RISE.

1893. MILLIKEN, *'Arry Ballads*, 70. As to my chance of a RISE wot do you think, old pal!

Verb. (colloquial).—1. To play into one's hands; to listen credulously.

1856. WHYTE-MELVILLE, *Kate Coventry*, xvi. John ROSE freely in a moment . . . he burst out quite savagely.

2. *See* RAISE.

TO GET (HAVE or TAKE) A RISE OUT OF ONE, *verb. phr.* (common).—To mortify; to make ridiculous; to outwit.

1600. KEMP, *Dance to Norwich* [OLIPHANT, *New Eng.*, ii. 52. The new substantives are pipe, a RISE (leap); whence comes "GET A RISE OUT OF HIM"].

*d.*1859. DE QUINCEY, *Spanish Nun*. Possibly TAKING A RISE out of his worship the Corregidor.

1901. *Sporting Times*, 6 Ap., 1, 4. But, I don't care how hard he tries, He out of me can't TAKE A RISE.

PHRASES.—TO RISE A BARNEY (showmen's) = to collect a crowd; TO RISE ARSE UPWARDS = 'A sign of good luck' (RAY).

RISING, *quasi-adv.* (colloquial).—1. Upwards of; and (2) approaching to.

1853. BRADLEY, *Verdant Green*, 1. 7. When Mr. Verdant Green was [in stable language] RISING sixteen.

RISPIN. *See* RESPIN.

RITES OF LOVE, *subs. phr.* (conventional).—Copulation: *see* GREENS.

*d.*1638. CAREW, *The Rapture*. We only sin when LOVE'S RITES are not done.

1733. BAILEY, *Coll. Eras.*, 'The Uneasy Wife.' There are some Women who will be querulous, and scold even while the RITES OF LOVE are performing.

RIVER LEA, *subs. phr.* (rhyming).—The sea.

RIVER-RAT, *subs. phr.* (common).—A riverside thief: specifically one who robs the corpses of men drowned.

RIVER TICK. *See* TICK.

RIVET, *subs.* (common).—In *pl.* = money: *see* RHINO.

Verb. (colloquial).—To marry; TO HITCH (*q.v.*); TO SPLICE (*q.v.*).

1700. CONGREVE, *Way of the World*, i. 2. "Sir, there's such coupling at Pancras that they stood behind one another as 'twere in a country dance . . . so we drove round to Duke's Place, and there they were RIVETTED in a trice."

RIZ. *See* RAISE.

RIZZLE, *verb.* (provincial).—*See* quot.

1890. *Cassell's Sat. Jour.*, 2 Aug., 1068, 1. The newest of new verbs is the verb to RIZZLE . . . to enjoy a short period of absolute idleness after a meal.

R.M.D., *phr.* (common).—Ready Money Down; immediate payment.

ROACH. *See* SOUND.

ROAD, *subs.* (venery).—1. The female *pudendum*: also ROAD TO HEAVEN (or PARADISE): *see* MONOSYLLABLE. Whence ROAD-MAKING (or ROAD UP FOR REPAIRS) = menstruation. Also (2) a harlot.

1598. SHAKSPEARE, *2 Hen. IV.*, ii. 2, 182. This Doll Tearsheet should be some ROAD.

*c.*1796. BURNS, *Merry Muses*, 112.

TO TAKE TO THE ROAD, *verb. phr.* (various).—To turn highwayman (THE ROAD also = highway robbery); footpad; beggar; tramp; or commercial. Whence ROAD-AGENT, GENTLEMAN (or KNIGHT) OF THE ROAD = (1) a highwayman, and (2) a commercial traveller.

1704. [ASHTON, *Social Life, &c.*, II. 242]. There is always some little Trifle given to Prisoners, they call Garnish; we OF THE ROAD are above it.

1730. SWIFT, *Capt. Creichton* [OLIPHANT, *New Eng.*, ii. 162. Among the verbs are . . . GO UPON THE ROAD (as a highwayman) . . .].

1749. SMOLLETT, *Gil Blas* [ROUTLEDGE], 13. I do not think you are fool enough to make any bones about consorting with GENTLEMEN OF THE ROAD.

1883. STEVENSON, *Silverado Squatters*, 15. The highway robber—ROAD-AGENT, he is quaintly called.

1893. *Standard*, 29 Jan., 2. Now suppose we are ON THE ROAD . . . and we meet a josser policeman.

1895. MARRIOTT-WATSON [*New Review*, July, 8]. But if a GENTLEMAN OF THE ROAD must be hindered by the impudent accidents of the weather, he had best . . . settle down with empty pockets afore a mercer's counter.

ROAF, *adj.* (back slang).—Four. Hence ROAF-YANNEPS = fourpence; ROAF-GEN = four shillings.

ROACH-AND-DACE, *subs. phr.* (rhyming).—The face: *see* DIAL.

ROADSTER, *subs.* (hunting).—A person who prefers the road to cross country riding.

1885. *Field*, 4 Ap. Once in a way the ROADSTERS and shirkers are distinctly favoured.

ROARER, *subs.* (common).—Anything especially loud: *e.g.* (1) = a broken-winded horse (GROSE); (2) a pushing newsvendor; (3) a stump-orator. Hence ROAR = (1) to breathe hard: of horses; (2) to RANT (*q.v.*); ROARING = the disease in horses causing broken wind.

1752. JOHNSON, *Rambler*, No. 144. The ROARER . . . has no other qualifications for a champion of controversy than a hardened front and a strong voice.

1837. PEAKE, *Quarter to Nine*, 1. His horse is neither a crib biter nor a ROARER.

*d.*1841. HOOK, *Man of Many Friends*. His stalls at Melton inhabited by slugs and ROARERS.

1841. THACKERAY, *Sketches*, 'A Night's Pleasure.' Cox's most roomy fly . . . in which he insists on putting the ROARING gray horse.

1847. ROBB, *Traits of Squatter Life*, 64. Ben was an old Mississip' ROARER.

1850. STOWE, *Uncle Tom's Cabin*, viii. Tom's a ROARER when there's any thumping or fighting to be done.

1865. *Evening Citizen*, 7 Aug. One of a class of men known as ROARERS went round with a few evening papers which he announced to be "extraordinary editions."

1872. *Figaro*, 30 Nov. Greeley's too great a ROARER, and depended too much on the stump.

1872. ELIOT, *Middlemarch*, xxiii. The horse was a penny trumpet to that ROARER of yours.

1883. *D. Telegraph*, 5 Jan., 2, 6. Prosecutor, after paying for the mare, discovered her to be a ROARER.

ROARATORIO, *subs.* (old).—An oratorio.—GROSE (1785).

ROARING, *adj.* and *adv.* (common).—Brisk; successful; strong: *see* DRIVE, HUMMING, &c.

1831. PLANCHE, *Olympic Revels*, 3. But what a ROARING trade I'm driving, burn me! But I can scarcely tell which way to turn me.

1837. MARRYATT, *Snarleyow*, xii. You've got a ROARING fire, I'll bet.

1883. *Referee*, 20 May, 2, 4. Rain having kindly come to the rescue of managers on Whit-Monday, most theatres did a ROARING trade.

ROARING-BOY (-BLADE, -GIRL, -LAD, -RUFFIAN, &c., or **ROARER**), *subs. phr.* (old).—A street bully: late 16th and 17th centuries: also OATMEAL (*q.v.*) and TERRIBLE-BOY (*q.v.*). Also ROAR, *verb.* = to riot; to swagger; ROARING = riotous. As *adv.* = extravagantly, noisily, superbly.—B. E. (*c.*1696); GROSE (1785).

*c.*1600. *Brave English Gypsey* [COLLIER, *Roxburghe Ballads* (1847), 185]. Our knockers make no noise, We are no ROARING BOYES.

1603. DEKKER, *London's Tempe*. The gallant ROARS; ROARERS drink oathes and gall.

1609. SHAKSPEARE, *Tempest*, i. 1. What care these ROARERS for the name of King?

1610. BEAUMONT and FLETCHER, *Philaster*, v. 4. We are thy myrmidons, thy guard, thy ROARERS. *Ibid.* (1616), *Widow*, ii. 3. Two ROARING-BOYS of Rome that made all split.

1611. MIDDLETON, *THE ROARING GIRL* [Title]. *Ibid.* (1617), *A Faire Quarrell*, v. i. I saw a youth, a gentleman, a ROARER.

*c.*1620. *Court and Times James I.* [OLIPHANT, *New Eng.*, ii. 58. The new cant word ROARING BOY comes up in p. 322].

1630. TAYLOR, *Works* [NARES]. Virago ROARING GIRLES, that to their middle, To know what sexe they were, was halfe a riddle.

1640. HUMPHRY MILL, *Night's Search*, Sect. 8, 42. Two ROARING BLADES being on a time in drink.

1640. *The Wandering Jew*. "I am a man of the Sword; a Battoon Gallant, one of our Dammees, a bouncing Boy, a kicker of Bawdes, a tyrant over Puncks, a terrour to Fencers, a mewer of Playes, a jeerer of Poets, a gallon-pot-flinger; in rugged English, a ROARER."

1658. ROWLEY [NARES], i. 2. One of the country ROARING LADS; we have such, as well as the city, and as arrant rakehells as they are.

1659. MASSINGER, *City Madam*, iii. 1 know them, swaggering, SUBURBIAN ROARERS, Sixpenny truckers.

1664. COTTON, *Virgil Travestie* (1st ed.), 10. A Crew of drunken ROARING RUFFINS.

*d.*1680. ROCHESTER, *Song* [*Works*]. Room for a bold blade of the Town That takes delight in ROARING.

1697. VANBRUGH, *Prov. Wife*, iii. 2. We's got a' ROARING FOW.

1759. TOWNLEY, *High Life Below Stairs*, i. 2. We'll have a ROARING night.

1791. BURNS, *Tam o'Shanter*. That every naig was ca'd a shoe on The smith and thee gat ROARING FOU on.

1822. SCOTT, *Fort. of Nigel*, xvii. The tarnished doublet of bald velvet . . . will best suit the garb of a ROARING BOY.

1834. MARRYAT, *Peter Simple*, xxviii. Three of our men whom he had picked up, ROARING DRUNK.

ROARING BUCKLE. *See* BUCKLE.

ROARING-FORTIES, *subs. phr.* (nautical).—The degrees of latitude between 40° and 50° N—the most tempestuous part of the Atlantic: also, occasionally to the same zone in the South Atlantic.

1883. BUCHAN [*Ency. Brit.*, xvi. 146, 2. The region of the 'brave west winds,' the ROARING FORTIES of sailors.

1884. LADY BRASSEY, *The Trades, Tropics, and* 'ROARING FORTIES' [Title].

1893. J. A. BARRY, *Steve Brown's Bunyip*, 165. They found the ROARING FORTIES quite strong enough for them.

ROARING GAME (THE), *subs. phr.* (Scots'). — Curling. [BURNS: 'The curlers quest their ROARING PLAY.']

ROARING MEG, *subs. phr.* (old).—(1) A very famous piece of ordnance; whence (2) anything loud, efficient, or extraordinary.

1575. CHURCHYARD, *Chipper*, 'Siege of Edenbrough Castell.' With thondryng noyes was shot of[f] ROERING MEG.

1602. MIDDLETON, *Blurt. Master Constable*, ii. ii. O, Cupid, grant that my blushing prove not a lintstock, and give fire too suddenly to the ROARING MEG of my desires.

1621. BURTON, *Anat. of Melan.* A ROARING MEG against melancholy, to rear and revive the languishing soul.

1623. FLETCHER and ROWLEY, *Maid of the Mill*, III. ii. I'll sell my mill, and buy a ROARING MEG; I'll batter down his house.

1630. TAYLOR, *Works* [NARES]. Thy name and voice, more fear'd then Guy of Warwick, Or the rough rumbling, ROARING MEG of Barwicke.

1638. WHITING, *Albino ana Bellama*. Beates downe a fortresse like a ROARING MEG.

ROAST, *verb.* (old).—1. To ridicule; TO QUIZ (*q.v.*).—GROSE.

*d.*1732. ATTERBURY, *Epist. Corr.*, ii. 417. Bishop Atterbury's ROASTING lord Coningsby about the topick of being priest-ridden.

1751. SMOLLETT, *Peregrine Pickle*, lxxi. Who no sooner entered the room than the mistress of the house very kindly desired one of the wits present to ROAST the old put.

1780. LEE, *Chapter of Accidents*, iii. 1. But I must keep my own counsel, or my old beau of a brother will ROAST me to death on my system of education.

1854. WHYTE MELVILLE, *General Bounce*, xiii. "Let them but lay a finger on my 'Medea,' and I'll give them such a ROASTING as they haven't had since the days of the 'Dunciad.'"

1897. MITFORD, *Romance of Cape Frontier*, I. ix. Poor Allen was ROASTED unmercifully on the strength of it.

2. (thieves').—(*a*) To watch closely; TO STALL (*q.v.*). Also TO ROAST BROWN and TO GET (or GIVE) A ROASTING: Fr. *pousser de la ficelle*. Thus (old) TO SMELL OF THE ROAST = to get into prison.—B. E. (*c.*1696); GROSE (1785).

1587. *Mirour for Magistrates* [NARES]. My souldiers were slayne fast before mine owne eyes, Or forc'd to flie, yeilde, and SMELL OF THE ROST.

1879. HORSLEY, *Jottings from Jail* [*Mac. Mag.*, xl. 504]. I see a reeler giving me a ROASTING, so I began to count my pieces for a jolly.

1888. SIMS, *Plank Bed Ballad* [*Referee*, 12 Feb.]. A reeler was ROASTING ME BROWN.

PHRASES.—TO RULE THE ROAST = to lead, to domineer (B. E., GROSE); TO CRY ROAST MEAT = to chatter about one's good fortune (B. E., GROSE); TO MAKE ROAST MEAT FOR WORMS = to kill; TO GIVE ROAST MEAT AND BEAT WITH THE SPIT = 'to do one a Curtesy, and Twit or Upbraid him with it' (B. E.); TO ROAST SNOW IN A FURNACE = to attempt the unnecessary or absurd. Also PROVERBIAL SAYINGS:—'Set a fool to ROAST eggs, and a wise man to eat them'; 'You are in your ROAST MEAT when others are in their fod'; 'There's reason in ROASTING of eggs'; 'Great boast and small ROAST make unsavoury mouths.' *Cf.* RIB-ROASTER.

*c.*1380. *Debate of the Carpenters' Tools* [HAZLITT, *Early Pop. Poet*, i. 85]. My mayster yet shall REULE THE ROSTE.

*d.*1529. SKELTON, *Why Come Ye not to Court*. He RULETH all THE ROSTE With bragging and with boste.

1594. SHAKSPEARE, *2 Henry IV.*, i. 1. "Suffolk, the new-made duke, that RULES THE ROAST." *Ibid.* (1608), *Pericles*, i. 3. *Pand.* The poor Transylvanian is dead, that lay with the little baggage. *Boult.* Ay, she quickly poop'd him; she made him ROAST MEAT FOR WORMS.

1606. CHAPMAN, *Gentleman Usher*, v. Ah, I do domineer, and RULE THE ROAST.

1634. LENTON, *Innes of Court Anag.* [NARES]. They boast Of dainty cates, and afterwards CRY ROAST.

*d.*1662. GAUDEN, *Tears of the Church*, 682. He might . . . not have PROCLAIMED on the housetop to all the world the ROST-MEAT he hath gotten.

1670. COTTON, *Scoffer Scofft* [*Works* (1725), 256]. Why then, if I may RULE THE ROAST, I affect naked Women most.

1719. DURFEY, *Pills*, iii. 22. When you GIVE a Man ROAST-MEAT, AND BEAT WITH THE SPIT.

1748. SMOLLETT, *Rod. Random*, li. Who was hand and glove with a certain person who RULED THE ROAST. *Ibid.* (1749), *Gil Blas* [ROUTLEDGE], 362. She began to see that there was REASON IN ROASTING OF EGGS.

1749. FIELDING, *Tom Jones*, IV. v. To trumpet forth the praises of such a person would . . . be CRYING ROAST MEAT.

1809. LAMB, *Christ's Hospital*. The foolish beast, not able to fare well but he must CRY ROAST MEAT . . . would needs proclaim his good fortune to the world below.

1829. MONCRIEFF, *Giovanni in London*, i. 3. Now, sirs, I hope you'll own we are your wives, the rulers of the ROAST.

ROAST-AND-BOILED, *subs. phr.* (old).—The Life Guards: 'who are mostly substantial house-keepers, and eat daily of ROAST AND BOILED' (GROSE).

ROASTER, *subs.* (Irish).—*See* quot.

1888. *D. Tel.*, 29 Nov. The meaning of "ROASTERS" was turnspits for landlords; that the names of the "ROASTERS" were kept; that when particular "ROASTERS" were to be boycotted it was the League that boycotted them; and that he dare not work for the men whose names were on the list.

ROASTING-JACK, *subs. phr.* (venery).—The female *pudenaum*: *see* MONOSYLLABLE.

ROAST-MEAT CLOTHES, *subs. phr.* (old).—Sunday or holiday gear (B. E., GROSE).

ROB. *See* BARN, PETER.

ROBA. *See* BONA-ROBA.

ROB-ALTAR, *subs. phr.* (old).—A sacrilegious plunderer.

*d.*1655. ADAMS, *Works*, i. 179. What law can be given to ROB-ALTARS?

ROBBERY. EXCHANGE IS NO ROBBERY, *phr.* (old).—An excuse for a forced or jesting imposition.—HEYWOOD (1546); RAY (1760).

1749. SMOLLETT, *Gil Blas* [ROUTLEDGE], 35. Since you have taken a fancy to it, an EXCHANGE IS NO ROBBERY . . . a genteel way enough of making a present.

ROB-DAVY (or **ROB-O'-DAVY**), *subs. phr.* (old colloquial).—Metheglin.

1630. TAYLOR, *Works* [NARES]. Peter-see-mea, or headstrong Charnico, Sherry, nor ROB-O'-DAVY here could flow.

ROBE. GENTLEMAN OF THE LONG ROBE, *subs. phr.* (old).—A lawyer: *see* LONG ROBE for addit. quots.

1677. YARRANTON, *Eng. Impr.*, 34. Three worthy GENTLEMEN OF THE LONG ROBE.

1702. STEELE, *Grief-a-la-Moae*, Pref. Far be it from any Man's Thought to say there are not MEN of strict Integrity OF THE LONG ROBE, tho' it is not every Body's good Fortune to meet with them.

1856. MOTLEY, *Dutch Republic*, I. 377. Rich advocates, and other GENTLEMEN OF THE ROBE.

1863. THACKERAY, *Roundabout Papers*, xviii. His honour being even then a GENTLEMAN OF THE LONG ROBE.

ROBERD'S-MAN (-KNAVE, or **ROBERTS'-MAN)**, *subs. phr.* (old).—'The third (old) Rank of the Canting Crew, mighty Thieves, like Robin-hood.'—B. E. (*c.*1696); GROSE (1785).

1362. LANGLAND, *Piers Plowman*, 3. In glotonye . . . Go thei to bedde, And risen with ribaudie Tho ROBERDES KNAVES.

1838. TOMLINS, *Law. Dict.*, s.v. ROBBERSMEN, or ROBBERDSMEN were a sort of great thieves mentioned in the statutes (5 Edw. 3, &c.] . . . of whom Coke says, that Robin Hood lived in the reign of King Richard I., on the borders of England and Scotland by robbery, burning of houses, rapine and spoil, &c., and that these ROBBERDSMEN took name from him.

ROBERT (or **ROBERTO**), *subs.* (common).—A policeman.

1870. *Figaro*, 18 Nov. That intolerable nuisance, the "British Peeler"—who is always poking his nose where he is not wanted, and is never to be found when he is—is, after all, a sensitive creature. The blood of the ROBERTS is at length aroused.

1880. SIMS, *An Awful Character*. The guilt of one person is well to the fore, For our ROBERTS so terribly fly are.

ROBIN, *subs.* (common).—A penny: *see* RHINO.

1894. *Chatham and Rochester News*, 20 Jan., 7, 5. Witness asked him how much he got, and he said "Seventeen and a ROBIN."

2. (American). — 'A flannel under-shirt.'—BARTLETT.

See ROUND ROBIN.

ROBIN HOOD. Many phrases trace back to the legend of this heroic thief. Thus ROBIN HOOD, *subs.* = a daring lie; ROBIN HOOD'S PENNYWORTH (*see* quots. 1662 and 1682); 'GOOD EVEN, GOOD ROBIN HOOD' (said of civility extorted by fear); 'Many talk of ROBIN HOOD that never shot in his bow' = Many speak of things of which they have no knowledge; 'Tales of ROBIN HOOD are good enough for fools.'

1509. BARCLAY, *Ship of Fooles* (1570), fol. 250. I write no ieste ne TALE OF ROBIN HOOD.

*d.*1529. SKELTON, *Why Come Ye, &c.*, 193. Is nat my reason good? GOOD EUYN, GOOD ROBYN HOOD! Some say yes, and some Syt styll as they were dom.

16[?]. *Star Chamber Case* [*Camden Soc.*, 117]. "Walton the Bayliffe leavyed of the poore mans goods 77*li* att ROBIN-HOOD'S PENIWORTHS."

1633. T. NEWTON, *Lennie's Touchstone of Complexions*, 129. Reporting a flim-flam TALE OF ROBIN HOOD.

1652. ASHMOLE, *Theat. Chem. Brit.*, 175. Many man spekyth wyth wondreng Of ROBYN HODE, and of his bow, Whych never shot therin, I trow.

1662. FULLER, *Worth. Eng.*, 315. To sell ROBIN HOODS PENNYWORTHS.—It is spoken of things sold under half their value; or if you will, half sold half given. ROBIN HOOD came lightly by his ware, and lightly parted therewith; so that he could afford the length of his Bow for a yard of Velvet.

1682. BARNARD, *Life of Heylin*, cxli. Soldiers seized on all . . . for the use of the Parliament (as they pretended) but sold as they passed along to any chapman, inconsiderable rates, ROBIN HOOD'S PENNYWORTHS.

1705. WARD, *Hud. Rediv.*, I. viii. 8. Many Fools, their Parts to show Will TALK OF ROBIN AND HIS BOW That never, by Enquiry, knew Whether 'twas made of Steel or Yew.

ROBIN REDBREAST, *subs. phr.* (old).—A Bow-street runner: also ROBIN and REDBREAST.

ROBIN'S-EYE, *subs. phr.* (common).—A scab.

ROBINSON. *See* JACK ROBINSON.

ROB-POT, *subs. phr.* (old). — A drunkard; a MALT-WORM (*q.v.*).

1622. MASSINGER, *Virgin Martyr*, ii. 1. Bacchus, the god of brew'd wine and sugar, grand patron of ROB-POTS.

ROB-THE-RUFFIAN, *subs. phr.* (venery).—The female *pudendum: see* MONOSYLLABLE.

ROB-THIEF, *subs. phr.* (old).—*See* quot.

*d.*1655. ADAMS, *Works*, i. 195. Now he plays ROB-THIEF, and steals from himself.

ROBY DOUGLAS, *subs. phr.* (nautical).—The breech: *see* MONOCULAR-EYEGLASS.

ROCHESTER-PORTION, *subs. phr.* (old).—'Two torn Smocks, and what Nature gave.'—B. E. (*c.* 1696); GROSE (1785).

ROCK, *subs.* (common).—Generic for hard eatables:—(1) = a cheese made from skim-milk, and said to be 'used in making pins to fasten gates' (Hampshire); (2) a kind of hard sweetmeat; (3) school bread as distinguished from 'baker's-bread' (Derby School); (4) a hard kind of soap: *see* quot. 18 . .; &c., &c.

1857. KINGSLEY, *Two Years Ago*, xv. Promising them ROCK and bull's-eyes.

1885. W. L. CARPENTER, *Soap and Candles*, 254. Calcium stearate and oleate are formed . . . These . . . when mixed together constitute an insoluble soap, technically called ROCK.

1888. *Harper's Mag.*, lxxvi. 625. Pieces of peppermint ROCK . . . prized by youthful gourmands.

5. (common).—A rock pigeon.

1885. *Field*, 4 Ap. Being a bit slow in firing, a fast ROCK escaped him.

6. (American).—In *pl.* = money. Hence POCKETFUL OF ROCKS = flush; ON THE ROCKS = STRANDED (*q.v.*).

1846. *Pickings from the New Orleans Picayune.* Spare my feelings, Squire, and don't ask me to tell any more. Here I am in town without a ROCK in my pocket, and without a skirt to my coat, or crown to my hat.

1847. ROBB, *Squatter Life*, 165. You know if I had a POCKET FULL OF ROCKS you should share them.

7. (American).—A pebble; a stone (at Winchester = a medium-sized stone): as *verb.* = to throw stones.

18 [?]. *Jonesborough* (Tenn.) *Whig* [BARTLETT]. They commenced ROCKING the Clay Club House in June, on more occasions than one, and on one occasion threw a ROCK in at the window.

1848. *Georgia Scenes*, 193. S—— came home in a mighty bad way, with a cold and a cough; so I put a hot ROCK to his feet, &c.

1872. O. W. HOLMES, *Poet at Breakf. Table*, xii. The boys would follow . . . crying, 'ROCK him!' . . . He's got a long-tailed coat on.

1893. BRET HARTE, *Soc. on the Stanislaus.* Nor should the individual . . . Reply by heaving ROCKS at him.

8. (common).—A cause of difficulty, defeat, or annoyance: as an over-trump at cards, an obstacle suddenly placed in one's way, and so forth.

1601. SHAKSPEARE, *Henry VIII.*, i. 1, 113. Lo, where comes that ROCK, That I advise your shunning. [*Enter Cardinal Wolsey.*]

*d.*1654. SELDEN, *Table Talk*, 57. Every Church govern'd itself, or else we must fall upon that old foolish ROCK, that St. Peter and his Successours govern'd all.

THE ROCK, *subs. phr.* (common).—Gibraltar.

TO DO BY ROCK OF EYE AND RULE OF THUMB, *verb. phr.* (tailors').—To substitute guess-work for exact measurement.

See BEDROCK, ROCKER.

ROCKER (or **ROKKER**), *verb.* (tramps': originally Gypsy).—1. To understand; (2) to speak.

1876. HINDLEY, *Cheap Jack*, 231. Can you ROCKER Romany, Can you patter flash?

1893. *Standard*, 29 Jan., 2. We have to be out in the road early, you know, to secure our "Toby" (great laughter). That's plain. We don't ROCK Romany all day long (laughter).

1894. A. MORRISON [*Strand Mag.*, July, 60]. Hewitt could ROKKER better than most Romany chals themselves.

ROCKETER, *subs.* (sporting).—A flushed pheasant, rising quick and straight; ROCKETTING = rising straight.

1869. *Quarterly Rev.*, cxxvii. 387. The driven partridge and the ROCKETING pheasant are beyond the skill of many a man who considers himself a very good shot.

1884. *Field*, 6 Dec. It is nonsense to say that a ROCKETER is easily disposed of.

1888. *Harper's Mag.*, lxxvii. 182. Presently an old cock-pheasant came ROCKETING over me.

ROCK-SCORPION, *subs. phr.* (naval and military).—A mongrel Gibralterine: Spanish, Portuguese, French, Genoese, Barbary Hebrew, Moorish, negro—a mixture of all mettles.

ROCKY (**ROCKED**, or **ROCKETTY**), *adj.* (common).—1. Broken: by drink, illness, poverty; and (2) difficult; dubious; debateable. Hence TO GO ROCKY = to go to pieces; to go wrong. Whence ROCKINESS = (1) craziness; (2) incapacity, utter or partial; OFF ONE'S ROCKER = crazy; ROCKED IN A STONE KITCHEN = 'the person spoken of is a fool, his brains having been disordered by the jumbling of his cradle' (GROSE).

1885. *D. Telegraph*, 28 Dec. Let him keep the fact of things having gone ROCKY with him as dark as he can.

1892. *Nat. Observer*, 20 Feb., 352, 1. Though the morals were ROCKY . . . the society was very good.

1896. CRANE, *Maggie*, xiv. I call it ROCKY treatment for a fellah like me.

1897. *Sporting Times*, 13 Mar., 1, 2. It dawned upon the crowd that he was a bit ROCKY in his aspirates.

ROD, *subs.* (common).—An angler.

1886. *Fishing Gazette*, 30 Jan. The late Sir F. Sykes, a first-rate ROD.

2. (venery).—The *penis: see* PRICK: also FISHING-ROD. Hence as *verb.* = to copulate.

See BREACH, PICKLE, TAIL.

ROD-MAKER, *subs. phr.* (Winton).—'The man who made the rods used in BIBLING (*q.v.*).—MANSFIELD (*c.*1840).

RODNEY. A REGULAR RODNEY, *subs. phr.* (old).—An idle fellow; a lazybones.

RODOMONTADE, *subs.* (old colloquial: now recognised).—Boasting; swagger. Hence RODOMONT = a boaster. [A character in Ariosto.]

ROE, *subs.* (venery).—The semen: *see* CREAM. Hence TO SHOOT ONE'S ROE = to emit.

ROF-EFIL, *subs. phr.* (back slang).—A life sentence; 'for life.'

ROGER, *subs.* (Old Cant).—1. A portmanteau; a POGE (*q.v.*).—B. E. (*c.*1696); GROSE (1785).

2. (Old Cant).—A goose: also ROGER (or TIB) OF THE BUTTERY.—HARMAN (1567); DEKKER (1609); B. E. (*c.*1696); GROSE (1785).

1622. FLETCHER, *Beggar's Bush*, v. 1. Margery praters, ROGERS, and Tibs o' th' Buttery.

3. (venery).—The *penis: see* PRICK. Hence as *verb.* = to copulate: *see* RIDE. [*Cf.* ROGER = ram, and 'ROGER a name frequently given to a bull' (B. E., GROSE).]

1653. URQUHART, *Rabelais*, I. xi. Taking you know what between their fingers and dandling it. And some of the . . . women would give these names, my ROGER . . . smell-smock . . . lusty live sausage.

1720. DURFEY, *Pills*, *&c.*, vi. 201. And may Prince G——'s ROGER grow stiff again and stand.

1750. ROBERTSON of Struan, *Poems*, 98. Dear sweet Mr. Wright . . . Go RODGER to-night Your Wife, for ye want her.

1794. BURNS, *The Summer Morn.* [*Merry Muses* (*c.*1800), p.]. To ROGER Madam Thetis. *Ibid.* (*b.*1796), 'We're a' gaun Southie, O.' Bonie lassie, braw lassie, 'Will ye hae a sodger?' Then she took up her duddie sark, An' he shot in his ROGER.

1885. BURTON, *Thousand Nights*, iii. 304. I will not ROGER thee. *Ibid.* (1890), *Priapeia*, xii. Thou shalt be pedicate, (lad) thou also (lass!) shalt be ROGERED.

4. (nautical).—A pirate flag: also JOLLY ROGER.—GROSE (1785).

5. (old).—A ROGUE (*q.v.*).

ROGERIAN, *subs.* (old).—A kind of wig.

1599. HALL, *Virgid*, III. v. 16. The sportfull winde to mocke the headlesse man, Tosses apace his pitch'd ROGERIAN.

ROGUE (**ROGE** or **ROGER**), *subs.* (Old Cant).—1. A professed beggar; 'the fourth Order of Canters' (AWDELEY, HARMAN, B. E., GROSE). Whence (2) WILD ROGUE (*see* quot. 1567), and (3, modern) = a knave or rascal; A ROGUE IN GRAIN = 'a great rogue, or a corn-chandler' (GROSE); A ROGUE IN SPIRIT = 'a distiller or brandy-merchant' (GROSE). As *verb* = to beg.

1531-47. COPLAND, *Spyttel Hous* [HAZLITT, *Early Pop. Poet.*, iv. 44]. These ROGERS that . . . foot and frydge.

1567. AWDELEY, *Warning*, *&c.* . . . A WILDE ROGE is he that is borne a Roge: he is more subtil and more geuen by nature to all kinde of knauery than the other. I once rebuking a wyld roge because he went idelly about he shewed me that he was a begger by enheritance—his grandfather was a begger, his father was one, and he must nedes be one by good reason.

1605. SHAKSPEARE, *Lear*, iv. 7, 39. To hovel thee with swine and ROGUES forlorn.

1611. COTGRAVE, *Dict.*, s.v. *Divague.* Raunging, ROGUING about.

1619. FLETCHER, *Wildgoose Chase*, ii. 3. *Ros.* 'Tis pity such a lusty fellow should wander up and down, and want employment. *Bel.* She takes me for a ROGUE.

[*Passim* in English literature to the present time.]

2. (colloquial).—Anything vicious; bastard; or unstandardized. Thus ROGUE-ELEPHANT = an evil-minded murderous male or female; ROGUE'S-BADGE = blinkers for a vicious horse. [*Cf.* ROGUE (christened Roger) Riderhood, DICKENS, *Mutual Friend.*]

1859. DARWIN, *Origin of Species*, 42 and 43. When a race of plants is . . . established the seed-raisers do not pick out the best plants, but . . . pull up the ROGUES, as they call the plants that deviate from the proper standard . . . The destruction of horses under a certain size . . . may be compared to the ROGUING of plants.

1888. *Referee*, 11 Dec. Admiral Benbow is a ROGUE, but he was tried exceedingly well in the summer time.

1891. *Lic. Vict. Gaz.* He wore the ROGUE'S BADGE, but is built on racing lines.

3. (colloquial).—An endearment. Whence ROGUISH = playfully mischievous. Also = a wag.

1596. SHAKSPEARE, *Hamlet*, ii. 2, 197. The satirical ROGUE says here that old men have grey beards. *Ibid.* (1598), *2 Hen. IV.*, ii. 4, 233. Ah, you sweet little ROGUE, you!

1607. BEAUMONT and FLETCHER, *Woman Hater*, v. 5. Come, come, little ROGUE, thou art too maidenly [*et passim*].

1733. POPE, *Imit. of Horace*, I. vii. 27. What, rob your boys? those pretty ROGUES.

*b.*1796. BURNS, *Cessnock Banks.* An' she has twa sparkling ROGUEISH een.

DERIVATIVES.—ROGUE'S-GALLERY = a collection of photographs of convicted prisoners; ROGUE-HOUSE = a prison or lock-up; ROGUE-MONEY (Scots') = an assessment for police purposes; ROGUE'S-MARCH = the DRUMMING OUT (*q.v.*) of a disgraced soldier or sailor; ROGUE'S-YARN = a worsted thread, varying in color in each dockyard, woven in each strand of rope to prevent theft and to trace defective manufacture.

1886. BESANT, *World went very well Then*, xxi. As for the Hue and Cry, leave that to me. I will tackle the Hue and Cry, which I value not an inch of ROGUES' YARN.

1891. *Century Dict.*, s.v. ROGUE . . . In rope made in United States navy-yards the ROGUE'S YARN is twisted in a contrary direction to the others, and is of manila in hemp rope, and of hemp in manila rope.

ROGUE-AND-PULLET, *subs. phr.* (thieves').—A man and woman in confederacy as thieves.

ROGUE-AND-VILLAIN, *subs. phr.* (rhyming).—A shilling: *see* RHINO.

1887. HORSLEY, *Jottings from Jail.* Come, cows-and-kisses, put the battle of the Nile on your Barnet fair, and a ROGUE AND VILLAIN in your sky-rocket.

ROGUESHIP. *See* SPITTLE ROGUESHIP.

ROISTER (**ROYSTER DOISTER**, **ROYSTER**, **ROISTERER**, &c.), *subs.* (old).—(1) A swaggerer (B. E., GROSE); and (2) a frolic. Whence as *verb.* (also ROIST) = to swagger; ROISTING (ROISTERING, ROISTERLY, or ROISTEROUS) = uproarious.

1553. UDALL, *ROISTER DOISTER*, Prol. The vayne glorious . . . Whose humour the ROYSTING sort continually doth feed.

1577. HARRISON, *England*, 149. They ruffle and ROIST it out.

1602. SHAKSPEARE, *Troilus and Cress.*, ii. 2, 208. I have a ROISTING challenge sent amongst The dull and factious nobles of the Greeks.

1630. *Time's Whistle* [E. E. T. S.], 60. They must not part till they have drunk a barrell, Or straight this ROISTER will begin to quarrel.

1749. SMOLLETT, *Gil Blas* [ROUTLEDGE], 175. This is beyond all bearing, screamed out the young ROYSTER.

1809. IRVING, *Knickerbocker*, 92. An honest social race of jolly ROYSTERS, who had no objection to a drinking bout, and were very merry in their cups. *Ibid.*, 348. A gang of merry ROISTERING devils.

1843. CARLYLE, *Past and Present*, ii. 15. ROYSTEROUS young dogs; carolling, howling, breaking the Lord Abbot's sleep.

1855. TENNYSON, *Maud*, xiv. 2. Her brother lingers late with the ROYSTERING company. *Ibid.* (1859), *Geraint.* A rout of ROISTERERS femininely fair And dissolutely pale.

ROKER, *subs.* (schools).—A ruler; a stick; a poker. FLAT-ROKER = a flat ruler. [*Roke* (HALLIWELL) = to stir a fire, a liquid, &c.]

ROLAND (or **ROWLAND**) **FOR OLIVER**, *subs. phr.* (old).—(1) A match; a tit for tat; six of one and half a dozen of the other: a fanciful or practical proof of equality.—B. E. and GROSE. Fr. *Guy Contre Robert.*

[. . .]. *MS. Cantab*, Ff. ii. 38, f. 109. Soche strokys were never seen in londe Syth OLYVERE dyed AND ROWLONDE.

1542. HALL, *Henry VI.*, f. But to have a ROWLAND TO resist AN OLIVER, he sent solempne ambassadors to the kyng of Englande, offeryng hym hys doughter in marriage.

1565. CALFHILL, *Treat. of Cross*, 374. Have a quarrel to ROWLAND AND fight with OLIVER.

1598. SHAKSPEARE, *1 Hen. VI.*, i. 2. England all OLIVERS AND ROLANDS bred.

1612. *Court and Times James I.*, 187. There is hope you shall have AN OLIVER FOR A ROLAND.

1706. WARD, *Wooden World*, 68. By the help of some twopenny Scribbler she will always return him A ROWLAND FOR HIS OLIVER.

1820. COMBE, *Syntax*, II. iii. I shall be able . . . to bestow . . . a quid pro quo; Which I translate for Madam, there, A ROWLAND FOR YOUR OLIVER.

1901. *D. Telegraph*, 18 Nov., 7, 3. Oh, we are getting on splendidly! (Laughter.) That IS A ROLAND FOR AN OLIVER.

ROLY-POLY, *subs. phr.* (old).—1. A country bumpkin.

1602. DEKKER, *Satiromastix*, iii. 116. These two ROLLY POLLIES.

2. (common). — A jam roll pudding; DOG-IN-A-BLANKET: also ROLL.UP. As *adj.* = round and fat.

1841. THACKERAY, *Great Hoggarty Diamond*, xii. You said I make the best ROLY-POLY puddings in the world. *Ibid.* (1848), *Book of Snobs*, i. As for the ROLY-POLY, it was too good.

1851. MAYHEW, *Lond. Lab.*, I. 207. Sometimes made in the rounded form of the plum-pudding; but more frequently in the ROLY-POLY style.

1852. MRS. CRAIK, *Agatha's Husband*, xii. Cottages, in the doors of which a few ROLY-POLY, open-eyed children stand.

1860. ELIOT, *Mill on Floss*, i. 6. I know what the pudden's to be—apricot ROLL-UP—O my buttons!

1882. WORBOISE, *Sissie*, xix. Squashy ROLYPOLY pudding.

3. (common).—*See* quots.

1713. ARBUTHNOT, *Hist. John Bull.* Let us begin some diversion; what d'ye think of ROULYPOULY or a country dance?

1851-61. MAYHEW, *Lond. Lab.*, III. 145. When I danced it was merely a comic dance—what we call a ROLEY-POLEY.

4. (venery).—The *penis*: *see* PRICK.

ROLL, *subs.* (common).—In *pl.* = a baker: *see* BURNCRUST. Also MASTER OF THE ROLLS.

Verb. (old).—A verb of spirit: generic (1) = to gad; (2) to rollick in one's walk; and (3) to swagger: also TO ROLL ABOUT. Whence TO ROLL IN BUB (or GRUB) = to have plenty to eat (or drink); TO ROLL IN GOLD = to be monstrous rich; TO ROLL IN ONE'S IVORIES = to kiss; TO ROLL IN EVERY RIG = to be "up-to-date"; TO ROLL THE LEER = to pick pockets; TO HAVE A ROLL ON = to swagger, to put on SIDE (*q.v.*); TO ROLL ONE'S HOOP = to go ahead, to be on the safe side; ROLLING = smart, ready; ROLLING KIDDY = a clever thief; ROLLICK (or ROLLOP) = to romp along.

1383. CHAUCER, *Cant. Tales*, *Prol. Wife of Bath's Tale*, 6235. Man shal not suffer his wif go ROULE about.

1542. UDALL, *Apoph.*, 243 [OLIPHANT, *New Eng.*, i. 490. A bombastic orator ROLLS (exults) in painted terms; hence our 'ROLL IN WEALTH,' and the later ROLLICK].

1567. HARMAN, *Caveat*, 20. These unruly rascals in their ROLLING disperse themselves into several companies.

1775. *Old Song*, 'The Potato Man' [FARMER, *Musa Pedestris* (1896), 55. I am a saucy ROLLING blade.

1780. TOMLINSON, *Slang Pastoral*, viii. To ROLL IN HER IVORY, to pleasure her eye.

1789. PARKER, *Life's Painter*, 'The Happy Pair.' Moll Blabbermares and ROWLING Joe. [Note, a kind of fellow who dresses smart or what they term natty.] *Ibid.* Then we'll all ROLL IN BUB AND GRUB. *Ibid.* Up to St. Giles's they ROLL'D, sir.

1790. *Old Song*, 'The Flash Man of St. Giles' [*The Busy Bee*]. We ROLL IN EVERY knowing RIG.

*c.*1824. EGAN, *Boxiana*, iii. 621, 622. The boldest lad That ever mill'd the cly, or ROLL'D THE LEER. *Ibid.* With ROLLING KIDDIES, Dick would dive and buy.

1830. LYTTON, *Paul Clifford* (1854), 18. He merely observed by way of compliment, that Mr. Augustus and his companions seemed to be ROLLING KIDDIES.

1836. DICKENS, *Sketches*, 'Characters,' vii. That grave, but confident, kind of ROLL peculiar to old boys in general.

1837. HOOK, *Jack Brag* [LATHAM]. He described his friends as ROLLICKING blades.

1865. G. MEREDITH, *Rhoda Fleming*, xxix. He had not even money enough to pay the cabman . . . He ROLLICKED in his present poverty.

1877. PASCOE, *Everyday Life, &c.* Anything approaching swagger is severely rebuked; there is no more objectionable quality than that understood by the expression, "He's GOT such A horrid ROLL ON."

1893. MILLIKEN, *'Arry Ballads.* It sets a chap fair ON THE ROLL.

ROLLER, *subs.* (Oxford University). —1. A roll-call.

2. (Stock Exchange).—In *pl.* = United States Rolling Stock.

3. (old).—In *pl.*, the horse and foot patrols. — GROSE (1785); VAUX (1812).

4. (old).—A go-cart.

1660. SMITH, *Lives of Highwaymen*, II. 50. He could run about without a ROWLER or leading-strings.

5. (common). — A big wave coming in from a distance, and so with an enormous energy: also RUNNER.

1855. KINGSLEY, *Westw. Ho*, xxxii. ROLLERS of the vast Atlantic . . . with a thousand crests of flying foam.

ROLLEY, *subs.* (common). — A vehicle.

ROLLICKERS, *subs.* (military).—The 2nd Bat. The Princess Victoria's Royal Irish Fusiliers (formerly the Eighty-Ninth Foot). Also (1798) 'Blayney's Blood-hounds.'

ROLLING-PIN. *See* PIN.

ROLL-ME-IN-THE-DIRT, *subs. phr.* (rhyming).—A shirt.

ROLL-UP. *See* ROLY-POLY.

ROM. *See* ROMANY.

ROMANCE, *subs.* (colloquial).—A lie; a tarradiddle. Hence, as *verb* = 'to lie pleasantly, to Stretch in Discourse.'—B. E. (*c.*1696).

1651. EVELYN, *Diary*, 6 Sep. The knight was . . . not a little given to ROMANCE when he spake of himselfe.

*d.*1721. PRIOR, *An Eng. Padlock.* A Staple of ROMANCE and Lies, False Tears and real Perjuries.

*d.*1742. BAILEY, *Erasmus*, I. 53. I hear others ROMANCING about Things they never heard nor saw . . . with that Assurance that . . . they persuade themselves they are speaking Truth all the While.

ROMAN-FALL, *subs.* (obsolete).—A posture (*c.*1868) in walking: the head well forward and the small of the back well in: *see* GRECIAN BEND.

1870. *Orchestra*, 25 Mar., 'Grand Comic Concert.' The ladies have their Grecian bend, our typical gentlemen explains a correspondent masculine affectation which he dubs The ROMAN FALL.

1890. *Answers*, 8 Feb., 172, 2. Livingstone noticed that among the young bloods and sable patricians of Loanda a sort of ROMAN FALL seems to be practised, which consists of hobbling along as though encumbered by a load of ornaments.

ROMANY (ROMMANY or ROM), *subs.* (common).—1. A gypsy; and (2) the language spoken by gypsies. Whence TO PATTER ROMANY = 'to talk the gypsy flash' (GROSE); ROMANY RYE = a gentleman who talks and associates with gypsies (GROSE; VAUX). [A few Romany words have passed into English, but the only European tongues on which the Gipsy has had much influence are those of the Peninsula. In Spanish and Portuguese almost all the slang is Gipsy and almost all the Gipsy is slang. Our chief authorities, apart from personal knowledge, are J. Fitzmaurice Kelly, Esq., James Platt, Jr., Esq., and *El Gitano* by Francisco Sales Mayo (Madrid, 1870)].

1749. GOADBY, *Moore-Carew*, 'Oath of Cant. Crew.' No dummerar, or ROMANY.

1834. AINSWORTH, *Rookwood* (1864), 175. I'm dumb founded if he can't patter ROMANY as vel as the best on us!

1851. BORROW, *Lavengro*, xvii. 'We were talking of languages, Jasper . . . Yours must be a rum one?' 'Tis called ROMMANY.' . . . 'And you are what is called a Gypsy King?' 'Ay, ay; a ROMMANY kral.' *Ibid.* Rum and dree, Rum and dry, Rally round the ROMANY RYE.

1871. MEREDITH, *Harry Richmond*, xlv. I recognized a strange tongue in the cry, but too late that it was ROMANY to answer it.

1883. G. R. SIMS, *THE ROMANY RYE* [Title].

1893. EMERSON, *Signor Lippo*, xx. My old man was a ROMANY . . . but he was an awful boozer.

See RUM.

ROMBELOW. *See* RUMBELOW.

ROMBOYLE (or **ROMBOYLES**), *verb.* (Old Cant).—To make hue and cry; TO WHIDDLE BEEF (*q.v.*). Fr. *battre morasse* (B. E., GROSE). Whence ROMBOYL'D = WANTED (*q.v.*).

ROME. *See* RUM, *passim.*

ROMER (or **ROMEKIN**), *subs.* (Old Cant).—A drinking glass (or can). —B. E. (*c.*1696).

ROME-VILLE, *subs. phr.* (Old Cant). —London. [*See* RUM].

ROMFORD. *See* RUMFORD.

ROMP, *subs.* (old: now recognised). —A boisterous girl; a TOMBOY: *see* RAMP and quot. 1698 (B. E., GROSE). Also as *verb.* = (1) to LARK (*q.v.*); to play the RIG (*q.v.*); to wanton; and (2) TO ROMP IN = to win easily (racing).

1647. FLETCHER, *Mad Lover*, i. 1. How our St. Georges will bestride the dragons, The red and RAMPING dragons.

1698. COLLIER, *Eng. Stage* [OLIPHANT, *New Eng.*, ii. 128. The *a* changes to *o*, for the noun ROMP is formed from the verb RAMP].

1711. STEELE, *Spectator*, 187. The air she gave herself was that of a ROMPING girl. Ibid., *Tatler*, No. 15. My cousin Betty, the greatest ROMP in nature.

1730. THOMSON, *Autumn*, 528. ROMP-loving miss Is haul'd about, in gallantry robust.

1761. CHURCHILL, *Rosciad.* First, giggling, plotting chamber-maids arrive, Hoydens and ROMPS, led on by Gen'ral Clive.

1882. "THORMANBY," *Famous Racing Men*, 16. The north-country horse . . . could not touch Eclipse, who simply ROMPED IN, the easiest of winners.

1891. *Sporting Life*, 20 Mar. I recall his recent half-mile at Oxford, when he ROMPED home in the easiest possible manner.

1894. MOORE, *Esther Waters*, xxx. Favourites ROMPING in one after the other.

RONCHER (or **ROUNCHER**), *subs.* (American). — Anything of exceptional size or quality.

ROOK, *subs.* (old).—1. A cheat: spec. gaming: also ROOKER: *cf.* sense 2 and PIGEON. Hence ROOKERY (or ROKING) = swindling; ROOKY (or ROOKISH) = rascally, scampish; as *verb.* = to cheat, to swindle (B. E., DYCHE, GROSE, VAUX, BEE). Hence ROOKERY = (1) a gambling hell; and (2) any place of ill repute: *e.g.*, (*a*) a brothel, (*b*) subalterns' barrack quarters, and (*c*) a neighbourhood occupied by a criminal or squalid population, a SLUM (*q.v.*).

1590. *Sir Thomas More* [Shakspeare Soc.] [OLIPHANT, *New Eng.*, ii. 8. There are the new verbs ROOKE (plunder) and *sharke* (prey) . . .].

1603. DEKKER, *Wonderful Year* [GROSART, *Works*, i. 89]. ROOKES, catchpolls of poesy, That feed upon the fallings of hye wit.

1609. JONSON, *Epicœne*, i. 1. Such a ROOK . . . that will betray his mistress to be seen.

1641. MILTON, *Ref. in England*, i. A band of ROOKING officials. *Ibid.*, ii. The Butcherly execution of Tormentors, ROOKS and Rakeshames sold to lucre.

1672. WYCHERLEY, *Love in a Wood*, iii. 4. I dare no more venture myself with her alone, than a cully that has been bit dares venture himself in a tavern with an old ROOK.

*d.*1697. AUBREY, *Lives*, 'Sir J. Denham.' He was much ROOKED by gamesters.

1705. WARD, *Hud. Rediv.*, I. ix. 22. For like a ROOK at Gaming-Table . . . he . . . cheats all sides with equal zeal.

1748. SMOLLETT, *Rod. Random*, xlviii. He would not lend him money to squander away upon ROOKS. *Ibid.* (1751), *Peregrine Pickle*, lxxxviii. Having lost a few loose hundreds in his progress through the various ROOKERIES of the place.

1760. LUCAS, *Gamesters*, 125. ROOKS are grown of late so intolerably Rude and Insolent.

1821. EGAN, *Life in London*, II. iii. Guv'nur, how long are ve to be kept in this here ROOKERY, before you give us a sight of this phenomony?

1836. DICKENS, *Sketches by Boz*, 105. That classical spot adjoining the brewery at the bottom of Tottenham-court-road, best known to the initiated as the ROOKERY.

1840. THACKERAY, *Captain ROOK and Mr. Pigeon* [Title].

1869. *Gent. Mag.*, July, 231. No opportunity of pigeon-plucking is lost by the majority of [billiard] markers . . . still he is not the worst form of ROOK.

1883. *Sat. Review*, 31 March, 398, 1. The registered lodging-houses are more decent than the old ROOKERIES, but the people who live in the new buildings differ little, if at all, from those who lived in the old.

1884. SPENCER, *Man v. State*, 54. The misery, the disease, the mortality of ROOKERIES.

2. (old). — A simpleton; a PIGEON (*q.v.*). [One fit for ROOKING: *see* sense 1].

1596. JONSON, *Every Man in His Humour*, i. 1. Hang him, ROOK! he! why he has no more judgment than a malt horse. *Ibid.* (1599), *Every Man Out of His Humour*, i. 1. A tame ROOKE, you'l take him presently. *Ibid.* (1602), *Poetaster*, i. 1. What? shall I have my son a Stager now? an Enghle for Players? a Gull? a ROOKE? a Shot-clog? to make suppers, and bee laught at?

1607. DEKKER, *Westward Ho*, v. 1. Let's be wise, and make ROOKS of them that, I warrant, are now setting purse-nets to conycatch us.

1611. CHAPMAN, *May-Day*, iii. An arrant ROOK, by this light, a capable cheating stock; a man may carry him up and down by the ears like a pipkin.

3. (common).—A clergyman: *see* SKYPILOT: Fr. *corbeau.*

4. (tailors').—A sloven.

5. (thieves').—A housebreaker's JEMMY (*q.v.*); a CROW (*q.v.*).—GROSE.

Verb. 1. *See* subs. 2.

2. (gaming).—To win heavily.

1887. *Sporting Times*, 12 March, 2, 1. We play nap, and ROOK George Fredericks all the way.

ROOKERY, *subs.* (old).—*See* ROOK, 1.

2. (colloquial). — A scolding-match.

ROOKY (or **ROOKEY**), *subs.* (military).—A recruit: *see* SNOOKER, and ROOK, *subs.* 1.

1893. KIPLING, *Many Inventions*, "His Private Honour." "'Tis a hundred and thirty-seven ROOKIES to the bad, son." . . . You can't ride, you can't walk, you can't shoot,—you,—you awful ROOKIES.

ROOM. TO LEAVE THE ROOM, *verb. phr.* (conventional school).—To go to the W.C.

Verb. (colloquial).—To inhabit. Hence ROOMER = a lodger: spec. one occupying a single apartment.

1864. *Daily Telegraph*, 26 July. It's risky, I know, but I'll try him. I never did ROOM with a Rooshian before, and I'd like to know them stript.

1869. STOWE, *Oldtown*, 418. I am . . . living at the minister's! and then I ROOM with Esther.

18[?] *The Standard* (*Century*). The mother . . . occupies herself more with the needs of the ROOMERS, or tenants, and makes more money.

See APARTMENTS.

ROOMBELOW. *See* RUMBELOW.

ROORBACK, *subs.* (American).—1. A journalistic, or printed lie.

1876. *Providence Journal*, 9 May. Another infamous Democratic ROORBACK!

1876. *New York Tribune*, 14 Ap. The manufacture of ROORBACKS against Mr. Blaine, though active, is not very successful in producing a merchantable article.

ROOSHER, *subs.* (thieves').—A constable: *see* NARK.

ROOST, *subs.* (colloquial).—1. Bed: also ROOSTING-PLACE: also as *verb.* = (1) to sleep, and (2) to lodge.

1749. SMOLLETT, *Gil Blas* [ROUTLEDGE], 29. I . . . slunk to my ROOSTING-PLACE where I fell asleep like a man.

1821. EGAN, *Life in London*, II. ii. Mammy Brimstone . . . has also "toddled" in to have a "flash of lightning" before she goes to ROOST.

1843. MONCRIEFF, *Scamps of London*, i. 2. You can go to ROOST whenever you like.

1847. LYTTON, *Lucretia*, II. vii. And always give a look into my room every night before you go to ROOST.

1857. O. W. HOLMES, *Autocrat*, vi. The world has a million ROOSTS for a man, but only one nest.

1899. WHITEING, *John St.*, ix. You must do like them, ROOST in the open air.

Verb. (colloquial).—1. *See* subs.

2. (military).—To imprison.

3. (common).—To cheat: TO ROOST OVER ONE = to get a RISE (*q.v.*).

ROOSTER, *subs.* (American).—A euphemism for 'cock'—(a word impossible on the lips of any delicate American female)—the male of the barndoor hen.

1838. NEAL, *Charcoal Sketches* [BARTLETT]. As if the flourish of a quill were the crowing of a ROOSTER.

1855. IRVING, *Woolfert's Roost*, 17. The Skinners and Cowboys of the Revolution, when they wrung the neck of a ROOSTER, did not trouble . . . whether they crowed for Congress or King George.

1870. JUDD, *Margaret*, II. 1. A huge turkey gobbling in the road, a ROOSTER crowing on the fence.

1870. WHITE, *Words and Their Uses* [WALSH]. All birds are ROOSTERS . . . hens . . . as well as the cocks. What . . . delicacy then . . . in calling the cock a ROOSTER.

1880. *Scribner's Mag.*, 770. The crow of an early-rising ROOSTER.

2. (old: now American).—A street brawler; a rough.

1821. EGAN, *Life in London*, II. v. ROOSTERS and the 'peep-o'-day boys' were out on a prowl for a spree.

1885. *N. Am. Rev.*, cxli. 434. The toughest set of ROOSTERS that ever shook the dust of any town.

3. (venery).—The female *pudendum*: *see* MONOSYLLABLE.

See QUEER.

ROOST-LAY, *subs. phr.* (old).—Poultry stealing: *see* LAY.—GROSE.

ROOT (THE), *subs.* (common).—1. Money. ['The root of all Evil.']

1899. *D. Telegraph*, 7 Ap., 8, 3. All the week they do their little bit o' graft . . . an' take home THE ROOT on Sat'days to the missus or the mam.

2. (venery).—The *penis*: *see* PRICK. Also MAN-ROOT.

Verb. (common). — To kick. Whence (The Leys School) ROOT-ABOUT = promiscuous football practice: also as *verb*.

ROOTER, *subs.* (colloquial). — A superlative: as a brutal attack; a very smart dress; a priceless gem; a flagrant untruth, and so forth: *see* WHOPPER.

ROOTLE, *verb.* (venery).—To copulate: *see* RIDE. Also TO DO A ROOTLE.

ROOTY, *subs.* (military).—*See* quot.

1883. G. A. S[ALA], in *Illustr. L. News*, 7 July, 3, 3. [A correspondent in S. Travancore says that in Tamil and Teluga "Rôtie" means a loaf of bread.] Long since Private Tommy Atkins, returning from Indian service, has acclimatised "Rôtie" (pronounced "ROOTY") in the vocabulary of the British barrack. At least eight years ago I heard of a private soldier complaining in his barrack-room that he had not had his "proper section of ROOTY," *i.e.*, his proper ration of bread.

ROPE, *subs.* (football).—1. In *pl.* = a half-back.

2. (old).—A trick or knack; spec. (nautical) TO KNOW THE ROPES (or TO BE UP TO THE ROPES) = (1) to be expert, and (2) to be artful, FLY (*q.v.*); TO PULL (or WORK) THE ROPES = to control or direct; TO ROPE IN (or ROPE) = (1) to lose a race by PULLING (*q.v.*) or other foul means; (2) to decoy (in a mock-auction, gambling-den, &c.): hence ROPER-IN = a decoy; and (3) to pull (or gather) in: as TO ROPE IN THE PIECES = to make money. Hence PLENTY OF ROPE = lots of choice; AT THE END OF ONE'S ROPE = exhausted, done for.

1623. MABBE, *English Rogue* [OLIPHANT, *New Eng.*, ii. 83. Among the verbs we see . . . GIVE HIM LINE.

1670. RAY, *Proverbs* [BELL], 176. I thought I had given her ROPE enough, said Pedley, when he hanged his mare. *Ibid.*, 59. Let him alone with the saints' bell and give him ROPE enough.

1840. DANA, *Two Years before the Mast*, ix. The captain, who had been on the coast before, and KNEW THE ROPES, took the steering oar.

1854. *Cruise in Undine*, 15. I don't mind young fellows having PLENTY OF ROPE.

*c.*1859. *New York Tribune* [BARTLETT]. Mr. A—— complained that a ROPER-IN of a gambling-house had enticed him away, by whose means he had lost all his money.

1863. *Fraser's Magazine*, Dec., 'The English Turf.' An order to pull a horse back, *i.e.*, to 'ROPE' him, or, as in a late suspicious case it was expressed, to 'put the strings on,' is seldom resorted to.

1877. BESANT and RICE, *Golden Butterfly*, xiii. You've sought me out, and gone about this city with me; you've put me UP TO ROPES.

1882. MCCABE, *New York*, xxxix. The visitors to these establishments are chiefly strangers in the city, who are lured, or ROPED, into them by agents of the proprietors.

1888. BOLDREWOOD, *Robbery Under Arms*, xliv. He KNEW THE ROPES better than he did.

1889. *Snacks*, July, No. 1. He were sixty-nine year old—'n' got ROPED IN by a young widow, 'n' chouseled out of twenty-six thousan' dollars.

1892. ANSTEY, *Voces Populi*, 'Free Speech,' 103. Fellow-Citizens, I appeal to you, GIVE THIS MAN ROPE—he's doing our work splendidly!

1897. MITFORD, *Romance of Cape Frontier*, I. xxi. I dare say 'e's bin PUTTING YOU UP TO THE ROPES.

1900. BOOTHBY, *Maker of Nations*, i. You *do* require to KNOW THE ROPES. And what is more, you require to be very careful *how* you PULL THOSE ROPES when you are familiar with them.

Verb. (old).—1. To hang: *see* LADDER. Whence ROPE-TRICKS (ROPING or ROPERY) = roguery; ROPE-RIPE = fit for hanging; TO CRY ROPE = to warn, to bid beware; 'give ROPE [or LINE] enough and he'll hang' = 'He'll decoy himself to his undoing' (B. E.); MR. ROPER (or THE ROPER) = the hangman; THE ROPE-WALK = the Old Bailey; TO GO INTO THE ROPE-WALK = to take up criminal practice.

1553. WILSON, *Arte of Rhetorique* [NARES]. ROPE-RIPE chiding [of very foul and abusive language].

1584. *Three Ladies of London* [NARES]. Thou art very pleasant, and full of thy ROPERY.

1592. SHAKSPEARE, *1 Henry VI.*, i. 3, 53. Winchester Goose, I CRY A ROPE! a rope! *Ibid.*, 1593, *Taming of the Shrew*, 1, 2. She may perhaps call him half a score knaves or so: an' he begin once, he'll rail in his ROPE-TRICKS. *Ibid*, (1595), *Rom. and Juliet*, ii. 4, 154. What saucy merchant was this that was so full of his ROPERY.

1611. CHAPMAN, *May Day*, iii. 1. Lord, how you roll in your ROPE-RIPE terms!

1620. FLETCHER, *Chances*, iii. 1. You'll leave this ROPERY, When you come to my years.

1660. HOWELL, *Lex. Tet.* A ROPE-RIPE-ROGUE ripe for the rope, or deserving hanging.

1663. BUTLER, *Hudibras*, I. i. Could tell what subtlest parrots mean That speak, and think, contrary clean; What member 'tis of whom they talk When they CRY ROPE . . .

*d.*1705. DORSET [CHALMERS, *Eng. Poets*, viii. 345]. The queen, overhearing what Betty did say, Would send MR. ROPER to take her away.

1848. RUXTON, *Far West*, 14. Maybe you'll get ROPED.

1871. *Temple Bar*, xxxi. 321. In the law, for instance, a barrister is said to have GONE INTO THE ROPE-WALK, when he has taken up practice in the Old Bailey.

1882. SERJ. BALLANTINE, *Experiences*, viii. What was called the ROPE-WALK [at the Old Bailey] was represented by a set of agents clean neither in character nor person.

2. (old).—To beat with a rope: hence ROPE'S-END = a thrashing.

*c.*1460. *Book of Precedence* [E.E.T.S.] [OLIPHANT, *New Eng.*, i. 297. There are ROPPYS END, coke fyghtynge, callot . . .].

1593. SHAKSPEARE, *Com. of Errors*, iv. 4, 46. Mistress . . . respect your end; or rather . . . beware the ROPE'S-END.

PHRASES.—A ROPE OF SAND (RAY) = (1) a feeble hold, and (2) an endless or unprofitable task; ON THE HIGH ROPES = elated, arrogant: *see* HIGH HORSE (B. E., GROSE); 'What a ROPE!' = 'What the devil'; TO PUT A ROPE TO THE EYE OF A NEEDLE = to attempt the impossible or absurd; also the proverbial saying, 'A ROPE and butter: if one slip, the other may hold.'

ROPER (MRS.), *subs.* (naval).—*See* quot. TO MARRY MRS. ROPER = to list in the Marines.

1868. BREWER, *Phrase and Fable*, s.v. "MISTRESS ROPER." The Marines, or any one of them: so called by the regular sailors, because they handle the ropes like girls, not being used to them.

ROPPER, *subs.* (tramps').—A scarf; a comforter. [?'Wrapper.']

1873. GREENWOOD, *In Strange Company*. A great deal of the lower part of the face hidden in the thick folds of a ROPPER.

RORAM (or ?**ROLAND**), *subs.* (old).—The sun: *cf.* OLIVER = moon.—TUFTS.

RORITORIOUS, *adj.* and *adv.* (old).—Uproarious: *cf.* 'rory-tory' (Devon) = showy, dashing.

1821. EGAN, *Real Life*, I. 619. The Randallites were RORITORIOUS and flushed with good fortune.

RORTY (or **RAUGHTY**), *adj.* (costers').—Of the very best. Hence RORTY-TOFF = an out-and-out swell; RORTY-DASHER = a fine fellow; TO DO THE RORTY = to have a good time.

*c.*1864. VANCE, *Chickaleary Cove*, 1. I have a RORTY gal. *Ibid.*, 2. The vestat with the bins so RORTY.

1887. HENLEY, *Culture in Slums*, 'Rondeau,' 3. For in such RORTY wise doth Love express His blooming views.

1893. MILLIKEN, *'Arry Ballads*, 31. We'd a rare RORTY time of it. *Ibid.*, 69. A doin' the RORTY.

1899. WHITEING, *John St.*, 49. She is Boadicea . . . no 'British warrior queen' of nursery recitation, but a right-down RAUGHTY gal leading her alley to battle against the Roman 'slops.'

RORY-O'-MORE, *subs. phr.* (rhyming).—(1) The floor; (2) a whore; and (3) a door. Also RORY.

1892. MARSHALL, *Rhyme of the Rusher* [*Sporting Times*, 29 Oct.]. I fired him out out of the RORY quick.

RORYS (THE), *subs.* (military).—The Princess Louise's (Argyll and Sutherland Highlanders).

ROSARY, *subs.* (old).—A base coin (*temp.* Ed. I.), resembling the current silver penny. [It bore (verso) a rose or rosette.]

ROSE, *subs.* (showmen's).—1. A bitch.

2. (Stock Exchange).—In *pl.* = Buenos Ayres and Rosario Railway Ordinary Stock.

3. (venery).—The female *pudendum*: *see* MONOSYLLABLE; and (4) a maidenhead. To PLUCK A ROSE = (1) to take a maidenhead, and (2) a woman's euphemism for micturition or defecation in the open air: *cf.* TO PICK A DAISY (GROSE, HALLIWELL).

1730. SWIFT, *Pan. on Dean* [CHALMERS, *Eng. Poets*, xi. 489]. The bashful maid, to hide our blush . . . unobserved she boldly goes . . . to PLUCK A ROSE.

UNDER THE ROSE, *phr.* (colloquial).—Secretly; in confidence (DYCHE, GROSE).

1546. DYMOCKE, *Letter to Vaughan* [WALSH]. And the sayde questyon were asked with lysence, and that yt should remayn UNDER THE ROSSE, that is to say, to remain under the bourde and ne more to be rehersyd.

1616-25. *Court and Times James I.* [OLIPHANT, *New Eng.*, ii. 71. As to the prepositions we see UNDER THE ROSE].

1625. JONSON, *Staple of News*, ii. You are my lord, The rest are cogging Jacks, UNDER THE ROSE.

1632. CHAPMAN, *Ball*, ii. 2. UNDER THE ROSE the lords do call me cousin.

*c.*1707. *Old Song*, 'Praise of the Dairy Maid' [DURFEY, *Pills*, &c. (1707), i. 12. Such bliss ne'er oppose If e'er you'll be happy —— I SPEAK UNDER THE ROSE].

1753. *Adventurer*, No. 98. UNDER THE ROSE, I am a cursed favourite amongst them.

1821. LAMB, *Elia (Mrs. Battle).* All people have their blind side—their superstitions; and I have heard her declare, UNDER THE ROSE, that Hearts was her favourite suit.

18[?] SNELLING, *Coins*, 2. The rose . . . symbol of secrecy . . . [was] used with great propriety on privy seals, which came into use about the middle of the twelfth century.

1868. OUIDA, *Under Two Flags*, iv. All great ladies gamble in stock nowadays UNDER THE ROSE.

1892. NISBET, *Bushranger's Sweetheart*, 37. I no longer wondered that he should have quitted England UNDER THE ROSE.

A ROSE BETWEEN TWO THORNS (or NETTLES), *phr.* A woman sitting between two men: the usual retort is, ***mutatis mutandis***, as in quot.

1708-10. SWIFT, *Polite Conversation*, i. [*Miss, sitting between* Neverout *and the* Colonel.]—*Miss.* Well; here's A ROSE BETWEEN TWO NETTLES. *Neverout.* No, Madam; with submission, here's A NETTLE BETWEEN TWO ROSES.

TO STRIKE WITH A FEATHER AND STAB WITH A ROSE, &c., &c., *phr.* (colloquial).—To chastise playfully. A Music Hall refrain (*c.* 1888), but *see* quot.

1612. WEBSTER, *White Devil*, IV. iv. *Mar.* If I take her near you, I'll CUT HER THROAT. *Flam.* WITH A FAN OF FEATHERS.

ROSEBERYS, *subs.* (Stock Exchange).—London County Council $2\frac{1}{2}$ per cent. Stock. [Lord Rosebery was the first Chairman of the Council.]

ROSEBUD, *subs.* (common).—A débutante.

1847. TENNYSON, *Princess*, Prol. A ROSEBUD set with little wilful thorns, And sweet as English air could make her, she.

1885. *Century*, xl. 582. They flutter their brief hour in society. . . . Some of them hold on like grim death to ROSEBUD privileges.

ROSH (or **ROUSH**), *verb.* (Royal Military Academy).—To hustle; to horse-play. Hence STOP ROSHING! = an injunction to silence.

ROSIN (**ROZIN** or **ROZIN-THE-BOW**), *subs.* (old).—1. A fiddler; and (2) fiddler's lap. Whence as *verb.* = (1) to fiddle; and (2) to drink: ROSINNED (HALLIWELL) = drunk.

1607. DEKKER, *Westward Hoe*, v. 1. They are butt ROSINING, sir, and they'll scrape themselves into your company presently.

1870. *Figaro*, 31 Oct. They playfully call me "ROSIN," and . . . yet I must, perforce, go on with my playing.

1892. WATSON, *Wops the Waif*, iii. A short lame man, with a violin under his arm, suggesting the identity with the ROZIN announced.

ROSSER. *See* ROZZER.

ROST. TO TURN BOAST TO ROST, *verb. phr.* (old).—To turn from swagger to humility (HALLIWELL).

ROSY, *subs.* (common).—1. Drink; and (2) blood: *i.e.*, CLARET (*q.v.*). Hence ROSY-DROP = a grog blossom. Also THE RUBY.

1840. DICKENS, *Old Curiosity Shop*, vii. "Fred," said Mr. Swiveller, "remember the once popular melody of *Begone, Dull Care*, . . . and pass the ROSY WINE." . . . "The ROSY WINE was, in fact, represented by one glass of cold gin and water." . . . Richard Swiveller finished THE ROSY, and applied himself to the composition of another glassful." *Ibid.*, lvi. "I shall wear this emblem of woman's perfidy, in remembrance of her with whom I shall never again thread the windings of the mazy; whom I shall never more pledge in THE ROSY; who during the short remainder of my existence will murder the balmy."

1854. MARTIN and AYTOUN, *Bon Gualtier*, "Lay of the Love-Lorn." Comrades, you may pass THE ROSY.

1891. *Sporting Life*, 25 Mar. Goddard was smothered in THE ROSY as he went to his chair.

ROSY ABOUT THE GILLS, *phr.* (old).—(1) 'fresh-coloured' (B. E., GROSE), (2) = sanguine: *cf.* WHITE ABOUT THE GILLS. Also ROSY = favourable, auspicious, healthy: whence THE ROSY = good fortune.

1885. *Field*, 3 Oct. The future looks most ROSY.

1893. MILLIKEN, *'Arry Ballads*, 69. A doin' the rorty and ROSY as lively as 'Opkins's lot. *Ibid.*, 77. Not my idea of THE ROSY.

ROT, *subs.* (common).—Nonsense; BOSH (*q.v.*): also TOMMY-ROT (*q.v.*). As *verb.* = to humbug; to bully; ROTTER = a good-for-nothing.

1861. H. C. PENNELL, *Puck on Pegasus*, 'Sonnet by M. F. Tupper.' A monstrous pile of quintessential ROT.

1879. BRADDON, *Cloven Foot*, iv. I thought he despised ballet-dancing, yet this is the third time I have seen him looking on at this ROT.

1888. BOLDREWOOD, *Robbery Under Arms*, xliii. Half what them fellows puts down is regular ROT.

1891. *Harry Fludyer at Cambridge*, 106. Everybody here would have ROTTED me to death.

1892. HENLEY and STEVENSON, *Deacon Brodie*, III. i. 30. Oh, ROT, I ain't a parson.

1894. MOORE, *Esther Waters*, xxxix. All bloody ROT; who says I'm drunk? *Ibid.*, xi. A regular ROTTER; that man is about as bad as they make 'em.

1899. *Critic*, 18 Mar., 13, 2. ROTTER, at both our seats of learning, is applied indiscriminately to all persons prone towards intellectual levity. But the word must have an elastic meaning; for it embraces quacks and impostors who pass through existence with their tongue in their cheek.

ROT IT (or ROT 'UM), *intj. phr.* (common).—Hang it! damn it!

1664. COTTON, *Virgil Travestie*, 75. Where once your what shals' cal' ums—(ROT UM! It makes me mad I have forgot 'um).

1682. DRYDEN, *Prol. to Southern's Loyal Brother*, 5. Both pretend love, and both (plague ROT 'EM!) hate.

1742. FIELDING, *Joseph Andrews*, III. x. I don't care to abuse my profession; but, ROT ME, if in my heart I am not inclined to the poet's side.

1759. STERNE, *Tristram Shandy*, I. xvi. ROT the hundred and twenty pounds—he did not mind it a rush.

1806. LAMB, *Mr. H.*, i. 1. ROT his impertinence! bid him . . . not trouble me with his scruples.

1854. MARTIN and AYTOUN, *Bon Gaultier Ballads*, 'Lay of the Lovelorn.' Sink the steamboats! cuss the railways! ROT, oh ROT the Three-per-Cents!

ROTAN, *subs.* (old).—Any wheeled vehicle (GROSE).

ROT-GUT, *subs. phr.* (old).—Poor drink: generic; spec. bad beer or alcohol: also ROTTO (B. E., DYCHE, GROSE).

1597. HARVEY [*Ency. Dict.*]. They overwhelm their panch daily with a kind of flat ROT-GUT, we with a bitter dreggish mall liquor.

1633. HEYWOOD, *Eng. Traveller*, iv. 5, 226 (Mermaid). Let not a tester scape To be consumed in ROT-GUT.

1789. PARKER, *Life's Painter*, 40. That . . . is better than all the ROT-GUT wine that ever came from Popish grounds.

1796. WOLCOT, *P. Pindar* [1830], 53. A poor old woman, with diarrhœa, Brought on by slip-slop tea and ROT-GUT beer, Went to Sangrado with a woeful face.

1830. MARRYAT, *King's Own*, xxxiv. The master requested a glass of grog, as the ROT-GUT French wines had given him a pain in the bowels.

1856. HUGHES, *Tom Brown's School-Days*, I. vi. Drinking bad spirits and punch, and such ROT-GUT stuff.

1892. HENLEY and STEVENSON, *Deacon Brodie*, iv. 13. What brings the man from stuff like this to ROT-GUT and spittoons at Mother Clarke's.

1895. *Pall Mall Gaz.*, 19 Sept., 9, 1. I armed myself with a supply of the fieriest ROT-GUT . . . and set out to wish him good-bye.

ROTHSCHILD. *See* COME.

ROTTEN-ROW. TO BELONG TO ROTTEN-ROW, *verb. phr.* (naval). To be laid up as past service: of ships.

ROTTEN-SHEEP, *subs. phr.* (Fenian).—*See* quot.

1889. *Daily News*, 3 July, 6. Sir Richard Webster suddenly asked him if ROTTEN SHEEP was a Fenian expression. It would mean traitor or a useless fellow, said Mr. Davitt, adding that he himself had used it in a letter.

ROUGE, *subs.* (Eton).—A point in the Eton game of football: 3 ROUGES = 1 goal.

ROUGH, *subs.* and *adj.* (old colloquial: now largely recognised).—A ruffian: *see* quot. 1868. As *adj.* = 'uncouth, hard' (B. E.), severe: also (of fish) coarse or stale. Also TO CUT (or TURN) UP ROUGH (or TO ROUGH UP) = (1) to be annoyed, and (2) to use strong language; TO ROUGH ONE = to vex; TO ROUGH IT (or LIE ROUGH) = (1) to endure hardship (GROSE); (2) to take pot-luck; and (3) to sleep in one's clothes (B. E., GROSE); ROUGH-AND-READY = unpolished, happy-go-lucky; ROUGH ON = hard, severe.

1814. AUSTEN, *Mansfield Park*, xxxix. Take care of Fanny, mother. She is tender, and not used to ROUGH IT like the rest of us.

1843. *Punch*, iv. 254. He has, to use his own expression, ROUGHED-IT all through his life.

1851-61. MAYHEW, *London Lab.*, i. 55. The poorer classes live mostly on fish, and the "dropped" and "ROUGH" fish is bought chiefly for the poor.

1857. LAWRENCE, *Guy Livingstone*, iv. There was a railway in progress near, and the navvies and other ROUGHS came flocking in by hundreds.

1857. F. LOCKER, *Mabel.* My jealous Pussy CUT UP ROUGH The day before I bought her muff With sable trimming.

1858. TROLLOPE, *Dr. Thorne*, xxii. He was not going to hang back . . . he had always been ROUGH AND READY when wanted—and then, he was as READY as ever, AND ROUGH enough, too, God knows.

1860-5. MOTLEY, *Un. Netherlands*, IV. 138. The great queen . . . was besought . . . to name the man to whom she chose that the crown should devolve. 'Not to a ROUGH,' said Elizabeth, sententiously and grimly.

1861. HUGHES, *Tom Brown at Oxford*, iii. Drysdale seemed to prick up his ears and get combative whenever the other spoke, and lost no chance of ROUGHING HIM in his replies.

1868. DICKENS, *All Year Round*, 10 Oct. I entertain so strong an objection to the euphonious softening of ruffian into ROUGH, which has lately become popular, that I restore the right word to the heading of this paper.

1870. BRET HARTE, *Luck of Roaring Camp.* Yet a few of the spectators were, I think, touched by her sufferings. Sandy Tipton thought it was ROUGH ON Sal.

1872. *Judy*, 29 May, 59, 2. Have the ornaments handy, in case he should TURN UP ROUGH.

1883. BLACK, *Yolande*, l. A lot of English servants, who don't know what ROUGHING IT in a small shooting-box is like?

1889. *Pall Mall Gazette*, 18 Nov., 1, 3. It must have been during the early months of 1852 that Lord Salisbury "ROUGHED IT" on the colonial goldfields.

1893. MILLIKEN, *'Arry Ballads*, 80. Going to ROUGH UP. *Ibid.*, 40. PLAYING IT ROUGH.

1900. WHITE, *West End*, 355. She'll cut up ROUGH. But when she hears what you expect . . . she'll have a different feeling about it.

ROUGH ON RATS, *phr.* (common).—A hard case.

See RUFF.

ROUGH-AND-TUMBLE, *subs. phr.* (common).—1. A free fight; a mellay: as *adj.* = boisterous.

1838. HALIBURTON, *Clockmaker*, 2 S., I. "Fair fight, or ROUGH AND TUMBLE,—we've whipped 'em, that's a fact."

1873. *Conservative*, 15 Feb. His talent for ROUGH AND TUMBLE does not hold his own against the more scientific style and larger frame of the Oxford Pet.

1883. PAYN, *Thicker than Water*, xiv. Ralph foresaw that there might be . . . "A ROUGH AND TUMBLE" with his young relative.

1883. *The Lute*, 15 Jan., 20, 1. "That Dreadful Boy" is, in point of fact, an old-fashioned ROUGH-AND-TUMBLE farce.

1888. BOLDREWOOD, *Robbery Under Arms*, xxxvii. Moran after his ROUGH AND TUMBLE with Jim . . . was ready for anything.

2. (venery).—The female *pudendum*: *see* MONOSYLLABLE: also THE ROUGH-AND-READY. Hence A BIT OF ROUGH = a woman.

ROUGH-DIAMOND, *subs. phr.* (common).—A person of heart but no manners.

1753. *Adventurer*, No. 64. He married a lady, whose influence would have polished the ROUGH DIAMOND by degrees.

1853. LYTTON, *My Novel*, v. xiv. And believe me, though I'm a ROUGH DIAMOND, I have your true interest at heart.

ROUGH-FAM (or **ROUGH-FAMMY**), *subs. phr.* (old).—A waistcoat pocket.—VAUX (1812).

ROUGH-MALKIN, *subs. phr.* (venery).—The female *pudendum*: *see* MONOSYLLABLE.

1538. LYNDSAY, *Works* [LAING, I. 131, 91]. I dreid ROUCH MALKIN die for droute.

ROUGH-MUSIC, *subs. phr.* (common).—A clatter of sticks, pots, pans, and musical instruments: for the annoyance of offenders outraging public prejudice. Sometimes accompanied by a burning in effigy.

ROUGHRIDER'S-WASHTUB, *subs. phr.* (military).—The barrack water-cart.

ROUGHSHOD. TO RIDE ROUGHSHOD (OVER, or DOWN).—To domineer; to be void of GUTS (*q.v.*) or BOWELS (*q.v.*).

1881. *Nineteenth Century*, XXVI. 894. Henry [VIII.], in his later proceedings, RODE ROUGHSHOD over the constitution of the Church.

1892. LOWE, *Bismarck*, I. 283. The Chamber had again been RIDING ROUGHSHOD over His Majesty's schemes of army reform.

ROUGH-UP, *subs. phr.* (pugilists').—A fight at short notice.

1889. *Referee*, 26 Jan. It may be remembered that only a few weeks ago, in a similar ROUGH UP with the gloves to that under notice.

ROUND, *subs.* (colloquial).—An appointed and established circuit of travel: generic: *cf.* ROUNDER. Hence GENTLEMAN OF THE ROUND = an officer of the watch. Thus (1) ROUND (topers') = (*a*) liquor enough to go round the table, and (*b*) a toast drunk round; (2) ROUND (gamesters') = (*a*) cards to all, and (*b*) a hand in which all the players deal in turn; (3) an habitual course of visits, calls for orders, inspection; (4) a shot, a cartridge; and (5) archery = a competition; (6) (pugilists'—old) = the successive periods of action in a mill: between fall and fall; and (pugilists'—new, under Queensbury Rules) = so many encounters so many minutes long.

1596. JONSON, *Every Man in his Humour*, iii. 2. He had writhen himself into the habit of one of your poor infantry, your decay'd, ruinous, worm-eaten GENTLEMEN OF THE ROUND. *Ibid.* (1609), *Epicœne*, iv. 2. He walks the ROUND, up and down, through every room of the house.

1620. FLETCHER, *Philaster*, ii. 4. Come, ladies, shall we take a ROUND? as men Do walk a mile, women should talk an hour After supper.

*d.*1667. JER. TAYLOR, *Works* (1835), I. 615. Them that drank the ROUND, when they crouned their heads with folly and forgetfulness.

1714. *Spectator*, 597. Those noisy slaves . . . take their early ROUNDS about the city in a morning.

1715. ADDISON, *Freeholder*, No. 8. The Tories . . . can scarce find beauties enough . . . to supply a single ROUND of October.

*d.*1735. GRANVILLE, *Epigrams, &c.* [*Century*]. Women to cards may be compar'd; we play A ROUND or two, when us'd, we throw away.

*d.*1790. B. FRANKLIN, *Auto.*, 239. They . . . would salute with some ROUNDS fired before my door.

1827. KEBLE, *Christian Year*, 'Morning.' The trivial ROUND, the common task.

1836. LANE, *Mod. Egyptians*, I. 143. They accompany the military guards in their nightly ROUNDS through . . . the metropolis.

1847-8. THACKERAY, *Vanity Fair*, xxxiv. The Banbury man . . . polished him off in four ROUNDS.

1851-61. MAYHEW, *London Lab.*, i. 55. The costermongers . . . have mostly their little bit of a ROUND; that is, they go only to certain places.

1852. JUDSON, *Myst., &c., of New York*, I. 113. Taking a cruise about town, or going on a spree, is called taking a ROUND.

1860. *Punch*, xxxviii. 169. How many ROUNDS do you say these ruffians fought?

1868. WHYTE-MELVILLE, *White Rose*, I. iii. The start . . . would have ensured a ROUND of applause from any audience in Europe.

1879. THOMPSON, *Archery*, 12. The 'National ROUND' shot by the ladies of Great Britain . . .

1880. *Scribner's Mag.*, 499. Taking his ROUNDS periodically, giving ample warning of his approach.

1888. H. ADAMS, *Albert Gallatin*, 540. The second ROUND in this diplomatic encounter closed with the British government fairly discomfited.

2. (tramps').—Trousers: short for ROUND-THE-HOUSES (*q.v.*).

1893. EMERSON, *Lippo*, xiv. One day he walked straight into this kitchen clobbered in a black pair of ROUNDS, tight to his legs.

Adj. (old colloquial). — A general qualitative: = simple, straightforward, unmistakeable. Thus A ROUND SUM = (1) a large amount (B. E., GROSE), and (2) a sum stated in one term: *e.g.*, thirty pounds, thirty shillings, three pence; A ROUND ANSWER = plain speech; ROUND-DEALING = honest trading (B. E., GROSE); ROUND TROT = a good pace; ROUND TALE = the unvarnished truth; ROUND OATH = a swingeing expletive; ROUND-REPLY = a straight answer; ROUNDLY = plainly, vehemently, briskly; ROUND (or BROWN) DOZEN (*see* BROWN).

1240. *Middle English Poem* [E. E. T. S.: *The Ayenbyte, &c.*, 234]. The tale of an hondred betokneth ane ROUNDE FIGURE.

1593. HARVEY, *Pierces Superog.* [*Wks.*, ii. 49]. Hee it is, that hath it rightly in him indeede; and can ROUNDLY doe the feate, with a witnesse.

1596. SHAKSPEARE, *M. of Venice*, i. 3, 104. Three thousand ducats; 'tis a good ROUND SUM. *Ibid.* (1598), *Hen. V.*, iv. 1. Your reproof is something too ROUND. *Ibid.* (1602), *Hamlet*, iii. 2. Let her be ROUND with him. *Ibid.* (1602), *Othello*, i. 3, 90. I will a ROUND un-

varnish'd TALE deliver. *Ibid.* (1605), *King Lear*, i. 4. He answered me in the ROUNDEST manner, he would not.

1598. FLORIO, *Worlde of Wordes*, s.v. *Crollare il pero* . . . To tickle a woman ROUNDLIE.

1620. FLETCHER and MASSINGER, *Little Fr. Lawyer*, iii. 2. What a bold man of war! he invites me ROUNDLY.

*d.*1626. BACON, *Works* (1887), 'Truth.' Clear and ROUND DEALING is the honour of man's nature. *Ibid.* (JOHNSON). The Kings interfered in a ROUND and princely MANNER. *Ibid.*, *Polit. Fables*, ii. He ROUNDLY and openly avows what most . . . conceal.

1646. BROWNE, *Vulg. Err.*, vi. 1. The age of Noah is delivered to be just five hundred when he begat Sem; whereas perhaps he might be somewhat above or below that ROUND and complete NUMBER.

1700. CENTLIVRE, *Perjured Husband*, iv. 2. Suppose I help you to a lady with a ROUND SUM; you'd keep your word, and marry her?

1751. FIELDING, *Amelia*, VII. ix. I began to entertain some suspicions, and I took Mrs. Ellison very ROUNDLY to task upon them.

1779. SHERIDAN, *Critic*, i. 1. He ROUNDLY asserts that you had not the slightest invention or original genius.

1815. SCOTT, *Guy Mannering*, xliii. It's likely he might be brought to pay a ROUND SUM for restitution. *Ibid.* (1818), *Rob Roy*, vii. The self-willed girl told me ROUNDLY, that my dissuasions were absolutely in vain.

1847. BRONTE, *Jane Eyre*, xxvii. You found ready and ROUND ANSWERS.

1851-61. MAYHEW, *London Lab.*, II. 526. This . . . pursuing the ROUND NUMBER system would supply nearly five articles, &c.

1859. TENNYSON, *Geraint*. ROUND was their pace at first, but slackened soon.

18[?]. SHARP, *Sermons*, IV., ser. 18. Either a ROUND OATH or a curse.

1882. BERESFORD HOPE, *The Brandreths*, I. v. Remonstrating . . . in ROUND, bold, unconventional LANGUAGE.

*c.*1891. *Lancet* [*Century*]. The destructors now consumed, ROUNDLY, about 500 loads of refuse a week.

*d.*1898. GLADSTONE, *Might of Right*, 175. [The United States] has risen, during one simple Century of freedom, in ROUND NUMBERS, from two millions to forty-five.

2. (tailors').—Languid; MONDAYISH (*q.v.*)

Verb. (colloquial).—1. To betray; to PEACH (*q.v.*); (2) to turn upon and berate: also TO ROUND ON.

1864. *Cornhill Magazine*, vi. 646. ROUNDING or treachery is always spoken of very indignantly, and often severely, and even murderously punished.

1877. *Five Years' Penal Servitude*, i. Both desisted from their own recriminations as to ROUNDING and "blowing" on each other.

1882. *D. Telegraph*, 6 Oct., 6, 2. The prisoner . . . denied the charge, but afterwards asked who had ROUNDED.

1889. *Answers*, 11 May, 380. He ROUNDED on the warder, and the Governor, to catch the officer, ordered the prisoner to act as if the discovery had not been known.

1897. MAUGHAM, *Liza of Lambeth*, xi. They've all ROUNDED on me except you, Tom.

TO ROUND UP, *verb. phr.* (colonial).—To collect cattle: for inspection, branding, &c.: also as *subs.* Whence (general) = to complete; to take stock.

1881. GRANT, *Bush Life*. ROUND THEM UP, if possible, and let them stand a few minutes to breathe.

1886. ROOSEVELT, *Hunting Trips*, ii. [A ranchman's] hardest work comes during the spring and fall ROUND-UPS.

1886. *Philadelphia Times*, 3 May [*Century*]. That exception . . . will probably be included in the general ROUND-UP [of an agreement among railroads] to-morrow.

1887. FRANCIS, *Saddle and Moccasin*. As soon as the ROUND UP was completed, the branding was to take place.

TO BET ROUND, *verb. phr.* (racing).—To bet upon (or against) several horses in a race.

ROUND-ABOUT, *subs.* (old).—1. *See* quot. *c.*1548. Also (2: modern) = a short, close-fitting jacket: also ROUNDER.

*c.*1548. LATIMER, *Sermons and Remains* (PARKER, *Works*, 108). [OLIPHANT, *New Eng.*, i. 516. The huge farthingales worn by women are called ROUND-ABOUTS].

1848. DURIVAGE, *Stray Subjects*, 81. One of the party in a green ROUND-ABOUT.

1893. MILLIKEN, *'Arry Ballads*, 24. That's me in plaid dittos and ROUNDER.

3. (thieves').—A female thief's all-round pocket.

4. (common).—1. A horizontal wheel or frame, turned by a small engine, and furnished with wooden horses or carriages; a merry-go-round.

1872. BESANT & RICE, *R. M. Mortiboy*, xxiii. He got . . . a Punch and Judy, swing-boats, a ROUNDABOUT, and a performing monkey.

5. (prison).—A treadmill; the EVERLASTING-STAIRCASE (*q.v.*).

6. (thieves').—A housebreaker's tool: it cuts a round piece, about five inches in diameter, out of a shutter or door; also ROUND ROBIN (GROSE).

ROUND-AND-SQUARE, *phr.* (rhyming).—Everywhere.

ROUND-BETTING. *See* ROUND.

ROUNDEM, *subs.* (thieves'). — A button.

ROUNDER, *subs.* (common).—1. A whoremaster: *see* MUTTON-MONGER: spec. a FANCY-MAN (*q.v.*).

2. (common). — A person or thing taking or making a ROUND (*subs.*, senses 1-6).

3. (common). — A round of cheers.

1882. BLACKMORE, *Christowell*, xxxiii. Was off amid a ROUNDER of 'Thank'e, ma'am, thank'e.'

4. (common).—A big oath.

1886. CAMPBELL-PRAED, *Head Station*, 33. We can all swear a ROUNDER in the stock-yard.

5. (American).—A man who goes habitually from bar to bar.

1883. *Century*, xxxvi. 249. Midnight ROUNDERS, with nose laid over . . . as evidence of their prowess in bar-room mills and paving-stone riots.

1886. *Philadelphia Times* [*Century*]. G . . . had made himself conspicuous as a ROUNDER.

1887. *Christ. Union*, 25 Aug. A very large proportion . . . are old ROUNDERS, who return again and again.

TO ROUND (or ROUND IN THE EAR), *verb. phr.* (old). — To whisper.

1604. SHAKSPEARE, *Winter's Tale*, i. 2, 217. They're . . . whispering, ROUNDING.

1611. COTGRAVE, *Dict.*, s.v. S'ACCOUTER A L'OREILLE.

See ROUND, *subs.* and *adj.*, and ROUND-ABOUT.

ROUNDHEAD, *subs.* (old colloquial). —A PURITAN (*q.v.*). [The hair was worn closely cropped.] To ROUND THE HEAD = to cut the hair round.—B. E., GROSE.

ROUNDY (or **ROUNDY-KEN**), *subs. phr.* (old).—A watch-house; a lock-up.

1828. EGAN, *Finish to Life in London*, 245. To avoid a night's lodging in the ROUNDY-KEN.

ROUND MOUTH (THE), *subs. phr.* (old). — The fundament: also BROTHER ROUND-MOUTH. 'BROTHER ROUND-MOUTH SPEAKS' = 'He has let a fart' (GROSE).

ROUND O, *subs. phr.* (old).—A thumping lie: *see* WHOPPER.

1605. *London Prodigal*, iii. 2. Howsoever the Devonshire man is, my master's mind is bloody, that's a ROUND O [*aside*], and, therefore, Sir, entreaty is but vain.

ROUND ROBIN, *subs. phr.* (old).—1. *See* quots.

1563. FOX, *Acts and Monuments*, 523. [OLIPHANT, *New Eng.*, i. 550. Scurrilous Protestants used to call the Host ROUND ROBIN; we apply the phrase to petitions.]

*d.*1569. COVERDALE, *Works*, i. 426. Certain fond talkers . . . invent and apply to this most holy sacrament names of despite and reproach, as to call it Jack-in-the-Box and ROUND-ROBIN.

1661. HEYLIN, *Reformation*, i. 99. Reproached it [the Sacrament] by the odius names of Jack-in-a-box, ROUND ROBIN, Sacrament of the Halter . . .

2. (old).—A religious (= political) brawler.

1692. HACKET, *Life of Williams*, ii. 177. These Wat Tylers and ROUND ROBINS being driven . . . out of Whitehall.

3. (colloquial). — *See* quots. (GROSE).

1626. *Court and Times Chas. I.*, i. 187. [OLIPHANT, *New Eng.*, ii. 75. We find the first instance of a ROUND ROBIN in 1626; sailors write their names and marks in a good round circular form so that none might appear for a ringleader.]

1660. *Rump Songs*, i. 66. The ROUND-ROBIN by a like fate, Is Victor in the Tubb.

1755. *World*, 146. A ROUND ROBIN . . . of above a thousand of the most respectable names.

1776. FORBES [BOSWELL, *Johnson* (HILL), III. 83]. A ROUND ROBIN, as the sailors call it . . . so as not to let it be known who puts his name first or last to the paper.

1838. LYTTON, *Alice*, IV. iii. The whole country shall sign a ROUND ROBIN to tell him it's a shame.

1886. *D. Telegraph*, 24 Feb. The members of the Royal Commission sent to Sir George Grey a sort of ROUND-ROBIN.

4 and 5. (thieves').—*See* quot. and ROUNDABOUT.

1889. CLARKSON and RICHARDSON, *Police*, 341. Go in for a ROUND ROBIN, or good heavy swindle.

ROUND-SHAVING, *subs. phr.* (colloquial).—A reprimand.

ROUND-THE-HOUSES, *subs. phr.* (rhyming). — Trousers: *cf.* ROUNDS.

1892. MARSHALL, *The Rusher* [*Sporting Times*, 29 Oct.]. My ROUND-THE-HOUSES I tried to dry, By the Anna Maria's heat.

1898. *Pink 'Un and Pelican*, 153. Mr. Commissioner Kerr . . . once informed a snip who was after a chap for the price of a couple o' pair o' light ROUND-MY-HOUSES . . . that there was no such thing as *taking* credit.

RONNY, *subs.* (old).—A potato; a MURPHY (*q.v.*).

1821. HAGGART, *Life*, 90. A field where some coves were rousting RONNIES.

ROUSE, *subs.* (old).—(1) A large glass full of liquor; a big bumper; (2) a carouse.

1596. SHAKSPEARE, *Hamlet*, i. 4. The king doth wake to-night, and take his ROUSE.

1609. JONSON, *Silent Woman*, iii. 2. We will have a ROUSE in each of them.

1609. DEKKER, *Guls Hornbook* [NARES]. Tell me, thou soveraigne skinker, how to take the German's upsy-freeze, the Danish ROUZA, the Surtyer's stoop of Rhenish.

1618. DRAYTON, *Verses in Chapman's Hesiod*. To fetch deep ROUSES from Jove's plenteous cup.

1618. FLETCHER, *Loyal Subject*, iv. 5. Take the ROUSE freely, sir, 'Twill warm your blood, and make you fit for jollity. *Ibid.* (1624), *Wife for a Month*, ii. 6. We'll have a ROUSE before we go to bed, friends.

*c.*1620. HEALEY, *Disc. of New World*, 84. Gone is my flesh, yet thirst lies in the bone, Give me one ROUSE, my friend, and get thee gone.

1623. MASSINGER, *Duke of Milan*, i. 1. Your lord, by his patent, stands bound to take his ROUSE.

1840. TENNYSON, *Vision of Sin*. Fill the cup and fill the can, Have a ROUSE before the morn.

3. (thieves').—*See* quot.

1888. *Ev. Standard*, 26 Dec. If the constable did not allow him to go to the station in a cab he would ROUSE (a slang term for fighting).

ROUSER, *subs.* (common).—Generic for anything exceptional. Hence ROUSING = very, great, startling, exciting.

1677. COLES, *Eng.-Lat. Dict.* A ROUSING lye, *mendacium magnificum*.

1719. DURFEY, *Pills to Purge*, i. 264. She grown coy, Call'd him Boy, He getting from her cry'd, Zoons, you're a ROUZER.

1767. STERNE, *Tristram Shandy*, vi. 109. A Jew . . . had the ill-luck to die . . . and leave his widow in possession of a ROUSING trade.

1868. *Putnam's Mag.*, Jan. He is a ROUSER at making punch.

1893, MILLIKEN, *'Arry Ballads*, 64. We made the whole place ring a ROUSER, till Jolter implored us to stop.

2. (old).—A tremendous fart.

1731. SWIFT, *Strephon and Chloe*, . . . Let fly a ROUSER in her face.

ROUST, *subs.* (old).—1. The act of kind; whence, as *verb.* = to copulate: *see* GREENS and RIDE.

1599. HALL, *Satires*, iv. 1. And with her cruel lady-star uprose She seeks her third ROUST on her silent toes.

Verb. (old).—1. *See* subs.; (2) to frisk; to disturb; to shift; (3) to steal: *see* ROUSTABOUT.

1599. HALL, *Satires*, iv. 2. While yet he ROUSTETH at some uncouth signe

1821. HAGGART, *Life*, 66. She raised the doun that the swag was ROUSTED. *Ibid.*, 90. Some coves were ROUSTING ronnies.

ROUSTABOUT (ROUSE-ABOUT or ROUSER), *subs.* (common).—1. *See* quots.; (2) a fidget, and (3) a term of contempt.

1868. *Putnam's Mag.*, Sept., 'On the Plains.' As the steamer was leaving the levée, about forty black deck-hands or ROUSTABOUTS gathered at the bow, and sang a rude Western sailor's song.

1871. DE VERE, *Americanisms*, 225. The Western rough is frequently a ROUSTABOUT—a term evidently derived from the old English ROUST, quoted by Jamieson as meaning to disturb. He is noisy, but not necessarily a rowdy, and frequently a useful member of society in some capacity which requires hard work and constant exposure.

1883. EDW. E. MORRIS [*Longman's Mag.*, June, 178]. This poor young man had been a ROUSTABOUT hand on a station [in Australia] (a colonial expression for a man who can be put to any kind of work).

1890. *New York Sun*, 23 Mar. An old Mississippi ROUSTABOUT.

1894. *Sydney Morning Herald*, 6 Oct. A rougher person—perhaps a happier—is the ROUSEABOUT, who makes himself useful in the shearing shed . . . sometimes . . . spoken of as a ROUSTABOUT.

[?]. *American* [*Century*]. Men . . . who used to be ROUSTERS, and are now broken down and played out.

ROUT, *subs.* (old).—1. A fashionable party; and (2) 'a card party at a private house' (GROSE). As *verb.* = to assemble in company.

1775. SHERIDAN, *Rivals*, i. 1. A tall Irish baronet she met . . . at Lady Macshuffle's ROUT.

18[?]. MACAULAY [TREVELYAN, i. 265]. I have attended a very splendid ROUT at Lord Grey's.

ROUTER, *subs.* (old).—A cow: hence ROUTER-PUTTERS = cows'-feet (HAGGART).

ROVE, *verb.* (old: now recognised).—'To wander idly up and down.'—B. E. (*c.* 1696).

ROVER, *subs.* (American).—1. *See* quot.

1889. LELAND, in *S. J. & C.*, s.v. ROVERS . . . Young and good-looking women who go into brokers' shops, law-offices, stores, . . . many employed by churches, hospitals, &c.; others are cheats, who have many ingenious devices to obtain money . . . Also largely employed for purposes of intrigue.

2. (old).—A pirate; a free-booter; (formerly: now recognised) a 'wanderer; a vagabond.'—B. E., GROSE. Also (B. E.) TO RUN (or SHOOT) AT ROVERS = 'to run wild, to act at random.'

1440. *Prompt. Parv.*, 437. Robare . . . yn the see (ROVARE, or thef of the se).

d. 1512. FABYAN, *Chronicle*, 359. The best men of ye cytie by thyse ryotous persones were spoyled and robbid; and by the ROUERS also of ye see.

1611. *Bible*, 1 Chron. xii. 21. And they helped David against the band of the ROVERS.

1715. SOUTH, *Sermons* [*Century*]. Providence never SHOOTS AT ROVERS.

d. 1765. POCOCK, *Desc. of East*, II. i. 51. The Maltese ROVERS take away every thing that is valuable both from Turks and Christians.

1827. COOPER, *Red ROVER*, ii. The ship of that notorious pirate, the Red ROVER.

3. (common).—In *pl.* = the thoughts (JAMIESON).

ROW, *subs.* (originally University: now general).—1. A disturbance; a SHINDY (*q.v.*); boisterous talk: also ROWING: hence (2) a mob (Univ.). Whence ROWING-MAN (*ow* as *ough* in 'bough') = a SPREESTER (*q.v.*). Also as *verb.* = (1) to abuse; to create a disturbance (*see* quot. 1825); TO GET INTO A ROW = to get into trouble; [GROSE: s.v. ROUT, 'shortened into ROW, Cambridge slang.']

1794. *Gent. Mag.*, 1085. And was very near rustication [at Cambridge], merely for kicking up a ROW after a beakering party.

1820. BYRON [to Mr. Murray, 20 May]. Tell [Campbell] all this, and let him take it in good part; for I might have rammed it into a review and ROWED him.

1823. *Hints for Oxford*, 6. Faultless and frowning beings, who must needs be ever ROWING you at lecture.

1825. *English Spy*, I. 158 [Note, 'Oxford.'] ROWING A FELLOW—going with a party in the dead of night to a man's room, nailing or screwing his oak up, so as it cannot be opened on the inside, knocking at his door, calling out fire, and when he comes to the door, burning a quantity of shavings . . . to impress him with the idea that the staircase . . . is on fire. And when he is frightened almost out of his senses, setting up a most hideous horse-laugh and running away.

1826. CROKER [*Croker Papers*, i. 331]. Where there was a smart young waiter, whom, however, these two Englishmen used to ROW exceedingly.

1837. BARHAM, *Ingoldsby Leg.*, i. 35. Next morning there was a great ROW about it.

1852. BRISTED, *Five Years in Eng. Univ.* More disposed to ROWING than reading.

1864. *Eton School Days*, II. Chudleigh was going to speak . . . when Chorley cried, Hold your ROW, will you?

1883. *Punch*, 11 August, 72, 2. My sire will ROW me vigorously, My mother sore complain.

1889. *Time*, Aug., 149. I have a reminiscence of ROWING her for growing as tall as myself. *Ibid.*, 151. He ROWS her so fearful that Kitty thinks he'll be sure to desert her now.

THE ROW, *subs. phr.* (common).—1. Rotten Row, Hyde Park; and (2) Paternoster Row (booksellers').

1812. COMBE, *Syntax*, *Picturesque*, c. xxiii. 'Tis not confined, we all must know, To vulgar tradesmen in THE ROW.

1879. DICKENS, *Dict. of London*, s.v. BOND STREET. Those who would see the lounger of the present day must look for him in THE ROW.

PHRASES. A HARD (or LONG) ROW TO HOE = a difficult task; TO HOE ONE'S OWN ROW = to mind one's own business; TO ROW IN THE SAME BOAT = to share.

1840. CROCKETT, *Tour Down East*, 69. Gentlemen, I never opposed Andrew Jackson for the sake of popularity. I knew it was a HARD ROW TO HOE.

1847. ROBB, *Squatter Life*, 122. God help that poor creatur, she's GOT A HARD ROW TO HOE.

1871. MULFORD in *San Francisco Chronicle*. Now that I have HOED MY OWN ROW and rumor gives me a false condition, they deluge me with congratulations.

1892. GUNTER, *Miss Dividends*, iv. I am afraid Harry Lawrence has A HARD ROW TO HOE.

ROWDY, *subs.* (common).—1. A blackguard; and (2) a political brawler (American). Hence ROWDY (ROWDY-DOWDY, or ROWDY-DOW) = blackguardly, turbulent, vulgar; ROWDYISM (ROWDY-DOW, or ROWDINESS) = blackguardism.

1842. DICKENS, *American Notes*, xiii. Two . . . demi-johns, were consigned to the least ROWDY of the party for safe-keeping

1852. BRISTED, *UpperTenThousand*, 33. Whose team is that? Some ROWDY'S, I perceive. *Ibid.*, 69. My red wheels . . . are rather ROWDY, I must own; not exactly the thing for a gentleman.

1852. *Cadger's Ball* [LABERN, *Comic Song Book*]. Jane of the Hatchet-face divine Just did the ROWDY-DOWDY poker.

1857. KINGSLEY, *Two Years Ago*, x. A drunken, gambling, cut-throat ROWDY.

1857. *Baltimore Clipper*, 8 Sept. 'Convention of Baltimore ROWDIES.' [Title.]

1859. BARTLETT, *Dict. Americanisms*, s.v. ROWDY. The ROWDY nomenclature of the principal cities may now be classified as follows:—NEW YORK.—Dead Rabbits; Bowery Boys; Forty Thieves; Skinners; Robin Hood Club; Huge Paws; Short Boys; Swill Boys; Shoulder-hitters; Killers. PHILADELPHIA.—Killers; Schuylkill Annihilators; Moyamensing Hounds; Northern Liberty Skivers; and Peep of Day Boys. BALTIMORE.—Plug-Uglies; Rough Skins; Double Pumps; Tigers; Black Snakes; Stay Lates; Hard Times; Little Fellows; Blood Tubs; Dips; Ranters; Rip-Raps; and Gladiators.

1866. HOWELLS, *Venetian Life*, xx. The *lasagnone* is a loafer . . . but he cannot be a ROWDY,—that pleasing blossom on the nose of our fast, high-fed, thick-blooded civilisation.

1871. *Observer*, 24 Dec. Everything seems to be ROWDY, and to have about it a flavour of brandy-and-water; yet the people are industrious and well-ordered.

1882. ANSTEY, *Vice-Versa*, v. "I was strolling down Petty Cury with two other men, smoking (Bosher of 'Pothouse,' and Peebles of 'Cats,' both pretty well known up there for general ROWDINESS, you know—dear old friends of mine)."

1884. *D. Telegraph*, 11 Feb., 5, 2. His methods of controversy have been coarse; his Republicanism has been pushed to ROWDYISM.

1892. *Pall Mall Gaz.*, 12 Mar., 6, 2. I have never heard him use any bad language, or behave in any ROWDY kind of way.

3. (common).—Money: *see* RHINO: *cf.* RUDDY.

1841. LEMAN REDE, *Sixteen String Jack*, i. 4. *Theo. (aside.)* What's ROWDY, I wonder?

1842. EGAN, *Bould Yeoman* [Capt. Macheath]. I will not down you, if you will but disburse your ROWDY with me.

1849. THACKERAY, *Pendennis*, lxxv. From your account of him he seems a muff and not a beauty. But he has got THE ROWDY, which is the thing.

1856. *Punch*, xxxi. 79. The Queen of Oude, May spend her ROWD, Y, careless and *sans souci*.

ROWL, *verb.* (American University).—To recite well: *cf.* RUSH.

2. (old).—Money: *see* RHINO.

ROYAL, *subs.* (dockers').—*See* quot.

1883. SIMS, *How the Poor Live*, 96. Regular men, called ROYALS, are pretty sure to be taken on, their names being on the ganger's list and called out by him as a matter of course. *Ibid.*, 98. It is when the ROYALS are exhausted that the real excitement begins.

ROYAL-GOATS, *subs. phr.* (military).—The Royal Welsh Fusiliers (formerly the Twenty-third Foot.) Also "Nanny-goats." [A goat is kept as a regimental pet.]

ROYAL-IMAGE, *subs. phr.* (old).—In *pl.* = money: *see* RHINO.

1749. SMOLLETT, *Gil Blas* [ROUTLEDGE], 287. Poor Gil Blas was left behind, without a ROYAL IMAGE in his pocket.

ROYAL POVERTY, *subs. phr.* (old).—Gin: *see* WHITE SATIN.—BAILEY (1728).

ROYAL-SCAMP, *subs. phr.* (old).—A GENTLEMAN OF THE ROAD (*q.v.*) as distinguished from a foot-pad (GROSE).

ROYSTER. *See* ROISTER.

ROZIN. *See* ROSIN.

ROZZER, *subs.* (thieves').—A policeman: *see* BEAK.

18[?] *Globe* [S. J. & C.]. The prisoner, seeing a detective watching him, called out to a companion, "There's a ROSSER!" The term is, as the magistrate opined, a new one.

1893. EMERSON, *Signor Lippo*, xviii. If the ROZZERS was to see him in bona clobber they'd take him for a gun. *Ibid.*, xx. So I took on knocker up, but when I began the ROZZERS was down on me.

1898. *Pink 'Un and Pelican*, 237. What does she do? Lor' doomy! she acksherly sticks 'er 'ead out o' winder an' calls up a ROZZER!

1901. *Sporting Times*, 6 Ap., i. 4. From calmness I don't mean to lapse, I scorn you counterjumping chaps, Or you're some ROZZER'S nark, perhaps.

R'S. *See* THREE R'S (THE).

RUB, *subs.* (colloquial).—1. An obstacle; a disputable point; a difficulty: also (Old Cant) = a hard shift (B. E., GROSE). Hence, as *verb.* = to hinder, to obstruct. Also RUBBER.

1590. NASHE, *Pasquil's Apologie* [*Works*, i. 214]. Some small RUBS, as I heare, haue been cast in my way to hinder my comming forth, but they shall not profit.

1599. SHAKSPEARE, *Henry V.*, ii. 2. We doubt not now But every RUB is smoothed on our way. *Ibid.* (1602-3), *Hamlet*, iii. 1. To die, to sleep; To sleep: perchance to dream: ay, there's the RUB. *Ibid.* (1605), *Lear*, ii. 2. 'Tis the duke's pleasure, Whose disposition, all the world well knows, Will not be RUBB'D nor stopped.

1606. DAY, *Ile of Guts*, ii. 4. The duke is comming to bowles, and I would not for halfe mine office you should be a RUB in the way of his patience.

1613. PURCHAS, *Pilgrimage*, 243. Perceiuing that their power and authoritie would be a perillous RUB in his way.

1684. BUNYAN, *Pilgrim's Progress*, II. We have met with some notable RUBS already, and what are yet to come we knew not.

1724. HARPER in *Harlequin Sheppard*. He broke thro' all RUBBS in the whitt.

1762. GOLDSMITH, *Life of Nash* [*Works*, 552 (Globe)]. But he experienced such RUBS as these, and a thousand other mortifications, every day.

1840. DICKENS, *Old Curiosity Shop*, vii. 'Look at the worst side of the question then,' said Trent. . . . 'Suppose he lives.' 'To be sure,' said Dick, 'There's the RUB.'

1880. TROLLOPE, *Duke's Children*, lxxi. He who lives on comfortable terms with the partner of his troubles can afford to acknowledge the ordinary RUBS of life.

2. (military).—A loan: as of a newspaper.

Verb. (venery).—1. To masturbate; TO FRIG (*q.v.*): also TO RUB UP (or OFF); also *subs.* = an act of masturbation. Hence RUBBER-UP = a masturbator;

RUBBING-UP = masturbation; TO DO A RUB UP = to masturbate. Fr. *se branler*, *se coller une douce*, &c. Also (2) to copulate: *see* RIDE.

1599. JONSON, *Ev. Man Out of His Humour*, iv. 4. *Carlo.* Let a man sweat once a week in a hot-house and be well RUBBED and froted, with a good plump juicy wench, and sweet linen, he shall ne'er have the pox.

1656. FLETCHER, *Martiall*, xi. 30. Thus Phillis RUB ME UP, thus tickle me.

1700. CONGREVE, *Way of the World*, i. 9. They must wait a RUB OFF, if I want appetite.

1772. BRIDGES, *Burlesque Homer*, 5. Thou that RUBS UP the girls of Lilla. *Ibid.*, 42. Ever since I saw . . . Thetis stroking your knees, as on the ground you sat, And RUBBING UP, the LORD knows what.

3. (old).—To run or take away. Also to RUB OFF; TO RUB TO THE WHITT = to send to Newgate (B. E., GROSE).

*c.*1550. BANSLEY, *Pryde of Women* [HAZLITT, *Pop. Poet.*, iv. 238]. RUBBE forthe, olde trottes, to the devyl worde.

1676. *Warening for Housekeepers* [FARMER, *Musa Pedestris* (1896), 30.] O then they RUB us to the whitt.

1688. SHADWELL, *Squire of Alsatia*, i. The Captain whipt his Porker out, and away RUBB'D Prigster and call'd the watch.

*c.*1704. *Gentleman Instructed*, 351. In a huff he . . . RUB'D OFF, and left the field to Eusebius.

1737. *Old Ballad*, '*Black Procession* [*Bacchus and Venus*]. Toure you well; hark you well, see Where they are RUBB'D.

1859. MATSELL, *Vocabulum*, 'Hundred Stretches Hence.' Some RUBBED to whit had napped a winder.

COLLOQUIALISMS. — TO RUB ALONG (ON or OUT) = (1) to manage somehow, to live indifferently, and (2) = to live tolerably well (B. E., *c.*1696); TO RUB DOWN = 1 (police) to search: the prisoner's arms are raised, the vest unbuttoned, and the officer's hand passed over the body: also TO RUN THE RULE OVER; (2) to scold, rate, or take to task; TO RUB IN = (1) to nag, annoy, or aggravate persistently: Fr. *monter une scie*; (2) to peg away, insist, or exaggerate; TO BE RUBBED ABOUT = to be made a convenience; TO RUB OUT (tailors') = to cut out, also (2—colloquial) to forget old grievances, to cancel a debt: also TO RUB OFF; TO RUB OUT = to kill: hence RUBBED OUT = dead; TO RUB UP = (1) to refresh the memory (B. E., *c.*1696, GROSE), (2) to polish (B. E., *c.* 1696: now recognised), and (3) to touch a tender point or remembrance: hence TO RUB UP THE WRONG WAY = to irritate, to annoy: also TO RUB ON THE GAULE; TO GIVE A RUB OF THE THUMB = to explain or show the way.

1461-73. *Paston Letters.* I wyll RUBBE ON.

1546. HEYWOOD, *Proverbs.* RUB HIM ON THE GALL.

1610. *Mirr. Mag.*, 463. Enough, you RUB'D the guiltie ON THE GAULE.

*d.*1704. BROWN, *Works*, i. 193. Our affairs have made a shift TO RUB ON without any great conjuring. *Ibid.*, ii. 118. With a little RUBBING UP my memory I may be able to give you the lives of all the mitred hogs.

1778. SHERIDAN, *Rivals*, iii. 4. I must RUB UP my balancing, and chasing, and boring.

*a.*1790. FRANKLIN, *Autobiog.*, 73. We had nearly consumed all my pistoles, and now just RUBBED ON from hand to mouth.

1816. SCOTT, *Old Mortality*, xliii. Evandale is the man on earth whom he hates worst, and . . . were he once RUBBED OUT of the way, all, he thinks, will be his own.

1842. *Punch's Almanac.* You see Jinks with a three days' beard—you RUB OUT the slates—forget his action, and—.

1848. RUXTON, *Far West*, 65. Inarticulate words reached the ears of his companions as they bent over him. RUBBED OUT at last, they heard him say.

1850. TENNYSON, *In Memoriam*, lxxxix. We RUB each other's angles DOWN.

1863. READE, *Hard Cash*, I. 46. What I have got to RUB UP is my Divinity and my Logic; especially my Logic. Will you grind Logic with me?

1868. WHYTE MELVILLE, *White Rose*, I. xxv. It is no unusual drawback to married life, this same knack of RUBBING THE HAIR THE WRONG WAY.

1870. *D. News*, 26 May. 'Metropolitan Police.' RUBBING IT IN well is a well-known phrase amongst the doubtful portion of the constabulary.

1877. BESANT and RICE, *Golden Butterfly*, vii. Clawed I should have been, mauled I should have been, RUBBED OUT I should have been, on that green and grassy spot, but for the crack of Mr. Dunquerque's rifle.

1879. JAMES, *Bundle of Letters*, No. IV. She is for ever throwing Boston up at me; I can't get rid of Boston. The other one RUBS IT INTO me, too; but in a different way.

1883. J. HAWTHORNE, *Dust*, 291. Philip . . . was always RUBBED THE WRONG WAY by Lady Flanders.

1888. ROLF BOLDREWOOD, *Robbery Under Arms*, xxix. I suppose he'd RUB THEM OUT, every mother's son, if he could.

1892. NISBET, *Bushranger's Sweetheart*, 86. We managed to RUB ALONG on our fifteen shillings per week.

1898. *Pink 'Un and Pelican*, 163. Jubber was neither hard nor remorseless as a rule unless they RUBBED HIM THE WRONG WAY.

1900. WHITE, *West End*, 25. I knew this was the aspect which he desired to see, so I RUBBED it as bright as I could and held it up [speaking of patronage].

1902. *Pall Mall Gaz.*, 24 Jan., i. 2. Mr. Rowe . . . will RUB this fact INTO them before they are much older.

RUBBACROCK, *subs.* (colloquial).—A filthy slattern; a PUZZLE (*q.v.*).

RUBBAGE (or **RUBBIDGE**), *subs.* (vulgar).—Rubbish.

RUBBER, *subs.* (gaming). — 1. A round of three games: also RUB (B. E., GROSE).

1635. QUARLES, *Emblems*, i. 10. It is the trade of man, and ev'ry sinner Has play'd his RUBBERS; every soul's a winner.

1680. AUBREY, *Eminent Men* [OLIPHANT, *New Eng.*, ii. 121. Among new words are . . . RUBBER (of a game . . .)].

1753. *Adventurer*, 35. Mrs. Overall, the housekeeper, having lost three RUBBERS at whist running.

1843. DICKENS, *Martin Chuzzlewit*, xi. I've seen him play whist, with my father for a partner; and a good RUBBER, too.

1869. THACKERAY, *What Makes my Heart to Thrill and Glow?* 7. Why was it that I laughed and grinned at whist, although I lost the RUB?

2. (old). — A slight reproof; 'reflections upon any one . . . a rencounter with drawn swords.'—B. E. (*c.*1696). Also RUB.

3. (American).—In *pl.* = India-rubber over-shoes; goloshes.

1888. *Detroit Free Press*, 8 Dec. When I was a young man I had to slosh around dark, wet nights in RUBBERS that didn't fit.

4. (old).—*See* quot.

1606. DECKER, *Seven Deadly Sinnes*, 32 (ARBER'S ED.). A number of poore handy-crafts-men, that before wrought night and day, made stocks to themselves of ten groates, and crownes a peece, and what by Betting, Lurches, RUBBERS, and such tricks, they never took care for a good daies worke afterwards.

RUBBER-NECK (or **RUBBER**), *verb. phr.* (American). — *See* quots. Also TO RUBBER AROUND.

1901. FLYNT and WALTON, *The Powers that Prey*, 34. He was perfectly at a loss what to do next, except as he phrased it TO RUBBER AROUND, which is technical and esoteric for keeping his eyes and ears open. *Ibid.*, 60. They RUBBER so that they aint thinkin' 'bout their leathers . . . they'll screw their necks till you'll think they was never goun' to get 'em in shape again. *Ibid.*, 121. You RUBBER too much with your neck, you do.

1902. *Pall Mall Gaz.*, 8 Mar., 10, 1. It required considerable craning and stretching, or, as the Americans pithily describe it, RUBBER-NECKING, to allow even an occasional glimpse.

RUBBISH, *subs.* (old). — Money: generic: *see* RHINO.

1821. EGAN, *Real Life*, I. 142. She shall stump up the RUBBISH before I leave her.

RUBICON, *subs.* (gaming).—Used as in quot.

1896. FARJEON, *Betray. John Fordham*, III. 288. "RUBICON'D agin!" cried Maxwell with a oath, dashin' 'is fist on the table. *Ibid.*, 292. Eight fifty. Double the stake if you like. Thirteen 'underd. Another RUBICON . . . Luck wos agin me last night; looks as if it wos turning.

RUBIGO, *subs.* (old Scots').—The *penis*: *see* PRICK.

*c.*1584. R. SEMPILL, *Leg. of the Bischop, &c.* His RUBIGO began to ryiss.

RUBRIC. IN (or OUT OF) THE RUBRIC, *phr.* (old).—In (or out of) holy orders.

1699. FARQUHAR, *Constant Couple*, i. 1. Who would have thought to find thee OUT OF THE RUBRIC so long? I thought thy hypocrisy had been wedded to a pulpit cushion long ago.

RUB-RUB, *phr.* (old).—'Us'd on Greens when the Bowl Flees too fast, to have it forbear, if Words wou'd do it.'—B. E. (*c.*1696).

RUBY, *subs.* (colloquial).—1. Blood; CLARET (*q.v.*). Hence RUBY-FACE = 'a very red face' (B. E., GROSE); whence (2) RUBY = a GROG-BLOSSOM (*q.v.*).

*c.*16[?]. *Rox. Ballads* [Brit. Mus., C 20, f. 7, 214], 'The Little Barly-Corne,' II. It will inrich the palest face, and with RUBIES it adorne.

1839. AINSWORTH, *Jack Sheppard*, II. v. Jolly nose, the bright RUBIES that garnish thy tip.

1860. *Chambers' Journal*, xiii. 348. The fluid of which Harvey demonstrated the circulation in the human body, he speaks of as 'claret,' or 'carmine,' or RUBY,

1886-9. MARSHALL ['*Pomes*,' 49], *Honest Bill.* You'd be sure to nark the RUBY round his gilt.

1888. *Sporting Life*, 11 Dec. Saunders stopped a flush right-hander with his organ of smell, the RUBY duly making its appearance.

RUCK, *subs.* (colloquial).—1. The mob (B. E., *c.*1696); whence (2) = rubbish. Hence TO COME IN WITH THE RUCK (or TO RUCK IN) = to come in unnoticed, or (racing) unplaced.

1846. *Punch*, xi. 15. Who floored Sir Robin? . . . Who headed the RUCK? "I," said Lord George so able, Racy speech and mind stable, "And I headed the RUCK."

1857. HOLMES, *Autocrat of the Breakfast Table*, iv. First turn in the race . . . Several shew in advance of the RUCK.

1864. *Derby Day*, 18. It will be unpleasant for me if Ascapart is in the RUCK.

1874. COLLINS, *Frances*, xxiii. I don't care for Americans myself, men or women . . . the RUCK want educating.

1879. *Scrib. Mag.*, VIII. 159. He's stuck up and citified, and wears gloves . . . and all that sort of RUCK [*Century*].

1893. MILLIKEN, *'Arry Ballads*, 75. A Missus with money, and RUCKS IN along o' the rest.

*d.*1893. BAKER, *Heart of Africa*, 112. I soon found myself in the RUCK of men, horses, and drawn swords.

Verb. (common).—1. To inform; TO SPLIT (*q.v.*); (2) = to turn RUSTY (*q.v.*); and (3) to drag or crease.

1884. *D. News*, 20 Sept., 2, 2. I told the prisoner that I was not going to RUCK ON an old pal.

1889. *Answers*, 13 Ap., 313. To such of their own fraternity who RUCK or "blab" upon them, they most certainly entertain feelings of the deepest hatred.

1893. MILLIKEN, *'Arry Ballads*, 71. Mine RUCKED when I turned up in trousers in checks.

1894. EGERTON, *Keynotes*, 177. They [trousers] RUCK UP at the knees.

TO RUCK (or RUCKET) ALONG, *verb. phr.* (Oxford University).—To walk quickly.

RUCTION, *subs.* (common).—An uproar.—HALLIWELL (1847).

1833. NEAL, *Down-Easters*, II. 14. Ryled, all over, inside and out—Ryled—RUCTIONS.

1884. *Echo*, 19 March, 2, 3. The police, when there is a RUCTION, drop quietly over a wall into the midst of the combatants.

1894. *Sheffield Daily Telegraph*, 29 Mar., 4, 7. The RUCTIONS at the Freeman meeting yesterday.

1900. WHITE, *West End*, 124. RUCTIONS took place . . . and . . . he went so far as to tell his wife that "he didn't care a damn what she did."

RUDDER, *subs.* (venery). — The *penis*: *see* PRICK. Also (Somerset) = copulation.

*d.*1638. CAREW, *Rapture.* My RUDDER with thy bold hand . . . thou shalt steer and guide . . . into Love's channel.

1760. ROBERTSON of Struan, *Poems*, 95. Sure Venus never can be tir'd While pow'rful Mars directs the RUDDER.

RUDDOCKS (or **RED**, or **GOLDEN**, **RUDDOCKS**), *subs.* (old).—Money: specifically gold: also RUDDY. [Formerly gold was conventionally "red" ('a girdle of gold so red' and 'good red gold'—*Percy Rel.*).] *Cf.* RIDGE and REDGE.

1570. TURBERVILLE [CHALMER'S, *Poets*, ii. 647]. The greedie carle came . . . and saw the pot behind Where RUDDOCKS lay, but RUDDOCKS could not find.

1585. *Choise of Change* [*Cens. Literaria*, ix. 435]. He must have his RED RUDDOCKES ready.

1598. FLORIO, *Worlde of Wordes*, s.v. *Zanfrone.* Used also for crownes, great pieces of gold, as our countrymen say RED-RUDDOCKES.

1600. MUNDAY and DRAYTON, *Oldcastle*, i. 2. My fingers' end do itch To be upon those golden RUDDOCKS.

1607. HEYWOOD, *Fair Maid* [*Works*, II. 277]. I believe they be little better than pirates, they are so flush of their RUDOCKS.

RUDESBY, *subs.* (old colloquial).—A rude boisterous person. [JOHNSON (1745) 'a low word.'] *Cf.* SNEAKSBY, IDLESBIE, WIGSBY, &c.

1593. SHAKSPEARE, *Taming of the Shrew*, iii. 2. A mad-brain RUDESBY, full of spleen. *Ibid.* (1602), *Twelfth Night*, iv. 1. Be not offended, dear Cesario,—RUDESBY, begone.

RUDGE-GOWN, *subs.* (old). — An outcast: also RUG-GOWN. Whence RUG-GOWNED = meanly; RUG-HEADED = shock-headed.

1597. SHAKSPEARE, *Richard II.*, ii. 1, 156. We must supplant these rough RUG-HEADED kerns.

1622. FLETCHER and MASSINGER, *Prophetess*, ii. 2. I had rather meet An enemy in the field than stand thus nodding Like to a RUG-GOUNED watchman.

1654. *Witt's Recr.* [NARES]. A RUDG-GOWNS ribs are good to spur a horse.

RUE, *subs.* (colloquial).—Repentance: as RUE-QUARREL, *verb.* = to repent and withdraw; RUE-BARGAIN = smart-money.

1827. SCOTT, *Rob Roy*, xxvii. He said it would cost him a guinea of RUE-BARGAIN to the man who had bought his pony before he could get it back again.

*c.*1852. *Traits of Amer. Humour*, I. 226. I'm for no RUES and after-claps.

RUFF, *subs.* (old). — 'An old-fashioned double band.'—B. E. (*c.*1696).

2. (old).—A court card: hence TO RUFF = to trump. [RUFF = a game similar to whist, 'in which the greatest sorte of sute carrieth away the game.'—PEELE, I, 211, note.] *See* TRUMP.

1593. FLORIO, *Worlde of Wordes*, s.v. *Ronfar.* A game at cardes called RUFFE or trump.

1611. COTGRAVE, *Dict.*, s.v. *Ronfle.* Hand-RUFF at cards.

1837. DICKENS, *Pickwick*, xxxv. Miss Bolo would inquire . . . why Mr. Pickwick had . . . RUFFED the spade, or finessed the heart.

3. (old).—*See* quots.

1592. HARVEY, *Four Letters.* He . . . in the RUFF of his greatest jollity was fain to cry M. Churchyard a mercy to print.

1610. *Mirr. Mag.*, 607. In the RUFFE of his felicitie . . . he began disdaine His bastard lord's usurp'd authority.

4. (racing).—RUFF'S *Guide to the Turf.*

THE WOODEN RUFF, *subs. phr.* (old).—The pillory.

RUFFIAN, *subs.* (old).—1. Spec. the Devil: also OLD RUFFIAN. Whence (2) anyone behaving roughly or severely: as a magistrate, and esp. a pimp (*see* PONCE) or bawdy-house bully, 'a brutal bully or assassin' (B. E., ROWLANDS, COLES, GROSE), also a pugilist all spirit and no science; and so forth. Hence as *adj.* = (1) wanton (GROSE); (2) = brutal; and (3) = violent. As *verb.* = (1) to pimp, (2) to bully, and (3) to maul. Also RUFFIANLY (or RUFFINOUS) = wanton, outrageous. 'RUFFIAN cook RUFFIAN, he scalded the devil in his feathers' (GROSE), said of a bad cook. RUFFIAN'S-HALL (*see* quot. 1679). *Cf.* ROUGH.

*c.*1450. *York Plays* [Shakspeare Soc.], i. 17. [OLIPHANT, *New Eng.*, i. 288. The Devil is spoken of as RUFFYNE, which perhaps led to our RUFFIAN.]

*d.*1556. UDALL [RICHARDSON]. Repent of light RUFFIANYNG and blasphemous carnal gospelling.

1567. HARMAN, *Caveat*, 86. Gerry gan, the RUFFIAN clye thee. A torde in thy mouth, the deuyll take thee.

1593. HARVEY, *Four Letters* [*Century*]. RUFFIANLY hair, unseemly apparel, and more unseemly company.

1593. SHAKSPEARE, *Com. Errors*, ii. 2, 135. That this body, consecrate to thee, By RUFFIAN lust should be contaminate. *Ibid.* (1598), *2 Hen. IV.*, iii. 1, 22. The winds, Who take the RUFFIAN billows by the top. *Ibid.*, iv. 5, 125. Have you a RUFFIAN that will swear, drink, dance, Revel in the night? *Ibid.* (1602). If it hath RUFFIAN'D so upon the sea, What ribs of oak . . . can hold the mortice?

1598. FLORIO, *Worlde of Wordes*, s.v. *Ruffiano*, a RUFFIN, a swagrer, a swashbuckler. *Ibid.*, *Ruffo*, a RUFIAN, a ruffling roister; . . . also rude, RUFFE, or rough.

1603. CHAPMAN, *Iliad*, vi. 456. To shelter the sad monument from all the RUFFINOUS pride Of storms and tempests.

1609. DEKKER, *Lanthorne and Candlelight* [GROSART, *Wks.* (1886), iii. 203]. The RUFFIN cly the nab of the Harman beck.

1622. FLETCHER, *Beggar's Bush*, 'Maunder's Initiation.' Strine and trine to the RUFFIN (justice of peace).

1657. SMITH, *Sermons*, 208. She could not mince finer . . . nor carry more trappings about her, than our RUFFIANS and wantons do at this day.

*d.*1679. BLOUNT [HALLIWELL]. RUFFIANS HALL.—So that part of Smithfield was antiently called, which is now the horse-market, where tryals of skill were plaid by ordinary RUFFIANLY people with sword and buckler.

1819. MOORE, *Tom Crib*, 57. Hammering right and left with ponderous swing, RUFFIAN'D the reeling youngster round the ring.

1834. AINSWORTH, *Rookwood*, III. ii. 'Not now, in the devil's name!' said Turpin, stamping impatiently. 'We shall have OLD RUFFIN himself amongst us presently, if Peter Bradley grows gallant.'

RUFFLE, *subs.* (Old Cant). — A handcuff: usually in *pl.* (GROSE, VAUX).

1826. *Old Song*, 'Bobby and His Mary' [*Univ. Songst.*, iii. 108]. And RUFFLES soon they popped on.

1839. AINSWORTH, *Jack Sheppard*, II. ix. 'I'll accommodate you with a pair of RUFFLES,' and he proceeded to handcuff his captive.

THE RUFFLE, *subs. phr.* (conjurors').—The flourish to a trick at cards: the deck held firmly at the lower end by the left hand is rapidly manipulated by the right hand with a crackling noise.

See RUFFLER.

RUFFLER (RUFFLE, or RUFFLING ROISTER), *subs.* (old).—1. Spec. as in quot. 1565 (in Statue 27 Hen. VIII. = a sham soldier or sailor): whence (2) a bully, cheat, or violent or swaggering blackguard (AWDELEY, HARMAN, B. E., COLES, GROSE). RUFFLE (also RUFFLER), *verb.* = (1) to plunder, to rob: spec. with menaces and imprecations; and (2) to swagger, flaunt it, put on SIDE (*q.v.*) or be turbulent; RUFFLERY = violence; RUFFERED = boisterous; and RUFFLE = to dispute.

*c.*1537-50. *Old Poem* [OLIPHANT, *New Eng.*, i. 512. There are the Dutch words RUFFLE (brag), and *trick up* (ornare).]

1565. HARMAN, *Caveat*, 29. Now these RUFFLARS, the out castes of seruing men, when begginge or crauinge fayles, then they pycke and pylfer, from other inferiour beggeres that they méete by the waye, as Roages, Pallyardes, Mortes, and Doxes. *Ibid.* A RUFFLAR . . . wretchedly wanders aboute the most shyres of this realme; and with stoute audacyte demaundeth where he thinketh he may be bolde, and circomspecte ynough as he sethe cause to aske charitie.

1579. *Mariage of Witt and Wisdome.* My man Lobb Is become a jolly RUFFLER.

1582. STANIHURST, *Æneid*, iii. But neere ioynctlye brayeth with RUFFLERYE rumboled Ætna.

1593. SHAKSPEARE, *Titus And.*, i. 2. One fit to bandy with thy lawless sons, And RUFFLE in the Commonwealth of Rome. *Ibid.* (1605), *King Lear*, iii. 7. I am your host, With robber's hands, my hospitable favours You should not RUFFLE thus. *Ibid.* (1609), *Lover's Compl.* Sometime a blusterer, that the RUFFLE knew Of court and city.

1598. FLORIO, *Worlde of Wordes*, s.v. *Ruffo* . . . Also a RUFFLING ROISTER or ruffian, a swaggrer.

1600. JONSON, *Cynthia's Revels*, iii. 3. Lady, I cannot RUFFLE IT in red and yellow.

1610. *Mirr. for Mag.*, 473. And what the RUFFLER spake, the lout took for a verdite, For there the best was worst, worst best regarded. *Ibid.*, 165. To Britain over seas from Rome went I, To quaile the Picts, that RUFFLED in that ile.

1611. MIDDLETON, *Roaring Girl* [DODSLEY, *Old Plays* (REED), vi. 108]. Brother to this upright man, flesh and blood, RUFFLING Tear-cat is my name; and a RUFFLER is my stile, my title, my profession.

1614. FLETCHER, *Wit without Money*, v. 3. Can I not go about . . . But such companions as you must RUFFLE me.

1641. MILTON, *Ref. in Eng.*, i. Revil'd and RUFFL'D by an insulting . . . Prelate.

1712. STEELE, *Spectator*, 132. Our company was so far from being soured by this little RUFFLE that Ephraim and he took particular delight in being agreeable to each other for the future.

1818. SCOTT, *Midlothian*, xxv. A gude fellow that has been but a twelvemonth on the lay, be he RUFFLER or padder. *Ibid.* (1821), *Kenilworth*, xiii. He looked like a gay RUFFLING servingman.

1830. LYTTON, *Paul Clifford*, xvi. Oh, what a beast is a niggardly RUFFLER, Nabbing—grabbing all for himself.

1890. *Answers*, 27 Dec. In this fashion I RUFFLED like a prince for six years on a regular income of nothing per annum.

RUFFMANS, *subs.* (Old Cant).—A hedge: *cf.* quot. 1610 (HARMAN, B. E., HALL, GROSE).

1565. HARMAN, *Caveat*, 86. We wyll fylche some duddes of the RUFFEMANS.

1608. DEKKER, *The Beggars' Curse* [GROSART, *Works*, iii. 203]. If we mawnd Pannam, lap, or Ruff-peck, Or poplars of yarum: he cuts, bing to the RUFFMANS. *Ibid.* (1612), *O, per se O* [FARMER, *Musa Pedestris* (1896), 12]. We did creepe, and plant in RUFFE-MANS low.

1610. ROWLANDS, *Martin Mark-all*, 40 (H. Club, 1874). RUFFMANS, not the hedge or bushes as heretofore: but now the eauesing of houses or roofes: *Cragmans* is now vsed for the hedge.

1611. MIDDLETON and DEKKER, *Roaring Girl*, v. 1. I woud lib all the lightmans . . . under the RUFFEMANS.

1622. FLETCHER, *Beggar's Bush*, iii. 3. To mill from the RUFFMANS commissions and slates.

RUFF-PECK, *subs. phr.* (Old Cant). —Bacon. — HARMAN (1567); ROWLANDS (1610); HEAD (1665); B. E. (*c.*1696); COLES (1724).

1608. DEKKER, *The Beggars' Curse* [GROSART, *Works*, iii. 203]. If we maund Pannam, lap, or RUFF-PECK.

1641. BROME, *Jovial Crew*, 'The Merry Beggars.' Here's RUFFPECK and Casson, and all of the best.

1707. SHIRLEY, *Triumph of Wit*, 'Rum-Mort's Faithless Maunder.' RUFF-PECK still hung on my back.

RUFTY-TUFTY, *adj.* and *adv.* (old). —Rough; boisterous; indecent. Also as *intj.* = hey-day.

1592. BRETON, *Pilgrimage to Paradise*, 16. To sweare and stare until we come to shore, then RIFTY-TUFTY each one to his skore.

1606. CHAPMAN, *Gentleman Usher*, v. 1. Were I as Vince is, I would handle you In RUFTY-TUFTY wise.

1606. *Wily Beguiled* [HAWKINS, *Eng. Drama*, iii. 302]. RUFTY, TUFTY, are you so frolick?

*d.*1821. KEATS, *Cap and Bells*, 86. RUFFY-TUFFY heads Of cinder wenches meet and soil each other.

RUFUS, *subs.* (venery).—The female *pudendum*: *see* MONOSYLLABLE.

RUG, *subs.* (Rugby School).—A Rugbeian.

1892. *Evening Standard*, 25 Nov., 4, 5. The controversy was started by the death of one who succumbed to his exertions. "An Old Medical RUG" describes the sufferings he endured.

2. (old).—A sort of drink.

1653. TAYLOR, *Certaine Travailes*, *&c.* And . . . of all drinks potable, RUG is most puisant, potent, notable.

3. (old).—A tug. Whence as *verb.* = to pull roughly; TO GET A RUG = to get a share; to get THERE (*q.v.*).

13[?]. *York Plays*, 286. No ruthe were it to RUG the and ryue the in ropes.

1734. POPE, *Donne*, iv. 134. He knows . . . who GOT his pension RUG.

1814. SCOTT, *Waverley*, xlii. The gude auld times of RUGGING and riving . . . are come back again. *Ibid.* (1824), *Redgauntlet*, xi. Sir John . . . voted for the Union, having GOTTEN it was thought, A RUG OF the compensations.

ALL RUG, *phr.* (Old Cant).— All right; certain (B. E., GROSE).

1714. LUCAS, *Gamesters*, 104. His great dexterity of making ALL RUGG at Dice, as the Cant is for securing a Die between two fingers.

See BUG and RUGGINS.

RUGE. *See* ROUGE.

RUGGER, *subs.* (schools').—Football: the Rugby game.

1902. *Pall Mall Gaz.*, 2 Jan., 9, 2. The article which, so far as figures go, proves to the hilt England's degeneracy at RUGGER, and most lucidly gives the reason why.

RUGGIN'S, *subs.* (Old Cant).—Bed; AT RUG = asleep: *e.g.*, 'the whole gill is safe AT RUG' = 'the household are asleep' (GROSE).

1828. LYTTON, *Pelham*, lxxxii. Stash the lush . . . ay, and toddle off to RUGGINS.

RUIN. *See* BLUE RUIN.

RULE. TO RUN THE RULE OVER, *verb. phr.* (thieves').—*See* quot; TO FRISK (*q.v.*).

1879. J. W. HORSLEY [*Macm. Mag.*, xl. 504]. I am going to RUN THE RULE OVER (search) you.

1886. *D. News*, 30 Sept., iii. 2. When paraded each man has THE RULE RUN OVER HIM, *i.e.*, searched.

1886-96. MARSHALL, *He Slumbered* ['Pomes,' 118]. A lady . . . RAN THE RULE through all His pockets for her cheek was fairly tall.

RULE-OF-THREE (THE), *subs. phr.* (venery).—1. The *penis* and *testes*; and (2) copulation: *cf.* ADDITION, MULTIPLICATION, and SUBTRACTION.

*c.*1720. DURFEY, *Pills, &c.*, vi. 329. This accountant will come without e'er a Fee, And warrants a Boy by his RULE OF THREE.

RULE OF THUMB, *subs. phr.* (colloquial). — A rough-and-ready way: practical rather than exactly scientific (GROSE).

1809. SYDNEY SMITH, *To Francis Jeffrey*, 3 Sep. We'll settle men and things by RULE OF THUMB.

1864. *D. Review*, 17 Oct. The result, we trust, will exemplify the value of Science *versus* RULE OF THUMB in politics.

RUM (ROME, ROOME, or RAM), *adj.* (Old Cant).—1. A generic appreciative; good; fine; clever; excellent; strong, &c.: *cf.* sense 2 and QUEER; RUMLY = bravely, cleverly, delicately. Thus RUM-BEAK (or -BECK) = a Justice of the Peace; RUM-BING (or -BUNG) = a full purse; RUM-BIT (or -BITE) = (1) a clever rogue, and (2) a smart trick; RUM BLEATING-CHEAT = a fat wether; RUM-BLOWEN (or -BLOWER) = a handsome mistress; RUM-BLUFFER = a jolly host; RUM-BOB = (1) a young apprentice, (2) a clever trick, and (3) a smart wig; RUM-BOOZE (-BOUSE, -BUSE, -BUZE, or BOUZE) = (1) wine, or (2) good liquor of divers kinds; RUM-BOOZING-WELT = a bunch of grapes; RUM-BUBBER = a good thief; RUM-BUFFER (or -BUGHER) = a valuable dog; RUM-CHANT = a good song; RUM-CHUB = (butchers') an ignorant buyer; RUM-CLANK = a gold or silver cup; RUM-CLOUT (or WIPE) = a silk handkerchief; RUM-COD = (1) a full purse, and (2) a large sum of money; RUM-COLE = new money; RUM-COVE (or -CULL) = (1) a clever rogue, (2) a rich man, (3) a lover, and (4) an intimate: also RUM-CULL (theatrical) = a manager, or boss; RUM-DEGEN (-TOL, or -TILTER) = a splendid sword; RUM-DELL (-DOXY or -MORT) = a handsome whore; RUM-DIVER = a clever pickpocket; RUM-DRAWERS = silk stockings; RUM-DROPPER = a vintner; RUM-DUKE = (1) a handsome man, (2) a jolly companion, and (3) *see* quot. 1696 and also sense 2; RUM-DUCHESS = a handsome woman; RUM-DUBBER (or -FILE) = an expert picklock; RUM-FAM (or FEM) = a diamond ring; RUM-FUN = a clever fraud; RUM-GELT (or -GILT) = new money; RUM-GILL = (1) a clever thief, and (2) a handsome man; RUM-GAGGER = a whining beggar; RUM-GLYMMER = a chief link-boy; RUM-GOING = fast trotting; RUM-GUTLERS = canary; RUM-HOPPER = an innkeeper; RUM-KICKS = silver or gold-braided breeches; RUM-KEN = a popular inn or brothel; RUM-KIN = a large mug; RUM-MAUNDER = a clever beggar; RUM-MIZZLER = a thief expert at CLEARING (*q.v.*); RUM-MORT = a lady; RUM-ONE = a settling blow; RUM-NAB = a good hat; RUM-NANTZ = brandy; RUM NED = a rich fool; RUM-PAD = the highway; RUM-PADDER = a highwayman; RUM-PEEPER = a silver looking-glass; RUM-PECK = good food; RUM-

PRANCER = a fine horse; RUM-QUIDDS = a large booty; RUM-RUFFPECK = Westphalian ham; RUM-SQUEEZE = fiddlers' drink in plenty; RUM-SNITCH = a hard blow on the nose; RUM-TOPPING = a rich head-dress; RUM-VILLE = London.—AWDELEY (1560); HARMAN (1567); ROWLANDS (1610); HEAD (1665); B. E. (*c*.1696); COLES (1724); BAILEY (1726); PARKER (1781); GROSE (1785); VAUX (1812); BEE (1823).

1567. HARMAN, *Caveat*, 86. Byng we to ROME-VYLE.

1607. DEKKER, *Jests to make you Merie* in *Wks.* (GROSART), II. 308. A RUM COVES BUNG (so called in their canting vse of speech) (and as much as to say in ours, a rich chuffes purse).

1610. ROWLANDS, *Martin Mark-All*, 'Toure Out Ben Morts.' For all the ROME COUES are budgd a beake. *Ibid.* The quire coves are budgd to the bowsing ken As ROMELY as a ball.

1611. MIDDLETON and DEKKER, *Roaring Girl*, v. I. So my bousy nab might skew ROME BOUSE.

1612. DEKKER, *O per se O*, 'Bing Out, Bien Morts.' On chates to trine, by ROME-COUES dine for his long lib at last. *Ibid.* Bingd out bien morts, and toure, and toure, bing out of the ROME-VILE; . . . And Jybe well Ierkt, tick ROME-COMFECK.

1641. BROME, *Jovial Crew*, 'Morts' Drinking Song.' This bowse is better than ROM-BOWSE.

1653. URQUHART, *Rabelais*, II. i. Note. *Piot* a common cant word used by French clowns and other tippling companions; it signifies RUM-BOOZE as our gypsies call good-guzzle.

1656. BLOUNT, *Gloss.*, 538. RAMBUZE. A compound drink at Cambridge, and is commonly made of eggs, ale, wine, and sugar; but in summer, of milk, wine, sugar, and rose-water.

1664. COTTON, *Virgil Travestie* (1st ed.), 108. With that she set it to her Nose, And off at once the RUMKIN goes.

1665. HEAD, *Eng. Rogue* [RIBTON-TURNER, 621]. We straight took ourselves to the Boozing ken; and having bubb'd RUMLY, we concluded an everlasting friendship.

1688. SHADWELL, *Sq. of Alsatia*, ii. [*Works* (1720), iv. 47]. *Belf. Sen.* . . . Here's a nabb! you never saw such a one in your life. *Cheat.* A RUM NABB: it is a beaver of £5.

c.1696. B. E., *Dict. Cant. Crew*, *passim*. Also, more particularly, s.v. RUM-DUKES, c. the boldest or stoutest Fellows (lately) amongst the *Alsatians, Minters, Savoyards, &c.* Sent for to remove and guard the Goods of such Bankrupts as intended to take Sanctuary in those Places. *Ibid.*, s.v. PECK. The Gentry Cove tipt us RUM PECK and rum Gutlers, till we were all Bowsy, and snapt all the Flickers.

1706. FARQUHAR, *Recruiting Officer*, ii. 3. You are a justice of peace, and you are a king, and I am a duke, and a RUM DUKE, a'n't I?

1707. SHIRLEY, *Triumph of Wit*, 'Rum-Mort's Praise of Her Faithless Maunder.' By the RUM-PAD maundeth none, . . . Like my clapper-dogeon.

1724. HARPER, in *Harlequin Sheppard*, 'Frisky Moll's Song.' I Frisky Moll, with my RUM COLL.

1760. *Old Song*, 'Come All You Buffers Gay' [*The Humourist*, 2]. Come all you buffers gay, That RUMLY do pad the city. *Ibid.* If after a RUM CULL you pad.

1781. PARKER, *View of Society*, II. 174. RUM-MIZZLERS. Fellows who are clever in making their escape. *Ibid.* (*b*.1789), *Cantata*, 'The Sandman's Wedding.' For he's the kiddy RUM and queer.

1819. MOORE, *Tom Crib*, 76. The brandy and tea, rather thinnish, That knights of the RUMPAD so rurally sip. *Ibid.* Thus RUMLY floored.

c.1819. *Song*, 'The Young Prig' [FARMER, *Musa Pedestris* (1896), 83. But my RUM-CHANTS ne'er fail, sirs; The dubsman's senses to engage.

1821. EGAN, *Life in London*, II. iii. From a RUM KEN we bundled.

1823. MONCRIEFF, *Tom and Jerry*, ii. 6. Now, your honours, here's the RUM PECK, here's the supper.

1825. JONES, *Old Song*, 'The True Bottom'd Boxer' [*Univ. Songst.*, ii. 96]. Spring's the boy for RUM GOING and coming it. *Ibid.* You'll find him a RUM-'UN, try on if you can.

1830. MONCRIEFF, *Heart of London*, ii. I. We frisk so RUMMY. *Ibid.* We chaunt so RUMMY. *Ibid.*, i. 2. Good night, my RUM-'UNS. *Ibid.*, i. I. RUMMY Spitalfields wipes.

1834. AINSWORTH, *Rookwood* (1864), 180. RUM GILLS and Queer Gills, Patricos, Palliards, &c. *Ibid.*, 60. With them the best RUMPADS of England are not to be named the same day! *Ibid.*, 199. I want a little ready cash in RUMVILLE—beg pardon, ma'am, London I mean. *Ibid.*, 190. I know you can throw off a RUM CHANT . . . I heard you sing last night at the hall.

1844. SELBY, *London by Night*, i. 2. What's in the wind, my RUM CULL.

1851-61. MAYHEW, *Lond. Lab.*, I. 341. Not one swell in a score would view it in any light than a REAM concern.

1886. STEPHENS and YARDLEY, *Little Jack Sheppard*, 37. Farewell to Old England for ever, Farewell to my RUM CULLS as well.

2. (common).—In modern slang (by inversion) RUM = indifferent; bad; questionable; odd: as *adj.* RUMMY (or RUMLY). Whence (3) RUM = anybody or anything odd or singular in habit, appearance, &c.; RUM-NED = a silly fellow (B. E.); RUM DUKE = a half-witted churl (but *see* sense I); TO COME IT RUM = to act (or talk) strangely.

1729. SWIFT, *Grand Question Debated*. A rabble of tenants and rusty dull RUMS.

1772. BRIDGES, *Burlesque Homer*, 155. Well said, Ulysses, cries the king (A little touch'd tho' with the sting Of this RUM speech).

17 [?]. *Old Song* [*N. & Q.*, 7 S., ix. 97. Although a RUMMY codger, Now list to what I say.

1781. PARKER, *View of Society*, I. 48. 'Blow me up (says he) if I have had a fellow with such RUM TOGGYS cross my company these many a day.'

1803. SHARPE [*Correspondence* (1888), i. 18]. They were angry with RUMS, they were troubl'd with bores.

1812-15. NICHOLS, *Lit. Anec.*, v. 471. The books which booksellers call RUMS appear to be very nnmerous, . . . yet they are not really so.

1819. MOORE, *Tom Crib*, 'Jack Holmes's Song.' Some wonder, too, the tits that pull This RUM concern along, so full.

1829. SOMERSET, *Day After the Fair*. Well, dang it! though she's a RUM one to look at, she's a good one to go.

1836. DICKENS, *Pickwick*, xvi. "You're a RUM 'un to look at, you are," thought Mr. Weller.

1840. BARHAM, *Ingoldsby Legends* (*Hamilton Tighe*). And the neighbours say, as they see him look sick, "What a RUM old covey, is Hairy-faced Dick!"

1877. BESANT and RICE, *Son of Vulcan*, II. xxvii. How much? It's a RUMMY ramp—but how much?

1882. ANSTEY, *Vice-Versa*, xi. There's young Tom on the box; don't his ears stick out RUMMILY?

1888. BOLDREWOOD, *Robbery Under Arms*, i. What a RUM thing a man should laugh when he's only got twenty-nine days more to live.

1892. KIPLING, *Barrack Room Ballads*, 'Route Marchin'.' There's that RUMMY silver grass.

1899. WHITEING, *John St.*, v. RUMMY lot dahn there.

RUMBLE, *subs.* (colloquial).—A seat for servants at the back of a carriage: also RUMBLE-TUMBLE (which likewise [GROSE and VAUX]) = a stage coach. *See* DICKEY and quot. 1830.

1830. LYTTON, *Paul Clifford*, xxv. His favourite servant sat in the dickey in front (RUMBLE-TUMBLES not being then in use). *Ibid.* (1858), *What Will He Do, &c.*, I. 15. From the dusty height of a RUMBLE-TUMBLE . . . Vance caught sight of Lionel and Sophy.

1848. THACKERAY, *Vanity Fair*, xiv. A discontented female in a green veil and crimped curls on the RUMBLE.

Verb. (old).—To try; to search; to handle.

1821. HAGGART, *Life*, 14. I was RUMBLING the cloys of the twigs.

1886-96. MARSHALL, *Beautiful Dreamer* ['Pomes,' 65]. I RUMBLED the tip as a matter of course.

1898. *Pink 'Un and Pelican*, 209. I soon RUMBLED he was in it when I heard Bull givin' him the 'me lord' for it.

RUMBLER, *subs.* (old).—A hackney coach. Hence RUMBLER'S-FLUNKEY = (1) a footman and (2) a cab-runner; RUNNING-RUMBLER = a carriage thief's confederate.

c.1816. MAHER, *Song*, 'The Night Before Larry was Stretched.' The RUMBLER jugg'd off from his feet, And he died with his face to the city.

c.1819. *Old Song*, 'The Young Prig' [FARMER, *Musa Pedestris* (1896), 82]. I first held horses in the street, But being found defaulter, Turned RUMBLER'S FLUNKEY for my meat.

1823. MONCRIEFF, *Tom and Jerry*, ii. 4. A rattler . . . is a RUMBLER, otherwise a jarvey, better known, perhaps, by the name of a rack.

RUMBLING, *subs.* (Old Cant: now recognised).—'The rolling of Thunder, motion of a Wheel-barrow, or the noise in the Gutts.'—B. E. (*c*.1696).

RUM-BLOSSOM (or **-BUD**), *subs. phr.* (common).—A nasal pimple: *cf.* GROG-BLOSSOM.

1889. BUSH, *Effects of Ardent Spirits*. Redness and eruptions generally begin with the nose . . . they have been called RUM-BUDS, when they appear in the face.

RUMBO, *subs.*—I. Rum grog: also RUMBULLION and RUMBOWLING: *cf.* RUM-BOOZE (GROSE).

1651. *MS. Descrip. oj Barbadoes* [*Academy*, 5 Sep., 1885, 155]. The chief fudling they make in the island is RUMBULLION, alias Kill-Divil, and this is made of sugar canes distilled.

1751. SMOLLETT, *Per. Pickle*, ii. He and my good master . . . come hither every evening, and drink a couple of cans of RUMBO a-piece. *Ibid.* (1762), *Sir L. Greaves*, I. i. Three of the travellers . . . agreed to pass the time . . . over a bowl of RUMBO.

1821. SCOTT, *Pirate*, xxxix. Regaling themselves with a can of RUMBO.

1885. *D. News*, 12 August, 5, 2. When sailors speak of their grog as RUM BOWLING the expression is really a survival of the old word [*i.e.*, RUMBULLION, supposed to be the original name of "Rum," and of which the tatler is a corruption].

2. (old).—A prison: also RUMBO-KEN.

3. (dockyard).—Stolen rope (CLARK RUSSELL).

Adj. (old).—Good; plenty.

1870. HAZLEWOOD and WILLIAMS, *Leave it to Me*, i. Fifty pounds! Oh, what a coal and tater shop I will have. . . . Is that RUMBO? (*holds out his hand*).

1876. HINDLEY, *Cheap Jack*, 192. Mo exclaimed to his man, 'Chuck RUMBO (eat plenty), my lad.'

1895. *Pall Mall Gaz.*, 21 Dec., 8, I. But if the carts are all RUMBO, and the 'orses was all RUMBO, and there was no tickets and no jumpers.

RUMBO-KEN, *subs. phr.* (old).—I. A pawnbroker's shop.

2. (old).—A prison: also RUMBO.

1724. HARPER [*Harlequin Sheppard*, 'Frisky Moll's Song']. But filing of a RUMBO KEN, My Boman is snabbled again.

RUMBOWLINE (or **RAMBOWLINE**), *subs.* (nautical).—I. Condemned stores: rope, canvas, &c.; whence (2) anything inferior or deteriorated: as *adj.* = adulterated.

See RUMBO.

RUMBUSTICATE, *verb.* (venery).—To copulate: *see* GREENS and RIDE.

RUMFORD. TO RIDE TO ROMFORD, *verb. phr.* (old).—To get new breeched. [GROSE: 'Rumford was formerly a famous place for leather breeches: a like saying is current of Bungay.'] Also *see* quot.

1708-10. SWIFT, *Pol. Conv.*, ii. One may RIDE TO RUMFORD upon this knife, it is so blunt.

RUM-GAGGER, *subs. phr.* (nautical).—'A sailor who begs' (CLARK RUSSELL).

RUMGUMPTION, **RUMBUMPTION**, &c., *subs.* and *adj.* (common).—A class of colloquialisms compounded with an intensive prefix: (I) RAM (imitatively varied by RUM) = very, strong; and (2) RUM (*q.v.*) = good, fine, &c.: also *cf.* RAMP as in RAMPAGEOUS. Thus RAMBUNCTIOUS (or RAMBUSTIOUS) = noisy, 'high-and-mighty'; RAMBUSTION = a row; RAMBUMPTIOUS = conceited, self-assertive (GROSE); RUMBUMPTION = conceit, cock-sure-ness; RUMGUMPTION = mother-wit; RAMGUMPTIOUS = shrewd, bold, rash (GROSE); RAMFEEZLED = exhausted; RAMBUSKIOUS = rough; RAMGUNSCHOCH = rough; RAMSHACKLE = ricketty, crazy. Substantives are similarly formed: *e.g.*, RAMBUNCTION, RAMBUMPTION, RAMGUMPTION, &c., whilst such variants as RUMMEL-FUMPTION, RUMBLE-GUMPTION, RUMSTRUGENOUS, and the like are coined at will. Also RUMBUSTICATOR = a man of means, and RAMSTAM = a headlong fool, and as *adj.* = deliberately or undilutedly silly.

1768. ROSS, *Helenore*, 'Beattie's Address.' They need not try thy jokes to fathom, They want RUMGUMPTION.

1778. FOOTE, *Trip to Calais*, i. The sea has been rather RUMBUSTIOUS, I own.

d.1796. BURNS, *To James Smith*. The hairum-scairum, RAM-STAM boys.

1817. SCOTT, *Rob Roy*, xxviii. If we gang RAM-STAM in on them [we'll get] a broken head to learn us better havings.

1819. T. MOORE, *Tom Crib's Memorial*, 3. Has thought of a plan, which—excuse his presumption—He hereby submits to your Royal RUMGUMPTION.

1822. HOGG, *Perils of Man*, I. 78. Ye sud hae stayed at hame, an' wantit a wife till ye gathered mair RUMMELGUMPTION.

1823. GALT, *Entail*, III. 70. Wattie is a lad of a methodical nature, and no a hurly-burly RAM-STAM.

1823. LOCKHART, *Reg. Dalton*, I. 199. This will learn you again ye young RAMSHACKLE.

1844. SURTEES, *Hillingdon Hall*, v. 21. The RUMBUSTICAL apologies for great coats that have inundated the town of late years.

1847. PORTER, *Big Bear*, 120. He's as RAMSTUGENOUS an animal as a log-cabin loafer in the dog-days.

1847. G. ELIOT [*Life* (1885), I. 168]. All those monstrous ROMBUSTICAL beasts with their horns.

1847. THACKERAY, *Cane-Bottom'd Chair*, st. 5. And 'tis wonderful, surely, what music you get From the rickety, RAMSHACKLE, wheezy spinet.

1850. SMEDLEY, *Frank Fairlegh*, ix. He boldly inquired whether . . . "I had not been a-enhaling laughing gas, or any sich RUM-BUSTICAL wegitable?"

1853. LYTTON, *My Novel*, XI. xix. As for that white-whiskered alligator . . . let me get out of those RAMBUSTIOUS, unchristian, filbert-shaped claws of his.

1860. DICKENS, *Uncommercial Traveller*, xviii. The RAMSHACKLE vetturino carriage in which I was departing.

1882. *Athenæum*, I Ap. A RAMSHACKLE wagon, rough men, and a rougher landscape.

1883. CLEMENS, *Life on Mississippi*, xlviii. Strung along below the city, were a number of decayed, RAM-SHACKLY, superannuated old steamboats.

RUM-HOLE, *subs. phr.* (American).—A grog-shop: *see* LUSH-CRIB.

RUM-HOMEE (or -OMEE) OF THE CASE. *See* OMER.

RUM-JOHNNY, *subs. phr.* (Anglo-Indian).—I. A native wharf laborer.

2. (naval and military).—A prostitute: *see* TART.

RUMKIN, *subs.* (old).—1. A drinking vessel.

1636. DAVENANT, *The Wits*, iv. 2. Wine ever flowing in large Saxon ROMEKINS About my board.

2. (old).—A tailless fowl.

RUMLY (or **ROMELY**). *See* RUM.

RUMMAGE, *verb.* (venery). — To grope (or possess) a woman; TO FIRKY-TOODLE (*q.v.*).

RUMMY. *See* RUM.

RUM-MILL, *subs. phr.* (American). —A grog-shop; a LUSH-CRIB (*q.v.*).

RUMP, *subs.* (vulgar).—1. The posteriors: *see* BUM. Hence as *verb* = (1) to slight; (2) to FART AT (*q.v.*); (3) to SHIT ON (*q.v.*); (4) to flog (VAUX, 1812), and (5) (venery) to copulate; whence LOOSE IN THE RUMP = wanton; RUMP-SPLITTER = (1) the *penis*: *see* PRICK; and (2) a whoremaster. Also *subs.* (2) = fag end: spec. (political) the remnant of the Long Parliament after Pride's Purge (1653); whence RUMPER = a Long Parliamentarian. Again RUMP (3) = a whore; RUMPER = a whoremaster; RUMP-WORK = copulation; and *verb.* = to possess, to FUCK-BUTTOCK. 'He hath eaten the hen's RUMP' (RAY), said of a person full of talk.

*c.*1635. *Broadside Ballads*, 'Scotch Moggy's Misfortune' [*Pepy's Collect.* (Bodleian), iii. 288]. Robin he chast me about the stack, Robin laid me on my back, Robin be made my RUMP to crack.

1653. URQUHART, *Rabelais*, I. xi. Some of the women would give these names . . . my crimson chitterling, RUMP-SPLITTER, shove-devil.

1660. PEPYS, *Diary*, 7 Mar. Sir Arthur appeared at the House; what was done I know not, but there was all the RUMPERS almost come to the House to-day.

1661. *Old Song*, 'There was three Birds' [FARMER, *Merry Songs and Ballads* (1897), i. 141]. There was three birds that built on a stump, The first and the second cry'd, have at her RUMP, The third he went merrily in and in.

1662. *The Rump* [Title].

1708-10. SWIFT, *Pol. Conv.*, Int. The art of blasphemy or free-thinking . . . first brought in by the fanatic faction . . . and . . . carried to Whitehall by the converted RUMPERS.

1711. DURFEY, *The Fart* [*Pills to Purge* (1719), i. 28]. Gave a proof she was LOOSE IN HER RUMP.

1807. SOUTHEY, *Letters*, iv. 501. An old friend RUMPED him, and he winced under it.

1814. COLEMAN, *Poetical Vagaries*, 129 [2nd ed.]. He RUMPS us quite, and won't salute us.

RUMP-AND-DOZEN, *subs. phr.* (old). —An Irish wager: *i.e.*, 'A rump of beef and a dozen of claret' (GROSE).

RUMP-AND-KIDNEY MEN, *subs. phr.* (old).—'Fidlers that Play at Feasts, Fairs, Weddings, &c., And Live chiefly on the Remnants, or Victuals' (B. E., GROSE).

RUMP-AND-STUMP, *phr.* (colloquial).—Entirely; completely.

RUMPTY, *subs.* (Stock Exchange).— The thirty-second part of a pound sterling; a TOOTH (*q.v.*).

RUMPUS, *subs.* (common).—(1) A row; a noise; a disturbance: also as *verb.* and *adj.* (GROSE); (2) = a masquerade (VAUX, 1812).

1763. FOOTE, *Mayor of Garratt*, ii. 2. Oh Major! such a riot and RUMPUS!

1819. MOORE, *Tom Crib*, 6. And, setting in case there should come such a RUMPUS.

1830. BUCKSTONE, *Wreck Ashore*, i. 2. There never shall be no disgraceful RUMPUSSES, now I'm come into power.

1850. STOWE, *Uncle Tom's Cabin*, xxiv. And Marie routed up Mammy nights, and RUMPUSSED and scolded.

1876. ELIOT, *Daniel Deronda*, xii. She is a young lady with a will of her own, I fancy. Extremely well-fitted to make a RUMPUS.

RUM-SLIM (or **RUM-SLUM**), *subs. phr.* (old).—Punch.

1789. GEO. PARKER, *Life's Painter*, 162. Bobstick of RUM SLIM. That is, a shilling's worth of punch.

1821. EGAN, *Life in London*, I. 131. He was up to the RUM-SLUM.

RUM-SUCKER, *subs. phr.* (American). — A toper; LUSHINGTON (*q.v.*).

1858. *New York Tribune*, 9 July. An acquired appetite as strong as that of a RUM-SUCKER.

RUM TOM PAT, *subs. phr.* (old).— A clergyman.

1781. PARKER, *Variegated Characters.* "What, are Moll and you adamed?" "Yes, we are, and by a RUM TOM PAT too."

RUMTITUM, *adj.* (old).—'On prime twig, in fine order or condition: a flash term for a game bull' (GROSE).

RUM-UN. *See* RUM.

RUN, *subs.* and *verb. phrs.* (colloquial).—Generic for freedom or continuance. Thus (*subs. phrs.*), RUN (OF DICE, CARDS, OR LUCK) = a spell or period of good or bad fortune; RUN (of a play, book, fashion, &c.) = the course of representation, sale, popularity; THE RUN OF THINGS = the state of affairs; THE RUN OF A PLACE = freedom of range; THE RUN OF ONE'S TEETH (or KNIFE AND FORK) = victuals for nothing; A RUN ON A BANK = a steady call, through panic, on its resources; CATTLE-RUN = a farm where cattle roam at will; A RUN TO TOWN (or INTO THE COUNTRY) = a trip; TO HAVE (or LOSE) THE RUN = to lose sight of; TO GET (or HAVE) THE RUN ON = (1) to turn a joke on, and (2) to have the upper hand; TO HAVE A RUN = (1) to take a walk, a CONSTITUTIONAL (*q.v.*); (2) to get an opportunity: *see* P.P.; and (3) to make a fight for anything; TO RUN = to manage; TO RUN A BLUFF = to carry things with a high hand; TO RUN A BUCK (*see* BUCK); TO RUN FOR OFFICE (PARLIAMENT, CONGRESS, &c.) = to start as a candidate; TO RUN A RIG = to play a trick; TO RUN A CHANCE (or RISK) = to take the odds; TO RUN A TILT AT = to attack; TO RUN THE CUTTER = to smuggle; TO RUN AN EYE OVER = (1) to glance at; TO RUN THE GAUNTLET (*see* GAUNTLET); TO RUN ACROSS = to meet casually; TO RUN AFTER = to court; TO RUN AGAINST = (1) to come in collision with, (2) to calumniate, (3) to attack, and (4) to meet casually; TO RUN AMUCK (*see* AMUCK); TO RUN AWAY WITH = (1) to elope, (2) to steal; TO RUN AWAY WITH A NOTION = to be over credulous; TO RUN BIG = to be out of training; TO RUN COUNTER = to oppose; TO RUN DOWN = to pursue, depreciate, attack; TO RUN DRY = to give out; TO RUN FOUL OF = to attack or antagonise; TO RUN HARD = (1) to threaten, endanger, make difficult, and (2) to equal or almost achieve; TO RUN HIGH

= (1) to be violent, (2) to excel in a marked degree; TO RUN IN = (1) to arrest, and (2) to introduce; TO RUN IN ONE'S HEAD = (1) to bear in mind, (2) to remember; TO RUN INTO THE GROUND = to carry to excess; TO RUN IT (American cadets') = to go beyond bounds; TO RUN LIKE MAD = to go at the top of one's speed: Fr. *ventre à terre*; TO RUN LOW = (1) to diminish, (2) to be of little account; TO RUN MAD AFTER = to have a strong desire for; TO RUN OFF = (1) to repeat, (2) to count; TO RUN OFF WITH = (1) to elope, (2) to carry beyond bounds; TO RUN OFF THE STRAIGHT (*see* STRAIGHT); TO RUN ON = to keep going: spec. to chatter; TO RUN ON ALL FOURS (*see* FOURS); TO RUN ON PATTENS (*see* PATTENS); TO RUN ON THE HIRL = to gad, to LOAF (*q.v.*); TO RUN ONE'S FACE (or SHAPE) = to obtain credit; TO RUN ONE'S HEAD INTO A NOOSE = to fall into a snare; TO RUN ONE'S TAIL = to live by prostitution; TO RUN ONE'S WEEK (Am. Univ.) = to trust to chance for success; TO RUN ONE WAY AND LOOK ANOTHER = to play a double game; TO RUN OUT = (1) to end, (2) to have had one's day, (3) to be lavish; TO RUN OUT ON = to enlarge on; TO RUN OVER = (1) to count, (2) to call to mind, (3) to examine, (4) to describe, and (5) to sum up; TO RUN RIOT = (1) to be violent, (2) to exaggerate, (3) to have plenty, (4) to be active, (5) to disobey; TO RUN RUSTY (*see* RUSTY); TO RUN SLY (*see* SLY); TO RUN SMOOTH = to be prosperous; TO RUN THIN = to back out of a bargain; TO RUN TO = (1) to risk, (2) to suffice, (3) to afford; TO RUN TOGETHER = to grow like; TO RUN TO SEED = (1) to age, (2) to deteriorate; TO RUN THROUGH = (1) to be uniform, (2) to pervade, (3) to be present, (4) to kill, and (5) to be prodigal; TO RUN UP = (1) to increase, (2) to build, and (3) *see* RUNNER-UP; TO RUN UP AN ACCOUNT = (1) to get credit, (2) get into debt, and (3) to charge; TO RUN UP BILLS = to obtain goods with no intention of paying; TO RUN UPON = (1) to quiz, (2) to require; TO RUN TO WASTE = (1) to empty, (2) to fritter away; TO RUN WILD = (1) to ROMP (*q.v.*), and (2) to riot; BY (or WITH) A RUN = suddenly; A RUN FOR ONE'S MONEY = a good time in exchange for a certain expenditure of energy and cash; RUN OFF ONE'S LEGS = (1) exhausted, (2) bankrupt; A NEAR RUN = (1) a close finish, (2) a bare escape, (3) cheek by jowl; RUN AFTER = in repute; RUN DOWN = seedy, poor. Also proverbs and sayings, 'To RUN through thick and thin'; 'His shoes are made of RUNNING leather'; 'To RUN a wild-goose chase'; 'The Coaches won't RUN over him' (*i.e.*, 'He's in gaol'); 'He that RUNS may read' (said of things unmistakeably plain); 'To RUN where the devil drives'; 'RUN tap, RUN tapster' (RAY: 'of a tapster that drinks so much himself and is so free to others that he is fain to run away'); 'To hold with the hare and RUN with the hounds' (HEYWOOD, 1546). [Many of these colloquialisms are found *passim* in English literature, and, though fitly mentioned in this place, do not require extended illustration. Therefore, only early or striking quotations are given.]

*d.*1400. CHAUCER, *Rom. of Rose.* [OLIPHANT, *New Eng.*, i. 400. There are . . . RUN DOWN his fame, valour (in the new sense of *worth*) . . .].

*c.*1500. DUNBAR [OLIPHANT, *New Eng.*, i. 363. Among the verbs are RUN DOWN a man, take thy choice . . .].

1577. HARRISON, *Description of England.* [OLIPHANT, *New Eng.*, i. 595. The verb RUN is applied in a new sense; a range of hills RUNS in a certain direction.]

1605. JONSON, *Volpone*, iii. 6. So of the rest till we have quite RUN THROUGH, And wearied all the fables of the gods. *Ibid.* (1601). *Poetaster*, ii. 1. These courtiers RUN IN MY MIND still.

1613. PURCHAS, *Pilgrimage*, 196. And because these praiers are very many, therefore they RUN them OUER.

*c.*1617. HOWELL, *Letters*, I. v. 7. Jack Stanford would have RUN AT him, but was kept off by Mr. Nicholas.

1678. BUTLER, *Hudibras*, III. 2, 11. That first RUN all religion DOWN.

1694. PENN, *Rise and Prog. of Quakers*, v. Some . . . who, through prejudice or mistake, RAN AGAINST him.

1705. FARQUHAR, *Twin Rivals*, *Pref.* One reason that the galleries were so thin during the RUN of this play.

1709. STEELE, *Tatler*, 27. His desires RAN AWAY WITH him.

1710-3. SWIFT, *Stella* [OLIPHANT, *New Eng.*, ii. 150. A book has a RUN like the old course; there is also a RUN of ill weather.]

1711. *Spectator*, 262. I RUN OVER in my mind all the eminent persons in the nation. *Ibid.* (1712), 390. This creature, if not in any of their little cabals, is RUN DOWN for the most censorious dangerous body in the world. *Ibid.* (1714), 592. Several of them lay it down as a maxim, that whatever dramatic performance has a LONG RUN, must of necessity be good for nothing; as though the first precept in poetry were not to please.

1726. POPE, *Dunciad*, i. 113. Now (shame to Fortune) an ILL RUN at play Blank'd his bold visage.

1736. FIELDING, *Pasquin*, i. I read your comedy over last night . . . if it RUNS as long as it deserves, you will engross the whole season to yourself.

1748. SMOLLETT, *Rod. Random*, xlvii. I would not have you RUN your head precipitate'y INTO A NOOSE.

1812. AUSTEN, *Pride and Prejudice*, liii. I will not spend my hours in RUNNING AFTER my neighbours.

1837. DICKENS, *Pickwick*, x. You have RUN OFF WITH this lady for the sake of her money. *Ibid.* (1843), *Martin Chuzzlewit*, xxx. I think of giving her a RUN in London for a change. *Ibid.* (1846), *Cricket on Hearth*, i. 'Busy . . . Caleb?' 'Pretty well, John . . . There's rather a RUN ON Noah's Arks at present.'

1847. PORTER, *Quarter Race*, 23. I would not advise any man to try to RUN OVER me.

1848. RUXTON, *Far West*, 103. From the RUN of the hills, there must be plenty of water.

*c.*1854. MACAULAY, *Montgomery's Poems.* The publications which have had a RUN during the last few years.

*c.*1860. *Music Hall Song*, 'Drink under the Licensing Act.' It may be your fate, If not walking quite straight, By blue Guardians to be RUN IN.

1861. KINGSLEY, *Ravenshoe*, xxxvii. If any . . . burglar had [cracked] that particular crib . . . and got clear off with the swag he . . . might have been RUN . . . for Congress in a year or two.

1861. *Times*, 23 July. Is there such a thing as a RUN in calamity? Misfortunes, they say, never come single.

1864. LAURENCE, *Guy Livingstone*, xii. Livingstone headed the list, though Fallowfield RAN him HARD.

1865. KINGSLEY, *Hillyars & Burtons*, lix. He might have his RUN swept by fire . . . and be forced to hurry his sheep down to the boiling house.

1866. ELIOT, *Felix Holt*, xx. There was a great RUN on Gottleb's bank in '16. *Ibid.*, xxv. For a man who had long ago RUN THROUGH his own money, servitude in a great family was the best kind of retirement after that of a pensioner.

1869. STOWE, *Oldtown*, 29. She had the in and out of the Sullivan house, and kind o' kept the RUN o' how things went and came into it.

1877. *North Am. Rev.*, July, 5. They assumed the functions of all offices, including the courts of justice, and in many places they even RUN the churches.

1879. HOWELLS, *Lady of the Aroostook*, vii. "Every novelist RUNS a blonde heroine; I wonder why."

1879. *Auto. of Thief* [Macm. Mag., xl. 506]. 'I got RUN IN, and was tried at Marylebone.'

1880. SIMS, *Ballads of Babylon (Forgotten).* I made a success, and was lucky, the play RAN half a year.

1883. *Referee*, 29 April, 7, 2. American evangelists and speculators who RUN salvation on much the same lines as Barnum runs his menagerie.

1883. *D. Telegraph*, 28 August, 5, 1. It does not always follow that the silly backers get a RUN FOR THEIR MONEY. The horse . . . may be scratched a few hours before the race. *Ibid.* (1883), 4 Oct., 3, 2. What I should like is a nice pair of spectacles, and, as far as my money would RUN TO IT, everything else accordin', sir. *Ibid.* (1885), 1 July. Marchant being foolishly RUN OUT. *Ibid.* (1886), 8 Feb. Coming down to the ground WITH A RUN.

1885. *Money Market Review*, 29 Aug. We were unable to RUN the mill.

1885. *Echo*, 8 Sep. The RUN upon the Bank of Ireland and the Provincial Bank was very severe.

1886. PALMER, *New and Old*, 62. If I had had time to follow his fortunes, it was not possible to keep the RUN of him.

1887. FRANCIS, *Saddle and Moccasin.* I RAN A BLUFF on 'em. They said they wasn't driving 'em anyhow, but they got started in the trail ahead of 'em, and it wasn't their business to turn 'em.

1888. BRYCE, *American Commonwealth*, I. 84. It is often said of the President that he is ruled—or, as the Americans express it, RUN—by his Secretary.

1888. *Sp. Life*, 10 Dec. His opponent eventually RAN OUT a winner by 319 points.

1889. MARRIOTT - WATSON, *Australian Wilds*, 135. Drummond, a young squatter in Otago, had succeeded to the management of the RUN on the death of his father.

1889. *Globe*, 11 Feb. Of late they have had a long RUN OF LUCK.

1890. *Pall Mall Gaz.*, 3 Mar., 5, 2. Mr. Depew asserts that he is RUNNING A RAILROAD and not a Presidential boom.

1892. NISBET, *Bushranger's Sweetheart*, 22. Sailors, as a rule, are not friends of bailiffs or Custom House officers, and thus appreciate RUNNING THE CUTTER.

1893. MILLIKEN, *'Arry Ballads*, 14. Bald buffers seem fair IN THE RUN. *Ibid.*, 8. Cremorne's regular OUT OF THE RUN.

1893. EMERSON, *Signor Lippo*, xiv. Alright, give me due beonck quatro soldi per RUN and I'll bring you the duckets.

1895. IOTA, *Comedy in Spasms*, iv. It will give a fellow quite an added cachet . . . TO RUN so fine a woman as that, and pay off some old scores into the bargain.

1899. WHITEING, *John St.*, i. A coral island . . . RUN on principles of almost primitive Christianity.

1900. WHITE, *West End*, 40. I always had an idea that the Guv'nor had some money, but I didn't imagine it would RUN TO this. *Ibid.*, 157. 'Cricket tour,' said he, indignantly. 'I must get fit first. I feel quite RUN DOWN.'

RUNABOUT, *subs.* (old).—A gad-about; a vagabond.

1607. MARSTON, *What You Will*, iii. 1. A RUNNE-ABOUT, a skipping Frenchman.

RUNAWAY PRESTON-PANS (THE GREAT), *subs. phr.* (military).—The 13th Hussars. [A panic seized some of the men in the fight with the Jacobite rebels]. Also "The Green Dragoons"; "The Ragged Brigade"; "The Evergreens," and "The Geraniums."

RUN-DOWN, *subs. phr.* (conjurors').—The bridge between stage and auditorum: Fr. *practicable* and *pont*.

RUN-GOODS, *subs. phr.* (venery).—'A maidenhead, being a commodity never entered.'—GROSE.

RUNNER, *subs.* (printers').—1. *See* quot.

1892. JACOBI, *Some Notes on Books and Printing*, 47. RUNNERS, s.v. Figures or letters placed down the length of a page to indicate the particular number or position of any given line.

2. (various). — A tout: *e.g.* (Stock Exchange) = a broker's assistant with a private canvassing connection; (racing) = a messenger stationed at a telegraph office to get early information; (old gaming) = *see* quot. 1731 (BAILEY); (American) = (1) a steamboat and railroad tout: *see* TICKET-SCALPER; and (2) a commercial traveller.

1731. *St. James's Evg. Post* [SYDNEY, Eng. in 18th Cent., i. 229]. List of officers attached to the most notorious gaming houses . . . a RUNNER, who is to get intelligence of the justices' meetings, and when the constables are out.

1828. SMEATON, *Doings in London*, 'Humours of the Fleet.' Now mean as once profuse, the stupid sot Sits by a RUNNER'S side and damns his lot.

1869. *Fraser's Mag.*, 'British Merchant Seamen.' The "touter," whose business it is to attract the sailor to his master's lodgings by the judicious loan of money, the offer of grog or soft tack (bread); the RUNNER, who volunteers to carry his box of clothes and bedding free of charge to the same destination.

3. (old).—A police officer: also BOW-STREET RUNNER: in quot. 1383 = a sheriff's officer.

1383. CHAUCER, *Canterbury Tales*, 'Friar's Tale,' Prol. 19. A Sompnour is a RENNER up and down.

*c.*1820. T. HUDSON . . . They straightway sent to Bow-street for the famous old RUNNER, Townsend.

1825. SCOTT, *St. Ronan's Well*, iii. Constables, Bow-street RUNNERS, and such like.

1839. DICKENS, *Oliver Twist*, xxx. 'It's the RUNNERS,' cried Brittles . . . 'The what?' . . . 'The Bow-street officers, sir.'

4. (common). — A wave: *cf.* ROLLER.

5. (nautical). — A smuggler. Also a crimp; a single rope rove through a moveable block; and (formerly) a vessel sailing without a convoy in time of war. [CLARK RUSSELL].

*c.*1730. NORTH, *Lives of the Norths*, II. iii. The unfair traders and RUNNERS will undersell us. *Ibid.*, *Examen*, 490. RUNNERS and trickers . . . that cover a contraband trade.

RUNNER-UP, *subs. phr.* (common).—1. In coursing the hound taking second prize, losing only the final course against the winner; whence (2) any competitor running second or taking second place; whence RUN-UP = the race from the slips to the first turn of the hare: *see* TO RUN UP.

1884. *Field*, 6 Dec. The falling together of last year's winner and RUNNER-UP.

RUNNING, *subs.* (racing).—Pace; staying power. Whence, IN (or OUT) OF THE RUNNING = (1) in (or out) of competition; (2) qualified (or not); (3) likely to win (or not); TO MAKE GOOD RUNNING = to do well; TO MAKE GOOD ONE'S RUNNING = to do as well as one's rival; TO MAKE THE RUNNING = to force the pace; spec. (racing) to start a second-rate horse at a high speed with a view of giving a better chance to a 'stayer' belonging to the same owner; TO TAKE UP THE RUNNING = (1) to increase one's pace, (2) to take the lead or most active part.

1858. TROLLOPE, *Dr. Thorne*, v. But silence was not dear to the heart of the honourable John, and so he TOOK UP THE RUNNING. *Ibid.* (1864). *Small House at Allington*, ii. The world had esteemed him when he first MADE GOOD HIS RUNNING with the Lady Fanny.

1861. KINGSLEY, *Ravenshoe*, xxxvi. Ben Caunt was to MAKE THE RUNNING for Haphazard.

1889. *Bird o' Freedom*, 7 Aug., 3. Stewart MADE THE RUNNING so fast that I couldn't see the way he went.

1892. *Tit-Bits*, 17 Sep., 423, 2. There is a striking variation in the periods at which women retire from the RUNNING, if we may be permitted to make use of a sporting phrase in speaking of such a subject.

Adj. (old).—Hasty.

1601. SHAKSPEARE, *Henry VIII.*, i. 4. Had the Cardinal But half my lay thoughts in him, some of these Should find a RUNNING banquet ere they rested. *Ibid.*, v. 4, 69. There they are like to dance these three days; besides the RUNNING banquet of two beadles that is to come.

Prep. (old). — Approaching; going on for: *cf.* RISING.

17[?]. *Laird of Wariestoun* [CHILD, *Ballads*, III. 112]. I hae been your gud wife These nine years, RUNNING ten.

RUNNING - GLASIER, *subs. phr.* (old).—A thief: a sham glazier.

RUNNING-HORSE, *subs. phr.* (old).—A CLAP (*q.v.*); a gleet (GROSE).

RUNNING - LEATHER. TO HAVE SHOES OF RUNNING LEATHER, *verb. phr.* (common). — To be given to rambling.

RUNNING- (or FLYING) PATTERER (or STATIONER), *subs. phr.* (old).—A hawker of ballads, dying-speeches, newspapers, and books: *cf.* PINNER-UP (B. E., and GROSE).

1851-61. MAYHEW, *London Lab.*, I. 228. The latter include the RUNNING PATTERERS, or death-hunters; being men (no women) engaged in vending last dying speeches and confessions.

1864. HOTTEN, *Slang Dict.*, s.v. RUNNING STATIONER. Persons of this class formerly used to run, blowing a horn. Nowadays . . . these peripatetic newsmen bawl in quiet London thoroughfares, to the disturbance of the residents.

RUNNING-RUMBLE. *See* RUMBLER.

RUNNING - SMOBBLE, *subs. phr.* (old).—'Snatching goods off a counter, and throwing them to an accomplice, who brushes off with them' (GROSE).

RUNNING-SNAVEL, *subs. phr.* (old).—A thief whose speciality is the KINCHIN - LAY (*q.v.*): *see* SNAFFLE.

RUNT, *subs.* (old).—A term of contempt: specifically of an old woman. Whence RUNTY = surly; boorish. Also a short, squat man or woman [*cf.* WELSH RUNTS = small cattle].

1614. FLETCHER, *Wit without Money*, v. 2. Before I buy a bargain of such RUNTS, I'll buy a college for bears, and live among 'em.

1711. ADDISON, *Spectator*, No. 108. This overgrown RUNT has struck off his heels, lowered his foretop, and contracted his figure, that he might be looked upon as a member of this newly erected Society [The Short Club].

1721. CENTLIVRE, *Artifice*, iii. This city spoils all servants: I took a Welsh RUNT last spring.

1848. JONES, *Sketches of Travel*, 115. 'No indeed,' ses another little RUNTY-lookin' feller—we 've got enuff to do to take care of our own babys in these diggins.

RUN-TO-SEED, *phr.* (colloquial).—Pregnant; in POD (*q.v.*).

RUOF, *adj.* (back slang).—Four.

RURAL, *subs.* (old colloquial).—A rustic.

1604. MIDDLETON, *Father Hubbard's Tales.* Amongst RURALS verse is scarcely found.

1656. FORD, *Sun's Darling*, ii. Beckon the RURALS in; the Country-gray Seldom ploughs treason.

TO DO A RURAL, *verb. phr.* (common).—To ease oneself in the open: *cf.* TO PLUCK A ROSE.

RUSH, *subs.* and *verb.* (common).—Generic for violence. Whence (1) as *subs.* (old) = robbery wth violence: distinguished from a RAMP (*q.v.*), which might refer to the 'lifting' of a single article, whereas THE RUSH involves CLEANING OUT (*q.v.*); hence (2) any swindle; and, as *verb.* = to rob, to cheat, to extort (*e.g.*, 'I RUSHED the old girl for a quid'): also THE RUSH-DODGE, and TO GIVE ONE THE RUSH (PARKER, GROSE, VAUX). Into modern colloquial usage RUSH enters largely: as *subs.* = (1) extreme urgency of affairs; (2) a great demand, a RUN (*q.v.*); (3) a stampede of horses or cattle; (4) a mellay; (5) in Amer. schools = (*a*) a gabbled or brilliant recitation, and (*b*) a very successful 'pass'; (6) a forward's work at football: whence a SCRIMMAGE (*q.v.*). or play in which the ball is forced. As *verb.* = (1) to hurry, to force (or advance) a matter with undue haste; (2) to go for an opponent blindly: chiefly pugilists'; (3) to charge or attack wildly; and (4) at football = (*a*) to force a ball, (*b*) to secure a goal by forcing. Also TO DO A RUSH (racing) = to back a SAFE-'UN (*q.v.*), and (among bookmakers' touts) TO BET FLASH (*q.v.*), to induce business, TO BONNET (*q.v.*). Whence RUSHER = (1) a cheat, a thief (spec. a thief working a house insufficiently guarded); (2) a man of sensational energy, as a ranting divine, a bawling politician, a reckless punter, a wild-hitting pugilist; and (3) a forward good at running ball in hand or forcing the play (football). Also, TO ROAM ON THE RUSH (racing) = to swerve from the straight at the spurt for the finish; ON (or WITH) A RUSH = with spirit, energetically; ON THE RUSH = on the run, hard at it; TO RUSH THE SEASON = to anticipate social and other functions; TO DO A RUSH UP THE STRAIGHT (the FRILLS, or PETTICOATS) = to possess without further ado a yielding woman: *see* GROPE; TO RUSH A BILL (parliamentary) = to put a bill through, (*a*) without debate, or (*b*) by closuring the Opposition.

1595. SHAKSPEARE, *Rom. and Juliet*, iii. 3, 25. The kind prince, Taking thy part, hath RUSH'D aside the law.

1825. JONES, *True Bottom'd Boxer* [*Univ. Songst.*, ii. 96]. For taking and giving, for sparring and RUSHING it. *Ibid.* With chancery suiting, and sparring and RUSHING.

18[?]. *Brunonian* [BARTLETT]. A RUSH is a glib recitation, but to be a DEAD RUSH it must be flawless, polished, and sparkling like a Koh-i-noor.

18[?]. *Yale Lit. Mag.* [BARTLETT]. It was purchased by the man, who "really did not look" at the lesson on which he RUSHED.

1871. DE VERE, *Americanisms*, 171. The miner in California and Nevada has been known, in times of a RUSH, to speak of a place where he could stand leaning against a stout post, as his diggings for the night.

1872. *Daily Telegraph*, 9 Feb. The place was RUSHED—an expressive word, which signifies that the diggers swarmed to the spot in such crowds as to render merely foolish any resistance which an owner might be inclined to make. *Ibid.* (1874), 4 Aug. A number of bills are RUSHED through Parliament. *Ibid.* (1883), 22 May, 2, 3. The sore point of intrigue and bribery too well known by those familiar with the RUSHING of private bills through the American Senate as existing in that Assembly.

1881. GRANT, *Bush Life.* A confused whirl of dark forms swept before him, and the camp so full of life a minute ago is desolate. It was a RUSH a stampede.

1885. *Punch*, 24 Jan., 42. But, in affairs of empire, Have you been fogged—or RUSHED?

1887. PAYN, *Glow Worm Tales*, 123. That a fraud had been committed on us was certain, and a fraud of a very clumsy kind . . . he had RUSHED us as the phrase goes.

1888. BOLDREWOOD, *Robbery Under Arms*, xxiii. I've known cases where a single bushranger was RUSHED by a couple of determined men. *Ibid.*, xxiii. It's no use trying the RUSH DODGE with them.

1888. BESANT, *Fifty Years Ago*, 137. Peeresses . . . occupied every seat, and even RUSHED the reporters' gallery.

1889. *Illustrated Bits*, 13 July, 3. A girl of sixteen who receives calls from admirers, is commonly considered to be RUSHING THE SEASON. She is precocious and the reverse of passée.

1889. *Lic. Vict. Gaz.*, 4 Jan. Ain't that the swine of a snob that RUSHED me at Battersea?

1890. *Nineteenth Century*, xxvi. 854. There was a slight boom in the mining market, and a bit of a RUSH on American rails.

1892. KIPLING, *Barrack Room Ballads*, 'Fuzzy Wuzzy.' A happy day with Fuzzy ON THE RUSH.

1892. NISBET, *Bushranger's Sweetheart*, 96. "Jim always meant business wherever he went," she said confidently, "and we should be sure to hear of that RUSH if he had taken it up."

18[?] *N. A. Review* [*Century*]. Hazing, RUSHING, secret societies, society imitations and badges . . . are unknown at Oxford and Cambridge.

18[?] *Sci. American* [*Century*]. In RUSHING, as well as in following or heading off . . . the front lines get the most shocks.

1897. KENNARD, *Girl in Brown Habit*, x. She's a RUSHER, and just the animal to stick her forefeet into a drain like this, especially when she got excited.

1901. *D. Telegraph*, 9 Nov., 7, 2. At the next lecture the Swami made a dead RUSH to get those present to join.

7. (old).—The lowest minimum of value: *cf.* STRAW, RAP, CENT, &c. [*See* quot. 1591.]

1362. LANGLAND, *Piers Plowman*, 2421. And yet yeve ye me nevere The worthe of a RISSHE.

*c.*1440. *Generydes* [E.E.T.S.], l. 1680. Of all his payne he wold not sett a RISSH.

*c.*1540. *Doctour Doubble Ale*, 279. By them I set not a RYSH.

1591. LYLY, *Sappho and Phaon*, ii. 4. But bee not pinned alwayes on her sleeves; strangers have greene RUSHES, when daily guests are not worth a RUSH.

1593. SHAKSPEARE, *Com. of Errors*, iv. 3. A RUSH, a hair, a drop of blood, a pin, a nut, a cherry-stone.

1719. DURFEY, *Pills*, iii. 9. But the fool for his labour deserves NOT A RUSH, For grafting a Thistle upon a Rose Bush.

1767. STERNE, *Tristam Shandy*, ix. 17. I would not, my good people! give a RUSH for your judgment.

RUSH-RING. TO MARRY WITH A RUSH-RING, *verb. phr.* (old).—1. To marry in jest; and (2) to feign marriage. *See* quot. 1776.

1579. SPENSER, *Shepheards Calender*, Nov., 114. Where bene . . . The knotted RUSH-RINGES, and gilt rosemaree.

1598. SHAKSPEARE, *All's Well*, ii. 2, 22. As fit . . . as Tib's RUSH for Tom's forefinger.

*c.*1610. FLETCHER, *F. Shepherdess*, i. 3. Or gather RUSHES to make many a RING, For thy long finger.

1668. DAVENANT, *Rivals*. I'll crown thee with a garland of straw then, And I'll MARRY thee WITH A RUSH-RING.

1684. DURFEY, *Winchester Wedding* [*Several New Songs*]. And Tommy was so to Katty, And WEDDED her WITH A RUSH-RING. . . . And thus of Fifty fair Maids . . . Scarce Five of the Fifty was left ye, That so did return again.

1776. BRAND, *Pop. Antiq.*, ii. 38. A custom . . . appears anciently to have prevailed, both in England and in other countries, of marrying with a RUSH RING; chiefly practised, however, by designing men, for the purposes of debauching their mistresses, who sometimes were so infatuated as to believe that this mock ceremony was a real marriage.

RUSH-BUCKLER, *subs. phr.* (old).—A violent bully.

1551. MORE, *Utopia*, ii. 4. Take into this number also their servants: I mean all that flock of stout bragging RUSH-BUCKLERS.

RUSSIA, *subs.* (thieves').—A pocket-book; a READER (*q.v.*).

1877. *Five Years' Penal Servitude*, iii. 244. It was the swell's RUSSIA—a RUSSIA, you know, is a pocket-book.

RUSSIAN-LAW, *subs. phr.* (old colloquial).—*See* quot.

1641. JOHN DAY, *Parliament of Bees*, 65 (BULLEN). This three-pile-velvet rascall, widows decayer, The poore fryes beggerer and rich Bees betrayer, Let him have RUSSIAN LAW for all his sins. *Dic.* What's that? *Imp.* A 100 blowes on his bare shins.

RUST, *verb.* (streets').—*See* quot.

1884. *Cornhill Mag.*, June, 620. So far as Slinger has any business, it is that of RUSTING, *i.e.*, collecting—on the *chiffonier* system—old metal and disposing of it to the marine-store dealers . . . though RUST is the primary object of his explorations of rubbish heaps, all is fish that comes to his net.

TO NAB THE RUST, *verb. phr.* (old).—1. To take offence; to get restive: *cf.* RUSTY.—GROSE (1785).

ENGLISH SYNONYMS.—To chew oneself; to comb one's hair; to cut up rusty; to get dandered (or one's dander up); huffed or huffy; in a pelter; in a scot; in a wax; one's mad up; on the high ropes; the needle; the monkey up; the monkey on one's back; popped; shirty; the spur; waxy; to have one's bristles raised; one's shirt or one's tail out; to lose one's vest; to be miffed; to pucker up; to squall; to stand on one's hind leg; to throw up buckets.

FRENCH SYNONYMS.—*Avoir mangé de l'oseille; avoir son cran; avoir son arnaud* (also *être arnaud*); *en rester tout bleu; avoir son bœuf; gober sa chèvre; entrer en tempête; monter à l'arbre* or *l'eschelle.*

SPANISH SYNONYMS.—*Amontanar; atocinar; barba; desbantizarse despampanar; embersencharse; escamonearse; mosquear.*

2. (old).—To receive punishment unexpectedly.

3. (old).—*See* quot.

1858. A. MAYHEW, *Paved with Gold*, III. v. There's no chance of NABBING ANY RUST (taking any money).

RUSTIC, *subs.* (old: now recognised).—'A clownish Country Fellow.'—B. E. (*c.*1696).

RUSTICATE, *verb.* (University).—To banish by way of punishment; TO SEND DOWN (*q.v.*). Hence RUSTICATION (GROSE).

1714. *Spectator*, 596. After this I was deeply in love with a milliner, and at last with my bedmaker, upon which I was sent away, or, in the university phrase, RUSTICATED for ever.

1779. JOHNSON, *Life of Milton*, 12. It seems plain . . . that he had incurred RUSTICATION . . . with perhaps the loss of a term.

1794. *Gent. Mag.*, 1085. And was very near RUSTICATION, merely for kicking up a row after a beakering party.

1841. LEVER, *Charles O'Malley*, lxxix. Cecil Cavendish . . . has been RUSTICATED for immersing four bricklayers in that green receptacle of stagnant water and duckweed yclept "the Haha."

1843. THACKERAY, *Fitz-Boodle's Confess.* Then came demand for an apology; refusal on my part; appeal to the dean; convocation; and RUSTICATION of George Savage Fitz-Boodle.

1853. BRADLEY, *Verdant Green*, iv. Our hero . . . missed the moral of the story and took the RUSTICATION for a kind forgiveness of injuries.

1885. *D. Telegraph*, 29 Oct. Students who are liable at any moment to be RUSTICATED.

RUSTLE, *verb.* (American).—To bestir oneself; to grapple with circumstances; to rise superior to the event. Whence RUSTLER

= (1) an energetic resourceful man; and (2) a rowdy, a desperado: spec. (Western States) a cattle-lifter. RUSTLING = active, energetic, SMART (*q.v.*).

1872. S. L. CLEMENS, *Innocents at Home*, 20. Pard, he was a RUSTLER.

1882. *Century Mag.*, Aug., 508. I'll RUSTLE AROUND and pick up something. *Ibid.* RUSTLE the things off that table. *Ibid.* To say that a man is a RUSTLER is the highest indorsement a Dakotan can give. It means that he is pushing, energetic, smart, and successful.

1884. *Century*, xxxvii. 770. They're a thirsty crowd, an' it comes expinsive; but they're worth it, fer they're RUSTLERS, ivery wan of thim.

1887. MORLEY ROBERTS, *Western Avernus*. I tell you he was a RUSTLER . . . It means a worker, an energetic man, and no slouch can be a RUSTLER.

1889. *Cornhill*, July, 62. I was out one day after antelope (I RUSTLED all my meat, except a ham now and then as a luxury), when I happened to come across a large patch of sunflowers.

1889. *Harper's Mag.*, lxxi. 190. RUSTLE now, boys, RUSTLE! for you have a long and hard day's work before you.

1892. *Scotsman*, 7 May, 'RUSTLERS' and '*Regulators.*' The lawless element . . . not content with stealing cattle, openly defied the authorities. In June . . . an expedition started . . . and the result was that sixty-one thieves were hanged, after a pitched battle between the cattle men and the RUSTLERS.

RUSTY, *subs.* (thieves').—An informer.

1840. LYTTON, *Paul Clifford*, xxxiv. He'll turn a RUSTY, and scrag one of his pals!

Adj. (also **RESTY**) (colloquial).—Ill-tempered; sullen; restive; insolent; or (GROSE) 'out of use': whence TO RIDE RUSTY or NAB THE RUST: *see* RUST; and RUSTY-GUTS (B. E., GROSE) = a churl.

1362. LANGLAND, *Piers Plowman*, 3941. Robyn the ribaudour For hise RUSTY wordes.

[?]. *Coventry Myst.* [Shakspeare Soc.], 47. RUSTYNES of synne is cawse of these wawys.

*c.*1625. *Court and Times Chas. I.*, i. 36. In the meantime, there is much urging and spurring the parliament for supply and expedition, in both which they will prove somewhat RUSTY.

1649. MILTON, *Iconoclastes*, xxiv. The master is too RUSTY or too rich to say his own prayers.

1662. FULLER, *Worthies*, ii. 293. This Nation long restive and RUSTY in ease and quiet.

1706. WARD, *Wooden World*, 22. If he stand on his Punctilio's . . . he is immediately proclaimed throughout the Fleet a REISTY Puppy.

1772. BRIDGES, *Burlesque Homer*, 74. They're not to blame for being crusty, 'Twould make a Highlander RIDE RUSTY.

*d.*1794. COLMAN, *The Gentleman*, No. 5. His brown horse, Orator, took RUST, ran out of the course, and was distanced.

1815. SCOTT, *Guy Mannering*, xxviii. The people got RUSTY about it, and would not deal. *Ibid.* (1821), *Pirate*, xxxix. Even Dick Fletcher RIDES RUSTY on me now and then.

1851-61. MAYHEW, *Lond. Lab.* . . . If then she [a cat] TURNS RUSTY . . . he'll [a monkey] . . . give her a nip with his teeth.

1860. *Punch*, xxxix. 177. He don't care in whose teeth he RUNS RUSTY.

1863. READE, *Hard Cash*, xlv. They watched the yard till dusk, when its proprietor RAN RUSTY and turned them out.

1864. *Eton School Days*, xix. What is the good of turning RUSTY? with me, too. I haven't done anything.

1866. ELIOT, *Felix Holt*, xi. Company that's got no more orders to give, and wants to TURN UP RUSTY to them that has, had better be making room for filling it.

1892. HENLEY and STEVENSON, *Deacon Brodie*, vii. 16. Confound it, Deacon, Not RUSTY.

RUSTY-FUSTY-DUSTY, *adj.* and *adv.* (old colloquial).—Begrimed; malodorous and dirty.

1630. TAYLOR, *Works*, ii. 24. Our cottage that for want of use was musty, And most extremely RUSTY-FUSTY-DUSTY.

RUSTY BUCKLES (THE), *subs. phr.* military).—The Second Dragoon Guards (Queen's Bays): also "The Bays."

RUTTISH, *adj.* (venery).—Lecherous (GROSE): also IN RUT and RUTTY. Hence RUTTING (or RUTTING-SPORT) = the deed of kind; RUT, *verb.* (*see* quot. 1679); and RUTTER (*q.v.*).

1598. SHAKSPEARE, *All's Well*, iv. 3, 243. A foolish idle boy, but for all that very RUTTISH.

1670. COTTON, *Scoffer Scofft* [*Works* (1725), 192]. What with some Goddess he'd have bin Playing, belike, at In-and-In, And would be at the RUTTING-SPORT?

1679. DRYDEN, *Ovid's Metam.*, x. What piety forbids the lusty ram, Or more salacious goat, TO RUT their dam?

TO KEEP A RUT, *verb. phr.* (colloquial).—To play the meddler; to make mischief.

RUTAT (or **RATTAT**), *subs.* (back slang).—A potato; a 'tatur.'

RUTTER, *subs.* (venery).—1. A man or woman IN RUT (*q.v.*); and (2) Elizabethan for the German *reiter*.

1596. LODGE, *Wit's Miserie*. Some authors have compared it to a RUTTER'S codpiece.

*c.*1618. FLETCHER, *Custom of Country*, iii. 3. The RUTTER, too, is gone. *Ibid.* (*c.*1620), *The Woman's Prize*, i. 4. Such a regiment of RUTTERS Never defied men braver.

RY, *subs.* (Stock Exchange).—A dishonest practice; a sharp dodge.

RYDER, *subs.* (common).—A cloak.

RYE. *See* ROMANY.

RYE-BUCK, *adv.* (American).—All right; O. K. (*q.v.*).

SA, *adj.* (showmen's).—Six.

1893. EMERSON, *Lippo*, xx. Vell, when I got well I was hired out to a woman for SA soldi a day.

SABBATH-DAY'S JOURNEY, *subs. phr.* (colloquial).—A short walk: also (ironically) an excuse for not stirring.

SABE (SAVE, or SAVVY), *subs.* (American).—Shrewdness; NOUS (*q.v.*); GUMPTION (*q.v.*).

SABLE-MARIA. *See* BLACK MARIA.

SABIN, *subs.* (old).—A whimster.

1637. HOLLAND, *Camden*, 542. Grimsby, which our SABINS, or conceited persons dreaming what they list . . . will have to be so called of one Grimes a merchant.

SACCER, *subs.* (Harrow School).—The sacrament: *cf.* SOCCER, RUGGER, BREKKER, COLLECKER, &c.

SACHEVEREL, *subs.* (old).—'The iron door, or blower, to the mouth of a stove: from a divine of that name who made himself famous for blowing the coals of dissension in the latter end of the reign of Queen Ann' (GROSE, HALLIWELL).

SACK, *subs.* (Old Cant).—A pocket. As *verb* = to pocket; TO DIVE INTO A SACK = to pick a pocket.—B. E. (*c.* 1696); DYCHE (1748); GROSE (1785); VAUX (1812); EGAN (1823). *Cf.* DOODLESACK.

1858. MAYHEW, *Paved with Gold*, III. iii. I've brought a couple of bene coves, with lots of the Queen's pictures [money] in their SACKS.

PHRASES are: TO GIVE (or GET) THE SACK (BAG, BILLET, BULLET, CANVAS, KICK-OUT, MITTEN, PIKE, or ROAD) = to give or get discharge: from employment, office, position, &c.: *see* BAG: also TO SACK and TO BESTOW (or GET) THE ORDER OF THE SACK; TO BUY THE SACK = to get drunk (GROSE); TO BREAK A BOTTLE IN AN EMPTY SACK = 'a bubble bet, a sack with a bottle in it not being an empty sack' (GROSE); MORE SACKS TO THE MILL! = (1) Pile it on! a call to increased exertion, and (2) plenty in store.

1607. DEKKER and WEBSTER, *Westward Hoe*, ii. 1. There's other irons i' th' fire, MORE SACKS are coming TO THE MILL.

1623. MIDDLETON and ROWLEY, *Spanish Gypsy*, iv. 1. *Soto.* MORE SACKS TO THE MILL. *San.* More thieves to the sacks.

1837. DICKENS, *Pickwick Papers*, xx. I wonder what old Fogg would say? . . . I should GET THE SACK, I suppose.

1837. BARHAM, *Ingoldsby Legends*, II. 247. Don't . . . fancy, because a man's nous seems to lack, That whenever you please, you can GIVE HIM THE SACK.

1864. YATES, *Broken to Harness*, xxi. If it rested with me, doctor, I'd give him unlimited leave, confer on him THE ORDER OF THE SACK.

1867. *All Year Round*, 13 July, 55. When hands are being SACKED.

1895. *Standard*, 18 Ap., 1, 1. Thus GIVING THE SACK arose from the fact that masters or mistresses gave dismissed servants a rough bag in which to pack up their belongings, in order to expedite their departure.

1900. KIPLING, *Stalky & Co.*, 10. You must SACK your keeper. He's not fit to live in the same country with a God-fearing fox.

SACRIFICE, *subs.* (Trade Cant).—The surrender, or loss of profit: as *verb* = to sell regardless of cost.

1844. DICKENS, *Chimes*, ii. It's patterns were last year's and going at a SACRIFICE.

SAD, *adj.* and *adv.* (colloquial).—Mischievous; troublesome; of little account; merry; fast: as A SAD DOG = (1) 'a wicked debauched fellow' (GROSE), and (2) a playful reproach.

1706. FARQUHAR, *Recruiting Officer*, iii. 2. *Syl.* . . . you are an ignorant, pretending, impudent coxcomb. *Braz.* Ay, ay, a SAD DOG.

1713. SWIFT, *Stella* [OLIPHANT, *New Eng.*, ii. 150. The word SAD is much used; a man is a SAD DOG; sour grapes are SAD things].

1713. STEELE, *Spectator*, No. 448. Then does he begin to call himself the SADDEST fellow, in disappointing so many places.

1726. VANBRUGH, *Provoked Husband*, iii. 1. When a SAD wrong word is rising just to one's tongue's end, I give a great gulp, and swallow it.

1748. SMOLLETT, *Rod. Random*, xvi I suppose you think me a SAD DOG . . . I . . . confess that appearances are against me.

1759. GOLDSMITH, *Bee*, No. 2. You have always been a SAD DOG—you'll never come to good, you'll never be rich.

1771. MACKENZIE, *Man of Feeling*, xiv. I have been told as how London is a SAD place.

1836. DICKENS, *Sketches by Boz*, 141. Mr. Tones used to poke him in the ribs, and tell him he had been a SAD DOG in his time.

SADDLE, *subs.* (venery).—1. The female *pudendum*: *see* MONOSYLLABLE: *cf.* RIDE. Hence, IN THE SADDLE = mounted.

1611. CHAPMAN, *May-day*, iii. 2. Mine uncle Lorenzo's maid, Rose . . . he will needs persuade me her old master keeps her for his own SADDLE.

1621. BURTON, *Anat. Melan.*, III. III. i. 2. The adulterer sleeping now was riding on his master's SADDLE.

d. 1704. BROWN, *Works*, ii. 312. Damme, if I car'd a rush who rode in my SADDLE.

2. theatrical).—*See* quot.

1781. PARKER, *View of Society*, I. 54. His conscience carried him to extort two guineas on each person's benefit by way of SADDLE (which among theatrical people is an additional charge upon the benefits).

PHRASES.—TO PUT THE SADDLE ON THE RIGHT HORSE = (1) to blame (or praise) where justly due, and (2) to cast a burden where best borne; TO SUIT ONE AS A SADDLE SUITS A SOW = to become ill; to be incongruous; TO SADDLE A MARKET (Amer. Stock Exchange) = to foist a stock on the market; TO SADDLE ONE WITH A THING = to impose a thing on, to constrain to accept an unwelcome gift; 'He has a SADDLE to fit every horse' = 'He has a salve (or remedy) for every sore (or mishap)'; TO SADDLE THE SPIT = to give a dinner or supper (GROSE); TO SADDLE ONE'S NOSE = to wear spectacles (GROSE); TO SADDLE A PLACE (or PENSION) = 'to oblige the owner to pay a certain portion of his income to someone nominated by the donor' (GROSE); SADDLE-LEATHER = the skin of the posteriors; SADDLE-SICK = galled by riding (GROSE).

1607. DEKKER and WEBSTER, *Westward Ho*, v. 1. How say you, wenches? Have I SET THE SADDLE ON THE RIGHT HORSE?

c. 1616. *Court and Times James I.* [OLIPHANT, *New Eng.*, ii. 70. We see SET THE SADDLE ON THE RIGHT HORSE . . .].

1668. DRYDEN, *All for Love*, Preface. A wiser part to SET THE SADDLE ON THE RIGHT HORSE.

1708-10. SWIFT, *Polite Conversation*, ii. *Ld. Smart.* Why, he us'd to go very fine, when he was here in Town. *Sir John.* Ay; and IT BECAME HIM, AS A SADDLE BECOMES A SOW.

1744. NORTH, *Lord Guildford*, I. 314. His . . . lordship had done well to have shown . . . what was so added, and then THE SADDLE WOULD HAVE FALLEN ON THE RIGHT HORSE.

1837. CARLYLE, *Diamond Necklace*, i. Roland . . . was SADDLE-SICK, calumniated, constipated.

SADDLEBACK, *subs.* (common).—A louse: *see* CHATES.

SADLY, *adv.* (colloquial).—Indifferent in health.

1866. ELIOT, *Felix Holt*, xxvii. Mr. Holt, miss, wants to know if you'll give him leave to come in. I told him you was SADLY.

SAFE, *adj.* (occasionally colloquial).—Trustworthy; certain: *e.g.*, 'So-and-so's SAFE enough' = 'He is certain to meet his engagements'; SAFE to be hanged = sure of the gallows; SAFE AS HOUSES (THE BELLOWS, COONS, THE BANK—ANYTHING) = perfectly sure; A SAFE-CARD = a wide-awake fellow; A SAFE-UN = a horse not meant to run, nor, if he runs, to win; also STIFF-'UN (*q.v.*), DEAD-'UN (*q.v.*), or STUMER (*q.v.*): with such an entry a bookmaker can SAFELY operate.

1624. MIDDLETON, *Game at Chess*, ii. 1. To sell away all the powder in a kingdom To prevent blowing up: that's SAFE.

1851. MAYHEW, *London Lab.*, II. 154. If you was caught up and brought afore the Lord Mayor, he'd give you fourteen days on it, AS SAFE AS THE BELLOWS.

1854. WHYTE-MELVILLE, *General Bounce*, xiii. But here we are at Tattersall's; . . . so now for good information, long odds, a SAFE man, and a shot at the favourite!

1864. *Derby-day*, 51. We're all ruined AS SAFE AS COONS.

1864. YATES, *Broken to Harness*, x. I shall be county-courted, AS SAFE AS HOUSES. *Ibid.* (1866), *Land at Last*, I. 173. One or two more of the same sort are SAFE to make him an associate.

1867. *London Herald*, 23 Mar., 221, 3. We're SAFE to nab him; SAFE AS HOUSES.

1871. "HAWK'S-EYE," *Turf Notes*, 11. Most assuredly it is the bookmakers that profit by the SAFE UNS, or "stiff uns," as, in their own language, horses that have no chance of winning are called.

1890. ALLEN, *Tents of Shem*, xxviii. You may make your forgery itself as SAFE AS HOUSES.

1894. MOORE, *Esther Waters*, xxx. I overlaid my book against Wheatear; I'd heard that she was AS SAFE AS 'OUSES.

SAILS, *subs.* (naval).—A sailmaker.

1835. DANA, *Two Years Before Mast*, xxviii. Poor 'Chips' could eat no supper . . . SAILS tried to comfort him, and told him he was a bloody fool.

PHRASES.—TO SAIL IN = to put in an appearance, or take part in a matter; TO TAKE THE WIND OUT OF ONE'S SAILS = to run foul of, to spoil sport; TO SAIL NEAR (CLOSE TO, or TOO NEAR THE WIND) = (1) to run risks, (2) to act with caution, (3) to live closely to one's income, and (4) to verge upon obscenity; 'HOW YOU SAIL ABOUT' (B. E.) = How you saunter about.'

1860. THACKERAY, *Lovel the Widower.* Lady B. SAILED IN . . . many brooches, bangles, and other gimcracks ornamenting her plenteous person.

1888. *Harp. Mag.*, lxxviii. 561. A man must dismiss all thoughts of . . . common-sense when it comes to masquerade dresses, and just SAIL IN and make an unmitigated fool of himself.

1891. *M. Advertiser*, 30 Mar. John Harvey called William Tillman a liar 150 times, . . . and offered to lick him 104 times. At the 104th William . . . thrashed John. The verdict of the jury was that William ought to have SAILED IN an hour and a half earlier.

SAILOR'S-BLESSING, *subs. phr.* (nautical).—A curse.

SAILOR'S-PLEASURE, *subs. phr.* (nautical).—'Yarning, smoking, dancing, growling, &c.' (CLARK RUSSELL).

SAILOR'S-WAITER, *subs. phr.* (nautical).—*See* quot.

1835. DANA, *Two Years*, &c., iii. The second mate . . . is neither officer nor man . . . The crew call him the SAILOR'S-WAITER, as he has to furnish them with spun yarn, marline, and all other stuffs that they need in their work . . .

SAINT, *subs.* (old).—'A piece of spoiled timber in a coachmaker's shop, like a saint, devoted to the flames' (GROSE).

PHRASES and DERIVATIVES.—ST. ANTHONY'S PIGS (*see* quot. 1662); ST. GEOFFREY'S DAY = never (GROSE): *see* QUEEN DICK; ST. GILES'S BREED = 'Fat, ragged, and saucy' (GROSE); ST. GILES'S GREEK = Cant, SLANG (*q.v.*), PEDDLER'S FRENCH (GROSE); ST. LAWRENCE'S TEARS (*see* quot. 1874); ST. LUBBOCK'S DAY = a bank-holiday; ST. LUKE'S BIRD = an ox (GROSE); ST. MARGET'S ALE = water: *see* ADAM'S ALE; ST. MARTIN'S EVIL = drunkenness; ST. MARTIN'S RING = a copper-gilt ring; ST. MARTIN'S LACE = imitation gold lace, stage tinsel: *see* quot. 1607 (DEKKER); ST. MONDAY = 'a holiday taken on Monday to recover from the effects of the Sunday's rest' (GROSE): whence MONDAYISH = lazy: *see* COBBLER'S SUNDAY and SHOEMAKER'S HOLIDAY; ST. NICHOLAS (*see* NICHOLAS); ST. PATRICK (or ST. PATRICK'S WELL) = the best whiskey; ST. JOHN TO BORROW (*see* BORROW); TO DINE WITH ST. ANTHONY (*cf.* DUKE HUMPHREY); RIDING ST. GEORGE = 'the woman uppermost in the amorous congress, that is the dragon on St. George' (GROSE): whence ST. GEORGE A-HORSE-BACK = the act of kind (*see* quot. 1617); THE 'SPITAL STANDS TOO NIGH ST. THOMAS A' WATERINGS = 'Widows who shed most tears are sometimes guilty of such indiscretions as render them proper subjects for the public hospitals' (HAZLITT); SAINT OF THE SAUCEPAN = an expert cook.

1600. MUNDAY and DRAYTON, *Oldcastle*, iv. 4. If ye burn, by this flesh I'll make you drink their ashes in SAINT MARGET'S ALE.

. . . . *Plaine Percivall* [BRAND, *Pop. Antiq.*, II. 27, note]. I doubt whether all be gold that glistereth, sith SAINT MARTIN'S RINGS be but copper within, though they be gilt without.

1607. *Puritan*, i. 1. Here's a puling . . . my mother weeps for all the women that ever buried husbands . . . Alas! a small matter lucks a handkerchief! and sometimes THE 'PITAL STANDS TOO NIGH SAINT THOMAS A' WATERINGS.

1607. DEKKER, *Westward Ho*, ii. 1. You must to the Pawn to buy lawn; to SAINT MARTIN'S for LACE.

c. 1617. FLETCHER, *Mad Lover*, i. 1. How our SAINT GEORGES will BESTRIDE THE DRAGONS, The red and ramping dragons.

1632. MASSINGER, *Fatal Dowry*, iii. 1. *Charal.* You did not see him on my couch within, Like GEORGE A-HORSEBACK, on her, nor a-bed?

1648. *A Brown Dozen of Drunkards* . . . By one that hath drunk at ST. PATRICK'S WELL [*Title*].

1662. FULLER, *Worthies* (London), i. 65. Nicholas Heath . . . noted for one of SAINT ANTHONIE'S PIGS therein (so were the Scholars of that school [City of London] commonly called, as those of St. Paul, *Paul's Pigeons*).

1749. SMOLLETT, *Gil Blas* [ROUTLEDGE], 42. That SAINT OF THE SAUCEPAN . . . leaving him . . . to . . . his usual nap after dinner, we took away, and demolished the remainder with appetites worthy of our master. *Ibid.*, *Gil Blas* (1812), II. viii. Comedians . . . do not travel a-foot, and DINE WITH ST. ANTHONY.

1791. LACKINGTON, *Letter*, iii. [*Life*, 1803]. While he was keeping SAINT MONDAY, I was with boys of my own age, fighting, cudgel-playing, wrestling, &c.

1823. MONCRIEFF, *Tom and Jerry*, 5. Flash, my young friend, or slang, as others call it, is the classical language of the Holy Land; in other words, ST. GILES'S GREEK.

1874. *Eng. Mechanic* [DAVIES]. The familiar shower of shooting stars [9th to 11th Aug.] known of old as ST. LAURENCE'S TEARS, but now termed—rather more scientifically—the Perseides, from the point in the heavens whence they appear to radiate.

1882. RIDDELL, *Weird Stories, The Open Door.* We were always counting the weeks to next ST. LUBBOCK'S DAY.

1884. *D. News*, 22 July, 5, 3. It was evident that universal homage was being paid to SAINT MONDAY. Working London proclaimed a general holiday.

1902. *Pall Mall Gazette*, 26 July, 3, 1. It [Coronation day] will be the most memorable Bank Holiday that has yet figured in the annals of ST. John LUBBOCK.

SAKE. FOR SAKE'S SAKE (ANY SAKE, GOODNESS SAKE, &c.), *phr.* (colloquial).—A strong appeal. FOR OLD SAKE'S SAKE = for 'auld lang syne.'

1670. HOWARD, *Committee*, iii. Run after him, and save the poor fellow FOR SAKE'S SAKE.

1857. HUGHES, *Tom Brown's School-days*, I. iii. Us be cum to pay 'e a visit . . . FOR OLD SAKE'S SAKE.

1863. KINGSLEY, *Water Babies.* Yet FOR OLD SAKE'S SAKE she is still, dears, The prettiest doll in the world.

SAL, *subs.* (old colloquial).—1. Salivation; IN A HIGH SAL = 'in the pickling tub' (GROSE).

2. (theatrical).—Salary.

1885. *Household Words*, 29 August, 350. I say that part of this money shall be shared among us as SALS, and some of the remainder shall be used for mounting the guv'nor's panto.

SALAD, *subs.* (nautical).—1. *See* quot.

1877. *Notes & Queries*, 5 S., viii. 269. When an officer on board ship is wakened and fails to obey the snmmons, but has another nap, it is called TAKING A SALAD.

2. (colloquial).—A lettuce.

SALAD-DAYS (or **STAGE**), *subs. phr.* (colloquial).—The days of youthful simplicity; inexperience.

1608. SHAKSPEARE, *Ant. and Cleop.*, i. 5, 73. My SALAD DAYS, When I was green in judgement.

1892. ANSTEY, *Voces Populi*, 'At a Parisian Café Chantant,' 85. The diners in the gallery at the back have passed THE SALAD STAGE.

1893. *Chambers's Jour.*, 25 Feb., 125. Having in his SALAD DAYS made trial of a cheap cigar, the result somehow satisfied him that tobacco was not in his line.

SALAMANDER, *subs.* (colloquial).—1. Anything fire-proof, and (2) a fire-eating juggler (circus).

1886. BESANT, *Children of Gibeon*, I. vi. We ain't a show. Lotty ain't a clown; I ain't a jumping-horse; Liz ain't a SALAMANDER.

SALE. HOUSE OF SALE, *subs. phr.* (old).—*See* quot. and NANNY-HOUSE.

1596. SHAKSPEARE, *Hamlet*, ii. 1, 60. I saw him enter such a HOUSE OF SALE, Videlicet, a brothel.

See WASH-SALE.

SALESMAN'S-DOG, *subs. phr.* (old).—A shop tout; a BARKER (*q.v.*).—GROSE.

SALISBURY, *subs.* (political: obsolete).—*See* quots.

1890. *Standard*, 3 Mar., 3, 4 [*Mr. Labouchere loquitur*]. Some time ago they invented a word for the Marquess's statements. They said, "When you are telling a lie and want to tell it civilly, say you are telling a SALISBURY."

1890. *Pall Mall Gaz.*, 1 Mar., 5, 1. Lord Salisbury's evasion, which past experience, even without the facts, suggested was a SALISBURY. *Ibid.*, 6, 1. The famous SALISBURY about the Secret-Treaty . . . must henceforth be read "*cum grano salis*-bury."

SALLY. *See* AUNT SALLY.

SALLY-PORT, *subs. phr.* (venery).—The female *pudendum*: *see* MONOSYLLABLE.

1656. FLETCHER, *Martiall.* Torches can Best enter at the SALLI-PORT of man.

SALLINGER'S- (or **SALLENGER'S**—*i.e.*, **ST. LEGER'S**) **ROUND.** TO DANCE SALLINGER'S-ROUND, *verb. phr.* (old).—To wanton; to copulate: *cf.* THE TUNE OF THE SHAKING OF THE SHEET. [SALLENGER'S ROUND = a loose ballad and tune, *tempus* Elizabeth.]

1698. *London Spy* [NARES]. It will restore an old man of threescore, to the juvenallity of thirty, or make a girle at fourteen, with drinking but one glass, as ripe as an old maid of four and twenty. 'Twill make a parson DANCE SALLINGER'S-ROUND, a puritan lust after the flesh.

SALMAGUNDY (or **SALMON-GUNDY**), *subs.* (old).—1. *See* quot. Hence (2) = a cook.

1748. SMOLLETT, *Rod. Random*, xxvi. Ordering the boy to bring a piece of salt beef from the brine, cut off a slice, and mixed it with an equal quantity of onions, which seasoning with a moderate proportion of pepper and salt he brought it into a consistence with oil and vinegar. Then tasting the dish, assured us, it was the best SALMAGUNDY that he had ever made.

SALMON (or **SALOMON**), *subs.* (Old Cant).—The mass; 'the Beggers Sacrament or Oath.' [SMYTH-PALMER, *Folk Etymology*: 'probably a corruption of Fr. *serment*'; OLIPHANT, *New Eng.*, i. 384, 'Henry VIII., when surprised, cries *by the mass* (ELLIS, *Letters*, III. i. 196, 1513-25); this was to become a common oath all through the country.'] (HARMAN, DEKKER, ROWLANDS, HEAD, B. E., BAILEY, GROSE, EGAN, BEE.)

*c.*1536. COPLAND, *Spyttel-hous* [HAZLITT, *Pop. Poet.*, iv.]. By SALMON, and thou shall pek my jere.

1611. MIDDLETON, *Roaring Girl*, v. 1. I have, by the SALOMON, a doxy that carries a kinchin-mort in her slate at her back.

1614. OVERBURY, *Characters*, 'A Canting Rogue.' He will not beg out of his limit though hee starve; nor break his oath if hee sware by his SALOMAN . . . though you hang him.

1622. FLETCHER, *Beggar's Bush*, 'Maunder's Initiation.' I . . . stall thee by the SALMON into clowes.

1641. BROME, *Jovial Crew*, ii. By SALAMON, I think my mort is in drink.

1707. SHIRLEY, *Triumph of Wit*, 'Maunder's Praise of His Strowling Mort.' Doxy, oh! thy glaziers shine As glimmar; by the SALOMON!

1749. MOORE-CAREW, *Oath of Canting Crew.* And as I keep to the foregone, So may help me SALAMON!

1815. SCOTT, *Guy Mannering*, xxxiv. She swore by the SALMON.

SALMON-AND-TROUT, *subs. phr.* (rhyming).—The mouth: *see* POTATO-TRAP.

SALT, *subs.* (common).—1. A sailor: esp. an old hand: also SALT-WATER.

1835. DANA, *Two Years*, i. My complexion and hands were enough to distinguish me from the regular SALT.

1839. AINSWORTH, *Jack Sheppard*, vi. And why not, old SALTWATER? inquired Ben, turning a quid in his mouth.

1844. SELBY, *London By Night*, i. 1. I am too old a SALT to allow myself to drift on the quicksand of woman's perfidy.

1861. HUGHES, *Tom Brown at Oxford*, viii. He can turn his hand to anything, like most old SALTS.

1884. RUSSELL, *Jack's Courtship*, xxiii. The crew in oilskins, the older SALTS among them casting their eyes to windward at the stormy look of the driving sky.

1885. *D. Telegraph*, 11 Sept. An old SALT sitting at the tiller.

2. (common).—Money: specifically (Eton College) the gratuity exacted at the now obsolete triennial festival of the MONTEM (*q.v.*). Also (generic) = a measure of value.

1886. BREWER, *Phrase and Fable*, s.v. SALTHILL. At the Eton Montem the captain of the school used to collect money from the visitors on Montem day. Standing on a mound at Slough, he waved a flag, and persons appointed for the purpose collected the donations. The mound is still called SALT-HILL, and the money given was called SALT . . . similar to the Lat. *salarium* (salary) the pay given to Roman soldiers and civil officers.

1890. *Speaker*, 22 Feb., 210, 2. In lively, but worldly fashion we go to Eton, with its buried Montem, its "SALT! your majesty, SALT!" its gin-twirley, and its jumping through paper fires in Long Chamber.

3. (old).—Pointed language; wit: whence SALT-PITS (old Univ.) = 'The store of attic wit' (GROSE).

1580. BARET, *Alvearie*, s.v. SALT, a pleasaunt and merrie word that maketh folks to laugh, and sometime pricketh.

1635. QUARLES, *Emblems* [NARES]. Tempt not your SALT beyond her power.

1639. MAYNE, *Citye Match*, 15. She speaks with SALT.

Adj. (old).—1. Wanton; amorous; PROUD (*q.v.*). Also, as *subs.* = (1) HEAT (*q.v.*), and (2) = the act of kind; as *verb* = to copulate (B. E., GROSE). Whence SALT-CELLAR = the female *pudendum*: *see* MONOSYLLABLE; and SALT-WATER = urine.

1598. FLORIO, *Worlde of Wordes*, s.v. *Esser in frega*, to be proud or SALT as a bitch, or a catterwalling as cats.

1599. JONSON, *Ev. Man Out of His Humour*, iv. 4. Let me perish, but thou art a SALT one. *Ibid.* (1605), *Fox*, ii. 1. It is no SALT desire Of seeing countries . . . hath brought me out.

1599. HALL, *Satires*, IV. 1. He lies wallowing . . . on his brothel-bed Till his SALT bowels boile with poisonous fire.

1602. SHAKSPEARE, *Othello*, ii. 1, 244. For the better compassing of his SALT and most hidden loose affection. *Ibid.* (1608), *Antony and Cleopatra*, ii. 1. All the charms of love, SALT Cleopatra, soften thy wan lip.

1607. TOPSELL, *Beasts*, 139. Then they grow SALT, and begin to be proud.

1647-8. HERRICK, *Parting Verse* [*Hesperides*, 186]. The expressions of that itch And SALT which frets thy suters.

*d.*1704. BROWN, *Works*, ii. 202. It is not fit the silent beard should know how much it has been abus'd . . . for, if it did it would . . . make it open its sluice to the drowning of the low countries in an inundation of SALT-WATER.

2. (colloquial).—Costly; heavy; extravagant: generic for excess: *e.g.*, AS SALT AS FIRE = as salt as may be. Also SALTY.

1847. ROBB, *Squatter Life*, 142. Well, that thar was a SALTY scrape, boys.

1887. *Fun*, 21 Sept., 126. A magistrate who was lately fined 20s. for striking a man in the street, seemed somewhat astonished on hearing the decision, and remarked, "It's rather SALT."

Verb. (common).—To swindle: specifically to cheat by fictitiously enhancing value; *e.g.*, to SALT books = (1) to make bogus entries showing extensive and profitable

business; to SALT an invoice = to charge extreme prices so as to permit an apparently liberal discount; to SALT a mine = to sprinkle (or PLANT, *q.v.*) a worn-out or bogus property with gold dust, diamonds, &c., with a view to good sales, and so forth. Hence SALTER = a fraudulent vendor.

1872. *Civil Service Gaz.*, 28 Dec. The magnificent Californian diamond fields are nowhere . . . only SALTED with diamonds and rubies bought in England, according to the well-known process of SALTING.

1883. PAYN, *Canon's Ward*, xlviii. Your two friends had . . . been SALTING the mine. There is a warrant out for Dawson's apprehension on a much more serious charge.

1885. *D. Telegraph*, 22 Sept. One of the first to practise the art of SALTING sham goldfields.

1892. PERCY CLARKE, *New Chum in Australia*, 72. A SALTED claim, a pit sold for a £10 note, in which a nugget worth a few shillings had before been planted.

1894. *Pall Mall Gaz.*, 22 Dec. 'The art of SALTING a mine' [Title]. *Ibid.* Even experienced mining men and engineers have been made victims by SALTERS.

*d.*1901. BRET HARTE . . . . And the tear of sensibility has SALTED many a claim.

2. (American colloquial).—To be-jewell profusely: *see* sense 1, TO SALT A MINE.

1873. *Times*, 20 Jan. 'WELL SALTED.' An American paper states that Colorado ladies wearing much jewelry are said to be WELL SALTED.

3. (old).—*See* quot.

1636. [MARTIN, *Life of First Lord Shaftesbury*, i. 42]. On a particular day, the senior undergraduates in the evening called the freshmen to the fire, and made them hold out their chins; whilst one of the seniors with the nail of his thumb (which was left long for that purpose) grated off all the skin from the lip to the chin, and then obliged him to drink a beer glass of water and SALT.

1850. *Notes and Queries*, 1 S., i. 390. 'College SALTING and Tucking of Freshmen.'

PHRASES.—WITH A GRAIN OF SALT = under reserve: Lat.; NOT WORTH ONE'S SALT = unworthy of hire; TO EAT ONE'S SALT = to be received as a guest or under protection: SALT also = hospitality; TO PUT (CAST, or LAY) SALT ON THE TAIL = to ensnare, to achieve: as children are told to catch birds; TO COME AFTER WITH SALT AND SPOONS ('of one that is none of the Hastings,' B. E.); MAN OF SALT = a man of tears.

1580. LYLY, *Euphues* [OLIPHANT, *New Eng.*, i. 607. Among the verbs are . . . LAY SALT ON A BIRD'S TAILE].

1608-11. HALL, *Epistles*, Dec. i., Ep. 8. Abandon those from your table and SALT whom . . . experience shall descrie dangerous

1664 BUTLER, *Hudibras*, II. i. 278. Such great atchievements cannot fail To CAST SALT ON A WOMAN'S TAIL.

1809. WELLINGTON [GLEIG, *Life*, 702]. The real fact is . . . I have EATEN the King's SALT. On that account I believe it to be my duty to serve without hesitation . . .

1824. SCOTT, *Redgauntlet*, xi. Were you coming near him with soldiers, or constables . . . you will never LAY SALT ON HIS TAIL.

1854. DICKENS, *Hard Times*, xvii. He is a dissipated extravagant idler; he is NOT WORTH HIS SALT. *Ibid.* (1861), *Great Expectations*, iv. Plenty of subjects going about for them that know how TO PUT SALT UPON THEIR TAILS.

1855. THACKERAY, *Newcomes*, v. One does not EAT A MAN'S SALT as it were at these dinners. There is nothing sacred in this kind of London hospitality.

SALT-BOX, *subs.* (thieves').—A prison cell: specifically (Newgate) = the condemned cell (GROSE, VAUX). Fr. *abattoir.*

1820. *London Mag.*, I. 29. Leaving the stone-jug after a miserable residence in the SALT-BOXES, to be topp'd in front of the debtors' door.

SALT-BOX-CLY, *subs. phr.* (Old Cant).—An outside pocket with a flap (GROSE, VAUX).

SALTEE (or **SAULTY**), *subs.* (theatrical).—A penny: *see* RHINO.

1861. READE, *Cloister and Hearth*, lv. It had rained kicks all day in lieu of SALTEES.

1875. FROST, *Circus Life*, 306. SAULTY may be derived from the Italian *soldi*, and *duey* SAULTY and *tray* SAULTY are also of foreign origin.

SALT-EEL, *subs. phr.* (old naval).—A rope's-end; TO HAVE SALT-EEL FOR SUPPER = to be thrashed (B. E., GROSE).

1695. CONGREVE, *Love for Love*, iii. 7. *Ben.* An' he comes near me, may hap I may giv'n A SALT EEL FOR'S SUPPER for all that.

1752. SMOLLETT, *Per. Pickle*, xl. If so be as how you have a mind to give him a SALT-EEL FOR SUPPER.

SALT-HORSE (or **SALT-JUNK**), *subs. phr.* (nautical).—Salt beef: also OLD-HORSE (or -JUNK) which *see*.

1837. MARRYATT, *Snarley Yow*, xii. So while they cut their raw SALT JUNKS, with beef you will be crammed.

1874. SCAMMON, *Marine Mammals*, 123. Substantial fare called SALT-HORSE and hard-tack.

1880. *Blackwood's Mag.*, Jan., 59. 'Let me give you some SALT JUNK.' John was hungry, and rather enjoyed the salt beef.

1884. RUSSELL, *Jack's Courtship*, i. SALT-HORSE works out of the pores.

SALTIMBANCO, *subs.* (showmen's).—A street clown; A JIM CROW; A BILLY BARLOW. Fr. *pitre*.

SALT RIVER, *subs. phr.* (American).—*See* quots.

1848. BARTLETT, *Dict.* [quoting J. INMAN]. TO ROW UP SALT RIVER . . . there is a small stream of that name in Kentucky . . . difficult and laborious by its tortuous course as by shallows and bars. The application is to the unhappy wight who has the task of propelling the boat up the stream; but, in political or slang usage, it is to those who are rowed up.

c. 186 [?]. *Burial of Uncle Sam* [quoted by DE VERE]. "We thought . . . That Sag-Nichts and strangers would tread o'er his head, And we up the SALT RIVER billows."

1871. DE VERE, *Americanisms*, . . . It has become a universal cant phrase to say, that an unlucky wight, who has failed to be elected to some public office, was ROWED UP SALT RIVER. If very grievously defeated, they were apt to be ROWED UP TO THE VERY HEADWATERS OF SALT RIVER.

1877. *New York Tribune*, 28 Feb. Put away his empty barrel; Fold his Presidential clothes; He has started up SALT RIVER, Led and lit by Cronin's nose.

SALTS-AND-SENNA, *subs. phr.* (common).—A doctor: *see* TRADES.

SALUBRIOUS, *adj.* (common).—1. Drunk: *see* SCREWED; (2) = 'Pretty well, thank you.'

SALVE, *subs.* (common).—Praise; GAMMON (*q.v.*): *cf.* LIP-SALVE.

SAM, *subs.* (provincial).—A Liverpudlian: also DICKY SAM.

TO STAND SAM, *verb. phr.* (common).—To pay the shot; TO TREAT (*q.v.*).

1823. MONCRIEFF, *Tom and Jerry*, iii. 5. Landlady, serve them with a glass of tape, all round; and I'll STAND SAMMY.

1834. AINSWORTH, *Rookwood*, IV. ii. I must insist upon STANDING SAM upon the present occasion.

1876. HINDLEY, *Cheap Jack*, 123. He had perforce to STAND SAM for the lot.

1885. BLACK, *White Heather*, xxxii. There's plenty ready TO STAND SAM, now that Ronald is kent as a writer o' poetry.

1887. HENLEY, *Villon's Good-Night*, 2. Likewise you molls that flash your bubs For Swells to spot and STAND YOU SAM.

1890. *Lic. Vict. Gaz.*, 8 Feb. I'll STAND SAM for a week at Brighton for both of us.

1893. MILLIKEN, *'Arry Ballads*, 36. If sometimes P. J. do STAND SAM, why I ain't one to give myself hairs.

SAMBO, *subs.* (old).—A negro: generic: *c.* 1558 (ARBER, *Garner*, v. 95) a tribe of Africans is called SAMBOSES.

1862. *Punch*, Aug., *Jon. Appeal*. Now, SAMBO, darn it . . . You know how we in airnest air, From slavery to ease you.

SAMMY (or **SAMMY-SOFT**), *subs. phr.* (common).—A fool: *see* BUFFLE. Also as *adj.* = foolish (GROSE).

1837. PEAKE, *Quarter to Nine*, 2. What a SAMMY, give me a shilling more than I axed him!

1843. MONCRIEFF, *Scamps of London*, ii. 1. I'm a ruined homo, a muff, a flat, a SAM, a regular ass.

SAMPLE, *verb.* (common).—1. To drink: *see* LUSH. Hence SAMPLE-ROOM = a drinking bar.

1847. PORTER, *Quarter Race*, 118. Old T. never SAMPLES too much when on business.

18 [?]. H. PAUL, *World Upside Down* [BARTLETT]. John opened a SAMPLE-ROOM, and served out beer and gin.

2. (venery).—To fumble, or occupy a woman for the first time.

SAMPLE-COUNT, *subs.* (commercial).—A traveller; an AMBASSADOR OF COMMERCE (*q.v.*).

1894. EGERTON, *Keynotes*, 72. An ubiquitous SAMPLE-COUNT from Berlin is measuring his wits with a . . . merchant.

SAMPLE OF SIN, *subs. phr.* (old).—A harlot: *see* TART.

1749. SMOLLETT, *Gil Blas* [ROUTLEDGE], 105. That delicate SAMPLE OF SIN, who depends on her wantonness for her attractions.

SAMPLER, *subs.* (venery).—The female *pudendum*: *see* MONOSYLLABLE.

SAMSON (or **SAMPSON**), *subs.* (common).—1. A drink made of brandy, cider, sugar, and a little water (HALLIWELL).

2. (Durham School).—A baked jam pudding.

SAMSON AND ABEL, *subs. phr.* (Oxford University).—A group of wrestlers in the quadrangle of Brasenose. [Some said it represented Samson killing a Philistine; others Cain killing Abel: the matter was compromised.]

SAMSON'S-POSTS, *subs. phr.* (common).—A mousetrap so constructed that the capture is crushed to death.

SAND, *subs.* (old).—1. Moist sugar (GROSE, VAUX).

2. (American).—*See* quots.

1847. ROBB, *Squatter Life*, 73. He set his brain to work conning a most powerful speech, one that would knock the SAND from under Hoss.

1884. CLEMENS, *Huck. Finn*, viii. When I got to camp I warn't feeling very brash, there warn't much SAND in my craw; but I says, this ain't no time to be fooling around.

1892. J. L. HILL, *Treason-Felony*, 22. You're a long-winded old fraud, Mac, with a bonnet full of bees, and a head full of maggots, but you've got the SAND.

1896. LILLARD, *Poker Stories*, 19. SAND enough and money enough to sit out the game.

TO EAT SAND, *verb. phr.* (old).—*See* quot.

1743. *Memoirs of M. du Gue-Trouin* (2nd ed.), 95. Now it is very common for the man at the helm to shorten his watch by turning the glass before it is quite run out, which is called EATING OF SAND . . . as we had not seen the sun for nine days

together . . . it happened, that the helmsmen had EATEN SO MUCH SAND, that at the end of nine days they had changed the day into night, and the night into day.

SANDBAG, *subs.* (thieves').—1. A long sausage-like bag of sand dealing a heavy blow that leaves no mark. Also as *verb.*, and SANDBAGGER.

1895. POCOCK, *Rules of the Game*, II. vii. The other burglar, who looked like a mechanic, had now come up behind, and was brandishing a SAND-BAG.

2. (military).—In *pl.* = The Grenadier Guards. Also OLD EYES, COALHEAVERS, HOUSEMAIDS' PETS, and BERMUDA EXILES (*q.v.*).

SANDBOY. AS HAPPY (JOLLY or MERRY) AS A SANDBOY, *phr.* (old).—'All rags and all happiness . . . a merry fellow who has tasted a drop' (BEE).

1840. DICKENS, *Old Cur. Shop*, xvii. I put up at the JOLLY SANDBOYS, and nowhere else.

1900. BOOTHBY, *Maker of Nations*, iv. He had had a fairly rough time of it, but the men seemed as jolly as SANDBOYS.

SANDGATE-RATTLE, *subs. phr.* (provincial).—A quick and violent stamping dance.

SAND-MAN (or **SANDY-MAN**), *subs. phr.* (nursery).—When sleepy children begin to rub their eyes 'THE SAND-MAN (or DUSTMAN) IS COMING.'

SANDPAPER, *verb.* (common).—*See* quots.

1889. *Answers*, 9 Feb. "You will have to enact three parts in the 'Silent Foe' to-night." "Can't do it," said Lancaster, "and I hope to be SANDPAPERED if I try."

1901. *D. Telegraph*, 14 May, 10, 7. Let the American grass-widow with the broad and exasperating accent, which she takes no pains to SANDPAPER, be reduced to a minimum.

SANDWICH, *subs.* (common).—1. *See* quots.: also SANDWICH MAN: *see* TOAD-IN-THE-HOLE.

1836. DICKENS, *Boz*, 147. He stopped the unstamped advertisement—an ANIMATED SANDWICH, composed of a boy between two boards.

1880. *Scribner's Mag.*, Aug., 607. The double sign-boards, or SANDWICHES [incorrectly used] which conceal his body. *Ibid.*, 609. The SANDWICH-MAN carries in glass cases sample boots, sample shirts, &c.

2. (common).—A gentleman between two ladies: *cf.* BODKIN; THORN BETWEEN TWO ROSES, &c. Fr. *âne à deux pannières*.

1848. THACKERAY, *Vanity Fair*, lviii. A pale young man . . . came walking down the lane EN SANDWICH—having a lady, that is, on each arm.

Verb. (colloquial).—To insert between dissimilars.

1886. *Referee*, 18 April. These proceedings were SANDWICHED with vocal and instrumental selections.

SANDWICH-BOAT. *See* BUMPING-RACE.

SANDY, *subs.* (Scots' colloquial).—A Scot: short for Alexander.

1500. DUNBAR, *Works* [PATERSON], 251 [OLIPHANT, *New Eng.*, i. 362. Alexander appears as SANDY; Englishmen on the other hand, dock the last half of the Greek word, and make it *Alick*].

d. 1555. LYNDSAY, *Kitty's Confessioun* [LAING], i. 136. Ane plack I will gar SANDY, Gie the agane with Handie-Dandie.

1885. *Sportsman*, 28 July, 2, 1. Scotland has been troubled by a great and mighty heat, which has scorched SANDY'S brow and burnt the colour out of his kilt.

SANDY-PATE, *subs.* (old).—'One red-hair'd' (B. E., GROSE).

SANGAREE, *subs.* (old).—1. A drunken bout (HALLIWELL).

SANGUINARY JAMES. *See* BLOODY.

SANK (**SANKY**, or **CENTIPERS**), *subs.* (old).—A soldiers' tailor (GROSE): whence SANK-WORK (*see* quot).

1851-61. MAYHEW, *Lon. Lab.*, i. 377. She's gone almost as blind as myself working at the SANK WORK (making up soldiers' clothing).

SAP (**SAPHEAD**, **SAP-PATE**, or **SAPSCULL**), *subs.* (old).—1. A fool: *see* BUFFLE. Whence SAPPY (or SAPHEADED, &c.) = foolish; namby-pamby; lazy (B. E., DYCHE, MARTIN, GROSE, BEE).

1665. HEAD, *English Rogue* (1874), I. v. 48. *Culle* a SAP-HEADED fellow.

1815. SCOTT, *Guy Mannering*, xlviii. "They're sporting the door of the Custom-house, and the auld SAP at Hazlewood House has ordered off the guard." *Ibid.* (1817), *Rob Roy*, xix. He maun be a soft SAP.

1840. HALIBURTON, *Clockmaker*, 3, v. v. Talkin' cute, looks knavish; but talkin' soft, looks SAPPY.

1856. BRONTE, *Professor*, iv. If you are patient because you think it a duty to meet an insult with submission, you are an essential SAP.

1884. CLEMENS, *Huck. Finn*, iii. You don't seem to know anything, somehow—perfect SAP-HEAD.

1886. *The State*, 20 May, 217. A SAP-HEAD is a name for a fool.

1887. BRET HARTE, *Cons. of Excelsior*, II. i. These SAP-HEADED fools.

1893. MILLIKEN, *'Arry Ballads*, 70. Sour old SAP.

2. (common).—A hard worker: (school) a diligent student; a HASH (Charterhouse). Also as *verb.* = to read hard; to SWOT.

1827. LYTTON, *Pelham*, ii. When I once attempted to read Pope's poems out of school hours, I was laughed at, and called a SAP.

1848. KINGSLEY, *Yeast*, i. SAPPING and studying still.

1850. SMEDLEY, *Frank Fairlegh*, 117. They pronounced me an incorrigible SAP.

1853. LYTTON, *My Novel*, I. xii. He was sent to school to learn his lessons, and he learns them. You calls that SAPPING—I call it doing his duty.

1856. WHYTE-MELVILLE, *Kate Coventry*, xvii. At school, if he makes an effort at distinction in school-hours, he is stigmatised by his comrades as a SAP.

1888. GOSCHEN, *Speech at Aberdeen*, 31 Jan. Epithets applied to those who . . . commit the heinous offence of being absorbed in it [work]. Schools and colleges . . . have invented . . . phrases, semi-classical or wholly vernacular, such as a "SAP," "smug," "swot," "bloke," "a mugster."

1891. *Harry Fludyer at Cambridge*, 46. I . . . haven't to go SAPPING round to get it when I want my own tea.

3. (common).—Ale: *see* DRINKS. Hence, as *verb.* = TO BOOZE (*q.v.*): SAPPY-DRINKING = excessive drinking.

SAPPY, *adj.* (Durham School).—1. Severe; of a caning.

2. *See* SAP, *subs.* 1.

SARAHS, *subs.* (Stock Exchange).—Manchester, Sheffield, and Lincoln Deferred Stock.

SARAH'S BOOTS, *subs. phr.* (Stock Exchange).—Sierra Buttes Gold Mining Co.'s Shares.

SARD, *verb.* (old).—To copulate: *see* GREENS and RIDE.

1539. LYNDSAY, *Thrie Estaitis* [LAING], 3027, 8. Quhilk will, for purging of their neirs SARD up ae raw, and doun the uthir.

1598. FLORIO, *Worlde of Wordes* s.v. *Fottere*. To iape, to SARD, to fucke, to swive, to occupye.

1617. HOWELL, *Letters*, 17. Go, teach your grandam TO SARD, a Nottingham proverb.

SARDINE, *subs.* (American). — 1. A sailor: *spec.* an old whaling hand. [The living space on board a whaler is limited.] Whence (2) one of the crowd: *see* HERRING. PACKED LIKE SARDINES = huddled.

c.184 [?]. *New Haven, J. C.* [BARTLETT]. We 'Old Whalers,' or as we are sometimes called 'SARDINES.'

3. (Stock Exchange).—In *pl.* = Royal Sardinian Ry. Shares.

SARK, *verb.* (Sherborne School).—To sulk.

SASSENGER (or **SASSIGER**), *subs.* (vulgar).—A sausage.

SATAN'S BONES. *See* BONES.

SATCHEL-ARSED. *See* ARSE.

SATE-POLL, *subs. phr.* (common).—A stupid person: *see* BUFFLE.

SATIN. *See* WHITE SATIN.

SATURDAY - NIGHTER, *subs. phr.* (Harrow School).—An exercise set for Saturday night.

SATURDAY-SCAVENGER (or **-SCARAMOUCH**. *See* WEEKLY SCARIFIER.

SATURDAY - SOLDIER, *subs. phr.* (common).—A volunteer.

1890. *Globe*, 11 Aug., 3, 2. A slight selection of the epithets which he showered on the citizen defender: "Catshooter," SATURDAY SOLDIER.

SATURDAY-TO-MONDAY, *subs. phr.* (colloquial). — 1. A week-end jaunt; and (2) a week-end woman.

SATYR, *subs.* (Old Cant). — A cattle-thief.

SAUCE (SARSE, SASS, or **SAUCINESS)**, *subs.* (colloquial). — 1. Impudence; assurance (*see* quot. 1555). Hence SAUCY (*adj.*) = (1) impudent, bold, presuming; and (2) SMART (*q.v.*); as *verb.* (or TO EAT SAUCE) = to abuse, TO LIP (*q.v.*); SAUCE-BOX (SAUCE-PATE, SAUCELING, or SAUCE-JACK) = an impertinent: *see* JACK-SAUCE (B. E., GROSE).

*d.*1529. SKELTON, *Bowge of Courte*, 71. To be so perte . . . she sayde she trowed that I had ETEN SAUCE; she asked yf euer I DRANKE of SAUCYS CUPPE. *Ibid.*, *Magnyfycence*, 1421. Ye haue ETEN SAUCE, I trowe, at the Taylors Hall.

*d.*1555. LATIMER, *Sermons*, 182. When we see a fellow sturdy, loftie, and proud, men say, this is a SAUCY fellow . . . whiche taketh more upon him than he ought to doe. *Ibid.* He that will be a Christian man . . . must be a SAUSIE fellow: he must be well powdered with the SAUSE of affliction.

1587. STANIHURST, *Desc. of Ireland*, I. 13. *Ineptus* is as much in English, in my phantasie, as SAUCIE or malapert.

1588. *Marprelate's Epistle* (ARBER), 6. This is a pretie matter yat standers by must be so busie in other men's games: why SAWCEBONES must you be pratling?

1594. TYLNEY, *Lochrine*, iii. 3. You, master SAUCEBOX, lobcock, cockscomb.

1595. SHAKSPEARE, *Romeo and Juliet*, ii. 4, 153. What SAUCY merchant was this, that was so full of his ropery? *Ibid.* (1596), *As You Like It*, iii. 5. I'll SAUCE her with bitter words. *Ibid.* (1600), *Merry Wives*, iv. 3. I'll make them pay: I'll SAUCE them. *Ibid.*, *Lear* (1605), i. 1. This knave came somewhat SAUCILY into the world before he was sent for.

1598. LAYDOCK, *Lomatius on Painting* [NARES]. Nothing can deterre these SAUCIE doultes from this their dizardly inhumanite.

1614. JONSON, *Barth. Fair.* The reckonings for them are so SAUCY, that a man had as good licke his fingers in a baudy house.

1620. FLETCHER, *Philaster*, ii. 1. They were grown too SAUCY for himself.

1630. TAYLOR, *Works*, i. 113. JACK SAWCE, the worst knave amongst the pack.

1638. PEACHAM, *Truth of Our Times.* In Queene Elizabeth's time were the great bellied doublets, wide SAWCY sleeves, that would be in every dish before their masters.

1663. KILLEGREW, *Parson's Wedding*, iii. Why, goodman SAUCE-BOX, you will not make my lady pay for their reckoning, will you?

1689. *Satyr Against Hypocrites* [NARES]. Then, full of SAWCE and zeal, up steps Elnathan.

1705. WARD, *Hud. Rediv.*, i. i. 28. No SAUCEBOX, sure, by way of Farce, Will bid his Pastor Kiss his Arse.

1732. FIELDING, *Mock Doctor*, 2. What's that to you, SAUCE-BOX? Is it any business of yours.

1839. AINSWORTH, *Jack Sheppard*, II. xii. How do you like your quarters, SAUCEBOX? asked Sharples, in a 'eering tone.

*c.*1838. *East End Tailor's Broadside Advt.* Kicksies made very SAUCY.

1843. MONCRIEFF, *Scamps of London*, iii. 1. I've got a SARCY pair.

1856-7. ELIOT, *Amos Barton*, vii. Nanny . . . secretly chuckled over her outburst of SAUCE as the best morning's work she had ever done.

1862. LOWELL, *Biglow Papers.* We begin to think it's nater To take SARCE, and not be riled.

*c.*1871. *Siliad*, 17. Yankee impudence and SASS.

1890. *M. Advertiser*, 4 Nov. The witness denied that she SAUCED him or that she was drunk.

1897. MAUGHAM, *Liza of Lambeth*, xi. I won't kill yer, but if I 'ave any more of your SAUCE, I'll do the next thing to it.

2. (old: now American). — Vegetables: whence GARDEN-SAUCE = a salad; LONG-SAUCE = carrots, parsnips, beet, &c.; SHORT-SAUCE = potatoes, turnips, onions, &c. Whence any accessory or sequel.

1705. BEVERLEY, *Hist. of Virginia.* Roots, herbs, vine fruits, and salad flowers . . . very delicious SAUCE to their meats.

1833. NEAL, *Down Easters*, vii. 91. That ain't the kind o' SARSE I wanted, puddin' gravy to corn-fish! . . . I wanted cabbage or potaters, or most any sort o' garden SARSE.

184 [?]. *Widow Bedott Papers*, 88. If I should stay away to tea . . . don't be a lettin' into the plum SASS and cake as you did the other day.

3. (venery).—Pox (*q.v.*) or CLAP (*q.v.*).

1697. VANBRUGH, *Provok'd Wife*, iv. 3. I hope your punks will give you SAUCE to your mutton.

3. (old).—Money: *see* RHINO.

1749. SMOLLETT, *Gil Blas* (1812), I. ii. Having paid SAUCE for a supper which I had so ill digested. *Ibid.*, II. vii. Having breakfasted, and paid SAUCE for my good cheer, I made but one stage to Segovia.

PHRASES.—TO SERVE WITH THE SAME SAUCE = to minister or retaliate in kind; 'WHAT'S SAUCE FOR THE GOOSE IS SAUCE FOR THE GANDER' = TIT-FOR-TAT (*q.v.*); CARRIER'S- (or POOR MAN'S-) SAUCE = hunger: *cf.* 'Hunger is the best SAUCE'; 'MORE SAUCE THAN PIG' = 'exceeding bold' (B. E.).

1609. *Man in the Moone* [NARES]. After him another came unto her, and SERVED her WITH THE SAME SAUCE: then a third: at last she began to wax warie.

1700. COLLIER, *Short Def. of Short View*, 37. THAT'S SAWCE FOR A GOOSE IS SAWCE FOR A GANDER.

1703. WARD, *Lond. Spy* [NARES]. If he had been strong enough I dare swear he would have SERV'D him THE SAME SAUCE.

1708-10. SWIFT, *Polite Conversation*, ii. *Neverout* [*giving Miss a pinch* (*in return*)]. Take that, Miss; WHAT'S SAUCE FOR A GOOSE IS FOR A GANDER.

1749. SMOLLETT, *Gil Blas* [ROUTLEDGE], 367, s.v. SAUCE FOR GOOSE, SAUCE FOR GANDER.

1896. COTSFORD DICK, *Way of World*, 44. Let the SAUCE good FOR THE GANDER Then be seasoned, without slander, FOR THE GOOSE!

SAUCEPAN. TO HAVE THE SAUCEPAN ON THE FIRE, *verb. phr.* (old).—To be set on a scolding bout.

THE SAUCEPAN RUNS (or BOILS) OVER, *phr.* (old).—'You are exceeding bold.'—B. E. (*c.* 1696).

SAUCEBOX, *subs.* (common).—The mouth.

2. *See* SAUCE.

SAUCERS, *subs.* (common).—Eyes: spec. large, wide-opened eyes: also SAUCER-EYES.

1599. HALL, *Satires*, VI. i. Her eyes like silver SAUCERS faire beset.

1636. SUCKLING, *Goblins*, iv. Had we no walking fire, Nor SAUCER-EYED devil of these woods that led us.

1655. MASSINGER, *A Very Woman*, ii. Upon my conscience, she would see the devil first, With eyes AS BIG AS SAUCERS; when I but named you.

1697. VANBRUGH, *Relapse*, v. 3. Stare you in the face with huge SAUCER-EYES.

1751. SMOLLETT, *Peregrine Pickle*, xiii. Damn'd if it was not Davy Jones himself. I know him by his SAUCER-EYES.

1864. MARK LEMON, *Jest Book*, 185. I always know when he has been in his cups by the state of his SAUCERS.

SAUCY GREENS, *subs. phr.* (military).—The 2nd Bat. Worcester Regiment, formerly the Thirty-Sixth Foot. [From the facings 1742-1881.]

SAUCY-JACK. *See* SAUCY, and JACK, *subs.*, sense 8.

SAUCY POMPEYS. *See* POMPADOURS.

SAUCY SIXTH (THE), *subs. phr.* (military).—The Royal Warwickshires, formerly The 6th Foot. Also "Guise's Geese"; and "The Warwickshire Lads."

SAUCY SEVENTH (THE OLD).—The Seventh (The Queen's Own) Hussars (in the Peninsula): also "The Lily-white Seventh," "Young Eyes," "Old Straws," and "Strawboots."

SAUNTER, *verb.* (old: now recognised).—'To loiter Idly' (B. E.).

SAUSAGE (or **LIVE-SAUSAGE**), *subs.* (venery).—The *penis*: *see* PRICK.

1653. URQUHART, *Rabelais*, I. xi. Some of the other women would give these names, my Roger . . . my lusty LIVE SAUSAGE, my crimson chitterling.

1759-67. STERNE, *Tristram Shandy*, IX. 7. She made a feint, however, of defending herself by snatching up a SAUSAGE. Tom instantly laid hold of *another*—But seeing Tom's had more gristle in it—She signed the capitulation—and Tom seal'd it; and there was an end of the matter.

SAVAGEROUS, *adv.* (American).—Savage.

1847. PORTER, *Big Bear*, 121. Well, Capting, they war mighty SAVAGEROUS arter likher.

1848. BURTON, *Waggeries*, 24. They growed so darned SAVAGEROUS that I kinder feared for my own safety.

*c.*1852. *Traits of Amer. Humour*, 53. I looked at him sorter SAVIGEROUS like.

SAVE, *verb.* (racing).—To set part of one bet against another; TO HEDGE (*q.v.*). [Two persons back different horses agreeing, if either wins, to give the other, say £5, who thus SAVES a 'fiver.' Also, as in pool, to SAVE the stakes. Likewise to keep a certain horse on one side, not betting against it, SAVING it as a clear winner for oneself. Hence SAVER = a bet so made.

1869. BRADWOOD, *The O. V. H.*, xx. Most who received the news at least SAVED themselves upon the outsider.

1891. GOULD, *Double Event*, 301. The fact of the matter was, Kingdon had determined to make a £10,000 book for Mohican, or, in other words, to SAVE that horse to run for him. *Ibid.*, 123. I've put a SAVER on Caloola.

HANG SAVING, *phr.* (old colloquial).—'Blow the expense.'

1708-10. SWIFT, *Polite Conversation*, ii. *Lord Smart.* Come, HANG SAVING: bring us a Halfporth of Cheeze.

See BACON.

SAVE-ALL, *subs. phr.* (common).—A stingy person; a miser (GROSE).

SAVERS, *intj.* (boys').—'Halves!'

SAVE-REVERENCE. *See* SIR-REVERENCE.

SAVING-CHIN, *subs. phr.* (old).—A projecting chin: 'that catches what may fall from the nose': *cf.* NUTCRACKERS (GROSE).

1772. BRIDGES, *Burlesque Homer*, 56. It had your phizz and toothless jaws, And SAVING-CHIN and pimpl'd nose.

SAVEY (or **SAVVY**), *subs.* and *verb.* (American).—1. As *verb* = to know; as *subs.* = understanding; wit; NOUS (*q.v.*).

1833. CARMICHAEL, *West Indies* [BARTLETT]. When I read these stories, the Negroes looked delighted, and said: "We SAVEY dat well, misses."

1884. *Graphic*, 18 Oct., 418, 2. "Because no can SAVVEY if Chinaman like it," was the answer.

1888. BOLDREWOOD, *Robbery Under Arms*, xiv. If George had had the SAVEY to crack himself up a little.

1893. MILLIKEN, *'Arry Ballads*, 11. Fur too much SAVVY to frown.

2. (Pidgin). — To have; to know; to do; and all the other *verbs* that be.

SAW, *subs.* (whist).—The alternate trumping by two partners of suits led for the purpose; a RUFF. Also SEE-SAW, and as *verb.*

1755. *Connoisseur*, No. 60. A forces B, who, by leading Spades, plays into A's hand, who returns a Club, and so they get to a SAW between them.

2. (American).—A hoax: also as *adj.* and *verb.* Fr. *scie.*

1847. PORTER, *Quarter Race*, 68. 'Running a SAW' on a French gentleman.

1847. DARLEY, *Drama in Poterville*, 68. The manager was SAWED, as certainly as that Mr. Waters was not slain. *Ibid.* The thoroughly SAWED victim made way for him as if he had been the cholera incarnate.

SAW YOUR TIMBER! *phr.* (common).—Be off! Cut your STICK (*q.v.*).

HELD AT THE (or A) LONG SAW, *phr.* (old).—Held in suspense.

1742. NORTH, *Lord Guildford*, i. 148. Between the one and the other he was HELD AT THE LONG SAW over a month.

SAWBONES, *subs.* (common).—A surgeon; FLESH-TAILOR (*q.v.*).

1836. DICKENS, *Pickwick*, xxx. 'What! Don't you know what a SAWBONES is, sir?' inquired Mr. Weller. 'I thought everybody know'd as a SAWBONES was a Surgeon.'

1849-50. THACKERAY, *Pendennis*, II. xviii. She has taken on with another chap—another SAWBONES.

SAWDER (or **SOFT-SAWDER**), *subs.* (common).—Soft speech; BLARNEY (*q.v.*).

1853. LYTTON, *My Novel*, III. xiii. You've got SOFT SAWDER enough.

1863. READE, *Hard Cash*, xli. She sent in a note explaining who she was, with a bit of SOFT SAWDER.

1866. ELIOT, *Felix Holt*, xxi. My Lord Jermyn seems to have his insolence as ready as his SOFT SAWDER.

1896. ALLEN, *Tents of Shem*, x. I didn't try bullying; I tried SOFT SAWDER.

SAWDUST (or **SAWDUSTY**), *subs.* (common).—1. Humbug: also as *adj.*

1884. *Punch*, 11 Oct. Fancy, old chump, Me doing the SAWDUSTY reglar, and follering swells on the stump.

1893. MILLIKEN, *'Arry Ballads*, 41. That's true poetry, ain't it Not SAWDUST and snivel.

2. (American).—A variety of the confidence trick.

1888. *Pittsburg Times*, 8 Feb. He is implicated in the robbery of 10,000 dollars from William Murdock on Saturday a week ago. Murdock was drawn into a SAWDUST game in an office whose location he could not remember, on Grant street.

1888. *New Orleans Times Democrat*, 6 Feb. The prominent men you speak of are never at the front in any of these SAWDUST transactions . . . The courts find it very difficult to send a man to State prison for this kind of swindling, and the SAWDUST man who fights hard is generally certain of acquittal.

SAWNEY (or **SAWNY**), *subs.* (old).—1. A lout: *see* BUFFLE (B. E.). As *adj.* = stupid.

1567. EDWARDS, *Damon and Pithias* [DODSLEY, *Old Plays* (HAZLITT), iv. 74]. [OLIPHANT, *New Eng.*, i. 566. A servant speaks French to astonish a friend, and calls him *petit* ZAWNE (zany or sawny).]

1871. MRS. H. WOOD, *Dene Hollow*, viii. That wench Pris . . . she's a regular SAWNEY, though, in some things.

1873. MISS BROUGHTON, *Nancy*, vii. The bronze of his face is a little paled by emotion, but there is no SAWNY sentiment in his tone, none of the lover's whine.

2. (Scots').—A Scot; SANDY (*q.v.*).—B. E., GROSE.

d. 1704. BROWN, *Highlander* [*Works*, i. 127]. And learn from him against a time of need To husband wealth, as SAWNY does his weed.

1714. GAY, *Shep. Week*, vi. 115. He sung of Taffy Welch, and SAWNEY Scot.

1748. SMOLLETT, *Rod. Random*, xiii. [Addressing a Scotchman] 'Is it oatmeal or brimstone, SAWNEY?' said he.

1772. BRIDGES, *Burlesque Homer*, 138. A queer look'd whelp, called SAWNEY Dunn; His men from Caledonia came. *Ibid.* As firm as SAWNEY's rubbing post.

1822. SCOTT, *Fortunes of Nigel*, ii. Jockey . . . a name which at that time was used, as SAWNEY now is, for a general appellative of the Scottish nation.

1892. HENLEY and STEVENSON, *Deacon Brodie*, Tabl. II. ii. Jock runs east, and SAWNEY cuts west.

3. (common).—Bacon; also stolen cheese; hence, SAWNEY-HUNTER = a bacon thief: Fr. *spec.*—GROSE, VAUX.

1851-61. MAYHEW, *London Lab.*, i. 275. Of very ready sale "fish got from the gate" (stolen from Billingsgate; SAWNEY (thieved bacon). *Ibid.*, *Gt. World of London* (1856), 46. SAWNEY-HUNTERS, who purloin cheese or bacon from cheesemongers' doors.

SAWNEYING, *adj.* (old).—Soft-speaking; pimping; CARNEYING (*q.v.*).

1808. SOUTHEY, *Letters*, ii. 63. It looks like a sneaking SAWNEYING Methodist parson.

SAWYER, *subs.* (American).—A snag: a fallen tree, rising and falling with the waves.

1847. ROBB, *Squatter Life*, 106. Snags and SAWYERS, just thar, wur dreadful plenty.

1884. CLEMENS, *Huckleberry Finn*, and *Life on the Mississippi* (1883), *passim*.

SAY. *See* APE'S PATERNOSTER; BOH; JACK ROBINSON; KNIFE; MOUTH; NOTHING; PARSON; PRAYERS; TE DEUM; THING; WHEN.

SAY-SO, *subs. phr.* (colloquial).—An assertion; also a mild oath: ON MY SAY-SO = 'On my word of honour': also SAMMY SAY-SO.

1885. CRADDOCK, *Proph. of Great Smoky Mountains*, xii. Pete Cayce's SAY-SO war all I wanted.

1890. BARR, *Friend Olivia*, xvii. Kelderby stands in the wind of Charles Stuart's SAY-SO.

YOU SAY YOU CAN, BUT CAN YOU? *phr.* (American).—'You lie.'

SCAB, *subs.* (old).—1. A rascal: spec. a constable or sheriff's officer: often jocular. Hence SCABBY (or SCAB) = contemptible; beggarly; SCABBY-SHEEP = a ne'er-do-weel; SCABILONIAN (*see* quot. 1600).

1591. LYLY, *Endimion*, iv. 2. *Pages.* What are yee, SCABS? *Watch.* The Watch: this the Constable.

1594. GREENE, *Frier Bacon* [GROSART, *Works*, XIII. 9]. Loue is such a proud SCAB, that he will never meddle with fooles nor children.

1598. SHAKSPEARE, *2 Hen. IV.*, iii. 2. Wart, thou art a good SCAB. *Ibid.* (1600), *Much Ado*, iii. 3. *Bora.* Comrade, I say! *Con.* Here, man; I am at thy elbow. *Bora.* Mass, and my elbow itched; I thought there would a SCAB follow. *Ibid.* (1601), *Twelfth Night*, ii. 5. *Sir To.* Out, SCAB! *Fab.* Nay, patience, or we break the sinews of our plot.

1600. THOMAS HILL, *Cath. Religion* [NARES]. With the introduction of the Protestant faith were introduced your galligascones, your SCABILONIANS, your St. Thomas onions, your ruffees, your cuffees, and a thousand such new devised Luciferan trinckets.

1608. MIDDLETON, *Trick to Catch the Old One*, ii. 1. He? he's a SCAB to thee.

1630. TAYLOR, *Works*, ii. 111. A whore . . . growes pocky proud . . . That such poore SCABS as I must not come neere her.

1664. COTTON, *Virgil Travestie* (1st ed.), 15. A huffing Jack, a plund'ring Tearer, A vap'ring SCAB, and a great Swearer.

*c.*1696. B. E., *Dict. Cant. Crew*, s.v. SCAB, a sorry Wench, or Scoundril-Fellow.

1701. DEFOE, *True Born Englishman*, I. The Royal Branch, from Pict land did succeed, With troops of Scots, and SCABS from North-by-Tweed.

1751. SMOLLETT, *Peregrine Pickle*, xxi. A lousy, SCABBY, nasty, scurvy, skulking, lubberly noodle.

1851-61. MAYHEW, *London Lab.*, i. 20. He's a regular SCAB. *Ibid.*, iii. 107. I was the SCABBY SHEEP of the family, and I've been punished for it.

1861. MEREDITH, *Evan Harrington*, vi. A SCABBY sixpence?

1900. KIPLING, *Stalky and Co.*, 71. You're three beastly SCABS.

2. (artisans').—A workman who refuses to join, or continues at work during a strike; a BLACKLEG (*q.v.*); generally applied to all non-Union men. Fr. *flint*.

3. (tailors').—A button-hole.

SCABBADO, *subs.* (old).—Syphilis.

1725. BAILEY, *Erasmus's Colloq.* (1900), ii. 23. The new SCABBADO.

SCABBARD, *subs.* (venery).—The female *pudendum*: *see* MONOSYLLABLE.

SCABBY, *adj.* (printers').—Unevenly printed; blotchy.

SCABBY-NECK, *subs. phr.* (nautical).—A Dane.

SCAB-RAISER, *subs. phr.* (military: obsolete).—A drummer. [One of whose duties was to wield the cat.]

SCAD, *subs.* (American).—An abundance: hence in *pl.* = money; resources.

SCADGER, *subs.* (common).—A mean fellow; a CADGER (*q.v.*).

SCAFF, *subs.* (Christ's Hospital: obsolete).—A selfish fellow: the *adj.* forms are SCALY and SCABBY = mean; stingy.

SCAFF-AND-RAFF, *subs. phr.* (Scots' colloquial).—Refuse, rabble, RIFF-RAFF (*q.v.*).

SCAFFOLDERS, *subs.* (old).—Spectators in the gallery; THE GODS (*q.v.*).

1599. HALL, *Satires*, I. iii. 28. He ravishes the gazing SCAFFOLDERS.

SCALAWAG (or **SCALLAWAG**), *subs.* (American).—(1) Anything low class; and spec. (2) as in quot. 1891. As *adj.* = wastrel; shrunken; profligate: *cf.* CARPET-BAGGER.

1855. HALIBURTON, *Human Nature*, [BARTLETT]. You good-for-nothin' young SCALAWAG.

1870. *Melbourne Argus*. A new term has been added to the descriptive slang of the loafing classes of Melbourne. Vagrants are now denominated SCALAWAGS.

1877. *North Am. Rev.*, July, 5. [The carpet-baggers] combining with a few SCALAWAGS and some leading Negroes to serve as decoys for the rest . . . became the strongest body of thieves that ever pillaged a people.

1884. *Chambers's Journal*, 1 March, 139, 1. [Colorado man *loquitur*.] We are here to discuss the existence of thieves and SCALLAWAGS amongst us.

1891. *Century Dict.*, s.v. SCALAWAG. Used in the Southern States, during the Reconstruction period (1865-76) in an almost specific sense, being opprobriously applied by the opponents of the Republican party to native Southerners who acted with that party, as distinguished from Carpet-bagger, a Republican of Northern origin.

SCALD, *verb.* (venery).—(1) To infect; and (2) to wax amorous. SCALDER = a clap (GROSE). As *adj.* = (1) infected, and (2) contemptible; scoundrel. CUPID'S SCALDING-HOUSE = a brothel.

1563-4. *New Custom* [NARES]. Like lettuce like lips, a scab'd horse for a SCALD squire.

1592. NASH, *Piers Penniless* [HALLIWELL]. Other news I am advertised of that a SCALD, trivial, lying pamphlet is given out to be of my doing.

1599. MIDDLETON, *Old Law*, iii. 2. My three court codlings that look parboil'd, As if they came from CUPID'S SCALDING HOUSE.

1599. SHAKSPEARE, *Hen. V.*, v. 1, 31. Will you be so good, SCAULD knave, as eat it? *Ibid.* (1609), *Timon of Athens*, ii. 2. She's even setting on water to SCALD such chickens as you are.

1647-8. HERRICK, *Hesperides*, 'To Blanch.' Blanch swears her husband's lovely, when a SCALD Has blear'd his eyes.

1678. COTTON, *Virgil Travestie* [*Works* (1725), 63. For that which stabb'd her was his Weapon, For which she did so SCALD and burn, That none but he could serve her turn.

SCALDABANCO, *subs.* (old colloquial).—*See* quots.

1598. FLORIO, *Worlde of Wordes*, s.v. SCALDABANCO, one that keepes a seate warme, but ironically spoken of idle lectures that possesse a pewe in the schooles or pulpet in churches, and baffle out they know not what; also a hot-headed puritane.

1692. HACKET, *Williams*, ii. 182. The Presbyterians, those SCALDA-BANCOS, or hot declaimers, had wrought a great distast in the Commons at the king.

SCALDER, *subs.* (common).—*See* quot., and SCALD.

1892. SYDNEY WATSON, *Wops the Waif*, iv. I'm good at a hoperation, I can tell yer, when it's on spot and SCALDER (which being interpreted, meant cake and tea).

SCALDINGS! *intj.* (Winchester).—Be gone! 'Be off!' Also a general warning, 'Look out!'

1748. SMOLLETT, *Roderick Random*, xxv. The boy . . . returned with it full of boiled peas, crying, 'SCALDINGS,' all the way.

SCALD-RAG, *subs. phr.* (old).—A dyer.

1630. TAYLOR, *Works*, II. 165. As much impeachment as to cal a justice of the peace, a beadle; a dyer, a SCALD-RAGGE; or a fishmonger, a seller of gubbins.

SCALDRUM-DODGE, *subs. phr.* (tramps').—*See* quot. and FOX-BITE; SCALDRUM = a beggar.

1851-61. MAYHEW, *Lond. Lab.*, I. 262. By these Peter was initiated into the SCALDRUM-DODGE, or the art of burning the body with a mixture of acids and gunpowder, so as to suit the hues and complexions of the accident to be deplored.

SCALE, *verb.* (venery).—To MOUNT (*q.v.*): *see* GREENS and RIDE.

1607. W[ENTWORTH] S[MITH], *Puritan*, i. 1. I, whom never man as yet hath SCALED.

SCALES. *See* SHADSCALES.

SCALLOPS, *subs.* (old).—An awkward girl (HALLIWELL).

SCALP, *verb.* (American).—To sell under price; to share commission or discount: *e.g.*, TO SCALP STOCK = to sell stock regardless of value; TICKET-SCALPING = the sale of unused railway tickets, or tickets bought in quantities as a speculation, at a cheaper than the official rate; TICKET-SCALPER = a ticket broker.

1882. *Nation*, 5 Oct., 276. With the eternal quarrel between rail oads and SCALPERS, passengers have nothing to do.

1892. *Pall Mall Gaz.*, 1 Nov., 2, 1. TICKET-SCALPING . . . has reference to the transferability or otherwise of tickets rather than to their date of expiry.

1894. *Standard*, 3 May, 7, 1. These huge grouped tenderings on a preconcerted plan . . . when successful merely represent a SCALPING of the Stock at the expense of the genuine investor.

2. (American party-politician's).—(*a*) To ostracise for rebellion, and (*b*) to ruin one's influence.

SCALY, *adj.* (common).—Shabby; mean; FISHY (*q.v.*).—GROSE.

1821. EGAN, *Life in London*, II. iii. If you are too SCALY to tip for it, I'll shell out, and shame you.

1843. DICKENS, *Martin Chuzzlewit*, xxviii. Don't you remember hold mother Todgers's? . . . a reg'lar SCALY old shop, warn't it?

1848. LOWELL, *Biglow Papers*, I. 99. The SCALIEST trick they ever played wuz bringin' on me hither.

1851-61. MAYHEW, *Lond. Lab.*, I. 85. They and the ladies their hardest of SCALIEST customers.

1880. J. B. STEPHENS, *Poems*, 'To a Black Gin.' Methinks that theory is rather SCALY.

1883. PAYN, *Thicker than Water*, xlv. Do you mean to say he never gave you nothing? . . . SCALY varmint!

SCALY-FISH, *subs. phr.* (nautical).—'A honest, rough, blunt sailor' (GROSE).

SCAMANDER, *verb.* (common).—To LOAF (*q.v.*).

SCAMMERED, *adj.* (common).—Drunk: *see* SCREWED.

1891. CAREW, *Auto. of a Gipsy*, 435. He'll think he was SCAMMERED over night.

SCAMP, *subs.* (Old Cant).—1. A highway robber (also SCAMPSMAN); and (2) highway robbery (also SCAMPERY). Whence as *verb* = to rob on the highway; ROYAL-SCAMP = 'a highwayman who robs civilly'; ROYAL-FOOT-SCAMP = 'a footpad behaving in like manner'; DONE FOR A SCAMP = convicted (GROSE, PARKER, VAUX). *See* quot. 1823.

1754. *Disc. of John Poulter*, 42. I'll SCAMP on the panney.

1781. MESSINK, *Choice of Harlequin*. 'Ye SCAMPS, ye pads, ye divers.'

1823. BEE, *Dict. Turf*, s.v. SCAMP . . . Beggars who would turn their hands to any thing occasionally, without enquiring in whom the thing is vested, are said to GO UPON THE SCAMP. Fellows who pilfer in markets, from stalls or orchards, who snatch off hats, cheat publicans out of liquor, or toss up cheatingly—commit SCAMPING tricks.

*c.*1824. EGAN, *Boxiana*, iii. 622. And from the start the SCAMPS are cropp'd at home.

1830. MONCRIEFF, *Heart of London*, ii. 1. Cracksmen, . . . SCAMPSMEN, we; fol de rol, &c.

1834. AINSWORTH, *Rookwood*, 'The Game of High Toby.' Forth to the heath is the SCAMPSMAN gone. *Ibid.*, III. 5. A rank SCAMP, cried the upright man.

1842. EGAN, *Captain Macheath*, v. A SCAMPSMAN, you know, must always be bold.

3. (common).—A rogue; an arrant rascal; sometimes (colloquial) in jest. Hence SCAMPISH = roguish, tricky; SCAMPERY = roguery.

*c.*1835. DANA, *Before the Mast*, 84. Among the Mexicans . . . every rich man looks like a grandee, and every poor SCAMP like a broken-down gentleman.

1849-50. THACKERAY, *Pendennis*, xiii. The impudent bog-trotting SCAMP.

1854. WHYTE-MELVILLE, *General Bounce*, ii. Tom Blacke was a SCAMP of the first water.

*d.*1859. DE QUINCEY, *Works*, II. 43. He has done the SCAMP too much honour. *Ibid., Spanish Nun*, 23. The alcaïde personally renewed his regrets for the ridiculous scene of the two SCAMPISH occulists.

1879. PAYN, *High Spirits (Finding his Level)*. Vulgar dukes or SCAMPISH lords.

1883. *Graphic*, 24 Feb., 199, 3. All the SCAMPERY of Liverpool seems to be present.

1902. *D. Mail*, 14 Jan., 6, 3. Of all the SCAMPISH SCAMPS unhung this specimen of perverted culture beats all.

Verb. (common).—2. To do carelessly and ill; to give bad work or short measure.

1851-61. MAYHEW, *Lond. Lab.*, III. 240. SCAMPING adds at least 200 per cent. to the productions of the cabinet-maker's trade.

1862. *London Herald*, 27 Dec., 'Answers to Corresp.' Find out, if it is an estate where any SCAMPING is allowed to create heavy ground rents.

1881. PAYN, *Grape from a Thorn*, xlii. The idea of SCAMPING her work . . . had no existence for her.

1883. TROLLOPE, *Autobiog.*, I. 164. It is not on my conscience that I have ever SCAMPED my work. My novels, whether good or bad, have been as good as I could make them.

1886. *D. Telegraph*, 1 Jan. The work is as often . . . SCAMPED as it is well done.

SCAMPER, *verb.* (old: B. E., *c.*1696).—'To run away, or Scowre off, either from Justice, as Thieves, Debtors, Criminals, that are pursued; or from ill fortune, as Soldiers that are repulst or worsted.'

SCANDAL-BROTH (CHATTER, or WATER), *subs. phr.* (common).—Tea; CAT-LAP (*q.v.*).—GROSE.

SCANDALOUS, *subs.* (old).—'A Periwig.'—B. E. (*c.*1696).

SCANDAL-PROOF (old).—1. 'A thorough pac'd Alsatian, or Minter, one harden'd or past Shame,' B. E. (*c.*1696); and (2) 'one who has eaten shame and drank after it, or would blush at being ashamed,' GROSE (1785).

SCANMAG, *subs.* (common).—Scandalous jobber; pettifogging slander; talk. [Short and derisive for *Scandalum magnatum.*]

1883. G. A. S[ALA] [*Illustr. London News*, 31 March, 310, 3]. The audience have to listen to the bucolic drolleries of his groom, Saul Mash, and the provincial SCANMAG of the notabilities of the little country town. *Ibid.* (1861), *Twice Round the Clock*, One p.m., Par. 2. The swarms of flies . . . inebriating themselves with saccharine suction in the grocers' shops, and noisily buzzing their SCANMAG in private parlours.

SCANT-OF-GRACE, *subs.* (colloquial).—A scapegrace.

1821. SCOTT, *Kenilworth*, iii. You associate yourself with a sort of SCANT-OF-GRACE.

SCAPE, *subs.* (old).—1. A cheat.

1599. HALL, *Satires*. Was there no 'plaining of the brewer's SCAPE, Nor greedy vintner mixed the strained grape.

*d.*1634. CHAPMAN, *Hom. Hymn to Apollo*. Crafty mate What other SCAPE canst thou excogitate?

2. (old).—A fart.

1611. COTGRAVE, *Dict.*, s.v. *Pet.* A SCAPE, tayle-shot, or cracke.

1598. FLORIO, *Worlde of Wordes*, s.v. *Pettare.* To let a SCAPE or a fart.

3. (old).—An act, or effect, of fornication.

1594. SHAKSPEARE, *Lucrese*, 749. Day . . . night's SCAPES doth open lay. *Ibid.* (1604), *Winter's Tale*, III. 3, 73. Sure some SCAPE . . . I can read waiting-gentlewoman in the SCAPE.

Verb. (artists').—'To neglect one's brush' (BEE).

SCAPE-GALLOWS, *subs. phr.* (old).—One who deserves but has escaped the gallows (GROSE).

1839. DICKENS, *Nich. Nickleby*, xliv. Remember this SCAPE-GALLOWS . . . if we meet again . . . you shall see the inside of a gaol once more.

SCAPE-GRACE (or **-THRIFT**), *subs. phr.* (old).—A good-for-nothing; a ne'er-do-well (GROSE).

1577-87. HOLINSHED, *Hist. Scot.*, an. 1427. For shortlie vpon his deliuerance, he gathered a power of wicked SCAPETHRIFTS, and with the same comming into Inuernes, burnt the towne.

1862. THACKERAY, *Philip*, ii. I could not always be present to guard the little SCAPE GRACE.

1885. *D. Telegraph*, 29 Sept. The SCAPE-GRACES and ne'er-do-wells you considered dead a generation since.

SCARAMOUCH, *subs.* (old).—1. A buffoon; whence (2) = a disreputable rascal. [STANFORD: It. *Scaramuccia*, the braggart buffoon of Italian comedy.]

1662. DAVIES, *Ambass. Trav.* (1669), VI. 283. Countenances and Postures, as SCARAMUZZA himself would be much troubled to imitate.

1673. WYCHERLEY, *Gentleman Dancing Master*, iii. 1. Ah, le brave SCARAMOUCHE!

1673. DRYDEN, *Epilogue to Univ., Oxford*, 15 (Globe Ed., p. 422). Stout SCARAMOUCHA with rush lance rode in, And run a tilt at centaur Arlequin.

1707. WARD, *Hud. Rediv.*, II. v. 5. Dress'd up in Black, like SCARAMOUCHES.

1711. *Spectator*, No. 83. The third artist that I looked over was Fantasque, dressed like a Venetian SCARAMOUCH.

*c.*1720. *Broadside Ballad*, 'The Masquerade' [FARMER, *Merry Songs and Ballads* (1897), iii. 233]. A SCARAMOUCH is nimble, Tho' lazy he appears.

1716. WILKINS, *Palit. Bal.* (1860), II. 175. The SACRAMOUCHES everywhere, With open throats bawled out.

1725. BAILEY, *Coll. Eras.*, 'Penitent Virgin.' O these SCARAMOUCHES, how they know to wheedle the poor people!

1824. IRVING, *Tales of a Trav.* (1849), 322. He swore no SCARAMOUCH of an Italian robber would dare to meddle with an Englishman.

2. (showmen's).—A puppet.

1851-61. MAYHEW, *Lond. Lab.*, III. 60. This here's the SCARAMOUCH that dances without a head.

SCARBOROUGH-WARNING (LEISURE, SCRABBLING), &c., *subs. phr.* (old).—*See* quots.

1546. HEYWOOD, *Proverbs* [OLIPHANT, *New Eng.*, i. 504. SCARBOROUGH WARNING (the blow before the word) is found in page 76].

1557. HEYWOOD, *Old Ballad* [*Harl. Misc.* (PARK), x. 258]. This term, SCARBOROW WARNING, grew (some say) By hasty hanging, for rank robbry theare.

1580. TUSSER, *Husbandry*, x. 28, 22 [E. D. S.]. Be suretie seldome (but neuer for much) for feare of purse penniles hanging by such; Or SKARBOROW WARNING, as ill I beleeue, when (sir I arest yee) gets hold of thy sleeue.

1582. STANYHURST, *Ænid*, iv. 621. Al they the lyke poste haste dyd make with SCARBORO' SCRABBLING.

1589. PUTTENHAM, *Eng. Poesy*, B. iii. c. SKARBOROW WARNING, for a sodaine commandement, allowing no respect or delay to bethinke a man of his business.

1591. HARINGTON, *Ariosto*, xxxiv. 22. They tooke them to a fort, with such small treasure And in so SCARBOROW WARNING they had leasure.

1593. HARVEY, *Pierces Supererog.* [GROSART, *Works*, ii. 225]. He meaneth not to come upon me with a cowardly stratageme of SCARBOROUGH WARNING.

1603. T. MATHEW (Bishop of Durham), *Letter* 19, Jan. [NARES]. I received a message from my lord chamberlaine, that it was his majesty's pleasure that I should preach before him upon Sunday next; which SCARBOROUGH WARNING did not only perplex me, but so puzzel me.

1616. *Letter* [quoted by NARES]. I now write upon SCARBOROUGH WARNING.

1670. RAY, *Proverbs*, 263. This proverb took its original from Thomas Stafford, who in the reign of Queen Mary, 1557, with a small company seizd on SCARBOROUGH Castle (utterly destitute of provision for resistance) before the townsmen had the least notice of his approach. [This is taken from FULLER'S *Worthies*: *cf.* STAFFORD LAW and *see* quots. 1546 and 1557 which show the phrase in earlier use.]

1787. GROSE, *Prov. Glossary* (1811), 94. A SCARBOROUGH WARNING. That is, none at all, but a sudden surprise.

1843. HALLIWELL, *Archaic Words, &c.*, s.v. SCARBOROUGH . . . SCARBOROUGH LEISURE, no leisure at all.

SCARCE. TO MAKE ONE'S SELF SCARCE, *verb. phr.* (colloquial).—To retire (GROSE).

1749. SMOLLETT, *Gil Blas* [ROUTLEDGE], 374. It was my fixed purpose to MAKE MYSELF SCARCE at Seville.

1812. MARGRAVINE OF ANSPACH [C. K. SHARPE'S *Correspondence* (1888), ii. 20]. I shall MAKE MYSELF VERY, VERY SCARCE, and live only for myself.

1821. SCOTT, *Kenilworth*, iv. MAKE YOURSELF SCARCE—depart—vanish!

1836. M. SCOTT, *Cruise of Midge*, 114. My fine fellow, you are a little off your cruising ground, so be MAKING YOURSELF SCARCE—Bolt—vanish—get on deck with you.

1840. BARHAM, *Ingolds. Leg.* (*Lay of St. Odille*). Come, MAKE YOURSELVES SCARCE!—it is useless to stay.

1851-61. MAYHEW, *Lond. Lab.*, I. 265. I had warned her to MAKE HERSELF SCARCE at her earliest possible convenience.

1891. *Lic. Vict. Gaz.*, 16 Jan. Now, bobbies, MAKE YOURSELVES SCARCE . . . you know this is a gentleman's private apartment, and you're trespassers.

SCARE. TO SCARE UP, *verb. phr.* (colloquial).—To find; to discover: *e.g.*, 'TO SCARE UP money.'

SCARECROW, *subs.* (thieves').—*See* quot.

1884. GREENWOOD, *Little Ragamuffins.* The SCARECROW is the boy who has served him [a thief] until he is well known to the police, and is so closely watched that he may as well stay at home as go out.

SCAREHEAD, *subs.* (journalists').—A line in bold type calculated to arrest attention.

1900. WHITE, *West End*, 339. One of our calm days, unbroken by SCAREHEADS in the newspapers, or by the croakings of nervous critics.

SCARLET. TO DYE SCARLET, *verb. phr.* (old).—*See* quot.

1598. SHAKSPEARE, *1 Hen. IV.*, ii. 4. They call drinking deep, DYEING SCARLET.

TO WEAR SCARLET, *verb. phr.* (old).—1. To win the higher University degrees; (2) to attain sheriff or aldermanic rank. [Which were scarlet-robed.]

1610. JONSON, *Alchemist*, i. 1. This summer he will be of the clothing of his company, and next spring CALLED TO THE SCARLET.

1613. WEBSTER, *Devil's Law-Case*, ii. 3. Your patience has not ta'en the right degree OF WEARING SCARLET; I should rather take you For a bachelor in the art, than for a doctor.

SCARLET-FEVER, *subs. phr.* (common).—Flirtation with soldiers: Fr. *culotte-* (or *pantalon-*) *rouge*: *cf.* YELLOW-FEVER.

1862. MAYHEW, *Lon. Lab.*, IV. 235. Nurse-maids . . . are always ready to succumb to the SCARLET-FEVER. A red coat is all powerful with this class.

SCARLET-HORSE, *subs. phr.* (old).—*See* quot.

1785. GROSE, *Vulg. Tongue*, s.v. SCARLET HORSE. A *high-red*, hired or hack horse: a pun on the word.

SCARLET LANCERS (THE). *See* RED LANCERS.

SCARLET-RUNNER, *subs. phr.* (old).—1. A Bow-street officer; a ROBIN-REDBREAST (*q.v.*). [They wore scarlet waistcoats.]

2. (common).—A footman.

SCARLET-TOWN, *subs. phr.* (provincial).—Reading [Berks.]

SCARLET-WOMAN, *subs. phr.* (religious).—The Church of Rome.

SCARPER, *verb.* (showmen's).—To run away: *see* SKEDADDLE.

1844. SELBY, *London by Night*, ii. 1. Vamoose—SCARPER—fly!

SCAT, *verb.* (common).—Begone!

1880. HARRIS, *Uncle Remus*, xxii. W'en ole man Rabbit say 'scoot,' dey scooted, en w'en ole Miss Rabbit say 'SCAT,' dey SCATTED.

1892. *Nat. Observer*, 20 Aug., 356, 1. There is a village somewhere West of Devonshire whose inhabitants are universally called '—— SCAT-UPS.' For . . . once at a volunteer review they could be induced to 'dismiss' only by an impassioned cry of 'SCAT UP!'

1896. LILLARD, *Poker Stories*, 210. We chucked him two watches and 380 dollars in cash quicker'n SCAT.

SCATE, *subs.* (provincial).—A lightheels (HALLIWELL).

Verb. (provincial).—To be loose in the bowels (HALLIWELL).

SCATTERATION, *subs.* (American).—A commotion; a dispersal. Hence SCATTERATIONIST = a politician running his personal fads without reference to either party or public.

1878. *N. A. Rev.*, cxxvi. 244. Some well-directed shots . . . sent wagons flying in the air, and produced a SCATTERATION.

1888. BOLDREWOOD, *Robbery Under Arms*, xiii. I did see one explode at a review in Melbourne—and, my word! what a SCATTERATION it made.

SCATTERBRAIN, *subs.* (colloquial).—An unreasoning ass; SCATTER-BRAINED = giddy.

1849. KINGSLEY, *Alton Locke*, xii. A certain SCATTER-BRAINED Irish lad.

1857. HUGHES, *Tom Brown's Schooldays*, I. ii. A . . . tearful SCATTER-BRAINED girl.

*d.*1884. C. READE, *Art*, 23. Poor Alexander, he is a fool, a SCATTERBRAIN . . . but he is my son.

SCATTERGOOD, *subs.* (old).—A spendthrift.

1577. KENDALL, *Epigrammes*, 56. A mery jest of a SCATTERGOOD.

1653. SANDERS, *Physiognomie.* Which intimates a man to act the consumption of his own fortunes, to be a SCATTER-GOOD; if of honey colour or red, he is a drunkard and a glutton.

SCATTER-GUN, *subs. phr.* (American).—A shot-gun.

SCATTERLING, *subs.* (old colloquial).—A vagabond.

*d.*1599. SPENSER, *State of Ireland* [*Century*]. Many of them be such losells and SCATTERLINGS as that they cannot easely . . . be gotten.

SCAVENGER'S-DAUGHTER, *subs. phr.* (old).—An instrument of torture invented by Sir W. Skevington, Lieutenant of the Tower of London, *temp.* Hen. VIII.: *see* quot. 1889.

1580. *Dia. Rerum gestarum in Turri Londiniensi*, 10 Dec. Thomas Cotamus et Lucas Kirbæus presbyteri, SCAVINGERI FILIAM ad unam horum et amplius passi; ex quo prior copiosum sanguinem e naribus emisit.

1604. *Commons Journal*, 14 May. [The Committee] found in Little Ease in the Tower an engine of torture . . . called SKEVINGTON'S DAUGHTERS.

1840. AINSWORTH, *Tower of London*, xxiii. We will wed you to the SCAVENGER'S DAUGHTER, my little man.

1889. *Answers*, 9 Feb. The SCAVENGER'S DAUGHTER was a broad hoop of iron, consisting of two parts, fastened by a hinge. The prisoner knelt on the pavement, and the executioner having introduced the hoop under his legs, compressed the victim, till he was able to fasten the extremities over the small of the back. The time allotted was an hour and a half, it commonly happened that the blood started from the nostrils; sometimes, it was believed, from the extremities of the hands and feet.

SCEW. *See* SKEW.

SCELLUM, *subs.* (Old Cant).—A thief: *cf.* SKELLUM.

1630. TAYLOR, *Works*, ii. 123. None holds him, but all cry, Lope, SCELLUM, lope!

SCENE, *subs.* (colloquial).—An exhibition of feeling or temper.

1847. BRONTE, *Jane Eyre*, xxvii. You have no desire to expostulate, to upbraid, to make a SCENE.

1862. THACKERAY, *Philip*, xxvii. Hush! hush! . . . she must be kept quiet . . . There must be no more SCENES, my fine fellow.

BEHIND THE SCENES, *phr.* (colloquial).—Having access to information not open to the general public; in the KNOW (*q.v.*).

SCENE-RAT, *subs. phr.* (theatrical).—An "extra" in ballet or pantomime.

SCEPTRE, *subs.* (venery). — The *penis*: *see* PRICK. Also CYPRIAN SCEPTRE.

1653. URQUHART, *Rabelais*, I. xi. One of them would call it her fiddle-diddle, her staff of love . . . her CYPRIAN SCEPTRE.

1772. BRIDGES, *Burlesque Homer*, 47. Now night came on, The thund'rer led His helpmate to her wicker bed; There they agreed, and where's the wonder, His SCEPTRE rais'd she soon knock'd under.

SCHEME, *subs.* (Winchester).—*See* quot.—MANSFIELD (*c.* 1840).

1891. WRENCH, *Word Book*, s.v. SCHEME . . . The candle on reaching a measured point ignites paper, which by burning a string releases a weight; this falls on the head of the boy to be waked.

SCHISM-SHOP, *subs. phr.* (old).—A dissenting meeting-house; SCHISM-MONGER = a dissenting parson (GROSE): amongst Catholics any Protestant church or chapel.

1840. HALIBURTON, *Clockmaker*, 3 S., iv. "Stickin' a subscription paper into a very strait-laced man, even for building a SCHISM-SHOP for his own folks, is like stickin' a needle behind an ox's ear, it kills him dead on the spot."

1852. SHIRLEY BROOKS, *Miss Violet and her Offers*, vi. "The tenants-at-will who vote for church candidates ——." "By the tenants-at-won't, who go in for the SCHISM-SHOP"—dashed in the smart barrister.

SCHITT, *subs.* (Winchester). — A goal: at football: *see* GOWNER. [WRENCH: This was the word in general use till 1860, when it was superseded by 'goal.']

SCHLIVER, *subs.* (old).—A clasp-knife (BEE).

SCHOL, *subs.* (Harrow). — 1. A scholar; and (2) a scholarship.

SCHOOL, *subs.* (old).—'A party of persons met together for the purpose of gambling' (GROSE, VAUX). Also (modern) any small band of associates, as thieves or beggars working together, a set of passengers travelling regularly by the same train, &c. Hence SCHOOLMAN = a companion, a mate.

1851-61. MAYHEW, *London Lab.*, i. 234. Some classes of patterers, I may here observe, work in SCHOOLS or 'mobs' of two, three, or four.

1866. *London Miscellany*, 3 Mar., 57. We don't want no one took in that's on the square. The governor's promised the SCHOOL as strangers shant use the house.

SCHOOLING, *subs.* (thieves').—A term of confinement in a reformatory.

1879. *Auto. of Thief* [*Macm. Mag.*, xl., 501]. She is young—just come from a SCHOOLING.

2. (thieves').—*See* quot.

1888. *Globe*, 25 Mar. A batch of these grimy ones being brought up the other day for playing pitch and toss—in the local vernacular, SCHOOLING—in a public place, their counsel argued that they were driven to it by destitution.

SCHOOL-BUTTER, *subs. phr.* (old).—A flogging (B. E., GROSE).

SCHOOLMASTER. 1. *See* BILK.

2. (racing).—A horse good at jumping: generally ridden with one in training.

SCHOOL OF VENUS, *subs. phr.* (old).—A brothel: *see* NANNY-HOUSE (B. E., GROSE).

SCHOOL-STREET, *subs. phr.* (old University: Oxon.).—The University.

SCHOONER, *subs.* (American).—A tall glass: containing twice the quantity of an ordinary tumbler: THREE-MASTED SCHOONER = a SCHOONER of extra size.

1888. *Texas Siftings*, 30 June. Thanks, old hoss fly, what do you say to taking a SCHOONER of beer at my expense?

1889. *D. Telegraph*, 8 Feb. There is a coloured man at Derby who can swallow two quarts of molasses with as much ease as a Whyo can drink a SCHOONER of beer, and in about the same time.

See PRAIRIE SCHOONER.

SCHWASSLE-BOX. *See* SWATCHEL-COVE.

SCISSOREAN-OPERATION, *subs. phr.* (literary).—Gutting a book.

SCISSORS. TO GIVE ONE SCISSORS, *verb. phr.* (common).—To pay out; to CUT UP (*q.v.*). Also SCISSORS! = an exclamation of disgust or impatience.

1843. SELBY, *Antony and Cleopatra*. Oh, SCISSORS; insinuate that it takes nine of us to make a man!

1847. ROBB, *Squatter Life*, 64. I grabbed his slick har, and may be I didn't GIN HIM SCISSORS.

1893. MILLIKEN, *'Arry Ballads*, 33. Oh, SCISSORS! jest didn't we give 'em tantivy.

SCISSORS-AND-PASTE, *subs. phr.* (literary).—Compilation: as distinguished from original work. Fr. *travailler à coups de ciseaux* = to compile.

SCOB, *subs.* (Winchester College).—'An oak box with a double lid, set at the angles of the squares of wooden benches in school: used as desk and book-case. [Probably the word has been transferred from the bench itself, and comes from Fr. *escabeau*, Lat. *scabellum.*]'—WRENCH.

1620. *Account* [to J. Hutton at his entrance into the College]. For a SCOBB to hold his books, 3s. 6d.

1890. G. ALLEN, *Tents of Shem*, xlii. Parker's SCOB was 270.

SCOFF (or **SCORF**), *verb.* (nautical).—1. To eat: also as *subs.* = food. [*Cf.* Scots' *scaff* = food of any kind.]

1893. FLYNT, *Tramping with Tramps*, II. iii. SCOFF'S always more plenty than money.

1901. WALKER, *In the Blood*, iv 'Those birds kill snakes do they?' . . . 'Rather . . . They goes down themselves and SCOFFS them.'

2. (American).—To run away; TO SKEDADDLE (*q.v.*): also TO SCOFF (or SCUFF) AWAY.

SCOFFER, *subs.* (thieves').—Plate.

1891. CAREW, *Auto. of a Gipsy*, 416. I gets clean off with the SCAWFER.

SCOLDRUM. *See* SCALDRUM.

SCHOLLARD, *subs.* (vulgar). — A scholar.

1708-10. SWIFT, *Polite Conversations*, Intro. Happily sings the Divine Mr. Tibbald's . . . I am no SCHOLLARD; but I am polite: Therefore be sure I am no Jacobite.

SCOLOPENDRA, *subs.* (old). — A harlot: *i.e.*, a ramping thing with a sting in its tail: *see* TART (HALLIWELL).

b. 1660. DAVENANT, *The Siege*, v. 1. Go, bring a barrel hither! Why? when you SCOLOPENDRA.

SCOLD'S CURE, *subs. phr.* (old).—A coffin: 'the blowen has napped the SCOLD'S CURE; the wench is in her coffin' (GROSE).

SCONCE, *subs.* (old).—1. The head (GROSE, HALLIWELL = 'Old Cant'); whence (2) sense, judgment, brains.

1567. *Damon and Pithias* [DODSLEY, *Old Plays*, iv.].

1593. HARVEY, *New Letter* [GROSART, *Wks.*, i. 283]. That can play vpon his warped SCONCE, as vpon a tabor, or a fiddle.

1598. FLORIO, *Worlde of Wordes*, 82. A head, a pate, a nole, a SCONCE.

1602. SHAKESPEARE, *Hamlet*, v. 1. Why does he suffer this rude knave now to knock him about the SCONCE with a dirty shovel?

1611. BARRY, *Ram Alley*, xii. 436. I say no more, But 'tis within this SCONCE to go beyond them.

1642. DR. H. MORE, *Psychodia*, iii. 13. Which their dull SCONCES cannot eas'ly reach.

1655. FANSHAWE, *Lusiad*, viii. 51. Th' infused poyson working in his SCONCE.

1664. COTTON, *Scoffer Scofft* [*Works* (1725), 179]. I go, and if I find him once, With my Battoon I'll bang his SCONCE.

1771. SMOLLETT, *Humphry Clinker*, lxiii. And, running into the house, exposed his back and his SCONCE to the whole family.

1840. THACKERAY, *Paris Sketch Book*, 110. At last Fips hits the West Indian such a blow across his SCONCE, that the other grew furious.

1856. R BURTON, *El-Medinah*, 357. Though we might take advantage of shade . . . we must by no means cover our SCONCES.

1895. MARRIOTT-WATSON [*New Review*, July, 7]. I've a mind to open that ugly SCONCE of yours.

2. (old: now University).—A fine; a score. Hence TO BUILD A SCONCE (or TO SCONCE) = (1) to run up a score: spec. with no intention of paying; (2) to be mulcted in fines; and (3) TO SCONCE also = to pay out, to chastise (B. E., DYCHE, GROSE, BEE, HOTTEN).

1630. RANDOLPH, *Aristippus* [HAZLITT, *Works* (1875), 14. 'Twere charity in him TO SCONCE 'em soundly.

1632. SHIRLEY, *Witty Fair One*, iv. 3. I have had a head in most of the butteries of Cambridge, and it has been SCONCED to purpose.

c. 1640. [SHIRLEY], *Capt. Underwit* [BULLEN, *Old Plays*, ii. 323]. I can teach you to build a SCONCE, Sir.

d. 1704. T. BROWN, *Works*, ii. 282. I never parted with any of my favours, nay, not . . . a clap gratis, except a lieutenant and ensign . . . once . . . BUILT UP A SCONCE, and left me in the lurch.

1730. MILLER, *Humours of Oxford*, i. I understand more manners than to leave my friends to go to church—no, though they SCONCE me a fortnight's commons, I'll not do it.

1760. JOHNSTON, *Chrysal*, xxviii. These youths have been playing a small game, cribbing from the till, and BUILDING SCONCES, and such like tricks.

1764. COLMAN, *Terræ Filius*, No. 1. Any SCONCE imposed by the proctors.

1768. FOOTE, *Devil on Two Sticks*, ii. 1. She paid my bill the next day without SCONCING off sixpence.

1821. *The Etonian*, ii. 391. Was SCONCED in a quart of ale for quoting Latin, a passage from Juvenal; murmured, and the fine was doubled.

1883. ELLACOMBE [*N. & Q.*, 6 S., viii. 326]. Men were SCONCED if accidentally they appeared in hall undressed. I think the SCONCE was a quantity of beer to the scouts. The SCONCE-table was hung up in the buttery.

1899. *Answers*, 14 Jan., i. 1. The average freshman is not very long at Oxford before he is acquainted with the mysteries of SCONCING. A SCONCE is a fine of a quart of ale, in which the unlucky fresher is mulcted for various offences in Hall.

Verb. (common).—4. To reduce; to discontinue: *e.g.*, TO SCONCE ONE'S DIET = to BANT (*q.v.*): TO SCONCE THE RECKONING = to reduce expenses.

5. (Winchester).—To hinder; to get in the way: as of a kick at football, a catch at cricket, &c.: *e.g.*, "If you had not SCONCED, I should have made a flyer."

1899. *Pub. School Mag.*, Dec., 476. Opponents who get in each others way and SCONCE the kicks.

SCONICK, *verb.* (American).—To hurry about; to SHIN ABOUT (*q.v.*): also TO SCONICK ROUND.

1833. NEAL, *Down Easters*, vii. 108. I could see plain enough which side you was on, without SKONICKIN' round arter you much further.

SCOOP, *subs.* (American).—1. A big haul; an advantage: spec. (journalists') news secured in advance of a rival, a series of BEATS (*q.v.*). Also (2) on 'Change, a sudden breaking down of prices, enabling operators to buy cheaply, followed by a rise. As *verb.* = (1) to make a big haul: and (2) to get the better of a rival.

1882. MCCABE, *New York*, 160. He runs seventy 'busses on this line, and SCOOPS IN three 'r four hundred a day.

1888. *Detroit Free Press*, 22 Sep. Mr. Terada, the editor, is in jail for fourteen months for getting a SCOOP on the government.

1889. *Referee*, 6 Jan. He is SCOOPING IN the shekels.

1890. *Answers*, 25 Dec. Last night he slept in his bed when we walked the streets . . . To think that he should SCOOP us!

1896. LILLARD *Poker Stories*, 26. As a rule he SCOOPED the pot.

3. (common).—To fetch, to fit.

1888. *Sporting Life*, 7 Dec. It would better SCOOP the situation if it were described as 'goloptious.'

Verb. (whalers').—1. *See* quot.

1891. *Century Mag.*, s.v. SCOOPING. The right [whalebone] whale gets into a patch of food or brit (resembling sawdust on the surface of the water) . . . goes through it with only the head out and mouth open. As soon as a mouthful of water is obtained the whale closes its lips, ejects the water, the feed being left in the mouth and throat [Sailors' slang].

ON THE SCOOP, *phr.* (common).—On the drink, or a round of dissipation.

1893. MILLIKEN, *'Arry Ballads*, 47. An English milord ON THE SCOOP carn't be equalled at blueing a quid.

SCOOT (SKOOT or **SKUTE),** *verb.* (common).—To move quickly; ON THE SCOOT = on the run; SCOOTER = a restless knockabout; SCOOT-TRAIN = an express.

1838. J. C. NEAL, *Charcoal Sketches* 'Pair of Slippers.' Notwithstanding his convulsive efforts to clutch the icy bricks, he SKUTED into the gutter.

18 [?]. HILL, *Yankee Stories* [BARTLETT]. The fellow sat down on a hornet's nest; and if he didn't run and holler, and SCOOT through the briar bushes, and tear his trowsers.

1848. LOWELL, *Biglow Papers*. An send the Ensines SKOOTIN' to the bar-room with their banners.

1858. *Atlantic Monthly*, Mar. The captain he SCOOTED round into one port an' another.

1869. *Quart. Rev.*, cxxvi. 371. The laugh of the gull as he SCOOTS along the shore.

1871. *Philadelphia Age*, Feb. An Iowa man, instead of going to the expense of a divorce, gave his wife a dollar, and told her to SCOOT.

1880. HARRIS, *Uncle Remus*, xxii. W'en ole man Rabbit say 'SCOOT,' dey SCOOTED, en w'en ole Miss Rabbit say 'scat,' dey scatted.

1888. *Puck's Library*, May 18. SCOOT DOWN and buy like the devil!

1886-96. MARSHALL, *He Slumbered* ['Pomes,' 118]. So she SCOOTED from the shanty.

1894. *Sketch*, 461, 1. Once settled there, we SCOOTED around for members, but there was at that time no subscription.

SCORCHER, *subs.* (common).—Anybody or anything severe, eccentric, or hasty. Spec. TO SCORCH = to ride a bicycle, drive a motor, &c., at top speed: whence SCORCHING = HOT (*q.v.*).

1876. HINDLEY, *Cheap Jack*, 36. It was a very fine hot day — a regular "SCORCHER."

1885. HAWLEY SMART, *Post to Finish*, 361. It's a SCORCHER . . . and Mr. Elliston not 'weighing-in' with the Caterham money of course makes it rather worse for us.

1889. *Cornhill Mag.*, July, 62. The next day was a SCORCHER.

1890. PENNELL, *Cant. Pilgrimage, Preface.* We were pilgrims, not SCORCHERS.

1890. *Polytechnic Mag.*, 13 Mar., 5, 1. An impromptu SCORCH was started by trying to keep behind a really fast cabby to obtain shelter from the wind.

1893. MILLIKEN, *'Arry Ballads*, 22. They're regular SCORCHERS, these women.

1897. *Ally Sloper's Half-Holiday*, Oct. 23, 338, 3. The SCORCHER charges, without remorse, At all the people who cross his path.

1897. *Referee*, Oct. 24, 3, 1. A said-to-be SCORCHING play entitled "At the Foot of the Altar."

1901. *D. Telegraph*, 7 Jan., 8, 3. As a result of complaints as to the excessive speed at which motor-cars are driven . . . the police have been keeping a sharp look-out for SCORCHERS.

SCORE, *verb.* (common).—To get the better of: also TO SCORE OFF ONE.

SCORF. *See* SCORF.

SCORPION-OF-THE-BROW, *subs. phr.* (literary). — *See* quot. (R. BURTON).

1885. BURTON, *Thousand Nights*, i. 168. Note 3.—In other copies of these verses the fourth couplet swears BY THE SCORPIONS OF HIS BROW, *i.e.* the *accroche-cœurs*, the beau-catchers, bell-ropes or "aggravators."

SCOT, *subs.* (old).—1. A person easily vexed; esp. one given to resent company sport; the diversion is called GETTING ONE OUT (or ROUND THE CORNER). Also (2) = temper; a PADDY (*q.v.*); Scottish = fiery, easily provoked. [GROSE: 'A SCOT is a bullock of a particular breed which affords superior diversion when hunted; BEE: 'A butcher's term'].

SCOTCH, *subs.* (colloquial). — 1. Scotch whiskey: *cf.* IRISH.

1886-96. MARSHALL, *He Slumbered* ['Pomes,' 118]. In the early evening watches he had started well on SCOTCHES.

1893. CRACKANTHORPE, *Wreckage*, 125. Mary, two bitters and a small SCOTCH to the Commercial Room, and a large Irish for Mr. Hays here.

2. *See* SCOTCH-PEG.

PHRASES.—SCOTCH-BAIT = 'A halt and a resting on a stick as practised by pedlars (GROSE); SCOTCH-CASEMENT = the pillory; SCOTCH-CHOCOLATE = 'brimstone and milk' (GROSE); SCOTCH-COFFEE = hot water

flavoured with burnt biscuit; SCOTCH-FIDDLE = the itch; TO PLAY THE SCOTCH-FIDDLE = 'to work the index finger of one hand like a fiddle-stick between the index and middle finger of the other' (DYCHE, GROSE); SCOTCH GREYS = lice: hence HEADQUARTERS OF THE SCOTS' GREYS = a lowsy head (GROSE); SCOTCH-HOBBY = 'a little sorry, scrubbed, low Horse of that country' (B. E.); SCOTCH-MIST = a soaking rain (B. E., GROSE); SCOTCH-ORDINARY = 'the house of office' (RAY); SCOTCH-PEG = (rhyming) a leg: also SCOTCH; SCOTCH-PINT = 'a bottle containing two quarts' (GROSE); SCOTCH-PRIZE = a capture by mistake (GROSE): *cf.* DUTCH; SCOTCH-SEAMANSHIP = all stupidity and main strength; SCOTCH-WARMING-PAN = (1) a chambermaid, and (2) a fart (*q.v.*—RAY, B. E., GROSE); TO ANSWER SCOTCH FASHION = to reply by asking another question; *cf.* YANKEE FASHION.

1675. EARL OF ROCHESTER, *Tunbridge Wells*, June 30. And then more smartly to expound the Riddle Of all his Prattle, gives her a SCOTCH FIDDLE.

1762. *London Register* [*Notes and Queries*, 3 S., v. 14.] "THE SCOTCH FIDDLE," by M'Pherson. Done from himself. The figure of a Highlander sitting under a tree, enjoying the greatest of pleasures, scratching where it itches.

1834. MICHAEL SCOTT, *Cruise of Midge*, 231. What ship is that? This was answered SCOTCH FASHION—What felucca is that?

1851-61. MAYHEW, *London Lab.*, i. 357. But mind, if you handle any of his wares, he don't make you a present of a SCOTCH FIDDLE for nothing.

1868. *Temple Bar*, xxv. 76. The SCOTS GREYS were frequently on the march in the clothes of the convicts.

1886. MARSHALL, *Pomes*, 23. But some buds of youthfull purity, with undisplayed SCOTCH PEGS. *Ibid. Giddy* (70). With that portion of his right SCOTCH PEG supposed to be his calf.

1900. *St. James's Gazette*, 9 Ap. 3, 1. The superiority of resources on our side is so overwhelming that we must win if only by what the sailors call SCOTCH SEAMANSHIP.

1883. CLARK RUSSELL, *Sailor's Language*, 121. SCOTCHMAN. A piece of wood fitted to a shroud or any other standing rope to save it from being chafed.

SCOTCHMAN, *subs.* (Colonial).—A florin.

1886. RIDER HAGGARD, *Jess*, x. Jantjé touched his hat, spat upon the SCOTCHMAN, as the natives of that part of Africa [Transvaal] call a two-shilling piece, and pocketed it. [(1) Because once upon a time a SCOTCHMAN made a great impression on the simple native mind in Natal by palming off some thousands of florins among them at the nominal value of half-a-crown.]

FLYING SCOTCHMAN, *subs. phr.* (common).—The daily 2 p.m. express from Euston to Edinburgh and the North. *Cf.* WILD IRISHMAN.

1885. G. DOLBY, *Dickens as I knew him*, 33. A railway carriage which was being dragged along at the rate of fifty miles an hour by the FLYING SCOTCHMAN.

THE SCOTCHMAN HUGGING THE CREOLE, *phr.* (West Indian). —*See* quot.

1835. M. SCOTT, *Tom Cringle*, xiv. The SCOTCHMAN HUGGING THE CREOLE; look at that tree . . . It was a magnificent cedar . . . covered over with a curious sort of fret-work, wove by the branches of some strong parasitical plant . . .

SCOTS (THE), *subs.* (military).—The 1st Batt. Cameronians (Scottish Rifles), formerly The 26th Foot: *circa* 1762.

SCOTT. *See* GREAT SCOTT.

SCOUNDREL, *subs.* (old: now recognised). — 1. 'A Hedge-bird or sorry Scab' (B. E.); (2) 'a man void of every principle of honour' (GROSE).

SCOUR, *verb.* (old). — 1. To run away: also TO SCOUR AWAY (or OFF).—GROSE.

2. (venery).—To copulate: *see* GREENS and RIDE.

1656. FLETCHER, *Martiall*, II. 56. She is not wont To take, but give for SCOURING of her ——.

TO SCOUR THE DARBIES (or CRAMP-RINGS), *verb. phr.* (Old Cant).—To go (or lie) in chains [HARMAN (1573), HEAD, B. E., COLES, GROSE].

1608. DEKKER, *The Beggar's Curse* [GROSART, *Works*], iii. 203. Then to the quier ken, to SCOURE THE CRAMP-RING.

1707. SHIRLEY, *Triumph of Wit*, 'Rum-Works Faithless Maunder.' Thou the Cramp-rings ne'er did SCOWRE.

1815. SCOTT, *Guy Mannering*, xxxviii. No wonder that you SCOUR THE CRAMP-RING and trine to the cheat sae often.

SCOURER (or **SCOWRER**), *subs.* (old). — 1. 'Drunkards, beating the Watch, breaking Windows, clearing the Streets, &c. (B. E.: also GROSE): whence (2) a night-thief. Hence TO SCOUR THE STREETS = to act riotously.

*c.*1700. *Gentleman Instructed*, 491 [10 ed., 1732]. He spurr'd to London, and . . . Here he struck up with sharpers, SCOURERS, and Alsatians.

1712. STEELE, *Spectator*, 324. Bullies and SCOWERERS of a long standing.

1712. GAY, *Trivia*, iii. 325. Who has not heard the SCOWERERS midnight fame? Who has not trembled at the Mohock's name?

SCOUT, *subs.* (Oxford Univ.).—1. A college servant—a valet, waiter, messenger, &c., in one (GROSE).

1750. *The Student*, i. 55. My SCOUT, indeed, is a very learned fellow.

1822. SCOTT, *F. of Nigil*, xvi. No SCOUT in Oxford, no gyp in Cambridge, ever matched him in speed and intelligence.

1841. HEWLETT, *Peter Priggins, College SCOUT, &c.* [Title].

1853. BRADLEY, *Verdant Green*, iii. Mr. Robert Filcher, the excellent, though occasionally erratic SCOUT.

1884. JULIAN STURGIS *in Longmans'*, v. 65. The old don went back to his chair . . . as his SCOUT came in with a note.

2. (old). — A watchman, or (modern) a spy, esq. a police spy. Hence SCOUT-KEN = a watch-house (POULTER (1754), GROSE, VAUX).

1800. PARKER, *Life's Painter*, 116. There's no hornies, traps, SCOUTS, nor beak-runners amongst them.

1821. EGAN, *Life in London*, II. iii. Turning the corner of Old Bedlam, A SCOUT laid me flat upon my face.

3. (old).—A watch (B. E., GROSE).

1688. SHADWELL, *Squire of Alsatia*, ii. Sirrah! here's a SCOUT; what's a clock, what's a clock, Sirrah.

1821. HAGGART, *Life*, 28. Sporting an elegant dress SCOUT, drag, and chates.

4. (old).—A mean fellow; a SCAB (*q.v*).—B. E.

1749. SMOLLETT, *Rod. Random*, xv. Though I be a poor cobbler's son, I am no SCOUT.

Verb. (Sporting). — To shoot pigeons outside a gun-club enclosure.

TO SCOUT ON THE LAY, *verb. phr.* (thieves').—To go in search of booty.

*c.*1787. *Kilmainham Minit* [*Ireland Sixty Years Ago*, 88]. The scrag-boy may yet be outwitted, And I SCOUT again ON DE LAY.

SCOWBANK, *subs.* (nautical).—A term of contempt to a sailor (C. RUSSELL).

SCRAG (or **CRAG**), *subs.* (old).—The neck; COLQUARRON (*q.v.*): as *verb.* = (1) to hang; and (2) to throttle. Hence SCRAGGING

= an execution: SCRAG-BOY = the hangman; SCRAGGING-POST (SCRAG-SQUEEZER or SCRAG) = the gallows; SCRAGG-'EM FAIR = a public execution (GROSE, PARKER, VAUX).

*d.*1555. LYNDSAY, *Thrie Estaitis* [E. E. T. S., 4031]. Allace! Maister, ye hurt my CRAG.

1579. SPENSER, *Shep. Calendar*, Feb., 89. Thy Ewes that woont to haue blowen bags, Like wailefull widdowes hangen their CRAGS.

1653. MIDDLETON, *Changeling*, i. 2. The devil put the rope about her CRAG.

1780. TOMLINSON, *Slang Pastoral*, 10. What Kiddy's so rum as to get himself SCRAGG'D.

*c.*1787. *Kilmainham Minit* [*Ireland Sixty Years Ago*, 88]. But if dat de slang you run sly, The SCRAG-BOY may yet be outwitted, And I scout again on de lay.

1820. *London Mag.*, I. 26. The SCRAGGING-POST must have been his fate.

1827. LYTTON, *Pelham*, lxxxiii. If he pikes we shall all be SCRAGGED.

1829. *The Lag's Lament* [*Vidocq's Mem.*, iii. 169]. Snitch on the gang, that'll be the best vay To save your SCRAG.

1834. AINSWORTH, *Roohwood*, v. i. I wish I was as certain of my reward as that Turpin will eventually figure at the SCRAGGIMG-POST.

1836. MILNER, *Turpin's Ride to York*, i. 3. I shall never come to the SCRAGGING-POST, unless you turn topsman.

1837. BARHAM, *Ingoldsby Leg.* So out with your whinger at once And SCRAG Jane, while I spiflicate Johnny.

1838. DICKENS, *Oliver Twist*, xviii. Indicating, by a lively pantomimic representation, that SCRAGGING and hanging were one and the same thing.

1843. MONCRIEFF, *Scamps of London*, ii. 3. He was three times lagged, and werry near SCRAGGED.

1883. *D. Telegraph*, 7 August, 6, 2. His waistcoat was of the tight up round the SCRAG pattern.

1887. HENLEY, *Villon's Straight Tip.* Until the squeezer nips your SCRAG, Booze and the blowens cop the lot.

1893. MILLIKEN, *'Arry Ballads*, 61. A crusher's 'ard knuckles a crunching yer SCRAG.

1900. KIPLING, *Stalky & Co.*, 46. Don't drop oil over my 'Fors,' or I'll SCRAG you.

2. (colloquial).—A raw-bones. Hence SCRAGGY = lean; thin (GROSE).

3. (Shrewsbury School).—*See* quot.

1881. PASCOE, *Public Schools.* The highest mark is twenty with a cross . . . and so down to a huge duck's egg and a rent across the paper entitled a SCRAG.

TO SCRAG A LAY, *verb. phr.* (old).—'To steal clothes put on a hedge to dry' (TUFTS); TO GO SNOWY-HUNTING (*q.v.*).

SCRAGG'S HOTEL, *subs. phr.* (tramps').—*See* quot.

1886. *D. Telegraph*, 1 Jan., 1. It looked very much as though we should be obliged to put up at SCRAGG'S HOTEL—the Work'us, if you like it better.

SCRAMBLE, *subs.* (common).—A feed of any kind: usually with a qualifying *subs.*: as TEA-SCRAMBLE, MUFFIN-SCRAMBLE, TOFFEE-SCRAMBLE, &c.

1901. *Troddles*, 46. 'Rats! . . . didn't you ever have a TOFFEE SCRAMBLE?'

SCRAN, *subs.* (beggars').—(1) Food: spec. broken victuals; (2) = refuse; also (3, military) = a meal. Hence SCRAN-BAG = a haversack, or TOMMY-BAG (*q.v.*); ON THE SCRAN = begging. BAD SCRAN TO YE! (Irish) = a mild malediction.

1724. HARPER, *Frisky Moll's Song* [FARMER, *Musa Pedestris* (1896), 41. But ere for the SCRAN he had tipt the cole, The Harman he came in.

1821. EGAN, *Life in London*, 207. If you open your peepers you'll go without SCRAN.

1841. LEVER, *Charles O'Malley*, lxxxv. BAD SCRAN TO ME if I wouldn't marry out of a face this blessed morning just as soon as I'd look at ye.

1851. MAYHEW, *London Lab.*, i. 466. Most of the lodging-house keepers buy the SCRAN of the cadgers.

*c.*1876. *Music Hall Song*, 'Uncle Attend to Tommy.' And if he gets no SCRAN, I soon shall see him wollop me As hard as ever he can.

1883. *D. Telegraph*, 8 Feb., 3, 2. She used to buy the contents of their SCRAN BAGS of 'em. The broken wittles was no good to them, and they'd let it go cheap.

1893. EMERSON, *Lippo*, xviii. Thin BAD SCRAN TO HER. Is the 'onerable Mrs. Putney in town? The bark again consulted his book.

4. (common).—The reckoning at a public-house.

SCRAP, *subs.* (common).—(1) A fight; a ROUGH-AND-TUMBLE (*q.v.*): also SCRAP-UP: hence SCRAPPING (or SCRAPPING-MATCH) = prize-fighting or boxing; SCRAPPER = a pugilist. Also (2) = a blow: *see* quot. 1610.

1610. ROWLANDS, *Martin Mark-All*, 40 (H. Club's Repr., 1874). SCRAPPES, fatte and glorious bittes: sound blowes and bangings. The muggill will tip you fat SCRAPS and glorious bits, the Beadle will well bumbast you.

1885. G. DOLBY, *Dickens as I knew him*, 102. An effect . . . resembling a SCRAP in a game of football.

1886-96. MARSHALL, *Sad Heart* ['Pomes,' 76]. Why, he can't SCRAP for nuts.

1887. *D. News*, 3 Feb., 7, 1. He put his hat down in the hall, and said, "You want to SCRAP." (Laughter.)—Mr. D'Eyncourt: SCRAP! What does that mean?—Defendant: It is some boxing term, sir. He came squaring up to me in a fighting attitude, and then I admit I did the best I could.

1893. EMERSON, *Lippo*, xvii. I could put up my dooks, so I backed to SCRAP a cove bigger nor me for a finnif a side. The SCRAP came off down the river at a place near Erith.

1896. CRANE, *Maggie*, i. He murmured with interest, 'a SCRAP, Gee!' He strode over to the cursing circle. *Ibid.*, vi. Dat mug SCRAPPED like a dago. He tau't he was a SCRAPPER. But he foun' out diff'ent.

3. (old).—'A villainous scheme or plot': TO WHIDDLE THE WHOLE SCRAP = 'to discover the plot' (GROSE).

SCRAPE, *subs.* (colloquial). — 1. Trouble; a difficulty (GROSE).

1741. WARBURTON, *Divine Legation*, II. The too eager pursuit of his old enemy has led him into many of these SCRAPES.

1748. SMOLLETT, *Rod. Random*, ix. He got himself into a SCRAPE by pawning some of his lordship's clothes. *Ibid.* (1749), *Gil Blas* [ROUTLEDGE], 188. By this device I got out of the SCRAPE.

1754. *Connoisseur*, No. 6. I had, indeed, like to have got into some unlucky SCRAPES.

1767. STERNE, *Tristram Shandy*, i. 12. This unwary pleasantry of thine will . . . bring thee into SCRAPES and difficulties.

1778. SHERIDAN, *Rivals*, v. 1. Have they drawn poor . . . Sir Lucian into the SCRAPE.

1790. BRUCE, *Source of Nile*, II. 456. The Naybe Musa . . . found into what a terrible SCRAPE he had got.

1797. M. G. LEWIS, *Castle Spectre*, v. i. He'd be in a terrible SCRAPE if you began knocking down his walls.

1818. SCOTT, *Rob Roy*, viii. Jobson, however, was determined that Morris should not back out of the SCRAPE or easily. *Ibid.* (1819), *Lammermoor*, viii. Unless you be in the Jacobite SCRAPE already, it is quite needless for me to drag you in.

2. (common).—An obeisance: also as *verb* = to salute by scraping the feet; SCRAPE-SHOE = a sycophant: *see* LEG.

1632. MASSINGER [?], *City Madam*, iv. 1. Live, SCRAPE-SHOE, and be thankful.

*c.*1840. MANSFIELD, *School Life in Winchester*. When a Præfect wished to go out of School he SCRAPED with his foot till he got a nod from the Master.

1851. HAWTHORNE, *Seven Gables*, xi. He took off his Highland bonnet, and performed a bow and SCRAPE.

3. (common).—A shave: hence SCRAPER = (*a*) a razor, and (*b*) a barber; and as *verb* = to shave.

1869. *Public Opinion*, 19 June. The beard and moustache which the sailors in the Royal Navy will be permitted to wear, thereby doing away with the objection that blue-jackets have to the SCRAPER.

4. (school). — Cheap butter: whence BREAD AND SCRAPE = (*a*) bread very thinly spread with butter, and (*b*) short commons. SCRAPE also = short shrift.

1873. BROUGHTON, *Nancy*, xlvii. Some people have their happiness thinly spread over their whole lives, like BREAD AND SCRAPE!

1899. *Pall Mall Gazette*, 5 Ap., 2, 1. From the French adventurers he was only likely to get what schoolboys call SCRAPE, for though musical boxes and patent armchairs are all very well in the way, they do not serve to check a Dervish attack or to keep wild Somalis in subjection.

5. (old).—A turn at fiddling: also SCRAPING; as *verb* = to fiddle; SCRAPER (or GUT-SCRAPER) = a fiddler. *See* CAT-GUT SCRAPER.

1607. DEKKER and WEBSTER, *Westward Hoe*, v. 1. 'They are but rosining, sir, and they'll SCRAPE themselves into your company presently' . . . 'Plague a' their cat's-guts and their SCRAPING.'

1611. CHAPMAN, *May-day*, iv. 1. Strike up, SCRAPERS!

*d.*1667. COWLEY [JOHNSON]. Out! ye sempiternal SCRAPERS.

1785. BURNS, *Jolly Beggars*. Her charms had struck a sturdy Caird, As weel's a poor GUT-SCRAPER.

6. (old). — A miser: also SCRAPER, SCRAPE-PENNY, SCRAPE-ALL, SCRAPESCALL, and SCRAPEGOOD. As *verb* = to stint, to deny.

1631. G. HERBERT, *Temple*, 'Church Porch.' Never was SCRAPER brave man.

1653. URQUHART, *Rabelais*, III. iv. A pinch-penny, a SCRAPE-GOOD wretch.

*c.*1696. B. E., *Dict. Cant. Crew*, s.v. SCRAPE ALL, a Money-Scrivener: also a miserable Wretch, or gripping Fellow.

TO SCRAPE THE ENAMEL, *verb. phr.* (cyclists').—To scratch the skin: by a fall.

See ACQUAINTANCE; LEG.

SCRAPER, *subs.* (nautical). — A cocked hat (C. RUSSELL).

See SCRAPE, CATGUT-SCRAPER, ELBOW-SCRAPER.

SCRAPING, *subs.* (old).—*See* quot.

1785. GROSE, *Vulg. Tongue*, s.v. SCRAPING. A mode of expressing dislike to a person, or sermon, practised at Oxford by the students, in SCRAPING their feet against the ground during the preachment; frequently done to testify their disapprobation of a proctor who has been, they think, too rigorous.

SCRAPE-TRENCHER, *subs. phr.* (old).—A glutton.

1772. FOOTE, *Nabob*, iii. So, Mr. SCRAPETRENCHER, let's have no more of your jaw.

SCRAPPY (SCRAPPINESS, and **SCRAPPILY)**, *adj.*, *subs.* and *adv.* (colloquial).—Made up of odds and ends; in driblets; without system.

1872. ELIOT, *Middlemarch*, ii. Balanced . . . neatness . . . conspicuous from its contrast with . . . SCRAPPY slovenliness.

1886. *Cont. Rev.*, xlix. 779. [Carlyle] was still a raw, narrow-minded, SCRAPPILY educated Scotchman.

1890. *Academy*, 12 Ap., *Adv.* iv. Well graduated and sufficiently long to avoid SCRAPPINESS.

SCRATCH, *subs.* (old Scots').—1. *See* quot.: also SCRAT (COLES).

1560. LINDSAY, of Pitscottie, *Cronicles* (Edinburgh, 1883), I. 162. There was one borne quhich had the memberis both of male and female, called in oure language ane SCRATCH.

2. (old).—A swaggerer (HALLIWELL).

3. (old).—The itch (HALLIWELL). Hence SCRATCHLAND = Scotland: *cf.* SCOTS GREYS.

4. (old). — A miserly man (HALLIWELL).

5. (sporting). — In handicaps (*a*) a starting line for those contestants allowed no odds, (*b*) the time of starting, (*c*) a start, (*d*) contestants starting from the SCRATCH-line. In boxing, a line drawn across the RING (*q.v.*) to which boxers are brought for a SET-TO (GROSE). Hence TO COME (or BRING) UP TO (or TOE) THE SCRATCH = to be ready, willing.

1819. MOORE, *Tom Crib*, 51. Sprightly to the SCRATCH both buffers came.

1821. EGAN, *Life in London*, I. i. I challenge thee to the SCRATCH! 'Tis one of the Fancy calls!

1825. JONES, 'True Bottom'd Boxer' [*Univ. Songst.*, ii. 96]. He's for the SCRATCH, and COME UP TOO IN TIME.

1827. SCOTT, *Two Drovers*, ii. "How would you fight then?" said his antagonist; "though I am thinking it would be hard to BRING YOU TO THE SCRATCH anyhow."

1834. AINSWORTH, *Rookwood*, IV. ii. Bold came each buffer to the SCRATCH.

1857. BRADLEY, *Verdant Green*, II. iv. Wondering . . . if the gaining palms in a circus was the customary "flapper-shaking" before TOEING THE SCRATCH for business.

1880. *Athenæum*, 4 Sept., 316, 2. A young lady, apparently of about thirteen years of age, who comes on the stage in a short frock, BRINGS a timid and recalcitrant lover TO THE SCRATCH.

1885. *M. Post*, 5 Feb. The former starting from SCRATCH, and the latter in receipt of 200 points.

1885. *Century Mag.*, xl. 207. The SCRATCH, or line from which the jump is taken is a joist some five inches wide, sunk flush with the ground

1892. ANSTEY, *Voces Populi*, 'At the Military Tonrnament,' 97. (The chestnut is at length brought UP TO THE SCRATCH snorting, etc.)

6. (billiards).—A FLUKE (*q.v.*).

Adj. (colloquial).—Generic for chance: hap-hazard, hasty, 'first come, first served.' Thus a SCRATCH-CREW (-TEAM, or -COMPANY) = a crew, &c., got together at short notice and without special selection; SCRATCH-RACE = a contest, unrestricted by conditions, a 'Go-as-you-please' affair; A SCRATCH-MEAL = a PICK-UP (*q.v.*) meal; &c., &c. Also TO SCRATCH ALONG = to manage somehow.

1859. LEVER, *Davenport Dunn*, lvi. Gathered together like what jockies call a SCRATCH-TEAM,

1869. *Orchestra*, 18 June. There is no English company—not the best—worthy of comparison with Félix's SCRATCH TROUPE in respect of *ensemble*, of accurate detail.

1870. *Figaro*, 15 Feb. I do not much like the look of the SCRATCH COMPANY that Messrs. Montague, James. and Thorne have got together.

1874. COLLINS, *Frances*, xlii. Frances and Cecilia, coming down, found a hasty luncheon, and everybody busy at it . . . When this SCRATCH LUNCHEON was over, everybody went out.

1883. OLIPHANT, *Altiora Pets*, I. xvi. 261. A coarse-fibred, stumpy little man . . . whose vulgarity would have fatally handicapped any other woman than his lovely and talented wife in the social SCRATCH RACE.

1885. *Field*, 4 Ap. Notwithstanding their long preparation and perfect coaching [they] looked like SCRATCH CREWS.

1888. *Harper's Mag.*, lxxvii. 88. I suspect we'll SCRATCH ALONG all right.

Verb. (colloquial).—1. To expunge; to blot-out; spec. (*a*) to reject a horse, a candidate, &c.; and (*b*) to retire.

1860. W. H. RUSSELL, *Diary in India*, I. 189. His last act is to try and get his name SCRATCHED.

1868. WHYTE - MELVILLE, *White Rose*, I. xiii. How's the hoose? . . . You haven't SCRATCHED him, have ye?

1884. *D. Telegraph*, 25 August, 3, 4. An acceptance of fourteen has already been cut down to a dozen by the SCRATCHING of Jetsam and Loch Ranza. *Ibid.* (1885), 6 Oct. One of his owner's first actions . . . was to SCRATCH the horse.

1885. *D. Chronicle*, 3 July. The Eton boys . . . made up their minds on Wednesday evening to SCRATCH.

1888. *D. Chronicle*, 10 Dec. Grimsby Town received a bye, Gainsborough Trinity having SCRATCHED to them.

1888. *Sp. Life*, 18 Dec. As she was clearly handicapped out of the race at Wye I had no option but to SCRATCH her.

2. (colloquial).—To scribble: as *subs.* = a scrawl. SCRATCHER (U. S.) = a daybook.

*d.*1745. SWIFT [*Century*]. If any of their labourers can SCRATCH out a pamphlet, they desire no wit, style, or argument.

1172. ELIOT, *Middlemarch*, lxxv. This is Chichely's SCRATCH. What is he writing to you about.

1887. PHIL. LEDGER, 30 Dec. He [a bank teller] would not enter deposits in his SCRATCHER after a certain hour.

PHRASES. — NO GREAT SCRATCH = of little value; OLD SCRATCH (*q.v.*); TO SCRATCH ONE'S WOOL (tailors') = to try one's memory, to puzzle out; 'SCRATCH my breech and I'll claw your elbow' (KA ME, KA THEE, *q.v.*); NOT A SIXPENCE TO SCRATCH HIS ARSE WITH = penniless.

1844. *Major Jones's Courtship Detailed*, 136. There are a good many Joneses in Georgia, and I know some myself that ain't NO GREAT SCRATCHES.

SCRATCHED, *adj.* (Old Cant).—Drunk: *see* SCREWED. [TAYLOR, *'Vater Poet*, 1630].

SCRATCHER, *subs.* (American).—1. An independent elector; a BOLTER (*q.v.*).

1883. *Atlantic Monthly*, LII. 327. To whom a SCRATCHER is more hateful than the Beast.

See SCRATCH, *verb.* 2.

SCRAWNY, *subs.* (American).—A thin, ill-made man or woman; A RASHER OF WIND (*q.v.*).

1890. *Detroit Free Press*, 21 June, 5, 3. If the line is to be drawn between the SCRAWNY and the adipose, the SCRAWNIES have it. They are full of delightful possibilities.

SCREAMER, *subs.* (common).—1. An exceptional person or thing: hence SCREAMING = first - rate, splendid: spec. as causing screams of laughter.

1846. THORPE, *Backwoods* [*Century*]. If he's a specimen of the Choctaws that live in these parts, they are SCREAMERS.

1847. PORTER, *Quarter Race*, 189. 'Now look out for a SCREAMER!'

1853. WH. MELVILLE, *Digby Grand*, xx. I am in for a SCREAMER, and the bill for which I am arrested is only a ruse to prevent my leaving England.

1864. HOTTEN, *Slang Dict*, s.v. SCREAMING . . . Believed to have been used in the Adelphi play - bills: "a SCREAMING farce," one calculated to make the audience SCREAM with laughter.

1874. *Siliad*, 49. There'll be no child's play in the Russian dug, 'Twill be a SCREAMER, and a frightful tug.

1879. BRADDON, *Cloven Foot*, vi. "Well," cried the manager, radiant, "a SCREAMING success. There's money in it. I shall run this three hundred nights."

1883. *D. Telegraph*, 19 Jan., 3, 5. A more amusing half-hour could not be spent than under the influence of this farce, which, in the old Adelphi days would most emphatically have been called a SCREAMER. *Ibid.* (1888), 8 Dec. The 'Deputy-Registrar' is a SCREAMER indeed.

1888. RUNCIMAN, *Chequers*, 38. She's a SCREAMER, she's a real swell.

1891. *Sporting Life*, 25 Mar. The piece, which is of the SCREAMING order of farce, certainly produces abundant laughter.

1893. MILLIKEN, *'Arry Ballads*, 77. Yank on to one gal, a fair SCREAMER.

2. (thieves'). —A thief who, robbed by another thief, applies to the police; in American a SQUEALER (q.v.).

SCREECH, *subs.* (common).—Whiskey: *see* OLD MAN'S MILK.

SCREECHER, *subs.* (colloquial).—Anything harsh or strident. Hence SCREECHY = loud mouthed.

SCREED. SCREED O' DRINK, *subs. phr.* (Scots').—1. A full supply; whence (2) a drinking bout.

1815. SCOTT, *Guy Mannering*, xxv. Naething confuses one, unless it be a SCREED O'DRINK at an oration.

SCREEN, *subs.* (old).—A bank note (GROSE, VAUX). Hence SCREEN-FAKING = fingering notes; QUEER SCREENS = counterfeit paper: *cf.* SCREEVE.

1821. EGAN, *Life in London*, II. v. Vy, it's full of pot-hooks and hangers—and not a SCREEN [£1 note] in it.

1830. MONCRIEFF, *Heart of London*, II. I. A little SCREEN-FAKING, that's all.

1834. AINSWORTH, *Roodwood*, 'Nix my Dolly.' Readily the QUEER SCREENS I then could smash.

1840. LYTTON, *Paul Clifford*, xxxi. Stretched for smashing QUEER SCREENS.

SCREEVE (or **SCREAVE**), *subs.* (old). 1. Anything written: a begging letter, a testimonial, chalk pavement work, &c. Also (2) a bank note (Scots): *cf.* SCREEN; SCREEVETON = the Bank of England. As *verb.* = to write, or draw; SCREEVER (or SCREEVE-FAKER) = (1) a cheeky beggar (GROSE, VAUX), and spec. (2) a pavement-'artist.'

1821. HAGGART, *Life*, 25. The SCREAVES were in his benjy cloy.

1851-61. MAYHEW, *Lond. Lab.*, I. 339. Professional beggars are . . . those who 'do it on the blob' (by word of mouth), and those who do it by SCREEVING, that is, by petitions and letters. *Ibid.* I. 341. Such a 'fakement' [a begging petition, &c.], put into the hands of an experienced lurker, will bring the 'amanuensis,' or SCREEVER, two guineas at least, and the proceeds of such an expedition have in many cases averaged £60 per week. *Ibid.*, I. 542. His chief practice was SCREEVING or writing on the pavement. *Ibid.* (1862), IV. 442. The next SCREEVE takes the form of a resolution at a public meeting.

1857. *Punch*, 31 Jan., 49. It's agin the rules is SCREEVIN' to pals out o' gaol.

1866. *London Miscellany*, 3 Mar., 57. "You'd better be a SCREEVER if they ask you," said he. "That'll account for your hands, you know." "You mean a begging-letter writer?"

1883. *Punch*, 14 July, 13, 2. Here is a brilliant opening for merry old Academicians, festive flagstone SCREEVERS, and "distinguished amateurs."

1884. *World*, 16 April, 15, 1. A correspondent writes: "*Apropos* of SCREEVER . . . does it get its derivation from the Italian *scrivere*, to write?"

1887. HENLEY, *Villon's Straight Tip*, 1. Suppose you SCREEVE or go cheap-jack.

1889. *Answers*, 27 July, 136, 2. A list of subscribers to a charity is carefully cut out by the SCREEVERS and studied. *Ibid.* A clerk is frequently called a SCREEVER, but a SCREEVER proper (or improper) is such a remarkable person.

SCREW, *subs.* (colloquial).—1. An extortioner; a miser. As *verb.* = to coerce into paying or saving money, or making a promise, yielding one's opinion, vote, person, &c.: also TO SCREW UP (or OUT), and TO PUT ON (or UNDER or TURN) THE SCREW (B. E., GROSE); SCREWY (or SCREWING) = mean.

*c.*1696. B. E., *Dict. Cant. Crew*, s.v. SCREW, TO SCREW ONE UP, to exact upon one, or Squeeze one in a Bargain or Reckoning.

1781. COWPER, *Truth*, 385. Strained to the last SCREW he can bear.

1847. THACKERAY, *Vanity Fair*, viii. They both agreed in calling him an old SCREW, which means a very stingy, avaricious person.

1851-61. MAYHEW, *Lond. Lab.*, I. 319. Mechanics are capital customers . . . They are not so SCREWY.

1852. DOW, *Sermons*, i. 302. Love strains the heart-strings of the human race, and not unfrequently PUTS THE SCREWS ON so hard as to snap them asunder.

1855. THACKERAY, *Newcomes*, xliv. Did you ever hear of *me* SCREWING? No, I spend my money like a man.

1857. *New York Times*, 15 Sep. Such TURNS OF THE SCREWS as we have had for the last three weeks, if continued, would bring almost every mercantile house in New York to wreck.

1859. KINGSLEY, *Geoffrey Hamlyn*, xxvii. However I will PUT THE SCREW ON them. They shall have nothing from me till they treat her better.

1860. *Cornhill Mag.*, II. 381. He was an immense SCREW at school.

1866. G. ELIOT, *Felix Holt*, xi. A SCREWING fellow, by what I understand—a domineering fellow—who would expect men to do as he liked without paying them for it.

1869. GREENWOOD, *Seven Curses, &c.*, 170. If I entrust my tailor with stuff for a suit, and it afterwards comes to my knowledge that he has SCREWED an extra waistcoat out of it.

1874. MRS. H. WOOD, *Johnny Ludlow*, 1st S., No. XVII. 301. For once in his SCREWY life, old Brown was generous.

1876. BRADDON, *Joshua Haggard*, xxx. He were so hard upon 'em, and that SCREWY, never a drop of milk or a fagot to give 'em.

1876. BURNABY, *Ride to Khiva*, ii. The Russians will not openly stop you, but they will PUT THE SCREW UPON our own Foreign Office and force the latter to do so.

1885. *Field*, 12 Dec. The utterly exorbitant rents that Scotch proprietors . . . have managed to SCREW OUT of sportsmen in the last few years.

1885. *D. Telegraph*, 12 Sep. He had little doubt of being able to PUT THE SCREW ON me for any amount I was good for.

2. (American collegiate).—(*a*) An unnecessarily minute examination; and (*b*) a SCREW. The instructor is often designated by the same name.—(HALL, *College Words.*)

18[?]. *Harvard Register*, 378 [BARTLETT]. One must experience the stammering and stuttering, the unending doubtings and guessings, to understand fully the power of a mathematical SCREW.

3. (common). — An old or worthless horse: whence (loosely) anything old. SCREWY = worn-out, worthless.

1835. APPERLEY, *Nimrod's Hunting Tour*, 215. Mr. Charles Boultbee, the best SCREW driver in England. (*Note.*) This is somewhat technical, and wants an explanation. A lame or very bad horse is called a SCREW.

1858. LYTTON, *What Will He Do with it*, VIII. vi. I suppose I was cheated and the brute proved a SCREW.

1869. WHYTE-MELVILLE, *M. or N.*, 61. The utmost speed attainable by a pair of high wheels, a well-bred SCREW, and a rough-looking driver.

1870. R. BROUGHTON, *Red as a Rose*, xix. The oldest and SCREWIEST horse in the stables.

1870. *Times*, 23 July, 'Speech of Lord Granville.' A considerable number of what are vulgarly called SCREWS have been bought at £20 a piece.

1874. COLLINS, *Frances*, xlii. Julian Orchard proved his skill as a whip by making four SCREWS do six miles in twenty-five minutes.

1897. KENNARD, *Girl in Brown Habit*, i. 4. A couple of likely-looking SCREWS.

4. (common).—*See* quot. 1851.

1851-61. MAYHEW, *Lond. Lab.*, I. 494. I never was admitted to offer them in a parlour or tap-room; that would have interfered with the order for SCREWS (penny papers of tobacco), which is a rattling good profit.

18[?] DICKENS, *Reprinted Pieces* (*Bill-Sticking*), 181. A pipe, and what I understand is called a SCREW of tobacco—an object which has the appearance of a curl-paper taken off the barmaid's head with the curl in it.

5. (common).—Money earned.

*c.*1860. *Music-hall Song*, 'The G.P.O.' He often thought of marriage, though his SCREW was low.

1872. *Figaro*, 18 May. The amateur element . . . takes paltry salaries (often none), and keeps down the SCREW of the actor.

1879. JUSTIN M'CARTHY, *Donna Quixote*, xvii. They get a good SCREW at the music-halls, I'm told.

1886. *D. Telegraph*, 25 Sep. £150 per annum is considered quite a good SCREW for a senior hand.

1886-96. MARSHALL, '*Pomes*,' 45. When he paid him his SCREW.

1892. *Ally Sloper*, 27 Feb., 71, 3. He had now the neat salary of £450 a year, and had come to the conclusion that a person with a SCREW like that might safely commit matrimony.

6. (old).—A turnkey (GROSE): Fr. *raf* and *griffleur*. As *verb.* = to imprison: also TO PUT UNDER THE SCREW; SCREWING = a term of imprisonment.

1821. EGAN, *Life in London*, I. ii. Washing the ivory with a prime SCREW under the spikes in St. George's Fields. *Ibid.*, II. vii. The officer, for his own safety, was compelled to PUT him UNDER THE SCREW. *Ibid.* (1st ed.), 219. If ever I am SCREWED UP within these walls.

1869. *Temple Bar*, xxvi. 72. He was a fool to let the SCREW see he had the snout.

1872. *D. Telegraph*, 4 July. The letter was produced . . . It was to the effect that the woman was to try her best with the SCREWS, and that there were plenty of "quids" to get her out of prison by next Monday.

1877. *Five Years' Penal Servitude*, ii. The slang name for all the officials is SCREWS.

1889. *Answers*, 9 Mar., 233, 3. Great excitement was caused . . . by an attempt made by a prisoner on the life of a warder. The SCREW was examining the man, who was working as a tailor, &c.

1890. *Sportsman*, 6 Dec. He was next trained to run at Haydock in September, and got a good SCREWING for an unfurnished puppy sixteen months old.

7. (old).—A skeleton-key: as *verb.* = to burgle: spec. by means of false keys; THE SCREW (or SCREW-GAME) = burglary; SCREWSMAN = a burglar (VAUX). Also 'to stand ON THE SCREW' = (GROSE) 'the door is not bolted merely locked.'

1852. JUDSON, *Myst. of New York*, II. ii. I sent on to have the SCREWS fitted, and somethin's leaked out, for they've put a glim inside.

1857. SNOWDEN, *Mag. Assistant* (3rd Ed.), 445. Housebreaking implements—SCREWS.

1868. *Temple Bar*, xxv. 543. From that I got to be a SCREWSMAN, and a cracksman.

1879. HORSLEY [*Macm. Mag.*, xl. 503]. I had the James and SCREWS on me . . . We went and SCREWED into his place, and got thirty-two quid. *Ibid.*, 505. I asked a SCREWSMAN if he would lend me some SCREWS.

1888. *Cassell's Sat. Jl.*, 22 Dec., 305. The SCREW fits the same as if it had been made for the back door.

1888. SIMS, *Plank Bed Ballad*, 5. With SCREWS and a james I was collared.

8. (old). — A prostitute: *see* TART. Whence, as *verb.* = to copulate: *see* RIDE (GROSE).

9. (common). — A dram; a PICK-ME-UP.

1877. *Five Years' Penal Servitude*, iii. It seems he was in the habit of taking every morning a SCREW in the shape of a little dose of bitters to correct the effects of the last evening's festivities.

10. (old).—A stomach ache (HALLIWELL).

A SCREW LOOSE, *verb. phr.* (old).—Something wrong (GROSE: 'a complete flash phrase').

1821. EGAN, *Life in London*, I. vii. The token was sufficiently impressive to remind him that if the LOOSE SCREW was not attended to the hinges would be ultimately out of repair.

1830. MONCRIEFF, *Heart of London*, ii. 2. His lordship seems hipped—something wrong in the House last night, I suppose—a SCREW LOOSE on the opposition benches.

1837. DICKENS, *Pickwick*, xlix. My uncle was confirmed in his original impression that something dark and mysterious was going forward, or, as he always said himself, that 'there was A SCREW LOOSE somewhere.'

1855. TROLLOPE, *The Warden*, viii. There's a SCREW LOOSE in their case, and we had better do nothing.

1872. *South London Press*, 17 Aug. Whether there was a SCREW LOOSE in the apparatus, or whether the man possessed nerves of more than ordinary power, I know not; but somehow or other the electricity had no effect.

SCREWED (or **SCREWY**), *adj.* (common).—Drunk; TIGHT (*q.v.*).

ENGLISH SYNONYMS. — [Further lists will be found under DRINKS, DRUNK, D.T's, GALLON-DISTEMPER, LUSH, LUSH-CRIB, and LUSHINGTON.] TO BE afflicted, afloat, alecied, all at sea, all mops-and-brooms, in one's armour, in one's altitudes, at rest, *Bacchi plenus*, battered, be-argered, beery, bemused, a bit on, blind, bloated, blowed, blued, boozed, bosky, a brewer, bright in the eye, bubbed, budgy, buffy, bung-eyed, candy, canon (or cannon), chirping-merry, chucked, clear, clinched, concerned, corked, corkscrewed, corky, corned, crooked, in one's cups, cup-shot, cut, dagged, damaged, dead-oh! disguised, disorderly, doing the Lord (or Emperor), done over, down (with barrel-fever: *see* GALLON-DISTEMPER), dull in the eye, full of Dutch-courage, electrified, elephant's-trunk (rhyming), elevated, exalted, far gone, feeling funny (or right royal), fettled (or in good fettle), fighting-tight (or drunk), flawed, floored, fluffed, flummoxed, flushed, flustered, flustrated, flying-high, fly-blown, fogged (or foggy), fou (Scots), on fourth, foxed, fresh, fuddled, full, full-flavoured, full to the bung, fuzzy, gay, gilded, glorious, grape-shot, gravelled, greetin'-fou', groggy, hanced, half-seas-over, happy, hard-up, hazy, heady, hearty, helpless, hiccius-doccius, hickey, high, hockey, hoodman, in a difficulty (*see* GALLON-DISTEMPER), incog, inspired, jagged, jolly, jug-bitten, kennurd (back slang = drunk), all keyhole, kisk, knocked-up, leary, lion drunk, in Liquor-pond Street-loaded, looking lively, lumpy, lushy, making indentures with one's legs, malted, martin-drunk, mashed, mellow, miraculous, mixed, moony, mopped, moppy, mortal, muckibus, muddled, mugged, muggy, muzzy, nappy, nase (or nazy), noddy-headed, noggy, obfuscated, oddish, off (off at the nail, or one's nut), on (also on the bend, beer, batter, fuddle, muddle, sentry, skyte, spree, etc.: *see* FLARE-UP and FLOORED), out (also out of funds, register, altitudes, &c.), overcome, overseen, overshot, over-sparred, overtaken, over the bay, palatic, paralysed, peckish, a peg too low, pepst, pickled, piper-drunk (or -merry), ploughed, poddy, podgy, potted-off, pot-shot, pot-sick, pot-valiant, primed, pruned, pushed, queered, quick-tempered, raddled, rammaged, ramping-mad, rather touched, rattled, reeling (or tumbling), ripe, roaring, rocky, salubrious, scammered, scooped, sewn up, shaky, three (or four) sheets in the wind, shot, shot in the neck, slewed, smeekit, smelling of the cork, snapped, snuffy, snug, so, soaked, sow-drunk, spiffed, spoony-drunk, spreeish, sprung, squiffed (or squiffy), stale-drunk, starchy, swattled, swiggled, swilled, swinnied, swine-drunk, swiped (or swipey), swivelly, swizzled, taking it easy, tangle-footed, tapshackled, taverned (also hit on the head by a tavern bitch, or to have swallowed a tavern token), teeth under, thirsty, tight, tipsy, top-heavy, topsy-boosy, tosticated, under the influence, up a tree, up in one's hat, waving a flag of defiance, wet, wet-handed, what-nosed, whipcat (FLORIO), whittled, winey, yappish (yaupy or yappy). Also, TO HAVE a guest in the attic, the back teeth well afloat, a piece of bread and cheese in the head, drunk more than one has bled, the sun in one's eyes, a touch of boskiness, a cup too much, a brick in the hat, a drop in the eye, got the flavour, a full cargo aboard, a jag on, a cut leg, the malt above the wheat, one's nuff, one's soul in soak, yellow fever. Also, TO HAVE BEEN barring too much, bitten by a barn mouse, driving the brewer's horse, biting one's name in, dipping rather deep, making M's and T's, paid, painting the town red, shaking a cloth in the wind. Also, to wear a barley cap, to cop the brewer, to let the finger ride the thumb, to lap the gutter, to need a reef taken in, to see the devil, to take a shard (or shourd), to shoe the goose, to see one apiece.

FRENCH SYNONYMS.—*S'allumer; s'attendrir; attraper un allumette rond, un coup de sirop,* or *une maculature;* AVOIR *son affaire, son allumette* (*son allumette ronde, de campagne,* or *de marchand de vin*), *une barbe, son caillon, un coup de bleu* (*de bouteille, chasselas, fard, feu, feu de société, picton, sirop,* or *soleil*), *son casque, sa chique, sa cocarde, son compte, sa cuite, une culotte, de gaz, un grain* (or *petit grain*), *son jeune homme, le mal Saint-Martin, le nez sale* (or *nez-de-chien*), *le panache, son paquet, sa pente, sa pistache, son plein, son plumet, sa pointe, son pompon, son poteau* (or *poteau télégraphique*), *du roulis, un sabre, le sac plein,* or *son toquel; avoir fumé un pipe neuve;* EN AVOIR *jusqu'à la troisième capucin, une charretée, une vraie muffée, plein son sac,* or *dans le toquet; battre la muraille; se cardinaliser; charmer les puces; se cingler le blair; se coaguler; se cocarder; se coller un coup de jus,* or *une biture; se culotter de la tête aux pieds; écraser un grain; s'embrouillarder; s'émécher; s'émérillonner; s'entuminer; s'empaffer; s'empoivrer;* ETRE *absinthé, allumé, asphyxié, bamboche, bien* (or *bien pensé*), *un brin en riole, dans les brindezingues, dans le brouillard, dans les broussilles, bu, casquette, chargé, en chérance, cinglé, complet, dessous, en drive, éméché, emu, dans un état voisin, fadé* (or *bien fadé*), *fier, gai, gavé, gris d'officier, humecté, lancé, en liche, louave, machabé, monté, mouillé, paf* (or *paf jusqu'à la troisième*), *dans* (or *de*) *la paroisse de Saint-Jean le Rond, parti* (or *parti pour la gloire*), *en patrouille, pavois, pion, plein* (or *plein comme un œuf, un sac*), *plombé pochard, poche, poivre, poussé raide* (or *raide comme la justice*), *riche, rond* (or *ronde comme une balle, une bourrique, une bourrique à Robespierre,* or *une boule*), *saoul*

comme un âne (*un hanneton, une grive, un Polonais,* or *trente milles hommes*), *slasse* (or *slaze*), *teinté, dans la terrine, en train, dans les vignes* (or *la vigne*) *du Seigneur,* and *vent dessus-dessous* (or *dedans*); *faire cracher ses soupapes; se farder; fêter la Saint-Lundi; se flanquer un coup d'arrosoir* (*une cuite, une Culotte,* or *une fameuse pétée*); *se foncer; se grimer; se grisotter; mettre son nez dans le bleu; se mettre en dedans; se mouiller; se paffer; se payer; se pincer* (or *se pincer un coup de sirop* or *le tasseau*); *se piquer le nez* (*le tasseau,* or *le tube*); *se pocharder; se poisser; se poivrotter; se pommader; prendre son allumette de campagne* (or *une barbe*); *ramponner; se salir le nez; schniquer; se schlosser; se sculpter une guende de bois; slasser; se tinter; ne pas trouver son niveau; voir en dedans.*

1837. BARHAM, *Ing. Leg.*, 'Witches' Frolic.' Like a four-bottle man in a company SCREW'D, Not firm on his legs, but by no means subdued.

1841. *Punch*, i. 278. We had a great night in London before I started, only I got rascally SCREWED: not exactly sewed up, you know, but hit under the wing, so that I could not well fly.

1843. DICKENS, *Martin Chuzzlewit*, xxv. She was only a little SCREWED.

1850. SMEDLEY, *Frank Fairlegh*, 133. If any of our party were in the condition expressed by the mysterious word SCREWED, it certainly was Lawless himself.

1855. THACKERAY, *Newcomes*, xlvii. Blest if I didn't nearly drive her into a wegetable cart. I was so uncommon SCREUEY!

1871. *All Year Round*, 18 Feb., 288. Awfully SCREWED. Been keeping it up with a fast lot at Gypsum.

1895. *Reynolds*, 18 Aug., 4, 7. A witness suggested that the prisoners were too drunk to know what they were doing. Mr. Gray: No. We admit being a little bit SCREWED, but we were not so bad as all that.

SCRIBBLER'S-LUCK, *subs. phr.* (common).—*See* quot.

1898. *Pelican*, 3 Dec., 11, 2. His purse is pretty full; mine, worse luck, is almost empty. SCRIBBLER'S LUCK, an empty purse and a full hand.

SCRIBE. *See* ONE-EYED SCRIBE.

SCRIMSHANKER, *subs.* (military).—A loafer: *cf.* BLOODSUCKER; whence SCRIMSHANK = to shirk duty.

SCRIMSHAW (or **SCRIMSHANDER**), *subs.* (nautical).—*See* quots. Also SCRIMSHON and SCRIMSHORN.

18[?]. *Fisheries of U.S.*, v. ii. 231-2. SCRIMSHAWING ... is the art, if art it be, of manufacturing useful and ornamental articles at sea.... We find handsome writing desks, toilet boxes, and work-boxes made of foreign woods, inlaid with hundreds of other pieces of precious woods of various shapes and shades.

1883. C. RUSSELL, *Sailors' Language*, s.v. SCRIMSHANDY. An Americanism signifying the objects in ivory or bone carved by whalemen during their long voyages.

SCRIP, *subs.* (old).—*See* quot. and BLOT THE SCRIP (GROSE).

*c.*1696. B. E., *Dict. Cant. Crew*, s.v. SCRIP, *c.* a shred or scrap of paper. 'As the Cully did freely blot the SCRIP, and sipt me 40 Hogs,' *c.* one enter'd into Bond with me for 40 Shillings.

SCROBY. TO BE TIPPED THE SCROBY (or CLAWS) FOR BREAKFAST, *verb phr.* (old).—'To be whipped before the justices' (GROSE).

SCROOF (or **SCROOFER**), *subs.* (American).—A parasite: as *verb* = TO SPONGE (*q.v.*).

SCROPE, *subs.* (old).—A farthing: *see* RHINO (HALL, GROSE).

SCROUGER, *subs.* (American).—Anything exceptional in size, quality, capacity, &c.

1847. ROBB, *Squatter Life*, 106. The gals among 'em warn't any on your pigeon creaturs ... but real SCROUGERS—any on 'em over fourteen could lick a bar easy.

*c.*1852. *Traits of Amer. Humour*, 265. A drum, and a regular SCROUGER at that.

SCROUPERIZE, *verb.* (venery).—To copulate: *see* GREENS and RIDE (RABELAIS).

SCROYLE, *subs.* (old).—A diseased wretch: Fr. *écrouelles* = King's-evil.

1596. SHAKSPEARE, *King John*, ii. 2. By heaven, these SCROYLES of Angiers flout you, kings.

1596. JONSON, *Ev. Man*, i. 1. To be a consort for every humdrum; hang 'em, SCROYLES! there is nothing in them in the world. *Ibid.* (1601), *Poetaster*, iv. 3. A better, prophane rascal! I cry thee mercy, my good SCROILE, wast thou?

SCRUB, *subs.* (old colloquial).—Any mean, or ill-conditioned person, or thing; as *adj.* = paltry, mean: also SCRUBBED, and SCRUBBY; SCRUB-RACE = a contest between contemptible animals; after FARQUHAR and *The Beaux' Stratagem* (1707).—B. E., GROSE.

1598. SHAKSPEARE, *Mer. of Venice*, v. 1, 162. A little SCRUBBED boy No higher than myself.

1621. BURTON, *Anat. of Mel.* (1836) I. II. III. XV. 201. Or if they keep their wits, yet they are esteemed SCRUBS and fools, by reason of their carriage.

1634. WITHAL, *Dict.* [NARES]. Promus magis quam condus: he is none of these miserable SCRUBS, but a liberall gentleman.

*c.*1696. B. E., *Dict. Cant. Crew*, s.v. SCRUB, a Ragamuffin.

1706. WARD, *Hudibras Redivivus*, I. vi. 6. Each member of the holy club, From lofty saint, to lowly SCRUB. *Ibid.* I. x. 10. Mounted on SCRUBS that us'd to Scour, Upon a Trot, eight Miles an Hour.

1730. SWIFT, *Traulus*, i. The SCRUBBIEST cur in all the pack Can set the mastiff on your back. Ibid., *Stella*, xxviii He finds some sort of SCRUB acquaintance.

1731. FIELDING, *Letter Writers*, ii. 2. 1. *Wh.* You stoop to us, SCRUB! 2. *Wh.* You a lord! You are some attorney's clerk, or haberdasher's 'prentice. *Ibid.* (1749), *Tom Jones*, VIII. iii. He is an errant SCRUB, I assure you.

1751. SMOLLETT, *Peregrine Pickle*, lxxxvii. You are worse than a dog, you old flinty-faced, flea-bitten SCRUB.

1766. GOLDSMITH, *Vicar of Wakefield*, x. We should go there in as proper a manner as possible; not altogether like the SCRUBS about us.

1814. AUSTEN, *Mansfield Park*, xxv. I could not expect to be welcome in such a smart place as that—poor SCRUBBY midshipman as I am.

1843. DICKENS, *Martin Chuzzlewit*, xxxv. No SCRUBS would do for no such a purpose. Nothing less would satisfy our Directors than our member in the House of Commons.

1848. THACKERAY, *Book of Snobs*, xviii. A SCRUBBY-looking, yellow-faced foreigner.

1852. *L'Allegro: As Good as a Comedy*, 109. There was to be a SCRUB race for sweepstakes, in which more than twenty horses had been already entered.

1861. BRADDON, *Trail of the Serpent*, I. iv. The dumb man was a mere SCRUB, one of the very lowest of the police-force. *Ibid.* (1868), *Dead Sea Fruit*, xxiii. I told you I knew a handy SCRUB of a man, good at picking up any out-of-the-way book I may happen to want.

1883. ROOSEVELT [*Century*, xxxvi. 200]. We got together a SCRUB wagon team of four as unkempt, dejected, and vicious-looking broncos as ever stuck fast in a quicksand.

2. (American Univ.).—A servant.

Verb. (Christ's Hospital).—1. To write fast: *e.g.*, 'SCRUB it down.' Also as *subs.* = handwriting. [Lat. *scribere.*] *See* STRIVE.

2. (colloquial).—To drudge.

SCRUBBADO, *subs.* (old).—The itch (B. E., GROSE).

SCRUBBER, *subs.* (Australian).—*See* quot.

1859. KINGSLEY, *Geoffry Hamlyn*, xxix. The Captain was getting in the SCRUBBERS, cattle which had been left, under the not very careful rule of the Donovans, to run wild in the mountains.

SCRUBBING, *subs.* (Winchester: obsolete).—A flogging of four cuts: *see Public School Word Book.*

*c.*1840. MANSFIELD, *School Life*, 109. The ordinary punishment was called SCRUBBING ... for a more serious breach of duty a flogging of six cuts was administered.

1864. *Blackwood's Mag.*, xcv. 79. The place of execution where delinquents are bibled ... six cuts ... four being the sum of a ... SCRUBBING.

SCRUBBING-BRUSH, *subs. phr.* (venery).—The pubic hair: *see* FLEECE.

SCRUDGE, *subs.* (provincial).—A harlot: *see* TART.

SCRUFF, *subs.* (colonial).—*See* quot.

1870. *Montreal News* [*Figaro*, 25 Nov., 'Codland Habits.' The best society is called 'merchantable,' that being the term for fish of the best quality; while the lowest stratum is 'SCRUFF' or 'dun.'

Verb. (old).—To hang: *see* LADDER.

SCRUMPTIOUS, *adj.* and *adv.* (colloquial)—First-class; nice; fastidious.

1835. HALIBURTON, *Clockmaker*, 1 S., xxiii. A little tidy, SCRUMPTIOUS-looking sleigh, a real clipper of a horse.

1841. LEMAN REDE, *Sixteen String Jack*, iii. 5. Will you dance, Christopher, my SCRUMTIOUS pet?

1870. JUDD, *Margaret*, 304. I don't want to be SCRUMPTIOUS, judge; but I do want to be a man.

1888. BOLDREWOOD, *Robbery Under Arms*, xx. We had a SCRUMPTIOUS feed that night.

1891. *Lic. Vict. Gaz.*, 23 Jan. SCRUMPTIOUS girls who danced at the Alcazar.

1900. KIPLING, *Stalky & Co.*, 7. 'Isn't it SCRUMPTIOUS? Good old sea!'

SCRUNCH, *subs.* (colloquial).—1. A hard bite; a crushing blow; and (figuratively) a complete effect of tyranny; as *verb.* = to crush, to grind down, to squeeze; SCRUNCHER = a glutton.

1851-61. MAYHEW, *Lond. Lab.*, II. 566. I ... SCRUNTCHED myself into a doorway, and the policeman passed four or five times without seeing on me.

1865. DICKENS, *Mutual Friend*, III. v. It's the same ... with the footmen. I have found out that you must either SCRUNCH them, or let them SCRUNCH you.

1869. STOWE, *Oldtown*, 480. We ... shouted 'Hurrah for old Heber!' as his load of magnificent oak ... came SCRUNCHING into the yard.

1888. *Fort. Rev.*, N.S., xliii. 627. At each step there is a SCRUNCH of human bones.

SCUD, *subs.* (common).—(1) A fast runner; and (2) a HOT SPIN (*q.v.*).

1857. HUGHES, *Tom Brown's Schooldays*, I. v. I say ... you ain't a bad SCUD.

2. (American).—In *pl.* = money: *see* RHINO.

Verb. (old).—'To Sail, Ride, or Run very fast' (B. E., *c.*1696).

SCUDDICK, *subs.* (old).—The smallest item of value (HALLIWELL): *see* quot. 1823.

1823. BEE, *Dict. Turf*, s.v. SCUDDICK—is used negatively; 'not a SCUDDICK'—not any brads, not a win, empty clies. 'Every SCUDDICK gone'; 'she gets not a SCUDDICK from me.' does not amend the matter from repetition.

1843. MONCRIEFF, *Scamps of London*, i. 1. Hasn't a mag left—not a SCUDDICK—is obliged to live on his wits.

SCUFF, *subs.* (thieves').—A crowd.

1879. *Macm. Mag.*, xl. 501. This got a SCUFF round us.

1888. SIMS, *Plank-Bed Ballad* [*Referee*, 12 Feb.]. A SCUFF came about me and hollared.

SCUFFLE-HUNTER, *subs. phr.* (obsolete).—*See* quot.

1797. *Police of the Met.*, 54. Those who are distinguished by the nickname of SCUFFLE-HUNTERS prowl about the wharfs, quays and warehouses under pretence of asking employment as porters and labourers, but their chief object is to pillage and plunder whatever comes in their way.

SCUFTER, *subs.* (provincial).—*See* quot.

1886. *Graphic*, 30 Jan., 130, 1. In the North a constable is or was known as a SCUFTER and a "bulky."

SCUG, *subs.* (Eton and Harrow).—A SNEAK (*q.v.*); a play-CAD (*q.v.*).

1880. C. T. BUCKLAND, *Eton Fifty Years Ago*. Bathing was always in great favour with the Eton boys. A boy who did not bathe was called a SCUG.

1889. DRAGE, *Cyril*, vii. Such a little SKUG, to use a word in use at my tutor's.

SCULDUDDERY (or **SKULDUGGERY**), *subs.* (old). — Bawdry; also as *adj.*

1713. CENTLIVRE, *The Wonder*, iii. 3. *Gibby*. To run three hundred mile to this wicked town, and, before I can well fill my weam, to be sent a whorehunting after this black she-devil! . . . there's na sic honest people here, or there wud na be sa mickle SCULDUDRIE.

1818. SCOTT, *Midlothian*, xvi. Can find out naething but a wee bit SCULDUDDERY.

1890. *Scots Observer*, 23 Aug., 346. Living in a state of liquor and SKULDUDDERY.

SCULL, *subs.* (University).—1. The head (or master) of a College (GROSE). Hence SCULL-RACE = an examination.

2. (colloquial). — In *pl.* = a waterman using a pair of sculls or short OARS (*q.v.*).—GROSE.

*c.*1704. [ASHTON, *Soc. Life in Reign of Q. Anne*, II. 144.] A cry of next 'Oars' or 'SCULLS'!

3. (old).—'A one-horse chaise or buggy' (GROSE).

SCULLERY-SCIENCE, *subs. phr.* (obsolete).—Phrenology.

1836. CHORLEY, *Mem. Mrs. Hemans*, i. 255. I did very much aggravate the phrenologist lately by laughing at the whole SCULLERY SCIENCE and its votaries.

SCULL-THATCHER, *subs. phr.* (common),—1. A wig-maker (GROSE); and (2) a hatter: *see* NOB-THATCHER.

SCULPIN, *subs.* (American).—'A mean or mischief-making fellow [Local slang, New Eng.]' (*Century*).

SCUM, *subs.* (old: now recognised). —'The Riff-Raff, or Tagrag and Long-tail' (B. E., GROSE).

Adv. (old).—Enough (*Street Robberies Considered*, 20).

SCUMBER (or **SCUMMER**), *subs.* (old).—Excrement: as *verb.* = to defecate (COTGRAVE, 1611, s.v. *Chier*).

1598. FLORIO, *Worlde of Wordes*, s.v. *Chinchimurra* . . . A SKAMMERING of a dog.

[?]. *Ulysses upon Ajax*, B.6. The picture of a fellow in a square cap SCUMMERING at a privy.

1630. MASSINGER, *Picture*, v. 1. Just such a one as you use to a brace of greyhounds, When they are led out of their kennels to SCUMBER.

1658. *Musar. Del.*, 'On Epsom Wells.' Old Ops . . . Is yellow, not with summer, But safronised with mortal SCUMMER.

SCUMBLE, *verb.* (artists'). — To glaze a picture.

SCURF, *subs.* (common).—*See* quot. 1851.

1851-61. MAYHEW, *London Lab.*, i. 20. They . . . burst out into one expression of disgust. "There's a SCURF!" said one; "He's a regular scab," cried another. *Ibid.*, ii. 262. The Saxon *Sceorfa*, which is the original of the English SCURF, means a scab, and scab is the term given to the "cheap men" in the shoemaking trade. Scab is the root of our word *Shabby*, hence SCURF and Scab, deprived of their offensive associations, both mean shabby fellows.

1870. LONGFELLOW, *Dante's Inferno*, xv. 111. That wretched crowd . . . If thou had hadst an hankering for such SCURF.

Verb. (thieves').—To arrest; to lay hold of (GROSE, VAUX).

SCURRICK, *subs.* (Old Cant).—A halfpenny (GROSE): *see* RHINO.

SCURRY, *subs.* (racing).—*See* quot.: *cf.* SCAB-RACE.

1889. KRIK, *Guide to the Turf*. In sporting [SCURRY] a short race run for amusement by inferior horses or non-winners.

1902. HEADON HILL, *Caged*, xv. It would have been all right if I hadn't been welshed over the last SCURRY.

SCUT, *subs.* (venery). — 1. The female *pudendum*: *see* MONOSYLLABLE; and (2) the pubic hair: *see* FLEECE (GROSE).

1596. SHAKSPEARE, *Merry Wives*, v. 5, 20. My doe with the black SCUT.

1664. COTTON, *Virgil Travestie* (1st ed.), 104. And likewise there was finely put, A Cushion underneath her SCUT.

*c.*1705. *Broadside Song*, 'Oyster Nan' [FARMER, *Merry Songs and Ballads* (1897), i. 177]. Come in, says he, you silly Slut, I'll lay the Itching of your SCUT.

1720. DURFEY, *Pills*, vi. 198. With her breast she does butt, and she bubs up her SCUT Wheu the bullets fly close by her ear.

1730. *Broadside Song*, 'Gee Ho, Dobbin,' 5. I rumpl'd her Feathers, and tickl'd her SCUTT.

SCUTE, *subs.* (old).—(1) A small coin: hence a low standard.

1596. NASH, *Letter* [NARES]. Worse than a SCUTE or a dandiprat.

15[?]. FORTESCUE, *Diff. Between Absolute and Limited Monarchy* [NARES]. Sum . . . that was wonte to pay . . . a SCUTE, payyth now . . . over that SCUTE, fyve SKUTS.

SCUTTLE, *subs.* (old). — 1. An affected gait (*see* quot. 1704); (2) a hasty move; a BOLT (*q.v.*): as *verb.* = (1) to run off (B. E. and GROSE).

*c.*1704. [ASHTON, *Social Life, &c.*, I. 92]. Shut myself in my Chamber, practised Lady Betty Modely's SCUTTLE.

*c.*1711. *Spectator* [*Century*]. She went with an easy SCUTTLE out of the shop.

*d.*1797. WALPOLE, *Letters*, II. 476. I have no inclination to SCUTTLE barefoot after a Duke of Wolfenbuttle's army.

1841. THACKERAY, *Comic Tales*, II. 164. But, oh horror! a scream was heard from Miss Binse who was seen SCUTTLING at double-quick time towards the schoolhouse.

1869. BROWNING, *Ring and Book*, I. 286. No . . . viper of the brood shall SCUTTLE OFF.

1872. *Brighton Daily News*, 4 Sep. The infant SCUTTLED into existence about midday.

1875. W. H. KINGSTON, *South Sea Whaler*, xiv. SCUTTLING away at a rapid rate.

Verb. (Christ's Hospital, Hertford).—2. To cry out, under oppression, to attract the attention of the authorities. Hence SCUTTLE-CAT = one who SCUTTLES (obsolete).

3. (venery). — To deflower. Hence, TO SCUTTLE A SHIP = to take a maidenhead.

4. (thieves').—To stab.

TO SCUTTLE A NOB, *verb. phr.* (pugilists').—To break a head.

*c.*1811. MAHER, *Night before Larry was Stretched*. I'll SCUTTLE YOUR NOB with my fist.

1818. RANDALL, *On R.'s fight with Turner*. As he offered to SCUTTLE A NOB o'er again.

ON THE SCUTTLE, *phr.* (common).—On a round of drinking or whoring.

SCUTTLING, *subs.* (Manchester).—*See* quots.

1890. *D. Telegraph*, 13 Dec. 'SCUTTLING in Lancashire.' SCUTTLING was a practice very prevalent within the county of Lancaster. The offence was committed by a body of young persons, male and female, belonging to one part of the city, who had a real or fancied grievance against another similar body of persons from an adjacent part. The opposing forces were armed with belts with large buckles to them, knives, pokers, stones, and the like, and the mobs so armed turned out at times for a regular affray, and inflicted serious injuries upon one another. Not only did these roughs enter into conflict with others of a similar class, but they frequently attacked unoffending passers-by.

18[?]. *Lancet*, 3499, 643. Manchester is becoming notorious for a form of street ruffianism known locally as SCUTTLING. It consists of gangs of youths going about certain districts ostensibly to fight with similar gangs of adjacent districts.

SCUTTLE-MOUTH, *subs. phr.* (costers').—*See* quot.

1851-61. MAYHEW, *Lond. Lab.*, I. 77. The "big trade" was unknown until 1848, when the very large shelly oysters, the fish inside being very small, were introduced from the Sussex coast. The costermongers distinguished them by the name of SCUTTLE-MOUTHS.

SEA. AT SEA, *adv. phr.* (colloquial).—Puzzled; WIDE (*q.v.*): *cf.* HALF-SEAS-OVER.

1864. *Cornhill Mag.*, Nov., 577. 'What is he?' I asked, still more AT SEA.

1889. *Polytechnic Mag.*, 24 Oct., 263. For the first ten minutes the B's were all AT SEA on the rough and peculiarly shaped ground.

PHRASES AND COMBINATIONS. — SEA-CRAB = a sailor (GROSE); SEA-DOG = (1) a privateer (*temp.* Eliz.), and (2) a sailor: spec. an old SALT (*q.v.*); SEA-GALLOPER = a special correspondent; SEA-GROCER = a purser; SEA-LAWYER = (1) a shark (GROSE), and (2) a captious or scheming fo'csle hand: whence SEA-LAWYERING = argument with officers; SEA-LEGS = ability to walk the deck of a rolling ship without staggering; SEA-WAG = an ocean-going vessel; SEA-RAT (old) = a pirate: *cf.* RIVER-RAT; SEA-ROVER = a herring: *see* ATLANTIC RANGER; SON OF A SEA-COOK = a nautical term of abuse; SEA-CONNIE (or CUNNIE) = (1) the helmsman on an Indian trader, and (2) = a Lascar quarter-master (CLARK RUSSELL); SEA-COAL = money.

*c.*1835. DANA, *Before the Mast*, ii. I had not got my SEA LEGS on, was dreadfully sick . . . and it was pitch dark.

1836. SCOTT, *Cringle's Log*, xvi. Ay, you supercilious SON OF A SEA-COOK, you may turn up your nose at the expression.

1864. KINGSLEY, *Hillyars*, xxiv. It made her stand firmer on her . . . had I been speaking of an English duchess I would have said her SEA LEGS.

1874. GREEN, *Short Hist.*, 406. The Channel swarmed with SEA-DOGS . . . who accepted letters of marque from the Prince of Condé.

1890. *Spectator*, 3 May, Rev. of 'Slang and its Analogues.' . . . The extraordinary 'bouncer' that a very common request at Lockhart's coffee-houses in London is for 'a doorstep and a SEA-ROVER.'

1899. WHITEING, *John St.*, xi. At the words 'doorsteps and SEA-ROVER,' the man at the bar produces a slice of bread and a herring.

1899. HYNE, *Furth. Adv. Captain Cuttle*, v. Robinson's a SEA-LAWYER, is he? Courts, he talks about.

1901. *Referee*, 7 Ap., 1, 2. Great care should be exercised so as to minimise chances of their being able to take two chances for their money, one in the game and the other by 'SEA-LAWYERING.'

1901. *Army and Navy Gaz.*, 13 July, 683, 2. Whether these SEA-GALLOPERS—to use Lord Spencer's historical designation—in the battleships will be able to see much of the fun is, we should imagine, doubtful.

SEAL, *subs.* (clerical).—1. *See* quot.

1853. DEAN CONYBEARE [*Edin. Rev.*, Oct., 295, *note*]. A preacher is said in this phraseology to be owned when he makes many converts, and his converts are called his SEALS.

2. (American).—*See* quot.

1850-1. STANSBURY, *Salt Lake Exp.*, 136. In Mormon phraseology, all wives taken after the first are called spiritual wives, and are said to be SEALED to the husband . . . under the solemn sanction of the church, and in all respects, in the same relation to the man as the wife that was first married.

3. (venery).—In *pl.* = the testes: *see* CODS.

Verb. (venery).—To impregnate; TO SEW UP (*q.v.*).

SEALER, *subs.* (old).—'One that gives Bonds and Judgments for Goods and Money' (B. E., GROSE): *see* SQUEEZE-WAX.

SEAM. *See* WHITE-SEAM.

SEAR, *subs.* (old).—The female *pudendum*: *see* MONOSYLLABLE, &c. [Properly the touch-hole of a pistol.] Hence LIGHT (or TICKLE) OF THE SERE = wanton; fond of bawdy laughter (HALLIWELL).

[?] *Commune Secretary and Jalowsye* [HALLIWELL]. She that is fayre, lusty, and yonge, And can comon in termes wyth fyled tonge, And wyll abyde whysperynge in the eare, Thynke ye her tayle is not LYGHTE OF THE SEARE.

1596. SHAKSPEARE, *Hamlet*, ii. 2, 336. The clown shall make those laugh whose lungs are TICKLE OF THE SERE.

1620. HOWARD *Defensative* [DOUCE, ii. 230]. Moods and humours of the vulgar sort . . . loose and TICKLE OF THE SEARE.

SEASON, *verb.* (venery).—*See* quot., GREENS and RIDE.

1559. ELIOTE, *Dict. Admissura*, SEASONING of a cow, and coverynge of a mare.

SEAT. *See* BACK-SEAT.

SEAT-OF-HONOUR (**SHAME** or **VENGEANCE**), *subs. phr.* (common).—The posteriors.

1725. BAILEY, *Erasmus*, 225. A question . . . the most honourable part of a man? One . . . made answer . . . the . . . part we sit upon; . . . when every one cried out that was absurd, he backed it with this reason, that he was commonly accounted the most honourable that was first seated, and that this honour was commonly done to the part that he spoke of.

1749. SMOLLETT, *Gil Blas* [ROUTLEDGE], 169. My SEAT OF VENGEANCE was firked most unmercifully.

*d.*1796. WOLCOT, *Pair of Lyric Epistles* [*Works* (Dublin, 1795), ii. 424]. Behold him seiz'd, his SEAT OF HONOUR bare.

1821. COOMBE, *Syntax*, III. 2. While with his spade the conqueror plied, Stroke after stroke, the SEAT OF SHAME, Which blushing Muses never name.

1836. MARRYAT, *Midshipman Easy*, xviii. The bullet having passed through his SEAT OF HONOUR, from his having presented his broadside as a target to the boatswain.

1856. *Punch*, xxxi. 213, 2. Now I can vouch that, from the earliest ages to . . . those of the present head-master, they have, one and all, appealed to the very SEAT OF HONOR.

SECESH. *See* BLUE BELLIES.

SECOND. *See* BOW, CHOP, FIDDLE (adding quot. *infra*), and STRING.

1749. SMOLLETT, *Gil Blas* [ROUTLEDGE], 378. I am quite at your service to play SECOND FIDDLE in all your laudable enterprises.

SECOND PEAL. *See* PEAL.

SECOND-TIMER, *subs. phr.* (prison).—A prisoner twice convicted.

SECRET, *phr.* (old). — LET INTO THE SECRET: 'When one is drawn in at Horse-racing, Cock-fighting, Bowling, and other Sports or Games, and Bit.' (B. E. and GROSE.)

IN THE GRAND SECRET, *phr.* (colloquial).—Dead (GROSE).

SEDGLEY-CURSE, *subs. phr.* (old).—*See* quots.

1632. MASSINGER, *City Madam*, ii. 2. May the great fiend, booted and spurred, With a sithe at his girdle, as the Scotchman says, Ride headlong down her throat.

1633. FLETCHER, *Tamer Tamed*, v. 2. A SEDGLY CURSE light on him, which is, Pedro, The fiend ride through him booted and spurred With a sythe at his back.

1636. SUCKLING, *Goblins*, i. 1. Now the SEDGLY CURSE upon thee, And the great fiend ride through thee Booted and spurr'd, with a scythe on his neck.

*d.*1660. HOWELL [RAY, *Proverbs*, Staffordshire. The devil, &c. . . . This is SEDGELY CURSE. *Mr. Howel.*]

SEE, *subs.* (common).—In *pl.* = the eyes (GROSE). Also SEER = the eye.

1819. MOORE, *Tom Crib*, 3 [Note]. To close up their eyes—alias, to sew up their SEES.

1827. LYTTON, *Paul Clifford*, lxxxii. Strike me blind if my SEES don't tout your bingo muns in spite of the darkmans.

2. (American). — A sight; a glance.

Verb. (colloquial).—1. To believe; to credit; to consent: *e.g.*, 'I don't SEE that.'

1882. ANSTEY, *Vice-Versa*, iii. If I were to go back to my governor now, he wouldn't SEE it. It would put him in no end of a bait.

2. (prostitutes').—To copulate: also TO SEE STARS LYING ON ONE'S BACK.

PHRASES. TO SEE IT OUT = (1) to finish a matter, (2) to keep up a carouse, and (3) to come to an understanding, or know the reason why; TO SEE ONE THROUGH = to help to a finish; TO SEE A MAN = to have a drink; TO SEE THE DEVIL = to get tipsy: *see* SCREWED; TO SEE THE BACK OF = to get rid of; TO SEE ONE COMING = to impose on; TO SEE DOUBLE = (1) to be drunk (*see* SCREWED), and (2) to squint; TO SEE ONE'S AUNT = to evacuate: *see* BURY A QUAKER; TO SEE AS FAR INTO A MILLSTONE (or MILESTONE) AS . . . = to be as able or cute as . . .; TO SEE STARS (SPOTS or CANDLES) = to be dazed: spec. from a blow. Also *see* BRICKWALL, ELEPHANT, SHOW, &c.

1546. HEYWOOD, *Proverbs*. She had SEENE FAR IN A MILSTONE.

1628. EARLE, *Micro-cosmog.*, ii. His eyes like a drunkard's SEE all DOUBLE.

1692. DRYDEN, *Juvenal*, vi. When vapours to their swimming brains advance, And DOUBLE tapers on their tables dance.

1710. CONGREVE, *Art of Love*. From all intemperance keep, Nor drink till you SEE DOUBLE, lisp, or sleep.

1716. ADDISON, *Freeholder*, 22. I had a mind to SEE him OUT, and therefore did not care for contradicting him.

1749. SMOLLETT, *Gil Blas* (1812), x. x. Falling into a passion he gave me half-a-dozen boxes on the face . . . that made me SEE more CANDLES than ever burnt in Solomon's temple. *Ibid.* (1751), *Peregrine Pickle*, c. Notwithstanding the disgrace and discouragement they had met with in their endeavours to serve our adventurer, they were still resolved to persevere in their good offices, or, in the vulgar phrase, to SEE him OUT.

1857. DICKENS, *Xmas Stories* (*Perils of Prisoners*), (Household ed.), 46. We SAW OUT all the drink that was produced, like good men and true, and then took our leaves, and went down to the beach.

SEED, *subs.* (venery).—The semen: *see* SPENDINGS. Hence SEED-PLOT (or SEED-LAND) = the female *pudendum*: *see* MONOSYLLABLE; RUN TO SEED = pregnant, LUMPY (*q.v.*)

1555. *A Pore Helpe*, 84. They saye ye leade euyll lyues With other mennes wyues . . . And so your SEDE is sowne In other mennes grounde.

1656. FLETCHER, *Martiall*, xi. 105. The Phrygian Boyes in secret spent their SEED As oft as Hector's wife rid on his steed.

1719. DURFEY, *Pills*, iii. 107. For there where other gardeners here been sowing their SEED . . .

1865. SWINBURNE, *Atalanta in Calydon*, 107. Thou, I say Althea, since my father's ploughshare, drawn Through fatal SEEDLAND of a female field, Furrowed thy body.

RUN TO SEED, *adv. phr.* (colloquial).—1. Shabby; gone off the bloom; SEEDY (*q.v.*).

1837. DICKENS, *Pickwick Papers* (1857), 20. Large boots RUNNING rapidly TO SEED.

1891. *Ally Sloper*, 4 Ap. He had RUN very much TO SEED: there was no gloss on his hat or boots, but any amount of it on the sleeves of his coat.

SEEDY, *adj.* and *adv.* (colloquial).—Generic for depreciation = (1) weak or out-of-sorts in health, (2) worn or out at elbows in dress, (3) poor in pocket, (4) suspicious or shady in character (GROSE). Hence, SEEDINESS.

1743. FIELDING, *Jonathan Wild*, I. xii. However SEEDY Mr. Bagshot may be now . . . when he is in cash, you may depend on a restoration.

1768. GOLDSMITH, *Good Natured Man*, iii. Little Flanigan here, to be sure, has . . . a very good face; but then, he is a little SEEDY, as we say among us that practise the law.

1789. PARKER, *Bunter's Christening* [Life's Painter]. A queer procession of SEEDY brims and kids.

1819. MOORE, *Tom Crib*, 27. The Prince of Rag Rhino, who stood . . . bail for the SEEDY Right Liners.

1835. FISHER, *Garland*. Oh, let my hat be e'er sae brown, My coat be e'er sae SEEDY, O!

1840. LYTTON, *Paul Clifford*, vi. You look cursed SEEDY to be sure.

1854. MARTIN and AYTOUN, *Bon Gualtier Ballads*, 'The Knight, &c.' I feel extremely SEEDY, Languishing in vile duresse.

1857-9. THACKERAY, *Virginians*, ix. A SEEDY raff who has gone twice or thrice into the Gazette.

1864. *Tangled Talk*, 169. One of the flattering unctions that I lay to my soul when it strikes me that I am becoming morally SEEDY is, that I have not lost the child's capacity for wonder.

1873. BLACKIE, *Self-culture*, 74. What is called SEEDINESS, after a debauch, is a plain proof that nature has been outraged, and will have her penalty.

1883. *D. Telegraph*, 6 Jan., 6, 1. Gradually his habiliments become what is vulgarly but expressively termed SEEDY.

1893. EMERSON, *Lippo*, xvi. The 'oss is very bad and very SEEDY.

1899. POT and SWEARS, *Scarlet City*, 119. I've sent a wire to old Dibbler the stage manager to say I'm SEEDY.

SEEK. TO SEEK OTHERS AND LOSE ONESELF, *verb. phr.* (old colloquial).—*See* quot.

1598. FLORIO, *Worlde of Wordes*, s.v. *Lanternare* . . . to play the foole, TO SEEKE OTHERS AND LOOSE HIMSELFE.

SEEK-SORROW (or -TROUBLE), *subs. phr.* (old).—A whining malcontent.

1580. SIDNEY, *Arcadia*, i. Afield they go, where many lookers be, And thou SEEK-SORROW Claius them among.

1902. DAUDET, *Sapho* [FARMER], xi. She was a SEEK-SORROW, a sappy mopester, a poor gutless doll.

SEELEY'S PIGS, *subs. phr.* (nautical).—Pig iron in Government dockyards. [Some of the yards were half paved with pigs, which waste was brought to public notice by Mr. Seeley, M.P. for Lincoln.]

SEE-SAW, *subs. phr.* (gaming).—A double RUFF (*q.v.*); a SAW (*q.v.*): at whist.

SEGGON, *subs.* (old colloquial).—A term of contempt: spec. a poor labourer. Also SEG-HEAD = a blockhead; SEG-KITE = an overgrown and greedy person [HALLIWELL].

1557. TUSSER, *Husbandrie*, 174. Poore SEGGONS halfe staured worke faintly and dull.

SELL, *subs.* (common).—A successful hoax; a swindle: *see* GAMMON. As *verb.* = to betray; to impose on; to swindle; *see* BARGAIN. Whence TO SELL A PUP = to fool; TO BE SOLD LIKE A BULLOCK IN SMITHFIELD (GROSE) = 'to fall badly by treachery'; SOLD AGAIN! = DONE! (*q.v.*),

1597. SHAKESPEARE, *Rich. III.* v. 3. Jockey of Norfolk, be not so bold, For Dickon thy master is BOUGHT AND SOLD.

1605. DRAYTON, *Mortimeriados*. Is this the kindness that thou offerest me? And in thy country am I BOUGHT AND SOLD.

1605. JONSON, *Volpone*, Argument. New tricks for safety are sought; they thrive: when bold, each tempts the other again, and all are SOLD.

1850. SMEDLEY, *Frank Fairlegh*, 145. He called it . . . 'no end of a something or other'—"SELL," suggested Freddy. *Ibid.* (1851), *Lewis Arundel*, xxiv. You're not going to try and cut out Bellefield . . . are you? I wish you would, it would SELL Bell so beautifully.

1856. (*Tales from Blackwood*) *Dreepdaily Burghs*, 2. I had been idiot enough to make my *debut* in the sporting world . . . and as a matter of course, was remorselessly SOLD by my advisers.

1864. *Glasgow Citizen*, 10 Dec. People pretend to have read Spenser and Chaucer, and it is rude . . . to SELL the affable pretender by getting him to remember non-existent passages and minor poems.

1874. MRS. H. WOOD, *Johnny Ludlow*, 1 S., XXVI., 465. It's an awful SELL . . . no hunting, and no shooting, and no nothing.

1883. *D. News*, 18 Ap. 5, 4. Lord Randolph Churchill has been making Mr. Gladstone the victim of what, in . . . Addison's time, would have been called a BITE, and what in . . . our own time is called a SELL.

1888. BOLDREWOOD, *Robbery Under Arms*, x. Some day he'll SELL us all, I really do believe.

1891. *Lic. Vict. Gaz.* 16 Jan. But suppose that he should take our money and SELL us.

SEMI-BEJAN. *See* BEJAN.

SEMINARY, *subs.* (venery).—The *pudendum*: *see* MONOSYLLABLE. [With a pun on semen = the *liquor seminale.*]

SEMPER, *adj.* (Winchester).—*See* quot.

*c.*1840. MANSFIELD, *School Life* (1866), 233. A very common prefix; *e.g.*, a boy was said to be SEMPER continent, tardy, or extrumps if he was often at Sick House, or late for Chapel, or habitually went up to Books without having looked at his lessons. An official who was always at the College meetings went by the name of SEMPER Testis.

SEND. TO SEND UP, *verb. phr.* (American).—To commit to prison; TO FULLY (*q.v.*).

1852. JUDSON, *Myst. of New York*, III. 7. They'd blow on me for some of my work, and I'd be SENT UP.

1879. *Scribner's*, viii. 619. Some of them seem rather proud of the number of times they have been SENT UP.

1888. *Detroit Free Press*, 20 Oct. They SENT me UP for thirty days.

TO SEND DOWN (or AWAY), *verb. phr.* (University). — 1. To expel; and (2) TO RUSTICATE (*q.v.*).

1714. *Spectator*, 596. After this I was deeply in love with a milliner, and at last with my bedmaker, upon which I was SENT AWAY, or, in university phrase, rusticated for ever.

1863. KINGSLEY, *Austin Elliot*, i. 179. How dare you say 'deuce' in my presence? You can GO DOWN, my Lord.

1891. *Harry Fludyer*, 89. Next day they were hauled and SENT down.

1891. *Felstedian*, Ap. 32. They SENT him DOWN for two terms for smashing a shop window.

TO SEND IN, *verb. phr.* (old).—'To drive or break in: Hand down the jemmy and SEND IT IN; apply the crow to the door and drive it in' (GROSE).

See COVENTRY; DAYLIGHT; FLEA IN EAR; GREEN RIVER; OWLS; PACKING; SALT RIVER; UP.

SEND-OFF, *subs. phr.* (colloquial).—A start; a God-speed. SEND-OFF NOTICE = an obituary.

1872. CLEMENS, *Roughing It*, 332. One of the boys has passed in his checks, and we want to give him a good SEND OFF.

1876. BESANT and RICE, *Golden Butterfly* . . . After the funeral Huggins . . . wrote a beautiful SEND-OFF NOTICE saying what a loss the community had suffered in Scrimmy's untimely end.

1889. *Pall Mall Gaz.*, 16 Nov., 6, 1. It looks as if Adelina Patti's SEND-OFF concert on Monday night would be a very brilliant affair.

1894. MORRISON, *Mean Streets*, 132. In the beginning [he] might even have been an office boy, if only his mother had been able to give him a good SEND OFF in the matter of clothes.

1897. *Referee*, 14 Mar. 1, 1. These departers were to be patted on the back, given a good SEND-OFF, and helped on the road.

SENDER, *subs.* (common).—A severe blow.

SENSATION, *subs.* (common).—A small quantity; as much as can be perceived by the senses: spec. a half-quartern.

SENSE, *verb.* (once literary; now American colloquial.—To feel; to take in; to understand.

1651. CARTWRIGHT, *Poems* [NARES]. 'Twas writ, not to be understood, but read, He that expounds it must come from the dead; and undertake to SENSE it true, For he can tell more than himself e'er knew.

1665. GLANVILLE, *Scepsis, Scientifica*, xxii. Is he sure that objects are not otherwise SENSED by others, than they are by him?

1885. MERRIAM, *S. Bowles*, I, 101. He . . . got at the plans of the leaders, the temper of the crowd, SENSED the whole situation.

SENTIMENTAL-CLUB (THE), *subs. phr.* (literary).—The Athenæum.

SENTIMENTAL - JOURNEY. TO ARRIVE AT THE END OF THE SENTIMENTAL JOURNEY, *phr.* (common).—To possess a woman [That, so it is said, being the finish of Sterne's novel—'I put out my hand and caught hold of the *fille - de - chambre's* ——. FINIS'].

SENTINEL, *subs.* (Irish).—A wake candle; a GLIM (*q.v.*). Fr. *une flambarde.*

SENTRY. ON SENTRY, *adv. phr.* (common). — Drunk: *see* SCREWED.

SENTRY-BOX. CHELSEA HOSPITAL TO A SENTRY-BOX, *phr.* (old).—A fanciful bet.

1891. *Lic. Vict. Mirror*, 30 Jan., 7, 2. Tom's hit of the opening round, and led Aaron's friends to call out in their jubilation: "It's all your own, my boy; CHELSEA HOSPITAL TO A SENTRY-BOX."

SEP, *subs.* (American cadet).—A cadet joining in September.

SEPARATE, *subs.* (prison). — *See* quot. 1877.

1862. *Cornhill Mag.*, vi. 640. [Criminals] count by many thousands ... In prison and out of it ... doing their SEPARATES at Pentonville and among the rocks of Gibraltar wherever they are they develop and increase criminal tendencies, and spread criminal knowledge.

1877. *Five Years' Penal Servitude*, v. 333. A new large prison at Dartmoor, in which convicts could be confined in cells to do their SEPARATES, as the first eleven or twelve months' probationary imprisonment is termed.

SERAGLIETTO, *subs.* (B. E., *c.*1696).—"A lowly, sorry Bawdy-house, a meer Dog-hole."

SERAGLIO, *subs.* (B. E., *c.*1696, and GROSE, 1785). — "A Bawdy-house; also the Great Turk's Palace."

SERENE. *See* ALL SERENE.

SERGEANT. *See* COME.

SERGEANT-MAJOR, *subs. phr.* (butchers').—A fat loin of mutton.

SERGEANT-MAJOR'S BRANDY AND SODA, *subs. phr.* (military).—A gold-laced stable jacket.

SERGEANT-MAJOR'S WASH CAT, *subs. phr.* (cavalry).—(1) A new kit; and (2) the troop store-man.

SERPENT. STUNG BY A SERPENT, *phr.* (old).—With child (RAY).

TO HOLD A SERPENT BY THE TAIL, *verb. phr.* (old).—To act foolishly.

SERVANT, *subs.* (venery).—1. A lover *en parade*; and (2) a STALLION (*q.v.*): *cf.* MISTRESS. Hence, SERVICE = copulation; TO SERVE = *subagitare.*

1369. CHAUCER, *Troilus*, v. 1345. If any SERVAUNT durst or oghte aryght Upon his lady pitously compleyne. *Ibid.* (*c.*1387), *Queen Annelida*, 293. He was SERVAUNT unto her ladyship ... she had him at her oune will.

1595. SHAKSPEARE, *Two Gent. Verona*, ii. 4. Too low a mistress for so high a SERVANT. *Ibid.* (1605), *Lear*, iii. 4, 87. A SERVING man ... that ... SERVED the lust of my mistress's heart, and did the act of darkness with her.

1609. BEAUMONT and FLETCHER, *Scornful Lady*, v. 1 Was I not once your mistress, and you my SERVANT?

1609. JONSON, *Epicœne*, ii. 2. Where the first question is—if her present SERVANT love her? next, if she shall have a new SERVANT? and how many.

1611. CHAPMAN, *May-Day*, v. 2. A woman of good parts ... helps maids to SERVICES, restores maidenheads, brings women to bed, and men to their bedsides. *Ibid.* (1612), *Widow's Tears*, ii. 4. Madam, I am still the same ... not pressing to your bed but your pleasure shall be first known, if you will command me any SERVICE.

*c.*1619. FIELD and MASSINGER, *Fatal Dowry*, ii. 2. The only distinction betwixt a husband and a SERVANT is, the first will lie with you when he pleases, the last shall lie with you when you please.

1635. DAVENANT, *News from Plymouth*, ii. 1. He loves and honours ladies; for whose SERVICE He's still a ready champion.

1685. CROWNE, *Sir Courtly Nice*, ii. 1. You may proclaime at Mercat-cross, how great an Adorer you are of such a Woman's Charms? how much you desire to be admitted into her SERVICE; that is, how lusty a Centaur you are.

1692. DRYDEN, *Juvenal*, x. In form of law, a common hackney-jade Sole heir for secret SERVICES is made.

1720. DURFEY, *Pills*, v. 227. To shew he could a Lady SERVE, As well as the Hollander.

1772. BRIDGES, *Homer Burlesque*, 392. And all the virgins in the town Expect they shall be ravished soon ... At any time they'll let you SERVE 'em.

SERVE, *verb.* (old).—1. To rob: *e.g.*, 'I SERVED him for his thimble' = 'I robbed him of his watch' (GROSE and VAUX).

2. *See* SERVANT and TIME.

3. (thieves').—'To find guilty, convict, and sentence' (GROSE).

4. (old).—To maim; to wound; to PUNISH (*q.v.*): whence TO SERVE OUT = to take revenge; TO SERVE OUT AND OUT = to kill (GROSE and VAUX).

1819. MOORE, *Tom Crib.* Whoso'er grew unpolite The well-bred champion SERVED HIM OUT.

1821. EGAN, *Life in London*, II. ii. Squinting Nan, full of jealousy ..., is getting over the box to SARVE HER OUT for her duplicity.

1837-40. HALIBURTON, *Clockmaker* (1848), 12. Now the bees know how to SARVE OUT such chaps, for they have their drones, too.

1853. BULWER, *My Novel*, xii. 25. The Right Honourable Gentleman had boasted he had served his country for twenty years ... He should have said SERVED HER OUT.

1868. GREENWOOD, *Purgatory of Peter the Cruel*, i. 22. I am doomed to become a blackbeetle because of the many of the sort I have hurt and smashed, and more especially because I SERVED this wretched cockroach OUT.

TO SERVE UP, *verb. phr.* (American). To ridicule.

See SLOPS.

SESSIONS, *intj.* (common). — An exclamation of surprise.

SET, *subs.* (cricketers').—1. A determined stand; TO GET SET = to 'collar' the bowling.

2. (common).—A grudge; a sustained attack: in argument or conduct. Also DEAD-SET.

PHRASES. TO SET THE HARE'S HEAD TO THE GOOSE GIBLETS = to balance matters; to give tit for tat; TO SET JEWELS (*see* quot. 1874); ALL SET = 'Desperate fellows, ready for any kind of mischief' (DUNCOMBE).

1607. DEKKER and WEBSTER, *Westward Hoe*, v. 3. They came to Brainford to be merry, you were caught in Birdlime, and therefore SET THE HARE'S HEAD AGAINST THE GOOSE GIBLETS.

1874. HOTTEN, *Slang Dict.*, s.v. SETTING JEWELS. The taking the best portions of a clever book not much known to the general public, and incorporating them quietly in a new work by a thoroughly original author. The credit of this term belongs to Mr. Charles Reade, who explained that the process is accountable for the presence of some writing by one Jonathan Swift, in a story published at Christmas, 1872, and called *The Wandering Heir.*

See CAP; DEAD-SET; EARS; HARD-SET; SHOULDER; WHEEL.

SET-BACK. *See* BACK-SET.

SET-DOWN, *subs. phr.* (colloquial).—1. A snub; an unexpected or overwhelming reply. Also as *verb.* = to take to task; to rebuff; to get the better of.

1749. SMOLLETT, *Gil Blas* [OLIPHANT, *New Eng.*, ii. 166. Among new substantives are a SET-DOWN, blinkers, ...].

2. (American tramps'). — *See* quot.

1900. FLYNT, *Tramps*, 105. He will almost always give a beggar a SET-DOWN (square meal).

SET-OFF, *subs. phr.* (colloquial).—1. A contrast; an alternative; a QUID PRO QUO (*q.v.*)

1749. SMOLLETT, *Gil Blas* [ROUTLEDGE], 151. As a SET-OFF against his hen-pecked cowardice ... he gave me fifty ducats. *Ibid.*, 249. You will not have much spare room ... but as a SET-OFF I promise that you shall be superbly lodged at Lisbon.

1844. MILL, *Polit. Econ.*, III. xii. 6. If the cheque is paid into a different bank, it will not be presented for payment, but liquidated by SET-OFF against other cheques.

*d.*1868. BROUGHAM [*Century*]. A poor SET-OFF against constant outrages.

1879. FROUDE, *Cæsar*, 454. He pleaded his desertion of Pompey as a SET-OFF against his faults.

2. (colloquial). — An adornment; an ornament.

1619. FLETCHER, *Wildgoose Chase*, iii. 1. This coarse creature That has no more SET-OFF but his jugglings, His travell'd tricks.

SET-OUT, *subs. phr.* (colloquial).—A company, clique, display, or turn-out—any arrangement, state of things, or event.

1816. AUSTEN, *Emma*, xlii. 'There shall be cold meat in the house.' 'As you please; only don't have a great SET-OUT.'

1851-61. MAYHEW, *Lond. Lab.*, II. 46. The whole SET-OUT ... pony included, Cost £50 when new.

1837. DICKENS, *Pickwick* (1857), II. "P.C.," said the stranger,—"queer SET OUT—old fellow's likeness, and P.C.—What does P.C. stand for—Peculiar coat, eh?" *Ibid.* (1854), *Hard Times*, i. 8. She must just hate and detest the whole SET-OUT of us.

1856. WHYTE MELVILLE, *Kate Coventry*, iv. As we pulled up in front of the Castle Hotel ... "Ere's a spicy SET-OUT, Bill," said one.

SETTA, *adj.* (theatrical).—Seven. Also SETTER.

1893. EMERSON, *Lippo*, xiv. Then he placed a large piece of boiled bacon and a dish of potatoes and a dish of greens before three road scavengers, and said, "I'll take SETTA soldi from you gents."

SETTER, *subs.* (old).—1. *See* quots.; also (modern) a police spy: *see* NARK (GROSE).

1591. GREENE, *Notable Discovery* [*Works*, x. 15]. The nature of the SETTER, is to draw any person familiarly to drinke with him, which person they call the bonie.

1598. SHAKSPEARE, *1 Hen. IV.*, ii. 2, 53. 'Tis our SETTER: I know his voice.

1607. DEKKER, *Jests to make you Merie* [*Wks.* (GROSART), II. 310]. Your theeues trauelling mort is partly a SETTER of robberies, partly a theefe herselfe.

1680. COTTON, *Complete Gamester*, 333. Shoals of huffs, hectors, SETTERS, gilts, pads, biters, &c., may all pass under the general appellation of rooks.

*c.*1696. B. E., *Dict. Cant. Crew*, s.v. SETTERS, or Setting-dogs, they that draw in Bubbles, for old Gamesters to Rook; also a Sergeant's Yeoman, or Bailiff's Follower, or Second, and an Excize-Officer to prevent the Brewers defrauding the King.

1714. *Memoirs of John Hall* (4th ed.), 7. There are also SETTERS of both Sexes, that make it their Business to go about upon Information, to pry into the Disposition and Avenues of Houses, and bring notice of the Booty.

*d.*1745. SWIFT, *Last Speech Eben. Elliston.* We had SETTERS watching in corners, and by dead walls.

1754. B. MARTIN, *Eng. Dict.* (2nd ed.), s.v. SETTER ... (3) an associate of sharpers to get them bubbles.

1866. LEMON, *Leyton Hall.* Old Crookfinger, the most notorious SETTER, barnacle, and foist in the city.

2. (auctioneers').—A runner-up of prices; a BONNET (*q.v.*).

CLOCK-SETTER, *subs. phr.* (nautical).—1. One who tampers with the clock to shorten his watch; also (2) a busy-body, a SEA-LAWYER (*q.v.*).—*Century.*

SETTLE, *verb.* (common).—1. To knock down; TO DO FOR (*q.v.*).—GROSE. TO SETTLE ONE'S HASH (*see* HASH). Hence SETTLER = (1) a knock-down blow; and (2) a finishing stroke.

1819. MOORE, *Tom Crib*, 15. He tipp'd him a SETTLER.

1827. *The Fancy*, 'King Tims the First.' That thrust you gave me, Tims, has proved a nettler. Your stab turns out, what I have been, a SETTLER!

1836. SCOTT, *Cruise of the Midge*, 102. Like a cannon-shot right against me, giving me such a SETTLER.

1845. BUCKSTONE, *Green Bushes*, ii. 2. Whoever that lady aimed at, she has certainly brought down.... She settled the SETTLER, and no mistake.

1857. HOLMES, *Autocrat of the Breakfast Table*, vi. That slight tension about the nostrils which the consciousness of carrying a SETTLER in the form of a fact or a revolver gives the individual thus armed.

*c.*1866. *Music Hall Song*, 'What a fool.' My darling wife and Ma-in-law Have nearly SETTLED me.

1877. *Five Years' Penal Servitude*, iii. "'E see the engine a coming, ... and chucked hisself bang in front of it, and it soon SETTLED 'im."

1888. *Sportsman*, 22 Dec. A mistake at the last hurdles proved a complete SETTLER, and he succumbed by six lengths.

2. (thieves').—To give (or get) penal servitude for life.

SETTLEMENT-IN-TAIL, *subs. phr.* (venery).—An act of generation: *see* GREENS and RIDE.

SETTLER, *subs.* (common).—1. A parting drink: *see* SCREWED.

2. *See* SETTLE, 1.

SET-TO, *subs. phr.* (pugilists').—1. A bout at fisticuffs, with, or without, the gloves. Whence (2) = determined opposition (GROSE). Also as *verb.*

1819. MOORE, *Tom Crib*, 'Account of the Grand SET-TO between Long, Sandy and Georgy the Porpus' [Title].

1825. SCOTT, *St. Ronan's Well*, xxx. The alacrity of gentlemen of the Fancy hastening to a SET-TO.

1837. BARHAM, *Ingoldsby Leg.*, I. 317. As prime a SET-TO And regular turn-up as ever you knew.

1859. WHITTY, *Political Portraits*, 217. The bludgeon blows of the old Parliamentary SET-TOS ended in hand-shaking.

1864. *London Society*, Dec. I generally warms up in the SET-TO with Judy, and by the time the ghost business comes on, I'm all of a glow.

1879. PAYN, *High Spirits* (*Finding His Level*). He had had it laid down with turf instead of a carpet, for the greater convenience of his SET-TOS.

1889. *Modern Society*, 19 Oct., 1294, 1. They settled the affair with a good SET-TO with raw potatoes.

1892. *National Observer*, 27 Feb., 378. Give me a snug little SET-TO down in Whitechapel.

SET-UP, *subs.* (colloquial). — 1. Port; bearing; carriage.

1890. T. C. CRAWFORD, *Eng. Life*, 147. [English soldiers] have a SET-UP not to be found in any of the soldiers of the Continental armies.

2. (American). — A TREAT (*q.v.*) to SET-UP = to 'STAND SAM': *cf.* SET-DOWN.

1887. T. STEVENS, *Around World on a Bicycle* ... They threaten to make him SET 'EM UP every time he tumbles in hereafter.

Adv. (American).—Conceited.

SEVEN. TO BE MORE THAN SEVEN, *phr.* (common). Wide-awake. Also, MORE THAN TWELVE.

*c.*1876. *Music Hall Song*, 'You're MORE THAN SEVEN' [Title].

1892. NISBET, *Bushranger's Sweetheart*, 195. Yes, I really do think that the naughty boy is MORE THAN SEVEN.

1898. GISSING, *Town Traveller*, viii. 'We all know that Mr. Gammon's MORE THAN SEVEN.'

SEVENDIBLE, *adj. adv.* (Irish).—'A very curious word, used only in the North of Ireland, to denote something particularly severe, strong, or sound. It is, no doubt, derived from sevendouble—that is, sevenfold—and is applied to linen cloth, a heavy beating, a harsh reprimand, &c.' (HOTTEN).

SEVEN-PENNORTH (or **SEVEN-PENCE**), *subs. phr.* (old).—*See* quot.

1821. EGAN, *Life in London*, II. iii. 'My lord, if I am to stand SEVENPENCE [7 yrs transportation], my lord, I hope you'll take it into your consideration.'

SEVEN-SIDED ANIMAL (or **SEVEN-SIDED SON OF A BITCH**), *phr.* (old).—'A one-eyed person: as as he has a right side and a left side, a front side and a back side, an inside and an outside, and a blind side' (GROSE).

SEVEN-YEAR, *subs. phr.* (old).—A long time: proverbial.

15[?]. *Four Elements* [HALLIWELL]. That is the best daunce without a pype that I saw this SEVEN YERE.

1579. *Mariage of Witt and Wisdome.* Thay ware not so hack this SEVEN YEERE.

1600. SHAKSPEARE, *Much Ado*, iii. 3. He has been a vile thief this SEVEN YEAR.

SEVERELY, *adv.* (colloquial).—A generic intensive: *e.g.*, 'to be left SEVERELY alone' = to be altogether neglected.

1854. WHYTE MELVILLE, *General Bounce*, xii. That officer has dined SEVERELY, as he calls it, and is slightly inebriated.

SEW. TO SEW UP ONE'S STOCKING, *verb. phr.* (C. READE).—To silence; to confute.

1859. READE, *Love Me Little*, xxvi. Eh! Miss Lucy, . . . but ye've got a tongue in your head. Ye've SEWED UP MY STOCKING.

SEWED UP, *adj. phr.* (common).—1. Pregnant; KNOCKED-UP (*q.v.*). To SEW UP = to get with child.

2. (pugilists').—Severely punished: spec. with bloated eyes.

3. (common).—Exhausted; drunk; sick.

1829. BUCKSTONE, *Billy Taylor. Kitty. (Aside, and taking out a vial.)* This liquid, sent me by Monsieur Chabert, The fire-king, will SEW HIM UP.

1836. DICKENS, *Pickwick*, lv. "Busy!" replied Pell; "I'm completely SEWN UP, as my friend the late Lord Chancellor many a time used to say to me."

1841. *Punch*, I., 278. We had a great night in London before I started only I got rascally screwed, not exactly SEWED UP, you know, but hit under the wing so that I could not very well fly.

1847. ROBB, *Squatter Life*, 33. A most excellent first number—just the thing—SEW the lower town UP.

1850. SMEDLEY, *Frank Fairlegh*, xiv. "She's in first-rate training, 'pon my word: I thought she'd have SEWN me UP at one time—the pace was terrific."

1860. HALIBURTON, *The Season-Ticket*, No. x. "Are you sure you wasn't drunk, uncle?" said I. "Quite certain," he said; "I might have been overtaken . . . but I am sure I wasn't SEWED UP."

1884. C. RUSSELL, *Jack's Courtship*, xiii. If Alphonso carried his daughter away from England, I should be SEWED UP, as Jack says, for want of funds to stick to his skirts.

1902. HEADON HILL, *Caged*, xxii. She's about SEWN-UP . . . tired herself out at the game.

4. (nautical).—Grounded: also SUED UP.

SEWER, *subs.* (London).—The Metropolitan and Metropolitan District Railways.

2. (Stock Exchange).—In *pl.* = The East London Railway shares.

COMMON SEWER, *subs. phr.* (common).—(1) An indiscriminate tippler; (2) the throat; and (3) *see* quot.

1749. SMOLLETT, *Gil Blas* [ROUTLEDGE], 90. You may truly be termed a COMMON SEWER of erudition.

SEX, *subs.* (venery).—1. The female *pudendum*: generic. *See* MONOSYLLABLE. 2. THE SEX = womankind.

SEY (**SE** or **SAY**) (back slang).—Yes: pronounced *See*.

SHAB, *verb.* (old colloquial).—1. TO GET (or MAKE) SHABBY, which = (1) 'in sorry rigging' (B. E. and GROSE), out-at-elbows; and (2) mean, base, SEEDY (*q.v.*). Whence SHABBAROON (SHABROON, SHABRAG, or SHABSTER) = a ragamuffin, 'a mean spirited fellow' (B. E. and GROSE). Also SHABBY-GENTEEL = aping gentility, but really shabby; TO SHAB OFF = 'to sneak or slide away' (B. E.).

1680. AUBREY, *Lives*, 'Lettes' [OLIPHANT, *New Engl.*, ii. 121.] Among new words are Sketch . . . SHABBY (from *scabby.*)

1688. CLARENDON, *Diary*, 7 Dec. They were very SHABBY fellows, pitifully mounted, and worse armed.

1691-2. WOOD, *Athenæ Oxon.*, II. 743. They mostly had short hair, and went in a SHABBED condition.

1698. FARQUHAR, *Love and a Bottle*, iv. 3. I would have SHABBED him OFF.

1703. WARD, *London Spy*, xv. 365. Some loose SHABROON in Bawdy-Houses Bred.

d. 1704. T. BROWN, *Works*, ii. 184. My wife, too, . . . let in an inundation of SHABROONS to gratify her concupiscence.

1729. SWIFT, *Hamilton's Baron.* The dean was so SHABBY, and look'd like a ninny.

1816. SCOTT, *Antiquary*, xv. He's a SHABBY body.

1823. MONCRIEFF, *Tom and Jerry*, ii. 6. We haven't had a better job a long vile nor the SHABBY GENTEEL lay.

1837. BARHAM, *Ingoldsby Legends*, 'Lay of St. Nicholas.' And how in the Abbey No one was so SHABBY, As not to say yearly four masses a head.

1840. THACKERAY, *Shabby Genteel Story* [Title].

1862. THACKERAY, *Philip*, xxii. Her mother felt more and more ashamed of the SHABBY fly . . . and the SHABBY cavalier.

1894. W. M. BAKER, *New Timothy*, 153. Keeping up a fragmentary conversation with the SHABBY gentleman.

2. (old).—To scratch oneself: like a lousy man or mangy dog.

SHABBY-WOMAN (THE), *subs. phr.* (literary).—*See* quot.

1864. *Athenæum*, 29 Oct., 'Rev. of Slang Dict.' There is the SHABBY WOMAN, a term pointing to the statue of Minerva which guards the portal of the Athenæum, and looks so little like 'Eve on hospitable thoughts intent,'—for since the Athenæum Club was established, no member has ever afforded the simplest rites of hospitality to a friend.

SHACK, *subs.* (old).—1. A shiftless fellow; a vagabond: also SHACKABACK, SHACKBAG, SHACKRAG, a SHAKERAG. As *verb.* = to go on tramp; to idle, to loaf. As *adj.* (also SHACKNASTY) = contemptible: *cf.* SHAGBAG.

1740. NORTH, *Examen*, 293. Great ladies are more apt to take sides with talking, flattering gossips than such a SHACK as Fitzharris.

18... *Widow Bedott Papers*, 34. Her father was a poor drunken SHACK, and her mother took in washin'.

1856. DOW, *Sermons*, III. General fly-offs and moral unhitches incident to poor SHACKLY mortality.

1865. *Good Words*, Feby., 125. What makes the work come so heavy at the end of the week, is, that the men are SHACKING at the beginning.

1882. W. ANDREWS, *Book of Oddities*, 84. 'Ripley ruffians, Butterley blacks, Swanwick bull-dogs, Alfreton SHACKS.'. . . For generations past Alfreton always had, down to twenty years ago, a notorious set

of idlers in it, ready for anything except working for an honest living—easily earning the cognomen of Alfreton SHACKS. . . . The date of the origin of the rhyme is probably about 1800.

1888. *Detroit Free Press*, 29 Sep. The meanest, wickedest, low-down, SHACKNASTY lot of heathens in America.

1896. OPPENHEIM, *False Evidence*, xxvi. What would you have me do? SHACK about with my hands in my pockets all day.

2. (American).—*See* quots. In Canada SHACK = dwelling.

1887. ROBERTS, *Western Avernus*. I . . . and Mitchell were in one of the SHACKS or huts.

1881. *New York Times*, 18 Dec. [quoted in '*Noll*' 6 S., v. 65. SHACK.—A log cabin. The average SHACK comprises but one room, and is customarily roofed with earth, supported by poles.

1882. *Century Mag.*, 511. A SHACK is a one-story house built of cotton-wood logs, driven in the ground like piles, or laid one upon another. The roof is of sticks and twigs covered with dirt, and if there is no woman to insist on tidiness, the floor will be of pounded earth.

3. (Post Office).—A misdirected or returned letter.

SHACKLE, *subs.* (American).—A raffle.

1885. *Western Gaz.*, 30 Jan. [*Notes and Queries*, 6 S., xi. 245]. [He] was asked by a young man to join in a SHACKLE for live tame rabbits.

SHACKLY (or **SHACKLING**), *adj.* (American).—Ricketty; RAMSHACKLE (*q.v.*).

1872. J. T. TROWBRIDGE, *Coupon Bonds*, 387. The gate itself was such a SHACKLING concern, a child couldn't have leaned on it without breaking it down.

1876. *Century*, xxv. 672. An unpainted and SHACKLY dwelling.

1884. CLEMENS, *Huck. Finn.*, xxi. All kinds of old SHACKLY wagons.

1885. J. W. PALMER, *New and Old*, 55. Very small mean, slender and brittle-looking, or what old coloured nurses call SHACKLY.

1900. SAVAGE, *Brought to Bay*, v. Caliente, a SHACKLY frontier settlement.

SHACK-STONER, *subs. phr.*—As in quot. [?6d.].

1893. EMERSON, *Signor Lippo*, xvii. Oh! I knows 'em all and can recon 'em up, from a SHACK-STONER to a cold 'tater. You see I've been at the stand for twelve years. *Ibid.*, xx. You see, if yer get a rozzer to call yer up he wants a SCHACK-STONER, but if I call 'em up I gets a thrummer a week.

SHAD, *subs.* (American).—A prostitute. *See* TART.

SHADBELLY, *subs.* (American).—A Quaker: the Quaker coat from neck to skirt follows the ventral line of the shad—hence SHAD-BELLIED = sloping in front like a Quaker coat. *Cf.* CUTAWAY.

1869. STOWE, *Oldtown*, 8. He was kind 'o mournfnl and thin and SHAD-BELLIED.

1870. JUDD, *Margaret*, i. 13. Three cornered hats, SHAD-BELLIED coats, shoe and knee buckles.

SHADE, *subs.* (common).—In *pl.* = wine-vaults: also as in quot. 1823.

1823. BEE, *Dict. Turf*, s.v. SHADES. The SHADES at London Bridge are under Fishmongers' Hall. . . . The SHADES at Spring Gardens is a subterranean ale-shop.

Verb. (thieves').—To conceal; to keep secret.

SHADKIN, *subs.* (American).—A marriage-broker.

SHADOW, *subs.* and *verb.* (old).—1. A spy or close attendant: *e.g.* (1) a detective; (2) *see* quot. 1869; (3) a bosom friend; and (4) a JACKAL (*q.v.*). As *verb.* = (1) to track, to spy, to DOG (*q.v.*); and (2) to be inseparable.

1607. TOURNEUR, *Revenger's Tragedy*, ii. 3. *Ven.* I'd almost forgot —— the bastard! *Lus.* What of him? *Ven.* This night, this hour, this minute, now—— *Lus.* What? what? *Ven.* SHADOWS the duchess——.

b. 1859. *Providence Jl.* [BARTLETT]. She was SHADOWED, and her ways of life ascertained.

1869. GREENWOOD, *Seven Curses of London.* She's a dress-woman . . . one . . . they tog out that they may show off at their best, and make the most of their faces. They can't trust 'em . . . you might tell that by the SHADDER.

1876. *New York Herald*, 23 Mar. Barr was decoyed . . . by a member of the secret service, who SHADOWED him.

1888. PINKERTON, *Midnight Express*, 23. A man had SHADOWED the detective since his departure from the railway office.

1891. G. F. GRIFFITHS [Tr. FOUARD, *Christ, The Son of God*, i. 238]. He was SHADOWED by spies, who were stirring up the crowd against Him.

1897. *Weekly Dispatch*, 24 Oct., 2. 4. They proved to be two well-known and expert burglars . . . and the SHADOWING was continued for several days, the police hoping to secure the receiver.

1902. LYNCH, *High Stakes*, xxviii. It is not a SHADOWING expedition. It is a hold-up.

2. (Westminster School).—*See* quot.

1867. COLLINS, *Public Schools*, 187. When a boy is first placed in the school, he is attached to another boy in the same form, something in the relation of an apprentice. The new boy is called the SHADOW, the other the 'substance.' In the first week the SHADOW follows the substance everywhere, takes his place next to him in class . . . and is exempt from any responsibility for his own mistakes in or out of school. During this interval of indulgence his patron is expected to initiate him in all the work of the school . . . in short to teach him by degrees to enter upon . . . a responsible existence of his own.

MAY YOUR SHADOW NEVER BE (OR GROW) LESS, *phr.* (colloquial).—May you prosper!

1887. *Referee*, 2 Jan. The recipients . . . hope that Sara's SHADOW MAY NEVER GROW LESS.

SHADRACH, *subs.* (founders').—A mass of badly smelted iron. [*Cf.* Daniel, iii. 26, 27.]

SHADSCALES (or **SCALES**), *subs.* (American).—*See* quot.

1875. *American English* [*Cham. Journal*, 25 Sept., 610]. Money has different names; as . . . SHADSCALES, charms . . .

SHADY, *adj.* and *adv.* (orig. University: now generally colloquial.)—Generic for decadence and deterioration, moral, physical, and material. Hence, ON THE SHADY SIDE OF [*e.g.*, 40] = beyond (or older) than 40 years of age; TO KEEP SHADY (American) = to keep in the background, to be cautious and reticent.

1852. BRISTED, *Five Years in an Eng. University*, 147. Some . . . are rather SHADY in Greek and Latin.

1862. CLOUGH, *The Bothee of Tober-Na-Vuolich.* SHADY in Latin, said Lindsay, but topping in Plays and Aldrich.

1863. KINGSLEY, *Austin Elliott*, xii. Hayton had come for his hour's logic . . . Hayton was the only SHADY man of the lot; the only "pass" man of the whole.

1864. *Spectator*, 1186. The University word SHADY meaning simply poor and inefficient, as when a man is said to be "SHADY in Latin but topping in Greek plays" is obviously University slang.

1874. HATTON, *Clytie*, III. xiii. No more seedy clients, no more SHADY cases; Simon Cuffing shall be known for his intense respectability.

1883. HAWLEY SMART, *At Fault*, III. vii. Mr. Andernore engaged in a good many transactions that, though not illegal exactly, were of the kind denominated SHADY.

1886. *D. Telegraph*, 11 Sep. The public might be misled into subscribing to a SHADY undertaking. *Ibid.* (1888), 30 Nov. Between these, however, and the SHADIEST pickpocket who calls himself a Count there are infinite degrees of assumption and sham.

1897. MARSHALL, '*Pomes*,' 8. If this isn't a SHADY lot. *Ibid.*, 9. And luck of the SHADIEST sort.

THE SHADY GROVES OF THE EVANGELIST, *subs. phr.* (London).—St. John's Wood. [A favourite haunt of loose women.]

SHADY SPRING, *subs. phr.* (venery). — The female *pudendum*: *see* MONOSYLLABLE.

1772. BRIDGES, *Homer Burlesque*, 62. Not that for Greece she car'd a f——t, But hated Paris in her heart, Because he'd seen her SHADY SPRING, And did not think it was the thing.

SHAFT. TO MAKE A SHAFT OR A BOLT OF IT, *verb. phr.* (old). —To take a risk for what it is worth; to venture.

1596. SHAKSPEARE, *Merry Wives*, iii. 4, 24. I'll MAKE A SHAFT OR A BOLT ON'T: 'slid, 'tis but venturing.

1617. HOWELL, *Letters*, I, iii. 24. The Prince is preparing for his journey; I shall to it again closely when he is gone, or MAKE A SHAFT OR A BOLT ON IT.

SHAFT OF CUPID (or **DELIGHT**), *subs. phr.* (venery).—The *penis*: *see* PRICK.

1719. DURFEY, *Pills*, iv. 72. It is a SHAFT OF CUPID'S cut, 'Twill serve to Rove, to Prick, to Butt.

1782. STEVENS, *Songs Comic and Satirycal*, 'The Picture.' For Cupid's Pantheon, the SHAFT OF DELIGHT must spring from the masculine base.

SHAFTSBURY, *subs.* (B.E. *c.*1696). 'A gallon-pot full of wine, with a Cock.'

SHAG, *subs.* (venery).—1. The act of kind; (2) = a PERFORMER (*q.v.*): *e.g.*, 'He's but a bad SHAG' = 'He's no able woman's man' (GROSE). As *verb.* = (1) to copulate: *see* GREENS and RIDE; and (2) TO FRIG (*q.v.*).

TO SHAG BACK, *verb. phr.* (hunting).—To hesitate; to hang back; to refuse a fence.

AS WET AS A SHAG, *phr.* (provincial).—As wet as may be. [SHAG = cormorant].

SHAG- (or **SHAKE-**) **BAG** (or **RAG**), *subs. phr.* (old).—1. 'A poor shabby fellow' (B. E.); 'a man of no spirit: a term borrowed from the cock-pit' (GROSE): originally as in quot. 1611. Also as *adj.* = mean; beggarly. *See* RAG.

1588. MARLOWE, *Jew of Malta*, Act IV. *Bara.* Was ever Jew tormented as I am? To have a SHAG-RAG knave to come, &c.

1611. COTGRAVE, *Dict*, s.v. *Guerluset*, somewhat like our SHAG RAG, a byword for a beggerlie souldier.

1611. CHAPMAN, *May-day*, Act II. 281 (*Plays*, 1874). If I thought 'twould ever come to that, I'd hire some SHAG-RAG or other for half a zequine to cut's throat.

1612. CHAPMAN, *Widow's Tears*, Act v., 338 (*Plays*, 1874). To send a man abroad under guard of one of your silliest SHACK-RAGS; that he may beat the knave, and run's way?

1615. *Exch. Ware at the Second Hand* [HALLIWELL]. A scurrie SHAG-RAGGE gentleman.

1616. SCOT, *Certain Pieces*, *&c.* For . . . honestie is fellow SHAKERAG with simplicitie.

1630. TAYLOR, *Urania*, 7. The SHAK-RAG shag-haird crue.

1641. BROME, *Jovial Crew*, iii. Do you talk SHAKE-RAG? heart! yond's more of 'em; I shall be beggar-mawl'd if I stay.

1665. R. HEAD, *English Rogue*, I. ix., 71 (1874). From what Dunghil didst thou pick up this SHAKERAG, this squire of the body?

1815. SCOTT, *Guy Mannering*, i. 269. He was a SHAKE-RAG like fellow.

2. (cockers': also colloquial). —A fighting-cock; and so, by implication, a 'hen of the GAME' (*q.v.*).

1700. CONGREVE, *Way of the World*, N. II. *Wit.* Come Knight . . . will you go to a cock-match? *Sir Wil.* With a wench, Tony? Is she a SHAKE-BAG, sirrah?

1771. SMOLLETT, *Humphrey Clinker* [1900], i. 68. 'I bless God . . . that Mrs. Tabitha Bramble did not take the field to-day!' I would pit her . . . against the best SHAKEBAG of the whole main.

SHAKE, *subs.* (venery). — 1. A whore, and (2) an act of coition. 3. (common) a standard of value, usually in the phrase NO GREAT SHAKES = anything of small account. 4. (American) = a show. Also FAIR SHAKES = a tolerable bargain or chance.

1819. MOORE, *Tom Crib*, 41. Though NO GREAT SHAKES at learned chat.

1820. BYRON, *Letter* [to Murray], 28 Sep. I had my hands full, and my head too just then, so it can be NO GREAT SHAKES.

1834. AINSWORTH, *Rookwood*, III. ii. I'll give you a chant composed upon Dick Turpin, the highwayman. It's NO GREAT SHAKES, to be sure, but it's the best I have.

1847. *Chron. of Pineville*, 34. Give Bill Sweeny a FAIR SHAKE, and he can whoop blue blazes out of ye.

1848. DURIVAGE, *Stray Subjects*, 56. The Museum . . . he didn't consider ANY very GREAT SHAKES.

1855. KINGSLEY, *Westward Ho*, xxx. NO GREAT SHAKES of a man to look to, nether.

*c.*1859. *Newspaper Cutting* ["S"], 200. "A SHAKE. Hope no offence; none so meant, mum. A SHAKE'S a party as is married and as isn't, if you understand me, mum. 'In keeping,' some calls it."

1865. GASKELL, *Wives and Daughters*, xxi. After all, a senior wrangler was NO GREAT SHAKES. Any man might be one if he liked.

1888. BOLDREWOOD, *Robbery Under Arms*, xxix. We didn't set up to be ANY GREAT SHAKES ourselves, Jim and I.

1891. NEWMAN, *Scamping Tricks*, 47. Here comes the SHAKE.

1898. *Pink 'Un and Pelican*, 24. He was NO GREAT SHAKES as a scholar, but he understood racing and human nature.

2. (various).—In *pl.* = generic for unsteadiness: specifically delirium tremens.

*b.*1859. *Western Gazetteer* [BARTLETT]. The springs fail once in a while since the SHAKES of 1812.

1884. *Cornhill Mag.*, June, 616. Until she is pulled up by an attack of delirium tremens, or, as she and her neighbours style it, a fit of THE SHAKES.

1898. *Man of the World*, 7 Dec., 5, 3. When John has a real attack of THE SHAKES, we fasten the churn handle to him, and he brings the butter inside of fifteen minutes.

1900. NISBET, *Sheep's Clothing*, IV. iv. All had experienced the SHAKES, and so were able to sympathise.

5. (common).—A fad. Also in combination: the MILK-SHAKE, the VEGETARIAN-SHAKE, &c. SHOOK ON = in love with.

1888. BOLDREWOOD, *Robbery Under Arms*, xxiv. He was awful SHOOK ON Madg; but she wouldn't look at him. *Ibid.*, xxxvi. I'm regular SHOOK ON the polka. *Ibid.*, xl. A steady-going he's a little—you understand—well, SHOOK ON me.

6. (colloquial). — Generic for quick action: *e.g.*, A GREAT SHAKE = a quick pace; IN A BRACE (or COUPLE) OF SHAKES (or IN THE SHAKE OF A LAMB'S TAIL) = instantly.

[?]. *Huntlyng of the Hare*, 96. Thei wente a nobull SCHAKKE.

1837. BARHAM, *Ingolds. Leg.* (*Babes in the Wood*). I'll be back in a COUPLE OF SHAKES.

1841. *Punch*, i. 135. A couple of agues Caught, to speak vulgarly, IN A BRACE OF SHAKES.

1854. MARTIN and AYTOUN, *Bon Gaultier Ballads*, 'Jupiter and the Indian Ale.' Quick! invent some other drink, Or, IN A BRACE OF SHAKES thou standest On Cocytus' sulph'ry brink.

1866. READE, *Cloister and Hearth*, xciii. Now Dragon could kill a wolf in a BRACE OF SHAKES.

Verb. (venery).—1. *See* quots., and (2) to masturbate.

[?]. *Nominale MSS.*, *Lascivus.* Anglice a SCHAKERE.

1847. HALLIWELL, *Arch. Words, &c.*, s.v. SHAKE . . . (5) Futuo. This seems to be the ancient form of *shag*, given by Grose.

2. (old).—To steal: *e.g.*, TO SHAKE A SWELL = to rob a gentleman; TO SHAKE A CHEST OF SLOP = to steal a chest of tea; TO BE SHOOK OF A SKIN = to be robbed of a purse; HAVE YOU SHOOK? = Have you stolen anything, &c. (GROSE and VAUX).

1859. KINGSLEY, *Geoffrey Hamlyn*, xix. I . . . got from bad to worse till I SHOOK a nag, and got bowled out and lagged.

1885. *Chambers's Journal*, 21 Mar., 190. Each man on the best stock-horse he could beg, borrow, or SHAKE.

1888. BOLDREWOOD, *Robbery Under Arms*, xxiv. Some well-bred horse you chaps have been SHAKING lately. *Ibid.*, xxxiv. I've two minds to SHAKE him and leave you my horse and a share of the gold to boot.

3. (common). — To shake hands; generally SHAKE!

1825. JONES, *True Bottom'd Boxer* [*Univ. Songst.*, ii. 96]. Spring's the boy for . . . SHAKING a flipper.

1891. NEWMAN, *Scamping Tricks*, 59. SHAKE! That's right. As we understand each other, I will now tell you how things ended.

1892. *Lippincott's*, Oct., 501. I'd cure thet kid, ef it bust the plan Of the whole durned universe. "SHAKE!" says Dan.

1900. SAVAGE, *Brought to Bay*, ii. 'SHAKE, honest Injun!' said the Texan.

4. (common).—To throw dice, or (printers') 'quads'; to gamble (GROSE): *see* JEFF; and TO SHAKE AN ELBOW (*q.v.*, adding to the latter the following earlier and later quotations).

1613. WEBSTER, *Devil's Law Case*, ii. 1. SHAKING YOUR ELBOW at the table-board . . . and resorting to your whore in hired velvet.

1891. *Lic. Vict. Gaz.*, 3 Ap. SHAKING HIS ELBOW at baccarat nearly every night.

5. (common).—To turn one's back on; to desert.

PHRASES and COLLOQUIALISMS. —MORE THAN ONE CAN SHAKE A STICK AT = past counting; NOTHING WORTH SHAKING A STICK AT = worthless; TO SHAKE A FOOT (TOE, or LEG) = to dance; TO SHAKE A LOOSE LEG (*see* LEG); TO SHAKE TOGETHER = to get on well or smoothly; TO SHAKE UP = to upbraid; TO SHAKE A FALL = to wrestle; TO SHAKE A TART = to possess a woman; TO SHAKE UP = (1) to scold, and (2) to masturbate; TO SHAKE A CLOTH IN THE WIND = to be hanged (GROSE); TO SHAKE DOWN = (1) (*see* SHAKE-DOWN), and (2) to accommodate oneself to, to settle down; TO SHAKE THE GHOST INTO ONE = to frighten; TO SHAKE THE BULLET (or RED RAG) = (1) *see* BULLET and RED, and (2) to threaten to discharge (tailors'); TO SHAKE UP = to get (American); 'You may go and SHAKE YOUR EARS' = advice to one who has lost his money' (RAY).

1602. SHAKSPEARE, *Twelfth Night*, ii. 1. Go, SHAKE YOUR EARS.

[16?]. HOLLAND, *Camden*, 628. Mabel did SHAKE UP in some hard and sharpe termes a young gentleman.

1826. NEAL, *Peter Brush.* I've . . . got more black eyes and bloody noses than you could SHAKE A STICK AT.

[?]. CROCKETT, *Tour*, 87. There was nothing to treat a friend to that was worth SHAKING A STICK AT.

1830. BUCKSTONE, *Wreck Ashore*, ii. 1. *Gaf.* Dance? I havn't SHAKEN A TOE these twenty years.

1854. COLLINS, *Hide and Seek*, II. I. I can't SHAKE UP along with the rest of you . . . I am used to hard lines and a wild country.

1861. HUGHES, *Tom Brown at Oxford*, I. xi. The rest of the men had SHAKEN well TOGETHER.

1865. MAJ. DOWNING, *May-day in New York.* New York is an everlastin' great concern, and . . . there's about as many people in it as you could SHAKE A STICK AT.

18[?]. THACKERAY, *Mr. Malony's Account of the Ball.* And I'd like to hear the pipers blow, And SHAKE A FUT with Fanny there.

1880. *Scribner's Mag.*, Mar., 655. I've heard my father play it at Arrah, and SHOOK A FOOT myself with the lads on the green.

1892. FENN, *New Mistress*, i. "I'm very, very glad to know you, my dear," she said warmly, "and I hope you'll come and see me often as soon as you gét SHAKEN DOWN."

1892. ANSTEY, *Voces Populi*, 'At the Military Exhibition,' 72. Ain't you shot enough? SHAKE A LEG, can't yer Jim?

SHAKE-BAG, *subs. phr.* (venery).— The female *pudendum*: *see* MONOSYLLABLE. *Cf.* SHAGBAG, 2.

SHAKE-BUCKLER, *subs. phr.* (old). —A swash-buckler; a bully.

*d.*1570. BECON, *Works*, ii. 355. Such Sim SHAKE-BUCKLERS as in their young years fall into serving, and in their old years fall into beggary.

SHAKE-DOWN, *subs. phr.* (common).—1. An improvised bed. Also as *verb.* = (1) to sleep on a temporary substitute for a bed.

*d.*1849. MISS EDGEWORTH, *Rose, Thistle, and Shamrock*, i. 3. I would not choose to put more on the floor than two beds and one SHAKE-DOWN.

1821. EGAN, *Real Life*, II. 164. Sure enough a SHAKE-DOWN is a two-penny layer of straw, and saving the tatters on my back, not a covering at all at all.

1838. MRS. HALL, *Irish Character*, 137. A SHAKE-DOWN had been ordered even in Mr. Barry's own study.

1851-61. MAYHEW, *London Lab.*, I. 272. In the better lodging-houses the SHAKEDOWNS are small palliasses or mattresses; in the worst they are bundles of rags of any kind; but loose straw is used only in the country for SHAKEDOWNS.

1858. DICKENS, *Great Expectations*, xli. He . . . advised me to look out at once for a "fashionable crib" near Hyde Park, in which he could have a SHAKE-DOWN.

1860. RUSSELL, *Diary in India*, I. 40. Five or six of us SHOOK DOWN for the night and resigned ourselves to the musquitoes and to slumber.

1869. MRS. WOOD, *Roland Yorke*, xxxi. "Where are you going to sleep?" . . . "I dare say they can give me a SHAKE-DOWN at the mother's. The hearth-rug will do."

1872. *Sunday Times*, 18 Aug., 'Fun and Riddle Club.' It was resolved: The members of this club do retire to their virtuous SHAKEDOWNS to pass the rest of the night in the arms of Morpheus.

1883. GREENWOOD, *Odd People*, 51. Two or three of missus's younger children . . . have a SHAKEDOWN on the pot-board beneath her, while father and mother share a mattress in the wash-house.

1886. *D. Telegraph*, 20 Mar. At night he had a SHAKE-DOWN in an adjacent outhouse.

1893. EMERSON, *Lippo*, xi. The butler made a collection for us and gave us a SHAKE DOWN in the stables on some nice clean hay.

1897. MITFORD, *Romance of Cape Frontier*, I. v. He had SHAKEN-DOWN in Hick's room, and the two had talked . . . themselves to sleep.

1901. *Troddles*, 122. Why not run on and get a SHAKEDOWN there. They'll do us decently and cheap if they are not already full.

2. (American thieves'). — A brothel kept by a PANEL-THIEF (*q.v.*).

3. (American). — A rough dance; a BREAK-DOWN (*q.v.*).

SHAKE-LURK, *subs. phr.* (old Cant). — A begging petition: specifically one on account of shipwreck: SHAKE-GLIM = one for fire.

1857-61. MAYHEW, *London Lab.*, i. 233. The patterer becomes a "lurker,"—that is, an impostor; his papers certify any and every ill that flesh is heir to. Shipwreck is called a SHAKE LURK.

SHAKER, *subs.* (common).—1. The hand: *see* DADDLE.

2. (common).—A shirt: *see* FLESHBAG (SNOWDON, *Mag. Assist.* (1857) 446).

3. (busmen's).—An omnibus.

SHAKERAG. *See* SHAGBAG.

SHAKESTER. *See* SHICKSTER.

SHAKE-UP, *subs. phr.* (colloquial).—A commotion; a disturbance.

SHAKY, *adj.* (colloquial). — Anything questionable: generic — unstable, insolvent, unwell, dishonest, immoral, drunken, ignorant. SHAKINESS = hesitancy, degeneracy.

1841. THACKERAY, *Gt. Hoggarty Diamond.* Our director was — what is not to be found in Johnson's Dictionary—rather SHAKY.

1853. LYTTON, *My Novel*, XI. xvii. I must be off presently to those three SHAKY voters in Fish Lane.

1854. WHYTE MELVILLE, *General Bounce*, x. Is it not a noble ambition to arrive at terms of apparent intimacy with this SHAKY grandee?

1858. *N. Y. Tribune*, 21 Jan. Four . . . adverse, and several others SHAKY.

1859. ELIOT, *Adam Bede*, xxviii. I feel terribly SHAKY and dizzy.

1861. KINGSLEY, *Ravenshoe*, xviii. Affairs are getting somewhat SHAKY there: Welter's tradesmen can't get any money.

1890. ALLEN, *Tents of Shem*, x. I expect your chances would have been SHAKY.

1900. SAVAGE, *Brought to Bay*, iv. A few women, faultless in attire, even if SHAKY in morals.

SHALER, *subs.* (common).—A girl.

SHALLEY-GONAHEY, *subs. phr.* (provincial). — A smock-frock (HOTTEN).

SHALLOW, *subs.* (old) — 1. An empty-headed Justice of the Peace. [*Cf.* SHAKSPEARE, 2 *Hen. IV.* iii. 2.] Whence (2) = a fool; also SHALLOW-LING and SHALLOW-PATE (B. E. and GROSE.)

1615. SYLVESTER, *Tobacco Battered* [Century]. — Can Wee suppose that any SHALLOWLING Can finde much good in oft-Tobaccoring.

1646. *British Bellman* [Harl. Misc., vii. 633. Whores, when they have drawn in silly SHALLOWLINGS, will ever find some trick to retain them.

1902. HEADON HILL, *Caged*, xxvi. The local SHALLOWS thought this mode of entrance added dignity.

3. (old).—A low-crowned hat; 'a whip-hat': whence LILLY-SHALLOW = a white whip-hat (GROSE and VAUX).

4. (costermongers').—(*a*) The peculiar barrow used by street traders (also TROLLEY and WHITECHAPEL BROUGHAM: *Fr. une bagnole*); and (*b*) *see* quot. 1851.

1851-61. MAYHEW, *London Lab.*, i. 29. The square and oval SHALLOWS are willow baskets, about four inches deep, and thirty inches long, by eighteen broad. *Ibid.*, i. 146. Two or three customers with their SHALLOWS slung over their back.

1875. GREENWOOD, *Low Life Depths.* Here they are after it—in vehicles for the greater part; in carts and half-carts, and SHALLOWS and barrows.

1876. HINDLEY, *Cheap Jack*, 184. With a proviso that he did not go travelling in the country with his SHALLOW.

1891. *M. Advertiser*, 30 Mar. The connexion between Lord Lonsdale's travels . . . and his capacity to drive anything on wheels from a Pickford's van to a costermonger's SHALLOW, is, one would fancy, remote enough.

1896. SALA, *London Up-to-date*, 45. The free and independent costermonger, with his pal in the SHALLOW.

1899. *Ev. Standard*, 13 March, 8, 2. 'A China Episode.' Mathew Leveret, a peripatetic dealer in crockery ware, was driving his pony and SHALLOW . . . laden with crockeryware of all kinds.

4. (tramps').—*See* quots. and SHIVERING JEMMY.

1851-61. MAYHEW, *London Lab.*, i. 262. He scraped acquaintance with a 'school of SHALLOW COVES'; that is, men who go about half-naked, telling frightful tales about shipwrecks, hair-breadth escapes from houses on fire, and such like aqueous and igneous calamities. . . . People got 'fly' to the SHALLOW BRIGADE, so Peter came up to London to 'try his hand at something else.'

1869. GREENWOOD, *Seven Curses of London.* The SHALLER, or more properly SHALLOW DODGE, is for a beggar to make capital of his rags, and a disgusting condition of semi-nudity. . . . A pouncing of the exposed parts with common powder blue is found to heighten the frost-bitten effect.

1877. TURNER, *Vagrants, &c.*, 641. I have been a SHALLOW-COVE, also a high-flyer.

1893. *Ripon Chronicle*, 23 Aug. 'A Queer Life Story.' Billy Brum has been RUNNING SHALLOW at intervals in these parts for the past five years. By RUNNING SHALLOW I mean that he never wears either boots, coat, or hat, even in the depths of the most dismal winter.

1893. EMERSON, *Signor Lippo*, x. I only DO THE SHALLOW on the pinch. I shall have to come back to the nigger business, its more respectable. *Ibid.*, x. One thing, I always go very 'spectable—clean collar, clean scarf, clean boots. It's far better to go that way than SHALLOW.

1900. FLYNT, *Tramps*, 240. One day he is a SHALLOW-COVE, or 'Shivering Jimmy.'

TO LIVE SHALLOW, *verb. phr.* (thieves').—To live quietly and in retirement, as when WANTED (*q.v.*)

SHAM, *subs. adj.* and *verb.* (old). —Generic for false. As *subs.* = (1) a cheat, a trick; (2) a substitute, as a pillow-sham, false sleeves, fronts, or cuffs. As *adj.* = spurious, counterfeit. As *verb.* = to cheat; to feign: also TO CUT A SHAM = 'to play a rogue's Trick' (B. E. and GROSE); SHAMOCRAT = one who apes rank or wealth.

1677. WYCHERLEY, *Plain Dealer*, iii. 1. SHAMMING is telling you an insipid dull Lie with a dull Face, which the sly Wag the Author only laughs at himself; and, making himself believe 'tis a good Jest, puts the SHAM only upon himself.

1689. PRIOR, *To Fleetwood Shepherd.* Your Wits that fleer and SHAM, Down from Don Quixote to Tom Tram.

1700. CONGREVE, *Way of the World*, v. 10. That SHAM is too gross to pass on me! *Ibid.*, i. 1. The discovery of your SHAM addresses to her, to Conceal your Love to her Niece, has provok'd this Separation.

1722. STEELE, *Conscious Lovers*, i. Wearing SHAMS to make linen last clean a fortnight.

1740. NORTH, *Examen*, 231. The word SHAM is true cant of the Newmarket breed. It is contracted of 'ashamed.' The native signification is a town lady of diversion in country maid's cloaths, who to make good her disguise, pretends to be so 'SHAM'D.' Thence it became proverbial . . . so annex'd to a plot it means one that is fictitious and untrue.

1778. SHERIDAN, *The Rivals*, i. 1. Why does your master pass only for ensign?—now if he had SHAMM'D general.

1790. FRANKLIN, *Auto.*, 257. He stayed some time to exercise the men in SHAM attacks upon SHAM forts.

1813. AUBREY, *Lives*, 'Henry Blount.' Two young gent. that heard Sr. H. tell this SHAM . . . rode the next day to St. Albans to enquire . . . 'twas altogether false.

1817. SCOTT, *Rob Roy*, xxxvii. He SHAMMED ill, and his death was given publicly out in the French papers.

3. (common). — Champagne; BOY (*q.v.*): also SHAMMY.

1849. THACKERAY, *Pendennis*, iv. A bottle of sherry, a bottle of SHAM, a bottle of port and a shass caffy, it ain't so bad, hay, Pen.?

See ABRAHAM; SNITE.

SHAMBLE, *subs.* (old).—In *pl.* = the legs. Whence SHAKE YOUR SHAMBLES = Begone! As *verb.* = 'to walk awkwardly'; SHAMBLE-LEGGED = shuffling (B. E. and GROSE).

SHAMBROGUE, *subs.* (old). —The Shamrock. Also SHAMROOT.

1613. WITHERS, *Abuses Stript and Whipt*, 71. And for my cloathing in a mantle goe, And feed on SHAM-ROOTS as the Irish doe.

1712. *Spectator*, 455. I could easily observe . . . the Spanish myrtle, the English oak, the Scotch thistle, the Irish SHAMBROGUE.

SHAMELESS, *subs.* (old: B. E., *c.* 1696).—'A bold forward Blade.'

SHAM-LEGGER, *subs. phr.* (common).—A man offering worthless stuff for sale cheap.

SHAMMOCK, *verb.* (old).—To LOAF (*q.v.*).

d. 1704. BROWN, *Works*, ii. 184. Pox take you both for a couple of SHAMMOCKING rascals.

SHAMROCK. TO DROWN THE SHAMROCK, *verb. phr.* (Irish).—To go drinking on St. Patrick's Day (Mar. 17th).

1888. *D. Telegraph*, 22 Mar. An Irishman of strong national instincts, and resident, or 'commorant,' in Edinburgh, on Saturday last resolved to DROWN THE SHAMROCK in the orthodox fashion.

SHAN (or **SHAND**), *subs.* (Old Cant). —Base coin. Hence as *adj.* = worthless (GROSE and VAUX).

1815. SCOTT, *Guy Mannering*, xxxii. 'I doubt Glossin will prove but SHAND* after a', mistress,' said Jabot, as he passed through the little lobby beside the bar; 'but this is a gude half-crown ony way.' * [Cant expression for base coin.]

SHANDRYDAN (or **SHANDRY**), *subs.* (Irish).—A light two-wheeled, one-horsed cart: hence, any old ricketty trap.

1843. THACKERAY, *Irish Sketch Book*, xii. Where all the vehicles, the cars, barouches and SHANDRYDANS, the carts, the horse- and donkey-men could have found stable and shelter, who can tell?

1861. *Cornhill Mag.*, v. 440. An ancient rickety-looking vehicle of the kind once known as SHANDRYDAN.

1863. GASKELL, *Sylvia's Lovers*, xxix. I ha' been to engage a SHANDRY this very morn.

1876. BRADDO, *Joshua Haggard*, iii. An ancient white pony, which the Squire drove himself in a SHANDRYDAN of the chaise tribe, completed the Pentreath stud.

1886. *D. Telegraph*, 10 Sep. Until an immense procession of buggies, wagonnettes, chaise carts, and SHANDRYDANS had rattled by.

1896. SALA, *London Up-to-date*, 43. I have done the Derby . . . in every style —gigs, landaus, barouches, hansoms, SHANDRYDANS. . . .

SHANDY-GAFF, *subs. phr.* (common). —Beer and ginger-beer.

1853. BRADLEY, *Verd. Green*, I. 118. 'He taught me to grill a devil.' 'Grill a devil,' groaned Miss Virginia. 'And to make SHANDY-GAFF and sherry cobbler, and brew bishop and egg flip: oh, its capital!'

1864 *Eton School Days*, v. Chorley took him up the river and inducted him into the mysteries of SHANDY-GAFF at Surly.

1871. *Chambers' Journal*, 9 Dec., 771. I am sitting with him drinking SHANDY-GAFF.

1872. *Fun*, 10 Aug. 'A Ditton Ditty.' So let us quaff Our SHANDY-GAFF.

1880. MORTIMER COLLINS, *Thoughts in my Garden*, ii. 198. They bear about the same resemblance to real literature as SHANDY-GAFF to dry champagne.

SHANEY (or **SHANNY**), *subs.* (common).—A fool.

d. 1823. BLOOMFIELD, *The Horkey.* And out ran every soul beside, A SHANNY-pated crew.

SHANGHAI, *subs.* (American).— 1. A tall dandy [BARTLETT: In allusion to the long-legged fowls from Shanghai, all the rage a few years ago].

1859. *Gt. Republic Mag.*, Jan., 70. I degenerated into a fop, and became a SHANGHAI of the most exotic breed.

2. (Australian).— A catapult: also as *verb.*

3. (American).—*See* quot.

1880. *Scribner's Mag.*, *Jan.*, 365. The SHANGHAI is the glaring daub required by some frame-makers for cheap auctions. They are turned out at so much by the day's labor, or at from 12 dollars to 24 dollars a dozen, by the piece. All the skies are painted at once, then all the foregrounds. Sometimes the patterns are stenciled. The dealer attaches the semblance of some well-known name, of which there are several, and without initials.

3. (American). — *See* quot. 1871.

1871. DE VERE, *Americanisms*, 347. SHANGHAI applied to sailors refers not to the bird, but, according to a seaman's statement, to the town of Shanghai, where the process so called is said to have been once very common. The latter consists in drugging the unlucky sailor, when he enjoys himself after a long cruise, on shore, and carrying him, while in a state of insensibility, to a vessel about to depart, where he finds himself upon his recovery, entered in all forms on the book.

1871. *New York Tribune*, 1 Mar. They would have been drugged, SHANGHAIED, and taken away from all means of making complaint.

SHANK, *subs.* (B. E. and GROSE).— In *pl.* = the legs; GAMS (*q.v.*). TO SHANK IT (or TO RIDE SHANKS'S MARE, or NAG) = (1) to go on foot or by the MARYLEBONE STAGE (*q.v.*): and (2) to leave without ceremony (B. E. and GROSE).

1302-11. *Political Songs* [Camden Soc.] 223. He [King Edward I] with the longe SHONKES.

d. 1529. SKELTON [DYCE, *Works*, i. 117]. Your wynde schakyn SHANKKES . . . crokyd as a camoke. *Ibid.* 168 [OLIPHANT, *New Eng.* i. 371. The word SHANK had not then the lowering idea of our days; it is applied to the limbs of Christ on the cross].

d. 1555. LYNDSAY, *Thrie Estaitis* [E.E.T.S. 469].

1598. FLORIO, *Worlde of Wordes*, s.v. *Gambe*, legges or SHANKES.

1600. SHAKESPEARE, *As You Like It*, ii. 7, 161. His youthful hose, well saved, a world too wide, For his skrunk SHANK.

1635. [GLAPTHORNE], *Lady Mother* BULLEN'S, *Old Plays*, ii. 131]. But come, stir your SHANKS nimbly or Ile hough ye.

1785. BURNS, *Epistle to J. Lapraik*, Postcript. The youngsters took the sands Wi' nimble SHANKS.

1818. SCOTT, *Rob Roy*, xxii. Sitting on the bed, to rest his SHANKS, as he was pleased to express the accommodation which that posture afforded him.

1843. THACKERAY, *Irish Sketch Book*, xvi. Along the banks you see all sorts of strange figures washing all sorts of wonderful rags, with red petticoats and redder SHANKS standing in the stream.

1847. PORTER, *Quarter Race*, 90. Dick and Jule had to ride SHANKS' MAR'.

1855. KINGSLEY, *Westward Ho*, xv. I am away to London town to speak to Mr. Frank!! "To London! how wilt get there?" "On SHANKS HIS MARE," said Jack, pointing to his bandy legs.

1857. HOOD, *Pen and Pencil Pictures*, 118. Three pairs of woollen socks . . . will cherish thy lean SHANKS, old fellow!

1885. *Chambers' Journal*, 2 May, 287. Your true swagsman detests the sight of a horse . . . give him SHANKS' MARE.

1891. *Lic. Vict. Gaz.*, 9 Jan. The distance had choked off those whose only mode of locomotion was SHANKS'S MARE.

1891. RUSSELL, *Ocean Tragedy*, 194. I could see his naked yellow SHANKS.

1891. *Globe*, 5 June, 3, 3. People would be deprived of their habitual method of locomotion. Some would solve the difficulty by staying at home. Others would resort to SHANKS'S PONY; and the minority to cabs.

1901. *D. Telegraph*, 28 Oct., 10, 5. He was much more interested in two old-fashioned animals, the horse and another strange animal enjoying the name—the origin of which he had never yet been able to discover—of SHANKS'S PONY.

2. (colloquial).—The fag end.

1880. HARRIS, *Uncle Remus*, xv. Bimeby, to'rds de SHANK er de evenin'.

1888. PATON, *Down the Islands*. The old Kentuckian who in the SHANKS of the evening was wont to maintain there was no such thing as bad Kentucky whiskey.

SHANKER, *subs.* (venery). — 'A little Scab or Pox on the Nut or Glans of the Yard.' (B. E.).

1660. *Old Ballad*, 'An Hist. Ballad' [*Ane Pleasant Garden* (*c.*1800)]. A SHANKER'S a damn'd loveing thing where it seizes.

1731. SWIFT, *Young Nymph Going to Bed*. With gentlest touch she next explores Her SHANKERS, issues, running sores.

1772. BRIDGES, *Homer Burlesque*, 491. But Ajax gave him two such spankers, They smarted worse than nodes and SHANKERS.

SHANNON. 'It is said, persons dipped in that river are perfectly and for ever cured of bashfulness' (GROSE).

SHANT, *subs.* (tramps').—A quart; a pot: e.g., SHANT OF GATTER = a pot of beer. Also SHANTY.

1851-61. MAYHEW, *London Lab.* i. 232. They have a SHANT of gatter at the nearest boozing ken.

1893. EMERSON, *Lippo*. v. I should just think you would beg my pardon, and to show you mean it stand a couple of SHANTS of bevarly to square the boys.

SHA'N'T, *verb.* (colloquial).—Shall not. NOW WE SHAN'T BE LONG = It's all right: a general note of satisfaction or agreement: a street catch of the late nineties.

1897. MAUGHAM, *Liza of Lambeth*, v. Now WE SHAN'T BE LONG! she remarked.

SHANTY, *subs.* (common).—1. A rough and tumble hut; 2. (Australian and showmen's) a public-house; (3) a brothel (sailors'); and (4) a quart; whence (5) beer money. Also as *verb.* = (1) to dwell in a hut, and (2) to take shelter.

1848. COOPER, *Oak Openings*, 26. This was the second season that le Bourdon had occupied 'Castle Meal,' as he himself called the SHANTY.

1857. HAMMOND, *Wild Northern Scenes*, 197. Mark Shuff and a friend . . . SHANTIED on the outlet, just at the foot of Tupper's Lake. *Ibid.* 212. We SHANTIED on the Ohio.

*b.*1859. *New York Courier* [BARTLETT]. The sportsmen . . . brace themselves to meet the rude exigencies of a tramp and SHANTEEING OUT for a few days.

1861. KINGSLEY, *Ravenshoe*, liv. There was weeping in the reed-thatched hovels of the Don, and in the mud-built SHANTIES of the Dnieper.

1878. *Century Mag.*, Dec., 510. These droll and dirty congeries of SHANTIES and shacks.

1886-96. MARSHALL, '*He Slumbered*' ['Pomes,' 118]. She scooted from the SHANTY.

1887. *All Year Round*, 30 July, 67. Inns do not exist in Australia, every house of refreshment is a 'hotel.' It may be only a wooden SHANTY up-country.

1889. HADDON CHAMBERS, *In Australian Wilds*, 53. I knew that there was no public house or SHANTY within twelve miles.

1890. DILKE, *Prob. Greater Britain*, iii. 1. Kimberley is still a huge aggregation of SHANTIES, traversed by tramways, and lit by electric light.

1892. NISBET, *Bushranger's Sweetheart*, 34. "Yes; and did you run that SHANTY long, Stringy?" For three months and more, and did a roaring trade besides.

1893. MILLIKEN, *'Arry Ballads*, 3. A sand-parlour'd SHANTY.

1893. EMERSON, *Lippo*, v. Any SHANTY in your sky-rocket? *Ibid.*, xiv. Then we went out for a SHANTY, and when we came back Blower and Bottlenose were clearing up.

2. *See* CHANTEY.

SHAP, *subs.* (venery). — 1. The female *pudendum*: *see* MONOSYLLABLE. Also SHAPE.

[?]. *Owayne Myles* [*MS.* Cott. Calig. A ii. 91]. And some were yn to SHAPPUS And some were vp to the pappus.

[?]. *Relig. Antiq.*, ii. 20. Semeramis hir name . . . Which wold no man in eny wyse denye, But wyth her croked SHAP encreece and multeply.

*d.*1529. SKELTON, *Elynour Rummyng*, 492. An old rybybe . . . had broken her shyn At the the threshold comying in, And fell so wyde open That one myght see her token . . . Said Elynour Rummyng . . . Fy, couer thy SHAP With sum flyp flap.

1530. PALSGRAVE, *Lang. Francoyse*, fol. xxvi. Count, a womans SHAPPE, *con.*

1538. ELYOT, *Dict.*, s.v. *Hippomares*. The SHAPE of a mare.

1847. HALLIWELL, *Arch. Words*, s.v. SHAPE. The A.S. *gesceapu*, verenda, pudenda . . . Still in common use in Lincolnshire, used especially in the case of infants and children.

2. (Western American).—*See* quot.

1885. STAVELY HILL, *From Home to Home*. A pair of SHAPS, or leather overalls, with tags and fringes down the seams.

SHAPE, *subs.* (vulgar).—In *pl.* = (1) an ill-made man (B. E.), and (2) a tight-laced girl (HALLIWELL). Hence TO SHOW ONE'S SHAPE = (1) to strip: specifically (old) 'TO PEEL (*q.v.*) at the whipping-post' (GROSE), and (2) to turn about and march off; STUCK ON ONE'S SHAPE = pleased with one's appearance; 'There's a SHAPE for you' = an ironical comment on a skeleton-like person or animal—a RACK-OF-BONES (*q.v.*); TO TRAVEL ON ONE'S SHAPE = to swindle, to live by one's appearance; TO SPOIL ONE'S SHAPE = to be got with child; SHAPE-SMITH = a stay-maker; IN GOOD SHAPE = quite correct; TO CUT UP (or SHOW) ONE'S SHAPE = to frolic.

1678. COTTON, *Virgil Travestie* [*Works* (1725), 74]. My son's so big (which rarely falls) About his ——, and Gentials, That I am half afraid lest he Should chance to SPOIL her Majesty.

*d.*1704. BROWN, *Works*, ii. 97. The French king who had SPOIL'D THE SHAPE . . . of several mistresses . . . had a mind to do the same by me.

1715. GARTH, *Claremont*, 98. No SHAPE-SMITH set up shop and drove a trade To mend the work wise Providence had made.

1896. CRANE, *Maggie*, vi. Say, Mag, I'm stuck on yer SHAPE.

Verb. (colloquial). — To turn out; to behave.

1369. CHAUCER, *Troilus*, ii. 61. So SHOP it that hym fil that day a tene In love, for whiche in wo to bedde he wente.

1605. SHAKSPEARE, *Cymbeline*, v. 5, 346. Their dear loss, The more of you 'twas felt, the more it SHAPED Unto my end of stealing them.

1888. BOLDREWOOD, *Robbery Under Arms*, xxxvii. 'Well, I'm in your power, now,' says he, 'let's see how you'll SHAPE.' *Ibid.*, xxii. We shall have to SHAPE after a bit.

1891. GOULD, *Double Event*, 123. I am very anxious to see how my horse SHAPES.

1893. MILLIKEN, *'Arry Ballads*, 71. Briggs or no Briggs I SHAPED spiffin.

1898. GOULD, *Landed at Last*, v. 'He SHAPES as well as ever' . . . 'Moves splendidly.'

1902. *Pall Mall Gaz.*, 7 Feb., 1, 2. We should wait to see how he SHAPED, before deciding whether he was a personage to be encouraged or taught his place.

1902. DELANNOY, *£19,000*, xxvi. How do you SHAPE? . . . without bedclothes and with rodent company, or will you give me the letter? *Ibid.*, xxix. He seems to be SHAPING himself for a straight jacket.

SHAPPO, *subs.* (old).—A hat, 'the newest Cant, Nab being very old, and grown too common' (B. E., *c.*1696); also SHAPPEAU, SHOPPO, SHOPO, SHAPO [Fr. *chapeau*].

SHARD. TO TAKE A SHARD, *verb. phr.* (provincial).—To get tipsy: *see* SCREWED.

SHARE, *subs.* (old).—The pubes.

[?]. *Ms. Porkington*, 10. Sychone se I nevere ere Stondynge opone SCHARE.

1609. HOLLAND, *Ammianus Marcell.* [NARES]. Arrayed from the heele to the SHARE in manner of a nice and pretie page.

1624. BURROUGHS, *Method of Physick* [NARES]. They cannot make water, the SHARE becometh hard, and hath vehement pain.

SHARE-PENNY, *subs. phr.* (old).—A miser; a SKINFLINT (*q.v.*)

1606. *Wily Beguil'd* [HAWKINS, *Eng. Drama*, iii. 299]. I'll go near to cozen old father SHAREPENNY of his daughter.

SHARGE, *verb.* (provincial).—To copulate: *see* GREENS and RIDE (HALLIWELL).

SHARK, *subs.* and *verb.* (old).—1. A greedy adventurer; a swindler: also SHARKER (B. E. and GROSE). As *verb.* (or TO LIVE ON THE SHARK) = to live by roguery or thieving. Whence SHARK-GULL = a FLAT-CATCHER (*q.v.*); TO SHARK UP = to press, to enlist on terms of piracy; SHARKING = (1) roguery, and (2) greedy, tricky.

1590. SIR THOMAS MORE [OLIPHANT, *New Eng.* ii. 8]. There are the new verbs *rooke* (plunder) and SHARKE (prey)].

1596. SHAKSPEARE, *Hamlet*, i. 1. Of unimproved mettle hot and full, Hath in the skirts of Norway, here and there, SHARK'D up a list of landless resolutes For food and diet.

1599. JONSON, *Ev. Man Out of His Humour*. Characters . . . *Shift*. A threadbare SHARK . . . His profession is skeldring and odling. *Ibid.* (1609) *Silent Woman*, iv. 2. A very SHARK; he set me in the nick t'other night at Primero.

1606-8. BEAUMONT and FLETCHER, *Love's Cure*. Dram. Pers. A SHARKING, panderly constable.

1608. DEKKER, *Belman of London* [GROSART, *Works*, III. 162]. A crue of SHARKING companions (of which there be sundry consorts lurking about the suburbs of this City).

1609. ROWLANDS, *Knave of Clubs* (Hunterian Club's Repr., 1872), 10. Two hungry SHARKES did trauell Paules, Vntill their guts cride out, And knew not how, with both their wits, To bring one meale about.

1611. CHAPMAN, *May-Day*, ii. (1874) 288. Though y'are sure of this money again at my hands, yet take heed how this same Lodovico get it from you, he's a great SHARKER.

1628. EARLE, *Micro-cosmog.* 14. A SHARKE is one whome all other means haue fayl'd, and hee now liues of himselfe. *Ibid.* [BLISS] 206 That does it fair and above-board, without legerdemain, and neither SHARKS for a cup or a reckoning.

*d.*1639. WOTTON, *Letter to M. Velserus*. "A dirty SHARKER about the Romish court, who only scribbles that he may dine."

1653. MIDDLETON, *Spanish Gipsy*, II. 1. A trade brave as a courtier's; for some of them do but SHARK, and so do we.

1678-1715. SOUTH, *Sermons*, ii. 214. "Wretches who live UPON THE SHARK, and other men's sins, the common poisoners of youth."

1748. SMOLLETT, *Rod. Random*, iii. We returned to the village, my uncle muttering all the way against the old SHARK.

1760. JOHNSTON, *Chrysal*, I. iv. Making my fortune a prey to every SHARKING projector who flattered my vanity with promises of success.

1815. SCOTT, *Guy Mannering*, xxx. 'We want our goods, which we have been robbed of by these SHARKS,' said the fellow.

1857. TROLLOPE, *Three Clerks*, iii. He expected to pay £200 a year for his board and lodging, which he thought might as well go to his niece as to some SHARK, who would probably starve him.

1891. NEWMAN, *Scamping Tricks*, 2. Is part of the stock of such rare old SHARKS.

1898. NISBET, *Hagar*, 8. 'You'd take my money to yourself,' interrupted Dix with irony. 'Not if I know it, you SHARK!'

2. (old). — 'A custom-house officer or tide-waiter' (GROSE). Also in *pl.* = the press-gang.

1828. DOUGLAS JERROLD, *Ambrose Gwinett*, i. 3. *Gil.* A word with you—the SHARKS are out to-night. *Label.* The SHARKS? *Gil.* Ay, the blue-jackets—the press-gang.

3. (old). — 'One of the first order of pickpockets. *Bow St. term*, A.D. 1785' (GROSE).

4. (military).—A recruit.

5. (American College). — At Yale = reckless absence from college duties: of persons and conduct.

6. (Western American).— A lean hungry hog (BARTLETT).

Verb. (colloquial). — 1. To fawn for a dinner.

2. *See subs.*

SHARP, *subs.* (old).—1. A swindler; 'one that lives by his Witts' (B.E.); a ROOK (*q.v.*): the opposite of FLAT (*q.v.*): also SHARPER: *cf.* SHARKER (GROSE and VAUX). As *verb.* = to cheat; SHARPING (or ON THE SHARP) *subs.* and *adj.* = swindling; SHARPER'S TOOLS = (1) fools, and (2) false dice (B. E. and GROSE). *See* BIBLE-SHARP; FLATS-AND-SHARPS.

1688. SHADWELL, *Squire of Alsatia* [*Works* (1720), iv. 18]. 'Tatts . . . what's that?' 'The tools of SHARPERS, false dice.'

1690. DRYDEN, *Don Sebastian*, Epilogue, l. 35. All these young SHARPERS would my grace importune. *Ibid.* (1691), *King Arthur*, Prol. 38. Among the rest there are a SHARPING set That pray for us, and yet against us bet.

1693. CONGREVE, *Old Batchelor*, *Dram. Pers.* SHARPER.

1706. MRS. CENTLIVRE, *Basset Table*, IV. 1. But if he has got the knack of winning thus, he shall SHARP no more here, I promise him.

1729. GAY, *Polly*, iii. 5. Death, sir, I won't be cheated. *Cul.* The money is mine. D'you take me for a SHARPER, sir?

1748. SMOLLETT, *Rod. Random*, lviiii. Who supported myself in the appearance of a gentleman by SHARPING and other infamous practices.

1749. LUCAS, *Gamesters*, 250. She would PLAY altogether ON THE SHARP.

1768. GOLDSMITH, *Good Natured Man*, i. How can I be proud of a place in a heart, where every SHARPER and coxcomb find an easy entrance.

1789. GEO. PARKER, *Life's Painter*, 142. SHARPS . . . This term is applied to SHARPERS in general.

1821. EGAN, *Life in London*, I. ii. From autumn to winter, from winter to June, The "flat" and the SHARP must still play the same tune.

1830. LYTTON, *Paul Clifford* (Ed. 1854), 190. 'They are both gone ON THE SHARP to-night,' replied the old lady.

1837. WARREN, *Diary of Physician*, xi. I began to suspect that he was neither more nor less than a systematic London SHARPER—a gamester—a hanger-on about town.

1843. DICKENS, *Martin Chuzzlewit*, xxxvii. Tom's evil genius did not . . . mark him out as the prey of . . . those bloodless SHARPERS.

1849. MACAULAY, *Hist. of Eng.*, xviii. The crowd of pilferers, ring-droppers, and SHARPERS who infested the capital.

1861. TROLLOPE, *Framley Parsonage*, xxxiii. What an ass I have been to be so cozened by a SHARPER.

1872. BESANT AND RICE, *R. M. Mortiboy*, xxiv. It is not usual to see men play in your fashion. You have SHARPED us, sir—SHARPED us.'

1886-96. MARSHALL, *Beautiful Dreamer* ['Pomes' 65]. The SHARPS tipped The Lump, and left Pip in the lurch.

2. (old).—A pointed weapon: a sword as contrasted with a foil.

. . . . . *Joseph of Arim.* [E.E.T.S.], 17. Mony swoughninge lay thorw schindringe of SCHARPE.

1679. BEHN, *Feigned Curtizan*, iii. These dangerous SHARPS I never lov'd,

1697. COLLIER, *Essays*, 'Duelling.' If butchers had but the manners to go to SHARPS, gentlemen would be contented with a rubber at cuffs.

1763. FOOTE, *Mayor of Garratt*, ii. Why lookye, Major Sturgeon, I don't much care for your poppers and SHARPS.

3. (American).—An expert.

*c.*1889. *Scientific Amer.* [*Century*]. One entomological SHARP, who is spoken of as good authority estimates the annual loss at 300,000,000 dols.

Adj. (B. E. *c.*1696, and GROSE). 'Subtil, ready, quick or nimble-witted. forward, of lively Apprehension; also Poor and Needy.'

Adv. (colloquial). — To the moment: *e.g.* 'I'll be there at five o'clock SHARP.'

1847-8. THACKERAY, *Vanity Fair*, xxvii. Captain Osborne . . . will bring him to the . . . mess at five o'clock SHARP.

MR. SHARP, *phr.* (traders').—A similar expression to 'TWO-PUN-TEN' (*q.v.*), to signify that a customer of suspected honesty is about. The shopman asks one of the assistants, in a voice loud enough to be generally heard, 'Has MR. SHARP come in yet?' The signal is at once understood, and a general look-out kept (HOTTEN).

SHARP AS THE CORNER OF A ROUND TABLE, *phr.* (common).—Stupid.

SHARP'S THE WORD! *phr.* (colloquial). — 1. 'Of anyone very attentive to his own interest, and apt to take all advantage': sometimes with 'AND QUICK'S THE MOTION' (GROSE); also (2) a call to brisk movement, or ready obedience.

1706. VANBRUGH, *Mistake* [*Old Dram.*, 448]. SHARP'S THE WORD [*i.e.*, watchword].

1708-10. SWIFT, *Polite Conversation*, iii. *Lady Answ.* . . . They must rise early that would cheat her of her Money; SHARP'S THE WORD with her; Diamonds cut Diamonds.

SHARP-AND-BLUNT, *subs. phr.* (rhyming).—The female *pudendum*; the CUNT (*q.v.*): *see* MONOSYLLABLE.

SHARP'S ALLEY BLOODWORMS, *subs. phr.* (old). — 1. Beef sausages; and (2) black puddings. [A noted abattoir near Smithfield.]

SHARP-SET, *adj. phr.* (B. E. and GROSE).—1. Hungry; (2) hard-driven.

1577. STANIHURST, *Ireland*, 19. So SHARPE SET as to eat fried flies, butterd bees, stued snailes.

1579-80. LYLY, *Euphues* [OLIPHANT, *New Eng.*, i. 611. He has the following phrases that only just appeared in English . . . *Clounish*, SHARP SET . . .].

*d.*1742. SOMERVILLE, *Officious Messenger*. The SHARP-SET squire resolves at last, Whate'er befall him, not to fast.

1749. SMOLLETT, *Gil Blas* [ROUTLEDGE], 58. My appetite was SHARP-SET for a comfortable meal.

SHARPSHIN, *subs.* (American).—The smallest quantity.

1854. KENNEDY, *Swallow Barn* [DE VERE]. This inconsiderable claim—for it is not the value of a SHARPSHIN.

SHARPSHOOTER, *subs.* (American).—A swift clipper-built schooner.

See DEVIL'S SHARPSHOOTERS.

SHARP STICK, *subs. phr.* (American).—Persecution; retribution.

1856. *Western Scenes* [DE VERE]. If you stay much longer, the old man will be after you with A SHARP STICK, and I don't know what you'll do to keep him from killing you.

1871. *Trenton State Sentinel*, 26 May. The New York *Tribune* is still after Senators Carpenter, Conkling, and others, with a VERY SHARP STICK, for their ridiculous course in the arrest and imprisonment of the *Tribune* correspondents, for daring to be true to the profession.

SHATTERBRAIN (or PATE), *subs.* (colloquial).— A giddy person: SHATTERBRAINED (or PATED) = heedless; weak in intellect. *See* SHITTERBRAIN and SHUTTLEHEAD.

SHAVE, *subs.* (common).—A narrow escape; a SQUEAK (*q.v.*): usually with 'close,' 'near,' &c. Whence TO MAKE A SHAVE (or TO SHAVE THROUGH) = to get through 'by the skin of one's teeth.'

1844. *Puck*, 14. Of all the men that with me read There's never one . . . But got thro', if he made a SHAVE on't.

1860. RUSSELL, *Diary in India*, xxi. 'By Jove! that was a near SHAVE!' . . . a bullet whistled within an inch of our heads.

1871. *Daily News*, 7 Mar. In those famous telegrams of the King the expression, "Danke nur Gott!" means "It was a close SHAVE!"

1876. BURNABY, *Ride to Khiva*, Intro: I had, as it is commonly termed, a much closer SHAVE for my life than . . . even if I had been taken prisoner by the most fanatical Turkomans in Central Asia.

1885. *Field*, 4 Ap. It was a desperately close SHAVE.

1898. GOULD, *Landed at Last*, vii. We've had some narrow squeaks of missing him . . . [a] narrow SHAVE was at York.

2. (common).—A false report; a practical joke; a SELL (*q.v.*)

1854. *Morning Chronicle*, 13 Dec. "According to camp reports or camp SHAVES, as they are more expressively termed."

1860. RUSSELL, *Diary in India*, xii. At first a SHAVE of old Smith, then a well authenticated report.

1874. *Siliad*, 29. The SHAVES are many; so the nests of mares.

1882. *D. Telegraph*, 3 Oct., 5, 7. Rumours of Turkish troops being landed as our allies adding to the SHAVES that hourly came out.

1884. G. A. SALA, *Ill. Lon. News*, 26 April, 391, 3. The legend is probably a mere barrack-room SHAVE, but it is worth noting. *Ibid.* (1883), *Living London*, 115. SHAVE for hoax first obtained currency during the Crimean War.

3. (Stock Exchange). — A money consideration paid for the right to vary a contract, by extension of time for delivery or payment, &c.

4. (theatrical).—The proportion of the receipts paid to a travelling company by a local manager.

See SHAVER.

Verb. (old).—To extort; to strip; to cheat (B. E.). Hence SHAVING (or SHAVERY) = (1) usury, and (2) overcharge (with drapers called SHAVING THE LADIES). Also SHAVER = (1) a cheat, a swindler; (2) a banker, broker, or money-lender given to usury; and (3) SHAVER (*q.v.*): whence SHAVING-SHOP = a WILD-CAT BANK (*q.v.*); SHAVING-TERMS = make all you can.

1548. LATIMER, *Sermons*, 100 [OLIPHANT, *New Eng.*, i. 515. Latimer coins SHAVERY, something like slavery; to express the robbery of the Church].

1603. KNOLLES, *Hist. Turks.* They fell all into the hands of the cruel mountain people, living for the most part by theft, . . . by these SHAVERS the Turks were stript of all they had.

1606. DEKKER, *Seven Deadly Sinnes* (ARBER'S) 40. Then haue you Brokers yat SHAUE poore men by most iewish interest . . . Then haue you the SHAUING of Fatherlesse children, and of widowes, and that's done by Executors. *Ibid.*, 39. The next . . . was . . . a SHAUER of yong gentlemen, before euer a haire dare peepe out of their chinnes; and these are Vsurers.

1638. FORD, *Lady's Trial*, ii. 1. Whoo! the brace are flinch'd, The pair of SHAVERS are sneak'd from us, Don.

1850. DICKENS, *David Copperfield*, xxii. 'He pays well, I hope' . . . 'Pays as he speaks . . . through the nose . . . None of your close SHAVERS the Prince ain't.'

*c.*1857. *Parody on Emerson's Brahma*, [BARTLETT]. If the stock broker thinks he SHAVES, Or if the victim think's he's SHAVED, Let both the rascals have their say, And he that's cheated let him pay.

1862. *North Am. Rev.*, July, 113. This Wall-Street NOTE-SHAVING life is a new field, a very peculiar field.

1863. *Once a Week*, viii., 179. We have all heard for instance of an operation called SHAVING THE LADIES, yet we doubt if any lady is aware of the very clean SHAVE she is constantly undergoing.

1864. SALA [*Temple Bar*, Dec., 40]. He is as dextrous as a Regent Street counter-jumper in the questionable art of SHAVING THE LADIES.

*c.*1870. *Life in New York* [BARTLETT]. Make your money by SHAVING notes or stock-jobbing, and every door is thrown open; make the same amount by selling Indian candy, and the cold shoulder is turned upon you.

1871. *D. Telegraph*, 6 Oct. 'Official Corruption in America.' Tax-gatherers, brokers, SHAVERS, &c., . . . pets of the Treasury.

1893. EMERSON, *Lippo*, xiv. What wages? says I. SHAVING TERMS, SHAVING TERMS, my boy, says he.

SHAVED, *adj.* (common).—Drunk: *see* SCREWED.

1598. SHAKSPEARE, 1 *Hen. IV.*, iii. 2. Bardolph was SHAVED . . . and I'll be sworn my pocket was picked.

1834. *Atlantic Club-book*, I. 138. When I met him, he was about—yes—just about HALF SHAVED.

1837-40. HALIBURTON, *Clockmaker* (1862), 102. They remind me of Commodore Trip. When he was about HALF-SHAVED he thought everybody drunk but himself.

SHAVELING (or **SHORLING**), *subs.* (old).—1. A monk: *cf.* BEARDLING. Also (2) *see* SHAVER.

*d.*1563. BALE, *Image of Both Churches*, xvii. 6. This Babylonish whore, or disguised synagogue of SHORLINGS, &c.

1577. KENDALL, *Epigrammes* [NARES]. Wouldst knowe the cause why Ponticus Abroade she doeth not rome? It is her use these SHAVELYNGS still With her to have at home.

1601. HEYWOOD, *Death Rob., Earl of Huntingdon*, F3. Through that lewd SHAVELING will her shame be wrought.

1630. TAYLOR, *Epig.*, 1. Curse, exorcise with beads, with booke and bell, Polluted SHAVELINGS.

1653. URQUHART, *Rabelais*, II, xxx. [Note]. Pope Alexander VI. who was *ras* [A SHAVELING] was poisoned by another *ras* [A SHAVELING] with rat's bane.

*d.*1657. J. BRADFORD, *Works* [Parker Soc. (1858)], II. 276. That is the prerogative of the priests and shaven SHORLINGS. *Ibid.*, 291. No matter . . . so thou have the favour of the pope and his SHAVELINGS.

1694. MOTTEUX, *Rabelais*, iv. 45. About him stood three priests, true SHAVELINGS, clean shorn and polled.

1767. STERNE, *Tristram Shandy*, vii. 16. A poor soldier shows you his leg, or a SHAVELING his box.

*d.*1859. MACAULAY, *Moncontour*. Alas! we must leave thee, dear desolate home, To the spearmen of Uri, the SHAVELINGS of Rome.

1883. GREEN, *Conq. of England*, ii. 63. Houses guarded only by priests and SHAVELINGS, who dared not draw sword.

SHAVER, *subs.* (old).—1. A fellow; a party: spec. (modern) = a more or less precocious youngster (B.E., MARTIN, and GROSE); (2) a child, but *see* quot. 1664. Also SHAVELING and SHAVE, *verb.*

1586. MARLOWE, *Jew of Malta*, iii. 3. *Bar.* Let me see, sirrah, are you not an old SHAVER? *Slave.* Alas, sir! I am a very youth.

*c.*1597. *Wily Beguiled* [HAWKINS, *Eng. Drama*, III. 376]. If he had not been a merry SHAVER, I would never have had him.

1630. CRIMSALL, *Kind-Hearted Creature* [*Rox. Ball.* (Brit. Mus.) iii. 166]. This bonny Lass had caught a clap It seems by some young SHAUER.

1635. CRANLEY, *Amanda* [NARES]. Thou art a hackney, that hast off beene tride, And art not coy to grant him such a favour, To try the courage of so young a SHAVER.

1654. WEBSTER, *Appius and Virginia*, ii. 2. Was't you, my nimble SHAVER that would whet Your sword 'gainst your commander's throat?

1655. *Hist. of Francion* [NARES]. There were some cunning SHAVERS amongst us, who were very well verst in the art of picking locks.

1664. COTTON, *Virgil Travestie* (1st ed.), 62. And said, My Mother's a mad SHAVER, No man alive knows where to have her.

*c.*1685. *Broadside Ballad*, 'The London Lasses Folly' [*Pepys Ball.* (Bodleian) iii. 236]. Now will I ramble up and down to find out this young SHAVER.

1698. FARQUHAR, *Love and a Bottle*, iii. 1. Who wou'd imagine now, that this young SHAVER cou'd dream of a woman so soon?

1748. SMOLLETT, *Rod. Random*, ix. He drew a pistol, and fired it at the unfortunate SHAVER, who fell flat on the ground without speaking one word.

*d.*1796. BURNS, *A Dream*. Funny, queer Sir John, He was an unco' SHAVER, For monie a day.

1834. SOUTHEY, *The Doctor*. No one has ever given him credit for being a cunning SHAVER.

1836. SCOTT, *Cruise of Midge*, 3. A sharpish sort of a SHAVER. *Ibid. Tom Cringle's Log* (1836), x. A smart dandified SHAVER.

1837. BARHAM. *Ingoldsby Legends* (1862), 315. And all for a "shrimp" not as high as my hat—A little contemptible SHAVER like that.

1843. DICKENS, *Martin Chuzzlewit*, xxxiii. 323. 'Not these,' he added, looking down upon the boys, 'ain't them two young SHAVERS as was so familiar to me.'

1854. WHYTE MELVILLE, *General Bounce*, xiv. The very youngest of the SHAVELINGS who aspire to dandyism call him "Buttercup" to his face.

1858. G. ELIOT, *Mr. Gilfil's Love-Story*, i. Mr. Gilfil called it his wonderful pocket, because, as he delighted to tell the young SHAVERS and "two-shoes" . . . whenever he put pennies into it, they turned into sugar-plums or gingerbread, or some other nice thing.

1874. WOOD, *Johnny Ludlow*, 1 S. 25. The two children (little SHAVERS in petticoats) set up a roar in court.

1880. *Time*, Aug., 153. The contemptible little SHAVER.

1893. EMERSON, *Lippo*, xvi. Well to see this young SHAVER pilot your horse to the post was a treat.

2. (common).—A short jacket; a BUM-PERISHER (*q.v.*)

3. *See* SHAVE.

SHAVING - BRUSH, *subs. phr.* (venery). — The female pubic hair: *see* FLEECE and LATHER.

SHAVINGS, *subs.* (old).—'The clippings of money' (B. E. and GROSE).

SHAY, *subs.* (common).—A chaise.

1840. LYTTON, *Paul Clifford*, xxxi. When I puts myself out of the way To obleedge you with a SHAY.

SHE, *subs.* (once literary: now vulgar).—A woman: also SHE-ONE: *cf.* HE = a man. Hence SHE-HOUSE (GROSE) = a house under petticoat rule; SHE-SCHOOL = a girls' school.

1602. SHAKSPEARE, *Twelfth Night*, i. 5, 259. Lady, you are the cruell'st SHE alive. *Ibid.* (1605) *Cymbeline*, i. 3. The SHES of Italy should not betray Mine interest and his honour.

1648-55. FULLER, *Ch. Hist.*, vi. 297. Nunneries also were good SHEE-SCHOOLS.

*d.*1650. CRASHAW, *To his Supposed Mistress*. That not impossible SHE That shall command my heart and me.

1704. STEELE, *Lying Lover*, i. 1. I . . . gaz'd . . . till I forgot 'twas winter, so many pretty SHE'S marched by me.

2. (Charterhouse). — A plum pudding: also SHEE: *cf.* HE.

SHEARER'S JOY, *subs. phr.* (Australian).—Colonial beer.

1892. GILBERT PARKER, *Round the Compass*, 22. It was the habit afterwards among the seven to say that the officers of the Eliza Jane had been indulging in SHEARER'S JOY.

SHEARS. PAIR OF SHEARS, *subs. phr.* (old).—A striking likeness; little or no difference: *e.g.*, 'There's a PAIR OF SHEARS' = 'They're as like as two peas.'

1603. SHAKSPEARE, *Measure for Measure*, i. 2. There went but A PAIR OF SHEERS between us.

1623. FLETCHER and ROWLEY, *Maid of the Mill*. There went but A PAIR OF SHEERS and a bodkin between them.

1630. OVERBURY, *Charact.*, 34. There went but A PAIRE OF SHEERES between him and the pursuivant of hell, for they both delight in sinne.

1630. TAYLOR, *Works*, i. 103. And some report that both these fowles have scene Their like, that's but A PAYRE OF SHEERES between.

1633. ROWLEY, *Match at Midnight* [DODSLEY, *Old Plays* (REED), vii. 367]. Why there goes but A PAIR OF SHEERS between a promoter and a knave.

See KNIGHT.

SHEATH, *subs.* (venery).—1. The female *pudendum* : *see* MONOSYLLABLE.

2. (venery).—The prepuce or foreskin.

SHEBANG, *subs.* (American). — *See* quots.

1861-5. [BARTLETT, *Dict. Americanisms*, s.v. SHEBANG]. A strange word that had its origin during the late civil war. It is applied alike to a room, a shop, or a hut, a tent, a cabin ; an engine-house.

1871. DE VERE, *Americanisms*, . . . SHEBANG . . . used even yet by students of Yale College and elsewhere to designate their rooms or a theatrical or other performance in a public hall, has its origin probably in a corruption of the French *cabane*, a hut, familiar to the troops that came from Louisiana, and constantly used in the Confederate camp for the simple huts, which they built with such alacrity and skill for their winter-quarters.

1872. CLEMENS, *Roughing It*, xlvii. There'll be a kerridge for you . . . We've got a SHEBANG fixed up for you to stande behind.

1899. BINSTEAD, *Houndsditch Day by Day*, 198. In a four-wheeled fever box you must take your beaver on your knees or get it hopelessly ruffled against the roof of the old SHEBANG.

1902. SAVAGE, *Brought to Bay*, ii. To-night, at your own SHEBANG, alone.

SHEBEEN, *subs.* (Irish and Scots').—(1) Any unlicensed place where excisable liquors are sold ; whence (2) a low (or wayside) public-house. Also as *verb.*, SHEBEENING, and SHEBEENER : the last term applies to persons frequenting as well as to those keeping a SHEBEEN.

*c.*1787. *Kilmainham Minit* [*Ireland Sixty Years Ago* (1847), 88]. With de stuff to a SHEBEEN we hied.

1818. LADY MORGAN, *Flora Macarthy*, I. ii. 105. Fitted up a couple of bedrooms in what had lately been a mere SHEBEEN house.

1841. LEVER, *Charles O'Malley*, vii. A little country ale-house, or in Irish parlance, SHEBEEN, which stood at the meeting of four bleak roads.

1845. BUCKSTONE, *Green Bushes*, i. 2. Have you been to the SHEBEEN.

1870. *Figaro*, 14 Dec. Three extensive captures of SHEBEENERS were made in Glasgow on Sunday. One hundred and twenty persons were found in the dens. . . . Why are SHEBEENS and SHEBEENERS so numerous in the North?

1873. *Scotsman*, 15 Feb. TO OWNERS of INNS, HOTELS, and PUBLIC-HOUSES.—XXX (who is a brother Innkeeper) thinks it high time that we form an ASSOCIATION to protect ourselves against Grocers, SHEBEENERS, and others who sell LIQUORS which are consumed on their Premises, and who hold no Licence to do so. Suggestions, &c. . . .

1883. JAY, *Connaught Cousins*, I. i. 22. There is a little SHEBEEN close by where we will take a rest.

1892. *D. Chronicle*, 17 Aug., 3, 7. CARDIFF. The designation of this town as "The City of Shebeens," was further justified to-day.

SHED, *verb.* (provincial).—TO PISS (*q.v.*) : also TO SHED A TEAR.

TO SHED A TEAR, *verb. phr.*—To take a drink : originally to take a dram of REAL OR SHORT (*q.v.*).

1876. HINDLEY, *Cheap Jack*, 156. I always made time to call in and SHED A TEAR with him for convenience and 'days o' lang syne.'

SHE-DRAGON, *subs. phr.* (colloquial).—1. A vixen ; an elderly termagant.

2. (old).—A kind of wig.

SHEENEY (or **SHENEY**).—1. A Jew ; a YID (*q.v.*) : used by Gentiles and by Jews (jocosely by the latter). Whence (2) a pawnbroker : pawnbroking, like the fruit and fish trade, is mainly (in London at least) in the hands of Jews. Also as *adj.* = base, Jewish, fraudulent : also SHEEN.

1847. THACKERAY, *Snobs*, xiv. SHEENEY and Moses are . . . smoking their pipes before their lazy shutters in Seven Dials.

1852. JUDSON, *Myst. New York*, iv. You hav'nt got no more stock than a broken-down SHEENEY.

1862. *Cornhill Mag.*, vi. 648. I shall let old Abraham, the SHEENEY, have it at four punt and a half a nob.

1866. SALA, *Trip to Barbary*, 16. He was manifestly a Jew . . . a most splendid SHEENY.

*c.*1870. *Broadside Ballad*, 'Talkative Man from Poplar.' Last Sunday he went down Petticoat Lane, Talked a SHEENEY out of his watch and chain.

1876. HINDLEY, *Cheap Jack*, 307. Tell him that the little SHENEY . . . don't forget his kindness.

1879. HORSLEY, *Auto. of Thief* [*Mac. Mag.*, xl. 501]. I took the daisies to a SHENEY down the gaff.

1888. PAYN, *Eavesdropper*, II. ii. 'Can you smash a thick 'un for me?' inquired one, handing his friend a sovereign. 'You're sure it ain't SHEEN?' returned the other, with a diabolical grin.

1891. *Lic. Vict. Gaz.* 3 Ap. Down went the East-ender smothered in gore, and . . . from all parts of the crowd there came shouts of, "the SHEENIE wins!" *Ibid.* The SHEENIES chuckled at the thought of the chosen race once more 'spoiling the Egyptians." *Ibid.*, 23 Jan. 'Don't like that SHEENEY friend of yours,' he said ; 'if you don't look out he'll have you.

1893. EMERSON, *Lippo*, xxi. I used to spend a couple of thick 'uns a Friday in fish and greenstuff, and then fill up with oranges and nuts for Sunday, going down the lane for them, buying from the SHEENEYS.

SHEEP, *subs.* (colloquial). — 1. SHEEP like PIGEON (*q.v.*) is commonly generic for timidity and basfulness. Thus, as *subs.* = a simpleton ; SHEEP-FACED (or SHEEPISH) = bashful (B. E. and GROSE) ; SHEEP'S-HEAD = a block-head (B. E., DYCHE, and GROSE) ; SHEEP-HEADED = stupid ; SHEEP'S HEART = a coward ; SHEEP-HEARTED = cowardly ; 'LIKE A SHEEP'S HEAD, ALL JAW' = 'said of a talkative person' (GROSE) ; OLD SHEEPGUTS = a term of contempt.

*d.*1556. UDAL, *Fras. Apoph.*, 122. Those pereones who were sely poore soules . . . wer euen then . . . by a common prouerbe called SHEPES HEADS or SHEPE.

1563. FOX, *Acts and Monuments*, iv. 51 [OLIPHANT, *New Eng.*, i. 542]. Orrmin's old SHEEPISH now gets the new sense of *stultus*.

1592. NASHE, *Piers Pennilesse*, 45. I haue read ouer thy SHEEPISH discourse . . . and entreated my patience to bee good to thee whilst I read it.

1593. SHAKSPEARE, *Com. Errors*, iv. 1. Thou peevish SHEEP. *Ibid.* (1595), *Verona*, i. 1. Twenty to one then he is slipp'd already, And I have play'd the SHEEP in losing him. *Ibid.* A silly answer, and fitting well a SHEEP.

1605. CHAPMAN, *All Fools*, ii. Ah, errant SHEEP'S HEAD, hast thou lived thus long, And darest not look a woman in the face?

1630. TAYLOR, *Works* [NARES]. Simple SHEEP-HEADED fools.

1632. MASSINGER, *Maid of Honour*, ii. 2. *Page.* You, sirrah SHEEP'S-HEAD, With a face cut on a cat-stick? You yeoman fewterer.

1693. LOCKE, *Education*, 70. A SHEEPISH or conceited creature.

1749. SMOLLETT, *Gil Blas* [ROUTLEDGE], 216. The SHEEPISH acquiescence of a man who stood in awe of an ecclesiastical rap on the knuckles.

1768. STERNE, *Sent. Journey*, 20. I never felt the pain of a SHEEPISH inferiority so miserably in my life.

1773. GOLDSMITH, *She Stoops to Conquer*, i. 1. Reserved and SHEEPISH ; that's much against him.

1775. SHERIDAN, *Rivals*, iv. 1. *Acres.* A vile, SHEEP-HEARTED blockhead ! If I hadn't the valour of St. George and the Dragon to boot—

1818. SCOTT, *Rob Roy*, ix. Why, thou SHEEP'S HEART, how do ye ken but we may can pick up some speerings of your valise.

1835. DANA, *Before the Mast*, 155 (July 18). They've got a *man* for mate of that ship, and not a bloody SHEEP.

1863. READE, *Hard Cash*, I. 137. He wore a calm front of conscious rectitude ; under which peeped SHEEP-FACED misgivings as to the result of their advance : for like all lovers, he was half impudence, half timidity, and both on the grand scale.

1878. JOHN PAYNE, tr. *Poems of Villon*, 87. My poor orphans, all the three, Are grown in age, and wit likewise, No SHEEPSHEADS are they, I can see.

1900. SAVAGE, *Brought to Bay*, vi. California mine manipulators going over . . . to shear those fat-witted SHEEP, the British investors.

2. (Aberdeen Univ.). — *See* quot.

1865. MACDONALD, *Alec Forbes of Howglen*, II. 5. At length a certain *semi* (second-classman, or more popularly SHEEP) stood up to give his opinion on some subject in dispute.

PHRASES and PROVERBS.—TO WASH SHEEP WITH SCALDING WATER = to act absurdly ; TO LOSE A SHEEP (erroneously SHIP) FOR A HALF-PENNY WORTH OF TAR = to go niggardly about a business ; 'as well be hung for a sheep as a lamb.'

SHEEP-BITER, *subs. phr.* (old).—1. A slinking thief ; also SHEEP-SHEARER and SHEEP-NAPPER (the latter spec. = a sheep-stealer) ; SHEEP-BITING = sneaking.

1588. LYLY, *Man in the Moone*. A sepulchre to seafish and others in ponds, moates, and rivers ; a sharpe SHEEP-BITER, and a marvellous mutton-monger, a gosbelly glutton.

1602. SHAKSPEARE, *Twelfth Night*, ii. 5, 6. Wouldst thou not be glad to have the niggardly rascally SHEEP-BITER come by some notable shame? *Ibid.* (1603), *Meas. for Meas.*, v. 1, 359. You baldpated lying rascal . . . Show your SHEEP-BITING face and be hanged an hour.

1611. CHAPMAN, *May-day*, iii. 1. I wish all such old SHEEP-BITERS might dip their fingers in such sauce to their mutton.

1620. MIDDLETON, *Chaste Maid*, ii. 2. SHEEP-BITING mongrels, hand-basket freebooters.

*d.*1704. L'ESTRANGE [*Century*]. There are political SHEEP-BITERS as well as pastoral, betrayers of public trust as well as of private.

1712. SHIRLEY, *Triumph of Wit*, 'The Black Procession,' vi. The sixteenth a SHEEP-NAPPER, whose trade is so deep, If he's caught in the corn, he's marked for a sheep.

2. (old). — 'A poor sorry, sneaking ill-lookt Fellow' (B.E.)

SHEEP-DOG, *subs. phr.* (colloquial). *See* quots.

1847. THACKERAY, *Vanity Fair*. II. ii. 'Rawdon,' said Becky . . . 'I must have a SHEEP-DOG' . . . 'What the devil's that?' said his Lordship. 'A dog to keep the wolves off me,' Rebecca continued, 'a companion.'

1882. JAMES PAYNE, *Thicker than Water*, viii. Under pretence of being my chaperon, or SHEEP-DOG, everyone knows that Mary is here for the protection of the public.

SHEEP'S-CLOTHING.—*See* WOLF.

SHEEP'S-EYES. TO CAST (or MAKE) SHEEP'S-EYES (or lamb's-eyes), *verb. phr.* (common).—To ogle ; to leer (GROSE) : formerly to look modestly and with diffidence but always with longing or affection. Fr. *gingìner ; lancer son prospectus*.

1500-13. SKELTON, *Works* (DYCE), 121. When ye kyst a SHEPYS IE.

1590. GREENE, *Francesco's Fortunes* [in *Wks.* VIII., 191]. That CASTING A SHEEPE'S EYE at hir, away he goes ; and euer since he lies by himselfe and pines away.

1600. T. HEYWOOD, 1 *Ed. IV.* [PEARSON, *Works* (1874), I. 51]. Go to, Nell ; no more SHEEP'S EYES ; . . . these be liquorish lads.

1611. COTGRAVE, *Dict.* . . . Affectionate winke, A SHEEPESEYE.

1614. JONSON, *Bartholomew Fair*, v. 3. Who chances to come by but fair Nero in a sculler ; And seeing Leander's naked leg and goodly calf, CAST at him from the boat A SHEEP'S EYE an' a half.

1632. MASSINGER, *Maid of Honour*, iv. 5. His brother, nor his favourite, Fulgentio, Could get a SHEEP'S EYE from you, I being present.

1651. CARTWRIGHT, *Ordinary* [NARES]. If I do look on any woman, nay, If I do cast a SHEEPSEYE upon any.

1673. WYCHERLEY, *Gentleman Dancing Master*, iv. 1. I saw her just now give him the languishing eye, as they call it, that is, the whiting's eye, of old called THE SHEEP'S-EYE.

1675. COTTON, *Scoffer Scofft* [Works (1725), 192]. Observing what SHEEPS-EYES he cast.

1708-10. SWIFT, *Polite Conversation*, i. Pray, Miss, how do you like Mr. Spruce? I swear I have often seen him cast a SHEEP'S EYE out of a Calf's Head at you.

1714. *Spectator*, No. 623. The steward was observed to cast A SHEEP'S EYE upon her, and married her within a month after the death of his wife.

1748. SMOLLETT, *Rod. Random*, xvi. There was a young lady in the room, and she threw . . . many SHEEP'S EYES at a certain person whom I shall not name.

1766. *Old Song*, 'The Butcher' [*The Rattle*], 3. Brisk Dolly, the Cookmaid . . . At whom the young Butcher soon cast A SHEEP'S EYE.

1837. BARHAM, *Ingoldsby Leg.*, II. 334. Her Charms will excuse one for casting SHEEP'S EYES at her.

1864. G. A. LAWRENCE, *Guy Livingstone*, vii. He would stand for some time casting LAMB'S-EYES at the object of his affections—to the amorous audacity of the full-grown SHEEP he never soared.

1892. *Tit-Bits*, 19 Mar., 425, 1. Sowerbutt had a silent regard for Ethel, . . . on more than one occasion . . . furtively casting SHEEP'S EYES at my darling.

SHEEPSKIN, *subs.* (common).—1. The diploma received on taking a degree ; also (2) a person who has taken a degree ; and (3) a deed or similar document [engrossed on parchment].

1843. CARLTON, *New Purchase*, i. 203. I can say as well as the best o' them SHEEPSKINS, if you don't get religion and be saved, you'll be lost teetotally and forever. *Ibid.* This apostle of ourn never rubbed his back agin a college, nor toted about no SHEEPSKINS,—no, never ! . . . How you'd a perished in your sins, if the first preachers had stayed till they got SHEEPSKINS !

1853. DICKENS, *Bleak House*, xxxii. The entanglement of real estate in the meshes of SHEEPSKIN.

SHEEPSKIN-FIDDLE, *subs. phr.* (old).—A drum. Hence, SHEEP-SKIN-FIDDLER = a drummer (GROSE).

SHEEPWALK, *subs.* (old). — A prison.

1781. MESSINK, *Choice of Harlequin*, 'Ye Scamps, &c.,' i. In Tothill-field's gay SHEEPWALK, like lambs ye sport and play.

SHEEPWASH, *verb.* (Winchester).—To duck.

SHEET-ALLEY, *subs. phr.* (common).—Bed ; BLANKET-FAIR (*q.v.*).

SHEETS, *subs.* (old).—Generic for sexual intercourse : thus, THE SHAKING OF THE SHEETS = the act of kind (orig. the name of an old country dance). Also BETWEEN THE SHEETS = in the act ; WHITE- (or COLD-) SHEETS = chastity ; STAINED (or FOUL) -SHEETS = fornication ; LAWFUL SHEETS = wedlock ; TO POSSESS A WOMAN'S SHEETS = to enjoy her.

1600. SHAKSPEARE, *Much Ado*, ii. 3. *Claud.* Now you talk of a sheet of paper, I remember a pretty jest your daughter told us of. *Leon.* O, when she had writ it and was reading it over, she found Benedick and Beatrice BETWEEN THE SHEET. *Ibid.* (1604), *Winter's Tale*, i. 2. The purity and WHITENESS OF MY SHEETS. *Ibid.* (1605), *Cymbeline*, i. 6. Should he make me live . . . betwixt COLD SHEETS whiles he is vaulting variable ramps? *Ibid.*, ii. 2. The chastity . . . WHITER THAN THE SHEETS! That I might touch! *Ibid.* (1605), *Lear*, iv. 6. Let copulation thrive; for Gloucester's bastard son Was kinder to his father than my daughters' Got 'tween the LAWFUL SHEETS. *Ibid.* (1596), *Hamlet*, i. 2. O, most wicked speed, to post With such dexterity to incestuous SHEETS. *Ibid.* (1602), *Othello*, ii. 3. *Iago.* He hath not yet made wanton the night with her; and she is sport for Jove . . . Well, happiness to their SHEETS.

*c.*1603. HEYWOOD, *Woman Kill'd with Kindness*, i. 1. Yes, would she dance THE SHAKING OF THE SHEETS But that's the dance her husband means to lead her.

1605. CHAPMAN, JONSON, &c., *Insatiate Countess*, ii. You must not think to dance THE SHAKING OF THE SHEETS alone, though there be not such rare phrases in't —'tis more to the matter.

1607. DEKKER and WEBSTER, *Westward Hoe*, v. 2. Scrapers appear under the wenches' . . . window . . . Cannot THE SHAKING OF THE SHEETS be danced without your town piping?

1611. BARRY, *Ram Alley*, v. i. The widow and myself Will scamble out THE SHAKING OF THE SHEETS Without Musick.

1612. CHAPMAN, *Widow's Tears*, i. 2. *Eu.* I'll have thee tossed in blankets. *Tha.* In blankets, madam? You must add your SHEETS, and you must be the tosser. *Ra.* Nay then, sir, y'are as gross as you are saucy. *Ibid. Ars.* Did not one of the Countess's serving men tell us . . . that he had already POSSESSED HER SHEETS.

1633. ROWLEY, *Match at Midnight*, iii. 1. Thee and I shall dance THE SHAKING OF THE SHEETS together.

1659. MASSINGER, *City Madam*, ii. 1. In all these places . . . after tenpound suppers The curtain's drawn, my fiddlers playing all night THE SHAKING OF THE SHEETS, which I have danced Again and again with my cockatrice.

1630. TAYLOR, *Works*, ii. 96. There are many pretty provocatory dances, as the kissing dance, the cushion dance, the SHAKING OF THE SHEETS, and such like, which are important instrumentall causes whereby the skilfull hath both clyents and custome.

1768. GAYTON, *Festivous Notes*, 25. But you Sancho, had the Austrian Donzella BETWIXT THE SHEETS, where I am afraid you did not behave so well as was wished.

A SHEET [or THREE, or FOUR SHEETS] IN THE WIND (or WIND'S EYE).—More or less tipsy; HALF SEAS OVER (*q.v.*): *see* SCREWED.

1821. EGAN, *Real Life*, I. 385. Old Wax and Bristles is about THREE SHEETS IN THE WIND.

1835. DANA, *Before the Mast*, 185. Though S. might be thought tipsy—A SHEET OR SO IN THE WIND—he was not more tipsy than was customary with him. He . . . seldom went up to the town without coming down THREE SHEETS IN THE WIND.

1847. PORTER, *Big Bear*, 172. When he gets THREE SHEETS spred, and is tryin' to unfarl the fourth, he can jist out-laugh the univarse.

1879. *Chambers' Jl.*, 14 June, 383. We had all messed together, and I'm afraid had got rather more than THREE SHEETS IN THE WIND, had aboard more than we could carry.

1883. STEVENSON, *Treasure of Franchard*, iv. [*Longman's Mag.*, April, 693]. Desprez was inclined to be A SHEET IN THE WIND'S EYE after dinner, especially after Rhône wine, his favourite weakness.

1892. HENLEY and STEVENSON, *Three Plays*, 209. *Kit.* What cheer, mother? I'm only a SHEET IN THE WIND; and who's the worse for it but me?

SHE-FAMILIAR, *subs. phr.* (old).—A kept mistress (HALLIWELL).

SHEFFIELD HANDICAP, *subs. phr.* (provincial).—A sprint race with no defined SCRATCH (*q.v.*). The scratch man receives an enormous start from an imaginary FLYER (*q.v.*).

SHE-FLUNKEY, *subs. phr.* (common).—A lady's maid.

1877. *Five Years' Penal Servitude*, iii. 244. She were a SHE-FLUNKEY, lady's maid, once—that's how she know'd all about being a swell lady.

SHEKEL, *subs.* (common).—In *pl.* = money: generic: *see* RHINO.

1886. *Fun*, 21 July, 29. Now that Henry Ward Beecher is over here, intent on making SHEKELS, the following anecdote concerning him is worth reviving.

1886-96. MARSHALL, *Pomes* [1897], 17. He'd a pedigree long, land and SHEKELS galore.

1889. *Referee*, 6 Jan. H. is scooping in the SHEKELS, but you mustn't infer from this that he is a "She"-nie.

1890. *New York Herald*, 16 April, 6. Mr. Philips's . . . novels bring him in as many SHEKELS as Ouida's.

1892. GUNTER, *Miss Dividends*, x. Plenty of SHEKELS to hire legal talent and pack juries.

1897. *Cassell's Saturday Journal*, 15 Sep. I do a great deal in the matrimonial line. One individual, more full of love than SHEKKELS, was in here just as the clock was striking nine one Saturday.

SHELF. ON THE SHELF, *phr.* (various).—1. (general) = laid aside, in reserve, past service: Fr. *brûlé*; 2 (military) = under arrest; 3 (old) = in pawn (GROSE); 4 (thieves') = transported; 5 (common) = dead: whence OFF THE SHELF = resurrected.

1587, GASCOIGNE, *Fruits of War*, 132 [CHALMERS, *Eng. Poets*, ii. 522, 2, 4]. And I that neuer yet was SET ON SHELF, When any sayld . . . Went after him.

1655. HEYWOOD, *Fortune by Land and Sea.* The fates have cast us ON THE SHELF To hang 'twix air and water.

1821. EGAN, *Life in London*, II. ii. Once a distinguished leader of fashion, . . . but he is ON THE SHELF now.

1833. O'CONNELL [*O'C. Correspondence* (1888), i. 387]. Lord Anglesey now is obliged reluctantly to retire. Blackburne will be put ON THE SHELF.

1842. *Comic Almanack*, 324. For though "six, seven, eight," have got, each of them, nicks, They, at last, lay the gambler undone ON THE SHELF.

1857. TROLLOPE, *Three Clerks*, iv. What, pension him! put him on half-pay —SHELF HIM for life, while he was still anxiously expecting . . . promotion.

*c.*1870. *Music Hall Song*, 'Hands Off.' Some fine day, when I'm . . . Put to bed with a spade in the usual way, And yourself ON THE SHELF a neglected old maid.

1894. *Illus. Bits*, 7 April, 4, 2. It should be explained here that [it] had been ON THE SHELF some time.

1902. HUME, *Crime of Crystal*, i. Tell 'em to get back into their graves at once . . . we don't take any folks OFF THE SHELF.

SHELL, *subs.* (military).—An undress jacket: also SHELL-JACKET.

1886. *St. James's Gazette*, 22 Dec. Tunics and SHELLS and messing-jackets and caps.

1889. *Harper's Mag.*, lxxx. 396. Three turbaned soldiers in tight SHELL-jackets and baggy breeches.

2. (school).—*See* quots.

1857. T. HUGHES, *Tom Brown's Schooldays*, i. 5. The lower fifth, SHELL, and all the junior forms in order.

1867. COLLINS, *Public Schools*, 178 (Westminster). At the end of this room [the schoolroom] there is a kind of semicircular apse, in which the SHELL form were formerly taught, and the shape of which is said to have given rise to this name, since adopted at several other public schools.

1875. JEAN INGELOW, *Fated to be Free*, xix. The SHELL [Harrow] . . . means a sort of class between the other classes.

3. (venery).—The female *pudendum*: *see* MONOSYLLABLE.

4. (old).—In *pl.* = money: *see* RHINO. Hence TO SHELL OUT = to pay. Fr. *allonger les radis.* SHELLING-OUT = 'clubbing money together' (GROSE).

1591. GREENE, *Notable Discovery* [*Works*, x. 38]. The purse, the Bong, The monie, the SHELS.

1611. MIDDLETON, *Roaring Girl*, v. 1. 'Tis a question whether there be any silver SHELLS amongst them, for all their satin outsides.

1819. MOORE, *Tom Crib*, 27. Who knows but if coax'd, he may SHELL OUT the shiners.

1821. EGAN, *Life in London*, II. iii. Another kevarten . . . and if you are too scaly to tip for it, I'll SHELL OUT.

1825. NEAL, *Bro. Jonathan*, III. xxxvii. Maybe you'll treat, won't you, if I SHELL OUT, fair; all't I know o' the matter?

1829. *Old Song*, 'The Prigging Lay' [*Vidocq's Memoirs*, iv.]. Quickly draw the bolt of your ken, Or we'll not SHELL OUT a mag.

1844. SELBY, *London by Night*, i. 1. By the bye, Shadrack, you must SHELL OUT at once for contingencies.

*d.*1849. EDGEWORTH, *Love and Law*, I. 1. Will you be kind enough, sir, TO SHELL OUT for me the price of a daacent horse fit to mount a man like me.

1855. BARNUM, *Autobiography*, 195. At the same time motioning to his trembling victim to SHELL OUT.

1860. *Cassell's Mag.*, 4 Jan., 211. The grave shan't keep me quieter than the fifty suverins which Mr. Hewitt . . . will SHELL OUT in the morning.

1892. NISBET, *Bushranger's Sweetheart*, 75. And after they have SHELLED OUT, what happens?

1902. HEADON HILL, *Caged*, xiii. Are you prepared to keep on SHELLING OUT over her till kingdom come?

5. (old).—A drinking glass.

See BROWN SHELL.

SHELL-BACK, *subs. phr.* (nautical). —A sailor: also OLD SHELL.

1883. *Graphic*, 12 May, 487, 3. The marine was described as a joey, a jolly, a SHELLBACK.

1884. RUSSELL, *Jack's Courtship*, i. It takes a sailor a long time to straighten his spine and get quit of the bold sheer that earns him the name of SHELL-BACK.

1885. RUNCIMAN, *Skippers and* SHELLBACKS [Title].

1901. WALKER, *In the Blood*, 29. All excepting the captain, who was a regular quiet old SHELL-BACK.

1902. *Athenæum*, 8 Feb., 176, 3. Any one of a dozen gaunt and hungry SHELL-BACKS in the forecastle would have supported him.

SHELL-OUT, *subs. phr.* (billiards). —A variety of pool.

1882. BRADDON, *Mount Royal*, xxv. Refraining from the relaxation of pool, or SHELL-OUT—opining that the click of the balls might have an unholy sound so soon after a funeral.

S'HELP. *See* S'WELP.

SHELTA. A kind of cryptic Irish spoken by tinkers and confirmed tramps; a secret jargon composed chiefly of Gaelic words disguised by changes of initial, transposition of letters, backslanging and similar devices. [Discovered by C. G. Leland and announced to the world in his book *The Gypsies* (1882); in 1886 there was a correspondence on the subject in *The Academy*; in 1889 The Gypsy Lore Society was started and several articles on Shelta appeared in its *Journal*; finally in *Chamber's Encyclopædia* (1902) there is a long account of this once mysterious but now fully explained speech.]

SHELVE, *verb.* (printers').—To hold over part of the weekly bill; the reverse of HORSING (*q.v.*).

SHEMOZZLE (SHIMOZZEL or **SHLEMOZZLE)**, *subs.* (East End). —A difficulty.

1899. BINSTEAD, *Houndsditch Day by Day.* It was through no recklessness or extravagance that he was in this SHLEMOZZLE.

1900. *From the Front*, 183. We might look upon this little CHIMOZZLE as a kind of misunderstanding.

1901. J. MACLAREN COBBAN, *Golden Tooth*, 170. If Will comes out of this SHEMOZZLE.

Verb. (East End).—To be off; to decamp.

SHENANIGAN, *subs.* (American).—Bounce; chaff; nonsense; trickery (BARTLETT, 1877.)

1893. MILLIKEN, *'Arry Ballads*, 80. Never mind their SHENANIGAN.

1901. WALKER, *In the Blood*, 332. We're mates all round, an' no more SHENANNIKIN.

1902. A. PRATT, *Great Push Exper.*, 77. A real gentleman and no SHENANIGAN.

1902. R. BARR, *The Victor*, 81. If I were to pay them they might think there was some SHENANIGAN about it.

SHE-NAPPER, *subs. phr.* (Old Cant). —'A Woman Thief-catcher; also a Cock (he) or Hen (she) Bawd, a Procuress and Debaucher of young Virgins; a Maiden-head-jobber' (B. E. and GROSE.)

SHE-OAK, *subs.* (Australian and New Zealand).—Colonial brewed ale.

SHEPHERD, *verb.* (colloquial).—To guard; to keep under surveillance; to chaperon: as a ticket-of-leave man (*see* NARK, *subs. and verb.*); an unmarried woman, or (mining) as in quot. 1863. Also (football) to head off whilst one's side is runuing or kicking. At Harrow, SHEPHERD, *subs.* = every sixth boy in the cricket-bill who answers for the five below him being present.

1863. *Once a Week*, VIII. 507. Having sunk their holes, each about a foot, and placed in them a pick or shovel as a sign of ownership, they devoted themselves to the laborious occupation of SHEPHERDING, which consists in sitting by a huge fire with a pipe in your mouth, telling or listening to interminable yarns, . . . grumbling at your present and regretting your past luck, diversified by occasionally lounging up to the sinking party for the purpose of examining the 'tack' thrown up, and criticising the progress made.

1886. PERCY CLARKE, *New Chum*, 71. The speculators who sat dangling their legs in their infant pits, SHEPHERDING their claims, awaiting with anxiety . . . the run of the vein.

SHERBETTY, *adv.* (common).—Drunk: *see* SCREWED.

1890. *Lic. Vict. Gaz.*, 8 Feb. By the time one got to bed Tom was a bit SHERBETTY.

SHERIFF. The chief officer of justice within a county is naturally found in combination: thus SHERIFF'S PICTURE FRAME = the hangman's noose: *see* NUBBING-CHEAT; SHERIFF'S-JOURNEYMAN = a hangman; SHERIFF'S BALL = an execution: whence TO DANCE AT THE SHERIFF'S BALL AND LOLL OUT ONE'S TONGUE AT THE COMPANY = to hang; SHERIFF'S BRACELETS = handcuffs; SHERIFF'S HOTEL = a prison (GROSE).

1824. EGAN, *Boxiana*, iii. 622. All in the SHERIFF'S PICTURE FRAME the call Exalted high, Dick parted with his flame, And all his comrades swore that he dy'd game.

SHERRY (or **SHIRRY**), *verb.* (old).—To run away: also TO SHIRRY OFF (GROSE): *see* ABSQUATULATE.

SHERRY-FUG, *verb.* (University).—To tipple sherry.

SHERRY-MOOR, *subs. phr.* (provincial).—A fright [HALLIWELL: From the battle of Sheriffe-muir when 'all was blood, uproar, and confusion'].

SHET. *See* SHUT.

SHEVVLE, *subs.* (obsolete).—*See* quot.

1864. *D. News*, 2 Dec. This is a term recently introduced as a genteel designation for cats' meat, and evidently derived from CHEVAL, French for horse, as mutton from *mouton*, &c.

SHICER (or **SHICE**), *subs.* (thieves').—1. Any worthless person or thing: generic for contempt. Also (2)

=nothing; NIX (*q.v.*): *e.g.* TO WORK FOR SHICE=to get no payment. Spec. SHICE = base money; and, as *adj.*, (1) spurious, shabby, bad: also SHICERY and SHICKERY; and (2) = tipsy.

1851-6. MAYHEW, *Lon. Lab.*, I. 472. The hedge crocus is SHICKERY togged.

1871. *Illus. Sydney News*, 21 Jan., 'The Digger.' The ne'er-do-wells . . . are . . . the first to rush to a new field, scrape it of its surface gold and then too lazy to seek further by deep sinking denounce the rush as a SHICER.

1877. *Five Years' Penal Servitude*, iii. 240. I ascertained while at Dartmoor that a very large 'business' is done in SHISE. *Ibid.*, ii. Seeing how the fellow was acting he sent him two SHISE notes, which gave him a dose that cooked him.

1899. BINSTEAD, *Houndsditch Day by Day*, 46. She comes over SHIKKUR and vants to go to shleeb.

1901. WALKER, *In the Blood*, 260. 'You're a damned good plucked un, Toby!' muttered Squiffy, 'an' ye're no SHICER.'

SHICKSTER (SHICKSER, or SCHICKSTER), *subs.* (common).—A woman: specifically (among Jews) = (1) a female servant not of the Jewish faith; and (2) a woman of shady antecedents. SHICKSTER-CRABS=ladies' shoes.

1857. SNOWDEN, *Mag. Assistant* (3rd Ed.), 446. A lady—A SHIKSTER.

1899. BINSTEAD, *Houndsditch Day by Day*, 91. 'No Mr. Motzaberger' says the schveet young SHIKSA.

1891. CAREW, *Autobiography of a Gipsy*, 414. As I was leavin' the court a reg'lar 'igh-flying SHICKSTER comes up.

SHIF, *subs.* (back slang).—Fish.

SHIFT, *verb.* (common).—1. To eat; and especially to drink. Hence SHIFTER = a drunkard.

2. (old).—To change one's smock; to change one's clothes.

1695. CONGREVE, *Love for Love*, i. 4. Bid Margery put more flocks in her bed, SHIFT twice a week, and not work so hard, that she may not smell so vigorously.

TO DO A SHIFT, *verb. phr.* (common).—1. To go away; to change one's quarters.

1892. *National Observer*, 27 Feb., 378. *But* if you arst me, *do* I ever DO A SHIFT? *Am* I particklerly partial to a fuss? . . . Speaking as one man *to* another,—Yuss!

2. (common).—To evacuate.

TO SHIFT ONE'S BOB. *See* BOB.

SHIFTER, *subs.* (old).—1. An intriguer: SHIFTY-COVE = a trickster (GROSE). Also (2) = a thief; (3) a sharper; and (4) a drunkard. Whence SHIFTY (or SHIFTING) = tricky (now recognised); SHIFTING = (1) shuffling, stealing, swindling; and (2) = drinking.

1567. AWDELEY, *Fraternitye of Vagabonds*. As well as of rufling Vacabondes, as of beggerley, . . . with a Description of the Crafty Company of Cousoners and SHIFTERS. [Title.]

1584. ROBINSON, *Pleasant Delights* [ARBER], 14. Maids must be manerly, not full of scurility, wherein I see you excel . . . You are a trim SHIFTER.

1593. SHAKSPEARE, *Com. of Errors*, iii. 2, 187. I see a man here needs not live by SHIFTS.

1598. FLORIO, *Worlde of Wordes*, *Bazaro* . . . a SHIFTER, a conicatcher . . . a haltersacke.

1601. JONSON, *Poetaster*, iii. 1. Thou art an honest SHIFTER; I'll have the statue repealed for thee.

1607. *Common Council Enactment.* SHIFTERS, people lyvinge by Cozeainge, Stealinge, and Imbeazellinge of Men's Goodes as opportunitye may serve them.

1608. WITHALS, *Dict.* A SHIFTER whome they call a cunny-catcher.

1610. *Mir. for Mags.*, 144. Nought more than subtill SHIFTINGS did we please, With bloodshed, craftie undermining men.

1616. *Richard Cabinet* [NARES]. SHIFTING doeth many times incurre the indignitie of reproch, and to be counted a SHIFTER, is as if a man would say in plaine tearmes a coosener.

1630. TAYLOR, *Works* [NARES]. And let those SHIFTERS their own judges be, If they have not bin arrant thieves to me.

1637. HEYWOOD, *Royal King* [PEARSON, *Works* (1874), VI. 38]. He scorns to be a changeling or a SHIFT.

1639. FLETCHER, *The Bloody Brother*, iv. 2. "They have so little As well may free them from the name of SHIFTER."

1659. MILTON, *Civil Power* [*Century*]. Sly and SHIFTING.

2. (thieves').—An alarm: as given by one thief in watching to another 'on the job.'—VAUX (1812).

SHIFTING-BALLAST, *subs. phr.* (old nautical).—Landsmen on board ship: spec. soldiers (GROSE).

SHIFT-WORK (or SERVICE), *subs. phr.* (venery).—Fornication.

SHIG, *subs.* (East End).—In *pl.* = money: specifically silver. At Winchester SHIG = a shilling (MANSFIELD, *c.* 1840).

SHIGGERS, *subs. pl.* (Winchester).—White football trousers costing 10s.: *see* SHIG.

SHIKERRY. *See* SHICER.

SHILLAGALEE, *subs.* (American).—A loafer.

SHILLING. TO TAKE THE KING'S (or QUEEN'S) SHILLING, *verb. phr.* (colloquial).—To enlist.

c. 1702. [ASHTON, *Social Life in the Reign of Queen Anne* (1882-3), II. 203]. The QUEEN'S SHILLING once being taken . . . there was no help for the recruit unless he was bought out.

1706. FARQUHAR, *Recruiting Officer*, ii. 3. *Capt. P.* Come my lads . . . the army is the place to make you men for ever. *Pear.* Captain, give me a SHILLING; I'll follow you.

SHILLING-SHOCKER (or -DREADFUL), *subs. phr.* (literary).—A sensation novel sold at a shilling: a fashion initiated (1887) by *The Mystery of a Hansom Cab*, by Mr. Fergus Hume: *cf.* PENNY-AWFUL.

1885. *Athenæum*, 14 Nov., 638. Mr Stevenson is writing another SHILLING-DREADFUL.

1887. *Ill. London News*, 17 Sept., 349, 1. The three-volume novel may be dying out, as they tell us; but we have the SHILLING SHOCKER rampant among us.

1890. *Academy*, 22 Feb., 130, 2. I have often wondered why the experiences of the Styrian arsenic-eaters . . . has not been utilised by the writer of some three-volume novel or SHILLING SHOCKER.

SHILLY-SHALLY (also SHALLY-SHALLY), *verb. phr.* (colloquial).—To trifle; not to know one's mind; TO STAND SHILLY-SHALLY = to be irresolute (GROSE). Hence SHILLY-SHALLY (or SHILLY-SHALLYING) = indecision [Shall I? Shall I?]; SHILLY-SHALLIER = a trifler.

1630. TAYLOR, *Works*, iii. 3. There's no delay, they ne're stand SHALL I SHALL I: Hermogenes with Dallila doth dally.

1665. HOWARD, *Committee*, iii. Tell her your mind! ne'er stand SHILLY SHALLY.

1699. CONGREVE, *Way of the World*, iii. 15. I don't stand SHILL I, SHALL I, then; if I say't, I'll do't.

1703. STEELE, *Tender Husband*, iii. 1. Why should I stand SHALLY-SHALLY like a Country Bumpkin.

1709. KING, *Eagle and Robin*, 92. Bob did not SHILL-I-SHALL-I go, Nor said one word of friend or foe.

1782. BURNEY, *Cecilia*, v. 119 [OLIPHANT, *New Eng.*, ii. 188. The SHILL I, SHALL I of Congreve becomes SHILLY SHALLY].

1809. MALKIN, *Gil Blas* [ROUTLEDGE], 27. I never STAND SHILLY-SHALLY: begone, you are free.

1830. LYTTON, *Paul Clifford* (1854), 177. Your friends starve before your eyes, while you are SHILLY-SHALLYING about your mistress.

1834. SOUTHEY, *The Doctor*, cv. He was no SHILLY SHALLIER.

1849. THACKERAY, *Pendennis*, xxxvii. I'll have no more letters nor no more SHILLY-SHALLY.

1883. JAMES PAYN, *Thicker than Water*, xvii. He says he will have no more SHILLY-SHALLYING, but will you take the Lady or will you not?

1884. *Sat. Review*, 8 March, 299, 2. He relapses into SHILLY-SHALLY under cover of General Graham's feat.

SHIMMY (or SHIMMEY), *subs.* (colloquial).—A chemise. Also (Felsted) = a shirt: obsolete.

1837. MARRYATT, *Snarley Yow*, xliv. We have nothing here but petticoats and SHIMMEYS . . . Never mind I'll lend you a SHIMMEY.

1856. DOW, *Sermons* [BARTLETT]. As interesting a sight . . . as a SHIMMEY in a wash-tub.

18 [?]. *A Tale of Sleepy Hollow* [BARTLETT]. The ghost was Aunt Kate's SHIMMEYS pinned on the line to dry.

SHIN, *verb.* (colloquial).—Generic for action: spec. to walk, to tramp: also TO SHIN IT. Hence TO SHIN UP = to climb; TO SHIN IT (SHIN ROUND, or BREAK SHINS) = to go a round of lenders: whence SHINNER = a borrower; TO SHIN OUT OF = to clear off; TO BREAK ONE'S SHINS (*see* above); also (2) to be in a hurry; and (3) to fall against, or over, a person or thing; AGAINST ONE'S SHINS = unwillingly (RAY). Also SHINNY (American) = a negro tramp: *cf.* HOBOE.

1836. DANA, *Before the Mast*, 284. We had to furl them again in a snow-squall, and SHIN UP and DOWN single ropes caked with ice.

1838. NEAL, *Charcoal Sketches, The Fleshy One*, II. 13. 'SHIN IT, good man,' ejaculated a good-natured urchin.

1845. *New York Com. Adv.*, 13 Dec. The Senator was SHINNING AROUND, to get gold for the rascally bank-rags.

1857. HUGHES, *Tom Brown's Schooldays*, i. 9. Nothing for it but the tree; so Tom laid his bones to it SHINNING UP as as fast he could.

18 [?]. *Pearl St.*, 123 [BARTLETT]. "Any thing over?" is an expression used by SHINNERS, on applying to their acquaintances for the needful; and if so, it is expected that you will oblige the SHINNER.

1868. C. READE and BOUCICAULT, *Foul Play*, 158. I know I didn't ought to ax a parson to SHIN UP a tree for me.

1871. DE VERE, *Americanisms* . . . To obtain money he has probably had much SHINNING to do, as slang calls the running about to friends and acquaintances.

1882. ANSTEY, *Vice-Versa*, xvi. SHIN OUT OF this, whatever y'are, we don't contrack to carry no imps on this line.

1884. CLEMENS, *Huck. Finn*, iv. I was up in a second and SHINNING DOWN the hill.

1891. RUSSELL, *Ocean Tragedy*, 86. I sprang and had soon SHINNED as high as the topgallant-yard.

1900. GUNTER, *Princess of C.*, 7. Lay low, but tell yer dad to SHIN UP here quick.

1900. FLYNT, *Tramps*, 109. My knowledge of the SHINIES is very meagre. *Ibid.*, 323. The 'blanket stiff,' the 'gay-cat,' 'THE SHINNY,' the 'Frenchy,' and the 'ex-prushun' were all there.

1902. HEADON HILL, *Caged*, xxxiv. Hill . . . make a rope of the bed-clothes and SHIN DOWN with her in his arms.

2. (common).—To kick on the shins.

1837. BARHAM, *Ingold. Leg.*, II. 351. A ring—give him room, or he'll SHIN you—stand clear.

1864. *Eton School Days*, xiii. He could not go out . . . without someone throwing a stone at him, or hissing, or SHINNING him if he passed near enough.

SHINDY, *subs.* (old).—1. A dance (GROSE): in Western America SHINDIG = a noisy dance.

2. (common).—A disturbance; a quarrel: also SHINTY. Whence (3) a boisterous SPREE (*q.v.*).

1821. EGAN, *Life in London*, II. iii. The Jack Tar is quite pleased with his night's cruise, and is continually singing out, "What a prime SHINDY, my messmates!"

1837. BARHAM, *Ingoldsby Legends* (1862), 204. —— he won't kick up such SHINDIES, Were she once fairly married and off to the Indies.

1841. *Comic Almanack*, 260. Vell, sartingly its vindy; and here's a pretty SHINDY.

1847. THACKERAY, *Vanity Fair*, II. xix. There's a regular SHINTY in the house; and everything at sixes and sevens.

1864. *Derby-day*, 8. He asked them if they wanted to insult him grossly, and there was a very comfortable little SHINDY over it.

1869. MRS. WOOD, *Roland Yorke*, xiii. "Which cheque?" . . . "The one there's all this SHINDY over at Greatorex and Greatorex's."

1889. *Cassell's Sat. Jl.*, 19 Jan., 398. It was safe to prophecy that there would shortly be a SHINDY somewhere.

1892. KIPLING, *Barrack Room Ballads*, 'The Legend of Evil.' He wint to stop the SHINDY, The Devil wid a stable-fork bedivillin' their tails.

1897. MITFORD, *Romance of Cape Frontier*, II. iii. Did you get hit in that SHINDY just now?

4. (American).—A liking; a fancy.

1859. HALIBURTON, *Human Nature*, 70. Father took a wonderful SHINDY to Jessie; for even old men can't help liking beauty.

SHINE, *subs.* (common).—1. A happening; a TO-DO (*q.v.*), whether warlike or not; specifically a frolic. Hence (2) = show, or display; and (3) a row, a SHINDY (*q.v.*). TO CUT A SHINE = to make a show; EVERY SHINE = every one. As *verb.* = (1) to make a stir, or impression, and (2) to raise or show money; TO TAKE THE SHINE OUT OF = (1) to outwit, and (2) put in the shade; TO SHINE UP (or TAKE A SHINE) TO = to make oneself agreeable; to have a fancy for.

1818. EGAN, *Boxiana*, I. 23. Who was selected to punish this Venetian for his vain-boasting, that he would TAKE THE SHINE OUT OF Englishmen! *Ibid.* (1842), *By-Blow of the Jug* [*Captain Macheath*]. To the end of your life CUT A SHINE.

1835. HALIBURTON, *Clockmaker* I S., xvi. They fairly TAKE THE SHINE off creation—they are actilly equal to cash.

1843. *Major Jones's Courtship*, ii. They was all comin' to me bout it, and SHININ' and disputin' so I couldn't hardly hear one from tother.

1847. ROBB, *Squatter Life*. To make a SHINE with Sally I took her a new parasol.

1847. THACKERAY, *Vanity Fair*, II. xxv. A long, thin, queer-looking, oldish fellow—a dry fellow though, that TOOK THE SHINE OUT OF a man in the talking line.

1848. BURTON, *Waggeries*, 78. Quite careless as to what 'didoes and SHINES' he might cut in future.

1848. RUXTON, *Far West*, 13. I say. It won't SHINE, and what's the dollars? *Ibid.*, 174. You can't SHINE.

1851. COBB, *Mississippi Scenes*, 155. I'm pretty much like the old man, only I took a sort o' SHINE to old Cass.

1852. DICKENS, *Bleak House*, lvii. There'd be a pretty SHINE made if I was to go a-wisitin them, I think."

1853. *Diogenes*, II. 46. And TAKE OUT THEIR SHINE With a jolly large fine.

1856. DOW, *Sermons*, I. I've seen some evening twilights that TAKE THE SHINE OFF everything below.

c. 1859. *New York Sp. of Times* [BARTLETT]. You will find heaps of bogus money here, but bogus men CAN'T SHINE.

1861. KINGSLEY, *Ravenshoe*, xli. There's mostly a SHINE of a Sunday evening.

1864. *Hertford Post*, 14 July. The public . . . will pronounce her the finest and most comfortable boat they have ever visited, and be satisfied that she is bound TO SHINE.

1866. *Major Downing's Letters*, 37. I'm sorry he didn't bring his pitch-pipe with him, just to take the SHINE of them 'are singers.

1869. STOWE, *Oldtown*, 235. She needn't think she's goin' to come round me with any o' her SHINES, . . . with lying stories about me.

1883. T. WINTHROP, *John Brent*, 17 I've TUK A middlin' SHINE TO you, and don't want to see yer neck broke.

1886. *Congregationalist*, 4 Feb. Mother was always hecterin' me about getting married, and wantin' I should SHINE up to this likely girl and that.

1886. MCCLINTOCK, *Beedle's Marr.* I TOOK A great SHINE TO the schoolma'am.

4. (common). — Money: generic: *see* RHINO.

1842. EGAN, *Bould Yeoman* [*Captain Macheath*]. Then the High-toby gloque drew his cutlass so fine; Says he to the farmer, you or I for the SHINE.

5. (venery).—In *pl.* = copulation: *see* GREENS and RIDE.

6. (military).—A flash: *e.g.*, from a rifle.

1892. KIPLING, *Barrack Room Ballads*, 'The Young Brotish Soldier.' Shoot low at the limbers an' don't mind the SHINE.

SHINER, *subs.* (old). — A coin: spec. a gold piece. In *pl.* = money: generic: Also SHINO and SHINERY.

1760. FOOTE, *The Minor*, ii. To let a lord of lands want SHINERS, 'tis a shame.

1781. MESSINK, *Choice of Harlequin*. 'Ye Scamps, &c.' First you touch the SHINERS.

1819. MOORE, *Tom Crib*, 27. Who knows but if coax'd he may shell out the SHINERS.

1834. AINSWORTH, *Rookwood*, III. i. But when from his pocket the SHINERS he drew, And offered to 'make up the hundred to two.'

1839. DICKENS, *Oliver Twist*, xix. 'Fagin,' said Sykes, 'is it worth fifty SHINERS extra, if it's safely done from the outside?'

1848. DURIVAGE, *Stray Subjects*, 82. In one corner . . . was stowed away a goodly quantum of the SHINERS.

1857. READE, *Never too Late to Mend*, i. We'll soon fill both pockets with the SHINERY in California.

1886-96. MARSHALL, '*Pomes' from the Pink' Un*, 8. I don't want a SHINER that's only splashed.

1892. CHEVALIER, *Idler*, June, 549. I've got a little nipper, when 'e talks, I'll lay yer forty SHINERS to a QUID, You'll take 'im for the father, me the kid.

1890. *Detroit Free Press*, 10 May. Come, down with the SHINO.

2. (old). — A looking-glass (GROSE and VAUX).

3. (common).—A silk hat.

1885. FRANCIS, *On Angling*, 179. A tall black hat, or one of the genus called SHINER, I do not recommend.

1902. *D. Telegraph*, 31 Oct. 10, 6. The little man with the tall SHINER.

4. (old).—A clever fellow.

5. (tailors').—A boaster. Also SHINE = to boast.

THE SHINERS, *subs.* (military). —The Northumberland Fusiliers, formerly The 5th Foot. [From smart appearance at the time of The Seven Years' War.]

SHINE- (or SHINEY-) RAG. To WIN THE SHINE-RAG, *verb. phr.* (old).—*See* quot.

1851-61. MAYHEW, *London Lab.*, 20 He lost again, and some one bantering said, 'You'll WIN THE SHINE-RAG, Joe,' meaning that he would be 'cracked up,' or ruined, if he continued.

SHINFEAST, *subs.* (provincial).—A good fire (HALLIWELL).

SHINGLE, *subs.* (American). — A signboard. To HANG OUT (or STICK UP) ONE'S SHINGLE = to start business; SHINGLE-SPLITTING (obs. Tasmanian), *see* quot.

1830. *Hobart Town Almanack*, 89. When a man gets behindhand with his creditors . . . and rusticates in the country . . . he is said to be SHINGLE-SPLITTING.

1848. *N.Y. Com. Adv.*, 24 Dec. Doctors and dentists from the U. S. have STUCK UP THEIR SHINGLES in Mexico.

1852. JUDSON, *Myst. of New York*, xiv. The legal gentleman had no particular office, nor HUNG he OUT A SHINGLE anywhere.

1884. BELLAMY, *Dr. Heidenhoff's Process*, 99. There was a modest SHINGLE bearing the name 'Dr. Gustav Heidenhoff' fastened up on the side of the house.

Verb. (common). To chastise.

To HAVE A SHINGLE SHORT, *verb. phr.* (Australian).—To be crazy; to have a tile loose.

SHINGLE-TRAMPER, *subs. phr.* (nautical).—A coastguardsman.

SHINING-LIGHT, *subs. phr.* (common).—An exemplar.

*d.*1796. BURNS, *Holy Willy's Prayer*. 2. A burnin' and a SHININ' LIGHT To a' this place.

1892. *Sala's Jour.*, 2 July, 220. They are simply following the example of other SHINING LIGHTS in the profession.

SHINKIN-AP-MORGAN, *subs. phr.* (old) —A Welshman.

*c.*1660. *Broadside Ballad*, 'A Beggar I'll Be' [FARMER, *Musa Pedestris* (1896), 29]. With SHINKIN-AP-MORGAN, with Blue-cap, or Teague, We into no Covenant enter, nor League.

SHINNER, *subs.* (old). *See* quots.

1585. *Nomenclator*, 167. An hose, a nether stocke, a SHINNER.

1598. FLORIO, *Worlde of Wordes*. *Calcette*, hosen, or neather stockings, or SHINNERS.

See SHIN, *verb*.

SHINNY (or **SHINY**), *adj.* (American).—Drunk: *see* SCREWED.

SHINPLASTER, *subs.* (American). —*See* quot. 1890.

1838. NEAL, *Charcoal Sketches*, II. 23. If you have no brass and no tin, give us a SHINPLASTER then—them's my terms.

1845. *New York Tribune*, 3 Dec. The people may whistle for protection, and put up with what SHINPLASTER rags they can get.

1848. DURIVAGE, *Stray Subjects*, 135. The cards were dealt, a brace of hands were played, and I won his '*Red Dog*' SHINPLASTER.

1848. LOWELL, *Biglow Papers* . . . If greenbacks ain't not just the cheese, I guess there's evils that's extremer; For instance,—SHINPLASTER idees, Like them put out by Gov'nor Seymour.

1852. *L'Allegro*: *As Good as a Comedy*, 60. A greasy citizen. holding out a couple of SHINPLASTERS of single dollar denomination.

1856. DOW, *Sermons*, I. 309. Hope's brightest visions absquatulate with their golden promises before the least cloud of disappointment, and leave not a SHINPLASTER behind.

1862. *Punch*, 19 July, *Yankee Stories*. King Dollar 'ginst us he may turn, But we have King SHINPLASTER.

*c.*1866. *The Disseminator*. A grocer of New York, who had set up an opposition to the whole batch of suspended banks, found his SHIN-PLASTERS returned to him in such quantities, that, on counting over his "money," he found that he had redeemed about 100 dols. more than he had ever issued.

1890. *Cent. Dict.* s.v. SHINPLASTER . . . A small paper note used as money; a printed promise to pay a small sum issued as money without legal security. The name came into early use in the United States for notes issued on private responsibility, in denominations of from three to fifty cents, as substitutes for the small coins withdrawn from circulation during a suspension of specie payments; people were therefore obliged to accept them, although very few of them were ever redeemed. Such notes abounded during the financial panic beginning with 1837, and during the early part of the Civil War of 1861-5. After the latter period they were replaced by the fractional notes issued by the Government and properly secured, to which the name was transferred.

SHIN-RAPPER, *subs. phr.* (knackers'). — 1. A disabling blow on the splint bone; also (2) one who delivers such a blow.

1885. *D. Tel.*, 30 Sep. Every great stable in England had the fear of the poisoner, the SHIN-RAPPER, and the nobbler constantly in view.

SHINSCRAPER, *subs.* (thieves').— The treadmill: *see* EVERLASTING-STAIRCASE.

SHIP, *subs.* (printers' colloquial).— A body of compositors working together; one acts as clicker, takes charge and makes out the general bill which is shared and shared alike. [An abbreviation of "companionship."]

Verb. (common.)—1. To dismiss; TO SACK (*q.v.*) Also (2) to expel; to rusticate (American Univ.); (3) to turn out of bed, mattress on top (Sherborne School); and (4) to turn back in a lesson (Shrewsbury School).

1857. TROLLOPE, *Three Clerks*, xviii. I'm to stay at the office till seven o'clock for a month, and old Foolscap says he'll SHIP me the next time I'm absent half-an-hour without leave.

SHIP BLOWN UP AT POINT NONPLUS, *phr.* (old).—'Exemplifies the quietus of a man when plucked penniless; or, genteelly expelled. Oxf. Univ. cant' (GROSE).

See ANNO DOMINI; HOME; PUMP.

SHIP-HUSBAND, *subs. phr.* (nautical).—*See* quot.

1842. MARRYAT, *Percival Keene*, xviii. He was, as we use the term at sea, a regular SHIP-HUSBAND—that is to say, he seldom put his foot on shore; and if he did, he always appeared anxious to get on board again.

SHIP-IN-FULL-SAIL, *subs. phr.* (rhyming).—A pot of ale.

SHIP OF THE DESERT, *subs. phr.* (common).—A camel.

1869. *Notes and Queries*, 4 S. iv. 3 July, 10. By whom was the camel first called "THE SHIP OF THE DESERT?"

SHIP-SHAPE, *adj.* (colloquial). — Spick and span; smart above and below: originally SHIP-SHAPE AND BRISTOL FASHION. [Bristol's fame as a port in early days was far higher than now] (GROSE).

1835. DANA, *Before the Mast*, 25 Aug. Everything was SHIP-SHAPE AND BRISTOL FASHION. There was no rust, no dirt, no rigging hanging slack, no fag ends of ropes and 'Irish pendants' aloft, and the yards were squared 'to a *t*' by lifts and braces.

1848. DICKENS, *Dombey and Son*, xxiii. Wal'r will have wrote home . . . and made all taut and SHIP-SHAPE.

1874. E. L. LINTON, *Patricia Kemball*, ii. Though we can go on very well as we are, she must have everything SHIP-SHAPE and nice when she comes.

1891. *Lic. Vict. Mirror*, 3 Jan. 7, 2. No time was lost in putting the ring SHIP-SHAPE.

SHIRK, *verb.* (Eton College: obsolete).—*See* quot.

1857-64. BRINSLEY RICHARDS, *Seven Years at Eton* (1883). SHIRKING was a marvellous invention. Fellows were allowed to boat on the river, but all the approaches to it were out of bounds; we might walk on the terrace of Windsor Castle, but it was unlawful to be caught in the streets of Windsor which led to the terrace . . . If, out of bounds, you saw a master coming, you had to SHIRK, which was done by merely stepping into a shop. The master might see you but he was supposed not to see you. The absurdity was . . . that to buy anything in the shops in High Street, where all the school tradesmen dwelt, we were obliged to go out of bounds.

To SHIRK IN, *verb. phr.* (Winchester).—To walk into water instead of plunging. To SHIRK OUT = to go out contrary to rules. Whence SHIRKSTER = one who shirks.

SHIRKER, *subs.* (hunting).—One who prefers the road to cross-country riding: *cf.* SKIRTER.

1885. *Field*, 4 Ap. Once in a way the roadsters and SHIRKERS are distinctly favoured.

SHIRALLEE, *subs.* (Australian).— SWAG (*q.v.*); a bundle of blankets.

SHIRT. TO GET ONE'S SHIRT OUT (or LOSE ONE'S SHIRT), *verb. phr.* (common).—To make (or get) angry. Hence, SHIRTY = angry, ill-tempered.

1851-61. MAYHEW, *London Lab.*, iii. 147. They knocked his back as they went over, and he got SHIRTEY.

1897. MAUGHAM, *Liza of Lambeth*, iii. You ain't SHIRTY 'cause I kissed yer?

COLLOQUIALISMS. — TO BET ONE'S SHIRT (or PUT ONE'S SHIRT ON) = to risk all; TO FLY ROUND AND TEAR ONE'S SHIRT = to bestir oneself; SHIRT (or FLAG) IN THE WIND = a fragment seen through the fly, or through a hole in the breech; 'THAT'S UP YOUR SHIRT' = 'That's a puzzler for you'; 'DO AS MY SHIRT DOES' = 'Kiss my arse!'

*c.*1707. *Ballad of Old Proverbs* [DURFEY, *Pills*, &c. (1707)], ii. 112. But if she prove her self a Flurt, Then she may DO AS DOES MY SHIRT.

See also BOILED SHIRT; BLOODY SHIRT; HISTORICAL (or ILLUSTRATED) SHIRT.

SHIRT-SLEEVIE, *subs. phr.* (Stonyhurst). — A dance: on winter Saturday evenings, and sometimes in the open air at the end of summer term. [The costume is an open flannel shirt and flannel trousers.]

SHISE. *See* SHICE.

SHIT (or **SHITE**), *subs.* (vulgar).— Excrement: as *verb.* = to ease the bowels. Whence, SHIT = violent abuse: generic. Thus SHITSACK = (1) 'a dastardly fellow,' and (2) a Nonconformist (GROSE): also SHIT-STICKS, SHIT-RAG, SHIT-FELLOW, &c.; SHITTEN = worthless, contemptible; SHIDDLE-CUM-SHITE (SHITTLE-CUM-SHAW or SHITTLETIDEE) = nouns or exclamations of contempt; SHIT-FIRE = a bully; SHITTERS = the diarrhœa; SHIT-BAG = the belly: in *pl.* = the guts; SHIT-HOUSE = a privy; SHIT-POT = a rotten or worthless humbug; SHIT-HUNTER (or STIR-SHIT) = a sod; SHIT-SHARK = a gold-finder; SHIT-SHOE (or SHIT-SHOD) = derisive to one who has bedaubed his boot; SHIT-HOLE = the rectum; and TO SHIT THROUGH THE TEETH = to vomit. Also PROVERBS and PROVERBIAL SAYINGS: 'SHITTEN-CUM-SHITE'S the beginning of love' (proverbial); 'Wish in one hand and SHIT in the other, and see which will first fill'; 'Only a little clean SHIT (*Scottice*, 'clean dirt')': derisive to one bedaubed or bewrayed; 'He (she, or it) looks as though the Devil had SHIT 'em flying': of things and persons mean, dwarfed, eccentric, or ridiculous; 'Like SHIT (sticking) TO A SHOVEL': very adhesive indeed; 'To swallow a sovereign and SHIT it in silver' = the height of convenience; 'SHIT in your teeth' (old) = a foul retort on somebody who does not agree with you; 'It shines like a SHITTEN barn-door' (GROSE); 'All is not butter the cow SH—TS'; 'Claw a churl by the breech (or culls—JONSON) and he'll SH— in your fist'; 'The devil SH—S upon a great heap'; 'SHITTEN luck's good luck'; 'Lincolnshire, where hogs SH—soap, and crows SH— fire'; 'Go and eat coke and SHIT cinders' (popular) = derisive and defiant; 'Thought lay abed and SHIT himself, and thought he hadn't done it.'

1576. *Merie Tales of Skelton*, ix. Skelton then caste the clothes, and the frere dyd lye starke naked : then Skelton dyd SHITE vpon the freeres nauil.

1598. FLORIO, *Worlde of Wordes. Dometa*, an old worde for a SHITTEN fellow, or goodman turde, for *meta* is a heape of turde. Ibid., *Cacastraccie*, a SHITE-RAGS, an idle lazie fellow. Ibid., *Cacastecchi* . . . a SHITE-STICKS.

*c.*1600. MONTGOMERY, *Poems* [S.T.S.], I. 85, 'Flyting.' Halland-shaker, draught-raiker, bannock-baiker, ale-BESHITTEN.

*c.*1616. JONSON, *Epigrams*, 'On the Famous Voyage.' Alas! they will BESHITE us. *Ibid.* And in so SHITTEN sort so long had used him.

16 [?]. TAYLOR and SHIPMAN, *Grobiana's Nuptials*, Sc. 7 [MS.(Bodleian) 30, leaf 21]. Is SHITTEN CUM SHITES THE BEGINNINGE OF LOVE? why then, Tantoblin, thou art happye, Grobiana's thyne, the proverbe gives it thee.

1653. URQUHART, *Rabelais*, I. iv. Such SHITTEN stuff! *Ibid.*, I. xi. He pissed in his shoes, SHIT in his shirt, and wiped his nose on his sleeve.

1656. *Muses Recr.* [HOTTEN], 24. Here have I seen old John Jones, From this hill, SHITE to yonder stones.

1658. PHILLIPS, *Mysteries of Love and Eloquence*, 169. *Q.* Why is 'sweet mistress' so usual a complement? *A.* Because SHITTEN COMES SHITES IS THE BEGINNING OF LOVE.

1662. *Rump Songs*, ii. 3. That of all kinds of Luck, SHITTEN LUCK is the best. *Ibid.*, ii. 24. For it SHIT from Portsmouth to Wallingford House.

1664. COTTON, *Virgil Travestie* (1st ed.), 97. The SHIT-BREECH'D elfe Would shoot like Robin-Hood himself.

1665. PEPYS, *Diary*, 6 Ap. Sir G. Carteret . . . called Sir W. Batten in his discourse at the table to us . . . SHITTEN FOOLE, which vexed me.

1678. COTTON, *Virgil Travestie* [*Works* (1725) 80]. Among his Mates, and wishes rather, (And so the Stripling told his Father) For noughty Vermin that would bite him, Or Throstle Neast though't did —— ——.

1647-80. ROCHESTER, *The Restoration.* Made them SHIT as small as rats.

*d.*1704. T. BROWN, *Works*, ii. 180. Knocking a SHITING porter down . . . in his own sir-reverence.

1706. WARD, *Wooden World*, 69. 'A Sailor.' No man can ever have a greater contempt for Death, for every day he constantly SHITS on his own grave. *Ibid.* (1718), *Helter Skelter.* I say, sir, you're a mean SHIT-FIRE.

1707. *Old Ballad*, 'As the Fryer he Went along' [DURFEY, *Pills*, &c. (1707), iii. 130]. The Maid she SH——, and a Jolly brown T—— out of her Jolly brown Hole.

1708-10. SWIFT, *Polite Conversation*, ii. The young Gentlewoman is his Sweetheart; . . . They say in our Country, that SHITTEN-CUM-SHITE IS THE BEGINNING OF LOVE.

*c.*1710. *Broadside Song*, 'The Lass with the Velvet Arse' [FARMER, *Merry Songs and Ballads* (1897), i. 214]. When E'er she went to SH—— If twas ne'er such a little bit . . . She always wiped it with brown Paper.

*c.*1714. SWIFT, *Miscell.*, 'On the Discovery of the Longitude.' Now Ditton and Whiston may both be be-pist on, And Whiston and Ditton may both be BE-SHIT on.

1719. DURFEY, *Pills to Purge*, iv. 112. SHITTEN COME SHITE THE BEGINNING OF LOVE is, And for her Favour I care not a Pin.

*c.*1731. *Windsor Medley*, 13. How the old Proverb lyes, that says, SH——N LUCK's good.

*b.*1749. ROBERTSON of Struan, *Poems.* To be strain'd in Marriage-Press Is honourable . . . I confess, But never when the Bed's BESHIT.

1772. BRIDGES, *Burlesque Homer*, 96. May I be trampl'd, pist, and SH—T on, If I don't think you're right.

1787. BURNS, *Death and Dr. Hornbook.* Just SHIT in a kail-blade and send't.

1826. BURTON, *Mugging Maid* [*Univ. Songst.*, iii. 103. Why lie ye in that ditch, so snug, With S—— and filth bewrayed.

1838. LUCIAN REDIVIVUS, *Paradise Lost*, 80. Fearing he had —— himself. *Ibid.*, 82. Don't make a bother, Wish in one hand, and —— in t'other, And which will fill the first, says I, You'll soon discover if you try.

SHIVAROO, *subs.* (Australian).—A spree : *see* quot.

1888. *Bulletin*, 6 Oct. Both these fair Toby Tosspots are well-known in the Upper Circles of the Beautiful Harbour, and are seen at Government House SHIVAROOS with the regularity of clockwork.

SHIVER, *subs.* (colloquial). — In *pl.* = the ague; chills.

See BEAT and TIMBERS.

SHIVERING JEMMY (or **JAMES**), *subs. phr.* (streets').—*See* quot.

1887. *Standard*, 20 June, 5, 2. The half-hearted beggars . . . are the 'Shallow Coves' and SHIVERING JEMMIES of London slang.

1900. FLYNT, TRAMPS, 240. One day he is a 'shallow cove' or a SHIVERING-JIMMY.

SHIVERY-SHAKY, *adv. phr.* (common). — Trembling; SHIVERY-SHAKES = chills.

1864. *Derby-day*, 54. He's all SHIVERY-SHAKY, as if he'd got the staggers, or the cold shivers.

SHO, *intj.* (American).—Pshaw!

1851. SEAWORTHY, *Bertie*, 36. 'True, as my name's James Ragsdale.' 'SHO!'

SHOARD. TO TAKE A SHOARD, *verb. phr.* (provincial).—To get tipsy : *see* SCREWED.

SHOAT (or **SHOTE**), *subs.* (American).—*See* quots.

18 [?]. HILL, *Stories* [BARTLETT]. Seth Slope was what we call Down East a poor SHOTE, his principal business being to pick up chips, feed the hogs, &c.

1856. DOW, *Sermons* [BARTLETT]. If you . . . make a proper use of your time, happiness, peace, and contentment are yours; if not, you will always be miserable SHOATS.

SHOCK, *subs.* (B. E., *c.*1696).—'A Brunt. To stand the SHOCK, to bear the brunt.' SHOCKING, what is offensive, grating, grievous, and espec. indecent.

SHOCKER, *subs.* (common).—Anything to surprise or startle. *See* SHILLING SHOCKER.

1898. GOULD, *Golden Ruin*, vii. 'This is a surprise . . . but I am heartily glad to see you' . . . 'Thought I should give you a SHOCKER.'

SHOCKING. *See* HAT.

SHOD. *See* SHOE.

SHODDY, *subs.* (colloquial). — 1. Old material—cloth, rags, &c.—ground up or shredded, and rewoven with a new warp. Hence (2) anything of poor quality or pretentious reputation : spec. (in derision) a workman in a woollen factory. Also as *adj.* = sham. Also derivatives such as SHODDYITE, SHODDYISE, &c.

1851-61. MAYHEW, *London Lab.*, ii. 34. The fabric thus snatched, as it were, from the ruins of cloth, is known as SHODDY.

1864. *Spectator*, 355. The mixture of good wool and rotten SHODDY we call broad-cloth.

1869. FROUDE, *Address at St. Andrews*, 12 Mar. We have false weights, false measures, cheating and SHODDY everywhere.

1871. LOWELL, *Study Windows*, 56. A horrible consciousness of SHODDY running through politics, manners, art, literature, nay, religion itself.

1872. *Ev. Standard*, 11 Dec. 'Ag. Lab. Movement.' There were things that Parliament could do. It could abolish the truck system, whether in SHODDY or in cider, and could provide that money should be paid in the coin of the realm.

1880. OUIDA, *Moths*, vii. In New York she and hers were deemed SHODDY—the very SHODDIEST of SHODDY—and were looked coldly on, and were left unvisited.

1881. D. M. WALLACE, *Russia*, 176. The Russian merchant's ostentation is . . . entirely different from English snobbery and American SHODDYISM . . . He never affects to be other than he really is.

1883. *Belfast Weekly Northern Whig*, 3 Feb. 1, 9. Cloaks lined with ostrich feathers are now in style, but the worst of this fashion is that if a woman leaves it unbuttoned, she is accounted a SHODDYITE, more anxious for vulgar display than comfort, while if she keeps it buttoned it might just as well be lined with red flannel for no one can see it.

1889. *Academy*, 11 May, 325. Philosophic SHODDY.

SHOE, *subs.* (old local).—A room in Southgate Debtors' Prison.

PHRASES, COLLOQUIALISMS, and PROVERBIAL SAYINGS—TO WIN ONE'S SHOES (old tournament) = to vanquish one's adversary; TO DIE IN ONE'S SHOES (or BOOTS) = to be hanged : *see* LADDER; TO SHOE THE WILD COLT = to be initiated, 'to exact FOOTING' (*q.v.*); also TO SHOE; TO SHOE ALL ROUND = to provide hat-band, gloves, and scarf at a funeral; many SHOEINGS being only partial (GROSE); TO MAKE CHILDREN'S SHOES = to look ridiculous; TO LICK ONE'S SHOES = to fawn on; to cringe; TO MAKE FEET FOR CHILDREN'S SHOES = to copulate : *see* GREENS AND RIDE; IN ANOTHER'S SHOES = in his place; TO PUT THE SHOE ON THE RIGHT FOOT = to lay blame (or praise) where justly due; TO TREAD ONE'S SHOE STRAIGHT = to do what is right and proper; TO TREAD ONE'S SHOE AWRY = (1) to play fast and loose; and spec. (2) to play the whore; TO SHOE THE GOOSE = to undertake anything absurd or futile : *cf.* 'He that will meddle with all things may go SHOE THE GOSLINS'; and (2) to get tipsy : TO SHOE THE COBBLER = to tap the ice quickly with the forefoot when sliding : *see* COBBLER'S-KNOCK; TO WAIT FOR DEAD MEN'S SHOES (*see* DEAD MEN'S SHOES); TO THROW AN OLD SHOE = 'to wish them Luck on their Business' (B. E.); 'THE SHOE PINCHES (of untoward circumstances or events); also 'No man knows where THE SHOE PINCHES but he who wears it' (B. E.); ANOTHER PAIR OF SHOES = something quite different : Fr. *une autre paire de manches*; OVER SHOES, OVER BOOTS = 'in for a sheep, in for a lamb'; 'ONE SHOE will not fit all feet' = 'People nor circumstances are not all alike'; 'He came in hosed and SHOD' = 'He was born to a good estate.'

[?] *MS. Lincoln.* A. I. 17 *f.* 149. How that thir Knyghtis have WONE THAIR SCHONE.

1383. CHAUCER, *Caste Tales*, 9426. I wot best, wher WRINGETH ME MY SHO.

*d.*1529. SKELTON, *Colyn Clout.* What hath lay men to do THE GRAY GOSE FOR TO SHO.

*c.*1530. *Parlament of Byrdes* [HAZLITT, *Early Pop. Poet.*, iii. 179]. Who wyll smatter what euery man doose, May go helpe TO SHOO THE GOOSE.

1546. HEYWOOD, 46, sign. C. [NARES]. Now for good lucke CAST AN OLD SHOE after me.

1573-9. HARVEY, *Letters* [Camden Soc. 83 [OLIPHANT, *New Eng.*, i. 591. Men know where THE SHOE PINCHETH; . . . substituted for Chaucer's *wringeth*].

1606. *Ret. from Parnassus* [NARES]. Linden may shortly THROW AN OLD SHOE after us.

1609. SHAKSPEARE, *Tempest*, iii. 2. How does thy honour. Let me LICK THY SHOE.

1611. COTGRAVE, *Dict.* [HALLIWELL]. A woman to play false, enter a man more than she ought, or TREAD HER SHOOE AWRY.

1613. FLETCHER, *Honest Man's Fort.*, v. 1. Captain. YOUR SHOES are old, pray put them off, And LET ONE FLING 'em after us.

1621. JONSON, *Masque of Gypsies.* Hard AFTER AN OLD SHOE, I'll be merry.

1630. TAYLOR, *Works*, ii. 145. For where true courage roots, The proverb says, ONCE OVER SHOES, O'ER BOOTS.

1633. MARMYON, *Fine Compan.* [NARES]. Well, mistresse . . . pray THROW AN OLD SHOE after us.

1653. URQUHART, *Rabelais*, IV., xlv. [BOHN]. Whoever refused to do this should presently swing for it and DIE IN HIS SHOES.

1663. STAPYLTON, *The Slighted Maid*, 30. I'll THROW MARC ANTONY'S OLD SHOE after you.

1663. KILLIGREW, *Parson's Wedding* [DODSLEY, *Old Plays* (REED), xi. 499]. Ay, with all my heart, there's AN OLD SHOE AFTER YOU.

1682. BEHN, *Roundheads* . . . *Hews.* "Who, pox! shall we stand MAKING CHILDREN'S SHOES all the year? No : let's begin to settle the nation, I say, and go through-stitch with our work."

1708-10. SWIFT, *Polite Conversation*, i. *Col.* . . . . Mr. *Buzzard* has married again! *Lady Smart.* This is his Fourth Wife; Then he has been SHOD ROUND.

*d.*1734. NORTH, *Life of Lord Guildford*, ii. 96. He used to say George (his son) would DIE IN HIS SHOES.

1742. BRANSTON [WALPOLE, *Lett. to Mann* (1833), I. 180]. At the end of the walk hung a rogue on a gibbet! He beheld it and wept, for it caus'd him to muse on Full many a Campbell, that DIED WITH HIS SHOES ON.

1809. MALKIN, *Gil Blas* [ROUTLEDGE], 146. I promised to place him IN MY LATE MISTRESS'S SHOES.

1840. BARHAM, *Ingold. Leg.* And there is Sir Carnaby Jenks, of the Blues, All come to see a man DIE IN HIS SHOES.

1842. TAYLOR, *Edwin the Fair*, iii. 8. Not alone them that were placed by Edred IN THE SHOES of seculars that by Edred were expulsed.

1861. DICKENS, *Great Expectations* . . . We'll show 'em ANOTHER PAIR OF SHOES than that, Pip, won't us?

1868. BREWER, *Phrase and Fable*, s.v. SHOEING THE WILD COLT. Exacting a fine called 'footing' from a new comer, who is called the 'colt.' Of course, the play is between the words 'shoeing' and 'footing.'

SHOE - BUCKLES. NOT WORTH SHOE-BUCKLES, *phr.* (old).—Of little account (RAY).

SHOE-HORN, *verb.* (old). — To cuckold.

*c.*1650. BRATHWAYTE, *Barnaby's Jl.* 1723), 45. Venus swore . . . She'd SHOOE-HORN her Vulcan's Forehead.

SHOEING-HORN, *subs. phr.* (old). —A pretext or incitement.

1562-3. STILL, *Gammer Gurton's Needle* [DODSLEY, *Old Plays* (REED). ii. 8]. Shall serve as a SHOING-HORNE, to draw on two pots of ale.

1592. NASHE, *Pierce Penilesse* [*Works*, ii. 81]. To haue some SHOOING HORNE to pull on your wine, as a rasher of the coles, or a redde herring, to stirre it about with a candles ende to make it taste better, and not to holde your peace whiles the pot is stirring.

*c.*1620. FLETCHER and MASSINGER, *False One*, iv. 2. They swear they'll flea us, and then dry our quarters, A rasher of a salt lover is such a SHOEING-HORN.

1621. BURTON, *Anat. Melan.*, 246. By little and little, by that SHOEING-HORN of idleness . . . melancholy . . . is drawn on.

16 [?]. *Haven of Health*, cxxxii. 134. Yet a gamond of bacon well dressed is a good SHOOING HORN to pull down a cup of wine.

*c.*1620. *Disc. of New World*, 68. Then, sir, comes me up a service of SHOOING-HORNES (do yee see) of all sorts; salt-cakes, red herrings, anchoves, and gammons of bacon—and aboundance of such pullers-on.

1712. *Spectator*, No. 536. Most of our fine young ladies . . . retain in their service, by some small encouragement, as great a number as they can of supernumerary and insignificant fellows, which they use like whifflers, and commonly call SHOEING-HORNS. These are never designed to know the length of the foot, but only, when a good offer comes, to whet and spin him up to the point.

1815. SCOTT, *Guy Mannering*, xxiv. This, and some other desultory conversation, served as a SHOEING-HORN to draw on another cup of ale.

SHOE-LEATHER! *intj.* (thieves').—A cry of warning; 'Look out!' Fr. '*Chou! chou!*' or '*Acresto!*'

SHOEMAKER. PHRASES, &c. 'Who goes worse shod than the SHOEMAKER'S WIFE' (B. E.) = an excuse for the lack of something one ought to possess; IN THE SHOEMAKER'S STOCKS = 'pincht with straight shoes' (B. E.); SHOE-MAKER'S PRIDE = creaking shoes; SHOE-MAKER'S HOLIDAY (*see* quot. 1793, and *cf.* CRISPIN'S HOLIDAY).

1793. *European Mag.*, 172. There was nothing which he [Oliver Goldsmith] enjoyed better than what he used facetiously to term a SHOEMAKER'S HOLIDAY. . . . Three or four of his intimate friends rendevoused at his chambers to breakfast about ten o'clock in the morning; at eleven they proceeded, by the City Road and through the fields, to Highbury Barn to dinner; about six o'clock in the evening they adjourned to White Conduit House to drink tea; and concluded the evening by supping at the Grecian or Temple Exchange coffee houses, or at the Globe in Fleet Street. . . . The whole expenses of this day's fête never exceeded a crown, and . . . oftener from three-and-sixpence to four shillings, for which the party obtained good air and exercise, good living, the example of simple manners, and good conversation.

SHOESMITH, *subs.* (colloquial).—A cobbler.

SHOESTRING, *subs.* (American).—A small bet run up to a large amount.

SHOFUL (SHOWFULL or SCHOFEL), *subs.* and *adj.* (common).—Generic for anybody or anything questionable. Spec. SHOFUL, *subs.* = (1) base money (also SHOFUL MONEY): whence SHOFUL-PITCHER = a dealer in counterfeit; SHOFUL-PITCHING = SHOVING THE QUEER (*q.v.*); SHOFUL-JEWELLERY = pinchbeck gauds. Also (2) = a hansom cab (*see* quot. 1851), and SHOVEL (*q.v.*).

1851-61. MAYHEW, *Lond. Lab.*, I. 26. SHOWFULLS, bad money. *Ibid.*, I. 279. A racketty place, sir [of a beer-shop], one of the SHOWFULLS; a dicky one; a free-and-easy. *Ibid.*, II. 554. I don't think those SHOFULS (Hansoms) should be allowed—the fact is, if the driver is not a tall man he can't see his horse's head. *Ibid.*, III. 363. The Hansom's, which are always called SHOWFULLS by the cabmen. SHOWFULL, in slang, means counterfeit, and the SHOWFULL cabs are an infringement on Hansom's patent. *Ibid.* (1856), *Gt. World of London*, 47. The SHOFUL-MEN, or those who plunder by counterfeits, as coiners and forgers of checks and notes, and wills.

1866. *London Miscellany*, 3 Mar., 57. That . . . is old Finlaison the fence. . . . He used to be a SHOFUL MAN once—dealt in bad money, you know.

1882. SMYTHE-PALMER, *Folk-Etymology*, s.v. SHOWFULL or SHOFUL. A cant term which originated amongst the Jews, and is the Heb. *Shafal* (or *shaphal*), low, base, vile, the word which David applied to himself when he danced before the ark.

1890. *Tit-Bits*, 15 Mar., 362. There wasn't a SHOFUL on the stand; so I works the oracle, and drives him off easy.

1891. CAREW, *Auto. of a Gipsy*, 417. Palmer got down and heaved the sackful o' SHOFUL into the river . . . and SHOFUL it were right enough hevery bloomin' hounce. *Ibid.*, 17. SHOFUL-PITCHING, fawney-rigging and the thousand and one ingenious devices whereby the impecunious endeavour to augment balances at their bankers.

1897. *D. Telegraph*, 14 Sept., 9, 3. There is plenty of room for improvement in the accommodation which 'growlers' and SHOFULS offer to the bicycle.

1899. POT and SWEARS, *Scarlet City*, 177. When I had despatched the telegram—I found Anthony ensconced in what he called a spicy SHOWFUL.

1901. BINSTEAD, *More Gal's Gossip*, 86. He stopped the shabby SHOFUL.

SHOG, *subs.* (old).—A jog: also as *verb.* = to be off.

1599. SHAKSPEARE, *Hen. V.*, ii. 3, 47. Shall we SHOG? The King will be gone from Southampton.

SHOLL, *verb.* (thieves').—To BONNET (*q.v.*); to crush the hat over the eyes.

SHOO! *intj.* (old).—Be off! Away! As *verb.* = to scare away. 'Cannot say SHOOH to a goose' (RAY) = a retort on timidity or bashfulness: *see* BOH.

1611. FLORIO, *Worlde of Wordes*, s.v. *Scioare*, to cry SHOOE, SHOOE, as women do to their hens.

1623. FLETCHER and ROWLEY, *Maid in the Mill*, v. 1. SHOUGH, SHOUGH: up to your coop, pea-hen.

1883. *Century Mag.*, xxxvii. 788. He gave her an ivory wand, and charged her, on her life, to tell him what she would do with it, and she sobbed out she would SHOO her mother's hens to roost with it.

SHOOK ON. *See* SHAKE.

SHOOL, *verb.* (old).—To loaf; to go on the tramp; to beg. Whence SHOOLING = idling; SHOOLMAN = a loafer or vagabond. Fr. *battre sa flême*.

1748. SMOLLETT, *Roderick Random*, xli. They went all hands to SHOOLING and begging.

*c.*1750. *Humours of the Fleet* [ASHTON, *Eighteenth Cent. Waifs*, 247]. Now mean, as once profuse, the stupid sot Sits by a Runner's side, and SHULES a Pot.

1842. LOVER, *Handy Andy*, xxxiv. 'Oh, you always make out a good rayson for coming; but we have nothing for you to-night.' 'Throth, you do me wrong,' said the beggar, 'if you think I came SHOOLING.'

SHOON, *subs.* (thieves').—A fool; a lout: *see* BUFFLE.

SHOOT, *subs.* (colloquial).—1. A shooting party.

1573. SIR T. MORE, *Cumfort against Tribulation*, fol. 33. We shall now meat for ye SHOOT.

1885. *Field*, 4 Ap. At a big SHOOT in Warwickshire.

1887. NORRIS, *Major and Minor*, xxv. At the great SHOOTS . . . he was wont to be present with a walking-stick in his hand.

2. (builders').—A vacant piece of ground: where rubbish is got rid of.

3. (American).—A fancy.

1847. ROBB, *Squatter Life.* That gal was the prettyest creatur I ever took a SHUTE after.

TO SHOOT A BISHOP, *verb. phr.* (venery).—To have a WET-DREAM (*q.v.*): also TO SHOOT.

THE SHOOT, *subs. phr.* (London).—The Walworth-road station on the S. E. & C. Ry. [A large number of workpeople alight there.]

PHRASES.—SHOOT as a generic verb of action is found in frequent combination: as TO SHOOT (JERK or WHIP) THE CAT = (1) to vomit; *see* CAT (GROSE), and (2) to sound a refrain in the infantry bugle call to defaulters' drill, which, it is fancied, follows the sound of the words 'SHOOT THE CAT—SHOOT THE CAT'; TO SHOOT THE CROW = to run off without paying, TO BILK (*q.v.*); TO SHOOT HORSES (*see* quot. 1872); TO SHOOT ONE'S LINEN = to jerk and display the cuffs; TO SHOOT ONE'S LINES = to declaim with vigour; TO SHOOT (BOLT or SHOVE) THE MOON = to remove furniture by night to prevent seizure for rent (GROSE): *see* MOON; TO SHOOT ONE'S BOLT = to exhaust one's credit or resources, to come to an end of things; TO GO THE WHOLE SHOOT = to risk all; TO SHOOT OFF ONE'S MOUTH (or JAW) = to abuse; TO SHOOT ONE'S ROE (or MILT) = to emit; TO DO A SHOOT UP THE STRAIGHT = to possess a woman; TO BE SHOT = (1) to make a disadvantageous bet which is instantly accepted (turf), and (2) to be photographed (photographers'): *see* SNAP-SHOT; TO SHOOT ON THE POST = to make a close win at the finish; TO SHOOT OVER THE PITCHER = to brag of one's shooting; TO SHOOT ONE'S STAR = to die; TO SHOOT THE SUN = to determine the longitude (nautical); TO SHOOT ONE'S GRANNY = to find a mare's nest; to be disappointed; TO SHOOT THE MARKET (Stock Exchange) =

'to make a man a close price in a stock without knowing if there would be a profit or loss on the bargain' (ATKIN, *House Scraps*); SHOOT THAT [HAT, MAN—anything]! = (1) a mild imprecation, 'Bother!'; SHOOT THAT! = an injunction to silence: *e.g.*, SHOOT THE SHOP; TO SHOOT IN THE EYE = to do an ill turn; TO BE SHOT IN THE NECK = to be drunk; TO SHOOT IN THE TAIL = (1) to copulate, and (2) to sodomise; TO SHOOT TWIXT WIND AND WATER = to pox or clap (B.E. and GROSE); and (2) to do the act of kind: also as *subs.*; 'I'LL (OR MAY I) BE SHOT IF ——' = a mild imprecation or strenuous denial. *See* also SHOT.

1695. CONGREVE, *Love for Love*, iii. 15, 'A Soldier and a Sailor' [DURFEY, *Pills* (1707), i. 227]. And then he let fly at her, A SHOT 'TWIXT WIND AND WATER, Which won this fair Maid's Heart.

1706. WARD, *Wooden World*, 45. 'The Surgeon.' His Captain, being disabled by some unlucky SHOT 'TWIXT WIND AND WATER, repairs to him for a Refitment.

1826. BUXTON, *Luke the Labourer*, iii. 1. *Bob.* He, he, he! I'LL BE SHOT IF Lunnun temptation be anything to this.

1837. LYTTON, *Ernest Maltravers*, I., xv. 'Excuse—' again began Maltravers, half interested, half annoyed. 'I'LL BE SHOT IF I do. Come.'

1853. DICKENS, Bleak House, vii. I'LL BE SHOT IF it ain't very curious.

1855. *Brooklyn Journal*, 18 Ap. The prisoners . . . had shot Under-Sheriff Hegeman in the head . . . Mr. Schumacher defended his client by observing that some of the attornies got as often SHOT IN THE NECK as the Under-Sheriff did in the head.

1867. BARTLETT, *Americanisms*, s.v. SHOT. A slang term of recent origin. To say, 'SHOOT THAT DRESS,' is meant to convey the idea that the dress is inferior; that it is not worth much; or, to use another slang expression, 'it is no great shakes' after all. *Ibid.* [Quotation from *Danbury News*.] *Mother.* Stand still, Tommy, or I won't get your hair combed in time for school. *Tommy* (superciliously). Oh, SHOOT THE SCHOOL. Ibid., *New York Herald.* One lady . . . with derisive scorn . . . observed in the language of the day, 'Oh, SHOOT THAT HAT!'

1870. *New Orleans Picayune*, 17 Mar. I found this man dead drunk in the gutter . . . he offered to fight me. saying that he was not drunk, but only SHOT IN THE NECK.

1872. *Echo*, 29 July, 'Railway Porters' Strike.' The prisoner urged the men to SHOOT THE HORSES in the vans . . . [*i.e.*] to take the horses out of the vans to prevent them from being unloaded. Prisoner was told if he had any grievances the SHOOTING OF THE HORSES was not the way to redress them.

1876. BURTON, *Songs* [BARTLETT]. The slang the gang is using now, You'll hear from every lip; It's SHOOT THE HAT! and get it boiled; And don't you lose your grip.

1878. YATES [*World*, 16 Jan.] Adjust your curls, YOUR LINEN SHOOT, your coat wide open fling.

1886. *Daily News*, 8 Oct. The boy who won never did anything in later life. He had SHOT HIS BOLT.

1887. FRANCIS, *Saddle and Mocassin.* If he could kill Indians SHOOTING OFF HIS MOUTH at them, he'd soon clean them out all there is.

1887. *Fun*, 8 June. 246. A canny Scot was recently sentenced to ten days' hard for SHOOTING THE CROW—*i.e.*, ordering half-a-quartern of whiskey, drinking it rapidly, and neglecting to pay.

1896. CRANE, *Maggie*, xi. Youse fellers er lookin' fer a scrap, an' it's like yeh'll fin' one if yeh keeps on SHOOTIN' OFF YER MOUT'S.

1897. *Pearson's Mag.*, Sep., 254. He thought he saw the means of getting square with the millionaire who had done him such an unscrupulous SHOT IN THE EYE.

1899. WHITEING, *John St.*, xxi. It it warn't ready, he give the shove to THE 'OLE SHOOT.

SHOOTABOUT, *subs.* (school: esp. Charterhouse).—An irregular form of football.

SHOOTER, *subs.* (colloquial).—Generic. Thus (1) = a revolver: also, according to capacity, a FIVE, SIX, or SEVEN-SHOOTER; (2) = the guard of a mail coach (old): he was armed with a blunderbuss; (3) = a shooting star; (4) = a shooting-stick (printers'); a piece of hard word or metal used with a mallet for tightening quoins in a chase; (5) = a ball (cricket) bowled full pitch but SHOOTING IN close to the ground; and (6) = a black morning coat (Harrow) as distinguished from the tail coat worn by the Fifth and Sixth Forms.

*d.*1633. G. HERBERT, *Artillery.* But I have also stars, and SHOOTERS too.

1840. THACKERAY, *Shabby Genteel Story.* He had a word for the hostler about that grey mare, a nod for the SHOOTER or guard.

1899. *Scarlet City*, 107. Miss Winks took the terrible SHOOTER with a trembling hand. 'You're sure it's not loaded?' she ejaculated.

SHOOTER'S-HILL, *subs. phr.* (venery).—The *mons veneris*: *see* VENUS. Hence, TO TAKE A TURN ON SHOOTER'S-HILL = to copulate: *see* GREENS and RIDE.

SHOOTING-IRON, *subs. phr.* (common).—A gun or revolver.

1847. PORTER, *Quarter Race*, 135. He said his old SHOOTING-IRON would go off at a good imitation of a bear's breathing!

1848. BURTON, *Waggeries*, 175. This antique SHOOTING-IRON had not been visible on board the boat.

1871. DE VERE, *Americanisms.* . . . His rifle . . . he loves with almost tender affection . . . and speaks of it as a SHOOTING-IRON. . . . The more recent revolver, now quite common in the West, is, on the other hand, his FIVE or SIX SHOOTER.

1888. *Harper's Mag.*, lxxvi. 78. Timothy . . . drew his SHOOTING-IRON . . . cocking it with a metallic click.

1888. BOLDREWOOD, *Robbery Under Arms*, xxx. Hev' ye nary SHOOTIN' IRON?

1894. *To-Day*, 21 Ap., 351, 1. Say, what's that for? you've emptied yure SHOOTING IRON into him; what's he done?

1897. MITFORD, *Romance Cape Frontier*, II. v. We'll just get out our SHOOTING-IRONS and go and see.

1902. KERNAHAN, *Scoundrels and Co.*, xxiii. Keep your SHOOTING IRONS, Mr. Hall . . . I've got a brace of my own in my pocket.

SHOOTING-STARS, *subs. phr.* (common).—Dizziness: as caused by a blow.

SHOP, *subs.* and *verb.* (colloquial).—1. Generic for a place: of residence, business, manufacture, engagement, or resort (in quot. 1590 = the body); and (2) one's profession, business or occupation. Spec. (old, and thieves') = (3) a prison (B. E. and GROSE): whence, as *verb.* = to imprison, to confine (B. E. and GROSE); 4. (army) = a guardroom: also *see* quot. 1890; and 5. (racing) a place: whence TO BE SHOPPED (or GET A SHOP) = to come in first, second, or third; and (6) to kill, TO BURKE (*q.v.*). Whence, TO TALK SHOP = to talk business in society: Fr. *parler boutique*; TO SINK THE SHOP = to refrain from SHOP-TALK; SHOPPY (or FULL OF THE SHOP) = wholly engrossed in business matters; THE OTHER SHOP = a rival (trader, establishment, &c.).

1548. PATTEN, *Exped. to Scotl.* [ARBER (*Eng. Garner*, iii. 86)]. They had likewise SHOPPED UP themselves in the highest of their house.

1563. FOXE, *Acts and Monuments* [CATTLEY] iv. 652 [OLIPHANT, *New Eng.* i. 541. Foxe wishes that More had kept himself in his own SHOP (profession); hence our 'TALK SHOP'].

1590. SPENSER, *Fairy Queen*, II. i. 43. Then [he] gan softly feel Her feeble pulse . . . he hoped faire To call backe life to her forsaken SHOP.

1610. SHAKESPEARE, *Coriol.*, i. 1, 137. I [the belly] am the storehouse and the SHOP Of the whole body.

*c.*1617. HOWELL, *Letters*, I. iii. 30. The Liver . . . the SHOP and source of the Blood.

1678. *Four for a Penny* [*Harl. Misc.* IV. 147]. A main part of his office [a bum-bailiff's] is to swear and bluster at their trembling prisoners, and cry, 'Confound us, why do we wait? Let us SHOP him!'

1821. EGAN, *Life in London*, II. iii. Public and other houses were explored without loss of time; and it was a poor SHOP indeed that did not produce some little amusement.

1838. DICKENS, *Oliver Twist*, xvi. It was Bartlemy time when I was SHOPPED . . . Arter I was locked up for the night, the row and din outside made the thundering old jail so silent, that I could almost have beat my brains out.

*c.*1840. A. CLOUGH, *Long Vacation Pastoral*. Three weeks hence we return to THE SHOP.

1847-8. THACKERAY, *Vanity Fair*, xxxiv. 'What is THE OTHER SHOP?' said the lady . . . 'Cambridge, not Oxford,' said the scholar. *Ibid.* (1855), *Newcomes*, xliv. Now, when will you two gents come up to my SHOP to 'ave a family dinner?'

1853. BRADLEY, *Verdant Green*, I. viii. Give us a song! It's the punishment for TALKING SHOP, you know.

1855. GASKELL, *North and South*, ii. I don't like SHOPPY people.

1860. *Punch*, xxxix. 177. He's staid and he's solemn, TALKS SHOP by the column.

1861. TROLLOPE, *Framley Parsonage* If we . . . have no voice of our own, I don't see what's the good of our going to THE SHOP [House of Commons] at all.

1861. G. P. MARSH, *Lect. on the Eng. Lang.*, xi. All men, except the veriest, narrowest pedants in their craft, avoid the language of the SHOP.

*d.*1864. JOSIAH QUINCY, *Figures of the Past*, 193. He SUNK THE SHOP; though this same SHOP would have been a subject most interesting.

1868. WHYTE-MELVILLE, *White Rose*, II. vii. Actors and actresses seem the only artists who are never ashamed of TALKING SHOP. *Ibid.* (1869), *M. or N.* If you was took and SHOPPED . . . I'd go to quod with you if they'd give me leave.

1888. BOLDREWOOD, *Robbery Under Arms*, xxiv. What sort of a SHOP is it? Are they getting much gold? *Ibid.*, vi. We'll all be SHOPPED if you run against the police like this.

1889. *Rialto*, 23 May. The latest term for the South African gold market is THE SHOP.

1890. *D. Chronicle*, 4 Apr., 7, 2. THE SHOP is the name given in the Royal Artillery and the Royal Engineers to the Establishment which turns out the bulk of the officers of those two distinguished corps.

1891. *Lic. Vict. Gaz.*, 3 Apr. Then he went a raker on the favourite for the St. Leger, but the brute was not even SHOPPED.

1892. *Cassell's Saty. Jl.*, 28 Sep., 27, 2. In the long summer months, when the actor is 'resting,' the artiste is frequently out of a SHOP, as he terms his engagement.

1897. MITFORD, *Romance of Cape Frontier*, II. iii. And one heard such a lot of war SHOP talked. *Ibid.*, II. xxiii. What was this cowardly, egotistical, SHOPPY preacher to him?

Verb. (workmen's).—To work in a shop; whence SHOPPED = (1) in work, also (2) discharged.

1867. *All Year Round*, 13 July, 56. There are many men who would regard themselves as ingrates, were they not to celebrate their being SHOPPED, after having been out of collar, by a spree.

PHRASES.—TO SHUT UP SHOP = (1) to come to an end, to retire; (2) to cease talking: (*cf.* SHOP = body, SHUT UP, *see* quot. 1570); and (3) to finish, to 'do for'; TO COME (or GO) TO THE WRONG SHOP = to make a mistake; ALL OVER THE SHOP = confused; awry.

*c.*1570. GASCOIGNE, *Works* [CHALMERS, ii. 571]. Beautie SHUT UP THY SHOP [i.e. mouth].

1630-40. *Court and Times Chas. I.*, II. 21. If it go on thus, the Commissioners may SHUT UP SHOP.

1657. MIDDLETON, *Women Beware Women*, ii. 2. I'll quite give o'er, and SHUT UP SHOP in cunning.

1836. DICKENS, *Sketches*, 289. And what does he want? . . . money? meat? drink? He's COME TO THE WRONG SHOP for that, if he does.

1884. *Pall Mall Gaz.*, 29 Oct. Our mercantile marine would SHUT UP SHOP.

1888. *Sp. Life*, 13 Dec. The left eye, which had till now gradually closed, SHUT UP SHOP altogether.

1893. MILLIKEN, *'Arry Ballads*, 63. Things seemed ALL OVER THE SHOP.

SHOPKEEPER, *subs.* (traders').—An article long in stock: sometimes OLD SHOPKEEPER.

SHOP-LIFT (-LIFTER, or -BOUNCER), *subs. phr.* (old).—'One that steals under Pretence of Cheap'ning' (B. E.: also HEAD, DYCHE, GROSE, and SNOWDEN): *cf.* LIFT. Hence SHOP-LIFTING and similar compounds.

1678. *Four for a Penny* [*Harl. Misc.* iv. 147]. He is the treasurer of the thieves' exchequer, the common fender of all balkers and SHOP-LIFTS in the town.

1703. WARD, *London Spy*, v. 108. The Light finger'd subtlety of SHOP-LIFTING.

1704. SWIFT, *Tale of a Tub*, Sect. VI. Like a discovered SHOP-LIFTER, left to the mercy of Exchange women.

1748. DYCHE, *Dictionary* (5th Ed.) s.v. LIFTER. Also one that goes into mercers or drapers shops under pretence of buying goods, and so conveys some away privately, is called a SHOP-LIFTER.

1759. STERNE, *Tristram Shandy*, I. xi. More honest, well-meaning people were bubbled out of their goods and money by it in one twelve-month than by pocket-picking and SHOP-LIFTING in seven.

1839. AINSWORTH, *Jack Sheppard*, II. viii. Sally Wells, who was afterwards lagged for SHOPLIFTING.

1855. THACKERAY, *Newcomes*, liii. There are children who are accomplished SHOP-LIFTERS and liars almost as soon as they can toddle and speak.

SHOPOCRACY, *subs.* (colloquial).—The world of shopkeepers: *cf.* MOBOCRACY, SHAMOCRACY, &c.

1853. MRS. GASKELL, *Ruth*, xxxiii. The belles of the SHOPOCRACY of Eccleston.

18[?]. *Notes and Queries* [*Ency. Dict.*]. SHOPOCRACY . . . belongs to an objectionable class of words, the use of which is very common at the present day.

SHOPPY, *adj.* and *adv.* (colloquial).—1. Commercial; (2) full of shops; and (3) *see* SHOP.

1851-61. MAYHEW, *Lond. Lab.*, I. 292. Thoroughfares which are well-frequented, but which . . . are not so SHOPPY as others.

1855. GASKELL, *North and South*, xi. You were always accusing people of being SHOPPY.

SHOP-SHIFT, *subs. phr.* (old).—A tradesman's trick (JONSON: 'There's a SHOP-SHIFT! plague on 'em!')

SHOP-'UN, *subs. phr.* (colloquial).—A 'boxed' or 'pickled' egg: as distinguished from 'new-laid.'

1878. BYRON, *Our Boys*, *Perkin Middlewick.* [*Looking at eggs*] . . . I knows 'em! SHOP-'UNS! Sixteen a shilling!

1893. MILLIKEN, *'Arry Ballads*, 62. About colds, and cock-salmons and SHOP 'UNS; it's one of the rummiest sights.

SHOREDITCH (THE DUKE OF).—A mock title: *see* quots.

*b.*1547. [ELLIS, *Hist. of Shoreditch*, 170]. When Henry VIII. became king he gave a prize at Windsor to those who should excel in this exercise [archery], when Barlo, one of his guards, an inhabitant of Shoreditch, acquired such honour as an archer that the king created him Duke of Shoreditch on the spot. This . . . title continued so late as 1683.

1603. *Poore Man's Peticion to the Kinge.* Good king, make not good Lord of Lincoln DUKE OF SHORDITCHE, for he is a . . .

SHOREDITCH-FURY, *subs. phr.* (obsolete).—A harlot: *see* TART.

1599. HALL, *Satires*, I. ix. 21. What if some SHOREDITCH FURY should incite some lust-stung lecher.

SHORES, *subs.* (Stock Exchange).—Lake Shore Ry. shares.

SHORT, *subs.* (gaming).—1. A card (all below the eight) prepared so that nothing above the eight can be cut: by which the chances of an honour turning up are reduced to two to one: *cf.* LONG and BRIEF.

1837. BARHAM, *Ingoldsby Legends* (1862), 253. Ye youths, oh, beware, Of liquor, and how you run after the fair! Shun playing at SHORTS.

2. (common).—In *pl.* = knee breeches; small clothes.

1837. DICKENS, *Pickwick*, xxxiii. A little emphatic man with a bald head and drab SHORTS.

1888. BESANT, *Fifty Years Ago*, 49. The little old gentleman . . . follows him in black SHORTS and white silk stockings.

3. (Stock Exchange).—A BEAR (*q.v.*); one who has 'sold short,' and whose interest is to depress the market. As *adj.* or *adv.* = (1) not in hand when contracting to deliver; or (2) unable to meet one's engagements: *e.g.*, 'SHORT of Eries, Brighton A's,' &c.

1888. *D. Telegraph*, 13 Oct. The market continued to improve . . . coupled with SHORTS covering freely.

1902. *D. Mail*, 17 Nov., 2, 5. Wheat opened steady . . . SHORTS covering, and light acceptances.

4. (school).—In *pl.* = flannel trousers; CUTS (*q.v.*).

Adj. (common).—1. Unadulterated; NEAT (*q.v.*). As *subs.* = 'a dram [spec. of gin] unlengthened by water' (GROSE).

1837. DICKENS, *Pickwick Papers* (1857), 388. If you'll order waiter to deliver him anything SHORT, he won't drink it off at once, won't he!—only try him!

1841. REDE, *Sixteen String Jack*, I. 2. Nelly, toddle to the bar, and be continually drawing drops of SHORT.

1851-61. MAYHEW, *London Lab.* i. 54. Saveloys, with a pint of beer or a glass of SHORT, is with them another common week-day dinner.

1858. *M. Chronicle*, 8 Nov. A young man offered her some coffee, but she said she would prefer something SHORT.

1858. TROLLOPE, *Dr. Thorne*, xvii. Come, Jack, let us have a drop of some'at SHORT.

1883. *D. Telegraph*, 2 July, v. 3. All these are SHORT drinks—that is to say, drams.

1902. HEADON HILL, *Caged*, xvii. She wanted him to have a drop of something SHORT, which he refused.

3. (commercial). — 'A term used by cashiers of banks, in asking how a cheque is to be paid, 'How will you take it?' *i.e.*, in gold or notes? If in notes, 'Long or SHORT?' *i.e.*, in notes for small or large amounts (HOTTEN).

4. (old).—Hard up; 'SHORT of cash.'

1603. DEKKER, *Batchelars Banquet*, iv. They . . . if their father keepe them SHORT, will find some other friends that shall affoord it them.

1605. CHAPMAN, &c. *Eastward Ho*, v. And I not able to relieve her, neither, being kept so SHORT by my husband.

1608. DAY, *Law Trickes*, ii. And if your pursse grow SHORT, Rather then spend the publique treasurie, Ile lend your grace a brace of thousand pounds.

1700. FARQUHAR, *Constant Couple*, ii. v. I am very SHORT . . . at present.

1857. BRADLEY, *Verdant Green*, II. v. I wrote to her and said, 'I'm very SHORT; please to send me two ponies;' meaning, of course, that I wanted fifty pound.

PHRASES and COLLOQUIALISMS.—TO COME SHORT HOME = to be imprisoned; TO BITE OFF SHORT (tailors') = to dismiss abruptly, or refuse curtly; TO CUT IT SHORT = to be as brief as may be; SHORT AND SWEET = a jesting regret, or sarcastic comment: frequently with the addi-

tion, LIKE A DONKEY'S GALLOP; THE SHORT AND LONG (or THE SHORT AND PLAIN) = (1) the whole truth: now usually THE LONG AND THE SHORT: also (2) a couple of persons, one of dwarf and one of giant stature walking together; SHORT AND THICK, LIKE A WELSHMAN'S PRICK = a person very short and broad in the beam; SHORT OF PUFF = winded; SHORT (or SHORT-WAISTED) = crusty, irritable; SHORT OF A SHEET = crazy; FOR SHORT = for brevity's sake; 'A SHORT horse is soon curried' = a simple matter is soon disposed of; SHORT COMMONS = not too much to eat; SHORT-LIMBERED = touchy; A SHORT SHRIFT AND A LONG ROPE = instant despatch; A SHORT MEMORY = forgetfulness.

. . . . *Int. of Four Elements* [HALLIWELL]. Yf ye will nedys know at SHORT AND LONGE, It is evyn a woman's tounge.

1383. CHAUCER, *Cant. Tales* [OLIPHANT, *New Eng.* i. 123. We have, this is THE SHORT AND PLAIN (LONG AND SHORT of it).]

1577. STANIHURST, *Desc. Ireland* [OLIPHANT, *New Eng.* i. 599. A man is said to be in talk, SHORT AND SWEET].

1592. SHAKSPEARE, *Mid. Night's Dream*, iv. 2. The SHORT AND THE LONG is, onr play is preferred. *Ibid.* (1596), *Merry Wives*, ii. 1. He loves your wife; there's THE SHORT AND THE LONG. *Ibid.* (1600), *As You Like It*, iii. 5. I will be bitter with him and passing SHORT.

1602. MIDDLETON, *Blurt, Master Constable*, i. 2. The rogue's made of pie-crust, he's so SHORT.

1611. JONSON, *Cataline*, ii. 1. How, pretty sullenness, So harsh and SHORT!

1611. *Letter* [NARES]. In which service two or three of them CAME SHORT HOME.

*c.*1617. HOWELL, *Letters*, I. ii. 15. The French and English Ambassadors, interceding for a Peace, had a SHORT Answer of Philip II.

1636. HEYWOOD, *Love's Mistress*, 63. The SHORT AND THE LONG of 't is, she's an ugly creature.

1809. MALKIN, *Gil Blas* [ROUTLEDGE], 219. Don Alphonso CUT HIM SHORT in his explanation.

1837. BARHAM, *Ingolds. Leg.*, 'Brothers of Birchington.'—Father Dick, So they called him FOR SHORT.

1870. *Washington Watchman* [DE VERE]. My little gal's name is Helen, but we call her Heelen FOR SHORT.

SHORT-EAR, *subs. phr.* (American University).—A rowdy: *see* LAMB.

SHORTER, *subs.* (old).—One who dwindles the surface and the edges of coins by clipping, filing, shaking together in a bag, precipitation, or other means; a SWEATER (*q.v.*).

SHORT-HEAD, *subs. phr.* (racing).—A horse that fails by a short head.

1883. GREENWOOD, *Odd People*, 107. Fancy him having that horribly anathematized SHORT HEAD all his own, to revile it, and punch it . . . all the while with a firm grip on the cruel twitch attached to its nose.

SHORTHEELS, *subs.* (old).—A wanton: *see* TART. Hence, SHORT-HEELED = unchaste (GROSE).

1596. CHAPMAN, *Blind Beggar* [SHEPHEARD, *Works* (1874) 15]. Well, madam SHORT-HEELS, I'll be even with you. *Ibid.* (1611), *May-day*, iv. 4. Take heed you slip not, coz, remember y'are SHORT-HEELED.

SHORT-LENGTH, *subs. phr.* (Scots').—A small glass of brandy; a 'wee three.'

1864. *Glasgow Citizen*, 19 Nov. Is not the exhilarating SHORT-LENGTH of brandy known beyond our own Queen Street?

SHORT-ONE, *subs. phr.* (old coaching: obsolete).—A passenger whose name was not on the waybill; a SHOULDERSTICK (*q.v.*); a BIT OF FISH (*q.v.*).

SHORT-POT, *subs. phr.* (B. E. *c.*1696).—'False, cheating Potts used at Ale-houses, and Brandy-shops.'

SHORT-STAFF. *See* GENTLEMAN.

SHORT-STICK, *subs. phr.* (drapers').—*See* quot.

1863. *Once a Week*, viii. 179. All goods again that are sold in the piece run short: SHORT-STICK in fact is a slang term for insufficient lengths.

SHOT, *subs.* (old: still colloquial).—1. A reckoning; a share of expense (B. E. and GROSE). Hence (2) = money (generic): as SHOT IN THE LOCKER = money in hand, or at will. Also SHOT-BAG = a purse; SHOT-FREE = nothing to pay: also SCOT-FREE; SHOT-CLOG = a simpleton, tolerated because he is willing to pay reckonings; SHOT-FLAGON = 'the hosts' pot, given where the guests have drank above a shilling's-worth of ale' (HALLIWELL): whence SHOT-POT = one entitled to the SHOT-FLAGON; SHOT-SHIP = a company sharing and sharing alike; SHOT-SHARK = a waiter.

1591. GREENE, *Notable Discovery* [*Works*, x. 47]. There he bestowed cheare and ipocras vpon them, drinking hard til the SHOT came to a noble.

1595. SHAKSPEARE, *Two Gentlemen*, iii. 5. I'll to the alehouse with you presently; where for one SHOT of five pence, thou shalt have five thousand welcomes.

1598. FLORIO, *Worlde of Wordes*, s.v. *Pagare lo scotto*, to paie the SHOT or reckoning.

1596. JONSON, *Ev. Man in His Humour*, v. 4. Where be then these SHOT-SHARKS? *Ibid.* (1601), *Poetaster*, i. 1. A gull, a rook, a SHOT-CLOG, to make suppers and be laughed at.

1604. DEKKER, *Honest Whore* [*Works* (1873), ii. 51]. A brace of gulles, dwelling here in the city, came in, and paid all the SHOT.

1605. CHAPMAN, JONSON, &c., *Eastward Hoe*, i. 1. Thou common SHOT-CLOG, dupe of all companies.

..... *Amende for Ladies*, 51. Drawer, take your plate. For the reckoning there's some of their cloaks: I will be no SHOT-CLOG to such.

1630. T. ADAMS, *Fatal Banket* [The Title of the fourth part runs——] 'The SHOT, or the wofull price which the wicked pay for the Feast of Vanitie.'

1715. CENTLIVRE, *Gotham Election*, iv. We give the treat, but they shall pay the SHOT.

1800. C. LAMB, *Letter* [to Coleridge, 6 Aug.]. I have the first volume, and truth to tell, six shillings is a broad SHOT.

1821. SCOTT, *Kenilworth*, xix. Are you to stand SHOT to all this good liquor.

1836. M. SCOTT, *Tom Cringle's Log*, ii. I have wherewithal in the locker to pay my SHOT.

1837. BARHAM, *Ingoldsby Legends* (1862), 74. He bolted away without paying his SHOT, And the Landlady after him hurried.

1847-8. THACKERAY, *Vanity Fair*, xxvi. My wife shall travel like a lady. As long as there's a SHOT IN THE LOCKER she shall want for nothing.

1848. DURIVAGE, *Stray Subjects*, 57. Depositing the 'tin' in his SHOT-BAG.

1851. SEAWORTHY, *Bertie*, 42. I'll al'ays do the fair thing, and stan' SHOT till we git to Edentown.

1863. GASKELL, *Sylvia's Lovers*, xxxiv. Bring him some victual, landlord. I'll stand SHOT.

1880. SIMS, *Three Brass Balls*, Pledge xv. It shall never want a friend while I've a SHOT IN THE LOCKER.

3. (old).—A corpse.

4. (colloquial).—A guess; also (5) = an attempt, a venture.

1844. KINGLAKE, *Eothen*, viii. 137. I secretly smiled at this last prophecy as a bad SHOT.

1854. WHYTE-MELVILLE, *General Bounce*, xiii. But here we are at Tattersall's; . . . so now for good information, long odds, a safe man, and a SHOT at the favourite!

1857. BRADLEY, *Verdant Green*, II. xi. Without hazarding his success by making bad SHOTS, he contented himself by answering those questions only on which he felt sure.

1861. HUGHES, *Tom Brown at Oxford*. Yes, you would have said so . . . if you had seen him trying to put Jack up behind. He made six SHOTS.

1879. L. B. MILFORD, *Cousins*, i. It turned out to be a bad SHOT.

1891. N. GOULD, *Double Event*, 104. 'Won't you take a SHOT about Caloola, Mr. Marston?'

1900. FLYNT, *Tramps*, 281. They had just returned from the hop-country, and their money was well poised for another SHOT at the growler.

Adv. (common).—Drunk: *see* SCREWED. Also SHOT IN THE NECK: *see* SHOOT.

Verb (horse-copers').—To fake a horse: a dose of small shot gives a temporary appearance of sound-windedness.

TO PAY THE SHOT, *verb. phr.* (venery).—To copulate: *see* GREENS and RIDE. Also *see* subs. I.

*c.*1630. *Broadside Ballad*, 'The Jovial Companions' [*Bagford Ball.* (Brit. Mus.) i. 88.] He laid her on her Back, and PAID her THE SHOT Without ever a stiver of mony.

1635. *Broadside Ballad*, 'The Industrious Smith' [*Rox. Ball.* (Brit. Mus.), i. 159]. Old debts must be paid, O why should they not, The fellow went home to PAY THE old SHOT.

Intj. (Royal High School, Edin.).—A cry of warning at the approach of a master.

PHRASES. LIKE A SHOT = quickly, at full drive; SHOT IN THE NECK = drunk: *see* SCREWED; SHOT IN THE TAIL (or GIBLETS) = got with child; NOT BY A LONG SHOT = hopelessly out of reckoning: whence A LONG SHOT = a bold attempt or large undertaking. Also *see* SHOOT.

1853. WH.-MELVILLE, *Digby Grand*, x. An extremely abrupt conclusion . . . empties every bumper of blackstrap LIKE A SHOT.

1886-96. MARSHALL, 'Pomes' [1897], 27. So Zippy went in for A LONG SHOT.

1893. MILLIKEN, *'Arry Ballads*, 21. Put us all square LIKE A SHOT.

1897. MITFORD, *Romance of Cape Frontier*, I. i. Back I went LIKE A SHOT.

SHOT-CLOG. *See* SHOT, *subs.* 1.

SHOT-SOUP, *subs. phr.* (nautical).—Bad pea-soup.

SHOTTEN-HERRING, *subs. phr.* (old).—A term of contempt: spec. a lean meagre fellow (GROSE). Hence, SHOTTEN-SOULED = despicable.

1598. SHAKSPEARE, *I. Hen. IV.* ii. 4. 142. If manhood, good manhood, be not forgot upon the face of the earth, then am I A SHOTTEN HERRING.

1614. FLETCHER, *Wit without Money*, iii. 4. Upbraid me with your benefits, you pilchers, You SHOTTEN-SOUL'D, slight fellows.

1639. *Optick Glasse of Humours*, 27. His conceit is as lanck as a SHOTTEN HERRING.

1640. NABBES, *Bride*, sig. G ii. Thou art a SHOTTEN HERRING. Jackalent Spanyard.

SHOULDER, *verb.* (old coaching).—*See* quot. Hence SHOULDER-STICK = a passenger not on the way-bill: *see* SHORT-ONE and *cf.* SWALLOW.

1828. JON. BEE, *Picture of London*, 33. SHOULDERING, among coachmen and guards, is that species of cheating their employers in which they take the fares and pocket them, generally of such passengers as they overtake on the road, or who come across the country to the main road, and are not put down in the way-bill.

1886. *Athenæum*, 16 Jan., 99, I. Some amusing anecdotes of what was known as SHOULDERING are here related. This generation requires to be informed that the expression meant in coaching days allowing more than the number the coach authorized to carry was to ride in or upon

it. Of course such a permission meant extra fees and payment to the coachman and guard, and was a direct fraud on the proprietors.

1888. TRISTRAM [*Eng. Ill. Mag.*, June, 623]. SHOULDERING in the tongue of coachmen and guards meant taking a fare not on the way-bill, and unknown to the proprietor.

A SLIP OF THE SHOULDER, *subs. phr.* (old).—Seduction.

See COLD SHOULDER, WHEEL.

SHOULDER-CLAPPER, *subs. phr.* (old).—A bailiff; 'a member of the hold-fast club' (B. E. and GROSE); SHOULDER-CLAPPED = arrested.

1593. SHAKSPEARE, *Com. of Errors*, iv. 2. A back-friend, a SHOULDER-CLAPPER, one that countermandes The passages of alleys, creeks, and narrow lands.

1604. DEKKER and WEBSTER, *Westward Hoe*, v. 3. What a profane varlet is this SHOULDER-CLAPPER to lie thus upon my wife.

1611. CHAPMAN, *May-day*, iv. 2. These . . . pewter-buttoned SHOULDER-CLAPPERS.

1839. AINSWORTH, *J. Sheppard* (1840), 22. 'The SHOULDER-CLAPPERS!' added a lady, who . . . substituted her husband's nether habiliments for her own petticoats.

1886. SALA [*Ill. L. News*, 19 June, 644]. I do know that a sheriff's officer used to be called a SHOULDER-CLAPPER.

SHOULDER-FEAST, *subs. phr.* (old).—A dinner given to bearers after a funeral (GROSE).

SHOULDER-HITTER, *subs. phr.* (American).—A bully; a rowdy: spec. a gambling tout.

1858. *New York Tribune*, 30 Sep. A band of SHOULDER-HITTERS and ballet-box stuffers.

1871. DE VERE, *Americanisms*, 319. In the West a striker is not only a SHOULDER-HITTER, as might be suspected, but a runner for gambling establishments, who must be as ready to strike down a complaining victim as to ensnare an unsuspecting stranger.

1874. *N. Y. Commercial Advertiser*, 9 Sept. So long as substantial citizens choose to leave politics to SHOULDER HITTERS, rum-sellers and bummers of every degree, so long will they be robbed at every turn.

1886. SALA [*Ill. L. News*, 19 June, 644]. A certain variety of the New York rough is a SHOULDER-HITTER.

SHOULDER-KNOT, *subs. phr.* (common).—A footman.

SHOULDER-OF-MUTTON FIST, *subs. phr.* (common).—A coarse, big, broad hand: in contempt.

1876. HINDLEY, *Cheap Jack*, 17. Sold again, and to a gentleman with a SHOULDER-OF-MUTTON FIST, that has never been washed since he had it.

SHOULDER-PEGGED, *adj.* (common).—Stiff-limbed.

SHOULDER-SHAM, *subs. phr.* (B.E. *c.*1696).—'A Partner to a File.'

SHOUT, *subs.* (formerly Australian: now general).—A turn in paying for a round of drinks. Hence as *verb.* = to stand treat; SHOUTING = a general invitation to drink; TO SHOUT ONESELF HOARSE = to get drunk. *See* CHARTER THE BAR.

1859. KINGSLEY, *Geoffrey Hamlyn*, xxxi. I SHOUTED for him, and he for me, and at last I says, 'Butty,' says I, 'who are those chaps round here on the lay?'

1873. BRADDON, *Bitter End*, xxxix. When the lucky digger was wont to SHOUT—that is to say, pay the shot—for the refreshment of his comrades.

1881. GRANT, *Bush Life*, I. 243. He must drink a nobbler with Tom, and be prepared to SHOUT for all hands at least once a day.

1889. *Star*, 3 Jan. Good-natured, hearty Welsh diggers thronged in, and were willing to SHOUT for us as long as we would drink.

1900. NISBET, *Sheep's Clothing*, 196. They SHOUTED drinks for all who were present.

SHOUTING. ALL OVER BUT SHOUTING, *phr.* (common).—Said of anything obviously finished.

1891. *Lic. Vict. Gaz.*, 20 Mar. At Barnes it was estimated that he had a lead of 150 yards, and at this point, reached in 19 min. 50 sec., it looked ALL OVER BUT SHOUTING.

SHOVE, *verb.* (venery).—To copulate: *see* GREENS and RIDE; as *subs.* = the act of kind. Also (of women) TO GET A SHOVE IN ONE'S BLIND- (or THE BULL'S-) EYE. SHOVE-STRAIGHT (or SHOVE-DEVIL) = the *penis*: *see* PRICK.

16[?]. *Old Ballad*, 'King Edward and Jane Shore' [DURFEY, *Pills* (1707) iii. 20]. Joan could make them groan that ardently did love her, But Jane Shore . . . King Edward he did SHOVE her.

1653. URQUHART, *Rabelais*, I. xi. His governesses . . . would very pleasantly pass their time in taking you know what between their fingers . . . One . . . would call it her roger . . . lusty live sausage, SHOVE-DEVIL, &c.

1707. WARD, *Hud. Rediv.* II. ii. 21. If Holy Sister, wanting Grace, By Chance supplies a Harlot's Place, And takes a kind refreshing SHOVE Upon the Bed of lawless Love.

PHRASES. TO SHOVE FOR (or TO BE ON THE SHOVE) = to move, to try for; TO SHOVE THE MOON = to remove secretly, by night: *see* MOON; TO SHOVE THE TUMBLER = 'to be whipped at the cart's tail' (B. E. and GROSE); A SHOVE IN THE MOUTH = a dram (GROSE); TO SHOVE THE QUEER = to pass bad money; A SHOVE IN THE EYE = a punch in the eye: generic; TO GIVE THE SHOVE = to send packing; TO GET THE SHOVE = to be dismissed: *see* BAG.

1708. HALL, *Memoirs*, 15. Those cast for Petit-larceny SHOVE THE TUMBLER.

1821. EGAN, *Life in London*, II. iii. I vish'd to be a little curl to Dirty Suke, . . . so I gov'd her a SHOVE IN THE MOUTH.

1830. LYTTON, *Paul Clifford* (1854), 9. 'Tom Zobyson is a good-for-naught,' returned the dame, and deserves TO SHOVE THE TUMBLER; but, oh, my child be not too venturesome in taking up the sticks for a blowen.

1884. CLEMENS, *Huck. Finn.*, xxxviii. So Jim he was sorry, and said he wouldn't behave so no more, and then me and Tom SHOVED FOR bed.

1893. MILLIKEN, *'Arry Ballads*, 50. There is always some fun afoot there, as will keep a chap fair ON THE SHOVE.

1899. WHITEING, *John St.*, IV. Mind your own bloomin' business, or I'll give yer a SHOVE IN THE EYE. *Ibid.* x. Did you get THE SHOVE to-day? *Ibid.* xxi. If it warn't ready, he GIVE THE SHOVE to the 'ole shoot.

SHOVE-HALFPENNY (also **SHOVE-** [or **SHOVEL-**] **BOARD, SHOVE-GROAT, SLIDE-GROAT, SLIDE-THRIFT**, or **PUSH-PENNY**), *subs. phr.*—A gambling game, played on a table on which transverse lines have been drawn rather more than the width of a halfpenny apart. The play consists in sending a halfpenny by a smart stroke of the palm from the end of the table so as to make it rest in the compartments formed by the lines. [Ed. VI. shillings, as being smooth and easily pushed, were much in vogue as counters.]

1528. STANIHURST, *Chron. of Ireland*. When the lieutenant and he for their desporte were plaieing at SLIDEGROTE or SHOOFLEBOARD.

1596. JONSON, *Ev. Man in His Humour*, iii. 2. Made it run as smooth off the tongue as a SHOVE-GROAT shilling.

1598. SHAKSPEARE, *2 Hen. IV.*, ii. 4, 206. Quoit him down, Bardolph, like a SHOVE-GROAT shilling.

1630. TAYLOR, *Travels of Twelvepence* [NARES]. With me [a shilling of Ed. VI.] the unthrifts every day, With my face downward, do at SHOVE-BOARD play.

1801. STRUTT, *Sports and Pastimes*, 16. The game of SHOVELBOARD, though now considered as exceedingly vulgar, and practised by the lower classes of the people, was formerly in great repute amongst the nobility and gentry; and few of their mansions were without a SHOVEL-BOARD.

1841. *Punch*, I. 232. The favourite game of SHOVE-HALFPENNY was kept up till a late hour, when the party broke up highly delighted.

1851-61. MAYHEW, *London Lab.*, i. 14. SHOVE-HALFPENNY is another game played by them [costermongers].

SHOVEL, *subs.* (common).—A hat, broad-brimmed, turned up at the sides, and scooped in front, as worn by deans and bishops of the Established Church: also SHOVEL-HAT. Whence SHOVEL-HATTED.

1833-4. CARLYLE, *Sartor Resartus*, iii. 6. Whereas the English Jonson only bowed to every clergyman, or man with a SHOVEL-HAT, I would bow to any man with any sort of hat, or with no hat whatever.

1845. THACKERAY, *Cornhill to Cairo*, ii. The mitred bishops, the bigwigged marshals, the SHOVEL-HATTED abbés which they have borne. *Ibid.* (1855), *Newcomes*, xxvi. She was a good woman of business, and managed the hat-shop for nine years ... My uncle, the Bishop, had his SHOVELS there.

1849. BRONTE, *Shirley*, xvi. Looming large in full canonicals, walking as became a beneficed priest, under the canopy of a SHOVEL HAT.

1853. LYTTON, *My Novel*, xi. 2. The profession of this gentleman's companion was unmistakeable—the SHOVEL-HAT, the clerical cut of the coat, the neckcloth, without collar.

1857. HUGHES, *Tom Brown's School-days*, i. 2. A queer old hat, something like a doctor of divinity's SHOVEL.

1864. ALFORD, *Queen's English*, 228. I once heard a venerable dignitary pointed out by a railway porter as 'an old party in a SHOVEL.'

1871. *Parodies*, lxxxi. 297. Now about the same time the people of England were at loggerheads with the SHOVEL-HATTED gentry that infest the upper house of St. Stephen's.

2. (common).—A hansom-cab: *see* SHOFUL.

3. (nautical). — An ignorant marine engineer.

18 [?]. *Engineer* [*Century*]. In the early days after the Crimea war, the engineers in the Navy were a rough lot. They were good men but without much education. They were technically known as SHOVELS.

PHRASES. PUT TO BED WITH A SHOVEL (or SPADE) = buried (GROSE); 'He was fed with a SHOVEL (or FIRE-SHOVEL) = a jeer at a large mouth' (GROSE); 'That's before you bought your SHOVEL' = 'You are too previous,' 'That's up against you,' 'That settles your hash.'

1859. MATSELL, *Vocabulum*, 'Hundren Stretches,' 3. WITH SHOVELS they were PUT TO BED A hundred stretches since.

SHOVER, *subs.* (thieves').—One who utters base money; a SMASHER (*q.v.*); a SOUR-PLANTER (*q.v.*): also SHOVER OF THE QUEER.

1871. *Figaro*, 20 Feb. He established a saloon in New York which became the headquarters of all the counterfeiters and SHOVERS OF THE QUEER in the country.

SHOVE-UP, *phr.* (old).—'Nothing' VAUX (1812).

SHOW, *subs.* (colloquial).—1. An entertainment; a spectacle (as the LORD MAYOR'S SHOW); (2) one's business: *cf.* SHOP; and (3) a piece of work. Also SHOW-BOX (theatrical) = a theatre.

1530. TYNDALE, *Works* [OLIPHANT, *New Eng.*, i. 427. He loves SHEW as a synonym for *appearance* and *spectacle*].

1588-93. TARLETON, *Jests* (1844), 71. [OLIPHANT, *New Eng.*, ii. 12. The noun SHEW ... means a pageant.

1592. SHAKSPEARE, *Mids. Night's Dream.* The actors are at hand and by their SHOW You shall know all that you are like to know.

1613. DRAYTON, *Poly-Olbion*, xv. By this, the wedding ends, and brake up all the SHOW.

1811. MOORE, *Tom Crib*, 27. One of Georgy's bright ogles was put On the bankruptcy list, with its shop-windows shut; While the other soon made quite as tag-rag a SHOW.

1886. BESANT, *Children of Gibeon*, I. vi. We ain't a SHOW. Lotty ain't a clown; I ain't a jumping-horse.

1888. HAGGARD, *Mr. Meeson's Will* [*Ill. Lon. News*, Summer No., 28, 3]. Mr. John Short ... asked him the same question, explaining that their presence was necessary to the SHOW.

1891. NEWMAN, *Scamping Tricks*, 65. I would have stopped the SHOW.

1892. KIPLING, *Barrack Room Ballads*, 'The Widow's Party.' What was the end of all the SHOW, Johnnie, Johnnie?

1899. WHITEING, *John St.*, xx. When the SHOW was shut, I ... sits down to my toke and pipe.

1900. *Free Lance*, 6 Oct., 20, 2. There goes Amy Lester ... Just closed with 'The Face in the Lamplight.' That's the third SHOW she's queered this season.

4. (colloquial).—A chance; a turn; an opportunity.

c.1537-50. *Robin Conscience* [HAZLITT, Early Pop. Poetry, iii. 239]. Bvt and I liue another yeer, I will haue a better SHOWE; I will not goe thvs slvttishly, I trowe.

1886. BESANT, *Children of Gibeon*, II. xiv. Many young men are ardently desirous of distinction or even notoriety; they will stoop to tomfool tricks if they cannot get a SHOW by any other way.

1887. *Our American Cousins*, 267. Do you think there's any—any—any SHOW for me?

1893. EMERSON, *Lippo*, xii. If I could only have got his SHOW three turns nightly at fifteen pounds a turn!

1896. LILLARD, *Poker Stories*, 147. They told the management to trot out his wicker demijohn and give the sagebrushers a SHOW.

1901. *Troddles and Us*, II. You stick yourself down in the only decent chair ... you don't give a fellow a SHOW.

3. (women's: conventional).—The first signs of periodicity or parturition.

PHRASES AND COLLOQUIALISMS.—TO SHOW AWAY (or OFF) = to give oneself airs: hence SHOWING OFF = making the most of oneself; TO SHOW A LEG (nautical) = (1) to turn out; and (2) *see* LEG; TO SHOW UP = (1) to make an appearance (also TO SHOW ONESELF), and (2) to expose: also as *subs.* in both senses; TO SHOW THE DOOR (or THE OUTSIDE OF THE DOOR) = to dismiss without ceremony; TO BOSS THE SHOW = to manage; TO SHOW ONE LONDON = (school) to hold one by the heels upside down; TO SEE LONDON = to hang by the heels: as from a rail, trapeze; TO GIVE THE SHOW AWAY = to blab; &c. Also *see* AGILITY; COLD SHOULDER; ELEPHANT; HEELS; LEG; TEETH; WATER; WHITE FEATHER.

1554. TYTLER, *Ed. VI.* [OLIPHANT *New Eng.* I. 538. Charles V. SHOWS HIMSELF at a feast].

.... T. HALL, *Genuine Letters*, II. 45. Never give yourself airs: never press to SHEW AWAY as they call it.

1809. MALKIN, *Gil. Blas.* [ROUTLEDGE], 12. I boarded her [a kitchen-maid] with so little circumspection that Don Rodrigo ... twitted me with my low taste; and ... SHOWED the goddess of my devotions THE OUTSIDE OF THE DOOR.

1811. HAWKINS, *Countess and Gertrude* [OLIPHANT, *New Eng.* ii. 204. Certain phrases are marked to show that they are new; as ... SHEW HIMSELF (at a party).]

1819. MOORE, *Tom Crib*, 26. ... Could old Nap himself, in his glory, have wish'd To SHOW UP a fat Gemman more handsomely DISH'D?

1830. JON. BEE, *Samuel Foote*, lxxix. How far he was justified in SHOWING UP his friend Macklin may admit of question.

1848. THACKERAY, *Snobs*, xi. Instead of SHOWING UP the parsons, are we indulging in maudlin praises of that monstrous black-coated race.

1870. HUXLEY, *Lay Sermons*, 30. It would be unprofitable to spend more time ... in SHEWING UP the knots in the ravelled skeins of our neighbours.

1883. BLACK, *Yolande*, i. Don't you think it prudent of me to SHOW UP as often as I can in the House ... so that my good friends in Slagpool mayn't begin to grumble about my being away so frequently?

1886. *Times*, 29 Mar. Certain persons in high stations of life would be SHOWN UP.

1891. STEVENSON, *Kidnapped*, 287. Both got upon their knees to her; and the upshot of the matter was that she SHOWED both of them THE DOOR.

1899. WHITEING, *John St.*, vi. She wants yer TO SHOW UP at a sort o' bun struggle in 'er room.

1899. DELANNOY, *£19,000*, XXX. I didn't want to GIVE THE SHOW AWAY.

1900. SAVAGE, *Brought to Bay*, i. I'm all right, if I SHOW UP at eleven. *Ibid.*, Looks as if he could SHOW UP well in ... Le Sport.

SHOWER, *subs.* (colloquial). — A shower-bath.

1889. *Answers*, 9 Feb. After lunch comes the heavy work of the day. The crew assemble at the boathouse, and after going through exercise in a pair-oared boat, they carry out the eight. Returning to dinner after the refreshing 'SHOWER,' they have a good, plain repast.

SHOWING. A FRONT SHOWING, *subs. phr.* (military).—Parade at short notice: *i.e.* without time to properly prepare accoutrements and kit.

SHOWMAN, *subs.* (theatrical).—*See* quot.

1885. G. DOLBY, *Dickens as I knew Him*, 125. The SHOWMEN, as the managers of the theatres and caterers for public amusements are popularly termed.

SHOW - SUNDAY, *subs. phr.* (various).—Among the commonalty = Easter Sunday, when if you don't wear something new, 'the rooks will shit on you'; at Oxford, the Sunday in Commemoration Week (a kind of University Parade took place in the Broad Walk of Christ's, but the invasion of Town has stopped it); amongst artists, &c., the Sunday before sending-in day, when the studios are open to visitors and friends.

SHREDS (or **SHREDS** and **PATCHES**), *subs.* (old).—A tailor: *see* SNIP (B. E. and GROSE).

SHRIEKING (or **WHINING**) **SISTERHOOD**, *subs. phr.* (journalistic).—The world of women reformers: hence, busybodies.

1809. MALKIN, *Gil Blas* [ROUTLEDGE], 208. Yesterday Ambrose stumbled upon one of our WHINING SISTERHOOD.

1893. MILLIKEN, *'Arry Ballads*, 20. This yere SHRIEKING SISTERHOOD lay ain't 'arf bad.

SHRIMP, *subs.* (old). — 1. A drawf; a pigmy: in contempt (GROSE).

1383. CHAUCER, *Monk's Tale*, Prol., 67. We borel men been SHRYMPES; of fielde trees ther comen wrecched ympes.

1582. STANYHURST, *Æneis* [ARBER], 89. A windbeaten hard SHRIMP, With lanck wan visadge, with rags iags patcherye clowted.

1623. SHAKSPEARE, 1 *Henry VI.*, II. 3, 23. It cannot be, this weake and writhled SHRIMPE Should strike such terror to his enemies.

1772. GARRICK, *Irish Widow*, i. 1. *Whit.* Why, your wife is five feet ten! *Kec.* Without her shoes. I hate your little SHRIMPS.

1786. BURNS, *Jolly Beggars.* Despise that SHRIMP, that wither'd imp.

1840. BARHAM, *Ingolds. Leg.* (Aunt Fanny). And all for a SHRIMP not as high as my hat—A little contemptible shaver like that!!

1888. *Referee*, 11 Nov. Other nippers—little SHRIMPS of boys.

2. (old).—A prostitute: *see* TART.

1638. WHITING, *Albino and Bellama*, 52. Vat tough me vil not lye vit pimpes, And pend me's coyne on light-teale SHRIMPES.

SHRUBBERY, *subs.* (venery).—The pubic hair: *see* BUSH.

SHUCK, *subs.* (American).—The lowest standard of value; spec. the paper currency of the Confederate States. [At the close of the Civil War these notes became as valueless as pea-SHUCKS]. Hence, LESS THAN SHUCK = less than nothing; TO CARE (or BE WORTH) NOT A SHUCK = to care (or be worth) little; SHUCKLESS = worthless; SHUCKS! = Nonsense: a contemptuous denial or refusal.

Verb. (American). — To undress; TO PEEL (*q.v.*).

1847. ROBB, *Squatter Life* [BARTLETT]. If them thar is all he's got to offer, he ain't worth SHUCKS; and, if you don't lick him you ain't worth SHUCKS either.

1847. DARLEY, *Drama in Pokerville*, 68. Mr. Bagly was there with five more barrels [revolver] to do the same for any gentleman who might say 'SHUCKS!'

1848. JONES, *Sketches of Travel*, 117. I SHUCKED out of my old clothes, and got into my new ones.

1850. LONGSTREET, *Southern Sketches*, 31. He'd get mad as all wrath ... and the first thing you know'd, he'd SHUCK OFF his coat to fight.

c.1852. *Traits of Amer. Humour*, 56. Arch he hopped down off'n his ole hoss, an' commenced SHUCKIN' hisself fur er fight.

1856. *Major Jones's Courtship*, 48. One great, big, yellow cow, what wasn't worth SHUCKS to trail.

1888. *Detroit Free Press*, 8 Dec. Did you ever see a family which amounted to SHUCKS which didn't keep a dog? *Ibid.*, 29 Dec. Might hev bin the biggest lawyer or doctor or preacher in these Yunited Staits if he hadn't bin so slashin' SHUCKLESS.

SHUFFLE, *verb.* (GROSE).—1. 'To make use of false pretences or unfair shifts.' SHUFFLING-FELLOW (B. E. and GROSE) = 'A slippery, shiteing Fellow.'

2. (Winchester).—To pretend; to feign: as TO SHUFFLE sleep. Hence SHUFFLER.

SHUM, *subs.* (American Circus).—In *pl.* = money: *see* RHINO.

SHUNTER, *subs.* (Stock Exchange).—*See* quot.

1871. ATKIN, *House Scraps*, ... SHUNTER ... one who buys or sells stocks on the chance of undoing his business, on one of the provincial Stock Exchanges, at a profit.

SHURK, *subs.* (old).—A sharper (B. E.).

SHUT. TO SHUT UP, *verb. phr.* (old: now vulgar). — To hold one's tongue; to compel silence; TO DRY UP (*q.v.*). Also SHUT YOUR NECK (MOUTH, HEAD, or FACE; SHUT-UP! or SHUT IT!): Fr. *ferme ta boîte*. Hence, TO BE SHUT UP = to be silenced, exhausted, or done for.

1563. FOXE, *Acts and Monuments* [CATTLEY], viii. 216. I have SHUT UP your lips with your own book.

c.1570. GASCOIGNE, *Poems* [CHALMERS, *Eng. Poets*, ii. 571]. Beautie SHUT UP THY SHOP [mouth].

1605. SHAKSPEARE, *Lear*, v. 3, 155. SHUT YOUR MOUTH, dame, Or with this paper shall I stop it?

1614. JONSON, *Bartholomew Fair*, v. 3. Hold thy peace, thy scurrility, SHUT UP THY MOUTH.

1856. STOWE, *Dred.*, I. 312. This is the Lord's ground here; so SHUT UP your swearing, and don't fight.

1857. DICKENS, *Little Dorrit*, i. 13. It SHUTS THEM UP! They haven't a word to answer.

1858. MURSELL, *Lecture on Slang.* When a man speaks, he spouts; when he holds his peace, he SHUTS UP.

1865. *Fun*, 29 July, 'English Undefiled.' I sigh, "Carina! how I suffer; Be thou my Juliet! Be my queen!" She only says, "SHUT UP, you duffer!"

1877. JOWETT, *Plato*, III. 6. A mere child in argument, and unable to foresee that the next "move" (to use a Platonic expression) will SHUT HIM UP.

1886-96. MARSHALL, *Pomes* [1897], 54. Oh, SHUT IT! Close your mouth until I tell you when.

1888. RUNCIMAN, *Chequers*, 80. SHET YOUR NECK.

1892. KIPLING, *Barrack Room Ballads*, 'The Young British Soldier.' You SHUT UP your rag-box, an' 'ark to my lay.

1895. POCOCK, *Rules of the Game*, I. "SHUT YOUR MOUTH," he said, "or I'll knife you!

1896. CRANE, *Maggie*, ix. 'SHET YER FACE, an' come home yeh old fool!' roared Jimmie.

1897. MAUGHAM, *Liza of Lambeth*, v. SHUT IT! she answered, cruelly. *Ibid.* xi. "SHUT UP!" said Jim. . . . "I shan't SHUT UP."

1901. *Troddles and Us*, 75. Murray's pleasantry struck us as being untimely, and we told him to SHUT UP.

2. *verb.* (racing).—*See* quot.

..... KRIK, *Guide to the Turf.* To SHUT UP . . . to give up, as one horse when challenged by another in a race.

TO BE SHUT OF, *verb. phr.* (once literary: now vulgar).—To be rid of, freed from, quit of. As *subs.* (HALLIWELL) = a riddance.

1596. NASHE, *Haue with You*, To the Reader. And doo what I can, I shall not be SHUT OF him.

1639. MASSINGER, *Unnatural Combat*, iii. 1. We are SHUT OF HIM, He will be seen no more here.

1639. SHIRLEY, *Maid's Revenge*, ii. 2. We'll bring him out of doors—Would we were SHUT OF HIM.

d. 1704. L'ESTRANGE [BARTLETT]. We must not pray in one breath to find a thief, and in the next to get SHUT OF him.

1847. *Chronicles of Pineville*, 34. Never mind, doctor, we'll GET SHUT OF him.

1848. MRS. GASKELL, *Mary Barton*, v. And as for a bad man, one's glad enough to GET SHUT ON him.

1888. BOLDREWOOD, *Robbery Under Arms*, ii. Father was one of those people that GETS SHUT OF a deal of trouble in this world by always sticking to one thing.

1891. STEVENSON, *Kidnapped*, 96. What we want is to be SHUT OF him.

1896. KIPLING, *The Big Drunk Draf'.* I never knew how I liked the gray garron till I was SHUT OF him an' Asia.

SHUTS, *subs.* (Christ's Hospital).—A hoax, a SELL (*q.v.*). As *intj.* = 'Sold again!'

SHUTTERS. TO PUT UP THE SHUTTERS, *verb. phr.* (pugilists').—1. To 'bung up' an opponent's eyes.

2. (common). — To announce oneself a bankrupt; to stop payment.

SHUTTER-RACKET, *subs. phr.* (old).—'The practice of robbing houses or shops, by boring a hole in the window shutters and taking out a pane of glass' (GROSE and VAUX).

SHUTTLE-BAG. TO SWALLOW THE SHUTTLE-BAG, *verb. phr.* (provincial).—To get husky.

SHUTTLE-HEAD (-BRAIN, OR -WIT), *subs. phr.* (old).—An eccentric; a scatterling. Whence SHUTTLE-HEADED, &c. = flighty, scatter-brained; SHUTTLENESS = rashness, thoughtlessness. Also SHITTLE-HEAD, &c.

c. 1440. *Paston Letters*, I. 69. I am aferd that Jon of Sparham is . . . SCHYTTL-WYTTED.

1564. UDALL, *Erasmus*, 341. Metellus was so SHUTTLE-BRAINED that even in the middes of his tribuneship he left his office in Rome.

1580. BARET, *Alvearie* [HALLIWELL]. The vain SHITTLENESSE of an unconstant head.

1590. GREENE, *Quip for Upstart Courtier* [Harl. *Misc.*, v. 417]. Upstart boies, and SHITTLE-WITTED fools.

d. 1601. NASH, *Tom Nash his Ghost* [Old Book Coll. Misc.]. I would wish these SHUTTLE-HEADS that desire to take in the embers of rebellion, to give over blowing the coals too much.

1625-49. *MS. Poem* [HALLIWELL: *temp.* Chas. I.]. Nor can you deem them SHUTTLE-HEADED fellows Who for the Lord are so exceeding zealous.

1639-61. *Rump Songs* (1662), I. 7. Is it not strange that in their SHUTTLE-HEAD three Kingdoms ruines should be buried?

d. 1894. STEVENSON, *Olalla.* I wondered what had called forth in a lad so SHUTTLE-WITTED this enduring sense of duty.

SHY, *subs.* (colloquial).—Generic for a piece of action: as a throw, a chance, an attempt, a jibe. As *verb.* = to do, to make, to throw, and all other verbs of action (GROSE and BEE).

1824. EGAN, *Boxiana*, iv. 149. I like to have a SHY for my money.

1827. SCOTT, *Diary*, 26 Mar. I cannot keep up with the world without SHYING a letter now and then.

1849-50. THACKERAY, *Pendennis*, lxxv. I went with my last ten florin and had a SHY at the roulette. *Ibid.* (1854-5), *Newcomes*, xvi. There you go, Polly, you're always having a SHY at Lady Anne . . . 'A SHY! how can you use such vulgar words.'

1847. ROBB, *Squatter Life* [BARTLETT]. Just to make matters lively, I . . . SHIED a few soft things at her.

1857. READE, *Never Too Late*, xv. He . . . SHIED the pieces of glass carefully over the wall.

1859. LEVER, *Davenport Dunn*, xx. Though the world does take liberties with the good-tempered fellows, it SHIES them many a stray favour.

1863-4. CHAMBERS, *Book of Days*, I. 238. Where the cock belonged to some one disposed to make it a matter of business, twopence was paid for three SHIES at it, the missile used being a broom-stick.

1885. *D. Telegraph*, 17 Sep. With a grievous 'clod' in his hand TO SHY at it.

1888. BLACK, *Far Lochaber*, vi. He has an abject fear of cats . . . and if he can SHY a stone at one when it doesn't see him, that is delight.

1889. NORRIS, *Miss Shafto*, viii. An honest man has a much better chance on the turf than he has in the City . . . I've had a SHY at both.

Adj., *adv.* and *verb.* (colloquial).—1. Missing, hard to find: whence SHYCOCK = 'one who keeps within doors for fear of bailiffs' (GROSE). Hence (2) = 'coy, squeamish, cold, or averse' (B. E. and GROSE). *Cf. verb.* Also (3) of dubious repute or character. As *verb.* (in quot. 1796 = a wary man); TO FIGHT SHY OF = to keep out of the way, to abstain.

1796. REYNOLDS, *Fortune's Fool*, v. The members rose, lock'd the door, and call'd me a SHYCOCK.

1809. MALKIN, *Gil Blas* [ROUTLEDGE], 311. We have all our weak side . . . does he wench? . . . Do not FIGHT SHY I beseech you. *Ibid* (1771), *Humph. Clinker* (1900), 78. The doctor being a SHY COCK would not be caught with chaff.

1821. HAGGART, *Life*, 30. Although I had not been idle during these three months, I found my blunt getting SHY.

1825. JONES, *True Bottom'd Boxer* [*Univ. Songst.* ii. 96]. You SHY-COCKS, he shows 'em no favour, 'od rot 'em all.

1826. *Old Song*, 'Bobby and His Mary' [*Univ. Songst.* iii. 108]. The blunt ran SHY, and Bobby brush'd, To get more rag not fearing.

1840. BARHAM, *Ingolds. Legends* (*Old Woman Clothed in Grey*). That all who espied her, Immediately SHIED her, And strove to get out of her way.

1841. LEVER, *Charles O'Malley*, lxxix. His friends SHY him.

1849. THACKERAY, *Pendennis*, xxv. Mr. Wagg . . . said, 'Rather a SHY place for a sucking county member, ay, Pynsent?' *Ibid.* (1860), Philip, xix. The dinner, I own, is SHY unless I come and dine with my friends; and then I make up for banyan days.

1851-61. MAYHEW, *London Lab.* iii. 136. They bring 'em out, when business is SHY, for a draw, which they always find them answer.

1854. WHYTE MELVILLE, *General Bounce*, xiii. If 'Sennacherib' breaks down, and Blanche Kettering fights SHY, . . . have I not still got something to fall back upon?

1860. DICKENS, *Uncommercial Traveller*, x. 60. Nothing in SHY neighbourhoods perplexes my mind more than the bad company birds keep.

1864. H. J. BYRON, *Paid in Full*, v. Hadn't SHY turf-transactions been more than hinted at.

1865. *Glasgow Herald*, 23 Sept. The guests SHY all European topics.

1870. *D. Telegraph*, 7 Feb. The reader who wades through the rather hopeful jungle of the title-page, will certainly SHY at Mr. Beste's preface.

SHYSTER, *subs.* (American).—1. *See* quot. 1859. 2. (common) = a swindler, duffer, or vagabond: a generic term (1903) of contempt.

1857. *New York Tribune*, 13 Mar. The SHYSTERS or Tombs lawyers . . . sought to intercede for their clients; but the magistrates would listen to no appeals.

1859. BARTLETT, *Americanism* (1896), 590, s.v. SHYSTER, a set of men who hang about the police courts of New York and other large cities, and practise in them as lawyers, but who in many cases have never been admitted to the bar. They are men who have served as policemen, turnkeys, sheriff's officers, or in any capacity by which they have become familiar with criminals and criminal courts.

1864. *D. Telegraph*, 26 July. SHYSTER who goes to bed in his boots.

1871. DE VERE, *Americanisms*, . . . This is the SHYSTER . . . Ill-reputed men [who] offer their services to the new-comer, compel him to pay a fee in advance, and then—do nothing. On the contrary, they fight SHY of him, and hence they have obtained their name.

1877. MARK, *Green Past.*, xli. They held aloof from ordinary society—looked on a prominent civic official as a mere SHYSTER—and would have nothing to do with a system of local government controlled by 30,000 bummers, loafers, and dead-beats.

1882. MCCABE, *New York*, xxv. 417-8. If the prisoner has no money, the SHYSTER will take his pay out in any kind of personal property that can be pawned or sold.

1902. BOOTHBY, *Uncle Joe's Legacy*, 98. The SHYSTER lawyer, the bigamist Henry Druford, and last but not least . . . the company promoter.

SICE, *subs.* (Old Cant).—Sixpence: *see* RHINO (B. E. and GROSE).

1672. *Covent Garden Drollery*, 'Greenwich Strowlers.' The prizes they took, were a Londoner's groat, A Gentleman's SICE, but his skipkennel's pot.

1688. SHADWELL, *Squire of Alsatia.* [In list of cant words.]

d. 1704. BROWN, *Works*, ii. 266. Some pretty nymphs . . . but are sometimes forced to tick half a SICE a-piece for their watering.

1707. WARD, *Hud. Rediv.*, II. iii. 27. For who'd not readily advance A SICE to see the Devil dance.

1840. LYTTON, *Paul Clifford*, iii. As Mrs. Lobkins expressed it, two bobs for the Latin, and a SICE for the vartue!

SICK, *adj.* (colloquial). — In its primary, extended, and old literary sense (as in the Bible and Shakspeare), SICK (= disabled by disease or bad health) now borders on the colloquial, having been superseded by "ill," whilst SICK is confined to vomiting or nausea. There are also exceptional usages. Thus SICK (= muddy) WINE; SICK (= stale) FISH; A SICK HAND (at cards, esp. whist = without trumps); A SICK (= pale) LOOK; A SICK (= ruffled) TEMPER, &c. Also, 'IT MAKES ME SICK (or GIVES ME THE SICK)' = 'I am disgusted with it'; SICK AS A HORSE (DOG, RAT, CAT, CUSHION, or what not) = sick as may be (GROSE); SICK OF THE IDLES (THE LOMBARD FEVER, OF THE IDLE CRICK AND THE BELLY WORK IN THE HEEL, RAY) = 'a pretence to be idle upon no apparent cause'; TO SPEAK IN THE SICK TUNE = to affect sickness; SICKLY (*adv.*) = untoward or disgusting; SICKREL

(B. E.) = 'a puny, sickly Creature.' Also (American) = lacking, in need of: as paint-SICK, nail-SICK: *cf.* HOME-SICK, MOTHER-SICK, SLEEP-SICK, &c. Likewise (venery) SITTING UP WITH A SICK FRIEND = an excuse for marital absence all night.

1600. SHAKSPEARE, *Much Ado*, iii. 4, 44. Why, how now? Do you speak in the SICK TUNE?

1626. SYLVESTER, *Du Bartas*, I. 7. Such a SLEEP-SICK Elf.

1693. CONGREVE, *Old Batchelor*, ii. 3. I swear you'd MAKE ONE SICK to hear you.

1708-10. SWIFT, *Polite Conv.*, i. Poor Miss, she's SICK AS A CUSHION, she wants nothing but stuffing.

1759. STERNE, *Tristram Shandy*, VII. ii. I am SICK AS A HORSE, quoth I, already.

1870. MEDBERY, *Men and Mysteries of Wall St.* [BARTLETT]. When brokers hesitate to buy there is said to be a SICK MARKET.

1888. *D. News*, 4 Dec. When the barrel came to his place from Burton it was in a very dull condition, and was what was known as SICK.

1889. RIALTO, 23 Mar. Even Kaffirs raised their SICKLY heads.

1867. *Harper's Weekly*, xxxiv. 554. My boats kinder giv' out. She ain't nothin' mor'n NAIL-SICK, though.

1893. E. S. SHEPPARD, *Counterparts*, Intro. The Shelley [a boat], she lays down at it, SICK OF PAINT.

1895. POCOCK, *Rules of the Game*, i. I've quit reading lest I should find myself in print. MAKES ME SICK.

1897. MAUGHAM, *Liza of Lambeth*, i. IT GIVES ME THE SICK.

1900. KIPLING, *Stalky and Co.*, 25. Keep your eye on King, and, if he gives us a chance, appeal to the Head. That always MAKES 'EM SICK.

1902. HEADON HILL, *Caged*, xxxiv. You MAKE ME SICK with your silly fears.

SICKENER, *subs.* (common).—Too much (even of a good thing); a cause of disgust. *Cf.* BELLYFUL.

1809. MALKIN, *Gil Blas* [ROUTLEDGE], 180. Enough to have given a SICKENER to the inveterate stomachs of a regiment.

1818. EGAN, *Boxiana*, I. 267. Ward's friends were now in high spirits, and the betting went forwards, as it was thought that Dan had received rather a SICKENER.

1827. PEAKE, *Comfortable Lodgings*, i. 2. I took a favourable opportunity to insult him: this morning I gave him a SICKENER.

1884. RUSSELL, *Jack's Courtship*, xxxii. But sometimes you will get a dreary SICKENER betwixt the Channel and the parallel where the steady breeze is picked up.

1889. STEVENSON, *Master of Ballantrae*, ii. It was plain this lucky shot had given them a SICKENER of their trade.

SIDE, *subs.* (common).—SWAGGER (*q.v.*); conceit: thus, TO PUT ON SIDE = to 'give oneself airs': Fr. *se hancher.*

1878. HATTON, *Cruel London*, VIII. ii. Cool, downy cove, who PUTS SIDE ON.

1880. PAYN, *Confid. Agent*, xi. The captain sauntered up the mews, with a good deal of SIDE ON, which became a positive swagger as he emerged into the more fashionable street.

1880. HAWLEY SMART, *Social Sinners*, xiii. He has proved a most apt pupil in the acquisition of what, in the slang of the day, is denominated SIDE, which, translated into dictionary language, meaneth the conceit of the young.

1886-96. MARSHALL, *Pomes* [1897], 10. I'd no notion he be coming it with such a lot of SIDE.

1895. IOTA, *Comedy in Spasms*, i. Rugby boy, lately back from a seven years residence in England,—the possessor of unimpaired health, abounding SIDE, but limited sentiment.

1901. *Sp. Times*, 27 April, 1, 4. Her belief that she moves in a 'classy' set, And the SIDE . . . all are due to being badly bred.

Intj. (North Country).—Yes!

See BLANKET; BEST SIDE; BLIND SIDE; JACK; MOUTH; PULL; RIGHT SIDE; SEAMY; SET; SHADY; SHINNY; SPLIT; WRONG SIDE.

SIDEBOARD, *subs.* (obsolete).—1. A shirt-collar of the 'stand-up' order. Also (2) in *pl.* = whiskers, SIDE-WINGS, GILLS (*q.v.*).

SIDE-POCKET, *subs. phr.* (American).—An out-of-the-way drinking saloon.

WANTED AS MUCH AS A DOG (or A TOAD) WANTS A SIDE-POCKET, *phr.* (old).—'A simile used for one who desires anything by no means necessary' (GROSE). *See* also WIFE.

SIDE-SIM, *subs. phr.* (old).—A fool: *see* BUFFLE.

1612. *Passenger of Benevenuto* [NARES]. Reach me that platter there, you SIDE SIMME. This fellow the higher hee is in stature the more foole he grows.

SIDE-SLIP, *subs. phr.* (common).—bastard; a BYE-BLOW (*q.v.*)

1872. ELIOT, *Middlemarch*, xl. The old man . . . left it to this SIDE-SLIP of a son that he kept in the dark.

SIDE-SPLITTER, *subs. phr.* (colloquial).—A funny story. Hence, SIDE-SPLITTING = 'screamingly' funny.

1893. MILLIKEN, *'Arry Ballads*, 36. SIDE SPLITTERS, spice, and the like.

SIDETRACK, *verb.* (American).—To SHUNT (*q.v.*); to avoid; to place on one side; to discontinue.

1889. *Det. Free Press*, 12 Jan. Then he said to Beverly, who had been SIDE-TRACKED: 'Now I'll be Tucker for a while, and you can be Tucker's brother.'

1892. GUNTER, *Miss Dividends*, vi. Call me Buck! SIDE-TRACK the 'Mr. Powers'!

SIDE-WINDER, *subs. phr.* (pugilistic).—A heavy blow with the fist: also SIDEWIPE.

1850. *Southern Sketches* [BARTLETT]. Arch would fetch him a SIDE-WIPE on the head, and knock him into the middle of next week.

SIDLEDYWRY, *adj.* (old).—Crooked (GROSE).

SIDNEY-BIRD. *See* SYDNEY SIDER.

SIEGE, *subs.* (old colloquial).—1. Excrement; fæcal matter; (2) a jakes; and (3) defecation: as *verb.* = to stool (B. E., 1696).

1548. BARCLAY, *Ecloques* [CUNNINGHAM]. For sure the lord's SIEGE and the rural man's Is of like savour.

1603. JONSON, *Sejanus*, i. 2. I do not ask you of their urines, Whose smell's most violet, or whose SIEGE is best, Or who makes hardest faces on her stool.

1609. SHAKSPEARE, *Tempest*, ii. 2. How cam'st thou to be in the SIEGE of this mooncalf? Can he vent Trinculos.

1646. BROWNE, *Vulgar Errors.* It accompanieth the unconvertible part in the SIEGE.

SIEVE, *subs.* (old).—A loose-spoken person; a BLAB (*q.v.*): *cf.* 'As well pour water into a SIEVE as tell him' (RAY).

*d.*1701. DRYDEN, *Mock Astrologer*, i. 1. Why then, as you are a waiting-woman, as you are the SIEVE of all your lady's secrets, tell it me.

SIFT, *verb.* (thieves').—To embezzle small coins: such as might pass through a sieve.

SIFTER, *subs.* (American).—A drink composed of whiskey, honey, strawberry-syrup, lemon, and ice.

SIGHT, *subs.* (colloquial). — 1. Generic for magnitude (that is, something worth looking at): thus a SIGHT of people = a multitude; a SIGHT of work = untiring industry or 'enough and to spare'; a SIGHT of money = a large amount (BEE). Hence, OUT OF SIGHT = unrivalled, beyond comparison; A SMART (PRETTY, PRECIOUS, POWERFUL, &c.) SIGHT = a great deal; A SIGHT FOR SORE EYES = something to please: also in sarcasm.

1393. GOWER, *Conf. Amantis* (PAULI, I. 121). A wonder SIGHT of flowers.

1440-50. *Plumpton Papers* [OLIHANT, *New Eng.*, i. 268. There are the nouns karving knyves; a SIGHT (number) OF PEOPLE . . .].

*c.*14 [?]. [MARSH, *Eng. Lang.*, I. viii. Juliana Berners, lady prioress of the nunnery of Sopwell in the fifteenth century, informs us that in her time 'a bomynable SYGHT of monkes' was elegant English for a large company of friars].

1534. TYNDALE, *Bible*, Heb. xii. 22. Ye are come vnto the Mounte Sion . . . and to an innumerable SIGHT of angels.

1540. PALSGRAVE, *Acolastus.* Where is so great a strength of money, Where is so huge a SYGHT of mony.

1848. CARLETON, *New Purchase*, II. 74. Yes, Mr. Speaker, I'd a powerful SIGHT sooner go into retiracy . . . nor consent to that bill.

1857. HUGHES, *Tom Brown's Schooldays*, II. vii. It's a precious SIGHT harder than I thought.

1877. *Five Years' Penal Servitude*, iii. This 'ere Dartmoor is a BLESSED SIGHT better than Chatham, I can tell you.

1888. *Owosso* (Mich.) *Press*, April. Doctor, I'm a dead man! . . . NOT BY A BLANKETY BLANK BLANK SIGHT.

1893. MILLIKEN, *'Arry Ballads*, 14. That beats any sermon a SIGHT.

1899. MARSH, *Crime and Criminal*, xxiii. He was A SIGHT FOR SORE EYES . . . I like to see a man that is a man.

2. (colloquial). — An opportunity; a chance; a SHOW (*q.v.*). TO GET WITHIN SIGHT = to near the end.

3. (colloquial).—An oddity; a scarecrow: also contemptuously, 'Her new jacket was a perfect SIGHT,' or 'You've made yourself a regular SIGHT' = 'Not fit to be seen.'

1694. PENN, *Rise . . . of Quakers*, ii. It was not very easy to our primitive friends to make themselves SIGHTS and spectacles, and the scorn and derision of the world.

4. (American).—As far as can be seen at one time, as the reach of a river, or a bend in a road: thus, in directing a person, 'Go three SIGHTS on, and take,' &c. Also A LOOK.

5. (common).—A gesture of derision: the thumb on the nose-tip and the fingers spread fan-wise: also QUEEN ANNE'S FAN. A DOUBLE SIGHT is made by joining the tip of the little finger (already in position) to the thumb of the other hand, the fingers being similarly extended. Emphasis is given by moving the fingers of both hands as if playing a piano. Similar actions are TAKING A GRINDER (*q.v.*) or WORKING THE COFFEE-MILL (*q.v.*); PULLING BACON (*q.v.*); MAKING A NOSE (or LONG NOSE); COCKING SNOOKS, &c.

1702. *Eng. Theophrastus*, 'Frontispiece.' [Truth stripping a fine lady of her false decorations, with one hand removes a painted mask, and with the other pulls away her "borrowed" hair and head-dress, showing an ugly face, and a head as round and smooth as a bullet. Below there are four little satyrs, one of whom is taking a single SIGHT, or making "a nose" at the lady; whilst a second is taking a DOUBLE SIGHT, or "long nose," towards the spectator.—*N. & Q.*, 5 S., iii. 298.]

1712. *Spectator*, 354. The 'prentice speaks his disrespect by an extended finger, and the porter by stealing out his tongue.

1837. BARHAM, *Ingoldsby Legends*, 'Nell Cook.' He put his thumb unto his nose and spread his fingers out.

1840. DICKENS, *Old Curiosity Shop*, xxxviii. Even Mr. Chuckster would sometimes condescend to give him a slight nod, or to honour him with that peculiar form of recognition which is called TAKING A SIGHT.

1871. *Morning Advertiser*, 11 Sept. The fame of mighty Nelson shall not with his compare, Who . . . thrusts his tongue into his cheek, and TAKES A SIGHT at Death.

1875. *Notes and Queries*, 5 S., iii. 298. TAKING A SIGHT.—Pictorial illustrations of this gesture prior to the time of the Georges, are, I believe, not very common.

1886. *Household Words*, 2 Oct. 453. [This] peculiar action has, I believe, almost invariably been described as TAKING A SIGHT. A solicitor, however, in a recent police case at Manchester, described it as pulling bacon.

TO PUT OUT OF SIGHT, *verb. phr.* (common).—To eat; to consume.

SIGN. Here may be arranged two or three obsolete colloquialisms—SIGN OF A HOUSE TO LET = a widow's weeds (GROSE); the SIGN OF THE FEATHERS = a woman's best good graces; at THE SIGN OF THE HORN = in cuckoldom; the SIGN OF THE PRANCER = the Nag's Head; the SIGN OF THE THREE BALLS = a pawnbroker's; SIGN OF THE FIVE (TEN or FIFTEEN) SHILLINGS = The Crown (The Two Crowns or The Three Crowns).—GROSE (1785); TO LIVE AT THE SIGN OF THE CATS' FOOT = to be hen-pecked.

1567. HARMAN, *Caveat* (1869), 85. A bene mort hereby at THE SIGN OF THE PRAUNCER.

SIGNBOARD, *subs.* (common). — The face: *see* DIAL.

SIGN-MANUAL, *subs. phr.* (old).—The mark of a blow.

1822. SCOTT, *Fortunes of Nigel*, xxiii. I bear some marks of the parson about me . . . The man of God bears my SIGN-MANUAL too, but the Duke made us friends again.

SIKES. *See* BILL SIKES.

SIL. *See* SILVER-BEGGAR.

SILENCE, *verb.* (old: now recognised). — To knock down; to stun; to kill (GROSE). Whence SILENCER = a knock-down or stunning blow.

SILENCE IN THE COURT, THE CAT IS PISSING, *phr.* (old).—'A gird upon anyone requiring silence unnecessarily' (GROSE).

SILENT-BEARD, *subs. phr.* (venery). —The female pubic hair: *see* FLEECE.

*d.*1704. BROWN, *Works*, ii. 202. It is not fit the SILENT BEARD should know how much it has been abus'd . . . for, if it did, it would . . . make it open its sluice to the drowning of the low countries in an inundation of salt-water.

SILENT-FLUTE. *See* FLUTE.

SILK, *subs.* (common).—1. A King's Counsel; also SILK-GOWN. [The canonical K.C.'s robe is of silk; that of a Junior Counsel of stuff.] Hence TO TAKE SILK = to attain the rank of King's (or Queen's) Counsel. 2. (clerical) = a bishop: the apron is of silk.

1838. JERROLD, *Men of Character* (John Applejohn), viii. The finest lawn [bishop] makes common cause with any linen bands—the SILKEN APRON shrinks not from poor prunella.

1853. DICKENS, *Bleak House*, i. Mr. Blowers, the eminent SILK-GOWN.

1872. *Standard*, 16 Aug., Second Leader. Mr. J. P. Benjamin (an American gentleman) has, in the professional phrase, RECEIVED SILK; in other words has been raised to the rank of Queen's Counsel at the English Bar.

1889. *Pall Mall Gaz.*, 6 Nov., 6, 1. Some time ago the presence of a learned SILK was required in court at eleven o'clock.

1890. *Globe*, 6 May, 6, 1. Mr. Reid's rise has been steady and sure. Called at the age of twenty-five, he TOOK SILK only eleven years later, and is now a Bencher of his Inn at the age of forty-four.

TO CARRY (or SPORT) SILK, *verb. phr.* (racing).—To run (or RIDE) in a race.

1884. HAWLEY SMART, *Post to Finish*, 219. One thing he was clear about—that there could be no hope of his passing unrecognised if he WORE SILK on the Town Moor.

1889. *Lic. Vict. Gaz.*, 18 Jan. The largest number we saw CARRY SILK during the two days.

SILK-PETTICOAT. *See* SILK-STOCKING.

SILK POST, *subs. phr.* (GROSE).—'Assumption of a gentleman commoner's gown. *Oxf. Univ. Cant.*'

SILK-PURSE. *See* SOW'S-EAR.

SILK-SNATCHER, *subs. phr.* (GROSE).—'Thieves who snatch hoods or bonnets from persons walking in the streets.'

SILK-STOCKING, *subs. phr.* (old).—A rich man or woman. [Silken hose were regarded as extravagant and luxurious.] Hence, THE SILK-STOCKING GENTRY (or ELEMENT) = the wealthy classes; and SILKEN = luxurious; YOUR SILKINESS! = Mr. Luxury. Also SILK-PETTICOAT = a woman of fashion (in quot. 1706 = a whore of price).

1596. SHAKSPEARE, *King John*, v. 1, 70. A cocker'd SILKEN wanton.

1601. JONSON, *Poetaster*, iii. 1. Sir, YOUR SILKINESS clearely mistakes Mæcenas and his house.

1706. WARD, *Wooden World*, 62, 'A Midship-Man.' He will have a Whore . . . tho' he pay for it . . . SILK-PETTICOATS are not to be had for the uptaking.

SILKWORM, *subs.* (old).—*See* quot.

1712. STEELE, *Spectator*, No. 1564. The fellow who drove her came to us, and discovered that he was ordered to come again in an hour, for that she was a SILKWORM. I was surprised with this phrase, but found it was a cant among the hackney fraternity for their best customers, women who ramble twice or thrice a week from shop to shop, to turn over all the goods in town without buying anything. The SILKWORMS are, it seems, indulged by the tradesmen; for though they never buy, they are ever talking of new silks, laces, and ribbons, and serve the owners, in getting them customers.

SILLY, *subs.* (colloquial).—A simpleton: also SILLY-BILLY (or WILLY), *see* quot. 1851, SILLYTON and SILLIKIN. Hence TO KNOCK ONE SILLY = to hit out of time, or to affect *au possible*: *e.g.*, 'She KNOCKED HIM SILLY' = 'She sent him off his chump (wits, onion) about her.'

*c.*1620-50. *Percy Folio MS.*, 199. I . . . proffered him a favour; he kist me, and wisht me to beare with his behauior; but hie tro lolly lolly, le SILLY WILLY cold not doe, all content with him was spent.

1725. BAILEY, *Erasmus*, 586. SILLYTON, forbear railing, and hear what's said to you.

1851-61. MAYHEW, *Lond. Lab.*, I. 144. SILLY BILLY is a kind of clown, or rather a clown's butt; but not after the style of Pantaloon, for the part is comparatively juvenile. SILLY BILLY is supposed to be a schoolboy, although not dressed in a charity-boy's attire. He is very popular with the audience at the fairs; indeed, they cannot do without him.

*c.*1876. *Music Hall Song*, 'Blessed Orphan.' They think I am a SILLIKIN, But I am rather knowing.

1869. SPURGEON, *John Ploughman's Talk*, 101. Poor SILLIES they have wind on the brain.

SILLY-SEASON, *subs. phr.* (journalists').—The parliamentary recess: in the absence of debates, with a real or assumed dearth of news, the newspapers are driven to print all kinds of political and social twaddles: *cf.* GIGANTIC GOOSEBERRY, SHOWER OF FROGS, LORD ROSEBERY'S LATEST.

1882. PAYN, *For Cash Only*, viii. Sir Peter's eyes grew big as gooseberries in THE SILLY SEASON, in his earnest intentness.

1883. G. A. S[ALA] [*Ill. London News*, 22 Sep., 275, 1]. THE SILLY SEASON, forsooth! Why September is a month when, perhaps, the daily newspapers are fuller of instructive and entertaining matter than is the case at any other season of the year.

1892. *Pall Mall Gaz.*, 16 Aug., 4, 2. Signs of the so-called SILLY SEASON, which has been somewhat delayed this year owing to the political crisis, are now beginning to appear.

SILVER, *subs.* (Stock Exchange).—In *pl.* = India Rubber, Gutta Percha, and Telegraph Co. shares. [The works are at Silvertown.]

See PENNY.

SILVER-BEGGAR (or **-LURKER**), *subs. phr.* (common).—A tramp with BRIEFS (*q.v.*) or FAKEMENTS (*q.v.*) concerning bogus losses by fire, shipwreck, accident, and the like; guaranteed by forged signatures or SHAMS (*q.v.*) of clergymen, magistrates, &c., the false subscription-books being known as DELICATES (*q.v.*). Also SIL =(1) a forged document, and (2) a note on 'The Bank of Elegance' or 'The Bank of Engraving.'

1859. SALA, *Gaslight and Daylight*, xiii. Did you never hear of cadgers, SILVER-BEGGARS, shallow-coves?

SILVER-COOPER, *subs. phr.* (Scots').—*See* quot.

1815. SCOTT, *Guy Mannering*, xxxiv. You rob and you murder, and you want me to rob and murder, and play the SILVER-COOPER, or kidnapper, as you call it, a dozen times over, and then, Hagel and Sturm! You speak to me of conscience!

SILVER-FORK, *subs. phr.* (Winchester: obsolete).—A wooden skewer: used as a chop-stick when forks were scarce (MANSFIELD, *c.*1840).

THE SILVER FORK SCHOOL, *subs. phr.* (obsolete literary).—A school of novelists which laid especial stress on the etiquette of the drawing room: as Theodore Hook, Lady Blessington, Mrs. Trollope, and Lord Lytton. [It is only within the last forty years that the old two-pronged steel fork has been ousted by cheap four-prongs in imitation of silver ware.]

SILVER-GRAYS, *subs. phr.* (American).—At a convention of New York State certain measures being unacceptable, 'many withdrew whose locks were silvered by age,' drawing forth the remark, 'There go THE SILVER GRAYS!' 'The term remains and is the only one now (1859) used to distinguish one branch of the Whig party' (BARTLETT).

SILVER-HELL, *subs. phr.* (common).—A low-class gambling den: where silver is the usual stake.

1843. MONCRIEFF, *Scamps of London*, i. 1. He's the principal partner in all the SILVER HELLS at the West End.

SILVER-HOOK. TO CATCH FISH WITH A SILVER-HOOK, *verb. phr.* (anglers').—To purchase a catch in order to conceal unskilful angling: It. *pescar col hamo d'argenta* (RAY).

SILVER-LACED, *adj. phr.* (old).—Lousy: *e.g.*, 'The cove's kicksies are SILVER-LACED' = 'The fellow's breeches are covered with lice' (GROSE).

SILVER-SPOON. BORN WITH A SILVER SPOON IN ONE'S MOUTH, *adj. phr.* (colloquial). — Born rich: It. *aver la pera monda* (=to have his pear ready pared, RAY).

1830. BUCKSTONE, *Wreck Ashore*, i. 2. *Mag.* A branch of the aristocracy, and to be one of that order means a man born to a good place; or, as we say in the vulgar tongue, WITH A SILVER SPOON IN HIS MOUTH.

SILVER STATE (THE), *subs. phr.* (American).—Nevada.

SIM, *subs.* (Cambridge University).—A Simeonite, or member of the Evangelical section of the Church of England; a Low Churchman. The modern equivalent is PIMAN. [The Rev. Charles Simeon (1759-1836) was 54 years Vicar of Holy Trinity, Cambridge]: GROSE (1785).

1826. W. W. TODD, *The Sizar's Table* [WHIBLEY, *Cap and Gown*, 109]. Some carnally given to women and wine, Some apostles of SIMEON all pure and divine.

1851. BRISTED, *Eng. Univ.*, 39. While passing for a terribly hard-reading man, and a SIM of the straightest kind with the 'empty bottles.'

SIMKIN. *See* SIMPKIN and SIMPLE.

'SIMMON, *See* PERSIMMON.

SIMON, *subs.* (Old Cant).—1. Sixpence: *see* RHINO (B. E.; HALL, 1714; GROSE).

1885. *Household Words*, 20 June, 155. The old joke . . . about St. Peter's banking transaction, when he "lodged with one Simon a tanner." And this reminds us that SIMON is also a slang term for sixpence, and may possibly owe its origin to this play upon the other word.

2. (circus).—A trained horse.

3. (King Edward's School, B'gham). — A cane: obsolete. [*See* Acts ix. 43.]

SIMON PURE, *subs. phr.* (old).—The genuine article: also as *adj.*

1717. CENTLIVRE, *Bold Stroke for a Wife. Dram. Pers.* SIMON PURE. [*See* Act v. 1.]

1785. WOLCOT [P. Pindar], *Lyric Odes*, x. [*Wks.* (Dublin, 1795), i. 90]. Flattery's a mountebank so spruce — gets riches; Truth, a plain SIMON PURE, a Quaker Preacher.

1815. SCOTT, *Guy Mannering*, lvi. A young seafaring man came forward.—"Here," proceeded the counsellor, "is the real SIMON PURE——"

1839. LEVER, *Harry Lorrequer*, xvii. Fearing every moment the arrival of the real SIMON PURE should cover me with shame and disgrace.

1871. *Spectator*, 2 Dec., 'George Cruikshank.' Nagler, the author of the Kunstlerlexicon, studying the controversy about the Cruikshanks, read that 'George Cruikshank was the true SIMON PURE' with the utmost gravity, therefore catalogued him as 'Pure (Simon),' calling himself George Cruikshank.

1879. HOWELLS, *Lady of the Aroostook*, xxv. I should like to see what you call the SIMON-PURE American.

1883. *Century*, xxxvii., 337. The home of the SIMON-PURE wild horse is on the southern plains.

SIMKPIN (or **SIMKIN**), *subs.* (Anglo-Indian). — 1. Champagne. [A native pronunciation.]

1885. J. W. PALMER, *New and Old*. A basket of SIMKIN . . . behind the chariot.

1886. SALA [*Ill. Lon. News*, 24 July, 90]. There is a good deal of SIMPKIN or champagne consumed in the three Presidencies.

2. (theatrical).—The fool in comic ballets.

See SIMPLE.

SIMPLE, *subs.* (old).—In *pl.* = folly (B. E.), hence, as in proverb, 'To go to Battersea to be cut for the SIMPLES'=to take means to cure of foolishness (Battersea was famous for its herb gardens.). Also SIMPLETON (SIMKIN or SIMPLE SIMON) = a credulous person (B. E. and GROSE): 'SIMPLE SIMON Suck-egg Sold his wife for an addled duck-egg' (RAY).

*c.*1710. SWIFT, *Polite Conversation*, i. Indeed, Mr. Neverout, you should be CUT FOR THE SIMPLES this morning.

1834. SOUTHEY, *Doctor*, cxxxvi. What evils might be averted . . . in the Lords and Commons by clearing away bile . . . and occasionally by CUTTING FOR THE SIMPLES.

1876. HINDLEY, *Cheap Jack*, 7. Many more are CUT FOR THE SIMPLES.

SIMPLE ARITHMETIC. *See* ARITHMETIC.

SIMPLE INFANTICIDE, *subs. phr.* (venery). Masturbation: *see* FRIG.

SIMPSON (or **SIMSON**), *subs.* (obsolete).—1. Water: spec. when used for diluting milk; hence, Mrs. SIMPSON (or SIMPSON'S cow)=the pump; 'the cow with the iron tail.' Whence (2) = poor milk: *see* SKY-BLUE and CHALKERS.

1860. HOLMES, *Professor at the Breakfast Table.* It is a common saying of a jockey that he is all horse, and I have often fancied that milkmen get a stiff upright carriage, and an angular movement, that reminds one of a pump and the working of a handle.

1871. *Daily News*, 17 Ap. He had, he stated on inquiry, a liquid called SIMPSON on his establishment.

1871. *Standard*, 11 May. Police Report. If they annoyed him again he would christen them with SIMPSON, which he did by throwing a can of milk over the police.

1872. *Times*, 24 Dec. Police Report. His master supplied wholesale dealers, who, he believed, watered it. That was called SIMPSON. *Ibid.* Witness generally milked the cows for himself, and then added SIMPSON at discretion.

1872. *Standard*, 25 Dec. SIMPSON is . . . universally accepted as the title for that combined product of the cow natural and the "cow with the iron tail."

1880. *Punch*, 31 Jan., 48. In the first rank of the Committee of Management of The Householders' Pure Milk Supply Assn. stands the name of our old friend SIMPSON—SIMPSON, who has so often milked the cow with the iron tail, that in the language of the milk walk he has become identified with the animal Simpson-Pump!

SIN, *subs.* (colloquial).—The Devil: as the incarnation of evil.

1858. PRATT, *Ten Nights in Barroom*, i. 1. I'll defy SIN to say that I ever neglected my work.

SINBAD, *subs.* (nautical).—An old sailor.

SINES, *subs.* (Winchester).—Bread: A SINES = a small loaf.

SINEWS OF WAR, *subs. phr.* (old). Money: generic: *see* RHINO.

*d.*1626. BACON, *Works* (SPEDDING), x. 324. The proverb . . . taken first from a speech of Mucianus, that MONEYS ARE THE SINEWS OF WAR.

1653. URQUHART, *Rabelais*, I. xlvi. Coin is THE SINEWS OF WAR.

SING, *verb.* (common).—To cry: usually as a threat to a crying child, 'I'll give you something to SING for.'

PHRASES.—TO SING OUT=(1) to raise the voice; (2) to cry, or call out, from excess of emotion; and (3), *see* quot. 1815; TO SING SMALL = to lessen one's pretensions, to eat humble pie (GROSE); TO SING (or PIPE) ANOTHER SONG (or TUNE) = to modify one's conduct, manner, &c; TO SING THE SAME SONG = to repeat the weakness; TO SING IT = to exaggerate, to swagger, 'to chant the poker'; TO SING OUT BEEF (thieves') = to call out 'stop thief!' (GROSE). Also proverb, 'He could have SUNG well before he broke his left shoulder with whistling.' *See* BLACK PSALM; PLACEBO; TE DEUM.

1383. CHAUCER, *Cant. Tales*, 'Friar's Tale.' Certes, lecchours, did he gretest wo; They sholde SINGEN if that they were bent.

1530. PALSGRAVE, *Lang. Franc.* SYNGE OUT, chanter a playne voyx.

1609. HEYWOOD, *If you know not me* [*Works*, I. 207]. *Const.* The Queene must hear you SING ANOTHER SONG . . . *Eliz.* My God doth know I can no note but truth.

1753. RICHARDSON, *Grandison*, I. 120. I must myself SING SMALL in her company.

1815. SCOTT, *Guy Mannering*, xxviii. "But old Meg's asleep now," said another; "she grows a driveller, and is afraid of her own shadow. She'll SING OUT* some of these odd-come-shortlies, if you don't look sharp." *Ibid.* [Note]. *To SING OUT, or whistle in the cage, is when a rogue, being apprehended, peaches against his comrades.

1819. MOORE, *Tom Crib*, 24. His spunkiest backers were forced TO SING SMALL.

1830. LEVER. *Harry Lorrequer*, xvi. When the call-boy would SING OUT for Captain Beaugarde . . . we'd find that he had levanted.

1836. SCOTT, *Tom Cringle's Log*, i. Who's there? SUNG OUT the lieutenant.

1837. BARHAM, *Ingolds. Leg.*, 'Row in an Omnibus Box.' So after all this terrible squall, Doldrum and Fal-de-ral-tit SING SMALL.

1848. RUXTON, *Far West*, 3. They made 'em SING OUT.

1884. RUSSELL, *Jack's Courtship*, xiii. 'Read the letter aloud, Sophie,' said my uncle. 'SING IT OUT, my love.'

1885. CLEMENT SCOTT [*Ill. Lon. News*, 3 Oct., 339, 1]. There would not be so much reason for complaint, if heroism and virtue were not made to SING SMALL, by the side of this apotheosis of iniquity.

1902. HEADON HILL, *Caged*, xvi. Go and have a wash and SING OUT for that breakfast.

SINGED-CAT, *subs. phr.* (American).—*See* quots.

1839. HALIBURTON, *Old Judge*, I. 44. That critter is like a SINGED CAT, better nor he seems.

1858. *New Orleans Bulletin*, May. Parson Brownlow has found an antagonist in the Rev. Mr. Pryne, of Cincinnati . . . We reckon there'll be fun, as a Cincinnati paper says Pryne is a perfect SINGED CAT!

1859. BARTLETT, *Americanisms*, s.v. SINGED-CAT. An epithet applied to a person whose appearance does him injustice.

1876. CLEMENS, *Tom Sawyer*, 20. You're a kind of SINGED CAT, as the saying is.

SINGLE-BROTH (or **-TIFF**) *subs. phr.* (old). — Small beer: *see* SCREWED.

*d.*1635. CORBET, *On Dawson, the Butler of Christ Church.* And as the conduits ran with claret at the coronation so let your channels flow with SINGLE TIFF.

1654. *Witts Recreations*, 154. Sack's but SINGLE BROTH; Ale's meat, drink, and cloth.

SINGLE-PEEPER, *subs. phr.* (old.)—A one-eyed person (GROSE).

SINGLE-PENNIF, *subs. phr.* (back slang).—A five-pound note: *see* FINNUP.

1891. CAREW, *Auto. of Gipsy*, 416. I gets clean off with the scawfer and 'bout 'er thirty quid in SINGLE PENNIFS and silver.

SINGLE-SOLDIER, *subs. phr.* (old).—A private.

1816. SCOTT, *Old Mortality*, viii. I'se e'en turn a SINGLE SODGER mysell, or may be a sergeaunt or a captain.

SINGLETON, *subs.* (B. E.).—1. 'A very silly, foolish Fellow.'

2. (old).—A corkscrew: from the name of a Dublin cutler famous for his tempering (GROSE).

3. (gaming).—A single card of any suit in a hand: whist. Also a hand containing such a card.

1885. *Field*, 12 Dec. Nor was it to prove that the lead of a SINGLETON was sometimes good play.

1885. PROCTOR, *How to Play Whist*, Pref. Outside . . . modern signalling . . . and the absolute rejection of the SINGLETON lead there is very little difference between the whist of to-day and the whist of Hoyle and Mathews.

SINGLE-WOMAN, *subs. phr.* (old). *See* quot. and TART.

1530. PALSGRAVE, *Lang. Francoyse*, SYNGLE-WOMAN, a harlot, *putayn*.

1657. HOWELL, *Londinopolis*, 337. No Stew-holder, or his wife, should let or stay any SINGLE WOMAN to go and come freely at all times. No SINGLE WOMAN to take money to lye with any man except she lie with him all night till the morrow.

SING-SONG (various).—1. (old) = a poem; 2. (common) = a convivial meeting at a public house at which each person is expected to contribute a song; A FREE-AND-EASY (*q.v.*); 3. (nautical) = a Chinese theatre; and 4. (colloquial) = 'crooning.' As *adj.* = musical.

1656-61. *Choyce Drolleries* [EBSWORTH] [OLIPHANT, *New Eng.* ii. 97. The new substantives are blobber-lips, a SING-SONG (poem)].

*d.*1704. BROWN, *Works*, iii. 39. From huffing Dryden to SING-SONG Durfey.

1857. RITCHIE, *Night Side of London*, 192. The gay have their theatres—the philanthropic their Exeter Hall—the wealthy their "ancient concerts"—the costermongers what they term their SING-SONG.

1869. GREENWOOD, *Seven Curses*, 19. She has her 'young man' and accompanies him of evenings to SING-SONGS and raffles.

1877. TENNYSON, *Queen Mary*, ii. 1. You sit SING-SONGING here.

1891. STEVENSON, *Kidnapped*, 197. I was amazed at the clipping tones and the odd SING-SONG in which he spoke.

1893. MILLIKEN, *'Arry Ballads*, 3. A sand-parlour'd shanty devoted to SING-SONG.

1896. KIPLING, *Only a Subaltern*. The illustrated programme of the SING-SONG, whereof he was not a little proud.

1899. WHITEING, *John St.*, x. There's a little bit of a kick-up to-night with a few of us—sort of SING-SONG.

SINK, *subs.* (colloquial).—1. A slum; a ROOKERY: also SINK-HOLE. Also (2) a centre of anything disreputable.

1565. CALFHILL, *Aus. Martialls Treatise of the Cross* (Parker Soc.), 176. [The Palace] a SINK of sectaries.

1613. PURCHAS, *Pilgrimage*, 621. The SINKE of Fez, where every one may be a Vintner and a Bawde.

*d.*1842. CHANNING, *Perfect Life*, 70. The SINKS of intemperance . . . shops reeking with vapours of intoxicating drink.

3. (common).—A confirmed tippler; and (4) the throat: *see* SEWER. Hence TO FALL DOWN THE SINK = to take to drink.

5. (The Leys School).—A heavy feed; a STODGE (*q.v.*); and (6) = a glutton.

PHRASES. — TO SINK THE NOBLEMAN (LOVER, &c.) = to suppress, to keep in the background: *cf.* SHOP; SINK ME! = a mild imprecation.

1772. BRIDGES, *Homer Burlesqued*, 13. But SINK ME if I . . . understand.

1809. MALKIN, *Gil Blas* [ROUTLEDGE], 100. I am the idol of my wife, and I have not SUNK THE LOVER in the husband. *Ibid.*, 283. I . . . SUNK THE SECRETARY . . . till I should ascertain what solid profit might accrue from all my bows and scrapes.

1822. SCOTT, *Nigel*, xvii. You shall SINK A NOBLEMAN in the Temple Gardens, and rise an Alsatian at Whitefriars.

SINKER, *subs.* (old).—1. In *pl.* = base money (SNOWDEN, 1857).

2. (American), *see* quot.

1900. FLYNT, *Tramps*, 129. When he returned with a "poke out" (food given at the door) and a SINKER (dollar).

SINNER, *subs.* (common). 1. A publican: *cf.* Luke xviii.; 2. (old), a harlot: *see* TART. OLD SINNER = a jesting reproach.

1601. JONSON, *Poetaster*, iii. 1. *Tuc.* I would fain come with my cockatrice . . . and see a play if I knew when there were a good bawdy one. *Hist.* We have as much ribaldry in our plays . . . as you would wish, Captain: all the SINNERS in the suburbs come and applaud.

1809. MALKIN, *Gil Blas* [ROUTLEDGE], 106. Seasoned exactly to the taste of these OLD SINNERS.

SIP, *subs.* and *verb.* (back slang).—PISS (*q.v.*).

SIPPER, *subs.* (common).—Gravy.

SI QUIS, *subs. phr.* (old).—1. A public notice of ordination. [These commenced "SI QUIS," "If any"]. Whence (2) a candidate for holy orders; and (3) any public announcement. As *verb.* = to make hue and cry.

1599. HALL, *Satires*, II. v. Saws't thou ever SIQUIS patch'd on Paul's Church door, To seek some vacant vicarage before.

1607. MARSTON, *What You Will*, iii. My end is to paste up a SI QUIS.

1609. DEKKER, *Gulls Horne-Booke*, chap. iv. The first time that you venture into Powles, passe through the body of the Church like a Porter, yet presume not to fetch so much as one whole turne in the middle Ile, no nor to cast an eye to SI QUIS doore (pasted and plaistered up with Seruing-mens supplications) before you haue paid tribute to the top of Powles steeple with a single penny.

1704. *Gentleman Instructed*, 312. He may . . . SI QUIS me in the next Gazette.

SIR (SIR JOHN or MASS-JOHN), *subs.* (old).—A parson; spec. (B. E.) 'a country Parson or Vicar': *see* SKY-PILOT (GROSE). *See* JOHN.

1380. WICLIFFE, *Works* [E. E. T. S.], 192. [OLIPHANT, *New English*, i. 147. The priest SIR JOHN, becomes SIR JACKE . . . this change is unusual.]

1426. *Sir Jon Audlay* [*Percy Soc.*: the title of a description of a priest].

*c.*14[?]. *Tale of the Basyn* [HAZLITT, *Early Pop. Poet.*, iii. 47]. Hit is a preest, men callis SIR JOHN. *Ibid.* 49. SIR JOHN con wake, And nedis water he must make.

*d.*1555. LATIMER, *Works* [*Century*]. They hire a SIR JOHN which hath better skill in playing at tables . . . than in God's word.

1560. BECON, *Works* [Parker Soc.] 270. Hold up, SIR JOHN, heave it [the Host] a little higher.

1591. SPENSER, *Mother Hubb. Tale*, v. 390. But this good SIR did follow the plaine word.

1596. LAMBARD, *Peramb.*, 317. A poore Chapell, served with a single SIR JOHN, and destitute both of font and churchyard.

1602. SHAKSPEARE, *Twelfth Night*, iv. 2. Make him believe you are SIR Thopas, the curate. Do it quickly.

*c.*1609. FLETCHER, *M. Thomas*, v. 2. Close by the nunnery, there you'll find a night-priest, Little SIR Hugh, and he can say his matrimony, Over without book.

1633. JONSON, *Tale of a Tub*, i. 1. Though SIR Hugh of Pancras, Be hither come to Totten.

1648. HERRICK, *Hesperides*, 'The Tythe.' If children you have ten, SIR JOHN won't for his tenth part ask you one.

1817. DRAKE, SHAKSPEARE, &c., i. 88. The language of our Universities . . . confers the designation of Dominus on those who have taken their first degree of Bachelor of Arts; the word Dominus was naturally translated SIR, and, as almost every clergyman had taken his first degree, it became customary to apply the term to the lower class of the hierarchy.

SIR GARNET, *subs. phr.* (street's).—All right, or as it should be. [An echo of the days when Sir Garnet (now Viscount) Wolseley was in the forefront of military matters.]

1886-96. MARSHALL, *Une Affaire d'Honneur* ['Pomes,' 110], And the start was all SIR GARNET, Jenny went for Emma's Barnet.

SIR HARRY, *subs. phr.* (old).—A jakes: *see* MRS. JONES. TO VISIT (or GO TO) SIR HARRY = to evacuate the bowels.

SIR HUGH'S BONES. *See* BONES.

SIR JACK SAUCE. *See* JACK SAUCE and SAUCE.

SIR JOHN BARLEYCORN. *See* BARLEYCORN.

SIR JOHN LACK-LATIN. *See* LACK-LATIN and add earlier quot. *infra.*

1535. SIR FRANCIS BYGOD, 'Against Impropriations.' [OLIPHANT, *New Eng.*, i. 481. Bygod talks of a SIR JOHN LACKE-LATIN.]

SIR MARTIN WAGSTAFFE, *subs. phr.* (venery).—The *penis*: *see* PRICK.—URQUHART.

SIR OLIVER. *See* OLIVER.

SIR PETRONEL FLASH. *See* PETRONEL.

SIRRAH! *intj.* (old).—An angry, contemptuous, or jesting address: also (modern) SIRREE! (or SIRREE, BOB!)

1526. RASTELL, *Hundred Merry Tales*, 74. [The Sir is lengthened into] SIRRA.

1570. LEVINS, *Manip. Vocab.*, i. 6. SERRHA, heus, io.

1600. JONSON, *Cynthia's Revels*, ii, 1. Page, boy, and SIRRAH: these are all my titles.

1608. SHAKSPEARE, *Antony and Cleopatra*, v. 2, 229. SIRRAH Iras, go!

1617. MINSHEU, *Guide to Tongues*. SIRRA, a contemptuous word, ironically compounded of *Sir* and *a*, *ha*, as much as to say *ah*, *sir*, or *sir boy*, &c.

1615. DANIEL, *Hymen's Triumph*, 313. Ah, SIRRAH, have I found you? are you heere.

1688. SHADWELL, *Sq. of Alsatia*, ii. Look on my finger, SIRRAH, look here; here's a famble.

*d.*1721. PRIOR, *Cupid and Ganymede*. Guess how the goddess greets her son: Come hither, SIRRAH; no begone.

1848. RUXTON, *Far West*, 3. No SIRRE-E; I went out when Spiers lost his animals.

1857. *Baltimore Sun*, 30 Mar. 'Sir, are you drunk?' The juror . . . in a bold, half-defiant tone replied, 'No, SIRREE, BOB!' 'Well . . . I fine you five dollars for the 'REE' and ten for the 'BOB.'

1900. *Brought to Bay*, ii. 'So the title is secure?' . . . 'Yes, SIR-EE!'

SIRRETCH, *subs.* (back slang).—A cherry.

SIR- (or SAVE-) REVERENCE, *subs. verb*, and *intj.* (old colloquial).—1. An apology: the commonest of expressions, for nearly six centuries, on mentioning anything likely to offend, or for which an excuse was thought necessary. Whence (2) = excrement, a TURD (*q.v.*); and as *verb.* = (1) TO SHIT (*q.v.*), and (2) to excuse oneself. [Lat. *salvâ reverentiâ*, whence SA' REVERENCE, SUR-REVERENCE, and SIR-REVERENCE.]

1356. MANDEVILLE, *Travels*, 185. But aftre my lytylle wytt, it semethe me, SAVYNGE HERE REVERENCE, that it is more.

1586. WARNER, *Alb. Eng.*, ii. 10. And all for love (SURREVERENCE love!) did make her chew the cudde.

1592. GREENE, *Blacke Bookes Messenger* [*Works*, xi. 33]. His head, and his necke, were all besmeared with the soft SIRREVERENCE, so as he stunke worse than a Jakes Farmer.

1593. SHAKSPEARE, *Comedy of Errors*, iii. 2. A very reverend body: ay, such a one as a man may not speak of, without he say, SIR-REVERENCE. *Ibid.* (1595), *Romeo and Juliet*, i. 4. We'el draw you from the mire Of this SIR-REVERENCE, love, wherein thou stickest Up to the ears.

1594. LYLY *Mother Bombie*, i. 2. SAVING A REVERENCE, that's a lie!

1596. HARRINGTON, *Metam. Ajax* [Letter prefixed to]. The third I cannot name wel without SAVE-REVERENCE, and yet it sounds not unlike the shooting place.

1605. JONSON, CHAPMAN, &c., *Eastward Hoe*, iv. 1. We shall as soon get a fart from a dead man . . . Sister, SIR-REVERENCE!

1607. *Puritan*, iii. 1. A man that would . . . go ungartered, unbuttoned, nay (SIR-REVERENCE!) untrussed, to morning prayer.

1614. JONSON, *Bartholomew Fair*, iv. 1. His wife, SIR REVERENCE, cannot get him make his water, or shift his shirt, without his warrant.

1626. FLETCHER, *Fair Maid of the Inn*, iii. 1. The . . . suitors that attend to usher Their loves, SIR-REVERENCE, to your daughter.

1630. TAYLOR, *Epig.*, 40. If to a foule discourse thou hast pretence, Before thy foule words name SIR-REVERENCE.

*d.*1650. FLETCHER, *Poems*, 10. A puppy licks Manneia's lipps, the sense I grant, a dog may kiss—— SIR-REVERENCE.

1655. MASSINGER, *Very Woman*, ii. 3. The beastliest man . . . (SIR-REVERENCE of the company!)—a rank whoremaster.

1665. HEAD, *English Rogue* (1874), I. iii. 30. Another time SIRREVERENCING in a paper, and running to the window with it.

1662. *Rump Songs*, ii. 47. First with a SIRREVERENCE ushers the Rump.

1703. WARD, *London Spy*, II. 38. A narrow Lane, as dark as a Burying Vault, which Stunk of stale Sprats . . . and SIRREVERENCE.

*d.*1704. BROWN, *Works*, ii. 180. Knocking a shiting porter down, when you were drunk, back in his own SIR-REVERENCE.

1714. *Memoirs of John Hall* (4 Ed.), 15. The Lower-Ward [of Newgate], where the tight-slovenly Dogs lye upon ragged Blankets, spread near SIR-REVERENCE.

1771. SMOLLETT, *Humph. Clinker* (1900), i. 66. Asked if he did not think such a . . . mixture would improve the whole mass, 'Yes . . . as a plate of marmalade would improve a pan of SIR-REVERENCE.

1785. GROSE, *Vulgar Tongue*, s.v. REVERENCE. An ancient custom which obliges any person easing himself near the highway . . . on the word REVERENCE being given him by a passenger to take off his hat with his teeth, and without moving . . . to throw it over his head, by which it frequently falls into the excrement . . . A person refusing to obey might be pushed backwards. *Ibid.*, s.v. TARTADDLIN TART.

1847. HALLIWELL, *Arch. and Prov. Words*, s.v. REVERENCE. A woman of Devon describing something not peculiarly delicate, apologised with "SAVING YOUR REVERENCE." This is not uncommon in the country.

SIR SAUCE. *See* JACK SAUCE and SAUCE.

SIR SYDNEY, *subs. phr.* (old).—A clasp knife (GROSE and VAUX).

SIR THOMAS GRESHAM. TO SUP WITH SIR THOMAS GRESHAM, *verb. phr.* (old).—To go hungry: *see* DUKE HUMPHREY.

1628. HAYMAN, *Quidlibet* [Epigram on a Loafer]. For often with duke Humphrey thou dost dine, And often with SIR THOMAS GRESHAM SUP.

See PERTHSHIRE GREYBREEKS.

SIR TIMOTHY, *subs. phr.* (B. E. and GROSE.—'One that Treats every Body, and Pays the Reckonings every where.'

SIR TRISTAM'S KNOT, *subs. phr.* (old).—The hangman's noose: *see* LADDER and HORSECOLLAR.

[?]. WILYAM BULLEIN. Light fellows merrily will call . . . neckweede, or SIR TRISTAM'S KNOT.

SIR WALTER SCOTT, *subs. phr.* (rhyming).—A pot of beer.

SISERARA (SARSARA, SISERARA, SASARARA, &C,, *subs.* (old).—1. A writ of removal from a lower to a higher Court. Hence (2) = a blow, a scolding, an outburst; WITH A SARSARA = with a vengeance, suddenly.

1607. TOURNEUR, *Revenger's Mag.* [DODSLEY, *Old Plays* [REED), iv. 379]. Pray . . . that their sins may be removed by a writ of error, and their souls fetched up to heaven with a SASARARA.

1607. *Puritan*, iii. 3. If it be lost or stole . . . a cunning kinsman of mine . . . would fetch it again with a SESARARA.

1758. STERNE, *Tristam Shandy*, vi. 47. I fell in love all at once with a SISSERARA.

1766. GOLDSMITH, *Vicar*, xxi. Gentle or simple, out she shall pack with a SUSSARARA.

1771. SMOLLETT, *Humphrey Clinker*, i. 80. I have gi'en the dirty slut a SISERARY.

*d.*1832. SCOTT [*Century*]. He attacked it with such a SISERARY of Latin as might have scared the devil himself.

SISTER, *subs.* (old).—A disguised whore: *see* TART.

1607. DEKKER, *Westward Ho*, ii. 2. The serving-man has his punk, the student his nun . . . the Puritan his SISTER.

See BROTHER SMUT.

SISTERHOOD, *subs.* (old).—Harlotry in general.

1821. EGAN, *Life in London*, II. i. She certainly must be considered a female . . . materially different from THE SISTERHOOD in general.

SIT, *subs.* (American printers').—Situation: *e.g.* OUT OF A SIT= out of a job.

PHRASES.—TO SIT ON ONE'S KNEES=to kneel; TO SIT UNDER = to attend the ministry of some particular divine; TO SIT A WOMAN = to keep the NIGHT-COURTSHIP (*q.v.*): *cf.* BUNDLE; TO SIT ON (or UPON)=(1) to take to task, to snub—in anger, contempt, or jest: also SAT-UPON, *adj.*=reprimanded, snubbed; and (2) to allow milk to brim in the pan; TO SIT EGGS = to outstay one's welcome; TO SIT IN = to adhere firmly; TO SIT UP = to pull oneself together; TO MAKE ONE SIT UP=to astonish, disconcert, or get an advantage. *See* also BODKIN, SKIRTS.

1474-85. *Paston Letters* [ARBER] 235. [OLIPHANT, *New Eng.*, I, 341. Our slang use of SIT UPON is foreshadowed . . . the King intends TO SITTE UPPON a criminal; that is, in judgment.]

[?]. *Battle of Babrinnes* [CHILD, *Ballads*, VII. 229. When they cam to the hill againe They SETT DOUNE ON THAIR KNEES.

1644. MILTON, *Of Education*. There would then also appear in pulpits other visages, other gestures, and stuff otherwise wrought than what we now SIT UNDER.

1754. *Connoisseur*, No. 27. The . . . audience that SITS UNDER our preachers.

1821. SCOTT, *Kenilworth*, xxxii. I protest, Rulland, that while he SAT ON HIS KNEES before me . . . I had much ado to forbear cutting him over the pate.

1830. SOUTHEY, *Bunyan*, 25. At this time he SAT (in puritanical language) UNDER the ministry of holy Mr. Gifford.

1852. *Notes and Queries*, I S., iv. 43. It is said a young man is SITTING A YOUNG WOMAN when he is wooing or courting her.

1855. THACKERAY, *Newcomes*, ii. Each to SIT UNDER his or her favourite minister.

1876. C. H. WALL, *tr. Moliere*, i. 411. The jester shall be SAT UPON in his turn; he shall have a rap over the knuckles, by Jove.

1880. A. TROLLOPE, *The Duke's Children*, xxvi. Experience had taught him that the less people demanded the more they were SAT UPON.

1883. JAMES PAYN, *Thicker than Water*, xxi. The only person to whom he had ever known Mary distinctly antagonistic . . . He had seen her SIT UPON him . . . rather heavily more than once.

1883. *Referee*, March 25, 2, 4. In the years gone by when I was good, and used to SIT UNDER Newman Hall at Surrey Chapel.

1888. G. GISSING, *A Life's Morning*, iii. He allowed himself to be SAT UPON gracefully; a snub well administered to him was sure of its full artistic, and did not fail in its moral effect.

1891. *Harry Fludyer*, 15. I forgot to open last term's bills. I found them yesterday all stowed away in a drawer, and they MADE ME SIT UP.

1893. *Chambers's Jour.*, 25 Feb., 128. With that SAT-UPON sort of man . . . you never know where he may break out.

1902. *Free Lance*, 6 Oct., 4, 2. The fashion papers of Paris make even America SIT UP.

SITH-NOM, *subs. phr.* (back slang).—A month.

SIT-ON-A-ROCK, *subs. phr.* (American).—Rye whiskey.

SIT-STILL-NEST, *subs. phr.* (provincial).—A cow-turd; QUAKER (*q.v.*); PANCAKE (*q.v.*).

SITTER, *subs.* (Harrow).—A sitting room; *cf.* BREKKER, FOOTER, SACCER, &c.

SITTING-BREECHES. TO WEAR ONE'S SITTING BREECHES, *verb. phr.* (old).—'To stay long in company' (GROSE): also TO SIT LONGER THAN A HEN: *cf.* TO SIT EGGS.

SITUATION, *subs.* (racing). — A place.

1882. "THORMANBY," *Famous Racing Men*, 105. The three worst horses, probably, that ever monopolized the Derby SITUATIONS.

SIT-UPONS, *subs. phr.* (common).—Trousers: *see* KICKS.

1850. SMEDLEY, *Frank Fairlegh*, 25. I put a piece of cobbler's wax on the seat of Mildman's chair, and ruined his best Sunday-going SIT-UPONS.

1857. CUTHBERT BEDE, *Verdant Green*, II. x. I should advise you, old fellow, to get your SIT-UPONS seated with wash-leather.

SIVVY, *subs.* (common).—Word of honour; asseveration: *e.g.*, "'PON MY SIVVY' = 'It's true, Honour bright!' *Cf.* DAVY.

1883. GREENWOOD, *Tag, Rag, and Co.* 'PON MY SIVVY, if you were to see her pecking, you'd think she was laying on pounds weight in a day instead of losing.

1884. *Daily Telegraph*, 2 Feb., 3, 1. "You'll 'scuse the cheek I gave you just now, mister," the scowling young gentleman remarked, "but, 'PON MY SIVVY, we took you for the police."

1892. WATSON, *Wops the Waif*, II. Now I'll be as quiet as a dummy; I will, 'PON MY SIVY!

SIX, *subs.* (old).—1. Beer sold at 6s. a barrel; small beer: *cf.* FOUR-HALF and (modern) SIX ALE.

1631. *Clitus's Whimsies*, 97. How this threede-bare philosopher shrugges, shiffs, and shuffles for a cuppe of SIX.

1633. ROWLEY, *Match at Midnight*, i. I. Look if he be not drunk! The very sight of him makes one long for a cup of SIX.

2. (Oxford Univ.).—A privy.

AT SIXES AND SEVENS, *phr.* (old).—In confusion; at loggerheads (GROSE): also TO SET ON SEVEN = to confuse, to disarray.

*c.*1340. *Avowyne of King Arther*, 64 [Camden Soc., *Eng. Meln. Rom.*, 89]. Alle in sundur hit [a tun] brast IN SIX OR IN SEUYN.

1369. CHAUCER, *Troilus*, iv. 622. Lat not this wreched wo thyne herte gnawe, But manly, SET THE WORLDE ON SIX AND SEVENE.

[?]. *Morte Arthure* [E. E. T. S.], 2131. Thus he SETTEZ ON SEVENE with his sekyre knyghttes . . . And thus at the joyenyge the geauntez are dystroyede.

1596. NASHE, *Saffron Walden* [*Works*, iii. 38]. Caring for all other things else, sets his owne estate AT SIXE AND SEAUEN.

1597. SHAKSPEARE, *Richard II.*, ii. 2. All is uneven, And everything is left AT SIX AND SEVEN.

1598. FLORIO, *Worlde of Wordes*, s.v. *Asbaraglio* . . . at SIXE AND SEAUEN, in vaine.

1678. COTTON, *Virgil Travestie* [*Works* (1725) 73]. But, like a Dame of Wits bereaven, Let all Things go AT SIX AND SEVEN.

*d.*1704. BROWN, *Works*, i. 68. May thy Affairs . . . All the World o'er AT SIXES lie AND SEVENS.

1768. GOLDSMITH, *Good Natured Man*, i. Haven't I reason to be out of my senses, when I see things going AT SIXES AND SEVENS?

1772. BRIDGES, *Burlesque Homer*, 481. Whilst things went on AT SIX AND SEVEN, Jove smok'd a serious pipe in heaven.

1781. *Gentleman's Mag.*, li. 367. AT SIXES AND SEVENS, as the old woman left her house.

1790. D'ARBLEY, *Diary* (1876), iii. 240. All my workmen in the country are AT SIXES AND SEVENS, and in want of my directions.

1809. MALKIN, *Gil Blas* [ROUTLEDGE], 432. The affairs of the treasurer . . . are all AT SIXES AND SEVENS.

1816. SCOTT, *Antiquary*, xxii. All goes TO SIXES AND SEVENS—an universal saturnalia seems to be proclaimed in my peaceful and orderly family.

SIX OF ONE AND HALF A DOZEN OF THE OTHER, *phr.* (common).—Much alike; not a pin to choose between them; 'never a barrel the better herring.'

SIX-AND-EIGHTPENCE, *subs. phr.* (old). — 1. A solicitor: *see* GREEN-BAG (GROSE).

1756. FOOTE, *Englishman Ret. from Paris.* [An attorney is hailed as] Good SIX-AND-EIGHTPENCE.

2. (old).—*See* quot.

*c.*1696. B. E., *Cant. Crew*, s.v. SIX AND EIGHT-PENCE, the usual Fee given, to carry back the Body of the Executed Malefactor, to give it Christian Burial.

SIX-AND-TIPS, *subs. phr.* (Irish).—Whiskey and small beer (GROSE).

SIXER, *subs.* (thieves'). — 1. Six months' hard labour. Also 2. (prison) *see* quot. 1877.

1869. *Temple Bar*, xxvi. 75. The next bit I did was a SIXER.

1877. *Five Years' Penal Servitude*, iii. 194. He keeps a sharp eye on that man to see he does not "filch" a SIXER, as the six-ounce loaf, served with the dinner, is called.

1886-96. MARSHALL, *Bleary Bill* ['Pomes' 61]. I see what the upshot will be, Dear me! A SIXER with H.A.R.D.

SIX-FOOTER, *subs. phr.* (colloquial). A person six-feet (or more) in height.

*c.*1886. *Scientific American* [*Century*]. The centenarian is a SIX-FOOTER, chews tobacco, and loves a good story.

SIXPENCE. *See* SPIT.

SIXPENNY, *subs.* (Eton).—A playing field.

1864. *Eton School Days*, vi. If you are not in SIXPENNY after twelve, I will do my best to give you a hiding wherever I meet you.

Adj. (old). — Cheap; mean; worthless: generic. Hence SIXPENNY STRIKERS = petty footpads.

1598. SHAKSPEARE, I *Hen. IV.*, ii. I, 82. I am joined with no foot-land rakers, no long-staff SIXPENNY strikers.

1605. *London Prodigal*, v. I. I'll not let a SIXPENNY purse escape me.

*c.*1619. MASSINGER, &c., *City Madam*, iii. I. I know them, swaggering, suburbian roarers, SIXPENNY truckers.

SIX-SHOOTER, *subs. phr.* (common). A six chambered revolver. SIX-SHOOTER HORSE = a swift horse.

1887. FRANCIS, *Saddle and Mocassin*. A SIX-SHOOTER HORSE is a heap better than a six-shooter gun in these cases.

1894. W. M. BAKER, *New Timothy*, 177. 'The weapons of our warfare are not carnal' — bowie-knives, SIX-SHOOTERS, an' the like.

1900. SAVAGE, *Brought to Bay*, viii. With a quiet smile, he loaded his SIX-SHOOTER . . . 'for contingencies."

SIXTY, *subs.* (common).—Generic for magnitude.

1886. *Household Words*, 18 Sept., 415. "Like one o'clock," "Like winking," and "To go like SIXTY," all imply briskness and rapidity of motion.

SIXTY-PER-CENT, *subs. phr.* (old). — A usurer: also CENT-PER-CENT.

1616. FLETCHER, *Custom of the Country*, ii. 3. There are few gallants . . . that would receive such favours from the devil, though he appeared like a broker, and demanded SIXTY I' TH' HUNDRED.

1853. READE, *Gold*, i. I. What you do on the sly, I do on the sly, old SIXTY PER CENT.

1859. KINGSLEY, *Geoffry Hamlyn*, xiii. "Good night, old mole," said Hawker; "good night, old bat, old parchment skin, old SIXTY PER CENT. Ha, ha!"

1889. MARSH, *Crime and Criminal*, xii. Was he going to develop into a SIXTY PER CENT, and offer me a loan?

SIX-UPON-FOUR, *phr.* (nautical).—*See* quot.

1838. GLASCOCK, *Land Sharks and Sea Gulls*, II. 193. It was wicked work with them when it came to be SIX UPON FOUR, in other words, when long cruizes produced short commons.

1885. *Household Words*, 25 July, 260. In his time 'there were often SIX UPON FOUR aboard ship, and two banyan days in a week,' which being translated is, the rations of four men were served out amongst six, in addition to which, on two days in the week no rations were served out at all.

SIX-WATER GROG, *subs. phr.* (nautical).—Six of water to one of spirit.

1834. MARRYAT, *Peter Simple*, xxxv. "Take care I don't send for another helmsman, that's all, and give the reason why. You'll make a wry face upon SIX-WATER GROG to-morrow, at seven bells."

SIZE [*subs.* and *verb*, and **SIZAR**], *subs.* (Cambridge Univ. and Trin. Coll., Dublin).—1. *See* quots.: the grade no longer exists; practically speaking, it has ceased to exist for a century.

1592. NASHE, *Piers Pennilesse*, 45. [OLIPHANT, *New Eng.*, 2, 11. A Cambridge butler sets up a SIZE (allowance of bread); hence come SIZARS].

1594. GREENE, *Friar Bacon and Friar Bungay*. Friar Bacon's SUB-SIZER is the greatest blakhead in all Oxford.

1605. SHAKSPEAR, *Lear*, ii. 4, 178. 'Tis not in thee to grudge my pleasures . . . to scant my SIZES.

1606. *Ret. from Parnassus* [NARES]. So ho, maister recorder, you that are one of the divel's fellow commoners, one that SIZETH the devil's butteries.

1617. MINSHEN, *Guide unto Tongues*, s.v. A SIZE is a portion of bread or drinke, i. is a farthing, which Schollers in Cambridge haue at the butterie; it is noted with the letter S., as in Oxford with the letter Q. for halfe a farthing and q/u. for a farthing; and whereas they say in Oxford to Battle in the butterie booke, i. to set downe on their names what they take in Bread, Drinke, Butter, Cheese, &c., so in Cambridge they say to SIZE, i. to set downe their quantum, i. how much they take on their names in the Butterie booke.

1626. FLETCHER and ROWLEY, *Wit at Sev. Weapons*, ii. To be so strict A niggard to your Commons, that you're fain To SIZE your belly out with shoulder fees.

1630. RANDOLPH, *Aristippus* [HAZLITT, *Works* (1875), 14]. Drinking College tap-lash . . . will let them have no more learning than they SIZE.

1633. SHIRLEY, *Witty Fair One*, iv. 2. I know what belongs to SIZING, and have answered to my cue in my days; I am free of the whole university.

*d.*1635. CORBET, *Answ. to a Certain Poem.* How lackeys and SUB-SIZERS press And scramble for degrees.

1785. GROSE, *Vulg. Tongue*, s.v. SIZE. To sup at one's own expense. If a man asks you to sup, he treats you: if to SIZE, you pay for what you eat, liquor only being provided by the inviter. *Ibid.* SIZING-PARTY'S. A number of students who contribute each his part towards a supper.

1787. *Gentleman's Mag.*, 1147. The term SUB-SIZAR became forgotten, and the SIZAR was supposed to be the same as the servitor. *Ibid.* (1795), 21. In general, a SIZE is a small plateful of any eatable; and at dinner TO SIZE is to order for yourself any little luxury that may chance to tempt you . . . for which you are expected to pay the cook at the end of the term.

1798. *Laws of Harvard College* [HALL, *College Words and Customs*, 428]. When they come into town after commons, they may be allowed TO SIZE a meal at the kitchen.

18 . . . HAWKINS, *Orig. of Drama*, iii. 271. You are still at Cambridge with your SIZE cue

1811. *Laws of Yale College* [HALL, *College Words and Customs*, 428]. At the close of each quarter the Butler shall make up his bill against each student, in which every article SIZED, or taken up by him at the Buttery shall be particularly charged.

1824. *Gradus ad Cantab.*, s.v. SIZAR. The distinction between pensioners and SIZERS is by no means considerable . . . Nothing is more common than to see pensioners and SIZERS taking sweet counsel together, and walking arm-in-arm to St. Mary's as friends.

1848. THACKERAY, *Book of Snobs*, xiii. The unlucky boys who have no tassels to their caps are called SIZARS—servitors [*sic*] at Oxford . . . A distinction is made in their clothes because they are poor; for which reason they wear a badge of poverty, and are not allowed to take their meals with their fellow students.

185 . MACAULAY, *Oliver Goldsmith*. The SIZARS paid nothing for food and tuition, and very little for lodging; but they had to perform some menial services from which they have long been relieved. They swept the court; they carved up the dinner to the fellows' table, and changed the plates, and poured out the ale of the rulers of the society.

1851. BRISTED, *Eng. Univ.*, 20. 'Go through a regular second course instead of the SIZINGS.' *Ibid.*, 19. Soup, pastry and cheese can be SIZED for.

18... PEIRCE, *Hist. Harvard Univ.*, 219. We were allowed at dinner a cue of beer, which was a half-pint, and a SIZING of bread, which I cannot describe to you. It was quite sufficient for one dinner.

1861. O'CURRY, *Ancient Irish*, I. iv. Public schools where the sons of the lower classes waited on the sons of the upper classes, and received certain benefits (in food, clothes, and instruction) from them in return. In fact the SIZAR-SHIPS in our modern colleges appear to be a modified continuation of this ancient system.

1864. HOTTEN, *Slang Dict.*, s.v. SIZER. Poor scholars at Cambridge, annually elected, who got their dinners (including SIZINGS) from what was left at the upper, or Fellows' table, free, or nearly so. They paid rent of rooms, and some other fees, on a lower scale than the "Pensioners" or ordinary students, and were equal with the "battlers" and "servitors" at Oxford.

1889. *Cambridge Univ. Cal.*, 5. SIZARS are generally Students of limited means. They usually have their commons free, and receive various employments.

2. (old).—Half-a-pint (GROSE).

3. (colloquial).—Result; state; fact.

1861. BRADDON, *Trail of the Serpent*, IV, vii. "Dead?" said Richard . . . "That's about THE SIZE OF IT, sir," replied Mr. Peters.

1889. *Lic. Vict. Gaz.*, 8 Feb. They don't like to see a man's figure-head battered, that's about THE SIZE OF IT.

1891. GOULD, *Double Event*, 295. 'That's about THE SIZE OF IT,' said Jack, 'and I don't think you could do better.'

1893. MILLIKEN, *'Arry Ballads*, 22. That's THE SIZE OF IT, Charlie.

1902. HEADON HILL, *Caged*, xviii. That's about THE SIZE OF IT . . . I could have got away.

Verb. (colloquial).—To measure; to gauge; to reckon up: also TO SIZE UP.

1380. MIRK, *Inst. Parish Priests* [E. E. T. S.], 39. [OLIPHANT, *New Eng.*, i. 106. The old noun SYSE is used for measure; hence our to SIZE MEN on parade.]

1847. PORTER, *Big Bear*, 94. You see, Mr. Porter, I thot I'd SIZE her pile.

1889. *Puck's Library*, 25 Ap. If you want to know just how thoroughly the community has SIZED YOU UP, and to get the exact dimensions, ask for the best part in the amateur theatricals.

1891. MARRIOTT-WATSON, *Web of Spider*, xi. I haven't seen your little girl's face yet . . . It was dark . . . and I hadn't time to SIZE her.

1900. SAVAGE, *Brought to Bay*, i. The two . . . had SIZED UP the other guests as not worth . . . powder.

SKARY. *See* SKEER.

SKEDADDLE, *subs.* and *verb.* (common).—As *subs.* = hasty flight: also SKEDADDLING. As *verb.* = to scamper off; to scatter; to spill. For synomyns *see* BUNK.

1861. *New York Tribune* [BARTLETT]. With the South-east clear and General Price retiring into Arkansas in the South-west, we may expect to witness such a grand SKEDADDLE of Secesh and its colored property as was never seen before.

1861. *Missouri Democrat*, Aug. No sooner did the traitors discover their approach than they SKEDADDLED, a phrase the Union boys up here apply to the good use the Seceshers make of their legs in time of danger.

1862. *New York Tribune*, 27 May, 'War Correspondence.' Rebel SKEDADDLING is the next thing on the programme.

1864. HOTTEN, *Slang Dict.*, 292. Lord Hill wrote [to *The Times*] to prove that it was excellent Scotch. The Americans only misapply the word . . . in Dumfries—'to spill'—milkmaids . . . saying, 'You are SKEDADDLING all that milk.'

1874. BAKER, *Ismailia*, 211. Their noisy drums had ceased, and suddenly I perceived a general SKEDADDLE.

1877. *Atlantic Monthly*, xl. 234. We used to live in Lancashire and heard SKEDADDLE every day of our lives. It means to scatter, or drop in a scattering way.

1880. MORTIMER COLLINS, *Thoughts in my Garden*, i. 50. The burghers SKEDADDLED, and the Squire, thanks to his faint-hearted butler, had no chance of using his cavalry sword.

1890. *Pall Mall Gaz.*, 17 Oct., 2, 1. One fine day it happens that two Irish leaders SKEDADDLE in a trawler to the Continent.

1898. GOULD, *Landed at Last*, vii. They pays regular. There's no midnight SKEDADDLING about them.

1901. WALKER, *In the Blood*, 261. 'E's a "goner," buried in a fall of earth, blown up, killed, SKEDADDLED out o' this camp.

1902. HEADON HILL, *Caged*, xxxiv. And the bars, are they cut ready for a SKEDADDLE.

SKEER, *verb.* (American). — To scare. Hence SKEERY (SKARY, SCARY) = (1) dreadful; (2) frightened, nervous.

1582. STANIHURST, *Æneid*, iv. 438. But toe thee, poore Dido, this sight so SKEARVE beholding.

1825. NEAL, *Bro. Jonathan*, I. iv. Ye wasn't SKEERED, nor nothin', was ye, tho'.

1841. *The Kinsmen*, I. 150. 'Don't you be SCAREY,' said he.

1848. ROBB, *Squatter Life* [BARTLETT]. I got a little SCARY and a good deal mad.

1852. HALIBURTON, *Traits of Amer. Humour*, I. 222. He's the SCARIEST horse you ever saw.

1869. BLACKMORE, *Lorna Doone*, lix. The horses were a little SKEARY.

1880. *Scribner's Mag.*, Jan., 332. I seen they was mighty SKEERED.

1885. HAWLEY SMART, *Struck Down*, xi. Women get SKEARY, and desperate afraid of being compromised.

*d.*1892. WHITTIER, *Poems* [*Century*]. I'm SCARY always to see her shake Her wicked hand.

SKEESICKS, *subs.* (American).—A good-for-nothing; also like 'dog,' 'rogue,' 'rascal,' in playful address.—BARTLETT. [LELAND (S. J. & C.): 'I take it rather to mean a fidgetty, fussy, little fellow.']

1858. *Evening Star* (Washington), Nov. "Oh, he be d—d!" replied the fellow: "he's the little SKEEZICKS that told me to call for Long." This brought down the house.

1870. BRET HARTE, *Miggles* [*Century*]. Thar ain't nobody but him within ten miles of the shanty, and that ar' . . . old SKEESICKS knows it.

SKEET, *verb.* (old).—A variant of SCOOT (*q.v.*); to run, or decamp. As *adj.* and *adv.* (old literary) = swift, fleet.

*c.*1360. *Allit. Poems* [MORRIS], iii. 195. Thenne ascryed thay him SKETE.

*c.*1400. *Tale of Gamelyn*, 185. A steede ther sadeled smertely and SKEET.

*c.*1430. *Destr. of Troy* [E. E. T. S.], 13434. This Askathes, the skathill, had SKET sons thre.

1848. BURTON, *Waggeries*, 17. The critter . . . SKEETED over the side o' the ship into the water.

SKEETER, *subs.* (American). — A mosquito.

1852. STOWE, *Uncle Tom's Cabin*, xx. Law, Miss Feely whip!—[she] wouldn't kill a SKEETER.

SKELDER, *subs.* (old).—A rogue; a SPONGE (*q.v.*): as *verb.* = to cheat; to play the sponge: *cf.* SKELLUM. Hence SKELDERING = swindling; sponging.

1599. JONSON, *Ev. Man Out of Humour*. His profession is SKELDERING and odling. *Ibid.* (1601), *Poetaster*, iii. 4. A man may SKELDER ye now and then of half a dozen shillings or so. *Ibid.* i. There was the mad SKELDERING captain . . . that presses every man he meets, with an oath to lend him money.

1609. DEKKER, *Gulls Horne-Booke*, v. If he be poore, he shall now and then light upon some Gull or other, whom he may SKELDER (after the gentile fashion) of mony.

1611. MIDDLETON and DEKKER, *Roaring Girl*, v. 1. Soldiers? You SKELDERING varlets!

1633. MARMION, *Fine Companion*. Wandring abroad to SKELDER for a shilling Amongst your bowling alleys.

1773. HAWKINS, *Orig. Eng. Drama*, iii. 119. If SKELDRING fall not to decay, thou shalt flourish.

1823. SCOTT, *Peveril*, xxxviii. She hath many a thousand stitched to her petticoat; such a wife would save thee from SKELDERING on the public.

SKELETON. A SKELETON IN THE CUPBOARD (LOCKER, CLOSET, HOUSE), *subs. phr.* (colloquial).—A secret source of trouble, fear, or annoyance. Fr. *un cadavre.*

1855. THACKERAY, *Newcomes*, xvii. Barnes' SKELETON CLOSET [Title].

SKELLUM (or **SCELLUM**), *subs.* (Old Cant).—A rascal: a vagabond: *cf.* SKELDER.

1611. CORYAT, *Crudities*. He longs for sweet grapes, but going to steale 'em, He findeth soure graspes and gripes from a Dutch SKELUM.

1630. TAYLOR, *Works*, ii. 123. None hold him, but all cry, Lope, SCELLUM, lope!

1663. PEPYS, *Diary*, 3 Ap. He ripped up Hugh Peters (calling him the execrable SKELLUM), his preaching stirred up the maids of the city to bring their bodkins and thimbles.

1690. *Pagan Prince*. Let me send that SKELLUM to perdition.

1719. DURFEY, *Pills*, i. 210. Now to leave off writing, SKELLUMS pine and grieve, When we're next for Fighting We'll not ask you leave.

1791. BURNS, *Tam o'Shanter*. She tauld thee weel thou wast a SKELLUM, A blethering, blustering, drunken blellum.

SKELPER, *subs.* (provincial).—Anything big or striking: *see* SPANKER and WHOPPER. [SKELP = a blow, and as *verb.* to strike.]

SKELTER. *See* HELTER-SKELTER.

SKENSMADAM, *subs.* (provincial).—A show dish, sometimes real, sometimes sham.

SKERFER, *subs.* (pugilists'). — A blow on the neck.

SKET, *subs.* (thieves').—A skeleton-key.

SKEVINGTON'S - DAUGHTER (or **(-IRONS)**. *See* SCAVENGER'S-DAUGHTER.

SKEW, *subs.* (Old Cant).—1. 'A Begger's Wooden Dish or Cup' (B. E. and GROSE).

1641. BROME, *Jovial Crew*, ii. This is Bien Bowse . . . Too little is my SKEW.

1754. *Song* [*Scoundrels' Dict.*]. To thy Bugher and thy SKEW, Filch and Jybes, I bid adieu.

2. (Harrow). — An entrance examination at the end of term: that at the commencement is the 'dab,' after which there is no further chance; a shaky candidate tries the dab first. As *verb.* = to turn back, to fail.

SKEWER, *subs.* (American).—1. A sword. Hence, as *verb.* = (1) to run through; and (2) to impose on.

1848. DURIVAGE, *Stray Subjects*, 147. Our enterprising journal, which had purchased the news, in company with its sharp friends, had been SKEWERED.

2. (common).—A pen. Fr. *une griffarde* (or *griffonante*).

SKEW-FISTED, *adj. phr.* (old).—'Awkward, ungainly' (B. E.).

SKEW-GEE, *subs.* (colloquial).—A squint: as *adj.* = crooked, skew'd, squinting.

SKEWGY-MEWGY, *subs. phr.* (nautical).—*See* quot.

1886. *St. James's Gaz.*, 7 Ap. The skipper rejoices in a steady drizzling rain, which keeps a certain caustic composition, known to yachtsmen by the mysterious name of SKEWGY-MEWGY, damp and active under the scrubbing-brushes and holy-stones of her crew.

SKEWING, *subs.* (gilders). In *pl.* = perquisites; MAKINGS (*q.v.*). [Properly SKEW (gilders') = to remove superfluous gold leaf, and to make good defects.] Analogous terms are CABBAGE (tailors'); BLUE-PIGEON (plumbers'); MEN-AVELINGS (beggars'); FLUFF (railway clerks'); PUDDING, or JAM (common).

SKEW-THE-DEW, *subs. phr.* (common).—A splay-footed person; a BUMBLE-FOOT (*q.v.*).

SKEWVOW, *adj.* (old).—'Crooked, inclining to one side' (GROSE): also ALL ASKEW.

SKID (or **SKIV**), *subs.* (common).—A sovereign: *see* RHINO.

2. (American).—A volunteer; a militiaman.

TO PUT ON THE SKID, *verb. phr.* (colloquial).—To speak or act with caution.

1885. *Punch*, 31 Jan., 60. I could pitch you a yarn on that text; but I fear I must PUT ON THE SKID.

SKIFF, *subs.* (common).—A leg [?].

1891. *M. Advertiser*, 6 Ap. Now, 16s. 3d. wanted a lot of earning, more especially when a man had to drive an "old crock" with "skinny SKIFFS."—None of them could deny that the "S.T." cabs were horsed by very old racehorses, bad platers, and what were termed "chin backed horses."

SKIFFLE, *subs.* (common).—A great hurry: *cf.* SCUFFLE.

SKILL, *subs.* (football).—A goal kicked between posts.

SKILLET, *subs.* (nautical).—A ship's cook.

SKILLINGERS (THE), *subs.* (military). — The 6th (Inniskilling) Dragoons: also "The Old Inniskillings."

SKILLY (or **SKILLIGOLEE**), *subs.* (formerly nautical and prison: now common).—1. A thin broth or soup of oatmeal and water. Hence (2) anything of little or no value. SKILLY AND TOKE = prison fare.

1846. MARRYAT, *Peter Simple*, xi. I am not worth a SKILLAGOLEE, and that is the reason which induces me to condescend to serve his Majesty.

1857. SNOWDEN, *Magistrate's Assistant* (3rd Ed.), 446, s.v. SKILLY. The broth in prisons.

1870. *Chambers's Miscellany*, No. 77, 6. Burgoo, or as it was sportively called, SKILLAGALLEE, was oatmeal boiled in water to the consistency of hasty pudding.

1871. *Figaro*, 7 Oct. They christened the latter "Cardwell's SKILLY," and a course of it would soon turn our Life Guards into the lightest of cavalry.

1883. *D. Telegraph*, 19 May, 5, 4. England did not wish her to eat SKILLY, and to wear the "parish dress."

1889. *Sportsman*, 2 Jan. The worthy ones who play hole-and-corner with society are made to partake of the toke of contrition, and the SKILLY of repentance.

1902. DESART, *Herne Lodge Myst.*, xvi. The thought of SKILLY . . . I had very vague ideas . . . came into my mind.

SKILT, *subs.* (common).—In *pl.* = trousers: *see* KICKS.

SKIM, *subs.* (thieves').—*See* quot.

1869. *Daily News*, 29 July, 'Police Reports.' They thought it contained his SKIM (money). They took down the bag without wakening him, and found that, instead of SKIM, the parcel contained two revolvers.

SKIMBLE-SKAMBLE, *subs.*, *adj.*, and *adv.* (old colloquial).—Rigmarole, nonsense; wandering, confused; incoherently.

1598. SHAKSPEARE, 1 *Hen. IV.*, iii. 1, 154. Such a deal of SKIMBLE-SKAMBLE stuff.

1630. TAYLOR, *Works*, *Desc. of a Wanton.* Here's a sweet deal of SCIMBLE-SCAMBLE stuff.

SKIMMERY, *subs.* (Oxford Univ.). St. Mary's Hall.

1853. BRADLEY, *Verdant Green*, viii. I swopped the beggar to a SKIMMERYMAN.

1860. G. and P. WHARTON, *Wits and Beaux of Society*, 427. After leaving Westminster School he was sent to immortal SKIMMERY, Oxford.

SKIMMINGTON, *subs.* (old).—1. *See* quots: also TO RIDE THE SKIMMINGTON (or [Scots'] THE STANG). [For a long description see BUTLER, *Hudibras*, II. ii. 585.] Hence (2) a row, a quarrel.

1562. *Stowe's London* [STRYPE], B. ii, 258. Shrove Monday at Charing Cross was a man carried of four men, and before him a bagpipe playing, a shawm, and a drum beating, and twenty men with links burning round about him. The cause was his next neighbour's wife beat her husband; it being so ordered that the next should ride about to expose her.

1685. OLDHAM, *Satyrs.* When I'm in pomp on high processions shown, Like pageants of lord may'r, or SKIMMINGTON.

1753. WALPOLE, *Letters*, i. 289. There was danger of a SKIMMINGTON between the great wig and the coif, the former having given a flat lie to the latter.

1785. GROSE, *Vulgar Tongue*, s.v. RIDING SKIMMINGTON. A ludicrous cavalcade, in ridicule of a man beaten by his wife. A man behind a woman, face to horse's tail, distaff in hand, which he seems to work, the woman beating him with a ladle; a smock on a staff is carried before them denoting female superiority. They are accompanied by rough music, frying pans, bull's horns, marrowbones and cleavers, &c.—*Abridged.*

1822. SCOTT, *Fortunes of Nigel*, xxi. Note. The SKIMMINGTON has been long discontinued in England.

1865. *Exeter Police Report*, 9 Sep. Summary justice had been done by a SKIMMINGTON MATCH [*sic*], on two married persons, whose ill and faithless example had scandalised the neighbourhood.

SKIMP, *verb.* (colloquial). — To stint; TO SCAMP (*q.v.*). As *adj.* = insufficient, meagre; SKIMPING (or SKIMPY) = scanty, carelessly made, slightingly treated.

1864. *Sun*, 28 Dec., *Review Hotten's Slang Dict.* Mr. Hotten has made no mention of a dress that is describable as SKIMPY.

1879. BREWER, *Eng. Studies*, 444. The work was not SKIMPING work by any means.

1885. CRADDOCK, *Proph. Gt. Smoky Mountains*, iv. Grey hair drawn into a SKIMPY knot at the back of the head.

1888. EGGLESTON, *Graysons*, xix. The woman who has . . . schemed and SKIMPED to achieve her attire knows the real pleasure and victory of self-adornment.

SKIMSHANDER. *See* SCRIMSHAW.

SKIN, *subs.* (old).—1. A purse; a pocket-book; any receptacle for money. Thus A QUEER SKIN = an empty purse; FRISK THE SKIN = 'clean him out' (GROSE and VAUX).

1821. HAGGART, *Life*, 15. Young McGuire had taken some SKINS with a few shillings in each.

1852. JUDSON, *Myst. of New York*, vii. The offisare ave frisk me; he ave not found ze SKIN or ze dummy, eh?

1856. MAYHEW, *Gt. World of London*, iii. The London buzman can keep his pony by abstracting SKINS from gentlemen's pockets.

2. (old).—A sovereign; 20/-: *see* RHINO.

3. (old).—In *pl.* = a tanner (GROSE).

4. (American). *See* SKINNER.

5. (American).—A translation; a CRIB (*q.v.*); a BOHN (*q.v.*). Also as *verb.* = to copy a solution; and SKINNER = one using an irregular aid to study.

1851. BRISTED, *Five Years*, 394. Barefaced copying from books and reviews in their compositions is familiar to our students, as much so as SKINNING their mathematical examples. *Ibid.*, 457. Classical men were continually tempted TO SKIN the solution of these examples.

1855. *Yale College Songs.* 'Twas plenty of SKIN with a good deal of bohn.

18 [?]. *Yale Lit. Mag.* [BARTLETT]. Never SKIN a lesson which it requires any ability to learn.

1856. HALL, *College Words and Customs*, 430. In examinations . . . many . . . cover the palms . . . with dates, and when called upon for a given date they read it off . . . from their hands. Such persons SKIN.

18 [?]. TRUMBULL, *Story of the Sheepskin* [BARTLETT]. But now that last Biennial's past; I SKINNED and fizzled through.

6. (American).—Punch made in the glass: as a WHISKEY-SKIN, a RUM-SKIN, &c.

1871. HAY, *Little Breeches.* Says he, 'Young man, the Phins, know their own WHISKEY-SKINS.'

7. (common). *See* SKINFLINT.

Verb (old colloquial).—1. To rob; to strip; to CLEAN OUT (*q.v.*): spec. (racing) to win all one's bets; (bookmakers') SKIN THE LAMB (or HAVE A SKINNER) = to win with an unbacked horse; (2) = to swindle; and (3) = TO TAKE TOLL (*q.v.*). Hence SKIN-GAME (*e.g.*, SKIN-FARO: *see* quot. 1882) = a swindle: SKIN-HOUSE = a gambling den; SKINNER = (1) a sharping cheat, a thief: spec. (American) a looter infesting both camps; (2) a pirate; and (3) a race, which being won by a rank outsider, SKINS the ring.

1821. COOPER, *Spy*, i. This poor opinion of the SKINNERS was not confined to Mr. Cæsar Thompson.

1836. MILNER, *Turpin's Ride to York*, ii. 5. *Sam.* PEEL MY SKIN and dub up the browns! What do you mean? *Bal.* Just this—that if you do not hand over your money I shall blow out your brains!

1855. IRVING, *Wolfert's Roost*, 17. The SKINNERS and Cowboys of the Revolution, when they wrung the neck of a rooster, did not trouble . . . whether they crowed for Congress or King George.

1851-61. MAYHEW, *London Labour*, II. 81. Perhaps he gets SKINNED . . . and sells them for what he can.

1869. BRADWOOD, *O.V.H.*, xix. And a carefully roped and bottled animal, that dropped like a meteor upon the racing public for the Chester Cup, SKINNED THE LAMB for Mr. Bacon, landed every bet standing in his book.

1882. MCCABE, *New York*, xxxix. 545. SKIN-FARO the only game played here, offers no chance whatever to the player. In SKIN-FARO the dealer can take two cards from the box instead of one whenever he chooses to do so.

1883. *Sat. Review*, 28 April, 533, 2. His victory proved a gold mine to the professional bookmakers, many of whom did not bet against the horse at all, thus performing the profitable operation technically known in the betting-ring as SKINNING THE LAMB.

1883. *Graphic*, 21 April, 410, 2. The Ring are enormous winners on the race, the majority having SKINNED THE LAMB.

1883. GREENWOOD, *In Strange Company.* Amongst themselves they are SKINNERS, knock-outs, odd-trick men, and they work together in what . . . their profession calls a "swim."

1884. *Referee*, 10 August, 1, 1. The winner being found in Quilt, who had sufficient support to leave the result anything but a SKINNER for the bookmakers. *Ibid.* (1889), 2 June. They had made a little overtime at an inn near the station, and, by way of grace after meat, gone over the landlord, left him SKINNED, and the furniture smashed.

1890. *Atlantic Monthly*, lxvi. 511. There were two sets of these scapegraces—the 'Cow-boys,' or cattle thieves, and the SKINNERS, who took everything they could find.

1891. *M. Advtr.*, 21 Mar. The prisoner was entrusted with two tons of coal to deliver. Sergeant Hiscock, of the V division, watched his movements, and saw him SKINNING the sacks—that is, removing lumps from the tops and placing them in an empty sack.

1896. LILLARD, *Poker Stories*, 51. Southern planters used to lose money just like fun, and were SKINNED right and left.

1902. *D. Mail*, 17 Nov., 6, 1. What they shudderingly designate a SKINNER was enjoyed by a majority of the layers when old Fairyfield credited Mr. George Edwardes with the Belper Selling Plate.

2. (thieves'). — To SHADOW (*q.v.*): spec. when previous to arrest. *See* NARK.

3. (common). — To strip, TO PEEL (*q.v.*); and (venery), to retire the prepuce, TO SKIN THE LIVE RABBIT. Whence SKINNER (*see* quot. 1856).

1856. MAYHEW, *Gt. World of London*, 46. SKINNERS, or women and boys who strip children of their clothes.

1861. DICKENS, *Great Expectations*, xxxi. SKIN the stockings off . . . or you'll bust 'em.

1896. LILLARD, *Poker Stories*, 59. I have seen a game player just SKIN OFF his watch and ring and studs and play them in.

4. (gaming). — To PLANT A DECK (*q.v.*): *see* CONCAVE, BROADS, and REFLECTOR.

5. (common). — To abate a price; to lower a value: *cf.* SHAVING THE LADIES (s.v. SHAVE).

6. (common). — To thrash: also TO SKIN ALIVE.

1888. *Detroit Free Press*, 22 Dec. 'If yer don't stop your guzzum I'll SKIN YER ALIVE' . . . She flourished a skillet at him.

1895. *Idler*, Aug., 63. I'm sure that her parents would SKIN her, If they thought that she smiled on my suit.

1902. HEADON HILL, *Caged*, xxxiv. I'd have SKINNED the 'ussy if I'd caught her prying into my grounds.

OTHER COLLOQUIALISMS AND PHRASES. — BY THE SKIN OF ONE'S TEETH = a narrow escape, the closest of close shaves; TO SKIN OUT = to decamp; TO SKIN THE CAT (gynmasts') = to grasp the bar with both hands, raise the feet, and so draw the body, between the arms, over the bar; LIKE EELS, USED TO SKINNING = of good heart; TO SKIN THE EYES (*see* KEEP); ALL SKIN AND WHIPCORD = well-trussed; in good condition; IN (or WITH) A WHOLE SKIN = uninjured, with impunity; TO SAVE ONE'S SKIN = to escape unhurt: *see* BACON; TO SKIN A FLINT (*see* SKINFLINT); honest as the SKIN BETWEEN HIS BROWS (or HORNS): *see* BROW; TO SKIN A RAZOR = to drive a hard-and-fast bargain; TO SKIN ONE'S SKUNK = to do one's own dirty work; IN A BAD SKIN = angry (GROSE); CLEANSKIN (Australian) = an unbranded beast; *cf.* MAVERICK; TO LEAP (or JUMP) OUT OF ONE'S SKIN = to be startled or pleased; IN HER or HIS) SKIN = evasive as to a person's whereabouts.

16[?]. *Marq. of Huntley's Retreat* [CHILD, *Ballads*, vii. 271]. He had resolved that day To sleep IN A WHOLE SKIN.

1605. MARSTON, *Dutch Courtezan*, iii. 1. Blesse me, I was never so OUT OF MY SKINNE in my life.

1611. *Bible*, 'Authorised Version,' Job xix. 20. I am escaped WITH THE SKIN OF MY TEETH.

1616-25. *Court and Times Jas. I.* OLIPHANT, *New Eng.*, ii. 71. Amongst Romance words are SAVE HIS SKIN, refreshed with money . . .]

1664. COTTON, *Virgil Travestie* (1st ed.), 72. Æneas, was so glad on's kin, He ready was T'LEAP OUT ON'S SKIN.

*d.*1704. L'ESTRANGE, *Works* [*Century*]. Dangerous civilities, wherein 'tis hard for a man to SAVE both HIS SKIN and his credit.

1708. CENTLIVRE, *Busy-Body*, v. 1. Confirm it! Make me LEAP OUT OF MY SKIN.

1708-10. SWIFT, *Polite Conversation*, i. *Col.* Pray, Miss, where is your old Acquaintance, Mrs. Wayward. *Miss.* Why, where should she be? You must needs know; she's IN HER SKIN.

1798. G. COLMAN (the younger), *Blue Devils*, i. 1. Made me JUMP OUT OF MY SKIN with joy.

1809. MALKIN, *Gil Blas* [ROUTLEDGE], 26. At these words I was ready to JUMP OUT OF MY SKIN for joy.

1836. SCOTT, *Tom Cringle's Log*, i. Who says that EELS CAN NOT BE MADE USED TO SKINNING? The poor girls continued their preparations with an alacrity and presence of mind that truly surprised me. There was neither screaming nor fainting.

1841. THACKERAY, *Snobs*, xii. I should be ready to JUMP OUT OF MY SKIN if two Dukes would walk down Pall Mall with me.

1877. BESANT and RICE, *Golden Butterfly*, xxxiii. You jest gather up your traps and SKIN OUT of this.

1882. GRANT, *Bush Life*, I. 206. These CLEAN SKINS . . . are supposed to belong to the cattle owner, on whose run they emerge from their shelter.

1888. *Phil. Ev. Bulletin*, 23 Feb. Another Presidential candidate who is abroad, it will be remembered, utilized a pole daily for SKINNING THE CAT.

1888. BOLDREWOOD, *Robbery Under Arms*, xx. Brought out a horse—the same I'd ridden from Gippsland, saddled and bridled, and ready to JUMP OUT OF HIS SKIN.

1891. GOULD, *Double Event*, 101. The horse was regularly worked, and he looked in splendid health and condition, FIT TO JUMP OUT OF HIS SKIN, to use a racing term.

1896. SALA, *London up to Date*, 66. At the election I had no less than seventeen black balls; but . . . I got in by the SKIN OF MY TEETH.

SKIN-COAT, *subs. phr.* (venery).—The female *pudendum*: *see* MONOSYLLABLE. Hence SHAKING A SKIN-COAT = copulating.

1653. URQUHART, *Rabelais*, II. xvii. And by God, I will have their SKINCOAT SHAKEN once yet before they die.

TO CURRY ONE'S SKINCOAT, *verb. phr.* (old).—To thrash.

SKIN-DISEASE, *subs. phr.* (common).—Fourpenny ale.

SKINFLINT (or **SKIN**), *subs.* (old).—'A griping, sharping, close-fisted Fellow' (B. E., *c.*1696, and GROSE). As *verb.* (or TO SKIN, OF FLAY, A FLINT, FLY, STONE, &c.) = to pinch, to screw, to starve: *cf.* (proverbial) 'to skin a flea, and bleed a cabbage'; SKINNY = mean, stingy; THE SKINFLINTERIES = The Museum of Economic [now Practical] Geology, Jermyn St., W. *See* FILE, FLAY, FLEA, and FLINT for additional quots.

1761. MURPHY, *Citizen*, ii. An old miserly good-for-nothing SKIN-FLINT.

1789. PARKER, *Life's Painter*, 'The Masqueraders.' The miser, that SKIN-FLINT old elf.

1809. MALKIN, *Gil Blas* [ROUTLEDGE], 212. The SKINFLINT would not trust me for six ells of cloth.

1816. SCOTT, *Antiquary*, xi. It would have been long . . . ere my womankind could have made such a reasonable bargain with that old SKINFLINT. *Ibid. Fortunes of Nigel*, xxxi. 'Plague on ye,' he muttered, 'for a cunning auld SKIN-FLINT!'

1833. MARRYAT, *Peter Simple* (1846), II. 194. Report says she would SKIN A FLINT if she could.

1868. *Putnam's Mag.*, Jan. Old miser Dyser, SKIN a fly, Sir, Sell the skin and turn the money in.

1869. BYRON, *Not such a Fool as He Looks* [FRENCH], 12. Sharp old SKIN-FLINT, downy old robber as he is.

1884. *Century Mag.*, xxxix. 227. He would refer to . . . his former employer as that SKIN.

1889. *D. Tel.*, 11 May. It was suggested that the obstructive vehicles should stop in front of the Museum of Economic [*sic*] Geology—popularly known as THE SKINFLINTERIES.

1890. *Lancet*, II. 246. As a rule the whole of the men in a factory would contribute, and SKINNY ones were not let off easily.

1898. HUME, *Hagar*, i. He was . . . so avaricious that throughout the neighbourhood he was called SKINFLINT.

1900. SAVAGE, *Brought to Bay*, vi. This old SKINFLINT is such a character that you should keep all the working results sealed, till he certifies his own.

SKINFUL, *subs.* (common). — A bellyful—liquor or food.

1600. KEMP, *Dance to Norwich* [ARBER, *Eng. Garner*, vii.]. [OLIPHANT, *New Eng.*, ii. 52. A man takes a jump; he may have his SKINFULL of drink.]

1640-50. HOWELL, *Letters*, iii. 5. [Howell calls his body A SKINFULL OF BONES.]

1773. GOLDSMITH, *She Stoops to Conquer*, . . . I'll wager the rascals a crown, They always preach best with a SKINFUL.

1868. W. S. GILBERT, *Bab Ballads*, 'Sir Macklin.' He wept to think each thoughtless youth Contained of wickedness a SKINFUL.

1888. RUNCIMAN, *Chequers*, 85. They were reasonably anxious to secure a SKINFUL, and they feared lest my powers might prove abnormal.

1897. *D. Mail*, 25 Sep., 7, 3. The elastic skin man comes over here for the first time, and the Custom House authorities will need to look out that he is not employed for smuggling purposes—he has certainly been known many a time to have his SKINFUL.

SKINK, *verb.* (old).—Primarily to draw, serve, or offer drink. Whence as *subs.* = drink or LAP (*q.v.*); and SKINKER = (1) a tapster, or waiter (B. E.); (2) a landlord, and (3) *see* quots. 1785 and 1847.

1205. LAYAMON [MADDEN], 8124. Weoren tha bernes [men], I-SCÆNGTE mid beore, & tha drihliche gumen, weoren windrunken.

1383. CHAUCER, *Cant. Tales*, 'Merchant's Tale,' 478. Bacus the wyn hem SKYNKETH al aboute.

1582-7. HAKLUYT, *Voyages*, I. 480. For that cause called this new city by the name of Naloi: that is SKINCK or poure in.

1594. GREEN and LODGE, *Looking Glass for London and England*. I'll have them SKINK my standing bowls with wine. *Ibid.* Jack SKINKER, fill it full.

1600. HAUGHTON, *Grim the Collier* [DODSLEY, *Old Plays* (REED), xi. 222]. I must be SKINKER then . . . They all shall want ere Robin shall have none.

1601. JONSON, *Poetaster*, iv. 3. *Alb.* I'll ply the table with nectar, and make them friends. *Her.* Heaven is like to have but a lame SKINKER, then. *Ibid.* (1614), *Bartholomew Fair*, ii. Then SKINK out the first glass ever, and drink with all companies. *Ibid.* (*d.*1637), *Verses at Apollo*, vii. 295. Hang up all the poor hop-drinkers, Cries old Sym, the King of SKINKERS.

1606. MARSTON, *Sophon*, v. 2. Let me not drink 'Till my breast burst, O Jove, thy NECTAR SKINKE.

1609. DEKKER, *Gull's Hornbook*, 26. Awake thou noblest drunkard Bacchus—teach me, thou sovereign SKINKER.

1617. FLETCHER, *Knight of Malta*, iii. 1. Our glass of life runs wine, the vintner SKINKS it.

*c.*1650. BRATHWAYTE, *Barnaby's Jo.* (1723), 57. There I toss'd it with my SKINKERS, Not a drop of Wit remained Which the Bottle had not drained.

1652. SHIRLEY, *Impost.*, A5, 57. Such wine as Ganymede doth SKINKE to Jove.

1785. GROSE, *Vulg. Tongue*, s.v. SKINK . . . to wait on the company, ring the bell, stir the fire, and snuff the candles; the duty of the youngest officer in the military mess.

1818. SCOTT, *Rob Roy*, iv. I give my vote and interest to Jonathan Brown, our landlord, to be the King and Prince of SKINKERS, conditionally that he fetches us another bottle as good as the last.

1831. LAMB, *Satan in Search of a Wife*, II. xxvii. No Hebe fair stood cupbearer there, The guests were their own SKINKERS.

1847. HALLIWELL, *Arch. Words*, s.v. SKINK. In a family the person latest at breakfast is called the SKINK, or the SKINKER, and some domestic office is imposed or threatened for the day, such as ringing the bell, putting coal on the fire, or in other cases, drawing the beer for the family.

1852. HAWTHORNE, *Blithedale Romance*, 245. Some old-fashioned SKINKERS and drawers were spreading a banquet on the leaf-strewn earth.

SKIN-MERCHANT, *subs. phr.* (old). —A recruiting officer.

1783. BURGOYNE, *Lord of the Manor*, iii. 2. I am a manufacturer of honour and glory—vulgarly call'd a recruiting dealer, or more vulgarly still, a SKIN-MERCHANT.

SKINNED-RABBIT, *subs. phr.* (colloquial).—A very spare person.

SKINNER. 1. *See* SKIN.

2. (sporting). — A bird fat enough to burst its skin when shot.

SKIN-OF-THE-CREATURE (or **CRATER**), *subs. phr.* (Irish).—A bottle: *see* CREATURE.

SKIN-THE-LAMB, *subs. phr.* (old). —Lansquenet: *see* also SKIN, *verb.* 1.

SKIN-THE-PIZZLE. *subs. phr.* (venery).—The female *pudendum*: *see* MONOSYLLABLE.

SKINTIGHT, *subs.* (common).—A sausage.

SKINTLING, *adv.* (American).—*See* quot.

18[?]. *Science* [*Century*]. [The bricks] are carried in wheelbarrows, and set SKINTLING, or at right angles across each other.

SKIP, *subs.* (old).—1. A footman; a GRASSHOPPER (*q.v.*). Whence spec. 2 (Trin. Coll., Dublin), a college servant: *cf.* GYP and SCOUT. Also SKIPKENNEL (B. E. and GROSE).

1672. A. BROME, *Covent Garden Drollery*. The prizes they took were a Londoner's groat, A gentleman's size, but his SKIPKENNEL'S pot.

1703. WARD, *London Spy*, VII. 151. As a Courtier's Footman when he meets his Brother SKIP in the middle of Covent Garden.

*d.*1704. BROWN, *Works*, ii. 120. Pluto's SKIPKENNELS are not so insolent as yours are.

1721. AMHURST, *Terræ Fillius*. No. Z. Every scullion and SKIPKENNEL had liberty to tell his master his own.

1729. SWIFT, *Directions to Servants*, 'Footman.' My lady's waiting-woman . . . apt to call you SKIP-KENNEL.

1839. LEVER, *Harry Lorrequer*, xi. Conducting himself in all respects . . . as his . . . own man, SKIP, valet, or flunkey.

1842. *Tait's Mag.*, Oct., 'Rem. College Life.' The SKIP, or according to the Oxford etymology, 'the man vulture,' is not fit for his calling who cannot time his business so as to be present simultaneously at several places.

1845. THACKERAY, *Pendennis*, xx. His wounded tutor, his many duns, the SKIP and bedmaker who waited on him.

Verb. (common).—1. To decamp: *see* BUNK. Also TO SKIP OUT (or OFF), and TO DO A SKIP.

1872. CLEMENS, *Roughing It*, ix. The Indian had SKIPPED around so's to spile everything.

1888. *Detroit Free Press*, 19 Dec. I knew he was getting ready to SKIP OUT OF town the moment he saw the jig was up.

1889. *Ally Sloper*, 29 June. This base myrmidon of the law endeavoured to execute his task just as Andrew was about to lead a second bouncing bride to the altar. But Andrew espied him and quietly SKIPPED.

1892. KIPLING, *Barrack-Room Ballads*, 'Gunga Din.' With 'is mussick on 'is back, 'E would SKIP with our attack.

1895. POCOCK, *Rules of the Game*, II. 10. If I had known of this warrant, I'd have gone on my knees and implored him for your dear sake not to SKIP the train.

2. (common). — To die: *see* HOP THE TWIG.

1900. SAVAGE, *Brought to Bay*, xv. The dark pool of blood . . . told its awful story . . . SKIPPED OUT . . . game to the last, and never flinched.

3. (common).—To read hastily, picking out passages here and there. Hence 4 (University), to shirk work. Also SKIPPER = a hasty reader; and SKIPPABLE = easily and quickly read.

1884. *Pall Mall Gaz.*, 28 Feb. Two classes of readers, however, may get not a little that is interesting out of this book—the pachydermatous plodder and the judicious SKIPPER.

SKIP-BRAIN, *adj.* (old).—Flighty; volatile; fickle.

1603. DAVIES, *Microcosmus*, 30. This SKIPP-BRAINE Fancie.

SKIPJACK, *subs.* (old).—1. A horse-dealer's jockey (B. E. and GROSE).

1568. FULWEL, *Like will to Like* [OLIPHANT, *New Eng.*, i. 565. Here we see knave of clubs, SKIPJACK, snip-snap].

1608-9. DEKKER, *Lanthorne and Candlelight*, x. The boyes, striplings, &c., that have the riding of the jades up and downe are called SKIP-JACKES.

2.—A nobody; a trifler: also SKIPPER.

1580. SIDNEY, *Arcadia*, III. Now the devil, said she, take these villains. that can never leave grinning, because I am not so fair as mistress Mopsa; to see how this SKIP-JACK looks at me.

*d.*1592. GREENE, *Alphonsus*, i. What, know'st thou, SKIP-JACK, whom thou villain call'st.

1593. SHAKSPEARE, *Taming of Shrew*, ii. 1, 341. SKIPPER, stand back; 'tis age that nourisheth.

1611. COTGRAVE, *Nimbot*. A dwarfe, dandiprat, little SKIP-JACKE.

1670. COTTON, *Scoffer Scofft* [*Works* (1725), 190]. But till thou hadst this SKIP-JACK got.

SKIPPER, *subs.* (Old Cant).—1. A barn (AWDELEY, HARMAN, ROWLANDS, HEAD, B. E., and GROSE). Whence as *verb.* (or TO SKIPPER IT) = to sleep in the straw or in HEDGE SQUARE (*q.v.*); SKIPPER-BIRD = a barn-rooster or hedge-tramp.

1652. BROOME, *Jovial Crew*, ii. Now let each tripper Make a retreat into the SKIPPER.

1851-61. MAYHEW, *London Lab.*, ii. 83. When I get down I go to sleep for a couple of hours. I SKIPPER IT—turn in under a hedge or anywhere. *Ibid.*, i. 336. Here is the best places in England for SKIPPER-BIRDS (parties that never go to lodging-houses, but to barns or outhouses, sometimes without a blanket) . . . 'Keyhole whistlers,' the SKIPPER-BIRDS are sometimes called.

2. (common).—The Devil. For SYNONYMS *see* BLACK SPY.

3. (B. E. and GROSE: still colloquial).—'A Dutch Master of a Ship or Vessell'; in modern use any ship's captain; and (4) a leader or chief in any enterprise, adventure, or business. Hence 5. (general) a master, BOSS (*q.v.*), GOVERNOR (*q.v.*).

1485-1500. GARDNER, *Letters of Rich. III. and Hen. VII.* [OLIPHANT, *New Eng.*, i. 352. There is the SKIPPAR of a ship, and the Northern form *raid*]. *Ibid.* 341 (1509). [James IV. speaks of a crew as including] Master, 2 factours, SKIPPAR, sterisman.

1600. DECKER, *Show. Holiday* [GROSART, *Wks.* (1873), i. 30]. Do you remember the shippe my fellow Hans told you of, the SKIPPER and he are both drinking at the Swan?

1636. SUCKLING, *Goblins*, iv. With as much ease as a SKIPPER Would laver against the wind.

1699. CONGREVE, *Way of the World*, iii. 15. *Mrs. Mar.* No doubt you will return very much improv'd. *Witw.* Yes, refined like a Dutch SKIPPER from a whale fishing.

1710. GAY, *Wine* [*Wks.* (1811), 351]. Chase brutal feuds of Belgian SKIPPERS hence.

1751. SMOLLETT, *Per. Pickle*, xxxiv. By the SKIPPER'S advice the servants [carried] wine and provision on board.

1854. WHYTE MELVILLE, *General Bounce*, iv. The young SKIPPER exultingly stamped his foot on a deck he could really call his own.

*d.*1882. LONGFELLOW, *Wreck of Hesperus*. And the SKIPPER had taken his little daughter To bear him company.

6. (American). — The cheese-hopper: hence SKIPPERY = full of mites.

1856. DOW, *Sermons*, II. 258. The earth appears as animated as a plate of SKIPPERY cheese.

See SKIP and SKIPJACK.

SKIPPER'S-DAUGHTER, *subs. phr.* (common).—A crested wave; a WHITE-CAP (or HORSE).

*d.*1894. STEVENSON, *Education of an Engineer*. The swell ran pretty high, and out in the open there were SKIPPER'S DAUGHTERS.

SKIPPING, *adj.* (SHAKESPEARE).— Light, giddy, volatile.

1594. SHAKSPEARE, *Love's Labour Lost*, v. 2, 771. All wanton as a child, SKIPPING and vain. *Ibid.* (1598), *Merchant of Venice*, ii. 2, 196. Allay with some cold drops of modesty Thy SKIPPING spirit. *Ibid.* (1602), *Twelfth Night*, i. 5. 'Tis not that time of moon with me to make one in so SKIPPING a dialogue.

SKIRRY, *subs.* (old).—A run: also as *verb.* = to scurry (PARKER, 1781).

1821. HAGGART, *Life*, 36. He went into an entry as I SKIRRY'D past him. *Ibid.*, 37. The SKIRRY became general.

SKIRT, *subs.* (common).—In *pl.* = women (generic). Hence (venery) TO SKIRT (or FLUTTER A SKIRT) = to walk the streets; to DO A BIT OF SKIRT = to copulate: *see* RIDE and *cf.* PLACKET, PETTICOAT, MUSLIN, &c.

1899. HYNE, *Fur. Adv. Capt. Kettle*, xii. If . . . you rats of men shove your way down here . . . before all THE SKIRT is ferried across, you'll get knocked on the head.

TO SIT UPON ONE'S SKIRTS, *verb. phr.* (old).—To pursue.

1525-37. ELLIS, *Original Letters*, I. iii. She will SIT UPON MY SKYRTES.

1620. *Idle Houre* [HALLIWELL]. Cross me not, Liza, nether be so perte, For if thou dost, I'll SIT UPON THY SKIRTE.

1650. HOWELL, *Familiar Letters*. Touching the said archbishop, he had not stood neutrall as was promised, therefore he had justly SET ON HIS SKIRTS.

SKIRTER, *subs.* (hunting).—1. *See* quot; whence (2) a hunter who does not ride straight to hounds, but make short cuts: *cf.* SHIRKER.

1870. MAINE, *Ency. Rural Sports*, 386. A hound that has a habit of running wide of the pack is called a SKIRTER.

*d.*1875. KINGSLEY, *Go Hark!* Leave cravens and SKIRTERS to dangle behind.

SKIRT-FOIST, *subs. phr.* (old).—A general amorist; a POACHER (*q.v.*).

*d.*1652. WILSON, *Inconstant Lady* [NARES]. I think there is small good intended, that Emilia did prefer him. I do not like that SKIRT-FOIST.

SKIT, *subs.* (GROSE).—1. A jest, a satire: also as *verb.* (GROSE) = 'to wheedle.'

1779. MRS. COWLEY, *Who's the Dupe?* ii. 2. Come, come, none of your tricks upon travellers. I know you mean all that as a SKIT upon my edication.

1815. SCOTT, *Guy Mannering*, xxxii. But if he really shot young Hazlewood—But I canna think it, Mr. Glossin; this will be some o' yonr SKITS* now—I conna think it o' sae douce a lad;—na, na, this is just some o' your auld SKITS—ye'll be for having a horning or a caption after him. [*Tricks.]

1884. *Graphic*, 20 Sept., 299, 1. When will be produced the new Gilbert-Sullivan opera, which is reported to be a SKIT on "Thought-reading."

1885. *D. News*, 28 Sep. Of these many are SKITS at the expense of that unfailing object of Thackeray's love of banter.

2. *subs.* (old).—A wanton: *see* TART.

1583. HOWARD, *Def. agst. Superst. Prophesies.* [Herod] at the request of a dancing SKIT stroke off the head of St. John the Baptist.

SKITTER-BRAIN (or **-WIT**), *subs.* (common).—A flighty person. Also SKITTERBRAINED, &c.

SKITTING-DEALER, *subs. phr.* (Old Cant).—A sham dumby.

SKITTLES, *intj.* (common).—Nonsense!

Other COLLOQUIALISMS are—ALL BEER AND SKITTLES = Everything easy or to one's liking; ALL UP, AS SKITTLES WHEN DOWN = a difficulty, something to tackle or do again.

1864. *Orchestra*, 12 Nov., 106. 'To Correspondents.' *Se faire applaudir* is not "to make onesself applauded," and "joyous comedian" is simply SKITTLES.

1886. KIPLING, *Departmental Ditties*, 'Padgate, M.P.' 'Where is your heat?' said he. 'Coming,' said I to Padgate. 'SKITTLES!' said Padgate, M.P.

1889. *Lic. Vict. Gaz.*, 8 Feb. Plunging was NOT ALL BEER AND SKITTLES, as the Viscount had playfully and elegantly observed when a special pot had boiled over.

1890. *Pall Mall Gaz.*, 4 Nov., 3, 1. It would present a useful object lesson to those who think that the artist's life is ALL BEER AND SKITTLES.

1900. BOOTHBY, *Maker of Nations*, v. SKITTLES it would have been and of the most desperate description . . . I can tell you I was just about played out.

SKIV (or **SCIV**), *subs.* (common).—A sovereign; 20/-: *see* RHINO.

1870. *London Figaro*, 19 Dec. 'A Swell on Stalls.' I am anxious to pay more; indeed, what do I want with change? Assure you I should much prefer to pay HALF-A-SKIV, or even a "sov." for my seat.

1887. PAYN, *Glow Worm Tales*, 246. Please to send me the SKIV by return, for I sadly want some comfort.

SKOWBANKER, *subs.* (Australian).—A loafer; a hanger-on: also SHOWBANKER.

SKOWER. *See* SCOURE.

SKRIMP (or **SKRUMP**), *verb.* (provincial).—To steal apples.

SKRIMSHANKER, *subs.* (military).—*See* SCRIMSHANKER and add quots. *infra.*

1890. *Tit-Bits*, 26 Ap., 35, 1. Of course, besides the dread of being considered a SKRIMSHANKER, a soldier dislikes the necessary restraints of a hospital.

1893. KIPLING, *Many Inventions*, 'His Private Honour.' If Mulvaney stops SCRIMSHANKIN'—gets out o' . . . 'orspital . . . I lay your lives will be trouble to you.

SKRUNT, *subs.* (Scots').—A prostitute: *see* TART.

SKUE, *subs.* (old).—*See* quot.

1598. FLORIO, *A Worlde of Wordes*, *Codurza*, the rump or SKUE of a bird.

SKUG. *See* SCUG.

SKULKER, *subs.* (GROSE)—'A soldier who . . . evades his duty; a sailor who keeps below in time of danger; one who keeps out of the way when work is to be done. TO SKULK, to hide oneself; to avoid labour or duty.'

SKULL, *subs.* (University).—1. The head of a college: *see* GOLGOTHA; whence SKULL-RACE = a university examination. 2. (American) = any chief, as the President, the head of a business, the captain of a vessel, &c.

MY SKULL'S AFLY, *phr.* (old).—AWAKE (*q.v.*); FLY (*q.v.*)

SKULL AND CROSSBONES (THE), *subs. phr.* (military).—The 17th (The Duke of Cambridge's Own) Lancers. [The Regimental Badge.] Also "The Death or Glory Boys"; "Bingham's Dandies"; "The Gentlemen Dragoons"; and "The Horse Marines."

SKULLDUGGERY. *See* SCULLDUDDERY.

SKULL-THATCHER, *subs. phr.* (old).—1. A straw-bonnet maker; hence (2) a hatter; and (3) a wig-maker. SKULL-THATCH = a hat or wig.

1863. BRADDON, *Aurora Floyd*, xxiv. 'I'll find my SKULL-THATCHER if I can,' said Captain Prodder, groping for his hat amongst the brambles and the long grass.

SKUNGLE, *verb.* (American).—A generic verb of action: to decamp, to steal a watch, to gobble up food, &c.: *cf.* SKYUGLE.

SKUNK, *subs.* (American).—1. A mean, paltry wretch; a STINKARD (*q.v.*).

1841. *The Kinsmen*, I. 171. He's a SKUNK—a bad chap about the heart.

1876. BRET HARTE, *Gabriel Conroy*, I. i. 14. Ain't my husband dead, and isn't that SKUNK—an entire stranger—still livin'?

1884. *Referee*, 1 June, 7, 3. The bloodthirsty and cowardly SKUNKS, who rob servant girls in America of their money in order to blow servant girls in London to pieces.

2. (American). Utter defeat: as *verb.* = to disgrace: *cf.* SLAM.

1848. DURIVAGE, *Stray Subjects*, 135. In the second hand of the third game, I made high, low, game, and SKUNKED him, outright again.

Verb. 2. (American Univ.).—To neglect to pay.

SKY (or **SKI**), *subs.* (Westminster).—1. *See* quot. [An abbreviation or corruption of *Volsci*: the Westminster boys being *Romans*.]

1867. STANLEY, *Westminster Abbey*, 453. Conflicts between Westminster scholars and the SKYS of London, as the outside world was called.

2. *See* SKYROCKET.

Verb. (common).—1. To hang, throw, or hit high (*e.g.*, a picture at the Royal Academy: whence THE SKY = the upper rows of exhibitors; a ball at cricket: hence SKYER, OR SKYSCRAPER = a high hit). Whence (2) to spend freely till all's BLUED (*q.v.*). TO SKY A COPPER = to spin a coin.

1802. EDGEWORTH, *Irish Bulls.* 'Billy,' says I, 'will you SKY A COPPER.'

18[?]. REYNOLDS, *The Fancy*, Glossary. Toss for sides—the seconds SKY A COPPER, before every battle, to decide which man shall face the sun.

1874. COLLINS, *Frances*, xxvii. The ball had been struck high in air, and long-field had almost flown into air to meet it, catching it as it came down like a thunderbolt with his left hand only, and SKYING it at once with triumphant delight.

1881. JAS. PAYN, *Grapes from a Thorn*, ii. His pictures of the abbey having been SKIED in the Academy . . . made his humour a little tart that year.

1884. *Sat. Rev.*, 31 May. The high wind made SKYERS difficult to judge.

1885. SMART, *Post to Finish*, 134. Two or three more slashing hits, and then the Rector SKYED one which his opponents promptly secured.

1886-96. MARSHALL, *Pomes*, 40. With the takings safely SKYED.

1889. *Pall Mall Gaz.*, 23 Sept., 2, 1. "Lost ball!" was cried . . . When, overhead, supremely SKIED, I saw that awful ball descending.

1890. *Globe*, 7 May, 6, 1. It was SKIED at the Royal Academy last year.

2. (Harrow).—1. To charge, or knock down: at football. Also (2) to throw away.

IF THE SKY FALLS WE SHALL CATCH LARKS = a retort to a wild hypothesis: *cf.* 'if pigs had wings they'd be likely birds to fly.'

1654. WEBSTER, *Appius and Virginia* [DODSLEY, *Old Plays* (REED), iv. 124]. If hap THE SKY-FALL, WE MAY hap to HAVE LARKS.

SKY-BLUE, *subs. phr.* (old).—1. Gin (GROSE).

1755. *Connoisseur*, No. 53. Madam Gin has been christened by as many names as a German princess: every petty chandler's shop will sell you SKY-BLUE.

2. (common). — Diluted or 'separated' milk.

1800. BLOOMFIELD, *Farmer's Boy.* And strangers tell of three times skimmed SKY-BLUE.

*d.*1845. HOOD, *Retrospective Review.* That mild SKY-BLUE, That washed my sweet meals down.

1864. SALA, *Quite Alone*, xv. Cake and wine existed no more in her allure; she was suggestive only of bread and scrape and SKY-BLUE.

SKY-FARMER, *subs. phr.* (old).—*See* quot.: GROSE (1785).

1754. *Disc. John Poulter*, 39. SKY-FARMERS are People that go about the country with a false pass, signed by the Church Wardens and Overseers of the Parish or Place that they lived in, and some Justice of the Peace, but the Names are all forged; in this manner they extort money, under pretence of sustaining Loss by Fire, or the Distemper amongst the horned Cattle.

SKYGAZER, *subs.* (nautical). — A skysail

SKY-GODLIN, *adv.* (American).—Obliquely; askew.

1869. *Overland Monthly*, iv. 128. He will run SKY-GODLIN.

SKY-LANTERN, *subs. phr.* (old).—The moon: *see* OLIVER.

1843. MONCRIEFF, *Scamps of London*, i. 2. You won't want a light—you can see by the SKY-LANTERN up above.

SKYLARK, *subs.* (common).—Originally tricks in the rigging of H. M. Navy; hence any rough-and-tumble horseplay. As *verb.* = to frolic, to play the fool; SKYLARKING = boisterous merriment or fooling; and SKYLARKER = a practical joker.

1829. MARRYAT, *Frank Mildmay*, iv. I had become . . . so fond of displaying my newly acquired gymnastics, called by the sailors SKY-LARKING, that my speedy exit was often prognosticated. *Ibid.* (1834), *Peter Simple* (1846), I. 62. There was such bawling and threatening, laughing and crying . . . all squabbling or SKYLARKING, and many of them drunk.

1835. DANA, *Before the Mast*, xvii. We . . . ran her chock up to the yard. 'Vast there! vast!' said the mate; 'none of your SKYLARKING!

1836. M. SCOTT, *Cruise of Midge*, 188. Come on deck, man—come on deck—this is no time for SKYLARKING. *Ibid.* (1852), *Tom Cringle's Log*, iii. 'It's that SKY-LARKING son of a gun, Jem Sparkle's monkey, sir.'

1855. C. KINGSLEY, *Westward Ho*, xviii. Lucky for them . . . they were not SKYLARKING.

1858. *New York Courier.* 'Election.' There was a considerable amount of SKYLARKING carried on from sunset until midnight in the halls and passages of the building, hats were smashed, and members tumbled on the floor.

1863. KINGSLEY, *Austin Elliot*, iv. When his father wouldn't stand him any longer, he used to go out and SKYLARK with the clerks.

1871. *Morning Advertizer*, 2 Feb. Give warning of what is going on to "all husbands who SKYLARK around." The precise nature of the diversion, indicated by SKYLARKING AROUND, is a little foggy; but, taken in conjunction with the context, it is clearly not inconsistent with staying from home until the small hours.

1888. BOLDREWOOD, *Robbery under Arms*, xxiv. Talking and SKYLARKING, like a lot of boys.

1893. MILLIKEN, *'Arry Ballads*, 7. If yer don't find it a 'Oliday SKYLARK, wy, never trust 'Arry.

SKYLARKER, *subs.* (old thieves').—A housebreaker following bricklaying as a blind.

2. *See* SKYLARK.

SKYLIGHT, *subs.* (nautical).—The eye.

1836. SCOTT, *Tom Cringle's Log*, iii. After a long look through his starboard blinker (his other SKYLIGHT had been shut up ever since Aboukir) . . .

SKY-PARLOUR, *subs. phr.* (common).—A garret (GROSE).

1807-8. IRVING, *Salmagundi*, No. ii. I beg leave to repeat the advice so often given by the illustrious tenants of the theatrical SKY-PARLOUR to the gentlemen who are charged with the "nice conduct" of chairs and tables—"Make a bow, Johnny. Johnny, make a bow."

1821. EGAN, *Life in London*, II. v. Bob . . . proposed to see the author safe to his SKY PARLOUR.

1836. DICKENS, *Sketches by Boz*, 'First of May.' Now ladies, up in the SKY-PARLOUR; only once a year, if you please. *Ibid.* (1855), *Dorrit*, I. viii. She has a lodging at the turnkey's. First home there . . . SKY PARLOUR.

1847. RHODES, *Bombastes Furioso*, 15. My PARLOUR that's NEXT TO THE SKY I'd quit, her blest mansion to share.

1883. DOBSON, *Hogarth*, 43. The poor verseman, high in his Grub-Street or "Porridge-Island" SKY-PARLOUR.

1891. *Herald*, 31 May, 3, 1. SKY-PARLOURS may be very well, but I'm certain there is something wrong with my friend's "upper story."

1895. LE QUEUX, *Temptress*, iii. The necessaries of life which she would convey to his SKY PARLOUR.

SKY-PILOT, *subs. phr.* (common).—A clergyman: *see* BIBLE-POUNDER.

1889. *Sporting Times*, 29 June. The SKY PILOT, having regard to muttered remarks which might be heard emanating from the Englishman, gave his professional opinion that his service was anything divine.

1895. LE QUEUX, *Temptress*, ix. Have you seen the SKY PILOT?

SKYROCKET, *subs.* (rhyming).—1. A pocket: also SKY.

1879. J. W. HORSLEY in *Macm. Mag.*, xl. 502. A slavey piped [saw] the spoons sticking out of my SKYROCKET [pocket].

1893. EMERSON, *Lippo*, xiv. See everything is bono, and keep the split in your SKYROCKET. *Ibid.*, xx. I'd two bob in my SKY, so paid three night's letty.

1898. *Pink 'Un and Pelican*, 237. After thirty-six 'ands 'ad bin all over him, —why, even then we never found his SKY.

2. (old).—Eccentricity.

1690. DRYDEN, *Mistakes*, Prol. [*Works* (*Globe*), 473]. He's no highflyer—he makes no SKYROCKETS. His squibs are only levelled at your pockets.

SKYSCRAPER, *subs.* (common).—Generic for height: *e.g.* (1) a very tall man; (2) a very lofty building: spec. (American) erections sometimes twenty stories high; (3) a triangular sail set above the royals, a sky-sail, SKYGAZER, OR ANGEL'S FOOTSTOOL (*q.v.*); and (4) a SKIED ball. Hence SKYSCRAPING and other derivatives.

1815. SCOTT, *Guy Mannering*, v. Run out the bolt-sprit, up main-sail, top and top-gallant sails, royals, and SKYSCRAPERS, and away—follow who can!

1893. MILLIKEN, *'Arry Ballads*, 47. It's a bloominger SKY-SCRAPING Topper.

1902. *Free Lance*, 19 July, 364, 1. Unsightly blocks of SKY-SCRAPING buildings; vulgar self-advertisement, loudness, and beef Trusts, bluff and billionaires.

5. (old nautical).—A cocked hat.

6. (venery).—The *penis: see* PRICK and *cf.* HEAVEN = female *pudendum*.

SKYPPER. *See* SKIPPER, *subs.*, sense 1.

SKYTE, *subs.* (Shrewsbury).—*See* quot.: *cf.* Scots' SKYTE = fool.

1881. PASCOE, *Every-Day Life, &c.* Day boys . . . live or lodge in the town; and the designation of SKYTES was formerly applied to them.

Verb. (old).—1. SKITE (*q.v.*); and (2) SQUITTER (*q.v.*).

ON THE SKYTE, *phr.* (Scots').—Drunk: *see* SCREWED.

1872. *Paston Letters*, i. 85. Robert Weryngton to Thomas Daniel, May, 1449. And there I came about the Admirale, and bade them stryke in the Kyngys name of England, and they bade me SKYTE in the Kyngs name of England.

SKYUGLE, *verb.* (American).—*See* quots.

1873. *Tribune*, 27 Jan. Not knowing exactly what it is to SKYUGLE a message, we cannot say whether our reporter was guilty of that offence or not; but we have no hesitation in admitting that he procured a copy of the message in advance, and that our reporters do such things almost every day.

1880. COLLINS, *Thoughts in my Garden*, I. 49. The scoundrels SKYUGLED one excellent old gentleman's choice plate.

1864. *Army and Navy Journal* (American), 11 July. A corps staff officer informed me that he had been out on a general SCYUGLE; that he had SCYUGLED along the front, when the rebels SCYUGLED a bullet through his clothes; that he should SCYUGLE his servant; who, by the way, had SCYUGLED three fat chickens; that after he had SCYUGLED his dinner, he proposed to SCYUGLE a nap.

SKY-WANNOCKING, *subs. phr.* (common).—A drunken frolic.

SLAB, *subs.* (old).—1. A milestone (BEE).

2. (provincial).—A bricklayer's boy (HALLIWELL).

3. (common).—A thick slice of bread and butter: *cf.* DOORSTEP.

4. (Durham School).—In *pl.* = a flat cake.

TO SLAB OFF, *verb. phr.* (American).—To reject [BARTLETT].

1835. CROCKETT, *Tour Down East*, 212. You must take notice that I am SLABB'D OFF from the election, and am nothing but a voter.

SLABBERING-BIT, *subs. phr.* (old).—A neck-band: clerical or legal (GROSE).

SLABBERDEGULLION. *See* SLUBBERDEGULLION.

SLAB-SIDED, *adj.* (colloquial).—Tall; lank; 'up and down' in figure: also SLAP-SIDED.

1825. NEAL, *Brother Jonathan*, ii. Great, long, SLAB-SIDED gawkeys from the country.

1856. DOW, *Sermons*, II. 200. I like to see a small waist . . . and females with hour-glass shapes suit my fancy better than your Dutch-churn, soap-barrel, SLAB-SIDED sort of figures.

1856. LELAND, *New Sloper Sketches* [*Knickerbocker Mag.*, Mar.]. The real SLAB-SIDED whittler is indigenous to Varmount and New Hampshire.

1859. KINGSLEY, *Geoffrey Hamlyn*, 353. One of those long-legged, SLAB-SIDED, lean, sunburned, cabbage-tree hatted lads.

d. 1891. LOWELL, *Fitz-Adam's Story*. You didn't chance to run ag'inst my son, A long SLAB-SIDED youngster with a gun?

SLACK, *subs.* (common).—In *pl.* = overall trousers.

1883. GREENWOOD, *Odd People*. Unwashed, and in their working SLACKS and guernseys.

2. (pugilistic).—A smashing or knock-down blow. [Jack Slack, champion 1750-60, was known for his powerful delivery]. Also SLACK-'UN: *cf.* AUCTIONEER and MENDOZA.

3. (colloquial).—A slack time.

1851-61. MAYHEW, *Lond. Lab.*, III. 237. When there is a SLACK the merchants are all anxious to get their vessels delivered as fast as they can.

1861. HUGHES, *Tom Brown at Oxford*, II. xxi. Though there's a SLACK we haven't done with sharp work yet, I see.

Verb. (common).—To PISS (*q.v.*): also TO SLACK OFF.

TO HOLD ON THE SLACK, *verb. phr.* (nautical).—To skulk; to loaf.

SLACK-JAW, *subs. phr.* (American).—Impertinence.

1883. *Century Mag.*, xxxvii. 407. I mought do it fur you, bein' as how ye got so much SLACK-JAW.

SLAG, *subs.* (old).—'A slack-mettled fellow, one not ready to resent an affront' (GROSE).

SLAKE, *verb.* (provincial).—*See* quot.

1847. HALLIWELL, *Archaic Words, &c.*, s.v. SLAKE . . . 3. To lick . . . vulgarly used in the sense . . . of to kiss.

SLAM, *subs.* (old).—1. A trick (GROSE).

2. (cards').—At whist a game lost without scoring: also as *verb.* = to take every trick: *cf.* SKUNK (B. E. and GROSE).

[?]. *Loyal Songs* [*Ency. Dict.*]. Until a noble general came And gave the cheaters a clean SLAM.

3. (old).—A sloven: also SLAMKIN (GROSE: 'One whose clothes seem hung on with a pitchfork'); and (4) any ill-made, awkward, ungainly wretch.

1697. VANBRUGH, *Relapse*, v. 6. *Hoyd.* I don't like my lord's shapes, nurse. *Nurse.* Why in good truly, as a body may say, he is but a SLAM.

Verb. (common).—1. To brag; spec. (military) to feign drunkenness and boast of many drinks: *cf.* SLUM.

2. (strollers').—To PATTER (*q.v.*); to talk in the way of trade.

1884. HENLEY, *Villon's Good Night*. You swatchel coves that pitch and SLAM.

SLAM-BANG. *See* SLAP, *adv.*

SLAMKIN (SLAMMOCKS, or SLAMMERKIN), *subs.* (old).—A SLUT (*q.v.*). As *verb.* = to slouch.

SLAMMER, *subs.* (colloquial).—Anything exceptional: *see* WHOPPER. Hence SLAMMING (*adj.*) = large, exceptional.

SLAMPAM (SLAMPAINE, SLAMPAMBES, or SLAMPANT), *subs.* (old).—A blow: *see* WIPE. TO CUT OF (or GIVE THE) SLAMPAMBES = to circumvent; to get the better of.

c. 1563. *New Custome* [DODSLEY, *Old Plays* (REED), i. 230]. I wyll CUT HIM OF THE SLAMPAMBES, I hold him a crowne, Wherever I meete him, in countrie or towne.

1577-87. HOLINSHED, *Desc. Ireland*, iii. That one rascal in such scornefull wise should GIUE THEM THE SLAMPAINE.

1582. STANYHURST, *Æneid* [ARBER], 116. Shal hee scape thus? shal a stranger GEUE ME THE SLAMPAN?

SLAMTRASH, *subs.* (provincial).—A sloven (HALLIWELL).

SLANEY, *subs.* (thieves').—A theatre.

SLANG, *subs.*, *adj.*, and *verb.* (old: now recognised).—*See* TERMINAL ESSAY and quots. As *verb.* = (1) to speak slang; and (2) to scold or abuse. As *adj.* = (1) relating to slang; (2) = low, unrefined; and (3) = angry: also SLANGY and SLANGULAR. SLANGINESS = the state of being slangy; SLANG-BOYS (or BOYS OF THE SLANG) (*see* quot. 1789); SLANGSTER = a master of FLASH (*q.v.*); SLANG-WHANGER = a speaker addicted to slang: whence SLANGWHANGING, and SLANGWHANG, *verb.* = to scold; SLANGANDER (American) = to backbite; SLANGOOSING (American) = tittle-tattle, backbiting, esp. of women.

1743. FIELDING, *Jonathan Wild*, 'Advice to His Successor.' The master who teaches them [young thieves] should be a man well versed in the cant language, commonly called the SLANG patter, in which they should by all means excel.

1761. FOOTE, *Lyar.* [OLIPHANT, *New Eng.*, ii. 180. A man begs "in the College cant" to *tick* a little longer (remain in debt); this *cant* was soon to make way for SLANG]. *Ibid.* (1762), *Orators*, i. *Foote.* Have you not seen the bills? *Scamper.* What, about the lectures? ay, but that's all SLANG, I suppose, . . . no, no.

1785. GROSE, *Vulg. Tongue*, s.v. FLASH LINGO. The canting or SLANG language. *Ibid.*, GILES'. St. Giles Greek, the cant language, called also SLANG, Pedler's French, and Flash.

1789. PARKER, *Variegated Characters*. SLANG BOYS, fellows who speak the SLANG language which is the same as flash and cant.

1796. W. TAYLOR, *Monthly Rev.*, xx. 543-4. The personages have mostly the manners and language of elegant middle life, removed alike from the rant of tragedy or the SLANG of farce.

1798. *Anti-Jacobin*, 5 Mar. Stanzas . . . conceived rather in the SLANG or Brentford dialect.

1807. IRVING, *Salmagundi*, No. 14. It embraces alike all manner of concerns; . . . to the personal disputes of two miserable SLANGWHANGERS, the cleaning of the streets . . . *Ibid.* (1824). *T. Trav.*, I. 273. SLANG talk and cant jokes.

1809. MALKIN, *Gil Blas* [ROUTLEDGE], 47. He [a doctor] had got into reputation with the public by a certain professional SLANG.

1813. EDGEWORTH, *Patronage*, iii. The total want of proper pride and dignity . . . a certain SLANG and familiarity of tone, gave superficial observers the notion that he was good-natured.

1816. *Gentleman's Mag.*, lxxxvi, 418. Unwilling to be a disciple of the stable, the kennel, and the sty, as of the other precious SLANG, the dialect of Newgate.

1817. COLERIDGE, *Biog.*, II. xvi. To make us laugh by . . . SLANG phrases of the day.

1819. ROBERT RABELAIS THE YOUNGER, *Abeillard and Heloisa*, 35. For filthy talk and SLANG discourse, They every day grow worse and worse.

1820. *Blackwood's Mag.*, viii. 261. Living on the town, as it is SLANGISHLY called.

1821. DE QUINCEY, *Conf.* (1862), 234. According to the modern SLANG phrase.

1823. MONCRIEFF, *Tom and Jerry*, 5. Flash, my young friend, or SLANG, as others call it, is the classical language of the Holy Land; in other words, St Giles's Greek.

1824. SCOTT, *Redgauntlet*, xiii. What did actually reach his ears was disguised so completely by the use of cant words and the thieves'-Latin called SLANG, that even when he caught the words, he found himself as far as ever from the sense of their conversation.

1827. LYTTON, *Pelham*, xlix. We rowed, swore, SLANGED.

1830. KNIGHT, Tr. *Acharnians*, 106. Drunk he shall SLANG with the harlots.

1837. HOOD, 'Ode to Rae Wilson.' With tropes from Billingsgates' SLANG-WHANGING Tartars. *Ibid.* (1845), 36. *Tale of a Trumpet.* The smallest urchin whose tongue could tang Shock'd the dame with a volley of SLANG.

1840. HOOD, *Up the Rhine*, 62. In spite of a SLANG air, a knowing look, and the use of certain insignificant phrases that are most current in London . . .

1845. *N. Y. Com. Advtr.*, 10 Oct. Part of the customary SLANG-WHANGING against all other nations which is habitual to the English press.

1849. KINGSLEY, *Alton Locke*, ii. Be quiet, you fool . . . you're a pretty fellow to chaff the orator; he'll SLANG you up the chimney before you get your shoes on. *Ibid.* vi. A tall, handsome, conceited, SLANGY boy.

1851-61. MAYHEW, *Lond. Lab.*, III. 350. To SLANG with the fishwives.

1852. BRISTED, *Up. Ten Thousand*, 205. Here I have been five days . . . hazing—what you call SLANGING—upholsterers.

1853. DICKENS, *Bleak House*, xi. His strength lying in a SLANGULAR direction. *Ibid.* (1865). *Our Mutual Friend*, II. iv. Both were too gaudy, too SLANGY, too odorous of cigars, and too much given to horseflesh.

1857. H. REED, *Lect. Brit. Poets*, ix. 308. A freedom and coarseness of diction denominated SLANG, a word belonging to the very vocabulary it denotes.

1872. ELIOT, *Middlemarch*, xi. All choice of words is SLANG. . . . Correct English is the SLANG of prigs who write history and essays. And the strongest SLANG of all is the SLANG of poets.

1875. WHITNEY, *Life and Growth of Language*, vii. There are grades and uses of SLANG whose charm no one need be ashamed to feel and confess; it is like reading a narrative in a series of rude and telling pictures instead of in words.

1879-81. SKEAT, *Etymological Dict.*, s.v. SLANG . . . is from the Norwegian *sleng*, a slinging, a device, a burden of a song. *Slengja*, to sling; *slengja kieften*, TO SLANG, abuse (lit. to sling the jaw; SLENG-JENAMN, a *slang* (*i.e.*, an abusive name); *slengje-ord*, an insulting word; all from *slengja*, to *sling*.

1881-9. *Encyclopædic Dict.*, s.v. SLANG. A kind of colloquial language current amongst one particular class, or amongst various classes of society, uneducated or educated, but which, not having received the stamp of general approval, is frequently considered as inelegant or vulgar. Almost every profession or calling has its own SLANG . . . In this sense it means any colloquial words or phrases, vulgar or refined, used conventionally by each particular class of people in speaking of particular matters connected with their own calling. SLANG is sometimes allied to, but not quite identical with *cant*.

1884. H. JAMES, JR., *Little Tour*, 89. As the game went on, and he lost . . . he . . . SLANGED his partner, declared he wouldn't play any more, and went away in a fury.

1886. *D. Telegraph*, 11 Sep. A tipsy virago SLANGING the magistrate to the high amusement of the top-booted constables. *Ibid.*, 1 Jan. It is the business of SLANGINESS to make everything ugly. *Ibid.*, 13 Sep. 'Don't be so SLANGY, Julia,' remonstrates her father.

1888. *Poor Nellie*, 17. Looked awfully SLANGY then? I'm sure she was in a wax.

1898. *Century Dict.*, s.v. SLANG. 1. The cant words or jargon used by thieves, peddlers, beggars, and the vagabond classes generally. 2. In present use, colloquial words and phrases which have originated in the cant or rude speech of the vagabond or unlettered classes, or, belonging in form to standard speech, have acquired or have had given them restricted, capricious, or extravagantly metaphorical meanings, and are regarded as vulgar or inelegant . . . SLANG as such is not necessarily vulgar or ungrammatical; indeed, it is generally correct in idiomatic form, and though frequently censured on this ground, it often, in fact, owes its doubtful character to other causes.

1899. WHITEING, *John St.*, vi. A SLANGING MATCH . . . and the unnameable in invective and vituperation rises, as in blackest vapour from our pit to the sky.

1900. *Nation*, 9 Oct., 289. SLANG in the sense of the cant language of thieves appears in print as early as the middle of the last century [*see* quot. 1743 *supra*]. Scott when using the word felt the necessity of defining it; and his definition shows not only that it was generally unknown but that it had not then begun to depart from its original sense.

2. (old).—A leg iron; a fetter (GROSE and VAUX). [Formerly about three feet long, the SLANG being attached to an iron anklet rivetted on the leg: the SLACK (*q.v.*) was slung to the waistbelt.] Whence (3) = a watch-chain. In Dutch slang, SLANG = (1) a snake, and (2) a chain.

*c.*1790. *Kilmainham Minit* [*Ireland Sixty Years Ago*, 88]. If dat de SLANG you run sly, De scrag-boy may yet be outwitted, And I scout again on de lay.

*c.*1866. VANCE, *Chickaleary Cove.* How to do a cross-fan for a super or SLANG.

1877. HORSLEY, *Jottings from Jail.* Fullied for a clock and SLANG.

1900. MAJOR ARTHUR GRIFFITHS, *Fast and Loose*, xxxiii. If I am caught it'll mean a 'bashing' and the SLANGS.

1901. WALKER, *In the Blood*, 138. A watch and chain, or in thieves' language "white lot" and thimble and SLANG.

4. (old).—False weights and measures (*e.g.*, a slang quart = 1½ pts.). As *verb.* = to cheat by short weight or measure: also 'to defraud a person of any part of his due' (GROSE and VAUX). SLANGING-DUES (*see* quot. 1785).

1785. GROSE, *Vulg. Tongue*, s.v. SLANGING-DUES. When a man suspects that he has been curtailed of any portion of his just right, he will say, There has been SLANGING-DUES concerned.

1851-61. MAYHEW, *Lond. Lab.*, II. 104. Some of the street weights, a good many of them, are SLANGS.

5. (old).—A beggar's pass; a hawker's license: any official instrument. ON THE SLANG = begging or peddling. Hence (6) a pursuit; a LAY (*q.v.*); a LURK (*q.v.*).

1789. PARKER, *Variegated Characters.* How do you work now? Oh, upon THE old SLANG and sometimes a little bully-prigging.

7. (showmen's).—(*a*) A travelling show; a cheap-jack's van; and (*b*) a performance; a TURN (*q.v.*): *e.g.*, the first, second, or third SLANG = the first, second, or third HOUSE (*q.v.*), when more than one performance is given during the evening. Also THE SLANGS = (1) a collection of shows, and (2) the showman's profession; SLANGING and SLANG-CULL (*see* quot. 1789); SLANG-AND-PITCHER SHOP = (1) a cheap-jack's van, and (2) a wholesale dealer in cheap-jack wares; SLANG-TREE = (1) a stage, and (2) a trapeze: hence TO CLIMB UP THE SLANG TREE = (1) to perform, and (2) to make an exhibition of oneself.

1789. PARKER, *Var. Characters.* To exhibit anything in a fair or market, such as a tall man, or a cow with two heads, that's called SLANGING, and the exhibitor is called a SLANG-CULL.

1851-61. MAYHEW, *Lond. Lab.*, i. 353. The SLANG-COVES (the showmen) have . . . been refused.

1887. HENLEY, *Villon's Straight Tip*, 2. Pad with a SLANG, or chuck a fag.

1888. HOOD, *Comic Annual*, 52. There were all kinds of fakes on the SLANGS . . . amongst others some Chinese acrobatic work.

TO SLANG THE MAULEYS, *verb. phr.* (streets').—To shake hands. [That is TO SLING (*q.v.*)].

SLANGRILL (or **SLANGAM**), *subs.* (old).—A lout.

1592. GREENE, *Quip for Upstart Courtier* [*Harl. Misc.*, v. 407]. The third was a long leane, olde, slavering SLANGRILL.

1611. COTGRAVE, *Dict.*, s.v. *Longis.* A tall and dull SLANGAM, that hath no making to his height, nor wit to his making; also one that being sent on an errand is long in returning.

SLANT, *subs.* (colloquial).—1. An opportunity; a chance. [Originally nautical = a favourable wind: *e.g.*, 'a SLANT across the Bay.']

2. (American).—A side blow (BARTLETT).

Verb. (thieves').—1. To run away: *see* BOLT.

2. (colloquial). — To exaggerate; to 'draw the LONG BOW' (*q.v.*).

3. (racing).—To wager: *see* LAY.

SLANTENDICULAR, *adj.* (colloquial).—Indirect; a SLANT (*q.v.*). Also as *adv.*

1844. HALIBURTON, *The Attache*, xxviii. Pony got mad and sent the Elder right slap over his head SLANTENDICULARLY, on the broad of his back, into the river.

1872. DE MORGAN, *Budg. of Paradoxes*, 289. He must put himself [in the Calendar] under the first saint, with a SLANTENDICULAR reference to the other.

SLAP, *subs.* (old). — 1. Booty; plunder.

*c.*1790. *Kilmainham Minit* [*Ireland Sixty Years Ago*, 87]. And when dat he milled a fat SLAP, He merrily melted de winners.

2. (theatrical).—Make-up. Also as *verb.*: [*cf.* SLAP = to rough cast].

1897. MARSHALL, *Pomes*, 98. You could just distinguish faintly That she favoured the judicious use of SLAP.

Adj. (colloquial).—First-rate; SMART (*q.v.*); PRIME (*q.v.*): also SLAP-UP: *cf.* BANG-UP (GROSE). Whence SLAPPER = anything exceptional: *see* WHOPPER; SLAPPING = very big, excellent.

1851-61. MAYHEW, *Lond. Lab.*, II. 119. People's got proud now . . . and must have everything SLAP. *Ibid.*, 122. A smart female servant in SLAP-UP black.

1855. THACKERAY, *Newcomes*, xxxi. Might it not be more SLAP-UP still to have the two shields painted on the panels with the coronet over.

1859. MATSELL, *Vocabulum.* Kerseymere kicksies . . . built very SLAP with the artful dodge.

1865. DICKENS, *O. M. Friend.* A SLAP-UP gal in a bang-up chariot.

1880. AINSWORTH, *Auriol.* He's a regular SLAP-UP swell.

1885. *Stage*, 129. Whitechapel costers, who wore SLAP-UP kicksies.

Adv. (colloquial).—Violently; plump; offhand: also SLAP-BANG, SLAM-BANG and SLAP-DASH. As *subs.* = (1) careless work, and (2) indiscriminate action; as *verb.* = to go recklessly to work.

1671. BUCKINGHAM, *Rehearsal* [ARBER], 67. He is upon him, SLAP, with a repartee; then he is at him again, DASH, with a new conceit.

1693. CONGREVE, *Old Batchelor*, iv. 9. I am SLAP DASH down in the mouth, and have not one word to say.

1705. VANBRUGH, *Confederacy*, iv. Very genteel, truly! Go, SLAP DASH, and offer a woman of her scruples money, bolt in her face!

1712. CENTLIVRE, *Perpl. Lovers*, iii. If you don't march off, I shall play you such an English courant of SLAP DASH presently, that shan't out of your ears this twelvemonth.

1717. PRIOR, *Alma*, i. 17. And yet, SLAPDASH, is all again, In every sinew, nerve, and vein.

1753. RICHARDSON, *Grandison*, i. 170. In so peremptory, in so unceremonious a manner, SLAPDASH as I may say.

1759-67. STERNE, *Tristram Shandy*, III. 38. The whips and short turns which in one stage or other of my life have come SLAP upon me.

*c.*1790. *Kilmainham Minit* [*Ireland Sixty Years Ago*], 87. SLAP DASH tro de Poddle we lark it.

1809. MALKIN, *Gil Blas* [ROUTLEDGE], 42. He came down SLAP-DASH on all the rest of the dishes.

1837. BARHAM, *Ingoldsby Legends*, II. 143. His horse, coming SLAP on his knees . . . threw . . . him head over heels.

1853. LYTTON, *My Novel*, III. vi. It was a SLAPDASH style.

*c.*1866. VANCE, *Jolly Dogs.* SLAP-BANG, here we are again.

1882. LOWELL [*Century Mag.*, xxxv. 515]. The SLAPDASH judgments upon artists . . . are very characteristic.

1884. C. READE, *Art*, 20. He . . . executed a marvellously grotesque bow . . . this done, he . . . strode away again SLAP-DASH.

1885. *Weekly Echo*, 5 Sep. This most eccentric of quill-drivers gets up his facts in a SLAP-DASH fashion.

18... *Athenæum*, 3197, 146. As a specimen of newspaper SLAPDASH we may point to the description of General Ignatieff as 'the Russian Mr. Gladstone.'

A SLAP (or SLAT) IN THE FACE, *phr.* (colloquial).—A rebuff; a reproach (BEE).

See SLOP UP.

SLAP-BANG SHOP, *subs. phr.* (old). —1. *See* quot. 1785. Also SLAM-BANG SHOP (BEE).

1785. GROSE, *Vulg. Tongue*, s.v. SLAP-BANG SHOP. A petty cook's shop, where there is no credit given, but what is had must be paid for, down with the ready SLAP-BANG, *i.e.* immediately. This is a common appellation for a night cellar frequented by thieves.

1856. DICKENS, *Sketches by Boz*, 'Making a Night of it.' They dined at the same SLAP-BANG every day, and revelled in each other's company every night.

2. (old).—A stage coach, or caravan (GROSE).

See SLAP, *adv.*

SLAP-JACK. *See* FLAP-JACK.

SLAPPATY-POUCH (or **SLATTER-POUCH**), *subs.* (old). — Beating the arms on the chest to keep warm.

1654. GAYTON, *Festivous Notes*, 86. When they were boyes at trap, or SLATTERPOUCH They'd sweat.

*d.*1704. BROWN, *Works*, II. 126. We have . . . tir'd our palms and our ribs at SLAPPATY-POUCH.

SLAP-SAUCE, *subs. phr.* (old).—A hanger-on; a toady. As *adj.* = to SPONGE (*q.v.*).

1557. TUSSER, *Husbandrie*, 188. Ere tongue be too free, Or SLAPSAUCE be noted too saucie to bee.

1653. URQUHART, *Rabelais*, I. xxv. SLAPSAUCE fellows . . . lubbardly louts.

SLAP-SIDED. *See* SLAB-SIDED.

SLASH, *subs.* (thieves').—An outside pocket [*cf.* GROSE, s.v. SLIP, 'the SLASH pocket in the skirt of a coat behind.'].

Verb. (literary).—To criticise severely, sarcastically, or at random; TO CUT UP (*q.v.*).: also to SLASH IN. Hence SLASHING, *subs.* = damning criticism; as *adj.* = trenchent. harsh; SLASHER = a vigorous critic.

*d.*1859. DE QUINCEY, *Homer*, i. The Alexandrian critics with all their SLASHING insolence . . . groped about in twilight.

1874. MORTIMER COLLINS, *Frances*, xvii. The SLASHING writers who delight to cut up a book, especially if the author is a friend or a rival.

1888. *Athenæum*, 14 Jan., 43. He may be called the inventor of the modern SLASHING article.

SLASHER, *subs.* (old).—1. A bully; a bravo: *see* FURIOSO (GROSE and MATSELL). Also (2) a pounding pugilist, a HITTITE (*q.v.*); and (3) *see* SLASH.

1593. HARVEY [GROSART, *Works*, ii. 57]. That most threatening SLASSHER.

4. (old).—A sword.

1815. SCOTT, *Guy Mannering*, xxxiii. 'Had he no arms'? . . . 'Ay, ay, he was never without barkers and SLASHERS.

5. (colloquial).—Anything exceptional: *see* WHOPPER. Hence SLASHING = exceptionally brilliant, vigorous, successful, expert, &c. Also as *adv.*, as a SLASHING fine woman; a SLASHING good race; and so forth.

1854. DICKENS, *Hard Times* [*Ency. Dict.*]. A SLASHING fortune.

THE SLASHERS, *subs. phr.* (military).—The 1st Batt. Gloucestershire Regiment, formerly The 28th Foot. Also "The Old Braggs" and "The Right-abouts."

SLAT, *subs.* (old).—Half-a-crown: 2/6; *see* RHINO (GROSE); also (B. E.) SLATE.

Verb. (American).—To throw, beat, or move with violence.

1604. MARSTON, *Malcontent.* SLATTED his brains out, then soused him in the briny sea.

1846. *N. Y. Com. Advtr.*, 15 May. Aunt Nancy would retire to the kitchen, and taking up the dipper, would SLAT round the hot water from a kettle.

*c.*1859. *Layfayette Chronicle* [BARTLETT]. Suz alive! but warn't my dander up to hear myself called a flat? down I SLAT the basket, and upsought all the berries.

1865. *Major Jack Downing*, 200. With that I handed him my axe, and he SLATTED about the chamber a spell.

SLATE, *subs.* (Old Cant). — 1. A sheet (DEKKER and GROSE): also (B. E.) SLAT.

1567. HARMAN, *Caveat* [E. E. T. S.], 76. A kynching morte is a lytle gyrle; the Mortes their mothers carries them at their backs in their SLATES.

1611. MIDDLETON, *Roaring Girl*, v. 1. I have, by the Salomon, a doxy that carries a kinchin-mort in her SLATE at her back.

1622. FLETCHER, *Beggar's Bush*, iii. 3. To mill from the Ruffmans commission and SLATES.

2. (American political). — A preliminary list of candidates recommended to office; a party programme. [In practice a secret understanding between leaders as to the candidates they desire the nominating Convention to adopt.] To SMASH (or BREAK) THE SLATE = to defeat the wire-pullers; TO SLATE = (1) to prepare, and (2) to be included in such a list. SLATE-SMASHER = a leader who ignores the wishes of his party.

1877. *N. Y. Tribune*, 1 Mar. The facts about the latest Cabinet SLATE . . . are interesting as showing . . . the course of President Hayes in choosing his advisers.

Verb. (colloquial). — 1. To reprimand or criticise; TO CUT UP (*q.v.*). [Formerly SLAT = to bait.] Hence SLATING (or a SLATE) = a blowing up; severe censure; unsparing criticism.

*c.*1300. R. DE BRUNNE, *MS. Bowes*, 55. The apostille says that God thaim hatys, And over alle other with thaim SLATYS.

1889. BLACKMORE, *Kit and Kitty*, xxxi. And instead of being grateful you set to and SLATE me.

1890. KIPLING, *Light that Failed*, iv. None the less I'll SLATE him. I'll SLATE him ponderously in the cataclysm.

1902. KERNAHAN, *Scoundrels*, iv. If crimes were 'reviewed' in the same way as stories a critic might SLATE the two offences [lack of originality in crime and books] in almost identical words.

2. (HALLIWELL).—'A woman is said TO BE SLATED when her petticoat falls below her gown.'

3. (common). — To bash a man's hat over the eyes; TO BONNET (*q.v.*).

4. (sporting).—To bet heavily against an entry.

A SLATE OFF (LOOSE, &c.), *subs. phr.* (common).—Crazy; a TILE LOOSE (*q.v.*).

SLATER'S PAN, *subs. phr.* (obsolete).—'The gaol of Kingston in Jamaica; SLATER is the deputy provost-marshall' (GROSE).

SLATHERS, *subs.* (American).—Abundance; 'lashin's an' lavin's.'

1876. CLEMENS, *Tom Sawyer*, 75. I am going to be a clown at a circus. They get SLATHERS of money—most a dollar a day.

18 [?]. *New Princeton Rev.* [*Century*]. Mr. —— can repeat SLATHERS and SLATHERS of another man's literature.

SLAUGHTER, *verb.* (trade).—1. To sell at a SACRIFICE (*q.v.*). Hence SLAUGHTER-HOUSE = a shop or auction-room where goods are bought or sold for what they will bring; SLAUGHTERER = (1) a vendor at cost, and (2) a buyer for re-manufacture: as books for pulp, cloth for shoddy, &c.

1851-61. MAYHEW, *Lond. Lab.* . . . One East End SLAUGHTERER used habitually to tell that every Saturday afternoons . . . put £20 extra in his pocket . . . Under such circumstances the poor workman is at the mercy of the SLAUGHTERER.

SLAUGHTER OF THE INNOCENTS. *See* INNOCENT.

SLAVE-DRIVER, *subs.* (colloquial).—1. A harsh taskmaster; a strict master.

2. (Harrow cricket).—*See* quot.

1890. *Great Public Schools*, 95. The upper ground on these days is given up to practice at the nets for the eleven and the 'Sixth Form' game, and to practice in fielding and catching. Boys below the Removes have to fag for them, and these fags are managed by SLAVE-DRIVERS, three or four boys appointed for the purpose.

SLAVEY, *subs.* (common).—A drudge: male or female; 'a servant of either sex' (GROSE). Also (old) SLAVING-GLOKE.

1821. EGAN, *Life in London*, II. i. The SLAVEY and her master—the surgeon and the resurrection-man— . . . they are "all there."

1851-61. MAYHEW, *Lond. Lab.*, I. 472. The first enquiry is for the missus or a daughter, and if they can't be got at they are on to the SLAVEYS.

1855. THACKERAY, *Newcomes*, xi. The boy Thomas, otherwise called SLAVEY . . . has been instructed to bring soda whenever he hears the word SLAVEY pronounced from above.

1879. HORSLEY [*Macm. Mag.*, xl. 501]. I piped a SLAVEY come out of a chat, so when she had got a little way up the double, I pratted in the house.

1886. *D. Telegraph*, 1 Ap. No well-conducted English girl need be a SLAVEY at all.

1893. EMERSON, *Lippo*, xvi. She knew all the cant, and used to palarie thick to the SLAVEYS.

1901. *Free Lance*, 16 Mar., 586, 1. Joan Burnett . . . has inherited both her mother's and her father's talent, as all will have noticed who saw her play the curiously pathetic SLAVEY in "The Wedding Guest."

SLEDGE-HAMMER, *verb.* (colloquial).—To hit hard; to batter.

1834. LEWIS, *Letters*, 32. You may see what is meant by SLEDGE-HAMMERING a man.

SLEEK. *See* SLICK.

SLEEK-AND-SLUM SHOP, *subs. phr.* (BEE).—'A public house or tavern where single men and their wives resort.'

SLEEP, *verb.* (colloquial).—To provide sleeping accommodation: *cf.* ROOM.

1887. RIBTON-TURNER, *Vagrants and Vagrancy*, 399. They were to have a double row of beds, 'two tire' high, to admit of SLEEPING 100 men and 60 women.

TO SLEEP ON BONES, *verb. phr.* (old).—To sleep in a lap: *e.g.*, 'Let not the child sleep on bones, *i.e.*, in the nurse's lap' (RAY).

TO SLEEP ON BOTH EARS, *verb. phr.* (old).—To sleep soundly, without a care.

1633. MASSINGER, *Guardian*, ii. 2. SLEEP you secure ON EITHER EAR.

SLEEP-DRUNK, *adj. phr.* (colloquial).—Drowsy; confused: as on waking from heavy sleep.

SLEEPER, *subs.* (American).—A sleeping-car.

1886. *Referee*, 26 Dec. Our . . . SLEEPER as the natives prefer to call these much-vaunted American inventions.

2. (American gaming).—Unclaimed money.

SLEEPING-HOUSE, *subs. phr.* (B. E. *c.*1696).—'SLEEPINGE HOUSE, without Shop, Ware-House, or Cellar, only for a private Family.'

SLEEPING-PARTNER, *subs. phr.* (GROSE).—1. 'A partner in a trade, or shop, who lends his name and money, for which he receives a share of the profit, without doing any part of the business.'

2. (common).—A bed-fellow.

SLEEPY, *adj.* and *adv.* (old).—Much worn; threadbare: *e.g.*, a SLEEPY PEAR = a pear beginning to decay; a SLEEPLESS-HAT = shabby head-gear 'with nap worn off' (GROSE). *See* GOLGOTHA.

SLEEPY-HEAD, *subs. phr.* (common).—A dullard.

SLEEPY QUEENS (THE), *subs. phr.* (military).—The Queen's Royal Regiment, late the 2nd Foot.

SLEEPY-SEED, *subs. phr.* (nursery).—In *pl.* = The mucous secretion about the eyelids during sleep: *cf.* SAND-MAN.

SLEEVE. Here occur one or two PHRASES and COLLOQUIALISMS: TO HANG ON (or UPON) A SLEEVE = to be dependent; TO LAUGH IN ONE'S SLEEVES = to deride or exult in secret (B. E.); TO WEAR ONE'S HEART UPON ONE'S SLEEVE = to make no mystery, to be artless; IN (or UP) ONE'S SLEEVE = hidden, in reserve, ready for use; TO PIN TO ONE'S SLEEVE = to flaunt; TO HANG ON ANOTHER'S SLEEVE = to accept another's authority.

1546. HEYWOOD, *Proverbs.* To LAUGH IN MY SLEEVE.

1580. LYLY, *Euphues* [OLIPHANT, *New Eng.*, i. 607. Among the verbs are *match* (marry), PIN A MAN TO HER SLEEVE].

1589. PUTTENHAM, *Art of Eng. Poesy*, 251. The better to winne his purposes . . . to HAVE a journey or sicknesse IN HIS SLEEVE, thereby to shake off other importunities of greater consequence.

*d.*1600. HOOKER, *Eccles. Polity* [*Ency. Dict.*]. It is not . . . to ask why we should HANG our judgment UPON THE CHURCH'S SLEEVE.

1602. SHAKSPEARE, *Othello*, i. 1. I will WEAR MY HEART UPON MY SLEEVE for daws to peck at.

1713. ARBUTHNOT, *Hist. John Bull.* John LAUGHED heartily IN HIS SLEEVE at the pride of the esquire.

1809. MALKIN, *Gil Blas* [ROUTLEDGE], 79. I made him a thousand low bows though I felt for him IN MY SLEEVE the contempt and hatred, &c. *Ibid.*, 227. I could not help LAUGHING IN MY SLEEVE when I considered who and what they were.

1900. SAVAGE, *Brought to Bay*, ii. Sir Everard was a close enough old man . . . We, none of us, WEAR OUR HEARTS ON OUR SLEEVE. *Ibid.*, viii. He is the equal of any man. The sort of fellow who always has something UP HIS SLEEVE.

SLEEVEBOARD, *subs.* (tailors').—A hard word to pronounce; a JAW-BREAKER (*q.v.*).

SLEEVELESS, *adj.* (old).—Fruitless; inadequate; wanting a cover or excuse; 'impertinent or trifling' (BAILEY): now only in phrase, 'A SLEEVELESS ERRAND' = (B. E. and GROSE) 'a fool's errand, in search of what it is impossible to find,' CHAUCER, *Test. Love*, ii. 334.

14[?]. *Reliq. Antiq.*, I. 83. Syrrus, thynke not lonke, and y schall tell yow a SLEVELES RESON.

1579. LYLY, *Euphues*, 'Anat. of Wit,' 114. Neither faine for thy selfe any SLEEVELESS EXCUSE.

1593. *Passionate Morrice* [Shaks. Soc.], 63. Shee had dealt better if shee had sent himselfe away with a crabbed answere, then so vnmannerly to vse him by SLEEVELES EXCUSES.

1599. HALL, *Satires*, iv. 1. Worse than the logogryphes of later times, Or hundreth riddles shak'd to SLEEVELESSE RHYMES.

1602. SHAKSPEARE, *Troilus and Cressida*, v. 4, 10. That same young Trojan ass, that loves the whore there, might send that Greekish whoremasterly villain, with the sleeve, back to the dissembling luxurious drab, of a SLEEVELESS ERRAND.

*d.*1612. HARINGTON, *Epigrams*, III. 9. My men came back as from a SLEEVELESS ARRANT.

1620. FLETCHER, *Little French Lawyer*, ii. To be despatch'd upon a SLEEVELESS ERRAND, To leave my friend engag'd, mine honour tainted.

1630. TAYLOR, *Works*, II. iii. A neat laundresse, or a hearbwife can Carry a SLEEVELESS MESSAGE now and then.

1633. JONSON, *Tale of a Tub*, iv. 4. It [a coat] did play me such a SLEEVELESS ERRAND As I had nothing where to put mine arms in, And then I threw it off.

*d.*1680. BUTLER, *Works*, ii. 296. They are the likelier, quoth Bracton, To bring us many a SLEEVELESS ACTION.

*c.*1696. B. E., *Dict. Cant. Crew*, s.v. SLEEVELESS STORY, a Tale of a Tub, or of a Cock and a Bull.

1706. WARD, *Wooden World*, 22. He sends him upon a thousand SLEEVELESS ERRANDS to the great Consolation of the Footman.

1737-41. WARBURTON, *Div. Leg.*, iii. To save himself from the vexation of A SLEEVELESS ERRAND.

SLEWED, *adj.* (common).—Drunk: *see* SCREWED. Also SLUED.

1843. DICKENS, *Martin Chuzzlewit*, xxviii. He came into our place one night to take her home; rather SLUED, but not much.

1855. *Whig Almanack* [BARTLETT]. I went to bed SLEWED last night—didn't dream of such a thing in the morning.

SLEWER, *subs.* (American).—A servant-girl: *cf.* Dutch slang *sluer* (or *sloor*) = a poor, common woman.

SLIBBER-SLABBER, *adj.* (colloquial).—Careless.

SLICE. TO TAKE A SLICE, *verb. phr.* (venery).—To intrigue; 'particularly (GROSE) with a married woman, because a slice off a cut loaf is not missed.'

SLICK, *adv.* (Old English: then American).—1. Quick; bold; direct; perfect. Whence (2) = clever; plausible; expert; SMART (*q.v.*). Also SLEEK.

1605. JONSON, CHAPMAN, &c., *Eastware Hoe*, ii. 1. They be the smoothest and SLICKEST knaves in a country.

1832. HALIBURTON, *Traits of Am. Humour*, II. 18. Courtin' is the hardest thing in the world to begin, though it goes on so SLICK arterwards.

1835. CROCKETT, *Tour down East*, 120. The Senate could not pass Mr. Stevenson through for England . . . He was a-going through right SLICK till he came to his coat-pockets, and they were so full of papers written by Ritchie that he stuck fast.

1837. BARHAM, *Ingolds. Leg.*, I. 241. The hare, making play, Progress'd right SLICK away, As them tarnation chaps, the Americans, say.

1841. *Knickerbocker Mag.* [BARTLETT]. Singin' is a science which comes pretty tough at first, but it goes SLICK afterwards.

1844. *Major Jones's Courtship*, 94. I done it as SLICK as a whistle.

1847. *Blackwood's Mag.* The railroad company, out of sheer parsimony, have neglected to fence in their line, which goes SLICK through the centre of your garden.

1856. DOW, *Sermons* [BARTLETT]. Nobody can waltz real SLICK unless they have the spring-halt in one leg, as horses sometimes have.

1869. STOWE, *Oldtown*, 253. He [read] it off SLICKER than any on us could; he did—there wa'n't no kind o' word could stop him.

1896. LILLARD, *Poker Stories*, 243. One of the SLICKEST young fellows that ever turned a card . . . could work the shells and the elusive pea like a circus sharper . . .

TO SLICK UP, *verb. phr.* (American).—To TITTIVATE (*q.v.*); to smarten; to put in order.

1840. CLAVERS, *Montacute*, 211. Mrs. Flyer was SLICKED UP for the occasion, in the snuff-colored silk she was married in.

1843. CARLTON, *New Purchase*, I. 72. The caps most in vogue then were made of dark, coarse, knotted twine, like a cabbage-net, worn, as the wives said, to save SLICKING UP, and to hide dirt.

1865. MAJOR DOWNING, *Mayday*, 43. The house was all SLICKED UP as neat as a pin, and the things in every room all sot to rights.

SLICK-A-DIE, *subs. phr.* (thieves').—A pocket-book: *see* DEE.

SLICKER, *subs.* (Western American).—An overcoat: spec. a waterproof: also SLEEKER.

1882. ROOSEVELT [*Century Mag.*, XXXV. 864]. We had turned the horses loose, and in our oilskin SLICKERS covered, soaked and comfortless, under the lee of the wagon.

SLIDE, *verb.* (colloquial).—1. To decamp; TO SKIP (*q.v.*): also TO SLIDE OUT = (1) to leave stealthily; and (2) to shirk: by artifice.

18[?]. R. S. WILLIS, *Student's Song* [BARTLETT]. Broken is the band that held us, We must cut our sticks and SLIDE.

1896. LILLARD, *Poker Stories*, 150. He is supposed to gather his hat and coat, and SLIDE at once.

1899. WHITEING, *John St.*, xxi. Cheese it, an' SLIDE.

2. (colloquial).—To backslide; to WEAKEN (*q.v.*): *e.g.* from a resolution, attitude, or promise. As *subs.* = an error, a falling away; SLIDING = transgression.

1603. SHAKSPEARE, *Meas. for Meas.*, ii. 4, 115. Proved the SLIDING of your brother A merriment than a vice.

1620. FORD, *Line of Life* [*Century*]. The least blemish, the least SLIDE, the least error, the least offence, is exasperated, made capital.

TO LET SLIDE, *verb. phr.* (old colloquial).—To let go; to allow things to take care of themselves.

1369. CHAUCER, *Troilus*, v. 357. So sholdestow endure and LATEN SLYDE The time. *Ibid.* (1383), *Cant. Tales*, 'Clerkes Tale,' 26. Wel neigh all other cures let he SLIDE.

1420. PALLADIUS, *Hosbondrie* [E. E. T. S.], 64. Lette that crafte SLYDE.

1593. SHAKSPEARE, *Taming of Shrew*, Induct. i. 6. LET the world SLIDE.

TO DO A SLIDE UP THE BOARD (or STRAIGHT), *verb. phr.* (venery).—To copulate: *see* GREENS and RIDE.

SLIDE-GROAT, *subs. phr.* (old).—SHOVE-HALFPENNY (*q.v.*).

1528. HOLINSHED, *Chron. of Ireland.* The lieutenant and he for their disport were plaieing at SLIDE-GROTE or shooflebord.

SLIDER, *subs.* (old).—In *pl.* = drawers.

1700. DICKENSON, *God's Prot. Prov.* [*Century*]. A shirt and SLIDERS.

SLIDE-THRIFT. *See* SHOVEL-BOARD.

SLIM, *subs.* (Old Cant).—*See* quot.

1789. PARKER, *Variegated Characters*. . . . A bobstick of rum SLIM, a shilling's worth of rum

Adj. (colloquial).—Delicate; feeble.

1877. JEWETT, *Deephaven*, 169. She's had SLIM health of late years.

Adv. (colloquial).—Resourceful; SMART (*q.v.*). [In provincial English SLIM = sly, cunning, awry: the popular use of the word during the South African War, 1899-1902, largely, if not wholly = mere artfulness.]

SLIME, *verb*. (Durham School).—1. To 'cut' games. Also (2) to lounge, to loaf: *e.g.*, 'SLIMEING down town.'

3. (Felsted).—To sneak along; TO DO A SLIME = to take a crafty advantage.

4. (Harrow).—To go round quietly.

1898. WARNER, *Harrow School*, 282. His house-beak SLIMED and twug him.

5. (Harrow).—To make 'drops' at rackets.

SLING, *verb*. (common).—A generic verb of action. Thus 1 (thieves') = to throw away or pass to a confederate; and 2 (general) to do easily; TO SLING A POT = to drink; TO SLING THE BOOZE = to stand treat; TO SLING A BOB (a tanner—anything) = to give; TO SLING ONE'S HOOK (BUNK, or DANIEL) = to decamp; TO SLING A DADDLE = to shake hands; TO SLING A CAT = to vomit; TO SLING A TINKLER = to ring the bell; TO SLING ONE'S JUICE (or JELLY) = to masturbate; TO SLING A POEM, ARTICLE, or BOOK = to write; TO SLING A HAT = to wave one in applause; TO SLING THE SMASH = to smuggle tobacco to prisoners; TO SLING ABOUT = to loaf; TO SLING INK (or A PEN) = to write: hence INKSLINGER = a clerk or author; TO SLING A FOOT = to dance; TO SLING ONE IN THE EYE = to blacken it; TO KILL A CROW WITH AN EMPTY SLING (RAY) = to gain without effort; TO SLING OFF (or PATTER or JAW) = to talk, to abuse, to insinuate: *cf.* SLANG; TO SLING A SNOT = to blow one's nose with the fingers: also TO SLING; TO SLING (or JERK) A PART = to undertake a rôle: TO SLING A NASTY PART = to play so well that another would find it difficult to rival it; TO SLING ROUND ON THE LOOSE = to act recklessly; SLING YOURSELF (LET HER SLING!) = 'Bestir yourself.'

1835. CROCKETT, *Tour down East*, 37. We swung round the wharf; and when the captain told the people who I was, they SLUNG THEIR HATS and gave three cheers.

1864. BROWNE ('Artemus Ward'), *Works* (1870), 277. The chaps that write for the *Atlantic*, Betsy, understand their bisness. They can SLING INK, they can. *Ibid.*, 305. You ask me, sir, to SLING SOME INK for your paper.

1873. GREENWOOD, *In Strange Company*. He . . . swore . . . that if we did not that instant SLING OUR DANIELS . . . he would shy at us every heavenly article of crockery his apartment contained.

1884. CLEMENS, *Huckleberry Finn*. Teach singing . . . SLING A LECTURE sometimes.

1899. WHITEING, *John St.*, vi. Blow me if I shan't be sold up, too, if I don't soon SLING MY 'OOK. *Ibid.*, xxi. If ever I ketch yer messin' abaht wi' any o' them, I'll SLING him ONE IN THE EYE.

SLINGER, *subs*. (common).—A piece of bread floating in tea.

SLINGING, *adj*. (colloquial).—Covering; indefatigable; effortless.

1857. HUGHES, *Tom Brown's Schooldays*, I. 7. Two well-known runners . . . started off at a long SLINGING trot across the fields.

SLINK, *subs*. (common).—1. A sneak; (2) a greedy starveling (HALLIWELL); and (3) a cheat. Hence as *adj*. (or SLINKY) = (1) sneaky, mean; and 2 (America) = thin, lank (BARTLETT).

1816. SCOTT, *Antiquary*, xv. He has na' settled his account wi' my gudeman the deacon for this twalmonth; he's but SLINK, I doubt.

18 [?]. *Chronicles of Pineville*, 139 [BARTLETT]. I despise a SLINK.

4. (old).—A bastard: *cf.* SLINK = to miscarry (of beasts).

1702. COMBERBATCH, *Byron and Elms, Comberbatch*, 391. What did you go to London for but to drop your SLINK.

SLIP, *subs*. (old).—*See* quots.: also SLIP-COIN. Whence TO BE NAILED UP FOR SLIPS = to be tried and found wanting.

*d.*1592. GREENE, *Theeves Falling Out* [*Harl. Misc.*, viii. 399]. Certain SLIPS, which are counterfeit pieces of money, being brasse, and covered over with silver, which the common people call SLIPS.

1594. LYLY, *Mother Bombie*, ii. 1. I shall goe for silver though, when you shall be NAILED UP FOR SLIPS.

1595. SHAKSPEARE, *Romeo and Juliet*, ii. 4. *Rom.* What counterfeit did I give you. *Mer.* The SLIP, sir, the SLIP: can you not conceive?

*d.*1637. JONSON, *Epigrams*, 64. First weigh a friend, then touch and try him too, For there are many SLIPS and counterfeits.

*d.*1655. ADAMS, *Works*, i. 247. To take a piece of SLIP-COIN in hand.

2. (old).—A miscarriage; an abortion. Also as *verb*. = to miscarry.

PHRASES.—TO SLIP ONE'S CABLE (BREATH, or WIND) = to to die: *see* ALOFT; TO GIVE THE SLIP = to escape unobserved; A SLIP (or FALL) 'TWIXT CUP AND LIP = a thing not done may spoil in the doing; TO SLIP INTO = (1) to attack, and (2) to execute with vigour; TO SLIP UP = to err, to trip; A SLIP OF THE TONGUE = an inadvertency in speech; TO MAKE A SLIP = to give chastity the go-by: whence *see* SLIP, *ante* 2.

1563-4. EDWARDES, *Damon and Pithias* [DODSLEY, *Old Plays* (REED), iv.]. [OLIPHANT, *New Eng.*, i. 565. Among the verbs are GIVE HIM THE SLIP . .]

1570. LAMBARDE, *Peramb. of Kent*, 422. Many things happen BETWEENE THE CUP AND THE LIPPE.

1596. JONSON, *Ev. Man in Humour*, ii. 3. It's no matter . . . if I cannot GIVE him THE SLIP at an instant.

1599. CHAPMAN, *Hum. Day's Mirth* [*Works* (1874), 39]. He GAVE US THE SLIP before dinner.

*d.*1704. BROWN, *Works*, ii. 14. He had no sooner turn'd his back, but I pluck'd too the wicket, and GAVE him THE SLIP.

1726. VANBRUGH, *Provoked Husband*, ii. 1. A plague on him, the monkey has GIN US THE SLIP. *Ibid.*, v. 1. While she stood gaping, I GAVE her THE SLIP.

1751. SMOLLETT, *Peregrine Pickle*, lxxiii. I told him [a doctor] as how I could SLIP MY CABLE without his direction or assistance.

1772. BRIDGES, *Homer Burlesqued*, 109. Both those blades had SLIPT THEIR WIND, And in their rough fir coffins bound, Were safe from brabbles under ground.

*c.*1796. WOLCOT, *P. Pindar*, 69. And for their cats that happed TO SLIP THEIR BREATH, Old maids, so sweet, might mourn themselves to death.

1809. MALKIN, *Gil Blas* [ROUTLEDGE], 177. The sequel proved . . . that many things FALL OUT BETWEEN THE CUP AND THE LIP.

1827. LYTTON, *Pelham*, lxxvii. Oh, oh! Sir Reginald thought of GIVING ME THE SLIP, eh?

1856. READE, *Never Too Late, &c.*, x. Give him the right stuff, doctor . . . and he won't SLIP HIS WIND this time.

1883. *Century Mag.*, xxxvi. 279. SLIP UP in my vernacular? How could I? I talked it when I was a boy with the other boys.

1886. *Field*, 25 Sep. In agonies of fear lest our stag should GIVE US THE SLIP.

SLIP-ALONG. *See* SLIPSHOD.

SLIP-GIBBET (-HALTER, -ROPE, -STRING, or -THRIFT), *subs. phr.* (old).—A prodigal; one deserving of (or who has cheated) the gallows (GROSE).

[?]. *MS. Bright*, 170, f. 1. Such a SLIPPSTRING trick As never till now befell us heretofore.

1593. MARLOWE, *Lusts' Dominion* [DODSLEY, *Old Plays* (1876), xiv. 149.] As I hope for mercy, I am half persuaded that this SLIP-HALTER has pawned my clothes.

1594. LYLY, *Mother Bombie*, ii. 1. Thow art a SLIPSTRING I'le warrant.

1611. COTGRAVE, *Dict. s.v.* Young rascals or scoundrels, rakehells, or SLIP-STRINGS.

1619. FLETCHER, *A King and No King*, ii. Well, SLIP-STRING, I shall meet with you.

1621. GRANGER, *Eccles*, 273. Thus it is in the house of prodigals, drinking SLIPTHRIFTS, and Belials.

*d.*1637. DEKKER, *Londons Tempe*. We are making arrowes for my SLIP-STRING sonne.

SLIPPERY. *subs*. (thieves').—Soap: Fr. *glissant*.

Adj. and *adv*. (old colloquial: now recognised).—Untrustworthy; false; wanton. Also SLIPPER, SLIPPY, and SLIP-SKIN. Whence SLIPPERY-FELLOW (or -TRICK) = 'deceitful' (B. E.): 'one on whom there can be no dependance' (GROSE).

1553. J. BRENDE, Tr. *Quintus Curtius*, vii. Fortune . . . is SLIPPER, and cannot bee kept against her will.

[?]. *Political Poems* [E. E. T. S.], 60. He . . . of his herte . . . hath SLIPER holde.

[?]. TAVERNER, *Adag.*, C. 1. Let this example teach menne not to truste on the SLIPPERNESSE of fortune.

[?]. *Parad. of Dainty Devices*, E. 3. SLIPPER joy of certain pleasure here.

1579. SPENSER, *Shepheard's Kal.*, Nov. 153. And SLIPPER hope Of mortal men that swinck and sweate for nought. *Ibid.*, Sep. Long time he used this SLIPPERY prank.

1580. LYLY, *Euphues* [OLIPHANT, *New Eng.*, i. 606. Adjectives are employed in new senses as A SLIPPERY PRANKE, a broad jest . . .].

*d.*15[?]. PUTTENHAM, *Works*, i. 4. Because it is more currant and SLIPPER upon the tongue, and withal tunable and melodious.

1602. SHAKSPEARE, *Othello*, ii. 1, 246. A SLIPPER and subtle knave. *Ibid.* (1604), *Winter's Tale*, i. 2. My wife is SLIPPERY. *Ibid.* (1610), *Coriol.*, iv. 4. O world, thy SLIPPERY turns.

*d.*1607. BARNES, *Works*, 283. I know they bee SLIPPER that I have to do wyth, and there is no holde of them.

1619. FLETCHER, *King and No King*, ii. 1. Servants are SLIPPERY: but I dare give my word for her and her honesty [chastity].

1641-2. MILTON, *Animad. Rem. Defence*. A pretty SLIP-SKIN conveyance to sift mass into no mass. *Ibid.* (1641), *Prel. Epis.* Some bad and SLIPPERY men in that councell.

2. (common).—Quick.

1902. KERNAHAN, *Scoundrels*, vii. We must look SLIPPY about it . . . It's lucky I haven't far to go.

SLIP-SHOD, *adj*. (colloquial).—Careless; slovenly. [That is 'slipper-shod.'] Also SLIP-ALONG, SLIP-SLOP.

1605. SHAKSPEARE, *Lear*, i. 5. Thy wit shall ne'er go SLIPSHOD.

1818. SCOTT, *Heart of Midlothian*, i. A sort of appendix to the half bound, and SLIP-SHOD volumes of the circulating library.

1849. MAITLAND, *Reformation*, 559. It would be less worth while to read Fox's SLIP-ALONG stories.

1885. *D. Tel.*, 29 Aug. Stilted phraseology is preferable to SLIP-SHOD.

SLIP-SLOP, *subs. phr.* (colloquial).—1. A blunder. As *adj*. = slovenly, inaccurate: *cf.* SLIPSHOD.

1797. D'ARBLAY, *Diary*, iv. 14. He told us a great number of comic SLIP-SLOPS of the first Lord Baltimore, who made a constant misuse of one word for another.

1849. KINGSLEY, *Alton Locke*, xxxviii. His . . . SLIP-SLOP trick of using the word natural to mean, in one sentence, 'material,' and in the next, as I use it, only 'normal and orderly.'

2. (common).—In *pl.* = Shoes (or slippers) down at the heels: also (Norfolk) SLIP-SHOE.

Adj. (colloquial).—Here and there; 'all over the shop': also SLIP-SLAP and *verb*.

1721. CENTLIVRE, *The Artifice*, iii. I ha' found her fingers SLIP-SLAP this a-way and that a-way, like a flail upon a wheat-sheaf.

1870. FARJEON, *Griff*, 105. The dirty, broken bluchers in which Griff's feet SLIP-SLOPPED constantly.

See SLOP.

SLIP-THRIFT. *See* SLIP-GIBBET.

SLIT, *subs*. (venery).—1. The female *pudendum*: *see* MONOSYLLABLE (HALLIWELL).

1647-8. HERRICK, *Hesperides*, 'Upon Scobble.' Good Sir, make no more cuts i' th' outward skin, One SLIT's enough to let Adultry in.

2. (old).—A pocket.

12[?]. *King Horn* [E. E. T. S.], 61. Thu most habbe redi mitte Twenti Marc ine thi SLITTE.

SLITHER, *verb*. (common).—1. To slip; to make away; to smooth; and 3. (American) = to hurry. Also SLITHERY = SLIPPERY (*q.v.*).

1857. HUGHES, *Tom Brown's Schooldays*, II. iv. After getting up three or four feet they came SLITHERING to the ground, barking their arms and faces.

1857. KINGSLEY, *Two Years Ago*, xxiv. Gay girls SLITHERED past him, looked round at him, but in vain.

18 . . . TENNYSON, *Northern Cobbler*. Once of a frosty night, I SLITHERED and hurted my huck.

1886. *Field*, 13 Feb. You could not estimate the distance or direction to which your horse might SLITHER.

1901. WALKER, *In the Blood*, 244. They might 'a' SLITHERED with your goods if you 'adn't been so mighty sharp with your hands.

SLIVE, *verb*. (old colloquial).—To sneak or lounge away; to idle. SLIVE-ANDREW = a good-for-nothing; SLIVERLY = artful; SLIVING = idle. TO LET SLIVE (American) = to let fly.

1707. CENTLIVRE, *Platonick Love*, iv. I knew her gown agen: I minded her when she SLIV'D OFF. *Ibid.* (1710), *The Man's Bewitched*, iii. The SLIVING baggage will not come to a resolution yet.

1725. BAILEY, *Erasmus*, 41. What are you a SLIVING about, you drone? You are a year a lighting a candle.

1847. ROBB, *Squatter Life*. As soon as I clapped peeper on him I let SLIVER, when the varmint dropped.

SLOBBER, *subs*. (printers').—Badly distributed ink.

Verb. (colloquial).—1. To kiss effusively. Also as *subs*. and SLABBERING.

1583. STUBBES, *Amat. Abuses*, 114. What bussing, what smouching, and SLABBERING one of another.

*d.*1897. MARSHALL, *Pomes*, 36. The amatory SLOBBER which is comforting but low.

2. (colloquial).—To scamp work: also TO SLOBBER OVER.

SLOBBERDEGULLION. *See* SLUBBERDEGULLION.

SLOBBERER, *subs*. (provincial).—1. A slovenly farmer; and (2) a jobbing tailor (HALLIWELL).

SLOBGOLLION, *subs*. (nautical).—'Whaleman's term for an oozy, stringy substance found in sperm oil' (C. RUSSELL).

SLOG, *subs*. (common).—1. A blow; and (2) a bout of fisticuffs. As *verb*. = (1) to hit, or work hard; (2) to PUNISH (*q.v.*), to pound (pugilists'), and (3) to tackle a matter seriously. Whence SLOGGING-MATCH = a hard fight or tussle; SLOGGER = (1) a pugilist given to hard hitting, and (2) a steady worker; SLOGGING = a beating, a fight; and TO HAVE A SLOG ON = to put on a spurt. In America the spelling SLUG, SLUGGER, &c., is accepted.

1853. BRADLEY, *Verdant Green.* His whole person put in Chancery, slung, bruised, fibbed, propped, fiddled, SLOGGED, and otherwise ill-treated.

1857. HUGHES, *Tom Brown's School-days*, I. v. The SLOGGER pulls up at last . . . fairly blown.

1878. LANG, *Ballad of Boat-race.* They catch the stroke, and they SLOG it through.

1885. *Standard*, 1 Dec. He was a vigorous SLOGGER, and heartily objected to being bowled first ball.

1886. *Phil. Times*, 6 May. There was some terrible SLOGGING . . . Cleary planted two rib-roasters, and a tap on Langdon's face.

1887. *Fun*, 9 Nov., 201. He had a "merry mill" with a Thames bargee, known as "Jim the SLOGGER," and the SLOGGER . . . got the worst of the scrap.

1891. *Times*, 14 Sep. 'Capital Punishment.' They top a lag out here [W. Aus.] for SLOGGING a screw.

[?]. E. B. MICHELL, *Boxing and Sparring* [*Century*], 162. SLOGGING and hard hitting with the mere object of doing damage . . . earn no credit in the eyes of a good judge.

2. (public schools').—A large portion: spec. a big slice of cake.

SLOGGER, *subs.* (Camb. Univ.).—1. A boat in the second division: corresponding to the Oxford Torpids.

See SLOG.

SLOP, *subs.* (colloquial).—1. In *pl.* = liquid food: spec. weak tea: or 'any thin beverage taken medicinally' (GROSE): also SLIP-SLOP. As *adj.* = feeble, poor, weak; as *verb.* = to eat or drink greedily, TO MOP UP (*q.v.*): also TO SLOP (or SLAP) UP, or TO SLOP IT; SLOPPING-UP = a drinking bout; SLOP-FEEDER = a tea-spoon; SLOP-TUBS = tea-things; SLIP-SLOPPY = slushy, watery.

1515. *De Generibus Ebriosorum*, &c. [HODGKIN, *Notes and Queries*, 3 S. vii. 163. In this treatise occurs names of fancy drinks . . . I select a few of the most presentable] SLIP-SLOP . . . Raise-head . . . Swell-nose.

1566. STILL, *Gammer Gurton's Needle* [DODSLEY, *Old Plays* (REED), iii. 193]. To SLOP UP milk.

1675. COTTON, *Burlesque on Burlesque*, 187. No, thou shalt feed instead of these Or your SLIP-SLAPS of curds and whey On Nectar and Ambrosia.

1692. DRYDEN, *Juvenal*, vi. 772. But thou, whatever SLOPS she will have brought, Be thankful.

*d.*1704. LESTRANGE, *Works* [*Century*]. The sick husband here wanted for neither SLOPS nor doctors.

1821. COMBE, *Dr. Syntax*, III. i. At length the coffee was announced . . . 'And since the meagre SLIP-SLOP's made, I think the call should be obeyed.'

*a.*1832. EDGWORTH, *Rose, Thistle and Shamrock*, iii. 2. Does he expect tea can be keeping hot for him to the end of time? He'll have nothing but SLOP-DASH.

1837. BARHAM, *Ingold. Leg.*, II. 291. There was no taking refuge . . . On a SLIP-SLOPPY day, in a cab or a bus.

1900. FLYNT, *Tramps.* Yonkers Slim was going to meet him in Washington with some money, and the bums intended to have a great SLOPPIN'-UP.

2. (nautical).—In *pl.* = 'Wearing apparel and bedding used by seamen' (GROSE). Hence ready-made clothing. SLOP-SELLER = a dealer in ready-made clothes (GROSE); SLOP-CHEST = a ship's supply of clothes and bedding: usually doled out at cost price; SLOP-BOOK = the register of supplies; SLOP-WORK = (1) the cheapest: hence (2) any work poorly done; SLOPPY = ill-fitting. [Originally 'an outer garment made of linen' (WRIGHT)].

1530. PALSGRAVE, *Lang. Francoyse.* Payre of SLOPPE HOSES, *braiettes a marinier.*

1555. EDEN, *Works* [ARBER], 327. [OLIPHANT, *New English*, i. 535. We hear of mariner's SLOPPES; this old word for vestes seems henceforth to have been restricted to seamen.]

1772. BRIDGES, *Homer Burlesque*, 205. One kept a SLOP-SHOP in Rag Fair.

1851-61. MAYHEW, *Lon. Lab.*, II. 47. It was good stuff and good make . . . that's the reason why it always bangs a SLOP.

1882. *Queen*, 7 Oct. It must not be imagined that, to be easy, dress must necessarily be SLOPPY.

1886. *D. News.*, 3 Dec. The harsh oppressive middleman, and the heartless indifferent SLOPSELLER have sat for their portraits again and again.

1887. *Fish. of U. S.*, v. 2. 226 [*Century*]. If a poor voyage has been made, or if the man has drawn on the SLOP-CHEST . . . [so] as to ruin his credit, he becomes bankrupt ashore.

3. (common).—A tailor.

4. (back slang).—A policeman: a corruption of 'esclop.'

1851-61. MAYHEW, *Lond. Lab.* I wish I'd been there to have a shy at the ESCLOPS.

*c.*1870. *Music Hall Song* [S. J. & C.]. Never to take notice of vulgar nicknames, such at SLOP, "copper," "rabbit-pie shifter," "peeler."

1886. SIMS, *Ballads of Babylon* . . . I dragged you in here and saved you, and sent out a gal for the SLOPS.

1887. *Fun*, 9 Nov., 201. A vanishing point [is] the corner you bunks round when the SLOP's after yer.

1899. WHITEING, *John St.*, 49. She is Boadicea . . . a right-down raughty gal leading her alley to battle against the Roman SLOPS.

5. (Christ's Hospital).—A term of contempt.

Verb. (colloquial).—1. To make a mess; to walk or work in the wet.

1888. MURRAY, *Weaker Vessel*, xi. He came SLOPPING on behind me, with the peculiar sucking noise at each footstep which broken boots make on a wet and level pavement.

TO SLOP OVER, *verb. phr.* (colloquial).—To enter into with enthusiasm, and speak, write, or act like a fool; to put on SIDE (*q.v.*); to make a mistake.

1859. BROWNE, *Fourth of July Oration* [*Works* (1899), 124]. The prevailin' weakness of most public men is TO SLOP OVER . . . They get filled up and SLOP. They rush things. Washington never SLOPPED OVER.

1888. *Harper's Mag.*, lxxviii. 818. One of his great distinctions was his moderation . . . he never SLOPPED OVER.

SLOPE, *verb.* (common).—To run away; to BUNK (*q.v.*). As *subs.* = an escape: *e.g.*, TO DO A SLOPE.

18[?]. *Ballad of Blouzelinda* [BARTLETT]. He . . . made a SLOPE, and went off to Texas.

1844. HALIBURTON, *The Attache*, xxvii. They jist run like a flock of sheep . . . and SLOPE off, properly skeered.

1847. ROBB, *Squatter Life.* The Editor of the "Eagle" cannot pay his board bill, and fears are entertained that he will SLOPE without liquidating the debt.

*c.*1866. VANCE, *Chick-a-leary Cove.* Now, my pals, I'm going to SLOPE, See you soon again I hope.

1897. MARSHALL, *Pomes*, 17. So she SLOPED from her Brummy.

2. (Old Cant).—*See* quot.

1610. ROWLANDS, *Martin Mark-all* [Hunt. Club Rep. (1874), 38]. Cowch a hogshead . . . is like an Alminacke that is out of date; now the duch word TO SLOPE is with them vsed to sleepe, and liggen, to lie downe.

SLOPER'S ISLAND, *subs. phr.* (London).—A weekly tenement neighbourhood: spec. *c.*1870 the Artisan's Village near Loughborough Junction, originally in the midst of fields; now in the centre of a densely populated neighbourhood.

SLOPPER, *subs.* (The Leys School).—A slop basin: *cf.* FOOTER, BREKKER, &c.

SLOPPY, *adj.* (colloquial).—Loose; slovenly.

1890. *Academy*, 29 Mar., 218. [To] teach a great number of sciences and languages in an elementary and SLOPPY way.

SLOSH, *subs.* (common).—A drink.

1888. *Cornhill Mag.*, Oct. Barmeat and corn-cake washed down with a generous SLOSH of whiskey.

Verb. (American).—To go here and there; TO KNOCK ABOUT (*q.v.*).

1854. *Cairo* (Ill.) *Times*, Nov. To walk backward and forward through the crowd, with a big stick in his hand, and knock down every loose man in the crowd. That's what I call SLOSHING ABOUT.

1876. CLEMENS, *Tom Sawyer*, 67. How could [witches'] charms work till midnight?—and then it's Sunday. Devils don't SLOSH AROUND much of a Sunday.

1888. *Detroit Free Press*, 8 Dec. When I was a young man I had to SLOSH AROUND dark, wet nights in rubbers that didn't fit.

SLOSHER, *subs.* (Cheltenham College).—A boarding-house assistant: they are charged with superintending dormitories, the evening work, &c.

SLOUCH, *subs.* (old and still colloquial).—1. A clumsy lout, an idler; hence (2) anything indifferent: usually in phrase 'no SLOUCH'; and (3) an awkward lumpish gait. As *verb.* = to walk lumpishly or sullenly; SLOUCHING (or SLOUCHY) = awkward, ungainly, heavy (GROSE).

[?]. *MS. Gloucester* . . . SLOWCH, a lazy lubber, who has nothing tight about him, with his stockings about his heels, his clothes unbutton'd, and his hat flapping about his ears.

1570. LEVINS, *Manip. Vocab.* [E. E. T. S.], 217. A SLOUKE, iners, ertis, ignarus.

1578. WHETSTONE, *Promos and Cassandra*, 47. Thou filthie fine SLOUCH.

1633. JONSON, *Tale of a Tub*, iv. 5. I think the idle SLOUCH Be fallen asleep in the barn.

1705. WARD, *Hud. Rediv.*, I. vii. 20. You sooty, smutty, nasty SLOUCH.

1714. GAY, *Shepherd's Week*, i. Begin thy carols then, thou vaunting SLOUCH; Be thine the oaken staff, or mine the pouch.

*d.*1745. SWIFT, *Works* [*Century*]. Our doctor . . . hath a sort of SLOUCH in his walk.

1785. COWPER, *Task*, iv. 639. He stands erect; his SLOUCH becomes a walk.

1837. BARHAM, *Ingolds. Leg.*, ii. 374. In a few minutes his . . . figure was seen SLOUCHING UP the ascent.

1866. ELIOT, *Felix Holt*, Intro. The shepherd with a slow and SLOUCHING walk . . . moved aside, as if unwillingly.

1869. CLEMENS, *The Innocents at Home*, ii. He was always nifty himself, and so you bet his funeral ain't going to be no SLOUCH.

1870. *Chambers' Journal*, 9 July, 447. He sees a SLOUCHING, shambling hulk of a fellow standing listlessly in a doorway.

1877. *Scribner's Mag.*, Sep., 510. Bow-legged, SLOUCHY, ungraceful and inactive.

1877. *Century Mag.*, xxv. 176. Looking like a SLOUCHY country bumpkin.

1881. O. W. HOLMES, *Old Volume of Life*, 58. They looked SLOUCHY, listless, torpid—an ill-conditioned crew.

1885. *West. Rev.*, cxxv. 85. He had a long, strong, uncouth body; rather rough-hewn SLOUCHING features.

18[?]. H. KENDALL, *Billy Vickers.* He has, in fact, the SLOUCH and dress, Which bullock-puncher stamp him.

1885. *D. Tel.*, 14 Sep. A child taken by a SLOUCHING villain.

1887. MORLEY ROBERTS, *Western Avernus.* A rustler . . . means a worker, an energetic man, and no SLOUCH can be a rustler.

1899. WHITEING, *John St.*, xi. It is near bedtime, and those . . . to stay for the night are SLOUCHING to the lairs.

4. (common).—A slouch-hat (*i.e.*, a hat with a broad and drooping brim).

1818. SCOTT, *Midlothian*, xliii. Even the old hat looked smarter . . . instead of SLOUCHING backward or forward on the laird's head, as it was thrown on. *Ibid.*, iii. A sailor's cap SLOUCHED over his face.

1871. *Scribner's Mag.*, Sep. A big, farmer-looking fellow in a SLOUCH-HAT.

1889. *Harper's Mag.*, lxxix. 38. Middle-aged men in SLOUCH HATS lounge around with hungry eyes.

SLOUR, *adv.* (Old Cant).—'To lock up; to fasten; to button up one's coat; to make all secure' (GROSE).

1834. AINSWORTH, *Rookwood*, III. v. No SLOUR'D hoxter my snipes could stay.

SLOW, *subs.* (old colloquial).—A sluggard; a lazybones.

[?]. *M.S. Douce*, 52 [HALLIWELL]. Lothe to bedde and lothe fro bedde, men schalle know the SLOW.

Adv. (colloquial).—1. Stupid; spiritless; tedious.

1855. THACKERAY, *Newcomes*, xlix. The party was what you young fellows call SLOW.

186[?]. F. LOCKER, *Reply to a Letter.* The girls I love now vote me SLOW.

1874. *Siliad*, 97. Whither shall we go? The Judge and Jury? No, that's awful SLOW.

2. (Winchester).—Ignorant of Winchester NOTIONS (*q.v.*).

SLOW-BACK, *subs. phr.* (old).—A loafer.

1619. FAVOUR, *Antiq. Triumph over Novelty*, 63. The SLOW-BACKS and lazie bones uill none of this.

SLOWCOACH, *subs.* (colloquial).—1. A dullard; a lout. Also (2) a dawdler. Hence (3) an antique; a fossil.

1857. E. B. RAMSAY, *Scottish Life and Character*, 114. I dare say the girl you are sending will be very useful to us: our present one is a very SLOW-COACH.

SLOW-UP, *subs. phr.* (colloquial).—A slackening of speed. Also as *verb.* = to go easy.

SLUBBERDEGULLION, *subs.* (old).—'A slovenly, dirty, nasty Fellow' (B. E. and GROSE). Also SLABBERDEGULLION. As *adj.* = paltry, dirty.

1619. FLETCHER, *Custom of the Country*, i. 2. Yes, they are knit; but must this SLUBBERDEGULLION Have her maidenhead now?

1630. TAYLOR, *Laugh and be Fat*, 73. Contaminous, pestiferous, preposterous, stygmatical slavonians, SLUBBERDEGULLIONS.

1653. URQUHART, *Rabelais*, I. xxv. Calling them . . . slapsauce fellows, SLABBERDEGULLION druggels, lubbardly louts . . .

1656. *Mus. Del.*, 79. He's an oxe, and an asse, and a SLUBBERDEGULLION.

1663. BUTLER, *Hudibras*, I. iii. 885. Thow hast deserved, Base SLUBBERDEGULLION, to be served As thou didst vow to deal with me.

SLUED. *See* SLEWED.

SLUG, *subs.* (old colloquial).—Generic for sloth. Thus (1) = a drone, a lazybones: also SLUG-A-BED, and (now accepted) SLUGGARD; 2. (old) = a hindrance; and (3) = a slow-paced boat, horse, &c., or (B. E.) a dull-edged tool. As *adj.* (also SLUGGISH and SLUGGY) = lazy, slow; as *verb.* = (1) to laze, and (2) to hinder.

1383. CHAUCER, *Cant. Tales*, 'The Parson's Tale.' Then cometh . . . SLUGGY slumbring which maketh a man hevy.

1440. *Prompt. Parv.*, 460. SLUGGYN, desidio, torpeo.

14[?]. *Political Poems* [E. E. T. S.], 32. The SLUGGE lokyth to be holpe of God that commawndyth men to waake in the worlde.

1590. SPENSER, *Fairy Queen*, II. i. 23, 3. To SLUG in slouth and sensuall delights. *Ibid.* (*d.*1599), *State of Ireland.* He lay not all night SLUGGING in a cabin under his mantle.

1593. SHAKSPEARE, *Comedy of Errors*, ii. 2. Thou drone, thou snail, thou SLUG. *Ibid.* (1595), *Romeo and Juliet*, iv. 5, 2. Why, lamb! why, lady! fie, you SLUG-A-BED.

1605. BACON, *Adv. of Learning*. They are . . . hindrances to stay and SLUG the ship for further sailing. *Ibid.* (1597-1624), *Essays*, 'Of Usury.' Money would be stirring if it were not for this SLUGGE.

1611. COTGRAVE, *Dict.*, s.v. *Paresser*. To SLUGGE it, to laze it, to liue idly.

1621. BURTON, *Anat. Melan*, III. II. iii. I. A SLUG, a fat lustilugs.

1635. QUARLES, *Emblems* [NARES]. One spends his day in plots, his night in play; another sleeps and SLUGS both night and day. *Ibid.*, I. 13. Lord, when we leave the world and come to thee, How dull, how SLUG are we.

1641. MILTON, *Reformation in Eng.*, I. It is still episcopacy that . . . worsens and SLUGGS the most learned and seeming religions of our ministers.

1648. HERRICK, *Hesperides*, 'To Corinna Going a-Maying.' Get up sweet SLUG-A-BED, And see the dew bespangles herb and tree.

1652. SHIRLEY, *Brothers . . . Car.* Will none deliver me? *Lu.* They are somewhat SLUG.

1659. GAUDEN, *Tears of the Church*, 381. Which soon grew a SLUG, when once the North-wind ceased to fill its sailes.

1666. PEPYS, *Diary*, 17 Oct. His rendevouz for his fleet and for all SLUGGS to come.

1888. *Ency. Brit.*, xii. 199. A SLUG [horse] must be kept going, and an impetuous one restrained.

4. (old).—A dram. Hence TO FIRE (OR CANT) A SLUG=to drink (GROSE).

1762. SMOLLETT, *L. Greaves*, II. v. He ordered the waiter . . . to . . . bring alongside a short allowance of brandy or grog that he might CANT A SLUG into his breadroom.

5. (American). — An ingot of gold; a twenty-dollar piece (*Ency. Dict.*), but in *Century Dict.* 'a gold coin of the value of fifty dollars privately issued in San Francisco during the mining excitement of 1849.'

1890. *San Francisco Bulletin*, 10 May. An interesting reminder of early days in California in the shape of a round fifty-dollar SLUG. . . . But fifty of these round fifty-dollar pieces were issued when orders came from the East prohibiting private coinage.

SLUGGER. *See* SLOGGER.

SLUICE, *verb.* (common).—1. The mouth: also SLUICE-HOUSE. As *verb.*: *e.g.*, TO SLUICE THE BOLT (DOMINOES, GOB, OR IVORIES) = to drink heartily: *see* DOMINOES (GROSE). Whence SLUICERY = a public-house (GROSE).

1840. EGAN, *Book of Sports*. Sam's SLUICE-HOUSE was again severely damaged.

2. (venery).—The female *pudendum*: *see* MONOSYLLABLE.

*d.*1704. BROWN, *Works*, ii. 184. That whore, my wife . . . that us'd to open her SLUICE . . . to gratify her concupiscense.

Verb. (colloquial).—To paddle; to bathe (or wet) freely.

*d.*1859. DE QUINCEY, *Works* (*Century*). He dried his neck and face which he had been SLUICING with cold water.

1860. RUSSELL, *Diary in India*, I. 4. The great seas . . . SLUICING the decks with a mimic ocean.

TO SLUICE OFF, *verb. phr.* (American.)—To divert; to lay aside.

1862. *Congregationalist*, 3 June. Some of present earning must thus be SLUICED OFF, to repair the poverty of the past.

SLUM, *subs.* (old and thieves').—1. Nonsense; a trick; a swindle: *e.g.*, a sham begging letter, a roll of 'snide' notes, &c. Hence UP TO SLUM = knowing, not to be HAD (*q.v.*); TO FAKE THE SLUM = to do the trick. 2 (old) = idle talk (*see* quots. 1821 and 1823).

As *verb.* = (1) to trick, to cheat; and (2) to talk idly, or to speak slang.

*d.*1821. RANDALL, *Diary* (GROSE, 3rd ed. [1823]). And thus, without more SLUM, began.

1823. BEE, *Dict. Turf*, s.v. SLUM—loose ridiculous talk is all SLUM! 'None of your SLUM' is said by a girl to a blarneying chap . . . The gypsy *language*, or cant, is SLUM . . . Dutch Sam excelled in SLUMMERY—'Willus youvus givibus glasso ginibus.'

1851. MAYHEW, *Lond. Lab.* That was his leading SLUM, and pretty well he sponged them too. *Ibid.* (1856), *Gt. World of London*, 46. Screevers or the writers of SLUMS and fakements.

2. (old).—Originally a room [GROSE: also *see* quots. 1823, s.v. sense I and *infra*]. Also 3 (modern) = a squalid street or neighbourhood; a ROOKERY (*q.v.*): usually in *pl.* with 'back.' As *verb.* = (1) to explore poor quarters out of curiosity or charity; 2 (Univ.) to keep to back streets to avoid observation; and 3 (common) to keep in the background.

1823. BEE, *Dict. Turf*, s.v. SLUM . . . also the room in which persons meet who talk in that style [*see* sense I]; thus we may have 'the little SLUM,' or 'the great SLUM,' 'a dirty SLUM,' or 'a pretty SLUM,' 'the back SLUM,' and a SLUM in front. Derived from *slumber*, to sleep, the molls and coves napping nine winks at those places.

1823. MONCRIEFF, *Tom and Jerry*, ii. 3. Let's have a dive amongst the cadgers in the back SLUMS in the Holy Land.

1872. BLACK, *Adv. of Phaeton*, xviii. When one gets clear of the suburban SLUMS and the smoke of Liverpool, a very respectable appearance of real country-life becomes visible.

1884. *Referee*, 22 June. A wealthy lady went SLUMMING through the Dials the other day.

1885. *Echo*, 8 Sep. There is little in the author's observations on SLUMS and SLUM LIFE that has not been said before.

*d.*1894. YATES, *London Life*, I. ii. Gone is the Rookery, a conglomeration of SLUMS and alleys in the heart of St. Giles's.

1897. MARSHALL, *Pomes*, 74. It was really a SLUM, where the greens always hum. *Ibid.*, 97. But it [love] wouldn't be SLUMMED like a worm in the bud.

4. (thieves'). — A letter, a package: anything in hand.

5. (Punch and Judy). — The call; SLUM-FAKE = the coffin; SLUMMING = acting.

1872. BRADDON, *Dead Sea Fruit*, xiv. The gorger's awfully coally on his own SLUMMING, eh?

SLUMGULLION, *subs.* (American).—1. A representative; a servant [BARTLETT].

SLUMGUZZLE, *verb.* (American).—To deceive. Hence SLUMGUZZLING = humbuggery [BARTLETT].

SLUMMY, *subs.* (common).—A servant-girl.

SLUMP, *subs.* (Stock Exchange and colloquial).—1. A sudden fall: of prices; an ignominious failure: *e.g.*, a SLUMP in Kaffirs. As *verb.* = to fall heavily (Scots') SLUMP = all of a piece; to come down with a rush.

1888. HOWELLS, *Annie Kilburn*, xxv. What a SLUMP! . . . That blessed shortlegged little seraph has spoilt the best sport that ever was.

2. (common).—A gross amount; the whole: *e.g.* 'a SLUMP sum.' As *verb.*=to lump, or group together.

*d.*1856. SIR W. HAMILTON, *Works* (Century). The different groups . . . are exclusively SLUMPED together under that sense.

1870. W. MATHEWS, *Getting on in the World*, 20. SLUMPING the temptations which were easy to avoid with those which were comparatively irresistible.

3. (American College). — To recite badly; to fail; to bungle.

SLUNG. SLUNG OUT ON HANDS AND KNEES, *phr.* (tailors').—Instantly dismissed.

SLUR, *subs. verb.* (B. E. and GROSE).—1. 'A Cheat at Dice; also a slight Scandal or Affront.' Hence (2) to cheat.

1664. BUTLER, *Hudibras*, II. ii. What was the public faith found out for But to SLUR men out of what they fought for. *Ibid.*, *Remains*, 'Misc. Thoughts.' Some flug'ring trick or SLUR.

1680. *Compleat Gamester*, ii. SLURRING—that is by taking up your dice as you will have them advantageously lie in your hand, placing the one atop the other, not caring if the uppermost run a millstone . . . if the undermost run without turning.

SLUSH, *subs.* (nautical).—1. Food. Hence 2. (GROSE) = a foul feeder: also SLUSH-BUCKET; SLUSHER (OR SLUSHY), *see* quot. 1890. Also 3 (old)=a drunkard.

1890. *Argus*, 20 Sept., 13, 6. Sundays are the most trying days of all, say the cuisiniers . . . This man's assistant is called the SLUSHER.

1896. PATERSON, *Man from Snowy River*, 162. The tarboy, the cook, and the SLUSHY . . . with the rest of the shearing horde.

4. (American journalists').—Indifferent matter; PADDING (*q.v.*).

SLUT, *subs.* (old). — 1. A dirty housewife; (2) = an awkward person or thing; (3) a WENCH (*q.v.*): *cf.* QUEAN; (4) a bitch. As *verb.* = to befoul; SLUTTERY (also SLUTTISHNESS) = neglect; SLUTTISH = (1) wanton; and (2) untidy.

14[?]. *Babees Book* [E. E. T. S.], 158. Crabbe is a SLUTT to kerve, and a wrawd wight; Breke euery clawe a sondur.

1483. CHAUCER, *Cant. Tales*, 'Prol. to Canon Yeoman's Tale,' 83. Why is thy lord so SLUTTISH?

1596. SHAKSPEARE, *Merry Wives of Windsor*, v. v. 50. Our radiant queen hates SLUTS and SLUTTERY.

1615. SYLVESTER, *Tobacco Battered*. Don Tobacco's damnable Infection SLUTTING the Body.

1648. HERRICK, *Hesperides*, 'Excesse.' Excesse is SLUTTISH: keepe the meane; for why? Vertue's clean conclave is sobriety.

1664. PEPYS, *Diary*, 21 Feb. Our little girl Susan is a most admirable SLUT, and pleases us mightily, doing more service than both the others. *Ibid.* (1665), 7 Nov. He carried his glass with him for his man to let him drink out of at the Duke of Albemarle's, where he intended to dine, though this he did to prevent SLUTTERY.

*d.*1704. BROWN, *Works*, i. 338. The young SLUT never looked so gay and pleasant in her life.

1705. VANBRUGH, *Confederacy*, iii. 2. I have managed Master Gripe's little affairs for him these ten years, you SLUT, you!

1712. ADDISON, *Spectator*, No. 130. You see now and then some handsome young jades among them [gypsies]; the SLUTS have very often white teeth and black eyes.

1862. THACKERAY, *Philip*, xiii. I gave my cousin this dog . . . and the little SLUT remembers me.

SLY, *adj.* and *adv.* (GROSE).—'Under the rose; transacting business privately is frequently said to be done UPON THE SLY'; illicit: also BY THE SLY; TO RUN SLY = to escape, to evade.

*c.*1787. *Kilmainham Minit* [*Ireland Sixty Years Ago*, 88]. But if dat de slang you RUN SLY, The scrag-boy may yet be outwitted, And I scout again on de lay.

1851-61. MAYHEW, *Lon. Lab.*, I. 318. A SLY trade's always the best for paying, and for selling too.

1871-2. ELIOT, *Middlemarch*, lxxviii. Selling myself for any devil's change BY THE SLY.

1887. HENLEY, *Culture in the Slums*. I keeps a dado ON THE SLY.

SLYBOOTS, *subs.* (old).—A seemingly simple but really clever and designing fellow (B. E. and GROSE).

*c.*1680. NORTH, *Lives of the Norths*, 169. [Lord Guildford was nicknamed] SLYBOOTS.

1729. ADDISON, *Adv. of Abdalla*, 32. The frog call'd . . . several times, but in vain . . . though the SLY-BOOTS heard well enough all the while.

SMABBLED (or **SNABBLED**), *adj.* (GROSE).—Killed in battle.

SMACK (B. E. *c.*1686).—1. 'A Twang or ill Taste.'

2. (tailors'). — A liking; a fancy: *e.g.* 'He had a real SMACK for the old 'un': *cf.* (old colloquial) SMACKERING = 'a longing for' (BAILEY).

3. (colloquial).—A kiss: also SMACKER. Whence TO SMACK CALF'S SKIN (common) = to take oath.

1786. BURNS, *Jolly Beggars*. Ilk SMACK still, did crack still, Just like a cadger's whip.

1809. IRVING, *Hist. N. York*, 171. The gentlemen gallantly attended their fair ones to their respective abodes, and took leave of them with a hearty SMACK.

1860. DICKENS, *Uncom. Traveller*, 'Titbull's Almshouses.' Heard the sound of a SMACK—a SMACK which was not a blow.

SMACK SMOOTH, *phr.* (colloquial).—'Level with the surface; everything cut away' (GROSE).

1790. DIBDIN, *Poor Jack*. Though the tempest the topgallant mast SMACK SMOOTH should smite.

SMACKING-COVE, *subs. phr.* (Old Cant). — A coachman (B. E., BAILEY and Grose).

SMALL, *subs.* (colloquial).—1. In *pl.* = breeches: spec. the close-fitting knee-breeches of the 18th and early 19th centuries: also SMALL-CLOTHES [GROSE: 'A gird at the affected delicacy of the present age; a suit being called coat, waistcoat, and—articles or SMALL CLOTHES'].

1812. COOMBE, *Syntax*, i. 20. His SMALL-CLOTHES sat so close and tight, His boots, like jet, were black and bright.

1813. STEPHENS [Anti-Jacobin Rev. of *Life of Horne Took*, quoted by SOUTHEY, *Doctor*, Interchap. xx.] His breeches he [STEPHENS] calls SMALL CLOTHES; the first time we have seen this bastard term, the offspring of gross ideas and disgusting affectation, in print, in anything like a book.

1818. BYRON, *Beppo*, iv. You'd better walk about begirt with briars, Instead of coat and SMALL-CLOTHES.

1836. DICKENS, *Sketches*, 'The Last Cabdriver.' His boots were of the Wellington form, pulled up to meet his corduroy knee-SMALLS.

1840. HOOD, *Miss Kilmansegg*. Wear a negative coat and positive SMALLS.

1869. STOWE, *Oldtown*, 52. His well-brushed Sunday coat and SMALL-CLOTHES.

2. (Univ. Oxon).—In *pl.*, *see* quots. LITTLE-GO is the Cambridge equivalent. Properly 'Responsions.'

*c.*1840. E. A. FREEMAN [1823-92], *Cont. Rev.*, ii. 821. 'Greats,' so far as the name existed in my time, meant the Public Examination, as distinguished from Responsions, Little-go, or SMALLS.

1853. BRADLEY, *Verdant Green*, II. xi. The little gentleman was going in for his degree, *alias* Great-go, *alias* Greats; and our hero for his first examination *in literis humanioribus*, *alias* Responsions, *alias* Little-go, *alias* SMALLS.

1861. HUGHES, *Tom Brown at Oxford*, x. In our second term we are no longer freshmen, and begin to feel ourselves at home, while both SMALLS and greats are sufficiently distant to be altogether ignored if we feel that way inclined.

1863. READE, *Hard Cash* . . . Julia reminded her that SMALLS was the new word for little go.

1878. *Scribner's Mag.*, Dec., 283. Looking forward with annoyance to the rather childish first examination, in Oxford language known as SMALLS.

3. (theatrical). — A one-night performance in a small town or village by a minor company carrying its own 'fit-up.'

Adv. (colloquial). — Timidly; humbly: *e.g.* to SING (or SPEAK) SMALL (*q.v.*).

SMALL-AND-EARLY, *subs. phr.* (colloquial).—An evening party: informal and breaking up at an early hour.

1865. DICKENS, *Mutual Friend*, xi. For the clearing off of these worthies, Mrs. Podsnap added a SMALL AND EARLY evening to the dinner.

SMALL BEER. *subs. phr.* (colloquial).—1. Weak beer; hence (2) trifles. Whence TO CHRONICLE SMALL BEER = (1) to engage in trivial occupations, and (2) to retail petty scandal; TO THINK SMALL BEER OF ANYTHING = to have a poor opinion of it. Also SMALL THINGS. As *adj.* = petty.

1604. SHAKSPEARE, *Othello*, ii. 1, 161. To suckle fools and CHRONICLE SMALL BEER.

*d.*1666. A BROME, *Works* [CHALMERS, vi. 648, 1]. A dull SMALL-BEER sinner.

1712. ADDISON, *Spectator*, 269, 8. I allow a double quantity of malt to my SMALL BEER.

1832. SOUTHEY. *The Doctor*, Interch., xvi. He thought SMALL BEER at that time of some very great patriots and Queenites.

1840. DE QUINCEY, *Style* [*Works*, xi. 174]. Should express her self-esteem by the popular phrase, that she did not 'think SMALL BEER OF HERSELF.'

1844. THACKERAY, *Barry Lyndon*, xiv. All the news of sport, assize, and quarter-sessions were detailed by this worthy CHRONICLER OF SMALL BEER. *Ibid.* (1855), *Newcomes*, xxxix. She THINKS SMALL BEER of painters, J. J.—well, well, we don't THINK SMALL BEER of ourselves, my noble friend.

1853. LYTTON, *My Novel*, IV. xii. When I say that sum un is gumptious, I mean—though that's more vulgar like—sum un who does not THINK SMALL BEER of hisself.

1880. *Academy*, 25 Sep., 219. Two such chroniclers of SMALL BEER as Boswell and Erskine.

1902. *Pall Mall Gaz.*, 19 Sep., 1. 3. Vogler had reason to think no SMALL THINGS of himself. He was emphatically the popular man of his day; he was followed by enthusiastic admirers.

SMALL CAP O, *subs. phr.* (printers').—A second or inferior in command; an under overseer.

SMALL CHEQUE, *subs. phr.* (nautical).—A dram; a drink. To KNOCK DOWN A CHEQUE = to spend all in drink.

SMALL FRY, *subs. phr.* (colloquial).—Generic (1) for things little; and (2) for things trifling or valueless.

1888. BLACK, *Houseboat*, viii. While some of the SMALL FRY popped out their heads to have a look.

SMALL HOURS, *subs. phr.* (colloquial).—The first three or four hours after midnight: usually 'THE SMALL HOURS of the morning.' Also SHORT HOURS.

*d.*1796. BURNS, *Death and Dr. Hornbook*. Some wee SHORT HOURS ayont the twal'.

1903. *D. Telegraph*, 3 Jan., 9, 'Paris Day by Day.' An extraordinary assault has been committed in a third-class carriage of a train which left Paris in the SMALL HOURS of yesterday morning for Brussels.

SMALL POTATOES. *See* POTATO.

SMALL PILL, *subs. phr.* (The Leys School).—A diminutive football: used on runs.

SMART, *adj.* and *adv.* (colloquial).—Generic for superior, out of the common, distinguished. [In senses 1, 2, and 3 there is often, but not necessarily, an implied suspicion of something questionable.] (1)

= lively, witty, pert (B. E.): *e.g.*, A SMART (= clever) BOOK; A SMART (= ready) REPLY; A SMART (= bright) SAYING; A SMART (= sparkling) SPEECH; A SMART (= brisk) LAD, &c. 2. = well-dressed, fashionable, brilliant: *e.g.*, A SMART (= elegant and modish) FROCK; A SMART (= attractive and amusing) SHOW; SMART (= fashionable) SOCIETY: hence SMART, *subs.* = (1) a dandy (old), and (2) one in advance of the prevailing standard of good taste. 3. = quick, expert, shrewd: *e.g.*, A SMART (= precocious) CHILD; A SMART (= clever) WORKMAN; A SMART (= enterprising) TRADESMAN; A SMART (= capable, active and neat) SOLDIER, SAILOR, HAND, &c. 4 (American) = clever, knavish, and unscrupulous. 5 (prov.) = cold: *e.g.*, A SMART (= biting) MORNING. 6 (colloquial) = uncommon: *e.g.*, SMART (= hard) GOING; SMART (= resolute and lively) HITTING; SMART (= capable) WORK. As *adv.* = very, large, considerable, vigorously: with such derivatives and combinations as SMARTY (*subs.*), SMARTNESS (*subs.*), and SMARTISH (*adj.*).

[?]. *M.S. Cantab.*, Ff. ii. 38, f. 131 [HALLIWELL]. The swynehorde toke out a knyfe SMERT. *Ibid.*, Ff. v. 48, f. 110. SMERTLY then she callis a knave.

1383. CHAUCER, *Cant. Tales*, 'Gen. Prol.' 149. If men smot it with a yerde SMERTE.

[?]. *Book of Precedence* [E. E. T. S], i. 50. When thi seruantes haue do ther werke, To pay ther hyre loke thou be SMERTE.

1641. MILTON, *Def. of Humb. Remonstr.*, Pref. A voluble and SMART fluence of tongue.

1662. FULLER, *Worthies, Wiltshire*, iii. 335. Thomas of Wilton wrote also a SMART Book on this subject.

*d.*1699. STILLINGFLEET, *Sermons*, III. vii. These few words . . . contain a SMART and serious expostulation.

*d.*1701. DRYDEN, *Works* [*Century*]. After show'rs The stars shine SMARTER.

*c.*1704. *Gentleman Instructed*, 470. 'Sirrah,' says the youngster, 'make me a SMART wig, a SMART one, ye dog!' The fellow blessed himself: he had heard of a SMART NAG, a SMART MAN, &c., but a SMART WIG was Chinese to the tradesman. . . . Within two days he had a SMART WIG with a SMART PRICE in the box. The truth is, he had been bred up with the groom, and translated the stable dialect into the dressing room.

*d.*1704. BROWN, *Works*, ii. 123. I was a SMART child, and a smock-fac'd youth.

1705. VANBRUGH, *Confederacy*, v. 2. There's no need to be so SMART upon him . . . If he's not a gentleman, he's a gentleman's fellow.

1708-10. SWIFT, *Pol. Conv.*, Intro. So great a number of SMART TURNS of wit and humour as I have produced.

1715. ADDISON, *Drummer*, iii. 1. Thou'st very SMART my dear. But see! Smoke the doctor.

1739. TOWNLEY, *High Life Below Stairs*, ii. The gay sparkling Belle who the whole town alarms, And with eyes, lips, and neck, sets the SMARTS all in arms.

1740. RICHARDSON, *Pamela*, i. 51. I bought . . . two pairs of ordinary blue worsted hose that made a SMARTISH appearance with white clocks. *Ibid.* (1753), *Grandison*, iv. 292. Our cousin is looked upon amongst his brother libertines and SMARTS as a man of first consideration.

1742. FIELDING, *Joseph Andrews*, II. iv. All the SMARTS . . . were eclipsed in a moment. *Ibid.*, III. iii. I resolved to quit all further conversation with beaux and SMARTS of every kind.

1753. *Adventurer*, 100. The scale consists of eight: Greenhorn, Jemmy, Jessamy, SMART, Honest Fellow, Joyous Spirit, Buck, and Blood.

1785. COWPER, *Task*, iv. 468. And sighs for the SMART comrades he has left.

*c.*1812. MAHER, *The Night Before Larry was Stretched*. He fetched a SMART BLOW at his head.

1811. AUSTEN, *Sense and Sensibility*, xix. I always preferred the church . . . but that was not SMART enough for my family. They recommended the army, but that was a great deal too SMART for me.

1826. CROKER [*Croker Papers*, i. 331]. Where there was a SMART young WAITER, whom, however, these two Englishmen used to row exceedingly.

1833. MARRYAT, *Peter Simple*, iv. Come, heave ahead, my lads, and be SMART.

1835. HOFFMAN, *Winter in the West*. There's a SMART chance of cigars there in the bar.

1836. SCOTT, *Cruise of Midge*, 363. There's a SMART hand . . . a good seaman evidently by the cut of his jib.

1837. DICKENS, *Pickwick Papers*, ii. SMART chap that cabman . . . but . . . punch his head! *Ibid.* (1844), *Martin Chuzzlewit*, xxxiii. Scadder is a SMART man, sir . . . Scadder was a SMART MAN, and had drawed a lot of British capital that was as sure as sun-up . . . Wish he might be sifted fine as flour, and whittled small as chips; that if they didn't come off that fixing right SMART too, he'd spill 'em in the drink. *Ibid.* (1853), *Bleak House*, ix. I scarcely knew him again, he was so uncommonly SMART.

1843. CARLTON, *New Purchase*, I. 85. There was a SMART sprinkle of rattle-snakes on Red Rum, and a powerful nice day to sun themselves.

1844. HALIBURTON, *Attache*, ix. He has a SMART chance of getting a better character.

18[?]. MACAULAY [TREVELYAN, I. 202]. A SMART, impudent-looking young dog dressed like a sailor in a blue jacket and check shirt, marched up.

1849. BRONTE, *Shirley*, xxiv. This stout lady in a quaint black dress, who looks young enough to wear much SMARTER raiment if she would.

1852. *Stray Yankee in Texas* [BARTLETT]. A powerful SMART-looking chunk of a pony.

1854. OLMSTED, *Texas*, 301. Each man's rations consisting of a pint of mouldy corn and a RIGHT SMART chunk of bacon.

1856. STOWE, *Dred*, I. 209. She had RIGHT SMART of life in her.

1861. KINGSLEY, *Ravenshoe*, xxxv. He's a prig, and a SMART one, too.

1869. STOWE, *Oldtown*, 57. She was a little thin woman, but tough as Inger rubber, and SMART AS A STEEL TRAP.

1884. CLEMENS, *Huck. Finn*, v. 34. I'll lay for you, my SMARTY, and if I catch you about that school I'll tan you good.

1885. *Century Mag.*, xl. 271. For a time the Clays were seen and heard of, on the top wave of London's SMART SOCIETY.

1889. *Harper's Mag.*, lxxx. 'Lit. Notes.' The awfully SMART boy is only SMART—in the worst American sense of the word—as his own family make him so.

1889. KIPLING, *Rout of the White Hussars*. It was all the Colonel's fault . . . He said the regiment was not SMART enough.

1889. *Answers*, 27 July, 141, 1. He knew that if the manuscript got about the Yankees would think it a SMART thing to crib it.

1891. MARRIOT-WATSON, *Web of Spider*, xxii. 'SMART he was, but he had a SMARTER man against him.' . . . 'Yes, but you don't yet realise how SMART.'

1900. WHITE, *West End*, 19. Among the SMART SET, and under the surface, little is impossible.

1901. *Pall Mall Gaz.*, 28 Nov., 2, 3. There can be no question that the SMART tradesman of to-day thrusts himself upon the general notice with tiresome assiduity.

1903. *The Smart Set, a Magazine of Cleverness* [Title].

See SMART-MONEY.

SMART-MONEY, *subs. phr.* (old).—1. 'Given by the King, when a Man in Land or Sea-Service has a Leg Shot or Cut off, or is disabled' (B. E. and GROSE): hence (2) a fine; and (3) vindictive damages: also SMART.

SMASH, *subs.* (colloquial).—1. Iced brandy and water.

2. (common).—Mashed vegetables: potatoes, turnips, and the like (GROSE).

1851-61. MAYHEW, *Lond. Lab.* The sweep asked him what he was going to have. 'A two-and-a-half plate and a ha'p'orth of SMASH.'

3. (prison).—Tobacco: hence TO SLING THE SMASH = to pass tobacco to a prisoner.

Verb. (thieves').—To utter base coin. Hence SMASHER = (1) base coin or paper; and (2) one who passes base money into circulation (GROSE and VAUX). Also 2. (common) = to give change (BEE): as *subs.* = loose change.

1823. BEE, *Dict. Turf*, s.v. SMASHED . . . SMASHERS—passers of bad money were so called during the pest of the old smooth coin. The term was soon extended to bad notes of the Bank of England; and their occupation was called SMASHING from the resemblance each bore the other in morals.

1834. AINSWORTH, *Rookwood*, 'Jerry Juniper's Chaunt.' Readily the queer screens I then could SMASH.

1840. LYTTON, *Paul Clifford*, xxxi. Stretched for SMASHING queer screens.

1851-61. MAYHEW, *Lond. Lab.*, II. 488. Every coin . . . was bad — all SMASHERS.

1883. GREENWOOD, *Tag, Rag, and Co.* The individual mentioned on the paper was a SMASHER.

1886. *Ev. Standard*, 11 Jan. Paper of a kind commonly used by SMASHERS to wrap up their coins, to prevent their rubbing against each other.

1887. HENLEY, *Villon's Straight Tip*, 1. You pitch a snide, or SMASH a rag.

2. (common).—To ruinate, to go bankrupt: also (military) to be reduced or broke. As *subs.* (or SMASH-UP) = ruin, destruction, bankruptcy; ALL TO SMASH = all to pieces, completely.

*c.*1847. THACKERAY, *Letters*, 120. I have made an awful SMASH at the Literary Fund, and have tumbled into 'Evins knows where.

1849. BRONTE, *Shirley*, ii. Your hellish machinery is shivered to SMASH on Stilboro' Moor.

1861. BRADLEY, *New Rector*, x. There isn't a fellow at school can match me, Miss Moore! I beat them ALL TO SMASH!

1885. *D. Telegraph*, 28 Dec. If it . . . comes to out-and-out SMASH, and selling up.

1887. *St. James's Gaz.*, 22 Jan. There was a final SMASH-UP of his party as well as of his reputation.

1895. LE QUEUX, *Temptress*, iv. May this SMASH bring me good luck in the future. *Ibid.*, v. I tell you it is pay or SMASH with me.

3. (pugilists').—To beat badly; to double up (BEE). Hence SMASHER = a settling blow.

1832. EGAN, *Book of Sports*, s.v. All of a heap, and all of a lump, unmistakably doubled up by a SMASHER.

1866. *London Misc.*, 5 May, 202. Doubled you up, I mean, sir. SMASHED you.

4. (old).—To kick downstairs: *e.g.*, 'The chubbs toute the blosses, they SMASH, and make them brush' = The sharpers catch their Mistresses on the hop, kick them downstairs and make them clear out (B. E. and GROSE).

SMASHER, *subs.* (common). — 1. Anything exceptional; a settler: *see* WHOPPER. Whence SMASHING = crushing.

1854. FIELD, *Drama at Pokerville* [BARTLETT]. Put up your benefit for that night: and if you don't have a SMASHER . . . say I don't understand managing the theatres.

2. *See* SMASH, *verb.* 1.

3. (nautical).—A north country seaman (CLARK RUSSELL).

SMASH-FEEDER, *subs. phr.* (thieves'). — A Britannia-metal spoon.

SMATTERER, *subs.* (colloquial).—'One half-learned. A *Smattering*, a slight Tincture in any Skill or Learning' (B. E.).

SMEAR, *subs.* (old).—1. A plasterer (GROSE).

2. (American).—Food; hash; grub: espec. 'a society spread or supper' (BARTLETT).

SMEAR-GELT, *subs. phr.* (old).—A bribe (GROSE).

SMECTYMNUS (obsolete).—*See* quot.

1721. BAILEY, *Eng. Dict.*, s.v. SMECTYMNUS, A word made out of the first letters of the names of five presbyterian ministers, viz., Stephen Marshall, Edmund Culamy, Thomas Young, Mathew Newcomen, and William Spurstow, who wrote a book against Episcopacy, and the Common Prayer, A.D. 1641, whereupon they and their followers were called SMECTYMNIANS.

SMEEKIT, *subs.* (Scots).—Drunk: *see* SCREWED.

SMELL, *verb.* (old colloquial).—To investigate, to search; to NOSE (*q.v.*): also TO SMELL OUT. Hence SMELLING COMMITTEE = an investigating committee. [BARTLETT: 'the phrase originated in the examination of a convent in Massachusetts by legislative order.']. *See* SMELLER.

*d.*1555. LATIMER, *Sermons*, 335. From that time forward I began to SMELL the word of God, and forsook the school-doctors and such fooleries.

1600. SHAKSPEARE, *Much Ado*, iii. 2. Can you SMELL him OUT by that. *Ibid.* (1602), *Twelfth Night*, ii. 3. I SMELL a device. *Ibid.* (1604), *Winter's Tale*, iv. 3. I SMELL the trick of it. *Ibid.* (1605), *Lear*, i. 5, 22. What a man cannot SMELL OUT he may spy into.

1626. FLETCHER, *Noble Gentleman*, ii. 1. Come, these are tricks; I SMELL 'em; I will go.

1702. STEELE, *Grief-a-la-Mode*, iv. 1. I like this old fellow, I SMELL more money.

PHRASES and COLLOQUIALISMS.—*See* CORK; ELBOW-GREASE; FOOTLIGHTS; GREASE; INKHORN; LAMP; RAT; ROAST.

SMELLER, *subs.* (common).—1. The nose: *see* CONK (B. E. and GROSE): in *pl.* = nostrils. Also 2 (pugilists') = a blow on the nose; a NOSENDER, *q.v.* (BEE).

1678. COTTON, *Scarronides*, 64. For he on SMELLERS, you must know, Receiv'd a sad unlucky blow.

1840. COCKTON, *Val. Vox*, xxviii. There's a conk! there's a SMELLER.

1853. BRADLEY, *Verdant Green* . . . Come on, half-a-dozen of ye, and let me have a rap at your SMELLERS.

1901. WALKER, *In the Blood*, 20. I tipped 'im one on the SMELLER as soon as 'e said it.

3. (common).—In *pl.* = a cat's 'whiskers' (GROSE).

4. (common).—A spy; a PAUL PRY (*q.v.*).

SMELL-FEAST, *subs. phr.* (old).—1. A parasitic glutton; as *adj.* = sharking for victuals. Also (2) = a POINT (*q.v.*)-feast.

1599. HALL, *Virgid*, VI. i. 47. Nor now no more SMELL-FEAST Vitellio, Smiles on his master for a meal or two.

1609. HOLLAND, *Amm. Marcell* [NARES]. Mercurius called commonly captaine of SMELL-FEASTS, for that like unto a dogge . . . wagging his taile, he used to thrust himselfe often into feasts and companies. *Ibid.* These SMELL-FEAST parasites.

1621. BURTON, *Anat. Melan.*, II. III. viii. No SMELL-FEASTS . . . parasites, bawds, drunkards, whoremasters.

1633. HARRINGTON, *Epigrams*. What manner sprite these SMELLFEASTS had possest.

1648. HERRICK, *Hesperides*, 'Vpon Burr.' Burr is a SMELL-FEAST, and a man alone That (where meat is) will be a hanger on.

1653. URQUHART, *Rabelais*, I. liv. Fat chuffcats, SMELL-FEAST knockers, doltish gulls.

*d.*1704. LESTRANGE, *Works* [*Ency. Dict.*]. An intruder, and a common SMELL-FEAST that spunges upon other people's trenchers.

SMELLING-CHEAT, *subs. phr.* (Old Cant).—1. The nose: *see* CHEAT and SMELLER (HARMAN, DEKKER). 2 (Old Cant) = an orchard, garden, or nosegay (HARMAN, DEKKER, B. E., BAILEY, GROSE).

SMELL-SMOCK. *See* SMOCK.

SMELLY, *adv.* (colloquial).—Offensively odorous.

1863. KINGSLEY, *Water Babies*, 186. Nasty, dirty, frowzy, grubby, SMELLY old monks.

SMELL-POWDER, *subs. phr.* (old).—A duellist (BEE).

SMELT, *subs.* (old).—1. A gull: *see* BUFFLE. Hence (proverbial) 'Westward for SMELTS!' (old colloquial) = on the spree (*i.e.*, in search of conies, male or female).

*c.*1600. *Weakest to the Wall*, iii. 4. Now mine host rob-pot . . . gudgeon!—SMELT, I should say.

1600. JONSON, *Cynthia's Revels*, ii. 1. *Cup.* What's he, Mercury? *Mer.* A notable SMELT.

1607. DEKKER and WEBSTER, *Westward Ho*, iv. 2. To see how plain dealing women can pull down men! Moll, you'll help us to catch SMELTS, too? *Ibid.*, ii. 3. But wenches, with what pullies shall we slide with some cleanly excuse, out of our husbands suspicion; being gone WESTWARD FOR SMELTS all night?

1608. *Great Frost* [ARBER, *Garner*, i. 85]. Let your news be as country folk bring fruit to your markets, the small and good together. Say, have none 'gone WESTWARD FOR SMELTS,' as our proverbial phrase is.

1635. FLETCHER, *Love's Pilgrimage*, v. 2. Talk what you will, this is a very SMELT.

2. (Old Cant).—Half-a-guinea (B. E. and GROSE).

1822. SCOTT, *Fort. Nigel*, xxiii. You see . . . that noble Master Grahame, whom you call Green, has got the decuses and the SMELTS.

SMICKER, *verb.* (old).—To look wantonly: as *adj.* = amorous; SMICKERING = amorous inclination; SMICKLY = amorously.

1606. FORD, *Fame's Memorial*, 574. Regardful of his honour he forsook The SMICKER use of court humanity. *Ibid.* (1623-4), *Sun's Darling*, ii. 1. *Ray.* Who is he that looks so SMICKLY? *Fol.* One that loves mutton so well that he always carries capers about with him.

1608. *Cobler of Canterburie* [HALLIWELL]. The smith seeing what a SMICKER wench the coblers wife was . . . wished that he could finde meanes to have such a one his friend.

*d.*1625. LODGE, *Poems*, 'Coridon's Song' [*Rept.*, 106]. A SMICKER boy . . . a SMICKER swaine; That in his love was wanton faine.

1701. DRYDEN, *To Mrs. Steward*, Let. 35. We had a young doctour, who . . . seem'd to have a SMICKERING to our young lady of Pilton.

SMICKET, *subs.* (old).—A smock or shift.

1719. DURFEY, *Wit and Mirth*, . . . Touch but her SMICKET and all's your own.

1820. COOMBE, *Syntax*, ii. 5. The roaring, dancing bumpkins show, And the white SMICKETS wave below.

SMIGGINS, *subs.* (obsolete prison).—Hulk soup.

SMILE, *subs.* (American).—A drink: as *verb.* = to drink, spec. in company: *cf.* SHOUT.

1855. *N.Y. Tribune*, 31 Jan. The 'crowd' was invited into the Fifth Ward Hotel, and one general SMILE entirely absorbed the fee.

1858. *Baltimore Sun*, 23 Aug. There are many more fast boys about—some devoted to "the sex," some to horses, some to SMILING, and some to "the tiger."

1870. *Browne, Artemus Ward, His Book*, 36, Note. 'Tods' a shortening of toddy . . . Recently, however, TO SMILE has taken its place.

1887. FRANCIS, *Saddle and Mocassin*. With what exquisite feeling will he graduate his cup from the gentle SMILE of early morning to the potent 'smash' of night.

SMILING. TO COME UP SMILING, *verb. phr.* (common).—To rise superior to the moment.

SMIRK, *subs.* (B. E. and GROSE).—'A finical spruce Fellow. To SMIRK, to smile or look pleasantly.'

SMISH, *subs.* (Old Cant).—A chemise; a shirt: *cf.* CAMESA and MISH (GROSE and VAUX).

SMITE, *verb.* (old).—To get money; to RUSH (*q.v.*): 'Academic term' (GROSE).

SMITER, *subs.* (old).—1. A sword.

1591. LYLY, *Endimion*, i. 3. It is my *smiter*; which I by construction often studying to bee compendious, call my SMITER.

1611. COTGRAVE, *Dict.*, s.v. *Cimeterre*. A Scymitar, or SMYTER, a kind of short and crooked sword, much in use among the Turks.

1633. JONSON, *Tale of a Tub*, iv. 3. Then, Basket, put thy SMITER up, and hear; I dare not tell the truth to a drawn sword.

1659. *Leg. of Capt. Jones.* His fatal SMITER thrice aloft he shakes.

2. (old).—An arm (B. E. and GROSE).

SMITHEREENS (or **SMITHERS**), *subs.* (common).—Small fragments. ALL TO SMITHEREENS = all to SMASH (*q.v.*).

1855. TENNYSON, *Northern Cobbler*, xviii. 'Smash the bottle to SMITHERS, the Divil's in 'im,' said I.

1872. BLACK, *Adv. of a Phaeton*, iii. Knocked heaps of things to SMITHEREENS

SMITHFIELD-BARGAIN, *subs. phr.* (old).—*See* quots.

1598. SHAKSPEARE, 2 *Hen. IV.*, i. 2, 56. *Page.* He's gone into SMITHFIELD to buy your worship a horse. *Falst.* I bought him in Paul's. and he'll buy me a horse in SMITHFIELD; an I could get me but a wife in the stews, I were manned, horsed, and wived.

1621. BURTON, *Anat. Melan.*, III. III. iv. 2. He that . . . buys a horse in SMITHFIELD . . . shall likely have a jade.

1662. WILSON, *Cheats*, v. 5. If this is not better than a SMITHFIELD BARGAIN—give me so much money, and my horse shall leap thy mare.

*d.*1704. BROWN, *Works*, iii. 54. By the procurement of these experienc'd matrons, a marriage is struck up like a SMITHFIELD BARGAIN. There is much higling and wrangling for t'other ten pounds.

1731. WARD, *Terræfilius*, 4, 29. He can no more speak without breaking the fourth commandment than a SMITHFIELD jockey can sell a horse without giving the purchaser a lye into the BARGAIN.

1753. RICHARDSON, *Grandison* (1812), vi. 44. Women when . . . urged to give way to a clandestine or unequal address . . . are pleaded with to rise against the notions of bargain and sale, SMITHFIELD BARGAINS you Londoners call them.

1772. GRAVES, *Spir. Quixote*, v. xv. The devil take me if I would marry an angel upon the footing of a mere SMITHFIELD BARGAIN.

1776. FOOTE, *Bankrupt*, ii. 1. You deposit so much money, and he grants you such an annuity; a mere SMITHFIELD BARGAIN, that is all.

1785. GROSE, *Vulg. Tongue*, s.v. SMITHFIELD BARGAIN. A bargain whereby the purchaser is taken in. This is likewise frequently used to express matches, or marriages, contracted solely on the score of interest, on one or both sides, where the fair sex are bought and sold like cattle in Smithfield.

1881. DAVIES, *Supp. Glossary*, s.v. SMITHFIELD BARGAIN . . . A marriage of interest, where money is the chief consideration: the allusion is to buying a wife in Smithfield. *Cf.* BRETON, *Olde Man's Lesson* (1605), p. 7: 'Fie on these market matches, where marriages are made without affection.'

SMOCK, *subs.* (old).—A woman: *cf.* PETTICOAT, PLACKET, SKIRT, MUSLIN, &c. Hence, in combination = pertaining to, or connected with women. Thus SMOCK-AGE = the use of the sex; SMOCK-ALLEY = the female *pudendum*: *see* MONOSYLLABLE; SMOCK-FACE = an effeminate: SMOCK-FACED = 'snout-fair' (B. E.), 'fair-faced' (GROSE), smooth-faced; SMOCK NIGHT-WORK (SERVICE, or EMPLOYMENT) = copulation; SMOCK-LOYALTY = constancy; SMOCK-TREASON = adultery; SMOCK-SERVANT = (1) a mistress, and (2) a lover; SMOCK-AGENT = a bawd; SMOCKSTER (SMOCK-MERCHANT, SMELL-SMOCK, or SMOCK-TEARER) = a whoremonger: SMELL-SMOCK also = the *penis*, and as *adj.* = wanton; SMOCK-VERMIN = a contemptuous address; SMOCK-TOY

= a fancy PIECE (*q.v.*), male or female; SMOCK-SECRET = intrigue; SMOCK-HOLD = tenure during a wife's lifetime; SMOCK-GOVERNMENT (or SMOCK-LED) = petticoat rule; SMOCK-PENSIONER = a male KEEP (*q.v.*): also SMOCK-SQUIRE; SMOCK-HUNTING = whoring; SMOCK-LOOSE = wanton; IN HER SMOCK = intimately; SMOCK-RACE (*see* quot. 1801); &c. As *verb.* = to copulate (FLETCHER): *see* RIDE.

1582. STANYHURST, *Æneid*, iv. 222. Now this SMOCK-TOY Paris with berdlesse company wayted.

1585. *Nomenclator*, 528. *Mulierarius*, one given to love women, a SMELL-SMOCKE.

1595. SHAKSPEARE, *Romeo and Juliet*, ii. 4, 109. [*Enter Nurse and Peter*]. *Mer.* A sail, a sail! *Ben.* Two, two; a shirt and a SMOCK. *Ibid.* (1598), *All's Well*, ii. 1, 30. I shall stay here, the forehorse to a SMOCK. *Ibid.* (1608), *Antony and Cleopatra*, i. 2, 172. If there were no more women but Fulvia, then had you indeed a cut, and the case to be lamented; this grief is crowned with consolation; your old SMOCK brings forth a new petticoat.

1599. CHAPMAN, *Humorous Day's Mirth* [SHEPHERD, *Works* (1874), 35]. He was taken learning tricks at old Lucilla's house, the muster-mistress of all the SMOCK-TEARERS in Paris. *Ibid.* (1605), *Al Fooles*, v. 1. Some wealth without wit, some nor wit nor wealth, But good SMOCK-FACES. *Ibid.* (1612), *Widow's Tears* [SHEPHERD, *Works* (1874), 314]. Shalt hold thy tenement, to thee and thine heers for ever, in free SMOCKAGE, as of the manner of panderage.

1611. JONSON, *Cataline*, iv. 5. *Sem.* There are of us can be as exquisite traitors As e'er a male conspirator of you all. *Cet.* Ay, at SMOCK-TREASON, matron, I believe you. *Ibid.* (1632), *Magnetic Lady*, iv. 2. Keep these women matters SMOCK-SECRETS to ourselves.

1611. COTGRAVE, *Dict.* s.v, *Brigaille*. A noteable SMELSMOCKE, or mutton-mungar, a cunning solicitor of a wenche.

1624. MASSINGER, *Renegado*, ii. 1. 'Tis but procuring a SMOCK-EMPLOYMENT. *Ibid.* (1632), *Maid of Honour*, ii. 2. You are not the man; much less employ'd by him As a SMOCK-AGENT to me. *Ibid.* iii. 1. Peace, thou SMOCK-VERMIN! *Ibid.* (1637), *Guardian*, iii. 5. Now I think I had ever a lucky hand in such SMOCK NIGHT-WORK.

[?]. *Cat. of Books of the Newest Fashion* [Harl. Misc., v. 287]. SMOCK-PECK'D S——.

1630. TAYLOR, *Works*, ii. 167. This theame of SMOCKE is very large and wide . . . But I thinke best a speedy end to make, Lest for a SMELSMOCKE some should me mistake.

1653. URQUHART, *Rabelais*, I. xi. And some of the . . . women would give these names, my Roger . . . SMELL-SMOCK . . . lusty live sausage.

1657. MIDDLETON, *More Dissemblers, &c.*, i. 4. If thou dost not prove as arrant a SMELL-SMOCK as any the town affords in a term time I'll lose my judgement.

1663. *Unfortunate Usurper* [NARES]. SMELL-SMOCK Sardanapalus would have given The moiety of his kingdom to be his pupil.

1680. DRYDEN, *Spanish Friar*, ii. 1. Plague . . . on his SMOCK-LOYALTY. *Ibid.* (1692), *Juvenal*, x. 491. Young Endymion, your smooth SMOCK-FAC'D boy.

*d.*1704. BROWN, *Works*, ii. 123. I was a smart child, and a SMOCK-FAC'D youth.

1706. WARD, *Wooden World*, 69. If ever he's troubled with Dreams . . . then truly he oft fancies himself a mauling off the Roast-meat in SMOCK-ALLEY. *Ibid.* (1709), *Works*, i. 173. Skilful SMOCKSTERS . . . Tell us that Love's a drowthy exercise.

1746. *Poor Robin.* A whoremaster hath a SMELL-SMOCK nose which for the most part in process of time proves bridge-fallen.

1801. STRUTT, *Sports and Pastimes*, 476. SMOCK RACES are commonly performed by the young country wenches, and so-called because the prize is a holland SMOCK, or shirt, usually decorated with ribbands.

1809. MALKIN, *Gil Blas* [ROUTLEDGE], 136. Pacheco did not know what to make of so SMOCK-FACED a young spark.

1879. LECKY, *English in 18th Cent.*, iv. Among other amusements SMOCK-RACING by women was kept up there [Pall Mall] till 1733.

SMOKE, *subs.* (old).—1. A chimney. Hence (modern) THE SMOKE = any large city: spec. London: also THE GREAT SMOKE.

*d.*1687. PETTY, *Pol. Surv. of Ireland*, 9. Dublin hath Houses of more than one SMOAK.

2. (common).—A cigar: also the act of smoking. DRY-SMOKE = an unlighted cigar or pipe between the lips.

1860. RUSSELL, *Diary in India*, xxvii. Soldiers . . . lounging about, taking an early morning SMOKE.

*c.*1885[?]. JENNY HILL, '*'Arry.*' 'Arry likes a twopenny SMOKE.

3. (colloquial). — Idle talk; vanity; anything of little or no value. TO END IN SMOKE = to serve or come to no useful end.

1594. SHAKSPEARE, *Lucrece*, 1027. This helpless SMOKE of words doth me no right.

1603-15. *Court and Times of Jas. I.*, 291. [A project] GOES AWAY IN SMOKE.

Verb. (old).—1. To examine; to suspect; to observe; to discover; to understand; TO TWIG (*q.v.*): *cf.* SMELL, NOSE, &c. Whence SMOKY = (1) suspicious, inquisitive; and (2) = jealous (B. E., GROSE, BEE).

1280. *Ancren Riwle*, 316. Schrift get schal beon naked; thet is naked liche imaked, and nout bisaumpled feire, ne hendeliche ISMOKED. [Confession must be naked, that is made nakedly, not speciously palliated, nor gently touched on.]

1596. JONSON, *Ev. Man in His Hum.*, iv. 8. I'faith, I am glad I have SMOKED you yet at last. *Ibid.* (1622), *Masque of Augurs*, [*Works*] (MOXON), 230. Sir, we do come from among the brew-houses, . . . that's true, there you have SMOKED us.

1598. SHAKSPEARE, *All's Well*, iii. 6. He was first SMOKED by the old Lord Lafew—when his disguise and he is parted, tell me what a sprat you shall find him.

1607. DEKKER, *Jests*, &c. [GROSART, *Works*, ii. 329]. Kinchen, the coue towres, which is as much as, Fellow, the man SMOKES or suspects you. *Ibid.* (1620), *Lauthorne*, &c. The two freebooters, seeing themselves SMOAK'D.

1611. MIDDLETON and DEKKER, *Roaring Girl* [*Works*] (1873), III. 220. Wee are SMOAKT . . . wee are boyld, pox on her!

1614. CHAPMAN, *Odysseys*, iv. 337. And yet through all this difference, I alone SMOKED his true person.

1624. MASSINGER, *Renegado*, iv. 1. All's come out, sir. We are SMOK'D for being coney-catchers. *Ibid.* (1659), *City Madam*, iii. 1. I'll hang you both . . . you for a purse you cut In Paul's at a sermon; I have SMOAKED you, ha!

*c.*1650. BRATHWAYTE, *Barnaby's Jl.* (1723), 21. An apt one . . . Punk unto a Captain; I embrac'd . . . But Door creak'd and Captain SMOAK'T IT.

1693. CONGREVE, *Old Bach.*, iii. 6. I begin to SMOKE ye: thou art some forsaken Abigail. *Ibid.* (1694), *Double Dealer*, iii. 3. Should she SMOKE my design upon Cynthia I were in a fine pickle.

1705. VANBRUGH, *Confederacy*, iii. I'm thinking—hum—she'll SMOKE that though. *Ibid.* (1726), VANBRUGH and CIBBER, *Prov. Husband*, ii. He seems a little SMOKY.

1708-10. SWIFT, *Pol. Conv.* i. Pray, madam, SMOKE miss yonder, biting her lips, and playing with her fan.

1715. ADDISON, *Drummer*, iii. 1. Thou'rt very smart, my dear. But see! SMOKE the doctor.

1715-16. ADDISON, *Freeholder* [*Ency.*]. I began to SMOKE that they were a parcel of mummers.

1733. SWIFT, *Ans. to Sheridan's New Simile.* With which he made a tearing show; And Dido quickly SMOK'D the beau.

1753. FOOTE, *Eng. in Paris*, i. 1. A SMOAKY fellow this classic. *Ibid.* (1762), *The Liar*, i. 1. People in this town are more SMOAKY and suspicious.

1772. BRIDGES, *Burlesque Homer*, 75. The witch of Endor, Soon SMOK'D th' affair, and like a prophet, Got up and told the meaning of it.

1774. KELLY, *School for Wives*, iii. 5. Who the devil could think that he would SMOKE us in this disguise.

*d.*1859. DE QUINCEY, *Works*, xi. 86. The orator grew urgent; wits began to SMOKE the case, as active verbs—the advocate to smoke, as a neuter verb.

1877. *Five Years Penal Serv.*, iii. He stayed in a place doing the grand, and sucking the flats, till the folks began to SMOKE him as not 'all there.'

1900. SAVAGE, *Brought to Bay*, The secret reports of the head porter proved that no one could SMOKE OUT the aristocratic invalid.

2. (school).—To blush.

3. (old). — To ridicule; TO QUIZ (*q.v.*). Whence SMOKER = a mocker, a practical joker; SMOKING = bantering.

1698-1700. WARD, *Lond. Spy*, ix. 197. We SMOAK'D the Beaux almost as bad as unlucky schoolboys us'd to do the coblers, till they sneak'd off one by one.

1700. CONGREVE, *Way of World*, iii. 15. This is a vile dog; I see that already. No offence! . . . to him, Petulant, SMOKE him.

1782. BURNEY, *Cecilia*, vi. 11. You never laugh at the old folks, and never fly at your servants, nor SMOKE people before their faces.

1814. COLMAN, *Poet Vagaries*, 150. These quizzers, queerers, SMOKERS.

*d.*1840. D'ARBLAY, *Diary* (1842), ii. 69. What a SMOKING did Miss Burney give Mr. Crutchley.

4. (B. E.).—'To affront a Stranger at his coming in.'

5. (venery). — To copulate (FLETCHER): *see* RIDE.

6. (old).—To raise a dust by beating: *cf.* TO DUST ONE'S JACKET.

1596. SHAKSPEARE, *K. John*, ii. 1, 139. I'll SMOKE your skin-coat, an I catch you right.

7. (Australian).—To decamp: *see* ABSQUATULATE.

1893. *Sydney M. Herald*, 26 June, 8, 8. He said to the larrikins, . . . 'You have killed him.' 'What!' said one of them, 'do not say we were here. Let us SMOKE.'

PHRASES. LIKE SMOKE = rapidly: *see* LIKE; ALL SMOKE, GAMMON, AND SPINACH = all nothing; 'No SMOKE, but there's fire' (or 'Where there's SMOKE there's fire') 'of a thing that will out' (B. E.). *See* KNOCK; PIPE; TAKE.

1851-61. MAYHEW, *Lond. Lab.*, III. 105. Taking money LIKE SMOKE.

SMOKER (or **SMOKE-SHELL**), *subs.* (common). 1. A chamber-pot: *see* IT.

2. (B. E.). — 'A Vessel to Blind the Enemies, to make way for the Machine to play.

3. (colloquial). — A smoking-carriage: *see* SMOKE 3. Also 4. (old) = a tobacconist (B. E. and GROSE).

5. (old). *See* quot.

1847. HALLIWELL, *Arch. Words*, s.v. SMOKER. At Preston, before the passing of the Reform Bill in 1832, every person who had a cottage with a chimney and used the latter, had a vote, and was called a SMOKER.

SMOKE-STACK, *subs. phr.* (nautical).—A steam-boat.

1902. *Athenæum*, 8 Feb., 177, 1. The author shows the proper sailor-man's contempt for SMOKE-STACKS, and to this day would sooner travel in a "wind-jammer" than a P. & O. boat—or one of his readers is mistaken.

SMOOTH, *subs.* (American). — A meadow; a grass-plot; a lawn.

1870. JUDD, *Margaret*, i. 2. Get some plantain and dandelion on the SMOOTH for greens.

SMOOTHER, *subs.* (old).—*See* quot.

1653. URQUHART, *Rabelais*, III. iii. My claw-backs, my SMOOTHERS, my parasites.

SMOTHERATION, *subs.* (American). —1. Suffocation.

2. (American).—A dish (pork or beef) smothered with potatoes [*cf.* SMOTHER, an old cookery term—'rabbits SMOTHERED in onions'].

SMOUCH, *subs.* (old).—1. A low-crowned hat (HALLIWELL).

2. *See* SMOUS.

Verb. (old).—1. To kiss: as *subs.* (or SMOUCHER) = a kiss.

1578. WHETSTONE, *Promos and Cassandra*, 47. Come, smack me; I long for a SMOUCH.

1583. STUBBES, *Anat. Abuses*, 114. What bussing, what SMOUCHING, and slabbering one of another.

1600. *Weakest to Wall*, i. 3. You will love me, SMOUCH me, be my secret vriend.

1600. HEYWOOD, *1 Ed. IV.* [PEARSON, *Works* (1874), i. 40]. I had rather than a bend of leather, Shee and I might SMOUCH together.

1606. *Ret. from Parnassus.* Why how now pedant Phœbus, are you SMOUTCHING Thalia on her tender lips?

2. (old). — To chouse; to trick; to take an unfair advantage.

SMOUS (or **SMOUCH**), *subs.* (old).—A Jew (GROSE). Also (2) a sharper.

1705. BOSMAN, *Description of Guinea*, Letter XI. As impertenant and noisy as the SMOUSE or German Jews at their synagogue at Amsterdam.

1760. JOHNSTON, *Chrysal*, i. 228. I saw them roast some poor SMOUCHES at Lisbon because they would not eat pork.

1764. C. MACKLIN, *Man of the World*, ii. 1. Ha, ha, ha! . . . I honour the SMOUSE.

1837. BARHAM, *Ingolds. Leg.*, 'Mer. of Venice.' You find fault mit ma pargains, and say I'm a SMOUCH.

SMOUTING, *subs.* (old printers').—*See* quot: now GRASSING (*q.v.*).

1688. R. HOLME, *Academy*, *&c.* Workmen, when they are out of constant work, sometimes accept of a day or two's work or a week's work at another printing house; this by-work they call SMOUTING.

SMOUZE, *verb.* (American).—'To demolish; as with a blow' (BARTLETT).

SMUG, *subs.* (old).—1. A blacksmith (B. E. and GROSE).

1611. ROWLAND, *Knave of Clubs.* A SMUG of Vulcan's forging trade.

1629. DEKKER, *Londons Tempe.* I must now A golden handle make for my wife's fann, Worke, my fine SMUGGES.

1709. WARD, *Works*, i. 133. You're an impudent slut, cries the SMUG at his bellows.

2. (common). — An affectedly proper or self-satisfied person. Hence as *adj.* (B. E. and GROSE: now accepted) = 'Neat and spruce.'

3. (school and university).—*See* quot. As *verb.* = to work hard.

1888. GOSCHEN, *Speech at Aberdeen*, 31 Jan. The heinous offence of being absorbed in it [work]. Schools and Colleges . . . have invented . . . phrases, semi-classical, or wholly vernacular, such as 'sap,' 'SMUG,' 'swot,' 'bloke,' 'a mugster.'

1889. *Lancet*, II. 471. Students . . . continually at study . . . absent-minded . . . often offended at . . . a joke. They become labelled SMUGS and are avoided by their class-mates.

Verb. (common).—1. To pilfer; to snatch: in quot. 1633 = to sneak into favour. Hence SMUGGINGS (*see* quot. 1847). SMUG-LAY (old thieves'), *see* quots. *c.*1696 and 1785: also SMUGGLER.

*c.*1633. FLETCHER [HALLIWELL]. Thou mayst succeed Ganymede in his place, And unsuspected SMUG the Thund'rers face. O happy she shall climbe thy tender bed, And make thee man first for a maidenhead.

*c.*1696. B. E., *Dict. Cant. Crew*, s.v. SMUG-LAY. Those that Cheat the King of his Customs by private Imports and Exports.

1785. GROSE, *Vulg. Tongue*, s.v. SMUG-LAY. Persons who pretend to be smugglers of lace and valuable articles; these men borrow money of publicans by depositing these goods in their hands; they shortly afterwards decamp, and the publican discovers too late that he has been duped, and on opening the pretended treasure he finds trifling articles of no value.

1847. HALLIWELL, *Arch. Words*, s.v. SMUGGING. Games had . . . times or seasons . . . when any game was out, as it was termed, it was lawful to steal the thing played with . . . 'Tops are in, spin 'em again; Tops are out, SMUGGING's about.'

1851-61. MAYHEW, *Lond. Lab.*, II. 508. I shouldn't mind his licking me; I'd SMUG his money, and get his halfpence, or somethink. *Ibid.* After that he used to go SMUGGLING, running away with other people's things.

2. (thieves').—To hush up; (3) to steal; and (4) to apprehend.

1857. *M. Chron.*, 3 Oct. She wanted a guarantee the case should be SMUGGED, or in other words compromised.

1877. HORSLEY, *Jottings from Jail.* Then two or three more coppers came up, and we got SMUGGED, and got a sixer each.

SMUGGLE, *verb.* (old colloquial).—1. To cuddle; to fondle: *cf.* SNUGGLE.

1698. FARQUHAR, *Love and a Bottle*, i. 1. Oh, the little lips! and 'tis the best-natured little dear [SMUGGLES and kisses it].

1709. WARD, *Works*, i. 68. You may SMUGGLE and grope . . . But must pay for the ultimate favour.

2. (schools'). — To sharpen a pencil at both ends. Hence SMUGGLER = a pencil thus sharpened.

SMUGGLING-KEN, *subs. phr.* (old). —A bawdy house (GROSE).

SMULKIN, *subs.* (old).—A brass farthing (Irish): *temp.* Eliz.

SMUSA, *verb.* (GROSE). — 'To snatch or seize suddenly.'

SMUT, *subs.* (colloquial).—1. Obscenity; ribaldry. Hence SMUTTY = lewd, obscene, NUTTY (*q.v.*); SMUTTINESS = bawdry (B. E. and GROSE).

1698. COLLIER, *Eng. Stage*, 6. SMUTTINESS is a fault in behaviour as well as in religion. *Ibid.*, 24. There are no SMUTTY songs in their plays, in which the English are extremely scandalous.

*d.*1704. BROWN, *Works*, i. 237. The Judge gravely tells them, Look ye, Ladies we have a SMUTTY Tryal coming on . . . yet the Devil a Lady will flinch.

1709. WARD, *London Terræfilius*, 2. 12 [*Works* (1709), i.] She . . . has as many SMUTTY stories at her tongue's end as an old parish clerk.

*d.*1719. ADDISON, *The Lover*, 39. He . . . will talk SMUT, though a priest and his mother be in the room.

1722. STEELE, *Conscious Lovers*, Prol. Another SMUTS his scene.

1734. POPE, *Satires*, Prol. Spite, or SMUT, or rhymes, or blasphemies.

1746. SMOLLETT, *Advice*, 172. The SMUTTY joke, ridiculously lewd.

1857. *Punch*, 31 Jan., 'The Stone Jug.' A goney . . . As ain't up to our lurks, our flash patter and SMUT.

2. (various). — (*a*) A copper boiler (GROSE, VAUX, and HOTTEN); (*b*) = a grate (GROSE; in VAUX = a furnace); (*c*) = old iron (GROSE).

See BROTHER SMUT.

SNABBLE, *verb.* (old).—1. Generic for force: *e.g.* to rifle or plunder, to arrest, to kill; to eat greedily (GROSE).

1724. HARPER [*Harlequin Sheppard*, 'Frisky Moll's Song']. But fileing of a rumbo ken, My Boman is SNABBLED again.

1752. SMOLLETT, *Faithful Narrative*, *Wks.* (1901, xii. 184). The very cull who hath a warrant against me for SNABBLING his peeter and queer joseph.

2. (venery). — To copulate: *see* RIDE.

SNABBY (or **SNAB**), *adj.* (American). — Stylish ; tasteful ; good-looking [BARTLETT : 'a college word'].

SNACK, *subs.* (colloquial).—1. A share ; a portion : TO GO SNACKS (or TO SNACK) = to share ; to divide (B. E., GROSE and BEE).

1675. WYCHERLEY, *Country Wife*, iii. 2. Who is that that is to be bubbled? Faith, let me SNACK ; I ha'n't met with a bubble since Christmas.

1701. FARQUHAR, *Sir Harry Wildair*, iv. 2. Well, Monsieur, 'tis about a thousand pounds ; we GO SNACKS.

*d.*1704. LESTRANGE, *Works* [*Century*]. If the master gets the better on't, they come in for their SNACK.

*d.*1704. BROWN, *Works*, ii. 108. The Cardinal d'Estrée being passionately in love with the marchioness de Cœuvres who was supposed to have granted the duke de Sceaux the liberty of rifling her placket, was resolved to put in for his SNACK.

1719. SMITH, *Highwaymen*, i. 85. He and his comrades coming to an inn to SNACK their booty.

1734. POPE, *Satires*, Prol. All my demurs but double his attacks ; At last he whispers, 'Do, and we GO SNACKS.'

1789. PARKER, *Life's Painter*, 149. SNACK the bit.

*c.*1790. *Ireland Sixty Years Ago*, 'Kilmainham Minit,' 87. He merrily melted de winners, To SNACK wi' de boys of de pad.

1809. MALKIN, *Gil Blas* [ROUTLEDGE], 378. You shall GO SNACKS in all that we can squeeze out of the old fellow.

2. (colloquial).—A hasty meal ; a BITE (*q.v.*).—BEE.

1763. FOOTE, *Mayor of Garratt*, i. Come, son Bruin, we are all seated at table, man ; we have but just time for a SNACK.

1818. SCOTT, *Midlothian*, xxxviii. The cloth is laid . . . it is past three o'clock . . . I have been waiting this hour for you, and I have had a SNACK myself.

3. (common).—An innuendo ; a jibe : *e.g.* 'That's a NASTY SNACK for you.' As *verb.* = to QUIZ ; TO ROAST (*q.v.*). *Cf.* SNAG.

1897. MARSHALL, *Pomes*, 112. It gives no ground for spiteful SNACKS.

4. (Winchester College).—A racket ball.

SNAFFLE, *subs.* (old).—Talk : spec. conversation uninteresting or unintelligible to those present : *cf.* SHOP.

Verb. (old). — 1. To steal. Whence SNAFFLE (or SNAFFLER) = a thief : spec. a highwayman ; SNAFFLING-LAY = highway robbery ; SNAFFLED = arrested.

1724. HARPER, 'Frisky Moll's Song' [*Harlequin Jack Sheppard*]. From priggs that SNAFFLE the prancers strong.

1751. FIELDING, *Amelia*, i. 3. I thought by your look you had been a clever fellow, and upon the SNAFFLING LAY at least ; but . . . I find you are some sneaking-budge rascal.

2. (thieves').—To arrest ; TO PULL UP (*q.v.*).

SNAG, *subs.* (common). — 1. A tooth : spec. a long, irregular tooth (B. E. and GROSE) : also SNAGGLER : *see* GRINDERS. Whence SNAG-CATCHER = a dentist.

1717. PRIOR, *Alma*, ii. 148. In China none hold women sweet, Except their SNAGS are black as jet.

2. (common).—An unsuspected hindrance or set-back. [Orig. American = a half sunken tree impeding river navigation.] Hence, as *verb.* = to embarrass. To CATCH A SNAG = to get a rebuff, to get snubbed : *cf.* SNACK.

1881. W. PHILLIPS, *Speeches*, 38. Stagnant times have been when a great mind, anchored in error, might SNAG the slow moving current of society.

1901. *Free Lance*, 30 Nov., 220, 1. The nasty little SNAGS the average man of business is apt to encounter daily.

3. (old).—A snail (B E. and GROSE).

To SNAG ON, *verb. phr.* (American).—To attach oneself to another.

SNAGGLE, *verb.* (common). — To angle for poultry.

SNAIL, *subs.* (colloquial).—A drone : *cf.* SLUG. Hence as *verb.* (or TO GO AT A SNAIL'S PACE or GALLOP) = to move very slowly.

1582. STANYHURST, *Æneid*, iv. 689. This sayd shee trots on SNAYLING, lyk a toothshaken old hagge.

1593. SHAKSPEARE, *Comedy of Errors*, ii. 2, 196. Thou drone, thou SNAIL, thou slug, thou sot.

1725. BAILEY, *Erasmus*, i. 73. I see what Haste you make, you are never the forwarder, you go A SNAIL'S GALLOP.

1748. RICHARDSON, *Clarissa*, iv. 124. SNAIL ON in a track we are acquainted with.

1821. COOMBE, *Dr. Syntax*, III. iii. He, by degrees, would seldom fail T'adopt THE GALLOP OF A SNAIL.

SNAKE, *subs.* (old).—1. 'A term of contempt ; 2 (colloquial) = a secret plotter, a hidden foe : *e.g.*, 'a SNAKE in the grass.'

1600. SHAKSPEARE, *As You Like It*, iv. 3. Well, go your way to her, for I see love hath made thee a tame SNAKE.

1612-3. FLETCHER, *Captain*, i. 3. Admit 'em ; but no SNAKES to poison us With poverty.

*c.*1620. HEALY, *Disc. New World*, 114. The poor SNAKES dare not so much as wipe their mouthes unless their wives bidde them.

1636. *Clitus's Whimzies*, 67. For those poore SNAKES who feed on reversions, a glimpse through the keyhole, or a light through the grate, must be all their prospect.

1638. RANDOLPH, *Muses' Looking Glass* [DODSLEY, *Old Plays* (REED), ix. 228]. But I have found him a poor baffled SNAKE.

1677. COLES, *Eng.-Lat. Dict.* A poore SNAKE, *Iries.*

3. (tailors').—A skein of silk.

Verb. (thieves').—1. To steal warily : *cf.* SNEAK.

2. (American).—To beat ; to thrash.

18[?]. LEADSTREET, *Southern Sketches*, 120. Any gal like me . . . ought to be able to SNAKE any man of her heft.

PHRASES.—TO SNAKE OUT (ALONG or UP) = to drag or worm out ; TO SNAKE IN = to steal in, to draw in ; TO GIVE ONE A SNAKE = to vex ; TO SNAKE THE POOL = to take the pool (billiards') ; A CAUTION TO SNAKES = a matter of surprise, something singular, a REVELATION (*q.v.*) ; SNAKES IN THE BOOTS = delirium tremens : also TO SEE SNAKES ; 'As sure as there's SNAKES in Virginny' = as sure as may be.

1848. LOWELL, *Biglow Papers*. Pomp he SNAKED UP behind, And creeping gradually close to . . . Jest grabbed my leg.

1877. *Boston Bulletin*, Feb. Although they could not open the doors of the Church to him, perhaps he might be SNAKED IN under the canvas.

1883. *Phil. Press*, 2810, 4. Unless some legal loophole can be found through which an evasion or extension can be successfully SNAKED.

1884. CLEMENS, *Huck. Finn.* Well, it beats me, and SNAKED a lot of letters OUT of his pocket.

1893. *Sci. Amer.*, N. S., lxix. 265. After mining the log is easily SNAKED OUT of the swamp.

1897. MARSHALL, *Pomes*, 'Her Sunday Clothes,' 105. Her Sunday best was her week-day worst, 'Twas simply A CAUTION TO SNAKES.

SNAKE-IN-THE-GRASS, *subs. phr.* (rhyming).—A glass.

See SNAKE.

SNAKESMAN. *See* SNEAK.

SNAM, *verb.* (thieves').—To steal : spec. to snatch from the person : also ON THE SNAM.

1887. HENLEY, *Villon's Good Night*. Likewise you copper's narks and dubs What pinched me when UPON THE SNAM.

SNAP, *subs.* (old).—1. A sharper ; a pilferer ; a cheat : spec. a thief claiming a share of booty (in quot. 1731 = a sharking lawyer). Also SNAPPER and SNAPPER-UP. As *verb.* = to claim a share ; TO NAP THE REGULARS (*q.v.*) ; ON THE SNAP = (1) waiting a chance of robbery ; and 2 (modern) looking out for odd jobs.

1604. SHAKSPEARE, *Winter's Tale*, iv. 3, 26. A SNAPPER-UP of unconsidered trifles.

1611. MIDDLETON, *Roaring Girl* [*Old Plays*, vi. 113]. Then there's a cloyer, or SNAP, that dogs any new brother in that trade, and SNAPS—will have half in any booty.

1622. FLETCHER, *Spanish Curate*, ii. 1. Take heed of a SNAP, sir ; h'as a cozening countenance.

1653. WILSON, *James I.* Butler, being a subtle SNAP, wrought so with his companion, with promises of a share, that he got the possession of it.

*d.*1704. LESTRANGE, *Works* [*Ency. Dict.*]. He had no sooner said out his say but up rises a cunning SNAP then at the board

*d.*1731. WARD, *Honesty in Distress*. Brother SNAP . . . here's a welcome guest.

2. (old).—A scrap ; a portion ; a share : *cf.* SNACK. Hence a small standard of value : *e.g.*, NOT A SNAP = nothing ; NOT WORTH A SNAP = worthless.

1561. AWDELEY, *Frat. Vacabondes*, 4. [OLIPHANT, *New Eng.*, i. 575. A man gets a share or SNAP unto himself ; hence comes TO GO SNACKS, with the usual interchange of *c* and *p*].

1648-58. FULLER, *Holy and Prof. States*, v. xiv. 1. Alms of learning, here a SNAP, there a piece of knowledge.

3. (common).—A project ; a business—any happening : *e.g.*, A COLD SNAP = a sudden spell of cold weather ; A SOFT SNAP = a pleasant time, a profitable affair ; TO GIVE THE SNAP AWAY = to discover. Also SNAP (theatrical) = a short engagement.

1886. *Field*, 9 Jan. If we are to be interned for a cold SNAP it will be a pleasure to think of this Tuesday's sport.

1887. FRANCIS, *Saddle and Mocassin*. I want fifty dollars for an hour or two . . . I've got a SOFT SNAP on, can't miss it.

18[?]. FREUND, *Music and Drama*, XIV. xvi. 3. Actors and actresses who have just come in from summer SNAPS, to prepare for the work of the coming season.

4. (common).—A hasty meal ; a SNACK (*q.v.*).

*d.*1880. ELIOT, *Janet's Repentance*, i. Two hearty meals that might have been mistaken for dinners if he had not declared them to be SNAPS.

5. (American). — Knowledge ; energy, GO (*q.v.*) ; SNAPPY = lively, amusing.

18[?]. *Book of Sports* [*Century*], 118. [Lacrosse] . . . a game well suited to the American taste, being short, SNAPPY and vivacious, from beginning to end.

1885. G. S. MERRIAM, *S. Bowles*, II. 375. The vigorous vernacular . . . gave zest and SNAP to many a paragraph.

1888. LESTER WALLACK [*Scribner's Mag.*, iv. 722]. That act went with the most perfect SNAP.

1896. LILLARD, *Poker Stories*, 90. I thought you had more business SNAP.

Adj. (colloquial).—On the spur of the moment ; without preparation : as *subs.* = a chance (or SCRATCH) comer, player, crew, team, &c.). Thus, a SNAP-DIVISION = an unexpected vote ; SNAP-JUDGMENT = a verdict hastily got or given ; SNAP-SHOT = (1) a shot fired without deliberate aim, and (2) a photograph taken unawares. As *verb.* = to take an instantaneous photograph with a hand camera : also TO SNAP-SHOT.

1860. RUSSELL, *Diary in India*, I. 346. Our appearance attracted SHOTS from all quarters. Fellows took SNAPS at us from balconies, from doors, on the roofs of houses.

1888. *Nineteenth Century*, xxiii. 252. The previous assent of the Chair to the motion for closure would prevent SNAP-DIVISIONS.

1889-90. *St. Nicholas*, xvii. 1034. A painter . . . hit upon the plan of using a hand camera with which he followed the babies about SNAPPING them in their best positions.

1896. LILLARD, *Poker Stories*, 130. My . . . friend had brought him along as a SNAP . . . I supposed of course that he was all right, or his friend would not have invited him in the game.

PHRASES. — TO SNAP THE GLAZE = 'to smash shop windows' (GROSE) ; TO SNAP THE EYE = to wink ; ON THE SNAP = on the look out, on the MOUCH (*q.v.*).

SNAPPED, *adj.* (American). — 1. Drunk : *see* SCREWED.

1844. *Major Jones's Courtship*, 102. He got SNAPT on egg-nog.

2. (old). — 'Taken, caught' (B. E.).

SNAPPER, *subs.* (old).—1. A pistol (GROSE). Also (2) = a castanet ; and (3) = a cracker bonbon.

1587. HARRISON, *Desc. of England* [OLIPHANT, *New Eng.*, ii. 2. Amongst the new substantives are SNAPPER (pistol) butt-end . . .].

1615. SANDYS, *Travels*, 172. Their musicke is answerable ; the instruments no other than SNAPPERS, gingles, and round bottomed drums.

1837. BARHAM, *Ingolds. Leg.*, 'Wedding-day.' And nasty French lucifer SNAPPERS with mottoes.

4. (American).—A braggart : also SNAPPERHEAD.

THE SNAPPERS, *subs. phr.* (military).—The East Yorkshire Regiment, formerly The 15th Foot. Also "The Poona Guards."

SNAPPISH, *adj.* (B. E.).—'Peevish, quarrelsome (a Man) ; apt to Bite (a Dog).'

SNAP-SHOT. *See* SNAP.

SNARLER, *subs.* (common). — A dog.

SNATCH, *subs.* (old).—1. A shuffling answer ; an evasive reply.

1603. SHAKSPEARE, *Meas. for Meas.*, iv. 2, 6. Come, sir, leave me your SNATCHES, and yield me a direct answer.

2. (old).—A hasty meal ; a SNACK (*q.v.*) : also SNATCH AND AWAY.

1573. TUSSER, *Husbandrie*, 168. A SNATCH and to worke, fellowes tarrie not here.

1585. *Nomenclator*. Prandium statarium . . . Manger debout ou en pied. A standing dinner, which is eaten in haste ; a SNATCH AND AWAY.

1623. MASSINGER, *Duke of Milan*, iii. 2. I fear you'll have cold entertainment . . . 'twere discretion to take a SNATCH by the way.

3. (venery).—A hasty act of kind ; a FLYER (*q.v.*).

1621. BURTON, *Anat. of Melan.*, III. II. v. 3. They had rather go to the stews, or have now and then a SNATCH as they can come by it, borrow of their neighbours, than have wives of their own. *Ibid.* I could not abide marriage, but as a rambler I took a SNATCH when I could get it.

IN (or BY) SNATCHES, *phr.* (colloquial).—By fits and starts ; spasmodically : also SNATCHY.

1573-9. HARVEY, *Letters* (Camden Soc.), 178. I purpose to heare M. Doctor Bing and "get" gleane as mutch as I can BI SNATCHES.

1865. DICKENS, *Mutual Friend*, ii. 4. Transactions of business . . . at untimely hours . . . and in rushes and SNATCHES.

1883. *Cambridge Sketches*, 16. The modern style seems short and SNATCHY ; it has not the long majestic sweep of former days.

SNATCH-BLATCH, *subs. phr.* (venery).—The female *pudendum* : *see* MONOSYLLABLE.

SNATCHER, *subs.* (old).—A thief: spec. a camp-follower. SNATCH-CLY = a pickpocket (GROSE).

1599. SHAKSPEARE, *Hen. V.*, i. 2. We do not mean the coursing SNATCHERS only.

1820. SCOTT, *Monastery*, i. They would have fallen a speedy prey to some of the SNATCHERS in the neighbourhood.

See BODYSNATCHER.

SNATCH-PASTRY, *subs. phr.* (HALLIWELL).—A greedy fellow.

SNAVEL, *verb.* (old).—To steal: spec. by snatching or PICKING (*q.v.*): *cf.* SNABBLE (BEE) and *see* RUNNING SNAVEL.

SNEAK, *subs.* (common).—A petty thief: also SNEAK-THIEF, SNEAKING-BUDGE, and SNEAKSMAN: *see* quot. 1819, AREA-SNEAK, and *cf.* RAMP and RUSH. Hence MORNING-SNEAK = an EARLY BIRD (*q.v.*); EVENING-SNEAK = a night thief; UPRIGHT SNEAK = a thief preying on potboys (B. E., GROSE and VAUX). As *verb.* = to pilfer, to steal: spec. 'to walk about undefinedly, to see what may be picked up' (BEE); SNEAKING ON THE LURK (or ON THE SNEAK) = prowling for booty.

1744. FIELDING, *Jonathan Wild*. Wild . . . looked upon borrowing . . . as . . . the genteelest kind of SNEAKING-BUDGE. *Ibid.* (1751), *Amelia*, i. 3. I find you are some SNEAKING-BUDGE rascal.

1819. VAUX, *Memoirs*, s.v. SNEAK. The SNEAK is the practice of robbing houses or shops, by slipping in unperceived, and taking whatever may lay most convenient; this is commonly the first branch of thieving, in which young boys are initiated, who, from their size and activity, appear well adapted for it. To SNEAK a place, is to rob it UPON THE SNEAK. A SNEAK is a robbery effected in the above manner. One or more prisoners having escaped from their confinement by stealth, without using any violence, or alarming their keepers, are said to have SNEAK'D 'EM, or given it to 'em UPON THE SNEAK.

1829. *Life and Death of James Wilson*. That awful monster, William Burke, Like Reynard SNEAKING ON THE LURK.

1834. AINSWORTH, *Rookwood*, III. v. Until at last there was none so knowing, No such SNEAKSMAN or buz-gloak going.

1897. MARSHALL, *Pomes*, 31. My 'Arry SNEAKS my cady on the sly. *Ibid.*, 32. The elder of the twain Had . . . SNEAKED a quid. *Ibid.*, 107. Strictly speaking, it was SNEAKING (He preferred the term 'convey').

1899. WHITEING, *John St.*, v. They ain't no class . . . Fancies theirselves burglars—Nothin' o' the sort—SNEAK THIEVES.

1902. LYNCH, *High Stakes*, xx. I believe it will be best . . . to keep to the SNEAK-THIEF theory.

2. (thieves').—*See* quot.

1873. GREENWOOD, *In Strange Company*. SNEAKS . . . are shoes with canvas tops and india-rubber soles.

3. (cricketers').—A ground ball having no pitch whatever; A DAISY-TRIMMER (or CUTTER); GRUB; or UNDERGROUNDER (*q.v.*).

SNEAKBILL. *See* SNEAKSBY.

SNEAK-CUP, *subs. phr.* (old).—One who shies his drink: hence, a paltry fellow: also SNEAK-UP.

1598. SHAKSPEARE, *1 Hen. IV.*, iii. 3. How? The prince is a Jack, a SNEAK-CUP.

SNEAKER, *subs.* (old).—1. A small bowl (B. E. and GROSE): *e.g.*, a SNEAKER of punch.

2. (cricketers'). — A SNEAK, *subs.* sense 3.

SNEAKING, *adj.* (colloquial).—Unavowed; undemonstrative: *e.g.*, a 'SNEAKING kindness' ('liking,' or 'preference').

1753. RICHARDSON, *Grandison*, i. 290. You, my dear, shall reveal to me your SNEAKING passion, if you have one, and I will discover mine.

1812. COOMBE, *Dr. Syntax*, I. vii. For they possess'd, with all their pother, A SNEAKING kindness for each other.

SNEAKSBY (**SNEAKBILL**, or **SNEAKSBILL**), *subs.* (old). — A sneak: *cf.* IDLESBY, SURESBY, RUDESBY, LEWDSBY, WIGSBY, &c. (GROSE). Also SNEAKING (B. E.) = 'sheepish or mean spirited'; SNEAKBILL (*adj.*) = sneaking.

1577. KENDALL, *Floures of Epigrammes*. Perchaunce thou deemst me in thy minde Therefore a SNEEKBILL snudge unkinde.

1611. COTGRAVE, *Dict.* [HALLIWELL]. A checheface, mecher, SNEAKEBILL, wretched fellow, one out of whose nose hunger drops. *Ibid.* A meacocke, milkesop, SNEAKSBIE, worthlesse fellow.

1651. CARTWRIGHT, *Ordinary*. A base thin-jaw'd SNEAKSBILL, Thus to work gallants out of all.

1653. URQUHART, *Rabelais*, I. xxv. Scurvy SNEAKSBIES, fondling fops, base loons.

1685. BARROW, *Sermons*, III. xxxiv. A demure SNEAKSBY, a clownish singularist.

SNECK-DRAWER, *subs. phr.* (Scots').—A latchlifter; a slyboots. SNECK-DRAWING = crafty, cheating.

*c.*1401. *Political Poems*, ii. 98. [OLIPHANT, *New Eng.*, i. 192. Among the nouns SNECK-DRAWER; used by Scott.]

*d.*1796. BURNS, *Address to the Deil*. And you, ye auld SNECK-DRAWING dog, Ye came to Paradise incog.

1817. SCOTT, *Rob Roy*, xxxviii. Sydall is an auld SNECK-DRAWER.

SNECK UP! *intj.* (old).—Go hang! Also SNICK UP.

1599. *Two Angry Women of Abingdon* [NARES]. If they be not, let them GO SNICK UP.

1602. SHAKSPEARE, *Twelfth Night*, ii. 3, 101. We did keep time, sir, in our catches. SNECK UP!

1610. BEAUMONT and FLETCHER, *Knight of Burning Pestle*, iii. 1. Let him go SNICK UP!

1611. CHAPMAN, *Mayday*, iv. But for a paltry disguise she shall go SNICK UP.

*c.*1620. HEALEY, *Disc. New World*, 106. I am in great perplexitie, least my country-women should have any understanding of this state; for if they have, wee may go SNIC UP for any female that will bide among us.

1630. HEYWOOD, *Fair Maid of West* [PEARSON, *Works* (1874), II., 268]. She shall not rise, sir, goe, let your Master SNICK-UP!

1630. TAYLOR, *Praise of Hempseed*. A Tiburne hempen-candell will e'en cure you: It can cure traitors, but I hold it fit T' apply 't ere they the treason do commit. Wherefore in Sparta it ycleped was SNICK-UP, which is in English gallow-grass.

1638. FORD, *Lady's Trial*, iii. 2. Dost want a master? If thou dost, I'm for thee; Else choose, and SNECK UP!

1666. *Wily Beguil'd* [HAWKINS, *Orig. Drama*, iii. 342]. If my mistress would be ruled by him, Sophos might GO SNICK UP.

SNEE. *See* SNICK-AND-SNEE.

SNEERG, *subs.* (back slang).—Greens.

SNEERING, *adj.* (B. E. and GROSE).—'Jeering, flickering, laughing in scorn.'

SNEEZE, *subs.* (old).—1. Snuff: also SNISH.

2. (common).—The nose: *see* SNEEZER.

TO SNEEZE AT, *verb. phr.* (common). — To despise; to scorn: usually in phrase 'not to be SNEEZED AT' = worth having or considering.

1820. COOMBE, *Syntax*, ii. 5. A . . . dame . . . who wish'd . . . to change her name, And . . . would NOT perhaps HAVE SNEEZED AT mine.

1823. BEE, *Dict. Turf*, s.v. SNEEZE. A handsome girl with a few thousands tacked to her arse is NOT TO BE SNEEZED AT.

1837. BARHAM, *Ingolds. Leg.*, 'The Coronation.' If any bould traitour or infarior craythur SNEEZES AT THAT, I'd like to see the man.

1855. HALIBURTON, *Human Nature*, 173. My knowledge of horse-flesh AIN'T TO BE SNEEZED AT.

1857. A. H. ELTON, *Below the Surface*, xxvii. My professional reputation is NOT TO BE SNEEZED AT.

SNEEZE- (or **SNUFF-**) **LURKER**, *subs. phr.* (thieves'). — A thief working with snuff, pepper, and the like. TO GIVE ON THE SNEEZE (or SNUFF) RACKET = 'to dose a man in the eyes, and then rob him' (GROSE).

SNEEZER, *subs.* (common). — 1. Severe weather: as a hard frost or a violent gale. Whence (2) = anything exceptional — a stiff glass, a knock-out blow: *see* WHOPPER. Also (army) = a martinet.

*c.*1812. MAHER, *The Night Before Larry was Stretched*. He'd fence all the duds that he had, To help the poor dog to a SNEEZER.

1855. HALIBURTON, *Human Nature* [BARTLETT]. It's awful to hear a minister swear; and the only match I know for it is to hear a regular SNEEZER of a sinner quote Scripture.

1878. *Century Mag.*, Dec., 602. Caught in a north-west SNEEZER.

1902. DOWLING, *Tempest Driven*, xxiv. 'It will be a SNEEZER,' said the boatman.

2. (common).—The nose: also SNEEZE: *see* CONK. Whence (3) = a pocket-handkerchief; and (4) = a snuff-box: also SNEEZING COFFER (GROSE and VAUX.)

1834. AINSWORTH, *Rookwood*. Fogles and fawnies soon went their way To the spout with the SNEEZERS in grand array.

1838. DICKENS, *Oliver Twist*, xliii. To think of . . . the Artful Dodger going abroad for a common twopenny-halfpenny SNEEZE-BOX.

1861. H. KINGSLEY, *Ravenshoe*, xxxv. 'What is cly-faking,' said Charles. 'Why, a prigging of wipes, and SNEEZE-BOXES . . . and such.'

SNEEZY, *subs.* (old).—The second month [*Brumaire* = foggy] of the French Republican Calendar.

SNELL, *subs.* (hawkers'). — A needle. Hence SNELL-FENCER = a needle-hawker. [*Cf.* (Scots') SNELL = sharp.]

1891. CAREW, *Auto. Gipsy*, 415. A chiv, blink and SNELL-FENCER.

SNIB, *subs.* (Scots').—A PRIG, *q.v.* (GROSE).

Verb. (venery).—To copulate: *see* RIDE.

SNICKER, *subs.* (old).—1. A drinking cup; HORN-SNICKER = a drinking-horn (HOTTEN).

2. (old).—A glandered horse (GROSE). *See* also SNIGGER.

SNICKERSNEE, *subs.* (nautical).—1. A knife; and (2) a combat with knives: also SNICK-AND-SNEE.

*c.*1617. HOWELL, *Letters*, I. i. 41. None must carry a pointed knife about him [in Genoa]; which makes the Hollander, who is used to SNIK AND SNEE, to leave his Horn-sheath and knife a shipboard when he comes ashore.

1673. *Norfolk Drollery*, 64. But they'l ere long come to themselves you'l see, When we in earnest are at SNICK A SNEE.

1698. *Fatal Friendship*. What hand that can design a history Wou'd copy lowland boors at SNICK A SNEE.

*d.*1701. DRYDEN, *Parallel of Poetry and Painting*. The brutal sport of SNICK-OR-SNEE, and a thousand other things of this mean invention.

1707. WARD, *Hud. Rediv.* By their sides knives for SNICK-A-SNEE.

1869. THACKERAY, *Little Billee*. 'Make haste, make haste,' says Guzzling Jimmy, While Jack pulled out his SNICKERSNEE.

SNICK-FADGE, *subs. phr.* (thieves').—A petty thief.

SNICKLE, *verb.* (thieves').—To inform; to PEACH (*q.v.*).

1859. MATSELL, *Vocabulum*. If the cove should be caught in the hock [imprisoned] he won't SNICKLE.

SNICKTOG, *verb.* (thieves').—To go shares.

SNIDE (or **SNID**), *subs.* (Scots').—1. Sixpence: *see* RHINO.

2. (common).—Anything mean or spurious: as a contemptible wretch, counterfeit coin, &c. As *adj.* (also SNIDDY or SNIDEY) = bad, wretched, contemptible, or (army) dirty. SNIDE-PITCHING (*see* quot. 1868).

1868. *Temple Bar*, xxxiv. 538. SNYDE-PITCHING is passing bad money, and it is a capital racket.

1876. A. MURSELL, *Shady Pastorals*. Sometimes the police will help the thieves by getting SNIDE witnesses . . . who will swear anything according to instructions.

1887. HENLEY, *Villon's Straight Tip*. Or PITCH A SNIDE, or knap a yack.

1887. FRANCIS, *Saddle and Mocassin*. These 'ere men don't want none of your SNIDE outfits, but just good bronchos and a waggon, and strong harness.

1891. CAREW, *Auto. of a Gipsey*, 416. When I put the hacid on it hevery bloomin' hounce was SNIDE. *Ibid.*, 418. Nat said, 'S'trewth when Griffin seen the plate turn up agen, like a SNIDE midgie, his face were a picter.'

1897. MARSHALL, *Pomes*, 50. The SNIDE 'uns in the race of life don't always canter in. *Ibid.*, 89. His pockets she tried, Which is wifely, though SNIDE.

1900. FLYNT, *Tramps*, 277. "Utica," he said, "if you intend gettin' your breakfast there in the morning, is a sort of a SNIDE place this time of the year."

SNIFFY, *adj.* (American).—Disdainful.

SNIFTER, *subs.* (common).—1. A long-drawn breath.

2. (common).—A dram; a GO (*q.v.*).

3. (American).—A blizzard.

SNIFTY, *adj.* (American).—Pleasant smelling.

SNIGGER (or **SNICKER**), *verb.* (B. E. and GROSE). — 'To laugh privately or in one's sleeve'; 'ill suppressed laughter' (BEE).

SNILCH [*sic.*], *verb.* (Old Cant).—To see; to watch closely (B. E. and GROSE).

SNIP, *subs.* (old).—1. A share; a piece; a SNACK (*q.v.*). TO GO SNIPS = to share. Hence 2, (racing) = a good tip. Also SNIPPET = a small piece; SNIPPY (or SNIPPETY) = fragmentary, absurdly small.

1621. SYLVESTER, *Du Bartas*, ii. Her lips two SNIPS of crimson Sattin are.

*c.*1640. BUTLER, *Nye's Beard*. For some have doubted if [the beard] 'twere made of SNIPS Of sables, glew'd and fitted to the lips.

1668. DRYDEN, *Ev. Love*, v. Pray, sir, let me GO SNIP with you in this lye.

*d.*1704. LESTRANGE, *Works* [*Century*]. The SNIP that he . . . expected on the dividend.

1725. BAILEY, *Erasmus*, II. 5. The Gamester . . . promises I shall GO SNIPS with him in what he shall win.

1809. MALKIN, *Gil Blas* (1812), VII. xii. Let me know what is the business, and I promise you shall get some SNIPS out of the minister.

1880. *Ch. Times*, 9 Ap. Variety is pleasant, SNIPPETINESS is not.

1884. *Sat. Rev.*, 12 Jan., 62. If the editor had confined himself to one period he might have made a useful book . . . he has produced a collection of SNIPPETS.

1886-96. MARSHALL, '*Pomes*' ['The Age of Love'], 26. He's the winner right enough! It's the one sole SNIP of a lifetime—simply the cop of one's puff.

3. (common).—A tailor: also SNIPPER, SNIP-CABBAGE, and SNIPLOUSE (BEE). *Cf.* SNIPPERADO, quot. 1605, SNIPRS = scissors (VAUX). *See* TRADES.

1600. *Weakest to Wall*, i. 3. Beest thou a snyder? SNIP, snap, mette shears.

1605. CHAPMAN [B. DOBELL, on *Newly Discovered Documents of the Elizabethan and Jacobean Periods* (*Athenæum*, 13 Ap., 1901, 466, 1)]. Taylors and Shoo-makers, and such SNIPPERADOS.

1643. RANDOLPH, *Muses' Looking Glass. Lup.* Where's my wife? *Colax.* Shee's gone with a young SNIP, and an old bawd. *Ibid.*, iv. 3. Sir, here's SNIP the taylor charg'd with a riot.

*d.*1701. DRYDEN, *Hist. of League*, Postscr. Our SNIPPERS go over once a year into France, to bring back the newest mode.

1709. WARD *Terræfilius* [*Works*, i. 5, 35]. Poor Crespin was laugh'd at thro' the whole parish, . . . and the Gentleman and yonder SNIP-CABBAGE his Taylor, commended for their Ingenuity.

1772. BRIDGES, *Burlesque Homer*, 529. He swears . . . (Like SNIP the tailor with his suit) He'll find some way to piece it out.

1849. KINGSLEY, *Alton Locke*, xiii. Alton, you fool, why did you let out that you were a SNIP?

1852. BRISTED, *Eng. Univ.*, 292, Note. A fashionable SNIP . . . 'breeches-maker to H.R.H. Prince Albert.'

1898. *Pink 'Un and Pelican*, 153. Mr. Commissioner Kerr . . . once informed a SNIP . . . that there was no such thing as *taking* credit.

SNIPE, *subs.* (old). — 1. A thin thing, male or female: in America = a small child. 2 (old) = a simpleton; SNIPE-KNAVE (COTGRAVE): 'So called because two of them are worth but one SNIPE.'

1602. SHAKSPEARE, *Othello*, i. 3. I mine own gained knowledge should profane, If I would time expend with such a SNIPE.

1859. KINGSLEY, *Geof. Hamlyn*, xxxi. I sat there like a great SNIPE.

3. (old).—A lawyer: hence (4) a long bill.

5. (thieves'). — In *pl.* = the fingers.

1834. AINSWORTH, *Rookwood*, III. v. No slour'd hoxter my SNIPES could stay.

6. (Old Cant). — Scissors (GROSE).

7. (American street).—A half-smoked cigar.

8. (American S. Exchange).—A curbstone broker; a GUTTER-SNIPE (*q.v.*).

1870. MEDBERY, *Wall St.*, 131. Solid brokers . . . scoffingly declare its [the Open Board] members . . . are simply SNIPES and lame ducks.

Verb. (military).—To fire at random into a camp.

SNIPPER-SNAPPER, *subs.* (common).—An insignificant person; a WHIPPER-SNAPPER (*q.v.*).

1677. *Poor Robin's Visions*, 12. This seeming gentile WHIPPER-SNAPPER vanisht . . . and I was left alone.

SNIPPY (SNIPENNY, SNIPTIOUS, or SNIPPISH), *adj.* (American).—Vain; conceited; pert.

SNIP-SNAP, *subs. phr.* (colloquial).—A neat verbal effect. As *adj.* = quick, sharp, SMART (*q.v.*).

1594. SHAKSPEARE, *Love's Lab. Lost*, v. i. A sweet touch, a quick venue of wit! SNIP SNAP, quick and home! it rejoiceth my intellect.

1597. HARVEY, *Works* [GROSART, iii. 72]. If heer I have been too prodigall in SNIP-SNAPS, tell me of it.

1728. POPE, *Dunciad*, ii. 240. SNIP-SNAP short, and interruption smart.

1870. JUDD, *Margaret*, iii. I recollect . . overhearing . . . a sort of grave SNIP-SNAP about Napoleon's return from Egypt . . . and what not.

SNIRP, *subs.* (old).—An undersized, contemptible wretch.

SNITCH, *subs.* (thieves').—1. In *pl.* = handcuffs: also SNITCHERS.

2. (old).—'A Filip on the Nose': also SNITCHEL (B. E.); also the nose.

Verb. (thieves').—1. To inform. Hence SNITCHER = an informer. Also (2) = TO NARK (*q.v.*).—GROSE and BEE.

*c.*1812. JOHN JACKSON [quoted by BYRON in *Don Juan*, xi. 19.] Then your blowing will wax gallows haughty, When she hears of your scaly mistake, She'll surely turn SNITCH for the forty, That her Jack may be regular weight.

1819. VAUX, *Memoirs*, s.v. SNITCH; to impeach, or betray your accomplices is termed SNITCHING UPON them. A person who becomes King's evidence on such an occasion is said to have turned SNITCH; an informer, or tale-bearer, in general, is called a SNITCH, or a SNITCHING-RASCAL, in which case SNITCHING is synonymous with nosing or coming it.

1829. *The Lag's Lament* [*Vidocq's Mem.*, iii. 169]. SNITCH on the gang, that'll be the best vay To save your scrag.

SNITCHED, *adj.* (horsedealers').—*See* quot.

1876. HINDLEY, *Cheap Jack* . . . A horsedealer . . . was showing a farmer a horse that was SNITCHED, that is glandered.

SNITE, *verb.* (Old Cant).—To wipe: TO SNITE A CANDLE = to snuff it; 'SNITE his Snitch = Wipe his Nose or give him a good Flap on the Face' (B. E.).

14 [?]. *Babees Book* [E. E. T. S.], 13. Fro spettyng & SNETYNG kepe the also.

1599. HALL, *Satires*, VI. i. 104. He . . . wrings and SNITES, and weeps and wipes again.

1701. GREW, *Cosmo Sacra*, I. v. Nor would anyone be able to SNITE his nose, or to sneeze.

SNIV, *verb.* (Old Cant). — 1. To hold one's tongue: *e.g.* SNIV THAT! (GROSE). Also 2 (VAUX) = BENDER! (*q.v.*)

SNIVEL, *subs.* (colloquial).—Hypocrisy; CANT (*q.v.*): as *verb.* = to complain; to BLEAT (*q.v.*). Hence SNIVELLER (or SNIVELARD) = a whining malcontent; SNIVELLING = hypocritical repentance (B. E. and GROSE).

1440. *Promp. Parv.*, 461. SNYVELARD, or he that spekythe yn the nose.

*c.*1520. *Coventry Myst.*, 'Assumption,' 396 [OLIPHANT, *New Eng.*, i. 397. There is SNEVELER used in scorn.]

1767. STERNE, *Tristram Shandy*, ix. 12. 'That SNIVELLING virtue of meekness,' as my father would always call it.

1771. SMOLLETT, *Humphrey Clinker*, Lett. v. I have received a SNIVELLING letter from Griffin.

1780. SHERIDAN, *The Camp*, i. 1. Come forward, you SNIVELLING, sneaking sot, you.

1809. MALKIN, *Gil Blas* [ROUTLEDGE], 224. Indeed am I punished for having preposterously lowered myself to the level of a dirty SNIVELLING adventurer.

1886. *St. James's Gaz.*, 9 Feb. The cant and SNIVEL of which we have seen so much of late.

1886. BESANT, *World Went Very Well Then*, ii. Would'st not surely choose to be a sneakin' SNIVELLING quill-driver in a merchant's office?

1888. WHIPPLE, *Essays and Reviews*, II. 117. He SNIVELS in the cradle, at the school, at the altar . . . on the death-bed.

1898. GOULD, *Landed at Last*, xviii. You SNIVELLING coward.

SNIVEL-NOSE, *subs. phr.* (old).—A niggard (HALLIWELL).

SNOACH, *verb.* (old).—To speak through the nose; to snuffle (GROSE).

SNOB, *subs.* (old). — 1. A shoemaker (GROSE); spec. a journeyman cobbler (HALLIWELL).

1808. J. MAYNE, *Siller Gun*, III. 133. Counter to a mandate clear, Ane of the SNOBS Vain as a peacock, strutted here, In crimson robes.

1837. BARHAM, *Ing. Leg.*, II. 220, note. The Shoemaker, born a SNOB.

2. (old Univ.: then general).—An inferior: *see* quots.

1822. DE QUINCEY, *Conf.* (1862), 120. Base SNOBS who would put up with a vile Brummagen substitute. *Ibid.* (1849), *Eng. Mail Coach* (*Wks.*, 1854, iv. 293). If

our dress and bearing sheltered us, generally, from the suspicion of being "raff" (the name at that period for SNOBS), we really were such constructively, by the place we assumed. [*Note.*—SNOBS, and its antithesis, 'nobs' arose amongst the internal factions of shoemakers, perhaps ten years later [*i.e.*, apparently, *c.*1815]. Possibly enough, the terms may have existed much earlier, but they were then first made known, picturesquely and effectively, by a trial at some assizes which happened to fix the public attention.]

1824. *Gradus ad Cantab.*, s.v. SNOBS. A term applied indiscriminately to all who have not the honour of being members of the university; but in a more particular manner to the *profanum vulgus*, the tag-rag and bob-tail, who vegetate on the sedgy banks of Camus.

1837. DISRAELI, *Henrietta Temple*, VI. xviii. Of all the great distinctions in life none perhaps is more important than that which divides mankind into the two great sections of Nobs and SNOBS . . . Captain Armine was a Nob, and the poor tradesman a SNOB.

1840. DICKENS, *Old Curiosity Shop*, xxxviii. "Pull up, SNOBBY," cried Mr. Chuckster, addressing Kit, "You're wanted inside here." . . . "Ask no questions, SNOBBY."

*c.*1845. HOOD, *Tale of a Trumpet*, xxxviii. Whether she listened to Hob or Bob, Nob or SNOB.

1855. THACKERAY, *Newcomes*, II. 177. An English SNOB with a coat of arms bought yesterday.

1863. READE, *Hard Cash*, I. 228. Once more . . . a motley crew of peers and printers . . . of nobs and SNOBS, fought and scrambled . . . to get rich in a day.

1870. *Figaro*, 18 July. Is it more cruel for a SNOB to shoot a sea-bird in the breeding season than it is for a nob to shoot pigeons in the breeding season, thereby starving all their young?

1878. *Masque of Poets*, 183. The SNOB Made haste to join the fashionable mob.

3. (colloquial).—A toadying or blatant vulgarian: *see* quots. 1843 and 1861. Also as *adj.* with numerous derivatives: *e.g.*, SNOBBERY, SNOBBISHNESS, and SNOBBISM; SNOBBESS; SNOBBISH, SNOBBISHLY, and SNOBBY; SNOBLING; SNOBOCRACY; SNOBOGRAPHER; and SNOBOGRAPHY.

1843. THACKERAY, *Irish Sk. Bk.* (*Wks.*, 1879, xviii), iii. A vulgar man in England . . . displays his character of SNOB by assuming as much as he can for himself, swaggering and showing off in his coarse dull stupid way. *Ibid.* (1848), *Bk. of Snobs*, ii. He who meanly admires mean things is a SNOB—perhaps that is a safe definition of the character.

1844. DICKENS, *Martin Chuzz.*, xxvi. These lions' heads was made for men of taste: not SNOBS.

1859. SMILES, *Self Help*, xiii. (1860), 352. He who bullies those who are not in a position to resist, may be a SNOB but cannot be a gentleman.

1861. LEVER, *One of Them*, xxxix. Ain't a SNOB a fellow as wants to be taken for better bred, or richer, or cleverer, or more influential than he really is?

1863. BRADDON, *J. Marchmont's Leg.*, I. ii. 42. "What a SNOB I am," he thought, "always bragging of home.'

1871. J. LEIGHTON, *Paris under Commune*, lxviii. 245. Is it nothing . . . to be no longer subjected to the oppression of SNOBS, reactionnaires and traitors?

1866. CARLYLE, *Remin.* (1881), II. 189. What of SNOB ambition there might be in me, which I hope was not very much.

1883. *Congregationalist*, May, 377. The SNOB nature comes out in strange ways.

1884. *Pall Mall G.*, 1 Mar., 4, 2. Admiral Maxse's French guest was strongly impressed with the healthy hatred in which three things—the "quack," the "humbug," and the SNOB—are held by the Englishmen with whom he associated in England. On being asked here what a SNOB is he said, "an individual who would enjoy living in a dirty hole provided it had a fine frontage, and who is absolutely incapable of valuing moral or mental greatness unless it is first admired by big people."

3. (workmen's). — A BLACKLEG, KNOBSTICK, RAT, SCAB (*q.v.*).

4. (provincial).—Mucus; SNOT (*q.v.*)—HALLIWELL.

Verb. (tailors'). — To sloven one's work: *cf.* SNOBBERY.

SNOBBERY, *subs.* (tailors').—Bad work; slack trade, &c. *Cf.* SNOB, sense 3 and *verb.* TO HIDE THE SNOBBERY = to conceal imperfections or cover up inferior work.

SNOB'S-BOOT, *subs. phr.* (tailors').—Sixpence: *see* RHINO.

SNOB'S-CAT.—In *phr.* (BEE) 'like a SNOB'S-CAT, full of piss and tantrums.' *Cf.* BARBER'S CAT.

SNOB'S-DUCK, *subs. phr.* (common).—A leg of mutton, stuffed with sage and onions.

SNOBSTICK, *subs.* (workmen's).—A black-leg; RAT, KNOBSTICK (*q.v.*): also SNOB.

SNOCK, *verb.* (American). — To 'land' a blow: *e.g.* TO SNOCK ON THE GOB = to punch one in the mouth.

SNODDY, *subs.* (common). — A soldier.

SNOOK, *subs.* (common).—In *pl.* = the imaginary name of a practical joker; also a derisive retort on an idle question—SNOOKS!

Verb. (common).—To pry; to watch; TO DOG (*q.v.*): also SNOOP: which also = (American) TO PICK (*q.v.*). Hence SNOOK (SNOOP, SNOOKER, or SNOOPER) = a spy; a sneak; a PAUL PRY (*q.v.*).

1653. BROME, *New Acad.*, ii. 1. I must not lose my harmlesse recreations Abroad, to SNOOK over my wife at home.

TO CUT (or COCK) SNOOKS, *verb. phr.* (common). — *See* SIGHT.

SNOOKER, *subs.* (Royal Military Academy).—A cadet-student of the fourth class; a freshman.

SNOOZE, *subs.* (colloquial). — 1. Sleep: spec. a NAP (*q.v.*): also SNOOZEM; also (2) = a bed: *see* KIP. As *verb.* (or SNOOZLE) = to nestle; SNOOZER = (1) a sleepy-head, and (2) a domiciled boarding-house or hotel thief (American); SNOOZING = sleep; SNOOZE-KEN (or SNOOZING-KEN) = (1) a bed, (2) a bed-room, (3) a lodging-house, (4) a brothel; SNOOZE-CASE = a pillow-slip (GROSE, BEE, VAUX). SNOOZY (Old Cant) = a night watchman or constable (GROSE).

1819. MOORE, *Tom Crib*, 28. What with SNOOZING, high-grubbing and guzzling like Chloe.

1838. BECKETT, *Paradise Lost*, 39. For when —— went to SNOOZEM Their din incessant sure must rouse him.

1847. BRONTE, *Wuthering Heights*, iii. A dog SNOOZLED its nose overforwardly into her face.

1855. THACKERAY, *Newcomes*, xlix. SNOOZE gently in thy arm-chair, thou easy baldhead.

1862. BROWNE, *Artemus Ward, His Book* [*Works* (1899), 41. I spose I'd been SNOOZIN half an hour when I was woke up by a noise at the door.

1874. *Siliad*, 61. Kamdux had SNOOZED, but now his fat sides shook.

18[?]. STEVENSON, *Treas. of Franchard.* The same SNOOZING countrified existence.

1880. BRET HARTE, *A Quiet Ride.* Bully place for a nice quiet SNOOZE—empty stage, sir!

1886. *E. Telegraph*, 1 Dec. The last surreptitious SNOOZE in which he was wont to revel.

SNOPSY (SNOPS or SNAPS), *subs.* (American).—Gin [*i.e.*, Schnaps].

SNORK, *verb.* (Shrewsbury School).—To excel; to surpass: *e.g.*, to do the whole of an examination paper, or to cap another in argument or repartee.

SNORT, *verb.* (colloquial). — To laugh in derision.

1835. HALIBURTON, *Clockmaker*, I. xix. I thought I should have SNORTED right out two or three times . . . to hear the critter let her clapper run that fashion.

1865. *Major Downing's Letters*, 15. We all SNORTED and snickered.

1885. *Century Mag.*, xli. 340. 'Such airs!' he SNORTED.

SNORTER, *subs.* (American). — 1. Anything large or exceptional: spec. a gale of wind, a heavy snow-storm: *cf.* SNEEZER: *see* WHOPPER.

18 [?]. *Cape Ann Fisherman* [BARTLETT]. The skipper said . . . we must make all snug, fur we're going to have a SNORTER.

1870. THORPE, *Backwoods*, 183. 'I'm a roaring earthquake in a fight,' sung out one of the . . . fellows, 'a real SNORTER of the universe.'

1891. MARRIOTT-WATSON, *Web of Spider*, xv. 'What's to become of me, then?' asked Ida. 'Well,' he said, 'that's rather a SNORTER. I dunno' where we could put you.'

1897. KENNARD, *Girl in Brown Habit*, i. Some of these fences are regular downright SNORTERS.

2. (common).—The nose: *see* CONK.

SNOT, *subs.* (vulgar). — 1. Nasal mucus. Hence 2 (common) = a contemptible wretch: also (2) SNOTTER and SNOTTIE = (naval) a midshipman. Whence as *verb.* = (1) to blow the nose, and (2) to act scurvily; SNOTTERY = filth; SNOTTY = running at the nose, mean, dirty; SNOTTY-NOSED = contemptible, filthy; SNOT-GALL (or SNOTTER) = the nose; SNOT-RAG (SNOTTINGER, or SNOTTER) = (1) a pocket-handkerchief; and (2) the nose (also SNOT- and SNOTTLE-BOX): SNOTTER also = a handkerchief thief; SNOTTER-HAULING = sneaking of WIPES (*q.v.*); SNOTTED = reprimanded: Fr. *mouché*.

1598. MARSTON, *Scourge of Villanie*, ii. To purge the SNOTTERY of our slimy time.

1601. JONSON, *Poetaster*, v. 1. Teach thy incubus to poetize, And throw abroad thy spurious SNOTTERIES.

*d.*1633. G. HERBERT, *Jacula Prudentum*. Better a SNOTTY child than his nose wiped off.

1685. *Poor Robin's Alman.* Three kisses, four Busses, and five licks under the SNOT-GALL.

1692. WOOD, *Athenæ Oxon*, ii. The continual importunities of his covetous and SNOTTY wife.

1725. BAILEY, *Erasmus*, II. 32. Linen rags . . . retaining still the Marks of the SNOT.

1823. BEE, *Dict. Turf*, s.v. WIPE—a pocket-handkerchief . . . When this kind of article is in the last stages of consumption they scoff at it, as a SNOTTER.

SNOUT, *subs.* (colloquial).—1. The nose: in contempt. 2. = the face: also SNOUT-PIECE (GROSE); SNOUT-FAIR = pretty, comely (HARMAN and GROSE).

*c.*1610. *Masque of Twelve Months.* Lady Pigswiggin the only SNOUT-FAIRE of the fairies.

1621. BURTON, *Anat. Melan.*, III. III. iv. 2. A modest Virgin, well-conditioned, to such a fair SNOUT-PIECE, is much to be preferred. *Ibid.*, III. III. i. 2. He that marries a wife that is SNOWY FAIR [? SNOUT FAIR] alone, let him . . .

1653. BROME, *Court Beggar*, ii. 1. Shee be SNOUT-FAIRE, and has some wit.

1663. BUTLER, *Hudibras*, I. iii. 357. Her subtle SNOUT Did quickly wind his meaning out.

2. (prison). — Tobacco: *see* WRIGHT and TRAFFICKING; also (itinerants') a cigar.

SNOW, *subs.* (Old Cant).—Linen: spec. linen hung out to dry: also SNOWY. Hence SNOW-GATHERER (or DROPPER) = a hedge-thief: also SNOW-DROPPING (GROSE and VAUX).

1877. HORSLEY, *Jottings from Jail.* We used to go and smug SNOWY that was hung out to dry.

SNOWBALL, *subs.* (venery).—1. A seminal globule: *see* CREAM and LETCHWATER.

*d.*1680. ROCHESTER [*Works* (1718), 87]. Priapus, squeez'd, one SNOWBALL did emit.

2. (old).—A negro (GROSE). Fr. *boule de neige*.

SNOW-BROTH, *subs. phr.* (B. E.).—'Snow-water.' Also (modern) = cold LAP (*q.v.*).

1603. SHAKSPEARE, *Meas. for Meas.*, i. 458. A man whose blood Is very SNOW-BROTH.

*d.*1796. BURNS, *Brigs of Ayr.* In mony a torrent doun his SNA-BROO rowes.

1870. JUDD, *Margaret*, i. 6. 'This is none of your SNOW-BROTH, Peggy,' said the mother; 'it's warming.'

SNUB, *verb.* (B. E. and GROSE).—To check, to rebuke.

See SNOB.

SNUB-DEVIL, *subs. phr.* (old).—A parson.

SNUB-NOSE, *subs. phr.* (GROSE).—'A short nose turned up at the end.'

SNUDGE, *subs.* (old).—1. A miser; a curmudgeon. Hence as *adj.* (SNUDGE-LIKE, or SNUDGING) = miserly, mean, crabby; as *verb.* = to grasp, to screw; SNUDGERY = meanness.

1531-47. COPLAND, *Hyeway to Spitel Hous.* Scrapynge and SNUDGYNGE without ony cease.

1544. ASCHAM, *Toxophilus*, i. Your husbandry . . . is more like the life of a covetous SNUDGE that ofte very evill proves.

1553. SIR T. WILSON, *Rhetorike.* SNUDGYNGE wittely rebuked . . . she beeyng greved charged hym . . . that he should saie she was such a pinchpeny as would sell her olde showes for mony.

1562. LEWICK, *Titus and Gisippus.* What man wold judge Titus to have been such a SNUDGE.

1577. KENDALL, *Floures of Epig.* Thou deemst me in thy minde . . . a sneekbill SNUDGE unkinde.

1579. NORTH, *Plut.*, 135. This bribing wretch was forced for to holde A tippling boothe, most like a clowne or SNUCHE.

1581. HAKLUYT, *Voyages*, I. 240. They may not say, as some SNUDGES in England say, I would find the Queene a man to serue in my place.

1587. HOLINSHED, *Descr. Ireland*, iii. SNUDGING peniefathers would take him vp verie roughlie.

1597. GERARD, *Herbal*, Verses prefixed. Of his faire flowring brats she [Mother Earth] is no SNUDGE.

1599. NASHE, *Lenten Stuffe* [Harl. Mis., vi. 147]. Their miserable SNUDGERY.

1600. DEKKER, *Old Fortunatus* [*Anc. Drama* (1814), iii. 124]. SNUDGES may well be called jailers.

1602. HEYWOOD, *How a Man may Choose a Good Wife from a Bad.* My master . . . is such an old SNUDGE, he'll not lose the droppings of his nose.

1694. MOTTEUX, *Rabelais*, v. xvi. We find that the filthy SNUDGE is yet more mischievous and ignorant than these ignorant wretches here.

2. (old). — A thief concealing himself under a bed (B. E. and GROSE).

SNUDGE-SNOUT, *subs. phr.* (old).—A dirty fellow.

1606. *Wily Beguild* [HAWKINS, *Eng. Dr.*, iii. 303]. That puck-fist, that SNUDGE-SNOUT, that coal-carrierly clown.

SNUFF, *subs.* (old).—The drainings of a glass; HEEL-TAPS (*q.v.*).

1641. BRAITHWAITE, *Penitent Pilgrim.* Those very SNUFFS which your excess procured, would have been sweet drops to many . . . who for want of drink have fainted.

Verb. — To be testy, easily offended: also TO TAKE SNUFF, or TO SNUFF PEPPER: *see* PEPPER. Whence IN SNUFF =

in dudgeon; TO GIVE SNUFF = to reprimand, to rebuke, to scold; SNUFFY = (1) offended, and (2) = drunk (BEE); as *subs.* SNUFF = a PET (*q.v.*).—(GROSE).

1584. ROBINSON, *Pleasant Delights* [ARBER], 35. Huffing and SNUFFING deserveth blame.

1593. HOLLYBAND, *Dict.* To spite, to anger, to take a matter IN SNUFFE.

1598. SHAKSPEARE, *1 Hen. IV.*, i. 3, 41. Who therewith angry, when it next came there, Took it IN SNUFF.

1601. JONSON, *Poetaster*, ii. 1. I take it highly IN SNUFF to learn how to entertain gentlefolks of you, at these years, i' faith. *Ibid.* (1609), *Silent Woman*, iv. 2. He went away IN SNUFF.

1611. *Bible*, Authorised Ver., Mal. i. 13. Ye said, what a weariness is it, and ye have SNUFFED at it.

1625. HALL, *Thanksgiving Sermon*, 29 Jan. Do the enemies of the church rage, and SNUFF, and breathe nothing but threats and death?

16 [?]. *Rox. Ballads* [B.M., C20, f. 8, 407], 'The Scolding Wife.' They was not so soon out of the Quire, ee'r She began TO SNUFF.

*c.*1630. TAYLOR, *Laugh and be Fat*, 69. No man's lines but mine you TAKE IN SNUFF.

1688. *Cap of Gray Hairs, &c.*, 113. If IN SNUFF and distaste you may fling away from such *re infecta*, a little patience and good words may do your business.

*d.*1704. L'ESTRANGE, *Works* [*Century*]. Jupiter TOOK SNUFF at the contempt, and punished him.

1891. *Harry Fludyer*, 30. He rather GAVE ME SNUFF about my extravagance, but I was prepared for that.

PHRASES.—UP TO SNUFF = not to be deceived, WIDEAWAKE (*q.v.*), KNOWING (*q.v.*); TO SNUFF OUT = to silence, settle, annihilate; TO SNUFF IT = to die: *see* ALOFT. *See* SNEEZE-LURK.

1785. GROSE, *Vulg. Tongue*, s.v. UP TO SNUFF. Synonymous with the above phrase ['Up to slum']; and is often rendered more emphatic by such adjuncts as 'UP TO SNUFF and twopenny,' 'UP TO SNUFF, and a pinch above it.'

1811. POOLE, *Hamlet Travestie.* He knew well enough The game we're after: zooks, he's UP TO SNUFF.

1823. BYRON, *Don Juan*, xi. 60. 'Tis strange the mind, that fiery particle, Should let itself be SNUFF'D OUT by an article.

1830. MONCRIEFF, *The Heart of London*, ii. 1. I nose: UP TO SNUFF.

1837. BARHAM, *Ingoldsby Leg.*, i. 295. Lady A., who is now what some call UP TO SNUFF.

1837. DICKENS, *Pickwick.* He was one too many for you warn't he? UP TO SNUFF, and a pinch or two over.

1838. BECKETT, *Paradise Lost*, 39. And being UP TO SNUFF in this, He turns his bottom, and says "kiss."

1876. HINDLEY, *Cheap Jack.* Having travelled all my lifetime, was better UP TO SNUFF than an ordinary man would be at fifty.

1885. SIMS, *Rogues and Vagabonds.* Josh Heckett isn't going to SNUFF IT just for a crack on the head.

1887. *D. Teleg.*, 15 Feb. They will be SNUFFED OUT; nobody will listen to them before seven, or after nine.

1891. NEWMAN, *Scamping Tricks*, 120. Now it is only fair to say the assistant knew his book, and was UP TO SNUFF.

SNUFFLE, *subs.* (B. E. and GROSE).—In *pl.* = a cold in the head: as *verb.* = to speak gruffly or through the nose.

1789. D'ARBLAY, *Diary*, iii. 180. First the Queen deserts us; then Princess Royal begins coughing; then Princess Augusta gets THE SNUFFLES.

SNUFFLER, *subs.* (common).—A preacher. Hence SNUFFLING = canting.

1861. HUGHES, *Tom Brown at Oxford*, xliv. You know I never was a SNUFFLER; but this sort of life makes one serious, if one has any reverence at all in one.

SNUFFY, *adj.* (common).—Tipsy: *see* SCREWED (GROSE).

SNUG, *verb.* (venery).—To copulate: *see* RIDE.

Adj. (common).—Drunk: *see* SCREWED.

ALL SNUG, *phr.* (GROSE).—All's quiet.

See BUG.

SNUGGERY, *subs.* (common).—A comfortable privacy: as a woman's boudoir, a man's smoking den, a bar-parlour.

1837. DICKENS, *Pickwick*, xlv. 'Vere are they?' said Sam . . . 'In the SNUGGERY,' rejoined Mr. Weller.

1872. ELIOT, *Middlemarch*, xvii. Knowing . . . Mr. Farebrother was a bachelor he had thought of being ushered into a SNUGGERY, where the chief furniture would probably be books.

1886. *Field*, 13 Feb. We in Meath had a pleasant time in Miss Murphy's SNUGGERY.

1898. *Pink 'Un and Pelican.* Give me the old-fashioned waiter . . . who becomes a part and parcel of the house. Simpson's, and that older SNUGGERY, the "Cheshire Cheese," have had many such.

SNYDER (or **SNIDER**), *subs.* (old).—A tailor: *see* TRADES.

*c.*1600. *Weakest to Wall*, i. 3. Beest thou a SNYDER? snip, snap, mette sheers.

SO, *adv.* (colloquial).—1. Drunk: *see* SCREWED. Also SO-SO.

1809. MALKIN, *Gil Blas* [ROUTLEDGE], 50. We drank hard, and returned to our employers in a pretty pickle, that is to say SO-SO in the upper story.

2. (conventional: women's).—Pregnant; LUMPY (*q.v.*).

3. (*Ibid.*).—In courses, UNDER REPAIR (*q.v.*).

Intj. (colloquial).—A questioning reply to a positive statement: *e.g.*, 'The King returns to town to-day' 'So?'

SO-AND-SO, *subs.* (colloquial). —1. Somebody or something indefinite; and (2) in place of a thing forgotten, or which it is not desired to mention: *e.g.*, Mr. SO-AND-SO.

SO LONG, *intj.* (common).—Good bye!

1902. LYNCH, *High Stakes*, xxxii. I'm off for change of air . . . Sow LONG. I'll see ye later.

SO-SO, *adj.* and *adv.* (colloquial). — Ordinary; mediocre; nothing to speak of.

1530. PALSGRAVE, *Lang. Francoyse*, 445. *Tellement quellement, je me porte*, SO SO.

*c.*1537. *A Pore Helpe* [HAZLITT, *Early Pop. Poet.*, iii. 263], 300. A noble teacher, And SO-SO a preacher.

1595. SHAKSPEARE, *Two Gent.*, i. 2. 'What thinkest thou of the rich Mercatio?' 'Well of his wealth; but of himself, SO-SO.' *Ibid.* (1600), *As You Like It*, v. i. 29. So So is good, very good, very excellent good; and yet it it is not; it is but SO-SO.

*d.*1703. PEPYS, *Diary.* She is a mighty proper maid, and pretty comely, but SO-SO; but hath a most pleasing tone of voice, and speaks handsomely.

*d.*1704. BROWN, *Works*, I. 173-4. Their outsides wondrous fine, their Pockets lined within but SO-SO.

*c.*1784. DR. S. PARR [*N. and Q.*, 7 S., x. 274]. Dr. Taylor read the service but SO-SO.

1797. LAMB, *Correspondence*, 'Coleridge,' xix. The remainder is only SO-SO.

1810. RHODES, *Bombastes Furioso.* Only SO-SO. O, monstrous doleful thing!

1837. BARHAM, *Ingoldsby Legends*, I. 73. That illustrious lady, who, after leading but a SO-SO life, had died in the odour of sanctity.

1857. F. LOCKER, *Reply to a Letter.* I trembled once beneath her spell Whose spelling was extremely SO-SO.

1888. BOLDREWOOD, *Squatter's Dream*, vi. He had . . . agreed . . . to sell this year's clip in the colony, as the washing and getting up were only SO-SO, and wool was high.

SOAK, *subs.* (common). — 1. A drinking bout; (2) a hard drinker: also SOAKER. As *verb.* = to steep oneself in drink; TO BOOZE (*q.v.*). Whence SOAKING = hard drinking; SOAKED = drunk: *see* SCREWED: TO SET SOAKING = to ply the pot (B. E., BAILEY, and GROSE).

1700. CONGREVE, *Way of the World*, iv. 10. The Sun's a good Pimple, an honest SOAKER; he has a Cellar at your Antipodes.

*d.*1704. LOCKE, *Works* [*Ency. Dict.*]. The tickling of his palate with a glass of wine, or the idle chat of a SOAKING club.

1709. DAMPIER, *Voyages*, I. 419. Scarce a ship goes to China but the Men come home fat with SOAKING this Liquor [Arrack].

*d.*1716. SOUTH, *Sermons*, VI. iii. By a good natur'd man is usually meant neither more nor less than a good fellow; a painful, able, and laborious SOAKER.

1766. GOLDSMITH, *Vicar of Wakefield*, xxi. You do nothing but SOAK with the guests all day long.

1772. BRIDGES, *Burlesque Homer*, 58. On this th' old SOAKER said no more.

1837. BARHAM, *Ingold. Leg.*, 'Milkmaid's Story.' That particular day, As I've heard people say, Mr. David Pryce had been SOAKING his clay.

1848. THACKERAY, *Van. Fair*, lxvi. Her voice is as cracked as thine, O thou beer-SOAKING Renowner.

1855. PARSONS, *Inside View of Slavery* [BARTLETT]. When a Southron intends to have a SOAK, he takes the bottle to his bedside, goes to bed, and lies there till he gets drunk.

Verb. (common).—1. To pawn: also TO PUT IN SOAK.

2. (anglers').—To be lavish of bait.

3. (common).—To sit lazily over the fire (HALLIWELL).

SOAKER, *subs.* (colloquial). — A heavy rain. *See* SOAK.

1851-61. MAYHEW, *Lond. Lab.*, I. 314. Well, sir, suppose it's a SOAKER in the morning . . . then, maybe, after all, it comes out a fine day.

1883. GREENWOOD, *Tag, Rag & Co.* That countryman was right when he prognosticated a SOAKER.

SOAP, *subs.* (common).—1. Flattery: also SOFT-SOAP: *cf.* SOFT-SAWDER. As *verb.* = to flatter; TO CARNEY (*q.v.*); SOAPY = smooth-tongued.

1840. *Widow Bedott Papers*, 308. You don't catch me a slanderin' folks behind their backs, and then SOFT SOAPIN' them to their faces.

1843. WALSH, *Speech* [BARTLETT]. I am tired of this system of placemen SOFT-SOAPING the people.

1853. BRADLEY, *Verdant Green*. The tailor and robemaker . . . visibly SOAPED our hero in what is understood to be the shop sense of the word.

1861. HUGHES, *Tom Brown at Oxford*, xxxiii. He and I are great chums, and a little SOFT-SOAP will go a long way with him.

1865. DICKENS, *Dr. Marigold* . . . These Dear Jacks SOAP the people shameful, but we Cheap Jacks don't.

1876. DIPROSE, *Laugh and Learn*. Flattery is the confectionery of the world. In polite society it goes by the name of SOAP, and in general is designated soft-sawder.

1902. DELANNOY, *£19,000*, xxxix. 'Mrs. Depew, you're the most sensible woman I've ever met.' 'None of your SOFT-SOAP, now.'

2. (old). — Money: generic: spec. secret service money. As *verb.* = to bribe.

1834. MARRYATT, *Peter Simple*, iv. Well, Reefer, how are you off for SOAP?

1884. *Boston* [Mass.] *Globe*, 7 Oct. 'Sinews of war,' and 'living issues,' SOAP, and other synonyms for campaign boodle are familiar.

18 [?]. *Mag. Amer. Hist.* [*Century*]. SOAP—Originally used by the Republican managers during the campaign of 1880, as the cipher for money in their telegraphic despatches. In 1884 it was revived as a derisive war cry aimed at the Republicans by their opponents.

3. (Royal Military Academy). —Cheese.

SOAP-AND-BULLION, *subs. phr.* (nautical).—*See* quot.

1883. CLARK RUSSELL, *Sailor's Language*, xii. I have known many a strong stomach, made food-proof by years of pork eaten with molasses, and biscuit alive with worms, to be utterly capsized, by the mere smell of soup-and-bouilli. Jack calls it 'SOAP-AND-BULLION, one onion to a gallon of water,' and this fairly expresses the character of the nauseous compound.

SOAP-CRAWLER, *subs. phr.* (common).—A toady.

SOAP-LOCK (or CURL), *subs. phr.* (American).—A soaped lock of hair on the temple.

1844. *Major Jones's Courtship* [BARTLETT]. The way my last letter has cradled off the SOAPLOCKS, and imperials, and goatlocks . . . is truly alarming.

2. (American). — A rowdy (BARTLETT).

SOAP-SUDS, *subs. phr.* (old).—'Gin and water, hot, with lemon and lump sugar' (BEE).

SOAP-TRICK, *sub. phr.* (American thieves').—A variety of the well-known purse swindle. A cake of soap is sold for a dollar to a gull who thinks he has that one he has wrapped a five-dollar bill in, and marked himself. Hence SOAPER = a soap-trick swindler.

SOARY, *adj.* and *adv.* (American). —Inclined to 'draw the long bow'; HIGH-FALUTIN' (*q.v.*).

SOBERSIDES, *subs.* (colloquial).—A sedate person.

1852. BRONTE, *Villette*, xxviii. You deemed yourself a melancholy SOBERSIDES enough! Miss Fanshawe there regards you as a second Diogenes in his tub.

SOBER-WATER, *sub. phr.* (common).—Soda-water.

SOC, *subs.* (printers').—'Society': non-Soc-man = a RAT (*q.v.*), a blackleg, a non-Union-man.

SOCIUS, *subs.* (Winchester). — A chum; a companion. As *verb.* = to accompany. [The School precept is *Sociati omnes incedunto.*]

SOCK, *subs.* (Old Cant).—1. A pocket: 'Not a rag in my sock' = penniless (B. E.).

2. (Eton College).—Edibles of any kind: spec. dainties, TUCK (*q.v.*). As *verb.* = (1) to eat outside regular meals; (2) = TO TREAT (*q.v.*); whence (3) = to give.

*c.*1550. MACHYN, *Diary* [Camden Soc.] [OLIPHANT, *New Eng.*, i. 534. The substantive SUCKETT appears for dainty . . . hence, perhaps, the SOCK so dear to Etonians.]

1881. PASCOE, *Every-day Life, &c.* The consumption of SOCK, too, in school was considerable, and on occasion very conspicuous.

1883. BRINSLEY RICHARDS, *Seven Years at Eton*. We Eton fellows, great and small SOCKED prodigiously.

1889. BUCKLAND, *Eton Fifty Years Ago* [*Macm. Mag.*, Nov.]. My governor has SOCKED me a book . . . A boy has also been heard to ask another TO SOCK him a construe of his lesson.

3. (common). — Credit; JAWBONE (*q.v.*): also as *verb.* = (1) to get credit, and 2 (American) = to pay: also TO SOCK DOWN.

4. (common).—An overgrown baby [*Ency. Dict.*].

5. (old).—A comedy. [The SOCK, an ancient emblem of Comedy; the BUSKIN = Tragedy.] Whence SOCK-AND-BUSKIN = (1) THE PROFESSION (*q.v.*).

1590. SPENSER, *Tears of the Muses*, 176. Where be the sweete delights of learnings treasure, That wont with Comick SOCK to beautefie The painted Theaters.

1637. MILTON, *L'Allegro*, 132. Then to the well-trod stage anon, If Jonson's learned SOCK be on.

1809. MALKIN, *Gil Blas* [ROUTLEDGE], 107. The gentlemen of THE SOCK AND BUSKIN are not on the best possible terms with the church. *Ibid.*, 190. My kindred of THE SOCK AND BUSKIN. *Ibid.*, 249. I knew perfectly that my sister of THE SOCK AND BUSKIN had entrapped this nobleman.

1817. BYRON, *Beppo*, xxxi. He was a critic upon operas, too, And knew all niceties of THE SOCK AND BUSKIN.

Verb. (old).—1. To beat; to drub (B. E.); to press hardly: also as *subs.*: *e.g.*, 'SOCK IT him' or 'Give him SOCK (or SOCKS)' = 'Pitch into him, dress him down.' Whence SOCKER = a heavy blow. Also 2 (American) = to smash a hat over head and ears, TO BONNET (*q.v.*). [*Cf.* (provincial) SOCK = to strike hard.]

1890. KIPLING, *The Oont* [*Scots Observer*]. We SOCKS him with a stretcher-pole, and 'eads him off in front. *Ibid.*, "*C.B.*" Drunk and resistin' the guard; 'Strewth! but I SOCKED at 'em 'ard.

1897. MARSHALL, *Pomes*, 87. He SOCK'D her in the eye at times, and stars she'd often view.

1898. *Illust. Bits*, Xmas No., 50. Then Maudie . . . jumps across the floor, And ketches me a . . . rousin' SOCKER on the jore.

1903. *D. Tel.*, 19 Jan. 'Police Report.' Then, said the witness, occurred the most dreadful SOCKING he had ever seen in the course of a long experience of street rows. It was literally a case of 'fur and feathers flying'—the hair was torn . . . in handfuls from the scalp.

2. (Winchester).—To hit hard: spec. at cricket. Also to defeat.

3. (old).—To sew up.

1584. R. SCOT, *Disc. of Witchcraft* [*N. and Q.*, 6 S., xi. 268]. Needels wherewith dead bodies are sowne or SOCKT into their sheets.

1604. MIDDLETON, *Witch*, i. 2. The same needles thrust into their pillows That sews and SOCKS up dead men in their sheets.

SOCKDOLOGER (**SOCDOLOGER**, **STOCKDOLOGER**, **SLOGDOLOGER**, or **SOGDOLOGER**), *subs.* (American).—1. Anything overwhelming or exceptional: from a repartee to an earthquake: generic. Also as *verb.* [*Cf.* SOCK.]

18 [?]. CROCKETT, *Bear Hunt* [BARTLETT]. . . . I gave the fellow a SOCDOLAGER over his head with the barrel of my gun.

1862. *Punch*, Aug., 'Jonathan's Appeal to Sambo.' Up, niggers! slash, smash, sack, and smite, SLOGDOLLAGIZE, and slay 'em.

1883. LOWELL, *To Mr. John Bartlett* [who had sent a 7-lb. trout]. Fit for an Abbot Theleme . . . He lies there, the SOGDOLOGER!

1884. CLEMENS, *Huck. Finn*. The thunder would go rumbling and grumbling away, and quit — and then rip comes another flash and another SOCKDOLOGER.

SOCKER, *subs.* (common). — 1. A fool, sloven, or lout: a general term of contempt. Also SOCKIE and SOCKHEAD.

1772. BRIDGES, *Burlesque Homer*, 4. The rabble then began to swear, What the old SOCKER said was fair.

2. (originally Harrow: now general).—Association Football: *cf.* RUGGER. Also SOCCER.

1896. *Tonbridgian*, 339. Hartley has been playing very well this season, and has also become a great half-back at SOCKER.

1897. *Felstedian*, Nov. 194. In SOCCER, with old Blues up, we ought to be very strong.

1902. *Pall Mall Gaz.*, 2 Jan., 9, 2. The article, which deals with both forms of the English game—SOCCER and rugger—proves to the hilt, &c.

SOCKET, *subs.* (venery).—The female *pudendum*: *see* MONOSYLLABLE. *See* SOCKET-MONEY.

1621. JONSON, *Masque of Gypsies* [GIFFORD, *Works*, iii. 144]. And sounding the SOCKETS Of simper-the-cockets.

*c.*1650. BRATHWAYTE, *Barnaby's Jo.* (1723), 93. Her I caught by you know what-a, Having boldly thus adventur'd, And my Sara's SOCKET entered.

BURNT TO THE SOCKET, *phr.* (old).—Dying (RAY).

SOCKET-MONEY, *subs. phr.* (old).—'Demanded and spent upon Marriage' (B. E.); 2 (GROSE) = 'money paid by a married man caught in an intrigue'; 3 (old) = 'a whore's fee' (GROSE). Hence SOCKETER = a blackmailer.

1772. BRIDGES, *Burlesque Homer*, 127. We'll take her, be she wife or whore; But we must likewise come upon ye, By way of costs, for SOCKET-MONEY.

SOD, *subs.* (common). — 1. A sodomist; hence (2) a violent term of abuse.

SODGER. *See* SOGER.

SODOM, *subs.* (Oxford Univ.).— 1. Wadham College.

2. (old).—London: *cf.* BABYLON.

SOFT, *subs.* (thieves').—Bank notes (GROSE): generic: also SOFT-FLIMSY. TO DO SOFT = to utter counterfeit notes.

Adj. (old).—(1) Foolish; easy-going (B. E. and BEE); and (2) choice, exquisite (*see* quot. 1596): originally effeminate. As *subs.* (SOFTY, or SOFT-HORN) = a simpleton; as *adj.* (SOFTISH, or SOFT-HEADED) = weak-minded, silly (BAILEY).

*d.*1536. TYNDALE, *Works*, ii. 258. [OLIPHANT, *New Eng.*, i. 428. An Emperor who gave in to the Pope is called a SOFT man.]

1596. SHAKSPEARE, *Hamlet*, v. 2, 110. Laertes . . . an absolute gentleman, full of most excellent differences, of very SOFT SOCIETY and great showing.

1621. BURTON, *Anat. Melan.*, 209. What cannot such scoffers do, especially if they find a SOFT creature on whom they may work. *Ibid.*, 149. He made . . . SOFT fellows stark noddies.

1809. MALKIN, *Gil Blas* [ROUTLEDGE], 13. You are young, and seem a little SOFT.

1828. BEE, *Liv. Pict. Lond.*, 45. If you appear tolerably SOFT, and will 'stand it,' he perhaps refuses these also, after having rung the changes once more. This is called a double do.

1859. ELIOT, *Adam Bede*, ix. If you've got a SOFT to drive you, he'll soon turn over into the ditch.

1863. MRS. GASKELL, *Sylvia's Lovers*, xv. Nancy . . . were but a SOFTY after all.

1864. BRADDON, *Aurora Floyd*, xvii. 'I've mashed the tea for 'ee,' said the SOFTY.

1888. MRS. H. WARD, *Robert Elsmere*, iii. He is a kind of SOFTIE—all alive on one side of his brain, and a noodle on the other.

1897. MARSHALL, *Pomes*, 73. Called the beak 'a balmy kipper,' dubbed him 'SOFT about the shell.'

1902. LYNCH, *High Stakes*, xxxii. I . . . heard them calling me SOFTY, and other . . . names, before I had fairly turned my back on them.

PHRASES. SOFT-HEARTED = yielding, piteous, tender; 'HARD (ARSE) OR SOFT?' = 'Third class or first?'; SOFT FOOD = pap; SOFT = hash; SOFT IS YOUR HORN = 'You make a mistake' (BEE); A SOFT THING = (1) an easy or pleasant task, and (2) a facile simpleton; A BIT OF HARD FOR A BIT OF SOFT (venery) = copulation; SOFT DOWN ON = in love with. *See* HARD-SHELL; HARD-TACK; SAWDER (adding quot. 1844 *infra*); SNAP; SOAP; SPOTS; TACK.

1844. HALIBURTON, *Attache*, 19. I don't like to be left alone with a gall; it's plaguy apt to set me a SOFT-SAWDERIN', and a courtin'. *Ibid.* (1855), *Human Nature*, 311. Sam Slick said he trusted to SOFT SAWDER to get his wooden clocks into a house.

SOFT-BALL, *subs. phr.* (Royal Military Academy).—Tennis.

SOFT-HORN, *subs. phr.* (common).—An ass, whether quadruped or biped.

SOFT-HORSE, *subs. phr.* (racing).—A horse lacking stamina.

SOFTLING, *subs.* (old).—A voluptuary.

1576. WOOLTON, *Christ. Manual.* Effeminate and SOFTLINGS cause the stoute man to waxe tender.

SOFT-SOAP. *See* SOAP.

SOFT-SHELL, *subs. phr.* (obsolete American political).—*See* quots. and HARD-SHELL. Also SOFTS and SOFT-SHELL Democrats.

1858. *Report of Meeting Co. of Orleans*, Sept., *Resolved.* That the terms Hunker, Barnburner, SOFT-SHELL, and Hardshell have become obsolete, and hereafter we will be known only by the term Democrat.

1899. *Century Dict.*, s.v. SOFT. II. 2. In U.S. Politics: (*a*) A member or an adherent of that one of the two factions into which in 1852 and succeeding years the Democratic party in the State of New York was divided which was less favourable to the extension of slavery. (*b*) A member of the pro-slavery wing of the Democratic party in Missouri about 1850.

SOFT-TACK (or **-TOMMY**), *subs. phr.* (nautical). — Bread: as distinguished from biscuit, which is 'Ship's bread.'

1878. GILBERT, *H.M.S. Pinafore.* I've treacle and toffee, and excellent coffee, SOFT TOMMY, and succulent chops.

1883. GREENWOOD, *Odd People.* The SOFT-TACK and the green vegetables the bumboat people bring alongside ships that have been long absent on sea service.

SOG, *subs.* (school).—1. A sovereign; 20/-.

2. (American). — A swoon; lethargy.

1865. S. O. JEWETT [*Scribner's Mag.*, II. 738. Old Ezra Barnet . . . waved a limp hand warningly toward the bedroom door, 'She's layin' in a SOG,' he said, hopelessly.

SOGER (SOJER, or SODGER), *subs.* (colloquial).—1. A soldier. [*Cf. sawgeoure* (*miles*) Townley Myst. (*c.*1401), p. 310].

[?]. *Chronicon, Mirab.*, 109. A SOGER of the armé.

*d.*1796. BURNS, *Jolly Beggars*, 'Soldier Laddie,' iii. He ventur'd the soul, and I risked the body, 'Twas then I prov'd false to my SODGER laddie.

1864. BROWNE, *Works* (1870), 257. We certainly don't lack brave SOJERS—but there's one thing I wish we did lack, and that is, our present Congress.

*d.*1868. LOVER, *The Bould Soger Boy* [Title].

1899. WHITEING, *John St.*, 217. Won't it be fine to see the SOJERS on 'orseback? I hope its the Reds.

2. (nautical).—*See* quots.

1835. DANA, *Before the Mast*, 25. All hands are engaged upon it [reefing], and after the halyards are let go, there is no time to be lost—no SOGERING, or hanging back. *Ibid.*, 117, Note. SOGER (soldier) is the worst term of reproach that can be applied to a sailor. It signifies a *skulk*, a *sherk*—one who is always trying to get clear of work, and is out of the way, or hanging back, when duty is to be done. "Marine" is applied more particularly to a man ignorant and clumsy about seaman's work—a green-horn—a land-lubber. To make a sailor shoulder a handspike, and walk fore and aft the deck, like a sentry, is the most ignominious punishment that could be put on him; inflicted upon an able seaman in a vessel of war, would break his spirit down more than a flogging.

1881. WARNER, *Winter on the Nile*, 248. The two long lines of men attached to the ropes . . . stretch out . . . so far that it needs an opera-glass to discover whether the leaders are pulling or only SOLDIERING.

1883. CLARK RUSSELL, *Sailor's Language*, xiii. Many an old prejudice survives in sea-language . . . SOGER . . . is as strong a term of contempt as one sailor can fling at another, whilst SOGERING means to loaf, to skulk . . . as if . . . characteristic of a soldier.

3. (Winchester). — *See* quot. and PERCHER.

1880. *Music of a Merry Heart*, 55. The books went up and in due time were returned to us after examination, with the most startling faults indicated by a good big cross in the margin, which crosses for some reason, were known as SODGERS.

SOILED-DOVE, *subs. phr.* (obsolete).—A prostitute: *see* TART.

SOLACE, *subs.* (old printers').—A penalty; a fine (MOXON, 1683).

SOLD. *See* SELL.

SOLDIER, *subs.* (common).—1. A red herring; and (2) a boiled lobster (GROSE and BEE).

Verb. (Australian). — 1. 'To make temporary use of (another man's horse). Thus a man wanting a mount catches the first horse he can, rides it to his destination, and then lets it go' (*Century*).

2. (old).—To bully; to hector (HALLIWELL).

3. (military).=To do routine work, as cleaning accoutrements, fatigue duty, anything irksome in a soldier's life.

PHRASES and COMBINATIONS.—SOLDIER'S-BOTTLE (B. E. and GROSE) = a large bottle; SOLDIER'S-MAWND=(1) 'a counterfeit Sore or Wound in the left Arm' (B. E.), and (2) 'a pretended soldier, begging with a counterfeit wound, which he pretends to have received at some famous siege or battle' (GROSE); SOLDIER'S JOY = masturbation; SOLDIER'S POMATUM=a piece of tallow (GROSE); SOLDIER'S THIGH = an empty pocket; A SOLDIER'S WIND = a fair wind either way, consequently (C. RUSSELL) 'a beam wind'; OLD SOLDIER = (1) an empty bottle: *cf.* MARINE, and (2) *see* OLD SOLDIER. *See* COME and FRESH-WATER SOLDIER.

1853. KINGSLEY, *Westward Ho*, xix. The breeze blowing dead off the land was 'a SOLDIER'S WIND there and back again,' for either ship.

SOLEMNCHOLY. *subs.* (common).—Seriousness; gravity: *cf.* 'melancholy.'

SOLE-SLOGGER, *subs.* (common).—A shoemaker.

SOL-FA, *subs.* (old).—A parish clerk (GROSE).

SOLID, *adj.* (*Century*: Am. polit. slang). — United; unanimous. Thus, a SOLID vote=a unanimous vote; THE SOLID SOUTH (American)=the Southern States during reconstruction: from their uniform support of the Democratic party; A SOLID PARTY=a united party; TO MAKE ONESELF SOLID WITH=to come to an agreement with, &c.

1884. *Century Mag.*, xxxvii. 30. We thus succeeded in making ourselves SOLID with the administration before we had been in a town or village forty-eight hours.

1888. HOWELLS, *Annie Kilburn*, xviii. I'm SOLID FOR Mr. Peck every time.

1898. WALSH, *Lit. Curios.*, 1019. SOLID SOUTH . . . The first occurrence of the phrase in the modern sense may be traced back to *circa* 1868 . . . The persistent solidarity of action of the Southern States . . . found expression in it as a term of reproach.

SOLITARY, *subs.* (prison).—Solitary confinement.

1901. WALKER, *In the Blood*, 156. We done a bit o' SOLITARY once or twice.

SOLO, *subs.* (Winchester).—A solitary walk, without a SOCIUS (*q.v.*).

SOLOMON (or **SOLLOMON**). *See* SALMON.

SOLUTION OF CONTINUITY, *subs. phr.* (venery). — The female *pudendum*: *see* MONOSYLLABLE (URQUHART).

SOME, *subs.* and *adv.* (American).—Somewhat; a certain amount; a great deal: *cf.* FEW and *see* PUMPKIN.

1598. SHAKSPEARE, *2 Hen. IV.*, v. 5. Bate me SOME, and I will pay you SOME.

1847. RUXTON, *Far West*, 54. When a boy, our trapper was 'SOME' . . . with the rifle, and always had a hankering for the West.

1849. *New York Tribune*, 15 May. Admitted by the oldest inhabitant to be 'SOME' in the way of cold winters.

1856. *Knickerbocker Mag.*, Mar. He was SOME on horses . . . immense at ten-pins.

1896. LILLARD, *Poker Stories*, 178. I used to play cards SOME before I was married.

SOMETHING. *See* DAMP and SHORT.

SOMEWHERES, *adv.* (vulgar). — Somewhere; about: *e.g.*, 'SOMEWHERES along of fifty quid.'

SON. In combination, thus—SON OF APOLLO = a scholar (B. E.); SON OF A BITCH (SOW, WHORE, &c.) = a term of violent abuse; SON OF A BACHELOR=a bastard; SON OF A GUN (or SEA-COOK) = (1) a soldier's bastard, and (2) a term of contempt (*see* quot. 1867); SON OF MARS=a soldier (B. E.); SON OF MERCURY=a wit (B. E.); SON OF PARCHMENT = a lawyer (B. E.); SON OF PRATTLEMENT = an advocate (GROSE); SON OF WAX = a cobbler; EVERY MOTHER'S SON = everybody; A FAVOURITE SON (*see* quot. 1888); SON OF VENUS = a wencher.

*c.*1330. *Auchinleck MS.* [HORSTMANN, *Altenglische Legenden*, 253]. [OLIPHANT, *New Eng.*, i. 18. There is the new phrase mani a moder child; whence comes EVERY MOTHER'S SON.]

1592. SHAKSPEARE, *Mid. Night's Dream*, i. 2, 80. That would hang us, EVERY MOTHER'S SON.

1611. CHAPMAN, *May Day*, ii. 2. The SON OF A SOW-GELDER that came to town . . . in a tattered russet coat . . . must needs rise a gentleman.

*d.*1704. BROWN, *Works*, I. 121. Get thee gone from my Door, Like a SON OF A WHORE. *Ibid.*, III. 41. Certain SONS OF PARCHMENT called Sollicitors and Barristers.

1705. VANBRUGH, *Confederacy*, iii. 2. Here's a SON OF A W——.

1748. SMOLLETT, *Random*, iii. Lookee, you lubberly SON OF A W——E, if you can athwart me . . . ; I'll be foul of your quarter, d——n me. *Ibid.*, xxvii. Lazy lubberly SONS OF BITCHES . . . good for nothing on board but to eat the King's provision, and encourage idleness in the skulkers.

1772. BRIDGES, *Burlesque Homer*, 'Publisher to the Reader.' They called one another rogue, rascal, and SON OF A BITCH very cordially.

1830. LYTTON, *Paul Clifford*, x., 'Fighting Attie's Song.' Pass the bingo—OF A GUN, You musky, dusky, husky SON.

1833. MARRYAT, *Peter Simple* (1834), 446. You are the SON OF A BITCH. *Ibid.*, xii. Take that—and that—and that . . . you damn'd hay-making SON OF A SEA-COOK.

1835. DANA, *Two Years Before Mast*, xiv. He was not the man to call a sailor a SON OF A B——H, and knock him down with a handspike.

1837. BARHAM, *Ingolds. Leg.* A stupid, old snuff-coloured SON OF A GUN.

1867. AD. SMYTH, *Sailors' Word Book*, s.v. SON OF A GUN. An epithet conveying contempt in a slight degree, and originally applied to boys born afloat, when women were permitted to accompany their husbands to sea; one admiral declared he literally was thus cradled, under the breast of a gun-carriage.

1888. BRYCE, *American Commonwealth*, II. 153. A FAVOURITE SON is a politician respected or admired in his own State, but little regarded beyond it.

1899. WHITEING, *John St.*, xvi. They have that to give which is wanted by EVERY MOTHER'S SON.

SONG, *subs.* (common).—A trifle; a nominal sum or price: also an OLD (or MERE) SONG.

1598. SHAKSPEARE, *All's Well*, iii. 2, 8. I know a man that had this trick of melancholy sold a goodly manor for A SONG.

*d.*1719. ADDISON, *Works* [*Ency. Dict.*]. A hopeful youth, newly advanced to great honour, was forced by a cobbler to resign for AN OLD SONG.

1888. *Globe*, 2 Sep. Evergreen, who was bought for A MERE SONG.

1901. *St. James's Gaz.*, 5 Mar., 5, 1. Ships, like everything else, grow old. Though they cost a round million to build, they are sold for a SONG when obsolete.

TO CHANGE ONE'S SONG (or SING ANOTHER SONG), *verb. phr.* (common).—To tell a different tale (GROSE): *see* SING. Also 'His morning and evening SONG do not agree' = 'He tells another yarn at night to the one in the morning.'

SONKEY, *subs.* (common). — A clumsy fellow; a lout: also SONK, SONKY, and SONKIE.

SONNIE (SONNY or **SONNIKIN)**, *subs.* (common).—An affectionate or familiar address: with no necessary reference to age or relationship. Also (nautical) SONNIWAX or SONNYWAX.

1542. UDAL, *Erasmus*, 233. This word *paidion*, SONNEKIN . . . tripped a little in his tongue.

1896. PATERSON, *Man from Snowy River*, 10. Weel, weel, don't get angry, my SONNY.

SOOL, *verb.* (Australian).—1. To excite a dog; to set him on. 2. = to worry, as a dog a cat.

1896. MRS. PARKER, *Aus. Leg. Tales*, 90. She went softly towards her camp, calling softly . . . 'SOOL 'EM, SOOL 'EM' . . . the signal for the dogs to come out.

SOOT-BAG, *subs. phr.* (HOTTEN).—A reticule.

SOOTERKIN, *subs.* (old).—1. *See* quot. 1755 (B. E.). Hence (2) an abortive proposal or scheme.

1673. DRYDEN, *Remarks on Emp. of Morocco.* He has all the pangs and throes of a fanciful poet, but is never delivered of any more perfect issue of his phlegmatick brain than a dull Dutch woman's SOOTERKIN is of her body.

1678. BUTLER, *Hudibras*, III. ii. 146. For knaves and fools b'ing near of kin, As Dutch boors are t'a SOOTERKIN.

1726. POPE, *Dunciad*, i. 126. All that on Folly Frenzy could beget, Fruits of dull heat, and SOOTERKINS of wit.

1755. JOHNSON, *Eng. Dict.*, s.v. SOOTERKIN. A kind of false birth fabled to be produced by Dutch women from sitting over their stoves.

SOP, *subs.* (old).—1. A bribe; *e.g.*, a SOP TO CERBERUS = a doorkeeper's or porter's TIP (*q.v.*).

1513. DOUGLAS, *Æneis*, vi. 6o. Cerberus, the hiddus hund . . . Quham til the prophetes . . . A SOP stepit intill hunny . . . gan cast.

1670. HOWARD, *Committee*, iv. 1. You unconscionable Rascal . . . do you want some Fees? I'll perish . . . before throwing SOPS to such Curs.

1695. CONGREVE, *Love for Love*, i. 4, 17. If I can GIVE THAT CERBERUS A SOP, I shall be at rest for one day.

1697. DRYDEN, *Æneis*, Postscr. Even Cerberus when he had received the SOP, permitted Æneis to pass.

*d.*1745. SWIFT, *Works* [*Century*]. To Cerberus they give a SOP, His triple barking mouth to stop.

1773. FOOTE, *Nabob*, i. There is but one way of managing here: I must GIVE THE CERBERUS A SOP, I suppose.

1825. H. SMITH, *Gaities and Grav.* I will throw down a napoleon AS A SOP TO CERBERUS.

2. (old).—A small piece; a thing or matter of little value.

1362. LANGLAND, *Piers Plowman* (B), xiii. 124. For one Piers the Ploughman hath inpugned vs alle, And sette alle sciences at a SOPPE saue loue one.

3. (common).—A simpleton; a 'milk-SOP.'

A SOP IN THE PAN, *subs. phr.* (colloquial).—1. A dainty; and (2) a favour.

1621. FLETCHER, *Pilgrim*, iii. 7. Stir no more abroad, but tend your business; You shall have no more SOPS I' THE PAN else.

SOPH, *subs.* (Cambridge Univ.).—A sophister: in U.S.A. sophomore; 'a student beyond his first year' (GROSE). The terms are 1st year, Freshman; 2nd year, Junior SOPH; 3rd year, Senior SOPH. *See* HARRY SOPH.

1719. DURFEY, *Wit and Mirth*. I am a jolly SOPH.

1726. POPE, *Dunciad*, ii. 379. Three Cambridge SOPHS and three past Templars came.

1870. GOODRICH [WEBSTER *Unabridged*, s.v. SOPHOMORE]. This word, generally considered an American barbarism, was probably introduced at a very early period from the Univ. of Cambridge, England. Among the cant terms at that University as given in the 'Gradus ad Cantab' [1803] we find SOPHMOR. It is added that MOR=Gr., *moria* introduced at a time when the *Enconium Moriæ*, the *Praise of Folly* by Erasmus was so generally used. The ordinary derivation of the word from *sophos* and *moros* would seem, therefore, to be incorrect [*Abridged*].

SORE-FIST, *subs. phr.* (tailors').—A bad workman: *cf.* TO WRITE A POOR HAND (*ibid.*)=to sew badly.

SORE LEG, *subs. phr.* (military).—1. German sausage. Also 2. (streets') = a plum-pudding; SPOTTED-DOG (*q.v.*).

SORREL-PATE, *subs. phr.* (B. E. and GROSE). — A red-haired man; CARROTS (*q.v.*).

SORROWFUL TALE, *subs. phr.* (rhyming).—Three months in jail.

SORRY, *adj.* (GROSE). — 'Vile, mean, worthless: a sorry fellow or hussy, a worthless man or woman.'

Intj. (colloquial).—'I beg your pardon.'

SORT, *subs.* (colloquial).—SORT (= kind) in its colloquial usages is frequently elliptical. Thus, 'THAT'S YOUR SORT' (of method, fancy, thing, &c.); 'AFTER A SORT' (of fashion—'well enough of its kind'); A GOOD (or BAD) SORT (of man, fellow, lot, &c.). OUT OF SORTS=(1) SEEDY (*q.v.*); (2) = cross, depressed; and (3)=old, destitute. SORTER (American) = sort of.

*d.*1536. TYNDALE, *Works*, i. 274. [OLIPHANT, *New Eng.*, i. 433. SORT stands for *homo*, much as we say he is a bad lot.]

1590. E. WEBBE, *Travels* (ARBER), 34. Now to . . . declare vnto you in what SORT I imploide my selfe since my first entring into Englande.

1595. SHAKSPEARE, 3 *Hen VI.*, v. 5. Now march we hence: discharge the COMMON SORT with pay and thanks. *Ibid.* (1609), *Tempest*, ii. 1, 102. Is not, sir, my doublet as fresh as the first day I wore it? I mean, IN A SORT.

1603-15. *Court and Times Chas. I.*, I. 6. The Duke's journey to France is laid down: and yet they say the business goeth on IN A SORT.

1622. FLETCHER, *Prophetess*, iii. 1. Give your petitions in seemly SORT, and keep your hats off decently.

1678. RAY, *Proverbs*, 304. Many a man of good extraction coming home from far voyages, may chance to land here, and, being OUT OF SORTS, is unable for the present time and place to recruit himself with clothes.

1680. BETTERTON, *Revenge*, iv. Why girl . . . you're all OUT OF SORTS: I thought thy tongue and heels could never have been idle.

1779. D'ARBLAY, *Diary*, Jan., 'To Mr. Crisp.' I was most violently OUT OF SORTS, and really had not spirits to answer it.

1782. BURNEY, *Cecilia* (1778), v. 308. [OLIPHANT, *New Eng.*, ii. 192. Men are described as being OUT OF SORTS, a new phrase.]

1792. HOLCROFT, *Road to Ruin. Gold.* (*passim*). THAT'S YOUR SORT!

1817. SCOTT, *Rob Roy*, xxvi. He has a kind o' Hieland honesty—he's honest AFTER A SORT, as they say.

1847. PORTER, *Big Bear*, 126. He was breathin' SORTER hard.

1851. HAWTHORNE, *Seven Gables*, viii. No wonder you are OUT OF SORTS, my little cousin. To be an inmate with such a guest may well startle an innocent young girl.

1859. THACKERAY, *Virginians*, xv. 'You were hurt by the betting just now?' 'Well,' replied the lad, 'I am SORT O' hurt.'

SO-SO. *See* SO.

SOSS, SOSSLE, &c. *See* SOZZLE.

SOTWEED, *subs.* (old).—Tobacco (GROSE). Hence SOTWEED-DEALER and SOTWEED-PLANTER.

*d.*1704. BROWN, *Works*, I. 126. When the stew'd SOTWEED in his Mouth has lain So long, till spiting does its Virtues drain.

1705. WARD, *Hud. Rediv.*, I. 2, 22. I scarce had fill'd a pipe of SOTWEED, And by the Candle made it Hotweed.

1708. COOK, *SOT-WEED Factor*, 2. These SOTWEED planters crowd the shoar. *Ibid.* (1730), *SOT-WEED Redivivus*, 9. When aged Roan . . . Left SOTWEED Factor in the Lurch.

SOU, NOT A SOU (or **SOUSE**), *subs.* (B. E. and GROSE).—Nothing.

1761. CHURCHILL, *Rosciad*, 310. Next came the treasurer of either house, One with full purse, t'other with NOT A SOUSE.

1812. COLMAN, *Poet. Vag.*, 30. That, you may tell me, matters NOT A SOUSE.

1837. BARHAM, *Ingoldsby Legends*. NOT A SOU had he got, not a guinea or note.

SOUL. SOUL IN SOAK, *phr.* (nautical). — Drunk: *see* SCREWED (GROSE).

SOUL-CASE, *subs. phr.* (GROSE).—The body.

SOUL-DRIVER, *subs. phr.* (old).—A parson (B. E.).

SOUND, *verb.* (GROSE and VAUX).—To examine; TO TRY (*q.v.*); to extract information artfully; TO PUMP (*q.v.*). TO SOUND A CLY = to 'try' a pocket.

1597. SHAKSPEARE. *Richard III.*, iii. 1, 169. Go, gentle Catesby, And as it were, far off, SOUND thou Lord Hastings, How he doth stand affected to our purpose.

1626. BACON, *Negotiating* (1887). It is better to SOUND a person with whom one deals, afar off, than to fall upon the point at first, except you mean to surprise him by some short question.

1768. GOLDSMITH, *Good Natured Man*, ii. I have SOUNDED him already at a distance, and find all his answers exactly to our wish.

1885. *Ev. Standard*, 3 Oct. His Holiness, however, on being SOUNDED on the subject, by the Spanish Ambassador in Rome, declined.

SOUND AS A ROACH (TROUT, BELL, &c.), *phr.* (old).—Perfectly sound. [Roche = rock].

1697. VANBRUGH, *Provoked Wife*, iv. 6. *Lady B.* I hope you are not wounded? *Sir J.* SOUND AS A ROACH, wife.

See GOOSE.

SOUP, *subs.* (legal).—1. A brief for the defence given to a junior in court by the Clerk of the Peace or Arraigns.

2. (printers').—Bad ink.

3. (thieves'). — Melted plate: also WHITE SOUP. Whence SOUP-SHOP = A FENCE (*q.v.*); melting-pots are kept going, no money passing from fence to thief until identification is impossible.

IN THE SOUP, *adv. phr.* (American).—In a pickle, or difficulty; LEFT (*q.v.*).

SOUPER, *subs.* (common).—1. A cadger for soup-tickets.

2. (thieves').—A SUPER (*q.v.*).

SOUR, *subs.* (thieves'). — 1. Base silver money. TO PLANT THE SOUR = to 'utter' SNIDE (*q.v.*) silver; whence SOUR-PLANTER. *See* SHOVER.

1883. GREENWOOD, *Tag, Rag, and Co.* The individual mentioned . . . was a smasher, or in other words, a dealer in . . . . SOURS. *Ibid.*, 34. It is not in paltry pewter SOURS with which the young woman has dealings, but in dandys which . . . mean imitation gold coin.

2. (American). — An acid punch: thus WHISKEY-SOUR = whiskey and lemon.

Adj. (B. E.).—'Crabbed, surly, ill-conditioned.'

TO SOUR ON, *verb. phr.* (American).—To treat unkindly.

SOUR-ALE. TO MEND LIKE SOUR-ALE IN SUMMER, *verb. phr.* (colloquial).—To get worse.

SOUR-CUDGEL, *subs. phr.* (old).—A severe beating (WITHAL, 1608).

SOUSE-CROWN, *subs. phr.* (B. E.).—A fool: *see* BUFFLE.

SOUTHERLY BUSTER, *subs. phr.* (Australian). — A sudden gale from the southward: *cf.* BRICK-FIELDER.

1863. F. FOWLER [*Athenæum*, 21 Feb., 264, 1.] The brickfielder is the cold wind or SOUTHERLY BUSTER which . . . carries a thick cloud of dust across the city.

1878. *Australian*, i. 587. *SOUTHERLY BUSTERS* by '*Ironbark*' [Title].

1883. *Times*, 27 Sep., 9. The port is exposed to sudden gales known as SOUTHERLY BUSTERS.

1885. FINCH-HATTON, *Advance Australia*. A SOUTHERLY BUSTER sweeps up from the ice-fields of the Southern Sea.

1889. ZILLMANN, *Australian Life*, 40. It is no mere pastime to be caught in a SOUTHERLY BUSTER.

1893. *The Australasian*, 12 Aug., 302, 1. You should see him with Commodore Jack out in the teeth of 'the hard glad weather,' when a SOUTHERLY BUSTER sweeps up the harbour.

1896. H. A. HUNT, *Essay on SOUTHERLEY BUSTERS* [Title].

SOUTH JEOPARDY, *subs. phr.* (GROSE). — 'Terrors of insolvency. *Oxf. Univ. Cant.*'

SOV, *subs.* (common).—A sovereign; 20/-: *see* RHINO.

SOW, *subs.* (old).—1. A fat woman; hence (2) = a general term of abuse: *cf.* BITCH. SOW-CHILD = a girl baby (B. E. and GROSE); SOW'S BABY = a sucking pig.

1702. WARD, *Works*, i. 5, 27. She looks . . . like a sow in petticoats.

1725. BAILEY, *Erasmus*, 'Epithal. Petrus Ægidius.' The wife [has been called] SOW, Fool, Dirty Drab.

PHRASES and PROVERBS. TO GREASE A FAT SOW ON THE ARSE = to be insensible to kindness; TO COME SAILING IN A SOW'S EAR (RAY); TO GET THE RIGHT (or WRONG) SOW BY THE EAR = to make a right (or wrong) conclusion (B. E. and GROSE); 'You cannot make a silk-purse of a SOW'S EAR=a retort on the impossible' (RAY): *cf.* 'You cannot make a horn of a pig's tail' and 'An ass's tail will not make a sieve.' *See* DAVID'S SOW; HEMPSEED; SADDLE; WILD OATS.

1596. JONSON, *Ev. Man in Humour*, ii. 1. He has THE WRONG SOW BY THE EAR, i' faith; and claps his dish at the wrong man's door.

1605. CHAPMAN and JONSON, *Eastward Ho*, ii. 1. YOU HAVE THE SOW BY THE RIGHT EAR, sir.

1664. BUTLER, *Hudibras*, II. iii. 580. You have a WRONG SOW BY THE EAR.

*d.*1731. WARD, *Merry Observations*, June. Those that happen to HAVE THE WRONG SOW BY THE EAR will be very apt to curse the shortness of the Vacation.

1771. SMOLLETT, *Clinker* [SAINTSBURY (1900), i. 81]. You know, my dear friend, how natural it is for us Irishmen to blunder, and TO TAKE THE WRONG SOW BY THE EAR.

1834. MARRYATT, *Peter Simple*, xii. The man was very well, but having been brought up in a collier, he could not be expected to be very refined; in fact . . . 'it was IMPOSSIBLE TO MAKE A SILK-PURSE OUT OF A SOW'S EAR.'

SOW'S-BABY, *subs. phr.* (old).—Sixpence: *see* RHINO and *cf.* HOG = 1/-.

SOW-BELLY, *subs. phr.* (military and naval).—Salt-pork.

SOW-DRUNK, *adj.* (common). — Beastly drunk: *see* DRUNK AS DAVID'S-SOW.

1857. TENNYSON, *Northern Cobbler.* Soa SOW-DROONK that tha doesn not touch thy 'at to the Squire.

SOZZLE (SOSSLE, SOSS, or SOZZ), *subs.* (colloquial).—Generic for lumpishness. Thus (1) = a lout: also SOSS-BELLY; (2) a heavy fall; a FLOP DOWN; (3) a muddle; a mess. As *verb.* = (1) to flop; (2) to toss at random; and (3) to slush about. As *adj.* (or SOSS-BELLIED) = ponderously fat; SOSS-BRANGLE = (1) a slattern, and (2) a big horse-godmotherly whore; SOSSLY (or SOZZLY) = wet, sloppy: SOSSLED = drunk.

1549. BALE, *Dict. of Bonner's Articles*, 29. Thou SOS-BELY swil-bol.

1557. TUSSER, *Husbandrie*, Ap., 48, 20. Her milke-pan and creame-pot so slabbered and SOST.

1566. STILL, *Gammer Gurton's Needle*, v. 4. [DODSLEY, *Old Plays* (HAZLITT), iii. 183]. To dig and delve, in water, mire, and clay, SOSSING and possing in the dirt.

1611. COTGRAVE, *Dict.* s.v. A great, unweldie, long, mishapen, ill-favoured, or ill-fashioned man or woman; a luske, a slouche; a SOSSE.

1710-11. SWIFT, *Letter to Stella*, 10 Mar. I went to-day into the city, but in a coach, and SOSSED up my leg on the seat. *Ibid.* SOSSING in an easy chair.

1767. STERNE, *Tristram Shandy*, III. xxiv. She fell backward SOSS against the bridge.

1870. JUDD, *Margaret*, 8. She sat down and SOZZLED her feet in the foam.

1873. WHITNEY, *Other Girls*, xiii. Folks grow helplesser all the time, and the help grows SOZZLIER. *Ibid.*, *Leslie Goldthwaite*, xii. The woman . . . had always hated . . . anything like what she called a SOZZLE . . . always screwed-up and sharp-set to hard work.

1897. MARSHALL, *Pomes*, 75. She was thick in the clear, Fairly SOSSELLED on beer.

SPADE, *subs.* (old). — A eunuch: also SPADO (*q.v.*). Hence as *verb.* = to unsex.

1612. CHAPMAN, *Widow's Tears*, v. 5. I'll have all young widows SPADED for marrying again.

TO CALL A SPADE A SPADE, *verb. phr.* (old). — To speak plainly; to eschew paraphrasis and ambiguity.

*c.*1588. *Mar-Prelate's Epitome*, 2. I am plaine, I must needs CALL A SPADE A SPADE, a pope a pope.

1621. BURTON, *Anat. Melan.*, Pref. I CALL A SPADE A SPADE; I respect matter, not words.

1630. TAYLOR, *Works*. And CALL A SPADE A SPADE, a sicophant A flatt'ring knave. *Ibid.*, ii. 92. I think it good, plaine English, without fraud, To CALL A SPADE A SPADE, a bawd a bawd.

1706. WARD, *Hudibras Redivivus.* Hush, says my friend, mind what you say . . . We must not CALL A SPADE A SPADE.

1725. BAILEY, *Erasmus*, 'Philetymus and Pseudochius.' But this art is what we dullards call theft, who CALL a fig a fig, and A SPADE A SPADE.

1809. MALKIN, *Gil Blas* [ROUTLEDGE], 147. Don Gonzales . . . could not stomach those beauties who CALL A SPADE A SPADE . . .; the rites of Venus must be consummated in the temple of Vesta.

1862. THACKERAY, *Philip*, xxiii. Chesham does not like to CALL A SPADE A SPADE. He calls it a horticultural utensil.

See SHOVEL.

SPADGE, *subs.* (Christ's Hospital).—An affected walk. Formerly merely = to walk.

SPADGER, *subs.* (provincial).—A sparrow.

SPADO, *subs.* (old).—1. A sword: 'that is (GROSE) *spadone*.'

1711. CENTLIVRE, *Marplot*, i. 1. By St. Anthony you shall feel what mettle my SPADO is made of.

2. (old).—An eunuch. Hence SPADONIC = eunuchistic; and SPADONISM = eunuchry. In civil law (modern) = an impotent: also (provincial) = a gelding.

SPAIN. A CASTLE IN SPAIN, *subs. phr.* (old).—A day-dream; idle fancies. Thus TO BUILD A CASTLE IN SPAIN (IN THE AIR, THE SKIES, or TO BUILD A CASTLE) = to indulge in visionary projects or schemes; to romance. Fr. *château en Espagne, en Asie, en Albanie*, &c. *See* AIR.

*c.*1400. *Rom. Rose*, 2573. Thou shalt make CASTELS thanne IN SPAYNE, And dreme of joye, alle but in vayne.

1475. CAXTON, *Jason*, 19. He began to make CASTELLIS IN SPAYGNE as louers doo.

1586. T. B., *La Primand Fr. Acad.*, ii. 182. Some . . . have their wittes a wool-gathering, and as wee use commonly to say, are building of CASTLES IN SPAINE.

1611. COTGRAVE, *Dict.*, s.v. *Faire des chasteaux en Espaigne*, TO BUILD CASTLES IN THE AIRE (say we).

1809. MALKIN, *Gil Blas* (1812), VII. x. I was gradually lulled with so much wealth, and fell asleep in the very act of building CASTLES IN SPAIN.

1860. MOTLEY, *Netherlands*, iv. 282. The explosion of the Gunpowder Plot blowing the CASTLES IN SPAIN into the air.

1871. M. COLLINS, *Marquis and Merchant*, II. vii. 203. We have all had our CASTLES IN SPAIN.

SPALPEEN, *subs.* (Irish). — A generic term of contempt.

1809-12. EDGEWORTH, *Love and Law*, i. 4. The SPALPEEN! turned into a buckeen that would be a squireen, but can't.

*d.*1845. HOOD, *Irish Schoolmaster*. How many pigs be born to each SPALPEEN?

1857. KINGSLEY, *Two Years Ago*, xix. I've brought away the poor SPALPEEN of a priest, and have got him safe in the house.

SPAN- (SPANDY-, or SPANFIRE-) NEW. *See* SPICK-AND-SPAN.

SPANGE, *adj.* and *adv.* (Royal Military Academy).—New; dressy; SMART (*q.v.*): *e.g.* a SPANGE uniform = a new outfit; or 'You look SPANGE enough.'

SPANGLE, *subs.* (obsolete). — A seven-shilling piece: *see* RHINO (GROSE and VAUX).

SPANGLE-SHAKER (or **-GUTS**), *subs. phr.* (theatrical).—A harlequin.

SPANIEL, *subs.* (old).—A parasite: as *adj.* = servile: as *verb.* = to fawn, to be obsequious.

1601. SHAKSPEARE, *Julius Cæsar*, iii. 1, 43. Low crooked court'sies, and base SPANIEL-FAWNING.

1638. FORD, *Fancies*, iii. 3. He unhappy man! whom your advancement Hath ruin'd by being SPANIEL to your fortunes, Will curse he train'd me hither.

SPANISH. SPANISH, like DUTCH (*q.v.*), IRISH (*q.v.*), &c., contributes to colloquial English. Thus SPANISH = (1) money, spec. ready money: in America silver only; and (2) 'fair words and compliments' (B. E. and GROSE); SPANISH-FAGOT = the sun (GROSE); SPANISH-GOUT

(NEEDLE, or POX) = syphilis: *see* FRENCH-GOUT and LADIES'-FEVER; SPANISH-PADLOCK = 'a kind of girdle contrived by jealous husbands of that nation to secure the chastity of their wives' (GROSE); SPANISH-PIKE = a needle; SPANISH-PLAGUE = building (RAY); SPANISH-TRUMPETER (or KING OF SPAIN'S TRUMPETER, *i.e.*, DON KEY) = a braying ass (GROSE); TO WALK SPANISH = to be seized by the scruff and the seat, and thus forced along; hence, to act under compulsion; TO RIDE THE SPANISH MARE (nautical) = a punishment in which the offender was set astride a beam with the guys loosed, when the vessel was in a sea-way.

1656. FORD, *Sun's Darling*, ii. 1. A French gentleman, that trails a SPANISH PIKE; a tailor.

1837. BARHAM, *Ingoldsby Leg.* Save its synonyms SPANISH, blunt, stumpy and rowdy.

SPANK, *subs.* (colloquial). — A sounding thwack: spec. on the buttocks (GROSE): also SPANKER. As *verb.* = to strike. Whence SPANKING = a beating.

1772. BRIDGES, *Burlesque Homer*, 491. But Ajax gave him two such SPANKERS, They smarted worse than nodes and shankers.

1857. TENNYSON, *Northern Cobbler*. An' 'e SPANKS 'is 'and into mine.

1869. L. M. ALCOTT, *Little Women*, xxxviii. Meg led her son away, feeling a strong desire TO SPANK the little marplot.

1883. *Century Mag.*, xxvii. 743. My mother lifted me cleverly, planted two SPANKS behind, and passed me to the hands of Madame.

1885. *Queen*, 28 Sept. Suggested SPANKING all round as a cure for the evil.

Verb. (old). — 1. 'To run neatly along between a trot and a gallop' (GROSE), to move quickly and briskly: usually with 'along.'

SPANKING, *adj.* = (1) big, jolly, sprightly: as a SPANKING lass (BAILEY); (2) large, big (BAILEY and GROSE), STUNNING (*q.v.*), WHOPPING (*q.v.*); and (3) dashing, free-going. Hence SPANKER = anything of exceptional size, pace, figure, or merit: *cf.* SKELP, 'He's a SPANKER to go.' SPANKY = showy, SMART (*q.v.*).

1751. SMOLLETT, *Pereg. Pickle*, lxxxvii. His desire being titillated by the contact of a buxom wench . . . he . . . suddenly broke out . . . ''Sblood, I believe master thinks I have no more stuff in my body than a dried haddock, to turn me adrift in the dark with such a SPANKER.'

1772. BRIDGES, *Burlesque Homer*, 501. So spread a table . . . Whereon she placed a SPANKING dish.

1790. DIBDIN, *Sea Songs*, '. . . . . I've a SPANKING wife at Portsmouth gate, A pigmy at Goree.

1802. COLMAN, *Poor Gentleman*, iv. 2. There are four SPANKING greys ready harnessed . . . that shall whisk us to town in a minute.

1840. THACKERAY, *Shabby Genteel Story*, v. How knowingly did he SPANK the horses ALONG. *Ibid.* (1860), *Lovel the Widower*. Here a Gentleman in a natty gig, with a high trotting horse, came SPANKING towards us over the common.

1885. *Cassell's Sat. Jo.*, 19 Sep., 802. We SPANKED ALONG, rapidly accelerating our pace.

2. (thieves'). — To break, to smash: *e.g.*, TO SPANK THE GLAZE (*see* quot. 1785); also ON THE SPANK.

1785. GROSE, *Vulg. Tongue*, s.v. SPANK is, to break a pane in a shop window and to snatch some article, having tied the shop door to prevent pursuit (*Abridged*).

SPANKER, *subs.* (old).—1. In *pl.* = money: generic: spec. gold (GROSE).

2. (nautical).—A fore-and-aft gaff sail on the mizzen mast of a ship or barque (CLARK RUSSELL). Hence SPANKING = sailing swiftly along with the wind so quartered as to keep the SPANKERS full.

See SPANK.

SPARK, *subs.* (old).—1. A dandy: masc. or fem.: also SPARKLE; (2) a lover, and spec. (American) a sweetheart; and (3) a man or woman of pluck and parts. As *verb.* = to court, to gallant, *e.g.*, to SPARK a girl, or to SPARK a girl home. SPARKISH = (1) spirited: also SPARKFUL and SPARKY; and (2) = showy, dandified, gay (B. E. and GROSE).

1362. LANGLAND, *Piers Plowman* [SKEAT], C. xxi. 12. SPRAKLICHE he lokede.

[?]. *Robin Hood* [CHILD, *Ballads*, v. 358]. Robbin Hood upon him set With his couragious SPARKES.

1601. JONSON, *Poetaster*, i. 1. Thy son's a gallant SPARK, and must not be put out of a sudden.

1605. CAMDEN, *Remains*, 'Languages.' Hitherto will our SPARKEFULL youth laugh at their great grandfather's English.

1612. CHAPMAN, *Widow's Tears*, i. I will wed thee To my great widdowes daughter and sole heire, The lovely SPARKE, the bright Laodice.

1632. MASSINGER [?], *City Madam*, iv. 2. Shew yourself city-SPARKS, and hang up money.

1633. MARMION, *Antiquary*, i. What pretty SPARKLE of humanity have we here?

*d.*1643. CARTWRIGHT, *Ordinary*, iii. 5. Save you, boon SPARKS! Will't please you to admit me.

[?]. BISHOP, *Marrow of Astrology*, 55. When Venus is ill-placed she inclines men to be . . . lustful, followers of wenches . . . a fantastic SPARK . . . coveting unlawful beds . . . , if a woman, very impudent in all her ways.

1654. WEBSTER, *Appius and Virginia* [DODSLEY, *Old Plays* (HAZLITT), iv. 112]. But stay: behold the peerless SPARKS, whereof my tongue did talk.

1662. PEPYS, *Diary*, 7 Sep. Here I also saw Madame Castlemaine, and . . . the King's bastard, a most pretty SPARKE.

1675. WYCHERLEY, *Country Wife*, iv. 2. I have been detained by a SPARKISH coxcomb.

1687. BROWN, *Works*, I. 94, 'The Saints in an Uproar.' Those old-fashioned SPARKS yonder.

1692. LESTRANGE, *Æsop* [*Century*]. A daw, to be SPARKISH, trick'd himself up with all the gay feathers he could muster.

1693. DRYDEN, *Love Triumph*, Prol. 24. No *double entendres*, which you SPARKS allow, To make the ladies look—they know not how.

1709. WARD, *Works*, I. v. 6. Some Associate who . . . will very readily swear she is both a Whore and a Pick-pocket, which terrible Accusation soon frights away her SPARK. *Ibid.* (1711), *Don Quixote*, 10. The gay Damsel that is taught, By some loose SPARK to know what's what.

1749. FIELDING, *Hist. Foundling*, VIII. ii. I'd rather have the soldiers than officers; for nothing is ever good enough for those SPARKS.

1773. GOLDSMITH, *She Stoops*, &c., iii. Fly to your SPARK; he'll tell you more of the matter.

1777. SHERIDAN, *School for Scandal*, i. 2. Their worthy father . . . was . . . nearly as wild a SPARK.

1801. DIBDIN, *Il Bondocani*, iii. 3. None of your wishy-washy SPARKS that mince their steps.

1820. IRVING, *Sketch Book*, 432. A sure sign that his master was courting, or as it is termed SPARKING.

1832. LONGSTREET, *Southern Sketches*, 120. Some think I ought to get married, and two or three have tried TO SPARK IT with me.

1840. BARHAM, *Ingoldsby Leg.*, 'St. Gengulphus.' A spruce young SPARK of a Learned Clerk Had called on his Lady, and stopped to tea.

1844. THACKERAY, *Barry Lyndon*, i. The company of . . . two or three other young SPARKS of the town.

1846. KIRKLAND, *West. Clearings*, 16. That was the way young men cast sheep's eyes when they went a SPARKING.

1888. EGGLESTON, *Graysons*, xxxiii. The boys that do a good deal of SPARKING, and the girls that have a lot of beaux don't always get married first.

1897. MARSHALL, *Pomes*, 48. He found her at supper with some other SPARKS.

2. (thieves'). — A diamond: also SPARKLE. A SPARK-PROP = a diamond breast-pin.

1879. HORSLEY, *Auto. of Thief* [*Macmillan Mag.*, xl. 506]. Pipe his SPARK PROP.

Verb. (Australian thieves').—To watch closely.

1901. WALKER, *In the Blood*, 113, All you've got to do is to be sure o' your John, an' learn the time 'e comes round, SPARK him well away and do yer little does in the blooming hinterval.

A SPARK IN THE THROAT, *subs. phr.* (old).—Chronic thirst (GROSE).

SPARKLER, *subs.* — Anybody or anything brilliant, gay, or lively: *see* SPARK.

1713. ADDISON, *Guardian*, No. 120. What would you say, should you see a SPARKLER shaking her elbow for a whole night together.

1879. H. W. WARREN, *Astronomy*, 113. [Mercury] keeps so near the sun . . . that very few people have ever seen the brilliant SPARKLER.

SPARROW. MUMBLING A SPARROW, *phr.* (old).—*See* quot.

1785. GROSE, *Vulg. Tongue*, s.v. SPARROW. A cruel sport practised at wakes and fairs: a booby, hands tied behind, has the wing of a cock-sparrow put into his mouth; without any other assistance than the motion of his lips he is to get the sparrow's head into his mouth; the bird defends itself surprisingly, pecking the mumbler till his lips are covered with blood and he is obliged to desist; to prevent the bird getting away he is fastened to the booby's coat.—[*Abridged.*]

SPARROW-CATCHING, *subs. phr.* (venery).—Walking the streets; doing a FLUTTER (*q.v.*).

SPARROWGRASS (or **SPARAGRAS**), *subs.* (old colloquial).—Asparagus: polite in the 18th Century; now vulgar.

1649. BLYTHE, *Eng. Improver Impr.* (1652), 237. [The Hop plant] comes up with several sprouts like SPARROWGRASS.

1667. PEPYS, *Diary* (1879), IV. 307. Brought with me from Fenchurch Street, a hundred of SPARROWGRASS.

1706. PHILLIPS, *Dict.*, s.v. ASPARAGUS, a Plant call'd SPARROW-GRASS by the Common People.

1711. GREENWOOD, *Eng. Gram.*, 190. Sperage, which the vulgar wrest to SPARROGRASS, or SPARROWGRASS.

1763. FOOTE, *Mayor of Garratt*, ii. 1. I should recommend the opening of a new branch of trade, SPARAGRASS, gentlemen.

1801. SOUTHEY [C. SOUTHEY, *Life*, II. 134]. SPARAGRASS (it ought to be spelt so) and artichokes, good with plain butter.

SPARROW-MOUTH, *subs. phr.* (old).—'One whose mouth cannot be enlarged without removing the ears'; as *adj.* = wide-mouthed: 'such persons do not hold their mouths by lease but have it from (y)ear to (y)ear' (GROSE).

1621. BURTON, *Anat. Melan.*, III. II. v. 3. She . . . if she do but laugh or smile, makes an ugly SPARROW-MOUTHED face.

1725. BAILEY, *Erasmus* (1877), 31. Can you fancy that black-a-top, snub-nosed, SPARROW-MOUTH, paunch-bellied creature?

SPARROW-TAIL, *subs. phr.* (common).—A dress-coat; a SWALLOW-TAIL, CLAWHAMMER (*q.v.*).

1888. EGGLESTON, *Graysons*, xxvi. The lawyers in their blue SPARROW-TAIL coats, with brass buttons, which constituted then [*c.*1840] a kind of professional uniform.

SPAT, *subs.* (American). — 1. A slap; a light blow; and (2) = a petty quarrel; a snarling-match. Also as *verb.* = (1) to slap; and (2) to dispute, to quarrel. [WEBSTER: 'A low word.']

1869. STOWE, *Old Town Folks*, 33. They was pretty apt to have SPATS.

1870. JUDD, *Margaret*. The little Isabel leaped up and down SPATTING her hands.

1887. AMER. CORRESPONDENT, *Notes and Queries*, 12 Mar., 206. A SPAT between the feminine heads of two families.

SPATCH-COCK, *subs. phr.* (GROSE).—1. 'A fowl killed, dressed, and broiled at short notice'; SUDDEN DEATH (West Indies).

2. (military).—To insert hurriedly; to SANDWICH (*q.v.*).

1901. SIR R. BULLER, *Speech* [*Times*, 11 Oct., 10, 2]. I therefore SPATCHCOCKED into the middle of that telegram a sentence in which I suggested it would be necessary to surrender.

SPEAK, *verb.* (old thieves').—To steal: also TO SPEAK WITH: *see* PRIG. TO MAKE A GOOD (or RUM) SPEAK = to make a good (or bad) haul; SPOKEN TO = robbed: also SPOKE TO ON THE SCREW, CRACK, SNEAK, HOIST, BIG, &c. (*see* the nouns).—GROSE and VAUX.

PHRASES.—SPOKEN TO (thieves') = dying (VAUX); TO SPEAK TO (colloquial) = to admonish; TO SPEAK AT THE MOUTH = to talk freely; to say one's say; TO SPEAK DAGGERS (*see* DAGGER); 'Ale that would make a cat SPEAK' = strong ale; 'SPEAKS the parrot' = a taunting reply: *cf.* SKELTON, *Speke Parrot*; TO SPEAK (or TALK) BIG = to boast, to talk loudly; TO SPEAK FAIR = to use soft words.

1581. J. BELL, *Haddon's Answ. Osor.*, 360*b*. They . . . fashion theyr voyces BIGGE like olde men.

1591. LYLY, *Endimion*, v. 3. *Cynth.* SPEAKES THE PARROT? . . . cut off her tongue, nay, her head.

1591. SPENSER, *Virgil's Gnat.*, ii. This Muse shall SPEAK IN BIGGER notes.

1656. DUGARD, *Gate Lat. Unl.*, 701. The voice of striplings before they begin to SPEAK BIGG.

1709. *Colonial Records*, Penn., II. 501. It was necessary to TALK BIGG.

1872. INGELOW, *Off the Skelligs*, xix. 'Papa . . . will you SPEAK TO Giles? . . . If this sort of thing is allowed to go on . . . it will perfectly ruin the independance of my character.'

SPEARMEN. THE DELHI SPEARMEN, *subs. phr.* (military).—The 9th Lancers.

SPEC, *subs.* (common).—1. Speculation (BEE). Hence ON SPEC = on chance; on the hazard of the die.

1834. SOUTHEY, *Doctor*, clxxiii. He had engaged in this adventure (by which better word our forefathers designated what the Americans call a SPEC) with the hope of increasing his fortune.

1837. DICKENS, *Pickwick*, xxxiv. They said what a wery gen'rous thing it was o' them to have taken up the case ON SPEC, and to charge nothing at all for costs unless they got 'em out of Mr. Pickwick.

1837. KINGSLEY, *Two Years Ago* xxv. If tradesmen will run up houses ON SPEC in a water meadow who can stop them.

1873. GREENWOOD, *Strange Company*. Hundreds . . . had heard [it was] the best SPEC out.

2. (common).—In *pl.* = spectacles.

1837. BARHAM, *Ingoldsby Leg.*, 'Knight and Lady.' He wore green SPECS with a tortoise-shell rim.

1838. NEAL, *Charcoal Sketches*. My ma' was used to put on her SPECS.

3. (racing).—*See* quot.

1869. GREENWOOD, *Seven Curses*. Throughout lower London, and the shady portion of its suburbs, the window of almost every public-house and beershop was spotted with some notice of these SPECS . . . They all meant . . . a lottery, conducted on principles more or less honest, the prize to be awarded according to the performances of certain horses.

4. (Winchester College).—Anything enjoyable or pleasant; a good thing. ON SPEC = in consequence.

1891. WRENCH, *Winchester Word Book*, s.v. SPEC. What a SPEC! My pitch-up have turned up, and I've got leave out ON SPEC.

5. (Edinburgh Advocates').—The Speculative Society.

SPECIAL, *subs.* (old).—1. A paramour, male or female: *cf.* PARTICULAR.

*c.*1350. *Tale of the Basyn* [HAZLITT, *Early Pop. Poet.*, iii. 52], xxii. The wenche was his SPECIALL.

1440. *Prompt. Parv.*, 468. SPECYAL, concubyne, the womann (SPECIALL or leman). *Concubina.*

[?]. *Lytell Geste of Robin Hode* [CHILDE, *Ballads*, v. 123]. Syr Roger of Donkester That was her owne SPECIALL.

2. (colloquial).—By ellipsis a particular person or thing: *e.g.*, a SPECIAL train, SPECIAL Scotch, a SPECIAL constable, a SPECIAL edition, &c.

1890. *Lancet*, II. 796. What are known as SPECIALS are being held this week. These are for men who partially failed at the last regular examinations.

1897. MARSHALL, *Pomes*, 16. But Rosette for a potman's regard didn't care; She preferred her swell SPECIALS.

SPECK, *subs.* (costers').—In *pl.* = damaged oranges.

SPECKLEBELLY, *subs.* (provincial).—A dissenter. [HOTTEN: 'Used in Worcester and the North.']

SPEECH, *subs.* (racing).—Information: spec. a TIP (*q.v.*): *e.g.*, TO GIVE (or GET) THE SPEECH. Fr. *tuyau.*

SPEECHER, *subs.* (Harrow).—1. Speech-day: usually the first Thursday in July. THE SPEECHER = The Speech-room: built 1871.

SPEEDYMAN, *subs.* (Winchester: obsolete).—The herald of news of a vacancy at New College, Oxford. Whence SPED TO NEW COLLEGE = elected to a scholarship.

SPEEL, *verb.* (common).—To decamp: *see* ABSQUATULATE. TO SPEEL THE DRUM = to make off to the highway.

SPEELER, *subs.* (American).—A gambler. Also SPEEL (*see* quot.).

1896. LILLARD, *Poker Stories*, 151. We bet our money. They bet all they had, including a roll of bogus bills, called SPIELS, used for that kind of work [railway sharping], and pocketed all the money.

SPEG, *adj.* (Winchester: obsolete).—Smart.

SPELL, *subs.* (colloquial).—1. A turn of work [BAILEY: 'A sea term']. Hence 2. (spec. Australian) a turn of rest. Also (3) a period of love, weather, adventure, sickness, luck, temper, and so forth (*see* quot. 1869). As *verb.* = (1) to relieve; and (2) = to rest.

*c.*1586. HAKLUYT, *Voyages* [ARBER, *Eng. Garner*, 5, 514]. [OLIPHANT, *New Eng.*, ii. 6. Men work by SPELLS . . . there was an old English *spelung* (turn, change)].

1602. CAREW, *Survey of Cornwall*, fol. 11. Their toyl is so extreame as they cannot endure it above foure houres in a day, but are succeeded by SPELS.

1706. WARD, *Wooden World*, 25. He . . . believes there is no more Sin in taking a SPELL with a Whore, than in pumping a leaky Vessel.

1775. WASHINGTON, *Letter* 'To J. Reed,' 25 Dec. Nothing new has happened . . . except the setting in of a severe SPELL of cold weather, and a considerable fall of snow.

1823. *Jamaica Planters' Guide*, 340. Sometimes there are two ostensible boilers TO SPELL and relieve one another. When one is obliged to be SPELLED for the purpose of natural rest, he should leave his injunctions to a judicious negro.

1829. B. HALL, *Travels in N. A.*, I. 188. A poor old negro . . . offered to give me a SPELL when I became tired.

1835. CROCKETT, *Tour Down East*, 90. He had come home from the South, where he had been peddling a SPELL.

1846. J. L. STOKES, *Disc. in Australia*, II. 42. In order to SPELL the oars, we landed at a point on the east side.

1856. KANE, *Arctic Expl.*, I. 182. A gentle, misty air . . . makes me hope that we are going to have a warm SPELL.

1865. *Major Downing's Letters*, 35. Public affairs go on easier than they did a SPELL ago.

1869. STOWE, *Oldtown*, 171. When Hepsy does get beat out she has SPELLS, and she goes on awful, and they last day arter day.

1873. TROLLOPE, *Australia and New Zealand*, I. 84. Having a SPELL—what we should call a short holiday.

1877. R. W. DIXON, *Hist. Ch. Eng.*, xix. After a grievous SPELL of eighteen months on board the French galleys.

1880. G. N. OAKEY, *Victoria in 1880*, 114. He SPELLED upon the ground; a hollow Gum Bore up his ample back, and bade him rest.

1887. C. C. WARNER, *Pilgrimage*, 145. No, I hain't got a girl now. I had one a SPELL, but I'd rather do my own work.

1887. HOWELLS, *Annie Kilburn*, xvi. Don't you want I should SPELL you a little while, Miss Kilburn?

1890. BOLDREWOOD, *Colonial Reformer*, xxiv. 328. There's a hundred and fifty stock-horses there, SPELLING for next winter's work.

1896. BALD. SPENCER, *Horne Exp.*, 48. Beside a water-pool . . . we SPELLED for a day.

Verb. (thieves').—To advertise: SPELT IN THE LEAR = WANTED (*q.v.*).

TO SPELL FOR (or AT), *verb. phr.* (colloquial).—To desire; to hanker after: indirectly.

1821. COOMBE, *Syntax*, III. iv. Syntax with native keenness felt At what the cunning tradesman SPELT.

See BAKER; BACKWARD; SPELLKEN.

SPELL-BINDER, *subs. phr.* (American).—A speaker who holds (or thinks he holds) his hearers 'spell-bound.'

SPELL-KEN (SPELL or SPEELKEN), *subs. phr.* (old).—A theatre (GROSE and VAUX).

*c.*1800. JACKSON [quoted by BYRON in notes to *Don Juan*, xi. 19]. If you at the SPELLKEN can't hustle, You'll be hobbled in making a Clout.

1819. VAUX, *Memoirs*, s.v. Push . . . When any particular scene of crowding is alluded to, they say, the push . . . at the SPELL doors; the push at the stooping-match.

1823. BYRON, *Don Juan*, xi. 19. Who in a row like Tom could lead the van, Booze in the Ken, or at the SPELLKEN hustle?

SPEND. TO SPEND THE MOUTH, *verb. phr.* (old).—To give voice; to talk; and (of dogs) to bark.

1593. SHAKSPEARE, *Venus and Adonis*, 695. Then do they SPEND THEIR MOUTHS.

SPEND-ALL, *subs. phr.* (old).—A prodigal; a spendthrift.

1591. LYLY, *Man in the Moone*. Thy wife shall be enamoured of some SPEND-ALL, which shall wast all as licentiously as thou hast heaped together laboriously.

1598. FLORIO, *Worlde of Wordes*, s.v. *Allarga la mano*, a SPEND ALL, a wast-good.

SPENDINGS, *subs. phr.* (venery).—Semen; CREAM (*q.v.*). Hence TO SPEND = to ejaculate.

1598. SHAKSPEARE, *All's Well*, ii. 3, 296. He wears his honour in a box unseen, That hugs his kicky-wicky here at home, SPENDING his manly marrow in her arms.

*d.*1680. ROCHESTER, *Works* (1718), 'The Debauchee,' 143. I SPEND in her hand and spue in her lap. *Ibid.*, 'A Ramble,' &c., 82. A passive pot for fools to SPEND in. *Ibid.*, 'The Disappointment.' May'st thou ne'er piss that did'st refuse to SPEND.

1772. BRIDGES, *Burlesque Homer*, 196. With such a tool I thought he'd split her . . . she held it fast, and made it stand, And SPEND its venom in her hand.

*d.*1892. WHITMAN, *Children of Adam*. My love-SPENDINGS.

SPESS, *subs.* (Felsted School).—*See* quot.

1899. *Felstedian*, July, 66. Others . . . calling out . . . 'frightful SPESSES,' which word is 'specimens.'

SPEW, *verb.* (venery).—To ejaculate; TO SPEND (*q.v.*). Whence SPEW ALLEY = the female *pudendum*: *see* MONOSYLLABLE.

*d.*1680. ROCHESTER, *Works*, 'Tunbridge Wells' (1718), i. 29. Importance, thinks too, tho' she'd been no sinner To wash away some dregs he had SPEWED in her.

TO SPEW OAKUM, *verb. phr.* (nautical).—A ship spews oakum when the seams start.

SPEW ALLEY, *subs. phr.* (common).—The throat: *see* GUTTER LANE.

SPHERE, *subs.* (athletic).—A football.

SPICE, *verb.* (thieves').—To rob: hence, THE SPICE (or HIGH TOBY SPICE) = highway robbery; SPICER (or SPICE-GLOAK) = a footpad (GROSE and VAUX).

*c.*1800. JACKSON [quoted by BYRON in *Don Juan*, Notes to Canto xi.]. On the HIGH TOBY SPICE flash the muzzle.

SPICE-ISLAND, *subs. phr.* (old).—1. The rectum; and (2) = a privy; STINK-HOLE BAY; DILBERRY CREEK (GROSE). Whence (3) = any filthy, stinking neighbourhood (BEE).

SPICK-AND-SPAN NEW, *adj.* (colloquial).—Quite fresh; brand new: as a 'spike and chip' from the workman's hands. Also SPICK-AND-SPAN; SPICK-SPAN NEW; SPAN-NEW; and SPAN-FIRE NEW. Also SPICK-AND-SPAN (SPAN, or SPANDY), *adv.* = quite; wholly.

1369. CHAUCER, *Troilus*, iii. 1665. This tale ay was SPAN-NEWE to beginne.

1614. TOMKIS, *Albumazar* [DODSLEY, *Old Plays* (REED), vii. 161]. Of a stark clown I shall appear SPECK AND SPAN gentleman.

1614. JONSON, *Barthol. Fayre*, iii. 5. Sir, this is a spell against them, SPICK AND SPAN NEW.

1619. FLETCHER, *False One*, iii. 2. Am I not totally a SPAN-NEW gallant, Fit for the choicest eye?

1628. FORD, *Lover's Melancholy*, ii. 1. 'Tis a fashion of the newest edition, SPICK AND SPAN NEW, without example.

*c.*1630. HOWELL, *Letters*, I. iv. 2. Blackfriars will entertain you with a Play SPICK AND SPAN NEW, and the Cockpit with another.

1663. BUTLER, *Hudibras*, I. iii. 398. The honour thou hast got Is SPICK AND SPAN NEW, piping hot.

1718. BUCKINGHAM, *Rehearsal*. Why madam, an intire SPICK AND SPAN NEW piece of doctrine of my own invention.

*d.*1779. GARRICK [W. COOKE, *Memoirs of S. Foote*, I. 107. From our poetic storehouse we produce A couple SPICK AND SPAN for present use.

1824. SCOTT, *Redgauntlet*, xi. In the same doings to make a SPICK-AND-SPAN new world.

1857. TENNYSON, *Northern Cobbler*. Look at the cloaths on 'er back, thebbe ammost SPICK-SPAN-NEW.

1877. TROLLOPE, *South Africa*, II. vi. The Dutch Boer will not endure over him . . . a SPICK-AND-SPAN Dutch Africander from the Cape Colony.

1884. JAMES, *Little Tour*, 178. Beside my hotel rose a big SPICK-AND SPAN church.

1887. *Referee*, 27 Feb. The SPICK-AND-SPAN appearance presented by Marlow after their journey.

1888. L. M. ALCOT, *Hospital Sketches*, 319. Thirty gentlemen with SPANDY clean faces and hands were partaking of refreshment.

SPICY, *adj.* (common).—1. Racy; FULL-FLAVOURED (*q.v.*); SMUTTY (*q.v.*); NUTTY (*q.v.*). 2. = showy, handsome, SMART (*q.v.*).

1844. *Puck*, 14. The milliners' hearts he did trepan, My SPICY, swell small-college man.

1868. WHYTE MELVILLE, *White Rose*, I. xiii. Bless'd if there isn't Snipe . . . there's a drummer holding his nag. What a SPICY chestnut it is.

*d.*1872. LEVER, *Rent in a Cloud*, 58. A SPICY bit of scandal.

1897. MARSHALL, *Pomes*, 88. Their jokelets more SPICY than witty.

3. (venery).—JUICY (*q.v.*): of women.

SPIDDOCK-POT LEGS, *subs. phr.* (old). — Large awkward legs (HALLIWELL).

SPIDER, *subs.* (common).—Claret and lemonade.

TO SWALLOW A SPIDER, *verb. phr.* (old). — To go bankrupt (RAY).

SPIDER-CATCHER, *subs. phr.* (B. E.). —'A Spindle of a Man.' Also (HALLIWELL)=a monkey.

SPIDER-CLAW, *verb. phr.* (venery). —To grasp and roke the *testes* in the palm and fingers.

SPIDER-SHANKED, *adj. phr.* (old). —Long legged (GROSE). SPIDER-SHANKS = a lanky fellow: *see* LAMP-POST.

1827. LYTTON, *Pelham*, lxxxii. The tallest of the set, who bore the euphonious appellation of SPIDER-SHANKS.

SPIDER-WEB, *subs. phr.* (B. E.).— 'The subtilties of Logic, which, tho' artificial to sight, were yet of no Use.'

SPIDIREEN, *subs.* (nautical).—An imaginary vessel figuring in an unwilling reply: 'What ship do you belong to?' 'The SPIDIREEN frigate, with nine decks, and ne'er a bottom.'

SPIEL. *See* SPIELER.

SPIERIZE, *verb.* (Oxf. Univ. Cant). —To have one's hair cut and dressed. [Spiers was a barber in The High.]

SPIFFING, *adj.* (common). — A generic intensitive: of pleasure or admiration: used for anything or anybody out of the common: *e.g.*, a SPIFFING TIME OR GIRL; awfully SPIFF; 'How SPIFF you look'; 'How are you?' 'Pretty SPIFF'; and so forth. Also SPIFF, *subs.* = a swell.

1891. *Harry Fludyer*, 119. Pat of course looked as if he had just walked out of a ban-box, and the Mater and the girls looked SPIFFING.

2. (drapers').—In *pl.* = a percentage on the sale of old or 'dead' stock.

SPIFFED, *adj.* (common).—Drunk: *see* SCREWED.

SPIFLICATE (**SPIFFLICATE**, or **SMIFLIGATE**), *verb.* (common).— To confound; to crush; to SMASH (*q.v.*). Hence SPIFLICATION = confusion; annihilation (GROSE). *See* quot. 1823.

1823. BEE, *Dict. Turf*, s.v. SPIFLICATE. To SPIFLICATE a thief is to spill him, or betray the subject of his roguery.

1837. BARHAM, *Ingoldsby Leg.* So out with your whinger at once And scrag Jane, while I SPIFLICATE Johnny.

1856. R. F. BURTON, *El. Medinah*, I. 264. Whose blood he vowed to drink—the Oriental form of threatening SPIFLICATION.

1873. *Brit. Quart. Rev.*, lvii. 276. The way in which the learned, racy old Hector smashes and SPIFLICATES scientific idiots . . . is delicious.

1899. HYNE, *Furth. Adv. Captain Kettle*, ix. 'Very well. Den we shall SPIFLICATE you until you do.' 'I wonder what SPIFLICATION is,' mused Kettle.

1901. WALKER, *In the Blood*, 170. Then they threatened to SPIFLIGATE him if he stirred, and made off.

SPIGOT, *subs.* (venery).—The *penis*: *see* PRICK.

1653. URQUHART, *Rabelais*, I. iii. Honest widows may without danger play at the close-buttock game with might and main for the . . . first two months . . . If the devil would not have them to bag, he must wring hard the SPIGOT, and stop the bung-hole.

SPIGOT-SUCKER, *subs. phr.* (old).— *See* quot., LUSHINGTON, and KNIGHT.

1611. COTGRAVE, *Dict.*, s.v. *Pinteur*. A tippler, pot-companion, SPIGGOT-SUCKER.

2. (venery).—A mouth-whore; a STAND (*q.v.*): *cf.* SPIGOT.

SPIKE, *subs.* (tramps').—A casual ward. SPIKE-RANGER=a tramper from ward to ward.

1866. *Temple Bar*, xvi. 184. Let the SPIKES be what they may they were a great deal better than the padding-kens.

1897. *Quiver*, 846. I sat there for two hours anxiously looking for a typical SPIKE-RANGER—one . . . who can tell you with amazing accuracy precisely what you may expect at any given workhouse.

1900. FLYNT, *Tramps*, 260. The next two nights of our stay as tramps in London were spent in the Notting Hill . . . SPIKE as it is called in tramp parlance.

2. (venery).—An erection: *see* HORN. As *verb.*=to copulate: *see* RIDE; SPIKE-FAGGOT = the *penis*.

SPIKE-PARK, *subs. phr.* (obsolete). —The Queen's Bench prison.

SPILL, *subs.* (old).—1. A small fee, reward, or gift of money (B. E.).

1726. AYLIFFE, *Parergon*. The bishops who consecrated the ground were wont to have a SPILL or sportule from the credulous laity.

2. (colloquial). — A fall; a tumble. As *verb.*=to throw; to fall; to overturn (GROSE and BEE). Also (3)=to betray (BEE).

1881. BURROUGHS, *Pepacton*, 217. Its body slumps off, and rolls, and SPILLS down the hill.

1886. *Field*, 2 Jan. A quick drive along the frosty road, ending in a harmless SPILL.

TO SPILL STOCK, *verb. phr.* (American).—*See* quot.

1870. MEDBERY, *Men, &c., in Wall St.* [BARTLETT]. To SPILL STOCK is to throw great quantities upon the market, sometimes from necessity, but often in order to 'break' the price.

SPILL-GOOD, *subs. phr.* (old).—A spendthrift (MINSHEU).

SPILLSBURY, *subs.* (old).—Failure: *e.g.*, 'to come by SPILLSBURY': *cf.* BEDFORDSHIRE, PECKHAM, CLAPHAM, &c.

1692. HACKET, *Williams*, i. 208. They might seek their fortune . . . and come home by SPILLSBURY.

SPILL-TIME, *subs. phr.* (old).—An idler.

1362. LANGLAND, *Piers Ploughman*, C. vi. 28. A splendour that spende mot other a SPILLE-TYME.

SPILT-MILK. TO CRY OVER SPILT-MILK, *verb. phr.* (colloquial).— To lament what is past recovery or mending.

1877. *New York Tribune*, 10 Mar. 'Letter from Washington.' The Democrats . . . are CRYING, and cursing too, OVER SPILLED MILK.

1900. DOWLING, *Tempest Driven*, vi. There's no use crying over SPILT MILK. What we have to ask ourselves is: How can it be best faced?

SPIN, *subs.* (colloquial).—A brisk run, a smart canter, a spurt. As *verb.*=to go quickly: usually TO SPIN ALONG.

1854. WILKIE COLLINS, *Hide and Seek*, ii. 4. While it [money] lasts, make it SPIN.

1883. S. LANIER. *Eng. Novel*, 3. The locomotive SPINS ALONG no less merrily because ten car-loads of rascals may be profiting by its speed.

1884. *Field*, 6 Dec. After a short undecided SPIN, Athos took a good lead.

Verb. (Royal Military Academy).—To reject; TO PLOUGH; TO PLUCK (*q.v.*). Also TO GET A SPIN.

1868. WHYTE MELVILLE, *White Rose*, I. x. Don't you funk being SPUN?

PHRASES. TO SPIN A YARN= to tell a story: originally nautical; TO SPIN STREET-YARN=to gad, to LOAF (*q.v.*); TO SPIN A FAIR THREAD=to busy oneself about trifles (RAY); TO SPIN OUT = to prolong unreasonably; 'She'd rather kiss than SPIN' (of a wanton).

*d.*1704. LESTRANGE, *Works* [*Century*]. By one delay after another, they SPIN OUT their whole lives.

1779. SHERIDAN, *Critic*, i. 1. Do you mean that the story is tediously SPUN OUT?

1837. PRESCOTT, *Ferd. and Isabella*, ii. 13. He endeavoured, however, to gain further time by SPINNING OUT the negotiation.

18 [?]. *Widow Bedott Papers*, 149. They say when Sally Hugle ain't a SPINNIN' street-yarn, she don't do nothing but write poetry.

1885. *Observer*, 20 Dec. The YARN IS SPUN by Ben Campion, the old salt who was its hero.

SPINDLE, *subs.* (venery). — The *penis*: *see* PRICK.

TO MAKE (or SPIN) CROOKED SPINDLES, *verb. phr.* (old).—*See* quot.

1598. FLORIO, *Worlde of Wordes*. A woman that MAKES or SPINS CROOKED SPINDLES, that is, maketh her husband cuckold.

SPINDLE-LEGS (or **-SHANKS**), *subs. phr.* (colloquial).—1. Long, thin legs: hence (2) a tall, slender person; a LAMP-POST (*q.v.*). Also as *adj.* (or SPINDLY) = thin, slim (GROSE).

1570. *Marr., Wit and Science* [DODSLEY, *Old Plays* (HAZLITT), ii. 336]. But what, if she find fault with these SPINDLE-SHANKS.

1703. STEELE, *Tender Husband*, i. 1. A Weezel-faced cross old Gentleman with SPINDLE-SHANKS.

1715. ADDISON, *Drummer*, i. 1. This SPINDLE-SHANKED fellow.

1723. SWIFT, *Mary the Cookmaid's Letter* [CHALMERS, *Eng. Poets*, xi. 433]. My master is a personable man, and not a SPINDLE-SHANKED hoddy-doddy.

1888. *Pop. Sci. Monthly*, xxxvi. 556. The effect of all this may be easily imagined —a SPINDLY growth of rootless ideas.

SPINK, *subs.* (Royal Military Academy).—Milk: new or condensed.

SPINNING- (or **SPIN-**) **HOUSE**, *subs. phr.* (old).—A house of correction or Bridewell for loose women. [The task work consisted of spinning or beating hemp.] Hence SPINSTER = a harlot. [The term is still applied to the prison for disorderly women attached to the Vice-Chancellor's Court at the University of Cambridge.]

1622. FLETCHER, *Prophetess*, iii. 1. We are no SPINSTERS; nor if you look upon us, So wretched as you take us.

1641. EVELYN, *Diary*, 19 Aug. As we returned we stepp'd in to see the SPINHOUSE, a kind of Bridewell, where incorrigible and lewd women are kept in discipline and order.

1662. FULLER, *Worthies of England*, Kent. Many would never be wretched SPINSTERS were they spinsters in deed, nor come to so public and shameful punishments.

SPINNIKEN (tramps').—St. Giles' Workhouse; LARGE HOUSE (*q.v.*).

SPINSRAP, *subs.* (back slang).—A parsnip.

SPINTEXT, *subs.* (old).—A parson; spec. a prosy preacher.

1693. CONGREVE, *Old Bachelor*, i. 1. SPINTEXT! Oh, the fanatic one-eyed parson.

*d.*1704. BROWN, *Works*, ii. 236. Mr. SPINTEXT the preacher, or Mr. Lovelady the chaplain.

*c.*1712. WARD, *Works* (1718), iii. 'Libertine's Answ. to his Uncle.' I . . . cannot but believe you have been at the expence of imploying some superannuated SPINTEXT, to rattle off your poor nephew.

1788. V. KNOX, *Winter Evenings*, ix. The race of formal SPINTEXTS, and solemn saygraces is nearly extinct.

SPIRIT. TO SPIRIT AWAY, *verb. phr.* (old).—To kidnap (B. E. and GROSE). Hence SPIRITER= an abductor.

1675. COTTON, *Burlesque on Burlesque*, 257. While the poor boy half dead with fear, Writh'd back to view his SPIRITER.

*c.*1730. ARBUTHNOT and POPE [*Ency. Dict.*]. The ministry had him SPIRITED AWAY, and carried abroad as a dangerous person.

SPIRITUAL FLESH-BROKER, *subs.* (old).—A parson: *see* BLACK-SPY (B. E. and GROSE).

SPIRIT OF HARTSHORN. *See* HORN.

SPIT, *subs.* (colloquial). — 1. A speaking likeness; orig. 'as like as if he'd spit it'; usually in phrase 'the SPIT of (someone named).'—GROSE. Fr. *C'est son père tout craché.*

1602. BRETON, *Merry Wonders*, 8. Twoo girles . . . the one as like an owle, the other AS LIKE an urchin, AS IF they had beene SPITTE OUT OF THE MOUTHS of them.

1675. COTTON, *Burl. on Burl.*, 278. Nay, I'm as like my dad, in sooth, As he had SPIT ME OUT ON'S MOUTH. *Ibid.*, *Virgil Travestie*, iv. (1770), 60. I dare be sworn 'twas thou did'st get him, He's e'en as like thee as th' had'st SPIT him.

1698. FARQUHAR, *Love and a Bottle*, i. 1. Poor child! he's as like his own dadda as if he were SPIT OUT OF HIS MOUTH.

1751. SMOLLETT, *Per. Pickle*, xiii. He is the very moral of you, and as like as if he had been SPIT OUT OF YOUR OWN MOUTH.

1851-61. MAYHEW, *Lond. Lab.*, II. 488. The very SPIT of the one I had for years; it's a real portrait.

2. (Old Cant). — A sword (GROSE).

1613. PURCHAS, *Pilgrimage*, 309. Going naked with a SPIT on his shoulder.

3. (printers').—An obelisk or dagger; †: used as a reference mark.

*d.*1656. HALL, *To Hugh Cholmley* [LATHAM]. Either your starres or your SPITS . . . shall be welcome to my margent.

Verb. (colloquial).—1. To show signs of rain: also as *subs.*= drops of rain.

1818. FERRIER, *Marriage*, vii. 'And' —putting her hand out of the window—'I think it's SPITTING already.'

*d.*1870. DICKENS, *Sketches*, *Tales*, vii. It had been SPITTING with rain for the last half-hour, and now began to pour in good earnest.

1887. WARNER, *Pilgrimage*, 175. SPITS of rain dashed in their faces.

2. (venery).—To foraminate a woman.

PHRASES.—A SPIT AND A STRIDE = a very short distance; TO SPIT AT ONE = to insult; TO SPIT IT OUT = to speak plainly; TO SPIT WHITE (WHITE BROTH, or SIXPENCES)=to expectorate from a dry but healthy mouth: Fr. *cracher des pièces de dix sous*; TO PUT FOUR QUARTERS ON THE SPIT = to know carnally.

1594. LYLY, *Mother Bombie*, iii. 1 [NARES]. That makes them SPIT WHITE BROATH, as they do.

1598. SHAKSPEARE, 2 *Hen. IV.*, i. 2, 237. If it be a hot day, and I brandish anything but a bottle, I would I might never SPIT WHITE again.

1603. *Measure for Meas.*, ii. 1. As she SPIT IN HIS FACE, so she defied him.

1622. MASSINGER, *Virgin Martyr*, iii. 3. 'Had I been a pagan still, I should not have SPIT WHITE for want of drink.

1772. GRAVES, *Spiritual Quixote*, IV. vi. He had thought it rather a dry discourse; and beginning to SPIT SIXPENCES (as his saying was), he gave hints to Mr. Wildgoose to stop at the first public-house they should come to.

1809. MALKIN, *Gil Blas* [ROUTLEDGE], 371. You have no one to quarrel with but yourself; for I do not see so much as a cat TO SPIT AT you.

1897. MARSHALL, *Pomes*, 123. 'You must SPIT IT OUT a bit!' I yelled, and Ike began once more.

SPITALFIELD'S BREAKFAST, *subs. phr.* (East London).—No breakfast at all; 'a tight necktie and a short pipe': *cf.* IRISHMAN'S DINNER, DUKE HUMPHREY, &c.

SPIT-CURL, *subs. phr.* (costers').—A curl lying flat on the temple; a SOAP-CURL (*q.v.*): *see* AGGERAVATORS.

SPITE, *verb.* (Winchester).—*See* quots.

*c.*1840. MANSFIELD, *School Life* (1866), 235. When a boy suffered some injury himself, in order to spite another person; or, having in some way injured another, received punishment, he was said to be SPITING Gabell. Dr. Gabell was formerly Head-master, and the extreme inexpediency of attempting to annoy him gave rise to the proverb.

1891. WRENCH, *Winchester Word Book*, s.v. SPITE. The word in Wykehamical usage generally connoted the frame of mind rather than the acts in which it finds expression. But the phrase 'TO SPITE GABELL,' describes the act popularly known as 'cutting off your nose to spite your face.'

SPITFIRE, *subs.* (old).—A hot tempered person: *see* FURIOSO (GROSE).

1623. MABBE, *Guzman* [OLIPHANT, *New Eng.*, ii. 83. There are the phrases . . . a brown study . . . FIRE SPITTING DEVILS, whence comes our SPITFIRE].

1687. BROWN, *Works*, i. 87. 'Tis some comfort to me . . . Bully SPIT-FIRE, that thou canst not abuse me without falling foul upon my Country.

1695. CONGREVE, *Love for Love*, ii. 3. But there's but one virgin among the twelve signs, SPITFIRE, but one virgin.

1891. MARRIOT-WATSON, *Web of Spider*, xii. Foster was right . . . She is a little SPITFIRE.

1899. HYNE, *Furth. Adv. Captain Kettle*, ix. It was clear that this little SPITFIRE of a sailor, with his handy pistol, daunted him.

SPIT-FROG, *subs. phr.* (old).—A small sword.

1630. TAYLOR, *Works*. I would not see thy spightfull SPIT-FROG drawn.

1677. *Wrangling Lovers*. And each a little SPIT-FROG by his side.

SPITHEAD-NIGHTINGALE, *subs. phr.* (nautical).—A bo'sun or bo'sun's mate.

SPITTER, *subs.* (common).—Slight rain: *see* SPIT, *verb.*

SPITTLE (or **SPITAL**), *subs.* (old).—A hospital or lazar-house. Hence, SPITTLE-WHORE (or SINNER) = a foundered harlot; a SPITTLE-ROGUE (or MAN) = (1) a gaolbird; and (2) a diseased outcast: whence a general term of contempt.

1580. BARET, *Alvearie*. SPITTLE WHORE, a very common whore.

1607. DAVIES, *Summa Totalis*, 26. Good preachers that liue ill (like SPITTLE-MEN) Are perfect in the way they neuer went.

1632. MASSINGER, *Fatal Dowry*, iii. 1. I will rather choose a SPITTLE SINNER . . . though three parts rotten. *Ibid.* (1632), *City Madam*, iii. 1. *Ramb.* Rank and rotten, is she not? *Shave.* Your SPITTLE-rogueships.

SPITTOON, *subs.* (BEE: now recognised).—'An utensil mostly used in public-houses for the reception of smokers' expectorations.'

SPLASH, *subs.* (common).—1. Face powder; SLAP (*q.v.*). As *verb.* = TO MAKE UP (*q.v.*).

2. (common).—Display; exertion; effort. Hence, SPLASH UP = in good style; quick time; BANG-UP (*q.v.*)

1885. *D. Telegraph*, 28 Dec. Enable him to have a rattling good SPLASH for it somehow—break or make.

1885. SALA [*D. Tel.*, 1 Sep., 5, 4]. I should like to see the Australian Crœsusses spending their money. Why don't they cut a SPLASH with their magnificent revenues?

1900. WHITE, *West End*, 16. 'What a big SPLASH your uncle will make, Atherton,' said he. 'Of course it isn't for me to advise; but if you want him to arrive soon you had better get a real flyer to take your aunt in hand.'

1902. KERNAHAN, *Scoundrels*, xv. I've got the loan of a big hall . . . and I intend to make a bit of a SPLASH.

SPLASHER, *subs.* (military).—In *pl.* = The Wiltshire Regiment, late The 62nd Foot.

SPLATHERS. HOLD YOUR SPLATHERS, *phr.* (tailors').—'Hold your tongue!' SPLATHEVER = a braggart; a great talker.

SPLATTERDASH, *subs.* (colloquial).—A bustle; an uproar.

SPLATTER-FACE, *subs. phr.* (common).—A broad-faced man or woman; also as *adj.*

1861. HUGHES, *Tom Brown at Oxford* (1861), vi. A SPLATTER-FACED wench neither civil nor nimble.

SPLAY-FOOT, *subs. phr.* (colloquial).—A person with flat, awkward, or spreading feet: SPLAY-FOOTED = awkward in gait, heavy-footed. SPLAY-MOUTH = (1) a large, wide, grinning mouth; hence (2) a grimace.

1588-93. TARLETON, *Jests* [HALLIWELL (1844)]. [OLIPHANT, *New Eng.*, ii. 13. Amongst the romance words are undecentnes . . . SPLAIE-FOOTED.]

1608. MACHIN, *Dumb Knight*, iv. 1. Sure I met no SPLEA-FOOTED beggar.

1633. FORD, *Broken Heart*, v. 1. The doublers of a hare, or in a morning Salutes from a SPLAY-FOOTED witch.

1692. DRYDEN, *Persius*, i. Hadst thou but, Janus like, a face behind, To see the people when SPLAY MOUTHS they make.

*d.*1704. BROWN, *Works*, ii. 271. These solemn SPLAY-MOUTHED gentlemen, Madam, says I, only do it to improve in natural philosophy.

SPLENDIFEROUS, *adj.* (colloquial).—Splendid. Also SPLENDACIOUS; SPLENDIDOUS; and SPLENDIDIOUS.

1538. BALE, *Enterlude Johan Bapt.* [Harl. Misc., i. 113]. O tyme most ioyfull, daye most SPLENDIFERUS.

1605. JONSON, *Fox*, ii. 1. Worshipful merchants, ay, and senators too . . . have detained me to their uses by their SPLENDIDOUS liberalities.

1605. DRAYTON, *Moses, &c.*, B iii. His brows encircled with SPENDIDIOUS rays.

1630. TAYLOR, *Works*. To the mirror of time, the most refulgent SPLENDIDIOUS reflecting court animal, don Archibald Armstrong.

1855. HALIBURTON, *Human Nature*, 280. To my mind a SPLENDIFEROUS woman and a first-chop horse are the noblest works of creation.

1856. DOW, *Sermons*, I. 69. The SPLENDIFEROUS splendours that decorate the opposite shore ['of the gulf of death'].

1863. READE, *Hard Cash*, xxviii. Where is all your gorgeous attire . . . I see the SPLENDIFEROUS articles arrive, and then they vanish for ever.

SPLICE, *verb.* (common).—1. To marry: of the agent; and 2. (venery) = to copulate. TO BE SPLICED = to get married. Also SPLICE, *subs.* = a wife (GROSE).

1751. SMOLLETT, *Per. Pickle*, vii. Trunnion! Trunnion! turn out and be SPLICED, or lie still and be d——ed.

1839. AINSWORTH, *Jack Sheppard* (1889), 20. Tomorrow we'll go to the Fleet, and get SPLICED.

1852. BRONTE, *Villette*, xl. We never meant to be SPLICED in the humdrum way of other people.

1857. WHITTY, *Bohemia*, I. 205. 'Is this the confidence of married life?' 'Not SPLICED yet you know.'

1858. LYTTON, *What Will He Do With It*, IV. ix. If you advise me to be SPLICED, why don't you get SPLICED yourself? . . . you can be at no loss for a heiress.

1897. MARSHALL, *Pomes*, 31. He's fond of something tasty, so to speak, For me and him was SPLICED last Monday week.

1901. WALKER, *In the Blood*, 282. Suppose a feller goes on the racket when e's young, what's to prevent 'im SPLICING 'imself to 'is own daughter when she gets to years o' discretion or indiscretion?

2. (Winchester).—To throw; to fling.

TO SPLICE THE MAIN BRACE, *verb. phr.* (nautical).—To drink: orig. to serve out extra grog. WITH MAIN BRACE WELL-SPLICED = drunk: *see* SCREWED.

SPLIT, *subs.* (thieves').—1. A detective; a police spy: also as *verb.* (or TO TURN SPLIT) = to inform; to NOSE; to SNITCH (*q.v*): *see* NARK and *cf. verb.* sense 1.

2. (acrobats').—In *pl.* = a sitting posture, the legs extended laterally on the ground. Whence WELL-SPLIT UP = long in limb; SPLIT-UP = a lanky fellow: *see* LAMP-POST.

1851-61. MAYHEW, *Lond. Lab.*, II. 569. He taught me to put my leg round my neck, and I was just getting along nicely with the SPLITS when I left him.

3. (common).—(*a*) A small bottle of ærated water; also as *adv.* = divided: *e.g.*, 'two Scotches and a soda (or small soda) SPLIT.' (*b*) a half glass of spirits; a dram.'

Verb. (venery).—To copulate: *see* RIDE and *cf.* SPLIT-ARSE MECHANIC = a whore. Also BEARD-SPLITTER = a whoremaster; SPLIT-MUTTON = a woman; SPLIT-RUMP = the *penis* (URQUHART).

PHRASES.—TO MAKE ALL SPLIT = to make a disturbance or commotion; TO SPLIT ALONG (or GO LIKE SPLIT) = (1) to stride, to run quickly; and (2) to move or work with vigour; AT FULL SPLIT = as hard as may be; TO SPLIT ONE'S SIDES (or TO SPLIT) = to burst with laughter; TO SPLIT THE EARS = to deafen; TO SPLIT HAIRS = to cavil about trifles, to be over-nice in argument: hence HAIR-SPLITTER (or SPLITTER) = a PRECISIAN (*q.v.*), the reverse of LUMPER (*q.v.*); TO SPLIT ON A ROCK = to fail, to come to grief; TO SPLIT ON ONE (or TO SPLIT) = to betray confidence: *see* subs. 1; TO SPLIT FAIR = to tell the truth; TO SPLIT OUT (thieves') = to separate; TO SPLIT WITH ONE = to quarrel; 'SPLIT my windpipe!' = 'a foolish kind of a curse among the Beaux' (B. E.).

1592. SHAKSPEARE, *Mid. Night's Dream*, i. 2. I could play Ercles rarely, or a part to tear a cat in, TO MAKE ALL SPLIT. *Ibid.* (1596), *Hamlet*, iii. 2. To SPLIT THE EARS of the groundlings.

1609. BEAUMONT and FLETCHER, *Scornful Lady*, ii. 3. Two roaring boys of Rome that MADE ALL SPLIT.

1611. MIDDLETON, *Roaring Girl* [DODSLEY, *Old Plays* (REED), vi. 89]. If I sail not with you both 'TILL ALL SPLIT, hang me up at the main yard and duck me.

1612. CHAPMAN, *Widow's Tears* [DODSLEY, *Old Plays* (REED), vi. 153]. To prepare my next encounter, but in such a way as shall MAKE ALL SPLIT.

1693. CONGREVE, *Old Bachelor*, ii. 2. Now I must speak; it will SPLIT A HAIR, by the Lord Harry.

1734. POPE, *Satires*, VI. 131. Each had a gravity would make you SPLIT.

1809. MALKIN, *Gil Blas* [ROUTLEDGE], 51. I was in danger more than once of SPLITTING MY SIDES with laughing. *Ibid.*, 373. He laughed ready TO SPLIT HIS SIDES. *Ibid.*, 56. They would not SPLIT A HAIR about the loss of a wife.

1837. BARHAM, *Ingolds. Leg.*, 'Babes in the Wood.' His man being caught in some fact . . . When he came to be hanged for the act SPLIT, and told the whole story to Cotton.

1838. DICKENS, *Oliver Twist*, xxv. I might have got clear off if I'd SPLIT UPON her.

*d.*1841. HOOK, *Sutherlands*. Don't let Emmy know that we've SPLIT, else she'll be savage with us.

1844. *Major Jones's Courtship* [BARTLETT]. I set the niggers a-drummin' and fifin' as hard as they could SPLIT.

1862. BROWNE, *Artemus Ward, His Book* [*Works* (1870), 47]. You wood have SPLIT YOUR SIDES larfin to see the old man jump up.

1865. DOWNING, *May Day*, 64. There was no end to the one-horse teams, goin' LIKE SPLIT all over the city.

1877. HORSLEY, *Jottings from Jail*. There is a reeler over there who knows me. We had better SPLIT OUT.

1884. GREENWOOD, *Little Ragamuffins*. If I tell you all about it, will you promise that you won't SPLIT.

1888. A. L. GORDON, *Poems*, 'Wolf and Hound.' We had run him for seven miles and more, As hard as our nags could SPLIT.

1897. OUIDA, *Massarenes*, i. We won't do that, Boo. Mummy's a bad un TO SPLIT ON.

1899. WHITEING, *John St.*, v. You see if the baby farm was TO SPLIT ON Ikey, he might SPLIT ON the baby farm.

SPLIT-ARSE MECHANIC, *subs. phr.* (venery).—A harlot. Also SPLIT-MUTTON = (1) the *penis*; and (2) generic for the female sex.

SPLIT-ASUNDER, *subs. phr.* (rhyming).—A costermonger.

SPLIT-CAUSE, *subs. phr.* (old).—A lawyer (GROSE): also (B. E.) SPLITTER OF CAUSES.

SPLIT-FIG, *subs. phr.* (old).—A grocer (B. E. and GROSE).

SPLIT FOOT (or **OLD SPLIT FOOT**), *subs. phr.* (common).—The Devil.

1848. LOWELL, *Biglow Papers*, . . . An' make ole SPLIT FOOT wince and squirm.

SPLITTING, *adj.* (colloquial).—Extreme; severe: *e.g.*, a SPLITTING (= very quick) PACE; A SPLITTING (= painfully throbbing) HEAD-ACHE, &c. *See* SPLIT.

1868. WHYTE MELVILLE, *White Rose*, II. xv. Though stout he was no mean pedestrian; and on he ran at a SPLITTING pace.

SPLODGER, *subs.* (common).—A lout. SPLODGY = awkward (in gait), coarse (in complexion).

SPLOSH, *subs.* (common).—Money: generic: *see* RHINO.

1893. GUS ELEN, *'E Dunno Where 'E Are.* Since Jack Jones come into that little bit o' SPLOSH.

1902. BOOTHBY, *My Strangest Case*, 166. I reckon we ain't a-goin' to see no SPLOSH this 'ere trip.

Adv. (common).—Plump.

1891. *Harry Fludyer*, 47. Such larks when you heard the ball go SPLOSH on a man's hat!

SPLURGE, *subs.* (colloquial).—Generic for effort and effect. As *verb.* = to make the most and do the showiest; SPLURGY = ON IT (*q.v.*).

18[?]. *Widow Bedott Papers*, 67. Did you see Major Coon's wife? . . . Didn't she CUT A SPLURGE?

1844. *Major Jones's Courtship*, 101. Cousin Pete was thar SPLURGIN' ABOUT . . . with his dandy-cut trowsers and big whiskers.

1845. *New York Com. Adv.*, 13 Dec. Members of Congress should not forget when Senator Benton was shinning around, making what they call in Missouri a great SPLURGE, to get gold.

1860. PORTER, *Tales of South-west*, 54. Well, them was great times, but now the Settlements is got too thick for them TO SPLURGE.

1885. *D. Telegraph*, 28 Dec. The great SPLURGE made by our American Cousins when . . . they completed another connection with the Pacific.

1887. WARNER, *Pilgrimage*, 114. You would be surprised to know the number of people who . . . SPLURGE OUT for a year or two, then fail or get tired of it, and disappear.

SPOFFLE, *verb.* (colloquial). — To fuss; to bustle. SPOFFISH (or SPOFFY) = fussy; bustling; smart. Also SPOFFY, *subs.* = a busybody.

1836. DICKENS, *Sk. by Boz*, 'Horatio Sparkins.' A little SPOFFISH man with green spectacles. *Ibid.* (1838-40), *Sketches, Tales*, vii. He invariably spoke with astonishing rapidity; was smart, SPOFFISH, and eight and twenty.

SPOFFSKINS, *subs.* (common).—A prostitute: *see* TART.

SPOIL, *verb.* (various).—In addition to the sense (now accepted) given by GROSE ('to mar, to place obstacles in the way') there are colloq. usages as follows:—To SPOIL FOR = to be eager for: as 'SPOILING for a fight,' and SPOILING to be invited; TO SPOIL ONE'S SHAPE = to be got with child; TO SPOIL ONE'S MOUTH = to damage the face. Also in sarcastic combination, SPOIL-BREAD = a baker; SPOIL-BROTH = a cook; SPOIL-IRON = a smith (GROSE); SPOIL-PAPER = a scribbler; SPOIL-PUDDING = a long-winded preacher (GROSE); SPOIL-SPORT = an unfriendly or dispirited associate or intruder: hence TO SPOIL SPORT = (1) to dishearten, and (2) to prevent; SPOIL-TRADE = an unscrupulous competitor; SPOIL-TEMPER = an exacting superior.

1280. [OLIPHANT, *New Eng.*, i. 427. All through the century [16th] new words formed like the SPILBRED of 1280 (not *bread-spiller*) were coming in.]

1597-8. HAUGHTON, *Woman will have her Will* [DODSLEY, *Old Plays* (1874), x. 537]. The rogue is waiting yet to SPOIL YOUR SPORT.

1611. HOLLAND [DAVIES, *Scourge of Folly*, 81]. My Satyre shall not touch such sacred things . . . As some SPOILE-PAPERS have dearly done of late.

1678. COTTON, *Virgil Travestie* [*Works* (1725), 74]. That I am half afraid lest he Should chance to SPOIL her Majesty.

1694. MOTTEUX, *Rabelais*, iv. xlvii. He spied his wife lying on the ground piteously weeping and howling . . . 'He has SPOILED me. I am undone.'

d. 1704. BROWN, *Works*, ii. 97. The French king who had SPOIL'D THE SHAPE . . . of several mistresses . . . had a mind to do the same by me.

1821. SCOTT, *Kenilworth*, xxviii. Mike Lambourne was never a make-bate, or a SPOIL-SPORT, or the like.

1821. EGAN, *Life in London*, II. iv. 'Hang you! . . . if you don't hold that are red rag of yours, I'll SPOIL YOUR MOUTH.'

1864. *Derby Day*, 52. It will SPOIL SPORT to call in the bobbies.

1901. *D. Telegraph*, 6 Nov., 'Racing in the Fog.' Fog as a SPOIL-SPORT is less recurrent than snow and wind.

SPOKE. TO PUT A SPOKE IN ONE'S WHEEL (or CART), *verb. phr.* (old).—To do an ill turn. Occasionally (by an unwarrantable inversion) = to assist.

1661-91. *Merry Drolleries* [EBSWORTH, 1875], 224. He . . . lookt to be made an emperor for't, But the Divel did SET A SPOKE IN HIS CART.

1689. *God's Last Twenty-Nine Years Wonders* [WALSH]. Both . . . bills were such SPOKES IN THEIR CHARIOT-WHEELS that made them drive much slower.

1809. MALKIN, *Gil Blas* [ROUTLEDGE], 19. Rolando put a SPOKE IN THEIR WHEEL by representing that they ought at least to wait till the lady . . . could come in for her share of the amusement.

1855. THACKERAY, *Newcomes*, ix. There's a SPOKE IN YOUR WHEEL, you stuck-up little Duchess.

1872. ELIOT, *Middlemarch*, xiii. It seems to me it would be a very poor sort of religion TO PUT A SPOKE IN HIS WHEEL by refusing to say you don't believe.

1898. WALSH, *Lit. Curios.*, 1030. When solid wheels were used, the driver was provided with a pin or SPOKE, which he thrust into one of the three holes made to receive it, to skid the cart when it went down hill.

SPOKE-BOX, *subs. phr.* (colloquial). —The mouth.

1874. *Siliad*, 206. Do I, for this, his brows with wreaths adorn, And lubricate his SPOKE-BOX every morn.

SPONDULICS (SPONDOOLICKS or SPONDULACKS), *subs.* (American). —Money: generic: originally (*Century*) paper money.

1863. SALA [*Illust. Lond. News*, 1883, 8 Dec. 547]. I first became acquainted with the word in the United States just twenty years ago. SPONDULICS was . . . an enlarged vulgarisation of greenbacks. It may also have been applied to the nickel cents used in small change.

1876. *Harper's Mag.*, April, 790. Now let's have the SPONDULICKS, and see how sweet and pretty I can smile on you.

1884. CLEMENS, *Huck. Finn.* I'm derned if I'd live two mile out of town . . . not for his SPONDULICS.

1897. MARSHALL, *Pomes*, 113. SPONDULICS quite sufficient to ensure her a position.

1901. WALKER, *In the Blood*, 329. 'Thish place fair schmells of blooming SPONDULICKS!' said Ikey.

SPONGE (SPONGER, or SPUNGE), *subs.* (old).—1. A parasite (B. E. and GROSE); also (2) = 'a thirsty fellow' (B. E.), a drunkard. As *verb.* = to take kicks and lick dishes for a living. Whence SPONGING = (1) CADGING (*q.v.*); and (2) extortion: *e.g.*, a SPONGING-HOUSE = a bailiff's pound in which arrested debtors were SQUEEZED (*q.v.*) pending transfer to a regular prison.

1598. SHAKSPEARE, *Mer. Venice*, i. 2. 101. I will do anything, Nerissa, ere I'll be married to a SPONGE.

1640. *Two Lancashire Lovers*, 24. Or from the wanton affection, or too profuse expense of light mistresses, who make choice of rich servants to make SPONGES of them.

1641. MILTON, *Ref. in England*, ii. Better a penurious kingdom then where excessive wealth flowes into the gracelesse and injurious hands of common SPONGES to the impoverishing of good and loyal men.

1692. LESTRANGE, *Æsop* [*Ency. Dict.*]. A generous and rich man, that kept a splendid and open table, would try which were friends, and which only trencher flies and SPUNGERS.

1697. SOUTH, *Sermons*, I. xii. How came such multitudes of our own nation . . . to be SPUNGED of their plate and money?

1709. WARD, *Terræfilius*, ii. 9. [*Works*, i.]. I'll warrant he has been SPUNGING a Morning's Draught out of the Poor's Box.

1727. SWIFT, *Richmond Lodge and Marble Hill.* Here wont the Dean, when he's to seek, To SPUNGE a breakfast once a week.

1749. SMOLLETT, *Gil Blas* (1812), III. iii. 'Gil Blas,' said he, 'who is that tall SPUNGER in whose company I saw thee today.

1762. GOLDSMITH, *Citizen of the World*, xxvii. They SPUNGED up my money while it lasted, borrowed my coals and never paid for them, and cheated me when I played at cribbage.

1809. MALKIN, *Gil Blas* [ROUTLEDGE], 89. We went there . . . both in ecstasy at having an opportunity of SPUNGING on a citizen. *Ibid.* (174). One of your shabby fellows always SPUNGING on his friends.

1814. AUSTEN, *Mansfield Park*, x. 'What else have you been SPUNGING,' said Maria.

1843. CARLETON, *New Purchase*, II. 240. These preachers dress like big bugs, and go riding about on hundred-dollar horses, A-SPUNGIN' poor priest-ridden folks.

1848. THACKERAY, *Book of Snobs*, xxi. Bull passes the season in London, SPONGING for dinners, and sleeping in a garret near his club.

1849-61. MACAULAY, *Hist. Eng.*, ii. From all the brothels, gambling-houses, and SPUNGING-HOUSES of London, false witnesses poured forth to swear away the lives of Roman Catholics.

1862. BROWNE, *Artemus Ward, His Book* [*Works* (1870), 51]. He leaves orf workin . . . and commensis SPUNGIN his livin out of other people.

1879. *Chambers' Jo.*, July, 408. He . . . had no business to come SPONGING on Mr. King.

1887. HENLEY, *Villon's Good-Night*, i. You SPONGES miking round the pubs.

TO THROW UP THE SPONGE, *verb. phr.* (orig. technical: now general).—To acknowledge defeat. [The sponge used in cleansing a combatant's face was chucked up in sign of submission.]

1899. HYNE, *Further Adv. of Captain Kettle*, vi. Don't THROW UP THE SPONGE until someone else does it for you.

SPONGE-WIT, *subs. phr.* (old).—A plagiarist.

SPOOF, *subs.* (common).—Deception, a swindle: also the SPOOF-GAME. Also as *verb.* (or TO PLAY SPOOF).

1897. MARSHALL, *Pomes*, 10. Then 'e sets the gals a-screaming with a caper known as SPOOF, Playing monkey games on my old Uncle John.

SPOOK, *subs.* (colloquial).—A ghost. Whence SPOOKISH (or SPOOKY) = ghostly.

SPOON, *subs.* (common).—1. A simpleton: spec. an absurd whole-hearted lover: also SPOONEY; A RANK SPOON = 'a prating shallow fellow' (VAUX). Hence (2) = calf-love: *e.g.*, a CASE OF SPOONS. As *verb.* (TO COME THE SPOON, or TO BE SPOONS ON) = to make love openly, innocently, and ridiculously. Also SPOONY = stupidly fond; SPOONINESS = foolish fondness (GROSE, VAUX, BEE).

1837. BARHAM, *Ingolds. Leg.*, 'Witches' Frolic.' But you'll find very soon, if you aim at the moon, In a carriage like that, you're a bit of a SPOON.

1838. BECKET, *Paradise Lost*, 67. And I, at that time not suspicious . . . Suck'd in her gammon like a SPOONY.

d. 1845. HOOD, *Morning Meditations.* A man that's fond precociously of stirring must be a SPOON.

1847. BRONTE, *James Eyre*, xv. In short I began the process of ruining myself in the received style, like any other SPOONIE.

1848. THACKERAY, *Vanity Fair*, xxxiv. What the deuce can she find in that SPOONEY of a Pitt Crawley? . . . The fellow has not pluck enough to say Bo to a goose.

1855. TOM TAYLOR, *Still Waters*, iii. 'A coolness, a self-possession . . . I never should have expected from—from ——' 'From such a SPOON—that's what you mean, isn't it?'

1859. LEVER, *Davenport Dunn*, lx. Not actually in love . . . but only SPOONY.

1863. READE, *Hard Cash*, Prol. What a good-natured SPOON that Dodd is!

1869. *Macm. Mag.*, Nov., 65. Yes, Captain Waldron averred, he was a SPOONEY; that was the right name for a man who let himself be played with as she had played with him.

1885. HAWLEY SMART, *Struck Down* xi. A girl would rather make her way out by herself than with a fellow she's SPOONS on.

1887. HENLEY, *Culture in Slums.* Was it not prime—I leave you all to guess How prime! to have a jude in love's distress Come SPOONING round.

1888. *Harper's Mag.*, lxxviii. 749. I ought to remember, for I was SPOONS ON you myself for a week or two.

1897. MARSHALL, *Pomes*, 38. 'Twas an instance . . . Of the danger attending unlimited SPOONS.

Verb. (American). — 1. To nestle; to lie close; and 2. (venery). = to copulate while lying SPOON-FASHION, *i.e.*, the bowl of one spoon in the other's.

1888. *Harper's Mag.*, lxxvii. 49. 'Now SPOON me.' Sterling stretched himself out on the warm flag-stone, and the boy nestled up against him. *Ibid.* (1886), lxxiv. 781. Two persons in each bunk, the sleepers SPOONING together, packed like sardines.

3. (cricketers').—To hit with a 'slack and horizontal' bat, causing the ball to rise in the air.

PHRASES.—TO STICK ONE'S SPOON IN THE WALL = to die; *see* HOP THE TWIG; TO FILL THE MOUTH WITH EMPTY SPOONS = to go hungry (RAY); TO TAKE WITH A BIG (or LITTLE) SPOON = to take in large (or small) quantities: *see* SILVER SPOON, and WOODEN SPOON.

SPOONAGE, *subs.* (old).—Liquid food; PAP (*q.v.*).

1586. WARNER, *Albions England*, II. x. And suck she might a teat for teeth, And SPOONAGE too did faile.

SPOONY DRUNK, *adj. phr.* (common).—Sentimentally drunk: *see* SCREWED.

SPOORAN, *subs.* (venery).—The pubic hair: *see* FLEECE.

SPOOPS (or **SPOOPSIE**), *subs.* (American). — A simpleton: *see* BUFFLE. SPOOPY = silly, foolish.

SPORT, *subs.* (old).—1. Copulation: also THE SPORT OF VENUS (or VENEREAL SPORT). Hence as *verb.* = to wanton; SPORTIVE (or SPORTFUL) = lecherous; SPORTSWOMAN (or SPORTING-PIECE) = a harlot; SPORTSMAN = a MUTTONMONGER (*q.v.*); SPORTSMAN'S GAP = the female *pudendum*; SPORTSMAN'S TOAST = 'pointer and stubble'; &c.

1570. *Marr. Wit and Science* [DODSLEY, *Old Plays* (1874), ii. 326]. What though I be too young to show her SPORT in bed, Yet there are many in this land that at my years do wed.

1593. SHAKSPEARE, *Taming of the Shrew*, ii. 1, 263. Let Kate be chaste, and Dian SPORTFUL. *Ibid.* (1597), *Richard III.*, i. 1. I, that am not shaped for SPORTIVE tricks. *Ibid.* (1598), *Sonnets*, cxxi. Why should others' false adulterate eyes Give salutation to my SPORTIVE blood? *Ibid.* (1602,) *Othello*, ii. 1, 230. When the blood is made dull with the ACT OF SPORT. *Ibid.*, ii. 3, 17. He hath not yet made wanton the night with her, and she is SPORT, for Jove. *Ibid.* (1603), *Measure for Meas.*, iii. 2. Ere he would have hanged a man for the getting a hundred bastards, he would have paid for the nursing a thousand: he had some feeling of the SPORT.

c. 1600. JONSON, *Frag. Petron. Arbiter Translated.* Doing, a filthy pleasure is, and short; And done, we straight repent us of the SPORT.

1621. BURTON, *Anat. Melan.* III. III. i. 2. When . . . he did not play the man as he should do, she fell in league with a good fellow, and whilst he sat up late at his study . . . she . . . continued at her SPORT.

1629. MASSINGER, *Picture*, iii. 6. This ring was Julietta's, a fine piece, But very good at the SPORT.

1673. COTTON, *Scoffer Scofft* [1770], 239. He comes i' th' middle of their SPORT . . . Took the poor Lovers in the Manner.

1700. DRYDEN, *Wife of Bath's Tale.* The widow's wish was oftentimes to wed; The wanton maids were all for SPORT a-bed.

d. 1704. BROWNE, *Works*, ii. 204. An old fornicatrix, who can part with her money as freely at one SPORT as she got it at another.

c. 1709. WARD, *T— B——'s Last Letter.* If . . . you have not the gift of continence . . . match your cock with the next fair SPORTSWOMAN you meet. *Ibid.* (*d.* 1731), *Terræfilius*, v. 25. Good enough to solemnize her VENEREAL SPORTS upon a tavern chair. *Ibid.*, 27. She is of the true colour for the SPORT OF VENUS. *Ibid.*, *Infernal Vision*, III. Or Money gained admission to her Beard . . . What she first thought on't, How she lik'd the SPORT? Whether it pleas'd her well, or if it hurt?

1740. RICHARDSON, *Pamela*, ii. 35. A poor SPORTING-PIECE for the great.

1772. BRIDGES, *Burlesque Homer*, 4. In England, if you trust report, Whether in country, town or court, The parsons daughters make best SPORT.

c. 1796. MORRIS, *The Plenipotentiary.* As he knew in our state that the women have weight, He chose one well-hung for the SPORT, sirs.

2. (turf, &c.).—A professional sportsman: a pugilist, bookmaker, jockey, &c.: also SPORTING-MAN. Whence SPORTING-HOUSE = a public-house frequented by sportsmen.

1877. *New York Tribune*, April. I know two or three thousand SPORTS floating now on the sea of adversity.

1896. LILLARD, *Poker Stories*, 50. Those were the days, my boy . . . every SPORT with stuff in his pockets, and lots of good clothes.

2. (colloquial). — Mischief; horseplay.

Verb. (old).—Generic for display: 'the word . . . was in great vogue in . . . 1783 and 1784' (GROSE); now-a-days still general, but spec. a public school and university usage. Thus TO SPORT (or BAULK) a report = to publish far and wide; TO SPORT (= drive) A GIG; TO SPORT (= wear) NEW TOGS; TO SPORT IVORY = to grin; TO SPORT (=exhibit) TEMPER; TO SPORT OAK (TIMBER, OR TO SPORT IN) = to deny oneself to callers by closing an outer door: *see* OAK; TO SPORT AN ÆGROTAT (*see* ÆGROTAT); TO SPORT OFF = to do with ease; TO SPORT (= provide) A DINNER; TO SPORT LITERATURE = to write a book; TO SPORT (= spend) MONEY, ONE'S SALARY, &c.; TO SPORT (= express) AN OPINION; TO SPORT A NESCIO (*see* NESCIO); TO SPORT SILK (racing)=to ride a race; TO SPORT (=indulge or engage in) SMOKING, WALKING, &c. Whence (Winchester) A SPORTING ACTION=an affected manner, gesture or gait, or a betrayal of emotion. [*Cf.* SPORT (var. dial.) = to show, to exhibit.] SPORTINGS (Charterhouse) = clothes worn at the EXEAT (*q.v.*).

1794. *Gent. Mag.*, 1085. They [at Cambridge] SPORTED an Ægrotat, and they SPORTED a new coat.

1825-7. HONE, *Ev.-Day Book*, Feb., 22. Shutting my room door, as if I was SPORTED IN, and cramming Euc.

1830. LYTTON, *Paul Clifford* (1854), 29. Paul, my ben cull . . . I doesn't care if I SPORTS you a glass of port.

1848. THACKERAY, *Book of Snobs*, xx. Beaux . . . of society who SPORT a lace dickey and nothing besides.

1853. MRS. GASKELL, *Cranford*, i. By-and-by, Captain Brown SPORTED a bit of literature.

1859. KINGSLEY, *Geof. Hamlyn*, xxxi. I took him for a flash overseer, SPORTING HIS SALARY, and I was as thick as you like with him.

1882. *Punch*, lxxxii. 147, 2. Anybody can enter here who chooses to SPORT his blunt.

1885. *D. Chron.*, 28 Dec. Duly qualified by age TO SPORT SILK and satin on the public racecourse.

*d.*1890. J. H. NEWMAN, *Works* [*Century*]. A man . . . must SPORT AN OPINION when he really had none to give.

1896. LILLARD, *Poker Stories*, 246. For two days those fellows SPORTED it on that dollar.

1896. FARJEON, *Betray. of John Fordham*, III. 279. Louis had plenty of money to SPORT; e'd been backin' winners.

1897. MARSHALL, *Pomes*, 46. She SPORTED her number one gloss on her hair, And her very best blush on her cheek. *Ibid.*, 68. That O. P. fairy . . . SPORTS a real diamond ring.

1900. TOD, *Charterhouse*, 102. The splendour of Exeat garb defies description. It is enough to say that the Carthusian's apparel then is as costly as his purse will buy, and that he calls it SPORTINGS.

SPOT, *subs.* (venery).—1. The female *pudendum*: *see* MONOSYLLABLE.

1705. WARD, *Hud. Rediv.*, I. x. 18. They hide that tempting SPOT, That caus'd old Adam's Fall.

2. (American). — Shares (or goods) ready for delivery: that is 'on the SPOT.'

1902. *D. Mail*, 17 Nov., 2, 2. The quotation for two months' forward delivery declined 1-16d. to 22 11-16d., but was unchanged at 22⅝d. for SPOT.

3. (American gaming). — A dollar: *e.g.*, FIVE SPOT = five dollars; $5.

1896. LILLARD, *Poker Stories*, 246. But one single dollar remained of that FIVE SPOT.

Verb. (colloquial). — 1. To recognise; to take note of; to discover. Also 2. (thieves')=to detect, to come upon: hence SPOTTER=a detective: Fr. *indicateur*: whence SPOTTED=known to the police (TUFTS, 1791); and

3. (racing)=to pick out, to choose, to chance upon: *e.g.*, TO SPOT THE WINNER.

1851-61. MAYHEW, *Lond. Lab.*, I. 484. At length he became SPOTTED. The police got to know him, and he was apprehended, tried, and convicted.

1857. *M. Chron.*, 22 June. Having met with tolerable success in SPOTTING the winners.

1861. HOLMES, *Elsie Venner*, xxi. The Widow Leech . . . rang three times . . . but all in vain; the inside Widow having SPOTTED the outside one through the blinds.

1877. *Five Years' Penal Scrvitude*, i. 33. The officer SPOTTED him directly, and . . . would mark him for the attention of someone else.

1885. *Field*, 4 Ap. The hounds SPOTTED him, and he became food and trophy two minutes later.

1896. FARJEON, *John Fordham*, III. 279. The minute I saw 'm I SPOTTED wot they wos up to.

1898. WHITEING, *John St.*, v. I've SPOTTED her many a time when she didn't think I was lookin'.

1902. *Free Lance*, 19 July, 377, 1. To hear you laugh is as good as SPOTTING A WINNER.

1903. *Punch's Almanack*, 12, 1. B. P. gives a thrilling example of experiment on this line. Got up a tree and watched how many passers-by SPOTTED him.

4. (common).—To gamble.

PHRASES AND COMBINATIONS. —A SOFT SPOT=an easy, comfortable, or desirable berth, thing, or circumstance: *see* HUNT; TO KNOCK SPOTS OUT OF (*see* KNOCK); ON (or OFF) THE SPOT = alert, dead certain; IN SPOTS = by snatches; TO HAVE A VACANT SPOT = to be crazy.

1887. HENLEY, *Villon's Straight Tip*. Palm and be always ON THE SPOT.

SPOTTED-DOG, *subs. phr.* (common). —1. A plum or currant dumpling: SPOTTED DONKEY = plum pudding; and 2. (military) a sausage or saveloy.

SPOTTED MYSTERY, *subs. phr.* (military).—Tinned beef.

SPOUT, *subs.* (common). — 1. A pawnbroker's shoot or lift from shop to store-room; whence (2) = a pawnbroker's. As *verb.* = to pawn; UP THE SPOUT (or SPOUTED)=pawned: in America 'gone where the WOODBINE (*q.v.*) twineth' (GROSE and BEE). Also UP THE SPOUT = imprisoned, in hospital (BEE).

ENGLISH SYNONYMS. — To blue; to bullock's-horn (rhyming =pawn); to flue (or put up the flue); to lay up in lavender; to lug; to lumber; TO MOSKENEER (*q.v.*); to put away; to send to uncle's; to soak; to spout; to sweat; to vamp; to warehouse.

FRENCH SYNONYMS.—*Accrocher chez sa tante* (= UNCLE, *q.v.*); *enclouer*; *guinaliser*.

1837 BARHAM, *Ingoldsby Leg.*, II. 16. His pockets, no doubt, Being turned inside out, That his mouchoir and gloves may be put UP THE SPOUT.

1861. HUGHES, *Tom Brown at Oxford*, II. i. The dons are going to SPOUT the college plate.

1864. ART. WARD, *Among the Mormons* [*Works*, 257]. Even if she [the Goddess of Liberty] don't have to SPOUT the gold stars in her head band.

1887. HENLEY, *Villon's Straight Tip*. It's UP THE SPOUT and Charley-wag.

1889. *Notes and Queries*, 7 S, vii. 56. Pawnbrokers . . . before SPOUTS were adopted, used a hook to lift the articles.

1897. MARSHALL, *Pomes*, 71. He asked her if she'd seen his watch about; She said . . . 'It may be half-way UP THE giddy SPOUT.'

Verb. (old).—To talk, speechify, or declaim for effect (GROSE, VAUX, and BEE). Hence SPOUTER =(1) a mouthing talker; whence (2) a fourth-rate speaker or actor. TO SPOUT BILLY=to earn a living

by reciting Shakspeare in taprooms (BEE); SPOUTING-CLUB ='a rehearsal club' (GROSE); IN GREAT SPOUT = noisy, in high spirits. Also TO SPOUT INK = to write: *cf.* SLING INK.

1599. NASHE, *Lenten Stuffe* [GROSART, *Works*, v. 232]. Never since I SPOUTED incke, was I of woorse aptitude to goe thorow with such a mighty March brewage as you expect.

1610. BEAUMONT and FLETCHER, *Coxcomb*, iv. 4. Pray SPOUT some French, son.

1673. COTTON, *Scoffer Scofft* [1770], 202. His mouth will one day be a SPOUT Of Eloquence, without a doubt.

1771. SMOLLETT, *Humph. Clinker*, 'To Sir Watkin Phillips, 30 April.' Mr. Gwynn . . do, pray, SPOUT a little the Ghost of Gimlet.

1781. KNOX, *Liberal Education*, 20. Introduce him to SPOUTING clubs or disputing societies. *Ibid.* (1788), *Winter Evenings*, xxxii. The quoters imitate parrots or professed SPOUTERS in committing words only to memory purposely for the sake of ostentation.

1792. *Advt.* in *Dupes of Fancy* [HOGG]. The New SPOUTERS' Companion [Title].

1796. REYNOLDS, *Fortune's Fool*, iv. 1. In the garret is a SPOUTING author.

1797. D'ARBLAY, *Diary*, vi. 187. These and his SPOUT of satire are mere quizziness.

1809. MALKIN, *Gil Blas* [ROUTLEDGE], 246. Phenecia prevailed on me to repeat the lines I had already SPOUTED. *Ibid.*, 372. The major-domo, a great SPOUTER, undertook to train me for the stage.

1814. AUSTEN, *Mansfield Park*, xiii. For anything of acting, SPOUTING, reciting kind I think he has always a decided taste.

1827. LYTTON, *Pelham*, l. He SPOUTS at the 'Ciceronian' for half a crown a night.

1837. BARHAM, *Ingolds. Leg.*, 'Milkmaid's Story.' With scorn on her lip, And a hand on each hip, SPOUT herself till her nose grew red at the tip.

1858. MURSELL, *Lecture on Slang*. When a man speaks, he SPOUTS; when he holds his peace, he shuts up.

1886. *D. Telegraph*, 12 Jan. The women's rights agitator, the platform SPOUTER in petticoats. *Ibid.*, 9 Feb. Listening to the more forcible than polite SPOUTINGS of rabid 'fair traders' and Socialists. *Ibid.*, 14 Oct. While SPOUTING the most intolerant rubbish that can be endured.

1897. MARSHALL, *Pomes*, 87. She blewed it on a gent who SPOUTED in the Park.

1903. *Morning Advertiser*, 4 Feb. SPOUTING agitators who never did a honest day's work in their lives.

SPOUTER, *subs.* (nautical). — *See* quot. and SPOUT.

1835. DANA, *Before the Mast*, Nov., 14. The SPOUTER, as the sailors call a whaleman, had . . . made signal for us to heave to. *Ibid.*, 8 Sep. One . . . had been in a SPOUTER, and of course, had all the whaling stories to himself.

SPRAT, *subs.* (common).—1. *See* quots.

1857. SNOWDEN, *Mag. Assist.* (3rd ed.), 444. Sixpence, downer, also SPRAT.

1857. *M. Chron.*, 2 Dec. Several Lascars were charged with passing SPRATS, the slang term applied to spurious fourpenny pieces, sixpences, and shillings.

1898. *Sporting Times*, 19 Feb., 1, 5. I don't mean lunch with only two and a SPRAT in my clothes; have a drink?

2. (common).—A sweetheart: *cf.* BLOATER, DUCK, PIPPIN, &c.

3. (common).—In *pl.* = furniture; effects: *cf.* MARBLES, STICKS, &c.

4. (old). — An undersized or mean-looking man or boy; a SCARECROW (*q.v.*): also JACK SPRAT (*q.v.*).

1598. SHAKSPEARE, *All's Well*, iii. 6, 112. When his disguise and he is parted, tell me what a SPRAT you shall find him.

SPREAD, *subs.* (colloquial).—1. A meal; a feast.

1827. BARHAM, *Ingoldsby Leg.*, II. 51. After giving one SPREAD, With fiddling and masques at the Saracen's Head.

1848. MRS. GASKELL, *Mary Barton*, ix. We had such a SPREAD for breakfast as th' Queen herself might ha' sitten down to.

1873. GREENWOOD, *In Strange Company*. Next day I was present at a SPREAD at the Mission Hall of a much more gratifying description.

1897. MARSHALL, *Pomes*, 11. 'E didn't even give me an invite To 'is New Year's SPREAD.

2. (old).—Butter (GROSE and VAUX: *cf.* SCRAPE.

3. (old).—An umbrella (GROSE).

4. (common).—A lady's shawl (HOTTEN).

5. (Old Cant). — A saddle (TUFTS, 1798).

6. (Stock Exchange). — An option; a STRADDLE (*q.v.*).

Verb. (venery).—To open up (of women), or to lay out (of men) for SERVICE (*q.v.*).

1692. DRYDEN, *Juvenal*, vi. Many a fair nymph has in a cave been SPREAD, And much good love, without a featherbed. *Ibid.* What care our drunken dames to whom they SPREAD?

TO SPREAD ONESELF, *verb. phr.* (American).—To push, to come out strong, TO SWAGGER (*q.v.*).

1832. LONGSTREET, *Southern Sketches* [BARTLETT]. Hoss Allen mounted the balcony of the hotel, and rolling up his sleeves, SPREAD HIMSELF for an unusually brilliant effort.

1848. HAMMOND, *Wild Northern Scenes*, 266. We despatched Cullen to prepare a dinner. He had promised . . . TO SPREAD HIMSELF in the preparation of this meal.

1876. CLEMENS, *Tom Sawyer*, 46. At school, on great occasions before company, the Superintendent . . . had always made this boy come out and SPREAD HIMSELF.

1887. FRANCIS, *Saddle and Mocassin*. For the benefit of the tenderfoot he SPREAD HIMSELF.

SPREAD-EAGLE, *subs. phr.* (old).—1. A posture: arms (wings or fins) and legs extended: *e.g.*, a soldier lashed to the halberts (GROSE), or a sailor to the rigging; a fowl split down the back for broiling; fish split and laid out to dry; and (2) a figure in skating imitating the heraldic 'Eagle displayed' [*i.e.*, with wings and legs extended on each side of the body]. As *verb.* =(1) to tie up for punishment; (2) to prepare poultry or fish for broiling or drying; and (3) in racing to scatter the FIELD (*q.v.*).

*d.*1701. DRYDEN, *Post. History of the League*, II. 469. A kind of SPREAD-EAGLE plot was hatched, with two heads growing out of the same body.

1835. DANA, *Two Years*, xv. Answer my question, or I'll make a SPREAD EAGLE of you! I'll flog you, by G—d! . . . SPREAD EAGLES were a new kind of bird in California.

1885. *D. Chron.*, 27 Oct. Caltha SPREAD-EAGLED her field a long way from home.

1887. *Notes and Queries*, 7 S., iv. 278. Cod—as well as haddock and ling . . . may be seen SPREAD-EAGLED across transverse sticks to dry.

1900. KENNARD, *Right Sort*, xxv. Young Rassington's horse shot out like an arrow from a bow, and SPREAD-EAGLING his field in a style not often seen.

2. (Stock Exchange). — *See* quots.

18[?]. HUNT, *Merch. Mag.* (*Century*). This term [SPREAD EAGLE] is frequently used among stock speculators. A broker, satisfied with small profits . . . sells say one hundred shares Eric Railroad stock at fifty-eight, buyer sixty days, and at the same time buys the same quantity at fifty-seven, seller sixty days. The difference is . . . one per cent, which would be so much profit, without any outlay of capital, provided both contracts run their full time. Having sold buyer's option sixty days, and bought seller's option sixty days, the time is equal, but . . . he does not control the option in either case. The buyer can call when he pleases, which will compel the SPREAD-EAGLE operator to deliver; and the seller may deliver any time, which would compel the broker to receive. If he had capital to carry the result would not differ from that anticipated; if not he may be caught in a tight place.

1882. BIDDLE, *Stockbrokers*, 74. SPREAD EAGLE is where a broker buys a certain stock at seller's option, and sells the same at seller's option within a certain time, on the chance that both the contracts may run the full time, and he gain the difference.

Adj. (American).—Bombastic; espec. in reference to national vanity. Whence SPREAD-EAGLEISM = patriotic brag. As *verb.* = to play the good American till all is split.

1858. *N. Am. Rev.*, Oct, SPREAD-EAGLE style—a compound of exaggeration, effrontery, bombast and extravagance, mixed metaphors, platitudes, defiant threats thrown at the world, and irreverent appeals flung at the Supreme Being.

1871. LOWELL, *Study Windows*, 375. We Yankees are thought to be fond of the SPREAD-EAGLE style.

1873. *Hist. Mag.*, Sept., 'Rev. of Mission of N. Amer. People.' A very singular [volume] . . . with very much of that slam-bang, SPREAD-EAGLE literature which has made George Francis Train so notorious the world over.

1884. CLEMENS, *Huck. Finn.* Read the parts over in the most splendid SPREAD-EAGLE way.

1885. *D. Tel.*, 29 Nov. A fact resented by the SPREAD-EAGLEISM of the place in journalistic leaders.

1887. *Fort. Rev.*, N. S., XLI. 330. When we talk of SPREAD-EAGLEISM, we are generally thinking of the United States.

SPREE, *subs.* (old).—1. A frolic. As *verb.* = to carouse; SPREEISH = drunkish: *see* SCREWED (GROSE and BEE).

1821. EGAN, *Life in London*, II. v. Roosters and the 'peep-o'-day boys' were out on a prowl for a SPREE.

1825. SCOTT, *St. Roman's Well*, xx. John Blower, honest man, as sailors are aye for some SPREE or another, wad take me ance to see ane Mrs. Siddons.

1844. *Puck*, 14. The Proctor caught him in a SPREE, Asked his name . . . with courtesie.

1847. *Ireland Sixty Years Ago*, 15. The SPREE would probably have ended in the total sacking of Flattery's house.

1852. JUDSON, *Myst., &c., of New York*, I. 113. Taking a cruise about town, or going on a SPREE.

1856. DOW, *Sermons*, . . . If a young man creates his own ruination by going it loose and SPREEING it tight, it is surely a disgrace.

1859. *Punch*, xxxvii. 22. Our friend prone to vices you never may see, Though he goes on the loose, the cut, or the SPREE.

1866. WINTHROP, *Love and Skates.* He . . . took to SPREEIN' and liquor, and let down from a foreman to a hand.

1871. *All Year Round*, Sep. Out on the rampage, the loose, or the SPREE.

1885. *D. Tel.*, 16 Nov. He was always of the devil-may-care sort, fond of SPREEING about and lively company.

1892. KIPLING, *Barrack Room Ballads*, 'Gentlemen Rankers.' Gentlemen rankers out on the SPREE, Damned from here to eternity.

Adj. (Winchester). — 1. Conceited; stuck-up; of persons; (2) smart, stylish, befitting a Wykehamist. SPREE-MESS (*see* quot. *c.*1840).

*c.*1840. MANSFIELD, *School Life* (1866), 72. At the end of the half-year we used to have large entertainments called SPREE-MESSES, between Toy-time and Chapel, consisting of tea, coffee, muffins, cakes, &c., the funds for which were generally provided by fines inflicted during Toy-time for talking loud, slamming the door, coming in without whistling (to show that it was not a Master entering), improper language, &c., &c. Sometimes a SPREE-MESS was given by the boys about to leave that Half.

1881. PASCOE, *Public Schools.* Deprive a Wykehamist of words . . . such as quill . . . pruff . . . SPREE . . . cad . . . And his vocabulary becomes limited.

SPRIG, *subs.* (common).—A young dandy; any well-groomed youngster.

1637. SHIRLEY, *Hyde Park*, i. 1. A SPRIG of the nobility, That has a spirit equal to his fortunes.

1812. COOMBE, *Dr. Syntax in Search of Picturesque*, xix. An arch young SPRIG, a banker's clerk.

SPRING, *verb.* (colloquial).—(1) To bring to notice suddenly; (2) to pay out, to give alms; (3) to provide; and (4) to extort. To SPRING TO = to be able to accomplish, pay, give, &c., &c.

1614. JONSON, *Barthol. Fair*, v. 3. I may, perhaps, SPRING a wife for you anon.

*d.*1701. DRYDEN, *Ovid*, x. [CHALMERS, *Eng. Poet.*, xx. 511, 2, 1]. Surprised with fright, She starts, and leaves her bed, and SPRINGS a light.

1851-61. MAYHEW, *Lond. Lab.*, I. 53. It's a feast at a poor country labourer's place when he SPRINGS sixpenn'orth of fresh herrings.

1878. J. F. SULLIVAN, *The British Working Man, &c.* Wot's 'e SPRUNG?

1885. *D. Tel.*, 21 Nov. Such a man is not likely to SPRING UPON his associates and allies a scheme of English surrender to Irish demands.

1901. *Troddles and Us*, 106. It's seven pound fifteen, and we can SPRING TO that between us.

SPRINGAL (SPRING or SPRINGER), *subs.* (old).—A youth.

1535. COVERDALE, *Tr. Bible* [OLIPHANT, *New Eng.*, i. 443. Among his Romance phrases Coverdale has . . . SPRYNGALD (juvenis).]

*d.*1555. LATIMER, *Sermons*, 190 b. Joseph when he was sold to Potiphar . . . was a faire young SPRINGALL.

1570. LEVINS, *Manip. Vocab.* [E. E. T. S.], 16. A SPRINGALD, adolescens.

1578. NORTH, *Plutarch*, 90 E. He commaunded the women to departe, and . . . put lusty beardles SPRINGALLES into their apparell.

1585. NOMENCLATOR, *Adolescens*, . . . Un jouvenceau. A lad; a youth; a SPRINGALL.

1590. SPENSER, *Muiopotmus*, 292. The one his bowe and shafts, the other SPRING A burning Teade about his head did move. *Ibid.* (1596), *Fairy Queen*, v. v. 6. Amongst the rest . . . There came two SPRINGALS of full tender years.

1606. WILY, *Beguiled* [HAWKINS, *Orig. Dr.*, iii. 332]. Pray ye, maid, bid him welcome . . . he is a good proper SPRINGOLD.

1611. BEAUMONT and FLETCHER, *Kn. of Burning Pestle*, ii. 2. Sure the devil . . . is in this SPRINGALD.

1657. MIDDLETON, *More Dissemb. Beside Women*, v. 1. Ha, well done! excellent boy! dainty, fine SPRINGAL.

1661. DAVENPORT, *City Night Cap* [DODSLEY, *Old Plays* (REED), xi. 325]. That lusty SPRINGAL, Millicent, is no worse man Than the duke of Milan's son.

1692. DRYDEN, *Juvenal*, x. Your SPRINGAL, by his beauty curst . . . His form procures him journey-work; a strife Betwixt town madams and the merchant's wife.

SPRING-ANKLE WAREHOUSE, *subs. phr.* (old). — A prison: spec. Newgate (GROSE).

SPRINGERS (THE), *subs.* (military). —The Lincolnshire Regiment, formerly The 10th Foot: the nickname is also borne by the late 62nd Foot.

SPRINGER-UP, *subs. phr.* (HOTTEN).—A slop-tailor. SPRUNG-UP CLOTHES = garments 'blown' together.

SPRINKLE, *verb.* (colloquial).—To christen.

SPROUT, *subs.* (American).—1. A course of severe discipline; a birching. Also 2. (Yale) = a department of study—classics, mathematics, &c.; and 3. (in *pl.*) = a bunch of twigs. A BUNCH OF SPROUTS = (1) the closed fist, and (2) the chambers of a revolver.

SPRUG. To SPRUG UP, *verb. phr.* (provincial).—To dress neatly; to spruce.

SPRUNG, *adj.* (common).—Drunk: *see* SCREWED.

1856. MRS. STOWE, *Dred*, I. 87. He reckoned they were a little bit SPRUNG.

1870. JUDD, *Margaret*, I. 13. Ex-Corporal Whiston with his friends sallied from the store well-SPRUNG.

SPRUNT. TO SPRUNT UP, *verb. phr.* (American).—To bristle up; to resent suddenly.

SPRUSADO, *subs.* (nonce-word).—A dandy.

1665. *Com. on Chaucer* [Quoted in TODD'S JOHNSON]. The answer of that SPRUSADO to a judge . . . a rigid censor of men's habits; who, seeing a neat, finical divine come before him in a cloak lined through with plush, encountered him.

SPRY, *adj.* (American).—Active; lively; SMART (*q.v.*).

SPUD, *subs.* (common).—1. A potato: *see* MURPHY. Hence SPUDDY (costers') = a baked-potato man.

1887. *Field*, 12 Mar. But it was evidently a 'speed the plough,' a speed the SPUDS, and the seeds day.

1901. *Troddles and Us*, xix. Enough to revolt an Irishman's pig, and set him against SPUDS for the rest of his natural life.

1901. *Sp. Times*, 27 Ap., 1. 4. Annie used to fetch the SPUDS and greens.

2. (common). — A dwarf; a short thickset person.

3. (nursery).—A baby's hand.

4. (American).—In *pl.* = money: *see* RHINO.

5. (common).—A spade.

SPUDGEL, *verb.* (American).—To decamp: *see* ABSQUATULATE.

SPUNK, *subs.* (old).—1. Mettle; spirit; pluck (GROSE). Hence SPUNKIE (Scots) = (*a*) a plucky fellow, a lad of mettle; and (*b*) a will-o'-the-wisp; SPUNKY = spirited; TO SPUNK UP = to show fight.

1772. BRIDGES, *Burlesque Homer*, 262. Whether quite sober or dead drunk, I know, my dear, you've too much SPUNK.

1773. GOLDSMITH, *She Stoops to Conquer*, i. 2. The Squire has got SPUNK in him.

1784. BURNS, *Jolly Beggars*, Sir Violino, with an air That show'd a man of SPUNK. *Ibid.* (1786), *Address to the Deil.* An' aft your moss-traversing SPUNKIES, Decoy the wight that late and drunk is. *Ibid.* (*d.*1796), *Prayer to Sc. Reps.* Erskine, a SPUNKIE Norland billie.

1789. PARKER, *Happy Pair* [FARMER, *Musa Pedestris* (1896), 68]. With SPUNK let's post our neddies.

*c.*1790. *Ireland Sixty Years Ago*, 88. We saw de poor fellow was funkin', De drizzle stole down from his eye, Do we tought he had got better SPUNK in.

1796. WOLCOT ('Peter Pindar'), *Works*, i. 245. In that snug room where any man of SPUNK Would find it a hard matter to get drunk.

1819. MOORE, *Tom Crib*, 24. His SPUNKIEST backers were forced to sing small.

1838. BECKET, *Paradise Lost*, 11. They'll show more SPUNK, And fight much better when half drunk.

1853. LANDOR, *Imag. Conv.* 'Wm. Penn and Lord Peterborough.' Grave dons . . . grown again as young and SPUNKY as undergraduates.

1869. STOWE, *Oldtown*, 67. Parsons is men, like the rest of us, and the doctor had got his SPUNK up.

1896. LILLARD, *Poker Stories*, 143. I admire your SPUNK . . . most women faint when they see me.

2. (street and Scots).—In *pl.* = matches. SPUNK-FENCER = a match-vendor. Hence = a spark.

1815. SCOTT, *Guy Mannering*, xi. A SPUNK o' fire in the red room.

3. (venery).—The seminal fluid; METTLE (*q.v.*).

SPUR, *verb.* (thieves').—To annoy. TO GET THE SPUR = to be annoyed: *see* NEEDLE.

1877. HORSLEY, *Jottings from Jail.* The only thing that SPURRED me was being such a flat to bring them home.

SPY, *subs.* (old).—The eye.

1590. SPENSER, *Fairy Queen*, III. i. 36. With her two crafty SPYES She secretly would search each daintie lim.

1609. SHAKSPEARE, *Tempest*, v. 1. 259. If these be true SPIES which I wear in my head, here's a goodly sight.

SQUAB, *subs.* (old).—1. Anything fat, short, and dumpy. Hence (2) a fat sofa or well-filled bed. As *adj.* (SQUABBY, SQUADDY, SQUATTY, SQUABBISH, &c.) = fat and short, heavy, bulky (in quot. 1756 = short, abrupt).—GROSE. As *verb.* = to fall heavily, to plump down.

1593. GREENE, *News from Heaven and Hell.* A fatte SQUADDY monke that had been well fedde in some cloyster.

1666. HARVEY, *Of Consumption.* Diet makes them of a SQUABBISH or lardy habit of body.

1675. WYCHERLEY, *Country Wife*, iv. 3. A little SQUAB French page who speaks no English.

1692. L'ESTRANGE, *Æsop.* The eagle took the tortoise up in the air, and dropt him down, SQUAB, upon a rock.

*c.*1708. POPE, *Artemisia* [CHALMERS, *Eng. Poets*, xii. 211]. 'Artemisia.' On her large SQUAB you find her spread, Like a fat corpse upon a bed.

1712. BETTERTON, *Miller of Trompington.* Nor the SQUAB daughter nor the wife were nice.

1714. ADDISON, *Spectator*, 529. Seated . . . upon a SQUAB.

1716. POPE, *Letter*, 'To Lady M. W. Montague,' 18 Aug. We shall then see how the prudes of this world owed all their fine figure only to their being a little straiter laced; and that they were naturally as arrant SQUABS as those that went more loose.

1759. GOLDSMITH, *Bee*, No. 2. A French woman is a perfect architect in dress . . . She never tricks out a SQUABBY Doric shape with Corinthian finery.

1756. WALPOLE, *To Mann*, 25 July, iii. 125. We have returned a SQUAB answer.

1855. GASKELL, *North and South*, xii. Bessie, herself, lay on a SQUAB, or short sofa, placed under the window.

1865. MAJOR DOWNING, *May-Day.* I had hardly got seated when in came a great, stout, fat, SQUADDY woman.

1870. JUDD, *Margaret*, ii. 11. Ladies in . . . short cloaks, with hoods SQUABBING behind.

1885. *D. Tel.*, 10 Sep. The SQUABBY stone structure.

2. (colloquial).—An inexperienced person; a fledgling. As *adj.* = CALLOW (*q.v.*), coy, quiet.

1635. BROME, *Sparagus Garden*, ii. 2. *Brit.* Is he a trim youth? *Mon.* We must make him one, Jacke; 'tis such a SQUAB . . . such a lumpe.

1689. NAT. LEE, *Princess of Cleves*, iii. 1. Your demure ladies that are so SQUOB in company are devils in a corner.

*d.*1712. W. KING, *The Old Cheese* [CHALMERS, *Eng. Poets*, ix. 297. Why must old pigeons, and they stale, be drest, When there's so many SQUAB ones in the nest.

1781. COWPER, *Prog. of Error*, 218. Gorgonius sits, abdominous and wan, Like a fat SQUAB upon a Chinese fan.

Verb. (King Edward's School, B'gham).—To squeeze by: also SQUOB: with foot on wall or desk, and back against the victim who is similarly treated on the other side, or pressed against the opposite wall. Also SQUAB-UP = to push.

SQUABASH, *verb.* (old colloquial). —To crush. As *subs.* = a flattening out; SPIFLICATION (*q.v.*).

1827. SCOTT, *Diary*, 17 Jan. His satire . . . SQUABASHED at one blow, a set of coxcombs who might have humbugged the world long enough.

1830. *Intelligencer*, 11 Ap. Compared with the sarcastic irony which SQUABASHES poor Mr. Nicholas Carlisle.

1833. *M. Advtr.*, 1 July. A SQUABASH of the growing incumbrance of chivalrous novels.

1837. BARHAM, *Ingolds. Leg.*, 'House Warming.' Harry the Sixth who, instead Of being SQUABASHED, as in Shakespeare we've read, Caught a bad influenza, and died in his bed.

SQUABBLED, *adj.* (printers').—'Broken': of type which, after 'setting,' has been knocked so much awry that it is a painstaking job to prevent it going to PI (*q.v.*).

SQUADDLE, *verb.* (American).—To decamp; TO ABSQUATULATE (*q.v.*).

SQUAIL (also **SQUAILER**), *verb.* and *subs.* (old).—*See* quot. 1847. Also SQUAWL.

1651. [HUNT, *Bristol*, quoted in *Notes and Queries*, 7 S., iv. 169]. SQUAILING a goose before his door, and tossing cats and dogs on Shrove Tuesday.

*c.*1696. B. E., *Dict. Cant. Crew*, s.v. SQUAWL—To throw awry.

1834. SOUTHEY, *Doctor*, clxiv. You SQUAIL at us on Shrove Tuesday . . . and arm us with steel spurs that we may mangle and kill each other for your sport.

1847. HALLIWELL, *Arch. Words*, s.v. SQUAIL. To throw sticks at cocks. SQUAILER, the stick thrown. Mr. Akerman says SQWOILING is used for throwing, but the thing thrown must be some material not easily managed; with a stick sometimes made unequally heavy by being loaded with lead at one end. SQUAILING is often very awkwardly performed, because the thing thrown cannot be well directed; hence the word SQUAILING is often used in ridicule of what is done awkwardly, untowardly or irregularly shaped. "She went up the street SQUAILING her arms about, you never saw the like:" an ill shaped loaf is a SQUAILING loaf; Brentford is a long SQUAILING town; and, in Wiltshire, Smithfield Market would be called a SQUAILING sort of a place.—[*Abridged*].

1881. *D. Tel.*, 30 Nov. Now that the trees are bare and the leaves have fallen, the idlers of the county towns may perhaps sally forth armed with SQUAILERS, an ingenious instrument composed of a short stick of pliant cane and a leaded knob, to drive the harmless little squirrel from tree to tree, and lay it a victim at the feet of a successful shots.

SQUALL, *subs.* (old).—A girl.

1593. HOLYBAND, *Dict.* *Tu es un cainar*, thou art a SQUALL.

1607. MIDDLETON, *Michælmas Term*, i. 2. A pretty, beautiful, juicy SQUALL.

1611. COTGRAVE, *Dict.*, s.v. *Obeseau*, a young minx or little proud SQUALL.

1630. TAYLOR, *Works*. The rich gull gallant Call's her deare and love, Ducke, lambe, SQUALL, sweet-heart, cony, and his dove.

Verb. (B. E.).—'To cry a loud.'

TO LOOK OUT FOR SQUALLS, *verb. phr.* (colloquial).—To be on guard.

SQUANTUM, *subs.* (American).—1. The imaginary name of a place 'very far way back' from whence rustics and HAYSEEDS (*q.v.*) come. Also (2) = a picnic.

SQUARE, *adj.*, *verb.*, and *adv.* SQUARE, like ROUND (*q.v.*), has lived many lives in slang: in fact, it has 'boxed the compass,' and now means the antipodes of what it meant in Shakspeare's time.

Verb. (old).—1. To disagree, to quarrel or be at variance: hence SQUARER = a quarreller; while OUT OF SQUARE = (1) at variance, and (2) dishonest; TO BREAK (or BREED) SQUARES = to give offence; AT SQUARE = angry, at enmity; TO SQUARE UP TO = to assume a fighting attitude (BEE); TO SQUARE UP AND DOWN = to strut; TO SEE HOW SQUARES GO = to watch events, 'to see how the cat will jump.'

1551. *State Trials*, 'Gardiner,' 5 Ed. VI. He said he had often SQUARED WITH me but he loved me never the worse.

1555. R. EDEN to Francisco Lopez [*First Books on America* (ARBER), 346]. He speaketh not greatly OUT OF SQUARE.

1577. HOLINSHED, *Hist. Engl.*, iv. 8. She falling AT SQUARE with hir husband.

1578. WHETSTONE, *Promos and Cassandra*, ii. 4. Marry, She knew you and I were AT SQUARE; At least we fell to blowes.

1592. SHAKSPEARE, *Mid. Night's Dream*, ii. 1. And now, they never meet . . . But they do SQUARE. *Ibid.* (1593), *Tit. And.*, ii. 1, 100. Are you such fools To SQUARE FOR this. *Ibid.* (1600), *Much Ado*, i. 1, 82. Is there no young SQUARER now that will make a voyage with him to the devil. *Ibid.* (1608), *Anthony and Cleop.*, iii. 11. Mine honesty and I begin TO SQUARE.

1592. GREENE, *Quip for Upst. Courtier.* To SQUARE it UP AND DOWNE the streets before his mistresse.

1594. HOOKER, *Eccles. Polity*, iii. 1. In St. Paul's time the integrity of Rome was famous; Corinth many ways reproved; they of Galatia much more OUT OF SQUARE.

*d.*1612. HARINGTON, *Epigrams*, I. 37. Once, by mishap, two poets fell A-SQUARING.

*d.*1657. BRADFORD, *Plymouth Plantation*, 269. At length they . . . resolved to send Mr. Winslow . . . into England, TO SEE HOW YE SQUARS WENTE.

1696. LESTRANGE, *Æsop*. One frog looked about him TO SEE HOW SQUARES WENT with their new king. *Ibid.* I will BREAK NO SQUARES whether it be so or not.

1902. *D. Mail*, 13 Nov., 3, 4. The men SQUARED UP to each other, and Martin struck Drew a violent blow in the face which felled him.

2. (colloquial).—To be entirely in agreement, to arrange, to accommodate. Whence ON (or UPON) THE SQUARE (or SQUARELY, *adv.*) = absolutely dependable; ALL SQUARE (or SQUARES) = all right; SQUARE TO (BY THE SQUARE, or IN SQUARE) = suitable, exact, in amity or agreement; TO KEEP SQUARE = to lead a straight life. Also in combination: amongst others, SQUARE BACKDOWN = a palpable retreat; SQUARE PIECE = a decent girl; SQUARE ANSWER = an unmistakable reply; SQUARE CLOBBER = respectable clothes; SQUARE CRIB = 'a house of good repute' (GROSE); SQUARE TATS = honest dice; SQUARE DRINKER = a steady toper; SQUARE EATER = a hearty feeder; SQUARE THING = the truth: *see* quot. 1785: also SQUARE HEAD (thieves') = an honest man; SQUARE MEAL = a substantial repast; SQUARE PLAY = fair play; SQUARE-RIGGED = well-dressed, &c., &c.

1589. PUTTENHAM, *Arte of Eng. Poesie* [ARBER], 113. A constant minded man, euen egal and direct on all sides, and not easily ouerthrowne by euery little aduersitie . . . a SQUARE MAN.

1604. SHAKSPEARE, *Winter's Tale*, v. 1. O, that ever I Had SQUARED me to thy counsel. *Ibid.* (1608), *Anthony and Cleop.*, ii. 2, 190. She's a most triumphant lady if report be SQUARE to her. *Ibid.*, ii. 36. Read not my blemishes in the world's report: I have not KEPT MY SQUARE; but that to come shall all be done by the rule. *Ibid.* (1609), *Timon of Athens*, v. 4, 36. It is not SQUARE to take On those that are revenges.

1611. COTGRAVE, *Dict.* s.v. *Vn ferial beuveur.* A SQUARE DRINKER . . . one that will take his liquor soundly.

1616. FLETCHER, *Bonduca*, ii. 3. By Heaven, SQUARE EATERS! . . . Upon my conscience, The poor rogues have not eat this month.

1628. FORD, *Lover's Melancholy*, iv. 2. Then they . . . steal women's hearts; with them and theirs The world runs round; yet they are SQUARE MEN still.

16[?]. MILTON, *Ans. to Salmasius*, x. They chose rather to be lorded over . . . by a tyrant . . . than endure their brethren and friends to be ON THE SQUARE with them.

1640. SHIRLEY, *Love's Cruelty*, ii. 3. Should he retain a thought not SQUARE of her, This will correct all.

1642. SIR T. BROWNE, *Religio Medici*, i. 5. There is no Church whose every part so SQUARES unto my conscience.

1644-5. HOWELL, *Letters*, I. vi. 46. He could never SQUARE well with his Eminence the Cardinal.

1662. FULLER, *Worthies*, I. xv. Both being put together may SQUARE out the most eminent of the ancient gentry in some tolerable proportion.

1677. WYCHERLEY, *Plain Dealer*, i. 1. Telling truth is . . . as prejudicial to a man that would thrive in the world as SQUARE PLAY to a cheat.

1692. DRYDEN, *Juvenal*, iii. 179. We live not ON THE SQUARE with such as these.

*d.*1704. BROWN, *Works*, i. 46. If they dealt SQUARELY with me they'd scarce at all wonder.

*d.*1718. PENN, 'To his Wife and Children' [*Century*]. Keep UPON THE SQUARE, for God sees you.

1726. VANBRUGH, *Provoked Husband*, v. 1. Marriage is at worst but playing UPON THE SQUARE.

1782. COWPER, *Charity*, 559. No works shall find acceptance in that day That SQUARES not truly with the Scripture plan.

1785. GROSE, *Vulg. Tongue*, s.v. SQUARE. All fair, upright and honest practices are called THE SQUARE, in opposition to the cross. A . . . person who is considered by the world to be honest, and who is unacquainted with family people, and their system of operation, is by the latter emphatically styled a SQUARE COVE; whereas an old thief who has acquired an independance, and now confines himself to SQUARE practices is called, by his old pals, a flash cove who has tyed up prigging.

1809. MALKIN, *Gil Blas* [ROUTLEDGE], 86. I never split hairs, but deal UPON THE SQUARE.

1823. BEE, *Dict. Turf*, s.v. SQUARE . . . Anything you have bought, or acquired honestly, is termed a SQUARE ARTICLE; and any transaction which is fairly and equitably conducted, is said to be a SQUARE CONCERN.

1826-9. OLIVER, *Signs and Symbols*, 190. You must keep within the compass, and act UPON THE SQUARE with all mankind, for your masonry is but a dead letter if you do not habitually perform its reiterated injunctions.

1864. BROWNE, *Artemus Ward Among the Mormons* [*Works* (1899), 231]. That was the SQUAREST meal on the road except at Weber. *Ibid.*, 288. A good SQUARE, lively fite.

1866. ELIOT, *Felix Holt*, xx. If a man's got a bit of property . . . he'll want to keep things SQUARE. *Ibid.* (1866), xxi. 'Was the marriage all right then?' 'Oh, all ON THE SQUARE—civil marriage, church—everything.

1866. *London Miscellany*, 3 Mar., 57. We don't want no one took in that's ON THE SQUARE. The governor's promised the school as stranger's shan't use the house.

1869. MCCLURE, *Rocky Mountains*, 30. The transition from the luxurious tables of the East to the SQUARE MEALS of the West is fortunately gradual.

1885. *Field*, 3 Oct. James again brought matters SQUARE on the fifth. *Ibid.* (1886), 25 Sep. Mr. Laidlay won with six, and SQUARED matters.

1886. *D. Tel.*, 17 Feb., 5. The question will now come SQUARELY before the House.

1887. HENLEY, *Villon's Straight Tip*. Suppose you try a different tack, And ON THE SQUARE you flash your flag.

1896. LILLARD, *Poker Stories*, 240. The games played there were not what are known as SQUARE games.

1900. FLYNT, *Tramps*, 278. But I've given many a lad a ride, and I'm always willing to be square to a SQUARE PLUG (fellow).

1901. WALKER, *In the Blood*, 106. His SQUARE-CLOBBER or respectable clothes. *Ibid.*, 259. I don't call it actin' ON THE SQUARE to Susie.

3. (colloquial).—To bribe; to pay. Thus TO SQUARE MATTERS = to pay off: also TO SQUARE THE YARDS (nautical); TO SQUARE UP = to settle a bill.

1835. DANA, *Before the Mast*, xxvi. Many a delay and vexation . . . did he get to pay up the old scores, or 'SQUARE THE YARDS with the bloody quill-driver.'

1845. DISRAELI, *Sybil*, III. 2. There will be enough to pay all our debts and pay us all SQUARE.

1859. LEVER, *Davenport Dunn*, xi. The horses he had 'nobbled,' the jockeys SQUARED, the owners 'hocussed.'

1879. HUXLEY [*Pop. Sci. Monthly*, XXXV. 609]. How D—— was SQUARED, and what he got in . . . these transactions does not appear.

1886. *Globe*, 10 Mar. They have squandered enormous sums of money in SQUARING a huge army of committee men, collectors, and other hangers-on.

1893. EMERSON, *Lippo*, v. To show you mean it stand a couple of shants of bevarly TO SQUARE the boys.

4. (colloquial).—To assume a rigid or set attitude: as TO SQUARE ONE'S SHOULDERS = (1) to stand (or sit) bolt upright, and (2) to show disgust; TO SQUARE ONE'S ELBOWS = to give free play in driving (BEE); TO SIT SQUARE = to sit straight; TO SQUARE OUT = to lay out; TO SQUARE ROUND = to make room.

1850. THACKERAY, *Pendennis*, xxxviii. 'Wanted to fight the Frenchman'; . . . and he laughed, and he SQUARED with his fists.

1854. W. COLLINS, *Hide and Seek*, i. 12. Here Zack came in with the gloves on, SQUARING on the most approved prize fighter principles as he advanced.

1861. DICKENS, *Great Expect.*, xliii. I planted myself side by side with Mr. Drummie, my shoulders SQUARED and my back to the fire.

1878. STEVENSON, *Inland Voyage*, 50. He who can sit SQUAREST on a three-legged stool, he it is who has the wealth and glory. *Ibid.*, Epil. He again SQUARED HIS ELBOWS over his writing.

5. MISCELLANEOUS PHRASES.—TO SQUARE THE CIRCLE = to achieve the impossible; 'How go SQUARES?' = 'How do you do?'; A SQUARE PEG IN A ROUND HOLE = anything misplaced or incongruous; STRAIGHT DOWN THE CROOKED LANE AND ALL ROUND THE SQUARE = a humorous way of setting a man on his word; ALL FAIR AND SQUARE = above board, dependable.

SQUARE-CAP, *subs. phr.* (old).—A London apprentice.

1651. CLEAVELAND, *Poems* [NARES]. But still she repli'd, good sir, la-bee, If ever I have a man, SQUARE-CAP for me.

SQUARE-FACE, *subs. phr.* (common).—An inferior gin made, chiefly in Germany, for barter with and consumption by savages.

SQUAREHEAD, *subs.* (Australian).—1. Formerly a free emigrant; now (2) a German or Scandinavian.

See SQUARE.

SQUARE-TOES, *subs. phr.* (old).—An old man (GROSE); a FOGEY (*q.v.*); a PRECISIAN (*q.v.*); also OLD SQUARETOES. Hence SQUARE-TOED = formal, prim, testy.

1771. SMOLLETT, *Humph. Clinker* (1900), i. 65. He seems to have a reciprocal regard for OLD SQUARETOES, whom he calls by the familiar name of Mathew.

1772. BRIDGES, *Burlesque Homer*, 23. OLD SQUARE-TOES . . . Call'd silence; but he first with care Lifted his buttocks off his chair.

1860-3. THACKERAY, *Roundabout Papers*, xi. Have we not almost all learnt these expressions of old foozles, and uttered them ourselves when in the SQUARE-TOED state. *Ibid.* (1862), *Philip*, xv. I have heard of an OLD SQUARETOES of sixty who learned very satisfactorily to dance.

SQUARSON, *subs.* (common).—*See* quots., SQUISHOP, and PORTMANTEAU-WORD. Whence SQUARSONAGE = a parsonage.

1886. A. LANG, *Mark of Cain*, ix. He held the sacrosanct position of a SQUARSON, being at once Squire and Parson of the parish of Little Wentley. *Ibid.* She left the gray old SQUARSONAGE, and went to London.

1888. *Living Church*, 25 Aug. The . . . Rev. W. H. Hoare, of Oakfield, Sussex . . . was the original of the well-known expression, invented by Bishop Wilberforce, SQUARSON, by which he meant a landed proprietor in holy orders.

SQUARUM, *subs.* (shoemakers').—A lapstone.

SQUASH, *subs.* (colloquial).—1. A smash, a soft or flat mass; and (2) a mellay: spec. (Harrow), *see* quot. 1876. As *verb.* = (1) to crush or smash: also TO GO SQUASH = to collapse; and (2) to silence by word or deed. Hence SQUASHER, SQUASHINESS, and SQUASHY.

1726. SWIFT, *Gulliver*, ii. 1. One of the reapers approaching . . . made me apprehend that with the next step I should be SQUASHED to death under his foot. *Ibid.*, ii. 7. My fall was stopped by a terrible SQUASH.

1824-9. LANDOR, *Imag. Conv.*, 'Southey and Porson,' ii. Give a trifle of strength and austerity to the SQUASHINESS of our friend's poetry.

1854. DICKENS, *Hard Times*, xi. Wet through and through; with her feet squelching and SQUASHING in her shoes whenever she moved.

1876. COLLINS, *Public Schools* [Harrow], 312. The gravel cut the leather case of the ball occasionally, as well as the hands and faces of those who scrambled over it in a SQUASH . . . which Rugby men know as a 'scrummage' and Etonians as a 'rouge.'

1884. *Harper's Mag.*, lxxviii. 80. It seemed churlish to pass him by without a sign, especially as he took off his SQUASH of a hat to me.

1898. NISBET, *Sweet Sinner*, vi. George Keath was a stalwart man . . . and the like of this music teacher he could have settled and SQUASHED in half a minute.

3. (Harrow).—Racquets played with a soft india-rubber ball: the ball is also known as a SQUASH.

SQUAT, *subs.* (colloquial).—1. A short thick-set person. SQUATTY (or SQUADDY) = lumpish, dumpy.

1881. J. BURROUGHS, *Pepacton*, iii. A few yards away stood another short, SQUATTY hemlock, and I said my bees ought to be there.

2. (American Stock Exchange).—*See* quot.

1870. MEDBERY, *Men and Mysteries of Wall St.*, 168. He extricated himself from serious difficulties by . . . what is known in the street as SQUATTING. In other words, he dishonored his own contracts, and entered upon a lawsuit to cover his duplicity.

SQUATTER, *subs.* (old colloquial: now general).—1. A settler on public land without title or license; hence (2) any domiciliary usurper. Also (3) in Australia a pastoral tenant of the Crown. Whence SQUAT, *verb.* = (1) to settle on land without title: *e.g.*, on a common, and (2) as in *subs.* senses 2 and 3. Derivatives are numerous: *e.g.*, SQUATTAGE = a squatter's station; SQUATTOCRACY (SQUATTERARCHY or SQUATTERDOM) = the world of squatters: spec. rich landowners in pastoral districts: *cf.* MOBOCRACY, COTTONOCRACY, SLAVEOCRACY, &c., &c.

1829. CAPT. BASIL HALL, *Trav. in N. Amer.*, II. 297. A wooding station owned by what is called a SQUATTER.

1835. T. A. MURRAY, *Evidence before Legislative Council of New South Wales on Police and Gaols.* There are several parties of SQUATTERS in my neighbourhood. I detected, not long since, three men at one of their stations in the act of slaughtering one of my own cattle. I have strong reason to suspect that these people are, in general, illicit sellers of spirits.

1840. F. P. LABILLIERE, *Early History of Victoria* (1878), ii. 189. The SQUATTERS of New South Wales, a class of persons whom it would be wrong to confound with those who bear the same name in America, . . . generally persons . . . who have taken unauthorized possession of land. Among the SQUATTERS of New South Wales are the wealthiest of the land, occupying, with the permission of the Government, thousands and tens of thousands of acres.

1846. HODGSON, *Reminisc.*, 118. English are the most numerous, then the Scotch, then the Irish amongst the SQUATTOCRACY.

1854. *Melbourne Morning Herald*, 18 Feb., 4, 5. *SQUATTOCRATIC IMPUDENCE* [Title].

1861. MCCOMBIE, *Australian Sketches*, 128. SQUATTER was applied in the first instance to signify, as in America, such as erected huts on unsold land. It thus came to be applied to all who did not live on their own land, to whom the original and more expressive name of settler continued to be applied.

1868. BONWICK, *John Batman*, 94. Writes to another at a distance upon the subject of SQUATTERDOM.

1872. C. H. EDEN, *Wife and I*, 59. The howl for the abolition of the SQUATTOCRACY had not yet been fostered under the malign influence of short-sighted politicians.

1885. CAMPBELL-PRAED, *Head Station*, 35. The bloated SQUATTOCRACY represents Australian Conservatism.

1890. BOLDREWOOD, *Squatter's Dream*, iv. 42. He trusted to pass into the ranks of the SQUATTOCRACY.

1897. *Austr. Steam Nav. Co. 'Guide Book,'* 29. The term SQUATTER, as applied to the class it now designates—without which where would Australia now be?—was not in vogue till 1842.

Verb. (old).—To move briskly or noisily through mud and water.

1598. FLORIO, *Worlde of Wordes*, s.v. *Squaecarare.* To SQUATTER; to lash it out behind after a purgation. *Ibid.*, *Squaechera*, a soft SQUATTERING turd.

*d.*1796. BURNS, *Address to the Deil.* Amang the springs, Awa' ye SQUATTER'D, like a drake, On whistling wings.

1852. BRONTE, *Villette*, xxv. A little callow gosling SQUATTERING out of bounds.

SQUATTEZ-VOUS, *intj. phr.* (common).—'Sit down!'

1900. KIPLING, *Stalky and Co.*, 179. 'Be quick, you ass! . . . SQUATTEZ-VOUS on the floor, then!

SQUATTLE, *verb.* (American).—To decamp: *see* ABSQUATULATE.

SQUAWK, *subs.* (colloquial).—1. A harsh noise or voice: also as *verb.*

1856. *Widow Bedott Papers*, 208. The way she SQUAWKED it out was a caution to old gates on a windy day!

1861. C. READE, *Cloister and Hearth*, xxvi. Gerard gave a little SQUAWK, and put his fingers in his ears.

2. (American).—A bad failure.

SQUEAK, *subs.* (colloquial). — A narrow escape; a close SHAVE (*q.v.*).—GROSE.

1889. O'REILLY, *Fifty Years on the Trail.* It was a NARROW SQUEAK for me, as the bullet cut off a lock of my hair.

1898. GOULD, *Landed at Last*, vii. We've had some NARROW SQUEAKS of missing him . . . [a] narrow shave was at York.

Verb. (old).—1. To talk; and (2) to betray confidence; TO SQUEAL, TO PEACH (*q.v.*). Hence SQUEAKER = (1) a BLAB (*q.v.*), and (2) an informer; TO SQUEAK BEEF = to cry 'Stop thief': *see* BEEF (B. E. and GROSE).

1690. DRYDEN, *Don Sebastian*, iv. 3. If he be obstinate, put a civil question to him on the rack, and he SQUEAKS, I warrant him.

*c.*1725. *Retoure my dear Dell* [*Canting Dict.*]. I never will whiddle, I never will SQUEAK.

1815. SCOTT, *Guy Mannering*, xxxiv. That's another breaker ahead, Captain! Will she not SQUEAK, think ye!

1834. AINSWORTH, *Rookwood*, III. v. Never blow the gab or SQUEAK.

3. (old).—To shirk: an obligation, debt, &c.

SQUEAKER, *subs.* (old). — 1. A child: spec. (B. E. and GROSE) a BYE-BLOW (*q.v.*); also SQUEALER. TO STIFLE THE SQUEAKER = (1) to procure abortion; and (2) to get rid of a bastard.

2. (old).—In *pl.* = organ pipes (GROSE).

3. (old).—A pig.

4. (old).—A young bird; a CHIRPER; a PEEPER; a SQUEALER (*q.v.*).

1876. GREENER, *The Gun* (1884), 535. Mr. Campbell succeeded in bagging 220 grouse by evening; every SQUEAKER was, however, counted.

SQUEAL, *verb.* (thieves').—1. To inform; TO PEACH; TO SQUEAK (*q.v.*). Hence SQUEALER = an informer: *see* NARK (GROSE).

1870. *New York Tribune*, 27 Oct. G. R—— is caught, and may SQUEAL on us.

1882. *Century Mag.*, xxxv. 649. The first step . . . is to spread abroad the rumour that this, that, or the other confederate is about to SQUEAL; . . . it will be but a few days before one of the rogues will . . . anticipate the traitors by turning State's evidence.

1896. LILLARD, *Poker Stories*, 52. The planter was clean 'cornered,' but he was working George on a dead sure thing and couldn't SQUEAL.

1900. FLYNT, *Tramps*, 128. If they SQUEAL, as the tramp says, they are sure to be rewarded.

1902. LYNCH, *High Stakes*, xxiii. When he drew a fare and got well treated, he was not the man TO SQUEAL.

SQUEALER, *subs.* (common).—1. *See* quot., SQUEAKER, and SQUEAL.

1881. *Century Mag.*, xxxiii. 100. When ready to leave the nest and face the world for itself, it [a young pigeon] is a SQUEALER, or, in market parlance, a squab.

2. (Wellington School). — A small boy.

SQUEEMISH, *adj.* (B. E.).—'Nice.'

SQUEEZE, *subs.* (common). — 1. Silk.

1877. HORSLEY, *Jottings from Jail.* Me and another screwed a place at Stoke Newington, and we got some SQUEEZE dresses, and two sealskin jackets, and some other things.

2. (common).—A crowd; a PUSH (*q.v.*); crowding.

1862. THACKERAY, *Philip*, xxvi. Four and twenty hours of SQUEEZE in the diligence.

3. *See* SQUEEZER.

Verb. (B. E.).—'To gripe, or skrew hard.' Also (colloquial) = to extort, to coerce, TO BEST (*q.v.*). As *subs.* = (1) a hard bargain; (2) HOBSON'S CHOICE (*q.v.*); and (3) a RISE (*q.v.*). Whence SQUEEZABLE, SQUEEZABILITY, &c.

1670. MILTON, *Hist. Britain*, vi. He [Canute] SQUEEZED out of the English, though now his subjects, not his Enemies, 72, some say 82, thousand pound.

1809. MALKIN, *Gil Blas* [ROUTLEDGE], 378. You shall go snacks in all that we can SQUEEZE OUT of the old fellow.

1852. SAVAGE, *Reuben Medlicott* (1864), i. 9. You are too versatile and too SQUEEZABLE . . . you take impressions too readily.

1890. PEACOCKE, *Descript. of the East*, i. 171. The little officers oppress the people; the great officers SQUEEZE them.

1892. LOWE, *Bismarck*, II. 230. The peace-of-mind-at-any-price disposition of that Cabinet had rendered it SQUEEZABLE to any extent.

1900. FLYNT, *Tramps*, 308. And then there is a celebration over having SQUEEZED another Railroad company.

SQUEEZE-EM-CLOSE, *subs. phr.* (venery).—Copulation: *see* GREENS.

SQUEEZER (or **SQUEEZE**), *subs.* (old).—1. The neck (GROSE and VAUX). Also (2) = the hangman's noose.

*c.*1811. MAHER, *The Night Before Larry was Stretched.* For Larry was always the lad, When a friend was condemned to the SQUEEZER, He'd fence all the togs that he had, Just to help the poor boy to a sneezer.

*c.*1866. VANCE, *Chickaleary Cove.* The stock around my SQUEEZE of a guiver colour see.

1887. HENLEY, *Villon's Straight Tip.* Until the SQUEEZER nips your scrag, Booze and the blowens cop the lot.

3. (American).—In *pl.* = playing cards with the values marked in the top left hand margins. Also SQUEEZE, *verb.*, *see* quot.

1896. LILLARD, *Poker Stories*, 23. Gen. Schenck, like all great poker players, used to SQUEEZE his hand, that is, arrange them so that only the indicators at the corners were visible.

SQUEEZE-WAX, *subs. phr.* (old).—A surety (B. E. and GROSE).

SQUELCH (or **SQUELSH**), *subs.* (old).—A hard hit, a heavy fall; espec. one under something or somebody: also SQUELCHER. As *verb.* = to crush, to SQUASH (*q.v.*).

1624. MIDDLETON, *Game at Chess*, v. 3. This fat bishop hath so overlaid me, So SQUELCH'D and squeezed me.

1663. BUTLER, *Hudibras*, I. ii. 933. But Ralpho, who had now begun T'adventure resurrection From heavy SQUELCH, and had got up.

*d.*1687. COTTON, *Works* (1734), 242. And yet was not the SQUELCH so ginger, But that I sprain'd my little finger.

. . . . . *St. George for England*, Part II. But George he did the dragon fell, And gave him a plaguy SQUELCH.

1853. BRADLEY, *Verdant Green.* There's a SQUELCHER in the bread-basket that'll stop your dancing, my kivey!

1866. [Quoted by BROWNE in *Artemus Ward Among the Fenians*, 'Preliminary.'] SQUELCHED, exterminated . . . and extinguished the cantankerous Senators.

1886. J. W. PALMER, *After his Kind*, 120. Luke gazed shamefaced at the nosegay in his button-hole and was SQUELCHED.

1902. *Pall Mall Gaz.*, 4 Dec., 2, 2. Politicians in Dublin have been experiencing a delirious titillation of the bump of combativeness by an announcement that Mr. Redmond is to descend upon Dundalk with a design to SQUELCH Mr. Healy.

SQUENCH, *verb.* (vulgar). — To quench.

1600. *Contention*, I. 59. Fetche pitch and flaxe, and SQUENCH it.

SQUIB, *subs.* (GROSE). — 1. 'A small satirical or political temporary jeu d'esprit, which, like the fire-work of that denomination, sparkles, bounces, stinks, and vanishes.'

2. (artists').—A brush.

3. (old).—*See* quot.

1731. *St. James's Evg. Post* [SYDNEY, *Eng. in 18th Century*, i. 229], 'List of Officers attached to Gaming-houses' . . . 4. Two Puffs, who have money given them to play with. . . . 6. A SQUIB who is a puff of a lower rank, who serves at half salary while he is learning to deal.

4. (costers'). — In *pl.* = asparagus.

Verb. (old).—To lampoon.

SQUIBOB, *subs.* (American). — A finniking, fussy person: in contempt.

SQUIFFED, *adj.* (colloquial). — Drunk: also SQUIFFY: *see* SCREWED.

1900. KIPLING, *Stalky & Co.*, 17. I never got SQUIFFY but once . . . an' it made me horrid sick.

1901. WALKER, *In the Blood*, 256. He had often been outspoken enough about anybody being SQUIFFY.

SQUIGGLE, *verb.* (American).—To evade; to wriggle; TO SQUIRM (*q.v.*).

SQUINNY-EYES, *subs. phr.* (old).—A squinting man or woman: also SQUIN-EYES, SQUINT-A-PIPES, and SQUINT-A-FUEGO. As *adj.* = squinting; TO SQUINNY (or SQUIN) = to squint; and (American) to laugh, wink, or smile.

1602. HEYWOOD, *How to Choose a Good Wife.* Gold can make limping Vulcan walke upright, Make SQUIN-EIES looke straight.

1605. SHAKSPEARE, *Lear*, iv. 6. I remember thine eyes well enough. What, dost Thou SQUINY at me?

1609. ARMIN, *Ital. Taylor and his Boy.* As doctors in their deepest doubts, Stroke up their foreheads hie; Or men amazde, their sorrow flouts By SQUEANING with the eye.

1692. DRYDEN, *Persius*, v. 271. The timbrel, and the SQUINTIFEGO maid Of Isis, awe thee.

1785. GROSE, *Vulg. Tongue*, s.v. SQUINT-A-PIPES . . . said to be born in the middle of the week, and looking both ways for Sunday; or born in a hackney coach, and looking out of both windows; fit for a cook, one eye in the pot, and the other up the chimney; looking nine ways at once.

SQUINSY. HEMPEN SQUINSY, *subs. phr.* (old). — A hanging: *see* HEMPEN FEVER and LADDER.

SQUINT, *verb.* (tailors').—To lack: food, material, money, anything.

SQUINTER, *subs.* (common).—In *pl.* = the eyes: *see* GLIM.

SQUINT-MINDED, *adj.* (old).—Deceitful; crooked; with TWISTED VISION (*q.v.*).

1653. URQUHART, *Rabelais*, II. xxxiv. You and I both are far more worthy of pardon than a great rabble of SQUINT-MINDED fellows, dissembling and counterfeit saints.

SQUIRE, *subs.* (old).—1. A gallant; a woman's man; a SERVANT (*q.v.*): also LOVE-SQUIRE, and SQUIRE OF DAMES. Hence APPLE-SQUIRE (*q.v.*) and SQUIRE OF THE BODY = a STALLION (*q.v.*). As *verb.* = (1) TO SERVE (*q.v.*); (2) to PIMP (*q.v.*); and (3) to gallant.

1383. CHAUCER, *Cant. Tales*, 5, 884. Our prentis Jankin . . . SQUIERETH me both up and doun, Yet hast thou caught a false suspection: I wol him nat, though thou were ded to-morwe.

1590. SPENSER, *Fairy Queen*, II. i. 21, 8. And eke himselfe had craftily devised To be her SQUIRE, and do her Service well aguised.

1599. JONSON, *Out of Humour*, 'Characters—Shift.' His chief exercises are taking the whiff, SQUIRING a cockatrice, and making privy searches for imparters.

1611. CHAPMAN, *May-Day*, ii. 4. Now for a far-fetched device to fetch over my LOVE-SQUIRE.

1632. MASSINGER, *Emperor of the East*, i. 2. Marry, there I'm call'd The SQUIRE OF DAMES, or Servant of the Sex.

1639. MAYNE, *City Match*, 35. And spoile your SQUIRING in the dark.

1665. R. HEAD, *English Rogue*, I. ix. 71 (1874). From what Dunghil didst thou pick up this shakerag, this SQUIRE OF THE BODY?

1675. WYCHERLEY, *Country Wife*, iv. 3. To SQUIRE women about for other folks is as ungrateful an employment as to tell money for other folks.

1678. COTTON, *Virgil Travestie* (1770), 90. Turning To look for Dido and her SQUIRE, All in a chamber finely matted, He very fairly spy'd 'em at it.

1708-10. SWIFT, *Polite Conversation*, i. *Neverout*. . . . I'll go to the Opera to-night, . . . for I promised to SQUIRE the Countess to her Box.

1900. SAVAGE, *Brought to Bay*, II. vi. It was no light-minded SQUIRE OF DAMES who sat alone in the smoking-room.

3. (American).—*See* quot.

1862. BROWNE, *Artemus Ward, His Book*, 'The Octoroon.' It is a middlin fine day, SQUIRE. [Note.—SQUIRE in New England phraseology, a magistrate, or justice; but throughout the States, a very general complimentary title, varied occasionally by major, colonel, general, &c.]

4. (various).—*See* quots. *c.*1696 and 1785: also BROOM, GALLIPOT, and PAD.

1688. SHADWELL, *SQUIRE OF ALSATIA* [Title].

*c.*1696. B. E., *Dict. Cant. Crew*, s.v. SQUIRE OF ALSATIA, a Man of Fortune, drawn in, cheated, and ruin'd by a pack of poor, lowsy, spunging, bold Fellows that liv'd (formerly) in White-Fryers. The SQUIRE, a Sir Timothy Treat-all; also a Sap-pate. SQUIRISH, foolish, also one that pretends to Pay all Reckonings, and is not strong enough in the Pocket. A fat Squire, a rich Fool.

1785. GROSE, *Vulg. Tongue*, s.v. SQUIRE OF ALSATIA. A weak profligate spendthrift, the SQUIRE OF THE COMPANY; one who pays the whole reckoning, or treats the company, is called STANDING SQUIRE.

SQUIREEN, *subs.* (Irish).—A term of contempt: *see* quot. Also (general) SQUIRELET.

1812. EDGEWORTH, *Absentee*, vii. SQUIREENS are persons who, with good long leases or valuable farms, possess incomes of from three to eight hundred a year, who keep a pack of hounds, take out a commission of the peace, sometimes before they can spell . . . and almost always before they knew anything of law or justice.

1839. CARLYLE, *Misc.*, III. 56. A Scottish SQUIRELET, full of gulosity and gigmanity.

1857. KINGSLEY, *Two Years Ago*, viii. A small SQUIREEN cursed with six or seven hundreds a year of his own, never sent to school, college, or into the army, he had grown up in a narrow circle of SQUIREENS like himself.

1873. *Fraser's Mag.*, May, 647. The family of Bodley belonged to that class of SQUIRELETS . . . of which Devonshire in the days of Elizabeth was very full.

SQUIRESS, *subs.* (colloquial).—A squire's wife.

1827. LYTTON, *Pelham*, vii. The one milliner's shop was full of fat SQUIRESSES, buying muslin ammunition.

SQUIRISH, *adj.* (GROSE).—Foolish.

SQUIRM, *subs.* (public schools').—A small obnoxious boy: *cf.* SQUIRT.

Verb. (colloquial).—To wriggle; to shudder: mentally or physically. Whence (American) TO GET A SQUIRM ON = to bestir oneself; and SQUIRMY = (1) crooked, deceitful; and (2) ALL-OVERISH (*q.v.*).

1859. HON. MR. PITT [BARTLETT]. We have declared an intention, and now, when we come to publish it, some gentleman is suddenly seized with the "retrenchment gripes," and SQUIRMS around like a long red worm on a pin-hook.

1857. HOLMES, *Autocrat*, v. You never need think you can turn over any old falsehood without a terrible SQUIRMING.

1862. BROWNE, *Artemus Ward, His Book*, 44. I give Uriah a sly wink here, which made the old feller SQUIRM like a speared eel.

1874. *Siliad*, 205. I rage, I SQUIRM . . . I say rude things, but no one cares a bit.

1902. KERNAHAN, *Scoundrels and Co.*, v. I SQUIRM under the cold kiss that a revolver's ugly lips press to my forehead.

SQUIRREL, *subs.* (old).—A harlot; 'because she (GROSE), like that animal, covers her back with her tail.'

SQUIRT, *subs.* (American).—1. A dandified PUPPY (*q.v.*); an upstart; a cad. Whence SQUIRTISH = dandified, self-assertive, caddish. In contempt.

1844. *Major Jones's Courtship*, 160. If they won't keep company with SQUIRTS and dandies, who's going to make a monkey of himself?

1847. ROBB, *Squatter Life*, 73. It's my opinion that these slicked-up, SQUIRTISH kind of fellars ain't particular hard baked, and they always goes in for aristocracy notions.

1854. NORTH, *Slave of the Lamp*, 25. He's a galvanized SQUIRT, and, as the parson said, "the truth ain't in him."

2. (public schools').—An obnoxious boy: *cf.* SQUIRM.

3. (old colloquial).—A spurt.

1759-67. STERNE, *Tristram Shandy*, iii. 28. How different from the rash jerks, and hare-brained SQUIRTS thou art wont, Tristram, to transact it with in other humours.

4. (old).—(*a*) In *pl.* = diarrhœa: *cf.* SQUITTERS; and (*b*) a chemist or apothecary.

1551. STILL, *Gammer Gurton's Needle*, i. 2. *Hodge*. See, so I am arrayed with dabbling in the dirt! She that set me to ditching, I would she had THE SQUIRT.

1678. COTTON, *Virgil Travestie* (1770), 12. As if . . . troubl'd with the SQUITTERS.

1696. MOTTEUX, *Rabelais*, 'Pant. Prog.,' iii. Troubled with the thorough-go-nimble, or wild SQUIRT.

1712. GAY, *Trivia*, ii. 563. Pleas'd sempstresses the Lock's fam'd Rape unfold; and SQUIRTS read Garth till apozems grow cold.

18 [?]. *Dispensary*, Dram. Pers. SQUIRTS, an apothecary's boy.

5. (Harvard).—'A showy recitation' (HALL).

Verb. (old).—To BLAB (*q.v.*).

TO SQUIRT ONE'S DYE, *verb. phr.* (American).—To seize an opportunity.

TO DO A SQUEEZE AND A SQUIRT, *verb. phr.* (venery).—To copulate: *see* GREENS and RIDE. Also TO SQUIRT ONE'S JUICE.

SQUISH, *subs.* (public schools').—1. Marmalade; also (Winchester) = weak tea.

SQUISHOP, *subs.* (common). — A bishop who is also a landed proprietor: *cf.* SQUARSON.

SQUIT, *subs. phr.* (provincial).—A young woman not over pleasing and small (HALLIWELL).

SQUITTERS, *subs. pl.* (common).—Looseners of the bowels: *cf.* SQUIRT.

SQUO, *subs.* and *adj.* (Charterhouse).—Racquets played with a soft ball: *e.g.*, SQUO-COURT, SQUO-BALL, &c.: *cf.* SQUASH, 3.

SRES-WORT, *subs. phr.* (back slang).—Trousers.

SRET-SIO, *subs.* (back slang).—Oysters.

'STAB, *subs.* (printers').—'Establishment': *e.g.*, ON THE 'STAB = in regular work at fixed wages: as opposed to piece-work.

Verb. (venery).—To copulate: also TO STAB IN THE THIGH: *see* GREENS and RIDE.

TO STAB THE DICE, *verb. phr.* (old gaming).—*See* quot.

1674. COTTON, *Complete Gamester* (1680), 12. STABBING, that is, having a smooth box and small in the bottom, you drop in both your dice in such manner as you would have them sticking therein . . . the dice lying one upon another; so that, turning up the box, the dice never tumble . . . by which means you have bottoms according to the tops you put in: for example, if you put in your dice so that two fives or two fours lie a top, you have in the bottom turn'd up two twos, or two treys; so if six and an ace a top, a six and an ace at bottom.

TO STAB ONESELF AND PASS THE DAGGER, *verb. phr.* (theatrical).—To help oneself and send the bottle round.

STABLE, *subs.* (military).—1. In *pl.* = routine duty at the stables.

1885. *M. Post*, 5 Feb. They seem always at STABLES, on parade, or out doing field-firing.

2. (racing).—The horses in a racing establishment.

1887. *Referee*, 24 Ap. They can insure a straight run for their money in connection with this STABLE.

TO SHUT THE STABLE DOOR WHEN THE STEED IS STOLEN, *verb. phr.* (old).—To set a guard after a mischief is done.

1509. BARCLAY, *Ship of Fools* (1874), i. 76. WHEN THE STEDE IS STOLYN, TO SHYT THE STABLE DORE.

STABLE-MY-NAGGIE. TO PLAY AT STABLE-MY-NAGGIE, *verb. phr.* (venery). — To copulate: *see* GREENS and RIDE.

STAB-RAG, *subs. phr.* (common).—A tailor: also RAG-STABBER (*q.v.*): *see* TRADES.

STAB-SHOT, *subs. phr.* (billiards').—A stroke where the ball stops 'dead' (or nearly so) on the spot occupied by the object ball.

STACIA. LIKE STACIA, *adv. phr.* (provincial).—A term of comparison: *e.g.*, 'to do it LIKE STACIA'; 'as drunk AS STACIA,' &c. (HALLIWELL).

STACK, *subs.* (common).—A large quantity: *e.g.*, STACKS OF THE READY = plenty of money.

Verb. (gaming).—To 'make' cards in a pre-arranged manner for a crooked game; TO PACK (*q.v.*); TO STOCK (*q.v.*).

1896. LILLARD, *Poker Stories*, 54. The cards were STACKED and marked on the back, so that he didn't have any chance at all to win.

STAFF, *subs.* (venery).—The *penis*: also STAFF OF LIFE and STAFF OF LOVE: *see* PRICK. Hence STAFF-BREAKER (or CLIMBER) = a woman.

1653. URQUHART, *Rabelais*, I. xi. One of them would call it her fiddle-diddle, her STAFF OF LOVE . . . her Cyprian sceptre.

1686. DORSET, *Faithful Catalogue* [Rochester, *Roscommon, &c.* (1718), II. 33]. Well has his STAFF a double use supplied.

PHRASES. TO PUT DOWN (or SET UP) ONE'S STAFF = to rest; to take up residence (RAY); TO KEEP STAFF IN HAND = to retain possession; TO PART WITH ONE'S STAFF = to get rid of one's substance; TO ARGUE FROM STAFF TO CORNER = to raise a question other than that under 'discussion,' to draw a red herring across the trail; TO HAVE THE BETTER (or WORSE) END OF THE STAFF = to get the best (or worst) of a matter: *see* STICK.

1564. UDAL, *Apoph. Erasmus*, 340. A rief thyng it is to see feloes enough of the self same suite, which as often as thei see theim selfes TO HAUE THE WORSE ENDE OF THE STAFFE in their cause, doen make their recourse wholly vnto furious brallyng.

1625-30. *Court and Times, Chas. I.*, II. 94. And so now ours seem TO HAVE THE BETTER END OF THE STAFF.

*d.*1655 [?]. ADAMS, *Works* [NICHOLS, *Puritan Divines*, 1861-2], i. 185. If Cleanthes open his shop he shall have customers; many a traveller there SETS DOWN HIS STAFF.

*d.*1663. BRAMHALL, *Works* [Ang. Cath. Lib.], ii. 94. This is an argument FROM THE STAFF TO THE CORNER. I speak of a succession of Holy Orders, and he of a succession of opinions.

1753. RICHARDSON, *Grandison*, ii. 122. Miss Byron, I have had THE BETTER END OF THE STAFF, I believe?

1766. BROOKE, *Fool of Quality*, i. 370. There are few men now at liberty near so wealthy as this gentleman who has done us the honour TO SET UP HIS STAFF of rest in our house.

1773. GRAVES, *Spiritual Quixote* (1808), VIII. x. As the evening now came on, and the two pilgrims were much fatigued . . . they thought it best TO SET UP THEIR STAFF at the public-house where they had preached.

1782. WALPOLE, *Letters*, iv. 326. I did not think a wife was the stall where he would SET UP HIS STAFF.

STAFF OF LIFE, *subs. phr.* (common).—1. Bread.

ENGLISH SYNONYMS (*see* also GRUB). MELTON (*q.v.*); penny-starver (= penny roll); soft-tack (or -tommy); tack; toke; tommy; pannum.

FRENCH SYNONYMS. *Artic*; *arton*; *boule* (prison: also *boule de son*); *bissard* (= brown bread); *boucle zoze* (thieves' = brown bread); *bricheton*; *briffe*; *brignolet*; *bringue*; *bronté*; *cholet*; *graigaille*; *grignolet*; *gringue*; *gros Guillaume*; *lartif*; *lartie*; *larton*; *mousseline* (= white bread); *pierre dure*.

2. *See* STAFF.

STAFFORD COURT. TO BE TRIED IN STAFFORD COURT, *verb. phr.* (old).—To be beaten or ill-treated. Hence STAFFORD LAW = violence, lynch law.

1598. FLORIO, *Worlde of Wordes*, s.v. *Braccesca licenza*, as we say STAFFORD'S LAW.

1599. BRETON, *Wil of Wit*, 2, 'The Scholler and Souldier.' Among souldiers, STAFFORD LAW, martiall law, killing or hanging, is soon learned.

1611. COTGRAVE, *Dict.*, s.v. *Il a este au festin de Martin baston*, he hath had A TRIALL IN STAFFORD COURT, or hath received Jacke Drums intertainment.

1647. MILES CORBET, *Speech* [Harl. Misc., i. 273]. We have unlawfully erected marshall law, club law, STAFFORD LAW, and such lawless laws as make most for treason.

STAFFORDSHIRE KNOTS (THE), *subs. phr.* (military).—The 2nd Batt. of The South Staffordshire Regiment, formerly The 81st Foot. [The regimental badge is a knotted cable.]

STAFF-STRIKER, *subs. phr.* (old).—A sturdy beggar; a tramp.

STAG, *subs.* (old).—1. An informer; a SNITCH (*q.v.*): also STAGGER.

2. (Stock Exchange). — An applicant for shares in new issues, who has no intention of holding, but prefers to forfeit the deposit money if unable to sell at a premium on allotment. Hence (3) any irregular 'outside' dealer. Also as *verb*.

1849. KINGSLEY, *Yeast*, ii. If the Stock-Exchange and railway STAGGING . . . are not The World, what is? *Ibid.*, xii. The slipperiness, sir, of one STAGGING parson has set rolling this very avalanche.

1871. ATKINS, *House Scraps*. A STAG there was—as I've heard tell, Who in an attic used to dwell . . . And being blest, like many I know, With little conscience, and less rhino, Took to that frailest of all frail ways.

4. (old).—A professional bailsman or *alibi* (BEE).

5. (common).—A shilling: *see* RHINO.

1887. HENLEY, *Villon's Straight Tip*. You cannot bank a single STAG.

6. (provincial). — A romping girl.

7. (common).—A male. Whence STAG-DANCE = a man's dance; a BULL-DANCE (*q.v.*): also STAG-PARTY; STAG-MONTH = the month of a woman's lying-in; STAG-WIDOW = a man whose wife is in childbed.

18 [?]. *West Point* [U. S. Mil. Acad.] *Scrap Book*. After supper a universal STAG DANCE of not less than fifty couples came off . . . The dancers arrange themselves in two long lines, facing each other, inside of a lane of candles, half buried in the ground, and above these three muskets forming a tripod, and each bayonet having a candle spluttering on its point. Drums, fires, and violins formed the orchestra. The cadets started with a simultaneous bound, involving themselves inextricably, and at last it became a mere competition who should work his legs and feet most excruciatingly.

1854. *Baltimore Sun*, 13 Nov. The prisoners in the jail at Lafayette, Indiana, have been provided with a violin; and, one of the number being a good player, they have frequent STAG-DANCES.

1856. MACE SLOPER (C. G. LELAND), *Knickerbocker Mag.*, April. I lose myself in a party of old bricks, who, under pretence of looking at the picture, are keeping up a small STAG-PARTY at the end of the room.

Adj. (old).—*See* quot.

1602. DEKKER *Satiromastix* [HAWKINS, *Eng. Dr.*, iii. 141]. Come, my little cub, do not scorn me because I go IN STAG, in buff.

Verb. (old).—1. To find, to watch closely, TO DOG (*q.v.*): *e.g.*, TO STAG A THIEF = to look on and spoil his game; TO STAG THE PUSH = to watch the crowd; 'Who's that STAGGING?' = 'Who's following?' (GROSE, BEE). Also STAGGER = a spy.

1827. LYTTON, *Pelham*, lxxxiii. Bess STAGS you, my cove! Bess STAGS you.

1828. BEE, *Living Picture*. Lest the transaction may have been STAGGED by some impertinent bystander or a trap, he mounts his box and drives away.

1859. KINGSLEY, *Geoffrey Hamlyn*, v. So you've been STAGGING this gentleman and me, and listening, have you

2. (common). — To dun; to beg.

STAGE-FEVER, *subs. phr.* (colloquial).—A craze for the boards: hence STAGE-STRUCK.

*c.*1710. [ASHTON, *Soc. Life in Reign of Queen Anne*, II. 21.] He was intended for the Church, but he caught STAGE-FEVER, ran away from school at the age of 17, and joined the theater at Dublin.

1821. SCOTT, *Pirate*, xxxix. The false tones and exaggerated gesture of the STAGE-STRUCK pirate.

1851-61. MAYHEW, *Lond. Lab.*, III. 142. Some of the young fellows stick in their parts. They get the STAGE FEVER, and knocking in the knees.

STAGER (or **OLD STAGER**), *subs. phr.* (colloquial).—1. A person of experience: *cf.* STAGER = a player; whence (2) anything long in use or evidence.

1563. FOXE, *Acts and Monuments* [CATTLEY] [OLIPHANT, *New Eng.*, i. 549. Amongst Romance words are . . . mummery, OLD STAGER . . .].

1748. CHESTERFIELD, *Letters*, 20 Dec. Here let me, as an OLD STAGER on the theatre of the world, suggest one consideration to you.

1809. MALKIN, *Gil Blas* [ROUTLEDGE], 69. She is an OLD STAGER, a veteran in the service of the apothecarie's wife.

1884. *Field*, 6 Dec. While Sabrina and Ripple, OLD STAGERS at the game, slid along the shore.

1897. MARSHALL, *Pomes*, 108. The same young lady, I will wager, But her escort's not the same; Methinks he is a younger STAGER.

STAGGER, *subs.* (common).—In *pl.* = a drunken fit.

See STAG, *verb*.

STAGGERER, *subs.* (common). — Anything overwhelming; a poser.

1889. *Athenæum*, 26 Oct., 560. This was a STAGGERER for Dive's literary 'gent,' and it took him nearly six weeks to get over it and frame a reply.

STAGGERING BOB, *subs. phr.* (common).—1. A newly dropped calf (HALLIWELL); and (2) meat unfit for human food because the knife has only anticipated death from accident or disease; also (GROSE) STAGGERING BOB WITH HIS YELLOW PUMPS.

STAG-MAG, *subs. phr.* (theatrical). —A stage manager. Also as *verb.* = to stage manage.

STAINES. AT STAINES, *adv. phr.* (old).—*See* quot.

1785. GROSE, *Vulgar Tongue*, s.v. STAINES, a man who is in pecuniary distress is said to be AT STAINES, or at the Bush, alluding to the Bush Inn at that town.

STAIRS. THE STAIRS WITHOUT A LANDING, *subs. phr.* (thieves').—The treadmill: *see* EVERLASTING STAIRCASE.

1884. GREENWOOD, *Little Ragamuffins*. He's lodging now at Coldbaths Fields—getting up THE STAIRS WITHOUT A LANDING.

STAKE, *subs.* (old).—*See* quot.

1785. GROSE, *Vulg. Tongue*, s.v. STAKE. A booty acquired by robbery . . .; and, if considerable, a PRIME STAKE, or a HEAVY STAKE. A person alluding to anything . . . comparatively . . . invaluable, would say, I consider it a STAKE . . . a valuable or acceptable acquisition of any kind is emphatically called a STAKE, meaning a great prize.

Verb. (American).—To provide for.

TO LOSE THE MATCH AND POCKET THE STAKES, *verb. phr.* (venery).—To be got with child.

STALE, *subs.* (old).—1. A pretence, a fraud, a theft. As *verb.* = to deceive, to rob.

1033 [?]. KENNETT, *MS. Lansd.*, f. 392. A STALE or pretence, a fraud or deceit.

1340. *Ayenbyte of Inwyt* [E. E. T. S.], 9. Ine these heste is norbode roberie, thiefte, STALE and gauel, and bargayn with othren.

2. (old).—Any object of contempt, deception, or ridicule. As *verb.* = to ridicule or abuse.

*c.*1400. *Chester Plays* (Shakspeare Soc.), i. 173. So shall you meete with that STALL, That woulde my kingdome clayme and call.

1593. SHAKSPEARE, *Tam. of Shrew*, i. 1. I pray you, sir, is it your will To make a STALE of me among these mates?

1620. FLETCHER, *Little French Lawyer*, iii. Are we made STALES to one another?

1633. FORD, *Love's Sacrifices*, ii. 1. A subject fit TO be the STALE of laughter.

1635. RULTEN, *Shepheard's Holyday*, sig. G 1. Before I could get earnest of any ones love, To whom I made addresse, even she would say, You have another mistresse, go to her, I will not be her STALE.

3. (old).—A decoy; a stalking horse: hence ambush. As *verb.* = to hide, to lie in wait, to ensnare.

1530. PALSGRAVE, *Lang. Francoyse*, s.v. STALE for foules takynge.

1548. HALL, *Union*, 'Hen. IV.', f. 31. He ordeined certain of his men to geve assaulte to the toune of Guisnes while he stode in a STALE to lie in waite for the relefe that might come from Callis.

1577. STANIHURST, *Descr. Ireland*, 21. Laie in STALE.

1577. HELLOWES, Fr. of *Guevara's Letters*, 42. When he happened to fall into the STALL of his enimies.

1588. GREENE, *Dorastus and Fawnia*, 38. The lyon never prayeth on the mouse, nor faulcons stoupe not to dead STALES. *Ibid.*, *Penitent Palmer's Ode*. Her ivory front, her pretty chin, Were STALES that drew me on to sin.

1590. SPENSER, *Fairy Queen*, II. i. 4. Still as he went, his craftie STALES did lay, With cunning traynes him to entrap unware. *Ibid.* (1596), VI. x. 3. Would never more delight in painted show Of such false blisse as there is set for STALES, T' entrap unwary fooles.

1593. SHAKSPEARE, *Com. of Errors*, ii. 1. But, too unruly deer, he breaks the pale, And feeds from home, poor I am but his STALE. *Ibid.*, iii. 2. 'Twere good to STEAL our marriage. *Ibid.* (1609), *Tempest*, iv. 1. The trumpery in my house, go bring it hither, For STALE to catch these thieves.

1597. BACON, *Essays*, xi. Profess it plainly, and declare it, together with the reasons that move thee to change, and do not think to STEAL it.

1601. JONSON, *Poetaster*, iii. 1. Make them STALLS to his lewd solecisms and worded trash. *Ibid.* (1605), *Fox*, iv. 5. And with this strumpet, The STALE to his forg'd practice. *Ibid.* (1611), *Catiline*. Dull stupid Lentulus, my STALE with whom I stalk.

1610. *Mirr. Mag.*, 366. This find I true, for as I LAY IN STALE, To fight with the duke Richard's eldest son, I was destroy'd, not far from Dintingdale.

1622. MARMION, *Holland's Leaguer*, ii. 1. I'll make a STALE, to take this courtier in a freak. *Ibid.* (1633), *Fine Companion*, iii. 4. Captain Whibble, the toun STALE For all cheating employments.

1626. FLETCHER, *Wit at Several Weapons*, ii. 2. Why, thou wert but the bait to fish with, not The prey; the STALE to catch another bird with.

1640. *Two Lancashire Lovers*, 21. Must an husband be made a STALE to sinne, or an inlet to his owne shame?

1688. *Cap of Grey Hairs*, &c., 96. If it be a solitary beauty you court, which as yet is *intemerata virgo*, so that none beside take to the scent, she will not long be so, for your attendance will be but like the fowlers STALE, the appearance of which brings but others to the net.

4. (old).—A common whore: *see* TART.

1600. SHAKSPEARE, *Much Ado*, iv. 1. I stand dishonour'd, that have gone about To link my dear friend to a common STALE.

1641. MILTON, *Reformation in Eng.*, i. Common STALES to countenance . . . every Politick Fetch that was then on foot.

5. (Old Cant). — An accomplice: 'a STALE for a foist or pickpocket': now (also STALL) a confederate working either before (FRONT-STALL or FORE-STALL) or behind (BACK-STALL) the actual thief, to cover his movements, and assist in his escape (*see* quot. 1785): also STALLSMAN. As *verb.* = to screen: also TO CHUCK A STALL, and TO STALL OFF; also to FENCE (*q.v.*): whence STALLING-KEN = a mart for stolen goods (HARMAN, B. E., and GROSE): also (HARMAN) = 'a tippling-house.' Also TO STALL OFF = to excuse plausibly; to escape wilily.

1610. ROWLANDS, *Martin Mark-all* [Hunt. Club Rept.], 39. STAWLING-KEN, a house to receive stolen goods.

1630. TAYLOR, *Works*, 'Brood of Cormorants,' 8. Lives like a gentleman by sleight of hand, Can play the foist, the nip, the STALE, the stand.

1671. HEAD, *English Rogue*, 'Canting Song.' So she and I did STALL and cloy whatever we could catch.

1785. GROSE, *Vulg. Tongue*, s.v. STALL-UP. To STALL a person up . . . is to surround him in a crowd, or in the open street, force his arms up, and keep them in that position while others of the gang rifle his pockets at pleasure, the cove being unable to help or defend himself; this is what the newspapers denominate hustling, practised where the general anxiety to push forward, or to obtain a view, forms a pretext for jostling.

1827. LYTTON, *Pelham*, lxxxiii. Plant your stumps, Master Guinea Pig; you are going to STALL OFF the Daw's baby in prime twig.

1884. GREENWOOD, *Seven Years Penal Servitude*. I said to my pal, 'CHUCK ME A STALL and I'll have that.' What did I mean? Why, keep close to me and cover what I'm doing.

1885. *Daily Tel.*, 12 Nov. Lovely drew out, and STALLING OFF the challenge of the ungenerous Duke of Richmond won by two lengths.

TO STALL ONE'S MUG, *verb. phr.* (old).—To be off.

TO STALL A DEBT, *verb. phr.* (old).—To forbear it.

See STALL.

STALE BEAR (or **BULL**), *subs. phr.* (Stock Exchange).—A BEAR (or BULL) *q.v.* who has long been short of (or has long held) stock.

STALE-DRUNK, *adj. phr.* (common). —A man is said to be STALE-DRUNK when again in liquor before complete recovery from a previous bout: *see* SCREWED (GROSE).

STALK (THE), *subs.* (Punch and Judy).—The gallows: *see* NUBBING CHEAT.

TO STALK A JUDY (THE STREETS, &c.), *verb. phr.* (venery).—To run a woman down; to quest for MEAT (*q.v.*); TO GROUSE (*q.v.*).

STALL, *verb.* (Old Cant).—1. To install; to initiate (HARMAN, DEKKER, B. E.).

1567. HARMAN, *Caveat*. When an upright man mete any beggar, whether he be sturdy or impotent, he will demand of him whether ever he was 'STALLED TO THE ROGE,' or no. If he say he was, he will know of whom, and his name yt stalled him. And if he be not learnedly able to shew him the whole circumstance thereof, he will spoyle him of his money, either of his best garment, if it be worth any money, and haue him to the bowsing-ken; which is, to some typling house next adjoyninge, and layth there to gage the best thing that he hath for twenty pence or two shillings; this man obeyeth for feare of beatinge. Then dooth this upright man call for a gage of bowse, which is a quarte potte of drink, and powres the same vpon his peld pate, adding these words,—I, *G.P.*, do stalle thee, *W.T.*, to the Roge, and that from henceforth it shall be lawfull for thee to cant, that is, to aske or begge for thi liuing in al places.

2. (theatrical).—To take a part.

3. (common).—To lodge, or put up at a public house.

See STALE.

STALLION, *subs.* (old).—A whoremonger (B. E.): spec. (GROSE) 'a man kept by an old lady for secret purposes.'

1605. CHAPMAN, *All Fools*, iii. 1. Thou play'st the STALLION ever where thou comest; . . . no man's bed secure; No woman's unattempted by thee.

1622. MARMION, *Holland's Leaguer*, i. iv. Their [women's] unjust desires would ask the labours of some ten STALLIONS.

1678. COTTON, *Virgil Travestie* (1770), 32. And if thou stay'st that Rogue Pygmalion Intends to use thee like a STALLION.

1686. DORSET, *Faithful Catalogue* [Rochester, *Roscommon*, &c., II. 44]. Ne'er was a truer STALLION to his cost.

1686. ROCHESTER, *Works* (1718), 'Lais Junior,' I. 75. Disabling sluts and STALLIONS every hour. *Ibid.*, I. 167, 'Rochester's Farewell.' Of numerous STALLIONS let her not despair.

1694. MOTTEUX, *Rabelais*, v. vii. Don't you STALLIONISE it sometimes? Ibid., *Pantag. Prognos*, v. Smockers, STALLIONS and belly-bumpers.

1697. VANBRUGH, *Provoked Wife*, iv. *Sir John.* That goat; that STALLION there, is ready to run me through the guts.

1705. WARD, *Hud. Rediv.*, II. ii. 15. And pick his Pocket, to supply Some starving STALLION of the Town. *Ibid.*, 'Hypocrisy Lampoon'd.' The Mourning Widow too can play The Hypocrite with Vail on, And most devoutly kneel and pray, Tho' 'tis but for a STALION.

1772. BRIDGES, *Burlesque Homer*, 216. As to that copper-nosed rabscallion, Venus's bully-back and STALLION.

STALL-WHIMPER, *subs. phr.* (Old Cant).—A bastard: *see* BYE-BLOW (B. E. and GROSE).

STAM-BANG, *adv.* (provincial).—Plump down.

STAM FLASH, *verb. phr.* (Old Cant).—To cant (B. E. and GROSE).

STAMMEL (or **STRAMMEL**), *subs.* (old).—'A brawny, lusty, strapping Wench' (B. E. and GROSE).

STAMMER, *subs.* (Old Cant).—An indictment (GROSE).

STAMP, *subs.* (Old Cant).—1. In *pl.* = the legs; (2) = shoes (HARMAN, B. E., GROSE, and VAUX); and (3) 'carriers' (B. E.). Also STAMPERS. Whence STAMP-DRAWERS = stockings.

1620. DEKKER, *Lanthorne and Candlelight*, sig. C., iii., s.v.

1641. BROME, *Jovial Crew*, i. Strike up, Piper, a merry, merry dance, That we on our STAMPERS may foot it and prance.

1828. EGAN, *Finish in Tom and Jerry*, 309. My padders, my STAMPERS, my buckets, otherwise my boots.

4. (old).—A coin of small value: spec. (HALLIWELL) a halfpenny. In *pl.* (American) = paper money; SHINPLASTERS (*q.v.*). Also generic for money.

1628. MIDDLETON, *Widow*, ii. 1. *Ric.* Oh cruel, merciless woman, To talk of law, and know I have no money. *Val.* I will consume myself to the last STAMP Before thou gett'st me.

1877. *Providence Jo.*, 5 Feb. The patience with which he waited in the box-office to rake in all the STAMPS led his audience to form a fair estimate of his appreciation of the almighty dollar.

1899. HYNE, *Further Adven. Captain Kettle*, xi. He's the flat. Cranze is the — er — his friend who stands to draw the STAMPS.

5. (printers').—In *pl.* = type.

1563. FOXE, *Acts and Monuments* [OLIPHANT, *New Eng.*, i. 540. Among new substantives are STAMPS (types) . . . the bench (magistrates).

Verb. (old).—*See* quot.

1785. GROSE, *Vulg. Tongue*, s.v. STAMP. A particular manner of throwing the dice out of the box, by striking it with violence against the table.

STAMP-CRAB, *subs. phr.* (common).—A lumpish walker; a BEETLE-CRUSHER (*q.v.*).

STAMP-IN-THE-ASHES, *subs. phr.* (old).—*See* quot.

1515. *De Generibus Ebriosorum, &c.* [HODGKIN, *Notes and Queries*, 3 S., vii. 163. In this treatise occurs names of fancy drinks . . . I select a few of the most presentable slip-slop . . . STAMP-IN-THE-ASHES . . . Swell-nose.

STANCHEOUS, *adj.* and *adv.* (Western American).—Strong; durable.

1844. *Major Jones's Courtship*, 33. I tell you what, it's a mighty STANCHEOUS-looking building, and looks far off at a distance when you're going up to it.

STAND, *subs.* (venery). — 1. An *erectio penis*: also STANDING-WARE; likewise as *verb.* Thus TO MAKE STANDING ROOM FOR ONE = to receive a man: hence UNDERSTANDINGS = a woman's conquests. *See* HORN. Also (proverbial) 'STAND always, as the girl said'; *cf.* NILNISISTANDO. STAND also = a mouth whore.

*d.*1529. DUNBAR, *Works*, 'Twa Marrit Wemen,' s.v.

*c.*1593. NASH, *Choise of Valentines*, 131. 'Unhappie me,' quoth shee, 'and will't not STAND? Com, let me rubb and chafe it with my hand!'

1598. FLORIO, *Worlde of Wordes*, s.v. *A conscienza vitta* . . . with a stiffe STANDING pricke. *Ibid. Priapismo* . . . the STANDING of a man's yard.

1601. MUNDAY and CHETTLE, *Death of Robert, Earl of Huntingdon* [DODSLEY, *Old Plays* (1874), viii. 309]. Except you use that trick to conjure doun the STANDING spirit of my lord the king That your good mother there, the Abbess, uses To conjure down the spirit of the monk.

1606. CHAPMAN, *Gent. Usher*, ii. 1. Perhaps some tender lady will squat here, And if some STANDING rush should chance to prick her.

1616. DRUMMOND [CHALMERS, *Eng. Poets*, v. 666]. I wish you not a hundred arms nor hands, But hundred things like those With which Priapus in our garden STANDS.

1686. ROCHESTER, 'The Happy Night' [*Works* (1718), I. 36]. Then binds his wounds up with a busy hand And with that Balm enables him to STAND.

1705. WARD, *Hud. Rediv.*, I. ix. 6. Till she had burnt with Claps and Poxes, More STANDING WARE than Sampson's Foxes. *Ibid.*, *T[om] B[rown]'s Last Letter.* Stroke with warm Hand . . . To make what's pendant STAND erected.

1774. BRIDGES, *Burlesque Homer*, 132. Knowing a touch of her soft hand . . . will make him STAND. *Ibid.*, 196. But she . . . in sweaty palm, There held it fast and made it STAND, And spend its venom in her hand.

1786. CAPT. MORRIS, *Lyra Urbanica* (1840), 'Billy's too Young to Drive Us.' Here's Britannia! And may he never stand at her head, Who never could STAND at her tail.

*d.*1796. BURNS, *Merry Muses*, 'Here's his Health in Water.' He followed me baith out an' in, Wi' a stiff STANIN' pillie. *Ibid.*, 'Act Sederunt' (1793). STANIN' pricks are fau'tors a'.

2. (Old Cant).—*See* quot. 1548. Also STANDING.

1548. LATIMER, *Sermons and Remains* (Parker Soc.). [OLIPHANT, *New Eng.*, i. 515. There are hanger-on, a STANDING (thieves' station)].

3. (various).—A cheap-jack's, coster's, or street-vendor's PITCH (*q.v.*). Also (colloquially) A SHOP (*q.v.*); A SHOW (*q.v.*).

1902. LYNCH, *High Stakes*, xxiii. The lady . . . came . . . with the best of home and foreign recommendations, began business at her present "STAND," and has flourished mightily.

4. (theatrical touring). — A visit; a RUN (*q.v.*).

1900. *Free Lance*, 6 Oct., 20, 1. This year I'm going with Grady—north and south—right through the big two week STANDS.

5. (American). — Situation: *e.g.*, 'The Astor House is a good STAND for a hotel' (BARTLETT).

Verb. (colloquial).—To endure, put up with, forbear.

1383. CHAUCER, *Miller's Tale*, 644. But STONDE he moste unto his owene harm.

1705. WARD, *Hud. Rediv.*, I. ix. 13. After she has STOOD the thrust To satisfy her Master's Lust.

PHRASES.—STAND is frequently colloquial. Thus TO STAND READY AT THE DOOR = to be handy for use; TO STAND TO A CHILD = to act as sponsor; TO STAND BUFF (or BLUFF) = to swear to, to outface, to take the consequences; NOT A FOOT (or LEG) TO STAND ON = at the end of one's resources, or one's repute; TO STAND IN = (1) to take side (or lot) with, to share, and (2) to cost; TO STAND ON ONE'S HIND LEGS = to show temper, to take in bad part; TO STAND ON ONE'S HEAD (EARS, &c.) = to be in good spirits; TO STAND UP TO THE RACK = to take rough and smooth; TO STAND UP TO = to put oneself in fighting attitude (BEE): whence a STAND-UP FIGHT = a bout where the contestants manfully face each other; TO STAND UP WITH = (1) to dance, and (2) to act as bridesmaid or groomsman; TO STAND HOLES (*see* quot. 1847). Also *see* PAD; PATTER; RACKET; SAM; TREAT; VELVET.

. . . . . *Towneley Mysteries* (Camden Soc.), 310. They have NO FETE TO STANDE.

1628. EARLE, *Microcos* [ARBER, 32], 10, 'A Church Papist.' He bates her in tyres what she STANDS HIM IN religion.

*c.*1680. BUTLER, *Hudibras's Epitaph*. For the good old cause STOOD BUFF 'Gainst many a bitter kick and cuff.

1698. VANBRUGH, *Prov. Wife*, i. 1. Would my courage come up to a fourth part of my ill-nature, I'd STAND BUFF to her relations, and thrust her out of doors. *Ibid.*, v. 2. The marriage knot . . . may STAND BUFF a long time.

1701. COLLIER, *M. Anton.* (1726), 219. To STAND BUFF against danger and death.

1732. FIELDING, *Misc.*, II. i. I must even STAND BUFF and outface him.

1777. SHERIDAN, *Sch. Scandal*, ii. 3. Ha! ha! ha! that he should have STOOD BLUFF to an old bachelor so long, and sink into a husband at last!

1812. AUSTEN, *Mansfield Park*, xii. If you want to dance, Fanny, I will STAND UP WITH you.

1827. SCOTT, *Diary* [LOCKHART (1839), IX. 146]. It is best to STAND BUFF to him.

1832. CROCKETT, *Tour Down East*, 137. I begun a new campaign at Washington. I had hard work, but I STOOD UP TO THE RACK, fodder or no fodder.

1844. *Major Jones's Courtship*, 64. It was the hottest night's work ever old Wolf undertook; and it tuck a mighty chance of hollerin' to make him STAND UP TO HIS RACK as well as he did.

1847. HALLIWELL, *Arch. Words, &c.*, s.v. STAND-HOLES. "I'LL STAND HOLES," I will hold to my bargain; sometimes thus limited, "I'LL STAND HOLES till next Wednesday." It seems borrowed from the game kit-cat, or bandy wicket, at which if a player indicate an intention of running indiscreetly in the opinion of another, the latter will fix him to his position by roaring out "STAND HOLES."

1848. THACKERAY, *Vanity Fair*, xxxiv. He STOOD UP TO the Banbury Man for three minutes, and polished him off in four rounds.

1853. WINTHROP, *Hist. New England*, i. 55. Every bushel of wheat meal STOOD US IN fourteen shillings.

1872. HOLMES, *Poet at Breakfast Table*, i. His face marked with strong manly furrows, records of hard thinking, and square STAND-UP FIGHTS with life.

1877. HORSLEY, *Jottings from Jail*. If I lend you these I shall want to STAND IN; but I said I can't stand you at that; I will grease your dukes if you like.

STANDER, *subs.* (Old Cant).—A sentinel.

1607. ROWLANDS, *Hist. Rogues* [quoted by RIBTON-TURNER, *Vagrants, &c.*, 583]. And so was faine to liue among the wicked sometimes a STANDER for the padder.

STANDER-UP, *subs. phr.* (American thieves').—A thief whose speciality is robbing drunken men under pretence of helping them home.

STAND-FAR-OFF (or **STAND-FURTHER-OFF**), *subs. phr.* (old).—*See* quots.

1630. TAYLOR, *Works* [NARES]. Certaine sonnets, in praise of Mr. Thomas the deceased; fashioned of divers stuffs, as mockado, fustian, STAND-FURTHER OFF, and motley.

1665. FULLER, *Ch. Hist.*, vi. 332. False miracles, . . . like the stuffe called STAND-FARRE-OFF, must not have the beholder too near, lest the coursnesse thereof doth appeare. *Ibid.* (1662), *Worthies* 'Norwich.' In my child-hood there was one [cloth] called STAND-FAR-OFF (the emblem of Hypocrisie), which seemed pretty at competent distance, but discovered its coarseness when nearer to the eye.

STAND-FURTHER, *subs. phr.* (provincial).—A quarrel, tiff, or disagreement: *e.g.*, 'There's quite a STAND-FURTHER between them.'

STANDING. *See* STAND.

TO TAKE STANDING, *verb. phr.* (colloquial).—To accept or endure with composure [as one would take a 'high jump' without a run in]: hence, without ado.

1901. *Free Lance*, 27 Ap., 77, 2. Like a philosophical American, he TOOK IT STANDING, merely remarking to an English friend that it was "just as cheap as Monte Carlo, and a durned sight pleasanter."

STANDING-DISH, *subs. phr.* (colloquial). — Any person or thing making a frequent appearance: *e.g.*, a sponging diner-out; a stock play; &c., &c.

STANDING-PATTERER, *subs. phr.* (streets').—A street-vendor who, taking a STAND (*q.v.*), 'slings the patter' to sell his wares: almost obsolete since police control under the Metropolitan Streets' Act, 1867: *cf.* RUNNING PATTERER.

STAND-OFF, *subs. phr.* (colloquial).—Polarity; a holding off. As *adj.* = distant, reserved; also STAND-OFFISH and STAND-OFFISHNESS.

1873. ROBINSON, *Her Face was Her Fortune*, v. If the landed gentry were STAND-OFFISH . . . Miss Shaldon . . . was all the more grateful for their reserve.

1888. WARD, *Robert Elsmere*, i. 2. People generally like the other two much better. Catherine is so STAND-OFF.

1888. D. C. MURRAY, *Weaker Vessel*, xxxii. I told him I did not like this pride and STAND-OFFISHNESS between man and man.

1890. *Atlantic Mag.*, lxvi. 672. The preferences of other clients, perhaps equal in number and value, who are fighting with Fabian tactics, make a complete STAND-OFF.

STAND-UP, *subs. phr.* (colloquial).—1. A meal or SNACK (*q.v.*) taken standing; a PERPENDICULAR (*q.v.*).

2. (venery).—An act of coition against a wall, tree, post, &c.; a KNEE-TREMBLER: a PERPENDICULAR (*q.v.*).

STANG. RIDING THE STANG, *subs. phr.* (old).—*See* quots. and SKIMMINGTON. Hence STANGEY = a hen-pecked husband.

1674. RAY, *Proverbs*, 44. This word is still used in some colleges in the University of Cambridge: TO STANG scholars in Christmas being to cause them to ride on a coltstaff or pole for missing of chappel.

1782. CALLANDER, *Two Ancient Scottish Poems*, 154. A custom [is] still prevalent among the country people of Scotland: who oblige any man, who is so unmanly as to beat his wife, to ride astride on a long pole, borne by two men, through the village, as a mark of the highest infamy. This they call RIDING THE STANG; and the person who has been thus treated seldom recovers his honour in the opinion of his neighbours. When they cannot lay hold of the culprit himself, they put some young fellow on the STANG or pole, who proclaims that it is not on his own account that he is thus treated, but on that of another person, whom he names.

1847. HALLIWELL, *Archaic Words*, s.v. RIDING THE STANG . . . [One] cry or proclamation is as follows:—Ran, Tan, Tan, the sign of the old Tin Can; Stephen Smith's been paying his daughter Nan: He paid her both behind and before, He paid her 'cause she wouldn't be his whore. He lick'd her neither with stake nor stower, But up wi' his fist and knock'd her ower. Now if Steenie Smith don't mend his manners, The skin of his prick shall go to the tanner's; And if the tanner don't tan it well; Skin, tanner, and prick shall go to hell.

1892. SYDNEY, *England and the English*, ii. 255. RIDING STANG was another local punishment inflicted occasionally upon the intemperate, particularly in the county of Cheshire.

STANGEY, *subs.* (common).—1. A tailor: *see* TRADES.

2. (old).—*See* STANG.

STAR, *subs.* (common).—1. A white 'blaze' on a horse's forehead.

1845. LONGFELLOW, *Spanish Student*, iii. 6. Onward, caballito mio, With the white STAR in thy forehead.

2. (printers'). — An asterisk: *cf.* DAGGER, SPEAR, &c. FRENCH-STARS = ***: a mark of division between paragraphs, &c.

3. (auctioneers'). — An article introduced into a sale after the catalogue has been printed: marked in the official copy by a STAR, sense 2.

4. (theatrical).—A distinguished singer or player. Hence TO STAR THE PROVINCES (or THE HALLS) = to go on tour (or make the round of the music halls) as the chief attraction (or as an important TURN, *q.v.*); STAR-ENGAGEMENT = an important or chief part; STAR-QUELLER = a player whose bad business spoils the efforts of better players.

1903. *Referee*, 8 Feb., 2, 4 I would like once more to record my astonishment that only STARS have pantomime benefits.

5. (venery).—The female *pudendum*: *see* MONOSYLLABLE: also THE STAR OVER THE GARTER: *cf.* LADY-STAR.

17[?]. LORD CORK, *The Bumper Toast.* Give me THE STAR that shines OVER THE GARTER. *Ibid.* A STAR . . . is the emblem of Cunt.

Verb. (common).—To strike a window, mirror, &c., so that cracks radiate from a common centre. Also (thieves') = to smash a window and rob its contents: spec. as in quot. 1856, or by striking a dab of putty with a life-preserver: also TO STAR THE GLAZE. Hence DONE FOR A STAR = convicted for window smashing; THE STAR-LAY = window robbery (GROSE).

1838. BECKETT, *Paradise Lost*, 16. To mill the glaze, and STAR the lamps.

1856. G. L. CHESTERTON, *Revelations of Prison Life.* Some crack a pane in a shop-front and by passing the wet thumb along, they can direct the crack as they please; then removing the glass they can remove the goods.

1870. DIPROSE, *Laugh and Learn.* So, in fractional arithmetic, it is considered highly improper to STAR THE GLAZE, in falling through the sashes of a grapery. when on the look-out for grapes.

TO BLESS (or THANK) ONE'S STARS, *verb. phr.* (colloquial).—To thank for one's good fortune.

1633. MARMION, *Antiquary*, i. I THANK MY STARS he has improved his time.

1706. WARD, *Wooden World*, 27. He has oft-times THANKED HIS good STARS for it.

*c.*1845. HOOD, *Pauper's Christmas Carol.* Ought not I to BLESS MY STARS?

MY STARS! *phr.* (colloquial).—An exclamation of surprise: also 'MY STAR AND GARTER!'

1726. VANBRUGH, *Provoked Husband*, iii. MY STARS! and you would really live in London half the year, to be sober in it.

STAR-BASON, *subs. phr.* (common).—An impudent-looking fellow (HALLIWELL).

STARCH. TO TAKE THE STARCH OUT OF, *verb. phr.* (venery).—1. To receive a man: *see* GREENS and RIDE.

2. (colloquial).—To mortify; to humiliate; to abase another's honour or dignity.

1888. *Cornhill Mag.*, 375. The free-born Westerner thinks the blamed Yankee puts on a yard too much style—the Boys don't approve of style—and suavely proposes TO TAKE THE STARCH OUT OF HIM.

STARCHED, *adj* (B. E. and GROSE).—Affected, proud, stiff: also STARCHY. Hence STARCH, *subs.* = a stiff, formal manner.

1599. JONSON, *Every Man Out of Humour*, i. 1. Look with a good STARCHED face, and ruffle your brow like a new boot.

1704. SWIFT, *To Rev. Dr. Tisdall*, 20 Ap. I might . . . talk STARCHLY, and affect ignorance of what you would be at.

1711. ADDISON, *Spectator*, 305. This professor is to give the society their stiffening, and infuse into their manners that beautiful political STARCH which may qualify them for levees, conferences, visits.

1872. ELIOT, *Middlemarch*, xxii. Nothing like these STARCHY doctors for vanity.

STARCHER, *subs.* (common).—A stiff white tie.

STARCHY, *adj.* (common).—Drunk: *see* SCREWED. Also *see* STARCHED.

STARE, *verb.* (Old Cant).—To swagger; to bully (HALLIWELL: 'a cant term').

STARE-CAT, *subs. phr.* (women's).—A meddlesome or inquisitive neighbour.

STARF. STARF TAKE YOU, *intj*, (provincial).—An imprecation; 'the devil take you' (HALLIWELL).

STAR-GAZER, *subs. phr.* (common).—1. A hedge whore: *see* TART (GROSE); and (2) a *penis* in erection. TO GO STARGAZING ON ONE'S BACK = to copulate: *see* RIDE.

*c.*1704. WARD, *Works*, 'T[om] B[rown]'s Last Letter.' If . . . the Label of Mortality . . . begins to turn STAR-GAZER, venture half a crown.

3. (old).—'A horse holding its head well up while trotting' (GROSE).

4. (nautical).—An imaginary sail, a SKYSCRAPER (*q.v.*).

5. (old).—An astrologer: also an astronomer: in contempt or jest. Also STAR-CLERK, STAR-CONNER, STAR-DIVINE, STAR-SHOOTER, and STAR-MONGER. Hence STAR-CRAFT = astrology.

*c.*1572. GASCOIGNE [CHALMERS, *Eng. Poets*], 'The Fruites of Warre,' 15. If Mars mooue warre, as STARCONNERS can tel.

1583. *Bible, Isaiah* xlvii. 13. Let now the astrologers, the STARREGASERS, and prognosticatours stand vp.

1599. JONSON, *Every Man Out of Humour*, iii. 2. Tut, these STARMONGER knaves, who would trust them.

1621. SYLVESTER, *Du Bartas*, III. i. 494. If, at the least, STAR-CLARKS be credit worth. *Ibid.*, IV. i. 134. So many stars, whose greatnes doth exceed So many times (if STAR-DIUINES say troth) The greatnes of the earth and ocean both.

1708. SWIFT, *Elegy on Partridge* A cobler, STAR-MONGER and quack. *Ibid.* The cobling and STAR-GAZING part.

1742-4. NORTH, *Life of Lord Guildford*, ii. 253. His lordship received him with much familiarity, and encouraged him to come and see him often . . . The STAR-GAZER was not wanting to himself in that.

18[?]. TENNYSON, *Lover's Tale*, i. Under the selfsame aspect of the stars (O falsehood of all STAR-CRAFT) we were born.

STARING QUARTER, *subs. phr.* (GROSE).—'An ox cheek.'

STARK-NAKED, *subs. phr.* (common).—NEAT (*q.v.*) gin (GROSE): orig. STRIP-ME-NAKED (RANDALL, *Diary*, 1820): also as *adj.* = unadulterated.

1830. LYTTON, *Paul Clifford.* His "bingo" was unexceptionable; and as for his STARK-NAKED, it was voted the most brilliant thing in nature.

STARLING, *subs.* (old colloquial).—1. *See* quots.

11[?]. *Robert of Gloucester*, 563. The King of is tresorie 'eche yer him sende A certein sume of STERLINGS, to is liue's ende.

1383. CHAUCER, *Cant. Tales*, 12,841. Min holy pardon may you all warice, So that ye offre nobles or STARLINGES, Or elles silver broches, spones, ringes.

1657. HOWELL, *Londonopolis*, 25. The lesser payments were in STARLINGS, which was the only coin then current, and stamp'd, which were pence so call'd: the probablest Reason that is given, why it was STARLING money, was, because in the ring or border of the peny, there was a starre stamped.

2. (police).—A marked or 'starred' man.

See BROTHER STARLING.

STAR OF THE LINE (THE), *subs. phr.* (military).—The 2nd Batt. Worcestershire Regiment, late The 36th Foot.

STAR-PITCH, *subs.* (tramps').—Sleeping in the open; a 'doss in HEDGE SQUARE' (*q.v.*).

STARPS, *subs.* (back slang).—In *pl.* = sprats.

STARS-AND-STRIPES, *subs. phr.* (American).—The United States flag: THE GRIDIRON; THE STAR-SPANGLED BANNER. STARS-AND-BARS = the flag of the Southern Confederacy, 1861-5.

1777. *Act of Congress.* "*Resolved*, That the flag of the thirteen United Colonies be THIRTEEN STRIPES alternately red and white; that the Union be THIRTEEN STARS, white in a blue field, representing a new constellation."

1812. F. S. KEY, '*The Star-Spangled Banner.*' Oh! say, does that STAR-SPANGLED BANNER yet wave O'er the land of the free and the home of the brave?

*c.*1861. *Confederate Song* [BARTLETT]. Our Southern boys are brave and true, and are joining heart and hand, And are flocking to the STARS AND BARS, as they are floating o'er our land.

START (THE), *subs. phr.* (tramps' and thieves').—1. London; and (2) The Old Bailey (also THE OLD START).—GROSE.

1851-61. MAYHEW, *London Lab.* I got fullied. I was tried at THE START.

1891. CAREW, *Auto. of a Gipsy*, 413. When I come out of steel I padded the hoof to START. *Ibid.*, 434. It ain't no manner of use goin' to the hexpense of bringin' a fust-class cracksman all the way from START.

3. (old).—*See* quot.

*c.*1696. B. E., *Dict. Cant Crew*, s.v. START, (Drink) Brewers emptying several Barrels into a great Tub, and thence conveying it through a Leather-pipe down the Cellar into the Butts.

4. (colloquial).—A happening: *e.g.*, A RUM START = an odd occurrence.

PHRASES. TO START IN (or UP) = to begin; TO START A VESSEL FROM THE STUMP = to outfit completely; TO START ON = to beat, bully, quiz, or take in hand.

STARTER, *subs.* (B. E.).—1. A question.

2. (old).—A milksop, a poltroon, a WHITE-LIVER (*q.v.*): 'I'm no STARTER' = 'I shan't flinch' (B. E. and GROSE).

*c.*1604. HEYWOOD, *If You Know not Me* [PEARSON, *Works*, i. 213]. Nay, nay, you need not bolt and lock so fast; she is no STARTER.

STARTLER, *subs.* (colloquial).—1. Generic for intensive surprise: *see* WHOPPER.

1864. ARTEMUS WARD, *Among the Mormons* (*Works*, 1899), 204. To a young person fresh from the land of greenbacks this careless manner of carting off solid silver is rather of a STARTLER.

START-UP, *subs. phr.* (old).—1. An upstart; 'no-one-knows-who': also as *adj.* = obscure; mushroom.

1600. SHAKSPEARE, *Much Ado*, i. 3. That young START-UP hath all the glory of my overthrow.

1653. R. BROME, *Queen and Concubine*, ii. 1. Upon my life, his marriage with that START-UP, That snake this good queen cocker'd in her bosom.

1704. SWIFT, *Tale of a Tub*, 1. Two junior START-UP societies.

1764. WALPOLE, *Castle of Otranto*, iv. Father Falconara's STARTUP son.

2. (old).—In *pl.*, *see* quots. 1575 and 1611.

1575. THYNNE, *Debate*, 33. A payre of STARTUPPES had he on his feete, That lased were up to the small of the legge; Homelie they were, and easier then meete, And in their soles full many a wooden pegge.

1586-1606. WARNER, *Albion's Eng.*, IV. xx. 95. And of the bacon's fat to make his STARTOPES black and soft.

1592. GREENE, *Quip*, &c. [Harl. Misc., v. 329]. But Hob and John of the country, they stept in churlishly in their high STARTUPS.

1599. HALL, *Satires*, vi. i. And in high START-UPS walk'd the pastur'd plaines, To tend her tasked herd that there remaines.

1605. DRAYTON, *Eclogues*, ix. (1753), 1,429. When not a shepherd any thing that could, But greaz'd his STARTUPS black as autumn's sloe.

1608. WITHAL, *Dict.*, 211. In a maner all husbandmen doe weare START-UPS, sunt omnes pene agricolæ soccati.

1611. COTGRAVE, *Dict.*, s.v. *Guestres*, START-UPS; high shooes, or gamashes for countrey folks.

1614. *Terence in English.* Some of my men comes running to me, and pulls of my STARTUPS, others I see hasting to make readie supper and to lay the cloath.

1629. MASSINGER, *Picture*, v. 1. Fie upon 't, what a thread 's here! a poor cobler's wife Would make a finer to sew a clown's rent STARTUP.

1821. SCOTT, *Kenilworth*, xxiv. A stupid lout . . . in a grey jerkin, with his head bare, his hose about his heels, and huge START-UPS upon his feet.

STARVATION, *subs.* (old: now recognised).—*See* quots. [Latham's edition (1866) of Todd's *Johnson* was the first English Dictionary to include this word.]

1775. DUNDAS, *Speech on American Affairs.* I shall not wait for the advent of STARVATION from Edinburgh to settle my judgment.

1781. WALPOLE, *Letters*, 'To Rev. W. Mason,' 25 April. STARVATION Dundas, whose pious policy suggested that the devil of rebellion could be expelled only by fasting.

1851. MITFORD, *Correspond. of Walpole* [CUNNINGHAM, viii. 30. Note]. STARVATION was an epithet applied to Mr. Dundas, the word being, for the first time, introduced into our language by him, in a speech in 1775 in an American debate, and thenceforward became a nickname.

1899. *Century Dict.*, s.v. STARVATION. The word is noted as one of the first (*flirtation* being another) to be formed directly from a native English verb with the Latin termination—*ation* . . . first used or brought into notice by Henry Dundas, first Viscount Melville.

STARVE 'EM, ROB 'EM, AND CHEAT 'EM, *phr.* (old nautical and military).—Stroud, Rochester, and Chatham: *cf.* THE LONDON SMASH 'EM AND DO-FOR-'EM RY. = The L.C.D.R.

STASH, *verb.* (common).—To desist; to set aside; TO STOW IT: *e.g.*, TO STASH PRIGGING = to turn honest; TO STASH ONE'S PATTER = to hold one's tongue; TO STASH THE LUSH = to stop BOOZING (*q.v.*).

1785. GROSE, *Vulg. Tongue*, s.v. WANTED . . . It becomes the latter [a thief] to keep out of the way . . . until he . . . can find means to STASH the business through the medium of Mr. Palmer.

1827. LYTTON, *Pelham*, lxxxii. STASH the lush . . . and toddle off to Ruggins.

1830. JON BEE, *Living Picture of London.* What to the heel do you STASH at? I'll chive you.

1841. LEMAN REDE, *Sixteen String Jack*, i. 6. STASH your patter and come along.

STATE NICKNAMES. The colloquial designation of various States and peoples of the American Union is as follows:—BADGER STATE = Wisconsin; BAY STATE = Massachusetts; BAYOU STATE = Mississippi; BEAR STATE = (1) Arkansas, (2) California (*Century*), and (3) Kentucky (*Century*); BIG BEND STATE = Tenessee: *people* = MUDHEADS; BLUE HEN STATE = Delaware: *people* = BLUE HEN'S CHICKENS; BLUE-LAW STATE = Connecticut: also *infra*; BUCK-EYE STATE = Ohio; BULLION STATE = Missouri: *people* = PUKES; CENTENNIAL STATE = Colorado: *people* = CENTENNIALS; CORN-CRACKER STATE = Kentucky: *people* = CORNCRACKERS; CRACKER STATE = Georgia: *people* = CRACKERS; CREOLE STATE = Louisiana: also *infra*;

THE DARK AND BLOODY GROUND = Kentucky : also *supra;* DIAMOND STATE = Delaware : also *supra;* EMPIRE STATE = New York : also *infra : people* = KNICKERBOCKERS ; EMPIRE STATE OF THE SOUTH = Georgia : *people* = CRACKERS ; EXCELSIOR STATE = New York : also *supra;* FREESTONE STATE = Connecticut : also *supra* and *infra;* GARDEN STATE = Kansas : also *infra;* GOLDEN STATE = California : also *supra;* GOPHER STATE = Minnesota ; GRANITE STATE = New Hampshire ; GREEN MOUNTAIN STATE = Vermont ; GULF STATE = Florida : also *infra;* HAWKEYE STATE = Iowa : *people* = HAWKEYES ; HOOSIER STATE = Indiana : *people* = HOOSIERS ; KEYSTONE STATE = Pennsylvania ; LAKE STATE = Michigan : *people* = WOLVERINES ; LAND OF STEADY HABITS = Connecticut : also *supra;* LITTLE RHODY = Rhode Island ; LONE STAR STATE = Texas : *people* = BEEFHEADS ; LUMBER STATE = Maine ; also *infra;* MOTHER OF PRESIDENTS (or STATES) = Virginia : also *infra;* MUDCAT STATE = Mississippi : also *supra;* NEW ENGLAND OF THE WEST = Minnesota : also *supra;* OLD COLONY = Massachusetts : also *supra;* OLD DOMINION = Virginia : also *supra;* OLD LINE STATE = Maryland ; OLD NORTH STATE = North Carolina : also *infra;* PALMETTO STATE = South Carolina ; PAN HANDLE STATE = West Virginia ; PELICAN STATE = Louisiana : also *supra;* PENINSULAR STATE = Florida : also *supra;* PINE TREE STATE = Maine : also *supra;* PRAIRIE STATE = Illinois : also *infra;* SAGE-HEN STATE (or SILVER STATE) = Nevada ; SQUATTER STATE = Kansas : also *supra;* SUCKER STATE = Illinois : also *supra;* TURPENTINE STATE = North Carolina : *people* = TAR-HEELS : also *supra;* WEB-FOOT STATE = Oregon ; WOLVERINE STATE = Michigan : *people* = WOLVERINES ; WOODEN NUTMEG STATE = Connecticut : also *supra.*

1835. HOFFMAN, *Winter in the West*, 210. There was a long-haired HOOSIER from Indiana, a couple of smart-looking SUCKERS from Illinois, a keen-eyed, leather-belted BADGER from Wisconsin : and who could refuse to drink with such a company?

18[?]. *Am. Congress*, 'Am. Rejected Addresses.' Broad Indiana's HOOSIER sons her fame must needs keep good.

1848. *New York Herald*, 13 June. Thank God, in my own State, in the BULLION STATE, they did not succeed in depreciating our majority.

1849. WHITTIER, *Voices of Freedom.* What means the OLD DOMINION? Hath she forgot the day, When o'er her conquered valleys swept the Briton's steel array? *Ibid.* Lift again the stately emblem on the BAY STATE'S rusted shield, Give to Northern winds the pine-tree on our banner's tattered field!

1850. ALLIN, *Yankee Ballads.* The EMPIRE STATE is your New York ; I grant it hard to mate her ; Yet still give me the NUTMEG STATE, Where shall we find a greater?

1856. STOWE, *Dred.*, i. 152. I was amused enough, said Nina, with Old Hundred's indignation at having got out the carriage and horses to go over to what he called a CRACKER funeral.

1859. BARTLETT, *Americanisms*, s.v. BEAR STATE. I once asked a Western man if Arkansas abounded in bears, that it should be designated as the "Bear State." Yes, said he, it does ; for I never knew a man from that State but he was a BAR, and in fact the people are all BARISH to a degree.

1861. *Charleston Mercury*, 'War Song.' March, march on, brave PALMETTO BOYS, Sumter and Lafayette, forward in order.

1861. *Delaware Inquirer*, 5 May. Delaware's honor is in your hands . . . BLUE HEN'S CHICKENS to the front! Forward! March!

1861. *N. York Observer*, 26 Dec. A young lady from the rural districts of HOOSIERDOM lately visited Chicago with her beau.

18[?]. *Voice from the South*, 53. Let us not forget the cynosure of Independence [*i.e.* Massachusetts] ; but bid her a kind farewell for her pilotage through the breakers of the Revolution—put the LONE STAR in its place.

*c.*1861-5. MASON, *Southern Poems of the War*, 95. And Texans will fight, 'Neath the flag of the LONE STAR, For God and their right.

1865. WHEELER, *Dict.* s.v. DARK AND BLOODY GROUND (The). An expression formerly much used in allusion to Kentucky, of which name it is said to be a translation. The phrase is an epitome of the early history of the State, of the dark and bloody conflicts of the first white settlers with their savage foes ; but the name originated in the fact that this was the grand battle-ground between the Northern and Southern Indians.

1872. EGGLESTON, *Hoosier Schoolmaster.* It has been in my mind since I was a HOOSIER boy to do something toward describing life in the back-country districts of the Western States.

1877. HALE, *Adv. of a Pullman*, 30. So they whirled relentlessly across the PAN-HANDLE, by which domestic name that funny strip of Western Virginia is known that shoots up like an inverted icicle between Pennsylvania and Ohio.

1877. PRES. HAYES, *Speech* [Providence, 28 June]. I ask every lady and gentleman to consider that here and now I give you a hearty BUCKEYE shake. *Ibid.* [Louisville, 17 Sep.] The once DARK AND BLOODY GROUND of Kentucky, no longer so, but, as I trust in God, here and elsewhere a land of peace, prosperity, and happiness.

1877. *New York Tribune*, 6 July. old church in Nassau Street (New York) was dedicated in 1732 . . . The congregation was composed of the wealthiest and most prominent people of Manhattan Island—the veritable KNICKERBOCKERS.

*d.*1891. LOWELL, *Poems.* When first the Pilgrims landed on the BAY STATE'S iron shore, The word went forth that slavery should one day be no more.

1896. LILLARD, *Poker Stories*, iii. The game, as she is played in the LAND OF STEADY HABITS . . .

TO LIE IN STATE, *verb. phr.* (GROSE).—'To be in bed with three regular harlots.'

IN A STATE OF ELEVATION, *verb. phr.* (common).—More or less drunk : *see* SCREWED.

1749. SMOLLETT, *Gil Blas* (1812), II. iv. We drank hard, and went home in a STATE OF ELEVATION, that is half-seas over.

IN A STATE OF NATURE. *See* NATURE'S GARB.

STATES OF INDEPENDENCY, *subs. phr.* (GROSE).—'Frontiers of Extravagance. *Oxf. Univ. Cant.*'

STATIONERY, *subs.* (theatrical).—Free passes ; PAPER (*q.v.*).

STAVE, *verb.* (American).—To press onwards regardless of everything : generic for vigorous action. Hence STAVING = (1) dashing, active, and (2) great, strong, &c.—a general intensive. STAVER = anybody or anything exceptionally active, brilliant, or dashing ; a ROUSER (*q.v.*). Also TO RIP (*q.v.*) AND STAVE.

1842. KIRKLAND, *Forest Life* [BARTLETT]. Hilloa, Steve! where are you STAVING to? If you're for Wellington, scale up here, and I'll give you a ride.

1848. *Am. Review*, June. A president of one of our colleges once said to a graduate at parting, "My son, I want to advise you. Never oppose public opinion. The great world will STAVE right on!"

*c.*1850. *Cincinnatti Times* [BARTLETT]. A STAVING dram put him in better humour. Strange what arguments some people require.

1869. STOWE, *Oldtown Folks*, 117. Miss Asphyxia's reputation in the region was perfectly established. She was spoken of with applause, under such titles as a STAVER, a pealer, a roarer at work.

1884. *Century Mag.*, xxxviii. 41. He . . . went STAVING down the street as if afraid to look behind him.

STAY, *subs.* (old).—1. A cuckold (GROSE).

2. (colloquial).—Half a meal : also STAY-BELLY. Also as *verb.* (or TO STAY THE STOMACH).

1610. JONSON, *Alchemist*, iii. 2. A piece of gingerbread to be merry withal, And STAY YOUR STOMACH lest you faint with fasting.

1899. WHITEING, *John St.*, xi. I could eat both portions four times over, of course, but the meal as it stand is a STAY.

Verb. (colloquial). — To endure, last out, or persevere : as an athlete in exercise, a horse in racing, an author in public favour. Hence STAYER = anybody or anything capable of holding on for a long time ; STAYING-POWER = capacity for endurance.

1885. *D. Tel.*, 14 Sep. He won at Lincoln . . . and would STAY better than Pizarro. *Ibid.*, 11 Nov. Doubts are also entertained concerning her ability to STAY the course.

1885. *Field*, 3 Oct. Monolith has never been thought such a genuine STAYER as to prefer two miles to one.

1898. GOULD, *Landed at Last*, iv. Workman was certainly a horse to inspire confidence, being well-shaped and built like a STAYER. *Ibid.* Not one of my horses has failed through lack of STAYING POWER, or because he was not fit.

PHRASES, &c.—TO STAY PUT = to remain as placed ; TO STAY WITH = to court (American) ; TO STAY OUT (Eton : *see* quot.) ; COME TO STAY = said of anything meeting a public need, or with approval or favour ; TO UNLACE ONE'S STAYS = to copulate : *see* GREENS and RIDE.

1857-64. BRINSLEY RICHARDS, *Seven Years at Eton.* Sometimes Blazes had a lazy fit, and put himself on the sick list for a day. This was called STAY OUT, for the reason that one had to stay in.

1870. "MAC," *Sketchy Memories of Eton.* Many things at Eton were called by misnomers, in the construction of which the *lucus a non lucendo* principle came out very strong. Thus, when we stayed in, we said we were STAYING OUT ; when "absence" was called, we had to be present.

1876. WHITNEY, *Sights and Insights*, 37. We piled our bags and baskets . . . 'If they will only STAY PUT,' said Emery Ann.

1901. *Athenæum*, 13 Ap., 455, 1. The issue . . . of Byron's letters will leave very little doubt in the mind of the reading public of the new century that Lord Byron as a letter-writer has COME TO STAY.

1903. *Referee*, 8 Feb., 7, 4. No one with half a grain of sense could for a moment question the autocars' many merits, nor their having COME TO STAY and become a great power in the land.

STAY-AT-HOME, *subs. phr.* (colloquial).—A person of domestic tastes ; a HOME-BIRD (*q.v.*). ; a HOUSE-DOVE (*q.v.*) ; as *adj.* = fond of remaining at home ; the reverse of GAD-ABOUT (*q.v.*).

1814. AUSTEN, *Mansfield Park*, v. A talking pretty young woman like Miss Crawford is always pleasant society to an indolent, STAY-AT-HOME man.

1855. KINGSLEY, *Westward Ho*, xv. Go forth and find us STAY-AT-HOMES new markets for our ware.

1863. GASKELL, *Sylvia's Lovers*, ix. "Cold!" said her father, "what do ye STAY-AT-HOMES know about cold?"

1883. *Pall Mall Gaz.*, 2 Nov. The quantity of admiration might make a modest STAY-AT-HOME dizzy to contemplate.

STAY-TAPE, *subs. phr.* (old).—A tailor : *see* TRADES. [GROSE : 'from that article and its coadjutor buckram, which formerly made no small figure in the bills of these knights of the needle'].

STEADY HABITS. THE LAND OF STEADY HABITS, *subs. phr.* (American). — Connecticut : *see* STATE NICKNAMES. [BARTLETT : 'On account of the staid deportment and excellent morals of the people.']

1896. LILLARD, *Poker Stories*, iii. The most interesting jack-pot in the history of the game, as she is played in THE LAND OF STEADY HABITS, has been raked into the coffers of the Goddess of Justice in a lively Connecticut borough.

STEAL. *See* BREWER'S-BASKET, and STALE.

STEAM, *subs.* (colloquial).—Force ; energy ; GO (*q.v.*).

STEAM-ENGINE, *subs. phr.* (Manchester).—Potato-pie (HOTTEN).

STEAMER, *subs.* (old).—A pipe : a SWELL-STEAMER = a long pipe (GROSE).

STEAMING, *subs.* (military). — A steamed pudding.

STEAM-PACKET, *subs. phr.* (rhyming).—A jacket.

STEEL, *subs.* (old).—The House of Correction, Coldbath Fields, London (GROSE) : latterly, any prison or lock-up. [Originally (HOTTEN) The Bastille].

1851-61. MAYHEW, *Lond. Lab.*, i. 457. The only thing that frightens me when I'm in prison is sleeping in a cell by myself—you do in the Old Horse and the STEEL.

1877. *Five Years Penal Servitude*, i. The STEEL, a slang name for the large metropolitan prisons.

1888. J. GREENWOOD, *Dick Temple.* "And the STEEL—the place to which Mr. Eggshells alludes in connection with his retirement?" "Coldbath Fields," responded Mr. Badger, promptly, "quod—gaol—prison—that's the STEEL."

1889. THOR FREDUR, *Sketches from Shady Places.* He pitched into the policeman, was lugged off to the STEEL, had up before the magistrate, and got a month.

STEELBACKS (THE), *subs. phr.* (military). — 1. The 1st Batt. Northamptonshire Regiment, the late 48th Foot ; and (2) The 1st Batt. Middlesex Regiment, the late 57th Foot.

STEEL-BAR, *subs. phr.* (old).—A needle. Hence STEEL - BAR DRIVER (or FLINGER) = a needle-man (or woman) : spec. a journeyman tailor (GROSE). *See* TRADES.

STEEL-BOY, *subs.* (Irish). — *See* quot.

1772. [THACKERAY, *Barry Lyndon*, xvi.] The kingdom of Ireland was at this period ravaged by various parties of banditti ; who, under the name of White-boys, Oakboys, STEELBOYS, with captains at their head, killed proctors, fired stacks, houghed and maimed cattle, and took the law into their own hands.

STEEL-PEN COAT, *subs. phr.* (common).—A dress coat : a SWALLOW-TAIL (*q.v.*).

STEENKIRK, *subs.* (old).—'A Muslin neckcloth carelessly put on,' 'from the manner in which the French officers wore their cravats when they returned from the Battle of Steenkirk' [1692], 'afterwards a Fashion for both sexes' (B. E. and GROSE). Likewise applied to other articles of dress, as wigs, buckles, &c.

STEEP, *adj.* and *adv.* (colloquial).—A general intensive : *cf.* TALL. Thus a STEEP (= high) price ; STEEP (= excessive) damages ; a STEEP (= a difficult or forlorn) undertaking ; a STEEP (= heavy) tax, &c. TOO STEEP = too absurd (bad, idiotic, or impudent) for acceptance. Hence, in the same sense PRECIPITOUS (*q.v.*). Fr. *raide.*

1841. EMERSON, *Essays*, 1 S., 302. Perhaps if we should meet Shakspeare we should not be conscious of any STEEP inferiority.

1857. *Chicago Tribune*, 17 Oct. At the election in Minnesota, one hundred and ten Winnebago Indians . . . voted the Democratic ticket ; but the agent thought this was rather STEEP, so he afterwards crossed that number from the list.

1858. *Baltimore Sun*, 23 Aug. The verdict by twelve of seventeen of a jury giving 150,000 dollars as damages to a Land and Water-Power Company, at the Great Falls of the Potomac . . . is regarded as decidedly STEEP.

1882-3. FROUDE, *Sketches*, 164. Neither priest nor squire was able to establish any STEEP difference in outward advantages between himself and the commons among whom he lived.

STEEPLE, *subs.* (old colloquial).—A woman's head-dress: 14th Century. Also, later, a steeple-crowned hat for either sex (*see* quot. 1583).

1583. STUBBES, *Anat. of Abuses* (1585), f. 21. Long hats pearking up like the spere or shaft of a STEEPLE, standyng a quarter of a yarde above the croune of their headës, some more, some lesse, as please the phantasies of their inconstant mindes.

1601. WRIGHT, *Passions of the Mind* (1621), 330. STEEPLED HATS.

*c.*1704. [ASHTON, *Queen Anne*, II. 138]. The women wearing the old country STEEPLE-CROWNED HAT and simply made gowns.

1706. WARD, *Hudibras Redivivus*. The good old dames . . . In stiffen-body'd russet gowns, And on their heads old STEEPLE-CROWNS.

1837. BROWNING, *Strafford*. An old doublet and a STEEPLE HAT.

1888. *Ency. Brit.*, VI. 469. Some of the more popular of these strange varieties of headgear have been distinguished as the 'horned,' the 'mitre,' 'the STEEPLE'—in France known as the 'hennin'—and the butterfly.

STEEPLE-FAIR, *subs. phr.* (old).—The simoniacal mart: in quot. 1599 = St. Paul's. [Formerly church doors were plastered with all kinds of miscellaneous advertisements: *see* SIQUIS.]

1599. HALL, *Satires*, III. v. 7. Thou servile foole, why couldst thou not repaire To buy a benefice at STEEPLE-FAIRE.

1606. *Return from Parnassus*, iv. 2. Are not you the young drover of livings Academico told me of that haunts STEEPLE-FAIRS?

STEEPLE-HOUSE, *subs. phr.* (old Quakers').—A church (GROSE).

*d.*1690. FOX, *Journal* (Philadelphia), 167. The reason why I would not go into their STEEPLE HOUSE was because I was to bear my testimony against it, and to bring all off from such places to the Spirit of God, that they might know their bodies to be the temples of the Holy Ghost.

1890. WHITTIER, *Poems*, 'The Old South.' There are STEEPLE-HOUSES on every hand, And pulpits that bless and ban; And the Lord will not grudge the single church, That is set apart for man.

STEER, *verb.* (nautical).—STEER has furnished one or two colloquialisms: thus TO STEER A TRICK = to take a turn at the wheel; TO STEER SMALL = to exercise care or skill; TO GIVE A STEER = to give a TIP (*q.v.*).

STEERER. *See* BUNCO-STEERER.

STEERING-COMMITTEE, *subs. phr.* (American political). — A committee of direction; WIREPULLERS (*q.v.*).

STEEVER. *See* STIVER.

STEM, *subs.* (colloquial).—In *pl.* = the legs.

STEM-WINDER, *subs. phr.* (American).—Anything well-finished: hence, the best of its kind. [STEM-WINDER = keyless watch: at the time a new and exquisite improvement.]

STEP, *verb.* (colloquial).—To make off: also TO STEP IT: *see* ABSQUALULATE. Also (military) = to desert.

TO STEP OUT, *verb. phr.* (common).—To die: *see* ALOFT.

STEP DOWN AND OUT! *intj. phr.* (American).—"Shut up!" "Stow it!" "You're done!"

STEPHEN (or STEVEN), *subs.* (old).—Money: generic. 'STEPHEN'S at home' = 'He's got 'em' (GROSE and VAUX).

1834. AINSWORTH, *Rookwood*, 'Double Cross.' I rather fancies that it's news, How in a mill, both men should lose; For vere the odds are thus made even, It plays the dickens with the STEVEN.

ST. STEPHEN'S LOAF, *subs. phr.* (old).—*See* quot.

1696. MOTTEUX, *Rabelais*, v. 42. Having said this, he took up one of ST. STEPHEN'S LOAVES, *alias* a stone, and was going to hit him with it about the middle.

STEPMOTHER, *subs.* (colloquial).—A horny filament growing up the side of the finger-nail. STEPMOTHER'S BLESSING = a 'hangnail.'

STEPPER, *subs.* (prison).—1. The treadmill; the EVERLASTING STAIRCASE (*q.v.*).

2. (colloquial).—A high-spirited or full-actioned horse: also REGULAR STEPPER and HIGH-STEPPER. Hence anybody or anything more than usually good of its kind. *Cf.* HIGHFLYER.

1886. *Field*, 16 Jan. The man who wants a pair of STEPPERS.

STEPPING-KEN, *subs. phr.* (chiefly American). — Dancing rooms: espec. such as are frequented by sailors.

STEREO, *subs.* (printers').—Stale news: *see* GEORGE HORNE.

STERLING. *See* STARLING.

STERN, *subs.* (colloquial).—The backside; THE BUM (*q.v.*). Hence STERN-FOREMOST = backwards, arse-first; ASTERN = behind; STERN-UPPERMOST = on one's face; STERN-CHASE = a pursuit; STERN-CHASER = a sodomite.

1590. SPENSER, *Fairy Queen*, I. xi. 8. He . . . gan his sturdy STERNE about to weld.

1836. M. SCOTT, *Tom Cringle's Log*. Steer clear of the stem of a sailing ship, or the STERN of a kicking horse, Tom.

1868. FURNIVALL [*Book of Precedence* (E. E. T. S.) *Forewords*, xxiii.]. We don't want to deceive ourselves about them, or fancy them cherubs without STERNS.

1902. *Athenæum*, 8 Feb., 176, 3. He was taught nothing, except that jumping to any word of command saved his bows from cuffing, his STERN from kicking.

TO BRING A SHIP DOWN BY THE STERN, *verb. phr.* (nautical).—To over officer.

1835. DANA, *Before the Mast*, xiv. We had now four officers, and only six in the forecastle. This was BRINGING HER too much DOWN BY THE STERN for our comfort.

STERN-POST, *subs. phr.* (venery).—The *penis*: *see* PRICK.

STEVEN. *See* STEPHEN.

STEVER. *See* STIVER.

STEW, *subs.* (old colloquial and literary).—1. A fish-pond. Whence 2. (colloquial and literary), in *pl.* = a brothel, or a street of brothels. STEW (old) = a harlot is rare, and may very well be an effect of ignorance or affectation on the user's part. But STEWISH (or STEWED), *adj.* = bordelesque, whorish, harlotry (in the worst sense).

1362. LANGLAND, *Piers Plowman*, 3936. Jonette of the STUWES.

1383. CHAUCER, *Cant. Tales*, 'Friars Tale.' Wommen of the STIVES. *Ibid.* (C) xxiii. 159. Sleuthe . . . wedded one Wanhope, a wenche of the STEWES.

*c.*1520. *Hick Scorner* [DODSLEY, *Old Plays* (HAZLITT), i. 180]. My mother was a lady of the STEWS . . . And . . . my father wore an horne.

*c.*1520. *Mayd Emlyn* [HAZLITT, *Pop. Poet.*, iv. 96]. And bycause she loued rydynge, At the STEWES was her abydynge.

*d.*1529. SKELTON, *Bowge of Courte*, 400. Now renne muste I to the STEWYS syde, To wete yf Malkyn, my lemman, haue gete oughte: I let her to hyre, that men may on her ryde.

1530. PALSGRAVE, *Lang. Francoyse*, s.v. STEWES, a place for commen women, *bordeau*.

1535. *Bible* [COVERDALE], Ezek. xvi. 39. [They] shal breake downe thy STEWES, and destroy thy brodel houses.

1546. *Proclamation* [*MSS. note* by R. SMITH quoted by HEARNE, *Diary*, Oct. 12, 1713]. These abhominable STEWHOUSES were kept in Southwark . . . being whited houses, painted with signes to know them. These bawdy houses were tollerated, and had lawes and orders made for the STEW-HOLDERS to observe.

1550. CROWLEY, *Epigrams*. The bawds of the STEWS be turned al out; But some think they inhabit al England throughout.

1564. UDAL, *Apoph. Eras.* O Aristippus thou art a greate medler with this woman, beyng a STEWED strumpette.

1566. STILL, *Gammer Gurton's Needle* [DODSLEY, *Old Plays* (HAZLITT), iii. 217]. Where is the strong STEWED whore?

1573. BARET, *Alvearie*. The STEWES, or place without the wals of the citie where bawderie was kept.

1578. WHETSTONE, *Promos and Cass*, I. iv. 3. And shall Cassandra now be termed, in common speeche, a STEWES.

1596. JONSON, *Every Man in Humour*, ii. 1. And here, as in a tavern, or a STEWES, He and his wild associates spend their hours.

1597. SHAKSPEARE, *Rich. II.*, v. 3, 16. He would unto the STEWS, And from the common'st creature pluck a glove and wear it as a favour. *Ibid.* (1598), *2 Hen. IV.*, i. 2. An I could get me but a wife in the STEWS.

1599. HALL, *Satires*, i. 9. Rhymed in rules of STEWISH ribaldry.

1621. BURTON, *Anat. Melan.*, I. II. ii. 4. A . . . Priest that, because he would neither willingly marry, nor make use of the STEWS, fell into grievous melancholy. *Ibid.*, III. II. i. 2. In Italy and Spain they have their STEWS in every great city.

1633. HEYWOOD, *Eng. Trav.*, i. 2. His modest house Turn'd to a common STEWES.

[?]. BISHOP, *Marrow of Astrology*, 57. Venus denotes in houses, all places belonging to women, as garnished beds, STEWS.

1650. SIR A. WELDON, *Court James I.*, 146. Instead of that beauty he had a notorious STEW sent to him.

1683. *England's Vanity*, 55. You may find them, as Solomon sayes, not in the corner of the streets onely, but thick in the very midst of them, and turning the whole city into a STEWS.

*d.*1704. BROWN, *Works*, ii. 107. What Montaigne said formerly of the women, I now say of the priests . . . they send their conscience to the STEWS, and keep their countenance within rule.

1733. POPE, *Imit. Horace*, I. vi. 130. And shall we every decency confound? Through taverns, STEWS, and bagnios take our round?

3. (colloquial).—Worry; fuss; mental disturbance.

1837. BARHAM, *Ingolds. Leg.*, 'M. of Venice.' And Antonio grew, In a deuce of a STEW For he could not cash up, spite of all he could do. *Ibid.*, i. 104. And he, though naturally bold and stout, In short, was in a most tremendous STEW.

1838. BECKETT, *Paradise Lost*, 62. Now Adam, in a plaguey STEW, Cried 'Zounds and blood, what must we do?'

Verb. (Stonyhurst College).—To study: hence STEW-POT = a hard-working student.

TO STEW (FRY OF MELT) IN ONE'S OWN (or ANOTHER'S) JUICE (GREASE, FAT, OR GRAVY), *verb. phr.* (common). — To be left vindictively or resentfully alone.

1383. CHAUCER, *Cant. Tales*, 'Wife of Bath's Prol.' But certainly I made folk such chere, That IN HIS OWN GREES I made him FRIE.

1596. SHAKSPEARE, *Merry Wives*, iii. 5. I was more than HALF-STEWED IN GREASE.

1774. BRIDGES, *Burlesque Homer*, 8. By Sol's hob hot beams so sore were pelted, That IN OUR GREASE we're almost MELTED.

1843. G. P. R. JAMES, *Forest Days*. If yonder cooks have not done their duty and got all ready, I will FRY them IN their OWN JUICE.

STEWARD, *subs.* (American Cadet).—A doctor.

STEWED QUAKER. *See* QUAKER.

STIBBER-GIBBER, *adj. phr.* (Old Cant).—Used as in quot.

1560-1. AWDELEY, *Fraternitye of Vacabondes*, 'XXV. Orders of Knaues,' 12. Proctour is he, that will tary long, and bring a lye, when his Maister sendeth him on his errand. This is a STIBBER GIBBER knaue, that doth fayne tales.

STIBBLER, *subs.* (Scots).—A clerical probationer; a GUINEA-PIG (*q.v.*). *See* STICKIT.

1815. SCOTT, *Guy Mannering*, xlvi. Listen, ye stickit STIBBLER, to what I tell ye, or ye sall rue it.

STICHEL, *subs.* (old).—A term of contempt.

*c.*1620. *Lady Alimony*, I 4b. Barren STICHEL! that shall not serve thy turn.

STICK, *subs.* (old).—1. In *pl.* = furniture; MARBLES (*q.v.*): also STICKS AND STONES (GROSE, VAUX, BEE).

1883. SIMS, *How the Poor Live*. To tide over till then is a work of some difficulty, but the STICKS and the "wardrobe" of the family have paid the rent up to now.

1883. GREENWOOD, *Tag, Rag, & Co.* None will permit him to occupy a room in a private house, unless he has at least a few STICKS by way of security for the payment of a week's rent.

1890. WHITEING, *John St.*, ii. What rent kin yer affawd . . . have yer got any STICKS?

2. (Old Cant).—In *pl.* = pistols; POPS (*q.v.*); 'STOW YOUR STICKS' = 'hide your pistols' (GROSE and VAUX).

3. (colloquial).—An awkward, dull, or stupid person: in contempt. Usually POOR STICK. A RUM (or ODD) STICK = an oddity.

1803. EDGEWORTH, *Belinda*, xx. "You . . . will go and marry, I know you will, some STICK of a rival." . . . "I hope I shall never marry a STICK."

1814. AUSTEN, *Mansfield Park*, xiii. I was surprised to see Sir Henry such a STICK; luckily the strength of the piece did not depend upon him.

1847. BRONTE, *Jane Eyre*, xvii. The poor old STICK used to cry out, "Oh you villains childs," and then we sermonised her on the presumption of attempting to teach such clever blades as we were, when she was herself so ignorant.

1855. *New York Tribune*, 4 Sep. About the poorest STICK for a legislator ever elected.

1886. *D. Teleg.*, 13 July. A great actor may not exhibit himself as a STICK for half-an-hour together, and claim to redeem his fame by a few magnificent moments.

1899. KERNAHAN, *Scoundrels*, xxi. The STICK will find himself . . . cold-shouldered, and the assumer of 'side' may think himself lucky if he be allowed to depart unbaited.

1900. WHITE, *West End*, 131. 'Elsenham's a STICK.' 'He is rather,' said my aunt. 'But he is heir to one of the oldest earldoms in the kingdom.

4. (thieves').—A crowbar; a JEMMY (*q.v.*).

1877. HORSLEY, *Jottings from Jail*. "What tools will you want?" "We shall want some twirls and the STICK."

5. (silversmiths').—(*a*) A candlestick; and (*b*) a candle.

6. (cricketers').—In *pl.* = the stumps.

7. (common). — In *pl.* = the legs; STUMPS (*q.v.*).

8. (printers').—A hard or otherwise badly printing ink-roller.

9. (athletic).—In *pl.* = hurdles. Hence STICK-HOPPER = a hurdle-racer.

10. (nautical).—A mast: *e.g.*, 'She has handsome STICKS' = 'She is finely sparred.'

11. (colloquial).—Hesitation; demur. Hence TO STICK AT = to BOGGLE (*q.v.*).

1678. BUNYAN, *Pilgrim's Progress*, vi. When he came to the Hill Difficulty he made no STICK at that.

THE STICK, *subs. phr.* (venery).—A venereal disease: clap, shanker, or pox; LADIES' FEVER (*q.v.*).

Verb. (venery).—To copulate: *see* GREENS and RIDE.

2. (colloquial).—To kill: spec. (India) to spear wild hogs.

PHRASES and COLLOQUIALISMS are numerous. Thus TO BE STUCK ON THE DEAL = to pay too much, to be swindled; TO STICK ON THE PRICE = to overcharge; TO STICK FOR DRINKS = to win the toss; TO STICK IT UP = to get credit; TO STICK UP (a bank, a train, a caravan) = to rob; TO BE STUCK ON ONE'S LINES (theatrical) = to forget; TO STICK UP TRICKS (POINTS, RUNS, GOALS, &c.) = to score; TO STICK UP = to take one's own part, or another's; TO STICK IN A PIN = to make a note of, to take heed; TO STICK TO = to stand by; TO STICK AT = to be scrupulous; TO STICK AT NOTHING = to be utterly without scruple; TO STICK IN ONE'S STOMACH (or GIZZARD) = to rankle; TO STICK TO = to back through thick and thin, to follow closely; TO STICK ONE'S SPOON IN THE WALL = to die; TO CUT ONE'S STICKS = to decamp; TO HAVE THE FIDDLE BUT NOT THE STICK = to have the means without sense to use them; TO GO TO STICKS AND STAVES (or NOGGIN STAVES) = to go to ruin; TO BEAT ALL TO STICKS = to vanquish utterly; TO STICK A POINT = to settle a matter; TO STICK IN (cricket) = to play carefully. so as to keep up the wicket; TO STICK ONESELF UP = to assert oneself, to SPREAD OUT (*q.v.*); TO STICK TO ONE'S FINGERS = to remain in possession unlawfully; TO STICK OUT FOR = to contend obstinately; TO STICK AND LIFT = to live from hand to mouth. Also STUCK ON ONE'S SHAPE = pleased with one's appearance; STUCK IN THE MUD = CORNERED (*q.v.*); STUCK FOR THE READY = penniless; STUCK BY ONE'S PAL = deceived, deserted, DONE (*q.v.*); STUCK IN ONE'S FIGURES (FACTS, or CALCULATIONS) = mistaken, at a loss; DEAD STUCK = completely disappointed, flabbergasted, or ruined; STUCK ON A JUDE = enamoured; STUCK UP = conceited, proud. Also AS CROSS AS TWO STICKS = fully angered; STICK-AND-STONE = everything: *cf.* ROOT AND BRANCH, STOCK AND BLOCK; IN QUICK STICKS (or CHISEL) = instantly; WRONG END OF THE STICK = (1) the worst of a position; and (2) the false of a story. 'Any STICK (or STAFF) suffices to beat the dog' (RAY).

1337. BRUNNE, *Handlyng Synne* (HEARNE), 113. [Castles] are won ilka STIK.

1448-60. *Paston Letters*, 462. EVERY STONE AND STIKKE thereof.

1544. *Exped. in Scotland* [ARBER, *Eng. Garner*, i. 120]. We brake down the pier of the haven of Perth, and burnt every STICK of it.

1564. UDAL, *Erasmus's Apoph.*, 215. So in fine were thei beaten doune, their citee taken, spoiled, and destroyed bothe STICKE AND STONE.

1569. *Marriage of Wit and Science* [DODSLEY, *Old Plays* (HAZLITT), ii. 342]. I know a younker that will ease you . . . That will not STICK TO marry you within this hour.

1594. SHAKSPEARE, 2 *Hen. VI.*, iii. 1. The ancient proverb will be well effected: 'A STAFF is quickly found to beat a dog.' *Ibid.* (1598), 2 *Hen. IV.*, i. 2. And yet he will not STICK TO say his face is a face-royal.

1611. BEAUMONT and FLETCHER, *Knight of B. Pestle*, ii. 1. And this it was she swore, never to marry But such as one whose mighty arm could carry (As meaning me, for I am such a one) Her bodily away through STICK AND STONE.

1648-55. FULLER, *Church Hist.*, vi. 268. This quaternion of subscribers have STICK'N THE POINT dead with me that all antient English monks were Benedictines.

16[?]. PEPYS, *Diary*, IV. 141. To serve him I should, I think, STICK AT NOTHING.

1743. FIELDING, *Jon. Wild*, I. xiii. It was his constant maxim, that he was a pitiful fellow who would STICK AT a little rapping for his friend.

*d.*1796. BURNS, *To William Simpson*, Postsc. Folk thought them ruined STICK-AN'-STONE.

1824. FERRIER, *Inheritance*, i. 95. She married a Highland drover or lacksman, I can't tell which, and they went ALL TO STICKS and staves.

1837. BARHAM, *Ingolds. Leg.*, 'Lay of St. Aloys.' Lastly, as to the Pagan who played such a trick, First assuming the tonsure, then CUTTING HIS STICK. *Ibid.*, 'St. Odille.' Many ladies in Strasburg were beautiful, still They were BEAT ALL TO STICKS by the lovely Odille.

1840. DICKENS, *Old Curiosity Shop*, xl. And now that the nag has got his wind again . . . I'm afraid I must CUT MY STICK.

1841. *Punch*, I. 136. If we were speaking of an ordinary man, and not a monarch, we should have rendered by the familiar phrase of CUT HIS STICK.

1843. THACKERAY, *Lyra Hibernica*, 'Battle of Limerick.' The best use Tommy made Of his famous battle blade Was to CUT HIS OWN STICK from the Shannon shore. *Ibid.* (1862), *Philip*, xl. Heard him abuse you to Ringwood. Ringwood STUCK UP FOR you . . . spoke up like a man—like a man who STICKS UP FOR a fellow who is down.

1846. STOKES, *Discoveries in Australia*, ii. xiii. 502. It was only the previous night that he had been STUCK UP with a pistol at his head.

1851-61. MAYHEW, *Lond. Lab.*, II. 18. The pawnbrokers have been so often STUCK with inferior instruments that it is difficult to pledge even a really good violin. *Ibid.*, III. 142. Some of the young fellows STICK IN THEIR PARTS. They get the stage fever and knocking in the knees.

1855. HOWITT, *Two Years in Victoria*, ii. 187. Unless the mail came well armed, a very few men could STICK IT UP without any trouble or danger.

1855. KINGSLEY, *Westward Ho*, v. Silence, or my allegory will GO TO NOGGIN-STAVES. *Ibid.* (1857), *Two Years Ago*, i. In a few minutes Tom came in. "Here's a good riddance! . . ." "What?" "CUT HIS STICK, and walked his chalks, and is off to London."

*d.*1859. DE QUINCEY, *Roman Meals*. All which remained for a decayed poet was respectfully to CUT HIS STICK, and retire.

1860-3. MOTLEY, *Un. Netherlands*, II. 87. One third of the money sent by the Queen for the soldiers STUCK IN HIS FINGERS.

1867. *Week in Wall Street*, 47. As soon as the whole class of small speculators perceived they had been STUCK, they all shut their mouths; no one confessing the ownership of a share.

1872. BESANT and RICE, *Ready Money Mortiboy*, xlii. "You won't pay her any more attentions, for you shall come out of this place IN QUICK STICKS," said Mrs. Bowker.

1877. HORSLEY, *Jottings from Jail*. Now don't STICK ME UP; meet me at six to-night.

*c.*1880. C. SHEARD, *Music Hall Song*, 'I'm a Millionaire.' Though some STICK IT UP, now I'll pay money down.

1881. GRANT, *Bush Life in Queensland*. Why, they STUCK UP Wilson's Station there, and murdered the man and woman in the kitchen; they then planted inside the house, and waited until Wilson came home at night with his stockman.

1882. ANSTEY, *Vice Versa*, vii. 'Why, you are STICKING UP FOR him now!' said Tom . . . astonished at this apparent change of front.

1885. *Leisure Hour*, Mar., 192. Having attacked, or, in Australian phrase, STUCK UP the station, and made prisoners of all the inmates.

1885. *Field*, 3 Oct. Two gentlemen, fishing at Aldermaston, STUCK TO IT all day.

1886. *Graphic*, 10 Ap., 399. An actor who forgets his words is said to STICK or be corpsed.

1887. G. L. APPERSON, *All the Year Round*, 30 July, 68, 1. In times gone by, it was by no means an uncommon occurrence [in Australia] for a coach to be STUCK UP by a band of bushrangers. . . . But a coach is now seldom interfered with, and to STICK UP is applied to less daring attempts to rob.

1888. BOLDREWOOD, *Squatter's Dream*, 47. Well, then, I'll CUT MY STICK; you won't want the pair of us. *Ibid.*, 204. A note to settle our little account IN QUICK STICKS.

1890. WHITEING, *John St.*, xxvii. Her tiny chum sometimes comes home at night, CROSS AS TWO STICKS, and resists every attempt to cheer her.

1899. HYNE, *Further Adv. Captain Kettle*, vi. When it comes to STICKING UP the cable station you'll see him do the work of any ten like us.

1903. *D. Tel.*, 11 Feb., 7, 1. I said, "Are you going to STICK me UP for this money?" He gave an indefinite sort of the shoulders, and returned no answer.

STICKER, *subs.* (common).—1. A pointed question, an apt and startling comment or rejoinder, an embarrassing situation; a STUMPER (*q.v.*).

2. (anglers').—A gaff.

3. (common).—A plodder.

4. (colloquial).—A lingering guest.

1712. ARBUTHNOT, *John Bull* [ARBER, *Eng. Garner*, vi.], s.v.

STICK-IN-THE-MUD, *subs. phr.* (colloquial).—A fogey; a slowcoach.

1823. MONCRIEFF, *Tom and Jerry*, ii. 4. *Tom.* Good night, old STICK-IN-THE-MUD.

1855. HALIBURTON, *Human Nature*, 132. "Well, arter all this palaver," said old STICK-IN-THE-MUD, "what are you arter?"

1861. HUGHES, *Tom Brown at Oxford*, x. This rusty-coloured one is that respectable old STICK-IN-THE-MUD, Nicias.

1880. *Punch*, 10 Jan., 6. Shut up, old STICK IN THE MUD, and let's join the ladies.

6. (tradesmen's: Am.).—An article which won't sell; a SHOP-KEEPER (*q.v.*).

7. (American tramps').—*See* quot.

1900. FLYNT, *Tramps*, 131. This is also true of the office-beggar, or STICKER as he calls himself.

8. (common).—A knife.

1899. WHITEING, *John St.*, iv. There warn't no time to square up to 'im when I see the STICKER in his 'and.

STICK FLAMS, *subs. phr.* (Old Cant).—A pair of gloves (B. E. and GROSE).

STICKING, *subs.* (common.)—In *pl.* = Coarse, bruised, inferior meat: spec. the portions damaged by the butcher's knife. *See* CLODS and STICKINGS.

STICKING-PLACE (or **-POINT**), *subs. phr.* (old colloquial).—The point of election: usually in phrase 'to come to THE STICKING-POINT.'

1606. SHAKSPEARE, *Macbeth*, i. 7, 60. But screw your courage to THE STICKING PLACE, and we'll not fall.

1833. DISRAELI, *Alroy*, i. 2. On sight of thee would nerve me to the STICK ING POINT.

STICK-IN-THE-RIBS, *subs. phr.* (common).—Thick soup; GLUE (*q.v.*).

STICKIT-MINISTER, *subs. phr.* (Scots').—A disqualified candidate for holy orders: spec. a sucking-parson, who, breaking down at his first sermon, never attempts another.

1815. SCOTT, *Guy Mannering*, ii. But, alas . . . he became totally incapable of proceeding in his intended discourse—gasped, grinned, hideously rolled his eyes till the congregation thought them flying out of his head—shut the Bible—stumbled down the pulpit-stairs, trampling upon the old women who generally take their station there—and was ever after designated a STICKIT-MINISTER.

1893. CROCKETT, *The Stickit Minister* [Title].

STICKLER, *subs.* (old).—An obstinate or trifling contender; a zealot; a PRECISIAN (*q.v.*): also STIFFLER. [Orig. an umpire].

*d.*1575. PARKER [DAVIES], *Works*, 252. The drift was, as I judged, for Dethick to continue such STIFFLERS in the College of his pupils, to win him in time by hook or crook the master's room.

1813. AUBREY, *Lives*, 'William Aubrey.' He was one of the delegates . . . for the Tryall of Mary, Queen of Scots, and was a great STICKLER for the saving of her life.

1885. *Field*, 4 Ap. The Englishman—in his own country greatest of all STICKLERS for the correct thing in raiment.

1900. KERNAHAN, *Scoundrels and Co.*, xv. I'm a bit of a STICKLER for what's gentlemanly myself.

STICK-SLINGER, *subs. phr.* (thieves').—*See* quot.

1856. MAYHEW, *Great World of London*, 46. Those who plunder with violence; as . . . bludgers or STICK-SLINGERS, who rob in company with low women.

STICK-UP, *subs. phr.* (common).—In *pl.* = a high-standing collar; GILLS (*q.v.*).

1884. *D. Tel.*, 8 July, 5, 4. Lord Macaulay wore to the close of his life, STICK-UPS or gills.

STICKY, *subs.* (common).—Sealing-wax.

STIFF, *subs.* (Old Cant).—1. A bill of exchange; negotiable paper; THICK (*q.v.*). TO TAKE (or GIVE) THE STIFF = to receive (or pay) in paper (GROSE); TO DO A BIT OF STIFF = to accept a bill.

1828. BEE, *Living Picture of London*. [He] could not otherwise obtain his share of the plunder than by taking paper from P., *i.e.*, STIFF in the form 'I promise to pay.'

1854-5. THACKERAY, *Newcomes*, vi. I wish you'd DO ME A BIT OF STIFF, and just tell your father if I may overdraw my account, I'll vote with him.

1899. MARSH, *Crime and Criminal*, xviii. 'I must be unknown . . . or he would never lend.' 'Can't you DO anything on A BIT OF STIFF.'

2. (thieves').—Forged bank notes.

3. (old).—A corpse: also STIFF ONE (GROSE).

1871. JOHN HAY, *Myst. of Gilgal*. They piled the STIFFS outside the door—They made, I reckon, a cord or more.

4. (racing).—A horse certain not to run, nor if it run, to win: also DEAD-UN, SAFE-UN, STUMER, &c. (*q.v.*). BOOKMAKERS STIFF = a horse nobbled at the public cost in the bookmakers' interest. Also as *adj.* (Australian) = dead certain to win; *e.g.*, 'Grand Flaneur is STIFF for any race for which he may enter.'

1871. "HAWK'S-EYE," *Turf Notes*, 11. Most assuredly it is the bookmakers that profit by the safe uns, or STIFF UNS, as, in their own language, horses that have no chance of winning are called.

1897. [Advt. on front fly of *Pomes*] *The Rialto* . . . Do not invest money Until you read The Rialto. Never on STIFF 'UNS, wrong 'uns, or dead 'uns.

5. (prison).—A clandestine letter.

1900. GRIFFITHS, *Fast and Loose*, xxxiii. Will your pal trust me,' says I. 'Yes, if I send him a bit of a STIFF.'

Adj. and *adv.* (colloquial).—A general intensive: *cf.* STEEP, TALL, WIDE, &c. Thus a STIFF (= a strong or long) drink; a STIFF (= a cramped) style; a STIFF (= a formal) manner: also crusty, whence TO CUT UP

STIFF = to turn testy; a STIFF (= strong and steady) breeze; STIFF (= incredible) news; a STIFF (= difficult) examination; a STIFF (= high) price: *cf.* STEEP: also, a price (or a market) STIFFENS = goes higher: TO PAY STIFFLY = to pay expensively; a STIFF (= firm, unyielding) market; a STIFF UPPER LIP = courageous; TO CUT UP STIFF = to leave a large estate: *cf.* WARM and *supra.*

1608. SHAKSPEARE, *Ant. and Cleop.*, i. 2, 104. Labienus—this is STIFF news—hath with his Parthian force Extended Asia from Euphrates.

1620. FLETCHER, *Philaster*, iii. 1. With a STIFF gale their heads bow all one way.

1711. ADDISON, *Spectator*, 119. This kind of good manners was perhaps carried to an excess, so as to make conversation too STIFF, formal and precise.

1784. COWPER, *Tirocinium*, 671. And his address, if not quite French in ease, Not English STIFF, but frank, and form'd to please.

1855-7. THACKERAY, *Misc.*, II. 272. The old gent CUT UP uncommon STIFF.

1885. *D. News*, 28 Sep. The STIFFNESS of country rates also tends to give firmness to the attitude of staplers.

1842. TENNYSON, *Will Waterproof.* But, tho' the port surpasses praise, My nerves have dealt with STIFFER.

1887. *D. Chron.*, 21 Mar. Yarns were very STIFF.

1893. *Harper's Mag.*, lxxxvi. 447. We now left the carriages and began a STIFF climb to the top of the hill.

1899. WESTCOTT, *David Hume*, xvi. He's got a pretty STIFF UPPER LIP of his own, I reckon.

2. (venery).—(1) Wanton: *e.g.*, A STIFF QUEAN = a harlot (RAY); and (2) priapic: *see* STAND. THE STIFF DEITY (or THE STIFF AND STOUT) = the *penis* in erection.

1653. URQUHART, *Rabelais*, i. xi. And some of the women would give these names, my Roger . . . my STIFF AND STOUT. *Ibid.* (MOTTEUX), iv. v. The STIFF DEITY, Priapus . . . remained sticking in her natural Christmas box.

1720. DURFEY, *Pills, &c.*, vi. 201. And may Prince G——'s Roger grow STIFF again and stand.

STIFFLER. *See* STICKLER.

STIFF-FENCER, *subs. phr.* (streets').—A hawker of writing paper.

STIFF-RUMPED, *adj. phr.* (colloquial). — Proud; stately (B. E. and GROSE).

*d.*1704. BROWN, *Works*, iii. 196. Our STIFF-RUMPED Countesses in their silks and sattins.

STIFFY, *subs.* (American).—A well-dressed conceited boy (BARTLETT).

STIFLER, *subs.* (thieves').—1. The gallows: also STIFLES: *see* LADDER and NUBBING CHEAT. Hence TO NAB THE STIFLER = to be hanged; TO QUEER THE STIFLER = to escape the rope.

1818. SCOTT, *Midlothian*, xxiii. I think Handie Dandie and I may QUEER THE STIFLER for all that is come and gone.

2. (provincial).—A busybody (HALLIWELL).

3. (common).—A severe blow.

STIGMATIC, *subs.* (old). — 1. A branded criminal; (2) anyone deformed; and (3) a contemptible wretch.

1598. SHAKSPEARE, *2 Hen. IV.*, ii. 2, 136. But, like a foul, mis-shapen STIGMATIC.

1601. CHETTLE and MUNDAY, *Death of R. Earl of Huntingdon*, 76. That prodigious bloody STIGMATIC . . . portendeth still Some innovation, or some monstrous act.

1616. *Philomythic* [NARES]. Convaide him to a justice, where one swore He had been branded STIGMATIC before.

STILE. TO HELP A LAME DOG OVER A STILE, *verb. phr.* (common).—To give a hand; to assist in a difficulty; to bunk up. Fr. *sauver la mise à quelqu'un.*

1546. HEYWOOD, *Proverbs.* TO HELP A DOGGE OVER A STILE.

1605. MARSTON, *Insatiate Countess*, ii. 2. Here's A STILE so high as a man cannot HELP A DOG OVER IT.

1670. RAY, *Proverbs* (1893), 168. HELP THE LAME DOG OVER THE STILE.

1710. SWIFT, *Pol. Conv.*, i. Madam, I know I shall always have your good word; you love to HELP A LAME DOG OVER THE STILE.

*d.*1721. PRIOR, *Viceroy.* But for this horrid murder vile None did him prosecute. His old friend HELPED HIM O'ER THE STILE; With Satan who'd dispute?

1857. KINGSLEY, *Two Years Ago*, xxv. I can show my money, pay my way, eat my dinner, kill my trout, hunt my hounds, HELP A LAME DOG OVER A STILE (which was Mark's phrase for doing a generous thing), and thank God for all.

LET THE BEST DOG LEAP THE STILE FIRST, *phr.* (old).—'Let the best take lead' (RAY).

STILL, *subs.* (undertakers').—A still-born infant. Also (American firemen's) = a still alarm: *i.e.*, an alarm given other than by the regular signal service.

STILL-SOW, *subs. phr.* (old).—*See* quots.

1598. FLORIO, *Worlde of Wordes*, 9. A close, slie lurking knave, a STIL SOW, as we say.

1598. SHAKSPEARE, *Merry Wives*, iv. 2. STILL SWINE eat all the draff.

STILTING, *subs.* (thieves'). — *See* quot.

1884. GREENWOOD, *Little Raga-muffins.* You are a nice sort of chap to try your hand at STILTING!" (first-class pocket-picking).

STILTON (THE), *subs. phr.* (common). — The correct thing: a variant of THE CHEESE (*q.v.*).

STIMBLE, *verb.* (provincial).—To urinate; TO PISS (*q.v.*).—HALLIWELL.

STING, *verb.* (old).—To rob; to trick (GROSE and VAUX). 'That cove is fly; he has already been STUNG' = 'The man is on his guard; he has been robbed before.'

STING-BUM, *subs. phr.* (old).—A niggard (B. E. and GROSE).

STINGER, *subs.* (common).—Generic for anything exceptional: *e.g.*, a heavy blow, a sharp rebuke, a vexatious occurrence, &c., &c. Hence STINGING = keen, sharp, telling.

1613. WEBSTER, *Devil's Law Case*, iv. 2. That's a STINGER: be a good wench, be not daunted.

1657. MIDDLETON, *More Dissemblers Besides Women*, iii. 2. That malice Wears no dead flesh about it, 'tis a STINGER.

1863. READE, *Hard Cash*, xliii. Rooke . . . received a STINGER that staggered him, and nearly closed his right eye.

1873. O. W. HOLMES, *Address* on opening Fifth Av. Theatre. The STINGING lash of wit.

1888. *Sporting Life*, 21 Nov. Planted a couple of well-delivered STINGERS on Harris's nasal.

STINGO, *subs.* (old).—Strong liquor: spec. HUMMING ALE (*q.v.*).—B. E. and GROSE.

1638. RANDOLPH, *Hey for Honesty*, ii. 6. Come, let's in, and drink a cup of STINGO.

1661. *Merry Drolleries* [OLIPHANT, *New Eng.*, ii. 98. Among the substantives are . . . STINGO, brimmer, Jew's harp].

*c.*1650. BRATHWAYTE, *Barnaby's Jl.* (1723), 125. I drank STINGO With a Butcher and Domingo.

1697. *Praise of YORKSHIRE STINGO*, 29. Such STINGOE, nappy, pure ale they have found.

1774. BRIDGES, *Burlesque Homer*, 79. He best can understand their linguo And tell 'em where to find good STINGO.

1821. EGAN, *Real Life*, vii. Let us fortify . . . with a horn or two of humming STINGO.

1840. BARHAM, *Ingoldsby Leg.*, 'St. Dunstan.' Thys Franklyn, syrs, he brewed goode ayle, And he called it rare goode STYNGO.

STINGY, *adj.* (B. E.).—'Covetous, close-fisted, sneaking.'

STINK, *subs.* (old). — 1. Any disagreeable exposure: spec. (thieves') *see* quot. 1785. TO STIR UP A STINK = to expose; and as *verb.* = to have a bad reputation.

1647. FLETCHER, *Humorous Lieut.*, iii. 7. Fall Fate upon us, Our memories shall never STINK behind us.

1785. GROSE, *Vulg. Tongue*, s.v. STINK. When any robbery of moment has been committed, which causes much alarm, or of which much is said in the daily papers, the family people will say there is a great STINK about it.

1851-61. MAYHEW, *Lond. Lab.*, I. 250. The newspapers of the district . . . had raised . . . what the patterers of his class proverbially call a STINK . . . had opened the eyes of the unwary to the movements of Chelsea George.

2. (scholastic).—In *pl.* = (*a*) chemistry: hence STINK-CUPBOARD = a close chamber for evil-smelling or obnoxious chemical experiments; and (*b*) a lecturer on chemistry. TO GO OUT IN STINKS = to take a degree in natural science (Cambridge).

1903. *Pall Mall Gaz.*, 19 Feb., 7, 1. The branch of learning facetiously denominated "STINKS," at Oxford, is by now beginning to boast the sanctifying prestige of time.

TO TAKE A STINK FOR A NOSEGAY, *verb. phr.* (old).—To be extremely gullible; to mistake egregiously.

1809. MALKIN, *Gil Blas* [ROUTLEDGE], 173. We had our hands to play against a novice at the game. Simple and cullible, so far from smelling out the rat, HE TOOK HIS STINK FOR A NOSEGAY.

STINK-A-PUSS, *subs. phr.* (provincial). — A term of contempt (HALLIWELL).

STINKARD, *subs.* (old).—A mean wretch: also STINKER: a general term of contempt. Hence STINKARDLY = mean.

1598. DEKKER, *Works* (GROSART), i. 77. And no more learning than the most errand STINKARD, that (except his owne name) could never find anything in the Horne-book.

1601. JONSON, *Poetaster*, iii. 1. You have Fortune and the good year on your side, you STINKARD. *Ibid.* (1609), *Epicœne*, iv. 1. You notoriously STINKARDLY bearward.

1612. CHAPMAN, *Widow's Tears*, i. 4. Only your block-headly tradesman . . . your unapprehending STINKARD is blessed with the sole perogative of his wife's chamber.

1630. TAYLOR, *Works*, ii. 145. For now the STINKARDS in their irefull wraths, Repelted me with lome, with stones, and laths.

1633. MARMYON, *Fine Companion.* How slave, and STINKARD, since you are so stout, I will see your commission ere I part.

1677. COLES, *Eng.-Lat. Dict.*, s.v. A STINKARD, homo fœtidus.

1700. CONGREVE, *Way of the World*, iv. 11. Your Mussulman is a dry STINKARD. No offence, aunt.

1732. MORGAN, *Phœnix Brit.*, 28. No more learning than the most errand STINKARD.

1748. SMOLLETT, *Rod. Random*, xxxiv. He asked with great emotion if I thought him a monster and a STINKARD.

STINKER, *subs.* (Old Cant).—1. A black eye (GROSE).

2. (various).—Anything offensive: *e.g.*, a stinkpot, a filthy person, in *pl.*, bad coal; spec. (modern) = a motor car: also STINK-CAR. *See* STINKARD.

1901. *Sporting Times*, 27 Ap., 2, 1. The advent of the STINK-CAR was almost as mournful a feature in the proceedings as was the mob of habitual bookmakers "resting" by the bars.

STINKFINGER. TO PLAY AT STINKFINGER, *verb. phr.* (venery).—To grope a woman; 'to go BIRDS-NESTING' (*q.v.*).

STINKIBUS, *subs.* (old).—Bad LAP (*q.v.*); ROT-GUT (*q.v.*).

1706. WARD, *Wooden World*, 70. He shall gulph thee down the rankest STINKIBUS with as good a Gusto as a Teague does Usquebaugh, and not be a Doit the worse for it.

STINKING FISH. TO CRY STINKING FISH, *verb. phr.* (common).—To run down one's own affairs; 'to foul one's own nest' (RAY).

STINKIOUS, *subs.* (old).—Gin: 18th century.

STINKOMALEE, *subs.* (obsolete).—*See* quot.

1864. HOTTEN, *Slang Dict.*, s.v. STINKOMALEE, a name given to the then New London University by Theodore Hook. Probably because some cow-houses and dunghills stood on the original site. Some question about Trincomalee was agitated at the same time. It is still applied by the students of the old Universities, who regard it with disfavour from its admitting all denominations.

STINKY, *subs.* (military).—A farrier.

STIPE, *subs.* (common).—A stipendiary magistrate.

STIR, *subs.* (thieves').—A prison: also STIRABEN (gypsy).

1851-61. MAYHEW, *Lond. Lab.*, I. 469. I was in Brummagen, and was seven days in the new STIR.

1897. MARSHALL, *Pomes*, 123. I didn't hear the reason why the lad was booked for STIR.

1901. *Referee*, 28 Ap., 9, 3. Mr. Patrick M'Hugh, M.P. for North Leitrim, has gone to STIR for six months for a seditious libel.

2. (common).—A crowd; a PUSH (*q.v.*).

TO HAVE PLENTY TO STIR ON, *verb. phr.* (colloquial).—To be wealthy.

See STUMPS.

STIRRUP-OIL, *subs. phr.* (old).—A sound beating; a drubbing.

1677. COLES, *Eng.-Lat. Dict.* To give one some STIRRUP-OYL. *Aliquem fustigare.*

STIR-UP-SUNDAY, *subs. phr.* (clerical).—The Sunday before Advent. [The collect for the day commences: 'Stir up, we beseech Thee, O Lord.']

STITCH, *subs.* (old).—1. A tailor: *see* TRADES (B. E. and GROSE).

2. (common).—Clothing: *e.g.*, 'not a dry STITCH about her.'

1888. *Field*, 4 Ap. With every STITCH of clothing wet, and no facilities for drying them.

PHRASES.—TO GO THROUGH STITCH = to accomplish, to bring to a finish; TO GO A GOOD STITCH = to go a good way; STOP STITCH WHILE I PUT A NEEDLE IN = a proverbial phrase applied to any one when one wishes him to do anything more slowly (HALLIWELL).

1611. COTGRAVE, *Dict.*, s.v. *Passe-partout*, a resolute fellow, one that GOES THROUGH-STITCH with every thing hee undertakes, one whose courses no danger can stop, no difficultie stay.

1631. CHETTLE, *Hoffman*, f. iii. Now wee are in, wee must GOE THROUGH STITCH.

1653. URQUHART, *Rabelais*, I. xlvii. And in regard of the main point that they should never be able to GO THROUGH STITCH with that war.

1677. COLES, *Dict.* TO GO THOROW-STITCH with the work, *opus peragere.*

1678. COTTON, *Virgil Travestie* (1770), 91. Who means to conquer Italy, Must with his Work GO THOROUGH STITCHES And not be running after Bitches.

1684. BUNYAN, *Pilgrim's Prog.*, ii. 148. I promise you, said he, you have GONE A GOOD STITCH: you may well be aweary; sit down.

Verb. (venery).—To copulate (DORSET): *cf.* SEW UP = to get with child, NEEDLE = *penis*, and NEEDLE-CASE = female *pudendum*: *see* GREENS, PRICK, MONOSYLLABLE, and RIDE.

STITCH-BACK, *subs. phr.* (B. E.).—Very strong ale; STINGO (*q.v.*).

STITCH-LOUSE, *subs. phr.* (common).—A tailor: also PRICK-LOUSE. *See* TRADES.

1838. BECKETT, *Paradise Lost*, 59. Why can't we with fig-leaves make breeches? . . . Who's the best STITCH-LOUSE.

STIVE, *verb.* (old).—To crowd, to make hot in a sultry atmosphere. STIVED UP = stifled.

1865. DOWNING, *Mayday in New York*. "Oh, marcy on us," said a fat lady, who was looking for a house, "this 'll never do for my family at all. There's no convenience about it, only one little STIVED-UP closet. . . . And the bed-rooms, —she would as soon sleep in a pig-pen, and done with it, as to get into such little, mean, STIVED-UP places as them."

1870. JUDD, *Margaret*, ii. 8. 'Things are a good deal STIVED UP,' answered the Deacon.

1876. ELIOT, *Daniel Deronda*, liv. I shall go out in a boat . . . instead of STIVING in a damnable hotel.

Verb. (American).—To run; to move off [BARTLETT: 'a low word used in the Northern States'].

See STEW.

STIVER (STEEVER, STINNER, &c.), *subs.* (old).—1. A Dutch coin value 1d.; hence (2) a small standard of value, a STRAW, a FIG (*q.v.*); and (3) generic for money. Hence STIVER-CRAMPED = needy (GROSE).

1535. JOY, *Apology to Tyndale*, 22 [OLIPHANT, *New Eng.*, i. 472. The Dutch coin STEEVER appears].

1630. TAYLOR, *Works*, ii. 3. Through thy protection they are monstrous thrivers, Not like the Dutchmen in base doyts and STIVERS.

*c.*1630. *Broadside Ballad* [*Bagford* (Brit. Mus.), i. 88]. He . . . paid . . . the shot Without ever a STIVER of money.

1693. DAMPIER, *Voyages*. They will not budge under a STIVER.

1700. FARQUHAR, *Constant Couple*, i. 1. I there had a Dutch whore for five STIVERS.

1853. LYTTON, *My Novel*, ix. 3. Entre nous, mon cher, I care not a STIVER for popularity.

*d.*1891. LOWELL, *Fitz Adam's Story*. 'There's fourteen foot and over,' says the driver. 'Worth twenty dollars ef it's worth a STIVER.'

1892. ZANGWILL, *Children of the Ghetto*. A SHTIBBUR for a blind man.

1902. LAWSON, *Children of the Bush*, 94. I ain't got a lonely STEEVER on me.

STIZZLE, *verb.* (Tonbridge School).—To hurt.

STOCK, *subs.* (old).—1. Cheek; impudence; BRASS (*q.v.*).

2. (old). — Anything inert: hence = (1) a fool, a BLOCKHEAD (*q.v.*), and (2) in contempt: spec. in compounds (mostly recognised) such as laughing-STOCK, jesting-STOCK, courting-STOCK, &c. Whence STOCKISH = silly, lumpish; STOCKISHNESS = stupidity.

1593. SHAKSPEARE, *Taming of Shrew*, i. 1, 31. Let's be no stoics nor no STOCKS. *Ibid.* (1598), *Merchant of Venice*, v. 1, 81. Nought so STOCKISH, hard, and full of rage.

1607. BEAUMONT and FLETCHER, *Woman Hater*, iii. 3. All accounted dull, and common JESTING-STOCKS for your gallants.

1624. FLETCHER, *Rule a Wife*, iii. 5. Thou art the STOCK of men, and I admire thee.

1630. JONSON, *New Inn*, i. 1. And therefore might indifferently be made the COURTING-STOCK for all to practise on.

1766. BROOKE, *Fool of Quality*, iii. Such a STOCK of a child, such a statue! Why he has no kind of feeling either of body or mind.

1778. SHERIDAN, *Rivals*, iii. 1. What a phlegmatic sot it is! Why, sirrah, you'r an anchorite!—a vile insensible STOCK.

1837. BROWNING, *Strafford*, iii. 3. Friend, I've seen you with St. John—O STOCKISHNESS! Wear such a ruff, and never call to mind St. John's head in a charger.

STOCK AND BLOCK, *subs.* and *adv. phr.* (colloquial). — The whole; completely (GROSE). Also LOCK-STOCK-AND-BARREL, and (American) STOCK-AND-FLUTE: *cf.* STICK-AND-STONE, ROOT-AND-BRANCH, &c.

1725. BAILEY, *Erasmus*, 181. Before I came home I lost all, STOCK AND BLOCK [orig. *sors et usura* = capital and interest].

1861. *New York Tribune*, Oct. In other words, Tammany Hall is sold out STOCK AND FLUKE to Fernando Wood.

PHRASES.—TO TAKE STOCK IN = to have faith in; TO TAKE STOCK OF = to scrutinize, TO SIZE UP (*q.v.*); ON THE STOCKS = in hand, in preparation.

*d.*1704. BROWN, *Works*, iv. 42. I am told Mr. Dryden has something of this nature new UPON THE STOCKS.

1865. DICKENS, *Mutual Friend*, ii. In TAKING STOCK of his familiarity, worn . . . clothes, piece by piece, she TOOK STOCK of a formidable knife in a sheath at his waist.

1889. *Harper's Mag.*, Oct., 'Lit. Notices.' Captain Polly gives the right hand of fellowship to two boys, IN whom nobody else is willing TO TAKE STOCK, and her faith in them saves them.

See BROAD; WATER.

STOCK-BLIND, *adj.* (colloquial).—Quite blind; blind as a stock or block: *cf.* STONE-BLIND.

1675. WYCHERLEY, *Country Wife*, ii. 1. True lovers are blind, STOCK-BLIND.

STOCKDOLLAGER. *See* SOCKDOLAGER.

STOCK DRAWERS, *subs. phr.* (old). —Stockings (B. E. and GROSE).

STOCK EXCHANGE TERMS. [The following list is imperfect, but it contains the better known and older colloquialisms. The Stock Exchange, admittedly a 'close' corporation, is, in fact, so close that not only was direct official information refused, but also an appeal to be put into communication with some member interested in Stock Exchange colloquialisms was declined. Perhaps, however, subscribers will be good enough to help to a supplementary list as an Appendix.]—ALES = Messrs. S. Allsopp and Sons shares; APES = The Atlantic and North Eastern Railway first mortgage bonds; AYRSHIRES = Glasgow and South-Western Railway stock; BABY WEE-WEES = Buenos Ayres Water Works shares; BAYS = Hudson Bay Company shares; BERTHAS = London Brighton and South Coast Railway stock; BERWICKS = North Eastern Railway Ordinary stock; BONES = (1) North British 4 per cent. 1st Preference shares: *see* BONETTAS, and (2) Wickens, Pease and Company shares; BONETTAS = North British 4 per cent. 2nd Preference shares; BOTTLES = Barrett's Brewery and Bottling Company shares; BRUMS = London and North Western Railway stock (formerly London and Birmingham Railway); BULGARIAN ATROCITIES = Varna and Rutschuk Railway 3 per cent. Obligations; CALEYS = Caledonian Railway Ordinary stock; CASHELS = Great Southern and Western of Ireland Railway stock; CATS = Atlantic Cable 2nd Preference stock; CHATS = London Chatham and Dover Railway stock; CHINAS = Eastern Extension Australian and China Telegraph shares; CLARAS = Caledonian Railway Deferred and Ordinary stock; COFFINS = The Funeral Furnishing Company shares; COTTONS = Confederate Bonds; CREAMJUGS = Charkoff-Kremenlsching Railway bonds; DINAHS = Edinburgh and Glasgow Railway Ordinary stock; DOGS = Newfoundland Land Company shares; DORAS = South Eastern Railway Ordinary "A" stock; DOVERS = South Eastern Railway Ordinary stock; DUCKS = Aylesbury Dairy Company shares; FLOATERS = Exchequer bills; GORGONZOLA HALL = The HOUSE (*q.v.*); GOSCHENS = The $2\frac{3}{4}$ per cent. Government Stock; GUINNESS'S = Guinness and Company shares; HADDOCKS = North of Scotland Railway Ordinary stock; KAFFIRS = generic for South African Mining shares: whence KAFFIR CIRCUS = the South African Market in a state of excitement; KISSES = Hotchkiss Ordinance Company shares; KNACKERS = Harrison, Barber, and Company shares; LEEDS = Lancashire and Yorkshire Railway Ordinary stock; MAILS = Mexican Railway shares: *see* MEGS; MATCHES = Bryant and May's shares; MEGS = Mexican Railway 1st Preference shares: *see* MAILS; METS = Metropolitan Railway Co. shares; MIDDIES = Midland Railway Ordinary stock; MONAS = The Isle of Man Railway shares; MUTTONS = Turkish Loans of 1865 and 1873; NEW BILLINGSGATE = The HOUSE (*q.v.*); NEW PLATES = English Bank of the River Plate shares: *see* OLD PLATES; NORAS = Great Northern Railway Deferred Ordinary stock; NUTS = Barcelona Tramway shares; OLD PLATES = London and River Plate Bank shares; PIGTAILS = Chartered Bank of India, Australia, and China shares; POTS = Staffordshire Railway stock; SARAHS = Staffordshire and Lincoln Railway Deferred stock; SARAH'S BOOTS = Sierra Buttes Gold Mining Company shares; SARDINES = Royal Sardinian Railway shares; SEWERS = East London Railway shares; SILVERS = India Rubber, Gutta Percha, and Telegraph Company shares; SUNSHADES = The Sunhales Extension Buenos Ayres and Resario Railway Company shares; TERRORS = Northern Territories Co. shares; VESTAS = Railway Investment Company Deferred stock; VIRGINS = Virginia New Funded Bonds; WHIPSTICKS = Dunaberg and Witepsk Railway shares; WESTRALIANS = generic for Western Australian Mining shares. Also *see* BEAR; BUCKET-SHOP; BULL; COCKY; FIDDLE; FOURTEEN-HUNDRED; FUTURES; GUTTERSNIPE; HAMMER; HOUSE; JAM-TART; KERBSTONE-BROKER; KIDNEY; LAME-DUCK; LET-UP; LOAD; LONG; OMNIUM; ORCHID; PEG; PICKER-UP; PUT; RAID; RUSH; SCALP; SCOOP; SET-UP; SHOOT; SHORT; SHUNTER; STAG; STATE; SWEATER; SWIMMING; TAPES; TAPEWORM; TEN-UP; TIGHT; TWIST; UNLOAD; WADDLE; WATER; WASH-SALE; WIREWORM.

STOCKING. IN ONE'S STOCKINGS (or STOCKING-FEET), *adv. phr.* (colloquial).—Without shoes.

1809. IRVING, *Knickerbocker*, 168. The mistress and chambermaid visited the house once a week . . . leaving their shoes at the door, and entering devotedly in their STOCKING-FEET.

1854-5. THACKERAY, *Newcomes*, viii. Binnie found the Colonel in his sitting-room, arrayed in what are called in Scotland his STOCKING-FEET.

LONG-STOCKING, *subs. phr.* (common). — Means in plenty; resources.

STOCK-IN-TRADE, *subs. phr.* (colloquial).—The privities, male and female.

STOCK-JOBBER (STOCK-JOBBING, &c.), *subs. phr.* (old: now recognised).—*See* quots.

*c.*1696. B. E., *Dict. Cant. Crew*, s.v. STOCK-JOBBING, a sharp, cunning-cheating Trade of Buying and Selling Shares of Stock in East India, Guinea and other Companies; also in the Bank, Exchequer, &c.

1703. STEELE, *Tender Husband*, ii. 1. Public Knaves and STOCK-JOBBERS pass for Wits at her end of the Town, as common Cheats and Gamesters do at yours.

1785. GROSE, *Vulg. Tongue*, s.v. STOCK JOBBERS. Persons who gamble on the Stock Exchange pretending to buy and sell public funds, but only betting that they will be at a certain price at a particular time; possessing neither stock to be sold, nor money to make good the payments, known [as] bulls, bears and lame ducks.—[*Abridged.*]

STOCKPORT-COACH, *subs. phr.* (old).—A horse with two women riding sidewise.

Adj. (colloquial).—Very; completely: usually in combination: thus STOCK-STILL = entirely at rest; STOCK-BLIND = absolutely sightless, &c. · *cf.* STONE.

1675. WYCHERLEY, *Country Wife*, ii. 1. True lovers are blind, STOCK-BLIND.

1759. STERNE, *Tristram Shandy*, i. 22. If he begins a digression from that moment, I observe, his whole work stands STOCK-STILL.

1809. MALKIN, *Gil Blas* [ROUTLEDGE], 91. I stood STOCK-STILL in the street, not a little stiffened at this vision.

STOCKY, *adj.* (colloquial). — 1. Short and stout; lumpy; STUMPY (*q.v.*).

1712. ADDISON, *Spectator*, 433. They had no titles of honour among them but such as denoted some bodily strength or perfection; as, such a one 'the tall,' such a one 'the STOCKY,' such a one 'the gruff.'

1856. EMERSON, *Eng. Traits*, iv. It is the fault of their forms that they grow STOCKY, and the women have that disadvantage—few tall slender figures of flowing shape, but stunted and thick-set persons.

2. (provincial). — 'Irritable, headstrong and contrary, combined' (HALLIWELL). Also (3) impudent, BRASSY (*q.v.*).

1856. ELIOT, *Amos Barton*, v. He was a boy whom Mrs. Hackit in a severe mood had pronounced STOCKY.

STODGE, *subs.* (common).—1. Food; (2) a heavy meal; and (3) the crumb of new bread (Charterhouse). As *verb.* = to gorge; TO STUFF (*q.v.*). Hence STODGY (or STODGE-FULL) = distended, lumpy, crammed; STODGER = (1) a gormandiser; and (2) a penny bun.

1860. ELIOT, *Mill on the Floss*, i. 5. 'You don't know what I've got in my pockets' . . . 'No,' said Maggie. 'How STODGY they look, Tom.'

Verb. (Tonbridge School).—To hurt.

STOGY, *adj.* (colloquial).—Generic for coarseness: thus STOGY-SHOES (or STOGIES) = heavy shoes; STOGY-CIGAR = a rough coarse cigar.

STOKE, *verb.* (common).—To eat: spec. (1) to eat without appetite; and (2) TO WOLF (*q.v.*).

1901. *Troddles*, 47. To my mind, Troddles STOKED-UP on bread-and-butter pudding to such an extent that I wondered how on earth he could . . . expect to . . . drag himself about . . . after it.

STOLL, *verb.* (North Country Cant). —1. To understand (HOTTEN).

2. (common).—To tipple; TO BOOZE (*q.v.*). STOLLED=drunk: *see* SCREWED.

STOMACH, *subs.* (old colloquial).—Generic for disposition: *e.g.*, (*a*) spirit, compassion; (*b*) courage, temper; and (*c*) pride. Hence A PROUD STOMACH = a haughty disposition; STOMACH-GRIEF = anger. As *verb.* = (1) to endure, to encourage, (2) to resent, to disgust; TO STICK IN THE STOMACH = to remember with anger or disgust; STOMACHFUL=(1) stubborn, and (2) angry; STOMACHY = proud, irritable.

1383. CHAUCER, *Cant. Tales*, 'Friars Tale,' 143. STOMAK ne conscience ne know I noon.

1553. SIR T. WILSON, *Art of Rhetoric.* STOMACKE GRIEF is when we wil take the matter as hot as a toste.

*d.*1556. UDAL [ELLIS, *Lit. Letters*, 4]. Your excellente herte and noble STOMAKE.

*d.*1563. BALE, *Select Works*, 313 When he had STOMACHED them by the Holy Ghost . . . He went forward with them . . . conquering in them the prince of this world.

1570. ASCHAM, *Scholemaster*, 123. Many learned men have written . . . with great contrarietie and some STOMACKE amongest them selues.

1582. HAKLUYT, *Voyages*, ii. 23. King Richard, mooued in STOMACKE against King Philip, neuer shewed any gentle countenance of peace & amitie.

*c.*1589. GREENE, *Alphonsus*, iii. If that any STOMACH this my deed, Alphonsus can revenge my wrong with speed.

1596. JONSON, *Every Man in Humour*, iii. 2. O plague on them all for me! . . . O, I do STOMACH them hugely.

1601. SHAKSPEARE, *Hen. VIII.*, iv. 2, 34. He was a man of an unbounded STOMACH.

1608. CAPT. JOHN SMITH, *True Travels*, I. 39. Swift, STOMACKFULL . . . horse.

1641. BAKER, *Chronicles*, 50. He was able to pull down the high STOMACHS of the Prelates.

1677. WYCHERLEY, *Plain Dealer*, iii. 1. If I had but any body to stand by me, I am as STOMACHFULL as another.

*d.*1704. BROWNE, *Works*, ii. 70. I have not had an opportunity till now, of telling you what STICKS IN MY STOMACH.

1821. SCOTT, *Pirate*, xviii. Truths which are as unwelcome to a PROUD STOMACH as wet clover to a cow's.

1856. MOTLEY, *Dutch Repub.*, I. 76. The priests talk . . . of absolution in such terms that laymen can not STOMACH it.

1857. DICKENS, *Little Dorrit.* He has a proud STOMACH, this chap.

1866. HOWELLS, *Venetian Life*, vi. If you wipe your plate and glass carefully before using them, they need not STOMACH you.

STOMACH-TIMBER, *subs. phr.* (old). —Food: *cf.* BELLY-TIMBER.

1820. COOMBE, *Syntax*, II. vii. As Prior tells, a clever poet . . . The main strength of every member Depends upon the STOMACH TIMBER.

STOMACH-WORM, *subs. phr.* (old). —Hunger: 'the STOMACH-WORM gnaws' = I am hungry (GROSE)

STONE, *subs.* (vulgar).—In *pl.* = the testes. Hence STONE-HORSE = a STALLION (*q.v.*); STONE-PRIEST = a lascivious cleric; STONE FRUIT = children. TO TAKE A STONE UP IN THE EAR (venery) = to play the whore; TWO STONE UNDER WEIGHT (or WANTING) = castrated.

1598. FLORIO, *Worlde of Wordes*, s.v. *Coglioni*, the STONES or testicles of a man.

*c.*1600. HAUGHTON, *Grim the Collier*, v. But ne'er hereafter let me take you With wanton love-tricks, lest I make you Example to all STONE-PRIESTS ever, To deal with other men's loves never.

*c.*1600. *Merry Devil of Edmonton*, iv. 1. The STONE PRIEST steals more venison than half the country. *Ibid.*, iv. 2. I would to God my mill were an eunuch, And wanted her STONES, so I were hence.

1602. MARSTON, *Ant. and Mellida*, ii. 1, 3. My grandfathers great STONE-HORS, flinging up his head, and jerking out his left leg.

1605. CHAPMAN, *Eastward Ho*, iv. 1. Farewell, thou horn of destiny, th' ensign of the married man! Farewell, thou horn tree, that bearest nothing but STONE-FRUIT.

1608. *Merry Devil of Edmonton* [DODSLEY, *Old Plays*, xi. 155]. The villainous vicar is abroad in the chase this dark night: the STONE-PRIEST steals more venison than half the county.

1609. JONSON, *Silent Woman*, v. 1. *Damp.* Your ladyship sets too high a price on my weakness. *Han.* Sir, I can distinguish gems from pebbles ——. *Damp.* Are you so skilful in STONES? [*Aside.*]

1611. COTGRAVE, *Dict.*, s.v. *Entier . . . cheval entier*, a STONE-HORSE. *Ibid.*, s.v. *Couillon*, STONED; or that wants not his STONES. *Ibid.*, s.v. *Couillon*, a cod, STONE, testicle, cullion.

1622. MARMION, *Holland's Leaguer*, v. 4. When her husband has followed Strange women, she has turned him into a bezar [goat], And made him bite out his own STONES.

1678. COTTON, *Virgil Travestie* (1770), 68. I hate a base cowardly drone, Worse than a Rigil with one STONE.

1704. BROWN, *Works*, i. 60. My spouse, alas! must flaunt in silks no more, Pray heav'n for sustenance she turn not whore; And daughter Betty too, in time, I fear, Will learn to TAKE A STONE UP IN HER EAR.

Adj. (old).—In combination = quite; wholly: *e.g.*, STONE-blind, STONE-cold, STONE-dead, STONE-still, &c.: *cf.* STOCK (B. E. and GROSE).

*c.*1330. *Romance of Seven Sages* [WEBER, *Metrical Romances*, iii.]. [OLIPHANT, *New Eng.*, i. 16. Among the adjectives we find BLIND SO STON. *Ibid.* The substantive qualifies the adjective as STANE STILL (p. 141).]

[?]. *Perceval*, 841. Ever satt Percyvelle STONE-STILLE, And spakke nothynge.

[?]. *Rom. of Partenay* [E.E.T.S], 3121. The Geant was by Gaffray don bore, So discomfite, STANDEDE, and all cold.

1597. SHAKSPEARE, *Richard III.*, iv. 4, 227. The murderous knife was dull and blunt Till it was whetted on thy STONE-HARD heart.

1605. JONSON, *Volpone*, i. 1. He cannot be so stupid, or STONE-DEAD.

1609. DAVIES, *Humour's Heauen on Earth*, 47. For the contagion was so violent (The wil of Heau'n ordaining so the same) As often strook STONE-DED incontinent.

*d.*1618. SYLVESTER, *Du Bartas*, v. i. 434. The Remora fixing her feeble horn Into the tempest-beating vessel's stern, Stayes her STONE-STILL.

1647-8. HERRICK, *Appendix*, 451. Loue will part of the way be mett, or sitt STONE-STILL.

1856. ELIOT, *Mr. Gilfil*, xviii. I thought I saw everything, and was STONE-BLIND all the while.

COLLOQUIALISMS.—TO KILL TWO BIRDS WITH ONE STONE = to do (or achieve) a double purpose: *cf.* (FOXE) 'to stop two gaps with one bush'; TO LEAVE NO STONE UNTURNED = to spare no endeavour; TO MARK WITH A WHITE STONE = to single out as lucky or esteemed; TO LIVE IN A GLASS HOUSE AND YET THROW STONES = to lay oneself open to blame or attack.

1623. MABBE, *Spanish Rogue* (1660). He THREW STONES on my housetop, but when he found his own [tiles] to be of glass, he left his flinging.

1650-5. HOWELL, *Letters*, 91. He who hath glasse windows of his own, should take heed how he THROWES STONES at those of his neighbours.

1656. HOBBES, *Liberty* (1841), 117. T. H. thinks to KILL TWO BIRDS WITH ONE STONE, and satisfy two arguments with one answer.

1697. DRYDEN, *Æneid*, ii. 133. New crimes invented, LEFT UNTURN'D NO STONE To make my guilt appear, and hide his own.

1709 [?]. WARD, *Terræfilius*, iii. 22. Her most Topping School is among the Meeting-House Allies in Moorfields . . . that the Saints may KILL TWO BIRDS WITH ONE STONE, and tumble out of the School of Piety into that of Debauchery.

1774. BRIDGES, *Burlesque Homer*, 180. Thus swimmingly the knave went on, And KILLED TWO BIRDS WITH EVERY STONE.

STONE-BEE. *See* BEE.

STONE-BROKE (STONEY or STONY-BROKE), *adj. phr.* (common).—Penniless; HARD-UP (*q.v.*); PEBBLE-BEACHED (*q.v.*).

1891. *Harry Fludyer*, 122. Pat said he was STONEY OR BROKE or something but he gave me a sov., which was ripping of him.

1897. MARSHALL, *Pomes*, 106. Full of fixes, assets 'nixes,' STONEY-BROKE, and hence these tears. *Ibid.*, 120. On his right a STONEY-BROKE-ER In bad financial health.

1899. WHITEING, *John St.*, xxviii. You're a toff, STONE-BROKE—that's what you are.

1901. WALKER, *In the Blood*, 159. 'Twon't be a bad lay fer us when we're STONEY BROKE down 'ere.

STONE-DOUBLET (-JUG, -PITCHER, or -TAVERN), *subs. phr.* (old).—A prison: spec. Newgate (B. E., GROSE, and VAUX). Also JUG (*q.v.*).

1653. URQUHART, *Rabelais*, IV. xii. In danger of miserably rotting within a STONE DOUBLET, as if he had struck the King.

*d.*1704. BROWN, *Works*, ii. 300. Once more . . . observe . . . for I am not at leisure to trifle any longer with you: otherwise a STONE DOUBLET is the word.

1834. AINSWORTH, *Rookwood*, 'Jerry Juniper's Chant.' In a box of the STONE-JUG I was born.

1836. DICKENS, *Sketches by Boz*, 'Prisoner's Van.' Six weeks and labour . . . and that's better than the STONE JUG anyhow. *Ibid.* (1838), *Oliver Twist*, viii. "Was you never on the mill?" "What mill?" enquired Oliver. "What mill! why the mill—the mill as takes up so little room that it 'll work inside a STONE-JUG."

1856. READE, *Never too Late to Mend.* I will sell the bed from under your wife's back, and send you to the STONE-JUG.

STONE-FENCE, *subs. phr.* (common).—Brandy and ale; BREAKY-LEG (*q.v.*).

1862. E. MACDERMOTT, *Pop. Guide to Int. Exhib.*, 1862, 185. An American bar where visitors may indulge in . . . eye-openers, STONE FENCES, and a variety of similar beverages.

STONE-WALL, *subs.* (Australian).—1. Parliamentary obstruction: also as *verb.* Hence (2) *verb.* = to obstruct business at any meeting, chiefly by long-winded speeches; and (3) to play a slow game at cricket, blocking balls rather than making runs.

1876. *Victorian Hansard*, Jan., xxii. 1387. Mr. G. Paton Smith wished to ask the honourable member for Geelong West whether the six members sitting beside him (Mr. Berry) constituted the 'STONE WALL' that had been spoken of? Did they constitute the STONE WALL which was to oppose all progress.

1884. G. W. RUSDEN, *History of Australia*, iii. 405. Abusing the heroic words of STONEWALL Jackson, the Opposition applied to themselves the epithet made famous by the gallant Confederate General.

1885. CAMPBELL PRAED, *Head Station*, 35. He is great at STONE-WALLING tactics, and can talk against time by the hour.

1894. *Argus*, 26 Jan., 3, 5. The Tasmanians [sc. cricketers] do not as a rule STONEWALL.

AS ABLE TO SEE AS FAR THROUGH A STONE WALL AS ANYONE, *phr.* (common).—As capable of understanding—a retort on depreciation or doubt of one's abilities.

1900. KENNARD, *Right Sort*, xxii. I lay claim to no such exalted pretensions . . . although I flatter myself I can SEE THROUGH A STONE WALL AS CLEARLY AS MOST PEOPLE. Still that's not saying much.

STOOBS, *subs.* (back slang).—Boots.

STOOK, *subs.* (thieves').—A pocket-handkerchief: STOOK-HAULER = a handkerchief thief.

1893. EMERSON, *Signor Lippo*, xiv. All I get is my kip and a clean mill tog, a pair of pollies and a STOOCK, and what few meddays I can make out of the lodgers and nudies, and what I earn for keeping the grubs—a soldi from each as I told you.

STOOL, *subs.* (American).—A decoy: *see* STALE and STALL. Also (common) STOOL-PIGEON = a cardsharper's accomplice: *cf.* PIGEON and ROOK.

TO FALL BETWEEN TWO STOOLS, *verb. phr.* (old).—To hesitate between alternatives and lose (or be disappointed in) both.

1546. HEYWOOD, *Proverbs.* BETWENE TWO STOOLS MY TAILE GOES TO THE GROUND.

1696. MOTTEUX, *Rabelais*, v. xliv. She ordered him to sit down, BETWEEN TWO STOOLS . . . his arse on the ground.

1748. SMOLLETT, *Rod. Random*, xxxiii. Between the pride of one and the insolence of another the enterprise miscarried, according to the proverb, 'BETWEEN TWO STOOLS THE BACKSIDE FALLS TO THE GROUND.'

1867. TROLLOPE, *Last Chronicle of Barset*, xxxv. Lily was aware . . . that she was like to FALL TO THE GROUND BETWEEN TWO STOOLS—having two lovers, neither of whom could serve her turn.

TO LAY THE STOOL'S FOOT IN WATER, *verb. phr.* (old).—To make much preparation to receive a guest.

STOOP, *subs.* (old).—The pillory. 'The cull was served for macing and napped the STOOP (or was set on the STOOP)' = 'The swindler was convicted and pilloried.' STOOPING-MATCH = a pillory exhibition; STOOP-NAPPER = one under punishment (GROSE and PARKER).

TO GIVE THE STOOP, *verb. phr.* (old).—To yield; to KNOCK UNDER (*q.v.*).

1692. HACKET, *Williams*, ii. 186. O that a king should GIVE THE STOOP to such as these.

STOOP-GALLANT, *subs. phr.* (old). —*See* quot.

1611. COTGRAVE, *Dict.*, s.v. *Trousse-galant.*

STOP, *verb.* (pugilists').—To ward off; to parry.

1860. *Chambers' Jo.*, xiii. 347. He is initiated into all the mysteries of hitting and counter-hitting, STOPPING and infighting.

*d.*1870. A. L. GORDON, *In Utrumque Paratus.* Don't STOP with your head too frequently.

COLLOQUIALISMS.—TO STOP ONE'S MOUTH = to silence: spec. with a sop or bribe; TO STOP OUT (theatrical) = to cover teeth with black wax to make them invisible; TO STOP OFF (or OVER) = to make a break in a journey: also as *subs.*, *e.g.*, a STOP OFF in Philadelphia (American); STOP MY VITALS = 'A silly Curse in use among the Beaux' (B. E.); STOP THIEF (rhyming) = beef: *see* BEEF IT.

1628. FORD, *Lover's Melancholy*, iv. 1. Let repentance STOP YOUR MOUTH; Learn to redeem your fault.

1673. WYCHERLEY, *Gentleman Dancing Master*, v. 1. If you would have her silent STOP HER MOUTH with that ring.

STOP-DICE, *subs. pl.* (old).—A kind of false dice (PALSGRAVE, 1540).

STOP-HOLE ABBEY, *subs. phr.* (Old Cant).—*See* quot.

*c.*1696. B. E., *Dict. Cant. Crew*, s.v. STOP-HOLE ABBEY, the Nick-name of the chief Rendezvouz of the Canting Crew of Gypsies, Beggers, Cheats, Thieves, &c.

STOPPER, *subs.* (common). — A FINISHER (*q.v.*) ; a SETTLER (*q.v.*) : *see* WHOPPER.

1836. DANA, *Before the Mast*, 304. The last resort, that of speculating upon the future, seemed now to fail us, for our discouraging situation, and the danger we were really in (as we expected every day to find ourselves drifted back among the ice) "clapped a STOPPER" upon all that.

1887. *Field*, 19 Feb. Here we come immediately upon a STOPPER, unless it can be happily shunted.

STOPPING OYSTER. *See* OYSTER.

STORRAC, *subs. pl.* (rhyming). — Carrots.

STOREKEEPER, *subs.* (American). — An unsaleable article : a SHOP-KEEPER (English), which *see*.

STORY, *subs.* (colloquial). — 1. A falsehood : euphemistic. Whence STORY-TELLER = a liar.

1840. BARHAM, *Ingolds. Leg.* I wrote the lines . . . owned them ; he told STORIES.

1848. THACKERAY, *Vanity Fair*, xliv. Becky gave her brother-in-law a bottle of white wine, some that Rawdon had brought with him from France . . . the little STORY-TELLER said.

1887. *Referee*, 17 April. As they can't all be true some of them must be STORIES.

BLIND STORY, *subs. phr.* (old). — A pointless narrative.

1699. BENTLEY, *Phal.*, Pref., 64. He insinuates a BLIND STORY about some-body and something.

1762-71. WALPOLE, *Vertue's Anec. Paint.* (1786), II. 75. This STORY which in truth is but a BLIND one.

See UPPER STORY.

STOTER (or **STOTOR**), *subs.* (Old Cant). — A violent blow : *e.g.*, 'Tip him a STOTER in the halter-ing place' = 'Give it him under the left ear' (B. E. and GROSE). Hence a SETTLER (*q.v.*).

STOUPE, *verb.* (old).—To give up [HALLIWELL : 'A cant term'].

STOUT, *subs.* (B. E.).—1. 'Very strong Malt-drink' [LATHAM : Note to quot. 1720 in SWIFT, *Works* (1744) : 'a cant word for strong beer'].

2. (Stock Exchange).—In *pl.* = Guinness's shares.

STOUT ACROSS THE NARROW, *phr.* (common).—Full bellied ; corpulent.

1901. *Troddles*, xix. Troddles really is RATHER STOUT ACROSS THE NARROW, you know.

STOVE-PIPE (or **STOVE-PIPE-HAT**), *subs. phr.* (common).—A tall hat ; a CHIMNEY-POT (*q.v.*). Fr. *tuyan de poële.*

1867. *Galaxy*, 632. Pickpockets re-joice in neatly fitting suits, spotless linen, sparkling pins and ornaments, and STOVE-PIPE HATS, tall and glossy . . . worn jauntily on one side.

STOW, *verb.* (Old Cant).—1. To hold one's tongue ; to keep quiet ; to leave off : *e.g.*, 'STOW IT !' = 'Be quiet' ; 'STOW YOUR WHIDDS AND PLANT 'EM ; FOR THE COVE OF THE KEN CAN CANT 'EM' = 'Take care what you say, for the Master of the House understands you' (HAR-MAN, B. E., GROSE, and VAUX). Also Stowmarket (BEE).

1838. DICKENS, *Oliver Twist.* 'STOW that gammon,' interposed the robber.

1887. GILBERT, *Ruddigore.* But 'tain't for a British seaman to brag, so I'll just STOW my jawin' tackle, and belay.

STOZZLE, *verb.* (American).—To drink. Hence STOZZLED = drunk ; *see* SCREWED.

END OF VOL. VI.

A Dictionary of Slang and its Analogues.

TRADA REALE HIGHLANDERS, *subs. phr.* (military). — The 1st Batt. Gordon Highlanders, late The 75th Foot (KING). [In 1812 the regiment was detailed for Mediterranean service, and for some time formed the Main Guard of the Governor's residence in the Strada Reale, Valetta.]

STRADDLE, *subs.* (Stock Exchange). —A contract in which the holder can call for (or the signatory can deliver) stock at a fixed price : a speculation covering both a PUT and a CALL (*q.v.*) : *cf.* SPREAD-EAGLE. Also as *verb.*

Verb. (American political). — To adopt a non-committal atti-tude ; to favour both sides ; 'to sit on the FENCE' (*q.v.*) : also as *subs.*

1884. *Nation*, 3 July, 4. The plat-form contains the well-known plank STRADDLING the tariff question.

STRAIGHTS (THE), *subs.* (old London). — *See* quot. 1816.

[NARES : 'formerly frequented by profligates ; a Cant name.] *See* BERMUDAS.

1614. JONSON, *Bartholomew Faire*, ii. 6. Look into my angle o' the towne (the STREIGHTS, or the Bermudas) where the quarrelling lesson is read. *Ibid.* Turn pirates here at land, Ha' their Bermudas, and their STRAIGHTS i' th' Strand.

1816. GIFFORD, *Jonson.* Note to above. Cant names then given to the places frequented by bullies, knights of the post, and fencing masters. . . . These STREIGHTS consisted of a nest of obscure courts, alleys, and avenues, running be-tween the bottom of St Martin's Lane, Half Moon, and Chandos Street.

Adj. (colloquial).—STRAIGHT, generic for honesty, has, like ROUND (*q.v.*), and SQUARE (*q.v.*), a large colloquial vogue. Thus a STRAIGHT (= an exact) thinker ; a STRAIGHT (= a chaste) PIECE (*q.v.*) ; a STRAIGHT (= an out - and - out) TORY : hence STRAIGHT-OUT = thorough-going ; STRAIGHT (= NEAT : also duty-paid) WHISKEY ; STRAIGHT (= candid) SPEECH ; STRAIGHT (= honest) PEOPLE, LIVING, etc. ; STRAIGHT (= honestly acquired) GOODS : also of persons = SQUARE (*q.v.*) ; a STRAIGHT (= a trust-worthy) TIP, GRIFFIN, etc. (*q.v.*) ;

a STRAIGHT (= an unsmiling) FACE ; STRAIGHT (or STRAIGHT-OUT = outright, thorough ; STRAIGHT UP AND DOWN (IN THE STRAIGHT, or ON THE STRAIGHT) = plain, honest, free from crooked-ness of all kinds ; OUT OF THE STRAIGHT = dishonest, crooked.

1848. LOWELL, *Biglow Papers*, 88. I'm a STRAIGHT-spoken kind o' creetur, That blurts right out what's in his head.

1856. *New York Courier*, Sept. In the Presidential contest of 1844, no man was more fierce in his hostility to Henry Clay than the present candidate of the STRAIGHT Whigs for the Vice-Presidency.

1872. *New York Tribune*, 7 Mar. When . . . Blair . . . declared, in a speech from the steps of the Manhattan Club, that the main plank in the Demo-cratic platform was whiskey STRAIGHT, he probably shocked a few of his more orthodox and respectable hearers.

1886. *Fort. Rev.*, N.S., xxxix. 76. Dissipating their rare and precious cash on whiskey STRAIGHT in the ever-recurring bar-rooms.

1886. *St James's Gaz.*, 11 Nov. 'The husband of Lady Usk, a virtuous lady, who, as we are frequently told, is perfectly STRAIGHT and all that sort of thing.'

1887. *Referee*, 17 Ap. 'But going to first principles, nothing can be STRAIGHT-ER or more likely to work to an employer's interest than for his jockey to back his own mount.'

1872. *Nation*, 22 Aug., 113. Other STRAIGHT-OUTS, as they call themselves . . . cannot take Grant and the Re-publicans. *Ibid.* (1888), 6 Dec., 459. He shows himself to be a man of wide reading, a pretty STRAIGHT thinker, and a lively and independent critic.

1891. GOULD, *Double Event*, 22. He's got the STRAIGHT griff for something.

1897. MARSHALL, *Pomes*, 9. 'If that isn't a good 'un,' the bookie cried, 'I'll forfeit a fiver, STRAIGHT.'

1901. *Free Lance*, 30 Nov., 217. 1. Uncommonly sharp sons, who, if they live, and run STRAIGHT, may get into the Cabinet or do anything else.

1902. LYNCH, *High Stakes*, xxix. When he had me locked in with him he gave me the STRAIGHT tip.

1903. KENNEDY, *Sailor Tramp*, xix. What do I know about him ? Why that he's all right. That he's STRAIGHT GOODS.

IN THE STRAIGHT, *adv. phr.* (common).—Nearing the end ; within sight of a finish ; orig. a racing term.

1903. *T. P.'s Weekly*, 2 Jan., 248. 1. Good, I'm IN THE STRAIGHT now . . . Thank Heaven that's done.

STRAIGHT AS A POUND OF CANDLES (or AS A LOON'S LEG), *adv. phr.* (common).—As honest as may be. Also 'as STRAIGHT as the backbone of a herring (RAY), as a die, arrow,' etc.

1748. SMOLLETT, *Rod. Random*, xiii. My hair . . . hung down upon my shoulders, as lank and STRAIGHT AS A POUND OF CANDLES.

1865. DOWNING, *Letters*, 42. They were puzzled with the accounts ; but I saw through it in a minit, and made it all as STRAIGHT AS A LOON'S LEG.

STRAIGHT ! *intj.* (common).— Fact ! Honest Injun !

1890. CHEVALIER, *Coster's Court-ship.* STRAIGHT ! ses I, I'm on the job for better or for wuss.

STRAIGHT-LACED, *adj. phr.* (B. E. and GROSE).—'Precise, squeem-ish, puritanical, nice.'

STRAIN, *verb.* (venery).—To copulate : *see* RIDE.

1383. CHAUCER, *Cant. Tales*, (TYRWHITT), 9627. 'Merchant's Tale.' He that night in armes wold hire STREINE.

1601. SHAKSPEARE, *Hen. VIII.*, iv. 1. Our King has all the Indies in his arms, And more and richer when he STRAINS that lady.

TO STRAIN HARD, *verb. phr.* (B. E.)—'To ly heavily.'

SLANG AND ITS

ANALOGUES

PAST AND PRESENT

A DICTIONARY HISTORICAL AND COMPARATIVE OF THE HETERODOX SPEECH OF ALL CLASSES OF SOCIETY FOR MORE THAN THREE HUNDRED YEARS

WITH SYNONYMS IN ENGLISH, FRENCH, GERMAN, ITALIAN, ETC.

COMPILED AND EDITED BY

JOHN S. FARMER & W. E. HENLEY

VOL. VII.—STRA–Z

PRINTED FOR SUBSCRIBERS ONLY

MCMIV.

TO STRAIN ONE'S TATERS, *verb. phr.* (common).—To urinate: *see* PISS.

STRAM, *subs.* (colloquial). — 1. A walk; spec. a society parade. As *verb*=to walk stiffly: also (provincial: HALLIWELL)=to dash down violently, to beat.

1869. STOWE, *Oldtown*, 508. I hed sech a STRAM this mornin'.

2. (venery).—*See* STRUMPET.

STRAMASH, *subs.* (colloquial).—A disturbance; a ROUGH AND TUMBLE (*q.v.*). As *verb*=to beat, bang, destroy.

1837. BARHAM, *Ingolds. Leg.* 'House Warming.' More calling and bawling, and squalling and falling, Oh, what a fearful STRAMASH they're all in.

1855. KINGSLEY, *Ravenshoe*, xxxvi. I and three other University men . . . had a noble STRAMASH on Folly Bridge. That is the last fighting I have seen.

STRAMMEL. *See* STRUMMEL.

STRAMMER, *subs.* (colloquial).—Anything exceptional: *see* WHOPPER. STRAMMING=huge, great.

STRANDED, *adj.* (colloquial).—Penniless; friendless.

1897. MARSHALL, *Pomes*, 26. Now, the bank was a trifle dyspeptic—a quid was its longest reach—And Yiffler could see himself STRANDED, for he sighted a pebbly beach.

STRANGER, *subs.* (common).—1. A sovereign: formerly a guinea (GROSE): *see* RHINO.

2. (common.)—A visitor: *cf.* the folk-saying of a badly burning candle, or a stalk in tea: 'A stranger's coming.'

STRANGLE-GOOSE, *subs. phr.* (old). —A poulterer (GROSE).

STRAP, *subs.* (old).—1. A barber. [Poetry, Strap, a barber in SMOLLETT'S *Roderick Random*, 1748.]

2. (common).—Credit: orig. credit for drink. ON STRAP= 'on TICK' (*q.v.*); STRAPPED= penniless, bankrupt. *See* HARD-UP.

1857. *Nat. Intelligencer*, Oct. Lowndes is STRAPPED; had to pay his wife's cousin's last quarter's rent, which consumed what he had reserved for current expenses.

1903. KENNEDY, *Sailor Tramp*, I. ix. 'Say, . . . are you STRAPPED?' 'Oh . . . I'm not hard up. I'm all right.' *Ibid.*, II. i. Why didn't you come to me when you were STRAPPED?

Verb. (venery).—1. 'To lie with a woman': see GREENS and RIDE (B.E. and GROSE).

2. (common).—To flog; to beat. Hence STRAPPING (or A DOSE OF STRAP-OIL or OIL OF STRAP'EM) = a thrashing; an April fool joke is to send a lad for 'a penn'orth of STRAP OIL': *cf.* STIRRUP-OIL.

3. (Scots).—To hang.

1825. SCOTT, *St Ronan's Well*, xiv. It's a crime baith by the law of God and man, and mony a pretty man has been STRAPPED for it.

4. (old).—To work (GROSE).

See BLACKSTRAP.

STRAPPADO, *subs.* (old).—A form of torture: the culprit, his legs tied, was hoisted by a rope fastened to his arms behind his back, and was given a rapid descent stopped so suddenly that the jerk often dislocated the joints of arms and shoulders. This was repeated once or twice. *Cf.* SCAVENGER'S DAUGHTER.

1587. HAKLUYT; *Voyages*, II. 253. It was told vs we should have ye STRAPPADO.

1598. SHAKSPEARE, *Hen. IV.*, ii. 4. An I were at the STRAPPADO, or all the racks in the world, I would not tell you on compulsion.

c. 1603. HEYWOOD, *Woman Killed*, etc. [PEARSON, *Works* (1874), II. 141]. I would . . . Be rack'd, STRAPPADO'D, put to any torment.

1613. PURCHAS, *Pilgrimage*, 341. They vse also the STRAPPADO, hoising them vp and downe by the armes with a corde.

1622. MARKHAM, *Epist. of Warre.* STRAPPADO [enumerated with] gallow, gibbets, and scaffolds [which the Provost Marshall was bound to provide on occasion.]

1633. CALLOT, *Misères.* [In this work there is a sketch of a culprit suspended from a high beam, the executioner holding with both hands the end of one of four spokes which act like a wheel and lever for hoisting or lowering the culprit, the executioner's right foot pressing against a lower spoke, his left foot on the ground.]

1688. R. HOLME, *Acad. Armory*, III. vii. 310. [Holme writes as though the STRAPPADO were still in use in the army] the jerk not only breaketh his arms to pieces, but also shaketh all his joynts out of joint; which punishment is better to be hanged, than for a man to undergo.

STRAPPER, *subs.* (old).—'A swingeing two-handed woman' (B. E. and GROSE); anything big or bulky: *cf.* WHOPPER. STRAPPING=tall, robust, well-made.

1678. COTTON, *Virgil Travestie* [*Works* (1725), iv. 105]. At last a crew of STRAPPING jades, That were, or should have been her maids.

1681. RADCLIFFE, *Ovid Travestie*, 3. Has he not got a Lady that's a STRAPPER? *Ibid.*, 26. A STRAPPING LASS, She must be marry'd, or she'll grow too busy.

1694. CONGREVE, *Double Dealer*, iii. 10. Then that other great STRAPPING Lady.

1700. FARQUHAR, *Constant Couple*, i. 1. There are five-and-thirty STRAPPING officers gone this morning.

1751. SMOLLETT, *Pereg. Pickle*, lxxxvii. Ah, you STRAPPER, what a jolly bitch you are.

1778. DARBLAY, *Diary* (1893), i. 88. 'You who are light and little can soon recover, but I who am a gross man might suffer severely.' . . . Poor Lady Sadd, who is quite a STRAPPER, made no answer.

1847. BRONTË, *Jane Eyre*, xx. 'She's a rare one, is she not, Jane?' 'Yes, sir.' 'A STRAPPER, a real STRAPPER, big, brown and buxom.'

1885. *D. Tel.*, 25 Aug. 'The police, fine STRAPPING fellows, usually Irish, wear white ducks in fine weather.'

STRAVAG (or **STRAVAIG**), *verb.* (Scots and Irish).—To tramp; to loaf; to abscond. Hence STRAVAIGER=a vagabond.

1887. HENLEY, *Villon's Straight Tip.* Your merry goblins soon STRAVAG.

1888. BLACK, *Far Lochaber*, vii. Prancing down to the shore and back from the shore—and STRAVAYGING about the place.

STRAW, *subs.* (old).—1. Generic for worthlessness. Thus, NOT WORTH A STRAW=of no appreciable value; TO CARE NOT A STRAW=to care not at all; A MAN (or FACE) OF STRAW=a man of no standing or substance, a sham: in quot. 1700=a fumbler; STRAW-BAIL = professional security; STRAW-SHOES (MAN or WITNESS) =a perjured witness; STRAW-BID=a fictitious offer; STRAW-BIDDER=a buyer who cannot fulfil his contract; STRAW-VOTE =a snatch vote; STRAWYARDER (nautical)=a land-lubber playing the sailor; spec. a blackleg doing shipboard duty during a strike.

d. 1400. CHAUCER, *Tale of Melibeus.* And whan that they ben accompliced, yet ben they NOT WORTH A STRE.

. . . *Nugæ Poeticæ*, 48. Whatesoevery he be, and yf that he Whante money to plede the lawe, Do whate he cane in ys mater than Shale NOT prove WORTHE A STRAWE.

c. 1500. *Roberte the Deuyll* [HAZLITT, *Early Pop. Poetry*, i. 229, 261]. The Duke . . . asked Robert, iff he woulde lyue vnder awe Of God, and the order of knight-hode beare, He aunswered: I sett NOT thereby A STRAWE.

1534. UDAL, *Ralph Roister Doister* [DODSLEY, *Old Plays* (1874), iii. 128]. Then A STRAW for her. . . . She shall not be my wife were she never so fair.

c. 1540. *Doctour Doubble-Ale*, 10. Popish lawes; That are NOT WORTH TWO STRAWES, Except it be with dawes.

1604. SHAKSPEARE, *Winter's Tale*, iii. 2. Mistake me not; no life, I prize it NOT A STRAW, but for mine honour.

1675. WYCHERLEY, *Country Wife*, iv. 3. I will not be your drudge by day, to squire your wife about, and be your MAN OF STRAW or scarecrow only to pies and jays that would be nibbling at your forbidden fruit.

1700. DRYDEN, *Wife of Bath's Tale.* When you my ravish'd predecessor saw You were not then become this MAN OF STRAW.

1705. WARD, *Hud. Rediv.*, I. i. 9. No Zealot valu'd if A STRAW. But mounted . . . like Hunter's o'er a five-barr'd Gate.

1740. NORTH, *Examen*, 508. Off drops the vizor, and a FACE OF STRAW appears.

1753. RICHARDSON, *Grandison*, vi. 387. All those, however, were MEN OF STRAW with me.

1754. FIELDING, *Jon. Wild*, I. ii. . . . He had likewise the remarkable honour of walking in Westminster Hall with a STRAW in his shoe.

1772. BRIDGES, *Burlesque Homer*, 198. To me how all your matters go, Don't signify a single STRAW.

1809. MALKIN, *Gil Blas* [ROUTLEDGE], 104. The players are not MEN OF STRAW as I foolishly believed.

1827. LYTTON, *Pelham*, iii. He CARED NOT A STRAW that he was a man of fortune, of family, of consequence; he must be a man of *ton*, or he was . . . no man.

1848. THACKERAY, *Snobs*, xviii. Why the deuce should Mrs Botibol blow me a kiss? . . . I don't CARE A STRAW for Mrs Botibol.

1876. *Telegram* from Washington, 13 Mar. [BARTLETT]. The House post-office committee has agreed to report Luttrell's bill to prevent STRAW-BIDDING for mail contracts, and to punish STRAW-BIDDERS when caught.

1892. SYDNEY, *England and English*, ii. 275. Perjury at this time [*c.* 1750] was a regular trade. . . . The lawyer who required convenient witnesses . . . going into Westminster Hall . . . would address a STRAW-MAN with a 'Don't you remember?' (at the same time holding out a fee).

1902. *Sp. Times*, 1 Feb., 2 i. I DO NOT CARE TWO STRAWS what alleged people write about myself.

2. (common).—A long clay pipe; a churchwarden.

3. (common).—A straw hat. Also STRAWYARD, and (schools) STRAWER.

PHRASES. IN THE STRAW= in childbed (GROSE); TO BREAK A STRAW=to quarrel; TO LAY A STRAW=to pause; TO DRAW (or PICK) STRAWS=to show signs of sleep; A PAD IN THE STRAW= anything amiss; TO THROW STRAWS AGAINST THE WIND (COLES) = to essay the impossible. Also (proverbial) 'A STRAW shows which way the wind blows'; 'He gives STRAW to his dog, and bones to his ass' (of one given to absurdities); 'To make a block of a STRAW'; 'To stumble at a STRAW and leap over a block,' etc., etc.

1526. *Pilgr. Perf.* [W. de W., 1531], 93. Lest of a STRAWE we make a block.

1551. STILL, *Gammer Gurton's Needle*, v. 2. Ye perceive by this lingring there is a PAD IN THE STRAW.

15 [?] COLLIER, *Old Ballads* [HALLIWELL]. Here lyes in dede the PADDE WITHIN THE STRAWE.

1562. J. HEYWOOD. *Prov. and Epig.* (1867), 76. s.v. Ye stumbled at a STRAWE, and lept ouer a blocke.

1564. UDAL, *Erasmus's Apoph.*, 68. I prophecie (quoth he) that Plato and Dionysius wil erre many daies to an ende BREAKE A STRAWE betwene them.

1637. HOLLAND, *Camden*, 141. But LAY A STRAW here, for in a trifling matter others as well as myselfe may thinke these notes sufficient, if not superfluous.

1662. FULLER, *Worthies*, 'Lincoln.' Our English plain Proverb *de Puerperis*, 'they are IN THE STRAW,' shows Feather-Beds to be of no ancient use among the common sort of our nation.

1705. WARD, *Hud. Rediv.*, I. iv. 18. We sipp'd our Fuddle As Women IN THE STRAW do Caudle.

1710. SWIFT, *Pol. Conv.*, iii. *Lady Ans.* I'm sure 'tis time for all honest folks to go to bed. *Miss.* Indeed my eyes DRAW STRAWS. (She's almost asleep.)

1785. GROSE, *Vulg. Tongue*, s.v. STRAW. One eye DRAWS STRAW, and t'other serves the thatcher.

1786. BURGOYNE, *Heiress*, i. 1. *Mrs Blandish.* You take care to send to all the lying-in ladies? *Prompt.* At their doors, madam, before the first load of *straw*. (Reading his memorandum, as he goes out.) Ladies IN THE STRAW, ministers, etc.

1796. WOLCOT, *Peter Pindar*, 213. Their eyelids did not once PICK STRAWS, And wink and sink away; No, no, they were as brisk as bees.

1839. HOOD, *Miss Kilmansegg.* Although, by the vulgar popular saw, All mothers are said to be IN THE STRAW, Some children are born in clover.

STRAWBERRY, *subs.* (common).—A nevus; a birthmark.

c. 1866. BURNAND and SULLIVAN, *Box and Cox.* Have you a STRAWBERRY MARK on your left arm? No! Then you are my long lost brother.

TO CUT DOWN AN OAK, AND SET UP A STRAWBERRY, *verb. phr.* (old).—To waste; *cf.* Ital. *Cavar un chiodo e piantar una cavicchia* (=To dig up a nail and plant a pin).

STRAWBERRY-LEAVES, *subs. phr.* (common).—A dukedom: a ducal coronet is ornamented with eight strawberry-leaves.

STRAWBERRY - PREACHER, *subs. phr.* (old).—A non-resident; one who visited his cure only once a year.

STRAWBOOTS, *subs.* (military).—1. The 7th Dragoon Guards; also Old Strawboots, and The Straws. Also (2) the 7th Hussars. [Tradition says from these regiments having been employed in quelling agricultural riots.]

STRAW-CHIPPER, *subs. phr.* (old). —A barber; *cf.* STRUMMEL-FAKER and NOB-THATCHER.

1823. MONCRIEFF, *Tom and Jerry*, i. 5. Our dashing STRAW-CHIPPERS . . . in Burlington Arcade.

STRAWING, *subs.* (streets').—See quot.

1851-61. MAYHEW, *Lond. Lab.*, I. 229. STRAWING, or selling straws in the street, and giving away with them something that is really or fictionally forbidden to be sold, as indecent papers, political songs, and the like.

STRAW-RIDE, *subs. phr.* (American).—A driving excursion in a STRAWED-down van or sleigh.

STRAWYARD, *subs.* (tramps'). — *See* quot.

1851-61. MAYHEW, *Lond. Lab.*, II. 138. They come back to London to avail themselves of the shelter of the night asylums or refuges for the destitute (usually called STRAW-YARDS by the poor).

Hence, LIKE A STRAWYARD BULL, *phr.* (common).—A jocose retort to the question, 'How are you?' 'Like a STRAWYARD BULL, full of fuck and half-starved.'

See STRAW, *subs.* 3.

STREAK, *subs.* (American).—1. A mental peculiarity: *cf.* TWIST, KINK, etc. Also a fit of temper: whence STREAKY, *adj.* = (1)

irritable; short-tempered; (2) mean; (3) FLABBERGASTED (*q.v.*); and (4) variable. Also STREAKED.

1647. COWLEY, *The Mistress*, 'Wisdom.' Some STREAKS, too, of Divinity ran, Partly of Monk, and partly Puritan.

1848. LOWELL, *Biglow Papers.* I S. ii. But wen it comes to bein' killed, I tell ye I felt STREAKED, The fust time 'tever I found out wy baggonets wuz peaked.

1855. HALIBURTON, *Human Nature*, I S. Daniel Webster was a great man, I tell you; he'd talk King William out of sight in half an hour. If he was in your house of Commons, he'd make some of your great folks look pretty STREAKED.

18[?]. *Widow Bedott Papers*, 121. You know almost everybody has their queer STREAKS.

1856. STOWE, *Dred*, I. 120. Just act, now, as if you had got a STREAK of something in you, such as a man ought for to have who is married to one of the very first families in old Virginia.

1888. EGGLESTON, *The Graysons*, xviii. Mrs Button had been churning, and the butter 'took a contrary STREAK,' as she expressed it, and refused to come.

2. (common). — A run; a sequence of prosperities or adversities.

Verb. (common).—To decamp swiftly; to go with a rush: also TO MAKE STREAKS, TO STREAK OFF LIKE GREASED LIGHTNING, or TO GO LIKE A STREAK.

1604. HEYWOOD, *If You Know Not Me* [PEARSON, *Works* (1874) I. 292]. Have you beheld the like [a blazing star]? Look how it STREAKS.

1768. ROSS, *Helenore.* O'er hill and dale with fury she did dreel, A' roads to her were good and bad alike; Nane o't she wyl'd, but forward on did STREAK.

1843. CARLTON, *New Purchase*, I. 78. I was certain it wasn't no fox or wolf, but a dog; and if I didn't STREAK OFF like greased lightnin'.

1845. SIMMS, *Wigwam and Cabin*, 85. 'Twas a satisfaction to have such a horse, and 'twas a pleasure to crop him, and STREAK IT away, at a brushing canter, for a good five miles at a stretch.

1847. RUXTON, *Far West*, 79. What brings a duck a STREAKING IT down stream, if humans ain't behind her? and who's in these diggins but Indians?

1850. PORTER, *Tales of South-west*, 165. When I did get near, he'd stop and look, cock his ears, and give a snuff, as if he'd never seen a man afore, and then STREAK IT off as if I had been an Indian.

1855. HALIBURTON, *Human Nature*, 59. As soon as I touched land, I STREAKED IT for home, as hard as I could lay legs to the ground.

1856. DOW, *Sermons*, III. 108. The way they are STREAKING IT down the dark road to ruin is sorrowful to steam locomotives.

1865. DOWNING, *Letters*, 91. I STREAKED IT for Washington, and it was well-nigh upon midnight when I reached the White House.

1869. STOWE, *Oldtown*, 172. They jest STREAKED IT out through the buttery-door.

1886. *Field*, 25 Sep. Mayflower, first to take the breeze, went STREAKING away from Galatea.

STREAMERS, *subs. pl.* (common).—The Aurora Borealis; Northern Lights.

1805. SCOTT, *Lay of Last Minstrel*, ii. 8. He knew, by the STREAMERS that shot so bright, That spirits were riding the northern light.

STREAM'S-TOWN, *subs. phr.* (venery). — The female *pudendum*: *cf.* MONOSYLLABLE (GROSE). *See* TIPPERARY FORTUNE.

STREET, *subs.* (old colloquial).—1. The people living in a street.

1594. SHAKSPEARE, *Love's Lab. Lost*, iv. 3, 281. The STREET should see as she walk'd overhead.

1620. MIDDLETON, *Chaste Maid*, v. 2. All the whole STREET will hate us, And the world point me out cruel.

2. (colloquial). — A capacity, a method; a LINE (*q.v.*): *e.g.* 'That's not in my STREET' = 'I am not concerned' or 'That's not my way of doing,' etc.; IN THE SAME STREET = (1) on (or under) the same conditions; and (2) equal with.

1362. CHAUCER, *A.B.C.*, 70. Than makest thou his pees with his sovereign, And bringest him out of the croked STREETE.

1900. KENNARD, *Right Sort*, xx. Though not IN THE SAME STREET with King Olaf, it won't do to estimate Singing Bird's chance too lightly.

THE STREET, *subs. phr.* (old). —A centre of trade or exchange; spec. (American) Wall Street; *cf.* HOUSE, LANE, etc.

1612. PETER MARTYR [tr. EDEN, *First Books on America* [ARBER], 186]. Common places whyther marchauntes resort as to the burse or STREATE.

See GRUB STREET; KEY; QUEER STREET; SPIN.

STREET-GANGER, *subs. phr.* (thieves').—A beggar.

STREET-HOUND, *subs. phr.* (American).—A rough, bully, or loafer.

1872. *Sacremento Weekly Union*, 24 Feb., 2. Pettifoggers, polite loafers, STREET-HOUNDS, hoodlums, and bummers.

STREET-PITCHER, *subs. phr.* (common).—Anyone who stands, or takes a PITCH (*q.v.*), in the streets—vendor, mendicant, etc.

STREET-WALKER, *subs. phr.* (common).—1. A harlot working on the pavement; *see* TART. Hence STREET-WALKING = questing for men.

2. (old).—*See* quot.

1618. MYNSHUL, *Essays on a Prison* (1821), 59. [OLIPHANT, *New Eng.*, ii. 64. He has the new substantives key-turner (turnkey) and STREET-WALKER; these are both used of jailers.]

STRENGTH. ON THE STRENGTH, *phr.* (colloquial: military).—On the muster roll.

1889. FORBES [*Eng. Illus. Mag.*, vi. 525]. The colonel had put the widow woman ON THE STRENGTH; she was no longer an unrecognised waif, but had her regimental position.

STREPEROUS. *See* OBSTREPEROUS.

STRETCH, *subs.* (Old Cant).—1. A yard.

1785. GROSE, *Vulg. Tongue*, s.v. STRETCH . . . The cove was lagged for prigging a peter with several STRETCH of dobbin from a drag.

2. (thieves').—A year; THREE STRETCH = three years' imprisonment.

1877. HORSLEY, *Jottings from Jail.* I did not fall again for a STRETCH. This time I got two moon for assaulting the reelers when canon.

1888. GREENWOOD, *Undercurrents of Lond. Life.* 'All right, Sam.' 'How much, Toby?' 'Three STRETCH,' by which the sympathetic Sam knows his friend means 'three years.'

1893. EMERSON, *Signor Lippo*, xiv. Before you can open a paddin-ken, you must get a licence from the charpering carsey which lasts for a STRETCH.

1897. MARSHALL, *Pomes*, 116. I wished I'd been doing a STRETCH, sir, the year that we nobbled the crack.

1900. GRIFFITHS, *Fast and Loose*, xix. You know me; if you don't you ought, for I got you that last STRETCH in Tothill Fields.

3. (orig. University: now general).—A walk. TO STRETCH A LEG (or ONE'S LEGS) = to walk.

1653. WALTON, *Complete Angler*, 43. I have STRETCHED MY LEGS up Tottenham Hill to overtake you.

Verb. (old).—1. To hang; to SWING (*q.v.*): *see* LADDER. STRETCHING (STRETCHING-MATCH, or STRETCHING-BEE) = a hanging (B. E. and GROSE).

1623. MABBE, *Spanish Rogue* (1630), 7. He should STRETCH for it.

c. 1816.] MAYER, *Song*, 'The Night Before Larry was STRETCHED.' The rumbler jugg'd off from his feet, And he died with his face to the city.

2. (old).—To exaggerate; to lie: 'He STRETCHED hard' = 'He told a whistling lie' (B. E. and GROSE). Hence STRETCHER = an exaggeration, a falsehood.

d. 1844. FIELD, *Drama at Pokerville.* Whenever Mrs Oscar Dust told a STRETCHER, old Waters was expected to swear to it.

d. 1879. CLIFFORD, *Lectures*, I. 229. It is only by a STRETCH of language that we can be said to desire that which is inconceivable.

ON (or AT) A STRETCH, *adv. phr.* (colloquial).—Continuously; at one and the same time.

c. 1832. HALIBURTON, *Traits of American Humour.* Chunky used to whistle three days and nights ON A STRETCH.

1841. BULWER, *Night and Morning*, ii. 8. She could not entertain the child long ON A STRETCH.

1885. *St James's Gaz.*, 23 Sep. Drivers and others frequently make twenty-four hours AT A STRETCH.

TO STRETCH LEATHER, *verb. phr.* (venery). — To possess a woman: *see* RIDE. LEATHER = MUTTON (*q.v.*); LEATHER-STRETCHER = the *penis*: *see* PRICK and *cf.* KID-STRETCHER.

1653. URQUHART, *Rabelais*, I. vi. note. The vigour and STRETCHING-LEATHERNESS of the suffering part; for we see but very few women, however weakly they be, but what happily get over the condition you are in.

1678. COTTON, *Virgil Travestie* (1725), iv. 74. If they once do come together, He'll find that Dido's REACEING LEATHER.

TO STRETCH ONE'S LEGS ACCORDING TO THE COVERLET, *verb. phr.* (old).—To adapt oneself to circumstances; 'to cut one's coat according to the cloth' (RAY).

TO STRETCH (or STRAIN) A POINT, *verb. phr.* (colloquial).—To exceed a limit: *see* POINT.

STRETCHER, *subs.* (common).—1. In *pl.* = braces. Hence STRETCHER-FENCER = a vendor of braces.

2. (University).—A University Extension student.

3. *See* STRETCH.

4. (B. E.).—'The piece of Wood that lies cross the Boat where on the Water-man rests his Feet.'

STRETCH-HALTER (or **HEMP**), *subs. phr.* (old).—A scoundrel; one who badly needs a hanging: *cf.* CRACK-ROPE, WAG-HALTER; SCAPE-GALLOWS, etc.

1604. HEYWOOD, *If You Know Not Me* [PEARSON, *Works* (1874), I. 283]. Look here, I know this is the shop, by that same STRETCH-HALTER.

1629. *School of Good Manners* [quoted by NARES]. To mocke anybody by blabboring out the tongue is the part of STRETCH-HALTERS and lewd boyes, not of well mannered children.

STRETCHY, *adj.* (colloquial).—Sleepy; languid; inclined to stretch and yawn.

1872. CLEMENS, *Roughing It*, xxvii. In the night the pup would get STRETCHY and brace its feet against the old man's back.

'STREWTH, *intg.* (common).—'God's truth!'

1892. KIPLING, *Barrack Room Ballads*, 'C. B.' Drunk and resistin' the guard! 'STREWTH! but I socked at 'em 'ard.

1897. MARSHALL, *Pomes*, 7. 'Strewth! I'll have a drink, And wish all pals a prosperous New Year.

STRIDE, *subs.* (theatrical).—In *pl.* = trousers: *see* KICKS.

TO STRIDE A POT, *verb. phr.* (common).—To piss (of women): hence AS GOOD AS EVER STRODE A POT = as good as ever PISSED (*q.v.*).

TO TAKE IN ONE'S STRIDE, *verb. phr.* (common). — To do easily, and without an effort, as a hunter or a steeple-fencer takes a fence.

STRIDE-WIDE, *subs. phr.* (Old Cant). — Ale. [HALLIWELL: 'mentioned in HARRISON'S *England*, 202'.]

STRIKE, *subs.* (common).—A sovereign; 20*s.* (GROSE).

2. (American political).—*See* quot 1890. Whence STRIKER = a blackmailer.

1883. *Nation*, 6 Sep., 200. If he can elect such a ticket even in Virginia alone he will take the field after election as a STRIKER, and will offer his electoral votes to whichever candidate will give the highest terms.

1890. *Century Dict.*, s.v. Strike, *n.* 13. Any unscrupulous attempt to extort money or to obtain other personal advantage by initiating an attack with the intention of being bought off, as by introducing a bill into a legislature hostile 'to some moneyed interest, with the hope of being paid to let the matter drop.'

Verb. (old).—Generic for getting money: to steal (HARMAN, B.E.); to beg, to borrow (*e.g.* 'to STRIKE (or SPRING, *q.v.*) a man for a quid'); to get into debt (*cf.* TO STRIKE A LIGHT = to run up an alehouse score): *see* quot. *c.* 1696. Hence STRIKING = a robbery, swindle, or imposition; and STRIKER = a robber with violence.

1591. GREENE, *Art of Cony Catching* [NARES]. The cutting a pocket, or picking a purse, is called STRIKING.

1598. SHAKSPEARE, I *Hen. IV.*, ii. I. 82. I am joined with no foot-land rakers, no long-staff sixpenny STRIKERS.

1628. EARLE, *Microcos*, Appen. 254. 'Now we have well bousd, let us STRIKE some chete.'

1655. SHIRLEY, *Gent. of Venice* [NARES]. I must borrow money, And that some call a STRIKING.

c. 1696. B. E., *Dict. Cant. Crew*, s.v. STRIKE . . . STRIKE all the Cheats, c. Rob all you meet. STRIKE the Cull, c. Beg of that Gentleman. STRIKE the Cly, c. get that Fellow's Money from him. He has STRUCK the Quidds, c. he has got the Cole from him. He STRIKES every Body, c. he borrows Money every where, he runs in every one's Debt.

2. (venery).—To copulate: *see* RIDE. Hence STRIKER = a wencher.

1620. BURTON, *Anat. Melan.*, III. III. iv. I. Gave her a familiar touch with his wand, which she mistaking for her lover, said Ah, Landre, a good Knight should STRIKE before, and not behind.

1639. MASSINGER, *Un. Combat*, iv. 2. That, if the sign deceive me not, in time, Will prove a notable STRIKER, like his father.

STRIKE ME BLIND! *intj.* (common).—An oath.

STRIKE ME LUCK (or LUCKY), *phr.* (old).—Originally used in clenching a bargain: the hands were struck together, and the buyer left a luck-penny in the hands of the seller. Hence oath or ejaculation (BEE).

1616. BEAUMONT and FLETCHER, *Scornful Lady*, ii. Come STRIKE ME LUCK with earnest and draw the writings. There's a God's-penny for thee.

1664. BUTLER, *Hudibras*, II. i. 540. But if that's all you stand upon, Here, STRIKE ME LUCK, it shall be done.

TO MAKE A STRIKE, *verb. phr.* (colloquial).—To achieve, succeed, or be lucky: at ninepins: to knock all the pins down with one ball.

See BRIGHT; HEAP; JIGGER; OIL; RICH; ROSE.

STRIKE-ME-BLIND, *subs. phr.* (nautical).—Rice.

STRILL, *subs.* (provincial).—A cheating lie (HOTTEN).

STRING, *subs.* (printers').—A hoax; a discredited story. Hence as *verb*=to hoax, to deceive. Also (BEE) ON A STRING (or LINE)=hoaxed, bamboozled; STUFFED (*q.v.*).

1897. MARSHALL, *Pomes*, 68. You can't kid me ... they've been having you ON STRING.

Verb. (billiards).—To cast for play: each player to the top of the table to return to balk; the one nearest the bottom cushion has then the choice.

IN A STRING, *phr.* (old).—At command.

1706. WARD, *Wooden World*, 27. 'A Sea Lieutenant.' In fine, he is the Captain's humble Pig IN A STRING.

TO HARP UPON ONE STRING, *verb. phr.* (colloquial).—To repeat incessantly (HEYWOOD, *Proverbs*, 1546).

1640. *Two Lancashire Lovers*, 14. But her parents, ever HARPING UPON ONE STRING, expounded this aversenesse and declining of hers to a modest bashfull shame.

TO FEEL LIKE GOING TO HEAVEN IN A STRING, *verb. phr.* (old).—To feel blindly and confusedly happy.

STRINGER, *subs.* (old). — 1. A wencher: see MUTTON-MONGER.

1611. BEAUMONT and FLETCHER, *Kn. Burning Pestle*, i. 1. A whoreson tyrant, hath beene an old STRINGER in his days, I warrant.

2. (cricket).—A difficult ball to play.

STRINGY-BARK, *subs. phr.* (Australian).—See quot.

1890. A. J. VOGAN, *Black Police*, 217. STRINGY-BARK, a curious combination of fusil oil and turpentine, labelled 'whisky.'

Adj. (Australian). — Rough, uncultured; hence mean, ne'er-do-weel: equivalent to 'bush,' and usually in contempt.

1833. *New South Wales Magazine*, Oct., i. 173. I am but, to use a colonial expression, a STRINGY-BARK carpenter.

1853. C. RUDSTON READ, *Australian Gold Fields*, 53. After swimming a small river about 100 yards wide he'd arrive at old Geordy's, a STRINGY-BARK settler.

1892. NISBET, *Bushranger's Sweetheart*, 30. He was a Larikin of the Larikins, this tiny STRINGY-BARK, who haunted my thoughts.

STRIP, *verb.* (old).—1. See quot.

c.1696. B. E., *Dict. Cant. Crew*, s.v. STRIP, c. to Rob or Gut a House, to unrig any Body, or to Bite them of their Money. STRIP THE KEN, c. to Gut the House. STRIP THE TABLE, c. to Winn all the Money on the Place. *Ibid.* 'Poor, naked': *e.g.* 'We have STRIPT the Cull'='We have got all the Fool's Money'; 'The Cove's STRIPT'='the Rogue has not a Jack left to help himself.'

STRIPE, *subs.* (colloquial). — A characteristic; kind; KIDNEY (*q.v.*). Spec. (American)=persons of the same political colour.

1613. W. BROWNE, *Britannia's Pastorals*, i. 2. I shall go on; and first in differing STRIPE The flood-god's speech thus tune an oaten pipe.

1856. *New York Herald*, 7 July. The call of the Soft-shell Convention was signed by twelve men of the Free-Soil Buffalo STRIPE.

1875. STEDMAN, *Vict. Poets*, 256. Various poems are of a democratic, liberal STRIPE.

THE STRIPES, *subs. phr.* (American).—Short for 'STARS AND STRIPES' (*q.v.*).

STRIP-ME-NAKED, *subs. phr.* (old). — Gin. Also STARK-NAKED (*q.v.*).

c.1820. EGAN, *Randle's Diary*. Then shall young Bacchus see his glittering shrine Delug'd with STRIP-ME-NAKED 'stead of wine.

STRIPPED, *adj.* and *adv.* (colloquial). — Unadulterated; NEAT (*q.v.*).

STRIPPER, *subs.* (gaming).—In *pl.* =high cards cut wedge-shape, a little wider than the rest, so as to be easily drawn in a crooked game: *cf.* CONCAVES and CONVEXES, LONGS and SHORTS, etc.

STRIVE, *verb.* (Christ's Hospital).—To write with care: *cf.* SCRUB.

STROKE, *verb.* (venery).—1. To copulate: see RIDE; also as *subs.*=the act of kind (GROSE).

2. (venery). To grope (*cf.* STERNE, *Tristram Shandy*, viii., xxii.).

STROKER, *subs.* (old).—A flatterer; a sycophant.

1632. JONSON, *Magnet. Lady*, iv. 1. Dame Polish, My lady's STROKER.

STROLLER, *subs.* (B. E. and GROSE).—See quots.

c.1696. B. E., *Dict. Cant. Crew*, s.v. STROWLERS, c. Vagabonds, Itinerants, Men of no settled Abode, of a Precarious Life, Wanderers of Fortune, such as, Gypsies, Beggers, Pedlers, Hawkers, Mountebanks, Fidlers, Country-Players, Rope-dancers, Juglers, Tumblers, showers of Tricks, and Raree-show-men.

1785. GROSE, *Vulg. Tongue*, s.v. STROLLER ... itinerants of different kinds.

STROLLING-MORT, *subs. phr.* (Old Cant).—See quot. 1696 (HARMAN, GROSE).

c.1696. B. E., *Dict. Cant. Crew*, s.v. STROWLING-MORTS, c. pretending to be Widows, sometimes Travel the Countries, making Laces upon Ewes, Beggers-tape, &c. Are light Finger'd, Subtil, Hypocritical, Cruel, and often dangerous to meet, especially when a Ruffler is with them.

1707. SHIRLEY, *Triumph of Wit*, 'Maunder's Praise of His STROWLING MORT. Doxy, oh! thy glaziers shine As glimmar; by the Salomon!

STROMMEL, *subs.* (Old Cant).—1. Straw (HARMAN, DEKKER, B.E., and GROSE). Also STRAMMEL.

1567. HARMAN, *Caveat*, 84. Bene Lightmans to thy quarromes, in what lipken hast thou lypped in this darkemans, whether in a lybbege or in the STRUMMELL?

1641. BROME, *Jovial Crew*, ii. The bantling's born; the doxy's in the STRUMMEL, Laid by an Autumn mort of their own crew That served for midwife.

1815. SCOTT, *Guy Mannering*, xxviii. Sleep on the STRAMMEL in his barn.

2. (old).—Hair (GROSE and VAUX). Hence TO HAVE ONE'S STRUMMEL FAKED IN TWIG=to have it dressed in style; STRUMMEL-FAKER = a barber: *cf.* STRAW-CHIPPER.

1834. AINSWORTH, *Rookwood*. 'Jerry Juniper's Chant.' With my STRUMMEL FAKED IN the newest TWIG.

STRONG. See COME and GO.

STRONG MAN. TO PLAY THE PART OF THE STRONG MAN, *verb. phr.* (old).—'To be whipped at the cart's tail'; *i.e.*, 'to push the cart and horses too' (GROSE).

STRUE, *verb.* (schools').—'Construe.'

STRUM, *subs.* (old).—1. A wig (B. E.). [GROSE: 'Cambridge'.]

2. See STRUMPET.

Verb. (GROSE).—'To play badly on the harpsichord or any other stringed instrument. A strummer of wire, a player on any instrument strung with wire.'

STRUMPET (or STRUM), *subs.* (old).—A harlot: see TART (B. E. and GROSE). As *adj.*=wanton; as *verb*=(1) to play the whore; and (2) to hold up to contempt as a strumpet; also STRUM = to copulate (GROSE and BYRON); STRUMPETOCRACY = government by the privities; and THE STRUM (or STRAM), *subs.*=street-walking.

1593. SHAKSPEARE, *Com. Errors*, ii. 2. 146. STRUMPETED by the contagion. *Ibid.* (1602). *Othello*, v. 1. 'I am no STRUMPET; but of life as honest, As you that thus abuse me.'

1594. NASHE, *Unf. Trav.* (1890), 101. Out whore! STRUMPET ... away with her to prison.

1598. FLORIO, *Worlde of Wordes*, Palandrina, a common queane, a harlot, a STRUMPET, a gill.

1608. MIDDLETON, *Trick to Catch*, v. 1. Daintily abus'd! you've put a just upon me—a common STRUMPET.

1611. COTGRAVE, *Dict.*, s.v. *Gaultière*, A whore, drab, queane, STRUMPET.

1622. MARMION, *Holland's Leaguer*, ii. 2. Didst thou think that I could be corrupted To personate a STRUMPET's dalliance?

1630. *Times Whistle* [E. E. T. S.], 88. Shameless STRUMPETS, whose vncurbèd swing Many poor soules vnto confusion bring.

1633. FORD, *Broken Heart*, iv. 2. Poor Penthea's name is STRUMPETED.

1681. RADCLIFFE, *Ovid Travestie*, 75. You now Have caught a most notorious STRUMPET.

d.1704. BROWN, *Works*, ii. 52. Keeping a saucy STRUMPET under my nose.

1818. BYRON, *Beppo*, ii. Guitars, and every other sort of STRUMMING. *Ibid.* 'To Thomas Moore.' Guitarring or STRUMMING, now? O, Thomas Moore.

c.1857. CARLYLE, *Misc.*, iv. 80. The STRUMPETOCRACY sits at its ease, in high-cushioned lordliness.

1887. HENLEY, *Villon's Good Night*. You judes that clobber for the STRAM.

STRUNT, *subs.* (Old Cant).—The penis: see PRICK.

1608. MIDDLETON, *Epig. and Satyres*. Consenting she, his art'rizde STRUNT he drew, And to 'es venereous game he hastily flew.

2. (Scots).—Liquor.

1787. BURNS, *Hallowe'en*, xxviii. Syne, wi' a social glass of STRUNT, They parte' aff careerin'.

STRUT-NODDY, *subs. phr.* (old).—A mincing fool.

STUB, *subs.* (old).—1. A fool: see BUFFLE.

1632-74. MILTON, *Letters on Education*. Our dullest and laziest youth, our stocks and STUBS.

2. (American).—A counterfoil of a cheque. Hence STUB-BOOK=a book of counterfoils of cheques or other duplicate records.

1886. *Report of Secretary of Treas.*, 700. The filed STUB-BOOKS of stamps.

1896. LILLARD, *Poker Stories*, 136. Miss Hill's attorney ... endeavoured to have produced in court, in evidence of Senator Sharon's maintenance of the plaintiff, the millionaire's check STUBS.

Verb. (Felsted).—To kick a football about.

STUBBLE, *subs.* (venery). — The pubic hair: see FLEECE. TO SHOOT OVER THE STUBBLE (or IN THE BUSH)=to ejaculate before intromission; TO TAKE A TURN IN THE STUBBLE=to copulate: see RIDE and GREENS. *Cf.* The Sportsman's Toast: 'POINTER AND STUBBLE.'

TO STUBBLE ONE'S WHIDDS (or TO STUBBLE IT), *verb. phr.* (Old Cant). — To hold one's tongue (B. E. and GROSE).

1827. LYTTON, *Pelham*, lxxxii. STUBBLE IT, you ben, you deserve to cly the jerk for your patter. *Ibid.* (1830) *Paul Clifford.* STUBBLE YOUR WHIDS, you wants to trick I.

STUBBS, *adv.* (Old Cant).—Nothing (GROSE and VAUX).

STUB-FACED, *adj. phr.* (old).—Pitted with small pox (GROSE).

STUCK. See STICK in various senses: also PIG.

STUCK-UP, *adj. phr.* (colloquial).—Conceited; purse-proud; assuming airs, dignity, or importance. Also (rare) as *subs.*

18[?]. *Betsy Bobbet*, 272. She was dressed up like a doll, but she didn't act STUCK-UP a mite.

1839. DICKENS, *Nicholas Nickleby*, ix. 'He's a nasty STUCK-UP monkey, that's what I consider him,' said Mr Squeers, reverting to Nicholas. 'Supposing he is,' said Squeers, 'he's as well STUCK-UP in our schoolroom as anywhere else.'

1847. A. SMITH, *The Natural History of STUCK-UP People* [Title].

1863. OLIPHANT, *Salem Chapel*, i. Them STUCK-UP ways may do with the Church folks as can't help themselves, but they'll never do with us Dissenters.

1879. EGGLESTON, *Hoosier Schoolmaster.* She was so dog on STUCK-UP that she turned up her nose ... because I tuck a sheet off the bed to splice out the tablecloth.

1892. MILLIKEN, *'Arry Ballads*, 68. These STUCKUPPY snipsters as jaw about quiet and peace.

1899. WESTCOTT, *David Harum*, xii. Mr Robinson instantly arrived at the determination that the stranger was STUCK-UP.

STUDY, *subs.* (B. E.).—'A Closet of Books.'

See BROWN STUDY.

STUFF, *subs.* (once literary, now colloquial). — 1. Belongings: furniture, goods, utensils: generic. The literary usage lingers in 'household-STUFF,' and in such a tributary sense as 'food-STUFFS,' 'bread-STUFFS' (=raw material).

1360. *Anturs of Arther and Sir Amadace* [Camden Soc.], 21. [OLIPHANT, *New Eng.*, i. 67. STUFFE stands for equipment; this led to its sense of *furniture*.]

1427-9. *Wills and Inventories* [Surtees Soc.], 75. STUFFE of myn houses of offices as panetre and buttre.

c.1430. *Destr. Troy* [E.E.T.S.], 5775. Assemblit were some the same in the fight, And restorit full stithly the STUFF of the Grekes.

1593. SHAKSPEARE, *Comedy of Errors*, iv. 4. 162. Away, to get our STUFF aboard. *Ibid.* (1609), *Tempest*, i. 2. Rich garments, linens, STUFFS, and necessaries.

2. (old colloquial).—Money: generic (BEE).

1774. BRIDGES, *Burlesque Homer*, 261. Hector had got no great store of STUFF Called cash, but ancient blood enough.

1778. SHERIDAN, *Rivals*, i. 1. Has she got the STUFF, Mr Fag? Is she rich, hey?

1891. GOULD, *Double Event*, 160. When his party plank the STUFF down it's generally a moral.

1896. LILLARD, *Poker Stories*, 136. Every sport with STUFF in his pockets and lots of good clothes.

1903. KENNEDY, *Sailor Tramp*, I. iv. The sailor had spent over ten dollars by this time. 'How did—did yoush get the STUFF, Sailor?' he asked.

3. (old: still colloquial).—In contempt for anything to be swallowed: spec. medicine.

1605. SHAKSPEARE, *Cymbeline*, v. 5. 255. A certain STUFF, which being ta'en, would cease The present power of life.

1819. MOORE, *Tom Crib*, 17. Sandy tipp'd him a dose of that kind, that, when taken, It isn't The STUFF, but the patient that's shaken.

1851-61. MAYHEW, *Lond. Lab.*, i. 429. They carry . . . pint bladders of STUFF, or jigger-STUFF (spirit made at an illicit still) . . . and a tidy sale some of them had.

1897. MARSHALL, *Pomes*, 114. I was to doctor the STUFF, And be somewhere on hand with a pistol if the hocussing turned out a muff.

4. (colloquial). — Twaddle; fustian; trash—spoken or written. Spec. in such phrases as 'STUFF!' = 'Rubbish!' 'STUFF AND NONSENSE!' = 'What ROT' (*q.v.*)! (B. E. and GROSE). As *verb* = to GAMMON (*q.v.*): to fill full of lies, prejudice, statistics, victuals, etc. Whence STUFFING (journalists') = superfluous matter, used to fill a given space; PADDING (*q.v.*).

1579. GOSSON, *School of Abuses* [ARBER], 66. What STUFFE is this?

1701. FARQUHAR, *Sir Harry Wildair*, iii. 1. *Sir Harry.* There is a repose, I see, in the next room. *Lady Lure.* Unnatural STUFF! *Sir Harry.* . . . As fulsome as a sack-posset.

1725. BAILEY, *Erasmus*, I. 278. A Deal of such STUFF they sung to the deaf Ocean.

1770. FOOTE, *Lame Lover* [OLIPHANT, *New Eng.*, ii. 184. Some is pronounced to be NONSENSE AND STUFF; here we transpose].

1802. W. TAYLOR, *Roberds, Men.*, i. 425. If these topics be insufficient habitually to supply what compositors call the requisite STUFFING, recourse is to be had to amusive anecdotes.

1809. MALKIN, *Gil Blas* [ROUTLEDGE], 109. If they commended a piece I was ravished . . . but suppose they pronounced it bad? why, then I maintained that it was infernal STUFF.

1823. BEE, *Dict. Turf*, s.v. STUFF. . . . Ridiculous or deceitful talk . . . if meant to harm another . . . is bloody STUFF. She hearkened to his STUFF, and got ruinated. . . . Bawdry is STUFF, that's certain.

1853. TAYLOR, *Still Waters*, i. You'll allow me to observe it's anything but STUFF AND NONSENSE. . . . I have not paid a farthing of the money yet. . . .

1899. WHITEING, *John St.*, xix. It's all STUFF to say Sally's shoulders are too much loaded.

5. (prison).—Tobacco.

6. (American).—(*a*) A simpleton, a weakling; and (*b*) a respectable citizen (thieves').

7. (legal).—A Junior Counsel: as distinguished from SILK (*q.v.*): also STUFF-GOWN.

1903. *Pall Mall Gaz.*, 19 Feb., i. 2. 'Silk and STUFF' [Title of Legal Column].

Verb. (colloquial).—To gorge; TO WOLF (*q.v.*).

1809. MALKIN, *Gil Blas* [ROUTLEDGE], 31. My drinking kept pace with my eating, and when I could STUFF no longer, I went to bed.

1838. BECKETT, *Paradise Lost*, 58. He eat as long as he could STUFF.

1868. W. S. GILBERT, *Etiquette*. He longed to lay him down upon the shelly bed, and STUFF; He had often eaten oysters, but had never had enough.

TO STUFF A BALLOT-BOX, *verb. phr.* (American political).—To tamper with returns by the surreptitious introduction into the ballot-box of bogus voting papers. Hence STUFFER = a cheating teller.

STUFFER. *See* HEELER, quot. 1888, and STUFF.

STUFFING. *See* KNOCK and STUFF, sense 4.

STUFFY, *adj.* (American). — 1. Angry, sulky, obstinate.

2. (colloquial).—Close; airless; malodorous.

STULING-KEN. *See* STALL, *subs.* 5.

B

STUMBLE. *See* TRUCKLE-BED.

STUMER, *subs.* (common).—Generic for sham: spec. a worthless cheque.

1897. MARSHALL, *Pomes*, 8. 'The Merry STUMER' . . . STUMER tricks . . . STUMER stake . . . STUMER note . . . STUMER cheque.

1902. *Sp. Times*, 1 Feb., 3. 1. He had borrowed a few hundred franks from her, and had given her as security a STUMER in the shape of an unfinished history of Corsica.

STUMP, *subs.* (old).—1. In *pl.* = legs. As *verb* = to walk: spec. stiffly, heavily, or noisily; whence TO STIR ONE'S STUMPS = to bestir oneself, to increase one's speed.

c. 1609. WEBSTER, *Appius and Virginia*, ii. 3. I can bestir my STUMPS as soon as another, if fit occasion be offered.

1617. BRAITHWAITE, *Law of Drinking*, 70. His long practice of the pot has exempt him from being prest a souldier: hee has quite lost the use of his STUMPS, how should he then possibly keepe his march?

1633. JONSON, *Tale of a Tub*, iii. 1. How should we bustle forward? Give some counsel How to BESTIR OUR STUMPS in these cross ways.

1640. *Two Lancashire Lovers*, 262. This makes him STIRRE HIS STUMPS, and to answer her letter with such speedy cheerefulnesse, as Mellida can expect no lesse then all successe to her desires.

1663. BUTLER, *Hudibras*, I. ii. 926. Getting up on STUMP and huckle, He with the foe began to buckle.

1675. COTTON, *Burl. on Burl.* (1770), 247. Those fat STUMPS thou walkst upon.

1705. WARD, *Hud. Rediv.*, I. ii. 17. I had not long, on City Stones, BESTIRR'D MY STUMPS and Marrowbones.

1774. BRIDGES, *Burlesque Homer*, 5. Then cease your canting sobs and groans, And STIR YOUR STUMPS to save your bones.

1798. MORTON, *Secrets Worth Knowing*, i. 1. A parcel of lazy chaps, I dare say—but I'll make them STIR THEIR STUMPS.

1809. MALKIN, *Gil Blas* [ROUTLEDGE], 344. The reader may guess whether I did not STIR MY STUMPS.

1818. SCOTT, *Heart of Midlothian*, xii. He rose from his seat, STUMPED across the room.

1835. HALIBURTON, *Clockmaker*, 1 S. xxvi. I guess our great nation may be STUMPED to produce more eleganter liquor than this here. It's the dandy, that's a fact.

1841. LYTTON, *Night and Morning*, ii. 2. STUMP IT, my cove; that's a Bow-street runner.

1857. HUGHES, *Tom Brown's Schooldays*, i. 4. The guard picks him off the coach top, and sets him on his legs, and they STUMP off into the bar.

1860. *Funny Fellow*, 7 May, 1. Hallo, my kiddy, STIR YOUR STUMPS. . . . Make haste, young chip, my boots to shine.

1891. MARRIOTT-WATSON, *Web of Spider*, xiii. I'll go bail we wouldn't ha' got another half-mile on our STUMPS.

2. (old). — Money: generic; also STUMPY (GROSE). Hence as *verb* (or TO STUMP UP) = to pay; STUMPED (or PUT TO ONE'S STUMPS) = poor, hard-up, put to shift (GROSE); TO PAY ON THE STUMP = to disburse readily and promptly.

1821. EGAN, *Real Life*, I. 142. She shall STUMP UP the rubbish before I leave her.

1836. DICKENS, *Sk. by Boz*, 'Walkins Tottle.' Why don't you ask your old governor to STUMP UP? *Ibid.*, 'First Cab-driver.' Reduced to despair, they ransomed themselves by the payment of sixpence a head, or, to adopt his own figurative expression . . . forked out the STUMPY.

1837. BARHAM, *Ingolds. Leg.* 'Old Woman in Grey.' (Save its synonyms, 'Spanish,' 'Blunt,' 'STUMPY,' and 'Rhino'), II. 47. [He] . . . was STUMPED and hard up. *Ibid.*, 48. My trusty old crony, do STUMP UP three thousand once more as a loan.

183[?]. HOOD, *Tale of a Trumpet.* But common prudence would bid you STUMP IT, For not to enlarge, It's the regular charge At a Fancy Fair for a penny trumpet.

1835. HOOK, *Gilbert Gurney*, III. ii. 'Don't you know our history?—haven't you heard, my dear fellow, we are STUMPED!' 'STUMPED,' said I, almost unconsciously repeating the quaint, but wofully expressive word. 'Positively STUMPED,' said Daly. 'Don't speak loud. I thought, of course, you had heard of it. Blinkinsop has bolted.'

1849. KINGSLEY, *Alton Locke*, ii. Down with the STUMPY; a tizzy for a pot of half-and-half.

1882. BLACKMORE, *Christowell*, I. xxiii. How much is the captain going to STUMP UP?

1897. MARSHALL, *Pomes*, 63. In the annals of the absolutely STUMPED.

3. (common).—A blockhead: *see* BUFFLE.

4. (venery).—The *penis*: *see* PRICK. Also CARNAL STUMP.

1694. MOTTEUX, *Rabelais*, v. xlv. I hope To see some brawny, juicy rump Well tickled with my CARNAL STUMP.

Verb. (old).—1. To boast; to SWAGGER (*q.v.*). Hence STUMPER = a braggart (BAILEY and DYCHE).

1748. DYCHE, *Dict.*, s.v. BOUNCE . . . to swagger, boast, crack, STUMP, or pretend to great matters.

2. (colloquial).—To challenge, defy, puzzle, or confound; and (in an absolute sense) to ruin. As *subs.* (AMERICAN) = an attempt to puzzle or confound; STUMPER = a puzzler; UP A STUMP = confounded, UP A TREE (*q.v.*).

1837. BARHAM, *Ingolds. Leg.* To be all 'abroad,' to be STUMPED, not to know where To go, so disgraced as not to be 'placed,' Or, as Crocky would say to Jem Bland, 'to be nowhere.'

1838. NEAL, *Charcoal Sketches.* Instead of STUMPING his antagonist by launching out his cash, he shakes a portentous fist under his nose, and the affair is settled.

1844. *Major Jones's Courtship*, 135. Heavens and earth! thinks I, what does all this mean? I knowed I hadn't done any thing to be put in prison for, and I never was so STUMPED.

1847. ROBB, *Squatter Life.* My note was a STUMPER to Sally; so she got Jess to explain it.

1853. BRADLEY, *Verdant Green*, II. xi. That beastly Euclid altogether STUMPS me. . . . *Ibid.* They say it ain't a bad thing . . . to get your head shaved. . . . I think I shall try the dodge . . . when I've STUMPED the examiner I can wear my own . . . locks again.

1900. SAVAGE, *Brought to Bay*, ii. 'And my father and mother?' breathlessly demanded Julian. 'There I'm STUMPED,' carelessly answered Sir Aubrey.

3. (American).—To travel the country for the purpose of making partizan or personal speeches from stumps or other improvised platforms. Originally backwoods electioneering, and spec. on one's own account: now general. Frequently, but not necessarily, in a derogatory sense. Also TO GO ON THE STUMP (or TO TAKE THE STUMP). Hence STUMPER (STUMP ORATOR or STUMP-SPEAKER) = (1) an electioneer; and (2) a bombastic SPOUTER (*q.v.*), with such derivatives as STUMP-ORATOR, STUMP-SPEECH, etc. [WORCESTER: 'A cant phrase'.]

1843. CARLTON. *New Purchase*, I. 211. We had of course a passion for STUMP SPEAKING. But, recollect, we often mount the stump only figuratively; and very good STUMP SPEECHES are delivered from a table, a chair, a whiskey-barrel, and the like. Sometimes we make the best STUMP SPEECHES on horseback.

1848. *New York Herald*, 21 June, 'Letter from Washington.' The Hon. W. R. Thompson of Indiana, one of the most popular STUMP SPEAKERS of the day.

1856. DOW, *Sermons*, I. 132. When you see a politician extra full of patriotism, and stuffed with STUMP SPEECHES, you may take it for granted he wants office either for himself or for some particular friend.

1862. *Punch*, 5 Ap. Though not clear which STUMP I'LL TAKE, That STUMP shall be colossal; Whether I'm Slavery's advocate, Or Liberty's apostle.

1872. *Figaro*, 30 Nov. Greeley's too great a roarer, and depended too much ON THE STUMP.

1884. PHILLIPPS-WOLLEY, *Trottings of a Tenderfoot.* If a constitution was to grow up strong, it didn't want forcing with a lot of STUMP-SPOUTER'S rubbish, and so on, and so on.

1884. *Punch*, 11 Oct. Fancy, old chump, Me doing the sawdusty reglar, and follering swells ON THE STUMP.

STUMP AND RUMP, *adv. phr.* (colloquial). — Completely: *cf.* STOCK AND BLOCK; ROOT AND BRANCH; STICK AND STONE, etc.

STUMPER, *subs.* (Tonbridge School). — 1. Small cricket: played with a stump. At Harrow STUMPS.

2. (colloquial). — A wicket-keeper.

3. (common).—Anything that bowls out; a CORKER (*q.v.*): *see* WHOPPER.

See STUMP.

STUMP-OF-THE-GUTTER, *subs. phr.* (old).—*See* quot. with an eye on STUMPY = short, squat, dumpy.

1764. O'HARA, *Midas*, i. 5. You STUMP-O'-THE-GUTTER, you hop-o'-my-thumb, A husband must for you from Liliput come.

STUMP-TAIL CURRENCY, *subs. phr.* (American).—Currency issued by certain banks of doubtful credit prior to the Civil War (BARTLETT).

STUN, *verb.* (thieves').—To cheat; to DO (*q.v.*). TO STUN OUT OF THE REGULARS = to swindle a man of his share of booty.

STUNLAW, *subs.* (back slang).—Walnuts.

STUNNER, *subs.* (colloquial). — Generic for astonishment: *see* WHOPPER. STUNNING = amazing, strikingly large, good, etc.; TO PUT THE STUNNERS ON = to perplex, confound, astonish.

1848. THACKERAY, *Snobs*, xxv. For the performance of 'Gettin' up Stairs,' I have no other name but that it was a STUNNER.

1851-61. MAYHEW, *Lond. Lab.*, I. 471. He wears a STUNNING fawny on his finger.

1853. BRADLEY, *Verdant Green.* You get on STUNNINGLY, Giglamps.

1857. WHITTY, *Fr. Bohemia.* 193. 'He had seen her at the Crystal Palace? and she was sure he had applauded—so kind!' 'Why—yes,' said Jack . . . 'I think you are a STUNNER.'

1863. OUIDA, *Held in Bondage*, I. 245. The girl is STUNNING, the blokes say.

1874. *Siliad*, 102. 'Golden Nell,' the idol of the West, the peerless belle . . . she is a STUNNER.

1877. *Boston Jo.*, 19 May. This is a STUNNER,—a sockdolager, so to speak.

1890. BOLDREWOOD, *Squatter's Dream*, 29. She's a smart gin when she's away from grog, and a STUNNER at cutting out on a camp.

1900. *Free Lance*, 6 Oct., 16. 1. *Lady Dashout.* 'Those short skirts . . . must be simply delightful to walk in.' *Lady Jack.* 'They're perfectly STUNNING.'

STUPID (or **STUPE**), *subs.* (colloquial).—A blockhead: *see* BUFFLE.

1762. BICKERSTAFF, *Love in a Village*, ii. 2. Was ever such a poor STUPE?

1860. ELIOT, *Mill on the Floss*, i. 9. Tom . . . inconsiderately laughed . . . and told her she was a STUPID.

STURDY-BEGGAR, *subs. phr.* (Old Cant).—'The fifth and last of the most ancient Order of Canters' (B. E.); 'beggars that rather demand than ask' (GROSE).

1569. STRYPE, *Order of City of London*. Those that were Vagabonds, and STURDY BEGGARS, they were to carry to Bridewel.

1572. [*Encyclo. Dict.*, s.v.]. A term occurring in the Act 14 Eliz., c. 5, and used to distinguish 'beggars able to work' from 'beggars impotent to serve'; hence=a vagrant or tramp. By a statute of the Commonwealth, 1656, 'all and every idle and dissolute persons, vagrant and wandering from their usual place of living or abode without sufficient cause or business, and fiddlers and minstrels,' were adjudged rogues, vagabonds, and STURDY BEGGARS within the meaning of the Act of Elizabeth.

STURIBEN (or **STURIBIN**), *subs.* (thieves').—A prison; spec. (American) a State prison. Also STIR.

STYX, *subs.* (The Leys School).—A urinal.

SUB, *subs.* (colloquial).—(1) A subaltern; (2) a subordinate; (3) a subscription; (4) a subject; and (5) *see* quot. 1866. As *verb* (workmen's)=to draw money in advance.

1838. BECKETT, *Paradise Lost*, 8. No longer was he heard to sing, Like loyal SUBS, 'God Save the King!'

1862. THACKERAY, *Philip*, xxvi. When we were SUBS together in camp in 1803.

1866. HARRIS [*Evidence before Totness Election Commission*]. The voters ask for SUB, which is the term used here for money, as sugar and paint are used elsewhere.

1887. HENLEY, *Villon's Good-Night*, 2. You bleeding bonnets, pugs, and SUBS.

SUB-BEAU (or **DEMI-BEAU**), *subs. phr.* (B. E.).—'A wou'd-be-fine.'

SUBLIME RASCAL, *subs. phr.* (old).—A lawyer: *see* GREENBAG.

SUB ROSA, *subs. phr.* (colloquial).—Secretly; confidentially.

SUBSTANCE. *See* SHADOW.

SUBURB, *subs.* and *adj.* (old colloquial).—Generic for disorder and loose-living. [*See* quot. 1822.] Thus HOUSE IN THE SUBURBS = a brothel; SUBURB-WENCH (DRAB, SINNER, etc.)=a whore; SUBURB (=wanton) TRICKS; SUBURB(=blackguard) HUMOUR; MINION OF THE SUBURBS = a STALLION (*q.v.*); SUBURB-TRADE = harlotry; SUBURB-JUSTICE = 'money is right'; SUBURB-GARDEN (or GARDEN-HOUSE)= a *petite maison*: (*a*) a lodging for a KEEP (*q.v.*), and (*b*) a private FUCKERY (*q.v.*); SUBURBAN-ROARER=a bawdy-house bully. *See* quots.

1583. STUBBS, *Anat. Abuses*, 57. In the fields and SUBURBES of the cities, they have GARDENS wherein they may (and doubtless do) many of them play the filthy persons.

1596. JONSON, *Ev. Man in Humour*, i. 2. It will do well for a SUBURB HUMOUR.

1603. SHAKSPEARE, *Measure for Measure*, i. 2. But shall all our houses of resort in the SUBURBS be pulled down? *Ibid.* (1607), *Julius Cæsar*, ii. 1. Dwell I but in the SUBURBS of your good pleasure? If it be no more, Portia is Brutus' harlot, not his wife.

1605. *London Prodigal*, v. 1. Sweet lady, if you have any friend, or GARDEN-HOUSE, I am yours to command in all secret service.

1607. BEAUMONT, *Woman Hater*, ii. This is no GARDEN-HOUSE, in my conscience she went forth with no dishonest intent.

1614. JONSON, *Bartholomew Fair*, ii. 1. Ay, ay, gamesters, mock a plain, plump, soft WENCH OF THE SUBURBS, do; because she's juicy and wholesome.

1632. MASSINGER, *Emp. of the East*, i. 2. *Infor.* The MINION OF THE SUBURBS. *Pul.* What hath he to do in Constantinople? *Ibid.* (1659). *City Madam*, iii. I know them, swaggering, SUBURBAN ROARERS, Sixpenny truckers.

1632. ROWLEY, *New Wonder*, i. Come, we'll dine together, after walk abroad Unto my SUBERB GARDEN; where, if thou'lt hear, I'll read my heart to thee.

1633. MARMION, *Fine Companion*, iv. 1. There's a wench has her SUBURB TRICKS about her, I warrant you.

1640. BROME, *Sparagus Garden*, ii. 3. Some SUBURBE JUSTICE that sits o' the skirts o' the city and lives by't.

1661. MIDDLETON, *Mayor of Quin.* [DODSLEY, *Old Plays* (REED), xi. 120.] Man, who in some GARDEN-HOUSE, Taking his lustful time, Surprizes her.

1678. COTTON, *Virgil Travestie* (1770), 132. Or else some dirty SUBURB-DRAB, Has help'd the Rascal to a Clap.

1682. RADCLIFFE, *Poems*, 25. A Guiney to me was no more Than Fifteen Pence to a SUBURB WHORE.

1822. NARES, *Glossary*, s.v. SUBURBS. In the SUBURBS the citizens had their GARDENS and banqueting HOUSES, where, unless they are much slandered, many ntrigues were carried on.

SUCCUBA, *subs.* (venery).—A mistress; a harlot.

1610. JONSON, *Alchemist*, ii. 1. My glasses Cut . . . to multiply the figures, as I walk Naked between my SUCCUBÆ.

SUCCUBUS, *subs.* (old).—A thieving hanger-on; a scoundrel.

1700. FARQUHAR, *Constant Couple*, iv. 3. Here's an old SUCCUBUS, madam, that has stole two silver spoons.

SUCK, *subs.* (Old Cant).—1. 'Wine or strong Drink' (B. E. and GROSE). Also (2) a small draught: *see* quot. 1625. Hence RUM-SUCK = excellent tipple; SUCKY=drunkish; SUCK-SPIGOT (-PINT, -POT, -BOTTLE, or -CAN) =a confirmed tippler: also SUCKER; SUCKERDOM=the world of topers; SUCK-CASA=a public house. As *verb*=to tipple, to SOAK (*q.v.*). Also TO SUCK ONE'S FACE='to delight in drinking' (B. E.); SUCTION=BOOZE (*q.v.*): hence TO LIVE ON SUCTION=to drink hard; POWER OF SUCTION=capacity for BOOZING.

1585. *Nomenclator.* Ebriosus . . . A dronkard: a SUCKSPIGGET: a great drinker.

1611. COTGRAVE, *Dict.*, s.v. *Humeur*, a SUCKE-PINTE or swill-pot, a notable drunkard.

c. 1696. B. E., *Dict. Cant. Crew*, s.v. SUCK. We'll go and SUCK OUR FACES, but if they toute us, we'll take rattle and brush, c. let's go to Drink and be merry, but if we be Smelt, by the People of the House, we must Scower off.

c. 1709. WARD, *Terræfilius*, ii. 9. Out upon you, for a Damn'd Derby-Ale Sot . . . such a Swill-Belly SUCK-BOTTLE.

1836. DICKENS, *Pickwick*, xxiii. Wery good power o' SUCTION, Sammy.

1862. *N. Y. Tribune* [BARTLETT]. In resisting the tax on whiskey, it has been shown that one distiller in Ohio, who makes 8000 gallons a day, would pay into the treasury $375,600 a year, if SUCKERDOM continued thirsty.

2. (old).—A breast pocket (GROSE).

1625. MASSINGER, *New Way*, etc., i. 1. 'No house? nor no tobacco?' 'Not a SUCK, sir; nor the remainder of a single can.'

3. (University).—A toady: *cf.* SUCKER. Whence TO SUCK UP TO=to insinuate into one's good graces: *cf.* BUMSUCKER.

1900. KIPLING, *Stalky & Co.*, 43. That little swine Manders . . . [is] always SUCKIN' UP TO King.

4. (common).—A cheat; a trick: also SUCK-IN. TO SUCK IN=to TAKE IN (*q.v.*); and SUCKER (*q.v.*)=a greenhorn, a dupe: *see* SUCKING.

d. 1758. RAMSAY, *General Mistake*. This SUCKER thinks nane wise But him than can to immense riches rise.

1842. CLAVERS, *Forest Life*, I. 109. 'I ain't bound to drive nobody in the middle of the night,' said the driver; 'so you don't try to SUCK me IN there.'

1856. DOW, *Sermons*, II. 316. I can't help saying it confidentially, and before man alone, that life is all moonshine,—a monstrous humbug,—a grand SUCK IN.

1887. FRANCIS, *Saddle and Mocassin*. Such men always take it for granted that an Englishman is a SUCKER.

1887. *New York Semi-Weekly Tribune*, 11 Jan. The . . . SUCKERS . . . despite . . . oft-repeated warnings, swallowed the hook so clumsily baited.

1888. *Cincinnatti Enquirer.* The goldasted . . . mugwump has made SUCKERS of us again with his cracks about coming into the league.

1896. LILLARD, *Poker Stories*, 54. A SUCKER had no more chance against those fellows than a snowball has in a red-hot oven. Every deck was marked.

1900. SAVAGE, *Brought to Bay*, v. Anyone who will get those French and English SUCKERS to invest good money out here, *ought to live*.

Verb. (common).—1. To extract ideas or money; TO PUMP (*q.v.*): *e.g.* TO SUCK ONE'S BRAINS = to find out all one knows (GROSE). *See* SUCKER, *subs.* 1.

2. (American University).—To use a CRIB (*q.v.*). Hence SUCKER = a PONY (*q.v.*).

TO TEACH ONE'S GRANDMA (or GRANNIE) TO SUCK EGGS, *verb. phr.* (common).—To instruct an expert; to talk old to one's elders (RAY, *Lex. Bal.*). *See* GRANDMOTHER and *add* the following quotation and analogous PHRASES:—TO TEACH one's GRANNIE to grope her ducks, to sup sour milk, to sard or to spin; to TEACH ONE'S FATHER to get children. Also *Il ne faut pas apprendre aux poissons à nager*= You must not TEACH FISH to swim.

1897. MARSHALL, *Pomes*, 23. Some buds of youthful purity . . . Were engaged TO LECTURE GRANDMAS ON THE ART OF SUCKING EGGS.

See MONKEY and SUGAR-STICK.

SUCKER, *subs.* (common).—1. A parasite; a SPONGER (*q.v.*). Also BUMSUCKER (*q.v.*). Spec. (American political) = a blackmailer. Also SUCK, *verb*=to sponge upon: whence TO SUCK DRY=to exhaust: *cf.* proverbial saying, 'Children SUCK the mother when young, and the father when old.'

1856. DOW, *Sermons*, III. Of the scaly tribe, I may mention those SUCKERS belonging to the body loaferish, that never rise to the surface of respectability, whose sole study appears to be to see how much they can get without the least physical exertion.

2. (trade).—A SUCKING pig. Also (old)=any youngling: *e.g.* a RABBIT-SUCKER = a young rabbit, etc.

1591. LYLY, *Endymion*, v. 2. I prefer an olde cony before a RABBET-SUCKER, and an ancient henne before a young chicken peeper.

1598. SHAKSPEARE, 1 *Hen. IV.*, ii. 4. If thou dost it half so gravely, so majestically, both in word and matter, hang me up by the heels for a RABBIT-SUCKER.

1599. PORTER, *Two Angry Women of Abingdon* [STEEVENS]. Close as a RABBIT-SUCKER from an old coney.

1882. *Standard*, 3 Sep. For SUCKERS the demand was not very brisk.

3. (American).—A native of Illinois (which = the SUCKER STATE: *see* STATE).

1848. DURIVAGE, *Stray Subjects*, 79. There is a swarm of SUCKERS, hoosiers, buckeyes, corncrackers and wolverines eternally on the *qui vive* in those parts.

1854. *N. Y. Tribune*, 19 Oct. A band of music was sent thirty miles to wake up the sleepy SUCKERS, and draw them, by the magic of their music, to the Douglas gathering at Quincy, Illinois.

4 (venery).—The *penis*: *see* PRICK. Also SUCK-AND-SWALLOW=the female privity.

1730. *Broadside Song*, 'Gee ho, Dobbin' [FARMER, *Merry Songs and Ballads* (1897), ii. 204]. I worked at her pump till the SUCKER grew dry, And then I left pumping a good Reason why.

See SUCK and SUCKING.

SUCK-FYST, *subs.* (old).—A parasite (COTGRAVE, s.v. *Hume-vessie*).

SUCKING, *adj.* (old colloquial).—Young, unexperienced, callow: *cf.* SUCKER = a greenhorn, and SUCKING DOVE=a dupe or simpleton (GROSE and BEE). *Cf.* SUCKING-NELSON (=a midshipmite), POET-SUCKER, etc.

1680. DRYDEN, *Spanish Friar*, iii. 2. This is no Father Dominie, no huge overgrown abbey-lubber; this is but a diminutive SUCKING FRIAR.

1668. DRYDEN, *All for Love*. Preface. My enemies are but SUCKING criticks, who would fain be nibbling ere there teeth are come.

1849. BRÖNTE, *Shirley*, xiv. The very curates . . . she . . . looked upon as SUCKING SAINTS.

1849. THACKERAY, *Pendennis*, xxv. Mr. Wagg . . . said, 'Rather a shy place for a SUCKING county member, ay, Pynsent?' *Ibid.* (1855), *Newcomes*, v. I suppose you're a young barrister, SUCKING LAWYER, or that sort of thing, because you was put at the end of the table, and nobody took notice of you.

SUCKSTER (and **SUCKSTRESS**), *subs.* (venery).—A practitioner of irrumation; a CUNNILINGIST (*q.v.*).

SUCTION, *subs.* (Winchester).—Sweetmeats: *cf.* (prov.) SUCKER and SUCKET.

SUCTION. *See* SUCK.

SUDDEN DEATH, *subs. phr.* (common).—*See* quot.

b. 1842. MAGINN, *Bob Burke's Duel.* . . . Which is it to be—two out of three, as at Newmarket, or the first toss to decide? SUDDEN DEATH, said I, and there will soon be an end of it.

2. (University).—A crumpet or Sally Lunn.

3. (colonial).—*See* SPATCHCOCK.

SUDS. IN THE SUDS, *phr.* (old).—Troubled; perplexed; angry (GROSE).

1617. *Letter* [Nares]. The lord Coke is left IN THE SUDS, but sure it is Gods doing, according to the old saying, Perdere quos vult Jupiter prius dementat.

1619. FLETCHER, *Wild Goose Chase*, ii. 3. Will you forsake me now and leave me I' THE SUDS?

1622. *Good Newes and Bad Newes*. Now land is sold, and money gone in goods, He calls out, Andrew, I am IN THE SUDDES.

1706. WARD, *Wooden World*, 7. How fond soever . . . of his dear Duck's Company, he makes no tiresome stay with her . . . so taking . . . Farewell, he leaves her IN THE SUDDS.

1730. SWIFT, *Death and Daphne*. Away the frighted spectre scuds, And leaves my lady IN THE SUDS.

1737. FIELDING, *Tumble-down Dick, or Phaeton* IN THE SUDS. [Title.]

1774. BRIDGES, *Burlesque Homer*, 459. Whene'er he wanted to deceive you, And helpless IN THE SUDS to leave you.

SUETTY-ISAAC, *subs. phr.* (prison).—Suet pudding: also SOAPY-ISAAC.

SUFFER, *verb.* (colloquial).—In mock pity—'Do you SUFFER much?'

SUFFERER, *subs.* (common).—1. A tailor.

2. (common).—A loser.

SUGAR, *subs.* (common).—1. Money: generic: *see* RHINO. Also (rhyming) SUGAR-AND-HONEY.

1862. *Cornhill Mag.*, Nov. 648. We have just touched for a rattling stake of SUGAR at Brum.

1887. BONWICK, *Romance of Wool Trade*, 273. I hear him sing out 'sold again, and got the SUGAR'; 'half a sheep for a shilling.'

2. (old).—Flattery; GAMMON (*q.v.*). Also as *verb*, etc.

1596. SHAKSPEARE, *Hamlet*, iii. 1. 48. With devotion's visage And pious action we do SUGAR o'er The devil himself.

Verb. (rowing).—To malinger at the oars; to shirk while pretending to row hard.

TO SUGAR OFF, *verb. phr.* (American).—To amount to: in speaking of large sums of money.

SUGAR-CANDY, *subs. phr.* (rhyming).—Brandy.

SUGAR-BASIN. *See* SUGAR-STICK.

SUGARED, *adj.* (common).—Astonished; perplexed; GAMMONED (*q.v.*).

1901. *Troddles*, 38. He stood there aghast with his mouth wide open . . . and ever and again he murmured in profound astonishment . . . 'Well — I'm — SUGARED!'

SUGAR-LOAF, *subs. phr.* (old).—A high-crowned hat: conical like a SUGAR-LOAF.

SUGAR-STICK, *subs. phr.* (venery).—The *penis*: *see* PRICK (GROSE). SUGAR-BASIN = the female *pudendum*: *see* MONOSYLLABLE. TO SUCK THE SUGAR-STICK = to receive a man.

SUGAR-STICK BRIGADE, *subs. phr.* (military).—The Ordnance Store Corps.

SUICIDE, *subs.* (old). — Four horses driven in a line; HARUM-SCARUM. *See* TANDEM, RANDOM, UNICORN, etc. (GROSE).

SUIT, *subs.* (old).—1. *See* quot.

1785. GROSE, *Vulgar Tongue*, s.v. SUIT. In general synonymous with game; as, what SUIT did you give it to 'em upon? in what manner did you rob them, or upon what pretence, etc., did you defraud them? One species of imposition is said to be a prime SUIT, another a queer SUIT: a man describing the pretext he used to obtain money from another, would say, I draw'd him of a quid upon the SUIT of so and so, naming the ground of his application. A person having engaged with another on very advantageous terms to serve or work for him, will declare that he is upon a good SUIT. To use great submission and respect in asking any favour of another, is called giving it to him upon the humble SUIT.

2. (thieves').—*See* quot.

1839. AINSWORTH, *Jack Sheppard*. Bargaining with a pickpocket for a SUIT, or to speak in more intelligible language, a watch and seals.

3. (colloquial). — Generic for completeness: *e.g.* a SUIT (= full head) OF HAIR; A SUIT (= a complete set) OF TEETH; A SUIT OF MOURNING = two black eyes (GROSE). *See* subs. 2.

1870. JUDD, *Margaret*, ii. 1. The face of this gentleman was strikingly marked by a SUIT of enormous black WHISKERS that flowed together and united under his chin.

SUIT-AND-CLOAK, *subs. phr.* (Old Cant).—'Good store of Brandy or any agreable Liquor, let down Gutter-lane' (B. E. and GROSE).

SUIT TO A HAIR. *See* HAIR.

SUKEY, *subs.* (common).—1. A kettle (BEE).

2. (common). — A common name for a general servant or SLAVEY (*q.v.*): *cf.* JEAMES = footman. SUKEY-TAWDRY = 'a slatternly female in fine tawdry' (GROSE).

SULKY, *subs.* (old).—'A one-horse chaise or carriage, capable of holding but one person: called by the French a *désobligeante*' (GROSE).

d. 1892. WHITTIER, *Countess*. The country doctor's ancient SULKY.

SULLEN, *subs.* (colloquial).—In *pl.* = the sulks. SICK OF THE SULLENS (or SULLEN-SICK) = very gloomy.

1580. LILY, *Euphues*, 258. [A lady is] SICK OF THE SOLENS.

1597. SHAKSPEARE, *Rich. II.*, ii. 1. 139. Let them die that age and SULLENS have.

1632. MASSINGER, *Emp. of East*, iii. 4. If she be not SICK OF THE SULLENS, I see not the least infirmity in her.

1650. FULLER, *Pisgah Sight*, II. vii. 7. On the denyall Ahab falls SULLEN-SICK.

d. 1655. ADAMS, *Works*, i. 330. If the state . . . lie SULLEN-SICK of Naboth's vineyard, the lawyer is perchance not sent for, but gone to.

1692. HACKET, *Williams*, i. 84. If his Majesty were moody, and not inclin'd to his propositions, he would fetch him out of that SULLEN with a pleasant jest.

1833. LAMB, *Pop. Fallacies*, xvi. A long and desperate fit of THE SULLENS.

SULTRY, *adj.* (colloquial).—Lively, exciting, perhaps unpleasant: *cf.* HOT, WARM, etc.

1901. WALKER, *In the Blood*, 156. Anyway, the possession of it will make it more SULTRY for you.

SUMMER-COMPLAINT, *subs. phr.* (colloquial).—Diarrhœa.

SUMMER-BIRD, *subs. phr.* (old).—A cuckold [CUCKOO, *q.v.*]. Also SUMMER-CABBAGE = a woman [*cf. supra* and CABBAGE (or GREENS) = copulation].

1560. *Scholehouse of Women*, 317. Some other knave Shall dub her husband a SUMMER-BIRD.

1673. *Sackful of News*. So the poor man was cruelly beaten, and made a SUMMER'S BIRD.

SUMMER-GAME, *subs. phr.* (American gaming).—A game for amusement only, or with another's money.

SUMMER'S-DAY. AS NICE (PROPER, GOODLY, etc.) AS ONE CAN SEE IN A SUMMER'S-DAY, *phr.* (old).—As nice (proper, etc.) as may be: *cf.* DAY'S-MARCH.

1592. SHAKSPEARE, *Mid. Night's Dream*, i. 2. A proper man AS ONE SHALL SEE IN A SUMMER'S DAY. *Ibid.* (1599), *Henry V.*, iii. 6. As prave words AS YOU SHALL SEE IN A SUMMER'S DAY.

1594. LILY, *Mother Bombie* (1632), § x. They say hee is as goodly a youth at the pridge AS ONE SHALL SEE IN A SUMMER'S DAY.

1742. FIELDING, *Joseph Andrews*, IV. xv. AS FINE a fat thriving child AS YOU SHALL SEE IN A SUMMER'S DAY.

SUMPH, *subs.* (Scots).—A simpleton: *see* BUFFLE. Hence SUMPHISH = stupid.

1821. SCOTT, *Pirate*, i. 104. 'And you, ye silly SUMPH,' she said to poor Yellowley, 'what do ye stand glowering there for?'

1837. BARHAM, *Ingolds. Leg.*, 'Lord of Thoulouse.' Put your conjuring cap on, consider and see, If you can't beat that stupid old SUMPH with his tea.

1844. NAYLOR, *Reynard the Fox*, 37. A very SUMPH art thou, I wis.

1849-50. THACKERAY, *Pendennis*, Captain SUMPH (one of the characters in this novel).

SUMPSIMUS. *See* MUMPSIMUS.

SUMPSY, *subs.* (legal).—An action of *assumpsit*.

SUN. BEEN IN THE SUN (or SUNSHINE, or GOT THE SUN IN ONE'S EYES), *phr.* (common).—Drunk: *see* SCREWED (RAY, GROSE).

1840. DICKENS, *Old Curiosity Shop*, ii. Last night he had had 'the SUN very strong IN HIS EYES'; by which expression he was understood to convey to his hearers, in the most delicate manner possible, the information that he had been extremely drunk.

1857. ELIOT, *Janet's Repentance*, i. He was in that condition which his groom indicated with poetic ambiguity by saying that 'master HAD BEEN IN THE SUNSHINE.'

1897. MARSHALL, *Pomes*, 75. She was thick in the clear, fairly sosselled on beer.—IN THE SUN is poetical license.

TO MAKE HAY WHILE THE SUN SHINES, *verb. phr.* (old proverbial).—To seize an opportunity.

1509. BARCLAY, *Ship of Fools* (1874), ii. 45. BE BESY about your hay WHILE PHEBUS IS SHINING.

1546. HEYWOOD, *Proverbs*. When the SUNNE SHINETH, MAKE HAY.

1809. MALKIN, *Gil Blas* [ROUTLEDGE], 296. MAKE HAY WHILE THE SUN SHINES. You are on the high road to fortune; push forward.

TO GET THE SUN OVER THE FOREYARD, *verb. phr.* (nautical). To drink before noon.

See KNIGHT; SHOOT.

SUNBURNT, *adj.* (old colloquial). 1. Superficial; hackneyed; unbeautiful.

1570. ASCHAM, *Schoolmaster*, 137. But to dwell in epitomes and books of common places, and not to bind himself daily by orderly study . . . maketh so many seeming and SUNBURNT ministers as we have; whose learning is gotten in a summer heat, and washed away with a Christmas snow again.

1612. WEBSTER, *White Devil*, v. 1. It is a dowry, Methinks should make that SUN-BURNT proverb false, And wash the Æthiop white.

1881. DAVIES, *Supp. Glossary*, s.v. SUNBURNT. Ascham applies the word curiously to superficial scholars, whose mind receives as transient an impression from what they read as the face does from exposure to the summer sun.

2. (old).—'Having many (male) children' (B. E. and GROSE); and (3) 'CLAPPED' (GROSE).

SUNDAY. *See* SHOW-SUNDAY; MONTH OF SUNDAYS and QUEEN DICK.

SUNDAY-BEST (or -CLOTHES), *subs. phr.* (colloquial).—1. Clothes kept for use on Sundays and holidays; best clothes.

1838. BECKETT, *Paradise Lost*, 30. In his SUNDAY JACKET drest, And perch'd up higher than the rest.

1866. GASKELL, *Wives and Daughters*, xlv. Mrs Gibson was off, all in her SUNDAY BEST.

1897. MARSHALL, *Pomes*, 'Her SUNDAY CLOTHES,' 105. Her SUNDAY BEST was her week-day worst, 'Twas simply a caution to snakes.

2. (venery).—An *erecto penis*: as in the phrase, 'the old man (= the *penis*) has got his Sunday clothes on': *see* HORN.

SUNDAY FACE, *subs. phr.* (common).—The posteriors: *see* BUM.

SUNDAY-MAN, *subs. phr.* (old).—1. 'One who goes abroad on that day only, for fear of arrests' (GROSE).

2. (common).—A prostitute's bully. Also SUNDAY GIRL = a WEEK-END (*q.v.*) mistress.

SUNDAY-SAINT, *subs. phr.* (common). — One who roisters through the week and pulls a long face on Sunday.

SUNDAY'S-FELLOW, *subs. phr.* (old).—*See* quot.

1611. TARLETON, *Jests*. One asked Tarlton why Munday was called *Sundaies fellow?* Because he is a sausie fellow, saies Tarlton, to compare with that holy day. But it may be Munday thinkes himselfe Sundayes fellow because it followes Sunday, and is next after; but he comes a day after the faire for that.

SUNDERLAND-FITTER, *subs. phr.* (provincial).—The Knave of Clubs (HALLIWELL).

SUN-DODGER, *subs.* (military).—A heliographer.

1900. *Illust. Bits*, 22 Dec., 10. A first-class trooper with over three years' service to his name, and a qualified SUN-DODGER according to the regimental signalling instructor.

SUN-DOG, *subs. phr.* (nautical).—A mock sun.

189[?]. KIPLING, *Three Sealers* [*Works* (1898), xi. 256]. The good fog heaved like a splitten sail, to the right and left she bore, And you saw the SUNDOGS in the haze.

SUNDOWNER, *subs.* (Australian).—*See* quots. and OVERLANDMAN.

1880. OAKLEY, *Victoria in 1880*, 114. [Title of poem] THE SUNDOWNER.

1888. MACDONALD, *Gum Boughs*, 32. When the real SUNDOWNER haunts these banks for a season, he is content with a black pannikin, a clasp knife, and a platter whittled out of primæval bark.

1890. *Argus*, 20 Sept., 13. 5. SUNDOWNERS are still the plague of squatocracy, their petition for 'rashons' and a bed amounting to a demand.

1891. ADAMS, *John Webb's End*, 34. 'Swagsmen' too, genuine, or only 'SUNDOWNERS,'—men who loaf about till sunset, and then come in with the demand for the unrefusable 'rations.'

1892. *Scribner's Magazine*, Feb., 143. They swell the noble army of swagmen or SUNDOWNERS, who are chiefly the fearful human wrecks which the ebbing tide of mining industry has left stranded in Australia. [This writer does not differentiate between SWAGMAN (*q.v.*) and SUNDOWNER.]

1893. *Sydney Morning Herald*, 12 Aug., 8. 7. Numbers of men who came to be known by the class name of SUNDOWNERS, from their habit of straggling up at fall of evening with the stereotyped appeal for work; and work being at that hour impossible, they were sent to the travellers' hut for shelter and to the storekeeper or cook for the pannikin of flour, the bit of mutton, the sufficiency of tea for a brew, which made up a ration.

1896. *Windsor Magazine*, Dec., 132. 'A SUNDOWNER?' I queried. 'Yes; the lowest class of nomad. . . . They approach a station only at sunset, hence the name.'

SUNNY-BANK, *subs. phr.* (old).—'A good rousing winter fire' (B. E. and GROSE).

SUNNY SOUTH, *subs. phr.* (rhyming).—The mouth.

1887. *Referee*, 7 Nov., 7. 3. She'd a Grecian, 'I suppose,' And of 'Hampstead Heath' two rows, In her SUNNY SOUTH.

SUNSHADES, *subs. pl.* (Stock Exchange).—The Sunchales Extension of the Buenos Ayres and Rosario Railway Company shares.

SUNSHINE. *See* SUN.

SUPE (or SUPER), *subs.* (theatrical).—1. A supernumerary: whence SUPER-MASTER = the director of the supernumeraries: also as *verb*. 2. (Australian) = the superintendent of a station.

1870. GORDON, *Bush Ballads*, 23. What's up with our SUPER to-night? The man's mad.

1884. YATES, *Fifty Years of London Life*, I. ii. Preternaturally stupid people as . . . the SUPERS are found to be.

1890. BOLDREWOOD, *Colonial Reformer*, ix. That SUPER'S a growlin' ignorant beggar as runs a feller from daylight to dark for nothing at all.

1890. *Argus*, 10 June, 4. 1. He . . . bragged of how he had bested the SUPER who tried to 'wing him' in the scrub.

3. (old).—A watch: SUPE AND SLANG = watch and chain; SUPER-SCREWING = stealing watches.

c. 1866. VANCE, *Chickaleary Cove*. How to do a cross-fan for a SUPER or a slang.

4. (American University).—A toady: spec. one who BUM-SUCKS (*q.v.*) the professors.

SUPERANNUATE, *verb.* (Winchester).—*See* quot.

*c.*1840. MANSFIELD, *School Life* (1866) 237. SUPERANNUATE—a boy who was obliged to leave at Election, owing to his being past eighteen years of age. Founders were not SUPERANNUATE till they were twenty-five.

SUPERFINE REVIEW, *subs. phr.* (literary).—*The Saturday Review.* [A coinage of Thackeray's (1860–3) in *The Roundabout Papers.*]

SUPERNACULUM, *subs. and adv.* (old).—1. *See* quots. [Garden Latin: *super naculum*=on the nail.] Whence (2) right liquor; and (3) *see* quot. 1823.

1592. NASHE, *Pierce Pennilesse*, G. 2 v. a. Drinking SUPER NAGULUM, a devise of drinking new come out of Fraunce: which is, after a man hath turned up the bottom of the cup, to drop it on his naile, and make a pearle with that is left; which if it slide, and he cannot make it stand on, by reason ther's too much, he must drinke againe for his penance.

1598. JONSON, *Case is Altered*, viii. 348. I confess Cupid's carouse, he plays SUPER-NEGULUM with my liquor of life.

1617. BRAITHWAITE, *Law of Drinking*, 17. They without any difficulty at all can soake and sucke it ἐν τοῦ νῦν, to a nayle [margin, SUPER-NACULUM].

1622. MASSINGER, *Virgin Martyr*, ii. 1. Bacchus, the god of brewed wine and sugar, grand patron of rob-pots, upsy-freesy tipplers, and SUPER-NACULUM takers, headwarden of Vintners' Hall, ale-conner.

. . . . *Timon* [DYCE], 38. I drinke this to thee SUPER NACULUM.

1630. TAYLOR, *Works*, 2,AAA, 3, r° 1. As when he drinkes out all the totall summe, Gave it the stile of SUPERNACULUM.

1678. COTTON, *Virgil Travestie* (1770), 61. Says, Look, here's SUPERNACULUM.

c. 1696. B. E., *Dict. Cant. Crew*, s.v. SUPERNACULUM, not so much as a Drop left to be poured upon the Thumb-nail, so cleaverly was the Liquor tipt off.

1704. KING, *Orpheus.* Their jests were SUPERNACULUM, I snatch'd the rubies from each thumb.

1719. SWIFT, *To Dr. Sheridan*, Dec. 14. But I doubt the oraculum is a poor SUPERNACULUM.

1746. *De* SUPERNACULO *Anglorum.* 'Est vox hybrida, ex Latina prepositione *super* et Germano *nagel* (a nail) composita'; [NARES: which agrees with the account in Pierce Penilesse, and accounts for the *nagulum*, and *negulum*].

1785. GROSE, *Vulg. Tongue*, s.v. SUPERNACULUM. Good liquor, of which there is not even a drop left sufficient to wet one's nail.

1822. BYRON, *Werner*, i. 1. The SUPERNACULUM! twenty years of age, if 'tis a day.

1823. BEE, *Dict. Turf*, s.v. SUPERNACULUM. Any article of consumption unusually good—as a superior pinch of snuff, a 'drop of brandy like a nosegay,' or port vintage 1816.

1835. *Edin. Rev.*, lxii. 41. Drinking SUPERNACULUM.

d. 1891. LOWELL, *Eurydice.* And empty to each radiant summer A SUPERNACULUM of summer.

SUPERSTITIOUS-PIE, *subs. phr.* (old).—*See* quot.

c. 1696. B. E. *Dict. Cant. Crew*, s.v. SUPERSTITIOUS-PIES, Minc'd, or Christmas-Pies, so Nick-nam'd by the Puritans, or Precisians, tho' they can Eat em, but affecting to be singular, make them a Month or six Weeks before Christmas, or the Feast of Christ.

SUPOUCH, *subs.* (Old Cant).—'An Hostess or Landlady' (B. E.).

SUPPER, *subs.* (venery).—1. The female *pudendum*: *see* MONOSYLLABLE. TO GIVE THE OLD MAN HIS SUPPER=to confer the conjugal embrace; TO WARM THE OLD MAN'S SUPPER=to sit before the fire with petticoats lifted: Fr. *faire petite chapelle.*

TO SET ONE HIS SUPPER, *verb. phr.* (colloquial).—To perform a feat impossible for another to imitate.

SUPPLE. TO SUPPLE BOTH ENDS OF IT, *verb. phr.* (Scots venery).—To knock down a PRICK (*q.v.*).

d. 1796. BURNS [*Merry Muses* (1800), 93]. I SOUPLED it Tho bauldly he did blatter.

SUPPLE TWELFTH, *subs. phr.* (military).—The 12th Lancers.

SURAT, *subs.* (provincial).—*See* quot.

1864. HOTTEN, *Slang Dict.*, s.v. An adulterated article of inferior quality. Since the American Civil War, it has not been unusual for manufacturers to mix American cotton with SURAT, and, the latter being an inferior article, the people in Lancashire have begun to apply the term SURAT to any article of inferior or adulterated quality.

SURE. TO MAKE (or BE) SURE TO, *verb. phr.* (old colloquial.—To betroth; to be engaged to marry.

d. 1535. SIR T. MORE, *Hist. Rich. III.* The King was SURE TO Dame Elizabeth Lucy, and her husband before God.

1608. MIDDLETON, *Trick*, etc., iii. 1. I am but newly SURE yet TO the widow.

1611. COTGRAVE, *Dict.*, s.v. *Accordailles* . . . The betrothing or MAKING SURE of a man and woman together.

1665. J. COTGRAVE, *Wits Interpreter*, 177. She's that's MADE SURE to him she loves not well, Her banes are asked here, but she weds in hell.

1632. BROME, *Northern Lass.* I presumed you had BEEN SURE, as fast as faith could bind you.

SURE AS THE CREED (AS EGGS, FATE, DEATH, A GUN, etc.), *phr.* (colloquial).—As sure as may be; of a certainty. [*See* EGGS and GUN for numerous quots.]

1393. GOWER, *Confessio Amantis.* SIKER AS THE CREDE.

1672. RAY, *Proverbs*, 'Prov. Similes.' As SURE as check or Exchequer pay. This was a proverb in Queen Elizabeth's time; the credit of the Exchequer beginning in, and determining with her reign, saith Dr Fuller. *Ibid.* As SURE (or as round) as a juggler's box. . . . As SURE as a louse in bosom. . . . As SURE as a louse in Pomfret. . . . As SURE as a coat on one's back.

1703. STEELE, *Tender Husband*, iii. 2. She's distracted, AS SURE AS A GUN.

1772. BRIDGES, *Burlesque Homer*, 439. But SURE AS EGGS, whilst folks are sleeping We both again should catch thee peeping.

d. 1774. GOLDSMITH [OLIPHANT, *New Eng.*, ii. 188. I may mention as idioms of this age . . . AS SURE AS EGGS IS EGGS, handsome is as handsome does . . . from Goldsmith].

1809. MALKIN, *Gil Blas* [ROUTLEDGE], 143. As SURE AS A GUN then he is going to make a night of it.

SURE CARD (or **THING**), *subs. phr.* (colloquial).—A certainty; anything entirely trustworthy (B. E.).

1537. *Thersites* [DODSLEY, *Old Plays* (HAZLITT), i. 363]. This is a SURE CARD, this piece of work.

1579. LYLY, *Euphues* (1636), A. iv. A cleere conscience is a SURE CARD.

1589. R. HARVEY, *Plain Perc.*, 12. To get a SURE CARD on their side, Either calles for Iustice.

1593. SHAKSPEARE, *Tit. Andron.* v., 1. 100. As SURE A CARD as ever won the set.

1613. FLETCHER, *Captain* [quoted by Gifford, *Jonson*, ii. 284]. *For.* You know the juggling captain? *Clown.* Ay; there's a SURE CARD.

1672. RAY, *Proverbs*, 'Entire Sentences.' A clear conscience is a SURE CARD.

c. 1696. B. E., *Dict. Cant. Crew*, s.v. A SURE CARD, a trusty Tool, or Confiding Man.

1725. BAILEY, *Erasmus*, i. 'Of a Soldier's Life.' To be sure that Christopher the Collier was a SURE CARD to trust to.

1742. FIELDING, *J. Andrews*, iv. iii. We have one SURE CARD, which is to carry him before Justice Frolick.

SURESBY, *subs.* (old).—A dependable person: *cf.* RUDESBY, WIGSBY, etc.

1586. WITHALS, *Dict.*, 564. Lydius sive Herculeus lapis; here is a SURESBY.

1611. CORYAT, *Crudities*, i. 42. Old SURESBYES, to serue for all turnes.

1614. *Terence in English.* You are the same man that you were: old SUREBIE, no flinsher.

*d.*1657. BRADFORD, *Sermons* [Rept.]. Yes, there is one which is SURESBY as they say, to serve if anything will serve.

SURF, *sub.* (theatrical).—A half-and-half PROFESSIONAL (*q.v.*) player or musician: combining some daily occupation with nightly duty on or in connection with the boards.

SURLY, AS SURLY AS A BUTCHER'S DOG, *phr.* (old).—Very surly (RAY).

SURLY-BOOTS (or **SURLING**), *subs. phr.* (old).—A grumpy morose fellow: *cf.* LAZY-BOOTS.

*d.*1623. CAMDEN, *Remains*, 176. And as for these sowre SURLINGS, they are to be commended to Sieur Gaulard.

1812. COOMBE, *Syntax*, I. xxii. A sudden jolt their slumbers broke, They started all, and all awoke; When SURLY-BOOTS yawn'd wide and spoke.

SURPRISERS (THE), *subs. phr.* (military).—The 46th Foot, now the 2nd Batt. of the Duke of Cornwall's Light Infantry.

SURTOUT, *subs.* (B. E.).—'A loose, great, or riding Coat' (B. E.).

SURVEYOR OF THE HIGHWAY, *subs. phr.* (old).—A man reeling drunk (GROSE): *see* INSPECTOR.

SURVEYOR OF THE PAVEMENT, *subs. phr.* (old).—A man in the pillory (GROSE and BEE).

SUSPENSE. IN DEADLY SUSPENSE, *adv. phr.* (old).—Hanged (GROSE).

SUS. PER COLL., *phr.* (old).—'Hanged by the neck'—Lat. *suspensus per collum.* [GROSE: 'persons who have been hanged are thus entered in the jailer's books.']

1850. THACKERAY, *Pendennis*, II. xxv. That lamentable note of SUS. PER COLL. at the name of the last male of her line. *Ibid.* (1867), *Denis Duval*, i. None of us Duvals have been SUSPERCOLLATED to my knowledge.

SUSPICION, *subs.* (colloquial).—A very small quantity: *cf.* Fr. *soupçon.*

1863. HAWTHORNE, *Our Old Home.* A mere spice or SUSPICION of austerity which made it all the more enjoyable.

1867. TROLLOPE, *Last Chronicles of Barset*, xlix. He was engaged in brushing a SUSPICION of dust from his black gaiters.

1886. *D. Tel.*, 25 Sep. With just a SUSPICION of Irish brogue that only serves to increase the interest of her piquancy and fun.

Verb. (American).—To suspect.

1889. *Harper's Mag.*, lxxx. 349. They somehow SUSPICION'D he wasn't quite sound on hell.

1899. WESTCOTT, *David Harum*, i. Didn't ye SUSPICION nuthin' when he took ye up like that?

SUT, *adj.* (tailors').—Satisfactory; fortunate.

SWAB, *subs.* (old).—1. *See* SWABBER.

2. (nautical).—A naval officer's epaulet: jocose or in contempt: *cf.* SWABBER, sense 1.

SWABBER, *subs.* (old).—1. 'The sorriest sea-men put to wash and clean the ship' (B. E. and GROSE: in this sense good Shakspearean English); hence (2) a term of contempt. Also SWAB.

1602. SHAKSPEARE, *Twelfth Night*, i. 5. 216. *Mar.* Will you hoist sail, sir? . . . *Vio.* No, good SWABBER; I am to hull here a little longer. *Ibid.* (1609), ii. 2. 48. The master, the SWABBER, the boatswain, and I.

1609. BEAUMONT and FLETCHER, *Scornful Lady*, iii. 1. My lady speaks with no such SWABBERS.

1634. FORD, *Perkin Warbeck*, i. 1. More fit to be a SWABBER to the Flemish, After a drunken surfeit.

1678. COTTON, *Virgil Travestie* (1770), 33. This being said, our lusty SWABBER Groan'd like a Woman in her Labour.

1725. BAILEY, *Erasmus*, 42. I am his SWABBER . . . his brawl, his errand boy.

1748. SMOLLETT, *Roderick Random.* xxiv. He swore accordingly at the lieutenant, and called him . . . SWAB and lubbard.

1886. BESANT, *World Went Well*, etc., xxix. Luke was a grass comber and land SWAB.

3. (old).—'The ace of hearts, knave of clubs, ace and deuce of trumps at whist' (B. E. and GROSE): the holder was entitled to a portion of the stakes. [These four cards were only incident to betting at whist.]

c. 1700. SWIFT [quoted by STRUTT, *Sports and Pastimes* (1801, etc.), 436]. The clergymen used to play at whist and SWOBBERS; playing now and then a sober game at whist for pastime, it might be pardoned; but he could not digest those wicked SWOBBERS.

1754. FIELDING, *Jonathan Wild*, I. iv. As whisk and SWABBERS was the game then in the chief vogue, they were oblig'd to look for a fourth person, in order to make up their parties.

1817. SCOTT, *Rob Roy*, I. 225. The society of half a dozen of clowns to play at whisk and SWABBERS would give her more pleasure than if Ariosto himself were to awake from the dead.

SWACK, *subs.* (Christ's Hospital).—Deception. Hence TO SWACK UP=to deceive; TO TAKE IN (*q.v.*). Also SWACK-UP = a falsehood.

SWAD, *subs.* (old).—1. A reproach: generic; spec. (1) a rustic or clodhopper; and (2) a disbanded soldier (GROSE), now-a-days a militiaman. Also SWADDER, SWADKIN, SWADGILL, and SWADDY.

1534. HOLINSHED, *Chron. of Ireland.* Three drunken SWADS that kept the castell thought that this showt was nought else but a dreame.

1588. GREENE, *Perimedes.* Let countrey swaines and silly SWADS be still; To court, yoong wag, and wanton there thy fill.

1592. LYLY, *Midas*, iv. 3. I'll warrant, that was devised by some country SWAD.

1593. PEELE, *Honour of the Garter.* There came a pilfring SWAD And would have prayd upon this ornament.

1606. *Return from Parnassus.* But hang them, SWADDS, the basest corner in my thoughts is too gallant a roome to lodge them in.

1622. TAYLOR, *Motto.* I have opinion, and have ever had, That when I see a stagg'ring drunken SWAD, Then that a man worse then an asse I see.

1633. JONSON, *Tale of a Tub*, ii. 1. Now I remember me, There was one busie fellow was their leader, A blunt squat SWAD.

1638. BRAITHWAITE, *Survey of History.* A squeazed SWAD without either meanes, manners, or mannor.

1640. *Two Lancashire Lovers*, 22. How should the reasonable soule (unlesse all his prime faculties were drowned and drenched in the lees of sense) affect such a SWAD?

1656. BLOUNT, *Glossog.*, 627. SWAD, in the North, is a pescod shell; thence used for an empty shallow-headed fellow.

*d.*1701. DRYDEN, *Counter Scuffle* [Misc., iii. 340]. Wer't not for us, thou SWAD, quoth he, Where wouldst thou fog to get a fee?

2. (common).—A lump, bunch, crowd, mass: also SWOD.

1840. HALIBURTON, *The Clockmaker*, 3 S. vi. How is a colonist able to pay for this almighty SWAD of everlasting plunder, seein' he has no gold or silver?

1865. *Major Downing's Letters*, 35. There was a SWAD of fine folks, and the house was well-nigh upon chuck full.

1869. *Overland Monthly*, iii. 131. A Texan never has a great quantity of any thing, but he has scads of it or oodles or dead oodles, or scadoodles, or SWADS.

SWADDER, *subs.* (Old Cant).—1. *See* quot.

1567. HARMAN, *Caveat*, 72. These SWADDERS and Pedlars be not all evil, but of an indifferent behaviour.

2. *See* SWAD.

SWADDLE, *verb.* (old).—To cudgel; to rope's end (B. E. and GROSE); to swathe round with lash or stick. Hence SWADLER (Old Cant) = 'The tenth Order of the Canting Tribe' (B. E.) 'who not only rob, but beat and often murder passengers' (GROSE).

*c.*1570. *Wife Lapped in Morels Skin*, 845. [HAZLITT, *Early Pop. Poet.*, iv. 214]. I sweare by God, and by saynt John, Thy bones will I SWADDLE, so have I blisse.

1611. COTGRAVE, *Dict.*, s.v. *Chaperon*. Hee bangde, belammed, thumped, SWADLED her.

1612–3. FLETCHER, *Captain*, ii. 1. Were it not for taking So just an execution from his hands, . . . I would SWADDLE ye, 'Till I could draw off both your skins like scabbards.

1636. DAVENANT, *Wits*, iii. 1. (1673). How now, housewife? Do you slight authority? Behold this staff! in very truth I shall SWADDLE you with the King's wand of office.

1663. BUTLER, *Hudibras*, I. i. v. 23. Great on the bench, great in the saddle, He could as well bind o'er as SWADDLE.

*d.*1701. DRYDEN, *Counter-Scuffle* [Misc., iii. 347]. Behind the door he stood to hear, For in he durst not come, for fear Of SWADLING.

SWADDLER, *subs.* (Irish).—1. A Methodist (GROSE). Hence spec. (2) those who in winter play the Protestant, for the sake of the blankets, coals, etc., given by proselytisers. Also (3), in America, a street preacher, spec. (American thieves') a preaching confederate.

1820. SOUTHEY, *Life of Wesley*, ii. 153. It happened that Cennick, preaching on Christmas Day, took for his text these words from St. Luke's Gospel, 'And this shall be a sign unto you; ye shall find the babe wrapped in swaddling-clothes, lying in a manger.' A Catholic who was present, and to whom the language of Scripture was a novelty, thought this so ridiculous that he called the preacher a SWADDLER in derision.

1845. COKE and MOORE, *Life of Wesley*, 288. Butler and his mob were now in higher spirits than ever; they scoured the streets day and night, frequently hallooing as they went along, 'Five pounds for a SWADDLER'S head!'

1889. *Academy*, 11 May, 317. To revive Sir W. Petty's Colony by importing Northern Presbyterians and Cornish SWADDLERS.

2. *See* SWAD and SWADDLE.

SWAG, *subs.* (Old Cant). — 1. A shop: spec. a mart for stolen goods. Whence a RUM-SWAG = 'a shop full of rich goods' (B. E.); and SWAG-BARROW = a coster's cart. Hence (2) generic for property; spec. booty: *see* quots. 1785, 1819, and 1823. Also SWAG-CHOVEY BLOKE = a marine store dealer; SWAGSMAN = (1) a receiver of stolen goods, and (2) a miscellaneous dealer in 'City penn'orths' and other cheap stuff, wholesale or retail.

1785. GROSE, *Vulg. Tongue*, s.v. SWAG, a bundle, parcel, or package; as a SWAG of SNOW, etc. The SWAG, is a term used in speaking of any booty you have lately obtained, be it of what kind it may, except money, as Where did you LUMBER THE SWAG? that is, where did you deposit the stolen property? To carry THE SWAG is to be the bearer of the stolen goods to a

place of safety. A SWAG of any thing, signifies emphatically a great deal. To have knap'd a good SWAG, is to have got a good booty.

1819. VAUX, *Memoirs*, s.v. SWAG. Wearing-apparel, linen, piece-goods, etc., are all comprehended under the name of SWAG, when describing any speak lately made, etc., in order to distinguish them from plate, jewellery, or other more portable articles.

1823. BEE, *Dict. of Turf*, s.v. SWAG (the)—store of money. 'The SWAG lies upstairs, in a chest of drawers. . . . Rum-SWAG—A good deal of it.

1827. CUNNINGHAM, *Two Years in New South Wales*, ii. 59. A number of the slang phrases current in St. Giles's Greek bid fair to become legitimatized in the dictionary of this colony: plant, SWAG, pulling up, and other epithets of the Tom and Jerry school, are established—the dross passing here as genuine, even among all ranks.

1837. MUDIE, *Felonry of New South Wales*, 181. In short, having brought with her a supply of the SWAG, as the convicts call their ill-gotten cash, a wife seldom fails of having her husband assigned to her, in which case the transported felon finds himself his own master.

1838. DICKENS, *Oliver Twist*, xix. 'It's all arranged about bringing off the SWAG, is it?' asked the Jew. Sikes nodded.

1840. BARHAM, *Ingolds. Legends*, 'Misadv. at Margate.' He said 'he'd done me wery brown, and neatly stowed the SWAG.'

1851–61. MAYHEW, *London Lab.*, ii. 93. SWAGMEN who sell low-priced millinery.

1856. READE, *Never too Late*, etc., xlvi. He will shake all that nonsense to blazes when he finds himself out under the moon with the SWAG on one side and the gallows on the other.

1861. KINGSLEY, *Ravenshoe*, xxxvii. If any enterprising burglar had taken it into his head to crack that particular crib known as the Bridge Hotel, and got clean off with the SWAG, he might have retired on the hard-earned fruits of a well-spent life into happier lands.

1897. MARSHALL, *Pomes*, 121. The gentleman swore he'd been bested, And Sam had passed on the SWAG.

1900. FLYNT, *Tramps*, 282. 'It ain't such a bad lot,' he said; 'I chew every day, get a big SWAG once in a while.'

3. (Australian). — A tramp's bundle in a BLUEY (*q.v.*); hence personal luggage; TRAPS (*q.v.*). As *verb* = to tramp the bush carrying a SWAG; SWAGMAN (SWAGGER or SWAGGIE) = a man travelling in search of work: *cf.* SUNDOWNER.

1853. SIDNEY, *Three Colonies*, 361. His leathern overalls, his fancy stick, and his SWAG done up in mackintosh.

1861. MCCOMBIE, *Australian Sketches*, 5. There was the solitary pedestrian, with the whole of his supplies, consisting of a blanket and other necessary articles, strapped across his shoulders: this load is called the SWAG and the mode of travelling SWAGGING it.

1865. J. O. TUCKER, *Australian Story*, i. 86. The cumbrous weight of blankets that comprised my SWAG.

1873. TROLLOPE, *Australia and New Zealand*, i. 285. SWAG, which consists of his personal properties rolled up in a blanket.

1875. LADY BARKER, *Station Amusements in New Zealand*, 154. Describing the real SWAGGER, clad in flannel shirt, moleskin trowsers, and what were once thick boots.

1879. J. BRUNTON STEPHENS, *Drought and Doctrine* (*Works*, 309). Rememberin' the needful, I gets up an' quietly slips To the porch to see—a SWAGSMAN—with our bottle at his lips.

1883. KEIGHLEY, *Who are You?* 36. Then took a drink of tea . . . Such as the SWAGMEN in our goodly land Have with some humour named the post-and-rail.

1890. *Argus*, 2 Aug., 4, 2. He strapped the whole lot together, SWAG-like. *Ibid.* (1896), The Argus, 23 March, 5, 1. The minister's house is the sure mark for every stone-broke SWAGGER in search of clothes or victuals.

1891. BOLDREWOOD, *A Sydney-side Saxon*, 156. We pulled up a SWAGMAN. He was walking very slow; he was a bit lame too. His SWAG wasn't heavy, for he had only a rag of a blue blanket, a billy of water in his hand, and very little else.

1902. *Pall Mall Gaz.*, 26 July, 2. 1. The unmarried shearer, roaming, SWAG on back, from station to station, chasing summer down the latitudes, leads an active, pleasant life enough.

SWAG-BELLY, *subs. phr.* (old).—A very fat man or woman; a swing-paunch. [SWAG = to weigh heavily.] Hence SWAGGY (or SWAG-BELLIED) = fat, FORTY-GUTTED (*q.v.*).

1530. PALSGRAVE, *Langue Francoyse*. I SWAGGE, as a fatte persons belly swaggeth as he goth.

1602. SHAKSPEARE, *Othello*, ii. 3. I learned it in England, where, indeed, they are most potent in potting: your Dane, your German, and your SWAG-BELLIED Hollander . . . are nothing to your English.

1646. BROWNE, *Vulg. Errors*, III. iv. His SWAGGY and prominent BELLY.

1694. MOTTEUX, *Rabelais*, v. 'Pant. Prog.,' v. However, so many SWAGBELLIES and puff-bags will hardly go to St Hiacco, as there did in the year 524.

1886. OLIPHANT, *New English*, i. 462. The *swagge* of 1303 [*see* quot. 1530] is here used of a fat man's belly; hence the swag-bellied Hollander, and also the later SWAGGER.

SWAGGER, *subs.* and *verb.* (once literary: now colloquial: B. E. and GROSE).—Bluster; bravado; roaring insolence; SIDE (*q.v.*). As *verb* = to strut defiantly; to boast; to bluster; to affect or obtrude superiority: *see* quot. 1898. Also derivatives such as SWAGGERER and SWAGGERING.

1598. FLORIO, *Worlde of Wordes*, s.v. *Ruffo* . . . Also a ruffling roister or ruffian, a SWAGGRER.

1598. SHAKSPEARE, 2 *Hen. IV.*, ii. 4. Your ancient SWAGGERER comes not in my doors. *Ibid.* (1599), *Hen. V.*, iv. 7. 131. A rascal that SWAGGERED with me last night.

1607. DEKKER, *Northward Ho*, iv. 1. A SWAGGERING fellow, sir, that speaks not like a man of God's making, swears he must speak with you, and will speak with you.

1612. ROWLANDS, *Hist. Rogues* [RIBTON-TURNER, 582]. They chose a notable SWAGGERING rogue called Puffing Dicke to reuell over them.

c. 1622. HEYWOOD, *Fair Maid of the West* [PEARSON, *Works*, (1894), ii. 279]. Can we not live in compasse of the Law, But must be SWAGGERED out on't?

1636. DAVENANT, *Wits*, i. 2. And SWAGGER in the wool [that] we shall borrow from our own flocks.

1678. CUDWORTH, *Intellectual System*, 61. It was Atheism openly SWAGGERING, under the glorious appearance of wisdom and philosophy.

1699. DRYDEN, *Cox and Fox*, 443. [He] SWAGGERETH like a lord about his hall.

1725. SWIFT, *Will Wood's Petition*. The butcher is stout, and he values no SWAGGER. *Ibid. Court and Empire of Japan.* He would SWAGGER the boldest man into a dread of his power.

1765. GOLDSMITH, *Essays*, x. The bunters who SWAGGER in the streets of London.

1809. MALKIN, *Gil Blas*, 136. She could put on as brazen-faced a SWAGGER as the most impudent dog in town.

1835. MARRYATT, *Pacha of Many Tales*. 'The Water Carrier.' It requires but an impudent SWAGGER and you are taken on your own representation.

1844. THACKERAY, *Barry Lyndon*, xv. As for the SWAGGER . . . I deny it *in toto*, being always most modest in my demeanour.

1880. PAYN, *Confid. Agent*, xi. The captain [put] . . . a good deal of SIDE ON, which became a positive SWAGGER as he emerged into the more fashionable street.

1898. WARNER, *Harrow School*, 280. The rules of 'SWAGGER' or [SIDE] are most complex . . . And a new boy is apt to find himself entangled. He goes out with his umbrella rolled up . . . or carries it by its middle, or under his arm, or he walks on the middle terrace after chapel, or he innocently wears his 'blues' open when it is hot, or turns his trousers up when it is wet, and . . . he is SWAGGERING. Lady visitors sometimes think small boys at Harrow rude . . . to stick close to the wall . . . and shoulder the world into the gutter—it is modesty; to walk in the road is SWAGGER. To loiter at the house door, or to sing or whistle in the passages, and to wear a hat in the house are also forms of SWAGGER.

1901. WALKER, *In the Blood*, 107. He wore a new cricketing belt round his loins, as low down as he could get it to go; the lower down the greater assumption of 'push' SWAGGER.

Adj. (common). — TIP-TOP (*q.v.*); SWELL (*q.v.*); extremely new.

1886. *New York Tribune* (Semi-Weekly), 2 Nov. His gambling parties were so SWAGGER that rich money-lenders who wanted to extend their social relations did not mind to what extent they . . . lost money at them.

1897. OUIDA, *Massarines*, 8. Lord, ma'am, they'll pocket the marrons glacés at the table d'hôte and take the matches away from their bedrooms; but, then, you see, ma'am, them as are SWAGGER can do them things.

1900. WHITE, *West End*, 43. 'We are now living in a very different style.' . . . 'It looks a great deal more SWAGGER certainly.'

SWAINING, *subs.* (common). — Love-making; SPOONING (*q.v.*).

1839. MRS. TROLLOPE, *Michael Armstrong*, i. His general manner had a good deal of what in female slang is called SWAINING.

SWALLOW, *subs.* (once literary: now vulgar or colloquial).—1. The throat: also SWALLOW-PIPE; (2) the act of swallowing; and (3) a mouthful: hence (4) taste, relish, inclination, or capacity. As *verb* = to receive, endure, or embrace credulously, patiently, without examination, scruple or reserve; occasionally TO SWALLOW WHOLE. (B. E.). Hence SWALLOWABLE = credible.

1596. SHAKSPEARE, *King John*, iv. 2. 195. I saw a smith stand . . . With open mouth SWALLOWING a tailor's news. *Ibid.* (1603), *Meas. for Meas.*, iii. 1. 235. Left her . . . SWALLOWED his vows whole, pretending in her discoveries of dishonour.

1613. PURCHAS, *Pilgrimage*, 92. The mother (not able to SWALLOW her shame and grief) Cast herselfe into the lake to bee swallowed of the water.

1616–25. *Court and Times Jas. I.*, ii. 442. [A man] SWALLOWS indignities.

1690. LOCKE, *Human Understanding*, IV. xx. 4. Here men . . . must . . . SWALLOW down opinions as silly people do empiric pills, without knowing what they are made of.

1703. FARQUHAR, *Inconstant*, iii. 1. I have SWALLOWED my words already; I have eaten them up.

1796. WOLCOT ('Peter Pindar'), *Works*, 147. Each paunch with guttling was so swelled, Not one bit more could pass your SWALLOW-PIPE.

1834. WILSON, *Noctes Ambros.*, Dec. Attend to the differences between a civilized SWALLOW and a barbarous bolt.

1841. *Punch*, i. 169. Men with SWALLOWS like Thames Tunnels, in fact accomplished gaggers and unrivalled wiry watchers.

1849. MAITLAND, *Essays on the Reformation*, 315. An anecdote in its hundredth edition, and its most mitigated and SWALLOWABLE form.

1885. BUCK, *Handbook of Med. Sci.*, v. 4. A SWALLOW or two of hot milk sometimes aids in coughing up tenacious mucus.

1899. WESTCOTT, *David Harum*, xxiii. She took a SWALLOW of the wine. 'How do you like it?' asked David.

PHRASES. — 'One SWALLOW does not make a spring' (HEYWOOD, 1546 = proverbial); TO SWALLOW A SPIDER = to become a bankrupt (RAY); 'You say true; will you SWALLOW my knife?' (a sarcastic retort on an impossible story); TO SWALLOW A TAVERN TOKEN = to get drunk; TO SWALLOW THE CACKLE = to learn a part (theatrical); 'He has SWALLOWED a stake, and cannot stoop' (of a very upright unbending person).

1596. JONSON, *Ev. Man in Humour*, i. 3. Drunk, sir! you hear not me say so: perhaps he SWALLOWED A TAVERN TOKEN or some such device.

SWALLOW-TAIL, *subs. phr.* (old).—1. *See* quot. 1544.

1544. ASCHAM, *Toxophilus* [GILES, ii. 130]. Having two points or barbs, looking backward to the stele and the feathers, which surely we call in English a broad arrow head, or a SWALLOW-TAIL.

1828. SCOTT, *Fair Maid of Perth*, ii. 223. The English then strode forward, . . . and sent off their volleys of SWALLOW-TAILS before we could call on St. Andrew.

2. (nautical).—The points of a burgee.

3. (common).—A dress coat; a STEEL-PEN COAT (*q.v.*).

1886. *Referee*, 29 Aug. He is stripped of his SWALLOW-TAIL and his pseudonym, and marched off to the guard-room again.

1888. BESANT, *Fifty Years Ago*, 50. Here is one of the new police, with blue SWALLOW-TAIL COAT tightly buttoned, and white trousers.

1902. LYNCH, *Unseen Hand*, i. He passed his hand caressingly over the lapel of an immaculate SWALLOW-TAIL.

4. (? punning nonce-word).—A tongue always wagging.

1690. D'URFEY, *Collin's Walk*, i. He'd tire your ear with pentagons . . . And all your outworks would assail With his eternal SWALLOW'S TAIL.

SWAN. I SWAN, *intj.* (American).—'I swear!' Also (more emphatically), 'I SWAN TO MAN!'

1842. CLAVERS, *Forest Life*, I. 29. 'Well, I SWAN!' exclaimed the mamma, giving a round box on the ear to a dirty little urchin.

1862. LOWELL, *Biglow Papers*, 2 S. i. But they du preach, I SWAN TO MAN, it's puf'kly indescrib'le. *Ibid.* vi. I SWAN, You half forgit you've gut a body on.

1899. WESTCOTT, *David Harum*, xiv. 'You c'n git round on your pins 'bout's lively's they make 'em, I guess, I SWAN,' he exclaimed.

SWANK, *verb.* (public school).—To work hard: *cf.* SWINK. SWANKER = a hard-working student.

SWANKEY, *subs.* (common).—Any weak tipple: spec. small beer. Also (fishermen's) a mixture of water, molasses, and vinegar.

SWANNERY. TO KEEP A SWANNERY, *verb. phr.* (old).—To boast of one's own doings, possessions, etc.; to make out that all one's geese are swans (GROSE).

SWAN-SLINGER, *subs. phr.* (theatrical.—A player fond of or famous for SPOUTING BILL (*q.v.*); a Shakspearean actor: the same as 'slinging the Swan of Avon.'

SWAP (or **SWOP**), *subs.* (colloquial).—An act of barter; an exchange. As *verb* = to exchange; to strike a bargain. (B.E.) GROSE [= 'Irish Cant.'] and BEE.

1360. *Sir Gawayn* [E.E.T.S]. 35. [OLIPHANT, *New. Eng.*, i. 58. The old SWAP gets the new sense of 'make an exchange.'

1594. LYLY, *Mother Bombie*, v. 3. Soft, 'I'le not SWAP my father for all this.' . . . 'What, doe you thinke I'le be coz'ned of my father?'

1692. DRYDEN, *Cleomenes.* I would have SWOPP'D Youth for old age, and all my life behind, To have been then a momentary man.

1707. WARD, *Hud. Red.*, II. ii. 5. Those, who to preserve their Health, Had SWOP'D their little Store of Wealth.

1724. SWIFT, *Wood's Half-pence.* A fine lady SWAPPING her moles for the mange.

1781. PARKER, *View of Society*, II. 48. The hostler then says he has a choice nag or daisy-kicker to sell or SWAP.

1819. SCOTT, *Bride of Lammermoor*, xxvi. For the pouther, I e'en changed it . . . for gin and brandy . . . a gude SWAP too.

1830. COBBETT, *Rural Rides*, (1886), I. 199. It is barter, truck, change, dicker, as the Yankees call it, but as our horse jockies call it, SWAP, or chop.

1853. READE, *Gold*, i. Carry out a cargo of pea-jackets and four-penny bits to SWAP for gold dust.

1862. LOWELL, *Biglow Papers*, 2 S. v. We'd better take maysures for shettin up shop, And put off our stock by a vendoo or SWOP.

1887. EGGLESTON, *Graysons*, x. Farmers frequented the town, to meet old friends and get the better of them in SWAPPING horses.

1894. BAKER, *New Timothy*, 187. Not even the greasy cards can stand against the attractions of a SWAP of horses, and these join the group.

1899. WHITEING, *John St.*, xiv. You two countries ought to SWAP grandmothers, and then you'd match.

1900. SAVAGE, *Brought to Bay*, ii. Don Andrès proposes to SWAP herd for herd, taking our cattle as they run, at fifteen dollars, and giving us half-breed sheep at three.

TO GET THE SWAP (or SWOP), *verb. phr.* (common). — To be dismissed.

TO SWAP OFF, *verb. phr.* (American). — To cheat; TO SELL (*q.v.*).

1880. HARRIS, *Uncle Remus*, iv. Den Brer Fox know dat he been SWAP OFF mighty bad.

SWAPPER, *subs.* (common).—Anything large or big: *see* WHOPPER. Hence SWAPPING = huge; strong; A1.

1589. *Countercuffe given to Martin Junior.* A filch-man in his hande, a SWAPPING ale dagger at his back, containing by estimation some two or three pounds of yron in the hyltes and chape.

1624. MIDDLETON, *Game at Chess*, iv. 2. Ay, marry, sir, here's SWAPPING sins indeed.

SWARM, *verb.* (colloquial). — To climb; TO SHIN UP.

. . . *Syr Isumbras*, 351. He SWARMED UP into a tree, Whyle eyther of them might other se.

1888. *Spectator* [*Century Dict.*]. SWARMING UP the lightning conductor of a great church to fix a flag at the top of the steeple.

SWARRY, *subs.* (common). — A boiled leg of mutton and trimmings.

1837. DICKENS, *Pickwick*, xxxviii. Honourably accounts for Mr. Weller's absence by describing a . . . SWARRY . . . a boiled leg of mutton, hot, with caper sauce, turnips, and potatoes.

SWARTWOUT, *verb.* (American).—To abscond. [From the name of a public defaulter in New York.]

SWASH, *verb.* (old).—1. To make a noise: *see* quot. 1662. Hence SWASH - BUCKLER (SWASH, SWASHER or SWINGE-BUCKLER) = a sworder good at a lively peal on his opposite's target; and, therefore, by implication, a ruffler, bully, Hector. As *subs.* = bluster, vapouring, roaring; SWASHING (or SWASHY) = (1) noisy (a SWASHING blow); and (2) = loud-mouthed and quarrelsome.

1560. PILKINGTON, *Works* [PARKER], 151. A drunkard, a whore-hunter, a gamer, a SWASH-BUCKLER, a ruffian to waste his money in proud apparel.

1577–87. HOLINSHED, *Chron. Ireland*, 87. Whereby a man maie see how manie bloudie quarels a bralling SWASH-BUCKLER maie picke out of a bottle of haie, namelie when his braines are forebitten with a bottle of nappie ale.

1582. STANYHURST, *Æneid*, ii. 220. Their tayls with croompled knot twisting SWASHLYE they wrigled.

1595. SHAKSPEARE, *Romeo and Juliet*, i. 1. Draw, if you be men—Gregory, remember thy SWASHING blow. *Ibid.* (1598), 2 *Henry IV.*, iii. 2. 24. *Shallow.* You had not four such SWINGE-BUCKLERS in all the inns o' court again. *Ibid.* (1599), *Henry V.*, iii. 2. As young as I am, I have observed these three SWASHERS [Nym, Pistol, and Bardolph]. I am boy to them all three. *Ibid.* (1601), *As You Like It*, i. 3. We'll have a SWASHING and a martial outside, As many other mannish cowards have.

1598. FLORIO, *Worlde of Wordes*, 74. A bravo, a SWASH-BUCKLER, one that for mony and good cheere will follow any man to defend him and fight for him, but if any danger come, he runs away the first and leaves him in the lurch. *Ibid.*, 127. To fence, TO SWASH with swords, to swagger.

1609. HOLLAND, *Am. Mar.* Leo, a notarie afterwards, master of the offices, a very SWASH-BUCKLER at every funerall, a knowne robber, and a Pannonian; one who breathed foorth of his savage mouth crueltie, and yet was neverthelesse greedie still of mans bloud.

1611. CORYAT, *Crudities*, I. 54. Their men are very ruffians and SWASH-BUCKLERS, having exceeding long blacke haire curled, and swords or other weapons by their sides.

1611. COTGRAVE, *Dict.*, s.v. *Bravache.* A roister, cutter, swaggerer, SWASH BUCKLER, one thats ever vaunting of his owne valour.

1625, JONSON, *Staple of News*, v. 1. I do confess a SWASHING blow.

1636. HEYWOOD, *Love's Mistress*, 25. *Ille ipse*, the same; I desire no more than this sheep-hook in my hand to encounter with that SWASH-BUCKLER.

1637. DAVENANT, *Brit. Triumph.* [NARES.] With courtly knights, not roaring country SWASHES.

1662. FULLER, *Worthies*, 'London.' A ruffian is the same with a swaggerer, so called, because endeavouring to make that side to swag or weigh down whereon he ingageth. The same also with SWASH-BUCKLER, from swashing or making a noise on bucklers.

1677. *Ovid de Arte Amandi*, 141. Or score out husbands in the charcoal ashes, With country knights, nor roaring city SWASHES.

1809. MALKIN, *Gil Blas* [ROUTLEDGE], 143. The lovely Aurora metamorphosed herself in a twinkling, and resumed her SWASHING outside.

SWASH-BUCKET, *subs. phr.* (common).—A slattern.

SWAT, *subs.* (old).—1. A blow. As *subs.* = to strike; to hit.

Verb. (school). — To work hard; TO SWEAT (*q.v.*). [Orig. dialectical.] Also as *subs.* = hard study: spec. (Royal Military Academy) = mathematics.

SWATCHEL, *subs.* Hence (Punch and Judy).—Punch. Hence SWATCHEL (or SCHWASSLE)-BOX = the Punch and Judy show; SWATCHEL-COVE = a Punch and Judy man: spec. the patterer. The other terms connected with this drama of the streets are:—MOZZY = Judy; DARKEY = the negro; VAMPO = the clown; VAMPIRE = the ghost; BUFFER = the dog; BUFFER-FIGURE = the dog's master; CROCODILE = the demon; FILIO = the baby; THE FRAME = the street arrangement; PEEPSIES = the panpipes; NOBBING-SLUM = the bag for collecting money; THE LETTER CLOTH = the advertisement; TAMBOUR = the drum; THE STALK (or PROP) = the gallows; THE SLUM FAKE = the coffin; THE SLUM = the call.

1887. HENLEY, *Villon's Good Night.* You SWATCHEL-COVES that pitch and slam.

SWATTLED, *adj.* (common).—Drunk: *see* Screwed.

SWEAR, *subs.* (colloquial).—An oath; a CUSS (*q.v.*): also SWEAR-WORD. Also (colloquial) TO SWEAR AT (said of anything incongruous): *e.g.* 'His frock coat SWORE at his bowler-hat; TO SWEAR LIKE A LORD (TROOPER, etc.) = to volley oaths, TO MAKE THE AIR BLUE (*q.v.*); TO SWEAR THROUGH A NINE INCH PLANK (nautical) = to back up any lie (C. RUSSELL: 'a favourite expression of Lord Nelson when referring to American skippers').

1531. ELYOT, *Governour* (1834), 87. He that sweareth deep, SWEARETH LIKE A LORD.

1651. CARTWRIGHT, *Ordinary* [DODSLEY, *Old Plays* (REED), x. 295]. Gull'd by my SWEAR; by my SWEAR, gull'd. *Ibid.* I lose the taking, by my SWEAR, of taking As much, whiles that I am receiving this.

1672. RAY, *Proverbs*, 'He'll SWEAR through a nine inch board, a dagger out of sheath, the devil out of hell, 'till he's black in the face.'

1756. FOOTE, *Eng. Returned from Paris.* [To] SWEAR LIKE A TROOPER.

18[?]. *Elect. Review* (Amer.). [*Century.*] There has been in the past an immense quantity of scolding, occasionally a SWEAR WORD.

1887. *St. James's Gaz.*, 4 June. It is a dreadful thing to say, but I felt that if I didn't utter a big SWEAR at that moment something would happen.

1889. *Harper's Mag.*, lxxviii. 258. What is new in it . . . may SWEAR AT the old furniture and the delightful old portraits.

SWEAT, *verb.* (once literary; now colloquial).—1. To work hard; to drudge; to put in LICKS (*q.v.*); also TO SWEAT ONE'S GUTS OUT. *Cf.* modern (public school) SWAT (or SWOT) = fagging, hard study, especially mathematics, whence SWOT also = a mathematician; and as *verb*, to fag, or study hard (see quot. 1864).

1551. ROBYNSON, *More's Utopia*, ii. II. Watching, waiting, and SWEATING; hoping shortly to obtain it.

1597. SHAKSPEARE, *Richard III.*, v. 3. 255. If you do SWEAT to put a tyrant down, You sleep in peace the tyrant being slain.

1612. CHAPMAN, *Widow's Tears*, v. 5. Come, brother, thank the Countess; She hath SWEAT to make your peace.

1622. FLETCHER, *Spanish Curate*, iii. 3. I could out-plead An advocate, and SWEAT as much as he Does for a double fee.

d. 1667. COWLEY, *Tree of Knowledge*, 4. Henceforth, said God, the wretched Sons of Earth Shall SWEAT for Food in vain.

1864. HOTTEN, *Slang Dict.*, s.v. SWOT. This word originated at the Royal Military College, Sandhurst, in the broad Scotch pronunciation of Dr. Wallace, one of the Professors, of the word 'SWEAT.'

1881. PASCOE, *Everyday Life in Our Public Schools.* So much for work or SWOT, as the Harrovian, in common with other boys, somewhat inelegantly terms the more important part of instruction he receives at school.

1900. KIPLING, *Stalky and Co.*, 135. Fags bully each other horrid; but the upper forms are supposed to be SWOTTIN' for exams.

2. (common).—To suffer; to pay the penalty. Also (*trans.*) to beat; to pay out.

1610. BEAUMONT and FLETCHER, *Coxcomb*, v. 1. Well, Jarvis, thou hadst wrongs, and, if I live, Some of the best shall SWEAT for't.

3. (old).—*See* quots.

1712. STEELE, *Spectator*, 332. These SWEATERS . . . seem to me to have at present but a rough kind of discipline among them.

c. 1780. *Ireland Sixty Years Ago*, (1847), 13. Others were known by the sobriquet of 'SWEATERS and Pinkindindies.' It was their practice to cut off a small portion of the scabbards of the swords which every one then wore, and prick, or 'pink' the persons with whom they quarrelled with the naked points, which were sufficiently protruded to inflict considerable pain, but not sufficient to cause death.

1823. GROSE, *Vulg. Tongue* (3rd ed.), s.v. SWEATING. A diversion practised by the bloods of the last century, who styled themselves Mohocks: these gentlemen lay in wait to surprise some person late in the night, when surrounding him, they with their swords pricked him in the posteriors, which obliged him to be constantly turning round: this they continued till they thought him sufficiently SWEATED.

4. (common).—To extort, lose, or squander money freely; TO FLEECE (*q.v*). ; TO BLEED (*q.v.*): *see* quot. 1784. Also TO SWEAT ONE'S PURSE = to cause one to spend everything.

1784. *Ireland Sixty Years Ago*, (1847), 14. They determined to amuse themselves by SWEATING him, *i.e.*, making him give up all his fire-arms.

5. (common).—To work for (or employ labour at) starvation wages; to submit to extortion (or to extort). Hence SWEATER = an employer of underpaid labour: usually a middleman between the actual employer and employed; a grinding taskmaster. Whence SWEATING - SYSTEM, SWEATER, SWEATED, etc.

1850. C. KINGSLEY, *Cheap Clothes and Nasty.* At the honourable shops the master deals directly with his workmen; while at the dishonourable ones, the work is let out to contractors or middle-men—

'SWEATERS,' as their victims significantly call them—who, in their turn, let it out again, sometimes to the workmen, sometimes to fresh middle-men, so that out of the price paid for labour on each article, not only the woikmen, but the SWEATER, and perhaps the SWEATER'S SWEATER, and a third, and a fourth, and a fifth, have to draw their profit.

1851-61. MAYHEW, *Lond. Lab.*, I. 64. I have many a time heard both husband and wife—one couple especially who were SWEATING for a gorgeous clothes emporium—say that they had not time to be clean.

1882. *Contemp. Review*, lvi. 880. It is possible that several of the minor industries of the East End are absolutely dependent upon the fact that a low type of SWEATED and overworked labour is employed at starvation wages.

1883. *Pall Mall Gaz.*, 29 Oct. SWEATERS' hacks turning out frockcoats.

1886. *Echo*, 1 Dec. Recently a trade journal published a list of SWEATING firms in the clothing trade, each of which probably has grounds of action.

1887. *Nineteenth Century*, xxii. 489. They declared that they were being SWEATED, that the hunger for work induced men to accept starvation rates.

6. (old).—To pawn.

c. 1811. MAHER, *The Night Before Larry was Stretched*. A bit in their sacks, too, they fetched; They SWEATED their duds till they riz it.

PHRASES.—IN A SWEAT=(1) in a hurry, and (2) in a state of terror, impatient; TO SWEAT COINS=to remove part of the metal from coins (chiefly gold) by friction or acids, yet in such a manner that the depreciation is imperceptible.

1785. GROSE, *Vulg. Tongue*, s.v. SWEATING. A mode of diminishing the gold coin, practised chiefly by the Jews, who corrode it with aqua regia.

1796. WOLCOT, *Peter Pindar*, 109. His each vile sixpence that the world hath cheated, And his art that every guinea SWEATED.

1875. JEVONS, *Money and Mech. of Exch.*, 115. No one now actually refuses any gold money in retail business, so that the SWEATER, if he exists at all, has all the opportunities he can desire.

18[?]. THOR FREDUR, *Sketches from Shady Places* [S. J. and C.]. By far the most scientific form of smashing is that which is called SWEATING—the modern equivalent for the ruder art of 'clipping,' so fully described in Macaulay's History. Here the galvanic battery is brought into requisition, the metal being dissolved equally from all the surfaces of the coin operated upon, and that, too, without impairing the sharpness of 'image or superscription.' Sufficient metal for the SWEATER'S purpose being removed, the coin is polished afresh.

SWEAT-BOX, *subs. phr.* The cell used for prisoners while awaiting appearance before a magistrate.

SWEATER, *subs.* (Winchester).—1. A servant. Hence SWEAT-GALLERY=fagging juniors. *See* SWEAT and SWOT.

2. (athletic).—A thick coat (or flannel jersey) worn by contestants after a finish until they can be rubbed down.

3. (Stock Exchange). — *See* quot.

1871. ATKIN, *House Scraps* [SWEATER]. A broker who works for such small commissions as to prevent other brokers getting the business, whilst hardly being profitable to himself.

4. *See* SWEAT in all senses.

SWEAT-PITS, *subs. pl.* (old).—The arm-pits.

c. 1709. WARD, *Terræfilius*, v. 27. By nature she is almost as rank as a Red Herring, yet . . . she so Rectifies the Effluvia that arises from her SWEAT-PITS, that she smells as fragrant as a Perfumer's-Shop next Door to a Tallow-Chandler's.

SWEEP, *subs.* (colloquial).—1. A sweepstakes.

2. (common).—A term of contempt: *e.g.* 'What a SWEEP the man is'; 'You dirty SWEEP.'

TO SWEEP THE BOARD, *verb. phr.* (orig. gaming: now general).—To take everything; to pocket all the stakes. Also TO MAKE A CLEAN SWEEP=TO CLEAN OUT (*q.v.*); to remove entirely. Also SWEEP=at whist, taking all the tricks in the hand; a SLAM (*q.v.*).

1680. COTTON [SINGER, *Hist. Cards* (1816), 346]. He who hath five cards of a suit . . . SWEEPS THE BOARD.

1711. POPE, *Rape of Lock*, iii. 50. Spadillio first . . . Led off two captive trumps, and SWEPT THE BOARD.

1822. SCOTT, *Fort. Nigel*, xxi. 'Tis the sitting gamester SWEEPS THE BOARD.

1868. BLUNT, *Ref. Church England*, 316. The CLEAN SWEEP which had been made of so many ancient rights.

1869. STOWE, *Oldtown*, 163. They [Indians] burnt thirty-two houses in Springfield . . . MADE A CLEAN SWEEP on't.

THE SWEEPS, *subs. phr.* (military).—The Rifle Brigade. [Their facings from formation (1800) have been black.]

SWEEP'S-FRILL, *subs. phr.* (common).—Beard and whiskers worn round the chin, the rest of the face being clean shaven.

1892. *Tit Bits*, 19 March, 421, 2. The SWEEP'S FRILL would, I imagine, have made the Antinous, or the Apollo Belvedere, look undignified and slovenly.

SWEET, *adj.* (old and thieves').—1. Gullible; easily deceived. 2. Expert, dextrous, clever: *e.g.* 'SWEET'S your hand' (said of a clever thief). Hence, TO SWEETEN A VICTIM=to allay his suspicions (GROSE); to decoy, draw in, and bite (B. E. and GROSE): *see* SWEETENER.

SWEETBREAD, *subs.* (old). — A bribe; a TIP (*q.v.*).

1692. HACKET, *Williams*, ii. 163. A few SWEETBREADS that I gave him out of my purse.

SWEETBRIAR, *subs.* (venery).—The female pubic hair: *cf.* GROVE OF EGLANTINE (CAREW). *See* FLEECE.

SWEETEN, *subs.* (Old Cant).—A beggar. Also as *verb*=to give alms (GROSE).

Verb. (cards: espec. poker).—To contribute to the pool. Hence SWEETENING=money paid into the pool or kitty.

1896. LILLARD, *Poker Stories*, 191. Then along came a big jack pot that had been enlarged by repeated SWEETENINGS.

TO SWEETEN AND PINCH, *verb. phr.* (old).—*See* quot.

1678. *Four for a Penny* (Harl. Misc., iv. 147). A main part of his [a bumbailiff's] office is to swear and bluster . . . and cry, 'Confound us, why do we wait? let us shop him'; whilst the other meekly replies, 'Jack, be patient, it is a civil gentleman, and I know will consider us; which species of wheedling, in terms of their art, is called SWEETEN AND PINCH.

SWEETENER, *subs.* (Old Cant).—1. A GUINEA-DROPPER (*q.v.*): [A coin is PLANTED (*q.v.*), and a likely passer-by is offered a share because present at the discovery; to get change, 'drinks' are suggested, and the victim goes out fleeced].—(B. E. and GROSE).

1699. *Country Gentleman's Vade Mecum*, 97. Guinea dropping or SWEETNING is a paultry little cheat that was recommended to the world about thirty years ago by a memorable gentleman that has since had the misfortune to be taken off, I mean hang'd, for a misdemeanour upon the highway.

2. (auctioneers').—A RUNNER-UP (*q.v.*) of prices; a BONNET (*q.v.*).

3. (common). — In *pl.* = the lips. TO FAKE THE SWEETENERS=to kiss.

4. (old).—'One who decoys persons to game' (BAILEY). Also SWEETEN, *verb* (B. E. and GROSE)=to decoy, to draw in.

SWEETHEART, etc., *subs.* (old colloquial and literary).—1. A mistress, *pour le bon motif*; and (2) *see* quots. Also variants: SWEET, SWEETING, SWEETKINS, SWEETLIPS, etc. Also SWEETKIN, *adj.* =delicate, dainty; and SWEET ON=in love with; partial to.

c. 1534. *Milner of Abington* [HAZLITT. *Early Pop Poet.*, iii. 113]. Now, I pray you, my lemman free, A gowne cloath then buie you me . . . By Jesu, he saide, my SWEETING, I have but three shylling.

1552. HULOET, *Abecdarium*, s.v. Darlynge, a wanton terme used in veneriall speach, as be these: honycombe, pyggisnye, SWETEHERT, true love.

1593. NASHE, *Choise of Valentynes*, 89. Sweete heart, . . ., but thy self, true lover I haue none . . . With that she wanton faints, and falle's vpon hir bedd.

c. 1696. B. E., *Dict. Cant. Crew* . . . TO BE SWEET ON, cant, to coakse, wheedle, entice or allure.

1785. GROSE, *Vulg. Tongue*, s.v. SWEET-HEART . . . a girl's lover or a man's mistress. *Ibid.* s.v. SWEETNERS . . . TO BE SWEET UPON; to coax, wheedle, court or allure. He seemed SWEET UPON that wench; he seemed to court that girl.

1823. BEE, *Dict. Turf*, s.v. SWEET (TO BE)—to talk kind, conciliating to the other sex.

1865. DICKENS, *Mutual Friend*, iv. 15. Missis is SWEET enough ON you, Master, to sell herself up, slap, to get you out of trouble.

1895. OPPENHEIM, *Peer and the Woman*, II. ii. I don't know that we should have stopped so long, only Brown's rather SWEET ON the place.

SWEETHEART AND BAG-PUDDING! *phr.* (old: RAY).—Said of a girl got with child.

1608. DAY, *Humour out of Breath*, ii. 1. Farewell, SWEET HEART.—God a mercy, BAG-PUDDING.

SWEETIES, *subs. pl.* (common).—Sweetmeats: also SWEET-STUFF.

d. 1758. RAMSAY, *Poems*, II. 547. SWEETIES to bestow on lasses.

1851-61. MAYHEW, *Lond. Lab.*, I. 216. The SWEET-STUFF maker (I never heard them called confectioners) bought his 'paper' at the stationer's, or the old book-shops.

1863. THACKERAY, *Roundabout Papers*, x. Instead of finding bonbons or SWEETIES in the packets which we pluck off the boughs, we find enclosed Mr. Carnifex's review of the quarter's meat.

SWEET-LIPS, *subs. phr.* (common).—1. An epicure; a glutton.

2. *See* SWEETHEART.

SWEET-MEAT, *subs. phr.* (venery).—1. The *penis*: *see* PRICK. Also (2) a kept mistress of tender years.

SWEET MEAT MUST HAVE SOUR SAUCE, *phr.* (old).—*See* quot. It. *Se à mangiate le candele ora caga gli stoppini.*

1726. BAILEY, *Eng. Dict.* s.v. SWEET . . . AFTER SWEET MEAT COMES SOUR SAUCE . . . an excellent monition to temperance and sobriety.

SWEET-PEA, *subs.* (women's). — Urination: spec. in the open air. Hence, TO PLANT (or DO) A SWEET PEA=TO PISS (*q.v.*): *cf.* TO PLUCK A ROSE. Also in Conundrums: 'What's the sweetest flower in the nursery?' or 'What flower does a woman like after a long walk?' *Ans.* A sweet-pea.

SWEET-SCENTED HOLE, *subs. phr.* (venery). — The female *pudendum*: *see* MONOSYLLABLE.

1690. MOTTEUX, *Rabelais*, v. xxx. With his nervous horn he removed all the infection that might be lurking in some blind cranny of the . . . SWEET-SCENTED HOLE.

SWEET-TOOTH, *subs. phr.* (colloquial).—A liking for sweet things or sweetmeats.

SWELL, *subs.* (old).—1. *See* quots. 1785 and 1890. Hence, as *adj.* (also SWELLISH) = (1) elegant, stylish, dandified; and (2) first-rate, TIP-TOP (*q.v.*). Also derivatives and combinations such as SWELLDOM = the world of fashion; TO LIVE IN SWELL-STREET=to reside in the West End; A SWELL HUNG IN CHAINS =a bejewelled man or woman; A HOWLING SWELL (*see* HOWLING); SWELL-HEAD (or BLOCK) =a vain coxcomb (Amer.).

1785. GROSE, *Vulg. Tongue*, s.v. SWELL, a gentleman; but any well-dressed person is emphatically termed a SWELL, or a RANK SWELL. A family man who appears to have plenty of money, and makes a genteel figure, is said by his associates to be in SWELL STREET. Any thing remarkable for its beauty or elegance, is called a SWELL article; so a SWELL crib is a genteel house; a SWELL mollisher, an elegantly-dressed woman, etc. Sometimes, in alluding to a particular gentleman, whose name is not requisite, he is styled, THE SWELL, meaning the person who is the object of your discourse, or attention; and whether he is called THE SWELL, the cove, or the gory, is immaterial, as in the following (in addition to many other) examples:—I was turned up at China-street, because THE SWELL would not appear; meaning, of course, the prosecutor: again, speaking of a person whom you were on the point of robbing, but who has taken the alarm, and is therefore on his guard, you will say to your pall, It's of no use, the cove is as down as a hammer; or, We may as well stow it, the gory's leary.

1811. *Lexicon Balatronicum*, s.v. CADGE the SWELLS, beg of the gentlemen.

1819. MOORE, *Tom Crib's Memorial*. . . . What madness could impel So rum a flat to face so prime a SWELL.

1823. BEE, *Dict. Turf*, s.v. NOB. A . . . nob . . . differs from SWELL, inasmuch as the latter makes a show of his finery; whereas the nob, relying upon intrinsic worth, or bonâ-fide property, or intellectual ability, is clad in plainness.

1823. BYRON, *Don Juan*, xi. 17. Poor Tom was once a kiddy upon town, A thorough varmint and a real SWELL. *Ibid.*, xi. 19. So prime, so SWELL, so nutty, and so knowing.

1835. HOOK, *Gilbert Gurney*, III. ii. At the ball, my eldest girl danced with the Secretary of State for Foreign Affairs, and found him very chatty, though a bit of a SWELL.

1840-45. BARHAM, *Ingoldsby Legends* (1862), 70. No! no!—The Abbey may do very well For a feudal nob, or poetical 'SWELL.'

1851-61. MAYHEW, *Lond. Lab.*, I. 341. Not one SWELL in a score would view it in any light than a ream concern.

1854. THACKERAY [*Leech's Pictures* in *Quarterly Review*, No. 191]. Corinthian, it appears, was the phrase applied to men of fashion and ton . . . they were the brilliant predecessors of the SWELL of the present period. *Ibid.* (1855), *Newcomes*, xliii. This isn't the moment, when all SWELLDOM is at her feet, for me to come forward. *Ibid.* (1862), *Philip*, xxiii. The lady in the SWELL carriage, the mother of the young SWELL with the flower in his buttonhole.

c. 1864. VANCE, *Chickaleary Cove*. My tailor serves you well, from a perger to a SWELL.

1877. *Five Years' Penal Servitude*, iii. 244. It was the SWELL'S russia—a russia, you know, is a pocket-book.

1888. RUNCIMAN, *Chequers*, 38. She's a screamer, she's a real SWELL.

1890. T. R. OLIPHANT, *Eton College*. It is very hard to define exactly what is meant by a SWELL at Eton; but it usually implies a boy who, brought into notice either by athletic prowess or scholarship, or high standing in the school, by this means becomes acquainted with the leading members of the school, and is found on acquaintance to develop considerable social qualities, which make him hand and glove with all the Eton magnates.

1897. MARSHALL, *Pomes*, 41. The merest fool could tell that the lady was a SWELL.

1900. BOOTHBY, *Maker of Nations*, ix. I'm no end of a SWELL at politics.

2. (Winchester).—In *pl.* = Sunday Services; Saints' days, etc.: when surplices are worn.

Verb (Winchester).—To bathe; 'to swill.'

SWELL-HEAD, *subs. phr.* (common).—1. A drunken man: *see* LUSHINGTON.

2. *See* SWELL and SWOLLEN HEAD.

SWELL-MOBSMAN, *subs. phr.* (common).—A well-dressed pick-pocket. Hence SWELL-MOB.

1843. *Punch*, iv. 129. Rich Charities the Chapel throng, The SWELL MOB they are there, The Bishop's sermon is not long, The fogle-hunter ware!

1851-61. MAYHEW, *Lond. Lab.*, II. 417. SWELL-MOBSMEN, and thieves, and housebreakers, and the like o' that ere.

1856. *Quarterly Rev.*, June, 182. The SWELL MOBSMAN'S eye is for ever wandering in search of his prey.

c. 1860. DICKENS, *Three Detective Anecdotes*, ii. Some of the SWELL MOB . . . kidded us.

1866. HOTTEN, *Slang Dict.*, s.v. Public patterers, SWELL MOBSMEN who pretend to be Dissenting preachers, and harangue in the open air to attract a crowd for their confederates to rob.

SWELLED-NOSE, *subs. phr.* (old).—Ill temper. 'DOES YOUR NOSE SWELL (or ITCH) at that?' = 'Are you riled?'

SWELL-NOSE, *subs. phr.* (old).—Strong ale; STINGO (*q.v.*).

1515. *De Generibus Ebriosorum*, etc. [HODGKIN, *Notes and Queries*, 3 S. vii. 163. In this treatise occurs names of fancy drinks . . . I select a few of the most presentable] slip-slop . . . raise-head . . . SWELL-NOSE.

S'WELP, *intj.* (common).—'So help': usually in the adjurations, 'S'WELP ME BOB,' or 'S'WELP MY TATERS' (BOB, GREENS, etc.).

1837. BARHAM, *Ingolds. Leg.* (*Dead Drummer*). For his jaw-work would never, I'm sure, S'ELP ME BOB, Have come for to go for to do sich a job!

c. 1850. *Old Rhyme.* S'ELP ME BOB, My mother's a snob, My father takes in washin'.

1851-61. MAYHEW, *Lond. Lab.*, iii. 144. They'll say, too, S'ELP MY GREENS! and 'Upon my word and say so.'

1880. JAS. PAYN, *Confid. Agent*, xix. 'Not another word will I say, S'HELP ME BOB.'

1888. RUNCIMAN, *Chequers*, 86. I'll pay it back, S'ELP ME GORD.

1891. *Lic. Vict. Gaz.*, 13 Jan. Well, S'ELP ME GREENS . . . if you ar'n't the greatest treat I ever did meet.

1891. CHEVALIER, *Mrs 'Enery 'Awkins.* SELP ME BOB, I'm crazy, Liza, you're a daisy.

1893. EMERSON, *Signor Lippo*, xiv. So HELP MY BLESSED TATER if this isn't our old Jose.

1897. MARSHALL, *Pomes*, 30. If I wasn't sich a lidy, S'ELP ME BOB, I'd give the bloomin' magistrate a job.

1899. WHITEING, *John St.*, vi. SWELP ME LUCKY, I ain't tellin yer no lie.

SWIFT, *subs.* (printers').—A quick-working compositor (SAVAGE, 1841, *Dict.*).

SWIG, *subs.* (colloquial).—A deep draught: also as *verb* = to drink heartily. (B. E. and GROSE); TO PULL hard (*q.v.*) Hence SWIGGED = drunk: *see* SCREWED.

1623. MABBE, *Spanish Rogue*, (1630), ii. 208. [OLIPHANT, *New Eng.*, ii. 82. Bale's swink (bibere) becomes SWIGGE.]

1627. MIDDLETON and ROWLEY, *Changeling*, iv. 2. But one SWIG more, sweet madam.

c. 1650. *Roxburgh Ballads* [Brit. Mus., C. 20, f. 8. 236], 'Jolly Welsh Woman.' Now while she had gotten the jugg at her snout, . . . Hur gave it a tug, till hur SWIGG'D it half out.

c. 1670. *Old English Ballads* [Brit. Mus., C. 22, e. 2. 43]. 'Dead and Alive.' He never left off SWIGGING, Till he had suckt all out.

d. 1701. CREECH, *Virgil*, 'Eclogues,' iii. The flock is drained, the lambkins SWIG the teat, But find no moisture, and then idly bleat.

1706. WARD, *Wooden World*, 38. Not but that he can fight, and that very heartily too, after a lusty SWIG at the Brandy.

1772. BRIDGES, *Burlesque Homer*, 246. When my landlord does not nick me . . . But very fairly fills it full, I just can SWIGG it at one pull.

1819. MOORE, *Tom Crib*, 39. The Hero that sits there, SWIGGING blue ruin in that chair.

1835. MARRYAT, *Pacha Many Tales*, 'English Sailor.' The sailor having taken a SWIG at the bottle.

1838. BECKETT, *Paradise Lost*, 19. Half-cocked with SWIGGING ale and beer.

1851. HAWTHORNE, *Seven Gables*, xi. The jolly toper SWIGGED lustily at his bottle.

1885. *Harper's Mag.*, lxxi. 192. Take a little lunch . . . and a SWIG of whiskey and water.

1899. WHITEING, *John St.*, xi. I buy a ha'porth of bread, take a SWIG at a fountain, and tramp the East End parks to kill time.

SWIGMAN, *subs.* (Old Cant).—*See* quots. (AWDELEY, HARMAN, DEKKER, B. E., and GROSE).

1567. AWDELEY, *Frat. of Vacabondes*, 5. A SWYGMAN goeth with a pedlers pack.

c. 1696. B. E., *Dict. Cant. Crew*, s.v. SWIG-MEN, c. the 13th Rank of the Canting Crew, carrying small Habberdashery-Wares about, pretending to sell them to colour their Roguery.

SWILL, *verb.* (old colloquial: now vulgar).—To drink (and, occasionally, to eat) piggishly: hence as *subs.* = BOOZE (*q.v.*), the lap, or the act: in contempt. SWILL-BOWL (SWILLER, SWILL-POT, SWILL-TUB, or SWILL-BELLY) = a heavy toper (or glutton); SWILLED = drunk: *see* SCREWED (B. E. and GROSE).

1530. *Jyl of Brentford's Testament* [FURNIVALL], 7. [OLIPHANT, *New Eng.*, i. 466. The verb SWYLL takes a new meaning, that of bibere.]

1542. UDAL, *Erasmus's Apophth.*, 367. Lucious Cotta . . . was taken for the greatest SWIELBOLLE of wine in the woorlde.

d. 1563. BALE [*Works* (Parker Soc.), 193]. Their oiled SWILL-BOWLS and blind Balaamites.

1580. BARET, *Alvearie.* SWILBOLLES, *potores bibuli.*

1593. HARVEY, *Pierce's Supererogation*, ii. 141. Wantonness was never such a SWILLBOWL of ribaldry.

1597. SHAKSPEARE, *Richard III.*, v. 2. 9. The . . . usurping boar . . . SWILLS your warm blood like wash.

1616. R. C., *Times Whistle* [E. E. T. S.], 20. They which on this day doe drink and SWILL In such lewd fashion.

1652. BROME, *Jovial Crew*, II. As Tom or Tib When they at bowsing ken do SWILL.

1653. URQUHART, *Rabelais*, I. xxxiii. What doth that part of our army in the meantime which overthrows that unworthy SWILL-POT Grangousier?

1725. BAILEY, *Erasmus*, 198. The husband, instead of my dear soul, has been called blockhead, toss-pot, SWILL-TUB, and the wife sow, fool, dirty drab.

1775. SHERIDAN, *Duenna*, iii. 5. Ye eat, and SWILL, and sleep, and gormandize, and thrive.

1808. SCOTT, *Marmion*, i. 22. Let Friar John, in safety, still . . . Roast hissing crabs, or flagons SWILL.

1866. ELIOT, *Felix Holt*, xi. SWILLING themselves with ale.

1899. WYNDHAM, *Queen's Service*, xxxvi. He was SWILLING beer in the canteen as if he had never done anything else in his life.

SWIM, *subs.* (common).—One's particular pursuits, PITCH (*q.v.*), or fancy. Hence in a good (or bad) SWIM = lucky (or unlucky).

1883. GREENWOOD, *In Strange Company.* Amongst themselves they are skinners, knock-outs, odd-trick men, and they work together in what . . . their profession calls a 'SWIM.'

1900. *Free Lance*, 6 Oct., 16. 1. *Lady Dashout.* 'The pity of it is that we can't always keep the SWIM to ourselves. The rich third-raters will dive in, make the waters muddy, and copy our frocks. I should like to make my own SWIM!'

IN THE SWIM, *phr.* (common).—Participant in the times. Hence (2) = in the 'inner circle' or THE KNOW (*q.v.*); (3) = associated in any undertaking; and spec. (4) = a long time out of the hands of the police (thieves'). Fr. *dans le mouvement* (or *le train*).

1869. *Macm. Mag.*, Nov., 71. 2. A man is said to be IN THE SWIM when any piece of good fortune has happened, or seems likely to happen, to him. To have rowed one's college-boat to the head of the river, to have received a legacy, to have made a good book on the Derby, are any of them sufficient to have put one IN THE SWIM. The metaphor is piscatorial, 'SWIM' being the term applied by Thames fishermen to those sections of the river which are especially frequented by fish. The angler who casts his bait into these may depend upon sport, whereas his neighbour at a little distance may not have a nibble, being OUT OF THE SWIM.

1874. *Siliad*, 30. 'He's IN THE SWIM,' another Swift replies: 'Hot wather, thin, he loiks,' Obroian cries.

1889. *Harper's Mag.*, lxxviii. 313. His neighbourhood is getting INTO THE SWIM of the real-estate movement.

1897. OUIDA, *Massarenes*, 24. Never remind me of anything I said. I can't endure it: I believe you want to get IN THE SWIM.

1900. *Free Lance*, 6 Oct., 16. 1. *Hon. Mrs. Worldley.* 'Sounds distinctly appetising. Well, wherever *I* go, I want to be IN THE SWIM.'

TO SWIM IN GOLDEN GREASE (OIL, LARD, etc.), *verb. phr.* (old).—To 'roll' in bribes: *see* GREASE.

1605. JONSON, *Fox*, i. 1. When you do come to SWIM IN GOLDEN LARD.

TO MAKE A MAN SWIM FOR IT, *verb. phr.* (thieves').—To cheat a pal out of his share of booty.

HOW WE APPLES SWIM, QUOTH THE HORSE-TURD (RAY). *See* APPLES.

SWIMMER, *subs.* (Old Cant).—1. 'A Counterfeit (old) Coyn' (B. E. and GROSE).

2. (old).—*See* quot. (also TO HAVE A SWIMMER).

1785. GROSE, *Vulg. Tongue*, s.v. SWIMMER, a guard-ship, or tender; a thief who escapes prosecution, when before a magistrate, on condition of being sent on board the receiving-ship, to serve His Majesty, is said by his palls to be SWIMMERED.

SWIMMING, *adj.* (common).—Generic for plenty: thus a SWIMMING (= a full or brisk) MARKET: *cf.* SICK; a SWIMMING (= an overfull) DISH; a SWIMMING (= an extremely pleasant) TIME, etc. Hence SWIMMINGLY = successfully, prosperously.

1622. FLETCHER, *Prophetess*, i. 3. *Max.* Can such a rascal as thou hope for honour? . . . *Geta.* Yes; and bear it too, And bear it SWIMMINGLY.

1774. BRIDGES, *Burlesque Homer*, 180. Thus SWIMMINGLY the knave went on, And killed two birds with every stone.

1809. IRVING, *Knickerbocker*, 233. And now, for a time, affairs went on SWIMMINGLY.

1809. MALKIN, *Gil Blas* [ROUTLEDGE], 441. Your business is going SWIMMINGLY.

SWINDLE, *subs.* (common).—1. Originally (and properly) a fraud or imposition (in which sense *see* SWINDLER). Also 2 (loosely *and* frequently), any speculation or matter of chance: *e.g.*, a lottery, a toss for drinks, a sweepstakes, a race, etc.; also (more loosely still) any transaction in which money passes: *e.g.* 'What's the SWINDLE' = 'What's to pay (or the damage)?'

'Why don't you pay the girl her SWINDLE?' = 'Why don't you give the girl her price?' SWINDLER (*q.v.*) is quite another matter, and all quots. for it, for *subs.* 1, and the *verbal* sense are there given for the sake of distinction.

1870. *Legal Reports*, 'Decision of PIGOTT, J.' As to the second plea that SWINDLE had not a libellous meaning, this was in a great measure carried out by the plaintiff himself, who had advertised that he was getting up a SWINDLE. In sporting circles they certainly did deal with an extraordinary vocabulary, and apparently did not use this word SWINDLE in Dr. Johnson's sense. *Ibid.* 'Evidence in Davey *v.* Walmsley.' Mr. Hawkins—'Is the word SWINDLE commonly applied to things like "specs."?' Witness (Mr. Paul Walmsley, Editor, *Racing Investigator*)—'Certainly! I never heard them called by any other name. It is a regular byword with us as a racing phrase. Lotteries are announced and commonly known as SWINDLES.'

SWINDLER, *subs.* (old).—A cheat; a rogue: spec. one who employs petty or mean artifices, legal or illegal, for defrauding others. Hence SWINDLE, *subs.* = a fraud, a deception, an imposition; and SWINDLE, *verb* = to cheat, to defraud. Whence, also, derivatives such as SWINDLEABLE, SWINDLERY, SWINDLING, etc. [Orig. used of German Jews who settled in London, *circa* 1762. Also by soldiers in the Seven Years' War.]—GROSE and BEE.

1776. FOOTE, *Capuchin*, ii. After that you turned SWINDLER, and got out of gaol by an act for the relief of insolvent debtors.

1785. GROSE, *Vulg. Tongue*, s.v. SWINDLER . . . used to signify Cheats of every kind.

1785-6. VARENNE, [CARLYLE, *Diamond Necklace*, xvi., quoted in note 9]. 'Lamotte . . . under pretext of finding a treasure . . . had SWINDLED one of them out of 300 livres.'

1837. CARLYLE, *French Revol.*, II. vi. SWINDLERY and blackguardism.

1849. MACAULAY, *Hist. Eng.*, ii. Bedloe, a noted SWINDLER, followed.

1866. HOWELLS, *Venetian Life*, i. Let us take, for example, that pathetic SWINDLE, the Bridge of Sighs.

d. 1876. M. COLLINS, *Thoughts in my Garden*, i. 283. I look easily SWINDLEABLE.

1882. WEDGWOOD, *Eng. Etym.*, s.v. Swindle. In a figurative sense the German *schwindel* is applied to dealings in which the parties seem to have lost their head, as we say, to have become dizzy over unfounded or unreasonable prospects of gain. The word may be translated madness, delusion. Then, in a factitive sense, schwindeler, one who induces delusions in others. '*Einem etwas abschwindeln*,' to get something out of another by inducing delusions; to SWINDLE him out of something.

SWINE, *subs.* (common).—A term of the utmost contempt. Hence SWINISH (B. E.) = 'greedy, gluttonous, covetous.'

1597. SHAKSPEARE, *Richard III.*, v. 2. 10. This foul SWINE Lies . . . Near to the town of Leicester. [The boar was Richard's cognisance.]

1889. *Lic. Vict. Gaz.*, 4 Jan. 'Aint that the SWINE of a snob that rushed me at Battersea?

1899. WHITEING, *John St.*, ix. 'Git out, yer silly SWINE,' is the maiden's reply.

1903. KENNEDY, *Sailor Tramp*, II. iii. Sailor, it looks as if we were done for . . . That SWINE'LL surely make us get off.

PHRASES and PROVERBIAL SAYINGS. 'Like a SWINE, never good until he come to the knife' (of a covetous person); TO SING LIKE A BIRD CALLED A SWINE = to grunt (RAY); TO CAST PEARLS BEFORE SWINE (of unappreciated action or effort).

SWINE-DRUNK, *adj. phr.* (old).—Beastly drunk: *see* SCREWED.

1592. NASHE, *Works* [GROSART, ii. 82]. Ape drunke . . . Lion drunke . . . SWINE DRUNKE . . . Sheepe drunke. . . .

1598. SHAKSPEARE, *All's Well*, iv. 3. 286. Drunkenness is his best virtue, for he will be SWINE-DRUNK.

SWING, *subs.* (colloquial).—Bent; a free 'hand' or course: *e.g.* TO HAVE (or TAKE) ONE'S SWING (or FULL SWING)=to do as one likes. Also TO SWING (a matter) OVER ONE'S HEAD, SHOULDERS, etc.=to manage easily; TO SWING A BUSINESS (MARKET, PRICES, etc.)=to control; to manage.

1530. TYNDALE, *Works* [Parker Soc.], i. 530. The sect [of heretics] goeth now in her FULL SWING. *Ibid.*, ii. 219. The devil hath a great SWING among us.

1542. HALL, *Henry VIII.*, f. 5. And there for a certayne space loytred and lurked with Sir Thomas Broughton knyght, whiche in those quarters bare great SWYNGE, and was there in great auctoritie.

1592. HARVEY, *Four Letters*. Let them have their SWING that affect to be terribly singular.

1610. SACKVILLE, *Ind. Mirr. Mag.*, 260. That whilom here bare SWINGE AMONG the best.

1620. FLETCHER, *Little Fr. Lawyer*, ii. 3. Take your whole SWING of anger; I'll bear all with content.

1622. DENT, *Pathway*, 58. If they will needs follow their lustes, their pleasures, and their owne SWINGE, yet in the end, he will bring them to judgement.

1698. FARQUHAR, *Love and a Bottle*, ii. 3. The fellow will have his SWING though he hang for't.

1805. GODWIN, *Fleetwood*, vii. To thrust the world aside and take his SWING of indulgence.

1809. MALKIN, *Gil Blas* [ROUTLEDGE], 267. It was my full determination . . . to take my SWING about town, and look at men and manners a little.

1837. LYTTON, *Maltravers*, IV. ix. Your time is up . . . you have had your SWING.

1877–85. DIXON, *Hist. Ch. of England*, ii. Sacrilege was in full SWING.

1881. J. C. SHAIRP, *Aspects of Poetry*, 132. In the great chorus of song with which England greeted the dawn of this century individuality had FULL SWING.

Verb. (common). — 1. To hang; *see* LADDER. Hence, THE SWING=the gallows: *see* NUBBING CHEAT (GROSE).

1542. UDALL, *Erasmus* [OLIPHANT, *New Eng.*, i. 486.] 'Among the verbs are to gossip . . . SWING in a halter, take his heels,' etc.

1801. *Poetry of Anti-Jacobin* (4th ed.), 7. For this act Did Brownrigg SWING. Harsh laws! But time shall come When France shall reign, and laws be all repeal'd.

1836. DICKENS, *Boz*. 'Drunkard's Death.' If I'm caught, I shall SWING; that's certain.

1837. BARHAM, *Ingolds. Leg.*, i. 229. And now they tried the deed to hide; For a little bird whispered, 'Perchance, you may SWING.' *Ibid*. 'The Execution.' But to see a man SWING At the end of a string, With his neck in a noose, will be quite a new thing.

1887. HENLEY and STEVENSON, *Deacon Brodie*, iv. And is he thundering well corpsed? . . . Then, damme, I don't mind SWINGING.

TO SWING THE MONKEY, *verb. phr.* (nautical).—*See* quot.

1883. CLARK RUSSELL, *Sailor's Language*, s.v. SWING THE MONKEY . . . striking with knotted handkerchiefs a man who swings to a rope made fast aloft. The person the 'monkey' strikes whilst swinging takes his place.

SWINGE, *verb.* (old literary).—1. To beat; to thrash; to chastise; to punish (B. E. and GROSE). Hence (Charterhouse) SWINGER (*q.v.*) = a box on the ears. SWINGEING = a thrashing; SWINGE-BUCKLER (*see* SWASH).

c. 1280. *Havelok the Dane* [SKEAT, E.E.T.S. (1868), 214]. An ofte dede him sore SWINGE, And wit hondes smerte dinge; So that the blood ran of his fleys, That tendre was, and swithe neys.

1579. *Mariage of Witt and Wisdome*. O, the passion of God! so I shalbe SWINGED; So, my bones shalbe bang'd! The poredge pot is stolne: what, Lob, I say, Come away, and be hanged!

D

1590. SPENSER, *Fairy Queene*, I. xi. 26. The scorching flame sore SWINGED all his face.

1595. SHAKSPEARE, *Two Gentlemen* ii. 1. 87. I was in love with my bed: I thank you, you SWINGED me for my love. *Ibid.* (1596), *King John*, ii. 1. 288. Saint George that SWINGED the dragon. *Ibid.* (1598), 2 *Hen. IV.*, v. 4. I will have you . . . soundly SWINGED for this . . . if you be not SWINGED I'll forswear half kirtles.

1599. GREENE, *George a Greene*. Once he SWING'D me till my bones did ake.

1607. *Devil's Charter* [STEEVENS]. When I was a scholar in Padua, faith, then I could have SWINGED A SWORD AND BUCKLER.

1611. COTGRAVE, *Dict.*, s.v. *Dober*. To beat, SWINGE, lamme, bethwacke.

1614. FLETCHER, *Wit Without Money*, iv. 5. Be not too bold; for, if you be, I'll SWINGE you, I'll SWINGE you monstrously, without all pity.

1621. SYLVESTER, *Du Bartas* [NARES]. Then often SWINDGING, with his sinnewy train, Somtimes his sides, somtimes the dusty plain.

1637. DAVENANT, *Brit. Triumphans*, [*Dram. Rest.*, DAVENANT, ii. 282]. In Gaul he SWINGED the valiant Sir Amadis.

1663. BUTLER, *Hudibras*. Whether it be direct infrynging An oath if I should waive this SWINGING.

1709. SWIFT, *Stella*, xxxix. Walpole, late secretary of war, is to be SWINGED for bribery.

1763. FOOTE, *Mayor of Garratt*, i. I would . . . SWINGE and leather my lambkin.

2. (venery).—To copulate: *see* RIDE. Hence SWINGER=a PERFORMER (*q.v.*).

153[?]. LYNDSAY, *Descriptioun* [LAING, I. 156, 17]. Ane SWYNGEOUR coffe amangis the wyvis.

1622. FLETCHER, *Beggar's Bush*, iii. 1. Give her cold jelly To take up her belly, And once a day SWINGE her again.

1668. DRYDEN, *Enemy's Love*, v. And that baggage, Beatrix, how I would SWINGE her if I had her here.

SWINGED OFF, *adv. phr.* (old).—*See* quot.

c. 1696. B. E., *Dict. Cant. Crew*, s.v. SWINGING. . . . He is SWING'D OFF, damnably Clapt.

SWINGING (SWINDGING or SWINGEING), *adj.* (old).—Huge, astonishing: generic for size: anything that beats all else: *see* SWINGE, *verb*. Hence SWINGER =anything of size; a WHOPPER (*q.v.*). Spec. an unblushing falsehood.

1623. MABBE, *Spanish Rogue* (1630), ii. 144. A SWINGING pastie.

1624. FLETCHER, *Rule a Wife*, iv. 3. A SWINGING storm will sing you such a lullaby.

1648. HERRICK, *Twelfe Night*. Thus ye must doe To make the wassaile a SWINGER.

1672. DRYDEN, *Assignation*, iii. 8. Yours were but little vanities; but I have sinn'd SWINGINGLY against my vow.

1694. MOTTEUX, *Rabelais*, v. xviii. A SWINGEING ass's touch-tripe fastened to his waist.

c. 1696. B. E., *Dict. Cant. Crew*, s.v. SWINGING. Clap, Lye, Fellow, a very great one. I SWING'D HIM OFF, I lay'd on and beat him well-favoredly. He is SWING'D OFF, damnably Clapt.

1703. FARQUHAR, *Inconstant*, i. 1. We have rid a SWINGING pace from Nemours since two this morning.

1720. ECHARD, *Obs. Cont. Clergy*, 159. How will he rap out presently half a dozen SWINGERS, to get off cleverly.

1725. BAILEY, *Erasmus*, I. 271. Did I not tell you a SWINGEING Lie, then?

1730. NORTH, *Lives of Norths*. [A certain monstrous proposition is called] a SWINGER.

1734. CAREY, *Chronon.*, 3. Now, . . . for a SWINGEING lye.

1742. FIELDING, *Joseph Andrews*, ii. 5. If your jury were Christians, they must give SWINGEING damages, that's all.

1859. SALA, *Twice Round Clock*, 4 A.M. 17. Retailing the fish at a SWINGEING profit.

1872. C. D. WARNER, *Blacklog Studies*, 264. A placid, calm, SWINGEING cold night.

1884. *Pall Mall Gaz.*, 7 July. A good SWINGEING agitation against the House of Lords.

SWING-TAIL, *subs. phr.* (old).—A hog (GROSE).

SWINNY, *adj.* (common).—Drunk: *see* SCREWED. Also SWINNIED.

SWIPE, *subs.* (old: now colloquial). —1. A blow delivered with the full length of the arm. As *verb* =to DRIVE (*q.v.*); to bang. Hence SWIPER=a hard hitter, a SLOGGER (*q.v.*), a KNOCKER-OUT (*q.v.*). At Harrow=to birch.

c. 1200. *Life St. Katherine* [E.E.T.S.], 2452. SWIPTE hire of that heaned.

1857. HUGHES, *Tom Brown's Schooldays*, II. viii. Jack Raggles, the long-stop, toughest and burliest of boys, commonly called SWIPER Jack . . . The first ball of the over, Jack steps out and meets, SWIPING with all his force.

1886. *Field*, 4 Sep. In driving for Tel-el-Kebir, Kirk had a long SWIPE off the tee.

1901. *Free Lance*, 9 Mar., 558, 2. I am indebted to Mr. Gilbert Jessop, the well-known bowler and SWIPER (I hope the word has not gone out), for the excellent and temperate article which he contributes to another part of this number.

1903. *Punch's Almanack*, 11. Dicky Sinclair . . . hit a tremendous SWIPE, and ran eight before they had the sense to call 'Lost Ball.'

2. (common).—In *pl.*=thin, washy beer; small beer: also (schools) any poor tipple. As *verb* =to drink. Hence SWIPEY (or SWIPED)=drunk; and SWIPES= a potman (GROSE). Also *see* PURSER'S SWIPES.

1824. SCOTT, *Redgauntlet*, xiii. Small SWIPES—more of malt than hop—with your leave I'll try your black bottle.

1838. BECKETT, *Paradise Lost*, 32. I have nought to drink but SWIPES.

1843. DICKENS, *Chuzzlewit*, xxviii. He's only a little SWIPEY, you know.

Verb. (American).—To steal: *see* PRIG.

1900. FLYNT, *Tramps*, 43. Some one suggested a clever plan by which even a can of preserves could be 'SWIPED' as they called it.

1903. KENNEDY, *Sailor Tramp*, I. iv. That is rotten hard work. It's a job I'd SWIPE from no man.

SWISH, *verb.* (common).—To flog. Hence SWISHING=a thrashing.

1855–7. THACKERAY, *Misc.*, ii. 470. I pity that young nobleman's or gentleman's case: Dr. Wordsworth and assistants would SWISH that error out of him in a way that need not here be mentioned.

d. 1876. M. COLLINS, *Thoughts in my Garden*, ii. 22. He has been known to argue with the head-master as to whether he ought to be SWISHED.

1884. YATES, *Auto.*, I. ii. To smoke a penny cigar with constant anticipation of being caught and SWISHED.

1891. *Harry Fludyer*, 47. He complained of us and Tipkins, and I got SWISHED the other day.

SWISHED, *adj.* (old). — Married (GROSE).

SWISH-SWASH, *subs. phr.* (old).— Any weak beverage; SLOPS (*q.v.*).

1577. HARRISON, *Descr. Eng.* [HOLINSHED], 170. There is a kind of SWISH-SWASH made also in Essex, and diverse other places, with honicombs and water, which the homelie countrie wives, putting some pepper and a little other spice among, call mead, verie good in mine opinion for such as love to be loose-bodied at large, or a little eased of the cough; otherwise it differeth so much from the true metheglin as chalke from cheese.

1884. DOWELL, *Taxes in England*, iv. 55. The small sour SWISH-SWASH of the poorer vintages of France.

SWISH-TAIL, *subs. phr.* (old poachers'). — 1. A pheasant (GROSE). Also (2) a horse with undocked tail; and (3) a schoolmaster, a BUMBRUSHER (*q.v.*).

SWISS ADMIRAL, *subs. phr.* (naval). —A pretender to naval rank: *cf.* Fr. *amiral suisse*=a naval officer solely employed on shore, or who has never been to sea.

SWITCH, *verb.* (venery).—To copulate: *see* RIDE and *cf.* SWINGE.

1772. BRIDGES, *Burlesque Homer*, 297. If Paris had not got enough Of trimming her bewitching buff, But longs to SWITCH the gypsy still.

TO SWITCH IN, *verb. phr.* (American).—To be expeditious in movement.

SWIVE, *verb.* (venery). — To copulate: *see* RIDE (GROSE). Hence SWIVER=a performer (*q.v.*), a WENCHER (*q.v.*); QUEEN OF SWIVELAND=Venus.

. . . . *MS. Cantab.*, Ff. ii. 38, f. 136. A! seyde the pye, by Godys wylle, How thou art SWYVED y schalle telle.

. . . . *MS. Lincoln*, A. i. 17, f. 149. And now ere sary SWYWERS brokyne owte of bande, Thay fille alle fulle this Ynglande, and many other lande. In everilk a toune ther es many one, And everilk wyfe wenys hir selfe thar scho hafes one.

1383. CHAUCER, *Cant. Tales*, Miller's Tale, 666 [SKEAT (1895), I. v., 111]. Thus SWYVED was the carpenteres wyf, For al his keping and his Ialousye; and Absolon hath kist hir nether ye. *Ibid.*, l. 4178. Yon wench wol I SWIVE, etc.

c. 1508 [?], *Colyn Blowbols Testament*, [*MS. Rawl.*, C. 86, fol. 106, verso]. Alle tho that ben very good drynkers, And eke also alle feeble SWYVERS, And they also that can lyft a bole.

1598. FLORIO, *Worlde of Wordes*, s.v. *Fottere*. To iape, to sard, to fucke, to SWIVE, to occupy. [Also *see*=*Fottarie, Fottetrice, Fottitire*, and *Fottitura*.]

1612. COTGRAVE, *Dict.* s.v. *Chevaucherie*. A riding, a SWIVING.

c. 1620. *Percy Folio MS.*, 455. Of all the fishes in the Sea Give me a woman's SWIVING.

1656. FLETCHER, *Martiall*, xi. 98. I can SWIVE four times in a night; but thee Once in four years I cannot occupie. *Ibid.*, *Poems*, 101. Nor will I SWIVE thee though it bee Our very first nights jollitie. Nor shall my couch or pallat lye In common both to thee and I.

1659. *Legend Capt. Jones* [HALLIWELL]. Knights, squires, fools, In every town rejoice at his arrival, The townsmen where he comes their wives do SWIVE all.

d. 1680. ROCHESTER, *Ramble* (*Works*, 1718). And so may that false woman thrive That dares prophane the c—t I SWIVE.

1686. DORSET, *Faithful Catalogue* [*Works* (1718), ii. 33]. And from St James's to the land of Thule, There's not a Whore who SWIVES so like a Mule.

1741. *Voyage to Lethe*, 7. The Charming Sally, built by the celebrated Herman SWIVEITT, on the River Medway.

SWIVEL-EYED, *adj. phr.* (old).— Squinting (GROSE). Hence SWIVEL-EYE=a squint-eye; a BOSS-EYE (*q.v.*).

1865. DICKENS, *Mutual Friend*, ii. 12. She found herself possessed of what is colloquially termed a SWIVEL-EYE.

SWIVELLY, *adj.* (common). — Drunk: *see* SCREWED.

SWIZZLE (or SWIZZY), *subs.* (common). — 1. Generic for drink; also (2) various compounded drinks—rum and water, ale and beer mixed, and (West Indies) what is known in America as a cock-tail. As *verb*=to tope, to SWILL (*q.v.*); and SWIZZLED = drunk; also *see* SCREWED.

1850. HANNAY, *Singleton Fontenoy*. 'It serves me right for deserting rum, my proper tipple. Boy, the amber fluid!' Here Mr. Snigg mixed himself some SWIZZLE and consoled himself.

SWOBBER. *See* SWABBER.

SWODDY. *See* SWAD.

SWOLLENHEAD. TO HAVE A SWOL-LEN HEAD, *verb. phr.* (common). —1. To put on airs; to be filled with a violent sense of one's own importance. Also (2) to be drunk: *see* SCREWED. Also SWELLED-HEAD.

1898. GOULD, *Landed at Last*, vi. You have got a SWOLLEN HEAD this morning. . . . Had too much to drink last night.

1900. NISBET, *In Sheep's Clothing*, iv. iii. The candid friend is like a black draught; wholesome, perhaps, during periods of plethora and SWOLLEN HEAD, but decidedly debilitating if too long continued.

SWOP. *See* SWAP.

SWORD-RACKET, *subs. phr.* (old). —Enlisting in different regiments, and deserting after taking the bounty.

SWOT. *See* SWEAT.

IN A SWOT, *phr.* (Shrewsbury). —In a rage.

SYDNEY-SIDER (or BIRD), *subs. phr.* (Australian). — A convict. [Sydney was originally a convict settlement.]

SYEBUCK, *subs.* (old).—Sixpence (GROSE).

SYNTAX, *subs.* (old).—A schoolmaster (GROSE).

O A T, *phr.* (colloquial).—Exactly; to a nicety; as true as an angle drawn with a T-square.

1698. FARQUHAR, *Love and a Bottle*, iv. 3. He answered the description the page gave TO A T, sir.

1700. *Labour in Vain* [*Harl. Misc.*, vi. 387]. Having cajoled my inquirer, and fitted his humour TO A T.

1759-67. STERNE, *Tristram Shandy*, ii. 5. We could manage this matter TO A T.

1899. MARSH, *Crime and Criminal*, xxii. Levett turned out a regular trump, and they hit it off together TO A T.

TO BE MARKED WITH A T, *verb. phr.* (old).—Known as a thief. [Formerly convicted thieves were branded with a 'T' in the hand.]

T. T., *phr.* (American).—'Too thin' or 'too transparent': *e.g.* 'The story is T. T.'

TAB, *subs.* — 1. A check; an account. TO KEEP TAB=to keep watch.

1884. *Century*, xxxviii. 882. There are fellows in the office quietly keeping TAB on them.

2. (tailors').—In *pl.*=the ears.

TO DRIVE TAB, *verb. phr.* (old). —'To go out on a party of pleasure with a wife and family' (GROSE).

THE TAB, *subs. phr.* (London). —The Metropolitan Tabernacle in Newington Causeway.

TABARDER, *subs.* (Univ.). — A scholar on the foundation of Queen's College, Oxford.—WOOD, *Athen. Oxon.* (1692).

1822. NARES, *Glossary*, s.v. TABARD. The name of TABARDER is still preserved in Queen's College, Oxford, for scholars, whose original dress was a tabard. They are part of the foundation, which consists of, a provost, 16 fellows, 2 chaplains, 8 tabarders, 12 probationary scholars, and 2 clerks.—*Oxf. Univ. Cal.*

TABBY, *subs.* (colloquial).—1. An old maid; hence (2) a spiteful tattler: *cf.* CAT (GROSE). TABBY-PARTY = a gathering of women.

1761. G. COLMAN, *Jealous Wife*, ii. 3. I am not sorry for the coming in of these old TABBIES, and am much obliged to her ladyship for leaving us to such an agreeable tête-à-tête.

1774. BRIDGES, *Burlesque Homer*, 246. This made th' old TABBIES swear they'd never Fall out, but live good friends for ever.

d.1855. ROGERS [TREVELYAN, *Macaulay*, i. 241]. When he can get into a circle of old TABBIES, he is just in his element.

TABERNACLE, *subs.* (religious).— *See* quot.

1872. HALL, *False Philology*, 24, Note. The shed in Moorfields which Whitefield used as a temporary chapel was called 'The Tabernacle'; and, in the scornful dialect of certain Church-of-England men, Methodist and such-like places of worship have, since then, been known as TABERNACLES.

See TIN TABERNACLE and TAB.

TABLE. TO TURN THE TABLES, *verb. phr.* (colloquial). — To reverse matters (B. E.).

1692. LESTRANGE, *Fables*. They that are honest would be arrant knaves, if the TABLES WERE TURNED.

1694. CONGREVE, *Double Dealer*, iv. 13. I have an after-game to play that shall TURN THE TABLES.

d. 1701. DRYDEN [*Century Dict.*]. If it be thus the TABLES would BE TURNED upon me; but I should only fail in my vain attempt.

1809. MALKIN, *Gil Blas* [ROUTLEDGE], 217. The gang upon whom we TURNED THE TABLES were people of very bad character.

1885. *D. News*, 28 Sept. The west countrymen being victorious, but THE TABLES WERE TURNED in three following years.

TABLE-CLOTH (THE), *subs. phr.* (colonial).—A white cloud covering the top of Table Mountain.

TACE. TACE IS LATIN FOR A CANDLE, *phr.* (old). — A cant phrase in the 18th century suggesting the expediency of silence. [Latin, *tacēre*. GROSE.]

1710. SWIFT, *Polite Cond.*, ii. Brande is Latin for a goose, and TACE IS LATIN FOR A CANDLE.

1751. FIELDING, *Amelia*, I. x. TACE, Madam, answered Murphy, IS LATIN FOR A CANDLE; I commend your prudence.

TACH, *subs.* (back slang).—A hat: *see* GOLGOTHA.

TACHS, *subs.* (Tonbridge School). —A fad; a mental eccentricity. [*Cf.* quots.]

1822. NARES, *Glossary*, s.v. TADE or TATCH. A blot, spot, stain, or vice.

1847. HALLIWELL, *Archaic Words*, s.v. TACHE . . . A quality or disposition; a trick; enterprise.

TACK, *subs.* (common).—Generic for food: specifically (1)='bad food' or 'bad malt liquor' (HALLIWELL). Hence (2), in combination: *e.g.* HARD-TACK = coarse fare or (army and navy) biscuit as distinguished from bread; SOFT-TACK = (a) good fare, and (b) bread. Also TACKLE. At Sherborne School TACK=a feast in one's study.

18[?]. *Fish. of U. States*, v. ii. 228. For supper in the cabin: salt beef and pork, warm SOFT TACK, butter, sugar, tea, etc.

TO TACK TOGETHER, *verb. phr.* (common).— To marry: *cf.* HITCH, SPLICE, NOOSE, etc.

1754. FOOTE, *Knights*, ii. She falls in love with . . . her father's chaplain; . . . I slips on Dominie's robes . . . passed myself on her for him, and we were TACKED TOGETHER.

TACKER, *subs.* (provincial).—A great falsehood (HALLIWELL).

TACKET, *subs.* (provincial).—The *penis*: *see* PRICK.

TACKLE, *subs.* (old).—1. A mistress: *see* TART (B. E. and GROSE).

2. (old).—'Good clothes' (B. E. and GROSE).

3. (venery).—The *penis* and *testes*: *see* CODS and PRICK.

4. (thieves').—A watch chain: a RED TACKLE=a gold chain.

1877. HORSLEY, *Jottings from Jail*. One day I went to Croydon and touched for a red toy and RED TACKLE, with a large locket.

1888. SIMS, *Plank Bed Ballad* [*Referee*, 12 Feb.]. A toy and a TACKLE —both red-'uns.

Verb. (colloquial). — To do with energy; to set to work; to cope with; to attack: generic. Thus TO TACKLE (=to attempt the solution of) A PROBLEM; TO TACKLE (=to attempt) A WOMAN: TO TACKLE (=to close with) A BURGLAR, etc.

1844. *Major Jones's Courtship*, 53. It tuck a feller mighty wide between the eyes to TACKLE that tree, for it was a whopper.—*Ibid.*, *Travels* [BARTLETT]. I shook the two fellows off my trunks monstrous quick, and was going to TACKLE the chaps what had my carpet-bag.

1858. *New York Times*, 9 Aug. The people are no ways backward about discussing the subject of Mormonism. . . . One of the gentry TACKLED Governor Powell the other day, determined to make a convert.

1862. THACKERAY, *Philip*, xxi. TACKLE the lady, and speak your mind to her as best you can.

d.1868. S. LOVER [*Imp. Dict.*]. The old woman . . . TACKLED TO for a fight in right earnest.

1869. STOWE, *Oldtown*, 168. They was resolute, strong, hard-workin' women. They could all TACKLE a hoss, or load and fire a gun.

1885. *Field*, 4 April. A paid collector would be infinitely more successful than any number of printed appeals signed by gentlemen who could not TACKLE people personally.

1887. *Punch*, 10 Sep. 111. If a feller would TACKLE a feminine fair . . . he 'as got to be dabs at the cackle.

TAD, *subs.* (American).—"Perhaps an abbreviation of 'tadpole.' A very small boy, especially a small street-boy" (*Century*); "little TADS, small boys; old TADS, graybeards, old men" (BARTLETT).

2. (provincial). — Excrement (HALLIWELL).

3. (American).—A wencher; a MUTTON-MONGER (q.v.).

TAF, *adj.* (back slang).—Fat; *e.g.*, TAF ENO=a fat man or woman (lit.=fat one).

TAFF, *subs.* (Christ's Hospital).—A potato.

TAFFY, *subs.* (old).—1. A Welshman. Hence TAFFY'S DAY=St. David's Day, the 1st March (B. E. and GROSE). [A Welsh pronunciation of 'Davy.']

1577. HARRISON, *Descr. Eng.* 206. [OLIPHANT, *New Eng.* i. 595. A Welshman is called a David (TAFFY)].

1661. *Merry Drollery* [EBSWORTH]. TAFFIE [a Welshman].

. . . *Old Rhyme*. TAFFY was a Welsham; TAFFY was a thief.

2. (American). — Flattery; BLARNEY (q.v.), SOFT-SOAP (q.v.). As *verb* = to flatter. [Taffy=toffee.]

1879. *New York Tribune*, 16 Sep. There will be a reaction, and the whole party will unite in an offering of TAFFY.

TAG, *subs.* (Winchester football).— An off-side kick: also as *verb*.

c.1840. MANSFIELD, *School Life* (1866), 237. TAG . . . When a player has kicked the ball well forward, and has followed it, if it was then kicked back again behind him by the other side, he was then obliged to return to his original position with his own side. If the ball had, in the meantime, been again kicked in front of him, before he regained his position, and he was to kick it, it would be considered unfair, and he would be said TO TAG.

TAG, RAG, AND BOBTAIL *See* RAG, senses 1, 2, 3, and add the following quots.

d.1599. SPENSER, *State of Irelana*. They all came in both TAGGE AND RAGGE.

1610. JONSON, *Alchemist*, i. 5. Gallants, men and women, and All sorts, TAG-RAG.

1637. HEYWOOD, *Royal King* [PEARSON, *Works* (1894), vi. 14]. Stood I but in the midst of my followers, I might say I had nothing about me but TAGGE AND RAGGE.

183[?]. GREVILLE, *Memoirs*, 19 Jan. He [William IV.] lives a strange life at Brighton, with TAGRAG AND BOBTAIL about him, and always open house.

1837. BARHAM, *Ingolds. Leg.* II. 109. TAG, RAG, AND BOBTAIL are capering there.

TAG-END, *subs. phr.* (colloquial).—The fag-end; the concluding portion.

1891. E. L. BYNNER, *Begum's Daughter*, xix. She heard the TAG-END of the conversation.

TAGLIONI, *subs.* [obsolete]. An overcoat: named after the dancer.

1837. BARHAM, *Ingolds. Leg.*, 'S. Romwold.' I've bought to protect myself well, a Good stout Taglioni and gingham umbrella.

TAGRHYME, *subs.* (old).—A rhymester.

1698. FARQUHAR, *Love and a Bottle* ii. 3. I long to see Mr. Tagrhyme . . . these poets must have something extraordinary in their faces.

TAGSTER, *subs.* (provincial).—A scold, a virago (HALLIWELL).

TAGTAIL, *subs.* (colloquial).—A parasite; a hanger-on.

TAIL, *subs.* (vulgar).—1. The lower or latter end; the BEHIND (*q.v.*): *see* ARSE. Hence, KISS MY TAIL = Kiss my arse: a contemptuous retort; TO TURN TAIL = (1) to turn one's back on; (2) to run away, to shirk; TOP OVER TAIL = arse over head; THE TAIL END = the FAG-END (*q.v.*).

. . . *Chester Plays*, ii. 176. Thou take hym by the toppe and I by the TAYLE, A sorrowfull songe in faith he shall singe.

. . . *MS. Harl.*, 1701, f. 59. Wyth here kercheves the devylys sayle, Elles shul they go to helle bothe TOP AND TAYLE.

[?]. *MS. Cantab.*, Ff. ii. 38. f. 76. Soche a strokk he gaf hym then, that the dewke bothe hors and man turned TOPPE OVYR TAYLE.

14[?]. *Turnament of Totenham* [HAZLITT, *Early Pop. Poet.*, iii. 97]. Thei did but ran erswad, And ilke a man went bakward TOPPE OUER TAYLE.

1460. *Frere and Boye* [HAZLITT, *Early Pop. Poet.*, iii. 79]. Lowde coude she blowe. Some laughed without fayle, Some sayd: dame, tempre thy TAYLE.

d. 1529. SKELTON, *Bouge of Court.* [CHALMERS, *Eng. Poets*, ii. 253]. What reuell route quod he, and gan to rayle How ofte he hit Ienet on the TAYLE . . . How ofte he knocked at her klycket gate. [Possibly sense 2.]

1551. STILL, *Gammer Gurton's Needle* [DODSLEY, *Old Plays* (HAZLITT), iii. 216]. Thou wert as good kiss my TAIL.

1562. *Jack Juggler* [DODSLEY, *Old Plays* (HAZLITT), ii. 130]. *Jack Jugg.* . . . thy wits do thee fail. *Care.* Yea, marry, sir, you have beaten them down into my TAIL.

d. 1586. SIR P. SIDNEY (LATHAM). Would she TURN TAIL . . . and fly quite out another way.

1595. SHAKSPEARE, *Two Gent.* ii. 3. *Pan.* Where should I lose my tongue? *Launce.* In thy tale, Pan, In thy TAIL!

1598. FLORIO, *Worlde of Wordes*, s.v. *Culo.* The arse, TAIL, fundament, or bum.

1599. HALL, *Satires*, I. i. 11. Nor can I crouch and writhe my fawning TAYLE. *Ibid.*, IV. ii. And seven more plod at a patron's TAYLE.

1611. COTGRAVE, *Dict.*, s.v. *Cul.* An arse, bumme, TAYLE, nockandroe, fundament.

1621. SYLVESTER, *Du Bartas.* 'The Furies.' Our Sire . . . TURN'D TAIL to God, and to the Fiend his face.

1632. JONSON, *Magnetic Lady*, v. 4. Would thou had'st a dose of pills . . . to make thee TURN TAIL t'other way. *Ibid.* (1633), *Tale of a Tub*, iii. 3. *Pup.* Let me take this rump out of your mouth. *Dame T.* What mean you by that, sir? *Pup.* Rump and TAILE's all one . . . I would not say sur-reverence, the tale Out of your mouth, but rather take the rump.

1653. URQUHART, *Rabelais*, i. 117. Barytonising with his TAIL.

1663. BUTLER, *Hudibras*, I. iii. Yet shame and honour might prevail To keep thee thus from TURNING TAIL.

1673. COTTON, *Burlesque upon Burlesque* (1770), 260. And every Goddess lay her TAIL As bare and naked as my Nail.

1678. COTTON, *Virgil Travestie*, i. (1770), 9. He was, in fine, the loud'st of Farters, Yet could . . . Correct his TAIL, and only blow If there Occasion were, or so.

1695. CONGREVE, *Love for Love*, i. 1. Without a whole tatter to her TAIL.

d. 1704. BROWN, *Works*, i. 164. Several TAILS turned up at Paul's School, Merchant Taylors, etc., for their Repetitions.

c. 1709. WARD, *Terræfilius*, ii. 28. Let your Servants do their Business without your Watching at their TAILS.

1771. SMOLLETT, *Humph. Clinker* (1900), 105-9. An't you ashamed, fellow, to ride postillion without a shirt to cover your backside from the view of the ladies? . . . Try if you cans't make peace with my sister. Thou hast given her much offence by showing her thy naked TAIL.

1774. BRIDGES, *Burlesque Homer*, 53. Upstarts the king, and with his nail Scratch'd both his head, and ears, and TAIL.

1872. BLACK, *Phaeton*, xxii. The TAIL-END of a shower caught us.

1874. *Siliad*, 15. A general Hubbub all the force misled, And one, a Highland Chief, TURNED TAIL and fled.

2. (venery).—(*a*) The *penis*: *see* PRICK; (*b*) the female *pudendum*: *see* MONOSYLLABLE; (*c*) a harlot: *see* TART (GROSE). Also (*penis* or *pudendum*) TAIL-GAP, TAIL-GATE, TAIL-HOLE, TAIL-PIKE, TAIL-PIN, TAIL-PIPE, TAIL-TRIMMER, TAIL-TREE or TAIL-TACKLE (*penis* and *testes*). Hence TAIL-FEATHERS = the pubic hair: *see* FLEECE; TAIL-FLOWERS = the menses; TAIL-FRUIT = children; TAIL-FENCE = the hymen; TAIL-JUICE = (*a*) the semen and (*b*) urine: also TAIL-WATER; TAIL-WORK (or TAIL-WAGGING) = copulation; TO TAIL ('to make a SETTLEMENT IN TAIL,' 'to go TAIL-TICKLING' or TWITCHING, 'to play at UP-TAILS ALL,' 'to TURN UP ONE'S TAIL,' or to 'GET SHOT IN THE TAIL') = to copulate; TAIL-TRADING = prostitution; A TENANT-IN-TAIL = (1) a whore (a WAG-TAIL), (2) a KEEPER (*q.v.*) and (3) the *penis*; LIGHT (HOT, or WARM) IN THE TAIL = wanton; HOT-TAILED (or WITH TAIL ON FIRE) = infected. *See* SQUIRREL.

1363. LANGLAND, *Piers Plowman*, 1619. For she is tikel of hire TAIL . . . As commune as a cartway.

1383. CHAUCER, *Cant. Tales*, 6047-8. For al so siker as cold engendreth hayl, A likerous mouth most han a likerous TAYL.

c. 1400. *Coventry Myst.*, 134. Of his TAYLE oftetyme be lyght, And rygh tekyl undyr the too.

[?]. *Commune Secretary and Jalowsye* [HALLIWELL]. She that is fayre, lusty, and yonge . . . Thynke ye her TAYLE is not lyght of the seare.

d. 1529. SKELTON, *Bouge of Court* [CHALMERS, *Eng. Poets*, ii. 253]. I lete her to hyre that men may on her ryde . . . She hath got me more money with her TAYLE Than hath some shyppe that into bordews sayle.

15[?]. *MS. Poem* [Dr. BLISS], quoted by HALLIWELL. Alyed was countess would be, For she would still be TENAUNT IN TAILE To any one she could be.

1599. HALL, *Satires*, IV. iv. The maidens mocke, and call him withered leeke, That with a greene TAYLE hath an hoary head.

1647-80. ROCHESTER, *Poems.* Then pulling out the rector of the females, Nine times he bath'd him in their piping TAILS.

16[?]. *Old Song*, 'John Anderson, my Jo.' John Anderson, my Jo, John, When that ye first began, Ye hae as guid a TAIL-TREE As ony ither man.

1694. MOTTEUX, *Rabelais*, v. xxi. They were pulling and hauling the man like mad, telling him that it is the most grievous . . . thing in nature for the TAIL to be on fire. *Ibid.* xxx. I saw some . . . more diligent in TAILWAGGING than any water-wagtail. *Ibid.* (1694), *Pant. Prog.* Hedgewhores, WAGTAILS, cockatrices.

1697. VANBRUGH, *Prov. Wife*, iv. 6. You slut you—you wear an impudent lewd face; a damned designing heart; and a TAIL—a TAIL full of—— (*Falls fast asleep*).

c. 1704. WARD, *Merry Observations*, 88. TAIL-TRADING tenants will have so little to do that they won't be able to earn a Week's Rent in ready Money in a month. *Ibid.* (*c.* 1709), *Terræfilius*, iii. 39. Destroys the Worm call'd *Friskin*, very troublesome to the TAILS of most young Women.

d. 1704. BROWN, *Works*, i. 170. Women . . . busy with their Heads in the Day-time, and TAILS in the evening. *Ibid.* ii. 104. Your lover, fair lady, is so fast link'd to his old Duegna's TAIL [Madame Maintenon] that he thinks no more of you. *Ibid.* 187. 'Tis enough to put musick into the TAIL of an old woman of fourscore. *Ibid.* ii. 262. After a good week's work send her home with foul linen . . . no money, and perhaps a hot TAIL into the bargain.

d. 1742. SOMERVILE, *Incurious Bencher* [CHALMERS, *Eng. Poets*, xi. 238]. If you will burn your TAIL to tinder, Pray what have I to do to hinder?

d. 1744. POPE [CHALMERS, *Eng. Poets*, xii. 281]. 'To Mr. John Moore.' The nymph whose TAIL is all on flame, Is aptly termed a glow-worm.

1774. BRIDGES, *Burlesque Homer*, 103. We all are mortal men and frail, And oft are guided by the TAIL.

1782. STEVENS, *Songs Comic and Satirycall*, 'The Sentiment Song.' The nick makes the TAIL stand, the farrier's wife's mark!

1785. GROSE, *Vulg. Tongue*, s.v. CAB . . . Mother, how many TAILS have you in your cab? how many girls have you in your nanny house?

3. (colloquial).—A woman's dress: espec. when trailing on the ground.

1774. BRIDGES, *Burlesque Homer*, 264. Brimstones with their sweeping TAILS.

1883. *Century*, XXXVI. 128. He crossed the room, stepping over the TAILS of gowns, and stood before his old friend.

4. (common).—The reverse of a coin: spec. the side opposite to that bearing a HEAD (*q.v.*): chiefly in phrase 'heads or tails' in tossing. Hence NEITHER HEAD NOR TAIL = neither one nor the other; quite different.

1774. BRIDGES, *Burlesque Homer*, 115. 'Tis heads for Greece, and TAILS for Troy . . . Two farthings out of three were TAILS.

1785. GROSE, *Vulg. Tongue*, s.v. HARP . . . is also the Irish expression for 'woman' or 'TAIL' used in tossing up in Ireland.

1809. MALKIN, *Gil Blas* [ROUTLEDGE], 212. The horse was laden besides with a large bundle of stuffs, of which we could make neither HEAD NOR TAIL. . . . He had rather toss up heads or TAILS with them than oblige a plain citizen in an honest way.

1821. EGAN, *Life in Lond.* 279. Note. If the party . . . calls heads or TAILS, and all three coins are as he calls them, he wins.

5. (common).—In *pl.* = a tail-coat, as distinguished from a jacket. CHARITY-TAILS (Harrow) = a tail-coat worn by a boy in the Lower School who is considered by the Headmaster to be tall enough to require them.

1888. *St. Nicholas*, xiv. 406. Once a boy has reached the modern remove [Harrow], he puts on his TAILS or tail-coat.

6. (common).—A girl's hair, curled, plaited, etc., and allowed to hang down the back in a single strand.

1887. *Congregationalist*, 4 Aug. I noticed half a dozen groups of slender damsels with short frocks and long TAILS.

7. (colloquial.—A line of persons waiting in rank; a queue: as outside a theatre, booking-office, etc.

8. (old colloquial).—*See* quots.

1363. LANGLAND, *Piers Plowman* (C), iii. 196. Ich haue no tome to telle the TAIL that hem folweth.

1633. JONSON, *Tale of a Tub*, ii. 1. Why should her worship lack Her TAIL of maids, more than you do of men?

1814. SCOTT, *Waverley*, xvi. 'Ah! . . . if you . . . saw but the Chief with his TAIL on!' 'With his TAIL on?' echoed Edward. . . . 'Yes—that is, with all his usual followers, when he visits those of the same rank.'

d. 1845. HOOD, *Tale of a Trumpet.* Ay, now's the nick for her friend Old Harry To come with his TAIL like the bold Glengarry.

9. (Old Cant).—A sword (B. E. and GROSE); TAIL-DRAWER = 'a sword stealer' (B. E.).

10 (cricket).—The last two or three men in a batting eleven to go to the wickets.

Verb. (Australian).—To tend sheep; to herd cattle.

1844. *Port Phillip Patriot*, 5 Aug. 3, 6. I know many boys, from the age of nine to sixteen years, TAILING cattle.

1855. MUNDY, *Our Antipodes*, 153. The stockman, as he who tends cattle and horses is called, despises the shepherd as a grovelling, inferior creature, and considers 'TAILING sheep' as an employment too tardigrade for a man of action and spirit.

1890. BOLDREWOOD, *Colonial Reformer*, xix. 239. The cattle, no longer 'TAILED,' or followed daily, as a shepherd does sheep.

PHRASES AND COMBINATIONS. TAIL OF THE EYE = the outer corner of the eye; COW'S-TAIL (nautical) = a frayed rope's-end, one not properly knotted: hence HANGING IN COW'S TAILS (said of a badly kept ship); TAIL-END = the latter part, the wind-up; WITH ONE'S TAIL BETWEEN ONE'S LEGS = cowed, humiliated, conscious of defeat: also WITH TAIL DOWN; WITH TAIL UP = in good form or spirits; WITH TAIL OUT = angry; WITH TAIL IN THE WATER = thriving; TO FLEE THE TAIL = to near the end; TO TWIST THE LION'S TAIL = to gird at England (or the English people); TO CAST (LAY or THROW) SALT ON THE TAIL (*see* SALT, and *add* special quots. *infra*—GROSE).

1670. RAY, *Proverbs* [Bohn], 427. It is a foolish bird that stayeth the LAYING SALT UPON HER TAIL.

1838. BECKETT, *Paradise Lost*, 66. Or catching birds, which never fails, If you PUT SALT UPON THEIR TAILS.

1859. READE, *Love Me Little*, xiv. Miss Lucy noticed this out of the TAIL OF HER EYE.

1894. BAKER, *New Timothy*, 264. Tzed and Toad come, and very much as if with their TAILS BETWEEN THEIR LEGS.

1899. WHITEING, *John Street*, vii. Covey stands at the street corner with his hands in his pockets, and observes out of the TAIL OF HIS EYE.

Also PROVERBS AND PROVERBIAL SAYINGS: 'The devil wipes his TAIL with the poor man's pride' (RAY); 'BETWEENE two stools my TAILE goes to the ground' (HEYWOOD); 'To make a rod for one's own TAIL' (HEYWOOD); 'Like lambs, you do nothing but suck and wag your TAILS'; 'She goes as if she cracked nuts with her TAIL'; 'To look like a dog that has lost its TAIL'; 'She's like a cat, she'll play with her own TAIL'; 'Make not thy TAIL broader than thy wings' (= Keep not too many attendants); 'His TAIL will catch the chin-cough' (said of one sitting on the ground); 'As hasty as a sheep, as soon as the TAIL is up the turd is out'; 'As free as an ape is of his TAIL'; 'He that aught the cow gangs nearest her TAIL'; 'He holds the serpent by the TAIL' (of anything absurd or foolish); 'To grow like a cow's TAIL' (*i.e.* downwards); 'Lay the head of the sow to the TAIL of the grice'; 'To have a slippery eel by the TAIL' (of anything uncertain); 'It melts like butter in a sow's TAIL'; 'To swallow an ox, and be choked with the TAIL'; 'The higher the ape goes, the more he shows his TAIL'; 'There is as much hold of his word as of a wet eel by the TAIL'; 'He hath eaten a horse and the TAIL hangs out of his mouth.'

TAIL-BLOCK, *subs. phr.* (nautical).—A watch.

TAIL-BOARD, *subs. phr.* (nursery).—The back flap of a little girl's breeches.

TAIL-BUZZER, *subs. phr.* (thieves').—A pickpocket.

TAILER (or **TAYLOR**), *intj.* (old).—A fall on the breech; a PRAT-FALL (*q.v.*); and (2) an exclamation on falling, or unexpectedly sitting down on one's TAIL (*q.v.*). [*Cf.* CRUPPER (or CROPPER), HEADER, etc.].

1592. SHAKSPEARE, *Mid. Night's Dream*, ii. 1. Sometime for three-foot stool [she] mistaketh me, Then slip I from her bum, down topples she, And, TAILER, cries!

TAILOR. NINE (TEN, or THREE) TAILORS MAKE A MAN, *subs. phr.* (old).—*See* quots.

1605. SHAKSPEARE, *Lear*, ii. 2. 60. *Kent.* A tailor made thee. *Corn.* Thou art a strange fellow: A TAILOR MAKE A MAN?

1607. DEKKER, *Northward Hoe*, ii. 1. They say THREE TAILORS GO TO the making up of A MAN, but I am sure I had FOUR TAILORS AND A HALF WENT TO THE MAKING OF ME thus.

1630. TAYLOR, *Works*, iii. 73. Some foolish knave (I thinke) at first began The slander that THREE TAYLERS ARE ONE MAN.

1635. GLAPTHORNE, *The Lady Mother*, i. 1. He was by trade a taylor, sir, and is the TENTH PART of the bumbast that goes to the setting forth OF A MAN.

1635. QUARLES, *Emblems*, iv. 15. The nine sad knells of a passing bell.

d. 1643. NABBES [quoted by NARES]. I would take the wall of THREE TIMES THREE TAILORS, though in a morning, and at a baker's stall.

1663. BUTLER, *Hudibras*, I. ii. The foe, for dread Of YOUR NINE-WORTHINESS, is fled.

d. 1665. T. ADAMS, *Soul's Sickness* [*Works*, i. 487]. God made him a man, he hath made himself a beast; and now THE TAILOR (scarce a man himself) MUST MAKE HIM A MAN again.

1671. BUCKINGHAM, *Rehearsal*, iii. 1. Why . . . marry? If NINE TAYLORS MAKE but ONE MAN; and one woman cannot be satisfi'd with nine men: what work art thou cutting out for thy self?

c. 1709. WARD, *Terræfilius*, v. 31-33. An old Wealthy Limb-trimmer . . . the very NINTH PART OF A MAN that put the jest upon a Shoe-maker.

1763. FOOTE, *Mayor of Garratt*, ii. A journeyman tailor . . . who is but THE NINTH PART OF A MAN.

1767. RAY, *Proverbs* [Bohn], 135. NINE TAILORS MAKE but ONE MAN.

1785. GROSE, *Vulg. Tongue*, s.v. Tailor. . . . A London tailor rated to furnish HALF A MAN to the trained bands, asking how that could possibly be done, was answered, by sending FOUR JOURNEYMEN AND AN APPRENTICE.

1822. NARES, *Glossary*, s.v. Tailor, How old the sarcasm of NINE TAILORS MAKING A MAN may be, does not appear; but it is very old.

1833-4. CARLYLE, *Sartor Resartus*, III. xi. An idea has gone abroad . . . that Tailors are . . . not Men, but fractional Parts of a Man. . . . [Did not] Queen Elizabeth, receiving a deputation of Eighteen Tailors, address them with a 'Good morning, gentlemen both'? Did not the same virago boast . . . a Cavalry Regiment, whereof neither horse nor man could be injured; her Regiment, . . . of Tailors on Mares?

1838. DESMOND, *Stage Struck*, i. Instead of gallivanting a goddess to our shores I had . . . to usher from the boat THE NINTH PART OF A MAN.

1868. BLACKLEY, *Word Gossip*, 76. NINE TAILLERS (itself corrupted from tellers) MAKE IT A MAN [*i.e.* nine counting strokes at the end of a knell proclaim the death of a male adult].

1877. JEWITT, *Half-Hours Eng. Antiq.* 176. At Woodborough the Passing bell consists of THREE TOLLS THRICE repeated FOR A MAN, and two tolls thrice repeated for a woman.

1882. *Spectator*, 26 Aug., 1111. 'How many TELLERS MAKE A MAN?' asked a clergyman of a working man, as they listened to the tolling of a death-bell. 'NINE,' replied he promptly.

1899. WHITEING, *John St.* vii. A wrangling discussion . . . between '48 and a tailor . . . who . . . it appears is the NINTH OF A Conservative working MAN.

THE FAG-END OF A TAILOR, *subs. phr.* (old).—*See* quot.

1600. *Weakest to Wall*, i. 3. Zounds! twit me with my trade? I am THE FAG END OF A TAILOR, in plain English, a botcher.

PHRASES. 'A TAILOR'S shreds are worth the cutting'; 'Like the TAILOR who sewed for nothing, and found the thread himself'; 'Thieving and TAILOR go together'; 'Put a TAILOR, a miller, and a weaver into a sack, shake them well, and the first that puts out his head is certainly a thief' (GROSE).

16[?]. *Pasquil's Nightcap* [Rept.], 1. Theeving is now an occupation made, Though men the name of TAILOR do it give.

TAILORING. TO DO A BIT OF TAILORING, *verb. phr.* (venery).—To get with child; TO SEW UP (*q.v.*).

TAIL-PIPE, *verb* (colloquial).—1. To fasten anything to the tail of a cat or dog; hence (2) to annoy.

1857. KINGSLEY, *Two Years Ago*, ii. Even the boys . . . TAIL-PIPED not his dog.

1876. BLACKMORE, *Cripps the Carrier*, xxix. He might have been TAIL-PIPED for seven leagues, without troubling his head about it.

TAIL-PULLING, *subs. phr.* (publishers'). The publication of books of little or no merit, the whole cost of which is paid by the author: *cf.* BARRABAS.

TAKE, *verb* (colloquial). — To please; to succeed. Hence TAKING (or TAKY) = attractive, captivating. Also TO TAKE TO (or WITH) or TO HAVE A TAKE.

1340. HAMPOLE, *Works* [E. E. T. S.], 2. With whas lufe it es TAKYN.

1607. BEAUMONT, *Woman Hater*, iv. 2. So I shall discourse in some sort TAKINGLY.

1609. JONSON, *Epicœne*, i. 1. Such sweet neglect more TAKETH me Than all the adulteries of art.

1614. ANON., *Faithful Friends*, iii 3. There's something in thee TAKES MY FANCIES so I would not have thee perish for a world.

1625-30. *Court and Times Charles I.*, I. 101. A young man . . . tenderly and firmly affectionate where he TAKES.

d. 1667. JER. TAYLOR, *Artif. Hand.* 41 [LATHAM]. All outward adornings . . . have something in them of a complaisance and TAKINGNESS.

1677. COTTON [WALTON, *Angler*, ii. 237]. To say the truth it is not very TAKING at first sight.

1680. AUBREY, *Lives*, 'Samuel Butler.' He printed a witty poem called Hudibras; the first part . . . TOOKE extremely. *Ibid.* 372. A TAKING doctrine.

c. 1696. B. E., *Dict. Cant. Crew*, s.v. TAKE-TIME . . . VERY TAKING, acceptable, agreeable or becoming. IT TAKES WELL, or, the Town TAKES it, the Play pleas'd, or was acted with Applause, or the Book sells well. No doubt but it will TAKE, no question but it will sell.

d. 1732. ATTERBURY, *Sermons*, I. iii. He knew what would TAKE and be liked; and he knew how to express it after a TAKING manner.

1821. LAMB, *Mrs. Battle on Whist.* She . . . was never greatly TAKEN with cribbage.

1854. COLLINS, *Hide and Seek*, i. 9. Putting in TAKY touches, and putting in bits of effect.

1857. KINGSLEY, *Two Years Ago*, vii. The style TAKES; the style pays; and what more would you have?

1869. STOWE, *Old Town Folks*, 32. Somehow or other, she TOOK to Ruth, and Ruth TOOK to her.

1872. HOLMES, *Poet at Break. Table*, iii. Why do . . . your digestive contrivances TAKE kindly to bread rather than toadstools?

1889. OLIPHANT, *Poor Gentleman*, xxxiv. She's dreadful TAKING . . . When she gets talking, you could just stop there forever.

2. (old colloquial).—To blight; to injure: by infection, disease, grief, etc. As *subs.* = a witch's charm. Hence TAKING = infections (still colloquial or provincial).

c. 1332. *Joseph of Arimathie* [E. E. T. S.], 47. John Popes wyfe of comtone Had a yong chylde, that was TAKEN sodenly.

1596. SHAKSPEARE, *Merry Wives*, iv. 4. 32. He blasts the tree and TAKES the Cattle. *Ibid.* (1596), *Hamlet*, i. 1. No fairy TAKES. *Ibid.* (1605), *Lear*, ii. 4. 166. Strike her young bones, You TAKING airs, with lameness.

1619. FLETCHER, *False One*, iv. 3. Come not near me, For I am yet too TAKING for your company.

d. 1649. WINTHROP, *Hist. New England* [SAVAGE], I. 201. Two shallops . . . were TAKEN in the night with an easterly storm.

1678. *Quack's Acad.* [Harl. Misc. ii. 34.] He hath a TAKE upon him, or is planetstruck.

1768. GOLDSMITH, *Good Natured Man*, i. A plague TAKE their balderdash.

3. (old colloquial).—To deliver a blow; to strike.

c. 1430. *Destr. Troy* [E. E. T. S.], 6394. Ector . . . TOKE his horse with his helis.

1619. FLETCHER, *Humourous Lieut.* ii. 2. A rascal TAKES him o'er the face, and fells him.

1625-30. *Court and Times Charles I.* I. 156. Mr. William Vaux TOOK Mr. Knightly a blow on the face.

4. (conventional.)—To admit to sexual intercourse (of women): also TO TAKE UP ONE'S PETTICOATS TO = to receive a man: *see* RIDE and GREENS for numerous combinations. *See* CARROTS.

1672. RAY, *Proverbs*, 'Proverbial Sentences.' A maid that TAKETH yieldeth. *Ibid.* A maid that laughs is half TAKEN. *Ibid.* Do as the maids do, say no, and TAKE IT.

5. (conventional).—To be got with child: *see* HOLD.

PHRASES AND COLLOQUIALISMS.—TAKE has been, and still is, much in colloquial use. Thus, TO TAKE BACK = to retract; TO TAKE A BREATH = to consider, to seek advice; TO TAKE AFTER = to resemble; TO TAKE ABOUT THE NECK = to embrace; TO TAKE ANYONE FORTH = to teach, to give a start; TO BE TAKEN BY THE FACE = to be put to the blush; TO TAKE BEEF = to run away; TO TAKE DOWN = (1) to humiliate (*see* PEG); (2) to best (Australian); TO TAKE UP = to reprove (also TO TAKE TO DO, TO TASK, and A TALKING TO); TO TAKE HEART = to pluck up courage; TO TAKE TO HEART = to grieve; TO TAKE IT OUT = (1) to get value, to extort or compel satisfaction or reparation; and (2) = to exhaust; TO TAKE ONE (or IT) = to understand; TO TAKE IN = (1)

to deceive, to swindle (whence a TAKE-IN (BEE) = fraud, humbug); (2) = to believe; (3) = to capture, subdue, seize (B. E); TO TAKE OFF = (1) to kill (TAKING-OFF = death); (2) = to ridicule, to mimic (TAKE-OFF = a caricature); TO TAKE OUT = to copy; TO TAKE ON (or BY) = (1) to grieve, to show emotion (hence TAKING = a to-do); and (2) = to simulate; TO TAKE ONE (or A MATTER) ON = (1) to engage, to accept as an opponent, (2) to undertake; TO TAKE TO (or UP) = generic for doing (*e.g.*, to take to gambling, early rising, women, etc.); TO TAKE TO ONE'S LEGS (A SHUTE, WATER, etc.) = to fly: *see* HEELS, adding quots. *infra*; TO TAKE UP (old = TO TAKE) = (1) to arrest; (2) to stop; (3) to reform; (4) to clear up (prov. of the weather); (5) to protect, to defend; (6) to borrow; (7) to rally, to snub; and (8) to understand; TO TAKE UPON = to suspect; TO TAKE UPON ONESELF = to arrogate authority, dignity, etc.; TO TAKE WITH = to side with; TO TAKE UP WITH = (1) to consort with; (2) to court; (3) to endure; and (4) to adopt; TO TAKE THE GLOSS OFF = to detract in value; TO TAKE THE FIELD = to bet against the favourite; TO TAKE UP ONE'S CONNECTIONS (Amer. Univ.) = to leave college; TO TAKE AN OATH = to take a drink; TO TAKE ONE ALONG (or WITH ONE) = to make understand; TO TAKE ONE'S TEETH TO ANYTHING = to set to heartily; TO TAKE A STICK TO = to beat; TO TAKE (or SIT AT) ONE'S EASE IN ONE'S INN = to enjoy oneself: as if one were at home (hence, TAKING IT EASY = drunk); TAKE IT AS YOU LIKE = be angry or not—as you please (BEE). Also (proverbial) 'To TAKE from one's right side to give to one's left'; 'To TAKE ONE UP before he is down' 'To TAKE the bird by the feet'; 'TAKE all, and pay the baker'; 'To TAKE a Burford bait' (= to get drunk); 'To TAKE a dagger and drown oneself'; 'To TAKE A HAIR (*q.v.*) of the same dog'; 'To TAKE a thing in SNUFF' (*q.v.*); 'To TAKE a WRONG SOU (*q.v.*) by the ear'; 'To TAKE counsel of one's pillow'; 'To TAKE heart of grace'; 'To TAKE Hector's cloak' (= to deceive a friend); 'To TAKE one a PEG (*q.v.*) lower'; 'To TAKE physic before one is sick'; 'Who TAKES an eel by the tail and a woman by her word, may say, that he holds nothing.' *See* HUFF; PEPPER; TEA.

c. 1440. *Merlin* [E. E. T. S.], i. 13. As soone as the Iuges knowe ther-of, they well make yow TO BE TAKE FOR couetyse of your londes and herytage, and do Iustice vpon yow.

1470. *Rev. Monk Evesham* [ARBER], 72. [OLIPHANT, *New Eng.* i. 322. TAKE stands for *intelligere*, as in our 'I TAKE IT.']

1530. PALSGRAVE, *Lang. Francoyse*, etc. [HALLIWELL, s.v. Sterracles]. I TAKE ONNE, as one dothe that playeth his sterakels, je tempeste. *Ibid.* TAKE him UP (= reprove).

1569-70. *Wit and Science* [DODSLEY, *Old Plays* (HAZLITT), ii. 350]. Marry, sir, indeed she talks and TAKES ON her, Like a dame, nay like a duchess or a queen.

. . . *Political Poems* [E. E. T. S.], 73. Of verry righte he may be called trewe, and soo muste he be TAKE in every place.

. . . BACON, *Holy War* [*Century*]. You TAKE me right, Eupolis.

1591. GREENE, *Farw. to Folly* [STEEVENS]. The beggar Irus that haunted the palace of Penelope, would TAKE HIS EASE IN HIS INNE, as well as the peers of Ithaca.

1593. PEELE, *Edward I.*, p. 395. I'll TAKE YOU DOWN a button-hole.

1594. SHAKSPEARE, *2 Hen. VI.* ii. 5. How will my mother, for a father's death, TAKE ON with me, and ne'er be satisfied? *Ibid.* (1596), *Hamlet*, i. 1. This I TAKE IT Is the main motive of our preparations. *Ibid.* (1596), *Merry Wives*, iii. 3. What a TAKING was he in when your husband asked who was in the basket. *Ibid.* (1598), *All's Well*, ii. 3. Yet art thou good for nothing but TAKING UP; and that thou'rt scarce worth. *Ibid.* (1598), *2 Hen. IV.* i. 2. And if a man is thorough with them, in honest TAKING UP, then they must stand upon security. *Ibid.* (1598), *1 Hen. IV.* iii. 3. Shall I not TAKE MINE EASE IN MINE INN, but I shall have my pocket picked? *Ibid.* (1600), *As You Like It*, v. 4. *I.* And how was that TAKEN UP? *C.* Faith, we met and found the quarrel was upon the seventh cause. *Ibid.* (1602), *Othello*, iii. 4. Sweet Bianca, TAKE me this work OUT . . . ere it be demanded . . . I'd have it copied. *Ibid.* (1605), *Lear*, v. 1. 65. Let her who would be rid of him devise His speedy TAKING OFF.

d. 1599. SPENSER, *State of Ireland*. Doe you thinke . . . it is soe harde to TAKE HIM DOUNE as some suppose?

1599. JONSON, *Every Man out of Humour*, i. 1. I will TAKE UP, and bring myself in credit, sure. *Ibid.* (1605), *Volpone*, v. 1. I will have thee put on a gowne And TAKE UPON THEE as thou wert mine heir. (1609), *Epicœne*, i. 4. And now I can TAKE UP, at my pleasure. Can you TAKE UP ladies, sir? No, sir, excuse me, I meant money. *Ibid.* (1630), *New Inn*. i. 3. If I have got A seat to sit AT EASE HERE I' MINE INN, To see the comedy.

1601. HOLLAND, *Pliny* [STEEVENS]. Nicophanes gave his mind wholly to antique pictures, partly to exemplify and TAKE OUT their patterns.

c. 1603. HEYWOOD, *Woman Killed* [PEARSON (1876), II. 94]. In a good time that man both wins and wooes That TAKES his wife DOWNE in her wedding shooes. *Ibid.* (1607), *Fair Maid* (PEARSON, *Works* (1894), II. 280]. Because of the old proverbe, What they want in meate, let them TAKE OUT in drinke.

1607. DEKKER and WEBSTER, *Northward Hoe*, ii. 1. My father could TAKE UP, upon the bareness of his word, five hundred pound, and five too. *Ibid.* They will TAKE UP, I warrant you, where they may be trusted.

1611. COTGRAVE, *Dict.* s.v. TANSER, to chide, rebuke, checke, taunt, reprove, TAKE UP.

1616. *Times' Whistle*, [E.E.T.S.], 24. And TAKES UPON HIM in each company As if he held some petty monarchy.

1628. EARLE, *Micro-cosmog.* 2. He TAKES ON against the Pope without mercy, and ha's a iest still in lauender for Bellarmine.

d. 1631. DONNE, *Letters*, xlvii. Sir, it is time to TAKE UP.

1632. MASSINGER, *Emp. of East*, i. 1. If he owe them money . . . never Appoint a day of payment; so they may hope still. But if he be to TAKE UP more, his page May attend them at the gate. *Ibid.* (1636), *Gt. Duke*, etc., i. 2. *Coz.* Be not rapt so. *Cont.* Your Excellence would be so had you seen her. *Coz.* TAKE UP, TAKE UP! *Ibid.* (1637), *Guardian*, i. 1. When two heirs quarrel, The swordsmen of the city, shortly after Appear in plush, for their grave consultations In TAKING UP the difference.

. . . *Apologie for Ajax*, D. D. 1 b. At last, to TAKE UP the quarrel, M. A. and M. R. S. set downe their order that he should not be called any more captaine Ajax.

. . . *New Acad. Compliments* [NARES] All their beds were TAKEN UP; and he had ne'er a room to spare neither, but one.

1641. BAKER, *Chronicles*, 163. A Maid called La Pucelle, TAKING UPON HER to be sent from God for the Good of France.

1651. CARTWRIGHT, *Royall Slave*. *Arc.* Sirrah gaoler, see you send mistris Turnkey your wife to TAKE US UP whores enough.

d. 1657. BRADFORD, *Plym. Plan*, 10. Some were TAKEN and clapt up in prison.

1657. MIDDLETON, *Wom. Bew. Women*. She intends To TAKE OUT other works, in a new sampler.

1669. EARL OF WORCESTER, *Apoth.* God was fain to deal with wicked men as men do with frisking jades in a pasture, that cannot TAKE THEM UP till they get them to a gate; so wicked men will not be taken up till the hour of death.

1672. WYCHERLEY, *Love in a Wood. Ded.* Madam, TAKE IT from me, no Man . . . is more dreadful than a Poet.

1703. FARQUHAR, *Inconstant*, iv. 3. Tis my turn now to be upon the sublime; I'll TAKE HER OFF, I warrant her.

1704. STEELE, *Lying Lover*, ii. 1. My dear friend, you don't TAKE ME—Your friendship outruns my explanation.

1731. SWIFT, *Death of Dr. Swift*. He TAKES UP WITH younger folks, Who for his wine will bear his jokes. *Ibid.* (1710), *To Archbishop King*. We must TAKE UP WITH what can be got.

1743. POCOCKE, *Descr. East*, I. 165. An officer . . . TAKES UP all persons he finds committing any disorders, or that cannot give an account of themselves.

1749. SMOLLETT, *Gil Blas* (1812), I. iii. Everyone BETAKING himself TO HIS HEELS for safety.

1753. RICHARDSON, *Grandison*, i. 39. TAKEN IN, as he calls it, rather by the eyes than by the understanding.

1763. FOOTE, *Mayor of Garratt*, ii. Don't all the world cry, . . . 'Miss Molly Jollop to be married to Sneak; to TAKE UP at last WITH such a noodle as he'?

1766. BROOKE, *Fool of Quality*, i. 370. He . . . perfectly counterfeited or TOOK OFF, as they call it, the real Christian.

1777. SHERIDAN, *School for Scandal*, iii. 1. The great point, as I TAKE IT, is to be exorbitant enough in your demands. *Ibid.* (1778), *Rivals*, iii. 1. An obstinate, passionate, self-willed boy!—Who can he TAKE AFTER? *Ibid.* (1779), *Critic*, i. 1. A band of critics, who TAKE UPON them to decide for the whole town.

1782. BURNEY, *Cecilia*, v. 55. You TAKE me? [on propounding a pun]. *Ibid.*, A TAKE-IN.

d. 1797. WALPOLE, *Letters*, II. 28. She has lived so rakish a life that she is forced to go and TAKE UP.

1809. MALKIN, *Gil Blas* [ROUTLEDGE], 13. Why do you TAKE ON so? . . . You ought rather to bless your stars for your good luck. *Ibid.* 15. Leonarda and Domingo were completely TAKEN IN.

1812. COOMBE, *Syntax*, i. 4. *Hostess.* I took you in last night, I say. *Syntax.* 'Tis true; and if this bill I pay You'll TAKE ME IN again to-day.

1814. AUSTEN, *Mansfield Park*, v. I know so many who have married . . . who have found themselves entirely deceived. . . . What is this but a TAKE IN? . . . But I would not have him TAKEN IN: I would not have him duped.

1817. SCOTT, *Rob Roy*, xv. I dinna believe he speaks gude Latin neither; at least he disna TAKE ME UP when I tell him the learned names of the plants. *Ibid.* (1828), SCOTT, *Aunt Margaret's Mirror*, i. Her sister hurt her own cause by TAKING ON, as the maid-servants call it, too vehemently.

1837. DICKENS, *Pickwick*, xlii. Mr Mivvins, who was no smoker . . . remained in bed, and, in his own words, 'TOOK IT OUT in sleep.'

1843. MACAULAY, *Mirabeau* [*Edin. Rev.*]. They TOOK UP WITH theories because they had no experience of good government.

1847. ROBB, *Squatter Life*. 'Why, Polly, what's the matter, gal?' inquired he; 'what in thunder makes you TAKE ON so?'

1851-61. MAYHEW, *Lond. Lab.* I. 31. If . . . I catch him, I TAKE IT OUT OF him on the spot. I give him a jolly good hiding. *Ibid.* I. 326. Anybody that looks on the board looks on us as cheats and humbugs, and thinks that our catalogues are all TAKES-IN.

1852. *Bee* (Boston), 29 July. The 'Life Boat,' a weekly sheet in this city, TAKES the 'Bee' TO DO for its course in relation to the Liquor Law.

1857. HUGHES, *Tom Brown's Schooldays*, I. vii. They tried back slowly . . . beginning to feel how the run had TAKEN IT OUT OF them.

1865. DICKENS, *Mutual Friend*, iv. 13. Mr. and Mrs. Boffin . . . TOOK IT OUT OF [the baby] in a shower of caresses.

1867. MACLEOD, *Starling*, v. 'I do not TAKE YOU UP, sir,' replied the Sergeant.

1868. WHYTE-MELVILLE, *White Rose*, II. xxii. There's Missis walking about the drawing-room, TAKING ON awful.

1873. CARLETON, *Farm Ballads*, 19. And all of them was flustered, and fairly TAKEN DOWN, And I for a time was counted the luckiest man in town.

1878-80. M'CARTHY, *Hist. Own Times*, xli. Some critics declared that Mr. Cobden had been simply TAKEN IN; that the French Emperor had 'bubbled' him.

1883. *Gentleman's Mag.*, June, 569. It is curious that so able a man could have believed that he could in this way TAKE IN the British public.

d. 1884. C. READE, *Art*, 174. She was always mimicking. She TOOK OFF the exciseman, and the farmers, and her grandmother, and the very parson—how she used to make us laugh!

1885. HOWELLS, *Silas Lapham*, xv. I've disgusted you—I see that; but I didn't mean to. I—I TAKE IT BACK.

1887. A. JESSOPP, *Arcady*, ii. He TOOK UP £500 of Lawyer X . . . and then somehow he war bankrupt.

18[?]. W. S. GILBERT, *Phrenology*. Policeman, TAKE ME UP—No doubt I am some criminal.

1895. *Argus* [Melbourne], 5 Dec., 5. 2. [The defendant] accused hir of having TAKEN HIM DOWN, stigmatised him as a thief and a robber.

1897. MARSHALL, *Pomes*, 107. He was 'dicky,' She was tricky—TOOK HIM IN, and cleared him out.

See ABACK; BACK-SEAT; BEARD; BEEF; BIT; BOOK; BOSOM; BULL; BUSH; BUTTON-HOLE; CAKE; EARTH BATH; EASE; FRENCH LEAVE; GRINDER; GROUND SWEAT; HEELS; HOOK; MEASURE; NAPPING; PEG; PEPPER; POT-LUCK; RAG; RISE; ROAD; RUNNING; SHILLING; SHINE; SIGHT; SILK; SNUFF; STARCH; SUN; TOLL; TURN; VAIN; WIND.

TAKE-A-FRIGHT, *subs. phr.* (rhyming).—Night.

TAKER, *subs.* (sporting).—One who accepts a bet; a BOOKIE (*q.v.*).

1898. GOULD, *Landed at Last*, v. The offer was not accepted, or the TAKER would have lost his money.

TAKING, *subs.* (colloquial).—In *pl.* = receipts.

1851-61. MAYHEW, *Lond. Lab.* II. 528. [Crossing sweepers] at one period have considered fifteen shillings a bad week's work. But now the TAKINGS have very much reduced.

1889. *Sci. American* [*Century*]. The average TAKINGS are $1250 a week.

TALE, *subs.* (colloquial).—An incredible story; a marvellous narration: also OLD WIFE'S (or OLD MAN'S) TALE: *see* BULL and TUB. Whence TALE-TELLER (B. E. and GROSE) = 'Persons said to have been hired to tell wonderful stories of giants and fairies, to lull hearers to sleep.' Also TO TELL TALES OUT OF SCHOOL = (1) to romance, and (2) to play the informer: TELL-TALE (or TELL-TALE-TIT) = an informer; to TELL A TALE = to turn a matter to profit; 'HIS TALE IS TOLD' = 'It is all over with him'; TO BE IN A TALE = to agree: also TO JUMP IN ONE TALE; THEREBY HANGS A TALE, or TELL THAT FOR A TALE (the retort suggestive) = 'That's another story'; TO PITCH A TALE = to spin a yarn: hence TALE-PITCHER = a romancing talker or chattering malcontent.

1469. *Cov. Myst.* [OLIPHANT, *New Eng.* i. 316. We see the phrases: take it or ellys lef . . . TELLE NO TALYS].

d. 1536. TYNDALE [OLIPHANT, *New Eng.* i. 429]. To TELL TALES OUT OF SCHOOL.

1546. HEYWOOD, *Proverbs*. To TELL TALES OUT OF SCHOOLE.

1590. PEELE, OLD WIVES' TALE [BULLEN], 99. I am content to drive away the time with AN OLD WIVES' winters' TALE.

1592. NASHE, *Piers Pennilesse*, 66. Not two of them IUMPE IN ONE TALE.

1596. SHAKSPEARE, *Merry Wives*, iv. 1. *Quick.* Have not your worship a wart above your eye? *Fent.* . . . What of that? *Quick.* Well, THEREBY HANGS A TALE . . . we had an hour's talk of that wart. *Ibid.* (1600). *Much Ado*, iv. 2. 33. 'Fore God, they ARE both IN A TALE. *Ibid.* (1602), *Twelfth Night*, ii. 1. Mine eyes will TELL TALES of me. *Ibid.*, *Winter's Tale*.

1621. BURTON, *Anat. Melan.*, III. II. ii. 4. Whether this be a true story or a TALE, I will not much contend.

1625-30. *Court and Times Charles I.* II. 65. We have some news . . . I must not TELL TALES FORTH OF SCHOOL.

1633. FORD, *'Tis Pity*, i. 3. I find all these but dreams, and OLD MEN'S TALES, To fright unsteady youth.

1729. SWIFT, *Adv. to Ser.* 'Gen. Direct.' The only remedy is to bribe them with goody goodies, that they may not TELL TALES to papa and mamma.

1809. MALKIN, *Gil Blas* [ROUTLEDGE], 378. If ever I find that you TELL TALES OUT OF SCHOOL I will give you such a basting as you never had in your life.

TALESMAN, *subs.* (old).—'The author of a story or report: I'll tell you my TALE and my TALESMAN' (B. E. and GROSE).

TALENT (THE), *subs.* (racing).—In sing. = a BACKER (*q.v.*): as opposed to a layer or bookmaker.

1885. *Field*, 3 Oct. All the TALENT were discomfited, though; as they often are in nurseries.

TALK, *verb.* (stable).—To ROAR (*q.v.*): of horses. Hence TALKER = a ROARER.

COLLOQUIAL PHRASES, etc.—TO TALK ONE DOWN = to silence; TO TALK ONE OUT OF = to dissuade; TO TALK OVER = (1) to persuade: also TO TALK INTO; and (2) to review; TO TALK ROUND = to review a subject; TO TALK UP = (1) to speak plainly (or defiantly); and (2) = to discuss with a view to promotion; TO TALK ONE UP = to urge; TO TALK OUT = to exhaust patience, time, etc.; TO TALK TO = to chide: hence TALKING-TO = a reprimand; TO TALK AT = to gird or chide covertly: talking of a person who is present to another; TO TALK THE HIND LEG OFF A JACKASS (COW, HORSE, etc.) = to seduce, to wheedle, to charm: also TO TALK ONE MAD, TO DEATH, INTO A THING, FEVER, etc.; TO TALK GREEK, DUTCH (or DOUBLE DUTCH) = to talk nonsense; TO TALK THROUGH ONE'S NECK (American) = to talk foolishly; TO TALK TURKEY = to say pleasant things. Also 'TALK of the Angels (or the Devil) and you'll hear the rustling of their wings (or see his horns). *See* BIG; DUTCH-UNCLE; SHOP; TALL-TALK.

1600. SHAKSPEARE, *Much Ado*, ii. 1. 369. If they were but a week married they would TALK THEMSELVES MAD.

1693. VANBRUGH, *Old Bachelor* TALK of the Devil see where he comes. *Ibid.* (1706), *Mistake*. [We will] TALK HIM INTO [it].

1699. BROWN, *Works*, i. 206. I was within an ace of being TALKED TO DEATH.

1704. SWIFT, *Tale of a Tub*, 'Author's Pref.' He may ring the Changes as far as it will go, and vary his phrase till he has TALKED ROUND.

1717. PRIOR [MANLEY, *Lucius*, Epil.]. We'll . . . TALK YOU ALL TO DEATH.

1777. SHERIDAN, *School for Scandal*, iv. 3. And now . . . we will TALK OVER the situation of your affairs with Maria.

1816. AUSTEN, *Emma*, xvii. She had talked her into love; but, alas! she was not so easily to be TALKED OUT OF IT.

1838. BECKETT, *Paradise Lost*, 84. Prithee, good woman, leave your mag off; By George, you'd TALK A DOG'S HIND LEG OFF.

1847. TENNYSON, *Princess*, v. Her that TALK'D DOWN the fifty wisest men.

1859. BARTLETT, *Americanisms*, s.v. TALK . . . The story is an old one, —that an Indian and a white man, after a day's hunting, had only a *turkey* and a *partridge* to show for game. The white man proposed to divide them, and said to the Indian, "Take your choice. You can have the partridge, and I'll take the turkey; or *I'll* take the turkey, and *you* may have the partridge." "Ugh!" said the Indian, "you DON'T TALK TURKEY TO ME any."

1864. *New Haven Register* [BARTLETT]. They are not the only ones who TALK TURKEY, and rob the soldiers of what is contributed for their benefit.

18[?]. MCCLINTOCK, *Beedle's Marriage*. Polly Bean was not the first girl I run against, by a long shot; and I was plaguy apt to TALK TURKEY always when I got sociable, if it was only out of politeness.

TALKEE-TALKEE, *subs. phr.* (colloquial).—1. A corrupt dialect; jargon. Whence (2) chatter; verbiage. Also TALKY-TALKY.

1810 SOUTHEY, *To John May*, 5 Dec. The TALKEE TALKEE of the slaves in the sugar islands.

c. 1812. EDGEWORTH, *Vivian*, x. There's a woman, now, who thinks of nothing living but herself! All TALKEE TALKEE! I begin to be weary of her.

1854. PHILLIPS, *Essays*, ii. 280. A style of language for which the inflated bulletins of Napoleon, the TALKEE-TALKEE of a North American Indian, and the song of Deborah might each have stood as a model.

1883. *Sat. Rev.*, 10 Feb., 189. These Essays . . . are very TALKY-TALKY.

TALKER, *subs.* (Harrow).—1. *See* quot.

1898. HOWSON AND WARNER, *Harrow School*, 208. Then followed solos from those who could sing, and those who could not—it made no difference. The latter class were called TALKERS, and every boy was encouraged to stand up and TALK IT OUT.

2. *See* TALK, *verb*.

TALKING-IRON, *subs. phr.* (American).—A gun or rifle: also SHOOTING-IRON (*q.v.*).

1843-4. HALIBURTON, *Attaché*, ii. I hops out of bed, feels for my trunk, and outs with my TALKIN'-IRON, that was all ready loaded.

TALL, *adj.* (old colloquial).—1. Generic for worth. Thus TALL (=seemly) PRAYERS; A TALL (=valiant) MAN; TALL (=fine) ENGLISH; a TALL (=courageous) SPIRIT; A TALL (=celebrated) PHILOSOPHER; TO STAND TALL =to rely boldly; TALLY (=becomingly or finely) ATTIRED; a TALL (=great) COMPLIMENT, etc. [*Century*: 'the word TALL (= high, lofty) as applied to a man has been confused with TALL, fine, brave, excellent': *cf.*, however, sense 2]. Whence TALL FOR HIS INCHES=plucky for size.

c. 1430. *Destr. Troy* [E. E. T. S.], 3098. Ho tentit not in Tempull to no TALL prayers.

c. 1360. *William of Palerne* [E. E. T. S.], 1706. Sche went forthe stille . . . and TALLICHE hire a-tyred tiȝlli there-inne.

1364. CHAUCER, *Compl. Mars*, 38. She made him at her lust so humble and TALLE.

1440. *Prompt. Parv.* 486. TAL, or semely. Decens, elegans.

1448-60. *Paston Letters*, 224. One of the TALLEST (=fine) young men.

1595. SHAKSPEARE *Rom. and Juliet*, ii. 4. The pox of such antic, lisping, affecting fantasticoes; . . . By Jesu, a very good blade! a very TALL man. . . . *Ibid.* (1599), *Henry V.*, ii. 1. 72. Thy spirits are most TALL. *Ibid.* (1602), *Twelfth Night*, i. 3. 20. He's as TALL a man as any's in Illyria . . . he has three thousand ducats a year. *Ibid.* (1600), *As You Like It*, iii. 5. 118. He is not very TALL, yet for his years he's TALL.

1596. JONSON, *Ev. Man in Humour*, iv. 6. A TALL man is never his own man till he be angry.

d. 1597. PEELE, *David and Bathsheba*, xiii. Well done, TALL soldiers!

c. 1600. *Merry Devil of Edmonton*, iii. 2. 162. He is mine honest friend and a TALL keeper.

1613. FLETCHER, *Captain*, ii. 2. And you, Lodovic, That stand so TALLY on your reputation. *Ibid.* (1619), *Hum. Lieut.*, i. 4. We fought like honest and TALL men.

d. 1665. ADAMS, *Works*, II. 443. We are grown to think him that can tipple soundly a TALL man.

1699. BENTLEY, *Dis. Ep. Phalaris* (1817), 398. A TALL compliment.

1755. BOLINGBROKE, *Frag. Essays*, 65. Sounding imaginary fords, that are real gulfs, and wherein many of the TALLEST philosophers have been drowned.

1809. MALKIN, *Gil Blas* [ROUTLEDGE], 175. Young Pedro was what we call a TALL FELLOW FOR HIS INCHES.

1886. OLIPHANT, *New Eng.*, I. 46. We still hear people talk of TALL (fine) English.

2. (modern colloquial).—Anything out of the common: *e.g.* a TALL (=severe) FIGHT; TALL (=extravagant) TALK: whence TO TALK TALL=to GAS (*q.v.*); a TALL (= a great) PACE, etc. Hence as *adv.*, very, exceedingly. Also, TO WALK TALL=to carry one's head high; to put on SIDE (*q.v.*).

d. 1704. BROWN, *Works*, ii. 134. I for my part was to write BILLS as TALL as the monument, and charge them with the most costly medicines.

1844. KENDALL, *Santa Fé Exped.*, I. 398. Stump straightened up, and started at a pace that would have staggered . . . the greatest pedestrian mentioned in the annals of 'TALL WALKING.'

1846. THORPE, *Backwoods*, 131. I will walk TALL into varmint and Indian: it's a way I've got. *Ibid.*, *Big Bear of Arkansaw* [BARTLETT]. The live sucker from Illinois had the daring to say that our Arkansaw friend's STORIES smelt rather TALL.

1847. ROBB, *Squatter Life* [BARTLETT]. I seed Jess warn't pleased; but I didn't estimate him very TALL, so I kept on dancin' with Sally, and ended by kissin' her good-by, and making him jealous as a pet pinter.

1855. HAMMOND, *Wild Northern Scenes*, 211. It had a mighty big pile of the TALLEST kind of land layin' around waitin' to be opened up to the sunlight.

1869. STOWE, *Oldtown*, 72. I'm 'mazing proud on't. I tell you I WALK TALL—ask 'em if I don't, round to the store.

1891. *New York Times*, 26 Jan. A TALL YARN about the Jews wanting to buy the Vatican copy of the Hebrew Bible.

1897. MARSHALL, *Pomes*, 118. Her cheek was fairly 'TALL.'

1900. KERNAHAN, *Scoundrels*, xv. Public men who TALK TALL about the sacredness of labour.

1901. *Free Lance*, 16 Mar., 582. I. The 'boundary' has absolutely nothing to do with TALL SCORING.

1903. *D. Tel.*, 7 Ap., 9. 1. There is even TALL TALK about extending the strike to other countries, if negotiations fail.

TALL-BOY, *subs. phr.* (old).—1. A wine-glass: large, high-stemmed, and showy; spec. (B. E.) A Pottle or two Quart-pot full of Wine.

1694. MOTTEUX, *Rabelais*, v. xliii. She then ordered some cups, goblets, and TALLBOYS, of golde, silver and crystal to be brought, and invited us to drink.

2. (common). — A very tall chimney-pot.

1884. *D. Tel.*, Jan. This was but one of many scores of pots, TALLBOYS, cowls . . . swept from the chimney-stacks of the Metropolis on Saturday night.

TALL-MEN, *subs. phr.* (old gaming). —HIGHMEN (*q.v.*).

TALLOW, *subs.* (old).—A term of contempt. Thus TALLOW-KEECH (TALLOW-FACE or TALLOW-BREECH) = a very fat person: whence TALLOW-FACED=sickly, pale, undermade; TALLOW-GUTTED=pot-bellied; TALLOW-BREECHED=fat-arsed.

1595. SHAKSPEARE, *Romeo and Juliet*, iii. 5. 158. Out, you baggage! You TALLOW-FACE! *Ibid.* (1598), I *Henry IV.*, ii. 4. Thou whore-son, obscene, greasy, TALLOW-KEECH.

1621. BURTON, *Anat. Mel.*, 519. Every lover admires his mistress, though she be wrinkled, pimpled . . . TALLOW-FACED.

TO PISS ONE'S TALLOW, *verb. phr.* (old).—To leacher oneself lean: like a stag after rutting time.

1596. SHAKSPEARE, *Merry Wives*, v. 5. I am here a Windsor stag; and the fattest, I think, i' the forest. Send me a cool rut-time, Jove, or who can blame me to PISS MY TALLOW.

1694. MOTTEUX, *Rabelais*, v. xxviii. He is nothing but skin and bones, he has PISSED HIS TALLOW.

TALLY (or **TO LIVE TALLY**), *verb.* (provincial). — To live in concubinage; TO DAB IT UP (*q.v.*): chiefly in mining districts. Also to make a tally-bargain.

1890. *Notes and Queries*, 7 S. x. 297. They're LIVING TALLY is the way neighbours speak of them to enquiring visitors. . . . TO LIVE TALLY is quite a common expression amongst the working classes in all parts of Lancashire, as is also TALLY-WOMAN.

TALLY-MEN, *subs.* (old: now recognised). — 'Brokers that let out Cloths at moderate Rates to wear per Week, Month, or Year' (B. E.); 'that let out clothes to the women of the town' (GROSE).

TALLYWAG, *subs.* (venery). — The *penis*: *see* PRICK.

TAME. TO RUN TAME, *verb, phr.* (old).—'To live familiarly in the family with which one is upon a visit' (GROSE). *Cf.* TAME CAT.

TAME-ARMY, *subs. phr.* (old).—The London Trained Bands (GROSE). [*Cf.* Foote's description (*Mayor of Garratt*) of the 'London Regiments' as 'holiday soldiers,' 'never wet to the skin in their lives' except 'as a matter of accident.']

TAME-CAT, *subs. phr.* (common).— A woman's fetch-and-carry; a hearthrug saint.

TAME-GOOSE, *subs. phr.* (old).—A foolish fellow: a simpleton; also TAME-FELLOW (B. E.) = 'tractable, easy, manageable.'

c. 1598. JONSON, *Case is Altered* (1605). I say cast away; yea, utterly cast away upon a noddy, a ninny-hammer, a TAME-GOOSE.

TAMPER, *verb.* (B. E.). — 'To practise upon anyone.'

TAN, *subs.* (old).—To flog; to thrash. Hence TANNING = a beating. Also TO TAN ONE'S HIDE.

. . . *Robin Hood and Tanner* [CHILD, *Ballads*, v. 229]. *Tan.* If he be so stout, we will have a bout, And he shall TAN MY HIDE too.

1731. COFFEY, *Devil to Pay*, 5. Come, and spin, you drab, or I'll TAN YOUR HIDE for you.

1862. WOOD, *The Channings*. The master couldn't TAN him for not doing it.

1884. CLEMENS, *Huck. Finn*, v. 32. If I catch you about that school I'll TAN you good.

TO SMELL OF THE TAN, *verb. phr.* (literary).—To smack of the ring; to be circussy: *cf.* LAMP.

TANDEM, *subs.* (orig. Univ.: now recognised).—1. *See* quot. 1785 and 1890. Hence (2) a carriage so drawn; and (3) a bicycle for two riders.

1785. GROSE, *Vulg. Tongue*, s.v. TANDEM. A two-wheeled chaise, buggy, or noddy, drawn by two horses, one before the other; that is, *at length*.

1831. DISRAELI, *Young Duke*, i. 2. The Duke of St James . . . found sufficient time for his boat, his TANDEM, and his toilette.

1885. PENNELL, *Cant. Pilgr.* Two rode a TANDEM; the third a bicycle.

1890. *Century Dict.*, s.v. TANDEM. A humorous application, prob. first in university use, L. tandem, at length, with reference to time, taken in the E. use with reference to space, 'at length, stretched out in a single file . . . one behind the other . . . as TO DRIVE TANDEM' (that is, with two or more horses harnessed singly, one before the other instead of abreast).

TANGIERENES (THE), *subs.* (military).—1. The Queen's (Royal West Surrey Regiment), late the 2nd Foot: 2. The King's Own (Royal Lancaster Regiment), late the 4th Foot. [Tangiers formed part of the dowry of Catherine of Braganza, the Queen of Charles II.: the regiments were raised for the defence of that possession.]

TANGLE, *subs.* (Scots). A tall, lanky person.

TANGLEFOOT (or **TANGLELEG**), *subs.* (American).—Any intoxicating liquor. TANGLEFOOTED =drunk: *see* SCREWED.

1862. *Punch*, 26 July. Eye-brightener And LEG-TANGLER, And scores of other compounds known To each 'cute bar-room dangler.

1871. *Hartford Courant*, 17 Mar. He proceeded leisurely toward a neighboring saloon in quest of TANGLE-FOOT.

TANK, *verb.* (King Edward's School, Birm.).—To cane; TO COSH (*q.v.*). [Prov. TANK=a blow.]

TANKARD. TEARS OF THE TANKARD, *subs. phr.* (old).—Drippings of liquor on the waist-coat (RAY, B. E. and GROSE).

TANNER, *subs.* (old).—Sixpence: 6d.: *e.g.* 'The Kiddy tipt the rattling-cove a TANNER for luck' ='The lad gave the coachman sixpence for drink' (GROSE): *see* RHINO. Hence TANNERGRAM =a telegram: when the minimum cost was reduced from 1s. to 6d.

1843. DICKENS, *Martin Chuzzlewit*, xxxvii. The Man in the Monument replied a TANNER. It seemed a low expression compared with the Monument.

1877. *Five Years' Penal Servitude*, iii. 239. A 'shise' half-bull, and a 'duffing' TANNER.

1896. *Oamuru* (N.Z.) *Mail*, 13 June. TANNERGRAMS is the somewhat apt designation which the new sixpenny telegrams have been christened in commercial vernacular.

1897. MARSHALL, *Pomes*, 31. This worn-out TANNER 'Arry gave me once, To show his love was true, and not no bunce.

1899. WHITEING, *John St.*, xxviii. 'There's a whole TANNER'S worth for nix . . .' as she makes me a giant button-hole from the wild growths.

1901. WALKER, *In the Blood*, 20. On this trip Billy had pinched a TANNER dropped in the gutter.

TANNIKIN, *subs.* (old).—A Dutch placket; maid, wife, whore, or widow.

1605. MARSTON, *Dutch Courtezan*, i. 1. A pretty nimble-eyd Dutch TANAKIN.

1608. ARMIN, *Nest of Ninnies*. Out she would, tucks up her trinkets, like a Dutch TANNIKIN sliding to market on the ise, and away she flings.

TANQUAM, *subs.* (Old Cant).—*See* quot. 1681.

1662. FULLER, *Worthies* [1840], II. 359. Thomas Dove, D.D., was . . . bred a TANQUAM in Pembroke Hall in Cambridge.

1681. BLOUNT, *Gloss.* TANQUAM is a Fellow's fellow in our Universities.

TANTADLIN. *See* TANTOBLIN.

TANTARABOBS, *subs.* (provincial). —The Devil (HALLIWELL).

TANTIVY, *subs.*, *adj.*, *verb* and *intj.* (old).—Primarily a hunting call: a note on the horn. As *subs.* =(1) full chase; (2)=violent movement; (3) a fox-hunting parson; and (4) *temp.* Charles II., a High Tory: also TANTIVY-BOY. As *adj.*=swift. As *verb* =to racket, to gallop, to rush.

c. 1602. [*Scotland Charact.* (1701), Harl. Misc., vii. 380]. In the time of King James I., soon after his coming into England, one of his own country thus accosted him: Sir (says he), I am sorry to see your majesty so dealt with by your prelatical TANTIVIES.

1641. BROME, *Jovial Crew*, iv. 1. He is the merriest man alive, Up at five a' Clock in the morning . . . and TANTIVY all the country over.

d. 1658. CLEVELAND, *Works*, xxi. Sir, I expected to hear from you in the language of the lost groat, and the prodigal son, and not in such a TANTIVY of language.

1690. *Pagan Prince* [NARES]. How the palatine was restor'd to his palatinate in Albion, and how he RODE TANTIVY to Palpimania.

1694. MOTTEUX, *Rabelais*, v. 'Pant. Prognos.' Braggadocios, tory-rory rakes and TANTIVY BOYS; peppered, clapped, and poxed dabblers.

c. 1696. B. E., *Dict. Cant. Crew*, s.v. TANTIVY-BOIES, high-Flyers, or High-flown Church-men, in opposition to the moderate Church-men; or Latitudinarians, a lower sort of Flyers, like Batts, between Church-men and Dissenters.

1697. VANBRUGH, *Æsop*, ii. 1. *Æsop*. To boot and saddle again they sound. *Rog*. Ta ra! tan tan ta ra! . . . TANTIVE! TANTIVE! TANTIVE!

172[?]. SWIFT, *Stella*, xxxii. An ambitious TANTIVY, missing of his towering hopes of preferment in Ireland is come over to vent his spleen on the late ministry.

d. 1735. ARBUTHNOT [MASON, *Johnson*, 'Suppt.']. This sort . . . is not in esteem with the HIGH TANTIVEE scaramouches.

1740. NORTH, *Examen*, I. ii. 130. About half a dozen of the TANTIVIES were mounted on the Church of England, booted and spurred, RIDING it, like an old hack, TANTIVY to Rome. This . . . led to a common use of slighting and opprobrious words, such as Yorkist. . . . Then they came to TANTIVY, which implied RIDING post to Rome.

1796. DARBLAY, *Camilla*, III. viii. Pray, where are they gone TANTIVYING?

1843. MACAULAY, *Essays*, 'Comic Dramatists of the Restoration.' Collier . . . was a Tory of the highest sort, such as in the cant of his age was called a TANTIVY.

1854. THOREAU, *Walden*, 125. The TANTIVY of wild pigeons, flying by twos and threes athwart my view.

1876. ELIOT, *Daniel Deronda*, xxxi. Being Lady Certainly—and Lady Perhaps—and grand here—and TANTIVY there.

1893. MILLIKEN, *'Arry Ballads*, 33. Oh, scissors! jest didn't we give 'em TANTIVY.

TANTOBLIN, *subs.* (old).—Excrement; SHIT (*q.v.*). Also (GROSE) TANTADLIN and TANTADLIN TART.

1768. GAYTON, *Festivious Notes*, 73. I'll stick, my dear, to thee, and cling withall, As fast as e'er TANTOBLIN to a wall.

TANTONY (or **TANTONY PIG**) *subs. phr.* (old).—1. The smallest pig in a litter: hence a favorite. TO FOLLOW LIKE A TANTONY PIG = to follow closely. Hence TANTONY (2) = a servile follower; a petted retainer; TANTONY-POUCH (*see* quot. 1892).

1594. LYLY, *Mother Bombie*, ii. 1. At the dudgen dagger, by which hangs his TANTONIE POUCH.

1598. STOWE, *Surv. London* (1633), 190. The Officers . . . of the Markets [London] . . . did take from the Market people Pigs starved, or otherwise unwholesome for Man's sustenance. One of the Proctors for St Anthonies tyed a Bell about the neck, and let it feed on the Dunghills; no man would hurt or take it up; but if anyone gave to them bread, or other feeding, such would they know, watch for and daily follow. . . . Whereupon was raised a Proverbe, Such an one will FOLLOW such an one, and whine AS IT WERE AN ANTHONIE PIG.

1659. GAUDEN, *Tears of the Church*, 595. Some are such COSSETS and TANTANIES that they congratulate their oppressors and flatter their destroyers.

1700. CONGREVE, *Way of World*, iv. xi. I'll follow thee, my Anthony, my TANTONY. Sirrah thou shalt be my TANTONY, and I'll be thy PIG.

1710. SWIFT, *Polite Conv.*, i. Lord! she made me follow her last week through all the shops LIKE A TANTONY PIG.

1753. *Chambers' Cyclo.*, Suppt., s.v. ANTHONY. In several places, they [Romanists] keep at common charges a hog denominated ST ANTHONY'S HOG.

1867. *Standard*, 24 May. 'What is an ANTHONY?' 'The littlest pig, your honour. The little pig is always "ANTHONY."'

1892. FAIRHOLT [LILLY, *Works*, ii. 272. Note]. TANTONY-POUCH—I imagine the allusion is to a pouch or purse . . . having a cross . . . on the reverse . . . known as St Anthony was by his cross. This familiar mode of using the saint's name is preserved in the saying, 'He follows him like a TANTONIE PIG,' the saint always being pictured with one of these animals.

2. *See* SAINT.

TANTRUM, *subs.* (colloquial).—1. Usually in *pl.* = a PET (*q.v.*); the sullens; angry whims (GROSE).

1754. FOOTE, *Knights*, ii. I am glad here's a husband coming that will take you down in your TANTRUMS; you are grown too headstrong and robust for me.

1796. BURNEY, *Camilla*, III. v. He was but just got out of one of his TANTARUMS.

1820. GREVILLE, *Memoirs*, 20 Nov. He threw himself into a terrible TANTRUM . . . they were obliged to let him have his own way for fear he should be ill.

1844. THACKERAY, *Barry Lyndon*, xvii. If in any of her TANTRUMS or fits of haughtiness . . . she dared, etc.

1853. LYTTON, *My Novel*, XI. ii. He has been in strange humours and TANTRUMS all the morning.

d. 1876. READE, *Art*, 250. She went into her TANTRUMS and snapped at and scratched everybody else that was kind to her.

2. (venery).—The *penis*; *see* PRICK.

1675. COTTON, *Scoffer Scofft* [*Works* (1770), 282]. Twixt some twelve and one o'clock, He tilts his TANTRUM at my nock.

TAOC, *subs.* (back slang).—A coat. Thus KOOL THE DELO TAOC = Look at the old coat: also in contemptuous reference to the wearer. TAOC-TISAW = a waistcoat; and TAOC-ITTEP = petticoat.

TAP, *subs.* (GROSE: now recognised).—1. 'A gentle blow.' Whence TO TAP (or TAP ON THE SHOULDER) = to arrest (GROSE); TAPPER = a bailiff: also SHOULDER-TAPPER.

2. (old).—In *pl.* = the ears: *see* HEARING CHEATS.

3. (Eton College).—The only place, recognised by the authorities, where a boy can get beer.

Verb. (colloquial).—Out of TAP = to broach, also TO TAP ONE'S CLARET = to draw blood (*see* CLARET); TO TAP THE WIRES = to intercept a telegram; TO TAP A JUDY = to deflower (GROSE); TO TAP A HOUSE = to burgle; TO TAP THE ADMIRAL (*see* ADMIRAL); TO TAP A GUINEA = to change it (GROSE).

1853. BRADLEY, *Verdant Green*, xi. He was thoroughly conversant with the sporting slang of Tintinnabulums Life when he told Verdant that his CLARET had been repeatedly TAPPED.

TO BE ON ONE'S TAPS, *verb. phr.* (American).—On the alert; on one's feet, ready to move.

TO GET THE TAP, *verb. phr.* (tailors').—To get the upper hand.

ON TAP, *adv. phr.* (colloquial).—Available; at hand; on view.

TAPE, *subs.* (old).—1. Spirits: hence RED-TAPE = brandy; WHITE (or BLUE) TAPE = gin: *cf.* RIBBON (GROSE).

1755. *Connoisseur* [*Notes and Queries*, 7 S. x. 78]. Every night cellar will furnish you with HOLLAND TAPE [gin] three yards a penny.

1823. EGAN, *Randall's Scrap Book*. With TAPE in the morning, and punch in the night. *Ibid*. The TAPE I pour into the glass.

1830. LYTTON, *Paul Clifford*. Oh! those jovial days are ne'er forgot! But the TAPE lags. *Ibid.*, 80. RED TAPE those as likes it may drain.

TAPE-WORM, *subs. phr.* (Stock Exchange).—An official who collects the prices of stock for transmission on the TAPE.

TAPLASH, *subs.* (old).—1. Bad, thick beer: cask-dregs or tap-droppings. Hence, as *adj.* = poor, washy, trivial (B. E. and GROSE). Hence (2) a publican: in contempt.

. . . *Clitus's Cater Char.*, 32. Whatever he drains . . . goes in muddy TAPLASH down gutter-lane.

1630. RANDOLPH, *Artistippus* [HAZLITT, *Works* (1875), 14]. Drinking College TAP-LASH . . . will let them have no more learning than they size.

1630. TAYLOR, *Works*, III. 5. Fac'd with the TAP-LASH of strong ale and wine.

1640. *Witts Recr.*, C. 4b, Ep. 25. What, must we then a muddy TAPLASH swill, Neglecting sack?

c. 1648. *Eng. Ballads* [Brit. Mus., C. 22, e, 2.67]. 'No Money, no Friend.' Each TAP-LACH . . . Would cringe and bow, and swear to be My Servant to Eternity.

1673. PARKER, *Reproof Rehear. Transp.* iii. Did ever any man run such TAPLASH as this at first broaching? *Ibid.* [TODD], Bandied up and down by the schoolmen, in their TAPLASH disputes.

1793. O'KEEFE, *The London Hermit*, i. 1. They've rare things at home, yet come drinking our TAPLASH.

TAP-PICKLE, *subs. phr.* (Scots).—'The grain at the top of the stalk' (T. F. HENDERSON). By implication = a girl's maidenhead, or even favour.

1786. BURNS, *Hallowe'en*, vi. Her TAP-PICKLE maist was lost When kittlin' in the fause-house wi' him that night.

TAPPY. ON THE TAPPY, *phr.* (common).—Under consideration; on the *tapis*.

1690. CLARENDON, *Diary*. [They] gave no votes in the matter which was UPON THE TAPIS.

TAP-SHACKLED, *adj. phr.* (old).—Drunk; *see* SCREWED.

1610. HEALEY, *Disc. New World*, 82. Being truly TAPP-SHACKLED, mistook the window for the dore.

TAP-TUB (THE), *subs. phr.* (obsolete literary). — The *Morning Advertiser*: also *The Gin and Gospel Gazette*.

1823. BEE, *Dict. Turf*, s.v. TAP-TUB . . . *Morning Advertiser* . . . because that print catcheth the drippings of yesterday's news, and disheth it up anew.

TAR, *subs.* (old).—A sailor: also TARPAULIN (of which TAR is an abbreviation), JACK TAR (B. E. and GROSE), TARBREECH (or TARRYBREEKS), and TARBARREL. Hence TAR-TERMS (B. E.) = 'proper Sea Phrases or Words.' TAR-HOOD = the navy.

1582. STANYHURST, *Æneid*, iv. 393. Fro the shoare late a runnygat hedgebrat, A TARBREECHE quystroune dyd I take, with phrensye betrasshed.

1672. PHILLIPS, *Maronides*, 117. A young TARPAULIN Jack-a-lent.

1677. WYCHERLEY, *Plain Dealer*, ii. 1. Dear TAR, thy humble servant.

1695. CONGREVE, *Love for Love*, iii. 7. If I were a man—you durst not talk at this rate . . . you stinking TAR-BARREL.

[?]. *Turkish Spy*, i. The Archbishop of Bourdeaux is at present General of the French naval forces, who, though a priest, is yet permitted to turn TARPAULIN and soldier.

1701. BROWN, *Works*, i. 151. They'll provide for our TARRS, and settle the nation.

1706. WARD, *Wooden World*. 'To Reader.' The most glorious Piece of the Creation, called a TAR.

1725. BAILEY, *Erasmus*, I. 277. *Adol.* If you won't consent we'll throw you and your Cabinet into the Sea together. *Ant.* Spoken like a TARPAULIN.

1749. WALPOLE, *Letters*, 'To Mann,' ii. 285. A sea-piece . . . in which his own ship in a cloud of cannon was boarding the French Admiral. This . . . has been so ridiculed by the whole TARHOOD that the romantic part has been forced to be cancelled.

1786. BURNS, *A Dream*. Young royal TARRY BREEKS [Prince William Henry, afterwards William IV.].

1790. DIBDIN, *Sea Songs*, 'Tom Bowling.' Thus Death, who kings and TARS dispatches, In vain Tom's life has doffed.

1849. MACAULAY, *Hist. Eng.*, iii. To a landsman these TARPAULINS, as they were called, seemed a strange and half savage race. *Ibid.* xiv. His TARS passed their time in rioting among the rabble of Portsmouth.

1855. KINGSLEY, *Westward Ho*, xxx. No old TARRY-BREEKS of a sea-dog, like thy dad!

TO TAR OUT, *verb. phr.* (old).—To punish; to serve out. TO TAR AND FEATHER = a practice of great antiquity, but rare nowadays: heated tar is poured over a person, who is then covered with feathers.

TARRED WITH THE SAME BRUSH, *phr.* (common).—Alike.

TAR-BOX, *subs. phr.* (common).—A shepherd: in contempt. Hence the proverbial sayings, 'TO LOSE A SHEEP (erron. SHIP) FOR A HA'PORTH OF TAR' (GROSE); and 'To caper like a fly in a TAR-BOX.'

1672. RAY, *Proverbs*. Ne'er lose a hog for a HALFPENNY-WORTH OF TAR. A man may spare in an ill time; as some who will rather die than spend ten groats in physic. Some have it, Lose not a sheep, etc. Indeed, TAR is more used about sheep than swine. Others say, Lose not a ship, etc.

TAR-BRUSH, *subs. phr.* (common).—Black blood: in contemptuous reference to colour; A TOUCH OF THE TAR-BRUSH = a dash of the negro.

1785. GROSE, *Vulg. Tongue*, s.v. BLUE-SKIN . . . A person begotten on a black woman by a white man; any one having . . . A LICK OF THE TAR-BRUSH.

1899. HYNE, *Furth. Adv. Capt Kettle*, viii. Snuff-and-butter ladies . . . ignore their own lick of the TAR-BRUSH.

TARE-AND-TRET, *subs. phr.* (old).—'City bon-ton for—a Rowland for an Oliver, no matter the juxtaposition of the two matters. To give as good as is brought' (BEE).

TAR-FINGERS, *subs. phr.* (old).—A petty pilferer: *see* PITCH-FINGERS. Hence TARRY = thievish.

1822. GALT, *Sir Andrew Wylie*. The gypsies hae TARRY fingers . . . ye need an e'e in your neck to watch them.

TARGET, *subs.* (venery). The female *pudendum*: *see* MONOSYLLABLE.

TARLEATHER, *subs.* (old).—In quot. = a woman: in contempt.

1551. STILL, *Gammer Gurton's Needle*. HAZLITT, iii. 218. Thou'se pay for all, thou old TARLETHER.

TARDY, *adj.* (Winchester College).—Late: *e.g.* 'I was TARDY task' = 'I was late with my work.'

1803. *Gradus ad Cantab.*, s.v. TARDY. To be noted for coming late into Chapel.

TARHEEL, *subs. phr.* (American).—An inhabitant of S. Carolina. [Tar is one of the chief products of the State.]

TARNATION (and **TARNAL**), *adj.* and *adv.* (American). 'Damnation'; 'eternal'; mild oaths. As *adj.* = great, very, etc.: *e.g.* TARNATION strange, a TARNAL time, etc.

1839. HOOD, *Sailor's Apology*. And her TARNATION hull a-growing rounder!

1837. BARHAM, *Ingolds. Leg.*, 'Bagman's Dog.' Extremely annoyed by the 'TARNATION whop.'

1848. LOWELL, *Biglow Papers*, I S. ii. I darsn't skeer the TARNAL thing.

1853. LYTTON, *My Novel*, v. 8. A TARNATION long word.

1901. *Free Lance*, 30 Nov., 220. 2. This TARNATION old country.

TARPAULIN. *See* TAR.

TARRADIDDLE, *subs.* (old).—A fib; a yarn. As *verb* = to hoax (GROSE).

TARRIWAG, *subs.* (old).—In *pl.* = the *testes*: the BALLS (*q.v.*).

1622. TAYLOR, *Laugh and Be Fat* (1724), 5. I would not lose my TARRIWAGS for the best . . . in Christendom.

1838. BECKETT, *Paradise Lost*, 82. By gum, my arse is bare! I wish I had a clout, or rags, Just to wrap up my TARRIWAGS.

TARSE, *subs.* (venery).—The *penis*; the TAIL (*q.v.*): see PRICK. Hence TO STRIP ONE'S TARSE IN = *subagitare*: see GREENS and RIDE; and TARSANDER = a STALLION (*q.v.*).

14[?]. *Porkington MS.*, 10. Now 3e speke of a TARSE, In alle the warld is not a warse Thane hathe my hosbond.

1686. DORSET, *Faithful Catalogue* [ROCHESTER, *Works* (1718), II. 32]. Her rapacious arse Is fitter for thy sceptre than thy TARSE. *Idem*, 35. How often praised thy dear curvetting TARSE.

1682. *Juvenalis Redivivus*, 7. Let's draw our pens and quit TARSANDER'S praise. [See also Note 7, page 31.]

TART, *subs.* (common).—Primarily a girl, chaste or not; now (unless loosely used) a wanton, mistress, 'GOOD-ONE' (*q.v.*). Hence TARTLET (a diminutive).

ENGLISH SYNONYMS. [*Note*: The distinction between Woman, Wife, Concubine, Mistress, Harlot, and Bawd is very loosely observed in literary and popular usage, both in English and French.] Abandoned woman (or, generic, abandoned habits, *q.v.*); abbess; academician; ammunition wife (or whore); anonyma; aphrodisian dame; artichoke; article; Aspasia; Athanasian wench; aunt (SHAKSPEARE); autem-mort.

Baby; badger; baggage; bangster; Bankside lady; barber's chair; barrack-hack; bat; bawd; bawdy-basket; bedfagot; bed-fellow; bed-maker; bed-thrall (W. MORRIS); beef; best girl; bird (SHAKSPEARE); bird-of-the-game; bit; bit of stuff (mutton, fish, muslin, calico, etc.); bitch; bite; bloss; blouzalinda; blouzabella; blowze; blow; blowen (or blowing); bobtail; bona; bona-roba (SHAKSPEARE, FLETCHER, etc.); brevet-wife; brim; brimstone; brown Bess; bulker; bum- (or bottom-) worker; bunter; burerk (or burick); bussbeggar; buttered-bun; buttock; buttock-broker; buttock-and-file (whore and pickpocket); buttock-and-twang (or -sham file = whore and no pickpocket).

Cab-moll; canary; canary-bird; carrion; carry-knave; case-vrow; cast-off; cat; chauvering donna (or moll); chopper; cleaver; cockatrice; cock-chafer; cocktail; coleman hedge (HALLIWELL); Columbine; commodity (DEKKER); common Jack; common sewer; concubine; convenient; cooler; cottontop; Covent-garden nun (vestal, or abbess); cow; crack; cracked

pitcher; croshabell (GREENE); cruiser; cunt; curbstone sailor; cut; cyprian.

Dart (SKELTON); dasher; dalilah; daughter-of-Eve; dell; demi-mondaine; demi-rep; dickey-bird; disorderly; dolly; dolly-mop; dona; donny (HALLIWELL); dopey; doorkeeper (DEKKER); double-barrelled gun; dove; dowsabel; dowse; doxy; drab; drap; dragon (FLETCHER); dress-lodger; dromaky; drurylane vestal; dulcibel; dulcinea; dutch; dutch widow.

Easy virgin; easy virtue (or woman); evening-star; everlasting daughter-of-Eve.

Fad-cattle (generic); fagot; fancy-fagot; family of love (generic); fancy-piece; fancy-woman; feather-bed and pillows; fen; file (LANGLAND); filth (SHAKSPEARE); fire-ship (= a rotten whore); flag-about; flagger; flapper; flash-mollisher; flashtail; Fleet-street houri (or dove); flesh-broker; fling-dust; flip-flap; flirt-gill (SHAKSPEARE, SCOTT); flirt-gillian; Flirtina Cop-all; florence; fly-by-night; fly-girl (-donna, or -dame); foreskinhunter; frigate; free-lance; froe; fuckstress; Fulham virgin.

Gal; gallimaufry (SHAKSPEARE); game (generic); game-hen (-pullet, or woman); gamester (SHAKSPEARE, JONSON); garrison-hack; gay-girl (-bit, piece or woman: CHAUCER); gear (SHAKSPEARE: generic); gig (CHAUCER); giggler; giglet (UDAL, SHAKSPEARE, MASSINGER); gill (FLORIO); gill-flirt (FLORIO, COTGRAVE); girl; gixie (FLORIO, COTGRAVE); goat-

milker; gobble-prick (GROSE); go-between; good-girl (or good-one: COTGRAVE); gook; graduate; grass-widow; GREEN-GOODS (*q.v.*); green-goose (SHAKSPEARE, FLETCHER); guineahen; guttersnipe.

Hackney (or HACKSTER: SHAKSPEARE, NASH); hair (generic); harlotry (generic and individual: SKELTON, WYCHERLEY, CONGREVE); harridan (GROSE); Haymarket-ware; hedge-creeper (BIRD, -whore, etc.: FLORIO); hen; hen-of-the-game; high-flyer; high-roller; hightytighty; high-priestess of Paphos; hiren (SHAKSPEARE, POOLE, ADAMS, SYLVESTER); hiver; hobby-horse (CHAUCER, SHAKSPEARE); hogoninny; holer (CHAUCER); hooker; hop-picker; hopping wife; horse-breaker; hot-'un; houri; house-bit (-dove, or -piece); house-keeper; housewife; hunt-about; hurry-whore (TAYLOR); hussy.

Impure; incognita.

Jack's delight; jack-whore; jade; jam; jamtart; jay (SHAKSPEARE); jerker; jezebel; jill; jomer; jude; judy; jug (ROWLEY, CENTLIVRE); junt (MIDDLETON).

Kate (Scots); keep; keptwoman (or wench); kiddleywink; KIDLEATHER (*q.v.*); kindhearted wench; kittie (DUNBAR, LYNDSAY); kittock (DUNBAR); knock-em-down.

Laced mutton (SHAKSPEARE, *cum suis*); lady of accommodating morals (of easy virtue, of the lake, of pleasure, of more complaisance than virtue, etc.; DAVENANT, BUTLER); lady-bird; Lais; lakerlady (= a player's harlot: JONSON,

BROME); land-carrack (DAVENANT); laundress (BRERETON, BURTON, DAVENANT); left-handed wife (KILLIGREW); leman; lift-skirts; ligby; light-frigate; light-heels; light-o'-love (NASH, FLETCHER); light skirts; lindabrides (KILLIGREW, SCOTT); lioness (DAVIES); little girl; lone duck (or dove); loose woman; loose-bodied gown (DEKKER); loose kirtle; loteby (CHAUCER).

Mab; MACKEREL (*q.v.*); madam (RANDOLPH, DURFEY); Madam Van (or Ran); magdalen (CONGREVE); maggie; magpie; maid marian (SHAKSPEARE); maid-of-all-work; mare; MARK (*q.v.*); market-dame (WARD); maux (or mawkes); mean bit (MEAN, *q.v.*); mermaid (MIDDLETON); merry-bit; merry-arsed Christian (GROSE: also of a wencher); merry-legs; Messalina; minx (FLORIO, SHAKSPEARE); miss (EVELYN, BUTLER, DRYDEN); mistress; misswoman (or missliver: TYNDALE); mob; moll (GROSE); molly (DURFEY); mollisher; moonlighter; mopsy; morsel (DUNBAR, SHAKSPEARE, MARMION); mort (DEKKER, MIDDLETON, JONSON, FLETCHER, etc.); mort wap-apace; moth; mother (or mother of the maids); mount; Mrs Lukey Props (a tramp's bawd); MUTTON (generic: GREENE, SHAKSPEARE, *cum suis*); mutton-broker.

Nag (MARSTON, SHAKSPEARE); nanny; natural (SHADWELL); naughty dickey-bird; naughty-pack (ADDLINGTON, ROWLEY, SWIFT, etc.); necessary; needlewoman (CARLYLE); nestcock; nescock; nestlecock

(FULLER); niece; niggler; night-bird; night-cap; night-gear; night-hawk; night-hunter; nightingale; night-piece; night-poacher; night-shade (FLETCHER); night-snap; night-trader (MASSINGER); night-walker (DURFEY); nit; nockstress; nocturne; noffgur; nug; nun (FOOTE); nurse; nymph of darkness (or of the pavement).

Occupant (MARSTON); omnibus; one of my cousins (of us, of them); one and thirty; open-arse (SHAKSPEARE); out; owl.

Pack; pagan (SHAKSPEARE, MASSINGER); palliasse; panel; paphian; parnel (or pernel: LANGLAND); particular; partridge; peculiar (HERRICK); perfect lady; petticoat (DEKKER, PRIOR, SMOLLETT); pheasant; Phryne; pick-up; piece (SHAKSPEARE, JONSON, SMOLLETT); pillow-mate; pinch-prick; pinnace (DEKKER, CONGREVE); pintle-bit (fancier, maid, or ranger); piper's wife; pirate; placket (SHAKSPEARE); placket-lady; play-fellow (SHAKSPEARE); plaything (SMOLLETT); pleasure-lady (or merchant); plover (JONSON); poke; poker; poker-breaker; pole-climber; pole-cat (SHAKSPEARE); poll; polly; princess; presbyteress (BALE); presenterer; prancer; pretty dear (SMOLLETT); prettyhorsebreaker; prick-climber; priest's niece; prim; pross; prugge; public ledger; pug (MARSTON, COTGRAVE, DRYDEN); punk (SHAKSPEARE, *cum suis*); pure; purest pure; pure one; Puritan; purse-finder; pusher; put; puttock; puzzle.

Quædam; quail; quean; queen's (or king's) woman; quiet mouse; quicumque vult.

Rabbit-pie; ragtime girl; rainbow; ramp (CHAUCER, STILL, SHAKSPEARE); ram-skyt; randy-dandy (or ranty-tanty); rannel (HARVEY); rantipole; real lady; receiver-general; rep (or rip); ribaude (ribald, ribold or ribaud); rig (or rigol); rigmutton; rigsby; road (SHAKSPEARE); rover; rump.

Sad cattle (generic); St. John's Wood vestal; sample of sin; Saturday-to-Monday; scolopendra; Scotch warming-pan (= a chambermaid); screw; scrudge; sempstress; shake; shakester; she familiar; she-napper; schickster (or schiksa); shoful-pullet; Shoreditch fury (HALL); short-heels (CHAPMAN); silk-petticoat (WARD); single-woman (PALSGRAVE); sinner (JONSON); sister (DEKKER); sister of charity; skainsmate (SHAKSPEARE); smock-servant (agent, piece, toy, etc.); soiled dove; sparrow; special; spigot-sucker; spinster (FLETCHER, FULLER); spital-whore (or sinner); skit; split-arse mechanic; spoffkins; sporting-piece; sportswoman; squirrel; stammel (or strammel); STAND (*q.v.*); star-gazer; stew; stingtail; strawfagot; street walker; strum (or strumpet: SHAKSPEARE, FLORIO, COTGRAVE); suburban; summer-cabbage; Sunday-girl; swallow-cock; sweetheart; sweetmeat.

Tackle; tail; tailist; tail-trader; tail-worker; tally-woman; tart (or tartlet); tenant-in-tail; tender parnell; termer (or term-trotter); Thais; thing; thorough good-natured wench; threepenny up-righter (GROSE); tib; tickletail; tiffity-taffity; tit (or titter); trat (back slang); traviata; treble-

cleft; treddle; trigmate (provincial); trillbye (old: trill = the *anus*: *cf.* DOUBLE-BARRELLED); trollop; truck; trug; trull; trumpery; twang; tweak; twigger; twofer.

Under bed-blanket; underwear; unfortunate.

Vestal; vestal of Pickthatch; virgin-pullet; vroe (or vrow).

Wagtail; waistcoateer; walking mort; wallop; wanton; warm-'un; week-end girl (or mistress); wench; wench of the game; Whetstone-park deer; whipster; white-apron (POPE); willing tit; wife in water-colours; woman; woman-of-all-work; woman of pleasure; woman of the town; wren; wriggler; wrong-'un.

FRENCH SYNONYMS. [R. = Rabelais.] *Accrocheuse* (R.); *agenouillée*; *Agnès*; *aimeuse*; *alicaire* (R.: Lat. *alicaria*); *almanach de trente-dix mille adresses*; *ambubage* (R.: Lat. *ambubaia*); *andre*; *Arthurine*; *asticot* (also = *penis*); *ancelle* (Lat. *ancilla*); *autel de besoin*.

Bachelière (a student's mistress); *badine*; *bagasse* (R.: also *baiasse* and *bajasse*); *bague*; *baladeuse*; *balance de boucher* (*qui pèse toutes sortes de viandes* —R.); *balayeuse*; *baleine*; *belle*; *belle de nuit*; *belle enfant*; *belle petite*; *bezoche* (R. and ROQUEFORT: *besogner* + argot termination -*oche*: also *besoche* and *besochée*); *la bicherie* (generic: *la haute bicherie* = fashionable whoredom; [*la basse*] *bicherie* = slum harlotry); *blanc*; *blanchisseuse de tuyaux de pipe* (R.); *blanchisseuse en chemise*; *boîte* (also *boîte à jouissance*, and *boîte à vérole ; bonne amie ; bonne foutée ; bonne jouissance ; bonsoir* (R.); *bordelière* (=cab-moll); *boulevardière* (=suburban); *boule rouge ; boulonnaise ; boutonnière en pantalon ; bourre de soie ; bourbeteuse ; bourdon ; braydonne* (R.); *brimballeuse ; bringuenaudée* (COTGRAVE); *bru* (Old Fr.).

Cabaque ; cagne ; caignardière (R.); *caille* (QUAIL, *q.v.*); *calège* (VIDOCQ); *calicote ; cambrouse* (R.); *camélia ; le monde camelotte* (generic); *canicule* (R.); *cantonnière* (R.); *carabine* (=a sawbones' mistress); *carcan à crinoline ; carne ; carogne ; cascadeuse ; casserole ; catin* (also *catan* and *cathos*=KITTY); *chahuteuse ; chameau ; chamègue ; champisse* (R.); *chausson ; [femme de] chemin* (R.); *cité d'amour ; citrière* (R.); *cloistrière* (R.); *cocatrix* (R.); *cocotte* (*cocotterie*= generic); *coignée* (R.); *colombe ; connaissance ; consœur ; coquine* (BALZAC); *coureuse* (also *coureuse ;* RABELAIS, SCARRON, MOLIÈRE); *cousine de vendange* (=hop-picking wife); *crampeuse ; crevette ; croupière* (=buttock); *cul crotté ; cul terreux.*

Dame de joie (=lady of pleasure); *dame aux camélias* DUMAS *fils*); *dame à quatre* (*sous ; dehanchée ; dehoussée* (R.); *demi-castor ; demi-mondaine ; demoiselle du bitume ; demoiselle du Marais* (R.); *demoiselle du Pont-Neuf ; dessalée ; donde ; donzelle ; dossière ; drogue ; drôlesse ; drouine* (R.); *droule ; drue* (R.); *duchesse* (BERANGER).

Ecremeuse ; ensoignante (R.); *éponge ; espèce ; étudiante* (a student's whore).

Farceuse ; femme facile ; femme galante ; femme inconséquente (BALZAC); *femme comme il en faut ; femme de cavoisi ; femme de mal récapte ; femme de péché ; femme de vie* (*i.e. vit*) ; *femme de terrain ; fenêtrière ; feuille ; fesse* (=buttock); *feuilletée ; fillasse ; fille ; fille de Cypris ; fille de joie* (VOLTAIRE); *fille de métier ; fille du tiers-ordre ; fille d'amour ; fille publique ; fille de feu ; fille de jubilation ; fille à parties ; fille en carte ; fille en brème ; fille de barrière ; fille de trottoir ; fille de tourneur ; fille de maison ; fille de numéro ; fillette de pis* (R.); *fleur de macadam ; folieuse* (R.); *fripesauce* (Old Fr.): *friquenelle* (R. and BALZAC).

Galante ; galoise (R., COTGRAVE); *galupe ; galvaudeuse ; gamelle ; garce* (R.=wench); *garçonnière ; gaultière* (Old Fr.); *gaupe* (R.); *gaure ; génisse ; gibier de bordel ; gibier de maquerelle ; gibier de Saint-Lazare ; gigolette ; goipeuse ; gonzesse ; gothon ; gouapeuse ; goudine ; gouine ; goudinette* (R.); *gouge* (R.); *gouine* (Old Fr.); *gourgandine* (R.: also *gourgande*); *gouvernante* (=housekeeper); *goyne* (R.); *grenier à coups de sabre ; grenouille ; gripette ; grisette ; grue* (R.); *guenille* (R.); *guenippe* (R.); *guenon ; guenuche ; gueule ; gueuse : guimpe ; guinche.*

Harrebane (R.); *hirondelle de goguenot ; hollière* (R.: O. Fr. *holler*=to run); *hore* (R.: =whore); *horizantale ; hourière* (R.: also *hourieuse*).

Impure.

Jacqueline ; Jeannette ; Jeanneton (R., BÉRANGER, HUGO); *joueuse de flûte ; jouisseuse ; journalière.*

Lame ; lampe de couvent ; lanterne ; laqueuse ; lard ; larguèpe ; largue ; latine (=a harlot living in the Quartier Latin); *laisée ; latrine ; lésébombe ; lescheresse* (R.); *lévrier d'amour* (R.: =a bawd); *levrière* (R.: also *levrette*); *lice* (R.: also *lyce*, O. Fr.); *linge ; linotte coiffée ; lipète ; lolo ; lorette ; loudière* (R.); *Louis ; louille ; louve ; loupeuse* (R.); *lutainpem.*

Maca (also *maquerelle*=a bawd); *Madame* (=a bawd: generic); *Madame Diogène* (*'qui plante des hommes'*); *Madame de rébut ; magnée ; magnuce ; magneuse ; mal peignée ; mangeuse de blanc* (or *de viande cru*); *manuelle ; maquillée ; Marane* (R.); *marcheuse ; Margot* (also *Margotin* : generic ; *la margot*=whoredom); *marmite ; marneuse ; marquise ; martingale* (R.); *matelassière ; matelas ambulant ; maxima* (R.); *membre de la caravane ; menesse ; meschine ; mignonne ; mimi ; moché* (R.); *moclonneuse ; mome ; momentanée ; morceau* (=PIECE, *q.v.*); *morue ; mouquette ; musardine* (old: an habituée of the Concerts-Musard); *musequine* (R.).

Ningle ; nymphe.

Offre à tous (s') ; omnibus ; ordure (R.); *ouvrière.*

Paillarde (VILLON, R.); *paillasse ; paillasse à troufion ; paillasse de corps de garde ; pailletée ; pannanesse* (R.); *pantame ; panturme ; papillonne ; particulière ; pas grand'chose ; pantonnière* (R.); *peau ; peau de chien ; pêche à quinze sous* (DUMAS *fils*); *[femme de] péchié* (R.); *pélérine de Venus* (R.); *pélican ; pellice* (R.); *persilleuse, pétasse ; petite dame ; pieuvre* (BALZAC); *pigéon voyageur ; pinerie* (=prickery, *i.e.*=harlotry); *pierreuse ; piqueuse de trains ; planche à boudin ; polissonne* (BÉRANGER); *polisseuse de tuyaux de pipe ; polisseuse de mâts de cocagne en chambre ; ponifle ; Pont-Neuf ; postiqueuse* (R.); *pompe funèbre ; pontonnière ; pont d'Avignon ; portion ; poufiasse ; poule ; poulette ; poupée ; poupoule ; poupine ; poupinette ; prat ; présentière ; prêtresse de Venus* (RABELAIS, LA FONTAINE); *princesse* (or *princesse de l'asphalte*); *pucelle de Marolles* (or *de Belleville*); *punaise ; putain* (VILLON = whore: also *pute ; putanisme, puterie*, or *putage*=lechery).

Raccrocheuse ; racoleuse ; rafaitière (R.); *ragasie* (R.); *rameneuse ; redresseuse* (R.); *religieuse ; rempardeuse ; retapeuse ; reveleuse* (R.); *ribaude* (R.); *ricalde* (R.); *rigobette* (R.: also *rigobète*); *rivette ; robe ; roufle ; roti ; rouche ; roulette ; rouleuse ; rouloure ; rousse-caigne* (R.); *roustisseuse* (=buttock-and-file); *rutière.*

Safrette (R.); *salope ; saucisse ; sauterelle ; scaldrine* (R.); *serraine ; servante-maitresse ; [fille du] siècle* (R.); *sirène ; siroteuse ; sœur ; sommier de caserne ; sougnant* (R.); *souillon ; soupeuse ; sourditte* (R.); *sucrée ; suivante de Vénus* (R.).

Tapeuse de tal ; taupe ; terrière ; terreuse ; terrinière ; tireuse de vinaigre (R.); *tonton* (GAVARNI, LA FONTAINE); *torchon ; torpille d'occasion ; toupie* (R.); *tourterelle ; touse* (R.); *traînée ; traîneuse ; travailleuse ; tripière ; trottière ; truande ; trumeau ; trusseresse ; trychine.*

Usagère (R.).

Vache ; vache à lait ; vadrouille ; veau ; vendangeuse d'amour ; vendeuse de tendresse ; véroleuse ; verticale (=uprighter); *vesse* (=bladder); *vessie ; vésuvienne ; vestal ; vézon ; viagère* (R.); *viande ; [femme de] vie* (*i.e. vit* — R.); *vielle garde ; villotière* (COTGRAVE); *voirie ; volaille* (=pullet); *voyagère* (R.: also *voyageuse*).

Wagon ; wauve.

Zona.

18[?]. *Bird o' Freedom* [quoted in *S. J. & C.*]. Wrong 'uns at the Wateries, Noffgurs at the Troc, Coryphyées by Kettner, TARTLETS anywhere.

1896. MARSHALL, *Pomes*, 48. His years were in number some threescore and three, And Flossie ye TARTE of his bosom was she.

Adj. (B. E. and GROSE: now recognised).—'TART DAME [*sic*], sharp, quick' (B. E.); 'TART, sour, sharp, quick, pert' (GROSE).

TARTAR, *subs.* (old).—1. A bad or awkward tempered person: male or female. TO CATCH A TARTAR =(1) to be caught in one's own trap; and (2) to get more than one bargained for, or the worst of an encounter (B. E. and GROSE). [*Ency. Dict.*: Properly *Tatar*. 'The *r* was inserted in mediæval times to suggest that the Asiatic hordes who occasioned such anxiety to Europe came from hell (Tartarus), and were the locusts of Revelation ix.'] Hence (2) an adept: *e.g.*, 'He is quite a TARTAR at cricket or billiards' (GROSE).

1663. BUTLER, *Hudibras*, I. iii. Now thou hast got me for a TARTAR, To make m' against my will take quarter.

1748. SMOLLETT, *Rod. Random*, xxx. The captain . . . looking at me with a contemptuous sneer, exclaimed, 'Ah! ah! have you CAUGHT A TARTAR?'

1772. FOOTE, *Nabob* [OLIPHANT]. [One man may] CATCH A TARTAR [in another].

1772. BRIDGES, *Burlesque Homer*, 171. He turn'd him back and stole the cart, And strait despatch'd it to his quarters For fear of Justice Fielding's TARTARS.

1862. THACKERAY, *Philip*, xiv. A TARTAR that fellow was, and no mistake.

1868. WHYTE-MELVILLE, *White Rose*, II. i. This disconsolate sailor, whose first wife had been what is popularly called a TARTAR.

1901. *Free Lance*, 9 Mar., 558. 1. Occasionally, of course, Barabbas CATCHES A TARTAR who threatens legal proceedings and demands to inspect the publisher's books. Needless to say, the books were 'cooked' from the first in view of such an eventuality.

3. *See* TARTARIAN.

TARTARIAN (or **TARTAR**), *subs.* (Old Cant).—A thief: spec. a strolling vagabond; 'a sharper' (B. E.).

1596. SHAKSPEARE, *Merry Wives*, i. v. 18. Here's a Bohemian TARTAR.

c. 1600. *Merry Devil of Edmonton* (*Temple*), i. 1. 10. There's not a TARTARIAN, Nor a carrier, shall breathe upon your geldings.

1640. *Wandering Jew*, 3. And if any thieving TARTARIAN shall break in upon you, I will, with both hands, nimbly lend a cast of my office to him.

TARTUFFE, *subs.* (colloquial).—A hypocrite; a pretender. [From the character in Molière's comedy.] Hence TARTUFFISH= hypocritically precise; and TARTUFFISM=hypocrisy.

d. 1768. STERNE [*Ency. Dict.*]. She has some mother-in-law, or TARTUFISH aunt, or nonsensical old woman, to consult upon the occasion as well as myself.

TASSY, *subs.* (Australian).—Tasmania.

1894. *Argus*, 26 Jan., 3, 5. To-day TASSY—as most Victorian cricketers and footballers familiarly term our neighbour over the straits—will send a team into the field.

TASTE, *verb.* (venery).—To know carnally; TO ENJOY (*q.v.*). Hence TASTY-BIT (or MORSEL)= a JUICY wench (*q.v.*).

1602. SHAKSPEARE, *Othello*, iii. 3. 345. I had been happy, if the general camp . . . had TASTED her sweet body, So I had nothing known. *Ibid.* (1605), *Cymbeline*, ii. 4. 57. If you can make't apparent That you have TASTED her in bed, my hand And ring is yours.

1628. EARLE, *Micro-cosmog.*, 1. A Childe is a Man in a small Letter, yet the best Copie of Adam before hee TASTED of Eve, or the Apple.

1638. CAREW, *Counsel to a Young Maid*, No. 2 [EBSWORTH, 22]. So shalt thou be despis'd, fair maid, When by the sated lover TASTED.

d. 1704. BROWN, *Works*, i. 74. Then having let us see, pray let us TASTE Those dear conceal'd Delights below the Waste.

TASTE OF THE CREATURE, *subs. phr.* (old).—A dram; a drink; esp. of whiskey. *See* CRATER, and *add* quots., *infra.*

c. 1570. *Pride and Lowliness.* The CREATURE [wine] of the proper kind Was good, though use offenden therewithal.

1604. SHAKSPEARE, *Othello*, ii. 3. 313. Come, come, good wine is a good familiar CREATURE, if it be well us'd.

1638. PENKETHMAN, *Artach.*, Kiij. The moderate use of the CREATURE, and sparing Dyet, which is very little practised.

1690. DRYDEN, *Amphit.*, iii. 1. My master took too much of the CREATURE last night.

1694. MOTTEUX, *Rabelais*, v. xxxvi. This was the place where we were to have a TASTE OF THE CREATURE.

1758. SMOLLETT, *Fathom*, xiii. The German . . . never went to bed without a full dose of the CREATURE.

1827. HONE, *Ev. Day Book*, II. 286. His followers . . . take a little CRATHUR.

1888. *Standard*, 14 Aug., 2. Says he, 'Maggie,' have a drop of the CRATUR.

A NASTY TASTE IN ONE'S MOUTH, *subs. phr.* (colloquial).—An unpleasant feeling: regret, loathing, anxiety, etc.

1899. WHITEING, *John St.*, xxv. Never before have I heard such a speech . . . 'Sort o' gives a NASTY TASTE IN YOUR MOUTH,' says Low Covey.

TASTER, *subs.* (colloquial).—A small quantity; a taste: in quot. a small glass of ice-cream.

1901. *D. Tel.*, 21 May, 10. The irate signor . . . produced—not a halfpenny TASTER for the policeman, but a tattered copy of a work called 'Law without Lawyers.'

TASTY, *adj.* (common).—1. FULL-FLAVOURED (*q.v.*); NUTTY (*q.v.*); SPICY (*q.v.*); THICK (*q. v.*). Hence (2) of the best; RIPPING (*q.v.*).

1897. MARSHALL, *Pomes*, 31. He's fond of something TASTY . . . me and him was spliced last Monday week.

1899. WHITEING, *John St.*, vii. Nice and TASTEY, observes my friend . . . as he points to a leg that seems to fear nothing on earth . . . not even Lord Campbell's Act.

TAT, *subs.* (Old Cant).—1. In *pl.* =dice. Whence TAT BOX=a dice box; TAT-MONGER (or TATOGEY)=a sharper or cheat using loaded dice; TAT'S-MAN= a dicing gambler; TAT-SHOP=a gambling den (B. E. and GROSE): *see* IVORIES.

1887. HENLEY, *Villon's Straight Tip.* Rattle the TATS, or mark the spot.

2. (Old Cant).—A rag: MILKY TATS=white linen. Also as *verb* =to collect rags; and TATTER= a rag-gatherer.

1851-61. MAYHEW, *Lond. Lab.*, I. 417. He goes TATTING and billy-hunting in the country. *Ibid.*, 424. I'll tell you about the TAT-GATHERERS, buying rags they call it, but I call it bouncing people.

3. (colloquial).—An abbreviation of 'tattoo.'

TIT FOR TAT. *See* TIT.

TA-TA, *intj.* (common).—A salutation; 'Good-bye'!

18 [?]. STEVENSON, *Treas. of Franchard.* And so, TA-TA! I might as well have stayed away for any good I have done.

TATARWAGGES. *See* TATTERS.

TATER (or **TATUR**), *subs.* (vulgar).—A POTATO (*q.v.*). Whence TATER-TRAP=the mouth; TATER-AND-POINT=a meal of potatoes: *see* POINT. Also as noteworthy, one or two phrases: *e.g.*, TO SETTLE ONE'S TATERS=to settle one's hash; TO STRAIN ONE'S TATERS =TO PISS (*q.v.*); S'WELP MY TATERS (*see* SWELP).

1838. BECKETT, *Paradise Lost*, 57. Taste this . . . 'Twill to your TATER-TRAP prove nice.

1856. MAYHEW, *World of London*, 6, note. On this principle . . . the mouth has come to be styled the TATER-TRAP.

1869. *Echo*, 9 Sept. 'Life of London Boys.' They . . . would climb anywhere—where they would nick the TATERS, or apples, or onions, or anything else.

1891. *Notes and Queries*, 7 S. xi. 29. Uncommon fine TATERS them, sir.

TATOL, *subs.* (Winchester).—A tutor in Commoners.

TATTERDEMALION, *subs.* (old).—A ragged wretch: a general term of contempt: also TATTER, and RAGS-AND-TATTERS: *see* quot. 1696. TATARWAGGS and TATTERWALLOPS = ragged clothes (GROSE). *See* TAT, 2. As *adj.* = ragged.

1360. CHAUCER, *Romaunt of the Rose*. [TYRWHITT, (ROUTLEDGE), 7259.] And with graie clothis nat full clene, But frettid full of TATARWAGGES.

1608. SMITH, *True Travels*, I. 40. Those TATTERTIMALLIONS will have two or three horses . . . as well for service as for to eat.

1617. BRATHWAITE, *Smoaking Age*, 47. Whole families shall maintaine their TATTERDEMALLIONS, with hanging thee out in a string.

1622. MASSINGER, *Virgin Martyr*, iii. Why . . . should thou and I onely be miserable TATTERDEMALIONS, rag-a-muffins, and lowsy desperates?

1626. SMITH, *Eng. Sea Terms*, 864. TATTERTIMALLION [appears amongst new substantives].

1633. HEYWOOD, *Royal King* [PEARSON, *Works*, 1874, vi. 31]. A TATTERDEMALEAN that stayes to sit at the Ordinary to-day.

1638. RANDOLPH, *Hey for Honesty*, iii. 1. Well spoke, my noble English TATLER.

1677. *Poor Robin's Visions*, 73. I have carried a great many in my wherry, males and females, from the silken whore to the pitifull poor TATTERDEMALION.

1678. COTTON, *Virgil Travestie* (1770), 10. There are a few TATTER-DE-MALLIONS, That (with a Pox) would be Italians.

1687. BROWN, *Saints in an Uproar* [*Works*, i. 82]. The women . . . exclaim against Lobsters and TATTERDEMALLIONS. *Ibid.*, ii. 181. A couple of TATTERDEMALION hobgobblings.

1694. MOTTEUX, *Rabelais*, v. xxix. I wonder . . . what pleasure you can find in talking thus with this lousy TATTERDEMALLION of a monk.

c. 1696. B. E., *Dict. Cant. Crew.* s.v. TATTER-DE-MALLION, a ragged tatter'd Begger, sometimes half Naked, with design to move Charity, having better Cloths at Home. *In Tatters*, in Raggs. *Tatter'd and Torn*, rent and torn.

1700. CONGREVE, *Way of the World*, iii. 5. I'll reduce him to frippery and rags, a TATTERDEMALION! I hope to see him hung with TATTERS, like a . . . gibbet thief.

1771. SMOLLETT, *Humph. Clinker* (1900), i. 106. Mrs. Bramble . . . said she had never seen such a filthy TATTERDEMALION, and bid him begone.

1887. HENLEY and STEVENSON, *Deacon Brodie.* Crime's rabble, hell's TATTERDEMALION.

TO TATTER A KIP, *verb. phr.* (old).—To wreck a brothel.

1766. GOLDSMITH, *Vicar*, xx. My business was . . . to assist at TATTERING A KIP, as the phrase was, when he had a mind for a frolic.

TATTLE-BOX, *subs. phr.* (common).—A chatterbox: also TATTLER= a gossip: *see* TITTLE-TATTLE.

c. 1709. WARD, *Terræfilius*, I. iv. 36. She is an invidious TATTLE-BOX that rattles people out of their Senses.

1834. AINSWORTH, *Rookwood*, iv. vi. Oliver Whiddles—the TATLER old! Telling what best had been left untold.

TATTLE-DE-MOY, *subs. phr.* (? nonce-word).—*See* quot.

1676. [SOUTHEY, *Doctor* (1834) xciv.]. A TATTLE-DE-MOY . . . was a new-fashioned thing in . . . 1676, 'much like a saraband, only it had in it more of conceit and of humour. . . .' Thomas Mace invented it . . . and he called it a TATTLE-DE-MOY 'because it tattles and seems to speak those very words or syllables.'

TATTLER, *subs.* (Old Cant).—A watch (GROSE); spec. 'an Alarm, or Striking Watch or (indeed) any' (B. E.). Hence TO FLASH A TATTLER=to wear a watch; TO SPEAK TO A TATTLER=to steal a watch: Also TATTLE.

1781. MESSINK, *Choice of Harlequin*, 'Frisky Moll's Song' A famble, a TATTLE, and two pops Had my bowman when he was ta'en.

1823. EGAN, *Dict. Turf*, s.v. TATTLER . . . Doughey drew a gold TATTLER, and got two p'nd ten of the fence for it; so my regulars is ten bob.

1878. HINDLEY, *Catnach*. . . . Speak to the TATTLER, bag the swag, And finely hunt the dummy.

TATTLING FELLOW (or **WOMAN**), *subs. phr.* (old: B. E.).—'Prating, impertinent.'

TATTOO. *See* DEVIL'S TATTOO, *adding* GROSE (1785) and quot. *infra* as authorities.

1841. LYTTON, *Night and Morning*. Mr. Gawtrey remained by the fire beating the DEVIL'S TATTOO upon the chimney-piece, and ever and anon turned his glance towards Lilburne, who seemed to have forgotten his existence.

TAUNTON-TURKEY, *subs. phr.* (American).—A herring: *cf.* BILLINGSGATE-PHEASANT, GLASGOW-MAGISTRATE, etc.

1850. ALLIN [MRS. A. A. CURTIS], *Home Ballads*. Our fisheries o'er the world are famed, The mackerel, shad, and cod! And TAUNTON TURKEYS are so thick, We sell them by the rod!

TAUT, *adj.* (nautical).—Severe. Hence TAUT HAND=a disciplinarian (CLARK RUSSELL).

TAVERN (THE), *subs.* (Oxford Univ.).—New Inn Hall. [A punning allusion: also because the buttery is open all day long.]

1853. BRADLEY, *Verdant Green*, III. xi. Little Mr. Bouncer had abandoned his intention of obtaining a *licet migrare* to THE TAVERN, and had decided . . . to remain at Brazenface.

TO HUNT A TAVERN FOX (or TO SWALLOW A TAVERN TOKEN), *verb. phr.* (old).—To get drunk. Hence 'the TAVERN BITCH has bit him in the head' (or TAVERNED)=drunk: *see* SCREWED. Also TAVERNER=a tippler.

1340. *Ayenbite of Inwyt*, 51. [OLIPHANT, *New Eng.*, i. 30. We light upon the TAVERNYER or TAVERN-HAUNTER; this has given rise to an English surname.]

1596. JONSON, *Every Man in Humour*, i. 3. Drunk, sir! you hear not me say so; perhaps hes SWALLOWED A TAVERN TOKEN, or some such device.

1602. DEKKER, *Honest Whore*, i. 4. s.v.

1630. TAYLOR, *Old Parr* [Harl. Misc., vii. 76]. Else he had little leisure time to waste, Or at the ale-house huff-cap ale to taste; Nor did he ever HUNT A TAVERN FOX.

TAVISTOCK (or **TAWSTOCK**) **GRACE**, *subs. phr.* (HALLIWELL).—'Finis.'

TAW, *subs.* (old).—*See* quots. TAWLINGS (or TAW)=the line from which the marble is shot: hence (American), TO COME TO TAW=to come to SCRATCH (*q.v.*), to be called to account; TO BE ON ONE'S TAW='a species of threat' (GROSE).

1764. CHURCHILL, *Candidate*. To whip a top, to knuckle down at TAW.

1784. COWPER, *Tirocinium*, i. 307. To kneel and draw The chalky ring, and knuckle down at TAW.

1801. STRUTT, *Sports and Pastimes*, 491. TAW, wherein a number of boys put each of them one or two marbles in a ring and shoot at them alternately with other marbles, and he who obtains most of them by beating them out of the ring is the conqueror.

1819. VAUX, *Memoirs*, ii. 193. ONE UPON YOUR TAW, a person who takes offence at the conduct of another, or conceives himself injured by the latter, will say, never mind, I'll be ONE UPON YOUR TAW; or, I'll be a MARBLE ON YOUR TAW; meaning I'll be even with you some time.

1837. DICKENS, *Pickwick*, xxxiv. He [inquired] whether he had won any alley TORS or commoneys lately.

1842. TENNYSON, *Will Waterproof*. A . . . pottle-bodied boy That knuckled at the TAW.

1857. HUGHES, *Tom Brown's School-days*, i. 3. His small private box was full of peg-tops, white marbles (called 'alley TAWS' in the Vale).

1883. *Century Mag.*, xxxvi. 78. Their cries of 'rounses,' 'TAW,' 'dubs,' . . . might be heard there before and after school hours.

Verb. (old).—1. To beat; to scourge (GROSE); and (2) to torment. [A.S. *tawian*=to beat.] Also TAWS (or TAWSE)=a leather strap, slit or fringed at one end, used by schoolmasters (SCOTS).

1549. CHALONER, *Moriæ Enc.*, G 2. They are not TAWED, nor pluckt asunder.

1607. MARSTON, *What You Will*, E 2. For Ile make greatness quake, Ile TAWE the hide Of thick-skin'd Hugenes.

1609. *Ammianus Marcellinus* [NARES]. When he had been well TAWED with rods, and compelled to confesse.

1613. FLETCHER, *Captain*. He's to be made more tractable . . . if they TAW him as they do whit-leather.

1656. *Men Miracles*, 45. They TAW'D it faith, their gunnes would hit, As sure as they had studied it.

TAWDRY, *adj.* (old colloquial: now recognised in its debased sense).—1. Orig. fine, elegant, trim; whence (2) cheaply showy, ignorantly fine; *see* quots. 1696 and 1822. Also derivatives such as TAWDERED, TAWDRILY, TAWDRINESS, etc. TAWDRY-LACE (or TAWDRY)=a rustic necklace or girdle; TAWDRUMS = fal-lals. Hence, by implication = bawdy (*see* quot. 1759–62): *see* TOL-TAWDRY.

1530. PALSGRAVE, *Lang. Francoyse*. SEYNT AUDRIES LACE ['whence (OLIPHANT) came TAWDRY in later times'].

1548. PATTEN [ARBER, *Garner*, iii. 71]. [OLIPHANT, *New Eng.*, i. 519. We read of TAUTHRIE LACES in a list of superstitious trumpery; these were sold at St Audrey's fair at Ely.]

1579. SPENSER, *Shepheard's Calendar*, Ap., 133. Gird your waste, For more fineness, with a TAWDRIE lace.

1604. SHAKSPEARE, *Winter's Tale*, iv. 3. Come, you promised me a TAWDRY LACE, and a pair of sweet gloves.

1605. MARSTON, *Dutch Courtezan*, v. No matter for lace and TAWDRUMS.

1610. FLETCHER, *Faithful Shepherd*, iv. 1. The primrose chaplet, TAWDRY LACE, and ring.

1612. DRAYTON, *Polyolb.*, ii. 686. Of which the Naiads and the blue Nereids make Them TAUDRIES for their necks. *Ibid.*, iv. 727. They curl their ivory fronts; and not the smallest beck But with white pebbles makes her TAUDRIES for her neck.

1670. *Moral State of England*, 161. A kind of TAWDRINESS in their habits.

c. 1696. B. E., *Dict. Cant. Crew*, s.v. TAUDRY, garish, gawdy, with Lace or mismatched and flaring Colours: A Term borrow'd from those times when they Trickt and Bedeckt the Shrines and Altars of the Saints, as being at vye with each other upon that occasion. The Votaries of St *Audrey* (an Isle of *Ely* Saint) exceeding all the rest in the Dress and Equipage of her Altar, it grew into a Nay-word, upon anything very gawdy, that it was all Taudry, as much as to say all ST AUDREY.

1716. MONTAGUE, *Letters*, 22 Aug. Dirty people of quality TAWDERED OUT.

1736. PULTENEY, *To Swift*, 21 Dec. A rabble of people, seeing her very oddly and TAWDRILY dressed, took her for a foreigner.

1759–67. STERNE, *Tristram Shandy*, v. 59. There is nothing in this world I abominate worse than to be interrupted in a story, and I was that moment telling Eugenius a most TAWDRY one.

1762. CHURCHILL, *Prophecy of Famine*. All that artificial TAWDRY glare, Which Virtue scorns, and none but strumpets wear.

1822. NARES, *Glossary*, s.v. TAWDRY. A vulgar corruption of saint Audrey, or Auldrey, meaning saint Ethelreda, [implying] that things so called had been bought at the fair of saint Audrey, where gay toys of all sorts were sold. This fair was held in the Isle of Ely . . . on the . . . 17th of October. . . . An old historian makes saint Audrey die of a swelling in her throat, which she considered as a particular judgment, for having been in her youth much addicted to wearing fine necklaces. NICH. HARPSFIELD (1622), *Hist. Eccl. Anglicana*.

TAWNY-COAT, *subs. phr.* (old).—An ecclesiastical officer. [From the livery.]

. . . [DODSLEY, *Old Plays* [REED], vi. 99]. Husband, lay hold on yonder TAWNY COAT.

c. 1577. HARRINGTON, *Catal. Bishop* (PARK), ii. 22. It happened one day, bishop Elmer [? Aylmer] of London, meeting this bishop [Whitgift, then bishop of Worcester] with such an orderly troope of TAWNY COATS, demaunded of him, 'How he could keepe so many men?' he answeared, 'It was by reason he kept so few women.'

1592. SHAKSPEARE, 1 *Hen. VI.*, iii. 1. 174. Down with the TAWNY-COATS!

TAWNYMOOR, *subs.* (old).—A mulatto.

1717. *Centlivre, Bold Stroke for a Wife*, i. 1. There's a black, a TAWNYMOOR, and a Frenchman.

TAX-COLLECTOR, *subs. phr.* (old).—A highwayman.

T-BEARD, *subs. phr.* (old colloquial).—A fashion in trimming the beard; a beard cut T-wise.

1618. FLETCHER, *Queen of Corinth*, iv. 1. Your T-BEARD is in fashion.

TEA, *subs.* (old).—Urine: *see* COLD-TEA, LONG-TEA, and TEA-VOIDER.

1712. GAY, *Trivia*, ii. 297. Who 'gainst the sentry's box discharge their TEA.

Verb. (colloquial).—1. To take tea: *cf.* 'dine,' 'lunch,' 'sup,' etc. (all recognised).

1837. BARHAM, *Ingoldsby Leg.*, III. 255. Unless . . . you'd TEA with your wife.

1839. DICKENS, *Nicholas Nickleby*, ix. Father don't TEA with us.

2. (common).—To engage with, encounter, go in against.

1896. KIPLING, *Seven Seas*, 'The Lost Legion.' And some share our tucker with tigers, And some with the gentle Masai (Dear boys!), TAKE TEA WITH the giddy Masai.

TEACH. *See* GRANDMOTHER and SUCK.

TO TEACH IRON TO SWIM, *verb. phr.* (common).—To achieve the impossible.

TEACH-GUY, *subs. phr.* (back slang).—Eight shillings.

TEACUP. STORM (or TEMPEST) IN A TEACUP (or teapot), *subs. phr.* (common).—Much ado about nothing: *cf.* 'a tide and flood though it be but in a basin of water' (BENTLEY, *Phalaris*, 1699, 399).

1885. *D. Tel.*, 30 Sep. The 'échauffourée' in 'Southern Bulgaria' will prove a mere STORM IN A TEACUP.

TEA-FIGHT, *subs. phr.* (common).—A tea party: *cf.* MUFFIN-WORRY; TOFFEE-SCRAMBLE, etc.

1885. *North Am. Rev.*, cxli. 242. Gossip prevails at TEA FIGHTS in a back country village.

1899. WHITEING, *John Street*, vi. 'Kind of a TEA-FIGHT,' he returns. . . . I looked to Tilda . . . 'Come to tea next Sunday,' says the girl.

TEA PARTY. *See* BOSTON TEA-PARTY and NICE.

TEAGUE, *subs.* (old).—An Irishman: in contempt. Hence TEAGUELAND = Ireland (B. E. and GROSE).

1661. *Merry Drollery* [EBSWORTH], 335. TEG [stands for an Irishman].

1671. *Bagf. Ballads.* With Shinkin ap Morgan, with blew Cap or TEAGUE.

1672. RAY, *Proverbs.* Like TEAGUE'S cocks, that fought one another, though all were of the same kind.

c. 1686-8. *Old Song*, 'Lilibulero.' Ho, brother TEAGUE.

d. 1704. BROWN, *Works*, iv. 275. Excuse me from TEAGUELAND and slaughter.

d. 1706. DORSET, *Antiquated Coquet.* To TEAGULAND we this beauty owe, TEAGUELAND her earliest charms did know . . . The TEAGUES in shoals before her fell.

1706. WARD, *Wooden World*, 70. He shall gulph ye down the rankest Stinkibus with as good a gusto as a TEAGUE does Usquebaugh.

1733. SWIFT, *To Grant* [SCOTT, *Swift*, xviii. 203]. I was a year old before I was sent to England; and thus I am a TEAGUE, or an Irishman.

TEAICH-GIR, *adj.* and *adv.* (back slang).—'Right': pronounced 'tadger.' Hence TADGING = TIP-TOP (*q.v.*).

TEAM, *subs.* (colloquial).—Two or more persons associated for some purpose: *e.g.*, a football side, a cricket eleven, a coach's pupils, etc. [Properly of animals harnessed together.] Hence TEAM-WORK = work in company.

1622. MASSINGER, *Virgin Martyr*, iv. Hear me, my little TEAM of villains, hear me.

1852. BRISTED, *Eng. Univ.*, 191. A mathematical tutor can drive a much larger TEAM than a classical.

1885. *Echo*, 7 Sep. The football season in the North and Midlands is in full swing, and it is therefore little matter for wonder that the country TEAMS bear away the laurels every year from the metropolis.

TEAR, *subs.* (common).—A boisterous jollification; a SPREE (*q.v.*). As *verb.* (colloquial) = to move, speak, or act violently; to rant; to fume. Hence TEARER or TEAR CAT or TIMOTHY TEARCAT = (1) a blusterer; a bully; a ROARER (*q.v.*); and (2) anything violent. TEARING = violent, raving, etc.; TEAR-MOUTH (or TEAR-THROAT) = a ranting actor: and a *adj.* = vociferous; TO TEAR CHRIST'S BODY (old colloquial) = to blaspheme. TO TEAR ONE'S BEARD (or HAIR) = a simile of violent emotion.

1383. CHAUCER, *Cant. Tales*, 13,889. His oathes been so great and so damp-nable, That it is grisly for to hiere him swere Our blisful LORDE'S BODY thay TO TERE.

1563. FOXE, *Acts and Monuments*, viii. 641. [He speaks of swearers as] TEARERS OF GOD.

1592. SHAKSPEARE, *Mid. Night's Dream*, i. 2. I could play *Ercles* rarely, or a part to TEAR A CAT IN. *Ibid.* (1610), *Antony and Cleop.*, iv. 12. In the midst a TEARING groan.

1601. JONSON, *Poetaster*, iii. 1. You grow rich, you do, and purchase, you TWO-PENNY TEAR-MOUTH.

1606. DAY, *Isle of Guls*, Induction. I had rather heare two good jests, than a whole play of such TEAR-CAT thunder-claps.

1611. MIDDLETON, *Roaring Girl.* TEAR-CAT, a ruffian (Dram. Pers.).

1630. TAYLOR, *Works* [NARES]. The majesticall king of fishes . . . keepes his court in all this hurly-burly, not like a tyrannical TEAR-THROAT in open arms, but like wise Diogenes in a barrell.

1672. WYCHERLEY, *Love in a Wood* [ROUTLEDGE], 17, 41. [OLIPHANT, *New Eng.*, ii. 107-8. We have seen a TEARING groan about 1610; we read of TEARING (boisterous) wits, and of TEARING ladies; hence come our TEARING spirits.]

1672. C. COTTON, *Scarronides* (1725), I. 9. A huffing Jack, a plund'ring TEARER, A vap'ring Scab, and a great SWEARER.

1692. LESTRANGE, *Fables.* This bull that ran TEARING mad for the pinching of a mouse.

1713. ADDISON, *Cato*, ii. 5. Gods! I could TEAR MY BEARD to hear you talk.

1767. STERNE, *Tristram Shandy*, vii. 19. Though you do get on at a TEARING rate, yet you get on but uneasily.

1819. SCOTT [LOCKHART (1902), vi. 41], *Letter to Southey.* Such a letter as Kean wrote t'other day to a poor author, who . . . had, at least, the right to be treated as a gentleman by a copper-laced two-penny TEARMOUTH.

1843. DICKENS, *Christmas Carol*, iii. And now two smaller Cratchits, boy and girl, came TEARING IN.

1847-8. THACKERAY, *Vanity Fair*, lx. Immense dandies . . . driving in TEARING cabs.

1852. BRISTED, *Upper Ten Thousand*, 17. He TEARS along BEHIND him a sleigh.

1867. BROWN, *Capt. Smith and Poch.* [BARTLETT]. But the lofty chief's fair daughter Told her Pa he hadn't oughter; And the way she TORE AROUND induced him to behave.

1869. STOWE, *Oldtown*, 525. Aunt Lois, she's ben . . . TEARIN' ROUND 'nough to drive the house out o' the winders.

TO TEAR ONE'S SEAT, *verb. phr.* (tailors').—To attempt too much.

TEAR-PUMP. TO WORK THE TEAR-PUMP, *verb. phr.* (common).—To weep; 'to turn on the water-works.'

TEASE. ON THE TEASE, *phr.* (old).—Uneasy; fidgety.

1706. CENTLIVRE, *Basset-Table*, iii. There's one UPON THE TEIZE already.

See TEASER.

TEASER, *subs.* (pugilists').—1. A disturbing blow. TO TEASE (or TEAZE) = to flog (GROSE and VAUX); TO NAP THE TEAZE = to be flogged.

1840. EGAN, *Book of Sports.* The latter planted a TEASER on Sam's mouth, which produced the claret in streams.

2. (colloquial). — Anything difficult or perplexing.

1823. BEE, *Dict. Turf*, s.v. TEASER —a hit on some queer point, as on the tip of the nose. Also, 1st. A summons to little chancery. 2nd. A talking fellow who haunts another. 3rd. An old horse belonging to a breeding stud—'though devoid of *fun* himself, he is the cause of it in others.

1857. LAWRENCE, *Guy Livingstone*, ix. The third is a TEASER—an ugly black bullfinch with a ditch on the landing side.

TEASER OF THE CATGUT. *See* CATGUT-SCRAPER.

TEA-VOIDER, *subs. phr.* (old).—A chamber pot (GROSE).

TEA-WAGGON, *subs. phr.* (obsolete nautical).—An East Indiaman.

1836. DANA, *Two Years*, xxxiv. Like a true English TEA-WAGON; and with a run like a sugar-box.

TEAZLE, *subs.* (venery). — The female *pudendum*: *see* MONO-SYLLABLE.

TEC, *subs.* (common). — A deTECtive: *see* NARK.

1886. *Echo*, 4 Dec. I went to Dartford, in Kent, to Whistler's, so that we should not get picked up by the TECS.

1897. MARSHALL, *Pomes.* I went to the bank with the paper cash, And they said they'd send for a 'TEC.

1899. WHITEING, *John St.*, v. 'TECS down, one day, from Scotland Yard to look for dynamit'. *Ibid.*, viii. The depleted brood resist but rarely, for to them the TEC is fate.

1901. *Pall Mall Gaz.*, 11 May, 2. 3. This sham 'TEC is in refreshing contrast, considered as an artist, to the sham aristocrat with a preposterous title unknown to Debrett.

TEDDY. TEDDY MY GODSON, *phr.* (Irish).—'An address to a simple fellow or ninny' (GROSE).

TEDDY HALL (Oxford Univ.).—St. Edmund's Hall, Oxford.

TE DEUM *See* BACKWARDS.

TEEJAY, *subs.* (Winchester College).—A new boy; a *pro*TEGÉ: placed for a time under the care of older scholars. *Cf.* SHADOW and SUBSTANCE.

TEEK (or **TIQUE**), *subs.* (Harrow school).—Mathematics.

TEENY (or **TEENY-WEENY**), *adj.* (colloquial).—Tiny.

TEETH, *subs.* (various colloquial).—PHRASES. IN SPITE OF ONE'S TEETH = in defiance of; IN THE TEETH = to one's face; FROM THE TEETH = apparently, not seriously; TO CAST IN THE TEETH = to taunt, to reproach; TOOTH AND NAIL = whole-hearted, desperate, thorough; TO SHOW ONE'S TEETH = to get angry; TO HAVE THE TEETH WELL AFLOAT (or UNDER) = to be drunk; TO THE HARD TEETH = very severely; 'He ought to have his TEETH drawn' = 'He should be deprived of the power of doing mischief;' TO GO TO GRASS WITH TEETH UPWARDS = to be buried; TO DRAW TEETH = to wrench off knockers (old: medical students'). *See* TURD.

1542. UDAL, *Erasmus*, 355. Cicero mocked her TO THE HARD TEETH.

1593. SHAKSPEARE, *Comedy of Errors*, ii. 2. Dost thou jeer, and flout me IN THE TEETH? *Ibid.* (1596), *Hamlet*, iv. 7. It warms the very sickness in my heart, That I shall live and tell him TO HIS TEETH, Thus didest thou. *Ibid.* (1598), 2 *Henry IV.*, v. 3. 96. PUFF IN THY TEETH, most recreant coward base! *Ibid.* (1608), *Antony and Cleop.*, iii. 4. 8. When the best hint was given him, he not took't, Or did it FROM HIS TEETH.

1603. *Court and Times James I.* [Among the verbs is] SHOW OUR TEETH.

1663. DRYDEN, *Wild Gallant* [LITTLEDALE, *Dyce's Glossary*]. I am confident she is only angry FROM THE TEETH outwards.

1885. *D. Teleg.*, 6 Nov. A desperate TOOTH-AND-NAIL encounter raged for some moments before the tomb.

TEETHWARD, *adv.* (old). — *See* quot.

1593. HOLLYBAND, *Dict.* He is clarke to the TEETHWARD, he hath eaten his service book; spoken in mockage by such as maketh shew of learning and be not learned.

TEETOTAL, *adj.* (old).—*See* quots. [as applied to total abstinence, now recognised.]

1827. [REV. JOEL JEWELL, *Letter to Cent. Dict.*] In 1818 a temperance society at Hector, New York, pledged themselves to abstain from distilled spirits only, but in Jan. 1827 another pledge bound all syners to total abstinence. The two classes were distinguished by the initials O.P. (Old Pledge) and T. (Total): T = total became a familiar allocution.

1829. SPENCE, *Tour in Ireland* [EDWARDS, *Words, Facts and Phrases*, 561. He speaks of the word] 'TEETOTALLY' . . . in every-day use by the working classes.

1830-5. [WALSH, *Lit. Curios*, 1049.] It is said that Richard Turner, an English temperance orator, who had an impediment in his speech, would invariably speak of T-T-TOTAL abstinence.

1843. CARLTON, *New Purchase*, ii. 245. Stranger, I'm powerful sorry, but we're TEETOTALLY out: he took every bit of food with him.

1843-4. HALIBURTON, *Attaché*, xii. The meetin' houses on one side of the water, how TEETOTALLY different they be!

1856. DOW, *Sermons*, I. I wouldn't have you think that I am TEETOTALLY opposed to dancing in every shape, for the reason that I used to heel and toe it a trifle myself, when young.

d. 1859. DE QUINCEY, *Dinner*, etc. Dinner was an ugly little parenthesis between two still uglier clauses of a TEETOTALLY ugly sentence.

1861. THACKERAY [in *Cornhill Mag.*, iv. 758]. This giant had quite a small appetite . . . and was also a TEA-TOTALLER.

1882. SMYTH-PALMER, *Folk Etymology*, 385. TEA-TOTALERS, an occasional misprint of TEE-TOTALERS, as if it meant those who were TOTALLY FOR TEA. It is more likely to be an intensive reduplication . . . as in tip-top for first-rate. *Ibid.*, 655. It may be noted that TEE-TOTAL is the reduplication of a reduplication.

TEETOTAL HOTEL (THE), *subs. phr.* (thieves').—A prison.

TEIGNTON-SQUASH, *subs. phr.* (provincial).—Perry.

1834. SOUTHEY, *Doctor*, Interchapter, xvi. Cokaghee or foxwhelp, a beverage as much better than champagne as it is honester, wholesomer, and cheaper. Or PERRY, the TEIGNTON-SQUASH. These are right old English liquors, and I like them all.

TEIZE. *See* TEASE.

TEJUS, *adv.* (vulgar).—Tedious; extremely; wearyingly, tiresomely: *e.g.*, TEJUS good, bad, quick, slow, etc.

TELEGRAPH. *See* MILK and UNDERGROUND.

TELESCOPE, *verb.* (Australian).—To silence.

TELL, *subs.* (American).—A story; a *bon mot*; spec. one worth telling. Also, ACCORDING TO THEIR TELL = 'Upon their making out.'

1743. WALPOLE, *To Mann*, 4 Ap. There, I am at the end of my TELL! If I write on, it must be to ask questions.

18[?]. *Betsy Bobbet*, 101. I told Josiah that, ACCORDIN' TO THEIR TELL, I had got every disease under the sun, unless it was the horse-distemper.

18[?]. HUMPHREYS, *Yankee in England.* In his dealings with the other sex, he is a little twistical, ACCORDING TO THEIR TELL.

1882. EGGLESTON [*Century*, xxxv. 44]. Little Barb'ry's the very flower of the flock, ACCORDIN' TO MY TELL.

See MARINES; NOSES; TALES.

TELL-CLOCK, *subs. phr.* (old).—An idler.

d. 1639. WARD, *Sermons*, 131. Is there no mean between busy-bodies and TELL-CLOCKS, between factotums and faineants?

TELLER, *subs.* (pugilists').—A well-delivered blow; anything that scores; hence TELLING (colloquial) = effective, to the point.

1834. AINSWORTH, *Rookwood.* Ven luckily for Jem a TELLER Vos planted right upon his smeller.

1832. EMERSON, *Burns.* Not Latimer, not Luther, struck more TELLING blows against false theology than did this brave singer.

1888. *Academy*, 1 Dec. 345. Put TELLINGLY and persuasively.

2. *See* TAILOR.

TELL-TALE, *subs. phr.* (nautical).—An inverted compass fixed in a cabin. Also (general) any recording device: usually automatic: *e.g.*, a turnstile, an organ bellows-indicator, etc.

TELLING. THAT'S TELLINGS, *phr.* (common).—Said in reply to a question that one ought not, or that one does not wish, to answer.

TELL-TRUTH, *subs. phr.* (old colloquial).—A plain speaker; one who does not mince matters.

1650. FULLER, *Pisgah Sight*, II. iv. 3. Caleb and Joshua, the only two TELL-TROTHS, endeavoured to undeceive and encourage the people.

d. 1667. TAYLOR, *Works* (1835), II. 99. The rudeness of a Macedonian TELL-TRUTH is no apparent calamity.

d. 1704. BROWN, *Works*, iii. 20. A great many bold TELL-TRUTHS are gone before you.

TEMPEST, *subs.* (old).—*See* quot.

1746. SMOLLETT, *Advice*, Note to line 30. Drum: This is a riotous assembly of fashionable people, of both sexes, at a private house, consisting of some hundreds; not unaptly styled a drum, from the noise and emptiness of the entertainment. There are also drum-major, rout, TEMPEST, and hurricane, differing only in degrees of multitude and uproar.

See TEA CUP.

TEMPLE, *subs.* (Winchester College).—1. *See* quot.

1881. PASCOE, *Ev. Day Life*. On the last night of term there is a bonfire in Ball Court, and all the TEMPLES or miniature architectural excavations in 'Mead's' wall are lighted up with candle-ends.

TEMPLE OF BACCHUS, *subs. phr.* (old).—*See* quot.

1785. GROSE, *Vulg. Tongue*, s.v. TEMPLE OF BACCHUS. Merry-making after getting a liceat. *Oxf. Univ. Cant.*

TEMPLE OF VENUS, *subs. phr.* (venery).—1. The female *pudendum*: *see* MONOSYLLABLE; and (2) a brothel.

TEMPLE - PICKLING, *subs. phr.* (B. E.).—'The Pumping of Bailives, Bumms, Setters, Pick-pockets, etc.'

TENANT AT WILL, *subs. phr.* (old).—'One whose wife usually fetches him from the ale-house' (GROSE).

TENANT FOR LIFE, *subs. phr.* (old).—'A married man; *i.e.*, possessed of a woman for life' (GROSE).

TENANT-IN-TAIL. *See* TAIL.

TEN BONES (or **COMMANDMENTS**), *subs. phr.* (old).—The ten fingers: spec. of a woman. Also BY THESE TEN BONES! (once a common oath: in punning reference to the Mosaic Decalogue).

c. 1485. *Digby Myst.* (1882), 4, note. By thes BONYS TEN thei be to you vntrue.

c. 1540. HEYWOOD, *Four P's*. [DODSLEY, *Old Plays* (REED), i. 92]. Now ten tymes I beseche hym that hye syttes, Thy wives TEN COMMANDEMENTS may serch thy five wyttes.

1542. UDAL, *Erasmus*, 27. [Socrates is advised to use his TENNE COMMAUNDEMENTES in a brawl.]

1562. *Jacke Juggeler* [DODSLEY, *Old Plays* (HAZLITT), ii. 125]. I am a servant of this house, BY THESE TEN BONES.

c. 1575. *Ane Ballat of Matrymonie* [LAING, *Early Pop. Poet. Scotland*, ii. 76]. She . . . pylled the barke even of hys face With her COMMAUNDEMENTS TEN.

1589. *Pappe with Hatchet*, Ciiij. b. Martin swears BY HIS TEN BONES.

1593. SHAKSPEARE, 2 *Henry VI.*, i. 3. Could I come near your beauty with my nails, I'd set my TEN COMMANDMENTS in your face. *Ibid.*, i. 4. BY THESE TEN BONES, my lord [*holding up his hands*], he did speak to me in the garret one night.

1595. *Locrine* [SHAKS., *Suppt.*, ii. 242]. I trembled, fearing she would set her TEN COMMANDMENTS in my face.

1597. LYLY, *Woman in Moon*, v. Now he swears BY HIS TEN BONES.

1607. DEKKER, *Westw. Hoe*, v. 3. Your harpy that set his TEN COMMANDMENTS upon my back.

1609. FLETCHER, *Monsieur Thomas*, iv. 2. BY THESE TEN BONES, sir, if these eyes and ears Can hear and see. *Ibid.* (*c.* 1613), *Woman's Prize*, i. 3. I'll devil em, BY THESE TEN BONES, I will.

1621. JONSON, *Masque of Gipsies*, vi. 84. I swear BY THESE TEN You shall have it again.

1648. HERRICK, *Hesperides* [HAZLITT, i. 209]. Skurffe by his NINE-BONES swears, and well he may, All know a fellon eate the TENTH away.

1814. SCOTT, *Waverley*, xxx. I'll set my TEN COMMANDMENTS in the face of the first loon that lays a finger on him.

1830. MARRYAT, *King's Own*, xl. I'll write the TEN COMMANDMENTS on your face.

1842. LONGFELLOW, *Sp. Student*, iii. 3. In with you, and be busy with the TEN COMMANDMENTS, under the sly.

1903. *Pall Mall Gaz.*, 6 Ap. 2. 3. The mother attacked the unfortunate master, and began the time-honoured but painful ceremony of setting her TEN COMMANDMENTS in his face, while her hopeful offspring got the school cane and belaboured his instructor.

TENCH, *subs.* (old).—1. A prison; a 'peni(TENTI)ary.' At one time applied to the Clerkenwell House of Detention, now the Central Depôt of the Parcels Post.

1859. *Broad Arrow*, ii. 32. Prisoners' barracks, sir—us calls it TENCH [the Hobart Town Penitentiary].

1877. HORSLEY, *Jottings from Jail*. I fell at Isleworth for being found in a conservatory adjoining a parlour, and got remanded at the TENCH.

2. (venery). — The female *pudendum*: *see* MONOSYLLABLE.

TENDER. TENDER PARNEL, *subs. phr.* (old).—1. A mistress; also PARNEL, PERNEL; *see* TART. Hence (2) 'a very nicely Educated creature, apt to catch Cold upon the least blast of wind' (B. E.), 'AS TENDER as PARNELL, who broke her finger in a posset drink' (GROSE). Also 'as TENDER AS A CHICKEN,' and 'AS TENDER AS A PARSON'S LEMAN. (RAY.)

1362. LANGLAND, *Piers Plow.*, 2790. Dame PERNELE a priestes fyle . . . she hadde Child in Chirie-tyme.

1546. HEYWOOD, *Proverbs*, 45. [OLIPHANT, *New Eng.*, i. 505. The morals of the clergy are glanced at where a woman is said to be 'TENDER AS A PARSON'S lemman.'

1560. BECON, *Prayers* [*Works* (Parker Soc.), 267]. Pretty PARNEL [speaking of] a priest's whore.

d. 1575. PILKINGTON, *Works*, 56. But these TENDER PERNELS must have one gown for the day, another for the night.

TENDERFOOT, *subs.* (American and Colonial).—A new comer: as *adj.* = raw, inexperienced.

1875. L. SWINBURNE [*Scribner's Monthly*, II. 508]. Pilgrim and TENDERFOOT were formerly applied almost exclusively to newly-imported cattle, but by a natural transference they are usually used to designate all new-comers, tourists, and business men.

1885. STAVELEY-HILL, *Home to Home*. I put my naked foot on a cactus . . . and I realised in a substantial form the nick-name that is given to the new-comer out West of TENDER-FOOT or pilgrim.

1885. PHILLIPS-WOLLEY, *Trottings of a Tenderfoot*. How an American ever expects to digest his food is a problem to a TENDERFOOT as they call us new-comers.

1885. ROOSEVELT, *Hunting Trips*, 32. Hunters . . . who bedizen themselves in all the traditional finery of the craft, in the hope of getting a job at guiding some TENDERFOOT.

1886. *D. Tel.* 25 Jan. Before long the TENDERFOOT'S too fleet pony brings him abreast of the flying cow.

1896. LILLARD, *Poker Stories*, 86. The TENDERFOOT had announced his determination of relieving a few of the miners of what spare change they happened to have about them.

1901. WALKER, *In the Blood*, 59. 'Well, you keep your eyes open for a TENDERFOOT, an' that's a fact,' said Wallaby Dick.

TEN-FORTY, *subs. phr.* (American).—A five per cent. bond issued in 1864 by the U.S. Government, redeemable at any time after ten years and payable in forty years (*Century*).

TEN-IN-THE-HUNDRED, *subs. phr.* (old).—A usurer; a SIXTY-PER-CENT. (*q.v.*). [NARES: from their commonly exacting such interest for their money, before the legal limitation to five] (GROSE).

1594. *Death of Usury*, sig. B 4. He that puts forth money dare not exceede the rate of 10 IN THE 100, but he that uttereth ware doth make his rate to his owne contentment.

d. 16[?]. [BRATHWAITE [?], *Epitaph on John-a-Combe*. TEN IN THE HUNDRED lies here in-grav'd, 'Tis a hundred to ten that his soul is not sav'd.

1625. JONSON, *Staple of News*, ii. 1. Although your grace be fallen off TWO IN THE HUNDRED, In vulgar estimation; yet am I Your grace's servant still. [In 1624 the legal rate was reduced from ten to eight per cent.]

1648. HERRICK, *Hesperides* [HAZLITT, ii. 37]. Snare TEN I' TH' HUNDRED calls his wife, and why? She brings in much by carnal usury.

TENNER, *subs.* (common).—1. A ten pound note; £10: *cf.* FIVER.

1861. HUGHES, *Tom Brown at Oxford*, xix. 'No money?' 'Not much: perhaps a TENNER.'

1871. BRADDON, *Rupert Godwin*, I. 221. And you don't like me well enough to borrow a few TENNERS just to carry on the war with?

2. (thieves').—Ten years' imprisonment.

TENPENCE. ONLY TENPENCE IN THE SHILLING, *phr.* (common).—A description of weak intellect. Also TENPENNY = in contempt.

1607. DEKKER, *Westward Hoe*, iv. 2. If all the great Turk's concubines were but like thee, the TENPENNY infidel should never need keep so many geldings to neigh over 'em.

TENT, *subs.* (old).—The *penis*: *see* PRICK.

TENTERBELLY, *subs.* (old).—A glutton; one who distends his belly by gross feeding.

1621. BURTON, *Anat. Melan.*, III. II. v. 1. Not with sweet wine, mutton and pottage, as many of those TENTERBELLIES do.

TENTERHOOKS. ON TENTER-HOOKS (or TENTERS), *adv. phr.* (old).—In suspense; anxious; on the rack (or stretch).

1607. HEYWOOD, *Fair Maid* [PEARSON, *Works*, II. 25]. How, upon the TENTERS? indeed, if the whole peece were so stretcht, and very well beaten with a yard of reformation, no doubt it would grow to a goodly breadth.

d. 1774. GOLDSMITH, *Sequel to Poetical Scale* . . . . It was gallantry that suited her own maiden loftiness, ever stretched upon the TENTERS of punctillio.

1809. MALKIN, *Gil Blas* [ROUTLEDGE], 102. I was too much ON THE TENTERHOOKS about the result to mind his orders. *Ibid.*, 236. One must sit on the TENTERHOOKS of self-denial.

1868. WHYTE-MELVILLE, *White Rose*, II. xxviii. I know Dolly's ON TENTER-HOOKS now.

TENTOES. *See* BAYARD.

TENUC, *subs.* (back-slang).—The female *pudendum*: *see* MONOSYLLABLE.

TERCEL-GENTLE, *subs. phr.* (old colloquial). — 'A Knight or Gentleman of a good estate; also any rich Man' (B. E.). Also TASSEL-GENTLE [*Tercel* (COTGRAVE and RANDLE HOLMES) = the male of the peregrine falcon.] Hence FALCON 'GAINST TERCEL (or AS TERCEL) = 'One's as good as t'other.'

1595. SHAKSPEARE, *Romeo and Juliet*, ii. 2. 160. *Jul.* Hist! Romeo. hist! O! for a falconer's voice, To lure this TASSEL-GENTLE back again. *Ibid.* (1602), *Troilus*, iii. 2. 56. The FALCON AS THE TERCEL for all the ducks i' the river.

1820. SCOTT, *Abbot*, iv. I marvel what blood thou art—neither Englander nor Scot—fish nor flesh. Marry, out upon thee, foul kite, that would fain be a TERCEL-GENTLE!

TERMER, *subs.* (old colloquial).—A visitor to London at term time; specifically one whose object was intrigue, knavery, or sport. [The law terms marked the fashionable seasons.] Also TERM-TROTTER.

1608. DEKKER, *Belman of London*, H3. Some of these boothalers are called TERMERS, and they ply Westminster hall; Michaelmas term is their harvest, and they sweat in it harder than reapers or hay-makers doe at their works in the heat of summer.

1611. MIDDLETON, *Roaring Girl*, Preface. Single plots, etc.—those are fit for the times and the TERMERS.

1616. JONSON, *Epigrams*, 3. Nor have my title leaf on posts or walls, Or in cleft sticks advanced to make calls For TERMERS, or some clerk-like serving man.

1628. EARLE, *Micro-cosmog.*, 18. A gallant . . . obserues London trulier than the TERMERS.

1636. SUCKLING, *Goblins*, iii. Court ladies, eight; of which two great ones. Country ladies, twelve; TERMERS ALL.

1639. BANCROFT, *Epigrams*, i. 176. On Old Trudge, the TERMER. Thy practice hath small reason to expect Good termes, that doth faire honesty neglect.

TERRÆ FILIUS, *subs. phr.* (old colloquial).—1. A person of mean or obscure birth.

2. (university). — A scholar whose special duty was to make satirical speeches at the *Encænia*: full advantage being ever taken of his license to satirize, and generally rip up, authority.

1669 EVELYN, *Diary*, 10 July. The TERRÆ FILIUS (the Universitie Buffoone) entertain'd the auditorie with a tedious abusive, sarcastical rhapsodie, most unbecoming the gravity of the universitie.

c. 1709. WARD, *Terræ filius* [Title].

TERRA FIRMA, *subs. phr.* (B. E. and GROSE).—An estate in land.

TERRIBLE BOY. *See* ROARING BOY, adding quot. *infra*.

1609. JONSON, *Silent Woman*, i. 1. The doubtfulness of your phrase would breed you a quarrel once an hour with the TERRIBLE BOYS.

TERTIAN, *subs.* (Aberdeen Univ.).—A student of the third year.

TESTER (or **TESTON**), *subs.* (old).—1. A silver coin: orig. (*a*) the silver currency of Louis XII. of France (bearing the head of that prince, and worth (COTGRAVE) 18d. sterling); (*b*) the brass silvered shilling of Henry VIII. (worth, *temp.* Ed. VI., 9d.); and (*c*) the Elizabeth sixpence. Hence (2) a sixpence (GROSE): *see* TIZZY. As *verb* = to fee.

1577. HOLINSHED, *England*, 218. [Elizabeth] restored sundrie coines of fine silver, as peeces of halfepenie farding, of a penie, of three halfe pence, peeces of two pence, of three pence, of foure pence (called the groat), of sixpence, usuallie named the TESTONE.

1594. WILSON, *Cobler's Prophecy*. Tales, at some tables, are as good as TESTERNS.

1595. SHAKSPEARE, *Two Gentlemen*, i. 1. 153. You have TESTERNED me; in requital, whereof, henceforth carry your letters yourself. *Ibid.* (1598), 2 *Henry IV.*, iii. 2. Hold, there's a TESTER for thee.

1599. HALL, *Satires*, II. i. Lo, what it is that makes white rags so deare, That men must give a TESTON for a queare.

1599. JONSON, *Ev. Man Out of Humour*. 'Characters.' Takes up single TESTONS upon oaths till dooms-day, falls under executions of three shillings, and enters into five-groat bonds.

1602. DEKKER, *Honest Whore.* Ipocras, there then, here's a TESTON for you, you snake.

1605. CHAPMAN, *Eastward Ho*, i. 1. Wipe thy bum with TESTONES, and make ducks and drakes with shillings.

1608. DAY, *Law Trickes*, iii. Win, prethee give the Fidler a TESTAR and send him packing.

1611. TARLETON, *Jests.* Tarlton, seeing himself so over-reacht, greatly commended the beggers wit, and withall, in recompence thereof, gave him a TEASTER.

1613. FLETCHER, *Honest Man's Fort.*, iii. 3. There's a TESTER . . . now I am a wooer, I must be bounteful.

1633. HEYWOOD, *Eng. Traveller*, iv. 5, 226 (Mermaid). Let not a TESTER scape To be consumed in rot-gut.

1636. DAVENANT, *Wits*, i. 1. Together with his wife's bracelet of mill-TESTERS.

1698. FARQUHAR, *Love and a Bottle*, i. Who throws away a TESTER and a mistress loses sixpence.

1709. SWIFT, *Polite Conversations*, i. They say he that has lost his wife and sixpence has lost a TESTER.

1822. LAMB, *Chimney Sweepers.* If it be starving weather . . . thy humanity will surely rise to a TESTER.

1822. SCOTT, *Fort. Nigel*, xxvii. Dr R. who buckles beggars for a TESTER.

TETBURY PORTION, *subs. phr.* (old).—*See* quot., and *cf.* WHITE-CHAPEL TIPPERARY, and ROCHESTER PORTION, etc.

1785. GROSE, *Vulg. Tongue*, s.v. TETBURY PORTION. A . . . and a clap.

TEVISS, *subs.* (coster).—A shilling: *see* RHINO.

TEXAS, *subs.* (American).—The upper (or third) deck of a Mississippi steamboat. Hence Texas-TENDER = a waiter serving on the TEXAS.

1875. CLEMENS [*Atlantic Monthly*, Jan. and Feb.]. The boiler deck, the hurricane deck, and the TEXAS DECK are fenced and ornamented with white railings.

Ibid. We had a tidy, white-aproned, black TEXAS-TENDER to bring up tarts and ices and coffee during mid-watch day and night.

1877. HALE, *Adv. Pullman*, 45. His companion joined him, pausing a minute on the step-ladder which leads to the pilot-house from the roof of the TEXAS.

THAMES. SETTING THE THAMES ON FIRE, *phr.* (old).—A simile for the impossible: *see* quots.

1363. LANGLAND, *Piers Plowman.* C. vii. 335. Wickede dedes Fareth as a fonk of fuyr that ful a-myde TEMESE. [Wicked deeds fare as a spark of fire that falleth into the Thames.]

1546. HEYWOOD, *Proverbs.* 'As well cast water in TEMS as give him alms.'

1672. RAY, *Proverbs.* 'Joculatory Proverbs.' I care no more for it than a goose-turd for the THAMES.

1777. FOOTE, *Trip to Calais.* He won't SET FIRE TO THE THAMES.

1785. GROSE, *Vulg. Tongue*, s.v. THAMES. He will not find out a way to SET THE THAMES ON FIRE; he will not make any wonderful discoveries, he is no conjuror.

1868. BREWER, *Phrase and Fable*, s.v. THAMES. An active man would ply the TEMSE so quickly as to set fire to the wooden hoop at the bottom; but a lazy fellow would never SET THE TEMSE ON FIRE. The play on the word temse has given rise to many imitations: as, He will never set the Seine on fire (the French *seine* = a drag-net).

1884. *Notes and Queries*, 6 S., ix. 14 (Correspondent). To a practical man a grain-riddle firing would sound most absurd. If you say to a Lancashire labourer, 'Tha'll ne'er SET TH' TEMS AFIRE,' a hundred to one he would understand the River Thames. *Ibid.* (Editorial). The ordinarily accepted supposition is that it is equivalent to saying that an idle fellow will not accomplish a miracle.

THARBOROUGH. *See* THIRD-BOROUGH.

THARY, *verb.* (tramps').—To speak.

1891. CAREW, *Auto. Gipsy*, 412. You sonnied the bloke as THARIED you just as the rattler was startin'. *Ibid.*, 419. I grannied some of what you were a-THARYIN' to your cousin.

THAT, *pron.* (euphemistic).—1. The *penis*: *see* PRICK; 2. the female *pudendum*: *see* MONOSYLLABLE; and (3) the virginity. Fr. *ça*.

1898. *Pink 'Un and Pelican*, 227. 'Well, THAT'S gone!' as the girl said to the soldier in the park, when she lost her certificate from the Billericay Sunday-School.

AT THAT, *phr.* (American).—A pleonastic intensive.

1855. *Blackwood's Mag.*, Sept. 'Notes on North-Western States.' 'Liquor up, gentlemen.' We bowed. 'Let me introduce you to some of the most highly esteemed of our citizens.' We bowed again. 'Now then, Mister,' turning to the man at the bar, 'drinks round, and cobblers AT THAT.'

1859. BARTLETT, *Americanisms*, s.v. AT THAT. He's got a scolding wife, and an ugly one AT THAT.

1888. KEIGHLEY GOODCHILD, 'The Old Felt Hat.' So we'll drain the flowing bowl, 'Twill not jeopardise the soul, For it's only tea, and weak AT THAT.

THATCH, *subs.* (old).—Hair: spec. (*a*) the hair of the head; and (*2*) the pubic hair. Hence THATCHED HOUSE UNDER THE HILL = the female *pudendum*. *See* FLEECE and MONOSYLLABLE. As *verb* = to cover with (or wear) hair.

1609. SHAKSPEARE, *Timon*, iv. 3. 144. THATCH your poor thin roofs With burdens of the dead.

1630. DRAYTON, *Muse's Elysium*, iv. Thro' the thick hair that THATCH'D their browes Their eyes upon me stared.

1772. STEVENS, *Songs Comic and Satyrical. The Thatched House Under the Hill* [Title].

THATCHED-HEAD, *subs. phr.* (old).—An Irishman: in contempt. [NARES: 'one wearing the hair matted together, as the native Irish in times past.']

1612. BEAUMONT and FLETCHER, *Coxcomb*, ii. Ere ye go, sirrah THATCH'D-HEAD, would'st not thou Be whipp'd, and think it justice.

THATCH-GALLOWS, *subs. phr.* (old). — A worthless fellow (GROSE).

THEG (OR TEAICH) GEN, *subs. phr.* (back slang).—Eight shillings; THEG (or TEAITCH) YANNEPS = eightpence.

THERE, *adv.* (common).—Colloquial for SMART (*q.v.*): *e.g.*, ALL THERE = (1) alert, first-rate, up to the mark, nothing wanting. Also TO GET THERE = (1) to achieve; and (2) TO MAKE ONE'S JACK (*q.v.*): also TO GET THERE WITH BOTH FEET.

1821. EGAN, *Life in London*, II. i. The slavey and her master—the surgeon and the resurrection-man— . . . they are ALL THERE.

1877. *Five Years' Penal Servitude*, iii. 220. He stayed . . . doing the grand and sucking the flats till the folks began to smoke him as not ALL THERE.

1880. *Punch*, 7 Aug., 59. ALL THERE! *Clerk* (*who has called to see the gas-meter*). 'Is yours a *wet*, or a *dry* meter, madam?' *Young Wife* (*who does not like to show ignorance*). 'Well, it *is* rather *damp*, I'm afraid!'

1883. PAYN, *Thicker than Water*, xx. It was his excusable boast . . . that when anything was wanted he was ALL THERE.

1887. FRANCIS, *Saddle and Mocassin.* He said as he'd been gambling, and was two hundred dollars ahead of the town. He GOT THERE WITH BOTH FEET at starting.

1888. *New York Herald*, 29 July. Although not a delegate he GOT THERE all the same.

1901. *Free Lance*, 27 Ap., 79. 1. She was ALL THERE, and when she found that robbery was meant she made a stout resistance.

THETA. TO MARK WITH THETA, *verb. phr.* (old).—To condemn to death. [The first letter ('the unlucky letter') of Gr. θάνατος = death.]

THICK, *subs.* (colloquial). — 1. Generic for obtuseness: *e.g.*, as *subs.* = stupid fellow; a block-

head: also THICK-HEAD, THICK-SKULL, THICK-PATE, THICK SCONCE, THICK-SKIN, THICK-WITS, etc. The corresponding adjectival forms = dull, stupid, hidebound.

1582. STANYHURST, *Ded.* [ARBER], 9. What thinck you of thee THICK SKYN that made this . . .

1592. SHAKSPEARE, *Mid. Night's Dream*, iii. 2. 13. The shallowest THICK-SKIN of that barren sort. *Ibid.* (1598), 2 *Henry IV.*, ii. 4. 262. He a good wit? hang him, baboon! his wit's as THICK as Tewkesbury mustard.

1599. HALL, *Satires*, i. 8. THICK-SKIN ears, and undiscerning eyne.

1603. HAYWARD, *Answer to Doleman*, iv. I omit your THICK errour in putting no difference between a magistrate and a king.

c. 1616. DRAYTON, *Sacrifice to Apollo.* The THICK-BRAIN'D audience lively to awake.

1668. DRYDEN, *All for Love*, iii. 1. This THICK-SKULLED hero. (1679), *Persius*, i. 166. Pleas'd to hear their THICK-SKULLED judges cry, Well movd!

d. 1718. PENN, *Liberty of Conscience*, v. What if you think our reasons THICK, and our ground of separation mistaken.

1857. HUGHES, *Tom Brown's School-days*, I. vii. I told you how it would be. What a THICK I was to come!

1897. MARSHALL, *Pomes*, 75. She was THICK . . . fairly sosselled on beer.

2. (common).—Porter: ironically said to be 'a decoction of brewers' aprons.'

3. (streets').—Cocoa.

Adj. (colloquial).—1. Intimate or (Scots) 'chief': *e.g.*, 'As THICK AS THIEVES,' 'as THICK AS INKLE-WEAVERS,' *q.v.* (GROSE).

1525-37. ELLIS, *Letters* [OLIPHANT, *New Eng.*, i. 475. We see the expression] the THICKEST OF THE THEVES.

1835. DANA, *Before the Mast*, 68. I told the second mate, with whom I had been pretty THICK when he was before the mast, that I would do it.

1837. BARHAM, *Ingoldsby Legends*, I. 270. He . . . was thought to be THICK with the Man in the Moon,

1854-5. THACKERAY, *Newcomes*, xxiv. Newcome and I are not very THICK together.

1860. ELIOT, *Mill on the Floss*, ii. 6. Don't you be getting too THICK with him—he's got his father's blood in him too.

Adv. (colloquial).—Out of the common; extraordinary; a general intensive (in quot. 1563 = solid). Hence TO LAY IT ON THICK = to exaggerate; to surfeit with praise: also TO LAY IT ON WITH A TROWEL: *cf.* WIDE; GOT 'EM THICK = very drunk: *see* SCREWED; A BIT THICK = rather indecent.

1563. FOXE, *Acts and Monuments* [CATTLEY], 260. [Something cost] a hundred pounds THICK.

1655. FULLER, *Ch. Hist.* III., iv. 24. His reign was not onely long for continuance, fifty-six years, but also THICK for remarkable mutations happening therein.

1874. *Siliad*, 204. He complains I LAY IT ON TOO THICK.

1885. *New York Herald*, 22 June. The Know-Nothings were . . . LAYING IT ON THICK that 'Americans shall rule America.'

1888. WARD, *Elsmere*, xviii. He had been giving the squire a full and particular account . . . Henslowe LAYS IT ON THICK—paints with a will.

1893. EMERSON, *Lippo*, xvi. She knew all the cant, and used to palaver THICK to the slaveys.

1897. MARSHALL, *Pomes*, 63. The exercise required of him was THICK. *Ibid.*, 76. The fun . . . was the THICKEST I've met. *Ibid.*, 95. I've got 'em THICK he said . . . And . . . went upstairs to bed.

THROUGH THICK AND THIN, *phr.* (colloquial).—Thoroughly; steadily; at all costs. Hence THICK-AND-THIN (*adj.*) = sincere, OUT-AND-OUT (*q.v.*). [Orig. over rough or smooth places; *i.e.*, through coppice or sparse land.]

1359. GAYTRIGG, *Relig. Pieces* [E.E.T.S.], 99. [Fiends will not cease] FOR THIN NE THIK,

1380. *Kyng and Hermyt* [HAZLITT, *Early Pop. Poet.*, i. 15. And chasyd hym ryght fast, Both THOROW THYKE AND THINE.

1383. CHAUCER, *Cant. Tales*, 'Reeves Tale,' 146. Forth with 'We hee,' THURGH THIKKE AND THURGH THENNE.

1590. SPENSER, *Fairy Queen*, III. iv. 46. THROUGH THICK AND THIN . . . Those two great champions did attonce pursew The fearefull damzell.

1621. BURTON, *Anat. Melan.*, III. II. iii. 1. If once enamoured . . . THROUGH THICK AND THIN he will go to her.

1678. COTTON, *Virgil Travestie* (1770), 5. THRO' THICK AND THIN; Half-roasted now, now wet to th' Skin.

1774. BRIDGES, *Burlesque Homer*, 7. THROUGH THICK AND THIN he swore he'd dash on.

c. 1780. CAPTAIN MORRIS, *The Plenipo.* THROUGH THICK AND THROUGH THIN he bored his way in.

1809. MALKIN, *Gil Blas* [ROUTLEDGE], 237. One of those spoiled actors who are applauded THROUGH THICK AND THIN.

1838. BECKETT, *Paradise Lost*, 10. Yet swear THROUGH THICK AND THIN they hate thee.

1860-5. MOTLEY, *Hist. Netherlands*, II. 311. To lie daily, THROUGH THICK AND THIN . . . was the simple rule prescribed by his sovereign.

1887. *St James's Gazette*, 26 May. We again see that he is one of the most THICK-AND-THIN adherents of the neo-French technique.

THICKER, *subs.* (Harrow).—Thucydides: the translation of which is set in the Upper School.

THICKLIPS, *subs.* (old).—A negro (in quot. = a Moor). Whence THICK-LIPPED.

1593. SHAKSPEARE, *Tit. Andron.*, iv. 3. 175. Come on, you THICK-LIPP'D slave. *Ibid.* (1602), *Othello*, i. 1. 66. What a full fortune does the THICK LIPS owe, If he can carry't thus.

THICK-'UN, *subs. phr.* (common).—A sovereign; 20s.: also a crown piece; 5s. Hence TO SMASH (= change) or BLUE A THICK-'UN.

1863. *Cornhill Mag.*, vi. 648. If you like . . . I will send a few THICKUNS.

1871. AITKEN, *House Scraps.* Have you sufficient confidence in me to lend me a sovereign? Oh! yes, I've the confidence, but I haven't the THICK 'UN.

1886. P. CLARKE, *New Chum in Australia*, 143. If . . . he has a drought within him, and a friend or a THICK 'UN to stand by him, he is a poor weak . . . fool to refuse.

1888. PAYN, *Eavesdropper*, II. ii. 'Can you smash a THICK-'UN for me?' inquired one, handing his friend a sovereign.

1896. FARJEON, *Betrayal of John Fordham*, III. 277. With three peas and a thimble I've earnt many a THICK 'UN.

1897. MARSHALL, *Pomes*, 26. He wanted his THICK 'UN to canter home with forty or fifty more.

THIEF, *subs.* (old).—A term of reproach: not necessarily a robber. Thus (GROSE): 'You are a murderer and a THIEF, you have killed a baboon and stolen his face; vulgar abuse.'

1440. *Sir Perceval* [Camden Soc.], 923. Fiftene ȝeres es it gane Syne me my brodire hade slane, Now hadde the THEEFE undirtane, To sla us alle thenne.

1603. SHAKSPEARE, *Meas. for Meas.*, v. 1. 40. Angelo is an adulterous THIEF.

2. (old).—A mushroom growth on a burning wick which makes the candle gutter; a waster: *see* BISHOP (GROSE)

[1598. FLORIO, *Worlde of Wordes*, s.v. *Fungo*, that firy round in a burning candle called a BISHOP.]

1622. MAY, *Virgil*, 'Georgic,' i. Their burning lamps the storm ensuing show, Th' oil sparkles, THIEVES about the snuff do grow.

d. 1635. GIBBES, *Works*, iv. 355. Many break themselves by intemperate courses, as candles that have THIEVES in them.

1636. WARD, *Coal from the Altar* [*Sermons*]. The least known evil unrepented of is as a THIEF IN THE CANDLE.

1642. HOWELL, *Forraine Travell* [ARBER], 77. If there bee a THEEFE IN THE CANDLE . . . there is a way to pull it out; and not to put out the candle.

1644. QUARLES, *Judgment and Mercy* (1807), 132. If a THIEF be IN HIS CANDLE blow it not out.

1669. BROOKS, *Cabinet of Choice Jewels* (*Works*, iii. 295). A CANDLE will never burn clear while there is a THIEF in it.

d. 1797. WALPOLE, *Letters* (CUNNINGHAM), ii. 200. Un voleur! un voleur! cried Mrs Nugent at an assembly. It turned out to be a THIEF IN THE CANDLE.

2. (provincial).—A bramble: *cf.* BRAMBLE=country lawyer, keeping in mind the A.S. *thefethorn*=bramble.

3. SYNONYMS FOR THIEF [=a person guilty of larceny, robbery, swindling, or crookedness of any kind: the following list runs up and down the whole gamut of roguery].

Aaron; abacter; abaddon; abandanad; abraham-cove; ackman; ack-pirate; acquisitive cove; Adam; Adam Filer; adept; affidavit-man; afflicke; alsatian; ambidexter; amuser; anabaptist; angler; angling-cove; arch-cove; arch-dell; arch-doxy (GROSE); arch-gonnof; arch-rogue; area-sneak; ark-pirate; ark-ruff; artful-dodger; autem-diver; avoirdupois-man.

Babe; back-jumper; back-stall; badger; baggage-smasher; baldover; bank-sneak; barabbas; barnacle; baster; beak; beaker-hauler; beaker-hunter; bearer-up; beau-trap (GROSE); bene-feaker; bene-gybe; bester; bilk (SHERIDAN); bilker; Billy Buzman; billy-fencer; birdlime; bite; bit-faker; bit-make; black-leg; blasted-fellow; bleating-cull; blowed-in-the-glass-stiff (American tramps'); bludger; bludget; blue-pigeon flyer; bluey-hunter; bob; bobby-twister; bonnet; boodler; bookkeeper; bouncer; boung-nipper; bowman; bridle-cull; brief-snatcher; broad cove; broadsman; bubber; bubble; bubbler; budge; buffer; buffer-napper; bugger; bug-hunter; bulk; bulk-and-file; bull-trap; bully-buck; bully-cock; bunco-steerer; bunco-man; bung; bung-napper; bunter; burner; buster; buttock-and-file; button; buttoner; buzbloke; buz-cove; buz-faker; buzman; buzzer; buzzlock.

Canter (CANTING CREW= generic for thieves, rogues, and beggars); Captain Sharp; carrier: cat-and-kitten nipper; chariot-buzzer; charley-pitcher; chaunting-cove; chive or (chiff) thief; chouse; chouser; christener; circling-boy; clank-napper; clicker; clink-rigger; cloak-twitcher; clouter; cloy; cloyer; cly-filcher; cogger; collector; colt; cork; conveyancer; conveyor; coney-catcher; counterfeit-crank; cover; coverer; crack; cracksman; crony; crook; cross-bite; cross-biter; cross-famker; crib-cracker; cross; cross-cove; crossman; cross-mollisher; crow; cruiser; cunning-man; curtall; cut-purse; cutter.

Damber (GROSE); damned soul; dancer; darkman's budge; dead-nap; deeker; deep-one; diddler; dimber-damber (GROSE); ding-boy; dinger; dip; dipper; dipping-bloke; dive; diver; dog-buffer; dragsman; drag-sneak; draw-latch; drop-cove; dropper; dromedary; drummer; drunken tinker; dubber; dudder; duffer; dummerer; dummy-hunter; dunaker.

Eriff; eves-dropper (GROSE).

Facer; fagger; family (generic); father; fawney-rigger; fence; fencing-cully; ferret; fiddle; fidlam-bens; figger; filcher; filching-cove; filching-mort; file; finder; finger-smith; fire-prigger; fish-hook; flash-cove; flashman (GROSE); flash-gentry (generic); flat-catcher; fleecer; flimper; flying-cove; fobber; fogle-hunter; foist; foot-pad; fore-beggar; fork; forker; frater; free-booker; free-booter; freshwater-warmer; frisker; funker.

Gagger; gallows-bird; gambler (GROSE); garreteer; garrotter; geach; gentleman of the road; gentleman's master; gentry (generic); gilt; gin-spinner; glasier; gleaner; glimmerer; gold-dropper; gonnof; goodfellow; grafter; Greek; groaner; gun; gutter-prowler.

Hawk; heaver; hedge-creeper; highpad; high-tober (or toby); hoist; hoister (or hoyster); hook; hooker; hoveller; Hugh Prowler.

Ingler; innocent; int; Irish toyle (B. E.).

Jack-in-a-box; Janus-mug; jarkman; jerry-sneak; Jew; jilter; jingler; jockey; jumper.

Ken-cracker; ken-miller; kiddy (GROSE); kiddy-nipper; kidsman; kinchin-cove; kite; kirk-buzzer; kitchener; klep; knap; knight; knight of the road; knight of St Nicholas; knowing one; knuck; knuckler.

Ladrone; lag; landloper; landlubber; landpirate; land-shark; lark; latch-drawer; leatherhead; leg; legger; lift; lifter; little-sneaksman; lob-crawler; lob-sneak; lully-prigger; lumberer; lumper.

Mace-cove; magsman (MAYHEW, MATSELL, HENLEY); maker; mill-ben; money-dropper; mounter; mocher.

Nabber; nabbler; nailer; napper; nasty-man; natty-lad; needle; needle-point; Newgate-bird (or nightingale); New-market-heath Commissioner; nibbler; nibbling-cull; nicker; nick-pot; nickum; night-bird (cap, hawk, hunter, poacher, snap, trader or walker); nigler (=a sweater); nimmer; nip; nipping Christian; nobbler; nob-pitcher; nose (GROSE).

Office-sneak; old bird (or hand); olli compolli; ostler; out-and-outer; outrider.

Pad; pad-borrower; padder; paddist; palmer; panel dodger; panel-thief; pannyman; parlour-jumper; pea-rigger; pea-man; peter (=a safe thief); peter-biter; peter-claimer; peter-hunter; peterman; picaro; picaroon; picker; picker-up; pickereer; pick-penny; pick-pocket; pie-man; pigeon; pinch-gloak; pitch-fingers; poacher; pocket-book dropper; poulterer; practitioner; prig; prigger; prigman; Prince Prig; prinado; prowler (or Hugh Prowler); propnailer; pudding-snammer; puller-up; purple dromedary; puffer; puggard; push (generic); pushing tout.

Quarrel picker; queer bail (or bird); queer-bit-maker; queer bluffer; queer cole fencer; queer cole maker; queer plunger; queer-prancer; queer shover.

Ramper (ramp, or rampsman); ranger; rank-rider; rapparee; rascal (GROSE); reader-hunter; reader-merchant; repeater and revolver (American tramps'); resurrectionist; ring-dropper; ring-faller; river-rat; road-agent; roberd's-man (or knave); rob-thief; rogue; rook; rover; royal scamp; royal foot-scamp; rumbler; runner; running glasier; running-snavel.

Saint Peter's son; St Nicholas's clerk; St Nicholas's clergyman; salter; satyr (=cattle thief); sawny-hunter; scamp; scamps-man; screwsman; scuffle-hunter; setter; shark; sharp; sharper; shaver; sheep-biter; sheep-napper; sheep-shearer; she-napper; shifter; shoful-pitcher; shop-bouncer; shop-lift; shop-lifter; shoulderer; shoulder-sham; shover; shark; shutter-racket worker; shyce; shyster; silk-snatcher; silver cooper; skylarker; slink; smasher; smugger; snabbler; snaffle; snaffler; snaggler; snakesman; snammer; snap; snapper; snapper-up; snatch-cly; snatcher; sneak; sneak-thief; sneaking-budge; sneaksman; sneck-drawer; sneeze-lurker; snick-fudger; snide-pitcher; snow-dropper; snow-gatherer; snudge; soaper; sourplanter; son of St Peter; spice-gloak; stall (or stale); stallsman; stander-up; standing-budge; stook-hauler; sutler; swagsman; sweetener; swigman; swimmer; swindler.

Tail-buzzer; thimble-rigger; thimble-twister; till-sneak; tinny-hunter; toby-gill; toby-man; tool; tooler; top-sawyer; tosher; toy-getter; tradesman; traveller; tripper-up; Tyburn-blossom.

Uncorn; unregenerate; up-right-man.

Vamper; village bustler; voucher.

Walking poulterer; watch-maker; waterpad; water-sneak; water-sneaksman; welcher; wheedle; whipster; whispering dudder; whyo; wild rogue; wipe-drawer; workman; wrong 'un.

Ziff.

THIEF-TAKERS, *subs.* (old).—'Fellows who associate with all kinds of villains, in order to betray them, when they have committed any of those crimes which entitle the persons taking them to a handsome reward, called blood money. It is the business of these thief-takers to furnish subjects for a handsome execution at the end of every sessions' (GROSE). Also (B. E.), 'who make a Trade of helping People (for a gratuity) to their lost Goods, and sometimes for Interest or Envy snapping the Rogues themselves; being usually in fee with them and acquainted with their Haunts.'

THIEVES. THIEVES' LATIN, *subs. phr.* (old).—The cant terms and slang used by thieves; ST GILES' GREEK; PEDDLAR'S FRENCH (*q.v.*) etc.

1855. KINGSLEY, *Westward Ho.* '"Go away," I heard her say, . . . And then something about a "queer cuffin," that's a justice in these carters' THIEVES' LATIN.'

THE MURDERING THIEVES, *subs. phr.* (military).—The Military Train; the title from 1857 to 1860 of The Army Service Corps.

Other nicknames (also derived from the initials) are The London Thieving Corps (1855–7); The Moke Train (1857–60), etc.

SAFE AS A THIEF IN A MILL, *phr.* (old).—Very secure.

1630. TAYLOR, *Works*, iii. 9. There she may lodge, and trade too if she will, As sure and SAFE AS THEEVES ARE IN A MILL.

1694. MOTTEUX, *Rabelais*, v. iv. Your gaol birds . . . are as SAFE AS THIEVES IN A MILL within this sanctuary.

THIEVING-IRONS, *subs. phr.* (old).—Scissors.

THIMBLE, *subs.* (old).—A watch; a YACK (*q.v.*): hence THIMBLE-TWISTER=a watch thief; THIMBLE AND SLANG=watch and chain (GROSE, VAUX).

1834. AINSWORTH, *Rookwood*, III. v. With my THIMBLE [watch] of ridge.

1901. WALKER, *In the Blood*, 138. Obtained in the form of silver money and a watch and chain, or, in thieves' language, 'white lot' and THIMBLE AND SLANG.

KNIGHT OF THE THIMBLE, *subs. phr.* (common).—A tailor: *see* TRADES.

1838. GRANT, *Sketches in London*, III. 119. You'll do what, sir? observed the Man with the Mac'intosh, eyeing the KNIGHT OF THE THIMBLE steadily.

THIMBLED, *adj.* (old).—Arrested; laid by the heels (BEE).

THIMBLE AND BODKIN ARMY, *subs. phr.* (old).—The Parliamentary Army: in contempt.

1884. DOWELL, *Taxes in England*, II. 3. The nobles [were] profuse in their contributions of plate for the service of the king at Oxford, while on the parliamentary side the subscriptions of silver offerings included even such little personal articles as those that suggested the term THE THIMBLE AND BODKIN ARMY.

THIMBLEFUL, *subs.* (old).—A small quantity; as much as may be contained in a thimble: spec. a dram of spirits.

1690. DRYDEN, *Amphityron*, iv. 1. Yes, and measure for measure . . . a THIMBLEFULL of gold for a THIMBLEFULL of love.

1709. WARD, *Clubs* (1756), 16. Refusing all Healths, each taking off his THIMBLEFULL . . . paying . . . what himself calls for.

1886. *D. Tel.*, 11 Sep. Had the credit of suggesting the addition of a THIMBLEFUL of Veuve Cliquot.

THIMBLE-PIE, *subs. phr.* (women's).—Rapping the head with a thimbled finger.

THIMBLE-RIG, *subs.* (common).—A sharping trick: a pea placed on a table is quickly covered, in irregular succession, by three small cups, the operator betting against the discovery of the pea; as this is easily 'palmed,' a successful guess is at the option of the sharper and only allowed for the due 'landing' of the victim. Hence such derivatives as THIMBLE-RIG (or -MAN), THIMBLE-RIGGING, and as *verb.*

1835. HOOK, *Gilbert Gurney*, vii. I will appear to know no more of you than one of the cads of the THIMBLE-RIG knows of the pea-holder.

1841. *Blackwood's Mag.*, l. 202. Buttoners are those accomplices of THIMBLE-RIGGERS . . . whose duty it is to act as flat-catchers or decoys, by personating flats.

1843. DICKENS, *Martin Chuzzlewit*, xxxvii. Tom's evil genius did not . . . mark him out as the prey of ring-droppers, pea and THIMBLE RIGGERS, . . . or any of those bloodless sharpers, who are . . . better known to the police.

1851–61. H. MAYHEW, *London Lab. and Lon. Poor*, III. 121. Then the THIMBLE-RIGGER turns to the crowd, and pretends to be pushing them back, and one of the confederates, who is called a 'button,' lifts up one of the THIMBLES with a PEA under it, and laughs to those around, as much as to say, 'We've found it out.' Abridged.]

1864. *Glasgow Daily Mail*, 9 May. All kinds of cheats, and THIMBLE-RIGGERS, and prigs.

1868. WHYTE-MELVILLE, *White Rose*, II. iv. A merry blue-eyed boy, fresh from Eton, who could do THIMBLE-RIG, prick the garter, bones with his face blacked, and various other accomplishments.

1877. GREENWOOD, *Dick Temple*. The poor trumpery beggars—converted clowns, and dog-stealers, and tramps, and THIMBLE-RIGGERS—a poor out-at-elbows crew.

1883. J. BURROUGHS [*Century Mag.*, xxvii. 926]. The explanation of these experts is usually only clever THIMBLE-RIGGING.

1887. *D. Teleg.*, 15 Mar. THIMBLE-RIGGERS abounded, and their tables were surrounded by 'bonnets.'

THIN, *adj.* (colloquial).—One or two modern usages of THIN verge on the colloquial: *e.g.*, a THIN (=poor) EXCUSE; a THIN (=gutless) PLAY; a THIN (=trashy) NOVEL; TOO THIN (or T. T.)= frivolous, inadequate, insufficient to deceive, etc. Also (proverbial), 'As THIN as a lath'; 'As THIN as the last run of shad.'

1601. SHAKSPEARE, *Henry VIII.*, v. 3. 125. You were ever good at sudden commendations . . . now . . . they are TOO THIN and bare to hide offences.

1734. POPE, *Satires*, 93. Throned in the centre of his THIN designs.

1751. SMOLLETT, *Peregrine Pickle*, xxvi. This pretext was TOO THIN to impose upon her lover.

1763. FOOTE, *Mayor of Garratt*, i. *Sneak*. You see . . . I am almost as THIN AS A LATH. *Bruin*. An absolute skeleton.

1889. *Mod. Soc.*, 13 July, 852. 'Christopher's Honeymoon,' by M. Malcolm Watson, produced at the Strand, on Wednesday, is not wholly bad, but it is TOO THIN.

THIN RED LINE (THE), *subs. phr.* (military).—The Princess Louise's (Argyll and Sutherland Highlanders): of the 2nd battalion, late The 93rd Foot.

1901. FARMER, *Regimental Records of the British Army*, 207. Who amongst us does not remember, or who has not heard of that 'THIN RED LINE' drawn up by Colin Campbell to resist the onslaught of the Russian horse at Balaclava? how the 93rd stood their ground, successfully stemming, and finally repulsing that memorable charge? how it alone of all regiments of foot enjoys the proud distinction of 'Balaclava' on its colours?

THING, *subs.* (old colloquial).—1. In familiar usage (admiration, pity, scorn, or endearment)=a living creature, male or female: *e.g.*, SWEET THING (an old endearment); a POOR THING (a pitiful object); 'YOU THING!'; a THING OF A MAN (contemptuously: also A THING TO THANK GOD ON (SHAKSPEARE); a MERE THING in one's hands=a puppet, a nonentity; ALL THAT SORT OF THING=hardly worth notice, NO CLASS (*q.v.*), etc., etc.

c. 1440. *Eglamour* [Camden Soc.], 616. Seyde Organata that SWETE THYNGE, Y schalle geve the a gode golde rynge, Wyth a fulle ryche stone.

,, . . . *MS. Cantab.*, Ff. ii. 38. f. 176. Gye starte to that maydyn ȝynge, And seyde, Make no dole, my SWETE THYNGE.

1363. LANGLAND, *Piers Plowman* [E. E. T. S], 262. [A beggar is called] 'a POURE THING.'

d. 1536. TYNDALE, *Works*, ii. 120. [Tyndale speaks of Christ as] 'a THING soft and gentle.'

1542. UDAL, *Erasmus*, 270. Augustus beyng yet a YOUNG THING vnder mannes state.

1565. ASCHAM, *Schoolmaster* (1711), i. 42. If he be bashful, and will soon blush, they call him a babish and ill brought up THING.

1598. SHAKSPEARE, 1 *Henry IV.*, iii. 3. 129. For womanhood Maid Marian may be the deputy's wife of the ward to thee; go, YOU THING, go.

1633. FORD, *Broken Heart*, ii. 3. THING of talk, begone! Begone without reply.

1707. WARD, *Hud. Rediv.*, II. v. 24. You little Thingum of a THING.

2. (venery).—(*a*) The *penis*: *see* PRICK; (*b*) the *pudendum*: *see* MONOSYLLABLE. Hence (GROSE) 'Mr Thingstable, a ludicrous affectation for Mr CONSTABLE.' Fr. *chose*.

1610. JONSON, *Alchemist*, v. 1. Sure he ha' got some bawdy pictures . . .; or the new motion Of the knight's courser covering the parson's mare; The boy of six years old with the great THING.

d. 1631. DONNE, *Satires*, vi. [CHALMERS, *Eng. Poets*, v. 160. 2]. I found him thoroughly taught In curing burns. His THING had had more scars Than T . . . himself.

1653. URQUHART, *Rabelais*, i. xi. Madam, do you cut little children's THINGS? Were his cut off, he would be then Monsieur Sans-queue.

1700. FARQUHAR, *Constant Couple*, iv. 3. *Lady L.* And what shall I give you for such a fine thing [a ring]? *Sir H.* You'll give me another, you'll give me another fine THING.

17[?]. POPE, *Sober Advice from Horace* (WARTON, vi.). Did I demand in my most vigorous hour A THING descended from the Conqueror ('*Magno prognatum deposco connile cunnum*')?

1707. WARD, *Terræfilius*, I. v. 7. Pray Mr Whorehound of a THING-STABLE. . . .

1772. BRIDGES, *Burlesque Homer*, 62. [She] hated Paris in her heart, Because he'd seen her shady spring, And did not think it was THE THING . . . no matter whether They'd singly shew'd or both together.

3. (colloquial).—In *pl.*= (*a*) belongings; STICKS (*q.v.*); TRAPS (*q.v.*); and (*b*) clothes: as in the phrase 'Put on your THINGS.'

1383. CHAUCER, *Cant. Tales*, 'Second Nun's Tale,' 540. And hem she yaf hire mebles and hire THING.

c. 1400. *Towneley Myst.* [Camden Soc.], 47. [OLIPHANT, *New. Eng.*, i. 200. Property appears as] our THYNGES.

1593. SHAKSPEARE, *Taming of the Shrew*, iv. 3. Ruffs and cuffs and farthingales and THINGS.

1775. SHERIDAN, *Duenna*, i. 3. I suppose you don't mean to detain my apparel—I may have my THINGS, I presume?

1899. WHITEING, *John St.*, iv. By this time the heroine of the adventure has gathered up her 'THINGS.'

THE THING, *subs. phr.* (colloquial).—1. What is right, proper, becoming, fashionable, etc.

1759-62. GOLDSMITH, *Citizen of the World*, lxxvii. It is at once rich, tasty, and quite THE THING.

1781. JOHNSON [BOSWELL, *Life*, viii. 64]. A bishop's calling company together in this week is, to use the vulgar phrase, not THE THING.

1809. MALKIN, *Gil Blas* [ROUTLEDGE], 136. Young men of fashion are THE THING for me.

1814. AUSTEN, *Mansfield Park*, xii. It is quite delightful, ma'am, to see young people so properly happy, so well suited, and so much THE THING.

1823. *Song* [quoted by BEE in *Dict. Turf*]. I know I'm THE THING, And I wish I may swing, If I arn't now a nice natty crop.

1834. AINSWORTH, *Rookwood*, iii. 5. Just twig his swell kicksies and pipes; if they ain't THE THING, I'm done.

1863. DORAN, *Their Majesties' Servants*, I. 182. It was THE THING to look upon the company unless some irresistible attraction drew attention to the stage.

1868. WHYTE - MELVILLE, *White Rose*, I. v. Tangible advantage was THE THING after all.

1873. ARNOLD, *Literature and Dogma*, Pref. [A state church] is in itself . . . unimportant. THE THING is to re-cast religion.

1882. *Punch*, lxxxii. 193. They had low foreheads, and had big buttonholes . . . it was 'THE THING' to wear.

1901. *Free Lance*, 9 Feb., 470. 2. By the time the boom was at its height it had become THE THING for ladies . . . to gamble in 'Chartereds,' and 'Goldfields,' and 'Simmers.'

2. (thieves').—In *pl.*=base coin.

See KNOW; SOFT; HANDSOME (adding quot. *infra*), and GOOD THING.

1857. HUGHES, *Tom Brown's Schooldays*, i. 5. You see I'm doing the HANDSOME THING by you, because my father knows yours.

THINGUMBOB, *subs.* (common).—1. Used for the proper name of a person or thing, (*a*) when forgotten; or (*b*) when it is not desired to specifically name. Variants are numerous: *e.g.*, THINGUMAJIG, THINGUM, THINGUMMY, THINGAMY, THINGUMBEE, THING-A-MERRY, THINGUMMITE, THINGOMIGHTUM, etc. (GROSE and BEE). *See* JIGGUMBOB and WHAT'S-ITS-NAME.

1751. SMOLLETT, *Pickle*, ii. In a laced doublet and THINGUMBOBS at the wrists.

1831. LYTTON, *Eug. Aram*, I. ii. You will then see in the middle of a broad plain a lonely grey house, with a THINGUMBOB at the top: a 'servatory they call it.

1861. THACKERAY, *Philip*, I. 101. What a bloated aristocrat THINGAMY has become since he got his place.

1883. *Century Mag.*, xxxvii. 913. He got ther critter propped up an' ther THINGERMAJIG stropped on ter 'im.

1890. JAMES, *Prin. of Psychology*, I. 463. A polyp would be a conceptual thinker if a feeling of 'Hollo! THINGUMBOB again!' ever flitted through its mind.

2. (venery).—Euphemistic for (*a*) the *penis*: *see* PRICK; and (*b*) the female *pudendum*: *see* MONOSYLLABLE. Also (3) in *pl.*= the *testes*: *see* CODS.

THIN-GUTS, *subs. phr.* (old).—A starveling.

1631. MASSINGER, *Believe as You List*, iii. 2. Thou THIN-GUT!

THINK. *See* PENNY; SMALL BEER.

THIN-'UN, *subs. phr.* (common).—A half sovereign; 10s.; *cf.* THICK-'UN.

THIRDING, *subs.* (University).—A custom practised at the Universities, where two-thirds of the original price is allowed by the upholsterers to the students for household goods returned to them within the year (*Gradus ad Cantab*, 1803).

THIRTEEN (or THIRTEENER), *subs.* (old).—An Irish shilling=13d.: also THIRTEEN.

1837. BARHAM, *Ingoldsby Legends*, 'Coronation.' For the Earl of Surrey, all in his hurry, Throwing the THIRTEENS, hit him in his eye.

1847. THACKERAY, *George de Barnwell* [*Punch*, Ap. 3 to 17]. By Wood's THIRTEENERS, and the devil go wid 'em.

1851-61. MAYHEW, *Lond. Lab.*, I. 484. It was a shillin' he gave me . . . I niver heard it called a THIRTEENER before, but mother has.

1886. *Notes and Queries*, 7 S. i. 77. Colloquially it [the Irish shilling current prior to 1825-6] continued to be called a THIRTEEN . . . so late as 1835 to my knowledge.

THIRTEEN CLEAN SHIRTS, *subs. phr.* (prison).—Three months' imprisonment.

THIRTEEN - PENCE HALFPENNY, *subs. phr.* (old).—Hangman's wages (GROSE).

1602. DEKKER, *Honest Whore*, ii. [*Works* (1873), ii. 171]. Why should I eate hempe-seed at the hangman's THIRTEEN-PENCE-HALFE-PENNY ordinary?

1608. DAY, *Humour out of Breath*, F 3. If I shold, he could not hang me for't; 'tis not worth THIRTEEN PENCE HALF-PENNY.

1633. ROWLEY, *Match at Midnight* [DODSLEY, *Old Plays* (REED), vii. 357]. 'Sfoot, what a witty rogue was this to leave this fair THIRTEEN PENCE HALFPENNY, and this old halter, intimating aptly, Had the hangman met us there, by these presages, Here had been his work, and here his wages.

1659. *Hangman's last Will* [*Notes and Queries*, 2 S xi. 316]. For half THIRTEEN PENCE HALFPENNY wages I would have cleared out all the town cages.

THIRTY-POUND KNIGHT *subs. phr.* (old).—A creation of James I. [NARES: 'He created the order of baronet, which he disposed of for a sum of money; and it seems that he sold common knighthood as low as THIRTY POUNDS, or at least it was so reported.'

1605. CHAPMAN, *Eastward Ho* [DODSLEY, *Old Plays* (REED), iv. 261. Farewell, farewell; we will not know you for shaming of you. I ken the man well; he is one of my THIRTY-POUND KNIGHTS.

THOKE, *subs.* (Winchester College and prov.).—Rest: spec. lying in bed. Hence as *verb*=to lie in bed late. THOKESTER=an idler; THOKY (or THOKISH)= idle. Also TO THOKE UPON=to anticipate with pleasure: *e.g.*, 'I'm THOKING on next week; what a THOKE it will be, with a Leave out day, a Hatch-THOKE, and a half remedy' (WRENCH).

1899. *Public School Mag.*, Dec., 465. He attributed his success—or, at any rate, his long survival—to the art of THOKING: . . . which he had laboriously acquired during his first years of office.

THOMAS. MAN (or JOHN-) THOMAS, *subs. phr.* (venery).—The *penis*: *see* PRICK (URQUHART).

1619. FLETCHER, *Monsieur Thomas*. My MAN THOMAS did me promise He would visit me to-night.

THOMAS COURTEOUS, *subs. phr.* (old). — A churl [TYNDALE, *Works*, ii. 182].

THORNBACK, *subs.* (old). — 'An old Maid; also a well-known Fish, said to be exceedingly Provocative' (B. E. and GROSE). [*Cf.* Scots, *maiden - skate* = the thornback, *Raia clavata*.]

d. 1704. BROWN, *Works*, ii. 186. You were always very careful of your lord's health, and never brought anything to his embraces but unpenetrated maids, or very sound THORNBACKS.

THORNS. TO BE (or SIT) UPON THORNS, *verb. phr.* (old). — To be uneasy, anxious, impatient (GROSE).

1555. CAVENDISH, *Cardinal Wolseley* [OLIPHANT, *New Eng.*, i. 533. There are the phrases] SIT ON THORNS . . . broken English . . . etc.

THOROUGH CHURCHMAN, *subs. phr.* (GROSE).—'A person who goes in at one door of a church, and out at the other, without stopping.

THOROUGH-COUGH, *subs. phr.* (old).—'Coughing and breaking wind backwards at the same time' (B. E. and GROSE).

THOROUGH - GO - NIMBLE, *subs.* (old). — An attack of the SQUITTERS (*q.v.*); a BACK-DOOR TROT (*q.v.*). Also JERRY-GO-NIMBLE (*q.v.*) (GROSE and HALLIWELL).

1694. MOTTEUX, *Rabelais*, 'Pant. Prog.,' iii. Those who are troubled with the THOROUGH-GO-NIMBLE, or wild-squirt, will often prostitute their blind-cheeks to the bog-house.

THOROUGH-PASSAGE, *subs. phr.* (B. E.).—'In at one ear, and out at t'other.'

THOROUGH-STITCH. *See* THROUGH-STITCH.

THOUSAND. ANOTHER THOUSAND A YEAR! *phr.* (common).—A pledge in drinking: also ANOTHER TEN THOUSAND A YEAR—any sum indeed.

See BRICKS and UPPER TEN.

THRAPPLE, *subs.* (old). — The throat: also THROPPLE. *See* GUTTER-ALLEY.

THREAD. TO SPIN A GOOD THREAD, *verb. phr.* (colloquial).—To succeed.

TO THREAD THE NEEDLE, *verb. phr.* (venery).—To possess a woman: *see* RIDE.

THREAD-AND-THRUM, *subs. phr.* (old).—Everything; all: even to the fringe of threads left on the loom when the web has been removed.

1592. SHAKSPEARE, *Mid. Night's Dream*, v. 1. 291. O Fates, come, come; Cut THREAD AND THRUM.

THREADNEEDLE ST. *See* OLD LADY.

THREAD-PAPER. *See* HOP-POLE.

THREE. ONE (or TWO'S) COMPANY—THREE'S NONE! *phr.* (colloquial).—A suggestion to a second or third party that 'their room is preferred before their company.'

1430. *Babees Book* [E. E. T. S.], 307. Be not the THRYD FELAW for wele ne wo; Thre oxen in plowgh may never wel drawe.

CUBE OF THREE, *subs. phr.* (old).—*See* quot.

1705-6. HEARNE, Jan. 30 [*Reliquiæ*, i. 93]. The great health now is, The CUBE OF THREE, which is the number 27, *i.e.*, the number of the protesting lords.

THREE TIMES THREE! *phr.* (colloquial).—Three cheers, thrice repeated.

1850. TENNYSON, *In Memoriam*, Concl. Again the feast, the speech, the glee. . . . The crowning cup, the THREE TIMES THREE.

1857. HUGHES, *Tom Brown's School-days*, i. 6. I must give you a toast to be drunk with THREE TIMES THREE and all the honours.

TO PLAY THREE TO ONE, *verb. phr.* (venery).—To copulate: *see* RIDE. Also TO PLAY THREE TO ONE AND SURE TO LOSE (GROSE).

[?]. *Old Song*. 'As I cam o'er the Cairney Mount' [BURNS, *Merry Muses* (*c.* 1800), 45]. A famous battle then began, Wi' equal courage and desire, Altho' he struck me THREE TO ONE.

See SHEET.

THREE BALLS. THE SIGN OF THE THREE BALLS (BRASS, GOLDEN or BLUE BALLS), *phr.* (old).—A pawnbroker's: *see* UNCLE.

1748. SMOLLETT, *Roderick Random*, xvi. He at length unbuckled his hanger, and, showing me the SIGN OF THE THREE BLUE BALLS, desired me to carry it thither and pawn it for two guineas.

c. 1845. HOOD, *Pawning Watch*, ix. I've gone to a dance for my supper; And now must go to THREE BALLS!

1861. SALA, *Twice Round Clock*, 180. The brethren of the THREE GOLDEN BALLS.

1880. SIMS, *Three Brass Balls* [Title].

THREE-BY-NINE SMILE, *subs. phr.* (American).—A broad laugh (? a pun on 'benign').

THREE-CORNERED SCRAPER, *subs. phr.* (old).—A cocked hat.

THREE-DECKER, *subs.* (orig. nautical: now general).—1. A man-of-war carrying guns on three decks: whence (2) a piece of furniture, pulpit, etc., in three tiers (in a pulpit the *clerk's* place was at the bottom, the reading-desk on the second stage, and the pulpit highest of all); (3) a three-volume novel, or three-act play; and (4) a coat having three capes round the shoulders.

1814. AUSTEN, *Mansfield Park*, xli. Before the gentlemen . . . could . . . settle the number of THREE-DECKERS now in commission, their companions were ready to proceed.

1855. TENNYSON, *Maud*, II. ii. 4. Cataract seas that snap The THREE-DECKER'S open spine.

1885. *D. Teleg.*, 20 Oct. The modest pulpit of an English church is as yet a rarity, for the complicated and extensive 'THREE-DECKER' is still in use all over the country.

1888. W.S. OGDEN, *Antique Furniture*, 32. A THREE-DECKER sideboard, about 1700.

1896. KIPLING, *Seven Seas*, 'The Three-Decker' [Title *et passim*].

THREE-DRAWS-AND-A-SPIT, *subs. phr.* (common).—A cigarette.

THREE F'S (THE), *subs. phr.* (political).—1. The demands of the Irish Land League: Free Sale, Fixity of Tenure, and Fair Rent: practically conceded by Mr Gladstone's Land Act (1881).

2. (vulgar).—'Fuck, Fun, and a Footrace.'

THREE-LEGGED STOOL. TO COMB ONE'S HEAD WITH A THREE-LEGGED STOOL (or JOINT-STOOL), *verb. phr.* (old).—A humorous threat of punishment. For quots. *see* COMB ONE'S HAIR.

THREE TREES (THE), *subs. phr.* (old).—The gallows (B. E. and GROSE). Also THREE-LEGGED STOOL; THREE-CORNERED TREE; THREE-LEGGED MARE (also TWO-LEGGED MARE, and MARE WITH THREE LEGS), THE TYBURN TREE, and TRIPLE TREE: *see* NUBBING-CHEAT. [Executions at Tyburn were abandoned in 1783, and thenceforward (in London) till 1868 took place in front of Newgate: *see* quot. 1785.]

1582. BRETON, *Toyes of an Idle Head*, 28. For commonly such knaues as these Doe end their lyves vpon THREE TREES.

1654. *Witts Recreations* [NARES]. And from the fruit of the THREE CORNER'D TREE, Vertue and goodness still deliver me.

1685. BROWN, *Works*, iv. 243. If your sadness does proceed from fear Of being mounted on a THREE-LEGG'D MARE.

1694. MOTTEUX, *Rabelais*, v. iv. Gaol birds . . . made to ride the TWO or THREE-LEGGED MARE that groans for them.

1785. GROSE, *Vulg. Tongue*, s.v. THREE-LEGGED MARE. . . . This clumsy machine has given place to an elegant contrivance called the *new drop*, by which the use of that vulgar vehicle, a cart, or mechanical instrument a ladder, is also avoided; the patients being left suspended by the dropping down of that part of the floor on which they stand. This invention was first made use of for a peer.

1834. AINSWORTH, *Rookwood*, 'The Game of High Toby.' For the MARE WITH THREE LEGS, boys, I care not a rap.

189[?]. HENLEY, *Carmen Patibulare*. TREE, old TREE OF THE TRIPLE CROOK, And the Rope of the Black Election.

THREE-OUT. *See* OUT.

THREE-PENNY (or THREE-HALF-PENNY), *adj. phr.* (old).—Common, vulgar; in little esteem; of little worth: *cf.* 'three-inch fool' (SHAKSPEARE, *Tam. Shrew*, iv 1). Hence THREE-PENNY PLANET = an unpropitious augury; THREE-HALF-PENNY-HORSE-LOAF (in contempt of an undersized person).

d. 1555. LATIMER, *Remains* [PARKER], 29. [A curate's wages, nine or ten pounds may be earned by some] THREE-HALFPENNY priest.

1630. TAYLOR, *Works* [NARES]. Some men (being borne under a THREE-PENNY PLANET) can neither by paines, watching, labour, or any industry, be worth a groat.

THREEPENNY UPRIGHT (or BIT) (venery).—An act of coition taken standing with a threepenny whore: *cf.* PERPENDICULAR and KNEE-TREMBLER (GROSE).

THREE-PLY, *subs.* (American).—A Mormon having three wives.

THREE-QUARTERS OF A PECK, *subs. phr.* (rhyming).—The neck: amongst experts THREE QUARTERS and written '$\frac{3}{4}$.'

THREE STRIDE BUSINESS, *subs. phr.* (hurdle-racers').—Three strides between each hurdle: the crack style.

THREE R'S (THE). *subs. phr.* (common).—Reading, 'riting, and 'rithmetic; a jesting toast proposed by Sir William Curtis, Lord Mayor of London in 1795, at a dinner given by the Board of Education.

THREE TENS (THE), *subs. phr.* (military).—The 1st battalion East Lancashire Regiment, late The 30th Foot. Also The Triple X's.

THREE SHEETS. *See* SHEETS.

THREESWINS, *subs.* (old).—Three-pence.

THREE-THREADS (or THIRDS), *subs. phr.* (obsolete).—*See* quots.

c. 1696. B. E., *Dict. Cant. Crew*, s.v. THREE-THREADS, half common Ale, and the rest Stout or Double Beer.

1698. SORBIÈRE, *Journey to London* [*Notes and Queries*, 6 S. xii. 167]. He answered me that he had a thousand such sorts of liquors, as . . . THREE THREADS, Four Threads, old Pharaoh . . .

d. 1704. BROWN, *Works*, ii. 286. Ezekiel Driver . . . with too plentiful a morning's draught of THREE-THREADS and old Pharaoh, had the misfortune to have his cart run over him.

1874. *Chambers' Encyclop.*, s.v. PORTER . . . THREE THREADS is a corruption of three thirds, and denoted a draught, once popular, made up of a third each of ale, beer, and 'two-penny,' in contradistinction to 'half-and-half.' This beverage was superseded in 1722 by the very similar porter or 'entire.'

1881. DAVIES, *Supplemental Glossary*, s.v. THREE-THREADS. Half common ale mixed with stale and double beer. [So also *Ency. Dict.*]

1899. *Century Dict.*, s.v. THREE . . . THREE THREADS, a mixture of three malt liquors, formerly in demand, as equal parts of ale, beer, and twopenny.

THREE-UP, *subs. phr.* (streets').—A gambling game. Three half-pennies are 'skied' to a call: if they do not 'fall' alike, the cry is void, and the operation is repeated. When the three coins 'come off' (*i.e.*, fall alike), bets are decided. If two play, it is 'up for up,' *i.e.*, they toss and cry alternately: if three or more join in, it is a school, and one, a 'pieman,' cries to the halfpence of the others until he loses, when the winner of the toss becomes 'pieman' in turn: *see* SCHOOL and SCHOOLING.

THREE X'S (THE), *subs. phr.* (military).—The 1st battalion East Lancashire Regiment, late The 30th Foot.

THREP (THRIP or THRUPS), *subs.* (old).—Three-pence (B. E. and GROSE).

1888. J. C. HARRIS [*Harper's Mag.*, lxxvi. 703]. He was not above any transaction, however small, that promised to bring him a dime, where he had invested A THRIP.

THRESHER. CAPTAIN THRESHER, *subs. phr.* (obsolete).—In 1806 an Irish Catholic organization was formed to resist the payment of tithes: threats and warnings were sent out signed 'CAPTAIN THRESHER.'

THROAT. THROAT occurs in a few colloquialisms: *e.g.*, TO LIE IN ONE'S THROAT = to lie flatly: an expression of extreme indignation; TO CUT ONE ANOTHER'S

THROATS = to engage in CUT-THROAT (*q.v.*) competition or conduct ruinous to either; TO CUT ONE'S OWN THROAT (or TO CUT THE THROAT OF) = to ruin oneself, to shipwreck chances or interests; TO HAVE ONE'S THROAT LINED = to be void of taste; to wish for A THROAT A MILE LONG AND A PALATE AT EVERY INCH OF IT (= a modern echo of Rabelais: *see* quot. 1694). *See* BONE; STICK.

1637. HUMPHREY, *St Ambrose*, Pref. This CUTS THE THROAT of that misconceived opinion.

1648. TAYLOR, *Travels . . . to Isle of Wight*, 14. And therefore, reader, understand and note, Whoever sayes I lye, he LIES IN'S THROAT.

1692. SIMON PATRICK (Bp. of Ely), *Answ. Touchstone*, 10. This, which CUTS THE THROAT of the Roman cause.

1694. MOTTEUX, *Rabelais*, v. xlii. Tell me, noble strangers, are your THROATS LINED, paved, or enamelled . . . that you can have missed the taste, relish, and flavour of this divine liquor? *Ibid* Oh! that to keep the taste longer, we gentleman topers had but NECKS SOME THREE CUBITS LONG or so.

1824. STANHOPE, *Greece*, 12. Generals . . . who CUT THEIR OWN THROATS by word of command.

1867. FROUDE, *Short Studies* (2nd ed.), 114. They . . . believed that Elizabeth was CUTTING HER OWN THROAT.

1886. *St James's Gaz.*, 12 Ap. Gentlemen who supply, or try to supply, the public with cheap literature seem specially fond of that curious amusement known as CUTTING ONE ANOTHER'S THROATS.

THROTTLE (or THROPPLE), *verb.* (colloquial).—To strangle (GROSE).

THROUGH. Colloquialisms range themselves under THROUGH as follows: TO BE THROUGH = (1) to have finished: as of a meal, 'Are you THROUGH?'; (2) to be acquitted (old thieves': GROSE); (3) to complete a bargain; TO HAVE BEEN THROUGH THE MILL = to have learned by experience. Also *see* ALPHABET, THICK, WATER, and other nouns.

TO GO THROUGH A WOMAN, *verb. phr.* (venery).—To possess carnally.

THROUGHSHOT, *adj.* (colloquial).—Spendthrift: *e.g.*, A THROUGH SHOT sort of fellow.

THROUGH-STITCH, *adj. phr.* (old). Thorough; complete; 'over Shoes, over Boots' (B. E.); 'to stick at nothing' (GROSE): 'a tailor's expression' (BEE). Hence TO GO THROUGH STITCH (*see* quot. 1611).

1611. COTGRAVE, *Dict. Achever*. To atchieve; to end, finish, conclude (fully); to dispatch, effect, performe (throughly); to perfect, consummat, accomplish, GO THROUGH-STITCH WITH.

1630. TAYLOR, *Works* [NARES]. The taylers hell, who indeed are accounted the best bread men in the ship, and such as GOE THROUGH STITCH with what they take in hand.

1631. CHETTLE, *Hoffman*. *O. Stilt.* Mas he saies true son; but what's the remedy? *Stilt.* None at all father, now wee are in, wee must GOE THROUGH STITCH.

1634. FORD, *Perkin Warbeck*, ii. 3. He that threads his needle with the sharp eyes of industry shall in time GO THROUGH-STITCH with the new suit of preferment.

1662. *Rump Songs*. If any taylor have the itch, Your black-smith's water, as black as pitch, Will make his fingers go THOROUGH-STITCH. Which nobody can deny.

1690. *Pagan Prince* [NARES]. For when a man has once undertaken a business, let him GO THOROW STITCH with it.

1759-67. STERNE, *Tristram Shandy*, iii. 30. His book may properly be considered, not only as a model, but as a THOROUGH-STITCHED Digest and regular institute of noses.

THROW. Among SLANG and COLLOQUIAL USAGES may be enumerated: TO THROW A LEVANT = to make off: *see* BUNK; TO THROW A SOP TO CERBERUS (*see* SOP); TO THROW COLD WATER = to discourage, 'to damp'; TO THROW DUST (or PEPPER) IN THE EYES = to mislead, to dupe; TO THROW OFF = (1) to do or talk offhandedly: spec. to convey unpleasant allusions under a mask of pleasantry (GROSE); (2) 'to brag of past booty' (thieves': GROSE); (3) to discard; and (4) to start the pack (fox-hunters'); TO THROW ONESELF INTO = to do zealously; TO THROW OUT = to expel with violence; TO THROW OVER = to desert; TO THROW OVERBOARD = to abandon; TO THROW TOGETHER = (1) to do hastily, and (2) to bring together frequently: as 'their marriage came about through being THROWN much TOGETHER'; TO THROW UP = to resign; to desist; to CHUCK UP (*q.v.*); TO THROW UP THE SPONGE (*see* SPONGE); TO THROW ABOUT = to seek an opportunity, to try expedients; TO THROW BACK = to revert; TO THROW IN FOR = to enter: as for a race; TO THROW TO THE DOGS = to put aside as valueless; TO THROW OFF THE BELT = to stop; TO HAVE A THROW AT = to attack; TO THROW SNOT ABOUT = to weep; TO THROW (or THROW DOWN) A PAPER (LESSON, EXAMINATION, etc.) = TO FLOOR (*q.v.*).

1591. SPENSER, *Mother Hubbard's Tale*, 80. Now unto despaire I 'gin to growe, And meane for better winde ABOUT TO THROWE.

1698. COLLIER, *Short View*, 101. The Old Bachelour has a THROW at the Dissenting Ministers.

1712. ADDISON, *Spectator*, 105. I could not forbear THROWING TOGETHER such reflections as occurred to me on that subject.

1785. GROSE, *Vulg. Tongue*, s.v. THROW. . . . To talk flash of robberies past, or in contemplation, when in company with family people, is also termed THROWING OFF; meaning to banish all reserve, none but friends being present; also, to sing when called on by the company present.

1808. *Trial Gen. Whitelocke* (MOTTLEY), II. 442. He had stated that I was THROWING COLD WATER ON everything he did.

1809. MALKIN, *Gil Blas* [ROUTLEDGE], 168. THROWING TO THE DOGS all the mental physic they poured in; they would have none of it.

1842-3. THACKERAY, *Fitz-Boodle's Confession*. I at once THREW UP my hopes of military distinction, and retired into civil life.

1844. DISRAELI, *Coningsby*. They say the Rads are going to THROW us OVER.

1868. WHYTE - MELVILLE, *White Rose*, II. xi. A vast number of engagements, any of which . . . he was ready to THROW OVER at a moment's notice.

1870. *English Gilds* (E.E.T.S.), Int. It would be well to THROW his notes and materials INTO some SHAPE.

1883. MRS BISHOP [*Leis. Hour*, 86. 2]. Who THREW COLD WATER on the idea.

1886. DOBSON, *Steele*, Int. xxx. Often Addison's most brilliant efforts are built upon a chance hint THROWN OFF at random by Steele's hurrying pen.

1891. *Harry Fludyer*, 98. These blessed exams. are getting awfully close now; but I think I shall floor mine, and Dick's sure TO THROW his examiners DOWN.

THROW THE FEET, *verb. phr.* (American tramps'). *See* quot.

1900. JOSIAH FLYNT, *Tramping with Tramps*, 397. To beg, 'hustle,' or do anything that involves much action.

THROW-BACK, *subs. phr.* (common).—A set-back; a reversion; also TO THROW BACK = to revert to type.

H

1890. *Athenæum*, 3229, 351. She is personally a THROW-BACK to an angel.

THRUM, *verb.* (GROSE).—1. 'To play on any instrument stringed with wire'; to strum. Hence THRUMMER.

1550. UDAL, *Roister Doister*, ii. 1. Anon to our gittern, *thrumpledum, thrumpledum*, THRUM.

2. (venery). To possess a woman (HALLIWELL): *see* STRUM and RIDE.

1772. BRIDGES, *Homer Burlesque*, 22. Expect . . . to keep you safe to THRUM my harlot: Not I, by Jove. *Ibid.*, 95. Paris, says he, we know you can The wenches THRUM.

Subs. (old).—In *pl.* = threepence; THREPS (*q.v.*): *see* RHINO (B. E. and GROSE). Also THRUMBUSKINS and THRUMMOP.

THREAD AND THRUM. *See* THREAD.

THRUM-CAP, *subs. phr.* (old).—Rough headgear. [Properly a rugged rocky headland swept by the sea.]

1694. MOTTEUX, *Rabelais*, v. Pant. Prog. Scourers of greasy THRUM CAPS, stuffers, and bumbasters of pack saddles.

1772. BRIDGES, *Burlesque Homer*, 10. Smite my THRUM-CAP, and noddle too.

THUG, *subs.* (American political).—1. A nickname for a member of the native American party; (2) a cut-throat ruffian.

1883. *Century Mag.*, June, 230. Affrays were still common; the Know-Nothing movement came on, and a few THUGS terrorized the city with campaign broils, beating, stabbing, and shooting. *Ibid.* (249). During our civil war, the regiments which were composed of plug-uglies, THUGS, and midnight rounders, with noses laid over to one side as evidence of their prowess in bar-room mills and paving-stone riots, were generally cringing cowards in battle.

THUMB, *verb.* (old).—1. To drain a glass upon the thumb-nail: the glass must be emptied so that there remains only a drop that will not run off the nail. *See* SUPERNACULUM.

2. (common).—(*a*) To paw, to MESS ABOUT, TO GROPE A WOMAN; and (*b*) to possess one carnally: hence a WELL-THUMBED GIRL = a foundered whore. Also THUMBLE.

1606. *Wily Beguiled* [HAWKINS, *Eng. Drama*, iii. 317. Well, I'll not stay with her: stay, quotha? To be yauld and jaul'd at, and tumbled and *thumbled*, and tost and turn'd as I am by an old hag.

Among COLLOQUIAL PHRASES are: A THUMB UNDER THE GIRDLE = an indication of gravity or sadness; RULE OF THUMB (*q.v.*), adding quot. *infra*; ALL HIS FINGERS ARE THUMBS (of a clumsy person: also THUMBLESS); TO BITE THE THUMB (*see* BITE); UNDER ONE'S THUMB = under complete control, subservient; FINGER AND THUMB = inseparable, with tied navels. (It. '*Hanno legato il bellico insieme.*') Further, a WELL-THUMBED book = a rough-handled book; one 'thumbed' out of respectability; THUMB-MARKED = bearing unmistakable traces of an individual artist, reader, performer, etc. Also PROVERBIAL (and other) SAYINGS: 'When you come to this place of ease, Place your elbows on your knees, Behind your ears stick both your THUMBS, Give a heave, and out it comes.' 'If you BITE YOUR THUMB there's hell to pay.' (*See* BITE).

1534. UDAL, *Roister Doister*, i. 3. Ah, ECHE FINGER IS A THOMBE to-day me thinke.

1614. OVERBURY, *Characters*. They call the THUMB UNDER THE GIRDLE gravity, and because they can hardly smell at all, their posy's are under their girdles.

1639. *Optick Glasse of Humours*. Of all men wee count a melancholicke man the very sponge of all sad humours, the aqua-fortis of merry company, A THUMBE UNDER THE GIRDLE, the contemplative slumberer, that sleepes waking, etc.

1648. HERRICK, *Hesperides*, 333. When to a house I come and see The genius wastefull more than free; The servants THUMBLESSE, yet to eat With lawlesse tooth the floure of wheat.

1753. RICHARDSON, *Grandison*, v. 56. She remembers her delinquency, so she is obliged to be silent: I have her UNDER MY THUMB.

1809. MALKIN, *Gil Blas* [ROUTLEDGE], 277. The tenants were all UNDER MY THUMB. *Ibid.*, 378. He is an old hunks who wants to keep me UNDER HIS THUMB.

1859. KINGSLEY, *Geof. Hamlyn*, ix. He is UNDER THE THUMB of that doctor.

1861. HUGHES, *Tom Brown at Oxford*, xxi. We never learnt anything in the navy when I was a youngster, except a little RULE-OF-THUMB mathematics.

THUMBER, *subs.* (common).—(1) A sandwich; and (2) a slice of bread and meat carved and eaten between finger and thumb.

THUMBING, *subs.* (provincial).—A Nottingham phrase, used to describe that species of intimidation practised by masters on their servants: when the latter are compelled to vote as their employers please, under pain of losing their situations (HALLIWELL).

THUMB-OF-LOVE, *subs. phr.* (venery).—The *penis*: *cf.* WHITMAN (*Children of Adam*) and SHAKSPEARE (POTATO-FINGER, *q.v.*).

THUMP, *subs.* (old: now recognised).—A heavy blow with club, fist, or anything that resounds: also as *verb* (GROSE). [*Century*: Not found in Middle English; apparently a variant of *dump.*] Hence THUMPER. Also 'This is better than a THUMP on the back with a stone' (GROSE: said on giving a drink of good liquor on a cold morning); 'Thatch, thistle, thunder, and THUMP' (GROSE: 'words to the Irish, like the Shibboleth of the Hebrews').

1596. SPENSER, *Fairy Queen*, VI. ii. 10. He with his speare . . . Would THUMPE her forward and inforce to goe.

1607. DEKKER, *Northward Ho*, iv. 1. As though my heart-strings had been cracked I wept and sighed, and THUMPED and THUMPED, and raved and randed and railed.

c. 1618. FLETCHER, *Mad Lover*, v. O let me ring the fore bell, and here are THUMPERS.

1628. FORD, *Lover's Melancholy*, i. 1. When blustering Boreas . . . THUMPS a thunder-bounce.

d. 1771. GRAY, *Letters*, I. 71. With these masqueraders that vast church is filled, who are seen THUMPING their breasts, and kissing the pavement with extreme devotion.

Verb. (obscene).—To possess a woman.

1604. SHAKSPEARE, *Winter's Tale*, iv. 4. 195. Delicate burthens of dildos and fadings, 'jump her and THUMP her.'

THUMPER (THUMPING, ETC.), *subs.* (common).—1. Anything impressive: *cf.* WHOPPER; THUMPING = unusually large, heavy, etc. (GROSE).

c. 1709. WARD, *Terræfilius*, ii. 5. Here comes a THUMPING Brother of . . . the Law.

1710-13. SWIFT, *Journ. to Stella* [OLIPHANT, *New English*, ii. 150. The word THUMPER stands for *mendacium*].

d. 1763. BYROM, *Critical Remarks* [CHALMERS, *Eng. Poets*, xv. 236. 1]. Small as you will, if 'twas a bumper, Centum for one would be a THUMPER.

1774. GOLDSMITH, *Retaliation*. One fault he had and that one was a THUMPER.

1798. O'KEEFE, *Fontainebleau*, iii. 1. You've run up a THUMPING bill.

1809. MALKIN, *Gil Blas* [ROUTLEDGE], 358. Antonia has not a THUMPING fortune to bring with her.

1902. *Pall Mall Gaz.*, 24 Jan., i. 3. A THUMPING majority.

2. (showmens').—In *pl.* = dominoes.

THUMPKIN, *subs.* (thieves').—A barn filled with hay.

THUNDER! *intj.* (common).—A mild oath: also THUNDERATION! THUNDER - AND - LIGHTNING! and THUNDER - AND - TURF! BY THUNDER = By God, and the Devil, and what comes between.

1837. BARHAM, *Ingoldsby Legends*, 'The Ingoldsby Penance.' Now THUNDER AND TURF, Pope Gregory said.

1847. ROBB, *Squatter Life*. WHAT IN THUNDER makes you take on so?

18[?]. BRET HARTE, *Chiquita*. An' twelve hundred dollars of hog's-flesh afloat, and a drifting to THUNDER.

1887. HENLEY, *Hospital Outlines*. It looked like fighting, And they meant it too, BY THUNDER.

1896. LILLARD, *Poker Stories*, 95. THE THUNDER, you say . . . some of you must remind the Sheriff to shoot him on sight.

TO COLLAR (or STEAL) ONE'S THUNDER, *verb. phr.* (common).—*See* quot.

c. 1709. DENNIS [WALSH, *Lit. Curios*, 1052. John Dennis, critic and dramatist . . . was the inventor of a new species of stage thunder which was used for the first time in a play of his own . . . coldly received and speedily withdrawn. Shortly afterwards (so Spence tells us), he heard his own thunder made use of. 'Damn them!' he cried, 'they will not let my play run, but they STEAL MY THUNDER! So also POPE: see *Dunciad*, ii. 223, Note].

THUNDERBOMB (H.M.S.), *subs. phr.* (nautical).—An imaginary ship of enormous dimensions.

18[?]. BUCKSTONE, *Billy Taylor*. Straightway made her first lieutenant Of the gallant THUNDERBOMB.

THUNDERER (THE), *subs. phr.* (journalists').—*The Times* newspaper.

1874. *Siliad*, 201. If a small cloud doth in the East appear, Then speaks THE THUNDERER, and all men hear.

THUNDERING, *adj.* (common).—A strong intensive: great, large, tremendous, etc.

1597. HALL, *Satires*, i. Graced with huff-cap terms and THUNDERING threats. [Possibly a connecting link between the two senses.]

d. 1655. ADAMS, *Works*, II. 420. He goes a THUNDERING pace that you would not think it possible to overtake him.

1678. COTTON, *Virgil Travestie*, (1770), 59. And in they brought a THUNDERING Meal.

d. 1704. BROWN, *Works*, i. 249. I was drawing a THUNDERING fish out of the water.

d. 1743. HERVEY, *Memoirs Court of George II.* [Mention is made of Queen Caroline's indignation at the infliction of] a THUNDERING long sermon.

1772. BRIDGES, *Burlesque Homer*, 36. No sooner he the priest did spy, But up he brought a THUNDERING lie.

1840. CROCKETT, *Tour down East*, 61. I was told that Faneuil Hall was called the 'cradle of liberty.' I reckon old King George thought they were THUNDERING fine children that were rocked in it.

1844. *Major Jones's Courtship*, 82. If a chap only comes from the North, and has got a crop of hair and whiskers, and a coat different from everybody else, and a THUNDERIN' great big gold chain . . . he's the poplerest man among the ladies.

1848. LOWELL, *Biglow Papers*, I. i. Haint they cut a THUNDERIN' swarth?

1883. GREENWOOD, *Tag, Rag, and Co.* He took me into his confidence, with the professed object, as he himself declared, of proving to me 'what a THUNDERING fool he had been.'

1888. BOLDREWOOD, *Squatter's Dream*, iii. 24. If I had had my way, I'd have burned down the THUNDERING old place long ago.

THUNDER-MUG, *subs. phr.* (old).—A chamber-pot; *see* IT.

THUSNESS. WHY THIS THUSNESS? *phr.* (common).—A pleonastic 'Why'?

THWACK, *subs.* and *verb.* (B. E. and GROSE).—'To Beat with a Stick or Cudgel' (B. E.); 'a great blow with a stick across the shoulders' (GROSE); THICK-THWACK = blow after blow.

1574. *Appius and Virginia* [DODSLEY, *Old Plays* (HAZLITT), iv. 123]. With THWICK THWACK, with thump thump.

d. 1618. STANYHURST, *Conceites* [ARBER], 138. With peale meale ramping, with THWICK THWACK sturdelye thundring.

THWACKER, *subs.* (colloquial).—Anything very much out of the common; THWACKING = tremendous, great: *see* WHOPPER.

1620. MIDDLETON, *Chaste Maid*, v. 3. *Sec. Ser.* A bonfire, sir? *Sir Ol.* A THWACKING one, I charge you.

TIB, *subs.* (old).—1. A woman: generic (*cf.* TOM = man), a usage that long lingered (B. E. and GROSE); hence (2) a term of endearment (HALLIWELL): also a calf; and (3) contemptuously, a wanton. *Cf.* TIB OF THE BUTTERY = goose (sometimes = an endearment).

1582. STANYHURST, *Æneid* [ARBER], 102. A coy TYB . . . That the plat of Carthage from mee by coosinage hooked . . . Hath scorned my wedlock.

1598. SHAKSPEARE, *All's Well*, ii. 2. 22. As fit as your French crown for your taffeta punk, as TIB'S rush for Tom's forefinger. *Ibid.* (1609), *Pericles*, iv. 6. 176. Every coistrel That comes inquiring for his TIB.

1652. BROME, *Jovial Crew*, ii. As Tom or TIB When they at bowsing ken do swill.

1677. COLES, *Lat.-Eng. Dict.* A TIB, *mulier sordida*.

1693. *Cambridge Dict.*, TIB. TIB, a poor sorry woman; *mulier-cula impura*.

4. (provincial).—The *anus*: *see* BUM.

5. (back slang).—A bit: hence TIB FO OCCABOT = a bit of tobacco.

TO TIB OUT, *verb. phr.* (Charterhouse).—To go beyond bounds.

1854-5. THACKERAY, *Newcomes*, xli. When I was a boy I used what they call to TIB OUT, and run down to a public-house in Cistercian Lane, the Red Cow, sir.

TIB-OF-THE-BUTTERY (or **TIB**), *subs. phr.* (Old Cant).—A goose; *cf.* TIB (HARMAN, B. E. and GROSE).

1622. FLETCHER *Beggar's Bush*, v. 1. Margery praters, Rogers, and TIBS O' TH' BUTTERY.

1641. BROME, *Jovial Crew*, ii. Here's grunter and bleater with TIB OF THE BUTT'RY, And Margery Prater, all dress'd without slutt'ry.

1725. *Song* [*New Canting Dict.*]. On red shanks and TIBS thou shalt every day dine.

TIBB'S-EVE, *subs. phr.* (old).—An indefinite date (GROSE: 'Irish' . . . 'ST TIBB'S EVENING, the evening of the last day or day of judgment; as He will pay you on ST TIBB'S EVE'). *See* QUEEN DICK.

TIBBY, *subs.* (B. E. and GROSE).—1. A cat.

2. (common).—The head; TO DROP ON ONE'S TIBBY = to take unawares.

c. 1866. VANCE, *Chickaleary Cove.* For to get me on the hop, or on my TIBBY drop, You must wake up very early in the mornin'.

TICHBORNE'S OWN, *subs. phr.* (military).—The 6th Dragoon Guards (Carabineers): *c.* 1871-4, at the time of the Tichborne trial, Sir Roger Tichborne having (1849) served in the regiment.

TICK (or **TICKET**), *subs.* (old).—A word regarded as slang to-day (or verging thereon) that can boast of considerable (and, indeed, honourable) antiquity: an abbreviation of TICKET = a tradesman's bill, formerly written on slips of paper or cards. Hence TICK (or TICKET) = credit, a debt; as *verb* = to buy or take on trust, to run a score; TO TICK UP (or TO HAVE THE RUN OF THE TICKET) = to put to account, to run in debt (Fr. *avoir l'ardoise* = to slate); WHAT'S THE TICKET? = What's the price (Fr. *quelle est le marché du bœuf gras?*)—(B. E. and GROSE).

1609. DEKKER, *Gul's Hornbook*, vi. 145. No matter whether in landing you have money or no; you may swim in twentie of their boates over the river UPON TICKET.

1615. SHIRLEY, *Works*, iii. 56 [STEPHENS, *Characters*, 239]. [He] plaies UPON TICKET.

1633. MARMION, *Fine Companion*, v. 2. Yon courtier is mad to take up silks and velvets ON TICKET for his mistresse, and your citizen Is mad to trust him.

1638. RANDOLPH, *Hey for Honesty*, ii. 6. I am resolved to build no more sconces, but to pay my old TICKETS.

1648. FULLER, *Holy State*, 114. Though much indebted to his own back and belly, and unable to pay them, yet he hath credit himself, and confidently runs ON TICKET with himself.

1661. PRIDEAUX [Dean of Norwich], *Letter*, May. The Mermaid Tavern is lately broke, and our Christ Church men bear the blame of it, our TICKS, as the noise of the town will have, amounting to 1500*l.*

1663. BUTLER, *Hudibras*, I. iii. I'll . . . once more, for that carcass vile, Fight UPON TICK.

1668. SEDLEY, *Mulberry Garden.* I confess my TICK is not good, and I never desire to game for more than I have about me.

1668. DRYDEN, *Evening's Love*, iii. Play on TICK, and lose the Indies, I'll discharge it all to-morrow.

1683. OLDHAM, *Poems*, 174. Reduc'd to want, he in due time fell sick, Was fain to die, and be interr'd ON TICK.

c. 1700. *Diary of Ab. de la Pryme* [Surtees], 110. Every one runs UPON TICK and thou that had no credit a year ago has credit enough now.

d. 1704. BROWN, *Works*, ii. 266. Some pretty nymphs . . . but are sometimes forced TO TICK half a sice a-piece for their watering.

1713. ARBUTHNOT, *John Bull*, iii. 8. Paying ready money that the maids might not run TICK at the market. *Ibid.* The money went to the lawyers; counsel won't TICK.

d. 1729. STEELE, *Correspondence*, ii. 477. I shall contrive to have a quarter before-hand, and never let family TICK more for victuals, cloaths, or rent.

1785. GROSE, *Vulg. Tongue*, s.v. RIVER TICK. Standing debts, which only discharge themselves at the end of three years by leaving the Lake of Credit, and meandering through the haunts of 100 creditors. *Oxf. Univ. Cant.*

1809. MALKIN, *Gil Blas* [ROUTLEDGE], 169. Scarcely a day passed but he sinned ON TICK, and suffered by attorney.

1862. THACKERAY, *Philip*, xxxviii. Then the bills came down upon me. I tell you there are some of my college TICKS ain't paid now.

1880. *Punch's Almanack*, 3. Quarter-day, too, no more chance of TICK.

1899. WHITEING, *John Street*, xviii They're extremely nice people, and give one no end of TICK.

1901. *Sporting Times*, 17 Aug., i. 5. During my late Oxford days, I got put up to at least twenty different ways of getting TICK.

TO TICK AND TOY, *verb. phr.* (old).—To dally, to wanton.

1550. LATIMER, *Serm. before Ed. VI.* Stand not TICKING AND TOYING at the branches . . . but strike at the root.

1579. GOSSON, *School of Abuse* [HALLIWELL]. SUCH TICKING, SUCH TOYING, such smiling, such winking, and such manning them home when the sports are ended.

1614. *England's Helicon* [NARES]. Unto her repaire . . . Sit and TICK AND TOY till set be the sunne.

TICKER, *subs.* (common).—1. A watch (GROSE): also TICK. Fr. *tocante*.

1789. PARKER, *Varieg. Charac.* You know you'll buy a dozen or two of wipes, dobbin cants, or a farm, or a TICK with any rascal.

1829. MAGINN, *Vidocq's Slang Song* [FARMER, *Musa Pedestris* (1896), 107]. When his TICKER I set a-going, With his onions, chain, and key.

1830. EGAN, *Finish Life*, 217. I have lost my TICKER; and all my toggery has been boned.

1838. DICKENS, *Oliver Twist*, xviii. 'And always put this in your pipe, Nolly,' said the Dodger. 'If you don't take fogles and TICKERS . . . some other cove will.'

1877. *Five Years' Penal Servitude*, iv. 270. He listened to the tempter, 'filched the TICKER,' and was nailed almost immediately.

1887. HENLEY, *Villon's Straight Tip.* It's up the spout and Charley-wag, With wipes and TICKERS and what not.

1897. MARSHALL, *Pomes*, 71. He fished the TICKER out From her giddy little satchel right away.

1900. KIPLING, *Stalky & Co.*, 268. He'd . . . pledged the Government to all sorts of action. 'Pledged the States' TICKER, eh?' said M'Turk, with a nod to me.

2. (Stock Exchange and Post Office).—An automatic tape-machine.

3. (American University).—An ignoramus who talks for talking's sake.

4. (veterinary).—A crib-biting horse (LAWRENCE, *Horses* [1802], 218).

TICKET, *subs.* (old).—1. An account; a score: now TICK (*q.v.*).

2. (old).—A pass; a license: also TICKRUM (B. E. and GROSE): *cf.* approximation to Fr. *étiquette.* Hence (3) a visiting card: whence (from 2 and 3) THE TICKET = the correct thing; THAT'S THE TICKET = that's the thing, that's all right: also 'that's THE TICKET FOR SOUP' = 'You've got it—be off!'

[1611. CORYAT, *Crudities*, I. 57. The porter . . . gave me a little TICKET under his hand as a kind of warrant for mine entertainement in mine Inne.]

1782. BURNEY, *Cecilia*, I. iii. A TICKET is only a visiting card with a name upon it; but we call them TICKETS now.

1783-5. COWPER, *Task*, iii. Well dressed, well bred, Well equipaged, is TICKET good enough To pass us readily through every door.

1854-5. THACKERAY, *Newcomes*, vii. She's very handsome and she's very finely dressed, only somehow she's not—she's not THE TICKET, you see. *Ibid.* (1862), *Philip*, xiii. Poor dear Mrs Jones . . . still calls on the ladies of your family, and slips her husband's TICKET upon the hall table.

1862. TROLLOPE, *Orley Farm*, lxvii. That's about THE TICKET in this country.

1862. BRADLEY, *Tales of College Life*, 19. That's THE TICKET; that will just land me in time for gates.

1884. CLEMENS, *Huck. Finn.* ''Deed, that ain't THE TICKET, Miss Mary Jane,' I says, 'by no manner of means.'

4. (American political).—(*a*) A printed list of candidates in an election; (*b*) the candidates; and (*c*) a policy; A PLATFORM (*q.v.*). Whence STRAIGHT TICKET

= the party nominations, representing the official programme; SPLIT TICKET = a divided policy, a TICKET containing the names of candidates representing several differing interests or divisions; SCRATCHED-TICKET = a list of candidates from which names have been erased; MIXED TICKET = a list in which the nominations of different interests or parties have been blended. TO RUN AHEAD OF THE (or ONE'S TICKET), *see* quot. 1899.

1883. *Nation*, 6 Sep., 200. If he can elect such a TICKET even in Virginia alone, he will take the field after election as a striker.

1885. *D. Teleg.*, 17 Oct. To vote solidly the Parnell TICKET.

1899. *Century Dict.*, s.v. TICKET. TO RUN AHEAD OF THE TICKET, in U.S. politics, to receive a larger vote than the average vote polled by one's associates on the same electoral ticket. Similarly TO RUN BEHIND THE TICKET is to receive less than such an average vote.

A HARD TICKET, *subs. phr.* (American). — An unscrupulous man; a 'hard nut to crack.'

TO WORK THE TICKET, *verb. phr.* (military).—To procure discharge by being pronounced medically unfit.

1899. WYNDHAM, *Queen's Service*, xxxiii. There is still a good deal of malingering in the Service . . . it is a comparatively easy matter for a discontented man TO WORK HIS TICKET.

TICKLE, *adj. and adv.* (old and venery).—1. Wanton. Also as *verb* = (*a*) to grope; to FIRKYTOODLE (*q.v.*); (*b*) to FRIG (*q.v.*); and (*c*) to copulate. Hence TICKLE-TAIL = (*a*) a wanton and (*b*) the *penis*: also TICKLER, TICKLE-THOMAS (= female privity), TICKLE-PIECE, TICKLE-GIZZARD, TICKLE-FAGGOT and TICKLE-TOBY; TAIL-TICKLING = (1) copulation; (2) masturbation; TICKLE O' THE SERE = fond of bawdy laughter (HALLIWELL.)

1363. LANGLAND, *Piers Plowman*, 1619. For she is TIKEL of hire tail . . . As commune as a cartway.

[?]. *Coventry Myst.*, 134. Of hire tayle oftetyme be lyght, And rygh TEKYL.

1593. GREENE, *Gwydonius* [HALLIWELL]. Yet if she were so TICKLE, as ye would take no stand, so ramage as she would be reclaimed with no lure.

1598. FLORIO, *Worlde of Wordes. Fricciare* . . . to frig, to wriggle, to TICKLE.

1602. SHAKSPEARE, *Hamlet*, ii. 2. 336. The clown shall make those laugh whose lungs are TICKLE OF THE SERE. *Ibid.* (1602), *Troilus and Cressida*, v. 2. 57. How the devil Luxury, with his fat rump and potato-finger, TICKLES these together! Fry, lechery, fry!

1610. JONSON, *Alchemist*, v. 2. *Sub.* My bird o' the night! we'll TICKLE it at the Pigeons, When we have all . . . [*They kiss*].

1612. CHAPMAN, *Widow's Tears*, ii. 2. *Tha.* Hast thou been admitted? *Ars.* . . . ay, into her heart . . . I have set her heart upon as TICKLE a pin . . . that will never . . . rest till it be in the right position.

1620. HOWARD, *Defensative* [DRUCE, ii. 238]. Moods and humours of the vulgar sort . . . loose and TICKLE OF THE SEARE.

1652. SHIRLEY, *Brothers*, ii. 1. But these wives, sir, are such TICKLE Things, not one hardly staid amongst a thousand.

1653. URQUHART, *Rabelais*, i. xi. He had already begun to exercise the tools . . . One . . . would call it her pillicock, her fiddle-diddle, her staff-of-love, her TICKLE-GIZZARD.

1656. FLETCHER, *Martiall*, xi. 30. Thus Phillis rub me up, thus TICKLE me.

1672. COTTON, *Virgil Travestie*, 60. To Puss and to good company: And he that will not . . . name the words as I do barely, I do pronounce him to be no man, And may he never TICKLE woman.

1694. MOTTEUX, *Rabelais*, v. xlv. For, now I hope To see some brawny, juicy rump Well TICKLED with my carnal stump.

c. 1709. WARD, *Terræfilius*, ii. 11. A TICKLE TAIL Match between a Vigorous Whore-Master and a Desirous Young Damsel.

1730. *Broadside Song*, 'Gee ho, Dobbin' [FARMER, *Merry Songs and Ballads* (1897), ii. 203]. I rumpl'd her feathers, and TICKL'D her scutt.

1809. MALKIN, *Gil Blas* [ROUTLEDGE], 113. I know how to TICKLE a girl in a stiff gown, or an actress.

2. *See* TICKLISH.

Verb. (colloquial). — To chastise: frequently (as in TO TICKLE ONE'S TAIL) a humorous threat of punishment. Hence TICKLE-TAIL (TICKLETOBY, or TICKLER) =(*a*) a schoolmaster's rod; (*b*) a schoolmaster; (*c*) a whip or strap; (*d*) a small weapon carried on the person: a knife or pistol.

1598. SHAKSPEARE 2 *Henry IV.*, ii. 1. Away, you scullion! you rampallian! you fustilarian! I'll TICKLE YOUR CATASTROPHE. *Ibid.* (1602), *Twelfth Night*, v. 1. 196. If he had not been in drink, he would have TICKLED you othergates than he did.

c. 1600. *Merry Devil of Edm.*, ii. 1. A plague of this wind; O, it TICKLES OUR CATASTROPHE. *Ibid.*, v. 2. I'll TICKLE HIS CATASTROPHE for this.

1607. DEKKER, *Westward Hoe*, v. 3. If we find 'em to be malefactors, we'll TICKLE 'em.

1837. BARHAM, *Ingoldsby Legends*, 'The Ingoldsby Penance.' Come falchion in hand, I'll TICKLE the best Of all the Soldan's Chivalrie.

1861. DICKENS, *Great Expectations*, i. TICKLER was a wax-ended piece of cane, worn smooth by collision with my TICKLED frame.

2. (common).—To bribe; to fee: also TO TICKLE ONE'S PALM (or HAND).

1874. *Siliad*, 110. Brought by the din . . . to run him in; But, TICKLED by a shilling in his palm, Walked on discreetly blind, and sternly calm.

TICKLE-BRAIN, *subs. phr.* (old).—1. Strong drink; hence (2) a taverner: also TICKLE-PITCHER =a tosspot (B. E. and GROSE).

1598. SHAKSPEARE, 1 *Hen. IV.*, ii. 4. 438. Peace, good pint-pot: peace, good TICKLE-BRAIN.

TICKLER, *subs.* (colloquial).—1. A puzzler; anything difficult or perplexing: also (HALLIWELL) a shrewd cunning person.

2. (American). — A small pocket-ledger; also a banker's register: of bills (of exchange) payable and receivable, and daily cash balances.

1889. *Harper's Mag.*, lxxx. 464. The TICKLERS, showing in detail debts receivable in the future, those past due, and also the overdrafts, require explanation by the president.

3. (common).—A dram. Also (American)=a half pint flask of spirits.

1840. *Southern Sketches*, 33. Then he took out a TICKLER of whiskey; and, arter he'd took three or four swallows out'n it, says he, 'Oblige me by taking a horn.'

1888. *Harper's Mag.*, lxxix., 388. Whiskey was sold and drunk without screens or scruples. It was not usually bought by the drink but by the TICKLER.

1886. *Fort. Rev.*, N.S., xxxix. 77. It is too cold to work, but it is not too cold to sit on a fence chewing, with a TICKLER of whiskey handy.

4. (common).—A small poker: used to save a better one: *cf.* CURATE.

5. (American).—A bowie knife.

1843. DICKENS, *Martin Chuzzlewit.* One of which, for he was a man of pleasant humour, he was accustomed to call his ripper, the other his TICKLER.

6. *See* TICKLE, *verb.*

TICKLE-PITCHER. *See* TICKLE-BRAIN.

TICKLE-TEXT, *subs. phr.* (old).—A parson: *see* BIBLE-POUNDER.

TICK-TACK, *subs. phr.* (venery).—Copulation: *see* GREENS and RIDE.

c. 1550. WEAVER, *Lusty Juventus*, D i. verso. What a hurly burly is here! Smicke smacke, and all thys gere! You will to TYCKE-TACKE, I fere Yf thou had time.

TIDDIPOL, *subs.* (provincial).—'An overdressed fat young woman in humble life' (HALLIWELL).

TIDDLE, *verb.* (colloquial).—1. To advance by slow degrees, or small motions: *e.g.*, TO TIDDLE a ball, a marble, a wheelbarrow, etc. Also TO TIDDLE A GIRL=to master her inchmeal. Whence TIDDLING=getting on bit by bit. Also (=) to potter; to fidget.

1748. RICHARDSON, *Clarissa*, I. 322. To leave the family pictures from his sons to you, because you could TIDDLE about them, and though you now neglect their examples, could wipe and clean them with your dainty hands.

TIDDLIES. TO RUN TIDDLIES, *verb. phr.* (provincial).—To run over unsafe ice.

TIDDLYWINK, *subs.* (common).—An unlicensed house: a pawnbroker's (also LEAVING-SHOP, *q.v.*), a beershop, a brothel, etc.

Verb. (Australian).—To spend more than prudence or custom will sanction.

1888. BOLDREWOOD, *Squatter's Dream*, vii. He's going too fast, that new boss . . . I wonder what old Morgan would say to all this here TIDDLEY-WINKIN', with steam engine, and wire fences. . . .

TIDY, *subs.* (common).—An antimacassar.

Adj. (colloquial). — Considerable; pretty large, fine, healthy, comfortable, important, etc.

c. 1360. *William of Palerne* [E.E.T.S.], 5384. Al that touched ther to a TIDI erldome, To the kowherd and his wif the king ȝaf that time. *Ibid.*, 1338. For the TIDY tidinges that tiȝtly were seide.

1557. TUSSER, *Husbandrie*, August, 22. If weather be fair, and TIDY thy grain, Make speedily carriage, for fear of a rain.

1851-61. MAYHEW, *Lond. Lab.*, I. 408. May be after a TIDY day's work, I shall come home with 1s. in my pocket.

1887. *Field*, 23 July. There will probably be a TIDY little fleet, representatives of the Mersey Canoe Club.

1899. WHITEING, *John St.*, ix. Was you knocked about much when you was a young 'un? Pretty TIDY, only I alwiz stepped it when it got too 'ot.

Verb. (colloquial).—To put (or place) in order; to make neat: usually TO TIDY UP: TIDY, *adj.*=neat (GROSE) has long been recognised.

1853. DICKENS, *Bleak House*, xxx. I have TIDIED over and over again, but it's useless.

1863. GASKELL, *Sylvia's Lovers*, xliii. She found the widow with her house-place TIDIED UP after the mid-day meal.

1889. *Harper's Mag.*, lxxviii. 258. The small villages . . . have not the TIDINESS of the New England small villages.

TIE, *verb.* (old colloquial).—To marry; TO HITCH (*q.v.*); TO SPLICE (*q.v.*). Hence A KNOT TIED WITH THE TONGUE THAT CANNOT BE UNTIED WITH THE TEETH=matrimony.

1619. FLETCHER, *Wildgoose Chase*, iv. 1. I heartily desire this courtesy . . . This day, to see you TIED, then no more trouble you.

1668. ETHERIDGE, *She Would*, etc., i. 1. *Sir Oliv.* Well, a pox of this TYING men and women together, for better or worse.

Also PHRASES AND COLLOQUIALISMS: *e.g.*, TO TIE ONE'S HAIR (or WOOL)=to puzzle (tailors'); TO TIE UP=(1) to forswear: *e.g.*, TO TIE UP PRIGGING =to lead an honest life (thieves'); and (2)=to knock out (pugilists'); TIED-UP=(1) finished, settled; (2)=costive.

See APRON-STRINGS; RIDE; SAINT.

TIE-UP, *subs. phr.* (colloquial).—An obstruction; a blockade; a closure: *e.g.*, a strike, a blocked bill, etc.

TIFF, *subs.* (old).—(1) Small beer; SWIPES (*q.v.*). Hence (2) a moderate draught: A TIFF OF PUNCH=(GROSE) a small bowl of punch. As *verb* = to drink: TIFFING='eating and drinking out of meal time' (GROSE). Also TIFFIN (Anglo-Indian)=a meal between breakfast and dinner.

1654. *Witts Recreations.* As the conduits ran With claret, at the coronation, So let your channels flow with single TIFF.

1661. BROME, *Songs*, 165. That too shall quickly follow, if It can be rais'd from strong or TIFFE.

1703. PHILIPS, *Splendid Shilling*, 15. With scanty offals, and small acid TIFF.

1751. FIELDING, *Amelia*, VIII. x. What say you to a glass of white wine, or a TIFF OF PUNCH by way of whet?

1772. GRAVES, *Spiritual Quixote*, XI. xiv. Dr Slash . . . was smoaking his pipe over a TIFF OF PUNCH.

1812. COOMBE, *Syntax*, I. v. He TIFF'D his punch, and went to rest.

1815. SCOTT, *Guy Mannering*, i. 111. Sipping his TIFF of brandy punch with great solemnity.

1847-8. THACKERAY, *Vanity Fair.* iv. Let's have it for TIFFIN; very cool and nice this hot weather.

1884. BRASSEY, *Voy. Sunbeam*, II. xxi. After a pleasant chat we proceeded to the Hongkong hotel for TIFFIN.

2. (colloquial). — A slight quarrel. Also as *verb* = (*a*) to have words, and (*b*) to go peevishly; whilst TIFFY (or TIFFISH) = petulant; EASILY RILED (*q.v.*); TIFFING (GROSE) =disputing or falling out.

1700. CONGREVE, *Way of the World*, ii. 4. Poor Mincing TIFT and TIFT all the morning.

1753. RICHARDSON, *Grandison*, iv. 29. My lord and I have had another little —TIFF, shall I call it? it came not up to a quarrel.

1777. SHERIDAN, *School for Scandal*, i. 2. We TIFTED a little going to church, and fairly quarrelled before the bells had done ringing.

18[?]. LANDOR, *New Style.* She TIFF'D at Tim, she ran from Ralph.

1840. THACKERAY, *Shabby Genteel Story*, i. There had been numerous TIFFS and quarrels between mother and daughter.

1858. *Nat. Review*, vii. 395. In comparison with such words or gestures, George IV.'s quarrel with Brummel was an ordinary TIFF.

3. (venery).—To copulate; *see* RIDE (B. E. and GROSE): *cf.* TIFFITY-TAFFETY GIRLS.

TIFFITY - TAFFETTY GIRL (or TAFFETA PUNK), *subs. phr.* (old). —A courtesan. [TIFFANY= Epiphany: whence TIFFANY silk =a silk for holiday wear: a gauze-like material. TAFFETA also=a transparent silk. Hence TIFFITY-TAFFETY GIRL = one who discloses almost as much as she dissembles: *cf.* LOOSE-BODIED GOWN; TIFF, *verb*=to deck, to array; and TAWDRY.] Hence TIFFANY (or TAFFETY)=wanton, soft, yielding.

1598. SHAKSPEARE, *All's Well*, ii. 2. 22. As fit as ten groats is for the hand of an attorney, as your French crown for your TAFFETA PUNK.

1601. P. HOLLAND, *Plinie*, XI. xxii. The invention of that fine silke, TIFFANIE, sarcenet, and cypres, which instead of apparell to cover and hide, shew women naked through them.

1647-8. HERRICK, *Nuptiall Song.* Say . . . doe we not descrie Some Goddesse, in a cloud of TIFFANIE . . . the Emergent Venus from the Sea?

1769-78. TUCKER, *Light of Nature*, I. i. 5. Her desire of TIFFING out her mistress in a killing attire.

TIGER, *subs.* (colloquial).—A raff. TIGRISH=dissolute.

1849-50. THACKERAY, *Pendennis*, xix. A man may have a very good coat of arms, and be a TIGER, my boy . . that man is a TIGER, mark my word—a low man. *Ibid.* (1854), *Character Sketches*, 'The Artiste.' 'In France, where TIGERISM used to be the fashion among the painters, I make no doubt Carmine would have let his beard and wig grow, and looked the fiercest of the fierce.

1853. LYTTON, *My Novel*, VI. xx. Nothing could be more vagrant, devil-me-carish, and, to use the slang word, TIGRISH, than his whole air.

3. (common). — A smart-liveried boy-groom; 'a show' servant. [*Cf.* TIGER=generic for ornament: *e.g.*, TIGER-bittern, TIGER-cowry, TIGER-frog, TIGER-grass, etc.] Whence (loosely) a man's out-door servant in contra-distinction to a page=a ladies' attendant.

1827. LYTTON, *Pelham*, xlv. I sent my cab-boy (*vulgo* TIGER) to enquire . . . whether the horse was to be sold.

1837. BARHAM, *Ingoldsby Legends*, 'The Execution.' TIGER Tim was clean of limb, His boots were polished, his jacket was trim. With a very smart tie in his smart cravat, And a little cockade on the top of his hat, Tallest of boys or shortest of men, He stood in his stockings just four feet ten.

4. (American).—An intensive form of applause; an addition (*cf.* sense 3) thought to embellish the traditional 'three cheers': whence THREE CHEERS AND A TIGER=three cheers wound up by a growl, screech, or howl. [C. J. LELAND: new in 1842].

5. (navvies').—Streaky bacon.

TO FIGHT THE TIGER, *verb. phr.* (American). — To gamble with professionals; also (loosely) to play cards. Hence TIGER-HUNTER=a gambler.

1896. LILLARD, *Poker Stories*, 87. The game proceeded, but it was plainly evident that the unsophisticated young TIGER HUNTER had something on his mind.

See BENGAL TIGERS.

TIGERKIN, *subs.* (? nonce-word).—A cat.

1849. LYTTON, *Caxtons*, XIV. ii. Our domesticated TIGERKIN.

TIGHT, *subs.* (colloquial).—In *pl.* =closely fitting garments: *e.g.* (1) SMALL CLOTHES (*q.v.*); and (2) a garment fitting skin-tight to the legs or the whole body, either to display the form or for freedom of movement (chiefly theatrical).

1837. DICKENS, *Pickwick*, i. His elevated position revealing those TIGHTS and gaiters, which, had they clothed an ordinary man, might have passed without observation.

1869. BLACK, *In Silk Attire*, xxxvi And I shall be in TIGHTS and dance a breakdown.

1887. *D. Teleg.*, 15 Mar. Frozen in their TIGHTS or chilled to the bone in the midst of their carnivalesque revelry.

Adj. (old colloquial). — 1. Generic for merit. Thus A TIGHT (=strong or active) LAD; A TIGHT (=lively or pretty) WENCH; A TIGHT (=an adroit) QUESTION; A TIGHT (=well-built) SHIP; A TIGHT (=skilful) WORKMAN; A TIGHT (=pleasant) ISLAND, etc. Again, ALL TIGHT=in good health (or form); NEAT AND TIGHT=in good trim.

c. 1280. *Havelok the Dane* [E. E. T. S.], 1841. The laddes were kaske and TEYTE.

1553. DOUGLAS, *Bukes of Eneados*, xiii., Prol. Litill lammes. Full TAIT and trig.

1593. SHAKSPEARE, *Taming of Shrew*, ii. 1. 381. Three great argosies . . . two galliases, And twelve TIGHT gallies. *Ibid.* (1608), *Antony and Cleop.*, iv. 4. 15. My queen's . . . more TIGHT at this than thou.

d. 1656. HALL, *Naomi and Ruth.* Some TIGHT vessel that holds out against wind and water.

1681. DAMPIER, *Voyages.* While they are among the English they wear good cloaths, and take delight to go neat and TIGHT.

1707. FARQUHAR, *Beaux Stratagem*, i. 1. But you look so bright, And are dress'd so TIGHT.

1714. GAY, *What d'ye call it*, i. 1. I'll make a loving wife . . . day and night . . . and keep our children TIGHT. *Ibid.* (1714), *Shepherd's Week*, vi. Here the TIGHT lass, knives, combs, and scissors spies, And looks on thimbles with desiring eyes.

1748. THOMSON, *Castle of Indolence*, lxix. He had a roguish twinkle in his eye . . . If a TIGHT damsel chaunced to trippen by.

d. 1758. RAMSAY, *Auld Man's Best Argument*. Gie me the lad that's young and TIGHT. *Ibid.*, *Bessy Bell and Mary Gray*. Blythe as a kid, wi' wit at will, She blooming, TIGHT, and tall is.

c. 1796. DIBDIN, *The Snug Little Island*. O, 'tis a snug little island! A right little, TIGHT little island. *Ibid.* 'Poor Jack.' A TIGHT little boat and good sea room give me, And 'taint for a little I'll strike.

1822. SCOTT, *Fort. Nigel*, xxxi. Look at them—they are a' right and TIGHT, sound and round, not a doublet crept in amongst them.

1851. HAWTHORNE, *Seven Gables*, xiii. It will take a TIGHTER workman than I am to keep the spirits out of the seven gables.

1852. STOWE, *Uncle Tom's Cabin*, viii. A TIGHT, likely wench she was, too.

2. (colloquial).—Close; stingy; dear; hard-up. Hence A TIGHT (=straightened) MARKET; TIGHT (=scarce) MONEY; A TIGHT (=hard) BARGAIN; A TIGHT (=stingy) MAN: *cf.* EASY. Hence TO TIGHTEN=to become dear (of money).

18[?]. *Widow Bedott Papers*, 30. The Deacon was as TIGHT as the skin on his back; begrudged folks their victuals when they came to his house.

c. 1859. *N. Y. Tribune* [BARTLETT]. The money market, except on the best stocks, is getting TIGHT, and there is a general calling in of loans upon the 'fancies.'

1867. TROLLOPE, *Last Chron. of Barset*, xlii. I never knew money to be so TIGHT as it is at this moment.

1868. LEVER, *Bramleighs of Bishop's Folly*, I. xxi. A few curt sentences . . . told how matters stood in the City; money was TIGHT.

1883. *D. Teleg.*, 24 Nov. Lenders avoiding this class of paper from a belief that the market will, as usual, 'TIGHTEN up' towards the end of the year.

1891. *Harry Fludyer*, 49. Money is particularly valuable up here now—what the Pater calls 'TIGHT' when he speaks of the bank rate.

1900. WHITE, *West End*, 16. I cannot quite remember how Low brought Lady Elverton's name into the conversation, but I think it was in association with money being TIGHT.

3. (colloquial).—Severe; hard; difficult: *e.g.*, A TIGHT (=a straining) PULL; A TIGHT (=barely possible) SQUEEZE; A TIGHT (=awkward) POSITION (CORNER PLACE, etc.); a TIGHT=(hacking) COUGH.

1855. HALIBURTON, *Human Nature*, 217. It's a TIGHT SQUEEZE sometimes to scrouge between a lie and the truth in business.

4. (common).—Drunk; full of liquor: *see* SCREWED.

d. 1867. BROWNE, *Artemus Ward in London* (1899). Took to gin-and-seltzer, gettin' TIGHT every day afore dinner with the most disgustin' reg'larity.

186[?]. C. H. ROSS, *The Husband's Boat*. And now when he did get TIGHT, He used to go it proper right, Did grandfather!

1868. LEVER, *Bramleighs of Bishop's Folly*, II. iii. 'No, sir, not a bit tipsy,' said Harding, interpreting his glance; 'not even what Mr Cutbill calls TIGHT!'

1871. W. CARLETON, *Johnny Rich*. When you staggered by next night, Twice as dirty as a serpent and a hundred times as TIGHT.

1876. HABBERTON, *Barton Experiment*, 126. It's kinder discouragin' to lend a fellow that gets TIGHT a good deal . . . it's hard enough to get paid by folks that always keep straight.

1884. CLEMENS, *Huck. Finn*. In about half-an-hour they were as thick as thieves again, and the TIGHTER they got, the lovinger they got.

1889. *Echo*, 15 Feb. If rich, you may fuddle with Bacchus all night, And be borne to your chamber remarkably TIGHT.

1897. MARSHALL, *Pomes*, 29. But although he was full, he denied he was TIGHT.

1900. KIPLING, *Stalky & Co.*, 17. It's Heffelinga that 'as the evil mind,' Shouldn't wonder if he thought we got TIGHT.

5. (Winchester College).—*See* quot.

1891. WRENCH, *Winchester Word-Book*, s.v. TIGHT, fast, hard. A TIGHT bowler, etc. As superlative adverb now only used in TIGHT-junior. TIGHT-snob, TIGHT-rot, and other such uses are obsolete.

TIGHT-ARSED, *adj. phr.* (venery). — Chaste; *cf.* CLOSE-LEGGED (*q.v.*).

BLOW ME TIGHT! *See* BLOW.

TIGHT-CRAVAT, *subs. phr.* (old).—The hangman's noose: *see* HORSE-COLLAR.

TIGHTENER, *subs.* (common).—A hearty meal: *cf.* KAFFIR'S TIGHTENER. TO DO A TIGHTENER=to eat heartily.

1851-61. MAYHEW, *Lond. Lab.*, I. 70. For 2d. what is elegantly termed a TIGHTENER—that is to say a most plenteous repast—may be obtained.

1857. J. E. RITCHIE, *Night Side of London*, 193. Nommus (be off), I am going TO DO THE TIGHTENER.

TIGHT-FIT, *subs. phr.* (Vermont Univ.).—A good joke: the teller is said to be 'hard up.'

TIKE (or **TYKE**), *subs.* (old).—1. A dog: spec. a cur (a dog with a docked tail: *see* CURTAIL); a mongrel. Hence (2)=a clod-hopper, a churl, a mean snarling rascal: spec. a YORKSHIREMAN (*q.v.*).—(GROSE).

1363. LANGLAND, *Piers Plowman*, 13,026. The Jewes that were gentilmen . . . Now are thei lowe cherles . . . under tribut and taillage, As TIKES and cherles.

1440. *MS. Morte Arthure*, f. 91. Ȝone heythene TYKES.

1548. PATTEN, *Somerset's March into Scotland* [ARBER, *Eng. Garner*, iii. 114]. [Loon and] TYKE [are favourite words of abuse].

. . . *Gyre-Carling* [LAING, *Early Pop. Poet. Scotland*, ii. 20]. Wt all the TYKIS of Tervey come to thame that tyd.

1586-1606. WARNER, *Albion's England*, II. x. Battus, Medea-like, Did worke no lesse a cuer vpon This vaine vnwieldie TYKE.

1593. PEELE, *Edward I.* Sacrifice this TYKE in her sight . . . dip his foul shirt in his blood.

1599. SHAKSPEARE, *Henry V.*, ii. 1. Base TIKE, calls thou me host? *Ibid.* (1605), *Lear*, iii. 6. Bob-tail TIKE or trundle-tail.

1625. JONSON, *Staple of News*, v. 2. You are a dissembling TYKE, To your hole again.

1676. COTTON, *Virgil Travestie* (1770), 81. TYKES too they had of all sorts, bandogs, Curs, spaniels, water-dogs, and land-dogs.

d. 1697. AUBREY, *MS. Royal Soc.*, II. The indigenes of Yorkshire are strong, tall, and long legg'd; them call'em opprobriously long-legd TYKES.

1772. BRIDGES, *Burlesque Homer*, 2. At first approach he made a bow, Such as your Yorkshire TIKES make now. *Ibid.*, 151. A queer old TIKE, and full of jaw.

1795. BURNS, *Dumfries Volunteers*. Oh, let us not, like snarling TYKES, In wrangling be divided.

1821. EGAN, *Life in London*, I. ii. Hundreds of individuals . . . feel as much interest in matching their TYKES at Jem Rolfe's amphitheatre for a QUID or two.

1823. *Song* [BEE, *Dict. Turf*, s.v. HEN]. A TYKE and fighting cock, A saucy tip-slang moon-eyed hen.

1877. HORSLEY, *Jottings from Jail*. When I opened a door there was a great TYKE lying in front of the door, so I pulled out a piece of pudding and threw it to him, but he did not move.

1897. MARSHALL, *Pomes*, 60. And yet you seem out on the mike. . . . For a wonder you're minus your TYKE.

1901. WALKER, *In the Blood*, 113. An just tip a bait to the blooming TYKES.

TILBURY, *subs.* (old).—Sixpence; 6d.; *see* RHINO (GROSE, VAUX, HALLIWELL).

TILE, *subs.* (common).—A hat: spec. a tall silk-hat, or CHIMNEY-POT (*q.v.*): *see* GOLGOTHA. TILE-FRISKING = stealing hats from halls and lobbies (GROSE).

1837. DICKENS, *Pickwick*, xii. Afore the brim went it was a very handsome TILE.

1837. BARHAM, *Ingolds. Leg.*, 'Auto-da-Fé.' A feat which his Majesty deigning to smile on, Allowed him thenceforward to stand with his TILE on.

1854-5. THACKERAY, *Newcomes*, xxv. My uncle the bishop had his shovels there; and they used for a considerable period to cover this humble roof with TILES.

1891. *Notes and Queries*, 7 S. xii. 48. Short for 'chimney-pot hat,' less reverently known as a 'TILE.'

1897. MARSHALL, *Pomes*, 70. He was moist about the blinkers, and was bald upon the roof, Which was covered by a curate's giddy TILE.

A TILE LOOSE, *phr.* (common). —Silly; crazy.

ON THE TILES, *phr.* (common). —On the loose; caterwauling.

TILL, *subs.* (venery). The female *pudendum*: *cf.* MONEY-BOX: *see* MONOSYLLABLE.

TILL-SNEAK, *subs. phr.* (thieves').—A thief whose speciality is robbing shop-tills.

TILLY. EASY AS TILLY, *phr.* (old). —Very easy.

TILLY-VALLY, *phr.* (old). — Pish! nonsense! Bosh!

d. 1529 SKELTON, *Works* [DYCE], 35. Avent, avent, [avaunt] my popinjay, What will you do? nothing but play? TULLY VALLY, straw.

1551. MORE, *Utopia*, Int. xv. She used to say . . . TILLIE VALLIE, TILLIE VALLIE . . . will you sit and make goslings in the ashes?

1598. SHAKSPEARE, 2 *Henry IV.*, ii. 5. TILLY-FALLY, Sir John! never tell me; your ancient swaggerer comes not in my doors. *Ibid.* (1602), *Twelfth Night*, ii. 3. Am I not consanguinous? am I not of her blood? TILLY VALLEY, lady.

1816. SCOTT, *Antiquary*, vi. TILLEY-VALLEY, Mr Lovel . . . a truce to your politeness.

TILTER, *subs.* (Old Cant).—A sword: also TO TILT, *verb*=to fight with rapiers (B. E. and GROSE).

TIMBER, *subs.* (? nonce-word).—1. The stocks.

1838. D. JERROLD, *Men of Character*, 'Christopher Snub,' i. The squire gives me over to the beadle, who claps me here in the TIMBER.

2. (common).—In *pl.* = the legs. 'SHIVER (or DASH) MY TIMBERS! (a mock oath)'= Plague take my wooden legs: *see* DASH. Also TIMBER TOES=(1) a wooden-legged man; (2) a person wearing clogs (East End).

3. (American tramps'). *See* quot.

1900. JOSIAH FLYNT, *Tramping with Tramps*, 398. A clubbing at the hands of the toughs of a town unfriendly to tramps.

TAIL-TIMBER, *subs. phr.* (old).—BUM-FODDER (*q.v.*).

1678. LESTRANGE, *Quevedo's Visions*, 256. Into Lucifer's house of office where there was . . . many Tun of Sir Reverence, and Bales of flattering Paneygyricks . . . I could not but smile at this provision of TAIL-TIMBER.

TIMBER-MARE, *subs. phr.* (old).—*See* quot.

1755. JOHNSON, *Dict.* s.v. HORSE. A wooden machine which soldiers ride by way of punishment. It is sometimes called a TIMBER-MARE.

TIMBER-MERCHANT, *subs. phr.* (common). — A street match-seller; a SPUNK-FENCER.

TIMBERED. WELL (or CLEAN) TIMBERED, *adj. phr.* (old).—(*a*) Well made; and (*b*) WELL-HUNG (*q.v.*): TIMBER=strength, might. Also, How's HE TIMBERED?= how's he built? NOT TIMBERED UP TO MY WEIGHT=not my style.

14[?]. *Torrent of Portugal*, 99. Sith thy dwelling shalle be here, That thou woldist my son lere, Hys TYMBER ffor to asay.

1594. SHAKSPEARE, *Love's Labour Lost*, v. 2. I think Hector was not so CLEAN TIMBERED.

1605. JONSON, *Volpone*, iv. 2. That fine WELL-TIMBERED gallant.

1637. DRAYTON, *Poems*, 299. Alanson, a fine TIMB'RED man, and tall, Yet wants the shape thou art adorn'd withall: Vandome good carriage, and a pleasing eie, Yet hath not Suffolk's princely majestie.

TIMBER-TASTER, *subs. phr.* (trade). —A dockyard official who examines timber and decides on quality and fitness.

TIMBER-TUNED, *adj. phr.* (colloquial).—Heavy-fingered; wooden.

TIMBER-YARD, *subs. phr.* (cricketers').—The wicket.

1853. BRADLEY, *Verdant Green*, I. xi. Verdant found that before he could get his hand in, the ball was got into his wicket . . . and . . . there was a row in his TIMBER-YARD.

TIMBRELL, *subs.* (old).—The pillory (HOLLYBAND, 1593).

TIMDOODLE, *subs.* (provincial).—A silly fellow (HALLIWELL).

TIME, *subs.* (cabmen's).—*See* quot.

1864. HOTTEN, *Slang Dict.*, s.v. . . . To express 9s. 9d. they say that 'it is a quarter to ten'; if 3s. 6d., half-past three; if 11s. 9d., a quarter to twelve. Cab-drivers can hardly have originated a system which has been in existence as long as the adage, 'Time is money.' They have, however, the full use of the arrangement, which is perhaps the simplest on record.

THE TIME OF DAY, *subs. phr.* (common). — 1. The immediate trick; the latest dodge; the absolute aspect of affairs. Thus, TO PUT UP TO THE TIME OF DAY =to initiate; TO KNOW THE TIME OF DAY=to be fully informed, ON THE SPOT (*q.v.*); TO KNOW WHAT'S O'CLOCK (*q.v.*); THAT'S THE TIME OF DAY= 'That's how we DOES it!'

1687. BROWN, *Works*, i. 85. Your Dragons and flying Monsters won't go down at this TIME OF DAY.

1827. MAGINN, *Vidocq's Song*. Who should I meet but a jolly blowen Who was FLY TO THE TIME OF DAY.

1834. AINSWORTH, *Rookwood*, 'Nix my Dolly.' They PUT ME UP TO THE TIME OF DAY.

1838. DICKENS, *Oliver Twist*. Pop that shawl away in my castor, Dodger, so that I may know where to find it when I cut; THAT'S THE TIME OF DAY!

2. (pugilists').—A knock-out blow.

3. (old).—*See* quot.

1823. BEE, *Dict. Turf.*, s.v. TIME OF DAY . . . In the island (Wight) every good joke is 'THE TIME O' DAY.'

4. (old colloquial).—A salutation; a greeting; 'Good morning.' etc.

1609. SHAKSPEARE, *Pericles*, iv. 3. 35. Not worth THE TIME OF DAY.

1851-6. MAYHEW, *Lond. Lab.*, II. 489. The police . . . are very friendly. They'll pass THE TIME OF DAY with me.

1899. WHITEING, *John St.*, v. 'And the woman?' 'Back kitchen. Pass THE TIME O' DAY with 'er sometimes. No bizness o' mine.'

1900. SIMS, *London's Heart*, 4. I thought it was only right to pass THE TIME O' DAY to an old pal.

TO DO (or SERVE) TIME, *verb. phr.* (thieves').—To go to prison. Hence TIMER=a convict: *e.g.*, FIRST, SECOND, and THIRD TIMER =a prisoner serving for a first, second, or third stretch.

1898. GOULD, *Landed at Last*, vi. If it had not been for me you would have been DOING TIME before this.

1899. WYNDHAM, *Queen's Service*, 242. I . . . endorse the . . . opinion of one who had DONE TIME regarding this . . punishment.

TO KNOCK OUT OF TIME, *verb. phr.* (pugilists').—To hit out; so to punish an opponent that he cannot come up to the call of time.

ON TIME, *adv. phr.* (colloquial). —(1) Punctual; and (2) abreast of things.

IN GOOD TIME, *adv. phr.* (old colloquial).—Just so! Well and good! Fr. *à la bonne heure*.

1603. SHAKSPEARE, *Measure for Measure*, v. 1. 182. *Duke.* Leave me awhile with the maid . . . no loss shall touch her with my company. *Prov.* IN GOOD TIME. [See also v. 1. 284-7.]

1650. FULLER, *Pisgah Sight*, II. vi. 27. There, saith he, even at this day are shewed the ruines of those three tabernacles built according to Peter's desire. IN VERY GOOD TIME, no doubt!

d. 1663. SANDERSON, *Works* [Parker Soc.], i. 67. IN GOOD TIME! But I pray you then first to argue the cause a little . . . whether he deserve such honour?

See GOOD TIME; HIGH OLD TIME.

TIMOTHY, *subs.* (provincial).—The *penis*: of children (HALLIWELL).

TIMOTHY TEARCAT. *See* TEAR.

TIM-WHISKY (TIMMY-WHISKEY or **WHISKEY)**, *subs. phr.* (old).—A light one-horse chaise without a hood (GROSE).

1772. BRIDGES, *Burlesque Homer*, 481. In spite of him these youths so frisky, Went out and hir'd a TIMMY-WHISKY.

1774. FOOTE, *Cozeners*, i. A journey to Tyburn in a TIM-WHISKY and two would have concluded your travels.

d. 1832. CRABBE, *Works*, II. 174. WHISKEYS and gigs and curricles.

1834. SOUTHEY, *Doctor*, Interch. xiv. It is not like the difference between . . . a WHISKEY and a TIM-WHISKEY, that is to say, no difference at all.

1884. DOWELL, *Taxes in England*, III. 227. The increased taxation of the curricle had the effect of bringing into existence the less expensive gig, a development or an imitation of a two-wheeled carriage known in the country as a WHISKEY.

TIN, *subs.* (common.)—Money: generic: *see* RHINO. Hence TO TIN OUT=to pay.

1836. SMITH, *The Individual*, 'The Thieves' Chaunt,' 5. But because she lately nimm'd some TIN, They have sent her to lodge at the King's Head Inn.

1848. DURIVAGE, *Stray Subjects*, 57. Depositing the 'TIN' in his shot-bag.

1854. MARTIN and AYTOUN, *Bon Gualtier Ballads*. 'The Knyghte and the Taylzeour's Daughter.' Once for all, my rum 'un, I expect you'll post the TIN.

1855. TAYLOR, *Still Waters*, ii. 2. Divilish aisy to say 'buy,' but where's the TIN to come from?

1857. WHITTY, *Bohemia*, I. 166. No girls get married without TIN, little or great.

1872. BLACKIE, *Highlands and Islands*, 30. And is this all! And I have seen the whole, . . . 'Tis scantly worth the TIN, upon my soul.

1876. HINDLEY, *Cheap Jack*, 199. He started with a lot of TIN but had not sufficient brass or *physique* to stand the wear-and-tear.

1886. KENNARD, *Girl in Brown Habit*, i. How the dickens is he to get them, if he has no means of his own, except by marrying a woman with plenty of TIN?

1897. MARSHALL, *Pomes*, 76. Nothing mean about uncle—he squandered the TIN.

1901. *West. Gaz.*, 5 Mar., 8. 1. It is calculated to be nearly double that the traveller has to TIN OUT.

TIN-BELLIES, *subs. phr.* (military). —The 1st and 2nd Life Guards: from the cuirass.

TINCLAD, *subs.* (American).—A gunboat: spec. a musket-proof gunboat such as were used during the civil war on the western rivers: the armour plating of these was very light. Also (general)=any ironclad; a TIN-POT (*q.v.*).

TINGE, *subs.* (drapers').—A commission on the sale of out-of-date stock: *cf.* SPIFFINGS.

TINGER, *subs.* (provincial).—A great lie (HALLIWELL).

TINGLE-TANGLE, *subs. phr.* (old). —*See* quot.

1640. RANDOLPH, *Amyntas*. Now hang the hallowed bell about his neck, We call it a mellisonant TINGLE-TANGLE.

TIN-GLOVES, *subs. phr.* (Winchester).—*See* quot.

c. 1840. MANSFIELD, *School Life* (1866), 54. Other ordeals . . . were not quite so harmless . . . a pair of TIN GLOVES which Bully would furnish in the following manner. Taking a half-consumed stick from the fire, he would draw the 'red-hot end' down the back of Green's hand between each of the knuckles to the wrist, and having produced three lines of blisters, would make two or three transverse lines across. A scientifically fitted pair of gloves of this description was generally, if not pleasant wear, of great durability.

TINKARD, *subs.* (Old Cant).—A begging tinker.

1575. AWDELEY, *Frat. Vacabondes.* A TINKARD leaveth his bag a-sweating at the ale-house, which they terme their bowsing inne, and in the meane season goeth abrode a begging.

TINKER, *subs.* (colloquial).—1. An unskilful workman; a botcher. Also (2) a makeshift; a botch; a bungle. As *verb*= to make barely or rudely serviceable: *e.g.*, TO TINKER UP A PATIENT=to keep Death at arm's length; TO TINKER A FENCE=to stop a gap here and there; TO TINKER A BILL=to make it temporarily workable.

1857. HUGHES, *Tom Brown's School-days*, i. 1. They must speak their mind about it . . . and spend their time and money in having a TINKER at it.

1885. *Standard*, 11 Nov. I should oppose any mere TINKERING of its constitution which would retain the hereditary principles as its chief feature.

1890. DILKE, *Problems of Greater Britain*, vi. 6. The Victorian Act has been already TINKERED several times, and is not likely to last long in its present form.

TO SWILL LIKE A TINKER, *verb. phr.* (old).—To tipple without stint.

1694. MOTTEUX, *Rabelais*, v. v. Eat and drink bravely . . . SWILL LIKE TINKERS.

See LAZY, quot. 1811.

TINKER'S-BUDGET (or **-NEWS**), *subs. phr.* (old).—Stale news; PIPER'S NEWS (*q.v.*).

TINKER'S DAMN, *subs. phr.* (common).—A small standard of value: usually, in phrase, 'Not worth a TINKER'S DAMN' (or CURSE).

TINKLER, *subs.* (old).—1. A vagrant; whence (2) a runaway.

[?] *Sheriff-Muir* [CHILD, *Ballads*, vii. 161]. For Huntly and Sinclair, they both play'd the TINKLER.'

d. 1796. BURNS [*Merry Muses* (*c.* 1800), 122]. An' was rae Wattie a blinker? He maw'd-frae the queen to the TINKLER.

1847. BRONTË, *Jane Eyre*, xviii. 'Is there a tinkler in the library?' 'Yes, ma'am, but she looks such a TINKLER.'

2. (common).—A bell.

1838. DICKENS, *Oliver Twist*, xv. 'Jerk the TINKLER.' These words in plain English conveyed an injunction to ring the bell.

TINNY, *subs.* (Old Cant).—A fire; TINNY-HUNTER=a thief working at a conflagration (GROSE and VAUX).

TINPOT, *subs.* (naval).—An iron-clad: *cf.* TIN-CLAD.

Adj. phr. (colloquial).—Generic for shoddy. Thus A TIN-POT (=poor or pretentious) GAME; TIN-POT (=shabby) LOT; TIN-POT (=mean) COMPANY; IN A TIN-POT WAY=in poor or worthless fashion. Also (American) TIN-HORN.

1876. BESANT and RICE, *Golden Butterfly*. I shall have information of every dodge goin', from an emperor's ambition to a TIN-POT company bubble.

1887. FRANCIS, *Saddle and Mocassin.* They're A TIN-HORN LOT . . . on'y fit to take their pleasure in a one-horse hearse.

TIN-TAB, *subs. phr.* (Dulwich College).—The carpenter's shop.

TIN TABERNACLE, *subs. phr.* (common).—An iron-built church.

1898. LE QUEUX, *Scribes and Pharisees*, v. 54.

TIP, *subs.* (common).—1. Special information; private knowledge. Specifically an advice concerning betting or a Stock-Exchange speculation intended to benefit the recipient: THE STRAIGHT TIP =an absolute CERT (*q.v.*); in racing=direct advice from owner or trainer. Also (2) a horse, a stock, etc., specially recommended as a sound investment. As *verb*=to impart exclusive information. Hence TIPSTER (*see* quot. 1874): also TIPPER. 'THAT'S THE TIP'='That's the right thing'; TO MISS ONE'S TIP =to fail.

1567. HARMAN, *Caveat* [E. E. T. S.], 20. [Harman speaks of having coaxed his friends the beggars, and thus] attained to the TYP.

1842. *Quarterly Review*, clxiii. 175. It should be the first duty of consuls to keep the Foreign Office promptly supplied with every commercial TIP that can be of use to British trade.

1869. BYRON, *Not Such a Fool*, etc. [FRENCH], 8. Mr Topham Sawyer MISSED HIS OWN TIP as well as his victim's, and came down a cropper on a convenient doorstep.

1874. HENRY SAMPSON [*Slang Dict.* (HOTTEN), s.v. TIPSTER]. A 'turf' agent who collects early and generally special information of the condition and racing capabilities of horses in the training districts, and posts the same to his subscribers to guide their betting. There are, whatever non-racing men may think, many 'touts' whose information is valuable to even the 'best-informed' writers.

1881. A. C. GRANT, *Bush Life*, II. 33. He was a real good fellow, and would give them THE STRAIGHT TIP.

1885. *Field*, 3 Oct. Storm Light was a great TIP for the Snailwell Stakes.

1885. *Ev. Standard*, 3 Oct. The late Mr Segrott, who carried on the business of TIPSTER and sausage making, was the last year's winner of this plate.

1890. *Nineteenth Century*, xxvi. 846. The crowd of touts and TIPSTERS whose advertisements fill up the columns of the sporting press.

1891. GOULD, *Double Event*, 173. That's the rummiest TIP I ever got.

1898. GOULD, *Landed at Last*, iv. Tucka-Tucka's the place to breed good horses, take my TIP for it.

1897. MARSHALL, *Pomes*, 30. So, take my TIP and close your features now. *Ibid.*, 41. For the landlord had the pip, and required a first-rate TIP. *Ibid.*, 65. I rumbled the TIP as a matter of course.

1899. WHITEING, *John St.*, v. You kin take my TIP; there's some very respectable people in this place.

1900. LYNCH, *High Stakes*, xxiii. I guess Drexel will know whether it's a TIP or not.

1901. *Free Lance*, 9 Feb., 470. 2. [They] were pursued by their lady friends for TIPS as to what to buy or sell.

2. (colloquial).—A gratuity; a vail: spec. money in acknowledgment of service rendered or expected. Also (loosely), any gift of money. Likewise TIPPERY =payment. As *verb* TIP=(1) to give TIPS; and (2) to earn money (*see* quots. 1610 and 1772).

1610. ROWLANDS, *Martin Mark-all* (H. Club's Rept. 1874), 3. And TIP lowr with thy prat.

1707. FARQUHAR, *Beaux' Stratagem*, ii. 3. Then I, sir, TIPS me the verger with half-a-crown.

1727. GAY, *Beggar's Opera*, iii. 1. Did he TIP handsomely? How much did he come down with?

1772. BRIDGES, *Homer Burlesque*, 139. This job will TIP you one pound one.

1853. BRADLEY, *Verdant Green.* Mrs Tester . . . was dabbing her curtseys in thankfulness for the large amount with which our hero had TIPPED her.

1854-5. THACKERAY, *Newcomes*, xvi. Remember how happy such benefactors made you . . . and go off on the very first fine day and TIP your nephew at school. *Ibid.* What money is better bestowed than that of a schoolboy's TIP?

1857. DUCANGE ANGLICUS, *Vulg. Tongue*, 39. Lawyer Bob draws fakements up; he's TIPPED a peg for each.

1874. *Siliad*, 99. Gasmen assume respect, which costs them dear, 'Tis bought with TIPS to pay for quarts of beer.

1877. *Scribner's Mag.*, July, 400. This whole matter of TIPPING waiters, and of waiters expecting to be TIPPED, is a very marked manifestation of the poison of pauperism.

1884. GREENWOOD, *Little Ragamuffins*. 'Come on . . . TIP UP, Smiffield.' 'TIP UP!' I repeated, in amazement.' . . . 'Fork out,' said the boy.

1885. *D. Teleg.*, 16 Jan. Others declare that those only who display before-hand the alluring TIP catch the porter's eye.

1891. *Harry Fludyer*, 49. You get your pocket-money regularly, and I know the Pater TIPPED you at Christmas, and the Mater told me she gave you two pounds when you went back.

1898. GISSING, *Town Traveller*, xxiv. No doubt he was jolly frightened when you spotted him, and you know how he met you once or twice and TIPPED you.

3. (Felsted School).—(*a*) A false report; (*b*) a foolish blunder in translating.

1890. *Felstedian*, Feb. 3. Some one ventured to suggest that it was all a beastly TIP.

4. (old).—A draught of liquor; an abbreviation (B. E.) of TIPPLE (*q.v.*). TO TIP OFF= to drink (B. E. and GROSE).

Verb. (common).—Generic for doing: a verb of general application (HARMAN, B. E., GROSE, VAUX, HOTTEN). Thus TO TIP THE LOUR (COLE, BRASS, RHINO, etc.)=to pay, give, get or lend money (see *subs.* sense 2); TO TIP A SOCK=to land a blow; TO TIP A SETTLER=to knock-out; TO TIP TO ADAM TILER=to hand the swag to a confederate; TO TIP A MISH =to put on a shirt; TO TIP OFF =(1) to drink: *see* TIPPLE; (2) to die; TO TIP THE LION=to flatten one's nose with the thumb and extend the mouth with the fingers (GROSE); TO TIP A DADDLE (THE FIVES, or THE GRIPES IN A TANGLE)=to shake hands (GROSE); TO TIP A COPPER=to sky a coin; TO TIP A YARN=to tell a story; TO TIP THE TRAVELLER=to humbug, to romance; TO TIP THE WINK=

to wink (as a sign of caution, understanding, etc.); TO TIP THE RED RAG = to scold; TO TIP THE RAGS (or THE LEGS) A GALLOP (or THE DOUBLE) = to decamp (GROSE); TO TIP ALL NINE = to knock all the skittles down at once (GROSE); TO TIP THE VELVET = to tongue a woman (GROSE); TO TIP A STAVE = to sing; TO TIP THE LITTLE FINGER (Australian) = to drink; TO TIP THE GRAMPUS = to duck a man: a penalty for sleeping on watch (nautical); TO TIP ONE'S BOOM OFF = to hurry away (nautical); TO TIP THE LONG-'UN = to foraminate a woman; TO TIP A STAVE = to sing a song; TO TIP A NOD = to recognise; TO TIP A MORAL = to give the straight; TO TIP A RISE = to befool, etc.

1610. ROWLANDS, *Martin Mark-all*, 37. Cheates, which word is vsed generally for things, as TIP me that Cheate, Give me that thing.

1676. *Warning for Housekeepers*, 'Life and Death of the Darkman Budge.' For when that he hath nubbed us, And our friends TIP him NO COLE, He takes his chive and cuts us down, And TIPS us into the hole.

1692. DRYDEN, *Juvenal*, vi. She writes love letters to the youth in grace; Nay, TIPS THE WINK before the cuckold's face.

1694. MOTTEUX, *Rabelais*, iv. vi. The quarrel being hushed, Panurge TIPPED THE WINK upon Epistemon and Friar John . . . taking them aside.

c. 1696. B. E., *Dict. Cant. Crew*, s.v. TIP. TIP your Lour, or Cole or I'll Mill ye, c. give me your Money or I'll kill ye. TIP the Culls a Sock, for they are sawcy, c. Knock down the Men for resisting. TIP the Cole to Adam Tiler, c. give your Pick-pocket Money presently to your running Comrade. TIP the Mish, c. give me the Shirt. TIP me a Hog, c. lend me a Shilling.

d. 1704. BROWN, *Works*, i. 251. I now TIPP'D THE WINK, at her, and she as kindly returned it.

1709. ADDISON, *Tatler*, No. 86. The pert jackanapes, Nick Doubt TIPPED me THE WINK, and put out his tongue at his grandfather.

1731-5. POPE, *Moral Essays*, ii. 33. Sudden, she storms! she raves! You TIP THE WINK; But spare your censure: Silia does not drink.

174[?]. CIBBER, *Flora*, ii. 2. She TIPT THE WINK upon me, with as much as to say, desire him not to go till he hears from me.

1748. SMOLLETT, *Rod. Random*, xii. I began to smell his character, and, TIPPING Strap THE WINK, told the company, etc. *Ibid.* (1760-2), *Sir L. Greaves*, vi. Then, my lad, there would be some picking; aha! dost thou TIP ME THE TRAVELLER, my boy?

1772. BRIDGES, *Homer Burlesque*, 288. Nestor their meaning understood, And TIPT 'em all THE WINK it should.

1778. BURNEY, *Evelina*, lxxviii. 'Egad,' said Mr Coverley, 'the baronet has a mind to TIP us a touch of THE HEROICS this morning.'

c. 1780. *Ireland Sixty Years Ago*, 86. 'The Kilmainham Minit.' When to see Luke's last jig we agreed, We TIPPED him OUR GRIPES in a tangle. *Ibid.*, 87. We'd TIP him THE FIVES fore his det.

1809. MALKIN, *Gil Blas* [ROUTLEDGE], 309. Prowling about in masquerade, and TIPPING THE WINK to every blackguard who parades the street.

1819. MOORE, *Tom Crib*, 15. He TIPP'D HIM a settler.

1821. EGAN, *Anec. of Turf*, 183. She TIPPED THE party such a dish of RED RAG as almost to create a riot in the street.

1823. MONCRIEFF, *Tom and Jerry*, ii. 3. Hand us over three browns out of that 'ere tizzy; and TIP US THE HEAVY. (*Landlord receives money and delivers porter.*)

1824. *Sonnets for the Fancy* [*Boxiana*, iii. 622]. The knowing bench had TIPPED her buzzer QUEER.

1827. LYTTON, *Pelham*, lxxxiii. TIP him THE DEGAN, Fib, fake him through and through. *Ibid.*, xlix. I shall give you a cooling in the watchhouse if you TIPS us any of YOUR JAW.

1832. WILSON, *Noctes Ambrosianæ*, Sept. TIP THE captain one of your BROADSIDES.

1837. DISRAELI, *Venetia*, I. xiv. TIP me THE CLANK like a dimber mort.

1838. WRIGHT, *Mornings at Bow Street.* In plain words he fairly TIPP'D 'EM THE DOUBLE, he was vanished.

1839. AINSWORTH, *Jack Sheppard* [1889], 13. If he don't TIP THE COLE without more ado, give him a taste of the pump, that's all.

1851-61. MAYHEW, *Lond. Lab.* . . . Just by sweetening them, and then they don't mind TIPPING THE LOAVER.

1862. *Artemus Ward, His Book* (1899), 158. 'TIP US YER BUNCH OF FIVES, old faker!' said Artemus Junior.

1881. STEVENSON, *Treasure Island.* TIP US A STAVE.

1884. CLEMENS, *Huck. Finn.* If I could TIP her THE WINK, she'd light out and save me.

1897. MARSHALL, *Pomes*, 45. Our jockey pal TIPPED US THE WINK To denote that he'd done in the physic.

1899. WHITEING, *John St.*, xxi. So Bill TIPS me THE WINK not to tumble to their lingo.

1900. SAVAGE, *Brought to Bay*, v. The Frenchman, however, TIPPED Ross A WINK, which . . . was the beginning of a secret alliance.

1901. WALKER, *In the Blood*, 20. I TIPPED 'im ONE ON THE SMELLER, as soon as 'e said it. *Ibid.*, 21. I'll TIP my push THE WINK when you come up.

ON THE TIP OF THE TONGUE, *phr.* (colloquial).—On the point of speech; about to be said.

1843. DICKENS, *Martin Chuzzlewit*, xxix. It was ON THE TIP OF THE BOY'S TONGUE to relate what had followed; but . . . he checked himself.

TIPPER, *subs.* (old).—1. A special brew of ale: named after Mr Thomas Tipper: also BRIGHTON TIPPER.

1843. DICKENS, *Martin Chuzzlewit*, xxv. If they draws the BRIGHTON TIPPER here, I takes that ale at night.

d. 1876. LOWER [*Century Dict.*]. The peculiarity of [TIPPER] arises from its being brewed from brackish water, which is obtainable from one well only; and all attempts to imitate the flavour have hitherto failed.

2. *See* TIP, *subs.* 1 and 2.

TIPPERARY FORTUNE, *subs. phr.* (old).—'Two town lands, Stream's Town (= CUNT, *q.v.*) and Ballinocack (= ARSE-HOLE, *q.v.*); said of Irish women without fortune' (GROSE): *cf.* TETBURY PORTION.

TIPPERARY-LAWYER, *subs. phr.* (Irish).—A cudgel: *cf.* PLYMOUTH-CLOAK.

TIPPET, *subs.* (old).—A hangman's rope: also HEMPEN (ST JOHNSTONE'S or TYBURN) TIPPET. *See* HEMP (with all derivatives) and HORSE-COLLAR.

1586. MARLOWE, *Jew of Malta*, iv. 4. When the hangman had put on his HEMPEN TIPPET, he made such haste to his prayers as if he had had another cure to serue.

1816. SCOTT, *Old Mortality*, vii. Then it will be my lot . . . to be sent to Heaven wi' a ST JOHNSTONE'S TIPPET about my hause.

1899. *Century Dict.*, s.v. TIPPET. ST JOHNSTONE'S TIPPET . . . said to be named from the wearing of halters about their necks by Protestant insurgents of Perth (formerly also called St John's Town, St Johnston) in the beginning of the Reformation, in token of their willingness to be hanged if they flinched.

TO TURN TIPPET, *verb. phr.* (old).—To change right-about: *cf.* TURNCOAT and TURN CAT-IN-THE-PAN.

1562. HEYWOOD, *Epigrams* [OLIPHANT, *New English*, i. 561. Amongst the romance words are] TURN HIS TIPPET.

c. 1600. *Merry Devil of Edmonton* [TEMPLE], iii. 2. 137. Well, to be brief, the nun will soon at night TURN TIPPET; if I can but devise to quit her cleanly of the nunnery, she is my own.

1609. JONSON, *Case is Altered*, iii. A saint, Another Bridget, one that for a face Would put down Vesta; . . . You TO TURN TIPPET!

1609. FLETCHER, *Monsieur Thomas*, ii. 2. Ye stand now As if y' had worried sheep. You must TURN TIPPET, And suddenly, and truly, and discreetly, Put on the shape of order and humanity.

TIPPING, *adj.* (schools').—First-rate; jolly.

TIPPLE (or TIP), *subs.* (old).—1. Drink; (2) a drinking bout (B. E. and GROSE): also TIPLAGE and as *verb.* Whence not a few colloquial usages: *e.g.*, ON THE TIPPLE = on the BOOZE (*q.v.*); TO SPOIL A TIP = to interrupt while drinking; TIPPLER = (1) a toper; a fuddlecap, 'sots who are continually sipping' (B. E. and GROSE); and (2) a publican (the original meaning); TIPSY = fuddled, drunk, BOOSY (*q.v.*): also TIPPLED or TIPT (B. E.: 'a'most Drunk'). Also derivatives such as TIPPLING, TIPPLING-HOUSE, TIPSIFY, TIPSINESS, TIPSY-CAKE, etc.

1450. *Chester Myst.* [Shakspeare Soc.]. [OLIPHANT, *New Eng.*, i. 288. The Scandinavian words are *filly* and the verb TIPPLE.] [*Ency.* and *Century*: Norw. *tipla*, 'to drink little and often.']

c. 1520. *Wyf of Auchtermuchty*, 32. An husband, as I hard it tawld Quha weill cowld TIPPILL owt a can.

d. 1555. LATIMER, *Works* (1854-5), i. 133. They were but TIPPLERS, such as keep ale-houses.

1583. GRINDAL, *Remains* (1843), 138. No inn-keeper, ale-house keeper, victualler, or TIPLER shall admit or suffer any person or persons in his house or backside to eat, drink, or play at cards, tables, bowls, or other games, in time of Common Prayer.

1587. HARMAR, *Beza*, 313. Gamesters, TIPPLERS, tavern-haunters . . . and other dissolute characters.

1592. SHAKSPEARE, *Midsummer's Night's Dream*, v. 1. 48. The riot of the TIPSY Bachanals. *Ibid.* (1608), *Antony and Cleop.*, i. 4. 19. TIPPLING with a slave; To reel the streets at noon.

1601. [CAMDEN, *Hist. Queen Eliz.*]. Such kind of men who lurked in TIPPLING-HOUSES.

1611. COTGRAVE, *Dict.*, s.v. *Piailleur* . . . a TIPLER, bowser. *Ibid. Berlan*, a common TIPPLING HOUSE, a house of gaming, or of any other disorder.

1615. FLETCHER, *Nightwalker*, i. He's very merry, madam; . . . i' th' bottom o' the cellar; He sighs and TIPPLES.

1633. MARMION, *Antiquary*, iv. Why, they are as jovial as twenty beggars, drink their whole cups six glasses at a health, your master's almost TIPT already.

1653. URQUHART, *Rabelais*, II. i. Deific liquor which they call *piot*, or TIPLAGE.

d. 1655. ADAMS, *Works*, ii. 48. If the head be well TIPPLED [Satan] gets in and makes the eyes wanton, the tongue blasphemous and the hands ready to stab.

1672. COTTON, *Virgil Travestie* (1700), 128. Whil'st thou ly'st TIPPLED, or TIPPLING. *Ibid.*, *Scoffer Scofft*, 193. Wait her and fill me out my TIPPLE.

1693. DRYDEN, *Persius's Satires*, iv. 73. A peel'd slic'd onion eats, and TIPPLES verjuice.

1694. MOTTEUX, *Rabelais*, iv. 1. Having often renewed their TIPPLINGS, each mother's son retired on board his own ship.

c. 1696. B. E., *Dict. Cant. Crew*, s.v. Tip. *Don't spoil his* TIP, don't baulk his Draught, *A Tub of good* TIP (for TIPPLE) a Cask of strong Drink.

c. 1709. WARD, *Terræfilius*, ii. 10. This inordinate TIPPLE-PITCHER (notwithstanding his own Gluttony and Ebriety) so very busy on Sunday in persecuting all TIPPLERS. *Ibid.*, *Satyr against Wine* (*Works*, 1718, iii. 185). Both kind and TIPSIE lull'd themselves to Rest.

1710. SWIFT, *Polite Conv.*, ii. Miss (with a glass in her hand).—Hold your tongue, Mr Neverout, don't speak in my TIP.

1770. CHATTERTON, *Revenge*, ii. 4. I heard a voice within, or else I'm TIPSEY.

d. 1790. FRANKLIN, *Autobiog.*, 161. Walking the rounds was often neglected, and most of the nights spent in TIPPLING.

d. 1821. KEATS, *Lines on Mermaid Tavern.* Have ye TIPPLED drink more fine Than mine Host's Canary wine.

1834. AINSWORTH, *Rookwood*, i. ix. Famous wine this—beautiful TIPPLE—better than all your red fustian.

1847-8. THACKERAY, *Vanity Fair*, i. She was in such a passion of tears, that they were obliged to send for Dr Floss, and half TIPSIFY her with sal volatile.

1857. CARLYLE, *Miscell.*, iv. 95. The man was but TIPSIFIED when he went; happily when he returned, which was very late, he was drunk.

1886. *D. Teleg.*, 12 Jan. That apparently innocuous beverage which has hitherto passed itself off as the teetotaller's TIPPLE.

1888. DENTON, *Eng. in 15th Century*, 203. Still adulteration went on, and at almost every manor court the TIPPLERS . . . those who sold the ale not those who drank it . . . were fined.

TIPPYBOBS, *subs.* (American).—The wealthy classes (BARTLETT).

TIP-TOP, *subs. adj.* and *adv.* (colloquial).—The best; first rate; in the highest degree: hence TIP-TOPPER (GROSE).

ENGLISH SYNONYMS. A 1; about East; about right; above par; all brandy; all there; all the way; as good as they make it; as good as wheat; at par; bang up; Bible; bobbish; boiler-plated; bona; bully; cheery; the cheese; cheesy; chic; clean potato; clean wheat; clinking; clipping; crack; creamy; crushing; a corker; a daisy; dossy; downy; down to the ground; doubled-distilled; first chop; first-rate-and-a-half; fizzing; fly; gamey; hunky; jammy; jonnick; lummy; nap; out-and-out; pink; plummy; proper; pure quill; real jam; right as ninepence; ripping; rooter; rum; screaming; scrumptious; ship-shape; slap-up; slick; splash up; splendacious; splendiferous; to the knocker; to the nines; to rights; true marmalade; tsing-tsing; up to Dick. *See* also WHOPPER.

FRENCH SYNONYMS. *Abracadabrant; aux petits oignons; aux pommes; bath* (or *bate*); *du flan; hurf; un peu ça; bath aux pommes; chenâtre; chic* (or *chicque*); *chicard; chicancardo; chicandard; chocnoso; chocnosof; chocnosogue; koscnoff; chouette; chouettard; chouettaud; épatant; épataroufiant; farineux; flambant; frais* (ironically); *grand largue* (sailors'); *mirobolant; muche; numero un; obéliscal; ruisselant d'inouisme; rup* (or *rupin*); *schpile; sgoff; snoboye; superlifico* (or *superlificoquentieux*) = splendiferous; *tapé.*

d. 1720. VANBRUGH, *Provoked Husband*, iii. 1. Everything that accomplishes a fine lady is practised . . . she herself is at the very TIP TOP of it. . . . In TIP-TOP spirits.

1766. GOLDSMITH, *Vicar*, ix. What appeared amiss was ascribed to TIP-TOP quality breeding.

1772. BRIDGES, *Burlesque Homer*, 361. They're of the very TIP-TOP breed.

1849. THACKERAY, *Hoggarty Diamond*, iv. He was at the West End on Thursday, asked to dine, ma'am, with the TIP-TOP nobs.

1866. ELIOT, *Felix Holt*, xvii. That . . . Stake it, means the TIP-TOP—and nobody can get higher than that, I think.

1866. *London Misc.*, 3 Mar., 58. 3. No little let-down for a cove that's been TIP-TOPPER in his time.

1874. *Siliad*, 92. While shop-boys, trying TIP-TOP swells to be, Have robbed the till, and call for S. and B.

1882. *Century Mag.*, xxxv. 621. 'That suits us TIP-TOP, ma'am,' said the coxswain.

1885. *Field*, 26 Dec. Several other TIP-TOPPERS being behind the pair. *Ibid.* (1886), 23 Jan. I promised to provide them with TIP-TOP shooting for one season.

1891. CAREW, *Autobiog.*, 416. As fly a bewer she were, as ever chucked a stall, a reg'lar TIP-TOP tam-tart.

1899. WHITEING, *John St.*, v. You should see 'em goin' out o' Saturday nights. TIPTOP. Won't speak to nobody.

1900. LYNCH, *High Stakes*, xxxii. I've lost my bearings; used to know all the TIP-TOP fences—see!

TIQUE, *subs.* (Harrow).—1. Arithmetic; and (2) mathematics. [WARNER: from a French master's peculiar English.]

TIRE, *verb.* (American).—To alarm.

1887. MORLEY ROBERTS, *Western Avernus*. Then getting ferocious, 'Not that I'm scared at him.' . . . Nor of you either. I've seen cow-boys, bigger men than you, and with bigger hats too—but they didn't TIRE me.'

TIRED. BORN TIRED, *phr.* (common).—An excuse for assumed apathy or genuine disinclination.

1899. WHITEING, *John St.*, xxi. The fact is . . . I wos BORN TIRED, an' I don't seem ible to settle down to this 'ere ring-yer-in in the mornin', and ring-yer-out at night.

TIRLY-WHIRLY, *subs. phr.* (Scots).—The female *pudendum*: *see* MONOSYLLABLE (BURNS).

d. 1796. BURNS, *Court of Equity* [*MS.* in Brit. Mus.]. Ye wroucht a hurly-burly in Jeanie Mitchell's TIRLY-WURLIE.

TIRRIT, *subs.* (old).—Fright; terror.

1598. SHAKSPEARE, 2 *Henry IV.*, ii. 4. Here's a goodly tumult; I'll forswear keeping house, before I'll be in these TIRRITS and frights.

TIRY, *adj.* (old colloquial).—Tired.

1611. CORYAT, *Crudities*, I. 33. D. My horse began to be so TIRY that he would not stirre one foote.

'TISER, *subs.* (journalists').—*The Morning Advertiser*.

1874. *Siliad*, 10. The Victualler's anger, and the 'TISER's rage.

TISH, *subs.* (schools and university).—A cubicle; a partition.

TISTY-TOSTY, *adj. phr.* (old).—Swaggering; swashing (HALLIWELL). Also as in quot.

1570. *Marriage, Wit and Science* [DODSLEY, *Old Plays*, ii. 376]. Now mother, I must. Chalt be a lively lad with HEY TISTY-TUST.

TIT, *subs.* (old colloquial).—Orig. anything small: hence (1) a small horse; and (2) a girl; a young woman: *cf.* FILLY and TITTER.

1548. PATTEN, *Somerset's March*, 92 [OLIPHANT, *New Eng.*, 519. There is the Scandinavian TIT (equus), it means something very small].

1577-87. STANYHURST, *Desc. Ireland*, II. If he be broken accordinglie you shall haue a little TIT that will trauell a whole daie without anie bait.

1594. BARNEFIELD, *Helen's Rape* [ARBER], 39. But what spurres need now for an untam'd TITT to be trotting.

1600. JONSON, *Cynthia's Revels*, Ind. I wonder that any man is so mad, to come to see these rascally TITS play here.

1621. BURTON, *Anat. Melan.*, 524. A vast virago or an ugly TIT.

d. 1668. DENHAM, *Poems* [CHALMERS, *Eng. Poets*, vii. 245]. Being as worthy to sit On a nambling TIT As thy predecessor Dory.

1675. COTTON, *Scoffer Scofft* (1770), 267. The little wanton TIT . . . would both Home and Husband quit . . . To follow thee for dainty Bit.

1694. MOTTEUX, *Rabelais*, v. 'Pant. Prog.' Blowings, TITS, pure ones, concubines.

d. 1704. BROWN, *Works*, ii. Never trust any of your TITS into an inn of Court, for if you do they'll harass her about from chamber to chamber . . . and send her home with . . . perhaps a hot tail into the bargain. *Ibid.*, iii. 197. Not that thou art so willing a TIT neither, as to let every blockhead get up and ride for asking.

1706. WARD, *Hud. Rediv.*, I. x. 6. Mounted on Gallopers and TITS. *Ibid.* (*c.* 1709), *Works*, iii. (1718), 307. 'Spoken on the back of an Elephant.' 'Tis a strange TIT, he neither Trots nor Paces.

1707. FARQUHAR, *Beaux' Stratagem*, i. 1. As to our hearts, I grant ye, they are as willing TITS as any within twenty degrees.

1772. BRIDGES, *Burlesque Homer*, 123. I've been ten years his hackney jade, But now I'm weary of the trade; Brisk English TITS can't long bear hacking. *Ibid.*, 183. These little TITS of mine, I'm sure, Can trot eleven miles an hour.

1774. LLOYD, *The Poetry Professors*. 'Nay, should the TITS get on for once, Each rider is so grave a dunce.'

1785. GROSE, *Vulg. Tongue*, s.v. TIT. A horse: a pretty little TIT; a smart little girl. . . . TOMMY TIT, a smart lively little fellow.

1811. *Lex. Bal.*, s.v. KEEP. . . . Mother, your TIT won't keep; your daughter will not preserve her virginity.

3. (colloquial).—A small portion; a morsel: whence TIT-BIT = a choice piece; 'a fine snack' (B. E. and GROSE); anything specially selected.

1730. SWIFT, *Directions to Servants*, s.v.

1841. *Punch*, i. 6. The sneaking Whigs were helping themselves to all the fat TIT-BITS.

4. *See* TITMOUSE.

5. (Durham: local).—A student of Durham University: in contempt. Also 'VARSITY TIT.

TIT FOR TAT, *phr.* (colloquial).—Originally TAP FOR TAP (or TIP FOR TAP)=blow for blow; 'an equivalent' (GROSE); 'tant for tant (B. E.), TIT FOR TIT, and dash for dash.' Hence, TO GIVE TIT FOR TAT=to give as good as one gets.

1577. BULLINGER, *Works*, I. 283. Let every young man be persuaded . . . that his duty is . . . not to answer TIP FOR TAP, but to suffer much and wink thereat.

1598. SHAKSPEARE, 2 *Henry IV.*, 2. I. 205. This is the right fencing grace, my lord; TAP FOR TAP, and so part fair.

1607. DEKKER, *Northward Hoe*, ii. 1. *Doll.* Come TIT ME, come TAT ME, come throw a kiss at me—how is that? *Capt.* By Gad, I know not what your TIT-MEES and TAT-MEES are, but . . . I know what kisses be.

1766. COLMAN and GARRICK, *Clandestine Marriage*, v. 2. TIT FOR TAT, Betsey! You are right, my girl.

1772. BRIDGES, *Burlesque Homer*, 17. The general gave him TIT FOR TAT, And answered cocking first his hat. *Ibid.*, 117. Let him with Nell play TIT FOR TAT, And trim her till I eat my hat.

c. 1859. PALMERSTON [M'CARTHY, *Hist. Own Times*, xxiii.]. I have had my TIT-FOR-TAT with John Russell, and I turned him out on Friday last.

See TALE.

TITCH, *subs.* (Christ's Hospital).—A flogging: also as *verb.* [It has been suggested that TITCH=tight breeches: a portmanteau word.]

TITIVATE (or **TITTIVATE**), *verb.* (colloquial).—To spruce up; to put finishing touches to one's toilet.

1836. DICKENS, *Boz* ('Mr John Douce'). Regular as clockwork—breakfast at nine—dress and TITTIVATE a little.

1843-4. HALIBURTON, *The Attaché*, xxiii. Well, I'll arrive in time for dinner; I'll TITIVATE myself up, and down to drawin'-room.

1856. DOW, *Sermons*, I. 151. The girls are all so TITIVATED off with false beauty, that a fellow loses his heart before he knows it.

1857-9. THACKERAY, *Virginians*, xlviii. Call in your black man, and TITIVATE a bit.

TITIVIL, *subs.* (old).—A generic reproach: a knave; a jade. [Tom Titivil in old moralities = the Devil.]

1542. HALL, *Henry VI.*, f. 43. The devill hymself . . . did apparell certain catchepoules and parasites, commonly called TITIVILS and tale tellers, to sowe discord and dissencion.

1560. *Thersytes*, 67. Tynckers and tabberers, typplers, taverners, TYTTYFYLLES, fryfullers, turners and trumpers.

TITLEY, *subs.* (common).—Intoxicating liquor (HOTTEN).

TITMOUSE, *subs.* (venery).—The female *pudendum*: *see* MONOSYLLABLE. Also TIT and TIT-BIT (which last in quot. 1653= the *penis*).

[?] *Reliq. Antiq.* (1841), ii. 28 (HALLIWELL). Hir corage was to have ado with alle; She had no mynd that she shuld die, But with her prety TYTMOSE to encrece and multeply.

1653. URQUHART, *Rabelais*, I. 136. Another [called it] her Cyprian sceptre, her TIT-BIT.

d. 1704. BROWN, *Works*, II. 186. I hear you kept the poor TITMOUSE under such slavish subjection, that a peer of the realm . . . could not . . . come . . . to be brother-sterling with you.

TITTER, *subs.* (Old Cant).—A girl (GROSE): *cf.* TIT. [HOTTEN: 'a tramp's term.']

1887. HENLEY, *Villon's Good Night.* You flymy TITTERS full of flam.

TITTER-TATTER, *subs. phr.* (GROSE).—'One reeling and ready to fall at the least touch: also the childish amusement of riding upon the two ends of a plank, poised upon the prop underneath its centre; called also a see-saw.'

TITTLE-GOOSE, *subs.* (common).—A foolish blab.

TITTLE-TATTLE, *subs. phr.* (old).—1. Chatter; scandal; 'foolish impertinent talk' (B. E.); 'women's talk' (GROSE); and (2) a chatterbox, a gossip. As *verb.* =to gossip. Hence TITTLE-TATTLER and TITTLE-TATTLING. Also proverbial saying, 'TITTLE TATTLE, give the goose more hay.'

d. 1529. SKELTON [CHALMERS, *Eng. Poets*, ii. 292. 2]. I played with him [Philip Sparow] TITTEL TATTEL And fed him with my spattell.

1580. SIDNEY, *Arcadia*, ii. You are full in your TITTLE-TATTLINGS of Cupid.

1592. LYLY, *Midas*, iii. 2. O, sir, you know I am a barber, and cannot TITTLE TATTLE, I am one of those whose tongues are sweld in silence.

1604. SHAKSPEARE, *Winter's Tale*, iv. 4. You must be TITTLE TATTLING before all our guests.

1616. *Times' Whistle* [E. E. T. S.], 103. Dame Polupragma, gossip TITTLE-TATTLE Suffers her tongue let loose at randome, prattle.

1633. BROME, *Antipodes*, i. 6. The men do all the TITTLE-TATTLE duties.

1653. URQUHART, *Rabelais*, I. 113. The parchment whereon he wrote the TITTLE-TATTLE of two young mangy whores.

1675. COTTON, *Burlesque on Burlesque* (1770), 177. Come, come, I cannot stay to prattle, Nor hear thy idle TITTLE-TATTLE.

d. 1704. BROWN, *Works*, ii. 180. The merry subject of every tavern TITTLE-TATTLE.

1705. WARD, *Hud. Rediv.*, I. v. 9. For if bifarious TITTLE TATTLE, Could storm a Town, or win a Battel.

1709-11. ADDISON, *Tatler*, 157. Impertinent TITTLETATTLES who have no other variety in their discourse but that of talking slower or faster.

d. 1770. CHATTERTON, *Resignation.* The daily TITTLE-TATTLE of the court.

1809. MALKIN, *Gil Blas* [ROUTLEDGE], 4. I had been pestered with all the TITTLE-TATTLE of the town about this fellow.

1820. COOMBE, *Syntax*, ii. 31. The TITTLE-TATTLE town.

1890. *Academy*, 18 Oct., 336. Give all the facts and none of the TITTLE-TATTLE.

TITTUP (or **TITUP**), *subs.* (old).—1. 'A gentle hand-gallop or canter' (GROSE). Hence TITUPPING (or TITUPPY)=(1) lively, gay, frisky; and (2) shaky, ticklish.

c. 1704. [ASHTON, *Queen Anne*, I. 84]. Citizens in Crowds, upon Pads, Hackneys, and Hunters; all upon the TITTUP.

1818. AUSTEN, *Northanger Abbey*, ix. Did you ever see such a little TITUPPY thing in your life? There is not a sound piece of iron about it.

1825. SCOTT, *St Ronan's Well*, xiii. It would be endless to notice . . . the 'Dear mes' and 'Oh laas' of the TITUPPING misses, and the oaths of the pantalooned or buckskinn'd beaux.

1868-9. BROWNING, *Ring and Book*, I. 212. Walked his managed mule, Without a TITTUP, the procession through.

2. (colloquial).—The THING (*q.v.*). Thus THAT'S THE TITTUP =that's the thing; THE CORRECT TITTUP=the correct thing.

TITTERY, *subs.* (old).—Gin: *see* WHITE SATIN and DRINKS.

1725. G. SMITH, *Compleate Distiller* [DOWELL, *Taxes in England*, iv. 103]. Gin . . . sold under the names of double geneva, royal geneva, celestial geneva, TITTERY . . .

1731. BAILEY, *Eng. Dict.*, s.v. TITYRE, a nickname for the liquor called geneva, probably so called because it makes persons merry, laugh, and TITTER.

TITTERY-TU (or **TITYRE-TU**), *subs. phr.* (old).—A roaring boy; a street-ruffian; a MOHAWK (*q.v.*). [*Century*: In some fanciful allusion to the first line of the first Eclogue of Virgil,—*Tityre tu patulæ recubans, etc.*]

1616-25. *Court and Times James I.* [OLIPHANT, *New Eng.*, ii. 73. Young gentlemen form themselves into a club bearing the name of TITYRE TU; these rioters kept the name until the Restoration].

1630. TAYLOR, *Works* [NARES]. Roaring boyes, and rough-hewd TITTERY-TUES.

1647-8. HERRICK, *Hesperides*. 'New Year's Gift . . . to Sir Simeon Steward.' No noise of late-spawned TITTYRIES.

d. 1826. GIFFORD [Note on FORD'S *Sun's Darling*, I. 1]. Some of the TITYRE-TU'S, not long after the appearance of this drama (1624), appear to have been brought before the Council.

TIVY (or **TIVVY**), *subs.* (venery).—The female *pudendum*: *see* MONOSYLLABLE.

Adv. (hunting).—TANTIVY (*q.v.*)!

1669. DRYDEN, *Tyrannick Love*, iv. 1. In a bright moonshine while winds whistle loud, TIVY, TIVY, TIVY, we mount and we fly.

TIZZY, *subs.* (common).—A sixpence: *see* RHINO (GROSE). Hence TIZZY-POOLE (WINCHESTER)=a fives ball (costing 6d. and formerly sold by a head porter named Poole); TIZZY-TICK (Harrow)=an order on a tradesman to the extent of 6d. a day.

1823. MONCRIEFF, *Tom and Jerry*, ii. 3. Hand us over three browns out of that 'ere TIZZY.

1849. LYTTON, *Caxtons*, v. 1. There's an old 'oman . . . who will show you all that's worth seeing—the walks and the big cascade—for a TIZZY.

TO, *prep.* (American: vulgar).—At; in (of places): thus 'I shall be TO hum' (home); 'He lives TO Boston.'

1837. HALIBURTON, *Sam Slick* [BARTLETT]. I have forgot what little I learnt TO night-school.

1858. *Rome Sentinel*, Sept. The boiler . . . passed through the main building . . . without injuring the workmen there, although men were TO work on each side of where the boiler passed.

TOAD, *subs.* (old).—1. A term of contempt; and (2) a jocular address: *e.g.* 'You little TOAD': *cf.* MONKEY, ROGUE, etc. Also TOADLING.

1621. BURTON, *Anat. Melan.*, II. III. iii. Thou discontented wretch, thou coveteous niggard . . . thou ambitious and swelling TOAD.

1774. BRIDGES, *Barlesque Homer*, 203. Æneas swore it was not fair One man should box with such a pair Of ill-look'd TOADS.

1779. JOHNSON [D'ARBLAY, *Diary*, I. 133]. Your shyness, and slyness, and pretending to know nothing never took me in . . . I always knew you for a TOADLING.

1847. BRONTË, *Jane Eyre*, iii. If she were a nice pretty child one might compassionate her forlornness, but one can not really care for such a little TOAD as that.

PHRASES. 'She sits like a TOAD on a chopping block' (of a horsewoman with a bad seat); 'As much need of it as a TOAD of a side-pocket'=no need at all; 'As full of money as a TOAD is of feathers' = penniless (GROSE); 'Like a TOAD under a harrow'= on the rack.

TOADY, *subs.* (old).—A servile dependant; a LICKSPITTLE (*q.v.*); a BUM-SUCKER (*q.v.*). Also (GROSE and BEE) TOAD-EATER. Hence as *verb* (or TOAD-EATING) =to do dirty or 'reptile' service, to fawn, to lay it on THICK (*q.v.*): Fr. *avaler des couleuvres*. As *adj.* (TOADYISH, HATEFUL or UGLY AS A TOAD)=repulsive, SOAPY (*q.v.*), blandiloquent; TOADYISM (or TOAD-EATING)=servile adulation or service, SNOBBERY (*q.v.*), TUFT-HUNTING (*q.v.*), FLUNKEYISM (*q.v.*). [SMYTH-PALMER: TOADY has perhaps nothing to do with TOAD-EATER . . . originally TO BE TOADY, *i.e.* obliging, officiously attentive: in prov. Eng., TOADY=quiet, tractable, friendly, a corruption of *towardly*, the opposite of one who is *froward*, stubborn, perverse: but *see* quots. 1744 and 1785.]

d. 1572. KNOX, *Spirit of Despotism*, 20. A corrupted court formed of miscreant TOAD-EATERS.

c. 1628. FELTHAM, *Resolves*, i. 13. Vice is of such a TOADY complexion that she naturally teaches the soul to hate her.

1742. WALPOLE, *Letters*, i. 186. Lord Edgcumbe's [place] . . . is destined to Harry Vane, Pulteney's TOAD-EATER. *Ibid.*, II. 52. I am retired hither like an old summer dowager; only that I have no TOAD-EATER to take the air with me . . . and to be scolded.

1744. SARAH FIELDING, *David Simple*. TOAD-EATER . . . It is a metaphor taken from a mountebank's boy eating toads, in order to show his master's skill in expelling poison; it is built on a supposition that people who are so unhappy as to be in a state of dependence are forced to do the most nauseous things that can be thought on, to please and humour their patrons.

1785. GROSE, *Vulg. Tongue*, s.v. TOAD-EATER. A poor female relation, and humble companion or reduced gentlewoman, in a great family, the standing butt, on whom all kinds of practical jokes are played off, and all ill-humours vented.

1802. COLMAN, *Poor Gentleman*, ii. 2. How these tabbies love to be TOADIED.

1843. MACAULAY [BOSWELL'S *Johnson*]. Without the officiousness, the inquisitiveness, the effrontery, the TOAD-EATING, the insensibility to all reproof, he never could have produced so excellent a book.

1848. THACKERAY, *Book of Snobs*, v. Boys are not all TOADIES in the morning of life . . . The tutors TOADIED him. The fellows in hall paid him great clumsy compliments. *Ibid.*, iii. TOADYISM, organized — base man-and-mammon worship, instituted by command of law: snobbishness, in a word.

d. 1884. W. PHILLIPS, *Speeches*, 135. What magic wand was it whose touch made the TOADYING servility of the land start up the real demon that it was?

2. (Scots).—A coarse peasant-woman.

TOADSKIN, *subs.* (American).—*See* quot.

1867. LUDLOW, *Little Brother*. 'Don't you know what a TOADSKIN is?' said Billy, drawing a dingy five-cent stamp from his pocket. 'Here's one.'

PHRASE. 'His purse is made of TOAD'S SKIN' (of a covetous person: RAY).

TOAD-STICKER, *subs. phr.* (American). — A sword [BARTLETT: 'almost universal during the war' (1861–5)].

TOAST, *subs.* (old colloquial: now recognised). — 1. Originally, a lady pledged in drinking; subsequently (2) any person, cause, or thing to which success is drunk;

(3) a call to drink, and (4) the act of drinking. Also (Scots) TOSS, and as *verb* (B. E. and GROSE). Hence TOP-TOAST = a reigning belle: *cf.* TOP (=leading) LADY; TOASTER = the proposer of another's health.

1663–4. BUTLER, *Hudibras* [OLIPHANT, *New Eng.*, ii. 104. One way of winning the love of ladies is said to be] swallowing TOASTS of bits of ribbon; [TOAST was soon to stand for a lady].

c. 1696. B. E., *Dict. Cant. Crew*, s.v. TOST, to name or begin a new Health. Who TOSTS now? Who Christens the Health? An old TOST, a pert pleasant old Fellow.

1700. CONGREVE, *Way of World*, iii. 10. More censorious than a decayed beauty, or a discarded TOAST. *Ibid.*, iv. 5. To drink healths, or TOAST fellows.

1704. CIBBER, *Careless Husband*. [A lady's reputation is said to be the common TOAST of every public table.]

1707. FARQUHAR, *Beaux's Stratagem*, iii. 1. The gentleman has . . . TOASTED your health.

c. 1708. PRIOR, *Female Phaeton*. What has she better, pray, than I, What hidden charms to boast, That all mankind for her should die Whilst I am scarce a TOAST! *Ibid.*, *Chameleon*. Five deep he TOASTS the towering lasses.

1709. *Tatler*, No. 24, 4 June. A celebrated beauty was in the Cross-Bath, and one of her admirers took a glass of the water in which the fair one stood, and drank her health in the company. A gay fellow, half fuddled, offered to jump in, and swore, though he liked not the liquor, he would have the TOAST. This whim gave foundation to the present honour which is done to the lady we mention in our liquors, who has ever since been called a TOAST. [*Abridged.*]

1710. STEELE, *Tatler*, 95. Her eldest daughter was within half-a-year of being a TOAST.

1725. YOUNG, *Love of Fame*, vi. For Hervey the first wit she cannot be, Nor, cruel Richmond, the first TOAST for thee.

1777. SHERIDAN, *School for Scandal*, iii. 3. Let the TOAST pass—Drink to the lass, I'll warrant she'll prove an excuse for the glass.

d. 1796. BURNS, *Poems* (GLOBE), 254. My bonie sel' The TOSS of Ecclefechan.

d. 1797. BURKE, *Petition of Unitarians*. These insect reptiles while they go on caballing and TOASTING, only fill us with disgust.

1885. *D. Chron.*, 7 Sept. The TOAST of the Emperor, proposed by Dr. Stephan, was received with enthusiasm, all the guests standing.

2. (old).—A toper: *see* LUSHINGTON. Also TOAST AND BUTTER: in contempt.

1598. SHAKSPEARE, 1 *Henry IV.*, iv. 2. 22. None but such TOASTS-AND-BUTTER with hearts in their bellies no bigger than pins' heads.

1614. FLETCHER, *Wit without Money*, iv. 2. They love young TOASTS AND BUTTER, Bowbell suckers.

1668. LESTRANGE, *Quevedo* (1678), 306. How often must I be put to the Blush too, when every OLD TOAST shall be calling me Old Acquaintance.

1673. COTTON, *Voyage to Ireland*, iii. When having half din'd, there comes in my host, A catholic good and a rare drunken TOAST. *Ibid.* (1677), *Burlesque upon Burlesque*, 243. A Toss-pot and a drunken TOAST.

ON TOAST, *adv. phr.* (common).—1. Cornered; swindled; DONE (*q.v.*).

1886. *St. James's Gazette*, 6 Nov. The judges in the High Court are always learning some new thing. Yesterday it was entered on the record that the court took judicial cognizance of a quaint and pleasing modern phrase. They discovered what it was to be HAD ON TOAST.

1896. FARJEON, *Betray. John Fordham*, III. 288. 'It's my night,' I sed. 'Didn't I tell yer? I've got 'im ON TOAST.'

1900. KIPLING, *Stalky & Co.*, 64. Mason turned white with joy. He thought he had us all ON TOAST.

2. (American).—Nicely served: of food, etc.

TOASTING-FORK (or -IRON), *subs. phr.* (military). — A sword (GROSE): also CHEESE-TOASTER (*q.v.*).

1596. SHAKSPEARE, *King John*, iv. 3. Put up thy sword betime; Or I'll so maul you and your TOASTING-IRON, That you shall think the devil is come from hell.

1849–50. THACKERAY, *Pendennis*, xxii. I served in Spain with the king's troops, until the death of my dear friend Zumalcarreguy, when I saw the game was over, and hung up my TOASTING-IRON.

1861. HUGHES, *Tom Brown at Oxford*, xli. If I had given him time to get at his other pistol, or his TOASTING-FORK, it was all up.

1900. BOOTHBY, *Maker of Nations*, ix. One of the officers drew his sword . . . 'You can put up that TOASTING-FORK,' said Durrington, coolly.

TOASTY, *adj.* (artists'). — Warmly tinted.

TOBACCANALIAN (**TOBACCONER** or **TOBACCHIAN**), *subs.* (old).—A smoker. Also TOBACCONING =smoking.

1615. SYLVESTER, *Tobacco Battered*, s.v.

1621. VENNER, *Treat. Tobacco* (1637), 411. You may observe how idle and foolish they are, that cannot travell without a tobacco pipe at their mouth; but such (I must tell you) are no base TOBACCHIANS: for this manner of taking the fume, they suppose to bee generous.

d. 1656. HALL, *Hard Measure* [*Century*]. Musketeers, waiting for the major's return, drinking and TOBACCONING as freely as if it [the Cathedral] had turned ale-house.

1854–5. THACKERAY, *Newcomes*, xxv. We get very good cigars for a bajoccho and a half—that is, very good for us cheap TOBACCANALIANS.

See PIPE.

TOBY (or **TOBER**), *subs.* (Old Cant).—1. The road; the highway. Whence HIGH-TOBY = a main road; THE TOBY (TOBY-LAY or TOBY-CONCERN)=highway robbery (*see* quot. 1785); TOBY-GILL (or TOBY-MAN) = a road thief; HIGHTOBYMAN = a mounted highwayman, LOW-TOBYMAN=a footpad; TO TOBY =to rob on the highway; and DONE FOR A TOBY=convicted for highway robbery. *Cf.* gypsy TOBER=road.

1785. GROSE, *Vulg. Tongue*, s.v. THE TOBY applies exclusively to robbing on horseback; the practice of footpad robbery being properly called *the spice*, though it is common to distinguish the former by the title of HIGH-TOBY, and the latter of LOW-TOBY.

1830. LYTTON, *Paul Clifford*. You are a capital fellow . . . the bravest and truest gill that ever took to THE TOBY. *Ibid.* All the most fashionable prigs, or TOBY-MEN, sought to get him into their set.

1834. AINSWORTH, *Rookwood* (1884), 95. Believe me, there is not a game, my brave boys, To compare with the game of HIGH TOBY; No rapture can equal the TOBY-MAN'S joys.

2. (showmen's).—A pitch for a travelling show.

1893. *Standard*, 29 Jan., 2. We have to be out in the road early, you know. to secure our 'TOBY.'

3. (old: eighteenth century).—A drinking jug or mug: usually a grotesque figure of an old man in a three-cornered hat.

1840. DICKENS, *Barnaby Rudge*, iv. A . . . jug of well-browned clay, fashioned into the form of an old gentleman. 'Put TOBY this way, my dear.' This TOBY was the brown jug.

4. (venery).—The female *pudendum*: *see* MONOSYLLABLE.

1678. COTTON, *Virgil Travestie* (1770), 57. That Fame and Honour she may go by, And let Æneas firk her TOBY.

TOBY-TROT, *subs. phr.* (common). A simpleton (HALLIWELL).—

K

TOCO (or **TOKO**), *subs.* (common). —Chastisement: hence TO GIVE TOCO=to thrash.

1823. BEE, *Dict. Turf*, s.v. TOCO. If . . . Blackee gets a whip about his back, why he has caught TOCO.

1857. HUGHES, *Tom Brown's School-days*, I. v. The school leaders come up furious, and administer TOCO to the wretched fags.

1893. MILLIKEN, *'Arry Ballads*. When a reglar Primroser gits TOKO, one wonders wot next there will come.

TOD, *subs.* (American).—A drink; a 'toddy.'

1861. WINTHROP, *Cecil Dreeme*, xiv. Selleridge's was full of fire-company boys, taking their TODS after a run.

1862. *Artemus Ward: His Book* (1899), 37. Ef your peple take their TODS, say Mister Ward is as Jenial a feller as we ever met. *Ibid.*, 82. He liked his TODS too well, however.

TO-DAY. *See* BAKER.

TODDLE, *subs.* (colloquial). — A walk, a saunter: also as *verb* (or TO DO A TODDLE)=(1) to be off (GROSE), and (2) to totter along: as an invalid or child. Hence TODDLES (TODDLEKINS or LITTLE TODDLER)=an endearment to a little child.

1783. JOHNSON [BOSWELL, *Life*, ætat 74]. I should like . . . to have a cottage in your park, TODDLE about, live mostly on milk and be taken care of by Mrs. Boswell.

1785. GROSE, *Vulg. Tongue*, s.v. TODDLE . . . The cove was touting, but stagging the traps he TODDLED.

1816. SCOTT, *Antiquary*. xliv. And the bits o' weans that come TODDLING to play wi' me.

1823. EGAN, *Randall's Scrap Book*. Oft may we hear thy cheerful footsteps sound, And see us TODDLE in with heart elate. *Ibid.* (1827), *Anec. Turf*, 179. She was just about to TODDLE to the gin-spinners for the ould folks and lisp out for a quartern of Max.

1829. *Vidocq's Memoirs*, 'On the Prigging Lay' [FARMER, *Musa Pedestris* (1896), 107. I stops a bit: then TODDLED quicker, For I'd prigged his reader, drawn his ticker.

1855. THACKERAY, *Newcomes*, liii. Children who are accomplished shop-lifters and liars almost as soon as they can TODDLE and speak. *Ibid.* (1862), *Philip*, xvi. One of the children . . . was TODDLING by her side.

1856. ELIOT, *Janet's Repentance*, iii. When I was a little TODDLE Mr. and Mrs. Crewe used to let me play about in their garden.

1862. TROLLOPE, *Orley Farm*, xv. Her daily little TODDLE through the town.

1872. BLACKMORE, *Maid of Sker*, v. What did the little thing do but . . . set off in the bravest TODDLE.

1885. *Queen*, 26 Sept. A few tolerable TODDLEKINS in the intermediate cabins.

1891. *Pall Mall Gaz.*, 3 July, i. 2. The 'great Trek' . . . has TODDLED out of the little end of the horn.

1901. *Referee*, 14 Ap., 9. 2. Hundreds of tiny TODDLES in their white pinnies . . . were dancing together to a piano-organ.

1901. WALKER, *In the Blood*, 113. So ter-morrer me and Joe, my mate, do a little TODDLE round arter we see the lights go out.

TODDY, *subs.* (GROSE and BEE).—Originally, the juice of the cocoa tree; afterwards, rum, water, sugar, and nutmeg; now generic for a hot drink of any kind of spirits, as whiskey-TODDY, rum-TODDY, gin-TODDY, etc.

TODDY-BLOSSOM, *subs. phr.* (common).—A GROG-BLOSSOM (*q.v.*); a RUM-BUD (*q.v.*).

TODDY-STICK, *subs. phr.* (common). —A muddler.

TODGE, *subs.* (provincial).—Stodge: as *verb*=to smash; to pulp (GROSE).

To-do, *subs. phr.* (colloquial).—Ado; a fuss; a commotion; a set-out: *cf.* Fr. *affaire* (*à faire*).

1330. *Romance of Seven Sages* [Weber, iii. 73]. Make moche to done.

1675. Evelyn, *Diary*, 22 Mar. 'What a to-do is here!' would he say; 'I can lie in straw with as much satisfaction.'

1695. Congreve, *Love for Love*, iii. 1. What's here to do? O the Father! A man with her! . . . O you young harlotry.

1837. Dickens, *Pickwick*, iv. The next day there was another visit to Doctors' Commons, and a great to-do with an attesting ostler.

Toe, *verb* (common).—1. To kick: *e.g.* 'I'll toe your bum for you.'

2. (colloquial).—To reach (or touch) with the toes: *e.g.* to toe a line (a mark, or the scratch)=(1) to stand at attention (or at the start); (2)=to be fully prepared for a struggle or contest; (3) to come up to one's obligations; and (4) to border on.

1835. Dana, *Before Mast*, xiv. He was a man to toe the mark, and to make every one else step up to it.

1857. Bradley, *Verdant Green*, II. iv. The customary 'flapper-shaking' before toeing the scratch for business.

1881. Burroughs, *Pepacton*, 244. Then more meadow-land . . . and then the little grey school-house itself toeing the highway.

Phrases. To turn up the toes=to die: *see* hop the twig; to tread on one's toes=(1) to vex; and (2) to interfere.

1861. Reade, *Cloister and Hearth* xxiv. Several arbalestriers turned their toes up.

1868-9. Browning, *Ring and Book*, i. 130. He could not turn about Nor take a step i' the case, and fail to tread on some one's toes.

1900. Savage, *Brought to Bay*, vii. I only hope that he will soon turn up his toes was the wrathful speculator's adjuration.

Toe-fit-tie, *subs. phr.* (Winchester: obsolete).—*See* quot.

1881. *Felstedian*, Nov., 84. It was that brute A—— who 'to-fitti-ed' me last night . . . Let me explain . . . it is nothing more or less than the commencement of a line in the old, familiar, '*As in præsenti perfectum format in avi*' . . . 'to fit-ti,' in reference to verbs of the third conjugation transferred from the similarity of sound to the schoolboy's toe; it consisted in tying a running noose on a piece of string, cunningly turning up the bedclothes at the foot, putting it round the big toe of an unconscious sleeper, running the noose up tight, and pulling till the victim followed the direction of the string from the pain getting farther out of bed, and nearer the floor till released.

Toe-ragger, *subs. phr.* (Australian).—A term of contempt: *cf.* Toey.

1896. *Truth* (Sydney), 12 Jan. The bushie's favourite term of opprobrium 'a toe-ragger' is Maori. . . . The nastiest term of contempt was *tua rika rika*, or slave. The old whalers on the Maoriland coast in their anger called each other toe-riggers, and to-day the word in the form of toe-ragger has spread thoughout the whole of the South Seas.

Toey, *subs.* (Australian).—A swell; a toff (*q.v.*): a New South Wales localism.

Toff, *subs.* (common).—1. A gentleman, a fop, a swell (*q.v.*): *cf.* Toft and Tuft; (2)=a superior, a man of grit. Hence toffer=a fashionable whore; tofficky = dressy, showy, gritty (*q.v.*): toffishness= side (*q.v.*).

c. 1868. Arthur Lloyd, *Music Hall Song*, '*The Shoreditch* Toff' [Title].

1868. *Temple Bar*, xxiv. 538. 9. Moll . . . a flashtail . . . who goes about the streets at night trying to pick up toffs.

1873. Greenwood, *Strange Company*. Slices . . . under an inch thick would be regarded with contempt . . . perhaps with an uncomfortable suspicion . . . of the detestable ways of gentility. He [a coster] calls it toffishness.

1879. *Punch*, 3 May, 201. 1. If the Toffs took a fancy for chewing a stror or a twig . . . Pall Mall would be jolly soon gay.

1883. Sala [*Illust. Lond. News*, 21 Ap., 379. 2]. Fops flourished before my time, but I can remember the dandy, who was superseded by the count, the toff, and other varieties of the swell.

1897. Marshall, *Pomes*, 83. (*Loud cheers, and a voice, 'Gladstone's an old* toff'.)

1899. Wyndham, *Queen's Service*, 248. Such appellations as 'Toff Smith' or 'Dandy Jones.'

1899. Whiteing, *John St.*, xxviii. You're a toff, stone-broke—that's what you are . . . I ain't no class for you, I never can be.

1901. Walker, *In the Blood*, 27. 'I've lived here for six weeks like a toff, old man,' said Jack Oswald.

1902. *D. Telegraph*, 16 Sep., 5. 4. He held out his wrists to be handcuffed, and exclaimed, 'Now I'll die like a toff.' *Ibid.* (1903), 10 Feb., 6. 4. Over six thousand of us, I mean genuine out-of-works. Of course, there'll be loafers . . . and supposing the toffs of Pall-mall come along, welcome to them.

Toffee-scramble, *subs. phr.* (schoolboys'). — Toffee-making: *cf.* Tea-fight, Bun-worry; Muffin-circus, etc.

1901. *Troddles*, 46. . . . 'Foot sugar, my boy.' 'What do you do with it—make it into a poultice?' 'Rats! . . . didn't you ever have a toffee scramble?'

Toft, *subs.* (Hotten).—'A showy individual, a swell': *cf.* Tuft and Toff.

Togger. *See* Torpid.

Tog (or **Togs**). *See* Togman.

Togman (**Toge**, **Togemans**, or **Tog**), *subs.* (Old Cant).—A coat, a cloak, a gown (Harman, B. E., Grose, Bee, Hotten): sometimes togger, toggy, and (*Tufts*) long tog. [Latin, *toga* = a mantle; lit. a covering.] Also togs (*pl.*)=clothes: *see* toggery, *infra*; Sunday togs = best clothes; toged (or togged)= cloaked, gowned, togated, or equipped; togged out=carefully dressed; togged up to the nines = dressed to kill (*q.v.*), full-rigged; toggery= (1) clothes: *see* togs, *supra*; (2) harness, equipment, belongings; (3) worn-out clothes (Halliwell); long-togs (nautical)= shore clothes; upper tog (or upper togger) = an overcoat. As *verb*=to dress, to clothe, to equip.

1465-70. *Morte Arthure* [E.E.T.S.], 178. Alle with taghte mene and towne in togers fulle ryche.

1567. Harman, *Caveat* [E.E.T.S. (1869), 85]. I toure the strummel upon thy nabchet and Togman. *Ibid.*, 105. For want of their Casters and Togemans.

1602. Shakspeare, *Othello*, i. 1. 25. The toged consuls [in 1st quarto: other editions=*tongued*]. *Ibid.* (1610), *Coriolanus*, ii. 3. 122. Why in this woolvish toge should I stand here? [a modern reading; 1st Folio=*tongue*; other editions =*gown*].

c. 1696. B. E., *Dict. Cant. Crew*, s.v. Nim. Nim a togeman—to steal a cloak. *Ibid.*, s.v. Togeman . . . 'Tis a rum-togemans, 'tis a good Camlet-Cloak.

1785. Grose, *Vulg. Tongue*, s.v. Tog. They are said to be well or queerly togged, according to their appearance.

c. 1811. *Vidocq's Song*. Next slipt off his bottom clo'ing, And his ginger head topper gay. Then his other toggery stowing . . .

1820. *London Mag.*, i. 25. He was always togged out to the nines.

1823. Moncrieff, *Tom and Jerry*, 5. This toggery will never fit—you must have a new rig-out.

1823. Egan, *Randall's Scrap Book*. And with his upper togger gay, Prepared to toddle swift away.

1825. Scott, *St. Ronan's Well*, iv. He was tog'd gnostically enough.

1835. Dana, *Before Mast*, 131. I took no long togs with me; . . . being dressed like the rest, in white duck trousers, blue jacket, and straw hat.

1837. Barham, *Ingoldsby Legends*, 'St. Romwold.' Had a gay cavalier thought fit to appear In any such toggery . . . He'd have met with a highly significant sneer.

1838. Dickens, *Oliver Twist*, xvi. Look at his togs, superfine cloth and the heavy swell cut.

1844. Selby, *London by Night*, ii. 1. My togs being in keeping with this nobby place.

1869. Greenwood, *Seven Curses of London*. She's a dress-woman . . . one . . . they tog out that they may show off at their best, and make the most of their faces. *Ibid.* (187). *Night in a Workhouse*. Your suit of toggery ain't a very flash 'un.

1872. Blackmore, *Maid of Sker*, vii. What did I do but go to church with all my topmost togs.

1879. *Chambers' Jo.*, 368. Scrumptious young girls you tog out so finely.

1884. James, *Little Tour*, 150. Two . . . were gendarmes in full toggery.

1889. Thor Fredur, *Sketches*. In London many female servants seldom remain long in one situation; just long enough to get togged and fed up.

1898. Marshall, *Pomes*, 8. I took these togs to pawn, But uncle only looked at me and swore. *Ibid.*, 88. He was togged in his best, and so were the rest, Of his pals.

1900. Savage, *Brought to Bay*, v. Julian sported his . . . English togs, and Texas Dave was again a typical cowboy.

1900. Flynt, *Tramps*, 130. Wimmens'es togs haint up ter the men's.

1901. *Free Lance*, 9 Feb., 459. 1. No 'quick-change artist' could have had a larger assortment of 'togs.'

Toheno (or **Tohereno**), *adj.* (back slang).—Very nice. [That is, 'hot one.']

Toke, *subs.* (common).—Generic for food; grub (*q.v.*): spec. bread. Also (rare) = a piece, lump, portion.

1877. *Five Years' Penal Servitude*, i. Some prisoner who . . . had forgotten to eat what in prison slang is called his toke or chuck.

1898. Marshall, *Pomes*, 62. To a coffee-house he hied, And consumed some unkind Mocha, half a haddock, and some toke.

1899. Whiteing, *John St.*, xx. When the show was shut, I . . . sits down to my toke and pipe.

Verb (The Leys School).—To loaf (*q.v.*); to idle.

Token, *subs.* (venery).—1. The female *pudendum*: *see* Monosyllable. Also the token (Grose)=venereal disease: *e.g.* 'She tipped him the token' (='She gave him a clap or pox').

d. 1529. Skelton, *Elynour Rummyng*, 492. An old rybybe . . . At the threshold comying in, And fell so wyde open That one myght see her token . . . Said Elynour Rummyng . . . Fy, couer thy shap.

2. (old).—The plague (B. E. and Grose): also the characteristic spots of the disease on the body.

3. (old).—A farthing: hence a small standard of value (B. E.). [Properly a tradesman's 'small change,' of the nominal values of 1d., ½d., and ¼d.] Also Tom-fool's token=money (B. E.).

Toko. *See* Toco.

See Bullock's Heart.

Tol, *subs.* (back slang).—Lot of stock; share.

1851-61. Mayhew, *Lond. Lab. and Lond. Poor*. How is a man to sell fine cherries at 4d. when there's a kid alongside of him a selling his tol at 2d. a pound?

1877. Diprose, *London Life*. I've been doing awful dab with my tol, haven't made a yennep.

See Toledo.

Told. I told you so, *phr.* (old).—The retort provocant: in modern phrase, 'So like a woman to say, "I told you so!"'

1412. Occleve, *De Reg. Princ.* (Roxburgh), 26. I tolde hym so.

1609. Jonson, *Silent Woman*, iv. 2. *True.* I told you so, sir, and you would not believe me. *Mor.* Alas, do not rub those wounds . . . to blood again.

To be told, *verb. phr.* (Tonbridge School).—To obtain one's colours in a school team.

Toledo (or **Tol**), *subs.* (old).—A sword-blade: manufactured at Toledo in Spain, whence in fifteenth and sixteenth centuries came the finest tempered weapons: *cf.* Fox. Hence a rum-tol=a silver-hilted sword; a queer-tol=a very ordinary weapon (B. E. and Grose).

1596. Jonson, *Ev. Man in Humour*, iii. 1. A most perfect Toledo, I assure you, sir . . . This a Toledo, pish!

1612. Webster, *White Devil*, v. 2. O what blade is't? A Toledo, or an English fox?

1834. Ainsworth, *Rookwood*. His tol by his side, and his pops in his pocket.

Tolerable, *adj.* (colloquial).—In fair health; pretty well: *cf.* Toll-ollish.

1847. Brontë, *Jane Eyre*, xxvi. We're tolerable, sir, I thank you.

Toll. To take toll, *verb. phr.* (colloquial).—To pilfer; to 'pick and steal': *cf.* custom of millers taking a portion of grain as compensation for grinding. Also to get (or take) more than a proper share.

[1596. Shakspeare, *King John*, iii. 1. 154. No Italian priest shall tithe or toll in our dominion.]

1809. Malkin, *Gil Blas* [Routledge], 42. His hand shook . . . the table-cloth and napkin took toll [of soup].

Tolliban Rig, *subs. phr.* (old).—'A species of cheat carried on by a woman, assuming the character of a dumb and deaf conjuror' (Grose).

Tol-loll (or **Tol-lollish**), *adj. phr.* (common). — Tolerable; pretty good; 'nothing to grumble at.'

18[?]. Gilbert [*Encyclop. Dict.*]. Lord Nelson, too, was pretty well—That is, tol-lol-ish!

1901. *Free Lance*, 20 Sep., 4. 3. Oh, I feel tol-lollish enough to go through with that little bit of circus business.

Tolly, *subs.* (public schools').—1. A candle: spec. a 'tallow' candle. To tolly up (Harrow) =to light candles surreptitiously after the gas has been put out. *Cf.* Brolly, Yolly, etc.

2. (Stonyhurst). — The flat instrument used in caning the hand: also taps. Hence tolly-shop=a Præfect's room where corporal punishment is administered; and tolly-ticket=a good conduct card, given as a reward for specially good work, which, presented when punishment is ordered, secures immunity except for too grave an offence. [This system of accumulated merit, now almost obsolete, is precisely similar to one described by Mr. Kegan Paul in his *Memories* as existent at Eton in the forties.]

The Tolly (Rugby).—*See* quot. and sense 1.

1900. *Athenæum*, 16 June, 743. The chapel rather loses by its stunted head, especially as a fine tapering spire (disrespectfully known as 'THE TOLLY') appears at the back of the Close.

TOLOBEN (TOLLIBON or TULLIBON), *subs.* (Cant).—The tongue: hence TOLOBEN-RIG = fortune telling.

TOLSERY, *subs.* (provincial).—A penny. [HALLIWELL: 'A cant term.'] *See* RHINO.

TOM, *subs.* (colloquial).—1. A generic slight: *e.g.* TOMBOY, TOM-DOUBLE, TOM-FARTHING, TOM-FOOL, TOM-NODDY (all of which *see*): in quot. a contemptuous reference to the use of bells in the ceremonial of the mass.

1648-55. FULLER, *Church Hist.*, v. iv. 28. Item, That the singing or saying of masse, mattens, or evensong is but a roreing, howling, whisteling, mumming, TOMRING, and jugling.

2. (old).—A deep-toned bell: *e.g.* Great (or Big) TOM of Oxford, Lincoln, Exeter: probably onomatopœia. Whence AFTER TOM = after 9. p.m.: at that hour Big TOM of Christchurch, Oxford, strikes one for every student in residence (101); when it ceases the gates are closed and late comers are fined on a sliding scale up to midnight, after which delinquents are GATED (*q.v.*).

1630. WHITE [RIMBAULT, *Rounds, Catches*, etc. 30]. Great TOM is cast; And Christ Church bells ring . . . And TOM comes last.

1635. *Tom a Lincolne*, ii. [THOMS, *Early Eng. Prose Romances*, ii. 246]. Hee sent . . . a thousand pounds . . . to be bestowed upon a great bell to be rung at his funerall, which bell he causeth to be called TOM a Lincolne after his owne name, where to this day it remaineth in the same citie.

1648. CORBET, *On Great Tom of Christchurch*. And know, when TOM rings out his knells, The best of you will be but dinner-bells.

1807. SOUTHEY, *Don Espriella's Letters*. We ascended one of the other towers afterwards to see Great TOM, the largest bell in England.

1880. *Sat. Rev.*, l. 670. No one knows why TOM should have been twice selected for great bells . . . Indeed TOM of Oxford is said to have been christened Mary, and how the metamorphosis of names and sexes was effected is a mystery.

1882. SMYTH PALMER, *Folk Etymology*, 397. TOM . . . seems . . . imitative of the booming resonance of its toll . . . TOM-TOM, a drum . . . so 'Ding-dong, bell (*Tempest*, i. 2. 403), and Dr Cooke's round, 'Bim, Bome, bell.'

1900. FARMER, *Public School Word Book*, s.v. TOM . . . The great bell of Christ Church formerly belonged to Oseney Abbey, and weighs about 17,000 lbs.

3. (provincial).—A close-stool (HALLIWELL).

TOMAHAWK, *verb.* (Australian).—To bungle the shears in fleecing sheep.

1859. KINGSLEY, *Geoffrey Hamlyn*, 147. Shearers were very scarce, and the poor sheep got fearfully TOMAHAWKED by the new hands.

1872. EDEN, *My Wife and I in Queensland*, 96. Some men never get the better of this habit, but TOMAHAWK as badly after years of practice as when they first began.

1896. PATERSON, *Man from Snowy River*, 162. The 'ringer' that shore a hundred, as they never were shorn before, And the novice who toiling bravely Had TOMMYHAWKED half a score.

TO BURY (or DIG UP) THE TOMAHAWK, *verb. phr.* (colloquial).—To make peace (or go to war); to settle a difference (or to dispute): it was the custom of the North American Indians to BURY THE TOMAHAWK during time of peace: *see* HATCHET.

TOM-AND-JERRY DAYS, *subs. phr.* (obsolete).—The period of the Regency (1810-20): also 'when George IV. was king.' [An allusion to Pierce Egan's *Life in London*, published in 1821: in it Corinthian Tom and Jerry Hawthorn 'see life,' much of it of a 'low' or 'fast' order.

TOM-AND-JERRY SHOP, *subs. phr.* (old).—A low drinking-shop: *see* previous entry.

TOM ASTONER, *subs. phr.* (nautical).—A dashing fellow; a bold blade; a devil-may-care.

TOM-A-STYLES, *subs. phr.* (old).—Anybody; MR. THINGAMY (*q.v.*): *cf.* JOHN-A-NOAKES.

1772. STEVENS, *Songs Comic and Satyrical*, 246. From John-a-Nokes to TOM-A-STYLES, What is it all but fooling?

1785. GROSE, *Vulg. Tongue*, s.v. *Nokes*. John-a-Nokes and TOM-A-STYLES, two honest peaceable gentlemen, repeatedly set together by the ears by lawyers . . . two fictitious names commonly used in law proceedings.

TOM-A-THRUMS. *See* WISE.

TOMATO CAN VAG, *subs. phr.* (American tramps').—*See* quot.

1900. FLYNT, *Tramping with Tramps*, 398. The out-cast of Hoboeland; a tramp of the lowest order, who drains the dregs of an empty beer-barrel into a TOMATO-CAN, and drinks them; he generally lives on the refuse that he finds in scavengers' barrels.

TOMBOY, *subs.* (old colloquial).—1. A boisterous boy: *see* TOM; (2) a romping girl, a hoyden; whence (3) a strumpet: also TOM-RIG (B. E.). As *adj.* = rough, boisterous, wanton.

1550. UDALL, *Royster Doister*, ii. 4. Is all your delite and ioy In whyskyng and ramping abroade like a TOM BOY.

1605. SHAKSPEARE, *Cymbeline*, i. 6. 122. A lady, So fair . . . to be partner'd With TOMBOYS hired . . . with diseased ventures That play with all infirmities for gold.

1605. VERSTEGAN, *Rest. Dec. Intelligence* (1628), 234. TUMBE. To Dance . . . hereof we yet call a wench that skippeth or leapeth like a boy, a TOMBOY.

c. 1617. FLETCHER, *Kn. of Malta*, ii. 1. This is thy work, woman . . . you filly, You tit, you TOMBOY.

1637. DAVENANT, *Brit. Triumph.*, 'Mock Romanza.' *Giant.* I'll teach thee play the TOM-BOY, her the Rig.

1657. HOWELL, *Londonopolis*, 399. Some at stool-ball, though that stradling kind of TOMBOY sport be not so handsome for Mayds.

d. 1734. DENNIS, *Pope's Rape of Lock*, 16. The author represents Belinda a fine, modest, well-bred lady, and yet in the very next canto she appears an arrant ramp and TOM-RIG.

1885. *Century Mag.*, xli. 562. Just think of me at that age—what a TOMBOY I was.

TOM BRAY'S BILK, *subs. phr.* (old gaming).—'Laying out ace and deuce at cribbage' (VAUX).

TOM BROWN, *subs. phr.* (old gaming).—'Twelve in hand, or crib' (VAUX).

TOMBS (THE), *subs. phr.* (American).—The New York city prison: its style of architecture is heavy Egyptian. Hence TOMB'S LAWYER = a thieves' advocate: *cf.* OLD BAILEY PRACTITIONER.

TOMBSTONE, *subs.* (common).—1. A projecting tooth, a SNAGGLE-TOOTH (*q.v.*): *see* GRINDERS.

2. (common).—A pawn-ticket; a MORTGAGE DEED (*q.v.*).

c. 1889. *Sporting Times* [*S. J. and C.*]. The collection for master amounted to 4½d., and a TOMBSTONE for ninepence on a brown Melton overcoat.

TOMBSTONE-STYLE, *subs. phr.* (printers').—A fashion in 'composition': spec. of 'displayed' advertisements, these resembling (or are supposed to resemble) monumental inscriptions.

TOM CONEY, *subs. phr.* (old).—A blundering idiot; a thundering fool (B. E. and GROSE).

TOM COX'S TRAVERSE, *subs. phr.* (nautical).—'TOM COX'S TRAVERSE, three turns round the long boat, and a pull at the scuttle butt': said of a shirker feigning busy.

1835. DANA, *Before Mast*, xii. Every man who has been three months at sea knows how to work 'TOM COX'S TRAVERSE.' This morning everything went in his way. *Sojering* was the order of the day.

TOM, DICK, AND HARRY (or TOM AND DICK), *subs. phr.* (common).—Everybody and anybody: *cf.* 'all the world and his wife.' As *adj.* = commonplace.

[*c.* 1693. BROWN, *Works*, III. 72. Offended to hear almost every gentleman call one another JACK, TOM AND HARRY? They first dropt the distinction proper to men of quality, and scoundrels took it up and bestowed it upon themselves.]

1733. MALLET, *Verbal Criticism* [CHALMERS, II. ii. 1]. Rivalling the critic's lofty style, Mere TOM AND DICK are Stanhope and Argyll.

1886. STEVENSON, *Kidnapped*, 287. He rode from public house to public house and shouted his sorrows into the lug of TOM, DICK AND HARRY.

1901. *Free Lance*, 30 Nov., 224. i. Such a performance would be monstrous, blasphemous, and indefensible . . . exposed to the critical comments of TOM, DICK, AND HARRY.

TOM-DOODLE, *subs. phr.* (common).—A simpleton: *see* BUFFLE.

c. 1709. WARD, *Terræ-filius*, v. 10. That one TOM-DOODLE of a Son, who . . . if he happens to be Decoy'd . . . to fling away Two Pence in Strong Drink, he Talks of nothing but his Mother.

TOM-DOUBLE, *subs. phr.* (old).—A double-dealer; a shuffler.

1705. *Harl. Misc.*, ii. 355. 'Character of a Sneaker.' He is for a single ministry, that he may play the TOM-DOUBLE under it.

TOM DRUM. *See* JACK DRUM'S ENTERTAINMENT.

TOM-FARTHING, *subs. phr.* (common).—A fool: *see* BUFFLE.

TOM-FOOL, *subs. phr.* (common).—A thundering fool: an intensive: *see* TOM and JACK-FOOL (JACK, 8). Hence TOM-FOOLERY (TOM-FOLLY, or TOM-FOOLISHNESS) = nonsense, trash, anything ridiculous or trifling; TOMFOOLISH = ridiculously absurd; TOM-FOOL'S colours = scarlet and yellow (the ancient motley—'Red and yellow, TOM-FOOL'S colour'); 'More know TOM FOOL than TOM FOOL knows' (a sarcastic retort on failing to recognise, or professing to be unacquainted with, a person saluting).

1565. CALFHILL, *Treat. on Cross* (PARKER), 226, s.v.

c. 1709. WARD, *Infernal Vision*, 1. St. Barth'lomew's Physicians next came up, Some bred TOM-FOOLS, and some to Dance the Rope.

1824. LANDOR, *Imag. Conv.*, 'Archd. Hare and W. Landor.' 'Foolery' was thought of old sufficiently expressive; nothing short of TOMFOOLERY will do now.

18[?]. SOUTHEY, *Nondescripts*, viii. A man he is by nature merry, Somewhat TOM-FOOLISH, and comical, very.

1838. BECKETT, *Paradise Lost*, 63. I thought that all who saw me In such a TOM-FOOL'S dress would jaw me.

1848. THACKERAY, *Snobs*, xxxvi. The bride must have a trousseau of laces, satins, jewel-boxes and TOMFOOLERY, to make her fit to be a lieutenant's wife.

1851. BORROW, *Lavengro*, lxvii. The subjects . . . college education, priggism, church authority, TOMFOOLERY, and the like.

1882. *D. Teleg.*, 8 Nov. Guy Fawkes's Day would cease to be one of the recognised seasons for TOMFOOLERY in England.

1886. BESANT, *Children of Gibeon*, II. xiv. Many young men . . . will stoop to TOMFOOL tricks if they cannot get a show by any other way.

1888. BLACK, *In Far Lochaber*, xiv. He had resolved to treat these TOM-FOOLS with proper contempt, by paying no more heed to them.

1890. BROUGHTON, *Alas!* xxix. 'And leave you to go TOMFOOLING out there again?' asks Jim.

1899. WYNDHAM, *Queen's Service*, 228. Why the deuce don't you speak English then, without any of your dashed medical TOMFOOLERY about it?

TOM LONG, *subs. phr.* (old).—A prosy talker; a BORE (*q.v.*): a WINDBAG (*q.v.*). Also TO WAIT FOR TOM LONG THE CARRIER = to wait to no purpose (B. E., RAY and GROSE); 'That's COMING BY TOM LONG THE CARRIER (of anything long expected).

TOMMY, *subs.* (common).—1. Orig. a penny roll; hence (2) = bread, food: specifically a workman's daily allowance carried in a handkerchief; (3) = goods supplied to a workman in lieu of wages; (4) = the TRUCK-SYSTEM (*q.v.*); (5) = a shop run on truck lines: also TOMMY-SHOP (or STORE); and (6) = a baker's shop. Whence also SOFT (or WHITE) TOMMY (nautical) = (1) bread: as distinguished from biscuit or HARD-TACK (*q.v.*); and (2) soft solder (jewellers'); BROWN-TOMMY (GROSE) = ammunition bread for soldiers, or that given to convicts on the hulks; TOMMY-BAG = a workman's scran-bag (or handkerchief); and TOMMY MASTER = an employer who pays in kind or by orders on tradesmen with whom he shares profits. As *verb*, TOMMY = to enforce (or defraud by means of) the TOMMY-SYSTEM.

1845. DISRAELI, *Sybil*, III. i. The fact is, we are TOMMIED to death.

d. 1859. DE QUINCEY, *Casuistry Roman Meals* [*Works*, iii. 254]. It is placed in antithesis to soft and new bread, what English sailors call SOFT TOMMY.

1866. HARLAND, *Lancashire Lyrics*, 292. There'll be plenty o' TOMMY an' wark for us a', When this 'Merica bother gets o'er.

1875. HINTON, *Eng. Rad. Leaders*, 145. The employers . . . supplied them [miners] with food in order that they might spend no money save in the truck-shops or TOMMY-SHOPS.

18[?]. *Macmillan's Mag.* [ANNANDALE]. Halliwell sets down the word TOMMY, meaning provisions, as belonging to various dialects. It is now current among the 'navvy' class. . . . Hence . . . the store belonging to an employer, where his workmen must take part of their earnings in kind, especially in TOMMY or food, whence the name of TOMMY-SHOP.

1884. GREENWOOD, *Little Ragamuffin*. Coffee wirrout TOMMY don't make much of a breakfast.

7. (provincial).—A simpleton: a TOM-FOOL (*q.v.*).

8. *See* TOMMY ATKINS.

9. (Dublin University).—A sham shirt-front; a DICKEY (*q.v.*). [*Cf.* Gr. τομή = a section.]

10. (common).—A tomato: usually in plural.

c. 1889. *Daily Telegraph* [*S. J. and C.*]. Now that 'love-apples' have become cheap, the masses may be seen continually munching them, 'not only because the TOMMIES are nice, but because they are red.

TOMMY ATKINS (MR. ATKINS or **TOMMY)**, *subs. phr.* (common).—(1) A soldier (of privates only); and (2) among soldiers themselves = a private's pocket account-book. [On attestation forms and other documents occurs the sample name 'THOMAS ATKINS.' 'I, "THOMAS ATKINS," swear to do so-and-so.' The same bogus name appears in the Mutiny Act; it is, in fact, a tradition of a century, and was popularised by Rudyard Kipling in *Barrack-room Ballads.*] Fr. *Dumanet.*

1883. G. A. S[ALA] [in *Illustr. L. News*, 7 July, 3, 3]. In Tamil and Teluga 'Rôtie' means a loaf of bread. Long since Private TOMMY ATKINS, returning from Indian service, has acclimatised the word.

1892. KIPLING, *Barrack Room Ballads*, 'TOMMY' [Title]. *Ibid.* God bless you, TOMMY ATKINS, We're all the world to you (?).

1899. HYNE, *Furth. Adv. Captain Kettle*, iii. I am coming back again to give your . . . TOMMIES bad fits.

1899. WYNDHAM, *Queen's Service*, 303. The British soldier—I hate the term 'TOMMY ATKINS,' it is an impertinence and the expression of the shop-boy.

1901. *Pall Mall Gaz.*, 28 Nov., 2. 2. A nonconformist minister of the Colonial Missionary Society paid a high and well-merited tribute to MR. ATKINS last night.

1902. *Free Lance*, 4 Jan., 346. 1. The Sisters of Nazareth . . . have done splendid work at the war, and not an officer or a TOMMY fails to bless the Sisters in black and blue.

TOMMY-AXE, *subs. phr.* (Australian).—A corruption of TOMAHAWK (*q.v.*): an instance of the law of HOBSON-JOBSON (*q.v.*); but *see* quot.

1759. JOHNSON, *Idler*, No. 40. An Indian dressed as he goes to war may bring company together; but if he carries the scalping-knife and TOM-AX . . . many . . . will . . . never see him but through a grate.

TOMMY DODD, *subs. phr.* (common).—1. The odd man: in tossing, either winner or loser of a 'call,' according to agreement; also (2) the mode of tossing. [It was the refrain of a Music Hall song, *circa* 1866—'Heads or tails are sure to win, TOMMY DODD, TOMMY DODD.']

TOMMY O' RANN, *subs. phr.* (rhyming).—Scran; food.

TOMMY-ROT, *subs. phr.* (common).—Drivelling nonsense; BOSH (*q.v.*); GAMMON (*q.v.*). As *verb* = to fool, to humbug; TOMMY-ROTICS = obscenity, erotic balderdash.

1887. *Punch*, 10 Sept., 111. Gladstone's gab about 'masses and classes' is all TOMMY ROT.

1897. MARSHALL, *Pomes*, 8. I ain't dealing in TOMMY ROT. *Ibid.*, 68. Well, really, mater, you're the green 'un to believe such TOMMY ROT.

1901. CLEEVE, *As Twig is Bent*, 199.

TOMMY TRIPE, *verb phr.* (rhyming).—To observe; to PIPE (*q.v.*): also TOMMY. TOMMY his plates = Look at his feet.

TOM-NODDY (or TOMMY-NODDY), *subs. phr.* (common).—A fool: *see* NODDY and BUFFLE.

TOM O' BEDLAM. *See* BEDLAM BEGGAR and ABRAHAM-MAN.

TO-MORROW COME NEVER, *phr.* (old).—Never; at the Greek calends: *see* QUEEN DICK (GROSE).

1710. SWIFT, *Polite Conv.*, i. No, Miss, I'll send it you to-morrow. Well, well, to-morrow's a new day, but I suppose you mean TO-MORROW COME NEVER.

1725. BAILEY, *Erasmus*, 34. *Ra.* He shall have it in a very little Time. *Sy.* When? TO-MORROW COME NEVER.

1797. COLMAN, *Man and Wife*, iii. *Sally.* You married . . . ! When will that be? *Marc.* Very soon, my dear! To-day or to-morrow perhaps. *Sally.* TO-MORROW COME NEVER, I believe.

TOM-PAT, *subs. phr.* (Cant).—1. A shoe: in Gypsy = a foot.

2. (Old Cant).—A parson; a PATRICO (*q.v.*); RUM TOM-PAT = a clerk in holy orders: patrico = (properly) a sham or hedge-priest.

TOM PEPPER, *subs. phr.* (nautical).—A liar (CLARK RUSSELL).

TOMPION, *subs.* (old).—A watch. [Thomas Tompion, a celebrated watchmaker, died in 1669.]

1727. POPE, *Treatise on the Bathos.* Lac'd in her cosins new appear'd the bride, A bubble-bow and TOMPION at her side.

TOM-PIPER, *subs. phr.* (old).—A piper: *cf.* nursery rhyme, 'Tom, TOM, the PIPER's son.'

1616. W. BROWNE, *Brit. Pastorals*, ii. 2. So have I seene TOM-PIPER stand upon our village greene.

TOM-POKER, *subs. phr.* (nursery).—A bugbear.

TOM-RIG. *See* TOMBOY.

TOM TELL-TRUTH (or TOM TRUTH), *subs. phr.* (old).—1. *See* TELL-TRUTH, adding quot. *infra.* Also (2) = a honest man, a trusty fellow (RAY); and (3) 'a true guesser' (HALLIWELL).

1564. UDAL, *Erasmus Apoph.*, 202 This Demochares was . . . called . . . in their language, *Parrhesiastes* (as ye would say in English), THOM TROUTH or *plain Sarisbuirie.*

TOM THUMB, (old).—A dwarf; a thumbling (Fr. *petit poucet*); a HOP-O'-MY-THUMB (*q.v.*).—B. E. and GROSE.

1592. NASHE, *Piers Pennilesse.* [For this and innumerable contemporary references *see* HAZLITT, *Early Pop. Poet.*, ii. 167.]

1621. JOHNSON, *Tom Thumb*, Introd. Nor shall my story be made of Tom of Bethlem, Tom Lincoln, or Tom a Lin, the devil's bastard . . . but of an older Tom, a Tom of more antiquity . . . I mean little Tom of Wales, no bigger than a miller's thumb, and therefore, for his small stature, surnamed TOM THUMB.

1630. *Life and Death of* TOM THUMB [ROBERTS *Ballads*, 82]. In Arthur's court TOM THUMB did live.

d. 1704. BROWNE, *Works*, ii. 23. Thou pigmy in sin, thou TOM THUMB in iniquity.

1733. FIELDING, TOM THUMB *the Great* [Title].

1734. HEARNE, *Reliquiæ*, iii. 138. What makes me think TOM THUMB is founded on history is the method of those times of turning true history into little pretty stories.

TOM TIDDLER'S GROUND, *subs. phr.* (common).—Waste ground; unsettled acreage; a No-man's Land: properly a neutral or barren stretch of country between two kingdoms or provinces: *e.g.* the tract between Spain and the lines of Gibraltar.

TOM-TILER, *subs. phr.* (old).—A henpecked husband.

TOM TIT, *subs. phr.* (common).—A dwarf; an insignificant fellow: *see* HOP-O'-MY-THUMB.

TOM TITIVIL. *See* TITIVIL.

TOM-TOE, *subs. phr.* (provincial).—The great toe.

TOM TOPPER, *subs. phr.* (common).—A ferryman; a river hand: also TOM TUG.

TOM TOWLY, *subs. phr.* (old).—A simpleton: *see* BUFFLE.

1583. STANYHURST, *Æneid*, Dedic. What TOM TOWLY is so simple that wyl not attempt to be a rithmoure?

TOM-TROT, *subs. phr.* (common).—'A sweetmeat: sugar, butter, and treacle melted together' (HALLIWELL).

1844. DISRAELI, *Coningsby*, i. I want toffy; I have been eating TOM TROT all day.

TOM TUG, *subs. phr.* (rhyming).—1. A fool; a MUG (*q.v.*): *see* BUFFLE.

2. *See* TOM TOPPER.

TOM-TUMBLER, *subs. phr.* (old).—'? The name of a fiend. *See* SCOT, *Discoverie of Witchcraft*, 1584, as quoted in RITSON'S *Essay on Fairies*, p. 45' (HALLIWELL).

TOM TURDMAN. *See* TURD.

TOM TYLER, *subs. phr.* (old).—A common fellow; a MR. NOBODY: *cf.* SMITH and JONES.

1583. STANYHURST, *Æneid*, 154, s.v.

TON. *See* **BON-TON.**

TONE, *indef. pron.* (old literary: now vulgar).—That one: *see* TOTHER.

TONG, *subs.* (American).—1. In *pl.*, *see* quot. and KICKS.

1870. JUDD, *Margaret*, i. The boys dressed in TONGS, a name for pantaloons or overalls that had come into use.

2. (dentists' and medical).—In *pl.* = forceps: dental or midwifery.

PAIR OF TONGS, *subs. phr.* (common).—A lanky person; a LAMP-POST (*q.v.*): also TONGS! (a sarcastic address).

NOT TO BE TOUCHED WITHOUT A PAIR OF TONGS, *phr.* (common).—A simile of disgust: also EXCEPT AT THE END OF A BARGE-POLE.

1668. LESTRANGE, *Quevedo* (1678), 22. Your Beauties can never want gallants to lay their Appetites . . . Whereas NO-BODY WILL TOUCH the ill-favoured WITHOUT A PAIR OF TONGS.

HAMMER AND TONGS. *See ante*, s.v. HAMMER.

TONGUE, *subs.* (colloquial).—Generic for speech: esp. (1) gabble; (2) abuse, or (3) impudence. As *verb* (TO TONGUE IT, or TO FLASH THE TONGUE) = (1) to talk down; (2) to talk at, to chide; (3) TO MOUTH (*q.v.*); and (4) TO SAUCE (*q.v.*). Whence numerous DERIVATIVES AND COMBINATIONS: thus, TO TONGUE-BANG = to scold roundly, to rate: TONGUE-BANGER = a scold; TONGUE-BATTERY = a torrent of words, a flood of talk; TONGUE-BITER = an indistinct speaker: also TO BITE THE TONGUE = to keep silence; TONGUE-DOUGHTY = bragging, word-valiant; TONGUE-FENCE = debate, argument: TONGUE FENCER = (1) a master of words, and (2) a mouthing-speaker; TONGUE-LASHING = wordy abuse; TONGUE-MAN = (1) an orator, (2) a chatterbox, and (3) a scold: also TONGUE-PAD (*see* quot. 1696) and TONGUESTER; TONGUE-POWDER = fluency of phrase; TONGUE-SHOT = as far as the voice will reach: *cf.* 'ear-shot'; TONGUE-SORE = an evil tongue, ill-speaking; TONGUE-VALIANT = (1) free of talk: hence (2)

brave in word but cowardly in deed; TONGUEY = voluble, abusive; TO TONGUE-WALK = to abuse; TONGUE-WARRIOR = a boaster; TO TONGUE-WHIP = to lash with scorn; TONGUE-WAGGING = speech-making, verbosity, raillery: *cf.* 'He can WAG HIS TONGUE better than he can wield his sword, pen,' etc. (of one promising more than he can perform); TO WAG ONE'S TONGUE = to talk, to chatter; TONGUE-WORK = chatter: in quot. 1598 = philological studies; A LONG TONGUE = 'so full of talk that one can't get in a word edgeways'; AULD WIVES' TONGUES = scandal. Also PHRASES: ON (or AT) THE TIP (or END) OF THE TONGUE = on the point of speech, about to say (or tell); TO GIVE TONGUE = to blurt out; TO KEEP (or HOLD) ONE'S TONGUE = to be silent; TO WAG ONE'S TONGUE = to speak out of season; 'AS OLD AS MY TONGUE, AND A LITTLE OLDER THAN MY TEETH' = a dovetail to 'How old are you?' A TONGUE TOO LONG FOR ONE'S TEETH (or MOUTH) = indiscreet, over-ready of speech; TO FIND ONE'S TONGUE = to break silence; TO PUT ONE'S TONGUE IN ANOTHER'S PURSE = to silence; TONGUE ENOUGH FOR TWO SETS OF TEETH, said of a talkative person (GROSE); THE TONGUE OF THE TRUMP = the best, the most important thing or person: *see* TRUMP; 'MEW YOUR TONGUE' (old) = 'Shut your mouth!' THE VULGAR TONGUE (GROSE) = cant, slang, heterodox speech, etc.

1380. WYCLIF, *Bible*, Eccl. xxv. 27. As a graueli steezing vp in the feet of an old man so a TUNGY womman to a quyete man [A. V. As the climbing up a sandy way is to the feet of the aged, etc.].

1546. HEYWOOD, *Wit and Folly*, 11. So muche the bettyr, and yow so muche the wurs, That ye may now put YOUR TOONG IN YOUR PURS.

1564. UDALL, *Erasmus' Apoph.*, 24. He hath not learned to speake well. Imputing his TONGUESORE not vnto maliciousness, but vnto the default of right knowledge.

1593. SHAKSPEARE, *Taming the Shrew*, i. 1. 214. I will charm him first to KEEP HIS TONGUE. *Ibid.* (1596), *Hamlet*, iii. 4. 39. What have I done that thou darest WAG THY TONGUE In noise so rude against me? *Ibid.* (1598), 2 *Henry IV.*, i. 1. So York must sit, and fret, and BITE HIS TONGUE While his own lands are bargain'd for and sold. *Ibid.*, i. 1. 74. But Priam FOUND the fire ere he HIS TONGUE. *Ibid.* (1603), *Meas. for Measure*, iv. 4. 28. A deflower'd maid . . . But that her tender shame Will not proclaim against her maiden loss, How might she TONGUE me. *Ibid.* (1605), *Cymbeline*, v. 4. 147. Such stuff as madmen TONGUE and brain not.

1594. LYLY, *Mother Bombie*, ii. 1. MEW THY TONGUE, or wee'le cut it out.

1596. CHAPMAN, *Blind Beggar* [SHEPHEARD (1899), 16]. Do but TONGUE-WHIP him, madam, and care not, And so I leave him to the mercy of your tongue.

1598. FLORIO, *Worlde of Wordes*, 'To Reader,' xii. He may as justly stand vpon in this TOONG WORK as in Latin, Sir Thomas Eliot.

1603. DAVIES, *Microcosmos*, 22. Then come, sweet Prince, Wales wooeth thee by me, By me hir sorrie TONGS-MAN.

1607. MIDDLETON, *Michælmas Term*, iv. 4. I'll listen to the common censure now, How the world TONGUES me when my ear lies low.

1611. JONSON, *Cataline*, iv. 2. A boasting, insolent TONGUE-MAN.

c. 1620. FLETCHER, *Double Marriage*, iv. 3. Use more respect, and woman, 'twill become you; At least, less TONGUE.

1627. E. F., *Hist. Edward II.*, 55. I am no TONGUE-MAN, nor can move with language; but if we come to act I'll not be idle.

1634. WITHALS, *Dict.*, 562. *Lingua bellat*: hee layes it on with TONG-POWDER.

1644. MILTON, *Divorce*, ii. 21. An unseemly affront . . . to have her unpleasingness bandied up and down . . . in open court by those hir'd masters of

TONGUE-FENCE. *Ibid.* (1671), *Samson Agon.*, 404. With blandish parlies, feminine assaults, TONGUE-BATTERIES, she surceaseth not, day nor night, To storm me. *Ibid.*, 1180. TONGUE-DOUGHTY giant.

1679. DRYDEN, *Pref. Troil. and Cress.* Let his clack be set a-going, and he shall TONGUE IT as impetuously and as loudly as the arrantest hero of the play. *Ibid.* (1697), *Iliad*, i. 336. TONGUE-VALIANT hero, vaunter of thy might, In threats the foremost but the lag in fight. *Ibid.*, *Grounds of Criticism*. Let his clack be set a-going, and he shall TONGUE IT as impetuously as the arrantest hero of the play.

c. 1696. B. E., *Dict. Cant. Crew*, s.v. TONGUE-PAD, a smooth, Glib-tongued, insinuating Fellow.

1709-11. *Tatler* [*Century*]. She who was a celebrated wit at London is, in that dull part of the world, called a TONGUE-PAD.

d. 1719. ADDISON, *Pretty Disaffection.* Irritated from time to time by these TONGUE-WARRIORS.

1725. BAILEY, *Erasmus*, I. 116. Don't be sparing of your speech with one that is FULL OF TONGUE.

1740. RICHARDSON, *Pamela*, I. 205. God forgive me, but I had a sad lie AT MY TONGUE'S END.

d. 1796. BURNS, *Election Ballads*, ii. An' there will be black-lippit Johnnie, The TONGUE O' THE TRUMP to them a'.

1814. AUSTEN, *Mansfield Park*, viii. Mrs. Norris thought it an excellent plan, and had it at her TONGUE'S END, and was on the point of proposing it when Mrs. Grant spoke.

1843. DICKENS, *Martin Chuzzlewit*, xxix. It was ON THE TIP OF THE BOY'S TONGUE to relate what had followed, but he . . . checked himself.

1851. CARLYLE, *Life of Sterling*, v. In all manner of brilliant utterance and TONGUE-FENCE, I have hardly known his fellow.

1859. READE, *Love Me Little*, x. Hum! Eve, wasn't your TONGUE a little TOO LONG FOR YOUR TEETH just now? *Ibid.* (1861), *Cloister and Hearth*, lii. She would stand timidly aloof out of TONGUE-SHOT.

1862. LOWELL, *Biglow Papers*, 2 S. iii. He jes' ropes in your TONGUEY chaps an' reg'lar ten-inch bores, An' lets 'em play at Congress, ef they'll du it with closed doors.

1866. ELIOT, *Felix Holt*, xx. If a man takes to TONGUE-WORK, it's all over with him.

1876. TENNYSON, *Harold*, v. I. The simple, silent, selfless man Is worth a world of TONGUESTERS. *Ibid.*, *Northern Cobbler.* Then Sally she turn'd a TONGUE-BANGER, an' räated me.

1899. WYNDHAM, *Queen's Service*, 74. Beer has a marvellous effect in loosing tongues, and although there was not much . . . TONGUE-WAGGING, songs and toasts were very numerous.

TO TONGUE A WOMAN, *verb. phr.* (venery).—*See* VELVET.

TONIC, *subs.* (common).—1. A drink: spec. an appetiser.

2. (old).—A halfpenny: *see* RHINO (GROSE).

TONISH (TONY, etc.). *See* BON TON.

TONKABOUT, *subs.* (Charterhouse and Durham).—'Skying' a ball; to TONK=to drive a ball into the air: cricket.

TONNER, *subs.* (colloquial and nautical).—Usually in combination: *e.g.* a TEN-TONNER, etc. (of floating bottoms): *cf.* TWENTY-THOUSAND POUNDER (=a heiress: FARQUHAR, *Recruiting Officer*).

1889. *Scientific American* [*Century*]. Not so long ago a 1000 ton schooner was considered enormous. Now a 1500 TONNER is scarcely remarked.

TONY, *subs.* (common).—A simpleton: *see* BUFFLE (B. E.).

1668. DRYDEN, *All for Love*, Prol., 15. In short, a pattern and companion fit For all the keeping TONIES of the pit.

TONYGLE, *verb.* (Old Cant).—To copulate: *see* RIDE. [Thus given by HARMAN. Probably NIGGLE (*q.v.*), the '*to*' being the old and long obsolete intensive verbal affix, a form which survives Biblically: *see* Judges ix. 53.]

TOO. THIS IS TOO MUCH, *phr.* (colloquial).—The retort sarcastic or jocose: an echo of 'Artemus Ward among the Shakers.'

See BAG; BOOTS; THIN; TOO-TOO.

TOOL, *subs.* (colloquial).—1. A person employed by another (in reproach): a jackal, satellite, or dupe; a cat's-paw (B. E. and GROSE). Hence, a POOR TOOL =a clumsy worker, a bad hand at anything; A MERE TOOL= a sycophant. Also (old) TOOL= a useless, shiftless fellow.

1650. WELDON, *Court King James* (1817), 10. [A man is compared to] a TOOL in the workman's hand.

c. 1696. B. E., *Dict. Cant. Crew*, s.v. TOOL, an Implement fit for any Turn, the Creature of any Cause or Faction; a meer Property, or Cat's Foot.

1699. GARTH, *Dispensary*, III. Fools were promoted to the council-board, TOOLS to the bench, and bullies to the sword.

1775. SHERIDAN, *Duenna*, ii. 4. Oh, the easy blockhead! what a TOOL I have made of him!

1813. BYRON, *Bride of Abydos*, ii. 16. Such still to guilt just Alla sends—Slaves, TOOLS, accomplices—no friends!

1861. WINTHROP, *Cecil Dreeme*, v. He had been a clerk, TOOL, agent, slave, of the great Densdeath.

2. (old).—A weapon: spec. a sword.

c. 1360. *Sir Gawayne* [E.E.T.S.], 2261. Then the gome in the grene graythed hym swythe Gedere vp hys grymme TOLE, Gawayne to smyte.

1383. CHAUCER, *Cant. Tales*, 'Nun's Priest's Tale,' 96. Non niggard ne no fool, Ne him that is agast of every TOOL.

1582. STANYHURST, *Æneis* [ARBER], 63. Mye TOOLS make passadge through flame and hostilitye Greekish.

1595. SHAKSPEARE, *Romeo and Juliet*, i. 1. 37. *Gre.* Draw thy TOOL. . . . *Sam.* My naked weapon is out: quarrel, I will back thee.

3. (thieves').—Usually in *pl.* = (*a*) pistols; (*b*) housebreaking implements; (*c*) the hands, THE FORKS (*q.v.*); and (*d*) in *sing.* = a small boy employed to creep through windows, etc., to effect entry. Hence TO TOOL = to burgle, to pick pockets, to steal; FIXED FOR THE TOOLS = convicted for possession of illegal instruments; TOOLER=a burglar or pickpocket; MOLL-TOOLER= a female thief.

1890. BOLDREWOOD, *Squatter's Dream*, 157. He possessed himself of the sixteen-shooter, and handed the Snider to the Doctor. . . . We'll be a match for all the blessed traps . . . with these here TOOLS.

4. (colloquial).—Generic for equipment (*cf.* all senses): spec. (artists') = brushes; (authors')= books, especially works of reference; (medical)=surgical instruments (*see* quot. 1706, sense 6).

5. (driving).—A whip. Hence, as *verb*=to handle a team of horses skilfully; also (loosely)= to drive: applied to all means of locomotion—engine, cart, bicycle, motor-car, etc.; TO TOOL ALONG =to go quickly.

1849. LYTTON, *Caxtons*, xiii. 4. He could TOOL a coach.

1883. *Harp. Mag.*, lxv. 579. Only kept from stopping altogether . . . by the occasional idle play of Emerson's whip. . . . So we TOOLED on.

1885. *D. Teleg.*, 18 Nov. The crack coaches . . . were TOOLED by expert 'knights of the bench.'

1887. JESSOP, *Arcady*, i. The high-stepping mare that TOOLS him along through the village street.

1899. WHITEING, *John St.*, xiv. See about the coach for Ascot—driving down myself for the Nimrod. TOOL you down in style.

6. (venery).—The *penis*: also (in *pl.*)=the male privities: *see* PRICK. Hence TO GRIND ONE'S TOOL=to copulate: *see* GREENS and RIDE.

1640. *Ladies' Parliament. Stamford.* She is for the game, She saies her husband is to blame, For her part she loves a foole, If he hath a good TOOLE.

1653. URQUHART, *Rabelais*, I. xii. This little lecher was always groping his nurses and governesses . . . for he had already begun to exercise the TOOLS, and put his codpiece in practice.

1694. MOTTEUX, *Rabelais*, v. xxviii. *Pan.* What kind of TOOLS are yours? *Fri.* Big. . . . *Pan.* How many bouts a-nights? *Fri.* Ten. Catso! quoth Friar John, the poor fornicating brother is bashful. *Ibid.*, iv. Prol. What need you use a wooden TOOL? When lusty John does to me come, He never shoves but with his bum.

1706. WARD, *Wooden World*, 46, 'The Surgeon.' His TOOLS are of various Sorts and Sizes; his best he always carries in his Breeches. *Ibid.* (1707), *Hud. Redio*, II. ii. 22. And fire the TOOLS of Generation With Some Venereal Inflammation.

1772. BRIDGES, *Burlesque Homer*, 219. But in her hand, if I must tell ye, She caught my TOOL, and sav'd her belly.

d. 1796. BURNS [*Merry Muses* (*c.* 1800), 22]. 'Old Song Revised.' 'And noble TOOLS,' quo' she, 'by my faith!' And ay she waggit it wantonlie.

TOOLEY-STREET TAILOR, *subs. phr.* (obsolete).—A conceited, bumptious fellow. [HOTTEN: The 'three TAILORS OF TOOLEY STREET' immortalized themselves by preparing a petition for Parliament and presenting it with only their own signatures thereto, which commenced, 'We, the people of England'—so it is said.]

TOOT, *subs.* (provincial).—1. The Devil (prov. Eng.): *see* BLACK-SPY; and (2) a shiftless fellow, a good-for-nothing. Whence (American) ON A TOOT='raising the devil' (LELAND), 'on a spree' (BARTLETT).

1889. *Harper's Mag.*, lxxvii. 801. Marsh Yates, the 'shif'less TOOT,' and his beautiful, energetic wife.

1900. LYNCH, *High Stakes*, xxxii. I'd never 'a' carried 'em . . . if I 'adn't been ON A regular TOOT for the last week! It's a fool's trick to do.

See TOUT.

TOOTH (TEETH), *subs.* (colloquial).—A special taste, palate, or relish; a great liking. Hence TOOTHY (or TOOTHFUL)=palatable, to one's liking; THE RUN OF ONE'S TEETH = keep, maintenance; SOMETHING FOR THE TOOTH=(1) food, and (2) a tit-bit (GROSE); TO LOVE THE TOOTH =to gourmandise; TOOTH-MUSIC =mastication (GROSE).

1581. LYLY, *Euphues* [ARBER], 308. I am glad that my Adonis hath a sweete TOOTH in his head.

1607. DEKKER, *Northward Hoe*, iv. 4. Having met one fit for his own TOOTH, you see, he skips from us.

1610. HOLLAND, *Camden*, 543. Very delicate dainties . . . greatly sought by them that LOVE THE TOOTH so well.

1622. MASSINGER, *Virgin Martyr*, v. I. If so TOOTHFULL I will be banquetted.

1697. DRYDEN, *Persius's Satires*, iii. 229. These are not dishes for thy dainty TOOTH.

1769-78. TUCKER, *Light of Nature*, II. ii. xxiii. My compatriots . . . are too squeamish in their taste, and fonder of the TOOTHSOME than the wholesome.

1875. COLLINS, *Blacksmith and Scholar*, i. The splendid saddle (the Squire's own Southdowns), which melted so TOOTHSOMELY in the mouth.

c. 1885. *Alienist and Neurol.* [*Century*]. A certain relaxation . . . during which meat or game which is at first tough, becomes more tender and TOOTHY.

1889. *Harper's Mag.*, lxxviii. 867. Affable greetings, pressing invitations, great courtesy, but nothing, absolutely nothing, for the impatient TOOTH of a correspondent.

PHRASES AND COMBINATIONS.—HEN'S TEETH = anything imaginary or rare, a *rara avis*: *cf.* black swan; IN SPITE OF ONE'S TEETH=(1) in face of opposition; (2) under protest; IN THE TEETH =(1) with difficulty or much ado; (2) at long odds, or against the grain; and (3) to one's face; TO CAST (OR THROW) IN THE TEETH= to accuse, blame, or bring home to: *see* Matthew xxvii. 44; TO GRIND (OR SHOW) ONE'S TEETH=to take amiss, to get angry; TO SET ONE'S TEETH=to steel oneself, to put one's foot down; TO ONE'S TEETH = resolutely, boldly, openly; FROM ONE'S TEETH=reluctantly, as a matter of form, not seriously; TO HIT IN THE TEETH=to taunt, to twit; TO HIDE ONE'S TEETH=to dissemble, to feign friendship; TO LIE IN ONE'S TEETH=to tell unblushing falsehoods; WITH TEETH AND ALL (*see* TOOTH-AND-NAIL); BETWEEN THE TEETH = in a whisper, aside; TO SET THE TEETH ON EDGE = to repel, offend, or shock; TO TAKE THE BIT IN ONE'S TEETH, =to cast aside restraint, 'to kick over the traces'; TO HAVE CUT ONE'S EYE (OR HIGH) TEETH=to be cute or knowing, to know WHAT'S WHAT (*q.v.*); OLD IN THE TOOTH =advanced in years: spec. in contempt of old maids; ARMED TO THE TEETH = fully prepared, alert, AWAKE (*q.v.*); BY THE SKIN OF THE TEETH = barely, 'by a close shave'; CLEAN AS A HOUND'S TOOTH = as clean as may be, highly polished; TO CARRY A BONE IN THE TEETH (*see* BONE); TO HAVE THE TEETH WELL AFLOAT (OR UNDER) = to be drunk; TO THE HARD TEETH =very severely; TO GO TO GRASS WITH TEETH UPWARDS = to be buried; TO DRAW TEETH = (medical students': obsolete) to wrench off knockers; DOG'S-TOOTH=a snaggle tooth, a TOMB-STONE (*q.v.*); COLT'S-TOOTH (*see ante*); 'He ought to have his teeth drawn' = He should be curbed, SAT UPON (*q.v.*).

1542 UDAL, *Erasmus*, 355. Cicero marked her TO THE HARD TEETH.

1593 (and after). SHAKSPEARE [*see* quots. s.v. TEETH].

1596. DRAYTON, *Baron's Wars*, ii. 43. Mowbray in fight him matchless honour won: . . . Gifford seemed danger TO HER TEETH to dare.

1603. *Court and Times James I.* [Among the verbs is] SHOW OUR TEETH.

1614. FLETCHER, *Wit Sev. Weapons*, v. I. If you have done me a good turn do not HIT ME I' THE TEETH with 't; that's not the part of a friend.

1653. URQUHART, *Rabelais*, i. 49. Four brigades . . . had no sooner reached the top of the hill but they met Picrochole IN THE TEETH, and those that were with him scattered.

1663. DRYDEN, *Wild Gallant* [LITTLEDALE]. I am confident she is only angry FROM THE TEETH OUTWARDS.

d. 1713. ELLWOOD, *Life* [HOWELL], 322. The jailer . . . HID HIS TEETH . . . putting on a show of kindness.

1725. YOUNG, *Love of Fame*, i. 17. When the law SHEWS HER TEETH, but dare not bite.

1790. BRUCE, *Source of Nile*, I. 62. A strong, steady gale almost directly IN THEIR TEETH.

c. 1827. MACAULAY, *Hallam's Const. Hist.* As the oath taken by the clergy was IN THE TEETH of their principles, so was their conduct in the teeth of their oath.

1876. BLACKMORE, *Cripps the Carrier*, i. The carrier scarcely knew what to do IN THE TEETH of so urgent a message.

TOOTH AND NAIL, *adv. phr.* (colloquial).—In earnest; to the utmost: *i.e.*, even to biting and scratching. Also WITH TEETH AND ALL.

1550. *Jyl of Brentford's Testament* [FURNIVALL], 23. Fight with TOOTHE AND NAYLE.

1550. HUTCHINSON, *Works* (Parker Society), 213. [OLIPHANT, *New Eng.*, i. 527. Men attack something] TOOTH AND NAIL.

d. 1634. RANDOLPH, *Pot Good Ale* [*Century*]. And physic . . . will stand against physic both TOOTH AND NAIL.

1705. WARD, *Hud. Red.*, I. iii. 6. Does TOOTH AND NAIL so nobly stand By th' ancient Glories of the Land.

1706. HEARNE, *Reliquiæ*, i. 114. The bishop laboured TOOTH AND NAYLE to have brought in to have succeeded him a certain haughty Dr.

1749. SMOLLETT, *Gil Blas* (1812), II. i. He fell TOOTH AND NAIL upon this course.

1809. MALKIN, *Gil Blas* [ROUTLEDGE], 7. This Lucrece of the Asturias . . . defended her sweet person TOOTH AND NAIL.

1885. *D. Teleg.*, 6 Nov. A desperate TOOTH-AND-NAIL encounter.

TOOTH-CARPENTER, *subs. phr.* (common).—A dentist; a SNAGFENCER (*q.v.*).

TOOTH-DRAWER. LIKE A TOOTH-DRAWER, *phr.* (old). — Thin; meagre (RAY); bald.

1393. LANGLAND, *Piers Plowman* C.), vii. 370. Of portours and of pykeporses, and pyled (bald) TOTH-DRAWERS.

TOOTHER, *subs.* (pugilists'). — A blow on the mouth.

TOOTHFUL, *subs.* (common). — A dram; a nip: *cf.* THIMBLEFUL.

1868. WHYTE MELVILLE, *White Rose*, ii. I. Step round and take a TOOTHFUL of something short to our better acquaintance.

1885. *Field*, 4 April. A pull at the milk and soda water . . . or possibly a TOOTHFUL of something a little stronger.

TOOTHPICK, *subs.* (old).—1. 'A large stick' (GROSE). THE CRUTCH AND TOOTHPICK BRIGADE (modern) = foppish 'men about town': spec. (*c.* 1884) hangers-on at stage doors when burlesque was in full swing at the Gaiety: they affected, as the badge of their tribe, a crutch-handled stick and a toothpick.

2. (military).—*See* quot.

1901. *Graphic*, 15 June, 798. 2. These gallant gentlemen generally display sovereign contempt for the TOOTHPICK, as they dub the ornamental appendage to uniform . . . by the regulations.

Adj. (American). — Narrow and pointed, like a TOOTHPICK: spec. of footgear.

See ARKANSAS TOOTHPICK.

TOOTH-RAKE (or **SCRAPER**), *subs. phr.* (old).—A toothpick.

1696. *Nomenclator*, s.v. Dentiscalpium. *Curedent.* A TOOTH-SCRAPER, OR TOOTH-RAKE.

TOOTHY-PEG, *subs. phr.* (nursery). —A tooth.

1839. HOOD, *Miss Kilmansegg*. Turn we to little Miss Kilmansegg, Cutting her first little TOOTHY-PEG.

TOOTING-TUB, *subs. phr.* (old).—A church organ.

[?]. BROOKE, *Eastford*, 22. I've heard they're subscribing for an organ! Yes, an organ! What on earth will they do next? That ever I should live to see a Popish TOOTIN'-TUB stuck up in our gallery!

TOOTLE, *subs.* (University). — Trashy: spec. of immature literary effort.

1886. *Daily News*, 1 Dec. It will produce abundance of easy, loose, rhetorical amateur criticism — will produce TOOTLE, as it used to be called.

TOOTLEDUM-PATTICK, *subs. phr.* (provincial). — A fool: *see* BUFFLE.

TOO-TOO, *adv.* and *adj.* (old literary: now colloquial).—An intensive form of TOO: over-and-above, more than enough, very good, extreme, utter; spec. (modern but obsolete) of exaggerated æstheticism. [HALLIWELL: It is often nothing more in sense than a strengthening of the word *too*, but TOO-TOO was regarded by our early writers as a single word.]

1533. *Old Play*, quoted by OLIPHANT [DODSLEY, *Old Plays* (HAZLITT), i. 423]. It is TOO TOO, the pastime.

1587. HOLINSHED, *Hist. Ireland*, F6b, 2b. Adding further, that he was TOO TOO evill, that coulde not speake well.

1590. SPENSER, *Fairy Queen*, III. iv. 26. A lesson TOO TOO hard for living clay.

1596. SHAKSPEARE, *Hamlet*, i. 2. 129. Oh that this TOO TOO solid flesh would melt.

1605. SYLVESTER, *Du Bartas*, i. 6. Oh TOO-TOO happy!

1618. TAYLOR, *Pennilesse Pilgrimage* [*Notes and Queries*, 7 S. x. 498]. Their loues they on the tenter-hookes did racke, Rost, boyl'd, bak'd, TOO-TOO much white, claret, sacke.

1630. JONSON, *New Inn*, ii. 2. That joy is TOO-TOO narrow Would bound a love so infinite as mine.

1634. FORD, *Perkin Warbeck*, ii. 2. The rigour and extremity of law Is sometimes TOO-TOO bitter.

1891. *Notes and Queries*, 7 S. xi. 30. Let the exclusive TOO-TOO æsthetes tolerate the remark that music and painting do not exist for them . . . [alone]. . . .

TOOTSIE, *subs.* (common). — A foot: spec. of women and children.

1897. MARSHALL, *Pomes*, 46. Towards her two TOOTSIES . . . she gazed with a feeling of fear . . . But her hose were well veiled from man's sight.

TOP, *subs.* (old).—1. The head (*see* verb); (2) the hair, THE THATCH (*q.v.*): also TOP-DRESSING: spec. the forelock or TOPKNOT. Whence TOPPER = (1) a violent blow on the head, and (2) = a hat; TOP-LIGHTS = the eyes. Also phrases: TAIL OVER TOP = headlong; TOP OVER TAIL = TOPSY-TURVY (*q.v.*), rashly, hastily; FROM TOP TO TOE = wholly; TOP AND TAIL = everything.

c. 1360. *William of Palerne* [E.E.T.S.], 2776. Sche TOP OUER TAIL tombled ouer the hacches.

1373. CHAUCER, *House of Fame*, 880. Thow shalt . . . with thyn eres heren wel TOP AND TAIL, and every del. *Ibid.* (1383), *Cant. Tales*, 'Gen. Prol.,' 590. His TOP was dokked lyk a preest beforn.

c. 1400. *Chester Plays*, ii. 176. Thou take hym by the TOPPE and I by the tayle.

[?]. *MS. Cantab.*, Ff. ii. 38, f. 76. But syr James had soche a chopp, That he wyste not be my TOPPE, Whethur hyt were day or nyght.

[?]. *Political Poems* (FURNIVALL), 95. Be-hold me how that I ame tourne, For I ame rente fro TOPE TO TO.

15[?]. *Turnament of Totenham*, xv. Ilke man went bakward TOPPE OUER TAYLE.

1544. ASCHAM, *Toxoph.* [ARBER], 47. To tumble ouer and ouer, to TOPPE OUER TAYLE . . . may be also holesom for the body.

1605. SHAKSPEARE, *Lear*, ii. 4. 165. All the starred vengeance of heaven fall On her ingrateful TOP.

1706. WARD, *Wooden World*, 67. It costs him many a Rub with his Paws before he can make his TOP LIGHTS to shine clearly.

1834. AINSWORTH, *Rookwood*. Vile Jem, with neat left-handed stopper, Straight threatened Tommy with a TOPPER.

1874. J. B. STEPHENS, *Poems*, 'To a Black Gin.' The coarseness of thy tresses is distressing, With grease and raddle firmly coalescing, I cannot laud thy system of TOP-DRESSING.

1897. MARSHALL, *Pomes*, 62. A most successful raid On a swell's discarded TOPPER.

1900. *Free Lance*, 6 Oct., 4. 1. The origin of the TOPPER. . . . The Baroness Cecile de Courlot, Lady-in-Waiting to the Princess de Lamballe, Princess of Savoy-Carignan, . . . writing from Paris, 19th Nivoise XI., says, 'The latest thing for gentlemen on the Corso at a review at Longchamps was the new high hats. . . . Thiery, who invented them, made a wager that he would introduce the very most absurd shape imaginable, and it would become fashionable. He won his wager.'

3. (common). — In *pl.* = top-boots: *cf.* SMALLS and TRUNKS. Also (rarely) upper garments.

[1707. FARQUHAR, *Beaux's Stratagem*, iii. 1. He has TOPS to his shoes up to his mid-leg.]

1837. DICKENS, *Pickwick*, xiv. In a green coat, knee-cords, and TOPS. *Ibid.* v. Mr. Weller's TOPS were newly cleaned.

Verb (Old Cant). 1. To behead (the usage still lingers in agriculture); to hang. Whence TO BE TOPPED = to be hung: *see* LADDER; TOPPING-CHEAT = the gallows: *see* CHEAT; TOPPING-COVE (or TOPSMAN) = JACK KETCH (*q.v.*); also TOP, *subs.* = a dying speech, a croak (B. E. and GROSE).

2. (colloquial). — Generic for superiority: to excel, surpass, CAP (*q.v.*). Thus TO TOP ONE'S PART = (*a*) to surpass oneself, and (*b*) to do zealously. As *adj.* (or TOPPING) = prime, first-class, distinguished, thorough, extreme: *e.g.* TOP (= the best) ALE; a TOP (= a principal) CHARACTER, or PART; THE TOP OF THE TREE = preëminent socially, in wealth, in a profession, etc.; a TOP (= a favourite) TOAST; a TOP (= a titled or well-to-do) FAMILY; TOP (= full) SPEED; and so forth. TOPPINGEST (or TOPLESS) = the best, supreme; and TOPPINGLY = fine, very well; also (in a baser sense) arrogantly, assumingly, badly, vilely. Also TOPPER (or TOP-SAWYER) = anybody or anything exceptional: as the largest and best fruit: usually placed on top in packing: *cf.* HUMPHREY TOPPERS; an expert thief; a famous horse; a beautiful woman; a man of large means, exceptional influence, high position, or remarkable genius: also (of persons) TOPPING MAN or TOPPING FELLOW (B. E. and GROSE). TO COME OUT ON TOP = to be successful, TO GET THERE (*q.v.*); A LITTLE BIT OFF THE TOP = some of the best; THE TOP OF DESIRE = the height of ambition, all that one cares for: *cf.* TIP-TOP; TOP AND TOP-GALLANT (orig. nautical) = in full FIG (*q.v.*), rig, array, or force.

1557. TUSSER, *Husbandry*, April: 'Lesson for Dairy-Maid.' These TOPPINGLY guests be in number but ten.

1594. PEELE, *Battle of Alcazar*, iii. 3. He cometh hitherward amain, TOP AND TOP-GALLANT, all in brave array.

1602. SHAKSPEARE, *Troilus*, i. 3. 151. Sometimes, great Agamemnon, Thy TOPLESS deputation he puts on. *Ibid.* (1605), *Lear*, i. 2. 21. To TOP the legitimate. *Ibid.* (1606), *Macbeth*, iv. 3. 57. To TOP Macbeth. *Ibid.* (1610), *Coriolanus*, ii. 1. 23. TOPPING all others in boasting.

1608. BREWER, *Merry Devil of Edmonton* [DODSLEY, *Old Plays* (REED), xi. 131]. He'll be here TOP AND TOP-GALLANT presently.

1682. DRYDEN, *Mac Flecknoe*, 167. But write thy best and TOP; and in each line Sir Formal's oratory will be thine.

1694. MOTTEUX, *Rabelais*, IV. vi. They are . . . TOPPING sheep, fatted sheep, sheep of quality.

c. 1696. B. E., *Dict. Cant. Crew*, s.v. TOPPING-FELLOW, who has reacht the Pitch and greatest Eminence in any Art; the Master, and the Cock of his Profession.

1698. JEREMY COLLIER, *Short View*, 219. The fine Berenthia, one of the TOP-CHARACTERS, is impudent and profane.

1698. FARQUHAR, *Love and a Bottle*, iii. 2. I have a project of turning three or four of our most TOPPING FELLOWS into doggrel.

1703. STEELE, *Tender Husband*, v. 1. Well, Jenny, you TOPP'D your part, indeed.

d. 1704. BROWN, *Works*, ii. 258. The TOPPINGEST shop-keepers in the city us'd now and then to visit me.

1708. KING, *Art of Love*, v. Th' old man receiv'd her, and exprest much kindness for his TOPPING guest.

1709. DAMPIER, *Voyages*, II. i. 141. Some . . . were TOPPING merchants and had many slaves under them.

d. 1713. ELLWOOD, *Life* (HOWELL'S), 291. These two Baptists were TOPPING blades, that looked high and spake big.

1721. D'URFEY, *Pills*, ii. 22. When 'the world first knew creation A rogue was a TOP PROFESSION.

1725. BAILEY, *Erasmus*, 'Rich Beggars.' There are TOPPING citizens too, who imitate them.

1734. HEARNE, *Diary*, 23 Jan. TOPPING books formerly . . . greedily bought at great prices, . . . turn'd to waste paper.

c. 1738. GAY, *Squire and Cur*. That politician TOPS his part Who readily can lie with art.

1742. JARVIS, *Don Quixote*, I. III. xi. It is the TOPPINGEST thing I ever heard. *Ibid.*, II. III. xviii. I mean to marry her TOPPINGLY when she least thinks of it.

1743-5. POCOCKE, *Descr. East*, II. ii. 9. There being only a few of the TOP FAMILIES in the city who use horses.

1766. BROOKE, *Fool of Quality*, i. 364. Setting out at TOP speed, he soon overtook him.

1774. FOOTE, *Cozeners*, i. Master Moses is an absolute Proteus; in every elegance at the TOP OF THE TREE.

1782. BURNEY, *Cecilia*, IV. vi. You must needs think what a hardship it is to me to have him turn out so unlucky, after all I have done for him, when I thought to have seen him at the TOP OF THE TREE.

1785. GROSE, *Dictionary of the Vulgar Tongue*, s.v. TOP . . . The cove was TOPPED for smashing queer screens. *Ibid.*, s.v. TOP SAWYER signifies a man that is a master genius in any profession. It is a piece of Norfolk slang, and took its rise [?] from Norfolk being a great timber county, where the TOP SAWYERS get double the wages of those beneath them.

1809. MALKIN, *Gil Blas* [ROUTLEDGE], 94. You TOPPED your part to perfection, and I was not quite contemptible in mine.

1836. MILNER, *Turpin's Ride to York*, i. 3. I shall never come to the scragging-post, unless you turn TOPSMAN.

1837. BARHAM, *Ingolds. Leg.*, II. 56. A young dandified lawyer, Whose air, nevertheless, speaks him quite a TOP-SAWYER.

1838. DICKENS, *Oliver Twist*, xliii. Wasn't he always TOP-SAWYER among you all? Is there one of you that could touch him or come near him on any scent? *Ibid.* (1853), *Bleak House*, ii. My Lady Dedlock has been . . . at the TOP OF THE fashionable TREE.

1843. MONCRIEFF, *Scamps of London*, iv. Our hells are full of Greeks—they are the Corinthians of the order—the TOP SAWYERS.

1851-61. MAYHEW, *Lond. Lab.* III. 387. Thirty-six were cast for death, and only one was TOPPED.

1851-61. MAYHEW, *Lond. Lab.*, I. 61. Strawberry pottles are often half cabbage leaves, a few tempting strawberries being displayed on the top of the pottle. . . . Ask any coster that knows the world, and he'll tell you that all the salesmen in the market TOPS UP. *Ibid.*, II. 137. A big pottle of strawberries that was rubbish all under the TOPPERS.

1854-5. THACKERAY, *Newcomes*, xv. He had paid the postboys, and travelled with a servant like a TOP-SAWYER.

1862. CLOUGH, *The Bothee of Tober-Na-Vuolich*. Shady in Latin, said Lindsay, but TOPPING in Plays and Aldrich.

1864. *Spectator*, 1186. The University word shady meaning simply poor and inefficient, as when a man is said to be 'shady in Latin but TOPPING in Greek plays,' is obviously University slang.

1869. BLACKMORE, *Lorna Doone*, xxxvi. 'See-saw is the fashion of England always, and the Whigs will soon be the TOP-SAWYERS.' 'But,' said I, 'still more confused, 'the King is the TOP-SAWYER according to our proverb; how then can the Whigs be?'

1869. WHYTE-MELVILLE, *M or N.* 'I'll marry a TOP-SAWYER,' he used to say, whenever his uncle broached the question of his settlement in life.

1871. LOWELL, *Study Windows*, 326. Of all who have attempted Homer [Chapman] has the TOPPING merit of being inspired by him.

1872. HARDY, *Under Greenwood Tree*, iv. 4. I don't like her to come by herself, now she's not so terrible TOPPING in health.

1892. *Pall Mall Gaz.*, 17 Oct., 2. 1. The song 'If I was only long enough' landed me with one bound at the TOP OF THE TREE.

1898. GOULD, *Landed at Last*, iv. When I have been beaten I have always met a better horse than my own. This year I fancy I shall be ON TOP.

1901. JOHNSTON, *Old Dominion*, i. I have the most TOPPING fellow in all London for my guest.

3. (colloquial).—To put in a finishing touch; to conclude: spec. to drink (or toss off) a bumper, or to wind up a meal by a special course. Also TO TOP UP (or OFF).

1614. *Terence in English* [NARES]. Its no heinous offence . . . for a young man to hunt harlots, to TOPPE OFF a canne roundly; its no great fault to breake open dores.

1853. DICKENS, *Bleak House*, xi. Four engage to go half-price to the play at night, and TOP UP with oysters. *Ibid.* (1861), *Great Expectations*, x. What'll you drink, Mr Gargery; at my expense, to TOP UP with?

1885. *Century Mag.*, xli. 47. A heavy sleep evolved out of sauerkraut, sausages, and cider, lightly TOPPED OFF with a mountain of crisp waffles.

4. (old).—To snuff (a candle): also TOP THE GLIM (GROSE and CLARK RUSSELL). [Amongst work-people, one cried 'Top!' the others followed, the last having to do duty: long obsolete.] *See verb* 1.

1607. MIDDLETON, *Five Gallants*, i. 1. TOP the candle, sirrah! methinks the light burns blue.

5. (old).—'To cheat, to trick, to insult' (B. E. and GROSE); TO GET THE BETTER OF (or A BULGE ON) ONE (*q.v.*): spec. to cheat with dice: *see* quots.

1674. COTTON, *Complete Gamester* (1681), 11. That is, when they take up both dice, and seem to put them in the box, and shaking the box, you would think them both there, by reason of the ratling occasioned with the screwing of the box, whereas one of them is at the top of the box, between his two forefingers, or secured by thrusting a forefinger into the box.

c. 1696. B. E., *Dict. Cant. Crew*, s.v. TOP. What do you TOP upon me? c. do you stick a little Wax to the Dice to keep them together, to get the Chance, you wou'd have? He thought to have TOPT upon me, c. he design'd to have Put upon me, Sharpt me, Bullied me, or Affronted me.

6. (venery).—To copulate: *see* RIDE, and *cf.* TUP.

1602. SHAKSPEARE, *Othello*, v. 2. 136. *Othello.* Cassio did TOP her. . . . Thy husband knew it all. . . . *Emil.* That she was false to wedlock? *Othello.* Ay, with Cassio.

TO CRY IN TOP OF, *verb phr.* (old).—(1) To overrule; (2) to talk down, to outspeak.

1596. SHAKSPEARE, *Hamlet*, ii. 2. 459. Others whose judgments in such matters CRIED IN THE TOP OF mine.

TO TOP A CLOUT, *verb. phr.* (old).—'To draw the corner or end to the top of a person's pocket, in readiness for shaking or drawing, that is, taking out, when a favourable moment occurs, which latter operation is frequently done by a second person.' (VAUX).

TO-PAN, *subs.* (Winchester).—'A large basin of red earthenware placed in each chamber for washing the feet in' (MANSFIELD, *c.* 1840).

TOP-DIVER, *subs. phr.* (old).—'A Lover of Women. An old TOP-DIVER, one that has Lov'd Oldhat in his time' (B. E. and GROSE).

TOP-DRESSING, *subs. phr.* (journalistic). — An introduction to a report: usually written by an experienced hand and set in larger type.

TOPE, *verb.* (old: now colloquial).—To drink: spec. to drink hard. Hence TOPER = a confirmed tippler, a SOAKER (*q.v.*); TO TOPE IT ABOUT = to keep the bottle going briskly (B. E. and GROSE).

1675. COTTON, *Scoffer Scofft*, 'Juno and Jupiter.' A sturdy Piece of Flesh, and proper, A merry Grig, and a true TOPER.

d. 1680. BUTLER, *Epig.*, 'On Club of Sots.' The jolly members of a TOPING club.

1688. DRYDEN, *To Sir Geo. Etherege*, 59. If you TOPE in form, and treat, 'Tis the sour sauce to the sweet meat, The fine you pay for being great.

1694. MOTTEUX, *Rabelais*, v. xxii. They TOPED . . . cool sparkling . . . syrup; which went down like mother's milk. *Ibid.*, xlii. Oh! that . . . we gentlemen TOPERS had but necks some three cubits long.

1765. TUCKER, *Light of Nature*, I. 1. v. Sits among his fellow TOPERS at the twopenny club.

d. 1796. BURNS [*Merry Muses* (*c.* 1800), 118]. Three wives, Who . . . often met to TOPE and chat, And tell odd tales of men.

d. 1845. HOOD, *Don't You Smell Fire?* Was there ever so thirsty an elf?—But he still may TOPE on.

1877. BESANT and RICE, *Son of Vulcan*, Prol. i. In the public houses . . . the TOPERS . . . keep [New Year's Eve] as they keep every feast . . . by making it a day more than usually unholy.

TOP-HEAVY, *adj. phr.* (old). — Drunk: *see* SCREWED (RAY, B.E. and GROSE).

TOP-HONOURS, *subs. phr.* (old nautical).—Top-sails.

1700. PRIOR, *Carmen Seculare*, 36. Let all the naval World due Homage pay; With hasty Reverence their TOP-HONOURS lower.

TOP-JOINT. *See* TOP-O'-REEB.

TOPLIGHTS. *See* TOP, *subs.*

TOP-LOFTY, *adj. phr.* (American).—Pretentious; bombastic; HIGH-FALUTIN (*q.v.*): also TOP-LOFTICAL.

1879. *Congregationalist*, 17 Dec. TOPLOFTICAL talking . . . and inflammatory speeches.

TOP-O'-REEB, *subs. phr.* (back slang).—A pot of beer. TOP-JOINT = a pint of beer.

TOP OF THE MORNING, *subs. phr.* (common).—A cheery greeting.

1855. TAYLOR, *Still Waters*, ii. 2. The TOP OF THE MORNIN' to ye, my boy! I'll be off to the City.

TOPPER, *subs.* (tramps').—1. A cigar stump; and (2) a plug of tobacco at the bottom of a pipe. Hence TOPPER-HUNTER = a scavenger of half-smoked and refuse tobacco.

3. (common).—A lanky person; a LAMP-POST (*q.v.*).

4. *See* TOP, *subs.* and *verb.*

TOPPING-CHEAT. *See* TOP, *subs.* 1.

TOP-ROPES. TO SWAY AWAY ON ALL TOP-ROPES, *verb. phr.* (old).—To live riotously or extravagantly (GROSE).

TOPSAIL (or **TOPSAILS OVER**), *phr.* (old). TOPSY-TURVY (*q.v.*); heels over head.

c. 1430. *Destr. Troy* (E.E.T.S.), 1219. Mony turnyt with tene TOPSAYLES OUER That hurlet to the hard vrthe and there horse leuyt.

[?] *Rom. of Cheuelere Assigne* (E.E.T.S.), 320. And eyther of hem TOPSEYLE tumbledde to the erthe.

TO PAY ONE'S DEBTS WITH THE TOPSAIL, *verb. phr.* (nautical) (GROSE).—To go to sea leaving scores unpaid; *cf.* (military) 'to pay one's score with the drum' (= to march away).

TOPS-AND-BOTTOMS. TO PLAY AT TOPS-AND-BOTTOMS, *verb. phr.* (venery).—To copulate: *see* RIDE.

TOP-SAWYER. 1. *See* TOP, *subs.*

2. (tailors').—A collar. Also the front of a garment.

TO PLAY TOP-SAWYER, *verb. phr.* (venery).—To copulate: *see* RIDE.

TOP-SHUFFLE, *verb. phr.* (gaming).—To shuffle the lower half of a pack over the upper half without disturbing it. The cut, of course, buries it, but by a very simple movement the cards are forced back to their original condition. This is 'shifting the cut,' and can be done with one hand or two.

TOPSY-BOOSY, *adj. phr.* (common).—Drunk: *see* SCREWED

TOPSY-TURVY, *adv.* (old colloquial).—Upside down; upset; in confusion: also as *adj.*, *subs.*, and *verb*, with derivatives such as TOPSY-TURVILY, TOPSY-TURVINESS, TOPSY-TURVYDOM, TOPSY-TURVYFICATION, TOPSY-TURVIFY, and TOPSY-TURVYISM (GROSE). [Of uncertain but much-discussed derivation: the word also shows remarkable changes in form, many of which are given *infra*. The most recently accepted theory of probable derivation (HALL, SKEAT, and *Century*) is TOP + SO + TERVY (= overthrown), with confusion in some of the forms with kindred phrases, such as TOPSAILS OVER (*q.v.*).]

VARIANTS. — TOPSY-TERVY; TOPSY-TYRVY; TOPSIE-TURVIE; TOPSE-TORVE; TOPSY-TURVYE; TOPSIE-TURVY; TOPSY-TURVY; TUPSIE-TURVIE; TOPSI-TURVY; TOPSY-TURVEY; TOPSOLTIRIA (Scots); TAPSALTEERIE (Scots); TAPSIE-TEERIE (Scots); TOP-TURVYE; TOPSEY; TURVY-TOPSY; TOPSYD-TURVEY; TOP-SIDE-TURVEY; TOPSIDE-TURVY; TOPSYTURN; TOPSITURN; TOP-SIETURN; TOPSYTURNY; TOPSI-TURNIE; TOPSIETURN; TOPSI-TURN; TOPSIDE-TURNED; TOPSET-TORVIE; TOPSET-TURVIE; TOPSET-TIRVI; TOPSIDE THE OTHER WAY; TOPSIDE TOTHERWAY; TOPSIDE TURF-WAY; TOSSY-TAIL.

1528. ROY, *Rede Me, &c.* [ARBER], 51. He tourneth all thynge TOPSY TERVY.

1547. HEYWOOD, *Dialogues* [PEARSON, *Works* (1874), vi. 214]. [TOPSIDE-TURNED.]

1583. STANYHURST, *Æneis*, ii. [ARBER, 33, 59]. TOPSIDE TURVEY. *Ibid.* (1586), *Descr. Ireland*, 26. 2. The estate of that flourishing towne was turned arsie versie, TOPSIDE THE OTHER WAIE.

1586. [FOSTER, *Notes and Queries*, 5 S. II. 478. In Bodleian MS. Rawl. Poet. 25 (which is dated 1694–5, and is a copy of a MS. written not later than 1586), on the reverse of sign. E 7, eleventh line, I find the phrase TOPSIDE TURFWAY.]

1589. HUGHES, *Misf. Arthur* [DODSLEY, *Old Plays* (HAZLITT), iv. 324]. There fortune laid the prime of Britain's pride, There laid her pomp, all TOPSY-TURVY turn'd.

1594. KYD, *Cornelia* [DODSLEY, *Old Plays* (REED), ii. 301]. When thwarting destiny, at Africk walls, Did TOPSIDE-TURVEY turn their common-wealth.

1596. SPENSER, *Fairy Queen*, v. viii. 42. At last they have all overthrowne to grounde Quite TOPSIDE TURVEY.

1598. SHAKSPEARE, 1 *Henry IV.*, iv. 1. We shall o'er-turn it TOPSIE-TURVY down.

1605. SYLVESTER, *Du Bartas*, ii. His trembling tent all TOPSIE TURUIE wheels. *Ibid.*, 'The Vocation,' 744. He breaketh in through thickest of his foes And by his travail TOPSI-TURNETH them. *Ibid.*, 'Schisme,' 993. Now Nereus foams, and now the furious waues All TOPSIE-TURNED by the Æolian slaues Do mount and roule.

1606. RICH, *Farewell to Mil. Life* (1846), 29. Now, behoulde, all . . . my purposes tourned cleane TOPSE-TURVE.

1612. CHAPMAN, *Widows' Tears*, v. In this TOPSY-TURVY world friendship and bosom-kindness are but made covers for mischief.

1617. MINSHEU, *Guide to Tongues*, s.v. TOPSITURNIE, arsiversie.

1625. BURTON, *Anat. Melan.*, III. II. iii. 3. Would rather have the common-wealth turned TOPSIE TURVIE than her tires marred.

1653. URQUHART, *Rabelais*, i. xi. This little lecher was always groping his nurses and governesses, upside down, arsiversy, TOPSITURVY.

1654. H. L'ESTRANGE, *Reign K. Charles* (1655), 75. Thus were all things strangely turned . . . TOPSIDE THE OTHERWAIE.

1664. COTTON, *Virgil Travestie* (1770), 61. Then, turning TOPSEY on her Thumb, says, Look, heres Supernaculum. *Ibid.*, 288. If I had not knock'd him down, And turn'd him TOPSY-TURVY under.

1694. CONGREVE, *Double-dealer*, v. All turned TOPSY-TURVY, as sure as a gun.

1713. ADDISON, *Guardian*, 154. I found nature turned TOPSIDE TURVY; women changed into men, and men into women.

1740. RICHARDSON, *Pamela*, ii. 40. My poor mind is all TOPSY-TURVIED.

1759–67. STERNE, *Tristram Shandy*, iii. 169. With all my precautions how was my system turned TOPSIDE TURVY!

1765. TUCKER, *Light of Nature*, II. ii. 23. His words are to be turned TOPSIDE TOTHER WAY to understand them.

d. 1774. GOLDSMITH, *Hyperbole.* Here the winds not only blow together, but they turn the whole body of the ocean TOPSY-TURVY.

1796. REYNOLDS, *Fortune's Fool*, Epil. What a bonnet! why it looks quite scurvy, It's like a coal-scuttle turn'd TOPSY-TURVY.

d. 1796. BURNS, *Green Grow the Rashes*, 3. An' war'ly cares an' war'ly men May a' gae TAPSALTEERIE, O!

1834. SOUTHEY, *Doctor*, xxxix. In the TOPSY-TURVEYING course of time Hexthorp has become part of the soke of Doncaster.

1837. CARLYLE, *Fr. Revol.*, II. I. x. Then is it verily, as in Herr Tieck's drama, a *verkeherte welt*, or world TOPSYTURVIED.

1840. THACKERAY, *Paris Sketch Book*, 'Madame Sand.' 'Valentine' was followed by 'Lelia,' . . . a regular TOPSYTURVYFICATION of morality, a thieves' and prostitutes' apotheosis.

1851. HAWTHORNE, *Seven Gables*, i. The TOPSY-TURVY commonwealth of sleep.

d. 1878. BOWLES [MERRIAM, *Life*, II. 159]. It is very hard to keep it [optimistic faith] fresh and strong in the presence . . . of such TOPSY-TURNING of right and wrong.

1879. ELIOT, *Theoph. Such*, x. Insane patients whose system, all out of joint, finds matter for screaming laughter in mere TOPSY-TURVY.

1885. *D. Teleg.*, 26 Nov., 2. Vivisection is TOPSYTURVYFIED in a manner far from pleasing to humanity. *Ibid.* (1886), 5 Feb. Has done some clever things in his time, can sing a good song, and might well be employed for Faust viewed TOPSITURVILY.

1885. *Athenæum*, 21 Mar., 384. The view of cynical TOPSYTURVYDOM which has been so long worked with success at length shows signs of exhaustion.

1890. *Notes and Queries*, 7 S. x. 286. Under the heading TOPSY-TURVYDOM, the author says . . . the Japanese do many things in a way that runs directly counter to European ideas.

TOP-YOB, *subs. phr.* (back slang).—A pot-boy.

TORCH-CUL, *subs. phr.* (old).—BUMFODDER (*q.v.*)—B. E. and GROSE.

TORCH-RACE, *subs. phr.* (Winchester: obsolete). — Formerly, part of the breaking-up ceremony of the winter half-year. On the last morning the boys, after early chapel, rushed out of gates, each bearing a burning birch broom, up College Street and along the wall of the close up to the old White Hart Inn, where breakfast was prepared before the chaises started. This subsequently gave way to a race of Seniors in sedan chairs.

TORMENTOR, *subs.* (nautical).—1. A long iron fork: used by cooks at sea.

2. (theatrical).—A first groove wing.

3. (common). — A BACK-SCRATCHER (*q.v.*), sense 1.

TORMENTOR-OF-CATGUT, *subs. phr.* (old).—A fiddler; a CATGUT-SCRAPER (GROSE).

TORMENTOR-OF-SHEEPSKIN, *subs. phr.* (old).—A drummer (GROSE).

TORN-DOWN, *subs.* (prov. and American).—An unruly, unmanageable person: as *adj.*=(1) rebellious; (2) overpowering.

1870. BAKER, *New Timothy*, xxxii. You know I was a girl onst; led the General a dance of it, I tell you. Yes, a real TORN-DOWN piece I was.

TORPID (or **TOGGER**), *subs.* (Oxford).—(1) A second-class racing eight: corresponding to the Cambridge SLOGGER (*q.v.*); (2) one of the crew; and (3) in *pl.* the Lent races: also as *adj.*

1853. BRADLEY, *Verdant Green*, II. xii. The Misses Green [saw] their brother pulling in one of the fifteen TORPIDS . . . immediately in the wake of the other boats.

1861. HUGHES, *Tom Brown at Oxford*, xxvii. The TORPIDS being filled with the refuse of the rowing men—generally awkward or very young oarsmen—find some difficulty in the act of tossing.

1884. *Pall Mall Gazette*, 19 Feb. Twenty-six TORPID eights were out at Oxford in training for the races. *Ibid.*, 26 Feb. An undergraduate who is one of their best TORPIDS.

1889. *Felstedian*, Feb., 11. After the TORPIDS will come the Clinker Forms—an institution hitherto unknown in Oxford.

1890. DICKENS, *Dict. Oxford*, 18. The TORPID Races last six days.

1900. *Westminster Gazette*, 21 Feb., 8. 3. Oxford University TORPIDS. These races were concluded to-day.

1900. *St. James's Gaz.*, 19 Feb. 6. 2. The TORPID races were continued at Oxford on Saturday in fine and pleasant weather, the attendance being large.

4. (Harrow).—A boy who has not been two years in the school.

TORRAC, *subs.* (back slang).—A carrot. 'Ekat a TORRAC'=an obscene retort.

TORRIL, *subs.* (HALLIWELL).—A worthless woman, or horse.

TORTURER OF ANTHEMS, *subs. phr.* (old).—A chorister; a HALLELUJAH HOWLER (*q.v.*).

1809. MALKIN, *Gil Blas* [ROUTLEDGE], 170. 'I am perfectly well acquainted with that city,' said the brazen-lunged TORTURER OF ANTHEMS.

TORTLE, *verb.* (American: Philadelphia).—To shamble away.

1837. J. C. NEAL, *Charcoal Sketches*. Put on your skeets and TORTLE.

TORTOISE.—*See* PUMP AND TORTOISE.

TORY, *subs.* (old: long recognised).—(1) Orig. (Irish)=a marauder: spec. a bandit (16th century) who, to cover lawlessness, took up arms for the King. Hence (2) a bully, a 'terror'; and (3) a generic reproach: *e.g.*, (*a*) a sympathiser with, disbeliever in, or supposed abettor of the Popish plot; (*b*) one who refused to concur in the Exclusion Act confirming the succession to the throne to Protestants, a measure which was directly aimed at the Duke of York, afterwards James II.; and (*c*), collectively, the Court as distinguished from the Country party, or WHIGS (*q.v.*). Subsequently TORY assumed its modern meaning: *i.e.*, one upholding the existing order of things in Church and State, as opposed to LIBERAL, *i.e.*, one who sought, by experimental legislation, to remedy admitted or supposed disabilities. About 1832 TORY began to be superseded by 'Conservative'; indeed the march of time has now (1903) considerably modified the old TORY political ideas.

1566. *Irish State Papers*. That Irish Papists . . . have returned into Ireland, occasioning the increase of TORIES and other lawless persons.

[?] BISHOP, *Marrow of Astrology*, 43. And now I must leave the orb of Jupiter, and drop down a little lower to the sphere of Mars, who is termed a TORY amongst the stars.

1680. [PINNOCK, *Goldsmith's Hist. Eng.* (1873), 252. The year 1680 is remarkable for the introduction of the well-known epithets Whig and TORY. The former was given to the popular party, from their pretended affinity to the fanatical conventiclers of Scotland, who were known by the name of Whigs. The latter was given to the courtiers, from a supposed resemblance between them and the Popish banditti in Ireland, to whom the appellation of TORIES was affixed. Thus these two ridiculous words came into general use, and have continued ever since to mark rival parties, though with very different meanings.]

1681. DRYDEN, *Absalom and Achit.*, 'To Reader.' Wit and fool are consequents of Whig and TORY; and every man is a knave or an ass to the contrary side. *Ibid.*, *Kind Keeper*, iv. 1. Lift up your voices . . . you TORY-RORY jades.

1694. MOTTEUX, *Pant. Prog.* Braggadocios, TORY-RORY rakes and tantivy boys.

1695. *Laws of William III.* [RIBTON-TURNER, *Vagrants and Vagrancy*, 396]. The frequent robberies, murders, and other notorious felonies, committed by robbers, rapparees, and TORIES, upon their keeping hath greatly discouraged the replanting of . . . [Ireland].

c. 1696. B. E., *Dict. Cant. Crew*, s.v. TORIES, Zealous Sticklers for the Prerogative and Rights of the Crown, in behalf of the Monarchy; also Irish thieves, or *Rapparies*.

1706. PHILLIPS, *World of Words*, s.v. Moss-troopers, a sort of rebels in the northern part of Scotland, that live by robbery and spoil, like the TORIES in Ireland, or the banditti in Italy.

1714. HEARNE, *Diary*, 25 Sep. King George hath begun to change all the ministers, and to put in the whiggs . . . to the grievous mortification of that party called TORIES.

1719. DURFEY, *Pills to Purge*, etc., i. 43. To oagle there a TORY tall, or a little Whig, Defying the Pretender.

1725. SWIFT, *Letter*, 11 Sep. There is hardly a whig in Ireland who would allow a potato and butter-milk to a reputed TORY.

1785. GROSE, *Vulg. Tongue*, s.v. TORY. An advocate for absolute monarchy and church power: also, an Irish vagabond, robber, or rapparee.

1849. MACAULAY, *Hist. Eng.*, ii. At this time were first heard two nicknames which, though originally given in insult, were soon assumed with pride. . . . It is a curious circumstance that one . . . was of Scotch, and the other of Irish, origin. Both in Scotland and in Ireland, misgovernment had called into existence bands of desperate men, whose ferocity was heightened by religious enthusiasm. . . . Thus the appellation of Whig was fastened on the Presbyterian zealots of Scotland, and was transferred to those English politicians who showed a disposition to oppose the court, and to treat Protestant nonconformists with indulgence. The bogs of Ireland, at the same time, afforded a refuge to Popish outlaws, much resembling those who were afterwards known as Whiteboys. These men were then called TORIES. The name of TORY was therefore given to Englishmen who refused to concur in excluding a Roman Catholic prince from the throne.

1886. *Fortnightly Rev.*, xxxix. 136. It was never certain whether he was going to nobble the TORIES, or square the Radicals.

1887. *Contemp. Rev.*, ii. 4. The party led by Sir Robert Peel no longer called itself 'TORY,' but Conservative.

4. (American). — A loyalist: during the period of the War of Independence. Hence any one favouring the claims of Great Britain against the revolted Colonies.

1821. COOPER, *Spy*, xxix. Washington will not trust us with the keeping of a suspected TORY, if we let the rascal trifle in this manner with the corps. *Ibid.*, xxii. Surrender, you servants of King George . . . or I will let a little of your TORY blood from your veins.

1855–9. IRVING, *Life of Washington*, ii. 371. It was said that the TORIES were arming and collecting in the Highlands, under the direction of distinguished officers, to aid the conspiracies formed by Gov. Tryon and his adherents.

TOSH, *subs.* (public schools').—1. A bath, a foot-pan. Also as *verb* =to splash, to douse, to throw water over a person: *e.g.*, 'He TOSHED his house beak by mistake, and got three hundred'; TOSH-POND (Royal Military Academy)=the bathing-pond.

1881. PASCOE, *Life in Our Public Schools*. A TOSH PAN, an important utensil for periodical ablutions on stated nights, is also provided.

2. *See* TUSH.

3. (University). — Nonsense; ROT (*q.v.*): 'What frightful TOSH' (*Oxf. Mag.* 26 Oct. 1892).

TOSHER, *subs.* (Oxford University).—1. An unattached student.

2. (nautical).—A small fishing vessel.

1885. *Daily Telegraph*, 26 Nov. Thus a TOSHER is not a longshore driver, though both little vessels are employed in catching what they can close into the land.

3. (HOTTEN).—'A man who steals copper from ships' bottoms in the Thames.'

TOSH-SOAP, *subs. phr.* (public schools').—Cheese: *see* TOSH.

TOSS, *subs.* (old colloquial).—1. agitation, commotion, anxiety.

1666. PEPYS, *Diary*, 2 June. This put us at the Board into a TOSSE. *Ibid.* (1667), 10 Oct. Lord what a TOSSE I was for some time in, that they could not justly tell where it [gold that he had buried] was.

1870. JUDD, *Margaret*, ii. 5 'We are all in a TOSS in our neighbourhood,' said Mistress Pottle.

2. (Billingsgate).—A measure of sprats.

Verb. (colloquial).—To drink at a draught, to gulp: *e.g.*, to TOSS a can of beer: also to TOSS OFF: *cf.* TOAST. Hence TOSS-POT=a drunkard (GROSE): *see* LUSHINGTON; TOSSED (or TOSTICATED)=drunk: *see* SCREWED.

1560. PILKINGTON, *Sermons* (Parker Soc.) [OLIPHANT, *New Eng.*, i. 558. Among the new substantives are gamester . . . lip-labour] a TOSSPOT.

1582. HAKLUYT, *Voyages*, I. 253. They returne to their old intemperancie of drinking, for they are notable TOSSPOTS.

1583. ASCHAM, *Scholemaster*, iv. 35. A certain friar TOSSING THE POT, and drinking very often at the table was reprehended by the priour.

1592. NASHE, *Summer's Last Will* [DODSLEY, *Old Plays* (HAZLITT), viii. 59]. Rise up, Sir Robert TOSS-POT [*Here he dubs Will Summer with the Black-Jack*].

1599. HALL, *Satires*, I. ii. 26. Now TOSS they bowls of Bacchus' boiling blood.

[?] *Robin Hood* [CHILD, *Ballads*. v. 375]. For in a brave vein they TOSSED OFF the bouls.

d. 1637. P. HOLLAND, *Plinie*, XXIII. xviii. Our lustie TOSS-POTS and swill-bowls.

1648–50. BRAITHWAIT, *Barnaby's Jo.*, II. 57. There I TOSSED it with my Skinkers.

1653. URQUHART, *Rabelais*, I. v. Thus became TOM TOSSPOT rich.

1670. COTTON, *Virgil Travestie* (1770), 129. Away he flies Ere TOSS-POT could unglue his eyes.

1695. CONGREVE, *Love for Love*, iii. 15. I mean to TOSS A CAN, and remember my sweetheart afore I turn in.

1719. DURFEY, *Pills to Purge*, vi. 201. We TOSS about the never-failing Cann, We drink and piss . . . and drink to piss again.

1725. BAILEY, *Erasmus*, 'Epith. P. Ægidus.' The husband . . . has been call'd Blockhead, TOSS-POT, Swill-Tub.

1820. LAMB, *Two Races of Men*. A good part he drank away (for he was an excellent TOSS-POT).

1821. EGAN, *Life in London*, 75. The soldiers . . . were TOSSING OFF the heavy wet and spirits.

1837. MARRYAT, *Snarleyyow*, xxxii. The corporal produced the bottle and the glass, poured it out, made his military salute, and TOSSED IT OFF.

1841. DICKENS, *Barnaby Rudge*, xiii. To be looked upon as a common pipe-smoker, beer-bibber . . . and TOSS-POT.

Also COLLOQUIALISMS and PHRASES: TO TOSS OUT=(1) to dress hurriedly, and (2) to depart hastily; TO TOSS OFF=(1) *see verb supra*; (2) to do, execute, or turn out quickly: as TO TOSS OFF a poem, a task, or musical performance; (3) to while away (of time), to dispose of easily; and (4)=to masturbate (venery); TO TOSS UP (or TO TOSS)=(1) to decide a matter by 'skying' a coin (GROSE): also as *subs.* (or TOSS-UP)=an even chance, and TO WIN THE TOSS=to be successful; TO TOSS UP=(2) to prepare rough and readily (of food).

[?] *Richard Cœur de Leon* [WEBER, *Met. Rom.*, II. 170]. Lordynges, now ye have herd . . . How Kyng Richard with his maystry WAN THE TOSS off Sudan Turry.

c. 1692. KING, *Vestry*. On Saturday stew'd beef, with something nice, Provided quick, and TOSS'D UP in a trice.

1759. GOLDSMITH, *Bee*, No. 2. I . . . walked behind a damsel TOSSED OUT in all the gaiety of fifteen; her dress was loose, unstudied, and seemed the result of conscious beauty.

1809. MALKIN, *Gil Blas* [ROUTLEDGE], 407. It is a TOSS UP who fails and who succeeds: the wit of to-day is the blockhead of to-morrow.

1851. HAWTHORNE, *Seven Gables*, vii. Poor Hepzibah was seeking for some . . . tit-bit which . . . she might TOSS UP for breakfast.

1851–61. MAYHEW, *Lon. Lab.*, I. 206. TO TOSS THE PIEMAN is a favourite pastime with costermongers' boys, and all that class. If the pieman WINS THE TOSS he receives a penny without giving a pie; if he lose, he hands over a pie for nothing. *Ibid.* II. 412. They spend . . . what money they may have in TOSSING for beer, till they are either drunk or penniless.

1853. DICKENS, *Bleak House*, xiii. 'I haven't the least idea,' said Richard, musing, 'what I had better be. Except that I am quite sure I don't want to go into the Church, it's a TOSS-UP.'

1857. HUGHES, *Tom Brown's School-days*, i. 5. Hasn't old Brooke WON THE TOSS, with his lucky halfpenny, and got choice of goals?

1870. JUDD, *Margaret*, ii. 1. Have you read *Cynthia?* It is a delightful thing TO TOSS OFF a dull hour with.

1872. ELIOT, *Middlemarch*, lxxxiii. It is a mere TOSS-UP whether I shall ever do more than keep myself decently.

1882. ASHTON, *Social Life*, etc., II. 35. He TOSSED UP whether he should hang or drown. The coin fell on its edge in the clay, and saved his life for that time.

1884. *Century Mag.*, xxxviii. 856. One of the most earnest advocates of the measure said, 'Tis the TOSS of a copper.'

1885. *D. Teleg.*, 23 Sep. There may have been instances where juries have 'TOSSED UP' sooner than remain to convince an obstinate colleague.

1886. *Field*, 4 Sep. [It] looked a TOSS-UP as to which would arrive home first.

1888. KIPLING, *Only a Subaltern*. 'He'll do,' said the doctor quietly; 'it must have been a TOSS-UP all through the night.'

See BLANKET.

TOSS-PLUME, *subs. phr.* (old).—A braggart; a swaggerer.

TOSSY, *adj.* (colloquial).—Off-hand; careless: also TOSSILY, *adv.*

1849. KINGSLEY, *Yeast*, vii. Argemone answered by some TOSSY commonplace. *Ibid.* She answered TOSSILY enough.

TOSSY-TAIL, *adv. phr.* (provincial).—TOPSY-TURVY (*q.v.*).

TOSTICATION, *subs.* (old). — Perplexity; commotion: whence TOSTICATED=(1) restless, worried; and (2) 'intoxicated': also TOSSICATED. *See* TOSS, *verb*.

17[?]. SWIFT, *Jour. to Stella* [*Century*]. I have been so TOSTICATED about since my last that I could not go on in my journal manner.

1748. RICHARDSON, *Clarissa*, III. lxviii. I want those TOSTICATIONS (thou seest how women and women's words fill my mind) to be over . . . that I may sit down quietly, and reflect.

TOT, *subs.* (common).—1. Generic for anything small: spec. an endearment: *e.g.*, a wee TOT = a little child: *cf.* TODDLEKINS. Also (2) a measure holding a gill; whence a nip or dram, a GO (*q.v.*); as *verb*=to drink: *see* TOTE.

1725. RAMSAY, *Gentle Shepherd* [*Works*, II. 81]. Sic wee TOTS toolying at your knee.

1868. WHYTE MELVILLE, *White Rose*, II. i. He . . . often found himself pining for . . . the glare of the camp-fires, the fragrant fumes of the honey-dew, and the TOT of rum.

1886. *St. James's Gaz.*, 10 Sep. Haydn . . . liked company; but if a guest stayed beyond a certain period, the great composer would suddenly start up, tap his forehead and say, 'Excuse me, I have a TOT'; by which he meant that he had a thought, and must go to his study to jot it down. A minute after he would return, looking all the brighter; and as forgetful as the Irish judge of La Rochefoucauld's maxim—that you may hoodwink one person, but not all the world. The expression, 'a TOT of spirits,' is said to have had this respectable origin.

1900. SAVAGE, *Brought to Bay*, vii. Raoul told a tale of a repentant mother's interest in the child which she had left as a wee TOT of two.

1901. WALKER, *In the Blood*, 294. Up came the children, wild-eyed, unkempt, dirty, ragged, yet brown, hardy, and active little TOTS.

3. *See* TOTTERY.

4. (common).—A bone: spec. (army)=kitchen refuse and (general) all kinds of waste, or marine store stuff. Hence TOTTING=bone-picking, dust-heap sifting; TOT-PICKER (or RAKER)=a scavenger. THE OLD TOTS=the 17th Lancers; the 'Death or Glory' Boys: in allusion to the regimental badge of 'A Skull and Crossbones.'

1884. GREENWOOD, *Little Raga-muffins*. P'r'aps he's goin' A-TOTTIN' (picking up bones).

1899. WYNDHAM, *Queen's Service*, 22. Anything . . . left on the TOT, or bone, is the recognised perquisite of the orderly-man.

Verb. (colloquial). — (1) To count; to reckon: also TO TOT UP (or TOTE). Also (2)=to wager all: *cf.* TOTE *infra*. Hence as *subs.* = an exercise in addition;

TOT-BOOK=a book containing examples for practice; THE TOTE (or THE WHOLE TOTE)=all, everything; TO TOTE FAIR=to reckon accurately: hence (South and Western American)=to act honestly; to PLAY THE GAME (*q.v.*).

1766. BROOKE, *Fool of Quality*, ii. 211. These TOTTED together will make a pretty beginning of my little project.

[?]. THACKERAY [*Century*]. 'A Night's Pleasure.' Seventeen hundred and twenty-five goes of alcohol in a year, we TOTTED it UP one night at the bar. *Ibid.* (1860–3), *Roundabout Papers*, xix. The last two TOT UP the bill.

1852. SAVAGE, *R. Medlicott* (1864), III. ii. 'One thousand eight hundred,' said Hyacinth, TOTTING his entries.

18[?]. *Chicago Tribune* [BARTLETT]. The predicament [of assassination] in Texas can be avoided by always 'TOTING FAIR' with everybody. Indeed, if you TOTE FAIR, you need TOTE no weapons; that is, you can go unarmed.

1895. *Notes and Queries*, 2 S. viii. 338. I have frequently heard in Lincolnshire the phrase, 'Come, TOTE IT UP, and tell me what it comes to.'

1896. *Athenæum*, No. 3268, 757. Graduated Exercises in Addition (TOTS and Cross TOTS, Simple and Compound).

TOTE, *subs.* (common). — A teetotaller: also (in sarcasm, with a glance at TOT=to drink drams) =a hard drinker.

c. 1870. *Music Hall Song*, 'Hasn't got over it yet.' As well we'd another old chum, By all of his mates called the TOTE, So named on account of the rum He constantly put down his throat.

c. 1889. *Music Hall Song*, 'Toper and Tote.' You'll always find the sober TOTE With a few pounds at command.

See TOT.

Verb. (American).—To carry; to bear a burden; to endure. Hence TOTE-LOAD=as much as one can carry; TOTE-ROAD=a road or track.

18[?]. *Negro Melody*, 'Come back, Massa' [BARTLETT]. De 'possum and de coon are as sassy as you please, Since all de blooded dogs were TOTED off by fleas; De measles TOTED off all de cunnin' little nigs, An' de sojers ob de army hab TOTED off de pigs.

18[?]. *Old Negro Song* [BARTLETT]. Dey say fetch an' TOTE 'stead of bring and carry, An' dat dey call grammar!—by de Lawd Harry.

18[?]. *Pickings from the Picayune*, 120. The watchman arrested Mr. Wimple for disturbing the peace, and TOTED him off to the calaboose.

18[?]. *Chronicles of Pineville*, 169. My gun here TOTES fifteen buckshot and a ball, and slings 'em to kill.

1843. CARLTON, *New Purchase*, I. 167. Here a boy was ferociously cutting wood—there one TOTING wood.

1844. *Major Jones's Courtship*, 39. The militia had everlastin' great long swords as much as they could TOTE. *Major Jones's Travels*. I could never bear to see a white gall TOATIN' my child about, and waitin' on me like a nigger: it would hurt my conscience.

c. 1869. DONNELY, *Speech in Congress* [*S.J. and C.*]. I cannot think Mr. Ulysses S. Grant will degenerate into a kind of hand-organ to be TOTED around on the back of a gentleman from Illinois.

1870. *Science*, XI. 242. I should also like to know how much a man can TOTE, how much a woman can TOTE, and how long a time, without resting, the TOTING may go on.

1873. *Trans. Am. Philol. Soc.*, xiii. 211. His report of his having induced the aristocratic Navajos to TOTE his luggage was received from the mouth of Gen'l Kane with a good-natured amused derision.

1879. *Scribner's Mag.*, VIII. 496. Its forests are still so unbroken by any highways save the streams and the rough TOTE-ROADS of the lumber-crews that this region cannot become populous with visitors.

1884. CLEMENS, *Huck. Finn.* I TOTED UP a load, and went back and sat down on the bow of the skiff to rest.

1885. *Century Mag.*, xl. 224. The bullies used to . . . make them TOTE more than their share of the log.

1890. *Cent. Dict.*, s.v. TOTE. Origin unknown; usually said to be an African word introduced by Southern negroes, but the African words which have come into English use through Southern negroes are few and doubtful . . . and do not include verbs.

TOTER, *subs.* (old colloquial).—A piper [GIFFORD: a low term].

1633. JONSON, *Tale of a Tub*, iii. 3. His name was Vadian, and a cunning TOTER.

TOTHER (TONE), *indef. prons.* (once literary: now vulgar).—The other; the one (THE=*thet*, the old neuter article); TONE AND TOTHER=both; TOTHER-EMMY=the others.

[12[?]. *Old Eng. Homilies*, 2 S. 175. Þat ON is Seint Peter and Þat OÐER is Seint Andrew.]

1340. HAMPOLE, *Prose Treat.* [E.E.T.S.], 29. Thou sulde doo bathe . . . the TANE AND THE TOTHER.

1360. CHAUCER, *Rom. of Rose*, 5559. The TOON yeveth conysaunce, And the TOTHER ignoraunce.

1380. WYCLIF, *Bible*, Luke xvi. 13. He schal hate oon, and loue the TOTHER.

[?]. *MS. Cantab.*, Ff. ii. 38. f. 74. The TOTHER day on the same wyse, As the kynge fro the borde can ryse.

1530. TYNDALE [OLIPHANT, *New Eng.*, i. 429. Tyndale sometimes, like his enemy More, uses the old form of 1180, 'THE TONE, THE TOTHER.']

1551. MORE, *Worship of Images*, 'Utopia,' Int. xci. Many other thinges touchyng the pestilent secte of Luther and Tyndale, by the TONE bygone in Saxony: and by the TOTHER laboured to be brought into England.

1565-7. GOLDING, *Ovid*, 'Pref.,' sign. A7. And where the TONE gives place, There still the other presseth in his place. *Ibid.*, ii. 9. So was Licaon made a woolfe; And Jove became a bull, The TONE for using crueltie, the TOTHER for his trull.

1573. TUSSER, *Good Husbandrie*, 145. [OLIPHANT, *New Eng.*, i. 583. The old THE TONE (here followed by THE TOTHER) is contracted into TONE.]

d. 1586. Sir P. SYDNEY, *Harington's Ariosto*, Notes, Bxi. As far from want, as far from vaine expence; TONE doth enforce, the other doth entice.

1591. HARINGTON, *Ariost.*, i. 18. And that with force, with cunning, nor with paine, The TONE of them could make the other yield.

1727. GAY, *Beggars' Opera*, ii. 2. How happy could I be with either, Were T'OTHER dear charmer away.

ONE WITH OTHER, *subs. phr.* (venery). — Copulation: *see* GREENS and RIDE.

T'OTHER-DAY, *subs. phr.* (common). — Spec. the day before yesterday, but frequently used in an indefinite sense.

T'OTHER SCHOOL, *subs. phr.* (Winchester).—1. One's former school; (2) any school not a public school. As *adj.* = NON-LICET (*q.v.*), or unbecoming because more or less alien to Winchester. T'OTHER-UN (Charterhouse) = a private school.

T'OTHER-SIDER, *subs. phr.* (Victoria: now rare). — A convict: *see* SIDNEY-SIDER.

TOTTER, *verb.* (Old Cant). — To hang; to swing on the gallows.

1630. FLETCHER, *Night-Walker*, iii. 3. I would lose a limb to see their rogueships TOTTER.

TOTTERARSE, *subs.* (provincial).—Seesaw.

TOTTERY, *adj.* (colloquial). — Shaky; unsteady: also TOTTLISH (or TOTTY). Hence TOTTLE, *verb* = to walk unsteadily; TOTTY-HEADED = giddy, hare-brained (B. E. and GROSE); TOT =a simpleton: *see* BUFFLE.

1383. CHAUCER, *Cant. Tales*, 'Reeve's Tale,' 333. Myn heed is TOTY of my swynk to-night.

M

[?]. *MS. Rawl.*, C. 86. So TOTY was the brayn of his hede, That he desired for to go to bede.

1819. SCOTT, *Ivanhoe*, xxxii. I was somewhat TOTTY when I received the good Knight's blow.

1855. HAMMOND, *Wild Northern Scenes*, 207. Our little boat was light and TOTLISH; and, as I pressed the trigger of my rifle, it rolled slightly over.

1861. HUGHES, *Tom Brown at Oxford*, vi. When I looked up and saw what a TOTTERY performance it was, I concluded to give them a wide berth.

1895. *Harper's Mag.*, lxxxix. 116. I find I can't lift anything into this canoe alone—it's so TOTTLISH.

TOTTIE, *subs.* (common).—A high-class harlot: somewhat of an endearment: *cf.* TOT.

TOUCH, *subs.* (old).—1. Worth; value; cost: usually in combination, as a GUINEA-TOUCH=something costing a guinea; a PENNY-TOUCH = a penn'orth. Also (Eton)=a present of money.

1720. Sir ERASMUS PHILLIPP, *Diary*, 22 Sep. At night went to the ball at the Angel, a guinea-TOUCH.

d. 1745. SWIFT [*Century*]. Print my preface in such form as, in the bookseller's phrase, will make a sixpenny TOUCH.

1864. HOTTEN, *Slang Dict.*, s.v. TOUCH . . . Sometimes said of a woman to imply her worthlessness, as, 'Only a HALF-CROWN TOUCH.'

2. (old colloquial).—A trick; a dodge; a contrivance: *cf. verb.* 1. TO DO A TOUCH=to make shift; to manage somehow.

1530. PALSGRAVE, *Lang. Fran.* TOUCHE, a crafty dede, *tour*.

1535. JOY, *Apology to Tyndale* [ARBER], 25. [The word TOUCHE is used for *trick*.]

3. (colloquial). — Generic for the minimum of effort or effect: *e.g.*, a TOUCH (= suspicion) of frost; a TOUCH OF THE TAR-BRUSH = slightly coloured (of mixed white and black blood); a TOUCH (=a spice) of humour; a slight TOUCH = a gentle reminder: hence TO TOUCH UPON =to dwell lightly on a matter; a TOUCH (=a pricking) of conscience; a TOUCH (=a trace) of pity; a TOUCH (=a foretaste) of spring; a TOUCH (=a twinge) of pain; TO TOUCH OFF=to outline, draft, or produce hastily or by a few strokes of pen, pencil, or brush; TO TOUCH UP=(1) to gently jog the memory, (2) to urge, egg on, or spur forward, (3) to improve, mend, or add to (*cf.* TO TOUCH OFF and TOUCHY): also *see verb*. 4: hence TOUCH-UP, *subs.* =(1) a reminder, (2) a spur to action, (3) a finishing or improving stroke.

1597. SHAKSPEARE, *Richard III.*, i. 2. 71. No beast so fierce but knows some TOUCH of pity.

1648. GAUDEN, *Eikon Basilike*. I never bare any TOUCH of conscience with greater regret.

1715. ADDISON, *Freeholder*, No. 44. What he saw was only her natural countenance, TOUCHED UP with the usual improvements of an aged coquette.

d. 1774. GOLDSMITH, *Clubs*. I was upon this whispered . . . that I should now see something TOUCHED OFF to a nicety.

1821. GALT, *Ayrshire Legatees*, viii. He's such a funny man, and TOUCHES OFF the Londoners to the nines.

1851. HAWTHORN, *Seven Gables*, x. Give me a rose that I may press its thorns and prove myself awake by the sharp TOUCH of pain!

d. 1878. BRYANT, *Song Sparrow*. While the air has no TOUCH of spring. Bird of promise! we hear thee sing.

1886. *Field*, 22 Jan. A TOUCH of frost.

1890. *Notes and Queries*, 7 S., x. 118. Faint in some parts, very dark in others. If the plate was worn it has been TOUCHED afterwards.

See TOUCH-AND-GO.

Verb. (old colloquial). — 1. Generic for getting: spec. (GROSE) to get money in hand. Also in modern usage = to obtain speciously or secretly, by methods that will not bear too close a scrutiny; and hence (thieves') = to steal: in Australia to act unfairly: *cf. subs.*

1726. VANBRUGH and CIBBER, *Provoked Husband* [OLIPHANT, *New Eng.*, ii. 159. A man TOUCHES money (obtains it), a new sense of the verb].

1749. SMOLLETT, *Gil Blas* (1812), III. ii. All that I have been able to TOUCH being no more than three thousand ducats.

1771. SMOLLETT, *Humphry Clinker* (1900), ii. 134. England, I conceive, may TOUCH about one million sterling a year.

1796. HOLMAN, *Abroad and at Home*, i. 3. I could not go abroad without her, so I TOUCH'D father's cash.

1862. *Cornhill*, Nov., 648. We have just TOUCHED for a rattling stake of sugar at Brum.

1877. HORSLEY, *Jottings from Jail*. One day I took the rattler from Broad Street to Acton. I did not TOUCH them, but worked my way to Shepherd's Bush.

1879. *Macm. Mag.*, xl. 502. I TOUCHED for a red toy and red tackle.

1888. SIMS, *Plank Bed Ballad* [*Referee*, 12 Feb., 3]. A spark prop a pal . . . and I had TOUCHED.

1888. *St. Louis Globe Democrat*. A dip TOUCHED the Canadian sheriff for his watch and massive chain while he was reading the Riot Act.

c. 1889. *Bird o' Freedom* [S. J. and C.]. He ran against a wealthy friend whom he thought to TOUCH. 'No, my boy,' said the friend, 'I never give or lend money.'

1896. LILLARD, *Poker Stories*, 102. I knew a thing or two about poker, and it would have required George Appo himself to have TOUCHED me for my wad.

1897. MARSHALL, *Pomes*, 17. He lived upon credit, and what he could TOUCH.

2. (colloquial). — To be equal to, capable of, or bear comparison with. TO HAVE A TOUCH = to make an attempt.

1713. STEELE, *Guardian*, No. 82. Mr. William Peer distinguished himself particularly in two characters, which no man ever could TOUCH but himself.

1838. DICKENS, *Oliver Twist*, xliii. Wasn't he always top-sawyer among you all? Is there one of you that could TOUCH him, or come near him?

1851-61. MAYHEW, *Lond. Lab.* I. 162. I thought I'd have a TOUCH at the same thing. But you see I never could rise money enough to make a do of it.

1865. *Major Jack Downing*, 30. The children of Israel going out of Egypt with their flocks and their little ones is no TOUCH to it [*i.e.*, the first day of May in New York].

4. (venery). — To copulate: see RIDE: as *subs.* = the act of kind; whence TOUCH-HOLE = the female *pudendum*: see MONOSYLLABLE; TOUCH-TRAP = the *penis*: see PRICK; TOUCH-CRIB = a brothel. Also (5) (or TO TOUCH UP) to grope a woman; (6) to roke a man; TOUCHABLE = (1) RIPE (*q.v.*), and (2) in trim for the act; also TO TOUCH UP (GROSE) = to masturbate. 'Not to be TOUCHED with a pair of tongs' (of a foundered whore): see BARGE-POLE.

1603. SHAKSPEARE, *Meas. for Meas.* v. Free from TOUCH or soil with her.

1653. URQUHART, *Rabelais*, I. xii. His governesses burst out laughing. . . . One would call it her pillicock . . . her TOUCH-TRAP, her flap-dowdle.

1661. *Merry Drollery* [EBSWORTH], 229. No man will TOUCH her WITHOUT A PAIR OF TONGS.

1668. LESTRANGE, *Quevedo* (1678), 22. Your Beauties can never want gallants to lay their appetites. . . . Whereas nobody will TOUCH the ill-favoured WITHOUT A PAIR OF TONGS.

1670. COTTON, *Virgil Travestie* (1770), 80. If Æneas be a spark they there . . . May take a gentle TOUCH together: So each of other may have Proof.

1719. DURFEY, *Pills to Purge*, iv. 207. But give me the Buxom Country Lass . . . That will take a TOUCH upon the grass, Ay, marry, and thank you too.

1725. BAILEY, *Erasmus*, 'Lying-in Woman.' Would you have me persuade your Husband never to TOUCH you more?

1751. SMOLLETT, *Peregrine Pickle*, lxxxvii. He wrote a letter to Hatchway, desiring him to receive this hedge inamorata, and desired her to be cleaned and clothed in a decent manner . . . so that she should be TOUCHABLE on his arrival.

1772. BRIDGES, *Burlesque Homer*, 361. May I for cats and dogs turn butcher, If ever yet she'd let me TOUCH her.

7. (old). — To arrest (GROSE).

PHRASES AND COLLOQUIALISMS. IN TOUCH WITH = (1) in sympathy, and (2) near at hand; OUT OF TOUCH WITH = (1) antagonistic, and (2) out-of-the-way, un-get-at-able; TO TOUCH ONE = to affect, concern, or influence; TO TOUCH A SORE SPOT (UP, HOME, or ON THE RAWS, etc.), to irritate by allusion or joke, to rub up the wrong way, to clinch an argument, advice, or comment; TRUE AS TOUCH = absolutely true; TO TOUCH BOTTOM (or BEDROCK) = (1) to reach the lowest point, and (2) to get at the truth of matters; TO TOUCH HER UP (nautical) = to shake a vessel by luffing; 'TOUCH POT, TOUCH PENNY' = 'No credit given'; 'TOUCH BONE AND WHISTLE' (GROSE) = 'Anyone having broken wind backwards, according to vulgar law, may be pinched by any of the company till he has touched bone (*i.e.* his teeth) and whistled.'

c. 1400. GENERYDES (E. E. T. S.), 560. With that the quene was wroth in hir maner, Thought she anon this TOWCHITH me right near.

1549. LATIMER, *Serms. bef. Ed. VI.*, III. They keep no TOUCH; they will talk of many gay things; they will pretend this and that, but they keep no promise. *Ibid.* As the text doth rise, I will TOUCH AND GO a little in every place.

1592. SHAKSPEARE, 1 *Henry VI.*, iv. 1. 118. The quarrel TOUCHETH none but us alone.

1633. SHIRLEY, *Bird in a Cage*, iv. 1. If Florence now KEEP TOUCH, we shortly shall Conclude all fear with a glad nuptial.

1634. FORD, *Perkin Warbeck*, ii. 1. Beshrew me, but his words have TOUCH'D me home.

1720. SWIFT, *Elegy on Mr. Demar*. He TOUCHED THE PENCE when others TOUCHED the pot.

1772. GRAVES, *Spiritual Quixote*, iii. 2. We know the custom of such houses, continues he; 'tis TOUCH-POT, TOUCH-PENNY; we only want money's worth for our money.

1838. BECKETT, *Paradise Lost*, 97. He's told by Dominus Factotum, To TOUCH YOU UP about the bottom.

1856. B. TAYLOR, *Northern Travel*, 43. A handsome, lively boy, whose pride was a little TOUCHED by my remonstrances.

[?]. *New Princeton Rev.*, II. 47. We want, with our brethren of the working class, that which we have largely lost . . . that expressive thing which we call TOUCH.

1882. *Pall Mall Gaz.*, 14 Sep. There were frequent halts to enable the regiments to maintain TOUCH.

1889. *Academy*, 1 June, 371. The European in Morocco feels that when he is in company with a Barbary Jew he is IN TOUCH WITH Europe.

See TOUCHED.

TOUCH-AND-GO, *subs.* and *adj.* (colloquial). — 1. Uncertain; risky; nothing to spare; hasty; superficial: of persons and things. As *subs.* = (1) a narrow escape, a close shave; and (2) a trifle. Also A NEAR (or CLOSE) TOUCH (or TOUCHER); AS NEAR AS A TOUCHER = as near as may be,

very nearly. TO TOUCH AND GO (old coaching: *cf.* nautical phrase, TO TOUCH BOTTOM = to graze the shallows) = (1) to drive close enough to TOUCH and escape injury (HOTTEN: a trick of the old jarveys to show their skill); hence (2) applied to anything within an ace of ruin: *cf.* quot. 1549, s.v. TOUCH (phrases).

1831. FERRIER, *Destiny*, iii. So it was with Glenroy and his lady. It had been TOUCH-AND-GO with them for many a day, and now, from less to more, from bad to worse, it ended in a threatened separation.

1860. SALA, *Baddington Peerage*, I. 188. It was a near TOUCHER, though.

1865. DICKENS, *Mutual Friend*, iii. 18. And there we are in four minutes' time, as NEAR AS A TOUCHER. *Ibid.* [ANNANDALE]. The next instant the hind coach passed my engine by a near shave. It was the nearest TOUCH I ever saw.

1883. *Century Mag.*, xxxvi. 127. It was TOUCH AND GO to that degree that they couldn't come near them.

1887. *St. James's Gazette*, 25 Oct. Herr Ludwig had a TOUCH-AND-GO journey before he caught the *Servia*.

1888. *Academy*, 3 Mar., 148. The illusive TOUCH-AND-GO manner.

1889. OLIPHANT, *Poor Gentleman*, xli. It was as Rochford felt, TOUCH AND GO, very delicate work with Sir Edward.

TOUCHED, *adv.* (colloquial). — Slightly crazy; mentally impaired. Hence TOUCH, *subs.* = a kink, a twist: *cf.* Old Eng. *touch* = to infect, blemish, taint.

1704. STEELE, *Lying Lover*, v. 1. Pray mind him not, his brain is TOUCH'D. *Ibid.* (c. 1709), *Tatler*, 178. This TOUCH in the brain of the British subject is certainly owing to the reading newspapers.

1705. VANBRUGH, *Confederacy*, v. 2. Madam, you see master's a little—TOUCHED, that's all.

1897. MARSHALL, *Pomes*, 86. There were some who called her 'TOUCHED,' because she told them plump and plain that she wasn't going to be a fellow's chattel.

1899. WHITEING, *John St.*, ix. He is not to be judged by their law; he has been TOUCHED.

TOUCHER. See TOUCH-AND-GO.

TOUCH-MY-NOB, *subs.* (rhyming). — A shilling; A BOB (*q.v.*): see RHINO.

TOUCH-PIECE, *subs. phr.* (old). — A good-luck piece given by the sovereign to those they 'touched' for the cure of scrofula, or king's evil.

1882. *Athenæum*, 28 Oct. Before the reign of Charles II. no coins were struck specially for TOUCH-PIECES, the gold 'angel' having been used for the purpose. The TOUCH-PIECES are all similar in design. Those of the Pretenders, however, which were struck abroad, are of much better work than those made in England. . . . These TOUCH-PIECES (all of them perforated) are curious relics of a superstition which had existed for many centuries, and was only stamped out on the accession of the Brunswick dynasty.

TOUCHY, *adj.* (old and still colloquial). — 1. Irritable, apt to take offence, all 'angles and corners' [*i.e.*, tetchy]. [JOHNSON: 'a low word.'] Hence TOUCHINESS = sensitiveness, peevishness.

d. 1529. SKELTON, *Works*. [OLIPHANT, *New Eng.*, i. 373. The verb TOUCH gets the new sense of *irritare*; . . . hence our TOUCHY.]

1605. *King Leir and his Three Daughters*. She breeds yong bones, And that is it makes her so TUTCHY sure.

1611. COTGRAVE, *Dict.*, s.v. *Chatouilleux à la poincte*. Quick on the spurre . . . TICHY, that will not endure to be TOUCHED.

1611. FLETCHER, *Maid's Trag.*, iii. Y'are TOUCHIE without all cause.

1628. EARLE, *Microcos.*, 'A Blunt Man.' Hee is TEACHY himself, and seldome to his own abuses replyes but with his Fists.

1628. GAUDEN, *Eikon Basilike*. My friends resented it as a motion not guided with such discretion as the TOUCHINESS of those times required.

1651. RANDOLPH, *Hey for Honesty*, Introduction. This is no age for wasps; 'tis a dangerous TOUCHY age, and will not endure the stinging.

1727. GAY, *Fables*, iv. You tell me that you apprehend My verse may TOUCHY folks offend.

1742. RAY, *North Country Words*, 45. TECHEY for TOUCHY, very inclinable to Displeasure or Anger.

1831. SMITH, *Letters* [DAVIES] You have a little infirmity—tactility or TOUCHINESS.

1844. BARNES, *Poems in Dorset Dialect*, Glossary. TOUCHY . . . very irritable or sensitive, impatient of being even 'touched.'

1885. *Daily Teleg.*, 14 Oct. In South Australia he is exceptionally TOUCHY, and, in particular, you must not interfere with his pipe.

2. (artists'). — Descriptive of a style in which points, broken lines, or touches are employed, as distinguished from firm unbroken line work: *cf.* TOUCH, *verb.* 2.

3. (Christ's Hospital). — Rather: *e.g.*, TOUCHY A LUX = rather a good thing.

TOUGH, *subs.* (American). — A rough; a bully.

1879. *Scribner's Mag.*, viii. 692. The whole appearance of the young TOUGH changed, and the terror and horror that had showed on his face turned to one of low sharpness and evil cunning.

c. 1889. *D. Teleg.* [S. J. and C.]. The TOUGH, his northern appellation changed to "hoodlum," continues to flourish in San Francisco.

Adj. (colloquial). — Generic for difficult, trying, severe: *e.g.*, a TOUGH (= incredible) YARN: 'a long story' (GROSE); a TOUGH (= difficult) JOB; a TOUGH (= severe) REBUKE; a TOUGH (= violent) STORM; a TOUGH (= prolonged) SIEGE; a TOUGH (= stubborn) CUSTOMER: a hard nut to crack. Also TO MAKE IT TOUGH = (1) to raise difficulties, to make much of a small matter, and (2) to take excessive pains; AS TOUGH AS WHITELEATHER (RAY) = as tough as may be.

[?]. *MS. Cantab.*, Ff. v. 48, f. 53. To day thou gate no moné of me, Made thou it never so TOWȜ.

[?]. *Releg. Cent.* ii. 29. Befe and moton wylle serve wele enow; And for to seche so ferre a lytill bakon flyk, Which hath long hanggid, resty and TOW.

1383. CHAUCER, *Cant. Tales* [TYRWHITT], 13,309. And up he goth and maketh it ful TOUGH. *Ibid.*, *Troilus*, v. 101. If that I . . . make it to TOUGH. *Ibid.*, *Booke of Dutchess*, 531. And made it neyther TOUGH ne queint.

c. 1640. HOWELL, *Letters*, I. iv. 15. [Breda] has yielded . . . to Spinola's Hands, after a TOUGH Siege of thirteen months.

1781. COWPER, *Table Talk*, 458. Callous and TOUGH, the reprobated race grows judgment-proof.

1817. SCOTT, *Rob Roy*, xiv. I found Mr. Macready . . . a TOUGH, sagacious, long-headed Scotchman.

1837. BARHAM, *Ingolds. Leg.*, II. 69. 'My Lord,' said the King, 'here's a rather TOUGH JOB.'

See OLD TOUGHS.

TOUPEE, *subs.* (venery). — 1. The female pubic hair: see FLEECE; and (2) a MERKIN (*q.v.*): see LADY'S LOW TOUPÉE.

TOUR, *subs.* (old). — A turn or drive: spec. the fashionable promenade in Hyde Park: now (1903) THE Row (Rotten Row). Also as *verb*.

1665. PEPYS, *Diary*, 19 Mar. Mr Povy and I in his coach to Hyde Parke, being the first day of the TOUR there; where many brave ladies. *Ibid.* (13 Mar. 1668). Took up my wife and Deb., and to the park, where being in a hackney, and they undressed, were ashamed to go into the TOUR.

1706. CENTLIVRE, *Basset Table*, i. 2. The sweetness of the Park is at eleven, when the Beau-Monde make their TOUR there.

17[?]. [ASHTON, *Queen Anne*, II. 173.] You'll at least keep Six Horses, Sir Toby, for I wou'd not make a TOUR in Hyde Park with less for the World; for me thinks a pair looks like a Hackney.

See TOWRE.

THE GRAND TOUR, *subs. phr.* (old colloquial).—In 18th and early 19th centuries a continental tour embracing France, Switzerland, Italy, and Germany: regarded as an essential finish to the education of young men of rank.

TOUSLE (or **TOWSLE**), *verb.* (colloquial). — To rumple; TO PULL (or MESS) ABOUT (*q.v.*); to ransack; freq. with 'mousle.' Whence (venery) = to master a woman by romping. Also TOUSY = rough, dishevelled, unkempt. [*Cf.* TOUSE.]

1370. *Thornton Rom.* [Camden Soc.], 239. [OLIPHANT, *New Eng.* i. 81. The *l* is added, for the verb *tuse* becomes *tousel* (Scott's TOWZEL).]

1530. TYNDALE, *Works*, ii. 151. He TOWSETH and mowseth.

1695. CONGREVE, *Love for Love*, iii. 10. He'll TOUZLE her and mouzle her. The rogue's sharp set . . . what if he should . . . fall to without the help of a parson. ha?

1763. FOOTE, *Mayor of Garratt*, i. 1. You slut, how you've TOUSLED the curls.

1791. BURNS, *Tam o' Shanter.* A TOWZIE tyke, black, grim and large.

1791. *Old Song*, 'My Jockey is a Bonny Lad.' And then he fa's a kissing, clasping, hugging, squeezing, TOUSLING, pressing, winna let me be.

1816. SCOTT, *Old Mortality*, xiv. She loot Tam TOUSLE her tap-knots. *Ibid.* (1816), *Antiquary*, ix. After they had TOUZLED many a leather pokeful of papers.

1852. STOWE, *Uncle Tom's Cabin*, ix. A very heavy mat of sandy hair, in a decidedly TOUSLED condition.

1887. *Field*, 27 Mar. A large TOUSEY dog that can kill singly a fox or badger.

TOUT, *subs.* (Old Cant). — The posteriors; the BACKSIDE (*q.v.*), the BUM (*q.v.*).

1383. CHAUCER, *Canterbury Tales*, 3810, 'Miller's Tale.' The hote culter brenned so his TOUTE. *Ibid.* Thus swived was the carpentere's wif . . . And Absolon hath kist hire nether eye; And Nicholas is scalded in the TOUTE.

[?]. *MS. Ashmole.*, 61, f. 60. Rubyng of ther TOUTE.

1882. PAYNE, *Thousand Nights*, etc., 'Porter of the Three Ladies of Baghdad.' Thy caze, thy TOUT, thy catso, thy coney.

Verb. (Old Cant).—'To look out sharp, to be on one's guard' (B. E.): also TO KEEP TOUT: *see* NARK. Hence (HALLIWELL) = to follow; and (modern) = to canvass for custom as do hotel, coach, or steamer servants, to solicit employment as does a guide, or (racing: *see* TIP) to spy out special information concerning horses in training. A STRONG TOUT = strict observation, close watching (VAUX). As *subs.* = (1) a hotel, coach, or steamer runner, (2) a spy for thief or smuggler, (3) a racing agent or 'horse-watcher' (GROSE). Also TOUTING-KEN = a tavern-bar (B. E. and GROSE).

c. 1696. B. E., *Dict. Cant. Crew*, s.v. TOUT. Who TOUTS? c. who looks out sharp? TOUT the Culls, c. Eye those Folks which way they take.

1718. C. HIGDEN, *True Disc.*, 13. He is a pushing TOUTE, alias thieves' watchman, that lies scouting in and about the City to get and bring intelligence to the thieves, when and where there is a Push, alias an Accidental Crowd of People.

d. 1761. RICHARDSON, *Corresp.*, III. 316. A parcel of fellows, mean traders whom they call TOUTERS, and their business TOUTING—riding out miles to meet carriages and company coming hither, to beg their custom while here.

1785. GROSE, *Vulg. Tongue*, s.v. TOUT. A look-out house, or eminence. *Ibid.*, TOUTER . . . Men, who, on the sly, obtain the speed and capabilities of race-horses during their training, and give

information to certain persons . . . who bet their money with more certainty. *Ibid.*, TOUTING. Publicans forestalling guests, or meeting them on the road, and begging their custom; to be met with at Brighton, Margate, etc.

1827. LYTTON, *Pelham*, lxxxii. Bess, my covess, strike me blind if my sees don't TOUT your bingo muns in spite of the darkmans.

1837. DISRAELI, *Venetia*, 69. Come, old mort . . . TOUT the cobble-colter; are we to have darkmans upon us?

1837. BARHAM, *Ingoldsby Legends* (1842), 256. I have not a doubt, I shall rout every TOUT.

1843. DICKENS, *Martin Chuzzlewit*, xxxvii. Thimbleriggers, duffers, TOUTERS, or any of those bloodless sharpers, who are, perhaps, a little better known to the police.

1857. KINGSLEY, *Two Years Ago*, x. 'It suits my purpose to become the principal medical man in this neighbourhood—' 'And I am to TOUT for introductions for you?'

1863. *Law Mag. Rev.*, 22. Barristers' clerks TOUTING among prisoners and prosecutors.

1869. *Fraser's Mag.*, 'British Merchant Seamen.' The TOUTER, whose business it is to attract the sailor to his master's lodgings by the judicious loan of money, the offer of grog or soft tack (bread); the runner, who volunteers to carry his box of clothes and bedding free of charge to the same destination.

1869. HOTTEN, *Slang Dict.*, s.v. TOUT. An agent in the training districts, on the look-out for information as to the condition and capabilities of those horses entering for a coming race. TOUTS often get into trouble through entering private training-grounds. They, however, are very highly paid, some making 40*l.* or 50*l.* a week during the season.

1885. *Field*, 3 Oct. There had been a good deal of before-breakfast TOUTING on the Bury side of the town. *Ibid.* Everybody was industrious, the professional TOUTS being outnumbered by the amateurs. *Ibid.* (1886), 4 Sep. The gallops . . . are less liable to be TOUTED than any other training-ground.

1886. *Athenæum*, 3067. A species of racing TOUT enters the cottage of a female trainer.

TOW, *subs.* (Shrewsbury School).—1. A long run in: at hare and hounds.

1881. PASCOE, *Everyday Life.* After that last 'all up' there is a TOW or continuous run of from one to three miles.

2. (common). — Generic for money: *see* RHINO.

TO TOW OUT, *verb. phr.* (old).—To decoy: spec. to distract attention and thus pave the way for robbery by a confederate: also TOW-STREET (GROSE) and TOW-LINE (VAUX).

IN TOW, *phr.* (colloquial).—In hand, at one's apron strings, under one's influence, or at command: of persons and things; spec. of a woman who is said to have such and such an admirer IN TOW.

TOWARDS. I LOOKS (*sic*) TOWARDS YOU, *phr.* (common).—A toast.

1857. WHITTY, *Bohemia*, I. 166. Ladies, I LOOKS TOWARD YOU.

TOWEL, *subs.* (common). — 1. A cudgel: also OAKEN (or BLACKTHORN) TOWEL; as *verb* (TO GIVE A TOWELLING or TO RUB DOWN WITH A TOWEL) = to reprimand, scold, and (spec.) thrash (GROSE).

1771. SMOLLETT, *Humphry Clinker*, i. 83. Prankly, shaking his cane, bid him hold his tongue, otherwise he would dust his cassock for him. 'I have no pretensions to such a valet,' said Tom; 'but if you should do me that office, and overheat yourself, I have here a good OAKEN TOWEL at your service.'

1851-61. MAYHEW, *Lond. Lab.*, I. 469. I got a TOWELLING, but it did not do me much good.

2. (old).—The *anus*; fundament: *see* BUM: also TEWEL.

1383. CHAUCER, *Cant. Tales*, 7730, 'Sompnoures Tale.' And whan this sike man felte this frere About his TOWEL gropen ther and here, Amid his hond he let the frere a fart.

A LEAD (or LEADEN) TOWEL, *subs. phr.* (common).—A bullet.

1812. J. and H. SMITH, *Rejected Addresses*, 182. Make Nunky surrender his dibs, Rub his pate with a pair of LEAD TOWELS.

TOWER, *subs.* (old).—1. A fashion in feminine hair-dressing, *temp.* William III. and Anne: pasteboard, ribbon, and lace were built up in tiers, or in stiffened bows, and draped with a lace scarf or veil. Also (2) a wig or the natural hair built up in the same fashion; and (3) false hair worn on the forehead (B. E.).

1663. BUTLER, *Hudibras*, 'To his Lady,' 186. Lay trains of amorous intrigues In TOW'RS, and curls, and periwigs.

1675. *Woman Turn'd Bully* [NARES]. 'Tis a frightful thing to see some women . . . undress'd: I do not mean naked; but only their face without the TOOR, shades, locks, hollows, bullies, and some transitory patches.

1675. *Ape-Gentlewoman*, 1. Her greatest ingenuity consists in curling up her TOWRE, and her chiefest care in putting it on.

1676. ETHEREGE, *Man of Mode*, ii. 1. Her TOUR wou'd keep in curl no longer.

1681. RADCLIFFE, *Ovid Travestie*, 63. Should I adorn my head with curles and TOWERS, When a poor skipper's cap does cover yours?

1710. CONGREVE, *Ovid's Art of Love*, iii. And Art gives Colour which with Nature vyes: The well-wove TOURS they wear their own are thought.

1711. [SYDNEY, *England and English*, i. 90. About the year 1711 the good taste of the Queen induced her to discontinue wearing the . . . TOWER or Bow steeple, names which the wits bestowed in derision.]

Verb. (Old Cant). — (1) To watch closely; to see, observe, understand: as a hawk on the look-out for prey: also TOURE, TOUR, TWIRE, TWYRE; TO TOUR OUT = to go abroad in search of booty: hence to be off, to decamp (HARMAN, B. E. and GROSE). [GROSE: 'to overlook, to rise aloft, as in a high tower.' DYCE: 'a verb particularly applicable to certain hawks, etc., which TOWER aloft, soar spirally to a station high in the air, and thence swoop upon their prey.']

1567. HARMAN, *Caveat* (E.E.T.S.), 86. Now I TOWER that bene bouse makes nase nabes.

1607. DEKKER, *Jests to Make You Merie* [GROSART, *Works*, ii. 329]. Kinchen the coue TOWRES, which is as much as, Fellow the man smokes or suspects you.

1610. ROWLANDS, *Martin Mark-all.* 'TOWRE out ben Morts' [Title].

1737. *Old Ballad*, '*Black Procession*' [*Bacchus and Venus*]. TOURE you well; hark you well, see Where they are rubb'd.

1822. SCOTT, *Fort. Nigel.* TOUR the bien mort TWIRING the gentry cove.

1837. DISRAELI, *Venetia*, 71. Queer cuffin will be the word if we don't TOUR.

BEEN ROUND THE TOWER (Old Cant).—Clipped: of money (B.E. and GROSE).

TOWER-HILL-PLAY, *subs. phr.* (old).—'A slap on the Face and a kick on the Breech' (B.E. and GROSE).

TOWER-HILL VINEGAR, *subs. phr.* (old).—The swordsman's block. [Tower-hill was, for long, the place of execution.] Hence TO PREACH ON TOWER HILL = to be hanged. *See* TYBURN.

d. 1529. SKELTON, *Magnyfycence* [*Works* (DYCE), i. 295]. Some fall to foly them selfe for to spyll, And some fall PRECHYNGE ON TOWRE HYLL.

TOWERING, *adj.* (colloquial).—Extreme, violent, outrageous.

1713. ADDISON, *Cato*, ii. 1. All else is TOWERING phrenzy and distraction.

1849-61. MACAULAY, *Hist. Eng.*, xxii. Russell went into a TOWERING passion.

TOWHEAD, *subs.* (colloquial).—1. A flaxen-haired person; and (2) a rumple-head; in contempt. Whence TOW-HEADED = rough-headed, unkempt.

TOWN, *subs.* (old colloquial).—1. London: *e.g.* 'I go to (or leave) TOWN to-morrow'; 'So-and-so is in TOWN: *cf.* LANE, HOUSE, ALLEY, etc.: whence MAN ABOUT TOWN (*see* PHRASES).

1601. SHAKSPEARE, *Henry VIII.*, Prol. As you are known the first and happiest hearers of the TOWN.

1607. DEKKER and WEBSTER, *Westward Hoe*, iii. 1. *Ten.* I know not when he will come to TOWN. *Moll.* He's in TOWN; this night he sups at the Lion in Shoreditch.

1648. *Commons' Journals*, v. 245. That a letter be directed to the Vice-Admiral to desire him to suffer Prince Philip, brother to the Prince Elector, to come to TOWN.

1711. ADDISON, *Spectator*, No. 2. A baronet . . . Sir Roger de Coverley. When he is in TOWN he lives in Soho Square.

c. 1825. JENKINSON [DAVIES: Bp. Jenkinson of St. David's (1825-40) offered a curate in his diocese a living, and desired him to come to TOWN to be instituted. The curate expressed every willingness to obey the command, but added that his Lordship had omitted to mention the name of the town where his presence was required.]

2. (University and schools').—Townspeople, as distinguished from GOWN (*q.v.*) = the members of the University. [In early days Universities were subject to perpetual conflict—with the TOWN, the Jews, the Friars, and the Papal Court: *see* quot. 1853.]

Also TOWNSMAN and (Cambridge) TOWNEE (or TOWNER): Ger. *Philister.* TOWN-LOUT (Rugby) = a scholar residing in the town with his parents, and TOWNEY (Christ's Hospital) = (1) the antithesis of 'housey,' that is peculiar to the Hospital: whence (spec.) TOWNEYS = clothes more in accordance with modern taste for town wear than is the distinctive BLUE habit; also (2) a comrade from the same town or locality (army): Fr. *pays.*

1846. *Punch*, x. 163. For the gownsmen funk the TOWNSMEN, And the TOWNSMEN funk the gown.

1853. BRADLEY, *Verdant Green*, II. iii., Note. TOWN and Gown disturbances [date back to] 1238. They not unfrequently terminated fatally to some of the combatants: on St. Scholastica the Virgin, February 10th, 1345, several lives were lost on either side. Grostête, the Bishop [Lincoln], placed the townspeople under an interdict, [which lasted] till 1357, when the mayor and sixty of the chief burgesses were required every anniversary to attend St. Mary's Church and offer up mass for the souls of the slain scholars, and individually present an offering of one penny at the high altar, besides a yearly fine of 100 marks to the University, with the penalty of an additional fine of the same sum for every omission in attending at St. Mary's. This fell into abeyance at the Reformation. In 15 Eliz., however, the University claimed arrears, and it was decided that the town should continue the annual fine and penance, though the arrears were forgiven. The fine was yearly paid on the 10th of February until put an end to by Convocation in the year 1825.

1887. *Blue*, Nov. Mention is made of the time when a boy leaves the school. The consequent change of dress might be vulgarly expressed by 'exchanging houseys for TOWNEYS.'

1899. HEYWOOD, *Guide to Oxford.* Town and gown rows . . . nowadays . . . are happily unknown.

PHRASES, ETC.—TO COME TO TOWN = (1) to become common, and (2) to be born; ON THE TOWN = (1) getting a living by prostitution, thieving, or the like, and (2) in the swing of pleasure, dissipation, etc., London (*see subs.* 1) being regarded as the centre of national life; TO GO (or TAKE A TURN) ROUND THE TOWN = to seek amusement, spec. at night and by a round of 'the halls'; A MAN (or WOMAN) OF THE TOWN = a person whose living, occupation, or taste is more or less connected with the shady or 'fast' side of life (GROSE); TO PAINT THE TOWN RED (*see* RED); IN TOWN (BEE) = in funds; OUT OF TOWN = hard up, penniless.

1593. NASH, *Works* (GROSART), ii. 283. [NASH] I knew a MAN ABOUT TOWN.

1600. *MS.*, '*The Newe Metamorphosis.*' This first was court-like, nowe 'tis COME TO TOWNE; 'Tis common growne with every country clowne.

1640–50. HOWELL, *Letters*, ii. 89. [Howell calls himself] a YOUTH ABOUT THE TOWN.

1672. WYCHERLEY, *Love in a Wood*, ii. 1. A man may . . . bring his bashful wench, and not have her put out of countenance by the impudent honest WOMEN OF THE TOWN.

1686–7. AUBREY, *Gentilisme* (1881), 163. The TOWNE is full of wanton wenches, and . . . (they say) scarce three honest women in the TOWN.

d. 1704. BROWN, *Dial. of Dead* [*Works*, ii. 313]. I have been a MAN OF THE TOWN . . . and admitted into the family of the Rakehellonians.

1766. GOLDSMITH, *Wakefield*, xx. The lady was only a WOMAN OF THE TOWN, and the fellow her bully and a sharper.

1823. BEE, *Dict. Turf*, s.v. Highflyers—WOMEN OF THE TOWN, in keeping.

1823. BYRON, *Don Juan*, xi. 17. Poor Tom was once a KIDDY UPON TOWN, A thorough varmint and a real swell.

1842. EGAN, *Capt. Macheath*, 'Jack Flashman.' Jack long was ON THE TOWN, a teazer; Could turn his fives to anything, Nap a reader, or filch a ring.

1900. GRIFFITHS, *Fast and Loose*, xxii. He . . . aspired more and more to be thought a tip-top swell, a fashionable MAN ABOUT TOWN.

TOWN-BULL (RAKE, or STALLION), *subs. phr.* (old).—A common whoremaster, wencher, MUTTON-MONGER (*q.v.*) (B.E. and GROSE). [NARES: it was formerly the custom to keep a bull for common town use.] Hence, 'AS LAWLESS AS A TOWN-BULL' (RAY) = 'one that rides all the women he meets' (B.E.); and TOWN-HUSBAND = a parish officer whose duty it was to collect bastardy fees.

1611. CHAPMAN, *May-day*, iii. 1. *Ho.* TOWN-BULL government; do you not mean so, sir? *Lod.* Do you imagine he went about stealing of city venison?

1630. TAYLOR, *Works* [NARES]. This piece of officer, this nasty patch, (Whose understanding sleepes out many a watch), Ran like a TOWNE BULL, roaring up and downe, Saying that we had meant to fire the towne.

1636. DAVENANT, *Platonic Lovers*, iv. 1. My son hath turned . . . from a tame soldier to a TOWN BULL.

1664. BUTLER, *Hudibras*, II. i. This made the beauteous queen of Crete To take a TOWN-BULL for her sweet.

1681. RADCLIFFE, *Ovid Travestie*, 116. What think you, lady, of your Father Jove? Shew me a TOWN-BULL h'as been more in Love.

1689. *Princess of Cleve.* Believe me, sir, in a little time you'll be nick'd the TOWN-BULL.

1711. SWIFT, *Examiner*, 29. Lewdness and intemperance are not of so bad consequences in the TOWN-RAKE as in a divine.

TO ROAR LIKE A TOWN-BULL, *verb. phr.* (old). — 'To cry, or bellow aloud' (GROSE).

TOW-POW, *subs. phr.* (military).—In *pl.* = The Grenadier Guards (HOTTEN).

TOW-ROW, *subs. phr.* (common).—A noise; a RACKET (*q.v.*).

TOUZERY GANG (THE), *subs. phr.* (common).—Mock auction swindlers: they hire sale-rooms, usually in the suburbs, and advertise their ventures as 'Alarming Sacrifices,' 'Important Sales of Bankrupts' Stock," etc.

TOWZLE (or TOWSE). *See* TOUSLE, *verb.*

TOY, *subs.* and *verb.* (old).—Generic for wantonness: as *subs.* = (1) a lewd conceit, jest, or tale; a love poem; amorous sport; (2) a maidenhead; and (3) the female *pudendum.* As *verb* = to wanton, to dally: also TO TICK AND TOY. TOYFUL (TOYSOME, TOYISH, or TOYING) = amorous, wanton (BAILEY, 1731).

1303. MANNING [Robert of Brunne]. [OLIPHANT, *New Eng.*, i. 427. Manning used TOY for dalliance in 1303. *Ibid.*, i. 370. He (Skelton) has Manning's peculiar sense of TOY.]

d. 1529. SKELTON, *Works* [DYCE], 50. To TOYE with him.

1571. EDWARDS, *Damon and Pithias*, Prol. The matron grave, the harlot wild, and full of wanton TOYS.

1579. GOSSON, *School of Abuses.* Such ticking, such TOYING, such smiling, such winking, and such manning them home when the sports are ended.

15[?]. HARRISON, *Passion of Sappho* [NICHOLS, iv. 183]. Wanton Cupid, idle TOYER, Pleasing tyrant, soft destroyer.

1590. SPENSER, *Fairy Queen*, II. ix. 34–35. And eke emongst them little Cupid play'd His wanton sportes . . . But other some could not abide to TOY.

1596. NASH, *Saffron Walden*, iii. 44. [Nash confesses he was often obliged] to pen unedifying TOYS for gentlemen.

[?]. *Gilderoy* [CHILD, *Ballads*, VI. 199]. Aft on the banks we'd sit us thair, And sweetly kiss and TOY.

1614. *England's Helicon* [NARES]. Unto her repaire. . . . Sit and TICK AND TOY till set be the sunne.

c. 1650. BRATHWAYTE, *Barnaby's Jl.* (1723), 61. With me TOY'D they, buss'd me, cull'd me.

1667. MILTON, *Paradise Lost*, ix. 1034. So said he, and forebore not glance or TOY Of amourous intent.

1663. KILLIGREW, *Parson's Wedding*, i. 2. [TOY = maidenhead.]

1678. COTTON, *Virgil Travestie* (1770), 46. But we can cherish lusty Yeoman, And carry TOYS like other women.

1680. DRYDEN, *Spanish Friar*, iv. 2. O virtue, virtue, what art thou become, That man should leave thee for that TOY, a woman!

1693. CONGREVE, *Old Bachelor*, Epil. As a rash girl, who will all hazards run, And be enjoyed . . . Soon as her curiosity is over, Would give the world she could her TOY recover.

1707. WARD, *Hud. Rediv.*, II. ii. 8. Kisses, LOVE-TOYS, and am'rous Prattle.

1753. RICHARDSON, *Grandison*, v. 299. Two or three TOYSOME things were said by my lord (no ape was ever so fond!) and I could hardly forbear him.

1841. MACAULAY, *Warren Hastings.* A *roi fainéant* who chewed bang, and TOYED with dancing girls.

Hence (old colloquial) = (4) anything of casual or trifling interest, use, amusement, or adornment, of adventitious worth, as contrasted with serious, hard use, or intrinsic value: a nick-nack, *e.g.*, a trinket, an idle story, odd conceit, and spec. anything diminutive.

d. 1529. SKELTON, *Sclaunder and False Detractions.* Then let them vale a bonet of their proud sayle, And of their taunting TOIES rest with il hayle.

1530. TYNDALE, *Works.* [OLIPHANT, *New Eng.*, i. 427. Tyndale uses TOY much like children's play, ii. 11 (Last Part).]

1550. LATIMER, *Serm. bef. Ed. VI.* Here by the way I will tell you a merry TOY.

1564. UDAL, *Erasmus.* [OLIPHANT, *New Eng.*, i. 484. The word TOY had already meant a trifle or a folly; it now stands for a play on words, page 115, and in page xxiv. it expresses joke.]

1590. MARLOWE, *Tamburlaine*, i. 2. 'Tis a pretty TOY to be a poet.

1592. SHAKSPEARE, *Midsummer Night's Dream*, v. 1. 3. I never may believe these antique fables, nor these fairy TOYS. *Ibid.* (1592), *1 Henry VI.*, iv. 1. 145. A TOY, a thing of no regard. *Ibid.* (1604), *Winter's Tale*, iv. 4. 326. Any silk, any thread, Any TOYS for your head?

1594. HOOKER, *Eccles. Polity*, i. 15. A man whose wisdom is in weighty affairs admired would take it in some disdain to have his counsel solemnly asked about a TOY.

c. 1600. *Merry Devil of Edmonton*, iii. 1. 32. For your busk, attires and TOYS, Have your thoughts on heavenly joys.

d. 1719. ADDISON, *Italy* [*Works* (BOHN), I. 504]. One cannot but be amazed to see such a profusion of wealth laid out in coaches, trappings, tables, cabinets, and the like precious TOYS.

1888. BLACK, *Houseboat*, ii. Perched on the top of a hill was a conspicuous TOY of a church.

5. (old).—A whim, fancy, huff, offence, or caprice. Hence TO TAKE TOY = (1) to be huffish, whimsical, restless; and (2) to go at random, play tricks, act the fool: whence TOYSOME, etc: *cf.* HOITY-TOITY = thoughtless, giddy. TOYT-HEADED = feather-brained.

14[?]. *Babees Book* [E.E.T.S.], 332. Cast not thyne eyes to ne yet fro, As thou werte full of TOYES.

1596. SHAKSPEARE, *Hamlet*, i. 4. 77. The very place puts TOYS of desperation, Without more notice, into every brain.

1598. MARLOWE, *Hero and Leander*, v. To hear her dear tongue robb'd of such a joy, Made the well-spoken nymph TAKE SUCH A TOY. That down she sunk.

1598. FLORIO, *Worlde of Wordes*, s.v. *Capricciare*, to growe or be humourous, TOISH, or fantastical.

1605. JONSON, CHAPMAN, etc., *Eastward Ho!* iii. 2. A TOY, a TOY, runs in my head, i' faith.

1607. CHAPMAN, *Bussy D'Ambois*, i. 1. *Ta.* Why did the TOY TAKE him in th' head now? *Bu.* 'Tis leap-year, lady.

c. 1611. BEAUMONT and FLETCHER, *Two Noble Kinsmen*, v. 4. 65. The hot horse, hot as fire, TOOKE TOY at this.

1613. MARSTON, *Insatiate Countess*, i. *Men.* How now, my lady? does the TOY TAKE you, as they say? *Abi.* No, my lord; nor doe we TAKE YOUR TOY, as they say.

1625. JONSON, *Staple of News*, i. 2. The fool . . . can commit whom he will, and what he will, error, absurdity, as the TOY TAKES him.

1628. EARLE, *Microcos.* [ARBER], 63. She is indeed one that has TAKEN A TOY at the fashion of Religion, and is enamour'd of the New-fangle.

d. 1631. DONNE, *Prog. of Soul*, 46. It quickened next a TOYFUL ape.

d. 1663. SANDERSON, *Works*, i. 358. As they sometimes withdraw their love from their children upon slender dislikes, so these many times TAKE TOY at a trifle.

1665. GLANVILLE, *Scep. Sci.* Your society will discredit that TOYISHNESS of wanton fancy that plays tricks with words, and frolicks with the caprices of frothy imagination.

d. 1665. ADAMS, *Sermons*, 'The Fatal Banquet,' i. 221. These TOYTHEADED times.

d. 1667. JER. TAYLOR, *Works* (1835), II. 320. The contention is trifling and TOYISH.

d. 1703. POMFRET, *Dies Novissima.* Adieu, ye TOYISH reeds that once could please My softer lips, and lull my cares to ease.

1903. BOOTHBY, *Long Live the King*, viii. HOIGHTY-TOITY . . . what is the matter with you now?

6. (thieves').—A watch. Whence WHITE TOY = a silver watch; RED TOY = a gold watch; TOY AND TACKLE = watch and chain; TOY-GETTER = a watch-snatcher.

1877. HORSLEY, *Jottings from Jail.* He was very tricky at getting a poge or a TOY, but he would not touch TOYS because he was afraid of being turned over.

7. (Winchester). — In *pl.* = a bureau—desk and bookcase combined. Whence TOY-TIME = evening preparation.

1440. *Prompt. Parv.* TEVE, of a cofyr or forcer.

1881. PASCOE, *Everyday Life.* The clock striking seven, each junior retires to his TOYS or bureau for an hour and a half during what is known as TOY-TIME, when the work of the next morning and the week's composition have to be prepared.

1891. WRENCH, *Winchester Word-Book*, s.v. TOYS . . . The expression TOY-TIME suggests that the *s* has been added. If TOYS has not descended from this word [teye], it must have been transferred from the contents of the TOYS, and mean simply *one's belongings.*

TPROT, *intj.* (old).—An exclamation of contempt (WRIGHT, *Political Songs*, 381).

TRACE, *subs.* (colloquial).—In *pl.* = authority, work, guidance, restraint; hence IN THE TRACES = in HARNESS (*q.v.*), at steady work; TO KICK OVER THE TRACES = to set at defiance, run riot, take the law into one's own hands.

TRACK, *verb.* (Old Cant).—1. To go: hence TO TRACK UP THE DANCERS = 'to whip upstairs' (HEAD, 1671; B. E., *c.* 1696; GROSE, 1785). Also (modern) TO MAKE TRACKS = to go (or run) away: *see* BUNK; TO MAKE TRACKS FOR = (1) to proceed towards; and (2) to attack, TO GO FOR (*q.v.*).

1847. LYTTON, *Lucretia*, II. vii. 'Bob, TRACK THE DANCERS. Up like a lark—and down like a dump.' Bob grinned . . . and scampered up the stairs. *Ibid.* (1858), *What Will He Do With it?* III. xvi. Come, my Hebe, TRACK THE DANCERS.

1857. KINGSLEY, *Two Years Ago*, xiv. You will be pleased TO MAKE TRACKS, and vanish out of these parts for ever.

1887. *Field*, 28 Feb. On joining my friend, we at once MADE TRACKS FOR the camp, ready for what was to follow.

1888. WARD, *Rob. Elsmere*, xiii. I MADE TRACKS FOR that lad. . . . I found him in the fields one morning.

1897. MARSHALL, *Pomes.* He said he was a banker, did our smart Teutonic Max, And many a quid he'd given her, before he MADE HIS TRACKS.

2. (modern.) — In various phrases: *e.g.* IN ONE'S TRACKS = on the spot, as one goes, then and there; OFF THE TRACK = discursive, out of one's reckoning, at sea; INSIDE TRACK = the truth, BEDROCK (*q.v.*).

1884. *Century Mag.*, xl. 224. [The boy] was in for stealing horses, but I think the real thief swore it off on him. If he did, God forgive him; he had better have shot the boy IN HIS TRACKS.

TRADE, *subs.* (American colloquial).—1. An exchange: *e.g.* a swopping of knives. Also as *verb* = to exchange.

2. (Christ's Hospital). — *See* quot.

1900. *D. Teleg.*, 16 Mar. 'London Day by Day.' After the boys had concluded their simple repast of bread and butter, they formed up two-and-two, and bowed to the Lord Mayor, the different wards being headed by THE TRADES as the boys who carry the candlesticks, the bread-baskets, table-cloth, and cutlery are termed.

TRADE-MARK, *subs. phr.* (colloquial).—1. A scratch on the face; hence TO PUT ONE'S TRADE-MARK UPON ONE = to claw the face: spec. of women.

c. 1876. *Music Hall Song*, 'Father, take a run.' The old woman . . . pawns everything in the place; And if I correct her for what she has done, She DRAWS HER TRADE-MARK DOWN MY FACE.

2. (servants').—A cap.

TRADER, *subs.* (old).—A whore: *see* TART: also SHE-TRADER and TRADING DAME. Hence THE TRADE = harlotry.

1678. COTTON, *Virgil Travestie* (1770), 72. That she, Now car'd no more for her good Name Than any common TRADING DAME.

1681. RADCLIFFE, *Poems*, 45. Ah London th'adst better have built new Burdellos, T'encourage SHE-TRADERS and lusty young Fellows.

d. 1796. BURNS [*Merry Muses* (*c.* 1800), 52]. Our dame hauds up her wanton tail As due as she gaes lie, An' yet misca's a young thing, The TRADE if she but try.

TRADESMAN, *subs.* (old).—A thief (GROSE): *see* THIEF. Hence A REGULAR TRADESMAN=an expert thief: also (common) = a compliment applied to anyone who thoroughly understands his business whatever it may be.

TRADES UNION (THE), *subs. phr.* (military). — The First (The King's) Dragoon Guards. [At one time most of the officers were sons of tradesmen, which is still an offence in the Cavalry.]

TRADING, *subs.* (American political).—A veiled form of political treachery: a State Governor is to be elected, and at the same election, say, Presidential electors; the one party agree with their political enemies that, in return for votes for their own candidate for Governor, they will vote and procure votes for the others' candidate for President. The practice is susceptible of numerous combinations and devices (WALSH). Whence TRADING POLITICIAN= a corrupt, venal elector or candidate; one who is regulated by interest rather than principle.

1839-43. BROUGHAM, *Hist. Sketches*, 'Canning.' The common herd of TRADING POLITICIANS.

TRAGEDY JACK, *subs. phr.* (theatrical).—A heavy tragedian: in contempt.

TRAIL, *verb.* (old).—To quiz, befool, draw out, GET AT (*q.v.*): also as *subs.*

1847. BRONTË, *Jane Eyre*, xvii. I presently perceived she was (what is vernacularly termed) TRAILING Mrs. Dent: that is, playing on her ignorance; her TRAIL might be clever, but it was decidedly not good-natured.

1900. KERNAHAN, *Scoundrels and Co.*, xxi. To see the Ishmaelites TRAIL a sufferer from swelled head is to undergo inoculation against that fell malady.

TO TRASH A TRAIL, *verb. phr.* (Western American).—To take to water in order to destroy scent: of human beings as well as animals.

TRAIL-TONGS (or -TRIPES), *subs. phr.* (common). — A slatternly servant; a DIRTY PUZZLE (*q.v.*). Hence TRAILY=slovenly.

TRAIN, *verb.* (colloquial).—1. To travel by train, usually with it: *cf.* ''bus it,' 'foot it,' 'tram it,' etc. Whence TO TRAIN UP=to hurry.

1889. *Harper's Mag.*, lxxvii. 954. From Aberdeen to Edinburgh we TRAINED IT by easy stages.

2. (American). — To romp, 'carry on,' act wildly. [BARTLETT: 'almost peculiar to the girls of New England,' but *cf.* sense 3.]

3. (colloquial). — To consort with on familiar terms: *e.g.*, 'TRAINING with such a crowd does not suit me.'

TRAINER, *subs.* (American). — A militia-man; spec. when called out for periodical 'training.'

TRAITOR. THERE ARE TRAITORS AT TABLE, *phr.* (old).—Of a loaf turned the wrong side upwards.

TRAM, *subs.* (colloquial).—A tramway-car: *cf.* 'bus,' 'rail' 'motor,' etc.

TRAMP, *subs.* and *verb.* (old: now recognised).—1. 'On the look-out for employment; walking about from place to place. *Cant*' (GROSE).

2. (nautical). — A cargo boat seeking charter or cargo when and where obtainable; also TRAMP-STEAMER, and OCEAN TRAMP.

TRAMPER, *subs.* (workmen's).—A travelling mechanic.

TRAMPLER, *subs.* (old).—A lawyer: *see* GREENBAG.

1619. MIDDLETON, *World at Tennis*. Pity your TRAMPLER, sir, your poor solicitor.

1630. TAYLOR, *Works* [NARES]. The TRAMPLER is in hast, O cleere the way, Takes fees with both hands cause he cannot stay.

TRAMPOLIN, *subs.* (circus). — A double spring-board.

TRAMPOOSE, *verb.* (American).— To walk, tramp, wander about: *cf.* VAMOOSE. Also TRAMPOUS and TRAMPOOS.

d. 1818 [?]. D. HUMPHREYS, *Yankee in England*. Some years ago, I landed near to Dover, And seed strange sights, TRAMPOOSING England over.

1837. HALIBURTON, *Clockmaker*, 387. I had been down city all day TRAMPOOSING everywhere a'most to sell some stock. *Ibid.* (1843-4), *The Attaché*, ii. I felt as lonely as a catamount, and as dull as a bachelor beaver; so I TRAMPOUSSES off to the stable.

1850. PORTER, *Tales of the South and West*, 44. So we TRAMPOUSED along down the edge of the swamp, till we came to a track.

TRANEEN. NOT WORTH A TRANEEN, *phr.* (Irish).—Valueless; not worth a rush. [TRANEEN= the Traneen-grass].

TRANGDILLO. *See* TWANGDILLO.

TRANGRAM (TRANGAM or TRANKUM), *subs.* (old).—A trifle, fal-lal, ornament; anything or anybody of little or no value. *Cf.* reduplication, TRINKUM-TRANKUM.

1677. WYCHERLEY, *Plain Dealer*, iii. 1. But go, thou TRANGAME, and carry back those TRANGAMES, which thou hast stol'n or purloin'd.

1713. ARBUTHNOT, *Hist. John Bull*, II. vi. What's the meaning of all these TRANGRAMS and gimcracks?

1820. SCOTT, *Abbot*, xix. 'What, have you taken the chain and medal off from my bonnet?' 'And meet time it was when yon . . . rogue . . . began to inquire what popish TRANGAM you were wearing.' *Ibid.* (1825), *St. Ronan's Well*, xviii. The shawl must be had for Clara, with the other TRANKUMS of muslin and lace.

TRANKLEMENT, *subs.* (common).— In *pl.*=intestines, entrails: *cf.* TROLLY-BAGS.

TRANSCRIBBLER, *subs.* (old).—(1) A careless copyist: hence (2) a plagiarist.

1746. GRAY, *To Wharton*, 11 Sept. Thirdly, he [Aristotle] has suffered vastly from the TRANSCRIBBLERS, as all authors of great brevity necessarily must.

TRANSFISTICATED, *adj.* (old).— Pierced.

1600. *Letting of Humours Blood in the Head-Vaine*. For though your beard do stand so fine mustated, Perhaps your nose may be TRANSFISTICATED.

TRANSLATE, *verb.* (old).—To remanufacture selected parts of old boots and shoes. Also (tailors') to turn (or cut down) a coat or other garment. Whence TRANSLATOR=(1) a cobbler; (2) in *pl.* =re-made boots and shoes; and (3) a renovating tailor (B. E. and GROSE).

1694. MOTTEUX, *Rabelais*, 'Pant. Prog.' (1900), v. 214. Shoemakers and TRANSLATORS, tanners, bricklayers.

c. 1696. B. E., *Dict. Cant. Crew*, s.v. TRANSLATOR, Sellers of old Shoes and Boots, between Shoe-makers and Coblers.

d. 1704. BROWN, *Works*, iii. 73. The cobbler is affronted, if you don't call him Mr. TRANSLATOR.

1757. SEWELL, *Dict.*, s.v. TRANSLATOR, *Schoenlappen*.

1851-61. MAYHEW, *Lond. Lab.*, II. 40. Great quantities of second-hand boots and shoes are sent to Ireland to be TRANSLATED there. . . . 'TRANSLATION, as I understand it (said my informant), is this— to take a worn, old pair of shoes or boots, and by repairing them make them appear as if left off with hardly any wear—as if they were only soiled.' *Ibid.*, II. 110. Among these things are blankets . . . TRANSLATED boots, mended trousers. *Ibid.*, I. 51. To wear a pair of second-hand [boots] or TRANSLATORS . . . is felt as a bitter degradation.

1864. *Times*, 2 Nov. The clobberer, the reviver, and the TRANSLATOR lay hands on them . . . to patch, to sew up, and to restore as far as possible the garments to their pristine appearance.

1865. *Cassell's Paper*, 'Old Clo'.' They are now past 'clobbering,' 'reviving,' or 'TRANSLATING.'

188[?]. GREENWOOD, *Woodchopper's Wedding*. I interviewed the kind-hearted old TRANSLATOR . . . in his kitchen in Leather Lane.

c. 1889. *Sporting Times* [*S. J. and C.*]. Baeker had to limp in his socks to the New Cut, and purchase a pair of TRANSLATED crab-shells to go home in.

TRANSMOGRIFY (or TRANSMIGRIFY), *verb.* (old). — To transform, change, alter, or 'new vamp' (B. E. and GROSE). Also, as *subs.*, TRANSMOGRIFICATION.

1728. FIELDING, *Love in Sev. Masques*, v. 4. I begin to think . . . that some wicked enchanters have TRANSMOGRIFIED my Dulcinea.

1751-4. JORTIN, *Eccles. Hist.*, i. 254. Augustine seems to have had a small doubt whether Apuleius was really TRANSMOGRAPHIED into an ass.

1777. FOOTE, *Trip to Calais* [OLIPHANT, *New Eng.*, ii. 187. There is the curious TRANSMOGRIFY].

1836. SCOTT, *Tom Cringle's Log*, iii. Jonathan . . . let drive his whole broadside: and fearfully did it TRANSMOGRIFY us.

1837. BARHAM, *Ingoldsby Legends*, 'St. Aloys.' The TRANSMOGRIFIED Pagan performed his vow.

1884. *Nation*, 20 Mar., 250. But of all restorations, reparations, and TRANSMOGRIFICATIONS that inflicted upon the Cnidian Venus of the Vatican is the most grotesque.

TRANSNEAR, *verb.* (GROSE).—'To come up with any body.'

TRAP, *subs.* (old).—1. Sagacity, craft, contrivance, penetration. Hence TO UNDERSTAND TRAP= to be knowing, WIDE-AWAKE (*q.v.*), alive to one's own interest (GROSE); TO SMELL TRAP=to suspect: spec. of thieves in 'spotting' a 'tec. 'That TRAP is down'=The trick (or try-on) has failed, It's no go.

d. 1704. BROWN, *Works* (1705). Crying out, Split my Wind Pipe, Sir, you are a Fool, and DON'T UNDERSTAND TRAP, the whole world's a Cheat.

1740. NORTH, *Examen*, 203. It is almost impossible that all these circumstances . . . should be collected without some contrivance for purposes that do not obviously appear; and nothing but TRAP can resolve them. *Ibid.*, 549. Some cunning persons that had found out his foible and ignorance of TRAP, first put him in great fright.

1748. BOYER, *Dict.* You DO NOT UNDERSTAND TRAP, 'vous n'y entendez pas finesse.'

1760. FOOTE, *Minor*, ii. Our Minor was a little too hasty; he DID NOT UNDERSTAND TRAP, knows nothing of the game, my dear.

1821. SCOTT, *Pirate*, i. 51. His good lady . . . UNDERSTOOD TRAP as well as any woman in the Mearns.

1869. GREENWOOD, *Seven Curses of London*. They can discover the detective . . . by his step, or by his clumsy affectation of unofficial loutishness. They recognise the stiff-neck in the loose neckerchief. They smell TRAP and are superior to it.

1881. ROBSON, *Bards of the Tyne*, 275. Says, aw, 'Smash! thou is UP TO TRAP!' For he lets the folks byeth in and out.

2. (old).—A sheriff's officer, thief-taker, policeman, or detective (GROSE).

1705. WARD, *Hud. Rediv.*, I. iv. 8. TRAPS Divers, Punks, and Yeomen.

1800. PARKER, *Life's Painter*, 116. There's no hornies, TRAPS, scouts, nor beak-runners amongst them.

1819. VAUX, *Glossary*, s.v. TRAPS, police officers, or runners, are properly so called; but it is common to include constables of any description under this title.

1823. BEE, *Dict. Turf*, s.v. Item . . . I gave the item that the TRAPS were a coming.

1830. LYTTON, *Paul Clifford* (1854), 80. Where a ruffler might lie, without fear that the TRAPS should distress him.

1838. DICKENS, *Oliver Twist*, xiii. The TRAPS have got him, and that's all about it.

1839. AINSWORTH, *Jack Sheppard* (1889), 12. 'Where are the lurchers?' 'Who?' asked Wood. 'The TRAPS!' responded a bystander.

1841. REYNOLDS, *Pickwick Abroad*, xxvi. But should the TRAPS be on the sly, For a change we'll have a crack.

1859. KINGSLEY, *Geof. Hamlyn*, vi. Dick's always in trouble; . . . there's a couple of TRAPS in Belston after him now.

1867. *Victorian Song Book*, 'Where's your License?' 6. The little word Joe! which all of you know, Is the signal the TRAPS are quite near.

1885. *Leisure Hour*, Mar. 192. Meantime the Kellys had got to hear that the TRAPS were in search of them.

1890. BOLDREWOOD, *Squatter's Dream*, 157. We'll be a match for all the blessed TRAPS between here and Sydney with these here tools.

1895. MARRIOTT-WATSON [*New Review*, July, 2]. He . . . was very useful . . . both to us on the lay, and to the TRAPS.

3. (common).—A carriage; 'a fast name for a conveyance of any kind' (HOTTEN). [SALA: 'The old-fashioned gig had, under the seat, a sort of boot extending a few inches beyond the back of the seat. At the beginning of the century gigs were raised upon higher wheels than at present. On this raised vehicle the boot was lengthened behind, holding a brace of dogs for sporting purposes. In these "dog-carts" (thus named afterwards) the dogs were at first placed in the boot at the front, and I dare say that the "noble sportsmen" may occasionally have had their heels or their calves bitten by dogs with short tempers, and with scant liking for the confinement of the boot. This led to a great improvement, in the shape of an open latticed box, which was attached to the back of the body of the conveyance, and provided with a trap-door behind for the admission of the dogs. In process of time the latticed box was found very convenient for the carriage of other things besides dogs, and as everything conveyed in the cart (chattels, not people) had to be put in through the trap-door (soon curtailed into TRAP: compare "bus" for omnibus, "cab" for cabriolet), the conveyance itself was eventually termed TRAP.'] Hence TRAPPER=a horse used in a TRAP: *cf.* VANNER, BUSSER, CABBER, etc., on the model of 'hunter.'

1854-5. THACKERAY, *Newcomes*, lvii. Florac's pleasure was to drive his Princess with four horses into Newcome. He called his carriage his TRAPPE, his 'drague.'

1872. INGELOW, *Off the Skelligs*, xx. I think you must make room for me inside the TRAP. It is remarkable how much men despise close carriages, and what disrespectful epithets they invent for them.

1887. *St. James's Gaz.*, 2 Feb. The object of the Spring Show is to encourage generally the breeding of sound and shapely half-bred horses, ponies, nags, TRAPPERS, hacks, chargers, harness - horses, and hunters.

4. (colloquial). — Belongings; THINGS (*q.v.*); STICKS AND STONES (*q.v.*): usually in a measure of contempt, *cf.* RATTLE-TRAP.

1835. DANA, *Before the Mast*, xvii. A part of her crew . . . promised to conceal him and his TRAPS until the *Pilgrim* should sail.

1840. THACKERAY, *Comic Almanack*, 237, 'Cox's Diary.' Carry you, and your kids, and your TRAPS, etc. *Ibid.* (1854-5), *Newcomes*, xxx. A couple of horses carry us and our TRAPS.

1853. HALIBURTON, *Wise Saws*, etc. We call clothes and other fixins 'TRAPS' here, and sometimes 'duds' for shortness.

1857. KINGSLEY, *Two Years Ago*, xiv. On the first hint of disease, pack up your TRAPS and your good lady, and go and live in the watch-house across the river.

1869. STOWE, *Oldtown*, 147. The other was a sort of storeroom, where the old cap'n kep' all sorts o' TRAPS.

1877. HALE, *Adv. of a Pullman*, 143. A cheerful black boy followed with their other TRAPS, and so they crossed to the platform of the through-train.

1887. *D. Teleg.*, 3 Sep. As soon as the affair was over, the TRAPS were packed up as quickly as possible and the party drove away.

1900. NISBET, *Sheep's Clothing*, III. vii. He left his TRAPS at the wharf when he landed.

5. (Australian).—SWAG (*q.v.*).

6. (venery).—The female *pudendum*: also CARNAL TRAP: *see* MONOSYLLABLE and TRAPSTICK.

1653. URQUHART, *Rabelais*, II. xxi. Here within . . . showing his long codpiece, is Master John Thursday who . . . doth so well know how to find out all the corners . . . in your CARNAL TRAP.

TRAPAN, *subs.* and *verb.* (old: now recognised).—'He that draws in or wheedles a Cull, and Bites him. TRAPAN'D, c. Sharpt, ensnar'd'; 'to inveigle, to ensnare' (GROSE).

TRAPES (or TRAIPES), *subs.* (old). —1. A sloven, slattern, draggletail (B.E. and GROSE): a generic term of contempt for a woman; hence (2) a going or gadding about, in a more or less careless, objectless, or even lawless fashion: also TRAPESING. As *verb* (or TO TRAPE)=to gad about; to wander listlessly, or in a slovenly or bedraggled fashion: *cf.* TRESPASS, Fr. *trépasser*.

1673. COTTON, *Burlesque on Burlesque*, 274. I had not car'd If Pallas here had been preferr'd; But to bestow it on that TRAPES, It mads me.

1678. BUTLER, *Hudibras*, III. ii. 467. But when he found the solemn TRAPES. Possess'd with th' Devil, worms, and claps.

1705. VANBRUGH, *Confederacy*, ii. Has she not lost her diamond necklace? Answer me to that, TRAPES.

1715. GAY, *What d'ye call it*, i. 1. From door to door I'd sooner whine and beg . . . Than marry such a TRAPES.

1728. POPE, *Dunciad*, iii. 141. Lo, next two slip-shod muses TRAIPSE along, In lofty madness, meditating song.

1728. YOUNG, *Satires*, vi., 'On Women.' Since full each other station of renown, Who would not be the greatest TRAPES in town?

d. 1745. SWIFT, *Works* [*Century*]. I am to go TRAPING with Lady Kerry and Mrs. Pratt to see sights all this day.

1773. GOLDSMITH, *She Stoops to Conquer*, i. The daughter a tall, TRAPESING, trolloping, talkative maypole.

1843-4. HALIBURTON, *Attaché*, ii. So away goes lunch, and off goes you and the 'Sir' a-trampoosin' and a-TRAPESIN' over the wet grass agin.

1852. THACKERAY, *Esmond*, ii. 15. How am I to go TRAPESING to Kensington in my yellow satin sack before all the fine company?

1855. LELAND, *Meister Karl's Sketch-Book*, 259. It has happened more than once to Meister Karl, during his tourifications, TRAPESINGS, tramps, trudges, and travels, . . . to be thrown into many a canny country corner of New England.

1862. WOOD, *Channings*, 471. It's such a toil and a TRAPES up them two pair of stairs.

18[?]. PALMER, *Devonshire Courtship*, 14. It wasn't vor want o' a good will, the litter-legg'd TRAPES hadn't a' blowed a coal between you and me.

1885. *D. Chron.* 14 Oct. He would not be found TRAPESING about the constituency.

TRAPPER. *See* TRAP, *subs.* 3.

TRAPPING, *subs.* (old).—Blackmail; Fr. *chantage*.

[?]. *Countrey Gentleman's Vade Mecum.* And last for their art of TRAPPING. This is mystery that they commonly manage either by the assistance of a pregnant whore, or by the help of some letters, or papers, that they pick out of your pocket, that gives them an inlet into your affairs.

TRAPPY, *adj.* (colloquial).—Tricky, treacherous: also TRAPPINESS.

1882. *D. Teleg.*, 13 Nov. The fences might have increased in size, however, without being made TRAPPY.

1885. *Field*, 26 Dec. Once over this there were broad pastures and large banks and ditches, innocent of TRAPPINESS for the most part, before the riders.

TRAPSTICK, *subs.* (old).—1. In *pl.* =the legs (GROSE).

2. (venery). — The *penis*; MIDDLE-LEG (*q.v.*): *see* PRICK.

1673. COTTON, *Burlesque on Burlesque*, 283. Well, well! but he were best to take heed How he attacks my Maidenhead: His mighty TRAPSTICK cannot scare us.

1694. MOTTEUX, *Rabelais*, v. xlv. Ere long, my friends, I shall be wedded, Sure as my TRAP-STICK has a red head.

1772. BRIDGES, *Burlesque Homer*, 188. With his TRAPSTICK on the cock . . . With such a force he drove it in It made the light-heel'd gipsy grin.

TRASH, *subs.* (old colloquial).—1. Generic for trifles and worthlessness (now recognised): spec. a harlot: whence, TRASHERY (or TRASHTRIE)=rubbish, odds and ends; TRASHILY (or TRASHY)= worthless, useless; TRASH-BAG= a good-for-nothing; TRASHMIRE =a slattern; and (American) TRASH=a negro term of contempt: *see* WHITE TRASH.

1602. SHAKSPEARE, *Othello*, ii. 1. 312. This poor TRASH of Venice. *Ibid.*, v. 1. 85. I suspect this TRASH [a strumpet] To be a party in this injury.

c. 1622. HEYWOOD, *Fair Maid of the West* (1631), I. 35. I heare say there's a whore here that draws wine . . . And I would see the TRASH.

d. 1779. ARMSTRONG, *To a Young Critic.* Who riots on Scotch collops scorns not any Insipid, fulsome, TRASHY miscellany.

1787. BURNS, *Twa Dogs.* Wi' sauce, ragouts, and sic like TRASHTRIE, That's little short o' downright wastrie.

1813. SCOTT, *Bridal of Triermain*, ii. Who comes in foreign TRASHERY Of tinkling chain and spur.

2. (Old Cant).—Money: *see* RHINO.

c. 1590. GREENE, *James IV.*, iii. 1. Therefore must I bid him provide TRASH, for my master is no friend without money. *Ibid.*, *Alphonsus*, iii. 1. Nor would Belinus for King Crœsus' TRASH Wish Amurack to displease the gods.

1598. FLORIO, *Worlde of Wordes*, 93. Pelfe, TRASH, *id est*, mony.

1607. SHAKSPEARE, *Julius Cæsar*, iv. 3. 74. I had rather coin my heart, And drop my blood for drachmas, than to wring From the hard hands of peasants, their vile TRASH By any indirection.

1809. MALKIN, *Gil Blas* [ROUTLEDGE], 17. Money! said he, . . . you have a poor opinion of Spanish charity, if you think that people of my stamp have any occasion for such TRASH upon their travels.

TRAT, *subs.* (old).—An old woman; a witch (*q.v.*): in contempt: *cf.* TROT.

c. 1360. *William of Palerne* [E.E.T.S.], 4769. Tho two TRATTES that William wold haue traysted.

1383. CHAUCER, *Cant. Tales*, 'Freres Tale,' 7164. Come out, he sayd, thou olde very TRATE.

1512-13. DOUGLAS, *Virgil*, 122. Thus said Dido, and the tothir with that Hyit on furth with slaw pase like ane TRAT.

TRAV, *subs.* (Felsted School).—Travelling money.

TRAVEL, *verb.* (colloquial). — To walk: spec. to go quickly; usually with *along*: *e.g.* 'The motor TRAVELLED ALONG, and no mistake.'

TO TRAVEL OUT OF THE RECORD, *verb. phr.* (colloquial). To wander from the point at issue, or the matter under discussion.

1857. DICKENS, *Little Dorrit*, ii. 28. I have TRAVELLED OUT OF THE RECORD, sir, I am aware, in putting the point to you.

See BODKIN and TRAVELLER.

TRAVELLER, *subs.* (old). — 1. A highwayman. Hence TO TRAVEL THE ROAD=to take to highway robbery.

1707. FARQUHAR, *Beaux's Stratagem*, iv. 2. There's a great deal of address and good manners in robbing a lady; I am the most a gentleman that way that ever TRAVELLED THE ROAD.

2. (tramps').—A tramp.

1851-61. MAYHEW, *Lond. Lab.* There are many individuals in lodging-houses who are not regular patterers or professional vagrants, being rather, as they term themselves, TRAVELLERS.

3. (old).—A transported felon, a convict: also a TRAVELLER AT HIS (or HER) MAJESTY'S EXPENSE.

4. (common). — A *bonâ fide* traveller: *i.e.* a person who, under the Licensing Act, is entitled to demand refreshment during prohibited hours.

5. (thieves'). — A thief who changes his quarry from town to town.

6. (Australian).—A SWAGMAN (*q.v.*). Hence TRAVELLER'S-HUT=quarters on a station set aside for swagmen, stockmen, and others not eligible for the squatter's house.

1869. CLARKE, *Peripatetic Philosopher*, 41. At the station where I worked for some time (as 'knock-about-man') three cooks were kept during the 'wallaby' season—one for the house, one for the men, and one for the TRAVELLERS. Moreover, 'TRAVELLERS' would not unfrequently spend the afternoon at one of the three hotels (which, with a church and a pound, constituted the adjoining township), and having 'liqoured up' extensively, swagger up to the station, and insist upon lodging and food—which they got. I have no desire to take away the character of these gentlemen TRAVELLERS, but I may mention as a strange coincidence, that, was the requested hospitality refused by any chance, a bush-fire invariably occurred somewhere on the run within twelve hours.

1893. *Sydney Morning Herald*, 12 Aug., 8. 7. Throughout the Western pastoral area the strain of feeding the 'TRAVELLERS,' which is the country euphemism for bush unemployed, has come to be felt as an unwarranted tax upon the industry, and as a mischievous stimulus to nomadism.

1896. *Australasian*, 8 Aug., 249. 2. They never refuse to feed TRAVELLERS; they get a good tea and breakfast, and often ten to twenty are fed in a day. These TRAVELLERS lead an aimless life, wandering from station to station, hardly ever asking for and never hoping to get any work, and yet they expect the land-owners to support them.

TO TIP THE TRAVELLER, *verb. phr.* (common). — To humbug; to romance; to tell wonderful stories of adventure *à la Mun-*

chausen: also TRAVELLER'S-TALE and TRAVELLER'S TALENT (GROSE).

1760-62. SMOLLETT, *Greaves*, vi. Aha! dost thou TIP ME THE TRAVELLER, my boy?

TRAVELLING-PIQUET, *subs. phr.* (old).—'A mode of amusement, practised by two persons riding in a carriage, each reckoning towards his game the persons or animals that pass by on the side next them, according to the following estimation:—A parson riding on a gray horse, with blue furniture—game; an old woman under a hedge — ditto; a cat looking out of a window—60; a man, woman, and child in a buggy—40; a man with a woman behind him—30; a flock of sheep —20; a flock of geese—10; a postchaise—5; a horseman—2; a man or woman walking—1' (GROSE).

TRAVELLING SCHOLARSHIP, *subs. phr.* (University).—RUSTICATION (*q.v.*).

1794. *Gent. Mag.*, 1085. Soho, Jack! almost presented with a TRAVELLING SCHOLARSHIP? very nigh being sent to grass, hey?

TRAVELLING TRADESMAN, *subs. phr.* (common).—A respectable mechanic in search of work.

TRAVERSE. *See* CART and TOM COX'S TRANSVERSE.

TRAVIATA. *See* COME.

TRAY, *adj.* (thieves'). — Three spec. three months' imprisonment; TRAY SODDY MITS=threepence halfpenny. [It. *tre*, *soldi*, *mezza*.]

1897. MARSHALL, *Pomes*, 71. And the magistrate who interviewed her left but very little doubt That the moons she'd have to do would be a TRAY.

BEFORE ONE CAN SAY TREY-ACE, *phr.* (old).—In a moment.

TRAY TRIP, *subs. phr.* (old).—An ancient game like Scotch hop (or HOPSCOTCH), played on a pavement, marked out in chalk into different compartments.

TREACLE, *subs.* (common). — 1. Thick inferior port.

2. (common). Love-making, SPOONING (*q.v.*). TREACLE-MOON =the honeymoon.

TREACLE BOLLY. *See* BOLLY.

TREACLE-SLEEP, *subs. phr.* (colloquial).—*See* quot.

1849. CARLYLE [FROUDE, *Life in London*, viii.]. I fell first into a sluggish torpor, then into TREACLE-SLEEP, and so lay sound.

TREACLE TOWN, *subs. phr.* (common). — 1. Bristol: the city is an important centre of the sugar-refining industry. Also (2) = Macclesfield: in allusion to a hogshead of treacle which burst, and, for a time, filled the gutters.

TREACLE-WAG, *subs. phr.* (provincial).—Very small beer.

TREAD (or TREADLE), *subs.* (conventional). — The act of kind, properly of birds: as *verb* (or TO CHUCK A TREAD)=to copulate: *see* RIDE. TREADING=copulation; TREAD-FOWL=a cock-bird; and TREDDLE=a whore ('a cant term'—HALLIWELL).

1383. CHAUCER, *Cant. Tales*, 'Monk's Tale,' Prol., 57. Thow woldest han been a TREDEFOWEL aright.

1594. SHAKSPEARE, *Love's Lab. Lost*, v. 2. 915. When shepherds pipe on oaten straws; when turtles TREAD.

1594. LYLY. *Mother Bombie*, i. 3. Shee will choose with her eye, and like with her heart, before she consent with her tongue; shee will fall too where shee likes best; and thus the chicke scarce out of the shel, cackles as though shee had beene TRODEN with an hundredth cockes.

1612. CHAPMAN, *Widow's Tears*, i. 4. *Cers.* Did not one of the countess's serving gentlemen tell us . . . that he had already possessed her sheets? *To.* No . . . 'twas her blankets. *Cers.* Out, you young hedge-sparrow, learn to TREAD afore you be fledge!

1638. FORD, *Fancies*, iii. 3. Whore, bitch-fox, TREDDLE!

1692. DRYDEN, *Juvenal*, vi. And TREADS the nasty puddle of his spouse.

1694. MOTTEUX, *Rabelais*, v. ii. Kept, billed, and TROD their females like men, but somewhat oftener.

PHRASES. — TO TREAD ON ONE'S TOES = to vex, offend, or injure; TO TREAD ONE'S SHOES STRAIGHT = to go carefully, act discreetly, exercise caution.

1851–61. MAYHEW, *Lond. Lab.*, I. 318. I've heard the old man say . . . how he had to TREAD HIS SHOES STRAIGHT about what books he showed publicly.

1868–9. BROWNING, *Ring and Book*, I. 130. He could not turn about . . . Nor take a step . . . and fail to TREAD ON some ONE'S TOES.

See BLACK-OX; BOARDS.

TREADER, *subs.* (common). — A shoe.

TREASON, *subs.* (venery).—Adultery: also FLESHLY TREASON.

1607. DEKKER, *Westward Hoe*, v. 3. Those [diamonds] are they your husband . . . would have given to a niece of mine . . . to have committed FLESHLY TREASON with her.

TREASURE, *subs.* (venery). — The female *pudendum*: *see* MONOSYLLABLE.

1675. COTTON, *Scoffer Scoft* (1770), 261. Come, Ladies, blanch you to your Skins . . . And whilst your Judge with leering Eyes . . . I'll be so civil and so wise . . . To turn my back . . . And whilst your TREASURE you display Turn my Calves-head another way.

d. 1796. BURNS, *Merry Muses*, 'O saw ye my Maggy' (*c.* 1800), 61. My Maggy has a TREASURE, A hidden mine of pleasure.

TREASURY (THE), *subs.* (theatrical). —The weekly payment.

TREAT, *subs.* (old colloquial).—1. An entertainment or party; in modern usage spec. of children and schools. Hence (common) = something paid for by an elder or superior, or given as a token of good will and affection: *e.g.* a drink, a dinner, a theatre-ticket, an entertainment, or the like. Also (2) a turn in a round of drinks: 'It's my TREAT.' As *verb* (or TO STAND TREAT) = to bear the expense of refreshments, an outing, or an entertainment. Also 'It does me a TREAT' = 'That's O.K.; real jam, and no error.' *See* TREATING.

1660. PEPYS, *Diary*, I. 195. My wife and I by water to Captain Lambert's, where we took great pleasure in their turret-garden . . . and afterwards had a very handsome TREATE and good musique that she made upon the haipsicord.

1672. WYCHERLEY, *Love in a Wood*, i. 1. Did you ever know a woman refuse a TREAT? no more than a lawyer a fee. *Ibid.* Fetch us a TREAT, as you call it.

1695. PRIOR, *Prol. spoken in Westminster School.* Our generous scenes are for pure love repeated, And if you are not pleased at least you're TREATED. *Ibid.*, *Orphan*, 'Prologue.' Our gen'rous Scenes for Friendship we repeat; And if we don't Delight, at least we TREAT.

1706. *Fifteen Comforts of Matrimony.* Fine TREATS and balls she is invited to, And he, good man, consents that she shall go.

d. 1745. SWIFT, *Stella*, vii. I dined with Mr. Addison and Dick Stuart, Lord Mountjoy's brother: a TREAT of Addison's.

1748. SMOLLETT, *Rod. Random*, xlvii. I desired her, howevei, to sit, and TREATED her with a dish of tea. *Ibid.* (1749), *Gil Blas* (1812), II. ix. Thy uncle, the mercer, TREATED yesterday, and regaled us with a pastoral feast.

1848. THACKERAY, *Book of Snobs*, xxxv. We don't have meat every day . . . and it is a TREAT to me to get a dinner like this.

1855. HALIBURTON, *Human Nature* [BARTLETT]. I was never sold before, I vow; I cave in, and will stand TREAT.

1885. *Weekly Echo*, 5 Sep. She and the girl were attending with donkeys at the annual TREAT at a Convalescent Home for children.

1897. MARSHALL, *Pomes*, 39. He put down a sovereign to TREAT us, And I collared the change by mistake.

3. (common).—In sarcasm: a nuisance, a TERROR (*q.v.*), anybody or anything objectionable.

TREATING, *subs.* (political).—Bribery. [A candidate who corruptly gives, causes to be given, or is accessory to giving, or pays, wholly or in part, expenses for meat, drink, entertainment, or provision for any person, before, during, or after an election, in order to be elected, or for being elected, or for corruptly influencing any person to give or refrain from giving his vote, is guilty of TREATING, and forfeits £50 to any informer, with costs. Every voter who corruptly accepts meat, drink, or entertainment, shall be incapable of voting at such election, and his vote shall be void (*Abstract of Act of Parliament*).]

TREATING-HOUSE, *subs. phr.* (old). —A restaurant.

c. 1704. *Gentleman Instructed*, 287. The taverns and TREATING-HOUSES have eas'd you of a round income. *Ibid.*, 479. His first jaunt is to a TREATING-HOUSE; here he trespasses upon all the rules of temperance and sobriety.

TREBLE X'S (THE), *subs. phr.* (military).—The 30th Foot, now the 1st battalion East Lancashire Regiment. Also TRIPLE X'S.

TREDDLE. *See* TREAD.

TREE, *subs.* (old).—A gallows: also SUBSTANTIAL TREE, FATAL TREE, 'TREE that bears fruit all the year round,' the TREE with three corners, etc.; spec. (Biblical and colloquial) = the Cross. *See* TRIPLE-TREE and TYBURN-TREE.

1611. *Bible*, Acts x. 39. Whom they slew and hanged on a TREE.

c. 1690. BROWN, *Works*, i. 70. Tho' 'twas thy Luck to cheat the FATAL TREE.

1809. MALKIN, *Gil Blas* [ROUTLEDGE], 217. Tell us rather to wait for you under a more SUBSTANTIAL TREE.

d. 1892. WHITTIER, *Works* [*Century*]. But give to me your daughter dear, And, by the HOLY TREE, Be she on sea or on the land, I'll bring her back to thee.

Verb. — To perplex, get at one's mercy, put in a fix, drive to the end of one's resources. Whence, TREED (or UP A TREE) = cornered, obliged to surrender, DONE FOR (*q.v.*).

1847–8. THACKERAY, *Vanity Fair*, xxxiv. The dreadful predicament in which he found himself, in a house full of old women . . . 'Regularly UP A TREE.'

1859. KINGSLEY, *Geof. Hamlyn*, v. You are TREED, and can't help yourself.

PHRASES.—AT THE TOP OF THE TREE (*see* TOP); TO TREE ONESELF (American) = to conceal oneself, hide; LAME AS A TREE = very lame; TO BARK UP THE WRONG TREE (*see* BARK); 'Put not the hand between the bark and the TREE' = 'Meddle not in family matters': also BETWEEN BARK AND TREE (or WOOD) = a well-adjusted bargain.

1562. HEYWOOD, *Proverbs and Epigrams*, 67. It were a foly for mee, To put my hande BETWEENE THE BARKE AND TREE . . . Betweene you.

1600. HOLLAND, *Livy*, xxxvi. v. 921. To deale roundly and simply with no side, but to go BETWEEN THE BARK AND THE TREE.

1642. ROGERS, *Naaman*, 303. So audacious as to go BETWEENE BARKE AND TREE, breeding suspitions . . . betweene man and wife.

1804. EDGEWORTH, *Mod. Griselda* [*Works* (1832), v. 299]. An instigator of quarrels between man and wife, or, according to the plebeian but expressive apophthegm, one who would come BETWEEN THE BARK AND THE TREE.

1857. HUGHES, *Tom Brown's Schooldays*, I. vii. 'What a pull,' said he, 'that it's lie-in-bed, for I shall be as LAME AS A TREE, I think.'

Adj. (old). — Three: *e.g.*, TREEWINS = threepence; TREE-MOON = three months' imprisonment, etc. (GROSE): *see* TRAY.

TREE OF KNOWLEDGE, *subs. phr.* (Charterhouse: almost obsolete). —The tree under which books, etc., are piled in the interval between morning school and dinner.

TREER, *subs.* (Durham School: obsolete).—A boy who avoids organised sports, but plays a private game with one or two friends. [Presumably because played at the trees by the side of the ground.]

TREK, *verb.* (common). — To go away, run off, BUNK (*q.v.*): of South African origin, properly = to yoke oxen to a waggon.

TREMBLE, *subs.* (common). — Involuntary shaking; spec. when caused by excessive cold, fear, drinking, etc. Also, ALL OF A TREMBLE = agitated, excited, shivery-shaky.

1849. BRONTË, *Shirley*, xx. Mrs. Gill . . . came 'ALL OF A TREMBLE,' as she said herself.

1882. BLACKMORE, *Christowell*, xli. The housekeeper . . . to set a good example, ordered back her TREMBLES and came out.

TREMBLER, *subs.* (old).—In *pl.* = the extreme Protestant section of early Reformation days: *cf.* QUAKER.

1705. WARD, *Hudibras Redivivus*, I. x. 21. As thus I strol'd along the street, Such gangs and parcels did I meet Of these quaint primitive dissemblers, In old queen Bess's days call'd TREMBLERS; For their sham shaking, and their shivering.

See KNEE-TREMBLER.

TRENCH, *subs.* (venery). — The female *pudendum*: *see* MONOSYLLABLE.

1772. BRIDGES, *Burlesque Homer*, 35. The smooth rimm'd TRENCHES Of sooty, sweaty, negro wenches. *Ibid.*, 361. I'll give him seven wenches With fists so hard they've kept their TRENCHES From being storm'd.

TRENCHER, *subs.* (old). — 1. A square wooden platter: in general use before plates, and till lately at Winchester. Whence, TRENCHERING = eating; TRENCHER-BUFFON = a droll or butt whose place has been taken by the 'professional diner-out'; TRENCHER-CHAPLAIN = a domestic chaplain; TRENCHER-FLY (FRIEND, MAN, or MATE) = a hanger-on, smell-feast, parasite, or sponger: whence TO LICK THE TRENCHER = to sponge, to lickspittle; TRENCHER KNIGHT (or KNIGHT OF THE TRENCHER) = a serving man, or waiter at table: hence TRENCHER-CLOAK = a cloak worn by servants and apprentices; TRENCHER-MAN = (1) a hearty feeder (GROSE), one who 'plays a good knife and fork,' (2) = a cook, and (3) *see supra*; TRENCHER-LAW = the regulation of diet; TRENCHER-

CRITIC = an epicurean law-monger; TRIM AS A TRENCHER = as trim or exact as may be, as clean as a TRENCHER when licked.

1542. UDAL, *Eras. Apoth.*, 276. Filling vp as TRIMME AS A TRENCHER the space that stood voide.

1547. HEYWOOD, *Dialogues* [PEARSON, *Works* (1874), vi. 171]. His TRENCHER-FLIES about his table jearing.

d. 1586. SIDNEY, *Works* [*Ency. Dict.*]. Palladius assured him, that he had already been more fed to his liking than he could be by the skilfullest TRENCHER-MEN of Media.

1594. SHAKSPEARE, *Love's Labour Lost*, v. 2. 464. Some carry-tale, some please-man . . . some mumble-news, some TRENCHER-KNIGHT. *Ibid.* (1600), *Much Ado*, i. 1. He is a very valiant TRENCHER-MAN; he hath an excellent stomach. *Ibid.* (1609), *Timon of Athens*, iii. 6. Courteous destroyers, affable wolves, meek bears, You fools of fortune, TRENCHER-FRIENDS, time's flies.

1594. HOOKER, *Eccles. Politie.* These TRENCHER-MATES frame to themselves a way more pleasant.

1599. HALL, *Satires*, IV. iv. 221. When spleenish morsels cram the gaping maw, Withouten diet's care or TRENCHER-LAW; Tho' never have I Salerne rhymes profess'd To be some lady's TRENCHER-CRITIC guest. *Ibid.*, II. vi. 2. A gentle squire would gladly entertain Into his house some TRENCHER-CHAPPERLAIN.

1600. *Letting of Humours Blood in the Head-Vaine.* Spotted in divers places with pure fat, Knowne for a right tall TRENCHER-MAN by that.

1608. WITHALS, *Dict.*, 263. A fellow that can licke his lordes or his ladies TRENCHER in one smooth tale or merrie lye, and picke their purses in another.

1612. DAVIES, *Muse's Sacrifice*, Dedication. [Davies speaks of] TRENCHER-BUFFONS.

1678. COTTON, *Virgil Travestie* (1770), 134. The good TRENCHER-MAN, his nasty Sire.

1692. LESTRANGE, *Fables* [*Ency. Dict.*]. He tried which of them were friends, and which only TRENCHER-FLIES and spungers.

1847–8. THACKERAY, *Vanity Fair* [*Ency. Dict.*]. A led-captain and TRENCHER-MAN of Lord Steyne.

2. (University and schools).—A college cap, a MORTAR-BOARD (*q.v.*). [In shape thought to resemble an inverted trencher with a basin upon it.] Also TRENCHER-CAP.

1862. MRS. WOOD, *Channings*, 91. The college boys raised their TRENCHERS.

TREPAN. *See* TRAPAN.

TREY. *See* TRAY.

TREYNING-CHEAT. *See* TRINE.

TRIAL, *subs.* (Harrow). — An examination: hence TRIALS = the examinations at the end of the summer and winter terms.

TRIANGLE, *subs.* (military).—1. In *pl.* = a frame of three halberds stuck in the ground and bound at the top: to this soldiers were bound to be flogged: obsolete.

2. (common).—In *pl.* = delirium tremens: *see* JIM-JAMS.

TRIANTELOPE, *subs.* (Australian). —A comic variation of *Tarantula.* [Applied in Australia to a perfectly harmless spider (though popularly supposed to be poisonous), with mandibles, but which will attack nobody unless itself attacked.]

1846. HODGSON, *Reminiscences of Australia*, 173. The tarantulas, or 'TRIANTELOPES,' as the men call them, are large, ugly spiders, very venomous.

1860. ANON., *My Experiences in Australia*, 151. There is no lack of spiders either, of all sorts and sizes, up to the large tarantula, or TRI-ANTELOPE, as the common people persist in calling it.

TRIB, *subs.* (Old Cant).—A prison (B. E. and GROSE): *see* CAGE. [That is, *tribulation.*] He is in TRIB (B. E.) = 'he is layd by the Heels, or in a great deal of trouble.'

TRIBE, *subs.* (colloquial). — A number of persons: in contempt.

d. 1685. ROSCOMMON, *Prol. to Duke of Y. at Edinburgh*. Folly and vice are easy to describe, The common subjects of our scribbling TRIBE.

1859. TENNYSON, *Geraint*. A TRIBE of women dress'd in many hues.

TRIBUNE, *subs.* (Winchester: obsolete). — A large pew in ante-chapel: reserved for ladies.

TRIBUTE. TO DEMAND TRIBUTE OF THE DEAD, *verb. phr.* (old).— To attempt the impossible or absurd (RAY).

TRICK, *subs.* (old thieves')—1. A watch (TUFTS, 1798).

2. (nautical).—A turn; a spell: *e.g.* 'a TRICK at the helm.'

1835. DANA, *Before the Mast*, v. That night it was my turn to steer, or, as the sailors say, my TRICK at the helm for two hours.

3. (common).—In *pl.* = wantonness: spec. of women (BEE): whence TO GET UP TO TRICKS = to play the whore; BEEN PLAYING TRICKS = pregnant; TO DO THE TRICK = to get with child (*see* also PHRASES).

1681. RADCLIFFE, *Ovid Travestie*, 19. Had I been there you would have had the other bout. . . . Rise, said I, be very quick; This is no time for any wanton TRICK.

4. (Western American).—Belongings, THINGS (*q.v.*), BAGGAGE (*q.v.*).

PHRASES and COLLOQUIALISMS.—A TRICK WORTH TWO (or A BETTER TRICK) = (1) a better way, a smarter expedient, and (2) a slightly sarcastic refusal: *e.g.* 'No, thanks! It's all right, but I KNOW A TRICK WORTH TWO OF THAT'; TO DO THE TRICK = (1) to accomplish one's purpose, and (2) *see* TRICK, *subs.* 3; A TRICK WITH A HOLE IN IT (American), of anything extraordinary; TO TRICK AND TIE = (1) to be equal (sporting) and (2) to have something in reserve. Also (proverbial saying) 'TRICK FOR TRICK, and a stone in thy foot besides, quoth one, pulling a stone out of his mare's foot, when she bit him on the back, and he her on the buttock.'

1598. SHAKSPEARE, *1 Hen. IV.*, ii. 1. 41. Soft: I KNOW A TRICK WORTH TWO OF THAT.

d. 1704. BROWN, *Works*, i. 1. 'Go turn Country-Parson.' . . . 'Thanks to my stars, I KNOW A BETTER TRICK THAN THAT.' *Ibid.*, iii. 31. They KNOW A TRICK WORTH TWO OF HIS, and have often experimented, that if one won't another will.

1772. GRAVES, *Spiritual Quixote*, III. xv. 'Ah!' says she, 'it is as I feared; the key is gone!' I was thunder-struck at this news; but she said SHE KNEW A TRICK WORTH TWO OF THAT, and bidding me follow her, . . . she opened a door into the area.

1854-5. THACKERAY, *Newcomes*, i. Hear what he says of you, sir? Clive, best be off to bed, my boy—ho! ho! No, no. We KNOW A TRICK WORTH TWO OF THAT. We won't go home till morning, till daylight does appear.

1888. BOLDREWOOD, *Robbery Under Arms*, xxiv. We KNEW A TRICK WORTH TWO OF THAT.

1900. GRIFFITHS, *Fast and Loose*, xxxi. 'How many of you will there be?' 'Half a dozen TO DO THE TRICK.' More might attract suspicion.

See BAG-OF-TRICKS.

TRICK-AND-A-HALF, *subs. phr.* (old). — A master-stroke of roguery: *cf.* A-LIE-AND-A-HALF = the truth: in sarcasm.

TRICKETT, *subs.* (Australian).—A long drink of beer. [New South Wales, after Trickett, the champion sculler.]

TRICKY, *adj.* (colloquial).—Clever, smart, NEAT (*q.v.*): *cf.* TRICK (once literary) = neat, spruce, trim, elegant.

1877. HORSLEY, *Jottings from Jail*. He was very TRICKY at getting a poge or a toy.

TRIED VIRGIN, *subs. phr.* (old).— A harlot: *see* TART.

1694. MOTTEUX, *Rabelais*, v. 'Pant. Prog.' TRIED VIRGINS, *bona robas*, barbers'-chairs.

TRIG, *subs.* (old colloquial).—1. A cockscomb, a dandy; as *adj.* (also TRICK) = (1) neat, spruce, in good condition; whence (2) trustworthy, active, clever: also TRIG AND TRIM (or TRIG AND TRUE, TIGHT, etc.). [Obsolete, provincial, or colloquial in all uses.] Hence TRIGLY, TRIGNESS, and other derivatives.

c. 1200. *Ormulum*, 6177. Thin laferrd birrth the buhsumm beon & hold & TRIGG & TREWWE.

1512-13. DOUGLAS, *Virgil*, 402. In lesuris and on leyis litill lammes Full TAIT AND TRIG socht bletand to thare dammes.

1570. ELDERTON, *Lenten Stuffe* (HALLIWELL). So he that hathe a consciens cleere May stand to hys takkell TRYKLYE.

1610. JONSON, *Alchemist*, iv. 1. It is my humour: you are a pimp and a TRIG, And an Amadis de Gaul, or a Don Quixote.

1787. BURNS, *To W. Creech*. Auld Reekie aye he keepit tight, An' TRIG AND BRAW; But now they'll busk her like a fright, Willie's awa.'

1804. TARRAS, *Poems*, 124. O busk yir locks TRIGLY, an' kilt up yir coaties.

1816. SCOTT, *Antiquary*, xxiv. Fling the earth into the hole, and mak a' things TRIG again. *Ibid.* (1825), *St. Ronan's Well*, ii. 137. The younger snooded up her hair, and now went about the house a damsel so TRIG AND NEAT, that some said she was too handsome for the service of a bachelor divine.

1821. GALT, *Annals of Parish*, 29. The lassies who had been at Nanse Banks' school were always well spoken of . . for the TRIGNESS of their houses, when they were afterwards married.

1879. *Century Mag.*, xxviii. 541. The stylish gait and air of the TRIG little body.

1890. BARR, *Olivia*, xvil. I wish I was in mid-ocean all TRIG AND TIGHT, Then I would enjoy such a passion of wind.

2. (thieves').—'A bit of stick, paper, etc., placed by thieves in the keyhole of, or elsewhere about, the door of a house, which they suspect to be uninhabited; if the TRIG remains unmoved the following day, it is a proof that no person sleeps in the house, on which the gang enter it the ensuing night upon the screw, and frequently meet with a good booty, such as beds, carpets, etc., the family being probably out of town.' This operation is called 'TRIGGING the jigger' (GROSE).

Verb. (old).—1. To stop: as *subs.* = an obstacle, prop, or skid.

1630. TAYLOR, *Works* [NARES]. Yet I have heard some serjeants have beene mild, And us'd their prisoner like a Christian's child; Nip'd him in private, never TRIG'D his way.

1647. STAPYLTON, *Juvenal*, xvi. 62. Nor is his suite in danger to be stopt, Or, with the TRIGGS of long demurrers propt.

1651. CARTWRIGHT, *Poems*. Times wheels are TRIG'D, and brib'd to make a stand.

1870. JUDD, *Margaret*, iii. I stand ready to TRIG the wheels in all the steep places.

2. (old).—To trudge along, to hasten.

[?]. *Old Ballad*, 'Three Merry Butchers' [NARES]. As they rode on the road, And as fast as they could TRIG, Strike up your hearts, says Johnston, We'll have a merry jig.

1653. WILSON, *Inconstant Lady*. After such fearefull apparitions Hee TRIGGS it to Romilia's.

1676. ETHEREGE, *Man of Mode*, iii. 3. There's many of my own Sex With that Holborn Equipage TRIG to Gray's Inn Walks.

TO TRIG IT, *verb. phr.* (old: GROSE). — To play truant; to CHARLEY-WAG (*q.v.*).

TO LAY A MAN TRIGGING, *verb. phr.* (old: GROSE).—To knock down, TO FLOOR (*q.v.*).

TRIG-HALL, *subs. phr.* (old).—Open house; LIBERTY-HALL (*q.v.*).

TRIGIMATE (or **TRIGRYMATE**), *subs.* (old).—'An idle She-Companion' (B. E. and GROSE); 'an intimate friend' (HALLIWELL).

TRIKE, *subs.* (common).—A tricycle: *cf.* BIKE.

1901. *Pall Mall Gaz.*, 15 May, 1. 2. The commercial 'TRIKE' is, perhaps, the least supportable of the various tyrannies on wheels which it is the perambulating Londoner's lot to endure.

TRILL, *subs.* (old).—The *anus*: *see* BUM [HALLIWELL: 'a cant term'].

TRILLIBUB, *subs.* (old).—1. Tripe; hence (2) anything of trifling value or importance. Also TRILLABUB, TRULLIBUBBE, TROLLYBAG, etc. TRIPES AND TRULLIBUBS (GROSE) = a fat man.

1599. MASSINGER, *Old Law*, iii. 2. I hope my guts will hold, and that's e'en all A gentleman can look for of such TRILLIBUBS.

1614. JONSON, *Bartholomew Fair*, i. 1. There cannot be an ancient TRIPE AND TRILLIBUB in the town, but thou art straight nosing it.

1637. SHIRLEY, *Hyde Park*, iii. 2. But I forgive thee, and forget thy tricks And TRILLIBUBS.

TRILLIL, *verb.* (old).—To drink: onomatopœia.

1599. NASHE, *Lenten Stuffe* [Harl. Misc., vi. 166]. In nothing but golden cups he would drinke or quaffe it; whereas in wodden mazers and Agathocles' earthen stuffe they TRILLILD it off before.

TRIM, *subs.* (B. E. and GROSE: still colloquial). — Dress: spec. 'State dress' (GROSE). Hence as *adj.* (and *adv.*) = spruce, neat, WELL-GROOMED (*q.v.*); IN SAD TRIM = 'Dirty, Undrest'; A TRIM LAD = 'a spruce, neat, well-trickt Man' (B. E.); TO TRIM UP (or FORTH) = to dress, make clean and neat, set out: spec. to shave or clip the beard.

1530. PALSGRAVE, *Lang. Francoyse*, 762. I TRYMME, as a man dothe his heare or his busshe. . . . TRYMME my busshe, barber, for I intende to go amongest ladyes to-day.

1595. SHAKSPEARE, *Romeo and Juliet*, ii. 1. Young Adam Cupid, he that shot so TRIM. *Ibid.* (1601), *Henry VIII.*, i. 3. What a loss our ladies will have of these TRIM vanities. *Ibid.* (1608), *Antony and Cleopatra*, v. 2. I found her TRIMMING UP the diadem On her dead mistress.

1659-69. PEPYS, *Diary*, I. 187. Before I went to bed the barber come to TRIM me and wash me, and so to bed, in order to my being clean to-morrow.

1696. *Nomenclator* [NARES]. Their fronts or partes which are in sight, being smooth and TRIM on both sides, their naturall substance remaineth rough and unhewne, to stuffe and fill up the middest of a wall, etc.

Verb. (old colloquial).—1. To call to account, reprove, thrash; hence, TO TRIM ONE'S JACKET = to drub, 'dress down,' dust one's coat; TRIMMING = a beating, scolding, or jacketing; TRIMMER = (*a*) a severe disciplinarian, also of things, and (*b*) *see infra* (GROSE).

c. 1520. *Wife lapped in Morrell's Skin* [HAZLITT, *Early Pop. Poetry*, iv. 209], 717. For I will TRIM thee in thy geare, Or else I would I were cald a sow.

d. 1536. TYNDALE, *Works*, ii. 313. [OLIPHANT, *New Eng.*, i. 431. The priests propose to TRIM Queen Katherine.]

1611. CHAPMAN, *May-day*, iii. 2. I'faith we shall TRIM him betwixt us.

1772. BRIDGES, *Homer*, 157. But after that, I know it fact, He fifty blust'ring bullies thwack'd . . . He TRIMM'D their jackets every one.

1773. FOOTE, *Bankrupt*. [A severe leading article is called a TRIMMER].

1778. SHERIDAN, *Rivals*, ii. 1. *Fag.* So! Sir Anthony TRIMS my master; he is afraid to reply to his father; then vents his spleen on poor Fag.

1778. BURNEY, *Evelina*, xlvii. His mouth was wide distended into a broad grin at hearing his aunt give the beau such a TRIMMING.

18 . HOOD, *Trimmer's Exercise*. You've been spelling some time for the rod, And your jacket shall know I'm a TRIMMER.

2. (old). — To cheat; hence TRIMMING = 'Cheating People of their Money' (B. E.): *cf.* SHAVE.

3. (venery).—To deflower, to possess a woman: *see* RIDE: also TO TRIM THE BUFF. Hence UNTRIMMED = virgin, undeflowered.

1596. SHAKSPEARE, *King John*, iii. 1. 209. The devil tempts thee here, In likeness of a new UNTRIMMED bride.

1611. CHAPMAN, *May-day*, iv. 4. Twenty to one she is some honest man's wife of the parish, that he sits secure at home, little knowing, God knows, what hangs over his head.

c. 1620. FLETCHER and MASSINGER, *False One*, ii. 3. An she would be cool'd, sir, let the soldiers TRIM her.

1772. BRIDGES, *Homer*, 110. And he . . . has liberty to take and TRIM The buff of that bewitching brim. *Ibid.*, 112. Let him with Nell play tit for tat, And TRIM her till I eat my hat.

See TRIMMER.

TRIMMER, *subs.* (old).—1. Orig. nautical. Figuratively = a moderate man, one taking a middle course between two extremes. Hence (2) a waverer, apostate (GROSE), or time-server. Also TO TRIM, *verb*, and such derivatives as TRIMMING, etc. [In Eng. politics a party which followed the Marquis of Halifax (1680-96) in TRIMMING between the Whigs and the Tories: *see* quot. *infra*].

c. 1680. HALIFAX, *Character of a Trimmer*, Pref. The innocent word TRIMMER signifies no more than this: That if men are together in a boat, and one part of the company should weigh it down on one side, another would make it lean down as much to the contrary, it happens there is a third opinion, of those who conceive it would do as well if the boat went even without endangering the passengers.

c. 1680. NORTH, *Lives of the Norths*. [A certain party are called TRIMMERS.]

1682. DRYDEN, *Duke of Guise*, Epilogue. A TRIMMER cried (that heard me tell this story), Fie, Mistress Cooke! faith, you're too rank a Tory! Wish not Whigs hanged, but pity their hard cases.

c. 1680. [MACAULAY, *Hist. Eng.*, ii.] He was the chief of those politicians whom the two great parties contemptuously called TRIMMERS. Instead of quarrelling with this nickname, he [Halifax] assumed it as a title of honour. . . . Everything good, he said, TRIMS between extremes. . . . Thus Halifax was a TRIMMER on principle.

c. 1696. B.E., *Dict. Cant. Crew*. TRIMMER, a moderate Man, betwixt Whig and Tory, between Prerogative and Property. To TRIM, to hold fair with both sides. TRIM the Boat, poise it. TRIM of the Ship, that way she goes best.

1707. WARD, *Hud. Rediv.*, II. iv. 18. Let me know Whether . . . like TRIMMERS now-a-days . . . You equally extend both ways.

1710. HUGHES, *Hudibras Imitated*, 19. A creature of amphibious nature, That TRIMS betwixt the land and water, And leaves his mother in the lurch.

1809. IRVING, *Knickerbocker*, 270. He who perseveres in error without flinching gets the credit of boldness and consistency, while he who wavers in seeking to do what is right gets stigmatised as a TRIMMER.

1885. *D. Teleg.*, 6 Nov. Lord Hartington is not the sort of statesman to TRIM his opinions according to the expediency of conciliating or not conciliating.

1885. *D. Chron.*, 5 Oct. They wanted no such aristocrats or TRIMMING Whigs for that constituency.

See TRIM.

3. (colloquial).—Anything specially decisive, of good quality, or noteworthy; a SETTLER (*q.v.*): spec. (cricket) = a well-delivered ball. Hence TRIMMING = large, big, etc.

1816. SCOTT, *Antiquary*, xi. I will show you his last epistle, and the scroll of my answer—egad, it's a TRIMMER!

TRIMMING, *subs.* (colloquial).—1. In *pl.* = accessories: spec. those accompanying any dish or article of food.

1837. DICKENS, *Pickwick*, xxxvii. A boiled leg of mutton with the usual TRIMMINGS.

1839. KIRKLAND, *New Home* [BARTLETT]. A cup of tea with TRIMMINGS is always in season, and is considered as the orthodox mode of welcoming any guest.

1845. *Knickerbocker Mag.*, Aug. The party luxuriated at Florence's [eating-house] on lobster and TRIMMINGS.

1848. THACKERAY, *Snobs*, xx. Whenever I ask a couple of dukes and a marquis or so to dine with me, I set them down to a piece of beef, or a leg of mutton and TRIMMINGS.

1860. HOLMES, *Professor*, iii. Champion, by acclamation of the College heavy-weights, broad-shouldered, bull-necked, square-jawed, six feet and TRIMMINGS.

1899. WHITEING, *John St.*, xxi. Amerikins is all right . . . Theirs is a big country, too—bigger than ours: but we make it up in the TRIMMINS like.

2. *See* TRIM and TRIMMER.

TRIM-TRAM, *subs. phr.* (old).—A trifle; an absurdity; folly; nonsense. As *adj.* = foolish, nonsensical, trifling. Also (GROSE) 'like master, like man.'

1547. PATTEN [ARBER, *Eng. Garner*, iii. 70]. Our consciences, now quite unclogged from the fear of [the Pope's] vain terriculaments and rattle-bladders, and from the fondness of his TRIM-TRAMS and gewgaws.

1583. STANYHURST, *Æneid*, ii. 113. But loa to what purpose do I chat such janglerye TRIM TRAMS.

1760–2. SMOLLETT, *Sir L. Greaves*, xiii. They thought you as great a nincompoop as your 'squire—TRIM-TRAM, like master, like man.

1772. BRIDGES, *Homer*, 411. He's telling some long TRIM-TRAM story.

TRINCUM (or **TRINKUM**), *subs.* (old).—A trinket.

TRINE, *verb.* (Old Cant).—1. To hang: *see* LADDER (B. E. and GROSE). TRINING-CHEAT = the gallows. [That is, TRINE = three + CHEAT (*q.v.*), generic for thing.] Also TREYNE.

1567. HARMAN, *Caveat*, 31. Their end is either hanging, which they call TRINING in their language, or die miserably of the pox.

1610. ROWLANDS, *Martin Mark-all* (H. Club's Rpt., 1874), 37. If you will make a word for the gallows, you must put thereto this word, TREYNING, which signifies hanging; and so TREYNING CHEATE is as much to say, hanging things, or the gallows.

1612. DEKKER, *O per se O*, 'Bing Out, Bien Morts.' On chates to TRINE, by Rome-coues dine for his long lib at last.

2. (old).—To go.

1360. *Allit. Poems* (MORRIS). [We see the Danish TRINE (ire), which Scott used as a slang term, 'TRINE to the nabbing cheat.']

1609. DEKKER, *Lanthorne and Candlelight*. If we . . . dup but the gigger of a country-coves ken, from thence . . . we TRINE to the chats.

1622. FLETCHER, *Beggar's Bush*. And Herman Beck strine and TRINE to the Ruffin.

TRINGUM-TRANGUM, *subs. phr.* (old).—A whim, a fancy (B. E. and GROSE).

TRINKET, *subs.* (old: in some senses recognised).—1. In *pl.* = 'Porringers, and also any little odd thing, Toies and Trifles' (B. E.); 'toys, baubles, or nicknacks' (GROSE).

2. (venery).—The female *pudendum*: *see* MONOSYLLABLE.

1726. VANBRUGH, *Provoked Husband*, iii. 1. *Lord T.* Women sometimes lose more than they are able to pay, and if a creditor be a little pressing, the lady may be induced to try if, instead of gold, the gentleman will accept of a TRINKET. *Lady T.* My lord, you grow scurrilous.

TRIP, *subs.* (B. E. and GROSE: now recognised).—1. A short voyage or journey, an excursion: not in general use till 18th century: as *verb* (modern), or TO TRIP IT = to make short journeys; also TRIPPER (or TRIPPIST) = (1) an excursionist: often in the combination CHEAP TRIPPER. Also (2) a tram conductor, railway guard, or driver who gets paid by the trip (American).

c. 1360. *York Plays*, 142. And sertis I dred me sore To make my smal TRIPPE.

1698. FARQUHAR, *Love and a Bottle*, Epil. She, to return our foreigner's complaisance, At Cupid's call has made a TRIP to France. *Ibid.* (1699). *The Constant Couple, or A TRIP to the Jubilee* [Title].

1753. RICHARDSON, *Grandison*, v. 255. It will be but what mariners call a TRIP to England.

1886. *Modern Society*, 16 Jan., 117. With returning appetite came the desire to the convivial ocean TRIPPISTS to set sail again for the Mediterranean.

1887. *Referee*, 30 Oct. The unpromising outlook did not affect the attendance, which, as regards its day TRIPPERS, would not be stalled off by weather.

1890. *Academy*, 4 Jan., 3. The dialect is dying out in Manx before the inroads of the TRIPPER.

1890. BESANT, *Armorel*, ii. There are two men in her, and they've got no oars in the boat. Ignorant TRIPPERS, I suppose.

2. (old colloquial: now recognised).—A failure, mistake, or error: spec. the result of inadvertence or want of thought; 'an Error of the Tongue or Pen, a stumble, a false step, a miscarriage, or a Bastard' (B. E. and GROSE): *e.g.* She has made a TRIP = She has had a bastard.

1628. MILTON, *Vacation Exercise*, 3. And mad'st imperfect words with childish TRIPS.

1677. WYCHERLEY, *Plain Dealer*, v. 1. How, Cousin! I'd have you know before this *faux pas*, this TRIP of mine, the World cou'd not talk of me.

3. (old).—A moment; the 'twinkling of an eye.'

1726. VANBRUGH, *Provoked Husband*, 59. They'll whip it up in the TRIP of a minute.

4. (thieves').—A thief's woman; a FANCY PIECE (*q.v.*): *see* TART.

1877. HORSLEY, *Jottings from Jail*. It was at one of these places I palled in with a TRIP, and stayed with her until I got smugged.

c. 1888. *Referee* [*S. J. and C.*]. My TRIP—cuss the day as I seen her—She sold off my home to some pals in her mob For a couple of foont and ten deaner.

5. (theatrical).—The *pas de deux* by which harlequin and columbine introduce each scene in the harlequinade.

6. (American).—Threepence; 3d.: *cf.* THRIP, THREP, etc.

[?]. HILLS, *Vulg. Arith.* [*Century*]. The same vingten is woorth our TRIP, or Eng. 3d., or woorth halfe a Spanish royall.

TRIPE, *subs.* (once literary: now vulgar).—In *pl.* = the guts: whence the belly. Also in contempt both of persons and things; TRIPE-VISAGED = flabby, baggy, expressionless; MR. DOUBLE-TRIPE = a fat man: also TRIPES AND TRULLIBUBS (GROSE); TRIPE-CHEEK = a fat blowsy face.

1598. SHAKSPEARE, 2 *Henry IV.*, v. 4. 9. Thou . . . TRIPE-VISAGED rascal.

1614. JONSON, *Bartholomew Fair*, iv. 3. *Alice.* Thou sow of Smithfield, thou! *Urs.* Thou TRIPE of Turnbull.

c. 1630. HOWELL, *Letters*, ii. The Turk, when he hath his TRIPE full of Pelaw, or of Mutton and Rice, will go . . . either to the next Well or River to drink Water.

1834. HOOD, *Tylney Hall*, xxxv. I'm as marciful as any on 'em—and I'll stick my knife in his TRIPES as says otherwise.

TRIPLET, *subs.* (colloquial).—One of three at a birth; in *pl.* = three children at a birth.

1874. FLINT, *Physiology*, 941. We have in mind at this moment a case of three females, TRIPLETS, all of whom lived past middle age.

TRIPLE-TREE, *subs. phr.* (Old Cant).—The gallows: *see* NUBBING-CHEAT, LADDER, and TREE.

d. 1635. RANDOLPH [?], *Hey For Honesty*, iv. 1. This is a rascal deserves to ride up Holborn, And take a pilgrimage to the TRIPLE TREE, To dance in hemp Derrick's coranto.

1641. BROOME, *Jovial Crew*, i. What they may do hereafter under a TRIPLE TREE is much expected.

1694. MOTTEUX, *Rabelais*, IV. xvi. That very hour from an exalted TRIPLE TREE two of the honestest gentlemen in Catchpoleland had been made to cut a caper on nothing.

d. 1704. BROWN, *Works*, iii. 62. A wry mouth on the TRIPLE TREE puts an end to all discourse about us.

1855. LELAND, *Meister Karl*. For whether I sink in the foaming flood, Or swing on the TRIPLE-TREE, Or die in my bed as a Christian should, Is all the same to me!

TRIPLE X'S (THE), *subs. phr.* (military).—The 30th Foot, now the 1st battalion East Lancashire Regiment. Also TREBLE X'S.

TRIPOLY. TO COME FROM TRIPOLY, *verb. phr.* (old).—To vault or tumble; to perform with spirit (HALLIWELL).

TRIPOS, *subs.* (Cambridge Univ.).—Orig. the stool on which the champion of the University sat at the disputations held with the 'Father' in the Philosophy School on Ash Wednesday, at the admission of Bachelors of Arts to their degree; then it was transferred to the Bachelor himself; still later to the humorous, or, in some cases, scurrilous, speech with which 'MR. TRIPOS' opened the proceedings, and to the verses of the Bachelors at the Acts, each sheet of verses being called a TRIPOS or TRIPOS-paper. The honours-lists were printed (about 1747–8) on the backs of these verses, and so TRIPOS came to mean an honour-list, and, last of all, the examination itself. Until the year 1824 there was only one TRIPOS, the Mathematical; and up to 1850 only those who had obtained honours in mathematics were admitted to the Classical examination. The degree was not given for that examination

till a few years later. There are now nine TRIPOSES . . . founded in the following order: Mathematical, Classical, Moral Sciences, Natural Sciences, Theological, Law, History, Semitic and Indian Languages, with a Mediæval and Modern Languages TRIPOS from 1885.

TRIPPER. *See* TRIP.

TRIPPING UP. *See* CARRY THE STICK, adding quot. *infra.*

1887. *Daily Chronicle*, 18 Nov. A witness at the East End inquest yesterday alluded to 'TRIPPERS-UP,' as though everyone should know the n as they would bakers, butchers, grocers, or other tradesmen. To the Coroner's perplexed question, 'What is that?' Inspector Read answered: 'A man who TRIPS you up and robs you. If you make a noise they jump on you.'

TRISTRAM. SIR TRISTRAM'S KNOT, *subs. phr.* (old).—A halter; TO TIE SIR TRISTRAM'S KNOT = to hang: *see* LADDER.

TRIUMPH. TO RIDE TRIUMPH, *verb. phr.* (old colloquial).—To go helter-skelter, rough-shod, full tilt.

1759–67. STERNE, *Tristram Shandy*, iii. 157. So many jarring elements breaking loose, and RIDING TRIUMPH in every corner of a gentleman's house.

TRIVET. RIGHT AS A TRIVET, *phr.* (colloquial).—As right, secure, or good as may be. To SUIT TO A TRIVET = to suit perfectly. *See* RIGHT.

1837. BARHAM, *Ingoldsby Legends*, 'St. Romwold.' Go home! you'll find there all as RIGHT AS A TRIVET.

1843. DICKENS, *M. Chuzzlewit*, xxviii. He's all right now; you ain't got nothing to cry for, bless you! he's RIGHTER THAN A TRIVET. *Ibid.* (1865), *Mutual Friend*, ii. 14. 'As to the letter, Rokesmith,' said Mr. Boffin, 'you're AS RIGHT AS A TRIVET.'

1855. TAYLOR, *Still Waters*, ii. 2. 'How are you?' . . . 'RIGHT AS A TRIVET, my prince of prospectus mongers.'

TROC, *subs.* (London).—The Trocadero: formerly Music Hall, now Restaurant.

c. 1889. *Sporting Times*. 'Shall it be the Royal, Pav., or TROC?' And echo answered, 'TROC!'

1899. GOULD, *Racecourse and Battlefield*, viii. Come . . . we will celebrate my appointment in real good style. Where shall it be—the TROC, the Cri, the Princes, or the club?

TROJAN, *subs.* (Old Cant).—A term of commendation: (1) a plucky fellow, a STICKER (*q.v.*); and (2) a familiar address, either to equals or inferiors. Hence TRUSTY TROJAN (B. E. and GROSE) = a sure friend or confidant: also TRUSTY TROUT.

1594. SHAKSPEARE, *Love's Lab. Lost*, v. 2. 639. Hector was but a TROJAN in respect of this. *Ibid.* v. 2. 681. Unless you play the honest TROJAN.

1600. KEMP, *Dance to Norwich* [ARBER, *Eng. Garner*, vii. A good fellow is called a true TROJAN].

c. 1614. FLETCHER, *Night-walker*, ii. 1. Sam the butler's true, the cook a reverend TROJAN.

1628. FORD, *Lover's Melan.*, iv. 2. By your leave, gallants, I come to speak with a young lady, as they say, the old TROJAN's daughter of this house.

1837–8. THACKERAY, *Yellowplush Papers*, vii. He bore . . . [the amputation of his hand] in cors like a TROJIN.

(3).—A boon companion, a LOOSE FISH (*q.v.*); occasionally (but loosely) a thief.

1598. SHAKSPEARE, 1 *Henry IV.*, ii. 1. 77. Tut! there are other TROJANS that thou dreamst not of, the which, for sport's sake, are content to do the profession some grace. *Ibid.* (1599), *Henry V.*, v. 1. Dost thou thirst, base TROJAN, To have me fold up Parca's fatal web?

TROLL, *verb.* (B. E. and GROSE).—'To loiter or saunter about': *cf.* TRULL. As *subs.* (or TROLLOCKS)=a slattern: *see* TRULL.

TROLLOLL, *verb.* (old).—To sing in a jovial, rollicking fashion (B. E. and GROSE).

1740. NORTH, *Examen*, 101. They got drunk and TROLLOLL'D it bravely.

TROLLOP, *subs.* (old).—1. 'A lusty, coarse Ramp or Tomrig' (B. E. and GROSE); a hedge-whore: also (2) a generic reproach: of women. Whence TROLLOPING (TROLLOPISH or TROLLOPY)= wanton, filthy, draggletail. As *verb* (or TO TROLLOP ABOUT)=to gad about: spec. (modern)=to quest for men. Also TROLLOPEE =a loose dress for women: *cf.* LOOSE-BODIED.

c. 1641. MILTON, *Apol. for Smectym.* Does it not argue rather the lascivious promptnesse of his own fancy, who from the harmelesse mention of a Sleekstone could neigh out the remembrance of his old conversation among the Viraginian TROLLOPS?

1675. COTTON, *Burlesque upon Burlesque* (1770), 191. Had either so much Grace or Wit, Manners, or Shame, or altogether, As not to bring thy TROLLOPS hither.

d. 1704. BROWN, *Works*, ii. 273. I tell thee, thou insignificant north-country TROLLOP . . . that one soldier is better than a thousand . . . stiff-rump'd parsons.

1706. VANBRUGH, *Mistake*, i. We are no fools, TROLLOP, my master, nor me; And thy mistress may go—to the devil.

1754. LADY M. W. MONTAGU, *Letter*, 28 June. Yet the virtuous virgin resolves to run away with him, to live among banditti, to wait upon his TROLLOP, if she had no other way of enjoying his company.

1759. GOLDSMITH, *Bee*, No. 2. There goes Mrs. Roundabout—I mean the fat lady in the lute-string TROLLOPEE.

1771. SMOLLETT, *Humph. Clinker* (1900), i. 91. To take up with a dirty TROLLEP under my nose. . . . I ketched him in the very fact, coming out of the housemaid's garret.

1814. AUSTEN, *Mansfield Park*, xxxvii. A TROLLOPY-looking maid-servant, seemingly in waiting for them at the door, stepped forward.

1816. SCOTT, *Antiquary*, i. Yes, you abominable woman . . . all will see the like of it that have anything to do with your TROLLOPING sex.

TROLLYBAGS, *subs.* (provincial).—Tripe.

TROLLY-LOLLY, *subs. phr.* (old).—'Coarse Lace once much in fashion, now worn only by the meaner sort' (B. E., GROSE, and HALLIWELL).

TROLLYWAGS, *subs.* (common).—Trousers, breeches: *see* KICKS.

TROMBONING. TO GO TROMBONING, *verb. phr.* (venery).—To copulate: *see* RIDE.

TRONK, *subs.* (S. African).—A prison: *see* CAGE.

1875. LADY DUFF GORDON, *Letters from the Cape.* He informed me that he had just been in the TRONK, and on my asking why, replied, 'Oh, for fighting and telling lies.'

TROOPER, *subs.* (Old Cant).—A half-crown (B. E.).

PHRASES.—TO SWEAR LIKE A TROOPER (a simile of hard swearing), 'to volley oaths till the air is blue'; 'You'll die the death of a TROOPER'S horse' ('a jocular method of telling anyone he will be hanged, *i.e.* will die with his shoes on'—GROSE).

TRORK, *subs.* (back slang).—A quart.

TROS, *subs.* (back slang).—Sort: spec. of anything bad or not to one's liking. Thus TROSSENO= a bad day, coin, etc.; also DAB-TROS.

1866. *London Miscellany*, 3 Mar., 57. It was a regular TROSSENO. If it went on like that always, he said, he should precious soon nommus (cut it).

1851–61. MAYHEW, *Lond. Lab.* A regular scab! . . . and a coster declared he was 'a TROSSENO, and no mistake!'

TROT (or **TRAT**), *subs.* (old).—1. An old woman: in contempt: usually OLD TROT; a bawd: 'a sorry base old woman' (B. E.): 'a decrepit old woman' (GROSE).

1512–3. DOUGLAS, *Virgil*, B. iv. 96, l. 97. Out on the old TRAT agit wyffe or dame. *Ibid.*, 122, 39. Thus saith Dido, and the tother with that, Hyit or furth with slow pase like ane TROT.

1551. STILL, *Gammer Gurton's Needle*, i. 1. The OLD TROT sits groaning with alas and alas. *Ibid.*, ii. 2. I will have the young whore by the head and the OLD TROT by the throat.

1560. GASCOIGNE, *Supposes*, ii. 5. Goe: that gunne pouder consume the OLD TROTTE!

1570. TURBERVILLE, *Of a Contrerie Mariage.* Put case an aged TROT be somewhat tough? If coyne shee bring the care will be the lesse. *Ibid.* [CHALMERS, ii. 618]. A filthie Trull is yrksome to the eie. . . . An aged TROT to lyke is hard to finde.

c. 1586. WARNER, *Albion's England*, ii. 47. He got assurance to be wedded to the OLD deformed TROT.

1593. SHAKSPEARE, *Taming of Shrew*, i. 2. 80. Or an OLD TROT, with ne'er a tooth in her head, though she have as many diseases as two and fifty horses. *Ibid.* (1603), *Meas. for Meas.*, iii. 2. 52. What sayest thou, TROT? . . . Bawd is he doubtless, and of antiquity, too.

1593. CHURCHYARD, *Challenge*, 250. Awaie OLD TROTTS, that sets young flesh to sale.

1594. *Affectionate Shepheard.* This leare I learned of a beldame TROT, (When I was yong and wylde as now thou art).

1599. NASHE, *Lenten Stuffe.* A cage . . . roomsome enough to comprehend her, and the toothless TROT her nurse, who was her only chat mate and chamber maid.

1653. URQUHART, *Rabelais*, I. vi. An ugly OLD TROT in the company . . . had the reputation of an expert she-physician.

1678. COTTON, *Virgil Travestie* (1770), 138. The hobbling TROT limps down the Stairs.

2. (old).—An endearment: of a child learning to run.

1854–5. THACKERAY, *Newcomes*, x. Ethel romped with the little children, the rosy little TROTS.

1897. OUIDA, *Massarenes*, 10. She must not keep this bonbonnière; the contents are more than enough for a careless little TROT who knocks people about with her balloon.

3. (American schools').—A PONY (*q.v.*), CRIB (*q.v.*). Whence as *verb* (or TO TROT A LESSON) =to use a translation or other adventitious aid to study.

Verb. (thieves').—1. To steal in broad daylight.

2. (colloquial).—Generic for doing: thus TO TROT OUT (=express) AN OPINION; TO TROT OUT (=escort) A JUDY; TO TROT OUT (=sing) A SONG; TO TROT OUT (=spend) THE PIECES, and so forth. TO TROT ROUND=to take a turn round the town, the halls, etc.; ON THE TROT=on the GO (*q.v.*), pegging away; DOG-TROT ='a gentle pace' (GROSE); TO TROT UP (auctioneers')=to bid against, to run up prices.

1888. CHRISTIE MURRAY, *Weaker Vessel*, xiii. They would sit for hours solemnly TROTTING OUT for one another's admiration their commonplaces . . . until I tingled from head to foot.

1860. *New York Ev. Post*, 18 Feb. The friends of Alexander H. Stephens are making vigorous efforts to TROT HIM OUT for the Presidency.

TO TROT OUT (or FEED) ONE'S PUSSY, *verb. phr.* (venery).—To receive a man: *see* GREENS and RIDE.

PHRASE.—'He lies as fast as a dog can TROT' (of a persistent liar).

TROT-COSY, *subs. phr.* (old).—*See* quot.

1814. SCOTT, *Waverley*, i. 318. The upper part of his form . . . was shrouded in a large great-coat belted over his under habiliments, and crested with a huge cowl of the same stuff, which, when drawn over the head and hat, completely overshadowed both, and being buttoned beneath the chin was called a TROT-COZY.

TROTTER, *subs.* (old).—1. In *pl.* = the feet: orig. of sheep (B. E. and GROSE): whence SHAKE (BOX or MOVE) YOUR TROTTERS != 'Begone! troop off!' TO SHAKE ONE'S TROTTERS AT BILBY'S BALL (where the sheriff pays the fiddlers) =to be put in the stocks (GROSE: 'perhaps the Bilboes ball'). TROTTER-CASES (or BOXES) = boots or shoes.

1838. DICKENS, *Oliver Twist*, xviii. He applied himself to a process which Mr. Dawkins designated as 'japanning his TROTTER-CASES.'

1839. AINSWORTH, *Jack Sheppard*, ii. All's bowman, my covey! Fear nothing! We'll be upon the ban-dogs before they can SHAKE THEIR TROTTERS.

1892. WATSON, *Wops the Waif*, iv. Teddy, look out, yer-ve got yer hoof on my TROTTERS.

1899. WYNDHAM, *Queen's Service*, 52. That particular cut known as 'bell-bottoms' . . . technically known as 'having one's strides cut a bit saucy-like over the TROTTERS.'

2. (University).—A tailor's assistant: he goes on round for orders; also (dressmakers' and milliners') = a messenger: Fr. *trottin.*

1898. GISSING, *Town Traveller*, iv. Did she not well remember the day when the poverty of home sent her, a little girl, to be TROTTER in a workroom?

TROUBLE, *subs.* (various).—1. Imprisonment (thieves'); (2)=childbed, pregnancy (conventional); (3)=a TO-DO (*q.v.*): *e.g.* 'What's the TROUBLE?'='What's going on?' Hence IN TROUBLE=(1) arrested, QUODDED (*q.v.*); (2) pregnant, LUMPY (*q.v.*): spec. got with a bastard; TO GET INTO TROUBLE='to be found out and punished' (GROSE).

1555. CAVENDISH, *Cardinal Wolsey* [SINGER], 382. [The phrase] be IN TROUBLE [is used of a man imprisoned].

1871. *D. Teleg.*, 4 Dec. A friendly lead for the benefit of Bill, who is just out of his TROUBLE. *Ibid.* (1885), 16 Nov. He would have GOT INTO TROUBLE if the old people hadn't helped him out of it.

1899. JOHNSTON, *Old Dominion*, vii. My friend has been IN TROUBLE. . . . He will not make the worse conspirator for that.

1900. GRIFFITHS *Fast and Loose*, xxxi. 'It would be worse for everyone if I got into TROUBLE.' 'What are you talking about TROUBLE for? . . . While we are hustling the screws you . . . lead him off.'

Also in combination: TROUBLE-GUSSET (-GIBLETS or -GUTS)=the *penis*: *see* PRICK; TROUBLE-HOUSE = a disturber of family concord; TROUBLE-MIRTH = a wet-blanket, spoil-sport, mar-all; TROUBLE-REST = an element of discord, sickness, anything tending to unhappiness or discomfort; TROUBLE-STATE (or TOWN) = a rebel, an agitator, a 'drunk and disorderly.' Also PROVERBIAL SAYINGS, 'That horse is TROUBLED with corns' (*i.e.* foundered); 'TROUBLES never come singly' (*see* quot. 1509).

[1509. BARCLAY, *Ship of Fools* (JAMIESON, 1874), ii. 251. One myshap fortuneth never alone.]

1595–1609. DANIEL, *Civil Wars* [*Ency. Dict.*]. Those fair baits those TROUBLE-STATES still use.

1614. *I Would and Would not*, s.v. [TROUBLE-TOWN].

d. 1618. SYLVESTER, *Furies*, 328. Foul TROUBLE-REST, fantastik greedy-gut.

1635. QUARLES, *Emblems*, v. 14. Soul-boiling rage and TROUBLE-STATE sedition.

1653. URQUHART, *Rabelais*, I. xi. He had already begun to exercise the tools . . . and some of the women would give these names, my Roger . . . my smell-smock, TROUBLE-GUSSET, etc. *Ibid.*, I. liii. Ill-bred louts, simple sots, or peevish TROUBLE-HOUSES.

1821. SCOTT, *Kenilworth*, xxxvii. But once more to this same TROUBLE-MIRTH, this Lady Varney.

TROUNCE, *verb.* (once literary: now colloquial).—To vex, trouble, punish; now to beat severely. [B. E.: 'TROUNC'D, troubled, cast in Law, Punisht; I'll TROUNCE the Rogue, I'll hamper him': GROSE: 'to punish by course of law.'] Whence TROUNCING = a drubbing.

1551. *Bible*, Judges iv. 15. The Lord TROUNSED [*Auth. Ver.* 'discomfited'] Sisara and all his charettes.'

c. 1614. *Faithful Friends*, i. 2. Well, sir, you'll dearly answer this: My master's constable; he'll TROUNCE you for't.

1772. BRIDGES, *Homer*, 184. By Jove, for all their bouncing, I'll give their rogueships such a TROUNCING.

1887. *Scribner's Mag.*, July, 283. We threatened to TROUNCE him roundly when he got sober.

TROUT. *See* NORLOCH TROUT and PECULIAR RIVER.

TROWEL. TO LAY ON WITH A TROWEL, *verb. phr.* (old).—1. To flatter or exaggerate grossly; TO BUTTER (*q.v.*). Also (2) to lie (RAY); and (3) to use powder, paint, or the like, without stint.

1600. SHAKSPEARE, *As You Like It*, i. 2. Well said: that was LAID ON WITH A TROWEL.

1694. CONGREVE, *Double Dealer*, iii. 10. Paints, d'ye say? Why she LAYS IT ON WITH A TROWEL . . . has a great beard that bristles through it, and makes her look as if she were plastered with lime and hair.

TRUB, *subs.* (old colloquial).—A slattern; 'a short squat woman' (AINSWORTH). Also TRUBAGULLY = 'a short dirty ragged fellow, accustomed to performing the most menial offices' (HALLIWELL).

TRUCK, *subs.* (colloquial).—1. Intercourse, dealing: *e.g.* 'I'll have no TRUCK with you.' Orig. (and still colloquial American), exchange, trading, espec. the barter of small commodities; whence (in contempt) odds and ends, rubbish, and spec. bad food, CAGMAG (*q.v.*), MULLOCK (*q.v.*). Also (now recognised) TRUCK-SYSTEM (TRUCK-SHOP), etc.=the payment of wages in kind instead of money: illegal since 1870–5. As *verb* (originally and still literary) = 'to swop, barter, or exchange' (B. E. and GROSE).

c. 1608. [Capt. JOHN SMITH, *Works*, I. 82.] Much other TRUCKE we had, and after two dayes he came aboord, and did eate and drinke with vs very merrily.

1622. MOURT, *Journal* [App. *New England's Memorial*, 360]. Retaining Tisquantum to send from place to place to procure TRUCK for us.

1716. CHURCH, *Indian War.* Now they passed down into Punkatees Neck; and in their march they found a large wigwam full of Indian TRUCK, which the soldiers were for loading themselves with.

1778. *Annals of Salem* [BARTLETT]. About this time family stores were usually called TRUCK. . . . She looked out of the window for the market people, to ask them if they would take TRUCK for their produce.

18[?]. *Chronicles of Pineville*, 40. They purchased homespun, calico, salt, rum, tobacco, and such other TRUCK as their necessities called for.

1844. *Major Jones's Travels.* If the people of Georgia don't take to makin' homespun and sich TRUCK for themselves, and quit their everlastin' fuss about the tariff and free trade, the first they'll know, the best part of their population will be gone to the new States.

1848. LONGSTREET, *Georgia Scenes*, 192. 'What do the doctors give for the fever and ague?' 'Oh, they give abundance o' TRUCK.'

1884. CLEMENS, *Huck. Finn.* No use to take TRUCK and leave money.

1899. WHITEING, *John Street*, xxvi. Fust time in 'er life . . . she's ever 'AD ANY TRUCK with any of them sort.

2. (common). — In *pl.* = trousers: *see* KICKS.

3. (nautical). — A hat: *see* GOLGOTHA.

TRUCKLE-BED, *subs. phr.* (old).—In saying, 'To stumble at the TRUCKLE- (or TRUNDLE-) BED' = (RAY) 'to mistake the chambermaid's bed for his wife's.' [Formerly a low bed on small wheels or castors was trundled under a 'standing-bed' in the daytime, and drawn out at night for a servant to sleep on.]

1660-9. PEPYS, *Diary*, III. 269. My wife and I in the high bed in our chamber, and Willet in the TRUNDLE-BED, which she desired to lie in, by us.

TRUE, *adj.* (old colloquial).—Honest: usually in contrast with 'thievish,' or TRUE MAN *v.* thief. Also (proverbial) TRUE AS TRUE (AS THE GOSPEL, GOD IN HEAVEN, AS I STAND HERE, etc.) = as true as may be.

d. 1400. CHAUCER, *Good Women*, 464. For why a TREWE MAN, withouten drede Hath nat to parten with a theves dede.

1513-25. SKELTON, *Poems* [DYCE], ii. 321. TREWE AS THE GOSPELL.

1592. MARLOWE, *Edward II.* [DODSLEY, *Old Plays* (REED), ii. 362]. We will not wrong thee so, To make away a TRUE MAN for a thief.

1593. SHAKSPEARE, *Venus and Adonis*, 724. Rich preys make TRUE MEN thieves. *Ibid.* (1594), *Love's Lab. Lost*, iv. 3. 187. Whither away so fast? A TRUE MAN, or a thief, that gallops thus? *Ibid.* (1598), 1 *Henry IV.*, ii. 1. 98. The thieves have bound the TRUE MEN. *Ibid.*, iii. 3. Now, as I am a TRUE WOMAN, holland of eight shillings an ell. *Ibid.* (1608), *Ant. and Cleop.*, ii. 6. *En.* There is never a fair woman has a TRUE face. *M.* No slander. They steal hearts.

1610. *Mirr. for Mag.*, 277. The TRUE MAN we let hang some whiles, to save a thief.

TRUE-BLUE, *adj.* and *subs.* (old colloquial). — 1. Unmistakable, honest, staunch, dependable: as *subs.*, a thoroughly reliable, good fellow, a stalwart: also BLUE (*q.v.*). [Blue is regarded as the colour or emblem of constancy, but whether in reference to the blue of sky or sea (both proverbially deceitful) or the fastness of some dye (*e.g.* Coventry blue) is unknown.] Hence spec. (2) in 17th century = the Scotch Presbyterians or Whigs: the Covenanters had adopted BLUE as against the Royal *red*; in later times staunchly Liberal or Tory, according to the choice made of blue as a party-colour by either, but mostly Conservative.

[*c.* 1500. *Balade agst. Women Unconst.* [STOW, *Chaucer* (1561), 340]. To newe thinges your lust is euer kene In stede of BLEW, thus may ye were al grene.]

d. 1635. RANDOLPH [?], *Hey for Honesty*, ii. 3. Be merry, TRUE BLUE, be merry: thou art one of my friends too.

1663. BUTLER, *Hudibras*, I. i. 191. For his Religion . . . 'Twas Presbyterian TRUE BLUE.

1674. FAIRFAX, *Bulk and Selv.*, 171. It being TRUE BLEW Gotham or Hobbes ingrain'd, one of the two.

1705. HICKERINGILL, *Priest-cr.*, II. viii. 86. The old Beau is TRUE-BLEW . . . the Highflown Principles.

1762. *Gent. Mag.*, 442. Honest, TRUE BLUES, a staunch, firm, chosen band.

1785. BURNS, *Author's Earn. Cry*, xiii. Dempster, a TRUE BLUE Scot, I'se warrant.

1818. SCOTT, *Heart Mid.* (1873), 75. A tough TRUE-BLUE Presbyterian called Deans.

1860. TROLLOPE, *Framley Pars.*, i. 10. There was no part of the country more decidedly TRUE BLUE.

1866. ELIOT, *Felix Holt*, xvii. This gentleman . . . is one of ourselves: he is a TRUE BLUE.

TRUE INWARDNESS, *subs. phr.* (literary). — The real meaning, BOTTOM (*q.v.*) facts, final result or end of a matter.

TRUEPENNY, *subs.* (old). — A familiar address: in commendation, but sometimes loosely used (*cf.* CASAUBON, *De Quatuor Linguis Commentatio*, pars prior [1650], p. 362; TRUEPENIE is defined as 'veterator vafer,' that is, a sly, cunning fellow, an old soldier): also (as in 'old boy') OLD TRUEPENNY.

1596. SHAKSPEARE, *Hamlet*, i. 5. 150. 'Say'st thou so? art thou there, TRUEPENNY? Come on.'

1604. MARSTON, *Malcontent* [OLD TRUEPENNY].

1618. FLETCHER, *Loyal Subject*, i. 3. Go, go thy ways, OLD TRUE-PENNY! Thou hast one fault: Thou art even too valiant.

1830. FORBY, *Vocab. East Anglia*. TRUE-PENNY. 'Generally OLD-TRUEPENNY, as it occurs in Sh. *Hamlet*, where the application of it to the ghost is unseemly and incongruous, yet it has attracted no notice from any commentator. Its present meaning is, hearty old fellow; staunch and trusty; true to his purpose or pledge' (FORBY). This appears more to the purpose than the information given by Mr. Collier, 'it is a mining term, and signifies a particular indication in the soil of the direction in which ore is to be found.'

TRUFF, *verb.* (Scots).—To steal: *see* PRIG.

d. 1758. RAMSAY, *Lucky Spence* [*Century*]. Be sure to TRUFF his pocket-book.

TRUG (TRUGGE or TRUK), *subs.* (old).—1. A concubine, a harlot: *see* TART; (2) 'a dirty Puzzel, an ord'nary sorry Woman (B. E., *c.* 1696); (3) a catamite. Hence TRUGGING-KEN (or HOUSE) = a brothel: *see* NANNY-SHOP.

1592. GREENE, *Quip* [Harl. Misc., v. 405]. A bowsie bawdie miser, goode for none but himself and his TRUGGE. *Ibid.*, 406. The TRUG his mistress. *Ibid.*, *Theeves Falling Out* [Harl. Misc. (PARK), viii. 401]. One of those houses of good hospitallity whereunto persons resort, commonly called a TRUGGING-HOUSE, or to be plain, a whore-house.

1607. MIDDLETON, *Five Gallants*, i. 1. A pretty middle-sized TRUG.

1608. DEKKER, *Belman of London*. The whore-house, which is called a TRUGGING-PLACE.

1620. HEALEY, *Disc. New World*, 194. Every other house keepes sale TRUGGES or Ganymedes, all which pay a yearly stipen, for the licence they have to trade.

1630. TAYLOR, *Works* [NARES]. Besides, I found a cursed catalogue of these veneriall caterpillars, who were supprest with the monasteries in England, in the time of king Henry the eight, with the number of TRUGS which each of them kept in those daies.

1648-50. BRAITHWAIT, *Barnaby's Jo.*, iv. Steepy ways by which I waded, And those TRUGS with which I traded.

TRULL, *subs.* (old).—A wanton, a harlot: spec. a hedge-whore, a TROLLOP (*q.v.*); 'a soldier's, beggar's, or tinker's wife or wench' (B. E. and GROSE).

d. 1529. SKELTON, *Works* [OLIPHANT, *New Eng.*, i. 372. There is *trowle* (TRULL) from the High German.]

c. 1530. RASTELL, *Four Elements*. For to satisfye your wanton lust I shall apoynt you a TRULL of trust, not a feyrer in this towne.

1567. TURBERVILLE, *Poems* [CHALMERS, ii. 618]. A filthie TRULL is yrksome to the eie.

1569. PRESTON, *Cambyses* [DODSLEY, *Old Plays* (HAZLITT), iv. 181]. *Meretrix*. What, is there no lads here that hath a lust To have a passing TRULL?

1605. CHAPMAN, *All Fools*, iv. A beggar too, a TRULL, a blowse!

1610. FLETCHER, *Maid's Tragedy*, i. 2. This is no place for such youths and their TRULLS.

1611. CORYAT, *Crudities*, I. 104. I never saw in all my life such an ugly company of TRULS and sluts as their women were.

1637. DAVENANT, *Brit. Tri.* [*Dram. Rest.*, ii. 280]. Shall I grow weak as babe when ev'ry TRULL is So bold to steal my sloes?

1638. FORD, *Lady's Trial*, iii. 1. The wench is your TRULL, your blouze, your dowdie.

d. 1639. WOTTON [*England's Helicon*]. Be thy voyce shrill, be thy mirth scene: Heard to each swaine, scene to each TROLL.

1648-50. BRAITHWAIT, *Drunken Barnaby*, II. 61. Thence to Holloway, Mother Redcap, Where a troop of TRULLS I did hap.

1659. MASSINGER, *City Madam*, ii. 2. Tinker's TRULL, A beggar without a smock.

1678. COTTON, *Virgil Travestie* (1770), 126. Shall I invite to be my Spouse . . . Æneas' Leavings, or, like TRULL here Run away basely with this sculler?

1688. RAND. HOLME, *Acad. Armory*. Guteli, or trulli, are spirits like women, which show great kindness to men, and hereof it is that we call light women TRULLS.

1693. STEPNEY, *Juvenal*, viii. To make the world distinguish Julia's son, From the vile offspring of a TRULL, who sits By the town wall.

1694. MOTTEUX, *Rabelais*, v. xxviii. Buttock of a monk! . . . how plump these plaguy TRULLS, these arch semiquavering strumpets must be!

1700. CONGREVE, *Way of the World*, i. 8. These are TRULLS whom he allows coach-hire.

1707. WARD, *Hud. Rediv.*, II. ii. 15. This is the Charm that tempts rich Fools To marry worthless Jilts and TRULLS.

1727. SOMERVILE, *Fables*, etc., xiii. Leave, leave, for shame your TRULLS at Sh——er hall, And marry in good time or not at all.

1748. SMOLLETT, *Rod. Random*, xlvii. This friend is no other than a rascal who wants to palm his TRULL off upon you for a wife.

TRULY. *See* BY MY TRULY and YOURS TRULY.

TRUMP, *subs.* (colloquial).—1. A good fellow, a friend in need, 'one (GROSE) who displays courage on every suit': the highest measure of praise.

1774. BRIDGES, *Homer*, 26. But I, in spite of all his frumps, Shall make him know I'm king of TRUMPS.

1837. BARHAM, *Ingolds. Leg.*, 'The Execution.' What must I fork out tonight, my TRUMP, For the whole first-floor of the Magpie and Stump?

1843. DICKENS, *Chuzzlewit*, xxviii. I wish I may die if you are not a TRUMP, Pip.

d. 1849. POE, *Works*, IV. 211. Thingum, my boy, you're a TRUMP.

1857. HUGHES, *Tom Brown's Schooldays*, i. 6. Tom . . . took his three tosses without a kick or a cry, and was called a young TRUMP for his pains.

1873. CARLTON, *Farm Ballads*, 86. The editor sat in his sanctum, and brought down his fist with a thump: 'God bless that old farmer,' he muttered, 'He's a regular editor's TRUMP.'

2. (provincial).—A FART (*q.v.*): also as *verb*.

1774. BRIDGES, *Homer*, 456. To which her bum plaid double-bass And made such thund'ring as she TRUMP'D, Both Ajax and Achilles jump'd.

3. (Scots). — A Jew's harp. Whence TONGUE OF THE TRUMP = a chief, an essential: properly the steel spring or reed by which the sound is produced.

d. 1872. MACLEOD, *Life in a Highland Bothy*. He has two large Lochaber TRUM. S, for Lochaber trumps were to the Highlands what Cremona violins were to musical Europe. He secures the end of each with his teeth, and, grasping them with his hands so that the tiny instruments are invisible, he applies the little finger of each hand to their vibrating steel tongues.

PHRASES. — TO BE PUT TO ONE'S TRUMPS = to be in difficulties (GROSE), driven to the last shift, or full exertion of one's strength; TO TURN UP TRUMPS = to fall out fortunately: *e.g.* 'something may TURN UP TRUMPS' = something lucky may happen (GROSE): 'all his cards are TRUMPS' = he is exceedingly fortunate.

1593. PEELE, *Edward I.*, iv. Ay, there's a card which PUTS US TO OUR TRUMP.

1609. *Amm. Marc.* Upon this strange accident, and for feare of some greater mischiefe to ensue, he was PUT TO HIS TRUMPES.

1655. BRIAN, *Pisse-Prophet*, 27. Now I am like to have a hard task of it, and to be so PUT TO MY TRUMPS, that if I play not my cards sure, I shall lose the set.

1694. CONGREVE, *Double Dealer*, ii. 3. Though marriage makes man and wife one flesh, it leaves 'em still two fools. . . . 'Tis an odd game . . . [but] since we've shuffled and cut, let's even TURN UP TRUMP now.

TRUMPERY, *subs.* (old). — 'Old Ware, old Stuff, as old Hatts, Boots, Shoes, etc.' (B. E.); 'an old whore, or goods of no value, rubbish' (GROSE): also TRASH AND TRUMPERY, and (proverbial) 'For want of good Company, welcome Trumpery.' Whence (modern) generic for showy trashiness, and as *adj.* = meretricious, worthless.

c. 1574. *Mir. for Mag.* i. 397. Here to repeate the partes that I haue playd Were to vnrippe a trusse of TRUMPERY.

1609. SHAKSPEARE, *Tempest*, iv. 1. 186. The TRUMPERY in my house go bring hither, For stale to catch these thieves.

1637. HALL, *Sermons at Exeter*, Aug. What a world of fopperies there are, of crosses, of candles, of holy water, and salt, and censings! Away with these TRUMPERIES.

d. 1699. STILLINGFLEET, *Sermons*, II. viii. All the TRUMPERY of the Mass and Follies of their Worship are by no means superstitions because required by the Church.

1749. FIELDING, *Tom Jones*, v. iv. If I was as Mr. Jones I should look a little higher than such TRUMPERY as Molly Seagrim.

1821. LAMB, *Old Benchers*. Extinct be the fairies and fairy TRUMPERY of legendary fabling.

1835. HOOK, *Gilbert Gurney*, II. i. A very TRUMPERY case it is altogether, that I must admit.

1885. *Field*, 26 Dec. Through the gate on to the road, over the TRUMPERY gap staring you full in the face.

TRUMPET. TO BLOW (or SOUND) ONE'S OWN TRUMPET, *verb. phr.* (old).—To praise (or talk about) oneself, to brag (GROSE). Hence 'His TRUMPETER is dead' (of a braggart).

1871. *Times*, 4 Nov. When a gentleman began by BLOWING HIS OWN TRUMPET, it was not altogether jannock.

TRUMPETER, *subs.* (various phrases).—KING OF SPAIN'S (or SPANISH) TRUMPETER = a braying ass, *i.e.* Don Key (GROSE); 'His TRUMPETER is dead' (*see* TRUMPET); 'He would make a good TRUMPETER, for he smells strong' (GROSE): 'of one with fœtid breath.'

TRUNDLER, *subs.* (old).—In *pl.* = peas (B.E. and GROSE: 'obsolete').

TRUNDLING-CHEAT, *subs.* (Old Cant).—A wheeled vehicle; a cart or coach: *see* CHEAT.

1630. JONSON, *New Inn*, iii. 2. They'll steal to bed . . . in private . . . and pay the fiddlers . . . next morning . . . and pack away in their TRUNDLING-CHEATS like gipsies.

TRUNK, *subs.* (old).—1. A blockhead, a dunce (BLOUNT, 1656).

2. (common).—In *pl.* = trunk-hose: *cf.* SMALLS, TOPS, TIGHTS, etc. Also (modern) = (1) breeches: *see* KICKS, and (2) = bathing-drawers.

1613. BEAUMONT and FLETCHER, *Captain*, iii. 3. He look'd, in his old velvet TRUNKS And his slic'd Spanish jerkin, like Don John.

1851-61. MAYHEW, *Lond. Lab.*, III. 120. Red striped cotton stockings, with full TRUNKS dotted red and black.

3. (old).—A nose (B. E. and GROSE). 'How's your old TRUNK?' = a jeer at a big-nosed man; TO SHOVE A TRUNK = to poke one's nose in, 'to introduce oneself unasked into any place or company' (GROSE).

TRUNKMAKER-LIKE, *adj. phr.* (old).—More noise than work (GROSE).

TRUNK-WORK, *subs. phr.* (old).—Underhand (or secret) dealing: *cf.* BACK-DOOR WORK.

1604. SHAKSPEARE, *Winter's Tale*, iii. 3. This has been some stair-work, some TRUNK-WORK, some behind-door work.

TRUSTED ALONE, *phr.* (GROSE).—'This bit of flash is made use of in speaking of any knowing or experienced person, meaning that he is so deep as to the tricks of the town that he may be "TRUSTED ALONE" in any company without danger to himself.'

TRUSTY, *subs.* (Irish).—1. An overcoat.

18[?]. EDGEWORTH, *Limerick Gloves*, ii. 'There was a sort of a frieze TRUSTY.' 'A TRUSTY!' said Mr Hill, 'what is that, pray?' 'A big coat, sure, plase your honour.'

2. (American).—A convict with special privileges, such as a ticket of leave.

1884. *Century Mag.*, xxxviii. 448. By far the greater number of criminals confined in the jails of the Far West are there for a class of offences peculiar to the country. They are men dangerous in one direction, perhaps, but generally not depraved. The TRUSTIES are often domesticated upon ranches near the town, and apparently are unwatched, and on the best of terms with the ranchman's family.

See TROJAN.

TRUT, *intj.* (old).—An exclamation of contempt; SHIT! (MANNING (1337), 317; *Prompt. Parv.* (1440), 505).

TRUTH. TELL THE TRUTH AND SHAME THE DEVIL, *phr.* (old).—To reveal all at any cost.

[1469. *Cov. Myst.* [HALLIWELL], 367. TREWTH DYD nevyr HIS MAYSTIR SHAME.]

1548. PATTEN, *March into Scotland* [ARBER, *Garner*, iii. 61]. SAY TRUTH AND SHAME THE DEVIL.

1632. JONSON, *Magn. Lady*, iv. 1. TELL TRUTH, AND SHAME THE she-man-DEVIL in puffed sleeves; Run any hazard.

TRY, *subs.* (old literary: now colloquial).—An attempt, endeavour (GROSE), trial, experiment: espec. (modern) a TRY-ON = an attempt at BESTING (*q.v.*). Hence TO TRY IT ON = to seek to outwit, get the better of, fleece, cheat, etc.: *see* GAMMON. TO TRY IT ON A DOG = to experiment at another's expense or risk; TO TRY ON (thieves') = to live by thieving: COVES WHO TRY IT ON = professed thieves (GROSE); TO TRY IT ON WITH A WOMAN = to attempt the chastity (BEE).

1609. SHAKSPEARE, *Timon of Athens*, v. 1. This breaking of his has been but a TRY for his friends.

1848. GASKELL, *Mary Barton*, xxvii. Don't give it up yet. . . . Let's have a TRY for him.

18[?]. *Trying It On* [Title of a popular farce].

1874. *Siliad*, 57. We do not pardon the flagitious claims — Call them, or damages, 'TRIES-ON,' or shames.

1899. GOULD, *Racecourse and Battlefield*, vi. Owen Righton did have a TRY, but . . . Alec Medway brought him up short.

PHRASES AND COLLOQUIALISMS.—TO TRY A FALL WITH = to compete, contest; TO TRY BACK = to revert to, to retrace one's steps: as to a former position, standpoint, or statement, etc., with a view to recover something missed, or lost: hence TRYBACK (BEE).

1857. HUGHES, *Tom Brown's Schooldays*, i. 7. The leading hounds . . . are TRYING BACK.

1859. LEVER, *Davenport Dunn*, xi. She was marvellously quick to discover that she was astray and TO TRY BACK.

1887. *Nineteenth Century*, xxii. 812. Would it not be well then TO TRY BACK? to bear in mind . . . that meat is suitable for grown men, that milk is suitable for babes?

TRYNING. *See* TRINE.

TUB, *subs.* (old).—1. Formerly a cure for the *lues venerea*: also SWEATING-TUB and POWDERING-TUB. [The patient was disciplined by long and severe sweating in a heated tub, combined with strict abstinence: *cf.* SPENSER, *Fairy Queene*, I. x. 25, 26.] Hence TUB-FAST = the period of salivation.

1599. SHAKSPEARE, *Henry V.* ii. 1. 78. To the spital go, And from the POWDERING-TUB of infamy Fetch forth the lazar-kite of Cressid's kind. *Ibid.* (1603), *Meas. for Meas.*, iii. 2. 59. Troth, sir, she hath eaten up all her beef, and is herself in the TUB. *Ibid.* (1609), *Timon of Athens*, iv. 3. 87. Be a whore still; . . . bring down rose-cheeked youth To the TUB-FAST and the diet.

1639. MAYNE, *City Match* [DODSLEY, *Old Plays* (REED), ix. 377]. One ten times cur'd by sweating, and the TUB. *Ibid.* And coming to this cave, This beast us caught, and put us in a TUB, Where we these two months sweat, and should have done Another month, if you had not reliev'd us.

1647. CARTWRIGHT, *Ordinary* [DODSLEY, *Old Plays* (REED), x. 293]. Trust me, you will wish You had confess'd and suffer'd me in time, When you shall come to dry-burnt racks of mutton, The syringe, and the TUB.

1676. WISEMAN, *Surgery*, B. vii. 2. TUB and chair were the old way of sweating, but if the patient swoons in either of them, it will be troublesome to get him out.

1688. HOLME, *Acad. Arms and Blazon*, B. iii. II. 441. He beareth Argent, a Doctor's TUB (otherwise called a CLEANSING TUB), Sable, Hooped, Or. In this pockified and such diseased persons, are for a certain time put into, not to boil up to an heighth, but to parboil.

2. (old).—A pulpit. Hence TUB-DRUBBER (-POUNDER, -PREACHER, -THUMPER, or TUBSTER) = a ranting divine: spec., in reproach, of Dissenters (GROSE, 'a Presbyterian parson'): also TUB-THUMPING, *subs.* and *adj.*

1661. *Merry Drollery*, 176 [EBSWORTH]. [A TUB is connected with preaching.]

1661. *Semper iidem* [Harl. Misc. vii. 401]. George Eagles, sirnamed Trudge-over-the-World, who, of a taylor, became a TUB-PREACHER, was indicted of treason.

1692. HACKET, *Williams*, ii. 165. Here are your lawful ministers present, to whom of late you do not resort, I hear, but to TUB-PREACHERS in conventicles.

d. 1704. BROWN, *Works*, i. 194. The TUB PREACHERS are very much dissatisfy'd that you invade their prerogative of hell. *Ibid.*, iii. 68. He (says the TUBSTER) that would be rich according to the practice of this wicked age must play the thief or the cheat. *Ibid.*, iii. 198. Business and poetry agree as ill together as faith and reason; which two latter, as has been judiciously observ'd by the fam'd TUB-DRUBBER of Covent Garden, can never be brought to set their horses together.

1705. WARD, *Hud. Rediv.*, I. v. 17. The consecrated TUB, in which The Gospel Emp'rick was to teach.

1725. HEARNE, *Reliquiæ*, 4 Sep. The doctor . . . bred a presbyterian (as his brothers were also, his elder brother Samuel Mead having been a TUB-PREACHER).

1726. POPE, *Dunciad*, ii. 2. High on a gorgeous seat, that far out-shone Henley's gilt TUB, or Flecknoe's Irish throne.

1849. BRONTÉ, *Shirley*, viii. 'The Rev. Moses Barraclough, t' TUB ORATOR.' . . . 'Ah!' said the Rector . . . 'He's a tailor by trade.'

1885. *Observer*, 27 Sep. Our thoroughfares are needed, of course, to serve a much more useful class of people than the oleagineous TUB-THUMPERS.

1889. *Contemp. Review*, liv. 253. Very modest gifts, belonging to what may be called the TUB-THUMPING school of oratory, have been known to fill a large church with eager congregations.

3. (colloquial).—A bath: spec. a sponge-bath, but also (loosely) a DIP (*q.v.*). Also as *verb*.

1610. JONSON, *Alchemist*, iv. 1. In your bathada, You shall be soaked, and stroked, and TUBBED, and rubbed, And scrubbed, and fubbed, dear don.

1637. MASSINGER, *Guardian*, ii. 5. The silver bathing-TUB, the cambric rubbers.

1839. HOOD, *Black Job*. In spite of all the TUBBING, rubbing, scrubbing, The routing and the grubbing, The blacks, confound them! were as black as ever.

1857. HUGHES, *Tom Brown's Schooldays*, i. 2. She had it out of him in the cold TUB before putting him to bed.

1886. *Field*, 20 Feb. A good TUB and a hearty breakfast prepared us for the work of the day.

1899. WHITEING, *John St.*, iii. Morning devotions and . . . morning TUB. *Ibid.*, xix. I join the hero in a peg after his cold TUB.

1900. DESART, *Herne Lodge*, xxvi. A man should [not] make love before others [or] take his TUB in Hyde Park. TUBBING and love-making are innocent, of course, but you don't want to soap or spoon before your friends.

4. (common).—A broad-bottomed, slow-sailing boat; also (loosely) a vessel of any kind. At the Universities = a boat for rowing practice. Hence TUBBING = boating, rowing practice; TO GET TUBBED = to be taught to row.

1853. BRADLEY, *Verdant Green*. So to the river he next day went, and made his first essay in a TUB.

1857. HOOD, *Pen and Pencil Pictures*, 144. Awful muff! . . . he'd upset the veriest TUB on the river.

1878. *Scribner's Mag.*, Nov., 81. I laughed, for I knew the *Osceola*—an old TUB, built in East Boston—never made more than ten knots an hour.

1883. CLARK RUSSELL, *Sea Queen*, xvi. The name of this deep and wallowing TUB was the *Richard and Ann*.

1887. *D. Teleg.* 8 Feb. No other work in the eight was done during day, but some TUBBING was indulged in later in afternoon. *Ibid.* . . . Practice in gigs, or more technically styled TUBS (small boats to hold a pair of oarsmen, and in the stern of which the coach steers and advises the rowers).

1887. *Field*, 5 Mar. Alexander of Jesus, who has been TUBBED a good deal. *Ibid.* . . . A good deal of TUBBING has been got through in the mornings.

1889. *Morning Advertiser*. Passing our time between grinding hard and TUBBING on the river.

1898. *Stonyhurst Mag.*, Dec., 149. Every College is on the look-out for new oarsmen. . . . One is TUBBED . . . taught to row by members of the College eight in boats that are too TUB-like to be easily capsized.

1900. NISBET, *Sheep's Clothing*, I. ii. Dash me if ever I sail a TUB of his again.

1901. *Troddles*, 106. What sort of a TUB is it? It sounds good. . . . We can have no end of a lark with a boat of our own.

1903. DICKENS, *Dict. Oxford*, 17. The freshmen are put into harness in TUB-pairs or four-oars.

5. (common).—A low-wheeled and deep-welled gig (*cf.* sense 4) or village cart; a governess-car.

1849. FROUDE [CARLYLE, *Life in London*, xi.]. The brothers [Carlyle] went in a steamer from Liverpool to Bangor, and thence to Llanberis, again in a TUB-gig, or Welsh car.

6. (Winchester).—A chest in Hall into which DISPARS (*q.v.*) not taken by the boys were put. Whence PRÆFECT OF TUB = a præfect whose duty was to examine the quality of meat sent in by the butcher, and after dinner to supervise the collection and distribution of the remains: obsolete (COLLINS) *c.* 1870. Whence (also) TUB-MESS = the table at which the Senior Præfects sat in Hall (*see* FARMER, *Public School Word-Book*, S.V. TUB 2).

A TALE OF A TUB. *subs. phr.* (old).—Any kind of nonsense, fooling, or absurdity; a COCK-AND-BULL STORY (*q.v.*); ROT (*q.v.*).

1538. BALE, *Com. concern. Three Laws.* Ye say they follow your law, And vary not a shaw, Which is A TALE OF A TUB.

1546. HEYWOOD, *Proverbs*. A TALE OF A TUBBE.

1554. COVERDALE, *Exhort. to the Cross.* You shall see in us that we preached no lyes, nor TALES OF TUBS, but even the true word of God.

c. 1559. *Wit and Science* [DODSLEY, *Old Plays* (HAZLITT), ii. 335]. What, should I make a broad tree of every little shrub, And keep her a great while with a TALE OF A TUB?

1632. CHAPMAN, *Ball*, iii. 4. *Lu.* Do not I hear how desperate some ha' been? . . . *Wi.* This is a TALE OF A TUB, lady.

1633. JONSON, *Tale of a Tub*, Prol. No state-affairs . . . Pretend we in our TALE here, OF A TUB; But acts of clowns and constables to-day Stuff out the scenes of our ridiculous play.

1653. URQUHART, *Rabelais*, II., Prol. These are no flim-flam stories, nor TALES OF A TUB.

1690. HOWELL, *Lex. Tetra.* A TALE OF A TUB, chose ridicule, conte de cicogne, chanson de ricoche.

1699. SWIFT, *TALE OF A TUB* [Title].

d 1704. BROWN, *Works*, ii. 11. What other business can a man and woman have in the dark but . . . to make the beast with two backs? not to pick straws, I hope, or to tell TALES OF A TUB.

TO THROW A TUB TO A WHALE, *verb. phr.* (old).—(1) To bait the hook, give a sop, or make capital; (2) to throw dust in the eyes, to divert attention, to emphasize small matters so that attention is distracted from essentials.

1809. MALKIN, *Gil Blas* [ROUTLEDGE], 41. He . . . expatiated on the honours I had gained in the schools . . . as if it was necessary for a prebendary's footman to be as learned as his master. However . . . it served as A TUB TO THE WHALE.

A CAT UNDER A TUB, *phr.* (nautical American).—A supposed cause of delay.

EVERY TUB (VAT, etc.) SHOULD STAND ON ITS OWN BOTTOM, *phr.* (old).—A simile of independence.

1538. LAMBERT [ELLIS, *Letters*, 533]. EVERY VAT SHALL STAND ON HIS OWN BOTTOM.

1606. HOLLAND, *Sueton.*, 97. Hee had used also before, to STAND UPON HIS OWNE BOTTOM.

1630-40. *Court and Times Chas. I.* [OLIPHANT, *New Eng.*, ii. 87. Bunyan was later to quote the proverb, 'EVERY TUB MUST STAND ON ITS OWN BOTTOM'; here men are left to do the same.]

c. 1656. HALL, *Cont.*, 45. Man, though he . . . STAND UPON HIS OWN BOTTOME, yet [is] he not a little wrought upon by examples.

1680. MORDEN, *Geog. Rect.* (1685), 106. Everyone endeavours to STAND ON THEIR OWN BOTTOM.

1788. REID, *Aristotle*, VI. i. 129. When reason acquires such strength as to STAND ON ITS OWN BOTTOM.

See TUBBY.

TUBBING, *subs.* (thieves').—1. Imprisonment.

2. *See* TUB.

TUBMAN, *subs.* (old legal).—*See* quot. [The old Exchequer Court is now merged in the High Court of Justice, but the appointments are still made.]

1765–9. BLACKSTONE, *Com.*, III. iii. Note. In the courts of exchequer, two of the most experienced barristers, called the post-man and the TUB-MAN (from the places in which they sit), have also a precedence in motions.

TUBBY, *subs.* (Christ's Hospital).—1. A male servant of the school: his business was the care of the latrine tubs: the name is still retained for the lavatory-man.

2. (common).—A big-bellied man; FATTY (*q.v.*); FORTY-GUTS (*q.v.*). As *adj.* (or TUBBISH)=round-bellied, swag-bellied: like a tub.

1796. WOLCOT, *Works*, 136. You look for men whose heads are rather TUBBISH, Or drum-like, better formed for sound than sense.

1836. DICKENS, *Sketches by Boz*, 'Mr. John Dounce.' He was a short, round, large-faced, TUBBISH sort of man. *Ibid.*, 'Monmouth Street.' We had seen him coming up to Covent Garden in his green chaise-cart with the fat TUBBY little horse.

1901. *Troddles*, 36. A TUBBY and short-winded keeper.

1902. *Free Lance*, 11 Oct., 44. 1. I was particular to find out whether the double-breasted lounge was a favourite among short and 'TUBBY' men.

TUBS, *subs.* (common). A butterman.

TUCK, *subs.* (common).—1. Generic for edibles; (2)=an appetite: spec. (schools') pastry, sweet-stuff, and the like. Whence TUCK-SHOP = a pastrycook's; TUCK-PARCEL=(Charterhouse) a hamper from home: nearly obsolete. Also (Australian) TUCKER=(1) food, GRUB (*q.v.*), spec. (2) barely sufficient on which to live, 'bare bread-and-cheese.' As *verb* (or TO TUCK IN) =to eat heartily: TUCK-IN (or TUCK-OUT) = a 'square meal.' [*Cf.* TACK=generic for food, and which, at Sherborne School,=a feast in one's study].

1840. A. BUNN, *Stage*, I. 295. Nothing can stop the mouth of a TUCK-hunter.

1847–8. THACKERAY, *Vanity Fair*, v. His father . . . gave him two guineas publicly, most of which he spent in a general TUCK-OUT for the school.

1856. HUGHES, *Tom Brown's School-days*, I. vi. Come along down to Sally Harrowell's; that's our school-house TUCK-SHOP. She bakes such stunning murphies. *Ibid.*, I. v. The slogger looks rather sodden, as if he didn't take much exercise and ate too much TUCK.

1858. *M. Chron.*, 31 Aug. Diggers, who have great difficulty in making their TUCKER at digging.

1873. GREENWOOD, *In Strange Company*. A TUCK-OUT, which in Hale's Street is short and simple language for as much as can be eaten.

1874. GARNET WALCH, *Head over Heels*, 73. For want of more nourishing TUCKER, I believe they'd have eaten *him*.

1875. WOOD and LAPHAM, *Waiting for the Mail*, 33. We heard of big nuggets, but only made TUCKER.

1886. *D. Teleg.*, 1 Jan. They set me down to a jolly good TUCK-IN of bread and meat.

1890. *Argus*, 14 June, 14. 1. When a travelling man sees a hut ahead, he knows there's water inside, and TUCKER and tea.

1890. *St. Nicholas*, XVIII. 125. What a TUCK-OUT I had.

1891. BOLDREWOOD, *Sydney-side Saxon*, 83. I took my meal in the hut, but we'd both the same kind of TUCKER.

1899. WHITEING, *John St.*, iii. You get your TUCK-IN Sundays. Lord, give me a reg'lar sixpence every day for grub, and I'd warrant I'd never starve.

1901. WALKER, *In the Blood*, 39. And they were off for a day's holiday and a camp-out as long as they could run it, TUCKER being the one essential.

Verb. (old university).—*See* quot.

d. 1695. WOOD, *Life*, 45. If any of the Freshmen came off dull or not cleverly some of the . . . Seniors would TUCK them—that is set the nail of their Thumb to their chin, just under the Lipp, and by the help of their other fingers under the Chin, they would give him a mark which would sometimes produce Blood. *Ibid.*, 46. Nothing was given him but salted drink . . . with TUCKS to boot.

TO TUCK UP, *verb. phr.* (old).—1. To hang: *see* LADDER. Hence TUCKED UP=hanged; TUCK-'EM FAIR=an execution (B. E. and GROSE).

1740. RICHARDSON, *Pamela*, I. 141. I never saw an execution but once, and then the hangman asked the poor creature's pardon, and . . . then calmly TUCKED UP the criminal.

1789. PARKER, *Variegated Characters*. He was knocked down for the crap the last sessions. He went off at the fall of the leaf at TUCK'EM FAIR.

c. 1811. MAHER, *The Night before Larry was Stretched*. He was TUCKED UP so neat and pretty.

2. (colloquial).—To perplex, to put in a fix or difficulty, to cramp.

1886. *Field*, 13 Feb. They have been playing the old game of skirting, eventually to find themselves fairly TUCKED-UP by wire-fencing.

1887. BURY and HILLIER, *Cycling*, 189. A . . . fifty-eight inch racer will be noticeably too short in the reach . . . and he will feel that he is what cyclists call TUCKED-UP.

TO TUCK ON, *verb. phr.* (American).—To unduly increase or enhance: *e.g.* 'That horse is not worth half what you gave for him; the dealer has TUCKED IT ON to you pretty well': *cf.* 'STICK IT ON.' *See* TWOPENNY.

TUCKER. *See* TUCK.

TUCKERED. TUCKERED OUT, *phr.* (American).—Tired out.

c. 1840. *Story of Bee Tree* [BARTLETT]. I'm clear TUCKERED OUT with these young ones. They've had the agur this morning, and are as cross as bear cubs.

c. 1859. *N. York Family Comp.* [BARTLETT]. I guess the Queen don't do her eating very airly; for we sot and sot, and waited for her, till we got e'en a'most TUCKERED OUT.

18[?]. *Southern Sketches*, 123. We fought until we were completely TUCKERED OUT.

TUCKER-IN (or TUCKER-UP), *subs. phr.* (old).—A chamber-maid, 'a supposed mistress' (GROSE): *cf.* SCOTCH WARMING-PAN.

TUCK-MAN, *subs. phr.* (commercial).—A moneyed partner.

TUEL (or TEWEL), *subs.* (old).—The fundament (HALLIWELL).

TUFT, *subs.* (University).—1. A young nobleman: students of rank formerly wore a gold tuft or tassel in their cap: obsolete. Whence TUFT-HUNTER=a hanger on to a man of title, a sycophant, toady, lick-spittle; TUFT-HUNTING=SPONGING (*q.v.*) on men of title or means. *See* GOLD-HATBAND (GROSE).

1840. THACKERAY, *Shabby Genteel Story*, ii. The lad . . . followed with a kind of proud obsequiousness all the TUFTS of the University. *Ibid.* (1842), *Book of Snobs*, v. At Eton . . . Lord Buckram was birched with perfect impartiality. Even there, however, a select band of sucking TUFT-HUNTERS followed him. *Ibid.*, xiv. In the midst of a circle of young TUFTS.

1851. CARLYLE, *Life of Sterling*, II. iii. He was at no time the least of a TUFT-HUNTER, but rather had a marked natural indifference to TUFTS.

1852. BRISTED, *Eng. Univ.*, 176. The gold-TUFTED Cap, which at Cambridge only designates a Johnian or Small-College Fellow-Commoner is here [Oxford] the mark of nobility.

1853. BRADLEY, *Verdant Green*, I. vii., note. As TUFT and TUFT-HUNTERS have become household words, it is perhaps needless to tell anyone that the gold tassel is the distinguishing mark of a nobleman.

1902. *Free Lance*, 22 Nov., 169. 1. A writer in the *Sovereign*, adopting the happy pseudonym of 'Thomas TUFT-HUNT,' has commenced a series entitled 'Sovereigns I have Seen.'

2. (old colloquial). — An imperial, a goat's beard.

1842–3. THACKERAY, *Fitz-Boodle's Confessions*. Do you like those TUFTS that gentlemen sometimes wear upon their chins?

3. (venery).—The pubic hair: male or female: also (of women) TUFTED HONOURS and CLOVEN TUFT (TUFTED HONOURS also=the female *pudendum*).

1653. URQUHART, *Rabelais*, XV., note. Why *Callibistri* should signify a woman's TUFTED HONOURS I know not.

d. 1704. BROWN, *Works*, ii. 186. Get a good warm *Girdle* and tie round you. . . . Pox on you, how can a single girdle do me good when a *Brace* was my destruction? . . . a sacrifice to a CLOVEN TUFT.

TUG, *subs.* (Eton).—A Colleger; a scholar on the foundation. Hence TUGGERY=College. [*Gt. Public Schools*: from the *toga* worn by Collegers to distinguish them from the rest of the school.]

1881. PASCOE, *Everyday Life in our Public Schools*. The long-looked-for St. Andrew's Day arrives, when the great match of collegers, or, as the small oppidan would term it, TUGS, and oppidans is to be played.

1883. BRINSLEY RICHARDS, *Seven Years at Eton*. My interlocutor was a red-headed, freckled little boy of eleven, who had come from Aberdeen, 'to try for TUGGERY,' that is, to try and pass on to the foundation as a King's scholar.

1890. *Great Public Schools*, 52. The disrespect, almost bordering on contempt, with which the Oppidans used for many years to regard the TOGATI, or gown-wearing boys.

Adj. (Winchester). — Stale, ordinary, vapid, common. Whence TUGS=stale news; TUG-CLOTHES=everyday clothes; TUG-JAW=wearisome talk.

PHRASES.—TO HOLD ONE TUG=to keep busy; to task-drive; TO HOLD TUG=to stand hard work, or severe strain; TUG OF WAR (see WAR).

1667. WOOD, *Life*, 18 July, 206. There was work enough for a curious and critical Antiquary, that would HOLD HIM TUGG for a whole yeare.

TUG-MUTTON, *subs. phr.* (venery).—1. A whoremaster; MUTTON-MONGER (*q.v.*).

1630. TAYLOR, *Works* [NARES]. For though he be chaste of his body, yet his minde is onely upon flesh, he is the onely TUGMUTTON, or mutton-monger, betwixt Dover and Dunbarr.

2. (HALLIWELL).—A glutton.

TUI, *subs.* (Winchester).—Tuition.

TULIP. GO IT, MY TULIP, *phr.* (obsolete).—A characteristic street phrase: an echo of the tulipomania of 1842, itself a recrudescence of the great craze of 1634.

TULIP-SAUCE, *subs. phr.* (common).—A kiss; kissing.

TUM, *adj.* (American).—Stylish, proper, spiff, A1.

c. 1889. *Chicago Times* [*S. J. and C.*]. By the way, gold spoons and forks for dessert have come in again, and you get them everywhere. Indeed, no table seems to look quite TUM for a big occasion without them.

P

TUMBIES, *subs.* (University). — Ablutions; TUBBING (*q.v.*).

1853. BRADLEY, *Verdant Green*. Our hero soon concluded his TUMBIES and his dressing.

TUMBLE, *verb.* (old colloquial).—To dance. [Formerly *dance* and TUMBLE were popularly synonymous; moreover, the professional dancers of mediæval times were also acrobats; and, pictorially, Herodias' daughter is often represented as walking on her hands.] Hence TUMBLER (or TUMBESTER) =a female dancer, and (modern) an acrobat. As *subs.*=(1) a dance; and (2) a CATHERINE WHEEL (*q.v.*).

1380. WYCLIF, *Bible*. The douȝtir of Herodias daunside [ether TUMBLIDE, margin] in the myddil, and pleside Heroude.

[?]. *MS. Harl.*, 1701, f. 8. Herodias douȝter, that was a TUMBESTERE and TUMBLEDE byfore him. *Ibid.*, 19. Hyt telleth that Eroud swore To here that TUMBLED yn the flore.

1383. CHAUCER, *Cant. Tales*, 'Pardoner's Tale,' 15. Comen TOMBESTERES . . . the verray deueles officeres To kindle and blowe the fyr of [lecherye].

1605. JONSON, *Fox*, ii. 3. A common rogue, come fiddling in to the osteria with a TUMBLING whore.

1626. FLETCHER, *Noble Gentleman*, ii. 1. There is no TUMBLER runs through his hoop with more dexterity Than I about this business.

1801. STRUTT, *Sports and Pastimes*, 288. The TUMBLER is walking upon his hands.

1824–8. LANDOR, *Imag. Conv.*, 'General . . . Lacy and Cura Merina.' A TUMBLE of heels over head, a feat performed by beggar boys on the roads.

2. (colloquial). — To understand, perceive, assent to, accept: *cf.* 'fall in with,' 'concur,' and Fr. *tombre d'accord*.

1851–61. MAYHEW, *Lond. Lab.* I. 15. The high words in a tragedy we call jaw-breakers, and say we can't TUMBLE TO that barrikin.

1897. MARSHALL, *Pomes*, 12. The courtship was progressive, and you'll TUMBLE TO their bliss.

1898. *Pink 'Un and Pelican*, 73. You're labouring under a great misapprehension. You're only here by the month—not on a ninety-nine years' lease! Do you TUMBLE?

1899. KERNAHAN, *Scoundrels & Co.*, XX. As soon as the members TUMBLE TO it . . . the chairman will spring to his feet. . . .

1899. WHITEING, *John St.*, xxi. Bill tips me the wink to pretend not to TUMBLE TO their lingo.

1900. LYNCH, *High Stakes*, xxiii. He didn't TUMBLE TO all the cop's nice boch.

1902. *Free Lance*, 19 July, 362. 2. So be simple, even silly, and the public, willy-nilly, Most assuredly will TUMBLE to your jokelets.

3. (Stock Exchange).—To fall rapidly in value: of prices.

4. (venery).—(*a*) To rumple, TOUZLE (*q.v.*), MESS ABOUT (*q.v.*); (*b*) to possess a woman: also TO TUMBLE IN; A TUMBLE-IN=the act of kind; TO DO A TUMBLE (of women)=to lie down to a man, TO SPREAD (*q.v.*). TO TUMBLE TO PIECES=to be brought to bed; TUMBLING-RIPE = ready for the act, wanton, COMING (*q.v.*). Whence TO TUMBLE A BED=to pile in the act; TUMBLE-A-BED =(1) chambermaid: *see* SCOTCH WARMING-PAN; and (2) a whore.

c. 1615. FLETCHER, *Woman's Prize*, i. 1. Do all the ramping, roaring tricks a whore Being drunk and TUMBLING-RIPE.

1772. BRIDGES, *Burlesque Homer*, 4. What priest beside thyself e'er grumbl'd To have his daughter tightly TUMBL'D?

PHRASES.—TO TUMBLE IN=to go to bed; TO TUMBLE UP=(*a*) to rise from one's bed, and (*b*) to come, or move quickly: also TO TUMBLE ALONG; TO TUMBLE TO=to set to vigorously: also see *verb* sense **2**; TO TAKE A TUMBLE TO ONESELF=to take oneself to task; to KICK ONESELF (*q.v.*); TO TUMBLE TO THE RACKET (Am. pol.), *see* RACKET; TO TUMBLE ON ONE'S FEET=to escape without injury, to come out on TOP (*q.v.*).

1843. DICKENS, *Chuzzlewit*, xxviii. Mr. Bailey . . . giving Jonas a shake, cried, 'We've got home, my flower! TUMBLE UP then.'

1890. *New York Evg. Post* [*Century*], 29 Jan. To give the name of legislation to the proceedings at Albany . . . would be an abuse of language. The proper name was 'TUMBLING TO THE RACKET.' The Assembly passed the bill without debate . . . much as they might pass a bill authorising a man to change his name.

TUMBLER, *subs.* (old).—In various colloquial or semi-colloquial usages denoting instability or eccentric movement. Thus (1) a glass rounded or pointed at the bottom, so that it could not be set down except when empty—a silent reminder of 'no heeltaps!' and to 'pass the bottle': orig. 'a low Silver Cup to Drink out of' (B. E., *c.* 1696): nowadays applied to any glass that is cylindrical in shape, without a stem; (2) a variety of pigeon: in flight the bird often drops without wing-play; (3) a dog used in coursing rabbits, 'a Coney Dog' (B. E.): it tumbles about in a careless fashion until, within reach of its prey, it seizes it with a sudden spring; (4) a porpoise; (5) a variety of printing machine: from the rocking or tumbling movement of the cylinder towards the impression surface; etc. etc.

1616. W. BROWNE, *Britannia s Past.*, ii. 4. I have seene a nimble TUMBLER . . . Bend cleane awry his course, yet give a checke And throw himselfe upon a rabbit's necke.

1635. SWAN, *Spec. Mundi*, ix. 1. The TUMBLER and lurcher ought to be reckoned by themselves.

1707. FARQUHAR, *Beaux's Stratagem*, iv. 2. The plate stands in the wainscot cupboard. Ay. Knives and forks, and cups and cans, and TUMBLERS and tankards.

1837. DICKENS, *Pickwick*, lii. Mr. Stiggins, walking softly across the room to a well-remembered shelf in one corner, took down a TUMBLER, and with great deliberation put four lumps of sugar in it.

1862. THACKERAY, *Philip*, xxxviii. She . . . reminds him of days which he must remember when she had a wine-glass out of poor Pa's TUMBLER.

1885. *D. Tel.*, 17 Nov. The little TUMBLER flashing downward in the sunlight is something to watch and admire.

1901. WALKER, *In the Blood*, 262. 'Arf our 'ard-earned money goes that way. It's melted inter pewter pots an' TUMBLERS.

6. (Old Cant).—A cart: properly 'tumbrel.' Whence TO NAP THE FLOG AT (or TO SHOVE) THE TUMBLER=to be whipped at the cart's-arse (B. E. and GROSE): *see* SHOVE, adding quot. **1721**.

1721. *Remarkable Tryals*, 2. He was ordered to SHOVE THE TUMBLER.

1815. SCOTT, *Guy Mannering*, viii. Behind them followed the train of laden asses and . . . TUMBLERS.

7. (old).—'A sharper employed to draw in pigeons to game' (B. E. and GROSE).

8. (turf).—A worthless horse; a SCREW (*q.v.*).

9. (old).—A German Baptist or Dunker. [The sect was founded by Alexander Mack about A.D. 1708. Persecution drove them in 1723 to the United States, where they founded a church at a German town in Pennsylvania. They separate the sexes in worship, are vegetarians, and are

called TUMBLERS from their mode of baptism, which is by putting the person whilst kneeling head first under water.]

10. (old).—A street rowdy: early part of the eighteenth century: *see* quot.

1712. STEELE, *Spectator*, 324. A third sort are the TUMBLERS, whose office it is to set women on their heads.

TUMBLE-DOWN, *adj. phr.* (colloquial). — Dilapidated, ruinous, RATTLETRAP (*q.v.*).

1839. LONGFELLOW, *Hyperion*, ii. 9. A TUMBLE-DOWN old Lutheran church.

1859. KINGSLEY, *Geoffrey Hamlyn*, iii. You will be doing injustice to this boy if you hang on here in this useless TUMBLE-DOWN old palace.

1863. GASKELL, *Sylvia's Lovers*, xxiv. T'oud TUMBLEDOWN place is just a heap o' brick and mortar.

1881. FREEMAN, *Venice*, 340. Dirty-looking men assemble at the door of a TUMBLE-DOWN building.

1885. *D. Teleg.*, 16 Nov. They came so low as to live in a TUMBLE-DOWN old house at Peckham.

TUMMY, *subs.* (common). — The stomach: also TUM-TUM; hence (venery) TUMMY-TICKLING = copulation: *see* GREENS and RIDE.

TUMP, *verb.* (American).—1. To pull, to draw.

2. (venery).—To copulate; to give the PUSH (*q.v.*); TO POKE (*q.v.*).

TUMPTSNER, *subs.* (provincial).—A settler: *e.g.* 'That'll be a TUMPTSNER for the old gentleman.'

TUM-TUM, *subs. phr.* (Indian and Colonial).—A dog-cart.

See TUMMY.

TUN, *subs.* (common).—1. A tippler: *see* LUSHINGTON.

2. (Oxford Univ.).—At Pembroke a small silver cup containing half a pint; sometimes with a whistle handle, which cannot be blown till the cup is empty.

TUN-BELLY, *subs.* (old).—A fat, round-bellied man; a pot-belly, a CORPORATION (*q.v.*). Hence TUN-BELLIED = paunchy, very corpulent, bellied like a tun: *cf.* TUN-GREAT (quot. 1383)=with a circumference of the size of a tun.

[1383. CHAUCER, *Cant. Tales*, 'Knight's Tale,' 1996. Every piler the temple to sustene was TONNE-GRET.]

1550. LEVER, *Sermons* [ARBER], 119 [OLIPHANT, *New Eng.*, i. 524. There are the phrases greedygut and TUNNE BELYED].

1651. CARTWRIGHT, *Royall Slave*. Some drunken hymn I warrant you towards now, in the praise of their great huge, rowling, TUNBELLYED god Bacchus as they call him.

1687. SEDLEY, *Bellamira*. I must have no . . . TUN-BELLY'D rogues, that fright chair-men from the house.

d. 1704. BROWN, *Works*, iii. 152. He has swore to her by all that is good and sacred never to forgive the presumptuous wretch that should think irreverently of a double chin and a TUN BELLY.

TUND, *verb.* (Winchester). — To thrash; TUNDING=a thrashing.

1881. PASCOE, *Everyday Life*, etc. I never heard of any case in Eton like the TUNDING which, some years ago, brought our mother-school into disagreeable notice.

1883. TROLLOPE, *What I remember*. It was the prefect of hall who ordered the infliction of a public TUNDING. . . . Some dozen or so of boys, who had the best capacities for the performance, were appointed by him for the purpose, and the whole assembly stood around the dais, while the hymn *Te de profundis* was sung. When all were thus assembled, and before the singers commenced, the culprit who had been sentenced to a TUNDING stepped

out, pulled off his gown, and received from the hands of one deputed by the 'prefect of hall,' and armed with a tough, pliant, ground-ash stick, a severe beating.

c. 1890. *Punch* ['Confession by a Wykehamist']. I like to be TUNDED twice a day, And swished three times a week.

TUNE, *verb.* (old).—To beat: also TO TUNE UP: *e.g.* 'The old man TUNED HIM UP delightfully'=He got a good thrashing: *cf.* 'I'll make you sing another TUNE'= a threat of corporal punishment. (GROSE).

THE TUNE THE COW (or OLD COW) DIED OF, *phr.* (old).—1. A grotesque or unpleasant noise; (2) a homily instead of alms. [From an old ballad.]

COLLOQUIALISMS. — TO THE TUNE OF=to the sum, amount, or measure of [a stated figure, etc.]; TO CHANGE ONE'S TUNE (or NOTE)=to alter one's way of talking, manner, or demand; to change from laughter to tears; TO SING ANOTHER TUNE (*see* SING); TO TUNE UP=to commence.

1578. *Scot. Poems 16th Cent.* (1801), II. 185. Priestes CHANGE YOUR TUNE.

1694. MOTTEUX, *Rabelais*, v. ix. I'll make him CHANGE HIS NOTE presently.

1709. STEELE, *Tatler*, 31. You look as if you were Don Diego'd TO THE TUNE of a thousand pounds. *Ibid.*, 230. Will Hazard has got the hipps, having lost TO THE TUNE OF five hundr'd pounds.

TUNKER, *subs.* (common). — A street-preacher. [? Dunker: *see* TUMBLER, 9.]

TUNNEL, *subs.* (old).—A nostril.

1596. JONSON, *Ev. Man in Humour*, i. 3. It would do a man good to see the fume come forth at's TUNNELS.

TUNNEL-GRUNTER, *subs. phr.*—Usually in *pl.* =potatoes.

TUP, *verb.* (venery).—To copulate: *see* RIDE (B. E. and GROSE). [Spec. of a ram.] Hence as *subs.* (or A STRAY TUP ON THE LOOSE) =(1) a man questing for a woman; and (2) = a cuckold (GROSE).

1602. SHAKSPEARE, *Othello*, i. 1. 89. Even now, now, very now, an old black ram Is TUPPING your white ewe.

1610. JONSON, *Alchemist*, v. 3. Come on, you ewe, you have matched most sweetly, have you not? Did not I say, I would never have you TUPPED But by a dubbed boy.

1772. BRIDGES, *Burlesque Homer*, 2. Latona's son, that red-fac'd TUP. *Ibid.*, 34. Before our chief could TUP her . . . send home the dame As good a virgin as she came.

2. (provincial).—To salute in drinking.

VENISON OUT OF TUP-PARK, *subs. phr.* (old). — Mutton (B. E.).

TUPPENCE (or **TUPPENNY**). *See* TWOPENNY.

TUP-RUNNING, *subs. phr.* (old).—'A rural sport practised at wakes and fairs in Derbyshire; a ram whose tail is well soaped and greased, is turned out to the multitude; anyone that can take him by the tail, and hold him fast, is to have him for his own' (GROSE).

TU QUOQUE, *subs. phr.* (venery).—The female *pudendum*; 'the mother of all saints' (GROSE): *see* MONOSYLLABLE.

TURD, *subs.* (old literary: now vulgar).—1. A lump of excrement; and (2) a contemptuous address: *cf.* SHIT. Frequently in combination: *e.g.* NOT WORTH A TURD=the maximum of worth-

lessness; 'A TURD FOR YOU!'= 'Go to hell and stay there' (also A TURD IN THE MOUTH!); TO CHUCK A TURD = to evacuate, to rear; and so forth. Also PROVERBS and PROVERBIAL SAYINGS, 'Many women many words, many geese many TURDS'; 'He's fallen into a cow's TURD' (of a dirty unkempt man); 'He looks like a COW-TURD stuck with primroses'; 'There's not a TURD to choose, quoth the good wife, by her two pounds of butter'; 'There's 'struction of honey, quoth Dunkinly, when he lick'd up the hen-TURD'; 'A TURD'S as good for a sow as a pancake' (*i.e.* 'Good things are not fit for fools': *cf.* French *Truie aime mieux bran que roses*, Sp. *No es la miel para la boca del asno*); 'He that thatches his house with TURDS shall have more teachers than reachers'; 'He is all honey, or all TURD'; 'See how we apples swim, quoth the horse-TURD'; 'As rotten as a TURD'; 'A humble-bee (or a beetle) in a cow-TURD thinks himself a king'; 'Look high and fall into a cow-TURD.'

1380. WYCLIF, *Bible*, Luke xii. And he answeringe seide to him, Lord, suffre also this yeer: til the while I delue aboute, and sende TOORDIS [Auth. Ver., till I shall dig about it and dung it].

d. 1529. SKELTON, *Bouge of Courte* [CHALMERS, ii. 253. 1]. Fye on this dyce they be NOT WORTH A TURDE.

1567. HARMAN, *Caveat*, 86. Gerry gan, the ruffian clye thee. A TORDE IN THY MOUTH, the deuyll take thee.

1575. STILL, *Gammer Gurton's Needle*, i. 5. Not so much as a hen's TURD but in pieces I tare it. *Ibid.* Fie! it stinks: it is a cat's TURD. *Ibid.*, ii. 2. It is twenty pound to a goose-TURD my gammer will not tarry.

1614. JONSON, *Bartholomew Fair*, i. 1. A TURD IN YOUR little wife's TEETH, too . . . 'twill make her spit.

1653. URQUHART, *Rabelais*, I., Prol. A TURD FOR HIM. *Ibid.*, xxi. Then Panurge said unto her, A TURD FOR YOU.

1660. A. BROME, *Poems*, 'The Clown.' 'Tis not a TURD to choose.

1678. COTTON, *Works* (1770), 44. The Rogues threw COW-TURDS at us. *Ibid.*, 223. Basta! no more, you wrangling TURDS.

1694. MOTTEUX, *Rabelais*, v. vi. They . . . would make us believe that a TURD is a sugar loaf. *Ibid.*, xxii. Others made chalk of cheese, and honey of a dog's TURD.

c. 1700. BROWN, *Works*, i. 77. Two thousand Flies attack a new-fall'n TURD.

1707. WARD, *Hud. Rediv.*, II. iv. 19. Like Dung-hill Cocks o'er Stable TURDS. *Ibid.*, II. v. 25. Concluding with, Good Night, you TURD.

1774. BRIDGES, *Burlesque Homer*, 12. Nor know, for all your kick and bounce how many * * * *s will make an ounce. *Ibid.*, 213. (Which will turn out not worth a T—.)

1785. GROSE, *Vulg. Tongue*, s.v. Sir Reverence. Human excrement, a T—D.

TURF, *subs.* (common).—1. Generic for horse-racing: hence THE TURF=(1) the racecourse; and (2) racing as a profession; ON THE TURF=making one's living by racing (GROSE): *cf.* 'in the City'; TURFITE (or TURFMAN)= a racing man; TURFY=sporting.

1760. FOOTE, *Minor*. [Horses are kept for THE TURF.]

1783-5. COWPER, *Task*, ii. 227. We justly boast At least superior jockeyship, and claim The honours of THE TURF as all our own.

1843. DICKENS, *Martin Chuzzlewit*, xxvi. It was a . . . horsefleshy, TURFY sort of thing to do.

c. 1882. LORD GEORGE BENTINCK [ANNANDALE]. All men are equal on THE TURF or under it.

1887. *Field*, 16 July. The modern TURFITE, to use a common but by no means elegant expression, has quite enough to do to keep himself posted in the most recent doings of the horses of to-day.

2. (Winchester).—The pitch: at cricket, the ' field ' being ' long grass.'

3. (Felsted School). — The cricket field : always without the definite article.

1881. *Felstedian*, Nov., 75. There are (or were) six cricket pitches on TURF.

Verb. (Derby School). — 1. To send to bed at bedtime.

2. (Marlborough School).—To chastise.

TURK, *subs.* (old).—1. A sword : *cf.* ANDREW, FOX, TOLEDO.

1638. *Albino and Bellama*, 108. That he forthwith unsheath'd his trusty TURKE, Cald forth that blood which in his veines did lurk.

2. (old).—A savage fellow ; 'a cruel hard-hearted man' (B. E. and GROSE); a TARTAR (*q.v.*). Also TO TURN TURK = to turn renegade, to change for the worse, to GO OFF (*q.v.*). TO TURKISE = to play the Turk ; TURKISH TREATMENT = barbarous usage, 'very sharp or ill dealing in business' (B. E.); TURKISH SHORE = 'Lambeth, Southwark, and Rotherhithe sides of the Thames' (GROSE); TURK-A-TEN-PENCE = a term of contempt : *cf.* 'tenpenny infidel' (a term applied to the Turk in DEKKER'S *Westward Hoe*, 1607) and TURK, sense 1, with an eye on TENPENNY SWORD = a poor tool. In modern usage TURK has lost somewhat of its rigorous meaning, and is frequently employed as a half-jesting endearment to a mischievous, destructive boy : *e.g.* 'You young TURK !'

1596. SHAKSPEARE, *Hamlet*, iii. 2. 287. If the rest of my fortunes TURN Turk with me. *Ibid.* (1600), *Much Ado*, iii. 4. 57. An you be not TURNED Turk,

1602. DEKKER, *Satiromastix* [NARES]. TURK-A-TENPENCE.

1630. TAYLOR, *Works* [NARES]. He call'd thee Giaur, but thou so well didst answer (being hot and fierie, like to crabbed Cancer) That if he had a TURKE OF TEN PENCE bin, Thou toldst him plaine the errors he was in.

3. (old).—A target : a dummy made up of cloth and rags.

TURKEY. TO HAVE A TURKEY ON ONE'S BACK, *verb. phr.* (American). — To be drunk : *see* SCREWED.

See TALK.

TURKEY-MERCHANT, *subs. phr.* (old).—1. 'A driver of Turkies' (B. E.); 'a poulterer' (GROSE); a chicken-thief (tramps').

1837. DISRAELI, *Venetia*. We'll make a TURKEY-MERCHANT of you yet . . . never fear that.

2. (old).—A dealer in contraband silk.

TURK'S - HEAD, *subs. phr.* (common).—1. A long broom : used for sweeping ceilings and the like. *See* POPE'S-HEAD.

1853. LYTTON, *My Novel*, x. 20. Dick was all for sweeping away other cobwebs, but he certainly thought heaven and earth coming together when he saw a TURK'S-HEAD besom poked up at his own.

2. (nautical).—An ornamental knot worked on to a rope : in shape supposed to resemble a turban.

TURN, *subs.* (old colloquial).—1. A trick, stratagem, device. Hence as *verb* = to trick, beguile, cheat, GET AT (*q.v.*).

1383. CHAUCER, *Cant. Tales*, 'Canon Yeoman's Tale,' 160. Til he had TORNED him he coude rot blinne.

c. 1400. *Tale of Gamelyn*, 244. Of all the TORNES that he cowthe he schewed him bul oon.

2. (Old Cant).—An execution : formerly, the criminal stood on a ladder which, at a given signal, was TURNED over (*cf.* NEW-DROP): also TO TURN OFF (*q.v. infra*) and TO TURN OVER. TURNING-TREE = the gallows : *see* NUBBING CHEAT.

1542. HALL, *Henry VIII.*, f. 224. And at the last, she and her husband, as they deserved, were apprehended, arraigned, and hanged at the foresayd TURNYNG-TREE.

1603. SHAKSPEARE, *Meas. for Meas.*, iv. 2. 62. For your kindness I owe you a good TURN [DYCE : Here by TURN Pompey, with a quibble, means a TURN OFF the ladder].

1664. BUTLER, *Hudibras*, III. ii. 698. Criminals condemned to suffer Are blinded first, and then TURNED OVER. . . . And make him glad to read his lesson, Or take a TURN for't at the session.

1705. *Flying Post*, 11 Dec. Some minutes after he was TURNED OFF, a Reprieve came for him, and being immediately cut down he soon reviv'd to the admiration of all spectators.

3. (colloquial).—A walk : spec. a short walk involving a speedy return to the starting-point : as a promenade on the deck of a vessel, round a garden, etc. [In quot. *c.* 1700 = an extended journey.]

1601. SHAKSPEARE, *Henry VIII.*, v. 1. 94. You and I must walk a TURN together.

c. 1700. DARREL [?], *Gentlemen Instructed*, 14. Some years ago I took a TURN beyond the seas, and made a considerable stay in those parts.

d. 1704. BROWN, *Works*, i. 250. Last week Hippias and I were taking a TURN in the Park.

1714. ADDISON, *Spectator*, 269. His master . . . would be glad to take a TURN with me in Gray's-Inn walks.

1849. BRONTÉ, *Shirley*, xxviii. Moore left his desk . . . [for] one or two TURNS through the room.

4. (colloquial).—A spell of work or a job in rotation with others : *e.g.* (theatrical) = a public appearance on the stage, preceding or following others.

1859. LEVER, *Davenport Dunn*, v. Not able . . . to do a hand's TURN for myself.

1897. MARSHALL, *Pomes*. 'Twas plain that ere her TURN had ceased, Her talent had, on him at least, Created a most palpable impression.

5. (conventional).—In *pl.* = menses : *see* DOMESTIC AFFLICTIONS.

6. (American).—A bonus over and above the legal rate of interest : charged by bankers on advances against stock when money is tight.

7. (colloquial). — A nervous shock, a qualm, nausea. As *verb* = to make sick, disgusted, silly : also TO TURN UP or TO TURN THE STOMACH. Whence TURNED UP = queasy, ill, sick, as from a shock, sea-sickness, drinking, smoking, etc.

1605. SHAKSPEARE, *Lear*, iv. 6. 23. I'll look no more Lest my brain TURN.

1709. DAMPIER, *Voyages*, II. i. 30. They have many sorts of dishes that wou'd TURN THE STOMACH of a stranger, which yet they themselves like very well.

1734. POPE, *Satires*, Epil., ii. 182. This filthy simile, this beastly line, Quite TURNS MY STOMACH.

1846. DICKENS, *Cricket on Hearth*, ii. What a hard-hearted monster you must be, John, not to have said so at once, and saved me such a TURN.

1860. ELIOT, *Mill on Floss*, i. 7. Mrs. Tulliver gave a little scream . . . and felt such a TURN that she dropped the large gravy spoon into the dish.

8. (venery).—An act of coition. Hence TO TAKE A TURN (or TO TURN A WOMAN UP) = to copulate : *see* RIDE : also TO TAKE A TURN AMONG THE CABBAGES, UP ONE'S PETTICOATS (or AMONG ONE'S FRILLS), IN ABRAHAM'S BOSOM, IN LOVE LANE, BUSHEY-PARK, COCK-ALLEY, COCK-LANE, CUPID'S-ALLEY, CUPID'S-CORNER, HAIR-COURT, ON MOUNT PLEASANT, AMONG THE PARSLEY, THROUGH THE STUBBLE, or A TURN ON ONE'S BACK (of women).

TO TURN UP, *verb. phr.* (old).—1. To desist ; abandon an object, pursuit, or quest ; change one's habits or course of life. Thus TO TURN UP (= to forsake) A MISTRESS, to BURY A MOLL (*q.v.*); TO TURN UP (= cut) AN ACQUAINTANCE ; TO TURN UP (= cease dealing with) A TRADESMAN ; TO TURN UP (= quit) A CROWD ; TO TURN UP A FLAT SWEET = to leave a PIGEON (*q.v.*) in good humour after fleecing him, and so forth (GROSE).

2. (Marlborough School).—To chastise : with cane, stick, or fives-bat.

A GOOD (ILL, SHREWD, etc.) TURN, *subs. phr.* (old).—A kind (spiteful or clever, etc.) act or deed : also proverbially, 'One GOOD TURN deserves another' (also ILL TURN, etc.).

14[?]. *Babees Book* [E.E.T.S.], 106. In requtying a good TOURNE, shew not thyself negligent nor contrarye.

1509. BARCLAY, *Ship of Fooles* [JAMIESON, ii. 38]. One YLL TURNE requyreth another.

1603. SHAKSPEARE, *Measure for Meas.*, iv. v. 2. 62. For your kindness I owe you a GOOD TURN [see same quot. *subs.* sense 2].

1635. HEYWOOD, *Hier. of Angels*, 535. It is commendable in men to forget BAD TURNES done, but to bee mindefull of courtesies receiued.

c. 1620. FLETCHER, *Little French Lawyer*, iii. 2. One GOOD TURN requires another.

TURN occurs in a multitude of phrases, all more or less colloquial. Thus TO TURN (= to perfect or polish) A PHRASE, SENTENCE, etc. ; TO TURN OVER (= mentally consider) A MATTER : also TO TURN ABOUT ; TO TURN THE CORNER = to begin to mend in health, pocket, prospects, etc. ; TO TURN UPSIDE DOWN (INSIDE OUT, or THE HOUSE OUT OF WINDOWS, etc.) = to cause a commotion or disturbance, to search thoroughly ; TO TURN OVER A NEW LEAF = to reform, to make a fresh start ; TO TURN (= distract) ONE'S ATTENTION ; TO TURN ONE'S HEAD = to unbalance the judgment, make crazy, flighty, or arrogant ; TO TURN (or BE TURNED OF) FIFTEEN (or any age) = to pass (or have advanced beyond) one's fifteenth birthday, to be older than ; TO TURN AGAINST = to become unfriendly, hostile to ; TO TURN ONE'S FLANK = to circumvent, outwit ; TO TURN AWAY (or OFF) = to dismiss, SACK (*q.v.*) ; TO TURN (or SEND) DOWN (University) = (1) to rusticate, and (2) to snub, suppress (American) ; TO TURN OFF (= execute, accomplish, produce) A CONTRACT, DESIGN, or BOOK : *see subs.* 2, and TURN OUT, *infra* ; TO TURN OFF (= marry) A COUPLE ; TO TURN OFF (= foil, counteract, or ignore) A JOKE, SLIGHT, etc. ; TO TURN ONE'S COAT (see TURNCOAT) ; TO TURN ONE'S HAND TO = to apply (or adapt) oneself ; TO TURN OUT (= train) A SCHOLAR, SOLDIER,

etc. ; TO TURN OUT (= produce) so much in a week, month, etc. ; TO TURN OUT (= show) ONE'S HAND : spec. at cards ; TO TURN OUT (or BE TURNED OUT) = to dress (or be clothed by one's tailor) with care : whence WELL TURNED OUT = WELL-GROOMED (*q.v.*) : *see* TURN-OUT ; TO TURN OVER (= transfer) A BUSINESS ; TO TURN OVER (= sell) GOODS ; TO BE TURNED OVER (thieves') = (1) to be stopped by the police and searched, (2) to be remanded, and (3) to be acquitted for lack of evidence ; TO TURN ONE'S BACK ON (see BACK) ; TO TURN CAT IN THE PAN (see CAT) ; TO TURN THE COLD SHOULDER (see COLD SHOULDER) ; TO TURN THE PAUNCH = to vomit ; TO TURN THE STOMACH = to cause nausea : *see subs.* 7 ; TO TURN THE TABLES (see TABLE) ; TO TURN AN HONEST PENNY (see PENNY) ; TO TURN RUSTY (see RUSTY) ; TO TURN TO THE RIGHT-ABOUT = to dismiss summarily : *see* RIGHT ; TO TURN TURTLE (nautical) = to capsize : of a boat or vessel ; TO TURN UP ONE'S NOSE = to make a gesture of contempt, to show disgust ; TO TURN UP ONE'S EYES = to make a gesture of (1) surprise, and (2) of mock sanctity ; TO TURN UPON = (1) to retort, and (2) to show anger, resentment, or fight, to pay back as good as sent ; TO TURN UP ONE'S TOES = to die : *see* TOE ; TO TURN IN = to go to bed ; TO TURN OUT = (1) to rise, to get out of bed, (2) to come abroad, (3) to come out on strike (workmen's), and (4) to result, end, prove ; TO TURN TO = to set to work ; TO TURN TURK (see TURK) ; TO TURN UP = (1) to happen, to occur, (2) to arrest (thieves'), (3) to acquit (thieves') ; TO BE TURNED OVER : *see* TO TURN UP, *supra* ; NOT TO TURN A HAIR = to take things quietly ; TO TURN A CARTWHEEL : *see* CARTWHEEL ; TO TAKE A TURN = to join in : *see subs.* 8 ; TO TURN IT (or THE GAME) UP = to desist, quit, abscond, change one's tactics ; TO TURN UP A TRUMP = to meet with good fortune, to improve one's chances (GROSE) ; TO A TURN = to a nicety : as a roasted joint cooked to a 'TURN' of the spit ; TURNED-ROUND = at a loss, puzzled : spec. of that momentary mental ignorance of one's exact whereabouts which sometimes occurs in a place that is normally perfectly well known ; TURN AND TURN ABOUT = in regular succession, alternate duty, one resting while the other works.

1380. WYCLIF, *Bible*, Luke xv. 8. TURN THE HOUSE UPSODOWN [Auth. Ver., Sweep the house and seek diligently].

1596. SHAKSPEARE, *Merry Wives*, i. 3. 4. I must TURN AWAY some of my followers. *Ibid.* (1598), 1 *Henry IV.*, i. 11. This house is TURNED UPSIDE DOWN since Robin Ostler died.

1605. HEYWOOD, *If You Know not Me* [*Works* (1874), I. 257]. Bones a me, Ile TURN ANOTHER LEAFE.

1620. FLETCHER, *Philaster*, ii. 1. Let me be corrected . . . Rather than TURN ME OFF.

1628. EARLE, *Micro-cosm.*, 'A Shee Precise Hypocrite.' Her devotion at the Church is much in the TURNING UP OF HER EYE.

1640. HOWELL, *Letters*, i. 5. 13. TURN HIM OVER TO ME again when I come back.

1689. SELDEN, *Table Talk*, 63. The Master of the House may TURN AWAY all his servants, and take whom he please.

1695. DRYDEN, *Aurengzebe*, iv. 1. 'Tis well the debt in payment does demand, You TURN ME OVER to another hand.

1695. CONGREVE, *Love for Love*, iii. 15. I mean to toss a can, and remember my sweetheart before I TURN IN.

1703. STEELE, *Tender Husband*, ii. 1. A good servant shou'd TURN HIS HAND TO everything in a family. *Ibid.* (1710), *Tatler*, 127. For the benefit of such whose heads are a little TURNED [with] . . . this dangerous distemper [pride]. *Ibid.*, *Spectator*, 264. Irus, though he is now TURNED OF fifty, has not appeared in the world in his real character since five-and-twenty.

d. 1719. ADDISON [*Century*]. He TURNED OFF his former wife to make room for this marriage.

1729. SWIFT, *Direct. to Servants*, 'Gen. Direct.' The master storms, the lady scolds; stripping, cudgelling, and TURNING OFF is the word.

1743–5. POCOCKE, *Descr. East*, II. ii. 227. When they are TURNED OF thirty they begin to look thin.

1749. SMOLLETT, *Gil Blas* (1812), III. ii. I was deeply affected . . . resolving to TURN OVER A NEW LEAF, and live honestly.

1759. GOLDSMITH, *Bee*, 2. The spirit of public fanaticism TURNED their heads.

1777. SHERIDAN, *School for Scandal*, iii. 3. How your expectations will TURN OUT is more . . . than you can tell.

1809. MALKIN, *Gil Blas* [ROUTLEDGE], 54. We can TURN HIM ROUND OUR FINGER. *Ibid.*, 91. I have already introduced to her three well-furnished gallants, but she TURNED UP HER NOSE at them. *Ibid.*, 255. Pounding Lama's fair face to a jelly, and TURNING HER whole HOUSE OUT AT WINDOW.

1813. SYDNEY SMITH, *To John Allen*, 24 Jan. Those accidental visitations of fortune are like prizes in the lottery, which must not be put into the year's income till they TURN UP.

1835. DANA, *Before Mast*, 8. I found that no time was allowed for day-dreaming, but that we must TURN TO at the first light. *Ibid.*, 57. No man can be a sailor . . . unless he has lived in the fo'castle with them, TURNED IN and OUT with them, and eaten from the common kid.

1837–8. THACKERAY, *Yellowplush Papers*, ix. I saw them TURNED OFF at igsackly a quarter past twelve.

1843. DICKENS, *David Copperfield*, xi. I shall, please Heaven, begin to be beforehand with the world . . . if—in short, if anything TURNS UP.

1851–61. MAYHEW, *Lond. Lab.*, I. 353. I never had a wife, but I have had two or three broomstick marriages, though they never TURNED OUT happy.

1851. HAWTHORNE, *Seven Gables*, vii. She watched the fish . . . as if . . . her immortal happiness were involved in its being done precisely TO A TURN.

1855. GASKELL, *North and South*, xviii. 'What do you say to a strike, by way of something to talk about?' 'Have the hands actually TURNED OUT?'

1855. HOLLAND, *Sydney Smith*, viii. The struggle for his society . . . would have been quite enough to TURN any head less strong than his.

1857. HUGHES, *Tom Brown's Schooldays*, ii. 6. Tom felt at once that HIS FLANK WAS TURNED.

1860. HOLMES, *Professor*, viii. Here is a boy that loves to run, swim, kick football, TURN SOMERSETS.

1864. TENNYSON, *Enoch Arden*. To all things could he TURN HIS HAND. . . . 'This is my house, and this my little wife.' 'Mine too,' said Philip, 'TURN AND TURN ABOUT.'

1869. STOWE, *Oldtown*, 406. Tina is a little TURNED OF fifteen; she is going to be very beautiful.

1871. HORSLEY, *Jottings from Jail*. 'What catch would it be if you was to TURN ME OVER?' So I took him into a pub which had a back way out, and called for a pint of stout, and told the reeler to wait a minute.

1872. WARNER, *Backlog Studies*, 125. Then from every house and hamlet the men TURNED OUT.

1874. FISKE, *Cosmic Philos.*, i. 54. If a black swan TURNS UP. . . .

1881. G. S. HALL, *German Culture*, 306. The German official . . . is always appalled at the quantity of work his compeer here can TURN OFF in a given time.

1885. *Field*, 4 Ap. Information that TURNS OUT to be hardly correct.

1885. SIMS, *Rogues and Vagabonds*. Marston had long ago announced his intention to TURN THE GAME UP.

1887. *D. Tel.*, 28 Feb. We had not steamed two miles from that berg when it split in three portions with thunderous sounds, and every portion TURNED TURTLE.

1887. *St. James's Gazette*, 19 Dec. The doctors hope I have now TURNED THE CORNER, which has been a sharp one.

1887. *Field*, 19 Feb. [The manufacturers] TURN OUT somewhere about 5000 tons weekly.

1887. *Scribner's Mag.*, Aug., 492. We were thinking of TURNING IN for the night.

1888. BESANT, *Fifty Years Ago*. 105. The schools TURNED OUT splendid scholars.

1903. *Sporting Times*, 7 Sep., I. 3. He had given instructions, when they came to a certain point, to let go the anchor. In the meantime he had 'TURNED IN.'

TURNABOUT, *subs.* (old).—1. An innovator.

1692. HACKET, *Williams*, II. 36. Our modern TURNABOUTS cannot evince us but that we feel we are best affected, when the great mysteries of Christ are celebrated upon anniversary festivals.

2. (provincial).—A disease in cattle; THE STAGGERS (*q.v.*).

d. 1618. SYLVESTER, *The Furies*, 610. The TURNABOUT and murrain trouble cattel.

3. (common).—A merry-go-round; a run-around.

1889. *Harper's Mag.* lxxix. 560. The high swings and the TURNABOUTS, the tests of the strength of limb and lung.

TURN-BACK, *subs. phr.* (old).—A coward.

TURNCOAT, *subs.* (old).—A renegade, an apostate, 'he that quits one and embraces another party' (B. E.), 'one who has changed his party from interested motives' (GROSE). Hence TO TURN COAT (or A COAT) = to change, to pervert.

1576. TOMSON, *Calvin's Serm. Tim.*, 107. 2. We shall see these backesliders whiche knowe the Gospell, reuolt and TURNE THEIR COATES.

1600. SHAKSPEARE, *Much Ado*, i. 1. 125. *Beat.* Courtesy itself must convert to disdain if you come in her presence. *Ben.* Then is courtesy a TURNCOAT.

d. 1674. MILTON, *Ans. to Salmasius*, Pref., 13. Crafty TURN-COAT! Are you not ashamed to shift hands thus in things that are sacred?

1849. MACAULAY, *Hist. Eng.*, viii. The Chief Justice himself stood aghast at the effrontery of this venal TURNCOAT.

1871. GRENVILLE MURRAY, *Member for Paris*, xx. They blackguarded him . . . said he only wanted to get into the House to finger the salary and then TURN HIS COAT.

1888. *Westminster Rev.*, cxxviii. 526. Mr. Bright should be the last man to charge a political opponent with TURNING HIS COAT.

TURNING-TREE. *See* TURN, *subs.* 2.

TURNIP, *subs.* (old).—A watch: spec. an old-fashioned silver watch which in size approached a turnip: also FRYING-PAN (*see* WARMING-PAN).

PHRASES.—TO GIVE TURNIPS = to get rid of a person by hook or by crook; TO GET TURNIPS = to be taken in, jilted: a play on turn-up; ONE'S HEAD TO A TURNIP = a fanciful bet: *cf.* LOMBARD STREET TO A CHINA ORANGE, etc. Also *see* CRY.

1694. MOTTEUX, *Rabelais*, v. ii. You would have laid YOUR HEAD TO A TURNIP that they had been mere men.

TURNIP-PATED, *adj. phr.* (old).—White or fair-haired (B. E. and GROSE).

TURN-OUT, *subs. phr.* (colloquial).—1. A parade. Also (2) an assembly: spec. a number of people gathered together in the open air.

1847–8. THACKERAY, *Vanity Fair*, xxx. The bugles were sounding the TURN-OUT.

3. (workmen's). — A strike. Also (4) a striker (singly and collectively).

1855. GASKELL, *North and South*, xviii. All his business plans had received a check, a sudden pull-up, from this approaching TURN-OUT. *Ibid.*, xx. Those were no true friends who helped the TURN-OUTS.

5. (American).—A shunting-line, a side-track, a railway siding.

6. (common). — Production, output.

7. (colloquial).—A carriage, coach, or any vehicle with horses, harness, and other appointments; also (latterly) applied to motor-cars.

1835. HOOK, *Gilbert Gurney*. I rather prided myself on my TURN-OUT.

1884. DOWELL, *Taxes in England*, III. 50. The best TURN-OUT of the Coaching or Four-in-hand clubs.

1903. *Bazaar and Mart.* [Sub-title s.v. *Driving*] TURN-OUTS.

8. (colloquial).—Dress, GET-UP (*q.v.*): *cf.* TO TURN OUT.

1883. GREENWOOD, *Tag, Rag, & Co.* 'What would [it] cost a girl on an average who hired a full TURN-OUT on Monday and Saturday evenings?' 'If a regular customer . . . two shillings, ostrich and all.'

9. (theatrical).—An interval.

1851. MAYHEW, *Lond. Lab.* The 'Delphi was better than it is. I've taken 3s. at the first TURN-OUT!

TURNPIKE-MAN, *subs. phr.* (old).—'A parson: because the clergy collect their tolls at our entrance into and exit from the world' (GROSE).

TURNPIKE-SAILOR, *subs. phr.* (tramps').—A beggar posing as a distressed sailor.

1851. MAYHEW, *Lond. Lab.*, I. 415. I became a TURNPIKE SAILOR, as it is called, and went out as one of the Shallow Brigade.

TURN-TAIL, *subs. phr.* (common).—A coward, renegade, pervert. TO TURN TAIL = (1) to change sides, (2) to turn one's back upon, and (3) to run away, to shirk.

d. 1586. Sir P. SIDNEY (LATHAM). Would she TURN TAIL . . . and fly quite out another way.

1612. *Pasquil's Night Cap.* How brittle, fickle, wavering, false, and fraile, Like to a wethercocke, still TURNING TAILE.

c. 1612. CORBET, *Iter Boreale.* His mare . . . for conscience sake, unspurr'd, unbeaten, Brought us six miles, and TURN'D TAYLE at Nuneaton.

1621. SYLVESTER, *Du Bartas.* 'The Furies.' Our Sire . . . TURN'D TAIL to God, and to the Fiend his face.

1632. JONSON, *Magnetic Lady*, v. 4. Would thou had'st a dose of pills . . . to make thee TURN TAIL t'other way.

1663. BUTLER, *Hudibras*, I. iii. Yet shame and honour might prevail To keep thee thus from TURNING TAIL.

1874. *Siliad*, 15. A general Hubbub all the force misled, And one, a Highland Chief, TURNED TAIL and fled.

TURN-TIPPET, *subs. phr.* (old).—A time-server; TURNCOAT (*q.v.*). Hence TO TURN TIPPET = to change right about.

d. 1556. CRANMER, *Works*, II. 15 [Parker Soc.]. The priests for the most part were double-faced, TURN-TIPPETS, and flatterers.

1562. HEYWOOD, *Epigrams* [OLIPHANT, *New English*, i. 561. Amongst the romance words are] TURN HIS TIPPET.

d. 1575. PILKINGTON, *Sermons*, 211. All TURN-TIPPETS, that turn with the world and keep their livings still, should have no office in Christ's Church.

1587. GREENE, *Morando.* No doubt he would not onely TURNE HIS TIPPET, recant his hereticall opinion, and perswade others to honor beautie.

c. 1600. *Merry Devil of Edmonton*, [TEMPLE], iii. 2. 137. Well, to be brief, the nun will soon at night TURN TIPPET; if I can but devise to quit her cleanly of the nunnery, she is my own.

1609. JONSON, *Case is Altered*, iii. A saint, Another Bridget, one that for a face Would put down Vesta; . . . You TO TURN TIPPET!

1609. FLETCHER, *Monsieur Thomas*, ii. 2. Ye stand now As if y' had worried sheep. You must TURN TIPPET, And suddenly, and truly, and discreetly, Put on the shape of order and humanity.

TURN-UP, *subs. phr.* (old).—1. 'A fight produced from a hasty quarrel, a casual boxing-match' (GROSE); a shindy; a scrimmage.

1834. WILSON, *Noctes Ambros.* Dec. I have seen many a TURN-UP and some pitched battles among the yokels.

1837. BARHAM, *Ingoldsby Leg.* I'd describe now to you as 'prime a set-to,' and 'regular TURN-UP,' as ever you knew; not inferior in 'bottom' to aught you have read of.

2. (common).—An unexpected event or result; a chance encounter, spec. a sudden piece of luck: *see* TURN, *phrases*.

1878. *Century*, xxvii. 926. The type of men [Carlyle and Emerson] are comparatively a new TURN-UP in literature.

1885. *D. Chron.*, 19 Oct. This doubtless caused the fielders to take a firm stand on the chance of a TURN-UP.

TURPENTINE STATE, *subs. phr.* (American). — North Carolina: its people are TARHEELS (*q.v.*).

TURPIN, *subs.* (old). — A kettle. [HALLIWELL: 'A cant term.']

TURTLE. *See* TURN.

TURTLE DOVE, *subs. phr.* (rhyming).—In *pl.* = a pair of gloves: also TURTLES.

1893. EMERSON, *Signor Lippo*, xiv. A long-sleeve cadi on his napper, and a pair of TURTLES on his martins finished him.

TURVY-TOPSY. *See* TOPSY-TURVY.

TUSH (or **TWISH**). *intj.* (old colloquial).—An expression of impatience, contempt, or rebuke: also as *verb*, and TUSHING, *subs.*: *cf.* TUT.

c. 1400. *York Mysteries*, 324. [OLIPHANT, *New Eng.*, i. 195. There is the interjection TUSSCH! which took a hundred years to reach London.]

d. 1529. SKELTON, *Works*, s.v.

1586. STANIHURST, *Descr. Ireland*, i. There is a cholerike or disdainfull interiection vsed in the Irish language called Bosgh, which is as much in English as TWISH.

1598. FLORIO, *Worlde of Wordes*, s.v. *Zoccoli*, *zoccoli*, TUSHTUSH, awaie, in faith sir, no, yea, in my other hose.

1611. *Bible*, *Auth. Version*, Psalm lxxiii. 11. TUSH, say they, how should God perceive it.

1612. CHAPMAN, *Widow's Tears*, v. TUSH, man; in this topsy-turvy world friendship and bosom-kindness are but made covers for mischief.

1819. SCOTT, *Ivanhoe*, ii. 387. Cedric TUSHED and pshawed more than once at the message, but he refused not obedience.

TUSHEROON, *subs.* (common).—A crown piece; 5s.: *see* CAROON.

TUSSEY, *subs.* (provincial).—A low drunken fellow: *cf.* TOSTICATED.

TUSSICATED, *adj.* (provincial).—Driven about, tormented (HALLIWELL).

TUSSLE, *subs.* (colloquial). — A struggle; a contest; a TOUSLE (*q.v.*). Also as *verb* = to scuffle, to struggle.

[?]. [PERCY, *Reliques*], 'St. George for England.' Did TUSTLE with red-eyed pole-cat.

1709. CENTLIVRE, *Busybody*, 44. Muzzle and TUZZLE and hug thee.

1818. SCOTT, *Midlothian*, li. It is some comfort when one has had a sair TUSSEL . . . that it is in a fair leddy's service.

TUSSOCKER, *subs.* (New Zealand). —A SUNDOWNER (*q.v.*).

1889. PYKE, *Wild Will Enderby.* Now, a 'sun-downer,' or 'TUSSOCKER' . . . is a pastoral loafer; one who loiters about till dusk, and then makes for the nearest station or hut, to beg for shelter and food.

TUT, *intj.* (colloquial).—TUSH (*q.v.*), PISH (*q.v.*). Also TUTS! and as *verb*. TO MAKE TUTS FOR = to make light of.

c. 1500. DUNBAR, *Works* (PATERSON), 97. [OLIPHANT, *New Eng.*, i. 363. The new interjection TUT is seen.]

d. 1555. BRADFORD, *Repentance.* O hard hearts that we have, which MAKE TUTS for skin.

1597. SHAKSPEARE, *Richard II.*, ii. 3. 87. TUT, TUT! Grace me no grace, nor uncle me no uncle.

1605. JONSON, *Volpone*, ii. 3. TUT, I am confident in thee, thou shalt see't.

1849. LYTTON, *Caxtons*, VIII. iii. In another moment the member of Parliament had forgotten the statist, and was pishing and TUTTING over the Globe or the Sun.

A TUT FOR A TUSH, *phr.* (old). —A TIT FOR TAT (*q.v.*): *see* TUSH.

TUTIVILLUS, *subs.* (old).—An old name for a celebrated demon, who is said to have collected all the fragments of words which the priests had skipped over or mutilated in the performance of the service, and carried them to hell.

TUTTING, *subs.* (provincial).—'A tea-drinking for women, succeeded by stronger potations in company of the other sex, and ending in ribaldry and debauchery. So called only, I believe, in Lincoln; in other places in the county it is known as a bun-feast. Now obsolete, or nearly so' (HALLIWELL).

TUTTLE (or TUTTLE NASK), *subs.* (old). — 'The Bridewell in Tuttle-Fields' (B. E.): closed in 1878.

TUT-WORK, *subs. phr.* (workmen's). —Piece-work.

TUZ I, *phr.* (Felsted School).—The same as FAINITS (*q.v.*), BAGS I (*q.v.*).

TUZZYMUZZY, *subs.* (venery).— The female *pudendum*: *see* MONOSYLLABLE (BAILEY).

TWACHIL (or TWACHYLLE), *subs.* (old).—The female *pudendum*: *see* MONOSYLLABLE, and *cf.* TWAT.

TWADDLE (TWATTLE, etc.), *subs.* (old colloquial). — 1. Gabble, STUFF AND NONSENSE (*q.v.*); (2) a prosy chatterbox, babbler, driveller: also TWADDLER (TWATTLER, TWATTLE-BASKET, or TWATTLE-BRAINS). As *verb* = to clack, prate, rattle on; TWADDLING (or TWADDLEY) = (1) silly, loquacious, inane; (2) trifling, paltry, petty. Also reduplicated in TWITTLE-TWATTLE.

15[?]. *King and Miller of Mansfield* [CHILD, *Ballads*, VIII. 43]. You feed us with TWATLING dishes soe small.

1577. STANIHURST, *Descr. Ireland*, vi. Let vs in Gods name leaue lieng for varlets, berding for ruffians, facing for crakers, chatting for TWATTLERS. *Ibid.* (1582), *Æneid*, iv. [ARBER], 101. As readye forgde fittons as true tales vaynelye toe TWATTLE.

1634. WHATELEY, *Redemp. of Time*, 15. The apostle Paul finds fault with a certain sort of women who were prattlers, which would go from house to house, TWATTLING, and babbling out frothy speech that was good for nothing.

1653. URQUHART, *Rabelais*, III. xviii. They show him the short and TWATTLE verses that were written.

c. 1660. LESTRANGE, *Works* [*Century*]. It is not for every TWATTLING gossip to undertake.

d. 1691. BAXTER, *Self Denial*, xxvii. Idle persons that will spend whole hours together in TWATTLING.

1719. SWIFT, *To Dr. Sheridan*, 14 Dec. Such a TWATTLING with you and your bottling.

1785. GROSE, *Vulgar Tongue*, Pref., vii. The favourite expressions of the day . . . vanish without leaving a trace behind. Such were the late fashionable words, a BORE and a TWADDLE, among the great vulgar. *Ibid.*, s.v. BORE . . . much in fashion about the years 1780 and 1781.

1825. SCOTT, *St. Ronan's Well*, ii. 188. The devil take the TWADDLE! . . . I must tip him the cold shoulder, or he will be pestering me eternally.

1830. GREVILLE, *Memoirs*, 4 Ap. The cardinals appeared a wretched set of old TWADDLERS.

1837. DICKENS, *Pickwick Papers*, li. You will perhaps be somewhat repaid by a laugh at the style of this ungrammatical TWADDLER.

1849. KINGSLEY, *Alton Locke*, viii. Between conceit and disgust, fancying myself one day a great new poet, and the next a mere TWADDLER, I got . . . puzzled and anxious.

1853. THACKERAY, *Eng. Humourists*, v. The puny cockney bookseller, pouring endless volumes of sentimental TWADDLE. *Ibid.* (1857-9), *Virginians*, xviii. The soft youth in the good Bishop of Cambray's TWADDLING story.

1856. READE, *Never too Late*, etc. xxiii. An occasion for TWADDLING had come, and this good soul seized it, and TWADDLED into a man's ear who was fainting on the rack.

1864. LOWELL, *Fireside Travels*, 155. To be sure Cicero used to TWADDLE about Greek literature and philosophy, much as people do about ancient art nowadays.

d. 1875. HELPS, *Works* [*Century*]. Their lucubrations seem to me to be TWADDLY.

3. (old). — Perplexity, confusion; 'or anything else: a fashionable term that for a while succeeded that of *bore*' (GROSE).

4. (old).—A diminutive person.

TWANG, *subs.* (old: now recognised).—'A smack or ill Taste' (B. E.); hence (modern) = a decided flavour.

1707. FARQUHAR, *Beaux' Stratagem*, iii. 2. Doctor, you talk very good English, but you have a mighty TWANG of the foreigner.

1769-78. TUCKER, *Light of Nature*, II. II. xxiii. Though the liquor was not at all impaired thereby in substance or virtue, it might get some TWANG of the vessel.

1831. DISRAELI, *Young Duke*, iv. 6. Hot, bilious, with a confounded TWANG in his mouth.

1817. SCOTT, *Rob Roy*, xviii. They already began to have a TWANG of commerce in them.

TO GO OFF TWANGING, *verb. phr.* (old).—To go well, swimmingly: *cf.* (RAY) AS GOOD AS EVER TWANGED = as good as may be.

1629. MASSINGER, *Roman Actor*, ii. 2. Had he died . . . It had GONE OFF TWANGING.

TWANGDILLO (or TRANGDILLO). *See* TWANGLE.

TWANGEY (or STANGEY), *subs.* (old).—A tailor: north country (GROSE).

TWANGLE, *subs.* (colloquial). — That is 'twang': also TWANK, TWANGDILLO, TWANGLING, and as *verb.*

1593. SHAKSPEARE, *Taming of the Shrew*, ii. 1. Rascal fidler, TWANGLING Jack. *Ibid.* (1609), *Tempest*, iii. 2. Sometimes a thousand TWANGLING instruments Will hum about mine ears, and sometimes voices.

d. 1704. BROWN, *Works*, i. 62. Even d'Urfey himself and such merry fellows, That put their whole trust in tunes and TRANGDILLOES, May hang up their harps and themselves on the willows.

d. 1719. ADDISON, *Works* [*Ency. Dict.*]. A freeman of London has the privilege of disturbing a whole street with TWANKING of a brass kettle.

1762. COLLINS, *Misc.*, viii. Pleas'd with the TWANGDILLOWS of poor Crowdero in a country fair.

1812. COLMAN, *Poet. Vag.* iii. Loud, on the heath, a TWANGLE rush'd, That rung out Supper, grand and big, From the crack'd bell of Blarneygig

1840. THACKERAY, *Shabby Genteel Story*, ii. The young Andrea bears up gaily, however; TWANGLES his guitar.

TWANK, *verb.* (Durham School).— To cane [HALLIWELL: 'to give a smart slap with the flat of the hand, a stick, etc., *East*'].

TWANKING, *adj.* (common).—Big, unwieldy: a generic intensive.

TWAT, *subs.* (old).—The female *pudendum*: *see* MONOSYLLABLE. [HALLIWELL, s.v. TWATETH: 'A buck or doe TWATETH, *i.e.* makes a noise at rutting time.] Whence (venery) TO GO TWAT-RAKING = to copulate: *see* RIDE; TWAT-RUG = the female pubic hair: *see* FLEECE.

d. 1650. FLETCHER, *Poems*, 104. Give not male names then to such things as thine, But think thou hast two TWATS O wife of mine.

1727. BAILEY, *Dict.*, s.v. TWAT. *Pudendum muliebre.*

1890. *Century Dict.*, s.v. TWAT [Found by Browning in the old royalist rimes 'Vanity of Vanities,' and on the supposition that the word denoted 'a distinctive part of a nun's attire that might fitly pair off with the cowl appropriated to a monk,' so used by him in his 'Pippa Passes'].

TWATTERLIGHT. *See* TWITTERLIGHT.

TWATTLE. *See* TWADDLE.

TWEAGUE (or TWEAK), *subs.* (old). — Passion, peevishness: also TWEAGUY, *adj.*; IN A TWEAK = 'in a heavy taking, much vext, or very angry' (B. E. and GROSE).

1713. ARBUTHNOT, *Hist. John Bull*, ii. This put the old fellow in a rare TWEAGUE.

TWEAK, *subs.* (old colloquial).—1. A jerk, twinge, pinch: as *verb* = to twitch, pull, or snatch: usually in phrase TO TWEAK ONE'S NOSE (GROSE). TWEAKER (Felsted School: obsolete) = a catapult.

1420. PALLADIUS, *Husbondrie* [E.E.T.S.], 150. Voide leves puld to be . . . With fyngers lightly TWYK hem from the tree.

1632. JONSON, *Magnetic Lady*, iii. 4. Now TWEAK him BY THE NOSE—hard, harder yet.

1632. BROME, *Northern Lass*, ii. 5. TWEAKS BY THE NOSE, Cuffs o' the Ear, and Trenchers at my Head in abundance.

1663. BUTLER, *Hudibras*, I. ii. Quoth he, TWEAKING his nose, 'you are, great sir, A self-denying conqueror.'

1724. SWIFT, *Riddle*, 25. In passion so weak, but gives it a TWEAK.

1887. WINGFIELD, *Lovely Wang*, ii. Her old toes TWEAKED with corns.

2. (old).—A dilemma (PHILLIPS, 1706): also as *verb* = to perplex (BAILEY, 1731).

3. (venery).—(*a*) A wanton, a whore: *see* TART; and (*b*) a wencher: *see* MUTTONMONGER.

Q

[?]. *Honest Ghost*, 'Farew. to Poetry,' 110. Where now I'm more perplext than can be told, If my TWEAKE squeeze from me a peece of gold; For to my lure she is so kindely brought, I look'd that she for nought should play the nought.

1617. MIDDLETON and ROWLEY, *Fair Quarrel*, iv. 4. Your TWEAKS are like your mermaids, they have sweet voices to entice the passengers.

c. 1650. BRATHWAYTE, *Barnaby's Jl.* (1723), 101. From the Bushes . . . Rush'd a TWEAK in Gesture flanting, With a leering Eye and wanton.

See TWEAGUE.

TWEEDLE, *subs.* (thieves'). — A Brummagem ring of good appearance used for fraudulent purposes.

See TWIDDLE.

TWEEDLEDUM AND TWEEDLEDEE (THE DIFFERENCE BETWEEN), *subs. phr.* (common).—No difference at all, save in sound; a distinction without a difference. [*Ency. Dict.*: The expression arose in the eighteenth century, when there was a dispute between the admirers of Bononcini and those of Handel, as to the respective merits of those musicians. Among the first were the Duke of Marlborough and most of the nobility; among the latter the Prince of Wales, Pope, and Arbuthnot.]

c. 1730. BYROM, *Feuds between Handel*, etc. Some say, compared to Bononcini, That Mynheer Handel's but a ninny. Others aver that he to Handel Is scarcely fit to hold a candle. Strange all this difference should be 'Twixt TWEEDLEDUM and TWEEDLEDEE.

TWEENIE, *subs.* (colloquial).—A 'between-maid.'

1888. *Notes and Queries*, 7 S. vi. 458. In want of a girl to ease both the cook and the housemaid . . . a neighbour . . . replied, . . . 'You want a TWEENIE.'

TWELVE. AFTER TWELVE, *subs. phr.* (Eton).—From noon till 2 p.m.

1861. WHYTE MELVILLE, *Good for Nothing*, 39. I used to visit him regularly in the dear old college from the AFTER TWELVE.

1864. *Eton School-days*, vi. I tell you plainly if you are not in Sixpenny AFTER TWELVE, I will do my best to give you a hiding wherever I meet you.

1883. BRINSLEY-RICHARDS, *Seven Years at Eton.* One day AFTER TWELVE the three of us passed over Windsor Bridge in the same condition as the 'bold adventurers' alluded to in Gray's Ode.

TWELVE APOSTLES, *subs. phr.* (Cambridge University).—1. The last twelve in the Mathematical Tripos (GROSE).

2. (Stonyhurst). — The first TWELVE Stonyhurst students.

TWELVE GODFATHERS, *subs. phr.* (common).—A jury. [HOTTEN: they name the nature of a crime; murder or manslaughter, felony or misdemeanour.] 'You'll be christened by TWELVE GODFATHERS some day' (a taunt).

TWELVEPENNY, *adj.* (old). — Trifling, of small value: frequently contemptuous.

1614. JONSON, *Bartholomew Fair*, v. 3. Thou esquire of dames, madams, and TWELVEPENNY LADIES.

1644. HEYLIN, *Hist. of the Presbyterians*, 371. That men be not excommunicated for trifles, and TWELVE-PENNY MATTERS.

d. 1701. DRYDEN, *Works* [*Ency. Dict.*]. I would wish no other revenge from this rhyming judge of the TWELVE-PENNY gallery.

TWELVER, *subs.* (old).—A shilling; 1s. (B.E. and GROSE): *cf.* THIRTEENER.

1858. MAYHEW, *Paved with Gold*, III. ii. One of the men . . . had only taken three TWELVERS.

TWENTY, *subs.* and *adj.* (old).—1. An indefinite number: also TWENTY AND TWENTY.

1593. SHAKSPEARE, *Venus and Adonis*, 575. Under TWENTY locks kept fast.

1623. BACON, *Hist. Hen. VII.*, 350. As for Maximillian, upon TWENTY respects he could not have been the man.

1704. BROWN, *Works*, i. 153. The tallowchandlers such dutiful and loyal subjects that they don't care if there were TWENTY AND TWENTY birthdays in a year, to help off with their commodity.

1748. RICHARDSON, *Harlowe*, ii. 145. I have hinted it to you TWENTY AND TWENTY times by word of mouth. *Ibid.* (1753). I could satisfy myself about TWENTY AND TWENTY things that now and then I want to know.

2. (Rugby).—The Sixth Form.

TWENTY-TWO AND TWENTY-TWO, *subs. phr.* (Winchester).—Football: twenty-two a side.

TWIBILL, *subs.* (Old Cant).—A street ruffian; a ROARING-BOY (*q.v.*): seventeenth century.

TWICE. AT TWICE, *adv. phr.* (old and still colloquial).—On a second trial; in two distinct attempts: *cf.* 'You've guessed it in once.'

1611. CORYAT, *Crudities*, I. 220. I could hardly compasse one . . . AT TWICE with both my armes.

1628. MIDDLETON, *Widow*, iv. 2. I'll undertake your man shall cure you, sir, AT TWICE i' your own chamber.

[?]. *Ballad of Goulden Vanitee* [Mrs. GORDON (quoted by), *Christopher North*, 433]. He took out an Instrument, bored thirty holes AT TWICE, As they sailed to the Lowlands low.

1860. ELIOT, *Mill on Floss*, iii. 3. 'Did Mr. Tulliver let you have all the money at once?' said Mrs. Tulliver. . . . 'No; AT TWICE,' said Mrs. Moss.

1869. TROLLOPE, *Phineas Redux*, xxv. His Grace should have . . . a glass and a half of champagne. His Grace won't drink his wine out of a tumbler, so perhaps your ladyship won't mind giving it him AT TWICE.

TWICE-LAID, *subs. phr.* (common).—A hash-up of fish and potatoes: *cf.* RESURRECTION-PIE.

TWICER, *subs.* (printers'). — A printer who works at press as well as at case.

TWIDDLE (or **TWEEDLE**), *verb.* (colloquial).—1. To finger idly and lightly: usually in phrase, 'to TWIDDLE one's fingers'; to FIDDLE (*q.v.*), wriggle, or twist about; to be busy about trifles; to wheedle, to coax: *e.g.* 'She can TWIDDLE him round her little finger': *cf.* TWIRL.

1540. [COLLIER, *Dramatic Poetry*, ii.]. [OLIPHANT, *New Eng.*, i. 482. There is the verb TWYDLE, which seems to be connected with *twirl*.]

1568. *Wit and Science.* What unthryftnes therein is TWYDLYNGS?

1676. WISEMAN, *Surgery* [*Century*]. I pressed close upon it, and TWIDLED it in, first one side and then the other.

1715. ADDISON, *Freeholder*, 3. A fiddler brought in with him a body of lusty young fellows, whom he had TWEEDLED into the service.

d. 1800. COWPER, *Pairing Time.* Dick heard, and TWEEDLING, ogling, bridling . . .

1847-8. THACKERAY, *Vanity Fair*, xiv. 'Look out,' . . . said the mustachio TWIDDLER. *Ibid.* (1848), *Snobs*, xxiv. All the bugles in her awful head-dress began to TWIDDLE and quiver. *Ibid.* (1862), *Philip*, xiv. TWIDDLING a little locket which he wore at his watch chain.

1851-61. MAYHEW, *Lond. Lab.*, I. 481. Marm, I seed him a TWIDDLING with your gown.

1880. P. ROBINSON, *Under the Sun*, 72. Straw-coloured crickets that sit and TWIDDLE their long antennæ.

1886. *D. Teleg.*, 13 Jan. TWIDDLING their thumbs in front of comfortable fires.

1889. OLIPHANT, *Poor Gentleman*, ix. Then he sat silent for a moment, staring into the fire, and TWIDDLING his thumbs.

2. (venery).—To wanton; to TOUCH (*q.v.*); TO SLEUTHER (*q.v.*). TWIDDLE-DIDDLES = the *testes* (GROSE).

TWIDDLEPOOP, *subs.* (old).—An effeminate-looking fellow (GROSE).

TWIG, *subs.* (old). — 1. Style, fashion, method. Hence as *adj.* = stylish, handsome; IN GOOD (or PRIME) TWIG = clever, well-dressed, in good spirits (GROSE). TO PUT OUT OF TWIG = to alter, disguise, so to change as to make unrecognisable (VAUX).

1819. MOORE, *Tom Cub.* Never since the renown'd days of Brougham and Figg Was the fanciful world IN such very PRIME TWIG.

1820. EGAN, *Randall's Diary.* In search of lark, or some delicious gig, The mind delights on, when 'tis IN PRIME TWIG.

2. (Marlborough: obsolete).—The Headmaster [in whose authority rested the use of the birch].

Verb. (old).—1. To watch, observe, mark (GROSE). Also (2) to understand, SEE (*q.v.*), TUMBLE TO (*q.v.*). Whence (in humorous imitation of Fr. *comprenez-vous*) TWIGGEZ-VOUS. *See* TWUG.

1763. FOOTE, *Mayor of Garratt*, ii. 2. Now TWIG him; now mind him; mark how he hawls his muscles about.

1796. HOLMAN, *Abroad and at Home*, iii. 2. He TWIGS me. He knows Dicky here.

1835. T. HOOK, *Gilbert Gurney*, III, ii. Don't you TWIG?

1837. DICKENS, *Pickwick*, xx. 'They're a-TWIGGIN' you, sir,' whispered Mr. Weller. . . . All the four clerks were minutely inspecting the general appearance of the supposed trifler with female hearts.

1840. BARHAM, *Ingoldsby Legends*, 'Jackdaw of Rheims.' They can't find the ring! And the Abbot declared that, 'when nobody TWIGG'D it, Some rascal or other had popp'd in, and PRIGG'D it!'

1845. DISRAELI, *Sybil*, v. 10. 'I TWIG,' said Mick.

1853. READE, *Gold*, i. 1. If he is an old hand he will TWIG.

1858. Dr. J. BROWN, *Spare Hours*, 1 S. 306. I TWIGGED at once that he didn't himself know what it meant.

1872. *Figaro*, 22 June. A nattier rig you'll hardly TWIG.

1877. *Five Years' Penal Servitude*, iii. 245. Some feller in the shop TWIGGED my old girl as one he'd a-seen before.

1890. W. JAMES, *Principles of Psychology*, I. 253. That first instantaneous glimpse of some one's meaning which we have when in vulgar phrase we say, we TWIG it.

1896. FARJEON, *Betray. John Fordham*, III. 284. The job I 'ad to orfer yer wos to pick feathers. A fat pigeon with feathers of gold. Do yer TWIG?

1898. MARSHALL, *Pomes*, 74. So her clobber, you'll TWIG, was a second-hand rig.

1900. KIPLING, *Stalky & Co.*, 40. 'Now jump up, Pussy! Say, "I think I'd better come to life!" Then we all take hands, etc. . . . TWIGGEZ-VOUS?' 'NOUS TWIGGONS.'

1900. WHITE, *West End*, 130. 'How do you know?' 'I TWIGGED it from mother's manner.'

3. (thieves').—To snap asunder, break off: *e.g.* 'TWIG the darbies' = knock off the irons.

TO MEASURE A TWIG, *verb. phr.* (old). — To act absurdly (RAY).

See HOP THE TWIG.

TWIGGER, *subs.* (venery). —1. A harlot; (2) a wencher. [In TUSSER, *Husb.*, 'Jan.' = a good breeder.] TWIGLE = to copulate (HALLIWELL).

1612. *Pasquil's Night Cap.* Now, Benedicite, her mother said; And hast thou beene already such a TWIGGER.

c. 1613. MIDDLETON, *No Wit*, etc., iv. 1. The mother of her was a good TWIGGER the whilst.

1694. MOTTEUX, *Rabelais*, v., 'Pant. Prog.' TWIGGERS, harlots, kept wenches.

TWILIGHT, *subs.* (old).—A corruption of toilet: (old) a dressing-cloth, towel, or napkin.

1684. DRYDEN, *Disappointment*, Prol., 50. A TWILLET, dressing-box, and half a crown.

c. 1690. *Ladies' Dict.* A toilet is a little cloth which ladies use for what purpose they think fit, and is by some corruptly called a TWYLIGHT.

1706. *Fifteen Comforts of Matrimony.* Fine TWI-LIGHTS, blankets, and the Lord knows what.

1853. BRADLEY, *Verdant Green*, II. vii. It was no use doing the downy again, so it was just as well to make one's TWILIGHT and go to chapel.

TWINE, *verb.* (thieves').—TO RING THE CHANGES (*q.v.*).

TWINKLER, *subs.* (colloquial).—1. In *pl.* = the eyes. Also (2) a star, and (3) a light (thieves').

1380. WYCLIF, *Ecclus*, vii. 25. The TWYNCLERE with the eȝe forgeth wicke thingus.

d. 1704. BROWN, *Works*, i. 267. I no sooner saw your Ladyship, but those everlasting Murderers, your TWINKLERS, prick'd and stabb'd me in a thousand Parts of my body.

1705. VANBRUGH, *Confederacy*, iii. 2. *Aram.* The stars have done this. *Clar.* The pretty little TWINKLERS.

1813. SHELLEY, *Queen Mab*, ix. Such tiny TWINKLERS as the planet-orbs.

1837. MARRYAT, *Snarley-yow*, I. vii. Following me up and down with those TWINKLERS of yours.

TWINKLING. *See* BEDPOST.

TWINS. TO HAVE TWINS, *verb. phr.* (American).—To take dinner and tea at one meal; TO BOX HARRY (*q.v.*).

TWIRE (**TWEER, TOUR,** and **TOWRE**).—1. To peep, to look round cautiously, to peer: *cf.* TOWER. [TOUR (the canting form: *see* TOWER) possibly originated in TWIRE being carelessly written.] Whence (2) (old) = to leer, to 'make eyes.' As *subs.* = a glance, a leer. TWIREPIPE = a peeping Tom.

1598. SHAKSPEARE, *Sonnets*, 28. So flatter I the swart-complexion'd night; When sparkling stars TWIRE not, thou gildst the even.

1602. MARSTON, *Antonio and Mellida*, iv. In good sadness, I would have sworn I had seen Mellida even now; for I saw a thing stir under a hedge, and I peep'd, and I spied a thing, and I peer'd and I TWEER'D underneath.

1604. MOFFAT, *Father Hubbard's Tales.* The TWEERING constable of Finsbury.

1619. FLETCHER, *Monsieur Thomas*, iii. 1. You are . . . a TWIRE-PIPE, A Jeffrey John Bo-peep. *Ibid.* (*c.* 1620), *Women Pleased*, iv. 1. I saw the wench that TWIR'D and twinkled at thee The other day.

1637. JONSON, *Sad Shepherd*, ii. 1. Which maids will TWIRE at 'tween their fingers thus.

1676. ETHEREGE, *Man of Mode*, iii. 3. The silly By-words, and Amorous TWEERS in passing.

1722. STEELE, *Conscious Lovers*, i. 1. If I was rich I could TWIRE and loll as well as the best of them.

1822. SCOTT, *Fort. Nigel.* TOUR the bien mort TWIRING the gentry cove.

TWIRL, *subs.* (thieves').—A skeleton key: *see* JEMMY.

1877. HORSLEY, *Jottings from Jail.* He was very lucky at making TWIRLS, and used to supply them all with tools.

TO TWIRL ONE'S THUMBS, *verb. phr.* (colloquial).—To be idle: *cf.* 'cool one's heels': *cf.* TWIDDLE.

1889. NORRIS, *Miss Shafto*, xxiv. Upon my word, Walter, you are pretty cool! Will it amuse me, pray, to TWIRL MY THUMBS in your studio?

TWISH, *intj.* (colloquial).—An exclamation of contempt.

TWISS, *subs.* (old).—A chamber-mug; IT (*q.v.*). [GROSE: A Mr. Richard Twiss having . . . given a very unfavourable description of the Irish character some utensils were made with his portrait at the bottom, and the following, 'Let every one piss, On lying Dick Twiss.']

TWIST, *subs.* (old).—1. The fourchure, the crutch.

1586. HARRISON, *Desc. Britain*, v. A man of common heigth might easilie go vnder his TWIST, without stooping, a stature incredible.

1609. HEYWOOD, *Troia Britanica.* Typhon makes play, Jhove catcht him by the TWIST, Heaves him aloft.

2. (colloquial).—A bent, turn, cast: a variation from what is usually normal and proper. Thus A TWISTED VISION = a wrong or 'cussed' way of looking at things; A TWISTED (= a lying) TONGUE: whence TWISTER = a falsehood or gross exaggeration; TWISTED (= brogueish) SPEECH, etc. Also TWISTY (or TWISTICAL) = awkward, CROOKED (*q.v.*), FUNNY (*q.v.*); TWISTABLE = easily influenced.

1820. HUMPHREYS, *Yankee in England.* He may be straight-going, farzino, manwards; but, in his dealings with t'other sex, he is a leetle TWISTICAL, according to their tell. I wouldn't make a town talk of it.

1821. LAMB, *Mackery End.* Heads with some diverting TWIST in them.

1824. PEAKE, *Americans Abroad*, i. 1. Come . . . you are but an underlin', tho' you are so uppish and TWISTICAL.

1862. *New York Tribune*, 28 Mar. This amendment is TWISTABLE into an advice, an impertinent advice to a foreign nation.

1881. HUXLEY, *Science and Culture.* An exclusively scientific training will bring about a mental TWIST as surely as an exclusively literary training.

1887. *Field*, 26 Nov. The fox made his straight point, though by devious and TWISTY courses.

d. 1891. LOWELL, *FitzAdam's Story.* You might have called him with his humorous TWIST, A kind of human entomologist.

3. (colloquial).—An appetite; hence TO TWIST IT DOWN (or LUSTILY) = 'to feed like a Farmer' (B. E.), 'to eat heartily' (GROSE). Fr. *crampe au pylore.*

4. (old).—(*a*) A mixture of tea and coffee (B. E. and GROSE); also (*b*) brandy, beer, and eggs (GROSE); and (*c*) brandy and gin.

1849-50. THACKERAY, *Pendennis*, xxxix. When he went to the Back Kitchen that night . . . the gin TWIST and devilled turkey had no charms for him.

5. (Winchester). — A stick spirally marked by a creeper having grown round it: also TWISTER.

Verb. (old).—To hang: *see* LADDER (GROSE). Hence TWISTED = hanged.

1823. GROSE, *Vulg. Tongue* [EGAN], s.v. NOSE. His pall NOSED, and he was TWISTED for a crack.

6. (cricket).—A turn given to the wrist in delivery, so that the ball breaks from the straight. Whence TWISTER = a ball so delivered by the bowler (also, at billiards, a ball that SCREWS or spins along with a twist). Hence (figuratively) = anything that puzzles or staggers.

1857. HUGHES, *Tom Brown's Schooldays*, ii. 8. The cover-point hitter, that cunning man, goes on to bowl slow TWISTERS.

c. 1889. *Pop. Science Monthly* (Century). He has learned the trick of playing with a straight bat the examiner's most artful TWISTERS.

1898. MARSHALL, *Pomes*, 61. That blow was a TWISTER.

1903. *Punch's Almanack*, 14. 1. Saunders doth next (at TWISTERS who so skilled?) slay ('Bowl' wouldn't rhyme, unfortunately) Tyldesley.

A TWIST ON THE SHORTS, *phr.* (American Stock Exchange).—A Wall Street phrase, used where the SHORTS (*q.v.*) have undersold heavily, and the market has been artificially raised, compelling them to settle at ruinous rates (MEDBURY).

TO TWIST (or WIND) ROUND ONE'S FINGER, *verb. phr.* (colloquial).—To control or influence completely, to make submissive: usually of women.

See TAIL.

TWIT, *verb.* (originally and still literary).—'To hit in the Teeth' (B. E.); 'to reproach a person or remind him of favours conferred' (GROSE); TWITTY (colloquial) = cross, ill-tempered.

TWITCH. TO TWITCH A TWELVE, *verb. phr.* (American university).—To get the highest number of marks.

TWITCHER, *subs.* (provincial).—1. A severe blow.

2. (common).—In *pl.* = small pincers.

TWITCHETTY, *adj.* and *adv.* (colloquial):—Nervous, fidgety, uncertain: also TWITCHY.

TWITTER. ALL OF A TWITTER, *phr.* (colloquial).—Frightened, nervous, fidgety (GROSE): also IN (or ON) THE TWITTERS. TWITTERATION (or TWITTERS) = sexual desire: espec. of women.

1660. LESTRANGE, *Quevedo*. A widow which had a TWITTERING towards a second husband took a gossiping companion to manage the job.

1766. COLMAN, *Clandestine Marriage*, i. 1. I am ALL OF A TWITTER to see my old John Harrowby again.

TWITTER-LIGHT, *subs.* (old).—Twilight: also TWATTERLIGHT.

1607. MIDDLETON, *Five Gallants*, v. 1. Then cast she up Her pretty eye, and wink'd; the word methought was then, 'Come not 'till TWITTER-LIGHT.'

1606. *Wily Beguil'd* [HAWKINS, *Eng. Dr.*, iii. 331]. What mak'st thou here this TWATTER-LIGHT? I think thou'rt in a dream.

TWITTLE, *verb.* (old colloquial).—To chatter, babble, tattle. Hence TWITTLE-TWAT = a chatterbox; TWITTLE-TWATTLE = gabble, idle talk.

1582. STANIHURST, *Æneid* [ARBER], Int., xi. His hystorie ... TWITTLED ... tales out of school.

1619. HOLLAND, *Plutarch*, 85. All that ever he did was not worth so much as the TWITTLE-TWATTLE that he maketh.

1660. LESTRANGE, *Quevedo*. Insipid TWITTLETWATTLES, frothy jests, and jingling witticisms, inure us to a misunderstanding of things.

1660. *Rump Songs*. Next come those idle TWITTLE-TWATS, Which calls me many God-knows-whats.

TWITTOC, *adj.* (Old Cant).—Two (GROSE).

TWO, *adj.* (old colloquial).—Doubly: *e.g.* TWO FOOLS = twice foolish; TWO KNAVES = doubly knavish.

1571. EDWARDS, *Damon and Pithias* [DODSLEY, *Old Plays* (REED), i. 176]. A varlet died in graine, You lose money by him, if you sell him for one knave, For he serves for TWAINE.

[1595. SHAKSPEARE, *Two Gentlemen*, iii. 1. I am but a fool, look you; and yet I have the wit to think my master is a kind of knave; but that's all one, if he be but one knave.]

c. 1625. FLETCHER, *Elder Brother*, ii. 1. I grieve to find You are a fool, and an old fool, and that's two.

d. 1631. DONNE, *Works* (BELL), ii. 16. I am TWO FOOLS, I know, For loving, and for saying so In whining poetry.

TWO THIEVES BEATING A ROGUE, *subs. phr.* (old).—A man's arms when beating his sides for warmth; BEATING THE BOOBY (*q.v.*), CUFFING JONES (*q.v.*) (GROSE).

See Bow.

TWO-BACKED BEAST, *subs. phr.* (venery).—Two persons piled in the act: see BEAST.

1653. URQUHART, *Rabelais*, I. iii. These two did often do the TWO-BACKED BEAST together ... in so far that at last she became great with child.

TWOER, *subs.* (common).—1. A florin; (2) a hansom cab.

TWO-EYED STEAK, *subs. phr.* (common).—A bloater: see GLASGOW MAGISTRATE.

TWOFER, *subs.* (common).—A wanton, a harlot: see TART.

TWO FIVES (THE), *subs. phr.* (military).—The second battalion Border Regiment, formerly the 55th Foot.

TWO-FOOT RULE, *subs. phr.* (rhyming).—A fool: see BUFFLE.

TWO FOURS (THE), *subs. phr.* (military).—The first battalion Essex Regiment, late the 44th Foot.

TWO-HANDED, *adj. phr.* (old).—1. Great: spec. of a strapping fellow or wench (GROSE). Also (2) expert with the 'dukes' (boxing).

TWO-HANDED GAME, *subs. phr.* (common).—A matter in which the chances of success are equal or nearly so: *e.g.* 'I'll dust your jacket for you,' 'Well, that's a TWO-HANDED GAME.'

TWO-HANDED PUT, *subs. phr.* (venery).—The act of kind: see GREENS and RIDE (GROSE).

TWO-LEGGED CAT (Fox, etc.), *subs. phr.* (common).—A thief: usually as a retort to 'The cat had it,'—'A TWO-LEGGED CAT, then.'

1551. STILL, *Gammer Gurton's Needle*, v. 2. Thy neighbour's hens thou takest, and plays the TWO-LEGGED FOX.

TWO-LEGGED TREE, *subs. phr.* (common).—The gallows: see NUBBING-CHEAT.

TWO-LEGGED TYMPANY, *subs. phr.* (old).—A baby; spec. a bastard. [TYMPANY = DROPSY (*q.v.*).] Hence to have a TWO-LEGGED TYMPANY = to be got with child (RAY).

TWO-NICK, *subs.* (printers').—A girl baby: *cf.* ONE-NICK.

TWOPENCE (or TUPPENCE). See DONKEY and PENNY.

TWOPENNY, *subs.* (old).—1. Beer; sold at 2d. a quart: *cf.* FOURPENNY, etc.

1771. SMOLLETT, *Humphry Clinker*, ii. 69. When the Lowlanders want to drink a chearupping cup, they go to the public-house called the change-house, and call for a chopin of TWOPENNY, which is a thin yeasty beverage made of malt, not quite so strong as the table-beer of England.

1834. SOUTHEY, *Doctor*, cxlii. There are many things in these kingdoms which are greatly undervalued; strong beer for example in the cider countries, and cider in the countries of good strong beer; bottled TWOPENNY in South Britain, sprats and herrings by the rich.

1884. DOWELL, *Taxes in England*, iv. 122. [Pale ale] was principally consumed by the gentry; the victualler sold it at 4d. the quart, under the name of TWOPENNY.

2. (common).—The head: also TUPPENNY. 'Tuck in your TUPPENNY' = (1) an injunction to 'make a back' at leap-frog; and (2) to desist.

c. 1888. *Music Hall Song*, 'Lord Mayor's Coachman.' 'Why, you're going into Newgate Street,' the Lord Mayor bawls, But John said 'TUCK YOUR TWOPENNY in—I'm going around St. Paul's.'

3. (London).—An intermediary between pawnbroker and client; a professional pawner: the usual fee being twopence.

Adj. (old).—Mean; of little value: as only costing TWOPENCE: also (modern) TWOPENNY-HALFPENNY.

c. 1485. *Paston Letters*, 144. [A gravecloth] not worth 11d.

1872. ELIOT, *Middlemarch*, I. iii. He thinks a whole world of which my thought is but a poor TWOPENNY mirror.

1884. *Pall Mall Gaz.*, 17 July. The moderate TWOPENNY-HALFPENNY Redistribution Bill which Mr. Gladstone intends to introduce.

TWOPENNY DAMN, *subs. phr.* (old).—1. A variant of RAP, STRAW, CURSE, TINKER'S CURSE (or DAMN), and many others. Tradition asserts that Wellington once said he did not care a TWOPENNY DAMN what became of the ashes of Napoleon Buonaparte.

2. (literary).—*The Twopenny Damn* = The St. James's Gazette: on account of its strong language concerning Mr. Gladstone and the 'latter-day Radicals.'

TWOPENNY-HOP, *subs. phr.* (? obsolete).—A cheap dance. [HOTTEN: The price of admission was formerly twopence: the clog hornpipe, the pipe dance, flash jigs, and hornpipes in fetters, *à la* Jack Sheppard, were the favourite movements, all entered into with great spirit.]

1851-61. MAYHEW, *Lond. Lab.* The girl is invited to 'raffles,' and treated to TWOPENNY HOPS and half-pints of beer.

TWOPENNY-ROPE, *subs. phr.* (tramps').—A lodging-house: one in which the charge is (or was) twopence: sacking stretched on ropes served as a shakedown. TO HAVE TWOPENN'ORTH OF ROPE = to 'doss down' in such a place: Fr. *coucher à la corde.*

1837. DICKENS, *Pickwick*. 'The TWOPENNY ROPE, sir,' replied Mr. Weller, 'is just a cheap lodgin'-house. ... At six o'clock every mornin', they lets go the ropes at one end, and down falls all the lodgers.'

TWOPENNY-WARD, *subs. phr.* (old).—Part of a prison was formerly so called.

1605. JONSON, *Eastward Ho*, v. 1. He lies i' the TWOPENNY WARD.

TWO-PIPE SCATTERGUN, *subs. phr.* (American).—A double-barrelled rifle.

1885. PHILLIPPS-WOLLEY, *Trottings of a Tenderfoot*. 'Oh, durn your rifles!' said an old settler to me. 'Give me a TWO-PIPE SCATTER-GUN and a spike-tailed smell-damp and I'm fixed.'

TWO SEVENS (THE), *subs. phr.* (military).—The second battalion Duke of Cambridge's Own Middlesex Regiment, late the 77th Foot.

TWO-SHOES, *subs. phr.* (nursery).—A little girl: an endearment, usually 'little TWO-SHOES' (*cf.* GOODY TWO-SHOES = a kind of fairy god-mother).

1858. ELIOT, *Mr Gilfil's Love Story*, i. He delighted to tell the young shavers and TWO-SHOES ... whenever he put pennies into [his pocket] they turned into sugar-plums or gingerbread.

TWO SIXES (THE), *subs. phr.* (military).—The second battalion Princess Charlotte of Wales's Royal Berkshire Regiment, late the 66th Foot.

TWO TENS (THE), *subs. phr.* (military).—The Lancashire Fusiliers, late the 20th Foot.

TWO-TWOS, *subs. phr.* (common).—A moment; the shortest imaginable space of time; in a twinkling.

THE TWO TWOS, *subs. phr.* (military).—The Cheshire Regiment, late the 22nd Foot.

TWOSTER. See TWIST.

TWO-TO-ONE SHOP, *subs. phr.* (old).—A pawnbroker's; UNCLE'S (*q.v.*). [GROSE: 'alluding to the three blue balls, the sign of that trade; or perhaps to its being TWO TO ONE that the goods pledged are never redeemed.']

TWO UPON TEN (or TWO PUN' TEN), *phr.* (HOTTEN).—An expression used by assistants to each other, in shops, when a customer of suspected honesty makes his appearance. The phrase refers to 'two eyes upon ten fingers,' shortened as a money term to TWO PUN' TEN. When a supposed thief is present, one shopman asks the other if that TWO PUN' (pound) TEN matter was ever settled. The man knows at once what is meant, and keeps a careful watch upon the person being served. If it is not convenient to speak, a piece of paper is handed to the same assistant, bearing the, to him, very significant amount of £2, 10s. *Cf.* SHARP, JOHN ORDERLY.

TWUG, *ppl. adj.* (Harrow).—Caught: *i.e.* the past ppl. of TWIG (*q.v.*).

TWYFORD. MY NAME IS TWYFORD, *phr.* (old).—'I know nothing of the matter' (RAY): *cf.* Sp. *No se nada, de me vinas vengo* (a reply to an inconvenient question, or when nothing is wished to be known of a matter: lit. 'I have been absent at my vineyard.')

TYBURN, *subs.* (old).—The place of execution for Middlesex to 1783: after which the death penalty was enforced at Newgate till the demolition of the prison in 1903. The Tyburn gallows stood in the angle formed by the Edgware Road and Oxford Street. In 1778 this was two miles out of London. Hence TYBURN-BLOSSOM = a young thief: 'who in time will ripen into fruit borne by the deadly never-green' (GROSE); TYBURN-CHECK (PICKADILL, TIFFANY, or TIPPET) = a rope, a halter: TYBURN-TIPPET, 'rather obsolete in 1822' (EGAN); TYBURN-FAIR (-JIG, -SHOW, or

-STRETCH) = a hanging; TYBURN-FACE = a hangdog look; TYBURN-TICKET = an exemption (under 10 & 11 Will. III., c. 23, § 2) to prosecutors who had secured a capital conviction: it released 'from all manner of parish and ward offices within the parish wherein such felony was committed': the Act was repealed in 1818: TYBURN-TICKETS were transferable, and often sold for a high price [see *Notes and Queries* (2nd ser., xi. 395, 437)]; TYBURN-TREE = the gallows; TO PREACH AT TYBURN-CROSS (FETCH A TYBURN STRETCH, DANCE A TYBURN HORNPIPE ON NOTHING, THE PADDINGTON-FRISK, etc.) = to be hanged; TYBURN-SPECTACLES = the cap pulled over the face of a criminal before execution; and so forth. *See* LADDER and TREE.

[1377. LANGLAND, *Piers Plowman*, [E.E.T.S.], 11. Here occurs a reference to the hangman of TYBORNE.]

c. 1515. *Cocke Lorell's B.* (Percy Soc.), 11. TYBURNE COLLOPES and penny pryckers.

1549. LATIMER, *Sermons before Edward VI.*, ii. He should have had a TYBURN TIPPET, a halfpenny halter, and all such proud prelates. *Ibid.*, 5 f. 63 b. There lacks a fourth thing to make up the messe which, so God help me, if I were judge, should be hangum tuum, a TYBURNE TIPPET to take with him.

1557. TUSSER, *Husbandrie*, 214. Where cocking dads make sawsie lads, In youth so rage to begin age, Or else to fetch a TIBOURNE stretch, Among the rest.

1576. GASCOIGNE, *Steele Glas*, 55 That soldiours sterve or FRECHE AT TIBORNE CROSSE.

1613. ROWLANDS, *Knave of Hearts.* Never regarding hangman's feare, Till TYBURN-TIFFANY he weare.

1630. TAYLOR, *Praise of Hempseed.* Till they put on a TYBURNE-PICKADILL.

1695. CONGREVE, *Love for Love*, ii. vii. Has he not a rogue's face . . . a damned TYBURN FACE without the benefit o' the clergy?

1698. FARQUHAR, *Love and a Bottle*, ii. 2. Which is best, Mr. Nimblewrist, an easy minuet, or a TYBURN-JIG?

1727. GAY, *Beggar's Opera.* Since laws were made for every degree, To curb vice in others as well as in me, I wonder we ha'nt better company 'Neath TYBURN TREE.

1827. LYTTON, *Pelham*, lxxxii. The cove . . . is as pretty a TYBURN BLOSSOM as ever was brought up to ride a horse foaled by an acorn.

1861. *Notes and Queries*, 2 S. xi. 395. Last week, says the *Stamford Mercury* of March 27, 1818, a TYBURN-TICKET was sold in Manchester for 280*l.*

1892. SYDNEY, *England and English*, ii. 285. An execution-day at Tyburn was considered, to all intents and purposes, by the lower classes, as a holiday. TYBURN FAIR was one of the designations by which [it] was known. A 'hanging-match' was another.

1903. HYNE, *Filibusters*, i. There's no consolation prize to look for, except a platoon, or a cable of hempen tow, and a TREE.

TYBURNIA, *subs.* (obsolete).—A name given, about the middle of the nineteenth century, to the district lying between Edgware Road and Westbourne and Gloucester Terraces and Craven Hill, and bounded on the south by the Bayswater Road, and subsequently including (HOTTEN) the Portman and Grosvenor Square district: facetiously divided by Londoners into 'Tyburnia Felix,' 'Tyburnia Deserta,' and 'Tyburnia Snobbica': it soon fell into disuse. [From a brook called *Tyburn* (properly The Eye bourn), which flowed down from Hampstead into the Thames.]

TYE (or TIE), *subs.* (old: now re-cognised).—A neckcloth (GROSE). [HOTTEN (1864): Proper hosiers' term now, but slang thirty years ago, and as early as 1718.]

TYG, *subs.* (old and University).—A three-handled TYG, a drinking cup so handled that three different persons, drinking out of it, and each using a separate handle, brought their mouths to different parts of the rim. The name is still applied in Oxford to an ordinary round pot with three handles, much used for cups, etc.

TYKE. *See* TIKE.

TYLER. *See* ADAM TILER.

TYMPANY, *subs.* (colloquial).—Conceit, bombast: properly a species of dropsy in which the belly is stretched tight like a drum.

1610. HALL, *Short Answer*, Pref. In the first leaf of my defence, I foretold you so much; as finding nothing in that swollen bulk, but a meer unsound TYMPANIE, instead of a truly solid conception.

TWO-LEGGED TYMPANY, *subs. phr.* (old).—A baby; *spec.* a bastard: *see supra.* Hence TO BE CURED OF A TYMPANY WITH TWO HEELS = to be brought to bed; *cf.* 'a dropsy that will drop into the lap.'

TYPO, *subs.* (printers').—A compositor. Also TYPE-LIFTER (or -SLINGER) = an expert comp.: sometimes in contempt = a slovenly workman.

TZING-TZING, *adj.* (common).—Excellent, AI: obsolete.

**UGLY**, *subs.* (colloquial).—1. An ugly person: also in contemptuous address, 'Hallo, UGLY!' MR. UGLY, etc.

d. 1797. WALPOLE, *Letters*, II. 422. There were all the beauties and all the diamonds, and not a few of the UGLIES of London.

2. (old).—A bonnet shade: worn by women as an extra protection from the sun: middle 19th century.

1851. THACKERAY, *Kickleburys on the Rhine.* She and her sisters wore a couple of those blue silk over-bonnets, which have lately become the fashion. . . . 'We call those hoods UGLIES.'

3. (common).—In *pl.* = delirium tremens; the HORRORS (*q.v.*).

4. (provincial).—A beating, a round of abuse (HALLIWELL).

Adj. (colloquial).—Generic for disquiet or unpleasantness: *e.g.* an UGLY (= threatening) TONE; an UGLY (= dangerous) WOUND; an UGLY (= unpleasant) RUMOUR; an UGLY (= wrong) TURN; UGLY (= stormy) WEATHER; an UGLY (= awkward or malicious) CUSTOMER, OPPONENT; a source of danger, etc.; an UGLY (= troublesome) COUGH; an UGLY (= ill-natured) TEMPER; an UGLY (= quarrelsome) ATTITUDE. Hence TO COME THE UGLY = to threaten; TO CUT UP (or LOOK) UGLY = to show anger or resentment; TO CALL BY UGLY NAMES = to revile or abuse. Also UGLINESS (American) = ill-nature, crossness, perversity.

c. 1360. *Alliterative Poems* [E.E.T.S.], 64. Thay wern wakened al wrank that therein won lenged, Of on the VGLOKEST vnhap that euer on erd suffred.

1859. KENDALL, *Santa Fé*, I. 133. The questions of the spies were answered in a sullen, swaggering manner; so much so that Captain Caldwell at once remarked to his men, in a low tone and in English, that these fellows LOOKED UGLY and fighty.

c. 1865. HOLMES, *At the Pantomime.* The grisly story Chaucer told, And many an UGLY TALE beside.

1867. *Harper's Mag.*, xxxv. 341. It was as UGLY a little promenade as I ever undertook.

1869. STOWE, *Oldtown*, 196. He was jest the crossest, UGLIEST critter that ever ye, see, an' he was UGLY jest for the sake o' UGLINESS.

1870. WEATHERLEY, *Lamplighter*, 110. I'll not answer her back when she's UGLY to me.

1880. STEVENSON, *Will o' the Mill.* An UGLY THRILL spread from the spot he touched.

1887. *Field*, 24 Sep. There is an UGLY RUMOUR afloat that certain bookmakers who had laid heavily are directly responsible for Monday's outbreak.

18[?]. J. BROWN, *Rab and His Friends*, 6. He must have been a hard hitter if he boxed as he preached—what 'The Fancy' would call an UGLY CUSTOMER.

See PLUG-UGLY.

R

UGLYMAN, *subs. phr.* (thieves'). In garrotting the actual perpetrator of the outrage: his operations are covered in front by the FORE-STALL (*q.v.*), and in the rear by the BACKSTALL (*q.v.*): also NASTY-MAN: *see* STALE.

UHLAN, *subs.* (tailors').—A tramp.

ULLAGE, *subs.* (common).—In *pl.* = drainings, dregs of glasses or casks. [Properly the wantage in a cask of liquor.]

ULTIMATE FAVOUR (THE), *subs. phr.* (venery).—The surrender, by a woman, of her person; also THE LAST FAVOUR.

1694. CROWNE, *Married Beau*, ii. I own common favours: that's no matter, But if she ever grants me the LAST FAVOUR,—I give her leave to cast me off for ever.

ULTRAMARINE, *adj.* (common).—BLUE (*q.v.*).

ULTRAY, *adv.* (colloquial).—Very: a corruption of 'ultra.'

UMPIRE. HOW'S THAT, UMPIRE? *phr.* (common).—What do you say to that? How's that for high? What price? [An echo of football and cricket.]

UMBLE-PIE. *See* HUMBLE-PIE.

UN-, *prefix* (old). *See* BETTY; DUB; PAL; SLOUR; THIMBLE, etc. [A negation.]

UNBAKED, *adj.* (old).—Immature: *cf.* HARD-BAKED.

1598. SHAKSPEARE, *All's Well*, iv. 5. All the UNBAKED and doughy youth of a nation.

1625. FLETCHER, *Elder Brother*, ii. 2. Songs she may have, And read a little UNBAK'D poetry.

UNBEKNOWN (or UNBEKNOWNST), *adj.* (once literary: now colloquial or vulgar).—Unknown.

d. 1665. GODWIN, *Works*, III. 372. The same secret instinct . . . to sympathize . . . in praying for such a thing UNBEKNOWN to one another.

1800. PEGGE, *Anec. Eng. Lang.* [OLIPHANT, *New Eng.*, ii. 199. There are wrong forms in London use, as UNBEKNOWN . . . he knowed . . . they cotch].

1837. DICKENS, *Pickwick*, xxxiv. I was there UNBEKNOWN to Mrs. Bardell.

1879. PHELPS, *Sealed Orders* [*Century*]. So by and by I creep up softly to my own little room . . . UNBEKNOWNST to most.

UNBLEACHED AMERICAN, *subs. phr.* (American).—A negro; SNOWBALL (*q.v.*). [An echo of mock Northern sentiment during the War of the Secession.]

UNCERTAINTY, *subs.* (printers').—A girl baby: *cf.* CERTAINTY = a boy.

UNCLE, *subs.* (common).—1. A pawnbroker (GROSE): Fr. *tante.* [*Cf.* UNCLE = a mythical rich relative.]

[1607. DEKKER, *Northward Ho*, i. 2. Fourscore pounds draws deep . . . I'll step to my UNCLE not far off . . . and he shall bail me.]

1828. HOOD, *Miss Kilmansegg.* Brothers, wardens of City Halls, And UNCLES, rich as three golden balls From taking pledges of nations.

1843. DICKENS, *Martin Chuzzlewit*, i. We find him making constant reference to an UNCLE, in respect of whom he would seem to have entertained great expectations, as he was in the habit of seeking to propitiate his favour by presents of plate, jewels, books, watches, and other valuable articles.

1854-5. THACKERAY, *Newcomes*, xii. 'Dine in your frock, my good friend, and welcome, if your dress-coat is in the country.' 'It is at present at an UNCLE'S,' Mr. Bayham said with great gravity.

1891. *Harry Fludyer at Cambridge*, iii. For instance, when your aunt Sophia was with us last week it kept on yelling something about 'the pop-shop round the corner, and paying your UNCLE a visit.'

1897. MARSHALL, *Pomes*, 37. It's cold enough to freeze the golden balls off UNCLE'S door.

1901. *D. Telegraph*, 28 Oct., 11. 5. A pawnbroker stated that his name was 'Uncle.' *Mr. Fordham*: Baptismal or paternal? *Witness*: It is my surname. *Mr. Fordham*: And it could not have been more appropriate to your calling.

2. (American).—A familiar address: spec. of an old worthy negro: *cf.* AUNT. [PEGGE: the Cornish apply aunt and UNCLE to all elderly persons (p. 301).]

1852. STOWE, UNCLE *Tom's Cabin* [Title].

1876. BONNER, *Dialect Tales*, 121. From the darkey settlement . . . queer old aunties and UNCLES hobbled out to milk them.

YOUR UNCLE, *phr.* (common).—Myself: *e.g.* Your UNCLE'S the man to do it, *i.e.* 'I'll do it for you.'

PHRASE. 'If my aunt had been a man she'd have been my UNCLE' (RAY), in derision of those who make ridiculous surmises: *see* MAN.

See DUTCH UNCLE.

UNCLE SAM, *phr.* (American).—A humorous personification of the Government or people of the U[nited] S[tates]: *cf.* JOHN BULL. [Usually supposed to date back to the war of 1812.]

1835. DANA, *Before the Mast*, 127. She was called the Catalina, and like all the other vessels in that trade . . . her papers and colours were from UNCLE SAM.

1848. LOWELL, *Biglow Papers*. For I have loved my country since My eyeteeth filled their sockets, And UNCLE SAM I reverence, Partic'larly his pockets.

UNCOMMON, *adv.* (vulgar).—Very; exceedingly: *e.g.* UNCOMMON bitter; UNCOMMON cheap, etc.

UNCONSCIONABLE, *adv.* (old colloquial).—Enormous, vast, very. [JOHNSON: 'a low word.']

1849. ROBB, *Squatter Life* [BARTLETT]. 'That's an UNCONSCIONABLE slick gal of your'n,' says I; and it did tickle his fancy to have her cracked up, 'cause he thought her creation's finishin' touch,—so did I!

UNCORK, *verb.* (American).—To expose to view, to set forth, to cause to flow out: as when a cork is removed from a bottle: *e.g.* 'UNCORK the swag' (thieves') = 'Unlock the bag'; 'UNCORK your clack' = speak out!

UNCOUTH, UNKISSED, *phr.* (old).—A proverbial allusion to the custom of saluting friends and acquaintances at meeting, but not unintroduced strangers (NARES): also (HEYWOOD) UNKNOWN, UNKISSED.

1566. HEYWOOD, *Poems*, D4. UNKNOWNE, UNKIST; it is lost that is unsought.

1588–90. *Mar. Martine* [*Cens. Lit.*, ix. 59]. Thou caytif kerne, UNCOUTH thou art, UNKIST thou eke sal bee.

1627. HAWKINS, *Apollo Shroving*, D. 6b. He cannot be so uncivill as to intrude, unbid, UNCOOTH, UNKIST.

UNCTION. *See* BLUE-UNCTION.

UNCULAR, *adj.* (old).—Of or relating to an uncle: *cf.* AVUNCULAR.

d. 1859. DE QUINCEY, *Spanish Nun*, vi. His UNCULAR and rather angular breast.

UNDER, *subs.* (colloquial).—In *pl.* = the female privities. To LIE UNDER (of women) = to SPREAD (*q.v.*).

TO GO UNDER, *verb. phr.* (common).—1. To die: whence the UNDER-SIDE = the grave.

18[?]. *Hawkeye, the Iowa Chief*, 210. Poor Hawkeye felt, says one of his biographers, that his time had come, and knowing that he must GO UNDER sooner or later, he determined to sell his life dearly.

1849. RUXTON, *Far West*, 2. Them three's all GONE UNDER.

1888. *Daily Inter-Ocean*, Mar. All . . . vowed to see that the mine should be worked . . . for the benefit of the girl whether Jim lived or had GONE UNDER.

1899. HYNE, *Furth. Adv. Captain Kettle*, vi. As sure as you are living now, you'll finish out on the UNDER SIDE then.

1902. HUME, *Crime of the Crystal*, i. Mother Bunch's GONE UNDER, I s'pose. She was making fast for Golden Jerusalem when I was a bud.

2. (common).—To become submerged in difficulty or debt, to be ruined, to disappear from society.

1879. PAYN, *High Spirits*, 'Finding his Level.' Poor John Weybridge, Esq., became as friendless as penniless, and eventually WENT UNDER and was heard of no more.

1890. *Pall Mall Gaz.*, 29 May, 5. 1. He asks us further to state that the strike is completely at an end, the society having GONE UNDER.

UNDER A CLOUD, *adv. phr.* (old).—In difficulties or disgrace.

c. 1520. *Old Song of the Lady Bessy* [*Percy Soc.*], xx. 79. [A man in disgrace] comes UNDER A CLOWDE.

UNDER THE BELT, *phr.* (common).—In the stomach.

1815. SCOTT, *Guy Mannering*, xxxix. They got me down to Clerihugh's, and there we sat birling, till I had a fair tappit UNDER MY BELT.

See BELOW.

UNDER THE ROSE, *phr.* (colloquial).—Secretly; in confidence (DYCHE, GROSE).

1546. DYMOCKE, *Letter to Vaughan* [WALSH]. And the sayde questyon were asked with lysence, and that yt should remayn UNDER THE ROSSE, that is to say, to remain under the bourde and ne more to be rehersyd.

1616–25. *Court and Times James I.* [OLIPHANT, *New Eng.*, ii. 71. As to the prepositions we see UNDER THE ROSE].

1625. JONSON, *Staple of News*, ii. You are my lord, The rest are cogging Jacks, UNDER THE ROSE.

1632. CHAPMAN, *Ball*, ii. 2. UNDER THE ROSE the lords do call me cousin.

c. 1707. *Old Song*, 'Praise of the Dairy Maid' [DURFEY, *Pills*, *etc.* (1707), i. 12]. Such bliss ne'er oppose If e'er you'll be happy —— I SPEAK UNDER THE ROSE.

1753. *Adventurer*, No. 98. UNDER THE ROSE, I am a cursed favourite amongst them.

1762. SNELLING, *Coins*, 2. The rose . . . symbol of secrecy . . . [was] used with great propriety on privy seals, which came into use about the middle of the twelfth century.

1821. LAMB, *Elia* (*Mrs. Battle*). All people have their blind side—their superstitions; and I have heard her declare, UNDER THE ROSE, that Hearts was her favourite suit.

1868. OUIDA, *Under Two Flags*, iv. All great ladies gamble in stock nowadays UNDER THE ROSE.

1892. NISBET, *Bushranger's Sweetheart*, 37. I no longer wondered that he should have quitted England UNDER THE ROSE.

UNDER-DUBBER (or **-DUBSMAN**).—A warder other than a chief in command (GROSE): *see* DUBBER and DUBSMAN.

UNDERFELLOW, *subs.* (old).—A mean wretch; SNIDE (*q.v.*): *see* SIDNEY, *Arcadia*, ii.

UNDERGEAR, *subs.* (American).—Underclothing.

UNDERGRAD, *subs.* (University).—1. An undergraduate.

2. (racing).—A horse in training for steeplechasing or hunting.

UNDERGROUND-RAILWAY, *subs. phr.* (American).—An organization for assisting fugitive slaves to the free states and Canada. Many expedients and devices for the purpose were in vogue during the agitation for the abolition of slavery in the United States.

1856. STOWE *Dred*, ii. 302. It is probable that nothing has awakened more bitterly the animosity of the slave-holding community than the existence, in the Northern States, of an indefinite yet very energetic institution, known as the UNDERGROUND RAILROAD.

1857. *Albany Ev. Jo.*, Dec. And now, if we may believe the promises made by the Democrats for two years past, we are on the eve of a political millennium. . . . There is to be no more 'agitation' of the slavery question. The UNDERGROUND RAILROAD is to suspend running, and rejoicing hosts of Negroes are to return from the bleak wilds of Canada to the luxurious delights of life on the plantation.

1858. *New York Tribune*, June. He [Connelly] regarded the UNDERGROUND RAILROAD as a peculiarly Southern institution, taking away from the South every year thousands of the most intelligent, restless, and desperate Negroes, who would do infinitely more mischief if kept there.

UNDERGROUNDER, *subs.* (cricket).—A ball bowled without pitch, a DAISY-CUTTER (or -TRIMMER), SNEAK (*q.v.*).

UNDER-PETTICOATING (TO GO), *verb. phr.* (venery).—To whore, to quest for women, to copulate: *see* GREENS and RIDE.

UNDERPINNER, *subs.* (common).—In *pl.* = the legs: *cf.* PINS.

UNDER-SHELL, *subs. phr.* (Old Cant).—A waistcoat: *cf.* UPPER-SHELL and UPPER-STOCKS.

UNDER-SPUR-LEATHER, *subs. phr.* (old).—An underling, a subservient person.

d. 1725. J. JOHNSON, *Unbl. Sacr.*, Pref. xxx. A design was publickly set on foot, to dissolve the Catholic church into numberless clans and clubs; and to degrade priests into meer tenders, or UNDER-SPUR-LEATHERS to those clans and clubs.

UNDER-STAIR, *adj. phr.* (old).—Subordinate, low, mean: *cf.* BACK-DOOR.

d. 1655. ADAMS, *Works*, i. 500. Living in some UNDER-STAIR office, when he would visit the country, he borrows some gallant's cast suit of his servant, and therein, player-like, acts that part among his besotted neighbours.

UNDERSTANDING, *subs.* (common).—(1) In *pl.* = the legs: *cf.* UNDERPINNERS. Also (2) = boots or shoes.

1602. SHAKSPEARE, *Twelfth Night*, iii. 1. 80. *Sir To.* Taste your legs, sir; put them to motion. *Vio.* My legs do better UNDERSTAND me, sir, than I UNDERSTAND what you mean by bidding me taste my legs.

1886. *Field*, 20 Mar. Economy's UNDERSTANDINGS having given way soon after, he knew the silk no more.

UNDERSTUMBLE, *verb.* (old).—To understand: also UNDERCOMESTUMBLE.

c. 1710. SWIFT, *Pol. Conv.*, i. *Miss.* I UNDERSTUMBLE you, gentlemen, *Nev.* Madam, your humblecumdumble.

UNDISGRUNTLED. *See* DISGRUNTLED.

UNFORTUNATE, *subs.* (conventional).—A prostitute: spec. a homeless street-walker (GROSE). [Probably, in the first place, the popular usage arose from a misreading of Hood's lines.]

[1827. HOOD, *Bridge of Sighs*. One more UNFORTUNATE, Weary of breath, Rashly importunate, Gone to her death.]

1877. MALLOCK, *New Republic*, III. ii. Hoping I might see some UNFORTUNATE cast herself from the Bridge of Sighs.

UNGUENTUM-AURUM, *subs. phr.* (old).—A bribe, PALM-GREASE (*q.v.*).—GROSE.

UNHINTABLES. *See* UNMENTIONABLES.

UNICORN, *subs.* (orig. University).—1. A team of horses: two wheelers abreast with a leader in front (GROSE); and (2) such a TURNOUT (*q.v.*), a SPIKE-TEAM (American): *cf.* FOUR-IN-HAND, MANCHESTER, SUDDEN DEATH, TANDEM, etc.

1803. EDGEWORTH, *Belinda*, xvii. 'Let me drive you out some day in my UNICORN. . . . Bid my blockhead bring my UNICORN.' She, her UNICORN, and her blockhead were out of sight in a few minutes.

2. (old Scots).—A gold coin, value 23 shillings Scotch: *temp.* James III., IV. and V.: a unicorn figured on the obverse.

3. (thieves').—Two men and a woman (or *vice versâ*), working together.

UNIV, *subs.* (Oxford University).—University College.

UNIVERSAL-STAIRCASE, *subs. phr.* (thieves'). — The treadmill, WHEEL OF LIFE (*q.v.*): also EVERLASTING-STAIRCASE (*q.v.*).

1851–61. MAYHEW, *Lond. Lab.* Well, the beaks got up to the dodge, and all the Spanish lurksmen in their turns got to work the UNIVERSAL STAIRCASE.

UNLICKED CUB (or **CUB**), *subs. phr.* (common).—A raw, unmannerly youth; an uncultivated boor; also an awkward, sulky girl (GROSE). As *adj.* = ungainly, rough, rude. [A popular notion was that a bear gave birth to shapeless lumps of flesh which she licked into shape.] Also UNLICKED BEAR.

[1602. SHAKSPEARE, *Twelfth Night*, v. 1. 167. O thou dissembling CUB what wilt thou be When time has sow'd a grizzle on thy case.]

1626. FLETCHER, *Fair Maid of the Inn*, iii. Thou UNLICKT BEAR, dar'st thou yet stand by my fury.

1693. CONGREVE, *Old Bachelor*, iv. 8. A country squire, with . . . a wife and two daughters . . . oh, Gad! two such UNLICKED CUBS.

1762. FOOTE, *Liar*, II. ii. I don't reckon much upon him: for you know, my dear, what can I do with an awkward, raw, college CUB?

1773. GOLDSMITH, *She Stoops to Conquer*, iv. 1. 'A poor contemptible booby that would but disgrace correction.' . . . 'An insensible CUB.'

1880. TROLLOPE, *Duke's Children*, ix. And Tommy, you are an uncivil young,—young,—young,—I should say CUB if I dared, to tell me that you don't like dining with me any day of the week.

1855. THACKERAY, *Newcomes*, xxix. I don't see why that infernal young CUB of a Clive is always meddling in our affairs.

UNLOAD, *verb.* (American commercial).—To sell stocks, shares, goods, etc., that have been held on speculation. Also to empty one's pockets.

1888. *D. Teleg.*, 6 Jan. There being some pressure to UNLOAD.

UNLOCK. UNLOCK THE LANDS, *verb. phr.* (Victorian).—A political cry calling for the opening up for free-selection of lands held by squatters on lease.

1887. J. F. HOGAN, *The Irish in Australia*, 290. The democratic party, that had for its watchword the expressive phrase, 'UNLOCK THE LANDS.'

UNLOCKED. TO HAVE BEEN SITTING IN THE GARDEN WITH THE GATE UNLOCKED, *verb. phr.* (venery). — 1. To be got with child: spec. of a bastard; and (2) to have 'caught cold.'

UNMENTIONABLE, *subs.* (common).—In *pl.* = trousers, breeches. Variants, mostly introduced by Dickens, are—INEFFABLES; INEXPRESSIBLES; INDESCRIBABLES; INEXPLICABLES; UNHINTABLES; UNUTTERABLES; UNWHISPERABLES, etc.

1837. DICKENS, *Sketches by Boz* (Shabby-Genteel People). The knees of the UNMENTIONABLES, and the elbows of the coat, and the seams generally, soon began to get alarmingly white.

1885. *Field*, 19 Dec. Fishing stockings full of water, UNMENTIONABLES ditto.

[1903. *Globe*, 24 Oct., 1. 3. Bifurcated UNWHISPERABLES offer no resistance to the wind. To the woman, the skirt is not only a hampering garment; it is a sail against which the wind blows.]

UNPALLED, *adj.* (old). — A thief whose associates are all apprehended, or taken from him by other means, is said to be UNPALLED, and he is then obliged to work single-handed.

UNPARLIAMENTARY, *adj.* (colloquial).—Abusive, obscene, unfit for ordinary conversation.

UNPAVED, *adj.* (venery).—1. Castrated; STONED (*see* STONES).

1605. SHAKSPEARE, *Cymbeline*, ii. 3. 34. The voice of UNPAVED eunuch.

2. (common). — Rough; inflamed: spec. from excessive drinking.

UNREADY, *verb.* (old colloquial).—To undress: as *adj.* =undressed, naked.

1580. SIDNEY, *Arcadia*, 379. Hee remayned with his daughter, to give his wife time of UNREADYING herself.

1589. PUTTENHAM, *Art Eng. Poesie*, B. iii. 18. A young gentlewoman, who was in her chamber, MAKING HERSELF UNREADY.

1592. SHAKSPEARE, 1 *Henry VI.*, ii. 1. [*Enter, several ways, Bastard, Alencon, Reignier, half-*READY, *and half-*UNREADY.] . . . How now, my lords, what all UNREADY so?

1606. CHAPMAN, *Mons. d'Olive*, v. Why I hope you are not going to bed; I see you are not yet UNREADY. *Ibid.* (1607), *Bussy D'Ambois* [*Anc. Dr.*, iii. 277]. *Mont.* Good day, my love: what, up, and ready too? *Tam.* Both, my dear lord, not all this night made I Myself UNREADY, or could sleep a wink.

1608. MIDDLETON, *Trick to Catch*, iii. Take this warm napkin about your neck, sir, while I help to make you UNREADY.

1609. ARMIN, *Two Maids*, etc. 'Stage Direction.' [*Enter James*, UNREADY, in his night-cap, garterless.]

1621. FLETCHER, *Island Princess*, iii. Come, where have you been, wench? make me UNREADY, I slept but ill last night.

UNREGENERATE CHICKEN-LIFTER, *subs. phr.* (American).—A petty thief: *see* THIEF.

UNRIG, *verb.* (old colloquial).—To strip: *e.g.* 'UNRIG the drab'= pull the whore's clothes off (B. E. and GROSE); whence UNRIGGED =naked. Also (2) to plunder; and (3) 'of ships that are laid up' (B. E.).

1692. DRYDEN, *Juvenal*, xiv. Lest he should be stolen, or UNRIGG'D as Mars was.

1693. CONGREVE, *Old Bachelor*, v. 1. *Bell* (in fanatic habit). I would UNRIG. *Set.* I attend you, sir.

UNROVE. UNROVE HIS LIFE LINE, *phr.* (nautical).—Said of a man who has died (CLARK RUSSELL).

UNSLOUR, *verb.* (old).—To unlock, unfasten, or unbutton: *see* SLOUR. [Speaking of a person whose coat is buttoned, so as to obstruct the access to his pockets,

the knucks will say to each other, the cove is SLOUR'D UP, we must UNSLOUR HIM to get at his kickseys.—GROSE.]

UNSPEAKABLE, *adj.* (colloquial).—A general intensive: extremely bad. Thus an UNSPEAKABLE (=outrageous) FOOL; an UNSPEAKABLE (=' rotten') PLAY; the UNSPEAKABLE (= cruel) TURK. [A Carlyleism.]

1831. CARLYLE, *Miscell.* 'Nibelungen Lied.' That UNSPEAKABLE TURK, King Machabol. *Ibid.*, Letter to George Howard (24 Nov. 1876). The UNSPEAKABLE TURK should immediately be struck out of the question and the country left to honest European guidance.

UNSWEETENED, *subs.* (common).—Gin: *i.e.* unsweetened gin.

UNTHIMBLE, *verb.* (old).—To UNTHIMBLE, to rob, or otherwise deprive a man of his watch. UNTHIMBLED, robbed of one's watch.

UNTHRIFT, *subs.* (old).—A prodigal, spendthrift, WASTEGOOD (*q.v.*).

1590. GOLDINGE, *Cæsar*, fol. 76. A great multitude of UNTHRIFTS and cut throtes.

. . . TAVERNER, *Adagies*, A. 8b. UNTHRYFTES do gather together with UNTHRIFTES, and good fellowes, with such as be good fellowes, and so forthe.

1596. JONSON, *Ev. Man in His Humour*, iii. 7. If he were an UNTHRIFT, a ruffian, a drunkard, or a licentious liver, then you had reason.

1597. SHAKSPEARE, *Richard II.*, ii. 3. My rights and royalties Pluck'd from my arms perforce, and given away To upstart UNTHRIFTS. *Ibid.* (1598), *Sonnets*, ix. Look, what an UNTHRIFT in the world doth spend, Shifts but his place, for still the world enjoys it.

UNTO. TO GO IN UNTO, *verb. phr.* (conventional). — To copulate: *see* GREENS and RIDE.

UNTRIMMED. *See* TRIM.

UNTWISTED, *adj.* (old).—Undone, ruined (B.E. and GROSE).

UNWASHED (or **GREAT-UNWASHED**), *subs.* (common). — The mob, the rabble: orig. the artisan class. [First used by Burke, popularised by Scott.]

1889. *Pall Mall Gaz.*, 18 Oct., 6. 2. Was it not time . . . that THE GREAT UNWASHED should declare that the great unpaid were no longer at liberty to oppress them?

1892. WATSON, *Wops the Waif*, iii. iv. It is only when we have paid our 'tuppence' and ascended to the gallery just under the roof . . . that we begin to understand what is meant by the lowest classes, THE GREAT UNWASHED.

Adj. (old colloquial).—Vulgar, filthy. UNWASHED BAWDRY (B. E.)=rant, errant, fulsome, bawdry.

1596. SHAKSPEARE, *King John*, iv. 2. 201. Another lean, UNWASH'D artificer.

1605. JONSON, *Volpone*, Ded. Such foul and UNWASHED BAWDRY as is now made the food of the scene.

UP, *verb, adv., prep.*, and *subs.* (old).—1. In various elliptical and colloquial senses. As *verb*, generic for action: *cf.* DOWN. Thus TO UP with one's fist, a stick, etc.=to raise the hand, etc., for striking a blow; TO UP with the standard=to bear aloft the flag; 'UP guards, and at 'em'= 'Stand and charge the enemy,' and so on. *Adverbially* in many connections: as (1) out of bed; (2) on one's legs (ready to speak); in the saddle; under repair (of streets); advanced in rank, position, value, etc.; in revolt, a commotion, or the like; in progress or taking place (as a hunt); adjourned, at an end (as a sitting

of the House), etc. Also a scoring-limit at billiards (500 or 1000 UP); recorded on the 'telegraph' at cricket (Grace 100 UP=a century of runs made). Also in numerous phrases and combinations, 'What's UP'?=What's the matter, or What's going on; UP TO (or IN)=well-equipped, equal to, conversant with (the law, mathematics, tricks of trade, etc.); ALL'S UP (or UP WITH)=everything is lost, ruin stares one in the face: frequently UP is spelt as, it's all 'U-P'; TO GO UP=(1) to travel to London, Paris, etc. (as the centre and focus of national life): specifically (University) to return to Oxford or Cambridge, the antithesis in this case being 'going down' to London, home, etc.; (2) to offer oneself for examination; TO HAVE (or PULL UP)=(1) to summons, arrest, or bring before a magistrate; and (2) to check a downward course (as of drink, dissipation, or the like); UP AND DOWN (*See* UP-AND-DOWN); TO COME UP WITH =to overtake, catch up; TO LOOK UP=to improve in health, credit, value; UP TO=about to do, occur, or in preparation; UP A TREE (or TREED)=(1) done for, ruined, (2)=in a difficulty, CORNERED (*q.v.*), and (3) drunk; also UP IN ONE'S HAT: *see* SCREWED; TO UP JIB (THE STICKS, or THE STAKES)=to pack up and go, to be off: *see* BUNK; TO UP AND DUST=to hurry up, move fast; UP TO SNUFF (SCENT, or THE ROPES)=KNOWING (*q.v.*), WIDE-AWAKE (*q.v.*), cunning, sharp (GROSE); UP TO THE KNOCKER (DOOR, NINES, A THING OR TWO, etc.)=good, capital, excellent; UP THE SPOUT=(1) in pawn, (2) imprisoned (GROSE); UP TO ONE'S EARS (ELBOWS, THE HILT, etc.)=overwhelmed; UP TO THE HUB=to the extreme point; TO LIVE UP TO BLUE CHINA=to spend up to, or more than, one's income; UP TO SAMPLE=of good quality, O.K. (*q.v.*); UP TO DICK =rich, generous, wise, quick, in good health, jolly, well-dressed: generic for the best; UP TO DICTIONARY=learned, UP TO THE GOSSIP (CACKLE, TRY-ON, etc.)=prepared for any attempt at imposition, roguery, or trickery (GROSE); UP TO SLUM (GROSE)= proficient in roguery, good as a TRADESMAN (*q.v.*); THAT'S UP AGAINST YOU=What do you say to that? That will knock the stuffing out of you; UP IN THE STIRRUPS=with plenty of money (GROSE).

1340. *Gamelyn* [SKEAT], 20. He UP WITH his staf.

1360. *Allit. Poems.* [E.E.T.S.]. [The excitement at Sodom is described, it is said that the] borough was all UP. *Ibid.*, 67. [Abraham was] UP in the morning.

1387. TREVISA [HIGDEN, *Lat. Chronicle*], iii. 297. He UP with a staf and smoot.

1399. LANGLAND, *Richard the Redeles* [E.E.T.S.], 474. Myscheff was UP.

1401. *Townley Myst.* (Camden Soc.), 221. UP with the tymbre.

c. 1430. *Destr. Troy* [E.E.T.S.], 7207. The tru VP, Agamynon the Grekys gedrit in the fild.

1528-37. *Letters on Suppression of the Monasteries* [Camden Soc.], 245. [An abbot talks of coming UPWARDS; that is UP to London.]

1530. PALSGRAVE, *Lang. Fran.*, 417. [Palsgrave says that] is my lorde UP [is a peculiar English phrase].

1550. UDAL, *Roister Doister* [ARBER], 13. UP to the harde eares in love

1592. MARLOWE, *Edward II.*, i. 4. 'Tis treason to be UP against the King.

1593. SHAKSPEARE, *Titus Andron.*, ii. 2. The hunt is UP. *Ibid.* (1594), *Lucrece*, 1277. When went . . . Tarquin from hence? Madame, ere I was UP, replied the maid. *Ibid.* (1597), *Richard III.*, v. 3, 7. UP with my tent there! Here will I lie to-night.

c. 1605. HEYWOOD, *If You Know not Me*, ii. You are all larkes this morning, VP with the sun: You are stirring early.

1607. DEKKER, *Northward Ho*, i. 3. *May.* Where is your mistress, villain? when went she abroad? *Pren.* . . . Why, as soon as she was UP, sir.

1608. ARMIN, *Nest of Ninnies* (1842), 43. He UPS and tels [him].

1611. *Bible*, Psalm xii. 6 (Psalter). I will UP, saith the Lord.

c. 1620. FLETCHER, *Double Marriage*, v. 1. *Duke.* What, is the city UP?

1635. QUARLES, *Emblems*, ii. 14. The true bred-gamester UPS afresh, and then Falls to't again.

1639. MASSINGER, *Un. Combat*, ii. 1. Now my anger's UP.

c. 1650. COWLEY, *Chronicle*, iii. Till UP in Arms my Passions rose, And cast away her Yoke.

1672. RAY, *Proverbs* [BOHN], 61. UP with it, if it be but a gallon; it will ease your stomach.

1766. BROOKE, *Fool of Quality*, i. 82. She UPS with her brawny arm, and gave Susy a douse on the side of the head.

1799. SCOTT, *Gray Brother.* UP, UP, unhappy! haste, arise.

[?]. *Farmer's Old Wife* [CHILD, *Ballads*, viii. 258]. She UPS with her pattens and beat out their brains.

1837. BARHAM, *Ingoldsby Legends*, ii. 199. The Saint made a pause As uncertain, because He knew Nick is pretty well UP in the laws.

1843. DICKENS, *Martin Chuzzlewit*, xxvi. What are you UP to, old feller?

1848. THACKERAY, *Snobs*, xxi. He will scrape acquaintance with old Carabas before they make Ostend. . . . See, he is UP TO old Carabas already! I told you he would.

1849-61. MACAULAY, *History Eng.*, xvi. In twenty-four hours all Devonshire was UP.

1849. ROBB, *Squatter Life*, 31. 'Well, hoss, we expect you to be right co-chunk UP TO THE HUB on them thar questions, and pour it into the enemy in slashergaff style.'

1853. HALIBURTON, *Wise Saws*, 34. You mustn't wander away, and you mustn't declaim: if you do, their attention is off, the public see it, and you are UP A TREE.

1856. STOWE, *Dred*, i. 311. 'For my part,' said Abijah, grimly, 'if things was managed my way, I shouldn't commune with nobody that didn't believe in election UP TO THE HUB.'

1857. MACAULAY, *Goldsmith.* In his seventeenth year Oliver went UP to Trinity College, Dublin, as a sizar.

1863. JEAFFRESON, *Live it Down*, xxiv. I'll finish my cigar in the betting room and hear what's UP.

1863. GASKELL, *Sylvia's Lovers*, xix. It was late, it is true, but on a May evening even country people keep UP till eight or nine o'clock.

1865. KINGSLEY, *Hillyars and Burtons*, xxviii. I made them UP STICK and take me home.

1866. BAKER, *Heart of Africa*, 259. I saw that it was ALL UP WITH our animals.

1866. ELIOT, *Felix Holt*, Int. It was not so well for a lawyer to be over-honest, else he might not be UP TO other people's tricks.

1868. OUIDA, *Under two Flags*, v. UP TO every dodge on the cross that this iniquitous world could unfold.

1869. STOWE, *Oldtown*, 124. 'Here you are, you little minx. . . . What are you UP TO now?'

1869. BLACKMORE, *Lorna Doone*, lxviii. Before I knew what he was UP TO, [he] said, 'Arise, Sir John Rudd.'

1870. LE FANU, *Dragon Volant*, i. I was posting UP to Paris.

d. 1878. BRYANT, *Song of Marion's Men.* The woodland rings with laugh and shout, As if a hunt were UP.

d. 1879. CLIFFORD, *Lectures*, ii. 137. If an astronomer, observing the sun, were to record the fact that at the moment when a sun-spot began to shrink there was a rap at his front-door, we should know that he was not UP TO his work.

1885. *Field*, 25 Sep. M'Lawlay . . . got down with a fine put, and stood again one UP. *Ibid.* (1886), 20 Feb. Having found it and used it, you must UP STICKS and away in a day or two.

1886. MACDONALD *What's Mine's Mine*, 283. Come, Mercy, you are UP TO a climb I'm sure.

1886. *Daily News*, 14 Oct. Streets that are UP.

1887. *Standard*, 18 Oct. When Fordham was UP those who were interested in a horse's success felt confident.

1892. KIPLING, *Barrack-room Ballads*. 'Tommy.' The publican 'e UP an' sez, 'We serve no Red-coats here.'

1898. WHITEING, *John Street*, viii. You don't know! You shouldn't argue if you ain't UP TO things like that. *Ibid.*, xxiii. 'WHAT'S UP now?' says my myte as was standing guard over me with a cutlash.

2. (Harrow).—In school. To BE UP AT SECOND SCHOOL=to go to any one for work at 10 or 11 o'clock.

TO TIE UP, *verb. phr.* (venery).—To get with child, impregnate, SEW UP (*q.v.*). Also TO BE UP (or UP ONE'S FRILLS, or PETTICOATS)=to be piled in the act.

UP-A-DAISA (or **UPS-A-DAISY**), *intj.* (nursery).—Used in 'baby-jumping.'

UP-AND-DOWN, *subs. phr.* (colloquial).—1. Usually in *pl.*= the events of life, vicissitudes of fortune, alternate good and bad luck. As *adj.*=plain, downright, positive. As *adv.*=(1) thorough, completely, in every respect, DOWN TO THE GROUND (*q.v.*); (2)=bluntly, BRUTALLY (*q.v.*); and (3)=without favour, justly.

1542. UDAL, *Erasmus's Apophth.*, 324. He [Phocion] was euen Socrates VP AND DOWNE in this pointe and behalfe, that no man euer sawe hym either laughe or weepe.

1620. MIDDLETON, *Chaste Maid*, iii. 2. The mother's month, UP AND DOWN, UP AND DOWN.

1759. GOLDSMITH, *Bee*, No. 3. Every man who . . . has had his UPS AND DOWNS in life . . . must have frequently experienced the truth of this doctrine.

d. 1797. WALPOLE, *Letters*, II. 464. A mixture . . . all UPS that should be DOWNS.

1857. LOCKER, *Piccadilly*. Life is chequer'd; a patchwork of smiles and of frowns; We value its UPS, let us muse on its DOWNS.

1869. STOWE, *Oldtown*, 240. Talk about coddling! it's little we got o' that, the way the Lord fixes things in this world. . . . He's pretty UP AND DOWN with us by all they tell us. *Ibid.*, 291. Miss Debby was a well-preserved, UP-AND-DOWN, positive, cheery, sprightly lady.

1884. MILLIKEN [*Punch*, 11 Oct.]. ''Arry at a Political Picnic.' Went to one on 'em yesterday, Charlie; a regular old UP AND DOWN lark.

UP AND DOWN PLACE, *subs. phr.* (tailors').—A shop where a cutter-out is expected to fill up his time sewing.

See UPS AND DOWNS, *post.*

UPHILL, *subs.* (Old Cant).—In *pl.*= dice loaded to cast high numbers: *cf.* LOWMEN (B. E. and GROSE).

Adj. (old colloquial).—Difficult, severe, AGAINST COLLAR (*q.v.*).—GROSE. Hence (2)=hampered.

1748. RICHARDSON, *Clarissa*. What an UPHILL labour must it be to be a learner.

1881. STEVENSON, *Virginibus Puerisque*, iv. These will be UPHILL intimacies, without charm or freedom to the end.

1885. *D. Teleg.*, 1 Sep. Our Government is engaged in a very UPHILL task.

UPON. *See* CROSS; SAY-SO; SIVVY; SQUARE; SNIB.

UPPER. DOWN ON ONE'S UPPERS, *phr.* (common). — Poor, HARD-UP (*q.v.*), BROKE (*q.v.*).

1900. FLYNT, *Tramps*, 117. I'se been a moocher, an' now I's skatin' ON ME UPPERS.

1903. *Judy*, 9 Dec., 577. 1. 'Yes, that's bad enough! But what would you do if you were in my shoes?' 'Eh? Oh, then I should be fairly DOWN ON MY UPPERS.'

UPPER-BEN (or **UPPER-BENJAMIN**), *subs. phr.* (old).—A great coat (GROSE); also BENJY: orig. JOSEPH, but (HOTTEN) 'because of the preponderance of tailors named BENJAMIN, altered in deference to them.'

UPPER-CRUST, *subs. phr.* (pugilists').—The skin.

1832. EGAN, *Book of Sports*. Sam's nob had been in pepper alley, and his UPPER CRUST was rather changed.

2. *See* UPPER-TEN.

3. (common). — A hat: *see* GOLGOTHA.

UPPER-HAND. TO HAVE (HOLD, or GET) THE UPPER-HAND (FORTUNE, or WHIP-HAND), *verb. phr.* (old colloquial).—To have (hold or get) at one's command, in one's power, lead, or under control; to have the day as one's own; to have full play or advantage.

1525. TYNDALE, *New Test*, [OLIPHANT, *New Eng.*, i. 413. Orrmin's *oferrhannd* now becomes THE UPPER HANDE].

1613. FLETCHER, *Honest Man's Fortune*, i. 2. You HAVE THE UPPER FORTUNE of him.

1809. MALKIN, *Gil Blas* [ROUTLEDGE], 106. He challenged them to drink, and in every respect TOOK THE UPPER HAND.

1857-61. BUCKLE, *Hist. Civilization*, II. iii. The nobles thus attained THE UPPER HAND.

1886. STEVENSON, *Kidnapped*, 175. I was growing impatient to get back and have THE UPPER HAND of my uncle.

UPPER-LIP. TO KEEP A STIFF UPPER-LIP, *verb. phr.* (common).—To be courageous, self-reliant under difficulties, unflinching in quest.

1833. NEAL, *Down Easters*, ii. 15. KEEP A STIFF UPPER LIP; no bones broke—don't I know?

1835. HALIBURTON, *Clockmaker*, 1st S. xxxii. He was well to do in the world once, CARRIED A STIFF UPPER LIP, and keered for no one.

1847. *Chronicles of Pineville*, 150. Tut, tut, major, KEEP A STIFF UPPER LIP, and you'll bring him this time.

1850. STOWE, *Uncle Tom's Cabin*, xii. I hope you keep up good heart, and are cheerful. Now, no sulks, ye see; KEEP A STIFF UPPER LIP, boys; do well by me, and I'll do well by you.

1899. WESTCOTT, *David Harum*, xvi. He's got a pretty STIFF UPPER LIP of his own, I reckon.

UPPER-SHELL, *subs. phr.* (Old Cant).—A coat: whence UNDER-SHELL=a waistcoat: *cf.* UPPER-STOCKS.

UPPER - SIXPENNY, *subs. phr.* (Eton). — A playing field: *see* SIXPENNY.

UPPER - STOCK, *subs. phr.* (Old Cant). — In *pl.* = trunk hose, breeches: *see* KICKS.

1546. HEYWOOD, *Epigrams*. The UPPER-STOCKS be they stuft with silk or flocks.

UPPER-STOREY (-LOFT, -WORKS, etc.), *subs. phr.* (common).—The head, brain (GROSE). Hence UNFURNISHED (SOMETHING WRONG, or RATS) IN THE UPPER-STOREY =crazy, demented, ignorant, OFF ONE'S CHUMP (*q.v.*), drunk.

1751. SMOLLETT, *Peregrine Pickle*, vi. I'd have you take care of your UPPER WORKS. *Ibid.* (1771), *Humphry Clinker* (1900), i. 180. Which you imagine to be the new light of grace . . . I take to be a deceitful vapour glimmering through a CRACK IN YOUR UPPER STOREY.

1773. FOOTE, *Bankrupt*. [A man's head is called] his UPPER STOREY.

1809. MALKIN, *Gil Blas* [ROUTLEDGE], 50. We drank hard, and returned . . . in a pretty pickle, that is to say, so-so in THE UPPER STOREY. *Ibid.*, 87. Arsenia and Florimonde are not strong in their UPPER WORKS.

1890. *Harper's Mag.*, lxxx. 348. It knocked everything topsy-turvy in my UPPER STOREY.

UPPER-TEN, *subs. phr.* (common).—The aristocracy, landed gentry, world of fashion: also UPPER TEN THOUSAND, UPPER-TENDOM, and UPPER-CRUST. [Usually referred to N. P. Willis, and originally applied to the wealthy classes of New York as approximating that member.]

c. 1835. WILLIS, *Ephemera*. At present there is no distinction among the UPPER TEN THOUSAND of the city.

1843-4. HALIBURTON, *Attaché*. I want you to see Peel, Stanley, Graham, Shiel, Russell, Macaulay, old Joe, and so on. They are all UPPER CRUST here.

1848. LOWELL, *Fable for Critics*. Caring naught for what vengeance the mob has in store, Let that mob be the UPPER TEN THOUSAND or lower.

18[?]. *Doesticks*, 131 [BARTLETT]. At a ball for the benefit of the poor was a commingling of UPPERTENDOM with lower twentydom,—an avalanche of exclusiveness in a torrent of mobocracy.

18[?]. BUTLER, *Nothing to Wear*. Researches in some of the UPPER TEN districts Reveal the most painful and startling statistics.

1868. *Athenæum*, Nov., 719. To provide for the well-being of the children of affluent parents, our social reformers urge that the mothers of the UPPER TEN THOUSAND should put their nurseries under the control of a superior nurse.

1874. *Siliad*, viii. Yet much remains that stigmatize we must, And in our Siliad THE UPPER CRUST Will find some words to ponder carefully.

1877. DAVITT, *Prison Diary*. Most of these pseudo-aristocratic impostors had succeeded in obtaining admission to the stocking-knitting party, which, in consequence, became known among the rest of the prisoners as the 'UPPER TEN PUSH.'

1884. *Harper's Mag.*, lxxviii. 568. The favourite promenade of the UPPER TEN.

UPPISH, *adj.* (colloquial). — 1. Proud, arrogant, STUCK - UP (*q.v.*); 'rampant, crowing, full of money' (B. E. and GROSE); also (B. E.)=brisk. Whence UPPISHLY and UPPISHNESS. [JOHNSON: 'a low word.']

d. 1704. BROWN, *Works*, i. 154. Half-pay officers at the parade very UPPISH upon the death of the King of Spain.

1710. *Tatler*, 230. Other of that kidney are very UPPISH and alert upon't.

1710-13. SWIFT, *Jour. to Stella* [OLIPHANT, *New Eng.*, ii. 150. Among the Adjectives is UPPISH, a new word objected to by Swift. *Ibid.*, ii. 151. He turns an Adjective into a verb; I'll UPPISH you, for he disliked this new phrase].

1740. NORTH, *Examen*, 48. It seems daring to rail at informers, projectors, and officers was not UPPISH enough, but his Lordship must rise so high as daring to limit the power and revenue of the Crown.

1824. PEAKE, *Americans Abroad*, i. 1. You are but an underlin', tho' you are so UPPISH and twistical.

1839. MRS TROLLOPE, *Michael Armstrong*, iii. She is a bedridden woman, and ought to be in the workhouse; but she's UPISH, and can't abide it.

1880. STOCKTON, *Merry Chanter*, xvii. Americans are too UPPISH; but when you get hold of a man who is accustomed to being downtrodden, it's easy to keep him so.

1882. LOWELL, [*Century*, xxxv. 512]. I sometimes question whether that quality in [Landor] which we cannot but recognise and admire. his loftiness of mind, should not, sometimes, rather be called UPPISHNESS.

2. (old).—Tipsy: *see* SCREWED.

1726. VANBRUGH, *Jour. to London*, iii. 1. *Lady Head.* Not so drunk, I hope, but that he can drive us? *Sew.* Yes, yes, madam, he drives best when he's a little UPPISH.

UPRIGHT, *subs.* (American).—1. A leg.

2. (venery).—An act of coition taken standing; a KNEE-TREMBLER (*q.v.*).

GO UPRIGHT, *phr.* (Old Cant).—'Said by Taylers and Shoemakers, to their Servants, when any Money is given to make them Drink, and signifies, bring it all out in Drink, tho' the Donor intended less, and expects Change, or some return of Money' (B. E., 1696).

UPRIGHT-MAN, *subs. phr.* (Old Cant).—The leader of a gang of mendicants or thieves (*see* quot. 1561); 'the second rank of the Canting Tribes, having sole right to the first night's Lodging with the Dells' (B. E.); 'a thorough-paced and determined thief' (GROSE): *see* CURTAIL.

1561. AWDELEY, *Fraternitye of Vacabondes*. An VPRIGHT MAN is one that goeth wyth the trunchion of a staffe, which staffe they cal a Fellchman. This man is of so much authority that, meeting with any of his profession, he may cal them to accompt, and commaund a share or snap vnto him selfe of al that they haue gained by their trade in one moneth.

1567. HARMAN, *Caveat*, 75. A dell is a yonge wenche, able for generation, and not yet knowen or broken by the VPRIGHT MAN.

1611. MIDDLETON, *Roaring Girl* [DODSLEY, *Old Plays* (REED), vi. 108]. Brother to this UPRIGHT MAN, flesh and blood, ruffling Tear-cat is my name.

1622. FLETCHER, *Beggar's Bush*, ii. 1. Come, princes of the ragged regiment, You of the blood,—Prigg, my most UPRIGHT LORD.

UPROAR, *subs.* (old).—An opera: *cf.* ROARATORIO=oratorio.

1762. STEVENS, *Bartholomew Fair*. We poor folk . . . old English ballads can sing-o, As they at their OPPERORES outlandish ling-o.

UPS AND DOWNS (THE), *subs. phr.* (military).—The second battalion of The Welsh Regiment, formerly the 69th Foot, the number being read in position or upside-down.

UPSEE-DUTCH (UPSEE-ENGLISH, UPSEE-FREESE), *subs. phr.* (old).—Conjecturally a kind of heady beer qualified by the name of the brew. Hence UPSEE - FREESY, etc.=drunk: *see* SCREWED; TO DRINK UPSEE-DUTCH (ENGLISH, etc.)=to drink deeply, or in true toper fashion according to the custom of the country named. Also UPSEES.

1600. *Letting of Humours Blood in the Head-vaine*. Tom is no more like thee then chalks like cheese, To pledge a health or to drinke UP-SE FREESE.

1606. DEKKER, *Seven Deadly Sins* [ARBER], 12. Were drunke according to all the learned rules of drunkenness, as UPSY FREEZE, crambo, etc. *Ibid.* (1608), *Belman of London*, 26. Teach me—how to take the German's UPSY-FREEZE, the Danish rowsa, etc.

1610. JONSON, *Alchemist*, iv. 4. I do not like the dulness of your eye. It hath a heavy cast, 'tis UPSEE DUTCH.

[?]. *The Shrift* [ELLIS, *Spec.*, iii. 121]. For UPSE FREEZE he drank from four to nine, So as each sense was steeped well in wine.

1616. *Times Whistle* [E.E.T.S.], 60. He with his companions George and Rafe, Doe meet together to drink VPSE-FREEZE Till they have made themselves as wise as geese.

1622. MASSINGER, *Virgin Martyr*, ii. 1. Bacchus, the god of brew'd wine and sugar, grand patron of rob-pots, UPSY-FREESY tipplers, and super-naculum topers.

1622. FLETCHER, *Beggar's Bush*, iv. 4. The bowl, —— which must be UPSEY ENGLISH, strong, lusty, London beer. *Ibid.*, iii. 1. So, sit down, lads, And drink me UPSEY DUTCH.

1630. TAYLOR, *Works* [NARES]. This valiant pot-leach that upon his knees Has drunke a thousand pottles UP-SE-FREESE.

1635. HEYWOOD, *Philocothonista*, 45. One that drinks UPSE-FREEZE.

1809. SCOTT, *Lady of the Lake*, vi. 5. Yet whoop, Barnaby! off with thy liquor, Drink UPSEES out, and a fig for the vicar.

UPSET. See APPLE-CART.

UPSIDES. TO BE UPSIDES WITH, *verb. phr.* (colloquial).—To be even with, quits with, a match for.

1816. SCOTT, *Antiquary*, xxi. I'se be UPSIDES wi' him ae day.

1861. HUGHES, *Tom Brown at Oxford*, xxxix. Nay, 'twarn't altogether spite, tho' I won't say but what I might ha' thought o' BEIN' UPSIDES wi' them.

UPSITTING, *subs.* (old).—The sitting up of a woman to see her friends after her confinement; the feast held on such an occasion.

1607. DEKKER, *Westward Hoe.* The jest shall be a stock to maintain us and our pewfellows in laughing at christenings, cryings out, and UPSITTINGS this twelve month.

1641. BROME, *Jovial Crew*, ii. We will have such a lying-in, and such a christening; such UPSITTING and gossiping.

UPSKIP, *subs.* (old).—An UPSTART (*q.v.*).

1549. LATIMER, *Serm. Bef. Ed. VI.*, ii. Put it not to the hearing of these velvet coats, these UPSKIPS.

UPSODOWN, *adv.* (colloquial).—TOPSY-TURVY (*q.v.*), upside-down: also UPSET-DOWN. [SMYTH-PALMER: *Upside-down* is no doubt . . . a false light of old Eng. UP-SO-DOWN, *i.e.* UP *what* (was) DOWN, so being the old relative pronoun]. *Cf.* BACKSEVORE.

1340. HAMPOLE, *Prick of Conscience*, 673. What es man in shap bot a tre, Turned UP ÞET ES DOUN, als men may se. *Ibid.*, 7230. Þafor it es ryght and resoune þat þai be turned UP-SWA-DOUNE.

c. 1360. *Allit. Poems*, 99. 362. Truly þis ilk toun schal tylte to grounde, VP-SO-DOUN schal 3e dumpe depe to þe abyme.

[?]. *Apology for Lollards* [Camden Soc., 19]. Þat þe kirk performe it solemply, candel slekennid, bell ro[n]gun, and þe cros turnid VP SO DOUN.

1378. WYCLIFFE, *Bible*, Job xxx. 12. Thei turneden VPSEDOUN my feet. *Ibid., Unpub. Works* [E.E.T.S.], 119. Proude clerkis and coueitouse, thei clepen holy chirche to turnen alle þing VPSODOUN as anticristis disciplis.

1383. CHAUCER, *Cant. Tales*, 1379. 'Knight's Tale.' Shortly turned was al UP-SO-DOUN, Bothe habit and eek disposicioun Of him, this woful lovere, daun Arcite.

1481. CAXTON, *Reynard the Fox* [ARBER], 74. Me thynketh this court is al torned VP SO DOUN.

1481. *Cath. Ang.*, 397. To turne VP SO DOWN; *euerterre.*

1493. GOWER, *Confessio Amantis*, ii. The londe was tourned VPSO DOWNE.

[?]. *Ancient Ballads* [LILLY], 235. Turne their hartes quite VPSIDOWNE, To become true subjects.

1611. *Bible*, Authorised Version, Acts xvii. 6. These that haue turned the world VPSIDE DOWNE, are come hither also.

UPSTAIRS, *subs.* (London).—A special brand of spirits: a bottle usually kept on a shelf: *e.g.* 'a drop of UPSTAIRS.' The particular brand varies with the house.

TO GO UPSTAIRS OUT OF THE WORLD, *verb. phr.* (old).—To be hanged: *see* LADDER.

1695. CONGREVE, *Love for Love*, ii. 7. By your looks you should GO UPSTAIRS OUT OF THE WORLD.

UPSTART, *subs.* (B. E. and GROSE).—1. A person suddenly raised from poverty to wealth, from a humble position to consequence, or from servitude to power: now recognised.

1592. GREENE, *Quip for Upstart Courtier* [Harl. Misc., v. 402]. In faith, goodman goosecap, you that are come from the startups, and therefore is called ad UP-START, *quasi* START UP from clouted shoone.

S

UPSYTURVY, *adv.* (old).—TOPSY-TURVY (*q.v.*).

d. 1594. GREENE, *James IV.*, iii. 3. There found I all was UPSY-TURVY turned.

UPTAILS-ALL, *subs. phr.* (old).—1. Confusion, riot, high jinks; (2) revellers, good fellows, boon companions. Hence (3) wantonness, and *spec.* the act of kind; whence TO PLAY AT UPTAILS ALL=to copulate: *see* GREENS and RIDE: a play on this sense and the old card game of uptails all was frequent.

1602. DEKKER, *Satiromastrix* [HAWKINS, *Eng. Drama*, iii. 170]. Feel, my UPTAILS-ALL, feel my weapon.

1647-8. HERRICK, *Hesperides*, 265. Love he doth call For his UPTAILES ALL.

UP-TO-DATE, *adj.* (colloquial)—Of the latest: in fashion, fact, or philosophy; abreast of the times.

1888. *Academy*, 4 Feb., 822. A good UP-TO-DATE English work on the islands.

UPWAYS, *adv.* (colloquial).—Upward.

URCHIN, *subs.* (old and still colloquial).—1. A mischievous child; a half-chiding endearment; 'a little sorry Fellow' (B. E. and GROSE): and (2) an elf, fairy, or sprite: popularly supposed to take the form of a hedgehog, the original meaning. Hence as *adj.*=(1) roguish, mischievous; and (2) trifling, foolish, trumpery.

1566. Roy and Barlow, *Rede Me*, etc. [ARBER, 43]. I trowe the VRCHYN will clyme To some promocion hastily.

1596. SHAKSPEARE, *Merry Wives of Windsor*, iv. 4. Like URCHINS, ouphes and fairies. *Ibid.* (1609), *Tempest*, i. 2. 326. URCHINS shall . . . all exercise on thee.

1634. MILTON, *Comus*, 845. URCHIN blasts and ill-luck signs.

1692. HACKET, *Williams*, ii. 91. Our Bishop . . . made himself merry with the conceit how easie it was to stride over such URCHIN articles. No man would find leisure to read the whole 36, they are so frivolous.

d. 1721. PRIOR, *Venus Mistaken.* 'And who's blind now, mamma?' the URCHIN cried.

d. 1850. WORDSWORTH, *Michael.* There stood the URCHIN as you will divine.

URINAL, *subs.* (old). — 1. 'A chamber-pot, or glass' (B. E.). URINAL OF THE PLANETS = Ireland: 'because of its frequent and great rains, as Heidelberg and Cologn, in Germany, have the same Name upon the same Account' (B. E.).

U.S.-COVE, *subs. phr.* (American).—A soldier. U.S.-PLATE = handcuffs: *cf.* GOVERNMENT SECURITIES.

USE, *subs.* (American).—Liking.

c. 1889. *Trans. Am. Phil. Ass.* [Century]. I have no USE for him—don't like him.

Verb (old). — To copulate (CHAUCER): *see* GREENS and RIDE.

1613. WEBSTER, *Devil's Law-case*, i. 2. *Waiting woman.* Very well, sir, You may USE me at your pleasure. *Rom.* By no means, Winifred; that were the way to make thee travail again.

TO USE AT (or ROUND) A PLACE, *verb. phr.* (thieves').—To haunt, frequent.

1877. HORSLEY, *Jottings from Jail.* I got in company with some of the widest people in London. They used TO USE AT a pub. in Shoreditch.

TO USE UP, *verb. phr.* (colloquial).—To exhaust, wear out, DO FOR (*q.v.*): whence USED UP = broken-hearted, bankrupt, fatigued, vanquished, killed, etc. (GROSE).

1835. DANA, *Before the Mast*, xxviii. Such a sight I never saw before . . . 'cleaned out' to the last real, and completely USED UP.

1855. KINGSLEY, *Westward Ho*, i. Half were USED-UP . . . with the scurvy.

1855. HALIBURTON, *Human Nature*, 192. Well, being out night arter night, she got kinder USED UP and beat out, and unbeknownest to me used to take opium.

1856. KANE, *Arctic Exped.*, II. 100. Hans has been really ill; five days down with severe pains of the limbs have left him a 'little weak,' which with him means well USED UP.

1865. DOWNING, *May-day in New York.* Moving on the first day in May in New York has USED ME UP worse than building forty acres of stone wall.

1871. CALVERLEY, *Fly Leaves.* 'Beer.' But what is coffee but a noxious berry Born to keep USED-UP Londoners awake?

1876. GRANT, *One of the Six Hundred*, iii. His whole air had the USED-UP bearing of those miserable dundrearys who affect to act as if youth, wealth, and luxury were the greatest calamities that flesh is heir to.

1887. *D. Teleg.*, 5 Mar. We have USED UP no fewer than six Irish Secretaries in little more than as many years.

USHER, *intj.* (thieves').—Yes: *cf.* Yiddish *user*=it is so.

1877. HORSLEY, *Jottings from Jail.* When I got into Shoreditch I met one or two of the mob, who said, 'Hallo, been out to-day? Did you touch?' So I said USHER.

USUAL, *subs.* (colloquial). — The custom. AS PER USUAL = as usual: pleonastic.

1589. PUTTENHAM, *Art of Eng. Poesy*, 72. The staffe of seuen verses hath seuen proportions, whereof one onely is THE VSUALL of our vulgar.

1892. MILLIKEN, *'Arry Ballads.* 'At a Political Picnic.' Bin playing some dark little game? I'm keeping mine hup as PER USUAL.

UTTER, *subs.* (old and colloquial).—The extreme; the utmost: also (modern) QUITE TOO UTTERLY UTTER=very; THE BLOOMING UTTER=the utmost. As *adj.*= excellent, A1: a supreme intensive.

d. 1697. AUBREY, *Lives.* 'Walter Raleigh.' I take my leave readie to countervaile all your courtesies to THE UTTER of my power.

1887. HENLEY, *Culture in the Slums*, iii. I likes a merry little flutter, I keeps a Dado on the sly, In fact my form's THE BLOOMING UTTER.

UZZARD, *subs,* (provincial).—The letter Z.

 (old).—1. A symbol of cuckoldry, the letter being occasionally printed in that connection. Hence TO MAKE V = to make HORNS (*q.v.*): the first and second fingers are derisively forked out: *cf.* CUNNY-THUMB.

1611. CHAPMAN, *May-day*, iv. As often as he turns his back to me, I shall be here V with him.

2. (American).—A five-dollar note: v is marked prominently to indicate its value.

VAC, *subs.* (University and schools).—Vacation.

1891. *Harry Fludyer at Cambridge*, 2. The pater . . . told me every day last VAC he wouldn't have his house over-run with dogs.

1900. WHITE, *West End*, 18. Fork out . . . I'll pay you back in the VAC.

VAG, *subs.* (American).—A vagabond. Whence VAG-ACT (police)=the Vagabond Act.

VAGARIES, *subs.* (old—B. E.).— 'Wild rambles, extravagant Frolicks' (1696); to gad, to range; *see* VAGRANT. Hence VAGARIAN = a CRANK (*q.v.*); VAGARIOUS (or VAGARIST) = whimsical, capricious, irregular.

1611. COTGRAVE, *Dict.*, s.v. *Vaguer*, to wander, VAGARIE, stray, gad, roame, raunge, flit, remoue from place to place.

d. 1622. RICH, *Herodotus.* The people called Phœnices gave themselves to long VAGARIES, and continual viages by sea.

1640. BROME, *Sparagus Garden*, ii. 2. You have not dealt well with me to put this FAGARY into her foolish fancy.

c. 1796. WOLCOT, *Peter Pindar*, 305. His eyes are oft VAGARISH.

VAGRANT, *subs.* (old: now recognised). — 'A wandering Rogue, a strolling Vagabond' (B. E., *c.* 1696): also VAGANT. [*Century*: sometimes VAGARANT, apparently simulating VAGARY.] Whence VAGRANCY (or VAGANCY)=wandering, strolling; also VAGRANT, *adj.*=roving, erratic, vagabond.

1380. WYCLIF, *Bible*, Gen. iv. 14. Fro thi face I shal be hid, and I shal be VAGAUNT.

1641. BROME, *Jovial Crew*, v. Fie! Canst not yet leave off those VAGANCIES.

1685. BARRON, *Sermons*, xxxvi. Therefore did he spend his days in continual labour, in restless travel, in endless VAGRANCY, going about doing good.

1770. GOLDSMITH, *Deserted Village*, 149. His house was known to all the VAGRANT train.

VAIN. TO TAKE ONE'S NAME IN VAIN, *verb. phr.* (colloquial).—To name: a common dovetail on hearing one's name mentioned; *e.g.* 'Who's TAKING MY NAME IN VAIN?'

VAIN-GLORIOUS MAN, *subs. phr.* (B. E.).—'One that Pisses more than he drinks' (*c.* 1696).

VALLEY. See CASCADE, 2.

VALLEY-TAN, *subs. phr.* (American). A special manufacture of whiskey sold in Utah.

VAMOSE (VAMOS or **VAMPOOSE)**, *verb* (American). — To go, decamp, CLEAR OUT (*q.v.*): also (Western) TO VAMOSE THE RANCH. [Spanish.]

1840. *Southern Sketches*, 141. The Camanches came within a league of us, but VAMOSED THE RANCH when they learned that the rangers were here.

1844. SELBY, *London by Night*, ii. 1. VAMOOSE—scarper—fly!

1848. *Amer. Jour. Commerce*, June. Yankee Sullivan's house, corner of Frankfort and Chatham Streets, is in a dangerous condition. . . . Its occupants received some very ominous premonitions of a downfall, and forthwith VAMOSED with their baggage.

1848. *New York Mirror*, May. I couldn't stand more than this stanza, . . . and I accordingly VAMOSED.

1857. KINGSLEY, *Two Years Ago*, i. Has he VAMPOOSED with the contents of a till?

c. 1861. *Parody on Leigh Hunt's "Abou Ben Adhem."* The devil wrote, and VAMOSED. The next night He came again, —this time a little tight.

1876. WOOLSON, *Jupiter Lights*, xxxi. He was sincerely sorry that Hollis had VAMOSED in that way.

1878. *Scribner's Mag.*, Nov. 82. My precious partners had VAMOSED THE RANCH.

1880. *Scribner's Mag.*, Aug., 610. I finished the sign and then VAMOOSED.

VAMP, *subs.* (thieves'). — 1. A robbery. Hence IN FOR A VAMP = QUODDED (*q.v.*) for PRIGGING (*q.v.*); VAMPER (*q.v.*) = a thief.

2. (common). — In *pl.* = refooted stockings (B. E.): *see* VAMPER.

Verb. (American colloquial). — 1. To improvise a musical accompaniment: the key and time being known, a passable accompaniment is playable at sight by a system which, in America, is 'taught in eight lessons for $10.' Also as *subs.*, and VAMPER.

1851-61. MAYHEW, *Lond. Lab.*, iii. 201. As soon as I could get in to VAMP the tunes on the banjo a little.

1888. *Pall Mall Gaz.*, 31 Jan. [Advt.]. How to VAMP to songs, chords, etc.

2. (common). — To pawn, SPOUT (*q.v.*) (B. E. and GROSE).

VAMPER, *subs.* (veterinary). — 1. A swindling horse-dealer; a FAKER (*q.v.*) of unsound horses: also *see* VAMP, *subs.* and *verb.*

1876. GREENWOOD, *Undercur. London Life.* It is beyond dispute that in the hands of the experienced horse-VAMPER the most wretched used-up screw in existence may, for a brief hour or so, be made to exhibit an amount of fire and spirit that if persisted in for a longer period would inevitably shake its ramshackle carcass all to pieces.

2. (old). — In *pl.* = stockings (B. E).

VAMPIRE, *subs.* (Punch and Judy). — 1. The ghost: *see* SWATCHEL.

2. (American). — A blackmailer: Fr. *chanteur.*

VAMPO, *subs.* (theatrical). — The clown: *see* SWATCHEL.

VANDEMONIANISM, *subs.* (obsolete Australian). — Rowdyism: *i.e.* pertaining to Van Diemen's Land, the old name of Tasmania when a convict settlement, with a glance at 'demon.' Also VANDEMONIAN, *adj.*

1852. MUNDY, *Our Antipodes* (1855), 533. The VAN DIEMONIANS, as they unpleasingly call themselves, or permit themselves to be called, are justly proud of their horse-flesh.

1853. SIDNEY, *Three Colonies of Australia* (2nd edit.), 171. One of the first acts of the Legislative Assemblies created by the Australian Reform Bill of 1850 was to pass . . . acts levelled against VAN DIEMONIAN expirees.

1855. HOWITT, *Two Years in Victoria*, i. 367. Unquestionably some of the VAN DIEMENIAN convicts.

1863. *Victorian Hansard*, 22 April, ix. 701. Mr. Houston looked upon the conduct of hon. gentlemen opposite as ranging from the extreme of VANDEMONIANISM to the extreme of nambypambyism.

1867. *Cassell's Magazine*, 440. 'I never wanted to leave England,' I have heard an old VANDEMONIAN observe boastfully. 'I wasn't like one of these "Jemmy Grants" (cant term for 'emigrants'); I could always earn a good living; it was the Government as took and sent me out.'

VAN JOHN, *subs. phr.* (colloquial). — A corruption of *Vingt-et-un.*

VANNER, *subs.* (trade). — A van horse: *cf.* BUSSER, CABBER, WHEELER, etc.

1888. *Referee*, 8 Ap. [Advt.]. Twenty-five Welsh cobs, cabbers, and VANNERS.

VANTAGE, *subs.* (old printers'). — Good paying work, FAT (*q.v.*): a spec. colloquial usage of a recognised word.

VANTAGE-LOAF, *subs. phr.* (old colloquial). — The thirteenth loaf in a BAKER'S-DOZEN (*q.v.*).

VAPOUR, *subs.* (old colloquial). — 1. In *pl.* = bluster, ostentatious or windy talk, SWAGGER (*q.v.*). [The ROARING BOYS (*q.v.*) of Elizabethan times, to provoke a quarrel, were wont flatly and swaggeringly to contradict everything said, even that to which a bully had previously assented (*see* JONSON, *Bartholomew Fair*, iv. 3).] Hence as *verb* = to boast, swagger, bully, with such derivatives as VAPOURED, VAPOURER, VAPOURISING, VAPOURISE, etc. Also (2), in the eighteenth century, a fashionable term for AIRS (*q.v.*), SIDE (*q.v.*): spec. an exaggerated affectation of 'nerves' or BLUES (*q.v.*): also (3) whims, fancies, MAGGOTS (*q.v.*), and as *verb* = to fuss, fidget, make TO DO (*q.v.*).

1552. STRYPE, *Eccles. Mem.* A VAPOURING sort (which that nation was then much addicted to).

1570. CAMDEN, *Hist. Elizabeth.* A ruffian, a riotous spendthrift and a notable VAPOURER.

1614. JONSON, *Bartholomew Fair*, ii. Nay, then, pardon me my VAPOUR. I have a foolish VAPOUR, gentlemen: Any man that does VAPOUR me the ass—I do VAPOUR him the lie. *Ibid.* (1630), *New Inn*, iii. 1. *Pierce.* He's Barst's protection. *Fly.* Fights and VAPOURS for him.

1628. FORD, *Lover's Melancholy*, iv. 2. He VAPOURS like a tinker, and struts like a juggler.

1641. MILTON, *Apology for Smectymnus.* His designe was, if he could not refute them, yet at least with quips and snapping adagies to VAPOUR them out.

1660-9. PEPYS, *Diary*, II. 331. My Lord Berkeley hath all along been . . . one that is the greatest VAPOURER in the world.

1706. VANBRUGH, *Mistake*, iv. 1. Here, take thy satin pincushion, with thy curious half hundred of pins in't, thou madest such a VAPOURING about yesterday.

1748. RICHARDSON, *Clarissa*, II. xcvii. You will not wonder that the VAPOURISHNESS which has laid hold of my heart should rise to my pen.

1749. WHISTON, *Memoirs*, 18. I was become so VAPOURED and timorous at home that I was ready to faint away if I did but go a few stones'-cast from our own house.

1751. FIELDING, *Amelia*, iii. 7. A man had better be plagued with all the curses of Egypt than with a VAPOURISH wife.

1759-67. STERNE, *Tristram Shandy*, ix. 3. The corporal gave a slight flourish with his stick—but not VAPOURINGLY.

1796. D'ARBLAY, *Camilla*, v. vi. She VAPOURS me but to look at her.

1809. IRVING, *Knickerbocker*, 355. All these valourous VAPOURINGS had a considerable effect.

1819. CRABBE, *Tales of the Hall* [*Works*, vii. 63]. Nor to be fretful, VAPOURISH, or give way To spleen and anger as the wealthy may.

1886. *D. Teleg.*, 7 Ap. Despite the VAPOURING of the Minister of War.

1888. *D. Teleg.*, 7 Feb. He VAPOURED considerably.

VARDO, *subs.* (Old Cant). — A waggon. VARDO-GILL = a waggoner (GROSE).

Verb (streets and circus). — To look, see, observe: *e.g.* VARDO THE CARSEY = look at the house.

VARDY, *subs.* (common). — An opinion: *e.g.* 'That's my VARDY on the matter' = That's what I think. [A corruption of *verdict.*]

VARLET, *subs.* (old colloquial). — A generic reproach: a rogue, scoundrel, low fellow. Whence VARLETRY = the mob, rabble, crowd (B. E.). [Properly = a page, groom, or serving-man.]

1549. LATIMER, *Serm. Bef. Edward VI.*, iii. Was not this a seditious VARLET, to tell them this to their beards.

1608. SHAKSPEARE, *Antony and Cleop.*, v. 2. 56. The shouting VARLETRY of censuring Rome.

c. 1620. FLETCHER, *Women Pleas'd*, ii. 4. 'There's money for thee: thou art a precious VARLET, Be fat, be fat, and blow thy master backward.'

1610. JONSON, *Alchemist*, ii. 1. Ananias . . . the VARLET That cozened the apostles!

1778. SHERIDAN, *Rivals*, iv. 2. Well, I am glad you are not the dull, insensible VARLET you pretended to be.

1840. BROWNING, *Sordello*, vi. Gay swarms of VARLETRY that come and go.

VARMINT, *subs.* (common). — Anything troublesome or mischievous: also a half-jocular endearment to a child: *e.g.* 'You young VARMINT' [that is, *vermin*].

1826. COOPER, *Last of the Mohicans*, viii. Uncas, we have need of all our we'pons to bring the cunning VARMENT from his roost.

1863. GASKELL, *Sylvia's Lovers*, i. All regarded in the light of mean kidnappers and spies—VARMENT as the common people esteemed them.

2. (hunting). — A fox.

1888. *Field*, 4 Feb. Decided the hound in question to go for the VARMINT he had found.

Adj. (University). — Spruce, natty, good-all-round.

1823. *Gradus ad Cantab.* A VARMINT man spurns a scholarship, would consider it a degradation to be a fellow.

1827. *Alma Mater.* . . . The handsome man, my friend and pupil, was naturally enough a bit of a swell, or VARMINT man.

VARMINT-MAN, *subs. phr.* (University). — A hack or GHOST (*q.v.*): 'one who, like Jemmy Gordon, wrote themes for idle undergrads': *see* VARMINT, *adj.*

VARNISHER, *subs.* (thieves'). — One who utters base money, a SNIDE-PITCHER (*q.v.*).

VARSAL, *adj.* (old colloquial). — Universal: frequently as an intensive.

1710. SWIFT, *Pol. Conv.*, ii. I believe there is not such another in the VARSAL world.

1771. SMOLLETT, *Humph. Clinker*, i. 125. Here was flying without any broom-sticks or thing in the VARSAL world.

[?]. SCOTT [*Century*]. Every VARSAL soul in the library were gone to bed.

VARSITY, *subs.* and *adj.* (collegiate). — University; and spec. University College, Oxford: the reduction is also affected by American students.

1864. TENNYSON, *Northern Farmer*, New Style. 'E coom'd to the parish wi lots o' VARSITY debt.

1886. *D. Tel.*, 8 May. The parson —possibly an old 'VARSITY MAN.

VARSITY-TIT, *subs. phr.* (University). — A student of Durham University: in contempt.

VARYING, *subs.* (Winchester). — A VULGUS (*q.v.*) when done 'up to BOOKS' (*q.v.*).

VASELINE, *subs.* (Royal Military Academy). — Butter, CART-GREASE (*q.v.*).

VAUGHAN (THE), *subs. phr.* (Harrow). — The school library: named after Dr. Vaughan.

VAULTING-HOUSE (or **-SCHOOL**), *subs. phr.* (venery). — A brothel: *see* NANNY-SHOP. Hence VAULT, *verb* = to copulate, LEAP (*q.v.*); and VAULTER = a PERFORMER (*q.v.*): *see* GREENS and RIDE (B. E. and GROSE).

1598. FLORIO, *Worlde of Wordes*, p. 97, s.v.

[1599. SHAKSPEARE, *Henry V.*, v. 2. 145. If I could win a lady . . . by VAULTING into my saddle . . . I should quickly leap into a wife.] *Ibid.* (1605), *Cymbeline*, i. 6. 133. Should he make me Live, like Diana's priests, betwixt cold sheets, Whiles he is VAULTING variable ramps.

1607. DEKKER, *Westward Hoe*, iii. 2. Now were I in an excellent humour to go to a VAULTING-HOUSE, I would break down all their glass windows, . . . tear their silk petticoats. . . . O the Gods, what I could do. *Ibid.*, v. 3. She has tricks to keep a VAULTING HOUSE under the law's nose. *Ibid.* (1607), *Northward Hoe*, iii. 1. How many VAULTERS have I entertained.

1639. MASSINGER, *Un. Combat*, iv. 2. A . . . VAULTING HOUSE . . . Where I used to spend my afternoons, among suburb she-gamesters . . . I have cracked a ring or two there.

VEAL, *subs.* (old colloquial). — A calf: *cf.* MUTTON, BEEF: in English these terms are now restricted to the dead carcase and not applied to the living animal, as in French and other languages.

1611. COTGRAVE, *Dict.*, s.v. Veël, A calfe or VEALE.

PHRASES. 'VEAL will be cheap, calves fall' (a jeer at those with spindly legs); 'In a shoulder of VEAL, there are twenty and two good bits' (RAY: a piece of country wit—there are twenty [others say forty] bits in a shoulder of veal, and but two good ones).

VEALY, *adj.* (colloquial). — Immature, calfish, GREEN (*q.v.*).

1864. LOWELL, *Fireside Travels*, 248. Their VEALY faces mezzotinted with soot.

VECK, *subs.* (old). — An old woman.

1360. [CHAUCER], *Romaunt of the Rose*, 4495. A rympled VEKKE, ferre ronne in age.

VEGETABLE-BREAKFAST, *subs. phr.* (common). — A hanging, execution: *i.e.* an artichoke (hearty choke) and caper sauce: *see* LADDER.

VEIN-OPENERS, *subs. phr.* (military). — The first battalion of the Worcestershire Regiment, late the 29th Foot.

VELVET, *subs.* (Old Cant). — The tongue (B. E. and GROSE): 'especially the tongue of a magsman' (HOTTEN).

TO STAND ON VELVET, *verb. phr.* (racing).—To arrange one's bets so that loss is impossible.

1896. FARJEON, *Betray. John Fordham*, III. 289. I'd won a matter of five thousand quid. 'Now I'm on welvet,' said I, grinnin' and rubbin' my 'ands. 'Fortune o' war,' sed Maxwell.

TO PLAY ON VELVET, *verb. phr.* (gaming).—To gamble with winnings.

TO TIP THE VELVET, *verb. phr.* (venery).—To tongue a woman (B. E. and GROSE).

VELVET-CAP, *subs. phr.* (old).—A physician: a velvet-cap formed a distinctive part of a doctor's garb.

1606. *Ret. from Parnassus. Theod.* O monsier, I have a singular care of your valetudo. It is requisite that the French phisitions be learned and carefull; your English VELVET-CAP is malignant and envious.

VELVETEEN, *subs.* (common).—In *pl.* = a gamekeeper.

1885. *D. Teleg.*, 29 Dec. Were the English VELVETEENS less conservative and orthodox in his views of what the limits of his duties are, he might take a hint from the foreigner in trapping blue rocks.

VELVET-JACKET, *subs. phr.* (old colloquial). — A steward in a nobleman's family, a man in the King's service: in quot. = the mayor of a city.

1600. HEYWOOD, 1 *Edward IV.* [PEARSON, *Works* (1874), I. 17]. Spoken like a man, and true VELUET-IACKET, And we will enter and strike by the way.

VELVET-PEE, *subs. phr.* (old).—A velvet pea-jacket.

1607-8. BEAUMONT and FLETCHER, *Love's Cure*, ii. 1. Though now your blockhead be covered with a Spanish block, and your lashed shoulders with a VELVET-PEE.

VENTILATOR, *subs.* (theatrical).—A play, player, or management that empties a house.

VENTURE. As in the proverbial saying, 'I'll VENTURE it as Johnson did his wife, and she did well' (RAY).

VENTURER, *subs.* (old).—A harlot: *see* TART.

VENUS, *subs.* (venery).—Generic for sexuality: thus, VENUS'S-CURSE = syphilis: *see* LADIES'-FEVER; VENUS'S-CELL (or -MARK) = the female *pudendum*: *see* MONOSYLLABLE; also VENUS'S SECRET CELL (HIGHWAY or HONYPOT), VENUS'S-GAME (or RITES OF VENUS) = copulation: *see* GREENS and RIDE.

c. 1508. *Colin Blowbol's Testament* [HAZLITT, *Early Pop. Poet*, i. 94]. He gaf me many a good certacion, With right and holsome predicacion, That he had laboured in VENUS' SECRETE CELLE.

1719. DURFEY, *Pills*, i. 16. I've no SCARS OF VENUS there, Twiddle come Tweedle twee. *Ibid.*, iii. 342 [HOTTEN]. For when you have possession got Of VENUS'S MARK, or HONYPOT.

1772. BRIDGES, *Burlesque Homer*, 256. You whoring rascal, leave this job, And come along and bear a bob: Why can't you run the risk of SCARS In Mars' as well as VENUS' wars?

1809. MALKIN, *Gil Blas* [ROUTLEDGE], 147. He could not stomach these beauties who call a spade a spade. Such were not for his market; the RITES OF VENUS must be consummated in the temple of Vesta.

VERB- (or GERUND-) GRINDER, *subs. phr.* (common).—A schoolmaster or tutor: spec. a pedantic pedagogue (GROSE). Also GERUND-GRINDING = the study of grammar.

1759-67. STERNE, *Tristram Shandy*, IV. 112. Tutors, governors, GERUND-GRINDERS, and bear-leaders.

1788. KNOX, *Winter Evenings*, 59. A pedant, a mere plodder, a petty tyrant, a GERUND-GRINDER.

1809. MALKIN, *Gil Blas* [ROUTLEDGE], 168. The VERB-GRINDER engendered in his noddle a most ingenious device, by which to keep this troublesome young lordling in awe, without trenching on his foolish father's instructions.

1825-7. HONE, *Ev. Day Book*, II. 33. GERUND-GRINDING and parsing are usually prepared for at the last moment.

VERDANT, *adj.* (colloquial).—Simple, inexperienced, 'easily TAKEN IN' (*q.v.*), GREEN (*q.v.*). Whence VERDANCY = rawness, inexperience.

1853. BRADLEY, *Adv. of* VERDANT *Green* [Title].

1878. *Scribner's Mag.*, Oct., 790. Forget his VERDANCY and grotesque appearance.

VERGE, *subs.* (thieves').—A gold watch.

VERITES (Charterhouse).—A boarding-house. [A corruption of OLIVERITES, after Dr. Oliver Walford, 1838-55.]

VERT, *subs.* (colloquial).—A pervert or con-VERT: spec. one leaving the Church of England for the Roman Communion, or *vice versâ*. Also as *verb*.

1864. *Exper. of a* VERT [*Union Rev.*, May]. Old friends call me a pervert, new acquaintance a convert, the other day I was addressed as a VERT.

1888. *Echo*, 17 Mar. As a man he is welcome to VERT and re-VERT as often as he pleases.

VERTICAL - CAREGRINDER, *subs. phr.* (prison).—The tread-mill, HORIZONTAL-STAIRCASE (*q.v.*), WHEEL OF LIFE (*q.v.*).

VESSEL, *subs.* (Winchester College).—The half-quarter of a sheet of foolscap. [*Voc. East Anglia*: VESSEL was used for theme-papers formerly at Bury School.]

THE WEAKER VESSEL, *subs. phr.* (colloquial). — A woman: *see* 1 Peter iii. 7.

1600. SHAKSPEARE, *As You Like It*, ii. 4. I must comfort THE WEAKER VESSEL, as doublet and hose ought to show itself courageous to petticoat.

VEST. PULL DOWN YOUR VEST, *verb. phr.* (American).—A street catch-phrase of no special meaning.

1875-6. RICHMOND, *Burton's Events* [BARTLETT]. But the latest flash saying with which we are blest Is to tell a man quietly, 'PULL DOWN YOUR VEST.'

TO LOSE ONE'S VEST, *verb. phr.* (common).—To get angry, lose one's temper: *cf.* 'KEEP YOUR HAIR ON!'

VESTA, *subs.* (Stock Exchange).—In *pl.* = Railway Investment Company Deferred Stock.

VET, *subs.* (colloquial). — 1. A veterinary surgeon. Also 2. (American) = a VETERAN (*q.v.*).

1888. *Field*, 4 Feb. Show his horse's feet to a VET, and ask his opinion.

1890. *Atlantic*, lxvi. 114. Great pains are taken with the shoeing, which is under the direct charge of the accomplished VET employed by that department.

VETERAN, *subs.* (American). — A soldier listing for a second term of service: also VET. Whence VETERAN (or VETERANIZE), *verb* = to re-enlist.

VEX, *adv.* (Christ's Hospital).—So much the worse for: *e.g.* 'Vex for you': *cf.* CHAFF.

VIC, *intj.* (Felsted School).—1. A warning of a master's approach; Cave! Hence TO KEEP VIC = to be on the look-out.

2. (London). — The Victoria Theatre.

VICTUAL. IN ONE'S VICTUALS, *phr.* (provincial). — In favour, petted, cossetted: spec. of a mother and child.

VICTUALLER, *subs.* (old). — A pander: the legitimate trade of a tavern-keeper was frequently but a cloak for intrigue and bawdry; hence many equivocal allusions. Also VICTUALLING HOUSE = a house of accommodation.

1598. SHAKSPEARE, 2 *Henry IV.*, ii. 4. Marry, there's another indictment upon thee, for suffering flesh to be eaten in thy house, contrary to the law — *Hostess.* All VICTUALLERS do so. What's a joint of mutton or two in a whole Lent.

1661. WEBSTER, *Cure for a Cuckold*, iv. 1. This informer comes into Turnbull street, to a VICTUALLING HOUSE, and there falls in league with a wench.

VICTUALLING-DEPARTMENT (or **-OFFICE)**, *subs. phr.* (common).—The stomach, the BREAD-BASKET (*q.v.*), the DUMPLING-DEPÔT (*q.v.*). *Fr. panier au pain*; Ital. *fagiana* (= bean-box).

VIEWPOINT, *subs.* (colloquial).—A point of view.

1877. *Edin. Rev.*, cxlv. 499. The manner in which the details of a history are presented should be judged from the standpoint of the writer, from the general VIEWPOINT of the time.

VIEWY, *adj.* (colloquial).—1. Visionary, KINKY (*q.v.*), FUNNY (*q.v.*).

1848. NEWMAN, *Loss and Gain*, i. 3. He was VIEWY, in a bad sense of the word.

18[?]. *American* [*Century*]. A man's identification with the movement was taken as proof that he was VIEWY and unfit for leadership.

2. (colloquial).—Showy, calculated to 'catch the eye.'

1851-61. MAYHEW, *Lond. Lab.*, III. 230. [The chests of drawers] would hold together for a time . . . and that was all; but the slaughterers cared only to have them VIEWY and cheap.

VIGILANCE-COMMITTEE, *subs. phr.* (American).—Orig. Californian: a self-constituted body of men ostensibly for the purpose of administering justice or protecting the public interests in places where the regular authorities were either unable or unwilling to execute the laws: *cf.* LYNCH-LAW. Hence VIGILANT = a member of such a committee.

1858. *Baltimore Sun*, 1 July. A hand-bill calling a meeting to form a VIGILANCE COMMITTEE to suppress certain secret movements among the coloured population, and to stop outrages on private property, Governor Wise addressed a letter to Mayor Mayo, adding that he would use force in prohibiting such meeting from being held on the Capitol square. The Mayor in reply states that he considers himself a 'VIGILANCE COMMITTEE' enough for him and his comrades, and therefore deems it unnecessary to adopt any unusual measures against the proposed movement.

1858. *New York Tribune*, 30 Sep. A Protestant congregation was broken up and a part of its members marched on a Sunday from their place of worship to the town jail. The final proceedings of the civil authorities in the case were, according to our American notions of right and law, as gross a violation of justice as VIGILANCE COMMITTEE or lynching mob was ever guilty of.

c. 1859. *Annals of San Francisco*, 562 [BARTLETT]. Few people abroad, who had been trained from infancy to revere 'the majesty of the law,' and who had never seen any crime but what their own strong legal institutions and efficient police could detect and punish, could possibly conceive such a state of things as would justify the formation and independent action of an association which set itself above all formal law, and which openly administered summary justice, or what they called justice, in armed opposition and defiance to the regularly constituted tribunals of the country. Therefore, in other lands, it happened that the VIGILANCE COMMITTEE became often a term of

reproach, and people pointed to it as a sign that society in California was utterly and perhaps irredeemably impure and disorganised.

1885. PALMER, *New and Old*, 73. The first man hung by the San Francisco VIGILANCE COMMITTEE was dead before he was swung up, and the second was alive after he was cut down.

1882. ROOSEVELT [*Century*, XXXV. 505]. A little over a year ago one committee of VIGILANTES in Eastern Montana shot or hung nearly sixty [horse-thieves] —not, however, with the best judgment in all cases.

VILE, *subs.* (Old Cant).—A town: *cf.* Fr. *ville*. Hence ROME-VILE = London (*see* RUM, *adj.* 1): DEUCE-A-VILE = the country: also DEAUSEAVILLE and DAISY-VILLE.

1567. HARMAN, *Caveat*, 86. Byng we to ROME-VYLE.

1612. DEKKER, *O per se O.* 'Bing out, Bien morts.' Bing out bien morts, and toure and toure, bing out of the ROME-VILE.

1622. HEAD, *Eng. Rogue.* And prig and cloy so benshiply All the DEUCE-A-VILE within.

1834. AINSWORTH, *Rookwood* (1864), 199. I want a little ready cash in RUM-VILLE—beg pardon, ma'am, London, I mean.

1891. CAREW, *Auto. of a Gipsy*, 416. We made a long round back to VILE. *Ibid.*, 417. The VILE's readered all hover with these 'ere stiffs.

VILL, *subs.* (Felsted School).—Felsted village.

VILLADOM, *subs.* (colloquial).—The world of suburban residents; spec. the middle classes.

1886. *Fort. Rev.*, N.S., xl. 254. VILLADOM of the suburbs votes for the internal divisions of London, and again in the suburban boroughs.

1888. *Pall Mall Gaz.*, 29 Feb. The outlying districts are not sacred to VILLADOM.

VILLAGE (THE), *subs. phr.* (common).—London. Also the HARDWARE VILLAGE = Birmingham.

VILLAGE - BUSTLER, *subs. phr.* (old).—An active petty thief: a picker-up of trifles, unconsidered or the reverse.

VILLAIN, *subs.* (common). — A jocular self-reproach: *e.g.* 'I'm a bit of a VILLAIN myself, but ——'; or 'I'm as mild a VILLAIN as ever scuttled a ship.' Also as an endearment.

1604. SHAKSPEARE, *Winter's Tale*, i. 2. Sweet VILLAIN! most dearest! my collop.

VIM, *subs.* (common). — Spirit, activity, energy: orig. University slang [Latin].

1869. MCCLURE, *Tour through Rocky Mountains.* Virginia City is sobering down with the ebbing tide into substantial, legitimate business; but Helena has all the VIM, recklessness, extravagance, and jolly progress of a new camp.

1875. *New York Herald*, 17 Ap. Mr. Fullerton figuratively jumped into the ring, rolled up his sleeves, and squared off with a VIM and determination that sometimes makes victory half assured.

1876. *Providence Press*, 8 Jan. We are of those who believe that our system of school management can be improved, and made more efficient. We believe that more of VIM, snap, or activity can be infused into it, to the manifest advantage of every interest.

d. 1878. S. BOWLES [MERRIAM, *Life*, x. II. 7]. The men . . . have . . . a wide practical reach, a boldness, a sagacity, a VIM, that I do not believe can be matched anywhere in the world.

VINCENT'S-LAW, *subs. phr.* (gaming).—Cheating at cards.

VINEGAR, *subs.* (Old Cant).—A cloak (B. E.). Also *see* PEPPER.

VIOLET (or GARDEN-VIOLET), subs. (common).—1. An onion : spec. in pl.=spring onions used as a salad. Also (2), in pl.=sage-and-onion stuffing.

VIOLENTO, subs. (old).—A violent man : cf. FURIOSO, GLORIOSO, etc.

1662. FULLER, Worthies, 'Cumberland,' i. 236. In the Raign of Queen Mary he fled beyond the Seas, and was no VIOLENTO in the Troubles of Francford, but, with all meekness, to his might, endeavoured a pacification.

VIRAGO, subs. (B. E., c. 1696).—'A masculine woman, or a great two-handed female.'

VIRGIN, subs. (Stock Exchange).—In pl.=Virginia New Funded Stock.

VIRGINHEAD, subs. (old).—Virginity, the maidenhead.

1605. SYLVESTER, Eden, 662. Unlike it is Such blessed state the noble flowr should miss Of VIRGIN-HEAD.

1607. BEAUMONT, Woman Hater, i. 3. Thither must I To see my love's face, the chaste VIRGIN-HEAD Of a dear fish, yet pure and undeflower'd, Not known of man.

1611. DAVIES, Scourge of Folly, 23. Two foes of honord name in Honor's bed (The field) desirde (like virgins newly wiues) To lose their valour's lusty VIRGIN-HEAD.

VIRGINIA-FENCE, subs. phr. (American). — A zig-zag rail fence ; a WORM-FENCE (q.v.). TO WALK A VIRGINIA FENCE= to reel : of drunken men.

VIRGIN-KNOT, subs. phr. (venery).—The maiden-head, virginity, chastity. [In allusion to the girdle worn by Greek and Roman maidens when of marriageable age.]

1609. SHAKSPEARE, Tempest, iv. 1. Take my daughter : but If thou dost break her VIRGIN-KNOT before All sanctimonious ceremonies may With full and holy rite be minister'd.

VIRGIN MARY'S BODY-GUARD, subs. phr. (military).—The 7th Dragoon Guards. [They served under Maria Theresa of Austria, temp. George II.]

VIRGIN-TREASURE, subs. phr. (venery). — The female pudendum ; see MONOSYLLABLE.

d. 1638. CAREW, 'A Rapture.' There my enfranchised hand on every side Shall o'er thy naked polish'd ivory slide. No curtain there, though of transparent lawn, Shall be before thy VIRGIN-TREASURE drawn.

VIRTUE, subs. (common).—Smoking, drinking, whoring. When a man confesses to abstention from tobacco and intoxicating liquors he is perversely said to have no virtues.

VISH, adj. (Christ's Hospital).—Cross, 'vicious' : formerly PASSY (q.v.).

VISOR-MASK, subs. phr. (old).—A harlot : see TART.

1682. J. BANKS, Virtue Betrayed. Epilogue The VISOR-MASK that ventured her half-crown.

VIXEN (or FIXEN), subs. (colloquial).—An ill-natured, snarling man or woman, a termagant, a scold. Also VIXENISH (or VIXENLY) = ill-tempered, snappish, snarling, turbulent.

1563. Appius and Virginia [DODSLEY, Old Plays (HAZLITT), iv. 120]. By the gods, how ungraciously the VIXEN she chatteth.

1590. PEELE, Old Wives' Tale. I think this be the curstest quean in the world ; you see what she is, a little fair, but as proud as the devil, and the veriest VIXEN that lives upon God's earth.

1592. SHAKSPEARE, Mid. Night's Dream, iii. 2. 325. She was a VIXEN when she went to school ; And, though she be but little, she is fierce.

d. 1677. BARROW, Sermons, I. xvii. These fiery VIXENS . . . really do themselves embroil things, and raise miserable combustions in the world. Ibid., Pope's Supremacy. A VIXENLY pope.

1709. CONGREVE, Ovid's Art of Love. I hate a VIXON, that her Maid assails, And scratches with her Bodkin, or her Nails.

1816. SCOTT, Antiquary, xxii. His VIXEN brawls, and breaking God's peace and the King's.

1837. DICKENS, Pickwick, xiv. So Tom Smart and his clay-coloured gig with the red wheels, and the VIXENISH mare with the fast pace, went on together.

1849-61. MACAULAY, Hist. Eng., xv. 'That may be very honourable in you,' said the pertinacious VIXEN.

1850. HAWTHORNE, Scarlet Letter, Int. p. 4. VIXENLY as she looks many people are seeking . . . to shelter themselves under the wing of the federal eagle.

1866. ELIOT, Felix Holt, xi. The shrill biting talk of a VIXENISH wife.

VOCAB, subs. (Charterhouse).—A dictionary, 'VOCABULARY.'

VOCALIER, subs. (American).—A singer.

1876. BESANT and RICE, Golden Butterfly. Let things alone, and presently that young lady discovers that she is not likely to get cracked up as a VOCALIER.

VOL, adj. (Harrow School).—Voluntary : e.g. VOL-GYM.

VOLANT, subs. (old).—A Jack-of-both-sides, a trimmer. As adj.=giddy, flighty.

1740. NORTH, Examen, 63. And so they kept the VOLANT a good while, and did not declare on which side they would fall. Ibid., 474. The Dutch had acted the VOLANT, and done enough on the one side or the other to have kept the fire alive.

1753. RICHARDSON, Grandison, i. 274. Yes, my VOLANT, my self-conducted quill, begin with the sister.

1801. Poetry of Anti-Jacobin, 129. The eddying smoke, quick flame, and VOLANT spark.

VOLUNTARY, subs. (Winchester).—A copy of verses written occasionally by some in Sixth Book and Senior Part ex proprio motu (MANSFIELD, c. 1840).

VOUCHER, subs. (Old Cant).—A man or woman 'that passes off False Money for sham coyners' (B. E.) ; a SNIDE-PITCHER (q.v.).

c. 1680. 'Black Procession' [FARMER, MUSA PEDESTRIS]. The first was a Coiner, that stampt in a mould ; The second a VOUCHER, to put off his gold.

VOWEL, verb. (common).—To give an I.O.U. : e.g. TO VOWEL a debt.

VOWEL-MAULER, subs. phr. (common).—An indistinct speaker.

VOYAGE. HOBBE'S-VOYAGE, subs. phr. (venery).—The act of kind, copulation : see GREENS and RIDE.

1697. VANBRUGH, Provoked Wife, v. 3. Bel. Matrimony's the spot where I expect you. Heart. 'Tis enough, I'll not fail. (Aside) So now I am in for HOBBE'S VOYAGE ; a great leap in the dark.

VROW-CASE, subs. phr. (old).—A brothel : see NANNY-SHOP.

VULGUS, subs. (Winchester : obsolete).—A Latin epigram : four or six lines long. Hence VULGUS-BOOK=a CRIB (q.v.). [See FARMER, Public School Wordbook.]

1856. HUGHES, Tom Brown's Schooldays, II. iii. The VULGUS (commonly supposed to have been established by William of Wykeham at Winchester, and

imported to Rugby by Arnold, more for the sake of the lines which were learnt by heart with it than for its own intrinsic value, as I've always understood) . . . is a short exercise in Greek or Latin verse, on a given subject, the minimum number of lines being fixed for each form.

1883. TROLLOPE, What I Remember. The mention of a 'VULGUS requires some explanation. Every inferior, i.e. non-prefect, in the school was required every night to produce a copy of verses of from two to six lines on a given theme—four or six lines for the upper classes, two for the lowest. This was independent of a weekly verse task of greater length, and was called a VULGUS, I suppose, because everybody—the VULGUS—had to do it.

VUM. I VUM, phr. (American).—A mild expletive or oath, 'I vow' : cf. SWAN.

1856. DOW, Sermons, III. 265. What though, instead of saying, 'I swear to God,' you say, 'I declare to goodness?' It is as much the same thing as a bobolink with a new coat of feathers. I VUM is just the same in spirit as I vow, and a 'diabolical falsehood' is synonymous with a devilish lie.

1865. HOLMES, Deacon's Masterpiece. The Deacon swore (as Deacons do) With an 'I dew VUM,' or an 'I tell yeou.'

1870. JUDD, Margaret, 86. 'I VUM,' said he, 'I'm sorry ; what's the matter?'

 WABASH, verb (American).—To cheat, swindle, victimise.

WABBLE (or WOBBLE), verb (old, and still colloquial). — 1. To rock from side to side, move unsteadily, sway unevenly. Hence (2) to vacillate, play 'fast and loose,' 'blow hot and cold.' Whence as subs.=unsteady movement, fickleness, vacillation ; WABBLY =unsteady, shaky, ROCKY (q.v.) ; WABBLER=a waverer, shuffler, trimmer. Also WIBBLE-WABBLE (a reduplication). [JOHNSON : 'a low barbarous word.']

1862. SPENCER, First Principles, 170. When . . . the top falls on the table . . . it falls into a certain oscillation, described by the expressive though inelegant word—WOBBLING.

1876. Times, 21 Oct. The WABBLING of the shot, owing to the imperfect fit, has been the great drawback.

1879-89. GROVE, Dict. Music, III. 509. Ferri . . . made use of the tremolo upon every note, to such an extent that his whole singing was a bad WOBBLING trill.

1883. GURNEY [Nineteenth Century, xiii. 446]. Dismal sounds may express dismal emotions, and soft sounds soft emotions, and WABBLY sounds uncertain emotions.

1898. CLARK RUSSELL, Jack's Courtship, xx. The wind had raised a middling stiff WOBBLE on the water.

3. (Western American).—To make free use of one's tongue, to be ready of LIP (q.v.). Hence WABBLER=a fluent speaker, a chattering fool.

WABBLER, subs. (provincial).—1. A boiled leg of mutton.

2. See WABBLE.

WACK. See WHACK.

WAD, subs. (American).—A roll of bank-notes ; hence generic for money : see RHINO.

1887. FRANCIS, Saddle and Mocassin. Many scores of these philanthropists, who have spent their lives in looking for men to enrich, whilst anxious only to make a small WAD for themselves, have I encountered.

1896. LILLARD, Poker Stories, 102. Even in these days I knew a thing or two about poker, and it would have required George Appo himself to have touched me for my WAD.

WADDLE, verb (old).—'To go like a duck' (B. E.), to toddle, shamble, slouch. Hence, as subs. (or WADDLING)=an ungainly walk, a WABBLING (q.v.) gait. Also derivatives : WADDLER, WADDLY, WADDLINGLY, etc.

1595. SHAKSPEARE, Romeo and Juliet, i. 3. 37. Then she could stand alone ; nay, by the rood, She could have run and WADDLED all about.

1605. DRAYTON, Mooncalf. 'They tread and WADDLE all the goodly grass, That in the field there scarce a corner was Left free by them.'

1809. IRVING, *Knickerbocker*, 437. Every member WADDLED home as fast as his short legs could carry him, wheezing as he went with corpulency and terror.

1885. *D. Tel.*, 29 Sep. It knows it cannot move fast . . . and scorns to do more than WADDLE away moderately.

TO WADDLE OUT OF THE ALLEY, *verb. phr.* (old).—To make default on the Stock Exchange: *cf.* LAME DUCK.

1771. GARRICK, *Prologue to The Maid of Bath.* The gaming fools are doves, the knaves are rooks, Change-alley bankrupts WADDLE OUT lame ducks.

1787. *Whitehall Evening News* [quoted in FRANCIS, *Stock Exchange*]. There were no less than 25 lame ducks who WADDLED OUT OF THE ALLEY.

1846. MARRYAT, *Peter Simple*, III. xxv. 458. He was obliged to WADDLE: if I didn't know much about bulls and bears, I know very well what a lame duck is to my cost.

1860. PEACOCK, *Gryll Grange*, xviii. In Stock Exchange slang, Bulls are speculators for a rise, Bears for a fall. A lame duck is a man who cannot pay his differences, and is said to WADDLE OFF.

WADDLER, *subs.* (common).—A duck.

WADDY, *subs.* (Australian).—A walking-stick: properly a war-club.

1874. STEPHENS, *Poems* (*The Headless Trooper*). Thanks, generous colonial, Thou art very, very kind; Now pick a thickish WADDY up And plug my wound behind.

WADE, *subs.* (colloquial).—1. A ford; and (2) the act of wading. Also WADERS = long water-proof boots: used by sportsmen for wading through water.

1885. *Field*, 4 Ap. It was a WADE of nearly a mile, and every now and then the water just touched the ponies' bellies. *Ibid.*, 11 Sep. WADERS are of as much service on the swampy ground round the pool as for actually reaching fish rising some way out.

1888. *Fort. Rev.*, xliii. 632. An ardent votary of fly and bank-fishing, with WADERS and a two-handed rod.

WAFER-WOMAN, *subs. phr.* (old).—A bawd; procuress, go-between. Also WAFERER = a pander, a male bawd.

1607. BEAUMONT, *Woman-hater*, ii. 1. 'Twas no set meeting, Certainly, for there was no WAFER-WOMAN with her These three days, on my knowledge.

1765. BICKERSTAFF, *Maid of the Mill*, i. 3. Do you think me a babe? Am I not able, cousin, At my years and discretion, to deliver A letter handsomely? is that such a hard thing? Why, every WAFER-WOMAN will undertake it.

WAFFLE, *verb* (printers').—To talk incessantly, CLACK (*q.v.*), JAW (*q.v.*): at Durham School = to talk nonsense. [*Cf.* prov. Eng. WAFFLE = to bark, to yelp.]

1888. *D. Teleg.*, 3 Mar. Out they went into the bleak bitterness, the dogs running before them, and, as the people say, WAFFLING—that is, snuffing and whining—in their eagerness to get on.

WAFFLES, *subs.* (common).—A loafer, an idle sauntering person.

WAFRICAN, *subs.* (Stock Exchange).—In *pl.* = generic for West African stocks and shares: *cf.* WESTRALIAN.

1901. *West. Gaz.*, 7 Feb., 9. 1. WAFRICANS. One thing beloved in the Stock Exchange is abbreviation; and another is nickname. Kaffirs have been far too long established to lay any claim to the title Safricans, so that there is no danger of the use of the term to clash with WAFRICANS. There is already a WAFRICANA Syndicate, or something of the sort. Thus is the language murdered to the disgust of the purist.

WAG, *subs.* (old colloquial).—1. A buffoon, droll, practical joker. [Probably WAG-HALTER (*q.v.*) = a ROGUE (*q.v.*): *cf.* 'mad wag,' 'mad wag-halter,' etc.]. Also as a half-jocular, half-affectionate

slur. As *adj.* = 'Arch, Gamesome, Pleasant' (B. E.). As *verb* (or WAGGLE) = generic for (1) playful or sportive, and (2) mocking, scornful, or derisive motion. Hence WAGGERY, WAGGISHNESS, WAGGISH, etc.

c. 1550. UDAL, *Roister Doister* [K. O., i. 492].

1592. G. HARVEY, *Foure Letters*, Pref. But mildly and calmly shew how discredit reboundeth upon the anthors, as dust flyeth back into the WAG'S eyes that will needs be puffing it up.

1600. SHAKSPEARE, *Much Ado*, ii. 1. 119. I know you by the WAGGLING of your head. *Ibid.* (1601), *Henry VIII.*, v. 3. Let me see the proudest He, that dares most, but WAG his finger at thee.

1600. JONSON, *Cynthia's Revels*, ii. 1. A wanton WAGGING of your head. *Ibid.* (1609), *Epicœne*, v. 1. Let's wanton it a little and talk WAGGISHLY.

1607. HEYWOOD, *Fair Maid of the Exchange* [*Works*, II. 66]. And with the Nymphes that haunt the silver streames, Learne to entice the affable young WAGGE.

1607. DEKKER, *Northward Hoe*, iii. 2. WAG . . . WILT be secret?

1611. *Bible*, Matthew xxvii. 39. And they that passed by reviled him, WAGGING their heads.

1635. QUARLES, *Emblems*, ii. 12. Let ditch-bred wealth henceforth forget to WAG Her base though golden tail.

d. 1654. SELDEN, *Table Talk*, 97. He did by the Parliament as an Ape when he hath done some WAGGERY.

1655. *Com. Hist. Francion*, iv. 22. He said to the three buffles who stood with their hats in their hands, Tell me, you WAGGS, etc.

1677. WYCHERLEY, *Plain Dealer*, i. 1. Jack, thou thinkest thyself in the Forecastle, thou'rt so WAGGISH.

1710. STEELE, *Tatler*, 184. A WAG is the last order even of pretenders to wit and humour.

1726. VANBRUGH, *Journey to London*, iii. 1. *Sir Fran.* A prodigious civil gentleman, uncle; and yet as bold as Alexander upon occasion. *Unc. Rich.* Upon a lady's occasion. *Sir Fran.* Ha, ha, you are a WAG, uncle.

1820. IRVING, *Sketch-book*, 434. It left Brom no alternative but to draw upon the funds of rustic WAGGERY in his disposition.

1828. *Eng. Spy*, I. 189. The man upon that half-starved nag Is an ex-S——ff, a strange WAG, Half flash and half a clown.

1848. THACKERAY, *Book of Snobs*, xviii. She . . . WAGGLES her little hand before her face, as if to blow you a kiss, as the phrase is.

1851. LONGFELLOW, *Golden Legend*, vi. Let us see what the learned WAG maintains With such a prodigal waste of brains.

2. (school).—THE WAG = truancy. As *verb* (or TO PLAY, or HOP, THE WAG) = to be truant: also CHARLEY-WAG (*q.v.*).

1851-61. MAYHEW, *Lond. Lab.*, III. 207. They often persuaded me to HOP THE WAG.

1876. HINDLEY, *Cheap Jack*, 59. Readier to PLAY THE CHARLEY-WAG than to be . . . in any prominent position in his class or form.

1901. WALKER, *In the Blood*, 13. They had WAGGED it from school, as they termed it, which was an unvarying practice of theirs, and meant truancy in all its forms.

Verb (old).—1. *See* subs. *supra.*

2. (colloquial).—To stir, move, make way, progress.

1546. HEYWOOD, *Proverbs*. Let the world WAGGE and take mine ease in mine inne.

1600. SHAKSPEARE, *As You Like It*, ii. 7. Thus may we see, quoth he, how the world WAGS.

3. (colloquial).—To go, be off, depart, begone.

1589. PUTTENHAM, *Art of Eng. Poesie*, 194. It is said by maner of a prouerbial speach that he who findes himselfe well should not WAGGE.

1684. BUNYAN, *Pilgrim's Progress*, ii. They made a pretty good shift to WAG ALONG.

d. 1800. COWPER, *Yearly Distress*. Come, neighbours, we must WAG.

See AFRAID.

WAG-FEATHER, *subs. phr.* (common).—A silly swaggerer.

WAGGED-OUT, *adv.* (American).—Tired, worn out.

WAGGLE, *verb* (common).—1. To overcome, BEAT (*q.v.*), 'GET THE BETTER OF' (*q.v.*).

2. *See* WAG.

WAGGONER, *subs.* (old nautical).—A book of sea-charts: *cf.* LIDDEL AND SCOTT = a dictionary; CRUDEN = a concordance. [From Baron von Waegenaar's *Speculum Nauticum*, etc.]

1580. [EVANS, *Life Frampton*, 30.] The Captain . . . called for the WAGONER to enquire whether any rock had been observed by others that had formerly used those seas.

WAG-HALTER, *subs. phr.* (old).—A rogue, gallows-bird: *i.e.* one likely or deserving to wag in a halter; *cf.* CRACK-ROPE, HALTER-SACK, etc.

1594. LYLY, *Mother Bombie*, ii. v. I'le teach my WAG-HALTER to know grapes from barley.

1611. COTGRAVE, *Dict.*, s.v. *Babouin*. A craftie knave, a crack-rope, WAG-HALTER, unhappie rogue.

1611. TARLETON, *Jests*. A WAG-HALTER boy met Tarlton in the street, and said, Master Tarlton who lives longest?

1613. MARSTON, *Insatiate Countess*, i. I can tell you I am a mad WAG-HALTER.

1629. *Schoole of Good Manners*. To mocke anybody by blabboring out the tongue is the part of WAGHALTERS and lewd boyes, not of well mannered children.

1638. FORD, *Fancies*, ii. 2. Not so terrible as a cross-tree that never grows, to a WAG-HALTER page.

WAGON, *subs.* (American).—A bicycle.

WAG-PASTIE, *subs. phr.* (old).—A ROGUE, URCHIN, RASCAL (all of which *see*); an endearment.

1534. UDAL, *Roister Doister*, iii. 2. *M. Mery.* Maide, with whom are ye so hastie? *Tib.* Not with you, sir, but with a little WAGPASTIE, A deceiuer of folkes by subtill craft and guile.

WAGTAIL, *subs.* (old).—A term of familiarity or contempt: spec. a harlot (B. E. and GROSE): *see* TART. Hence, TO WAG THE TAIL (of women) = to wanton, to copulate: *see* GREENS and RIDE.

1605. SHAKSPEARE, *Lear*, ii. 2. Spare my grey beard, you WAGTAIL.

1607. MIDDLETON, *Michaelmas Term*, iii. 1. WAGTAIL, salute them all; they are friends.

WAG-WIT, *subs. phr.* (old).—A wag: in contempt.

1712. STEELE, *Spectator*, 354. All the WAGWITS in the highway are grinning in applause of the ingenious rogue.

WAISTCOAT. FŒTID WAISTCOAT, *subs. phr.* (obsolete—*c.* 1859).—A waistcoat of a flaunting and vulgar pattern.

WAISTCOATEER, *subs.* (old).—A harlot: *see* TART. [The waistcoat was formerly in use by both sexes: when worn by women without a gown or upper dress it was considered the mark of a mad, low, or profligate woman.]

1602. DEKKER, *Honest Whore* [DODSLEY, *Old Plays* (REED), iii. 291]. You'd best come like a mad-woman, without a band in your WAISTCOAT, and the linings of your kirtle outward.

c. 1614. FLETCHER, *Wit Without Money*, iv. 4. D'ye think you're here, sir, Among your WAST-COATEERS, your base wenches, That scratch at such occasions? you're deluded. *Ibid.* (1619), *Hum. Lieut.*, i. 1. Who keeps the outward door there? here's fine shuffling. You WASTCOATEER, you must go back.

1659. MASSINGER, *City Madam*, iii. 1. I knew you a WAISTCOATEER in the garden alleys, And would come to a sailor's whistle.

1712. HERRICK, *Poor Robin*. Some shall be so incentive to lust, that every woman shall be devil enough to tempt him, from the Covent Garden silk gowns, to the Wapping WASTCOATIERS.

WAISTER, *subs.* (obsolete nautical).—A seaman or boy of little use, a GREEN (*q.v.*) hand: if inexperienced or broken-down, such as these were placed in the waist of a man-of-war for duties not requiring much exertion or seamanship. Also (modern) = a new whaling hand.

WAIT. TO WAIT FOR DEAD MEN'S SHOES, *verb. phr.* (common).—To look forward to an inheritance.

d. 1660. FLETCHER, *Poems*, 256. And 'tis a general shrift, that most men use, But yet 'tis tedious WAITING DEAD MEN'S SHOES.

1758. MURPHY, *Upholsterer*, i. I grant ye, ma'am, you have very good pretensions; but then it's WAITING FOR DEAD MEN'S SHOES.

1764. WILKES [FITZGERALD'S *Life* (1888), i. 244]. As they have no other relation but Miss Wilkes, I therefore suppose they will leave everything to her, independent of me. Yet this is, after all, WAITING FOR DEAD MEN'S SHOES.

1878. WALL, *Molière*, ii. 218. Death is not always ready to indulge the heir's wishes and prayers, and we may starve while WAITING FOR DEAD MEN'S SHOES.

1902. *Pall Mall Gaz.*, 26 July, 2. 3. WAITING FOR DEAD MEN'S SHOES is a tedious business, especially when the shoes in question are a pair of Turkish slippers.

TO WAIT ON ONE, *verb. phr.* (colloquial).—To seek a chance of retaliation, revenge, or spite; to try and get one's own back.

WAITER. MINORITY-WAITER, *subs. phr.* (old).—A waiter out of employment: *i.e.* as one out of (political) office.

1778. SHERIDAN, *Rivals*, ii. 1. I told Thomas that your Honour had already inlisted five disbanded chairmen, seven MINORITY WAITERS, and thirteen billiard markers.

WAKE. TO WAKE SNAKES, *verb. phr.* (American).—1. To rouse oneself, to be up and doing; and (2) to get into trouble.

1848. LOWELL, *Biglow Papers*. This goin' where glory awaits ye hain't one agreeable featur'; And, if it warn't for WAKIN' SNAKES, I'd be home agin short metre.

1850. *Southern Sketches*, 119. Well, here I be: WAKE SNAKES, the day's a-breaking.

1855. HALIBURTON, *Human Nature*, 164. Come, WAKE SNAKES, and push off with the captain, and get the fish on board.

1863. *Punch*, Aug. 'Mexico and Monroe-Land.' So then, as Mexico's gone goose And WAKIN' SNAKES, it ain't no use; Agin old Bull let's vengeance vow, And take no action else just now.

TO WAKE UP THE WRONG PASSENGER, *verb. phr.* (American).—To make a mistake, 'get the wrong sow by the ear': *see* WRONG PASSENGER.

WALER, *subs.* (colonial).—Orig. a cavalry horse imported into India from New South Wales; now applied to all 'cattle' brought from Australia.

1863. HEYWOOD, *Vacation Tour at the Antipodes*, 134. Horses are exported largely from Australia to India even. I have heard men from Bengal talk of the WALERS, meaning horses from New South Wales.

1866. TREVELYAN, *Dawk Bungalow*, 223. Well, young Shaver, have you seen the horses? How is the WALER'S off foreleg?

1873. *Madras Mail*, 25 June. For sale. A brown WALER gelding (*Advt.*).

1888. KIPLING, *Plain Tales from the Hills*, 224. The soul of the Regiment lives in the Drum-Horse who carries the silver kettle-drums. He is nearly always a big piebald WALER.

1896. *Melburnian*, 28 Aug., 62. Gaunt won the Regimental Cup Steeplechase this year on an Australian mare of his own. Australian horses are called WALERS in India, from the circumstance of their being generally imported from New South Wales.

WALK, *subs.* (colloquial). — A special haunt, place of resort, or ROUND (*q.v.*): an extension of the ordinary usage. Thus a MILKMAN'S (CAT'S-MEAT-MAN'S, POSTMAN'S, etc.) WALK = the district habitually served by a salesman (postman, etc.); a BANK-WALK = the round of a banker's collecting clerk; THE WALK (Royal Exchange) = that portion of the promenade frequented by some particular clique or set of merchants.

1851-61. MAYHEW, *Lond. Lab.*, II. He had thoughts at one time of trying to establish himself in a CAT'S-MEAT WALK.

COCK (or HEN) OF THE WALK (club, school, etc.), *subs. phr.* (common). — A man (or woman) of parts, a worthy, a leader.

1711. *Spectator*, 131. Service to the knight. Sir Andrew is grown the COCK OF THE CLUB since he left us, and if he does not return quickly will make every mother's son of us commonwealth's men.

1729. SWIFT, *Grand Question Debated*. But at cuffs I was always the COCK OF THE SCHOOL.

1764. O'HARA, *Midas*, i. 1. COCK OF THE SCHOOL. He bears despotic rule.

1862. WOOD, *Channings*, xxix. Were I going in for the seniorship, and one below me were suddenly hoisted above my head, and made a COCK OF THE WALK, I'd know the reason why.

d. 1863. THACKERAY, *Miscellanies*, II. 275. There is no more dangerous or stultifying position for a man in life than to be a COCK OF SMALL SOCIETY.

1899. WHITEING, *John St.*, xxiii. This HEN OF THE WALK of our slum is really herself. . . . Who can jaw a copper like Tilda, or carney a Covent Garden salesman . . . or take the size out of a chaffing swell?

LADIES' (or GENTLEMEN'S) WALK, *subs. phr.* (American).— A W.C.: a euphemism (hotel-proprietors').

TO WALK THE STREETS, *verb. phr.* (common).—To frequent the streets for the purpose of prostitution; to make public quest for men.

1887. *St. James's Gazette*, 2 July. The other prisoner was in the habit of WALKING the Quadrant.

TO WALK INTO, *verb. phr.* (colloquial). — 1. To attack, assault, drub: also TO WALK INTO THE AFFECTIONS; (2)=to scold, RAG (*q.v.*), SLANG (*q.v.*); (3)=to demolish, overcome, get the best of; and (4) to eat heartily, to WOLF (*q.v.*).

1840. DICKENS, *Old Curiosity Shop*, lxviii. There is little Jacob, WALKING . . . INTO a home-made plum-cake, at a most surprising pace.

1840. HALIBURTON, *Sam Slick*, III. 122. To WALK INTO a Down-East land-jobber requires great skill, and a very considerable knowledge of human nature.

1853. BRADLEY, *Verdant Green*. When he told Verdant that . . . his bread-basket WALKED INTO, his day-lights darkened.

1858 *New York Herald*, 16 Sept. The way in which the *Courier* and *Enquirer* WALK INTO the character and reputation of some of their old associates in the Clay movement is a caution to respectable blackguards.

c. 1859. HIRAM BIGELOW [*Letter* in *Fam. Comp.*]. [BARTLETT]. I went into the dining-room, and sot down afore a plate that had my name writ on a card onto it, and I did WALK INTO the beef, and taters, and things, about east.

TO WALK THE CHALK, *verb. phr.* (orig. American).—1. To walk along a chalk line as a test of sobriety. Hence (2) to go straight in conduct, manners, or morals, to keep up to the mark.

1840. HALIBURTON, *Clockmaker*, 3 S., xi. The way she WALKS HER CHALKS ain't no matter. She is a regular fore-and-after.

1843. *Comic Almanack*, 366. And since my future walk's chalk'd out—at once I'll WALK MY CHALKS.

1871. DE VERE, *Americanisms*, 318. The President, in whom he is disappointed for one reason or another, does not come up to chalk; when he dismisses an official, he is made to WALK THE CHALK.

18[?]. *Simon Suggs* [BARTLETT], 89. 'The Tallapoosa volunteers,' said Captain Suggs; 'so let everybody look out and WALK THE CHALK.'

TO WALK ONE'S CHALKS (or TO WALK), *verb. phr.* (common).— To decamp, move on, go about one's business: *see* CHALK for suggested origin.

[*d.* 1599. SPENSER, *State of Ireland*. When he comes foorth, he will make theyr cowes and garrans to WALKE.]

1853. READE, *Gold*, iv. 2. There are riflemen among them that will bring you down like squirrels if you don't WALK YOUR CHALKS in good time.

1873. TROLLOPE, *Phineas Redux*, i. Browborough has sat for the place now for three Parliaments. . . . I am told that he must WALK if anybody would go down who could talk to the colliers every night for a week or two.

THE GHOST WALKS (or DOESN'T WALK), *phr.* (theatrical).—There is (or is not) money in the treasury.

1853. *Household Words*, 183. When no salaries are forthcoming the GHOST DOESN'T WALK.

1883. *Referee*, 24 June, 3, 2. An Actors' Benevolent Fund box placed on the treasurer's desk every day when THE GHOST WALKS would get many an odd shilling or sixpence put into it.

1885. *The Stage*, 112. The rogues seldom appear at a loss for a plausible story when it is time for the GHOST TO WALK. *Ibid.* The next day THE GHOST DECLINES TO WALK.

1889. J. C. COLMAN (in *Slang, Jargon, and Cant*), 405. GHOST-WALKING, a term originally applied by an impecunious stroller in a sharing company to the operation of 'holding the treasury,' or paying the salaries, which has become a stock facetiæ among all kinds and descriptions of actors. Instead of inquiring whether the treasury is open, they generally say—'Has the GHOST WALKED?' or 'What, has this thing appeared again?' (Shakspeare).

1890. *Illustrated Bits*, 29 Mar., 11. 1. And a few nights with empty benches LAID THE GHOST completely. It could not even WALK to the tune of quarter salaries.

TO WALK THE PLANK, *verb. phr.* (nautical).—To walk overboard, to die: formerly an old method of execution or vengeance, the victim being forced to walk blindfolded along a plank over the ship's side.

TO WALK INTO ONE'S AFFECTIONS, *verb. phr.* (common).— 1. TO WALK INTO (*q.v. supra*); and (2) to get into debt.

TO WALK OVER, *verb. phr.* (racing).—To win a race without opposition; hence to win easily. WALK-OVER = an unopposed success, complete triumph. [Spec. of a horse, coming alone, of all the entries, to the scratch; it has consequently but to WALK OVER the course at leisure to be entitled to the stake.]

c. 1859. *Vicksburg Herald* [BARTLETT]. What a difference it makes to a candidate, when he knows he is offered a WALK-OVER instead of a forlorn hope.

1884. *Century Mag.*, xxxviii. 403. That's the bay stallion there . . . and he's never been beaten. It's his WALK-OVER.

1887. *Field*, 13 Aug. He then proceeded to WALK OVER the imaginary course for the imaginary plate. *Ibid.*, 25 June. In cases where no second horse exists in racing law, either for want of placing or by reason of a WALK-OVER.

WALK, KNAVE, WALK, *phr.* (old).—'A rude phrase which parrots were taught to use' (FAIRHOLT).

1592. LYLY, *Mydas*, i. 2. *Pet.* That's a leaden dagger in a velvet sheath, to have a blacke tongue in a faire mouth. *Lecio.* Tush, it is not for the blacknesse, but for the babling, for every hour she will cry, WALKE, KNAVE, WALKE.

1663-78. BUTLER, *Hudibras*. [Who] could tell what subtlest parrots mean, That speak and think contrary clean; What member 'tis of whom they talk, When they cry *rope*, and WALK, KNAVE, WALK.

Also in VARIOUS PHRASES: Thus TO WALK ALONE = to be an outcast, forsaken, shunned; TO WALK THE HOSPITALS = to attend the medical and surgical practice of hospitals as a student under one of the qualified staff; TO WALK SPANISH = to be seized by the scruff and the seat and thus forced along, to act under compulsion; TO WALK ABOUT (military) = an occasional instruction from officers to sentinels for the purpose of waiving the ceremony of the salute; TO WALK THE PEGS (gaming) = to 'sharp' one's pegs forward or those of one's antagonist backward (cribbage); TO WALK (or JUMP) DOWN ONE'S THROAT = to rate, scold, abuse; TO WALK UP LADDER-LANE AND DOWN HEMP-STREET = to be hanged at the yardarm: *see* LADDER; TO WALK ROUND ONE = to get an advantage, or the bulge over.

1853. HALIBURTON, *Wise Saws*, 20. My ambassadors, said the President, may not dance as elegantly as European courtiers, but they can WALK ROUND them in a treaty, that's a fact.

WALKER, *subs.* (old). — 1. A prowler, MOUCHER (*q.v.*): spec. one questing for opportunities of theft or harlotry: also (later) NIGHT - WALKER and STREET-WALKER.

c. 1380. *P. Plowman's Crede* [E.E.T.S.], 90. Wepyng, y warne ȝow of WALKERS aboute; It beth enemyes of the cros that crist upon tholede.

1544. ASCHAM, *Toxophilus*. Men that hunt so be privy stealers, or NIGHT WALKERS.

1620. BEAUMONT and FLETCHER, *Chances*, ii. 1. Sure these fellows Were NIGHT SNAPS. *Ibid. The* NIGHT WALKER, *or the Little Thief* [Title].

1637. MASSINGER, *Guardian*, v. 2. *Ador.* You have been, Before your lady gave you entertainment, A NIGHT-WALKER in the streets. *Mirt.* How, my good lord! *Ador.* Traded in picking pockets.

1664. ETHEREGE, *Comical Revenge*, iv. 2. *Grace.* Do you take me for a NIGHT-WALKER, Sir?

1693. CONGREVE, *Old Batchelor*, i. 5. The knight was alone, and had fallen into the hands of some NIGHT-WALKERS, who, I suppose, would have pillaged him.

1708. HATTON, *New View of London* [quoted in ASHTON'S *Soc. Life in Reign of Q. Anne*], vii. 238. Loose and disorderly Servants, NIGHT-WALKERS, Strumpets.

c. 1707. DURFEY, *Pills to Purge*, iii. 99. Now Miss turn NIGHT-WALKER.

2. (old).—In *pl.* = the feet.

1603. CHAPMAN, *Iliad*, xx. 36. And with them halted down (Proud of his strength) lame Mulciber, his WALKERS quite misgrown.

3. (colloquial). — A postman [HOTTEN: from an old song called, 'WALKER, the twopenny postman.']

HOOKEY WALKER (or WALKER), *intj.* (common).—1. An ironical expression of incredulity, BENDER (*q.v.*), GAMMON (*q.v.*); also (2) Be off! Clear out! (GROSE, VAUX, *Lex. Bal.*).

1837. BARHAM, *Ingoldsby Legends*, 'Old Woman Clothed in Gray.' Her senses were wandering—she seem'd not to hear, Or, at least, understand—for mere unmeaning talk her Parch'd lips babbled now, such as 'Hookey,' and WALKER!

1843. DICKENS, *Christmas Carol* [1843], 169. 'Buy it,' said Scrooge. 'WALKER!' said the boy.

1840. 'Characters of Freshmen' (WHIBLEY, *Cap and Gown*, 183). The pestilent freshman . . . is very pugnacious, and walking in the streets suddenly turneth and asketh a huge snob 'what the deuce he meant by that?' Whereat the snob (having done nothing at all) coolly answereth (as the Pestilent Freshman intended he should) HOOKY WALKER, provocative of a combat.

WALKING-MORT, *subs. phr.* (Old Cant). — A tramp or gypsy's woman: *see* MORT.

WALKING-PAPERS (or -TICKET), *subs. pl.* (American).—Dismissal. Thus, TO GET ONE'S WALKING-PAPERS = to get the SACK (*q.v.*), to be sent about one's business, 'with (spec.) a flea in one's ear.'

1840. CROCKETT, *Tour Down East*, 30. Mr. Duane was ordered to remove the deposits. He answered that his duty did not require it. In a few hours, he got his WALKING TICKET that his services were no longer wanted.

1843. *Kingston Whig* (Canada), Dec. We can announce with certainty that the Honourable Mr. D—— has received his WALKING TICKET, accompanied with some correspondence with his Excellency that has given him offence.

18[?]. *Widow Bedott Papers*, 307. 'If you ever question me again,' said Mrs. Samsom Savage, 'you'll get your WALKING TICKET in short order.'

c. 1859. *New York Herald*, Letter from Washington [BARTLETT]. It is probable that WALKING PAPERS will be forwarded to a large proportion of the *corps diplomatique* during the session of Congress. B—— and B—— are already admonished to return, and the invitation will be pretty general.

WALL, *subs.* (Eton).—Two football games are played at Eton— one at the WALL, the other in the FIELD. The first is only played by a very limited number of boys, for there is but one wall; the game is of an intricate nature, and the uninitiated spectator cannot, as a rule, even see how a point, called a Shy, is obtained. Indeed, were it not for the time-honoured match between Collegers and Oppidans on St. Andrew's Day the game would probably become obsolete. The Eton FIELD game has many merits as a game for boys superior to those of any other kind of football. In it speed, and skilful dribbling, and accurate kicking have their due success, but strength and dogged perseverance are not left out in the cold (*Great Public Schools*).

Verb. (Oxford).—To confine to College bounds: *cf.* GATE.

1860. *Macmillan's Mag.*, II. 222. To gate or WALL a refractory student.

GO-BY-THE-WALL, *subs. phr.* (old).—Strong ale.

PHRASES. AT (or TO) THE WALL = in difficulties; TO GO TO THE WALL = to be slighted, ousted, put on one side, to succumb to force of circumstances, to go UNDER (*q.v.*); LAID BY THE WALL = dead, but unburied; TO DRIVE TO THE WALL = to force to give way, to crush; TO TAKE THE WALL = to walk nearest the wall in passing; hence TO GET THE BETTER OF (or the advantage): *cf.* 'to get to WINDWARD' (*q.v.*): THE WALL (=the right of choice of way) was in olden times the safest and cleanest; TO HANG BY THE WALL=to be neglected, remain disused; TO SEE AS FAR INTO A BRICK WALL (MILLSTONE or MILESTONE) as . . .=to be as able (or as cute) as . . .; 'Look on the WALL, and it will not bite you' (a jeer to one whose tongue has been bitten by mustard); 'WALLS have ears' ='Be careful, someone may be listening.'

1530. TYNDALE, *Works*, i. 329. HOLD heretics TO THE WALL [OLIPHANT, *New Eng.* i. 431. . . . the first hint of the place whither the weakest go].

1533. *Thersites* [DODSLEY, *Old Plays* (HAZLITT), i. 401]. They GIVE me THE WALL.

[1546. HEYWOOD, *Proverbs*, II. v. Fieldes have eies, and woodes have eares.] *Ibid.* She had seene far IN A MILSTONE. *Ibid.* DRIVE him TO THE WALL.

1579–80. LYLY, *Euphues*, 53. The weakest must still TO THE WALL. *Ibid.* (1594), *Mother Bombie*, ii. 1. *Lucio.* I see not yet what you goe about. *Dro.* Lucio, that can PIERCE A MUD WALL of twentie foot thicke, would make us beleeve hee cannot see a candle through a paper lanthorne.

1595. SHAKSPEARE, *Romeo*, i. 1. That shews thee a weak slave; for the weakest goes TO THE WALL. *Ibid.* Women being the weaker vessels are ever THRUST TO THE WALL. *Ibid.* I will TAKE THE WALL of any man or maid. *Ibid.* (1605), *Cymbeline*, iii. 4. I am richer than to HANG BY THE WALLS.

1605. HEYWOOD, *If You Know not Me*, i. Since you will needs HAUE THE WALL, Ile take the pains to thrust you into the kennel.

1672. WYCHERLEY, *Love in a Wood.* WALLS HAVE EARS.

WALLABY. ON THE WALLABY (or WALLABY-TRACK), *phr.* (Australian).—Tramping the country on foot looking for work. [MORRIS: WALLABY = a small kangaroo. Often in the bush the only perceptible tracks, and sometimes the only tracks by which the scrub can be penetrated, are the tracks worn down by the WALLABY, as a hare tramples its 'form.' These tracks may lead to water or they may be aimless and rambling. Thus the man ON THE WALLABY may be looking for food or for work, or aimlessly wandering by day and getting food and shelter as a SUNDOWNER (*q.v.*) at night.]

1869. CLARKE, *Peripatetic Philosopher* (Reprint), 41. The Wimmera district is noted for the hordes of vagabond 'loafers' that it supports, and has earned for itself the name of 'The Feeding Track.' I remember an old bush ditty, which I have heard sung when *I* was ON THE WALLABY. . . . At the station where I worked for some time (as 'knock-about man') three cooks were kept during the WALLABY season—one for the house, one for the men, and one for the travellers.

1890. BOLDREWOOD, *Colonial Reformer*, 82. 'What is the meaning of OUT ON THE WALLABY?' asked Ernest. 'Well, it's bush slang, sir, for men just as you or I might be now, looking for work or something to eat; if we can't get work, living on the country, till things turn round a little.'

1893. GILBERT PARKER, *Pierre and his People*, 242. The WALLABY TRACK? That's the name in Australia for trampin' west, through the plains of the Never Never Country, lookin' for the luck o' the world.

1894. LONGMANS, *Notes on Books* (31 May), 206. 'ON THE WALLABY: a Book of Travel and Adventure.'

1894. CARMICHAEL [*Australasian*, 22 Dec., 1127. 5]. A WALLABY Christmas, Jack, old man!—Well, a worse fate might befall us! The bush must do for our church to-day, And birds be the bells to call us.

1896. LAWSON, *When the World was Wide.* 134. Though joys of which the poet rhymes Was not for Bill an' me: I think we had some good old times Out ON THE WALLABY.

WALLAH. *See* COMPETITION WALLAH.

WALL-EYED, *adj. phr.* (colloquial).—1. Having eyes with an undue proportion of white; 'all white like a plastered wall' (GROSE): hence (2)=glaring, fierce, threatening. Any work irregularly or ill done is called a WALL-EYED job. It is applied also to any very irregular action.

1580. BARET, *Alvearie.* A horse with a WALL-EYE, glauciolus.

1596. SHAKSPEARE, *King John*, iv. 3. 49. This is . . . the vilest stroke That ever WALL-EYED wrath, or staring rage, Presented to the tears of soft remorse.

1600. JONSON, *Cynthia's Revels*, v. 2. A pair of WALL-EYES in a face forced.

1766. GOLDSMITH, *Vicar*, x. Blackberry was WALL-EYED, and the colt wanted a tail.

WALLFLOWER, *subs.* (common).—1. Orig. a lady unable to obtain a partner in a dance; now applied to anyone of either sex who goes to a ball but does not dance, whether from inability, choice, or neglect. As *adj.*=neglected, *passé.*

d. 1830. PRAED, *County Ball.* The maiden WALLFLOWERS of the room Admire the freshness of his bloom.

1860. HOLMES, *Professor*, vi. Men . . . have shown as much self-devotion in carrying a lone WALLFLOWER down to the supper-table as ever saint or martyr in the act that has canonized his name.

1881. BRADDON, *Asphodel*, xx. Whom he had incontinently left to her own reflections, or to such conversation as she might be able to find among sundry other dowagers arrived at the same WALLFLOWER stage of existence.

1902. *Free Lance*, 22 Nov., 192. 1. When the old formula of 'Ladies first' In good society will be reversed, And male WALL-FLOWERS sitting out at dances Will reckon up their matrimonial chances.

2. (common).—In *pl.*=second-hand garments exposed for sale: *cf.* HAND-ME-DOWNS, REACH-ME-DOWNS, etc.

WALLOP, *verb* (common).—To beat, flog, thrash. Also as *subs.* =a severe blow; WALLOPING= a good trouncing. Also WALLOPER.

1838. NEAL, *Charcoal Sketches.* All I know was WALLOPPING into me; I took larnin' through the skin. *Ibid.* (1850), *Orson Dabbs.* There's nothing like WALLOPPING for taking the conceit out of fellows who think they know more than their betters.

1843–4. HALIBURTON, *Attaché*, xviii. I grabs right hold of the cow's tail, and yelled and screamed like mad, and WALLOPED away at her like anything.

1851–61. MAYHEW, *London Lab.*, I. 468. He kept me without grub and WALLOPED me.

1861. *Times*, 'On American Affairs.' Let us WALLOP great Doodle now when he is down, If we WALLOPS him well we will do him up brown.

1888. *Scribner's Mag.*, Nov., 79. Trying to get at a good place to WALLOP you with his ferule.

2. (provincial).—Generic for great effort or agitation: *e.g.* (*a*) to boil and bubble: *see* POT-WALLOPER; (*b*) move or gallop quickly; (*c*) to tumble about. Also as *subs.*, with the usual derivatives.

c. 1360. *William of Palerne* [E.E.T.S], 1770. Or he wiste, he was war of the white beres, Thei went a-wai a WALLOP as thei wod semed.

c. 1400. *Generydes* [E.E.T.S.], 3325 And he anon to hym com WALOPING.

c. 1440. *Merlin* [E.E.T.S.], ii. 233. Than the Kynge rode formest hym-self a grete WALOP, for sore hym longed to wite how the Kynge Tradilynaunt hym contened.

c. 1440. *Morte Arthure* [E.E.T.S.], 2147. Swerdez swangene in two, Sweltand Knyghtez Lyes wyde opyne welterande one WALOPANDE stedes.

d. 1691. BARLOW, *Hasty Pudding*, i. The yellow flour . . . Swells in the flood and thickens to a paste, Then puffs and WALLOPS.

1816. SCOTT, *Antiquary*, xxx. She WALLOPPED away with all the grace of triumph.

WALLOPING, *adj.* (common).—Great, bouncing. Also WALLOPER=anything superlative: *see* WHOPPER.

1903. HYNE, *Filibusters*, xix. One day I got a bit of a cheerer. I came upon a WALLOPPING great stone, which I found that with a bit of a push would move.

WALLYFORD, *subs.* (Loretto).—The usual run on a wet whole school-day: about 3½ miles.

WALTHAM'S-CALF. AS WISE AS WALTHAM'S CALF, *phr.* (old).—Very foolish.

d. 1529. SKELTON, *Colin Clout.* . . . As WYSE AS WALTHAM'S CALF . . . He can nothing smatter Of logicke nor scole matter.

1567. *Disclosing of the great Bull* [*Harl. Misc.*, vii. 535]. Some running and gadding calves, WISER than WALTHAM'S CALFE that ranne nine miles to sucke a bull.

WALTZ. TO WALTZ ABOUT (or ROUND), *verb. phr.* (common).—To move in a sprightly fashion, to buzz round. Also to fuss about, make oneself a nuisance.

WAMBLE-CROPPED, *adj. phr.* (colloquial).—Wretched, humiliated: also WOMBLE-CROPPED.

18[?]. *Widow Bedott Papers*, 284. The Captain looked so awful WOMBLE-CROPT that I pitied him. I never saw such an uncomfortable-looking countenance.

1848. MAJOR DOWNING, *Letter from Baton Rouge*, June 15. I never saw Captain Jumper so wilted down before, and that made me feel so WAMBLE-CROPT I could not say a word.

WAME. TO NAIL TWA WAMES THEGITHER, *verb. phr.* (Scots venery).—To copulate: *see* GREENS AND RIDE. [WAME= belly.] Hence TO GET THE WAME UP=to be got with child, to be LUMPY (*q.v.*).

1568. *Bannatyne MSS.*, 'The Use o. Court' (Hunt. Club), 765. VP GETTIS HER WAME, Scho thinkis no schame For to bring hame The laird ane herne.

WAND, *subs.* (venery).—The *penis*: *see* PRICK (DUNELM).

WANGER. *See* WHANGER.

WANION, *subs.* (old).—Misfortune, calamity, mischief, a curse. Thus WITH (or IN) A WANION=(1) 'Mischief take you,' 'Blast you'; with a vengeance; and hence (2) summarily, emphatically: also WANIONS ON YOU! [*Cf.* M. E. WANIAND (with quots.) = the waning of the moon, and spec. regarded as presaging ill-luck.]

[1362. *York Plays*, 124. Be they kyngis or knyghtis, in care ȝe thaim cast; ȝaa, and welde tham in woo to wonne, IN THE WANYAND.]

[*c.* 1401. *Townley Mysteries*, 241. OLIPHANT, *New Eng.*, i. 202. There is the strange phrase IN THE WENYANDE; in the unlucky time when the moon wanes; hence the curse, 'with a wanion.']

1549. LATIMER, *Sermons*, 36b. Was not this a good prelate? He should have beene at home preaching in his dioces WITH A WANNION.

1570. FOX, *Eccles. Hist.*, II. 457. 1. The pope—sent into France Hildebrand, his cardinal chaplaine (as meet a mate for such a feat, as was in all Satan's court), and made him WITH A WANIE to come againe *coram nobis.*

1605. JONSON, *Eastward Ho*, iii. 2. Marry, hang you, westward, WITH A WANION to you. *Ibid.* (1625), *Staple of News*, iii. 5. Act fables of false news, in this manner, to the super vexation of town and country, WITH A WANION.

1609. SHAKSPEARE, *Pericles*, ii. 1. 17. Come away, or I'll fetch thee WITH A WANNION.

1611. BEAUMONT, *Kn. of Burn. Pestle*, ii. 1. I'll tell Ralph a tale in his ear, shall fetch him again WITH A WANION, I'll warrant him.

1663. DRYDEN, *Wild Gallant*, iii. I'll teach you to take place of tradesmen's wives, WITH A WANNION to you.

1694. MOTTEUX, *Rabelais*, IV. xlvii. Ho, clod-pate, where art thou? Come out with a vengeance, come out WITH A WANNION.

1820. SCOTT, *Abbot.* I sent him out of my company WITH A WANION. *Ibid.* (1822), *Fort. of Nigel.* Bide down with a mischief to you—bide down WITH A WANION.

WANKER, *subs.* (Felsted School).—A bloater. [A master supplies: 'From stinker—stwanker—wanker.']

1892. *Felstedian*, Oct., 105. My name it is WANKER; a leaner or lanker, Salter or ranker fish never swam. *Ibid.* (1897), June, 100. He sniffs. 'Eugh, WANKERS again.

WANKY, *adj.* (printers').—Spurious, bad, wrong: *e.g.* a WANKY tanner =a SNIDE (*q.v.*) sixpence.

WANT. *See* KNOW.

WA'N'T, *verb* (colloquial).—Was not: also WARNT.

1699. VANBRUGH, *False Friend.* WA'N'T.

WANTAGE, *subs.* (American).—A deficiency; a shortage.

1888–9. *New York Prod. Exch. Rept.*, 256. Inspectors and gaugers should make a detailed return of . . . the gauge, WANTAGE, proof, and number of proof gallons.

WANTED, *ppl. adj.* (euphemistic). —'WANTED' by the police. (GROSE).

1885. *D. Teleg.*, 19 Dec. Two men supposed to be on board of a vessel which was loading at Hebburn Coal staithes, were WANTED in Germany for murder.

1883. GREENWOOD, *Tag, Rag, & Co.* The police, on their part, caused it to be understood that until he was really WANTED on a specific charge, a thief should in no case be interfered with.

WANTER, *subs.* (old colloquial).—1. A person in need of anything: *cf.* HAVES and HAVE-NOTS. Also (2) spec. =an unmarried person, 'one in want of a mate' (HALLIWELL).

1611. DAVIES, *Scourge of Folly*, 21. The WANTERS are despised of God and men.

WANT-GRACE, *subs. phr.* (old).—A reprobate.

1603. DAVIES, *Microcosmos*, 57. And rather than they should not die by force, Or want a WANT-GRACE to performe the deede, Their Vncle and Protector must perforce Their crowne from head, and head from life diuorce.

WAP, *verb* (Old Cant).—1. To copulate: *see* GREENS and RIDE. Hence WAPPING-MORT (or DELL) =a harlot: *see* TART; WAPPENED =(1) deflowered, (2) wanton, and (3) foundered. [The uncertainty on the part of Shakspearean editors as to 'wappened' and 'wappered' would seem to be elucidated by the canting use of WAP and its obvious popularity as instanced by the quotations.—J.S.F.]

1609. SHAKSPEARE, *Timon of Athens*, iv. 3. [Gold] makes the WAPP'END widow wed again: She, whom the spital-house and ulcerous sores Would cast the gorge at, this embalms and spices To the April day again.

1610. ROWLANDS, *Martin Mark-all*, 39 (H. Club's Rept., 1874). Nigling, company keeping with a woman: this word is not used now, but WAPPING, and thereof comes the name WAPPING MORTS, Whoores.

c. 1611. BEAUMONT and FLETCHER, *Two Noble Kinsmen*, v. 4. We come towards the gods Young and UNWAPPER'D, not halting under crimes.

1612. DEKKER, '*Bingout, bien Morts*,' v. [FARMER, *Musa Pedestris* (1896), 11]. And WAPPING DELL that niggles well, and takes loure for her hire.

c. 1696. B. E., *Dict. Cant. Crew*, s.v. WAP c., to Lie with a Man. If she won't WAP for a Winne, let her trine for a Make, If she won't Lie with a Man for a Penny, let her Hang for a Half-penny. MORT WAP-APACE, a Woman of Experience, or very expert at the sport.

1707. SHIRLEY, *Triumph of Wit*, 'Maunder's Praise of Strowling Most.' WAPPING thou I know does love . . . then remove, Thy drawers, and let's prig in sport.

1725. *Canting Songs*. This doxy dell can cut been whids, And WAP well for a win, And prig and cloy so benshiply Each deuseavile within.

2. *See* WHOP.

WAPPER. *See* WHOPPER.

WAPPER-EYED, *adj. phr.* (B. E.).—'That has sore or running eyes.'

d. 1627. MIDDLETON, *Black Book*, 528. A little WAPPER-EYED constable, to wink and blink at small faults.

WAPS, *subs.* (common).—A wasp.

WAR. TUG-OF-WAR, *subs. phr.* (common). — A severe and laborious contest.

1671. LEE, *Alexander the Great*, iv. 2. When Greeks join'd Greeks, then was THE TUG OF WAR.

See BEFORE THE WAR.

WARDROBE, *subs.* (old).—A privy.

1383. CHAUCER, *Cant. Tales*, 'Prioress' Tale,' 120. I seye that in a WARDROBE they him threwe, Wher as thes Jewes purgen his entraille.

WARE, *subs.* (venery). — 1. The female privities; also LADY-WARE: *see* MONOSYLLABLE; (2) the *penis* and *testes*: *see* PRICK and CODS: hence STANDING WARE=an *erectio penis*; also occasionally (3) the paps. Hence TO HAWK ONE'S WARES = (1) to quest for men, and (2) to expose one's charms (of women).

1705. WARD, *Hud. Rediv.*, I. ix. 6. Till she had burnt with Claps and Poxes, More STANDING WARE than Sampson's Foxes.

1772. BRIDGES, *Burlesque Homer*, 4. Had well examined all her WARE. *Ibid.*, 60. Our money spent, and breeks so torn, That for my own part, I declare, I'm d——d hard switch'd to hide my WARE. *Ibid.*, 64. He huffd thy WARE as well as mine, And tho' in every part he'd seen us, He gave the prize to Madam Venus.

1809. MALKIN, *Gil Blas* [ROUTLEDGE], 148. As Beatrice was one of those ladies who was obliged to hawk their WARES . . . I was . . . shielded from any temptation to break the commandments.

WAREHOUSE, *verb* (society). — To pawn. Hence as *subs.* = a fashionable UNCLE (*q.v.*).

WAR-HAT. *See* WAR-POT.

WAR-HORSE, *subs. phr.* (common). —A veteran: soldier or politician.

WARLING, *subs.* (old).—Apparently =slave, drudge: only occurring in proverbial saying, 'It is better to be an old man's derling, than an old man's werling' (HEYWOOD, 1542; CAMDEN, 1605).

WARM, *adj.* (old and still colloquial).—Generic for *extra*-ordinary: *e.g.* a WARM (= intimate FRIEND; WARM (= sincere) THANKS; a WARM (= hearty) WELCOME; a WARM (= fresh) TRAIL: *cf.* 'hot,' 'warm,' and 'cold' in children's play of guessing or 'hide-and-seek'; WARM (=easy) CIRCUMSTANCES: whence TO CUT UP WARM=to

leave a good estate, to die rich; a WARM (=rich) MAN: 'well-lined or flush in the pocket' (B. E. and GROSE); WARM (in one's position, duty, etc.) = at home, conversant with, well adapted to: hence TO KEEP A PLACE, etc., WARM=to occupy it; a WARM (= unpleasant) POSITION: *e.g.* 'He's in a WARM corner'; a WARM (= zealous) OPINION; a WARM (= brisk) ENGAGEMENT; a WARM (=enthusiastic) PARTISAN; WARM (= quick) WORK; a WARM (=hasty) TEMPER: espec. when contradicted; WARM (=wanton) DESIRE: a WARM (=lecherous) MEMBER (or WARM-'UN): a harlot or whoremonger: *cf.* HOT-UN, SCORCHER (*q.v.*); also (2) WARM-MEMBER = an energetic, pushful, self-advertising person; WARM (=strong) LANGUAGE; a WARM (= hostile) RECEPTION: hence the place gets too WARM (= unpleasant) because of unpopularity or antagonism to authority, and so forth.

1377. CHAUCER, *Troilus* [OLIPHANT, *New Eng.*, i. 114. A prosperous man is said to sit WARM; hence our WARM (thriving) MAN, and our tenants sit at so much rent].

1551. TYTLER, *Edward VI.* [OLIPHANT, *New Eng.*, i. 528. The adjective WARM is employed for *iratus*].

1610. JONSON, *Alchemist*, ii. 1. A gentleman newly WARM in his land, sir.

1613. PURCHAS, *Pilgrimage*, 84. His brother . . . had a while WARMED the throne.

1662. MIDDLETON, *Anything for a Quiet Life*, i. 1. *Water Camlet*. Believe it, I am a poor commoner. *Sir F. Cres.* Come, you are WARM and blest with a fair wife.

1680. DRYDEN, *Spanish Friar*, i. 1. We shall have WARM WORK on't.

c. 1693. CONGREVE, *Juvenal*, xi. Their small stock of credit gone, Lest Rome should grow too WARM, from thence they run.

1728. SWIFT, *Death of Stella*. When she saw any of the company very WARM in a wrong opinion, she was more inclined to confirm them in it than oppose them.

1766. GOLDSMITH, *Vicar*, xvi. We have been thinking of marrying her to one of your tenants . . . a WARM man . . . able to give her good bread.

1809. IRVING, *Knickerbocker*, 409. Scarcely had the worthy Mynheer Beekman got WARM in the seat of authority . . . than enemies began to spring up all around him.

1809. MALKIN, *Gil Blas* [ROUTLEDGE], 85. This WARM old gentleman has the moderation to lend me money at twenty per cent. *Ibid.*, 192. I was a WARM widow with a comfortable jointure, and a person little, if anything, the worse for wear. *Ibid.*, 216. We feathered our nests pretty WARMLY.

1814. AUSTEN, *Mansfield Park*, xvi. I do not know the play; but . . . if there is anything a little too WARM . . . it can be easily left out.

c. 1827. MACAULAY, *Hallam's Constit. Hist.* The conduct of Hampden in the affair of the ship-money met with the WARM approbation of every respectable royalist in England.

1834. EDGEWORTH, *Helen*, xxvi. When people are WARM they cannot stand picking terms.

1865. DICKENS, *Mutual Friend*, III. vi. He's WARM—he's getting cold—he's getting colder and colder—he's freezing.

c. 1875. *Music Hall Song*, 'Keep it Dark.' Dr. Kenealy, that popular bloke, That extremely WARM member, the member for Stoke.

c. 1889. *Music Hall Song*, 'Salvation Sarah.' They call me Salvation Sarah, A WARM-'UN I have been; But now I am converted, I'll never go wrong again.

1897. MARSHALL, *Pomes*, 124. And, in a monetary sense, He looked on her as 'WARM.'

1901. *Sporting Times*, 27 April, 1. 4. 'I suppose . . . the pretty bird should be placed in a warm room, eh?' 'Oh, it don't siggernify, lady, . . . any room'll be WARM enough once he starts a-talkin'!'

1902. LYNCH, *High Stakes*, 122. Perry ran to earth . . . the fellow . . . who drove Bradish . . . It means that we are getting WARM.

PHRASES: TO WARM A HOUSE =to celebrate incoming by a feast: hence HOUSE-WARMING; TO WARM TO (a thing, one's work, etc.)=to become enthusiastic, to do vigorously; WARM WITH='WARM WITH sugar': *cf.* COLD WITHOUT; 'Out of God's blessing into the WARM SUN'=from better to worse. Also *see* WARMING.

1581. LYLY, *Euphues*, Z. 3. b. Therefore if thou wilt follow my advice, and prosecute thine owne determination, THOU SHALT COME OUT OF A WARME SUNNE INTO GOD'S BLESSING.

1605. SHAKSPEARE, *Lear*, ii. 2. Good King! that must approve the common saw, Thou OUT OF HEAVEN'S BENEDICTION COM'ST TO THE WARM SUN.

1608. HARINGTON, *Catal. of Bishops*, *Carlyle*. Marks—removed from Carlisle to Lamos in Greece; viz. OUT OF GOD'S BLESSING INTO A WARME SUNNE, as the saying is. *Ibid.* (1615); *Epigrams*, ii. 56. Pray God they bring us not, when all is done, OUT OF GOD'S BLESSING INTO THIS WARM SUN.

1616–25. *Court and Times James I.*, s.v. [We see] WARM A HOUSE [with a feast].

1836. DICKENS, *Sketches by Boz*. Two glasses of rum-and-water WARM WITH.

1894. BAKER, *New Timothy*, 73. As the minister WARMS TO his sermon, there come through these cracks frequent exclamations.

1885. *Home Tidings*, 369. The two contestants put up their dukes and soon WARMED UP to their work.

WARMING, *subs.* (common).—A beating, flogging, thrashing. Hence TO WARM (OR WARM ONE'S JACKET, *q.v.*) = (1) to beat, drub, TAN (*q.v.*); and (2) to rate, abuse roundly, 'call over the coals.' TO WARM THE WAX OF ONE'S EAR=to box the ears.

WARMING-PAN, *subs. phr.* (common).—1. A substitute; a *locum tenens*; a person occupying another's office, situation or post during absence or while qualifying for it. Also W. P.: spec. a clergyman holding a living under a bond of resignation; also as *adj.*, *e.g.* a WARMING-PAN rector: *see* WARM.

1883. *Pall Mall Gaz.*, 21 Jan. It is not usual to inform a man that you propose to use him as a WARMING-PAN, however excellently suited he may be for such a purpose.

2. (old).—A large, old-fashioned gold watch: *cf.* FRYING-PAN (*q.v.*) or TURNIP (*q.v.*)=a large silver watch (B. E. and GROSE).

3. (old).—A female bed-fellow (B. E. and GROSE); a NIGHT-PIECE (*q.v.*). Also SCOTCH WARMING-PAN=a wench: spec. a chambermaid.

1672. RAY, *Proverbs* [BOHN], 61. The story is well-known of the gentleman travelling in Scotland, who desiring to have his bed warmed, the servant-maid doffs her clothes, and lays herself down in it a while. In Scotland they have neither bellows, warming-pans, nor houses of office.

WARM-SIDED, *adj. phr.* (naval).—Said of a fort or ship mounting heavy batteries.

WAR-PAINT, *subs. phr.* (common). —Official costume, evening dress, or (theatrical) MAKE-UP (*q.v.*).

1884. HAGGARD, *Dawn*. *She.* 'Have you seen the hero of the evening?' *He.* 'Who? Do you mean the Portuguese governor in his WAR-PAINT?'

1888. *St. James's Gaz.*, 9 Ap. Sir William Jenner in his WAR-PAINT as president of the Royal College of Physicians.

WARPATH. ON THE WARPATH, *phr.* (colloquial). — In hostile mood or attitude; 'making fur and feathers fly'; angry.

WAR-POT (or WAR-HAT), *subs. phr.* (military).—A spiked helmet.

WARREN, *subs.* (venery).—1. A brothel: also CUNNY (cony) WARREN (B. E. and GROSE): *see* NANNY-SHOP. Also (2) a boarding-school (B. E. and GROSE).

3. (Old Cant).—'He that is Security for goods taken up on Credit by Extravagant young Gentlemen' (B. E.).

WARWICKSHIRE LADS (THE), *subs. phr.* (military). — The Royal Warwickshire Regiment, late the 6th Foot.

WASH, *subs.* (Stock Exchange).—1. A fictitious bargain or sale: a broker gets instructions from one client to buy, and from another to sell, a particular stock; instead of making separate transactions of the two commissions to the best advantage of each principal, he merely transfers from one to the other, putting the difference in his own pocket: the practice is against the rules. Hence WASHED as applied to stock sold or bought in this way. Also a bogus deal made for the sake of a fictitious quotation: one broker arranges with another to buy a certain stock when he offers it for sale, the effect, when not detected, being to keep it quoted, and, if the plotters buy and sell the stock to a high figure, to afford a basis for *bona fide* sales.

1870. MEDBERY, *Men and Mysteries of Wall St.*, 327 From the spring of '58 to '60, the Stock Board slowly recovered its old tone. The bear element was in its glory. Brokers had become fearful of forced quotations. WASHING had become a constant trick before the panic, and bids were now closely scrutinized.

1888–9. *New York Produce Exchange Report*, 265. WASHED or fictitious sales are positively forbidden, and will render the parties concerned liable to suspension or expulsion from the Produce Exchange.

2. (B. E.).—'Paint for faces.'

3. (common).—Very weak LAP (*q.v.*): spec. (Durham School)= school tea or coffee: *see* ROCK.

Verb (colloquial).—1. To bear investigation; stand testing; prove genuine, reliable or trustworthy: as good fabrics and fast dyes stand the operation of washing.

1857. HUGHES, *Tom Brown's School-days*, ii. 2. He's got pluck somewhere in him. That's the only thing after all that'l WASH, ain't it?

1876. HINDLEY, *Cheap Jack*. The conversation, as a rule, ended in Charley's giving them an order too. Of course this little caper would only WASH once.

2. (craftsmen's).—To signify doubt of an assertion, or disapproval of conduct by language or action more forcible than pleasant: *e.g.* printers bang and knock on the cases; tailors indulge in strong language, etc. *See* JERRY and WHACK!

TO WASH ONE'S HEAD, *verb. phr.* (old).—To insult, to put indignity on one. Hence WASHING-BLOW=a box on the ears, a blow on the head; and TO GIVE ONE'S HEAD FOR WASHING=to submit to overbearing insult.

1612. BEAUMONT and FLETCHER, *Cupid's Revenge*, iv. 3. So am I, and forty more good fellows, that will not GIVE THEIR HEADS FOR the WASHING, I take it.

1621. FLETCHER, *Wild Goose Chase*, v. 4. And give her but a WASHING blow.

1663. BUTLER, *Hudibras*, I. iii. 255. For my part, it shall ne'er be said, I for the WASHING GAVE MY HEAD.

1710. WARD, *Hudibras Rediv.*, 14. Some of the laundry were (no flashing) That would not GIVE THEIR HEADS FOR WASHING.

TO WASH (or SLUICE) THE IVORIES, *verb. phr.* (common).—To drink: Fr. *se rincer la dent.* Also TO WASH ONE'S NECK.

1823. MONCRIEFF, *Tom and Jerry*, ii. 6. *Mr. J.* VASH YOUR IVORIES, will you? *Green.* I've got no HIVERIES TO WASH. *Mr. J.* Drink, vill you? don't you understand Hinglish.

1882. *Punch*, lxxxii. 185. 2. I never heard of him SLUICING HIS IVORIES with what you call S. and B.

TO WASH ONE'S SHEEP WITH SCALDING WATER, *verb. phr.* (old). — To do the absurd: a simile of folly (RAY). Also TO WASH THE CROW (THE ETHIOPIAN, A BLACKAMORE, etc.), WHITE.

WASHICAL, *phr.* (old). — WHAT-D'-YE-CALL-IT (*q.v.*).

1551. STILL, *Gammer Gurton's Needle* [DODSLEY, *Old Plays* (REED), ii. 67]. Geve my gammer again her WASHICAL [meaning her needle] thou stole away.

WASHING. TO GIVE ONE'S HEAD FOR A WASHING. *See* WASH.

WASHMAN, *subs.* (Old Cant).—A beggar 'faked out' with sores; 'a WASHMAN is called a PALLIARD [*q.v.*], but not of the right making. He vseth to lye in the hye way with lame or sore legs or armes to beg. These men ye right Palliards wil often times spoile, but they dare not complayn. They be bitten with spickworts, and sometime with rats bane' (AWDELEY, *Frat. Vacabondes*, 1561).

WASH-POT, *subs. phr.* (Collegiate and University).—A hat, a MOAB (*q.v.*): *see* GOLGOTHA.

WASP. AS QUIET AS A WASP IN ONE'S NOSE, *phr.* (old).—Very much alive.

WASPISH, *adj.* (B. E.).—'Peevish.'

WASTE-BUTT, *subs. phr.* (thieves').—An eating-house, GRUBBING-KEN (*q.v.*), MUNGARLY-CASA (*q.v.*).

WASTER, *subs.* (once literary: now colloquial). — 1. A prodigal, a spendthrift; also WASTREL, WASTE-GOOD, WASTE-THRIFT. Also 2 (modern)=a generic form of contempt, a ne'er-do-well, BAD-EGG (*q.v.*), ROTTER (*q.v.*); 'a useless, clumsy, or ill-made person' (HOTTEN). WASTREL (*q.v.*) (modern) = a neglected child, street-ARAB.

1383. CHAUCER, *Cant. Tales*, 'Merchant's Tale,' 231. A cludestere or WASTOUR of thy good.

1534. UDAL, *Roister Doister*, i. 1. Sometime Lewis Loiterer biddeth us come near; Somewhiles Watkin WASTER maketh us good cheer.

1592. NASHE, *Pierce Pennilesse*, 18. A young . . . cockney, that . . . have playde the WASTE-GOOD at the Innes of the Court.

1592. GREENE, *Quip for Upstart Courtier* [*Harl. Misc.*, v. 420]. This first . . . is a WAST-GOOD and an unthrift.

1608. MIDDLETON, *Trick to Catch*, ii. 1. A WASTETHRIFT, a common surfeiter, and, to conclude, a beggar.

1610. BEAUMONT and FLETCHER, *Knight of the Burning Pestle*, i. 4. Thou art a WASTETHRIFT, and art run away.

1611. *Bible*, 'Authorised Version,' Prov. xviii. 9. He also that is slothful in his work is brother to him that is a great WASTER.

1619. HOLLAND, *Plutarch*, 36. If Lucullus were not a WASTER and a delicate given to belly-cheare.

d. 1697. AUBREY, *Lives*, 'John Popham.' He left a vast estate to his son Sr Francis (I think ten thousand pounds per annum), he lived like a hog, but his son John was a great WASTER.

1818. SCOTT, *Heart of Midlothian*, xxviii. Ye will think I am turned WASTER for I wear clean hose and shoon every day.

1886. *D. Telegraph*, 20 Mar. Sending out not WASTRELS, paupers, and ne'er-do-wells, but capable mechanics and labourers, to Australia.

d. 1895. HUXLEY, *Technical Education* [*Century*]. The veriest waifs and WASTRELS of society.

3. (old).—A lawless thieving vagabond.

1342. *Statue Edward III.*, an. reg. 5, c. xiv. Divers manslaughters, felonies, and robberies done by people that he called Roberdsmen, WASTOURS, and Drawbacches.

4. (common).—An imperfection in the wick of a candle, causing it to gutter or 'waste': also THIEF (*q.v.*): *cf.* sense 3, *supra.*

5. (old).—A cudgel: spec. a wooden sword used for practice.

1593. CHURCHYARD, *Challenge*, 84. And suddainly a stout cobler will lay down the WASTER, and yeeld to him that hath more practise.

1598. FLORIO, *Worlde of Wordes*, 95. WASTERS or cudgels used in fence-schooles.

1598. STOWE, *London*, 70. The youthes of this citie also have used on holy dayes after evening prayer, at their maysters dores, to exercise their WASTERS and bucklers.

1602. DEKKER, *Honest Whore* [DODSLEY, *Old Plays* (REED), iii. 410]. If o'er husbands their wives will needs be masters. We men will have a law to win 't at WASTERS.

1608. HARINGTON, *Brief View of the Church*, 22. With a good WASTER he so mortified this old Adam of his son-in-law squire that he needed no other penance than this. *Ibid.*, *Epigrams*, i. 16. A man and wife strove cant who should be masters, And having chang'd between them houshold speeches, The man in wrath brought forth a pair of WASTERS, And swore that these should prove who wore the breeches.

1619. BEAUMONT and FLETCHER, *Philaster*, iv. Thou wouldst be loth to play half a dozen of venies at WASTERS, with a good fellow, for a broken head.

1621. BURTON, *Anat. Melan.*, 348. Or as they that play at WASTERS exercise themselves by a few cudgells to avoid an enemies blows.

. . . *Mad Men of Gotham*, 19. Then one took a WASTER in his hand, and gave him a dozen stripes, saying at every blow, Here, sirrah, take this for a reward, and hereafter mock us no more.

d. 1655. ADAMS, *Works*, I. 42. As with wooden WASTERS men learn to play at the sharp, so practice in times of peace makes ready for the time of war.

6. (common). — A damaged manufactured article: also WASTREL.

1863. EDE [CAMPIN, *Mechan. Engin.*, 355[. Had I not taken these precautions, which some are apt to think too much trouble, I should have had many a WASTER.

7. *See* WAISTER.

WASTE-TIME, *subs. phr.* (old).—Idle, useless, or trivial employment: a play on pastime.

1662. FULLER, *Worthies*, 'Lincoln,' ii. 6. 'As mad as the Baiting Bull of Stamford.' . . . Some think that the Men must be mad as well as the Bull, who can take delight in so dangerous a WAST-TIME.

WAT, *subs.* (old sporting).—1. A hare: *cf.* PHILIP=sparrow, TOM=cat, NED=donkey, etc.

c. 1470. *Babees Book* [E.E.T.S], 404. I wold my master were a WATT & my boke a wyld Catt, & a brase of grehowndis in his toppe. I wold be glad for to se that!

1593. SHAKSPEARE, *Venus and Adonis*, 697. Poor WAT, far off upon a hill Stands on his hinder legs with listening ear.

1622. DRAYTON, *Polyolbion*, xxiii. 1115. The man whose vacant mind prepares him for the sport, The finder sendeth out, to seek the nimble WAT, which crosseth in each field, each furlong, every flat, Till he this pretty beast upon the form hath found.

d. 1635. RANDOLPH, *Poems* (1668), 94. WATT, though he fled for life, yet joy'd withall So brave a dirge sung forth his funeral.

d. 1650. R. FLETCHER, *Epigr.*, 139. Thus once concluded out the teazers run, All in full cry and speed 'till WAT'S undone.

2. (old).—A fellow; 'a wily, cautious man' (HALLIWELL).

c. 1400. *Coventry Mysteries*, 294. Ffor be my thryfte I dare sweryn at this seyl, ȝe xal fynde hym a strawnge WATT!

WATCH, *subs.* (Old Cant).—1. Self: the ancient equivalent of NIBS (*q.v.*). Thus HIS WATCH= the person referred to; MY WATCH=myself; YOUR WATCH =yourself; OUR WATCH=ourselves, us, etc.

c. 1530. COPLAND, *Hye Way to the Spyttel Hous.* The patryng coue in the darkman cace Docked the dell for a coper meke HIS WATCH shall feng a prounces nobchete.

1567. HARMAN, *Caveat* (1869), 86. The vpright man canteth to the Roge; Man! That is beneshyp to OUR WATCHE.

1622. HEAD, *English Rogue*, 'Canting Song.' I met a Dell, I viewed her well, She was benship to MY WATCH.

2. (Westminster).—A junior who has to remain in College during play-hours to answer inquiries, receive messages, and so forth, performing, in fact, the duties of a servant.

TO WATCH OUT, *verb. phr.* (Winchester, cricket).—To field.

c. 1840. MANSFIELD, *School Life*, 138. Football wasn't all beer and skittles to the Fags. There was an institution called 'Kicking in,' which, while it lasted, was much worse than WATCHING OUT at cricket.

PADDY'S WATCH. *See* PADDY-WHACK.

WATCH-AND-SEALS, *subs. phr.* (common).—A sheep's head and pluck.

WATCH-BIRTH, *subs. phr.* (old).—A midwife.

1605. SYLVESTER, *Du Bartas*, ii., 'Magnificence.' Th' eternall WATCH-BIRTHS of thy sacred Wit.

WATCHER, *subs.* (venery). — A person set to watch a DRESS-LODGER (*q.v.*).

1869. GREENWOOD, *Seven Curses of London.* Not alone. Dress lodgers are never allowed to do that, sir. I haven't been one long, but long enough to find that out. There's always a WATCHER. Sometimes it's a woman—an old woman, who isn't fit for anything else—but in general it's a man. He watches you always, walking behind you, or on the opposite side of the way. He never loses sight of you, never fear.

WATCHMAKER, *subs.* (thieves').—A thief whose speciality is stealing watches: also 'WATCHMAKER IN A CROWD' (HOTTEN).

WATER, *subs.* (Westminster School).—Boating; aquatics; the Eton WET-BOBBING (*q.v.*).

1881. PASCOE, *Everyday Life in our Public Schools.* WATER, as it is called at Westminster, is in a very flourishing condition.

Verb (old).—1. To drink: *see* LUSH.

1598. SHAKSPEARE, I *Henry IV.*, ii. 4. When you breathe in your WATERINGS, they cry 'hem!'

1607. DEKKER, *Westward Hoe*, ii. 1. A certain well where all the Muses WATERED.

2. (old). — To urinate; PISS (*q.v.*); also TO MAKE WATER, TO WATER THE DRAGON, and TO WATER ONE'S NAG. Whence (venery) WATERWORKS=the urinary organs male or female: also WATER-ENGINE (*see* WATER-DROP); WATER-BOX (GAP, COURSE, GATE, etc.)=the female *pudendum*: *see* MONOSYLLABLE; WATER-CASTER (-DOCTOR or WATEROLOGER)=a urine-inspecting physician: spec. a quack; TO CAST WATER = to diagnose by means of the urine.

c. 1350. *Tale of the Basyn* [HAZLITT, *Early Pop. Poetry*, iii. 47]. ȝif thu myȝ with any gynne The vessell owt of the chaumber wynne, The same that thei MAKE WATER in, And bryng it me, I the pray.

1598. MARSTON, *Satires*, iv. 125. Well, I have CAST THY WATER, and I see Th' art fall'n to wit's extremest poverty.

1598. FLORIO, *Worlde of Wordes* (1611), 185. [WATER-BOX = female *pudendum.*]

1606. SHAKSPEARE, *Macbeth*, v. 3. If thou could'st, doctor, CAST THE WATER of my land, find her disease.

1607. *Puritan*, iv. 1. There's physicians enough to CAST HIS WATER: is that any matter to us?

1630. TAYLOR, *Workes.* A face like rubies mix'd with alabaster, Wastes much in physicke and her WATER-CASTER. *Ibid.* Which was the fare of quack salvers, mountebankes, ratcatching WATER-CASTERS, and also for all botching artificers and cobling tradesmen.

1653. URQUHART, *Rabelais*, I. 20. I might have cleft her WATER-GAP, And joined it close with my FLIP-FLAP.

1678. *Quack's Academy* [*Harl. Misc.*, II. 34]. You must either pretend to be WATEROLOGERS . . . or star-wizards.

1706. WARD, *Wooden World*, 39. He is acquainted with the Nature and Depths of all Soundings but that of his Wife's WATER-COURSE.

CANTERBURY-WATER, *subs. phr.* (old).—The blood of Thomas à Becket diluted with water: Archbishop of Canterbury, murdered in 1170, canonised as a saint and martyr.

1849-54. ROCK, *Church of our Fathers*, III. i. 424. To satisfy these cravings, so as to hinder an uneasy feeling at the thought of tasting human blood, a tiny drop was mixed with a chalice-full of water, and in this manner given to those who begged a sip. This was the far-famed CANTERBURY-WATER.

BURNING-WATER (*q.v.*, vol. i. *ante*).

3. (commercial).—To increase nominal capital by the issue of shares for which, though they rank for interest, no additional increase in the actual capital has been provided: the practice, it is urged, is justified by profits already earned, or by a supposed enhancement of the value of the property, franchises, etc.; but watering is usually only resorted to by companies on the down grade. Hence as *subs.*=additional shares created in this way.

1878. *Scribner's Mag.*, Oct., 896. Those which relate to the betrayal of trusts, the WATERING of stocks.

1887. *North Am. Rev.*, cxliii. 92. By the much-abused word 'property' he referred, of course, to the fictitious capital, or WATER, which the gas companies had added to their real capital.

1888. *St. James's Gaz.*, 14 June. But it is said by the chairman of the Committee on Public Finance, that 'more than half of this stock is WATER, and could not have come into existence had not this business been superior to the control of competition.'

1888. *Fort. Rev.*, xliii. 857. The stock of some of the railways has been WATERED to an enormous extent by the issue of fictitious capital, existing only on paper, though ranking equally for dividend, when money for this is forthcoming. Usually the paper stock has been sold to unwary customers.

PHRASES. ABOVE WATER = unembarrassed, untroubled, in (or of) easy circumstances, mind, or the like: whence TO KEEP ONE'S HEAD ABOVE WATER = to struggle through (or overcome) financial difficulties; BETWEEN WIND AND WATER (*see* WIND); IN DEEP WATER = (1) in trial, trouble, distress; (2) impecunious, reduced in circumstances: hence DEEP WATERS = tribulation of sorts; OF THE FIRST WATER = the highest, A1: properly of a diamond free of blemish, flaw, colour, or any imperfection; TO MAKE A HOLE IN THE WATER = to fall in it: spec. to commit suicide by drowning: *cf.* 'to make a hole in the silence' = to speak; OIL ON TROUBLED WATERS = anything to allay, assuage: the practice is ancient, being known to the Greeks and Romans, and its efficacy is frequently tested by modern seamen; TO BE IN HOT WATER = to be in trouble, difficulties, or disgrace; TO SHOW WATER = to bribe, to produce a fee; TO CAST ONE'S WATER (*see verb.* 2); TO CAST WATER INTO THE THAMES = to do the unnecessary or useless (*see* THAMES); TO HOLD WATER = to prove serviceable or adequate; TO TAKE WATER = to back out (or down), to WEAKEN (*q.v.*): as a boat when allowed to fall in the wake of another in a race; TO DRAW WATER WITH A SIEVE = to act absurdly; TO THROW COLD WATER ON = to discourage, damp one's ardour, interest, or chances; WATER IN ONE'S SHOES = a cause of annoyance or discomfort; TO WATER ONE'S PLANTS = to shed tears. Also proverbially: 'My mouth WATERS' = a simile of strong appetite or longing desire: also said of the teeth; 'That's where the WATER sticks' = That's the point in dispute; 'All WATER runs to his mill' = 'Fortune smiles on him,' 'Everything goes his way'; 'No safe wading in an unknown WATER'; 'Often to the WATER, often to the tatter'; 'Foul WATER will quench fire'; 'Where the WATER is shallow no vessel will ride'; 'WATER breeds frogs in the belly, and wine cures the worms'; 'I'll make him WATER his horse at Highgate' (*i.e.* 'I'll sue him and make him take a journey up to London'—RAY); 'The malt's above the WATER' = He's drunk (*see* SCREWED).

1530. PALSGRAVE, *Lang. Francoyse.* My TETHE WATERS to see.

1546. HEYWOOD, *Proverbs*, 69. It is to give him (quoth I) as much almes or neede As CAST WATER IN TEMS, or as good a deede As it is to helpe a dogge over a stile.

1555. PETER MARTYR [EDEN, *First Books on America* (ARBER), 181]. In theyr mindes they conceaued a hope of a dainty banquet, And espying their enemies a farre of beganne to swalowe theyr spettle as their MOUTHES WATERED for gredines of theyr pray.

1581. LYLY, *Euphues*, 'To Philuntus,' M4. Neither WATER THOU THY PLANTS, in that thou departest from thy pigges nie, neither stand in a mammering, whether it bee best to depart or not.

1609. SHAKSPEARE, *Pericles*, iv. 2. A Spaniard's mouth so WATERED.

1611. *Bible*, Authorised Version, Psalm lxix. 14. Let me be delivered from them that hate me, and out of the DEEP WATERS.

1623. MABBE, *Guzman* (1630), ii. 79. [It] WILL NOT HOLD WATER.

1632. MASSINGER, *Maid of Honour*, i. 1. *F.* If you've a suit, SHEW WATER, I am blind else. *A.* A suit; yet of a nature not to prove The quarry that you hawk for. . . . One poor syllable Cannot deserve a fee.

1650. WELDON, *Court of King James* (1817), 19. All THE WATER RUNS TO THEIR MILLS [applied to the Howards, who got everything at Court].

d. 1663. BRAMHALL, *Works*, ii. 366. That the reader may see clearly WHERE THE WATER STICKS between us.

1698. FARQUHAR, *Love and a Bottle*, v. 1. O, my little green gooseberry; my TEETH WATERS at thee.

1742-4. NORTH, *Lord Guildford*, i. 295. They caressed his lordship very much as a new comer, whom they were glad of the honour to meet, and talked about a time to dine with him; all which (as they say) was WATER IN HIS SHOES.

1809. MALKIN, *Gil Blas* [ROUTLEDGE], 104. You have made my MOUTH WATER to serve such a worshipful fraternity. *Ibid.*, 254. The brilliants . . . made her eyes sparkle and her MOUTH WATER.

1846. *Punch's Almanack*, 29 Nov. The *Times* first printed by steam, 1814, and has kept the country IN HOT WATER ever since.

1864. MARK LEMON, *Jest Book*, 238. Show me the blade that is *not out of temper* when plunged into HOT WATER.

18[?]. W. S. GILBERT, *Etiquette.* For the thought of Peter's oysters brought the WATER TO HIS MOUTH.

d. 1884. C. READE (DIXON). One comfort, folk are beginning to take an interest in us. I see nobs OF THE FIRST WATER looking with a fatherly eye into our affairs.

1885. *Field*, 3 Oct. A number of struggling men, who have managed TO KEEP ABOVE WATER during the bad seasons, must now go under.

1886. WARD [*Ency. Brit.*, xx. 57]. The dog's MOUTH WATERS only at the sight of food, but the gourmand's MOUTH will also WATER at the thought of it.

1892. MILLIKEN, *'Arry Ballads*, 76. I should just make a HOLE IN THE WATER, if 'tworn't for the wife and the kids.

WATER-BEWITCHED, *subs. phr.* (common).—Weak LAP (*q.v.*) of any kind: spec. (modern) tea very much watered down, but orig. (RAY, 1672) very thin beer: also WATER-DAMAGED: *cf.* HUSBAND'S-TEA.

1709-10. SWIFT, *Pol. Conv.*, i. Your ladyship is very sparing of your tea; I protest the last dish I took was no more than WATER BEWITCHT.

1725. BAILEY, *Erasmus*, 376. As for the broth, it was nothing but a little WATER BEWITCHED (*mera aqua*).

1835. DANA, *Before the Mast*, 10 Nov. A tin pot full of hot tea (or as the sailors significantly call it, 'WATER BEWITCHED') sweetened with molasses. *Ibid.* Our common beverage—'WATER BEWITCHED, and tea begrudged,' as it was.

1845. CARLYLE, *Cromwell*, i. 13. Another book of Noble's called *Lives of the Regicides* . . . is of much more stupid character; nearly meaningless indeed, mere WATER BEWITCHED.

WATER-BUTT (or -BARREL), *subs. phr.* (common).—The stomach: spec. a CORPORATION (*q.v.*).

WATER-CAN, *subs. phr.* (colloquial).—In saying 'Jupiter Pluvius has got out (or put on) his WATER-CAN' = It is raining: spec. of a heavy shower.

WATER-COLOUR. *See* WIFE IN WATER-COLOURS.

WATER-DOCTOR, *subs. phr.* (colloquial).—1. A hydropathist. Also (2) a WATER-CASTER (*q.v.*, WATER, *verb* 2).

WATER-DOG, *subs. phr.* (common).—1. A sailor: spec. an old SALT (*q.v.*). Also (2) anyone completely 'at home' in, or on, the water.

1835. DANA, *Before the Mast*, 94. The Sandwich Islanders are complete WATER-DOGS, and therefore very good in boating.

3. (common).—A Norfolk dumpling.

WATER-DROP, *subs. phr.* (old colloquial).—A tear. Also WATERWORKS = the eyes, the TEAR-PUMP: whence TO TURN ON THE WATERWORKS = to cry: also *see* WATER, *verb* 2.

1605. SHAKSPEARE, *Lear*, ii. 4. 280. Let not women's weapons, WATER-DROPS, Stain my man's cheeks.

1857. HUGHES, *Tom Brown's Schooldays*, ii. 5. Sneaking little brute . . . clapping on the WATERWORKS just in the hardest place.

WATERFALL, *subs.* (various).—1. A neckcloth, scarf, or tie with long pendant ends. Also (2) a chignon: spec. a fringe of hair falling down the neck under the chignon.

1824. FERRIER, *Inheritance*, I. xi. A drooping FALL of Foyers-looking neckcloth.

1861. HUGHES, *Tom Brown at Oxford*, II. iii. A gaudy figured satin waistcoat, and WATERFALL of the same material.

1880. WHITNEY, *Leslie Goldthwaite*, iii. The brown silk net . . . had given way all at once into a great hole under the WATERFALL, and the soft hair would fret itself through, and threaten to stray untidily.

WATER-FUNK, *subs. phr.* (school).—A boy shy of water: either in the way of personal cleanliness or aquatics.

1900. KIPLING, *Stalky and Co.*, 68. King scowled. 'One of you was that thing called a WATER-FUNK. So now you wish to wash? It is well. Cleanliness never injured a boy, or—a house.'

WATER-GUNNERS (THE), *subs. phr.* (military). — The Royal Marines.

WATERIES (THE), *subs. phr.* (common).—The Naval Exhibition at South Kensington: *cf.* FISHERIES, COLINDERIES, etc.

WATERINGS. ST. THOMAS À WATERINGS (old).—A place of execution (for Surrey as TYBURN (*q.v.*) for Middlesex) situated at the second milestone on the road from London to Canterbury. Like BEGGAR'S-BUSH, WEEPING-CROSS, CLAPHAM, etc., the place-name was the basis of many a quibbling allusion and much conventional wit. [At this point is a brook, probably a place for WATERING horses, whence its name; dedicated, of course, to St. Thomas à Becket, being the first place of any note in the pilgrimage to his shrine.]

1383. CHAUCER, *Cant. Tales*, Prol. v. 827. And forth we riden a litel more than pas [little more than a foot's pace]. Unto the WATERING OF SEINT THOMAS, And ther our hoste began his hors arest.

. . . *Hycke Scorner* [HAWKINS, *Orig. of Drama*, i. 105]. For at SAYNT THOMAS OF WATRYNGE an they stryke a sayle, Than they must ryde in the haven of hepe [hempe] without fayle.

1607. *Puritan*, i. 1. Alas! a small matter bucks a handkerchief! and sometimes the 'spital stands too nigh ST. THOMAS À WATERINGS. [That is, 'A little matter will serve to wet a handkerchief; and sometimes shedding too many tears will bring a person to the hospital'; that is, 'will produce sickness.']

16[?]. *Owle's Almanacke*, 55. A faire pair of gallowes is kept at Tiburne, from yeares end to yeares end: and the like faire (but not so much resort of chapmen and crack-ropes) is at ST. THOMAS À WATERINGS.

1630. JONSON, *New Inn*, i. 3. To which, if he apply him, He may perhaps take a degree at Tyburn, A year the earlier, come to read a lecture Upon Aquinas, at ST. THOMAS À WATERING'S, And so go forth a laureat in hemp circle.

1786. [CAREY, *Map of 15 miles round London.* We have at the two mile-stone on the Kent road, WATERING'S Bridge, a remnant of the old name.]

WATER-LANGUAGE, *subs. phr.* (old).—Jocose abuse, CHAFF (*q.v.*).

1721. AMHERST, *Terræ Filius*, I. 'Twas all WATER LANGUAGE at these times, and no exceptions were to be taken.

WATERLOO-DAY, *subs. phr.* (military).—Pay-day: *cf.* BALACLAVA-DAY.

WATERMAN, *subs.* (old).—A blue silk handkerchief: *cf.* FOGLE. [HOTTEN: 'The friends of the Oxford and Cambridge boats' crews always wear these—light blue for Cambridge, and a darker shade for Oxford.'] Also WATERSMAN.

WATEROLOGER. *See* WATER, *verb* 2.

WATER-PAD (or -RAT).—A thief working on the water: spec. 'one that Robbs Ships in the Thames' (B. E., GROSE, and CLARK RUSSELL): *cf.* WATER-SNEAK.

WATER-PUSHER (or -TREADER), *subs. phr.* (colloquial).—A ship: sail or steam.

1614. CHAPMAN, *Odyssey*, XIV. 477. When the WATER TREADER far away Had left the land.

1899. HYNE, *Furth. Adv. Capt. Kettle*, xi. I've had enough of your airs and graces. I've paid for my passage on this rubbishy old WATER-PUSHER of yours.

WATER-SNEAK (THE), *subs. phr.* (old).—'Robbing ships or vessels on a navigable river or canal, by getting on board unperceived, generally in the night. The WATER-SNEAK is lately made a capital offence' (GROSE).

WATERWORKS. *See* WATER-DROP and WATER, *verb* 2.

WATLYNGE-STRETE, *subs. phr.* (old).—The Milky Way.

1373. CHAUCER, *House of Fame*, 939. Se yonder, lo the Galaxye, The which men clepe the Milky Weye, For hit ys white; and somme parfeye, Callen hyt WATLYNGE STRETE.

WATTLE, *subs.* (B. E.).—In *pl.* = 'Ears; also Sheep-folds.'

WAVE. TO WAVE A FLAG OF DEFIANCE, *verb. phr.* (common).—to be drunk: *see* SCREWED.

TO NUMBER THE WAVES, *verb. phr.* (old).—To do the unneedful, act foolishly (RAY).

WAVY. WAVY IN THE SYLS, *phr.* (theatrical).—Imperfect in one's lines.

WAVY-RULE. TO MAKE WAVY RULE, *verb. phr.* (printers').—To be staggering drunk. [〰〰〰]

WAX, *subs.* (common).—A rage, a passion, a TEAR (*q.v.*); also WAXINESS = vexation, and WAXY = angry: *cf.* Lowland Scotch *wex* = vex.

c. 1490. *Lancelot of the Laik*, 156. And mak thi self als mery as yhoue may, It helpith not thus fore to WEX al way.

1648. BELLENDEN, *Letter*, 9 July [*Hamilton Papers*, 229]. They wowld place such persons in inferior commandis as ar to deboch the affections of the salers, from which being discouerid be him makes him the moir WAXY.

1853. DICKENS, *Bleak House*, xxiv. It would cheer him up more than anything if I could make him a little WAXY with me: he's welcome to drop into me right and left, if he likes.

1861. KINGSLEY, *Ravenshoe*, v. She's in a terrible WAX, but she'll be all right by the time he comes back from his holidays.

Verb (American).—To overcome, surmount a difficulty, get the better of: by stratagem or NOUS (*q.v.*).

1876. *New York Herald*, 16 Mar. The trader at Fort Lincoln, fearing removal, Orville Grant's clerk at Standing Rock advised him to tell Grant, 'he can WAX you.'

A LAD (or MAN) OF WAX, *subs. phr.* (old).—A smart lad, a clever man.

1595. SHAKSPEARE, *Romeo and Juliet*. A man of WAX.

CLOSE AS WAX, *phr.* (common).—As miserly, niggardly, or secretive as may be.

1863. READE, *Hard Cash*, I. 231. Then commenced a long and steady struggle, conducted with a Spartan dignity and self-command, and a countenance as CLOSE AS WAX.

1898. GOULD, *Landed at Last*, v. Not much chance of drawing Sim Sharples when he's alone. He's AS CLOSE AS WAX, and so is Sam Rogers.

NEAT AS WAX. *See* NEAT.

WAXED, *adj.* (tailors').—Well-known: *e.g.* So-and-so has been well WAXED, *i.e.* We know all about him.

WAY, *subs.* (colloquial).—Health, condition, state, calling; *e.g.* IN A BAD WAY=shaky in health, pocket, or manner; ONLY HIS WAY = characteristic: *cf.* 'PRETTY FANNY'S WAY.' Also in PHRASES: 'To look BOTH (or NINE) WAYS for Sundays'=to squint; 'There are no TWO WAYS about it'=the fact is as stated, there's no mistake; OUT OF THE WAY (thieves': *see* quot. 1819); 'to note THE WAY THE CAT JUMPS=to watch the course of events; TO GO THE WAY OF NATURE (or ALL FLESH)=(1) to be fond of BELLY CHEER, and (2) to die: *see* HOP THE TWIG; TO KNOW ONE'S WAY ABOUT=to be well informed, experienced: *see* KNOW; WAY TO ST. JAMES' (or WALSINGHAM WAY)=the Milky way (FULKE, *Meteors*, 1670, p. 81). 'The LONGEST WAY ROUND is the shortest way there'=a warning to the unwary or ignorant that short cuts are proverbial pitfalls: *cf.* 'Better go about than fall into the ditch.'

1350. *Tale of the Basyn* [HAZLITT, *Early Pop. Poet.*, III. 45]. After a ȝere or two his wyfe he myȝt not pleese; Mycall of his lande lay to the preests ese Eche tawȝt hym euer amang HOW THE KATTE DID SNEESE.

1601. SHAKSPEARE, *Henry VIII.*, i. 3. 61. Men of his WAY should be most liberal.

1607. DEKKER, *Westward Hoe*, ii. 2. I saw him even now going the WAY OF ALL FLESH, that is to say, towards the kitchen.

1698. COLLIER, *Short View* (1698), 211. Whenever you see a thorough Libertine, you may always swear he is in a rising WAY, and that the poet intends to make him a great man.

d. 1717. PARNELL, *Elegy to a Beauty*. And all that's madly wild and oddly gay We call it only PRETTY FANNY'S WAY.

1763. FOOTE, *Mayor of Garratt*, i. 1. Thinking that this would prove a busy day in the justicing WAY, I am come, Sir Jacob, to lend you a hand.

1777. SHERIDAN, *School for Scandal*, i. 1. You must tell him to keep up his spirits; almost everybody is in the same WAY.

c. 1809. MALKIN, *Gil Blas* [ROUTLEDGE], 13. I heard that Don Rodrigo had gone the WAY OF ALL FLESH.

1819. VAUX, *Memoirs*, ii. 194. OUT OF THE WAY, a thief who knows that he is sought after by the traps on some information and consequently goes out of town, or otherwise conceals himself, is said by his pals to be OUT OF THE WAY FOR SO AND SO, naming the particular offence he stands charged with. [*See* WANTED.]

1825. *Universal Songster*, i. ('The Dog's-Meat Man'). He soon saw WHICH WAY THE CAT DID JUMP, And his company he offered plump.

1827. SCOTT, in *Croker Pap.* (1884), I. xi. 319. Had I time, I believe I would come to London merely TO SEE HOW THE CAT JUMPED.

1841. THACKERAY, *Great Hoggarty Diamond*, xiii. Is not Gus Hoskins, my brother-in-law, partner with his excellent father in the leather WAY?

1853. BULWER LYTTON, *My Novel*, IV. 228. 'But I rely equally on your friendly promise.' 'Promise! No—I don't promise. I must first SEE HOW THE CAT JUMPS.'

1855. HALIBURTON, *Human Nature*, 3 S. vii. Jist so, jist so, stranger: you are just about half right, and there's NO TWO WAYS ABOUT IT.

1856. HOFFMAN, *Winter in the West* [BARTLETT]. THERE'S NO TWO WAYS ABOUT THAT, sir; but ar'n't you surprised to see such a fine population?

1859. LEVER, *Davenport Dunn*, III. 229. You'll see with half an eye HOW THE CAT JUMPS.

1874. *Sat. Rev.*, 139. This dismays the humble Liberal of the faint Southern type, who thinks that there are subjects as to which the heads of his party need not wait to see HOW THE CAT JUMPS.

1887. 'Pol. Slang,' in *Cornhill Mag.*, June, 626. Those who sit on the fence—men with impartial minds, who wait to SEE, as another pretty phrase has it, HOW THE CAT WILL JUMP.

1867. *All the Year Round*, 13 July, 56. The tramp who KNOWS HIS WAY ABOUT knows what to do.

1892. MILLIKEN, *'Arry Ballads*, 36. KNOWS HER WAY ABOUT well, I can tell yer.

WAY-BIT (WEABIT or WEBIT), *subs.* (provincial).—A considerable though indefinite addition to a mile; a BITTOCK (*q.v.*).

1611. COTGRAVE, *Dict.*, s.v. *Huquée*. *It n'y a qu'vne huquée* (Much like our Northern WEE-BIT) You have but a little (saies the clown, when you have a great) way thither.

1617–30. HOWELL, *Letters*, iv. 28. In the North parts . . . there is a WEA-BIT to every mile.

1662. FULLER, *Worthies*, 'Yorkshire,' II. 494. 'An Yorkshire WAY-BIT.' That is, an Over-plus not accounted in the reckoning, which sometimes proveth as much as all the rest. *Ibid.*, II. 535. General Leslie, with his Scottish, ran away more than a Yorkshire mile and a WEE BIT.

1692. HACKET, *Life of Williams*, i. 59. I have heard him prefer divers, and very seriously, before himself, who came short a mile and a WAY-BIT.

WAY-GOOSE, *subs. phr.* (old).—An entertainment given by an apprentice to his fellow-workmen: spec. (printers') an annual dinner; *cf.* BEANFEAST (*q.v.*). [A corruption of WAYZ-GOOSE= stubble goose, a favourite dish at such festivals: nowadays, among printers, the funds are collected by stewards appointed by the CHAPEL (*q.v.*).]

1677–9. MOXON, *Mechanic Exercises*. The Master Printer gives them a WAY-GOOSE; that is, he makes them a good feast.

1839. C. H. TIMPERLEY, *Printers and Printing*, 516. The WAY-GOOSES were always kept about Bartholomew-tide; and till the master-printer have given this WAY-GOOSE the journeymen do not use to work by candle-light.

WEAK-BROTHER (or -SISTER), *subs. phr.* (religious cant).—An unreliable man (or woman). *Cf.* also (colloquial) WEAKLING (a diminutive), which, as *adj.*= puny, weak; WEAK-KNEED=uncertain, vacillating, purposeless.

1595. SHAKSPEARE, *3 Henry VI.*, v. I. 37. Thou art no Atlas for so great a weight: And, WEAKLING, Warwick takes his gift again.

1740. NORTH, *Plutarch*, 700. He was but WEAKLING and very tender.

1847. BRONTË, *Jane Eyre*, xxxiv. Jane is not such a WEAKLING as you would make her.

1861. *New York Tribune*, Dec. The rebels assert that the Union has no friends at the South. The assertion is false. There are white Unionists there, but they are WEAK SISTERS,—overawed, terrorized, silenced.

1885. *Field*, 4 April. This was a feat not to be attempted by a WEAKLING.

1888. *St. James's Gazette*, 14 Jan. Such another WEAK-KNEED effort . . . will lead to no good result.

1893. *Harper's Mag.*, lxxxvi. 570. The WEAKLING cry of children.

WEAKER-SEX, *subs. phr.* (colloquial).—Womankind: also (in singular) THE WEAKER VESSEL [*See* I Peter iii. 7].

1600. SHAKSPEARE, *As You Like It*, ii. 4. 6. I must comfort THE WEAKER VESSEL, as doublet and hose ought to show itself courageous to petticoat.

1719. DURFEY, *Pills to Purge*, v. 259.

WEANIE. *See* WEENIE.

WEAPON, *subs.* (venery).—The *penis*: *see* PRICK (HALLIWELL): *cf.* SHEATH=female *pudendum*.

1772. BRIDGES, *Burlesque Homer*, 132. She guides his WEAPON where she lists Knowing a touch of her soft hand . . . will make him stand. *Ibid.*, 178. If you meet the whoring goddess, Drive your stiff WEAPON through her boddice, But take great care the gypsy's eyes, Don't guide to where her mousetrap lies. *Ibid.* When she appears don't gasping stand, But use the WEAPON in your hand, If you exhibit any other Don't think that I my rage will smother.

WEAR. TO WEAR IT, *verb. phr.* (old).—'TO WEAR IT UPON a person (meaning to wear a nose, or a conk) is synonymous with nosing, conking, splitting, or coming it, and is merely one of those fanciful variations so much admired by FLASH PEOPLE' (GROSE).

PHRASES. TO WEAR THE HEART UPON THE SLEEVE (*see* SLEEVE); TO WEAR THE BREECHES (*see* BREECHES); TO WEAR THE WILLOW (*see* WILLOW); TO WEAR YELLOW STOCKINGS OR HOSE (*see* YELLOW); TO WEAR THE COLLAR= to be subject to control, or under the direction of another (chiefly political); TO WEAR THE BANDS (*see* BAND); TO WEAR ILL (or WELL)=to look older (or younger) than one's years. Also PROVERBIAL, 'Let every cuckold WEAR his own horns'; 'to wear Pannier-alley on one's back' (*see* PANNIER-MAN).

WEARY, *adj.* (common).—Drunk: *see* SCREWED.

WEASEL, *subs.* (old).—A mean, greedy, or sneaking fellow. Also as *adj.*

1599. SHAKSPEARE, *Henry V.*, i. 2. 170. To her unguarded nest the WEASEL Scot Comes sneaking.

See WHISTLE.

WEATHER. PHRASES: TO MAKE FAIR WEATHER=to flatter, coax, conciliate, make the best of things; TO KEEP THE WEATHER EYE OPEN=to be on one's guard, alert, watchful: *see* 'Keep one's eyes skinned'; UNDER THE WEATHER = seedy, ill, indisposed; THE CLERK OF THE WEATHER=an imaginary controller of temperature, rainfall, etc.

. . . *Cheeke to King Edward* [*Nugæ Ant.*, i. 20]. And if anye suche shall be, that shall of all things MAKE FAIR WEATHER, and, whatsoever they shall see to the contrarye, shall tell you all is well; beware of them, they serve themselves, not you.

1594. SHAKSPEARE, *2 Henry VI.*, v. I. But I must MAKE FAIR WEATHER yet awhile, 'Till Henry be more weak, and I more strong. *Ibid.* (1600), *Much Ado*, i. 3. He hath ta'en you newly into his grace; where it is impossible you should take root, but by the FAIR WEATHER THAT YOU MAKE yourself.

1598. MARSTON, *Scourge of Villanie*, i. And by an holy semblance bleare men's eyes When he intends some damned villanies. Ixion MAKES FAIRE WEATHER unto Jove, That he might make foule worke with his faire love, And is right sober in his outward semblance, Demure and modest in his countenance.

1865. DICKENS, *Mutual Friend*, II. v. KEEP YOUR WEATHER EYE AWAKE, and don't make any more acquaintances, however handsome.

d. 1878. BOWLES [*Merriam*, II. 49]. Since I went to Washington . . . I have been quite UNDER THE WEATHER, and have had to neglect everything.

1903. HYNE, *Filibusters*, iv. By way of being on the safe side I am going to KEEP MY WEATHER-EYE LIFTING for everything that's unpleasant.

WEATHER-BREEDER, *subs. phr.* (American).—A hot day: which often precedes and 'prepares' a storm.

1888. EGGLESTON, *Roxy*, xiii. 'It's a . . . nice day,' growled Adam, 'but a WEATHER-BREEDER.'

WEATHERCOCK, *subs.* (old colloquial).—A fickle, inconstant, vacillating person.

1596. SHAKSPEARE, *Merry Wives*, iii. 2. Where had you this pretty WEATHERCOCK?

1638. RANDOLPH, *Amyntas*, i. 1. What pretty WEATHERCOCKS these women are.

1672. DRYDEN, *Conquest of Granada*, I. iii. 1. The word which I have given shall stand like fate, Not like the King's, that WEATHER-COCK of State.

c. 1709. WARD, *London Spy* [*Century*]. They are Men whose Conditions are subject to more Revolutions than a WEATHER-COCK, or the Uncertain Mind of a Fantastical Woman.

WEATHERDOG, *subs.* (provincial).—A rainbow, fragmentary and only partly visible: regarded as a presage instead of a concomitant of rain.

WEATHERGAGE, *subs.* (old).—Advantage, the upper hand: *cf.* WINDWARD. Whence TO GET THE WEATHERGAGE = to command, control, have the best of.

1813. SCOTT, *Rokeby*, vi. 24. The line of Rokeby once combined with mine I gain the WEATHER-GAGE of fate. *Ibid.* (1819), *Ivanhoe*, i. 13. Take a turn round the back o' the hill to gain the wind on them; and when thou'st got the WEATHER-GAGE thou mayst drive them before thee.

WEATHER-HEADED. *See* WETHER-HEADED.

WEATHER-SCUPPER, *subs. phr.* (nautical).—'It is an old joke at sea to advise a greenhorn to get a handspike and hold it down hard in the WEATHER-SCUPPERS to steady the ship's wild motions' (CLARK RUSSELL).

WEATHER-SPY, *subs. phr.* (old).—A weather-prophet: spec. an astrologer.

d. 1631. DONNE, *Satires*, i. A gulling WEATHER-SPY.

WEAVE (HOTTEN).—I. When a knowing blade is asked what he has been doing lately, and does not choose to tell, he replies, 'WEAVING LEATHER APRONS.' (From the reports of a celebrated trial for gold robbery on the South-Western Railway.) Similar replies are, 'Making a trundle for a goose's eye,' or a 'whim-wham to bridle a goose.' Sometimes a man will describe himself as 'a doll's-eye WEAVER.'

Verb (common).—To roll the neck and body from side to side: of horses. Also (American)=to walk unsteadily, TO MAKE SNAKES (*q.v.*): as a shuttle in a loom: spec. of drunken men: usually with *along*, *about*, etc.

1884. CLEMENS, *Huckleberry Finn*. He began in earnest too; and went WEAVING first to one side of the platform and then the other.

WEAVING, *subs.* (gaming).—A card-sharping trick: cards are kept on the knee, or between the knee and the under side of the table, and used when required by changing them for cards held in the hand (HOTTEN).

WEB-FOOT STATE, *subs. phr.* (American).—Oregon.

WEDDING, *subs.* (old).—Cesspool emptying: 'because always done in the night' (GROSE).

WEDGE, *subs.* (Old Cant).—1. Generic for money: spec. silver, money or plate: *see* RHINO (GROSE). Hence WEDGE-FEEDER=a silver spoon; WEDGE-LOBB=a silver snuff-box; WEDGE-YACK=a silver watch; WEDGE-HUNTER = a thief, spec. one devoting attention to silver plate, watches, etc.; TO FLASH THE WEDGE=to FENCE (*q.v.*) the SWAG (*q.v.*).

1832. EGAN, *Book of Sports*. He valued neither cove nor swell, for he had WEDGE snug in his clie.

1839. AINSWORTH, *Jack Sheppard* [1889], 70. Near to these hopeful youths sat a fence, or receiver, bargaining with a clouter, or pickpocket, for a 'suit,' . . . two 'cloaks,' . . . and a WEDGE-LOBB.

1879. HORSLEY, *Jottings from Jail* [*Macm.*, xl. 500]. They told me all about the WEDGE, how I should know it by the ramp.

1891. CAREW, *Auto. of a Gypsy*, 417. Nat swore I must'er been scammered and 'ad made a mistake in sampling the WEDGE.

2. (Cambridge University).—The last in the classical TRIPOS (*q.v.*) list: also WOODEN WEDGE: in 1824, on the publication of the first list the position was occupied by a T. H. Wedgewood.

TO KNOCK OUT THE WEDGES, *verb. phr.* (American). — To desert, 'leave in the LURCH' (*q.v.*), abandon one in a difficulty.

THE THIN (or SMALL) END OF THE WEDGE, *subs. phr.* (colloquial). — A first move (or a beginning), seemingly trivial, but calculated to lead to important results, 'a finger in the pie,' a manœuvre, shift, artifice.

WEDLOCK, *subs.* (old).—A wife.

1601. JONSON, *Poetaster*, iv. 1. Which of these is thy WEDLOCK, Menelaus? thy Helen, thy Lucrece? that we may do her honour, mad boy.

WEE, *adj.* (colloquial). — Small, little, tiny: also WEENY (which also *see*).

1596. SHAKSPEARE, *Merry Wives*, i. 4. 22. No, forsooth: he hath but a little WEE face, with a little yellow beard, a Cain-coloured beard.

1814. SCOTT, *Waverley*, lxxi. I made up a WEE bit minute of an antenuptial contract.

WEED, *subs.* (common).—1. A cigar, a NEWTOWN PIPPIN (*q.v.*). Also THE WEED=tobacco: *cf.* CABBAGE.

1844. *Puck*, 14. With his WEED in his cheek and his glass on his eye, His cutaway neat, and knowing tie, The milliners' hearts he did trepan My spicy swell small-college man.

1856. DOW, *Sermons*, iii. By the appearance of the shirt-bosoms of some inveterate chewers of the WEED, I should judge they had been squirting their juice in the face of a north-easter.

1879. *Mysteries of New York*, 89. Those who were not dancing were seated around the room, some smoking, others chewing the WEED, still others drinking.

1888. H. JAMES [*Harper's Mag.*, lxxvii. 88]. Sir Rufus puffed his own WEED in solitude, strolling up and down the terrace.

1889. *Ally Sloper*, 6 July. Last week he offered me a WEED—A worse one no man's lips e'er soiled.

1901. *Troddles*, 77. He was fourteen . . . and produced his cigarette case and asked me to 'have a WEED.'

2. (colloquial). — Generic for sorryness or worthlessness: spec. a horse, unfit for stock, a SCREW (*q.v.*): *i.e.* (racing) an animal lacking the points of a thoroughbred. Whence WEEDY, *adj.*= worthless, unfit for stock purposes.

1859. LEVER, *Davenport Dunn*, ii. He bore the same relation to a man of fashion that a WEED does to a winner of the Derby.

1888. BOLDREWOOD, *Squatter's Dream*, 28. She pointed to her steed, a small violent WEED.

1888. *Harper's Mag.*, lxxvi. 625. A gypsy hostler would trot out a succession of the WEEDIEST of old screws.

3. (once literary: now colloquial in surviving sense).—In *pl.* =generic for clothes: spec. an outer garment: now only in phrase WIDOWS' WEEDS=mourning. Whence WEEDY=clad in mourning garments.

1320. GROSSETESTE, *Castel of Loue*, 658. Vnder vre WEDE vre kynde nom, And al sop-fast mon-bi-com [Under our garb he took our nature, and became very man].

. . . *Rom. of Partenay* [E.E.T.S.], 3416. The gret dispite which in hert he had Off Fromont, that in monkes WEDE was clade.

1369. CHAUCER, *Troilus*, iii. 1719. He spendeth, justeth, and maketh feastings, He geveth freely oft, and chaungeth WEDE.

1503. DUNBAR, *Thistle and Rose*, sub. init. Methocht freshe May befoir my bed upstude, In WEID depaynt of mony diverse hew.

1588. GREENE, *Friar Bacon*, 153. Tell me, Ned Lacy, didst thou mark the maid, How lovely in her country-WEEDS she look'd. *Ibid.* (1594), *Orlando Furioso* [GROSART], 1130 O sir, know that vnder simple WEEDS The gods haue maskt.

1590. SPENSER, *Faery Queen*, I. vii. 21. The woful dwarfe.—When all was past, took up his forlorne WEED.

d. 1634. CHAPMAN [JOHNSON]. Her own hands putting on both shirt and WEEDE.

1671. MILTON, *Paradise Regained*, i. 314. They who, to be sure of Paradise, Dying put on the WEEDS of Dominic.

1766. BROOKE, *Fool of Quality*, i. 191. I gave her twopence, reassumed my former garb, and left my WEEDS in her custody.

d. 1870. DICKENS [ANNANDALE]. She was as WEEDY as in the earlier days of her mourning.

Verb (old).—'To pilfer or purloin a small portion from a large quantity of any thing; often done by young or timid depredators, in the hope of escaping detection, as, an apprentice or shopman will WEED his master's lob, that is, take small sums out of the till when opportunity offers, which sort of peculation may be carried on with impunity for a length of time; but experienced thieves sometimes think it good judgment to WEED a place, in order that it may be good again, perhaps for a considerable length of time, as in the instance of a warehouse, or other depôt, for goods, to which they may possess the means of access by means of a false key; in this case, by taking too great a swag, at first, the proprietors

would discover the deficiency, and take measures to prevent future depredation. To WEED THE SWAG is to embezzle part of the booty, unknown to your palls, before a division takes place, a temptation against which very few of the family are proof, if they can find an opportunity. A flash-cove, on discovering a deficiency in his purse or property, which he cannot account for, will declare that he (or it, naming the article) has been wedded to the ruffian' (GROSE). Hence WEEDING-DUES: in speaking of any person, place, or property that has been weeded, it is said WEEDING DUES have been concerned.

WEE-JEE, *subs. phr.* (old).—1. A chimney-pot. Hence (2) a hat: *see* GOLGOTHA.

3. (common).—Anything superlatively good of its kind: spec. a clever invention: *e.g.* 'That's a regular WEE-JEE.'

WEEK. PHRASES, etc.: A WEEK OF SUNDAYS=an indefinite time: spec. seven Sundays, hence seven weeks: also MONTH OF SUNDAYS; THE INSIDE OF A WEEK=from Monday till Saturday; A PARSON'S WEEK=from Saturday to Monday; TO KNOCK ONE INTO THE MIDDLE OF NEXT WEEK=to punish severely, knock out of time, DO FOR (*q.v.*); AN ATTACK OF THE WEEK'S (or MONTH'S) END = impecuniosity, hard uppishness; WHEN TWO SUNDAYS COME IN A WEEK= never: a left-handed assent.

1800. PRICE, *Life of H. F. Carey*, i. 144. Get my duty done for a Sunday, so that I may be out a PARSON'S WEEK.

1850. *Southern Sketches* [BARTLETT]. Arch would fetch him a side-wipe on the head, and KNOCK HIM INTO THE MIDDLE OF NEXT WEEK.

1850. KINGSLEY, *Alton Locke*, xxvii. I haven't heard more fluent or passionate English this MONTH OF SUNDAYS.

1888. BOLDREWOOD, *Robbery Under Arms*, XL. 'I ain't been out of this blessed hole,' he says, 'for a MONTH OF SUNDAYS.'

1892. HENLEY and STEVENSON, *Deacon Brodie*, Sc. 2. p. 7. A MONTH OF SUNDAYS.

WEEKENDER, *subs.* (common).—1. A week-end mistress, a Saturday-to-Monday girl.

2. (common). — A week-end holiday.

WEENIE, *intj.* (telegraph clerks').—A warning that an inspector is coming.

WEEPER, *subs.* (colloquial). — A conventional badge of mourning: *e.g.* a white border of linen or muslin worn at the end of a sleeve, a long crape hatband as worn by men at a funeral, or the long veil of WIDOWS'-WEEDS (*q.v.*).

1759–62. GOLDSMITH, *Citizen of the World*, xcv. Mourners clap bits of muslin on their sleeves, and these are called WEEPERS. Weeping muslin; alas, alas, very sorrowful truly! These WEEPERS then it seems are to bear the whole burthen of the distress.

1760–62. SMOLLETT, *Sir L. Greaves*, iii. The young squire was even then very handsome, and looked remarkably well in his WEEPERS.

1862. THACKERAY, *Philip*, ii. It is a funereal street . . . the carriages which drive there ought to have feathers on the roof, and the butlers who open the doors should wear WEEPERS. *Ibid.*, *Bluebeard's Ghost*. She had her beautiful hair confined in crimped caps, and her WEEPERS came over her elbows.

1871–2. ELIOT, *Middlemarch*, lxxx. If anybody was to marry me, flattering himself as I should wear those hijeous WEEPERS two years for him, he'd be deceived by his own vanity, that's all.

TO WEEP IRISH, *verb. phr.* (old).—To lament prodigally, to wail: spec. without sincerity, to shed crocodile's tears.

1650. FULLER, *Pisgah Sight*, II. xii. 15. Surely the Egyptians did not WEEP-IRISH with faigned and mercenary tears.

1710. CENTLIVRE, *Bickerstaff's Burying*. What the devil can be the matter? why all this noise? here's none but friends; I don't apprehend that anybody can overhear you; this is something like the IRISH CRY.

WEEPING-CROSS. TO RETURN BY WEEPING-CROSS, *verb. phr.* (old).—1. To fail, suffer defeat, meet with repulse. Hence (2) to repent, to lament: *cf.* LOTHBURY. [NARES: Of the three places now retaining the name, one is between Oxford and Banbury; another very near Stafford, where the road turns off to Walsall; the third near Shrewsbury: these crosses being, doubtless, places where penitents particularly offered their devotions.]

1580. LYLY, *Euphues and his England*, D. ii. b. But the time will come when, comming home by WEEPING CROSSE, thou shalt confesse that it is better to be at home.

1605. DEKKER, *Eastward Hoe* [DODSLEY, *Old Plays* (REED), iv. 266]. Since they have all FOUND THE WAY BACK AGAIN BY WEEPING CROSS. But I'll not see them.

1605. HEYWOOD, *If You Know not Me* [*Works* (1874), i. 267]. Had you before the law foreseen the losse, You had not now COME HOME BY WEEPING CROSSE.

1612. WITHERS, *Prince Henrie's Obseq*. For here I mourne for your, our publike losse, And doe my pennance at the WEEPING CROSSE.

1614. FLETCHER, *Night Walker*, i. 1. One is a kind of WEEPING CROSS, Jack, A gentle purgatory.

1629. *Young Gallant's Whirligig*. For if hee straggle from his limits farre (Except the guidance of some happy starre Doe rectifie his steps, restore his losse), He may perhaps COME HOME BY WEEPING CROSSE.

1655. FANSHAWE, *Lusiad*, x. 64. The pagan king of Calicut take short, That would have past him; with no little loss SENDING HIM HOME AGAIN BY WEEPING CROSS.

1660. HOWELL, *Proverbs*, P. 3. b. He that goes out with often losse, At last COMES HOME BY WEEPING CROSSE.

WEGOTISM, *subs.* (literary).—The incessant use of 'WE' in journalism: *cf.* WEISM.

1881. JENNINGS, *Curiosities of Criticism*, 156. Individual merit would no longer be merged, as it is now, in what is called the WEGOTISM of the press.

WEIGHT, *subs.* (old).—1. The end of one's tether: 'it is often customary with the TRAPS (*q.v.*) to wink at depredations of a petty nature, and for which no reward would attach, and to let a thief go unmolested till he commits a capital crime; they then grab him and share a reward of 40*l.*, or upwards: therefore these gentry will say, Let him alone . . . till he weighs his WEIGHT' (GROSE).

2. (old).—Lust, wantonness, HEAT (*q.v.*).

1772. BRIDGES, *Burlesque Homer*, 2. I'm certain ne'er a parson's daughter (Though you went round the world to get her) Would carry WEIGHT, for inches, better.

WEIRD SISTERS (THE), *subs. phr.* (literary). — The Fates: also THREE WEIRD SISTERS.

1512–3. DOUGLAS, *Æneid*, iii. The remanant hereof, quhat euer be it, The WEIRD SISTERIS defendis that suld be wit.

1606. SHAKSPEARE, *Macbeth*, ii. 1. 20. I dreamt last night of the three WEIRD SISTERS.

WEISM, *subs.* (literary).—The excessive use of 'WE' in journalism: *cf.* WEGOTISM.

WELL, *adv.* (American).—An elliptical use of well is peculiar to American speech, especially at the beginning of sentences, as a mere expletive or in answer to questions. [LOWELL, *Biglow Papers*, Int.: 'Put before such a phrase as "How d'e do?" it is commonly short, and has the sound of *wul*; but, in reply, it is deliberative, and the various shades of meaning which can be conveyed by difference of intonation, and by prolonging or abbreviating, I should vainly attempt to describe. I have heard *ooahl*, *wahl*, *ahl*, *wăl*, and something nearly approaching the sound of *le* in *able*. Sometimes before "I" it dwindles to a mere *l*; as, "l *I* dunno." A friend told me that he once heard five "WELLS," like pioneers, precede the answer to an inquiry about the price of land. The first was the ordinary *wul*, in deference to custom; the second, the long, perpending *ooahl*, with a falling inflection of the voice; the third, the same, but with the voice rising, as if in despair of a conclusion, into a plaintive. nasal whine; the fourth, *wulh*, ending in the aspirate of a sigh; and then, fifth, came a short, sharp *wal*, showing that a conclusion had been reached.']

TO DIG A WELL AT A RIVER, *verb. phr.* (old).—To act the fool, do the unnecessary (RAY).

TO PUT ONE IN A WELL (IN THE GARDEN, or IN A HOLE), *verb. phr.* (old).—1. To defraud an accomplice of his share of booty: also TO WELL ONE (GROSE).

2. (common).—To inconvenience, nonplus, or get the better of.

WELL-IN, *adj. phr.* (Australian).—Well-off, well-to-do, wealthy.

1891. BOLDREWOOD, *A Sydney-side Saxon*, 1. He's a WELL-IN squatter that took up runs or bought them cheap before free-selection, and land-boards, and rabbits, and all the other bothers that turn a chap's hair grey before his time.

WELLINGTON, *subs.* (common).—In *pl.* = (1) long-legged boots largely worn in the early part of the last century: they came well up the leg, high enough in front to cover the knee and to the bend of the knee behind. Also (2) shorter boots of similar pattern covering the calf of the leg, and worn (usually) under the trousers: *cf.* BLUCHER, ALBERT, GLADSTONE, etc. [A favourite campaigning foot-gear of the Duke of Wellington.]

d. 1821. KEATS, *Modern Love*. Miss's comb is made a pearl tiara, And common WELLINGTONS turn Romeo boots.

1821. COOMBE, *Dr Syntax*, III. v. His gaiters, with dust covered o'er, Were seen upon his legs no more, But when he rode his top-boots shone, Or hussar'd *à la* WELLINGTON.

1884. YATES, *Fifty Years London Life*, I. ii. No gentleman could wear anything in the daytime but WELLINGTON boots, high up the leg, over which the trousers fitted tightly, covering most of the foot, and secured underneath by a broad strap.

X

WELSH, *verb* (racing and common).—To cheat: spec. to run away without settling. Hence WELSHER = an absconding bookmaker, a common cheat: also WELCHER.

1869. GREENWOOD, *Seven Curses of London*. Does the reader know what is a WELSHER, the creature against whose malpractices the sporting public are so emphatically warned? Probably he does not. It is still more unlikely that he ever witnessed a WELSHER hurt.

1883. *Punch*, 26 May, 252. 1. 'Look 'ere, this hinnocent cove has been trying a ramp on!' *Crowd*. WELSHER! kill him! WELSHER!

18[?]. *All Year Round* [*Century*]. The WELCHER, properly so called, takes the money offered him to back a horse, but when he has taken money enough from his dupes departs from the scene of his labours, and trusts to his luck, a dyed wig or a pair of false whiskers, not to be recognised.

1887. *St. James's Gazette*, 2 June. The public has always understood that the law cannot be made to touch a 'WELSHER'; and hence it is that forcible measures are often taken to inflict private vengeance.

1887. *D. Teleg.*, 12 Mar. He stakes his money with one of the book-makers whom he has seen at his stand for many years, with the certainty that he will receive his winnings, and run no risk of being 'WELSHED'—which would probably be his fate on an English racecourse—if he be astute or lucky enough to spot the right horse.

1889. *Nineteenth Century*, xxvi. 850. WELSHING was decided to be an indictable offence.

WELSH-AMBASSADOR, *subs. phr.* (old).—The cuckoo.

1608. MIDDLETON, *Trick to Catch*, iv. Thy sound is like the cuckoo, the WELCH AMBASSADOR.

WELSH-CRICKET, *subs. phr.* (old).—1. A louse: and (2) = a tailor: *cf.* PRICK-LOUSE: *see* next entry.

1592. GREENE, *Quip for Upst. Court.* [*Harl. Misc.*, v. 404]. Before he [the taylor] had no other cognizance but a plaine Spanish needle with a WELCH-CRICKET at top.

WELSH-FIDDLE, *subs. phr.* (old).—The itch (B. E. and GROSE): *cf.* SCOTCH-FIDDLE (s.v. SCOTCH).

WELSHMAN'S-HOSE. TO TURN A THING TO A WELSHMAN'S-HOSE, *verb. phr.* (old).—To suit to one's purpose.

d. 1529. SKELTON, *Boke of Colin Clout*. And MAKE A WALSHMAN'S HOSE Of the text and of the glose.

1606. *Mirr. for Mag.*, 278. The laws we did interpret, and statutes of the land, Not truly by the text, but newly by a glose: And words that were most plaine, when they by us were skan'd, We turned by construction TO A WELCH-MAN'S HOSE.

WELSH-RABBIT, *subs. phr.* (common).—A dish of toasted cheese. [SMYTH-PALMER: 'One of a numerous class of slang expressions—the mock-heroic of the eating-house—in which some common dish or product for which any place or people has a special reputation is called by the name of some more dainty article of food which it is supposed humorously to supersede or equal.'] *Cf.* GERMAN-DUCK, COBBLER'S-LOBSTER, NORFOLK-CAPON, BILLINGSGATE-PHEASANT, and many others (GROSE).

1772. GRAVES, *Spiritual Quixote*, VII. ix. Go to the tavern, and call for your bottle, and your pipe, and your WELSH RABBIT.

1854-5. THACKERAY, *Newcomes*, i. The goes of stout, the Chough and Crow, the WELSH RABBIT, the Red Cross Knight . . . the song and the cup, in a word, passed round merrily.

WELSH-WIG, *subs. phr.* (common).—A worsted cap.

WELSH-PARSLEY, *subs. phr.* (old).—Hemp: hence a hangman's rope.

1625-35. FLETCHER, *Elder Brother*, i. 2. In tough WELCH-PARSLY, which our vulgar tongue is Strong hempen halters.

1638. RANDOLPH, *Hey for Honesty*, iv. 1. This is a rascal deserves . . . to dance in hemp Derrick's coranto; let's choke him with WELSH PARSLEY.

WELT, *verb* (colloquial).—To beat severely. Hence WELTER = a stinging blow; and WELTING = a sound thrashing.

1900. KIPLING, *Stalky & Co.*, 49. He gave us eight cuts apiece—WELTERS—for—takin' unheard-of liberties with a new master.

WENCH, *subs.* (once literary: now colloquial).—Orig. a child of either sex: *cf.* girl, harlot, etc.; subsequently a young woman without any idea of bold familiarity or wantonness long afterwards and still frequently associated with the term. [*See* quot. 1363.] WENCH = a wanton, mistress, or harlot early came into vogue: nowadays a working girl or woman of humble station in life is usually implied, while in America the word (save in vulgar use) is confined to coloured women, especially those in service. As *verb* = to whore; WENCHER = a whoremonger, MUTTON MONGER (*q.v.*), WENCHLESS = harlot-free; WENCHING = whoring; and as *adj.* = lecherous.

c. 1280. *Ancren Riwle*, 334. He biscinte Sodome & Gomorre, were, & wif, & WENCHEL. [He sank Sodom and Gomorrah, man, woman, and child.]

c. 1360. *William of Palerne* [E.E.T.S.], 1901. William & his worthi WENCHE [of a princess].

1363. LANGLAND, *Piers Plowman* [E.E.T.S.]. [Goddes WENCH = Virgin Mary, s.v. 336. WENCH = harlot, s.v. 422].

1380. WYCLIF, *Bible*, Matthew ix. 24. Go ȝe awey, for the WENCHE is nat dead but slepith.

1383. CHAUCER, *Cant. Tales*, 'Merl chauntes Tale,' 10076. I am a gentiwoman, and no WENCHE. *Ibid.* 'Manciples Tale.' For that other is a powre woman, She shal be cleped his WENCHE and his lemman.

1530. PALSGRAVE. I iape a WENCH, *ie fout* and *ie bistocque*, it is better to iape a WENCH than to do worse.

c. 1561. *Nar. of Reform*, (Camden Soc.), 171. Before I removed from the sayde howse in London I hadde two chyldearne borne ther, a boy and a WHENCH.

1578. WHETSTONE, *Promos and Cassandra*. Therefore, sweet WENCH, help me to rue my woe.

1588-93. TARLETON, *Jests* [OLIPHANT, *New. Eng.*, ii. 13. Among the Verbs are, TO WENCH, *miss the likeness*, . . .].

1591. HARINGTON, *Ariost.*, v. 20. For Ariodant so lov'd the princely WENCH.

1593. SHAKSPEARE, *Titus Andron.*, iii. 1. Bear thou my hand, sweet WENCH, between thy teeth. *Ibid.* (1598), 1 *Henry IV.*, i. 2. A fair hot WENCH in flame-coloured taffeta. *Ibid.* (1602), *Othello*, v. 2. Now, how dost thou look now? O, ill-starr'd WENCH, Pale as thy smock. *Ibid.* (1602), *Troilus and Cressida*, v. 4. 35. What's become of the WENCHING rogues? *Ibid.* (1605), *Cymbeline*, iv. 2. Do not play in WENCH-like words with that Which is so serious. *Ibid.* (1609), *Pericles*, iv. 2. Mytilene is full of gallants. We lost too much money this mart by being too WENCHLESS. We have but poor three.

1590. SPENSER, *Faery Queen*, I. iii. 11. But the rude WENCH her answerd not at all; She could not heare, nor speake, nor understand.

1597. HALL, *Satires*, iv. 5. An horse-leech, barren WENCH, or gaping grave.

1598. FLORIO, *Worlde of Wordes*. *Biondella* . . . a golden-lockt WENCH, as we say a goldilocks.

1599. JONSON, *Every Man out of His Humour*, iv. 4. Let a man sweat once a week in a hot-house, and be well rubbed and froted with a plump juicy WENCH and clean linen. *Ibid.* (1605), *Eastward Hoe* [DODSLEY, *Old Plays*, iv. 221]. Thou art pandar to me for my WENCH, and I to thee for thy cousenage.

1601. HOLLAND, *Plinie*, XXXV. x. Given he was exceedingly to WENCHING.

1607. DEKKER, *Northward Hoe*, i. 2. A lodging of your providing! to be called a lieutenant's or a captain's WENCH.

1607. *How a Man May Choose a Good Wife*, etc., iv. 3 (DODSLEY, *Old Plays*, 4th ed., 1875, ix. 78). A huffing WENCH i' faith.

1611. *Bible*, 2 Samuel xvii. 17. A WENCH went and told them.

1630. TAYLOR, *Works*. But yet, me thinkes, he gives thee but a frumpe, In telling how thee kist a WENCHES rumpe.

1651. RANDOLPH, *Hey for Honesty*, iii. 3. The WENCHES will tumble and merrily jumble.

d. 1654. SELDEN, *Table Talk*, 'Clergy.' The fellow that was a great WENCHER.

1660-69. PEPYS, *Diary*, III. 207. My cozen Roger told us . . . that the Archbishop of Canterbury . . . is as very a WENCHER as can be.

1663. KILLIGREW, *Parson's Wedding* [DODSLEY, *Old Plays* (1875), xiv. 438]. Rather than marry, keep a WENCH.

1672. WYCHERLEY, *Love in a Wood*, ii. 1. A man . . . may bring his bashful WENCH, and not have her put out of countenance by the impudent honest women of the town. *Ibid.*, v. 6. *Dap.* Why she was my WENCH. *Gripe.* I'll make her honest then.

1686-7. AUBREY, *Gentilisme* (1881), 163. The towne is full of wanton WENCHES, and . . . (they say) scarce three honest women in the town.

1686. DURFEY, *Commonw. of Wordes*, i. 1. I hate your young WENCHES, Skitish Colts—they are so hard mouth'd, there's no dealing with 'em.

1702. STEELE, *The Funeral, or Grief à la Mode*, Act. i. This WENCH I know has played me false, and horned me in my gallants. [NOTE.—That the speaker is a female shows the word to have been transferable to the other sex.]

1711. STEELE, *Tatler*, 242. The WENCH in the kitchen sings and scours from morning till night. *Ibid.* (1711), *Spectator*, 2. He . . . can inform you from which of the French kings's WENCHES our wives and daughters had this manner of curling their hair.

1109. MALKIN, *Gil Blas* [ROUTLEDGE], 311. Is he fond of play? Does he WENCH?

1856. DOW, *Sermons*, III. 111. The blushing morn at length came travelling up from the oriental clime, and sowed the earth with pearls and diamonds, that glittered upon the dark bosom of night like jewels upon the brow of an Ethiopian WENCH.

WEST-CENTRAL, *subs. phr.* (common).—A water-closet: *i.e.* W.C.

WESTMINSTER-WEDDING, *subs. phr.* (old).—'A Whore and a Rogue Married together' (B. E. and GROSE).

WESTPHALIA, *subs.* (trade).—The backside; the BUM (*q.v.*): an allusion to Westphalia hams.

WEST-POINTER, *subs. phr.* (American).—A student, a graduate of the U.S. Military Academy at West Point.

WESTRALIA, *subs.* (commercial).—Western Australia. [MORRIS: The word was coined to meet the necessities of the submarine cable regulations, which confine messages to words containing not more than ten letters.]

1896. *Studio*, Oct., 151. The latest example is the El Dorado of Western Australia, or as she is beginning to be more generally called 'Westralia.'

1896. *Nineteenth Century*, Nov., 711. The WESTRALIAN Mining Boom [Title].

1901. *Pall Mall Gaz.*, 15 May, 4. 3. WESTRALIANS continue decidedly firm, notwithstanding the troubles of the markets and the slackness of business.

WESTY-HEAD, *adj. phr.* (old).—Dizzy, giddy (HALL, *Satires*).

WET, *subs.* (common).—Generic for drink, BOOZE (*q.v.*): spec. 'drink demanded or expected of anyone wearing new clothes' (GROSE). Whence TO WET A COAT (BARGAIN, DEAL, etc.) = to

TREAT (*q.v.*), to ratify by drinking success. As *verb*=to drink, LUSH (*q.v.*): also TO WET ONE'S WHISTLE (CLAY, SWALLOW, THE RED LANE, etc.): Fr. *se mouiller*: *see* WHISTLE and WHISTLE-DRUNK; TO WET THE OTHER EYE=to take one drink after another. As *adj.* (or WET-HANDED) =(1) addicted to drinking, (2)= drunk: *see* SCREWED; and 3 (American) = anti - prohibition; *e.g.* a WET-TOWN=a town opposed to prohibition in the sale of intoxicants: *cf.* 'dry': whence A WET=one opposed to prohibition. Also HEAVY-WET=porter; TWOPENNY - WET (*see* TWO-PENNY); A WET-HAND (WHETTER or WET-'UN)=a toper: *see* LUSH-INGTON; WET - BARGAIN (*see* BARGAIN); WET - NIGHT = an evening carousal; WET-GOODS= drink: *cf.* 'dry-goods'; WET-QUAKER=(1) a secret drinker, and spec. (2)='a Drunkard of that Sect' (B. E.); TO WET THE SICKLE=to drink out earnest money at harvest-time; WETTING THE BLOCK=a custom among shoemakers on the first Monday in March, when they cease from working by candlelight, and have a supper so called (HALLIWELL).

1383. CHAUCER, *Cant. Tales*, 'Reeves Tale.' As any jay she light was and jolyf So was his joly WHISTLE WEL ywet.

1530. PALSGRAVE, *Lang. Franc.*, 780. I WETE MY WHYSTELL, as good drinkers do. *Je crocque la pie.* Wyll you WETE YOUR WHYSTELL.

1622. FLETCHER, *Beggar's Bush*, iii. 1. Give the boy some drink there! Piper, WHET YOUR WHISTLE.

1653. WALTON, *Compleat Angler*, 86. I have not yet WETTED my line Since we met together.

d. 1692. SHADWELL, *Humours of the Navy*, ii. 3. Then we should have commissions to WET.

c. 1700. WARD, *England's Reformation*, ii. 175. Socinians and Presbyterians, Quakers, and WET-QUAKERS or Merry-ones.

1703. STEELE, *Tender Husband*, i. Then, harkye! brother; we'll go take a WET, and settle the whole affair. *Ibid.* (1710), *Tatler*, No. 141. The WHETTER is obliged to refresh himself every moment with a liquor, as the Snuff-taker with a powder. *Ibid.*, *Tatler*, 138. People . . . known by the name of WHETTERS who drink themselves into an intermediate state of being neither drunk nor sober before the hours of Exchange or business. *Ibid.* (1714), *Spectator*, No. 88. Three quarts to my new Lord for WETTING his title.

d. 1704. BROWN, *Works*, iii. 26. Would you buy any naked truth, or light in a dark lanthorn? Look in the WET-QUAKER'S walk.

d. 1721. PRIOR, *Celia to Damon.* When my lost lover the tall ship ascends, With music gay, and WET with jovial friends, The tender accents of a woman's cry Will pass unheard, will unregarded die.

1731. FIELDING, *Letter Writers*, ii. 2. A soph, he is immortal, And never can decay; For how should he return to dust Who daily WETS HIS CLAY?

1847-8. THACKERAY, *Vanity Fair*, xi. As he knew he should have a WET NIGHT, it was agreed that he might gallop back again in time for church on Sunday morning.

1864. LOWELL, *Fireside Trav.*, 119. When his poor old CLAY WAS WET with gin.

1871. *Echo*, 16 March. 'Are you going to have a WET, old boy?' one familiarly remarked.

1874. *Siliad*, 16. Bacchus is in an awful vinous sweat; His hot brow laves he with all sorts of WET.

1876. HINDLEY, *Cheap Jack*, 268. I shall be back again shortly, when we will WET THE DEAL.

1879. BRUNLEES PATTERSON, *Life in the Ranks.* Many are the schemes, contrivances, and devices of some of the old topers to obtain a WET or reviver, first thing in the morning.

1881. GRANT, *Bush-life in Queensland*, I. 30. No bargain could be completed without a WET, and no friendship or enmity forgotten without recourse to the bottle.

1897. MARSHALL, *Pomes*, 76. For no hot summer sun ever dried up the WET Like the lads did—why, some of 'em ain't sober yet.

Adj. (venery).—Spec. of women when secreting LETCH-WATER (*q.v.*). Also TO HAVE (DO OR PERFORM) a BOTTOM-WETTER (WET-'UN OR GET A WET BOTTOM)=to copulate: of women only: *see* GREENS and RIDE.

1772. BRIDGES, *Burlesque Homer*, 123. There's ne'er a rake in all the town Would tip you half of half a crown, Then you'll with aldermen be willing To earn a sixpence or a shilling, Or else in midnight cellars ply For twopence WET and two-pence dry.

WET-BLANKET. *See* BLANKET.

WET BOAT, *subs. phr.* (nautical).—A boat that is crank and ships water readily.

1859. READE, *Love me Little*, xvii. 'Why don't you go forward, sir? She is sure to wet us abaft.' . . . Thank you, but . . . (with an heroic attempt at sea slang) I like a WET BOAT.

WET-BOB. *See* BOB.

WET-FINGER. WITH A WET FINGER, *phr.* (old). — Easily, readily: as easy as turning over the leaf of a book, or rubbing out writing on a slate.

1561. *Burnynge of Paules Church.* There is to manye suche, though ye laugh, and beleve it not, and not hard to shewe them WITH A WET FINGER.

1593. HARVEY, *Pierces Superog.*, 21. I hate brawls with my heart, and can turn over a volume of wrongs WITH A WET FINGER.

1602. DEKKER, *Honest Whore* [DODSLEY, *Old Plays* (REED), iii. 255]. If ever I stand in need of a wench that will come WITH A WET FINGER, porter thou shalt earn my money. *Ibid.* (1609), *Guls Hornebook* [NOTT], 160. What gentlewomen or citizen's wives you can WITH A WET FINGER have at any time to sup with you.

1615. BEAUMONT and FLETCHER, *Cupid's Revenge*, iv. Take a good heart, man; all the low ward is ours WITH A WET-FINGER.

1630. TAYLOR, *Works* [NARES]. As bookes are leafe by leafe oft turn'd and tost, So are the garments of a whore (almost): For both of them, WITH A WET FINGER may Be folded or unfolded, night or day.

Also in proverbial wheeze (amongst children), 'See my finger WET (*licking the finger*), see my finger dry (*wiping it dry*), I'll cut my throat (*drawing finger across throat*) before I tell a lie' (a strong assurance of veracity).

WET-GOOSE, *subs. phr.* (provincial). —A poor simple fellow.

WETHERALL. GENERAL WETHERALL'S IN COMMAND, *phr.* (military).—Used when a parade is abandoned through inclement weather.

WETHER-HEADED, *adj. phr.* (old). —Silly, superstitious, a bit off: also WEATHER-HEADED. As *subs.* = a dolt, simpleton, fool: *cf.* MUTTON-HEAD.

1695. CONGREVE, *Love for Love*, II. 7. Sir, is this usage for your son?—for that old WEATHER-HEADED fool, I know how to laugh at him; but you, Sir——.

WET - NURSED, *adj. phr.* — 1. Coddled, SHEPHERDED (*q.v.*), BACKED (*q.v.*); *see* NURSE.

1874. *Siliad*, 109. Who, ere his whiskers had completely grown, Possessed a comic paper of his own; But though WET-NURSED by someone in Debrett, It died quite young.

18[?]. *Elec. Rev.* (*Century*). The system of WET-NURSING adopted by the Post-office authorities in the case of the telegraph service has not been one of uniform success.

WET-UN, *subs. phr.* (slaughterers'). —1. A diseased beast: *cf.* STAGGERING-BOB.

2. *See* WET, *adj.*

WE-UNS, *pr.* (American). — We, us: *i.e.* we ones: *cf.* YOU-UNS.

1885. MURFREE, *Prophet Great Smoky Mountains*, ix. Grind some fur WEE-UNS ter-morrer.

W. F.'S, *subs. phr.* (old Tasmanian). —Wild cattle.

1891. FENTON, *Bush Life in Tasmania Fifty Years Ago*, 24. Round up a mob of the wildest W.F.'s that ever had their ears slit. [Note]: This was the brand on Mr. William Field's wild cattle.

WHACK (or WACK), *subs.* (old).— 1. A heavy, smart, sounding blow. As *verb* = to beat, thwack. Also a heavy fall, and as *verb*=to fall.

1837. BARHAM, *Ingoldsby Leg.*, 'Lady Rohesia.' A blow descended, such as we must borrow a term from the Sister Island adequately to describe—it was a WHACK.

1851-61. MAYHEW, *Lond. Lab.*, II. 564. Sometimes a chap will give me a lick with a stick just as I'm going over; sometimes a reg'lar good hard WHACK.

1888. CLOUSTON, *Book of Noodles*, ii. A traveller, coming up, finds the missing man by WHACKING each of them over the shoulder.

1886. *D. Teleg.*, 21 Feb. Yet the Flannigans and the Murphys paid no heed to him, but WHACKED away at each other with increasing vigour.

1887. *Field*, 24 Sep. Father WHACKS her and the children in turns.

2. (common). — A share; piece; spec. an equal portion (GROSE): also WHACKING. As *verb* (or GO WHACKS)=(1) to divide, to share; and (2) to settle, pay up: *e.g.* WHACK the blunt =share the money; Give me my WHACK = Hand me my due. Also TO WHACK UP.

1840. THACKERAY, *Shabby Genteel Story*, v. This gay young bachelor had taken his share (what he called 'his WHACK') of pleasure.

1851-61. MAYHEW, *Lond. Lab.*, II. 152. They then, as they term it, WHACK the whole lot. *Ibid.*, II. 172. At last Long J—— and I got to quarrel about the WHACKING; there was cheatin' a-goin' on.

1877. HORSLEY, *Jottings from Jail.* So when we got there, there was some reelers there what knew me, and my pals said, 'You had better get away from us; if we touch you will take your WHACK just the same.'

1888. GREENWOOD, *Little Ragamuffin.* 'You agreed that we should GO WHACKS in everything,' I pleaded, appealing to his sense of justice. *Ibid.*, *A Converted Burglar.* The sound, old-fashioned principle of 'sharing the danger and WHACKING THE SWAG.'

1890. WALCH, *Australian Song*, 509. My word! he did more than his WHACK; He was never a cove as would shirk.

1891. *Elect. Rev.* (*Century*). The city has never WHACKED UP with the gas company.

3. (colloquial).—An attempt, a trial, a stroke.

4. (provincial). — Appetite, TWIST (*q.v.*).

TO WHACK IT UP, *verb. phr.* (venery). — To copulate: *see* GREENS and RIDE.

WHACK! *adj.* (printers').—An emphatic expression of doubt; a polite way of giving the lie direct.

WHACKER, *subs.* (common).—Anything very large, a big thing, a WHOPPER (*q.v.*). Whence WHACKING=very large.

1861. HUGHES, *Tom Brown at Oxford*, XXX. 'Look what WHACKERS, Cousin Tom,' said Charley, holding out one of his prizes by its back towards Tom, while the indignant cray-fish flapped its tail.

1871. ATKINS, *House Scraps.* 'How kind of them,' says he, 'to gi'e me 'em, Since they're at such a WHACKING premium.'

1887. *Field*, 14 Nov. Good half-pounders every one, with an occasional WHACKER of ten ounces.

WHACKY, *subs.* (tailors').—A term applied to anyone doing anything ridiculous or FOOLING ABOUT (*q.v.*).

WHALE, *subs.* (Cheltenham College).— 1. Codfish.

2. (Royal Military Academy). —A sardine.

3. (common). — In *pl.* = anchovies on toast.

Verb (common)—1. To beat, thrash, lash vigorously. Hence WHALING=a trouncing, WALLOPING (*q.v.*).

1847. *New York Tribune*, Aug. But it is possible that we may, at some future time, go to war with England, her writers and speakers having spoken disparagingly of us, while her actors, half-pay officers, and other travelling gentry, carry their heads rather high in passing through our country,—for which 'arrogant' demeanour we are bound to give her a WHALING!

1870. WINTHROP, *Canoe and Saddle*, xii. I have whipped you . . . but have I WHALED you?

1884. BRET HARTE, *Society on the Stanislaus.* But first I would remark, that it is not a proper plan For any scientific gent to WHALE his fellow man.

2. (American).—To talk vehemently, harangue, SPOUT (*q.v.*): also TO WHALE AWAY.

18[?]. *Widow Bedott Papers*, 289. Professor Stubbins is always a WHALIN' AWAY about the dignity of labor, and has been deliverin' a course o' lectures on the subject. *Ibid.*, 105. I went to Baptist meeting. The elder, as usual, WHALED AWAY through his nose, thumped the desk, and went over and over the same thing.

1848. LOWELL, *Biglow Papers*, I. 13. Their masters can cuss 'em, and kick 'em, and WALE 'em, An' they notice it less 'an the ass did to Balaam.

TO FISH FOR HERRING AND CATCH A WHALE (or SPRAT), *verb. phr.* (old).—1. To get a result other than that expected. Hence (2) to 'catch a TARTAR' (*q.v.*), fail miserably.

IT'S VERY LIKE A WHALE, *phr.* (old).—Ironical assent to a preposterous assertion: *see* quot.

1596. SHAKSPEARE, *Hamlet*, iii. 2. 392. *Ham.* Do you see yonder cloud that's almost like a camel? *Pol.* By the mass and 'tis a camel, indeed. *Ham.* Methinks it is like a weasel. *Pol.* It is backed like a weasel. *Ham.* Or like a WHALE. *Pol.* VERY LIKE A WHALE.

TO GO AHEAD LIKE A WHALE, *verb. phr.* (common).—To forge ahead, to act, speak, or write vigorously.

See TUB and WHALER.

WHALEBONE. AS WHITE AS WHALEBONE, *phr.* (old).—A common simile for whiteness. [HALLIWELL: Some writers imagined ivory, formerly made from the teeth of the walrus, to be formed from the bones of the whale.]

c. 1430. *Destruction of Troy* [E.E.T.S.], 3055. To telle of hir tethe that tryelly were set, Alse QWYTE & qwem AS ANY QWALLE BON.

1567. TURBERVILLE, *Poems*, S. 8 b. A little mouth, with decent chin, A corall lip of hue, With teeth AS WHITE AS WHALE HIS BONE, Ech one in order due.

1590. SPENSER, *Faery Queen*, III. i. 15. Whose face did seem as clear as crystal stone, And eke, through fear AS WHITE AS WHALE'S BONE.

1594. SHAKSPEARE, *Love's Lab. Lost*, v. 2. This is the flower that smiles on every one, To shew his teeth AS WHITE AS WHALE HIS BONE.

WHALER, *subs.* (American).—1. Anything extraordinary of its kind, also WHALE, *e.g.* 'a regular WHALE': *see* WHOPPER. Hence WHALING = overwhelming.

1848. LONGSTREET, *Georgia Scenes*, 184. 'He's a WHALER!' said Rory; 'but his face is mighty little for his body and legs.'

2. (Australian).—A SUNDOWNER (*q.v.*): *i.e.* one who cruises about.

1893. *Sydney Morning Herald*, 12 Aug., 8. 8. The nomad, the WHALER, it is who will find the new order hostile to his vested interest of doing nothing.

WHANG, *subs.* (common).—1. A blow, a whack; a beating, a banging. As *verb* = to flog, thrash. Also (2) a banging noise, and as *verb* = to clatter, throw with violence.

d. 1889. BROWNING, *Up at a Villa*. Bang, WHANG, WHANG, goes the drum.

1890. WARNER, *Pilgrimage*, 317. The WHANG of the bass drum.

3. (colloquial). — A slice, chunk, DOLLOP (*q.v.*). Also as *verb* = to cut in large strips, slices, or chunks.

1678. RAY, *Proverbs*, 386. Of other men's lether, men take large WHANGES.

d. 1796. BURNS, *Holy Fair*. Wi' sweet-milk cheese in mony a WHANG.

d. 1803. BEATTIE, *Tales*, 8. My uncle set it to his breast, And WHANG'D it down.

4. (American). — Formerly, in Maine and some other parts of New England, a house-cleaning party; a gathering of neighbours to aid one of their number in cleaning a house (*Century*).

See WHANGER.

WHANGBY, *subs.* (provincial). — Very hard cheese made of old or skimmed milk (HALLIWELL).

WHANGAM (WHANGDOODLE, etc.), *subs.* (? nonce words).—An imaginary animal: its precise nature, form, and attributes are seemingly left to individual fancy.

1759-62. GOLDSMITH, *Citizen of the World*, xcviii. A WHANGAM that eats grasshoppers had marked [one] for its prey.

1856. *Harp of a Thousand Strings*. 'Where the lion roareth, and the WHANGDOODLE mourneth for her first-born.' It was subsequently applied to political subjects, such as the Free Trade, Decompton Democracy, etc.

WHANGER (or WHANG), *subs.* (common). — Anything big or unusual of its kind: *see* WHOPPER. As *adj.* (or WHANGING) = large, strapping.

WHAP. *See* WHOP.

WHARF-RAT, *subs. phr.* (old).—A thief prowling about wharves; *cf.* WATER-RAT.

WHARL, *verb* (old).—To be unable to pronounce the letter R. Also as *subs.*

1662. FULLER, *Worthies*, II. 225. All that are born therein have a harsh and rattling kind of uttering their words with much difficulty and WHARLING in their throats.

1724-7. DEFOE, *Tour Thro' Great Britain*, iii. 233. The natives of [Northumberland] of the antient original Race or families are distinguished by a Shibboleth upon their Tongues in pronouncing the letter R, which they cannot utter without a hollow Jairing in the Throat, by which they are as plainly known as a Foreigner is by pronouncing the Th; this they call the Northumberland R or WHARLE; and the Natives value themselves on that Imperfection, because, forsooth, it shows the Antiquity of their Blood.

WHAT, *rel. pro.* (old).—1. That, or that which: still a vulgarism: *e.g.* I had a donkey WHAT wouldn't go.

1570. ASCHAM, *The Scholemaster*, 142. The matter WHAT other men wrote.

1593 PEELE, *Edward I.* (*Old Plays*), II. 37. Offer them peace or aught WHAT is beside.

1601. SHAKSPEARE, *Henry VIII.*, v. I. 126. I fear nothing WHAT can be said against me.

2. (colloquial).—How much.

1867. TROLLOPE, *Last Chronicle of Barsett*, xxxvii. When a man bets he does not well know WHAT money he uses.

Indef. pro. (old).—(*a*) A something, anything: *e.g.* I'll tell you WHAT (it is). Also a bit, portion, a thing: *e.g.* It's a WHANGAM (*q.v.*); It's WHAT?

1373. CHAUCER, *House of Fame*, 1741. Al was us never broche ne rynge, Ne ellis WHAT fro women sent. *Ibid.*, *Boethius*, iv. prose 6. Thanne she a lytel WHAT smylynge seyde.

d. 1513. FABYAN, *Chronicle*, clxxii. Then the kynge anone called his seruante that had but one lofe and a little WHATTE of wyne.

1596. SPENSER, *Faery Queene*, VI. ix. 7. They prayd him sit, and gave him for to feed Such homely WHAT as serves the simple clowne.

1597. SHAKSPEARE, *Richard III.*, iii. 2. 92. Wot you WHAT, my lord? To-day the lords you talk of are beheaded.

1622. MASSINGER, *Virgin Martyr*, iii. 3. I'll tell you WHAT now of the devil.

1869. STOWE, *Oldtown*, 518. I tell you WHAT—Ellery Davenport lays out to marry a real angel. He's to swear, and she's to pray.

WHAT'S-HIS-NAME, etc., *phr.* (old colloquial).—1. A locution in speaking of what one has either forgotten, thinks so trivial, or does not wish to mention. Also WHAT-D'YE-CALL-IT, WHAT-D'YE-CALL-'EM, LORD KNOW'S WHAT, WASHICAL, etc.: *cf.* THINGUMY.

1600. SHAKSPEARE, *As You Like It*, iii. 3. 74. Good even, good Master WHAT-YE-CALL'T; how do you, sir?

1664. COTTON, *Virgil Travestie*, 75. Where once your WHAT SHALS' CAL' UMS —(rot um! It makes me mad I have forgot 'um).

1706. WARD, *Wooden World*, 31. The ship's crew . . . often call his Words to account, and too often count his Sunday labour a Sham, and himself a sacred WHAT-YE-CALL-'EM.

1749. SMOLLETT, *Gil Blas* (1812), I. xv. Mr. WHAT-D'YE-CALL-'UM, I never exact too much.

1759-67. STERNE, *Tristram Shandy*, VIII. 19. There is no part of the body, an' please your honour [with] . . . so many tendons and WHAT-D'YE-CALL-EMS all about it.

1801. DIBDIN, *Il Bondocani*, ii. 2. I wouldn't keep signior WHAT-D'YE-CALL-HIM waiting for the world.

1811. HAWKINS, *Countess and Gertrude*, iii. 97. [An inferior is addressed as] MRS. WHAT'S-YOUR-NAME.

1888. *Detroit Free Press*, 8 Dec. 'Won't it be rather hard at first to give up all the pink suppers and kettledrums and afternoon WHAT-DO-YOU-CALL-'EMS?' with a suspicion of a grin on his face.

2. (venery). — The *penis*: *see* PRICK. WHAT'S-HER-NAME = the female *pudendum*: *see* MONOSYLLABLE: also WHAT'S-ITS-NAME, THE LORD KNOWS WHAT, etc.

1772. BRIDGES, *Burlesque Homer*, 42. E'er since I saw that . . . Thetis stroking your knees, as on the ground you sat, And rubbing up, THE LORD KNOWS WHAT. *Ibid.*, 117. I wish I'd never touch'd her WHAT-D'YE-CALLUM, But gone where damsels in the Park Watch to earn sixpence in the dark.

TO KNOW WHAT'S WHAT (WHAT'S O'CLOCK, etc.), *verb. phr.* (common).—To have knowledge, taste, judgment, or experience; TO BE WIDE-AWAKE (*q.v.*), equal to any emergency, FLY (*q.v.*).

1513-25. SKELTON, *Works* [DYCE], ii. 132. TO KNOW WHAT YS A CLOCKE.

c. 1520. *Chaucer's Dream*, 216. [There occurs] to KNOW WHAT WAS WHAT.

1534. N. UDALL, *Roister Doister*, i. 2, p. 17 (ARBER). Have ye spied out that? Ah sir, mary nowe I see you KNOW WHAT IS WHAT.

1563. GOOGE, *Eclogues*, vii. Our wyts be not so base, But what we KNOW as well as you WHAT'S WHAT in every case.

1609. JONSON, *Silent Woman*, v. *Daw.* O, it pleases him to say so, sir; but Sir Amorous KNOWS WHAT'S WHAT as well.

1679. W. WYCHERLEY, *Love in a Wood*, iii. I. But you, gossip, KNOW WHAT'S WHAT.

1711. *Spectator*, No. 132. This sly saint, who, I will warrant, UNDERSTANDS WHAT IS WHAT as well as you or I, widow, shall give the bride as father.

1773. GOLDSMITH, *She Stoops to Conquer*, v. 'Come, boy, I'm an old fellow, and KNOW WHAT'S WHAT as well as you that are younger.'

1809. MALKIN, *Gil Blas* [ROUTLEDGE], 330. As soon as we get settled we must stock our cellar, and establish a respectable larder, like people who KNOW WHAT IS WHAT.

1835. DICKENS, *Sketches by Boz*. Our governor's wide awake, he is. I'll never say nothin' agin him, nor no man; but he KNOWS WHAT'S O'CLOCK, he does, uncommon. *Ibid.* (1836), *Pickwick*, 364 (1857). 'Never mind, Sir,' said Mr. Weller with dignity, 'I KNOW WOT'S O'CLOCK.'

1849. THACKERAY, *Pendennis*, x. I'm not clever, p'raps; but I *am* rather downy; and partial friends say I know WHAT'S O'CLOCK tolerably well.

1874. *Siliad*, 172. And KNOW WHAT'S WHAT in England, and who's who.

1887. BAUMANN, *Londinismen*, *Slang u. Cant*, pref. vi. So from hartful young dodgers From waxy old codgers, From the blowens we got Soon to KNOW VOT IS VOT.

1888. BOLDREWOOD, *Robbery Under Arms*, xxvii. As for old Mullockson, he used to take a drive to Sawpit Gully, or Ten-Mile, as soon as ever he saw WHAT O'CLOCK it was—and glad to clear out, too.

WHAT NOT, *phr.* (colloquial).—Elliptical for 'What may I not say'; also as *subs.* = no matter what, what you please, 'etcetera.'

1592. HARVEY, *Four Letters*. If Mother Hubbard, in the vein of Chaucer, happened to tell one canicular tale, father Elderton and his son Greene, in the vein of Skelton or Scoggin, will counterfeit a hundred dogged fables, libels, calumnies, slanders, lies for the whetstone, WHAT NOT.

1602. COOKE, *How a Man may Choose a Good Wife*, etc. [DODSLEY, *Old Plays* (1874), ix. 78]. Why, you Jack-sauce! you cuckold! you WHAT-NOT.

1621. BURTON, *Anat. Melan.*, 150. Such air is unwholesome and engenders melancholy, plagues, and WHAT NOT.

1678. BUNYAN, *Pilgrim's Progress*, i. Lions, dragons, darkness, and in a word, death and WHAT NOT.

1862. THACKERAY, *Philip*, ix. I profess to be an impartial chronicler of poor Philip's fortunes, misfortunes, friendships, and WHAT-NOTS.

1887. *Contemp. Rev.*, li. 617. College A cannot compete with College B unless it has more scholarships, unless it changes the time of election to scholarships, or WHAT NOT.

1903. *D. Tel.*, 28 Dec., 5. I. British, Italian, French, Russians, and natives . . . and WHAT-NOT.

TO GIVE WHAT FOR, *verb. phr.* (common).—To reprimand, call over the coals, castigate, PUNISH (*q.v.*).

THE LORD KNOWS WHAT, *phr.* (colloquial).—1. 'Heaps'; plenty more; all sorts of things.

1691-2. *Gentlemen's Journal*, Mar., p. 3. Here's novels, and new-town adventures . . . and the LORD KNOWS WHAT not.

2. *See* WHAT'S-HIS-NAME, 2.

WHAT HO! *phr.* (old).—A summons or call: once the recognised formula: long disused save in melodrama and burlesque, but latterly recrudescent in vulgar salutation and expletive.

1598. SHAKSPEARE, I *Henry IV.*, ii. I. 52. *Gads.* WHAT HO! chamberlain! *Chamb.* [*Within*] At hand, quoth pick-purse.

1898. MARSHALL, *Pomes*, ii. Where 'e let me in for drinks all round, and as I'd but a bob, I thought, 'WHAT HO! 'Ow am *I* a-going on?'

WHAT PRICE——? *phr.* (racing and common). — How's that? What do *you* think? How much? What odds?

1893. EMERSON, *Signor Lippo*, xiv. WHAT PRICE you, when you fell off the scaffold?

1895. POCOCK, *Rules of the Game*, II. 10. WHAT PRICE Mr. Jack Hayles, eh, boys? That proves he's a thief.

1898. *Cigarette*, 26 Nov., 13. I. Ain't he gone on saucy colours, Eh? WHAT PRICE the green and red?

1899. WHITEING, *John St.*, I. ix. WHAT PRICE grammar? It don't seem to teach people to keep a civil tongue in their head.

1901. *Free Lance*, 13 Ap., 28. 2. 'It is all very well,' writes a traveller, 'to legislate with regard to pure beer, but WHAT PRICE pure wine?'

WHAT (WHO, WHEN, WHERE, or HOW) THE DEVIL, *phr.* (common).—An expletive of wonder, vexation, etc.

c. 1360. *Alliterative Poems* [MORRIS], 97. [Jonah is asked by his shipmates] WHAT ÞE DEVEL hatȝ þou don?

b. 1688, *d.* 1744. POPE [quoted in ANNANDALE]. The things we know are neither rich nor rare; But wonder HOW THE DEVIL they got there.

1776. DAVID GARRICK, *Bon Ton, or High Life Above Stairs*, ii. I. *Sir T.* Why, WHAT THE DEVIL do you make one at these masqueradings?

1780. MRS. COWLEY, *The Belle's Stratagem*, i. 3. *Har.* WHO THE DEVIL could have foreseen that?

1827. R. B. PEAKE, *Comfortable Lodgings*, i. 3. WHAT THE DEVIL is all this about?

1836. MICHAEL SCOTT, *Cruise of the Midge* [Ry. ed. 1860], 134. HOW THE DEVIL can you get anything out of an empty vessel?

WHATABOUTS, *subs.* (colloquial).—A matter in hand, something under consideration.

1830. SOUTHEY, *To G. C. Bedford*, 3 Mar. You might know of all my goings-on and WHATABOUTS and whereabouts from Henry Taylor.

WHAT-LIKE, *adj. phr.* (colloquial).—Of what kind.

1865. DICKENS, *Mutual Friend*, iii. 2. She knows Miss Abbey of old, remind her, and she knows WHAT-LIKE the home, and WHAT-LIKE the friend is likely to turn out.

WHAT-NOSED, *subs. phr.* (common).—Drunk, hot-nosed from drinking: *see* SCREWED.

WHATSOMEVER, *adv.* and *pro.* (once literary: now vulgar).—Whatsoever: also WHATSOMDEVER.

1360. CHAUCER, *Rom. of the Rose*, 5041. WHATSOMEVER woo they fele They wol not pleyne, but concele.

14[?]. *Babees Book* [E.E.T.S.], 45. Doughtir, loke that thou be waare, WHATSUMEUERE thee bitide, Mak not thin husbonde poore with spendinge ne with pride.

WHAY-WORM (or WHEY-WORM), *subs. phr.* (old).—A whim, crotchet, MAGGOT (*q.v.*).—SKELTON.

1542. HALL, *Edward IV.*, 33. And so marched toward London where the Essex men, havinge wylde WHAY-WORMES in their heddes joined them with him.

WHEAT. *See* CLEAN WHEAT.

WHEATON. TO WHEATON IT, *verb. phr.* (American: West Point).—To play sick. [BARTLETT: The term is derived from the name of old Dr. Wheaton, U.S.A., long stationed at West Point.]

WHEEDLE, *verb* (old: now recognised). — To coax, cajole, fawn on, TAKE IN (*q.v.*) [SKEAT: fr. Ger. *wedeln*. *Century*: It is not clear how a German word of this kind could get into English; but the German wars of the 17th century brought in a number of words, and this may have been taken up as a slang term. FARMER: in B. E., *Dict. Cant. Crew*, 1696, to cut a WHEADLE ='to decoy by Fawning and Insinuation.'] As *subs.* = (1) cajolery, a hoax; (2)=a flatterer, cajoler; and (3) a SHARPER (*q.v.*): WHEEDLER, WHEEDLESOME, WHEEDLING, and other derivatives follow as a matter of course.

1664. BUTLER, *Hudibras*, II. iii. 335. His business was to pump and WHEEDLE.

1667. HEAD, *Porteus Redivivus, or the Art of* WHEEDLING [Title]. *Ibid.* (1678), *Madam* WHEEDLE [Title].

1668. ETHEREGE, *She Would*, etc., i. 1. Don't thou think to pass these gross WHEADLES on me too? . . . I could never have had the face to have WHEADL'D the poor knight so.

1673. WYCHERLEY, *Gentleman Dancing-Master*, iv. 1. So young a WHEEDLE. *Ibid.* (1675), *Country Wife*, ii. 1. WHEEDLE her, jest with her, and be better acquainted one with another.

1692. LESTRANGE, *Fables*. A fox stood licking of his lips at the cock, and WHEEDLING him to get him down.

1700. CONGREVE, *Way of the World*, iii. I have a deed of settlement . . . which I WHEEDLED out of her. *Ibid.*, iii. 4. If that WHEADLING Villain has wrought upon Foible to detect me, I'm ruined. *Ibid.*, v. 1. I am not the first that he has WHEADLED with his dissembling Tongue.

1713. ROWE, *Jane Shore*, i. A laughing, toying, WHEEDLING, whimp'ring she.

1849-61. MACAULAY, *Hist. Eng.*, xviii. He WHEEDLED Tillotson out of some money.

1853. KINGSLEY, *Hypatia*, iv. In a fawning, WHEEDLING tone.

1876. ALCOTT, *Hospital Sketches*, 88. Anything more irresistibly WHEEDLESOME I never saw.

1885. CLEMENT SCOTT [*Ill. Lon. News*, 3 Oct., 339. 2]. The change from the carneying, WHEEDLING sneak to the cowardly bully, is extremely clever.

WHEEL, *subs.* (old).—1. A five-shilling piece; 5s.: *see* CARTWHEEL (GROSE). Also (*Tufts*) =a dollar.

2. (colloquial).—A bicycle, or tricycle; as *verb*=to ride a bicycle or tricycle. Hence WHEELMAN (or -WOMAN) = a cyclist: also KNIGHT OF THE WHEEL; WHEELING = cycling: also THE WHEELING WORLD (generic for 'cycledom').

1874. *Century*, xix. 496. In the parlors the costumes of the wheelmen seemed not so much out of place. *Ibid.* (1884), Sep., 643. One young girl . . . was attended by a youth on a bicycle, who WHEELED attentively at her side. *Ibid.*, 646. As WHEELMEN nowadays so greatly abound, the landlords profit by this arrangement.

1890. PENNELL, *Cant. Pilgrimage*. The ugly barracks and pretty cottages by which we WHEELED.

TO BREAK A FLY (or BUTTERFLY) ON A WHEEL, *verb. phr.* (common).—To punish unduly, without regard to the gravity of the crime, or the standing of the

offender; whence to use means altogether out of proportion to the end in view; to 'crack a nut with a Nasmyth hammer.'

1734. POPE, *Satires*, Prol., 308. Satire or sense, alas! can Sporus feel, Who BREAKS A BUTTERFLY UPON A WHEEL?

1857. DICKENS, *Little Dorrit*, II. 21. He was sorry . . . for the excellent people, and deplored the necessity of BREAKING mere house-FLIES ON THE WHEEL.

TO GREASE THE WHEELS, *verb. phr.* (common).—1. To furnish money for a specific object: *see* GREASE.

1809. MALKIN, *Gil Blas* [ROUTLEDGE], 74. Your uncle . . . regaled us yesterday . . . and paid the piper. . . . To-day the WHEELS ARE GREASED by your humble servant.

2. (venery). — In *sing.* = to copulate: *see* GREENS and RIDE.

TO GO (or RUN) ON WHEELS, *verb. phr.* (old).—1. To do with ease, expedition, without exertion.

2. (old).—Said of one suffering from the after-effects of drunkenness.

1772. BRIDGES, *Burlesque Homer*, 114. Strong liquor don't agree with me; My head's too heavy for my heels, And all the world RUNS ROUND ON WHEELS.

TO PUT ONE'S SHOULDER TO THE WHEEL, *verb. phr.* (colloquial).—To put one's heart into a matter, to buckle to, to do with spirit, resolution, or courage.

WHEELS WITHIN WHEELS, *subs. phr.* (colloquial).—Complication, intricacies, something other than that which is apparent at first sight. [*Cf.* Ezekiel i. 16.]

1730. NORTH, *Lord Guildford*, ii. 144. It was notorious that after this secretary retired the king's affairs went backwards; WHEELS WITHIN WHEELS took place; the ministers turned formalisers, and the court mysterious.

1760. JOHNSTON, *Chrysal*, II. 196. But, sir, is there not danger of their being provoked by such an attack to say something improper, and that they who made the contracts with them may do you an ill office on another occasion? They are WHEELS WITHIN WHEELS.

1837. DICKENS, *Pickwick Papers*, xl. 'And a birdcage, sir,' said Sam; 'VEELS VITHIN VEELS, a prison in a prison.'

TO STEER A TRICK AT THE WHEEL. *See* TRICK.

TO PUT A SPOKE IN ONE'S WHEEL (or CART), *verb. phr.* (old).—To do an ill turn. Occasionally (by an unwarrantable inversion)=to assist.

1661-91. *Merry Drolleries* [EBSWORTH, 1875], 224. He . . . lookt to be made an emperor for't, But the Divel did SET A SPOKE IN HIS CART.

1689. *God's Last Twenty-Nine Years' Wonders* [WALSH]. Both . . . bills were such SPOKES IN THEIR CHARIOT-WHEELS that made them drive much slower.

1809. MALKIN *Gil Blas* [ROUTLEDGE], 19. Rolando put a SPOKE IN THEIR WHEEL by representing that they ought at least to wait till the lady . . . could come in for her share of the amusement.

1855. THACKERAY, *Newcomes*, ix. There's a SPOKE IN YOUR WHEEL, you stuck-up little Duchess.

1872. ELIOT, *Middlemarch*, xiii. It seems to me it would be a very poor sort of religion TO PUT A SPOKE IN HIS WHEEL by refusing to say you don't believe.

1898. WALSH, *Lit. Curios.*, 1030. When solid wheels were used, the driver was provided with a pin or SPOKE, which he thrust into one of the three holes made to receive it, to skid the cart when it went down hill.

WHEEL-HAND IN THE NICK, *phr.* (old).— Regular Drinking over the left Thumb' (B. E.).

WHEELBARROW. AS DRUNK AS A WHEELBARROW (or AS THE DRUM OF A WHEELBARROW), *phr.* (old).—Very drunk indeed: *see* SCREWED (RAY).

1675. COTTON, *Burlesque upon Burlesque*, 243. Besides, if he such things can do, When DRUNK AS DRUM OF WHEELBARROW, What would not this God of October Perform, I prithee, when he's sober.

TO GO TO HEAVEN IN A WHEELBARROW, *verb. phr.* (old). —To go to hell. [In the painted glass at Fairford, Gloucestershire, the devil is represented as wheeling off a scolding wife in a barrow.]

d. 1655. ADAMS, *Works*, I. 144. This oppressor must needs GO TO HEAVEN! what shall hinder him? But it will be, as the by-word is, IN A WHEELBARROW; the fiends, and not the angels, will take hold on him.

WHEELER, *subs.* (coaching).—A horse driven in shafts or next to the wheels: *cf.* LEADER. Also OFF-WHEELER = a horse driven on the right-hand side, *i.e.* the side on which a postillion never rides; NEAR-WHEELER= the horse on the left-hand side.

1862. THACKERAY, *Philip*, xiii. We saw the vehicle turn over altogether, one of the WHEELERS down with its rider, and the leaders kicking.

WHEEL-HORSE, *subs. phr.* (American).—An intimate friend; one's right-hand man; a leading man (BARTLETT).

1877. *New York Tribune*, 26 Feb. It is probable that the only man put forward by the republican's WHEEL-HORSES of Illinois for high appointment under President Hayes will be the Honorable John A. Logan.

WHEEL-OF-LIFE, *subs.phr.* (prison). —The treadmill, the EVERLASTING-STAIRCASE (*q.v.*).

1883. *Echo*, Jan. 25, p. 2, col. 4. The treadmill, again, is more politely called . . . the WHEEL OF LIFE, or the vertical care-grinder.

WHEEZE, *subs.* (common).—Generic for a GAG (*q.v.*) of any description: *e.g.* interpolated lines (usually comic) in a play, a bit of BUSINESS (*q.v.*), a sidesman's PATTER (*q.v.*), a bon-mot, joke, and so forth. TO CRACK A WHEEZE=to originate (or adapt) a smart saying at a 'psychological' moment.

1897. MARSHALL, *Pomes*, 24. What laughter fills the Court, At the counsel's ribald attitude and tone! But each WHEEZE from legal throats, When to Parkinson it floats Is a groan.

1887. *Referee*, 1 May. The man who propounds conundrums to purzzle 'Brudder Bones,' and puts on the most solemn air of attention while the comic men spin out their 'WHEEZES.'

Verb (thieves').—To say, inform, PEACH (*q.v.*).

WHEEZY, *subs.* (journalists').—The first month of the French Republican year: a free translation of *Vindémiare*.

WHELK, *subs.* (common).—1. The female *pudendum*: *see* MONOSYLLABLE, and note the veiledly obscene street catch-phrase of the seventies, 'I'll have your WHELK.'

2. (provincial).—A blow (also WHELKER), fall, blister, mark, or stripe.

3. (provincial).—A large number, a quantity: whence WHELKING = very large, big, numerous.

WHELP, *subs.* (colloquial). — A youth, UNLICKED CUB (*q.v.*); PUPPY (*q.v.*): in contempt. As *verb* (vulgar)=to be brought to bed, to PUP (*q.v.*).

1593. SHAKSPEARE, *Titus Andron.*, ii. 3. Two of thy WHELPS, fell curs of bloody kind.

1854. DICKENS, *Hard Times*, iii. 7. On one of the back benches . . . sat the villainous WHELP, sulky to the last, whom he had the misery to call his son.

2. (old).—A ship of some kind.

1630-40. *Court and Times Chas. I.*, II. 186. Captain Plumley was sent thither with one of the ships royal and two WHELPS to seek out Nutt the pirate.

1635. [BRERETON, *Travels*, 164.] Aboard one of the king's ships called the ninth WHELP.

WHEN. SAY WHEN! *phr.* (common).—That is, 'Say when I shall stop': the dovetail reply is 'Bob!'

1889. *Modern Society*, 6 June. 'SAY WHEN,' said Bonko, taking up a flagon of whiskey and commencing to pour out the spirit into my glass. 'BOB!' replied I.

WHENNYMEG, *subs.* (provincial).—In *pl.*=the *testes*, CODS (*q.v.*): properly TRINKETS (*q.v.*).

WHERE. *See* YOU.

WHEREFORE. *See* WHY.

WHEREWITH (or WHEREWITHAL), *subs.* (colloquial).—The necessary, requisites: spec. money (generic): *see* RHINO.

[1390. MANDEVILLE, *Travels* [HALLIWELL], 3. A man that hath WHEROF (*opes*).]

1659. MILTON, *Touching Hirelings*. We ourselves have not WHEREWITHAL; who shall bear the charges of our Journey?

1809. MALKIN, *Gil Blas* [ROUTLEDGE], 260. How the devil doos she mean that I should get the WHEREWITHAL? . . . Does she take me for . . . treasurer to a charity?

1855. SPENSER, *Prin. of Sociology*, 15. Heavily taxed in providing the WHEREWITHAL to meet excessive loss.

1864. TENNYSON, *Enoch Arden*. The WHEREWITHAL to give his babes a better bringing-up.

1887. *D. Teleg.*, 8 Dec. M. ——, however, had not the WHEREWITHAL to furnish a marriage portion of seven camels.

WHERRET. *See* WHIRRIT.

WHERRY-GO-NIMBLE, *subs. phr.* (common).—A looseness of the bowels, a BACK-DOOR TROT (*q.v.*): *cf.* JERRY-GO-NIMBLE.

WHETING-CORNE, *subs. phr.* (old). —The female *pudendum* (HALLIWELL): *see* MONOSYLLABLE.

WHETSTONE. TO GIVE (DESERVE, WIN, LIE FOR, etc.) THE WHETSTONE, *verb. phr.* (old). — To give (get, or compete for) the prize for lying: a WHETSTONE, *i.e.* a wit-sharpener, regarded as a satirical premium for what nowadays would be called 'naked' (or 'monumental') lying. [NARES: There were, in some places, jocular games, in which the prize given for the greatest lie was a WHETSTONE. HALLIWELL: The liar was sometimes publicly exhibited with the whetstone fastened to him.]

. . . BULLEYN, *Prose Morality* [WALDRON, *Sad Sheph.*, 162. 220]. My name is Mendax, a younger brother, linially descended of an auncient house before the Conquest We geve three WHETSTONES in gules, with no difference.

1570. ASCHAM, *Scholemaster*, 26. I assure you there is no such WHETSTONE to sharpen a good witte and encourage a will to learnynge as is praise.

1580. LYLY, *Euphues and His England*, C. 4. If I met with one of Crete, I was readie to LIE with him FOR THE WHETSTONE.

1580. LUPTON, *Too Good to be True*, 80. Lying with us is so loved and allowed, that there are many tymes gamings and prizes therefore purposely, to encourage one to outlye another. *O.* And what shall he gaine that gets the victorie in lying? *S.* He shall have a silver WHETSTONE for his labour.

1591. HARINGTON, *Ariosto*, xviii. 36. Well might Martano beare away the bell, Or else a WHETSTONE challenge for his dew, That on the sodaine such a tale could tell, And not a word of all his tale was true. *Ibid.* [*Nugæ Antiquæ* (PARK), ii. 240]. Part whereof [*i.e.* of his sentence] being that the knight should publicklie acknowledge how he had slandered the archbishop, which he did in words conceived to that purpose accordingly; yet his friends gave out, that all the while he carried a long WHETSTON hanging out at the pocket of his sleeve, so conspicuous as men understood his meaning was to give himselfe the lye.

1592. HARVEY, *Four Letters*. If Mother Hubbard, in the vein of Chaucer, happened to tell one canicular tale, father Elderton and his son Greene, in the vein of Skelton or Scoggin, will counterfeit a hundred dogged fables, libels, calumnies, slanders, LIES FOR THE WHETSTONE, what not.

1599. HALL, *Satires*, iv. 6. The brain-sicke youth that feeds his tickled eare With sweet-sauc'd lies of some false traveller; Which hath the Spanish decades red awhile, Or WHETSTONE leasings of old Mandevile.

1600. JONSON, *Cynthia's Revels*, i. 5. Cos? how happily hath Fortune furnish'd him with a WHETSTONE. *Ibid.* (1614), *Barthol. Fair*, i. Good Lord! how sharp you are, with being at Bedlam yesterday! WHETSTONE has set an edge upon you.

c. 1603. BACON [Z. GREY, *Hudibras*, Note to II. i. 5. 60]. [NARES: Sir K. Digby boasted before King James of having seen the philosopher's stone in his travels, but was puzzled to describe it, when Sir Francis Bacon interrupted him, saying, 'Perhaps it was a WHETSTONE.']

d. 1634. RANDOLPH, *Works*, 330. I thought it not the worst traffique to sell WHETSTONES. This WHETSTONE [he continues] will set such an edge upon your inventions, that it will make your rusty iron brains purer metal than your brazen faces. Whet but the knife of your capacities on this WHETSTONE, and you may presume to dine at the Muses' Ordinarie, or sup at the Oracle of Apollo.

1792. BUDWORTH, *Ramble to the Lakes*, vi. It is a custom in the north, when a man tells the greatest lye in the company, to reward him with a WHETSTONE; which is called LYING FOR THE WHETSTONE.

d. 1822. SHELLEY, *To his Genius*. Let them read Shakspeare's sonnets, taking thence A WHETSTONE for their dull intelligence.

WHETSTONE - PARK, *subs. phr.* (old).—'A Lane betwixt Holborn and Lincoln's-Inn-Fields, fam'd for a Nest of Wenches, now (B. E., *c.* 1696) de-park'd.' Whence many allusions in the old dramatists: *e.g.* WHETSTONE-PARK DEER (MUTTON, etc.)=a whore.

WHETTER. *See* WET.

WHEW, *subs.* (old).—Influenza, the FLUE (*q v.*): *see* quot.

1420. [SIR H. MAXWELL, *Notes and Queries*, 10 Dec. 1901.] It is well known that the influenza is not an exclusively modern complaint, but I am not sure whether a curious reference to it by Bower, the continuator of Fordun's chronicle, has been noted. Writing of the year 1420 he says that among those who died in Scotland were Sir Henry St. Clair, Earl of Orkney, Sir James Douglas of Dalkeith, Sir William de Abernethy, Sir William de St. Clair, Sir William Cockburn, and many others, all by 'that infirmity whereby not only great men, but innumerable quantity of the commonalty perished, which was vulgarly termed le QUHEW.' Now 'quh' in Scottish texts usually represents the sound of 'wh' (properly aspirated); therefore it seems that in the fifteenth century the influenza was known as 'the WHEW,' just as it is known in the twentieth century as 'the Flue.' There seems little doubt that the disease was identical with that with which we are so grievously familiar.

WHEYWORM. *See* WHAYWORM.

WHIBLIN, *subs.* (old).—1. A eunuch.

1602. DEKKER, *Honest Whore* [DODSLEY, *Old Plays* (REED), iii. 257]. God's my life, he's a very mandrake; or else (God bless us) one of these WHIBLINS, and that's worse.

2. (old).—A sword.

1653. BROME, *Lovesick Court*, v. 1. Come, sir, let go your WHIBLIN [*snatcheth his sword from him*].

WHID, *subs.* (Old Cant).—1. A word (HARMAN, B. E., and GROSE): in *pl.* (modern)=patter, talk, jocular speech. Also (2) (Scotch)=a lie, fib; (3) (provincial)=a dispute or quarrel. As *verb* (Scots)=to lie. Also TO CUT WHIDS=to talk, to speak; TO CUT BIEN WHIDS=to talk fairly, softly, kindly; TO CUT QUEER WHIDS=to abuse, swear, BULLYRAG (*q.v.*); also WHIDDLE =to talk, tell or discover (B. E. and GROSE): spec. to reveal secrets, or give the game away: hence WHIDDLER=an informer.

1567. HARMAN, *Caveat*, 116. What! stowe your bene, cofe, and CUT BENAT WYDDS.

1622. HEAD, *English Rogue*. This doxie dell can CUT BIEN WHIDS, And drill well for a win.

1787. BURNS, *Death and Doctor Hornbook*. Even ministers they have been kenn'd In holy rapture, A rousin' WHID at times to vend, And nail 't wi' Scripture.

1821. SCOTT, *Kenilworth*, x. Credit me, the swaggering vein will not pass here; you must CUT BOON WHIDS.

1834. AINSWORTH, *Rookwood* (1864), 230. Here I am, pal Peter; and here are my two chums, Rust and Wilder. CUT THE WHID.

1876. HINDLEY, *Life of a Cheap Jack*. The WHIDS we used to crack over them.

WHIDDLE. *See* WHID and OLIVER.

WHIFF, *subs.* (colloquial).—1. A smell; as *verb*=to smell: *e.g.* How it WHIFFS.

[1783. COWPER, *Task*, iv. 459. A WHIFF Of stale debauch, forth issuing from the sties That Law has licensed.]

2. (old).—A draught, a drink, a GO (*q.v.*): as *verb*=to drink: also WHIFFLE.

1653. URQUHART, *Rabelais*, I. vi. I will yet go drink one WHIFF more. *Ibid.*, I. xxvii. In this season we might press and make the wine, and in winter, WHIFF it up. *Ibid.*, I. xxxix. Gargantua WHIFFED the great draught. *Ibid.*, III. Prol. Constrain an easy, good-natured fellow to WHIFFLE, quaff, carouse.

WHIFFET, *subs.* (American).—Anything or anybody worthless or insignificant, a WHIPPER-SNAPPER (*q.v.*).

1883. *Philadelphia Times*, 1 Aug. The sneaks, WHIFFETS, and surface rats.

WHIFFLE, *verb* (old).—1. Generic for trifling: to hesitate, talk idly, prevaricate, waver. Hence WHIFFLER=a trifler, a fickle or unsteady person; WHIFFLERY (WHIFFLING or WHIFFLE-WHAFFLE) = levity, nonsense; WHIFFLING, *adj.* = uncertain.

1607. DEKKER, *Northward Hoe*, ii. 1. Your right WHIFFLER indeed hangs himself in St. Martin's, and not in Cheapside.

1671-94. TILLOTSON, *Sermons*, xlv. Every man ought to be stedfast . . . and not suffer himself to be WHIFFLED . . . by an insignificant noise.

d. 1745. SWIFT, *Works* [*Century*]. Every WHIFFLER in a laced coat . . . shall talk of the constitution.

1741. WATTS, *Improvement of the Mind*, I. ix. 27. A person of a WHIFFLING and unsteady turn of mind.

c. 1834. CARLYLE [FROUDE, *Life in London*, iii.]. Life is no frivolity, or hypothetical coquetry or WHIFFLING.

2. (old).—To drink.

WHIG, *subs.* (old: long recognised).—1. Orig. (middle 17th century) a Presbyterian zealot, a conventicler: in contempt. Whence (2) the Country party (the successors of the Roundheads of the Civil War) as opposed to the Court party or TORIES (*q.v.*). of the Restoration. Both WHIG and Tory were first applied, about 1680, in contempt, and both were ultimately assumed with pride. The WHIGS favoured the Revolution of 1688-9, and were in power during a large portion of the eighteenth century. The Whigs may be regarded as the party of experimental progress. The curious similarity in the historical development of both WHIG and Tory is further accentuated by the fact that at the same time (Reform Bill, 1832) as the term 'Tory' began to be superseded by 'Conservative,' so likewise the WHIGS began to be called Liberals. Also WHIGLAND =Scotland (B. E.); the WHIG COLLEGE = the Reform Club; WHIGGISH (*see* quot. 1696), and the usual derivatives and combinations.

1680. [PINNOCK, *Goldsmith's Hist. Eng.* (1873), 252. The year 1680 is remarkable for the introduction of the well-known epithets WHIG and Tory. The former was given to the popular party, from their pretended affinity to the fanatical conventiclers of Scotland, who were known by the name of WHIGS. The latter was given to the courtiers, from a supposed resemblance between them and the Popish banditti in Ireland, to whom the appellation of Tories was affixed. Thus these two ridiculous words came into general use, and have continued ever since to mark rival parties, though with very different meanings.]

1681. DRYDEN, *Absalom and Achit.*, 'To Reader.' Wit and fool are consequents of WHIG and Tory; and every man is a knave or an ass to the contrary side.

c. 1696. B. E., *Dict. Cant. Crew*, s.v. WHIGGS, the Republicans or Commonwealths-men, under the name of Patriots, and Lovers of Property; originally the Field-conventiclers in the West of Scotland. *Ibid.* WHIGGISH, Factious, Seditious, Restless, Uneasy.

1712. HEARNE, *Reliquiæ*, Mar. 30. Young, lewd, debauched sparks [Mohawks], all of the WHIGGISH gang, and the WHIGGS are now so much ashamed of this great scandal (provided WHIGGS can be ashamed) that . . .

d. 1715. BURNET, *Own Times*, I. The south-west counties of Scotland have seldom corn enough to serve them all the year round, and the northern parts producing more than they used, those in the west went in summer to buy at Leith the stores that came from the north. From the word WHIGGAM, used in driving their horses, all that drove were called the WHIGGAMORS, contracted into WHIGS. Now in the year before the news came down of duke Hamilton's defeat, the ministers animated their people to rise and march to Edinburgh; and they came up, marching on the head of their parishes, with an unheard-of fury, praying and preaching all the way as the came. The marquis of Argyle and his party came and headed them, they being about 6000. This was called the 'Whiggamors' Inroad'; and ever after that all who opposed the court came in contempt to be called WHIGS.

1712. SWIFT, *Conduct of the Allies*, Appen. They will not recognise a..y government in Great Britain but WHIGGARCHY only.

1714. HEARNE, *Diary*, 25 Sep. King George hath begun to change all the ministers, and to put in the WHIGGS . . . to the grievous mortification of that party called Tories.

1719. DURFEY, *Pills to Purge*, etc., i. 43. To oagle there a Tory tall, or a little WHIG, Defying the Pretender.

1725. SWIFT, *Letter*, 11 Sep. There is hardly a WHIG in Ireland who would allow a potato and butter-milk to a reputed Tory.

1791. BURKE, *Appeal from New to Old* WHIGS. Attached to the WHIG party.

1817. SCOTT, *Rob Roy*, xxv. It isna good for my health to come in the gate o' the WHIGAMORE bailie bodies.

1848. *John Bull*, 29 Ap. Among . . . good things . . . is to be reckoned a new sauce from the laboratory of Professor Soyer, of THE WHIG COLLEGE, commonly called the Reform Club.

1849. MACAULAY, *Hist. Eng.*, ii. At this time were first heard two nicknames which, though originally given in insult, were soon assumed with pride. . . . It is a curious circumstance that one . . . was of Scotch, and the other of Irish, origin. Both in Scotland and in Ireland, misgovernment had called into existence bands of desperate men, whose ferocity was heightened by religious enthusiasm. . . . Thus the appellation of WHIG was fastened on the Presbyterian zealots of Scotland, and was transferred to those English politicians who showed a disposition to oppose the court, and to treat Protestant nonconformists with indulgence. The bogs of Ireland, at the same time, afforded a refuge to Popish Outlaws, much resembling those who were afterwards known as Whiteboys. These men were then called Tories. The name of Tory was therefore given to Englishmen who refused to concur in excluding a Roman Catholic prince from the throne.

3. (American).—During the war of the American Revolution, the terms WHIG and Tory were applied,—the former to those who supported the Revolutionary movement, the latter to the royalists, or those who adhered to the British government (BARTLETT).

WHIM, *subs.* (B. E.).—1. 'A Maggot.' Hence 'WHIMSICAL' ='Maggotish': *see* BEE IN BONNET and MAGGOT.

2. (old). *See* JIGGUMBOB, spec. quot. 1678 s.v.

3. (venery). — The female *pudendum*: *see* MONOSYLLABLE: also WHIM-WHAM.

1707. WARD, *Hud. Rediv.*, II. iii. 26. When I had view'd the Ladies Limbs, And all these Members, but their WHIMS. *Ibid.*, II. iv. 18. Let me know whether your WHIM be high or low. . . . The Fro believing from my Joaks, I fancy'd not her Butter-box, Cock'd up her Head, took leave in scorn.

WHIMLING, *subs.* (common).—A person childish, weak, or full of whims, a CROTCHETEER. WHIMMY=whimsical.

1610. BEAUMONT and FLETCHER, *Coxcomb*, iv. 7. Go, WHIMLING, and fetch two or three grating-loaves out of the kitchen.

WHIMPER. ON THE WHIMPER, *phr.* (colloquial).—Peevish, whining, crying. Also (B. E.) 'WHIMPER, a low or small cry. What a WHIMPERING you keep.'

1857-9. THACKERAY, *Virginians*, xii. Mrs. Mountain is constantly ON THE WHIMPER when George's name is mentioned.

WHIM-WHAM, *subs. phr.* (old).—1. A trinket, trifle, fal-lal. Hence (2) generic for rubbish, nonsense.

1500-13. SKELTON, *Poems* (DYCE), iii. With a WHYM WHAM, Knyt with a trym tram.

1604. MARSTON and WEBSTER, *Malcontent*, i. 3. Sir Tristam Tristam come aloft, jacke-a-napes, with a WHIM-WHAM.

1608. *Cobler of Canterburie*. Her kercher hung from under her cap, With a taile like a flie flap. And tyed it fast with a WHIM WHAM, Knit up againe with a trim tram.

1614. FLETCHER, *Night Walker*, i. Nay not that way, They'll pull ye all to pieces for your WHIM-WHAMS, Your garters, and your gloves.

1619. MASSINGER [?], *City Madam*, iv. 3. 'Tis more comely, I wis, than their other WHIM-WHAMS.

1630. TAYLOR, *Works* [NARES]. His Alkaron, his Moskyes are WHIM-WHAMS, False bug-beare babies, fables all that dams. *Ibid.* When with her flesh mans stomack she hath fed, She gives him ease and comfort in his bed; She yeelds no WHIM-WHAMS wavering on his crest, But she relieves him with repose and rest.

3. *See* WHIM, *subs.* 3.

WHINDLE, *subs.* (B. E.).—'A low or feigned crying.'

WHINE, *verb* (B. E.).—'To cry squeekingly, as at Conventicles.'

WHINER, *subs.* (common).—A word; in *pl.*=speech, talk, GAB (*q.v.*); spec. (thieves') prayers. TO CHOP THE WHINERS=to talk, to say prayers.

1830. BULWER LYTTON, *Paul Clifford*, p. 2, ed. 1854. I tell you, I vent first to Mother Bussblour's, who, I knows, CHOPS THE WHINERS morning and evening to the young ladies.

1857. *Punch*, 31 Jan. For them coves in Guildhall and that blessed Lord Mayor, Prigs on their four bones should CHOP WHINERS I swear.

WHIP, *subs.* (colloquial).—1. A driver, a coachman: also KNIGHT OF THE WHIP.

1778. SHERIDAN, *Rivals*, i. 1. None of the London WHIPS . . . wear wigs now.

1809–12. EDGEWORTH, *Absentee*, viii. Major Benson, who was a famous WHIP, took his seat on the box of the barouche.

1828. JON BEE, *Picture of London*, 27. To the practices and necessities of the coachmen and guard's *private trade*, we owe the increasing number and fresh supply of hangers-on, whose first business has been the performing fetch-and-carry services for those KNIGHTS OF THE WHIP.

1837. DICKENS, *Pickwick*, xiii. You're a wery good WHIP, and can do what you like with your horses.

1874. COLLINS, *Frances*, xlii. Julian Orchard proved his skill as a WHIP by making four screws do six miles in twenty-five minutes.

1888. BESANT, *Fifty Years Ago*, 50. This is the famous coaching baronet than whom no better WHIP has ever been seen upon the road.

2. (parliamentary).—A member who (unofficially) looks after the interests of his party; prob. from WHIPPER-IN [BRYCE: The WHIP'S duties are (*a*) to inform every member belonging to the party when an important division may be expected, and, if he sees the member in or about the House, to keep him there until the division is called; (*b*) to direct the members of his own party how to vote; (*c*) to obtain 'pairs' for them if they cannot be present to vote; (*d*) to 'tell,' *i.e.* count the members in every party division; (*e*) to 'keep touch' of opinion within the party, and convey to the leader a faithful impression of that opinion, from which the latter may judge how far he may count on the support of his whole party in any course he proposes to take.] Also (3) the call made for attendance at a division, etc.; and as *verb* (or TO WHIP IN, or UP).

1836. DICKENS, *Sketches by Boz*. Sir Somebody Something, when he was WHIPPER-IN for the Government, brought four men out of their beds to vote in the majority, three of whom died on their way home again.

1882. *Pall Mall Gaz.*, 9 Nov. The Liberal WHIPS have issued a somewhat similar invitation. *Ibid.* Urgent WHIPS have been issued by both sides.

c. 1888. *Standard* [S. J. and C.]. A four-line WHIP has been issued by the Government in opposition to the second reading of Lord Dunraven's Bill for the reform of the House of Lords.

4. (printers').—A compositor quick in setting type; a TYPE-SLINGER (which also *see*).

Verb (common).—1. To surpass, beat, defeat, overcome; hence WHIPPING=defeat: *e.g.* to WHIP the enemy (or give them a WHIPPING), to WHIP creation, etc.

d. 1859. DE QUINCEY, *Herodotus*. A man without a particle of Greek WHIPPED . . . whole crowds of sleeping drones who had more than they could turn to any good account.

1892. W. WILSON, *Cong. Govt.* The only bond of cohesion is the caucus, which occasionally WHIPS a party together for co-operative action.

2. (thieves').—To swindle.

3. (colloquial). — Generic for quick, smart action: *e.g.* to WHIP ON (UP, OFF, OUT, etc.): frequently with an idea of stealth. Also WHIP, *adv.* = quickly, instanter.

1360. *Sir Gawayn* [E.E.T.S.]. [OLIPHANT, *New Eng.*, i. 59. The words akin to the Dutch and German are . . . blubber . . . WHIP OFF.]

1563. FOXE, *Acts and Monuments* (CATTLEY), viii. 336. [I will] WHIP ON my clothes.

c. 1696. B. E., *Dict. Cant. Crew*, s.v. WHIP OFF, c. to steal, to Drink cleaverly, to snatch, and to run away. WHIPT THROUGH the Lungs, run through the Body with a Sword. WHIPT IN at the Glaze, c. got in at the window.

1700. FARQUHAR, *Constant Couple*, iii. 2. He WHIPS OUT his stiletto, and I whips out my bull-dog.

1715. CENTLIVRE, *Gotham Election*, i. 4. You all talk it well affore you get in, but you are no sooner chose in but WHIP! you are as proud as the devil.

1748. RICHARDSON, *Clarissa*, VIII. 267. When I came, WHIP was the key turned upon the girls.

1837. MARRYAT, *Dog Fiend*, xiii. [He] may . . . WHIP the whole boiling of US OFF to the Ingees.

TO DRINK (or LICK) ON THE WHIP, *verb. phr.* (common).—To get a thrashing, to taste the whip.

c. 1401. *Townley Mysteries*, 30. In fayth and for youre long tarying Ye shal LIK ON THE WHYP.

1576. GASCOIGNE, *Steel Glas* [ARBER], 68. Comes naked neede? and chance to do amisse? He shal be sure, to DRINKE VPON THE WHIPPE.

TO WHIP THE CAT, *verb. phr.* (old).—1. To pinch, to be parsimonious, mean, stingy.

2. (old).—To go from house to house to work: chiefly tailors', but the practice was more or less common to all trades. Hence WHIP-CAT=a tailor: *see* quot. 1871.

18[?]. GOODRICH, *Remin.*, I. 74. Twice a year, the tailor came to the house and fabricated the semi-annual stock of clothes for the male members, this being called WHIPPING THE CAT.

1870. JUDD, *Margaret*, iii. Mr. Hart made shoes, a trade he prosecuted in an itinerating manner from house to house, 'WHIPPING THE CAT,' as it was termed.

1871. DE VERE, *Americanisms*, 648. WHIPPING THE CAT: an old English phrase, used only by tailors and carpenters, has maintained its existence in New England, Pennsylvania, and a few other States, where it denotes the annual visit of a tailor to repair the clothes of a household. It is said to have originated in a very rough practical joke, which bears the same name in Hampshire, England, and of which, it is surmised, the tailor may have been the victim (J. R. Lowell). The simple tailors of former days liked thus to go from house to house in the rural districts, providing the families with clothing. The chief romance for the happy 'Schneider' was in the abundant and wholesome cheer of the farmer who employed him, and as his annual visits fell in the pudding and sausage season, he was usually crammed with that kind of 'vegetables,' as he facetiously called them, to his heart's content. The only objection made to CATWHIPPING, was that it afforded no opportunity to 'cabbage,' and in former days this was a serious grievance. The introduction of large manufacturing establishments, low-priced ready-made clothing, and the advent of the sewing-machine, have now nearly made an end to this itinerant occupation. The terms CATWHIPPER and CATWHIPPING were often facetiously, and sometimes very irreverently, applied to other itinerant professions: even 'Schoolmasters'—there were no 'teachers,' much less 'educators,' in those benighted days—were called CAT-WHIPPERS, when they boarded, as was quite usual, in turns with the parents of their scholars. Itinerating preachers also were, by the initiated, included in this category.

1888. *St. James's Gazette*, 2 May. Mr. Hugh Haliburton dilates upon the custom of 'WHIPPING THE CAT'—*i.e.* working for people at their houses, as was once the wont of Scottish tailors. A minister who fills another's pulpit (for a consideration) is equally said to 'flog pouss.'

3. (modern).—To idle on Monday; to keep St. Monday.

3. (common).—(*a*) To get tipsy: *see* SCREWED: also TO WHIP (JERK OF SHOOT THE CAT, OR TO CAT): also (*b*)=to vomit. Hence WHIPCAT, *adj.*=drunken (FLORIO), WHIPCAN (which *see*) =a toper: *cf. verb*, sense 3.

1582. STANYHURST, *Æneid*, iii. 367. With WHIPCAT bowling they kept a myrry carousing.

1609. ARMIN, *Maids of More-cl.* (1880), 70. Ile baste their bellies and their lippes till we haue IERK'T THE CAT with our three WHIPPES.

1630. TAYLOR, *Brood Cormor* [*Works*, III. 5. 1]. You may not say hee's drunke . . . For though he be as drunke as any rat He hath but catcht a fox, or WHIPT THE CAT.

1830. MARRYAT, *King's Own*, xxxii. I'm cursedly inclined to SHOOT THE CAT.

4. (old).—To indulge in practical jokes: spec. (B. E. and GROSE) 'a trick often practised on ignorant country fellows, vain of their strength; by laying a wager with them, that they may be PULLED THROUGH A POND BY A CAT; the bet being made, a rope is fixed round the waist of the party to be catted, and the end thrown across the pond, to which the cat is also fastened by a pack-thread, and three or four sturdy fellows are appointed to lead and whip the cat; these, on a signal given, seize the end of the cord, and pretending to whip the cat, haul the astonished booby through the water.'

1614. JONSON, *Barthol. Fair*, i. 4. I'll be DRAWN WITH A GOOD GIB CAT THROUGH THE GREAT POND at home.

TO WHIP THE DEVIL ROUND THE STUMP, *verb. phr.* (American).—To make false excuses to one's self and others for doing what one likes, to equivocate, to say, pretend, or do one thing, and mean, or act differently.

1857. *New York Evening Post* [BARTLETT]. Jones, you're a clever fellow, but . . . there is a want of candor now, I perceive, in the statement of your affairs . . . you are WHIPPING THE DEVIL AROUND THE STUMP: I see his foot.

WHIP-ARSE, *subs. phr.* (old).—A schoolmaster: *cf.* BUM-BRUSHER.

1611. COTGRAVE, *Dict.*, s.v. *Fessecul*, a pedantical WHIP-ARSE.

WHIP-BELLY, *subs. phr.* (provincial).—Thin weak liquor: spec. bad beer, SWIPES (*q.v.*): also WHIP-BELLY-VENGEANCE: *cf.* ROT-GUT.

1709–10. SWIFT, *Pol. Conv.*, ii. I believe the brewer forgot the malt, or the river was too near him. Faith, it's meer WHIP-BELLY-VENGEANCE.

WHIP-BROTH, *subs. phr.* (old).—A beating: *cf.* HAZEL-OIL, THIMBLE-PIE, etc.

1630. TAYLOR, *Works* [NARES]. Where I was ill thought of by my friends, scorned by my foes, and in conclusion, in a greater puzzell then the blinde beare in the midst of all her WHIP-BROTH.

WHIPCAN, *subs.* (old).—A toper, tippler, boon-companion: in orig. of quot. *fesse-pinte*. *See* WHIP THE CAT, 3.

1653. URQUHART, *Rabelais*, I. viii. He would prove an especial good fellow, and singular WHIPCAN.

WHIP-HAND. TO HAVE THE WHIP-HAND (or WHIP-HANDLE), *verb. phr.* (colloquial).—To have an advantage, to be in a position to command, to have the best of a matter.

1697. VANBRUGH, *Æsop*, v. 1. Now, what say you, Mr. Flamefire? I shall HAVE THE WHIPHAND OF YOU presently.

d. 1701. DRYDEN [*Century*]. The archangel . . . HAS THE WHIP-HAND OF HER.

1884. *Century Mag.*, xxxviii. 932. Why, what matter? They know that we shall KEEP THE WHIP-HANDLE.

1887. *Field*, 24 Dec. A scheme to get the WHIP-HAND over them.

WHIPHANDLE, *subs.* (old).—*See* quot.

1653. URQUHART, *Rabelais*, II. xxvii. These little ends of men and dandiprats (whom in Scotland they call WHIP-HANDLES (*manches d'estrilles*), and knots of a tar-barrel) are commonly very testy and choleric.

2. *See* WHIPHAND.

WHIP-HER-JENNY, *subs. phr.* (old).—A term of contempt.

WHIP-JACK, *subs. phr.* (old).—A beggar shamming shipwreck. Hence a generic term of contempt.

c. 1530. PONET [MAITLAND, *On Reformation*, 74]. Albeit one Boner (a bare WHIPPE JACKE) for lucre of money toke vpon him to be thy father, and than to mary thy mother, yet thou wast persone Savage's bastarde.

1611. MIDDLETON, *Roaring Girl*, V. 1. A mere WHIP-JACK, and that is, in the commonwealth of rogues, a slave that can talk of sea-fight.

c. 1696. B. E., *Dict. Cant. Crew*, s.v. WHIP-JACKS, c. the tenth Order of the Canting Crew; Counterfeit Mariners Begging with false Passes, pretending Shipwrecks, great Losses at Sea, etc., narrow escapes; telling dismal Stories, having learnt Tar-terms on purpose, but are meer Cheats.

1753. RICHARDSON, *Grandison*, vi. 156. Sir Charles Grandison is none of your gew-gaw WHIP-JACKS that you know not where to have.

1791. BAMFYLDE-MOORE CAREW, *Oath of Canting Crew*. Swaddlers, Irish toyls, WHIP-JACKS.

WHIP-KING, *subs. phr.* (old).—One who controls or compels a king; a 'king-maker.'

1610. HOLLAND, *Camden*, 571. Richard Nevill, that WHIP-KING.

WHIPMASTER, *subs.* (old).—A flagellator: the actual word in the orig. which has long been recognised as standard English: *see* WHIPPER.

1725. BAILEY, *Erasmus*, 56. Woe to our backsides, he is a greater WHIPMASTER than Busby himself.

WHIPPER, *subs.* (common, but old).—Anything super-excellent: *cf.* WHOPPER and WHIP, *verb*.

1530. HEYWOOD, *Four P.'s* [Palmer, Pardoner, Poticary, Pedlar], [DODSLEY, *Old Plays* (1744), I. 103]. Mark wel this, this relique heer is a WHIPPER, My freend unfayned, this is a slipper Of one of the seven slepers, be sure.

2. (old).—A flagellant: *see* WHIPMASTER.

d. 1656. HALL, *Women's Vail*, I. A brood of mad hereticks, which arose in the church; whom they called Flagellantes, 'the WHIPPERS.'

WHIPPER-IN, *subs. phr.* (political).—*See* WHIP.

WHIPPER-SNAPPER, *subs. phr.* (common).—'A very small but sprightly boy' (B. E., *c.* 1696); spec. a precocious callow youth, or pert girl: always more or less in contempt. As *adj.*=diminutive, insignificant: also WHIPPING-SNAPPING.

1707. WARD, *Hud. Rediv.*, II. iv. 4. No sooner had they fix'd their Peepers Upon the Lifeless WHIPPER-SNAPPERS.

1742. FIELDING, *Jos. Andrews*, IV. vi. A parcel of WHIPPER-SNAPPER sparks.

1834. SOUTHEY, *Doctor*, cxxvii. The dog was frequently detected in all its varieties, from the lap-dog, who had passed into the WHIPPER-SNAPPER *petit-maître*, and the turn-spit who was now the bandy-legged baker's boy, to the Squire's eldest son, who had been a lurcher.

1860-3. THACKERAY, *Roundabout Papers*, xv. Though they had seven-leagued boots, you remember all sorts of WHIPPING-SNAPPING Tom Thumbs used to elude and outrun them.

1871. BROWNING, *Balaustion's Adv.* There spoke up a brisk little somebody Critic and WHIPPER-SNAPPER in a rage To set things right.

WHIPPING-BOY, *subs. phr.* (old).—A boy, companion to a prince, educated with him, and punished in his stead.

2. (racing).—A horse finishing last.

WHIPPING-CHEER, *subs. phr.* (old).—Flogging, flagellation, punishment: *cf.* BELLY-CHEER.

1598. SHAKSPEARE, 2 *Henry IV.*, v. 4. She shall have WHIPPING-CHEER enough, I warrant her.

1616. *Times' Whistle* [E.E.T.S.], 13. Your works of supererogation, Your idle crossings, or your wearing haire Next to your skin, or all your WHIPPING-CHEER.

1647. HERRICK, *Noble Numbers*, 398. Hell is the place where WHIPPING-CHEER abounds.

1661. DAVENPORT, *City Night-Cap*, iv. Since there is no remedy but that WHIPPING-CHEER must close up my stomach, I would request a note from your grace to the carman to intreat him to drive apace; I shall never endure it else.

1675. COTTON, *Burlesque upon Burlesque*, 187. For better fare thou shalt find here Than that same sowre-sauc'd WHIPPING-CHEER.

WHIPPY, *subs.* (Scots).—A pert girl, forward young woman.

WHIP-ROUND, *subs. phr.* (common).—A subscription got up for any purpose: *see* WHIP, *subs.*

1887. *Echo*, 23 Nov. [Her] neighbours, who knew that she had no money, instituted a WHIP-ROUND, and soon raised the necessary amount.

WHIPSAW, *verb* (gaming).—At faro to win at one turn, to beat in two ways at once; hence to win 'hands down,' to beat an opponent willy-nilly.

1896. LILLARD, *Poker Stories*, 119. The blacklegs showed no mercy. They did not let him win even a few dollars to encourage him, but either booked the cards every trip, or else WHIPSAWED him until he was forced to drop.

WHIPSHIRE, *subs. phr.* (old).—Yorkshire (B. E., *c.* 1696).

WHIPSTER, *subs.* (thieves').—'A sharp or subtil Fellow' (B. E., *c.* 1696, and GROSE); 'a sharper' (BAILEY, 1731); a sly, cunning BLADE (*q.v.*): also (old) WHIP-STROKE (like WHIPSTER) = a term of abuse.

1530. *Jyl of Brentford's Testament* [OLIPHANT, *New Eng.*, i. 466. We see WHYPSTROKE].

1602. SHAKSPEARE, *Othello*, v. 2. Every puny WHIPSTER gets my sword.

d. 1650. FLETCHER, *Poems*, 64. From Memphis comes a WHIPSTER unto thee, And a Black Indian from the Red Sea.

1697. VANBRUGH, *Provoked Wife*, v. 3. That young liquorish WHIPSTER, Heartfree.

WHIP-STICKS, *subs. phr.* (Stock Exchange).—The Dunaberg and Witepsk Railway shares.

WHIRLIGIG, *subs.* (old colloquial).—1. A whim, caprice, MAGGOT (*q.v.*), BEE (*q.v.*).

1635. SHIRLEY, *Coronation*, iii. The WHIRLIGIGS of women.

d. 1655. ADAMS, *Works*, I. 180. That every novelist with a WHIRLIGIG in his brain must broach new opinions.

2. (old).—Change, 'the turn of the wheel,' the lapse of time: in quot. 1721 = Time or the World in the abstract.

1602. SHAKSPEARE, *Twelfth Night*, v. 1. And thus the WHIRLIGIG of time brings in his revenges.

d. 1721. PRIOR, *Ladle.* [The Gods] gave things their Beginning And set this WHIRLIGIG a spinning.

3. (provincial).—A carriage: also WHIRLICOTE.

1633. STOWE, *Survey of London*, 70. Of old time, Coaches were not known in this Iland, but Chariots or WHIRLICOTES, then so-called.

4. (common).—Applied to various toys or the like: *e.g.* (*a*) a top or top-like toy, (*b*) a teetotum, (*c*) a round-about or merry-go-round: also WHIRLER and WHIRL-ABOUT; and (*d*) a turnstile.

1530. PALSGRAVE, *Lang. Francoyse*, 762. I tryll a WHIRLYGIG round-aboute . . . *je pirouette* . . . I holde the a peny that I will tryll my WHIRLYGIG longer about than thou.

c. 1735. ARBUTHNOT and POPE, *Martinus Scriblerus.* He found that marbles taught him percussion and WHIRLIGIGS the axis in peritrochio.

5. (old military).—An instrument for punishing petty offenders: a kind of wooden cage, turning on a pivot, in which the culprit was whirled round with great velocity.

WHIRRIT (WHERRET or WHIRRICK), *subs.* (old).—A blow, slap, box on the ear. As *verb* = to box the ears.

1577. KENDALL, *Flowers of Epigrams.* And in a fume gave Furius A WHIRRET on the eare.

1607. *Puritan*, iv. 2. Troth, now I'm invisible, I'll hit him a sound WHERRET on the ear, when he comes out of the garden.

c. 1613. FLETCHER, *Nice Valour*, iv. How meekly This other fellow here receives his WHIRRIT.

d. 1713. ELLWOOD, *Life* (HOWELLS), 222. Following me at my heels and now and then giving me a WHIRRET on the ear.

1750. BROOKE, *Fool of Quality*, i. 21. Harry . . . gave master such a WHIRRICK that his cries instantly sounded the *ne plus ultra* to such kind of diversions.

WHISHLER, *subs.* (circus).—A ring-master.

WHISK, *subs.* (old).—1. A servant: in contempt.

1653. BROME, *Novella.* This is the proud braches WHISKE.

2. (provincial).—An impertinent fellow, SAUCEBOX (*q.v.*), BOUNCER (*q.v.*).

WHISKER-BED, *subs. phr.* (common).—The face.

1853. BRADLEY, *Verdant Green.* His ivories rattled, his nozzle barked, his WHISKER-BED napped heavily.

WHISKERS (or WHISKERANDO), *subs.* (common).—A whiskered person: a jocular salutation, 'Hallo, WHISKERS!' Also WHISKERY and WHISKERANDOED, *adj.* [From Don Ferolo WHISKERANDOS in SHERIDAN'S *Critic*, 1779.]

1834. SOUTHEY, *The Doctor*, clvi. To what follies and what extravagancies would the WHISKERANDOED macaronies of Bond Street and St. James's proceed, if the beard once more were, instead of the neck-cloth, to 'make the man.'

1848. THACKERAY, *Book of Snobs*, xli. The old lady is as ugly as any lady in the parish, and as tall and WHISKERY as a Grenadier. *Ibid.* (1862), *Philip*, xiii. The dumpy, elderly, square-shouldered, squinting, carroty, WHISKERANDO of a warrior who was laying about him so savagely.

WHISKEY (TIM-WHISKEY or TIMMY-WHISKEY), *subs.* (old).—A light one-horse chaise without a hood (GROSE).

1772. BRIDGES, *Burlesque Homer*, 481. In spite of him these youths so frisky, Went out and hir'd a TIMMY-WHISKY.

1774. FOOTE, *Cozeners*, i. A journey to Tyburn in a TIM-WHISKY and two would have concluded your travels.

1809. BYRON, *Childe Harold*, i. 69. Thy coach of hackney, WHISKEY, one-horse chair, And humblest gig through sundry suburbs whirl.

d. 1832. CRABBE, *Works*, II. 174. WHISKEYS and gigs and curricles.

1834. SOUTHEY, *Doctor*, Interch. xiv. It is not like the difference between . . . a WHISKEY and a TIM-WHISKEY, that is to say, no difference at all.

1884. DOWELL, *Taxes in England*, III. 227. The increased taxation of the curricle had the effect of bringing into existence the less expensive gig, a development or an imitation of a two-wheeled carriage known in the country as a WHISKEY.

WHISKEY-BLOAT, *subs. phr.* (American).—A person bloated from drinking whiskey.—(BARTLETT.)

WHISKEYFIED (or WHISKIFIED), *adj.* (common).—Drunk, bemused with whiskey: *see* SCREWED.

1857-9. THACKERAY, *Virginians*, xxxviii. The two WHISKEYFIED gentlemen are up with her, however.

1872. BLACK, *Adventures of a Phaeton*, xxviii. This person was a sort of WHISKIFIED Old Mortality, who claimed to have cut all manner of tombstones standing around.

WHISKEY-MILL, *subs. phr.* (American).—A grog-shop, a grocery with a license.

1870. M'CLURE, *Rocky Mountains*, 55. Platt City consists of one fair hotel, several small boarding-houses for operatives, several warehouses, as many stores, and about forty WHISKEY-MILLS, or small groceries where whiskey, tobacco, and portable eatables are sold at fabulous prices.

WHISKING, *adj.* (old).—Large, great, WHOPPING (*q.v.*).—BAILEY, 1731.

WHISK-TELT, *adj. phr.* (provincial).—Whorish, HOT (*q.v.*).

WHISKY-FRISKY, *adj. phr.* (old).—Flighty, MAGGOTY (*q.v.*).

1782. BURNEY, *Cecilia*, IX. iii. As to talking in such a WHISKY-FRISKY manner that nobody can understand him, why it's tantamount to not talking at all.

WHISPER, *subs.* (racing).—A secret TIP (*q.v.*): spec. information passed from mouth to mouth on the pretence of secrecy. Hence TO GIVE THE WHISPER = (1) to blaze abroad a supposed secret, and (2) to give a quick tip (HOTTEN); a WHISPER AT THE POST = an owner's final instructions to a jockey.

Verb (common).—To borrow: spec. small sums. Hence WHISPERER = a petty borrower.

ANGEL'S WHISPER, *subs. phr.* (military).—The call to defaulters' drill: usually extra fatigue duty.

1899. WYNDHAM, *Queen's Service*, xxxv. Effective measures are taken to prevent defaulters leaving barracks. . . . All day long, the bugle sounds at unexpected moments the . . . ANGEL'S WHISPER . . . when there is some extra fatigue to be performed.

PIG'S-WHISPER, *subs. phr.* (common).—1. A grunt; (2) = a very short space of time: that is, as brief as a grunt (BEE): also (American) PIG'S-WHISTLE.

1836. DICKENS, *Pickwick*, xxxii. You'll find yourself in bed in something less than a PIG'S WHISPER.

WHISPERING SYL.-SLINGER, *subs. phr.* (theatrical).—A prompter [that is, 'syllable'-slinger].

WHISTER-CLISTER (WHISTER-SNEFET, WHISTER-SNIVET, WHISTER-TWISTER, or WHISTER-POOP), *subs. phr.* (old).—A thumping blow: spec. a back-handed blow.

1542. UDAL, *Erasmus*, 112. A good WHISTERSNEFET, truelie paied on his eare.

WHISTLE, *subs.* (common).—1. The throat, RED-LANE (*q.v.*). Hence TO WET (OR WHET) ONE'S WHISTLE = to drink (*see* WET): Fr. *s'affûter le sifflet.*

1383. CHAUCER, *Cant. Tales*, 'Reeves Tale.' As any jay she light was and jolyf So was his joly WHISTLE WEL YWET.

c. 1400. *Townley Mysteries*, Pastores. Had she oones WETT HYR WHYSTYLL she couth syng fulle clere.

1530. PALSGRAVE, *Lang. Franc.*, 780. I WETE MY WHYSTELL, as good drinkers do. Je crocque la pie. Wyll you WETE YOUR WHYSTELL.

1618. FLETCHER, *Mad Lover*, ii. My WHISTLE once WET I'll pipe. *Ibid.* (1622), *Beggar's Bush*, iii. 1. Give the boy some drink there! Piper, WHET YOUR WHISTLE.

1653. WALTON, *Compleat Angler*, iii. Let's ev'n say grace, and turn to the fire, drink the other cup to WET OUR WHISTLES, and so sing away all sad thoughts.

d. 1796. BURNS, *Poems* (Globe), 150. But till we meet and WEET OUR WHISTLE, Tak this excuse for nae epistle.

2. (common).—A whim, fancy, caprice; whence TO PAY FOR ONE'S WHISTLE = to pay high (or dearly). [The allusion is to a story told (1779) by Dr. Franklin (*Works* [1836], II. 182) of his nephew, who set his mind on a common whistle, which he bought of a boy for four times its value.]

1876. ELIOT, *Daniel Deronda*, xxxv. I wouldn't destroy any old bits, but that notion of reproducing the old is a mistake, I think; at least, if a man likes to do it, he must PAY FOR HIS WHISTLE.

Verb (old).—To inform.

1815. SCOTT, *Guy Mannering*, xxxiii. I kept aye between him and her for fear she had WHISTLED.

TO WHISTLE AND RIDE, *verb. phr.* (tailors').—To work and talk.

PHRASES. TO GO WHISTLE = to go to the deuce, to be discomfited or disappointed; TO WHISTLE FOR A WIND = (1) old salts of a superstitious turn of mind will WHISTLE for a breeze during a calm: during a storm they would not dream of so doing: hence TO WHISTLE FOR = to stand small chance of getting; (2) = a jocular offer of aid to one long in commencing to urinate; AT ONE'S WHISTLE = at call; WORTH THE WHISTLE = worth notice, attention, or a call; TO WHISTLE DOWN THE WIND = to talk for talking's sake, to talk idly, or to no purpose; AS CLEAN AS A WHISTLE = NEAT (*q.v.*), SLICK (*q.v.*).

1547. HEYWOOD, *Dialogues.* It's a poor dog that is not worth the WHISTLING.

1604. SHAKSPEARE, *Winter's Tale*, iv. 4. 715. This being done, let the law GO WHISTLE.

1605. SHAKSPEARE, *Lear*, iv. 2. I have been WORTH THE WHISTLE.

1611. BEAUMONT and FLETCHER, *Two Noble Kinsmen*, iii. 5. *Ger.* Here's a woman wanting. *Count.* We may GO WHISTLE; all the fat's i' the fire.

1760. JOHNSTON, *Chrysal*, ii. 184. 'Do you not desire to be free?' 'Desire! aye, that I do; but I may WHISTLE FOR that wind long enough before it will blow.'

d. 1763. SHENSTONE, *Poet and the Dun.* Your fame is secure, bid the critics GO WHISTLE.

1772. BRIDGES, *Burlesque Homer*, 214. She went and fetch'd each nag his bridle, Then hung the reins upon her wrist, And WHISTLED while the horses pist.

1809. MALKIN, *Gil Blas* [ROUTLEDGE], 144. If an angel from heaven were to whisper wisdom in one ear, and your cousin her mortal chit-chat in the other, I am afraid the angel might WHISTLE FOR an audience.

1849–61. MACAULAY, *Hist. Eng.*, xiii. Ready AT HIS WHISTLE to array themselves round him in arms against the commander in chief.

1863. GASKELL, *Sylvia's Lovers*, iv. If Measter Cholmley don't do what I ax him, he may GO WHISTLE for my vote, he may.

1901. WALKER, *In the Blood*, 161. 'Well, I will,' replied Jim, 'when I've WET MY WHISTLE.'

WHISTLE-BELLY-VENGEANCE, *subs. phr.* (common).—Bad beer, SWIPES (*q.v.*); hence indifferent LAP (*q.v.*) of any kind: *cf.* WHIP-BELLY-VENGEANCE.

1861. HUGHES, *Tom Brown at Oxford*, xli. 'I thought you wouldn't appreciate the widow's tap,' said East, watching him with a grin: 'regular WHISTLE-BELLY VENGEANCE, and no mistake.'

WHISTLE-CUP, *subs. phr.* (common).—A drinking-cup with a whistle attached: the last toper capable of using the whistle received the cup as a prize. Also a tankard fitted with a whistle, so arranged as to sound when the vessel was emptied, thus warning the drawer that more liquor was required.

WHISTLE-DRUNK, *adj. phr.* (old).—Very drunk indeed.

1749. FIELDING, *Tom Jones*, XII. ii. He was indeed, according to the vulgar phrase, WHISTLE-DRUNK; for before he had swallowed the third bottle, he became so entirely overpowered, that though he was not carried off to bed till long after, the parson considered him as absent.

WHISTLE-JACKET, *subs. phr.* (provincial).—Small beer.

WHISTLER, *subs.* (common).—1. A broken-winded horse, a ROARER (*q.v.*).

2. (common).—An unlicensed vendor of spirits. Hence WHISTLING-SHOP = an illicit dram-shop.

1837. DICKENS, *Pickwick*, xlv. The turnkey knows beforehand, and gives the word to the WHISTLERS, and you may whistle for it wen you go to look. *Ibid.* A WHISTLING-SHOP, sir, is where they sell spirits.

WHISTLING- (or PUFFING-) BILLY, *subs. phr.* (common).—A locomotive.

WHISTLING-BREECHES, *subs. phr.* (common).—Corduroy trousers.

WHIT, *subs.* (Old Cant).—A prison: *see* CAGE: spec. NEWGATE.

1676. *Warening for Housekeepers* [FARMER, *Musa Pedestris* (1896), 30]. O then they rub us to the WHITT.

1724. HARPER, *Harlequin Sheppard.* He broke thro' all rubbs in the WHITT.

WHITE, *subs.* (common).—1. In *pl.* = leucorrhœa.

2. (old).—In *pl.* = white clothes, vestments, or goods.

1644. HEYLIN, *Life of Laud*, 262. The Dean of our chappel . . . in his WHITES.

d. 1655. ADAMS, *Works*, ii. 174. You clothe Christ with your blacks on earth, he will clothe you with his glorious WHITES in heaven.

1724–7. DEFOE, *Tour Through Great Britain*, i. 324. Long cloths for the Turkey trade called Salisbury WHITES.

1888. *Bicycling News*, 14 July, 19. Unless a man can combine cycling and boating, he should never . . . ride his machine in WHITES.

3. (old archery).—(*a*) The centre of a target: Fr. *blanc*: formerly painted white: *cf.* BULL'S-EYE. Whence (*b*) the object in view, a mark; TO HIT THE WHITE = to be right.

1580. LYLY, *Euphues and his England* [NARES]. An archer say you is to be knowen by his aime, not by his arrowe: but your aime is so ill, that if you knewe how farre wide from the WHITE your shaft sticketh, you would hereafter rather breake your bowe then bend it.

1593. SHAKSPEARE, *Taming of the Shrew*, v. 2. 'Twas I won the wager, though you HIT THE WHITE.

c. 1605. DRAYTON, *Mooncalf*, 509. Quoth mother Howlett, you have HIT THE WHITE.

1629. FELTHAM, *Parody Jonson's Ode on Leaving the Stage.* As oft' you've wanted brains And art to strike the WHITE, As you have levelled right.

1632. MASSINGER, *Emperor of the East*, iv. 4. The immortality of my fame is the WHITE I shoot at.

c. 1635. HOWELL, *Letters*, iii. 3. Church-Lands were made secular, which was the WHITE they levell'd at.

4. (colloquial).—In *pl.* = the white of the eyes.

1662. *Grim the Collier*, iii. And he, poor heart, no sooner heard my news, But turns me up his WHITES and falls down flat.

1682. BARNARD, *Heylin*, clxxx. Lifting up both his hands and WHITES to heaven.

1764. MACKLIN, *Man of the World*, iii. 1. Ay, and I turned up the WHITES of my eyes till the strings awmost cracked again.

Adj. (old and still colloquial in many senses).—1. Thus WHITE (= fair or specious) WORDS; WHITE (= lucky) DAY: *cf.* RED-LETTER DAY; WHITE (= excusable) LIE (GROSE); WHITE (= venial) CRIME; WHITE (= friendly) WITCH; WHITE (= honourable) MAN, formerly = fair, handsome; WHITE (= guiltless) WAY; WHITE (= auspicious) HOUR; WHITE (= beneficially levied) MAIL.

c. 1300. *Hymns to Virgin* [E.E.T.S.], 72. Y was stalworthe & WHITE.

1369. CHAUCER, *Troilus*, ii. 1062. Thou, Minerva the WHYTE, Gif thou me wit my letre to devyse. *Ibid.*, ii. 887. Ye ywis, quod fresshe Antigone the WHITE. *Ibid.*, iii. 1568. Ye caused al this fare, Trow I, quod she, for al your WORDES WHITE.

1606. *Returne from Parnassus*, ii. 6. When he returns, I'll tell twenty admirable lies of his hawk, and then I shall be his little rogue, and his WHITE VILLAIN, for a whole week after.

c. 1616. FLETCHER, *Knight of Malta*, ii. 5. In the WHITE WAY of virtue and true valour.

1630. SHIRLEY, *Grateful Servant*, ii. 1. Till this WHITE HOUR these walls were never proud T'inclose a guest.

1689. MATHER, *Witchcraft*, 5. There is mention of creatures that they call WHITE-WITCHES, which do only good turns for their neighbours.

1715. ADDISON, *Drummer*, ii. The common people call him a wizard, a WHITE-WITCH, a conjuror, a cunning man, a necromancer.

1789. D'ARBLAY, *Diary*, iv. 289. Sir George has told me a lie—a WHITE LIE, he says, but I hate a WHITE LIE; if you will tell me a lie, let it be a black lie.

1815. SCOTT, *Guy Mannering* [WEBSTER]. On the whole the Dominie reckoned this as one of the WHITE DAYS of his life. *Ibid.* (1821), *Kenilworth*, i. 170. He was what the vulgar call a WHITE-WITCH, a cunning man, and such like.

1834. EDGEWORTH, *Helen*, vi. I wish that word fib was out of the English language, and WHITE LIE drummed out after it.

1855. KINGSLEY, *Westward Ho*, i. When he had warts or burns, he went to the WHITE-WITCH at Northam to charm them away.

1861. READE, *Cloister and Hearth* lii. He spent much of his gains, however, in sovereign herbs and choice drugs, and would have so invested them all, but Margaret WHITE-MAILED a part.

1869. STOWE, *Oldtown*, 336. The Thanksgiving festival of that year is particularly impressed on my mind as a WHITE DAY.

1884. *Century Mag.*, xxxix. 523. Why, Miss, he's a friend worth havin', and don't you forget it. There ain't a WHITER MAN than Laramie Jack.

1887. *St. James's Gazette*, 21 May. At present, when an Irishman is accused in Ireland of what is called a WHITE-CRIME by his fellow-countrymen (such, for instance, as the murder of a caretaker or a landlord) the difficulty is not only with the jury but with the witnesses.

1898. GOULD, *Landed at Last*, iv. There goes a 'WHITE MAN' if ever there was one. . . . That beard [is] the only black thing about him.

1900. LYNCH, *High Stakes*, xliii. She is the one WHITE, beautiful, lovable creature in all the world—to me.

2. *See* WHITE-BOY.

3. *See* WHITE-LOT.

Verb (old).—To gloss over, to rehabilitate: also (modern) WHITEWASH, which spec. = to clear of debt by process of the Bankruptcy Court. Hence WHITEWASH, *subs.* = a veneer of respectability; with WHITEWASHER and WHITEWASHING as derivatives. Also TO USE ONE WHITE = (1) to deal fairly and justly, and (2) to act on the SQUARE (*q.v.*).

c. 1616. FLETCHER, *Bloody Brothers*, iv. 1. WHIT'ST over all his vices.

1773. FOOTE, *Bankrupt* [OLIPHANT, *New Eng.*, ii. 186. Among the verbs are WHITEWASH a creditor].

1817. SCOTT, *Rob Roy*, vii. A WHITE-WASHED Jacobite . . . had lately qualified himself to act as a justice, by taking the oaths to Government.

1844–8. LOWELL, *Tempora Mutantur.* WHITEWASHED, he quits the politician's strife At ease in mind, with pockets filled for life.

1888. *D. Teleg.*, 21 Mar. The impecunious man could get the Bankruptcy Court to WHITEWASH him.

1885. *Notes and Queries*, 28 Nov., 439. Attempts to WHITEWASH the character of Richard III. . . . have been frequent.

1885. *Academy*, 21 Nov., 342. I have not aimed altogether at a WHITEWASHING of Bramwell Brontë.

1888. *St. James's Gaz.*, 17 Mar. If the Sicilian Vespers . . . have not as yet taken their place in the record of virtue, it is probably because the WHITEWASHER has been too busy upon other undertakings.

1903. *D. Teleg.*, 22 May, 7. 3. I had not followed the case closely, and did not know that he was an undischarged bankrupt. Mr. White had WHITEWASHED him.

1900. LYNCH, *High Stakes*, xxix. I don't see why I should give away a fellow that's USED ME WHITE.

TO SPIT WHITE, *verb. phr.* (old).—To expectorate from a dry but healthy mouth: also to SPIT WHITE BROTH (or SIXPENCES). Fr. *cracher des pièces de dix sous.*

1594. LYLY, *Mother Bombie*, iii. 1 [NARES]. That makes them SPIT WHITE BROATH, as they do.

1598. SHAKSPEARE, 2 *Hen. IV.*, i. 2. 237. If it be a hot day, and I brandish anything but a bottle, I would I might never SPIT WHITE again.

1622. MASSINGER, *Virgin Martyr*, iii. 3. Had I been a pagan still, I should not have SPIT WHITE for want of drink.

1772. GRAVES, *Spiritual Quixote*, IV. vi. He had thought it rather a dry discourse; and beginning to SPIT SIXPENCES (as his saying was), he gave hints to Mr. Wildgoose to stop at the first public-house they should come to.

WHITE-APRON, *subs. phr.* (old).—A whore: *see* TART.

1599. HALL, *Satires*, iv. 1. Or midnight plays, or taverns of new wine, Hye ye, WHITE APRONS, to your landlords signe.

1733–7. POPE, *Imit. of Horace.* And some to hunt WHITE-APRONS in the park.

WHITE-ASH BREEZE, *subs. phr.* (boating).—The breeze caused by rowing: oars are generally made of white ash.

WHITEBOY, *subs.* (old).—1. A generic endearment: also (of a favourite son) WHITE SON: see WHITE, *adj.* 1.

1554–63. FOXE, *Acts and Monuments*, ii. 190. The Pope's own WHITE SON.

1588. GREENE, *Friar Bacon* [DYCE, *Works*, I. 174]. He is great Prince of Wales. . . . Then ware what is done, For he is Henry's WHITE SON.

1611. BEAUMONT, *Knight of Burning Pestle*, ii. 2. What says my WHITE BOY?

1633. FORD, *'Tis Pity*, i. 4. 'I know,' quoth I, 'I am his WHITEBOY and will not be gulled.'

1640. *Two Lancashire Lovers*, 19. Fie, young gentleman, with such a brave sparke as you, that is your mother's WHITE-BOY, undoe your hopes?

1641. MILTON, *Apol. for Smectymnus.* His first addresse was an humble remonstrance by a dutifull son of the Church, almost as if he had said her WHITE-BOY.

d. 1688. BUNYAN [ANNANDALE]. One of God's WHITEBOYS.

1774–81. WARTON, *Hist. Poet.*, iv. 65. [NARES: T. Warton adds, as an illustration, that Dr. Busby used to call his favorite scholars his WHITE BOYS; and says that he could add a variety of other combinations.]

2. (Irish political).—A member of a secret political society, agrarian in character (*c.* 1759–60). [LECKY: 'Their object was to do justice to the poor by restoring the ancient commons and redressing other grievances.' This they sought to accomplish by throwing down fences, levelling enclosures, and generally destroying the property of anyone—landlords, agents, Protestant clergy, tax or tithe collectors—who had made themselves obnoxious to the association. They styled themselves Whiteboys 'because during their nocturnal excursions they covered their usual attire with white shirts. This disguise was used principally to enable them while scouring through the darkness to recognise each other' (DANIM)].

3. (London).—London rioters.

1768. WALPOLE, *Letters*, III. 250. Those black dogs, the WHITEBOYS or coal-heavers, are dispersed or taken.

WHITECHAPEL, *subs. phr.* (common).—1. A light two-wheeled cart, a coster's barrow, a SHOFUL (*q.v.*): also WHITECHAPEL-CART, WHITECHAPEL-BROUGHAM, and CHAPEL-CART.

2. (streets').—Tossing 'two out of three': *cf.* SUDDEN DEATH.

3. *See* WHITECHAPEL-PLAY.

WHITECHAPEL-PLAY (WHITECHAPEL). Anything mean, paltry, or unsportsmanlike: *cf.* BUNGAY-PLAY.

WHITECHAPEL-PORTION, *subs. phr.* (old).—A clean apron and an umbrella; also 'a clean gown and a pair of pattens' (HOTTEN).

1891. CAREW, *Auto. of Gypsy*, 416. Though she brought me nathink but a WHITECHAPEL FORTIN' she were worth her weight in gold.

WHITECHAPEL-SHAVE, *subs. phr.* (common).—*See* quot.

1860. DICKENS, *Uncommercial Traveller*, xxv. Blue-bearded though they were, and bereft of the youthful smoothness of cheek which is imparted by what is termed in Albion a 'WHITECHAPEL SHAVE' (and which is, in fact, whitening judiciously applied to the jaws with the palm of the hand), I recognised them.

WHITE-CHOKER, *subs. phr.* (common).—1. A white tie: hence (2) a parson.

WHITE-CROW, *subs. phr.* (colloquial).—A rarity; hence an apparent contradiction in terms which is none the less a fact. [Albino crows are occasionally met with.]

WHITE-EYE, *subs. phr.* (American).—Maize whiskey.

WHITE-FEATHER. *See* FEATHER.

WHITEFRIARS. *See* ALSATIA.

WHITE-HORSE, *subs. phr.* (common).—A white-crested dancing wave.

1849. KINGSLEY, *Life*, i. 168. The bay is now curling and writhing in WHITE HORSES under a smoking south-wester.

d. 1888. MATTHEW ARNOLD [HOTTEN]. Now the wild WHITE HORSES play, Champ and chafe and toss in the spray. Children, dear, let us away, This way, this way.

TO BE WHITE-HORSED IN, *verb. phr.* (tailors').—To obtain a berth through influence.

WHITE-HOUSE, *subs. phr* (American colloquial).—The official residence of the President of the United States, Washington: from its colour. Its official designation is EXECUTIVE MANSION (*Century*).

WHITE-LIVERED, *adj. phr.* (colloquial).—Cowardly, mean. [An old notion was that cowards had bloodless livers.]

1548. LATIMER, *Sermons and Remains*, s.v.

1597. SHAKSPEARE, *Richard III.*, iv. 4. WHITE-LIVER'D runagate, what doth he there? *Ibid.* (1598), *Merchant of Venice*, iii. 2. How many cowards . . . inward searched Have LIVERS WHITE as milk?

1600. JONSON, *Cynthia's Revels*, iv. 1. When they come in swaggering company, and will pocket up anything, may they not properly be said to be WHITE-LIVERED?

1625. FLETCHER, *Elder Brother*, iv. 3. As I live, they stay not here, WHITE-LIVERED wretches.

WHITE-LOT, *subs. phr.* (thieves').—A silver watch and chain: or (old) WHITE-STUFF (or WEDGE); *cf.* RED. WHITE CLOCK (or WHITE-'UN) = a silver watch; WHITE JENNY = a foreign-made silver watch (HOTTEN). WHITE-MONEY = silver; THE WHITE AND THE RED = silver and gold. SMOOTH-WHITE = a shilling: *see* RHINO.

1369. CHAUCER, *Troilus*, iii. 1384. They shulle forgon THE WHYTE AND THE REDE.

1628. MIDDLETON, *Widow*, iv. 2. A WHITE thimble that I found.

1901. WALKER, *In the Blood*, 138. That night he started a new career, and 'went through' three drunken men lying out in the Silent Places to the relieving tune of four pounds sterling, obtained in the form of silver money and a . . . WHITE LOT.

WHITE MAN'S HANSOM WOMAN, *subs. phr.* (West Indian).—A 'brown' or 'yellow' mistress: a 'black' smock-servant = WHITE MAN'S WHORE: an echo of the 'colour' sentiment: *cf.* a negro 'as black as one's hat' calling another 'a damned black nigger.'

WHITE-MOOR, *subs. phr.* (old).—A Genoese.

1642. HOWELL, *Forraine Travell*, vii. It is proverbially said, there are in Genoa mountaines without wood, sea without fish, women without shame, and men without conscience, which makes them to be termed the WHITE MOORES.

WHITENESS, *subs.* (old).—1. Chastity: also WHITE (or COLD) SHEETS; (2) = nakedness.

1604. SHAKSPEARE, *Winter's Tale*, i. 2. The purity and WHITENESS OF MY SHEETS. *Ibid.* (1605), *Cymbeline*, i. 6. Should he make me live . . . betwixt COLD SHEETS whiles he is vaulting variable ramps? *Ibid.*, ii. 2. The chastity . . . WHITER THAN THE SHEETS! That I might touch!

1654. CHAPMAN, *Rev. for Honour*. 'Twas a rape Upon my honour, more then on her WHITENESSE. *Ibid.* And now I would not but this devil prince Had done this act upon Caropia's WHITENESS.

WHITE-POODLE, *subs. phr.* (obsolete tailors').—A rough woolly cloth.

WHITE-PROP, *subs. phr.* (thieves').—A diamond scarf-pin: also SPARKLE- (or SPARK-) PROP.

1879. HORSLEY, *Auto. of Thief* [*Macmillan's Mag.*, xl. 506]. Pipe his spark PROP.

1888. SIMS, *Plank Bed Ballad* [*Referee*, 12 Feb., 3]. A spark PROP a pal . . . and I Had touched.

WHITER, *subs.* (Harrow School).—A white waistcoat: permissible after three years at the school: *cf.* -ER.

WHITE-SATIN, (-LACE, -TAPE, -WINE, or **-RIBBON)**, *subs. phr.* (common).—Gin: *see* DRINKS and TAPE.

1820. EGAN, *Randall's Diary*. Jack Randall then impatient rose, And said, 'Tom's speech were just as fine If he would call that first of GOES By that genteeler name—WHITE WINE.'

1851-61. MAYHEW, *Lond. Lab.* The 'driz fencers,' or sellers of cheap lace, carried about their persons 'jigger stuffs,' or spirit made at an illicit still. They sold it, I've heard them say, to ladies that liked a drop on the sly. One old lady used to give three shillings for three yards of 'driz,' and it was well enough understood, without no words, that a pint of brandy was part of them three yards.

WHITE-SERGEANT, *subs. phr.* (common).—A 'breeches-wearing' wife: THE GENERAL (*q.v.*), THE GREY-MARE (*q.v.*).

WHITE-TRASH, *subs. phr.* (negro).—A poor white: Southern states: also POOR WHITE FOLK.

1856. OLMSTED, *Texas* [BARTLETT]. In social relations, the Negroes are sensitive to the overbearing propensities of a proprietary who are accustomed to regard all neighbors out of their own class as WHITE TRASH.

1856. STOWE, *Dred*, II. Of all the pizen critters that I knows on, these ere mean WHITE TRASH is the pizenest. They ain't got no manners and no bringing up. *Ibid.*, I. 271. 'The fact is,' said Mr. Gordon, 'what with niggers, and overseers, and WHITE TRASH, my chances of salvation are dreadfully limited.'

1866. *Atlantic*, xviii. 84. Tain't no use, honey; you don't 'pear to take no int'res' in yer own kith and kin, no more dan or'nary WHITE TRASH.

WHITEWASH. 1. *See* WHITE, *verb.*

2. (old).—'A glass of sherry as a finish, after drinking port or claret' (HOTTEN).

WHITEWASHERS, *subs.* (military).—The second battalion Gloucestershire Regiment, late the 61st Foot.

WHITHER-GO-THEE, *subs. phr.* (B. E., *c.* 1696).—A wife.

WHITING. TO LET LEAP A WHITING, *verb. phr.* (old).—To miss an opportunity.

WHITING-MOP, *subs. phr.* (old).—1. A young and pretty girl; hence (2) an endearment; also WHITING.

d. 1525. SKELTON, *Elinour Rumming*. That can my husband saye Whan we kysse and playe In lust and in likynge He calleth me his WHITING.

1637. MASSINGER, *Guardian*, iv. 2. I have a stomach, and could content myself With this pretty WHITING-MOP.

1665. *Homer à la Mode*. He bids thee without further stops, Arme th' Greekes, with heads like WHITING MOPS.

WHITING'S-EYE, *subs. phr.* (old).—An amorous glance, SHEEP'S-EYE (*q.v.*).

1673. WYCHERLEY, *Gentleman Dancing Master*, iv. 1. I saw him just now give her the languishing eye, as they call it, that is, the WHITING'S EYE, of old called the sheep's eye.

WHITSUN-ALE, *subs. phr.* (old).—*See* ALE. Hence WHITSUN-LORD = the master of ceremonies at a Whitsun merrymaking.

1633. JONSON, *Tale of a Tub*, Prol. A cooper's wit, or some such busy spark, Illumining the high constable and his clerk, And all the neighbourhood from old records Of antique proverbs, drawn from WHITSON-LORDS.

WHITTLE, *verb* (old).—1. To confess at the gallows. Also (thieves') TO NOSE (*q.v.*), TO PEACH (*q.v.*).

1727. SWIFT, *Clever Tom Flinch*. I must speak to the people a little, But I'll see you all damn'd before I will WHITTLE.

2. *See* WHITTLED.

WHITTLED, *adj.* (common).—Drunk, CUT (*q.v.*): *see* SCREWED. Hence WHITTLE, *verb* = to make tipsy, and as *subs.* = a merry-making, drinking-bout, etc.

1586. WITHALS, *Dict.*, 560. *In vino veritas*. When men are well WHITLED, their toungs run at randome.

1594. LYLY, *Mother Bombie*, iii. 3. The best was, our masters were as well WHITLED as wee, for they yet lie by it.

1609. HOLLAND, *Ammianus Marcel.* Within the province of Africanus, ruling over Pannonia Secunda, some boone companions in Sirmium having taken their cups very liberally untill they were well WHITLED, supposing no man to bee by for to heare their talke, fell freely to finding fault with the present government.

16[?]. *Owle's Almanacke*, 47. Taylors shall be patternes and presidents to sober men, a bushell of wheat to a tankard of beere, lest they cut their fingers when they are WHITTELD.

16[?]. HARSNETT, *Popish Impost.*, x. 3. A Christmas temptation, after the devil was well WHITLED.

1628. VERSTEGAN, *Rest. Dec. Intell.*, 230. After the Britans were wel WHITTLED with wine he fell to taunting and girding at them.

d. 1742. SOMERVILE, *Poems*, 'Yeoman of Kent.' A lying-in's expensive too, In cradles, WHITTLES, spice-bowls, sack.

WHIZZER, *subs.* (provincial).—A falsehood (HALLIWELL).

WHOBALL (JOHN), *proverb* (old).—*See* quot.

1614. *Terence in English*. Se deludi facile haud patitur. You cannot easily make him a foole. He is NONE OF JOHN WHOBALLS CHILDREN. Hee will be abused at no mans hands if he may.

WHOLE. *See* BOILING, TEAM, and all nouns in the various combinations.

WHOP, (WAP, WOPPE, WHAP), *subs.* (old literary: now colloquial).—A blow. As *verb* = to beat.

c. 1360. *Alliterative Poems* (MORRIS) [OLIPHANT, *New Eng.*, i. 63. We find the new verbs *shout* . . . WAPPE, our WHOP].

c. 1362. *York Plays*, 326. For a WHAPP so he whyned and weasid And ȝitt no lasshe to the lurdan was lente.

1862. THACKERAY, *Philip*, xviii. Bunch had put his boys to a famous school, where they might WHOP the French boys and learn all the modern languages.

Intj. (American).—WHACK! (*q.v.*), WHIP! (*q.v.*), BANG! (*q.v.*).

1840. CROCKETT, *Tour*, 109. But a day of payment is coming; and, if the money ain't forthcoming, out comes a Randolph writ, and WHAP goes your money and liberty.

1843-4. HALIBURTON, *Attaché*, ii. I began to think smokin' warn't so bad after all, when WHAP went my cigar right out of my mouth into my bosom.

WHOPPER (WHAPPER), *subs.* (common).—Anything very large, fine, good: a generic intensive (GROSE): also WHOPPING = extremely fine, very large, A1 (*q.v.*).

[1520. HAZLITT, *Pop. Poet.*, ii. 94. An admiring woman calls a stalwart youth a WHYPPER; in our day she would use WHOPPER or whacker.]

1706. WARD, *Wooden World*, 69. He looks then most formidable . . . in his Fur-cap and WHAPPING large Watch-coat.

1829. MARRYAT, *Fr. Mildmay*, xx. This is a WHOPPER that's after us.

1847. ROBB, *Squatter Life*, 61. A WHAPPIN' big pan of mush stood in the centre of a table, and a large pan of milk beside it, with lots of corn-bread and butter.

1856. DOW, *Sermons*, I. 91. Before you lie, brethren, make up your minds to go it strong; for a little callow fib stands but a small chance among the big WHOPPERS. *Ibid.*, III. 21. A few years ago, WHAPPING great sleeves and big antecedents were all the rage; and what a funny figure our bellies did then cut.

1861. HUGHES, *Tom Brown at Oxford*, xlvii. There's a WHOPPER rising not more than ten yards below the rail.

1865. MAJOR DOWNING, *Letters*, 67. We've got only one crib, and that's a WHAPPIN' one too.

1887. *Harper's Mag.*, lxxiii. 213. But he hardly deserves mercy, having told WHOPPERS.

1888. *St. James's Gaz.*, 2 Mar. Not content with two WHOPPERS, as Mr. Jo Gargery might call them, Surtees goes on to invent a perfectly incredible heraldic bearing.

1901. WALKER, *In the Blood*, 23. 'Blime, she's a WHOPPER!' says Billy.

WHOP-STRAW (or JOHNNY WHOP-STRAW), *subs. phr.* (common).—A countryman, rustic, CLOD-HOPPER (*q.v.*).

WHORE, *subs.* (once literary: now low or vulgar).—1. A woman (orig.) who SPREAD (*q.v.*) for hire; in modern use, a harlot, strumpet, adulteress, or fornicatress: *see* TART. Hence (2) a generic term of abuse: of a woman, chaste or unchaste: *cf.* BLOODY, BUGGER, FUCKING, and similar expletives. Also WHORE'S-BIRD (WHORESON; WHORECOP) = (1) bastard, and (2) a generic reproach); and numerous combinations.

1275. *Genesis and Exodus* [E.E.T.S.], 4072. The mestres of thise HORE-MAN . . . The bidde ic hangen that he ben.

1280. *Ancren Riwle*, 316. Ich am a ful stod mere, a stinckinde HORE [I am a foul stud mare, a stinking WHORE].

c. 1401. *Townley Mysteries*, 'Juditium.' Alle harlottes and HORRES And bawdes that procures, To bryng them to lures, Welcom to my See.

1440. *Prompt. Parvulorum*, s.v. HORE, woman, Meretrix. *Ibid.*, s.v. HOREL, or bullowre, Fornicator . . . leno mechus.

1595. SHAKSPEARE, *Romeo and Juliet*, iv. 4. Well said; a merry WHORESON, ha! *Ibid.* (1596), *Hamlet*, v. 2. 64. He that hath kill'd my King and WHORED my mother. *Ibid.* (1598), 2 *Henry IV.*, iii. 2. 193. A WHORESON cold, sir, a cough, sir. *Ibid.* (1602), *Othello*, v. 1. 116. This is the fruit of WHORING. *Ibid.* (1602), *Troilus and Cressida*, ii. 3. A WHORESON dog that shall patter thus with us. *Ibid.* (1603), *Meas. for M.*, v. 1. 521. Do not marry me to a WHORE.

1602. MARSTON, *Antonio and Mellida*, i. iv. 1. Your WHORISH love, your drunken healths, your bouts and shouts.

1607. DEKKER, *Northward Hoe*, ii. 2. The WHORESON rich innkeeper of Doncaster, her father, shewed himself a rank ostler to send her up at this time a year, and by the carrier too.

1610. FLETCHER, *Maid's Tragedy*, v. Thou keptst me brave at Court, and WHOR'D me, Then married me.

1611. COTGRAVE, *Dict.* s.v., *Madame de rebut*, a rascally drab, a WHORE.

[?]. *Mary Ambree* [CHILD, *Ballads*, vii. 113]. 'A mayden of England, sir, never will bee The WHORE of a monarche,' quoth Mary Ambree.

d. 1628. J. BEAUMONT, *Psyche*, iii. 184. Thou knowst my Wrongs, and with what Pain I wear the Name of WHORE his Preachment on me pinn'd.

d. 1655. ADAMS, *Sermons*, I. 223. Tamar would not yield to Judah without a hire. The *hire* makes the WHORE.

1694. *Plautus made English*, 9. They'd set some sturdy WHORE'S-BIRD to meet me, and beat out half a dozen of my teeth.

1713. ARBUTHNOT, *John Bull*. Frog was a sly WHORESON, the reverse of John.

c. 1716. CONGREVE, *Juvenal*, xi. A Vestal ravish'd, or a Matron WHOR'D, Are laudable Diversions in a Lord.

1772. BRIDGES, *Burlesque Homer*, 183. Brave Diomed, I see Two WHORES' BIRDS coming full at thee.

1772. GRAVES, *Spiritual Quixote*, IV. ix. Damn you all together for a pack of WHORES'-BIRDS as you are.

1857. HUGHES, *Tom Brown's School-days*, I. ii. 'Imp'dent old WOSBIRD!' says he, 'I'll break the bald head on un.'

WHY AND WHEREFORE (THE), *subs. phr.* (colloquial). — The reason, cause.

1593. SHAKSPEARE, *Comedy of Errors*. Every WHY hath a WHEREFORE.

1624. FLETCHER, *Rule a Wife*, iii. 1. Dispute learnedly the WHYS AND WHERE-FORES.

1809. MALKIN, *Gil Blas* [ROUTLEDGE], 373. When I let him into the WHY AND the WHEREFORE, he laughed ready to split his sides.

d. 1897. JEAN INGELOW [*Century*]. The WHY AND THE WHEREFORE of it all. Who knoweth?

WHY-NOT. TO HAVE (or BE) AT A WHY-NOT, *verb. phr.* (old).—To have, stand, or be in a dilemma; to pull up suddenly, to meet with a sudden check or reverse.

d. 1612. HARINGTON [*Nugæ Antiq.* (PARK), II. 144]. This game . . . was like to have been lost with a WHY-NOT.

1664. BUTLER, *Hudibras*, II. ii. 528. And snapp'd their canons with a WHY-NOT. *Ibid.* 'On Philip Nye's Thanksgiving.' When the church was taken with a WHY-NOT in the lurch.

1753. RICHARDSON, *Grandison*, VI. 156. Now, dame Sally, I have you at a WHY-NOT, or I have had.

WIBBLE, *subs.* (provincial).—Weak LAP (*q.v.*); any thin, weak beverage.

WIBBLE-WOBBLE, *adj. phr.* (colloquial).—Unsteadily.

WIBLING'S - WITCH, *subs. phr.* (HALLIWELL). — The four of clubs.

WICKED, *adj.* (colloquial). — 1. Roguish, mischievous; and (2) amorous, wanton, *e.g.* a WICKED twinkle in the eye, to look WICKED, etc.

1600. SHAKSPEARE, *As You Like It*, iv. 1 That same WICKED bastard of Venus.

1809. MALKIN, *Gil Blas* [ROUTLEDGE], 369. Our doctor is rubicund in the jowl, Efflorescent on the nose, with a WICKED EYE at a bumper or a girl.

1849-50. THACKERAY, *Pendennis*, xxvii. Pen looked uncommonly WICKED.

WICKET, *subs.* (venery).—1. The female *pudendum*: *see* MONO-SYLLABLE.

. . . *MS. Addit.*, 12195. A WEKET of the wombe.

2. (common). — The mouth, GUTTER-ALLEY (*q.v.*).

1557. TUSSER, *Husbandrie*, 169. With hir that will clicket make daunger to cope, Least quickly hir WICKET seeme easie to ope.

WIDDY, *subs.* (colloquial).—1. A widow.

1900. WHITE, *West End*, 354. If my name appears there, in the worst place—I mean, making you a WIDDY—you must write to old Rupert.

2. *See* WIDOW.

WIDDLE. *See* OLIVER.

WIDDY-WADDY, *adj. phr.* (colloquial).—Trifling, insignificant.

WIDE, *adv.* (common).—1. Well-informed, KNOWING (*q.v.*), keen, alert, up to SNUFF (*q.v.*): also WIDE-AWAKE and WIDO: *cf.* NARROW.

1834. AINSWORTH, *Rookwood*. Two milling coves, each VIDE AVAKE, Vere backed to fight for heavy stake.

1836. *The Thieves' Chaunt* [FARMER, *Musa Pedestris* (1896), 121]. She's WIDE-AWAKE, and her prating cheat, For humming a cove was never beat.

1836. DICKENS, *Sketches by Boz*, 'Watkins Tottle.' Our governor's WIDE AWAKE, he is: I'll never say nothin' agin him nor no man, but he knows what's o'clock, he does.

1841. CATLIN, *North Am. Indians*, I. 71. Bogard . . . was a Yankee and a WIDE-AWAKE fellow.

1854-5. THACKERAY, *Newcomes*, xx. 'Your aunt is a woman who is uncommon WIDE AWAKE, I can tell you.' 'I always knew, sir, that my aunt was perfectly aware of the time of day,' says Barnes, with a low bow.

1856. STOWE, *Dred*, I. 210. Miss Harriet had more clothes and more money than the rest; because she was always WIDE-AWAKE, and looking out for herself.

1874. MAHAFFY, *Social Life in Greece*, 48. The Homeric Greeks were too shrewd and WIDE-AWAKE a people to sow where they did not reap; and the increase of communication, and consequent frequency of visitors, were sure to close quickly the open door, and the unasked right of entry.

1877. HORSLEY, *Jottings from Jail*. I got in company with some of the WIDEST people in London.

1897. MARSHALL, *Pomes*, 8. But the knight of the pencil was WIDE-AWAKE, and was not to be had with 'kid.' *Ibid.*, 49. WIDE, sir? I believe yer! Far too WIDE for Honest Bill. *Ibid.*, 120. Although she was quite the lady In deportment and in dress, Were you asked, as a WIDE-'UN, 'Shady?' You would have to answer 'Yes.'

2. (old).—Indifferent, wide of the mark, out of the running, adrift: hence generic for bad.

1612-5. HALL, *Contempl.*, 'Aaron and Miriam.' God eyther denyes or defers the grant of our requests for our good; it were WIDE for us if our suites should be euer heard.

WIDE-AWAKE, *subs. phr.* (common).—A soft felt hat with a broad brim: 'So-called (GROSE) because it never had a nap and never wants one.'

1857. C. KINGSLEY, *Two Years Ago*, Int. 'Then the fairy knight is extinct in England?' asked Stangrave, smiling. 'No man less; only he . . . has found a WIDE-AWAKE cooler than an iron kettle.'

1861. H. KINGSLEY, *Ravenshoe*, xliii. She was one of the first who appeared in the Park in a low-crowned hat—a WIDE-AWAKE.

1884. CLARK RUSSELL, *Jack's Courtship*, iii. 'My democratic WIDE-AWAKE, and the republican cut of my jib,' said he, looking down at his clothes.

1890. *Daily Graphic*, 7 Jan., 9. 4. Then the crowd go mad. Up fly head-gear, chimney-pot, and WIDE-A-WAKE alike, their owners careless of their fate.

See WIDE.

WIDGEON, *subs.* (common). — A simpleton: *see* BUFFLE.

WIDOW, *subs.* (Old Cant).—The gallows: *see* NUBBING-CHEAT. Also (Scots) THE WIDDY, and Fr. *veuve* (formerly the gallows, now applied to the guillotine).

d. 1796. BURNS, *Poems* (Globe), 50. Her dove had been a Highland laddie, But weary fa' the waefu' WOODIE!

WIDOW-BEWITCHED, *subs. phr.* (old).—A woman separated from her husband: *cf.* GRASS-WIDOW.

1725. BAILEY, *Erasmus*, 136. They should see you divorced from your husband—a widow, nay, to live (a WIDOW BEWITCHED) worse than a widow; for WIDOWS may marry again.

1863. GASKELL, *Sylvia's Lovers*, xxxix. Who'd ha' thought of yo'r husband . . . makin' a moonlight flittin' and leavin' yo' to be a WIDOW-BEWITCHED.

WIDOW'S-MAN, *subs. phr.* (various).—*See* quots.

1749. FIELDING, *Tom Jones*, III. vi. As to Square, who was in his person what is called a jolly fellow, or a WIDOW'S MAN, he easily reconciled his choice to the eternal fitness of things.

1834. MARRYAT, *Peter Simple*, vii. WIDOW'S MEN are imaginary sailors, borne on the books, and receiving pay and prize money, which is appropriated to Greenwich Hospital.

WIDOW'S-WEEDS, *subs. phr.* (old).—1. An unmarried mother, a deserted mistress (B. E. and GROSE).

2. *See* WEED, 3.

WIFE, *subs.* (prison). — A leg-shackle.

AS MUCH NEED OF A WIFE AS A DOG OF A SIDE-POCKET, *phr.* (old). — 'Said of a weak, old debilitated man' (GROSE).

WIFE IN WATER-COLOURS, *subs. phr.* (common).—(1) A morganatic wife; and (2) a mistress or concubine: *cf.* Fr. *collage à la détrempe.*

WIFEY, *subs.* (colloquial).—A wife: an endearment.

1897. MARSHALL, *Pomes*, 66. As WIFEY was out.

WIFFLE-WOFFLE, *subs.* (common). —In *pl.* = the stomach-ache, sorrow, THE DUMPS (*q.v.*): generic.

WIG, *verb* (North Country Cant). —1. 'To move off, go away' (HOTTEN).

2. (colloquial).—To rate, scold, 'carpet': spec. 'to call over the coals' publicly. Whence WIGGING = a public rebuke or reprimand: EAR-WIGGING = a more or less private calling over the coals.

1837. BARHAM, *Ingoldsby Leg.*, II. 386. If you wish to 'scape WIGGING, a dumb wife's the dandy.

1888. *Echo*, 26 Mar. So alarmed at the prospect of being WIGGED from home.

1897. MARSHALL, *Pomes*, 84. They both had a WIGGING at Marylebone For attempting to kiss a policeman.

1902. *Pall Mall Gaz.*, 26 July, 2. 2. 'Discipline must be maintained,' and now that the lads know that they are not to suffer for a crime they never committed they will not mind the C.-in-C.'s WIGGING.

WIG-BLOCK, *subs. phr.* (common). —The head.

WIGSBY, *subs.* (old).—A jocular appellation for a man wearing a wig: *cf.* RUDESBY, FOUR-EYES, BARNACLES, etc. (GROSE).

WILD, *subs.* (tramps').—A village, the country: *cf.* 'WEALD.'

[1598. SHAKSPEARE, 1 *Henry IV.*, ii. 1. 60. A franklin in the WILD of Kent.]

WILD-BRAIN, *subs. phr.* (old).—A harebrain, silly, SOFT (*q.v.*) fellow.

1608. MIDDLETON, *A Mad World, My Masters*, i. 1. I must let fly my civil fortunes, turn WILD-BRAIN, lay my wits upo' th' tenters, you rascals.

WILD-CAT, *adj. phr.* (American commercial).—Reckless, hazardous, unsound: orig. applied to banking enterprises of doubtful (if of no worse) character: *cf.* BLUE-PUP, RED-DOG, etc. [BARTLETT: A bank in Michigan had a large vignette on its notes representing a panther, familiarly called a WILD-CAT. This bank failed, a large amount of its notes were in circulation, which were denominated WILD-CAT money, and the bank issuing them the WILD-CAT bank. Other banks stopped payment soon after, and the term became general in Michigan, to denote banking institutions of an unsound character.] Hence WILD-CAT CURRENCY, SCHEMES, etc.

1842. CLAVERS, *Forest Life*, I. 91. We had to sell some of our land to pay taxes on the rest,—and then took our pay in WILD-CAT MONEY that turned to waste paper before we could get it off our hands.

1858. *Baltimore Sun*, 8 July. Certain it is that we are overrun with a WILD-CAT CURRENCY.

1877. *Galaxy*, 632. When the Yankee mind stoops to criminal pursuits, it is likely to manifest itself in the way of bank forgeries, embezzlements, or the formation of petroleum bubbles or WILD-CAT BANKING institutions.

1896. LILLARD, *Poker Stories*, 56. He went to the bartender and got a lot of WILD-CAT MONEY, wrapped it around with a couple of twenties, and put some fives in the middle.

1901. *Free Lance*, 9 Feb., 471. 1. Old ladies sell out of Consols to raise money with which to gamble in a WILD-CAT mining company, and end as dependents on the charity of their friends.

WILD-DELL, *subs. phr.* (Old Cant). —A DELL (*q.v.*) or girl begotten and born under a hedge.

WILD - GOOSE, *subs. phr.* (old military).—A recruit for the Irish Brigade in the service of France in the seventeenth and eighteenth centuries.

WILD-GOOSE CHASE, *subs. phr.* (common).—The pursuit of anything unprofitable or absurd; a blind hunt. [DYCE: Orig. 'a kind of horse-race, in which two horses were started together, and whichever rider could get the lead, the other was obliged to follow him over whatever ground he chose to go.']

1595. SHAKSPEARE, *Romeo and Juliet*, ii. 4. If our wits run the WILD-GOOSE CHASE, I have done; for thou hast more of the wild-goose in one of thy wits, than I have in my whole five.

d. 1650. FLETCHER, *Poems*, 202. No hints of truth on foot? no sparks of grace? No late sprung light to dance the WILD-GOOSE CHASE?

WILD INDIANS (THE), *subs. phr.* (military).—The Prince of Wales's Leinster Regiment (Royal Canadians). Both battalions trace some sort of connection with the Indians of N. America and the 'Indians' of the East: the first battalion having formerly been the 100th Foot, an expression of Canadian loyalty at the time of the Mutiny, and the 2nd battalion, the 109th (Bombay Infantry) Regiment, originally raised by the Hon. East India Company.

WILD IRISHMAN (THE), *subs. phr.* (railway). — The evening mail train between Euston and Holyhead: *cf.* FLYING DUTCHMAN, etc.

WILD-MARE, *subs. phr.* (old).—The nightmare.

TO RIDE THE WILD MARE, *verb. phr.* (old).—To play at see-saw.

1580. SIDNEY, *Arcadia*, ii. With that, bestriding the mast, I gat by little and little towards him, after such manner as boys are wont, if ever you saw that sport, when they RIDE THE WILD MARE.

1598. SHAKSPEARE, 2 *Henry IV.*, ii. 4. 268. And RIDES THE WILD MARE with the boys.

1611. COTGRAVE, *Dict.* To RIDE THE WILD-MARE, as children who, sitting upon both ends of a long pole or timber-log (supported only in the middle), lift one another up and downe.

WILD-OATS, *subs. phr.* (colloquial).—1. Youthful pranks or folly; hence (2) a rake or debauchee. To SOW ONE'S WILD OATS=to indulge in folly or dissipation, and (by implication) to grow steady.

d. 1570. BECON, *Works* (1843), 240. The tailors now-a-days are compelled to excogitate, invent, and imagine diversities of fashions for apparel, that they may satisfy the foolish desire of certain light brains and WILD OATS, which are altogether given to new fangleness.

1573. TUSSER, *Husbandrie*, 17. Bridle WILD OTES fantasie.

1576. *Touchstone of Complexions*, 99. We meane that wilful and unruly age, which lacketh rypeness and discretion, and (as wee saye) hath not SOWED all THEYR WYELD OATES.

1602. *How a Man may Chuse a Good Wife* [NARES]. Well, go to, WILD OATS! spendthrift, prodigal.

1616–25. *Court and Times James I.*, ii. 85. [A youth is called] the WILD OATS of Ireland.

1670. RAY, *Proverbs* [BOHN (1893), 178], s.v.

1696. B. E., *Dict. Cant. Crew*, s.v. OATS. One that has SOLD HIS WILD OATS, or one having run out of all, begins to take up and be more staied.

b. 1707. DURFEY, *Pills to Purge, &c.* (1707), ii. 276. Sow your WILD OATS, And mind not her wild Notes.

1785. GROSE, *Vulg. Tongue*, s.v. OATS, HE HAS SOWED HIS WILD OATS, he is staid, or sober, having left off his wild tricks.

1858. LYTTON, *What Will He Do With It?* VIII. v. Poole had picked up some WILD OATS—he had SOWN them now.

1874. *Siliad*, 108. Assorted hosts Besiege the Hebes of the Old Blue Posts, Push in to patronise the Barnes called Ned—Barnes, where, alas! WILD OATS are garnered.

1891. *Lic. Vict. Gaz.*, 23 Jan. Dad's very kind, and makes me a good allowance that I may SOW MY WILD OATS, but I seem only to buy more.

WILD-ROGUE, *subs. phr.* (Old Cant).—A thorough-paced thief; a rogue brought up to stealing from infancy.

WILD TRAIN, *subs. phr.* (railway).—A train not on the time-tables of the road, and therefore irregular, and 'not entitled to the track,' as the railroad phrase is, as against a regular train.

WILLIAM, *subs.* (commercial).—An acceptance. To MEET SWEET WILLIAM=to meet a bill on presentation.

WILLOW, *subs.* (cricketers').—A bat.

1892. *Cassell's Sat. Jour.*, 21 Sep., 13. 2. For nearly ten years I earned a living—and a good one—by 'wielding the WILLOW' and hunting the leather.

2 (old). — Mourning. Hence TO WEAR THE WILLOW = to lament the dead.

1595. SHAKSPEARE, 3 *Henry VI.*, iii. 3. 228. Tell him, in hope he'll prove a widower shortly, I'll WEAR THE WILLOW garment for his sake.

c. 1615. FLETCHER, *Night Walker*, i. We see your WILLOW and are sorry for't, And though it be a wedding we are half mourners.

WILLY-NILLY (WILL I, NIL I, etc.), *phr.* (old).—Willing or unwilling, *nolens volens*, 'Whether I will or not.' As *adj.*=vacillating: *see* NILLY-WILLY and SHILLY-SHALLY.

1563. FOXE, *Acts and Monuments* (CATTLEY), 556. WIL'D SHE, NIL'D SHE.

1590. SPENSER, *Faery Queen*, I. iii. 43. With foule reproaches and disdaineful spight Her vildly entertaines; and WILL OR NILL, Beares her away upon his courser light.

1593. SHAKSPEARE, *Taming of Shrew*, ii. 1. Your father hath consented That you shall be my wife; your dowry 'greed on; And WILL YOU, NILL YOU, I will marry you.

1607. BEAUMONT, *Woman Hater*, iii. 4. WILL SHE, NILL SHE, she shall come Running into my house.

1857. KINGSLEY, *Two Years Ago*, x. If I thought myself bound to doctor the man WILLY-NILLY, as you do, I would certainly go to him.

1877. TENNYSON, *Harold*, v. 1. Some one saw thy WILLY-NILLY nun Vying a tress against our golden fern.

WILT, *verb* (London).—To run away, BUNK (*q.v.*).

WIN (or WYN, or WING), *subs.* (Old Cant).—A penny; 1d.: *see* RHINO and NOSE-AND-CHIN.

1608. DEKKER, *Lanthorne and Candlelight* [GROSART, *Works* (188), iii. 203]. Or nip a boung that has but a WIN.

1823. BEE, *Dict. Turf*, s.v. *Scuddick*—is used negatively; 'not a SCUDDICK'—not any brads, not a WHIN, empty clies.

1900. FLYNT, *Tramps*. Just go and get a shave now, Jim. I'll give you a WING (penny) if you will.

WINCHESTER-GOOSE, *subs. phr.* (old).—1. A bubo; (2) a person thus infected; and (3) generally in contempt. [The STEWS (*q.v.*) in Southwark were, in the 16th century, under the jurisdiction of the Bishop of Winchester.] Also WINCHESTER-PIGEON.

1585. *Nomenclator*, 439. A sore in the grine or yard, which if it come by lecherie, is called a WINCHESTER GOOSE, or a botch.

1594. SHAKSPEARE, 1 *Henry IV.*, vi. i. 3. [Of the Bishop of Winchester] WINCHESTER GOOSE, I say, a rope, a rope. *Ibid.* (1602), *Troilus and Cressida*. v. 11. It should be now, but that my fear is this, Some galled GOOSE OF WINCHESTER would hiss.

1606. CHAPMAN, *Mons. D'Olive*, iv. The court is the only school of good education, especially for pages and waiting women. Paris, or Padua, or the famous school of England called WINCHESTER (famous I mean for the GOOSE)—are but belfries to the body or school of the court.

1611. COTGRAVE, *Dict.*, s.v. *Clapoir* . . . WINCHESTER GOOSE.

1618. ROWLEY, *Cure for a Cuckold*, F. had belike some private dealings with her, and there got a GOOSE.—The cunning jade comes into court, and there deposes that she gave him true WINCHESTER measure.

d. 1637. JONSON, *Execr. of Vulcan* [*Works*, vi. 410]. The WINCESTRIAN GOOSE, Bred on the Bank in time of popery, When Venus there maintain'd her mystery.

WIND, *subs.* (old literary: now colloquial or vulgar).—1. Breath, lung-power; and 2. (pugilists') the stomach: *i.e.* 'below the belt,' a forbidden point of attack in legitimate boxing. Hence WINDER=anything that deprives one of the power of breathing; TO NAP A WINDER=(1) to be hung, and (2) get a SETTLER (*q.v.*).

c. 1362. *York Plays*, 258. Woman, thy wordis and thy WYNDE thou not waste. *Ibid.*, 335. [A man after hard work says that] me wantis WYNDE.

c. 1469. *Coventry Mysteries*, 226. My WYNDE is stoppyd, gon is my brethe.

. . . *Political Poems* [FURNIVALL], 79. Ye noye me soore in wastyng al this WYNDE For I haue seide y-noughe, as semethe me.

1525–37. [ELLIS, *Letters*.] My WIND was short.

1596. SHAKSPEARE, *Merry Wives*, iv. 5. 104. If my WIND were but long enough to say my prayers, I would repent. *Ibid.* (1598), 2 *Henry IV.*, i. 2. Is not your voice broken, your WIND short?

1859. MATSELL, *Vocab.*, 'Hundred Stretches.' Some rubbed to wit had NAPPED A WINDER.

1860. HOLMES, *Professor*, ii. How they spar for WIND, instead of hitting from the shoulder.

d. 1870. DICKENS [*Century*]. He pats him and pokes him in divers parts of the body, but particularly in that part which the science of self-defence would call his WIND.

PHRASES. To TAKE WIND=to be known, to transpire; TO SAIL NEAR (or CLOSE TO) THE WIND=(1) to take every risk, and (2) to border on malpractice; TO RAISE THE WIND=to borrow (or procure) money: usually by shift, FLYING A KITE (*q.v.*), or bills of accommodation; TO GO DOWN THE WIND=to decay; TO SLIP ONE'S WIND=to die; TO TAKE THE WIND=to gain an advantage; TO HAVE ONE IN THE WIND=to understand a person; 'Is the WIND in that door?'='Is that so?'; WIND ENOUGH TO LAST A DUTCHMAN A WEEK=enough and to spare; BETWEEN WIND AND WATER=in a vulnerable spot: spec. (venery) TO GET SHOT BETWEEN WIND AND WATER = to be seduced, to receive (or get) a man; DOWN THE WIND=verging towards ruin or decay; THE WAY THE WIND BLOWS=the position of a matter, the state of affairs; THREE (more or less) SHEETS IN THE WIND (*see* SHEETS); IN THE WIND=(1) astir, afoot; and (2) a matter of surmise or suspicion; TO CARRY THE WIND=to be high-spirited or mettlesome: properly of horses tossing the nose as high as the ears; TO HAVE THE WIND OF=to keep strict watch; TOO NEAR THE WIND=mean, stingy (nautical).

1546. HEYWOOD, *Proverbs*, 502. He KNEW WHICH WAY THE WINDE BLEW.

1564. UDAL, *Erasmus*, 318. 'Why,' quoth Pompeius, 'IS THE WINDE IN THIS DOORE, that except Lucullus were a man geuen to delices, Pompeius might in no wise continue alive?'

d. 1592. GREENE, *Looking-Glass for London*, 121. *Thras.* I am come to entreat you to stand my friend, and to favour me with a longer time, and I will make you sufficient consideration. *Usurer.* IS THE WIND IN THAT DOOR?

1593. SHAKSPEARE, *Titus Andron.*, iv. 2. My son and I will HAVE THE WIND OF you.

1609. JONSON, *Case is Altered*, iii. 3. Go to, there is SOMETHING IN THE WIND, I see.

1620. FLETCHER, *Philaster*, iv. 1. SHOT him BETWEEN WIND AND WATER.

d. 1663. BRAMHALL, *Works*, iii. 507. THE WIND IS GOTTEN INTO THE OTHER DOOR since we were prosecuted and decried as Pelagians and enemies of grace.

1680. FANNANT, *Hist. Edward II.*, 11. He had hit his desires in the Master-vein, and struck his former Jealousie BETWEEN WIND AND WATER, so that it sunk in the instant.

1742–4. NORTH, *Life of Lord Guilford*, i. 101. If the lords had sat in the morning, the design to be executed at one o'clock might have TAKEN WIND.

1809. MALKIN, *Gil Blas* [ROUTLEDGE], 55. Ordonnez had not GOT WIND OF our affair.

1810. CRABBE, *Borough*, Letter 3. *The Curate.* An angry dealer, vulgar, rich and proud, Thinks of his bill, and passing, raps aloud; The elder daughter meekly makes him way—'I want my money, and I cannot stay; My Mill is stopt; what, Miss! I cannot grind, Go tell your Father he must RAISE THE WIND.'

1812. J. and H. SMITH, *Rejected Addresses*, 136. So when to RAISE THE WIND some lawyer tries, Mysterious skins of parchment meet our eyes.

1821. COMBE, *Dr. Syntax*, III. iii. Fortune at present is unkind, And we, dear sir, must RAISE THE WIND.

1830. MARRYAT, *King's Own*, x. 'My master, who always looked out for a rainy day, had collected these rings as a sort of stand-by, to RAISE THE WIND when required.'

1836. DANA, *Before the Mast*, xxxiii. This was an immense sail, and held WIND ENOUGH TO LAST A DUTCHMAN A WEEK—hove to.

1837. BARHAM, *Ingoldsby Legends*. And turn up their noses at one who could find No decenter method of RAISING THE WIND?

1838. DICKENS, *Oliver Twist*. What the blazes is IN THE WIND now?

1853. *Notes and Queries*, 1 S. vi. 486. Seamen who whistle at sea TO RAISE THE WIND.

1859. FARRAR, *Julian Home*, iv. Miss Sprong . . . seeing HOW THE WIND LAY, had tried to drop little malicious hints.

1869. WHYTE-MELVILLE, *M or N*, 124. Dick . . . began to surmise that this young lady had been RAISING THE WIND, as he called it, and to wonder for what mysterious purpose she could want so large a sum.

1874. *Siliad*, 32. And though it's SAILING very NEAR THE WIND, Monarch's prerogative can loose or bind.

1885. *Field*, 17 Oct. Indications are not wanting to show WHICH WAY THE WIND BLOWS.

1892. *Cassell's Sat. Jl.*, 5 Oct., 43. 2. Half-a-dozen coats are of no immediate use to a man who is content with one, unless it be to RAISE THE WIND, and the same remark applies to boots.

1902. *Pall Mall Gaz.*, 10 Ap., 2. 2. Even our sardonic Chancellor of the Exchequer must have been moved to a grim smile at some of the extraordinary expedients for RAISING THE WIND with which he has been credited.

TO WIND ONE'S COTTON, *verb. phr.* (common).—To give trouble.

TO WIND UP THE CLOCK, *verb. phr.* (venery). — To possess a woman: *see* GREENS and RIDE (see *Tristram Shandy*).

WIND-BAG, *subs. phr.* (common).—An incessant frothy talker: also GAS-BAG.

1889. *Sportsman*, 19 Jan. Hereafter he can have the newspapers to himself, and with that WINDBAG Mitchell fill them with guff and nonsense, but I won't notice them.

WINDING-SHEET, *subs. phr.* (colloquial).—Grease (or wax) drippings guttering down the side of a candle: deemed an omen of death by the superstitious (GROSE): *cf.* THIEF.

1859. DICKENS, *Tale of Two Cities*, ii. 4. He . . . fell asleep . . . a long WINDING-SHEET in the candle dripping down upon him.

WIND-JAMMER, *subs. phr.* (nautical).—1. A sailing vessel: *cf.* SMOKE-STACK.

1902. *Athenæum*, 8 Feb., 177. 1.

1903. HYNE, *Filibusters*, xviii. As a purser on a steamboat I had always held a fine contempt for sailor-men on WIND-JAMMERS.

2. (theatrical).—A player on a wind instrument.

WINDMILL J.P., *phr.* (obsolete Australian).—Formerly used in New South Wales for any J.P. who was ill-educated and supposed to sign his name with a cross (×).

WINDOW, *subs.* (common).—1. In *pl.*=the eyes, the PEEPERS (*q.v.*).

2 (old).—A blank space in a writing.

d. 1556. CRANMER, *Works*, ii. 249. I will therefore that you send unto me a collection thereof, and that your said collection have a WINDOW expedient to set what name I will therein.

GOLDSMITH'S-WINDOW, *subs. phr.* (Australian mining). — A rich working in which the gold shows FREELY.

See TURN.

WINDOW-BAR, *subs. phr.* (old).—In *pl.* = Lattice-work on a woman's stomacher, or MODESTY-PIECE (*q.v.*).

1609. SHAKSPEARE, *Timon of Athens*, iv. 3. Those milk-paps That through the WINDOW-BARS bore at men's eyes.

WINDOW-BLIND, *subs. phr.* (common.—A periodicity-cloth, 'sanitary towel,' menstrual rag.

WINDOW-DRESSING, *subs. phr.* (commercial). — Manipulation of figures and accounts to show fictitious or exaggerated value: brought into prominence during the trial of Whitaker Wright for fraud in connection with the balance-sheets of the London and Globe Corporation (1904).

WINDOW-FISHING, *subs. phr.* (thieves').—Entering a house by means of a window.

WIND-PUDDING, *subs. phr.* (common).—Air. TO LIVE ON WIND-PUDDING=to go hungry.

1900. FLYNT, *Tramps*, 141. I have known them live on 'WIND PUDDIN'.'

WINDSTOPPER, *subs.* (thieves').—A garotter.

WINDSUCKER, *subs.* (old).—1. A querulous fault-finder, GRIZZLE-GUTS (*q.v.*); one ready to catch another tripping or to 'pick holes'; one on the lookout for a blemish or weak spot.

1603. CHAPMAN, *Iliad*, Preface. But there is a certain envious WINDSUCKER that hovers up and down.

1880. SWINBURNE, *Shakspeare*, 55. It would be something too extravagant for the veriest WINDSUCKER amongst commentators to start a theory that a revision was made of his original work by Marlowe after additions had been made to it by Shakspeare.

WINDWARD. TO GET TO THE WINDWARD (or WINDWARD SIDE) OF ONE, *verb. phr.* (common).—To get an advantage, the better of one, or the best position.

WINDY, *adj.* (colloquial).—Talkative, boastful, vain. WINDY-WALLETS=a noisy prater, vain boaster, romancing yarnster.

WINE, *subs.* (University).—A wine-drinking party.

1847. TENNYSON, *Princess*, iv. A death's-head at the WINE.

1849. KINGSLEY, *Alton Locke*, xiii. He disappeared every day about four to 'hall'; after which he did not reappear till eight, the interval being taken up, he said, in 'WINES' and an hour of billiards.

1887. *Echo*, 5 Sep. Surely such a WINE was never given at Oxford in any gentleman's room.

WINE-BAG, *subs. phr.* (common).—A drunkard who makes wine his special TIPPLE (*q.v.*).

WINEY, *adj.* (common).—Drunk: *see* SCREWED.

WING, *subs.* (prison).—1. A quid or thereabouts of tobacco.

1882. GREENWOOD, *Gaol Birds.* A piece as large as a horse-bean, called a 'chew,' is regarded as the equivalent for a twelve-ounce loaf and a meat ration, and even a morsel—a mere taste that can only be laid on the tongue and sucked like a small sweetmeat (it is called a WING, and is not larger or of more substance than a man's little finger-nail), is 'good' for a six-ounce loaf.

Verb (colloquial). — 1. To wound slightly: orig. to shoot in the arm or shoulder.

2. (theatrical).—To undertake a part at short notice and study it in the 'wings.'

WINK. *See* EYE; FORTY; TIP.

WINKER, *subs.* (common).—1. The eye; and (2) in *pl.*=eyelashes.

WINKING. LIKE WINKING, *adv. phr.* (common).—Very quickly.

1837. BARHAM, *Ingoldsby Leg.*, 'Witches' Frolic.' Old goody Jones All skin and bones, Follows LIKE WINKING.

d. 1845. HOOD, *Sailor's Apology for Bow-legs.* Both my legs began to bend LIKE WINKIN'.

1861. DICKENS, *Great Expectations*, xxi. Nod away at him, if you please, LIKE WINKING.

1883. *Graphic*, 17 March, 287. 1. Nevertheless, this solid fare disappeared, with the beer, LIKE WINKING.

WINKS, *subs. pl.* (streets').—Periwinkles.

WINTER-CRICKET, *subs. phr.* (common).—A tailor.

WINTER-HEDGE, *subs. phr.* (common).—A clothes-horse.

WIPE, *subs.* (old).—1. A handkerchief: orig. WIPER=a hand towel, but *see* quot. 1624 (B. E. and GROSE).

1624. JONSON, *Masque of Owls.* WIPERS for their noses.

1830. MONCRIEFF, *Heart of London*, i. 1. Rummy Spitalfields WIPES.

1837. BARHAM, *Ingoldsby Legends*, 'The Forlorn One.' This here warment's prigged your WIPE.

1838. DICKENS, *Oliver Twist*, ix. 'And what have you got, my dear?' said Fagin to Charley Bates. 'WIPES,' replied Master Bates, at the same time producing four pocket-handkerchiefs.

1861. KINGSLEY, *Ravenshoe*, xxxv. 'But what is *clyfaking?*' said Charles. 'Why, a prigging of WIPES, and sneeze-boxes, and ridicules, and such.'

2. (common).—A blow; literally or figuratively. As *verb*=to strike: *e.g.* a WIPE over (=a rap) over the knuckles.

1577. GUEVARA, *Letters* (HELLOWES), 235. Since you were the first that layde hand to weapon, the fault is not mine if I haue happened to giue you a WYPE.

1589. NASHE [GROSART, *Works*, i. 232]. A WIPE over the shins.

1695. CONGREVE, *Love for Love*, iv. He was woundy angry when I giv'n that WIPE, he hadn't a word to say, and so I left'n.

1705. VANBRUGH, *Confederacy*, v. 2. That's a WIPE for me now, because I did not give her a new year's gift.

1733. SWIFT, *On Poetry.* To statesmen would you give a WIPE, You print it in Italic type.

1772. BRIDGES, *Burlesque Homer*, 16. Or else your jaws may get a WIPE.

1843-4. HALIBURTON, *Attaché*, xxvi. Father . . . gave me a WIPE . . . that knocked me over and hurt me properly.

1900. KIPLING, *Stalky & Co.*, 224. 'Mary'll weep sore when she knows we're leaving,' said Beetle. 'She gave me a awfull WIPE on the head last time,' said Stalky.

PHRASES. TO WIPE ONE DOWN=(1) to flatter, (2) to pacify; TO WIPE OFF A SCORE=to pay one's debts; TO WIPE A PERSON'S EYE=(1) to shoot game which another has missed, (2) to gain an advantage through skilful manipulation; TO WIPE THE OTHER EYE=to take another drink; TO WIPE OUT=to kill, to exterminate; TO WIPE ONE'S NOSE=to cheat; TO WIPE UP THE FLOOR WITH ONE=to completely demolish an adversary; TO WIPE A PERSON'S NOSE (*see* NOSE, adding quots. 1611 and 1622).

1611. CHAPMAN, *May-day* [*Anc. Dr.*, iv. 110]. 'Sfoot, lieutenant, wilt thou suffer thy NOSE TO BE WIP'D of this great heir?

1622. FLETCHER, *Spanish Curate*, iv. 5. Most finely fool'd, and handsomely, and neatly, Such cunning masters must be fool'd sometimes, sir, And HAVE THEIR worship's NOSES WIP'D, 'tis healthful, We are but quit.

1854. *Report of Com. of Indian Affairs.* They [the Camenches, Apaches, and others] had met for the purpose of forming their own party, in order, as they in their strong language said, to WIPE OUT all frontier Indians they could find on the plains.

1858. *Alta Californian*, July. The Pima Indians have got up another quarrel with the Apaches, and have mustered upwards of a thousand warriors to give battle. It is their determination to WIPE OUT the Apaches, or, as they express it, to eat them up entirely, which is a consummation devoutly to be wished.

1857. *New York Times*, Nov. 'Letter from Utah.' The Mormon militia under Brigham Young intend to take a stand at the pass in the mountains near Bear River, with the certainty of WIPING OUT the U.S. forces sent against them.

1861-5. ROBINSON, *Kansas*, 222. We are coming to Lawrence, said the Missourians, in a few days, TO WIPE OUT the damned abolition city, and to kill and drive off every one of the inhabitants.

1870. MEDBURY, *Men and Mysteries of Wall Street*, 138. To WIPE OUT a stock operator is a Wall-Street phrase, and means to entangle him in a stock transaction until he loses his footing and fails utterly. It is one of the malignancies and cruelties of the street.

1887. HENLEY and STEVENSON, *Deacon Brodie*, i. 3. I'll MOP THE FLOOR UP WITH HIM any day, if so be as you or any on 'em 'll make it worth my while.

1888. *Detroit Free Press*, Aug. The Scroggin boy was as tough as a dog-wood knot. He'd WIPE UP THE GROUND WITH HIM; he'd walk all over him.

WIRE, *subs.* (colloquial).—1. A telegram. Also as *verb.*

2. (thieves').—An expert pick-pocket: *see* THIEF.

1851-61. MAYHEW, *Lond. Lab.*, i. 410. He was worth £20 a week, he said, as a WIRE.

1862. MAYHEW, *Crim. Prisons*, 46. Buzzers who pick gentlemen's pockets, and WIRES who pick ladies' pockets.

TO WIRE IN (or AWAY), *verb. phr.* (common).—To set to with a will, to apply oneself perseveringly and zealously.

1888. *Fort. Rev.*, N.S., xliii. 93. In one fashion or another he keeps WIRING AWAY.

1900. NISBET, *Sheep's Clothing*, 132. She's a fine girl . . . and I think Mr. Lupus won't object to me hanging my hat up there. I'll WIRE IN and convert her first, though.

WIRED UP, *adj. phr.* (American).—Irritated; provoked.

WIRE-PULLER (or **-WORKER**), *subs. phr.* (political).—A manipulator of party and other interests, working by means more or less secret; a political intriguer. Hence TO PULL THE WIRES=to exercise a commanding secret political influence. Also WIRE-PULLING, *subs.*

1848. *New York Mirror*, 5 June. Philadelphia . . . is filled with WIRE-PULLERS, public opinion manufacturers, embryo cabinet officers, future ambassadors, and the whole brood of political make-shifts.

1858. *Nat. Intell.*, 20 Sept. The WIRE-WORKERS in convention had a deep interest in a particular suit at law, to which their candidate was pledged to give a judgment in their favor, in case of being the judge.

1874. *Siliad*, 69. They and their fathers, and their fathers' sires, Had worked the oracle and pulled the WIRES.

1879. FROUDE, *Cæsar*, 369. It was useless now to bribe the Comitia, to work with clubs and WIRE-PULLERS.

WISHY-WASHY, *adj.* (colloquial).—Weak, insipid, ROTTEN (*q.v.*).

1748. SMOLLETT, *Rod. Random*, xxiv. A good seaman he is as ever stept upon forecastle, and a brave fellow as ever crackt bisket—none of your Guinea-pigs, nor your fresh-water WISHY-WASHY, fair-weather fowls.

1801. DIBDIN, *Il Bondocani*, iii. 3. None of your WISHY-WASHY sparks that mince their steps.

1855. KINGSLEY, *Westward Ho*, viii. If you are a coffin, you were sawn out of no WISHY-WASHY elm-board, but right heart-of-oak.

1857. TROLLOPE, *Barchester Towers*, xli. The WISHY-WASHY, bread-and-butter period of life.

1876. HINDLEY, *Cheap Jack*, 192. Mo and his man were having a great breakfast . . . off a twopenny buster and a small bit of butter, with some WISHY-WASHY coffee . . .

1881. BRADDON, *Asphodel*, xx. A year hence she will have lost all that brightness, and will be a very WISHY-WASHY little person.

1891. *Harry Fludyer at Cambridge*, 18. Papa did not care for it much when I sang it the first time, and said it was WISHY-WASHY; but he knows nothing whatever about music. The only song he ever did care about was 'Annie Laurie'; I think it was because mother always sang it.

WISKER, *subs.* (old).—A lie.

1694. *Plautus made English*, 9. Suppose I tell her some damned WISKER; why, that's but m' old Dog-trick.

WISP. TO GIVE (WEAR, or SHOW) A WISP, *verb. phr.* (old).—A wisp, or small twist, of straw or hay, was often applied as a mark of opprobrium to an immodest woman, a scold, or similar offenders; even the showing it to a woman was, therefore, considered as a grievous affront. It was the badge of the scolding woman, in the ceremony of SKIMMINGTON (*q.v.*).

1567. DRANT, *Horace*, vii. So perfyte and exacte a scoulde that women might give place, Whose tatling tongues had won a WISPE.

1595. SHAKSPEARE, 3 *Henry VI.*, ii. 2. A WISP of straw were worth a thousand crowns, To make this shameless callat know herself.

1628. EARLE, *Microcos.* (BLISS), 278. [Of a scold.] There's nothing mads or moves her more to outrage, then but the very naming of a WISPE, or if you sing or whistle while she is scoulding.

1632. ROWLEY, *New Wonder* [*Anc. Dr.*, v. 266]. Nay worse, I'll stain thy ruff; nay, worse than that, I'll do thus. [Holds a WISP.] *M. Fost.* Oh my heart, gossip, do you see this? was ever Woman thus abus'd?

WITTOL, *subs.* (old).—A husband who knows of, and endures his wife's unfaithfulness; a contented cuckold. As *verb*=to make a wittol. [SKEAT: From *woodwale* (a bird whose nest is often invaded by the cuckoo, and so has the offspring of another palmed off on it for its own; like *Cuckold*, from *Cuckoo*.]

1513-25. SKELTON *Works* (DYCE), ii. 178 [OLIPHANT, *New Eng.*, i. 394. The old WITTOL in the guise of a wetewold is now first used in its evil sense].

1596. SHAKSPEARE, *Merry Wives*, ii. 2. Amaimon sounds well; Lucifer, well; Barbason, well; yet they are devil's additions, the names of fiends! But cuckold, WITTOL, cuckold! The devil himself hath not such a name!

1597. HALL, *Satires*, i. 7. Fond WITTOL that would'st load thy witless head, With timely horns before thy bridal bed.

1611. COTGRAVE, *Dict.*, s.v. *Jannin.* A WITTALL; one that knowes, and bears with, or winks at, his wives dishonesty.

1621. BURTON, *Anat. Melan.*, 44. To see . . . a WITTOL wink at his wife's dishonesty, and too perspicuous in all other affairs.

1624. DAVENPORT, *City Nightcap*, i. 1. He would WITTOL me With a consent to my own horns.

1631. LENTON, *Characters*, 32. A cuckold is a harmelesse horned creature, but they [his horns] hang not in his eies, as your WITTALS doe.

1638. FORD, *Fancies*, ii. 1. Mark, Vespucci, how the WITTOL Stares on his sometime wife! Sure he imagines To be a cuckold by consent is purchase Of approbation in a state.

1641. *Wit's Recreations.* Thy stars gave thee the cuckold's diadem: If thou wert born to be a WITTOL, can Thy wife prevent thy fortune? foolish man!

1693. CONGREVE, *Old Batchelor*, v. 6. *Sharp.* Death! it can't be—an oaf, an ideot, a WITTAL.

WIWI, *subs.* (Australian).—A Frenchman. [That is, *Oui, Oui!*]

1845. WAKEFIELD, *Adventures in New Zealand*, i. 94. If I had sold the land to the white missionaries, might they not have sold it again to the WIWI (Frenchmen) or Americans?

1857. HURSTHOUSE, *New Zealand, the Britain of the South*, i. 14. De Surville's painful mode of revenge, and the severe chastisement which the retaliatory murder of Marion brought on the natives, rendered the WEE-WEES (*Oui, oui*), or people of the tribe of Marion, hateful to the New Zealanders for the next half-century.

1859. THOMSON, *Story of New Zealand*, i. 236. Before the WEWIS, as the French are now called, departed.

1873. CARLETON, *Life of Henry Williams*, 92. The arrival of a French man-of-war was a sensational event to the natives, who had always held the OUI-OUI's in dislike.

1881. *Percy Pomo*, 207. Has [sic] the WEEWEES puts it.

WOBBLE. *See* WABBLE.

WOBBLER, *subs.* (military).—An infantryman.

WOBBLE-SHOP, *subs. phr.* (common).—A shop where intoxicants are sold without a license.

WOLF, *verb* (common).—To devour ravenously: hence WOLFER = a greedy feeder or guzzling tosspot: also A WOLF IN THE STOMACH = famished; TO KEEP THE WOLF FROM THE DOOR = to keep hunger and want at bay.

1513-25. SKELTON, *Works* (DYCE), ii. 132. TO KEPE THE WOLFE FROM THE DORE.

1645. HOWELL, *Familiar Letters*. Indeed tis very fitting that hee or shee should have wherwith to support both, according to their quality, at least to KEEP THE WOOLF FROM THE DOOR, otherwise 'twere a meer madnes to marry.

1705. BUCKINGHAM, *Works*, II. 127. I am no stranger, says she, to your circumstances, and know with what difficulty you KEEP THE WOLF FROM YOUR DOOR.

1885. *Field*, 4 Ap. WOLFING down some food preparatory to fishing.

1897. MARSHALL, *Pomes*, 118. He just placed him 'gainst a shutter, and then fired' him in the gutter, But the worn-out whiskey WOLFER calmly slumbered through it all.

PHRASES. DARK AS A WOLF'S MOUTH (or THROAT) = pitch dark; TO CRY WOLF = to raise a false alarm; TO HAVE A WOLF BY THE EARS (*see quots.*); TO SEE A WOLF = (1) to lose one's voice, and (2) to be seduced (Fr. *avoir vu le loup*).

d. 1655. ADAMS, *Works*, III. 249. He that deals with men's affections HATH A WOLF BY THE EARS; if we speak of peace, they wax wanton; if we reprove, they grow desperate.

1742-4. NORTH, *Lord Guildford*, ii. 2. He found himself so intrigued that it was like A WOLF BY THE EARS; he could neither hold it, nor let it go; and, for certain, it bit him at last.

1767. FAWKES, *Idyll. Theoc.*, xiv. 'What! are you mute?' I said—a waggish guest, 'Perhaps she's SEEN A WOLF,' rejoin'd in jest.

1823. SCOTT, *Quentin Durward*, xviii. 'Our young companion has SEEN A WOLF,' said Lady Hameline, alluding to an ancient superstition, 'and has lost his tongue in consequence.'

WOLFE'S OWN, *subs. phr.* (military).—The first battalion of The Loyal North Lancashire Regiment, late the 47th Foot; the black worm in the gold lace is in memory of the Hero of Quebec.

WOLVERINE STATE (THE), *subs. phr.* (American).—Michigan: its inhabitants are WOLVERINES.

WOLLOP. *See* WALLOP.

2 A

WOMAN, *subs.* (colloquial).—1. A term of abuse; *spec.* a harlot. Whence TO WOMAN (or WOMANIZE) = (1) to scold or abuse, and (2) to whore; TO PLAY THE WOMAN = to be addicted to the practice of men; TO BE AS WOMEN WISH WHO LOVE THEIR LORDS = to be pregnant; TO MAKE AN HONEST WOMAN (*see* HONEST); WOMAN OF THE TOWN = a harlot; WISE WOMAN = a midwife; WOMAN'S BROKER = a bawd; TO MAKE ONE A WOMAN = to deflower; TO ENJOY A WOMAN = to possess her: *see* ENJOY.

1648-50. BRATHWAYTE, *Barnaby's Jo*, 9. Where I drank and took my Common In a Tap-house with my WOMAN.

1705. WARD, *Hud. Red.*, II. ii. 5. To starve, beg, steal, or PLAY THE WOMAN [*i.e.* the whore].

1740. RICHARDSON, *Pamela*, ii. 268. She called her another time fat-face, and WOMANED her most violently.

1809. MALKIN, *Gil Blas* [ROUTLEDGE], 392. Scipio and myself were ... very soon to have the satisfaction of becoming fathers: our lasses were as WOMEN wish to be who love their lords.

2. *See* TAIL.

WONNER. *See* ONE-ER.

WOODCOCK, *subs.* (old).—1. A simpleton: *see* BUFFLE.

1593. SHAKSPEARE, *Taming of Shrew*, i. 2. O this WOODCOCK! what an ass it is!

1614. OVERBURY, *Characters*, M. 2. He cheats young guls that are newly come to towne; and when the keeper of the ordinary blames him for it, he answers him in his owne profession, that a WOODCOCKE must be plucked ere it be drest.

2. (common).—A tailor.

WOODCOCK'S-CROSS, *subs. phr.* (old).—Penitence for folly: *cf.* WEEPING-CROSS.

1630. TAYLOR, *Works* [NARES]. At Westminster, where such a coyle they keepe: Where man doth man within the law betosse, Till some go croslesse home by WOODCOCKS CROSSE.

WOODCOCK'S-HEAD, *subs. phr.* (old colloquial).—A pipe. [Early pipes were frequently so fashioned.]

1599. JONSON, *Ev. Man Out of Humour*, iii. 3. *Sav.* O peace, I pray you, I love not the breath of a WOODCOCK'S HEAD. *Fastid.* Meaning my head, lady? [*i.e.*, meaning to call me a fool?] *Sav.* Not altogether so, sir; but as it were fatal to their follies that think to grace themselves with taking tobacco, when they want better entertainment, you see your pipe bears the true form of a WOOD-COCK'S HEAD.

WOODEN-FIT, *subs. phr.* (common).—A swoon.

WOODEN-LEGGED MARE, *subs. phr.* (old).—The gallows: *see* NUBBING-CHEAT.

WOODEN-NUTMEG STATE (THE), *subs. phr.* (American).—Cincinnatti.

WOODEN-OVERCOAT (or -SURTOUT), *subs. phr.* (old).—A coffin.

WOODEN-RUFF, *subs. phr.* (old).—The pillory.

WOODEN-SPOON, *subs.* (Cambridge).—The student last on the list of mathematical honours. *See* TRIPOS, GULF, TWELVE APOSTLES, WRANGLER, etc.

1823. GROSE, *Vulg. Tongue* [EGAN]. OPTIME. The senior and junior optimes are the second and last classes of Cambridge honours conferred on taking a degree. That of wranglers is the first. The last junior optime is called the WOODEN SPOON.

WOODEN-SWORD. TO WEAR THE WOODEN-SWORD, *verb. phr.* (provincial).—To overstand the market.

WOODMAN, *subs.* (common).—1. A carpenter, CHIPS (*q.v.*).

2. (old).—A wencher, MUTTON-MONGER (*q.v.*).

WOOL, *subs.* (common).—Hair: *cf.* the wheezes, 'He has no WOOL on the top of his head in the place where the WOOL ought to grow'; and 'Keep your WOOL on' = don't get angry, keep quiet. As *verb* = to rumple or towsle the hair.

PHRASES. MORE SQUEAK THAN WOOL = more noise than substance; GREAT CRY AND LITTLE WOOL = 'Much ado about nothing': *see* CIDER; TO PULL THE WOOL OVER ONE'S EYES = to impose upon, deceive, delude, or use the PEPPER-BOX (*q.v.*); TO GO WOOL GATHERING = to indulge in idle fancies, act stupidly.

c. 1475. FORTESCUE [*Notes and Queries*, 7 S. vi. 186]. And so his hyghnes shal haue thereoff but as hadd the man that sherid is hogge, MUCHE CRYE and LITILL WOLL.

1579. GOSSON, *School of Abuse* [OLIPHANT, *New Eng.*, i. 605. There occurs RUN A WOOLGATHERING].

1621. BURTON, *Anat.*, I. ii. His wits were WOOLGATHERING as they say.

d. 1655. ADAMS, *Works*, I. 477. But if you compare his threatenings and his after affections you would say of them, as that wise man shearing his hogs: Here is a GREAT deal of CRY, BUT a LITTLE WOOL.

1742-4. NORTH, *Lord Guildford*. For matter of title he thought there was MORE SQUEAK THAN WOOL. *Ibid.*, ii. 326. The stir about the sheriff of London ... was MUCH SQUEAK AND NO WOOL, but an impertinent contention to no profit.

c. 1796. WOLCOT, *Works*, 135. Yet thou may'st bluster like bull-beef so big; And, of thy own importance full, Exclaim, 'GREAT CRY AND LITTLE WOOL!' As Satan holla'd when he shaved the pig.

1809. MALKIN, *Gil Blas* [ROUTLEDGE], 201. At first there was MUCH CRY BUT LITTLE WOOL; for we had no luck at finding cullies.

1898. LILLARD, *Poker Stories*, 102. That bad Westerner was a bungler. I could have given him points at his own game. Nevertheless, he was clever enough to PULL THE WOOL way down OVER THE EYES of the three other men.

WOOL-BIRD, *subs. phr.* (common).—A sheep.

WOOLFIST, *subs.* (old).—A term of reproach.

1606. *Wily Beguilde*, Prol. Out, you sous'd gurnet, you WOOLFIST! begone, I say, and bid the players despatch, and come away quickly.

WOOL-HOLE, *subs. phr.* (tramps').—A workhouse: *see* LARGE HOUSE.

WOOSTON, *adv.* (Christ's Hospital).—Very: that is 'whoreson' (*see* WHORE): *e.g.* 'a WOOSTON jolly fellow,' 'I'm WOOSTON chaffy.'

WORD. A WORD AND A BLOW, *subs. phr.* (old).—Immediate action: as *adj.* = instantly.

1710. SWIFT, *Pol. Conv.*, i. *Nev.* Pray, Miss, why do you sigh? *Miss.* To make a fool ask, and you are the first. *Nev.* Why, Miss, I find there is nothing but a WORD AND A BLOW with you.

1753. RICHARDSON, *Grandison*, iv. 206. My cousins are grieved: they did not expect that I would be a WORD AND A BLOW, as they phrase it.

1839. MRS. TROLLOPE, *Michael Armstrong*, iv. Mr. Joseph Parsons had a Napoleon-like promptitude of action, which the unlearned operatives described by calling him A WORD-AND-A-BLOW.

WORK, *verb* (thieves').—To steal. Fr. *travailler*; Sp. *trabajar*.

PHRASES. TO MAKE WORK = to cause (or make) a disturbance, kick up a SHINDY (*q.v.*); TO WORK THE ORACLE = to manœuvre, to victimise.

WORLD. ALL THE WORLD AND HIS WIFE, *subs. phr.* (common).—Everyone.

1709-10. SWIFT, *Polite Conversation*, iii. *Miss.* Pray, Madam, who were the company? *Lady Sm.* Why there was THE WORLD AND HIS WIFE.

1766. *New Bath Guide*, Letter xiii. How he welcomes at once ALL THE WORLD AND HIS WIFE, And how civil to folk he ne'er saw in his life.

1865. DICKENS, *Our Mutual Friend*, I. xvii. ALL THE WORLD AND HIS WIFE and daughter leave cards. Sometimes THE WORLD'S WIFE has so many daughters that her card reads rather like a miscellaneous lot at an auction.

WORM, *subs.* (common).—A policeman.

WORM-CRUSHER, *subs. phr.* (military).—A foot soldier: *cf.* MUDCRUSHER.

WORM-FENCE, *subs. phr.* (American).—A zig-zag rail-fence; a VIRGINIA-FENCE (*q.v.*).

1839-40. IRVING, *Wolfert's Roost*, 251. We drove Master Jack about the common, until we had hemmed him in an angle of a WORM FENCE.

WORRICROW, *subs.* (old).—A scarecrow.

... NAYLOR, *Reynard the Fox*, 39. What a WORRICROW the man doth look!

WORTH. *See* BEAN; CANDLE; CENT; CRACKER; CURSE; FIG; FLY; GAME; LOUSE; NUTSHELL; PEAR; RAP; STRAW; TURD, etc., etc.

W. P. *See* WARMING-PAN.

WRAP-RASCAL, *subs. phr.* (Old Cant).—A cloak, or coat.

1753. *Adventurer*, 101. Some of them had those loose kind of great-coats on, which I have heard called WRAP-RASCALS.

1853. WH.-MELVILLE, *Digby Grand*, xix. Cram on a WRAP-RASCAL and a shawl choaker. Never mind the gold-laced overalls and spurs.

1860-3. THACKERAY, *Roundabout Papers*, xviii. There is the cozy WRAP-RASCAL, self-indulgence, how easy it is.

1898. WHITEING, *John St.*, xxiv. The humble individual in slouch felt and threadbare WRAP-RASCAL.

WREN, *subs.* (military).—A prostitute frequenting the Curragh Camp.

1869. GREENWOOD, *Seven Curses of London*. These creatures are known in and about the great military camp and its neighbourhood as WRENS. They do not live in houses or even huts, but build for themselves 'nests' in the bush.

WRETCH. POOR WRETCH, *subs. phr.* (provincial).—A term of endearment.

WRETCHCOCK (or WRECHOCK), *subs.* (old).—A puny, insignificant person, a poor wretch.

WRIGGLING-POLE, *subs. phr.* (venery).—The *penis*: *see* PRICK. TO WRIGGLE NAVELS = to copulate: *see* GREENS and RIDE.

c. 1720. DURFEY, *Pills to Purge*, etc. (1720), vi. 91. 'The Jolly Tradesmen.' But if my Oven be over-hot, I dare not thrust it in, Sir; For burning of my WRIGLING-POLE, My Skill's not worth a Pin, Sir.

WRIGHT (MR.), *subs. phr.* (prison).—A warder acting as go-between for a prisoner and his friends.

WRINGLE-GUT, *subs. phr.* (common).—A nervous, fidgety man.

WRINKLE, *subs.* (old).—A new idea, useful hint, cunning trick, smart dodge.

d. 1555. LATIMER, *Works*, ii. 422. And now what manner of man do you make me, Master N., when you note me to be so much abused by so ignorant a man, so simple, so plain, and so far without all WRINKLES?

15[?]. *Narratives of the Reformation* [*Camden Soc.*], 102. Palmer as he was a man symple and withoute all WRYNCLES off cloked colusy-one, opened to hym his whole intent.

1580. LYLY, *Euphues and his England*, 389. They are too experte in loue hauing learned in this time of their long peace euery WRINCKLE that is to be scene or imagined.

1709-10. SWIFT, *Pol. Conv.*, i. *Lady Ans.* Have a care, Miss; they say mocking is catching. *Miss.* I never heard that. *Nev.* Why then, Miss, you have one WRINKLE; more than ever you had before.

c. 1876. *Music Hall Song*, 'You're More Than Seven.' I know you're a little bit artful, old boy, And up to a WRINKLE or two.

WRITERLING, *subs.* (old). — An author of the baser sort, a petty journalist.

1802. TAYLOR [ROBBERD, *Memoir*, I. 420]. Every writer and WRITERLING of name has a salary from the Government.

WRITINGS. TO BURN THE WRITINGS, *verb. phr.* (old). — To quarrel.

WROKIN, *subs.* (old). — A Dutch woman.

WRONG. In various combinations and phrases: *e.g.* WRONG IN THE UPPER-STOREY = crazy; IN THE WRONG BOX = mistaken, embarrassed, in jeopardy; THE WRONG END OF THE STICK = the worst of a position, the false of a story; TO WAKE UP THE WRONG PASSENGER = to make a mistake in the individual, 'to get the wrong sow by the ear'; TO LAUGH ON THE WRONG SIDE OF THE MOUTH = to cry; TO GET OUT OF (or RISE OUT OF) THE WRONG [or RIGHT] SIDE OF THE BED (or RIGHT SIDE) = a happy augury (or the reverse).

1554. RIDLEY ('Foxe,' 1838), vi. 438. Sir, quoth I, if you will hear how St. Augustine expoundeth that place, you shall perceive that you are IN A WRONG BOX.

1588. J. UDALL, *Distrephes*, 31. I perceive that you and I are IN A WRONG BOX.

1596. JONSON, *Ev. Man in Humour*, ii. 1. He has THE WRONG SOW BY THE EAR, i' faith; and CLAPS HIS DISH AT THE WRONG MAN'S door.

1605. CHAPMAN and JONSON, *Eastward Ho*, ii. 1. YOU HAVE THE SOW BY THE RIGHT EAR, sir.

1607. MARSTON, *What you Will* [*Works* (1633), sig. Rb]. YOU RISE ON YOUR RIGHT SIDE to-day, marry.

1614. *Terence in English* [NARES]. *C.* What doth shee keepe house alreadie? *D.* Alreadie. *C.* O good God: WE ROSE ON THE RIGHT SIDE to-day.

c. 1620. FLETCHER, *Women Pleased*, i. [s.v., near end of act].

1633. MACHIN, *Dumb Knight*, iv. 1. Sure I said my prayers, RIS'D ON MY RIGHT SIDE . . . No hare did cross me, nor no bearded witch, Nor other ominous sign.

1664. BUTLER, *Hudibras*, II. iii. 580. You have a WRONG SOW BY THE EAR.

1714. LUCAS, *Gamesters*, 65. But tho' he laugh; 'twas on the WRONG SIDE OF HIS MOUTH.

d. 1731. WARD, *Merry Observations*, June. Those that happen to HAVE THE WRONG SOW BY THE EAR will be very apt to curse the shortness of the Vacation.

1751. SMOLLETT, *Peregrine Pickle*, xliii. 'That, I grant you, must be confessed: doctor, I'm afraid we have got INTO THE WRONG BOX.'

TO TAKE ONE X (or LETTER X), *verb. phr.* (police). — To secure a violent prisoner: two constables firmly grasp the collar with one hand, the captive's arm being drawn down and the hand forced backwards over the holding arms; in this position the prisoner's arm is more easily broken than extricated.

X-LEG, *subs.* (common).—In *pl.* = Knock knees.

XMAS, *subs.* (colloquial).—Christmas: frequently pronounced 'eksmas.' See CHRISTMAS.

1771. SMOLLETT, *Clinker* [SAINTSBURY (1900), i. 81]. You know, my dear friend, how natural it is for us Irishmen to blunder, and TO TAKE THE WRONG SOW BY THE EAR.

1811. *Lex. Bal.*, s.v. LAUGH.

1823. GROSE, *Vulg. Tongue*, s.v. LAUGH.

1826. BUCKSTONE, *Death Fetch*, i. 4. *Snapsch.* (*Aside.*) And have a pretty family of them about my ears the first time I'm left alone in the dark, who would soon make me LAUGH ON THE OTHER SIDE OF MY MOUTH, I fancy.

1836. MARRYAT, *Midshipman Easy*, x. 'Take care your rights of man don't get you IN THE WRONG BOX—there's no arguing on board of a man-of-war.'

1837. CARLYLE, *Diamond Necklace*, iii. By and bye thou wilt LAUGH ON THE WRONG SIDE OF THY FACE.

WRONG-'UN, *subs. phr.* (common). —Generic for anything bad: *e.g.* a spurious note, base coin, whore, welsher, a horse intended to be PULLED (*q.v.*), and so forth.

1889. *Sporting Times*, June 29. Isabel and Maudie knew the Turf and all its arts—They had often blewed a dollar on a WRONG 'UN.

1896. FARJEON, *Betray. John Fordham*, iv. 299. 'All wery true, guv'nor, wus luck—but it don't make black white, 'cause I'm a WRONG 'UN.'

1898. *Pomes from Pink 'Un* [Advt. facing front inside cover]. Do not invest money . . . on Stiff 'uns, WRONG 'UNS or Dead 'uns.

1902. *D. Telegraph*, 11 Feb., 10. 7. Do you consider that all possible precautions are taken against welshers?— Yes. A welsher can be had up for fraud, and anyone who is known as a WRONG ONE is excluded from the racecourse.

WROUGHT-SHIRT. See HISTORICAL SHIRT.

WRY-NOT. TO SHEAD WRY-NOT, *verb. phr.* (provincial).—To out-do the devil.

WUGGINS, *subs.* (Oxford University). — Worcester College; BOTANY-BAY (*q.v.*).

WUSSER, *subs.* (bargees').—A canal boat.

WUZZLE, *verb* (American).—To jumble, muddle, mix.

1869. STOWE, *Oldtown*, 63. He WUZZLED things up in the most singular way.

-Y, *insep. suffix* (Manchester Grammar School). — MATHY = mathematics; CHEMMY = chemistry; GYMMY = gymnastics; etc.

YACK, *subs.* (thieves').—A watch. TO CHURCH (or CHRISTEN) A YACK = to change the case, or substitute a fictitious inscription, in order to prevent identification.

1851-61. MAYHEW, *Lond. Lab.*, ii. 57. At last he was bowled out in the very act of nailing a YACK.

1857. DUCANGE ANGLICUS, *Vulg. Tongue*, 38. He told me as Bill had flimped a YACK.

1868. DORAN, *Saints and Sinners*, II. 290. The [thieves] CHURCH THEIR YACKS when they transpose the works of stolen watches to prevent identification.

YAFF, *verb* (colloquial).—To talk pertly: also YAFFLE. [Properly YAFF = to bark or yelp.]

YAFFLE, *subs.* (provincial).—An armful.

Verb (Old Cant).—1. To eat (HALLIWELL).

2. (colloquial).—To snatch, to pilfer, to take illicitly.

3. See YAFF.

YAHOO, *subs.* (common). — A generic reproach: spec. a rough, brutal, uncouth character. In America = a back-country lout, a greenhorn (BARTLETT). [A name given by Swift in his *Gulliver's Travels* (1726) to a race of brutes, described as having human forms and vicious and degraded propensities. They were subject to the Houyhnhnms, or horses endowed with human reason.] As *adj.* = boorish, loutish, uncouth.

1772. GRAVES, *Spiritual Quixote*, IV. x. To see a noble creature start and tremble at the passionate exclamation of a mere YAHOO of a stable-boy . . . equally excites my pity and my indignation.

d. 1790. WARTON, *Newmarket*, 170 That hated animal, a YAHOO squire.

1861. KINGSLEY, *Ravenshoe*, lv. 'And what sort of fellow is he?' said Lord Saltire; 'a YAHOO, I suppose?' 'Not at all; he is a capital fellow, a perfect gentleman.'

1900. SAVAGE, *Brought to Bay*, v. You frontier YAHOOS know nothing but herding cattle.

YALLOW. See YELLOW.

YAM, *subs.* (nautical).—Food; GRUB (*q.v.*). As *verb* = to eat.

YANK, *subs.* (American).—1. A YANKEE (*q.v.*): 'an abbreviation universally applied by the Confederates to the soldiers of the Union armies' (BARTLETT).

1890. *Scribner's Mag.*, 242. 'He'd ev shot him, if he hadn't skedaddled.' 'Well, *sir*! what fur?' 'Oh, jest jaw-hawkin' a YANK, and burnin' his heouse down.'

2. (provincial).—In *pl.* = leggings.

Verb (colloquial).—1. Generic for quick, sharp, or jerking motion; to bustle, twitch, snatch, move quickly, work smartly; usually with *along*, *over*, *out*, etc. As *subs.* (or YANKER) = a smart stroke, jerk, or twitch; YANKING = active, pushing, thorough-going; TO YANK THE BUN = 'to take the CAKE' (*q.v.*).

1818. HOGG, *Brownie of Bodsbeck*, xiv. I gae . . . him a YANK on the haffat tell I gart his bit brass cap rattle against the wa'.

1825. SCOTT, *St. Ronan's Well*, ii. I cannot bide their YANKING way.

1870. WHITNEY, *Sights and Insights*, xxix. A YANKING old horse and a wretchedly uncomfortable saddle.

1880. CLEMENS, *A Tramp Abroad.* He moistens his hands, grabs his property vigorously, YANKS it this way, then that.

1888. KIPLING, *Only a Subaltern.* When the butt of a room goes on the drink, or takes to moping by himself, measures are necessary to YANK him OUT of himself.

1890. WARNER, *Their Pilgrimage*, 201. I don't see the fun of being YANKED OVER all the United States in the middle of August.

1891. JANVIER, *Aztec Treasure-house*, x. I guess th' best thing we can do is t' YANK our traps OUT of that cave an' get started again.

1893. MILLIKEN. *'Arry Ballads*, 77. YANK ON to one gal, a fair screamer.

1900. FLYNT, *Tramps*, 278. The watchman scouted around, and found three of them in a box-car, and YANKED 'em all UP.

2. (colloquial).—To chatter, scold, nag; to talk fast and incessantly. Hence YANKIE = a chatterbox, one who talks 'nineteen to the dozen.'

YANKEE (YANKEY or YANKY), *subs.* (American).—1. A citizen of New England; 2. (mostly European) = a native of the United States: also YANKEE-DOODLE. Also as *adj.* with derivatives such as YANKEEDOM, YANKEEFIED, YANKEEISM, etc. [Of dubious and much-discussed derivation: *see* quots. and *adj.* sense.] YANKEE-NATION = the United States. [*Century*: The word acquired wide currency during the war of the rebellion as a nickname or contemptuous epithet among the Confederates for a Union soldier, the confederates themselves being in like spirit dubbed Johnnies or Rebs by the Union soldiers: *see* YANK.]

1765. *Oppression* [WEBSTER]. From meanness first this Portsmouth YANKEY rose, And still to meanness all his conduct flows.

1768. *Boston Jour. of the Times*, Sept. [The first mention in print of the famous air.] Those passing in boats observed great rejoicings, and that the YANKEE DOODLE song was the capital piece in the band of music.

1775. GORDON [*Letter* quoted in *Notes and Queries* (1852), 57]. They [the British troops at Concord and Lexington] were roughly handled by the YANKEES, a term of reproach for the New Englanders, when applied by the regulars.

1809. IRVING, *Knickerbocker*, 276. Codfish, tinware, apple-brandy . . . wooden bowls, and other articles of YANKEE barter.

1822. HECKEWELDER, *Indian Nations*, 132. No doubt the word was the first effort of the Indians to imitate the sound of the national name of the English, which they pronounced YENGEES. The Indians 'say they know the YENGEES [*i.e.* the New Englanders], and can distinguish them by their dress and personal appearance, and that they were considered as less cruel than the Virginians, or Long Knives. The English proper they call Saggenash.'

1848. COOPER, *Oak Openings*, xxviii. The sobriquet of YANKEES which is in every man's mouth.

1856. *Stray* YANKEE *in Texas*, 113. The Colonel whittled away at a bit of stick in the most YANKEEFIED way possible.

18[?]. TRUMBULL [BARTLETT]. The name [YENGEES or YENKEES] was originally given by the Massachusetts Indians to the English Colonists, being the nearest sound they could give for 'English.' It was afterwards adopted by the Dutch on the Hudson, who applied the term in contempt to all the people of New England. During the American Revolution, it was eagerly caught at by the British soldiers.

18[?]. TRUMBULL [BARTLETT]. When YANKIES, skill'd in martial rule, First put the British troops to school.

1848. LOWELL, *Biglow Papers*, 1 S., Int. We have the present YANKEE, full of expedients, half-master of all trades, inventive in all but the beautiful, full of shifts, not yet capable of comfort. *Ibid.* (1862), 2 S. iv. Ez ef we could maysure stupenjious events By the low YANKEE stan'ard o' dollars and cents.

d. 1852. MOORE, *Diary*, vii. 231. Approaching very fast the sublime of YANKEEISM.

d. 1859. DE QUINCEY, *Style*, Note 1. YANKEE, in the American use, does not mean a citizen of the United States as opposed to a foreigner, but a citizen of the northern New England states.

1861. *Death of Lincoln Despotism* [BARTLETT]. And hold them till Abe Lincoln, and all his Northern scum, Shall own our independence of YANKEE DOODLEDOM.

18[?]. *Nation* [BARTLETT]. The 'YANKS,' or the equally grovelling 'nigger,' one or the other, what we do not know, has corrupted 'Pollard of Richmond.'

c. 1889. LORD HOUGHTON, '*Knock at the Door*' [*Notes and Queries*, 7 S. xi. 106]. Examine him outside and in I'd thank ye, Morals, Parisian; manners, perfect YANKEE.

1890. BROUGHTON, *Alas*, viii. Hackneyed as only YANKEEDOM and Cockneydom, rushing hand-in-hand through all earth's sacrednesses can hackney.

3. (American).—A glass of whiskey sweetened with molasses.

Adj. and *adv.* (colloquial).—A generic intensive: spanking, excellent.

1713. [GORDON, *Hist. Am. War* (1789), I. 324.] You may wish to know the origin of the term YANKEE. . . . It was a cant favourite word with Farmer Jonathan Hastings of Cambridge about 1713. . . . The inventor used it to express excellency. A Yankee good horse, or Yankee cider and the like were an excellent good horse and excellent cider.

YANKER, *subs.* (common).—1. A great falsehood: *see* WHOPPER.

1822. HOGG, *Three Perils of Man*, I. 336. Ay, billy, that is a YANKER. . . . When ane is gaun to tell a lie, there's naething like telling a plumper at aince.

2. *See* YANK, *verb.*

YANKIE, *subs.* (Scotch).—1. A sharp, forward, clever woman.

2. *See* YANK, *verb* 2.

YANNAM. *See* PANNAM (of which YANNAM is probably a misprint).

YAP, *subs.* (provincial).—1. A yelp; 2 = a cur, a TYKE (*q.v.*); whence (3) = a countryman. Also as *verb* = to bark, yelp; YAPSTER = a dog (*Tufts*, 1798).

1866. ELIOT, *Felix Holt*, xlii. Moro YAPPED in a puppy voice at their heels.

1889. BLACKMORE, *Kit and Kitty*, xxiv. Presently he YAPPED as in hot chase of a rabbit.

1901. FLYNT and WALTON, *Powers that Prey*, 21. This YAP from the country. *Ibid.*, 60. These YAPS come to town and throw up their hands at sights that a Bowery kid wouldn't drop a cigarette snipe to see.

Verb (back slang).—To pay. Whence YAPPY = over-generous, SOFT (*q.v.*), foolish: *i.e.* paying mad.

YARD, *subs.* (venery).—The *penis*: *see* PRICK.

1598. FLORIO, *Worlde of Wordes*, s.v. *Priapismo.* The standing of a man's YARD, which is when the YARD is stretched out in length and breadth. . . . If it come with a beating and panting of the YARD the phisicians call it then Satiriasi.

THE YARD, *subs. phr.* (London).—1. Scotland Yard, the headquarters of the London police, now located at New Scotland Yard.

1901. *Pall Mall Gaz.*, 11 May, 2. 3. He gave plausibility to his proceedings by exhibiting a subscription list for a testimonial to a member of 'THE YARD,' who, said he, was about to retire.

2. (Durham School).—In *pl.* = the list of members originally of the First Game, but now of the Second Game—at football or cricket. [Formerly in the cricket season only a patch of ground thirty yards square was mowed. Those who had the privilege of playing on this were said to be on the YARDS.]

UNDER ONE'S YARD, *phr.* (old).—In one's power, subject to authority.

1383. CHAUCER, *Canterbury Tales*, 7893, 'Clerke's Tale.' Hoste, quod he, I am UNDER YOUR YERDE.

TO GET YARDS, *verb. phr.* (Harrow).—To get a catch at football and be allowed a free kick, not running more than can be covered in three running strides. Hence TO GIVE YARDS = to give such a catch; TO STEP YARDS = to cover the distance in 'kicking off YARDS' in three strides; TO KNOCK DOWN YARDS = to prevent another from 'taking YARDS.' [Orig. 'three yards.']

See KNIGHT.

YARDER, *subs.* (Harrow).—Cricket played in the school yard: in the summer term.

YARD-OF-CLAY, *subs. phr.* (common).—A long clay pipe; a CHURCHWARDEN (*q.v.*).

1859. FAIRHOLT, *Tobacco* (1876), 173. Such long pipes were reverently termed aldermen in the last age, and irreverently YARDS OF CLAY in the present one.

1866. *London Miscellany*, 19 May, 235. 2. Surely these men, who win and lose fortunes with the stolidity of a mynheer smoking his CLAY YARD, must be of entirely different stuff from the rest of us.

YARD-OF-PUMPWATER, *subs. phr.* (common).—A tall thin man (or woman): *cf.* RASHER-OF-WIND.

YARK, *verb* (Durham School).—To cane.

YARMOUTH-CAPON (or -BEE), *subs. phr.* (common).—A herring: *see* GLASGOW MAGISTRATE (B. E. and GROSE).

1662. FULLER, *Worthies*, 'Norfolk,' II. 126. A YARMOUTH CAPON. That is, a Red-herring. I believe few Capons (save what have more fins than feathers) are bred in Yarmouth. But, to countenance this expression, I understand that the Italian Friers (when disposed to eat the flesh on Fridays) call Capon *piscem e corte*, a fish out of the coop.

YARMOUTH-COACH, *subs. phr.* (old).—'A sorry, low Cart to ride on, drawn by one Horse' (B. E.).

YARMOUTH-MITTENS, *subs. phr.* (nautical).—Bruised hands.

YARN, *subs.* (colloquial).—A story, a tale: spec. an incredible, long, or marvellous narration spun out by a sailor. Hence as *verb* (or TO SPIN YARNS) = to romance,

'draw the long bow'; A SAILOR'S YARN = a traveller's story (*q.v.*); YARN-CHOPPER (or SLINGER) = (1) a long prosy talker; and (2) a fictional journalist.

1859. READE, *Love Me Little*, iii. It isn't everybody that likes these sea-YARNS as you do, Eve. No, I'll belay, and let my betters get a word in now.

1879. *Scribner's Mag.*, viii. 465. The first lieutenant is YARNING with me under the lea of the bulwarks.

1884. CLARK RUSSELL, *Jack's Courtship*, xxx. All the crew . . . YARNING and smoking and taking sailors' pleasure.

1885. *D. Teleg.*, 29 Dec. [He] who has YARNED aforetime 'On the Fo'k'sle Head,' and 'Round the Galley Fire.'

YARUM, *subs.* (Old Cant).—Milk. POPLARS OF YARUM = milk porridge (HARMAN, B. E., and GROSE).

1567. HARMAN, *Caveat*, 86. She has a cackling-chete, a grunting-chete, ruff pecke, cassan, and POPPLAR OF YARUM.

1608. DEKKER, *Lanthorne and Candlelight* [FARMER, *Musa Pedestris* (1896), 3]. The Ruffin cly the nab of the Harmanbeck, If we maund . . . POPLARS OF YARUM, he cuts, bing to the Ruffmans.

1641. BROME, *Jovial Crew*, ii. Here's Pannam and Lap, and good POPLARS OF YARRUM.

YAWNEY (or YAWNUPS), *subs.* (provincial).—A stupid fellow; BUFFLE (*q.v.*): *cf.* SAWNEY. Also YAWNEY-BOX = a donkey: *see* NEDDY.

YAW-SIGHTED, *adj. phr.* (nautical).—Squinting.

YAW-YAW, *subs. phr.* (nautical).—A Dutchman: any man who says 'YAW-YAW' for 'Yes' (CLARK RUSSELL).

YEA-AND-NAY, *adj. phr.* (colloquial).—Insipid, watery; *e.g.* a poor YAY-NAY sort of a person = a stupid, doltish block: one who can say but YEA or NAY to a question: *see* next entry.

c. 1780. DARBLAY, *Diary*, II. 288. She is a sort of YEA AND NAY young gentlewoman, to me very wearisome.

YEA-AND-NAY MAN, *subs. phr.* (old).—A Quaker (B. E.).

YEACK, *verb* (old).—'An imitative word to express the sound with which coachmen encourage their horses (?), unless it is another form of yerk' (DAVIES).

1606. DEKKER, *Seven Deadly Sins*, iii. Candle light's coach . . . is drawne (with ease) by two rats: the coachman is a chaundler, who so sweats with YEACKING them, that he drops tallowe, and that feedes them as prouender.

YEAR'S-MIND (or YEAR-MIND), *subs. phr.* (old colloquial).—A memorial, a mass, an anniversary: *cf.* MONTH'S-MIND.

YELLOW, *subs.* (old colloquial).—1. Generic for jealousy, envy, melancholy: also YELLOWS and YELLOWNESS: *cf.* BLUE, BROWN, RED, WHITE, etc. (B. E.). Also in frequent proverbial phrase: *e.g.* TO WEAR YELLOW HOSE (BREECHES OR STOCKINGS) = to be jealous; TO ANGER THE YELLOW HOSE, etc. = to provoke jealousy; TO WEAR YELLOW STOCKINGS = to be cuckolded: hence YELLOW-HAMMER (or -GLOAK) = (1) a cuckold, and (2) a jealous man or husband. [YELLOW STOCKINGS (*q.v.*) were once, for a long period prior to the civil wars, a fashionable article of dress: the fashion is still preserved amongst BLUES (*q.v.*) at Christ's Hospital.]

1596. SHAKSPEARE, *Merry Wives*, i. 3. III. I will incense Page to deal with poison. I will possess him with YELLOWNESS. *Ibid.* (1600), *Much Ado*, i. 1. Civil as an orange, and something of that jealous complexion. *Ibid.* (1602), *Twelfth Night*, ii. 4. With a green and YELLOW melancholy. *Ibid.* (1604), *Winter's Tale*, ii. 3. 107. 'Mongst all colours, No YELLOW in't, lest she suspect, as he does, Her children not her husbands.

1607. DEKKER, *Northward Hoe*, i. 3. Jealous men are either knaves or coxcombs; be you neither; you WEAR YELLOW HOSE without cause. *Ibid.* (1607), *Westward Hoe*, ii. 2. I'll make the YELLOW-HAMMER, her husband, know . . . that there's a difference between a cogging bawd, and an honest motherly gentlewoman.

1621. BURTON, *Anat. Melan.*, III. III. i. 2. At length he began to suspect, and turne a little YELLOW, as well he might, for it was his owne fault; and if men be jealous in such cases . . . the mends is in their owne hands. . . . The undiscreet carriage of some lascivious gallant . . . may make a breach, and by his over-familiarity, if he be inclined to YELLOWNESS, colour him quite out.

1623. MASSINGER, *Duke of Milan*, iv. 1. If I were The duke (I freely must confess my weakness) I should WEAR YELLOW BREECHES.

1633. BROME, *Antipodes*, L. (4to). But for his YELLOWS, Let me but lye with you, and let him know it, His jealousy is gone.

1640. *Two Lancashire Lovers*, 27. Thy blood is yet uncorrupted, YELLOWS has not tainted it.

16[?]. *Roxburgh Ballads*, ii. 61. If thy wife will be so bad . . . Why . . . WEARE STOCKINGS that are YELLOW? Tush, greeve no more, A cuckold is a good man's fellow.

1678. BUTLER, *Hudibras*, iii. 1. In earnest to as jealous piques; Which th' ancients wisely signify'd By th' YELLOW mantuas of the bride.

2. *See* YELLOWSTOCKINGS.

BABY'S YELLOW *subs. phr.* (nursery). — Excrement, SHIT (*q.v.*): spec. infantine fæcal matter.

YELLOW-ADMIRAL. *See* ADMIRAL.

YELLOW-BANDED ROBBERS (THE), *subs. phr.* (military).—The Prince Albert's Somersetshire Light Infantry, late the 13th Foot.

YELLOW-BELLY, *subs.* (provincial).—1. A Lincolnshire fen-man.

2. (American).—A half-caste: also YELLOW-BOY (*q.v.*) or YELLOW-GIRL.

3. (American). — A Dutchman.

YELLOW-BOY, *subs. phr.* (common).—A gold coin: spec. a sovereign, 20s.: formerly a guinea: Fr. *jaunet*: *see* RHINO (B. E. and GROSE). Also YELLOW-HAMMER (tailors'), YELLOW-MOULD, and YELLOW-STUFF (generic); YELLOW-FEVER = gold fever: *cf.* SCARLET-FEVER.

1633. SHIRLEY, *Bird in a Cage*, ii. Is that he that has gold enough? would I had some of his YELLOW-HAMMERS.

1661. MIDDLETON, *Mayor of Quinborough*, ii. *Simon the Tanner.* Now, by this light, a nest of YELLOW-HAMMERS. . . . I'll undertake, sir, you shall have all the skins in our parish at this price.

1663. DRYDEN, *Wild Gallant*, i. How now, YELLOW BOYS, by this good light! Sirrah, varlet, how came I by this gold?

1706. WARD, *Wooden World*, 24. No Liquor could overcome him, the last Remedy then was, to bring out some YELLOW BOYS.

1713. ARBUTHNOT, *Hist. John Bull*, i. 6. John did not starve his cause; there wanted not YELLOW-BOYS to fee counsel.

1751. SMOLLETT, *Peregrine Pickle*, viii. I wish both their necks were broke, though the two cost me forty good YELLOW BOYS.

1830. LYTTON, *Paul Clifford*. Fighting Attie, my hero, I saw you to-day A purse full of YELLOW BOYS seize.

1840. DICKENS, *Old Curiosity Shop*, xlii. 'The delight of picking up the money—the bright, shining YELLOW BOYS —and sweeping 'em into one's pocket!'

1861. M'COMBIE, *Australian Sketches*, 47. Evident symptoms of the return of the YELLOW FEVER, and a journey to the new goldfields seemed to be the only cure.

1884. CLEMENS, *Huckleberry Finn*. When they found the bag they spilt it out on the floor, and it was a lovely sight, all them YALLER BOYS.

2. (American).—A mulatto, or dark quadroon: also YELLOW GIRL.

YELLOW-COVER, *subs. phr.* (American).—A notice of dismissal from government employment: pron. *yaller kiver*. [From being usually enclosed in a yellow envelope.]

YELLOW - COVERED, *adj. phr.* (orig. American: now general). — Cheap, sensational, trashy. Also YELLOW-BACKS = a generic term for cheap board - bound railway novels.

YELLOW-DOG, *subs. phr.* (American). — A strong term of contempt.

YELLOW-FANCY, *subs. phr.* (pugilists').—A yellow silk handkerchief spotted white: *cf.* YELLOW-MAN.

YELLOW-FEVER. 1. *See* YELLOW-BOY.

2. (old nautical). — Drunkenness: *see* SCREWED. [Part of the punishment of drunkards at Greenwich Hospital consisted in wearing a YELLOW COAT.]

YELLOW-HAMMER. *See* YELLOW and YELLOW-BOY.

YELLOW JACK, *subs. phr.* (nautical).—Yellow fever. [A yellow flag (or jack) being generally displayed at naval hospitals, or from vessels at quarantine, to denote the existence of contagious disease.]

1848. DICKENS, *Dombey and Son*, x. His elder brother died of YELLOW JACK in the West Indies.

1857. KINGSLEY, *Two Years Ago*, iv. Have seen three choleras, two army-fevers, and YELLOW-JACK without end.

YELLOW-MAN, *subs. phr.* (pugilists').—A yellow silk handkerchief: *cf.* YELLOW-FANCY.

1832. EGAN, *Book of Sports*. Sporting the YELLOW MAN. The wipe was of bright yellow, made on purpose for him.

YELLOW-MOULD. *See* YELLOW-BOY.

YELLOW-PINE, *subs. phr.* (American). — A quadroon or light mulatto.

YELLOW-PLASTER, *subs. phr.* (provincial).—Alabaster: freq. pronounced 'YALLOW'-plaster.

YELLOW-SLIPPER, *subs. phr.* (common).—A very young calf.

YELLOW-STUFF. *See* YELLOW-BOY.

YELLOW - STOCKING, *subs. phr.* (old).—1. *See* YELLOW.

2. (London).—A BLUE (*q.v.*) -coat boy: also YELLOWS.

YENNEP, *subs.* (back slang).—A penny: 1d.: *see* RHINO.

1851-61. MAYHEW, *Lond. Lab.* 'All a fellow wants to know to sell potatoes,' said a master street seller to me, 'is to tell how many tanners make a bob, and how many YENNEPS a tanner.'

1877. DIPROSE, *Lond. Life.* I've been doing awful dab with my tol . . . haven't made a YENNEP.

YEOMAN OF THE MOUTH, *subs. phr.* (old).—'An officer belonging to his Majestis's Pantry' (B. E.).

YES SIREE, BOB! *phr.* (American). —*See* SIRRAH.

YID (or YIDDISHER), *subs.* (common).—A Jew [Ger. *Judischer*]. Whence YIDDISH = Jewish; and as *subs.* a dialect or jargon spoken by Jews mainly composed of corrupt Hebrew and German.

YOB, *subs.* (back slang). — BOY (*q.v.*).

1897. MARSHALL, *Pomes*, 76. And you bet that each gal, not to mention each YOB, Didn't care how much ooftish it cost 'em per nob.

YOKEL, *subs.* (common). — A countryman, bumpkin, lout: in contempt. Hence as *adj.* (or YOKELISH) = rustic.

1838. DICKENS, *Oliver Twist*, xxxi. 'This wasn't done by a YOKEL, eh, Duff?' 'Certainly not,' replied Duff. 'And translating the word YOKEL for the benefit of the ladies, I apprehend your meaning to be that this attempt was not made by a countryman?' said Mr. Losberne, with a smile. 'That's it, master,' replied Blathers.

18[?]. HOOD, *Row at the Oxford Arms*. Lord knows their names, I'm sure I don't, no more than any YOKEL.

1847-8. THACKERAY, *Vanity Fair*, Preface. YOKELS looking up at the tinselled dancers and poor old rouged tumblers.

1869. BLACKMORE, *Lorna Doone*, xl. Thou art not altogether the clumsy YOKEL and the clod I took thee for.

YOKUFF, *subs.* (back slang).—A large box, chest, 'coffer.'

YOLLY, *subs.* (Winchester College). —A post-chaise. [Yellow was a favourite colour for these vehicles.]

YONKER. *See* YOUNKER.

YOÔP, *subs.* (colloquial).—A word expressive of a hiccuping or sobbing sound: onomatopœa [THACKERAY].

YORK. AS LIKE AS YORK IS TO FOUL SUTTON, *phr.* (old).—As dissimilar as may be.

1544. ASCHAM, *Toxophilus*, 47. To tumble ouer and ouer, to toppe ouer tayle, . . . which exercises surelye muste nedes be naturall bycause they be so childisshe, and they may be also holesome for the body; but surely as for pleasure to the minde or honestie in the doinge of them, they be AS LYKE shotinge AS YORKE IS FOULE SUTTON.

See YORKER.

YORKER, *subs.* (cricketers').—A ball finding pitch very close to the bat. Hence YORK, *verb* = to bowl YORKERS.

1885. *D. Teleg.*, 1 July. [He] was clean bowled in playing late at a YORKER.

YORKSHIRE. It would appear that formerly (*see* quot. 1611) Yorkshire was more proverbial for dulness and clownishness than, as in modern phrase, for 'the boot to be on the other leg': *e.g.* to COME (or PUT) YORKSHIRE OVER (or TO YORKSHIRE ONE) = to cheat, take a person in, to prove too wide-awake for him. Also YORKSHIRE-BITE = a specially 'cute piece of overreaching, entrapping one into a profitless bargain. The monkey who ate the oyster and returned a shell to each litigant affords a good example. CONFIDENT AS A YORKSHIRE CARRIER = cocksure; YORKSHIRE COMPLIMENT = a gift useless to the giver and not wanted by the receiver: also NORTH-COUNTRY COMPLIMENT; A YORKSHIRE ESTATE = money in prospect, a CASTLE IN THE AIR (*q.v.*): *e.g.* 'When I come into my YORKSHIRE ESTATES' = When I have the means; YORKSHIRE-RECKONING = a reckoning where each one pays his share; YORKSHIRE-TYKE = 'a Yorkshire manner of Man' (B. E.); YORKSHIRE-HOG = a fat wether.

1611. DAVIES, *Paper Persecutors*, 81. England is all TURNED YORKSHIRE, and the age Extremely sottish, or too nicely sage.

1706. WARD, *Wooden World*, 39. All this put together must needs make him follow his nose with great boldness . . . no wonder . . . he's MORE CONFIDENT of his Way than a YORKSHIRE CARRIER.

1772. BRIDGES, *Burlesque Homer*, 2. At first approach he made a bow, Such as your YORKSHIRE TIKES make now. *Ibid.*, 478. A pastrycook That made good pigeon pye of rook, Cut venison from YORKSHIRE HOGS And made rare mutton-pies of dogs.

1796. HOLMAN, *Abroad and at Home*, i. 1. His YORKSHIRE simplicity will qualify him admirably for the profession.

1839. DICKENS, *Nicholas Nickleby*, xlii. 'Wa'at I say, I stick by.' 'And that's a fine thing to do, and manly too,' said Nicholas, 'though it's not exactly what we understand by "coming YORKSHIRE over us" in London.'

YORKSHIRE-HUNTERS (THE), *subs. phr.* (old military).—A regiment formed by the gentlemen of Yorkshire during the Civil War.

YOU. YOU'RE ANOTHER, *phr.* (old). —A *tu quoque*: *i.e.* ANOTHER liar, fool, thief—any imaginable term of abuse.

1534. UDAL, *Roister Doister*, iii. 5. *Roister.* If it were an other but thou, it were a knaue. *M. Mery.* YE ARE AN OTHER your selfe, sir, the lorde us both saue.

1561. PRESTON, *Cambyses* [DODSLEY, *Old Plays* (HAZLITT), iv. 220]. Thou call'st me knave, THOU ART ANOTHER.

1749. FIELDING, *Tom Jones*, ix. vi. 'I did not mean to abuse the cloth; I only said your conclusion was a non sequitur.' 'YOU ARE ANOTHER,' cries the sergeant, 'an' you come to that; no more a sequitur than yourself.'

1836. DICKENS, *Pickwick*, xv. 'Sir,' said Mr. Tupman, 'you're a fellow.' 'Sir,' said Mr. Pickwick, 'YOU'RE ANOTHER.'

1882. *Boston Lit. World*, 3 June, 184. 3. The argument of it is simply, 'YOU'RE ANOTHER,' a retort in dignified manner to . . . British critics.

1888. SIR W. HARCOURT, *Speech at Eighty Club*, 21 Feb. Little urchins in the street have a conclusive argument. They say 'YOU'RE ANOTHER.'

d. 1891. LOWELL, *Democracy*. I find little to interest and less to edify me in these international bandyings of YOU'RE ANOTHER.

YOU BET, *intj. phr.* (American).—You may depend on it; to be sure! certainly! the most positive of affirmations: also 'YOU BET your boots,' 'life,' 'bottom dollar,' and so on. [Originally a Californian phrase: it has also been given as a name in the form of UBET to a town in the Canadian Northwest.]

1870. BRET HARTE, *Poems, etc.*, *The Tale of a Pony*. Ah, here comes Rosey's new turn-out! Smart! You BET YOUR LIFE 't was that!

c. 1840. *Grandpa's Soliloquy* [BARTLETT]. To little Harry, yesterday,—My grandchild, aged two,—I said, 'You love Grandpa?' said he, 'YOU BET YOUR BOOTS I do.'

18[?]. *Buffalo Courier*, 'Mystified Quaker.' His answer's gross irrelevance I shall not soon forget, Instead of simply yea or nay, he gruffly said, 'YOU BET.'

1872. S. CLEMENS ('Mark Twain'), *Roughing It*, ii. 'The mosquitoes are pretty bad about here, madam!' 'YOU BET!' 'What did I understand you to say, madam?' 'YOU BET!'

c. 1882. STAVELY HILL, *From Home to Home*. We reached the settlement of UBET. The name had been selected from the slang phrase so laconically expressive of 'You may be sure I will.'

1888. *Daily Inter-Ocean*, 7 Mar. Congressional Report. *Mr. Boutelle.* That is the bravery to which you refer? (Applause on the Republican side.) *Mr. O'Ferrall.* Well, sir, it is the right kind of bravery: you may BET YOUR BOTTOM DOLLAR on that.

YOU-KNOW-WHAT, *subs. phr.* (schoolgirls' conventional).—The female *pudendum,* the PUSSY (*q.v.*): see MONOSYLLABLE.

c. 1650. BRATHWAYTE, *Barnaby's Jl.* (1723), 93. But tho' . . . fat-a Her I caught by you KNOW WHAT-A.

YOUNG, *adj.* (political).—Found in various CANTING (*subs.* 2) combinations: Thus, YOUNG ENGLAND = a set of young aristocrats, who tried to revive the courtly manners of the Chesterfield school: they wore white waistcoats, patronised the pet poor, looked down upon shopkeepers, and were imitators of the period of Louis XIV.: Disraeli has immortalised their ways and manners. YOUNG GERMANY = a literary school, headed by Heinrich Heine [*Hī-ny*], whose aim was to liberate politics, religion, and manners from the old conventional trammels. YOUNG IRELAND = followers of Daniel O'Connell in politics, but wholly opposed to his abstention from war and insurrection in vindication of 'their country's rights.' YOUNG ITALY = certain Italian refugees, who associated themselves with the French republican party, called the *Carbonnerie Democratique:* the society was first organised at Marseilles by Mazzini, and its chief object was to diffuse republican principles (BREWER).

YOUNG BUFFS (THE), *subs. phr.* (military).—The first battalion East Surrey Regiment, late the 31st Foot. [At Dettingen, George II., through the similarity of the facings, mistook it for the 3rd Foot or (Old) Buffs.]

YOUNG EYES (THE), *subs. phr.* (military).—The Seventh (The Queen's Own) Hussars.

YOUNG HOPEFUL, *subs. phr.* (colloquial).—A half jocular, half affectionate address. [*Cf.* PATTEN, *Somerset's March* (1548), in which young Edward VI. is said to be of great HOPE; *i.e.* he begets hope in others.]

YOUNG MAN, *subs. phr.* (once literary: now conventionally vulgar).—A sweetheart, lover.

1585. PUTTENHAM, *Art of Eng. Poesy* [ARBER], 66. [We hear of a girl's YOUNG MAN.]

YOUNGSTER (YOUNKER, YOUNKERKIN, etc.), *subs.* (old).—1. A lad, a young person: always more or less familiar, contemptuous, or colloquial. Also (2) a novice, an inexperienced youth, and (nautical) a raw hand; in modern naval usage = a junior officer. [SMYTHPALMER (s.v. YOUNGSTER): No doubt a corrupt form of YOUNKER, orig. (Germ.) a title of honour. TRENCH: The first example of YOUNGSTER which Richardson gives us is from the *Spectator* [No. 324]. If it exists at all in our earlier literature, it will hardly be otherwise than as the female correlative of the male younker or 'yonker,' a word of constant recurrence. *Contrariwise, see* quot. 1593; it is probably late Tudor, having birth at a time when it had been forgotten that the termination *-ster* was originally feminine only.] Hence to make a YOUNKER of one = to gull, cheat, deceive (for an innocent).

[1502–9. *Letters of Richard III. and Henry VII.* (GARDNER). We see the Dutch title of honour, YONKER.]

1530. PALSGRAVE, *Lang. Francoyse,* s.v. *Ung rustre* [an uncouth rustic, but note similarity to YOUNGSTER], YONKER.

c. 1530. *Christes Kirk on the Green* [OLIPHANT, *New Eng.,* i. 467. YOUNKER . . . did not come in long before that year.]

2 B

1562. BULLEYN, *Booke of Simples,* xxviii. verso. If there be any YONKERS troubled with idelnesse and loytryng.

1584. HOLINSHED, *Conquest of Ireland.* Such young novices and YONKERS as are of late gone thither.

1593. *Tom Tel-Troth's Message,* 601. This trull makes YOUNGSTERS spend their patrimonie In sauced meates and sugred delicates.

1594. BARNEFIELD, *Affectionate Shepherd.* Yet such sheep he kept, and was so seemelie a shepheard, Seemelie a boy, so seemelie a youth, so seemelie a YOUNKER, That on Ide was not such a boy, such a youth, such a YOUNKER.

1594. GREENE, *Friar Bacon,* etc., 175. Now lusty YOUNKERS, look within the glass, And tell me if you can discern your sires.

1595. SHAKSPEARE, *3 Henry VI.,* ii. 1. How well resembles it the prime of youth, Trimm'd like a YONKER, prancing to his love. *Ibid.* (1598), *Merchant Venice,* ii. 6. How, like a YONKER, and a prodigal, The skarfed bark puts from her native bay. *Ibid.* (1598), 1 *Henry IV.,* iii. 3. What, will you make a YOUNKER of me? Shall I not take mine ease in mine inn, but I must have my pocket picked for it?

1596. SPENSER, *Faery Queen,* iv. i. 11. Amongst the rest there was a jolly knight . . . But that same YOUNKER soone was overthrowne.

1599. HALL, *Satires,* iii. v. 18. There must my YONKER fetch his waxen crown.

1607. DEKKER, *Northward Hoe,* iv. 1. If I were a YOUNKER, it would be no immodesty . . . to be seen in my company; but to have snow in the lap of June, vile, vile!

1614. CHAPMAN, *Odyssey,* xiv. Ulysses slept there, and close by The other YOUNKERS.

c. 1625. FLETCHER, *Elder Brother,* iii. 5. Would he were buried! I fear he'll make an ass of me, a YOUNKER.

1626. SMITH, *English Sea Terms,* s.v. *Sayler* [an old hand as opposed to] YOUNKER, a fore-mast man.

1630–40. HOWELL, *Letters,* i. vi. 4. There was a Parliament then at Rheinsburgh, where all the YOUNKERS met.

1647–8. HERRICK, *Hesperides,* 'Upon Pagget.' This YONKER fierce to fight.

1670. COTTON, *Scoffer Scofft* [*Works* (1725), 249]. He is a very honest YOUNKER, A bonny Lad, and a great Punker.

d. 1684. OLDHAM, *Satires,* 223. The credit of the business and the state Are things that in a YOUNGSTER's sense sound great.

1706. WARD, *Wooden World,* 24. A hundred or two of these little YOUNKERS, with which he could fight better than with so many stout Tars in an Engagement.

1772. BRIDGES, *Burlesque Homer,* 137. As smooth as YOUNKERS slide on ice.

1809. MALKIN, *Gil Blas* [ROUTLEDGE], 31. By all that is sacred . . . it is plain you are no YOUNKER.

1822. LAMB, *Essays,* 'Chimneysweepers.' It was a pleasure to see the sable YOUNKERS tick in the unctuous meat.

1870. JUDD, *Margaret,* i. 6. The juveniles and YOUNKERS in the town.

YOUNG THING, *subs. phr.* (colloquial).—An immature girl: in mild contempt or pity: *e.g.* 'She's but a YOUNG THING.'

1360. *Syr Gawayn* [E.E.T.S.], 49 [OLIPHANT, *New Eng.,* i. 57. A lady calls herself 'a YOUNG THING,' a phrase not yet lost].

YOUR NIBS. See NIBS and WATCH.

YOURS TRULY, *phr.* (common).—A jocular mode of reference to oneself: *cf.* NIBS and WATCH.

1866. COLLINS, *Armadale,* II. 168. YOURS TRULY, sir, has an eye for a fine woman and a fine horse.

1899. KETTLE, *Furth. Adv.,* ix. You may take it as straight from YOURS TRULY that you'll go to your own funeral if trouble starts.

YOU-UNS, *pr.* (Southern U.S.).—You: *cf.* WEE-UNS.

1876. HAY, *Mystery of Gilgal.* But I'll tell the yarn to YOUANS.

1885. CRADDOCK, *Prophet Gt. Smoky Mountains,* i. Mirandy Jane . . 'pears like I hev hed the trouble o' raisin' a idjit in YOU-UNS.

YOXTER, *subs.* (old prison).—A convict returned from transportation before his time was up.

YUM-YUM, *adv. phr.* (common).—First-rate, excellent.

**ANY,** *subs.* (old).—1. Orig. a buffoon's foil: his office consisted in making awkward and ludicrous attempts to mimic the professional jester or clown. Hence (2) a mimic; and (3) an attendant. As *verb* = to play the fool, to mimic, to dance attendance (B. E. and GROSE); whence also such derivatives as ZANYISM. *Cf.* SAWNEY.

1567. EDWARDS, *Damon and Pithias* [DODSLEY, *Old Plays* (HAZLITT), iv. 74]. [OLIPHANT, *New Eng.,* i. 566. A servant speaks French to astonish a friend, and calls him *petit Zawne* (ZANY or sawny).]

1598. FLORIO, *Worlde of Wordes,* s.v. *Zane* . . . the name of John, in some parts of Lombardy, but commonly used for a silly John, a simple fellow, a servile drudge, or foolish clowne, in any comedy or enterlude play.

1599. JONSON, *Every Man Out of Humour,* iv. 2. For, indeed, He's like the ZANI to a tumbler, That tries tricks after him to make men laugh. *Ibid.* (1600), *Cynthia's Revels,* ii. 3. The other gallant is his ZANY, and doth most of these tricks after him, and sweats to imitate him in everything.

1602. SHAKESPEARE, *Twelfth Night,* i. 5. I take these wise men, that crow so at these set kind of fools, no better than the fools' ZANIES.

1602. MIDDLETON, *Blurt, Master Constable,* iii. 1. Imperia, the courtesan's ZANY hath brought you this letter from the poor gentleman in the deep dungeon, but would not stay till he had an answer.

1602. MARSTON, *Antonio and Mellida,* II. iv. 1. Laughs them to scorne, as man doth busie apes When they will ZANIE men,

c. 1605. DRAYTON, *Eleg.,* 1256. As th' English apes, and very ZANIES be, Of everything that they do hear and see.

c. 1618. FLETCHER, *Queen of Corinth,* i. 2. All excellence In other madams do but ZANY hers.

1632. HEYWOOD, *Four Prentises* [*Works* (1874), II. 203]. Ile teach thee: thou shalt like my ZANY be, And feigne to do my cunning after me.

d. 1658. LOVELACE, *Works,* II. 78. As I have seen an arrogant baboon, With a small piece of glass, your ZANY the sun.

1668. DRYDEN, *Evening's Love,* Pref. Approbation which those very people give, equally with me, to the ZANY of a mountebank.

1726. POPE, *Dunciad,* iii. 206. Preacher at once, and ZANY of thy age.

1849. COLERIDGE, *Course of Lectures,* ix. The caricature of his filth and ZANYISM proves how fully he both knew and felt the danger.

1856. MOTLEY, *Dutch Republic,* I. 402. [GRANVILLE] had been wont in the days of his greatest insolence, to speak of the most eminent nobles as ZANIES, lunatics and buffoons.

1869. *Edin. Rev.,* July. The ZANY in Shakspeare's day was not so much a buffoon and mimic as the obsequious follower of a buffoon, and the attenuated mime of a mimic.

ZEBRA, *subs.* (American).—A prison dress: because striped.

1900. FLYNT, *Tramps,* 144. Not long after this experience he got into limbo and had to wear the famous ZEBRA.

ZEDLAND, *subs.* (common).—The western counties of England: where, *dialectically,* S is pronounced as Z. Also IZZARDLAND, and (literary) the UNNECESSARIANS = Western folk.

1605. SHAKSPEARE, *Lear,* ii. 2. 68. Thou whoreson ZED, thou UNNECESSARY LETTER.

ZEMMIES-HAW, *intj.* (provincial).—An exclamation of surprise.

ZIFF, *subs.* (thieves').—A young thief: see THIEF.

ZOO, *subs.* (colloquial). — The Zoological Gardens, London: *cf.* POPS, HOPS, etc.

1902. *Pall Mall Gaz.,* 26 July, 2. 1. Then there are parks and gardens, picture galleries and museums, and a ZOO free on Sundays.

ZOTY, *subs.* (provincial).—A fool: see BUFFLE.

ZU-ZU, *subs. phr.* (American).—In *pl.* = The Zouave contingent in the Union Army during the Civil War, 1860–5.

c. 1861–5. *Comic Song* [BARTLETT]. My love is a ZU-ZU so gallant and bold; He's rough, and he's handsome, scarce nineteen year old. *Ibid., The Zoo-Zoo's Toast.* Once again!—the hours are fleeting; Drinking is the soldier's trick: Hark! the drum the roll-call's beating,—Scatter, ZOO-zoos, 'double quick!